2017 County and City Extra
Annual Metro, City, and County Data Book
25th Edition

2017 County and City Extra
Annual Metro, City, and County Data Book
25th Edition

Edited by Deirdre A. Gaquin
and Mary Meghan Ryan

Lanham, MD

Published by Bernan Press
An imprint of
The Rowman & Littlefield Publishing Group, Inc.
4501 Forbes Boulevard, Lanham, Maryland 20706

www.rowman.com
800-462-6420
info@bernan.com

ISBN: 978-1-59888-939-0

E-ISBN: 978-1-59888-940-6

ISSN: 1059-9096

∞ ™ The paper used in this publication meets the minimum requirements of American National Standard for Information Sciences—Permanence of Paper for Printed Library Materials, ANSI/NISO Z39.48-1992. Manufactured in the United States of America.

Contents

INTRODUCTION

County and City Extra is an annual publication that provides the most up-to-date statistical information available for every state, county, metropolitan area, and congressional district, as well as all cities in the United States with a 2010 census population of 25,000 or more. Data for places, including towns and cities with populations of fewer than 25,000 people are published by Bernan Press in a separate companion volume, *Places, Towns and Townships,* now in its sixth edition. These two volumes are designed to meet the needs of libraries, businesses, and other organizations or individuals who desire convenient and timely sources of the most frequently sought information about geographic entities within the United States. The annual updating of *County and City Extra* for 25 years ensures its stature as a reliable and authoritative source for statistical information.

Bernan Press also publishes a companion volume, the *State and Metropolitan Area Data Book,* previously published by the Census Bureau. The recently published second edition provides an expanded collection of data about states and metropolitan areas, including micropolitan areas and their component counties. Another recent addition is the *County and City Extra: Special Historical Edition, 1790-2010* with data from the earliest days of the nation, and states, counties, and cities from their beginnings.

County and City Extra; Places, Towns and Townships; and *State and Metropolitan Area Data Book* are large volumes, but are not big enough to accommodate the wealth of information from the decennial census and the American Community Survey. Two additional volumes in the *County and City Extra* series include this information. *County and City Extra—Special Decennial Census Edition* provides detailed population and housing data from the 2010 census and was published by Bernan Press in December 2011. *The Who, What, and Where of America—Understanding the American Community Survey*, recently released in its fifth edition, includes social and economic details from the ongoing American Community Survey, and the *County and City Extra* Series includes additional books on special topics, such as the recently published *Millennials in America.*

The American Community Survey (ACS) is a national survey that has replaced the census long form as the key source of detailed social and economic data. *County and City Extra* includes data from both the 2010 census and the ACS.

New and Updated Information for the 2017 Edition

This edition includes income tax data for counties from the Statistics of Income program of the Internal Revenue Service. ACS data on commuting and availability of computers and internet access are now included for cities. Updated data include 2016 population estimates for states, counties, metropolitan areas, and cities. Also included are the latest available data for education, vital statistics, income and poverty, employment and unemployment, residential construction, production by industry, health resources, crime, land use, city government finances, and many other topics.

Table E (Congressional Districts) includes a wide selection of 2015 American Community Survey data and Business Patterns data for the 115th Congress, as well as Social Security data and data from the 2012 Census of Agriculture for the congressional districts of the 114th Congress, along with the 115th Congressional representatives. Only four states had revised boundaries between the 114th and 115th Congresses.

In July 2015, the Office of Management and Budget released an updated list of Core Based Statistical Areas (metropolitan and micropolitan areas) based on the 2010 census and some changes in the way these areas are defined. These metropolitan areas are used in Table C. Appendixes B and C provide details about the component counties of these metropolitan and micropolitan areas and their 2010 census and 2016 estimated populations. Appendix D has a map for each state showing the metropolitan and micropolitan areas.

This edition includes data from the 2010 census, 2015 and 2016 population estimates, and the ACS. Annual ACS data are available for all states and almost all metropolitan areas (all geographic areas with populations of 65,000 or more), but five years are needed to build a sample large enough for reliable estimates for all counties The Census Bureau no longer releases 3-year data which were previously available for areas with populations of 20,000 or more. These have now been replaced with 1-year Supplemental Estimates which are used in this book for Table D, cities with populations of 25,000 or more.

With the now annual release of 1-year and 5-year estimates, *County and City Extra* uses ACS data for all geographic areas. ACS 1-year data for 2015 are included in Table A (States), Table C (Metropolitan Areas) and Table E (Congressional Districts)—all areas with populations of 65,000 or more. Table D (Cities) uses the 1-year supplemental estimates which are less detailed than the regular 1-year estimates. Table B (States and Counties) includes 5-year data (2011-2015). The release of 5-year data for even the smallest geographic areas means that annual social and economic characteristics are available for all counties and cities.

Although some of the state data are also included in Table B (States and Counties), the separate state data table offers several important features:

- Additional data not available at the county level are provided. Examples include population projections, health insurance coverage, number of immigrants, personal tax payments, information about health service firms not subject to federal tax, and exports by state of origin.

- Additional data that exceeds the space limitations for counties can be found for states. Examples are age of householder, more detailed information about employment in retail trade and services, and the expanded presentation of federal grants and payments to individuals by type.

- State totals can be found more quickly and compared more readily.

Appendix F, **Source Notes and Explanations**, includes internet references for all data sources. This is especially helpful in today's environment where the data sources are updated at a faster pace. The sources referenced here can be used to track down additional information too cumbersome for this book. Some of the data can be directly found in data tables on the websites; some can be assembled through on-line access tools; others can be obtained by downloading files and processing them with statistical software; and some need to be ordered from the agencies.

Rankings

The rankings present the geography types by various subjects, including population, land area, population density, population change, age, immigration, birth rate, housing characteristics, race, Hispanic origin, educational attainment, income, unemployment rate, per capita local taxes, poverty rate, defense contracts, value of agricultural products, and violent crime rate.

Subjects Covered and Volume Organization

A summary of the **subjects covered** in each of the five tables appears on **page xi**. The **colored map** portfolio begins on **page xiii**.

The main body of this volume contains five basic parts. Each part includes a table that is preceded by highlights and rankings, as well as the complete column headings for the table. **Part A**, which begins on **page 1**, contains data for states. **Part B**, beginning on **page 51**, contains information for states and counties. The county geography codes include county typology codes from the Economic Research Service of the Department of Agriculture. These codes characterize counties by size of the largest place as well as by other criteria for nonmetropolitan counties. (See Appendix A for the definition of each code.) **Part C**, beginning on **page 773**, contains information for metropolitan areas. Statistics for cities with a 2010 census population of 25,000 or more can be found in **Part D**, which begins on **page 895**. **Part E**, beginning on **page 1175**, contains data for the congressional districts of the 115th Congress.

A contents page preceding tables B through E lists the page number on which the data for a given geographic area begin. Counties and cities are listed alphabetically by state. Metropolitan areas are listed alphabetically, except that metropolitan divisions are listed alphabetically within the metropolitan statistical area of which they are components. Congressional districts are listed in numeric order within states.

The appendixes include definitions of geographic concepts (**Appendix A**), sources and definitions of each data item included in this volume (**Appendix F**), an alphabetical listing of metropolitan areas with their component counties delineated as of July 2015, with 2010 census populations (**Appendix B**), a listing of metropolitan and micropolitan areas and their component counties as of July 2015, with 2010 census populations and 2016 estimated populations (**Appendix C**), a list of cities by county (**Appendix E**), and maps showing congressional districts in the United States; and metropolitan areas, counties and selected places within each state (**Appendix D**).

Symbols

D Indicates that the number has been withheld to avoid disclosure of information pertaining to a specific organization or individual, or because the number does not meet statistical standards for publication.

NA Indicates that data are not available.

X Indicates that data are not applicable or are not meaningful for this geographic unit.

In this volume, a figure that is less than half the unit of measure shown will appear as zero.

Sources

All of the data in this volume have been obtained from federal government sources. For a complete list of these sources, see **Appendix F**.

Data included in this volume meet the publication standards established by the U.S. Census Bureau and the other federal statistical agencies from which they were obtained. Every effort has been made to select data that are accurate, meaningful, and useful. All data from censuses, surveys, and administrative records are subject to errors arising from factors such as sampling variability, reporting errors, incomplete coverage, nonresponse, imputations, and processing error. Responsibility of the editors and publishers of this volume is limited to reasonable care in the reproduction and presentation of data obtained from sources believed to be reliable.

County and City Extra: Annual Metro, City, and County Data Book is part of Bernan Press's *County and City Extra* series. The editors of *County and City Extra* acknowledge the contributions of the late Courtenay Slater and George Hall, the originators of this publication. Their initial contributions continue to enrich the *County and City Extra* series. As always, we are especially grateful to the many federal agency personnel who assisted us in obtaining the data, provided excellent resources on their websites, and patiently answered questions.

Deirdre A. Gaquin has been a data use consultant to private organizations, government agencies, and universities for over 30 years. Prior to that, she was Director of Data Access Services at Data Use & Access Laboratories, a pioneer in private sector distribution of federal statistical data. A former President of the Association of Public Data Users, Ms. Gaquin has served on numerous boards, panels, and task forces concerned with federal statistical data and has worked on five decennial censuses. She holds a Master of Urban Planning (MUP) degree from Hunter College. Ms. Gaquin is also an editor of Bernan Press's *The Who, What, and Where of America: Understanding the American Community Survey*; *Places, Towns and Townships*; *The Congressional District Atlas*, *The Almanac of American Education, Race and Employment in America,* and *the State and Metropolitan Area Data Book.*

Mary Meghan Ryan is the senior research editor for Bernan Press. She is also the editor for the *Handbook of U.S. Labor Statistics*, *State Profiles*, and the associate editor for *Business Statistics of the United States*.

SUBJECTS COVERED, BY GEOGRAPHY TYPE

State data begin on page 1
County data begin on page 51
Metropolitan area data begin on page 773
City data begin on page 895
Congressional district data begin on page 1175

Subject	Table A. States	Table B. States and Counties	Table C. Metropolitan Areas	Table D. Cities	Table E. Congressional Districts
Land area	1	1	1	1	1
Population					
Total persons, 1990	31				
Total persons, 2000	32	20	20	23	
Total persons, 2010	33	21	21	24	
Total persons, 2015					2
Total persons, 2016	2	2	2	2	
Rank, 2016	3	3	3	3	
Persons per square mile	4	4	4	4	
Race and Hispanic or Latino origin, 2010	45-50				
Race and Hispanic or Latino origin, 2015				5-10	4-11
Race and Hispanic or Latino origin, 2016	5–9	5-9	5-9		
Percent female	21	19	19	22	12
Foreign-born population	22			11	13
Percent born in state of residence	23				14
Immigrants	24				
Age distribution, 2010	52-61				
Age distribution, 2015				12-20	15-23
Age distribution, 2016	10-19	10-18	10-18		
Median age	20, 62			21	24
Percent population change, 1990–2000	34				
Percent population change, 2000–2010	35	22	22	25	
Percent population change, 2010–2016	36	23	23	26	
Components of population change	37-41	24-26	24-26		
Daytime population		33-34	33-34		
Population projections	42-44				
Households					
Total households, 2010	64				
Total households, 2015	25	27	27	27	28
Total households, 2011–2015		27-31			
Percent change in number of households	26, 65				
Household type	28-30, 67-68	29-31	29-31	29-30	30-33
Persons per household	27, 66	28	28	28	29
Persons in group quarters		32	32	31-34	34-39
Housing					
Housing units in 2010	69-78			47-49	
Housing units in 2015	79-92		89-96	50-58	40-45
Housing units in 2016		87-88	87-88		
Housing units in 2011–2015		89-96			
Percent change in number of housing units	70, 80	88	88	48	
Housing costs	73-77, 83-90	91-95	91-95	52	43-45
Substandard housing units	78, 91	96			
Percent with computer access			96	57-58	
Commuting patterns				55-56	
Percent who lived in same house one year ago	92			59	
Percent who lived in different place one year ago				60	
New residential construction	93-95	169-170	169-170	69-71	
Manufactured housing	96				
Vital statistics					
Births	97-98	35-36	35-36		
Deaths	99-103	37-38	37-38		

SUBJECTS COVERED, BY GEOGRAPHY TYPE — Continued

State data begin on page 1
County data begin on page 51
Metropolitan area data begin on page 773
City data begin on page 895
Congressional district data begin on page 1175

Subject	Column Number				
	Table A. States	Table B. States and Counties	Table C. Metropolitan Areas	Table D. Cities	Table E. Congressional Districts
Health					
Persons in nursing facilities				33	37
Medicare enrollees	106	41-43	41-43		
Persons lacking health insurance	104-105	39-40	39-40		59
Crime	107-110	44-47	44-47	35-38	
Education					
School enrollment	111-112	48-49	48-49		25
Educational attainment	113-116	50-51	50-51	39-41	26-27
Expenditures for education	117-118	52-53	52-53		
Income					
Personal income	134-149	62-71	62-71		
Per capita income	122, 136, 149	54, 64	54, 64		46
Household income	123-126	55-58	55-58	42-45	47-48
Poverty	127-133	59-61	59-61	46	49-50
Food stamps					51
Personal income by type	138-140	66-70	66-70		
Earnings by industry	150-158	72-83	72-83		
Transfer payments	141-146	71	71		
Gross state product	159				
Personal tax payments	147				
Disposable personal income	148-149				
Social Security	160-162	84-86	84-86		60-62
Individual income taxes		197-199	197-199		
Labor Force and Employment					
Labor force and unemployment	167-171	97-100	97-100	61-68	52-54
Employment in selected occupations	163-166	101-103	101-103		55-58
Employment by industry	172-183, 207-216	104-112	104-112		73-84
Exports of goods produced	119-121				
Establishments, employment, sales, and payroll					
Manufacturing	207-216	151-154	151-154	88-91	
Construction	217-221				
Wholesale trade	222-226	135-138	135-138	72-75	
Retail trade	227-235	139-142	139-142	76-79	
Information	236-246				
Utilities	247-251				
Transportation and warehousing	252-256				
Finance and insurance	257-261				
Real estate and rental and leasing	262-266	143-146	143-146	80-83	
Professional, scientific, and technical services	267-275	147-150	147-150	84-87	
Health care and social assistance	276-289	159-162	159-162	100-103	
Arts, entertainment and recreation	290-294			96-99	
Accommodation and food services	295-300	155-158	155-158	92-95	
Other services, except public administration	301-308	163-166	163-166	104-108	
Nonemployer businesses		167-168	167-168		
Government employment	309-314	171, 194-196	171, 194-196	108	
Government payroll	315-330	172-179	172-179	109-116	
Government finances	331-350	180-193	180-193	117-139	

xi

SUBJECTS COVERED, BY GEOGRAPHY TYPE — Continued

State data begin on page 1
County data begin on page 51
Metropolitan area data begin on page 773
City data begin on page 895
Congressional district data begin on page 1175

Subject	Column Number				
	Table A. States	Table B. States and Counties	Table C. Metropolitan Areas	Table D. Cities	Table E. Congressional Districts
Agriculture	184-202	113-132	113-132		63-72
Land and water	203-206	133-134	133-134		
Voting and elections	351-355				
Climate				140-146	

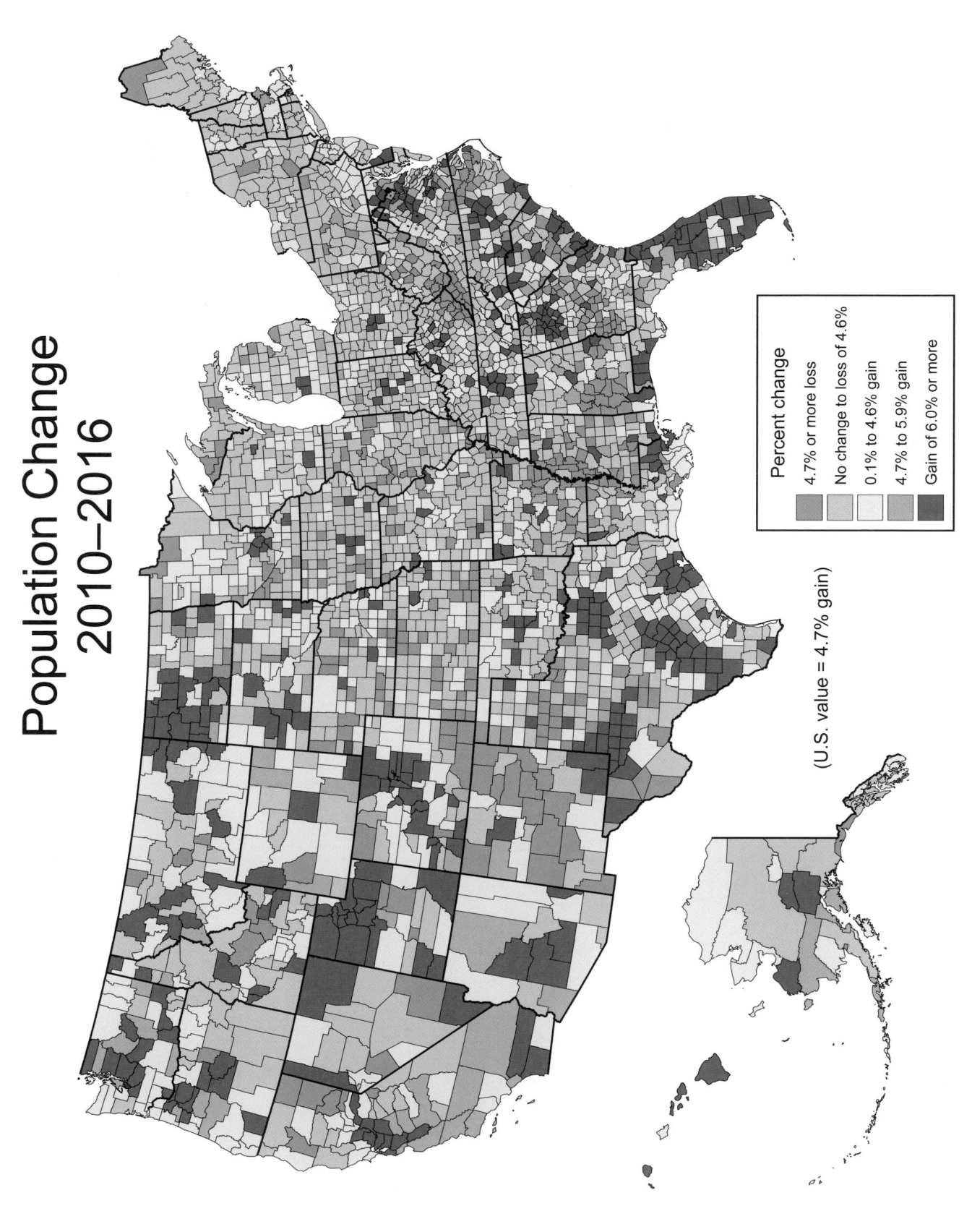

Population Change
2010–2016

Percent change

4.7% or more loss
No change to loss of 4.6%
0.1% to 4.6% gain
4.7% to 5.9% gain
Gain of 6.0% or more

(U.S. value = 4.7% gain)

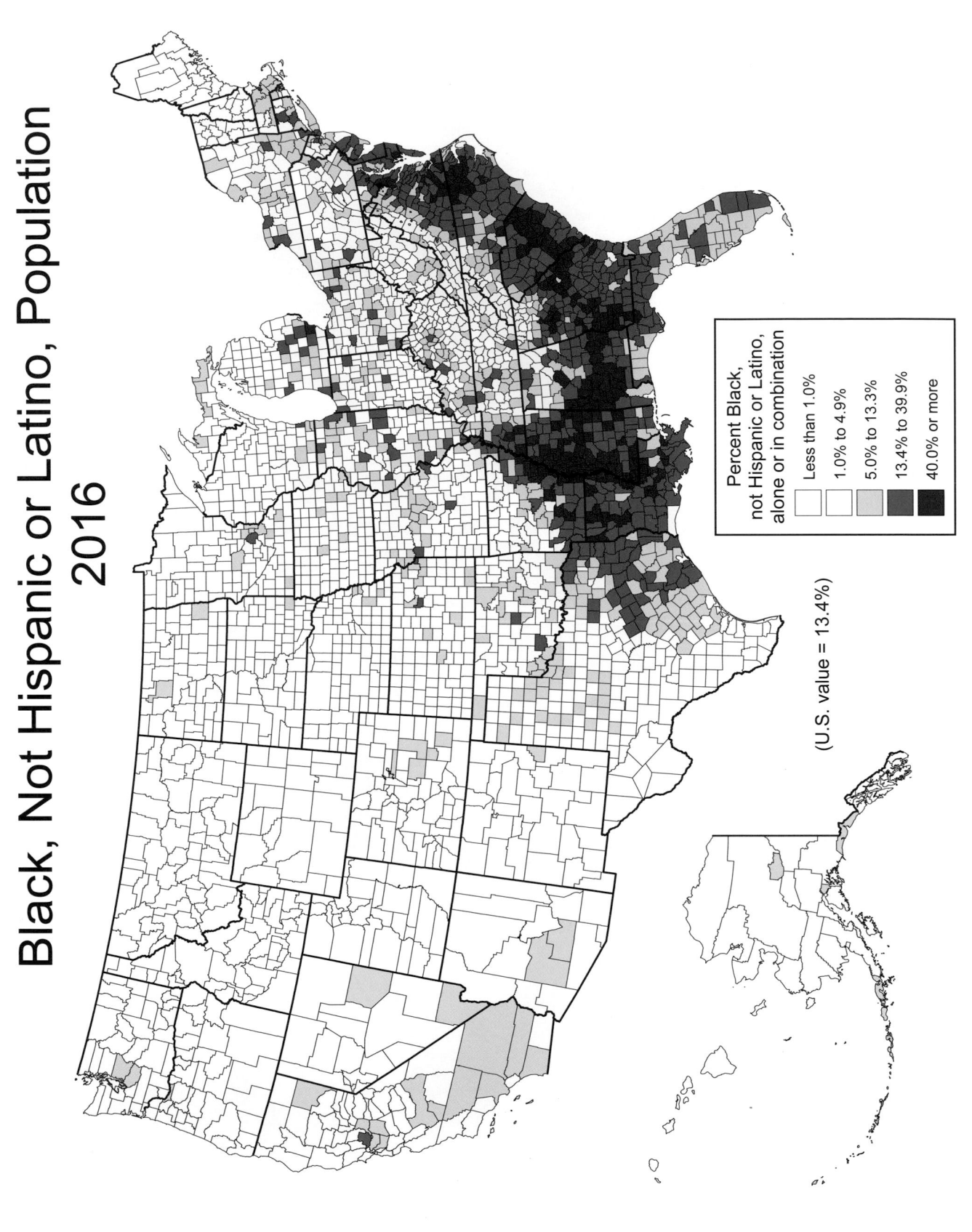

Black, Not Hispanic or Latino, Population
2016

Percent Black,
not Hispanic or Latino,
alone or in combination

Less than 1.0%
1.0% to 4.9%
5.0% to 13.3%
13.4% to 39.9%
40.0% or more

(U.S. value = 13.4%)

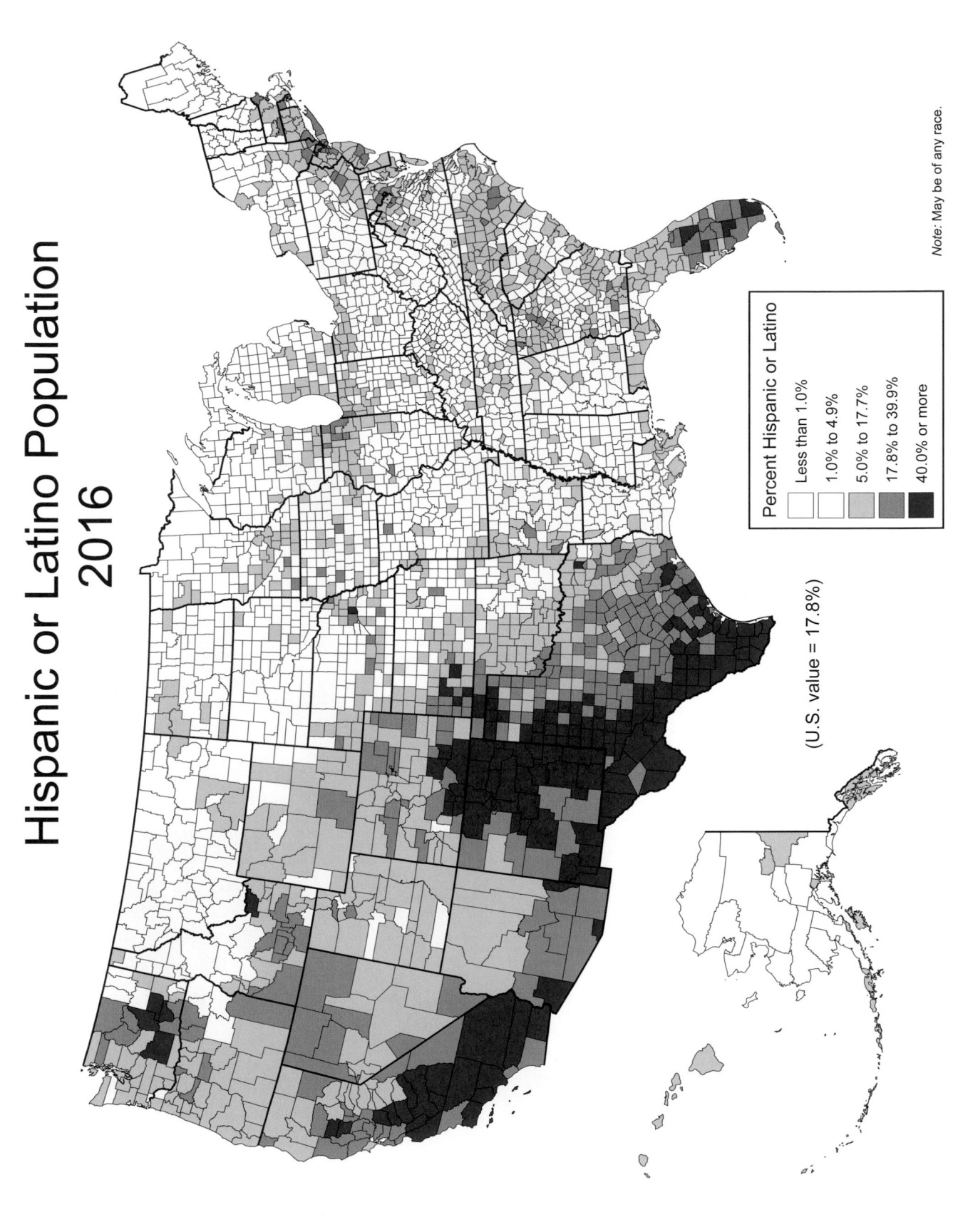

Hispanic or Latino Population
2016

Percent Hispanic or Latino

Less than 1.0%
1.0% to 4.9%
5.0% to 17.7%
17.8% to 39.9%
40.0% or more

(U.S. value = 17.8%)

Note: May be of any race.

Population Under 18 Years Old
2016

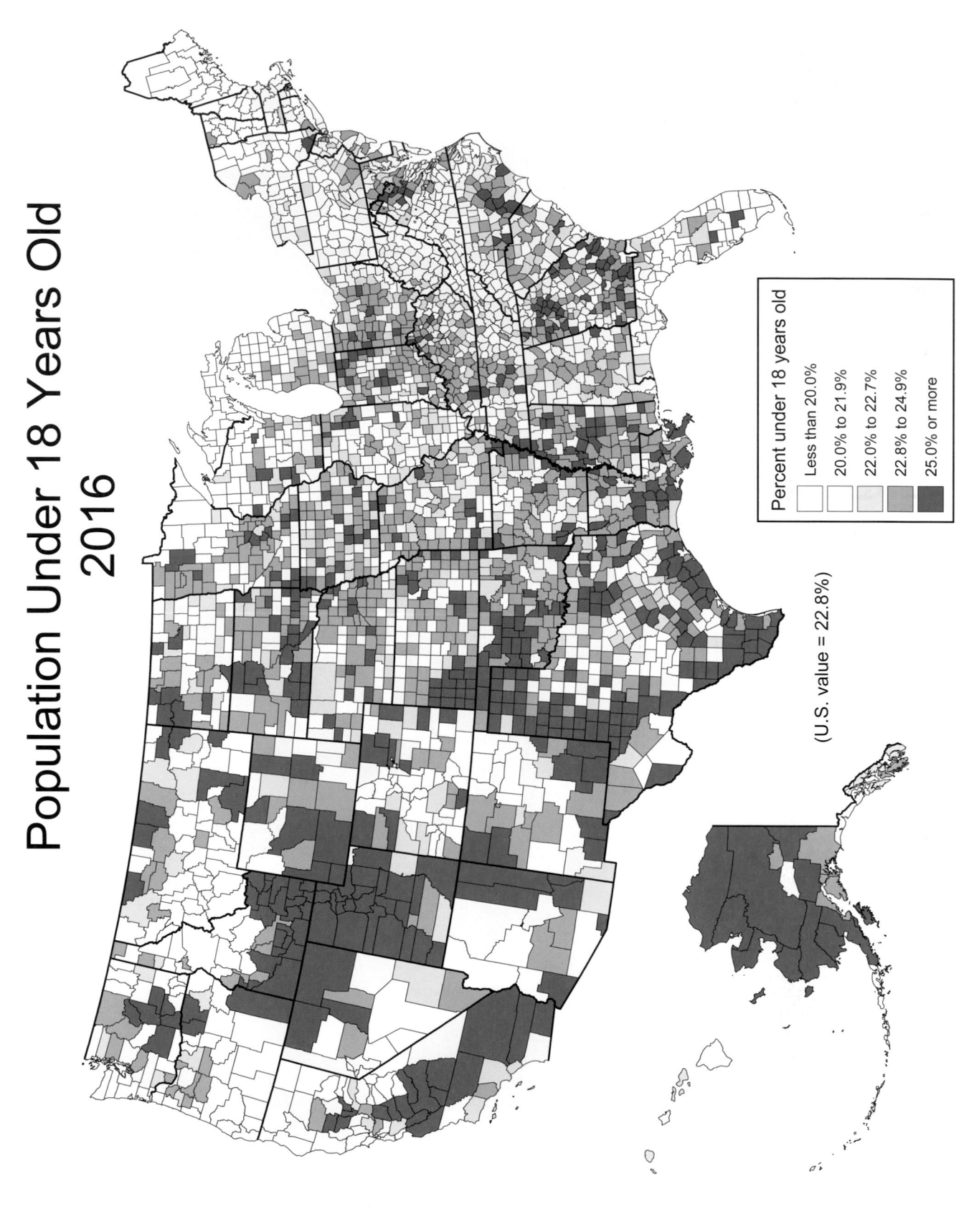

Percent under 18 years old

	Less than 20.0%
	20.0% to 21.9%
	22.0% to 22.7%
	22.8% to 24.9%
	25.0% or more

(U.S. value = 22.8%)

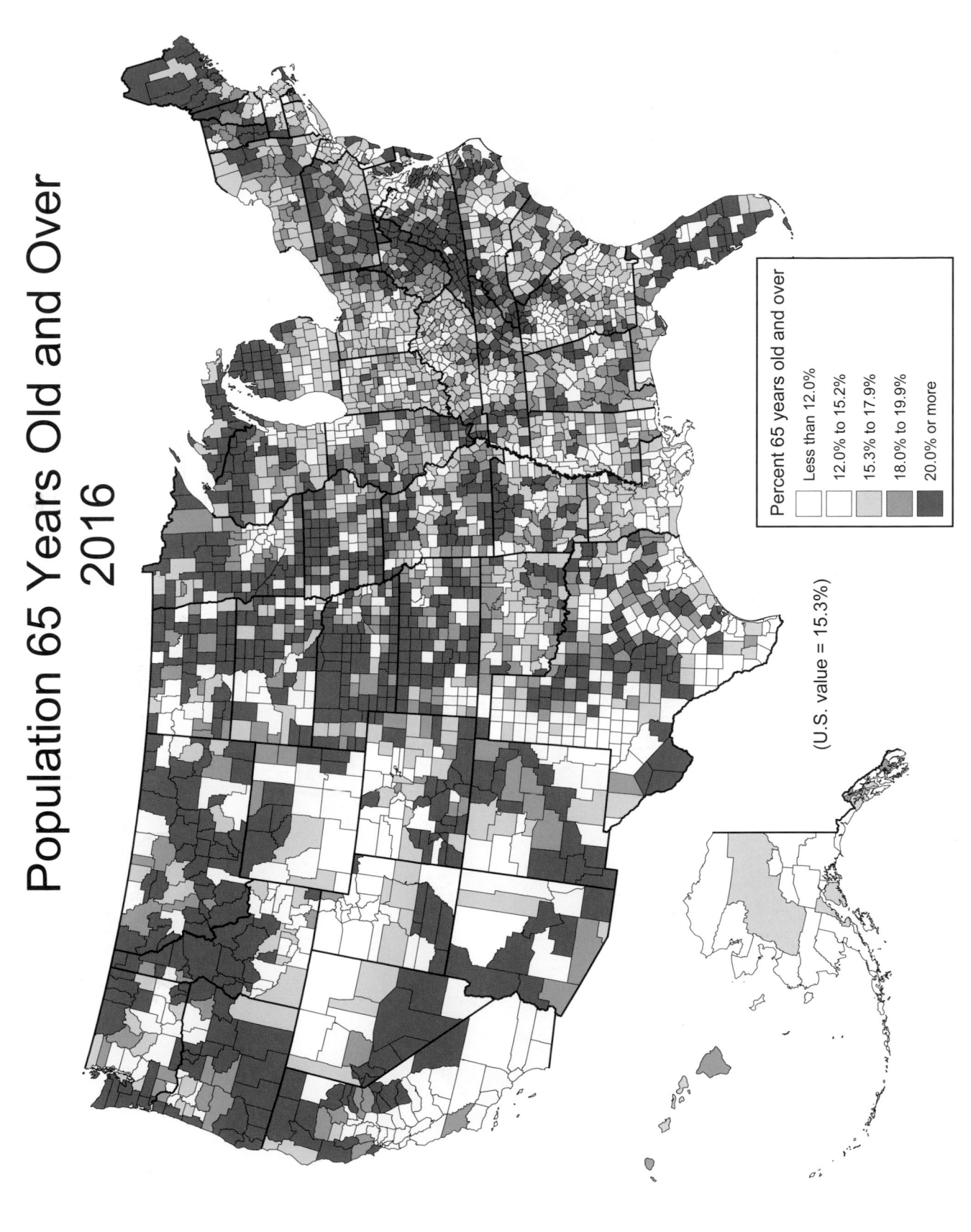

Population 65 Years Old and Over
2016

Percent 65 years old and over

Less than 12.0%
12.0% to 15.2%
15.3% to 17.9%
18.0% to 19.9%
20.0% or more

(U.S. value = 15.3%)

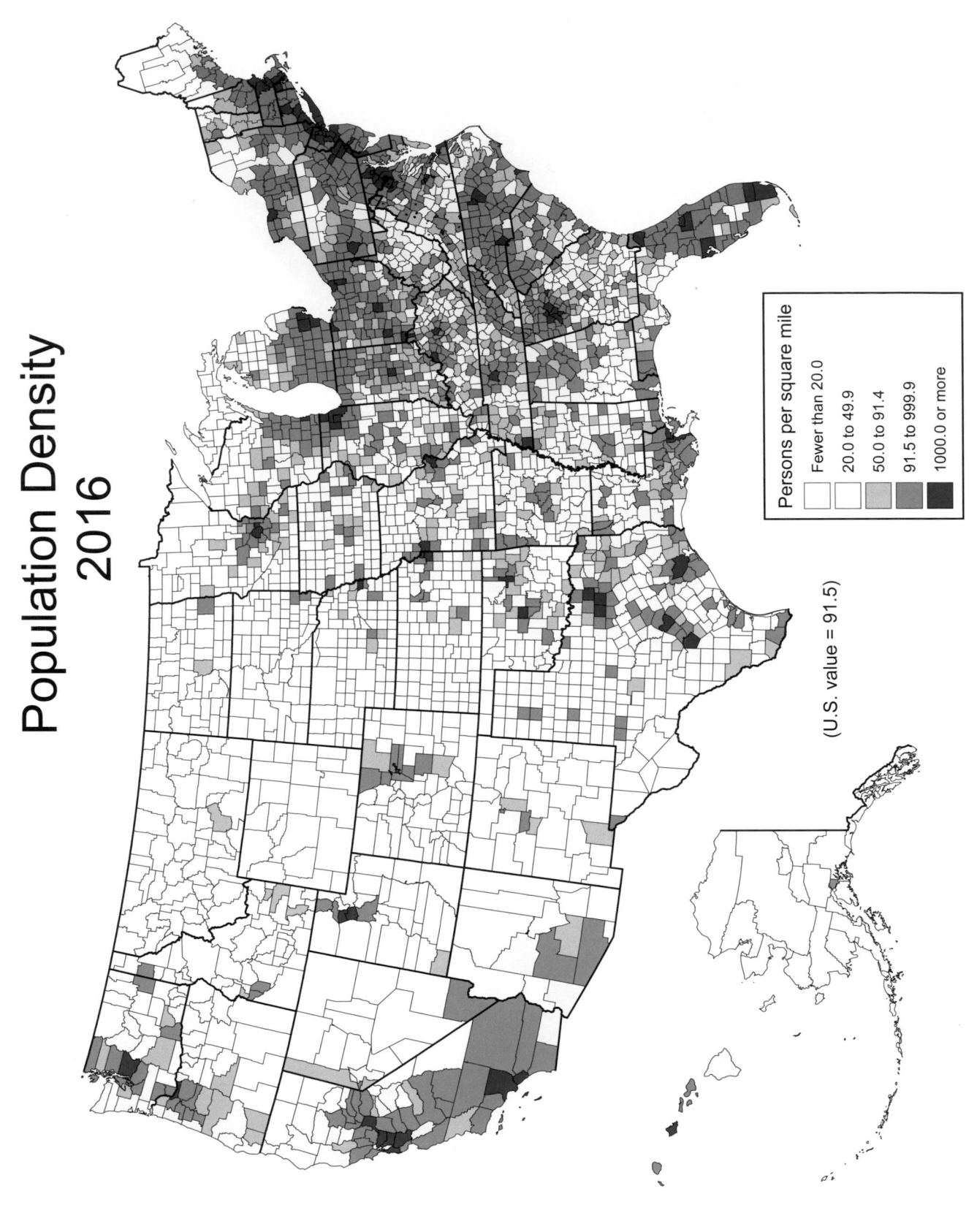

Population Density
2016

Persons per square mile

Fewer than 20.0
20.0 to 49.9
50.0 to 91.4
91.5 to 999.9
1000.0 or more

(U.S. value = 91.5)

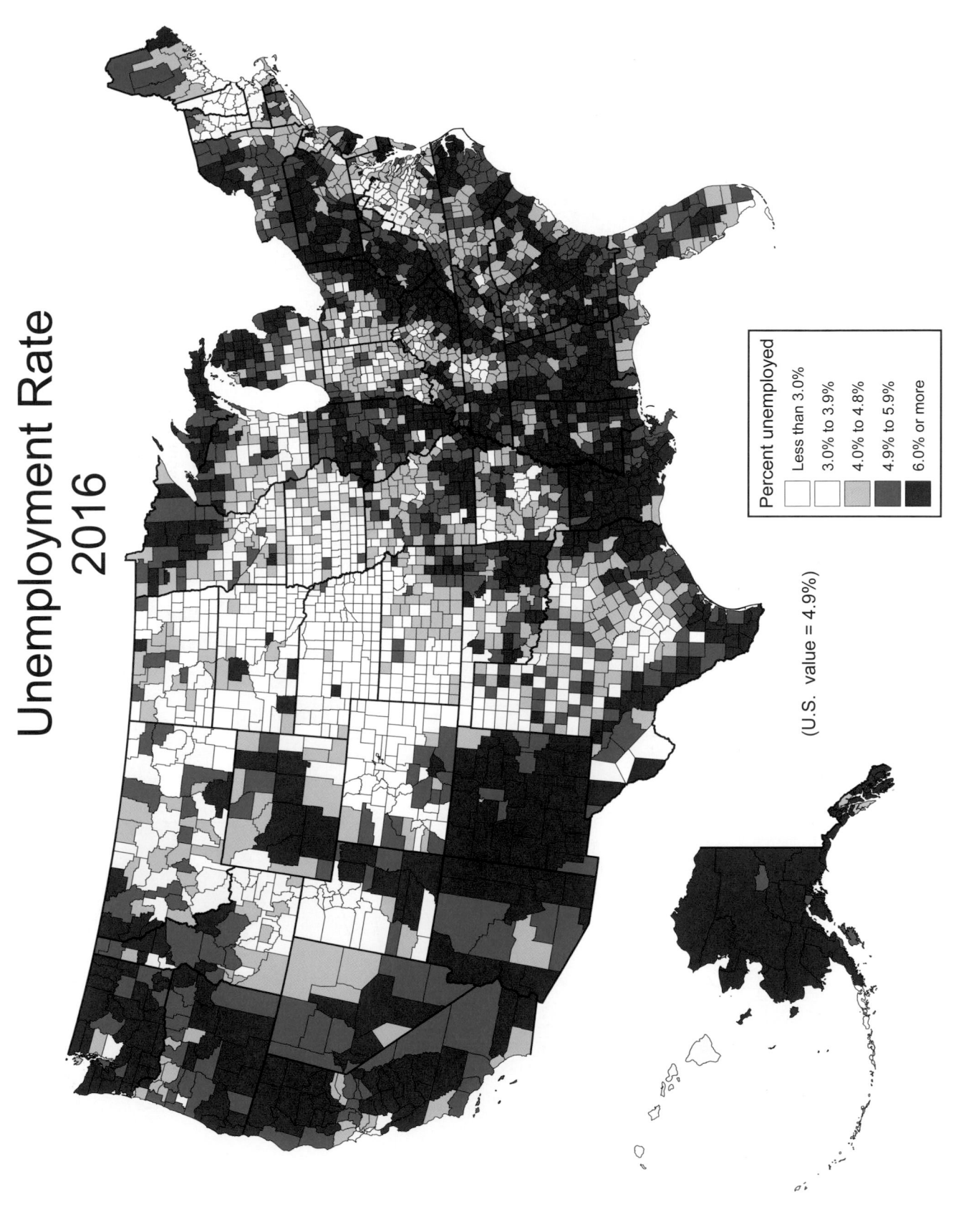

Unemployment Rate
2016

Percent unemployed

- Less than 3.0%
- 3.0% to 3.9%
- 4.0% to 4.8%
- 4.9% to 5.9%
- 6.0% or more

(U.S. value = 4.9%)

Educational Expenditures Per Student
2013–2014

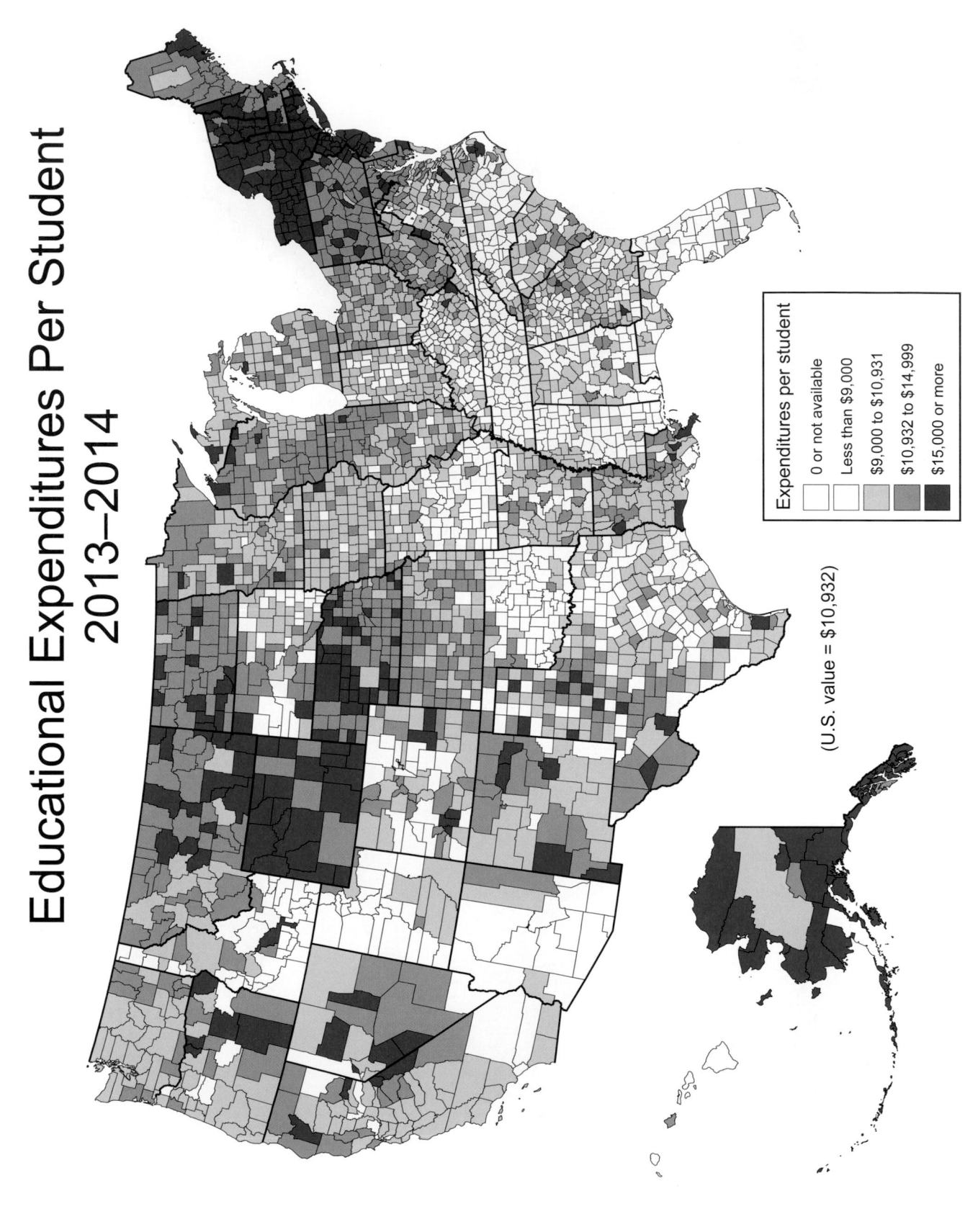

Expenditures per student

	0 or not available
	Less than $9,000
	$9,000 to $10,931
	$10,932 to $14,999
	$15,000 or more

(U.S. value = $10,932)

Population with High School Diploma or Less
2011–2015

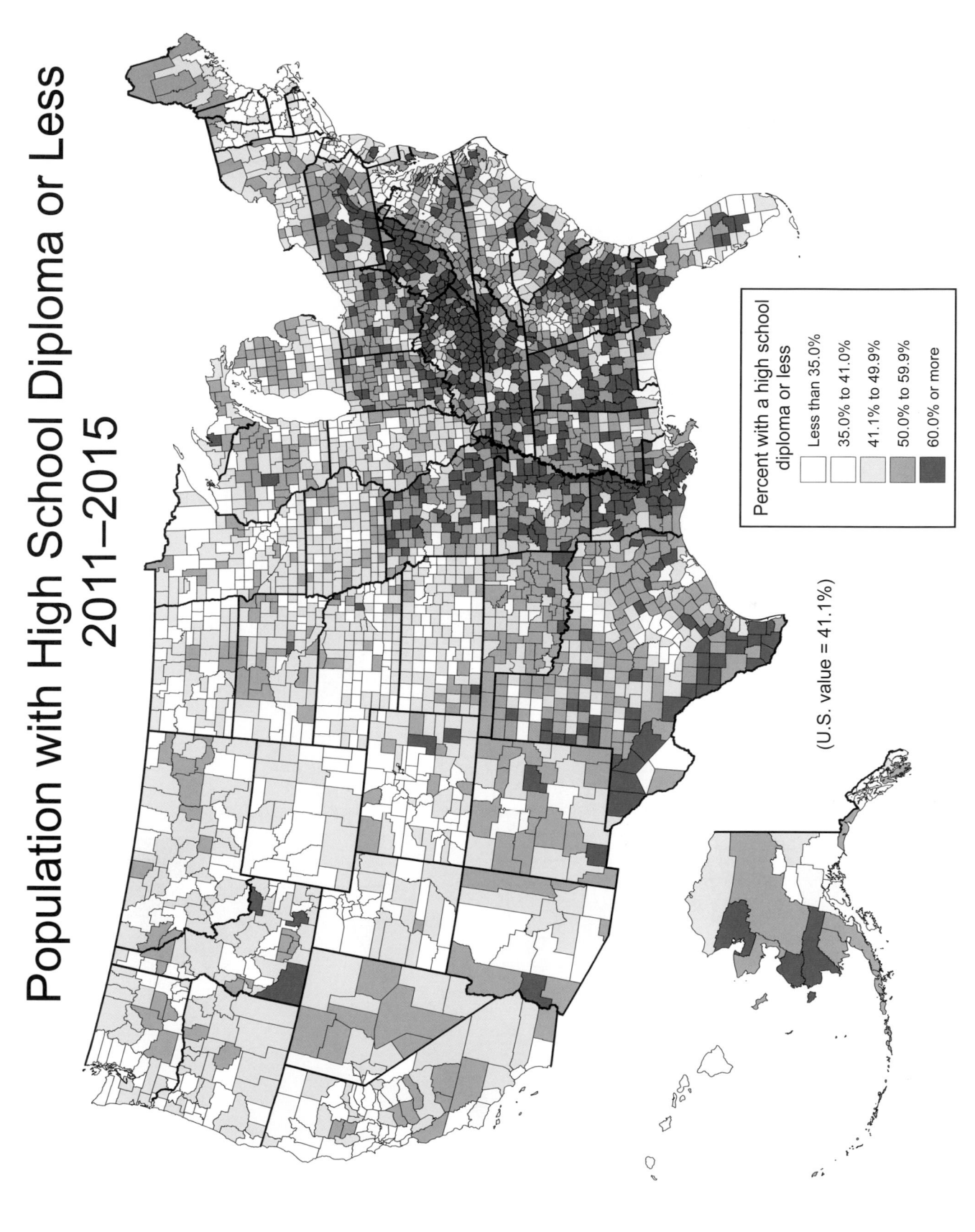

Percent with a high school diploma or less

- Less than 35.0%
- 35.0% to 41.0%
- 41.1% to 49.9%
- 50.0% to 59.9%
- 60.0% or more

(U.S. value = 41.1%)

Earnings from Manufacturing 2015

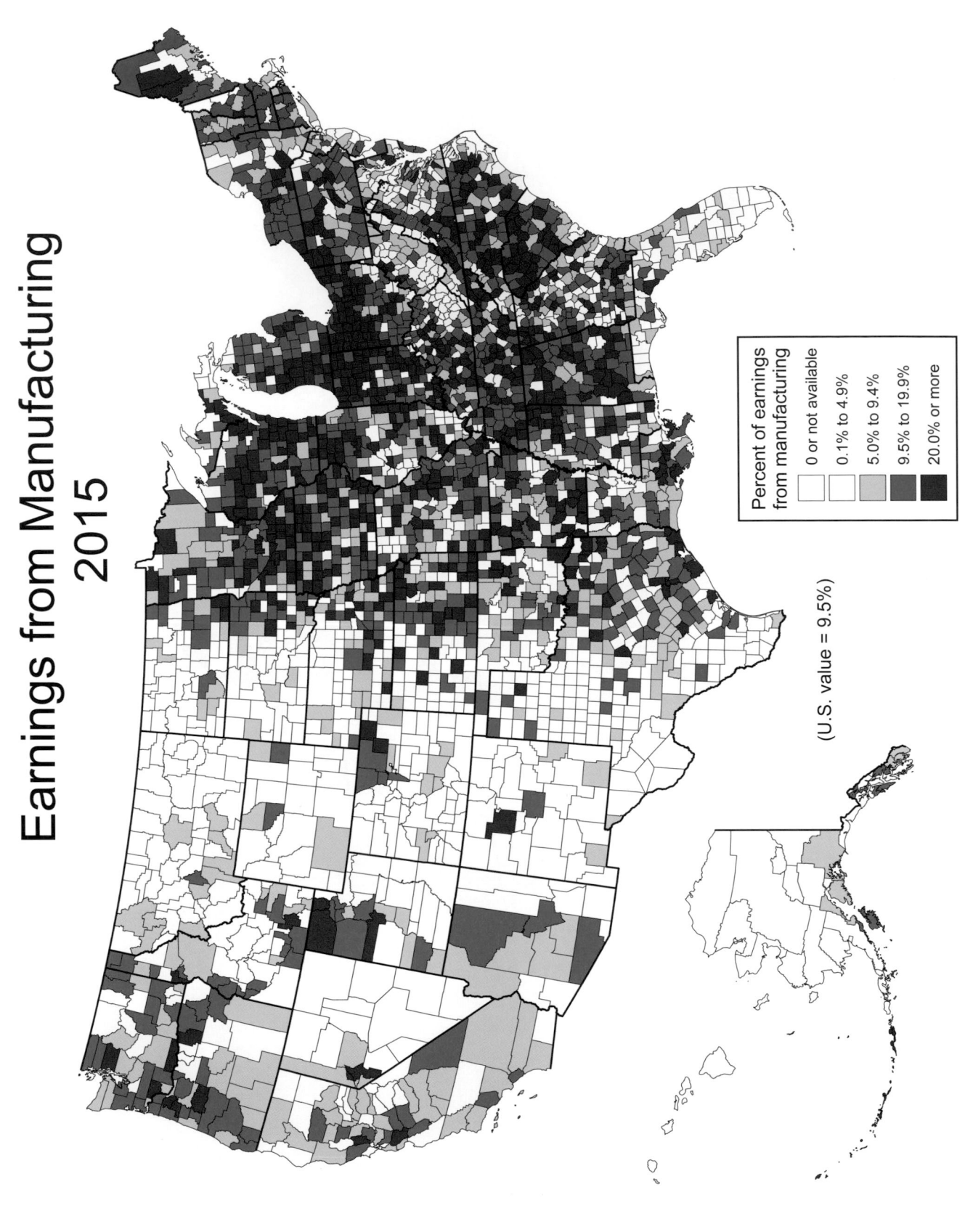

Percent of earnings from manufacturing

- 0 or not available
- 0.1% to 4.9%
- 5.0% to 9.4%
- 9.5% to 19.9%
- 20.0% or more

(U.S. value = 9.5%)

Employment in Management, Business, Science, and Arts Occupations: 2011–2015

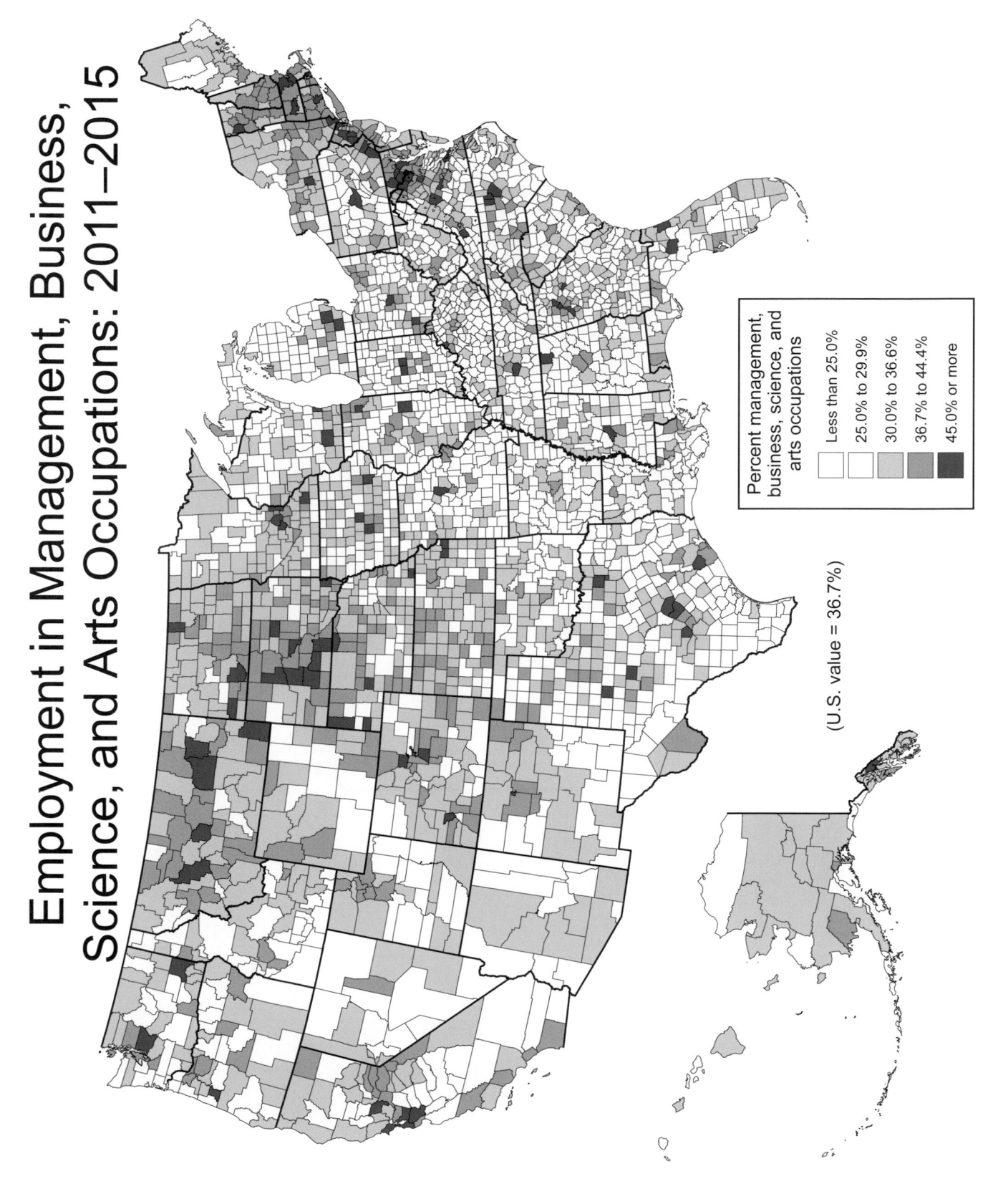

Percent management, business, science, and arts occupations

Less than 25.0%
25.0% to 29.9%
30.0% to 36.6%
36.7% to 44.4%
45.0% or more

(U.S. value = 36.7%)

Land in Farms
2012

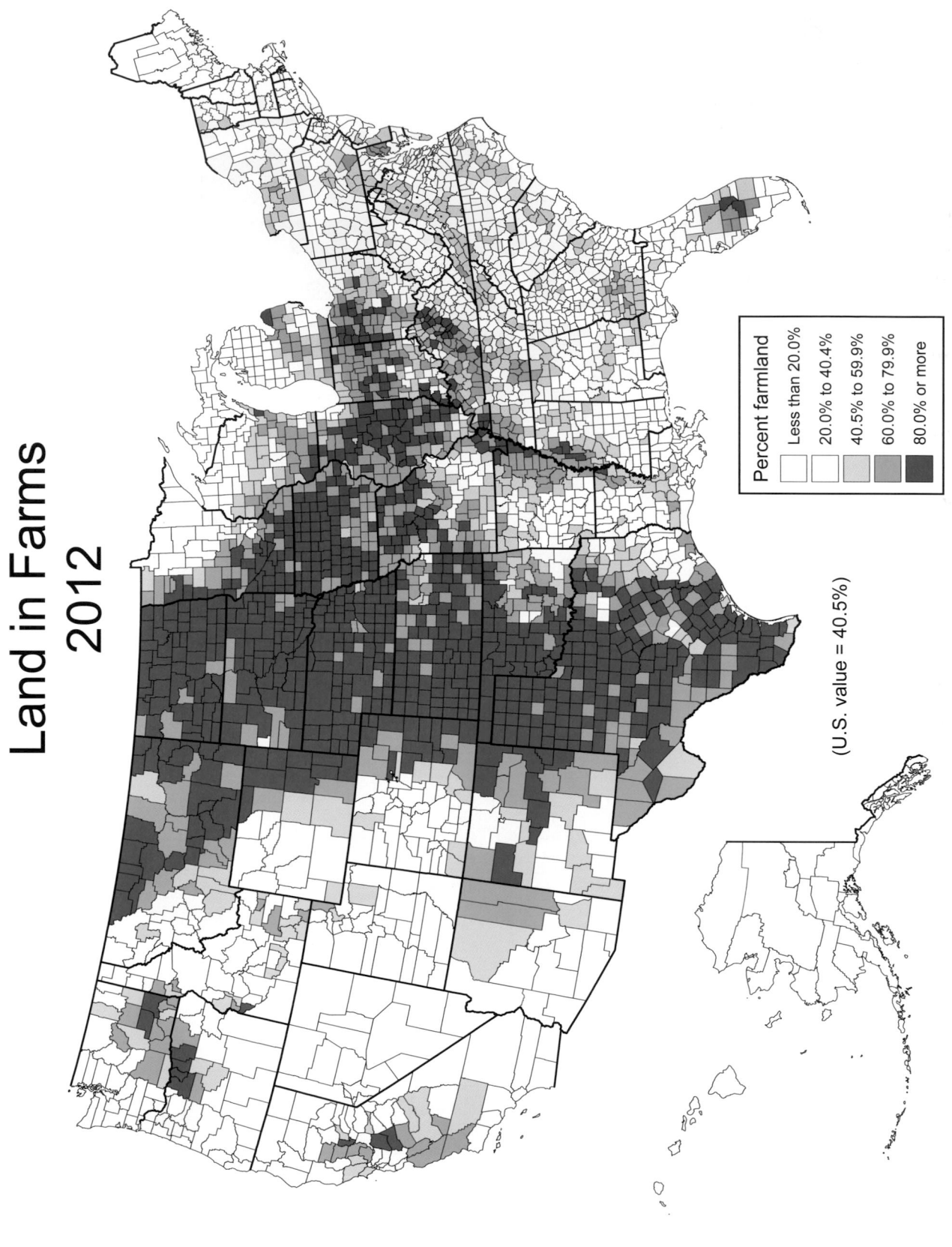

Percent farmland

Less than 20.0%
20.0% to 40.4%
40.5% to 59.9%
60.0% to 79.9%
80.0% or more

(U.S. value = 40.5%)

Persons Under Age 65 with No Health Insurance
2015

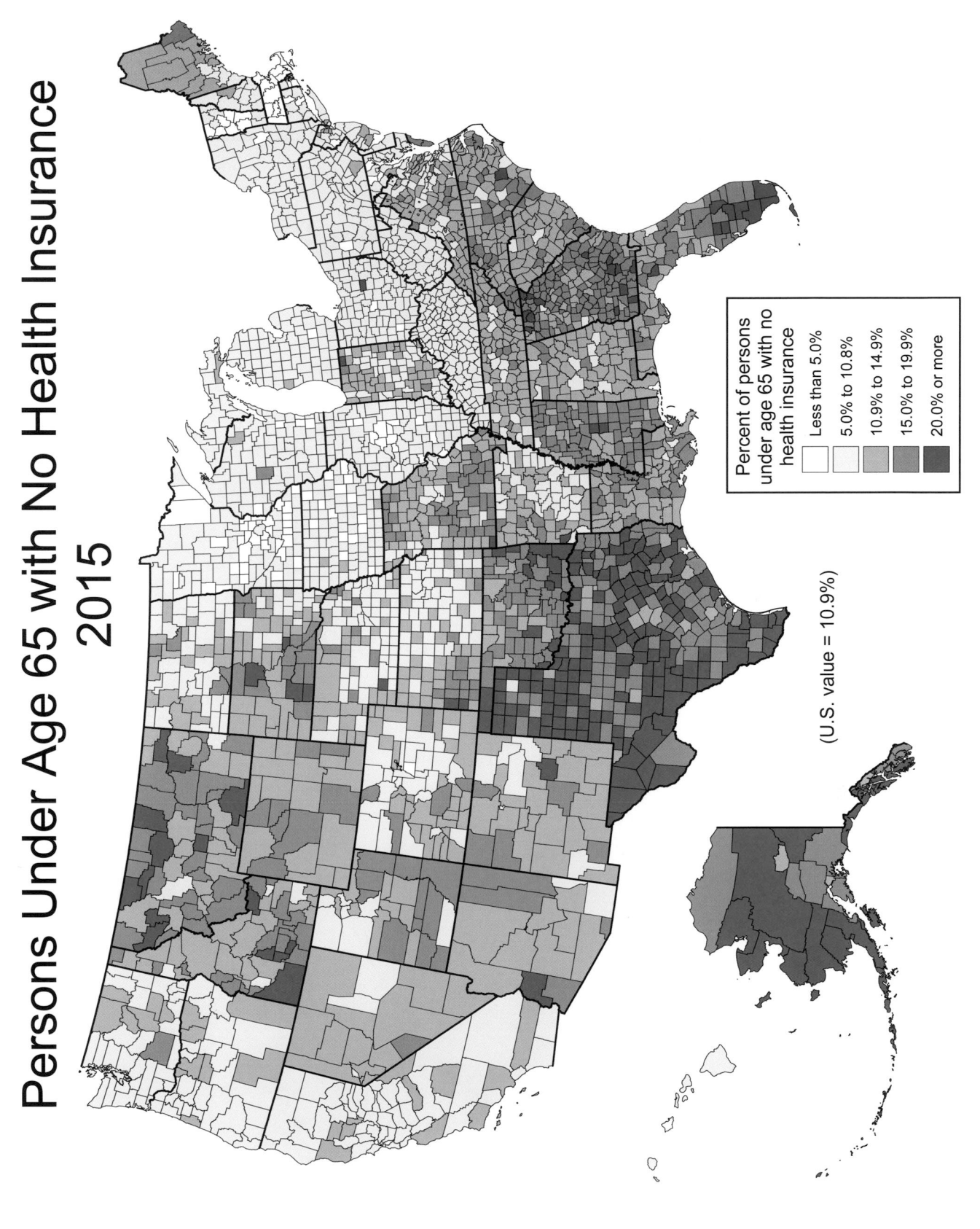

Percent of persons under age 65 with no health insurance

- Less than 5.0%
- 5.0% to 10.8%
- 10.9% to 14.9%
- 15.0% to 19.9%
- 20.0% or more

(U.S. value = 10.9%)

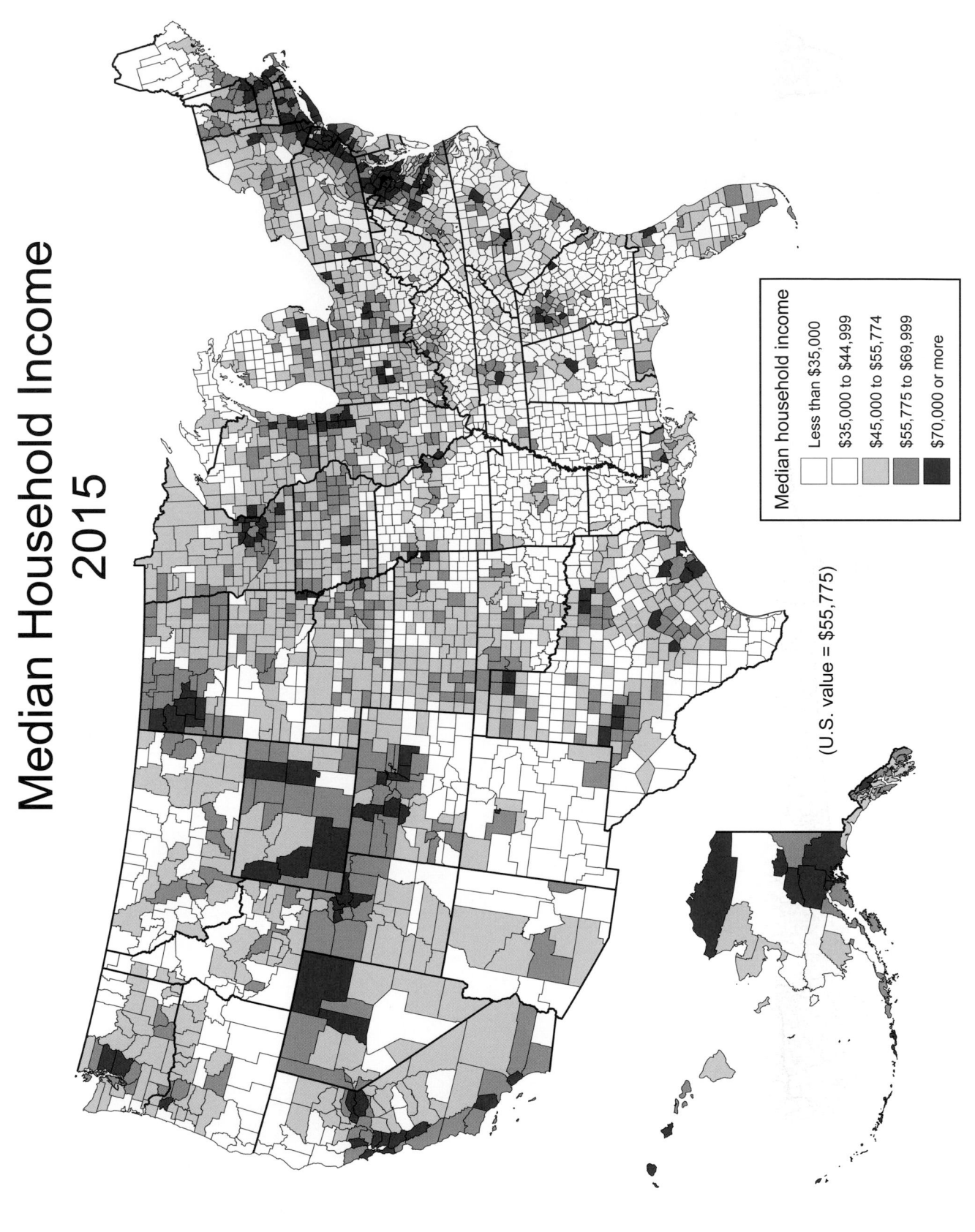

Median Household Income
2015

(U.S. value = $55,775)

Median household income

	Less than $35,000
	$35,000 to $44,999
	$45,000 to $55,774
	$55,775 to $69,999
	$70,000 or more

Percent in Poverty
2015

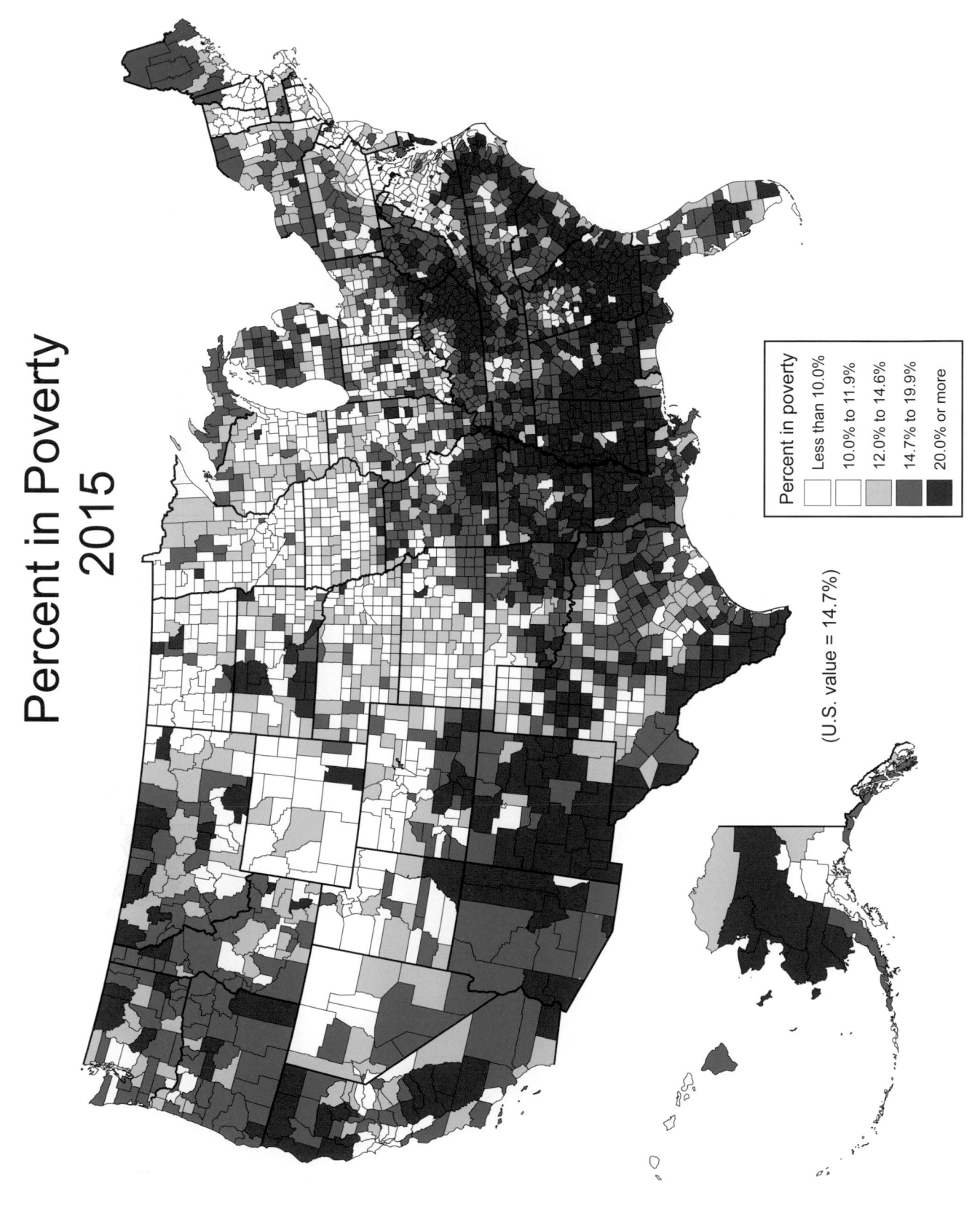

Percent in poverty

Less than 10.0%	
10.0% to 11.9%	
12.0% to 14.6%	
14.7% to 19.9%	
20.0% or more	

(U.S. value = 14.7%)

Median Value of Owner-Occupied Housing Units
2011–2015

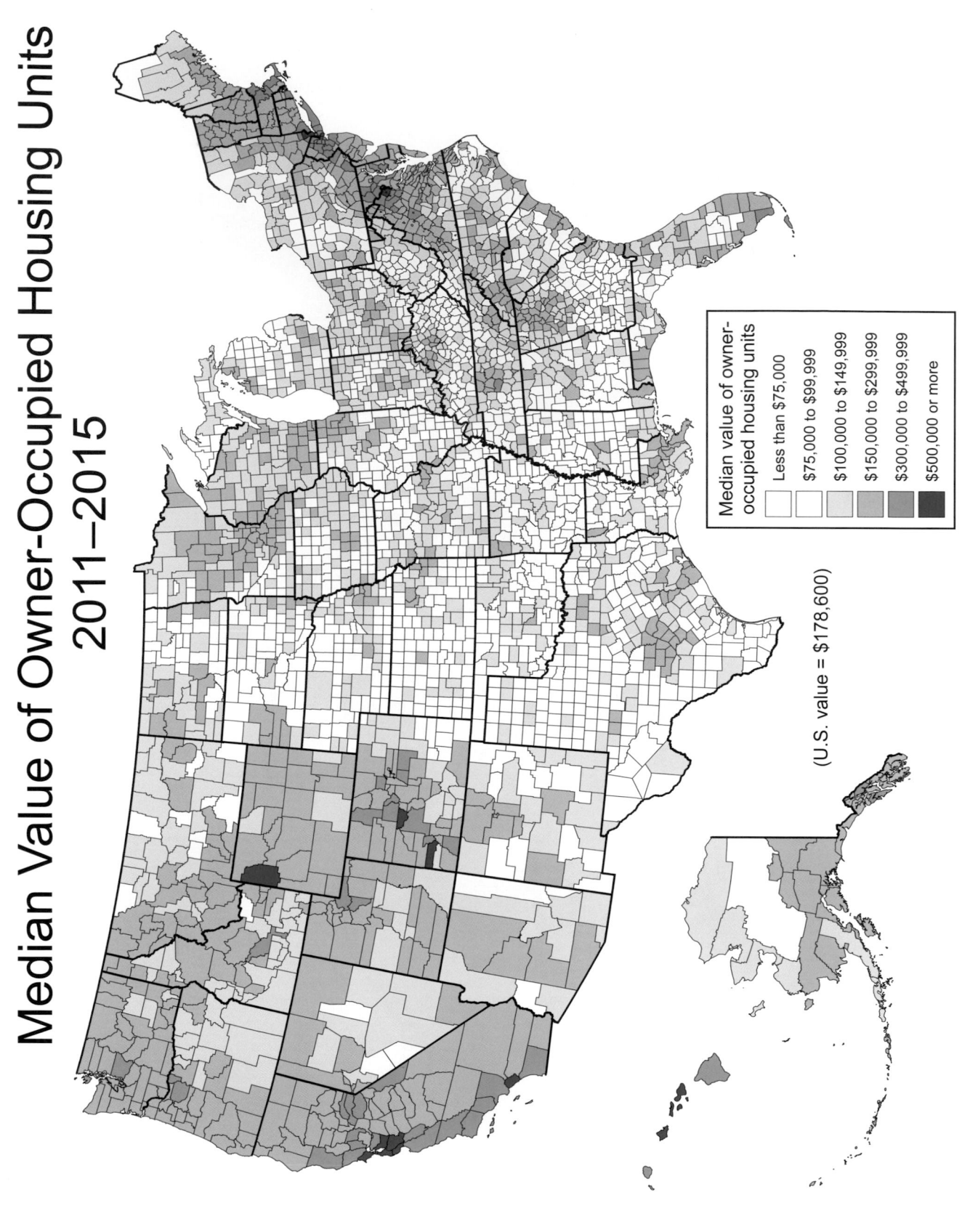

Median value of owner-occupied housing units

Less than $75,000
$75,000 to $99,999
$100,000 to $149,999
$150,000 to $299,999
$300,000 to $499,999
$500,000 or more

(U.S. value = $178,600)

States

(For explanation of symbols, see page viii)

Part A—States

1

State Highlights and Rankings

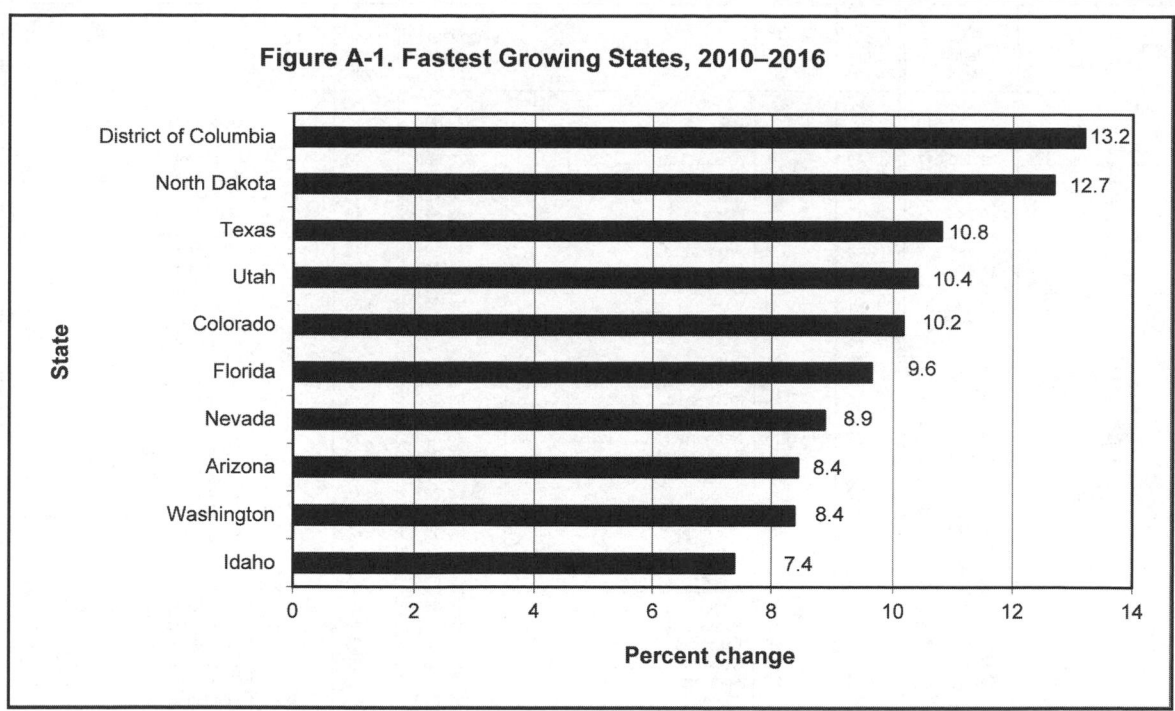

Figure A-1. Fastest Growing States, 2010–2016

State	Percent change
District of Columbia	13.2
North Dakota	12.7
Texas	10.8
Utah	10.4
Colorado	10.2
Florida	9.6
Nevada	8.9
Arizona	8.4
Washington	8.4
Idaho	7.4

There is no simple relationship between population size and land area for most of the geographic entities included in this publication. According to the Census Bureau's 2016 estimates, state populations ranged from a high of over 39 million in California to a low of 585,501 in Wyoming. (The median population for states—with half having a larger population and half having a smaller population—was over 4.4 million people.) California was also one of the largest states in land area (ranking third). Alaska was by far the largest state in area; it was more than twice the size of Texas, the second-largest state, even though its population rank was close to the bottom (ranked 48th). Texas was also the second-largest state in terms of total population with nearly 28.0 million residents. At the other end of the geographic size spectrum were many of the New England states (with Rhode Island ranking as the smallest), plus Delaware, Hawaii, and New Jersey. As a consequence of differing area size and population rank, New Jersey was the most densely settled state, with 1,216.0 persons per square mile while Alaska was the least densely settled, with about 1.3 persons per square mile. California, which had the largest population and third-largest land area, ranked 12th in terms of population density (251.9 persons per square mile). The 15 most populous states remained almost unchanged between 2010 and 2016—Arizona moved into the top 15 while Indiana dropped out—but there were changes within their ranks. Florida became the 3rd most populous state, pushing ahead of New York while Georgia became the 8th most populous state. North Carolina moved up to 9th place while Michigan dropped to 10th.

Not surprisingly, states with higher population density also had higher proportions of developed land. According to the Department of Agriculture's most recent National Resources Inventory, 35.4 percent of New Jersey's land was developed. Connecticut had the second highest proportion with 33.9 percent, followed by Massachusetts at 33.1 percent. Among the reporting states, Nevada had the lowest proportion of developed land, at just 0.8 percent, followed by Montana and Wyoming, with 1.1 percent

and 1.2 percent of their land developed. Nearly 85 percent of Nevada's land was owned by the federal government. This was by far the highest percentage in the nation. Federal land accounted for almost 21 percent of the United States' total land area. (Estimates are not available for Alaska, and the District of Columbia. See Appendix F for definitions and additional information.)

The total population of the United States increased 4.7 percent between 2010 and 2016, with 21 states matching or exceeding this rate of growth and the remainder growing more slowly. The District of Columbia and North Dakota experienced the highest growth rates (13.2 and 12.7 percent) even though they ranked 49th and 47th respectively in population among all the states. Despite its growth, North Dakota ranked 47th for total population and 48th for density. It was among three states with population densities of fewer than 10 persons per square mile. Texas and Florida ranked among the top 10 states for total population and for population growth from 2010 to 2016. Texas, with the second-largest population, grew by 10.8 percent, increasing its population by over 2.7 million people. Rhode Island and Vermont both ranked among the 10 least populous states, as well as among the 10 states with the lowest population growth between 2010 and 2016. While most states have increased their populations in the six years, the populations of West Virginia, Illinois, and Vermont declined by a small amount. Seven other states experienced increases below one percent. Louisiana's population has rebounded from a loss of about 250,000 residents after Hurricane Katrina hit the state in August 2005. Its 2016 population of over 4.6 million is slightly higher than its 2005 estimated population on July 1 of that year.

States and the District of Columbia, Selected Rankings

Population, 2016			Land Area, 2016				Population density, 2016			
Population rank	State	Population [col 2]	Population rank	Land area rank	State	Land area (square miles) [col 1]	Population rank	Density rank	State	Density (per square mile) [col 4]
	United States	323 127 513			United States	3 532 069			United States	91.5
1	California	39 250 017	48	1	Alaska	570 638	49	1	District of Columbia	11 140.2
2	Texas	27 862 596	2	2	Texas	261 250	11	2	New Jersey	1 216.0
3	Florida	20 612 439	1	3	California	155 793	43	3	Rhode Island	1 021.7
4	New York	19 745 289	44	4	Montana	145 547	15	4	Massachusetts	873.2
5	Illinois	12 801 539	36	5	New Mexico	121 302	29	5	Connecticut	738.5
6	Pennsylvania	12 784 227	14	6	Arizona	113 591	19	6	Maryland	619.6
7	Ohio	11 614 373	34	7	Nevada	109 780	45	7	Delaware	488.6
8	Georgia	10 310 371	21	8	Colorado	103 641	4	8	New York	419.0
9	North Carolina	10 146 788	51	9	Wyoming	97 091	3	9	Florida	384.3
10	Michigan	9 928 300	27	10	Oregon	95 987	6	10	Pennsylvania	285.7
11	New Jersey	8 944 469	39	11	Idaho	82 642	7	11	Ohio	284.2
12	Virginia	8 411 808	31	12	Utah	82 196	1	12	California	251.9
13	Washington	7 288 000	35	13	Kansas	81 758	5	13	Illinois	230.6
14	Arizona	6 931 071	22	14	Minnesota	79 627	40	14	Hawaii	222.4
15	Massachusetts	6 811 779	37	15	Nebraska	76 824	12	15	Virginia	213.1
16	Tennessee	6 651 194	46	16	South Dakota	75 811	9	16	North Carolina	208.7
17	Indiana	6 633 053	47	17	North Dakota	69 001	17	17	Indiana	185.1
18	Missouri	6 093 000	18	18	Missouri	68 747	8	18	Georgia	179.0
19	Maryland	6 016 447	28	19	Oklahoma	68 596	10	19	Michigan	175.6
20	Wisconsin	5 778 708	13	20	Washington	66 453	23	20	South Carolina	165.0
21	Colorado	5 540 545	8	21	Georgia	57 595	16	21	Tennessee	161.3
22	Minnesota	5 519 952	10	22	Michigan	56 547	41	22	New Hampshire	149.1
23	South Carolina	4 961 119	30	23	Iowa	55 857	26	23	Kentucky	112.4
24	Alabama	4 863 300	5	24	Illinois	55 517	13	24	Washington	109.7
25	Louisiana	4 681 666	20	25	Wisconsin	54 160	25	25	Louisiana	108.4
26	Kentucky	4 436 974	3	26	Florida	53 639	2	26	Texas	106.7
27	Oregon	4 093 465	33	27	Arkansas	52 036	20	26	Wisconsin	106.7
28	Oklahoma	3 923 561	24	28	Alabama	50 646	24	28	Alabama	96.0
29	Connecticut	3 576 452	9	29	North Carolina	48 619	18	29	Missouri	88.6
30	Iowa	3 134 693	4	30	New York	47 125	38	30	West Virginia	76.2
31	Utah	3 051 217	32	31	Mississippi	46 923	22	31	Minnesota	69.3
32	Mississippi	2 988 726	6	32	Pennsylvania	44 742	50	32	Vermont	67.8
33	Arkansas	2 988 248	25	33	Louisiana	43 207	32	33	Mississippi	63.7
34	Nevada	2 940 058	16	34	Tennessee	41 235	14	34	Arizona	61.0
35	Kansas	2 907 289	7	35	Ohio	40 862	33	35	Arkansas	57.4
36	New Mexico	2 081 015	26	36	Kentucky	39 485	28	36	Oklahoma	57.2
37	Nebraska	1 907 116	12	37	Virginia	39 482	30	37	Iowa	56.1
38	West Virginia	1 831 102	17	38	Indiana	35 827	21	38	Colorado	53.5
39	Idaho	1 683 140	42	39	Maine	30 844	42	39	Maine	43.2
40	Hawaii	1 428 557	23	40	South Carolina	30 063	27	40	Oregon	42.6
41	New Hampshire	1 334 795	38	41	West Virginia	24 041	31	41	Utah	37.1
42	Maine	1 331 479	19	42	Maryland	9 710	35	42	Kansas	35.6
43	Rhode Island	1 056 426	50	43	Vermont	9 218	34	43	Nevada	26.8
44	Montana	1 042 520	41	44	New Hampshire	8 953	37	44	Nebraska	24.8
45	Delaware	952 065	15	45	Massachusetts	7 801	39	45	Idaho	20.4
46	South Dakota	865 454	11	46	New Jersey	7 356	36	46	New Mexico	17.2
47	North Dakota	757 952	40	47	Hawaii	6 423	46	47	South Dakota	11.4
48	Alaska	741 894	29	48	Connecticut	4 843	47	48	North Dakota	11.0
49	District of Columbia	681 170	45	49	Delaware	1 949	44	49	Montana	7.2
50	Vermont	624 594	43	50	Rhode Island	1 034	51	50	Wyoming	6.0
51	Wyoming	585 501	49	51	District of Columbia	61	48	51	Alaska	1.3

States and the District of Columbia, Selected Rankings

Percent population change, 2010-2016				Percent Under 18 years old, 2016				Percent 65 years old and over, 2016			
Population rank	Percent change rank	State	Percent change [col 36]	Population rank	Under 18 years old rank	State	Percent under 18 years old [cols 10 + 11]	Population rank	65 years old and over rank	State	Percent 65 years old and over [cols 17 + 18 + 19]
		United States	4.7			United States	22.8			United States	15.3
49	1	District of Columbia	13.2	31	1	Utah	30.2	3	1	Florida	19.8
47	2	North Dakota	12.7	2	2	Texas	26.1	42	2	Maine	19.3
2	3	Texas	10.8	39	3	Idaho	25.9	38	3	West Virginia	18.7
31	4	Utah	10.4	48	4	Alaska	25.3	50	4	Vermont	18.1
21	5	Colorado	10.2	37	5	Nebraska	24.9	44	5	Montana	17.8
3	6	Florida	9.6	46	6	South Dakota	24.7	45	6	Delaware	17.5
34	7	Nevada	8.9	35	7	Kansas	24.6	6	7	Pennsylvania	17.4
14	8	Arizona	8.4	28	8	Oklahoma	24.5	14	8	Arizona	17.0
13	9	Washington	8.4	8	9	Georgia	24.3	40	8	Hawaii	17.0
39	10	Idaho	7.4	32	10	Mississippi	24.1	41	8	New Hampshire	17.0
23	11	South Carolina	7.3	17	11	Indiana	23.8	27	11	Oregon	16.9
27	12	Oregon	6.8	25	11	Louisiana	23.8	23	12	South Carolina	16.7
8	13	Georgia	6.4	51	13	Wyoming	23.7	36	13	New Mexico	16.5
9	14	North Carolina	6.4	33	14	Arkansas	23.6	43	13	Rhode Island	16.5
46	15	South Dakota	6.3	36	14	New Mexico	23.6	30	15	Iowa	16.4
45	16	Delaware	6.0	14	16	Arizona	23.5	33	16	Arkansas	16.3
44	17	Montana	5.4	22	17	Minnesota	23.4	24	17	Alabama	16.2
1	18	California	5.4	30	18	Iowa	23.3	29	17	Connecticut	16.2
12	19	Virginia	5.1	47	18	North Dakota	23.3	10	17	Michigan	16.2
40	20	Hawaii	5.0	1	20	California	23.1	7	17	Ohio	16.2
16	21	Tennessee	4.8	34	20	Nevada	23.1	18	21	Missouri	16.1
28	22	Oklahoma	4.6	21	22	Colorado	22.8	46	21	South Dakota	16.1
48	23	Alaska	4.5	5	22	Illinois	22.8	20	23	Wisconsin	16.0
37	24	Nebraska	4.4	26	22	Kentucky	22.8	15	24	Massachusetts	15.7
19	25	Maryland	4.2	18	25	Missouri	22.7	16	24	Tennessee	15.7
22	26	Minnesota	4.1	9	25	North Carolina	22.7	26	26	Kentucky	15.6
15	27	Massachusetts	4.0	16	27	Tennessee	22.6	9	27	North Carolina	15.5
51	28	Wyoming	3.9	24	28	Alabama	22.5	4	28	New York	15.4
25	29	Louisiana	3.3	7	28	Ohio	22.5	11	29	New Jersey	15.3
30	30	Iowa	2.9	19	30	Maryland	22.4	22	30	Minnesota	15.2
33	31	Arkansas	2.5	12	31	Virginia	22.3	39	31	Idaho	15.1
17	32	Indiana	2.3	13	31	Washington	22.3	32	31	Mississippi	15.1
26	33	Kentucky	2.2	20	31	Wisconsin	22.3	35	33	Kansas	15.0
35	34	Kansas	1.9	11	34	New Jersey	22.2	37	33	Nebraska	15.0
4	35	New York	1.9	10	35	Michigan	22.1	34	33	Nevada	15.0
24	36	Alabama	1.7	23	35	South Carolina	22.1	28	33	Oklahoma	15.0
18	37	Missouri	1.7	44	37	Montana	21.8	51	33	Wyoming	15.0
11	38	New Jersey	1.7	40	38	Hawaii	21.6	17	38	Indiana	14.9
20	39	Wisconsin	1.6	45	39	Delaware	21.5	13	39	Washington	14.8
41	40	New Hampshire	1.4	27	40	Oregon	21.3	5	40	Illinois	14.6
36	41	New Mexico	1.1	4	41	New York	21.2	19	40	Maryland	14.6
32	42	Mississippi	0.7	29	42	Connecticut	21.1	25	42	Louisiana	14.5
7	43	Ohio	0.7	6	43	Pennsylvania	21.0	47	42	North Dakota	14.5
6	44	Pennsylvania	0.6	38	44	West Virginia	20.5	12	42	Virginia	14.5
10	45	Michigan	0.5	3	45	Florida	20.2	1	45	California	13.6
43	46	Rhode Island	0.4	15	45	Massachusetts	20.2	21	46	Colorado	13.4
42	47	Maine	0.2	43	47	Rhode Island	19.7	8	47	Georgia	13.1
29	48	Connecticut	0.1	41	48	New Hampshire	19.5	2	48	Texas	12.0
50	49	Vermont	-0.2	42	49	Maine	19.1	49	49	District of Columbia	11.6
5	50	Illinois	-0.2	50	50	Vermont	19.0	31	50	Utah	10.6
38	51	West Virginia	-1.2	49	51	District of Columbia	17.8	48	51	Alaska	10.5

States and the District of Columbia, Selected Rankings

Percent born in state of residence, 2015				Number of immigrants, 2015				Birth rate, 2015			
Population rank	Born in state of residence rank	State	Percent born in state of residence [col 23]	Population rank	Immigrant rank	State	Number of immigrants [col 24]	Population rank	Birth rate rank	State	Birth rate (per 1,000 population) [col 98]
		United States	58.5			United States	1 051 031			United States	12.4
25	1	Louisiana	78.3	1	1	California	209 568	31	1	Utah	16.9
10	2	Michigan	76.6	4	2	New York	130 010	48	2	Alaska	15.3
7	3	Ohio	75.2	3	3	Florida	118 873	47	3	North Dakota	14.9
6	4	Pennsylvania	72.9	2	4	Texas	99 727	2	4	Texas	14.7
32	5	Mississippi	71.5	11	5	New Jersey	49 801	46	5	South Dakota	14.4
20	6	Wisconsin	71.4	5	6	Illinois	40 482	49	6	District of Columbia	14.2
30	7	Iowa	71.1	15	7	Massachusetts	28 535	37	7	Nebraska	14.1
24	8	Alabama	70.1	12	8	Virginia	27 622	25	8	Louisiana	13.9
38	9	West Virginia	69.7	8	9	Georgia	25 919	39	9	Idaho	13.8
26	10	Kentucky	69.6	6	10	Pennsylvania	24 969	28	10	Oklahoma	13.6
17	11	Indiana	68.4	13	11	Washington	24 765	35	11	Kansas	13.4
22	12	Minnesota	67.7	19	12	Maryland	22 627	51	12	Wyoming	13.2
5	13	Illinois	67.2	9	13	North Carolina	18 495	33	13	Arkansas	13.1
18	14	Missouri	66.1	10	14	Michigan	18 049	8	14	Georgia	12.9
37	15	Nebraska	64.9	14	15	Arizona	17 997	40	14	Hawaii	12.9
46	16	South Dakota	64.9	7	16	Ohio	16 050	32	16	Mississippi	12.8
42	17	Maine	64.1	22	17	Minnesota	14 737	17	17	Indiana	12.7
47	18	North Dakota	63.7	21	18	Colorado	12 661	22	17	Minnesota	12.7
4	19	New York	63.1	29	19	Connecticut	11 102	1	19	California	12.6
31	20	Utah	62.3	34	20	Nevada	11 053	30	19	Iowa	12.6
33	21	Arkansas	61.7	16	21	Tennessee	8 833	26	19	Kentucky	12.6
15	22	Massachusetts	61.6	27	22	Oregon	8 655	34	19	Nevada	12.6
28	23	Oklahoma	60.6	17	23	Indiana	8 554	14	23	Arizona	12.5
16	24	Tennessee	60.1	31	24	Utah	6 883	36	24	New Mexico	12.4
2	25	Texas	59.7	18	25	Missouri	6 731	16	24	Tennessee	12.4
35	26	Kansas	58.6	20	26	Wisconsin	6 655	13	24	Washington	12.4
23	27	South Carolina	57.7	40	27	Hawaii	6 513	24	27	Alabama	12.3
9	28	North Carolina	57.1	26	28	Kentucky	5 647	5	27	Illinois	12.3
43	29	Rhode Island	56.6	35	29	Kansas	5 419	19	27	Maryland	12.3
29	30	Connecticut	55.3	37	30	Nebraska	5 234	18	27	Missouri	12.3
8	31	Georgia	54.8	30	31	Iowa	5 047	12	27	Virginia	12.3
1	32	California	54.8	28	32	Oklahoma	4 880	21	32	Colorado	12.2
44	33	Montana	54.3	25	33	Louisiana	4 696	44	32	Montana	12.2
36	34	New Mexico	53.3	23	34	South Carolina	4 417	4	34	New York	12.0
40	35	Hawaii	53.0	24	35	Alabama	3 928	9	34	North Carolina	12.0
11	36	New Jersey	52.6	36	36	New Mexico	3 626	7	34	Ohio	12.0
50	37	Vermont	49.9	43	37	Rhode Island	3 610	23	37	South Carolina	11.9
12	38	Virginia	49.5	49	38	District of Columbia	2 976	45	38	Delaware	11.8
39	39	Idaho	48.0	33	39	Arkansas	2 814	20	39	Wisconsin	11.6
13	40	Washington	47.3	39	40	Idaho	2 531	11	40	New Jersey	11.5
19	41	Maryland	47.2	45	41	Delaware	2 168	10	41	Michigan	11.4
27	42	Oregon	45.9	41	42	New Hampshire	2 159	27	42	Oregon	11.3
45	43	Delaware	45.6	47	43	North Dakota	1 600	3	43	Florida	11.1
21	44	Colorado	42.7	32	44	Mississippi	1 587	6	44	Pennsylvania	11.0
41	45	New Hampshire	42.1	48	45	Alaska	1 572	38	45	West Virginia	10.7
48	46	Alaska	41.8	42	46	Maine	1 464	15	46	Massachusetts	10.5
51	47	Wyoming	40.7	46	47	South Dakota	1 265	43	47	Rhode Island	10.4
14	48	Arizona	39.2	50	48	Vermont	792	29	48	Connecticut	10.0
3	49	Florida	35.9	38	49	West Virginia	786	42	49	Maine	9.5
49	50	District of Columbia	35.8	51	50	Wyoming	539	50	50	Vermont	9.4
34	51	Nevada	25.8	44	51	Montana	519	41	51	New Hampshire	9.3

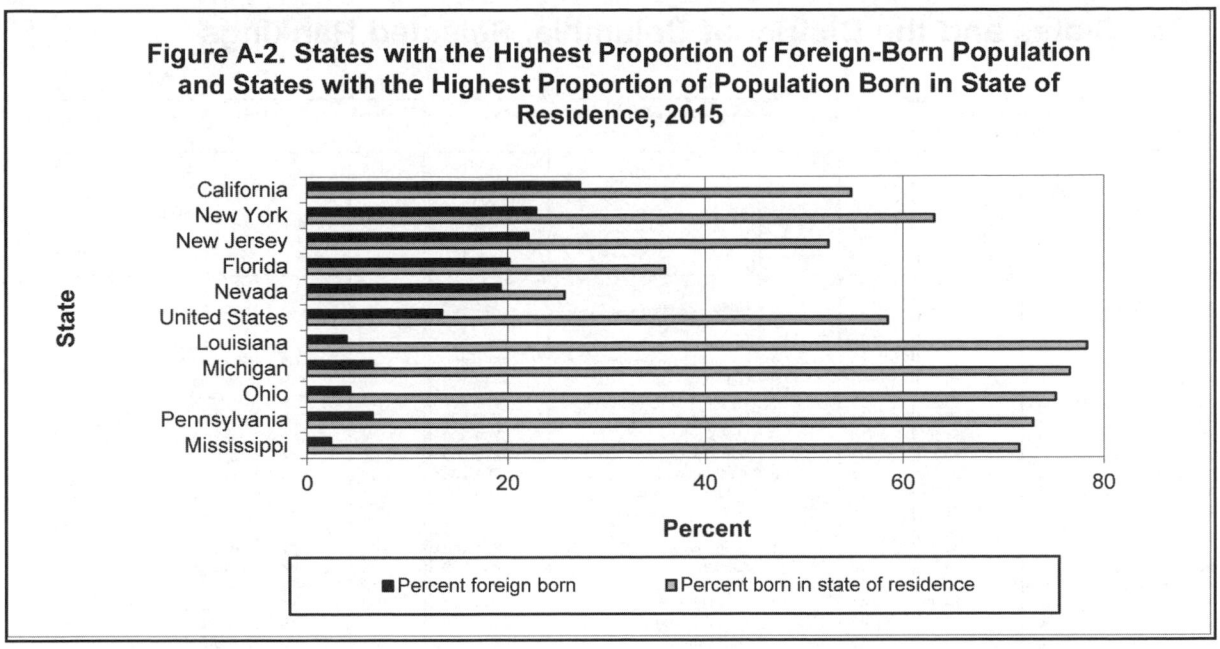

Figure A-2. States with the Highest Proportion of Foreign-Born Population and States with the Highest Proportion of Population Born in State of Residence, 2015

The U.S. median age increased slightly from 37.2 years in 2010 to 37.9 years in 2016, primarily caused by the aging Baby Boomer population. This increase was much less than the jump from 32.1 years to 35.3 years between 1990 and 2000. From 2010 to 2016, the population between 65 and 74 years showed the largest proportional increase, while the proportions between 5 and 17 years and 45 and 54 years showed the largest decreases. There were small increases in the young adult age groups, ages 18 to 34, with the 25 to 34 Millennial group now outnumbering the younger Baby Boomers in the 45 to 54 age group and the peak Baby Boomers in the 55 to 64 age group. The median age by state ranged from 30.8 years in Utah to 44.6 years in Maine. Utah had the highest proportion of young residents; in 2016, 30.2 percent of the state's population was younger than 18 years old. The population age 65 years and over ranged from 10.5 percent in Alaska to 19.8 percent in Florida. Alaska, North Dakota, Wyoming, and South Dakota had the lowest proportions of female residents, and were among just ten states in which men outnumbered women. The District of Columbia had the highest proportion of female residents with 52.5 percent, followed by Maryland, Delaware, and Alabama, all with 51.6 percent.

Natural growth is the difference between the number of births and the number of deaths. Vermont had the fewest births between 2010 and 2016. Maine and West Virginia were the only states to have more deaths than births. A net migration of more than 7,753 people prevented Maine from having a population loss from 2010 to 2016 but West Virginia did experience a population decline. California, the largest state in the nation, had over 1.5 million more births than deaths and 443,210 new residents through net migration. From 2010 to 2016, California gained 826,554 residents from foreign countries and lost 383,344 residents to other states. Texas and Florida each had a net gain of over 1.3 million new residents during this period. In Texas, 63.0 percent of these new residents were from other states; in Florida, over half were from other states. Fifteen states had a net loss of residents due to migration including New York which lost over 846,000 residents to other states but gained nearly 700,000 new residents from other countries.

In eight states, 70 percent or more of the residents were born in that same state. Louisiana ranked highest with 78.3 percent. The ten highest rates were mainly in the Midwest and the South. Fourteen states and the District of Columbia had proportions less than 50 percent. Nevada had the lowest proportion by far, with just 25.8 percent of its residents having been born in the state. Nationally, 58.5 percent of Americans lived in the state of their birth.

The U.S. birth rate in 2015 was 12.4 per 1,000 population, a slight decrease from 2014. Utah had the highest birth rate in the nation, with 16.9 births per 1,000 population. Alaska had the second highest birth rate at 15.3 followed by North Dakota with a birth rate of 14.9. Maine, Vermont, and New Hampshire had the lowest birth rates in the nation, all below 10 births per 1,000 population. Alaska had the lowest crude death rate with 5.6 deaths per 1,000 population followed by Utah at 5.7 deaths. However, both states had relatively young populations (in Utah, 41.5 percent of the population were under 25 years old while 35.4 percent of the population were under 25 in Alaska). Once adjusted for age, Alaska's death rate increased to 7.4, and Utah's to 7.1, just under the U.S. rate of 7.2. West Virginia, Alabama, and Arkansas had the highest crude death rates in the nation. Mississippi had the highest age-adjusted death rate followed by West Virginia, both with a mix of younger and older residents. Florida had, by far, the highest proportion of senior citizens. However, Florida also had a high proportion of younger people, which helped give the state a crude death rate of 9.3 per 1,000 population, ranking it 16th among the states. When Florida's death rate was age-adjusted, it dropped to 6.6, which was well below the national age-adjusted rate of 7.2 and among the lowest ten states. Hawaii had the lowest age-adjusted death rate at 5.9, one of 13 states with rates below 7.0. Alabama, Mississippi, and Oklahoma had the highest infant mortality rates, while California, New Hampshire, and Massachusetts had the lowest infant death rates.

States and the District of Columbia, Selected Rankings

Percent of owners with a mortgage paying 30 percent or more of income for housing expenses, 2015				Median value of owner-occupied housing units, 2015				Median gross rent of renter-occupied housing units, 2015			
Population rank	Percent of income for housing rank	State	Percent of income for housing [col 83]	Population rank	Median value rank	State	Median value (dollars) [col 88]	Population rank	Median rent rank	State	Median rent (dollars) [col 90]
		United States	29.4			United States	$194 500			United States	$959
40	1	Hawaii	39.8	40	1	Hawaii	$566 900	40	1	Hawaii	$1 500
1	2	California	39.3	49	2	District of Columbia	$551 300	49	2	District of Columbia	$1 417
11	3	New Jersey	39.2	1	3	California	$449 100	1	3	California	$1 311
4	4	New York	35.9	15	4	Massachusetts	$352 100	19	4	Maryland	$1 278
3	5	Florida	35.3	11	5	New Jersey	$322 600	11	5	New Jersey	$1 214
50	6	Vermont	34.6	19	6	Maryland	$299 800	4	6	New York	$1 173
29	7	Connecticut	33.2	4	7	New York	$293 500	15	7	Massachusetts	$1 164
15	8	Massachusetts	32.5	13	8	Washington	$284 000	48	8	Alaska	$1 163
27	9	Oregon	31.9	21	9	Colorado	$283 800	12	9	Virginia	$1 144
43	10	Rhode Island	31.8	29	10	Connecticut	$270 900	21	10	Colorado	$1 111
36	11	New Mexico	30.9	27	11	Oregon	$264 100	29	11	Connecticut	$1 108
45	12	Delaware	30.7	48	12	Alaska	$259 600	13	12	Washington	$1 080
32	13	Mississippi	30.1	12	13	Virginia	$257 800	45	13	Delaware	$1 049
34	14	Nevada	29.8	41	14	New Hampshire	$244 500	3	14	Florida	$1 046
14	15	Arizona	29.7	43	15	Rhode Island	$241 000	41	15	New Hampshire	$1 017
42	15	Maine	29.7	45	16	Delaware	$240 200	34	16	Nevada	$980
41	17	New Hampshire	29.6	31	17	Utah	$234 600	27	17	Oregon	$943
13	18	Washington	29.5	50	18	Vermont	$223 700	43	18	Rhode Island	$938
19	19	Maryland	29.4	34	19	Nevada	$221 400	5	19	Illinois	$936
44	19	Montana	29.4	51	20	Wyoming	$212 500	14	20	Arizona	$933
5	21	Illinois	29.1	44	21	Montana	$209 500	2	21	Texas	$932
39	22	Idaho	28.5	22	22	Minnesota	$200 000	31	22	Utah	$925
12	23	Virginia	28.1	14	23	Arizona	$194 300	50	23	Vermont	$923
23	24	South Carolina	28.0	47	24	North Dakota	$180 900	8	24	Georgia	$909
48	25	Alaska	27.9	5	25	Illinois	$180 300	22	25	Minnesota	$888
8	25	Georgia	27.9	42	25	Maine	$180 300	6	26	Pennsylvania	$868
21	27	Colorado	27.6	3	27	Florida	$179 800	9	27	North Carolina	$827
9	28	North Carolina	27.3	39	28	Idaho	$176 300	23	28	South Carolina	$819
6	29	Pennsylvania	27.2	6	29	Pennsylvania	$170 600	51	29	Wyoming	$815
2	30	Texas	26.7	20	30	Wisconsin	$168 300	10	30	Michigan	$803
49	31	District of Columbia	26.6	36	31	New Mexico	$164 100	25	31	Louisiana	$800
16	32	Tennessee	26.3	9	32	North Carolina	$160 100	42	32	Maine	$792
25	33	Louisiana	25.9	8	33	Georgia	$159 300	20	32	Wisconsin	$792
24	34	Alabama	25.0	25	34	Louisiana	$155 600	16	34	Tennessee	$785
10	34	Michigan	25.0	46	35	South Dakota	$152 800	36	35	New Mexico	$783
33	36	Arkansas	24.6	2	36	Texas	$152 000	35	36	Kansas	$782
28	36	Oklahoma	24.6	16	37	Tennessee	$150 600	47	37	North Dakota	$775
20	36	Wisconsin	24.6	23	38	South Carolina	$148 600	39	38	Idaho	$770
31	39	Utah	24.1	18	39	Missouri	$147 800	18	39	Missouri	$763
26	40	Kentucky	23.8	37	40	Nebraska	$141 600	44	39	Montana	$763
7	41	Ohio	23.7	35	41	Kansas	$141 200	28	41	Oklahoma	$759
18	42	Missouri	23.6	10	42	Michigan	$137 500	17	42	Indiana	$758
22	43	Minnesota	23.1	7	43	Ohio	$136 400	37	43	Nebraska	$750
51	44	Wyoming	23.0	30	44	Iowa	$136 100	7	44	Ohio	$746
46	45	South Dakota	21.8	24	45	Alabama	$134 100	24	45	Alabama	$729
35	46	Kansas	21.2	17	46	Indiana	$131 000	32	46	Mississippi	$724
38	47	West Virginia	21.1	26	47	Kentucky	$130 000	30	47	Iowa	$718
17	48	Indiana	21.0	28	48	Oklahoma	$126 800	26	48	Kentucky	$702
37	49	Nebraska	20.4	33	49	Arkansas	$120 700	33	49	Arkansas	$695
30	50	Iowa	19.9	32	50	Mississippi	$112 700	46	50	South Dakota	$675
47	51	North Dakota	16.3	38	51	West Virginia	$112 100	38	50	West Virginia	$675

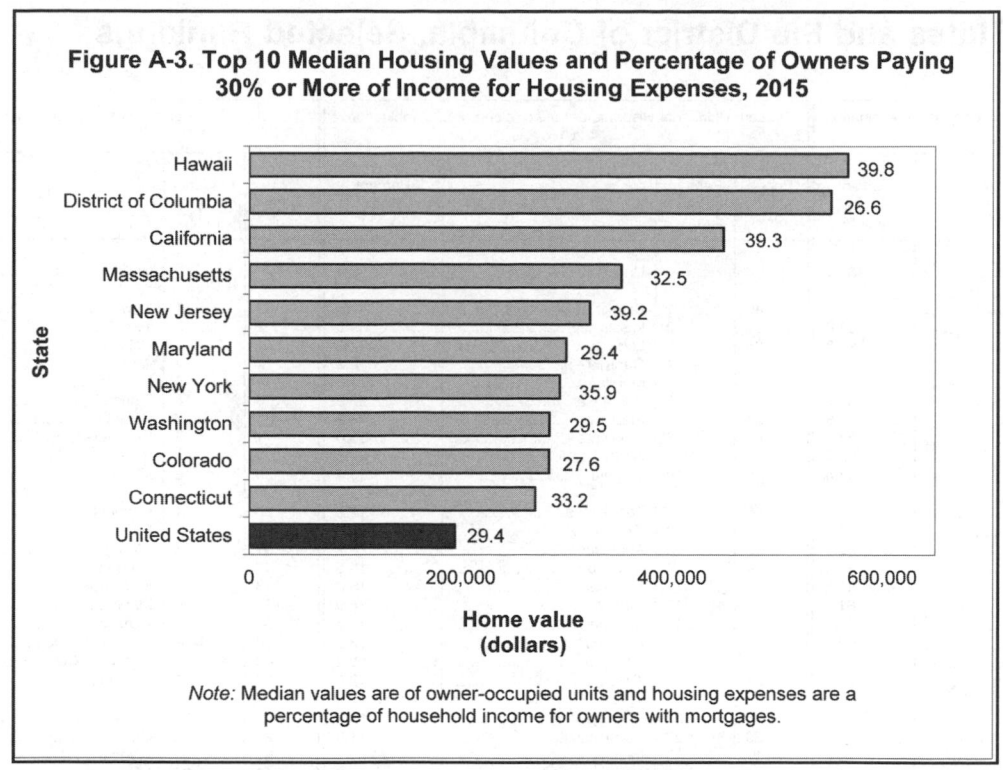

Figure A-3. Top 10 Median Housing Values and Percentage of Owners Paying 30% or More of Income for Housing Expenses, 2015

State	Percentage
Hawaii	39.8
District of Columbia	26.6
California	39.3
Massachusetts	32.5
New Jersey	39.2
Maryland	29.4
New York	35.9
Washington	29.5
Colorado	27.6
Connecticut	33.2
United States	29.4

Home value
(dollars)

Note: Median values are of owner-occupied units and housing expenses are a percentage of household income for owners with mortgages.

In 2015, homeowners with mortgages paid a median of 22.0 percent of their incomes for monthly owner costs (mortgage, insurance, taxes, utilities, fuel, etc.). This ranged from a high of 25.9 percent in California to 18.2 percent in North Dakota. Nationally, 29.4 percent of owners with a mortgage paid 30 percent or more of income for housing expenses in 2015. Hawaii and California had the highest proportion of mortgage holders paying 30 percent or more of their income with 39.8 and 39.3 percent respectively, followed by New Jersey at 39.2 percent, New York at 35.9 percent and Florida at 35.3 percent. In 37 states and the District of Columbia, less than 30 percent of all mortgaged owners paid this high level of owner costs. North Dakota had the lowest proportion in the nation with 16.3 percent. Four states and the District of Columbia had median home values exceeding $300,000 in 2015, led by Hawaii with a median home value of $566,900. Nationally, the median value of owner-occupied housing units was $194,500. Hawaii also had the highest median gross rent, at $1,500. The District of Columbia, Hawaii, California, Maryland, and New Jersey all had median gross monthly rents exceeding $1,200.

Many minority groups had above average growth rates since 2000. Currently, in four states and the District of Columbia, the minority population outnumbers the non-Hispanic White population. Nationally, 63.1 percent of the U.S. population were non-Hispanic White alone or in combination, but the racial and ethnic compositions of the states varied widely. In Hawaii, the state with the highest proportion of minorities, Asian and Pacific Islander alone or in combination was the largest race group, representing 75.1 percent of the state's population. Hispanic or Latino residents made up over 48 percent of New Mexico's population and over 38 percent of residents in both California and Texas. The District of Columbia had the highest proportion of Black residents at just under half the population at 47.5 percent, down from 60.5 percent in 2000. Among the states, Mississippi and Louisiana ranked first and second, with Black populations of 38.0 and 32.9 percent, respectively. Alaska had the highest proportion of American Indians and Alaska Natives, who made up 18.7 percent of the population. Montana, New Mexico, and South Dakota all had high proportions of American Indian populations. As might be expected, the states with the largest number of minorities were among the states with the highest total populations. New York was home to nearly 3.1 million Black residents, and California had the largest number of Hispanics, Asian and Pacific Islanders, and American Indians and Alaska Natives. California had over 390,000 non-Hispanic American Indian and Alaska Native residents, though they made up just 1.0 percent of the state's population. Despite having only about 83,000 Native American residents, South Dakota had the second highest proportion in the nation.

States and the District of Columbia, Selected Rankings

Percent White, not Hispanic or Latino, alone or in combination, 2016				Percent Black, not Hispanic or Latino, alone or in combination, 2016				Percent Hispanic or Latino,[1] 2016			
Population rank	Percent White rank	State	Percent White [col 5]	Population rank	Percent Black rank	State	Percent Black [col 6]	Population rank	Hispanic or Latino rank	State	Percent Hispanic or Latino [col 9]
		United States	63.1			United States	13.4			United States	17.8
42	1	Maine	95.1	49	1	District of Columbia	47.5	36	1	New Mexico	48.5
50	2	Vermont	94.8	32	2	Mississippi	38.0	2	2	Texas	39.1
38	3	West Virginia	93.8	25	3	Louisiana	32.9	1	3	California	38.9
41	4	New Hampshire	92.3	8	4	Georgia	32.2	14	4	Arizona	30.9
44	5	Montana	88.8	19	5	Maryland	31.0	34	5	Nevada	28.5
30	6	Iowa	87.7	23	6	South Carolina	27.9	3	6	Florida	24.9
47	7	North Dakota	86.8	24	7	Alabama	27.2	21	7	Colorado	21.3
26	8	Kentucky	86.6	45	8	Delaware	23.0	11	8	New Jersey	20.0
51	9	Wyoming	85.7	9	9	North Carolina	22.5	4	9	New York	19.0
46	10	South Dakota	84.4	12	10	Virginia	20.4	5	10	Illinois	17.0
39	11	Idaho	84.2	16	11	Tennessee	17.7	29	11	Connecticut	15.7
20	12	Wisconsin	83.2	3	12	Florida	16.4	43	12	Rhode Island	14.9
22	13	Minnesota	82.6	33	13	Arkansas	16.2	31	13	Utah	13.8
18	14	Missouri	81.6	4	14	New York	15.5	27	14	Oregon	12.8
17	15	Indiana	81.3	10	15	Michigan	15.0	13	15	Washington	12.4
7	15	Ohio	81.3	5	16	Illinois	14.9	39	16	Idaho	12.3
37	17	Nebraska	81.2	11	17	New Jersey	13.7	35	17	Kansas	11.6
31	18	Utah	80.7	7	17	Ohio	13.7	15	18	Massachusetts	11.5
27	19	Oregon	79.3	18	19	Missouri	12.6	49	19	District of Columbia	10.9
35	20	Kansas	78.6	2	20	Texas	12.5	37	20	Nebraska	10.7
6	21	Pennsylvania	78.5	6	21	Pennsylvania	11.8	40	21	Hawaii	10.4
10	22	Michigan	77.4	29	22	Connecticut	11.0	28	22	Oklahoma	10.3
16	23	Tennessee	75.8	17	23	Indiana	10.4	51	23	Wyoming	10.0
43	24	Rhode Island	75.1	34	24	Nevada	9.9	19	24	Maryland	9.8
33	25	Arkansas	74.6	26	25	Kentucky	9.1	8	25	Georgia	9.4
15	25	Massachusetts	74.6	28	26	Oklahoma	8.9	45	26	Delaware	9.2
13	27	Washington	73.1	15	27	Massachusetts	7.9	9	26	North Carolina	9.2
28	28	Oklahoma	71.2	22	28	Minnesota	7.1	12	28	Virginia	9.1
21	29	Colorado	70.7	20	28	Wisconsin	7.1	33	29	Arkansas	7.3
29	30	Connecticut	69.2	35	30	Kansas	7.0	48	30	Alaska	7.0
24	31	Alabama	67.2	43	30	Rhode Island	7.0	6	30	Pennsylvania	7.0
48	32	Alaska	67.1	1	32	California	6.5	17	32	Indiana	6.8
23	33	South Carolina	65.3	37	33	Nebraska	5.6	20	33	Wisconsin	6.7
9	34	North Carolina	65.1	14	34	Arizona	5.0	30	34	Iowa	5.8
45	35	Delaware	64.8	13	34	Washington	5.0	23	35	South Carolina	5.5
12	36	Virginia	64.7	21	36	Colorado	4.8	22	36	Minnesota	5.2
5	37	Illinois	63.1	48	37	Alaska	4.7	16	36	Tennessee	5.2
25	38	Louisiana	60.2	30	38	Iowa	4.4	25	38	Louisiana	5.0
32	39	Mississippi	57.8	38	38	West Virginia	4.4	10	38	Michigan	5.0
14	40	Arizona	57.2	47	40	North Dakota	3.4	24	40	Alabama	4.2
4	41	New York	57.1	40	41	Hawaii	3.0	18	41	Missouri	4.1
11	42	New Jersey	57.0	27	42	Oregon	2.6	7	42	Ohio	3.7
3	43	Florida	56.3	46	43	South Dakota	2.5	46	42	South Dakota	3.7
8	44	Georgia	54.9	36	44	New Mexico	2.3	44	44	Montana	3.6
19	45	Maryland	53.5	42	45	Maine	1.9	47	44	North Dakota	3.6
34	46	Nevada	52.7	41	46	New Hampshire	1.8	26	46	Kentucky	3.5
2	47	Texas	43.9	50	46	Vermont	1.8	41	46	New Hampshire	3.5
1	48	California	40.1	31	48	Utah	1.6	32	48	Mississippi	3.1
36	49	New Mexico	39.4	51	48	Wyoming	1.6	50	49	Vermont	1.9
49	50	District of Columbia	38.1	39	50	Idaho	1.1	42	50	Maine	1.6
40	51	Hawaii	36.3	44	51	Montana	1.0	38	51	West Virginia	1.5

1. May be of any race.

States and the District of Columbia, Selected Rankings

Percent high school graduates or more,[1] 2015

Population rank	Percent high school graduates rank	State	Percent high school graduates [col 115]
		United States	87.1
44	1	Montana	93.5
41	2	New Hampshire	93.1
22	3	Minnesota	92.8
48	4	Alaska	92.6
47	5	North Dakota	92.5
51	6	Wyoming	92.2
30	7	Iowa	91.7
42	7	Maine	91.7
50	7	Vermont	91.7
31	10	Utah	91.5
20	11	Wisconsin	91.4
21	12	Colorado	91.2
46	13	South Dakota	91.1
37	14	Nebraska	91.0
40	15	Hawaii	90.9
13	16	Washington	90.8
35	17	Kansas	90.3
29	18	Connecticut	90.2
15	18	Massachusetts	90.2
10	20	Michigan	90.1
39	21	Idaho	90.0
27	21	Oregon	90.0
49	23	District of Columbia	89.8
7	24	Ohio	89.7
6	24	Pennsylvania	89.7
19	26	Maryland	89.6
11	27	New Jersey	89.1
45	28	Delaware	88.9
18	28	Missouri	88.9
12	28	Virginia	88.9
5	31	Illinois	88.6
17	32	Indiana	88.2
43	33	Rhode Island	87.7
3	34	Florida	87.6
28	35	Oklahoma	87.3
9	36	North Carolina	86.6
23	37	South Carolina	86.3
14	38	Arizona	86.1
8	38	Georgia	86.1
16	38	Tennessee	86.1
4	41	New York	86.0
38	41	West Virginia	86.0
34	43	Nevada	85.6
33	44	Arkansas	85.4
26	45	Kentucky	85.1
24	46	Alabama	84.9
25	47	Louisiana	84.6
36	47	New Mexico	84.6
32	49	Mississippi	83.5
2	50	Texas	82.4
1	51	California	82.2

Percent college graduates (bachelor's degree or more),[1] 2015

Population rank	Percent college graduates rank	State	Percent college graduates [col 116]
		United States	30.6
49	1	District of Columbia	56.7
15	2	Massachusetts	41.5
21	3	Colorado	39.2
19	4	Maryland	38.8
29	5	Connecticut	38.3
11	6	New Jersey	37.6
12	7	Virginia	37.0
50	8	Vermont	36.9
41	9	New Hampshire	35.7
4	10	New York	35.0
22	11	Minnesota	34.7
13	12	Washington	34.2
5	13	Illinois	32.9
43	14	Rhode Island	32.7
1	15	California	32.3
27	16	Oregon	32.2
31	17	Utah	31.8
35	18	Kansas	31.7
40	19	Hawaii	31.4
45	20	Delaware	30.9
44	21	Montana	30.6
37	22	Nebraska	30.2
42	23	Maine	30.1
8	24	Georgia	29.9
48	25	Alaska	29.7
6	25	Pennsylvania	29.7
9	27	North Carolina	29.4
47	28	North Dakota	29.1
3	29	Florida	28.4
2	29	Texas	28.4
20	29	Wisconsin	28.4
10	32	Michigan	27.8
18	32	Missouri	27.8
14	34	Arizona	27.7
46	35	South Dakota	27.5
30	36	Iowa	26.8
7	36	Ohio	26.8
23	36	South Carolina	26.8
36	39	New Mexico	26.5
51	40	Wyoming	26.2
39	41	Idaho	26.0
16	42	Tennessee	25.7
17	43	Indiana	24.9
28	44	Oklahoma	24.6
24	45	Alabama	24.2
34	46	Nevada	23.6
26	47	Kentucky	23.3
25	48	Louisiana	23.2
33	49	Arkansas	21.8
32	50	Mississippi	20.8
38	51	West Virginia	19.6

Median household income, 2015

Population rank	Median income rank	State	Median income (dollars) [col 123]
		United States	$55 775
19	1	Maryland	$75 847
49	2	District of Columbia	$75 628
40	3	Hawaii	$73 486
48	4	Alaska	$73 355
11	5	New Jersey	$72 222
29	6	Connecticut	$71 346
15	7	Massachusetts	$70 628
41	8	New Hampshire	$70 303
12	9	Virginia	$66 262
1	10	California	$64 500
13	11	Washington	$64 129
21	12	Colorado	$63 909
22	13	Minnesota	$63 488
31	14	Utah	$62 912
45	15	Delaware	$61 255
4	16	New York	$60 850
47	17	North Dakota	$60 557
51	18	Wyoming	$60 214
5	19	Illinois	$59 588
43	20	Rhode Island	$58 073
50	21	Vermont	$56 990
6	22	Pennsylvania	$55 702
2	23	Texas	$55 653
20	24	Wisconsin	$55 638
37	25	Nebraska	$54 996
30	26	Iowa	$54 736
27	27	Oregon	$54 148
35	28	Kansas	$53 906
46	29	South Dakota	$53 017
34	30	Nevada	$52 431
42	31	Maine	$51 494
14	32	Arizona	$51 492
8	33	Georgia	$51 244
10	34	Michigan	$51 084
7	35	Ohio	$51 075
17	36	Indiana	$50 532
18	37	Missouri	$50 238
44	38	Montana	$49 509
3	39	Florida	$49 426
28	40	Oklahoma	$48 568
39	41	Idaho	$48 275
9	42	North Carolina	$47 830
16	43	Tennessee	$47 275
23	44	South Carolina	$47 238
25	45	Louisiana	$45 727
36	46	New Mexico	$45 382
26	47	Kentucky	$45 215
24	48	Alabama	$44 765
38	49	West Virginia	$42 019
33	50	Arkansas	$41 995
32	51	Mississippi	$40 593

1. Population 25 years and older.

States and the District of Columbia, Selected Rankings

Unemployment rate, 2016				Per capita state taxes, 2014				Exports of goods by state of origin, 2016			
Popu-lation rank	Unem-ployment rate rank	State	Unem-ployment rate [col 171]	Popu-lation rank	State taxes rank	State	State taxes per capita (dollars) [col 337]	Popu-lation rank	Exports rank	State	Exports (milions of dollars) [col 119]
		United States	4.9			United States	X			United States	1 454 624
36	1	New Mexico	6.7	47	1	North Dakota	8 277	2	1	Texas	232 588
48	2	Alaska	6.6	50	2	Vermont	4 728	1	2	California	163 616
25	3	Louisiana	6.1	48	3	Alaska	4 605	13	3	Washington	79 564
24	4	Alabama	6.0	29	4	Connecticut	4 431	4	4	New York	74 406
49	4	District of Columbia	6.0	40	5	Hawaii	4 250	5	5	Illinois	59 808
38	4	West Virginia	6.0	22	6	Minnesota	4 238	10	6	Michigan	54 451
5	7	Illinois	5.9	4	7	New York	3 898	3	7	Florida	52 033
32	8	Mississippi	5.8	51	8	Wyoming	3 875	7	8	Ohio	49 145
34	9	Nevada	5.7	15	9	Massachusetts	3 741	25	9	Louisiana	48 822
1	10	California	5.4	1	10	California	3 558	6	10	Pennsylvania	36 570
8	10	Georgia	5.4	45	11	Delaware	3 395	8	11	Georgia	35 723
6	10	Pennsylvania	5.4	11	12	New Jersey	3 321	17	12	Indiana	34 672
13	10	Washington	5.4	19	13	Maryland	3 167	16	13	Tennessee	31 466
14	14	Arizona	5.3	5	14	Illinois	3 042	23	14	South Carolina	31 270
43	14	Rhode Island	5.3	33	15	Arkansas	3 013	11	15	New Jersey	31 246
51	14	Wyoming	5.3	38	16	West Virginia	2 908	9	16	North Carolina	29 939
29	17	Connecticut	5.1	42	17	Maine	2 892	26	17	Kentucky	29 242
9	17	North Carolina	5.1	20	18	Wisconsin	2 850	15	18	Massachusetts	25 810
26	19	Kentucky	5.0	43	19	Rhode Island	2 811	14	19	Arizona	22 030
11	19	New Jersey	5.0	36	20	New Mexico	2 761	27	20	Oregon	21 953
3	21	Florida	4.9	13	21	Washington	2 754	20	21	Wisconsin	21 009
10	21	Michigan	4.9	6	22	Pennsylvania	2 674	24	22	Alabama	20 554
7	21	Ohio	4.9	30	23	Iowa	2 662	22	23	Minnesota	19 210
28	21	Oklahoma	4.9	44	24	Montana	2 594	12	24	Virginia	16 442
27	21	Oregon	4.9	37	25	Nebraska	2 592	29	25	Connecticut	14 403
4	26	New York	4.8	17	26	Indiana	2 554	18	26	Missouri	13 952
23	26	South Carolina	4.8	32	27	Mississippi	2 530	30	27	Iowa	12 129
16	26	Tennessee	4.8	35	28	Kansas	2 526	31	28	Utah	12 074
2	29	Texas	4.6	34	29	Nevada	2 516	32	29	Mississippi	10 513
18	30	Missouri	4.5	26	30	Kentucky	2 516	35	30	Kansas	10 168
45	31	Delaware	4.4	10	31	Michigan	2 503	34	31	Nevada	9 773
17	31	Indiana	4.4	27	32	Oregon	2 439	19	32	Maryland	9 314
19	33	Maryland	4.3	9	33	North Carolina	2 353	21	33	Colorado	7 551
35	34	Kansas	4.2	28	34	Oklahoma	2 347	37	34	Nebraska	6 370
44	35	Montana	4.1	7	35	Ohio	2 330	33	35	Arkansas	5 706
20	35	Wisconsin	4.1	12	36	Virginia	2 276	38	36	West Virginia	5 047
33	37	Arkansas	4.0	39	37	Idaho	2 246	28	37	Oklahoma	5 004
12	37	Virginia	4.0	21	38	Colorado	2 195	39	38	Idaho	4 876
42	39	Maine	3.9	31	39	Utah	2 145	45	39	Delaware	4 443
22	39	Minnesota	3.9	25	40	Louisiana	2 085	48	40	Alaska	4 371
39	41	Idaho	3.8	2	41	Texas	2 050	47	41	North Dakota	4 180
30	42	Iowa	3.7	14	42	Arizona	1 944	41	42	New Hampshire	4 143
15	42	Massachusetts	3.7	24	43	Alabama	1 916	36	43	New Mexico	3 629
31	44	Utah	3.4	46	44	South Dakota	1 885	50	44	Vermont	2 990
21	45	Colorado	3.3	18	45	Missouri	1 854	42	45	Maine	2 860
50	45	Vermont	3.3	23	46	South Carolina	1 848	43	46	Rhode Island	2 269
37	47	Nebraska	3.2	8	47	Georgia	1 845	44	47	Montana	1 342
47	47	North Dakota	3.2	16	48	Tennessee	1 803	49	48	District of Columbia	1 331
40	49	Hawaii	3.0	3	49	Florida	1 779	40	49	Hawaii	1 239
41	50	New Hampshire	2.8	41	50	New Hampshire	1 720	46	50	South Dakota	1 210
46	50	South Dakota	2.8	49	X	District of Columbia	X	51	51	Wyoming	1 104

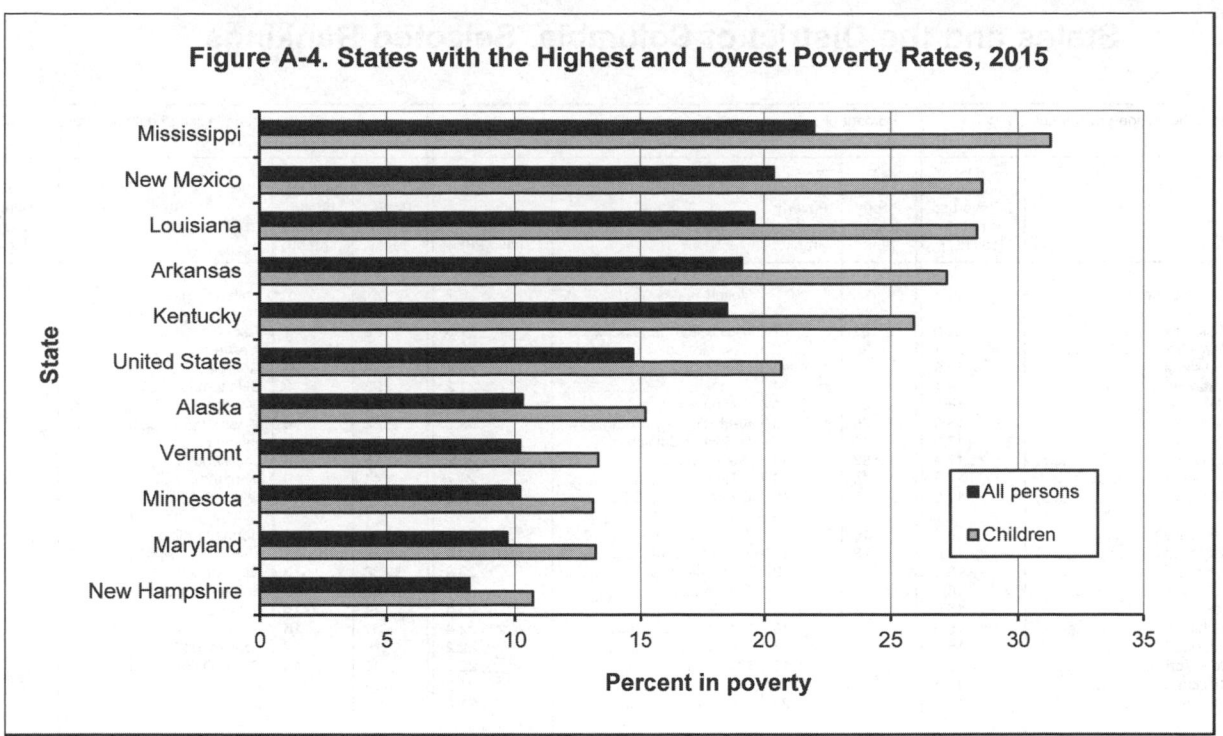

Figure A-4. States with the Highest and Lowest Poverty Rates, 2015

Nationally, 87.1 percent of the population 25 years old and over had graduated from high school. Twenty-three states had high school attainment levels of 90 percent or more, led by Montana with 93.5. percent. States in the Midwest and the West tended to have above average high school attainment rates although California had the lowest rate at 82.2 percent, followed by Texas at at 82.4 percent. States with above average high school attainment levels do not necessarily have high proportions of college graduates. Nationally, 30.6 percent of the population held bachelor's degrees. In the District of Columbia, 56.7 percent of the population had graduated from college. Even when compared with other large cities, the District of Columbia had among the 10 highest proportions of college graduates in the nation. Of the 50 states, Massachusetts, Colorado, Maryland, Connecticut, New Jersey, Virginia, New Hampshire, New York, and Vermont each had 35 percent or more of their populations holding bachelor's degrees or more. States in the Northeast tended to have above average college attainment levels, while states in the South had below average rates.

Median household income ranged from $40,593 in Mississippi to $75,847 in Maryland. Nationally, the median household income was $55,775. In two states—Mississippi and West Virginia, 30 percent or more of households had incomes below $25,000. The District of Columbia and Maryland had the highest proportions of households earning $100,000 or more, at 39.3 percent and 37.1 percent respectively, followed by New Jersey at 36.6 percent.

The poverty threshold for an individual was $12,082 in 2015. Mississippi had the highest poverty rate in the nation, with 22.0 percent of its population living in poverty. Arkansas, Louisiana, and New Mexico all had poverty rates of 19 percent or higher. The poverty threshold for a four-person family was $24,257. Among children under 18 years old, 20.7 percent were living in poverty. Over 30 percent of children in Mississippi lived in poverty. New Hampshire had the lowest proportion of children in poverty, at 10.7 percent. The District of Columbia had the highest proportion of residents 65 years and over living in poverty 15.2 percent followed by Louisiana at 12.8 percent.

The United States labor force increased by 1.3 percent between 2015 and 2016. From 2000 to 2008, it grew about an average of 1 percent a year but then declined from 2009 to 2011 followed by small increases in recent years. Ten states experienced a decline in their labor forces between 2015 and 2016. Louisiana experienced the largest decline, dropping 1.8 percent. Meanwhile, the labor forces in Utah and Oregon each grew by more than 3 percent in the same period. In 2016, the unemployment rate was 4.9 percent, down from 5.3 percent in 2015. Five states and the District of Columbia had an unemployment rate at 6.0 percent or higher. New Mexico had the highest unemployment rate in the nation at 6.7 percent followed by Alaska and Louisiana at 6.6 and 6.1 percent respectively. New Hampshire and South Dakota had the lowest unemployment rates in 2016, at 2.8 percent—the only states with unemployment rates below 3.0 percent.

States and the District of Columbia, Selected Rankings

Percent of persons below the poverty level, 2015				Percent of children under 18 years old below the poverty level, 2015				Percent of persons lacking health insurance, 2015			
Population rank	Poverty rate rank	State	Poverty rate [col 127]	Population rank	Poverty rate rank	State	Poverty rate [col 128]	Population rank	Percent lacking health insurance rank	State	Percent lacking health insurance [col 104]
		United States	14.7			United States	20.7			United States	9.4
32	1	Mississippi	22.0	32	1	Mississippi	31.3	2	1	Texas	17.1
36	2	New Mexico	20.4	36	2	New Mexico	28.6	48	2	Alaska	14.9
25	3	Louisiana	19.6	25	3	Louisiana	28.4	8	3	Georgia	13.9
33	4	Arkansas	19.1	33	4	Arkansas	27.2	28	3	Oklahoma	13.9
24	5	Alabama	18.5	24	5	Alabama	26.6	3	5	Florida	13.3
26	5	Kentucky	18.5	26	6	Kentucky	25.9	32	6	Mississippi	12.7
38	7	West Virginia	17.9	49	7	District of Columbia	25.6	34	7	Nevada	12.3
14	8	Arizona	17.4	38	8	West Virginia	25.2	25	8	Louisiana	11.9
49	9	District of Columbia	17.3	14	9	Arizona	24.7	44	9	Montana	11.6
8	10	Georgia	17.0	8	10	Georgia	24.5	51	10	Wyoming	11.5
16	11	Tennessee	16.7	16	11	Tennessee	24.2	9	11	North Carolina	11.2
23	12	South Carolina	16.6	23	12	South Carolina	24.0	39	12	Idaho	11.0
9	13	North Carolina	16.4	9	13	North Carolina	23.5	36	13	New Mexico	10.9
28	14	Oklahoma	16.1	3	14	Florida	23.1	23	13	South Carolina	10.9
2	15	Texas	15.9	2	15	Texas	23.0	14	15	Arizona	10.8
10	16	Michigan	15.8	10	16	Michigan	22.4	31	16	Utah	10.5
3	17	Florida	15.7	28	17	Oklahoma	22.2	16	17	Tennessee	10.3
4	18	New York	15.4	4	18	New York	22.0	46	18	South Dakota	10.2
27	18	Oregon	15.4	7	19	Ohio	21.3	24	19	Alabama	10.1
1	20	California	15.3	1	20	California	21.2	18	20	Missouri	9.8
39	21	Idaho	15.1	17	21	Indiana	20.9	17	21	Indiana	9.6
18	22	Missouri	14.8	34	21	Nevada	20.9	33	22	Arkansas	9.5
7	22	Ohio	14.8	27	23	Oregon	20.3	35	23	Kansas	9.1
34	24	Nevada	14.7	18	24	Missouri	20.2	12	23	Virginia	9.1
44	25	Montana	14.6	45	25	Delaware	19.4	11	25	New Jersey	8.7
17	26	Indiana	14.5	44	25	Montana	19.4	1	26	California	8.6
43	27	Rhode Island	13.9	6	25	Pennsylvania	19.4	42	27	Maine	8.4
46	28	South Dakota	13.7	43	25	Rhode Island	19.4	37	28	Nebraska	8.2
5	29	Illinois	13.6	5	29	Illinois	19.1	21	29	Colorado	8.1
42	30	Maine	13.4	46	30	South Dakota	18.1	47	30	North Dakota	7.8
6	31	Pennsylvania	13.2	39	31	Idaho	17.8	5	31	Illinois	7.1
35	32	Kansas	13.0	42	32	Maine	17.4	4	31	New York	7.1
37	33	Nebraska	12.6	35	33	Kansas	17.2	27	33	Oregon	7.0
45	34	Delaware	12.4	37	34	Nebraska	16.8	19	34	Maryland	6.6
30	35	Iowa	12.2	20	35	Wisconsin	16.4	13	34	Washington	6.6
13	35	Washington	12.2	11	36	New Jersey	15.6	7	36	Ohio	6.5
20	37	Wisconsin	12.1	13	37	Washington	15.5	6	37	Pennsylvania	6.4
21	38	Colorado	11.5	48	38	Alaska	15.2	41	38	New Hampshire	6.3
15	38	Massachusetts	11.5	30	39	Iowa	14.8	10	39	Michigan	6.1
31	40	Utah	11.3	15	39	Massachusetts	14.8	29	40	Connecticut	6.0
12	41	Virginia	11.2	12	39	Virginia	14.8	26	40	Kentucky	6.0
51	42	Wyoming	11.1	21	42	Colorado	14.7	38	40	West Virginia	6.0
47	43	North Dakota	11.0	29	43	Connecticut	14.5	45	43	Delaware	5.9
11	44	New Jersey	10.8	40	44	Hawaii	14.2	43	44	Rhode Island	5.7
40	45	Hawaii	10.6	50	45	Vermont	13.3	20	44	Wisconsin	5.7
29	46	Connecticut	10.5	19	46	Maryland	13.2	30	46	Iowa	5.0
48	47	Alaska	10.3	51	46	Wyoming	13.2	22	47	Minnesota	4.5
22	48	Minnesota	10.2	22	48	Minnesota	13.1	40	48	Hawaii	4.0
50	48	Vermont	10.2	31	49	Utah	12.9	49	49	District of Columbia	3.8
19	50	Maryland	9.7	47	50	North Dakota	12.1	50	49	Vermont	3.8
41	51	New Hampshire	8.2	41	51	New Hampshire	10.7	15	51	Massachusetts	2.8

States and the District of Columbia, Selected Rankings

	State government employment, 2015				Value of agricultural products sold, 2012				Violent crime rate, 2015		
Popu-lation rank	State government employment rank	State	State government employment [col 312]	Popu-lation rank	Agricultural sales rank	State	Value of sales (millions of dollars) [col 197]	Popu-lation rank	Violent crime rate rank	State	Violent crime rate (per 100,000 population) [col 108]
		United States	4 341 978			United States	394 644			United States	372.6
1	1	California	404 069	1	1	California	42 627	49	1	District of Columbia	1 269.1
2	2	Texas	304 337	30	2	Iowa	30 822	48	2	Alaska	730.2
4	3	New York	242 861	2	3	Texas	25 376	34	3	Nevada	695.9
3	4	Florida	178 754	37	4	Nebraska	23 069	36	4	New Mexico	656.1
6	5	Pennsylvania	163 446	22	5	Minnesota	21 280	16	5	Tennessee	612.1
10	6	Michigan	141 957	35	6	Kansas	18 461	25	6	Louisiana	539.7
11	7	New Jersey	140 977	5	7	Illinois	17 187	33	7	Arkansas	521.3
9	8	North Carolina	140 242	9	8	North Carolina	12 588	23	8	South Carolina	504.5
7	9	Ohio	138 032	20	9	Wisconsin	11 744	45	9	Delaware	499.0
8	10	Georgia	127 892	17	10	Indiana	11 211	18	10	Missouri	497.4
12	11	Virginia	127 181	47	11	North Dakota	10 951	24	11	Alabama	472.4
5	12	Illinois	123 953	46	12	South Dakota	10 170	3	12	Florida	461.9
13	13	Washington	122 216	7	13	Ohio	10 064	19	13	Maryland	457.2
15	14	Massachusetts	101 856	33	14	Arkansas	9 776	1	14	California	426.3
24	15	Alabama	89 469	8	15	Georgia	9 255	28	15	Oklahoma	422.0
17	16	Indiana	88 251	18	16	Missouri	9 165	10	16	Michigan	415.5
19	17	Maryland	87 591	13	17	Washington	9 121	2	17	Texas	412.2
18	18	Missouri	87 578	10	18	Michigan	8 678	14	18	Arizona	410.2
26	19	Kentucky	85 734	39	19	Idaho	7 801	15	19	Massachusetts	390.9
22	20	Minnesota	82 277	21	20	Colorado	7 781	35	20	Kansas	389.9
21	21	Colorado	80 650	3	21	Florida	7 702	17	21	Indiana	387.5
23	22	South Carolina	80 171	6	22	Pennsylvania	7 401	5	22	Illinois	383.8
14	23	Arizona	78 789	28	23	Oklahoma	7 130	46	23	South Dakota	383.1
16	24	Tennessee	78 383	32	24	Mississippi	6 441	4	24	New York	379.7
20	25	Wisconsin	74 383	24	25	Alabama	5 571	8	25	Georgia	378.3
25	26	Louisiana	74 118	4	26	New York	5 415	44	26	Montana	349.6
28	27	Oklahoma	68 922	26	27	Kentucky	5 067	9	27	North Carolina	347.0
27	28	Oregon	66 775	27	28	Oregon	4 884	38	28	West Virginia	337.9
29	29	Connecticut	63 528	44	29	Montana	4 230	21	29	Colorado	321.0
33	30	Arkansas	63 297	25	30	Louisiana	3 809	6	30	Pennsylvania	315.1
40	31	Hawaii	58 478	12	31	Virginia	3 753	20	31	Wisconsin	305.8
32	32	Mississippi	56 711	14	32	Arizona	3 732	40	32	Hawaii	293.4
31	33	Utah	55 355	16	33	Tennessee	3 611	7	33	Ohio	291.9
30	34	Iowa	50 303	23	34	South Carolina	3 040	30	34	Iowa	286.1
35	35	Kansas	50 155	36	35	New Mexico	2 550	13	35	Washington	284.4
36	36	New Mexico	45 909	19	36	Maryland	2 271	32	36	Mississippi	275.8
38	37	West Virginia	40 131	31	37	Utah	1 816	37	37	Nebraska	274.9
37	38	Nebraska	32 122	51	38	Wyoming	1 689	27	38	Oregon	259.8
34	39	Nevada	28 377	45	39	Delaware	1 274	11	39	New Jersey	255.4
48	40	Alaska	26 201	11	40	New Jersey	1 007	22	40	Minnesota	242.6
45	41	Delaware	26 144	38	41	West Virginia	807	43	41	Rhode Island	242.5
39	42	Idaho	23 430	50	42	Vermont	776	47	42	North Dakota	239.4
42	43	Maine	21 005	34	43	Nevada	764	31	43	Utah	236.0
44	44	Montana	20 877	42	44	Maine	763	51	44	Wyoming	222.1
47	45	North Dakota	19 339	40	45	Hawaii	661	26	45	Kentucky	218.7
41	46	New Hampshire	18 905	29	46	Connecticut	551	29	46	Connecticut	218.5
43	47	Rhode Island	18 370	15	47	Massachusetts	492	39	47	Idaho	215.6
50	48	Vermont	14 564	41	48	New Hampshire	191	41	48	New Hampshire	199.3
46	49	South Dakota	14 475	43	49	Rhode Island	60	12	49	Virginia	195.6
51	50	Wyoming	13 438	48	50	Alaska	59	42	50	Maine	130.1
49	X	District of Columbia	X	49	X	District of Columbia	X	50	51	Vermont	118.0

Table A. States — **Land Area and Population Characteristics**

State code	STATE	Land area,[1] 2016 (sq mi)	Total persons, 2016	Rank	Per square mile	Race alone or in combination, not Hispanic or Latino (percent)				Hispanic or Latino[2] (percent)	Age (percent)					
						White	Black	American Indian, Alaska Native	Asian and Pacific Islander		Under 5 years	5 to 17 years	18 to 24 years	25 to 34 years	35 to 44 years	45 to 54 years
		1	2	3	4	5	6	7	8	9	10	11	12	13	14	15

1. Dry land or land partially or temporarily covered by water. 2. May be of any race.

Table A. States — **Population Characteristics, Immigration, and Households**

STATE	Population characteristics, 2016 (cont.)									Households, 2015					
	Age (percent) (cont.)												Household type		
	55 to 64 years	65 to 74 years	75 to 84 years	85 years and over	Median age	Percent female 2015	Percent foreign born 2015	Percent born in state of residence 2015	Immigrants admitted to legal status, 2015	Number	Percent change, 2014–2015	Persons per house-hold	Married couple family	Female house-holder family[1]	House-holder living alone
	16	17	18	19	20	21	22	23	24	25	26	27	28	29	30

1. No spouse present.

Table A. States — **Population Change**

STATE	Population, 1990–2010			Population change, 1990–2016								Population, 2020–2030		
	Census counts			Percent change			Components of change, 2010–2016					Projections		
										Migration				
	1990	2000	2010	1990–2000	2000–2010	2010–2016	Births	Deaths	Net migration	Inter-national	Net internal	2020	2025	2030
	31	32	33	34	35	36	37	38	39	40	41	42	43	44

Table A. States — **Population Characteristics**

STATE	Population characteristics, 2010																		
	Race (percent)							Age (percent)											
	White alone	Black alone	American Indian, Alaska Native alone	Asian and Pacific Islander alone	Some other race or two or more races	Percent Hispanic or Latino[1]	Percent foreign born	Under 5 years	5 to 17 years	18 to 24 years	25 to 34 years	35 to 44 years	45 to 54 years	55 to 64 years	65 to 74 years	75 to 84 years	85 years and over	Median age	Percent female
	45	46	47	48	49	50	51	52	53	54	55	56	57	58	59	60	61	62	63

1. May be of any race.

Table A. States — **Households and Housing Units**

STATE	Households, 2010					Housing units, 2010									
				Percent				Occupied units							
									Owner-occupied				Renter-occupied		
										Median owner cost					
	Number	Percent change, 2000–2010	Persons per household	Female family householder[1]	One person households	Total	Percent change, 2000–2010	Total	Percent	Median value[2] (dollars)	With a mortgage	Without a mortgage[3]	Median gross rent[4] (dollars)	Median rent as a percent of income	Sub-standard units[5] (percent)
	64	65	66	67	68	69	70	71	72	73	74	75	76	77	78

1. No spouse present.   2. Specified owner-occupied units.   3. Median monthly costs is often in the minimum category—10.0 percent or less, which is indicated as 10.0 percent.
4. Specified renter-occupied units.   5. Overcrowded or lacking complete plumbing facilities.

Table A. States — **Housing Units**

STATE	Housing units, 2015													
			Occupied units											
					Percent who pay 30 percent or more of income for housing expenses[1]		Median owner cost as a percent of income							
	Total	Percent change, 2014–2015	Total	Percent owner-occupied	Owners with a mortgage	Renter	With a mortgage	Without a mortgage[2]	Median monthly housing costs (dollars)	Median value of units[3] (dollars)	Percent valued over $500,000	Median gross rent[4] (dollars)	Sub-standard units[5] (percent)	Percent living in a different house than 1 year ago
	79	80	81	82	83	84	85	86	87	88	89	90	91	92

1. Excludes units where owner costs or gross rent as a percentage of households income cannot be calculated.   2. Median monthly costs is often in the minimum category—10.0 percent or less, which is indicated as 10.0 percent.   3. Specified owner-occupied units.   4. Specified renter-occupied units.   5. Overcrowded or lacking complete plumbing facilities.

Table A. States — **Residential Construction, Vital Statistics, and Health**

STATE	Value of residential construction authorized by building permits, 2016				Births, 2015		Deaths, 2014					Percent lacking health insurance, 2015		
								Number		Rate				
										Total				
	New construction ($1,000)	Number of housing units	Percent single family	Average sales price of new manufactured housing units put in place, 2015	Total	Rate[1]	Total	Infant[2]	Crude[1]	Age-adjusted[1]	Infant[3]	All persons	Children under 18 years	Medicare beneficiaries 65 years and older, 2015
	93	94	95	96	97	98	99	100	101	102	103	104	105	106

1. Per 1,000 resident population.   2. Deaths of infants under 1 year old.   3. Deaths of infants under 1 year old per 1,000 live births.

Table A. States — **Crime and Education**

STATE	Serious crime known to police,[1] 2015				Public elementary and secondary school enrollment, 2014–2015		Educational attainment[3] (percent)				Local government expenditures for education, 2013–2014	
	Violent Crime		Property Crime				2010		2015			
	Number	Rate[2]	Number	Rate[2]	Total	Student/ teacher ratio	High school graduate or more	Bachelor's degree or more	High school graduate or more	Bachelor's degree or more	Total current expenditures (mil dol)	Current expenditures per student (dollars)
	107	108	109	110	111	112	113	114	115	116	117	118

1. Data for serious crimes have not been adjusted for underreporting; this may affect comparability between geographic areas and over time.   2. Per 100,000 population estimated by the FBI.   3. Persons 25 years old and over.

Table A. States — **Exports, Income, and Poverty**

STATE	Exports of goods by state of origin, 2016 (mil dol)			Income, 2015					Percent below poverty level, 2015							
					Households									Families with related children under 18		
	Total	Manu-factured	Non-manu-factured	Per capita income (dollars)	Median income (dollars)	Percent with income of $25,000 or less	Percent with income of $100,000 or more	Median income of family of four	All persons	Children under 18 years	Persons 65 years and over	All families	Married-couple families	Male house-holder[1] families	Female house-holder[1] families
	119	120	121	122	123	124	125	126	127	128	129	130	131	132	133

1. No spouse present.

Table A. States — **Personal Income**

STATE	Personal income, 2015												
			Per capita[1]		Sources of personal income (mil dol)								
									Transfer payments				
										Government payments to individuals			
	Total (mil dol)	Percent change, 2014–2015	Dollars	Rank	Wages and salaries[2]	Proprietors' income	Dividends, interest, and rent	Total	Total	Social Security	Medical payments	Income main-tenance	Unemploy-ment insurance
	134	135	136	137	138	139	140	141	142	143	144	145	146

1. Based on the resident population estimated as of July 1 of the year shown.   2. Includes supplements to wages and salaries.

Table A. States — **Personal Income and Earnings**

STATE	Personal tax payments, 2015 (mil dol)	Disposable personal income, 2015		Earnings, 2015										Gross state product, 2015 (mil dol)
						Percent by selected industries								
						Goods-related[2]		Service-related and other[3]						
		Total (mil dol)	Per capita[1] (dollars)	Total (mil dol)	Farm	Total	Manu-facturing	Total	Retail trade	Finance, insurance, real estate, rental and leasing	Health care and social assist-ance	Government	
	147	148	149	150	151	152	153	154	155	156	157	158	159

1. Based on the resident population estimated as of July 1 of the year shown.   2. Total includes mining, construction, and manufacturing.   3. Includes private sector earnings in forestry, fishing, related activities, and other; utilities; wholesale trade; transportation and warehousing; and information.

Table A. States — **Social Security, Employment, and Labor Force**

STATE	Social Security beneficiaries, December 2015			Civilian employment and selected occupations,[2] 2015					Civilian labor force (annual average), 2016				
					Percent							Unemployed	
	Number	Rate[1]	Supple-mental Security Income recipients, December 2015	Total	Management, business, science and art occupations	Services, sales, and office occupations	Construction and production occupations		Total (1,000)	Percent change, 2015–2016	Employed (1,000)	Total (1,000)	Rate[3]
	160	161	162	163	164	165	166		167	168	169	170	171

1. Per 1,000 resident population estimated as of July 1 of the year shown.   2. Persons 16 years old and over.   3. Percent of civilian labor force.

Table A. States — Nonfarm Employment and Earnings

STATE	Private nonfarm employment and earnings, 2016											
	Employed		Manufacturing			Employment (1,000)						
				Average earnings of production workers								
	Total (1,000)	Percent change, 2015–2016	Employment (1,000)	Hourly	Weekly	Construction	Transportation and public utilities	Wholesale trade	Retail trade	Information	Financial activities	Services[1]
	172	173	174	175	176	177	178	179	180	181	182	183

1. Includes professional and business services, educational and health services, leisure and hospitality, and other services.

Table A. States — Agriculture

STATE	Agriculture, 2012											
	Farms					Land in farms					Value of land and buildings (dollars)	
		Percent with:						Acres				
	Number	Fewer than 50 acres	500 acres or more	Farm operators whose principal occupation is farming (percent)	Government payments, average per farm (dollars)	Acreage (1,000)	Percent change, 2007–2012	Average size of farm	Total irrigated (1,000)	Total cropland (1,000)	Average per farm	Average per acre
	184	185	186	187	188	189	190	191	192	193	194	195

Table A. States — Agriculture, Land, and Water

STATE	Agriculture, 2012 (cont.)							Land, 2012			
	Value of machinery and equipment, average per farm (dollars)	Value of products sold				Percent of farms with sales of:					Water consumption, 2010 (mil gal per day)
				Percent from:							
		Total (mil dol)	Average per farm (dollars)	Crops	Livestock and poultry products	$10,000 or more	$100,000 or more	Cropland (percent)	Owned by the federal government (percent)	Developed (percent)	
	196	197	198	199	200	201	202	203	204	205	206

Table A. States — Manufactures and Construction

STATE	Manufactures, 2015										Construction, 2012			
	All employees			Production workers				Value added by manufacture (mil dol)	Value of shipments (mil dol)	Total cost of materials (mil dol)	Number of establishments	Employees		
						Wages								
	Number (1,000)	Percent change, 2014–2015	Annual payroll (mil dol)	Number (1,000)	Work hours (millions)	Total (mil dol)	Average per worker (dollars)					Number	Percent change, 2007–2012	Value (mil dol)	Annual payroll (mil dol)
	207	208	209	210	211	212	213	214	215	216	217	218	219	220	221

Table A. States — **Wholesale Trade and Retail Trade**

STATE	Wholesale trade, 2012					Retail trade,[1] 2012								
		Employees					Employees							
	Number of estab-lishments	Number	Percent change, 2007–2012	Sales (mil dol)	Annual payroll (mil dol)	Number of estab-lishments	Total	Percent change, 2007–2012	Motor vehicle and parts dealers	Food and beverage stores	Clothing and clothing accessory stores	General merchan-dise stores	Sales (mil dol)	Annual payroll (mil dol)
	222	223	224	225	226	227	228	229	230	231	232	233	234	235

1. Establishments with payroll.

Table A. States — **Information**

STATE	Information, 2012										
		Employees									
	Number of establishments	Number	Percent change, 2007–2012	Publishing, except Internet	Motion picture and sound recording	Broadcasting, except Internet	Internet publishing and broad-casting and web search portals	Telecom-munications	Data processing, hosting, and related services	Receipts (mil dol)	Annual payroll (mil dol)
	236	237	238	239	240	241	242	243	244	245	246

Table A. States — **Utilities, Transportation and Warehousing, and Finance and Insurance**

STATE	Utilities, 2012					Transportation and warehousing, 2012					Finance and insurance, 2012				
		Employees					Employees					Employees			
	Number of estab-lishments	Number	Percent change, 2007–2012	Receipts (mil dol)	Annual payroll (mil dol)	Number of estab-lishments	Number	Percent change, 2007–2012	Receipts (mil dol)	Annual payroll (mil dol)	Number of estab-lishments	Number	Percent change, 2007–2012	Receipts (mil dol)	Annual payroll (mil dol)
	247	248	249	250	251	252	253	254	255	256	257	258	259	260	261

Table A. States — **Real Estate and Rental and Leasing and Professional, Scientific, and Technical Services**

STATE	Real estate and rental and leasing, 2012					Professional, scientific, and technical services, 2012								
		Employees					Employees							
	Number of estab-lishments	Number	Percent change, 2007–2012	Receipts (mil dol)	Annual payroll (mil dol)	Number of estab-lishments	Total	Percent change, 2007–2012	Legal services	Accounting tax preparation, book-keeping, and payroll services	Architectural, engineering, and related services	Computer systems design and related services	Receipts (mil dol)	Annual payroll (mil dol)
	262	263	264	265	266	267	268	269	270	271	272	273	274	275

Table A. States — **Health Care and Social Assistance**

STATE	Health care and social assistance, 2012													
	Subject to federal tax							Tax-exempt					
		Employees							Employees				
	Number of estab-lishments	Total	Percent change, 2007–2012	Ambulatory health care services	Hospitals	Receipts (mil dol)	Annual payroll (mil dol)	Number of estab-lishments	Total	Percent change, 2007–2012	Ambulatory health care services	Hospitals	Receipts (mil dol)	Annual payroll (mil dol)
	276	277	278	279	280	281	282	283	284	285	286	287	288	289

Table A. States — **Arts, Entertainment, and Recreation and Accommodation and Food Services**

STATE	Arts, entertainment, and recreation, 2012					Accommodation and food services, 2012				
		Employees					Employees			
	Number of establishments	Number	Percent change, 2007–2012	Receipts (mil dol)	Annual payroll (mil dol)	Number of establishments	Total	Percent change, 2007–2012	Food services and drinking places	Receipts (mil dol)	Annual payroll (mil dol)
	290	291	292	293	294	295	296	297	298	299	300

Table A. States — **Other Services, Except Public Administration, and Government Employment**

STATE	Other services, except public administration, 2012								Government employment, 2015		
		Employees									
	Number of establishments	Total	Percent change, 2007–2012	Repair and maintenance	Personal and laundry services	Religious, civic, and similar services	Receipts (mil dol)	Annual payroll (mil dol)	Federal civilian	Federal military	State and local
	301	302	303	304	305	306	307	308	309	310	311

Table A. States — **State Government Employment and Payroll**

STATE	State government employment and payroll, 2015											
	State government employment, 2015			State government payroll, 2015		Full-time equivalent payroll (1,000 dollars)						
							Percent of total for:					
	Full-time equivalent employees	Full-time employees	Part-time employees	Full-time March payroll (1,000 dollars)	Part-time March payroll (1,000 dollars)	Total March payroll (1,000 dollars)[1]	Administration	Judicial and legal	Police	Corrections	Highways and transportation	Public Welfare
	312	313	314	315	316	317	318	319	320	321	322	323

1. Includes program categories not shown separately.

Table A. States — **State Government Employment and Payroll and State Government Finances**

	State government employment and payroll, 2015 (cont.)							State government finances, 2014							
	Full-time equivalent payroll (1,000 dollars) (cont.)							General revenue (mil dol)							
	Percent of total for:								From federal government		From own sources				
												Taxes		Taxes per capita[1] (dollars)	
STATE	Health	Hospitals	Social Insurance administration	Natural resources and parks	Utilities, sewerage, and waste management	Elementary and secondary education and libraries	Higher education	Total	Total	Per capita (dollars)	Total	Total	Sales and gross receipts	Total	Sales and gross receipts
	324	325	326	327	328	329	330	331	332	333	334	335	336	337	338

1. Based on resident population estimated as of July 1 of the year shown.

Table A. States — **State Government Finances and Voting**

	State government finances, 2014 (cont.)										Voting and registration, November 2016		Presidential election, 2016 (percent of vote cast)		
	General expenditures (mil dol)									Debt outstanding					
		Direct general expenditures			By selected function										
STATE	Total	To local governments	Total	Per capita[1] (dollars)	Education	Health and hospitals	Highways	Public safety	Public welfare	Natural resources, parks, and recreation	Total (mil dol)	Per capita[1]	Percent registered	Percent voted	Democratic	Republican	All other
	339	340	341	342	343	344	345	346	347	348	349	350	351	352	353	354	355

1. Based on resident population estimated as of July 1 of the year shown.

Table A. States — **Land Area and Population Characteristics**

State code	STATE	Land area,[1] 2016 (sq mi)	Total persons, 2016	Rank	Per square mile	White	Black	American Indian, Alaska Native	Asian and Pacific Islander	Hispanic or Latino[2] (percent)	Under 5 years	5 to 17 years	18 to 24 years	25 to 34 years	35 to 44 years	45 to 54 years
		1	2	3	4	5	6	7	8	9	10	11	12	13	14	15
0	United States	3 532 068.7	323 127 513	X	91.5	63.1	13.4	1.3	6.7	17.8	6.2	16.6	9.5	13.8	12.5	13.2
1	Alabama..............................	50 646.4	4 863 300	24	96.0	67.2	27.2	1.2	1.8	4.2	6.0	16.5	9.5	13.1	12.2	13.2
2	Alaska.................................	570 638.3	741 894	48	1.3	67.1	4.7	18.7	9.7	7.0	7.3	18.0	10.1	16.2	12.4	12.7
4	Arizona...............................	113 590.7	6 931 071	14	61.0	57.2	5.0	4.6	4.3	30.9	6.3	17.2	9.7	13.5	12.2	12.2
5	Arkansas............................	52 035.6	2 988 248	33	57.4	74.6	16.2	1.6	2.2	7.3	6.4	17.2	9.4	13.1	12.2	12.7
6	California............................	155 792.7	39 250 017	1	251.9	40.1	6.5	1.0	16.5	38.9	6.3	16.8	9.8	15.1	13.1	13.2
8	Colorado............................	103 641.2	5 540 545	21	53.5	70.7	4.8	1.3	4.3	21.3	6.1	16.7	9.6	15.2	13.4	13.0
9	Connecticut	4 842.7	3 576 452	29	738.5	69.2	11.0	0.6	5.3	15.7	5.2	15.9	9.8	12.4	11.8	14.7
10	Delaware............................	1 948.7	952 065	45	488.6	64.8	23.0	0.9	4.6	9.2	5.8	15.7	9.0	13.4	11.5	13.4
11	District of Columbia............	61.1	681 170	49	11 140.2	38.1	47.5	0.8	5.1	10.9	6.4	11.4	11.8	22.8	14.5	11.4
12	Florida................................	53 638.9	20 612 439	3	384.3	56.3	16.4	0.6	3.5	24.9	5.5	14.7	8.4	13.0	12.0	13.4
13	Georgia...............................	57 594.8	10 310 371	8	179.0	54.9	32.2	0.7	4.7	9.4	6.4	17.9	9.8	13.8	13.2	13.7
15	Hawaii.................................	6 422.5	1 428 557	40	222.4	36.3	3.0	1.7	75.1	10.4	6.4	15.2	9.0	14.6	12.4	12.5
16	Idaho	82 642.4	1 683 140	39	20.4	84.2	1.1	1.9	2.5	12.3	6.8	19.1	9.3	13.2	12.2	11.8
17	Illinois	55 517.1	12 801 539	5	230.6	63.1	14.9	0.5	6.1	17.0	6.0	16.8	9.5	13.9	12.9	13.4
18	Indiana................................	35 826.6	6 633 053	17	185.1	81.3	10.4	0.7	2.7	6.8	6.4	17.4	10.0	13.0	12.3	13.1
19	Iowa....................................	55 856.5	3 134 693	30	56.1	87.7	4.4	0.7	3.0	5.8	6.4	16.9	10.3	12.6	11.7	12.4
20	Kansas	81 758.4	2 907 289	35	35.6	78.6	7.0	1.8	3.6	11.6	6.7	17.9	10.2	13.2	11.9	12.2
21	Kentucky.............................	39 485.2	4 436 974	26	112.4	86.6	9.1	0.7	1.9	3.5	6.2	16.6	9.5	13.0	12.5	13.5
22	Louisiana............................	43 206.7	4 681 666	25	108.4	60.2	32.9	1.1	2.2	5.0	6.6	17.2	9.5	14.6	12.3	12.6
23	Maine..................................	30 843.9	1 331 479	42	43.2	95.1	1.9	1.4	1.7	1.6	4.9	14.2	8.3	11.8	11.3	14.3
24	Maryland.............................	9 709.6	6 016 447	19	619.6	53.5	31.0	0.8	7.5	9.8	6.1	16.3	9.1	13.9	12.7	14.2
25	Massachusetts	7 801.0	6 811 779	15	873.2	74.6	7.9	0.6	7.4	11.5	5.3	14.9	10.3	14.0	12.1	14.1
26	Michigan.............................	56 546.7	9 928 300	10	175.6	77.4	15.0	1.3	3.7	5.0	5.8	16.3	9.8	12.6	11.7	13.6
27	Minnesota...........................	79 626.7	5 519 952	22	69.3	82.6	7.1	1.7	5.6	5.2	6.4	17.0	9.2	13.6	12.3	13.2
28	Mississippi..........................	46 923.0	2 988 726	32	63.7	57.8	38.0	0.8	1.4	3.1	6.3	17.8	9.9	13.2	12.2	12.7
29	Missouri..............................	68 746.5	6 093 000	18	88.6	81.6	12.6	1.1	2.6	4.1	6.1	16.6	9.5	13.3	12.0	13.0
30	Montana..............................	145 547.0	1 042 520	44	7.2	88.8	1.0	7.7	1.5	3.6	6.0	15.8	9.5	12.8	11.5	12.1
31	Nebraska............................	76 823.8	1 907 116	37	24.8	81.2	5.6	1.4	3.0	10.7	7.0	17.9	10.1	13.3	12.1	12.0
32	Nevada...............................	109 780.2	2 940 058	34	26.8	52.7	9.9	1.5	11.1	28.5	6.3	16.8	8.5	14.6	13.2	13.4
33	New Hampshire...................	8 952.7	1 334 795	41	149.1	92.3	1.8	0.7	3.2	3.5	4.8	14.7	9.6	12.0	11.4	15.1
34	New Jersey.........................	7 355.5	8 944 469	11	1 216.0	57.0	13.7	0.5	10.4	20.0	5.8	16.4	8.8	13.0	12.8	14.5
35	New Mexico.........................	121 301.5	2 081 015	36	17.2	39.4	2.3	9.3	2.1	48.5	6.2	17.4	9.6	13.5	11.7	12.1
36	New York.............................	47 124.9	19 745 289	4	419.0	57.1	15.5	0.7	9.5	19.0	5.9	15.3	9.6	14.6	12.5	13.7
37	North Carolina....................	48 618.5	10 146 788	9	208.7	65.1	22.5	1.7	3.4	9.2	6.0	16.7	9.5	13.2	12.7	13.7
38	North Dakota.......................	69 001.0	757 952	47	11.0	86.8	3.4	6.1	2.1	3.6	7.3	16.0	12.0	15.0	11.4	11.3
39	Ohio....................................	40 862.4	11 614 373	7	284.2	81.3	13.7	0.7	2.7	3.7	6.0	16.5	9.3	13.0	11.9	13.3
40	Oklahoma...........................	68 596.4	3 923 561	28	57.2	71.2	8.9	12.4	3.0	10.3	6.8	17.7	9.8	13.9	12.2	12.1
41	Oregon	95 986.6	4 093 465	27	42.6	79.3	2.6	2.4	6.3	12.8	5.8	15.5	8.9	14.0	13.0	12.6
42	Pennsylvania......................	44 742.4	12 784 227	6	285.7	78.5	11.8	0.5	3.9	7.0	5.6	15.4	9.3	13.1	11.6	13.6
44	Rhode Island......................	1 033.9	1 056 426	43	1 021.7	75.1	7.0	1.1	4.2	14.9	5.2	14.5	10.8	13.5	11.6	13.9
45	South Carolina....................	30 062.6	4 961 119	23	165.0	65.3	27.9	0.8	2.1	5.5	5.9	16.2	9.4	13.2	12.1	13.1
46	South Dakota	75 810.5	865 454	46	11.4	84.4	2.5	9.6	1.9	3.7	7.1	17.6	9.8	13.0	11.4	11.8
47	Tennessee..........................	41 234.8	6 651 194	16	161.3	75.8	17.7	0.8	2.3	5.2	6.1	16.5	9.3	13.4	12.5	13.4
48	Texas..................................	261 249.7	27 862 596	2	106.7	43.9	12.5	0.7	5.4	39.1	7.2	18.9	9.9	14.7	13.4	12.6
49	Utah....................................	82 195.6	3 051 217	31	37.1	80.7	1.6	1.5	4.7	13.8	8.3	21.9	11.3	14.7	13.5	10.3
50	Vermont..............................	9 217.6	624 594	50	67.8	94.8	1.8	1.1	2.3	1.9	4.9	14.1	10.8	11.6	11.1	13.8
51	Virginia...............................	39 481.8	8 411 808	12	213.1	64.7	20.4	0.8	7.8	9.1	6.1	16.2	9.7	13.9	12.9	13.8
53	Washington	66 453.4	7 288 000	13	109.7	73.1	5.0	2.5	11.3	12.4	6.2	16.1	9.1	14.8	12.9	13.0
54	West Virginia.......................	24 040.9	1 831 102	38	76.2	93.8	4.4	0.7	1.2	1.5	5.5	15.0	8.8	12.0	12.2	13.3
55	Wisconsin...........................	54 159.9	5 778 708	20	106.7	83.2	7.1	1.4	3.3	6.7	5.8	16.5	9.7	12.6	11.9	13.5
56	Wyoming	97 091.2	585 501	51	6.0	85.7	1.6	2.9	1.6	10.0	6.5	17.2	9.4	14.0	12.2	11.8

1. Dry land or land partially or temporarily covered by water.   2. May be of any race.

Table A. States — Population Characteristics, Immigration, and Households

| STATE | Population characteristics, 2016 (cont.) | | | | | | | | | Households, 2015 | | | | | |
| | Age (percent) (cont.) | | | | Median age | Percent female 2015 | Percent foreign born 2015 | Percent born in state of residence 2015 | Immigrants admitted to legal status, 2015 | Number | Percent change, 2014–2015 | Persons per household | Household type | | |
	55 to 64 years	65 to 74 years	75 to 84 years	85 years and over									Married couple family	Female householder family[1]	Householder living alone
	16	17	18	19	20	21	22	23	24	25	26	27	28	29	30
United States	12.8	8.9	4.4	2.0	37.9	50.8	13.5	58.5	1 051 031	118 208 250	0.8	2.65	48.0	12.8	27.9
Alabama	13.3	9.6	4.8	1.8	38.9	51.6	3.5	70.1	3 928	1 846 390	0.3	2.57	46.8	14.7	29.9
Alaska	12.8	7.1	2.5	0.9	33.9	47.7	7.9	41.8	1 572	250 185	0.2	2.84	48.1	11.3	26.7
Arizona	12.0	9.9	5.1	2.0	37.6	50.3	13.4	39.2	17 997	2 463 008	1.4	2.71	46.8	12.5	27.6
Arkansas	12.7	9.5	4.9	1.9	38.0	50.9	4.8	61.7	2 814	1 144 663	1.2	2.53	49.0	13.1	28.4
California	11.9	7.9	3.9	1.8	36.4	50.3	27.3	54.8	209 568	12 896 357	1.1	2.97	49.2	13.3	24.0
Colorado	12.6	8.3	3.6	1.5	36.6	49.7	9.8	42.7	12 661	2 074 735	1.7	2.57	50.0	9.7	27.2
Connecticut	14.1	9.1	4.6	2.5	40.7	51.2	14.5	55.3	11 102	1 343 703	-0.9	2.59	48.2	12.7	28.5
Delaware	13.7	10.5	5.0	2.0	40.2	51.6	9.3	45.6	2 168	352 595	0.8	2.61	48.3	13.8	26.6
District of Columbia	10.3	6.7	3.2	1.7	33.9	52.5	14.1	35.8	2 976	281 787	1.6	2.24	25.5	15.1	42.0
Florida	13.2	11.0	6.1	2.7	42.1	51.1	20.2	35.9	118 873	7 463 184	1.8	2.66	46.2	13.4	28.9
Georgia	12.0	8.1	3.7	1.3	36.5	51.3	10.0	54.9	25 919	3 656 407	1.9	2.72	47.9	15.0	26.9
Hawaii	12.9	9.7	4.6	2.7	38.6	49.8	17.7	53.0	6 513	445 936	-1.1	3.11	52.1	11.7	23.4
Idaho	12.4	9.1	4.3	1.7	36.2	49.9	5.7	48.0	2 531	597 421	1.0	2.72	53.7	9.4	27.2
Illinois	12.9	8.4	4.2	2.0	37.8	50.9	14.2	67.2	40 482	4 794 523	0.5	2.62	47.7	12.5	29.4
Indiana	13.0	8.7	4.3	1.9	37.6	50.7	4.9	68.4	8 554	2 515 143	0.5	2.56	48.3	12.0	29.1
Iowa	13.3	9.0	4.9	2.5	38.0	50.3	4.8	71.1	5 047	1 247 249	0.5	2.42	50.4	9.2	29.1
Kansas	12.8	8.4	4.4	2.2	36.5	50.2	7.1	58.6	5 419	1 111 582	0.2	2.55	50.4	9.9	29.5
Kentucky	13.3	9.3	4.5	1.8	38.7	50.7	3.6	69.6	5 647	1 716 168	0.2	2.50	48.3	12.7	28.5
Louisiana	12.9	8.6	4.2	1.7	36.6	51.1	4.0	78.3	4 696	1 737 908	1.1	2.61	43.0	15.9	30.7
Maine	15.8	11.4	5.5	2.4	44.6	51.0	3.4	64.1	1 464	545 226	-0.8	2.37	48.5	9.8	29.6
Maryland	13.2	8.6	4.1	1.9	38.5	51.6	15.2	47.2	22 627	2 177 934	0.6	2.69	47.9	14.0	27.0
Massachusetts	13.5	9.0	4.4	2.3	39.4	51.5	16.1	61.6	28 535	2 559 951	0.4	2.56	46.4	12.5	28.8
Michigan	14.0	9.5	4.6	2.1	39.7	50.8	6.6	76.6	18 049	3 858 532	0.6	2.51	47.2	12.3	29.5
Minnesota	13.4	8.6	4.4	2.2	37.9	50.2	8.3	67.7	14 737	2 147 262	0.8	2.49	50.8	9.2	28.4
Mississippi	12.7	8.9	4.5	1.7	37.1	51.5	2.4	71.5	1 587	1 104 371	0.8	2.62	43.9	18.2	28.4
Missouri	13.4	9.2	4.8	2.1	38.4	50.9	4.0	66.1	6 731	2 374 180	0.8	2.49	47.9	11.8	29.7
Montana	14.6	10.6	5.0	2.2	39.8	49.7	2.1	54.3	519	414 804	0.9	2.42	48.9	8.4	31.5
Nebraska	12.6	8.4	4.4	2.2	36.3	50.2	6.8	64.9	5 234	744 159	0.5	2.48	49.6	9.5	30.0
Nevada	12.3	9.4	4.2	1.4	37.8	49.9	19.3	25.8	11 053	1 042 065	2.0	2.74	43.8	13.4	28.7
New Hampshire	15.4	10.2	4.6	2.2	43.0	50.5	6.0	42.1	2 159	517 615	-0.4	2.49	52.0	10.0	26.2
New Jersey	13.4	8.7	4.4	2.2	39.7	51.2	22.1	52.6	49 801	3 187 963	-0.2	2.75	51.2	13.1	25.9
New Mexico	13.1	9.8	4.8	1.9	37.6	50.5	9.4	53.3	3 626	761 797	0.1	2.68	44.9	13.1	30.6
New York	13.0	8.7	4.5	2.2	38.5	51.4	22.9	63.1	130 010	7 233 694	-0.7	2.66	43.6	14.5	30.1
North Carolina	12.8	9.3	4.4	1.8	38.7	51.4	7.9	57.1	18 495	3 843 745	1.4	2.55	47.6	13.2	28.8
North Dakota	12.5	7.8	4.3	2.4	34.8	48.7	3.8	63.7	1 600	313 475	2.6	2.33	47.9	7.8	30.4
Ohio	13.8	9.3	4.7	2.2	39.3	51.0	4.3	75.2	16 050	4 606 655	0.3	2.45	46.1	12.8	30.3
Oklahoma	12.4	8.7	4.5	1.8	36.4	50.5	6.0	60.6	4 880	1 465 951	0.4	2.59	48.7	12.2	28.0
Oregon	13.4	10.2	4.6	2.1	39.3	50.5	9.9	45.9	8 655	1 553 205	1.2	2.54	48.3	10.3	27.9
Pennsylvania	14.1	9.7	5.1	2.6	40.7	51.0	6.5	72.9	24 969	4 956 037	0.2	2.50	47.8	12.3	29.2
Rhode Island	13.9	9.2	4.6	2.7	40.0	51.4	13.5	56.6	3 610	407 484	-0.5	2.49	42.9	14.0	31.8
South Carolina	13.3	10.3	4.7	1.7	39.2	51.5	4.8	57.7	4 417	1 857 768	1.7	2.56	46.7	14.6	28.9
South Dakota	13.4	9.0	4.6	2.5	37.0	49.6	3.2	64.9	1 265	339 437	1.5	2.43	50.2	9.5	29.6
Tennessee	13.0	9.4	4.6	1.7	38.7	51.2	5.0	60.1	8 833	2 530 260	0.8	2.55	47.9	13.6	28.0
Texas	11.2	7.2	3.4	1.4	34.5	50.4	17.0	59.7	99 727	9 421 412	1.6	2.85	50.0	14.0	25.3
Utah	9.5	6.3	3.1	1.2	30.8	49.7	8.2	62.3	6 883	930 980	1.4	3.17	60.7	9.5	19.8
Vermont	15.5	10.8	5.0	2.3	42.7	50.6	4.5	49.9	792	254 865	-0.9	2.36	48.5	7.9	30.3
Virginia	12.8	8.7	4.1	1.7	38.1	50.8	12.2	49.5	27 622	3 106 895	0.7	2.62	49.9	11.9	27.1
Washington	13.0	9.0	4.0	1.8	37.7	50.0	13.7	47.3	24 765	2 728 573	1.8	2.58	50.0	10.0	27.0
West Virginia	14.5	11.1	5.5	2.1	42.2	50.5	1.6	69.7	786	734 536	-0.1	2.44	47.8	11.5	30.3
Wisconsin	14.0	9.2	4.6	2.2	39.3	50.3	4.8	71.4	6 655	2 319 538	0.5	2.42	49.0	9.8	29.1
Wyoming	13.9	9.1	4.1	1.8	37.1	48.9	3.8	40.7	539	228 937	-1.6	2.50	51.2	7.2	29.9

1. No spouse present.

Table A. States — **Population Change**

STATE	Population, 1990–2010			Population change, 1990–2016								Population, 2020–2030		
	Census counts			Percent change			Components of change, 2010–2016					Projections		
									Migration					
	1990	2000	2010	1990–2000	2000–2010	2010–2016	Births	Deaths	Net migration	International	Net internal	2020	2025	2030
	31	32	33	34	35	36	37	38	39	40	41	42	43	44
United States	248 709 873	281 421 906	308 745 538	13.2	9.7	4.7	24 762 895	16 235 690	5 842 203	5 842 203	(X)	335 804 546	349 439 199	363 584 435
Alabama	4 040 587	4 447 100	4 779 736	10.1	7.5	1.7	367 421	312 625	27 555	29 630	-2 075	4 728 915	4 800 092	4 874 243
Alaska	550 043	626 932	710 231	14.0	13.3	4.5	71 088	25 713	-13 454	13 791	-27 245	774 421	820 881	867 674
Arizona	3 665 228	5 130 632	6 392 017	40.0	24.6	8.4	539 307	320 404	305 233	81 853	223 380	8 456 448	9 531 537	10 712 397
Arkansas	2 350 725	2 673 400	2 915 918	13.7	9.1	2.5	238 842	187 626	21 775	19 238	2 537	3 060 219	3 151 005	3 240 208
California	29 760 021	33 871 648	37 253 956	13.8	10.0	5.4	3 135 219	1 563 968	443 210	826 554	-383 344	42 206 743	44 305 177	46 444 861
Colorado	3 294 394	4 301 261	5 029 196	30.6	16.9	10.2	411 768	213 620	306 202	62 531	243 671	5 278 867	5 522 803	5 792 357
Connecticut	3 287 116	3 405 565	3 574 097	3.6	4.9	0.1	228 277	185 383	-34 774	100 910	-135 684	3 675 650	3 691 016	3 688 630
Delaware	666 168	783 600	897 934	17.6	14.6	6.0	68 977	51 096	35 621	15 135	20 486	963 209	990 694	1 012 658
District of Columbia	606 900	572 059	601 723	-5.7	5.2	13.2	58 893	30 473	50 470	23 794	26 676	480 540	455 108	433 414
Florida	12 937 926	15 982 378	18 801 310	23.5	17.6	9.6	1 353 262	1 150 096	1 562 390	695 906	866 484	23 406 525	25 912 458	28 685 769
Georgia	6 478 216	8 186 453	9 687 653	26.4	18.3	6.4	817 366	468 825	263 358	144 659	118 699	10 843 753	11 438 622	12 017 838
Hawaii	1 108 229	1 211 537	1 360 301	9.3	12.3	5.0	117 502	68 045	20 050	48 549	-28 499	1 412 373	1 438 720	1 466 046
Idaho	1 006 749	1 293 953	1 567 582	28.5	21.1	7.4	142 224	76 045	47 053	9 986	37 067	1 741 333	1 852 627	1 969 624
Illinois	11 430 602	12 419 293	12 830 632	8.6	3.3	-0.2	992 140	649 058	-361 646	178 520	-540 166	13 236 720	13 340 507	13 432 892
Indiana	5 544 159	6 080 485	6 483 802	9.7	6.6	2.3	521 319	372 748	4 511	63 671	-59 160	6 627 008	6 721 322	6 810 108
Iowa	2 776 755	2 926 324	3 046 355	5.4	4.1	2.9	243 461	178 416	24 643	35 326	-10 683	3 020 496	2 993 222	2 955 172
Kansas	2 477 574	2 688 418	2 853 118	8.5	6.1	1.9	246 116	157 380	-34 632	35 867	-70 499	2 890 566	2 919 002	2 940 084
Kentucky	3 685 296	4 041 769	4 339 367	9.7	7.4	2.2	346 968	273 427	26 135	40 051	-13 916	4 424 431	4 489 662	4 554 998
Louisiana	4 219 973	4 468 976	4 533 372	5.9	1.4	3.3	393 453	267 075	21 958	44 308	-22 350	4 719 160	4 762 398	4 802 633
Maine	1 227 928	1 274 923	1 328 361	3.8	4.2	0.2	79 584	83 138	7 753	9 715	-1 962	1 408 665	1 414 402	1 411 097
Maryland	4 781 468	5 296 486	5 773 552	10.8	9.0	4.2	457 026	286 739	77 875	161 392	-83 517	6 497 626	6 762 732	7 022 251
Massachusetts	6 016 425	6 349 097	6 547 629	5.5	3.1	4.0	452 120	341 961	163 483	236 088	-72 605	6 855 546	6 938 636	7 012 009
Michigan	9 295 297	9 938 444	9 883 640	6.9	-0.6	0.5	710 867	573 859	-87 519	128 353	-215 872	10 695 993	10 713 730	10 694 172
Minnesota	4 375 099	4 919 479	5 303 925	12.4	7.8	4.1	431 430	254 314	42 028	80 206	-38 178	5 900 769	6 108 787	6 306 130
Mississippi	2 573 216	2 844 658	2 967 297	10.5	4.3	0.7	241 975	187 223	-35 013	14 296	-49 309	3 044 812	3 069 420	3 092 410
Missouri	5 117 073	5 595 211	5 988 927	9.3	7.0	1.7	470 801	356 501	-6 804	51 332	-58 136	6 199 882	6 315 366	6 430 173
Montana	799 065	902 195	989 415	12.9	9.7	5.4	76 644	58 129	33 673	3 945	29 728	1 022 735	1 037 387	1 044 898
Nebraska	1 578 385	1 711 263	1 826 341	8.4	6.7	4.4	163 686	96 895	14 572	24 303	-9 731	1 802 678	1 812 787	1 820 247
Nevada	1 201 833	1 998 257	2 700 551	66.3	35.1	8.9	222 508	134 927	146 626	42 594	104 032	3 452 283	3 863 298	4 282 102
New Hampshire	1 109 252	1 235 786	1 316 470	11.4	6.5	1.4	78 003	68 798	9 804	12 587	-2 783	1 524 751	1 586 348	1 646 471
New Jersey	7 730 188	8 414 350	8 791 894	8.9	4.5	1.7	649 061	447 845	-39 135	297 224	-336 359	9 461 635	9 636 644	9 802 440
New Mexico	1 515 069	1 819 046	2 059 179	20.1	13.2	1.1	165 723	106 138	-37 780	15 183	-52 963	2 084 341	2 106 584	2 099 708
New York	17 990 455	18 976 457	19 378 102	5.5	2.1	1.9	1 495 760	949 141	-147 221	699 448	-846 669	19 576 920	19 540 179	19 477 429
North Carolina	6 628 637	8 049 313	9 535 483	21.4	18.5	6.4	751 818	523 384	370 369	128 086	242 283	10 709 289	11 449 153	12 227 739
North Dakota	638 800	642 200	672 591	0.5	4.7	12.7	66 088	38 052	56 271	9 475	46 796	630 112	620 777	606 566
Ohio	10 847 115	11 353 140	11 536 504	4.7	1.6	0.7	865 493	706 188	-70 390	112 592	-182 982	11 644 058	11 605 738	11 550 528
Oklahoma	3 145 585	3 450 654	3 751 351	9.7	8.7	4.6	331 103	238 568	78 417	38 804	39 613	3 735 690	3 820 994	3 913 251
Oregon	2 842 321	3 421 399	3 831 074	20.4	12.0	6.8	284 655	210 571	184 204	38 917	145 287	4 260 393	4 536 418	4 833 918
Pennsylvania	11 881 643	12 281 054	12 702 379	3.4	3.4	0.6	887 430	804 358	11 424	195 038	-183 614	12 787 354	12 801 945	12 768 184
Rhode Island	1 003 464	1 048 319	1 052 567	4.5	0.4	0.4	68 094	60 437	-3 159	25 406	-28 565	1 154 230	1 157 855	1 152 941
South Carolina	3 486 703	4 012 012	4 625 364	15.1	15.3	7.3	358 823	277 145	243 861	36 963	206 898	4 822 577	4 989 550	5 148 569
South Dakota	696 004	754 844	814 180	8.5	7.9	6.3	75 478	45 707	21 072	9 563	11 509	801 939	801 845	800 462
Tennessee	4 877 185	5 689 283	6 346 105	16.7	11.5	4.6	502 451	392 451	191 384	55 613	135 771	6 780 607	7 073 125	7 380 634
Texas	16 986 510	20 851 820	25 145 561	22.8	20.6	10.8	2 437 794	1 117 880	1 375 776	508 843	866 933	28 634 896	30 865 134	33 317 744
Utah	1 722 850	2 233 169	2 763 885	29.6	23.8	10.4	321 460	99 031	65 017	32 159	32 858	2 990 094	3 225 680	3 485 367
Vermont	562 758	608 827	625 741	8.2	2.8	-0.2	37 939	34 505	-4 076	5 196	-9 272	690 686	703 288	711 867
Virginia	6 187 358	7 078 515	8 001 024	14.4	13.0	5.1	641 455	392 605	157 996	202 410	-44 414	8 917 395	9 364 304	9 825 019
Washington	4 866 692	5 894 121	6 724 540	21.1	14.1	8.4	549 553	323 987	333 395	142 595	190 800	7 432 136	7 996 400	8 624 801
West Virginia	1 793 477	1 808 344	1 852 994	0.8	2.5	-1.2	127 578	137 344	-10 139	6 564	-16 703	1 801 112	1 766 435	1 719 959
Wisconsin	4 891 769	5 363 675	5 686 986	9.6	6.0	1.6	419 490	307 115	-20 083	43 853	-63 936	6 004 954	6 088 374	6 150 764
Wyoming	453 588	493 782	563 626	8.9	14.1	3.9	47 402	28 731	2 864	3 181	-317	530 948	529 031	522 979

Table A. States — **Population Characteristics**

| | Population characteristics, 2010 | | | | | | | | | | | | | | | | | | | |
| | Race (percent) | | | | | | | Age (percent) | | | | | | | | | | | |
STATE	White alone	Black alone	American Indian, Alaska Native alone	Asian and Pacific Islander alone	Some other race or two or more races	Percent Hispanic or Latino[1]	Percent foreign born	Under 5 years	5 to 17 years	18 to 24 years	25 to 34 years	35 to 44 years	45 to 54 years	55 to 64 years	65 to 74 years	75 to 84 years	85 years and over	Median age	Percent female
	45	46	47	48	49	50	51	52	53	54	55	56	57	58	59	60	61	62	63
United States	72.4	12.6	0.9	5.0	9.1	16.3	12.9	6.5	17.5	9.9	13.3	13.3	14.6	11.8	7.0	4.2	1.8	37.2	50.8
Alabama...........................	68.5	26.2	0.6	1.2	3.5	3.9	3.5	6.4	17.3	10.0	12.6	13.0	14.5	12.3	7.8	4.4	1.6	37.9	51.5
Alaska.............................	66.7	3.3	14.8	6.4	8.9	5.5	6.9	7.6	18.8	10.5	14.5	13.1	15.6	12.1	5.0	2.1	0.6	33.8	48.0
Arizona............................	73.0	4.1	4.6	3.0	15.3	29.6	13.4	7.1	18.4	9.9	13.4	12.9	13.2	11.4	7.8	4.4	1.6	35.9	50.3
Arkansas.........................	77.0	15.4	0.8	1.4	5.4	6.4	4.5	6.8	17.6	9.7	12.6	12.6	14.0	12.0	8.0	4.6	1.8	37.4	50.9
California........................	57.6	6.2	1.0	13.4	21.9	37.6	27.2	6.8	18.2	10.5	14.2	13.9	14.1	10.8	6.1	3.7	1.6	35.2	50.3
Colorado.........................	81.3	4.0	1.1	2.9	10.6	20.7	9.8	6.8	17.5	9.7	14.4	13.9	14.8	11.9	6.2	3.4	1.4	36.1	49.9
Connecticut.....................	77.6	10.1	0.3	3.8	8.2	13.4	13.6	5.7	17.2	9.1	11.8	13.6	16.1	12.4	7.1	4.6	2.4	40.0	51.3
Delaware.........................	68.9	21.4	0.5	3.2	6.1	8.2	8.0	6.2	16.7	10.1	12.3	12.9	14.9	12.4	8.1	4.5	1.8	38.8	51.6
District of Columbia	38.5	50.7	0.3	3.6	7.0	9.1	13.5	5.4	11.3	14.5	20.9	13.4	12.6	10.6	6.1	3.5	1.8	33.8	52.8
Florida............................	75.0	16.0	0.4	2.5	6.1	22.5	19.4	5.7	15.6	9.3	12.1	12.9	14.6	12.4	9.2	5.7	2.4	40.7	51.1
Georgia...........................	59.7	30.5	0.3	3.3	6.1	8.8	9.7	7.1	18.6	10.0	13.6	14.4	14.4	11.0	6.3	3.1	1.2	35.3	51.2
Hawaii.............................	24.7	1.6	0.3	48.6	24.8	8.9	18.2	6.4	15.9	9.6	13.3	13.0	14.2	12.9	7.4	4.7	2.3	38.6	49.9
Idaho..............................	89.1	0.6	1.4	1.3	7.6	11.2	5.5	7.8	19.6	9.9	13.3	12.2	13.3	11.5	7.0	3.8	1.7	34.6	49.9
Illinois............................	71.5	14.5	0.3	4.6	9.0	15.8	13.7	6.5	17.9	9.7	13.9	13.5	14.6	11.5	6.6	4.0	1.9	36.6	51.0
Indiana...........................	84.3	9.1	0.3	1.6	4.7	6.0	4.6	6.7	18.1	10.0	12.7	13.0	14.6	11.9	7.0	4.3	1.7	37.0	50.8
Iowa...............................	91.3	2.9	0.4	1.8	3.6	5.0	4.6	6.6	17.3	10.0	12.6	12.0	14.4	12.2	7.4	5.0	2.5	38.1	50.5
Kansas............................	83.8	5.9	1.0	2.5	6.9	10.5	6.5	7.2	18.3	10.1	13.0	12.2	14.2	11.6	6.7	4.3	2.1	36.0	50.4
Kentucky.........................	87.8	7.8	0.2	1.2	3.0	3.1	3.2	6.5	17.1	9.5	13.0	13.3	14.8	12.4	7.5	4.2	1.6	38.1	50.8
Louisiana........................	62.6	32.0	0.7	1.5	3.1	4.2	3.8	6.9	17.7	10.5	13.7	12.5	14.4	11.8	6.9	3.9	1.5	35.8	51.0
Maine.............................	95.2	1.2	0.6	1.0	1.9	1.3	3.4	5.2	15.4	8.7	10.9	12.9	16.5	14.5	8.5	5.3	2.1	42.7	51.1
Maryland.........................	58.2	29.4	0.4	5.6	6.5	8.2	13.9	6.3	17.1	9.7	13.2	13.8	15.6	12.1	6.7	3.9	1 7	38.0	51.6
Massachusetts.................	80.4	6.6	0.3	5.3	7.3	9.6	15.0	5.6	16.1	10.4	12.9	13.5	15.5	12.3	7.0	4.6	2.2	39.1	51.6
Michigan.........................	78.9	14.2	0.6	2.4	3.8	4.4	6.0	6.0	17.7	9.9	11.7	12.9	15.3	12.7	7.3	4.5	1.9	38.9	50.9
Minnesota	85.3	5.2	1.1	4.0	4.3	4.7	7.1	6.7	17.5	9.5	13.5	12.8	15.2	11.9	6.7	4.2	2.0	37.4	50.4
Mississippi......................	59.1	37.0	0.5	0.9	2.4	2.7	2.1	7.0	18.4	10.3	12.6	12.6	14.1	11.7	7.2	4.1	1.5	36.0	51.4
Missouri..........................	82.8	11.6	0.5	1.7	3.4	3.5	3.9	6.5	17.3	9.8	12.9	12.5	14.8	12.1	7.5	4.5	2.0	37.9	51.0
Montana..........................	89.4	0.4	6.3	0.7	3.1	2.9	2.0	6.3	16.3	9.6	12.3	11.4	15.1	14.0	8.2	4.7	2.0	39.8	49.8
Nebraska.........................	86.1	4.5	1.0	1.9	6.5	9.2	6.1	7.2	17.9	10.0	13.2	12.1	14.2	11.7	6.7	4.7	2.2	36.2	50.4
Nevada...........................	66.2	8.1	1.2	7.8	16.7	26.5	18.8	6.9	17.7	9.2	14.3	14.2	13.9	11.7	7.3	3.6	1.1	36.3	49.5
New Hampshire	93.9	1.1	0.2	2.2	2.5	2.8	5.3	5.3	16.5	9.4	11.0	13.6	17.2	13.5	7.4	4.4	1.8	41.1	50.7
New Jersey.......................	68.6	13.7	0.3	8.3	9.1	17.7	21.0	6.2	17.3	8.7	12.6	14.1	15.7	11.9	7.0	4.5	2.0	39.0	51.3
New Mexico......................	68.4	2.1	9.4	1.5	18.7	46.3	9.9	7.0	18.1	9.9	12.8	12.1	14.2	12.5	7.5	4.3	1.5	36.7	50.6
New York.........................	65.7	15.9	0.6	7.3	10.4	17.6	22.2	6.0	16.4	10.2	13.7	13.5	14.9	11.9	7.0	4.5	2.0	38.0	51.6
North Carolina..................	68.5	21.5	1.3	2.3	6.5	8.4	7.5	6.6	17.3	9.8	13.0	13.9	14.4	11.9	7.3	4.1	1.6	37.4	51.3
North Dakota....................	90.0	1.2	5.4	1.0	2.3	2.0	2.5	6.6	15.7	12.0	13.1	11.2	14.4	12.2	7.0	5.1	2.5	37.0	49.5
Ohio...............................	82.7	12.2	0.2	1.7	3.2	3.1	4.1	6.2	17.4	9.5	12.4	12.8	15.1	12.6	7.4	4.7	2.0	38.8	51.2
Oklahoma........................	72.2	7.4	8.6	1.8	10.0	8.9	5.5	7.0	17.7	10.2	13.5	12.3	14.0	11.7	7.5	4.4	1.6	36.2	50.5
Oregon............................	83.6	1.8	1.4	4.0	9.1	11.7	9.8	6.2	16.4	9.4	13.7	13.0	14.1	13.3	7.6	4.3	2.0	38.4	50.5
Pennsylvania...................	81.9	10.8	0.2	2.7	4.3	5.7	5.8	5.7	16.2	9.9	11.9	12.7	15.3	12.8	7.7	5.3	2.5	40.1	51.3
Rhode Island....................	81.4	5.7	0.6	3.0	9.3	12.4	12.8	5.5	15.8	11.4	12.0	13.0	15.4	12.4	7.0	4.9	2.5	39.4	51.7
South Carolina..................	66.2	27.9	0.4	1.4	4.2	5.1	4.7	6.5	16.8	10.3	12.7	13.0	14.3	12.6	8.0	4.1	1.6	37.9	51.4
South Dakota...................	85.9	1.3	8.8	0.9	3.0	2.7	2.7	7.3	17.6	10.0	12.8	11.4	14.4	12.0	7.1	4.8	2.4	36.9	50.0
Tennessee	77.6	16.7	0.3	1.5	3.9	4.6	4.5	6.4	17.1	9.6	12.8	13.5	14.6	12.4	7.7	4.2	1.6	38.0	51.3
Texas..............................	70.4	11.8	0.7	3.9	13.2	37.6	16.4	7.7	19.6	10.2	14.3	13.8	13.7	10.3	5.9	3.3	1.2	33.6	50.4
Utah...............................	86.1	1.1	1.2	2.9	8.7	13.0	8.0	9.5	22.0	11.5	16.2	12.0	11.1	8.7	5.0	2.9	1.1	29.2	49.8
Vermont	95.3	1.0	0.4	1.3	2.0	1.5	4.4	5.1	15.5	10.4	11.2	12.5	16.4	14.4	7.9	4.5	2.1	41.5	50.7
Virginia...........................	68.6	19.4	0.4	5.6	6.1	7.9	11.4	6.4	16.8	10.0	13.8	14.3	15.2	11.9	6.9	3.8	1.5	37.5	50.9
Washington......................	77.3	3.6	1.5	7.8	9.9	11.2	13.1	6.5	17.0	9.7	13.9	13.5	14.7	12.4	6.8	3.7	1.8	37.3	50.2
West Virginia....................	93.9	3.4	0.2	0.7	1.8	1.2	1.2	5.6	15.3	9.1	11.7	12.8	14.9	14.3	8.8	5.2	2.0	41.3	50.7
Wisconsin........................	86.2	6.3	1.0	2.3	4.2	5.9	4.5	6.3	17.3	9.7	12.6	12.8	15.4	12.3	7.0	4.6	2.1	38.5	50.4
Wyoming..........................	90.7	0.8	2.4	0.9	5.2	8.9	2.8	7.1	16.9	10.0	13.6	11.9	14.8	13.0	7.0	3.8	1.6	36.8	49.0

1. May be of any race.

Table A. States — Households and Housing Units

STATE	Households, 2010 Number	Percent change, 2000-2010	Persons per house-hold	Female family house-holder[1]	One person house-holds	Housing units, 2010 Total	Percent change, 2000-2010	Occupied units Total	Percent	Median value[2] (dollars)	Median owner cost With a mort-gage	Without a mort-gage[3]	Median gross rent[4] (dollars)	Median rent as a percent of income	Sub-standard units[5] (percent)
	64	65	66	67	68	69	70	71	72	73	74	75	76	77	78
United States	116 716 292	10.7	2.58	13.1	26.7	131 791 065	13.7	114 567 419	65.4	179 900	25.1	12.8	855	31.6	3.9
Alabama............................	1 883 791	8.4	2.48	15.3	27.4	2 174 428	10.7	1 815 152	70.1	123 900	23.0	12.3	667	32.2	2.4
Alaska..............................	258 058	16.5	2.65	10.7	25.6	307 065	17.7	254 610	63.9	241 400	23.3	10.8	981	29.0	10.2
Arizona............................	2 380 990	25.2	2.63	12.4	26.1	2 846 738	30.0	2 334 050	65.2	168 800	26.5	11.3	844	31.6	5.1
Arkansas..........................	1 147 084	10.0	2.47	13.4	27.1	1 317 818	12.3	1 114 902	67.4	106 300	21.5	10.9	638	29.9	3.2
California..........................	12 577 498	9.3	2.90	13.3	23.3	13 682 976	12.0	12 406 475	55.6	370 900	30.6	11.4	1 163	33.8	9.1
Colorado..........................	1 972 868	19.0	2.49	10.1	27.9	2 214 262	22.5	1 960 585	65.9	236 600	25.2	10.7	863	31.2	3.2
Connecticut	1 371 087	5.3	2.52	12.9	27.3	1 488 215	7.4	1 358 809	68.0	288 800	26.8	17.6	992	32.1	2.4
Delaware..........................	342 297	14.6	2.55	14.2	25.6	406 489	18.5	328 765	73.0	243 600	24.8	11.8	952	32.3	2.9
District of Columbia..............	266 707	7.4	2.11	16.4	44.0	296 836	8.0	252 388	42.5	426 900	24.8	11.0	1 198	30.4	3.5
Florida	7 420 802	17.1	2.48	13.5	27.2	8 994 091	23.2	7 035 068	68.1	164 200	29.5	14.4	947	35.5	3.1
Georgia	3 585 584	19.3	2.63	15.8	25.4	4 091 482	24.7	3 482 420	66.2	156 200	25.2	12.3	819	32.4	3.2
Hawaii	455 338	12.9	2.89	12.6	23.3	519 992	12.9	445 812	58.0	525 400	30.1	10.1	1 291	33.5	9.1
Idaho	579 408	23.4	2.66	9.6	23.8	668 634	26.7	576 709	69.6	165 100	24.7	10.6	683	30.5	3.6
Illinois	4 836 972	5.3	2.59	12.9	27.8	5 297 077	8.4	4 752 857	67.7	191 800	25.9	13.8	848	31.5	3.1
Indiana............................	2 502 154	7.1	2.52	12.4	26.9	2 797 172	10.5	2 470 905	70.3	123 300	21.6	11.0	683	30.8	2.2
Iowa...............................	1 221 576	6.3	2.41	9.3	28.4	1 337 563	8.5	1 223 439	72.4	123 400	21.3	11.5	629	28.1	1.7
Kansas............................	1 112 096	7.1	2.49	10.4	27.8	1 234 037	9.1	1 101 658	68.1	127 300	21.8	11.8	682	28.1	2.2
Kentucky..........................	1 719 965	8.1	2.45	12.7	27.5	1 928 617	10.1	1 684 348	68.6	121 600	22.2	11.3	613	29.8	2.5
Louisiana..........................	1 728 360	4.4	2.55	17.2	26.9	1 967 947	6.5	1 689 822	67.6	137 500	21.6	10.5	736	31.7	3.7
Maine	557 219	7.5	2.32	10.0	28.6	722 217	10.8	545 417	72.7	179 100	24.1	13.9	707	29.8	2.5
Maryland	2 156 411	8.9	2.61	14.6	26.1	2 380 605	11.0	2 127 439	67.0	301 400	25.4	12.9	1 131	30.8	2.4
Massachusetts	2 547 075	4.2	2.48	12.5	28.7	2 808 727	7.1	2 520 419	62.2	334 100	26.1	15.3	1 009	30.4	2.0
Michigan...........................	3 872 508	2.3	2.49	13.2	27.9	4 531 231	7.0	3 806 621	72.8	123 300	24.6	13.9	730	33.3	2.1
Minnesota.........................	2 087 227	10.1	2.48	9.5	28.0	2 348 242	13.7	2 091 548	73.0	194 300	24.1	11.9	764	30.2	2.3
Mississippi........................	1 115 768	6.6	2.58	18.5	26.3	1 276 441	9.9	1 079 999	69.8	100 100	23.5	12.0	672	33.2	4.0
Missouri...........................	2 375 611	8.2	2.45	12.3	28.3	2 714 017	11.1	2 350 628	69.0	139 000	22.6	11.7	682	30.1	2.2
Montana...........................	409 607	14.2	2.35	9.0	29.7	483 006	17.1	402 747	69.9	181 200	24.1	11.3	642	28.3	2.8
Nebraska..........................	721 130	8.2	2.46	9.8	28.7	797 677	10.4	719 304	67.4	127 600	21.4	12.6	669	27.7	2.2
Nevada............................	1 006 250	34.0	2.65	12.7	25.7	1 175 070	42.0	989 811	57.2	174 800	28.1	12.2	952	31.6	5.0
New Hampshire	518 973	9.3	2.46	9.7	25.6	614 996	12.4	515 431	71.7	243 000	26.5	16.5	951	30.3	1.9
New Jersey........................	3 214 360	4.9	2.68	13.3	25.2	3 554 909	7.4	3 172 421	66.4	339 200	28.7	18.9	1 114	32.4	4.1
New Mexico.......................	791 395	16.7	2.55	14.0	28.0	902 242	15.6	765 183	67.9	161 200	24.3	10.0	699	29.3	4.7
New York..........................	7 317 755	3.7	2.57	14.9	29.1	8 108 211	5.6	7 196 427	54.3	296 500	26.3	15.5	1 020	31.7	5.5
North Carolina....................	3 745 155	19.6	2.48	13.7	27.0	4 333 479	23.0	3 670 859	67.2	154 200	24.0	12.5	731	31.3	2.8
North Dakota......................	281 192	9.3	2.30	8.2	31.5	318 099	9.8	280 412	66.9	123 000	19.6	10.0	583	25.8	1.3
Ohio................................	4 603 435	3.5	2.44	13.1	28.9	5 128 113	7.2	4 525 066	68.4	134 400	23.4	13.1	685	31.1	1.8
Oklahoma..........................	1 460 450	8.8	2.49	12.3	27.5	1 666 205	10.0	1 432 959	67.8	111 400	21.9	11.2	659	28.9	3.0
Oregon............................	1 518 938	13.9	2.47	10.5	27.4	1 676 476	15.4	1 507 137	62.5	244 500	27.3	12.9	816	32.7	3.4
Pennsylvania......................	5 018 904	5.1	2.45	12.2	28.6	5 568 820	6.1	4 936 030	70.1	165 500	23.8	13.7	763	30.4	1.6
Rhode Island......................	413 600	1.3	2.44	13.5	29.6	463 416	5.4	402 295	60.8	254 500	27.7	15.4	868	30.9	2.6
South Carolina	1 801 181	17.4	2.49	15.6	26.5	2 140 337	22.0	1 761 393	68.7	138 100	23.5	12.0	728	32.2	2.7
South Dakota	322 282	11.0	2.42	9.7	29.4	364 031	12.6	318 955	68.0	129 700	21.9	10.9	591	26.9	2.7
Tennessee	2 493 552	11.7	2.48	13.9	26.9	2 815 087	15.4	2 440 663	68.1	139 000	23.7	11.4	697	31.4	2.5
Texas..............................	8 922 933	20.7	2.75	14.1	24.2	9 996 209	22.5	8 738 664	63.6	128 100	23.4	12.5	801	30.2	5.8
Utah................................	877 692	25.2	3.10	9.7	18.7	981 821	27.7	880 025	69.9	217 200	24.8	10.0	796	29.5	4.6
Vermont............................	256 442	6.6	2.34	9.6	28.2	322 698	9.6	256 922	70.4	216 800	26.0	16.3	823	31.8	2.2
Virginia............................	3 056 058	13.2	2.54	12.4	26.0	3 368 674	16.0	2 992 732	67.7	249 100	24.7	11.4	1 019	30.2	2.6
Washington	2 620 076	15.4	2.51	10.5	27.2	2 888 594	17.9	2 606 863	63.1	271 800	26.7	12.1	908	30.6	3.4
West Virginia......................	763 831	3.7	2.36	11.2	28.4	882 213	4.5	741 940	74.6	95 100	20.1	10.0	571	29.7	1.8
Wisconsin..........................	2 279 768	9.4	2.43	10.3	28.2	2 625 475	13.1	2 279 532	68.7	169 400	24.5	14.0	715	29.8	2.2
Wyoming	226 879	17.2	2.42	8.9	28.0	262 286	17.2	222 803	69.7	180 100	22.0	10.0	693	25.3	2.8

1. No spouse present.   2. Specified owner-occupied units.   3. Median monthly costs is often in the minimum category—10.0 percent or less, which is indicated as 10.0 percent.
4. Specified renter-occupied units.   5. Overcrowded or lacking complete plumbing facilities.

Table A. States — Housing Units

STATE	Total	Percent change, 2014–2015	Total	Percent owner-occupied	Owners with a mort-gage	Renter	With a mort-gage	Without a mort-gage[2]	Median monthly housing costs (dollars)	Median value of units[3] (dollars)	Percent valued over $500,000	Median gross rent[4] (dollars)	Sub-standard units[5] (percent)	Percent living in a different house than 1 year ago
	79	80	81	82	83	84	85	86	87	88	89	90	91	92
United States	134 793 665	0.6	118 208 250	63.0	29.4	46.8	22.0	11.7	1 009	194 500	12.4	959	3.8	14.7
Alabama	2 218 391	0.5	1 846 390	67.9	25.0	42.7	19.8	10.6	727	134 100	3.8	729	2.1	14.3
Alaska	309 453	0.3	250 185	63.9	27.9	43.9	22.3	10.0	1 251	259 600	7.9	1 163	9.4	19.9
Arizona	2 929 173	0.7	2 463 008	61.9	29.7	44.9	21.7	10.0	953	194 300	8.4	933	5.1	18.0
Arkansas	1 347 598	0.5	1 144 663	65.2	24.6	41.8	19.6	10.2	681	120 700	3.3	695	3.2	16.9
California	13 988 399	0.6	12 896 357	53.6	39.3	52.9	25.9	11.0	1 438	449 100	43.2	1 311	8.8	13.5
Colorado	2 309 122	1.4	2 074 735	63.7	27.6	48.0	21.4	10.0	1 195	283 800	16.0	1 111	3.0	18.3
Connecticut	1 496 056	0.2	1 343 703	66.2	33.2	49.1	23.6	15.5	1 398	270 900	16.5	1 108	2.0	12.5
Delaware	421 734	1.0	352 595	70.8	30.7	44.0	22.0	10.8	1 098	240 200	7.2	1 049	2.4	14.4
District of Columbia	309 596	1.1	281 787	39.9	26.6	45.6	21.2	10.0	1 577	551 300	54.8	1 417	4.2	20.8
Florida	9 210 287	0.7	7 463 184	63.8	35.3	52.9	23.8	12.5	998	179 800	8.9	1 046	3.3	16.1
Georgia	4 182 228	0.7	3 656 407	61.8	27.9	45.8	21.1	10.8	947	159 300	6.5	909	2.8	15.8
Hawaii	532 413	0.4	445 936	56.6	39.8	52.4	25.7	10.0	1 533	566 900	58.2	1 500	10.1	14.7
Idaho	692 482	1.1	597 421	69.0	28.5	42.5	21.6	10.0	829	176 300	4.7	770	3.1	18.4
Illinois	5 317 618	0.2	4 794 523	65.3	29.1	45.6	22.1	13.0	1 052	180 300	8.4	936	3.0	13.2
Indiana	2 841 450	0.4	2 515 143	68.2	21.0	43.9	18.9	10.2	803	131 000	3.0	758	1.9	15.5
Iowa	1 369 379	0.5	1 247 249	70.7	19.9	40.1	19.0	11.4	777	136 100	2.8	718	1.8	15.7
Kansas	1 253 889	0.4	1 111 582	66.4	21.2	38.9	19.8	11.3	838	141 200	3.3	782	2.3	16.3
Kentucky	1 957 133	0.3	1 716 168	66.3	23.8	40.6	19.7	10.6	719	130 000	3.2	702	2.5	15.2
Louisiana	2 024 737	0.7	1 737 908	64.6	25.9	46.0	19.9	10.0	755	155 600	4.2	800	2.7	13.1
Maine	729 392	0.2	545 226	71.0	29.7	44.8	22.4	13.2	884	180 300	5.6	792	2.4	14.4
Maryland	2 434 465	0.5	2 177 934	65.9	29.4	47.7	22.5	10.9	1 440	299 800	18.8	1 278	2.7	14.4
Massachusetts	2 845 805	0.6	2 559 951	61.7	32.5	48.1	23.4	14.3	1 410	352 100	25.3	1 164	2.3	12.4
Michigan	4 550 324	0.2	3 858 532	70.4	25.0	46.1	20.0	12.6	846	137 500	3.6	803	2.1	14.4
Minnesota	2 397 081	0.5	2 147 262	70.9	23.1	44.0	20.3	10.9	1 016	200 000	6.5	888	2.6	14.8
Mississippi	1 300 932	0.5	1 104 371	67.4	30.1	43.6	21.4	11.3	678	112 700	2.0	724	3.4	13.7
Missouri	2 746 644	0.4	2 374 180	66.1	23.6	41.9	19.9	11.3	812	147 800	4.0	763	2.0	15.9
Montana	494 222	0.6	414 804	66.7	29.4	40.5	22.5	10.7	795	209 500	8.4	763	2.5	16.1
Nebraska	820 925	0.7	744 159	65.9	20.4	39.7	19.7	11.4	843	141 600	2.9	750	2.2	16.0
Nevada	1 209 864	0.9	1 042 065	54.0	29.8	46.8	22.6	10.0	1 026	221 400	7.9	980	4.6	19.9
New Hampshire	622 604	0.4	517 615	70.9	29.6	44.0	23.0	15.5	1 264	244 500	7.6	1 017	1.9	13.9
New Jersey	3 593 722	0.1	3 187 963	63.0	39.2	50.5	25.7	17.6	1 500	322 600	21.6	1 214	3.5	9.8
New Mexico	914 979	0.2	761 797	67.5	30.9	45.3	21.9	10.0	777	164 100	5.6	783	4.4	14.2
New York	8 207 161	0.2	7 233 694	53.1	35.9	50.2	24.1	14.0	1 255	293 500	25.1	1 173	5.8	10.5
North Carolina	4 491 090	0.9	3 843 745	63.9	27.3	44.9	21.0	11.4	866	160 100	5.9	827	2.7	15.6
North Dakota	362 889	3.5	313 475	61.7	16.3	36.2	18.2	10.0	773	180 900	3.8	775	2.5	18.4
Ohio	5 156 546	0.2	4 606 655	65.4	23.7	43.3	19.9	12.0	826	136 400	2.9	746	1.8	15.3
Oklahoma	1 711 515	0.7	1 465 951	65.3	24.6	39.7	19.9	10.2	756	126 800	3.0	759	3.1	17.1
Oregon	1 718 509	1.1	1 553 205	61.1	31.9	48.2	23.3	11.9	1 036	264 100	12.7	943	3.6	17.8
Pennsylvania	5 603 051	0.2	4 956 037	68.7	27.2	45.2	21.3	12.9	932	170 600	6.0	868	1.9	12.3
Rhode Island	462 555	0.0	407 484	59.0	31.8	44.6	23.5	14.6	1 145	241 000	10.3	938	2.0	13.8
South Carolina	2 210 150	1.0	1 857 768	68.1	28.0	43.8	20.9	10.7	813	148 600	6.1	819	2.2	15.2
South Dakota	380 307	1.1	339 437	68.2	21.8	37.2	20.0	10.3	747	152 800	3.7	675	2.6	17.2
Tennessee	2 892 407	0.8	2 530 260	65.8	26.3	43.5	20.9	10.2	798	150 600	5.1	785	2.3	15.1
Texas	10 588 236	1.5	9 421 412	61.1	26.7	43.9	21.1	11.4	968	152 000	6.1	932	5.4	16.1
Utah	1 038 065	1.5	930 980	68.9	24.1	41.5	21.2	10.0	1 048	234 600	8.3	925	3.8	17.4
Vermont	326 874	0.3	254 865	70.7	34.6	46.3	23.9	15.2	1 085	223 700	8.0	923	3.0	14.1
Virginia	3 468 952	0.6	3 106 895	65.0	28.1	46.0	22.1	10.3	1 210	257 800	18.1	1 144	2.3	16.1
Washington	2 991 584	1.0	2 728 573	62.4	29.5	45.4	22.7	11.2	1 200	284 000	18.8	1 080	3.8	18.5
West Virginia	885 539	0.1	734 536	72.3	21.1	38.7	18.3	10.0	572	112 100	2.0	675	2.1	11.7
Wisconsin	2 656 669	0.3	2 319 538	66.8	24.6	43.0	21.1	12.9	907	168 300	4.1	792	2.2	14.3
Wyoming	269 469	0.5	228 937	68.0	23.0	35.9	20.1	10.0	858	212 500	6.8	815	2.8	18.0

1. Excludes units where owner costs or gross rent as a percentage of households income cannot be calculated. 2. Median monthly costs is often in the minimum category—10.0 percent or less, which is indicated as 10.0 percent. 3. Specified owner-occupied units. 4. Specified renter-occupied units. 5. Overcrowded or lacking complete plumbing facilities.

Table A. States — **Residential Construction, Vital Statistics, and Health**

STATE	Value of residential construction authorized by building permits, 2016			Average sales price of new manu-factured housing units put in place, 2015	Births, 2015		Deaths, 2014					Percent lacking health insurance, 2015		Medicare beneficiaries 65 years and older, 2015
							Number		Rate					
									Total					
	New con-struction ($1,000)	Number of housing units	Percent single family		Total	Rate[1]	Total	Infant[2]	Crude[1]	Age-adjusted[1]	Infant[3]	All persons	Children under 18 years	
	93	94	95	96	97	98	99	100	101	102	103	104	105	106
United States	237 101 606	1 206 642	62.2	$68 000	3 978 497	12.4	2 626 418	23 215	8.2	7.2	5.8	9.4	4.8	43 882 917
Alabama............	2 722 956	15 001	77.9	$65 000	59 657	12.3	50 215	516	10.4	9.1	8.7	10.1	3.1	725 387
Alaska...............	369 042	1 503	68.9	NA	11 282	15.3	4 128	75	5.6	7.4	6.6	14.9	10.6	65 067
Arizona.............	8 044 524	35 578	69.9	$73 800	85 351	12.5	51 538	534	7.7	6.6	6.2	10.8	8.3	945 305
Arkansas...........	1 562 882	9 474	71.9	$65 800	38 886	13.1	30 467	290	10.3	8.8	7.5	9.5	4.9	453 261
California...........	24 045 190	102 350	49.2	$109 000	491 748	12.6	245 929	2 163	6.3	6.1	4.3	8.6	3.3	4 586 664
Colorado...........	8 928 897	38 974	55.4	$65 500	66 581	12.2	35 237	315	6.6	6.6	4.8	8.1	4.2	646 268
Connecticut.......	1 196 936	5 504	44.7	$75 300	35 746	10.0	29 860	176	8.3	6.5	4.9	6.0	3.3	513 832
Delaware...........	721 546	5 804	80.8	$90 600	11 166	11.8	8 260	74	8.8	7.3	6.7	5.9	3.0	149 441
District of Columbia..............	510 518	4 690	7.2	X	9 578	14.2	4 723	69	7.2	7.4	7.3	3.8	1.5	59 483
Florida..............	25 863 502	116 240	64.6	$70 700	224 269	11.1	185 956	1 333	9.3	6.6	6.1	13.3	6.9	3 426 364
Georgia............	9 380 677	51 675	70.6	$69 500	131 404	12.9	76 887	976	7.6	8.0	7.5	13.9	6.7	1 199 505
Hawaii..............	1 266 133	3 369	60.7	D	18 420	12.9	10 767	83	7.6	5.9	4.5	4.0	1.6	202 988
Idaho...............	2 367 554	12 165	80.1	$89 800	22 827	13.8	12 613	125	7.7	7.2	5.5	11.0	5.8	235 409
Illinois.............	4 388 478	22 603	45.1	$64 600	158 116	12.3	105 293	1 045	8.2	7.3	6.6	7.1	2.5	1 681 137
Indiana	3 875 847	18 713	75.2	$53 300	84 040	12.7	60 940	595	9.2	8.2	7.1	9.6	6.7	933 356
Iowa..................	2 660 753	14 317	57.3	$62 200	39 482	12.6	29 190	191	9.4	7.2	4.8	5.0	3.5	487 706
Kansas..............	1 769 452	9 807	53.3	$63 400	39 154	13.4	25 793	247	8.9	7.6	6.3	9.1	5.1	402 409
Kentucky...........	1 727 013	12 714	57.1	$63 500	55 971	12.6	44 838	398	10.2	9.1	7.1	6.0	4.2	643 852
Louisiana..........	2 766 650	14 503	86.3	$59 800	64 692	13.9	43 869	483	9.4	8.9	7.5	11.9	3.6	608 309
Maine	776 944	4 010	81.4	$72 700	12 607	9.5	13 510	85	10.2	7.4	6.7	8.4	5.7	240 818
Maryland	3 166 845	17 044	64.9	$68 400	73 616	12.3	45 867	478	7.7	7.0	6.5	6.6	3.9	733 399
Massachusetts....	3 946 447	16 288	46.9	$89 400	71 492	10.5	55 200	315	8.2	6.6	4.4	2.8	1.1	944 742
Michigan	4 271 807	20 408	71.2	$56 200	113 312	11.4	93 914	745	9.5	7.8	6.5	6.1	3.1	1 537 383
Minnesota.........	4 593 041	21 449	56.3	$69 500	69 834	12.7	41 445	352	7.6	6.5	5.0	4.5	3.1	768 619
Mississippi.........	1 125 912	6 886	89.2	$64 500	38 394	12.8	30 557	319	10.2	9.4	8.2	12.7	4.0	424 277
Missouri............	3 282 703	18 997	59.4	$64 100	75 061	12.3	58 320	457	9.6	8.1	6.1	9.8	5.7	902 964
Montana............	760 191	4 781	65.1	$90 700	12 583	12.2	9 381	68	9.2	7.3	5.5	11.6	7.6	169 395
Nebraska...........	1 306 195	8 078	62.9	$58 400	26 679	14.1	15 978	136	8.5	7.2	5.1	8.2	5.3	262 839
Nevada.............	2 871 930	17 952	63.4	$76 700	36 298	12.6	21 793	196	7.7	7.5	5.5	12.3	7.6	369 460
New Hampshire ...	759 526	3 796	70.6	$78 400	12 433	9.3	11 516	53	8.7	7.1	4.3	6.3	2.7	206 957
New Jersey	4 028 688	26 793	35.9	$86 000	103 127	11.5	71 316	454	8.0	6.7	4.4	8.7	3.7	1 209 017
New Mexico	907 006	4 863	78.5	$77 300	25 816	12.4	17 579	141	8.4	7.5	5.4	10.9	4.5	292 856
New York...........	6 045 261	33 711	30.4	$68 400	237 274	12.0	149 944	1 110	7.6	6.4	4.7	7.1	2.5	2 660 419
North Carolina.....	11 091 052	60 550	72.1	$67 700	120 843	12.0	85 367	857	8.6	7.8	7.1	11.2	4.4	1 436 632
North Dakota......	714 175	3 981	59.3	$71 700	11 314	14.9	6 184	57	8.4	6.9	5.0	7.8	7.9	101 143
Ohio..................	4 589 266	22 816	66.7	$58 000	139 264	12.0	114 509	956	9.9	8.1	6.9	6.5	4.4	1 744 373
Oklahoma..........	2 155 011	12 092	75.8	$66 300	53 122	13.6	38 464	434	9.9	9.0	8.1	13.9	7.4	538 141
Oregon.............	3 944 409	19 586	56.2	$83 800	45 655	11.3	34 151	234	8.6	7.1	5.1	7.0	3.6	630 284
Pennsylvania......	4 515 560	23 303	70.6	$68 100	141 047	11.0	128 434	838	10.0	7.5	5.9	6.4	4.1	2 060 323
Rhode Island......	236 512	1 226	75.0	$64 000	10 993	10.4	9 770	48	9.3	7.0	4.4	5.7	3.4	155 503
South Carolina	6 723 604	32 165	81.9	$67 900	58 139	11.9	45 454	372	9.4	8.3	6.5	10.9	4.1	756 952
South Dakota	883 698	5 686	56.2	$75 700	12 336	14.4	7 507	72	8.8	7.1	5.9	10.2	6.7	133 720
Tennessee.........	6 580 600	36 157	67.9	$65 500	81 685	12.4	64 661	564	9.9	8.8	6.9	10.3	4.2	970 390
Texas	29 242 398	165 853	64.2	$62 400	403 618	14.7	183 912	2 337	6.8	7.5	5.9	17.1	9.5	2 942 105
Utah..................	4 808 309	22 662	67.1	$80 000	50 778	16.9	16 719	251	5.7	7.1	4.9	10.5	7.2	280 010
Vermont.............	315 195	1 771	54.7	$72 200	5 903	9.4	5 623	28	9.0	6.9	4.6	3.8	1.0	105 435
Virginia.............	5 473 492	31 132	69.4	$68 900	103 303	12.3	63 598	595	7.6	7.2	5.8	9.1	4.9	1 081 829
Washington	9 116 339	44 077	51.0	$91 100	88 990	12.4	52 099	402	7.4	6.7	4.5	6.6	2.6	972 709
West Virginia......	397 382	2 544	78.4	$67 500	19 805	10.7	22 186	143	12.0	9.3	7.0	6.0	2.8	321 466
Wisconsin..........	3 732 635	19 274	57.1	$54 200	67 041	11.6	50 291	381	8.7	7.1	5.7	5.7	3.6	882 785
Wyoming	570 418	1 727	89.7	$80 400	7 765	13.2	4 666	49	8.0	7.4	6.4	11.5	7.8	80 229

1. Per 1,000 resident population.   2. Deaths of infants under 1 year old.   3. Deaths of infants under 1 year old per 1,000 live births.

Table A. States — **Crime and Education**

STATE	Serious crime known to police,[1] 2015				Public elementary and secondary school enrollment, 2014–2015		Educational attainment[3] (percent)				Local government expenditures for education, 2013–2014	
	Violent Crime		Property Crime				2010		2015			
	Number	Rate[2]	Number	Rate[2]	Total	Student/teacher ratio	High school graduate or more	Bachelor's degree or more	High school graduate or more	Bachelor's degree or more	Total current expenditures (mil dol)	Current expenditures per student (dollars)
	107	108	109	110	111	112	113	114	115	116	117	118
United States	1 197 704	372.6	7 993 631	2 487.00	50 312 581	16.1	85.6	28.2	87.1	30.6	553 501	11 066
Alabama...............	22 952	472.4	144 746	2 978.90	744 164	17.4	82.1	21.9	84.9	24.2	6 743	9 036
Alaska.................	5 392	730.2	20 806	2 817.60	131 176	16.9	91.0	27.9	92.6	29.7	2 418	18 466
Arizona...............	28 012	410.2	207 107	3 033.20	1 111 695	23.1	85.6	25.9	86.1	27.7	8 221	7 457
Arkansas.............	15 526	521.3	96 836	3 251.50	490 917	13.9	82.9	19.5	85.4	21.8	4 778	9 752
California.............	166 883	426.3	1 024 914	2 618.30	6 312 161	23.6	80.7	30.1	82.2	32.3	61 051	9 671
Colorado..............	17 515	321.0	144 136	2 641.50	889 006	17.3	89.7	36.4	91.2	39.2	7 924	9 036
Connecticut..........	7 845	218.5	65 066	1 812.00	542 678	12.9	88.6	35.5	90.2	38.3	10 050	18 401
Delaware.............	4 720	499.0	25 455	2 691.00	134 042	13.9	87.7	27.8	88.9	30.9	1 816	13 793
District of Columbia...........	8 531	1 269.1	31 435	4 676.20	80 958	12.3	87.4	50.1	89.8	56.7	1 608	20 577
Florida................	93 626	461.9	570 270	2 813.20	2 756 944	15.3	85.5	25.8	87.6	28.4	24 364	8 955
Georgia...............	38 643	378.3	308 723	3 022.30	1 744 437	15.6	84.3	27.3	86.1	29.9	15 922	9 236
Hawaii................	4 201	293.4	54 346	3 796.20	182 384	15.6	89.9	29.5	90.9	31.4	2 317	12 400
Idaho..................	3 568	215.6	28 858	1 743.80	290 885	18.6	88.3	24.4	90.0	26.0	1 950	6 577
Illinois................	49 354	383.8	255 729	1 988.60	2 050 239	15.5	86.9	30.8	88.6	32.9	27 290	13 213
Indiana...............	25 653	387.5	171 847	2 596.00	1 046 269	18.5	87.0	22.7	88.2	24.9	9 841	9 396
Iowa..................	8 936	286.1	63 957	2 047.30	505 311	14.2	90.6	24.9	91.7	26.8	5 355	10 647
Kansas................	11 353	389.9	79 199	2 720.10	497 275	13.2	89.2	29.8	90.3	31.7	5 083	10 240
Kentucky.............	9 676	218.7	96 362	2 177.60	688 640	16.6	81.9	20.5	85.1	23.3	6 375	9 411
Louisiana.............	25 208	539.7	156 629	3 353.40	716 800	15.5	81.9	21.4	84.6	23.2	7 721	10 853
Maine.................	1 729	130.1	24 327	1 830.00	182 470	12.2	90.3	26.8	91.7	30.1	2 441	13 267
Maryland..............	27 462	457.2	139 048	2 315.00	874 514	14.8	88.1	36.1	89.6	38.8	12 314	14 217
Massachusetts........	26 562	390.9	114 871	1 690.70	955 844	13.3	89.1	39.0	90.2	41.5	15 183	15 886
Michigan..............	41 231	415.5	187 101	1 885.60	1 537 922	18.1	88.7	25.2	90.1	27.8	16 494	10 649
Minnesota............	13 319	242.6	121 984	2 222.10	857 235	15.4	91.8	31.8	92.8	34.7	9 724	11 427
Mississippi...........	8 254	275.8	84 790	2 833.60	490 917	15.2	81.0	19.5	83.5	20.8	4 071	8 265
Missouri..............	30 261	497.4	173 642	2 854.20	917 785	13.6	86.9	25.6	88.9	27.8	9 126	9 938
Montana..............	3 611	349.6	27 100	2 623.60	144 532	14.1	91.7	28.8	93.5	30.6	1 577	10 941
Nebraska.............	5 212	274.9	42 495	2 241.10	312 635	13.6	90.4	28.6	91.0	30.2	3 654	11 877
Nevada................	20 118	695.9	77 137	2 668.30	459 189	21.2	84.7	21.7	85.6	23.6	3 739	8 275
New Hampshire	2 652	199.3	23 229	1 745.70	184 670	12.5	91.5	32.8	93.1	35.7	2 720	14 601
New Jersey	22 879	255.4	145 701	1 626.10	1 400 579	12.2	88.0	35.4	89.1	37.6	25 734	18 780
New Mexico	13 681	656.1	77 094	3 697.40	340 365	15.2	83.3	25.0	84.6	26.5	3 190	9 403
New York	75 165	379.7	317 529	1 604.00	2 741 185	13.5	84.9	32.5	86.0	35.0	55 081	20 156
North Carolina.......	34 852	347.0	276 183	2 750.10	1 548 895	15.6	84.7	26.5	86.6	29.4	12 685	8 287
North Dakota.........	1 812	239.4	16 020	2 116.50	106 586	11.8	90.3	27.6	92.5	29.1	1 251	12 032
Ohio...................	33 898	291.9	300 525	2 587.70	1 724 810	16.2	88.1	24.6	89.7	26.8	19 714	11 434
Oklahoma.............	16 506	422.0	112 878	2 885.90	688 511	16.4	86.2	22.9	87.3	24.6	5 451	7 995
Oregon...............	10 468	259.8	118 719	2 946.60	601 318	21.6	88.8	28.8	90.0	32.2	5 647	9 959
Pennsylvania.........	40 339	315.1	232 085	1 812.80	1 743 160	14.3	88.4	27.1	89.7	29.7	24 265	13 824
Rhode Island.........	2 562	242.5	20 043	1 897.50	141 959	15.0	83.5	30.2	87.7	32.7	2 183	15 372
South Carolina.......	24 700	504.5	161 245	3 293.30	756 523	15.3	84.1	24.5	86.3	26.8	7 164	9 608
South Dakota	3 289	383.1	16 680	1 943.00	133 040	13.8	89.6	26.3	91.1	27.5	1 183	9 036
Tennessee............	40 400	612.1	193 796	2 936.20	995 475	15.2	83.6	23.1	86.1	25.7	8 607	8 662
Texas..................	113 227	412.2	777 739	2 831.30	5 233 765	15.3	80.7	25.9	82.4	28.4	44 331	8 602
Utah...................	7 071	236.0	89 278	2 980.00	635 577	23.2	90.6	29.3	91.5	31.8	4 094	6 546
Vermont...............	739	118.0	8 806	1 406.60	87 311	10.6	91.0	33.6	91.7	36.9	1 602	18 066
Virginia...............	16 399	195.6	156 470	1 866.50	1 280 381	14.2	86.5	34.2	88.9	37.0	13 955	10 955
Washington	20 394	284.4	248 369	3 463.80	1 073 638	18.0	89.8	31.1	90.8	34.2	10 912	10 305
West Virginia.........	6 231	337.9	37 251	2 020.00	280 310	14.0	83.2	17.5	86.0	19.6	3 195	11 371
Wisconsin.............	17 647	305.8	113 924	1 974.00	871 432	14.9	90.1	26.3	91.4	28.4	9 920	11 345
Wyoming..............	1 302	222.1	11 151	1 902.60	94 067	12.4	92.3	24.1	92.2	26.2	1 467	15 903

1. Data for serious crimes have not been adjusted for underreporting; this may affect comparability between geographic areas and over time.   2. Per 100,000 population estimated by the FBI.   3. Persons 25 years old and over.

Table A. States — **Exports, Income, and Poverty**

STATE	Exports of goods by state of origin, 2016 (mil dol) Total	Manu-factured	Non-manu-factured	Income, 2015 Per capita income (dollars)	Median income (dollars)	Households Percent with income of $25,000 or less	Percent with income of $100,000 or more	Median income of family of four	Percent below poverty level, 2015 All persons	Children under 18 years	Persons 65 years and over	All families	Families with related children under 18 Married-couple families	Male house-holder[1] families	Female house-holder[1] families
	119	120	121	122	123	124	125	126	127	128	129	130	131	132	133
United States	1 454 624	1 051 267	153 467	29 979	55 775	22.0	24.8	82 508	14.7	20.7	9.0	10.6	7.7	20.5	39.2
Alabama.............................	20 554	18 764	1 119	24 769	44 765	29.1	17.3	70 056	18.5	26.6	9.9	13.7	8.9	26.4	47.7
Alaska...............................	4 371	322	3 983	34 352	73 355	13.9	34.0	96 612	10.3	15.2	4.5	7.0	4.5	20.4	26.6
Arizona..............................	22 030	13 132	3 250	26 721	51 492	23.2	20.8	71 154	17.4	24.7	9.0	12.5	11.1	22.6	40.1
Arkansas............................	5 706	3 809	600	23 589	41 995	29.5	14.8	66 645	19.1	27.2	10.3	13.7	10.5	28.6	46.2
California............................	163 616	103 406	19 790	31 587	64 500	19.4	31.6	83 012	15.3	21.2	9.9	11.3	9.7	21.0	37.0
Colorado............................	7 551	6 410	352	33 563	63 909	17.3	29.3	93 932	11.5	14.7	7.0	7.6	5.6	13.4	33.7
Connecticut.........................	14 403	12 103	907	39 430	71 346	17.6	35.6	111 996	10.5	14.5	7.2	7.4	3.7	15.9	32.6
Delaware............................	4 443	3 413	94	31 441	61 255	18.1	25.8	92 642	12.4	19.4	6.2	8.7	5.5	20.7	34.2
District of Columbia	1 331	1 221	64	50 187	75 628	20.3	39.3	112 064	17.3	25.6	15.2	14.0	4.5	19.2	40.3
Florida...............................	52 033	38 419	3 257	27 697	49 426	24.4	19.7	71 480	15.7	23.1	10.3	11.3	9.1	23.1	37.1
Georgia..............................	35 723	28 614	2 889	26 810	51 244	24.3	21.7	72 290	17.0	24.5	9.7	13.0	8.8	22.0	42.5
Hawaii...............................	1 239	1 035	137	31 052	73 486	15.3	34.7	96 837	10.6	14.2	7.8	6.9	4.6	20.5	26.2
Idaho.................................	4 876	3 351	530	24 273	48 275	24.6	17.5	70 308	15.1	17.8	8.7	10.9	8.1	18.2	43.4
Illinois...............................	59 808	44 052	4 787	31 867	59 588	20.9	27.2	90 080	13.6	19.1	8.5	9.8	6.9	17.1	38.8
Indiana	34 672	30 281	879	26 396	50 532	22.9	18.9	76 600	14.5	20.9	7.2	10.2	6.4	18.8	43.2
Iowa	12 129	9 944	1 786	28 628	54 736	21.1	20.3	82 481	12.2	14.8	7.0	7.7	4.7	19.7	36.8
Kansas	10 168	7 509	2 006	28 852	53 906	21.3	22.2	82 487	13.0	17.2	7.3	8.4	6.1	20.1	36.5
Kentucky	29 242	23 455	468	25 082	45 215	28.1	16.6	71 955	18.5	25.9	11.2	14.0	11.2	28.5	47.0
Louisiana	48 822	29 265	18 941	25 456	45 727	29.7	19.6	71 061	19.6	28.4	12.8	14.7	7.3	23.6	49.8
Maine.................................	2 860	1 685	949	28 437	51 494	24.3	18.9	80 929	13.4	17.4	8.8	8.9	5.4	21.7	37.1
Maryland	9 314	6 894	804	37 522	75 847	14.6	37.1	111 281	9.7	13.2	7.3	6.7	3.3	14.1	27.1
Massachusetts.....................	25 810	19 344	2 775	38 130	70 628	18.9	35.5	112 235	11.5	14.8	9.2	7.9	3.7	18.5	33.8
Michigan	54 451	46 185	2 221	27 865	51 084	23.8	20.5	81 951	15.8	22.4	7.8	11.1	7.7	23.1	44.2
Minnesota...........................	19 210	16 339	1 126	33 425	63 488	17.7	28.0	100 494	10.2	13.1	6.9	6.3	4.0	13.3	32.1
Mississippi	10 513	8 484	385	21 291	40 593	32.7	14.0	60 420	22.0	31.3	12.5	17.0	10.0	28.5	49.6
Missouri	13 952	12 078	1 057	27 384	50 238	23.9	19.6	80 161	14.8	20.2	8.5	10.2	6.4	20.5	41.3
Montana	1 343	765	285	27 735	49 509	24.8	18.2	78 933	14.6	19.4	7.6	9.3	6.4	23.2	45.3
Nebraska	6 370	5 156	972	29 000	54 996	21.0	22.2	82 676	12.6	16.8	7.4	8.5	5.8	24.2	38.0
Nevada	9 773	7 813	468	27 220	52 431	21.4	20.5	72 010	14.7	20.9	8.4	10.9	8.4	18.3	35.7
New Hampshire....................	4 143	3 388	184	35 925	70 303	15.7	32.4	107 348	8.2	10.7	6.1	5.0	2.4	8.0	30.3
New Jersey..........................	31 246	21 498	2 902	37 245	72 222	17.5	36.6	113 455	10.8	15.6	7.9	8.1	5.5	18.2	33.6
New Mexico.........................	3 629	1 876	119	24 388	45 382	29.0	17.9	59 505	20.4	28.6	11.1	14.8	15.1	20.9	43.9
New York	74 406	36 104	11 023	34 297	60 850	22.3	29.6	90 852	15.4	22.0	11.2	11.6	8.9	20.1	38.3
North Carolina	29 939	25 452	1 800	26 801	47 830	25.4	19.1	71 923	16.4	23.5	9.2	11.8	8.5	26.5	42.4
North Dakota	4 181	1 736	2 374	34 063	60 557	19.3	26.9	95 271	11.0	12.1	8.9	6.9	3.3	23.0	33.1
Ohio..................................	49 145	40 196	3 798	28 001	51 075	23.9	20.4	82 005	14.8	21.3	7.6	10.7	6.6	21.6	43.1
Oklahoma	5 004	4 009	320	25 762	48 568	25.4	18.3	68 201	16.1	22.2	8.4	11.7	8.5	23.0	42.1
Oregon	21 953	17 830	2 179	29 117	54 148	22.0	22.4	79 171	15.4	20.3	7.3	9.9	8.1	19.7	38.8
Pennsylvania.......................	36 570	28 606	3 124	30 384	55 702	21.8	23.8	89 690	13.2	19.4	7.8	9.1	5.6	19.1	39.2
Rhode Island.......................	2 269	1 555	506	31 888	58 073	22.9	26.6	99 216	13.9	19.4	10.3	10.1	4.7	15.0	40.6
South Carolina.....................	31 270	29 300	541	25 627	47 238	26.3	17.5	70 981	16.6	24.0	9.3	12.1	8.7	21.9	41.9
South Dakota.......................	1 210	1 119	65	27 624	53 017	21.7	18.9	80 494	13.7	18.1	8.3	8.3	6.0	19.1	34.3
Tennessee	31 466	23 098	1 193	26 216	47 275	26.1	18.0	68 298	16.7	24.2	9.8	12.3	9.0	27.9	42.7
Texas	232 588	163 046	21 630	28 210	55 653	21.6	24.9	75 885	15.9	23.0	10.3	12.2	9.5	19.0	39.9
Utah..................................	12 074	11 154	421	25 816	62 912	15.7	25.8	78 717	11.3	12.9	6.8	8.3	7.0	14.0	34.1
Vermont	2 990	2 083	76	31 216	56 990	21.2	23.0	91 793	10.2	13.3	6.6	5.8	3.9	15.4	32.8
Virginia..............................	16 442	12 401	2 400	34 780	66 262	17.7	31.8	96 513	11.2	14.8	7.3	7.8	4.5	16.8	33.3
Washington.........................	79 564	63 415	13 108	33 486	64 129	17.5	29.1	91 572	12.2	15.5	7.4	7.9	5.6	17.7	34.0
West Virginia	5 047	3 434	1 372	23 539	42 019	30.1	14.3	70 510	17.9	25.2	8.5	13.5	9.9	26.7	48.7
Wisconsin	21 009	18 164	1 234	29 563	55 638	20.4	21.4	88 133	12.1	16.4	7.1	7.9	5.0	17.4	36.7
Wyoming.............................	1 104	1 020	67	31 383	60 214	18.7	25.2	81 839	11.1	13.2	8.0	6.7	5.0	12.4	32.2

1. No spouse present.

Table A. States — **Personal Income**

	Personal income, 2015												
			Per capita¹		Sources of personal income (mil dol)								
								Transfer payments					
									Government payments to individuals				
STATE	Total (mil dol)	Percent change, 2014–2015	Dollars	Rank	Wages and salaries²	Proprietors' income	Dividends, interest, and rent	Total	Total	Social Security	Medical payments	Income maintenance	Unemployment insurance
	134	135	136	137	138	139	140	141	142	143	144	145	146
United States	15 463 981	4.5	48 190	(X)	7 848 555	1 394 466	2 908 467	2 678 606	2 604 945	871 793	1 195 026	268 869	32 490
Alabama.............................	184 785	3.2	38 070	48	88 319	12 908	31 888	42 899	41 783	15 945	16 553	4 709	231
Alaska.................................	41 461	3.1	56 202	6	21 211	3 320	6 908	6 609	6 442	1 286	2 395	843	95
Arizona...............................	267 361	4.5	39 217	43	134 025	17 562	49 793	56 304	54 735	18 714	24 275	4 910	351
Arkansas............................	113 924	2.2	38 257	47	52 465	8 343	23 047	27 309	26 629	9 462	11 867	2 518	270
California............................	2 103 669	6.4	53 949	11	1 066 514	202 834	416 270	323 786	314 779	82 561	158 738	35 918	5 274
Colorado.............................	277 732	4.2	50 971	14	146 574	29 743	57 312	36 881	35 626	12 071	16 171	2 939	519
Connecticut........................	246 709	2.9	68 822	2	112 327	27 871	52 179	31 690	30 873	10 793	15 028	2 600	617
Delaware............................	45 058	6.3	47 727	23	24 498	3 728	7 987	9 007	8 791	3 134	4 145	689	83
District of Columbia.............	49 276	6.1	73 505	1	67 557	6 328	9 145	6 256	6 108	1 108	3 615	987	56
Florida................................	900 636	5.5	44 487	29	403 927	52 390	235 263	180 329	175 659	63 951	75 549	17 262	639
Georgia...............................	411 721	5.0	40 367	41	224 339	30 914	68 783	72 940	70 600	24 937	27 592	9 337	445
Hawaii................................	69 129	4.8	48 506	21	34 578	4 960	14 284	10 872	10 546	3 790	4 382	1 301	144
Idaho.................................	63 535	4.6	38 440	45	27 837	7 948	13 080	11 812	11 430	4 529	4 443	1 019	127
Illinois.................................	646 789	3.5	50 377	16	350 206	48 801	122 541	99 401	96 449	33 344	43 385	11 079	1 790
Indiana...............................	277 629	4.0	41 984	38	138 591	26 078	42 212	54 532	53 021	20 118	22 990	4 943	362
Iowa...................................	143 394	3.8	45 930	27	70 124	16 396	25 827	24 677	23 967	9 324	10 389	1 969	402
Kansas...............................	137 316	2.0	47 241	24	66 666	16 159	26 155	21 256	20 590	8 054	8 519	1 894	260
Kentucky............................	170 756	4.4	38 592	44	85 339	11 048	26 231	42 201	41 191	13 557	19 556	4 125	319
Louisiana............................	200 594	3.2	42 963	32	97 087	21 014	33 557	40 818	39 747	11 996	19 433	4 552	262
Maine.................................	56 894	3.7	42 795	34	26 833	4 041	10 090	12 833	12 529	4 550	5 638	1 005	129
Maryland............................	336 187	4.1	56 078	7	162 273	25 336	63 904	46 673	45 294	14 825	21 648	4 397	670
Massachusetts....................	425 353	5.6	62 697	3	235 282	33 933	81 907	63 029	61 491	18 644	32 159	5 985	1 425
Michigan.............................	424 807	4.6	42 833	33	214 703	28 370	73 797	91 438	89 160	33 765	39 974	8 419	924
Minnesota...........................	279 263	4.2	50 938	15	153 846	22 841	50 923	44 234	42 976	14 975	20 177	3 950	741
Mississippi..........................	104 045	1.8	34 805	51	46 433	8 582	15 664	27 334	26 651	8 932	12 138	3 236	131
Missouri..............................	257 338	3.2	42 352	35	134 523	19 532	45 673	51 659	50 270	18 394	22 713	4 303	394
Montana.............................	43 187	4.0	41 845	39	19 271	4 608	9 797	8 088	7 852	3 073	3 048	624	120
Nebraska............................	92 048	1.2	48 606	19	45 743	13 809	16 831	13 452	13 018	4 900	5 324	1 143	94
Nevada...............................	121 096	5.4	41 992	37	60 874	6 033	27 094	20 713	20 042	7 263	8 480	2 069	384
New Hampshire	74 388	4.4	55 926	10	34 467	6 474	14 225	10 726	10 424	4 461	4 403	628	89
New Jersey	537 026	4.1	60 101	4	250 878	49 053	96 382	76 221	74 159	26 100	33 879	6 841	2 000
New Mexico	79 104	3.5	38 025	49	37 444	4 741	14 586	19 088	18 608	5 633	8 978	2 126	183
New York............................	1 161 414	3.8	58 814	5	626 912	98 615	236 861	201 039	196 522	54 141	106 012	22 096	2 315
North Carolina.....................	409 338	4.6	40 790	40	213 256	29 827	70 439	82 122	79 821	29 304	33 410	8 474	316
North Dakota.......................	42 350	-1.2	55 956	9	23 452	4 378	9 208	5 326	5 155	1 798	2 116	427	115
Ohio...................................	505 950	3.5	43 597	31	265 273	37 311	78 001	101 930	99 274	33 861	47 095	9 668	948
Oklahoma............................	178 250	1.8	45 619	28	76 876	32 364	30 499	31 253	30 360	10 917	12 522	3 033	351
Oregon...............................	176 401	6.5	43 830	30	91 124	14 136	34 064	35 702	34 775	12 205	15 740	3 245	554
Pennsylvania.......................	636 857	3.8	49 786	18	308 208	59 538	107 385	122 229	119 321	42 303	55 936	10 894	2 229
Rhode Island.......................	52 834	4.3	50 050	17	25 577	3 646	9 477	10 670	10 431	3 264	5 001	1 135	166
South Carolina	187 532	5.4	38 312	46	90 324	12 530	31 309	42 679	41 560	15 779	16 652	4 232	204
South Dakota	41 104	4.8	47 912	22	17 761	7 179	8 612	6 088	5 894	2 374	2 354	545	31
Tennessee	277 832	5.5	42 127	36	137 424	37 442	39 047	57 156	55 641	20 266	24 090	6 215	320
Texas.................................	1 289 604	4.5	47 015	25	661 654	186 307	210 222	190 023	183 708	56 293	84 667	21 580	2 835
Utah...................................	117 764	6.2	39 378	42	64 680	9 676	21 957	16 014	15 321	5 588	5 704	1 836	177
Vermont..............................	30 418	2.9	48 584	20	14 127	2 330	6 062	6 349	6 207	2 098	3 003	586	71
Virginia...............................	436 350	4.6	52 148	12	225 441	26 241	87 062	59 304	57 391	21 745	22 763	5 294	404
Washington	372 125	4.6	51 971	13	191 805	30 359	77 925	56 395	54 743	19 396	21 830	5 347	1 023
West Virginia.......................	67 787	2.5	36 820	50	30 238	4 165	9 818	19 118	18 695	6 844	8 133	1 714	245
Wisconsin............................	264 988	3.6	45 942	26	135 408	19 077	47 544	46 005	44 683	17 863	18 920	3 988	567
Wyoming	32 870	0.4	56 038	8	14 260	3 647	9 637	4 138	4 004	1 560	1 494	240	89

1. Based on the resident population estimated as of July 1 of the year shown.   2. Includes supplements to wages and salaries.

Table A. States — Personal Income and Earnings

STATE	Personal tax payments, 2015 (mil dol)	Disposable personal income, 2015		Earnings, 2015									Gross state product, 2015 (mil dol)
							Percent by selected industries						
						Goods-related[2]		Service-related and other[3]					
		Total (mil dol)	Per capita[1] (dollars)	Total (mil dol)	Farm	Total	Manu-facturing	Total	Retail trade	Finance, insurance, real estate, rental and leasing	Health care and social assist-ance	Government	
	147	148	149	150	151	152	153	154	155	156	157	158	159
United States	1 937 011	13 526 970	42 154	11 074 659	0.8	16.8	9.5	65.8	5.9	9.1	10.9	16.6	17 919 651
Alabama	17 749	167 036	34 413	122 154	1.3	20.7	14.3	57.2	6.5	6.7	11.3	20.7	199 656
Alaska	3 817	37 644	51 029	31 340	0.1	19.6	3.1	49.5	5.4	3.8	10.7	30.8	52 747
Arizona	27 234	240 127	35 222	180 699	0.7	14.0	7.9	68.3	7.7	10.0	12.4	16.9	290 903
Arkansas	11 570	102 353	34 371	72 669	2.4	19.3	12.8	60.7	6.9	5.8	12.2	17.6	118 907
California	306 832	1 796 838	46 080	1 521 817	1.2	14.6	9.2	67.2	5.7	8.5	9.3	17.0	2 481 348
Colorado	36 377	241 355	44 295	204 637	0.7	18.2	6.1	65.3	5.3	7.9	8.9	15.8	313 748
Connecticut	40 528	206 182	57 517	164 942	0.1	17.1	11.8	69.6	5.6	16.5	11.0	13.2	252 930
Delaware	5 103	39 955	42 322	34 272	1.0	12.4	6.7	71.0	5.8	17.6	13.2	15.4	68 724
District of Columbia	7 457	41 818	62 380	91 938	0.0	1.6	0.2	59.4	1.0	4.7	5.7	39.0	122 146
Florida	100 332	800 304	39 531	544 853	0.6	10.6	4.8	73.4	7.9	9.2	12.8	15.4	888 087
Georgia	47 420	364 302	35 718	304 778	0.8	14.4	9.2	68.3	6.2	8.0	9.8	16.5	497 944
Hawaii	7 406	61 723	43 309	49 622	0.6	9.5	1.8	59.1	6.1	6.0	9.8	30.9	80 376
Idaho	6 347	57 188	34 600	42 720	5.3	19.3	11.1	58.7	8.9	5.8	11.8	16.7	65 549
Illinois	87 000	559 789	43 600	477 651	0.1	16.2	11.1	69.6	5.3	10.7	10.2	14.1	776 882
Indiana	29 311	248 318	37 551	197 351	0.7	27.1	20.9	59.6	6.1	8.6	12.3	12.7	336 053
Iowa	15 508	127 886	40 963	103 479	5.7	24.1	16.8	54.3	5.7	9.6	10.0	15.9	174 030
Kansas	14 729	122 588	42 174	99 290	2.5	21.6	13.8	58.5	5.5	8.6	10.6	17.5	149 641
Kentucky	18 174	152 581	34 485	118 362	0.7	21.7	14.9	58.1	6.0	6.8	12.2	19.6	193 274
Louisiana	19 828	180 766	38 717	140 633	0.4	25.9	9.4	57.6	6.4	5.7	11.5	16.0	239 305
Maine	5 981	50 912	38 296	37 551	0.3	16.7	9.5	64.7	7.8	6.8	16.2	18.3	57 297
Maryland	46 446	289 741	48 331	227 570	0.1	10.9	4.3	64.3	5.3	8.9	11.2	24.6	365 356
Massachusetts	68 484	356 868	52 603	320 420	0.0	14.1	8.4	73.1	4.6	11.1	13.5	12.7	484 943
Michigan	49 041	375 767	37 888	292 034	0.5	22.0	16.5	63.4	5.9	7.2	12.4	14.1	468 334
Minnesota	39 315	239 948	43 767	209 481	1.7	19.0	12.8	66.2	5.4	10.2	12.6	13.1	328 340
Mississippi	8 850	95 195	31 844	66 123	1.7	21.1	13.2	54.6	7.7	5.2	11.3	22.6	105 819
Missouri	29 075	228 263	37 567	186 353	0.4	16.8	11.0	67.1	6.2	8.5	12.2	15.7	294 491
Montana	5 084	38 103	36 919	28 740	2.5	16.8	4.2	60.9	8.0	6.6	13.6	19.7	45 237
Nebraska	10 353	81 695	43 139	70 138	7.0	16.4	9.8	61.0	5.3	8.1	10.4	15.7	113 282
Nevada	12 691	108 405	37 592	82 638	0.2	12.0	3.6	70.8	6.9	5.5	9.4	17.0	139 724
New Hampshire	7 654	66 734	50 171	49 051	0.1	19.0	11.6	67.8	8.2	8.8	12.4	13.2	73 867
New Jersey	75 639	461 388	51 636	357 154	0.1	12.9	7.3	71.5	5.9	10.4	11.2	15.5	567 738
New Mexico	7 385	71 719	34 475	51 828	1.5	14.8	3.0	56.8	6.9	5.0	11.9	26.9	93 339
New York	196 367	965 047	48 870	880 576	0.1	9.1	4.5	74.3	5.0	17.8	10.7	16.5	1 433 531
North Carolina	46 335	363 004	36 173	293 173	1.2	17.5	11.6	62.3	6.2	8.2	10.2	19.1	495 402
North Dakota	5 007	37 343	49 340	32 892	1.2	25.6	5.7	57.3	6.6	7.1	10.8	16.0	55 860
Ohio	58 045	447 906	38 596	367 756	0.3	20.8	14.8	63.6	5.9	7.2	13.0	15.3	610 928
Oklahoma	17 519	160 731	41 135	128 083	1.6	25.0	8.2	55.8	5.7	5.1	9.5	17.5	185 981
Oregon	22 995	153 406	38 117	126 376	1.4	18.4	12.3	63.9	6.6	6.2	12.6	16.3	217 629
Pennsylvania	76 215	560 642	43 828	448 390	0.4	16.7	10.0	69.5	5.5	7.8	13.8	13.4	709 762
Rhode Island	6 197	46 636	44 179	35 458	0.1	14.2	8.7	68.4	6.3	9.9	14.3	17.1	56 052
South Carolina	18 755	168 777	34 481	124 999	0.1	20.2	14.2	59.1	6.9	7.4	9.5	20.6	201 005
South Dakota	3 881	37 223	43 388	29 483	6.3	18.3	11.3	59.4	7.6	10.0	13.7	16.1	47 244
Tennessee	24 051	253 781	38 481	204 878	0.2	18.3	11.9	67.8	6.9	7.3	16.1	13.8	315 857
Texas	137 989	1 151 615	41 984	985 468	0.6	25.2	9.1	60.3	5.8	8.1	8.9	13.8	1 630 082
Utah	13 281	104 483	34 937	90 130	0.5	18.7	10.1	63.6	7.8	9.0	8.4	17.2	147 503
Vermont	3 258	27 160	43 380	20 101	0.6	18.8	11.0	61.4	7.4	5.4	14.7	19.1	30 038
Virginia	56 275	380 075	45 422	305 268	0.1	11.5	5.9	64.7	5.2	6.8	9.0	23.7	481 084
Washington	40 730	331 395	46 282	265 947	1.7	16.9	10.4	62.7	7.3	6.5	10.0	18.7	445 413
West Virginia	6 806	60 981	33 123	42 243	-0.1	21.4	8.1	57.5	7.0	4.5	15.7	21.1	74 321
Wisconsin	30 874	234 113	40 589	189 248	1.4	24.2	18.2	59.4	6.0	7.6	12.3	15.0	302 076
Wyoming	3 708	29 162	49 717	21 904	1.2	27.4	4.1	47.2	5.7	5.1	6.9	24.3	39 864

1. Based on the resident population estimated as of July 1 of the year shown.   2. Total includes mining, construction, and manufacturing.   3. Includes private sector earnings in forestry, fishing, related activities, and other; utilities; wholesale trade; transportation and warehousing; and information.

Table A. States — Social Security, Employment, and Labor Force

STATE	Social Security beneficiaries, December 2015		Supplemental Security Income recipients, December 2015	Civilian employment and selected occupations,[2] 2015				Civilian labor force (annual average), 2016				
					Percent						Unemployed	
	Number	Rate[1]		Total	Management, business, science and art occupations	Services, sales, and office occupations	Construction and production occupations	Total (1,000)	Percent change, 2015–2016	Employed (1,000)	Total (1,000)	Rate[3]
	160	161	162	163	164	165	166	167	168	169	170	171
United States	58 444 059	182.1	8 308 531	150 534 773	37.1	41.6	21.3	159 187	1.3	151 436	7 751	4.9
Alabama............................	1 108 543	228.4	170 844	2 040 118	33.9	39.9	26.1	2 169	0.8	2 039	130	6.0
Alaska..............................	91 960	124.7	12 515	354 766	36.4	40.4	23.2	360	-0.6	337	24	6.6
Arizona.............................	1 241 101	182	119 715	2 937 510	34.6	46.1	19.3	3 238	2.3	3 066	172	5.3
Arkansas...........................	679 689	228.2	110 053	1 271 063	32.1	40.4	27.5	1 343	0.8	1 289	54	4.0
California...........................	5 651 601	144.9	1 292 302	18 045 450	37.7	41.7	20.6	19 103	1.1	18 065	1 038	5.4
Colorado...........................	813 266	149.3	72 806	2 765 115	41.2	40.6	18.3	2 891	2.0	2 795	96	3.3
Connecticut.......................	659 238	183.9	63 736	1 807 098	42.4	40.6	17.0	1 892	0.1	1 796	96	5.1
Delaware...........................	196 651	208.3	16 880	447 516	40.0	42.3	17.8	473	1.2	452	21	4.4
District of Columbia.............	80 546	120.2	26 886	361 179	61.8	32.7	5.5	392	1.5	369	24	6.0
Florida	4 334 337	214.1	571 293	8 990 221	34.5	47.1	18.4	9 839	2.3	9 359	480	4.9
Georgia	1 714 145	168.1	258 401	4 605 633	36.4	40.7	22.9	4 920	2.8	4 656	264	5.4
Hawaii	256 912	180.3	24 778	675 214	33.6	47.7	18.6	685	1.6	665	21	3.0
Idaho	315 571	190.9	30 774	744 228	33.7	42.1	24.3	815	2.2	783	31	3.8
Illinois	2 174 883	169.4	274 621	6 196 524	37.5	41.2	21.3	6 539	0.5	6 155	384	5.9
Indiana	1 301 948	196.9	128 781	3 119 966	32.9	39.3	27.8	3 327	1.7	3 180	147	4.4
Iowa.................................	622 906	199.5	51 059	1 599 893	34.4	39.0	26.6	1 701	-0.1	1 638	62	3.7
Kansas	528 174	181.7	48 360	1 417 069	37.3	39.1	23.6	1 484	-0.3	1 422	62	4.2
Kentucky	963 497	217.8	184 103	1 928 967	33.2	40.5	26.3	1 992	1.3	1 892	100	5.0
Louisiana	868 017	185.9	178 954	2 037 812	33.7	42.7	23.6	2 121	-1.8	1 992	129	6.1
Maine	329 559	247.9	37 328	648 414	36.5	41.5	21.9	691	1.2	664	27	3.9
Maryland	952 251	158.8	120 254	3 031 466	44.7	39.5	15.8	3 170	0.7	3 034	136	4.3
Massachusetts	1 236 248	182.2	188 207	3 522 203	44.9	39.6	15.5	3 589	0.2	3 456	133	3.7
Michigan	2 141 824	216	275 866	4 512 641	35.2	40.9	23.9	4 837	1.7	4 599	238	4.9
Minnesota	979 776	178.7	94 146	2 913 176	40.2	38.6	21.2	3 001	0.9	2 884	117	3.9
Mississippi.........................	647 420	216.6	123 207	1 206 679	30.8	41.2	28.1	1 280	0.8	1 206	75	5.8
Missouri............................	1 258 256	207.1	140 271	2 880 309	35.4	42.0	22.6	3 112	0.5	2 971	141	4.5
Montana	217 758	211	18 312	489 875	38.1	40.0	21.9	526	1.3	505	22	4.1
Nebraska...........................	330 309	174.4	27 909	986 789	36.6	40.0	23.4	1 011	0.3	979	32	3.2
Nevada.............................	492 121	170.7	53 440	1 331 796	27.4	53.7	19.0	1 427	0.9	1 346	81	5.7
New Hampshire	288 891	217.2	19 588	713 313	40.1	39.6	20.2	749	0.8	727	21	2.8
New Jersey........................	1 583 456	177.2	182 247	4 374 536	41.3	40.8	17.9	4 524	-0.1	4 300	224	5.0
New Mexico	408 931	196.6	64 175	879 807	34.5	45.4	20.1	927	0.4	865	62	6.7
New York	3 513 125	177.9	648 707	9 473 337	39.9	43.5	16.6	9 584	-0.1	9 121	463	4.8
North Carolina....................	1 984 962	197.8	235 704	4 550 972	36.6	40.1	23.3	4 876	2.3	4 629	246	5.1
North Dakota	125 786	166.2	8 198	404 589	35.3	38.8	26.0	416	0.5	403	13	3.2
Ohio.................................	2 290 813	197.4	312 351	5 489 742	35.7	40.6	23.6	5 713	0.4	5 431	282	4.9
Oklahoma..........................	758 912	194.2	96 921	1 753 445	33.6	41.8	24.6	1 828	-0.3	1 739	89	4.9
Oregon	818 228	203.3	86 153	1 881 255	37.7	41.4	20.9	2 055	3.9	1 955	100	4.9
Pennsylvania......................	2 744 424	214.5	368 212	6 109 670	37.4	40.7	21.9	6 472	0.7	6 120	352	5.4
Rhode Island	217 881	206.4	33 114	524 975	38.2	43.3	18.4	552	-0.3	523	29	5.3
South Carolina	1 066 150	217.8	118 080	2 165 702	33.8	42.5	23.6	2 298	1.2	2 187	111	4.8
South Dakota	168 626	196.6	14 834	436 852	33.8	40.9	25.3	453	0.5	440	13	2.8
Tennessee	1 392 164	211.1	181 992	2 998 814	34.3	41.1	24.6	3 135	2.1	2 984	151	4.8
Texas	3 928 648	143.2	666 218	12 693 901	35.3	41.6	23.1	13 285	1.8	12 672	613	4.6
Utah.................................	375 685	125.6	31 365	1 414 337	36.7	41.5	21.8	1 511	3.1	1 460	52	3.4
Vermont............................	142 755	228	15 664	327 841	41.1	38.5	20.5	345	-0.2	334	11	3.3
Virginia.............................	1 443 127	172.5	156 517	4 081 600	43.0	39.0	18.1	4 240	0.7	4 070	170	4.0
Washington	1 260 474	176	151 062	3 397 974	39.8	38.8	21.4	3 644	2.8	3 446	198	5.4
West Virginia......................	468 120	254.3	76 375	738 438	33.5	43.1	23.4	783	0.0	736	47	6.0
Wisconsin..........................	1 170 705	203	118 556	2 959 655	35.2	39.3	25.5	3 120	0.8	2 991	129	4.1
Wyoming	103 689	176.8	6 697	295 328	31.5	39.5	29.0	302	-0.9	286	16	5.3

1. Per 1,000 resident population estimated as of July 1 of the year shown.   2. Persons 16 years old and over.   3. Percent of civilian labor force.

Table A. States — Nonfarm Employment and Earnings

	Private nonfarm employment and earnings, 2016											
	Employed		Manufacturing			Employment (1,000)						
				Average earnings of production workers								
STATE	Total (1,000)	Percent change, 2015–2016	Employment (1,000)	Hourly	Weekly	Construction	Transportation and public utilities	Wholesale trade	Retail trade	Information	Financial activities	Services[1]
	172	173	174	175	176	177	178	179	180	181	182	183
United States	144 306	1.7	12 348	20.43	855.69	6 711.0	5 546.0	5 867.0	15 820.0	2 772.0	8 285.0	64 057.0
Alabama............................	1 976	1.4	261	19.38	821.71	84.3	73.7	73.7	232.9	20.6	96.5	744.6
Alaska...............................	332	-1.9	13	22.16	813.27	16.3	21.8	6.4	37.1	6.3	12.1	123.3
Arizona.............................	2 704	2.6	160	17.61	704.40	134.5	94.4	94.0	328.0	45.3	202.1	1 223.5
Arkansas...........................	1 228	1.5	155	15.84	636.77	50.3	63.9	46.3	142.0	13.5	51.2	486.7
California..........................	16 477	2.6	1 306	21.89	904.06	774.1	585.2	722.5	1 682.5	523.1	822.9	7 522.4
Colorado...........................	2 598	2.2	142	28.67	1 155.40	154.6	81.0	104.9	268.5	71.7	163.3	1 162.2
Connecticut	1 679	0.3	156	26.72	1 138.27	59.0	51.1	62.7	184.6	32.3	130.0	766.2
Delaware...........................	453	1.0	26	17.61	718.49	20.8	17.1	12.0	53.4	4.6	47.1	206.7
District of Columbia...........	782	1.7	1	—	—	15.2	4.8	5.0	22.7	17.0	30.0	447.1
Florida...............................	8 383	3.4	355	21.01	855.11	473.4	278.1	339.3	1 100.7	137.0	546.7	4 052.6
Georgia.............................	4 378	2.7	388	18.14	781.83	176.1	213.8	220.1	492.1	111.4	238.9	1 842.1
Hawaii...............................	648	1.4	14	21.4	849.18	37.8	31.4	17.9	70.6	8.8	28.5	312.3
Idaho.................................	696	3.5	65	19.74	791.57	41.7	23.6	28.8	85.3	9.0	34.1	283.8
Illinois...............................	6 013	0.7	574	20.25	864.68	217.0	289.7	299.5	619.6	98.7	383.2	2 693.6
Indiana..............................	3 083	1.5	523	18.89	785.41	130.6	144.3	118.3	332.5	32.5	133.8	1 232.9
Iowa..................................	1 570	0.6	213	18.66	776.26	80.7	66.3	67.0	182.7	22.5	108.5	569.1
Kansas..............................	1 410	0.5	160	19.0	796.10	61.2	57.7	59.7	149.5	20.7	85.6	552.4
Kentucky	1 914	1.5	249	20.41	893.96	77.0	107.1	76.1	214.0	22.9	93.6	745.6
Louisiana...........................	1 971	-1.2	136	22.11	921.99	140.6	82.6	70.6	234.7	23.6	92.2	827.9
Maine	617	1.1	51	21.28	878.86	27.4	18.5	20.0	82.0	7.7	30.9	277.7
Maryland............................	2 708	1.3	104	19.08	767.02	160.6	89.2	85.9	291.5	37.7	149.0	1 285
Massachusetts	3 562	1.7	246	22.79	945.79	145.8	94.5	124.6	354.6	89.0	223.7	1 827.3
Michigan............................	4 326	1.9	600	20.5	879.45	155.6	137.4	172.0	472.2	57.5	212.9	1 910.1
Minnesota..........................	2 896	1.4	318	20.03	815.22	116.2	101.7	132.0	298.4	50.6	175.6	1 273
Mississippi.........................	1 145	1.0	143	20.33	855.89	44.2	54.6	34.6	140.1	12.1	43.8	420.9
Missouri.............................	2 842	1.6	263	20.26	854.97	120.6	109.0	120.4	316.2	53.2	169.0	1 253.0
Montana.............................	468	1.3	20	18.69	713.96	27.2	18.3	17.4	59.5	6.4	23.8	197.4
Nebraska...........................	1 015	0.8	97	17.79	752.52	50.6	52.3	42.0	110.8	18.5	73.4	397.6
Nevada..............................	1 300	3.3	44	19.13	797.72	76.3	63.7	34.5	143.6	14.4	62.7	689.9
New Hampshire	668	1.9	68	20.67	866.07	25.6	16.3	27.8	95.9	12.5	37.0	293.4
New Jersey	4 076	1.5	242	21.26	856.78	153.0	188.8	215.7	461.5	73.1	248.4	1 877.6
New Mexico	831	0.3	27	16.87	656.24	43.4	24.4	21.4	93.1	12.8	33.5	364.1
New York	9 396	1.5	451	19.51	782.35	289.0	339.8	339.8	944.2	267.1	712.4	4 567.7
North Carolina...................	4 340	2.3	465	17.39	730.38	200.6	137.0	182.7	494.2	78.5	226.4	1 823.3
North Dakota......................	435	-4.1	25	20.61	808.30	32.1	22.7	24.6	49.2	6.7	24.1	152.2
Ohio...................................	5 481	1.1	686	20.59	877.13	205.7	211.1	235.1	574.4	72.3	299.8	2 409.4
Oklahoma..........................	1 652	-1.0	129	18.62	750.39	77.1	64.0	58.5	184.2	21.3	78.8	641.5
Oregon..............................	1 833	2.9	188	19.96	802.39	90.6	60.4	75.3	205.8	33.5	96.8	767.7
Pennsylvania.....................	5 884	0.8	558	19.29	796.68	238.5	275.0	219.5	633.2	84.6	316.7	2 829.5
Rhode Island.....................	490	1.0	40	18.22	710.58	18.2	11.5	16.7	48.2	8.0	33.4	253.0
South Carolina	2 054	2.4	238	19.26	808.92	94.8	75.1	72.2	247.2	27.1	100.0	831.2
South Dakota	433	1.0	42	18.59	780.78	22.9	13.4	21.2	53.8	5.8	29.3	164.6
Tennessee	2 966	2.5	343	18.58	798.94	115.2	163.3	119.9	333.8	45.5	152.8	1 260.5
Texas................................	12 028	1.3	847	22.66	976.65	701.6	521.2	582.2	1 318.3	201.9	732.5	4 977.8
Utah...................................	1 427	3.6	126	20.11	786.30	91.7	57.0	50.1	165.0	36.8	81.8	572.7
Vermont.............................	313	0.3	30	20.14	787.47	15.3	8.0	9.5	38.0	4.6	12.0	139.1
Virginia..............................	3 918	1.5	233	19.56	803.92	187.5	132.0	110.9	419.4	68.0	200.5	1 844.3
Washington........................	3 244	3.1	290	26.42	1 099.07	186.1	104.5	133.3	369.8	120.7	150.7	1 309.6
West Virginia.....................	748	-1.2	47	19.83	781.30	30.1	25.4	21.0	86.9	9.7	27.6	324.0
Wisconsin..........................	2 924	1.1	465	19.62	806.38	111.8	106.7	124.1	308.9	48.8	151.7	1 190.8
Wyoming............................	281	-3.9	9	21.99	853.21	21.2	14.5	8.6	30.7	3.7	10.8	91.9

1. Includes professional and business services, educational and health services, leisure and hospitality, and other services.

Table A. States — Agriculture

STATE	Agriculture, 2012											
	Farms					Land in farms					Value of land and buildings (dollars)	
		Percent with:						Acres				
	Number	Fewer than 50 acres	500 acres or more	Farm operators whose principal occupation is farming (percent)	Government payments, average per farm (dollars)	Acreage (1,000)	Percent change, 2007–2012	Average size of farm	Total irrigated (1,000)	Total cropland (1,000)	Average per farm	Average per acre
	184	185	186	187	188	189	190	191	192	193	194	195
United States	2 109 303	38.6	15.0	47.8	9 925	914 528	-0.8	434	55 822	389 690	1 075 491	2 481
Alabama	43 223	37.4	8.6	44.2	6 802	8 903	-1.4	206	113	2 759	547 524	2 658
Alaska	762	56.2	11.3	54.1	12 473	834	-5.4	1 094	2	84	681 479	623
Arizona	20 005	79.9	8.1	66.1	10 245	26 249	0.5	1 312	881	1 151	844 065	643
Arkansas	45 071	30.8	13.0	47.3	20 013	13 811	-0.4	306	4 804	7 931	807 965	2 637
California	77 857	64.8	9.9	54.5	19 349	25 569	0.8	328	7 862	9 592	2 061 792	6 278
Colorado	36 180	39.4	24.3	49.6	14 897	31 887	0.9	881	2 517	10 650	1 128 277	1 280
Connecticut	5 977	69.8	1.8	46.3	9 328	437	7.6	73	9	151	809 375	11 082
Delaware	2 451	56.5	9.8	63.9	10 553	509	-0.3	208	127	439	1 694 584	8 166
District of Columbia	X	X	X	X	X	X	X	X	X	X	X	X
Florida	47 740	68.6	5.6	48.0	10 158	9 548	3.4	200	1 493	2 744	1 040 259	5 201
Georgia	42 257	39.9	10.4	47.0	9 793	9 621	-5.2	228	1 125	4 191	702 282	3 085
Hawaii	7 000	88.1	2.6	52.0	8 325	1 129	0.7	161	82	174	1 461 342	9 058
Idaho	24 816	47.9	17.1	49.8	10 673	11 497	2.3	474	3 365	5 793	1 052 941	2 222
Illinois	75 087	34.1	20.4	50.4	9 829	26 775	0.6	359	522	23 753	2 261 778	6 305
Indiana	58 695	46.6	12.8	43.7	8 331	14 773	-0.4	251	437	12 591	1 342 826	5 354
Iowa	88 637	30.9	22.4	54.1	11 262	30 748	-0.4	345	172	26 256	2 207 220	6 389
Kansas	61 773	19.0	31.6	48.3	10 426	46 346	-0.4	747	2 881	28 503	1 218 662	1 632
Kentucky	77 064	36.5	6.2	41.7	5 087	13 993	-6.7	169	74	6 336	512 033	3 024
Louisiana	28 093	43.7	11.6	43.2	14 625	8 110	-2.6	281	1 093	4 276	718 179	2 554
Maine	8 173	43.0	6.7	48.5	7 629	1 348	7.9	178	31	477	410 633	2 308
Maryland	12 256	49.2	7.6	48.9	7 784	2 052	-1.0	166	105	1 396	1 148 268	6 930
Massachusetts	7 755	67.5	1.5	50.0	10 416	518	1.1	68	23	161	704 071	10 430
Michigan	52 194	43.9	8.8	48.4	7 567	10 032	-0.8	191	592	7 669	766 148	4 020
Minnesota	74 542	25.2	18.2	52.9	8 962	26 918	-3.3	349	524	21 597	1 474 057	4 220
Mississippi	38 076	28.1	11.8	43.0	10 983	11 456	-4.6	287	1 652	5 076	652 593	2 273
Missouri	99 171	25.5	13.7	44.2	7 834	29 027	-2.6	285	1 181	15 259	795 444	2 791
Montana	28 008	28.1	42.2	55.1	16 865	61 388	-2.7	2 134	1 903	17 022	1 674 568	785
Nebraska	49 969	23.3	37.7	59.7	11 436	45 480	-0.3	907	8 297	21 597	2 159 268	2 380
Nevada	4 137	53.2	18.9	53.0	9 566	5 865	0.8	1 429	688	757	1 324 673	927
New Hampshire	4 391	55.5	3.5	48.0	7 434	472	0.5	108	3	98	449 848	4 167
New Jersey	9 071	71.2	3.1	49.5	7 332	733	-2.5	79	88	457	1 008 402	12 792
New Mexico	24 721	51.3	25.3	50.1	12 829	43 238	-0.1	1 748	680	1 977	755 185	432
New York	35 537	32.6	8.4	57.4	7 955	7 175	0.1	202	60	4 217	525 587	2 600
North Carolina	50 218	48.1	6.8	48.9	8 332	8 475	-0.7	168	175	4 745	726 944	4 338
North Dakota	30 961	11.0	48.8	56.6	15 398	39 675	-1.0	1 268	218	27 147	1 808 801	1 426
Ohio	75 462	41.1	8.3	43.9	6 603	13 957	0.0	185	47	10 749	894 933	4 837
Oklahoma	80 245	25.0	19.0	42.1	8 634	35 087	-2.1	428	480	11 279	573 858	1 340
Oregon	35 439	61.5	10.6	49.9	16 054	16 400	-0.6	460	1 630	4 690	865 613	1 882
Pennsylvania	59 309	39.3	4.1	51.7	5 395	7 809	-1.3	130	39	4 546	704 712	5 425
Rhode Island	1 243	71.1	0.9	49.8	12 344	68	2.6	56	4	23	786 093	14 041
South Carolina	25 266	44.1	8.1	41.0	6 867	4 889	1.7	197	159	1 967	586 518	2 981
South Dakota	31 989	19.6	43.6	58.9	12 451	43 666	-0.9	1 352	379	19 147	2 281 026	1 687
Tennessee	68 050	39.4	5.5	41.8	4 184	10 970	-0.9	160	146	5 330	569 416	3 565
Texas	248 809	37.7	15.8	42.1	12 293	130 399	-0.2	523	4 489	29 148	876 614	1 676
Utah	18 027	57.9	12.3	38.5	8 584	11 095	-1.1	609	1 104	1 646	888 886	1 460
Vermont	7 338	39.2	7.3	51.5	8 929	1 233	1.5	171	4	488	546 627	3 205
Virginia	46 030	38.6	7.7	45.1	7 719	8 104	2.4	180	69	2 991	776 719	4 306
Washington	37 249	63.2	11.0	47.4	22 014	14 973	-1.5	396	1 634	7 527	910 249	2 299
West Virginia	21 489	28.3	5.8	42.6	3 203	3 698	-2.5	168	2	804	413 407	2 463
Wisconsin	69 754	32.2	8.8	49.8	6 093	15 191	-4.1	209	422	9 911	819 551	3 924
Wyoming	11 736	28.8	36.3	49.8	10 027	30 170	0.6	2 587	1 436	2 419	1 759 200	680

Table A. States — Agriculture, Land, and Water

STATE	Agriculture, 2012 (cont.)							Land, 2012			
	Value of products sold					Percent of farms with sales of:					
				Percent from:							
	Value of machinery and equipment, average per farm (dollars)	Total (mil dol)	Average per farm (dollars)	Crops	Livestock and poultry products	$10,000 or more	$100,000 or more	Cropland (percent)	Owned by the federal government (percent)	Developed (percent)	Water consumption, 2010 (mil gal per day)
	196	197	198	199	200	201	202	203	204	205	206
United States	115 706	394 644	187 097	53.8	46.2	43.4	18.4	18.7	20.9	5.8	351 417.1
Alabama	71 211	5 571	128 894	23.6	76.4	33.8	11.2	6.9	2.8	8.6	9 960.0
Alaska	87 445	59	77 329	42.2	57.8	42.3	11.4	NA	NA	NA	1 094.5
Arizona	63 624	3 732	186 559	55.6	44.4	20.3	7.3	1.2	41.5	2.9	6 088.2
Arkansas	115 438	9 776	216 897	49.5	50.5	44.0	16.7	21.0	9.6	5.4	11 327.0
California	124 720	42 627	547 510	71.2	28.8	57.0	26.4	9.0	46.7	6.2	37 962.2
Colorado	110 134	7 781	215 060	31.3	68.7	37.7	15.6	11.9	36.1	2.9	10 994.2
Connecticut	58 958	551	92 123	70.7	29.3	30.0	7.7	5.4	0.5	33.9	3 311.0
Delaware	161 559	1 274	519 794	33.7	66.3	64.6	41.7	26.8	1.6	19.0	717.5
District of Columbia	X	X	X	X	X	X	X	NA	NA	NA	0.1
Florida	60 845	7 702	161 322	77.5	22.5	34.3	11.0	7.6	10.3	14.6	14 936.0
Georgia	93 146	9 255	219 020	39.7	60.3	37.4	17.3	11.1	5.5	12.3	4 718.8
Hawaii	43 999	661	94 478	81.5	18.5	41.6	7.2	2.1	14.8	5.9	1 273.8
Idaho	143 835	7 801	314 372	44.1	55.9	44.3	20.5	10.1	62.5	1.7	17 230.5
Illinois	203 192	17 187	228 895	82.3	17.7	54.5	33.0	66.3	1.4	9.5	13 091.3
Indiana	143 252	11 211	191 001	67.2	32.8	48.3	24.4	57.5	2.1	10.9	8 643.0
Iowa	213 856	30 822	347 728	56.3	43.7	62.8	41.0	72.1	0.6	5.4	3 070.5
Kansas	156 740	18 461	298 845	37.8	62.2	56.0	25.5	49.1	0.9	4.0	4 004.8
Kentucky	70 190	5 067	65 755	45.0	55.0	36.5	8.2	21.1	4.9	8.2	4 326.5
Louisiana	104 418	3 809	135 600	73.1	26.9	33.0	11.7	15.8	4.0	6.1	8 540.3
Maine	69 780	763	93 364	62.1	37.9	34.6	9.5	1.7	1.0	4.1	449.3
Maryland	115 879	2 271	185 329	46.3	53.7	43.1	20.6	17.6	2.1	19.2	7 382.0
Massachusetts	53 948	492	63 470	77.8	22.2	32.7	9.8	4.1	1.4	33.1	2 995.9
Michigan	122 533	8 678	166 265	63.5	36.5	44.0	18.0	21.4	8.6	11.3	10 837.2
Minnesota	197 715	21 280	285 479	65.2	34.8	60.0	33.5	39.0	6.4	4.5	3 821.2
Mississippi	91 917	6 441	169 162	46.2	53.8	33.0	12.4	15.6	5.5	6.1	3 933.0
Missouri	88 960	9 165	92 415	49.8	50.2	46.8	12.5	31.3	4.5	6.7	8 568.5
Montana	137 625	4 230	151 031	53.3	46.7	50.4	26.2	15.4	28.7	1.1	7 645.2
Nebraska	230 222	23 069	461 661	49.3	50.7	68.5	43.0	40.4	1.2	2.4	8 036.3
Nevada	134 658	764	184 710	47.9	52.1	42.0	21.2	0.9	84.1	0.8	2 623.1
New Hampshire	56 439	191	43 477	52.8	47.2	26.6	6.0	2.0	13.5	12.3	1 214.6
New Jersey	81 470	1 007	111 006	88.5	11.5	36.1	12.3	9.3	3.4	35.4	5 670.7
New Mexico	60 610	2 550	103 157	24.2	75.8	24.4	7.0	2.0	33.9	1.7	3 161.0
New York	117 163	5 415	152 380	41.5	58.5	49.2	20.0	16.3	0.7	12.2	10 574.5
North Carolina	92 887	12 588	250 670	34.2	65.8	37.3	16.6	15.3	7.1	14.2	12 420.1
North Dakota	300 334	10 951	353 693	88.3	11.7	59.0	40.6	54.7	3.9	2.2	1 147.1
Ohio	116 899	10 064	133 366	65.6	34.4	47.4	20.3	42.0	1.4	15.8	9 442.8
Oklahoma	74 212	7 130	88 848	26.3	73.7	40.8	10.0	19.6	2.7	4.9	3 168.2
Oregon	90 222	4 884	137 805	66.5	33.5	35.6	13.1	5.6	51.7	2.3	6 734.5
Pennsylvania	89 735	7 401	124 783	37.6	62.4	48.1	19.9	17.4	2.3	15.2	8 134.9
Rhode Island	56 065	60	47 990	82.1	17.9	35.7	8.7	2.1	0.5	28.4	375.5
South Carolina	72 400	3 040	120 323	42.6	57.4	27.0	8.6	11.0	5.3	13.5	6 782.2
South Dakota	241 388	10 170	317 929	59.7	40.3	65.0	40.7	35.7	5.6	1.9	625.8
Tennessee	69 248	3 611	53 064	57.8	42.2	30.2	6.1	16.8	5.2	11.6	7 696.6
Texas	72 185	25 376	101 988	29.0	71.0	29.7	7.0	14.0	1.8	5.2	24 796.7
Utah	84 537	1 816	100 746	31.6	68.4	37.2	11.0	2.7	64.1	1.6	4 463.8
Vermont	86 947	776	105 765	22.9	77.1	40.6	15.1	8.6	7.4	6.5	430.5
Virginia	72 561	3 753	81 540	36.2	63.8	37.9	9.6	10.3	8.7	11.7	7 648.0
Washington	98 588	9 121	244 859	71.2	28.8	34.2	16.4	13.2	28.5	5.8	4 955.8
West Virginia	50 027	807	37 544	17.2	82.8	25.3	4.0	4.6	8.2	7.4	3 533.0
Wisconsin	129 561	11 744	168 370	39.2	60.8	52.3	24.6	28.9	5.1	7.7	6 157.6
Wyoming	114 212	1 689	143 952	26.0	74.0	48.8	23.5	3.4	47.2	1.2	4 701.5

Table A. States — Manufactures and Construction

	Manufactures, 2015										Construction, 2012			
	All employees			Production workers								Employees			
						Wages									
STATE	Number (1,000)	Percent change, 2014–2015	Annual payroll (mil dol)	Number (1,000)	Work hours (millions)	Total (mil dol)	Average per worker (dollars)	Value added by manu-facture (mil dol)	Value of ship-ments (mil dol)	Total cost of materials (mil dol)	Number of estab-lishments	Number	Percent change, 2007–2012	Value (mil dol)	Annual payroll (mil dol)
	207	208	209	210	211	212	213	214	215	216	217	218	219	220	221
United States	11 167	1.5	636 504	7 808	15 969	360 741	46 202	2 430 098	5 546 998	3 117 562	598 065	5 669 623	-22.5	1 366 427	272 546
Alabama	234	-0.7	11 989	176	367	7 733	43 984	45 183	129 827	84 638	6 865	78 615	-26.6	17 914	3 312
Alaska	13	-1.0	584	10	21	412	39 681	5 807	3 973	2 156	23 219	5.1	6 431	1 539
Arizona	134	-1.1	8 813	82	165	3 837	47 008	27 667	52 940	25 343	10 540	123 478	-44.3	26 211	5 560
Arkansas	150	1.5	6 671	120	244	4 731	39 311	25 468	59 267	33 706	4 739	42 539	-15.6	8 874	1 666
California	1 124	1.6	72 133	716	1 448	33 570	46 907	253 830	511 912	258 332	60 222	597 083	-31.7	148 808	30 402
Colorado	119	2.9	7 188	78	159	3 658	46 863	25 974	52 722	26 763	13 976	123 296	-29.0	29 762	5 868
Connecticut	156	-0.4	10 827	91	186	4 738	52 065	35 105	57 995	22 972	7 173	54 595	-23.8	14 952	2 949
Delaware	26	1.4	1 496	18	36	804	45 401	6 029	18 674	12 724	1 997	17 708	-31.0	3 821	868
District of Columbia	1	0.4	53	1	2	30	41 383		316	123	390	8 986	14.7	2 643	476
Florida	269	1.9	15 010	180	363	7 735	43 044	56 974	107 033	52 356	39 536	294 308	-37.9	66 489	11 621
Georgia	346	3.5	17 386	262	535	10 845	41 409	68 622	167 762	98 957	13 790	144 936	-35.2	36 691	6 376
Hawaii	11	-0.8	556	7	15	335	44 950		5 904	3 893	2 378	27 541	-22.5	7 939	1 564
Idaho	53	5.0	3 041	39	79	1 810	45 910	8 588	20 421	11 770	5 165	32 033	-36.4	6 573	1 116
Illinois	542	1.0	30 906	379	779	17 290	45 644	108 600	258 510	149 402	25 046	204 819	-24.9	54 281	11 446
Indiana	473	1.6	25 599	357	739	16 619	46 536	105 755	250 419	143 239	12 195	123 888	-16.0	27 325	6 178
Iowa	207	0.8	10 789	150	305	6 516	43 335	48 847	117 584	68 916	7 703	65 860	-6.4	15 586	2 939
Kansas	160	-1.1	8 934	115	233	5 453	47 578	34 517	88 193	53 429	6 070	58 461	-13.7	13 644	2 681
Kentucky	227	3.5	12 212	176	362	8 428	47 862	46 416	133 362	86 788	6 675	63 974	-23.1	13 949	2 760
Louisiana	121	-3.6	8 254	87	184	5 150	59 502	49 642	174 288	123 006	7 318	136 439	0.5	26 212	7 317
Maine	48	1.9	2 567	35	71	1 677	47 627	7 689	15 909	8 198	4 547	25 178	-15.8	4 546	1 011
Maryland	94	1.8	6 032	58	116	2 742	47 289	22 019	40 223	18 383	12 987	144 715	-24.3	37 372	7 421
Massachusetts	226	2.2	15 446	133	270	6 698	50 293	45 709	83 616	38 313	15 689	120 685	-10.9	34 227	6 857
Michigan	545	3.8	31 339	393	822	19 340	49 271	103 492	264 609	162 169	16 123	131 609	-17.8	32 535	6 370
Minnesota	292	2.4	16 327	195	394	8 751	44 903	55 699	119 852	64 297	14 615	113 633	-15.6	32 923	6 061
Mississippi	130	-0.6	6 160	102	207	4 191	41 067	21 572	58 500	36 537	3 736	41 520	-25.8	8 858	1 703
Missouri	248	2.3	13 739	184	364	8 884	48 207	54 050	121 666	69 106	12 435	110 274	-32.9	25 678	5 306
Montana	16	2.9	848	11	22	512	45 945	3 402	9 722	6 379	4 307	23 981	-21.0	5 149	970
Nebraska	94	1.5	4 394	72	148	2 954	41 307	19 289	56 703	37 377	5 676	40 562	-9.1	8 728	1 683
Nevada	40	1.7	2 244	27	54	1 273	47 082	8 249	16 216	7 966	4 335	54 321	-55.8	12 254	2 463
New Hampshire	66	1.0	4 071	40	80	1 808	45 636	11 015	20 288	9 414	3 710	24 409	-18.8	5 202	1 210
New Jersey	225	4.1	14 430	143	292	6 822	47 751	47 702	96 575	48 909	18 806	146 521	-18.7	39 872	8 053
New Mexico	23	-0.2	1 275	16	31	731	46 721	5 639	13 627	7 909	4 084	37 806	-31.3	6 997	1 520
New York	398	0.0	22 836	267	536	12 223	45 853	78 528	150 850	72 431	41 016	333 187	-4.6	87 292	18 169
North Carolina	408	2.4	19 968	304	615	12 181	40 071	107 969	214 445	106 726	18 294	180 433	-25.6	35 964	6 683
North Dakota	24	3.7	1 160	18	37	752	40 638	5 019	13 827	8 648	2 729	25 882	33.6	6 557	1 240
Ohio	649	2.4	35 884	466	961	21 825	46 872	130 628	325 674	194 066	18 439	180 735	-19.4	42 772	8 582
Oklahoma	128	-0.8	6 861	95	193	4 269	45 081	24 953	63 408	38 319	7 541	69 691	-0.2	16 229	3 004
Oregon	157	1.4	9 289	108	219	5 107	47 450	27 579	58 405	30 933	10 051	69 771	-32.2	16 562	3 296
Pennsylvania	531	1.4	29 616	368	753	17 203	46 688	108 333	224 894	116 273	24 874	237 969	-10.5	55 120	11 763
Rhode Island	37	-1.2	2 175	25	51	1 172	46 616	5 925	11 907	5 936	2 868	17 418	-19.6	4 760	850
South Carolina	219	5.9	11 768	163	340	7 471	45 908	45 054	112 930	68 172	8 136	68 679	-36.5	15 219	2 669
South Dakota	44	0.7	2 006	32	66	1 267	39 303	7 479	17 106	9 636	2 916	19 737	-4.2	4 189	757
Tennessee	303	4.1	15 580	224	458	9 745	43 512	63 708	144 722	81 204	8 627	103 474	-16.9	23 078	4 505
Texas	745	-1.6	45 047	513	1 067	25 072	48 835	219 272	566 356	343 403	34 641	572 922	-4.0	146 299	27 831
Utah	110	2.9	6 212	74	149	3 424	46 292	22 739	48 646	25 918	7 294	64 534	-27.4	16 329	2 716
Vermont	27	-3.0	1 502	19	37	827	44 372	4 134	8 579	4 388	2 596	15 667	-10.3	3 012	648
Virginia	230	1.8	12 587	165	334	7 532	45 685	57 468	101 654	44 189	17 108	177 074	-24.7	42 371	8 067
Washington	250	0.7	16 351	166	340	8 975	54 170	69 611	144 903	78 783	17 741	138 649	-30.3	33 760	7 086
West Virginia	44	-0.3	2 605	31	64	1 599	51 026	11 536	24 595	13 059	3 017	26 670	-16.6	4 975	1 116
Wisconsin	437	2.0	23 110	312	639	13 595	43 509	80 759	175 958	95 353	12 207	102 542	-18.8	25 625	5 063
Wyoming	9	-1.7	633	7	14	425	63 069	2 809	7 702	4 837	2 610	20 067	-10.9	3 966	877

Table A. States — Wholesale Trade and Retail Trade

STATE	Wholesale trade, 2012					Retail trade,[1] 2012								
	Employees						Employees							
	Number of establishments	Number	Percent change, 2007–2012	Sales (mil dol)	Annual payroll (mil dol)	Number of establishments	Total	Percent change, 2007–2012	Motor vehicle and parts dealers	Food and beverage stores	Clothing and clothing accessory stores	General merchandise stores	Sales (mil dol)	Annual payroll (mil dol)
	222	223	224	225	226	227	228	229	230	231	232	233	234	235
United States	419 464	5 881 913	-5.5	7 899 979	362 121	1 062 083	14 703 529	-5.2	1 709 998	2 864 650	1 664 114	2 772 612	4 219 822	369 001
Alabama	5 408	73 312	-9.6	75 845	3 669	18 211	218 531	-8.5	28 975	29 631	21 550	53 855	58 565	5 123
Alaska	743	8 740	-3.6	9 615	517	2 508	33 721	-3.6	3 772	7 386	2 228	8 225	10 474	977
Arizona	6 647	88 916	-13.0	96 619	5 159	17 479	286 184	-15.2	37 592	50 041	29 030	60 429	84 717	7 368
Arkansas	3 462	41 577	-13.3	61 692	2 068	10 923	135 448	-3.3	17 615	18 725	10 562	37 096	36 815	3 062
California	59 293	842 343	-5.1	969 250	58 755	106 419	1 540 055	-8.5	165 764	332 177	215 230	250 267	481 800	43 361
Colorado	7 224	92 714	-12.0	118 605	6 155	18 474	245 704	-6.2	29 189	47 396	24 058	45 245	67 815	6 509
Connecticut	4 324	75 460	-0.7	216 166	5 321	12 597	182 528	-6.9	20 097	43 566	24 279	23 858	51 632	4 975
Delaware	1 029	14 465	-25.6	20 474	1 106	3 616	51 711	-6.7	6 594	9 121	6 215	9 474	14 456	1 270
District of Columbia	430	4 259	-17.8	4 103	341	1 710	19 780	3.5	D	6 619	3 916	D	4 440	525
Florida	31 657	296 207	-9.4	342 238	15 394	71 189	947 877	-6.7	109 996	180 849	133 935	173 836	273 867	24 034
Georgia	13 151	184 561	-13.4	246 067	11 191	33 426	433 840	-8.7	D	83 727	48 250	D	119 801	10 290
Hawaii	1 751	18 761	-7.4	13 466	845	4 643	68 360	-3.3	5 981	13 474	13 170	12 784	18 902	1 835
Idaho	2 012	26 221	-1.1	24 397	1 233	5 815	72 980	-9.3	10 373	11 524	5 115	16 057	20 444	1 794
Illinois	19 302	314 389	-2.0	549 200	20 596	39 947	592 942	-7.2	65 978	111 600	68 011	118 814	166 635	14 576
Indiana	7 823	110 761	-4.4	127 024	5 791	21 601	309 552	-7.1	39 062	48 662	25 910	69 169	85 858	7 079
Iowa	4 992	67 124	3.4	76 728	3 263	12 046	174 556	-1.5	21 506	36 192	12 346	33 369	44 906	3 865
Kansas	4 565	65 118	13.1	103 968	3 701	10 548	145 480	-2.8	17 830	27 677	12 656	29 608	38 276	3 325
Kentucky	4 324	67 581	-4.7	100 077	3 679	15 224	202 615	-5.7	24 909	34 136	16 129	47 191	54 870	4 619
Louisiana	5 610	76 773	1.6	86 301	4 008	16 743	220 257	-4.8	27 024	33 458	21 780	50 414	61 396	5 335
Maine	1 550	16 759	-10.5	16 370	818	6 351	80 155	-3.8	9 746	18 108	5 918	11 905	21 522	1 885
Maryland	5 698	85 955	-13.7	84 734	5 379	18 179	281 678	-4.5	35 373	63 344	34 220	48 063	76 380	7 168
Massachusetts	8 061	139 520	-8.5	182 173	10 304	24 311	351 598	-2.4	32 685	99 593	45 747	40 988	92 915	9 162
Michigan	11 489	166 238	-3.5	254 319	9 800	34 858	441 190	-6.3	52 989	72 592	42 860	101 906	119 302	10 527
Minnesota	8 298	134 596	-3.0	167 376	9 335	19 109	288 888	-5.9	30 830	52 671	25 578	58 637	78 898	6 858
Mississippi	2 858	34 757	-6.6	35 523	1 583	11 594	136 032	-3.8	15 581	18 984	12 603	36 906	37 053	2 868
Missouri	7 955	126 328	-2.2	135 013	6 203	21 456	302 568	-4.6	37 602	47 881	26 145	64 255	90 547	7 278
Montana	1 530	14 443	1.8	15 764	650	4 831	55 418	-5.9	7 496	9 917	3 205	10 123	15 624	1 347
Nebraska	3 160	40 832	5.4	58 624	2 111	7 279	105 953	-2.1	12 622	19 100	7 872	19 657	30 471	2 440
Nevada	2 970	33 250	-20.2	28 436	1 890	8 135	129 977	-7.0	13 417	21 310	23 568	24 118	38 234	3 454
New Hampshire	1 865	24 558	-1.6	22 683	1 588	6 127	95 660	-2.7	11 462	23 302	8 438	14 559	26 018	2 404
New Jersey	14 661	263 316	-7.1	406 845	21 240	31 722	436 299	-5.3	42 776	104 425	63 756	61 632	133 666	12 676
New Mexico	1 937	21 929	-4.4	17 405	1 211	6 590	90 792	-6.8	12 096	13 431	7 112	21 333	25 179	2 215
New York	32 704	368 966	-10.7	434 354	23 106	77 463	905 325	1.4	71 441	211 095	149 390	124 135	251 168	23 641
North Carolina	11 830	172 760	-4.4	175 657	10 376	34 288	446 373	-4.3	57 916	83 490	44 074	91 034	120 691	10 421
North Dakota	1 618	21 533	22.4	32 269	1 223	3 185	47 186	7.1	6 651	7 231	3 332	8 654	15 520	1 204
Ohio	14 266	229 244	-5.9	252 195	12 812	36 531	549 152	-7.1	69 278	100 346	48 156	110 859	153 554	13 099
Oklahoma	4 660	60 195	-1.7	102 935	3 251	13 051	168 839	-1.3	23 146	21 534	14 904	40 799	50 256	4 055
Oregon	5 395 (r)	72 446 (r)	-6.6	70 111	4 163	13 879	187 402	-8.5	21 349	38 829	17 457	38 684	49 481	4 832
Pennsylvania	15 053	242 365	-1.6	295 599	14 996	43 952	643 903	-4.2	75 264	144 969	66 135	106 485	178 795	15 331
Rhode Island	1 367	20 235	-5.9	27 840	1 322	3 795	47 688	-6.2	4 992	12 033	5 213	6 112	12 064	1 207
South Carolina	5 027	64 418	-5.6	59 732	3 368	17 586	220 438	-4.9	26 447	42 487	23 822	45 385	58 094	4 955
South Dakota	1 487	17 702	13.1	25 292	827	3 843	49 867	-1.9	6 834	9 249	2 958	9 057	13 792	1 127
Tennessee	6 902	112 664	-8.8	169 781	6 170	22 615	306 078	-4.6	36 861	50 721	29 518	65 515	91 642	7 420
Texas	32 656	496 603	0.3	1 129 151	31 454	78 281	1 150 148	1.0	147 197	209 508	138 335	228 562	356 116	28 835
Utah	3 664	50 741	-4.1	43 854	2 791	9 095	133 535	-6.1	16 109	21 609	13 300	26 428	38 024	3 335
Vermont	809	10 742	1.1	12 850	566	3 509	38 910	-3.7	4 793	10 689	2 739	2 555	9 934	967
Virginia	7 381	106 428	-11.4	120 174	6 064	27 415	410 918	-4.8	51 166	78 937	44 208	78 638	110 002	10 008
Washington	9 361	121 805	-7.8	143 082	7 084	21 588	307 089	-6.4	37 871	60 125	30 279	60 723	118 924	8 723
West Virginia	1 553	19 901	-3.6	19 749	918	6 393	85 305	-7.5	11 506	13 183	5 563	19 982	22 638	1 908
Wisconsin	7 113	113 112	-3.9	111 021	6 250	19 272	296 956	-7.2	36 012	52 527	21 622	59 092	78 202	6 835
Wyoming	839	8 290	8.4	7 238	477	2 681	30 088	-6.1	4 324	5 469	1 717	5 745	9 446	796

1. Establishments with payroll.

Table A. States — Information

STATE	Information, 2012										
	Employees										
	Number of establishments	Number	Percent change, 2007–2012	Publishing, except Internet	Motion picture and sound recording	Broadcasting, except Internet	Internet publishing and broadcasting and web search portals	Telecommunications	Data processing, hosting, and related services	Receipts (mil dol)	Annual payroll (mil dol)
	236	237	238	239	240	241	242	243	244	245	246
United States	138 341	3 321 226	-5.0	876 286	304 497	278 168	183 436	1 134 466	497 300	1 238 463	269 070
Alabama	1 574	35 102	-12.4	9 500	1 978	D	224	16 043	3 940	NA	1 898
Alaska	399	6 523	-3.4	680	637	839	29	4 025	D	NA	395
Arizona	2 117	48 994	-6.8	12 950	4 561	D	684	16 008	11 055	NA	2 983
Arkansas	1 020	23 729	-9.0	5 710	D	D	61	7 958	6 554	NA	1 362
California	21 925	561 399	0.9	140 978	113 899	48 593	63 536	112 158	78 236	NA	70 662
Colorado	3 023	81 953	-3.1	16 527	4 294	3 720	2 938	39 441	14 723	NA	5 851
Connecticut	1 675	37 338	-7.5	8 690	2 609	4 887	2 386	12 652	4 534	NA	2 712
Delaware	417	6 964	-18.7	1 390	365	252	183	3 535	1 077	NA	403
District of Columbia	741	22 144	-9.6	7 781	1 035	4 712	2 189	4 136	1 084	NA	2 215
Florida	8 030	152 775	-12.9	36 131	11 716	14 729	3 032	67 240	18 959	NA	10 280
Georgia	4 155	123 145	0.5	20 111	6 875	12 686	5 706	58 004	19 011	NA	9 197
Hawaii	543	8 329	-17.4	1 510	1 034	D	99	4 051	771	NA	495
Idaho	654	12 264	-19.1	2 654	793	1 055	D	6 084	1 040	NA	557
Illinois	5 404	124 859	-8.6	35 176	9 134	8 037	9 424	42 171	19 375	NA	8 942
Indiana	2 183	42 361	-7.5	10 541	D	D	1 475	15 471	7 241	NA	2 299
Iowa	1 545	30 342	-11.8	9 799	D	D	405	9 876	5 668	NA	1 400
Kansas	1 406	34 052	-35.4	6 968	1 792	2 219	D	17 537	4 665	NA	2 026
Kentucky	1 552	33 009	-2.9	6 069	1 974	2 813	625	11 151	9 665	NA	1 393
Louisiana	1 426	24 743	-19.0	4 191	1 957	3 079	170	12 950	2 235	NA	1 274
Maine	845	11 952	-11.6	3 040	705	977	100	4 735	1 711	NA	538
Maryland	2 381	56 781	-10.0	12 898	3 321	5 392	1 057	22 691	9 865	NA	4 256
Massachusetts	3 673	115 614	5.1	46 869	4 771	4 691	8 714	26 157	22 905	NA	10 521
Michigan	3 294	67 232	-13.4	22 993	D	D	1 619	23 596	D	NA	4 349
Minnesota	2 655	63 187	-10.1	23 085	4 282	4 234	D	15 939	9 328	NA	4 534
Mississippi	926	13 879	-12.7	2 504	742	D	64	8 017	809	NA	605
Missouri	2 422	59 607	-18.4	15 435	D	D	1 318	22 894	11 355	NA	3 805
Montana	615	9 160	-3.6	2 657	653	D	116	3 897	879	NA	427
Nebraska	954	20 647	2.1	7 278	D	D	1 052	5 882	3 361	NA	1 180
Nevada	1 234	17 216	-3.9	3 444	D	D	568	7 165	2 095	NA	931
New Hampshire	802	13 731	-11.3	5 780	768	596	98	4 947	1 300	NA	1 050
New Jersey	3 705	119 179	-11.3	24 725	5 521	3 545	18 231	50 376	15 450	NA	9 815
New Mexico	764	12 516	-10.5	2 155	1 175	1 270	109	7 057	601	NA	536
New York	11 335	286 744	-4.8	71 481	32 463	43 156	20 452	73 996	32 436	NA	25 032
North Carolina	3 570	79 833	4.5	20 995	4 995	5 165	1 085	32 220	14 630	NA	5 181
North Dakota	361	7 052	-1.0	2 788	358	D	32	2 134	413	NA	391
Ohio	3 956	90 083	-7.5	29 098	5 242	6 759	4 857	32 372	11 193	NA	5 607
Oklahoma	1 497	28 890	-11.1	4 770	2 001	2 628	130	15 990	2 903	NA	1 377
Oregon	2 010	38 799	-1.2	12 409	3 040	2 874	1 459	11 826	7 031	NA	2 312
Pennsylvania	5 109	130 606	-4.7	38 947	6 549	8 123	2 309	51 934	17 445	NA	8 997
Rhode Island	435	7 236	-10.2	1 918	D	D	D	3 154	508	NA	445
South Carolina	1 436	34 056	3.0	8 022	D	D	214	17 331	3 208	NA	1 796
South Dakota	446	6 750	-7.5	1 829	D	1 108	D	2 577	600	NA	286
Tennessee	2 489	48 231	-5.0	9 733	5 219	5 435	653	20 647	6 336	NA	2 674
Texas	9 221	230 781	-7.8	42 166	17 247	16 362	4 957	99 015	48 907	NA	16 243
Utah	1 414	37 498	12.6	11 709	3 447	1 556	2 276	8 780	9 481	NA	2 241
Vermont	507	6 775	12.0	2 188	433	576	285	1 483	1 510	NA	370
Virginia	3 916	101 402	-2.6	24 116	5 102	6 648	4 123	41 053	19 447	NA	8 080
Washington	3 281	128 014	14.5	62 052	6 497	3 911	5 719	32 449	15 415	NA	15 482
West Virginia	673	10 945	6.4	2 082	592	1 385	D	5 914	843	NA	509
Wisconsin	2 295	52 807	-2.5	18 801	3 544	5 519	1 088	15 998	7 721	NA	2 982
Wyoming	331	3 998	-3.9	963	386	453	D	1 749	320	NA	173

Table A. States — Utilities, Transportation and Warehousing, and Finance and Insurance

STATE	Utilities, 2012					Transportation and warehousing, 2012					Finance and insurance, 2012				
	Number of establishments	Employees		Receipts (mil dol)	Annual payroll (mil dol)	Number of establishments	Employees		Receipts (mil dol)	Annual payroll (mil dol)	Number of establishments	Employees		Receipts (mil dol)	Annual payroll (mil dol)
		Number	Percent change, 2007–2012				Number	Percent change, 2007–2012				Number	Percent change, 2007–2012		
	247	248	249	250	251	252	253	254	255	256	257	258	259	260	261
United States	17 595	651 234	2.2	531 891	58 922 951	213 809	4 305 464	-3.3	730 541	183 841	468 183	6 040 880	-8.6	3 636 114	523 553
Alabama.............................	424	15 454	7.3	NA	1 361 953	2 836	57 835	-6.4	8 422	2 460	7 294	72 763	1.0	NA	4 466
Alaska.................................	86	2 025	17.0	NA	184 291	1 091	18 957	-5.9	5 176	1 183	740	7 215	-7.2	NA	433
Arizona...............................	265	12 185	1.9	NA	1 096 751	3 110	80 725	-3.6	13 864	3 442	9 196	128 762	-12.9	NA	7 847
Arkansas.............................	320	7 065	-0.9	NA	528 383	2 356	50 798	-15.5	7 945	2 047	4 319	35 504	-6.1	NA	1 924
California............................	1 143	66 836	4.5	NA	7 009 835	21 218	441 734	-2.3	78 926	19 716	48 523	601 858	-16.4	NA	57 898
Colorado.............................	365	8 498	0.4	NA	736 022	3 443	61 976	-4.3	13 963	2 851	9 828	98 761	-7.8	NA	7 418
Connecticut........................	153	10 545	3.3	NA	922 836	1 595	44 003	-0.3	5 114	1 681	6 108	119 326	-13.1	NA	16 627
Delaware.............................	48	2 622	0.3	NA	246 949	612	11 938	2.6	1 056	418	1 920	36 438	-14.1	NA	3 034
District of Columbia..............	47	D	NA	NA	D	193	8 483	-3.7	1 968	342	999	18 080	-7.2	NA	2 666
Florida	699	27 343	-11.6	NA	2 356 891	13 280	209 381	-4.0	49 159	8 958	30 653	338 872	-8.8	NA	22 758
Georgia...............................	599	22 615	-7.7	NA	1 991 441	5 972	154 248	-9.0	26 825	6 840	14 434	164 422	-8.2	NA	12 272
Hawaii................................	54	3 379	14.4	NA	289 114	847	26 839	-17.1	4 599	1 150	1 401	18 686	-9.9	NA	1 145
Idaho..................................	204	3 709	11.4	NA	287 206	1 736	17 195	1.2	2 390	588	2 793	21 698	-3.9	NA	1 035
Illinois................................	492	29 968	8.4	NA	3 044 699	13 251	230 695	-3.0	39 888	10 023	22 230	296 035	-15.0	NA	28 201
Indiana...............................	538	15 558	3.8	NA	1 293 728	5 096	118 242	0.1	16 995	4 438	9 692	96 927	-12.0	NA	5 866
Iowa...................................	272	7 656	-0.8	NA	570 315	3 499	55 762	2.4	7 641	2 111	6 071	91 750	0.7	NA	5 780
Kansas...............................	230	7 263	-20.7	NA	607 926	2 510	50 019	6.7	6 561	1 968	5 976	59 099	-4.1	NA	3 717
Kentucky	340	8 685	4.9	NA	699 968	2 910	84 757	7.4	12 816	3 859	6 346	67 888	1.6	NA	3 838
Louisiana............................	517	11 132	2.5	NA	884 069	3 764	70 059	-2.8	15 110	3 779	7 716	64 813	0.8	NA	3 643
Maine	99	2 363	-6.0	NA	169 783	1 175	14 908	-2.0	1 729	557	1 899	25 688	-4.8	NA	1 574
Maryland.............................	130	9 484	-5.7	NA	1 049 972	3 348	64 906	-3.6	8 719	2 701	7 583	100 204	-20.0	NA	8 630
Massachusetts	274	13 305	0.6	NA	1 324 451	3 558	77 843	-2.1	10 653	3 173 044	9 384	202 811	-8.8	NA	22 940
Michigan.............................	389	23 036	3.7	NA	2 030 234	5 699	106 324	-0.5	20 033	4 525 164	13 181	151 712	-13.5	NA	9 757
Minnesota...........................	320	12 802	8.7	NA	1 218 248	4 617	82 311	2.5	14 948	3 334 532	9 266	157 494	0.6	NA	13 450
Mississippi..........................	592	8 803	1.5	NA	607 227	2 019	33 100	-9.1	4 273	1 303 347	4 692	34 472	-4.0	NA	1 634
Missouri..............................	361	16 131	0.6	NA	1 381 461	4 543	82 336	-7.5	13 788	3 202 496	10 876	132 479	-3.5	NA	8 884
Montana..............................	204	2 925	5.9	NA	232 408	1 475	11 861	1.7	1 972	449 841	1 944	16 206	-4.7	NA	800
Nebraska.............................	115	930	-28.2	NA	77 087	2 283	26 879	-43.8	5 980	1 071 756	4 201	62 434	-3.2	NA	3 811
Nevada...............................	123	4 991	-6.3	NA	466 381	1 409	43 720	-9.6	5 570	1 631 242	4 053	34 396	-18.2	NA	1 982
New Hampshire	120	3 329	4.8	NA	294 495	804	13 787	8.5	1 244	441 785	1 889	24 252	-13.7	NA	1 760
New Jersey	406	20 304	10.7	NA	2 131 755	7 004	160 321	-11.7	26 485	7 078 122	11 927	198 724	-6.9	NA	20 350
New Mexico	234	4 880	-2.6	NA	376 693	1 384	17 510	1.8	2 678	703 942	2 674	22 709	-10.9	NA	1 228
New York	616	42 612	11.2	NA	3 882 982	12 312	240 587	-0.6	43 409	9 676 996	27 518	539 761	-8.6	NA	98 776
North Carolina.....................	478	20 114	-1.8	NA	1 849 812	5 393	108 760	-7.0	14 744	4 277 276	13 088	168 278	-12.5	NA	13 115
North Dakota.......................	124	D	NA	NA	D	1 641	18 847	83.7	4 639	962 681	1 755	17 199	6.0	NA	919
Ohio....................................	627	26 222	-1.1	NA	2 370 045	6 966	158 891	-10.5	23 709	6 649 313	17 443	241 719	-9.2	NA	16 209
Oklahoma............................	345	8 202	-16.5	NA	617 887	2 641	44 502	-7.4	9 571	2 144 251	6 691	57 760	-4.4	NA	3 078
Oregon	286	8 069	1.1	NA	697 565	2 991	52 351	-8.6	7 897	2 156 783	5 812	57 422	-13.9	NA	3 638
Pennsylvania.......................	757	30 687	5.2	NA	3 061 256	8 175	209 798	1.5	25 255	7 843 461	17 733	266 764	-4.5	NA	20 439
Rhode Island.......................	39	1 217	-5.1	NA	108 147	610	11 271	5.5	1 153	363 060	1 311	25 216	-19.7	NA	2 006
South Carolina	333	11 956	-1.5	NA	955 667	2 497	48 696	-13.1	5 443	1 859 027	7 204	66 331	-0.2	NA	3 510
South Dakota	158	2 216	4.4	NA	162 748	1 146	9 549	4.2	1 526	370 640	1 958	26 472	-11.2	NA	1 254
Tennessee	144	3 256	0.2	NA	201 896	4 047	132 825	0.6	18 040	5 168 090	9 726	112 241	-3.5	NA	7 171
Texas.................................	1 953	52 894	14.6	NA	4 467 197	16 998	386 767	3.6	79 794	19 206 695	39 037	481 749	3.5	NA	33 436
Utah...................................	214	4 319	-6.9	NA	374 644	2 177	45 945	-6.9	8 848	1 957 105	4 865	52 959	-9.7	NA	3 344
Vermont..............................	65	D	NA	NA	D	486	5 731	-8.2	677	200 358	990	9 039	-4.1	NA	570
Virginia...............................	314	15 065	-9.4	NA	1 398 172	4 779	90 068	-5.2	14 858	3 926 070	11 190	153 274	-9.0	NA	11 430
Washington.........................	297	9 213	58.3	NA	759 825	4 840	87 862	0.9	16 791	4 274 033	9 737	97 245	-18.4	NA	7 005
West Virginia.......................	221	5 849	-9.3	NA	453 649	1 234	15 705	-5.3	2 797	602 177	2 148	17 875	-10.5	NA	807
Wisconsin............................	323	14 046	-10.7	NA	1 247 335	5 251	97 724	-6.7	13 100	3 707 470	9 177	140 391	-2.9	NA	9 149
Wyoming.............................	138	2 435	8.9	NA	203 277	988	10 133	16.9	1 801	466 688	992	6 707	-2.1	NA	330

Table A. States — Real Estate and Rental and Leasing and Professional, Scientific, and Technical Services

STATE	Real estate and rental and leasing, 2012					Professional, scientific, and technical services, 2012								
	Number of establishments	Employees Number	Percent change, 2007–2012	Receipts (mil dol)	Annual payroll (mil dol)	Number of establishments	Total	Percent change, 2007–2012	Legal services	Accounting tax preparation, bookkeeping, and payroll services	Architectural, engineering, and related services	Computer systems design and related services	Receipts (mil dol)	Annual payroll (mil dol)
	262	263	264	265	266	267	268	269	270	271	272	273	274	275
United States	354 106	1 923 770	-12.1	487 655	85 326	856 463	8 203 735	4.2	1 148 683	1 443 462	1 354 603	1 473 241	1 480 277	581 406
Alabama	3 858	22 852	-15.7	3 919	820	9 109	89 988	-4.3	13 755	12 456	24 527	18 294	16 320	5 725
Alaska	872	4 212	-3.6	1 023	188	1 898	17 648	37.4	D	1 917	8 171	1 253	3 175	1 178
Arizona	8 089	40 479	-23.1	9 330	1 693	16 198	121 381	-6.2	17 690	20 352	21 731	22 873	19 268	7 379
Arkansas	2 802	12 867	-8.8	1 923	410	5 678	32 210	-0.5	D	6 889	5 762	2 813	4 528	1 567
California	49 276	273 511	-12.5	78 740	13 467	114 321	1 303 232	3.4	141 018	384 308	162 594	200 809	234 371	90 437
Colorado	9 295	38 706	-18.6	8 482	1 570	23 872	180 064	12.1	19 729	20 420	39 432	41 352	33 741	12 932
Connecticut	3 219	19 778	-11.9	5 349	958	9 220	97 578	-4.4	12 910	14 369	12 982	16 920	17 994	8 364
Delaware	1 111	5 402	-7.0	5 471	265	2 543	D	D	D	3 109	2 585	5 393		
District of Columbia	1 112	10 103	4.6	3 214	674	5 061	97 555	9.6	31 675	4 829	8 003	14 685	31 866	11 196
Florida	29 845	139 955	-18.1	30 560	5 337	70 785	440 858	2.5	93 530	73 188	60 374	76 034	70 176	27 100
Georgia	10 484	55 551	-15.7	14 232	2 704	28 112	D	D	31 571	42 729	33 823	56 588		
Hawaii	1 919	11 369	-32.2	3 411	484	3 226	21 629	-3.7	D	3 385	5 251	2 847	3 334	1 266
Idaho	2 033	6 268	-25.1	1 040	184	4 198	32 076	1.3	D	3 702	7 951	2 623	4 274	1 728
Illinois	12 035	76 794	-12.2	23 649	3 816	38 673	364 336	-1.3	57 212	62 779	44 413	62 613	70 263	28 315
Indiana	5 729	31 715	-7.5	6 548	1 172	12 829	99 962	3.9	14 668	19 194	18 906	12 437	14 702	5 491
Iowa	2 742	12 031	-18.0	2 268	426	6 204	48 521	14.5	7 489	9 878	5 908	7 957	6 421	2 467
Kansas	2 999	14 256	-6.0	2 743	508	7 110	60 989	8.3	7 462	12 290	12 765	8 129	8 716	3 596
Kentucky	3 534	18 250	-9.4	4 846	637	8 101	62 851	1.5	10 848	15 446	9 866	8 447	7 782	2 817
Louisiana	4 500	31 298	1.2	7 486	1 461	11 728	88 093	3.1	19 363	16 839	26 874	6 092	13 546	5 023
Maine	1 580	6 242	-10.1	1 100	221	3 492	22 943	3.2	4 025	3 317	4 866	2 813	3 353	1 238
Maryland	6 001	42 838	-13.9	13 410	2 253	19 714	244 710	-2.8	D	20 872	44 204	67 825	50 025	20 161
Massachusetts	6 485	42 788	-11.9	13 628	2 358	21 422	255 022	0.8	29 271	25 343	38 428	51 240	60 370	23 827
Michigan	7 826	48 706	-11.2	11 974	1 807	21 650	D	D	26 862	38 730	59 343	32 723	D	D
Minnesota	6 300	34 499	-12.5	7 828	1 396	16 348	140 927	-0.6	D	18 988	17 814	24 040	23 449	9 739
Mississippi	2 374	10 235	0.6	1 709	334	4 747	30 205	-2.6	D	6 904	5 529	3 438	4 023	1 450
Missouri	6 165	33 447	-15.6	6 730	1 298	13 279	137 981	4.3	21 063	22 228	18 976	30 349	24 293	8 615
Montana	1 726	5 207	-18.8	835	162	3 545	16 660	-1.4	2 972	3 236	4 129	1 185	2 192	799
Nebraska	2 001	10 068	0.9	1 732	389	4 448	74 514	82.5	D	42 825	5 660	8 215	5 727	2 832
Nevada	3 866	22 412	-29.1	4 981	815	8 102	47 934	-17.5	9 894	7 385	8 885	4 681	7 759	2 832
New Hampshire	1 338	7 044	-3.1	1 593	310	3 825	30 159	2.4	D	6 571	4 357	5 756	3 948	1 697
New Jersey	8 749	53 751	-16.0	17 328	2 813	29 390	307 549	-7.3	38 055	44 203	39 728	88 570	58 738	24 013
New Mexico	2 369	9 754	-16.5	1 960	369	4 687	44 175	-0.3	5 449	4 647	8 101	4 058	7 619	2 772
New York	32 033	166 315	-3.1	56 410	8 654	59 302	588 820	4.2	121 085	97 246	59 318	77 105	133 639	49 200
North Carolina	10 104	47 155	-12.0	9 302	1 943	22 855	196 287	6.1	23 399	29 415	28 778	36 677	31 948	12 940
North Dakota	912	5 157	37.6	1 445	248	1 722	13 715	40.0	1 902	1 821	3 213	2 586	1 847	736
Ohio	9 932	60 966	-9.1	16 133	2 442	23 961	233 876	2.3	34 707	36 624	40 381	39 420	35 971	14 220
Oklahoma	4 000	21 261	-14.6	4 270	898	9 470	71 997	9.3	12 250	11 842	21 414	7 113	10 991	4 115
Oregon	5 644	26 016	-16.0	4 650	903	11 663	84 493	-0.9	11 773	11 963	12 941	11 952	11 386	5 841
Pennsylvania	9 438	58 585	-15.0	13 364	2 618	29 297	316 658	6.0	51 348	50 126	58 713	42 585	54 834	22 622
Rhode Island	1 058	5 615	-13.5	1 120	219	2 997	21 165	-7.5	4 086	3 091	3 470	4 696	3 338	1 310
South Carolina	4 692	23 189	-23.8	4 334	826	9 721	79 824	6.5	13 690	11 165	20 796	10 923	12 722	4 817
South Dakota	962	3 526	-8.3	583	106	1 822	11 144	9.3	1 820	2 570	2 277	1 305	1 315	482
Tennessee	5 470	30 593	-18.9	6 178	1 220	10 863	104 552	3.7	D	22 269	18 445	11 327	14 200	6 129
Texas	26 639	169 941	-2.2	38 757	7 752	62 322	639 561	18.3	81 308	90 410	171 740	110 640	122 086	47 256
Utah	4 446	16 197	-20.7	3 226	605	9 009	76 345	11.5	9 137	16 734	11 239	10 085	10 555	3 909
Vermont	741	3 092	-8.9	510	104	2 113	15 948	-3.5	D	5 838	2 056	1 874	1 782	740
Virginia	8 862	54 246	-10.3	11 759	2 378	29 368	429 690	11.0	27 122	35 371	73 172	162 320	92 776	36 365
Washington	9 913	45 209	-11.7	9 695	1 895	20 047	167 512	4.9	D	20 084	30 768	32 431	28 284	11 977
West Virginia	1 405	6 011	-14.8	1 256	204	2 974	24 816	11.6	6 084	4 068	4 320	2 733	3 105	1 143
Wisconsin	4 509	23 762	-12.7	4 359	801	11 301	99 162	1.1	14 704	18 173	17 021	13 998	15 135	5 738
Wyoming	1 076	4 546	-2.3	1 259	216	2 141	9 134	3.5	D	1 324	2 603	419	1 297	467

Table A. States — **Health Care and Social Assistance**

STATE	Health care and social assistance, 2012												
	Subject to federal tax						Tax-exempt						
		Employees							Employees					
	Number of establishments	Total	Percent change, 2007–2012	Ambulatory health care services	Hospitals	Receipts (mil dol)	Annual payroll (mil dol)	Number of establishments	Total	Percent change, 2007–2012	Ambulatory health care services	Hospitals	Receipts (mil dol)	Annual payroll (mil dol)
	276	277	278	279	280	281	282	283	284	285	286	287	288	289
United States	690 525	9 542 138	14.7	5 687 621	677 114	1 008 745	409 812	140 778	8 872 619	4.8	787 378	5 074 227	1 031 697	391 428
Alabama..............................	8 489	142 386	5.5	76 205	20 349	14 628	5 995	1 816	100 808	-2.3	8 624	67 461	11 412	4 244
Alaska................................	1 851	21 389	38.7	12 315	1 849	2 810	1 098	581	27 312	8.4	4 359	12 617	3 565	1 336
Arizona..............................	15 041	184 186	19.6	106 247	15 871	20 221	7 975	1 831	130 921	4.9	13 850	79 719	16 835	6 261
Arkansas............................	5 936	86 999	12.7	42 556	12 408	8 541	3 496	1 549	79 456	5.0	6 689	42 744	7 252	2 823
California............................	89 999	1 005 201	13.8	630 526	66 982	127 356	48 373	13 208	771 239	8.8	72 024	466 701	121 598	42 767
Colorado............................	12 701	140 738	10.8	82 675	7 852	14 693	6 167	2 168	117 160	4.7	18 826	64 999	14 795	5 710
Connecticut........................	7 876	131 732	7.6	73 550		13 333	6 059	2 420	139 540	6.6	13 781	D	16 240	6 475
Delaware............................	1 964	30 400	20.1	18 888		3 174	1 435	560	31 497	7.1	2 618	D	3 830	1 561
District of Columbia............	1 353	24 356	23.6	13 997	3 244	2 871	1 203	712	43 386	4.9	2 717	23 473	6 093	2 393
Florida	51 567	614 004	14.1	360 507	77 106	76 786	27 914	5 092	377 250	3.1	34 574	224 905	47 276	16 521
Georgia..............................	20 166	256 945	12.2	158 607		28 196	11 171	2 568	191 515	0.7	11 486	134 809	23 604	8 344
Hawaii................................	2 794	26 788	-7.7	20 436		3 180	1 347	765	39 984	15.5	4 777	21 720	4 957	1 943
Idaho.................................	4 271	49 613	11.5	26 127	2 924	4 281	1 636	594	33 892	15.1	1 393	25 236	3 614	1 535
Illinois...............................	27 624	383 980	18.1	240 920	15 441	39 270	16 151	5 431	386 504	1.3	22 524	230 249	44 161	16 423
Indiana..............................	12 360	206 531	13.8	113 641	15 020	21 191	8 626	2 796	190 392	1.0	12 842	119 354	17 028	5 804
Iowa..................................	5 582	78 961	12.4	43 888		7 151	3 357	2 549	127 945	-0.1	7 799	D	D	D
Kansas..............................	5 977	93 121	11.5	52 953	6 761	9 678	3 955	1 957	99 151	4.4	6 359	51 968	6 152	2 429
Kentucky............................	9 449	127 446	10.2	69 066	8 611	11 985	5 178	1 976	124 432	4.0	11 499	80 486	11 418	3 868
Louisiana...........................	10 240	167 792	15.6	88 911	19 565	15 870	6 157	1 759	117 187	5.7	4 258	77 104	9 939	3 613
Maine................................	3 071	41 700	4.9	23 055		3 487	1 613	1 659	67 531	4.9	7 036	D	D	D
Maryland............................	13 217	168 241	17.1	105 879		18 823	7 785	2 783	191 493	11.3	9 804	D	D	D
Massachusetts	13 136	237 631	17.2	138 145	18 506	26 639	12 209	5 250	349 854	13.5	32 003	169 964	25 847	10 415
Michigan............................	21 447	270 655	18.4	173 860	14 278	27 435	11 944	4 784	314 875	-1.8	31 655	191 187	27 028	10 346
Minnesota..........................	11 233	189 308	20.6	108 030		15 774	7 259	3 874	250 887	9.5	23 077	D	D	D
Mississippi.........................	5 149	84 441	16.3	43 908	11 822	8 731	3 451	1 062	73 179	-1.5	3 226	54 427	6 833	2 684
Missouri.............................	14 644	184 918	15.9	95 013	14 471	17 917	7 525	3 122	215 022	6.0	18 417	129 225	17 263	6 202
Montana.............................	2 545	24 420	12.2	15 400		2 508	1 041	967	41 237	14.2	2 978	D	D	D
Nebraska............................	4 282	57 239	16.0	31 302	2 328	5 707	2 398	1 128	68 230	4.0	3 575	40 591	5 495	1 806
Nevada..............................	5 766	77 665	6.8	42 411	14 806	9 937	3 598	542	30 920	29.3	2 120	20 737	3 216	1 223
New Hampshire	2 775	35 400	8.2	21 181	2 347	444	1 770	803	51 699	1.4	9 014	25 218	5 615	2 317
New Jersey........................	23 088	297 847	17.7	198 143	10 677	1 468	13 028	3 847	243 028	-2.9	20 746	136 380	27 740	11 297
New Mexico	3 970	67 477	17.5	34 002	8 324	1 176	2 450	997	49 080	2.1	5 093	26 723	5 166	2 138
New York	43 548	540 067	17.4	397 708	3 366	237	22 401	13 186	928 920	7.3	102 840	443 108	100 067	42 779
North Carolina....................	19 152	292 709	2.0	168 931	7 693	1 090	11 432	3 825	236 861	0.2	16 895	151 084	27 922	10 325
North Dakota......................	1 235	15 038	6.4	9 934			776	621	41 601	9.3	1 630	D	3 609	1 638
Ohio..................................	22 945	393 909	13.7	231 564	12 043	1 530	15 471	5 292	404 861	2.5	32 022	254 046	46 278	17 670
Oklahoma...........................	8 868	128 437	6.0	63 736	19 773	3 626	4 996	1 786	84 789	6.5	5 726	49 730	9 413	3 293
Oregon	9 829	105 341	14.7	65 396			4 534	2 646	112 243	11.8	11 445	D	13 940	5 156
Pennsylvania......................	27 983	433 818	17.7	266 329	28 531	3 968	19 364	8 569	521 661	3.1	48 929	245 857	52 550	19 962
Rhode Island	2 470	35 597	2.4	20 571			1 536	766	48 470	2.7	4 687	D	4 756	2 020
South Carolina	8 346	132 360	14.4	70 689	16 924	2 886	5 385	1 502	80 084	-5.3	3 855	51 861	9 119	3 302
South Dakota	1 544	20 514	17.9	11 889			830	754	42 980	10.0	3 975	D	4 189	1 729
Tennessee.........................	12 286	220 313	18.7	123 165	30 315	4 700	9 564	2 611	160 140	5.2	13 454	100 602	17 842	6 664
Texas................................	55 176	945 659	21.2	552 817	118 155	20 879	36 493	6 166	400 005	3.6	30 342	268 014	51 047	18 077
Utah..................................	6 601	77 036	14.9	44 035	7 957	8 254	3 017	684	49 139	7.8	5 381	32 987	5 109	1 573
Vermont.............................	1 370	14 976	-2.6	8 847		1 297	578	726	29 222	10.1	6 615	D	D	D
Virginia..............................	16 070	236 459	15.9	139 138	17 223	25 556	10 868	2 704	174 649	4.5	13 334	102 848	15 825	5 535
Washington........................	16 888	194 136	12.9	115 714		20 414	8 703	2 945	180 091	4.0	23 965	D	D	D
West Virginia......................	3 734	57 400	10.8	27 271	5 215	5 125	2 108	1 205	71 675	14.0	8 152	43 463	5 810	2 094
Wisconsin..........................	11 460	175 153	6.1	99 434	1 679	16 357	7 785	3 199	210 988	3.3	23 362	112 126	17 578	5 514
Wyoming............................	1 457	13 706	17.3	8 109	1 159	1 486	608	441	17 634	0.4	1 026	9 743	1 408	561

Table A. States — Arts, Entertainment, and Recreation and Accommodation and Food Services

STATE	Arts, entertainment, and recreation, 2012					Accommodation and food services, 2012					
		Employees					Employees				
	Number of establishments	Number	Percent change, 2007–2012	Receipts (mil dol)	Annual payroll (mil dol)	Number of establishments	Total	Percent change, 2007–2012	Food services and drinking places	Receipts (mil dol)	Annual payroll (mil dol)
	290	291	292	293	294	295	296	297	298	299	300
United States	124 591	2 081 668	1.0	201 193	64 052	662 489	12 007 689	3.5	10 057 608	708 139	196 103
Alabama...........................	1 086	17 170	-4.5	1 194	297	8 339	157 337	4.3	142 339	7 576	2 071
Alaska.............................	545	5 055	13.4	407	91	2 126	26 836	4.7	20 057	2 221	626
Arizona............................	1 764	42 407	-8.8	3 810	1 263	11 669	251 455	0.3	203 083	13 997	4 030
Arkansas..........................	781	8 881	-3.6	704	160	5 473	95 854	6.6	85 388	4 307	1 183
California..........................	21 191	303 838	0.6	39 179	13 419	78 560	1 394 984	2.1	1 160 464	90 830	25 148
Colorado..........................	2 433	51 235	3.1	3 783	1 323	12 744	240 484	3.8	194 749	13 618	3 995
Connecticut	1 610	26 476	5.2	2 298	715	8 263	134 546	1.9	107 171	9 542	2 591
Delaware	409	8 102	18.2	651	208	1 987	35 609	10.6	31 519	2 148	567
District of Columbia.............	301	7 510	2.6	1 021	412	2 371	60 370	13.9	45 949	5 102	1 505
Florida.............................	7 562	169 796	1.8	16 453	4 904	37 118	786 082	5.3	621 439	49 818	13 598
Georgia............................	2 733	42 851	-4.9	3 780	1 262	18 815	353 638	-0.5	313 419	18 977	5 173
Hawaii	495	10 623	-11.4	844	249	3 518	98 364	0.0	59 938	9 537	2 536
Idaho	712	8 944	-0.8	455	138	3 564	54 257	-4.2	43 787	2 680	726
Illinois.............................	4 520	77 153	-3.1	7 401	2 348	27 117	469 870	0.2	415 659	27 937	7 707
Indiana............................	2 069	33 726	-6.0	3 652	941	13 057	255 223	0.4	224 519	13 077	3 433
Iowa................................	1 466	21 233	-2.0	1 626	364	7 047	115 134	-1.5	96 648	5 469	1 467
Kansas............................	1 000	14 341	-8.3	884	252	5 943	106 850	2.0	95 624	4 873	1 343
Kentucky	1 242	17 360	-6.4	1 207	349	7 678	156 965	3.6	143 432	7 500	2 084
Louisiana..........................	1 376	23 386	-5.6	2 661	720	9 019	193 928	7.6	157 059	11 698	3 111
Maine	849	7 305	-6.3	527	155	3 958	49 672	0.6	40 538	2 901	851
Maryland	1 960	35 932	-4.2	3 391	1 062	11 344	204 222	6.0	181 041	12 517	3 411
Massachusetts	3 130	55 585	5.4	5 012	1 788	16 898	273 185	6.2	243 840	17 509	5 020
Michigan	3 369	46 255	-16.1	3 709	1 416	19 491	347 337	2.4	302 053	17 962	4 872
Minnesota.........................	2 714	42 320	0.6	3 127	1 191	11 345	221 859	0.4	184 868	11 723	3 238
Mississippi........................	656	8 840	8.1	587	161	5 177	116 238	-2.8	82 085	6 999	1 765
Missouri...........................	2 095	38 190	1.8	3 716	1 341	12 459	239 264	-0.9	206 309	12 430	3 409
Montana...........................	1 126	10 903	5.9	785	170	3 458	46 251	0.2	35 921	2 420	650
Nebraska..........................	842	13 090	15.2	780	206	4 326	70 128	1.4	62 732	3 094	855
Nevada............................	1 290	26 705	-11.8	3 645	772	5 815	296 762	-8.8	102 621	27 482	8 556
New Hampshire	724	12 946	11.7	793	235	3 606	54 047	-2.2	44 957	2 942	891
New Jersey	3 421	56 427	10.5	4 632	1 606	20 127	291 933	0.2	233 932	19 674	5 387
New Mexico	652	12 259	-14.5	1 353	268	4 177	82 601	2.7	64 280	4 350	1 250
New York	11 615	162 729	2.8	21 929	6 900	49 731	679 146	14.8	584 408	49 286	13 734
North Carolina....................	3 471	58 185	5.2	4 774	1 535	19 496	358 602	4.5	318 217	18 622	5 041
North Dakota......................	421	4 901	7.0	242	64	1 935	35 698	17.8	26 990	2 045	521
Ohio................................	3 810	60 704	-7.1	5 432	1 977	23 432	437 293	0.2	403 421	20 653	5 743
Oklahoma.........................	1 052	26 375	0.5	2 791	672	7 403	143 561	11.2	125 756	7 121	1 908
Oregon	1 636	24 031	-1.2	1 607	570	10 610	150 482	0.0	126 327	8 467	2 438
Pennsylvania......................	4 402	99 568	19.1	8 748	2 742	27 646	439 159	4.5	386 349	23 504	6 377
Rhode Island......................	537	8 798	-0.4	780	216	2 973	44 063	-0.8	40 040	2 481	706
South Carolina	1 525	24 918	-1.5	1 813	432	9 828	185 282	1.3	158 300	9 764	2 650
South Dakota	668	6 204	-3.6	437	103	2 363	37 974	3.4	29 328	1 874	514
Tennessee	2 326	32 490	0.2	3 355	1 150	12 004	241 348	0.8	211 928	12 499	3 546
Texas..............................	6 304	119 132	8.6	10 287	3 309	48 721	976 390	12.7	868 360	54 481	14 744
Utah................................	923	20 749	12.2	1 181	401	5 108	95 933	4.5	78 587	4 789	1 363
Vermont...........................	451	7 147	-10.8	352	116	1 920	31 365	0.6	18 803	1 564	494
Virginia............................	2 744	54 248	6.0	4 244	1 268	16 832	320 514	6.0	273 558	17 796	4 909
Washington.......................	2 744	58 770	2.0	5 093	1 553	16 333	234 145	0.4	198 551	14 297	4 160
West Virginia......................	756	8 349	-22.7	632	128	3 629	66 302	7.4	52 982	4 036	976
Wisconsin.........................	2 655	43 555	1.8	3 182	1 053	14 137	221 567	-2.6	189 520	10 303	2 764
Wyoming...........................	428	3 971	-1.8	248	79	1 799	27 580	2.2	18 763	1 645	469

Table A. States — Other Services, Except Public Administration, and Government Employment

STATE	Other services, except public administration, 2012								Government employment, 2015		
		Employees									
	Number of establishments	Total	Percent change, 2007–2012	Repair and maintenance	Personal and laundry services	Religious, civic, and similar services	Receipts (mil dol)	Annual payroll (mil dol)	Federal civilian	Federal military	State and local
	301	302	303	304	305	306	307	308	309	310	311
United States	529 691	3 430 711	-1.4	1 194 122	1 349 371	887 218	426 694	108 186	2 811 000	1 955 000	19 376 000
Alabama..............................	6 087	37 291	-7.9	17 145	14 117	6 029	4 378	1 117	53 109	29 508	316 204
Alaska.................................	1 355	7 238	-4.3	2 579	2 228	2 431	905	236	14 964	26 034	63 572
Arizona...............................	8 503	62 073	-9.2	23 444	23 403	15 226	6 232	1 736	54 710	32 306	357 060
Arkansas............................	3 961	21 830	-5.9	8 514	8 577	4 739	2 339	586	20 339	16 839	193 000
California............................	57 009	395 836	-0.9	143 971	155 062	96 803	50 439	12 251	245 204	204 096	2 235 940
Colorado.............................	10 246	64 398	2.6	22 061	23 944	18 393	8 519	2 100	53 453	53 609	371 628
Connecticut	7 282	43 384	-9.6	13 274	20 799	9 311	4 904	1 382	17 781	13 712	228 224
Delaware............................	1 513	9 841	-1.7	2 963	4 705	2 173	975	290	5 668	8 566	60 333
District of Columbia.............	3 357	58 982	18.3	638	7 081	51 263	19 773	4 239	193 919	14 422	40 286
Florida	34 843	195 176	-3.2	60 133	84 877	50 166	20 799	5 415	134 252	94 025	937 309
Georgia	13 828	89 302	-8.9	35 769	36 220	17 313	10 617	2 703	99 029	94 611	572 337
Hawaii	2 808	19 348	-3.8	3 202	7 812	8 334	2 005	539	33 088	58 274	94 002
Idaho..................................	2 553	12 188	-10.9	5 569	4 257	2 362	1 118	311	12 630	8 772	106 892
Illinois.................................	23 334	165 366	-1.4	58 058	59 330	47 978	21 356	5 827	80 035	42 385	753 594
Indiana	10 777	72 937	-3.1	28 900	25 835	18 202	8 910	2 107	36 696	20 861	385 558
Iowa...................................	5 866	30 672	-3.8	11 925	11 612	7 135	3 343	848	17 555	11 706	237 829
Kansas...............................	5 147	29 521	-6.8	10 781	10 367	8 373	3 433	849	25 049	34 937	235 232
Kentucky	5 849	38 364	-6.3	16 863	14 589	6 912	4 071	1 090	36 648	48 037	273 056
Louisiana............................	6 293	43 500	3.0	21 958	14 140	7 402	5 409	1 479	30 243	36 715	295 913
Maine	2 786	13 755	3.4	4 907	4 517	4 331	1 463	376	14 520	6 936	84 726
Maryland.............................	9 978	79 391	2.6	25 219	31 858	22 314	10 880	2 929	173 183	50 284	344 059
Massachusetts	14 008	93 489	3.6	25 127	42 404	25 958	10 455	2 931	45 980	19 682	396 228
Michigan.............................	15 919	96 150	-5.3	37 715	37 999	20 436	10 408	2 720	51 545	17 943	534 668
Minnesota...........................	10 832	72 715	-11.1	22 221	29 525	20 969	7 877	2 017	31 599	19 967	370 038
Mississippi..........................	3 540	19 232	-5.8	8 304	6 723	4 205	1 952	549	25 295	27 515	221 679
Missouri..............................	10 357	62 825	-6.9	25 284	24 124	13 417	6 980	1 835	57 526	35 505	378 004
Montana..............................	2 278	10 917	5.8	4 644	2 731	3 542	1 222	303	13 055	7 857	74 814
Nebraska............................	3 989	21 832	-3.2	9 171	7 747	4 914	2 841	612	16 697	12 491	145 267
Nevada...............................	3 538	25 386	-6.8	8 561	12 023	4 802	2 609	706	18 543	17 910	132 984
New Hampshire	2 879	16 603	2.8	5 699	6 736	4 168	1 555	473	7 544	4 616	82 278
New Jersey	18 327	108 216	2.4	32 991	56 552	18 673	11 608	3 150	49 288	25 185	537 355
New Mexico	2 962	17 464	-3.3	7 474	5 336	4 654	1 799	501	29 200	16 917	162 440
New York	45 646	271 689	8.9	56 633	111 369	103 687	39 709	9 395	115 146	56 762	1 284 098
North Carolina.....................	13 716	80 710	-5.4	32 784	31 859	16 067	9 141	2 321	70 425	128 726	652 330
North Dakota.......................	1 716	9 232	-0.3	3 515	3 137	2 580	1 064	254	9 214	11 440	66 448
Ohio....................................	18 851	127 366	-5.8	44 260	55 364	27 742	13 221	3 491	76 607	35 702	682 926
Oklahoma............................	5 411	32 388	2.3	13 280	12 874	6 234	4 037	940	47 014	33 551	292 218
Oregon	6 894	37 941	-3.0	14 717	13 486	9 738	4 435	1 149	27 820	11 722	242 640
Pennsylvania.......................	25 231	154 319	0.0	51 110	63 740	39 469	17 737	4 367	96 059	35 786	642 693
Rhode Island.......................	2 276	13 046	-9.3	4 172	5 690	3 184	1 445	391	10 494	6 991	54 023
South Carolina	6 666	44 374	-2.5	19 017	15 909	9 448	4 465	1 302	32 872	53 382	319 402
South Dakota	1 805	8 371	-1.7	3 569	2 586	2 216	939	214	11 136	7 896	65 278
Tennessee	8 117	55 990	-10.3	20 581	23 773	11 636	6 526	1 711	49 614	21 650	371 541
Texas..................................	34 116	259 128	2.2	120 606	95 613	42 909	30 172	8 454	195 091	172 422	1 647 199
Utah....................................	4 259	26 026	-0.8	11 864	9 841	4 321	2 544	723	35 048	16 166	193 682
Vermont..............................	1 588	7 211	-0.8	2 223	2 032	2 956	755	199	6 794	4 370	47 114
Virginia...............................	14 726	112 430	1.2	34 521	41 520	36 389	17 079	4 471	196 453	139 516	536 052
Washington	12 425	69 976	-1.7	24 072	29 997	15 907	13 185	2 203	73 286	76 001	481 139
West Virginia.......................	2 661	16 583	0.3	6 969	5 759	3 855	1 773	444	23 310	8 753	123 118
Wisconsin............................	10 210	62 054	-6.5	21 698	25 964	14 392	6 407	1 732	28 898	15 938	389 220
Wyoming.............................	1 373	6 655	2.0	3 467	1 628	1 560	885	215	7 372	6 003	62 366

Table A. States — **State Government Employment and Payroll**

STATE	State government employment, 2015			State government payroll, 2015		Full-time equivalent payroll (1,000 dollars)						
									Percent of total for:			
	Full-time equivalent employees	Full-time employees	Part-time employees	Full-time March payroll (1,000 dollars)	Part-time March payroll (1,000 dollars)	Total March payroll (1,000 dollars)[1]	Administration	Judicial and legal	Police	Corrections	Highways and transportation	Public Welfare
	312	313	314	315	316	317	318	319	320	321	322	323
United States	4 341 978	3 754 288	1 598 689	19 369 134	2 222 088	21 591 222	5.4	4.9	3.1	10.2	6.5	4.9
Alabama...............................	89 469	78 795	30 953	354 423	32 150	386 572	3.7	4.2	1.5	5.1	5.1	3.9
Alaska..................................	26 201	24 260	5 087	138 496	6 517	145 013	7.8	6.8	3.2	8.5	13.3	6.6
Arizona................................	78 789	66 414	32 035	322 223	37 538	359 760	4.0	3.2	3.1	10.9	3.9	6.4
Arkansas..............................	63 297	57 951	17 340	231 863	14 978	246 840	5.5	2.1	2.0	7.5	5.9	5.6
California.............................	404 069	336 495	169 482	2 314 069	354 406	2 668 475	6.4	1.8	4.0	17.5	6.1	0.8
Colorado..............................	80 650	58 531	46 901	321 294	83 707	405 001	3.7	8.0	2.2	9.6	4.5	3.1
Connecticut..........................	63 528	53 902	24 393	338 915	43 049	381 964	6.7	9.4	4.0	10.4	5.7	9.8
Delaware..............................	26 144	23 003	8 488	105 659	11 990	117 650	4.1	7.9	7.2	11.3	9.7	4.9
District of Columbia..............	X	X	X	X	X	X	X	X	X	X	X	X
Florida.................................	178 754	159 899	47 208	693 513	57 878	751 390	4.5	11.6	2.4	11.1	4.6	4.2
Georgia................................	127 892	112 376	56 038	461 191	52 803	513 994	3.3	3.5	2.2	9.2	4.4	4.8
Hawaii..................................	58 478	52 499	19 544	243 114	20 667	263 781	2.6	5.1	0.0	5.1	4.0	0.8
Idaho...................................	23 430	20 303	10 359	99 021	11 191	110 212	7.7	4.8	2.3	11.7	5.4	6.2
Illinois.................................	123 953	104 032	51 566	599 665	88 715	688 380	6.1	3.9	3.5	11.3	6.5	9.2
Indiana................................	88 251	74 557	42 406	329 018	35 137	364 155	3.3	3.1	2.4	5.7	4.0	5.3
Iowa.....................................	50 303	40 760	28 963	255 161	24 231	279 392	3.5	4.9	2.1	5.4	4.4	5.2
Kansas.................................	50 155	44 525	17 979	199 872	19 287	219 159	4.2	4.5	2.2	5.5	5.2	3.7
Kentucky..............................	85 734	75 192	24 132	324 326	27 132	351 458	4.3	6.0	2.4	3.5	5.4	7.9
Louisiana.............................	74 118	66 443	20 999	305 133	20 578	325 711	6.9	2.5	3.7	7.6	6.6	5.2
Maine...................................	21 005	18 362	8 118	79 364	8 861	88 225	7.8	4.2	3.5	5.4	10.4	13.3
Maryland..............................	87 591	78 677	13 563	410 136	40 252	450 387	5.7	7.1	3.2	14.3	8.2	6.9
Massachusetts.....................	101 856	89 587	35 051	516 210	55 230	571 440	6.3	10.6	5.2	13.3	5.2	7.7
Michigan..............................	141 957	112 983	72 581	649 994	118 469	768 464	4.6	1.6	2.2	9.3	2.0	7.9
Minnesota............................	82 277	68 386	34 811	392 068	51 257	443 325	8.6	4.8	1.2	4.9	9.4	2.1
Mississippi...........................	56 711	51 936	13 482	196 744	13 194	209 938	4.1	1.2	2.3	3.7	5.1	6.1
Missouri...............................	87 578	77 626	28 982	297 663	26 116	323 779	4.4	5.5	3.5	11.0	6.1	6.4
Montana...............................	20 877	17 414	9 758	79 095	10 785	89 880	8.4	4.3	3.0	6.0	12.2	8.1
Nebraska..............................	32 122	26 763	10 234	113 686	11 922	125 608	3.7	3.6	3.2	9.3	7.1	6.8
Nevada.................................	28 377	25 246	9 859	121 623	11 234	132 857	9.8	3.9	4.3	12.8	6.2	6.8
New Hampshire	18 905	14 727	11 494	75 120	13 962	89 081	6.7	4.4	3.5	6.6	9.2	9.9
New Jersey...........................	140 977	127 809	29 656	797 886	48 678	846 564	4.3	10.0	3.7	6.5	12.1	6.5
New Mexico..........................	45 909	40 994	13 828	188 300	17 817	206 117	3.1	7.4	1.2	7.2	4.8	3.4
New York..............................	242 861	225 283	45 067	1 382 350	80 126	1 462 476	8.2	9.8	3.9	12.9	13.4	1.7
North Carolina......................	140 242	122 765	45 295	582 835	56 806	639 641	3.0	5.2	2.6	14.5	6.8	0.7
North Dakota........................	19 339	16 170	10 144	76 858	11 755	88 613	5.4	4.3	1.4	4.5	7.3	2.0
Ohio.....................................	138 032	108 641	76 069	570 552	87 517	658 069	6.9	3.0	2.4	10.1	4.7	2.5
Oklahoma.............................	68 922	60 749	26 247	254 330	23 633	277 963	5.3	5.0	4.1	6.2	4.3	8.7
Oregon.................................	66 775	59 468	24 916	292 847	33 450	326 297	8.0	5.2	2.5	8.3	6.4	10.1
Pennsylvania........................	163 446	141 622	64 895	713 808	111 867	825 675	5.7	3.8	5.8	12.2	7.3	5.9
Rhode Island........................	18 370	16 898	7 027	97 511	6 348	103 859	9.1	7.3	2.6	10.1	9.2	8.2
South Carolina	80 171	71 712	21 919	298 456	24 280	322 737	4.8	1.5	2.6	7.9	6.0	5.1
South Dakota	14 475	12 675	6 196	55 591	5 431	61 022	6.8	5.4	2.6	5.6	7.4	11.7
Tennessee	78 383	69 874	26 553	296 918	24 207	321 125	6.2	4.7	2.8	7.1	4.3	8.8
Texas	304 337	270 901	87 685	1 341 590	123 441	1 465 031	3.5	2.2	3.3	9.0	4.2	6.0
Utah.....................................	55 355	46 901	26 916	225 512	30 521	256 033	5.8	3.3	1.6	4.8	3.0	3.7
Vermont................................	14 564	13 348	4 039	66 935	6 937	73 872	7.7	5.1	5.1	7.5	7.6	10.7
Virginia................................	127 181	107 503	59 392	527 555	69 313	596 869	4.1	3.5	2.9	8.2	7.5	2.3
Washington	122 216	101 960	54 109	531 494	90 900	622 394	3.2	2.2	2.1	6.3	6.1	8.2
West Virginia........................	40 131	36 462	12 369	138 148	11 436	149 584	4.9	5.5	2.9	6.6	13.2	6.5
Wisconsin.............................	74 383	58 731	50 987	306 495	50 839	357 334	4.5	4.2	1.5	12.9	2.7	2.8
Wyoming..............................	13 438	12 178	3 574	54 503	3 551	58 054	8.4	5.2	2.5	8.5	13.1	4.1

State government employment and payroll, 2015

1. Includes program categories not shown separately.

Table A. States — State Government Employment and Payroll and State Government Finances

	State government employment and payroll, 2015 (cont.)							State government finances, 2014							
	Full-time equivalent payroll (1,000 dollars) (cont.)							General revenue (mil dol)							
	Percent of total for:								From federal government		From own sources				
												Taxes		Taxes per capita[1] (dollars)	
STATE	Health	Hospitals	Social Insurance administration	Natural resources and parks	Utilities, sewerage, and waste management	Elementary and secondary education and libraries	Higher education	Total	Total	Per capita (dollars)	Total	Total	Sales and gross receipts	Total	Sales and gross receipts
	324	325	326	327	328	329	330	331	332	333	334	335	336	337	338
United States	4.2	8.8	1.6	3.5	0.3	1.1	38.9	X	X	X	X	X	X	X	X
Alabama	4.7	14.1	0.9	2.2	-	-	48.5	22 948	8 135	1 678	14 813	9 294	4 813	1 916	992
Alaska	3.1	1.0	1.1	10.2	-	8.1	17.2	10 436	2 810	3 814	7 626	3 393	258	4 605	350
Arizona	3.1	9.3	1.8	2.3	-	-	44.6	29 350	10 951	1 627	18 399	13 084	7 760	1 944	1 153
Arkansas	6.0	10.3	1.9	3.8	-	0.1	43.7	18 058	6 097	2 055	11 961	8 937	4 324	3 013	1 458
California	3.9	10.8	2.8	4.4	0.2	-	35.3	230 742	63 517	1 637	167 225	138 070	50 002	3 558	1 289
Colorado	2.2	6.4	1.4	3.1	-	-	49.8	24 739	7 278	1 359	17 462	11 755	4 474	2 195	835
Connecticut	6.4	9.7	1.2	1.4	0.1	-	25.9	25 845	6 365	1 770	19 481	15 938	6 782	4 431	1 886
Delaware	7.4	4.3	1.0	2.4	0.5	-	30.6	7 605	2 102	2 246	5 504	3 176	480	3 395	513
District of Columbia	X	X	X	X	X	X	X	X	X	X	X	X	X	X	X
Florida	7.9	1.9	1.2	4.3	-	-	41.7	76 827	25 802	1 297	51 026	35 384	29 047	1 779	1 460
Georgia	3.7	6.4	0.9	4.7	-	-	52.5	39 007	14 612	1 447	24 395	18 629	7 310	1 845	724
Hawaii	4.0	9.3	0.4	1.8	-	39.9	19.8	11 304	2 811	1 980	8 494	6 033	3 848	4 250	2 710
Idaho	7.6	1.7	3.3	9.4	-	-	30.6	7 436	2 531	1 549	4 904	3 672	1 821	2 246	1 114
Illinois	2.7	8.7	1.6	2.5	-	-	36.8	66 637	18 227	1 415	48 409	39 183	15 759	3 042	1 223
Indiana	2.1	1.8	1.2	2.5	-	-	64.8	33 260	11 056	1 676	22 204	16 847	10 395	2 554	1 576
Iowa	0.9	16.7	1.1	3.5	-	-	44.5	18 889	6 219	2 001	12 670	8 272	3 772	2 662	1 214
Kansas	2.1	15.8	0.2	2.4	-	-	47.4	15 391	3 976	1 369	11 416	7 334	3 891	2 526	1 340
Kentucky	4.6	8.3	1.2	3.6	-	-	47.1	25 268	9 769	2 213	15 499	11 104	5 354	2 516	1 213
Louisiana	5.0	12.1	1.3	6.4	-	0.2	35.5	25 352	10 215	2 197	15 137	9 695	5 116	2 085	1 100
Maine	5.2	2.5	1.8	6.9	-	0.1	30.1	8 193	3 028	2 277	5 164	3 847	1 911	2 892	1 437
Maryland	6.8	4.0	1.0	2.8	-	-	30.0	36 281	11 038	1 847	25 242	18 929	8 023	3 167	1 342
Massachusetts	7.4	4.5	1.5	2.3	1.6	2.0	25.5	49 046	14 166	2 100	34 881	25 236	7 933	3 741	1 176
Michigan	3.6	10.2	0.6	2.5	-	-	51.7	54 834	17 930	1 809	36 905	24 804	12 310	2 503	1 242
Minnesota	4.2	4.4	1.2	4.4	1.0	-	44.7	37 646	9 838	1 803	27 808	23 129	9 759	4 238	1 788
Mississippi	5.6	18.2	1.0	5.1	0.2	-	40.2	17 576	7 378	2 464	10 199	7 575	4 705	2 530	1 571
Missouri	3.3	10.8	0.5	2.9	-	-	39.8	26 677	10 395	1 714	16 282	11 241	4 915	1 854	811
Montana	4.6	2.8	3.9	7.8	-	-	30.0	5 977	2 342	2 288	3 635	2 656	550	2 594	538
Nebraska	2.0	10.9	0.8	5.8	-	-	38.2	9 779	3 095	1 645	6 684	4 877	2 304	2 592	1 225
Nevada	5.1	4.9	1.5	3.7	0.2	-	32.0	11 480	3 021	1 064	8 459	7 143	5 714	2 516	2 013
New Hampshire	4.9	2.9	1.4	2.6	0.1	-	36.9	5 913	1 853	1 397	4 060	2 283	877	1 720	661
New Jersey	2.8	8.2	1.0	1.9	0.5	12.1	24.1	56 559	16 049	1 796	40 510	29 679	12 752	3 321	1 427
New Mexico	5.3	16.6	0.6	3.5	-	-	40.3	15 591	5 558	2 665	10 032	5 757	2 800	2 761	1 342
New York	3.5	15.4	2.9	2.0	1.0	-	19.5	146 853	49 114	2 487	97 739	76 979	23 545	3 898	1 192
North Carolina	1.6	12.7	0.9	3.6	0.3	-	42.2	46 909	15 643	1 573	31 266	23 397	9 978	2 353	1 003
North Dakota	8.2	3.3	1.7	6.2	-	-	44.3	8 850	1 534	2 074	7 316	6 120	1 848	8 277	2 499
Ohio	2.7	10.2	1.3	2.1	-	-	48.3	62 101	22 350	1 928	39 751	27 021	15 618	2 331	1 347
Oklahoma	8.3	2.3	1.3	2.9	1.6	-	43.6	21 441	7 410	1 911	14 032	9 103	3 989	2 347	1 029
Oregon	3.4	9.4	4.3	4.4	-	-	34.1	24 356	8 791	2 214	15 565	9 684	1 445	2 439	364
Pennsylvania	1.2	5.3	2.3	4.5	-	-	37.6	70 355	21 869	1 710	48 486	34 193	17 419	2 674	1 362
Rhode Island	5.5	4.4	2.0	2.5	1.9	2.0	21.6	7 117	2 510	2 379	4 607	2 966	1 566	2 811	1 484
South Carolina	6.1	7.1	1.2	2.9	4.0	-	44.7	23 076	7 640	1 581	15 436	8 933	4 628	1 848	958
South Dakota	4.4	2.1	1.5	6.4	-	-	36.7	4 162	1 574	1 844	2 588	1 608	1 297	1 885	1 520
Tennessee	6.1	4.5	1.3	5.7	-	-	42.6	26 493	10 645	1 625	15 848	11 806	8 758	1 803	1 337
Texas	6.4	6.8	1.0	3.9	-	-	49.5	121 679	40 561	1 505	81 118	55 261	45 747	2 050	1 697
Utah	3.4	16.5	1.7	2.5	-	-	47.5	14 974	4 211	1 431	10 763	6 312	2 682	2 145	911
Vermont	3.8	1.8	1.8	5.4	-	-	30.4	5 772	1 943	3 101	3 829	2 963	1 015	4 728	1 620
Virginia	4.1	11.4	0.9	2.7	-	-	46.0	41 469	10 028	1 204	31 441	18 949	6 063	2 276	728
Washington	5.1	9.2	2.8	4.3	0.5	-	44.7	38 296	11 475	1 625	26 821	19 448	15 210	2 754	2 154
West Virginia	1.9	3.1	1.2	5.3	-	-	39.3	12 247	4 350	2 351	7 896	5 380	2 561	2 908	1 384
Wisconsin	2.7	4.6	1.2	3.4	-	-	50.2	32 441	9 256	1 608	23 186	16 411	7 360	2 850	1 278
Wyoming	7.3	4.3	0.9	9.4	-	-	26.9	5 780	2 208	3 780	3 572	2 263	926	3 875	1 585

1. Based on resident population estimated as of July 1 of the year shown.

Table A. States — **State Government Finances and Voting**

STATE	General expenditures (mil dol)										Debt outstanding		Voting and registration, November 2016		Presidential election, 2016 (percent of vote cast)		
		To local govern-ments	Direct general expenditures		By selected function												
	Total		Total	Per capita[1] (dollars)	Educa-tion	Health and hospitals	High-ways	Public safety	Public welfare	Natural resources, parks, and recreation	Total (mil dol)	Per capita[1]	Percent registered	Percent voted	Demo-cratic	Repub-lican	All other
	339	340	341	342	343	344	345	346	347	348	349	350	351	352	353	354	355
United States	X	X	X	X	X	X	X	X	X	X	X	X	64.2	56.0	48.0	45.8	6.2
Alabama	28 128	6 474	18 028	3 717	10 367	2 706	1 685	7 058	6 619	262	8 908	1 837	68.0	56.4	34.4	62.1	3.6
Alaska	12 920	2 059	9 368	12 715	2 769	394	1 244	4 933	2 169	354	6 049	8 210	69.1	59.4	36.6	51.3	12.2
Arizona	33 231	7 448	21 645	3 216	9 714	2 896	1 758	12 803	9 081	263	14 316	2 127	60.5	53.3	45.1	48.7	6.2
Arkansas	20 410	5 199	13 359	4 503	7 611	1 247	1 373	5 123	5 713	256	4 533	1 528	65.7	56.0	33.7	60.6	5.8
California	284 556	91 869	142 962	3 684	79 813	18 665	12 632	106 212	83 486	3 720	156 808	4 041	53.8	48.2	61.7	31.6	6.7
Colorado	30 649	6 750	18 453	3 445	10 079	1 883	1 645	11 518	6 715	343	16 929	3 161	68.2	63.8	48.2	43.3	8.6
Connecticut	29 308	4 899	19 277	5 360	7 226	2 320	1 064	9 326	7 233	160	33 230	9 239	63.9	57.5	54.6	40.9	4.5
Delaware	8 787	1 391	6 587	7 041	2 842	488	531	4 126	2 142	88	5 354	5 723	66.8	57.2	53.4	41.9	4.7
District of Columbia	X	X	X	X	X	X	X	X	X	X	X	X	75.9	68.7	90.5	4.1	5.4
Florida	83 274	18 708	55 769	2 803	25 076	4 739	6 596	27 032	24 368	1 116	36 348	1 827	59.3	52.9	47.8	49.0	3.2
Georgia	45 452	10 558	28 491	2 822	17 402	2 330	2 300	17 711	11 742	452	13 380	1 325	64.1	55.7	45.6	50.8	3.6
Hawaii	12 379	256	10 789	7 600	3 276	1 347	414	2 517	2 583	112	8 427	5 936	49.8	43.3	61.0	29.4	9.6
Idaho	8 449	2 015	5 314	3 251	2 647	232	667	3 065	2 226	207	3 606	2 206	64.5	58.3	27.5	59.3	13.2
Illinois	77 319	16 924	46 456	3 607	17 696	3 415	5 259	18 863	21 228	281	65 832	5 111	68.5	58.8	55.8	38.8	5.4
Indiana	35 990	9 315	23 703	3 593	14 603	663	2 418	8 895	10 593	335	21 120	3 202	66.1	56.0	37.8	56.9	5.3
Iowa	21 214	4 964	13 634	4 388	6 729	1 842	1 807	3 869	5 538	301	6 343	2 042	69.2	60.7	41.8	51.2	7.1
Kansas	16 920	4 108	10 967	3 777	6 095	2 029	1 189	4 419	3 789	224	6 743	2 322	67.1	58.0	36.1	56.7	7.3
Kentucky	29 938	4 649	21 062	4 772	9 253	1 969	2 501	7 033	8 349	317	14 830	3 360	67.3	55.3	32.7	62.5	4.8
Louisiana	31 804	6 053	21 435	4 610	8 593	2 346	1 523	10 480	8 081	720	18 996	4 085	70.6	59.7	38.4	58.1	3.5
Maine	9 258	1 285	6 948	5 224	2 087	573	583	2 178	3 362	162	5 474	4 115	78.5	71.3	46.3	43.5	10.2
Maryland	41 309	8 734	27 303	4 568	11 985	2 698	2 186	19 742	10 834	470	26 379	4 414	67.3	59.2	60.3	33.9	5.8
Massachusetts	58 305	9 812	38 495	5 707	13 477	1 636	2 231	20 417	16 656	415	74 235	11 005	68.1	61.7	59.1	32.3	8.7
Michigan	63 862	19 779	35 509	3 583	23 549	4 526	2 628	23 040	15 680	302	31 528	3 181	71.3	61.8	47.3	47.5	5.2
Minnesota	41 845	12 621	23 878	4 375	14 696	784	2 763	9 633	12 442	702	15 818	2 899	72.9	65.3	46.4	44.9	8.6
Mississippi	20 013	4 920	12 353	4 126	5 507	1 534	1 364	4 929	5 809	264	7 104	2 373	78.3	66.7	40.1	57.9	1.9
Missouri	30 454	5 785	20 364	3 358	9 129	3 338	1 435	10 038	8 069	325	19 042	3 140	72.1	62.8	38.1	56.8	5.1
Montana	7 219	1 382	4 829	4 717	1 920	207	734	2 483	1 502	233	3 402	3 324	72.8	65.2	35.9	56.5	7.6
Nebraska	10 046	2 202	7 151	3 800	3 412	736	742	3 631	2 639	278	1 909	1 014	71.7	63.4	33.7	58.7	7.6
Nevada	13 217	4 169	6 610	2 328	4 460	615	495	3 633	2 720	103	3 521	1 240	61.4	53.5	47.9	45.5	6.6
New Hampshire	7 345	1 269	4 855	3 659	2 038	159	512	1 547	1 760	73	8 099	6 104	73.1	66.9	46.8	46.5	6.7
New Jersey	69 081	12 104	41 413	4 633	17 087	3 732	3 607	22 811	15 923	442	66 090	7 394	60.7	53.4	55.5	41.4	3.2
New Mexico	17 721	4 605	10 890	5 221	5 501	1 511	710	5 773	4 224	189	6 887	3 302	59.2	49.4	48.3	40.0	11.7
New York	178 325	58 135	86 298	4 370	41 599	14 024	4 746	41 199	54 150	390	136 441	6 910	59.0	50.7	56.1	32.4	11.5
North Carolina	51 113	13 173	31 944	3 212	19 054	3 016	3 753	18 405	12 722	467	17 853	1 795	68.1	61.6	46.2	49.8	4.0
North Dakota	7 486	2 262	4 553	6 157	2 124	198	1 347	1 221	1 059	327	1 887	2 552	72.8	62.1	27.2	63.0	9.8
Ohio	79 239	16 648	44 970	3 879	21 480	5 758	3 755	18 433	21 477	372	33 662	2 903	69.5	61.4	43.6	51.7	4.8
Oklahoma	23 378	4 279	15 848	4 087	7 553	1 201	1 888	7 842	6 523	225	9 047	2 333	63.7	53.2	28.9	65.3	5.7
Oregon	29 414	6 007	18 139	4 569	7 895	2 709	1 313	9 668	8 024	517	14 583	3 673	67.4	61.0	50.1	39.1	10.8
Pennsylvania	86 986	18 836	54 046	4 227	22 858	6 992	6 867	28 915	24 369	633	47 573	3 720	69.2	60.2	47.9	48.6	3.6
Rhode Island	8 334	1 198	5 647	5 352	2 026	233	339	2 593	2 538	49	9 388	8 897	64.4	55.5	54.4	38.9	6.7
South Carolina	28 904	5 581	18 102	3 746	8 702	2 586	1 101	6 760	6 658	214	15 089	3 122	69.0	59.8	40.7	54.9	4.4
South Dakota	4 521	746	3 293	3 860	1 278	211	615	1 622	986	179	3 239	3 797	69.3	57.3	31.7	61.5	6.7
Tennessee	30 519	7 222	20 861	3 185	10 115	1 078	1 640	11 757	10 922	294	6 049	924	64.3	52.0	34.7	60.7	4.6
Texas	130 574	29 192	85 452	3 170	50 420	8 350	8 711	45 897	32 834	1 073	41 855	1 553	58.1	47.7	43.2	52.2	4.5
Utah	17 040	3 266	11 881	4 037	7 026	1 663	828	4 597	3 147	177	7 327	2 490	66.7	58.9	27.5	45.5	27.0
Vermont	6 303	1 571	4 294	6 853	2 482	335	474	2 314	1 671	101	3 291	5 253	70.2	61.0	55.7	29.8	14.5
Virginia	48 188	11 793	31 406	3 772	14 825	5 143	4 284	22 741	10 218	245	27 739	3 332	69.4	62.6	49.8	44.4	5.8
Washington	47 971	10 439	30 026	4 252	16 189	4 719	3 023	12 967	9 771	955	31 601	4 475	69.9	60.5	52.5	36.8	10.6
West Virginia	13 241	2 414	9 265	5 007	4 285	464	1 119	3 769	3 719	228	7 987	4 316	63.6	50.4	26.5	68.6	4.9
Wisconsin	38 583	9 890	23 345	4 055	11 195	2 109	2 487	12 427	9 791	681	22 368	3 885	74.4	68.7	46.5	47.2	6.3
Wyoming	5 895	1 913	3 153	5 397	1 763	275	522	1 901	792	359	930	1 591	69.7	63.5	21.6	67.4	11.0

1. Based on resident population estimated as of July 1 of the year shown.

PART B.

States and Counties

(For explanation of symbols, see page viii)

Page

Part B—States and Counties

County Highlights and Rankings

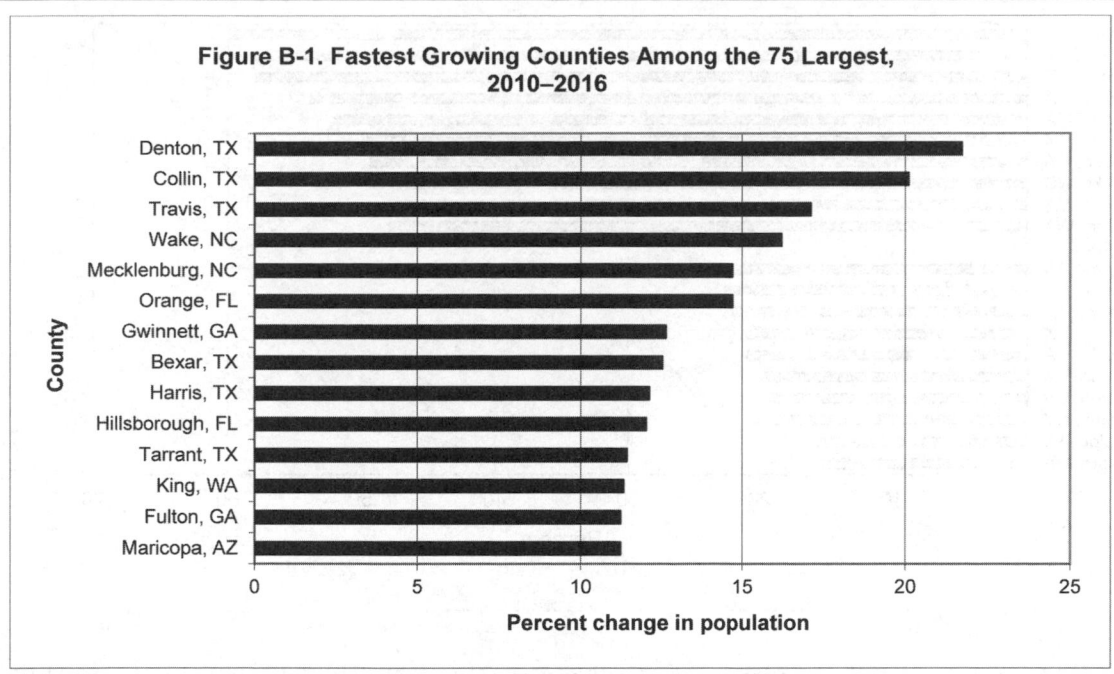

Figure B-1. Fastest Growing Counties Among the 75 Largest, 2010–2016

Six years after the 2010 census, the 2016 population estimates show that Los Angeles County, CA, remains, by far, the most populous county, with more than 10 million residents. Next is Cook County, IL, which includes Chicago, with over 5.2 million people. Its population declined 3.4 percent from 2000 to 2010 but increased 0.2 percent from 2010 to 2016. New York City consists of five counties (the five boroughs), with Kings (Brooklyn) and Queens each with over 2 million residents. Queens county moved out of the top 10 in 2014 but Brooklyn's 5.0 percent growth keeps Kings the 8th most populous county in the nation.

Among the 75 most populous counties, the highest growth rates from 2010 to 2016 were found in the South. From 2010 to 2016, the fastest-growing of these large counties was Denton, TX, in the Dallas-Fort Worth metropolitan area During the past six years, Denton County's population increased by 21.7 percent followed by Collin County, TX (also Dallas) at 20.1 percent. In 2016, Denton County ranked 75th among the most populous counties. Four other counties in Texas also had growth rates over 10 percent—Travis (Austin), Bexar County (San Antonio), Harris (Houston), and Tarrant (Fort Worth). Other large counties that experienced more than 10 percent growth in the five-year period were in North Carolina, Florida, Georgia, Washington, Arizona, and Nevada. Nearly 1,700 counties lost population during this period. The largest proportional losses were in counties with very small populations. Among the largest counties, only New Haven County, CT, Hartford County, CT, Cuyahoga County, OH (Cleveland), and Wayne County, MI (Detroit), declined in population between 2010 and

20165. One-hundred and ninety-one counties had population growth rates at or above 10 percent from 2010 to 2016, and 140 of these fast-growing counties had more than 50,000 residents while 114 counties had more than 100,000 residents.

Within states, the number and physical size of counties varied considerably: Delaware had three counties while Texas had 254 counties. For the 3,142 counties (and county equivalents —see Appendix A) in the United States, population in 2016 ranged from 10.1 million in Los Angeles, CA, to 88 in Kalawao County, HI. Other particularly large counties in terms of population are Cook County, IL (over 5.2 million people), encompassing Chicago and its suburbs, Harris County, TX (containing Houston) with more than 4.5 million people, and Maricopa County, AZ (containing Phoenix), with over 4.2 million people. There were 44 counties with a population of 1,000,000 or more; these counties combined contain more than one-fourth of the U.S. population. Over half of the U.S. population lived in the 150 largest counties, those with a population of 450,000 or more. At the other extreme, there were 35 counfies with fewer than 1,000 people in 2016. The median county population size was 25,771.

In terms of land area, counties range from the nearly 145,493 square miles of Yukon-Koyukuk Census Area, AK; to Kalawao County, HI, with 12 square miles; New York County, NY (Manhattan), with 22.7 square miles; Bristol County, RI, with 24.2 square miles; and Arlington County, VA, with 26 square miles.[1] Counties tend to be larger in the western United States (most of the largest 50 in size are in that

---

[1] Several independent cities in Virginia, which are treated as counties for tabulation purposes, were excluded here.

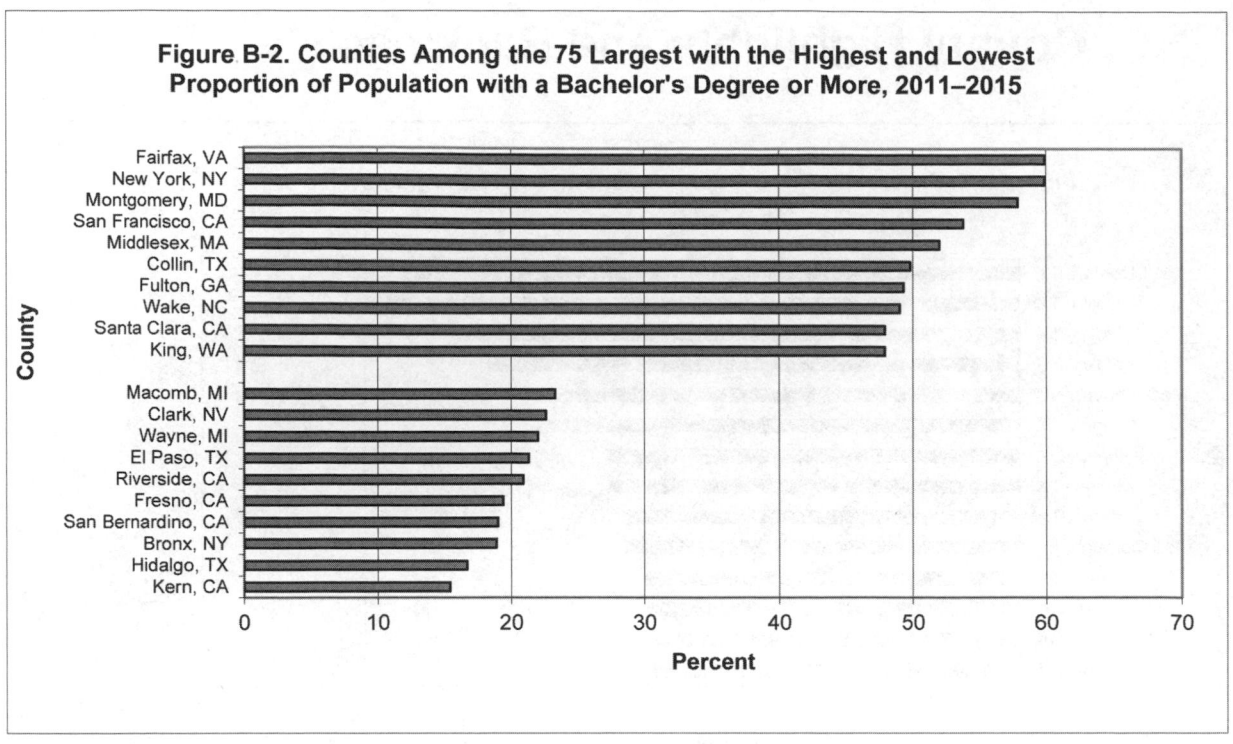

Figure B-2. Counties Among the 75 Largest with the Highest and Lowest Proportion of Population with a Bachelor's Degree or More, 2011–2015

region). The median land area for all U.S. counties was about 616 square miles in 2016.

While New York County, NY, had one of the smallest land areas, it had by far the highest population density among U.S. counties in 2016, with over 72,000 persons per square mile. No other county approached that density (although three other New York City boroughs were among the top five counties in population density). San Francisco had the highest population density outside of New York City, with Suffolk County, MA (Boston); Philadelphia County, PA; and Washington, DC, also among the top 10 counties. The median county had nearly 45 persons per square mile, with 264 counties having more than 500 persons per square mile. The nation's largest county in terms of population (Los Angeles) had a population density of 2,498 persons per square mile. This density ranked 20th among the 75 most populous U.S. counties.

Proportionally large year-to-year labor force changes are not unusual for counties with small populations. The 2016 annual averages reflect a national labor force that increased by 1.3 percent. Among the 75 most populous counties, 12 counties' labor forces grew by 30.0 percent or more between 2015 and 2016. Collin County, TX, and Denton County, TX, the two fastest growing counties also experienced the largest increase among the 75 most populous counties, both over 3.9 percent. Travis County, TX followed with an increase of 3.8 percent. Nearly 1200 counties experienced declines in their labor forces from 2015 to 2016, with 108 counties losing 5 percent or more. Among the most populous 75 counties, 8 counties had decreases in their labor forces,

led by Erie County, NY (Buffalo) at -0.7 percent and Kern County, CA (Bakersfield) at -0.4 percent.

The national annual average unemployment rate was 4.9 percent in 2016—the lowest it has been since 2007. The unemployment rate was down from 5.3 in 2015 and 6.2 in 2014. Nearly 1,600 counties had unemployment rates above the national average of 4.9 percent in 2016 and 67 counties had unemployment rates greater than 10 percent, down from 1,100 counties in 2010 and 82 counties in 2015. Of the 10 counties with the highest unemployment rates, only Imperial County, CA, and Yuma County, AZ, had populations over 100,000. Among the 75 most populous counties, 26 exceeded the national unemployment rate of 4.9 percent, with the highest in two California counties—10.3 percent in Kern county and 9.4 percent in Fresno county. Honolulu, HI had the lowest unemployment rate at 2.8 percent, followed by Middlesex, MA at 3.0 Among smaller counties in 2016, two counties each in North Dakota, South Dakota and Colorado and one in Montana had unemployment rates of 2 percent or less.

Among the 75 largest counties, the two counties with the highest unemployment rates, Fresno and Kern counties in CA, ranked among the top counties for agricultural sales. Meanwhile, Wayne County, MI which ranked second highest in manufacturing employment had the sixth highest unemployment rate among the 75 most populous counties. Three of the ten lowest unemployment rates were in the three counties that topped the rankings for employment in professional, scientific, and technical occupations (Fairfax County, VA, Montgomery County, MD, and San Francisco

County, CA). These three counties were also among the top counties for median household income and educational attainment, with more than 50 percent of residents holding bachelor's, master's, doctoral or professional degrees. Five large counties had college-educated proportions of less than 20 percent and four out of the five had the highest unemployment rates among the large counties. Nationally, 30.6 percent of the population held bachelor's degrees or higher in 2015.

75 Largest Counties by 2016 Population
Selected Rankings

Population, 2016			Land area, 2016				Population density, 2016			
Population rank		Population [col 2]	Population rank	Land area rank	County	Land area (Square miles) [col 1]	Population rank	Density rank	County	Density (per square kilometer) [col 4]
1	Los Angeles, CA	10 137 915	14	1	San Bernardino, CA	20 057	21	1	New York, NY	72 411.2
2	Cook, IL	5 203 499	4	2	Maricopa, AZ	9 199	8	2	Kings, NY	37 666.9
3	Harris, TX	4 589 928	44	3	Pima, AZ	9 187	26	3	Bronx, NY	34 577.7
4	Maricopa, AZ	4 242 997	62	4	Kern, CA	8 132	11	4	Queens, NY	21 443.5
5	San Diego, CA	3 317 749	12	5	Clark, NV	7 892	63	5	San Francisco, CA	18 569.0
6	Orange, CA	3 172 532	10	6	Riverside, CA	7 206	23	6	Philadelphia, PA	11 683.1
7	Miami-Dade, FL	2 712 945	47	7	Fresno, CA	5 959	2	7	Cook, IL	5 506.3
8	Kings, NY	2 629 150	5	8	San Diego, CA	4 207	29	8	Nassau, NY	4 780.5
9	Dallas, TX	2 574 984	1	9	Los Angeles, CA	4 058	54	9	Bergen, NJ	4 034.2
10	Riverside, CA	2 387 741	13	10	King, WA	2 116	6	10	Orange, CA	4 012.8
11	Queens, NY	2 333 054	27	11	Palm Beach, FL	1 970	50	11	Milwaukee, WI	3 938.1
12	Clark, NV	2 155 664	7	12	Miami-Dade, FL	1 899	49	12	Pinellas, FL	3 508.0
13	King, WA	2 149 970	68	13	Ventura, CA	1 843	9	13	Dallas, TX	2 949.2
14	San Bernardino, CA	2 140 096	3	14	Harris, TX	1 705	37	14	Fairfax, VA	2 912.9
15	Tarrant, TX	2 016 872	65	15	Pierce, WA	1 669	19	15	Wayne, MI	2 858.4
16	Bexar, TX	1 928 680	67	16	Hidalgo, TX	1 571	56	16	Du Page, IL	2 837.8
17	Santa Clara, CA	1 919 402	73	17	Worcester, MA	1 511	32	17	Cuyahoga, OH	2 732.6
18	Broward, FL	1 909 632	17	18	Santa Clara, CA	1 291	70	18	Middlesex, NJ	2 706.3
19	Wayne, MI	1 749 366	16	19	Bexar, TX	1 240	3	19	Harris, TX	2 692.2
20	Alameda, CA	1 647 704	18	20	Broward, FL	1 207	1	20	Los Angeles, CA	2 498.1
21	New York, NY	1 643 734	58	21	Erie, NY	1 043	31	21	Franklin, OH	2 375.1
22	Middlesex, MA	1 589 774	28	22	Hillsborough, FL	1 020	52	22	Marion, IN	2 374.4
23	Philadelphia, PA	1 567 872	69	23	El Paso, TX	1 013	15	23	Tarrant, TX	2 335.2
24	Sacramento, CA	1 514 460	36	24	Travis, TX	992	48	24	Westchester, NY	2 263.7
25	Suffolk, NY	1 492 583	24	25	Sacramento, CA	965	20	25	Alameda, CA	2 229.3
26	Bronx, NY	1 455 720	2	26	Cook, IL	945	34	26	Hennepin, MN	2 226.3
27	Palm Beach, FL	1 443 810	25	27	Suffolk, NY	912	42	27	Montgomery, MD	2 117.4
28	Hillsborough, FL	1 376 238	30	28	Orange, FL	903	60	28	Gwinnett, GA	2 107.7
29	Nassau, NY	1 361 500	75	29	Denton, TX	879	40	29	Mecklenburg, NC	2 014.6
30	Orange, FL	1 314 367	9	30	Dallas, TX	873	74	30	Hamilton, OH	1 993.3
31	Franklin, OH	1 264 518	33	31	Oakland, MI	868	45	31	St. Louis, MO	1 966.5
32	Cuyahoga, OH	1 249 352	15	32	Tarrant, TX	864	22	32	Middlesex, MA	1 944.2
33	Oakland, MI	1 243 970	53	33	Collin, TX	841	43	33	Fulton, GA	1 942.9
34	Hennepin, MN	1 232 483	41	34	Wake, NC	835	59	34	Prince George's, MD	1 881.2
35	Allegheny, PA	1 225 365	22	35	Middlesex, MA	818	64	35	Macomb, MI	1 811.2
36	Travis, TX	1 199 323	6	36	Orange, CA	791	72	36	Montgomery, PA	1 701.3
37	Fairfax, VA	1 138 652	55	37	Shelby, TN	764	35	37	Allegheny, PA	1 678.4
38	Contra Costa, CA	1 135 127	57	38	Duval, FL	763	46	38	Honolulu, HI	1 652.7
39	Salt Lake, UT	1 121 354	39	39	Salt Lake, UT	742	25	39	Suffolk, NY	1 637.0
40	Mecklenburg, NC	1 054 835	20	40	Alameda, CA	739	18	40	Broward, FL	1 582.1
41	Wake, NC	1 046 791	61	41	Hartford, CT	735	38	41	Contra Costa, CA	1 570.5
42	Montgomery, MD	1 043 863	35	42	Allegheny, PA	730	24	42	Sacramento, CA	1 569.6
43	Fulton, GA	1 023 336	38	43	Contra Costa, CA	723	16	43	Bexar, TX	1 555.5
44	Pima, AZ	1 016 206	51	44	Fairfield, CT	625	39	44	Salt Lake, UT	1 511.1
45	St. Louis, MO	998 581	19	45	Wayne, MI	612	51	45	Fairfield, CT	1 510.7
46	Honolulu, HI	992 605	66	46	New Haven, CT	605	17	46	Santa Clara, CA	1 486.5
47	Fresno, CA	979 915	46	47	Honolulu, HI	601	30	47	Orange, FL	1 455.1
48	Westchester, NY	974 542	71	48	Baltimore, MD	598	33	48	Oakland, MI	1 434.0
49	Pinellas, FL	960 730	34	49	Hennepin, MN	554	7	49	Miami-Dade, FL	1 428.8
50	Milwaukee, WI	951 448	31	50	Franklin, OH	532	66	50	New Haven, CT	1 417.5
51	Fairfield, CT	944 177	43	51	Fulton, GA	527	71	51	Baltimore, MD	1 388.7
52	Marion, IN	941 229	40	52	Mecklenburg, NC	524	28	52	Hillsborough, FL	1 348.9
53	Collin, TX	939 585	45	53	St. Louis, MO	508	41	53	Wake, NC	1 253.9
54	Bergen, NJ	939 151	42	54	Montgomery, MD	493	55	54	Shelby, TN	1 223.9
55	Shelby, TN	934 603	72	55	Montgomery, PA	483	57	55	Duval, FL	1 214.6
56	Du Page, IL	929 368	59	56	Prince George's, MD	483	61	56	Hartford, CT	1 214.0
57	Duval, FL	926 255	64	57	Macomb, MI	479	36	57	Travis, TX	1 209.2
58	Erie, NY	921 046	32	58	Cuyahoga, OH	457	53	58	Collin, TX	1 116.8
59	Prince George's, MD	908 049	48	59	Westchester, NY	431	13	59	King, WA	1 016.2
60	Gwinnett, GA	907 135	60	60	Gwinnett, GA	430	75	60	Denton, TX	917.7
61	Hartford, CT	892 389	74	61	Hamilton, OH	406	58	61	Erie, NY	883.3
62	Kern, CA	884 788	52	62	Marion, IN	396	69	62	El Paso, TX	827.0
63	San Francisco, CA	870 887	37	63	Fairfax, VA	391	5	63	San Diego, CA	788.7
64	Macomb, MI	867 730	56	64	Du Page, IL	328	27	64	Palm Beach, FL	732.9
65	Pierce, WA	861 312	70	65	Middlesex, NJ	309	73	65	Worcester, MA	542.6
66	New Haven, CT	856 875	29	66	Nassau, NY	285	67	66	Hidalgo, TX	541.0
67	Hidalgo, TX	849 843	49	67	Pinellas, FL	274	65	67	Pierce, WA	516.2
68	Ventura, CA	849 738	50	68	Milwaukee, WI	242	4	68	Maricopa, AZ	461.2
69	El Paso, TX	837 918	54	69	Bergen, NJ	233	68	69	Ventura, CA	461.1
70	Middlesex, NJ	837 073	23	70	Philadelphia, PA	134	10	70	Riverside, CA	331.3
71	Baltimore, MD	831 026	11	71	Queens, NY	109	12	71	Clark, NV	273.2
72	Montgomery, PA	821 725	8	72	Kings, NY	70	47	72	Fresno, CA	164.4
73	Worcester, MA	819 589	63	73	San Francisco, CA	47	44	73	Pima, AZ	110.6
74	Hamilton, OH	809 099	26	74	Bronx, NY	42	62	74	Kern, CA	108.8
75	Denton, TX	806 180	21	75	New York, NY	23	14	75	San Bernardino, CA	106.7

75 Largest Counties by 2016 Population
Selected Rankings

Percent population change, 2010-2016				Employment/residence ratio, 2011-2015				Percent White, not Hispanic or Latino, alone or in combination, 2016			
Population rank	Percent change rank	County	Percent change [col 23]	Population rank	Number of employees per resident rank	County	Number of employees per resident [col 34]	Population rank	White rank	County	Percent white [col 5]
75	1	Denton, TX	21.7	21	1	New York, NY	2.81	64	1	Macomb, MI	81.8
53	2	Collin, TX	20.1	43	2	Fulton, GA	1.80	35	2	Allegheny, PA	80.7
36	3	Travis, TX	17.1	63	3	San Francisco, CA	1.41	73	3	Worcester, MA	79.3
41	4	Wake, NC	16.2	34	4	Hennepin, MN	1.35	72	4	Montgomery, PA	78.0
30	5	Orange, FL	14.7	74	5	Hamilton, OH	1.32	58	5	Erie, NY	77.3
40	5	Mecklenburg, NC	14.7	52	6	Marion, IN	1.29	49	6	Pinellas, FL	76.5
60	7	Gwinnett, GA	12.6	9	7	Dallas, TX	1.27	22	7	Middlesex, MA	75.0
16	8	Bexar, TX	12.5	40	7	Mecklenburg, NC	1.27	33	8	Oakland, MI	74.5
3	9	Harris, TX	12.1	30	9	Orange, FL	1.25	39	9	Salt Lake, UT	73.8
28	10	Hillsborough, FL	12.0	32	10	Cuyahoga, OH	1.24	65	10	Pierce, WA	72.9
15	11	Tarrant, TX	11.4	56	11	Du Page, IL	1.21	34	11	Hennepin, MN	72.1
13	12	King, WA	11.3	45	12	St. Louis, MO	1.20	25	12	Suffolk, NY	69.3
4	13	Maricopa, AZ	11.2	31	13	Franklin, OH	1.19	56	13	Du Page, IL	68.9
43	13	Fulton, GA	11.2	57	13	Duval, FL	1.19	45	14	St. Louis, MO	68.4
12	15	Clark, NV	10.5	36	15	Travis, TX	1.18	74	15	Hamilton, OH	67.9
67	16	Hidalgo, TX	9.7	55	15	Shelby, TN	1.18	31	16	Franklin, OH	66.8
27	17	Palm Beach, FL	9.4	23	17	Philadelphia, PA	1.17	66	17	New Haven, CT	65.2
18	18	Broward, FL	9.2	61	17	Hartford, CT	1.17	13	18	King, WA	65.0
20	19	Alameda, CA	9.1	13	19	King, WA	1.16	51	19	Fairfield, CT	63.8
10	20	Riverside, CA	9.0	72	19	Montgomery, PA	1.16	61	20	Hartford, CT	63.6
39	21	Salt Lake, UT	8.9	3	21	Harris, TX	1.15	41	21	Wake, NC	62.3
9	22	Dallas, TX	8.8	35	21	Allegheny, PA	1.15	75	22	Denton, TX	62.2
31	23	Franklin, OH	8.7	39	21	Salt Lake, UT	1.15	29	23	Nassau, NY	61.8
7	24	Miami-Dade, FL	8.6	17	24	Santa Clara, CA	1.14	32	24	Cuyahoga, OH	61.1
65	25	Pierce, WA	8.3	33	25	Oakland, MI	1.13	53	25	Collin, TX	60.6
38	26	Contra Costa, CA	8.2	28	26	Hillsborough, FL	1.10	71	26	Baltimore, MD	59.9
63	26	San Francisco, CA	8.2	19	27	Wayne, MI	1.09	52	27	Marion, IN	58.5
17	28	Santa Clara, CA	7.7	22	27	Middlesex, MA	1.09	54	28	Bergen, NJ	58.3
42	29	Montgomery, MD	7.4	50	29	Milwaukee, WI	1.08	4	29	Maricopa, AZ	58.0
5	30	San Diego, CA	7.2	2	30	Cook, IL	1.07	27	30	Palm Beach, FL	57.0
57	30	Duval, FL	7.2	58	30	Erie, NY	1.07	57	31	Duval, FL	56.0
34	32	Hennepin, MN	7.0	6	32	Orange, CA	1.06	48	32	Westchester, NY	55.3
24	33	Sacramento, CA	6.7	7	32	Miami-Dade, FL	1.06	37	33	Fairfax, VA	54.3
22	34	Middlesex, MA	5.8	16	34	Bexar, TX	1.05	44	34	Pima, AZ	54.2
6	35	Orange, CA	5.4	41	34	Wake, NC	1.05	50	35	Milwaukee, WI	53.9
62	35	Kern, CA	5.4	1	36	Los Angeles, CA	1.03	28	36	Hillsborough, FL	52.0
37	37	Fairfax, VA	5.3	27	36	Palm Beach, FL	1.03	19	37	Wayne, MI	51.6
47	37	Fresno, CA	5.3	49	36	Pinellas, FL	1.03	36	38	Travis, TX	51.1
14	39	San Bernardino, CA	5.2	51	36	Fairfield, CT	1.03	15	39	Tarrant, TX	49.5
59	39	Prince George's, MD	5.2	4	40	Maricopa, AZ	1.02	24	40	Sacramento, CA	49.3
26	41	Bronx, NY	5.1	5	40	San Diego, CA	1.02	40	40	Mecklenburg, NC	49.3
8	42	Kings, NY	5.0	37	40	Fairfax, VA	1.02	5	42	San Diego, CA	48.9
49	43	Pinellas, FL	4.8	12	43	Clark, NV	1.01	21	43	New York, NY	48.6
69	44	El Paso, TX	4.7	24	43	Sacramento, CA	1.01	38	44	Contra Costa, CA	48.0
11	45	Queens, NY	4.6	62	43	Kern, CA	1.01	68	45	Ventura, CA	47.9
52	46	Marion, IN	4.2	44	46	Pima, AZ	1.00	42	46	Montgomery, MD	47.0
46	47	Honolulu, HI	4.1	46	46	Honolulu, HI	1.00	12	47	Clark, NV	46.5
54	48	Bergen, NJ	3.8	47	46	Fresno, CA	1.00	70	48	Middlesex, NJ	44.8
44	49	Pima, AZ	3.7	15	49	Tarrant, TX	0.99	63	49	San Francisco, CA	43.8
21	50	New York, NY	3.6	69	49	El Paso, TX	0.99	2	50	Cook, IL	43.7
33	51	Oakland, MI	3.5	20	51	Alameda, CA	0.97	6	51	Orange, CA	43.5
70	52	Middlesex, NJ	3.4	48	52	Westchester, NY	0.96	30	52	Orange, FL	43.1
1	53	Los Angeles, CA	3.3	67	52	Hidalgo, TX	0.96	43	53	Fulton, GA	41.5
64	54	Macomb, MI	3.2	70	52	Middlesex, NJ	0.96	60	54	Gwinnett, GA	40.3
68	54	Ventura, CA	3.2	54	55	Bergen, NJ	0.95	18	55	Broward, FL	38.9
71	54	Baltimore, MD	3.2	42	56	Montgomery, MD	0.94	10	56	Riverside, CA	38.2
51	57	Fairfield, CT	3.0	66	56	New Haven, CT	0.94	8	57	Kings, NY	37.3
23	58	Philadelphia, PA	2.7	14	58	San Bernardino, CA	0.91	55	57	Shelby, TN	37.3
48	58	Westchester, NY	2.7	18	58	Broward, FL	0.91	62	59	Kern, CA	36.5
72	58	Montgomery, PA	2.7	53	60	Collin, TX	0.89	23	60	Philadelphia, PA	36.4
73	58	Worcester, MA	2.7	68	60	Ventura, CA	0.89	20	61	Alameda, CA	35.4
29	62	Nassau, NY	1.6	25	62	Suffolk, NY	0.88	17	62	Santa Clara, CA	35.0
56	63	Du Page, IL	1.4	60	62	Gwinnett, GA	0.88	46	63	Honolulu, HI	32.1
74	64	Hamilton, OH	0.8	65	62	Pierce, WA	0.88	47	64	Fresno, CA	31.6
55	65	Shelby, TN	0.7	29	65	Nassau, NY	0.87	3	65	Harris, TX	31.5
50	66	Milwaukee, WI	0.4	71	65	Baltimore, MD	0.87	14	66	San Bernardino, CA	31.2
2	67	Cook, IL	0.2	73	65	Worcester, MA	0.87	9	67	Dallas, TX	30.9
35	67	Allegheny, PA	0.2	64	68	Macomb, MI	0.84	16	68	Bexar, TX	29.5
58	67	Erie, NY	0.2	10	69	Riverside, CA	0.81	1	69	Los Angeles, CA	28.2
25	70	Suffolk, NY	0.0	38	70	Contra Costa, CA	0.75	11	70	Queens, NY	26.5
45	70	St. Louis, MO	0.0	8	71	Kings, NY	0.74	59	71	Prince George's, MD	14.5
61	72	Hartford, CT	-0.2	59	72	Prince George's, MD	0.73	7	72	Miami-Dade, FL	14.3
66	73	New Haven, CT	-0.6	26	73	Bronx, NY	0.68	69	73	El Paso, TX	13.1
32	74	Cuyahoga, OH	-2.4	11	74	Queens, NY	0.66	26	74	Bronx, NY	9.9
19	75	Wayne, MI	-3.9	75	75	Denton, TX	0.65	67	75	Hidalgo, TX	6.7

75 Largest Counties by 2016 Population
Selected Rankings

Percent Black, not Hispanic or Latino, alone or in combination, 2016				Percent American Indian, Alaska Native, alone or in combination, 2016				Percent Asian or Pacific Islander, alone or in combination, 2016			
Population rank	Black rank	County	Percent black [col 6]	Population rank	American Indian Alaska native rank	County	Percent American Indian, Alaska native [col 7]	Population rank	Asian or Pacific Islander rank	County	Percent Asian or Pacific Islander [col 8]
59	1	Prince George's, MD	64.0	44	1	Pima, AZ	3.1	46	1	Honolulu, HI	78.2
55	2	Shelby, TN	54.4	65	2	Pierce, WA	2.7	17	2	Santa Clara, CA	38.7
43	3	Fulton, GA	44.8	4	3	Maricopa, AZ	2.2	63	3	San Francisco, CA	37.9
23	4	Philadelphia, PA	42.6	13	4	King, WA	1.7	20	4	Alameda, CA	33.6
19	5	Wayne, MI	40.0	24	5	Sacramento, CA	1.5	11	5	Queens, NY	27.9
40	6	Mecklenburg, NC	32.6	34	5	Hennepin, MN	1.5	70	6	Middlesex, NJ	25.4
8	7	Kings, NY	31.4	46	5	Honolulu, HI	1.5	6	7	Orange, CA	22.3
32	8	Cuyahoga, OH	30.9	62	8	Kern, CA	1.3	37	8	Fairfax, VA	21.8
57	9	Duval, FL	30.6	50	9	Milwaukee, WI	1.2	13	9	King, WA	20.9
26	10	Bronx, NY	30.3	12	10	Clark, NV	1.1	38	10	Contra Costa, CA	19.9
52	11	Marion, IN	29.5	19	10	Wayne, MI	1.1	24	11	Sacramento, CA	19.5
71	12	Baltimore, MD	29.4	39	10	Salt Lake, UT	1.1	54	12	Bergen, NJ	17.5
18	13	Broward, FL	29.1	47	10	Fresno, CA	1.1	42	13	Montgomery, MD	16.8
60	14	Gwinnett, GA	27.8	5	14	San Diego, CA	1.0	1	14	Los Angeles, CA	16.1
50	15	Milwaukee, WI	27.7	10	14	Riverside, CA	1.0	53	15	Collin, TX	15.4
74	16	Hamilton, OH	27.6	38	14	Contra Costa, CA	1.0	5	16	San Diego, CA	14.5
45	17	St. Louis, MO	25.3	75	14	Denton, TX	1.0	21	17	New York, NY	13.6
31	18	Franklin, OH	24.2	14	18	San Bernardino, CA	0.9	8	18	Kings, NY	13.4
2	19	Cook, IL	24.1	15	18	Tarrant, TX	0.9	12	19	Clark, NV	13.0
9	20	Dallas, TX	23.2	31	18	Franklin, OH	0.9	22	19	Middlesex, MA	13.0
30	21	Orange, FL	21.4	40	18	Mecklenburg, NC	0.9	56	21	Du Page, IL	12.7
41	22	Wake, NC	21.3	53	18	Collin, TX	0.9	60	21	Gwinnett, GA	12.7
42	23	Montgomery, MD	19.4	58	18	Erie, NY	0.9	47	23	Fresno, CA	11.2
3	24	Harris, TX	19.2	59	18	Prince George's, MD	0.9	65	23	Pierce, WA	11.2
27	25	Palm Beach, FL	19.1	64	18	Macomb, MI	0.9	29	25	Nassau, NY	10.4
11	26	Queens, NY	19.0	11	26	Queens, NY	0.8	75	26	Denton, TX	9.5
28	27	Hillsborough, FL	17.0	20	26	Alameda, CA	0.8	68	27	Ventura, CA	9.0
15	28	Tarrant, TX	16.9	23	26	Philadelphia, PA	0.8	14	28	San Bernardino, CA	8.3
7	29	Miami-Dade, FL	16.6	33	26	Oakland, MI	0.8	34	28	Hennepin, MN	8.3
33	30	Oakland, MI	15.0	41	26	Wake, NC	0.8	72	28	Montgomery, PA	8.3
35	31	Allegheny, PA	14.5	52	26	Marion, IN	0.8	2	31	Cook, IL	8.0
48	31	Westchester, NY	14.5	57	26	Duval, FL	0.8	23	31	Philadelphia, PA	8.0
34	33	Hennepin, MN	14.3	63	26	San Francisco, CA	0.8	33	31	Oakland, MI	8.0
61	34	Hartford, CT	14.1	68	26	Ventura, CA	0.8	10	34	Riverside, CA	7.9
58	35	Erie, NY	14.0	71	26	Baltimore, MD	0.8	41	35	Wake, NC	7.8
66	36	New Haven, CT	13.6	9	36	Dallas, TX	0.7	43	35	Fulton, GA	7.8
21	37	New York, NY	13.4	17	36	Santa Clara, CA	0.7	3	37	Harris, TX	7.7
12	38	Clark, NV	12.5	36	36	Travis, TX	0.7	36	37	Travis, TX	7.7
64	38	Macomb, MI	12.5	43	36	Fulton, GA	0.7	39	39	Salt Lake, UT	7.1
20	40	Alameda, CA	12.0	45	36	St. Louis, MO	0.7	48	40	Westchester, NY	7.0
29	40	Nassau, NY	12.0	49	36	Pinellas, FL	0.7	71	40	Baltimore, MD	7.0
24	42	Sacramento, CA	11.7	60	36	Gwinnett, GA	0.7	9	42	Dallas, TX	6.7
51	43	Fairfield, CT	11.6	74	36	Hamilton, OH	0.7	40	43	Mecklenburg, NC	6.5
49	44	Pinellas, FL	11.3	1	44	Los Angeles, CA	0.6	30	44	Orange, FL	6.4
37	45	Fairfax, VA	10.5	6	44	Orange, CA	0.6	15	45	Tarrant, TX	6.3
75	46	Denton, TX	10.4	8	44	Kings, NY	0.6	51	45	Fairfield, CT	6.3
53	47	Collin, TX	10.3	16	44	Bexar, TX	0.6	57	47	Duval, FL	6.0
72	48	Montgomery, PA	10.2	26	44	Bronx, NY	0.6	31	48	Franklin, OH	5.9
70	49	Middlesex, NJ	10.1	28	44	Hillsborough, FL	0.6	61	48	Hartford, CT	5.9
38	50	Contra Costa, CA	10.0	30	44	Orange, FL	0.6	62	50	Kern, CA	5.6
65	51	Pierce, WA	9.4	32	44	Cuyahoga, OH	0.6	73	51	Worcester, MA	5.5
14	52	San Bernardino, CA	9.1	37	44	Fairfax, VA	0.6	4	52	Maricopa, AZ	5.2
1	53	Los Angeles, CA	8.7	42	44	Montgomery, MD	0.6	59	53	Prince George's, MD	5.1
36	53	Travis, TX	8.7	55	44	Shelby, TN	0.6	45	54	St. Louis, MO	5.0
16	55	Bexar, TX	7.9	61	44	Hartford, CT	0.6	28	55	Hillsborough, FL	4.9
25	55	Suffolk, NY	7.9	66	44	New Haven, CT	0.6	50	56	Milwaukee, WI	4.8
13	57	King, WA	7.8	73	44	Worcester, MA	0.6	66	56	New Haven, CT	4.8
10	58	Riverside, CA	7.0	2	58	Cook, IL	0.5	18	58	Broward, FL	4.6
4	59	Maricopa, AZ	6.2	3	58	Harris, TX	0.5	25	58	Suffolk, NY	4.6
54	60	Bergen, NJ	6.0	18	58	Broward, FL	0.5	64	58	Macomb, MI	4.6
63	60	San Francisco, CA	6.0	21	58	New York, NY	0.5	26	61	Bronx, NY	4.3
62	62	Kern, CA	5.9	25	58	Suffolk, NY	0.5	35	61	Allegheny, PA	4.3
22	63	Middlesex, MA	5.8	35	58	Allegheny, PA	0.5	49	63	Pinellas, FL	4.2
5	64	San Diego, CA	5.7	69	58	El Paso, TX	0.5	58	63	Erie, NY	4.2
56	65	Du Page, IL	5.5	70	58	Middlesex, NJ	0.5	19	65	Wayne, MI	4.0
47	66	Fresno, CA	5.3	22	66	Middlesex, MA	0.4	44	66	Pima, AZ	3.9
73	66	Worcester, MA	5.3	27	66	Palm Beach, FL	0.4	32	67	Cuyahoga, OH	3.7
44	68	Pima, AZ	4.1	29	66	Nassau, NY	0.4	52	67	Marion, IN	3.7
46	69	Honolulu, HI	3.6	48	66	Westchester, NY	0.4	16	69	Bexar, TX	3.6
69	70	El Paso, TX	3.5	51	66	Fairfield, CT	0.4	27	70	Palm Beach, FL	3.4
17	71	Santa Clara, CA	3.0	56	66	Du Page, IL	0.4	74	71	Hamilton, OH	3.1
39	72	Salt Lake, UT	2.2	72	66	Montgomery, PA	0.4	55	72	Shelby, TN	3.1
68	72	Ventura, CA	2.2	54	73	Bergen, NJ	0.3	69	73	Miami-Dade, FL	1.9
6	74	Orange, CA	2.1	7	74	Miami-Dade, FL	0.2	67	74	El Paso, TX	1.7
67	75	Hidalgo, TX	0.5	67	75	Hidalgo, TX	0.1	67	75	Hidalgo, TX	1.0

75 Largest Counties by 2016 Population
Selected Rankings

Percent Hispanic or Latino,[1] 2016				Percent under 18 years old, 2016				Percent 65 years old and over, 2016			
Population rank	Hispanic or Latino rank	County	Percent Hispanic or Latino [col 9]	Population rank	Under 18 years old rank	County	Percent under 18 years old [cols 10 and 11]	Population rank	65 years old and over rank	County	Percent 65 years old and over [cols 17 and 18]
67	1	Hidalgo, TX	91.8	67	1	Hidalgo, TX	33.3	49	1	Pinellas, FL	23.8
69	2	El Paso, TX	82.2	62	2	Kern, CA	29.2	27	2	Palm Beach, FL	23.3
7	3	Miami-Dade, FL	67.7	47	3	Fresno, CA	28.7	44	3	Pima, AZ	19.1
16	4	Bexar, TX	59.9	39	4	Salt Lake, UT	27.9	35	4	Allegheny, PA	18.0
26	5	Bronx, NY	56.0	69	5	El Paso, TX	27.7	45	5	St. Louis, MO	17.3
14	6	San Bernardino, CA	52.8	60	6	Gwinnett, GA	27.4	72	6	Montgomery, PA	17.2
47	6	Fresno, CA	52.8	3	7	Harris, TX	27.0	29	7	Nassau, NY	17.1
62	6	Kern, CA	52.8	14	8	San Bernardino, CA	26.8	32	7	Cuyahoga, OH	17.1
1	9	Los Angeles, CA	48.5	9	9	Dallas, TX	26.7	58	7	Erie, NY	17.1
10	10	Riverside, CA	48.4	15	9	Tarrant, TX	26.7	46	10	Honolulu, HI	16.6
68	11	Ventura, CA	42.5	53	9	Collin, TX	26.7	54	11	Bergen, NJ	16.5
3	12	Harris, TX	42.4	16	12	Bexar, TX	26.0	71	11	Baltimore, MD	16.5
9	13	Dallas, TX	39.9	10	13	Riverside, CA	25.7	61	13	Hartford, CT	16.3
44	14	Pima, AZ	36.8	75	14	Denton, TX	25.5	64	14	Macomb, MI	16.2
6	15	Orange, CA	34.3	26	15	Bronx, NY	25.3	66	14	New Haven, CT	16.2
36	16	Travis, TX	33.8	55	16	Shelby, TN	25.2	48	16	Westchester, NY	16.1
5	17	San Diego, CA	33.5	52	17	Marion, IN	24.9	18	17	Broward, FL	16.0
12	18	Clark, NV	30.9	4	18	Maricopa, AZ	24.5	25	17	Suffolk, NY	16.0
4	19	Maricopa, AZ	30.7	41	18	Wake, NC	24.5	7	19	Miami-Dade, FL	15.9
30	20	Orange, FL	30.5	50	20	Milwaukee, WI	24.3	33	19	Oakland, MI	15.9
18	21	Broward, FL	28.7	40	21	Mecklenburg, NC	24.2	38	21	Contra Costa, CA	15.0
15	22	Tarrant, TX	28.4	19	22	Wayne, MI	24.0	21	22	New York, NY	14.9
11	23	Queens, NY	28.0	24	22	Sacramento, CA	24.0	73	22	Worcester, MA	14.9
28	24	Hillsborough, FL	27.6	37	24	Fairfax, VA	23.8	51	24	Fairfield, CT	14.8
21	25	New York, NY	26.0	65	25	Pierce, WA	23.7	63	24	San Francisco, CA	14.8
17	26	Santa Clara, CA	25.9	31	26	Franklin, OH	23.6	74	26	Hamilton, OH	14.7
38	27	Contra Costa, CA	25.4	12	27	Clark, NV	23.5	4	27	Maricopa, AZ	14.6
2	28	Cook, IL	25.3	68	27	Ventura, CA	23.5	22	27	Middlesex, MA	14.6
48	29	Westchester, NY	24.4	42	29	Montgomery, MD	23.4	42	27	Montgomery, MD	14.6
24	30	Sacramento, CA	23.0	74	30	Hamilton, OH	23.3	68	27	Ventura, CA	14.6
20	31	Alameda, CA	22.5	8	31	Kings, NY	23.2	19	31	Wayne, MI	14.4
27	32	Palm Beach, FL	21.5	38	32	Contra Costa, CA	23.1	56	31	Du Page, IL	14.4
60	33	Gwinnett, GA	20.8	51	32	Fairfield, CT	23.1	11	33	Queens, NY	14.2
70	34	Middlesex, NJ	20.7	28	34	Hillsborough, FL	23.0	70	33	Middlesex, NJ	14.2
51	35	Fairfield, CT	19.4	56	34	Du Page, IL	23.0	12	35	Clark, NV	14.1
54	35	Bergen, NJ	19.4	43	36	Fulton, GA	22.7	6	36	Orange, CA	13.9
8	37	Kings, NY	19.2	17	37	Santa Clara, CA	22.6	10	36	Riverside, CA	13.9
75	37	Denton, TX	19.2	57	37	Duval, FL	22.6	28	38	Hillsborough, FL	13.7
42	39	Montgomery, MD	19.1	6	39	Orange, CA	22.5	24	39	Sacramento, CA	13.6
25	40	Suffolk, NY	19.0	30	39	Orange, FL	22.5	2	40	Cook, IL	13.5
39	41	Salt Lake, UT	18.1	36	39	Travis, TX	22.5	57	40	Duval, FL	13.5
59	42	Prince George's, MD	17.8	48	39	Westchester, NY	22.5	5	42	San Diego, CA	13.4
61	43	Hartford, CT	17.6	59	39	Prince George's, MD	22.5	65	43	Pierce, WA	13.3
66	43	New Haven, CT	17.6	2	44	Cook, IL	22.3	34	44	Hennepin, MN	13.2
29	45	Nassau, NY	16.8	1	45	Los Angeles, CA	22.2	20	45	Alameda, CA	13.0
37	46	Fairfax, VA	16.1	34	45	Hennepin, MN	22.2	1	46	Los Angeles, CA	12.9
63	47	San Francisco, CA	15.2	45	45	St. Louis, MO	22.2	17	47	Santa Clara, CA	12.8
53	48	Collin, TX	15.1	23	48	Philadelphia, PA	22.0	23	47	Philadelphia, PA	12.8
50	49	Milwaukee, WI	14.8	5	49	San Diego, CA	21.9	8	49	Kings, NY	12.7
23	50	Philadelphia, PA	14.4	70	50	Middlesex, NJ	21.8	13	49	King, WA	12.7
56	51	Du Page, IL	14.3	25	51	Suffolk, NY	21.7	50	49	Milwaukee, WI	12.7
40	52	Mecklenburg, NC	13.0	29	51	Nassau, NY	21.7	55	52	Shelby, TN	12.5
73	53	Worcester, MA	11.0	72	51	Montgomery, PA	21.7	37	53	Fairfax, VA	12.4
65	54	Pierce, WA	10.6	71	54	Baltimore, MD	21.6	59	54	Prince George's, MD	12.3
52	55	Marion, IN	10.2	33	55	Oakland, MI	21.5	47	55	Fresno, CA	11.9
41	56	Wake, NC	10.0	54	55	Bergen, NJ	21.5	69	55	El Paso, TX	11.9
46	57	Honolulu, HI	9.7	64	55	Macomb, MI	21.5	26	57	Bronx, NY	11.8
13	58	King, WA	9.5	73	55	Worcester, MA	21.5	52	57	Marion, IN	11.8
49	59	Pinellas, FL	9.3	44	59	Pima, AZ	21.4	16	59	Bexar, TX	11.7
57	60	Duval, FL	9.2	46	59	Honolulu, HI	21.4	30	60	Orange, FL	11.3
22	61	Middlesex, MA	7.9	61	59	Hartford, CT	21.4	31	60	Franklin, OH	11.3
43	62	Fulton, GA	7.3	18	62	Broward, FL	21.3	14	62	San Bernardino, CA	11.1
34	63	Hennepin, MN	6.9	32	63	Cuyahoga, OH	21.2	43	63	Fulton, GA	11.0
55	64	Shelby, TN	6.1	20	64	Alameda, CA	20.9	67	63	Hidalgo, TX	11.0
19	65	Wayne, MI	5.8	13	65	King, WA	20.6	15	65	Tarrant, TX	10.8
32	66	Cuyahoga, OH	5.7	66	65	New Haven, CT	20.6	40	66	Mecklenburg, NC	10.6
31	67	Franklin, OH	5.3	58	67	Erie, NY	20.5	41	66	Wake, NC	10.6
58	67	Erie, NY	5.3	11	68	Queens, NY	20.4	53	68	Collin, TX	10.5
71	67	Baltimore, MD	5.3	7	69	Miami-Dade, FL	20.3	62	69	Kern, CA	10.4
72	70	Montgomery, PA	5.0	22	69	Middlesex, MA	20.3	9	70	Dallas, TX	10.1
33	71	Oakland, MI	3.9	27	71	Palm Beach, FL	19.4	39	70	Salt Lake, UT	10.1
74	72	Hamilton, OH	3.1	35	72	Allegheny, PA	18.9	3	72	Harris, TX	9.8
45	73	St. Louis, MO	2.8	49	73	Pinellas, FL	16.7	73	73	Denton, TX	9.4
64	74	Macomb, MI	2.5	21	74	New York, NY	14.6	60	74	Gwinnett, GA	9.3
35	75	Allegheny, PA	2.0	63	75	San Francisco, CA	13.6	36	75	Travis, TX	9.0

75 Largest Counties by 2016 Population
Selected Rankings

Percent female-headed family households, 2011–2015				Birth rate, 2016				Percent under 65 who have no health insurance, 2015			
Population rank	Female households rank	County	Percent female households [col 30]	Population rank	Live birth rate rank	County	Birth rate [col 36]	Population rank	No health insurance rank	County	Percent with no health insurance [col 40]
26	1	Bronx, NY	31.1	67	1	Hidalgo, TX	19.0	67	1	Hidalgo, TX	32.0
55	2	Shelby, TN	20.6	47	2	Fresno, CA	16.1	69	2	El Paso, TX	22.8
67	2	Hidalgo, TX	20.6	62	3	Kern, CA	16.0	9	3	Dallas, TX	22.6
23	4	Philadelphia, PA	20.5	3	4	Harris, TX	15.9	7	4	Miami-Dade, FL	21.2
59	5	Prince George's, MD	20.2	69	4	El Paso, TX	15.9	3	5	Harris, TX	21.1
8	6	Kings, NY	19.6	8	6	Kings, NY	15.8	60	6	Gwinnett, GA	17.8
19	7	Wayne, MI	19.5	39	6	Salt Lake, UT	15.8	15	7	Tarrant, TX	17.7
69	8	El Paso, TX	19.4	9	8	Dallas, TX	15.6	27	8	Palm Beach, FL	17.2
7	9	Miami-Dade, FL	18.2	52	9	Marion, IN	15.3	16	9	Bexar, TX	16.8
47	10	Fresno, CA	18.0	31	10	Franklin, OH	15.0	18	10	Broward, FL	16.5
14	11	San Bernardino, CA	16.9	16	11	Bexar, TX	14.7	36	11	Travis, TX	16.2
50	12	Milwaukee, WI	16.7	26	11	Bronx, NY	14.7	30	12	Orange, FL	15.7
16	13	Bexar, TX	16.6	14	13	San Bernardino, CA	14.6	28	13	Hillsborough, FL	14.7
62	13	Kern, CA	16.6	50	14	Milwaukee, WI	14.4	12	14	Clark, NV	14.5
52	15	Marion, IN	16.5	55	14	Shelby, TN	14.4	49	15	Pinellas, FL	14.3
11	16	Queens, NY	16.3	15	16	Tarrant, TX	14.2	43	16	Fulton, GA	14.0
9	17	Dallas, TX	16.2	23	17	Philadelphia, PA	14.1	52	17	Marion, IN	13.7
32	18	Cuyahoga, OH	15.9	40	18	Mecklenburg, NC	14.0	55	18	Shelby, TN	13.6
57	18	Duval, FL	15.9	36	19	Travis, TX	13.8	57	19	Duval, FL	13.2
1	20	Los Angeles, CA	15.6	57	19	Duval, FL	13.8	11	20	Queens, NY	12.9
3	20	Harris, TX	15.6	65	21	Pierce, WA	13.7	40	20	Mecklenburg, NC	12.9
18	20	Broward, FL	15.6	34	22	Hennepin, MN	13.6	75	20	Denton, TX	12.9
30	23	Orange, FL	15.4	74	22	Hamilton, OH	13.6	1	23	Los Angeles, CA	12.5
74	24	Hamilton, OH	15.3	5	24	San Diego, CA	13.5	4	23	Maricopa, AZ	12.5
2	25	Cook, IL	15.0	59	25	Prince George's, MD	13.4	39	25	Salt Lake, UT	12.2
24	25	Sacramento, CA	15.0	19	26	Wayne, MI	13.3	44	25	Pima, AZ	12.2
60	27	Gwinnett, GA	14.7	46	26	Honolulu, HI	13.3	59	27	Prince George's, MD	11.3
61	27	Hartford, CT	14.7	4	28	Maricopa, AZ	13.2	26	28	Bronx, NY	11.1
43	29	Fulton, GA	14.5	24	28	Sacramento, CA	13.2	23	29	Philadelphia, PA	11.0
28	30	Hillsborough, FL	14.4	2	30	Cook, IL	13.1	53	29	Collin, TX	11.0
40	30	Mecklenburg, NC	14.4	10	31	Riverside, CA	12.9	10	31	Riverside, CA	10.9
71	30	Baltimore, MD	14.4	11	31	Queens, NY	12.9	47	32	Fresno, CA	10.8
15	33	Tarrant, TX	14.3	43	31	Fulton, GA	12.9	2	33	Cook, IL	10.6
45	33	St. Louis, MO	14.3	60	34	Gwinnett, GA	12.8	8	34	Kings, NY	10.2
66	35	New Haven, CT	14.2	1	35	Los Angeles, CA	12.7	6	35	Orange, CA	10.0
31	36	Franklin, OH	14.1	12	35	Clark, NV	12.7	68	36	Ventura, CA	9.9
12	37	Clark, NV	13.9	30	35	Orange, FL	12.7	14	37	San Bernardino, CA	9.7
58	38	Erie, NY	13.8	28	38	Hillsborough, FL	12.6	41	37	Wake, NC	9.7
10	39	Riverside, CA	13.6	37	38	Fairfax, VA	12.6	62	37	Kern, CA	9.7
64	40	Macomb, MI	13.0	75	38	Denton, TX	12.6	70	37	Middlesex, NJ	9.7
48	41	Westchester, NY	12.9	42	41	Montgomery, MD	12.5	54	41	Bergen, NJ	9.6
4	42	Maricopa, AZ	12.8	17	42	Santa Clara, CA	12.4	5	42	San Diego, CA	9.5
44	42	Pima, AZ	12.8	41	43	Wake, NC	12.3	31	43	Franklin, OH	9.2
73	44	Worcester, MA	12.5	68	44	Ventura, CA	12.2	51	43	Fairfield, CT	9.2
20	45	Alameda, CA	12.4	6	45	Orange, CA	12.1	37	45	Fairfax, VA	8.8
68	45	Ventura, CA	12.4	20	45	Alameda, CA	12.1	50	46	Milwaukee, WI	8.6
38	47	Contra Costa, CA	12.3	13	47	King, WA	12.0	42	47	Montgomery, MD	8.5
46	47	Honolulu, HI	12.3	32	47	Cuyahoga, OH	12.0	19	48	Wayne, MI	8.4
51	47	Fairfield, CT	12.3	71	47	Baltimore, MD	12.0	45	49	St. Louis, MO	8.2
25	50	Suffolk, NY	12.2	53	50	Collin, TX	11.8	48	49	Westchester, NY	8.2
70	50	Middlesex, NJ	12.2	7	51	Miami-Dade, FL	11.7	21	51	New York, NY	7.9
5	52	San Diego, CA	12.1	18	52	Broward, FL	11.6	32	52	Cuyahoga, OH	7.8
27	52	Palm Beach, FL	12.1	44	52	Pima, AZ	11.6	74	53	Hamilton, OH	7.5
6	54	Orange, CA	12.0	45	52	St. Louis, MO	11.6	65	54	Pierce, WA	7.3
65	55	Pierce, WA	11.8	56	55	Du Page, IL	11.4	24	55	Sacramento, CA	7.2
29	56	Nassau, NY	11.7	38	56	Contra Costa, CA	11.3	64	55	Macomb, MI	7.2
35	56	Allegheny, PA	11.7	21	57	New York, NY	11.2	66	57	New Haven, CT	7.0
41	58	Wake, NC	11.6	70	57	Middlesex, NJ	11.2	25	58	Suffolk, NY	6.9
42	59	Montgomery, MD	11.5	22	59	Middlesex, MA	11.1	71	59	Baltimore, MD	6.8
21	60	New York, NY	11.4	58	60	Erie, NY	11.0	13	60	King, WA	6.5
54	61	Bergen, NJ	11.3	33	61	Oakland, MI	10.8	29	60	Nassau, NY	6.5
75	61	Denton, TX	11.3	35	61	Allegheny, PA	10.8	38	60	Contra Costa, CA	6.5
49	63	Pinellas, FL	11.2	48	61	Westchester, NY	10.8	33	63	Oakland, MI	6.4
36	64	Travis, TX	10.9	64	61	Macomb, MI	10.8	63	64	San Francisco, CA	6.3
39	65	Salt Lake, UT	10.7	72	65	Montgomery, PA	10.7	20	65	Alameda, CA	6.0
33	66	Oakland, MI	10.6	51	66	Fairfield, CT	10.6	35	65	Allegheny, PA	6.0
17	67	Santa Clara, CA	10.5	63	66	San Francisco, CA	10.6	17	67	Santa Clara, CA	5.9
34	68	Hennepin, MN	10.1	29	68	Nassau, NY	10.5	56	67	Du Page, IL	5.9
53	68	Collin, TX	10.1	61	68	Hartford, CT	10.5	34	69	Hennepin, MN	5.8
22	70	Middlesex, MA	9.7	73	68	Worcester, MA	10.5	61	69	Hartford, CT	5.8
72	71	Montgomery, PA	9.5	25	71	Suffolk, NY	10.3	58	71	Erie, NY	5.4
37	72	Fairfax, VA	9.2	27	72	Palm Beach, FL	10.2	72	72	Montgomery, PA	5.3
56	72	Du Page, IL	9.2	66	72	New Haven, CT	10.2	46	73	Honolulu, HI	4.4
13	74	King, WA	8.8	54	74	Bergen, NJ	9.9	22	74	Middlesex, MA	2.9
63	75	San Francisco, CA	8.3	49	75	Pinellas, FL	9.0	73	74	Worcester, MA	2.9

75 Largest Counties by 2016 Population
Selected Rankings

Percent college graduates (bachelor's degree or more), 2011–2015				Expenditures per student, 2013–2014				Per capita personal income, 2015			
Population rank	College graduates rank	County	Percent college graduates [col 51]	Population rank	Expenditures rank	County	Expenditures per student (dollars) [col 53]	Population rank	Per capita income rank	County	Per capita income (dollars) [col 64]
21	1	New York, NY	59.9	29	1	Nassau, NY	24 889	21	1	New York, NY	156 708
37	1	Fairfax, VA	59.9	48	2	Westchester, NY	24 141	51	2	Fairfield, CT	106 382
42	3	Montgomery, MD	57.9	25	3	Suffolk, NY	22 482	63	3	San Francisco, CA	103 529
63	4	San Francisco, CA	53.8	21	4	New York, NY	20 740	48	4	Westchester, NY	93 229
22	5	Middlesex, MA	52.0	8	4	Kings, NY	20 740	17	5	Santa Clara, CA	82 756
53	6	Collin, TX	49.8	11	4	Queens, NY	20 740	29	6	Nassau, NY	77 762
43	7	Fulton, GA	49.3	26	4	Bronx, NY	20 740	42	7	Montgomery, MD	76 863
41	8	Wake, NC	49.0	54	8	Bergen, NJ	18 061	54	8	Bergen, NJ	75 849
13	9	King, WA	47.9	51	9	Fairfield, CT	17 962	37	9	Fairfax, VA	74 923
17	9	Santa Clara, CA	47.9	61	10	Hartford, CT	17 708	22	10	Middlesex, MA	73 265
34	11	Hennepin, MN	47.0	66	11	New Haven, CT	17 186	13	11	King, WA	72 530
54	12	Bergen, NJ	46.9	72	12	Montgomery, PA	16 599	72	12	Montgomery, PA	71 306
72	12	Montgomery, PA	46.9	70	13	Middlesex, NJ	16 503	43	13	Fulton, GA	69 977
48	14	Westchester, NY	46.7	58	14	Erie, NY	15 652	27	14	Palm Beach, FL	68 743
56	14	Du Page, IL	46.7	22	15	Middlesex, MA	15 613	38	15	Contra Costa, CA	66 348
36	16	Travis, TX	46.0	35	16	Allegheny, PA	15 200	34	16	Hennepin, MN	65 231
51	17	Fairfield, CT	45.8	42	17	Montgomery, MD	15 181	56	17	Du Page, IL	64 059
33	18	Oakland, MI	44.4	56	18	Du Page, IL	15 041	33	18	Oakland, MI	63 454
20	19	Alameda, CA	43.0	2	19	Cook, IL	14 579	45	19	St. Louis, MO	62 194
29	20	Nassau, NY	42.8	59	20	Prince George's, MD	13 977	20	20	Alameda, CA	61 879
40	21	Mecklenburg, NC	42.3	37	21	Fairfax, VA	13 710	53	21	Collin, TX	59 532
45	22	St. Louis, MO	41.6	73	22	Worcester, MA	13 690	25	22	Suffolk, NY	59 484
75	23	Denton, TX	41.3	32	23	Cuyahoga, OH	13 483	61	23	Hartford, CT	59 240
70	24	Middlesex, NJ	41.0	71	24	Baltimore, MD	13 338	36	24	Travis, TX	58 362
38	25	Contra Costa, CA	39.6	23	25	Philadelphia, PA	12 900	6	25	Orange, CA	57 749
35	26	Allegheny, PA	37.8	45	26	St. Louis, MO	12 835	3	26	Harris, TX	55 088
6	27	Orange, CA	37.7	34	27	Hennepin, MN	12 471	2	27	Cook, IL	54 714
31	28	Franklin, OH	37.6	46	28	Honolulu, HI	12 458	71	28	Baltimore, MD	54 395
71	29	Baltimore, MD	36.6	63	29	San Francisco, CA	12 375	68	29	Ventura, CA	54 155
61	30	Hartford, CT	36.3	74	30	Hamilton, OH	11 794	35	30	Allegheny, PA	54 090
2	31	Cook, IL	35.8	31	31	Franklin, OH	11 706	1	31	Los Angeles, CA	53 521
5	32	San Diego, CA	35.7	33	32	Oakland, MI	11 412	70	32	Middlesex, NJ	53 467
74	33	Hamilton, OH	35.0	50	33	Milwaukee, WI	11 080	5	33	San Diego, CA	53 298
60	34	Gwinnett, GA	34.7	19	34	Wayne, MI	10 969	9	34	Dallas, TX	53 186
73	35	Worcester, MA	34.4	43	35	Fulton, GA	10 700	40	35	Mecklenburg, NC	52 129
25	36	Suffolk, NY	34.0	64	36	Macomb, MI	10 645	46	36	Honolulu, HI	52 122
66	36	New Haven, CT	34.0	13	37	King, WA	10 504	74	37	Hamilton, OH	52 081
27	38	Palm Beach, FL	33.6	65	38	Pierce, WA	10 199	66	38	New Haven, CT	51 835
8	39	Kings, NY	32.8	1	39	Los Angeles, CA	10 178	41	39	Wake, NC	51 776
46	40	Honolulu, HI	32.7	52	40	Marion, IN	10 067	73	40	Worcester, MA	51 370
39	41	Salt Lake, UT	32.1	17	41	Santa Clara, CA	9 814	75	41	Denton, TX	50 112
68	42	Ventura, CA	31.7	47	42	Fresno, CA	9 794	23	42	Philadelphia, PA	49 701
58	43	Erie, NY	31.6	62	43	Kern, CA	9 658	15	43	Tarrant, TX	48 727
30	44	Orange, FL	31.1	27	44	Palm Beach, FL	9 380	32	44	Cuyahoga, OH	48 506
59	44	Prince George's, MD	31.1	36	45	Travis, TX	9 265	49	45	Pinellas, FL	47 731
18	46	Broward, FL	30.8	60	46	Gwinnett, GA	9 240	52	46	Marion, IN	47 508
28	47	Hillsborough, FL	30.6	55	47	Shelby, TN	9 221	31	47	Franklin, OH	46 949
32	48	Cuyahoga, OH	30.5	67	48	Hidalgo, TX	9 216	58	48	Erie, NY	46 786
4	49	Maricopa, AZ	30.4	20	49	Alameda, CA	9 204	24	49	Sacramento, CA	46 539
11	49	Queens, NY	30.4	24	50	Sacramento, CA	9 183	55	50	Shelby, TN	45 153
1	51	Los Angeles, CA	30.3	5	51	San Diego, CA	9 151	18	51	Broward, FL	44 909
15	51	Tarrant, TX	30.3	38	52	Contra Costa, CA	9 145	59	52	Prince George's, MD	44 866
44	51	Pima, AZ	30.3	7	53	Miami-Dade, FL	9 106	39	53	Salt Lake, UT	44 692
55	54	Shelby, TN	30.2	49	54	Pinellas, FL	9 080	65	54	Pierce, WA	44 600
3	55	Harris, TX	29.5	68	55	Ventura, CA	9 020	28	55	Hillsborough, FL	43 435
9	56	Dallas, TX	29.1	10	56	Riverside, CA	8 947	7	56	Miami-Dade, FL	43 278
50	56	Milwaukee, WI	29.1	6	57	Orange, CA	8 890	50	57	Milwaukee, WI	43 020
49	58	Pinellas, FL	28.9	57	58	Duval, FL	8 831	8	58	Kings, NY	42 743
24	59	Sacramento, CA	28.8	69	59	El Paso, TX	8 824	16	59	Bexar, TX	42 702
52	60	Marion, IN	28.3	14	60	San Bernardino, CA	8 757	11	60	Queens, NY	42 288
57	61	Duval, FL	27.3	16	61	Bexar, TX	8 702	4	61	Maricopa, AZ	42 092
7	62	Miami-Dade, FL	26.9	28	62	Hillsborough, FL	8 685	64	62	Macomb, MI	41 847
16	63	Bexar, TX	26.7	18	63	Broward, FL	8 580	57	63	Duval, FL	41 339
23	64	Philadelphia, PA	25.4	30	64	Orange, FL	8 467	12	64	Clark, NV	40 652
65	65	Pierce, WA	24.7	9	65	Dallas, TX	8 412	30	65	Orange, FL	39 591
64	66	Macomb, MI	23.3	3	66	Harris, TX	8 406	44	66	Pima, AZ	38 536
12	67	Clark, NV	22.6	40	67	Mecklenburg, NC	8 264	19	67	Wayne, MI	38 512
19	68	Wayne, MI	22.0	15	68	Tarrant, TX	8 174	47	68	Fresno, CA	38 323
69	69	El Paso, TX	21.3	75	69	Denton, TX	8 131	62	69	Kern, CA	37 355
10	70	Riverside, CA	20.9	12	70	Clark, NV	8 074	60	70	Gwinnett, GA	37 106
47	71	Fresno, CA	19.4	53	71	Collin, TX	7 998	10	71	Riverside, CA	35 589
14	72	San Bernardino, CA	19.0	44	72	Pima, AZ	7 936	14	72	San Bernardino, CA	35 431
26	73	Bronx, NY	18.9	41	73	Wake, NC	7 770	69	73	El Paso, TX	32 614
67	74	Hidalgo, TX	16.7	4	74	Maricopa, AZ	7 156	26	74	Bronx, NY	32 442
62	75	Kern, CA	15.4	39	75	Salt Lake, UT	6 459	67	75	Hidalgo, TX	24 579

75 Largest Counties by 2016 Population
Selected Rankings

Median household income, 2015				Median value of owner-occupied housing units, 2011–2015				Median gross rent of renter-occupied housing units, 2011–2015			
Population income rank	Median income rank	County	Median income (dollars) [col 58]	Population rank	Median value rank	County	Median value (dollars) [col 91]	Population rank	Median rent rank	County	Median rent (dollars) [col 94]
37	1	Fairfax, VA	112 844	21	1	New York, NY	848 700	37	1	Fairfax, VA	1 747
17	2	Santa Clara, CA	102 191	63	2	San Francisco, CA	799 600	17	2	Santa Clara, CA	1 705
29	3	Nassau, NY	101 568	17	3	Santa Clara, CA	698 600	42	3	Montgomery, MD	1 627
42	4	Montgomery, MD	98 314	46	4	Honolulu, HI	580 200	29	4	Nassau, NY	1 578
63	5	San Francisco, CA	90 527	8	5	Kings, NY	570 200	46	5	Honolulu, HI	1 569
22	6	Middlesex, MA	90 025	6	6	Orange, CA	553 600	63	6	San Francisco, CA	1 558
54	7	Bergen, NJ	88 512	20	7	Alameda, CA	543 100	6	7	Orange, CA	1 548
25	8	Suffolk, NY	87 634	48	8	Westchester, NY	506 900	25	8	Suffolk, NY	1 544
53	9	Collin, TX	86 823	37	9	Fairfax, VA	501 200	21	9	New York, NY	1 519
51	10	Fairfield, CT	86 297	68	10	Ventura, CA	458 100	68	10	Ventura, CA	1 507
48	11	Westchester, NY	85 688	42	11	Montgomery, MD	454 700	38	11	Contra Costa, CA	1 426
72	12	Montgomery, PA	83 258	11	12	Queens, NY	450 300	11	12	Queens, NY	1 367
38	13	Contra Costa, CA	83 036	29	13	Nassau, NY	446 400	20	12	Alameda, CA	1 367
13	14	King, WA	81 816	1	14	Los Angeles, CA	441 900	48	14	Westchester, NY	1 364
56	15	Du Page, IL	81 616	54	15	Bergen, NJ	441 100	51	15	Fairfield, CT	1 348
20	16	Alameda, CA	81 462	38	16	Contra Costa, CA	439 900	54	15	Bergen, NJ	1 348
68	17	Ventura, CA	79 285	5	17	San Diego, CA	429 600	5	17	San Diego, CA	1 344
70	18	Middlesex, NJ	78 249	51	18	Fairfield, CT	416 000	22	18	Middlesex, MA	1 341
6	19	Orange, CA	78 002	22	19	Middlesex, MA	414 600	70	19	Middlesex, NJ	1 299
46	20	Honolulu, HI	76 544	13	20	King, WA	384 300	59	20	Prince George's, MD	1 294
59	21	Prince George's, MD	76 366	25	21	Suffolk, NY	375 100	1	21	Los Angeles, CA	1 231
75	22	Denton, TX	75 898	26	22	Bronx, NY	363 400	8	22	Kings, NY	1 215
21	23	New York, NY	75 136	70	23	Middlesex, NJ	323 300	13	23	King, WA	1 204
41	24	Wake, NC	70 629	72	24	Montgomery, PA	292 300	18	24	Broward, FL	1 191
33	25	Oakland, MI	70 150	56	25	Du Page, IL	278 500	10	25	Riverside, CA	1 179
61	26	Hartford, CT	69 260	59	26	Prince George's, MD	254 700	27	26	Palm Beach, FL	1 170
34	27	Hennepin, MN	68 902	10	27	Riverside, CA	253 200	71	27	Baltimore, MD	1 163
71	28	Baltimore, MD	68 317	73	28	Worcester, MA	252 600	72	28	Montgomery, PA	1 158
5	29	San Diego, CA	67 053	24	29	Sacramento, CA	248 400	56	29	Du Page, IL	1 143
73	30	Worcester, MA	65 621	71	30	Baltimore, MD	246 600	53	30	Collin, TX	1 119
39	31	Salt Lake, UT	65 549	66	31	New Haven, CT	245 200	14	31	San Bernardino, CA	1 116
36	32	Travis, TX	65 244	43	32	Fulton, GA	241 300	7	32	Miami-Dade, FL	1 112
60	33	Gwinnett, GA	61 797	36	33	Travis, TX	237 100	26	33	Bronx, NY	1 074
66	34	New Haven, CT	61 758	14	34	San Bernardino, CA	236 700	66	34	New Haven, CT	1 061
45	35	St. Louis, MO	61 569	61	35	Hartford, CT	236 400	36	35	Travis, TX	1 054
15	36	Tarrant, TX	60 735	39	36	Salt Lake, UT	234 700	60	36	Gwinnett, GA	1 043
11	37	Queens, NY	60 241	41	37	Wake, NC	234 000	24	37	Sacramento, CA	1 036
65	38	Pierce, WA	60 168	65	38	Pierce, WA	232 600	30	38	Orange, FL	1 033
43	39	Fulton, GA	59 911	34	39	Hennepin, MN	229 200	65	39	Pierce, WA	1 029
1	40	Los Angeles, CA	59 045	53	40	Collin, TX	223 400	43	40	Fulton, GA	1 001
24	41	Sacramento, CA	58 735	2	41	Cook, IL	218 700	12	41	Clark, NV	999
10	42	Riverside, CA	57 895	27	42	Palm Beach, FL	204 700	61	42	Hartford, CT	992
40	43	Mecklenburg, NC	57 029	7	43	Miami-Dade, FL	203 300	75	43	Denton, TX	991
2	44	Cook, IL	56 841	75	44	Denton, TX	197 600	2	44	Cook, IL	980
3	45	Harris, TX	56 670	47	45	Fresno, CA	194 600	28	45	Hillsborough, FL	965
27	46	Palm Beach, FL	56 638	4	46	Maricopa, AZ	187 100	4	46	Maricopa, AZ	962
4	47	Maricopa, AZ	56 017	18	47	Broward, FL	185 900	49	47	Pinellas, FL	952
64	48	Macomb, MI	54 939	40	48	Mecklenburg, NC	184 800	34	48	Hennepin, MN	951
35	49	Allegheny, PA	54 412	33	49	Oakland, MI	178 900	41	49	Wake, NC	948
31	50	Franklin, OH	53 939	45	50	St. Louis, MO	173 400	57	50	Duval, FL	943
18	51	Broward, FL	53 624	12	51	Clark, NV	170 400	33	51	Oakland, MI	942
14	52	San Bernardino, CA	53 526	60	52	Gwinnett, GA	167 700	40	52	Mecklenburg, NC	938
16	53	Bexar, TX	52 230	62	53	Kern, CA	167 400	39	53	Salt Lake, UT	936
58	54	Erie, NY	52 176	30	54	Orange, FL	163 800	73	54	Worcester, MA	934
9	55	Dallas, TX	51 824	44	55	Pima, AZ	159 900	23	55	Philadelphia, PA	922
28	56	Hillsborough, FL	51 710	28	56	Hillsborough, FL	159 200	15	56	Tarrant, TX	913
12	57	Clark, NV	51 624	50	57	Milwaukee, WI	151 700	9	57	Dallas, TX	907
62	58	Kern, CA	51 150	31	58	Franklin, OH	150 600	3	58	Harris, TX	906
74	59	Hamilton, OH	51 070	49	59	Pinellas, FL	150 200	62	59	Kern, CA	888
8	60	Kings, NY	51 026	23	60	Philadelphia, PA	145 300	47	60	Fresno, CA	886
30	61	Orange, FL	50 593	57	61	Duval, FL	142 300	45	61	St. Louis, MO	882
57	62	Duval, FL	49 565	74	62	Hamilton, OH	142 000	16	62	Bexar, TX	876
49	63	Pinellas, FL	47 591	15	63	Tarrant, TX	141 000	64	63	Macomb, MI	861
44	64	Pima, AZ	47 107	3	64	Harris, TX	137 800	55	64	Shelby, TN	859
55	65	Shelby, TN	46 998	9	65	Dallas, TX	132 700	31	65	Franklin, OH	845
47	66	Fresno, CA	46 608	55	66	Shelby, TN	130 800	44	66	Pima, AZ	816
50	67	Milwaukee, WI	45 905	58	67	Erie, NY	130 000	50	67	Milwaukee, WI	806
32	68	Cuyahoga, OH	45 506	35	68	Allegheny, PA	129 600	19	68	Wayne, MI	794
7	69	Miami-Dade, FL	43 687	16	69	Bexar, TX	129 400	52	69	Marion, IN	788
69	70	El Paso, TX	43 101	64	70	Macomb, MI	126 000	35	70	Allegheny, PA	780
19	71	Wayne, MI	41 585	32	71	Cuyahoga, OH	121 800	69	71	El Paso, TX	750
52	72	Marion, IN	41 407	52	72	Marion, IN	118 300	58	72	Erie, NY	739
23	73	Philadelphia, PA	41 210	69	73	El Paso, TX	113 900	32	73	Cuyahoga, OH	730
67	74	Hidalgo, TX	35 441	19	74	Wayne, MI	83 000	74	74	Hamilton, OH	709
26	75	Bronx, NY	35 102	67	75	Hidalgo, TX	79 200	67	75	Hidalgo, TX	661

75 Largest Counties by 2016 Population
Selected Rankings

Percent of population below the poverty level, 2015				Percent under 18 years old below the poverty level, 2015				Unemployment rate, 2016			
Population rank	Poverty rate rank	County	Poverty rate [col 59]	Population rank	Poverty rate for children rank	County	Poverty rate for children under 18 years [col 60]	Population rank	Unemployment rate rank	County	Unemployment rate [col 100]
67	1	Hidalgo, TX	31.1	67	1	Hidalgo, TX	42.9	62	1	Kern, CA	10.3
26	2	Bronx, NY	30.3	26	2	Bronx, NY	42.6	47	2	Fresno, CA	9.4
23	3	Philadelphia, PA	25.4	23	3	Philadelphia, PA	38.4	67	3	Hidalgo, TX	7.8
47	4	Fresno, CA	25.2	19	4	Wayne, MI	37.0	26	4	Bronx, NY	7.1
19	5	Wayne, MI	24.8	47	5	Fresno, CA	36.3	23	5	Philadelphia, PA	6.8
8	6	Kings, NY	22.3	8	6	Kings, NY	31.5	19	6	Wayne, MI	6.4
62	7	Kern, CA	21.9	55	7	Shelby, TN	31.4	65	7	Pierce, WA	6.3
52	8	Marion, IN	20.6	62	8	Kern, CA	31.3	2	8	Cook, IL	6.2
50	9	Milwaukee, WI	20.3	52	9	Marion, IN	31.0	10	9	Riverside, CA	6.1
69	9	El Paso, TX	20.3	50	10	Milwaukee, WI	29.5	12	10	Clark, NV	5.8
55	11	Shelby, TN	20.2	69	11	El Paso, TX	29.4	14	11	San Bernardino, CA	5.7
7	12	Miami-Dade, FL	20.0	44	12	Pima, AZ	27.7	55	12	Shelby, TN	5.5
14	13	San Bernardino, CA	18.9	7	13	Miami-Dade, FL	27.3	66	12	New Haven, CT	5.5
44	14	Pima, AZ	18.7	14	13	San Bernardino, CA	27.3	7	14	Miami-Dade, FL	5.4
32	15	Cuyahoga, OH	18.2	9	15	Dallas, TX	26.5	24	14	Sacramento, CA	5.4
9	16	Dallas, TX	17.9	32	16	Cuyahoga, OH	26.2	32	14	Cuyahoga, OH	5.4
21	17	New York, NY	17.6	57	17	Duval, FL	25.4	43	14	Fulton, GA	5.4
31	18	Franklin, OH	17.1	3	18	Harris, TX	25.3	3	18	Harris, TX	5.3
24	19	Sacramento, CA	16.9	21	19	New York, NY	24.9	8	18	Kings, NY	5.3
1	20	Los Angeles, CA	16.7	31	20	Franklin, OH	24.5	61	18	Hartford, CT	5.3
3	21	Harris, TX	16.6	58	21	Erie, NY	24.3	64	18	Macomb, MI	5.3
74	21	Hamilton, OH	16.6	43	22	Fulton, GA	23.8	1	22	Los Angeles, CA	5.2
4	23	Maricopa, AZ	16.3	1	23	Los Angeles, CA	23.5	35	22	Allegheny, PA	5.2
2	24	Cook, IL	16.2	2	23	Cook, IL	23.5	68	22	Ventura, CA	5.2
10	24	Riverside, CA	16.2	74	25	Hamilton, OH	23.1	50	25	Milwaukee, WI	5.1
43	26	Fulton, GA	16.0	4	26	Maricopa, AZ	23.0	57	26	Duval, FL	5.0
57	26	Duval, FL	16.0	24	27	Sacramento, CA	22.7	44	27	Pima, AZ	4.9
28	28	Hillsborough, FL	15.8	10	28	Riverside, CA	22.6	58	27	Erie, NY	4.9
16	29	Bexar, TX	15.6	12	28	Clark, NV	22.6	69	27	El Paso, TX	4.9
30	29	Orange, FL	15.6	30	28	Orange, FL	22.6	27	30	Palm Beach, FL	4.8
58	29	Erie, NY	15.6	16	31	Bexar, TX	22.2	51	30	Fairfield, CT	4.8
12	32	Clark, NV	15.4	28	32	Hillsborough, FL	21.4	56	30	Du Page, IL	4.8
40	33	Mecklenburg, NC	14.3	27	33	Palm Beach, FL	20.8	5	33	San Diego, CA	4.7
18	34	Broward, FL	14.0	49	34	Pinellas, FL	20.6	40	33	Mecklenburg, NC	4.7
5	35	San Diego, CA	13.9	18	35	Broward, FL	20.3	60	33	Gwinnett, GA	4.7
11	35	Queens, NY	13.9	66	36	New Haven, CT	20.0	18	36	Broward, FL	4.6
49	37	Pinellas, FL	13.6	11	37	Queens, NY	19.6	4	37	Maricopa, AZ	4.5
66	37	New Haven, CT	13.6	40	38	Mecklenburg, NC	19.1	11	37	Queens, NY	4.5
27	39	Palm Beach, FL	13.5	15	39	Tarrant, TX	18.4	21	37	New York, NY	4.5
36	40	Travis, TX	13.2	60	40	Gwinnett, GA	17.9	28	37	Hillsborough, FL	4.5
15	41	Tarrant, TX	13.1	5	41	San Diego, CA	17.8	71	37	Baltimore, MD	4.5
6	42	Orange, CA	12.7	36	41	Travis, TX	17.8	30	42	Orange, FL	4.4
60	43	Gwinnett, GA	12.6	6	43	Orange, CA	16.8	38	42	Contra Costa, CA	4.4
63	44	San Francisco, CA	12.4	64	43	Macomb, MI	16.8	49	42	Pinellas, FL	4.4
65	44	Pierce, WA	12.4	65	45	Pierce, WA	16.7	52	42	Marion, IN	4.4
35	46	Allegheny, PA	12.2	35	46	Allegheny, PA	16.5	59	42	Prince George's, MD	4.4
73	47	Worcester, MA	12.1	61	47	Hartford, CT	15.7	70	42	Middlesex, NJ	4.4
64	48	Macomb, MI	11.7	73	48	Worcester, MA	15.2	25	48	Suffolk, NY	4.3
20	49	Alameda, CA	11.5	41	49	Wake, NC	14.7	74	48	Hamilton, OH	4.3
41	50	Wake, NC	11.1	68	50	Ventura, CA	14.3	20	50	Alameda, CA	4.2
61	50	Hartford, CT	11.1	59	51	Prince George's, MD	14.2	33	50	Oakland, MI	4.2
34	52	Hennepin, MN	10.9	45	52	St. Louis, MO	14.0	41	50	Wake, NC	4.2
39	53	Salt Lake, UT	10.8	34	53	Hennepin, MN	13.9	45	50	St. Louis, MO	4.2
45	54	St. Louis, MO	10.3	20	54	Alameda, CA	13.8	48	50	Westchester, NY	4.2
38	55	Contra Costa, CA	10.2	63	55	San Francisco, CA	13.5	54	50	Bergen, NJ	4.2
48	56	Westchester, NY	10.1	48	56	Westchester, NY	13.1	72	50	Montgomery, PA	4.2
68	57	Ventura, CA	9.9	39	57	Salt Lake, UT	12.8	6	57	Orange, CA	4.0
13	58	King, WA	9.8	38	58	Contra Costa, CA	12.7	9	57	Dallas, TX	4.0
59	59	Prince George's, MD	9.5	71	59	Baltimore, MD	11.9	31	57	Franklin, OH	4.0
33	60	Oakland, MI	9.3	33	60	Oakland, MI	11.7	13	60	King, WA	3.9
46	61	Honolulu, HI	9.2	46	61	Honolulu, HI	11.5	15	60	Tarrant, TX	3.9
71	62	Baltimore, MD	9.1	51	62	Fairfield, CT	11.2	29	60	Nassau, NY	3.9
51	63	Fairfield, CT	9.0	70	63	Middlesex, NJ	10.8	73	60	Worcester, MA	3.9
70	64	Middlesex, NJ	8.5	25	64	Suffolk, NY	10.7	17	64	Santa Clara, CA	3.8
17	65	Santa Clara, CA	8.3	13	65	King, WA	10.6	16	65	Bexar, TX	3.7
75	66	Denton, TX	8.0	42	66	Montgomery, MD	10.5	53	66	Collin, TX	3.5
25	67	Suffolk, NY	7.8	56	67	Du Page, IL	9.2	34	67	Hennepin, MN	3.4
22	68	Middlesex, MA	7.6	17	68	Santa Clara, CA	9.0	75	67	Denton, TX	3.4
42	69	Montgomery, MD	7.5	75	68	Denton, TX	9.0	42	69	Montgomery, MD	3.3
54	70	Bergen, NJ	7.1	54	70	Bergen, NJ	8.6	63	69	San Francisco, CA	3.3
56	70	Du Page, IL	7.1	29	71	Nassau, NY	8.4	37	71	Fairfax, VA	3.2
53	72	Collin, TX	6.6	22	72	Middlesex, MA	8.2	39	71	Salt Lake, UT	3.2
72	72	Montgomery, PA	6.6	53	72	Collin, TX	8.2	36	73	Travis, TX	3.1
37	74	Fairfax, VA	6.2	37	74	Fairfax, VA	7.5	22	74	Middlesex, MA	3.0
29	75	Nassau, NY	6.1	72	74	Montgomery, PA	7.5	46	75	Honolulu, HI	2.8

75 Largest Counties by 2016 Population
Selected Rankings

Manufacturing employment as a percent of total nonfarm employment, 2015				Professional, scientific, and technical employment as a percent of total nonfarm employment, 2015				Per capita local government taxes, 2012			
Population rank	Manufacturing rank	County	Percent employed in manufacturing [col 107/ col 105]	Population rank	Professional services rank	County	Percent employed in professional services [col 110/ col 105]	Population rank	Local taxes rank	County	Per capita local taxes (dollars) [col 183]
64	1	Macomb, MI	23.1	37	1	Fairfax, VA	32.6	29	1	Nassau, NY	5 254
19	2	Wayne, MI	13.1	42	2	Montgomery, MD	17.5	48	2	Westchester, NY	5 135
73	3	Worcester, MA	11.2	63	3	San Francisco, CA	16.5	21	3	New York, NY	5 096
15	4	Tarrant, TX	10.8	70	4	Middlesex, NJ	14.9	8	3	Kings, NY	5 096
58	5	Erie, NY	10.4	21	5	New York, NY	14.2	11	3	Queens, NY	5 096
6	6	Orange, CA	10.3	33	5	Oakland, MI	14.2	26	3	Bronx, NY	5 096
20	6	Alameda, CA	10.3	22	7	Middlesex, MA	13.1	25	7	Suffolk, NY	4 295
61	6	Hartford, CT	10.3	17	7	Santa Clara, CA	13.1	63	8	San Francisco, CA	4 001
32	9	Cuyahoga, OH	10.2	43	9	Fulton, GA	12.5	54	9	Bergen, NJ	3 788
50	9	Milwaukee, WI	10.2	59	9	Prince George's, MD	12.5	51	10	Fairfield, CT	3 419
68	11	Ventura, CA	9.7	36	11	Travis, TX	11.9	42	11	Montgomery, MD	3 168
25	12	Suffolk, NY	9.4	41	12	Wake, NC	11.3	56	12	Du Page, IL	3 002
47	13	Fresno, CA	9.3	5	13	San Diego, CA	11.0	37	13	Fairfax, VA	2 810
66	14	New Haven, CT	9.2	28	14	Hillsborough, FL	10.2	43	14	Fulton, GA	2 802
14	15	San Bernardino, CA	9.0	1	15	Los Angeles, CA	9.9	2	15	Cook, IL	2 765
56	15	Du Page, IL	9.0	64	15	Macomb, MI	9.9	32	15	Cuyahoga, OH	2 765
1	17	Los Angeles, CA	8.7	53	17	Collin, TX	9.7	70	17	Middlesex, NJ	2 730
17	18	Santa Clara, CA	8.5	20	18	Alameda, CA	9.6	31	18	Franklin, OH	2 717
39	18	Salt Lake, UT	8.5	9	19	Dallas, TX	9.5	23	19	Philadelphia, PA	2 636
72	20	Montgomery, PA	8.4	2	19	Cook, IL	9.5	17	20	Santa Clara, CA	2 621
74	20	Hamilton, OH	8.4	34	19	Hennepin, MN	9.5	61	21	Hartford, CT	2 571
3	22	Harris, TX	8.3	13	22	King, WA	9.2	13	22	King, WA	2 543
34	23	Hennepin, MN	8.2	72	23	Montgomery, PA	8.9	27	23	Palm Beach, FL	2 542
5	24	San Diego, CA	8.1	6	24	Orange, CA	8.8	72	24	Montgomery, PA	2 541
51	25	Fairfield, CT	8.0	51	25	Fairfield, CT	8.7	22	25	Middlesex, MA	2 471
10	26	Riverside, CA	7.9	3	25	Harris, TX	8.7	36	26	Travis, TX	2 455
33	27	Oakland, MI	7.8	68	27	Ventura, CA	8.6	74	27	Hamilton, OH	2 403
49	28	Pinellas, FL	7.6	71	28	Baltimore, MD	8.5	53	28	Collin, TX	2 390
13	29	King, WA	7.5	39	28	Salt Lake, UT	8.5	58	29	Erie, NY	2 368
2	29	Cook, IL	7.5	40	30	Mecklenburg, NC	8.4	20	30	Alameda, CA	2 358
52	29	Marion, IN	7.5	74	30	Hamilton, OH	8.4	66	30	New Haven, CT	2 358
65	32	Pierce, WA	7.4	60	30	Gwinnett, GA	8.4	9	32	Dallas, TX	2 338
44	33	Pima, AZ	7.2	35	33	Allegheny, PA	8.2	35	33	Allegheny, PA	2 228
45	34	St. Louis, MO	7.1	27	34	Palm Beach, FL	8.1	3	34	Harris, TX	2 171
70	35	Middlesex, NJ	7.0	45	34	St. Louis, MO	8.1	45	35	St. Louis, MO	2 133
9	36	Dallas, TX	6.8	54	34	Bergen, NJ	8.1	7	36	Miami-Dade, FL	2 132
54	36	Bergen, NJ	6.8	29	34	Nassau, NY	8.1	15	37	Tarrant, TX	2 029
60	36	Gwinnett, GA	6.8	52	38	Marion, IN	7.8	40	38	Mecklenburg, NC	1 923
75	39	Denton, TX	6.5	23	38	Philadelphia, PA	7.8	71	39	Baltimore, MD	1 917
55	39	Shelby, TN	6.5	25	38	Suffolk, NY	7.8	34	40	Hennepin, MN	1 910
22	41	Middlesex, MA	6.4	18	41	Broward, FL	7.7	1	41	Los Angeles, CA	1 891
62	42	Kern, CA	6.3	49	42	Pinellas, FL	7.6	50	42	Milwaukee, WI	1 888
4	43	Maricopa, AZ	6.2	38	42	Contra Costa, CA	7.6	38	43	Contra Costa, CA	1 861
69	44	El Paso, TX	5.7	24	44	Sacramento, CA	7.5	55	44	Shelby, TN	1 828
31	45	Franklin, OH	5.2	56	44	Du Page, IL	7.5	30	45	Orange, FL	1 815
57	46	Duval, FL	5.1	4	46	Maricopa, AZ	7.1	6	46	Orange, CA	1 806
53	47	Collin, TX	5.0	7	46	Miami-Dade, FL	7.1	5	47	San Diego, CA	1 791
35	47	Allegheny, PA	5.0	58	46	Erie, NY	7.1	75	48	Denton, TX	1 790
16	49	Bexar, TX	4.6	30	49	Orange, FL	7.0	59	49	Prince George's, MD	1 761
36	49	Travis, TX	4.6	31	50	Franklin, OH	6.8	18	50	Broward, FL	1 742
38	49	Contra Costa, CA	4.6	48	50	Westchester, NY	6.8	16	51	Bexar, TX	1 675
71	49	Baltimore, MD	4.6	32	52	Cuyahoga, OH	6.5	68	52	Ventura, CA	1 650
40	53	Mecklenburg, NC	4.5	73	53	Worcester, MA	6.4	73	53	Worcester, MA	1 630
24	53	Sacramento, CA	4.5	19	53	Wayne, MI	6.4	49	54	Pinellas, FL	1 597
30	55	Orange, FL	3.8	61	55	Hartford, CT	6.2	57	55	Duval, FL	1 536
11	55	Queens, NY	3.8	57	55	Duval, FL	6.2	60	56	Gwinnett, GA	1 529
8	57	Kings, NY	3.7	16	57	Bexar, TX	6.1	65	57	Pierce, WA	1 521
28	57	Hillsborough, FL	3.7	62	57	Kern, CA	6.1	33	58	Oakland, MI	1 515
7	59	Miami-Dade, FL	3.5	12	59	Clark, NV	5.3	4	59	Maricopa, AZ	1 506
18	59	Broward, FL	3.5	44	60	Pima, AZ	5.2	19	60	Wayne, MI	1 499
23	59	Philadelphia, PA	3.5	15	60	Tarrant, TX	5.2	52	61	Marion, IN	1 447
67	59	Hidalgo, TX	3.5	46	62	Honolulu, HI	5.0	44	62	Pima, AZ	1 438
48	63	Westchester, NY	3.2	50	62	Milwaukee, WI	5.0	41	63	Wake, NC	1 436
29	64	Nassau, NY	2.9	75	64	Denton, TX	4.8	39	64	Salt Lake, UT	1 428
41	64	Wake, NC	2.9	69	65	El Paso, TX	4.6	12	65	Clark, NV	1 367
59	66	Prince George's, MD	2.7	66	66	New Haven, CT	4.2	62	66	Kern, CA	1 365
46	66	Honolulu, HI	2.7	55	67	Shelby, TN	4.2	10	67	Riverside, CA	1 362
43	68	Fulton, GA	2.5	47	68	Fresno, CA	4.1	28	68	Hillsborough, FL	1 359
27	68	Palm Beach, FL	2.5	65	69	Pierce, WA	3.8	24	69	Sacramento, CA	1 357
12	70	Clark, NV	2.4	8	70	Kings, NY	3.5	46	70	Honolulu, HI	1 348
26	71	Bronx, NY	2.3	10	70	Riverside, CA	3.5	69	71	El Paso, TX	1 318
42	72	Montgomery, MD	1.9	14	72	San Bernardino, CA	3.2	14	72	San Bernardino, CA	1 287
63	73	San Francisco, CA	1.3	67	73	Hidalgo, TX	3.1	47	73	Fresno, CA	1 131
37	74	Fairfax, VA	1.0	11	74	Queens, NY	2.9	64	74	Macomb, MI	1 112
21	75	New York, NY	0.8	26	75	Bronx, NY	1.6	67	75	Hidalgo, TX	1 071

75 Largest Counties by 2016 Population
Selected Rankings

	Violent crime rate, 2014 (violent crime known to police)			Military as a percent of all federal employment, 2015				Mean income tax, 2014			
Population rank	Violent crime rate rank	County	Violent crime rate per 100,000 population [col 46]	Population rank	Military employment rank	County	Percent military federal employment [col 195/col 194+195]	Population rank	Mean income tax rank	County	Mean income tax [col 199]
55	1	Shelby, TN	1 306	65	1	Pierce, WA	73.6	21	1	New York, NY	48 504
52	2	Marion, IN	1 226	69	2	El Paso, TX	69.4	51	2	Fairfield, CT	34 778
23	3	Philadelphia, PA	1 022	5	3	San Diego, CA	68.0	48	3	Westchester, NY	29 946
50	4	Milwaukee, WI	1 002	46	4	Honolulu, HI	64.5	63	4	San Francisco, CA	26 092
19	5	Wayne, MI	995	14	5	San Bernardino, CA	56.9	17	5	Santa Clara, CA	24 732
63	6	San Francisco, CA	802	12	6	Clark, NV	54.3	29	6	Nassau, NY	19 487
43	7	Fulton, GA	791	53	7	Collin, TX	53.3	37	7	Fairfax, VA	19 335
12	8	Clark, NV	743	60	8	Gwinnett, GA	51.7	54	8	Bergen, NJ	19 033
3	9	Harris, TX	718	75	9	Denton, TX	50.0	22	9	Middlesex, MA	18 945
57	10	Duval, FL	687	16	10	Bexar, TX	49.3	43	10	Fulton, GA	18 569
30	11	Orange, FL	682	72	11	Montgomery, PA	46.9	27	11	Palm Beach, FL	17 726
20	12	Alameda, CA	645	57	12	Duval, FL	46.3	13	12	King, WA	17 577
7	13	Miami-Dade, FL	633	70	13	Middlesex, NJ	45.4	72	13	Montgomery, PA	17 301
21	14	New York, NY	598	54	14	Bergen, NJ	41.8	42	14	Montgomery, MD	16 752
8	14	Kings, NY	598	68	15	Ventura, CA	41.4	53	15	Collin, TX	15 866
11	14	Queens, NY	598	51	16	Fairfield, CT	40.7	38	16	Contra Costa, CA	15 636
26	14	Bronx, NY	598	73	17	Worcester, MA	39.7	56	17	Du Page, IL	14 599
32	18	Cuyahoga, OH	561	44	18	Pima, AZ	39.1	33	18	Oakland, MI	14 004
2	19	Cook, IL	558	4	19	Maricopa, AZ	39.0	34	19	Hennepin, MN	13 915
40	20	Mecklenburg, NC	522	45	20	St. Louis, MO	37.9	36	20	Travis, TX	13 865
62	21	Kern, CA	510	26	21	Bronx, NY	37.3	45	21	St. Louis, MO	13 636
49	22	Pinellas, FL	506	8	22	Kings, NY	36.5	20	22	Alameda, CA	12 983
24	23	Sacramento, CA	503	18	22	Broward, FL	36.5	3	23	Harris, TX	12 888
47	24	Fresno, CA	471	41	24	Wake, NC	36.4	25	24	Suffolk, NY	12 397
59	25	Prince George's, MD	460	10	25	Riverside, CA	35.8	6	25	Orange, CA	12 299
74	26	Hamilton, OH	457	28	26	Hillsborough, FL	35.5	9	26	Dallas, TX	11 937
16	27	Bexar, TX	454	29	27	Nassau, NY	33.0	75	27	Denton, TX	11 804
27	28	Palm Beach, FL	452	6	28	Orange, CA	31.4	2	28	Cook, IL	11 269
71	29	Baltimore, MD	448	33	29	Oakland, MI	30.7	40	29	Mecklenburg, NC	11 097
9	30	Dallas, TX	443	40	30	Mecklenburg, NC	30.6	41	30	Wake, NC	10 874
44	30	Pima, AZ	443	39	31	Salt Lake, UT	30.3	61	31	Hartford, CT	10 401
58	32	Erie, NY	441	22	32	Middlesex, MA	30.0	1	32	Los Angeles, CA	10 365
65	33	Pierce, WA	432	67	32	Hidalgo, TX	30.0	71	33	Baltimore, MD	10 074
73	34	Worcester, MA	431	20	34	Alameda, CA	29.6	68	34	Ventura, CA	10 045
34	35	Hennepin, MN	427	3	35	Harris, TX	29.1	35	35	Allegheny, PA	9 938
1	36	Los Angeles, CA	422	27	36	Palm Beach, FL	28.8	15	36	Tarrant, TX	9 889
31	36	Franklin, OH	422	49	37	Pinellas, FL	28.3	74	37	Hamilton, OH	9 829
18	38	Broward, FL	409	56	38	Du Page, IL	28.0	5	38	San Diego, CA	9 808
35	39	Allegheny, PA	401	62	39	Kern, CA	27.8	70	39	Middlesex, NJ	9 789
15	40	Tarrant, TX	400	15	40	Tarrant, TX	27.4	66	40	New Haven, CT	9 416
14	41	San Bernardino, CA	392	7	41	Miami-Dade, FL	27.1	73	41	Worcester, MA	9 157
4	42	Maricopa, AZ	383	38	41	Contra Costa, CA	27.1	7	42	Miami-Dade, FL	9 104
69	43	El Paso, TX	364	13	43	King, WA	26.8	18	43	Broward, FL	8 966
36	44	Travis, TX	355	1	44	Los Angeles, CA	26.7	49	44	Pinellas, FL	8 868
39	45	Salt Lake, UT	350	34	45	Hennepin, MN	26.6	28	45	Hillsborough, FL	8 485
13	46	King, WA	334	66	46	New Haven, CT	26.1	4	46	Maricopa, AZ	8 340
66	47	New Haven, CT	333	17	47	Santa Clara, CA	25.3	32	47	Cuyahoga, OH	8 252
38	48	Contra Costa, CA	329	24	48	Sacramento, CA	25.1	55	48	Shelby, TN	7 942
67	48	Hidalgo, TX	329	48	49	Westchester, NY	25.0	39	49	Salt Lake, UT	7 773
5	50	San Diego, CA	325	61	50	Hartford, CT	24.6	12	50	Clark, NV	7 755
28	50	Hillsborough, FL	325	50	51	Milwaukee, WI	23.1	16	51	Bexar, TX	7 613
45	52	St. Louis, MO	307	2	52	Cook, IL	22.3	31	52	Franklin, OH	7 603
64	53	Macomb, MI	288	59	52	Prince George's, MD	22.3	30	53	Orange, FL	7 397
61	54	Hartford, CT	276	31	54	Franklin, OH	22.2	58	54	Erie, NY	7 237
10	55	Riverside, CA	269	55	54	Shelby, TN	22.2	8	55	Kings, NY	7 195
17	56	Santa Clara, CA	247	35	56	Allegheny, PA	21.7	46	56	Honolulu, HI	7 170
51	57	Fairfield, CT	246	11	57	Queens, NY	20.8	65	57	Pierce, WA	7 163
48	58	Westchester, NY	226	74	58	Hamilton, OH	19.9	57	58	Duval, FL	7 032
68	59	Ventura, CA	223	30	59	Orange, FL	19.2	24	59	Sacramento, CA	6 591
6	60	Orange, CA	198	36	59	Travis, TX	19.2	60	60	Gwinnett, GA	6 357
60	61	Gwinnett, GA	195	19	61	Wayne, MI	18.9	44	61	Pima, AZ	6 327
22	62	Middlesex, MA	190	64	61	Macomb, MI	18.9	50	62	Milwaukee, WI	6 315
33	63	Oakland, MI	174	25	63	Suffolk, NY	18.7	64	63	Macomb, MI	6 028
42	64	Montgomery, MD	169	9	64	Dallas, TX	18.6	52	64	Marion, IN	5 880
75	65	Denton, TX	167	32	65	Cuyahoga, OH	18.2	19	65	Wayne, MI	5 859
53	66	Collin, TX	159	37	66	Fairfax, VA	17.7	23	66	Philadelphia, PA	5 604
70	67	Middlesex, NJ	155	52	67	Marion, IN	17.5	47	67	Fresno, CA	5 490
29	68	Nassau, NY	153	58	68	Erie, NY	17.1	62	68	Kern, CA	5 479
72	69	Montgomery, PA	148	23	69	Philadelphia, PA	14.8	59	69	Prince George's, MD	5 236
41	70	Wake, NC	126	47	69	Fresno, CA	14.8	10	70	Riverside, CA	5 170
25	71	Suffolk, NY	122	71	71	Baltimore, MD	14.6	11	71	Queens, NY	5 105
37	72	Fairfax, VA	91	42	72	Montgomery, MD	14.4	14	72	San Bernardino, CA	4 655
56	73	Du Page, IL	83	43	73	Fulton, GA	10.8	69	73	El Paso, TX	4 034
54	74	Bergen, NJ	81	21	74	New York, NY	10.5	67	74	Hidalgo, TX	3 349
46	75	Honolulu, HI	72	63	75	San Francisco, CA	10.1	26	75	Bronx, NY	2 952

75 Largest Counties by 2016 Population
Selected Rankings

Nonemployer businesses, 2015

Population rank	Nonemployer Businesses rank	County	Nonemployer businesses [col 167]
1	1	Los Angeles, CA	1 022 938
2	2	Cook, IL	475 448
7	3	Miami-Dade, FL	462 297
3	4	Harris, TX	394 410
6	5	Orange, CA	300 969
4	6	Maricopa, AZ	298 614
5	7	San Diego, CA	268 900
8	8	Kings, NY	263 777
18	9	Broward, FL	252 153
11	10	Queens, NY	243 480
21	11	New York, NY	225 955
9	12	Dallas, TX	224 664
27	13	Palm Beach, FL	171 074
13	14	King, WA	166 065
15	15	Tarrant, TX	162 998
10	16	Riverside, CA	161 369
12	17	Clark, NV	154 711
14	18	San Bernardino, CA	141 417
20	19	Alameda, CA	139 261
17	20	Santa Clara, CA	139 245
29	21	Nassau, NY	136 547
22	22	Middlesex, MA	134 915
16	23	Bexar, TX	131 716
25	24	Suffolk, NY	127 010
19	25	Wayne, MI	126 572
30	26	Orange, FL	125 651
28	27	Hillsborough, FL	116 379
36	28	Travis, TX	116 321
26	29	Bronx, NY	114 788
33	30	Oakland, MI	113 364
42	31	Montgomery, MD	108 980
43	32	Fulton, GA	106 684
37	33	Fairfax, VA	104 930
34	34	Hennepin, MN	103 278
24	35	Sacramento, CA	101 015
60	36	Gwinnett, GA	99 862
63	37	San Francisco, CA	98 890
48	38	Westchester, NY	95 840
31	39	Franklin, OH	93 514
54	40	Bergen, NJ	92 417
51	41	Fairfield, CT	91 902
38	42	Contra Costa, CA	91 637
40	43	Mecklenburg, NC	91 430
32	44	Cuyahoga, OH	91 324
23	45	Philadelphia, PA	88 920
53	46	Collin, TX	85 086
41	47	Wake, NC	84 397
49	48	Pinellas, FL	82 176
39	49	Salt Lake, UT	82 040
56	50	Du Page, IL	81 992
35	51	Allegheny, PA	80 279
55	52	Shelby, TN	78 921
45	53	St. Louis, MO	74 431
59	54	Prince George's, MD	73 775
67	55	Hidalgo, TX	69 823
72	56	Montgomery, PA	69 365
68	57	Ventura, CA	67 736
57	58	Duval, FL	67 189
75	59	Denton, TX	66 761
71	60	Baltimore, MD	65 395
46	61	Honolulu, HI	64 258
44	62	Pima, AZ	64 179
64	63	Macomb, MI	62 979
52	64	Marion, IN	61 844
66	65	New Haven, CT	59 574
61	66	Hartford, CT	58 242
74	67	Hamilton, OH	57 438
69	68	El Paso, TX	56 344
70	69	Middlesex, NJ	55 578
73	70	Worcester, MA	51 541
47	71	Fresno, CA	50 405
58	72	Erie, NY	47 593
50	73	Milwaukee, WI	47 560
62	74	Kern, CA	45 226
65	75	Pierce, WA	42 238

Value of residential construction authorized by building permits, 2016

Population rank	Value ($-1,000) rank	County	Value ($1,000) rank [col 169]
4	1	Maricopa, AZ	5 918 178
1	2	Los Angeles, CA	4 910 545
3	3	Harris, TX	3 683 504
13	4	King, WA	3 375 978
53	5	Collin, TX	3 105 206
9	6	Dallas, TX	2 741 849
28	7	Hillsborough, FL	2 670 056
6	8	Orange, CA	2 445 261
30	9	Orange, FL	2 374 812
5	10	San Diego, CA	2 223 118
36	11	Travis, TX	2 211 377
15	12	Tarrant, TX	2 113 588
7	13	Miami-Dade, FL	2 088 260
41	14	Wake, NC	2 025 574
12	15	Clark, NV	2 016 831
75	16	Denton, TX	1 949 641
43	17	Fulton, GA	1 918 886
2	18	Cook, IL	1 909 931
10	19	Riverside, CA	1 625 917
40	20	Mecklenburg, NC	1 509 315
39	21	Salt Lake, UT	1 493 137
20	22	Alameda, CA	1 460 018
34	23	Hennepin, MN	1 294 844
27	24	Palm Beach, FL	1 272 494
17	25	Santa Clara, CA	1 176 448
63	26	San Francisco, CA	1 144 467
16	27	Bexar, TX	1 066 142
57	28	Duval, FL	969 645
31	29	Franklin, OH	917 019
65	30	Pierce, WA	907 635
22	31	Middlesex, MA	901 934
18	32	Broward, FL	846 723
14	33	San Bernardino, CA	821 694
24	34	Sacramento, CA	808 876
33	35	Oakland, MI	792 106
38	36	Contra Costa, CA	749 612
47	37	Fresno, CA	729 163
44	38	Pima, AZ	693 032
54	39	Bergen, NJ	656 798
69	40	El Paso, TX	656 311
25	41	Suffolk, NY	650 568
46	42	Honolulu, HI	641 470
67	43	Hidalgo, TX	637 566
51	44	Fairfield, CT	621 925
8	45	Kings, NY	619 962
60	46	Gwinnett, GA	613 000
21	47	New York, NY	540 463
23	48	Philadelphia, PA	534 322
26	49	Bronx, NY	531 101
62	50	Kern, CA	488 500
49	51	Pinellas, FL	478 582
45	52	St. Louis, MO	478 129
35	53	Allegheny, PA	437 576
42	54	Montgomery, MD	424 990
56	55	Du Page, IL	410 312
11	56	Queens, NY	403 536
64	57	Macomb, MI	400 845
59	58	Prince George's, MD	396 213
55	59	Shelby, TN	388 430
72	60	Montgomery, PA	380 261
37	61	Fairfax, VA	375 044
52	62	Marion, IN	365 995
19	63	Wayne, MI	358 370
58	64	Erie, NY	342 197
68	65	Ventura, CA	340 979
48	66	Westchester, NY	323 829
29	67	Nassau, NY	321 252
73	68	Worcester, MA	299 072
74	69	Hamilton, OH	255 373
50	70	Milwaukee, WI	249 316
70	71	Middlesex, NJ	243 010
71	72	Baltimore, MD	237 170
32	73	Cuyahoga, OH	207 582
61	74	Hartford, CT	193 675
66	75	New Haven, CT	147 953

Full-time equivalent government employees, 2012

Population rank	Government employees rank	County	Government employees rank [col 171]
21	1	New York, NY	411 393
8	1	Kings, NY	(included in
11	1	Queens, NY	New York,
26	1	Bronx, NY	NY)
1	5	Los Angeles, CA	386 456
2	6	Cook, IL	198 590
3	7	Harris, TX	166 045
4	8	Maricopa, AZ	129 919
9	9	Dallas, TX	105 099
7	10	Miami-Dade, FL	102 308
5	11	San Diego, CA	97 178
6	12	Orange, CA	85 251
16	13	Bexar, TX	76 821
15	14	Tarrant, TX	76 274
18	15	Broward, FL	73 864
10	16	Riverside, CA	68 997
14	17	San Bernardino, CA	68 989
13	18	King, WA	65 821
25	19	Suffolk, NY	63 444
32	20	Cuyahoga, OH	62 490
23	21	Philadelphia, PA	60 937
40	22	Mecklenburg, NC	60 489
29	23	Nassau, NY	60 368
17	24	Santa Clara, CA	59 919
20	25	Alameda, CA	56 184
19	26	Wayne, MI	52 078
12	27	Clark, NV	51 796
22	28	Middlesex, MA	51 015
24	29	Sacramento, CA	50 509
27	30	Palm Beach, FL	46 198
28	31	Hillsborough, FL	45 811
30	32	Orange, FL	45 111
36	33	Travis, TX	45 034
35	34	Allegheny, PA	43 945
31	35	Franklin, OH	43 936
43	36	Fulton, GA	43 801
37	37	Fairfax, VA	43 275
48	38	Westchester, NY	42 725
55	39	Shelby, TN	39 378
67	40	Hidalgo, TX	39 042
63	41	San Francisco, CA	38 712
42	42	Montgomery, MD	38 590
69	43	El Paso, TX	38 262
34	44	Hennepin, MN	35 312
58	45	Erie, NY	35 259
45	46	St. Louis, MO	35 141
47	47	Fresno, CA	34 954
56	48	Du Page, IL	34 627
39	49	Salt Lake, UT	34 230
52	50	Marion, IN	34 223
50	51	Milwaukee, WI	34 086
54	52	Bergen, NJ	32 531
62	53	Kern, CA	32 191
49	54	Pinellas, FL	32 162
33	55	Oakland, MI	32 137
51	56	Fairfield, CT	32 029
61	57	Hartford, CT	31 675
44	58	Pima, AZ	31 634
41	59	Wake, NC	31 235
38	60	Contra Costa, CA	31 030
74	61	Hamilton, OH	30 330
66	62	New Haven, CT	28 448
53	63	Collin, TX	28 433
73	64	Worcester, MA	28 380
60	65	Gwinnett, GA	27 778
68	66	Ventura, CA	27 714
59	67	Prince George's, MD	27 062
57	68	Duval, FL	26 681
70	69	Middlesex, NJ	26 592
71	70	Baltimore, MD	26 532
65	71	Pierce, WA	23 934
72	72	Montgomery, PA	23 690
75	73	Denton, TX	21 018
64	74	Macomb, MI	20 477
46	75	Honolulu, HI	9 304

75 Largest Counties by 2016 Population
Selected Rankings

Value of agricultural sales, 2012			Average agricultural sales per farm, 2012				Number of farms, 2012			
Value of sales rank	County	Value of sales (millions of dollars) [col 125]	Value of sales rank	Average sales rank	County	Average sales per farm (dollars) [col 126]	Value of sales rank	Number of farms rank	County	Number of farms [col 113]
1	Fresno, CA	4 973	28	1	Haskell, KS	5 400 412	50	1	San Diego, CA	5 732
2	Tulare, CA	4 017	22	2	Hartley, TX	4 630 969	1	2	Fresno, CA	5 683
3	Kern, CA	3 999	8	3	Imperial, CA	4 486 078	15	3	Lancaster, PA	5 657
4	Monterey, CA	2 980	32	4	Scott, KS	3 642 543	2	4	Tulare, CA	4 931
5	Merced, CA	2 968	46	5	Hansford, TX	2 977 973	7	5	Stanislaus, CA	4 143
6	San Joaquin, CA	2 250	40	6	Grant, KS	2 790 860	6	6	San Joaquin, CA	3 580
7	Stanislaus, CA	2 228	4	7	Monterey, CA	2 527 341	33	7	Sonoma, CA	3 579
8	Imperial, CA	1 889	19	8	Castro, TX	2 466 429	9	8	Weld, CO	3 525
9	Weld, CO	1 861	62	9	Wichita, KS	2 357 736	45	9	Stearns, MN	3 501
10	Kings, CA	1 829	18	10	Parmer, TX	2 332 523	12	10	Yakima, WA	3 143
11	Grant, WA	1 762	66	11	Moore, TX	2 318 107	67	11	Miami-Dade, FL	2 954
12	Yakima, WA	1 646	36	12	Gray, KS	2 247 407	26	12	Riverside, CA	2 949
13	Sioux, IA	1 613	17	13	Deaf Smith, TX	2 220 734	53	13	San Luis Obispo, CA	2 666
14	Madera, CA	1 603	3	14	Kern, CA	2 063 462	71	14	Marion, OR	2 567
15	Lancaster, PA	1 475	72	15	Sherman, TX	1 886 121	5	15	Merced, CA	2 486
16	Ventura, CA	1 440	49	16	Phelps, NE	1 824 185	29	16	Maricopa, AZ	2 479
17	Deaf Smith, TX	1 379	41	17	Finney, KS	1 822 062	16	17	Ventura, CA	2 150
18	Parmer, TX	1 330	58	18	Dallam, TX	1 756 642	3	18	Kern, CA	1 938
19	Castro, TX	1 312	31	19	Yuma, AZ	1 752 685	55	19	Rockingham, VA	1 902
20	Duplin, NC	1 276	10	20	Kings, CA	1 732 231	54	20	Chester, PA	1 730
21	Sampson, NC	1 259	35	21	Gooding, ID	1 581 904	13	21	Sioux, IA	1 618
22	Hartley, TX	1 181	34	22	Cassia, ID	1 427 737	23	22	Santa Barbara, CA	1 597
23	Santa Barbara, CA	1 178	24	23	Yuma, CO	1 379 309	11	23	Grant, WA	1 552
24	Yuma, CO	1 150	20	24	Duplin, NC	1 357 895	38	24	Benton, WA	1 509
25	Cuming, NE	1 081	5	25	Merced, CA	1 193 694	14	25	Madera, CA	1 507
26	Riverside, CA	1 039	21	26	Sampson, NC	1 179 750	30	26	Palm Beach, FL	1 409
27	Texas, OK	1 014	25	27	Cuming, NE	1 177 889	75	27	Allegan, MI	1 396
28	Haskell, KS	1 010	11	28	Grant, WA	1 135 499	42	28	Custer, NE	1 352
29	Maricopa, AZ	1 004	64	29	Jerome, ID	1 101 943	51	29	Kossuth, IA	1 349
30	Palm Beach, FL	999	14	30	Madera, CA	1 063 547	59	30	Plymouth, IA	1 331
31	Yuma, AZ	985	73	31	Swisher, TX	1 038 602	70	31	Polk, MN	1 322
32	Scott, KS	980	44	32	Dawson, NE	1 025 163	60	32	Glenn, CA	1 311
33	Sonoma, CA	974	13	33	Sioux, IA	996 964	68	33	Twin Falls, ID	1 294
34	Cassia, ID	954	27	34	Texas, OK	990 157	61	34	Holt, NE	1 279
35	Gooding, ID	943	37	35	Pinal, AZ	989 059	74	35	San Bernardino, CA	1 249
36	Gray, KS	939	1	36	Fresno, CA	875 073	39	36	Sussex, DE	1 214
37	Pinal, AZ	928	48	37	Franklin, WA	838 068	69	37	Mercer, OH	1 208
38	Benton, WA	923	65	38	Morgan, CO	816 073	56	38	Huron, MI	1 205
39	Sussex, DE	921	2	39	Tulare, CA	814 657	4	39	Monterey, CA	1 179
40	Grant, KS	918	39	40	Sussex, DE	758 755	47	40	Lincoln, NE	1 168
41	Finney, KS	909	23	41	Santa Barbara, CA	737 581	43	41	Lyon, IA	1 139
42	Custer, NE	845	43	42	Lyon, IA	734 068	21	42	Sampson, NC	1 067
43	Lyon, IA	836	30	43	Palm Beach, FL	709 041	52	43	Renville, MN	1 061
44	Dawson, NE	826	57	44	Platte, NE	692 256	10	44	Kings, CA	1 056
45	Stearns, MN	809	63	45	Martin, MN	690 708	27	45	Texas, OK	1 024
46	Hansford, TX	783	47	46	Lincoln, NE	670 087	57	46	Platte, NE	942
47	Lincoln, NE	783	16	47	Ventura, CA	669 829	20	47	Duplin, NC	940
48	Franklin, WA	740	52	48	Renville, MN	669 506	37	48	Pinal, AZ	938
49	Phelps, NE	739	6	49	San Joaquin, CA	628 536	25	49	Cuming, NE	918
50	San Diego, CA	726	42	50	Custer, NE	625 226	63	50	Martin, MN	897
51	Kossuth, IA	722	38	51	Benton, WA	611 771	48	51	Franklin, WA	883
52	Renville, MN	710	56	52	Huron, MI	543 207	24	52	Yuma, CO	834
53	San Luis Obispo, CA	665	7	53	Stanislaus, CA	537 807	44	53	Dawson, NE	806
54	Chester, PA	661	51	54	Kossuth, IA	535 440	65	54	Morgan, CO	754
55	Rockingham, VA	659	9	55	Weld, CO	527 863	34	55	Cassia, ID	668
56	Huron, MI	655	12	56	Yakima, WA	523 548	17	56	Deaf Smith, TX	621
57	Platte, NE	652	61	57	Holt, NE	497 540	35	57	Gooding, ID	596
58	Dallam, TX	652	69	58	Mercer, OH	493 681	18	58	Parmer, TX	570
59	Plymouth, IA	643	60	59	Glenn, CA	486 166	31	59	Swisher, TX	565
60	Glenn, CA	637	59	60	Plymouth, IA	483 173	60	60	Yuma, AZ	562
61	Holt, NE	636	74	61	San Bernardino, CA	466 156	64	61	Jerome, ID	560
62	Wichita, KS	625	68	62	Twin Falls, ID	463 355	19	62	Castro, TX	532
63	Martin, MN	620	70	63	Polk, MN	449 722	41	63	Finney, KS	499
64	Jerome, ID	617	75	64	Allegan, MI	416 071	8	64	Imperial, CA	421
65	Morgan, CO	615	29	65	Maricopa, AZ	404 790	36	65	Gray, KS	418
66	Moore, TX	605	54	66	Chester, PA	381 933	49	66	Phelps, NE	405
67	Miami-Dade, FL	604	26	67	Riverside, CA	352 306	58	67	Dallam, TX	371
68	Twin Falls, ID	600	55	68	Rockingham, VA	346 475	40	68	Grant, KS	329
69	Mercer, OH	596	33	69	Sonoma, CA	272 253	72	69	Sherman, TX	313
70	Polk, MN	595	15	70	Lancaster, PA	260 731	32	70	Scott, KS	269
71	Marion, OR	593	53	71	San Luis Obispo, CA	249 431	62	71	Wichita, KS	265
72	Sherman, TX	590	71	72	Marion, OR	230 953	46	72	Hansford, TX	263
73	Swisher, TX	587	45	73	Stearns, MN	230 933	66	73	Moore, TX	261
74	San Bernardino, CA	582	67	74	Miami-Dade, FL	204 549	22	74	Hartley, TX	255
75	Allegan, MI	581	50	75	San Diego, CA	126 657	28	75	Haskell, KS	187

75 Largest Counties by 2016 Population
Selected Rankings

Average size of farm, 2012

Value of sales rank	Size of farm rank	County	Average size of farm (acres) [col 119]
22	1	Hartley, TX	3 541
58	2	Dallam, TX	2 296
46	3	Hansford, TX	2 155
66	4	Moore, TX	2 006
28	5	Haskell, KS	1 944
72	6	Sherman, TX	1 863
62	7	Wichita, KS	1 750
32	8	Scott, KS	1 686
41	9	Finney, KS	1 635
24	10	Yuma, CO	1 623
17	11	Deaf Smith, TX	1 487
36	12	Gray, KS	1 309
27	13	Texas, OK	1 257
37	14	Pinal, AZ	1 252
8	15	Imperial, CA	1 225
47	16	Lincoln, NE	1 219
3	17	Kern, CA	1 202
42	18	Custer, NE	1 112
61	19	Holt, NE	1 106
40	20	Grant, KS	1 105
4	21	Monterey, CA	1 076
19	22	Castro, TX	1 030
18	23	Parmer, TX	971
73	24	Swisher, TX	966
34	25	Cassia, ID	915
65	26	Morgan, CO	858
70	27	Polk, MN	828
49	28	Phelps, NE	818
44	29	Dawson, NE	782
48	30	Franklin, WA	708
10	31	Kings, CA	638
11	32	Grant, WA	621
52	33	Renville, MN	586
12	34	Yakima, WA	566
9	35	Weld, CO	555
60	36	Glenn, CA	510
53	37	San Luis Obispo, CA	502
63	38	Martin, MN	478
38	39	Benton, WA	466
57	40	Platte, NE	453
51	41	Kossuth, IA	444
23	42	Santa Barbara, CA	439
14	43	Madera, CA	434
59	44	Plymouth, IA	407
35	45	Gooding, ID	402
25	46	Cuming, NE	395
5	47	Merced, CA	394
31	48	Yuma, AZ	382
56	49	Huron, MI	375
68	50	Twin Falls, ID	374
30	51	Palm Beach, FL	365
64	52	Jerome, ID	336
43	53	Lyon, IA	325
1	54	Fresno, CA	303
13	55	Sioux, IA	299
21	56	Sampson, NC	273
2	57	Tulare, CA	251
20	58	Duplin, NC	246
69	59	Mercer, OH	226
39	60	Sussex, DE	224
6	61	San Joaquin, CA	220
45	62	Stearns, MN	216
75	63	Allegan, MI	194
29	64	Maricopa, AZ	192
7	65	Stanislaus, CA	185
33	66	Sonoma, CA	165
16	67	Ventura, CA	131
26	68	Riverside, CA	117
55	68	Rockingham, VA	117
71	70	Marion, OR	111
54	71	Chester, PA	95
15	72	Lancaster, PA	78
74	73	San Bernardino, CA	62
50	74	San Diego, CA	39
67	75	Miami-Dade, FL	28

Average value of land and buildings per farm, 2012

Value of sales rank	land and buildings per farm rank	County	Average value per farm (dollars) [col 122]
8	1	Imperial, CA	8 577 865
3	2	Kern, CA	5 332 548
4	3	Monterey, CA	5 263 068
10	4	Kings, CA	3 847 243
49	5	Phelps, NE	3 684 978
22	6	Hartley, TX	3 557 855
52	7	Renville, MN	3 547 517
51	8	Kossuth, IA	3 380 844
14	9	Madera, CA	3 302 033
23	10	Santa Barbara, CA	3 233 061
5	11	Merced, CA	3 045 778
59	12	Plymouth, IA	2 992 740
37	13	Pinal, AZ	2 979 541
63	14	Martin, MN	2 931 235
31	15	Yuma, AZ	2 758 098
13	16	Sioux, IA	2 726 452
43	17	Lyon, IA	2 677 244
28	18	Haskell, KS	2 676 770
30	19	Palm Beach, FL	2 586 187
32	20	Scott, KS	2 556 929
1	21	Fresno, CA	2 509 484
44	22	Dawson, NE	2 429 274
33	23	Sonoma, CA	2 409 158
70	24	Polk, MN	2 403 190
62	25	Wichita, KS	2 375 048
41	26	Finney, KS	2 353 291
60	27	Glenn, CA	2 342 959
61	28	Holt, NE	2 314 973
57	29	Platte, NE	2 302 510
24	30	Yuma, CO	2 223 818
6	31	San Joaquin, CA	2 218 140
58	32	Dallam, TX	2 164 833
34	33	Cassia, ID	2 143 115
11	34	Grant, WA	2 128 600
25	35	Cuming, NE	2 120 511
53	36	San Luis Obispo, CA	2 115 410
42	37	Custer, NE	2 110 533
48	38	Franklin, WA	2 071 813
16	39	Ventura, CA	2 041 990
72	40	Sherman, TX	2 006 652
46	41	Hansford, TX	1 994 289
56	42	Huron, MI	1 952 800
2	43	Tulare, CA	1 893 271
66	44	Moore, TX	1 884 521
7	45	Stanislaus, CA	1 786 289
69	46	Mercer, OH	1 775 939
39	47	Sussex, DE	1 761 092
47	48	Lincoln, NE	1 749 910
36	49	Gray, KS	1 747 136
35	50	Gooding, ID	1 539 908
40	51	Grant, KS	1 471 553
17	52	Deaf Smith, TX	1 470 176
64	53	Jerome, ID	1 289 525
38	54	Benton, WA	1 276 306
54	55	Chester, PA	1 242 743
65	56	Morgan, CO	1 224 219
26	57	Riverside, CA	1 191 416
68	58	Twin Falls, ID	1 155 801
19	59	Castro, TX	1 131 530
9	60	Weld, CO	1 098 289
29	61	Maricopa, AZ	1 087 145
21	62	Sampson, NC	1 086 479
12	63	Yakima, WA	1 021 212
18	64	Parmer, TX	1 010 667
27	65	Texas, OK	1 005 370
20	66	Duplin, NC	1 001 313
15	67	Lancaster, PA	973 388
75	68	Allegan, MI	927 485
73	69	Swisher, TX	888 986
71	70	Marion, OR	885 406
45	71	Stearns, MN	844 095
74	72	San Bernardino, CA	831 612
55	73	Rockingham, VA	823 606
67	74	Miami-Dade, FL	699 727
50	75	San Diego, CA	694 313

Average value of land and buildings per acre, 2014

Value of sales rank	Value of land and buildings per acre rank	County	Average value per acre (dollars) [col 123]
67	1	Miami-Dade, FL	25 423
50	2	San Diego, CA	17 964
16	3	Ventura, CA	15 621
33	4	Sonoma, CA	14 620
74	5	San Bernardino, CA	13 455
54	6	Chester, PA	13 070
15	7	Lancaster, PA	12 529
26	8	Riverside, CA	10 212
6	9	San Joaquin, CA	10 090
7	10	Stanislaus, CA	9 636
13	11	Sioux, IA	9 105
1	12	Fresno, CA	8 286
43	13	Lyon, IA	8 245
71	14	Marion, OR	7 942
69	15	Mercer, OH	7 854
39	16	Sussex, DE	7 853
5	17	Merced, CA	7 737
14	18	Madera, CA	7 614
51	19	Kossuth, IA	7 608
2	20	Tulare, CA	7 535
23	21	Santa Barbara, CA	7 365
59	22	Plymouth, IA	7 352
31	23	Yuma, AZ	7 220
30	24	Palm Beach, FL	7 090
55	25	Rockingham, VA	7 055
8	26	Imperial, CA	7 002
63	27	Martin, MN	6 134
52	28	Renville, MN	6 055
10	29	Kings, CA	6 031
29	30	Maricopa, AZ	5 663
25	31	Cuming, NE	5 364
56	32	Huron, MI	5 202
57	33	Platte, NE	5 088
4	34	Monterey, CA	4 893
75	35	Allegan, MI	4 790
60	36	Glenn, CA	4 593
49	37	Phelps, NE	4 504
3	38	Kern, CA	4 435
53	39	San Luis Obispo, CA	4 212
20	40	Duplin, NC	4 076
21	41	Sampson, NC	3 975
45	42	Stearns, MN	3 901
64	43	Jerome, ID	3 840
35	44	Gooding, ID	3 830
11	45	Grant, WA	3 428
44	46	Dawson, NE	3 106
68	47	Twin Falls, ID	3 090
48	48	Franklin, WA	2 927
70	49	Polk, MN	2 902
38	50	Benton, WA	2 738
37	51	Pinal, AZ	2 379
34	52	Cassia, ID	2 343
61	53	Holt, NE	2 093
9	54	Weld, CO	1 979
42	55	Custer, NE	1 898
12	56	Yakima, WA	1 803
32	57	Scott, KS	1 517
41	58	Finney, KS	1 439
47	59	Lincoln, NE	1 436
65	60	Morgan, CO	1 426
28	61	Haskell, KS	1 377
24	62	Yuma, CO	1 370
62	63	Wichita, KS	1 357
36	64	Gray, KS	1 335
40	65	Grant, KS	1 332
19	66	Castro, TX	1 098
72	67	Sherman, TX	1 077
18	68	Parmer, TX	1 040
22	69	Hartley, TX	1 005
17	70	Deaf Smith, TX	989
58	71	Dallam, TX	943
66	72	Moore, TX	939
46	73	Hansford, TX	925
73	74	Swisher, TX	921
27	75	Texas, OK	800

Table B. States and Counties — **Land Area and Population**

STATE/ County code	CBSA code[1]	County type[2]	STATE County	Land area,[3] (sq mi) 2016	Population, 2016			Population and population characteristics, 2016											
								Race alone or in combination, not Hispanic or Latino (percent)						Age (percent)					
					Total persons 2016	Rank	Per square mile	White	Black	Amer- ican Indian, Alaska Native	Asian and Pacific Islander	Percent Hispanic or Latino[4]	Under 5 years	5 to 17 years	18 to 24 years	25 to 34 years	35 to 44 years	45 to 54 years
				1	2	3	4	5	6	7	8	9	10	11	12	13	14	15

1. CBSA = Core Based Statistical Area. See Appendix A for explanation. See Appendix B for list of metropolitan areas with component counties. 2. County type code from the Economic Research Service of USDA Rural-Urban Continuum Codes. See Appendix A for definition. 3. Dry land or land partially or temporarily covered by water. 4. May be of any race.

Table B. States and Counties — **Population and Households**

STATE County	Population, 2016 (cont.)				Population change and components of change, 2000–2016							Households, 2011–2015				
	Age (percent) (cont.)				Total persons		Percent change		Components of change, 2010–2016					Percent		
	55 to 64 years	65 to 74 years	75 years and over	Percent female	2000	2010	2000– 2010	2010– 2016	Births	Deaths	Net migration	Number	Persons per house- hold	Family house- holds	Female family house- holder[1]	One per- son
	16	17	18	19	20	21	22	23	24	25	26	27	28	29	30	31

1. No spouse present.

Table B. States and Counties — **Population, Vital Statistics, Health, and Crime**

STATE County	Persons in group quarters, 2016	Daytime population, 2011–2015		Births, 2016		Deaths, 2016		Persons under 65 with no health insurance, 2015		Medicare, 2015			Serious crimes known to police,[2] 2014	
													Total	
		Number	Employ- ment/ resi- dence ratio	Total	Rate[1]	Number	Rate[1]	Number	Percent	Total Beneficiaries	Enrolled in Original Medicare	Enrolled in Medicare Advantage	Number	Rate[3]
	32	33	34	35	36	37	38	39	40	41	42	43	44	45

1. Per 1,000 estimated resident population. 2. Data for serious crimes have not been adjusted for underreporting; this may affect comparability between geographic areas and over time.
3. Per 100,000 population estimated by the FBI.

Table B. States and Counties — **Crime, Education, Money Income, and Poverty**

STATE County	Serious crimes known to police, 2014 (cont.)[1]		Education							Money income, 2011–2015				Income and poverty, 2015		
	Rate[2]		School enrollment and attainment, 2011–2015				Local government expenditures,[5] 2013–2014					Households			Percent below poverty level	
			Enrollment[3]		Attainment[4] (percent)								Percent			
					High school grad- uate or less	Bach- elor's degree or more	Total current spending (mil dol)	Current spend- ing per student (dollars)	Per capita income[6] (dollars)	Median income (dollars)	with income of less than $50,000	with income of $200,000 or more	Median house- hold income (dollars)	All per- sons	Children under 18 years	Children 5 to 17 years in families
	Violent	Property	Total	Per- cent private												
	46	47	48	49	50	51	52	53	54	55	56	57	58	59	60	61

1. Data for serious crimes have not been adjusted for underreporting; this may affect comparability between geographic areas and over time. 2. Per 100,000 population estimated by the FBI.
3. All persons 3 years old and over enrolled in nursery school through college. 4. Persons 25 years old and over. 5. Elementary and secondary education expenditures.
6. Based on population estimated by the American Community Survey, 2011–2015.

Table B. States and Counties — **Personal Income**

STATE County	Personal income, 2015										Earnings, 2015		
	Total (mil dol)	Percent change, 2014–2015	Per capita[1]		Wages and salaries (mil dol)	Supplements to wages and salaries; employer contributions (mil dol)		Proprietors' income (mil dol)	Dividends, interest, and rent (mil dol)	Personal transfer receipts (mil dol)	Total (mil dol)	Contributions for government social insurance (mil dol)	
			Dollars	Rank		Pension and insurance	Government social insurance					From employee and self-employed	From employer
	62	63	64	65	66	67	68	69	70	71	72	73	74

1. Based on the resident population estimated as of July 1 of the year shown.

Table B. States and Counties — **Earnings, Social Security, and Housing**

STATE County	Earnings, 2015 (cont.)									Social Security beneficiaries, December 2015		Supplemental Security Income recipients, December 2015	Housing units, 2016	
	Percent by selected industries													
	Farm	Mining	Construction	Manufacturing	Information: professional, scientific, technical services	Retail trade	Finance, insurance, real estate and leasing	Health care and social assistance	Government	Number	Rate[1]		Total	Percent change, 2010–2016
	75	76	77	78	79	80	81	82	83	84	85	86	87	88

1. Per 1,000 resident population estimated as of July 1 of the year shown.

Table B. States and Counties — **Housing, Labor Force, and Employment**

STATE County	Housing units, 2011–2015									Civilian labor force, 2016				Civilian employment,[6] 2011–2015		
		Occupied units										Unemployment			Percent	
		Owner-occupied				Renter-occupied										
				Median owner cost as a percent of income												
	Total	Percent	Median value[1]	With a mortgage	Without a mortgage[2]	Median rent[3]	Median rent as a percent of income[2]	Sub-standard units[4] (percent)	Total	Percent change, 2015–2016	Total	Rate[5]	Total	Management, business, science and arts	Construction, production, and maintenance occupations
	89	90	91	92	93	94	95	96	97	98	99	100	101	102	103

1. Specified owner-occupied units. 2. A value of 10.0 represents 10 percent or less; a value of 50.0 represents 50 percent or more. 3. Specified renter-occupied units.
4. Overcrowded or lacking complete plumbing facilities. 5. Percent of civilian labor force. 6. Civilian employed persons 16 years old and over.

Table B. States and Counties — **Nonfarm Employment and Agriculture**

STATE County	Private nonfarm establishments, employment and payroll, 2015									Agriculture, 2012			
	Number of establishments	Employment						Annual payroll		Farms			
		Total	Health care and social assistance	Manufacturing	Retail trade	Finance and insurance	Professional, scientific, and technical services	Total (mil dol)	Average per employee (dollars)	Number	Percent with:		Farm operators whose principal occupation is farming (percent)
											Fewer than 50 acres	500 acres or more	
	104	105	106	107	108	109	110	111	112	113	114	115	116

Table B. States and Counties — Agriculture

STATE County	Agriculture, 2012 (cont.)															
	Land in farms					Value of land and buildings (dollars)		Value of machinery and equipment, average per farm (dollars)	Value of products sold				Percent of farms with sales of:		Government payments	
			Acres								Percent from:					
	Acreage (1,000)	Percent change, 2007–2012	Average size of farm	Total irrigated (1,000)	Total cropland (1,000)	Average per farm	Average per acre		Total (mil dol)	Average per farm (dollars)	Crops	Live-stock and poultry products	$10,000 or more	$100,000 or more	Total ($1,000)	Percent of farms
	117	118	119	120	121	122	123	124	125	126	127	128	129	130	131	132

Table B. States and Counties — Water Use, Wholesale Trade, Retail Trade, and Real Estate

STATE County	Water use, 2010		Wholesale trade,[1] 2012				Retail trade,[2] 2012				Real estate and rental and leasing,[2] 2012			
	Total water withdrawn (mil gal/day)	Gallons withdrawn per person per day	Number of establish-ments	Number of employees	Sales (mil dol)	Annual payroll (mil dol)	Number of establish-ments	Number of employees	Sales (mil dol)	Annual payroll (mil dol)	Number of establish-ments	Number of employees	Receipts (mil dol)	Annual payroll (mil dol)
	133	134	135	136	137	138	139	140	141	142	143	144	145	146

1. Merchant wholesalers, except manufacturers' sales branches and offices.   2. Employer establishments.

Table B. States and Counties — Professional Services, Manufacturing, and Accommodation and Food Services

STATE County	Professional, scientific, and technical services, 2012				Manufacturing, 2012				Accommodation and food services, 2012			
	Number of establish-ments	Number of employees	Receipts (mil dol)	Annual payroll (mil dol)	Number of establish-ments	Number of employees	Receipts (mil dol)	Annual payroll (mil dol)	Number of establish-ments	Number of employees	Sales (mil dol)	Annual payroll (mil dol)
	147	148	149	150	151	152	153	154	155	156	157	158

Table B. States and Counties — Health Care and Social Assistance, Other Services, Nonemployer Businesses, and Residential Construction

STATE County	Health care and social assistance, 2012				Other services, 2012				Nonemployer businesses, 2015		Value of residential construction authorized by building permits, 2016	
	Number of establish-ments	Number of employees	Receipts (mil dol)	Annual payroll (mil dol)	Number of establish-ments	Number of employees	Receipts (mil dol)	Annual payroll (mil dol)	Number	Receipts (mil dol)	New Construction ($1,000)	Number of housing units
	159	160	161	162	163	164	165	166	167	168	169	170

Table B. States and Counties — **Government Employment and Payroll, and Local Government Finances**

STATE County	Government employment and payroll, 2012									Local government finances, 2012				
			March payroll (percent of total)							General revenue				
													Taxes	
														Per capita[1] (dollars)
	Full-time equivalent employees	March payroll (dollars)	Administration, judicial, and legal	Police and Corrections	Fire Protection	Highways and transportation	Health and Welfare	Natural resources and utilities	Education and libraries	Total (mil dol)	Inter-governmental (mil dol)	Total (mil dol)	Total	Property
	171	172	173	174	175	176	177	178	179	180	181	182	183	184

1. Based on the resident population estimated as of July 1 of the year shown.

Table B. States and Counties — **Local Government Finances, Government Employment, and Income Taxes**

STATE County	Local government finances, 2012 (cont.)							Debt outstanding		Government employment, 2015			Individual income tax returns, 2014		
	Direct general expenditure														
			Percent of total for:												
	Total (mil dol)	Per capita[1] (dollars)	Education	Health and hospitals	Police protection	Public welfare	Highways	Total (mil dol)	Per capita[1] (dollars)	Federal civilian	Federal military	State and local	Number of returns	Mean adjusted gross income	Mean income tax
	185	186	187	188	189	190	191	192	193	194	195	196	197	198	199

1. Based on the resident population estimated as of July 1 of the year shown.

Table B. States and Counties — **Land Area and Population**

STATE/ County code	CBSA code[1]	County type[2]	STATE County	Population, 2016				Population and population characteristics, 2016										
								Race alone or in combination, not Hispanic or Latino (percent)					Age (percent)					
				Land area,[3] (sq mi) 2016	Total persons 2016	Rank	Per square mile	White	Black	American Indian, Alaska Native	Asian and Pacific Islander	Percent Hispanic or Latino[4]	Under 5 years	5 to 17 years	18 to 24 years	25 to 34 years	35 to 44 years	45 to 54 years
				1	2	3	4	5	6	7	8	9	10	11	12	13	14	15
00 000	...	0	UNITED STATES	3 532 068.7	323 127 513	X	91.5	63.1	13.4	1.3	6.7	17.8	6.2	16.6	9.5	13.8	12.5	13.2
01 000	...	0	ALABAMA	50 646.4	4 863 300	X	96.0	67.2	27.2	1.2	1.8	4.2	6.0	16.5	9.5	13.1	12.2	13.2
01 001	33860	2	Autauga	594.4	55 416	913	93.2	76.5	19.9	0.9	1.7	2.7	5.8	18.6	8.2	12.7	13.3	14.3
01 003	19300	3	Baldwin	1 589.8	208 563	314	131.2	84.7	9.7	1.4	1.5	4.4	5.6	16.1	7.4	11.4	12.1	13.5
01 005	21640	6	Barbour	884.9	25 965	1 565	29.3	47.2	48.2	0.7	0.7	4.2	5.2	15.9	8.3	14.2	12.4	13.3
01 007	13820	1	Bibb	622.6	22 643	1 703	36.4	75.2	22.0	0.8	0.4	2.5	5.6	15.1	8.1	15.0	13.5	14.9
01 009	13820	1	Blount	644.8	57 704	890	89.5	88.7	1.9	1.2	0.5	9.1	5.8	17.4	7.7	11.7	12.4	13.9
01 011	...	6	Bullock	622.8	10 362	2 398	16.6	22.3	69.7	0.6	0.5	7.8	5.8	15.5	8.5	14.6	12.9	13.1
01 013	...	6	Butler	776.8	19 998	1 829	25.7	53.1	44.6	0.7	1.2	1.3	6.0	17.6	8.0	11.6	11.6	12.1
01 015	11500	3	Calhoun	605.9	114 611	537	189.2	74.2	21.6	1.0	1.4	3.6	5.6	16.2	9.1	13.2	12.0	13.1
01 017	46740	6	Chambers	596.5	33 843	1 329	56.7	57.0	39.9	0.6	1.2	2.3	6.1	15.1	8.4	12.0	11.4	13.6
01 019	...	6	Cherokee	553.7	25 725	1 574	46.5	93.2	4.9	1.5	0.4	1.6	4.6	15.2	7.0	10.1	11.3	14.2
01 021	13820	1	Chilton	692.9	43 941	1 094	63.4	81.6	10.6	0.7	0.6	7.6	6.3	17.7	8.0	12.3	12.8	13.4
01 023	...	9	Choctaw	913.5	12 993	2 228	14.2	57.2	41.8	0.4	0.3	1.0	5.1	15.2	7.7	10.0	11.2	13.8
01 025	...	7	Clarke	1 238.5	24 392	1 626	19.7	53.6	44.5	0.7	0.7	1.4	5.7	16.2	8.8	10.5	11.9	13.7
01 027	...	9	Clay	604.0	13 492	2 196	22.3	82.2	15.0	1.2	0.4	3.0	5.4	15.4	8.1	10.8	11.6	14.2
01 029	...	8	Cleburne	560.1	14 924	2 101	26.6	93.8	3.7	0.8	0.4	2.5	5.9	17.2	7.3	11.4	11.9	13.8
01 031	21460	4	Coffee	679.0	51 226	972	75.4	72.9	18.3	2.1	2.4	7.0	6.1	17.6	8.2	12.6	13.1	13.4
01 033	22520	3	Colbert	592.6	54 216	927	91.5	80.4	16.8	1.3	0.8	2.5	5.6	15.6	7.8	12.3	11.7	13.8
01 035	...	7	Conecuh	850.2	12 395	2 268	14.6	51.0	46.9	0.8	0.4	2.0	5.4	15.7	8.1	10.6	10.8	12.8
01 037	45180	8	Coosa	650.9	10 581	2 385	16.3	66.6	31.0	1.0	0.4	2.2	4.6	12.9	7.6	10.1	11.2	15.7
01 039	...	6	Covington	1 030.5	37 458	1 235	36.3	84.6	13.4	1.2	0.6	1.6	5.8	16.2	7.3	11.7	11.3	13.0
01 041	...	8	Crenshaw	608.8	13 913	2 173	22.9	72.5	24.6	1.1	1.8	1.9	5.7	17.3	7.8	11.5	11.7	13.3
01 043	18980	4	Cullman	734.9	82 471	684	112.2	93.4	1.5	1.2	0.7	4.3	6.0	16.4	7.7	12.6	12.2	13.4
01 045	37120	4	Dale	561.1	49 226	998	87.7	71.6	21.0	1.5	2.1	6.1	6.6	16.5	8.8	14.3	12.0	12.5
01 047	42820	4	Dallas	978.7	40 008	1 174	40.9	28.3	70.3	0.4	0.6	1.1	6.1	18.5	9.2	11.7	11.1	12.3
01 049	22840	6	DeKalb	777.1	70 900	762	91.2	82.6	1.9	2.6	0.6	14.3	6.0	18.5	8.1	12.0	12.8	13.5
01 051	33860	2	Elmore	618.5	81 799	686	132.3	74.8	21.8	1.0	1.2	2.8	5.9	16.6	8.7	13.9	13.3	13.9
01 053	12120	4	Escambia	945.1	37 728	1 230	39.9	62.0	32.9	4.3	0.6	2.2	5.9	16.3	8.2	13.4	13.0	13.2
01 055	23460	3	Etowah	535.3	102 564	590	191.6	79.5	16.2	1.1	1.0	3.8	5.6	16.2	8.3	12.0	12.4	13.6
01 057	...	6	Fayette	627.7	16 546	2 006	26.4	86.0	12.6	0.7	0.4	1.6	5.5	15.6	8.2	11.0	11.1	13.6
01 059	...	6	Franklin	633.8	31 628	1 393	49.9	78.4	4.4	1.1	0.6	16.8	6.5	17.9	8.4	12.6	12.9	13.2
01 061	20020	3	Geneva	574.4	26 614	1 541	46.3	85.5	10.2	1.6	0.6	3.9	5.6	16.5	7.1	11.3	11.6	13.8
01 063	...	8	Greene	647.1	8 422	2 557	13.0	17.9	80.7	0.4	0.4	1.2	5.9	16.8	8.6	11.4	10.0	11.7
01 065	46220	3	Hale	643.9	14 952	2 099	23.2	40.7	57.7	0.5	0.5	1.4	7.0	16.8	8.8	11.3	11.0	12.3
01 067	20020	3	Henry	561.8	17 164	1 973	30.6	69.9	27.2	0.8	0.7	2.6	5.1	15.7	7.3	10.6	12.1	13.0
01 069	20020	3	Houston	579.9	104 056	578	179.4	68.6	27.6	1.0	1.4	3.2	6.0	17.4	7.8	13.1	12.4	13.3
01 071	42460	6	Jackson	1 077.9	52 138	959	48.4	91.9	3.9	3.2	0.7	2.8	5.2	16.0	7.5	11.2	12.4	13.6
01 073	13820	1	Jefferson	1 111.3	659 521	101	593.5	51.2	43.6	0.6	2.0	3.7	6.5	16.5	8.9	14.4	12.6	12.7
01 075	...	6	Lamar	604.8	13 918	2 171	23.0	87.5	11.4	0.8	0.4	1.5	5.0	16.3	6.9	11.0	11.7	13.3
01 077	22520	3	Lauderdale	667.7	92 318	634	138.3	86.1	10.8	0.9	1.0	2.6	5.1	15.0	11.4	11.8	10.9	13.0
01 079	19460	3	Lawrence	690.7	33 244	1 349	48.1	81.0	11.6	9.3	0.6	2.1	5.7	16.1	7.8	12.0	11.5	15.0
01 081	12220	3	Lee	607.6	158 991	407	261.7	68.9	23.9	0.7	4.3	3.8	5.8	15.6	18.9	14.5	12.0	11.8
01 083	26620	2	Limestone	559.9	92 753	630	165.7	78.7	14.1	1.4	2.0	5.8	5.6	17.4	7.6	13.1	13.6	15.1
01 085	33860	2	Lowndes	715.9	10 358	2 399	14.5	25.0	73.1	0.6	0.4	1.5	6.0	16.6	8.0	12.3	10.7	13.5
01 087	...	6	Macon	608.9	18 963	1 875	31.1	16.5	81.4	0.6	0.8	1.8	4.6	12.7	18.3	11.1	9.3	11.7
01 089	26620	2	Madison	801.6	356 967	194	445.3	67.1	25.5	1.6	3.6	4.8	5.8	16.2	9.6	13.9	12.1	14.5
01 091	...	7	Marengo	976.9	19 673	1 844	20.1	45.8	51.5	0.6	0.5	2.5	5.9	16.9	8.3	11.1	11.3	12.8
01 093	...	7	Marion	742.3	29 998	1 434	40.4	92.9	4.4	0.8	0.5	2.5	5.3	15.7	7.5	11.1	11.6	14.4
01 095	10700	4	Marshall	565.8	95 157	619	168.2	82.9	2.9	1.3	1.0	13.5	6.7	18.0	8.1	12.3	12.0	13.2
01 097	33660	2	Mobile	1 229.4	414 836	167	337.4	58.6	36.3	1.5	2.4	2.8	6.5	17.2	9.3	13.9	11.9	12.7
01 099	...	7	Monroe	1 025.7	21 530	1 751	21.0	56.1	41.6	1.9	0.7	1.3	5.4	17.3	8.7	10.5	11.5	13.3
01 101	33860	2	Montgomery	784.4	226 349	291	288.6	35.7	58.4	0.6	3.4	3.3	6.8	16.5	10.1	14.7	12.8	12.5
01 103	19460	3	Morgan	579.4	119 012	520	205.4	77.9	13.2	1.7	1.1	8.1	5.7	17.1	8.0	12.3	12.4	14.1
01 105	...	8	Perry	719.7	9 574	2 463	13.3	30.5	67.5	0.5	0.6	1.6	5.3	16.3	15.0	10.5	10.6	10.6
01 107	46220	3	Pickens	881.4	20 324	1 817	23.1	55.2	40.4	0.5	0.5	4.3	5.2	14.7	8.6	13.4	11.6	14.2
01 109	45980	6	Pike	672.1	33 286	1 348	49.5	57.5	38.2	1.3	2.6	2.2	5.6	13.6	23.1	11.9	9.9	10.3
01 111	...	6	Randolph	580.5	22 652	1 702	39.0	76.4	20.5	0.9	0.6	3.0	5.9	16.0	8.5	10.3	11.2	13.6
01 113	17980	2	Russell	641.2	58 172	887	90.7	48.9	45.1	1.1	1.7	5.5	7.5	17.6	8.6	15.1	12.7	12.9
01 115	13820	1	St. Clair	631.9	88 019	658	139.3	87.0	9.9	0.9	1.1	2.4	6.0	16.8	7.2	13.4	13.1	14.1
01 117	13820	1	Shelby	785.4	210 622	313	268.2	79.5	12.8	0.7	2.6	5.7	5.9	18.1	8.2	12.5	14.1	14.4
01 119	...	8	Sumter	903.9	13 040	2 227	14.4	25.3	72.3	0.3	1.6	1.1	5.8	14.0	19.3	9.5	8.8	11.2
01 121	45180	4	Talladega	736.8	80 103	700	108.7	64.4	33.2	0.9	0.9	2.2	5.3	16.4	8.3	12.6	12.2	13.9
01 123	10760	6	Tallapoosa	716.5	40 727	1 160	56.8	70.0	27.1	0.7	0.7	2.5	5.6	15.4	7.7	11.0	10.8	13.5
01 125	46220	3	Tuscaloosa	1 321.7	206 102	318	155.9	63.1	32.1	0.6	1.9	3.5	6.0	14.9	17.3	14.8	11.8	11.2
01 127	13820	1	Walker	791.2	64 967	814	82.1	90.4	6.9	1.0	0.7	2.5	6.1	16.1	7.8	11.6	11.7	13.6

1. CBSA = Core Based Statistical Area. See Appendix A for explanation. See Appendix B for list of metropolitan areas with component counties.   2. County type code from the Economic Research Service of USDA Rural-Urban Continuum Codes. See Appendix A for definition.   3. Dry land or land partially or temporarily covered by water.   4. May be of any race.

Table B. States and Counties — **Population and Households**

STATE County	55 to 64 years	65 to 74 years	75 years and over	Percent female	Total persons 2000	Total persons 2010	Percent change 2000–2010	Percent change 2010–2016	Births	Deaths	Net migration	Households Number	Persons per house-hold	Family house-holds	Female family house-holder[1]	One per-son
	16	17	18	19	20	21	22	23	24	25	26	27	28	29	30	31
UNITED STATES............	12.8	8.9	6.4	50.8	281 421 906	308 758 105	9.7	4.7	24 762 895	16 235 690	5 842 203	116 926 305	2.64	66.1	13.0	27.6
ALABAMA	13.3	9.6	6.6	51.6	4 447 100	4 780 131	7.5	1.7	367 421	312 625	27 555	1 848 325	2.55	67.0	15.1	28.8
Autauga........................	12.4	8.7	6.1	51.3	43 671	54 571	25.0	1.5	3 882	3 347	176	20 396	2.68	69.7	10.6	26.1
Baldwin........................	14.1	11.9	7.8	51.5	140 415	182 265	29.8	14.4	13 682	12 324	23 779	74 104	2.60	67.8	10.4	28.0
Barbour........................	12.7	10.9	7.1	46.9	29 038	27 457	-5.4	-5.4	1 764	1 980	-1 308	9 222	2.61	65.7	19.5	32.2
Bibb............................	12.4	9.2	6.2	46.4	20 826	22 919	10.0	-1.2	1 592	1 525	-321	7 027	2.95	75.4	15.1	22.1
Blount.........................	13.1	10.8	7.2	50.6	51 024	57 324	12.3	0.7	4 256	3 720	-212	20 816	2.74	75.1	10.0	22.7
Bullock........................	13.4	9.3	6.9	46.0	11 714	10 911	-6.9	-5.0	814	755	-622	3 683	2.73	63.3	25.9	31.9
Butler.........................	14.1	10.5	8.5	53.4	21 399	20 946	-2.1	-4.5	1 556	1 651	-835	8 056	2.49	65.4	18.7	30.9
Calhoun........................	13.9	10.1	6.8	51.9	112 249	118 586	5.6	-3.4	8 211	8 667	-3 373	45 154	2.52	67.7	16.6	27.8
Chambers.......................	14.4	11.2	7.8	52.0	36 583	34 170	-6.6	-1.0	2 548	2 843	-42	13 787	2.44	62.6	17.2	34.1
Cherokee.......................	15.5	13.8	8.2	50.4	23 988	25 986	8.3	-1.0	1 413	2 101	432	11 278	2.28	72.5	12.0	26.1
Chilton........................	13.5	9.7	6.3	50.8	39 593	43 631	10.2	0.7	3 455	3 020	-123	16 237	2.68	71.4	11.8	25.5
Choctaw........................	15.2	12.7	9.2	52.4	15 922	13 858	-13.0	-6.2	815	1 038	-635	5 575	2.37	63.7	14.8	33.9
Clarke.........................	14.0	10.7	8.4	52.7	27 867	25 833	-7.3	-5.6	1 731	1 824	-1 386	9 622	2.57	64.4	14.3	33.0
Clay...........................	13.9	12.0	8.6	51.0	14 254	13 932	-2.3	-3.2	874	1 175	-161	5 419	2.45	68.2	13.2	29.0
Cleburne.......................	13.7	11.1	7.7	50.3	14 123	14 972	6.0	-0.3	1 116	1 139	-76	5 776	2.57	70.5	11.0	26.5
Coffee.........................	12.5	9.7	6.7	50.6	43 615	49 948	14.5	2.6	3 903	3 128	519	19 160	2.62	67.9	13.6	28.5
Colbert........................	14.0	10.9	8.3	51.8	54 984	54 428	-1.0	-0.4	3 748	4 267	440	22 204	2.43	67.9	14.2	28.6
Conecuh........................	15.1	12.5	9.0	51.9	14 089	13 228	-6.1	-6.3	849	1 078	-601	5 168	2.48	66.4	16.4	31.4
Coosa..........................	17.9	12.6	7.3	49.3	12 202	11 758	-3.6	-10.0	597	779	-986	4 450	2.42	62.9	14.3	32.9
Covington......................	14.5	11.3	9.0	51.8	37 631	37 765	0.4	-0.8	2 779	3 132	10	14 949	2.49	69.6	15.3	27.3
Crenshaw.......................	14.0	11.1	7.5	51.2	13 665	13 898	1.7	0.1	924	1 083	172	5 383	2.56	66.2	16.6	31.3
Cullman........................	13.4	10.8	7.4	50.6	77 483	80 410	3.8	2.6	6 106	5 991	1 829	31 287	2.55	69.9	11.4	27.1
Dale...........................	13.1	9.4	6.8	50.7	49 129	50 247	2.3	-2.0	4 151	3 023	-2 168	19 018	2.56	66.3	13.8	28.9
Dallas.........................	14.3	10.0	6.8	53.8	46 365	43 820	-5.5	-8.7	3 300	3 275	-3 877	16 413	2.53	62.4	25.5	33.9
DeKalb.........................	12.8	10.0	6.4	50.5	64 452	71 115	10.3	-0.3	5 218	4 694	-651	25 013	2.81	70.4	9.7	27.2
Elmore.........................	12.7	9.1	5.7	51.5	65 874	79 296	20.4	3.2	6 060	4 640	949	28 651	2.65	72.1	13.9	25.2
Escambia.......................	12.9	10.0	7.1	48.6	38 440	38 319	-0.3	-1.5	2 805	2 822	-543	13 659	2.60	67.2	16.5	31.2
Etowah.........................	13.9	10.9	7.4	51.6	103 459	104 427	0.9	-1.8	7 290	8 690	-340	39 899	2.56	69.2	13.5	27.4
Fayette........................	14.3	11.9	8.7	50.6	18 495	17 241	-6.8	-4.0	1 109	1 459	-323	7 037	2.36	70.3	13.3	28.2
Franklin.......................	12.3	9.4	6.9	50.1	31 223	31 709	1.6	-0.3	2 522	2 427	-158	11 980	2.62	69.7	14.2	26.6
Geneva.........................	14.2	11.6	8.3	50.9	25 764	26 788	4.0	-0.6	1 893	2 198	146	10 754	2.47	69.9	15.1	25.6
Greene.........................	16.1	11.0	8.4	52.5	9 974	9 045	-9.3	-6.9	654	656	-611	3 201	2.70	59.3	22.6	38.8
Hale...........................	14.3	10.6	7.9	52.8	17 185	15 760	-8.3	-5.1	1 297	1 125	-1 016	5 927	2.53	65.8	20.5	31.7
Henry..........................	14.3	13.7	8.2	51.6	16 310	17 300	6.1	-0.8	1 088	1 334	113	6 894	2.47	65.9	11.5	31.0
Houston........................	13.2	9.9	7.0	52.1	88 787	101 555	14.4	2.5	8 067	6 524	1 028	39 197	2.62	66.5	16.3	29.2
Jackson........................	14.8	11.7	7.7	50.8	53 926	53 226	-1.3	-2.0	3 468	4 178	-338	20 431	2.56	69.7	9.9	25.8
Jefferson......................	13.3	8.7	6.4	52.7	662 047	658 348	-0.6	0.2	55 155	43 550	-9 204	260 929	2.47	63.8	18.1	31.5
Lamar..........................	14.6	11.9	9.4	51.3	15 904	14 564	-8.4	-4.4	869	1 236	-263	6 138	2.27	71.6	12.5	26.8
Lauderdale.....................	13.8	10.9	8.2	52.2	87 966	92 709	5.4	-0.4	5 845	6 761	600	38 612	2.35	65.5	11.4	29.9
Lawrence.......................	14.1	11.0	6.6	51.2	34 803	34 339	-1.3	-3.2	2 284	2 473	-875	13 537	2.46	71.5	13.4	25.4
Lee............................	10.4	6.9	4.1	50.7	115 092	140 296	21.9	13.3	11 163	6 234	13 421	57 171	2.54	62.9	14.0	27.2
Limestone......................	13.0	8.9	5.6	49.9	65 676	82 782	26.0	12.0	6 261	4 507	7 927	32 213	2.64	72.3	11.2	25.0
Lowndes........................	14.1	11.1	7.8	52.7	13 473	11 289	-16.2	-8.2	843	828	-990	4 282	2.49	66.2	25.9	32.0
Macon..........................	14.1	10.9	7.3	54.4	24 105	21 448	-11.0	-11.6	1 229	1 504	-2 223	8 009	2.24	58.4	24.7	37.0
Madison........................	13.4	8.2	6.2	51.2	276 700	334 811	21.0	6.6	25 922	17 610	13 302	137 767	2.46	65.0	12.5	30.4
Marengo........................	14.0	10.9	8.9	52.7	22 539	21 036	-6.7	-6.5	1 483	1 622	-1 275	8 281	2.42	61.9	16.9	35.6
Marion.........................	13.7	11.7	9.0	50.3	31 214	30 776	-1.4	-2.5	1 888	2 503	-140	12 714	2.34	71.3	13.3	25.0
Marshall.......................	12.8	10.0	6.9	50.7	82 231	93 019	13.1	2.3	7 999	6 787	863	34 261	2.72	71.4	12.5	25.6
Mobile.........................	13.2	9.2	6.2	52.2	399 843	413 143	3.3	0.4	34 956	26 603	-6 253	154 188	2.62	67.2	18.5	28.6
Monroe.........................	14.8	10.7	7.9	52.3	24 324	23 070	-5.2	-6.7	1 463	1 621	-1 336	8 406	2.62	63.7	13.3	34.5
Montgomery.....................	12.7	8.2	5.8	52.7	223 510	229 385	2.6	-1.3	19 691	12 877	-9 586	89 532	2.47	63.5	21.0	31.5
Morgan.........................	13.5	9.8	6.9	50.8	111 064	119 486	7.6	-0.4	8 753	7 702	-1 394	46 235	2.55	68.4	13.5	28.1
Perry..........................	13.2	10.3	8.3	52.9	11 861	10 581	-10.8	-9.5	714	848	-876	3 450	2.70	66.4	30.9	30.8
Pickens........................	14.1	10.4	7.8	50.0	20 949	19 746	-5.7	2.9	1 359	1 548	687	7 644	2.51	64.0	15.8	34.7
Pike...........................	10.8	8.7	6.1	52.2	29 605	32 899	11.1	1.2	2 407	2 039	-31	12 786	2.44	61.5	16.5	29.2
Randolph.......................	14.3	11.6	8.5	51.5	22 380	22 914	2.4	-1.1	1 605	1 747	-167	8 915	2.49	67.1	13.4	29.3
Russell........................	12.5	7.9	5.3	51.6	49 756	52 951	6.4	9.9	5 464	3 472	3 096	22 241	2.59	65.1	19.6	29.9
St. Clair......................	13.3	10.1	6.1	50.1	64 742	83 593	29.1	5.3	6 455	5 427	3 172	31 979	2.62	72.4	11.0	23.9
Shelby.........................	12.9	8.7	5.3	51.5	143 293	195 218	36.2	7.9	15 037	8 476	8 601	75 534	2.66	71.6	9.4	24.7
Sumter.........................	14.2	9.2	8.0	54.5	14 798	13 763	-7.0	-5.3	923	978	-684	4 815	2.61	57.0	24.2	37.4
Talladega......................	14.3	10.4	6.6	51.6	80 321	82 291	2.5	-2.7	5 398	6 090	-1 324	31 424	2.49	69.0	18.5	27.8
Tallapoosa.....................	15.2	12.5	8.2	51.4	41 475	41 618	0.3	-2.1	2 929	3 316	-501	16 323	2.48	70.2	16.7	26.9
Tuscaloosa.....................	11.5	7.5	4.9	51.8	164 875	194 657	18.1	5.9	15 320	10 503	6 650	69 128	2.75	66.5	15.5	27.4
Walker.........................	14.1	11.3	7.7	51.2	70 713	67 023	-5.2	-3.1	5 018	6 063	-1 038	25 602	2.54	70.2	15.3	26.2

1. No spouse present.

Table B. States and Counties — **Population, Vital Statistics, Health, and Crime**

STATE County	Persons in group quarters, 2016	Daytime population, 2011–2015 Number	Employ-ment/resi-dence ratio	Births, 2016 Total	Births, 2016 Rate[1]	Deaths, 2016 Number	Deaths, 2016 Rate[1]	Persons under 65 with no health insurance, 2015 Number	Percent	Medicare, 2015 Total Beneficiaries	Enrolled in Original Medicare	Enrolled in Medicare Advantage	Serious crimes known to police,[2] 2014 Total Number	Rate[3]
	32	33	34	35	36	37	38	39	40	41	42	43	44	45
UNITED STATES	8 079 879	316 515 021	1.00	3 977 745	12.3	2 746 013	8.5	29 165 227	10.9	52 386 554	34 036 390	18 350 164	9 443 212	2 962
ALABAMA	119 659	4 785 101	0.98	58 556	12.0	52 405	10.8	475 233	11.9	950 827	686 830	263 997	174 821	3 605
Autauga	455	44 322	0.55	631	11.4	494	8.9	4 431	9.4	9 192	5 977	3 215	1 769	3 241
Baldwin	2 341	179 013	0.81	2 274	10.9	2 113	10.1	18 751	11.5	44 243	28 689	15 554	4 227	2 189
Barbour	3 186	26 905	1.00	253	9.7	314	12.1	2 482	13.3	5 387	4 386	1 001	728	2 894
Bibb	2 252	19 202	0.58	266	11.7	237	10.5	2 027	11.9	4 600	2 718	1 882	248	1 171
Blount	489	45 286	0.43	663	11.5	622	10.8	6 609	14.0	9 311	5 258	4 053	1 379	2 376
Bullock	1 653	10 117	0.85	114	11.0	111	10.7	1 080	14.5	1 403	1 035	368	190	1 795
Butler	333	19 510	0.89	236	11.8	241	12.1	1 998	12.2	4 503	3 955	548	746	3 709
Calhoun	2 776	117 820	1.03	1 237	10.8	1 441	12.6	10 764	11.4	27 423	22 648	4 775	4 615	3 965
Chambers	458	28 893	0.62	419	12.4	476	14.1	3 662	13.3	8 655	6 947	1 708	1 394	4 077
Cherokee	290	22 167	0.61	208	8.1	331	12.9	2 355	11.7	5 731	4 233	1 498	842	3 204
Chilton	393	37 085	0.62	540	12.3	483	11.0	5 603	15.2	7 866	4 173	3 693	1 397	3 180
Choctaw	129	12 622	0.82	139	10.7	170	13.1	1 219	11.8	3 481	3 115	366	96	757
Clarke	280	25 335	1.03	297	12.2	313	12.8	2 505	12.6	6 527	4 902	1 625	337	1 362
Clay	255	12 587	0.81	136	10.1	202	15.0	1 542	14.4	3 306	2 817	489	148	1 105
Cleburne	178	11 921	0.47	171	11.5	202	13.5	1 465	12.1	3 216	2 724	492	299	1 992
Coffee	600	47 615	0.85	602	11.8	537	10.5	5 077	11.9	9 447	8 434	1 013	1 457	2 848
Colbert	474	56 031	1.08	582	10.7	661	12.2	4 651	10.6	12 691	10 750	1 941	2 353	4 313
Conecuh	45	12 493	0.90	115	9.3	191	15.4	1 457	14.7	3 282	2 817	465	333	2 720
Coosa	257	8 744	0.38	91	8.6	101	9.5	1 138	13.5	2 731	2 301	430	233	2 263
Covington	575	36 828	0.92	440	11.7	520	13.9	3 681	12.3	9 693	8 660	1 033	592	1 581
Crenshaw	132	12 341	0.71	145	10.4	193	13.9	1 458	12.8	3 303	2 599	704	279	2 067
Cullman	990	76 662	0.86	997	12.1	1 009	12.2	9 426	14.1	18 440	13 767	4 673	1 951	2 410
Dale	917	51 733	1.09	637	12.9	542	11.0	4 703	11.5	10 911	9 478	1 433	1 627	3 267
Dallas	856	41 589	0.96	465	11.6	545	13.6	4 119	12.1	10 643	7 828	2 815	2 867	6 896
DeKalb	782	67 653	0.88	796	11.2	771	10.9	10 467	17.6	13 884	10 697	3 187	1 396	2 454
Elmore	5 391	65 783	0.55	978	12.0	794	9.7	6 033	9.3	15 330	10 759	4 571	2 397	2 948
Escambia	3 280	38 286	1.03	440	11.7	458	12.1	4 388	15.5	8 156	6 612	1 544	919	2 423
Etowah	2 085	99 612	0.90	1 148	11.2	1 497	14.6	9 969	12.0	24 831	18 589	6 242	4 647	4 475
Fayette	290	14 892	0.67	170	10.3	234	14.1	1 580	11.9	3 916	3 353	563	172	1 022
Franklin	272	30 234	0.88	363	11.5	378	12.0	4 336	16.4	6 917	6 199	718	871	2 766
Geneva	229	22 554	0.59	284	10.7	358	13.5	3 356	15.7	6 513	5 738	775	627	2 346
Greene	45	8 198	0.79	99	11.8	91	10.8	830	12.1	2 031	1 831	200	262	3 244
Hale	221	12 766	0.51	226	15.1	197	13.2	1 481	12.1	4 205	3 824	381	176	1 364
Henry	199	14 679	0.62	166	9.7	209	12.2	1 820	13.5	4 282	3 287	995	318	1 895
Houston	1 420	110 380	1.16	1 282	12.3	1 121	10.8	10 048	11.7	21 106	17 481	3 625	2 668	2 560
Jackson	597	49 993	0.86	519	10.0	670	12.9	5 827	13.8	12 986	10 534	2 452	1 427	2 775
Jefferson	16 343	726 102	1.23	8 775	13.3	7 269	11.0	62 034	11.3	134 013	74 149	59 864	32 365	5 144
Lamar	217	12 925	0.77	135	9.7	197	14.2	1 374	12.6	3 910	3 548	362	124	875
Lauderdale	2 060	87 867	0.88	940	10.2	1 099	11.9	8 256	11.2	21 422	18 107	3 315	2 208	2 385
Lawrence	229	27 986	0.55	380	11.4	408	12.3	3 702	13.6	5 907	5 028	879	606	1 881
Lee	4 955	139 556	0.83	1 904	12.0	1 056	6.6	15 691	11.5	18 480	15 379	3 101	4 155	2 704
Limestone	2 728	76 857	0.68	1 013	10.9	787	8.5	9 188	12.1	13 422	10 628	2 794	1 645	1 820
Lowndes	96	9 792	0.71	123	11.9	148	14.3	1 023	12.0	2 261	1 314	947	NA	NA
Macon	1 690	18 710	0.82	186	9.8	269	14.2	1 527	10.8	4 447	3 193	1 254	988	5 129
Madison	8 107	380 172	1.21	4 249	11.9	3 069	8.6	30 501	10.3	57 914	47 169	10 745	14 404	4 117
Marengo	254	19 919	0.94	230	11.7	267	13.6	1 740	10.8	4 402	3 846	556	634	3 234
Marion	868	29 665	0.94	292	9.7	404	13.5	3 058	13.0	6 883	6 028	855	674	2 233
Marshall	1 061	94 570	1.01	1 280	13.5	1 145	12.0	12 095	15.5	20 866	17 375	3 491	3 046	3 199
Mobile	7 516	425 006	1.06	5 596	13.5	4 514	10.9	45 101	13.0	76 274	41 491	34 783	18 673	4 505
Monroe	230	22 214	1.00	229	10.6	267	12.4	2 492	14.2	4 708	3 948	760	690	3 273
Montgomery	8 876	264 393	1.37	3 170	14.0	2 171	9.6	22 761	12.2	39 804	27 282	12 522	10 314	4 563
Morgan	2 121	119 031	0.99	1 331	11.2	1 245	10.5	13 488	13.7	25 860	21 868	3 992	3 186	2 673
Perry	805	9 381	0.76	106	11.1	139	14.5	910	12.7	2 110	1 949	161	NA	NA
Pickens	1 842	17 308	0.61	216	10.6	262	12.9	1 893	12.5	4 642	4 252	390	NA	NA
Pike	2 258	35 223	1.15	392	11.8	339	10.2	3 667	13.8	5 968	4 544	1 424	1 374	4 107
Randolph	407	19 873	0.67	294	13.0	282	12.4	2 448	13.7	5 123	4 281	842	358	1 578
Russell	574	48 255	0.58	873	15.0	629	10.8	5 849	11.3	11 626	8 673	2 953	2 678	4 411
St. Clair	1 893	69 129	0.54	988	11.2	922	10.5	8 239	11.5	14 588	7 972	6 616	1 386	1 603
Shelby	2 703	183 614	0.80	2 384	11.3	1 527	7.2	14 942	8.4	21 065	11 786	9 279	NA	NA
Sumter	906	12 722	0.86	162	12.4	153	11.7	1 273	12.5	2 857	2 603	254	249	1 902
Talladega	2 805	81 129	0.99	846	10.6	1 053	13.1	7 297	11.2	18 128	12 804	5 324	3 576	4 420
Tallapoosa	576	39 348	0.88	450	11.0	543	13.3	3 873	12.0	10 467	8 783	1 684	1 263	3 085
Tuscaloosa	11 007	208 308	1.09	2 520	12.2	1 810	8.8	16 560	9.8	31 633	26 970	4 663	7 891	3 898
Walker	851	63 173	0.88	797	12.3	950	14.6	6 764	12.8	18 992	11 655	7 337	2 722	4 186

1. Per 1,000 estimated resident population.   2. Data for serious crimes have not been adjusted for underreporting; this may affect comparability between geographic areas and over time.
3. Per 100,000 population estimated by the FBI.

Table B. States and Counties — **Crime, Education, Money Income, and Poverty**

STATE County	Serious crimes known to police, 2014 (cont.)[1] Rate[2] Violent	Property	Education — School enrollment and attainment, 2011–2015 Enrollment[3] Total	Percent private	Attainment[4] (percent) High school graduate or less	Bachelor's degree or more	Local government expenditures,[5] 2013–2014 Total current spending (mil dol)	Current spending per student (dollars)	Money income, 2011–2015 Per capita income[6] (dollars)	Median income (dollars)	Households Percent with income of less than $50,000	with income of $200,000 or more	Income and poverty, 2015 Median household income (dollars)	Percent below poverty level All persons	Children under 18 years	Children 5 to 17 years in families
	46	47	48	49	50	51	52	53	54	55	56	57	58	59	60	61
UNITED STATES............	366	2 596	82 528 567	16.3	41.1	29.8	544 544.8	10 932	28 930	53 889	46.5	5.3	55 775	14.7	20.7	19.5
ALABAMA	427	3 178	1 206 014	14.0	46.8	23.5	6 728.2	9 017	24 091	43 623	55.4	2.7	44 833	18.5	26.5	25.2
Autauga...................	264	2 977	14 358	21.7	46.4	23.2	71.0	7 434	24 974	51 281	48.6	2.4	56 580	12.7	18.8	18.4
Baldwin...................	189	2 000	43 767	15.0	39.3	29.0	267.2	8 824	27 317	50 254	49.7	3.9	52 387	12.9	19.6	18.2
Barbour...................	374	2 520	5 821	10.1	61.2	12.5	34.1	8 918	16 824	32 964	67.5	0.7	31 433	32.0	45.2	43.9
Bibb.......................	109	1 063	4 943	8.1	61.4	10.6	28.0	8 107	18 431	38 678	62.0	0.7	40 767	22.2	29.3	28.5
Blount....................	215	2 161	12 634	6.4	54.9	12.9	75.7	7 780	20 532	45 813	53.5	0.9	50 487	14.7	22.2	21.3
Bullock...................	293	1 502	2 074	13.7	68.5	13.9	16.7	11 094	17 580	31 938	67.5	1.1	28 251	39.6	51.2	49.4
Butler.....................	567	3 143	4 385	8.2	59.8	14.5	28.4	8 622	18 390	32 229	68.1	0.5	33 868	25.8	36.0	34.9
Calhoun..................	618	3 348	29 048	9.6	50.9	17.6	166.0	9 003	21 374	41 703	58.0	1.3	42 091	20.0	30.7	29.8
Chambers................	497	3 579	7 415	9.6	59.5	11.6	42.8	9 133	21 071	34 177	65.6	1.4	35 560	22.4	34.4	34.1
Cherokee................	293	2 911	5 030	5.9	56.9	13.8	36.0	8 895	21 811	36 296	63.8	1.2	39 144	19.4	30.2	28.8
Chilton...................	314	2 866	9 704	8.8	60.8	14.1	61.5	8 016	21 399	41 627	57.9	1.0	42 767	20.2	28.1	26.3
Choctaw.................	134	623	2 891	26.9	60.4	11.8	15.2	9 102	20 755	33 536	64.3	1.3	35 089	24.4	33.5	30.8
Clarke....................	388	974	5 427	12.8	63.4	12.9	41.2	9 037	20 064	32 011	65.9	1.9	37 317	22.2	30.9	28.9
Clay.......................	314	791	2 735	13.0	61.2	9.6	17.2	8 565	18 905	35 327	67.1	0.6	38 908	18.4	27.3	26.3
Cleburne.................	87	1 906	3 296	9.9	63.1	12.1	23.5	8 826	20 151	38 056	61.8	1.5	42 136	18.9	27.7	25.0
Coffee....................	289	2 559	11 973	8.8	44.8	23.9	82.9	8 797	24 936	46 729	52.7	2.0	46 858	16.2	23.7	21.4
Colbert...................	453	3 860	12 289	5.8	50.7	18.6	80.3	9 711	22 546	40 576	58.5	1.1	41 171	18.1	26.9	25.4
Conecuh.................	425	2 295	2 610	12.8	66.4	8.2	18.5	11 862	15 968	24 900	72.6	0.5	29 981	28.3	41.0	38.6
Coosa....................	185	2 079	2 039	4.2	63.5	8.5	10.7	9 681	17 519	31 212	68.7	0.5	36 078	20.3	32.2	31.4
Covington...............	171	1 410	8 018	8.4	53.8	14.3	52.5	8 484	20 977	36 444	62.2	1.7	36 355	22.3	34.1	35.2
Crenshaw...............	496	1 571	3 008	12.7	60.1	14.3	19.0	8 477	20 585	36 022	62.9	2.2	36 759	19.9	29.6	28.2
Cullman.................	147	2 263	17 743	10.2	52.8	14.6	112.6	8 844	20 881	38 971	61.8	1.7	39 290	19.4	24.7	25.0
Dale.......................	309	2 958	12 367	10.3	46.8	16.4	57.1	8 863	22 566	45 028	55.2	1.3	45 294	18.5	29.0	28.1
Dallas....................	806	6 090	10 795	12.6	56.6	14.0	70.8	9 297	17 808	27 306	71.9	2.0	29 682	34.6	50.1	48.1
DeKalb...................	290	2 164	16 440	7.4	62.8	11.2	101.5	8 559	18 411	38 192	62.7	1.4	37 305	20.6	28.9	26.6
Elmore...................	229	2 719	19 744	19.8	48.8	21.4	102.7	7 803	24 381	53 555	47.0	2.1	53 548	14.0	19.9	18.5
Escambia................	422	2 001	8 037	11.3	62.2	12.5	53.3	9 452	17 045	32 330	66.7	1.2	36 840	24.4	32.0	32.1
Etowah...................	490	3 985	23 515	8.3	49.5	16.0	135.2	8 415	20 500	39 220	58.7	1.3	42 145	19.0	30.7	29.3
Fayette...................	154	867	3 743	8.1	61.2	14.1	21.8	8 964	19 545	34 680	66.2	1.5	37 085	20.4	29.4	26.3
Franklin..................	222	2 543	6 977	6.3	62.9	11.4	52.5	9 068	18 595	35 372	65.6	1.6	38 535	21.1	32.4	31.2
Geneva..................	397	1 949	5 442	5.1	58.0	12.3	33.3	8 277	20 224	36 024	64.3	1.2	36 289	22.4	34.8	34.1
Greene...................	718	2 526	2 010	8.7	63.0	10.9	13.2	10 950	13 611	20 541	83.1	0.6	25 398	37.7	54.7	53.3
Hale.......................	139	1 224	3 805	13.2	62.2	13.9	24.9	8 822	18 877	32 714	68.2	1.6	35 470	28.5	38.6	35.3
Henry....................	179	1 716	3 680	16.5	56.7	16.5	21.4	8 156	22 931	41 997	57.1	1.0	42 501	17.0	27.5	27.5
Houston..................	282	2 278	25 004	15.9	48.4	20.6	138.3	8 839	23 925	41 571	57.9	2.9	43 568	18.3	29.5	27.0
Jackson..................	311	2 464	11 132	9.2	63.0	12.4	77.4	9 252	20 066	37 745	63.0	1.5	40 201	18.4	26.9	26.4
Jefferson................	813	4 331	167 361	16.5	38.0	30.8	1 023.1	9 802	27 240	45 610	53.1	4.1	48 415	18.0	26.2	25.3
Lamar.....................	155	719	2 872	7.3	59.7	11.5	19.6	8 218	20 130	35 450	67.9	1.3	36 520	24.7	33.8	29.5
Lauderdale..............	270	2 115	22 788	11.5	49.8	21.8	117.6	9 033	24 215	43 125	56.5	2.0	43 008	17.3	23.9	22.7
Lawrence................	245	1 636	7 405	7.2	61.8	11.1	46.4	9 186	21 369	40 003	59.9	0.7	41 771	18.7	26.4	25.0
Lee........................	241	2 463	54 575	9.2	36.9	34.0	196.8	8 933	24 356	44 570	54.6	2.9	46 442	21.0	20.7	19.3
Limestone..............	129	1 691	21 315	12.9	49.4	23.2	113.7	9 280	25 569	49 570	50.5	3.3	55 060	14.3	18.8	18.1
Lowndes................	NA	NA	2 504	14.0	61.1	14.1	22.3	13 130	18 429	25 876	71.6	1.5	31 117	35.2	46.7	49.3
Macon....................	706	4 423	6 334	46.2	49.5	19.3	24.3	10 994	17 374	30 738	69.6	0.3	29 522	32.2	46.1	44.6
Madison..................	565	3 552	91 661	15.7	30.6	39.4	489.7	9 248	32 131	57 993	44.0	5.1	59 117	13.3	19.1	17.2
Marengo.................	469	2 765	5 054	13.4	57.3	15.3	36.0	8 971	21 471	32 042	66.2	1.5	35 389	23.3	34.8	34.2
Marion...................	295	1 938	6 349	8.4	56.4	11.5	41.2	8 653	20 042	32 299	67.8	1.8	34 977	19.8	30.4	28.6
Marshall.................	218	2 981	21 822	6.3	54.4	16.6	150.0	8 762	21 363	38 983	60.7	2.6	40 599	20.1	32.7	32.1
Mobile...................	510	3 994	105 910	20.4	47.5	22.0	563.2	8 839	22 953	43 809	55.3	2.3	42 530	18.4	26.9	24.7
Monroe...................	507	2 765	4 847	9.1	60.8	12.2	32.9	8 900	15 863	27 257	71.5	0.6	35 163	28.6	35.7	32.2
Montgomery............	472	4 092	62 667	24.3	40.7	31.1	266.7	8 385	25 138	44 369	54.8	3.3	42 666	22.8	33.8	35.0
Morgan..................	132	2 541	28 226	10.3	48.2	21.3	186.4	9 975	24 449	45 751	54.2	2.3	47 234	16.4	24.0	21.3
Perry......................	NA	NA	2 730	18.6	64.0	13.2	16.3	9 759	14 804	24 537	75.5	1.3	26 218	40.0	54.4	52.0
Pickens..................	NA	NA	4 417	15.1	63.5	9.9	24.9	9 195	17 957	30 330	67.9	1.0	33 160	24.3	35.3	33.4
Pike.......................	442	3 665	11 130	4.7	54.1	23.4	40.9	9 592	19 415	32 825	67.2	1.4	34 442	25.9	36.0	35.9
Randolph................	79	1 499	4 902	10.0	59.8	15.1	32.2	8 744	19 363	36 924	63.6	1.2	37 333	18.7	31.7	29.2
Russell...................	428	3 982	15 617	12.1	49.1	17.1	88.5	8 396	19 882	37 049	62.1	0.7	36 124	23.0	36.3	35.7
St. Clair..................	146	1 457	19 222	13.6	52.4	15.6	106.2	8 186	24 168	51 859	47.6	2.0	53 558	12.4	17.5	17.2
Shelby...................	NA	NA	55 277	21.0	30.0	40.8	262.1	9 059	33 494	70 187	35.1	6.1	70 879	8.5	10.2	9.4
Sumter...................	374	1 528	4 311	5.9	62.2	16.3	18.2	10 338	12 887	19 501	78.9	0.1	25 931	33.2	44.2	41.7
Talladega................	396	4 024	18 065	8.7	57.0	13.1	111.0	8 987	19 598	35 155	64.1	1.0	37 911	22.4	31.1	30.3
Tallapoosa..............	393	2 692	8 812	9.2	54.6	17.3	52.9	8 781	21 177	39 206	60.0	1.4	39 051	21.7	34.5	33.9
Tuscaloosa.............	409	3 490	60 360	8.8	43.5	28.5	256.9	9 145	23 124	46 565	52.7	2.8	47 868	20.0	25.1	23.5
Walker...................	401	3 785	13 839	7.8	58.2	10.8	97.9	9 040	20 166	35 843	63.1	1.4	37 305	20.6	31.1	29.5

1. Data for serious crimes have not been adjusted for underreporting; this may affect comparability between geographic areas and over time.   2. Per 100,000 population estimated by the FBI.
3. All persons 3 years old and over enrolled in nursery school through college.   4. Persons 25 years old and over.   5. Elementary and secondary education expenditures.
6. Based on population estimated by the American Community Survey, 2011–2015.

STATE County	Personal income, 2015										Earnings, 2015		
	Total (mil dol)	Percent change, 2014–2015	Per capita[1]		Wages and salaries (mil dol)	Supplements to wages and salaries; employer contributions (mil dol)		Proprietors' income (mil dol)	Dividends, interest, and rent (mil dol)	Personal transfer receipts (mil dol)	Total (mil dol)	Contributions for government social insurance (mil dol)	
			Dollars	Rank		Pension and insurance	Government social insurance					From employee and self-employed	From employer
	62	63	64	65	66	67	68	69	70	71	72	73	74
UNITED STATES	15 463 981	4.5	48 190	X	7 848 555	1 264 813	566 825	1 394 466	2 908 467	2 678 606	11 074 659	634 828	566 825
ALABAMA	184 785	3.2	38 070	X	88 319	14 365	6 561	12 908	31 888	42 899	122 154	7 928	6 561
Autauga	2 091	3.4	37 773	1 702	422	72	31	86	315	448	610	46	31
Baldwin	8 173	4.9	40 121	1 316	2 532	372	190	532	1 637	1 759	3 626	260	190
Barbour	833	2.9	31 443	2 658	308	58	23	78	125	270	468	31	23
Bibb	657	3.5	29 075	2 896	175	31	13	29	71	201	249	20	13
Blount	1 826	2.3	31 663	2 531	308	55	23	132	221	471	519	42	23
Bullock	277	1.0	25 929	2 987	96	20	7	21	41	93	144	9	7
Butler	676	1.7	33 518	2 288	244	44	19	50	99	215	357	24	19
Calhoun	3 864	2.7	33 418	2 324	1 729	353	131	229	695	1 130	2 442	161	131
Chambers	1 067	3.6	31 282	2 501	305	56	23	29	144	354	413	33	23
Cherokee	844	2.5	32 645	2 433	187	36	14	60	120	266	298	24	14
Chilton	1 379	3.6	31 380	2 724	352	62	26	70	169	384	510	40	26
Choctaw	409	2.5	31 046	2 682	175	27	12	40	56	161	254	19	12
Clarke	787	1.5	31 877	2 424	333	58	24	51	115	260	465	34	24
Clay	447	4.1	32 965	2 434	131	25	10	41	61	137	208	15	10
Cleburne	469	1.3	31 209	2 592	108	18	8	46	53	136	180	13	8
Coffee	1 994	3.3	38 929	1 326	544	95	42	170	364	461	851	54	42
Colbert	1 948	2.3	35 831	1 996	1 102	189	82	115	302	559	1 488	100	82
Conecuh	376	3.6	29 643	2 715	130	25	10	25	58	151	190	14	10
Coosa	307	4.0	28 651	2 977	52	10	4	9	45	100	76	7	4
Covington	1 195	1.1	31 581	2 519	442	84	34	91	176	392	650	46	34
Crenshaw	478	4.2	34 228	2 035	146	26	11	76	59	144	259	16	11
Cullman	2 946	3.8	35 923	1 846	1 095	175	82	305	393	765	1 657	110	82
Dale	1 691	1.6	34 107	2 232	1 198	289	104	104	307	457	1 694	92	104
Dallas	1 300	2.7	31 595	2 569	499	88	39	88	193	493	715	51	39
DeKalb	2 107	3.2	29 621	2 757	771	136	59	192	295	617	1 157	78	59
Elmore	3 060	3.9	37 561	1 683	705	130	54	127	476	693	1 015	74	54
Escambia	1 147	2.6	30 342	2 621	524	96	38	39	193	372	697	49	38
Etowah	3 513	3.1	34 086	2 217	1 347	217	102	230	514	1 084	1 897	137	102
Fayette	510	4.0	30 426	2 732	138	30	10	26	73	193	203	17	10
Franklin	1 002	3.6	31 614	2 650	368	71	28	68	134	285	535	36	28
Geneva	861	3.1	32 155	2 487	173	34	13	92	116	274	312	22	13
Greene	263	3.1	31 029	2 480	62	14	5	25	42	100	105	7	5
Hale	523	4.1	34 726	1 945	104	21	8	58	68	167	191	13	8
Henry	615	2.2	35 727	1 896	141	24	11	45	96	179	221	17	11
Houston	3 988	2.7	38 284	1 554	1 980	322	146	268	707	978	2 715	177	146
Jackson	1 779	2.1	33 930	2 186	603	109	47	113	312	495	872	62	47
Jefferson	31 512	2.8	47 718	453	19 321	2 757	1 388	3 272	6 274	5 811	26 737	1 678	1 388
Lamar	425	3.1	30 593	2 699	132	23	10	21	60	156	185	15	10
Lauderdale	3 258	2.0	35 189	2 125	1 058	180	79	212	636	826	1 530	111	79
Lawrence	1 070	0.2	32 320	2 498	175	33	13	65	119	310	286	25	13
Lee	5 278	5.1	33 622	2 268	2 169	408	159	249	957	956	2 985	187	159
Limestone	3 415	3.7	37 260	1 534	1 109	205	85	198	475	706	1 598	106	85
Lowndes	394	2.3	37 720	1 769	114	23	9	53	46	120	199	12	9
Macon	596	1.0	31 191	2 611	214	57	16	15	97	197	301	21	16
Madison	16 184	3.5	45 836	714	11 305	1 779	865	729	3 209	2 570	14 678	882	865
Marengo	716	1.1	35 761	1 564	288	51	21	54	112	227	414	29	21
Marion	874	2.5	28 972	2 850	339	60	26	72	141	285	497	35	26
Marshall	3 126	3.1	32 996	2 471	1 259	225	95	239	513	836	1 818	122	95
Mobile	14 684	3.5	35 348	1 933	8 181	1 262	607	1 079	2 311	3 707	11 129	721	607
Monroe	667	2.1	30 784	2 617	271	45	20	24	117	223	360	27	20
Montgomery	9 168	3.4	40 474	1 059	6 330	1 140	479	552	1 936	2 022	8 499	505	479
Morgan	4 346	3.1	36 345	1 906	2 106	351	157	252	719	1 035	2 865	189	157
Perry	284	2.8	29 414	2 770	73	16	6	32	38	114	127	9	6
Pickens	629	2.5	30 139	2 685	142	31	11	49	85	207	233	17	11
Pike	1 167	3.9	35 323	1 913	577	106	43	110	185	303	835	51	43
Randolph	729	2.7	32 119	2 506	168	32	13	57	104	233	269	20	13
Russell	1 730	3.7	29 001	2 819	527	89	39	42	246	543	698	51	39
St. Clair	2 995	3.6	34 400	2 328	734	119	55	155	343	687	1 063	80	55
Shelby	10 271	4.4	49 212	608	4 706	604	329	655	1 690	1 338	6 294	400	329
Sumter	402	-0.2	30 695	2 561	126	26	9	53	50	138	214	13	9
Talladega	2 572	2.7	31 805	2 551	1 389	225	104	92	329	793	1 810	125	104
Tallapoosa	1 468	2.7	35 942	1 886	473	81	37	83	266	455	673	51	37
Tuscaloosa	7 346	3.7	36 016	1 859	4 212	731	308	456	1 324	1 561	5 708	356	308
Walker	2 420	3.2	37 056	1 588	705	123	53	140	427	752	1 021	79	53

1. Based on the resident population estimated as of July 1 of the year shown.

Table B. States and Counties — Earnings, Social Security, and Housing

STATE County	Earnings, 2015 (cont.) Percent by selected industries									Social Security beneficiaries, December 2015		Housing units, 2016		
	Farm	Mining	Construction	Manu-facturing	Infor-mation: professional, scientific, technical services	Retail trade	Finance, insur-ance, real estate and leasing	Health care and social assistance	Govern-ment	Number	Rate[1]	Supple-mental Security Income recipients, December 2015	Total	Percent change, 2010–2016
	75	76	77	78	79	80	81	82	83	84	85	86	87	88
UNITED STATES............	0.8	1.5	5.8	9.5	13.5	5.9	9.1	10.9	16.6	58 444 059	182	8 308 531	135 697 926	3.0
ALABAMA	1.3	0.6	5.8	14.3	9.4	6.5	6.7	11.3	20.7	1 108 543	228	170 844	2 230 185	2.7
Autauga...............................	1.3	0.7	6.9	18.1	3.1	8.5	4.6	10.1	19.5	11 455	208	1 497	22 984	3.8
Baldwin................................	0.5	0.3	8.9	6.9	5.8	12.8	6.9	13.0	14.4	50 340	247	3 510	110 608	6.3
Barbour...............................	8.7	2.9	2.2	23.8	D	8.8	2.5	D	18.6	7 050	268	1 507	11 789	-0.3
Bibb....................................	1.2	D	24.6	7.9	D	6.1	1.9	D	26.7	5 630	250	1 002	8 997	0.2
Blount..................................	8.1	D	10.5	10.9	4.3	7.6	3.4	D	19.9	13 665	237	1 333	23 876	-0.1
Bullock................................	14.4	0.0	D	D	D	3.6	1.8	13.1	25.3	2 095	200	600	4 452	-0.9
Butler..................................	6.7	0.0	5.6	19.8	D	7.4	2.8	12.7	13.8	5 405	269	1 130	9 903	-0.6
Calhoun...............................	1.0	D	3.2	14.5	4.5	8.4	3.6	10.7	32.8	30 045	261	4 758	53 344	0.1
Chambers............................	3.9	D	3.5	24.9	2.8	7.4	2.3	D	23.3	9 865	290	1 529	16 869	-0.7
Cherokee.............................	8.6	0.1	4.0	17.8	D	10.9	3.5	6.7	21.4	7 800	303	901	16 239	-0.2
Chilton.................................	0.8	D	11.2	21.6	D	9.7	3.9	D	18.1	10 200	233	1 411	19 297	0.1
Choctaw..............................	1.4	0.2	D	D	1.8	6.5	2.0	D	9.4	4 305	326	833	7 227	-0.6
Clarke..................................	0.9	0.8	3.2	27.3	D	9.2	5.5	D	20.7	7 155	289	1 462	12 578	-0.5
Clay.....................................	9.0	0.0	3.8	36.3	D	4.6	D	D	21.3	3 970	294	518	6 726	-0.7
Cleburne..............................	13.6	0.0	26.3	11.4	D	8.0	2.0	2.0	22.1	3 940	263	530	6 684	-0.5
Coffee..................................	9.3	0.0	3.1	17.6	D	10.1	3.7	10.9	16.4	11 295	221	1 461	22 925	2.7
Colbert.................................	0.6	0.6	8.2	28.0	1.9	6.8	3.8	8.0	20.8	15 085	278	2 098	26 409	2.5
Conecuh...............................	7.3	D	2.4	14.9	1.5	3.9	1.2	D	20.4	4 005	318	746	7 053	-0.6
Coosa..................................	1.3	0.0	2.9	39.0	D	3.2	D	D	22.0	2 945	276	472	6 457	-0.5
Covington............................	5.3	D	5.7	14.6	3.2	9.5	4.7	D	16.6	10 595	281	1 470	18 762	-0.4
Crenshaw............................	20.0	0.0	4.0	24.3	1.5	2.7	2.6	D	11.7	3 875	279	666	6 698	-0.5
Cullman...............................	7.1	D	6.7	20.4	3.3	8.0	4.3	12.4	13.3	21 410	262	2 616	37 263	0.6
Dale.....................................	1.8	D	2.9	21.0	3.0	2.0	1.5	2.5	49.2	11 310	229	1 921	22 834	0.7
Dallas..................................	5.3	D	4.2	25.9	2.3	7.9	3.4	13.4	18.9	11 170	273	4 318	20 210	0.0
DeKalb................................	8.2	D	5.8	28.6	3.1	6.7	2.3	9.8	14.7	17 155	242	2 180	31 057	-0.2
Elmore.................................	0.2	D	7.6	16.5	4.9	10.7	4.5	9.6	23.9	18 000	222	2 335	33 741	3.4
Escambia.............................	0.9	3.1	4.3	19.7	2.0	8.0	3.9	7.8	31.2	9 960	263	1 508	16 401	-0.5
Etowah................................	0.8	0.2	5.3	16.0	3.7	8.5	5.1	22.4	15.0	28 650	278	4 763	47 540	0.2
Fayette................................	5.1	1.3	4.8	21.8	2.2	9.3	3.3	D	28.5	5 495	329	787	8 399	-0.5
Franklin...............................	4.5	0.9	3.5	37.0	D	5.7	4.1	D	18.5	7 695	244	1 179	14 081	0.4
Geneva................................	17.9	0.0	6.2	10.1	D	6.8	3.9	4.6	21.3	7 490	280	1 237	12 639	-0.4
Greene................................	20.7	0.0	1.3	20.2	D	4.2	D	D	29.4	2 560	303	795	4 991	-0.3
Hale....................................	27.1	D	4.8	16.7	1.3	4.5	2.7	D	23.0	4 620	306	1 113	7 638	-0.2
Henry...................................	7.0	0.0	7.7	14.0	D	5.1	2.5	D	15.9	5 055	294	629	8 982	1.0
Houston...............................	0.5	D	5.5	6.4	4.8	10.4	5.1	18.3	18.7	24 950	239	4 071	46 896	3.5
Jackson	3.6	D	5.5	30.9	2.8	8.1	3.1	D	21.5	14 400	275	1 714	24 806	0.1
Jefferson.............................	0.0	0.6	6.4	7.1	11.3	5.0	11.3	16.8	15.7	140 750	213	24 551	308 532	2.7
Lamar..................................	1.6	D	4.2	34.8	D	5.9	3.7	6.9	16.1	4 375	315	638	7 321	-0.4
Lauderdale...........................	0.8	D	7.8	10.8	5.0	11.2	5.5	17.4	18.7	23 660	256	2 680	44 579	1.8
Lawrence.............................	7.9	D	10.2	3.8	D	8.9	4.8	D	24.9	8 965	271	1 467	15 171	-0.4
Lee......................................	0.1	0.2	5.1	12.8	5.4	6.9	4.1	6.4	35.0	24 080	154	3 394	67 159	7.6
Limestone............................	1.8	D	15.1	13.1	4.4	9.3	2.5	4.1	33.0	18 375	201	2 141	35 759	2.2
Lowndes..............................	21.6	D	2.8	38.1	D	2.0	D	2.2	14.7	3 110	298	806	5 079	-1.1
Macon.................................	1.4	D	D	D	D	3.5	0.9	D	65.7	4 845	252	1 125	10 205	-0.5
Madison...............................	0.1	D	2.9	12.0	25.6	5.0	3.4	7.5	28.6	62 900	178	6 955	159 088	8.6
Marengo..............................	4.8	0.1	5.3	23.8	D	6.7	4.4	D	18.5	6 080	305	1 521	10 200	-0.4
Marion.................................	6.2	D	3.6	29.6	1.3	6.8	4.5	D	15.9	8 030	266	1 069	14 697	-0.3
Marshall..............................	3.3	D	6.4	26.1	4.1	9.3	3.7	6.6	17.9	22 550	238	3 144	40 339	0.0
Mobile.................................	0.3	0.4	7.3	15.9	8.8	6.6	6.9	12.2	15.3	89 650	216	15 281	182 642	2.5
Monroe................................	1.9	0.2	3.1	26.4	D	6.9	3.2	D	19.9	6 025	278	980	11 266	-0.6
Montgomery.........................	0.8	0.0	4.2	10.8	9.6	5.5	5.9	11.5	30.7	45 255	199	9 922	104 615	2.9
Morgan................................	0.8	0.1	7.7	33.1	4.8	6.4	4.0	7.6	13.9	28 030	235	3 322	51 689	1.0
Perry....................................	16.0	0.1	4.0	16.0	D	3.8	2.7	7.6	21.9	2 820	291	1 068	4 679	-1.2
Pickens................................	10.5	D	2.8	18.3	D	4.9	D	D	32.8	5 635	271	1 242	9 440	-0.5
Pike.....................................	5.0	0.2	2.7	24.0	3.0	5.1	4.3	7.8	21.9	6 790	203	1 629	15 844	3.8
Randolph.............................	10.6	D	5.6	19.2	2.9	7.5	3.7	D	21.5	6 175	272	871	11 914	-0.6
Russell................................	1.7	0.2	6.0	26.0	D	8.9	5.5	10.2	21.3	12 570	214	1 920	27 336	11.1
St. Clair...............................	2.0	D	9.6	18.9	4.8	8.3	4.0	8.8	15.4	19 105	220	2 022	36 017	1.3
Shelby	0.0	0.6	7.1	5.7	11.2	6.9	19.1	7.7	8.0	36 210	174	2 583	85 376	5.4
Sumter.................................	20.0	D	3.3	10.1	D	3.5	1.7	D	31.6	3 365	254	1 139	6 747	-0.6
Talladega.............................	0.3	D	4.0	42.5	2.8	4.7	2.0	8.0	15.1	21 460	266	4 137	37 206	0.3
Tallapoosa...........................	0.5	D	5.8	17.9	5.0	7.4	3.7	D	16.3	12 465	306	1 619	22 109	0.0
Tuscaloosa..........................	0.1	5.1	4.8	19.2	5.3	5.7	4.7	7.3	27.3	38 965	191	6 443	89 746	5.7
Walker.................................	0.9	2.8	5.4	9.8	3.8	12.3	4.5	D	16.2	20 295	311	3 392	30 663	-0.5

1. Per 1,000 resident population estimated as of July 1 of the year shown.

Table B. States and Counties — Housing, Labor Force, and Employment

STATE County	Housing units, 2011–2015								Civilian labor force, 2016		Unemployment		Civilian employment,[6] 2011–2015		
		Occupied units												Percent	
			Owner-occupied			Renter-occupied									
				Median owner cost as a percent of income											
	Total	Percent	Median value[1]	With a mortgage	Without a mortgage[2]	Median rent[3]	Median rent as a percent of income[2]	Substandard units[4] (percent)	Total	Percent change, 2015–2016	Total	Rate[5]	Total	Management, business, science and arts	Construction, production, and maintenance occupations
	89	90	91	92	93	94	95	96	97	98	99	100	101	102	103
UNITED STATES	116 926 305	63.9	178 600	23.1	12.1	928	31.0	3.7	158 741 980	1.1	7 729 204	4.9	145 747 779	36.7	21.1
ALABAMA	1 848 325	68.7	125 500	21.0	11.1	717	30.5	2.2	2 168 612	0.8	129 835	6.0	2 022 325	33.3	25.8
Autauga	20 396	73.9	141 300	21.1	10.0	883	32.8	2.7	25 649	1.4	1 352	5.3	23 986	33.2	25.6
Baldwin	74 104	71.5	169 300	22.3	10.5	879	30.3	1.5	89 931	2.5	4 870	5.4	85 953	33.1	22.0
Barbour	9 222	63.6	92 200	21.1	12.3	579	30.3	2.2	8 302	-4.0	718	8.6	8 597	26.8	33.9
Bibb	7 027	75.1	102 700	23.3	11.5	651	26.9	0.4	8 573	0.6	569	6.6	8 294	21.5	42.8
Blount	20 816	78.9	119 800	20.5	10.7	601	26.1	2.0	24 525	0.7	1 354	5.5	22 189	28.5	33.4
Bullock	3 683	70.8	68 600	25.6	13.2	570	30.3	3.2	4 811	0.7	345	7.2	3 865	18.8	46.5
Butler	8 056	70.1	78 900	23.0	13.5	575	30.9	3.1	9 132	-0.3	651	7.1	7 813	27.5	34.0
Calhoun	45 154	69.1	105 900	20.2	10.3	637	31.1	1.8	45 794	-0.6	3 067	6.7	47 401	27.3	30.9
Chambers	13 787	67.6	80 800	21.5	13.1	658	32.3	3.8	15 134	0.4	839	5.5	13 689	23.3	35.9
Cherokee	11 278	77.7	105 100	23.1	13.5	621	30.2	2.6	11 163	-0.4	582	5.2	10 155	29.3	35.2
Chilton	16 237	76.4	100 100	21.8	11.7	661	28.4	3.4	19 153	0.6	1 076	5.6	17 895	27.2	34.9
Choctaw	5 575	81.6	61 100	20.4	12.3	497	32.8	2.1	4 300	-2.2	382	8.9	4 405	24.9	40.2
Clarke	9 622	66.2	86 900	20.4	13.0	545	30.4	1.6	8 011	-0.2	893	11.1	8 161	21.1	38.5
Clay	5 419	74.3	84 100	25.0	10.0	451	25.9	4.0	5 558	-0.3	342	6.2	5 180	21.5	44.4
Cleburne	5 776	77.4	108 000	22.0	12.1	557	24.2	3.9	5 831	2.3	355	6.1	6 065	28.9	36.3
Coffee	19 160	67.6	142 400	19.7	10.0	683	27.0	1.9	20 402	0.2	1 235	6.1	20 912	32.2	26.5
Colbert	22 204	71.3	99 400	20.2	11.7	632	30.3	1.2	23 707	0.1	1 662	7.0	21 290	27.3	31.5
Conecuh	5 168	77.2	70 100	22.9	12.7	522	40.6	5.7	4 593	-2.3	396	8.6	3 718	19.4	39.2
Coosa	4 450	79.3	78 300	26.5	13.1	597	24.8	2.4	4 444	0.0	273	6.1	3 852	18.0	40.3
Covington	14 949	74.7	93 600	22.1	12.0	599	26.3	2.2	15 392	-0.9	1 077	7.0	14 200	26.2	34.6
Crenshaw	5 383	70.4	70 600	19.5	12.0	520	26.3	0.7	6 451	1.4	388	6.0	5 620	27.6	37.1
Cullman	31 287	75.3	115 200	23.1	12.3	625	29.6	2.1	37 715	3.3	1 923	5.1	32 282	28.5	32.1
Dale	19 018	62.0	101 700	19.3	10.0	629	27.2	2.0	20 078	0.8	1 188	5.9	18 735	27.1	30.9
Dallas	16 413	58.8	81 500	22.4	14.1	564	36.5	6.8	15 530	-0.8	1 459	9.4	14 094	26.5	34.6
DeKalb	25 013	73.2	98 500	22.3	11.6	540	22.9	3.5	29 016	0.4	1 800	6.2	27 778	24.2	38.8
Elmore	28 651	74.9	147 500	20.3	10.1	785	28.3	1.8	36 726	1.1	1 809	4.9	33 636	33.3	25.5
Escambia	13 659	71.6	93 800	20.9	13.4	560	31.1	3.0	14 633	-0.2	985	6.7	12 294	25.4	29.7
Etowah	39 899	71.4	100 400	21.5	12.4	621	30.5	2.0	43 887	1.6	2 618	6.0	41 236	28.7	31.5
Fayette	7 037	74.1	75 200	20.1	11.0	469	30.8	1.7	6 543	1.7	456	7.0	6 122	27.0	36.8
Franklin	11 980	67.6	85 600	20.3	12.7	534	26.5	4.2	13 723	0.0	837	6.1	12 249	21.4	45.6
Geneva	10 754	74.8	77 400	20.3	11.2	559	29.7	2.9	10 905	0.7	642	5.9	10 419	23.9	35.9
Greene	3 201	71.1	69 600	36.2	17.6	343	33.0	5.0	2 893	0.5	293	10.1	2 412	20.1	31.6
Hale	5 927	75.4	87 400	25.7	12.9	460	32.9	3.4	6 050	0.6	471	7.8	5 282	25.5	33.4
Henry	6 894	78.3	96 300	20.7	11.1	595	26.8	1.3	6 762	0.2	446	6.6	6 922	33.5	30.9
Houston	39 197	64.7	123 300	20.4	10.0	691	29.3	1.3	44 718	-0.1	2 629	5.9	44 067	31.1	24.3
Jackson	20 431	73.5	98 900	20.7	10.5	564	26.4	1.9	23 636	0.4	1 519	6.4	20 883	25.3	39.6
Jefferson	260 929	63.2	143 400	21.9	11.6	810	32.2	1.8	310 908	0.6	18 211	5.9	293 202	38.7	19.0
Lamar	6 138	71.6	67 900	18.8	11.2	426	28.0	1.4	5 708	1.2	325	5.7	5 391	25.9	39.4
Lauderdale	38 612	69.3	118 600	20.1	10.0	593	29.3	1.3	43 009	0.5	2 763	6.4	39 734	29.5	26.8
Lawrence	13 537	80.1	94 800	21.4	11.5	562	24.1	1.8	13 729	-0.4	966	7.0	12 704	25.1	41.8
Lee	57 171	59.0	154 300	20.5	10.5	792	36.2	2.2	72 893	1.8	3 827	5.3	68 614	39.7	21.3
Limestone	32 213	76.3	142 100	20.3	10.0	616	28.4	2.4	40 575	1.8	2 151	5.3	37 664	34.2	28.4
Lowndes	4 282	73.7	67 800	26.7	20.0	568	33.1	3.6	3 803	0.4	409	10.8	3 471	23.9	40.6
Macon	8 009	65.0	74 700	24.4	13.4	592	32.8	2.7	7 981	-0.1	617	7.7	7 585	26.7	27.6
Madison	137 767	67.7	167 900	18.6	10.0	765	28.5	1.5	173 295	1.6	9 016	5.2	163 753	44.6	16.6
Marengo	8 281	70.1	90 800	22.2	13.6	530	30.1	2.5	7 640	2.7	568	7.4	6 860	28.4	32.7
Marion	12 714	75.5	81 400	19.5	11.6	485	30.1	2.1	12 586	0.4	845	6.7	11 560	26.2	32.7
Marshall	34 261	71.8	115 500	22.0	11.0	594	27.8	3.5	41 255	1.8	2 261	5.5	38 140	28.1	34.6
Mobile	154 188	66.5	122 400	22.0	11.6	788	33.4	2.3	185 092	0.7	12 716	6.9	170 900	32.4	24.0
Monroe	8 406	66.2	81 200	23.4	11.5	537	28.9	1.4	7 281	-1.2	681	9.4	6 551	22.9	35.6
Montgomery	89 532	59.2	122 300	21.1	10.4	814	31.9	2.4	104 822	1.0	6 134	5.9	99 158	36.0	19.8
Morgan	46 235	70.7	123 500	19.9	10.0	599	27.1	2.5	55 331	-0.1	3 096	5.6	51 472	29.7	30.6
Perry	3 450	68.5	66 300	28.2	16.6	512	33.1	7.1	3 467	-0.8	367	10.6	2 865	26.5	26.3
Pickens	7 644	71.8	82 000	21.7	12.2	448	33.0	1.9	7 994	0.5	555	6.9	6 712	19.7	40.7
Pike	12 786	58.0	105 500	20.4	10.0	593	33.3	2.0	15 157	1.0	969	6.4	14 462	29.7	28.7
Randolph	8 915	71.3	85 800	23.0	10.8	603	32.6	4.5	9 491	0.2	539	5.7	8 630	27.6	39.2
Russell	22 241	58.8	111 000	23.6	12.8	732	29.5	3.0	24 007	-0.9	1 354	5.6	22 927	28.7	26.6
St. Clair	31 979	80.1	140 000	20.1	11.5	699	25.5	1.5	38 588	0.6	2 055	5.3	36 977	28.8	28.7
Shelby	75 534	78.9	192 800	20.4	10.0	944	27.0	1.3	108 320	0.7	4 765	4.4	101 343	42.8	15.6
Sumter	4 815	67.9	72 900	29.0	18.3	555	44.6	2.9	5 143	0.3	402	7.8	4 416	23.8	26.7
Talladega	31 424	71.1	93 400	22.2	12.3	584	31.0	2.5	34 781	-1.3	2 352	6.8	30 618	28.1	34.8
Tallapoosa	16 323	71.4	103 400	20.7	11.2	575	31.7	4.6	18 906	0.4	1 059	5.6	15 837	28.6	35.3
Tuscaloosa	69 128	63.9	156 500	21.3	10.4	785	32.5	2.1	98 533	0.4	5 685	5.8	87 695	35.1	25.0
Walker	25 602	74.0	82 800	20.4	11.7	584	30.5	2.0	25 658	0.9	1 952	7.6	24 043	25.4	31.7

1. Specified owner-occupied units.　　2. A value of 10.0 represents 10 percent or less; a value of 50.0 represents 50 percent or more.　　3. Specified renter-occupied units.
4. Overcrowded or lacking complete plumbing facilities.　　5. Percent of civilian labor force.　　6. Civilian employed persons 16 years old and over.

Table B. States and Counties — Nonfarm Employment and Agriculture

STATE County	Private nonfarm establishments, employment and payroll, 2015									Agriculture, 2012			
	Number of establishments	Employment						Annual payroll		Farms			
												Percent with:	
		Total	Health care and social assistance	Manufacturing	Retail trade	Finance and insurance	Professional, scientific, and technical services	Total (mil dol)	Average per employee (dollars)	Number	Fewer than 50 acres	500 acres or more	Farm operators whose principal occupation is farming (percent)
	104	105	106	107	108	109	110	111	112	113	114	115	116
UNITED STATES	7 663 938	124 085 947	19 221 864	11 605 501	15 704 167	6 135 914	8 798 260	6 253 488	50 396	2 109 303	38.6	15.0	47.8
ALABAMA	98 540	1 634 391	241 618	248 033	231 788	69 400	96 861	67 370	41 220	43 223	37.4	8.6	44.2
Autauga	844	10 454	1 618	971	2 631	375	240	321	30 747	389	31.6	14.4	51.2
Baldwin	5 127	58 868	7 507	4 248	13 794	1 590	1 927	1 887	32 059	989	52.6	8.1	45.8
Barbour	453	6 853	679	2 306	856	142	102	242	35 379	571	13.8	17.3	46.1
Bibb	280	3 421	620	329	498	76	110	127	37 129	189	29.6	13.8	38.6
Blount	654	6 508	958	1 034	1 221	195	258	193	29 667	1 241	40.6	3.1	48.8
Bullock	103	2 193	404	D	239	54	15	64	29 336	273	17.2	30.4	40.7
Butler	412	6 017	894	1 353	951	144	62	186	30 934	407	25.1	8.6	45.2
Calhoun	2 300	35 910	6 088	6 145	6 355	926	960	1 166	32 472	592	45.4	3.5	46.1
Chambers	546	5 990	673	1 737	1 109	156	150	195	32 630	301	22.6	15.6	38.9
Cherokee	355	3 903	449	1 073	922	128	52	119	30 613	561	32.1	11.6	45.6
Chilton	734	7 585	696	1 965	1 474	228	115	250	32 942	543	37.9	7.0	41.1
Choctaw	256	2 782	398	D	349	65	44	140	50 152	248	37.1	14.5	40.3
Clarke	590	7 089	913	1 834	1 601	339	80	243	34 330	263	38.8	9.9	35.4
Clay	190	3 165	505	1 648	295	84	59	93	29 443	401	24.7	7.7	39.7
Cleburne	160	1 800	67	313	266	55	12	72	39 759	341	36.7	5.3	47.8
Coffee	965	13 625	1 953	3 738	2 331	503	779	431	31 665	899	27.9	9.1	50.5
Colbert	1 222	21 311	2 727	6 812	2 926	651	295	817	38 336	687	39.6	9.0	36.7
Conecuh	198	2 622	417	503	277	45	29	82	31 444	346	19.1	8.4	44.8
Coosa	92	955	115	390	103	10	23	34	35 816	152	23.7	11.8	52.6
Covington	821	10 501	1 638	2 198	1 846	349	290	325	30 983	1 051	31.4	6.8	40.3
Crenshaw	210	3 281	460	1 348	267	103	29	113	34 348	575	21.6	12.3	40.2
Cullman	1 692	23 262	3 610	4 695	3 657	795	447	832	35 781	2 007	47.6	2.1	48.6
Dale	758	10 817	1 256	554	1 242	359	882	505	46 710	487	27.9	12.7	30.8
Dallas	738	10 418	1 820	2 932	1 658	308	218	343	32 909	506	22.9	25.7	45.7
DeKalb	1 073	17 898	2 495	7 179	2 351	445	376	580	32 384	2 035	44.9	3.4	50.7
Elmore	1 157	14 836	2 118	2 733	2 942	412	378	475	32 025	552	46.4	7.8	40.9
Escambia	728	10 327	1 223	2 270	1 717	395	166	344	33 354	454	44.1	13.9	39.6
Etowah	1 980	29 603	7 218	5 030	4 704	1 026	578	991	33 490	853	51.1	2.9	40.3
Fayette	306	3 077	717	815	598	78	35	98	31 869	414	24.6	8.0	38.9
Franklin	526	9 510	1 028	4 734	1 044	383	134	315	33 167	825	25.7	7.8	47.5
Geneva	398	3 672	552	684	797	127	108	117	31 803	1 017	31.6	9.8	43.1
Greene	106	1 279	338	425	167	33	7	43	33 372	304	26.0	24.0	50.3
Hale	190	1 911	412	489	273	69	13	64	33 460	456	27.0	16.0	49.8
Henry	301	2 669	180	372	342	95	129	97	36 336	498	19.5	17.1	43.0
Houston	2 703	43 013	9 491	4 028	7 868	1 121	1 098	1 666	38 741	816	38.8	12.3	44.5
Jackson	852	12 771	1 791	5 354	1 890	330	212	418	32 752	1 376	40.1	6.0	37.4
Jefferson	16 365	316 174	53 767	24 319	40 278	22 325	15 066	16 002	50 610	394	59.9	3.0	46.7
Lamar	238	3 022	314	1 353	304	106	53	118	38 883	353	31.7	8.5	33.4
Lauderdale	1 999	25 389	5 145	2 369	5 683	980	842	758	29 838	1 466	45.9	5.2	44.8
Lawrence	382	2 940	621	138	774	104	68	82	27 960	1 551	41.5	4.3	43.2
Lee	2 658	41 553	5 983	6 927	6 957	1 037	1 412	1 323	31 850	315	32.7	7.6	37.1
Limestone	1 314	16 293	2 452	3 390	2 784	365	775	582	35 702	1 230	40.6	6.9	46.6
Lowndes	102	1 621	D	735	174	26	11	79	48 606	441	24.5	21.8	48.5
Macon	205	5 407	1 661	608	429	48	27	214	39 603	352	26.4	15.9	48.3
Madison	8 213	155 894	22 970	16 219	20 081	3 569	35 736	7 741	49 652	1 033	48.4	8.0	49.5
Marengo	467	5 983	983	1 377	905	223	81	219	36 600	499	27.3	16.8	33.9
Marion	529	7 592	1 291	2 538	1 090	388	67	238	31 346	715	32.3	3.8	37.5
Marshall	1 790	30 086	3 803	10 240	4 718	772	616	974	32 367	1 505	53.2	3.1	41.9
Mobile	8 600	148 864	20 646	16 770	20 827	5 354	9 371	6 156	41 351	698	60.9	4.4	48.6
Monroe	392	5 323	652	1 238	892	165	39	213	40 094	480	37.1	12.1	44.6
Montgomery	5 568	103 062	16 981	13 014	12 822	4 102	5 904	4 196	40 716	603	28.0	19.2	50.4
Morgan	2 569	41 938	5 821	11 842	5 610	1 391	1 401	1 761	41 992	1 237	44.2	3.7	42.1
Perry	115	1 451	152	467	196	60	18	44	30 456	389	26.2	19.0	39.8
Pickens	272	2 705	549	576	381	133	82	83	30 830	433	28.4	9.9	46.9
Pike	644	10 788	1 105	2 206	1 543	357	461	399	36 941	600	21.5	14.7	39.5
Randolph	328	3 781	624	1 210	706	158	49	102	26 846	611	27.8	8.3	52.2
Russell	781	10 938	1 338	3 025	2 008	367	193	377	34 502	280	28.9	21.8	35.4
St. Clair	1 279	15 560	1 921	2 573	2 744	472	619	516	33 176	540	44.3	3.3	51.1
Shelby	4 995	80 862	6 734	5 552	8 800	10 306	5 073	3 976	49 165	401	45.4	6.7	44.6
Sumter	200	3 006	389	148	284	60	D	114	38 063	428	22.7	22.9	46.0
Talladega	1 235	23 303	2 745	9 177	2 645	554	472	1 060	45 483	519	38.2	8.5	50.3
Tallapoosa	715	10 904	2 247	2 370	1 555	235	221	330	30 248	345	35.1	5.5	42.0
Tuscaloosa	4 028	76 274	11 968	14 332	10 277	1 687	2 260	3 075	40 317	497	43.7	9.5	37.0
Walker	1 237	15 239	3 207	1 957	3 426	470	461	532	34 934	482	46.9	3.7	33.8

Table B. States and Counties — **Agriculture**

STATE County	Land in farms					Value of land and buildings (dollars)		Value of machinery and equipment, average per farm (dollars)	Value of products sold				Percent of farms with sales of:		Government payments	
			Acres								Percent from:					
	Acreage (1,000)	Percent change, 2007–2012	Average size of farm	Total irrigated (1,000)	Total cropland (1,000)	Average per farm	Average per acre		Total (mil dol)	Average per farm (dollars)	Crops	Live-stock and poultry products	$10,000 or more	$100,000 or more	Total ($1,000)	Percent of farms
	117	118	119	120	121	122	123	124	125	126	127	128	129	130	131	132
UNITED STATES............	914 528	-0.8	434	55 822.2	389 690.4	1 075 491	2 481	115 662	394 644.5	187 097	53.8	46.2	43.4	18.4	8 053 346	38.5
ALABAMA	8 903	-1.4	206	113.0	2 758.5	547 524	2 658	71 210	5 571.2	128 894	23.6	76.4	33.8	11.2	88 145	30.0
Autauga....................	112	0.9	287	1.6	41.3	655 057	2 285	73 658	19.8	50 928	D	D	33.7	6.9	1 245	31.9
Baldwin....................	192	1.3	194	7.7	100.9	773 980	3 980	107 905	135.6	137 070	85.3	14.7	35.2	11.7	2 649	26.7
Barbour....................	204	2.6	358	2.3	41.3	808 758	2 261	80 371	104.4	182 760	14.1	85.9	32.7	9.6	1 806	62.5
Bibb.........................	56	47.7	298	0.1	12.6	624 810	2 098	66 159	D	D	D	D	23.8	1.6	138	14.3
Blount.....................	146	-3.4	118	0.5	37.1	427 880	3 632	58 512	178.2	143 587	7.0	93.0	37.4	12.7	897	19.1
Bullock....................	165	22.9	603	1.4	26.1	1 312 890	2 178	107 813	54.5	199 813	62.0	38.0	38.8	13.6	721	31.5
Butler......................	88	-4.5	217	0.0	21.3	527 472	2 429	65 489	110.1	270 634	D	D	28.7	10.8	355	26.3
Calhoun...................	81	6.6	137	0.9	21.4	418 128	3 046	61 630	92.4	156 052	11.8	88.2	30.1	7.3	406	17.4
Chambers................	96	-8.2	320	0.1	15.3	832 784	2 602	61 761	8.3	27 708	24.3	75.7	35.2	5.3	397	15.6
Cherokee.................	124	-6.5	221	1.3	58.8	757 134	3 419	84 629	120.0	213 913	30.0	70.0	36.4	17.3	1 985	38.1
Chilton....................	91	-8.8	168	0.5	23.7	493 578	2 933	55 048	16.0	29 538	63.8	36.2	36.8	5.3	296	10.3
Choctaw..................	68	24.5	276	0.0	8.0	517 085	1 872	53 851	D	D	D	D	18.5	2.0	194	11.3
Clarke.....................	47	-35.6	181	0.0	7.7	369 251	2 045	38 399	2.6	9 863	49.1	50.9	24.3	0.8	153	17.5
Clay........................	78	4.6	194	0.0	13.0	480 421	2 474	54 217	58.1	144 850	1.8	98.2	38.4	8.7	585	19.5
Cleburne..................	50	1.4	147	0.3	7.7	404 111	2 745	60 522	3.9	247 170	3.9	96.1	45.2	18.5	106	12.6
Coffee.....................	202	-4.2	225	3.3	85.5	593 148	2 636	90 236	258.2	287 171	14.3	85.7	37.9	19.7	3 459	57.7
Colbert....................	153	18.5	222	3.7	65.7	626 991	2 820	80 017	67.0	97 531	54.3	45.7	32.3	8.7	1 996	31.4
Conecuh..................	94	8.6	271	0.1	20.1	539 208	1 991	72 494	16.4	47 436	44.6	55.4	35.0	6.4	770	41.0
Coosa......................	36	-20.8	236	D	4.3	489 967	2 072	52 934	2.1	13 763	D	D	30.3	2.0	39	5.9
Covington................	209	4.2	198	1.4	65.5	447 436	2 255	67 858	119.8	114 025	26.0	74.0	30.9	12.9	2 582	43.8
Crenshaw.................	130	-1.9	226	0.9	29.0	458 381	2 029	80 572	143.8	250 132	3.5	96.5	36.2	17.0	919	51.0
Cullman...................	194	-15.5	97	0.5	58.4	403 876	4 176	64 375	417.1	207 820	3.8	96.2	43.3	21.1	567	12.0
Dale........................	130	-6.1	267	2.6	49.6	668 934	2 510	86 197	118.0	242 400	21.6	78.4	32.6	15.8	1 495	55.6
Dallas......................	255	-0.7	504	2.0	76.8	925 310	1 835	106 532	70.2	138 800	39.5	60.5	32.6	12.3	2 616	45.8
DeKalb....................	229	-2.5	113	0.3	72.3	427 088	3 790	70 291	461.7	226 882	5.3	94.7	37.4	17.5	2 652	24.1
Elmore.....................	90	-12.1	164	3.1	30.2	519 685	3 175	64 795	26.5	47 986	65.6	34.4	29.3	4.3	959	15.9
Escambia.................	107	-4.8	236	0.8	47.7	537 068	2 271	93 018	40.9	89 991	88.5	11.5	28.4	11.5	2 602	48.9
Etowah....................	86	-8.6	101	0.1	19.5	359 368	3 559	51 635	83.7	98 161	6.5	93.5	27.8	8.2	450	11.8
Fayette....................	81	2.9	196	D	27.6	415 915	2 124	83 215	36.3	87 751	D	D	30.2	7.0	903	37.4
Franklin...................	150	6.8	182	0.8	35.0	383 861	2 104	57 796	132.7	160 807	5.6	94.4	39.3	13.8	782	21.8
Geneva....................	219	-0.8	215	2.7	93.1	465 026	2 161	89 514	178.5	175 499	26.4	73.6	36.0	15.6	4 741	59.2
Greene.....................	120	-11.3	396	0.3	21.8	803 934	2 030	58 648	22.4	73 658	7.7	92.3	28.0	9.2	790	35.5
Hale........................	161	-5.2	352	D	29.9	735 855	2 091	81 908	65.2	142 934	D	D	39.9	11.4	797	32.0
Henry......................	170	2.5	341	8.1	72.9	762 197	2 235	108 992	75.0	150 647	53.5	46.5	38.4	15.5	3 315	64.3
Houston...................	198	-3.3	243	9.1	97.4	631 875	2 604	89 566	89.2	109 336	71.7	28.3	31.1	14.8	5 065	59.3
Jackson....................	232	-4.5	168	0.4	89.4	440 304	2 613	65 429	117.2	85 181	30.5	69.5	35.0	8.6	1 849	34.4
Jefferson..................	39	-3.6	99	0.2	9.1	446 142	4 507	49 924	10.4	26 277	10.5	89.5	20.6	1.3	98	8.1
Lamar......................	82	-2.8	233	D	13.9	344 326	1 477	42 527	7.5	21 337	20.7	79.3	21.5	2.0	203	27.5
Lauderdale...............	212	-7.1	144	0.4	100.0	428 690	2 970	56 675	72.4	49 385	55.6	44.4	30.7	6.8	2 973	34.7
Lawrence.................	244	9.6	157	4.7	114.7	480 849	3 059	81 876	192.1	123 829	29.4	70.6	32.0	13.9	4 764	40.4
Lee.........................	59	-6.6	187	0.9	12.2	707 330	3 775	71 403	D	D	D	D	32.4	4.8	692	19.0
Limestone................	247	4.0	201	13.1	146.1	815 963	4 068	103 711	132.7	107 913	64.2	35.8	36.3	10.7	3 605	34.6
Lowndes..................	218	16.6	494	3.8	40.0	852 254	1 726	73 297	76.3	173 052	D	D	41.0	10.0	880	34.7
Macon.....................	103	-11.5	294	1.9	20.1	721 324	2 458	81 386	15.2	43 230	80.5	19.5	31.5	4.0	622	33.2
Madison...................	209	5.0	203	5.1	125.4	752 873	3 715	88 137	74.2	71 833	86.2	13.8	31.0	8.3	3 156	34.1
Marengo...................	165	-7.1	332	0.4	32.8	591 148	1 783	59 990	19.4	38 964	27.5	72.5	34.7	5.6	912	28.9
Marion.....................	114	-2.9	159	0.0	21.8	353 441	2 221	47 490	100.1	139 948	3.2	96.8	27.6	11.2	599	29.0
Marshall..................	163	5.5	108	0.2	46.7	410 550	3 791	61 688	256.5	170 433	2.9	97.1	34.2	12.3	2 102	23.7
Mobile.....................	89	-21.9	127	2.8	36.6	516 701	4 062	78 354	84.7	121 289	90.7	9.3	33.2	8.5	796	12.2
Monroe....................	141	18.3	293	0.2	53.9	576 181	1 967	103 242	44.5	92 663	72.1	27.9	34.6	10.0	2 925	59.2
Montgomery.............	220	-1.4	365	1.7	61.2	957 657	2 624	76 778	77.4	128 421	21.5	78.5	40.6	11.8	927	23.7
Morgan....................	153	-5.5	123	0.3	52.6	460 337	3 732	52 647	109.3	88 335	12.7	87.3	32.7	9.1	1 462	19.6
Perry.......................	157	-5.1	404	0.3	39.5	709 424	1 755	68 270	29.6	76 177	32.6	67.4	31.1	11.8	1 428	53.5
Pickens....................	103	-21.5	237	D	24.6	490 279	2 068	68 935	110.6	255 370	6.0	94.0	39.5	20.6	511	20.1
Pike........................	167	-6.6	279	3.2	35.2	635 038	2 278	66 467	130.4	217 322	8.9	91.1	42.5	16.0	1 573	54.2
Randolph.................	114	-0.7	186	0.1	14.4	523 882	2 810	66 257	111.5	182 509	1.9	98.1	40.4	13.9	831	21.1
Russell....................	117	24.6	419	3.4	29.4	947 768	2 261	83 646	28.9	103 057	56.0	44.0	29.6	8.6	738	34.6
St. Clair...................	67	-5.8	125	0.3	13.6	479 537	3 839	55 039	64.8	120 028	15.2	84.8	30.4	9.1	119	6.1
Shelby.....................	58	6.6	146	1.1	18.7	612 140	4 199	68 581	12.2	30 347	80.4	19.6	25.9	6.2	659	10.5
Sumter....................	240	32.5	560	1.5	33.3	797 215	1 423	58 586	30.5	71 199	D	D	33.2	10.0	1 057	36.4
Talladega.................	100	-16.1	192	4.8	39.7	559 618	2 909	63 229	40.7	78 428	41.8	58.2	28.3	5.8	717	17.1
Tallapoosa...............	61	-4.9	177	1.1	8.4	426 409	2 414	53 971	10.6	30 635	32.2	67.8	24.6	3.2	266	10.4
Tuscaloosa..............	86	-22.2	173	1.1	25.3	512 952	2 965	60 022	27.7	55 682	33.8	66.2	27.0	6.0	493	17.1
Walker....................	55	-22.5	113	0.0	13.1	291 614	2 578	51 429	33.1	68 683	11.4	88.6	24.3	5.6	105	4.8

Table B. States and Counties — Water Use, Wholesale Trade, Retail Trade, and Real Estate

STATE County	Water use, 2010		Wholesale trade,[1] 2012				Retail trade,[2] 2012				Real estate and rental and leasing,[2] 2012			
	Total water withdrawn (mil gal/day)	Gallons withdrawn per person per day	Number of establishments	Number of employees	Sales (mil dol)	Annual payroll (mil dol)	Number of establishments	Number of employees	Sales (mil dol)	Annual payroll (mil dol)	Number of establishments	Number of employees	Receipts (mil dol)	Annual payroll (mil dol)
	133	134	135	136	137	138	139	140	141	142	143	144	145	146
UNITED STATES............	351 417.1	1 138	355 983	4 880 666	5 208 023.5	287 549.6	1 062 083	14 703 529	4 219 821.9	369 001.4	354 106	1 923 770	487 655.2	85 326.0
ALABAMA	9 960.0	2 084	4 600	60 332	57 746.6	2 894.7	18 211	218 531	58 565.0	5 123.1	3 858	22 852	3 919.4	819.6
Autauga..............................	55.6	1 018	22	D	D	D	166	2 385	607.9	54.6	31	D	D	D
Baldwin..............................	64.4	353	175	1 868	1 118.2	84.1	950	12 072	3 145.8	280.0	292	1 760	250.3	53.8
Barbour..............................	11.1	402	16	181	114.0	4.0	94	868	206.5	18.2	15	20	3.3	0.6
Bibb	7.6	332	14	52	41.0	2.3	58	474	118.9	11.3	6	8	1.9	0.3
Blount	57.1	996	36	290	153.7	10.5	135	1 255	298.7	28.6	11	19	3.3	0.5
Bullock..............................	3.2	292	5	D	D	D	23	244	92.6	5.3	4	12	0.9	0.1
Butler	4.5	216	13	44	63.5	2.0	97	914	209.0	19.5	13	18	2.8	0.5
Calhoun.............................	29.3	247	97	1 792	1 808.8	73.6	477	5 954	1 463.5	134.1	73	299	48.9	8.0
Chambers...........................	5.4	158	13	104	32.6	4.2	120	1 172	282.0	23.6	14	50	5.1	0.9
Cherokee...........................	5.5	213	12	48	55.2	2.0	88	859	200.2	17.9	12	49	5.7	1.8
Chilton	7.3	168	20	320	260.5	12.6	152	1 397	442.8	32.0	19	52	6.4	1.2
Choctaw............................	42.9	3 095	9	D	D	D	54	337	100.0	7.1	6	D	D	D
Clarke...............................	24.3	941	13	126	75.2	3.8	138	1 311	341.0	28.4	13	48	6.6	1.2
Clay	2.5	180	6	D	D	D	34	291	67.7	5.4	6	9	0.6	0.1
Cleburne............................	1.8	120	5	49	6.6	0.8	36	275	64.0	6.9	3	4	0.5	0.2
Coffee	14.7	294	29	250	213.2	10.5	195	2 129	610.1	55.5	47	212	21.5	4.4
Colbert..............................	1 344.3	24 699	78	853	657.4	32.1	228	2 829	1 011.3	76.5	31	144	17.8	3.5
Conecuh............................	2.4	181	5	236	103.9	8.8	41	280	136.4	5.6	3	3	0.2	0.1
Coosa................................	0.9	81	5	D	D	D	22	161	37.9	3.5	3	1	0.6	0.1
Covington...........................	10.3	273	34	445	470.5	17.9	202	1 834	452.0	40.3	27	97	12.3	3.1
Crenshaw...........................	3.2	227	12	405	309.0	15.2	38	301	72.7	5.9	6	20	1.6	0.4
Cullman	37.9	471	93	896	1 068.8	37.9	332	3 264	896.4	76.1	47	195	21.6	5.6
Dale	10.3	204	18	169	41.0	4.3	138	1 170	323.5	26.4	30	199	33.7	7.4
Dallas	49.1	1 121	28	215	107.1	8.5	179	1 630	413.1	37.0	30	88	13.5	2.2
DeKalb...............................	11.9	168	37	415	161.0	13.7	246	2 173	579.7	53.2	24	140	9.3	3.3
Elmore	16.0	202	37	282	136.1	9.7	224	2 649	711.6	61.0	48	D	D	D
Escambia...........................	45.2	1 180	22	129	134.1	6.1	176	1 542	374.9	30.3	15	63	6.2	1.2
Etowah	146.3	1 401	82	837	549.9	31.2	392	4 675	1 236.5	96.1	62	367	57.2	10.5
Fayette	4.7	270	7	24	34.8	0.6	62	562	131.2	12.2	4	D	D	D
Franklin.............................	6.4	203	19	92	44.3	3.5	100	1 116	277.7	28.0	13	33	4.7	0.6
Geneva..............................	7.5	278	20	D	D	D	91	713	160.8	14.6	7	14	1.4	0.4
Greene	366.4	40 504	2	D	D	D	23	164	40.3	2.8	1	D	D	D
Hale	20.3	1 285	7	24	29.4	0.9	43	317	76.5	6.4	8	D	D	D
Henry	6.5	375	8	101	40.6	3.9	55	364	100.3	7.9	3	3	0.3	0.0
Houston.............................	118.0	1 162	168	D	D	D	570	7 598	2 164.9	182.5	100	423	73.0	16.0
Jackson	1 067.5	20 055	27	D	D	D	185	1 873	454.9	40.1	25	D	D	D
Jefferson............................	81.3	124	977	15 345	15 668.5	816.2	2 806	38 691	10 154.0	961.4	681	6 526	1 138.7	283.7
Lamar................................	2.1	143	7	D	D	D	51	344	80.9	7.1	3	D	D	D
Lauderdale	17.5	189	76	1 244	577.6	39.2	419	4 920	1 190.8	104.5	96	378	52.2	10.5
Lawrence............................	72.8	2 120	12	64	38.9	2.2	85	793	218.0	17.0	5	11	2.6	0.3
Lee	18.2	130	75	613	504.3	28.3	477	6 450	1 632.1	141.6	113	544	81.0	16.0
Limestone	2 744.2	33 150	45	447	332.7	17.3	261	2 804	777.1	64.3	52	166	30.7	5.5
Lowndes............................	4.5	394	2	D	D	D	21	177	100.8	3.2	2	D	D	D
Macon................................	7.1	333	6	D	D	D	45	392	93.2	7.1	5	18	1.1	0.3
Madison..............................	79.1	236	331	4 111	3 768.8	222.9	1 316	18 653	4 958.0	450.2	409	1 706	339.9	60.9
Marengo	25.1	1 191	19	151	105.9	5.3	102	883	199.7	17.8	10	72	20.9	2.9
Marion...............................	7.0	227	23	176	222.1	8.0	102	976	229.0	19.9	14	28	4.7	0.7
Marshall.............................	30.5	327	81	1 253	1 177.7	47.8	419	4 559	1 280.0	102.0	58	591	34.1	9.6
Mobile...............................	1 096.7	2 656	499	6 116	3 680.0	283.8	1 454	19 204	5 102.6	454.7	410	2 125	419.1	83.2
Monroe..............................	50.6	2 194	16	151	101.0	7.0	89	863	211.0	17.6	13	39	4.8	1.2
Montgomery	37.6	164	299	5 401	4 140.8	257.0	911	12 148	3 258.7	302.9	228	1 907	342.5	65.5
Morgan..............................	123.6	1 035	152	2 080	1 417.0	89.2	498	5 507	1 673.5	127.6	82	340	76.2	12.4
Perry.................................	10.8	1 023	5	59	14.7	1.5	32	174	34.7	3.6	4	D	D	D
Pickens..............................	6.2	312	10	69	29.8	2.2	59	427	100.6	9.0	2	D	D	D
Pike	7.8	237	29	D	D	D	143	1 465	373.6	31.3	26	91	17.8	2.0
Randolph............................	2.9	125	5	D	D	D	70	704	158.3	15.0	10	27	3.2	0.6
Russell...............................	40.7	768	13	D	D	D	155	1 810	499.7	40.7	39	D	D	D
St. Clair	18.1	216	69	1 160	476.4	49.2	223	2 613	704.4	56.9	36	101	22.6	3.3
Shelby	688.6	3 530	353	4 260	4 651.3	272.0	610	8 195	2 567.4	210.9	205	1 318	396.0	59.9
Sumter	8.6	628	11	105	60.2	3.5	46	283	62.1	4.4	7	16	1.9	0.3
Talladega............................	46.0	559	52	D	D	D	275	2 748	743.4	60.8	37	210	22.2	4.6
Tallapoosa..........................	12.1	290	20	D	D	D	169	1 503	361.8	32.3	27	92	20.9	3.6
Tuscaloosa..........................	39.2	202	143	1 681	1 180.8	83.5	733	9 622	2 619.3	218.3	182	1 485	164.6	44.3
Walker	955.0	14 248	44	406	279.4	18.2	297	3 216	963.5	78.7	38	158	28.5	5.5

1. Merchant wholesalers, except manufacturers' sales branches and offices.   2. Employer establishments.

— **Professional Services, Manufacturing, and Accommodation and Food Services**

STATE County	Professional, scientific, and technical services, 2012				Manufacturing, 2012				Accommodation and food services, 2012			
	Number of establish-ments	Number of employees	Receipts (mil dol)	Annual payroll (mil dol)	Number of establish-ments	Number of employees	Receipts (mil dol)	Annual payroll (mil dol)	Number of establish-ments	Number of employees	Sales (mil dol)	Annual payroll (mil dol)
	147	148	149	150	151	152	153	154	155	156	157	158
UNITED STATES............	856 463	8 203 735	1 480 277.1	581 406.1	297 191	11 214 165	5 696 729.6	593 397.0	662 489	12 007 689	708 138.6	196 103.3
ALABAMA	9 109	89 988	16 319.9	5 724.6	4 283	232 650	124 809.8	11 099.5	8 339	157 337	7 576.5	2 071.1
Autauga..............................	58	D	D	D	24	941	665.9	57.5	84	1 954	93.4	24.8
Baldwin..............................	450	1 899	211.5	86.2	146	3 780	1 438.8	166.8	462	10 726	560.6	161.1
Barbour..............................	39	105	16.6	3.9	25	2 837	735.1	103.3	49	596	26.2	6.4
Bibb	16	44	3.6	1.1	15	283	117.5	10.8	11	170	10.1	2.2
Blount	48	223	20.1	7.5	40	1 247	343.0	40.9	43	576	27.1	7.1
Bullock..............................	5	D	D	D	4	D	D	D	7	D	D	D
Butler................................	20	58	4.8	1.7	19	1 029	811.3	42.2	40	754	32.2	8.5
Calhoun.............................	167	1 140	137.1	43.1	114	5 957	2 713.2	256.9	212	4 673	199.1	53.0
Chambers..........................	32	134	15.4	4.3	21	1 513	474.0	58.3	49	566	30.3	7.5
Cherokee...........................	18	52	7.1	1.7	16	949	368.0	33.0	36	369	17.2	4.5
Chilton..............................	38	94	9.6	2.9	40	1 884	287.2	56.7	52	767	35.4	9.3
Choctaw	21	50	3.4	1.2	5	D	D	D	22	139	7.6	1.7
Clarke...............................	29	88	12.0	2.3	31	1 724	681.3	88.5	45	641	28.0	6.6
Clay..................................	11	56	3.5	1.6	10	1 161	D	40.9	10	117	4.8	1.2
Cleburne...........................	8	25	1.5	0.5	12	608	269.2	23.2	12	D	D	D
Coffee...............................	64	459	77.8	21.7	36	3 344	1 089.9	93.2	87	1 281	61.3	15.2
Colbert..............................	87	305	34.9	11.5	98	4 638	2 547.0	220.1	101	1 624	72.8	19.1
Conecuh............................	12	28	4.6	1.4	11	357	79.7	11.5	11	156	6.2	1.6
Coosa...............................	5	17	2.2	0.7	6	430	D	17.4	4	D	D	D
Covington	72	279	24.1	8.8	32	2 141	671.9	74.9	55	836	33.1	7.8
Crenshaw	12	32	2.9	0.8	9	1 082	D	38.7	12	D	D	D
Cullman.............................	110	455	40.2	13.4	105	4 041	1 880.8	175.9	131	2 298	111.2	29.7
Dale..................................	98	783	126.5	46.0	31	412	110.2	14.0	83	1 131	54.6	13.5
Dallas...............................	49	193	−14.1	5.4	41	3 065	1 309.9	131.0	52	873	36.1	8.7
DeKalb..............................	72	361	32.6	11.2	106	6 814	1 551.9	243.9	98	1 545	79.0	20.9
Elmore..............................	85	440	82.4	18.2	55	2 610	800.2	140.1	93	1 517	66.9	18.7
Escambia...........................	39	157	18.6	5.8	36	2 097	758.9	102.1	59	816	37.2	8.9
Etowah..............................	130	1 250	82.2	35.5	96	4 715	1 355.8	194.1	172	3 231	153.0	40.0
Fayette..............................	13	36	2.9	1.0	20	675	143.3	23.9	20	D	D	D
Franklin.............................	27	158	15.0	6.1	47	3 830	981.2	135.9	41	470	23.8	5.9
Geneva..............................	31	123	8.3	2.5	20	581	D	19.6	24	D	D	D
Greene..............................	3	D	D	D	7	379	102.2	12.5	2	D	D	D
Hale..................................	6	21	2.0	0.5	14	537	D	20.9	11	D	D	D
Henry................................	22	106	13.6	4.4	14	268	D	11.3	22	D	D	D
Houston.............................	208	1 130	140.6	52.7	98	3 985	1 390.8	151.8	234	4 602	213.0	57.0
Jackson.............................	60	243	23.4	8.7	69	5 196	1 540.4	196.5	75	1 151	49.0	12.7
Jefferson...........................	1 833	16 087	2 933.8	1 064.3	582	23 463	10 951.8	1 260.0	1 352	27 207	1 461.1	422.6
Lamar................................	15	50	3.7	1.7	16	1 035	334.2	48.5	18	D	D	D
Lauderdale	159	766	75.5	29.0	83	3 123	778.2	102.7	167	3 831	159.1	47.0
Lawrence...........................	32	122	15.7	6.6	20	1 039	D	D	41	D	D	D
Lee...................................	202	1 474	138.0	55.1	111	5 903	2 386.1	248.4	323	5 947	271.6	70.4
Limestone..........................	114	706	114.5	42.7	61	3 537	841.4	161.6	108	1 691	81.4	21.9
Lowndes............................	7	D	D	D	11	1 231	2 375.0	83.6	3	46	1.7	0.6
Macon...............................	13	D	D	D	9	728	D	25.3	29	509	29.0	8.0
Madison.............................	1 328	32 575	7 651.1	2 648.8	283	16 571	7 992.2	959.7	720	14 659	728.7	202.7
Marengo............................	17	80	10.0	2.9	23	1 356	557.0	63.5	41	466	20.3	5.1
Marion...............................	30	82	4.9	1.8	40	2 594	686.6	92.7	48	561	25.4	6.6
Marshall............................	124	558	50.7	18.8	107	10 666	3 234.5	327.5	180	2 936	124.4	33.9
Mobile...............................	850	9 039	1 175.1	474.0	343	16 063	10 562.7	886.3	671	13 684	617.9	167.9
Monroe..............................	17	41	4.8	1.3	17	975	423.0	67.1	30	361	15.3	3.8
Montgomery	606	6 178	1 307.8	403.9	197	12 585	10 786.6	615.4	491	9 986	474.5	130.9
Morgan..............................	198	1 361	152.1	62.7	182	11 009	D	D	202	D	D	D
Perry.................................	8	14	1.0	0.3	7	D	166.0	17.8	11	D	D	D
Pickens.............................	14	75	3.9	2.1	22	552	D	17.0	17	D	D	D
Pike	30	645	60.9	28.4	24	1 303	611.7	57.5	72	1 349	57.8	14.8
Randolph...........................	17	46	3.9	1.1	21	690	251.6	27.7	24	316	15.6	3.6
Russell..............................	51	215	17.5	5.1	42	2 697	1 209.2	130.6	77	1 440	70.2	16.7
St. Clair	98	648	63.4	17.4	77	2 884	931.3	134.8	120	1 969	89.8	24.7
Shelby	564	4 724	845.2	269.3	152	5 062	1 700.0	259.0	337	6 640	334.4	93.6
Sumter..............................	8	D	D	D	7	156	D	D	25	262	10.7	2.8
Talladega...........................	76	455	34.0	15.5	88	8 419	D	473.1	110	D	D	D
Tallapoosa.........................	52	216	26.2	9.2	30	2 239	456.3	79.3	57	863	37.0	10.6
Tuscaloosa........................	337	2 167	322.9	99.7	136	11 487	14 291.1	707.2	390	D	D	D
Walker	93	445	39.1	20.9	44	1 710	505.7	65.0	95	1 468	75.3	18.9

1. Establishment subject to federal tax.

Table B. States and Counties — Health Care and Social Assistance, Other Services, Nonemployer Businesses, and Residential Construction

STATE County	Health care and social assistance, 2012				Other services, 2012				Nonemployer businesses, 2015		Value of residential construction authorized by building permits, 2016	
	Number of establishments	Number of employees	Receipts (mil dol)	Annual payroll (mil dol)	Number of establishments	Number of employees	Receipts (mil dol)	Annual payroll (mil dol)	Number	Receipts (mil dol)	New Construction ($1,000)	Number of housing units
	159	160	161	162	163	164	165	166	167	168	169	170
UNITED STATES	831 303	18 414 757	2 040 441.2	801 239.5	529 691	3 430 711	426 693.7	108 185.7	24 331 403	1 148 715.5	237 101 606	1 206 642
ALABAMA	10 305	243 194	26 039.6	10 238.9	6 087	37 291	4 378.0	1 117.1	322 025	13 316.5	2 722 956	15 001
Autauga	95	1 580	119.4	46.2	58	D	D	D	3 149	116.1	45 256	169
Baldwin	444	7 029	622.5	265.3	269	1 203	110.5	31.9	17 876	863.8	490 227	2 520
Barbour	45	791	66.7	24.1	21	72	6.5	1.6	1 595	49.4	686	3
Bibb	29	D	D	D	20	D	D	D	1 177	49.6	2 356	10
Blount	48	D	D	D	64	D	D	D	3 609	136.3	2 815	14
Bullock	14	413	30.3	11.2	6	D	D	D	515	16.5	0	0
Butler	40	948	89.0	32.4	17	71	6.7	2.0	1 075	40.9	1 346	9
Calhoun	273	5 785	573.5	221.0	177	785	80.2	23.3	6 440	244.1	9 578	77
Chambers	59	1 247	99.1	40.9	33	141	12.2	3.7	2 347	58.8	1 832	12
Cherokee	41	406	35.7	14.7	19	73	5.9	1.7	1 509	70.6	609	6
Chilton	56	822	66.4	25.4	36	D	D	D	2 804	101.4	3 398	24
Choctaw	28	356	30.9	12.0	22	D	D	D	833	25.5	0	0
Clarke	53	882	68.2	29.3	36	126	11.5	3.0	1 592	56.9	919	5
Clay	21	D	D	D	11	D	D	D	767	32.7	0	0
Cleburne	10	D	D	D	9	45	4.8	1.3	931	36.0	170	1
Coffee	101	1 798	174.3	68.3	67	310	26.6	8.2	2 615	91.3	12 421	67
Colbert	128	2 620	281.6	110.9	71	D	D	D	3 627	137.7	16 250	136
Conecuh	16	336	31.6	12.9	14	D	D	D	668	20.9	175	2
Coosa	5	D	D	D	8	D	D	D	405	14.3	0	0
Covington	93	1 727	139.0	55.2	49	229	21.7	6.1	2 271	75.5	1 377	8
Crenshaw	14	489	28.7	14.4	13	D	D	D	863	28.6	870	4
Cullman	182	2 533	242.2	101.0	101	499	56.3	15.0	5 641	263.0	14 454	113
Dale	60	1 134	86.7	35.8	50	217	13.1	3.9	2 454	79.5	2 934	23
Dallas	102	2 011	173.5	65.6	51	375	30.0	8.3	2 384	73.9	3 337	25
DeKalb	123	2 294	189.2	73.9	51	181	16.8	5.0	4 616	201.5	3 473	22
Elmore	109	1 981	156.9	59.2	78	392	38.7	9.0	5 173	203.9	12 444	101
Escambia	67	1 265	105.7	42.7	46	198	17.7	4.3	2 127	63.3	1 260	9
Etowah	316	7 433	701.9	303.4	125	632	98.9	19.0	7 071	312.8	14 186	97
Fayette	50	801	54.1	23.5	22	D	D	D	1 075	36.5	600	2
Franklin	63	1 112	96.4	36.0	36	D	D	D	1 869	72.3	1 387	16
Geneva	33	632	42.9	19.4	20	D	D	D	1 615	63.4	1 403	10
Greene	13	290	16.8	7.9	5	D	D	D	476	14.6	522	5
Hale	17	445	28.1	11.0	7	10	1.2	0.2	747	24.7	940	6
Henry	28	466	22.4	10.9	16	D	D	D	1 062	37.4	2 519	19
Houston	314	9 145	1 061.9	455.9	185	1 056	115.5	27.6	7 183	332.3	68 154	331
Jackson	116	D	D	D	42	175	15.8	5.0	3 084	122.5	4 594	36
Jefferson	1 688	57 068	7 766.2	2 830.6	1 042	9 351	1 262.3	306.0	47 207	2 119.7	443 052	1 985
Lamar	22	346	18.6	8.5	11	D	D	D	991	41.5	0	0
Lauderdale	254	4 337	449.8	158.9	115	D	D	D	6 526	283.5	18 362	179
Lawrence	36	736	44.1	20.3	30	80	9.0	2.3	1 955	64.8	0	0
Lee	235	5 923	541.5	218.4	172	787	72.8	18.6	9 855	416.4	241 301	891
Limestone	121	2 163	170.1	74.9	82	512	46.6	13.8	5 768	214.5	22 347	117
Lowndes	5	90	5.5	2.3	4	D	D	D	661	20.2	0	0
Macon	24	D	D	D	15	D	D	D	1 042	26.0	255	1
Madison	932	21 762	2 475.1	985.4	474	3 503	570.6	126.8	23 532	947.8	361 782	2 875
Marengo	61	984	75.7	30.7	30	89	6.3	1.7	1 010	32.1	1 547	10
Marion	79	1 355	125.9	46.5	27	D	D	D	1 800	73.7	350	2
Marshall	191	3 727	336.0	124.7	84	370	26.4	7.4	7 150	330.6	6 777	38
Mobile	734	21 863	2 397.2	927.8	570	3 577	334.8	96.2	30 496	1 117.8	203 382	1 195
Monroe	30	709	50.6	21.3	18	D	D	D	1 303	46.2	0	0
Montgomery	666	16 589	1 780.7	762.2	429	3 172	404.6	113.9	15 560	678.6	95 438	535
Morgan	340	5 733	497.1	187.4	150	980	94.0	27.2	7 529	305.4	33 426	194
Perry	8	142	7.1	3.2	7	9	0.7	0.2	519	17.2	0	0
Pickens	25	705	44.7	20.6	17	D	D	D	1 067	35.4	1 584	9
Pike	63	1 156	91.7	39.4	39	139	10.2	2.8	1 800	70.5	4 454	33
Randolph	35	634	49.3	21.1	23	D	D	D	1 363	45.5	0	0
Russell	65	D	D	D	61	275	22.2	7.3	3 413	95.0	20 133	130
St. Clair	93	1 907	133.5	54.5	81	265	26.8	7.0	5 429	214.2	24 938	157
Shelby	439	6 297	583.4	240.5	281	1 792	215.0	56.1	16 644	862.6	246 648	1 114
Sumter	24	415	26.9	10.7	5	21	2.0	0.5	798	29.9	820	4
Talladega	160	D	D	D	66	D	D	D	3 994	153.6	11 569	72
Tallapoosa	88	2 181	186.3	78.2	44	169	14.8	3.9	2 500	112.5	28 056	114
Tuscaloosa	437	13 201	1 413.0	613.0	235	D	D	D	11 738	530.4	231 133	1 450
Walker	171	3 178	311.7	114.6	83	D	D	D	3 806	140.5	2 260	8

Table B. States and Counties — Government Employment and Payroll, and Local Government Finances

	Government employment and payroll, 2012									Local government finances, 2012				
			March payroll (percent of total)							General revenue				
												Taxes		
													Per capita[1] (dollars)	
STATE County	Full-time equivalent employees	March payroll (dollars)	Administration, judicial, and legal	Police and Corrections	Fire Protection	Highways and transportation	Health and Welfare	Natural resources and utilities	Education and libraries	Total (mil dol)	Inter-governmental (mil dol)	Total (mil dol)	Total	Property
	171	172	173	174	175	176	177	178	179	180	181	182	183	184
UNITED STATES......	X	X	X	X	X	X	X	X	X	X	X	X	X	X
ALABAMA	X	X	X	X	X	X	X	X	X	X	X	X	X	X
Autauga....................	1 582	5 202 816	4.0	9.6	6.8	2.7	1.7	5.0	67.1	125.4	65.8	41.7	751	262
Baldwin....................	7 374	22 581 577	7.4	8.0	2.9	4.3	20.7	5.6	47.7	640.7	189.9	231.1	1 211	537
Barbour....................	1 162	3 226 895	2.8	6.5	3.7	2.8	22.4	6.2	54.3	79.4	44.6	19.5	719	241
Bibb........................	837	2 413 468	3.7	5.9	0.0	3.6	26.0	2.1	58.0	59.5	31.7	7.9	351	147
Blount.....................	1 539	4 659 233	4.8	7.3	1.6	3.1	0.9	5.3	75.6	107.3	70.3	23.0	398	220
Bullock....................	552	1 468 315	4.4	5.2	0.0	4.7	37.7	0.1	46.6	28.4	20.9	4.8	454	337
Butler......................	934	2 423 650	4.8	7.9	2.9	6.4	14.6	5.7	55.8	65.7	35.4	23.2	1 142	306
Calhoun....................	5 708	17 129 463	3.6	6.8	2.8	2.8	32.2	7.0	43.2	507.7	169.3	112.4	958	366
Chambers..................	1 193	3 265 131	6.9	10.3	3.6	6.5	3.3	9.0	58.5	79.2	43.1	21.6	634	304
Cherokee...................	997	3 526 515	5.0	5.1	0.1	2.9	16.9	6.0	63.4	50.9	29.6	16.6	640	293
Chilton....................	1 218	3 862 506	5.9	8.9	0.5	4.3	1.4	6.0	72.4	95.1	55.9	25.1	572	321
Choctaw....................	383	970 992	9.1	5.8	0.0	6.4	0.0	1.9	74.4	27.8	15.9	7.3	536	470
Clarke.....................	1 107	3 358 366	4.7	9.6	0.0	3.2	12.7	8.4	59.5	70.9	38.1	25.5	1 015	336
Clay.......................	699	1 916 771	2.1	5.9	0.1	5.2	39.3	5.7	40.5	52.0	20.5	9.5	704	493
Cleburne...................	633	2 123 561	3.8	6.3	0.1	3.4	9.9	5.1	70.2	36.9	24.6	7.3	490	274
Coffee.....................	2 026	5 912 313	3.1	6.9	2.2	3.8	13.7	5.8	63.9	136.4	72.2	40.1	782	349
Colbert....................	3 178	10 303 212	2.2	5.5	2.5	2.4	36.7	11.6	37.7	258.1	88.3	46.3	850	424
Conecuh....................	486	1 319 565	6.8	10.8	0.0	6.5	1.3	10.9	62.6	33.3	20.8	7.6	588	279
Coosa......................	265	695 770	2.4	13.6	0.0	6.3	0.6	1.2	75.2	21.9	15.4	4.4	397	290
Covington..................	1 587	4 552 054	7.2	6.3	1.6	5.3	1.1	22.2	53.7	120.6	57.2	30.6	805	249
Crenshaw...................	472	1 600 404	4.4	5.5	0.0	6.3	0.9	7.4	75.5	27.8	16.6	6.6	471	206
Cullman....................	3 911	11 764 023	3.0	6.7	1.9	3.3	31.4	8.4	43.9	194.4	96.2	54.4	676	276
Dale.......................	1 600	4 956 908	3.8	7.4	2.7	2.6	26.4	5.1	50.9	131.8	55.8	34.7	688	250
Dallas.....................	1 746	4 733 521	4.8	9.2	3.2	2.5	1.5	6.4	67.0	113.7	68.6	33.9	791	371
DeKalb.....................	2 193	6 908 865	4.2	8.4	2.2	3.5	4.3	10.3	66.0	169.1	97.9	42.8	602	293
Elmore.....................	2 265	6 703 799	3.5	10.3	1.2	3.1	0.8	4.6	75.0	153.6	86.5	43.7	541	251
Escambia...................	1 604	4 378 782	4.5	9.0	2.3	4.4	15.2	2.8	58.4	116.3	47.9	27.6	726	330
Etowah.....................	3 980	11 900 349	4.3	10.5	6.2	3.7	6.9	8.4	56.6	284.1	137.1	99.7	955	293
Fayette....................	541	1 471 267	6.2	6.8	1.8	7.2	2.2	10.0	65.4	50.8	33.7	12.6	742	260
Franklin...................	1 331	3 838 038	4.8	7.1	2.1	3.7	3.3	12.5	65.2	84.8	50.1	15.5	488	176
Geneva.....................	1 102	3 351 087	3.2	5.0	0.1	3.9	27.3	3.4	56.6	106.8	34.4	20.2	751	302
Greene.....................	456	1 298 955	3.6	6.0	0.0	5.0	31.6	4.7	48.5	30.5	13.4	5.5	620	359
Hale.......................	605	1 537 609	4.7	7.4	0.0	3.8	23.7	1.0	59.3	51.7	27.1	9.4	613	301
Henry......................	549	1 493 829	6.9	8.0	2.0	5.6	2.8	4.3	68.4	33.3	19.9	9.4	546	269
Houston....................	5 714	19 682 365	3.7	6.6	3.6	2.3	45.1	5.9	30.9	590.6	124.8	126.4	1 222	429
Jackson....................	2 490	8 016 220	3.3	6.6	1.8	3.9	29.0	8.0	46.4	205.9	91.7	40.1	756	359
Jefferson..................	27 700	103 543 070	5.4	12.8	7.2	3.5	7.3	9.3	49.8	2 895.7	935.7	1 334.8	2 022	856
Lamar......................	454	1 337 464	7.1	9.0	0.8	4.9	2.6	9.6	64.8	31.4	20.5	6.5	457	274
Lauderdale.................	2 704	9 293 198	4.1	8.4	4.2	4.1	2.8	16.3	57.5	230.1	103.9	91.1	984	414
Lawrence...................	1 156	3 399 543	4.4	7.8	0.4	3.4	14.2	4.4	64.8	74.9	46.2	11.0	324	217
Lee........................	6 506	23 295 526	2.9	5.8	2.5	1.6	40.7	4.1	41.4	640.1	158.1	164.2	1 115	594
Limestone..................	2 694	10 450 795	2.4	6.2	1.4	1.9	21.8	7.7	57.3	213.7	86.7	39.0	445	236
Lowndes....................	502	1 360 565	8.1	8.4	0.0	4.3	0.5	2.4	75.6	38.0	25.6	9.0	830	443
Macon......................	731	2 048 937	7.8	7.7	2.4	4.5	1.6	16.0	58.1	49.6	28.9	15.3	746	268
Madison....................	17 330	64 421 407	3.9	6.3	3.3	2.9	40.3	7.4	32.3	1 978.9	813.4	389.2	1 134	579
Marengo....................	1 007	2 884 299	5.2	7.8	3.8	5.1	8.0	6.1	61.8	87.7	38.7	15.2	746	331
Marion.....................	992	2 975 924	4.1	7.5	1.3	5.2	1.2	15.9	64.8	75.9	39.2	22.6	745	282
Marshall...................	4 582	15 491 666	2.4	5.3	2.4	1.7	30.3	11.3	46.0	395.1	144.9	75.8	799	378
Mobile.....................	15 334	47 151 677	5.5	11.5	5.1	4.9	9.2	7.3	53.7	1 405.0	626.1	561.4	1 356	491
Monroe.....................	1 069	3 209 902	3.2	6.5	1.2	3.7	34.3	2.7	48.2	82.1	40.2	13.0	573	337
Montgomery	8 484	27 145 960	5.0	15.4	6.4	3.3	4.4	9.5	49.6	1 098.6	290.3	265.5	1 154	360
Morgan.....................	4 927	17 209 848	3.0	7.3	3.3	2.5	22.7	9.2	50.8	514.7	208.9	123.2	1 023	501
Perry......................	634	1 533 195	4.2	5.7	0.1	9.3	22.6	2.7	54.6	35.7	28.0	5.6	546	240
Pickens....................	699	1 770 074	5.4	8.5	0.0	6.6	2.9	6.6	68.1	65.0	32.5	7.6	389	243
Pike.......................	1 061	3 438 644	6.1	11.4	3.5	4.1	4.1	13.7	55.5	103.3	44.5	21.4	644	263
Randolph...................	771	2 493 832	3.6	8.3	0.1	4.4	13.3	1.8	67.8	67.1	30.1	11.3	500	257
Russell....................	2 491	7 257 682	19.9	8.4	3.1	2.7	1.7	7.6	53.3	148.3	81.2	49.2	851	413
St. Clair..................	2 191	7 157 617	7.3	9.7	4.9	3.2	0.1	3.1	71.1	184.8	107.5	55.3	649	287
Shelby.....................	5 778	16 879 679	6.7	14.3	5.9	3.1	2.9	4.8	60.5	441.4	172.8	191.6	954	567
Sumter.....................	560	1 553 057	5.4	7.7	1.9	5.9	1.9	7.7	67.6	34.6	20.5	8.9	664	293
Talladega..................	3 476	9 539 423	3.6	6.8	2.5	2.7	19.3	8.7	54.0	201.6	106.6	60.5	740	379
Tallapoosa.................	1 698	5 118 158	4.4	8.1	3.8	2.6	22.1	9.3	47.3	118.2	65.1	34.0	826	434
Tuscaloosa.................	10 215	37 068 838	3.6	7.2	3.6	3.5	48.2	3.7	29.3	991.4	234.1	212.4	1 070	420
Walker.....................	2 414	6 546 224	3.1	8.7	1.3	3.2	3.4	7.9	70.5	157.6	87.1	48.0	726	246

1. Based on the resident population estimated as of July 1 of the year shown.

— **Local Government Finances, Government Employment, and Income Taxes**

STATE County	Total (mil dol)	Per capita¹ (dollars)	Education	Health and hospitals	Police protection	Public welfare	Highways	Total (mil dol)	Per capita¹ (dollars)	Federal civilian	Federal military	State and local	Number of returns	Mean adjusted gross income	Mean income tax
	185	186	187	188	189	190	191	192	193	194	195	196	197	198	199
UNITED STATES	X	X	X	X	X	X	X	X	X	2 811 000	1 955 000	19 376 000	NA	NA	NA
ALABAMA	X	X	X	X	X	X	X	X	X	53 109	29 508	316 204	2 046 400	52 722	6 086
Autauga	119.9	2 161	60.8	0.1	7.0	0.5	2.9	149.8	2 699	78	247	2 158	23 820	51 951	5 003
Baldwin	700.0	3 669	34.5	19.2	6.1	0.1	7.7	911.0	4 775	334	898	8 876	90 890	57 717	7 109
Barbour	74.3	2 732	47.4	18.7	6.4	0.0	3.9	37.2	1 369	56	113	1 612	9 730	38 497	3 258
Bibb	57.9	2 564	51.4	26.2	4.4	0.0	4.1	55.2	2 445	77	90	1 199	7 980	45 825	4 466
Blount	108.1	1 870	72.0	0.8	5.8	0.3	6.1	48.6	841	89	254	1 833	21 900	47 095	4 256
Bullock	30.6	2 921	53.3	22.5	3.6	0.7	8.6	14.8	1 416	36	40	687	3 820	32 268	2 319
Butler	60.7	2 987	47.3	9.6	5.4	0.5	9.3	65.0	3 202	40	88	906	8 320	40 126	3 704
Calhoun	517.7	4 414	32.7	36.2	5.9	0.0	3.9	358.0	3 052	3 745	569	8 416	48 040	44 419	4 104
Chambers	78.6	2 308	50.4	1.2	8.3	0.3	7.0	72.0	2 112	50	150	1 830	14 690	35 135	2 493
Cherokee	48.3	1 856	75.1	0.1	4.8	0.0	4.5	60.1	2 309	48	114	1 241	9 180	41 957	3 600
Chilton	96.3	2 198	62.9	0.6	7.0	0.4	5.7	23.3	533	62	194	1 742	17 430	43 849	3 855
Choctaw	28.4	2 080	53.7	0.0	6.0	0.1	13.4	22.9	1 681	25	58	469	5 230	47 036	4 162
Clarke	67.0	2 664	60.9	0.3	7.8	0.2	6.2	111.3	4 422	81	108	1 722	10 280	47 029	4 676
Clay	70.4	5 240	51.0	26.2	4.1	0.1	4.4	26.5	1 971	51	59	898	5 460	40 641	3 362
Cleburne	41.7	2 813	52.6	0.1	4.4	17.0	6.0	35.4	2 387	42	66	731	5 700	43 606	3 627
Coffee	144.1	2 812	62.6	0.4	4.8	0.2	4.8	136.0	2 654	231	225	2 320	21 010	52 755	5 639
Colbert	259.3	4 762	32.1	37.0	3.6	0.2	3.5	178.7	3 282	689	240	4 119	23 690	49 362	5 387
Conecuh	37.1	2 859	59.4	0.0	8.0	0.6	6.4	64.7	4 982	29	56	709	4 910	37 252	3 002
Coosa	22.3	2 029	59.1	0.1	7.7	0.2	19.6	8.9	810	19	47	347	4 000	40 779	3 201
Covington	141.5	3 727	42.0	0.3	6.6	0.1	12.6	930.5	24 517	114	166	2 046	15 010	45 550	4 475
Crenshaw	29.8	2 119	65.1	6.8	9.7	0.0	3.3	16.9	1 199	37	62	578	5 760	41 401	3 540
Cullman	206.4	2 566	52.3	2.1	7.2	1.1	7.3	191.6	2 381	209	360	4 240	33 260	47 359	4 800
Dale	146.4	2 902	56.7	19.7	4.5	0.2	2.5	62.7	1 242	3 059	3 757	2 078	20 080	43 848	3 910
Dallas	143.5	3 347	61.4	0.1	8.3	0.4	3.2	105.2	2 455	161	179	2 637	16 500	36 502	2 996
DeKalb	174.9	2 461	64.2	3.0	8.3	0.4	7.1	113.8	1 602	162	313	3 196	26 820	38 567	3 170
Elmore	159.9	1 983	65.0	0.8	7.4	0.0	7.2	169.3	2 100	142	338	4 504	34 760	52 954	5 215
Escambia	124.2	3 269	45.2	24.5	6.3	0.4	4.3	40.7	1 071	57	153	4 129	14 360	43 659	4 188
Etowah	278.9	2 672	46.7	1.9	11.2	0.2	4.8	218.9	2 097	290	449	5 080	41 710	44 077	4 205
Fayette	33.4	1 968	66.1	1.2	2.5	0.0	10.0	12.4	731	36	73	1 242	6 250	41 997	3 446
Franklin	94.1	2 961	58.5	0.1	4.4	0.0	6.5	55.6	1 752	90	140	1 406	12 320	39 288	3 451
Geneva	79.5	2 953	44.2	28.4	5.0	0.2	5.9	34.0	1 262	56	118	1 406	10 220	38 924	3 334
Greene	31.5	3 551	49.2	28.3	3.2	0.5	3.8	17.4	1 960	23	38	643	3 480	30 236	1 918
Hale	48.8	3 170	51.5	17.8	6.3	0.0	12.3	13.5	876	49	66	851	6 390	36 568	2 698
Henry	34.2	1 979	64.6	0.0	6.7	0.7	13.2	44.3	2 565	44	76	633	7 050	43 520	4 037
Houston	591.0	5 716	25.3	46.6	3.9	0.1	3.3	407.2	3 938	299	491	8 255	44 650	50 467	6 156
Jackson	209.8	3 957	51.6	23.7	4.0	0.3	4.2	118.1	2 227	256	230	3 059	21 140	44 103	4 229
Jefferson	2 885.7	4 372	40.1	5.3	6.6	0.0	4.0	7 596.1	11 509	8 158	3 229	50 769	295 560	63 289	8 868
Lamar	32.3	2 262	61.7	0.0	6.4	0.4	4.7	29.7	2 081	39	61	564	5 290	41 248	3 230
Lauderdale	225.0	2 431	58.9	0.1	6.2	0.1	6.7	265.7	2 871	276	407	4 750	38 140	52 210	5 876
Lawrence	78.1	2 309	60.0	13.5	6.3	0.5	6.4	41.6	1 229	81	146	1 275	13 540	44 415	3 975
Lee	638.8	4 408	33.9	39.7	4.1	0.0	2.6	782.4	5 313	288	726	16 744	61 750	53 067	5 827
Limestone	276.5	3 155	51.2	23.1	4.8	0.2	3.7	282.8	3 227	1 548	395	5 272	37 590	57 861	6 299
Lowndes	39.8	3 667	69.6	0.0	5.6	0.0	9.7	34.2	3 148	28	46	519	4 960	35 753	2 765
Macon	52.1	2 539	58.2	0.3	5.4	0.0	2.5	68.8	3 349	873	85	2 094	8 180	32 924	2 509
Madison	1 830.4	5 335	30.6	39.1	3.7	0.0	2.5	1 931.7	5 631	17 900	2 334	24 094	163 260	65 773	8 568
Marengo	94.5	4 633	40.6	31.0	3.2	0.0	2.7	33.7	1 651	55	104	1 497	8 350	44 302	4 201
Marion	72.1	2 379	61.7	0.0	6.4	0.0	5.4	62.6	2 065	75	130	1 476	10 760	41 184	3 648
Marshall	395.8	4 177	40.0	33.4	5.5	0.2	1.9	306.5	3 234	266	417	5 838	39 280	44 248	4 462
Mobile	1 433.8	3 464	41.2	6.0	6.8	0.5	8.3	1 386.2	3 349	2 601	2 687	23 168	176 120	48 416	5 469
Monroe	83.9	3 713	40.0	33.9	5.1	0.1	8.3	7.6	334	53	95	1 387	8 330	44 991	4 598
Montgomery	1 084.1	4 711	25.4	43.2	5.2	0.3	2.1	1 050.3	4 564	6 152	3 563	26 297	100 620	51 755	6 261
Morgan	592.0	4 917	54.2	17.4	4.2	0.3	2.9	883.2	7 336	312	524	6 559	52 650	50 945	5 363
Perry	37.4	3 675	46.2	24.5	3.6	0.4	7.2	37.3	3 663	25	85	513	3 740	30 775	1 998
Pickens	72.8	3 752	37.4	29.1	3.2	0.1	5.3	52.7	2 716	304	83	906	7 530	40 058	3 371
Pike	119.3	3 594	39.5	22.5	7.4	0.0	3.2	140.0	4 218	95	142	3 120	12 620	43 754	4 766
Randolph	70.0	3 087	46.0	32.1	4.6	0.0	1.9	57.2	2 521	56	99	1 124	8 970	41 268	3 431
Russell	149.9	2 593	59.3	0.1	5.7	0.1	3.0	302.5	5 233	94	263	2 809	23 780	36 991	2 879
St. Clair	188.6	2 213	57.2	6.9	10.0	0.1	4.2	290.2	3 404	112	379	2 772	35 230	50 936	4 959
Shelby	463.8	2 308	61.2	1.7	10.9	0.2	3.8	773.4	3 849	358	916	8 220	92 570	75 792	10 660
Sumter	37.0	2 754	54.6	0.8	7.3	0.1	13.6	25.2	1 879	38	55	1 217	5 100	34 275	2 910
Talladega	213.4	2 610	55.2	4.8	7.5	0.4	5.6	225.8	2 762	464	346	4 578	32 740	42 242	3 746
Tallapoosa	123.8	3 008	45.4	17.8	6.1	0.0	4.1	118.8	2 886	87	179	1 986	17 270	43 703	4 032
Tuscaloosa	994.6	5 008	29.0	43.5	4.8	0.0	4.7	615.9	3 101	1 547	871	22 627	81 530	54 049	6 364
Walker	158.5	2 394	61.5	0.1	5.4	0.0	8.0	116.9	1 765	186	288	3 076	25 260	45 114	4 343

1. Based on the resident population estimated as of July 1 of the year shown.

Table B. States and Counties — **Land Area and Population**

STATE/ County code	CBSA code[1]	County type[2]	STATE County	Land area,[3] (sq mi) 2016	Total persons 2016	Rank	Per square mile	White	Black	American Indian, Alaska Native	Asian and Pacific Islander	Percent Hispanic or Latino[4]	Under 5 years	5 to 17 years	18 to 24 years	25 to 34 years	35 to 44 years	45 to 54 years
				1	2	3	4	5	6	7	8	9	10	11	12	13	14	15
			ALABAMA—Cont'd															
01 129	...	8	Washington	1 080.2	16 756	1 995	15.5	65.8	24.2	8.4	1.6	1.4	5.4	17.6	8.5	11.0	11.4	14.2
01 131	...	9	Wilcox	888.5	10 986	2 356	12.4	28.2	70.4	0.5	0.4	1.2	6.4	18.0	9.3	10.4	11.0	12.2
01 133	...	6	Winston	613.0	23 805	1 648	38.8	95.2	1.2	1.3	0.6	3.0	5.2	15.6	7.1	10.6	11.5	14.6
02 000	...	0	ALASKA	570 638.3	741 894	X	1.3	67.1	4.7	18.7	9.7	7.0	7.3	18.0	10.1	16.2	12.4	12.7
02 013	...	9	Aleutians East	6 982.0	3 296	2 954	0.5	13.3	10.2	20.2	46.1	13.5	2.4	6.5	10.7	16.1	20.1	22.6
02 016	...	9	Aleutians West	4 390.3	5 647	2 788	1.3	27.3	7.9	13.0	42.0	13.9	2.8	8.9	8.9	17.6	18.7	21.1
02 020	11260	2	Anchorage	1 706.6	298 192	231	174.7	64.9	7.4	11.9	14.8	9.0	7.3	17.5	10.5	17.5	12.7	12.7
02 050	...	7	Bethel	40 570.1	17 968	1 922	0.4	13.2	1.2	85.5	1.8	2.3	11.2	24.8	10.6	15.5	10.3	10.8
02 060	...	9	Bristol Bay	503.9	898	3 111	1.8	59.2	2.6	46.1	4.0	4.6	5.6	13.6	10.1	14.4	11.8	15.3
02 068	...	8	Denali	12 747.6	1 953	3 052	0.2	86.4	2.0	7.8	5.0	3.0	4.9	13.3	7.1	15.8	15.4	17.7
02 070	...	9	Dillingham	18 568.7	4 954	2 837	0.3	24.5	1.4	77.3	2.5	3.3	9.8	21.7	10.8	15.2	9.7	11.8
02 090	21820	3	Fairbanks North Star	7 343.3	100 605	594	13.7	75.8	6.3	10.7	5.7	7.9	7.8	16.6	13.9	18.8	12.1	10.8
02 100	...	9	Haines	2 320.2	2 496	3 006	1.1	84.9	1.6	15.4	2.6	3.1	3.7	14.3	6.2	10.8	10.1	15.3
02 105	...	9	Hoonah-Angoon	6 550.8	2 078	3 040	0.3	54.9	2.1	44.5	3.1	5.5	4.7	14.9	6.0	10.4	9.8	15.5
02 110	27940	5	Juneau	2 702.0	32 468	1 370	12.0	72.2	2.1	17.6	11.1	6.7	6.0	16.0	9.0	15.6	12.9	14.3
02 122	...	7	Kenai Peninsula	16 075.1	58 506	883	3.6	85.8	1.2	11.6	3.0	4.2	6.2	16.6	8.1	12.8	11.5	13.0
02 130	28540	7	Ketchikan Gateway	4 858.4	13 746	2 185	2.8	72.0	1.5	20.0	10.9	4.6	6.0	16.3	8.3	13.5	12.0	14.2
02 150	...	7	Kodiak Island	6 550.4	13 732	2 187	2.1	55.7	1.5	16.4	24.0	9.3	7.7	18.6	9.2	16.1	13.0	12.9
02 158	...	0	Kusilvak	17 081.4	8 049	2 594	0.5	5.8	0.6	93.8	0.7	1.5	13.0	27.8	11.6	15.4	8.6	9.6
02 164	...	9	Lake and Peninsula	23 450.2	1 562	3 076	0.1	31.8	2.6	69.9	3.5	2.9	9.2	19.2	10.3	14.8	12.6	11.1
02 170	11260	2	Matanuska-Susitna	24 607.9	104 365	577	4.2	85.6	2.0	10.8	3.7	4.8	7.2	20.0	8.7	14.3	13.1	13.0
02 180	...	7	Nome	22 963.0	9 917	2 438	0.4	20.4	1.0	80.4	2.4	2.3	10.6	24.7	10.1	15.3	10.8	10.8
02 185	...	7	North Slope	88 839.0	9 606	2 460	0.1	35.4	2.1	54.3	9.6	4.1	7.8	18.2	7.8	17.0	12.7	16.8
02 188	...	7	Northwest Arctic	35 635.4	7 673	2 616	0.2	16.2	1.7	83.5	2.1	2.5	10.8	25.0	10.4	15.9	10.3	11.0
02 195	...	9	Petersburg	2 917.6	3 149	2 959	1.1	77.6	2.7	15.1	5.4	6.1	6.6	15.9	8.4	12.0	11.8	14.3
02 198	...	9	Prince of Wales-Hyder	5 262.0	6 347	2 727	1.2	52.3	1.6	47.9	3.2	4.0	6.1	18.1	7.3	12.7	11.2	15.1
02 220	...	7	Sitka	2 870.4	8 830	2 520	3.1	68.9	1.9	21.3	10.1	6.9	5.0	17.3	7.8	14.1	14.0	12.5
02 230	...	9	Skagway	452.3	1 088	3 105	2.4	86.1	1.5	7.9	4.1	5.1	4.5	9.7	6.3	19.9	18.2	15.0
02 240	...	9	Southeast Fairbanks	24 767.6	6 876	2 685	0.3	78.3	2.5	15.4	3.0	5.7	7.3	18.4	7.9	13.5	12.1	13.2
02 261	...	9	Valdez-Cordova	34 238.3	9 355	2 477	0.3	75.8	1.4	18.3	6.3	4.7	6.6	17.3	7.7	13.5	11.8	14.2
02 275	...	9	Wrangell	2 541.5	2 411	3 012	0.9	77.0	2.1	24.1	5.5	2.4	5.2	15.6	7.8	10.2	8.7	13.1
02 282	...	9	Yakutat	7 649.5	601	3 133	0.1	46.3	6.8	47.1	11.0	4.5	6.7	13.5	10.3	12.3	10.8	16.8
02 290	...	9	Yukon-Koyukuk	145 493.0	5 526	2 800	0.0	26.6	1.3	74.0	1.4	2.4	8.0	19.7	8.5	13.1	10.6	10.8
04 000	...	0	ARIZONA	113 590.7	6 931 071	X	61.0	57.2	5.0	4.6	4.3	30.9	6.3	17.2	9.7	13.5	12.2	12.2
04 001	...	6	Apache	11 197.5	73 112	746	6.5	19.1	1.1	74.7	0.7	5.9	6.9	21.9	9.8	12.2	10.7	12.1
04 003	43420	3	Cochise	6 164.6	125 770	499	20.4	57.7	4.8	1.6	3.4	35.0	6.1	15.9	8.6	12.5	10.8	11.3
04 005	22380	3	Coconino	18 618.7	140 908	457	7.6	56.8	1.9	27.1	2.9	13.8	5.8	15.4	20.0	13.6	10.7	10.6
04 007	37740	4	Gila	4 758.0	53 556	938	11.3	63.8	0.9	16.8	1.1	18.6	5.9	14.5	6.7	9.7	8.3	11.2
04 009	40940	7	Graham	4 622.7	37 599	1 233	8.1	52.1	2.1	13.4	1.2	32.6	7.5	20.4	10.3	15.0	12.8	10.8
04 011	...	7	Greenlee	1 842.0	9 613	2 459	5.2	49.0	2.1	3.4	1.2	46.1	7.7	20.6	9.0	14.9	12.7	11.8
04 012	...	6	La Paz	4 499.6	20 317	1 818	4.5	59.5	1.4	13.3	1.1	26.9	4.9	12.3	6.3	8.6	7.6	9.2
04 013	38060	1	Maricopa	9 199.2	4 242 997	4	461.2	58.0	6.2	2.2	5.2	30.7	6.6	17.9	9.3	14.4	13.0	12.8
04 015	29420	3	Mohave	13 311.1	205 249	320	15.4	79.3	1.5	2.9	1.9	16.2	4.5	13.5	6.5	10.0	9.0	11.8
04 017	43320	4	Navajo	9 949.9	110 026	548	11.1	42.6	1.3	45.4	1.1	11.2	7.2	20.1	8.7	12.0	10.5	11.6
04 019	46060	2	Pima	9 187.2	1 016 206	44	110.6	54.2	4.1	3.1	3.9	36.8	5.8	15.6	12.0	12.3	11.2	11.4
04 021	38060	1	Pinal	5 365.8	418 540	165	78.0	59.4	5.2	5.3	2.7	29.4	5.9	17.5	7.7	13.0	13.0	11.1
04 023	35700	4	Santa Cruz	1 236.9	45 985	1 049	37.2	15.4	0.5	0.5	0.6	83.3	6.9	20.7	9.7	10.4	10.7	11.9
04 025	39140	3	Yavapai	8 123.5	225 562	292	27.8	82.3	1.1	2.3	1.7	14.4	4.3	12.4	6.6	9.1	8.7	11.3
04 027	49740	3	Yuma	5 514.0	205 631	319	37.3	32.9	2.3	1.4	1.8	62.8	7.3	18.1	11.6	13.5	10.7	10.6
05 000	...	0	ARKANSAS	52 035.6	2 988 248	X	57.4	74.6	16.2	1.6	2.2	7.3	6.4	17.2	9.4	13.1	12.2	12.7
05 001	...	6	Arkansas	988.8	18 214	1 905	18.4	71.6	24.9	0.8	1.1	3.1	6.8	16.1	7.9	11.2	12.0	12.7
05 003	...	7	Ashley	925.3	20 492	1 799	22.1	69.2	25.5	0.9	0.4	5.2	6.0	17.2	7.7	10.8	11.7	13.3
05 005	34260	3	Baxter	554.3	41 062	1 152	74.1	96.2	0.5	1.7	0.8	2.3	4.5	13.3	5.7	9.4	9.0	12.0
05 007	22220	2	Benton	847.5	258 291	263	304.8	76.2	2.2	2.7	4.9	16.4	7.1	19.6	8.1	14.6	14.1	12.8
05 009	25460	7	Boone	590.3	37 304	1 241	63.2	95.7	0.6	2.0	1.0	2.4	6.2	16.3	7.7	11.6	11.5	12.9
05 011	...	7	Bradley	649.2	10 996	2 355	16.9	56.7	28.3	0.9	0.5	14.9	6.2	17.7	7.5	11.6	11.9	13.0
05 013	15780	9	Calhoun	628.6	5 144	2 823	8.2	73.9	22.2	1.1	0.6	3.9	4.8	13.5	8.4	11.4	10.2	15.2
05 015	...	6	Carroll	630.0	27 646	1 507	43.9	82.0	0.9	2.2	1.8	15.0	5.6	16.5	6.9	10.6	10.8	12.3
05 017	...	7	Chicot	644.3	10 945	2 359	17.0	40.0	54.1	0.6	0.7	5.5	5.8	17.1	8.2	11.1	11.1	12.1
05 019	11660	7	Clark	866.1	22 657	1 700	26.2	70.2	24.6	1.1	0.9	4.8	5.3	13.8	21.7	10.7	9.9	10.8
05 021	...	7	Clay	639.4	14 920	2 104	23.3	96.9	1.1	1.1	0.3	1.9	5.3	15.6	7.7	11.0	11.6	13.7
05 023	...	6	Cleburne	553.7	25 264	1 597	45.6	96.2	0.7	1.6	0.6	2.3	4.6	14.6	6.4	9.9	10.4	13.0

1. CBSA = Core Based Statistical Area. See Appendix A for explanation. See Appendix B for list of metropolitan areas with component counties. 2. County type code from the Economic Research Service of USDA Rural-Urban Continuum Codes. See Appendix A for definition. 3. Dry land or land partially or temporarily covered by water. 4. May be of any race.

Table B. States and Counties — Population and Households

STATE County	55 to 64 years	65 to 74 years	75 years and over	Percent female	2000	2010	2000–2010	2010–2016	Births	Deaths	Net migration	Number	Persons per house-hold	Family house-holds	Female family house-holder[1]	One per-son
	16	17	18	19	20	21	22	23	24	25	26	27	28	29	30	31
ALABAMA—Cont'd																
Washington	14.1	10.7	7.1	51.0	18 097	17 583	-2.8	-4.7	1 070	1 238	-641	6 133	2.75	73.3	12.6	24.0
Wilcox	13.8	10.9	7.9	52.4	13 183	11 665	-11.5	-5.8	856	930	-619	3 843	2.86	63.2	24.4	34.1
Winston	14.4	12.5	8.5	50.6	24 843	24 484	-1.4	-2.8	1 525	1 920	-231	9 406	2.53	68.0	10.6	29.7
ALASKA	12.8	7.1	3.3	47.7	626 932	710 249	13.3	4.5	71 088	25 713	-13 454	250 969	2.81	66.8	11.2	25.7
Aleutians East	14.7	4.4	2.5	32.2	2 697	3 141	16.5	4.9	95	36	87	690	2.43	61.4	14.8	28.7
Aleutians West	15.7	5.2	1.1	33.0	5 465	5 561	1.8	1.5	198	67	-54	1 138	3.59	60.5	9.1	29.5
Anchorage	12.0	6.6	3.3	49.0	260 283	291 826	12.1	2.2	29 227	10 047	-12 561	105 175	2.77	66.2	12.3	25.7
Bethel	9.9	4.8	2.3	48.3	16 006	17 013	6.3	5.6	2 725	734	-1 026	4 488	3.86	74.9	17.7	16.7
Bristol Bay	18.3	6.9	4.1	46.0	1 258	997	-20.7	-9.9	70	46	-122	377	2.50	64.7	9.0	27.9
Denali	17.4	6.0	2.5	45.5	1 893	1 822	-3.8	7.2	127	43	31	681	2.34	59.5	3.5	33.0
Dillingham	12.4	5.5	3.2	49.1	4 922	4 847	-1.5	2.2	630	248	-276	1 349	3.56	70.3	17.0	27.0
Fairbanks North Star	11.1	6.2	2.7	45.9	82 840	97 585	17.8	3.1	10 636	2 895	-4 733	35 582	2.69	64.1	9.6	27.5
Haines	20.4	13.6	5.6	50.6	2 392	2 508	4.8	-0.5	118	111	-7	1 176	2.12	57.8	7.0	29.3
Hoonah-Angoon	20.9	11.9	5.9	47.9	NA	2 135	NA	-2.7	132	75	-124	892	2.26	62.0	10.2	32.7
Juneau	14.5	8.1	3.6	49.1	30 711	31 275	1.8	3.8	2 469	1 115	-85	12 114	2.62	65.9	11.2	26.2
Kenai Peninsula	16.4	10.6	4.9	47.6	49 691	55 400	11.5	5.6	4 482	2 534	1 253	21 485	2.57	64.0	8.3	29.7
Ketchikan Gateway	15.8	9.2	4.7	48.4	14 070	13 491	-4.1	1.9	1 105	550	-257	5 267	2.55	61.8	10.3	29.1
Kodiak Island	12.6	6.9	3.0	46.9	13 913	13 606	-2.2	0.9	1 407	356	-915	4 577	2.98	75.0	12.2	21.2
Kusilvak	8.3	4.0	1.8	47.8	7 028	7 459	6.1	7.9	1 416	429	-403	1 683	4.65	84.8	25.8	13.4
Lake and Peninsula	13.7	6.1	2.9	48.1	1 823	1 635	-10.3	-4.5	192	81	-186	491	2.90	68.2	17.5	27.1
Matanuska-Susitna	13.2	7.3	3.2	47.7	59 322	88 995	50.0	17.3	8 714	3 372	9 855	31 098	3.03	71.8	8.6	21.7
Nome	9.8	5.2	2.5	47.5	9 196	9 492	3.2	4.5	1 430	472	-550	2 925	3.26	75.1	18.9	20.9
North Slope	14.6	3.7	1.4	37.6	7 385	9 430	27.7	1.9	1 071	296	-561	1 962	3.28	75.8	23.2	19.6
Northwest Arctic	9.3	4.4	3.0	45.8	7 208	7 523	4.4	2.0	1 167	309	-709	1 903	3.97	79.7	20.7	14.9
Petersburg	16.8	9.8	4.2	47.3	NA	3 207	NA	-1.8	248	99	-201	1 284	2.40	62.5	9.4	26.6
Prince of Wales-Hyder	17.1	8.7	3.5	45.4	NA	6 172	NA	2.8	494	258	-23	2 268	2.77	63.1	11.6	30.1
Sitka	14.7	8.7	5.9	48.4	8 835	8 881	0.5	-0.6	600	391	-259	3 472	2.49	59.9	7.3	32.2
Skagway	15.3	7.4	3.6	48.2	NA	968	NA	12.4	64	15	78	406	2.15	49.3	4.4	35.0
Southeast Fairbanks	14.6	8.9	4.1	44.6	6 174	7 029	13.8	-2.2	718	270	-589	2 117	3.11	69.0	7.1	27.5
Valdez-Cordova	18.1	7.9	3.0	47.9	10 195	9 636	-5.5	-2.9	796	354	-715	3 010	3.10	69.5	11.1	24.4
Wrangell	20.9	11.7	6.8	48.4	NA	2 365	NA	1.9	154	112	2	1 127	2.08	55.4	7.0	35.8
Yakutat	15.3	8.7	5.7	43.8	808	662	-18.1	-9.2	51	15	-100	250	2.32	63.2	14.8	33.2
Yukon-Koyukuk	14.1	9.7	5.6	46.6	6 551	5 588	-14.7	-1.1	552	383	-304	1 982	2.81	62.9	17.0	31.9
ARIZONA	12.0	9.9	7.0	50.3	5 130 632	6 392 301	24.6	8.4	539 307	320 404	305 233	2 412 212	2.69	65.6	12.7	27.3
Apache	12.3	8.5	5.7	50.8	69 423	71 516	3.0	2.2	6 306	3 670	-960	19 272	3.67	68.7	21.6	27.5
Cochise	13.4	12.2	9.0	49.0	117 755	131 356	11.6	-4.3	10 347	7 775	-8 261	48 825	2.42	65.9	12.0	28.9
Coconino	11.9	7.6	4.3	50.7	116 320	134 437	15.6	4.8	10 636	4 778	556	46 619	2.70	64.1	13.0	23.7
Gila	15.9	16.4	11.5	50.4	51 335	53 597	4.4	-0.1	3 883	4 652	683	20 909	2.50	66.0	12.2	28.9
Graham	10.3	7.5	5.5	46.4	33 489	37 220	11.1	1.0	3 601	1 707	-1 520	10 959	3.02	70.9	12.2	25.6
Greenlee	11.4	6.8	5.1	48.3	8 547	8 437	-1.3	13.9	803	357	733	3 219	2.78	71.9	14.4	22.5
La Paz	13.4	19.1	18.7	49.0	19 715	20 489	3.9	-0.8	1 248	1 450	-15	9 365	2.14	60.5	9.3	33.3
Maricopa	11.4	8.5	6.1	50.6	3 072 149	3 817 357	24.3	11.2	342 110	172 943	248 848	1 442 518	2.75	65.5	12.8	27.1
Mohave	16.2	16.7	11.9	49.6	155 032	200 185	29.1	2.5	11 655	16 725	9 221	80 832	2.43	63.7	10.8	28.2
Navajo	12.9	10.4	6.5	49.9	97 470	107 489	10.3	2.4	10 151	5 886	-1 839	34 129	3.08	71.2	18.4	25.1
Pima	12.6	10.9	8.2	50.8	843 746	980 263	16.2	3.7	74 431	56 200	16 140	389 658	2.49	61.6	12.8	30.7
Pinal	11.7	12.4	7.6	48.1	179 727	375 770	109.1	11.4	28 917	16 536	28 105	127 599	2.87	71.6	11.9	23.6
Santa Cruz	12.4	10.1	7.2	52.2	38 381	47 420	23.6	-3.0	4 075	1 783	-3 869	15 359	3.04	75.3	16.0	21.2
Yavapai	17.5	18.0	12.1	51.2	167 517	211 015	26.0	6.9	11 670	17 156	19 101	92 310	2.30	63.4	9.4	30.1
Yuma	9.8	9.4	9.0	48.5	160 026	195 750	22.3	5.0	19 474	8 786	-1 690	70 639	2.77	76.8	12.9	19.0
ARKANSAS	12.7	9.5	6.8	50.9	2 673 400	2 916 025	9.1	2.5	238 842	187 626	21 775	1 138 025	2.53	66.8	13.2	28.2
Arkansas	14.9	10.3	8.2	51.8	20 749	19 018	-8.3	-4.2	1 541	1 448	-839	7 743	2.39	63.3	13.1	32.4
Ashley	13.9	11.6	7.7	51.3	24 209	21 853	-9.7	-6.2	1 615	1 573	-1 376	8 327	2.52	70.3	14.3	27.3
Baxter	15.5	16.7	13.9	51.6	38 386	41 513	8.1	-1.1	2 199	4 152	1 495	18 164	2.23	65.8	9.4	30.0
Benton	10.6	7.7	5.4	50.4	153 406	221 364	44.3	16.7	21 256	10 351	25 362	85 670	2.75	74.2	9.8	21.1
Boone	13.5	11.4	9.0	50.7	33 948	36 903	8.7	1.1	2 767	2 685	353	14 961	2.45	69.3	10.5	26.7
Bradley	13.5	10.1	8.5	51.2	12 600	11 508	-8.7	-4.4	853	942	-401	4 598	2.39	67.4	16.1	30.2
Calhoun	15.7	11.4	7.3	49.5	5 744	5 368	-6.5	-4.2	295	337	-200	2 125	2.40	71.4	10.5	27.4
Carroll	15.4	13.5	8.5	50.8	25 357	27 443	8.2	0.7	1 919	1 851	252	10 977	2.49	66.0	9.0	28.9
Chicot	15.2	10.1	9.4	50.4	14 117	11 800	-16.4	-7.2	876	953	-746	4 513	2.36	66.2	18.9	33.0
Clark	11.3	8.9	7.5	52.5	23 546	22 993	-2.3	-1.5	1 521	1 586	-283	8 681	2.28	61.4	14.1	33.6
Clay	13.5	12.1	9.6	51.0	17 609	16 083	-8.7	-7.2	843	1 474	-492	6 611	2.31	65.0	11.1	30.6
Cleburne	15.0	14.1	12.0	50.6	24 046	25 969	8.0	-2.7	1 508	2 270	81	10 157	2.50	68.8	9.7	28.1

1. No spouse present.

Table B. States and Counties — **Population, Vital Statistics, Health, and Crime**

STATE County	Daytime population, 2011–2015 Persons in group quarters, 2016	Daytime population, 2011–2015 Number	Daytime population, 2011–2015 Employ-ment/resi-dence ratio	Births, 2016 Total	Births, 2016 Rate[1]	Deaths, 2016 Number	Deaths, 2016 Rate[1]	Persons under 65 with no health insurance, 2015 Number	Persons under 65 with no health insurance, 2015 Percent	Medicare, 2015 Total Beneficiaries	Medicare, 2015 Enrolled in Original Medicare	Medicare, 2015 Enrolled in Medicare Advantage	Serious crimes known to police,[2] 2014 Total Number	Serious crimes known to police,[2] 2014 Total Rate[3]
	32	33	34	35	36	37	38	39	40	41	42	43	44	45
ALABAMA—Cont'd														
Washington	147	16 032	0.83	187	11.2	207	12.4	1 675	12.1	3 826	3 237	589	163	975
Wilcox	108	11 239	1.00	140	12.7	126	11.5	1 093	12.3	2 985	2 629	356	214	1 903
Winston	301	23 751	0.95	239	10.0	321	13.5	2 381	12.6	6 102	5 224	878	197	984
ALASKA	27 826	741 517	1.02	11 255	15.2	4 511	6.1	105 982	16.3	77 272	76 253	1 019	25 018	3 396
Aleutians East	1 726	3 466	1.06	15	4.6	6	1.8	1 149	37.4	NA	NA	NA	NA	NA
Aleutians West	2 520	6 521	1.22	30	5.3	8	1.4	1 129	21.8	D	D	D	NA	NA
Anchorage	8 126	308 297	1.06	4 560	15.3	1 774	5.9	35 930	13.6	31 340	30 914	426	14 136	4 692
Bethel	324	17 887	1.02	435	24.2	142	7.9	4 031	24.6	D	760	D	NA	NA
Bristol Bay	16	1 232	1.49	11	12.2	7	7.8	168	21.7	D	659	D	12	1 270
Denali	44	2 574	1.42	20	10.2	0	0.0	327	19.1	D	D	D	NA	NA
Dillingham	52	5 037	1.03	97	19.6	47	9.5	1 065	23.3	D	449	D	NA	NA
Fairbanks North Star	4 868	99 010	0.99	1 676	16.7	471	4.7	12 273	14.1	8 424	8 317	107	NA	NA
Haines	0	2 475	0.94	16	6.4	6	2.4	462	22.1	D	486	D	47	1 808
Hoonah-Angoon	0	2 116	0.99	18	8.7	15	7.2	431	24.4	D	87	D	NA	NA
Juneau	1 076	32 996	1.03	392	12.1	176	5.4	4 054	14.3	4 458	4 410	48	1 061	3 216
Kenai Peninsula	1 721	56 153	0.96	724	12.4	483	8.3	9 112	18.9	9 320	9 203	117	NA	NA
Ketchikan Gateway	275	13 964	1.04	168	12.2	76	5.5	2 201	18.8	2 090	2 067	23	NA	NA
Kodiak Island	391	14 284	1.04	223	16.2	50	3.6	2 594	21.0	878	864	14	NA	NA
Kusilvak	16	8 096	1.09	214	26.6	97	12.1	1 753	22.9	D	449	D	NA	NA
Lake and Peninsula	37	1 608	1.21	29	18.6	17	10.9	451	31.9	NA	NA	NA	NA	NA
Matanuska-Susitna	2 425	83 008	0.67	1 514	14.5	573	5.5	14 873	16.7	9 845	9 689	156	NA	NA
Nome	172	9 954	1.03	215	21.7	96	9.7	2 138	24.0	D	640	D	NA	NA
North Slope	2 652	18 276	2.58	161	16.8	66	6.9	1 657	18.1	D	386	D	185	1 909
Northwest Arctic	381	8 125	1.16	179	23.3	84	10.9	1 808	25.5	436	436	0	NA	NA
Petersburg	43	3 242	1.01	36	11.4	24	7.6	492	18.0	1 062	1 049	13	NA	NA
Prince of Wales-Hyder	50	6 380	1.00	75	11.8	46	7.2	1 398	25.2	D	649	D	NA	NA
Sitka	253	8 968	1.01	76	8.6	51	5.8	1 506	20.0	1 193	1 180	13	245	2 707
Skagway	32	1 002	1.00	12	11.0	12	11.0	159	16.8	D	536	D	18	1 804
Southeast Fairbanks	369	7 557	1.18	107	15.6	34	4.9	1 291	21.7	D	593	D	NA	NA
Valdez-Cordova	192	10 481	1.20	132	14.1	47	5.0	1 546	18.6	1 455	1 429	26	NA	NA
Wrangell	16	2 391	1.00	24	10.0	29	12.0	367	18.9	NA	NA	NA	29	1 204
Yakutat	18	649	1.02	10	16.6	0	0.0	176	33.9	NA	NA	NA	NA	NA
Yukon-Koyukuk	31	5 768	1.06	86	15.6	74	13.4	1 441	30.7	1 013	999	14	NA	NA
ARIZONA	156 879	6 616 867	0.99	87 204	12.6	56 564	8.2	710 610	12.8	1 092 787	633 290	459 497	242 156	3 597
Apache	993	70 708	0.92	1 005	13.7	680	9.3	10 583	17.5	9 203	8 413	790	510	703
Cochise	5 204	130 346	1.01	1 582	12.6	1 283	10.2	10 179	10.7	27 552	17 928	9 624	2 473	2 314
Coconino	11 485	136 276	0.99	1 683	11.9	869	6.2	16 458	14.6	20 593	17 140	3 453	4 877	3 529
Gila	962	53 683	1.03	615	11.5	832	15.5	5 137	13.6	15 071	12 304	2 767	1 414	2 702
Graham	3 121	36 154	0.89	581	15.5	270	7.2	3 423	11.6	5 202	3 310	1 892	NA	NA
Greenlee	35	10 912	1.58	152	15.8	51	5.3	608	7.3	1 166	970	196	110	1 183
La Paz	356	20 806	1.07	205	10.1	262	12.9	2 598	21.1	4 920	3 901	1 019	579	3 335
Maricopa	64 540	4 056 536	1.02	56 073	13.2	30 645	7.2	437 561	12.5	582 032	315 476	266 556	140 504	3 438
Mohave	4 622	193 418	0.85	1 879	9.2	3 101	15.1	20 035	14.0	56 378	39 304	17 074	6 743	3 364
Navajo	2 317	108 479	1.03	1 566	14.2	986	9.0	13 709	15.6	19 554	15 058	4 496	2 206	2 042
Pima	25 162	997 346	1.00	11 778	11.6	9 795	9.6	98 124	12.2	191 101	96 906	94 195	49 303	4 894
Pinal	24 001	341 122	0.63	4 543	10.9	3 021	7.2	38 345	12.6	57 901	32 635	25 266	8 316	2 131
Santa Cruz	387	47 446	1.02	601	13.1	321	7.0	5 758	15.0	8 132	3 534	4 598	845	1 798
Yavapai	4 154	212 166	0.95	1 944	8.6	2 886	12.8	20 512	13.2	64 387	44 511	19 876	NA	NA
Yuma	9 540	201 469	0.98	2 997	14.6	1 562	7.6	27 580	17.4	29 595	21 900	7 695	6 006	2 946
ARKANSAS	85 075	2 956 382	1.00	37 936	12.7	30 581	10.2	269 055	11.1	586 220	454 228	131 992	113 261	3 818
Arkansas	247	20 194	1.18	232	12.7	225	12.4	1 568	10.5	4 057	3 512	545	774	4 139
Ashley	191	21 190	0.99	237	11.6	263	12.8	1 684	10.1	4 963	4 410	553	749	3 545
Baxter	595	41 710	1.05	374	9.1	680	16.6	2 841	10.0	14 590	10 426	4 164	1 270	3 115
Benton	2 138	245 435	1.07	3 629	14.1	1 727	6.7	24 522	11.4	34 506	22 881	11 625	4 731	2 023
Boone	465	38 391	1.08	435	11.7	459	12.3	3 064	10.4	10 409	7 861	2 548	1 178	3 143
Bradley	224	10 964	0.94	126	11.5	135	12.3	1 322	14.9	2 518	2 178	340	158	1 413
Calhoun	175	4 889	0.84	47	9.1	48	9.3	394	9.9	995	838	157	57	1 093
Carroll	230	27 427	0.98	311	11.2	305	11.0	3 579	16.7	6 278	4 334	1 944	684	2 457
Chicot	771	11 296	0.98	125	11.4	154	14.1	970	11.8	2 708	2 265	443	448	3 996
Clark	2 826	22 310	0.95	244	10.8	247	10.9	1 701	10.4	4 640	3 651	989	572	2 523
Clay	125	14 108	0.79	165	11.1	217	14.5	1 407	12.0	3 998	3 435	563	179	1 175
Cleburne	339	24 929	0.92	226	8.9	374	14.8	1 962	10.5	7 407	6 302	1 105	910	3 557

1. Per 1,000 estimated resident population.   2. Data for serious crimes have not been adjusted for underreporting; this may affect comparability between geographic areas and over time.
3. Per 100,000 population estimated by the FBI.

Table B. States and Counties — **Crime, Education, Money Income, and Poverty**

STATE County	Serious crimes known to police, 2014 (cont.)[1] Rate[2] Violent	Property	School enrollment and attainment, 2011–2015 Enrollment[3] Total	Percent private	Attainment[4] (percent) High school graduate or less	Bachelor's degree or more	Local government expenditures,[5] 2013–2014 Total current spending (mil dol)	Current spending per student (dollars)	Money income, 2011–2015 Per capita income[6] (dollars)	Median income (dollars)	Households Percent with income of less than $50,000	with income of $200,000 or more	Income and poverty, 2015 Median household income (dollars)	Percent below poverty level All persons	Children under 18 years	Children 5 to 17 years in families
	46	47	48	49	50	51	52	53	54	55	56	57	58	59	60	61
ALABAMA—Cont'd																
Washington	180	796	3 966	5.6	65.6	9.9	27.2	8 832	19 743	42 811	58.6	0.9	42 658	22.4	31.5	28.6
Wilcox	578	1 325	2 530	15.0	64.0	12.5	19.0	10 143	14 170	23 750	76.5	0.6	23 014	33.2	49.2	46.3
Winston	90	894	5 247	5.3	59.3	11.4	39.8	9 288	18 808	33 194	66.6	0.9	36 497	18.9	29.3	27.6
ALASKA	636	2 760	195 151	12.5	35.7	28.0	2 404.0	18 359	33 413	72 515	33.6	6.1	73 391	10.4	14.5	13.3
Aleutians East	NA	NA	400	6.8	57.7	14.0	9.4	37 811	28 608	61 518	35.4	2.5	57 015	17.4	15.5	13.3
Aleutians West	NA	NA	1 159	4.0	53.1	14.7	12.8	25 643	31 754	84 306	28.2	7.2	80 695	8.5	8.5	7.9
Anchorage	865	3 827	81 388	14.1	31.2	33.2	758.6	15 641	36 920	78 326	30.1	7.9	77 791	8.7	12.4	11.2
Bethel	NA	NA	5 390	0.9	64.7	11.6	150.3	29 466	17 746	51 012	48.9	1.8	44 849	24.2	31.5	31.1
Bristol Bay	0	1 270	258	12.4	38.7	20.0	20.3	39 420	38 267	79 750	27.9	3.7	66 373	9.0	8.6	7.7
Denali	NA	NA	387	21.7	28.7	33.3	10.0	11 793	35 315	81 544	28.3	4.8	73 000	6.6	10.2	9.1
Dillingham	NA	NA	1 374	5.5	51.6	16.2	33.7	29 813	22 257	54 173	45.2	3.3	50 753	20.0	30.4	31.0
Fairbanks North Star	NA	NA	28 972	12.8	29.0	31.7	276.0	17 678	33 244	71 068	33.7	4.8	70 881	8.1	10.1	9.3
Haines	154	1 654	432	4.4	32.3	35.6	6.3	33 902	33 903	58 750	44.5	6.7	57 876	10.9	20.2	16.2
Hoonah-Angoon	NA	NA	368	13.3	40.9	26.6	9.1	33 793	30 943	52 419	46.6	2.7	53 726	16.2	29.2	26.0
Juneau	573	2 643	8 152	10.2	26.3	38.5	85.5	17 617	39 979	85 746	23.1	7.6	82 892	8.0	10.1	8.7
Kenai Peninsula	NA	NA	12 703	12.1	39.7	22.8	165.2	18 437	31 537	63 684	38.9	4.5	62 025	11.4	14.0	12.5
Ketchikan Gateway	NA	NA	3 032	12.5	40.9	23.8	42.1	18 364	32 021	64 222	38.8	5.1	65 314	10.3	14.4	13.0
Kodiak Island	NA	NA	3 660	13.7	36.9	24.7	51.3	20 336	30 657	70 887	35.9	5.0	67 515	7.5	9.3	8.6
Kusilvak	NA	NA	2 615	1.1	71.5	5.0	73.9	29 600	11 569	38 229	63.5	0.5	33 511	31.8	43.4	42.1
Lake and Peninsula	NA	NA	442	2.3	55.6	12.9	NA	NA	23 041	50 781	49.5	2.9	42 120	19.3	31.4	30.7
Matanuska-Susitna	NA	NA	26 448	15.5	39.4	20.7	273.0	15 349	29 913	72 983	33.2	4.9	76 601	9.8	11.8	10.3
Nome	NA	NA	2 877	1.4	56.7	14.1	81.2	31 209	19 804	48 868	51.1	2.8	52 952	21.4	27.6	26.2
North Slope	764	1 145	2 110	4.0	48.1	13.9	74.2	36 981	51 085	72 576	35.5	7.8	70 834	12.6	17.6	16.6
Northwest Arctic	NA	NA	2 194	2.5	64.9	10.6	67.6	32 679	21 101	63 648	38.1	3.8	53 774	26.3	34.9	32.0
Petersburg	NA	NA	754	10.2	37.2	25.3	13.5	25 030	34 884	67 935	36.1	4.1	63 098	7.9	10.3	9.8
Prince of Wales-Hyder	NA	NA	1 391	7.2	50.3	15.5	31.1	23 992	25 205	48 523	51.7	2.0	45 305	15.6	23.8	21.4
Sitka	66	2 641	2 180	10.4	29.3	31.2	26.4	14 989	33 890	70 376	32.8	4.5	68 472	9.2	10.4	9.0
Skagway	0	1 804	149	10.1	31.7	35.9	2.7	24 935	38 696	69 318	25.1	2.7	65 878	3.7	6.3	6.7
Southeast Fairbanks	NA	NA	1 786	20.9	41.1	17.9	27.1	21 574	30 079	62 670	39.5	3.4	60 203	13.5	21.4	20.6
Valdez-Cordova	NA	NA	2 497	14.5	34.7	28.7	31.5	22 678	33 293	78 810	32.9	8.4	70 101	9.5	12.2	11.7
Wrangell	208	996	440	4.1	45.4	19.9	8.0	23 308	30 089	48 603	50.8	2.9	54 500	12.0	16.0	13.4
Yakutat	NA	NA	138	3.6	50.2	15.3	3.0	31 082	33 159	72 500	36.8	1.2	53 795	15.4	26.1	26.3
Yukon-Koyukuk	NA	NA	1 455	4.7	57.8	11.2	60.3	10 819	20 698	38 491	59.5	1.1	37 755	23.4	34.4	31.6
ARIZONA	400	3 198	1 754 549	10.9	38.4	27.5	8 167.8	7 412	25 848	50 255	49.7	3.8	51 473	17.4	24.7	23.5
Apache	119	585	20 589	4.1	56.6	10.8	138.9	12 177	13 011	31 757	68.4	0.6	31 072	38.0	44.7	44.6
Cochise	283	2 032	31 939	9.6	36.8	22.9	158.8	8 084	23 506	45 075	54.2	2.7	43 451	16.9	25.7	24.9
Coconino	346	3 183	46 964	6.7	32.9	33.6	170.0	8 991	24 308	50 234	49.8	3.9	51 955	19.5	20.7	19.7
Gila	336	2 366	10 081	10.1	46.0	16.7	69.5	8 870	20 583	39 751	62.2	0.8	41 346	21.3	36.6	35.1
Graham	NA	NA	10 243	6.2	48.1	13.2	51.2	7 413	17 481	45 964	54.7	1.1	44 169	22.9	26.9	24.3
Greenlee	462	720	2 615	7.7	51.8	10.8	15.0	8 820	21 994	51 628	48.5	1.3	58 854	10.1	11.3	10.1
La Paz	202	3 133	3 260	3.5	60.6	9.9	24.1	9 638	20 439	34 466	68.1	0.6	34 835	22.2	36.9	35.0
Maricopa	383	3 055	1 091 346	11.5	36.3	30.4	5 144.8	7 156	27 832	54 229	46.0	4.8	56 017	16.3	23.0	22.0
Mohave	202	3 162	38 760	15.1	51.7	11.8	172.2	7 050	20 974	38 488	62.4	1.4	40 360	17.4	29.8	29.3
Navajo	313	1 729	29 213	6.1	48.0	14.7	177.1	9 619	16 486	35 921	62.6	1.4	37 658	28.1	36.7	34.7
Pima	443	4 451	265 511	10.6	35.2	30.3	1 149.6	7 936	25 729	46 162	53.4	3.1	47 107	18.7	27.7	25.5
Pinal	226	1 905	93 720	10.5	45.1	18.0	384.7	7 025	21 130	49 477	50.5	1.8	50 888	15.8	21.6	20.2
Santa Cruz	132	1 666	13 059	6.1	52.1	22.0	75.2	7 502	17 795	40 140	59.0	1.1	34 893	24.4	36.7	34.3
Yavapai	NA	NA	43 320	14.4	36.0	25.6	185.5	7 628	25 418	44 748	55.3	2.0	47 220	15.1	23.4	21.3
Yuma	370	2 576	53 929	6.3	53.9	14.4	251.2	6 748	19 102	40 743	59.6	1.9	40 426	21.1	30.8	31.0
ARKANSAS	480	3 338	750 024	11.0	50.2	21.1	4 688.2	9 568	22 798	41 371	58.1	2.4	42 046	18.7	26.4	24.5
Arkansas	460	3 679	4 173	7.2	60.4	12.4	27.9	9 190	22 473	36 411	65.8	2.4	41 179	20.7	30.5	28.2
Ashley	327	3 219	5 228	6.0	56.5	13.2	34.8	8 829	19 891	34 263	64.7	1.4	39 871	19.6	31.2	30.0
Baxter	140	2 975	7 447	9.2	48.1	17.9	46.0	8 909	22 475	35 396	65.8	1.5	36 902	16.4	28.5	24.7
Benton	235	1 788	60 307	13.5	44.0	30.2	378.3	9 173	27 934	56 239	44.0	5.1	60 294	10.8	15.3	13.5
Boone	413	2 729	8 414	7.8	50.1	14.7	54.5	8 688	21 946	39 251	62.1	2.3	40 909	16.5	25.1	22.5
Bradley	215	1 199	2 613	7.0	62.6	13.0	22.0	10 633	20 252	33 701	67.5	1.8	37 331	28.0	40.2	37.2
Calhoun	173	921	1 025	7.4	68.6	10.4	6.1	11 424	20 537	36 899	64.1	0.6	40 526	16.7	23.1	21.9
Carroll	312	2 144	5 304	13.4	51.8	16.7	36.9	9 262	20 195	36 897	66.0	0.9	37 587	16.6	27.7	25.5
Chicot	392	3 603	2 720	11.8	65.7	11.1	18.9	11 515	19 053	28 913	70.1	1.8	29 968	31.4	43.2	40.8
Clark	260	2 263	7 748	20.3	46.7	23.9	39.3	13 778	19 555	35 031	63.6	1.8	37 856	22.5	28.2	25.5
Clay	138	1 038	3 033	4.4	65.2	11.0	21.4	8 304	19 166	32 552	67.9	0.4	35 324	20.8	27.9	24.9
Cleburne	274	3 283	4 747	8.6	54.2	16.8	31.5	9 188	24 912	42 905	57.4	2.8	43 913	15.6	24.7	22.6

1. Data for serious crimes have not been adjusted for underreporting; this may affect comparability between geographic areas and over time.   2. Per 100,000 population estimated by the FBI.
3. All persons 3 years old and over enrolled in nursery school through college.   4. Persons 25 years old and over.   5. Elementary and secondary education expenditures.
6. Based on population estimated by the American Community Survey, 2011–2015.

Table B. States and Counties — **Personal Income**

STATE County	Personal income, 2015										Earnings, 2015		
	Total (mil dol)	Percent change, 2014–2015	Per capita[1]		Wages and salaries (mil dol)	Supplements to wages and salaries; employer contributions (mil dol)		Proprietors' income (mil dol)	Dividends, interest, and rent (mil dol)	Personal transfer receipts (mil dol)	Total (mil dol)	Contributions for government social insurance (mil dol)	
			Dollars	Rank		Pension and insurance	Government social insurance					From employee and self-employed	From employer
	62	63	64	65	66	67	68	69	70	71	72	73	74
ALABAMA—Cont'd													
Washington	571	2.8	34 007	2 197	212	43	15	31	66	163	302	21	15
Wilcox	311	2.4	28 128	2 931	122	23	9	21	48	140	175	13	9
Winston	777	2.3	32 545	2 766	254	46	20	88	120	245	407	29	20
ALASKA	41 461	3.1	56 202	X	21 211	5 234	1 575	3 320	6 908	6 609	31 340	1 586	1 575
Aleutians East	166	22.5	49 611	1 608	111	27	9	12	13	12	159	8	9
Aleutians West	300	-0.7	52 569	265	220	48	17	15	25	22	300	15	17
Anchorage	18 737	2.4	62 728	115	10 336	2 264	793	1 566	3 236	2 682	14 959	779	793
Bethel	715	3.8	39 827	1 590	316	126	21	19	65	223	482	20	21
Bristol Bay	59	-2.3	65 769	139	61	16	5	11	12	9	93	5	5
Denali	130	1.2	67 770	89	110	22	9	6	19	33	147	8	9
Dillingham	260	0.3	51 969	377	121	38	9	21	43	48	189	9	9
Fairbanks North Star	5 399	4.7	54 185	303	2 615	736	209	317	962	823	3 877	182	209
Haines	121	2.6	47 929	31	40	11	3	16	31	28	70	4	3
Hoonah-Angoon	115	2.8	53 956	407	31	12	2	13	24	27	58	3	2
Juneau	2 054	2.2	62 694	171	1 023	342	66	160	383	248	1 591	69	66
Kenai Peninsula	3 056	2.5	52 639	344	1 096	302	76	228	560	568	1 702	91	76
Ketchikan Gateway	867	3.2	63 235	160	382	115	28	128	142	145	653	32	28
Kodiak Island	808	2.0	58 162	244	376	104	30	118	142	112	628	31	30
Kusilvak	243	-0.1	29 896	2 852	70	44	4	5	21	107	123	4	4
Lake and Peninsula	87	1.9	55 385	538	35	15	2	8	18	17	61	3	2
Matanuska-Susitna	4 706	5.7	46 554	694	1 102	302	81	345	610	733	1 830	99	81
Nome	481	3.8	48 805	724	210	75	14	26	49	134	325	14	14
North Slope	357	2.2	36 883	2 109	1 722	253	111	9	75	60	2 094	113	111
Northwest Arctic	364	2.4	46 918	680	205	56	13	10	31	109	284	14	13
Petersburg	211	3.6	66 323	150	62	22	4	56	46	39	144	7	4
Prince of Wales-Hyder	255	2.3	40 205	1 499	91	38	6	25	43	60	160	7	6
Sitka	568	-0.3	64 122	114	227	68	17	89	119	77	399	19	17
Skagway	83	-5.6	78 171	34	40	10	3	7	15	9	60	3	3
Southeast Fairbanks	296	3.8	43 256	1 234	183	44	13	15	51	73	255	14	13
Valdez-Cordova	592	4.0	63 236	183	289	81	20	65	102	79	456	23	20
Wrangell	112	1.8	47 214	823	37	13	3	16	21	27	69	4	3
Yakutat	37	-6.6	60 333	646	12	5	1	9	5	7	27	1	1
Yukon-Koyukuk	285	-0.4	51 496	222	88	46	5	5	47	98	144	6	5
ARIZONA	267 361	4.5	39 217	X	134 025	19 496	9 616	17 562	49 793	56 304	180 699	11 358	9 616
Apache	2 115	4.4	29 597	2 880	775	192	59	36	293	935	1 063	68	59
Cochise	4 821	3.1	38 133	1 642	1 855	426	152	218	956	1 528	2 651	163	152
Coconino	5 705	4.7	41 018	1 293	2 702	546	200	338	1 208	1 097	3 786	222	200
Gila	1 917	4.4	36 066	2 034	634	120	47	70	380	778	870	66	47
Graham	1 120	0.6	29 731	2 828	378	74	27	56	132	388	535	35	27
Greenlee	355	1.8	37 240	1 535	318	48	21	12	31	85	398	23	21
La Paz	604	2.3	29 963	2 805	207	42	15	28	113	229	292	21	15
Maricopa	175 438	4.8	42 092	1 033	98 802	13 004	6 986	11 709	31 937	30 515	130 501	8 051	6 986
Mohave	6 041	5.2	29 505	2 938	1 830	301	137	378	1 019	2 139	2 646	218	137
Navajo	3 154	5.4	29 963	2 956	1 153	226	93	154	495	1 293	1 626	114	93
Pima	38 922	2.7	38 536	1 596	17 163	2 981	1 251	2 263	8 442	9 586	23 659	1 525	1 251
Pinal	11 255	5.9	27 682	3 037	2 494	478	181	649	1 469	3 297	3 801	278	181
Santa Cruz	1 563	0.7	33 646	2 695	632	127	50	197	311	391	1 006	65	50
Yavapai	7 900	5.5	35 545	2 319	2 383	398	175	556	2 058	2 479	3 512	279	175
Yuma	6 450	8.3	31 574	2 858	2 698	535	220	897	948	1 565	4 351	230	220
ARKANSAS	113 924	2.2	38 257	X	52 465	7 772	4 089	8 343	23 047	27 309	72 669	4 761	4 089
Arkansas	731	-2.1	39 643	889	424	63	35	87	95	183	608	38	35
Ashley	667	2.4	32 013	2 365	314	47	26	42	72	236	430	31	26
Baxter	1 427	4.5	34 751	2 201	532	87	42	77	279	519	739	61	42
Benton	17 923	3.0	71 787	66	6 701	723	474	536	8 856	1 623	8 434	536	474
Boone	1 197	1.4	32 166	2 371	540	89	42	83	182	379	754	54	42
Bradley	361	2.6	32 522	2 355	135	23	11	38	41	137	207	14	11
Calhoun	161	6.9	30 770	2 823	135	19	10	6	17	46	170	11	10
Carroll	846	-2.0	30 526	2 512	325	55	27	80	152	252	486	33	27
Chicot	356	-1.9	32 289	2 168	118	18	9	39	47	141	185	12	9
Clark	702	2.3	31 021	2 587	334	60	27	39	97	225	461	30	27
Clay	498	-1.6	32 938	2 197	121	20	10	51	63	170	202	14	10
Cleburne	850	0.3	33 379	2 121	236	40	20	64	174	282	360	29	20

1. Based on the resident population estimated as of July 1 of the year shown.

Table B. States and Counties — Earnings, Social Security, and Housing

STATE County	Earnings, 2015 (cont.) Percent by selected industries									Social Security beneficiaries, December 2015			Housing units, 2016	
	Farm	Mining	Construction	Manu-facturing	Infor-mation: professional, scientific, technical services	Retail trade	Finance, insur-ance, real estate and leasing	Health care and social assistance	Govern-ment	Number	Rate[1]	Supple-mental Security Income recipients, December 2015	Total	Percent change, 2010–2016
	75	76	77	78	79	80	81	82	83	84	85	86	87	88
ALABAMA—Cont'd														
Washington	4.2	D	5.0	40.6	D	2.3	D	D	14.3	4 730	280	715	8 382	-0.3
Wilcox	5.5	0.0	4.4	34.8	D	3.9	2.5	D	21.0	3 785	343	1 455	5 618	-0.5
Winston	4.9	D	4.9	36.1	D	6.2	3.8	D	14.3	6 855	287	1 013	13 412	-0.4
ALASKA	0.1	9.0	7.5	3.1	7.6	5.4	3.8	10.7	30.8	91 960	125	12 515	310 658	1.2
Aleutians East	0.0	0.0	D	D	D	1.4	D	D	13.2	175	53	13	755	1.1
Aleutians West	1.1	D	2.3	40.9	D	4.2	D	2.6	15.6	235	41	17	1 941	0.6
Anchorage	0.0	5.7	7.0	1.0	11.6	5.6	5.1	12.7	27.3	34 730	116	5 899	115 544	2.2
Bethel	0.0	D	2.8	D	D	5.0	5.2	D	46.7	1 710	95	411	5 990	1.2
Bristol Bay	0.0	0.0	D	D	D	D	D	D	23.4	120	135	9	966	-0.3
Denali	0.0	D	D	0.4	D	1.1	D	0.6	22.8	245	128	12	1 755	-0.8
Dillingham	0.0	D	0.6	D	D	3.8	D	25.6	29.4	535	107	99	2 444	0.7
Fairbanks North Star	0.1	2.4	10.9	1.1	4.1	5.5	2.8	9.4	46.4	10 360	104	1 055	41 557	-0.5
Haines	0.0	D	11.4	11.3	4.4	7.6	D	9.0	22.3	580	233	47	1 647	1.0
Hoonah-Angoon	0.0	0.0	D	3.3	D	4.1	D	D	46.4	465	220	45	1 763	0.4
Juneau	0.0	D	6.1	1.2	6.2	5.2	3.4	7.2	48.0	4 335	133	540	13 443	3.0
Kenai Peninsula	0.1	9.8	7.9	5.8	4.7	6.5	3.8	11.8	28.4	10 920	188	1 033	30 881	1.0
Ketchikan Gateway	0.0	D	8.2	5.2	2.6	7.6	4.3	9.6	33.4	2 320	169	249	6 278	1.7
Kodiak Island	0.0	0.1	4.4	17.6	1.8	3.0	2.4	8.4	31.8	1 580	115	150	5 340	0.7
Kusilvak	0.0	0.0	D	D	0.1	7.0	0.0	D	70.2	800	99	208	2 243	2.7
Lake and Peninsula	0.0	0.0	4.2	D	D	1.9	D	D	46.9	175	112	19	1 503	-0.1
Matanuska-Susitna	0.4	0.5	17.7	2.4	6.1	9.7	3.7	13.8	26.7	13 080	129	1 612	41 487	0.4
Nome	0.0	D	6.1	D	D	4.5	2.6	D	43.4	1 065	108	221	4 081	1.8
North Slope	0.0	66.3	D	D	D	0.7	D	D	10.0	645	67	28	2 600	4.0
Northwest Arctic	0.0	D	D	0.1	D	D	D	D	31.6	750	97	115	2 725	0.7
Petersburg	0.0	D	5.0	10.0	2.2	5.5	1.4	1.8	31.6	715	227	35	1 655	0.7
Prince of Wales-Hyder	0.0	D	3.3	4.4	D	7.3	2.8	3.7	50.8	990	156	116	3 353	-0.1
Sitka	0.0	-0.2	7.5	13.8	3.5	5.3	2.4	10.5	32.7	1 295	146	89	4 137	0.9
Skagway	0.0	0.0	12.2	4.3	D	14.3	D	0.9	27.0	115	109	0	667	4.9
Southeast Fairbanks	0.0	D	5.1	D	D	4.0	0.5	7.7	31.9	1 175	172	147	3 879	-0.9
Valdez-Cordova	0.0	D	6.4	7.6	3.9	4.3	D	4.8	28.7	1 400	150	117	6 072	-0.5
Wrangell	0.0	0.0	5.6	9.1	D	6.8	1.4	D	39.0	470	196	34	1 425	0.4
Yakutat	0.0	0.0	D	D	D	D	D	1.5	39.1	115	185	0	451	0.2
Yukon-Koyukuk	0.0	1.2	6.8	D	D	4.4	D	7.6	65.4	860	155	184	4 076	0.9
ARIZONA	0.7	0.9	5.2	7.9	10.2	7.7	10.0	12.4	16.9	1 241 101	182	119 715	2 961 003	4.1
Apache	-0.6	0.8	2.2	0.6	2.2	2.8	2.0	12.5	62.2	12 460	174	4 350	32 810	0.9
Cochise	2.2	0.2	4.2	1.1	8.2	5.8	2.8	7.7	50.9	31 020	245	3 086	60 873	3.1
Coconino	0.2	0.2	4.7	10.4	3.7	6.9	3.9	15.0	32.5	19 330	139	2 624	65 271	3.1
Gila	-0.1	11.1	4.9	14.7	D	6.6	1.8	10.2	31.8	16 875	318	1 446	33 371	2.1
Graham	2.6	D	4.0	1.7	14.9	8.5	2.1	11.4	33.8	6 145	163	787	13 437	3.5
Greenlee	1.1	D	4.1	0.0	D	1.5	D	D	7.9	1 475	155	112	4 447	1.7
La Paz	3.3	0.3	2.3	2.4	2.6	10.9	D	D	44.1	5 565	276	487	16 276	1.4
Maricopa	0.3	0.4	5.2	8.2	11.4	7.9	12.0	12.1	12.3	656 565	158	61 594	1 711 284	4.4
Mohave	0.4	0.3	6.5	6.2	4.7	11.5	5.5	20.8	17.8	64 295	315	4 681	113 809	2.6
Navajo	0.7	3.4	6.4	0.7	8.4	8.1	2.4	13.4	34.7	22 650	209	4 708	57 800	1.5
Pima	0.2	1.3	4.9	9.9	9.5	6.6	6.0	14.7	25.2	208 665	207	20 275	456 551	3.5
Pinal	5.6	2.5	6.9	5.8	3.7	6.6	3.5	6.4	34.9	77 320	190	6 091	170 711	7.2
Santa Cruz	0.4	D	4.0	2.3	D	8.7	2.7	3.9	35.7	9 115	198	1 398	18 251	1.3
Yavapai	0.2	2.9	9.4	5.5	5.7	9.5	5.1	15.1	19.7	74 885	338	3 713	114 798	4.0
Yuma	14.1	0.0	4.0	2.7	4.8	7.5	3.1	10.2	29.7	34 735	171	4 363	91 314	3.9
ARKANSAS	2.4	0.9	5.6	12.8	6.3	6.9	5.8	12.2	17.6	679 689	228	110 053	1 354 762	2.9
Arkansas	5.6	0.0	2.9	35.2	1.8	8.2	3.6	7.2	9.7	4 645	253	748	9 445	0.1
Ashley	2.1	0.1	9.8	35.1	D	5.7	2.4	9.3	12.5	5 800	279	963	10 087	-0.5
Baxter	0.3	0.4	5.1	17.3	4.9	9.6	8.0	26.2	11.8	16 090	392	1 042	22 662	0.4
Benton	1.1	0.1	4.8	6.9	8.1	5.1	2.6	5.8	6.7	42 635	170	3 487	102 139	9.7
Boone	1.7	D	5.1	12.5	4.2	9.1	4.0	9.4	22.0	11 005	296	1 144	16 925	0.6
Bradley	9.0	D	4.1	20.3	D	5.0	3.6	15.4	19.2	2 870	260	514	5 794	-1.1
Calhoun	0.7	D	3.5	71.6	D	D	D	2.0	7.5	1 355	260	165	2 882	-0.5
Carroll	9.3	D	6.8	27.1	2.6	6.8	4.8	9.0	12.4	7 760	280	601	13 597	0.3
Chicot	16.1	0.1	7.1	1.6	D	6.7	6.0	D	24.9	3 010	274	926	5 399	-0.4
Clark	1.6	0.0	2.1	20.8	3.8	8.4	3.3	D	24.5	5 045	223	788	10 418	0.3
Clay	19.2	0.0	4.7	7.1	2.1	6.7	4.1	9.2	19.5	4 695	312	662	8 025	-0.1
Cleburne	3.1	5.8	8.6	13.8	4.1	8.9	5.8	9.9	13.4	8 475	333	761	15 868	0.3

1. Per 1,000 resident population estimated as of July 1 of the year shown.

Table B. States and Counties — Housing, Labor Force, and Employment

STATE County	Housing units, 2011–2015								Civilian labor force, 2016		Unemployment		Civilian employment,[6] 2011–2015 Percent		
	Occupied units														
			Owner-occupied			Renter-occupied									
				Median owner cost as a percent of income											
	Total	Percent	Median value[1]	With a mortgage	Without a mortgage[2]	Median rent[3]	Median rent as a percent of income[2]	Substandard units[4] (percent)	Total	Percent change, 2015–2016	Total	Rate[5]	Total	Management, business, science and arts	Construction, production, and maintenance occupations
	89	90	91	92	93	94	95	96	97	98	99	100	101	102	103
ALABAMA—Cont'd															
Washington	6 133	83.9	85 700	19.1	11.9	569	25.5	2.6	6 776	1.1	592	8.7	5 656	20.3	45.0
Wilcox	3 843	68.8	77 300	23.5	16.6	424	29.4	1.8	2 809	-1.0	413	14.7	2 838	28.4	34.6
Winston	9 406	76.2	81 500	22.4	13.4	515	26.7	1.6	9 403	0.0	689	7.3	8 894	24.5	35.8
ALASKA	250 969	63.4	250 000	22.6	10.6	1 146	28.2	9.6	360 428	-0.6	23 807	6.6	351 108	36.2	23.6
Aleutians East	690	53.5	126 100	19.7	10.0	930	22.0	4.9	2 498	1.1	68	2.7	2 519	13.6	69.8
Aleutians West	1 138	32.2	217 500	21.3	14.1	1 270	19.4	11.0	3 907	-3.7	127	3.3	3 787	16.9	55.1
Anchorage	105 175	60.0	290 500	22.6	10.9	1 197	28.9	4.5	156 112	-0.3	8 226	5.3	152 355	39.7	18.7
Bethel	4 488	64.6	165 700	20.4	12.7	1 169	24.9	53.0	7 018	-4.4	989	14.1	6 232	35.2	21.1
Bristol Bay	377	54.1	187 500	20.2	10.0	1 063	21.4	9.3	403	5.8	28	6.9	541	33.1	27.7
Denali	681	75.3	190 200	20.6	10.0	1 044	11.9	21.0	1 107	3.7	95	8.6	1 210	30.3	26.7
Dillingham	1 349	60.3	195 100	22.7	11.8	950	24.2	30.6	1 983	-2.7	192	9.7	1 854	38.1	23.7
Fairbanks North Star	35 582	58.1	218 100	24.5	11.6	1 216	30.9	10.6	46 098	-0.5	2 607	5.7	46 661	36.6	23.0
Haines	1 176	69.0	211 400	23.8	10.0	868	32.2	16.9	1 077	-0.6	106	9.8	1 470	34.0	24.8
Hoonah-Angoon	892	66.3	233 400	24.6	10.0	725	22.2	11.2	1 202	6.4	138	11.5	1 086	35.6	29.7
Juneau	12 114	63.7	323 500	22.5	10.4	1 188	25.0	6.3	17 162	0.6	750	4.4	17 836	45.4	18.4
Kenai Peninsula	21 485	72.5	219 100	21.7	10.0	940	26.7	8.6	27 189	-1.4	2 217	8.2	25 637	29.9	28.9
Ketchikan Gateway	5 267	58.8	252 500	22.1	12.2	1 033	28.3	4.3	7 028	1.1	439	6.2	6 655	30.4	26.7
Kodiak Island	4 577	60.1	245 400	25.1	10.7	981	29.6	9.6	6 417	-2.9	319	5.0	7 032	27.1	32.3
Kusilvak	1 683	76.9	108 000	16.5	11.9	514	19.3	67.4	2 660	-5.0	566	21.3	2 067	29.9	24.9
Lake and Peninsula	491	65.6	145 000	18.8	11.6	707	15.7	22.0	633	-1.9	78	12.3	657	34.1	31.8
Matanuska-Susitna	31 098	75.7	224 900	22.3	10.0	1 073	28.9	8.9	46 065	-0.1	3 709	8.1	40 854	32.8	28.3
Nome	2 925	56.4	123 500	19.5	14.4	1 188	25.7	42.2	3 987	-2.1	499	12.5	3 654	34.7	20.9
North Slope	1 962	53.5	141 100	14.4	10.0	1 087	17.7	37.9	3 968	-7.7	257	6.5	5 499	24.0	42.5
Northwest Arctic	1 903	55.7	124 500	20.1	13.8	1 141	18.3	47.5	2 889	-0.4	455	15.7	2 593	33.8	25.7
Petersburg	1 284	67.3	218 800	18.0	10.8	938	26.3	3.2	1 450	-2.8	125	8.6	1 665	30.7	37.8
Prince of Wales-Hyder	2 268	71.6	162 600	19.5	10.0	811	23.0	10.7	2 780	0.9	324	11.7	2 819	27.0	36.6
Sitka	3 472	59.2	338 600	23.6	10.0	1 057	27.5	4.4	4 425	-3.7	192	4.3	4 756	37.6	22.4
Skagway	406	54.9	324 600	25.5	10.8	1 020	20.0	6.7	801	-1.1	85	10.6	676	27.5	34.6
Southeast Fairbanks	2 117	70.1	197 300	21.0	10.0	1 176	24.8	16.2	3 019	0.6	308	10.2	3 038	30.4	32.8
Valdez-Cordova	3 010	70.6	200 700	19.1	10.0	974	19.8	9.0	4 851	-0.4	398	8.2	4 415	35.4	26.7
Wrangell	1 127	66.1	171 400	23.1	10.0	732	28.7	7.1	1 047	1.7	76	7.3	1 088	30.2	30.0
Yakutat	250	54.4	166 000	17.8	10.5	945	25.3	9.6	247	-4.6	20	8.1	375	29.6	37.6
Yukon-Koyukuk	1 982	70.7	88 800	20.9	11.4	638	23.2	45.5	2 405	0.1	414	17.2	2 077	35.7	26.1
ARIZONA	2 412 212	62.8	167 500	23.0	10.5	913	30.1	5.0	3 237 865	2.3	171 600	5.3	2 813 406	35.1	18.8
Apache	19 272	76.6	83 300	22.8	10.0	523	18.0	26.9	20 064	-2.5	2 273	11.3	18 334	28.8	25.1
Cochise	48 825	68.0	143 900	21.2	10.1	802	29.2	4.0	50 187	-0.7	3 071	6.1	43 776	33.7	17.9
Coconino	46 619	59.8	219 300	22.6	10.0	1 003	32.6	9.9	74 287	1.4	4 397	5.9	64 844	34.7	19.3
Gila	20 909	72.7	134 200	24.1	11.7	742	29.1	5.1	20 976	-1.0	1 504	7.2	17 961	29.4	25.4
Graham	10 959	70.7	123 300	21.8	10.1	729	26.8	7.8	14 307	-1.3	955	6.7	11 954	29.8	28.0
Greenlee	3 219	46.4	82 500	20.8	10.0	415	10.0	8.0	3 898	-3.6	296	7.6	3 346	26.4	47.3
La Paz	9 365	74.4	69 100	23.7	10.0	592	26.4	7.4	8 493	4.0	508	6.0	6 386	25.2	31.3
Maricopa	1 442 518	60.7	187 100	22.7	10.4	962	29.9	4.7	2 076 894	2.9	93 738	4.5	1 821 038	36.6	17.9
Mohave	80 832	67.1	123 200	24.9	11.0	786	29.6	4.0	80 432	1.1	5 294	6.6	66 880	25.0	22.4
Navajo	34 129	70.0	104 400	22.0	10.0	656	28.6	14.7	41 331	1.7	3 364	8.1	31 955	28.5	23.2
Pima	389 658	61.2	159 900	23.3	10.9	816	31.8	4.3	472 015	1.2	23 078	4.9	422 371	36.0	17.3
Pinal	127 599	72.2	128 700	23.3	11.0	992	29.3	4.1	161 850	3.1	8 874	5.5	134 182	30.5	22.5
Santa Cruz	15 359	66.0	137 000	24.1	11.3	603	28.4	7.2	19 288	-2.8	1 911	9.9	17 246	26.8	23.0
Yavapai	92 310	69.9	188 200	26.7	11.4	857	31.5	3.3	99 838	3.5	4 851	4.9	81 511	31.3	21.8
Yuma	70 639	68.1	112 100	24.3	10.6	839	29.6	7.3	94 005	0.5	17 486	18.6	71 622	25.0	28.1
ARKANSAS	1 138 025	66.1	111 400	20.0	10.5	677	29.5	3.0	1 342 695	0.8	53 698	4.0	1 256 081	32.0	27.1
Arkansas	7 743	66.7	75 600	22.3	11.0	622	27.9	1.0	9 309	-1.9	322	3.5	8 088	26.8	35.4
Ashley	8 327	75.5	65 700	19.5	11.8	588	29.8	2.6	7 833	-3.9	495	6.3	7 840	28.0	35.8
Baxter	18 164	75.6	120 400	23.3	11.8	624	29.3	1.4	16 112	-0.8	698	4.3	15 229	29.2	27.7
Benton	85 670	67.0	150 800	19.0	10.0	796	24.2	3.2	126 311	3.7	3 683	2.9	109 788	35.2	24.8
Boone	14 961	71.2	111 700	20.3	10.3	596	28.6	3.5	16 013	1.0	592	3.7	15 368	30.7	25.0
Bradley	4 598	67.5	68 700	19.5	10.4	565	34.9	4.9	4 387	0.1	229	5.2	4 180	25.6	36.2
Calhoun	2 125	80.0	69 000	18.0	11.7	634	30.8	1.5	2 401	-0.3	113	4.7	2 243	22.0	44.4
Carroll	10 977	75.6	116 200	24.8	10.9	622	26.0	4.5	12 966	2.4	461	3.6	11 454	27.5	36.7
Chicot	4 513	67.6	57 300	21.8	14.9	575	31.6	3.9	3 587	-3.8	238	6.6	3 769	27.9	25.1
Clark	8 681	63.5	87 200	17.9	10.8	580	30.6	2.0	9 460	0.1	421	4.5	9 780	35.0	21.4
Clay	6 611	73.5	63 900	19.7	11.6	509	31.9	3.5	6 070	-3.6	345	5.7	6 283	22.6	37.9
Cleburne	10 157	76.2	126 500	20.1	10.1	660	29.0	2.5	9 534	-0.8	569	6.0	9 699	25.9	33.3

1. Specified owner-occupied units.   2. A value of 10.0 represents 10 percent or less; a value of 50.0 represents 50 percent or more.   3. Specified renter-occupied units.
4. Overcrowded or lacking complete plumbing facilities.   5. Percent of civilian labor force.   6. Civilian employed persons 16 years old and over.

Table B. States and Counties — Nonfarm Employment and Agriculture

	Private nonfarm establishments, employment and payroll, 2015									Agriculture, 2012			
		Employment						Annual payroll		Farms			
											Percent with:		
STATE County	Number of establishments	Total	Health care and social assistance	Manufacturing	Retail trade	Finance and insurance	Professional, scientific, and technical services	Total (mil dol)	Average per employee (dollars)	Number	Fewer than 50 acres	500 acres or more	Farm operators whose principal occupation is farming (percent)
	104	105	106	107	108	109	110	111	112	113	114	115	116

STATE County	104	105	106	107	108	109	110	111	112	113	114	115	116
ALABAMA—Cont'd												
Washington	207	5 726	299	4 242	259	57	31	399	69 624	371	31.3	6.2	43.4
Wilcox	186	1 742	273	D	273	87	20	83	47 707	316	30.7	24.1	44.9
Winston	447	6 311	732	2 731	790	178	83	189	29 921	520	32.3	3.3	51.0
ALASKA	20 907	267 999	49 240	12 294	35 221	7 340	18 662	15 643	58 371	762	56.2	11.3	54.1
Aleutians East	57	2 553	D	D	60	D	NA	77	30 025	NA	NA	NA	NA
Aleutians West	115	4 333	96	3 003	151	D	11	160	37 034	NA	NA	NA	NA
Anchorage	8 733	148 448	25 778	1 849	16 495	4 761	14 417	9 265	62 409	291	56.7	5.8	56.4
Bethel	247	3 222	1 101	D	852	34	21	135	41 834	NA	NA	NA	NA
Bristol Bay	75	382	D	86	39	D	D	49	128 720	NA	NA	NA	NA
Denali	101	503	12	NA	19	D	3	54	108 089	NA	NA	NA	NA
Dillingham	96	1 224	701	11	213	9	D	68	55 960	NA	NA	NA	NA
Fairbanks North Star	2 459	27 673	5 679	576	5 019	735	1 334	1 453	52 490	217	39.2	20.7	47.9
Haines	143	611	128	25	114	D	12	29	47 290	NA	NA	NA	NA
Hoonah-Angoon	76	226	31	D	66	NA	D	11	47 004	NA	NA	NA	NA
Juneau	1 147	11 272	2 312	260	1 833	361	530	571	50 675	52	92.3	0.0	63.5
Kenai Peninsula	2 061	15 353	3 800	676	2 634	298	530	819	53 317	162	67.9	4.9	57.4
Ketchikan Gateway	604	5 002	818	358	804	214	113	277	55 469	NA	NA	NA	NA
Kodiak Island	483	4 862	718	1 821	466	77	56	203	41 700	NA	NA	NA	NA
Kusilvak	73	672	D	D	303	D	NA	18	26 388	NA	NA	NA	NA
Lake and Peninsula	51	193	NA	55	16	D	NA	17	86 870	NA	NA	NA	NA
Matanuska-Susitna	2 154	17 795	3 935	246	3 611	495	754	903	50 757	NA	NA	NA	NA
Nome	175	2 300	D	D	369	29	16	110	47 996	NA	NA	NA	NA
North Slope	164	5 409	245	D	240	D	61	443	81 840	NA	NA	NA	NA
Northwest Arctic	75	1 987	D	96	138	D	D	159	80 032	NA	NA	NA	NA
Petersburg	177	958	172	NA	245	21	15	56	58 336	NA	NA	NA	NA
Prince of Wales-Hyder	145	934	205	138	201	29	NA	39	41 464	NA	NA	NA	NA
Sitka	371	2 875	803	380	407	66	55	136	47 199	NA	NA	NA	NA
Skagway	115	357	5	1	85	D	NA	26	71 459	NA	NA	NA	NA
Southeast Fairbanks	184	1 287	124	14	195	16	47	87	67 441	NA	NA	NA	NA
Valdez-Cordova	506	2 853	472	209	348	36	115	190	66 553	NA	NA	NA	NA
Wrangell	84	572	D	D	123	D	10	21	37 257	NA	NA	NA	NA
Yakutat	26	154	12	D	49	NA	NA	6	39 818	NA	NA	NA	NA
Yukon-Koyukuk	99	315	31	NA	125	NA	D	13	42 260	NA	NA	NA	NA
ARIZONA	136 352	2 295 186	338 701	140 742	314 461	141 104	144 711	102 671	44 733	20 005	79.9	8.1	66.1
Apache	455	6 839	2 813	84	1 247	70	126	251	36 747	5 591	85.6	4.2	73.3
Cochise	2 188	26 092	4 560	348	5 329	500	3 646	905	34 676	1 093	43.8	22.4	56.1
Coconino	3 527	50 051	8 007	5 480	8 063	830	1 708	1 933	38 627	2 239	92.0	3.8	72.5
Gila	1 006	11 572	2 206	181	2 156	188	254	491	42 443	195	65.6	13.3	58.5
Graham	473	6 682	1 503	224	1 624	114	433	237	35 505	412	61.4	15.8	45.4
Greenlee	91	3 883	130	NA	194	D	111	264	67 922	159	52.8	15.1	57.9
La Paz	345	3 804	568	184	962	59	41	111	29 091	125	35.2	28.8	73.6
Maricopa	88 900	1 571 313	217 313	97 400	203 089	118 028	112 270	75 271	47 903	2 479	84.6	5.7	50.9
Mohave	3 677	41 520	8 699	2 830	9 538	919	905	1 342	32 324	335	59.1	23.9	51.3
Navajo	1 725	18 576	4 317	328	4 068	355	423	641	34 525	3 846	91.3	3.4	75.5
Pima	20 152	310 979	59 120	22 501	47 724	12 914	16 236	12 162	39 107	855	79.4	9.4	49.0
Pinal	3 365	47 712	7 784	4 036	8 618	953	936	1 672	35 046	938	56.5	22.8	62.8
Santa Cruz	1 162	11 314	1 131	369	2 422	188	168	347	30 660	236	53.0	19.5	58.9
Yavapai	5 741	57 307	13 011	3 387	10 725	1 154	1 698	1 960	34 206	940	69.9	13.1	64.1
Yuma	2 942	41 516	7 181	3 390	8 294	1 102	1 390	1 360	32 754	562	64.4	14.4	54.8
ARKANSAS	65 175	1 003 113	168 568	155 487	143 230	36 327	36 828	39 451	39 329	45 071	30.8	13.0	47.3
Arkansas	511	8 252	934	3 445	1 165	230	80	309	37 496	492	17.9	41.7	53.7
Ashley	393	6 123	920	2 139	728	181	66	260	42 543	376	47.9	12.2	40.4
Baxter	1 037	13 082	3 680	2 520	2 256	523	469	438	33 508	561	38.5	6.4	44.9
Benton	5 768	107 465	8 819	9 922	12 158	2 753	7 681	6 302	58 646	2 157	43.2	5.1	47.8
Boone	870	11 839	2 213	1 759	1 989	418	217	413	34 859	1 282	32.2	9.2	52.7
Bradley	251	2 932	497	800	315	113	33	82	27 946	185	39.5	2.7	36.8
Calhoun	60	407	D	D	54	18	D	16	40 047	92	20.7	5.4	28.3
Carroll	691	8 067	775	3 145	1 123	221	135	225	27 919	1 126	27.5	10.7	49.4
Chicot	212	2 099	792	8	320	89	29	68	32 346	313	17.6	41.5	57.5
Clark	488	6 790	1 039	1 292	1 179	238	183	207	30 554	381	26.0	10.0	44.1
Clay	290	2 668	704	303	499	98	38	77	28 933	610	24.6	26.6	52.5
Cleburne	574	5 795	752	1 078	1 105	171	217	172	29 735	797	32.4	7.0	40.0

Table B. States and Counties — **Agriculture**

STATE County	Acreage (1,000) [117]	Percent change, 2007–2012 [118]	Average size of farm [119]	Total irrigated (1,000) [120]	Total cropland (1,000) [121]	Average per farm [122]	Average per acre [123]	Value of machinery and equipment, average per farm (dollars) [124]	Total (mil dol) [125]	Average per farm (dollars) [126]	Crops [127]	Live-stock and poultry products [128]	$10,000 or more [129]	$100,000 or more [130]	Total ($1,000) [131]	Percent of farms [132]
ALABAMA—Cont'd																
Washington	96	14.3	258	0.0	12.6	435 148	1 689	62 544	31.7	85 329	15.3	84.7	26.7	7.0	373	17.5
Wilcox	120	-29.2	379	D	22.3	636 839	1 682	51 880	D	D	D	D	25.9	3.2	1 142	44.9
Winston	58	-10.2	111	D	13.5	289 904	2 601	51 921	57.6	110 785	1.4	98.6	36.7	13.8	135	7.3
ALASKA	834	-5.4	1 094	2.5	84.1	681 479	623	87 445	58.9	77 329	42.2	57.8	42.3	11.4	2 432	25.6
Aleutians East	NA	NA	NA	NA	NA	NA	NA	NA	NA	NA	NA	NA	NA	NA	NA	NA
Aleutians West	NA	NA	NA	NA	NA	NA	NA	NA	NA	NA	NA	NA	NA	NA	NA	NA
Anchorage	36	-5.2	125	1.3	17.1	879 979	7 039	92 491	30.0	103 158	47.3	52.7	46.0	14.8	354	17.5
Bethel	NA	NA	NA	NA	NA	NA	NA	NA	NA	NA	NA	NA	NA	NA	NA	NA
Bristol Bay	NA	NA	NA	NA	NA	NA	NA	NA	NA	NA	NA	NA	NA	NA	NA	NA
Denali	NA	NA	NA	NA	NA	NA	NA	NA	NA	NA	NA	NA	NA	NA	NA	NA
Dillingham	NA	NA	NA	NA	NA	NA	NA	NA	NA	NA	NA	NA	NA	NA	NA	NA
Fairbanks North Star	100	-10.1	459	1.0	61.4	580 382	1 264	94 359	9.1	42 120	84.8	15.2	42.4	10.6	1 354	30.9
Haines	NA	NA	NA	NA	NA	NA	NA	NA	NA	NA	NA	NA	NA	NA	NA	NA
Hoonah-Angoon	NA	NA	NA	NA	NA	NA	NA	NA	NA	NA	NA	NA	NA	NA	NA	NA
Juneau	1	37.5	14	0.0	0.1	740 712	54 479	152 173	12.4	238 692	7.4	92.6	51.9	23.1	25	13.5
Kenai Peninsula	29	-23.9	180	0.1	4.5	435 877	2 423	46 315	D	D	D	D	30.9	3.7	353	33.3
Ketchikan Gateway	NA	NA	NA	NA	NA	NA	NA	NA	NA	NA	NA	NA	NA	NA	NA	NA
Kodiak Island	NA	NA	NA	NA	NA	NA	NA	NA	NA	NA	NA	NA	NA	NA	NA	NA
Kusilvak	NA	NA	NA	NA	NA	NA	NA	NA	NA	NA	NA	NA	NA	NA	NA	NA
Lake and Peninsula	NA	NA	NA	NA	NA	NA	NA	NA	NA	NA	NA	NA	NA	NA	NA	NA
Matanuska-Susitna	NA	NA	NA	NA	NA	NA	NA	NA	NA	NA	NA	NA	NA	NA	NA	NA
Nome	NA	NA	NA	NA	NA	NA	NA	NA	NA	NA	NA	NA	NA	NA	NA	NA
North Slope	NA	NA	NA	NA	NA	NA	NA	NA	NA	NA	NA	NA	NA	NA	NA	NA
Northwest Arctic	NA	NA	NA	NA	NA	NA	NA	NA	NA	NA	NA	NA	NA	NA	NA	NA
Petersburg	NA	NA	NA	NA	NA	NA	NA	NA	NA	NA	NA	NA	NA	NA	NA	NA
Prince of Wales-Hyder	NA	NA	NA	NA	NA	NA	NA	NA	NA	NA	NA	NA	NA	NA	NA	NA
Sitka	NA	NA	NA	NA	NA	NA	NA	NA	NA	NA	NA	NA	NA	NA	NA	NA
Skagway	NA	NA	NA	NA	NA	NA	NA	NA	NA	NA	NA	NA	NA	NA	NA	NA
Southeast Fairbanks	NA	NA	NA	NA	NA	NA	NA	NA	NA	NA	NA	NA	NA	NA	NA	NA
Valdez-Cordova	NA	NA	NA	NA	NA	NA	NA	NA	NA	NA	NA	NA	NA	NA	NA	NA
Wrangell	NA	NA	NA	NA	NA	NA	NA	NA	NA	NA	NA	NA	NA	NA	NA	NA
Yakutat	NA	NA	NA	NA	NA	NA	NA	NA	NA	NA	NA	NA	NA	NA	NA	NA
Yukon-Koyukuk	NA	NA	NA	NA	NA	NA	NA	NA	NA	NA	NA	NA	NA	NA	NA	NA
ARIZONA	26 249	0.5	1 312	880.6	1 150.8	844 064	643	62 708	3 732.1	186 559	55.6	44.4	20.3	7.3	31 329	15.3
Apache	5 598	D	1 001	9.8	26.5	192 667	192	18 893	24.2	4 327	54.5	45.5	7.5	0.6	973	14.9
Cochise	917	11.2	839	65.5	123.3	1 175 308	1 401	81 234	150.0	137 235	D	D	37.6	13.3	2 594	16.9
Coconino	5 816	-4.7	2 597	1.9	8.3	543 406	209	23 731	25.8	11 528	9.1	90.9	9.6	1.4	987	23.0
Gila	1 189	1.9	6 098	0.8	2.8	1 993 174	327	55 646	3.8	19 241	9.1	90.9	33.8	4.6	323	10.8
Graham	1 251	-7.0	3 037	36.9	41.7	1 752 109	577	143 189	170.9	414 769	97.1	2.9	33.5	15.8	3 056	38.3
Greenlee	52	48.5	329	5.4	5.2	514 126	1 561	70 818	9.7	61 239	24.8	75.2	32.7	15.1	337	32.7
La Paz	D	D	D	93.2	120.0	2 513 648	D	345 968	183.2	1 465 944	D	D	64.8	45.6	2 011	34.4
Maricopa	476	-2.0	192	192.9	222.5	1 087 145	5 663	113 576	1 003.5	404 790	44.5	55.5	32.2	14.1	5 379	9.7
Mohave	1 244	45.0	3 714	20.8	29.1	1 792 487	483	75 743	30.2	90 102	68.9	31.1	33.7	11.9	1 242	11.3
Navajo	4 323	-4.0	1 124	6.5	20.1	291 214	259	20 164	64.5	16 775	9.0	91.0	7.6	0.6	832	13.1
Pima	D	D	D	32.4	36.7	1 651 870	D	64 622	97.3	113 786	76.8	23.2	31.2	10.3	1 085	5.3
Pinal	1 175	12.2	1 252	223.6	302.6	2 979 541	2 379	188 860	927.7	989 059	34.0	66.0	49.7	30.0	9 558	27.8
Santa Cruz	215	65.9	911	1.8	1.2	1 390 784	1 527	35 631	14.7	62 110	4.7	95.3	43.6	12.7	996	15.7
Yavapai	825	29.0	877	7.6	10.7	1 382 518	1 576	51 250	41.6	44 285	25.5	74.5	32.2	12.0	141	3.2
Yuma	215	2.0	382	181.4	200.1	2 758 098	7 220	372 064	985.0	1 752 685	D	D	61.7	28.5	1 815	17.1
ARKANSAS	13 811	-0.4	306	4 803.9	7 931.1	807 965	2 637	115 436	9 775.8	216 897	49.5	50.5	44.0	16.7	262 967	29.2
Arkansas	402	-0.7	817	314.6	360.2	2 168 250	2 653	320 372	298.2	606 043	99.7	0.3	55.5	46.5	17 373	83.9
Ashley	112	-27.7	297	70.8	83.7	861 694	2 905	127 370	72.8	193 734	91.6	8.4	31.4	15.2	3 123	31.1
Baxter	92	-5.4	164	0.1	12.8	436 902	2 668	46 217	20.4	36 305	3.0	97.0	29.8	4.1	948	16.8
Benton	305	19.7	141	0.6	88.0	626 853	4 435	68 418	529.1	245 307	1.0	99.0	46.5	17.8	1 832	13.7
Boone	257	6.2	201	0.4	38.7	515 837	2 572	54 509	124.1	96 775	1.1	98.9	45.1	10.8	3 730	34.8
Bradley	20	-21.7	107	D	5.5	372 924	3 492	57 232	43.6	235 854	D	D	41.1	16.2	133	13.0
Calhoun	14	-15.4	151	0.1	3.4	370 859	2 459	57 957	6.0	64 761	6.5	93.5	28.3	7.6	32	21.7
Carroll	256	5.7	228	0.1	48.2	579 130	2 543	70 987	307.0	272 652	0.6	99.4	56.6	20.4	2 464	25.3
Chicot	290	1.4	925	197.1	254.9	2 465 096	2 665	340 051	204.7	654 054	96.4	3.6	60.4	44.7	7 640	83.7
Clark	90	10.3	237	D	26.5	437 554	1 848	53 113	15.1	39 588	13.9	86.1	34.6	5.0	342	22.8
Clay	331	0.3	543	235.6	298.0	1 737 748	3 198	263 780	246.2	403 561	98.6	1.4	48.9	32.0	9 792	77.2
Cleburne	157	21.3	198	0.8	37.0	540 846	2 738	62 587	47.9	60 064	2.5	97.5	33.9	6.9	1 013	23.5

Table B. States and Counties — Water Use, Wholesale Trade, Retail Trade, and Real Estate

STATE County	Water use, 2010 Total water withdrawn (mil gal/day)	Gallons withdrawn per person per day	Wholesale trade,[1] 2012 Number of establishments	Number of employees	Sales (mil dol)	Annual payroll (mil dol)	Retail trade,[2] 2012 Number of establishments	Number of employees	Sales (mil dol)	Annual payroll (mil dol)	Real estate and rental and leasing,[2] 2012 Number of establishments	Number of employees	Receipts (mil dol)	Annual payroll (mil dol)
	133	134	135	136	137	138	139	140	141	142	143	144	145	146
ALABAMA—Cont'd														
Washington	89.6	5 098	3	D	D	D	34	232	75.7	5.5	1	D	D	D
Wilcox	22.2	1 905	7	D	D	D	47	269	72.8	5.5	3	D	D	D
Winston	2.2	89	22	171	207.7	6.8	98	754	165.0	16.3	8	22	3.5	0.6
ALASKA	1 094.5	1 541	638	7 734	5 216.3	440.9	2 508	33 721	10 474.3	977.4	872	4 212	1 022.7	187.6
Aleutians East	3.7	1 172	1	D	D	D	8	D	D	D	3	7	1.3	0.2
Aleutians West	5.0	892	13	111	145.9	7.8	11	148	53.4	4.7	4	34	11.9	1.9
Anchorage	46.2	158	336	5 228	3 147.7	296.6	860	15 253	4 966.8	462.2	383	2 403	631.3	112.1
Bethel	0.5	28	5	28	6.9	0.6	54	855	162.8	15.4	7	D	D	D
Bristol Bay	0.2	191	4	D	D	D	9	52	15.8	1.6	1	D	D	D
Denali	24.2	13 237	NA	NA	NA	NA	13	99	13.4	1.1	NA	NA	NA	NA
Dillingham	0.4	80	2	D	D	D	18	214	58.4	4.6	6	D	D	D
Fairbanks North Star	53.6	549	69	666	413.5	36.5	301	4 758	1 732.5	153.1	144	661	159.6	33.2
Haines	44.4	17 699	1	D	D	D	19	115	21.6	3.5	5	3	0.8	0.1
Hoonah-Angoon	141.1	65 623	NA	NA	NA	NA	14	48	11.4	1.0	2	D	D	D
Juneau	58.8	1 880	36	265	196.9	12.8	142	1 821	491.4	53.0	61	249	42.2	7.0
Kenai Peninsula	28.0	506	44	383	262.4	18.2	266	2 482	804.2	69.7	66	238	68.9	12.7
Ketchikan Gateway	29.9	2 220	10	D	D	D	121	856	235.9	28.1	28	103	17.5	3.3
Kodiak Island	6.1	449	22	93	78.1	4.1	41	463	115.9	12.2	13	71	6.2	1.6
Kusilvak	0.5	68	2	D	D	D	25	339	46.6	4.6	2	D	D	D
Lake and Peninsula	0.5	294	1	D	D	D	4	D	D	D	4	8	1.0	0.1
Matanuska-Susitna	33.8	379	40	298	134.9	14.8	244	3 415	1 039.1	89.3	75	181	38.3	6.2
Nome	0.7	78	4	D	D	D	34	360	78.7	7.9	5	18	4.0	0.5
North Slope	221.2	23 453	9	234	354.0	19.2	20	240	94.9	6.8	8	49	10.9	2.5
Northwest Arctic	9.8	1 307	1	D	D	D	12	D	D	D	4	6	0.7	0.0
Petersburg	62.3	16 338	8	33	22.2	1.8	28	231	44.2	6.0	4	5	D	D
Prince of Wales-Hyder	73.7	13 254	2	D	D	D	25	204	48.2	5.1	3	D	D	D
Sitka	55.3	6 221	9	48	38.3	1.9	57	424	98.5	12.4	16	47	4.3	1.2
Skagway	8.7	8 988	2	D	D	D	38	118	32.2	4.3	2	D	D	D
Southeast Fairbanks	1.0	135	4	D	D	D	34	248	78.6	6.3	8	11	0.7	0.1
Valdez-Cordova	42.7	4 431	8	44	62.7	4.9	52	372	114.0	9.5	10	21	3.0	0.9
Wrangell	48.1	20 283	2	D	D	D	20	180	27.7	4.7	3	2	0.5	0.0
Yakutat	92.6	139 849	1	D	D	D	5	41	5.2	0.9	1	D	D	D
Yukon-Koyukuk	1.8	317	2	D	D	D	33	130	32.9	2.4	3	3	1.1	0.1
ARIZONA	6 088.2	952	5 570	73 496	69 437.3	4 144.3	17 479	286 184	84 716.5	7 367.8	8 089	40 479	9 329.7	1 693.2
Apache	49.0	685	15	D	D	D	105	1 133	324.3	22.2	12	D	D	D
Cochise	238.4	1 815	47	269	133.9	10.1	408	5 266	1 267.3	115.2	113	424	57.1	11.4
Coconino	52.2	388	95	738	439.3	33.8	590	7 337	1 896.5	164.8	188	667	137.3	28.1
Gila	34.7	647	23	169	68.5	8.6	169	2 005	486.0	46.0	61	149	27.0	4.1
Graham	176.2	4 734	15	D	D	D	93	1 524	381.8	33.6	25	80	17.4	2.6
Greenlee	25.9	3 069	3	D	D	D	16	143	44.2	3.1	3	D	D	D
La Paz	668.8	32 644	11	94	64.2	4.2	81	924	436.0	19.8	21	72	10.7	1.5
Maricopa	1 953.6	512	3 957	57 945	60 841.1	3 426.0	10 415	183 609	57 296.7	4 930.7	5 398	29 825	7 607.5	1 352.0
Mohave	121.2	605	114	816	391.1	30.5	593	8 918	2 712.7	211.4	199	628	83.2	15.6
Navajo	61.7	574	36	291	170.0	12.1	300	3 935	1 120.3	89.1	94	211	36.0	7.0
Pima	305.4	312	703	6 172	3 099.3	269.6	2 770	43 642	11 377.2	1 094.8	1 250	6 042	973.5	205.5
Pinal	1 130.1	3 007	101	1 633	785.6	123.5	484	8 142	2 375.2	184.3	180	574	105.4	15.6
Santa Cruz	17.4	368	150	D	D	D	219	2 344	498.3	47.8	45	192	23.9	3.2
Yavapai	92.3	437	163	1 385	880.4	59.1	787	9 854	2 504.3	233.3	341	941	153.0	27.7
Yuma	1 161.4	5 933	137	2 433	1 439.8	102.5	449	7 408	1 996.0	171.9	159	639	91.9	18.0
ARKANSAS	11 327.0	3 885	2 884	34 492	31 256.1	1 630.8	10 923	135 448	36 815.3	3 061.5	2 802	12 867	1 922.7	409.8
Arkansas	939.7	49 410	36	428	300.4	19.8	99	1 066	336.0	26.0	22	67	10.0	1.7
Ashley	205.2	9 388	12	136	198.7	6.8	85	863	185.2	17.2	12	26	3.1	0.8
Baxter	4.8	117	21	D	D	D	210	2 105	476.6	43.4	36	150	43.7	13.8
Benton	402.5	1 818	237	2 550	2 366.0	150.5	660	10 143	2 906.0	241.3	245	897	173.2	35.7
Boone	2.8	76	36	D	D	D	143	1 739	493.3	42.2	37	D	D	D
Bradley	2.1	180	10	96	54.9	3.0	39	338	98.9	7.6	7	14	0.8	0.2
Calhoun	0.7	121	2	D	D	D	17	78	17.8	1.5	1	D	D	D
Carroll	10.7	390	9	94	33.5	3.9	147	1 142	230.2	24.0	26	72	4.3	1.0
Chicot	273.1	23 140	12	109	169.1	6.4	49	379	75.9	7.6	11	D	D	D
Clark	11.6	505	10	D	D	D	96	1 158	273.7	27.0	29	94	10.9	1.5
Clay	407.5	25 337	15	258	192.9	8.3	55	485	179.4	11.4	6	D	D	D
Cleburne	26.0	999	21	D	D	D	108	1 052	313.1	23.4	21	D	D	D

1. Merchant wholesalers, except manufacturers' sales branches and offices.   2. Employer establishments.

Professional Services, Manufacturing, and Accommodation and Food Services

STATE County	Professional, scientific, and technical services, 2012				Manufacturing, 2012				Accommodation and food services, 2012			
	Number of establish-ments	Number of employees	Receipts (mil dol)	Annual payroll (mil dol)	Number of establish-ments	Number of employees	Receipts (mil dol)	Annual payroll (mil dol)	Number of establish-ments	Number of employees	Sales (mil dol)	Annual payroll (mil dol)
	147	148	149	150	151	152	153	154	155	156	157	158
ALABAMA—Cont'd												
Washington	13	50	6.4	3.5	14	3 022	D	236.0	11	D	D	D
Wilcox	10	D	D	D	8	471	D	32.9	12	D	D	D
Winston	28	78	8.5	2.4	53	2 624	608.2	79.4	36	D	D	D
ALASKA	1 898	17 648	3 175.2	1 178.3	527	12 450	D	514.5	2 126	26 836	2 221.3	626.0
Aleutians East	NA	NA	NA	NA	5	D	D	D	11	D	D	D
Aleutians West	1	D	D	D	15	2 120	598.5	81.6	7	118	14.2	4.1
Anchorage	1 141	13 516	2 523.8	958.8	182	2 049	479.8	95.7	788	14 957	1 106.2	338.1
Bethel	6	D	D	D	4	10	D	0.4	18	D	D	D
Bristol Bay	1	D	D	D	6	509	D	17.1	19	57	15.7	4.0
Denali	6	5	1.2	0.3	NA	NA	NA	NA	34	106	63.9	17.3
Dillingham	3	D	D	D	4	267	D	8.5	12	49	4.7	0.9
Fairbanks North Star	237	1 683	293.4	86.5	67	641	1 941.2	36.2	213	3 092	255.3	66.4
Haines	5	8	0.9	0.2	8	44	26.3	3.3	20	94	5.7	1.6
Hoonah-Angoon	NA	NA	NA	NA	NA	NA	NA	NA	16	48	8.4	1.8
Juneau	89	514	79.7	31.4	26	236	75.4	11.7	119	1 329	81.5	24.1
Kenai Peninsula	122	541	65.0	27.6	63	758	D	49.6	265	1 646	149.4	37.4
Ketchikan Gateway	28	93	12.7	4.6	11	648	152.4	27.0	66	560	45.7	11.8
Kodiak Island	24	72	26.5	5.7	22	1 744	D	59.6	47	453	31.5	8.7
Kusilvak	NA	NA	NA	NA	NA	NA	NA	NA	NA	NA	NA	NA
Lake and Peninsula	NA	NA	NA	NA	4	237	57.1	6.7	11	11	9.8	2.6
Matanuska-Susitna	165	915	122.7	45.4	45	222	53.8	9.1	200	1 782	135.5	35.3
Nome	6	7	1.4	0.5	3	D	D	D	18	176	14.8	3.4
North Slope	6	46	12.7	5.9	NA	NA	NA	NA	33	783	132.9	31.7
Northwest Arctic	3	D	D	D	NA	NA	NA	NA	7	99	6.1	2.1
Petersburg	5	10	0.5	0.2	8	D	104.9	9.8	16	63	5.2	1.1
Prince of Wales-Hyder	1	D	D	D	8	161	D	5.6	26	108	10.6	2.6
Sitka	18	74	5.5	2.0	14	325	D	11.8	39	358	30.3	7.9
Skagway	2	D	D	D	3	6	D	D	22	69	13.0	3.7
Southeast Fairbanks	8	25	4.0	2.0	6	23	D	0.8	24	212	16.5	4.8
Valdez-Cordova	17	90	17.6	5.0	14	385	D	14.7	72	462	41.4	10.1
Wrangell	3	D	D	D	4	59	D	D	6	31	2.9	0.7
Yakutat	NA	NA	NA	NA	NA	NA	NA	NA	6	14	3.7	0.9
Yukon-Koyukuk	1	D	D	D	NA	NA	NA	NA	11	54	5.1	1.1
ARIZONA	16 198	121 381	19 268.1	7 378.7	4 269	131 941	51 243.5	8 193.2	11 669	251 455	13 996.6	4 030.3
Apache	27	D	D	D	10	86	D	D	70	816	47.1	12.6
Cochise	217	4 592	586.7	254.7	43	279	141.0	14.2	277	3 875	173.4	48.4
Coconino	331	1 584	178.5	65.3	90	4 025	2 181.3	312.0	545	11 436	765.7	191.8
Gila	81	354	44.5	15.4	18	723	D	32.2	130	1 673	94.6	26.5
Graham	24	227	7.3	16.4	13	167	D	5.4	57	866	36.2	9.0
Greenlee	3	D	D	D	NA	NA	NA	NA	16	D	D	D
La Paz	13	D	D	D	12	199	D	D	79	D	D	D
Maricopa	11 557	90 488	15 557.1	5 822.6	2 889	91 348	34 583.4	5 426.8	6 776	159 029	9 105.9	2 655.2
Mohave	239	931	72.4	30.8	133	2 566	D	109.5	382	5 787	256.7	74.3
Navajo	113	364	30.7	9.8	31	402	179.8	22.1	225	3 197	186.6	48.1
Pima	2 531	16 514	2 241.1	940.0	640	24 297	8 686.6	1 906.7	1 787	42 311	2 154.7	637.4
Pinal	255	1 430	101.7	42.7	111	2 713	2 244.1	133.8	345	6 125	350.5	90.1
Santa Cruz	64	167	20.6	6.8	27	289	211.0	10.2	103	1 413	58.6	17.4
Yavapai	522	1 748	190.9	74.3	184	2 765	706.9	130.8	548	8 223	407.5	130.8
Yuma	221	1 364	132.3	68.0	68	2 084	884.3	79.8	329	5 736	307.5	76.2
ARKANSAS	5 678	32 210	4 528.0	1 567.0	2 688	153 706	62 712.9	6 290.8	5 473	95 854	4 307.3	1 182.5
Arkansas	23	78	9.6	2.4	27	3 628	1 927.2	126.1	39	D	D	D
Ashley	27	71	10.0	2.4	29	2 172	1 339.9	135.4	27	425	17.3	4.4
Baxter	75	401	30.1	12.1	50	2 201	574.4	86.7	99	1 372	61.6	16.1
Benton	619	6 232	1 062.7	402.1	160	9 219	D	363.0	401	8 290	366.8	105.1
Boone	61	D	D	D	54	1 700	493.7	69.0	68	D	D	D
Bradley	11	31	2.7	0.8	8	459	127.9	18.9	11	D	D	D
Calhoun	2	D	D	D	NA	NA	NA	NA	6	17	1.0	0.2
Carroll	36	130	9.7	3.4	32	3 546	741.9	102.5	133	1 185	56.7	17.0
Chicot	13	35	3.6	1.4	6	81	D	1.7	17	187	7.5	1.9
Clark	28	463	74.8	23.9	23	1 186	392.7	53.9	55	1 025	41.5	12.1
Clay	17	39	3.0	0.9	16	341	D	12.0	19	D	D	D
Cleburne	43	167	13.8	4.9	31	1 183	190.3	42.6	59	766	33.9	8.6

1. Establishment subject to federal tax.

STATE County	Health care and social assistance, 2012				Other services, 2012				Nonemployer businesses, 2015		Value of residential construction authorized by building permits, 2016	
	Number of establishments	Number of employees	Receipts (mil dol)	Annual payroll (mil dol)	Number of establishments	Number of employees	Receipts (mil dol)	Annual payroll (mil dol)	Number	Receipts (mil dol)	New Construction ($1,000)	Number of housing units
	159	160	161	162	163	164	165	166	167	168	169	170
ALABAMA—Cont'd												
Washington	19	D	D	D	9	D	D	D	1 060	30.6	520	3
Wilcox	18	262	16.0	6.7	8	31	3.1	0.8	622	18.5	0	0
Winston	36	684	57.9	21.4	20	D	D	D	1 642	72.9	330	3
ALASKA	2 432	48 701	6 375.5	2 434.2	1 355	7 238	904.6	235.8	55 521	2 601.8	369 042	1 503
Aleutians East	10	D	D	D	4	D	D	D	243	24.5	0	0
Aleutians West	14	D	D	D	6	D	D	D	236	13.9	392	4
Anchorage	1 165	25 616	3 656.2	1 347.8	580	3 863	514.2	136.0	20 364	1 067.2	259 216	930
Bethel	47	D	D	D	14	56	8.4	1.1	887	20.8	2 250	8
Bristol Bay	2	D	D	D	2	D	D	D	206	9.2	450	2
Denali	3	12	1.0	0.6	3	D	D	D	182	6.7	NA	NA
Dillingham	8	D	D	D	6	17	1.5	0.6	780	18.4	575	2
Fairbanks North Star	290	5 748	746.9	305.5	185	842	88.8	25.6	5 587	230.5	2 931	11
Haines	10	134	9.2	4.0	7	D	D	D	428	14.6	2 229	8
Hoonah-Angoon	7	44	3.6	1.5	3	D	D	D	278	11.1	500	3
Juneau	144	2 458	275.5	112.4	82	406	46.5	12.9	2 773	136.7	25 610	153
Kenai Peninsula	226	3 651	352.9	144.4	138	648	78.5	19.9	6 622	284.7	22 376	113
Ketchikan Gateway	36	799	90.1	39.3	42	142	14.1	3.8	1 311	74.0	10 092	38
Kodiak Island	39	733	79.7	35.4	30	150	19.1	4.4	1 498	77.7	3 688	18
Kusilvak	19	D	D	D	4	D	D	D	510	4.0	0	0
Lake and Peninsula	NA	NA	NA	NA	1	D	D	D	272	11.1	NA	NA
Matanuska-Susitna	267	3 621	411.5	161.6	123	572	64.4	16.7	6 940	311.1	16 976	116
Nome	27	D	D	D	13	D	D	D	504	15.6	1 119	9
North Slope	9	D	D	D	7	D	D	D	273	7.9	2 814	11
Northwest Arctic	4	D	D	D	9	D	D	D	252	8.1	2 506	6
Petersburg	11	176	17.5	6.4	13	D	D	D	775	53.5	2 094	6
Prince of Wales-Hyder	10	197	13.4	6.4	7	D	D	D	534	23.4	1 605	8
Sitka	25	937	111.5	47.7	25	100	8.3	2.3	1 327	71.3	5 931	24
Skagway	4	4	0.3	0.1	5	22	1.3	0.4	147	7.5	2 531	13
Southeast Fairbanks	11	D	D	D	7	D	D	D	529	16.6	NA	NA
Valdez-Cordova	24	455	46.1	18.7	28	109	10.7	3.4	1 191	52.2	2 437	13
Wrangell	7	D	D	D	7	D	D	D	360	14.0	530	6
Yakutat	3	D	D	D	NA	NA	NA	NA	124	5.1	191	1
Yukon-Koyukuk	10	32	2.3	1.2	4	D	D	D	388	10.3	0	0
ARIZONA	16 872	315 107	37 055.9	14 236.1	8 503	62 073	6 231.7	1 736.0	451 951	20 709.1	8 044 524	35 578
Apache	64	3 300	412.8	148.1	19	75	7.7	1.6	2 859	61.6	8 379	36
Cochise	273	4 896	408.9	167.4	150	684	53.1	16.1	6 628	206.3	21 936	149
Coconino	381	6 995	1 040.7	354.3	230	1 307	105.8	32.7	9 015	375.9	134 500	647
Gila	133	2 479	259.1	97.6	57	225	18.2	5.3	3 339	118.0	27 856	116
Graham	78	822	61.3	25.1	33	219	31.2	8.0	1 452	53.9	16 104	75
Greenlee	7	D	D	D	2	D	D	D	255	5.0	655	5
La Paz	21	D	D	D	15	D	D	D	802	32.0	4 695	28
Maricopa	10 811	199 139	23 736.9	9 260.4	5 265	42 665	4 489.1	1 246.0	298 614	14 750.9	5 918 178	25 856
Mohave	478	8 222	995.0	364.2	290	1 394	110.3	29.4	10 592	461.3	133 961	683
Navajo	241	3 832	439.1	177.5	117	525	46.0	11.4	5 359	173.5	40 684	221
Pima	2 777	56 539	6 617.5	2 441.8	1 483	10 691	1 008.6	281.2	64 179	2 556.9	693 032	2 466
Pinal	420	8 118	786.3	313.8	240	1 249	120.5	33.1	17 428	645.2	514 340	2 727
Santa Cruz	70	1 135	146.0	41.0	44	154	13.4	3.7	4 237	176.1	16 179	70
Yavapai	759	11 555	1 245.1	517.8	364	1 717	142.9	41.0	18 282	750.9	375 819	1 602
Yuma	359	7 092	794.1	282.4	194	1 099	77.8	25.0	8 910	341.6	138 205	897
ARKANSAS	7 485	166 455	15 792.6	6 318.7	3 961	21 830	2 339.4	586.3	198 380	8 380.3	1 562 882	9 474
Arkansas	46	988	63.6	27.6	30	112	7.6	3.0	1 358	62.3	960	8
Ashley	46	931	64.3	26.8	25	100	9.3	2.6	1 084	33.8	0	0
Baxter	170	3 490	337.5	133.3	80	326	25.4	6.5	3 023	126.3	4 834	24
Benton	472	8 091	751.6	281.5	256	1 613	145.1	44.1	17 040	750.8	587 311	2 883
Boone	126	2 336	195.6	74.3	48	227	24.5	6.5	2 799	113.8	1 560	8
Bradley	25	530	38.6	14.9	21	69	6.7	1.8	510	23.1	258	2
Calhoun	4	D	D	D	2	D	D	D	184	6.3	0	0
Carroll	50	752	57.9	24.0	39	114	10.7	2.8	2 492	85.1	2 382	27
Chicot	36	900	51.2	26.7	10	58	6.5	1.6	577	21.6	410	3
Clark	59	934	65.9	26.4	27	92	10.7	2.4	1 291	50.7	1 957	40
Clay	33	695	42.1	19.8	29	D	D	D	787	33.5	313	3
Cleburne	45	828	54.1	21.5	33	121	10.7	2.4	2 151	88.8	0	0

Table B. States and Counties — Government Employment and Payroll, and Local Government Finances

	Government employment and payroll, 2012									Local government finances, 2012				
			March payroll (percent of total)							General revenue				
												Taxes		
													Per capita[1] (dollars)	
STATE County	Full-time equivalent employees	March payroll (dollars)	Adminis-tration, judicial, and legal	Police and Corrections	Fire Protection	Highways and transpor-tation	Health and Welfare	Natural resources and utilities	Education and libraries	Total (mil dol)	Inter-govern-mental (mil dol)	Total (mil dol)	Total	Property
	171	172	173	174	175	176	177	178	179	180	181	182	183	184
ALABAMA—Cont'd														
Washington	673	2 075 254	4.0	4.1	0.0	2.0	21.7	3.3	64.7	40.9	25.0	11.8	691	514
Wilcox	583	1 459 476	6.1	7.4	0.0	6.3	11.1	6.3	60.3	29.0	18.4	7.7	674	358
Winston	1 387	3 355 200	3.1	5.2	0.8	2.7	29.1	3.2	54.4	62.5	36.3	16.1	667	283
ALASKA	X	X	X	X	X	X	X	X	X	X	X	X	X	X
Aleutians East	184	728 454	19.1	7.1	0.2	11.9	2.3	7.0	41.2	34.8	17.1	10.2	3 215	0
Aleutians West	278	1 422 298	17.8	11.2	3.2	9.9	3.0	15.4	24.7	56.1	18.9	21.5	3 872	853
Anchorage	10 003	52 917 485	4.5	7.7	6.5	5.4	2.3	9.8	62.6	1 313.0	582.8	546.6	1 831	1 623
Bethel	302	1 160 315	19.0	13.8	3.3	7.0	2.2	43.9	0.1	65.9	43.9	9.6	543	0
Bristol Bay	78	333 504	12.5	13.6	0.7	18.6	2.8	5.7	46.1	16.8	7.9	5.5	5 590	3 083
Denali	82	322 133	9.4	0.0	0.0	0.0	4.0	0.0	85.9	11.0	7.8	2.8	1 472	0
Dillingham	293	1 115 865	13.8	10.5	0.7	3.7	2.6	29.8	35.5	40.8	28.5	5.7	1 140	460
Fairbanks North Star	2 949	14 833 210	7.9	3.4	2.6	2.4	1.8	5.3	75.9	380.0	201.2	148.5	1 481	1 335
Haines	105	554 027	8.6	6.3	0.8	5.6	0.6	5.8	68.5	20.5	12.5	5.3	2 089	1 020
Hoonah-Angoon	90	310 388	14.5	8.3	2.0	8.6	2.0	9.8	54.0	12.4	8.3	1.7	814	39
Juneau	2 061	10 714 562	5.3	5.1	2.9	7.0	24.9	13.7	41.0	338.0	110.1	83.0	2 549	1 125
Kenai Peninsula	2 080	9 477 210	10.6	5.1	7.7	3.9	1.5	4.4	61.5	445.9	125.4	111.8	1 965	1 014
Ketchikan Gateway	699	3 359 138	10.3	7.2	4.6	11.2	1.5	15.2	47.8	123.4	42.9	28.8	2 087	994
Kodiak Island	637	2 986 849	7.4	6.7	2.5	6.1	0.9	9.3	64.9	102.4	55.1	27.0	1 893	1 004
Kusilvak	286	832 391	24.5	17.3	0.7	6.1	0.8	19.3	17.7	58.3	48.1	1.6	208	0
Lake and Peninsula	163	640 681	11.6	0.0	0.1	1.6	1.2	2.7	78.9	24.1	18.4	2.8	1 706	0
Matanuska-Susitna	2 847	12 057 275	8.3	3.7	1.6	2.4	3.8	2.2	76.5	386.7	229.3	136.9	1 458	1 165
Nome	378	1 484 923	12.5	9.6	0.1	4.9	2.6	23.5	37.5	50.2	28.5	9.5	963	231
North Slope	1 749	8 359 644	27.7	5.0	3.3	11.1	11.6	11.4	26.8	503.2	75.9	366.0	37 957	37 888
Northwest Arctic	630	2 686 215	7.5	8.0	1.7	3.7	1.1	9.5	61.6	100.8	72.5	4.2	541	0
Petersburg	512	2 386 453	4.4	6.0	0.8	10.0	32.9	10.6	32.3	82.3	42.5	9.6	2 490	1 229
Prince of Wales-Hyder	289	1 128 652	6.7	2.6	1.0	2.1	2.2	19.6	61.2	30.3	21.8	3.3	576	89
Sitka	525	2 686 315	6.2	5.6	2.0	2.6	30.9	12.2	35.9	89.4	30.2	15.4	1 705	671
Skagway	66	277 303	9.2	10.8	6.1	7.0	16.4	6.9	36.1	19.8	9.1	8.4	8 710	2 132
Southeast Fairbanks	12	40 359	51.1	0.0	0.0	7.5	18.3	0.0	17.1	1.8	1.3	0.0	0	0
Valdez-Cordova	506	2 285 718	8.9	9.3	3.5	9.2	14.4	12.9	38.6	103.7	27.4	50.7	5 213	4 747
Wrangell	NA	NA	NA	NA	NA	NA	NA	NA	NA	NA	NA	NA	NA	NA
Yakutat	56	174 101	20.5	10.7	0.0	9.9	2.5	2.0	50.3	6.3	4.3	1.3	1 936	647
Yukon-Koyukuk	365	1 481 198	10.8	1.7	0.6	2.6	1.1	7.6	73.3	41.9	35.8	0.9	148	52
ARIZONA	X	X	X	X	X	X	X	X	X	X	X	X	X	X
Apache	2 657	8 600 597	5.6	5.3	1.9	2.9	2.7	1.1	79.6	168.2	116.4	31.5	431	379
Cochise	4 879	16 984 358	11.7	10.2	5.2	2.9	3.0	3.3	61.1	397.9	175.5	144.2	1 092	821
Coconino	4 575	17 536 070	11.8	13.5	9.2	3.5	4.5	6.4	48.1	469.7	159.1	223.4	1 643	979
Gila	2 222	7 331 024	14.5	15.3	7.8	3.9	2.3	5.8	48.1	194.4	80.9	87.8	1 652	1 207
Graham	2 165	7 913 958	6.9	8.1	0.2	2.5	26.5	4.9	50.0	137.7	81.5	29.0	774	382
Greenlee	376	1 216 974	14.2	15.2	0.0	7.6	5.4	1.1	53.9	32.1	12.7	13.6	1 545	1 283
La Paz	799	2 443 896	12.2	19.6	6.3	4.6	4.4	6.2	44.6	60.9	26.7	21.8	1 075	779
Maricopa	129 919	553 767 788	8.2	13.2	5.3	2.8	6.3	12.4	50.5	14 121.0	4 763.7	5 936.1	1 506	958
Mohave	5 613	20 393 845	13.0	13.4	11.7	4.5	2.0	5.6	47.4	538.5	183.2	229.9	1 131	849
Navajo	4 056	13 281 721	8.7	9.6	5.1	2.8	1.5	3.5	67.5	523.9	174.9	109.2	1 020	745
Pima	31 634	115 785 276	10.5	14.5	6.6	3.5	2.2	7.1	52.9	3 257.1	1 214.5	1 427.3	1 438	1 057
Pinal	9 793	33 904 548	13.3	15.5	5.5	3.5	3.8	5.1	52.2	961.4	426.5	329.1	850	624
Santa Cruz	2 004	6 229 659	10.5	13.1	10.4	3.9	2.5	1.8	56.6	161.7	83.6	52.4	1 108	737
Yavapai	6 155	23 081 009	10.4	13.4	9.4	4.0	2.1	5.5	45.2	648.3	201.2	335.8	1 579	1 029
Yuma	7 924	25 609 990	12.0	12.1	3.1	2.2	2.4	7.3	59.9	638.9	314.0	221.6	1 108	716
ARKANSAS	X	X	X	X	X	X	X	X	X	X	X	X	X	X
Arkansas	988	2 636 492	5.7	8.3	2.3	3.4	19.7	5.4	51.8	59.0	32.8	17.1	906	316
Ashley	866	2 414 339	4.8	9.8	2.9	4.1	2.0	4.2	71.6	63.9	38.0	15.5	719	291
Baxter	1 228	3 503 816	4.6	8.5	3.2	6.2	1.3	7.6	68.0	81.3	46.3	22.7	553	251
Benton	7 214	24 863 912	5.8	8.5	5.2	2.0	0.5	6.6	70.3	624.9	346.9	196.3	845	405
Boone	1 391	3 599 052	4.9	7.8	2.9	3.4	0.3	7.1	72.7	96.8	61.2	19.7	527	210
Bradley	467	1 184 067	4.0	5.4	0.9	4.3	3.1	2.7	79.4	35.7	24.9	6.9	603	215
Calhoun	169	422 712	9.1	11.0	0.0	8.6	4.4	3.4	61.8	17.3	7.1	2.7	511	302
Carroll	1 012	2 598 555	4.9	8.8	2.4	5.9	2.4	9.3	64.4	71.0	38.3	16.2	585	295
Chicot	716	2 139 884	6.2	8.0	0.0	2.0	31.0	4.0	48.8	35.1	21.3	8.7	762	307
Clark	763	2 247 437	7.0	17.2	2.0	3.9	2.5	9.0	58.1	67.1	41.9	13.1	572	219
Clay	859	3 044 204	5.9	15.6	0.0	4.6	23.1	14.3	35.5	49.8	25.0	7.5	478	259
Cleburne	801	2 107 158	6.7	9.2	0.5	4.7	1.5	7.6	69.0	57.0	31.3	15.0	583	313

1. Based on the resident population estimated as of July 1 of the year shown.

Table B. States and Counties — Local Government Finances, Government Employment, and Income Taxes

STATE County	Local government finances, 2012 (cont.) Direct general expenditure — Total (mil dol)	Per capita[1] (dollars)	Educa-tion	Health and hospitals	Police protec-tion	Public welfare	High-ways	Debt outstanding Total (mil dol)	Per capita[1] (dollars)	Government employment, 2015 Federal civilian	Federal military	State and local	Individual income tax returns, 2014 Number of returns	Mean adjusted gross income	Mean income tax
	185	186	187	188	189	190	191	192	193	194	195	196	197	198	199
ALABAMA—Cont'd															
Washington	42.8	2 504	67.0	3.3	3.6	0.1	11.2	186.5	10 900	32	74	923	6 620	50 701	4 864
Wilcox	31.8	2 786	61.3	2.7	5.4	0.0	7.4	45.1	3 945	66	49	731	4 480	33 641	2 349
Winston	67.7	2 809	62.8	0.9	3.3	0.0	6.0	53.1	2 204	74	105	1 088	9 040	43 254	4 337
ALASKA	X	X	X	X	X	X	X	X	X	14 964	26 034	63 572	361 110	67 211	9 403
Aleutians East	35.1	11 095	24.9	0.3	3.1	0.0	6.3	40.2	12 717	22	11	253	1 000	41 746	3 978
Aleutians West	55.3	9 975	16.7	0.1	7.8	0.0	12.5	41.9	7 550	13	29	464	2 330	55 358	6 552
Anchorage	1 268.0	4 246	52.5	2.1	9.8	0.0	5.8	1 857.9	6 222	8 476	12 961	19 958	154 390	75 033	11 458
Bethel	70.7	3 986	0.0	0.1	6.7	0.0	3.2	8.4	476	71	122	2 934	7 050	37 154	3 641
Bristol Bay	15.8	15 960	28.3	4.7	6.6	0.0	2.4	1.0	993	50	D	184	530	51 613	6 717
Denali	10.7	5 696	75.8	0.1	0.0	0.0	0.0	0.0	0	200	24	154	1 150	67 916	9 247
Dillingham	39.6	7 872	29.2	2.5	8.2	2.1	5.2	15.1	2 990	47	34	675	2 390	44 682	4 567
Fairbanks North Star	342.4	3 415	63.0	1.6	2.3	0.0	6.2	170.2	1 698	2 945	9 019	7 921	48 140	64 566	8 494
Haines	15.3	5 980	38.0	1.6	3.3	0.0	6.3	16.4	6 424	D	18	176	1 360	50 122	5 584
Hoonah-Angoon	11.8	5 536	49.2	1.1	4.3	0.0	4.8	3.0	1 396	98	15	265	1 020	49 541	6 288
Juneau	318.0	9 768	26.7	30.7	5.4	0.0	4.2	225.5	6 927	698	462	5 972	17 540	71 527	9 930
Kenai Peninsula	437.7	7 692	32.5	38.4	2.0	0.0	2.4	171.8	3 019	357	484	4 452	29 020	66 253	9 193
Ketchikan Gateway	133.0	9 654	26.9	0.8	3.6	0.0	4.1	145.8	10 581	237	264	1 796	7 250	59 938	7 654
Kodiak Island	95.8	6 729	46.7	0.6	5.3	0.0	3.3	62.8	4 413	287	1 009	1 080	7 020	59 564	7 103
Kusilvak	70.2	8 985	80.8	0.2	1.6	0.0	1.3	3.8	489	19	56	1 570	3 260	23 554	1 309
Lake and Peninsula	20.2	12 184	72.3	0.1	0.5	0.0	0.8	3.8	2 267	39	11	391	750	37 580	3 668
Matanuska-Susitna	393.6	4 190	61.3	2.3	2.6	0.0	6.9	404.7	4 309	214	683	4 877	44 140	66 714	8 491
Nome	44.7	4 511	29.0	1.0	4.3	0.0	6.8	12.3	1 244	46	67	1 647	3 820	48 215	5 513
North Slope	459.1	47 609	17.7	2.7	3.1	1.5	3.7	510.2	52 913	21	49	1 949	3 860	51 578	6 458
Northwest Arctic	89.1	11 410	62.5	0.1	1.7	0.0	2.2	72.5	9 289	42	51	1 073	2 570	50 034	5 435
Petersburg	85.2	22 155	24.0	26.0	3.2	1.2	7.1	28.2	7 342	99	51	387	2 000	55 544	6 235
Prince of Wales-Hyder	28.0	4 867	53.2	1.1	4.5	0.0	2.7	4.0	704	88	44	973	2 430	47 824	5 295
Sitka	79.2	8 752	28.6	27.3	5.4	0.0	1.8	117.1	12 949	127	240	1 048	4 730	63 360	8 442
Skagway	17.6	18 327	12.7	9.9	7.3	0.1	9.4	6.5	6 776	53	D	133	770	56 590	7 408
Southeast Fairbanks	1.9	262	0.2	0.1	0.0	0.0	8.6	0.9	119	403	45	416	3 240	53 453	5 796
Valdez-Cordova	84.7	8 716	25.8	23.7	2.1	0.0	3.8	37.8	3 895	145	214	1 151	5 160	60 299	7 646
Wrangell	NA	NA	NA	NA	NA	NA	NA	NA	NA	51	16	262	1 190	49 634	5 318
Yakutat	6.6	9 847	45.8	2.9	9.1	0.0	7.6	1.0	1 548	22	D	108	290	47 017	4 724
Yukon-Koyukuk	46.4	8 035	79.2	0.3	1.0	0.0	1.2	6.9	1 200	86	38	1 303	2 840	33 519	2 984
ARIZONA	X	X	X	X	X	X	X	X	X	54 710	32 306	357 060	2 844 970	56 904	7 148
Apache	161.6	2 208	65.6	3.6	3.3	0.0	6.5	280.9	3 837	2 606	158	8 104	23 880	37 016	2 899
Cochise	407.1	3 082	44.0	3.5	12.3	4.9	7.3	161.6	1 223	5 101	4 254	6 385	52 000	46 526	4 433
Coconino	457.2	3 361	35.9	3.4	6.5	1.6	7.6	377.9	2 779	2 706	301	16 135	58 640	52 565	6 064
Gila	163.2	3 071	37.4	1.4	11.8	2.5	6.1	46.8	881	431	117	4 851	21 240	44 090	4 080
Graham	132.6	3 543	64.5	0.4	8.6	1.6	4.9	28.1	752	408	77	2 408	11 530	47 787	4 443
Greenlee	31.0	3 517	44.5	5.9	11.6	0.0	6.8	16.8	1 911	35	21	523	3 480	57 640	5 624
La Paz	82.5	4 069	27.8	3.1	9.7	0.6	7.2	44.7	2 204	316	44	2 071	6 520	35 659	2 999
Maricopa	13 916.1	3 530	41.6	5.1	8.2	1.5	4.1	27 988.0	7 100	20 167	12 887	194 164	1 780 700	61 720	8 340
Mohave	555.1	2 730	33.9	2.7	6.9	0.1	8.7	627.7	3 087	463	448	7 167	79 020	40 480	3 781
Navajo	397.5	3 712	44.4	24.0	5.0	0.8	4.3	156.9	1 465	1 660	237	7 888	37 850	39 951	3 209
Pima	3 531.8	3 559	37.0	3.1	9.1	2.7	5.3	5 788.9	5 833	12 506	8 041	67 320	434 040	54 350	6 327
Pinal	1 130.4	2 918	46.7	4.4	9.1	1.6	3.8	1 030.3	2 660	1 684	853	17 873	133 500	47 718	4 353
Santa Cruz	148.9	3 149	48.5	3.1	10.0	0.0	3.8	161.3	3 410	1 665	103	2 061	19 610	41 071	3 659
Yavapai	653.7	3 074	36.5	2.1	7.2	1.8	9.0	725.7	3 413	1 497	500	9 188	100 270	49 296	5 492
Yuma	616.3	3 081	47.8	2.1	6.0	2.5	4.6	668.5	3 342	3 465	4 265	10 922	82 770	39 369	3 414
ARKANSAS	X	X	X	X	X	X	X	X	X	20 339	16 839	193 000	1 223 070	53 219	6 287
Arkansas	54.5	2 887	54.8	0.8	6.7	0.0	6.5	53.2	2 814	192	78	952	8 030	47 952	5 587
Ashley	63.4	2 945	60.9	0.2	5.8	0.0	6.5	95.2	4 425	68	88	1 083	8 400	45 749	4 652
Baxter	82.1	2 001	58.9	0.0	7.5	0.1	8.6	143.9	3 507	132	173	1 546	17 680	45 366	4 721
Benton	620.5	2 672	61.2	0.2	5.6	0.0	5.6	1 204.1	5 184	451	1 058	9 375	105 520	91 415	14 709
Boone	94.8	2 540	65.0	0.1	4.7	0.0	4.2	59.7	1 600	148	157	3 058	15 220	44 871	4 373
Bradley	34.0	2 985	65.5	0.0	5.4	0.1	7.3	14.7	1 294	34	46	861	4 330	39 939	3 750
Calhoun	20.8	3 913	57.2	1.1	3.3	0.5	6.0	106.6	20 089	10	22	274	1 910	45 927	4 355
Carroll	75.8	2 746	55.7	0.1	5.3	0.0	7.5	76.9	2 784	86	117	1 122	12 120	37 361	3 186
Chicot	34.4	3 008	57.3	2.8	6.4	0.1	7.0	15.4	1 344	41	44	950	4 090	40 394	4 311
Clark	65.6	2 861	64.3	0.1	4.3	0.0	5.6	101.8	4 437	83	85	2 520	8 470	45 251	4 499
Clay	49.7	3 171	48.6	25.1	4.0	0.0	5.7	31.5	2 010	55	64	834	5 970	36 434	3 481
Cleburne	54.0	2 093	60.3	0.2	4.9	0.1	9.9	57.4	2 225	87	107	873	10 410	49 639	5 654

1. Based on the resident population estimated as of July 1 of the year shown.

STATE/ County code	CBSA code[1]	County type[2]	STATE County	Land area,[3] (sq mi) 2016	Total persons 2016	Rank	Per square mile	White	Black	American Indian, Alaska Native	Asian and Pacific Islander	Percent Hispanic or Latino[4]	Under 5 years	5 to 17 years	18 to 24 years	25 to 34 years	35 to 44 years	45 to 54 years
				1	2	3	4	5	6	7	8	9	10	11	12	13	14	15
			ARKANSAS—Cont'd															
05 025	38220	3	Cleveland	597.8	8 241	2 575	13.8	85.7	12.2	0.8	0.3	2.3	5.2	17.4	7.4	10.9	11.9	13.7
05 027	31620	7	Columbia	766.1	23 901	1 645	31.2	60.4	36.0	0.8	1.3	2.7	6.0	14.9	17.1	11.0	10.1	11.7
05 029	...	6	Conway	552.3	20 937	1 777	37.9	83.5	12.4	1.6	0.7	3.9	6.0	16.9	7.6	11.8	11.4	13.3
05 031	27860	3	Craighead	707.3	105 835	564	149.6	78.5	15.9	0.8	1.5	4.9	7.1	17.8	10.8	15.5	12.6	11.9
05 033	22900	2	Crawford	591.2	62 267	846	105.3	87.3	2.1	3.8	2.0	7.5	6.3	18.4	7.8	12.5	12.3	13.6
05 035	32820	1	Crittenden	610.3	49 235	997	80.7	43.6	53.6	0.6	0.9	2.5	7.8	20.1	9.1	13.2	11.9	12.8
05 037	...	6	Cross	616.4	17 037	1 978	27.6	73.8	23.7	0.8	0.9	2.0	6.5	17.7	8.1	11.1	12.3	13.1
05 039	...	6	Dallas	667.4	7 469	2 632	11.2	54.1	42.8	1.0	0.6	3.2	5.0	16.8	7.3	10.7	10.7	12.3
05 041	...	6	Desha	768.1	11 876	2 304	15.5	46.7	46.7	0.8	0.7	6.1	6.8	18.9	7.8	11.2	11.1	11.8
05 043	...	6	Drew	828.4	18 651	1 885	22.5	67.9	28.6	0.6	0.9	3.1	6.2	15.8	14.6	11.5	10.7	12.1
05 045	30780	2	Faulkner	647.9	122 227	512	188.7	82.5	12.4	1.2	1.9	4.0	6.2	17.3	15.3	14.6	12.3	11.9
05 047	...	6	Franklin	608.9	17 626	1 938	28.9	93.9	1.4	2.2	1.3	2.9	5.9	17.3	8.4	11.4	12.0	13.0
05 049	...	9	Fulton	618.2	12 123	2 287	19.6	97.0	1.2	1.5	0.6	1.4	5.2	15.4	6.3	9.0	9.5	13.0
05 051	26300	3	Garland	677.8	97 477	608	143.8	84.6	9.5	1.5	1.3	5.4	5.5	15.1	7.4	11.4	11.1	12.6
05 053	30780	2	Grant	631.8	18 082	1 916	28.6	93.9	3.1	1.2	0.6	2.5	5.5	17.5	7.5	12.0	12.8	14.0
05 055	37500	2	Greene	577.7	44 598	1 080	77.2	94.6	2.0	1.1	0.8	2.8	6.5	18.2	8.2	13.1	13.0	13.5
05 057	26260	6	Hempstead	727.5	21 974	1 728	30.2	56.6	30.7	1.1	0.9	12.6	7.1	18.9	7.9	11.2	11.6	12.6
05 059	31680	6	Hot Spring	615.2	33 374	1 345	54.2	84.3	11.9	1.4	0.8	3.4	5.0	15.8	8.2	12.7	12.4	14.0
05 061	...	6	Howard	588.6	13 377	2 206	22.7	65.9	21.2	1.5	0.9	12.2	7.2	18.7	7.9	12.0	10.8	13.4
05 063	12900	7	Independence	764.0	37 168	1 248	48.6	90.3	2.8	1.1	1.2	6.2	6.3	17.7	8.7	11.9	12.2	12.9
05 065	...	9	Izard	580.6	13 433	2 201	23.1	94.4	2.3	1.8	0.7	2.1	4.3	13.7	6.5	10.4	10.9	14.0
05 067	...	6	Jackson	633.9	17 221	1 966	27.2	78.4	18.4	1.3	0.8	2.7	5.5	14.7	7.8	14.6	13.2	13.7
05 069	38220	3	Jefferson	870.7	70 016	767	80.4	40.3	56.9	0.8	1.2	2.0	6.3	16.6	10.1	12.9	11.5	12.7
05 071	...	7	Johnson	659.9	26 176	1 554	39.7	81.8	2.1	1.9	2.2	13.9	6.7	17.8	9.2	13.1	11.7	12.7
05 073	...	8	Lafayette	528.3	6 847	2 689	13.0	59.9	37.3	0.7	0.6	2.6	4.8	14.6	7.9	9.8	10.4	14.0
05 075	...	6	Lawrence	587.6	16 735	1 998	28.5	96.8	1.4	1.4	0.4	1.4	5.7	16.3	9.8	11.2	11.2	12.9
05 077	...	7	Lee	602.6	9 310	2 481	15.4	42.2	54.7	1.2	0.7	2.6	5.1	13.9	8.3	15.2	13.1	12.9
05 079	38220	3	Lincoln	561.6	13 705	2 188	24.4	65.1	30.9	0.9	0.5	3.7	4.2	13.2	10.4	17.1	14.7	14.5
05 081	45500	3	Little River	532.3	12 451	2 264	23.4	74.6	20.6	2.5	0.7	3.7	5.6	16.2	7.4	10.8	12.1	13.3
05 083	...	6	Logan	708.1	21 792	1 737	30.8	92.5	2.0	2.1	2.3	2.9	5.7	16.3	8.0	10.9	11.3	14.2
05 085	30780	2	Lonoke	770.9	72 228	752	93.7	87.9	6.7	1.2	1.6	4.4	6.7	19.2	8.1	14.3	13.6	13.2
05 087	22220	4	Madison	834.3	16 072	2 035	19.3	91.4	0.8	2.5	1.6	5.5	6.2	17.4	7.5	11.1	11.5	13.5
05 089	...	9	Marion	597.0	16 325	2 021	27.3	96.1	0.7	2.0	0.7	2.2	4.6	13.0	5.8	9.2	9.0	12.7
05 091	45500	3	Miller	625.6	43 787	1 097	70.0	70.5	25.9	1.3	0.8	3.2	6.8	17.5	8.0	13.8	12.2	13.2
05 093	14180	4	Mississippi	900.6	42 835	1 115	47.6	59.8	36.2	0.7	0.7	4.1	7.2	19.3	9.1	12.9	12.1	12.6
05 095	...	7	Monroe	607.1	7 169	2 655	11.8	55.9	40.7	1.2	1.0	2.8	6.3	14.9	7.9	10.2	10.8	12.9
05 097	...	8	Montgomery	779.9	8 879	2 515	11.4	93.3	0.9	2.4	1.4	4.2	4.4	14.4	6.9	8.4	9.3	14.2
05 099	26260	7	Nevada	617.8	8 398	2 561	13.6	65.1	31.5	0.9	0.5	3.6	5.7	16.7	7.2	11.2	10.8	13.1
05 101	25460	9	Newton	820.9	7 936	2 603	9.7	96.4	0.9	2.7	0.5	1.7	4.6	15.3	6.2	9.8	10.0	12.4
05 103	15780	7	Ouachita	732.8	24 098	1 640	32.9	57.2	40.8	1.0	0.7	2.2	5.8	16.7	7.3	11.3	10.8	13.0
05 105	30780	2	Perry	551.6	10 132	2 426	18.4	94.2	2.4	1.9	0.6	2.9	5.7	16.5	7.4	10.9	11.9	14.6
05 107	25760	6	Phillips	695.6	18 975	1 873	27.3	35.7	62.1	0.6	0.6	2.0	7.3	19.1	9.1	10.8	10.3	11.9
05 109	...	6	Pike	600.6	10 832	2 369	18.0	88.6	4.0	1.6	0.7	6.7	5.4	16.8	8.1	10.7	12.3	13.6
05 111	27860	3	Poinsett	758.4	24 023	1 642	31.7	88.5	8.8	0.8	0.5	2.9	6.4	17.5	8.1	12.2	11.9	13.3
05 113	...	7	Polk	857.7	20 173	1 822	23.5	90.2	0.8	3.7	1.0	6.6	6.1	17.2	7.3	10.1	10.4	12.6
05 115	40780	5	Pope	812.6	63 779	831	78.5	86.1	3.8	1.7	1.6	8.8	6.3	16.6	13.2	13.7	11.2	12.3
05 117	...	8	Prairie	647.9	8 251	2 572	12.7	85.8	12.6	0.9	0.3	1.6	5.6	15.1	7.0	10.4	10.2	14.6
05 119	30780	2	Pulaski	758.6	393 250	176	518.4	54.5	37.7	1.0	2.8	6.1	6.8	16.8	8.8	14.9	12.7	12.5
05 121	...	7	Randolph	652.2	17 448	1 949	26.8	96.3	1.4	1.3	0.5	1.9	5.7	16.7	7.3	11.9	11.4	13.0
05 123	22620	6	St. Francis	634.8	26 196	1 552	41.3	41.3	53.1	0.9	0.9	5.0	6.2	15.9	8.3	14.6	14.4	12.8
05 125	30780	2	Saline	723.6	118 703	522	164.0	86.7	7.6	1.0	1.5	4.5	5.9	17.5	7.1	12.8	13.5	13.0
05 127	...	6	Scott	892.3	10 277	2 405	11.5	86.4	1.2	3.2	3.6	7.6	5.7	17.7	7.7	11.2	10.6	14.0
05 129	...	9	Searcy	666.1	7 967	2 601	12.0	95.9	0.8	2.9	0.7	2.0	5.2	15.2	6.4	10.2	10.0	13.2
05 131	22900	2	Sebastian	531.9	127 793	492	240.3	73.1	7.7	3.3	5.3	13.9	6.5	17.7	9.1	13.5	12.2	13.2
05 133	...	6	Sevier	565.1	16 910	1 983	29.9	59.9	4.7	3.2	1.4	33.0	7.6	20.7	9.4	11.8	12.5	12.5
05 135	...	7	Sharp	604.4	17 157	1 974	28.4	95.6	1.2	2.2	0.9	2.1	5.6	15.5	6.5	9.6	10.2	12.5
05 137	...	9	Stone	606.4	12 539	2 257	20.7	96.4	0.7	1.9	0.7	2.0	4.8	15.0	6.6	9.0	10.0	12.0
05 139	20980	7	Union	1 039.2	39 887	1 178	38.4	62.1	33.3	1.0	0.9	4.0	6.7	17.5	7.8	11.9	11.7	13.0
05 141	...	8	Van Buren	709.8	16 628	2 002	23.4	95.1	0.9	2.0	0.5	3.1	5.2	14.9	6.1	9.5	10.2	13.0
05 143	22220	2	Washington	942.0	228 049	286	242.1	74.4	4.1	2.3	5.4	16.4	7.0	17.7	14.8	15.2	12.9	11.2
05 145	42620	4	White	1 035.1	79 263	704	76.6	90.0	5.3	1.2	1.0	4.2	6.5	17.2	11.7	12.6	11.7	12.8
05 147	...	9	Woodruff	586.8	6 641	2 700	11.3	71.3	27.0	0.9	0.6	1.9	5.6	15.4	7.7	10.0	10.8	12.9
05 149	40780	6	Yell	930.2	21 552	1 750	23.2	77.2	1.9	1.2	1.4	19.5	6.0	18.4	8.0	11.3	11.9	13.7

1. CBSA = Core Based Statistical Area. See Appendix A for explanation. See Appendix B for list of metropolitan areas with component counties.   2. County type code from the Economic Research Service of USDA Rural-Urban Continuum Codes. See Appendix A for definition.   3. Dry land or land partially or temporarily covered by water.   4. May be of any race.

Table B. States and Counties — Population and Households

STATE County	55 to 64 years [16]	65 to 74 years [17]	75 years and over [18]	Percent female [19]	Total persons 2000 [20]	2010 [21]	2000–2010 [22]	2010–2016 [23]	Births [24]	Deaths [25]	Net migration [26]	Number [27]	Persons per household [28]	Family households [29]	Female family householder[1] [30]	One person [31]
ARKANSAS—Cont'd																
Cleveland	14.0	11.4	8.1	50.9	8 571	8 689	1.4	-5.2	519	593	-395	3 334	2.53	73.1	12.2	24.6
Columbia	12.3	9.0	7.9	51.7	25 603	24 552	-4.1	-2.7	1 845	1 931	-545	9 597	2.37	68.8	17.2	26.2
Conway	14.1	10.6	8.4	50.9	20 336	21 267	4.6	-1.6	1 614	1 569	-325	8 362	2.49	69.5	13.9	27.4
Craighead	10.9	7.8	5.6	51.3	82 148	96 443	17.4	9.7	9 055	5 503	5 705	38 724	2.52	66.6	14.5	25.8
Crawford	13.2	9.6	6.5	50.7	53 247	61 948	16.3	0.5	4 788	3 788	-650	23 649	2.58	75.5	13.4	22.0
Crittenden	12.2	7.6	5.2	52.3	50 866	50 902	0.1	-3.3	4 986	2 921	-3 659	18 348	2.67	68.5	24.6	26.4
Cross	13.2	10.7	7.2	51.7	19 526	17 866	-8.5	-4.6	1 393	1 343	-858	6 918	2.49	69.5	15.7	26.0
Dallas	15.8	11.7	9.7	51.0	9 210	8 116	-11.9	-8.0	500	656	-474	3 248	2.26	64.6	13.7	33.5
Desha	14.6	10.3	7.5	52.9	15 341	13 008	-15.2	-8.7	1 054	969	-1 226	5 272	2.33	63.7	20.4	33.3
Drew	12.6	9.0	7.6	51.5	18 723	18 509	-1.1	0.8	1 493	1 193	-150	7 314	2.43	67.6	14.8	24.2
Faulkner	10.6	7.3	4.6	51.1	86 014	113 242	31.7	7.9	9 645	5 443	4 640	43 204	2.65	66.8	11.3	24.8
Franklin	13.6	10.4	8.1	50.1	17 771	18 121	2.0	-2.7	1 253	1 394	-378	6 784	2.58	70.2	10.2	26.0
Fulton	15.2	15.2	11.1	50.4	11 642	12 245	5.2	-1.0	688	1 072	274	5 300	2.27	70.8	10.4	24.4
Garland	14.6	12.8	9.6	51.8	88 068	95 995	9.0	1.5	6 886	8 458	3 298	40 290	2.35	64.4	13.2	29.0
Grant	13.8	10.2	6.7	50.2	16 464	17 853	8.4	1.3	1 217	1 136	156	6 859	2.61	74.3	10.9	24.1
Greene	12.0	9.2	6.2	50.8	37 331	42 090	12.7	6.0	3 496	2 910	1 961	16 682	2.56	68.6	11.2	26.5
Hempstead	13.8	9.5	7.4	51.7	23 587	22 609	-4.1	-2.8	2 050	1 487	-1 161	7 823	2.81	66.5	15.6	31.4
Hot Spring	14.1	10.8	7.0	47.7	30 353	33 010	8.8	1.1	2 191	2 350	553	12 136	2.59	71.5	13.5	23.3
Howard	12.6	9.6	7.8	51.8	14 300	13 789	-3.6	-3.0	1 176	1 001	-564	5 049	2.65	70.3	18.1	26.9
Independence	13.1	9.7	7.5	51.2	34 233	36 647	7.1	1.4	2 889	2 600	309	14 238	2.52	69.2	11.9	26.2
Izard	15.2	14.0	11.1	48.0	13 249	13 696	3.4	-1.9	717	1 158	230	5 549	2.28	67.6	7.8	30.0
Jackson	13.5	10.0	6.9	50.5	18 418	17 998	-2.3	-4.3	1 211	1 397	-594	6 339	2.25	61.3	14.0	34.1
Jefferson	13.9	9.6	6.5	50.5	84 278	77 435	-8.1	-9.6	5 873	5 287	-8 051	28 119	2.41	62.0	18.9	34.4
Johnson	12.6	9.6	6.7	50.2	22 781	25 540	12.1	2.5	2 185	1 618	119	10 111	2.50	68.0	10.4	27.5
Lafayette	16.2	12.3	10.0	51.6	8 559	7 645	-10.7	-10.4	440	582	-626	2 830	2.52	63.4	17.2	31.8
Lawrence	13.1	10.7	9.0	50.7	17 774	17 411	-2.0	-3.9	1 167	1 456	-379	6 696	2.45	65.2	12.2	30.6
Lee	13.7	9.9	8.0	43.6	12 580	10 424	-17.1	-10.7	653	737	-1 017	3 605	2.34	61.6	18.8	35.1
Lincoln	11.4	8.1	6.3	38.3	14 492	14 134	-2.5	-3.0	783	745	-455	4 040	2.43	70.8	16.6	24.9
Little River	14.1	12.0	8.4	51.4	13 628	13 168	-3.4	-5.4	848	982	-572	5 251	2.39	65.4	16.1	30.5
Logan	13.9	11.2	8.4	50.3	22 486	22 350	-0.6	-2.5	1 622	1 777	-382	8 609	2.48	69.5	12.4	26.3
Lonoke	11.6	8.1	5.2	50.7	52 828	68 354	29.4	5.7	5 978	3 846	1 717	25 909	2.70	74.8	12.1	20.8
Madison	14.5	11.1	7.3	50.0	14 243	15 720	10.4	2.2	1 201	1 070	239	6 338	2.46	73.4	8.9	23.9
Marion	18.0	17.0	10.7	50.7	16 140	16 651	3.2	-2.0	960	1 509	300	6 701	2.43	68.5	7.0	26.8
Miller	12.8	9.3	6.5	50.7	40 443	43 462	7.5	0.7	3 803	2 705	-692	16 960	2.50	64.6	16.2	30.9
Mississippi	12.8	8.2	5.7	51.4	51 979	46 480	-10.6	-7.8	4 049	3 113	-4 530	17 141	2.57	68.1	18.9	28.1
Monroe	15.9	12.1	9.7	53.2	10 254	8 150	-20.5	-12.0	603	668	-862	3 364	2.27	60.1	18.0	35.6
Montgomery	15.9	14.6	11.8	50.3	9 245	9 487	2.6	-6.4	531	777	-334	3 892	2.33	66.4	6.8	29.1
Nevada	15.0	11.4	8.9	50.3	9 955	8 997	-9.6	-6.7	652	704	-546	3 472	2.48	62.3	10.2	35.8
Newton	15.9	15.8	10.1	49.4	8 608	8 330	-3.2	-4.7	459	596	-257	3 310	2.42	67.3	6.7	30.1
Ouachita	15.7	11.0	8.4	52.6	28 790	26 121	-9.3	-7.7	1 844	2 238	-1 580	10 552	2.34	64.9	16.3	32.9
Perry	14.8	10.8	7.5	50.6	10 209	10 441	2.3	-3.0	680	770	-245	3 847	2.62	69.0	7.0	25.3
Phillips	14.1	10.2	7.1	52.8	26 445	21 757	-17.7	-12.8	1 891	1 684	-3 019	8 135	2.48	62.9	24.6	32.2
Pike	13.9	11.2	8.1	50.1	11 303	11 291	-0.1	-4.1	712	875	-265	4 355	2.50	69.9	12.4	27.8
Poinsett	13.2	10.2	7.2	51.5	25 614	24 583	-4.0	-2.3	1 924	2 112	-357	9 286	2.57	69.8	17.4	28.2
Polk	14.1	13.0	9.2	50.9	20 229	20 662	2.1	-2.4	1 494	1 679	-270	7 911	2.56	67.1	13.2	29.5
Pope	11.9	8.6	6.1	50.3	54 469	61 754	13.4	3.3	4 925	3 572	771	22 645	2.62	68.2	10.4	26.9
Prairie	14.5	12.3	10.3	50.2	9 539	8 715	-8.6	-5.3	565	640	-399	3 826	2.16	68.6	13.2	26.9
Pulaski	13.0	8.6	5.9	52.2	361 474	382 788	5.9	2.7	35 045	22 174	-1 876	154 240	2.49	60.2	15.6	34.3
Randolph	13.4	11.5	9.1	50.4	18 195	17 970	-1.2	-2.9	1 225	1 472	-228	7 335	2.36	68.3	11.0	28.6
St. Francis	13.0	9.0	5.7	45.1	29 329	28 258	-3.7	-7.3	2 194	1 703	-2 515	9 430	2.51	62.7	20.2	33.0
Saline	12.4	10.7	7.2	51.0	83 529	107 141	28.3	10.8	8 367	6 344	9 379	42 299	2.66	71.5	11.5	24.3
Scott	13.8	11.2	8.1	49.0	10 996	11 208	1.9	-8.3	792	750	-966	4 055	2.66	74.4	12.6	21.5
Searcy	15.5	13.6	10.6	49.6	8 261	8 192	-0.8	-2.7	473	709	26	3 172	2.48	64.4	6.2	31.2
Sebastian	12.6	8.9	6.3	51.1	115 071	125 776	9.3	1.6	10 663	7 751	-871	49 579	2.53	65.2	12.9	30.1
Sevier	11.1	8.2	5.9	50.3	15 757	17 058	8.3	-0.9	1 662	970	-817	6 075	2.81	71.1	15.8	26.0
Sharp	14.5	14.8	10.8	50.3	17 119	17 267	0.9	-0.6	1 144	1 594	408	7 108	2.37	62.3	9.1	33.2
Stone	16.1	15.1	11.4	50.7	11 499	12 394	7.8	1.2	755	1 050	410	5 142	2.40	62.7	6.5	34.2
Union	14.2	9.6	7.5	51.2	45 629	41 639	-8.7	-4.2	3 274	3 277	-1 757	16 536	2.43	68.5	16.3	27.7
Van Buren	15.8	14.2	11.2	50.3	16 192	17 294	6.8	-3.9	1 071	1 397	-274	6 879	2.44	66.1	10.5	29.6
Washington	10.0	6.7	4.6	50.0	157 715	203 043	28.7	12.3	20 059	8 961	13 575	81 722	2.55	62.2	10.1	28.1
White	11.9	9.1	6.6	51.4	67 165	77 076	14.8	2.8	6 203	5 037	931	29 404	2.55	70.7	12.3	24.9
Woodruff	15.0	12.9	9.8	52.6	8 741	7 264	-16.9	-8.6	466	625	-460	2 911	2.36	60.3	15.8	37.2
Yell	13.0	9.9	7.8	50.0	21 139	22 185	4.9	-2.9	1 748	1 576	-851	7 687	2.80	69.9	10.5	26.5

1. No spouse present.

Table B. States and Counties — **Population, Vital Statistics, Health, and Crime**

STATE County	Persons in group quarters, 2016	Daytime population, 2011–2015 Number	Daytime population, 2011–2015 Employment/residence ratio	Births, 2016 Total	Births, 2016 Rate[1]	Deaths, 2016 Number	Deaths, 2016 Rate[1]	Persons under 65 with no health insurance, 2015 Number	Persons under 65 with no health insurance, 2015 Percent	Medicare, 2015 Total Beneficiaries	Medicare, 2015 Enrolled in Original Medicare	Medicare, 2015 Enrolled in Medicare Advantage	Serious crimes known to police,[2] 2014 Total Number	Serious crimes known to police,[2] 2014 Total Rate[3]
	32	33	34	35	36	37	38	39	40	41	42	43	44	45
ARKANSAS—Cont'd														
Cleveland	52	6 587	0.39	72	8.7	87	10.6	617	9.3	1 832	1 573	259	105	1 226
Columbia	1 817	24 189	0.99	301	12.6	296	12.4	2 046	11.0	5 074	4 355	719	539	2 246
Conway	285	20 455	0.92	244	11.7	230	11.0	1 873	11.0	5 193	4 038	1 155	691	3 256
Craighead	3 819	105 920	1.10	1 528	14.4	943	8.9	9 245	10.6	18 055	14 705	3 350	4 106	4 001
Crawford	540	54 998	0.73	777	12.5	623	10.0	6 272	12.1	12 334	7 319	5 015	1 747	2 841
Crittenden	953	45 768	0.80	790	16.0	495	10.1	3 574	8.5	8 192	6 517	1 675	2 969	6 010
Cross	225	16 557	0.87	216	12.7	207	12.2	1 510	10.7	3 705	2 967	738	843	4 829
Dallas	401	8 176	1.10	68	9.1	84	11.2	529	9.3	1 830	1 389	441	254	3 218
Desha	56	13 029	1.15	150	12.6	174	14.7	1 053	10.8	2 688	2 312	376	NA	NA
Drew	978	17 889	0.88	253	13.6	198	10.6	1 528	10.3	3 422	2 951	471	624	3 320
Faulkner	4 400	110 023	0.83	1 509	12.3	889	7.3	9 253	8.9	17 076	14 986	2 090	4 917	4 068
Franklin	448	16 699	0.81	207	11.7	200	11.3	1 640	11.4	3 889	2 686	1 203	390	2 168
Fulton	165	10 779	0.67	111	9.2	190	15.7	947	10.5	3 448	2 670	778	165	1 340
Garland	2 176	97 937	1.03	1 068	11.0	1 324	13.6	9 611	12.9	31 441	24 189	7 252	NA	NA
Grant	143	14 677	0.55	188	10.4	169	9.3	1 313	8.7	3 288	2 759	529	392	2 174
Greene	602	42 738	0.96	572	12.8	486	10.9	3 314	8.9	8 616	6 718	1 898	2 344	5 415
Hempstead	301	22 773	1.05	318	14.5	222	10.1	2 381	13.1	3 888	3 020	868	903	4 026
Hot Spring	2 279	30 224	0.76	340	10.2	382	11.4	2 289	9.0	6 783	5 449	1 334	NA	NA
Howard	181	15 500	1.36	188	14.1	168	12.6	1 562	14.4	3 203	2 609	594	308	2 280
Independence	1 025	38 799	1.12	457	12.3	419	11.3	3 210	10.7	8 383	7 425	958	1 494	4 037
Izard	1 008	13 100	0.92	104	7.7	192	14.3	1 239	13.5	3 722	2 959	763	357	2 688
Jackson	2 271	17 682	1.02	183	10.6	209	12.1	1 346	11.0	3 703	3 166	537	917	5 243
Jefferson	5 168	75 878	1.08	890	12.7	864	12.3	4 920	8.9	15 270	11 439	3 831	3 921	5 436
Johnson	580	25 994	1.01	335	12.8	252	9.6	3 213	15.0	4 929	3 617	1 312	645	2 490
Lafayette	113	6 535	0.70	73	10.7	76	11.1	673	12.5	1 571	1 342	229	133	1 859
Lawrence	653	16 171	0.86	180	10.8	245	14.6	1 249	9.6	4 736	3 831	905	212	1 256
Lee	1 757	9 501	0.84	105	11.3	116	12.5	659	10.5	1 815	1 313	502	184	1 856
Lincoln	3 805	13 381	0.81	127	9.3	129	9.4	934	11.4	2 093	1 707	386	140	999
Little River	123	11 865	0.82	130	10.4	163	13.1	1 013	10.2	2 945	2 412	533	338	2 678
Logan	573	20 277	0.80	271	12.4	299	13.7	1 947	11.3	5 427	3 989	1 438	NA	NA
Lonoke	572	54 996	0.51	931	12.9	669	9.3	5 137	8.3	11 450	9 316	2 134	1 925	2 703
Madison	79	13 013	0.60	190	11.8	154	9.6	1 897	14.8	4 101	2 682	1 419	185	1 179
Marion	141	15 435	0.82	156	9.6	256	15.7	1 262	10.8	4 575	3 243	1 332	391	2 390
Miller	1 472	39 584	0.77	586	13.4	471	10.8	3 755	10.5	8 278	6 458	1 820	2 358	5 442
Mississippi	807	48 382	1.21	649	15.2	518	12.1	3 499	9.5	8 290	6 359	1 931	2 571	5 800
Monroe	84	7 776	1.02	96	13.4	117	16.3	727	12.6	1 987	1 550	437	137	1 810
Montgomery	121	7 860	0.62	82	9.2	142	16.0	886	13.4	2 236	1 804	432	132	1 442
Nevada	157	8 054	0.77	88	10.5	105	12.5	684	10.2	2 061	1 606	455	185	2 115
Newton	51	6 891	0.63	74	9.3	101	12.7	671	11.4	2 134	1 604	530	98	1 226
Ouachita	352	23 905	0.89	271	11.2	342	14.2	1 639	8.4	6 154	4 433	1 721	NA	NA
Perry	152	7 965	0.43	110	10.9	120	11.8	822	9.9	2 474	1 931	543	302	2 929
Phillips	246	19 843	0.92	287	15.1	273	14.4	1 529	9.6	4 195	3 174	1 021	NA	NA
Pike	196	10 404	0.84	110	10.2	128	11.8	1 423	16.5	2 540	2 039	501	186	1 670
Poinsett	341	21 462	0.69	316	13.2	341	14.2	2 192	11.2	5 667	4 349	1 318	820	3 811
Polk	155	20 455	1.01	247	12.2	284	14.1	2 120	13.6	5 157	4 413	744	533	2 623
Pope	3 825	63 790	1.04	807	12.7	565	8.9	6 162	12.2	12 049	9 274	2 775	2 162	3 454
Prairie	131	7 144	0.63	91	11.0	106	12.8	844	13.3	2 030	1 745	285	121	1 460
Pulaski	9 043	457 446	1.37	5 444	13.8	3 663	9.3	33 094	10.0	75 973	60 219	15 754	26 679	6 791
Randolph	349	16 463	0.81	194	11.1	252	14.4	1 450	10.6	4 196	3 092	1 104	574	3 259
St. Francis	4 089	27 332	1.00	335	12.8	294	11.2	1 773	9.5	5 529	4 233	1 296	NA	NA
Saline	1 414	89 171	0.53	1 350	11.4	1 071	9.0	7 920	8.2	10 352	8 509	1 843	2 554	2 201
Scott	79	10 605	0.94	124	12.1	116	11.3	1 288	15.3	2 570	1 827	743	262	2 506
Searcy	71	7 187	0.72	72	9.0	109	13.7	769	13.0	2 462	1 853	609	32	401
Sebastian	2 383	142 347	1.28	1 712	13.4	1 236	9.7	13 915	13.0	23 997	16 280	7 717	5 896	4 647
Sevier	173	15 952	0.81	242	14.3	148	8.8	3 128	21.3	2 751	2 359	392	402	2 309
Sharp	189	15 658	0.75	205	11.9	250	14.6	1 627	13.1	5 758	4 555	1 203	NA	NA
Stone	151	12 127	0.91	115	9.2	153	12.2	1 261	13.9	3 664	3 200	464	297	2 355
Union	524	42 839	1.14	547	13.7	533	13.4	3 617	11.0	9 642	8 032	1 610	1 491	3 687
Van Buren	189	16 243	0.86	161	9.7	234	14.1	1 602	12.9	4 615	3 611	1 004	452	2 686
Washington	8 312	217 462	1.01	3 142	13.8	1 508	6.6	25 891	13.4	30 784	23 032	7 752	NA	NA
White	3 575	75 227	0.89	982	12.4	815	10.3	6 967	10.9	16 448	13 749	2 699	NA	NA
Woodruff	106	6 718	0.89	64	9.6	99	14.9	680	13.0	1 834	1 555	279	137	1 951
Yell	323	19 702	0.75	250	11.6	243	11.3	2 850	16.1	4 647	3 637	1 010	511	2 343

1. Per 1,000 estimated resident population.   2. Data for serious crimes have not been adjusted for underreporting; this may affect comparability between geographic areas and over time.
3. Per 100,000 population estimated by the FBI.

Table B. States and Counties — Crime, Education, Money Income, and Poverty

STATE County	Serious crimes known to police, 2014 (cont.)[1] Rate[2] Violent	Property	Education — School enrollment and attainment, 2011–2015 — Enrollment[3] Total	Percent private	Attainment[4] (percent) High school graduate or less	Bachelor's degree or more	Local government expenditures,[5] 2013–2014 Total current spending (mil dol)	Current spending per student (dollars)	Money income, 2011–2015 Per capita income[6] (dollars)	Households Median income (dollars)	Percent with income of less than $50,000	Percent with income of $200,000 or more	Income and poverty, 2015 Median household income (dollars)	Percent below poverty level All persons	Children under 18 years	Children 5 to 17 years in families
	46	47	48	49	50	51	52	53	54	55	56	57	58	59	60	61
ARKANSAS—Cont'd																
Cleveland	35	1 191	2 196	6.9	58.6	15.4	12.7	8 404	21 905	43 158	57.6	1.7	44 123	18.1	25.9	22.9
Columbia	292	1 954	6 967	5.0	54.0	20.0	35.7	9 260	20 045	36 619	60.8	1.0	38 057	23.8	32.8	31.2
Conway	226	3 030	4 635	11.8	57.8	16.5	42.9	13 271	21 897	37 732	59.4	2.1	43 702	17.8	29.1	27.6
Craighead	429	3 573	29 564	5.8	45.3	25.4	155.2	8 615	23 091	42 475	57.0	2.5	42 460	17.3	24.3	21.9
Crawford	289	2 551	15 575	7.1	53.2	14.5	99.4	8 900	20 849	41 268	59.8	1.9	46 545	14.4	22.5	20.5
Crittenden	1 073	4 937	14 092	5.7	55.3	16.4	96.1	9 147	19 682	38 004	59.5	1.7	37 371	25.9	37.3	34.6
Cross	773	4 055	4 059	3.6	65.7	13.7	31.5	9 176	19 543	38 103	63.5	1.7	39 132	21.5	31.8	31.0
Dallas	570	2 648	1 789	7.9	67.4	13.1	7.5	8 716	17 868	34 084	69.4	0.6	33 352	21.3	35.9	33.9
Desha	NA	NA	3 098	6.0	63.0	11.9	26.8	9 790	17 788	27 197	70.1	1.6	30 987	30.9	45.7	41.5
Drew	388	2 932	5 314	7.7	52.9	20.5	39.5	12 636	17 481	32 819	63.9	0.6	39 339	21.2	29.3	27.7
Faulkner	330	3 738	36 543	14.0	39.8	28.3	164.4	8 741	24 603	51 223	49.0	2.4	51 157	14.8	17.0	15.8
Franklin	361	1 806	4 202	8.2	58.3	12.3	27.9	10 054	19 550	39 285	60.9	0.9	41 933	18.2	26.9	24.2
Fulton	195	1 145	2 461	9.7	57.5	10.6	15.2	8 958	19 163	37 066	67.7	0.0	34 717	19.4	34.2	30.2
Garland	NA	NA	20 855	7.1	44.1	21.4	146.0	9 721	24 070	38 733	60.5	2.7	37 723	19.3	28.2	24.4
Grant	166	2 007	4 240	8.4	54.2	17.1	37.9	7 797	23 686	46 171	53.1	1.5	47 652	13.2	18.8	16.4
Greene	328	5 087	10 788	6.0	59.1	15.4	63.8	8 347	20 689	41 286	57.8	1.4	43 996	17.1	24.9	22.3
Hempstead	566	3 460	5 793	6.6	59.9	12.2	40.4	10 830	17 049	32 122	70.3	0.7	34 560	24.1	34.1	32.7
Hot Spring	NA	NA	7 727	6.8	57.4	13.0	49.4	9 168	18 956	40 000	61.0	0.8	39 851	20.8	28.1	26.1
Howard	104	2 176	3 355	5.7	55.4	15.1	27.5	9 282	21 273	34 229	64.2	2.4	33 199	18.7	30.7	28.5
Independence	497	3 540	8 978	9.5	55.9	15.9	58.5	9 172	20 242	36 265	63.1	1.9	38 241	18.0	26.8	24.8
Izard	188	2 500	2 524	5.9	57.9	12.7	20.4	11 343	18 995	32 630	67.9	1.1	35 355	19.8	31.4	28.4
Jackson	755	4 488	3 478	2.4	68.3	8.8	22.8	9 890	17 797	31 261	69.2	1.6	32 571	27.5	39.7	37.5
Jefferson	882	4 555	19 740	10.6	53.9	17.5	124.8	10 224	19 885	36 747	62.4	1.5	36 990	26.5	37.8	35.0
Johnson	220	2 270	5 768	12.9	61.9	17.1	40.2	8 800	19 341	34 139	67.0	2.1	35 877	21.8	29.1	26.9
Lafayette	224	1 636	1 492	13.1	64.9	11.8	7.2	10 109	20 904	31 194	68.7	2.1	33 864	22.7	36.3	33.5
Lawrence	213	1 043	4 240	12.8	60.6	12.9	34.3	10 522	17 312	32 379	70.2	0.4	34 808	23.7	33.5	30.1
Lee	232	1 624	2 041	12.5	70.7	7.9	11.2	11 474	14 298	28 393	75.5	1.2	28 481	35.9	48.7	45.9
Lincoln	128	871	2 505	13.5	69.6	8.9	16.5	9 916	14 377	32 580	64.5	2.1	40 216	25.1	27.4	24.9
Little River	143	2 536	2 924	4.4	55.7	10.0	19.0	9 545	19 858	36 205	62.7	0.8	39 265	19.9	28.2	25.7
Logan	NA	NA	4 922	7.2	61.2	12.6	37.1	9 259	20 011	35 325	67.0	2.1	37 924	20.5	30.5	29.6
Lonoke	312	2 392	19 199	10.0	46.8	19.1	117.7	8 501	23 555	53 631	45.6	1.0	56 240	11.9	16.7	15.5
Madison	236	943	3 237	8.0	67.6	10.7	20.9	9 066	20 693	37 691	60.9	1.3	41 007	18.8	29.1	27.2
Marion	336	2 054	2 720	3.5	58.0	13.2	21.6	13 040	17 779	34 195	70.3	0.2	34 946	18.8	34.7	31.9
Miller	600	4 842	9 796	11.8	54.0	14.3	64.3	9 519	21 104	40 317	59.9	1.2	39 005	22.3	31.5	29.0
Mississippi	970	4 830	11 420	5.0	56.9	13.2	78.2	9 619	19 073	34 612	65.1	1.7	34 888	26.3	37.6	39.2
Monroe	264	1 546	1 712	5.5	64.3	9.4	12.4	10 420	17 470	27 647	73.4	1.4	30 801	30.9	46.7	42.1
Montgomery	219	1 224	1 582	4.2	57.3	12.3	10.5	9 222	19 975	33 037	66.5	0.8	37 813	21.8	34.8	31.1
Nevada	194	1 920	1 948	6.8	59.5	14.1	13.7	9 730	17 277	30 691	72.6	1.4	35 914	24.0	35.6	34.2
Newton	275	951	1 688	3.3	60.4	14.6	14.9	11 303	18 038	34 536	69.3	0.8	33 679	24.2	37.1	33.7
Ouachita	NA	NA	5 699	3.8	57.2	16.1	40.6	10 307	19 810	31 293	66.1	1.4	37 987	22.8	35.1	33.0
Perry	514	2 415	2 382	6.3	60.8	11.5	14.0	8 533	22 328	42 346	58.2	1.2	43 020	16.8	25.9	23.9
Phillips	NA	NA	5 713	4.6	56.3	10.8	54.3	12 985	16 700	26 844	71.4	1.7	28 224	37.3	56.4	53.7
Pike	180	1 490	2 386	6.5	54.1	14.6	19.1	9 239	19 294	33 097	65.8	1.1	36 266	18.5	30.2	27.4
Poinsett	330	3 481	5 489	6.9	65.7	8.4	43.5	10 020	17 202	33 070	68.7	0.3	32 756	23.9	36.6	32.7
Polk	281	2 343	4 676	6.4	53.9	12.0	34.6	9 541	19 004	33 702	67.7	1.0	34 723	24.4	32.4	29.9
Pope	275	3 179	18 112	6.5	50.5	20.9	93.1	9 316	20 047	39 810	60.3	1.5	41 074	20.8	24.6	22.9
Prairie	193	1 267	1 813	7.0	62.6	10.3	11.6	9 423	19 329	35 833	69.9	0.1	39 518	19.6	28.5	26.3
Pulaski	1 010	5 781	100 255	20.1	37.3	32.9	646.4	10 970	27 708	46 140	53.5	4.0	46 473	19.4	27.7	26.7
Randolph	267	2 992	4 383	5.2	56.8	13.4	20.0	8 338	19 011	34 044	66.0	0.3	34 730	17.6	27.4	25.3
St. Francis	NA	NA	6 864	7.8	61.2	11.4	43.7	10 273	15 971	32 105	70.5	0.9	31 625	30.7	44.3	43.4
Saline	296	1 904	27 237	10.4	45.3	23.0	130.4	7 799	26 050	55 817	44.3	2.1	56 926	10.7	15.3	13.6
Scott	335	2 171	2 539	2.7	62.3	11.6	23.4	9 381	17 833	37 321	67.8	1.0	36 028	20.8	34.7	29.7
Searcy	113	288	1 663	15.0	58.3	13.9	17.3	11 107	18 533	33 083	70.3	1.3	30 427	22.2	39.1	38.0
Sebastian	625	4 022	32 091	9.3	49.7	19.2	188.8	9 318	23 182	38 575	60.1	3.0	41 452	22.1	29.9	28.4
Sevier	138	2 172	4 649	4.9	65.7	7.9	38.7	11 720	17 371	36 579	63.2	0.4	41 848	20.8	32.2	30.4
Sharp	NA	NA	3 530	8.1	62.7	9.9	25.3	8 616	16 848	30 691	72.9	0.8	32 095	24.6	39.2	36.1
Stone	151	2 205	2 737	10.0	56.3	15.9	15.5	8 889	18 944	29 264	72.7	1.0	32 023	21.5	36.3	33.8
Union	556	3 131	10 131	8.4	54.3	17.5	67.3	8 894	21 779	38 678	59.5	2.3	42 195	19.7	27.0	25.9
Van Buren	285	2 401	3 271	4.9	60.8	12.3	25.2	10 957	19 047	32 312	68.0	0.4	38 306	19.0	29.6	27.5
Washington	NA	NA	68 249	8.6	44.3	30.5	374.0	9 411	24 638	43 524	55.8	3.6	46 418	16.9	21.3	19.5
White	NA	NA	21 645	28.2	54.3	19.5	120.1	9 140	22 547	42 554	56.5	2.3	42 508	19.7	24.2	21.8
Woodruff	128	1 823	1 367	4.0	71.0	10.4	13.2	11 494	18 377	28 993	73.1	1.2	31 013	25.8	39.3	35.6
Yell	326	2 018	5 217	4.2	64.8	12.6	39.5	9 184	18 288	37 804	63.9	0.7	37 415	17.8	27.6	25.1

1. Data for serious crimes have not been adjusted for underreporting; this may affect comparability between geographic areas and over time.   2. Per 100,000 population estimated by the FBI.
3. All persons 3 years old and over enrolled in nursery school through college.   4. Persons 25 years old and over.   5. Elementary and secondary education expenditures.
6. Based on population estimated by the American Community Survey, 2011–2015.

Table B. States and Counties — **Personal Income**

STATE County	Personal income, 2015										Earnings, 2015		
	Total (mil dol)	Percent change, 2014–2015	Per capita[1] Dollars	Per capita[1] Rank	Wages and salaries (mil dol)	Supplements to wages and salaries; employer contributions (mil dol) Pension and insurance	Supplements to wages and salaries; employer contributions (mil dol) Government social insurance	Proprietors' income (mil dol)	Dividends, interest, and rent (mil dol)	Personal transfer receipts (mil dol)	Total (mil dol)	Contributions for government social insurance (mil dol) From employee and self-employed	Contributions for government social insurance (mil dol) From employer
	62	63	64	65	66	67	68	69	70	71	72	73	74
ARKANSAS—Cont'd													
Cleveland	291	-1.0	34 987	2 001	34	7	3	34	28	86	78	5	3
Columbia	810	0.5	33 601	1 938	355	60	27	56	131	248	500	34	27
Conway	779	0.8	37 053	1 751	276	44	22	86	105	219	428	28	22
Craighead	3 614	3.8	34 628	2 169	1 931	290	154	415	443	896	2 790	176	154
Crawford	1 846	2.0	29 917	2 664	736	107	61	78	207	559	981	71	61
Crittenden	1 672	1.1	34 148	2 221	666	101	55	161	181	480	984	65	55
Cross	594	-1.3	34 349	1 843	186	29	15	45	72	179	275	20	15
Dallas	229	2.8	30 068	2 727	93	14	8	6	27	94	122	9	8
Desha	448	-2.9	37 417	1 450	172	26	14	69	58	143	281	16	14
Drew	658	1.5	35 039	2 074	232	42	18	87	85	188	379	24	18
Faulkner	4 161	2.9	34 235	2 220	1 793	254	143	207	502	937	2 397	157	143
Franklin	530	0.3	29 961	2 674	178	35	14	43	76	170	270	19	14
Fulton	319	2.0	26 116	2 983	61	13	5	31	47	136	110	10	5
Garland	3 604	2.7	37 090	1 742	1 376	196	110	224	706	1 115	1 905	142	110
Grant	621	2.8	34 323	2 135	158	24	12	32	73	158	226	17	12
Greene	1 396	2.8	31 588	2 644	609	102	52	138	168	414	901	60	52
Hempstead	653	-1.6	29 591	2 677	281	49	22	54	75	217	407	26	22
Hot Spring	977	3.1	29 226	2 879	332	56	27	42	125	326	456	35	27
Howard	415	-2.8	31 230	2 412	237	42	20	55	50	133	354	21	20
Independence	1 206	2.5	32 542	2 387	577	93	48	111	154	367	829	55	48
Izard	390	1.9	28 971	2 886	110	21	9	33	54	153	173	14	9
Jackson	596	0.5	34 387	2 756	213	35	17	169	62	178	435	28	17
Jefferson	2 304	0.7	32 189	2 495	1 225	223	101	116	310	751	1 665	109	101
Johnson	685	0.9	26 218	3 020	293	47	24	58	80	227	423	29	24
Lafayette	234	-2.3	33 437	1 825	48	8	4	39	32	76	99	6	4
Lawrence	510	0.2	30 390	2 773	144	26	12	63	67	189	245	18	12
Lee	250	-3.0	25 940	2 908	80	14	6	26	37	99	126	9	6
Lincoln	346	-2.5	25 003	3 058	112	22	8	42	35	110	185	11	8
Little River	408	2.0	32 686	2 425	189	26	14	28	50	132	258	18	14
Logan	739	-2.2	34 032	2 095	192	35	15	88	85	251	329	22	15
Lonoke	2 537	1.6	35 413	1 953	517	75	40	114	324	588	747	55	40
Madison	494	-0.6	31 356	2 342	121	20	10	82	57	136	233	15	10
Marion	464	3.3	28 695	2 911	155	27	11	23	78	191	216	19	11
Miller	1 377	4.5	31 350	2 547	547	78	42	91	193	383	758	54	42
Mississippi	1 362	-4.6	31 150	2 315	806	115	64	62	163	436	1 046	69	64
Monroe	256	-2.1	34 618	1 842	76	12	6	34	33	92	128	8	6
Montgomery	248	0.2	27 684	2 935	46	9	4	28	36	97	87	7	4
Nevada	279	1.4	32 548	2 349	95	15	8	27	34	99	144	10	8
Newton	210	1.2	26 583	3 031	32	7	3	17	35	83	59	6	3
Ouachita	817	1.6	33 525	2 278	262	49	21	40	104	270	372	28	21
Perry	325	2.3	31 935	2 496	48	8	4	24	40	101	84	7	4
Phillips	619	-3.6	31 720	2 301	209	36	17	53	78	236	316	21	17
Pike	324	-0.2	29 898	2 746	80	14	6	32	52	110	132	10	6
Poinsett	714	-1.8	29 719	2 667	203	31	16	78	79	265	329	24	16
Polk	582	-0.7	28 776	2 820	194	36	16	68	88	208	314	22	16
Pope	2 072	2.9	32 684	2 443	1 136	180	93	113	257	549	1 522	98	93
Prairie	276	-1.9	33 346	2 130	60	9	5	39	35	86	113	7	5
Pulaski	18 008	2.7	45 862	570	13 178	1 986	1 028	1 484	3 337	3 580	17 677	1 076	1 028
Randolph	511	-3.4	29 256	2 795	137	26	12	50	66	201	225	18	12
St. Francis	696	2.4	26 176	3 054	306	57	25	68	84	260	456	30	25
Saline	4 388	3.9	37 360	1 771	882	127	71	230	504	1 044	1 310	103	71
Scott	303	-1.0	28 790	2 869	94	18	8	41	38	103	161	11	8
Searcy	217	0.7	27 524	2 933	47	9	4	18	34	92	79	7	4
Sebastian	4 853	2.2	37 983	1 502	2 902	419	229	561	798	1 129	4 111	262	229
Sevier	451	-1.8	26 058	3 007	174	29	15	54	50	136	273	17	15
Sharp	524	1.6	30 957	2 827	124	20	10	46	70	232	200	18	10
Stone	343	1.2	27 516	2 941	77	14	6	38	65	152	135	12	6
Union	1 772	-1.6	44 151	532	945	144	72	104	362	417	1 265	84	72
Van Buren	507	1.8	30 219	2 762	176	28	13	25	87	192	241	20	13
Washington	7 938	5.5	35 205	2 001	4 768	693	355	686	1 190	1 424	6 503	399	355
White	2 565	3.3	32 398	2 465	979	144	78	144	361	708	1 345	96	78
Woodruff	228	1.2	33 858	2 104	71	12	5	23	30	83	112	7	5
Yell	661	-1.0	30 441	2 600	209	38	17	65	82	205	329	22	17

1. Based on the resident population estimated as of July 1 of the year shown.

Table B. States and Counties — Earnings, Social Security, and Housing

STATE County	Earnings, 2015 (cont.)									Social Security beneficiaries, December 2015			Housing units, 2016	
	Percent by selected industries											Supplemental Security Income recipients, December 2015		Percent change, 2010–2016
	Farm	Mining	Construction	Manufacturing	Information: professional, scientific, technical services	Retail trade	Finance, insurance, real estate and leasing	Health care and social assistance	Government	Number	Rate[1]		Total	
	75	76	77	78	79	80	81	82	83	84	85	86	87	88
ARKANSAS—Cont'd														
Cleveland	33.6	0.0	3.9	4.5	D	2.0	D	5.2	20.6	2 115	255	277	4 045	-0.5
Columbia	2.6	11.2	3.7	27.7	D	5.7	4.7	D	19.8	5 825	241	1 264	11 588	-0.1
Conway	11.8	2.2	10.2	15.1	D	5.9	4.4	D	16.5	5 675	270	938	9 732	0.2
Craighead	1.8	D	6.5	13.8	4.3	7.9	5.0	22.1	15.5	20 100	193	4 024	44 394	9.6
Crawford	1.9	1.6	6.2	21.7	D	6.6	2.7	6.8	12.4	15 060	243	2 051	26 550	1.7
Crittenden	2.3	D	9.1	12.0	2.2	6.6	4.1	10.8	15.2	10 255	209	3 475	21 708	1.0
Cross	3.7	0.0	2.3	9.2	2.8	13.7	7.0	D	21.0	4 445	257	830	7 900	0.6
Dallas	0.6	0.0	4.2	21.9	D	8.8	3.6	D	12.8	2 225	293	416	4 282	-0.5
Desha	20.1	0.1	2.9	19.9	1.4	5.3	3.4	D	16.4	3 240	270	781	6 297	0.6
Drew	7.9	0.2	5.3	11.2	2.4	7.5	3.7	D	26.8	4 170	223	734	8 484	0.9
Faulkner	0.0	4.1	8.7	8.8	12.9	8.0	4.3	12.0	17.8	20 295	167	2 716	49 321	5.8
Franklin	9.3	7.1	4.1	17.6	D	6.8	2.6	D	20.6	4 625	261	556	8 013	-0.1
Fulton	15.0	D	5.0	4.2	2.8	4.3	4.9	14.5	27.0	3 885	319	461	6 761	-0.3
Garland	0.2	0.7	7.0	7.5	5.9	10.6	6.1	22.4	14.3	29 755	306	3 922	50 563	0.1
Grant	3.9	D	6.9	29.4	D	7.0	2.7	D	19.2	4 105	228	401	7 847	1.1
Greene	3.5	D	4.9	36.8	D	7.2	3.9	10.4	12.6	10 715	243	1 768	18 737	4.7
Hempstead	9.4	D	3.7	26.4	1.9	6.8	3.0	D	21.6	5 170	235	1 013	10 459	0.4
Hot Spring	0.2	D	6.4	18.6	D	5.6	3.1	D	21.7	8 670	259	1 212	14 307	-0.5
Howard	11.2	D	4.1	40.1	D	5.4	2.1	8.3	12.1	3 465	260	523	6 232	-0.1
Independence	3.1	0.7	3.7	20.0	D	6.7	5.3	20.8	13.2	9 500	256	1 250	16 335	0.9
Izard	8.4	D	7.0	7.8	1.6	6.9	4.8	15.3	27.9	4 275	318	576	7 213	-0.3
Jackson	8.5	D	2.5	30.4	2.2	5.5	3.0	D	16.0	4 260	246	766	7 587	-0.2
Jefferson	2.3	0.1	2.8	18.8	2.4	6.0	4.3	14.4	29.3	16 390	228	4 474	33 244	0.7
Johnson	5.8	0.1	4.1	27.0	1.6	6.1	3.4	D	14.9	6 245	239	949	11 393	0.7
Lafayette	32.5	6.9	8.8	2.4	D	D	2.2	D	16.4	2 015	289	443	4 340	-0.3
Lawrence	11.6	1.0	6.9	9.9	D	8.2	4.3	D	22.4	4 890	292	938	7 978	-0.3
Lee	12.1	0.0	D	D	D	5.9	6.1	D	29.1	2 240	232	758	4 356	0.0
Lincoln	17.7	D	3.9	8.3	D	3.3	2.3	D	35.6	2 675	193	539	4 850	-0.2
Little River	7.2	D	5.3	49.9	D	4.5	1.7	2.3	15.5	3 465	278	431	6 444	-0.2
Logan	16.9	2.9	6.9	17.6	3.0	6.9	3.4	9.0	19.4	6 265	287	882	10 122	0.1
Lonoke	3.1	D	9.9	14.0	4.1	8.8	7.4	9.3	19.5	13 830	193	1 880	29 165	7.1
Madison	23.4	D	D	22.7	4.1	6.6	2.0	4.1	13.2	4 165	265	445	7 485	0.0
Marion	1.5	D	5.2	34.5	D	6.3	4.6	5.9	12.5	5 705	352	547	9 352	0.0
Miller	0.0	0.5	7.9	24.3	D	5.3	3.9	D	15.1	9 435	215	2 144	19 447	0.9
Mississippi	1.2	0.0	5.2	43.7	1.3	4.3	2.8	D	12.6	10 080	231	3 213	20 531	0.4
Monroe	20.3	0.1	2.4	4.8	D	7.3	5.6	D	16.2	2 225	300	556	4 423	-0.7
Montgomery	17.8	D	7.8	2.1	D	4.9	4.4	4.0	28.1	2 855	318	321	5 745	-0.3
Nevada	9.8	0.1	D	D	D	4.8	2.1	9.0	14.0	2 405	281	481	4 534	-0.6
Newton	4.9	0.1	8.0	2.8	D	D	D	D	35.6	2 775	350	376	4 671	0.2
Ouachita	0.9	3.4	4.4	11.7	D	8.0	3.9	D	24.3	6 920	284	1 433	13 051	-0.5
Perry	10.5	D	12.8	2.5	D	4.2	D	D	22.3	2 830	278	383	4 901	-0.1
Phillips	11.2	0.0	2.3	6.3	D	7.4	4.2	14.2	21.1	4 985	255	1 914	10 199	0.7
Pike	11.7	D	7.7	6.5	D	7.4	8.3	D	21.4	3 040	280	372	5 569	-0.2
Poinsett	11.0	D	5.1	12.8	1.9	6.0	4.9	8.5	18.2	6 600	275	1 533	10 932	0.1
Polk	9.9	D	6.1	18.6	2.8	7.0	4.5	D	16.7	6 120	303	683	10 028	0.3
Pope	2.6	1.0	8.8	15.7	4.0	6.6	4.6	9.1	15.5	13 730	216	2 013	26 015	1.8
Prairie	28.4	0.1	7.8	1.4	D	5.5	2.9	7.7	15.9	2 310	279	333	4 498	-0.1
Pulaski	0.1	0.3	4.2	5.2	11.0	7.0	9.8	13.1	24.4	79 025	201	16 772	183 269	4.4
Randolph	4.9	D	7.3	11.1	D	7.5	5.3	D	22.4	5 220	299	680	8 567	0.6
St. Francis	6.1	D	D	D	2.0	7.4	3.3	D	31.3	5 650	213	2 034	10 905	0.0
Saline	0.1	0.2	13.4	6.7	5.1	12.7	5.1	12.4	20.0	25 990	221	2 694	47 858	6.8
Scott	16.7	0.0	D	D	D	5.1	2.0	D	19.4	2 960	282	431	5 210	0.5
Searcy	2.1	0.1	D	9.0	D	7.1	2.8	14.3	25.0	2 780	354	461	4 893	-0.1
Sebastian	0.7	2.6	4.1	17.9	5.2	6.3	9.0	17.2	11.3	27 910	219	4 376	56 562	3.5
Sevier	13.8	D	D	D	D	7.2	4.0	D	19.6	3 185	185	458	6 882	-0.1
Sharp	7.2	D	D	3.1	D	10.1	5.1	D	17.8	6 635	392	884	9 820	0.0
Stone	9.5	0.1	8.4	6.2	D	13.8	3.8	D	20.8	4 545	366	572	6 767	0.8
Union	0.3	3.0	11.4	21.7	2.2	5.6	3.5	10.1	10.2	10 830	270	1 874	19 792	0.7
Van Buren	1.0	15.4	3.9	1.9	D	7.2	2.9	D	14.7	5 595	333	612	10 340	0.0
Washington	1.2	0.1	5.9	11.6	5.4	6.7	4.9	13.1	18.7	34 400	153	4 505	92 028	4.8
White	0.4	3.8	7.7	9.7	3.4	8.7	4.9	16.1	14.0	18 190	230	2 682	33 345	2.6
Woodruff	21.2	D	3.0	10.2	D	3.9	3.4	8.0	20.6	2 050	305	422	3 876	-0.5
Yell	12.5	D	5.0	26.5	D	4.5	2.6	D	21.1	5 315	246	800	9 779	0.3

1. Per 1,000 resident population estimated as of July 1 of the year shown.

Table B. States and Counties — Housing, Labor Force, and Employment

STATE County	Housing units, 2011–2015								Civilian labor force, 2016				Civilian employment,[6] 2011–2015		
	Occupied units										Unemployment			Percent	
			Owner-occupied			Renter-occupied										
				Median owner cost as a percent of income											Con-struction, produc-tion, and mainte-nance occu-pations
	Total	Percent	Median value[1]	With a mort-gage	Without a mort-gage[2]	Median rent[3]	Median rent as a per-cent of income[2]	Sub-stand-ard units[4] (percent)	Total	Percent change, 2015–2016	Total	Rate[5]	Total	Manage-ment, business, science and arts	
	89	90	91	92	93	94	95	96	97	98	99	100	101	102	103
ARKANSAS—Cont'd															
Cleveland	3 334	78.5	84 700	17.9	10.7	627	21.4	1.2	3 335	-0.7	152	4.6	3 256	29.2	35.7
Columbia	9 597	68.2	79 000	18.7	11.1	599	31.9	1.9	9 289	-2.6	539	5.8	10 491	27.4	29.6
Conway	8 362	72.9	91 500	21.7	10.0	598	39.2	3.2	8 462	-2.1	489	5.8	8 306	28.8	33.7
Craighead	38 724	59.1	129 700	19.0	10.0	681	30.1	2.2	52 140	2.2	1 702	3.3	45 526	33.8	26.7
Crawford	23 649	76.7	108 600	21.1	11.0	637	28.2	4.4	26 876	0.1	1 059	3.9	25 099	28.0	30.5
Crittenden	18 348	57.2	104 600	20.7	11.9	686	32.9	4.8	21 535	0.5	988	4.6	20 336	29.5	26.6
Cross	6 918	64.0	82 400	19.4	12.1	645	29.2	1.5	7 961	-1.8	355	4.5	7 140	24.3	32.6
Dallas	3 248	66.0	62 000	18.6	10.0	521	26.5	3.3	2 917	1.5	147	5.0	3 031	19.8	37.9
Desha	5 272	57.5	59 300	19.2	12.0	537	32.0	2.6	5 477	-1.3	301	5.5	4 355	27.7	33.1
Drew	7 314	60.7	93 600	18.5	11.7	597	42.3	2.3	7 891	-0.5	458	5.8	7 361	36.0	25.6
Faulkner	43 204	63.2	146 100	19.4	10.0	731	29.1	2.6	60 491	0.9	2 316	3.8	57 108	34.5	22.8
Franklin	6 784	71.0	93 100	18.6	10.0	584	27.8	2.2	7 363	-0.7	302	4.1	6 592	26.0	33.7
Fulton	5 300	75.8	96 700	23.0	11.0	508	29.4	4.8	4 692	-1.4	205	4.4	4 498	26.6	32.5
Garland	40 290	67.3	130 700	21.8	10.3	712	32.8	2.8	40 148	0.5	1 742	4.3	39 729	31.5	22.8
Grant	6 859	77.3	108 300	18.8	10.7	695	23.5	2.1	8 320	0.7	302	3.6	7 608	29.1	33.6
Greene	16 682	64.7	107 700	19.5	11.4	670	28.4	1.9	19 877	-0.4	857	4.3	17 659	28.3	34.5
Hempstead	7 823	67.7	74 700	19.9	11.1	571	34.8	2.8	9 945	0.9	380	3.8	8 699	25.6	41.2
Hot Spring	12 136	72.0	83 300	19.1	10.1	657	33.1	2.1	14 132	-0.2	562	4.0	13 293	26.5	31.2
Howard	5 049	65.3	83 900	21.1	10.0	560	26.3	2.8	5 942	-1.9	198	3.3	5 596	25.6	40.5
Independence	14 238	71.4	96 000	21.9	11.0	573	30.2	3.6	16 008	2.1	798	5.0	15 303	28.2	34.0
Izard	5 549	78.1	78 000	23.5	10.7	508	33.5	2.5	4 989	0.2	281	5.6	4 607	33.1	30.7
Jackson	6 339	68.0	60 600	20.0	12.3	541	27.9	4.6	6 099	-1.5	381	6.2	5 585	22.0	39.7
Jefferson	28 119	64.0	82 000	20.5	11.6	669	32.2	2.1	28 590	-0.7	1 607	5.6	28 119	28.9	27.7
Johnson	10 111	71.2	89 900	20.7	10.0	605	31.3	4.4	10 518	1.1	505	4.8	10 376	25.5	39.6
Lafayette	2 830	71.8	61 400	21.6	12.1	470	28.4	1.4	2 576	-1.6	152	5.9	2 527	27.8	36.2
Lawrence	6 696	70.4	64 500	19.3	11.6	531	28.4	2.4	6 942	-1.5	303	4.4	6 527	25.5	32.6
Lee	3 605	56.9	59 500	23.5	12.6	533	32.7	1.2	3 130	-1.6	151	4.8	2 910	20.9	33.0
Lincoln	4 040	69.7	59 600	19.3	10.1	593	30.9	3.1	4 088	-1.0	201	4.9	3 666	29.2	34.0
Little River	5 251	73.5	75 500	19.5	10.6	530	31.9	1.4	5 655	1.1	265	4.7	4 805	26.0	35.7
Logan	8 609	73.6	83 200	19.6	10.6	549	27.5	3.2	9 164	0.0	423	4.6	8 718	28.2	31.1
Lonoke	25 909	70.4	126 900	19.5	10.0	714	26.5	2.9	33 267	0.8	1 120	3.4	31 944	34.1	25.3
Madison	6 338	76.1	96 100	21.3	10.0	621	29.9	4.0	7 283	2.8	232	3.2	6 751	27.1	38.8
Marion	6 701	79.0	102 900	22.8	11.9	553	30.0	3.9	6 556	0.5	263	4.0	5 679	19.4	34.7
Miller	16 960	64.4	94 600	19.6	10.3	708	30.7	2.8	20 104	0.9	840	4.2	18 429	26.8	30.5
Mississippi	17 141	57.6	79 600	18.8	11.7	624	31.0	2.9	18 216	-0.9	1 242	6.8	17 164	23.7	37.3
Monroe	3 364	61.9	55 000	19.2	11.3	497	31.2	2.6	2 888	-2.9	142	4.9	2 815	22.4	29.4
Montgomery	3 892	79.6	82 200	22.1	12.3	538	28.4	2.5	3 068	-4.9	164	5.3	3 636	27.6	36.9
Nevada	3 472	71.2	66 600	21.9	11.1	635	31.5	4.0	3 669	1.0	136	3.7	3 265	20.3	32.8
Newton	3 310	84.2	82 900	24.8	10.0	370	22.3	7.3	3 424	0.9	133	3.9	3 228	23.5	37.6
Ouachita	10 552	67.0	66 400	18.0	11.5	546	31.8	1.6	9 843	-0.4	501	5.1	10 415	24.5	35.2
Perry	3 847	79.9	84 200	19.8	10.0	621	24.5	5.2	4 208	0.1	202	4.8	4 184	29.3	33.7
Phillips	8 135	51.3	61 200	20.0	11.7	589	36.6	3.4	6 715	-4.0	399	5.9	6 932	26.6	25.2
Pike	4 355	75.7	74 700	21.8	10.2	489	26.6	2.1	4 184	0.3	181	4.3	4 476	25.2	37.6
Poinsett	9 286	61.6	74 200	19.6	12.0	516	30.5	4.7	10 214	1.5	436	4.3	9 053	24.2	35.6
Polk	7 911	79.0	84 300	25.0	10.1	484	26.3	5.5	8 197	-1.2	402	4.9	7 473	28.6	32.4
Pope	22 645	67.6	117 100	21.0	10.0	640	29.0	3.5	29 303	-1.3	1 358	4.6	27 407	28.8	30.1
Prairie	3 826	70.6	66 400	19.0	12.2	471	30.4	2.8	3 647	-2.2	143	3.9	3 513	27.8	33.3
Pulaski	154 240	60.2	142 400	20.7	10.9	779	30.0	1.8	187 667	0.8	6 709	3.6	180 430	40.3	17.0
Randolph	7 335	73.1	73 700	19.2	10.1	531	31.5	2.6	6 459	4.4	304	4.7	6 714	30.4	33.0
St. Francis	9 430	55.6	60 800	20.0	11.7	576	29.6	2.3	8 890	-0.7	465	5.2	9 259	23.7	30.8
Saline	42 299	77.0	141 400	20.3	10.0	808	26.2	2.4	56 518	0.9	1 782	3.2	53 363	33.9	22.2
Scott	4 055	74.2	76 800	18.5	10.0	512	31.7	3.4	4 463	-0.5	168	3.8	4 250	24.5	41.6
Searcy	3 172	80.7	86 300	24.2	10.0	421	34.5	3.8	3 033	0.2	137	4.5	2 836	27.7	34.4
Sebastian	49 579	60.7	114 600	20.7	10.0	631	30.1	2.6	57 943	0.3	2 161	3.7	54 852	29.9	28.2
Sevier	6 075	72.5	68 200	19.8	10.0	543	31.0	6.4	5 676	1.3	282	5.0	7 173	20.4	47.3
Sharp	7 108	77.5	74 800	22.3	11.2	578	33.4	4.6	6 049	0.7	331	5.5	5 764	27.7	34.4
Stone	5 142	75.9	92 700	32.3	11.2	518	27.7	3.8	4 723	0.4	246	5.2	4 332	31.4	32.9
Union	16 536	70.9	74 600	17.9	11.4	633	28.7	5.3	16 407	-2.8	906	5.5	16 418	30.8	29.8
Van Buren	6 879	76.9	89 900	22.0	12.2	596	32.1	3.8	6 076	-5.5	424	7.0	5 478	25.3	35.9
Washington	81 722	54.7	151 900	19.7	10.0	704	29.3	4.8	119 518	3.7	3 259	2.7	102 944	36.5	23.3
White	29 404	68.6	108 800	18.6	10.5	641	29.6	2.4	34 158	-1.1	1 785	5.2	32 318	30.5	28.6
Woodruff	2 911	61.3	60 000	19.7	12.1	468	32.3	2.7	3 000	-1.1	165	5.5	2 472	32.9	31.6
Yell	7 687	67.6	94 900	21.6	10.4	539	25.6	5.7	8 804	-1.6	393	4.5	8 567	24.3	41.1

1. Specified owner-occupied units.   2. A value of 10.0 represents 10 percent or less; a value of 50.0 represents 50 percent or more.   3. Specified renter-occupied units.
4. Overcrowded or lacking complete plumbing facilities.   5. Percent of civilian labor force.   6. Civilian employed persons 16 years old and over.

Table B. States and Counties — Nonfarm Employment and Agriculture

STATE County	Private nonfarm establishments, employment and payroll, 2015									Agriculture, 2012			
		Employment						Annual payroll		Farms			
												Percent with:	
	Number of establish-ments	Total	Health care and social assistance	Manufac-turing	Retail trade	Finance and insurance	Professional, scientific, and technical services	Total (mil dol)	Average per employee (dollars)	Number	Fewer than 50 acres	500 acres or more	Farm operators whose principal occu-pation is farming (percent)
	104	105	106	107	108	109	110	111	112	113	114	115	116
ARKANSAS—Cont'd													
Cleveland	75	626	124	D	59	D	D	19	30 490	211	39.8	2.8	58.8
Columbia	575	7 702	1 266	2 230	990	216	336	279	36 264	278	28.4	5.8	42.1
Conway	420	4 899	543	792	840	135	81	176	35 908	816	29.7	7.7	51.0
Craighead	2 451	40 662	10 018	5 567	6 918	999	915	1 463	35 978	583	38.6	29.5	52.0
Crawford	1 079	16 676	1 475	4 053	1 950	407	289	569	34 096	886	45.4	5.3	44.2
Crittenden	823	13 460	1 972	1 652	2 190	216	247	429	31 895	263	17.5	44.1	66.9
Cross	345	3 822	823	538	812	172	75	113	29 631	325	16.0	41.2	59.1
Dallas	181	2 324	711	579	351	68	15	68	29 290	90	18.9	11.1	51.1
Desha	292	3 646	494	1 007	646	140	51	121	33 262	244	20.5	43.4	64.8
Drew	401	4 564	921	751	989	163	102	146	32 025	308	27.3	17.2	42.9
Faulkner	2 501	35 107	5 443	4 002	6 010	1 004	991	1 289	36 729	1 288	40.7	6.2	33.8
Franklin	290	3 473	563	850	591	281	73	111	32 030	829	28.1	8.6	43.9
Fulton	162	1 409	564	118	227	74	30	37	25 911	753	20.5	13.9	47.4
Garland	2 697	32 412	7 369	2 371	6 009	972	1 470	1 032	31 825	361	49.3	2.5	55.4
Grant	260	3 432	314	1 281	508	73	89	112	32 712	257	37.4	5.8	44.4
Greene	779	13 695	1 687	5 536	1 975	599	350	468	34 152	711	37.6	15.3	40.6
Hempstead	384	6 439	1 131	2 195	886	232	122	195	30 285	748	25.1	15.2	54.4
Hot Spring	486	6 085	1 303	1 094	873	218	61	206	33 799	536	43.1	3.2	41.6
Howard	284	6 057	746	3 209	575	95	34	185	30 582	552	26.8	8.0	50.5
Independence	788	14 708	3 259	4 054	1 818	391	198	522	35 477	1 003	28.9	11.3	37.9
Izard	215	1 964	525	215	420	92	21	58	29 512	633	21.2	15.0	41.7
Jackson	331	3 770	717	1 048	804	100	115	128	33 979	437	18.5	31.8	51.0
Jefferson	1 361	20 836	4 060	5 157	3 475	817	323	741	35 580	444	35.4	26.8	52.3
Johnson	399	7 430	864	2 738	988	139	86	213	28 671	624	28.0	6.9	46.2
Lafayette	107	751	148	59	144	50	12	25	32 694	263	17.9	22.1	60.5
Lawrence	273	3 000	715	416	589	81	33	86	28 511	559	22.7	22.4	46.7
Lee	121	895	277	D	165	37	31	31	34 841	220	13.6	40.0	81.4
Lincoln	169	1 457	283	282	204	48	17	49	33 830	377	23.6	20.4	56.0
Little River	165	2 627	306	1 266	402	64	48	130	49 609	448	21.9	16.7	48.0
Logan	372	4 104	676	1 098	722	237	112	131	31 804	969	27.0	7.0	48.1
Lonoke	1 020	10 989	1 487	1 696	2 201	445	351	327	29 772	767	31.8	19.0	55.8
Madison	190	2 403	223	905	501	81	40	75	31 197	1 250	22.0	8.9	49.3
Marion	210	2 775	282	1 367	470	131	55	82	29 448	485	21.0	14.0	42.9
Miller	722	11 667	1 012	2 460	1 552	375	153	404	34 633	525	35.6	12.0	45.0
Mississippi	808	17 731	1 777	5 240	1 777	236	90	616	34 765	347	17.6	55.0	74.1
Monroe	185	1 662	302	101	320	63	19	51	30 761	230	20.0	51.3	64.8
Montgomery	137	800	68	39	130	D	18	25	31 464	449	24.1	5.3	50.1
Nevada	120	1 953	423	D	248	42	29	63	32 335	351	23.6	5.7	47.6
Newton	85	819	255	42	103	D	D	19	23 067	648	28.2	6.5	42.6
Ouachita	519	7 500	1 267	2 556	1 023	208	168	288	38 361	182	39.0	6.6	33.0
Perry	103	807	181	D	159	17	14	26	32 062	419	31.7	6.2	43.2
Phillips	401	3 884	974	276	854	112	82	122	31 336	282	13.5	50.7	68.8
Pike	201	1 865	254	237	338	58	49	48	25 559	346	24.0	8.7	55.8
Poinsett	357	3 515	638	640	722	117	47	111	31 660	397	22.2	53.4	66.2
Polk	435	5 070	1 129	1 283	865	123	82	144	28 395	893	38.4	4.4	42.6
Pope	1 594	23 454	3 315	4 820	3 483	928	762	829	35 357	977	36.6	6.3	48.2
Prairie	154	973	248	D	210	36	28	24	25 156	445	20.9	29.7	50.8
Pulaski	12 051	204 670	41 340	13 541	25 991	13 168	11 688	9 139	44 652	417	50.6	7.4	42.7
Randolph	329	3 543	965	639	732	109	71	95	26 896	667	21.0	15.4	39.7
St. Francis	443	5 485	1 331	819	1 055	181	111	158	28 804	326	21.2	37.1	65.3
Saline	1 866	20 438	4 473	1 380	3 949	506	611	627	30 658	386	52.8	4.9	46.9
Scott	138	1 821	236	837	276	33	13	52	28 822	602	25.6	5.3	49.8
Searcy	113	1 070	294	165	228	40	25	22	20 471	592	18.6	15.2	50.3
Sebastian	3 369	60 920	11 230	13 359	7 927	1 601	1 412	2 416	39 654	770	36.8	5.5	43.4
Sevier	261	3 960	541	D	729	121	62	128	32 263	543	28.4	6.4	44.8
Sharp	305	2 579	627	95	735	187	33	60	23 400	648	20.4	12.7	39.4
Stone	226	1 949	518	151	481	105	42	48	24 801	523	19.9	13.4	49.9
Union	1 118	17 295	2 153	3 130	2 173	428	467	779	45 066	280	34.3	5.7	48.6
Van Buren	331	3 810	687	87	529	92	47	150	39 332	587	21.8	7.7	47.5
Washington	5 150	84 477	14 105	12 754	12 693	2 292	3 722	3 334	39 463	2 502	43.2	4.1	42.3
White	1 533	22 915	4 438	2 207	3 921	612	475	742	32 383	1 836	35.6	7.3	35.9
Woodruff	133	1 207	114	244	267	51	11	49	40 577	217	14.7	48.8	60.8
Yell	300	4 836	1 015	1 763	560	165	99	145	29 897	794	29.7	8.3	47.9

Table B. States and Counties — **Agriculture**

STATE County	Land in farms Acreage (1,000)	Percent change, 2007–2012	Acres Average size of farm	Total irrigated (1,000)	Total cropland (1,000)	Value of land and buildings (dollars) Average per farm	Average per acre	Value of machinery and equipment, average per farm (dollars)	Value of products sold Total (mil dol)	Average per farm (dollars)	Percent from: Crops	Live-stock and poultry products	Percent of farms with sales of: $10,000 or more	$100,000 or more	Government payments Total ($1,000)	Percent of farms
	117	118	119	120	121	122	123	124	125	126	127	128	129	130	131	132
ARKANSAS—Cont'd																
Cleveland	27	-12.5	129	D	6.0	502 071	3 895	83 725	105.8	501 427	0.4	99.6	48.8	36.0	237	10.4
Columbia	46	-3.1	164	0.3	12.5	353 727	2 157	65 011	41.7	150 032	12.2	87.8	38.5	11.5	84	8.6
Conway	179	-4.2	220	14.8	76.4	568 464	2 587	77 902	161.6	198 098	10.3	89.7	44.6	16.9	1 554	17.4
Craighead	338	0.2	579	271.6	314.2	1 857 806	3 208	276 847	261.6	448 714	98.9	1.1	55.1	36.5	10 157	57.8
Crawford	125	5.1	141	4.5	48.6	424 447	3 001	59 635	67.4	76 081	33.4	66.6	32.6	7.8	342	8.7
Crittenden	338	7.7	1 285	173.3	306.5	3 568 985	2 778	506 837	215.0	817 551	99.8	0.2	71.9	52.5	6 850	76.4
Cross	279	-1.4	858	214.7	255.2	2 181 258	2 542	375 991	188.8	580 855	99.8	0.2	56.9	44.9	11 662	84.9
Dallas	21	6.7	236	D	3.2	377 989	1 600	49 933	1.3	14 500	59.5	40.5	31.1	1.1	54	26.7
Desha	267	-12.9	1 095	202.1	243.9	3 053 189	2 789	683 840	212.9	872 512	97.0	3.0	68.0	49.2	7 594	87.3
Drew	130	4.4	422	66.9	86.8	1 062 338	2 520	147 227	88.3	286 841	72.0	28.0	44.8	19.5	2 580	44.8
Faulkner	185	-2.7	144	6.8	54.5	470 804	3 279	52 585	26.3	20 386	38.3	61.7	30.4	2.6	1 254	13.8
Franklin	160	4.6	193	0.6	44.8	439 010	2 277	64 706	158.2	190 806	2.7	97.3	50.5	13.9	542	10.0
Fulton	204	15.3	271	0.0	25.9	434 740	1 601	44 228	27.7	36 819	4.0	96.0	42.0	5.8	1 708	21.9
Garland	36	-9.6	99	0.3	8.4	364 504	3 688	43 119	24.1	66 756	18.6	81.4	24.7	5.3	93	8.9
Grant	65	86.9	252	0.1	10.3	567 051	2 253	61 296	20.9	81 183	2.6	97.4	26.5	6.6	55	9.7
Greene	260	-2.6	366	166.0	216.6	1 251 740	3 418	167 745	177.3	249 404	94.3	5.7	37.1	18.3	8 391	53.4
Hempstead	196	-6.7	263	D	48.9	537 639	2 047	76 608	198.5	265 362	2.3	97.7	52.1	19.5	814	24.5
Hot Spring	69	-4.7	128	0.1	19.3	329 142	2 567	48 366	23.9	44 675	4.8	95.2	30.2	3.9	202	13.1
Howard	147	32.6	266	0.5	23.2	627 100	2 357	72 839	179.1	324 422	0.8	99.2	60.3	31.5	99	15.0
Independence	248	-0.7	247	32.7	87.2	517 500	2 094	76 524	131.9	131 473	25.7	74.3	44.5	8.5	1 541	17.0
Izard	173	1.3	273	0.3	28.3	481 487	1 766	56 648	49.4	78 044	D	D	41.7	6.2	2 095	30.8
Jackson	307	1.6	703	206.5	271.7	1 768 018	2 516	289 577	186.8	427 545	98.3	1.7	54.0	37.1	12 642	70.9
Jefferson	292	-3.8	657	207.5	257.5	1 905 205	2 900	305 345	215.3	484 831	91.2	8.8	45.0	30.9	10 681	71.2
Johnson	118	11.9	190	1.0	38.7	456 329	2 405	59 563	141.0	226 029	3.1	96.9	48.7	14.6	348	12.2
Lafayette	115	18.1	438	21.7	60.8	886 065	2 022	177 734	127.9	486 259	24.7	75.3	61.2	38.0	1 817	41.4
Lawrence	253	-4.1	452	130.3	179.2	1 208 589	2 673	190 691	149.1	266 798	84.6	15.4	50.4	24.7	7 345	49.0
Lee	261	-13.8	1 185	158.0	245.9	3 313 277	2 796	452 068	171.9	781 227	99.9	0.1	76.4	47.7	6 373	82.7
Lincoln	200	7.4	530	135.0	157.5	1 481 042	2 795	274 745	219.5	582 101	53.6	46.4	54.1	35.5	7 190	55.7
Little River	172	23.2	383	10.0	59.9	643 661	1 681	86 491	76.5	170 781	23.4	76.6	45.1	16.5	833	28.8
Logan	198	23.2	204	0.9	66.8	458 086	2 246	64 342	188.0	193 997	3.4	96.6	49.0	16.4	229	9.8
Lonoke	339	-8.8	442	199.6	274.6	1 228 919	2 781	204 691	223.4	291 236	85.6	14.4	39.5	19.0	12 927	51.4
Madison	269	3.8	216	0.5	57.5	585 871	2 718	63 058	208.2	166 530	1.5	98.5	48.3	14.0	2 670	24.7
Marion	137	4.8	282	D	19.3	567 852	2 014	58 499	39.7	81 788	1.4	98.6	39.8	7.4	1 159	26.6
Miller	164	-6.3	312	5.5	85.3	620 006	1 986	71 606	45.5	86 739	53.8	46.2	39.2	8.4	1 229	18.3
Mississippi	476	3.1	1 371	286.9	462.6	3 905 478	2 849	614 256	314.6	906 764	99.9	0.1	80.7	62.8	9 887	83.3
Monroe	268	10.8	1 167	199.5	248.9	2 804 648	2 404	458 365	194.4	845 100	D	D	64.8	54.3	8 137	84.3
Montgomery	74	1.0	166	0.3	20.8	415 392	2 506	56 347	42.1	93 871	2.1	97.9	40.5	12.0	464	16.7
Nevada	67	2.2	190	0.1	16.1	360 188	1 897	66 954	47.9	136 519	2.4	97.6	47.0	13.7	178	21.7
Newton	114	1.1	176	0.1	17.2	388 836	2 206	44 318	28.7	44 221	3.5	96.5	35.2	2.2	784	29.6
Ouachita	26	-20.0	143	0.0	6.9	318 632	2 228	55 341	16.5	90 467	2.5	97.5	26.4	4.4	113	19.8
Perry	70	-3.2	168	4.7	25.4	409 379	2 438	65 847	33.1	78 955	14.8	85.2	43.7	9.1	602	17.4
Phillips	352	-19.4	1 250	231.9	345.6	3 260 908	2 610	512 504	248.0	879 426	99.9	0.1	77.7	61.3	10 328	87.2
Pike	70	-16.2	202	1.0	14.9	431 405	2 132	65 754	82.3	237 962	0.7	99.3	52.0	22.0	201	21.1
Poinsett	385	13.1	970	310.0	369.8	2 978 222	3 069	481 224	287.4	723 980	99.8	0.2	67.3	57.2	15 715	83.1
Polk	119	-10.9	133	0.4	31.9	352 879	2 651	54 186	117.8	131 885	1.4	98.6	37.0	11.3	185	14.4
Pope	154	0.1	157	6.2	51.3	432 140	2 745	67 052	150.1	153 636	6.9	93.1	39.4	11.3	828	9.7
Prairie	275	-17.1	618	179.1	214.1	1 546 649	2 501	236 348	165.1	370 933	96.7	3.3	43.6	30.6	10 031	76.4
Pulaski	84	-11.4	202	21.5	47.9	692 978	3 438	77 942	40.0	95 851	75.4	24.6	30.5	8.4	1 439	18.9
Randolph	211	-16.6	316	56.9	89.9	636 148	2 015	92 799	79.6	119 318	72.1	27.9	44.1	10.3	3 472	29.4
St. Francis	300	17.5	919	209.3	273.3	2 175 083	2 366	355 064	189.9	582 448	99.5	0.5	60.1	42.0	7 971	72.1
Saline	45	0.1	116	0.4	12.1	408 819	3 519	61 010	4.5	11 645	40.6	59.4	26.7	1.6	55	8.0
Scott	100	4.0	167	0.0	30.1	365 899	2 197	57 341	132.0	219 276	1.0	99.0	54.7	16.3	283	11.0
Searcy	169	-13.4	285	D	25.0	475 546	1 668	49 813	13.0	22 024	7.8	92.2	42.1	3.9	2 000	27.7
Sebastian	119	13.8	154	0.0	35.0	411 097	2 663	53 995	97.4	126 507	2.5	97.5	37.7	11.2	374	6.1
Sevier	129	10.9	238	D	27.4	555 635	2 335	70 293	137.4	253 066	0.6	99.4	46.8	20.1	224	24.9
Sharp	158	-14.0	244	0.1	28.8	444 068	1 818	58 008	75.6	116 607	1.4	98.6	40.7	8.5	1 522	24.1
Stone	135	-5.1	259	0.2	22.1	504 455	1 951	69 801	53.7	102 608	1.6	98.4	44.6	10.7	1 122	32.5
Union	43	12.1	152	0.0	7.8	384 639	2 534	58 164	28.0	99 829	2.0	98.0	26.4	6.4	91	15.0
Van Buren	123	7.5	209	0.3	29.5	519 421	2 481	59 424	19.9	33 981	5.3	94.7	43.3	3.4	648	17.9
Washington	312	-4.7	125	0.6	83.5	512 264	4 111	57 567	443.0	177 068	1.6	98.4	41.4	11.6	1 611	14.1
White	356	-13.5	194	39.4	138.3	498 108	2 571	61 275	100.4	54 669	39.0	61.0	27.0	5.3	4 909	26.6
Woodruff	274	-0.1	1 263	197.0	246.0	3 152 682	2 495	489 051	167.6	772 295	D	D	60.4	48.4	6 684	88.9
Yell	160	-8.5	202	3.1	56.5	458 194	2 271	73 649	196.4	247 331	3.2	96.8	49.5	18.8	1 339	22.9

Table B. States and Counties — Water Use, Wholesale Trade, Retail Trade, and Real Estate

STATE County	Water use, 2010 Total water withdrawn (mil gal/day)	Gallons withdrawn per person per day	Wholesale trade,[1] 2012 Number of establishments	Number of employees	Sales (mil dol)	Annual payroll (mil dol)	Retail trade,[2] 2012 Number of establishments	Number of employees	Sales (mil dol)	Annual payroll (mil dol)	Real estate and rental and leasing,[2] 2012 Number of establishments	Number of employees	Receipts (mil dol)	Annual payroll (mil dol)
	133	134	135	136	137	138	139	140	141	142	143	144	145	146
ARKANSAS—Cont'd														
Cleveland	1.4	165	2	D	D	D	12	63	13.4	0.8	1	D	D	D
Columbia	11.3	458	22	D	D	D	103	1 010	197.0	20.1	28	139	20.1	5.4
Conway	29.2	1 371	15	212	150.8	6.7	78	903	287.6	19.8	8	43	5.0	1.7
Craighead	422.7	4 383	131	1 509	1 430.1	68.3	455	6 391	1 680.9	142.6	113	473	79.2	12.8
Crawford	34.7	561	62	775	380.8	29.6	153	1 922	525.4	42.0	40	198	32.4	7.6
Crittenden	219.7	4 317	57	987	1 938.0	42.7	144	2 158	813.3	44.7	38	180	22.0	5.3
Cross	561.7	31 433	17	268	265.7	11.4	70	789	180.8	16.5	19	101	9.5	2.3
Dallas	0.8	99	4	14	6.8	0.5	46	375	71.8	7.7	5	15	3.6	0.3
Desha	484.0	37 207	19	223	389.0	10.3	67	595	153.6	11.0	8	67	3.5	1.1
Drew	37.3	2 013	10	87	147.1	4.5	91	1 000	260.7	20.0	26	102	14.6	2.9
Faulkner	8.8	78	88	818	551.7	35.0	377	5 538	1 435.8	116.8	120	447	111.9	19.5
Franklin	11.1	615	6	14	3.8	0.4	51	450	163.0	11.3	6	12	0.9	0.2
Fulton	84.4	6 894	7	39	9.3	1.0	37	208	59.3	4.1	4	13	0.8	0.1
Garland	17.6	183	79	D	D	D	513	5 877	1 564.0	133.8	133	439	65.0	13.0
Grant	5.3	298	14	D	D	D	46	450	128.9	9.5	8	D	D	D
Greene	367.0	8 719	39	573	1 067.7	23.5	154	1 799	503.5	40.2	31	52	8.1	1.1
Hempstead	4.7	206	14	96	52.0	3.3	79	893	197.6	18.2	16	52	6.4	1.2
Hot Spring	125.0	3 797	11	D	D	D	89	903	254.2	19.9	16	44	4.1	1.0
Howard	4.4	321	11	63	34.2	3.1	66	619	162.5	13.4	11	23	2.2	0.3
Independence	156.7	4 276	26	D	D	D	164	1 703	441.1	37.3	23	88	10.8	2.3
Izard	4.6	339	5	D	D	D	50	401	108.7	8.2	6	50	5.6	0.7
Jackson	442.0	24 559	16	148	106.9	7.2	66	681	177.7	15.8	14	29	3.2	0.5
Jefferson	350.6	4 528	57	463	443.9	20.2	291	3 447	843.9	77.9	63	221	38.6	6.3
Johnson	5.6	218	5	D	D	D	72	903	237.3	19.6	18	32	5.1	0.8
Lafayette	25.1	3 286	NA	NA	NA	NA	21	142	30.5	2.3	2	D	D	D
Lawrence	198.5	11 401	18	162	159.1	5.8	58	615	196.3	14.4	10	28	3.0	0.6
Lee	307.0	29 451	9	109	123.5	4.6	19	166	43.8	3.7	10	28	4.6	0.8
Lincoln	224.2	15 862	6	D	D	D	26	209	57.5	3.7	6	D	D	D
Little River	105.2	7 986	4	D	D	D	39	383	104.2	8.7	2	D	D	D
Logan	4.2	187	8	43	7.4	0.7	66	658	152.8	13.9	11	18	1.7	0.4
Lonoke	489.5	7 161	36	291	217.9	12.2	171	2 265	613.4	49.6	49	127	16.7	3.9
Madison	1.8	113	3	D	D	D	32	402	130.2	9.5	6	11	1.2	0.2
Marion	2.0	122	8	18	16.5	0.8	36	444	94.8	8.7	11	13	1.6	0.3
Miller	15.5	357	38	579	308.2	31.3	125	1 393	435.7	30.7	27	D	D	D
Mississippi	381.2	8 201	48	D	D	D	166	1 748	437.8	40.1	36	137	30.5	3.3
Monroe	297.5	36 509	14	201	126.2	9.0	39	311	90.6	6.9	4	10	0.8	0.2
Montgomery	1.0	105	4	D	D	D	18	119	28.8	3.0	8	30	1.5	0.4
Nevada	1.4	150	5	15	8.6	0.4	25	277	159.1	5.3	5	11	0.6	0.2
Newton	1.4	163	3	D	D	D	17	86	17.0	1.5	1	D	D	D
Ouachita	43.4	1 663	22	D	D	D	108	1 104	222.0	21.2	21	D	D	D
Perry	2.0	193	2	D	D	D	18	153	30.5	2.5	2	D	D	D
Phillips	266.7	12 256	33	328	594.1	14.3	85	956	223.2	21.6	17	50	5.6	0.9
Pike	1.8	163	12	146	89.8	3.3	43	331	70.0	6.3	4	85	6.8	3.1
Poinsett	937.3	38 126	22	390	424.6	25.8	69	751	178.0	13.6	11	36	4.0	1.1
Polk	4.0	191	15	D	D	D	83	966	193.5	17.5	13	130	10.5	3.1
Pope	987.2	15 985	67	469	322.4	19.3	272	3 180	869.4	67.4	69	191	29.7	5.7
Prairie	334.2	38 344	8	65	67.2	2.9	33	206	54.3	3.3	3	D	D	D
Pulaski	82.1	215	659	11 024	8 414.5	576.5	1 715	25 070	7 234.4	622.7	592	3 397	606.5	119.4
Randolph	156.2	8 692	11	83	33.8	2.1	59	600	170.7	13.5	16	32	2.6	0.6
St. Francis	363.1	12 848	22	D	D	D	113	1 104	316.2	22.0	26	63	7.1	1.1
Saline	31.9	298	69	723	351.3	30.3	278	3 995	1 404.8	100.1	65	119	24.2	3.3
Scott	1.9	170	6	D	D	D	22	293	50.4	6.1	4	12	1.1	0.3
Searcy	1.8	221	2	D	D	D	34	265	49.8	4.7	5	D	D	D
Sebastian	3.7	30	194	2 362	1 713.4	105.7	574	7 899	1 944.5	174.1	170	888	133.9	28.2
Sevier	4.6	268	5	49	19.4	2.5	67	673	190.5	14.0	7	22	3.1	0.6
Sharp	3.5	203	6	D	D	D	58	650	152.6	12.1	10	20	1.7	0.5
Stone	2.8	225	7	59	34.1	1.2	46	526	107.5	12.1	6	6	0.6	0.1
Union	20.4	490	50	D	D	D	208	2 152	511.1	46.8	39	210	37.4	8.6
Van Buren	4.4	252	10	38	35.6	1.3	57	546	168.4	12.3	6	7	0.9	0.1
Washington	3.1	15	234	2 487	1 740.0	118.1	765	11 098	2 925.8	254.6	239	2 359	191.1	64.1
White	88.0	1 142	61	575	432.9	27.9	294	3 358	911.7	72.6	65	183	29.6	5.7
Woodruff	246.3	33 928	15	157	118.1	7.7	27	240	74.2	5.3	6	7	0.8	0.1
Yell	4.1	186	10	86	15.2	2.5	55	488	121.4	9.6	10	19	1.7	0.4

1. Merchant wholesalers, except manufacturers' sales branches and offices. 2. Employer establishments.

Table B. States and Counties — **Professional Services, Manufacturing, and Accommodation and Food Services**

STATE County	Professional, scientific, and technical services, 2012				Manufacturing, 2012				Accommodation and food services, 2012			
	Number of establish-ments	Number of employees	Receipts (mil dol)	Annual payroll (mil dol)	Number of establish-ments	Number of employees	Receipts (mil dol)	Annual payroll (mil dol)	Number of establish-ments	Number of employees	Sales (mil dol)	Annual payroll (mil dol)
	147	148	149	150	151	152	153	154	155	156	157	158
ARKANSAS—Cont'd												
Cleveland	1	D	D	D	3	72	D	2.0	3	11	0.6	0.1
Columbia	33	218	22.7	8.0	32	2 118	602.8	97.6	41	674	30.8	6.9
Conway	31	86	8.6	2.8	24	904	384.4	45.9	25	333	13.9	3.6
Craighead	173	876	125.8	46.0	99	5 254	2 101.7	221.2	212	D	D	D
Crawford	87	283	27.6	8.3	63	4 126	1 207.8	127.1	82	1 502	64.8	18.1
Crittenden	55	264	23.5	8.4	40	1 484	849.0	60.9	89	1 565	82.8	19.8
Cross	24	70	5.4	1.8	10	588	238.8	17.3	24	322	14.3	3.5
Dallas	6	16	1.2	0.3	7	504	194.2	18.4	8	121	4.7	1.2
Desha	21	51	11.6	1.6	10	724	407.0	34.9	34	305	12.9	3.4
Drew	26	108	11.7	4.3	20	550	D	23.1	36	D	D	D
Faulkner	223	D	D	D	89	3 707	1 203.0	175.9	212	4 745	198.7	53.7
Franklin	19	94	7.0	2.0	19	1 049	D	36.1	23	255	11.3	3.0
Fulton	10	36	2.8	1.1	12	137	10.7	3.3	17	149	5.7	1.7
Garland	217	1 160	91.1	40.4	90	2 180	476.9	95.1	274	5 162	218.0	63.4
Grant	18	81	21.6	3.6	13	1 180	603.2	D	19	D	D	D
Greene	52	430	39.4	18.8	53	4 743	1 840.7	189.6	64	1 114	49.1	13.3
Hempstead	14	70	4.9	2.1	26	2 086	786.9	71.0	32	483	22.7	5.8
Hot Spring	29	93	6.6	2.1	34	1 409	728.0	61.1	34	476	21.5	5.3
Howard	14	36	2.8	1.0	19	3 455	1 022.9	93.8	19	D	D	D
Independence	59	223	20.7	6.2	34	3 891	1 211.4	137.6	66	1 173	48.8	12.2
Izard	7	22	2.7	1.0	6	215	D	8.2	13	D	D	D
Jackson	23	85	7.0	2.9	20	989	425.0	42.9	28	308	14.9	3.5
Jefferson	79	577	65.1	27.8	61	5 118	2 113.6	225.4	120	D	D	D
Johnson	29	87	9.3	2.9	32	2 791	657.3	77.5	35	439	20.4	5.3
Lafayette	5	12	1.3	0.3	5	42	D	1.4	5	55	3.1	0.7
Lawrence	14	40	4.9	1.0	20	328	73.2	10.8	19	242	9.2	2.3
Lee	10	33	3.0	0.9	3	14	5.2	5.2	6	56	3.1	0.7
Lincoln	7	D	D	D	6	343	D	16.1	11	D	D	D
Little River	9	54	6.5	1.7	14	1 239	D	87.5	11	D	D	D
Logan	31	71	9.7	2.7	16	1 138	D	52.3	26	242	9.3	2.5
Lonoke	88	313	31.8	9.7	32	D	628.5	59.1	91	1 369	60.0	15.9
Madison	15	39	2.7	1.0	22	1 066	D	32.2	13	182	7.4	1.9
Marion	17	45	3.7	1.4	16	1 539	244.8	42.5	30	166	8.5	1.9
Miller	43	226	25.7	7.8	29	2 331	D	142.1	75	D	D	D
Mississippi	40	135	10.7	3.7	46	5 306	5 231.1	340.9	77	1 178	51.5	12.4
Monroe	9	22	1.2	0.5	6	132	48.5	4.7	18	246	9.9	2.6
Montgomery	6	10	0.8	0.3	8	143	D	3.4	17	204	23.2	5.7
Nevada	7	41	1.8	0.9	7	D	D	D	7	D	D	D
Newton	4	D	D	D	9	32	5.3	1.3	11	D	D	D
Ouachita	24	D	D	D	32	2 566	D	128.1	31	500	19.1	5.1
Perry	8	D	D	D	NA	NA	NA	NA	8	D	D	D
Phillips	26	68	9.4	2.1	12	D	D	D	22	345	13.6	3.2
Pike	4	37	1.4	0.5	14	192	39.5	6.1	14	189	7.0	1.8
Poinsett	15	40	3.3	1.0	21	656	224.0	24.2	36	D	D	D
Polk	27	83	5.4	2.1	32	1 195	D	40.0	39	499	18.1	5.2
Pope	145	468	50.0	15.3	60	4 626	1 506.7	164.4	115	D	D	D
Prairie	8	30	2.9	0.8	NA	NA	NA	NA	12	84	4.0	0.7
Pulaski	1 529	10 113	1 616.1	552.9	327	13 328	6 515.9	655.6	985	19 810	961.9	281.2
Randolph	23	71	7.2	2.5	27	594	115.0	16.4	23	329	14.7	3.5
St. Francis	31	120	18.9	4.0	6	754	D	21.1	39	590	27.8	6.9
Saline	146	558	77.6	22.2	77	1 403	D	58.4	146	2 825	128.3	33.0
Scott	9	12	1.2	0.3	14	1 193	297.8	32.5	12	130	4.7	1.6
Searcy	8	28	1.4	0.3	11	96	D	2.8	9	D	D	D
Sebastian	320	1 452	244.6	61.5	183	13 713	5 156.5	560.3	270	5 467	242.1	70.0
Sevier	14	46	3.4	1.0	6	D	D	D	24	251	10.3	2.6
Sharp	17	41	2.7	0.8	13	77	D	2.3	32	288	13.1	3.4
Stone	13	43	2.7	0.9	14	88	10.5	2.8	34	395	14.8	4.1
Union	68	250	28.6	9.5	45	2 961	4 719.2	161.3	74	970	45.4	11.6
Van Buren	16	45	4.6	1.6	10	44	D	1.8	23	371	15.8	4.1
Washington	579	3 044	345.7	137.8	204	12 207	3 487.0	440.2	503	9 220	399.4	113.7
White	109	515	45.5	16.9	60	2 300	1 031.0	98.1	133	2 543	113.6	27.8
Woodruff	10	12	1.5	0.4	7	342	D	9.2	8	D	D	D
Yell	19	54	3.5	1.2	18	1 962	571.0	55.5	20	D	D	D

1. Establishment subject to federal tax.

Health Care and Social Assistance, Other Services, Nonemployer Businesses, and Residential Construction

STATE County	Health care and social assistance, 2012				Other services, 2012				Nonemployer businesses, 2015		Value of residential construction authorized by building permits, 2016	
	Number of establishments	Number of employees	Receipts (mil dol)	Annual payroll (mil dol)	Number of establishments	Number of employees	Receipts (mil dol)	Annual payroll (mil dol)	Number	Receipts (mil dol)	New Construction ($1,000)	Number of housing units
	159	160	161	162	163	164	165	166	167	168	169	170
ARKANSAS—Cont'd												
Cleveland	6	120	3.6	2.7	6	D	D	D	365	14.1	0	0
Columbia	77	1 212	77.7	32.7	44	178	11.9	3.4	1 227	50.8	0	0
Conway	46	649	31.4	16.2	22	78	11.1	2.4	1 369	48.7	1 701	19
Craighead	359	8 701	921.0	362.1	125	805	83.9	23.2	7 620	365.8	104 651	1 021
Crawford	97	1 665	140.4	59.4	65	327	32.3	8.7	3 805	156.2	11 077	112
Crittenden	117	2 181	170.6	69.4	59	379	33.3	8.9	3 604	128.3	11 542	67
Cross	46	810	42.0	21.0	19	D	D	D	1 401	56.6	2 190	11
Dallas	24	785	34.3	15.0	14	43	3.4	1.0	355	12.4	267	4
Desha	28	589	43.5	18.4	14	34	2.9	0.7	722	32.2	0	0
Drew	46	1 054	72.6	30.5	20	53	5.6	1.2	1 088	53.0	1 185	10
Faulkner	291	5 108	450.6	173.8	157	783	69.2	16.7	8 160	316.1	58 062	319
Franklin	32	623	47.9	19.3	14	40	3.8	1.0	990	36.6	974	5
Fulton	29	561	38.8	14.7	9	D	D	D	778	27.2	0	0
Garland	319	7 374	717.5	275.4	161	766	53.3	16.2	7 961	329.6	14 287	45
Grant	22	D	D	D	20	D	D	D	1 167	45.0	2 128	14
Greene	96	1 558	140.5	50.2	42	175	14.5	3.9	2 791	134.4	17 600	149
Hempstead	51	1 119	62.9	27.6	34	133	17.9	4.5	961	35.8	465	5
Hot Spring	46	1 334	85.6	38.7	23	D	D	D	1 843	67.8	0	0
Howard	33	D	D	D	25	86	9.4	2.3	731	33.0	290	4
Independence	98	3 010	282.1	111.5	53	276	17.8	6.0	2 429	100.4	5 510	32
Izard	28	593	32.7	15.4	11	34	3.1	0.7	848	32.8	293	3
Jackson	52	825	76.1	29.6	18	63	4.8	1.3	824	32.3	857	9
Jefferson	215	4 384	399.6	161.6	84	D	D	D	3 795	128.3	4 318	46
Johnson	40	996	65.7	28.5	28	112	5.6	2.5	1 363	49.4	3 681	23
Lafayette	9	177	8.1	4.3	4	30	2.0	0.7	323	10.6	0	0
Lawrence	32	623	40.4	19.8	15	D	D	D	1 129	48.5	1 651	16
Lee	17	323	31.4	11.0	6	18	1.0	0.3	646	25.2	0	0
Lincoln	16	323	26.6	9.4	15	D	D	D	546	21.8	0	0
Little River	14	D	D	D	13	36	3.6	0.9	576	20.1	1 140	14
Logan	43	613	44.4	17.4	23	81	6.6	1.9	1 240	41.8	448	6
Lonoke	98	1 274	78.5	32.0	62	235	18.1	5.6	4 477	193.5	31 242	303
Madison	18	279	13.5	6.0	15	D	D	D	1 221	47.5	1 033	14
Marion	18	D	D	D	15	39	3.9	0.6	1 157	39.3	3 706	44
Miller	67	D	D	D	45	238	20.1	5.6	2 530	111.9	6 262	42
Mississippi	125	1 895	131.4	53.5	43	190	15.8	4.4	2 144	70.1	4 510	48
Monroe	20	313	18.0	7.5	12	D	D	D	508	24.8	125	3
Montgomery	11	D	D	D	8	25	1.5	0.4	736	26.5	NA	NA
Nevada	15	443	19.8	9.7	9	41	2.9	0.7	449	15.4	0	0
Newton	13	216	7.8	3.8	3	D	D	D	648	22.9	0	0
Ouachita	62	D	D	D	30	D	D	D	1 273	43.5	393	6
Perry	13	D	D	D	5	D	D	D	691	27.9	68	2
Phillips	64	1 045	73.4	30.4	29	100	10.8	3.0	1 418	47.7	887	40
Pike	13	296	14.5	6.6	9	18	2.0	0.5	837	34.6	NA	NA
Poinsett	46	648	37.7	16.3	26	D	D	D	1 428	53.7	965	7
Polk	46	983	67.9	28.5	31	104	6.1	1.6	1 482	53.1	100	2
Pope	165	3 073	218.2	80.0	91	513	35.0	11.5	3 684	144.0	10 569	107
Prairie	11	D	D	D	10	27	2.0	0.5	460	20.2	197	2
Pulaski	1 446	41 716	5 078.9	2 013.0	807	6 109	823.4	190.7	28 517	1 340.6	211 860	1 314
Randolph	46	867	57.9	25.9	19	D	D	D	1 264	54.8	1 248	18
St. Francis	58	1 106	82.6	35.6	20	130	9.5	4.5	1 769	61.3	320	3
Saline	197	4 120	277.2	129.7	127	D	D	D	7 916	322.6	64 540	375
Scott	16	239	15.2	8.0	11	46	2.3	1.7	605	20.1	266	4
Searcy	14	D	D	D	2	D	D	D	804	32.2	50	1
Sebastian	410	11 295	1 192.7	466.3	203	963	80.5	22.8	8 596	457.4	64 308	442
Sevier	31	506	42.7	14.6	24	D	D	D	774	33.8	283	6
Sharp	46	540	29.7	13.4	22	108	7.5	1.8	1 231	43.1	1 104	6
Stone	23	509	31.9	15.1	15	D	D	D	1 200	43.7	470	9
Union	127	2 169	213.7	80.2	81	387	51.6	12.0	2 787	111.4	5 763	86
Van Buren	36	731	44.0	18.0	19	D	D	D	1 248	40.5	839	3
Washington	568	14 228	1 525.8	614.1	308	1 955	320.9	52.9	15 579	709.7	292 118	1 523
White	164	4 429	360.8	146.6	98	514	45.4	14.1	5 398	219.2	14 357	116
Woodruff	15	D	D	D	6	D	D	D	402	15.7	0	0
Yell	42	934	52.6	24.9	13	55	4.6	1.1	1 194	46.0	994	16

		Government employment and payroll, 2012								Local government finances, 2012				
			March payroll (percent of total)							General revenue				
													Taxes	
													Per capita[1] (dollars)	
STATE County	Full-time equivalent employees	March payroll (dollars)	Adminis-tration, judicial, and legal	Police and Corrections	Fire Protection	Highways and transpor-tation	Health and Welfare	Natural resources and utilities	Education and libraries	Total (mil dol)	Inter-govern-mental (mil dol)	Total (mil dol)	Total	Property
	171	172	173	174	175	176	177	178	179	180	181	182	183	184
ARKANSAS—Cont'd														
Cleveland	330	806 962	9.0	5.0	0.0	5.3	0.7	2.9	76.0	20.0	15.3	2.4	280	186
Columbia	810	2 122 431	5.9	8.7	1.9	4.1	0.6	7.5	70.9	84.2	34.7	16.8	686	216
Conway	751	2 035 580	5.2	11.1	0.6	3.9	0.8	8.1	70.0	72.1	44.8	15.9	748	377
Craighead	3 565	10 924 637	4.8	9.2	2.9	3.7	1.2	10.0	67.7	285.0	164.7	77.8	780	344
Crawford	2 079	8 936 720	9.1	2.8	0.0	1.4	5.5	24.0	57.1	156.8	108.4	28.6	461	213
Crittenden	2 243	7 239 687	5.6	10.1	4.1	1.8	1.6	6.1	67.6	182.3	109.3	39.6	792	258
Cross	603	1 548 890	10.4	9.4	1.4	3.4	1.1	2.8	71.5	51.1	33.6	9.9	562	280
Dallas	261	612 066	9.1	13.5	0.3	5.1	2.7	7.1	61.9	19.8	11.6	4.3	544	186
Desha	795	2 143 489	5.0	5.6	0.5	2.7	22.4	3.6	59.5	57.2	28.7	12.9	1 031	405
Drew	969	2 684 507	3.1	4.7	1.1	2.3	30.7	2.1	55.8	79.4	41.6	12.6	671	211
Faulkner	3 393	11 696 206	5.6	8.1	3.7	2.3	1.7	2.7	75.5	324.2	171.2	77.9	656	297
Franklin	616	1 780 777	6.6	4.8	0.5	3.5	2.3	1.9	77.8	48.5	35.0	9.5	525	268
Fulton	446	1 158 320	4.4	3.4	0.7	4.9	23.0	2.8	60.2	31.9	18.9	3.9	319	163
Garland	2 929	9 379 603	4.7	8.8	4.0	3.5	3.4	5.5	68.3	270.5	155.0	62.1	640	262
Grant	736	2 167 090	4.0	5.7	0.2	2.7	0.5	2.6	83.3	54.6	40.7	8.6	480	234
Greene	1 593	4 613 388	4.1	5.9	2.2	3.0	2.1	8.3	68.5	112.0	67.4	19.6	455	189
Hempstead	991	2 866 901	6.3	9.8	1.5	3.8	2.3	7.5	64.3	63.0	40.8	14.1	629	190
Hot Spring	1 020	3 135 235	4.3	4.3	1.6	3.0	1.9	5.9	78.5	75.0	50.6	15.7	471	242
Howard	721	2 467 138	7.2	17.5	1.7	5.0	3.5	21.0	42.7	46.1	28.6	9.7	704	226
Independence	1 442	3 864 054	4.6	7.4	0.9	3.5	2.2	8.2	72.6	113.1	69.9	22.7	614	314
Izard	479	1 132 741	7.6	7.8	0.2	5.9	1.2	5.3	71.6	32.9	23.1	5.4	399	259
Jackson	623	1 641 667	7.2	8.7	4.1	4.3	2.8	5.1	65.5	43.2	27.4	9.3	528	229
Jefferson	2 803	8 103 678	6.2	13.3	4.7	3.4	1.8	1.9	66.2	217.6	136.9	51.2	686	285
Johnson	832	2 711 188	3.4	5.5	0.7	2.3	0.4	12.2	75.6	63.8	42.9	12.1	466	209
Lafayette	324	1 024 900	6.7	6.5	0.5	5.3	1.6	2.4	77.1	19.1	12.6	3.8	516	258
Lawrence	1 057	2 598 077	3.2	3.6	0.8	2.1	33.0	2.4	54.7	79.8	45.0	7.8	459	210
Lee	422	1 112 758	5.2	7.2	1.9	5.4	2.5	8.4	68.7	24.4	17.7	4.1	401	201
Lincoln	362	919 481	6.2	5.9	0.1	3.6	0.2	2.7	80.4	24.4	16.8	4.2	297	152
Little River	689	1 796 446	3.9	4.0	0.1	2.7	34.8	3.7	50.8	44.7	19.0	7.9	615	273
Logan	771	2 027 835	5.6	7.0	0.2	4.0	2.6	4.4	76.0	49.8	33.4	9.6	437	237
Lonoke	2 693	7 148 935	4.2	6.7	2.0	2.1	0.5	4.6	79.3	189.2	129.4	38.9	558	260
Madison	571	1 449 917	5.1	4.6	0.0	6.7	5.3	2.7	75.2	31.5	20.9	6.6	420	180
Marion	420	1 177 227	8.0	10.7	0.3	8.0	1.6	5.5	65.4	26.6	17.6	6.1	370	207
Miller	1 370	3 792 335	7.1	17.4	7.1	4.8	0.8	2.2	58.3	120.6	70.4	29.4	674	250
Mississippi	2 048	5 872 177	5.4	9.7	2.9	3.6	2.1	9.0	65.1	191.6	104.8	32.2	707	241
Monroe	360	1 055 919	8.0	11.9	0.8	5.2	0.9	10.4	61.7	25.7	17.8	4.5	571	283
Montgomery	294	752 749	7.1	6.2	0.0	6.4	2.9	4.0	72.7	19.1	14.5	3.0	317	201
Nevada	405	978 364	8.6	11.3	0.0	8.2	3.9	6.8	59.4	20.3	14.7	3.3	374	180
Newton	434	1 232 173	2.8	2.8	0.0	2.9	1.0	1.0	89.0	59.7	55.7	2.4	298	215
Ouachita	1 097	3 081 016	5.9	8.9	2.9	5.3	2.7	5.6	68.4	75.4	51.1	15.8	623	202
Perry	344	973 732	8.1	7.6	0.0	4.4	0.3	3.1	72.6	20.7	15.2	3.5	334	164
Phillips	872	2 319 840	6.4	8.7	2.9	4.6	0.0	7.6	68.3	70.5	48.6	14.3	689	239
Pike	507	1 198 447	2.9	2.6	0.0	2.3	0.6	3.0	88.0	32.5	23.2	6.0	533	207
Poinsett	959	2 599 342	5.4	11.1	1.0	3.7	0.5	5.4	72.6	69.5	51.1	10.0	411	173
Polk	1 139	3 233 326	3.5	4.4	0.5	3.3	0.1	3.1	84.0	84.7	45.1	10.6	516	173
Pope	2 245	7 108 185	4.8	9.2	3.2	2.4	3.2	4.5	71.3	165.6	100.1	42.3	674	270
Prairie	351	1 159 649	15.7	11.7	0.5	12.8	1.1	5.2	52.5	20.8	12.8	4.0	470	235
Pulaski	15 078	52 069 152	6.0	12.7	6.6	4.5	3.5	11.7	52.8	1 476.7	724.3	418.1	1 075	551
Randolph	552	1 387 909	7.5	7.1	2.0	4.5	1.7	6.7	68.7	37.2	24.0	9.9	551	358
St. Francis	1 036	3 954 323	5.7	6.9	1.6	2.0	2.7	7.1	73.4	75.8	52.5	14.7	527	164
Saline	2 671	8 478 497	6.2	7.9	4.2	2.4	0.6	6.1	71.0	238.1	147.9	54.6	489	267
Scott	364	909 428	4.1	3.6	0.0	5.1	1.8	4.7	79.2	25.0	18.3	4.3	391	127
Searcy	296	714 402	4.4	5.2	0.0	5.9	1.5	2.7	80.0	16.3	12.2	2.5	308	178
Sebastian	4 285	15 121 933	5.9	9.8	4.3	4.0	2.6	7.8	65.5	399.0	208.5	123.0	966	364
Sevier	764	2 036 880	4.0	5.6	0.4	2.6	1.5	12.6	72.8	59.3	43.9	8.4	490	157
Sharp	745	1 804 388	5.9	6.5	3.5	5.1	0.2	6.1	71.2	44.2	31.2	7.0	408	175
Stone	424	1 109 650	6.3	5.7	0.0	5.5	1.2	9.6	70.0	26.1	18.0	5.4	423	148
Union	1 719	4 970 357	4.4	7.3	4.6	3.5	2.6	4.4	72.2	125.7	71.2	35.1	859	292
Van Buren	757	1 902 959	7.4	21.6	1.0	6.7	1.1	2.5	58.5	49.1	26.5	14.0	822	502
Washington	7 560	23 284 035	5.1	10.7	3.9	4.1	1.3	4.1	69.5	691.8	396.1	183.9	870	333
White	2 609	7 296 125	4.8	6.2	2.5	2.4	2.0	5.5	75.7	192.0	122.5	42.8	545	227
Woodruff	367	874 741	9.7	5.0	0.3	4.3	1.5	8.7	68.2	25.9	19.0	3.7	521	309
Yell	877	2 241 720	3.8	7.4	0.3	4.0	0.5	4.0	79.4	58.7	42.0	10.7	489	268

1. Based on the resident population estimated as of July 1 of the year shown.

Table B. States and Counties — Local Government Finances, Government Employment, and Income Taxes

STATE County	Local government finances, 2012 (cont.)									Government employment, 2015			Individual income tax returns, 2014		
	Direct general expenditure							Debt outstanding							
			Percent of total for:												
	Total (mil dol)	Per capita[1] (dollars)	Educa-tion	Health and hospitals	Police protec-tion	Public welfare	High-ways	Total (mil dol)	Per capita[1] (dollars)	Federal civilian	Federal military	State and local	Number of returns	Mean adjusted gross income	Mean income tax
	185	186	187	188	189	190	191	192	193	194	195	196	197	198	199
ARKANSAS—Cont'd															
Cleveland	19.8	2 299	72.2	0.7	3.3	0.2	9.2	7.9	916	11	35	345	3 200	46 894	4 047
Columbia	85.3	3 484	43.3	28.4	3.6	0.1	3.9	107.4	4 388	37	96	1 942	9 210	50 533	5 634
Conway	70.4	3 308	65.7	1.5	5.0	0.2	8.3	39.8	1 868	59	89	1 463	8 470	52 641	6 374
Craighead	279.3	2 800	56.9	0.3	5.7	0.1	5.4	482.8	4 841	315	436	7 861	41 540	51 816	5 966
Crawford	160.3	2 588	67.2	0.0	5.0	0.0	7.4	203.0	3 277	96	261	2 119	23 800	44 437	3 869
Crittenden	177.1	3 540	57.7	0.2	7.9	0.0	4.9	305.8	6 114	94	206	2 723	21 180	40 993	3 832
Cross	50.3	2 847	65.6	4.4	4.9	0.2	5.5	15.3	867	52	73	1 087	7 290	41 861	3 938
Dallas	18.2	2 276	53.5	0.2	7.1	0.0	9.3	15.1	1 887	20	31	373	2 920	38 048	3 160
Desha	54.8	4 365	49.1	21.1	6.0	0.1	3.4	43.6	3 478	58	51	953	4 960	41 242	3 992
Drew	81.1	4 329	53.9	22.7	3.7	0.2	6.4	39.5	2 108	57	76	2 028	7 140	46 754	4 662
Faulkner	340.2	2 866	58.3	0.1	4.3	0.0	5.9	686.1	5 780	199	515	7 588	48 870	54 054	5 758
Franklin	46.2	2 558	73.0	3.3	3.8	0.3	6.5	43.4	2 406	152	74	860	6 730	43 769	3 904
Fulton	30.6	2 485	53.3	24.1	3.1	0.1	8.4	14.3	1 159	28	51	633	4 330	36 649	2 894
Garland	268.9	2 775	57.5	0.3	5.6	0.0	3.6	344.1	3 551	496	407	4 061	43 040	48 927	5 645
Grant	54.3	3 022	74.8	0.6	4.5	0.1	4.4	31.4	1 747	28	77	797	7 320	50 029	4 679
Greene	119.5	2 769	59.8	0.2	3.6	0.1	4.4	136.1	3 152	90	186	2 028	17 260	45 044	4 255
Hempstead	64.4	2 877	60.7	0.2	4.3	0.1	5.2	53.7	2 402	81	93	1 688	8 600	36 752	2 868
Hot Spring	76.2	2 283	72.0	1.7	3.4	0.1	4.0	94.3	2 823	66	133	1 978	12 360	42 102	3 524
Howard	46.0	3 350	63.9	0.8	4.9	0.1	4.2	74.9	5 451	65	56	853	5 500	37 815	3 157
Independence	118.5	3 202	52.8	0.2	3.5	0.1	6.2	274.1	7 403	106	154	2 160	14 610	45 201	4 476
Izard	33.6	2 497	65.3	1.3	4.8	0.2	6.9	26.2	1 942	26	53	1 024	4 570	38 889	3 102
Jackson	41.6	2 363	54.0	1.4	7.4	0.1	6.9	23.9	1 357	43	65	1 502	5 820	39 780	3 748
Jefferson	217.7	2 914	59.7	0.1	7.5	0.1	4.0	226.1	3 025	1 485	311	6 871	30 130	41 161	3 686
Johnson	65.1	2 514	63.3	0.2	4.4	0.0	7.2	48.8	1 883	86	109	1 087	9 740	39 682	3 282
Lafayette	20.9	2 805	68.4	0.2	6.4	0.1	6.3	10.0	1 344	25	29	318	2 590	39 814	3 634
Lawrence	75.1	4 412	56.5	22.2	3.3	4.3	3.1	40.2	2 361	52	69	1 168	6 160	37 502	3 015
Lee	21.6	2 110	53.3	0.4	9.2	0.2	10.8	5.6	551	36	34	705	3 020	40 435	4 763
Lincoln	25.2	1 788	68.0	0.1	4.2	0.0	7.9	12.9	913	21	43	1 258	3 980	42 145	3 604
Little River	45.4	3 511	41.4	20.9	4.1	6.7	4.1	77.9	6 027	43	53	816	4 960	43 027	3 639
Logan	50.5	2 295	64.1	5.2	5.3	0.1	5.4	41.6	1 893	97	90	1 341	8 460	40 535	3 320
Lonoke	184.1	2 636	69.9	0.2	4.3	0.0	2.8	172.0	2 463	115	304	2 706	29 470	51 950	4 968
Madison	31.6	2 021	66.4	3.3	5.6	0.0	11.6	24.7	1 576	41	67	555	6 200	41 575	3 798
Marion	28.0	1 688	60.5	0.2	8.4	0.2	11.9	19.4	1 172	31	69	552	6 300	36 344	2 906
Miller	112.1	2 568	56.8	0.3	9.6	0.0	4.3	109.3	2 504	61	181	1 986	17 530	44 933	4 623
Mississippi	189.3	4 154	49.4	0.5	5.1	0.1	2.9	796.0	17 471	106	184	2 744	17 330	41 059	3 785
Monroe	25.5	3 252	52.9	1.3	5.1	0.2	10.3	10.9	1 390	29	31	439	3 070	33 646	2 934
Montgomery	18.0	1 926	60.2	0.1	3.4	0.0	10.6	13.6	1 457	46	38	490	3 140	36 870	2 909
Nevada	20.5	2 300	61.8	0.3	6.5	0.2	8.5	12.4	1 394	26	36	447	3 430	37 335	2 800
Newton	30.3	3 746	81.8	0.1	1.5	0.1	7.3	72.1	8 919	48	34	456	2 860	35 349	2 459
Ouachita	71.1	2 801	66.5	0.1	4.9	0.0	5.4	60.6	2 386	93	103	1 860	9 740	43 954	4 168
Perry	19.2	1 861	72.5	0.1	5.9	0.3	7.5	14.0	1 359	19	43	401	4 000	43 302	3 781
Phillips	71.5	3 442	65.5	0.1	5.3	0.1	3.5	34.7	1 670	63	82	1 400	7 460	35 715	3 214
Pike	30.8	2 738	73.7	0.4	3.3	0.2	7.6	17.3	1 541	52	45	584	4 140	38 613	3 178
Poinsett	65.0	2 676	70.6	0.2	6.9	0.1	4.4	35.9	1 479	66	101	1 158	9 000	38 142	3 301
Polk	82.4	4 025	54.6	28.8	2.5	0.0	3.6	60.1	2 937	85	86	1 109	7 640	38 828	3 213
Pope	163.1	2 599	67.0	1.6	6.5	0.1	6.0	190.1	3 029	255	255	4 384	25 260	50 362	5 437
Prairie	19.8	2 343	62.2	2.0	6.4	0.0	9.5	17.3	2 050	40	35	328	3 310	41 234	3 792
Pulaski	1 448.1	3 723	46.0	4.2	6.9	0.0	3.8	1 780.8	4 578	9 220	6 006	44 648	182 160	62 440	8 616
Randolph	35.5	1 979	57.5	0.0	7.8	0.0	9.3	8.9	498	35	73	1 186	6 730	38 946	3 418
St. Francis	73.2	2 628	65.4	0.5	5.9	0.1	4.9	21.2	759	691	96	1 479	9 170	33 515	2 663
Saline	246.7	2 206	68.6	0.3	4.4	0.0	5.3	376.7	3 368	83	496	4 569	50 040	56 431	5 736
Scott	25.5	2 315	68.6	0.5	4.5	0.0	7.8	31.9	2 901	77	45	579	4 020	33 840	2 318
Searcy	16.1	2 010	62.9	0.2	4.8	0.2	10.4	2.8	353	40	33	429	2 890	31 012	2 512
Sebastian	398.6	3 131	51.6	0.2	5.7	0.1	6.2	717.8	5 639	939	574	6 635	53 660	53 111	6 538
Sevier	59.7	3 477	77.9	0.0	3.5	0.1	3.6	19.8	1 151	67	73	1 119	6 100	37 904	2 936
Sharp	43.7	2 563	62.6	0.1	5.0	0.0	10.0	23.8	1 398	48	71	786	6 300	35 725	2 814
Stone	24.5	1 931	63.3	0.1	5.7	0.2	9.7	8.6	681	63	53	563	4 570	36 045	2 909
Union	124.9	3 056	60.5	0.1	5.9	0.0	7.4	143.9	3 521	144	170	2 553	17 570	59 531	7 628
Van Buren	45.8	2 692	53.0	4.9	8.6	0.2	14.4	61.6	3 616	33	71	729	6 490	45 565	4 423
Washington	690.9	3 268	59.8	0.3	5.5	0.0	3.8	886.2	4 192	1 998	946	17 777	92 890	54 777	6 834
White	187.6	2 389	67.8	0.2	5.9	0.1	5.3	228.1	2 907	161	324	3 557	30 220	48 965	4 951
Woodruff	27.6	3 888	46.7	0.3	3.9	20.3	8.1	12.6	1 776	36	28	489	2 640	37 620	3 760
Yell	56.6	2 581	70.7	0.1	6.1	0.0	5.0	53.5	2 439	117	91	1 225	8 200	39 112	3 199

1. Based on the resident population estimated as of July 1 of the year shown.

Table B. States and Counties — **Land Area and Population**

STATE/ County code	CBSA code[1]	County type[2]	STATE County	Land area,[3] (sq mi) 2016	Total persons 2016	Rank	Per square mile	White	Black	American Indian, Alaska Native	Asian and Pacific Islander	Percent Hispanic or Latino[4]	Under 5 years	5 to 17 years	18 to 24 years	25 to 34 years	35 to 44 years	45 to 54 years
								Race alone or in combination, not Hispanic or Latino (percent)					Age (percent)					
				1	2	3	4	5	6	7	8	9	10	11	12	13	14	15
06 000	...	0	CALIFORNIA	155 792.7	39 250 017	X	251.9	40.1	6.5	1.0	16.5	38.9	6.3	16.8	9.8	15.1	13.1	13.2
06 001	41860	1	Alameda	739.1	1 647 704	20	2 229.3	35.4	12.0	0.8	33.6	22.5	5.9	15.0	8.6	16.6	14.8	13.7
06 003	...	8	Alpine	738.3	1 071	3 107	1.5	69.6	1.0	19.5	1.6	10.4	3.2	15.0	7.0	9.1	7.0	16.0
06 005	...	6	Amador	594.6	37 383	1 240	62.9	81.1	2.5	2.8	2.5	13.6	4.1	11.4	6.0	10.9	10.9	13.7
06 007	17020	3	Butte	1 636.5	226 864	289	138.6	76.0	2.5	3.0	6.3	16.0	5.5	14.6	14.6	12.8	10.5	10.9
06 009	...	6	Calaveras	1 020.0	45 171	1 070	44.3	84.5	1.3	2.9	2.8	11.6	4.1	13.1	6.5	9.2	9.0	13.0
06 011	...	6	Colusa	1 150.7	21 588	1 746	18.8	37.1	1.5	1.8	2.2	58.8	7.1	20.5	9.5	13.0	11.8	12.2
06 013	41860	1	Contra Costa	722.8	1 135 127	38	1 570.5	48.0	10.0	1.0	19.9	25.4	5.8	17.3	8.3	12.8	13.3	14.6
06 015	18860	7	Del Norte	1 006.2	27 540	1 511	27.4	66.6	3.8	9.4	4.5	19.7	5.9	15.2	7.9	14.2	12.7	12.9
06 017	40900	1	El Dorado	1 707.9	185 625	350	108.7	81.0	1.4	1.9	6.2	12.8	4.6	15.7	7.6	10.0	10.9	14.6
06 019	23420	2	Fresno	5 958.8	979 915	47	164.4	31.6	5.3	1.1	11.2	52.8	8.1	20.6	10.3	15.2	12.2	11.4
06 021	...	6	Glenn	1 313.9	28 085	1 487	21.4	53.0	1.3	2.4	3.3	41.7	7.1	19.4	9.3	12.5	11.5	11.9
06 023	21700	5	Humboldt	3 568.0	136 646	463	38.3	78.9	2.3	7.6	4.8	11.3	5.5	14.0	13.0	13.5	12.5	11.0
06 025	20940	3	Imperial	4 176.6	180 883	360	43.3	11.6	2.6	1.0	1.6	83.8	8.5	20.2	10.5	14.4	11.9	11.6
06 027	...	7	Inyo	10 180.9	18 144	1 910	1.8	65.5	1.4	11.8	2.4	21.4	6.0	14.5	6.8	10.9	10.6	11.8
06 029	12540	2	Kern	8 131.9	884 788	62	108.8	36.5	5.9	1.3	5.6	52.8	8.1	21.1	10.5	15.4	12.5	11.6
06 031	25260	3	Kings	1 389.4	149 785	438	107.8	34.6	6.8	1.4	5.2	54.2	7.8	19.5	11.3	16.8	13.5	12.0
06 033	17340	4	Lake	1 256.5	64 116	825	51.0	74.0	2.7	4.2	2.7	20.0	5.7	15.0	6.8	11.2	9.9	12.7
06 035	45000	7	Lassen	4 541.2	30 870	1 411	6.8	68.7	8.5	4.2	2.8	18.6	4.9	12.5	10.4	18.1	14.4	13.7
06 037	31080	1	Los Angeles	4 058.2	10 137 915	1	2 498.1	28.2	8.7	0.6	16.1	48.5	6.2	16.0	9.9	15.9	13.7	13.7
06 039	31460	3	Madera	2 137.1	154 697	420	72.4	36.0	3.6	1.8	2.7	57.4	7.5	20.0	9.8	13.8	12.4	11.8
06 041	41860	1	Marin	520.5	260 651	260	500.8	74.8	3.2	0.8	8.5	16.0	4.7	15.7	6.6	8.7	12.3	15.9
06 043	...	8	Mariposa	1 448.8	17 410	1 950	12.0	83.3	1.7	4.5	2.6	11.0	4.4	12.0	6.6	10.4	9.3	12.3
06 045	46380	4	Mendocino	3 506.4	87 628	661	25.0	68.1	1.4	5.5	3.0	25.0	6.0	15.7	7.4	11.4	11.7	12.0
06 047	32900	2	Merced	1 935.2	268 672	254	138.8	30.0	3.6	0.9	8.5	58.9	7.9	21.9	11.2	14.4	12.2	11.5
06 049	...	6	Modoc	3 915.4	8 795	2 523	2.2	79.3	1.8	4.4	1.9	15.2	4.6	15.0	6.5	10.2	10.6	12.4
06 051	...	7	Mono	3 049.0	13 981	2 166	4.6	67.1	1.4	2.6	3.4	27.7	5.0	14.1	8.9	15.0	12.9	14.2
06 053	41500	2	Monterey	3 280.6	435 232	162	132.7	32.2	3.2	0.9	7.9	58.3	7.4	18.9	10.3	14.6	12.9	12.0
06 055	34900	3	Napa	748.3	142 166	453	190.0	55.0	2.6	1.1	9.8	33.9	5.3	16.0	8.8	12.3	12.5	13.5
06 057	46020	4	Nevada	957.8	99 107	598	103.5	87.7	0.9	2.0	2.6	9.5	4.3	13.2	6.3	9.9	10.5	12.4
06 059	31080	1	Orange	790.6	3 172 532	6	4 012.8	43.5	2.1	0.6	22.3	34.3	6.0	16.5	9.5	14.3	13.0	14.4
06 061	40900	1	Placer	1 407.1	380 531	180	270.4	76.6	2.3	1.4	9.7	13.8	5.3	17.2	7.5	11.0	12.6	14.0
06 063	...	7	Plumas	2 553.1	18 627	1 887	7.3	86.4	1.8	3.9	2.2	9.0	4.2	12.9	6.5	9.6	9.3	11.7
06 065	40140	1	Riverside	7 206.3	2 387 741	10	331.3	38.2	7.0	1.0	7.9	48.4	6.6	19.1	10.0	13.8	12.6	12.8
06 067	40900	1	Sacramento	964.9	1 514 460	24	1 569.6	49.3	11.7	1.5	19.5	23.0	6.6	17.4	8.9	15.5	13.0	12.9
06 069	41940	1	San Benito	1 388.7	59 414	872	42.8	36.5	1.3	0.9	3.7	59.2	6.6	19.7	9.6	13.4	12.7	13.7
06 071	40140	1	San Bernardino	20 057.3	2 140 096	14	106.7	31.2	9.1	0.9	8.3	52.8	7.2	19.6	10.7	14.9	12.7	12.6
06 073	41740	1	San Diego	4 206.6	3 317 749	5	788.7	48.9	5.7	1.0	14.5	33.5	6.4	15.5	10.7	16.4	13.1	12.7
06 075	41860	1	San Francisco	46.9	870 887	63	18 569.0	43.8	6.0	0.8	37.9	15.2	4.6	9.0	7.3	23.4	15.7	13.5
06 077	44700	2	San Joaquin	1 392.4	733 709	88	526.9	35.5	8.1	1.2	17.7	41.2	7.1	20.3	9.9	13.9	12.8	12.6
06 079	42020	2	San Luis Obispo	3 300.6	282 887	242	85.7	71.6	2.2	1.3	5.3	22.3	4.8	13.2	15.4	11.5	10.6	11.5
06 081	41860	1	San Mateo	448.5	764 797	83	1 705.2	42.8	3.0	0.6	32.6	24.8	5.8	15.3	7.4	14.6	14.3	14.3
06 083	42200	2	Santa Barbara	2 735.1	446 170	157	163.1	47.1	2.4	1.0	6.9	45.1	6.5	15.9	15.8	13.3	11.2	11.3
06 085	41940	1	Santa Clara	1 291.2	1 919 402	17	1 486.5	35.0	3.0	0.7	38.7	25.9	6.2	16.4	8.6	15.8	14.5	14.1
06 087	42100	2	Santa Cruz	445.2	274 673	248	617.0	60.4	1.7	1.2	6.4	33.5	5.4	14.3	15.1	12.1	11.6	12.8
06 089	39820	3	Shasta	3 775.4	179 631	362	47.6	83.8	1.8	4.0	4.4	9.8	5.9	15.6	7.8	12.7	10.6	12.3
06 091	...	8	Sierra	953.2	2 947	2 976	3.1	86.1	1.3	2.8	1.3	11.0	3.6	11.6	5.9	7.0	9.9	12.5
06 093	...	6	Siskiyou	6 278.8	43 603	1 100	6.9	80.5	2.4	6.4	2.9	12.3	5.3	14.9	7.0	10.3	9.6	11.6
06 095	46700	2	Solano	821.8	440 207	160	535.7	42.9	15.9	1.4	19.5	26.2	6.1	16.4	9.1	14.6	12.2	13.3
06 097	42220	2	Sonoma	1 575.9	503 070	138	319.2	66.6	2.3	1.6	6.0	26.6	5.1	14.9	8.4	13.1	12.2	13.4
06 099	33700	2	Stanislaus	1 496.0	541 560	122	362.0	45.0	3.3	1.3	7.6	45.6	7.2	19.9	9.6	14.4	12.5	12.3
06 101	49700	3	Sutter	602.4	96 651	614	160.4	49.6	2.9	2.0	18.5	30.5	6.9	19.2	9.0	13.7	12.0	12.3
06 103	39780	4	Tehama	2 949.7	63 276	836	21.5	71.0	1.3	3.5	2.2	24.7	6.4	17.7	8.0	11.9	11.0	12.6
06 105	...	8	Trinity	3 179.3	12 782	2 242	4.0	86.5	1.3	7.0	2.2	7.3	4.4	12.7	6.0	8.9	10.4	12.6
06 107	47300	2	Tulare	4 824.4	460 437	149	95.4	30.5	1.6	1.2	4.1	64.1	8.4	22.8	10.3	14.1	12.4	11.2
06 109	43760	4	Tuolumne	2 220.9	53 804	935	24.2	82.8	2.4	2.9	2.3	12.2	4.5	12.2	7.2	11.8	10.4	12.1
06 111	37100	2	Ventura	1 843.0	849 738	68	461.1	47.9	2.2	0.8	9.0	42.5	6.1	17.4	9.6	13.2	12.4	13.8
06 113	40900	1	Yolo	1 014.8	215 802	306	212.7	50.7	3.2	1.3	17.3	31.5	5.8	15.5	19.9	13.7	11.6	11.0
06 115	49700	3	Yuba	632.0	75 275	732	119.1	59.8	4.9	3.4	9.0	27.8	7.9	19.4	10.1	15.6	12.1	11.3
08 000	...	0	COLORADO	103 641.2	5 540 545	X	53.5	70.7	4.8	1.3	4.3	21.3	6.1	16.7	9.6	15.2	13.4	13.0
08 001	19740	1	Adams	1 167.3	498 187	142	426.8	52.6	3.9	1.1	4.9	39.6	7.4	19.9	8.9	16.0	14.4	12.7
08 003	...	7	Alamosa	722.6	16 654	2 000	23.0	50.1	1.9	2.1	1.6	46.1	6.8	17.0	18.3	13.3	10.4	9.7
08 005	19740	1	Arapahoe	797.9	637 068	104	798.4	64.0	12.0	1.1	7.4	18.9	6.4	17.7	8.5	15.2	14.0	13.3
08 007	...	7	Archuleta	1 350.1	12 854	2 238	9.5	78.6	1.0	2.7	1.4	18.0	4.7	13.4	5.6	9.8	10.4	12.5
08 009	...	9	Baca	2 555.0	3 568	2 938	1.4	87.2	1.2	2.1	0.7	10.4	5.7	15.2	7.4	9.7	9.6	11.2
08 011	...	7	Bent	1 512.9	5 861	2 765	3.9	57.3	7.7	2.0	1.9	32.0	3.4	11.5	9.2	17.0	15.0	14.1

1. CBSA = Core Based Statistical Area. See Appendix A for explanation. See Appendix B for list of metropolitan areas with component counties. Service of USDA Rural-Urban Continuum Codes. See Appendix A for definition. 2. County type code from the Economic Research Service of USDA Rural-Urban Continuum Codes. See Appendix A for definition. 3. Dry land or land partially or temporarily covered by water. 4. May be of any race.

STATE County	55 to 64 years	65 to 74 years	75 years and over	Percent female	Total persons 2000	Total persons 2010	Percent change 2000–2010	Percent change 2010–2016	Births	Deaths	Net migration	Number	Persons per household	Family households	Female family householder[1]	One person
	16	17	18	19	20	21	22	23	24	25	26	27	28	29	30	31
CALIFORNIA	11.9	7.9	5.8	50.3	33 871 648	37 254 522	10.0	5.4	3 135 219	1 563 968	443 210	12 717 801	2.96	68.7	13.6	24.1
Alameda	12.2	7.7	5.3	50.9	1 443 741	1 510 261	4.6	9.1	121 894	60 212	78 585	558 907	2.78	66.0	12.4	25.6
Alpine	19.6	16.1	7.1	47.3	1 208	1 175	-2.7	-8.9	32	39	-104	358	3.06	62.8	9.5	34.4
Amador	17.2	16.2	10.0	46.8	35 100	38 091	8.5	-1.9	1 771	2 626	166	13 925	2.36	67.5	8.2	27.7
Butte	13.1	10.4	7.6	50.5	203 171	220 000	8.3	3.1	15 302	14 220	5 611	85 318	2.55	59.7	11.6	28.8
Calaveras	18.8	16.6	9.8	50.0	40 554	45 578	12.4	-0.9	2 176	3 008	509	18 060	2.45	67.2	7.9	26.9
Colusa	12.2	7.9	5.9	48.7	18 804	21 419	13.9	0.8	1 909	858	-836	6 966	3.04	77.2	10.7	19.5
Contra Costa	13.1	8.8	6.2	51.2	948 816	1 049 200	10.6	8.2	77 311	46 837	55 629	384 646	2.82	71.0	12.3	22.9
Del Norte	14.5	10.1	6.7	45.6	27 507	28 610	4.0	-3.7	1 987	1 700	-1 340	9 420	2.55	62.0	14.6	32.7
El Dorado	17.2	12.0	7.4	50.1	156 299	181 058	15.8	2.5	9 950	8 836	3 604	67 086	2.69	70.5	8.6	23.6
Fresno	10.4	6.9	5.0	50.1	799 407	930 491	16.4	5.3	99 284	40 558	-9 483	296 305	3.17	72.9	18.0	21.4
Glenn	12.8	8.8	6.7	49.4	26 453	28 122	6.3	-0.1	2 490	1 470	-1 041	9 497	2.92	68.5	10.4	27.5
Humboldt	13.9	10.4	6.1	50.1	126 518	134 623	6.4	1.5	9 357	8 089	943	53 036	2.47	57.8	11.7	31.2
Imperial	10.3	6.9	5.7	49.0	142 361	174 528	22.6	3.6	19 505	6 075	-7 347	46 452	3.61	77.2	19.5	19.5
Inyo	16.6	12.4	10.5	49.7	17 945	18 546	3.3	-2.2	1 339	1 126	-589	7 957	2.23	55.8	10.5	38.3
Kern	10.4	6.3	4.1	48.7	661 645	839 627	26.9	5.4	89 042	35 445	-7 445	259 700	3.21	75.5	16.6	19.5
Kings	9.4	5.6	4.1	44.9	129 461	152 982	18.2	-2.1	14 984	5 042	-13 302	41 554	3.19	76.7	18.4	17.6
Lake	16.7	13.7	8.2	50.1	58 309	64 665	10.9	-0.8	4 611	5 220	80	26 993	2.34	59.7	13.1	31.0
Lassen	12.5	8.2	5.3	37.7	33 828	34 895	3.2	-11.5	1 905	1 307	-4 647	9 707	2.24	65.2	8.4	28.2
Los Angeles	11.7	7.3	5.6	50.7	9 519 338	9 818 700	3.1	3.3	810 749	377 144	-100 271	3 263 069	3.02	67.0	15.6	25.7
Madera	11.1	8.2	5.4	51.7	123 109	150 843	22.5	2.6	14 523	6 594	-3 876	43 159	3.35	76.9	14.9	19.5
Marin	15.5	12.1	8.5	51.2	247 289	252 409	2.1	3.3	14 659	11 836	5 941	103 670	2.41	62.1	8.9	31.0
Mariposa	19.1	15.4	10.3	49.0	17 130	18 250	6.5	-4.6	909	1 070	-583	7 345	2.29	67.6	7.3	25.7
Mendocino	15.2	13.2	7.4	50.3	86 265	87 840	1.8	-0.2	6 615	5 301	-1 308	34 017	2.51	59.5	10.9	32.8
Merced	9.9	6.4	4.5	49.6	210 554	255 798	21.5	5.0	26 416	10 143	-3 129	77 692	3.32	76.7	18.7	18.6
Modoc	16.4	14.5	9.9	49.4	9 449	9 686	2.5	-9.2	475	658	-694	3 745	2.32	58.6	5.8	36.5
Mono	16.2	9.1	4.5	46.5	12 853	14 202	10.5	-1.6	898	283	-860	4 906	2.82	55.8	4.5	37.1
Monterey	11.1	7.3	5.4	49.1	401 762	415 055	3.3	4.9	41 336	15 211	-5 343	125 402	3.26	72.5	13.9	21.6
Napa	13.5	10.3	7.8	50.4	124 279	136 530	9.9	4.1	9 282	7 526	3 728	49 494	2.74	69.4	11.0	24.3
Nevada	18.0	15.7	9.8	50.8	92 033	98 748	7.3	0.4	5 097	5 995	1 531	40 993	2.38	63.7	8.2	28.8
Orange	12.3	7.9	6.0	50.7	2 846 289	3 010 261	5.8	5.4	238 043	117 213	43 160	1 009 353	3.04	72.0	12.0	21.2
Placer	13.5	10.8	8.2	51.3	248 399	348 494	40.3	9.2	23 296	18 405	26 464	135 456	2.67	70.1	9.6	24.1
Plumas	19.6	16.6	9.6	49.9	20 824	20 007	-3.9	-6.9	954	1 349	-906	8 217	2.26	59.8	7.6	33.3
Riverside	11.2	7.9	6.0	50.3	1 545 387	2 189 753	41.7	9.0	190 186	95 882	100 383	699 232	3.24	73.6	13.6	20.8
Sacramento	12.2	7.9	5.7	51.1	1 223 499	1 418 742	16.0	6.7	123 768	68 262	38 855	522 596	2.76	65.7	15.0	27.0
San Benito	12.2	7.4	4.8	49.7	53 234	55 269	3.8	7.5	4 571	1 837	1 463	17 198	3.33	79.8	13.8	15.8
San Bernardino	11.1	6.8	4.3	50.3	1 709 434	2 035 212	19.1	5.2	192 795	81 359	-7 085	614 325	3.33	75.6	16.9	19.6
San Diego	11.7	7.7	5.7	49.7	2 813 833	3 095 342	10.0	7.2	276 631	128 855	74 361	1 094 157	2.86	66.8	12.1	24.4
San Francisco	11.7	8.1	6.7	49.1	776 733	805 193	3.7	8.2	56 191	35 923	46 474	353 287	2.32	45.8	8.3	37.8
San Joaquin	11.1	7.3	5.0	50.1	563 598	685 308	21.6	7.1	63 542	32 847	16 893	219 073	3.16	74.8	15.9	19.9
San Luis Obispo	14.0	11.1	7.8	49.3	246 681	269 599	9.3	4.9	16 554	14 368	10 644	103 576	2.51	63.2	9.0	26.2
San Mateo	13.0	8.6	6.6	50.7	707 161	718 498	1.6	6.4	56 819	29 711	20 745	259 711	2.85	68.7	10.3	24.2
Santa Barbara	11.3	7.9	6.7	50.0	399 347	423 939	6.2	5.2	36 061	18 763	4 970	142 713	2.92	65.5	11.6	24.8
Santa Clara	11.6	7.2	5.6	49.5	1 682 585	1 781 672	5.9	7.7	148 588	60 931	53 051	621 463	2.95	71.9	10.5	21.2
Santa Cruz	13.8	9.5	5.4	50.5	255 602	262 362	2.6	4.7	19 105	10 917	4 129	94 802	2.72	62.9	10.6	26.4
Shasta	14.8	12.0	8.3	51.0	163 256	177 223	8.6	1.4	13 102	13 101	2 055	69 375	2.54	64.8	11.9	28.2
Sierra	20.6	18.7	10.2	49.1	3 555	3 240	-8.9	-9.0	119	208	-191	1 252	2.38	61.4	7.4	32.4
Siskiyou	17.2	14.9	9.2	50.2	44 301	44 900	1.4	-2.9	2 797	3 304	-705	19 133	2.26	62.2	9.2	31.1
Solano	13.5	8.9	5.7	50.3	394 542	413 344	4.8	6.5	32 406	19 292	13 319	143 612	2.89	71.8	15.8	22.1
Sonoma	14.7	11.1	7.1	51.1	458 614	483 880	5.5	4.0	32 093	25 136	11 677	187 782	2.59	63.1	10.8	28.3
Stanislaus	11.2	7.5	5.3	50.6	446 997	514 451	15.1	5.3	47 899	24 893	4 109	169 196	3.08	73.7	15.7	20.6
Sutter	11.7	8.5	6.7	50.2	78 930	94 743	20.0	2.0	8 178	4 768	-1 645	31 917	2.95	73.4	13.4	21.7
Tehama	13.9	10.8	7.7	50.3	56 039	63 440	13.2	-0.3	4 817	4 074	-855	23 704	2.63	69.0	12.6	25.3
Trinity	19.8	15.9	9.3	48.7	13 022	13 786	5.9	-7.3	694	1 011	-649	5 484	2.38	60.1	7.1	32.9
Tulare	9.8	6.5	4.5	50.0	368 021	442 182	20.2	4.1	48 587	18 088	-11 659	133 570	3.36	78.0	16.9	17.4
Tuolumne	17.1	14.8	9.9	48.0	54 501	55 365	1.6	-2.8	2 897	4 061	-366	22 133	2.28	65.7	10.7	27.8
Ventura	12.9	8.5	6.1	50.5	753 197	823 387	9.3	3.2	66 011	33 801	-6 044	268 969	3.08	73.6	12.4	20.7
Yolo	10.4	6.9	5.1	51.3	168 660	200 850	19.1	7.4	15 162	7 697	7 307	71 997	2.77	61.8	10.9	24.5
Yuba	11.5	7.5	4.6	49.4	60 219	72 148	19.8	4.3	7 545	3 483	-873	25 139	2.87	72.4	14.2	20.0
COLORADO	12.6	8.3	5.2	49.7	4 301 261	5 029 324	16.9	10.2	411 768	213 620	306 202	2 024 468	2.55	64.3	10.2	27.7
Adams	10.6	6.2	3.8	49.6	348 618	441 687	26.7	12.8	44 806	17 381	28 353	156 628	2.98	70.9	13.7	22.6
Alamosa	11.2	7.9	5.4	49.7	14 966	15 445	3.2	7.8	1 426	764	507	5 932	2.56	59.5	9.3	32.8
Arapahoe	12.3	7.7	4.8	50.6	487 967	572 155	17.3	11.3	49 340	22 608	37 945	229 601	2.63	66.2	12.1	27.4
Archuleta	19.2	16.7	7.7	49.8	9 898	12 084	22.1	6.4	708	550	652	5 334	2.25	68.9	8.6	27.4
Baca	15.4	12.6	13.3	49.8	4 517	3 788	-16.1	-5.8	252	348	-120	1 568	2.30	65.1	8.0	31.6
Bent	12.8	9.5	7.5	34.2	5 998	6 499	8.4	-9.8	249	339	-558	1 635	2.19	68.7	12.4	28.7

1. No spouse present.

Table B. States and Counties — Population, Vital Statistics, Health, and Crime

STATE County	Persons in group quarters, 2016	Daytime population, 2011–2015 Number	Daytime population, Employment/residence ratio	Births, 2016 Total	Births, 2016 Rate[1]	Deaths, 2016 Number	Deaths, 2016 Rate[1]	Persons under 65 with no health insurance, 2015 Number	Persons under 65 with no health insurance, 2015 Percent	Medicare, 2015 Total Beneficiaries	Medicare, 2015 Enrolled in Original Medicare	Medicare, 2015 Enrolled in Medicare Advantage	Serious crimes known to police,[2] 2014 Total Number	Serious crimes known to police,[2] 2014 Total Rate[3]
	32	33	34	35	36	37	38	39	40	41	42	43	44	45
CALIFORNIA	813 569	38 416 815	1.00	502 848	12.8	273 850	7.0	3 234 373	9.7	5 278 529	2 762 697	2 515 832	1 100 901	2 837
Alameda	36 415	1 565 592	0.97	20 018	12.1	10 695	6.5	84 805	6.0	199 820	102 351	97 469	67 976	4 236
Alpine	24	1 425	1.74	4	3.7	5	4.7	83	9.6	209	192	17	28	2 401
Amador	3 235	37 021	1.00	305	8.2	413	11.0	1 688	6.9	9 908	7 699	2 209	710	1 951
Butte	5 396	223 061	1.01	2 520	11.1	2 444	10.8	14 769	8.1	46 872	45 740	1 132	7 309	3 265
Calaveras	493	40 000	0.70	374	8.3	498	11.0	2 352	7.1	11 730	9 972	1 758	1 102	2 475
Colusa	268	21 790	1.05	295	13.7	127	5.9	2 250	12.3	3 326	3 060	266	390	1 818
Contra Costa	10 542	973 013	0.75	12 785	11.3	8 347	7.4	62 229	6.5	166 454	80 001	86 453	35 882	3 230
Del Norte	2 916	28 267	1.06	302	11.0	246	8.9	1 610	8.1	5 762	5 262	500	814	2 922
El Dorado	1 644	161 025	0.73	1 639	8.8	1 589	8.6	9 276	6.2	36 372	23 874	12 498	3 547	1 939
Fresno	17 435	957 693	1.00	15 767	16.1	7 049	7.2	91 282	10.8	118 408	77 591	40 817	37 082	3 837
Glenn	316	26 905	0.89	395	14.1	241	8.6	2 721	11.6	4 940	4 846	94	652	2 324
Humboldt	5 518	135 480	1.01	1 476	10.8	1 345	9.8	9 915	8.9	25 810	24 631	1 179	5 272	3 902
Imperial	8 870	177 885	0.99	3 201	17.7	1 019	5.6	15 794	10.6	25 245	22 980	2 265	6 119	3 577
Inyo	429	18 744	1.05	213	11.7	168	9.3	1 241	8.9	2 958	2 843	115	409	2 204
Kern	32 350	868 500	1.01	14 173	16.0	6 094	6.9	73 282	9.7	101 349	60 756	40 593	32 748	3 744
Kings	16 201	151 462	1.01	2 324	15.5	849	5.7	10 670	8.9	14 906	12 621	2 285	4 171	2 754
Lake	1 136	60 290	0.82	737	11.5	881	13.7	5 162	10.3	16 116	15 235	881	2 139	3 343
Lassen	7 682	33 886	1.14	316	10.2	181	5.9	1 089	5.7	4 449	4 306	143	661	2 085
Los Angeles	176 710	10 187 456	1.03	128 480	12.7	66 489	6.6	1 092 708	12.5	1 252 736	512 490	740 246	260 218	2 571
Madera	7 504	153 332	1.00	2 276	14.7	1 066	6.9	16 485	13.0	22 146	14 445	7 701	4 268	2 780
Marin	7 958	260 979	1.02	2 308	8.9	1 979	7.6	12 651	6.2	50 813	30 328	20 485	5 019	1 922
Mariposa	725	16 701	0.85	153	8.8	179	10.3	1 018	7.9	4 121	3 914	207	347	1 957
Mendocino	1 991	88 049	1.01	1 026	11.7	876	10.0	8 330	12.0	20 373	18 704	1 669	2 058	2 351
Merced	5 747	250 085	0.85	4 188	15.6	1 730	6.4	23 618	10.1	31 409	27 892	3 517	8 611	3 233
Modoc	357	8 938	0.92	67	7.6	105	11.9	712	10.7	2 178	1 999	179	215	2 372
Mono	322	14 845	1.10	137	9.8	44	3.1	1 427	12.0	2 560	2 473	87	220	1 560
Monterey	18 190	426 592	0.99	6 452	14.8	2 630	6.0	43 444	11.9	54 495	52 638	1 857	12 410	2 857
Napa	4 998	147 767	1.11	1 483	10.4	1 296	9.1	9 719	8.5	25 996	16 028	9 968	2 919	2 055
Nevada	1 204	94 791	0.91	847	8.5	960	9.7	6 012	8.1	23 934	20 078	3 856	1 899	1 926
Orange	42 892	3 198 870	1.06	38 433	12.1	20 520	6.5	271 391	10.0	425 459	195 503	229 956	61 011	1 933
Placer	3 766	362 800	0.98	3 705	9.7	3 253	8.5	16 403	5.4	72 996	38 320	34 676	7 239	1 937
Plumas	280	19 165	1.03	142	7.6	197	10.6	1 179	8.7	5 561	5 125	436	403	2 154
Riverside	33 834	2 126 971	0.81	30 845	12.9	17 092	7.2	218 225	10.9	313 612	117 303	196 309	67 694	2 907
Sacramento	22 572	1 470 749	1.01	19 978	13.2	12 123	8.0	92 561	7.2	210 711	101 227	109 484	47 698	3 222
San Benito	385	49 726	0.69	715	12.0	322	5.4	5 277	10.3	6 934	6 499	435	932	1 594
San Bernardino	37 630	2 023 029	0.91	31 183	14.6	14 506	6.8	179 718	9.7	246 651	82 959	163 692	63 059	2 986
San Diego	105 973	3 252 893	1.02	44 652	13.5	22 552	6.8	263 461	9.5	437 333	202 020	235 313	69 635	2 138
San Francisco	23 535	1 033 512	1.41	9 262	10.6	6 235	7.2	45 556	6.3	126 255	69 947	56 308	52 758	6 205
San Joaquin	15 110	679 185	0.89	10 239	14.0	5 701	7.8	53 841	8.6	94 535	56 113	38 422	30 438	4 271
San Luis Obispo	15 800	273 999	0.98	2 666	9.4	2 414	8.5	17 356	8.0	54 334	46 703	7 631	6 860	2 453
San Mateo	8 668	750 621	1.00	9 196	12.0	5 151	6.7	36 880	5.7	108 303	55 181	53 122	15 747	2 076
Santa Barbara	18 835	449 687	1.07	5 841	13.1	3 216	7.2	44 488	12.2	67 169	56 203	10 966	10 382	2 354
Santa Clara	30 498	1 990 696	1.14	23 834	12.4	10 944	5.7	98 375	5.9	226 162	104 136	122 026	47 760	2 524
Santa Cruz	13 656	258 272	0.91	3 006	10.9	1 877	6.8	17 542	7.8	41 497	37 348	4 149	9 260	3 398
Shasta	2 828	180 159	1.02	2 072	11.5	2 227	12.4	12 195	8.6	43 370	40 695	2 675	6 980	3 869
Sierra	33	2 758	0.75	22	7.5	31	10.5	205	9.6	817	786	31	40	1 324
Siskiyou	578	44 539	1.04	422	9.7	543	12.5	3 060	9.3	12 293	11 210	1 083	861	1 968
Solano	11 318	381 523	0.76	5 302	12.0	3 472	7.9	21 726	6.0	64 619	35 813	28 806	15 562	3 620
Sonoma	10 396	475 590	0.92	5 084	10.1	4 359	8.7	35 290	8.7	91 408	50 969	40 439	10 404	2 079
Stanislaus	6 413	509 370	0.91	7 708	14.2	4 281	7.9	39 586	8.5	76 544	40 820	35 724	21 385	4 027
Sutter	737	88 770	0.82	1 327	13.7	804	8.3	8 964	11.0	15 882	15 363	519	2 680	2 791
Tehama	846	59 540	0.84	824	13.0	657	10.4	4 734	9.2	11 727	11 481	246	1 910	3 019
Trinity	385	13 620	1.05	105	8.2	169	13.2	845	8.7	6 626	6 253	373	208	1 547
Tulare	4 808	445 316	0.95	7 575	16.5	3 119	6.8	45 247	11.2	54 396	45 924	8 472	13 301	2 895
Tuolumne	3 598	54 177	1.01	472	8.8	653	12.1	2 736	7.2	14 374	13 625	749	1 308	2 429
Ventura	11 204	797 191	0.89	10 348	12.2	5 996	7.1	71 633	9.9	126 228	85 093	41 135	18 702	2 206
Yolo	9 136	221 371	1.16	2 454	11.4	1 336	6.2	13 510	7.5	26 632	15 235	11 397	6 264	3 032
Yuba	1 279	71 142	0.91	1 175	15.6	555	7.4	6 047	9.4	10 706	9 894	812	2 431	3 286
COLORADO	118 125	5 265 634	0.99	67 453	12.2	37 121	6.7	428 602	9.2	747 532	442 768	304 764	152 064	2 839
Adams	4 085	420 982	0.78	7 197	14.4	2 998	6.0	55 165	12.6	50 024	21 052	28 972	15 449	3 228
Alamosa	1 275	18 414	1.35	225	13.5	112	6.7	1 679	12.9	2 761	2 018	743	NA	NA
Arapahoe	4 337	598 829	0.97	7 987	12.5	4 011	6.3	51 582	9.4	86 977	44 537	42 440	17 313	2 797
Archuleta	129	11 873	0.94	107	8.3	94	7.3	1 229	13.2	3 005	2 512	493	231	1 879
Baca	82	3 702	1.00	33	9.2	51	14.3	355	13.4	D	948	D	33	897
Bent	1 932	6 039	1.12	36	6.1	46	7.8	324	10.5	865	807	58	81	1 464

1. Per 1,000 estimated resident population.   2. Data for serious crimes have not been adjusted for underreporting; this may affect comparability between geographic areas and over time.
3. Per 100,000 population estimated by the FBI.

Table B. States and Counties — Crime, Education, Money Income, and Poverty

STATE County	Serious crimes known to police, 2014 (cont.)[1] Rate[2] Violent	Property	Education School enrollment and attainment, 2011–2015 Enrollment[3] Total	Percent private	Attainment[4] (percent) High school graduate or less	Bachelor's degree or more	Local government expenditures,[5] 2013–2014 Total current spending (mil dol)	Current spending per student (dollars)	Money income, 2011–2015 Per capita income[6] (dollars)	Households Median income (dollars)	Percent with income of less than $50,000	Percent with income of $200,000 or more	Income and poverty, 2015 Median household income (dollars)	Percent below poverty level All persons	Children under 18 years	Children 5 to 17 years in families
	46	47	48	49	50	51	52	53	54	55	56	57	58	59	60	61
CALIFORNIA	396	2 441	10 579 176	14.1	38.9	31.4	59 746.4	9 599	30 318	61 818	41.3	7.9	64 483	15.4	21.2	20.3
Alameda	645	3 591	417 716	15.2	31.5	43.0	2 052.5	9 204	37 285	75 619	34.3	11.5	81 462	11.5	13.8	13.4
Alpine	343	2 058	309	17.5	41.1	27.5	3.5	38 678	21 415	52 917	47.5	2.8	50 882	19.0	35.7	26.9
Amador	223	1 728	7 148	12.4	38.7	21.3	37.7	9 055	27 473	54 171	46.4	3.9	55 879	13.1	19.5	17.2
Butte	303	2 962	63 724	8.1	34.7	25.9	316.8	10 197	24 259	43 444	55.5	2.8	45 369	21.4	23.8	22.6
Calaveras	254	2 221	7 973	11.8	35.9	20.9	64.2	10 993	29 553	53 233	46.7	3.4	52 471	13.0	21.2	18.6
Colusa	186	1 632	5 853	8.1	53.5	14.6	51.2	10 861	21 897	52 168	47.4	2.7	51 118	13.2	19.4	18.0
Contra Costa	329	2 901	293 711	16.4	29.8	39.6	1 582.3	9 145	39 313	80 185	31.5	12.4	83 036	10.2	12.7	11.6
Del Norte	592	2 330	6 160	9.6	49.2	15.1	44.3	10 685	19 560	40 847	57.4	2.2	38 963	23.3	33.8	32.2
El Dorado	224	1 716	42 911	11.6	29.5	32.1	264.1	9 761	35 588	69 584	36.6	9.2	75 575	9.1	11.6	10.4
Fresno	471	3 367	288 605	8.0	49.3	19.4	1 911.6	9 794	20 408	45 233	53.9	3.2	46 608	25.2	36.3	33.6
Glenn	446	1 878	7 511	7.4	54.5	14.9	57.5	10 750	21 313	39 349	58.1	2.3	43 584	18.5	25.7	23.4
Humboldt	359	3 543	36 150	7.1	35.4	28.0	192.9	10 940	23 367	42 197	58.0	2.3	40 739	20.9	23.0	22.8
Imperial	341	3 236	53 420	5.8	55.5	14.1	376.5	10 183	16 143	41 079	57.4	2.0	39 925	24.3	31.4	32.1
Inyo	571	1 633	3 915	10.2	43.3	23.9	59.8	11 764	27 850	45 955	53.3	2.7	51 697	12.4	19.9	19.2
Kern	510	3 234	252 985	8.6	53.8	15.4	1 735.4	9 658	20 644	49 026	50.7	3.2	51 150	21.9	31.3	29.2
Kings	460	2 295	44 816	9.8	52.6	13.4	270.5	10 440	18 707	46 481	53.1	2.7	46 440	22.4	28.4	28.1
Lake	480	2 863	13 677	10.4	44.0	16.0	95.0	11 180	21 407	35 578	62.6	1.7	37 993	20.5	30.2	30.0
Lassen	442	1 643	6 508	23.3	48.8	12.3	36.5	8 655	19 274	51 555	48.2	1.7	54 670	17.1	19.7	18.1
Los Angeles	422	2 149	2 760 505	15.5	43.4	30.3	15 803.6	10 178	28 337	56 196	45.1	7.0	59 045	16.7	23.5	22.0
Madera	578	2 201	42 116	6.7	54.3	13.3	283.4	9 184	17 970	45 073	54.8	2.2	46 593	22.6	32.3	31.1
Marin	174	1 748	61 655	24.1	19.0	55.8	394.9	12 043	60 236	93 257	28.5	20.4	99 868	7.5	8.8	7.7
Mariposa	400	1 557	3 005	7.5	39.0	22.1	22.0	11 612	28 316	47 681	51.7	2.2	44 595	15.2	24.1	23.2
Mendocino	585	1 766	20 248	9.2	39.7	23.7	148.6	11 306	24 059	42 980	55.5	2.3	43 237	20.3	27.3	25.2
Merced	558	2 675	83 807	4.8	57.0	13.1	564.1	10 065	18 204	42 462	56.5	2.5	42 879	25.9	35.9	36.3
Modoc	541	1 832	1 717	13.9	39.3	18.0	14.5	14 984	21 001	37 860	65.0	0.9	38 402	20.3	31.1	26.8
Mono	255	1 304	3 390	4.1	31.9	32.3	30.9	15 425	29 437	56 944	40.9	3.3	53 992	11.2	17.3	16.7
Monterey	422	2 435	120 233	8.3	50.1	23.1	765.5	10 262	24 994	58 783	42.4	5.5	60 047	15.3	22.3	21.5
Napa	376	1 679	34 903	15.1	36.1	32.4	229.7	11 009	36 475	71 379	35.6	9.5	72 683	10.1	12.1	11.0
Nevada	312	1 614	20 313	12.5	26.3	33.7	170.5	10 461	32 442	56 521	44.9	4.4	57 627	12.4	16.4	14.8
Orange	198	1 735	865 733	14.9	33.4	37.7	4 450.8	8 890	34 817	76 509	33.1	11.1	78 002	12.7	16.8	16.2
Placer	159	1 777	96 972	13.5	25.3	36.4	563.7	8 586	36 022	73 948	33.6	7.8	76 203	8.6	9.0	8.1
Plumas	486	1 668	3 501	10.2	33.4	22.0	27.5	11 055	30 842	47 333	52.5	4.7	46 813	13.8	22.5	20.7
Riverside	269	2 638	660 858	11.7	45.7	20.9	3 813.6	8 947	23 783	56 603	44.6	4.2	57 895	16.2	22.6	21.5
Sacramento	503	2 718	411 108	12.4	35.6	28.8	2 184.8	9 183	27 315	55 987	45.0	4.3	58 735	16.9	22.7	21.8
San Benito	335	1 259	16 629	10.1	46.4	18.0	103.2	9 230	27 239	71 077	33.8	6.4	76 521	9.3	14.0	13.0
San Bernardino	392	2 594	627 868	11.0	47.7	19.0	3 604.3	8 757	21 352	53 433	46.6	3.4	53 526	18.9	27.3	26.4
San Diego	325	1 813	869 887	14.5	32.9	35.7	4 604.0	9 151	31 266	64 309	39.4	7.4	67 053	13.9	17.8	17.2
San Francisco	802	5 402	172 097	31.5	25.7	53.8	722.6	12 375	52 220	81 294	34.3	16.4	90 527	12.4	13.5	14.5
San Joaquin	750	3 521	208 310	12.5	48.4	18.4	1 262.6	9 081	22 645	53 274	46.9	3.5	53 341	17.5	23.7	23.1
San Luis Obispo	421	2 032	76 104	9.1	30.0	33.0	331.9	9 552	31 060	60 691	41.8	5.6	61 761	14.4	14.6	13.8
San Mateo	206	1 870	187 438	22.1	28.2	45.6	1 021.6	10 791	48 278	93 623	26.2	18.4	101 133	8.4	9.7	9.1
Santa Barbara	293	2 060	133 986	10.4	38.1	32.2	655.5	9 685	30 589	63 985	40.1	7.8	63 049	15.6	20.0	18.8
Santa Clara	247	2 277	506 050	20.5	28.4	47.9	2 705.7	9 914	43 880	96 310	27.0	18.2	102 191	8.3	9.0	8.5
Santa Cruz	418	2 980	78 851	11.0	29.5	38.2	417.6	10 238	33 241	67 256	38.4	9.2	64 841	15.4	17.6	16.5
Shasta	707	3 162	43 057	16.5	36.6	19.6	274.5	10 191	24 107	44 620	54.8	2.5	45 943	19.0	26.5	24.3
Sierra	364	960	410	15.6	41.8	18.9	6.6	17 379	29 986	42 833	55.2	4.3	47 535	13.8	17.4	14.5
Siskiyou	313	1 655	9 238	12.0	36.4	22.7	79.7	12 575	22 561	37 170	62.2	1.8	37 447	22.6	31.4	29.2
Solano	491	3 129	110 398	14.2	36.3	24.9	576.9	8 725	29 185	66 828	37.0	5.7	67 202	12.0	15.8	14.9
Sonoma	364	1 715	122 434	12.1	32.8	32.9	701.5	9 890	34 235	64 240	38.4	6.9	66 463	11.0	14.0	12.8
Stanislaus	532	3 495	150 422	8.8	51.1	16.5	1 006.6	9 643	21 922	50 125	49.9	3.1	51 949	19.5	26.6	25.3
Sutter	329	2 462	26 881	10.2	46.3	17.6	178.5	8 344	23 689	52 017	47.6	2.9	50 810	17.5	24.4	22.0
Tehama	507	2 512	15 105	8.1	48.2	14.4	114.6	10 914	21 263	41 001	58.4	2.5	40 292	22.5	32.1	29.5
Trinity	253	1 294	2 391	9.1	40.2	20.0	24.1	15 298	22 975	34 974	62.4	2.9	37 669	19.7	32.1	30.9
Tulare	414	2 481	139 963	6.5	56.8	13.8	978.7	9 681	17 876	42 031	57.3	2.4	42 637	27.2	36.3	34.6
Tuolumne	280	2 148	10 600	11.7	39.4	20.4	66.8	11 348	27 054	50 306	49.7	3.5	53 136	14.5	21.6	20.0
Ventura	223	1 983	230 114	15.1	35.8	31.7	1 280.6	9 020	33 435	77 348	31.8	9.9	79 285	9.9	14.3	13.5
Yolo	366	2 665	76 384	8.5	34.2	39.0	272.3	9 330	28 116	54 989	45.5	6.2	58 766	17.5	16.8	15.0
Yuba	400	2 886	21 403	8.8	44.2	14.3	135.4	9 750	20 471	46 892	53.5	1.8	46 500	21.6	31.7	29.6
COLORADO	309	2 530	1 395 787	13.1	31.1	38.1	7 843.3	8 953	32 217	60 629	41.5	5.8	63 945	11.5	14.8	13.6
Adams	342	2 886	127 655	10.5	46.5	22.2	736.8	8 456	25 039	58 946	41.8	3.2	62 991	12.8	17.3	16.3
Alamosa	NA	NA	5 674	9.8	41.0	25.5	24.6	10 369	19 524	32 395	64.5	2.3	40 067	24.0	30.2	29.8
Arapahoe	292	2 506	161 992	14.0	28.4	40.1	1 081.4	9 308	34 190	63 265	38.6	6.7	67 062	9.2	12.2	10.9
Archuleta	179	1 700	2 126	14.9	34.5	35.0	11.8	8 892	28 884	46 646	53.7	3.7	50 361	13.1	25.4	24.3
Baca	136	761	736	4.9	44.4	19.0	8.8	12 915	21 361	38 000	63.5	1.3	35 405	20.8	32.1	31.0
Bent	145	1 319	815	5.2	68.4	7.0	7.3	9 587	13 544	36 791	65.7	1.4	36 630	36.7	40.3	37.5

1. Data for serious crimes have not been adjusted for underreporting; this may affect comparability between geographic areas and over time.　2. Per 100,000 population estimated by the FBI.
3. All persons 3 years old and over enrolled in nursery school through college.　4. Persons 25 years old and over.　5. Elementary and secondary education expenditures.
6. Based on population estimated by the American Community Survey, 2011–2015.

Table B. States and Counties — Personal Income

| STATE County | Personal income, 2015 | | | | | | | | | | Earnings, 2015 | | |
	Total (mil dol)	Percent change, 2014–2015	Per capita[1] Dollars	Per capita[1] Rank	Wages and salaries (mil dol)	Supplements to wages and salaries; employer contributions (mil dol) Pension and insurance	Supplements to wages and salaries; employer contributions (mil dol) Government social insurance	Proprietors' income (mil dol)	Dividends, interest, and rent (mil dol)	Personal transfer receipts (mil dol)	Total (mil dol)	Contributions for government social insurance (mil dol) From employee and self-employed	Contributions for government social insurance (mil dol) From employer
	62	63	64	65	66	67	68	69	70	71	72	73	74
CALIFORNIA	2 103 669	6.4	53 949	X	1 066 514	181 338	71 131	202 834	416 270	323 786	1 521 817	84 514	71 131
Alameda	101 370	8.7	61 879	191	54 355	8 937	3 707	8 603	17 379	13 273	75 602	4 143	3 707
Alpine	77	7.1	69 705	107	43	9	2	3	22	15	57	3	2
Amador	1 547	5.7	41 807	1 248	531	161	34	120	334	392	847	52	34
Butte	9 010	7.0	39 971	1 600	3 349	786	241	810	1 733	2 441	5 185	315	241
Calaveras	2 075	6.9	46 289	836	352	102	24	148	497	512	626	48	24
Colusa	929	1.9	43 237	775	388	88	27	176	168	170	680	29	27
Contra Costa	74 757	7.5	66 348	96	24 427	4 118	1 688	4 846	14 491	8 860	35 079	2 069	1 688
Del Norte	903	6.0	33 129	2 659	312	117	19	66	156	333	514	30	19
El Dorado	10 909	5.6	59 145	174	2 624	538	186	783	2 022	1 599	4 131	261	186
Fresno	37 360	6.2	38 323	1 810	16 241	3 692	1 196	3 580	6 101	9 283	24 708	1 319	1 196
Glenn	1 103	6.7	39 375	1 424	358	89	26	182	204	275	655	32	26
Humboldt	5 636	5.7	41 525	1 485	1 926	519	135	728	1 177	1 431	3 308	193	135
Imperial	6 052	5.3	33 584	2 388	2 488	752	179	784	761	1 628	4 203	202	179
Inyo	962	3.4	52 668	709	347	112	22	190	174	211	671	35	22
Kern	32 953	2.8	37 355	1 753	15 561	3 540	1 096	3 698	4 849	6 598	23 895	1 231	1 096
Kings	5 001	2.0	33 126	2 391	2 301	674	169	386	832	1 106	3 531	162	169
Lake	2 442	6.4	37 807	1 897	602	165	43	193	446	823	1 003	72	43
Lassen	1 085	4.7	34 630	2 210	467	181	30	36	202	281	714	37	30
Los Angeles	544 325	6.1	53 521	418	272 320	46 404	18 744	66 157	107 759	93 618	403 625	22 527	18 744
Madera	5 450	3.0	35 165	2 272	1 976	495	143	1 014	824	1 215	3 628	170	143
Marin	28 493	5.8	109 076	7	7 961	1 273	527	3 655	9 172	2 056	13 416	752	527
Mariposa	808	5.9	46 069	962	209	60	15	69	157	209	353	24	15
Mendocino	3 843	5.2	43 845	1 241	1 247	311	90	489	898	1 054	2 136	133	90
Merced	9 714	5.6	36 185	2 138	3 180	848	223	1 478	1 393	2 477	5 729	258	223
Modoc	367	2.8	40 926	1 117	96	33	7	39	80	124	175	10	7
Mono	650	3.6	46 706	805	277	69	21	90	190	70	456	23	21
Monterey	21 624	8.0	49 836	592	9 082	1 984	681	3 265	4 757	3 153	15 011	709	681
Napa	8 759	7.6	61 483	218	4 120	810	298	1 427	2 023	1 157	6 655	356	298
Nevada	5 470	5.6	55 325	366	1 385	310	101	711	1 329	1 020	2 507	161	101
Orange	183 052	4.9	57 749	211	99 523	15 052	6 980	16 361	39 836	21 399	137 915	7 888	6 980
Placer	21 659	6.0	57 696	221	8 572	1 397	632	1 468	3 958	2 997	12 069	718	632
Plumas	877	2.3	47 615	635	262	85	19	75	233	251	441	28	19
Riverside	84 026	6.6	35 589	2 177	31 272	6 766	2 254	5 960	13 366	16 916	46 252	2 723	2 254
Sacramento	69 870	6.8	46 539	766	38 861	9 743	2 498	4 587	11 377	14 449	55 689	2 816	2 498
San Benito	2 566	8.5	43 643	1 011	743	170	55	243	403	389	1 211	66	55
San Bernardino	75 403	6.5	35 431	2 298	33 876	7 303	2 537	4 708	11 102	16 605	48 424	2 790	2 537
San Diego	175 859	5.2	53 298	315	92 225	17 182	6 656	12 146	37 800	25 715	128 209	7 026	6 656
San Francisco	89 533	7.7	103 529	12	70 282	9 067	4 057	12 498	19 942	7 319	95 904	5 120	4 057
San Joaquin	28 151	7.9	38 769	1 759	10 996	2 409	811	2 301	4 276	6 938	16 517	920	811
San Luis Obispo	14 034	6.2	49 873	600	5 384	1 250	378	1 624	3 427	2 167	8 636	487	378
San Mateo	74 641	7.1	97 553	14	42 215	4 567	2 307	6 229	18 349	4 773	55 319	3 141	2 307
Santa Barbara	24 208	5.8	54 428	357	10 788	2 148	760	2 883	7 020	3 129	16 579	877	760
Santa Clara	158 729	7.8	82 756	42	122 850	12 085	6 541	10 443	31 590	12 762	151 918	8 620	6 541
Santa Cruz	15 697	6.0	57 257	284	5 074	1 051	357	2 217	3 412	2 048	8 698	473	357
Shasta	7 340	6.3	40 882	1 467	2 771	644	204	564	1 381	2 307	4 183	268	204
Sierra	115	3.8	38 722	1 563	22	10	1	11	31	31	44	3	1
Siskiyou	1 715	7.0	39 381	1 601	540	150	42	107	401	600	839	58	42
Solano	19 408	8.3	44 504	945	8 020	1 682	576	1 005	3 229	3 607	11 283	654	576
Sonoma	26 875	7.2	53 520	431	10 648	1 990	774	3 309	6 235	4 128	16 720	968	774
Stanislaus	21 237	6.9	39 445	1 712	8 473	1 754	622	2 100	3 189	4 756	12 950	714	622
Sutter	3 908	7.0	40 514	1 335	1 235	261	90	439	655	852	2 026	113	90
Tehama	2 270	5.0	35 850	2 343	731	170	53	184	462	675	1 138	71	53
Trinity	466	5.9	35 627	2 407	106	36	8	35	120	178	184	14	8
Tulare	16 809	2.4	36 551	1 899	6 129	1 555	442	2 225	2 400	4 184	10 352	500	442
Tuolumne	2 243	6.8	41 770	1 372	748	205	51	165	538	639	1 170	76	51
Ventura	46 060	5.6	54 155	363	18 759	3 428	1 299	4 006	9 038	6 182	27 491	1 537	1 299
Yolo	10 451	7.1	49 063	668	5 801	1 671	368	1 052	1 957	1 525	8 892	402	368
Yuba	2 796	7.2	37 535	1 939	1 083	333	85	162	413	879	1 663	86	85
COLORADO	277 732	4.2	50 971	X	146 574	17 822	10 498	29 743	57 312	36 881	204 637	11 294	10 498
Adams	18 161	5.7	36 962	1 881	10 473	1 347	742	1 350	2 174	3 049	13 912	739	742
Alamosa	562	7.0	34 088	2 238	313	51	22	44	99	147	431	22	22
Arapahoe	33 161	3.4	52 545	189	20 898	2 161	1 488	2 602	7 129	4 001	27 149	1 567	1 488
Archuleta	498	6.8	40 307	1 653	141	20	10	78	144	112	250	15	10
Baca	136	-1.6	37 619	1 264	41	9	2	9	34	43	61	3	2
Bent	174	3.2	29 908	2 713	42	7	3	23	38	49	76	3	3

1. Based on the resident population estimated as of July 1 of the year shown.

Table B. States and Counties — Earnings, Social Security, and Housing

STATE County	Earnings, 2015 (cont.) Percent by selected industries									Social Security beneficiaries, December 2015		Supplemental Security Income recipients, December 2015	Housing units, 2016	
	Farm	Mining	Construction	Manu-facturing	Infor-mation: professional, scientific, technical services	Retail trade	Finance, insur-ance, real estate and leasing	Health care and social assistance	Govern-ment	Number	Rate[1]		Total	Percent change, 2010–2016
	75	76	77	78	79	80	81	82	83	84	85	86	87	88
CALIFORNIA	1.2	0.4	5.1	9.2	19.0	5.7	8.5	9.3	17.0	5 651 601	145	1 292 302	14 060 525	2.8
Alameda	0.0	0.0	6.4	11.0	19.5	5.4	4.1	10.5	16.6	209 210	128	51 926	599 732	3.0
Alpine	0.0	0.0	D	D	D	0.9	3.4	1.4	34.4	230	208	39	1 767	0.4
Amador	1.4	0.7	7.8	6.1	6.3	7.0	3.4	D	41.5	10 965	296	720	18 241	1.2
Butte	3.6	0.1	6.5	5.1	6.6	9.0	5.9	20.1	22.6	51 035	227	11 390	98 430	2.7
Calaveras	1.4	D	13.4	2.7	6.8	7.5	3.8	7.5	32.2	13 170	294	1 086	28 202	1.0
Colusa	23.2	D	2.3	12.8	1.1	4.1	5.1	D	22.0	3 635	171	576	8 014	1.7
Contra Costa	0.2	0.7	7.5	6.4	14.8	6.1	11.1	14.2	13.2	177 455	158	26 494	410 753	2.6
Del Norte	1.6	0.0	3.5	1.2	2.9	7.0	2.2	14.0	52.9	6 220	228	1 966	11 327	1.3
El Dorado	0.1	0.2	11.6	5.0	8.5	6.6	13.0	11.4	21.0	40 595	220	3 148	89 462	1.5
Fresno	6.2	0.2	5.2	6.6	6.0	6.7	5.5	13.9	22.8	132 645	136	43 429	327 780	3.9
Glenn	24.4	D	5.2	7.5	1.7	5.2	2.7	D	23.3	5 770	206	1 154	10 941	1.5
Humboldt	1.7	0.0	9.1	3.9	5.9	10.3	4.5	13.0	28.9	28 060	207	6 500	62 650	1.8
Imperial	12.7	0.9	3.6	1.7	2.3	7.9	2.6	6.0	38.8	30 815	171	10 421	57 384	2.3
Inyo	0.8	D	5.9	17.6	2.8	6.3	1.6	4.7	37.5	4 465	245	448	9 509	0.3
Kern	7.5	9.2	6.0	4.9	5.2	6.0	3.6	8.3	24.0	116 820	133	33 746	295 213	3.8
Kings	10.4	0.0	2.7	9.0	2.2	4.4	2.2	9.3	45.8	17 510	116	4 591	45 765	4.3
Lake	2.8	0.4	6.8	2.0	4.4	10.0	2.8	18.9	27.8	18 315	284	3 841	35 656	0.5
Lassen	3.3	D	1.9	0.3	D	4.6	1.6	D	68.4	5 175	165	988	12 722	0.1
Los Angeles	0.0	0.4	3.4	7.6	20.9	5.7	9.8	9.4	14.9	1 300 105	129	418 827	3 520 627	2.2
Madera	21.5	D	4.0	7.6	2.3	4.8	2.2	13.9	21.4	24 685	160	4 806	50 204	2.2
Marin	0.2	D	6.7	4.7	19.8	6.6	11.6	10.7	12.8	50 525	194	3 513	112 882	1.5
Mariposa	1.9	D	6.6	2.3	4.8	8.4	2.2	3.6	39.1	5 000	285	489	10 372	1.8
Mendocino	1.1	0.1	9.1	9.4	4.3	10.9	3.5	13.1	23.0	21 025	241	3 427	40 840	1.3
Merced	21.2	D	3.3	11.1	2.2	5.7	2.4	8.7	26.3	36 425	136	11 291	84 406	0.8
Modoc	18.6	0.1	3.0	0.9	D	4.6	3.9	D	43.9	2 595	290	429	5 247	1.1
Mono	1.9	D	7.7	2.0	D	6.2	D	2.7	33.4	1 505	108	101	14 053	1.0
Monterey	13.4	0.3	4.0	2.6	5.6	5.3	4.5	7.5	24.5	60 650	140	8 977	140 813	1.3
Napa	1.9	D	8.0	22.9	6.5	5.1	5.5	9.0	14.9	26 585	187	2 362	55 531	1.4
Nevada	0.0	D	18.3	4.3	9.5	7.9	6.6	13.1	20.1	27 255	276	2 002	53 535	1.8
Orange	0.0	0.1	7.0	11.1	16.2	5.8	14.3	8.8	10.9	433 330	137	74 589	1 090 054	3.9
Placer	0.0	0.1	10.4	5.8	10.1	8.4	11.1	16.5	13.4	75 325	201	5 655	161 415	5.7
Plumas	1.6	0.1	8.6	7.9	4.3	6.1	3.0	6.2	39.6	5 885	320	686	15 726	1.0
Riverside	0.8	0.3	10.3	6.5	5.5	8.5	4.6	10.8	24.2	355 815	151	62 097	831 375	3.8
Sacramento	0.1	0.0	5.5	4.0	11.4	5.1	6.6	11.5	37.3	234 660	157	67 886	565 815	1.8
San Benito	8.4	D	9.7	13.4	D	12.4	4.7	4.4	22.1	8 435	144	928	18 404	3.0
San Bernardino	0.2	0.2	6.2	8.0	5.0	7.5	4.3	12.3	24.4	283 675	134	73 399	714 302	2.1
San Diego	0.2	0.0	4.7	8.8	18.2	5.3	7.6	8.6	24.2	475 805	145	84 965	1 202 324	3.2
San Francisco	0.0	0.0	2.9	1.4	33.6	4.1	15.7	4.9	13.7	120 825	140	44 181	392 795	4.2
San Joaquin	5.0	0.1	5.2	8.1	4.0	7.0	4.5	12.2	22.0	107 155	148	29 502	240 582	2.9
San Luis Obispo	2.2	0.2	8.5	6.5	9.1	8.7	5.6	10.9	21.6	57 130	203	4 777	120 856	3.0
San Mateo	0.2	0.0	5.3	8.3	36.9	4.1	9.9	6.1	6.3	111 605	146	10 980	275 947	1.8
Santa Barbara	4.8	1.4	4.9	7.3	13.2	6.0	6.7	10.6	20.8	71 110	160	9 000	155 953	2.0
Santa Clara	0.1	0.0	3.4	21.5	35.3	3.8	5.2	6.4	6.5	229 055	120	47 249	665 061	5.2
Santa Cruz	4.2	D	12.1	7.1	8.9	7.1	6.0	12.6	19.0	44 385	162	5 928	105 649	1.1
Shasta	0.8	D	6.5	3.7	6.8	9.8	5.4	19.4	24.7	48 495	270	10 066	78 311	1.3
Sierra	11.1	D	D	D	D	2.3	D	3.0	53.9	895	300	92	2 342	0.6
Siskiyou	2.5	D	5.4	5.4	4.7	7.1	2.8	13.7	34.4	13 260	305	2 633	24 001	0.4
Solano	1.0	0.3	8.9	13.2	4.4	6.7	4.4	16.6	25.1	74 015	170	12 611	156 819	2.7
Sonoma	1.7	0.1	9.5	13.5	9.9	7.5	6.1	12.9	14.6	96 460	192	9 454	208 150	1.7
Stanislaus	8.2	0.0	6.1	13.3	4.0	7.6	4.1	16.2	18.2	85 825	160	22 102	180 825	0.7
Sutter	11.0	0.5	5.3	5.3	3.6	9.0	5.7	13.0	18.6	17 085	178	4 090	34 282	1.3
Tehama	10.0	0.0	7.3	10.0	2.1	6.9	2.6	11.7	23.8	15 405	244	3 225	27 334	1.3
Trinity	-1.8	D	9.6	7.9	4.6	9.7	2.3	D	43.4	3 870	296	690	8 817	1.6
Tulare	15.2	0.1	3.7	8.3	3.2	6.9	3.7	6.6	24.5	63 130	138	18 954	147 518	4.1
Tuolumne	0.6	0.5	6.3	4.8	5.8	8.1	4.1	16.8	35.3	15 835	295	1 682	31 423	0.6
Ventura	3.6	0.9	5.6	15.3	10.1	7.4	8.8	9.1	17.0	134 090	158	16 475	286 864	1.8
Yolo	3.8	0.2	5.1	5.5	6.5	4.5	3.2	6.4	43.4	27 785	131	5 551	77 166	2.8
Yuba	3.3	0.3	5.5	3.1	3.4	3.5	1.2	12.1	55.1	12 810	172	4 078	28 357	2.6
COLORADO	0.7	5.0	7.1	6.1	16.1	5.3	7.9	8.9	15.8	813 266	149	72 806	2 339 118	5.7
Adams	0.2	0.5	13.6	7.9	6.2	5.7	3.8	8.4	22.2	59 105	120	7 143	168 774	3.4
Alamosa	7.0	D	5.8	1.5	3.8	8.9	6.1	D	26.7	2 790	170	603	6 824	4.1
Arapahoe	0.0	3.0	6.8	2.3	20.6	6.0	14.3	10.6	9.8	83 255	132	7 343	246 702	3.5
Archuleta	3.0	1.1	16.9	1.7	9.1	11.1	7.9	D	18.7	3 385	273	124	9 143	4.3
Baca	13.1	0.5	D	D	D	5.3	D	45.4	D	995	276	74	2 224	-1.1
Bent	31.4	0.3	D	D	D	2.8	D	4.4	27.6	1 030	175	231	2 210	-1.4

1. Per 1,000 resident population estimated as of July 1 of the year shown.

Table B. States and Counties — Housing, Labor Force, and Employment

STATE County	Housing units, 2011–2015								Civilian labor force, 2016				Civilian employment,[6] 2011–2015		
			Occupied units								Unemployment			Percent	
			Owner-occupied			Renter-occupied									
				Median owner cost as a percent of income											
	Total	Percent	Median value[1]	With a mortgage	Without a mortgage[2]	Median rent[3]	Median rent as a percent of income[2]	Sub-standard units[4] (percent)	Total	Percent change, 2015–2016	Total	Rate[5]	Total	Management, business, science and arts	Construction, production, and maintenance occupations
	89	90	91	92	93	94	95	96	97	98	99	100	101	102	103
CALIFORNIA	12 717 801	54.3	385 500	27.3	11.2	1 255	33.7	8.6	19 102 734	1.1	1 037 687	5.4	17 246 360	37.3	20.2
Alameda	558 907	52.7	543 100	25.8	10.1	1 367	31.2	6.9	837 917	1.8	35 530	4.2	778 132	46.6	15.7
Alpine	358	78.8	295 000	40.0	12.2	913	37.3	2.2	556	1.8	36	6.5	408	37.3	24.5
Amador	13 925	76.0	251 000	26.7	13.4	1 047	36.4	1.4	14 646	2.1	862	5.9	12 573	30.9	20.9
Butte	85 318	58.6	221 700	25.5	11.6	905	36.7	3.7	102 319	1.0	6 693	6.5	89 411	34.6	18.5
Calaveras	18 060	79.0	243 800	28.7	14.1	1 038	31.8	2.2	20 914	1.6	1 177	5.6	16 248	36.1	24.2
Colusa	6 966	62.2	196 000	25.9	10.0	869	28.4	8.3	10 887	-1.6	1 691	15.5	8 837	24.7	40.3
Contra Costa	384 646	64.6	439 900	26.5	11.3	1 426	32.5	4.9	556 454	1.7	24 639	4.4	509 920	42.9	16.0
Del Norte	9 420	60.6	183 700	26.2	12.8	808	31.2	4.4	9 806	-0.7	731	7.5	8 612	33.9	15.8
El Dorado	67 086	74.3	363 000	26.8	13.3	1 054	31.7	2.5	89 737	1.6	4 547	5.1	79 568	40.2	15.7
Fresno	296 305	52.8	194 600	25.5	10.9	886	34.7	10.1	446 228	1.1	42 094	9.4	374 564	28.6	29.0
Glenn	9 497	61.7	204 400	27.9	12.8	725	30.1	5.3	13 091	0.8	1 075	8.2	10 523	21.9	38.3
Humboldt	53 036	54.9	279 300	28.9	11.2	892	36.5	5.0	62 674	0.4	3 060	4.9	58 449	34.0	20.2
Imperial	46 452	55.5	151 600	25.1	11.9	766	34.0	10.3	76 863	-1.6	18 079	23.5	58 391	23.5	27.3
Inyo	7 957	64.2	240 100	24.7	13.2	844	29.6	3.6	8 984	-1.3	470	5.2	8 370	31.5	20.4
Kern	259 700	56.7	167 400	24.3	11.1	888	32.7	9.5	389 091	-0.4	40 169	10.3	327 294	25.6	34.4
Kings	41 554	51.4	169 500	24.7	10.0	881	30.7	9.6	57 183	-1.2	5 699	10.0	50 960	25.1	33.1
Lake	26 993	63.0	164 300	31.3	15.5	891	38.6	3.8	29 378	1.1	1 951	6.6	23 011	27.1	23.9
Lassen	9 707	65.1	172 900	23.2	11.1	882	30.7	2.6	10 517	-2.5	724	6.9	9 082	29.1	22.4
Los Angeles	3 263 069	46.0	441 900	29.3	11.3	1 231	35.2	12.2	5 043 254	0.9	264 495	5.2	4 635 465	35.7	20.6
Madera	43 159	60.9	189 700	27.2	11.5	926	33.1	10.1	61 468	2.4	5 632	9.2	53 032	25.3	36.8
Marin	103 670	62.4	815 100	26.8	11.9	1 678	32.2	3.8	141 059	1.1	4 567	3.2	129 027	51.4	10.1
Mariposa	7 345	71.1	235 900	28.0	11.7	812	28.0	2.8	7 552	-5.9	521	6.9	7 329	31.2	17.4
Mendocino	34 017	57.9	308 400	29.9	12.8	960	36.6	6.0	39 865	-0.2	2 083	5.2	36 848	30.3	23.0
Merced	77 692	51.6	161 200	25.1	11.1	873	33.6	9.5	115 037	0.6	12 056	10.5	96 170	22.7	37.5
Modoc	3 745	73.9	153 100	28.0	11.2	653	39.3	2.7	3 327	0.7	260	7.8	3 334	40.7	26.5
Mono	4 906	59.5	313 000	35.3	13.3	1 068	23.6	2.5	8 406	1.8	448	5.3	7 061	42.1	14.0
Monterey	125 402	49.2	369 100	28.4	10.8	1 236	33.3	13.0	220 414	0.8	16 662	7.6	177 333	27.6	31.2
Napa	49 494	60.0	466 800	26.7	11.7	1 405	32.4	6.1	73 426	-0.7	3 127	4.3	68 587	34.8	22.4
Nevada	40 993	72.4	347 000	29.3	14.1	1 191	35.3	2.2	48 419	0.6	2 299	4.7	41 473	39.1	16.3
Orange	1 009 353	57.7	553 600	27.3	10.2	1 548	33.9	9.3	1 602 371	0.9	64 345	4.0	1 508 753	40.1	16.8
Placer	135 456	70.1	358 500	26.2	12.4	1 303	32.3	2.6	179 819	1.7	7 983	4.4	162 616	41.9	14.1
Plumas	8 217	72.3	217 200	27.6	13.8	836	30.1	3.0	7 873	-0.3	759	9.6	7 200	33.2	24.4
Riverside	699 232	64.8	253 200	28.1	13.2	1 179	35.3	7.6	1 051 815	1.6	63 782	6.1	920 603	29.0	24.3
Sacramento	522 596	55.4	248 400	25.7	10.2	1 036	33.2	5.2	697 427	1.7	37 318	5.4	633 897	37.7	16.9
San Benito	17 198	62.7	380 200	28.0	11.9	1 353	31.6	9.2	29 790	1.5	2 016	6.8	26 261	27.3	30.3
San Bernardino	614 325	59.7	236 700	27.2	11.7	1 116	35.7	9.0	935 579	1.6	53 398	5.7	829 145	28.7	26.9
San Diego	1 094 157	52.9	429 600	27.9	11.1	1 344	33.6	6.5	1 570 422	1.0	73 468	4.7	1 462 130	40.6	16.1
San Francisco	353 287	36.4	799 600	27.3	10.3	1 558	27.5	8.3	559 788	2.6	18 206	3.3	478 373	53.4	9.0
San Joaquin	219 073	56.6	223 000	26.3	11.7	1 024	34.5	7.6	319 187	1.3	25 729	8.1	280 460	28.0	29.4
San Luis Obispo	103 576	57.7	445 700	28.3	11.1	1 235	34.3	3.9	140 365	0.5	5 982	4.3	124 997	37.4	18.5
San Mateo	259 711	59.1	776 300	26.9	10.6	1 728	30.6	7.8	448 587	2.5	13 436	3.0	387 006	45.4	13.7
Santa Barbara	142 713	51.9	465 300	27.1	11.6	1 369	33.7	10.1	216 625	-0.5	10 846	5.0	203 616	35.2	22.3
Santa Clara	621 463	56.8	698 600	25.8	10.0	1 705	29.2	8.0	1 026 525	1.7	38 620	3.8	915 619	50.5	14.7
Santa Cruz	94 802	57.6	578 800	28.4	12.0	1 441	36.3	6.9	144 525	0.8	9 971	6.9	131 321	40.4	18.5
Shasta	69 375	62.5	216 600	26.1	13.3	926	35.3	3.6	74 700	0.5	5 167	6.9	69 261	31.4	19.7
Sierra	1 252	78.4	170 400	20.0	14.1	938	34.2	0.2	1 349	-0.5	102	7.6	1 110	33.9	36.1
Siskiyou	19 133	63.8	174 700	27.8	13.2	806	35.8	4.0	17 917	0.0	1 515	8.5	16 127	33.7	22.9
Solano	143 612	59.9	279 100	25.7	10.0	1 294	33.6	4.7	207 882	1.3	11 355	5.5	187 021	32.5	22.1
Sonoma	187 782	59.4	436 400	27.2	12.0	1 320	33.4	5.4	260 479	0.8	10 296	4.0	240 247	36.3	20.5
Stanislaus	169 196	56.7	190 800	26.1	11.3	989	34.5	7.1	244 500	1.2	20 845	8.5	208 428	26.4	31.1
Sutter	31 997	59.1	198 700	24.4	11.1	906	32.9	7.3	45 327	1.4	4 347	9.6	37 520	30.5	27.3
Tehama	23 704	67.5	171 500	27.3	11.7	782	32.3	5.0	25 201	0.5	1 788	7.1	23 127	26.1	29.0
Trinity	5 484	68.9	263 100	28.8	10.9	786	33.1	5.9	5 067	-1.5	358	7.1	4 832	29.8	18.1
Tulare	133 570	56.7	162 700	26.3	11.1	830	33.3	10.9	205 909	0.9	22 627	11.0	170 780	23.9	37.2
Tuolumne	22 133	68.4	259 300	27.4	13.3	917	33.8	3.7	21 858	1.3	1 345	6.2	19 477	33.9	19.6
Ventura	268 969	64.2	458 100	27.1	10.3	1 507	34.2	7.3	427 785	-0.1	22 149	5.2	398 116	37.2	21.5
Yolo	71 997	52.1	325 700	24.3	10.2	1 102	35.4	5.5	106 271	1.5	6 146	5.8	92 806	44.5	17.7
Yuba	25 139	58.0	172 100	26.0	12.0	885	34.4	7.8	28 319	1.6	2 411	8.5	25 499	28.1	26.3
COLORADO	2 024 468	64.3	247 800	22.7	10.0	1 002	30.6	2.9	2 891 051	2.0	95 814	3.3	2 624 436	40.4	18.3
Adams	156 628	64.5	198 800	23.7	10.6	1 039	31.0	5.1	253 515	2.0	9 190	3.6	229 743	29.5	27.2
Alamosa	5 932	57.1	144 300	23.8	10.0	635	33.2	3.0	7 906	3.0	326	4.1	6 283	30.2	25.0
Arapahoe	229 601	62.1	247 600	22.5	10.0	1 077	31.5	3.2	341 904	2.0	10 687	3.1	311 498	41.2	16.3
Archuleta	5 334	71.7	264 200	26.4	12.3	946	31.4	4.4	6 313	4.7	211	3.3	5 506	39.7	16.3
Baca	1 568	72.9	73 200	23.0	11.9	525	27.5	1.8	2 119	7.2	37	1.7	1 702	38.0	23.3
Bent	1 635	70.6	65 700	21.9	11.8	713	33.7	3.8	1 852	6.6	58	3.1	1 212	35.5	25.4

1. Specified owner-occupied units.   2. A value of 10.0 represents 10 percent or less; a value of 50.0 represents 50 percent or more.   3. Specified renter-occupied units.
4. Overcrowded or lacking complete plumbing facilities.   5. Percent of civilian labor force.   6. Civilian employed persons 16 years old and over.

Table B. States and Counties — **Nonfarm Employment and Agriculture**

STATE County	Private nonfarm establishments, employment and payroll, 2015									Agriculture, 2012			
		Employment						Annual payroll		Farms			
												Percent with:	
	Number of establishments	Total	Health care and social assistance	Manufacturing	Retail trade	Finance and insurance	Professional, scientific, and technical services	Total (mil dol)	Average per employee (dollars)	Number	Fewer than 50 acres	500 acres or more	Farm operators whose principal occupation is farming (percent)
	104	105	106	107	108	109	110	111	112	113	114	115	116
CALIFORNIA	908 120	14 325 377	1 873 857	1 162 646	1 690 005	591 037	1 258 225	856 954	59 821	77 857	64.8	9.9	54.5
Alameda	38 793	641 881	89 537	66 296	68 913	17 492	61 566	42 357	65 989	452	60.2	12.2	48.7
Alpine	37	511	D	D	4	D	D	7	14 673	3	0.0	33.3	0.0
Amador	811	8 130	1 234	945	1 575	187	269	293	36 011	461	47.7	11.3	49.2
Butte	4 663	59 475	14 232	4 534	10 954	2 405	2 398	2 177	36 612	2 056	66.8	7.0	59.4
Calaveras	894	6 108	994	394	1 296	149	198	197	32 333	663	60.0	10.0	46.6
Colusa	368	3 825	454	454	551	98	34	156	40 873	782	27.5	23.0	61.6
Contra Costa	23 184	315 385	52 282	14 571	45 530	23 880	23 878	20 699	65 630	602	73.3	8.0	52.0
Del Norte	424	4 121	1 255	106	978	88	123	123	29 922	121	59.5	6.6	57.9
El Dorado	4 332	43 288	6 486	2 474	6 094	3 470	2 259	1 897	43 831	1 358	78.4	3.0	52.1
Fresno	16 350	249 702	42 438	23 328	37 805	8 998	10 210	10 056	40 273	5 683	59.7	11.2	59.6
Glenn	457	4 890	474	722	742	122	301	248	50 626	1 311	51.3	15.3	62.9
Humboldt	3 132	33 302	6 812	2 007	6 804	1 036	1 790	1 157	34 749	930	54.0	15.5	56.1
Imperial	2 494	33 153	5 025	3 612	8 719	838	796	1 064	32 103	421	29.7	40.6	69.4
Inyo	510	5 309	1 151	171	930	74	120	193	36 363	125	50.4	31.2	63.2
Kern	12 642	194 840	29 994	12 248	31 869	5 869	11 808	8 445	43 345	1 938	40.6	26.6	63.2
Kings	1 585	23 393	4 519	4 236	4 192	546	681	908	38 830	1 056	51.2	18.6	66.0
Lake	1 047	9 631	2 390	316	2 263	250	234	349	36 197	838	68.7	5.1	43.9
Lassen	396	3 727	819	26	890	91	354	123	32 944	448	40.6	25.2	51.8
Los Angeles	265 112	4 007 163	523 703	350 520	424 218	155 521	397 181	212 874	53 123	1 294	88.9	2.9	60.6
Madera	1 929	26 580	5 789	3 829	3 790	442	460	1 054	39 660	1 507	44.8	14.3	57.9
Marin	9 926	100 498	15 246	2 160	14 723	5 701	9 470	6 283	62 516	323	39.9	34.1	58.5
Mariposa	344	3 074	442	87	431	30	43	100	32 435	364	37.9	23.6	51.9
Mendocino	2 465	22 779	4 364	2 672	4 645	550	631	818	35 931	1 220	48.8	14.3	49.8
Merced	2 969	42 036	6 977	8 621	8 456	980	780	1 606	38 217	2 486	56.7	12.8	64.5
Modoc	155	1 209	433	D	185	32	43	43	35 227	437	22.4	37.8	60.4
Mono	568	6 173	408	73	641	27	94	168	27 263	72	31.9	27.8	58.3
Monterey	8 557	106 652	15 875	7 750	17 003	2 843	7 088	4 637	43 477	1 179	42.0	26.4	61.7
Napa	4 160	62 275	10 016	11 592	6 991	1 389	1 874	3 149	50 567	1 685	71.9	5.3	34.9
Nevada	2 959	27 093	4 669	2 244	4 168	916	1 425	1 126	41 554	742	79.0	2.0	46.6
Orange	92 798	1 449 828	160 063	149 721	154 364	87 458	127 380	80 740	55 689	312	85.3	4.8	58.7
Placer	10 127	141 136	20 358	4 432	23 438	9 016	13 878	7 613	53 941	1 355	82.2	2.4	45.5
Plumas	598	3 874	961	452	553	126	133	156	40 259	141	37.6	34.0	44.0
Riverside	36 465	540 169	74 801	42 883	93 397	11 204	18 703	20 721	38 360	2 949	86.0	3.5	49.1
Sacramento	28 446	449 584	80 294	20 127	62 365	26 394	33 810	23 340	51 915	1 352	72.3	7.6	48.2
San Benito	956	11 064	1 403	2 756	1 375	253	234	474	42 810	628	51.6	23.2	58.3
San Bernardino	33 735	578 755	87 148	52 065	86 386	15 438	18 299	23 774	41 077	1 249	85.9	2.1	57.0
San Diego	81 710	1 239 334	162 748	100 268	154 012	52 423	135 903	66 592	53 732	5 732	91.6	0.9	47.6
San Francisco	34 011	611 140	62 710	7 723	48 234	50 699	100 781	59 332	97 085	6	100.0	0.0	83.3
San Joaquin	11 025	173 611	27 966	19 410	26 236	6 248	4 564	7 360	42 394	3 580	63.5	8.3	59.0
San Luis Obispo	8 164	91 540	15 394	6 489	14 883	2 299	4 766	3 727	40 719	2 666	55.8	12.2	47.0
San Mateo	21 101	376 743	33 725	23 771	34 451	16 836	38 924	42 199	112 009	334	61.7	6.3	56.0
Santa Barbara	11 455	146 504	22 182	14 223	20 336	4 268	9 630	7 278	49 675	1 597	63.9	11.3	51.7
Santa Clara	47 775	999 906	106 022	84 873	87 264	25 840	130 509	109 703	109 714	1 003	76.4	5.6	56.0
Santa Cruz	6 961	75 572	13 179	5 182	12 274	2 225	4 158	3 364	44 511	667	73.8	4.6	62.1
Shasta	4 141	49 163	10 429	2 058	9 647	1 892	2 263	1 877	38 174	1 544	72.9	6.1	44.9
Sierra	68	211	32	D	32	D	D	7	33 872	48	14.6	27.1	56.3
Siskiyou	1 065	8 356	1 550	751	1 550	214	353	285	34 071	929	35.5	22.5	58.2
Solano	6 855	107 550	22 405	9 760	19 539	4 203	3 376	5 250	48 811	860	62.9	11.7	53.7
Sonoma	13 746	166 604	25 550	20 322	25 726	5 456	9 216	8 170	49 038	3 579	71.3	6.0	51.3
Stanislaus	8 744	135 488	22 813	18 998	23 224	3 328	6 418	5 877	43 379	4 143	68.8	5.9	59.1
Sutter	1 724	20 653	3 628	1 540	4 523	786	687	824	39 912	1 358	51.8	14.1	64.4
Tehama	981	12 306	2 065	2 083	1 889	207	219	487	39 565	1 743	61.6	10.7	52.3
Trinity	248	1 529	316	201	422	40	77	52	34 134	247	55.5	8.1	48.6
Tulare	6 259	94 155	15 753	12 958	16 511	2 977	2 544	3 517	37 352	4 931	61.2	8.4	58.3
Tuolumne	1 278	12 400	2 764	817	2 350	303	473	481	38 785	391	53.5	9.7	40.7
Ventura	20 602	257 011	37 055	24 828	40 237	12 295	22 132	13 635	53 053	2 150	78.0	5.2	48.7
Yolo	3 984	63 422	6 895	7 298	7 889	1 392	3 427	3 002	47 340	1 011	47.5	14.7	59.1
Yuba	805	9 461	2 201	518	1 494	181	652	373	39 465	795	61.4	10.4	44.2
COLORADO	161 737	2 253 795	292 970	121 335	272 567	105 193	191 456	117 540	52 152	36 180	39.4	24.3	49.6
Adams	9 203	158 046	23 123	12 258	19 574	2 910	5 100	7 405	46 856	841	50.4	20.6	43.0
Alamosa	487	5 484	1 608	118	1 062	322	171	185	33 654	322	22.4	24.5	51.2
Arapahoe	18 129	276 753	36 234	6 740	34 214	22 985	24 377	16 330	59 006	755	65.4	10.9	39.3
Archuleta	494	3 286	358	97	740	82	129	88	26 785	372	34.9	22.3	54.0
Baca	88	516	D	D	122	22	D	16	30 926	737	3.4	62.0	48.4
Bent	58	565	81	D	81	47	7	19	34 065	277	15.9	46.6	53.4

Table B. States and Counties — **Agriculture**

STATE County	Land in farms Acreage (1,000)	Percent change, 2007–2012	Acres Average size of farm	Acres Total irrigated (1,000)	Acres Total cropland (1,000)	Value of land and buildings (dollars) Average per farm	Value of land and buildings (dollars) Average per acre	Value of machinery and equipment, average per farm (dollars)	Value of products sold Total (mil dol)	Value of products sold Average per farm (dollars)	Percent from: Crops	Percent from: Live-stock and poultry products	Percent of farms with sales of: $10,000 or more	Percent of farms with sales of: $100,000 or more	Government payments Total ($1,000)	Government payments Percent of farms
	117	118	119	120	121	122	123	124	125	126	127	128	129	130	131	132
CALIFORNIA	25 569	0.8	328	7 862.0	9 591.8	2 061 792	6 278	124 710	42 627.5	547 510	71.2	28.8	57.0	26.4	146 919	9.8
Alameda	178	-13.1	393	8.9	20.3	2 170 265	5 517	47 292	57.5	127 261	82.7	17.3	42.7	9.7	49	3.5
Alpine	D	D	D	0.2	0.6	1 800 000	D	20 333	0.3	88 333	D	D	100.0	33.3	0	0.0
Amador	155	-5.1	337	11.3	16.0	1 324 401	3 934	51 321	32.0	69 345	68.1	31.9	49.7	15.4	37	2.8
Butte	381	1.9	185	199.7	227.3	1 408 199	7 599	135 591	541.3	263 266	97.3	2.7	59.7	26.2	9 386	13.7
Calaveras	212	5.5	320	4.5	6.1	1 043 833	3 262	40 736	26.0	39 222	45.5	54.5	36.2	7.7	8	0.6
Colusa	453	-4.4	579	260.9	285.7	3 146 341	5 431	300 276	577.3	738 252	98.7	1.3	80.7	59.1	13 629	48.5
Contra Costa	128	-13.1	212	27.3	46.5	1 786 847	8 425	80 620	89.4	148 435	84.7	15.3	43.2	13.1	232	5.6
Del Norte	D	D	D	9.2	8.6	1 481 355	D	115 661	35.7	294 636	46.5	53.5	34.7	11.6	96	12.4
El Dorado	128	19.9	95	6.8	11.1	777 782	8 228	30 537	30.5	22 465	79.8	20.2	32.3	5.7	237	3.0
Fresno	1 721	5.2	303	968.7	1 153.4	2 509 484	8 286	161 509	4 973.0	875 073	74.4	25.6	71.9	41.9	10 149	9.0
Glenn	669	36.7	510	242.9	274.3	2 342 959	4 593	192 225	637.4	486 166	79.9	20.1	68.6	38.0	13 136	35.5
Humboldt	594	-0.6	638	17.1	20.9	1 649 520	2 584	57 685	203.3	218 559	D	D	45.4	16.8	1 242	8.8
Imperial	516	20.7	1 225	455.0	487.9	8 577 865	7 002	745 304	1 888.6	4 486 078	69.4	30.6	84.3	66.7	2 788	29.5
Inyo	331	13.1	2 647	23.8	18.7	2 062 976	779	86 688	19.6	156 904	34.6	65.4	40.8	16.0	D	1.6
Kern	2 330	-1.3	1 202	730.0	899.4	3 847 243	4 435	332 960	3 999.0	2 063 462	80.8	19.2	62.0	43.8	5 306	15.5
Kings	674	-1.0	638	407.4	501.5	3 847 243	6 031	340 454	1 829.2	1 732 231	46.7	53.3	68.3	45.1	7 901	36.4
Lake	151	21.4	180	13.5	29.1	1 095 199	6 089	55 516	99.5	118 691	98.0	2.0	52.6	13.6	100	4.8
Lassen	483	5.1	1 077	66.0	70.9	2 075 935	1 927	113 085	72.7	162 212	D	D	42.0	16.3	186	9.6
Los Angeles	92	-15.5	71	39.7	59.6	882 832	12 459	45 905	193.1	149 225	90.1	9.9	34.2	11.6	247	3.1
Madera	654	-3.8	434	292.3	304.2	3 302 033	7 614	182 022	1 602.8	1 063 547	77.4	22.6	70.2	46.8	2 400	11.4
Marin	171	28.2	529	3.7	14.4	3 295 415	6 229	69 226	91.8	284 238	9.3	90.7	64.1	34.1	1 283	16.4
Mariposa	284	33.4	779	1.8	12.6	1 638 973	2 104	44 742	22.3	61 321	11.7	88.3	37.1	8.8	515	7.4
Mendocino	770	26.5	631	25.7	49.3	2 533 399	4 013	51 877	148.9	122 047	92.1	7.9	50.2	16.9	426	2.3
Merced	979	-6.0	394	468.2	522.6	3 045 778	7 737	236 454	2 967.5	1 193 694	42.9	57.1	76.0	45.7	9 528	20.2
Modoc	524	-12.4	1 198	128.4	154.7	2 061 595	1 721	125 055	106.6	243 950	66.0	34.0	60.4	37.1	701	24.7
Mono	56	26.4	783	21.5	11.4	2 205 819	2 817	144 722	18.0	249 667	49.0	51.0	48.6	40.3	D	1.4
Monterey	1 268	-4.5	1 076	263.8	358.3	5 263 068	4 893	396 806	2 979.7	2 527 341	98.5	1.5	59.6	35.4	635	7.0
Napa	253	13.5	150	54.6	63.0	3 278 130	21 801	85 134	536.1	318 188	97.8	2.2	74.5	34.1	85	1.1
Nevada	42	-40.0	57	5.3	3.3	614 920	10 834	31 177	9.1	12 256	63.9	36.1	27.9	2.4	126	2.2
Orange	60	-30.8	194	8.1	15.2	4 237 538	21 854	70 968	158.5	508 055	99.0	1.0	41.3	18.3	43	4.8
Placer	91	-30.9	67	20.7	33.6	719 330	10 664	35 897	43.4	32 057	D	D	27.2	5.0	1 305	2.8
Plumas	174	44.9	1 236	19.1	26.0	2 194 518	1 776	95 652	22.6	160 404	19.7	80.3	51.8	22.0	0	0.0
Riverside	344	-3.0	117	146.0	227.2	1 191 416	10 212	76 009	1 038.9	352 306	71.7	28.3	50.2	13.9	2 189	4.7
Sacramento	247	-24.9	183	86.0	105.7	1 302 636	7 135	85 653	326.6	241 559	63.9	36.1	43.2	18.6	2 474	10.3
San Benito	604	4.2	962	19.2	38.5	2 737 111	2 844	93 435	164.0	261 198	76.9	23.1	50.2	18.9	174	7.5
San Bernardino	77	-85.0	62	21.8	29.8	831 612	13 455	83 151	582.2	466 156	11.5	88.5	42.4	16.7	849	4.1
San Diego	222	-27.1	39	45.2	68.2	694 313	17 964	34 672	726.0	126 657	89.3	10.7	42.9	9.1	451	1.7
San Francisco	0	71.4	2	0.0	0.0	252 167	126 083	52 000	D	D	D	D	0.0	0.0	0	0.0
San Joaquin	787	6.7	220	485.4	517.9	2 218 140	10 090	145 302	2 250.2	628 536	73.7	26.3	73.5	39.3	5 508	9.4
San Luis Obispo	1 339	-2.2	502	81.6	255.4	2 115 410	4 212	92 222	665.0	249 431	92.9	7.1	52.2	19.1	3 488	9.0
San Mateo	48	-15.6	144	2.8	8.5	1 629 243	11 299	69 497	75.9	227 213	96.4	3.6	49.1	14.7	182	4.2
Santa Barbara	701	-3.6	439	96.7	132.3	3 233 061	7 365	125 663	1 177.9	737 581	95.8	4.2	58.8	29.4	554	1.5
Santa Clara	230	-23.3	229	17.8	38.4	1 538 866	6 713	69 246	243.8	243 100	95.7	4.3	45.3	12.8	20	1.2
Santa Cruz	100	110.5	150	28.9	41.1	1 857 240	12 390	113 943	565.8	848 328	96.9	3.1	59.2	28.0	D	0.1
Shasta	376	-3.7	244	38.2	36.9	682 565	2 801	36 550	65.6	42 501	36.6	63.4	26.2	4.8	420	4.6
Sierra	39	36.0	815	9.7	4.0	1 226 333	1 504	92 896	D	D	D	D	62.5	22.9	D	2.1
Siskiyou	723	21.0	778	160.0	194.8	1 586 712	2 039	121 981	223.1	240 146	85.4	14.6	42.2	18.0	2 029	19.7
Solano	407	13.6	473	130.9	169.6	2 631 010	5 558	146 770	307.4	357 463	79.0	21.0	53.1	22.7	1 911	15.7
Sonoma	590	11.1	165	75.0	130.6	2 409 158	14 620	78 965	974.4	272 253	62.2	37.8	60.3	24.3	2 615	4.1
Stanislaus	768	-2.7	185	320.8	340.9	1 786 289	9 636	117 810	2 228.1	537 807	47.7	52.3	66.5	33.9	7 049	10.7
Sutter	375	4.3	276	244.3	275.8	1 828 515	6 619	179 143	508.2	374 208	98.8	1.2	77.1	40.8	11 326	27.1
Tehama	617	15.8	354	84.9	89.3	1 053 199	2 978	71 962	240.8	138 163	70.6	29.4	46.2	13.8	1 627	9.0
Trinity	176	40.8	712	1.6	2.1	811 870	1 140	29 838	5.2	20 895	D	D	23.1	2.0	247	12.1
Tulare	1 239	6.0	251	557.4	677.5	1 893 271	7 535	144 666	4 017.1	814 657	41.6	58.4	70.2	36.6	12 174	13.5
Tuolumne	88	-25.0	225	2.3	2.8	1 039 974	4 631	59 552	27.7	70 721	9.4	90.6	25.6	3.1	D	0.5
Ventura	281	8.5	131	87.1	101.1	2 041 990	15 621	94 136	1 440.1	669 829	99.3	0.7	65.1	24.7	154	2.0
Yolo	461	-4.0	456	229.9	306.9	2 571 454	5 642	218 361	561.2	555 135	93.6	6.4	61.7	34.2	6 240	28.1
Yuba	188	16.6	236	82.5	89.8	1 367 039	5 792	149 175	193.4	243 332	79.8	20.2	47.0	25.4	3 341	15.3
COLORADO	31 887	0.9	881	2 516.8	10 649.7	1 128 277	1 280	109 260	7 780.9	215 060	31.3	68.7	37.7	15.6	165 576	30.7
Adams	691	-1.6	821	17.6	550.3	1 179 177	1 436	121 985	116.5	138 483	88.0	12.0	31.6	15.2	5 479	40.7
Alamosa	182	3.3	567	68.6	71.5	825 866	1 458	154 025	92.5	287 354	87.5	12.5	46.0	23.0	821	29.8
Arapahoe	283	12.5	375	2.5	137.2	632 109	1 685	62 514	31.7	41 933	D	D	20.9	4.6	1 635	23.2
Archuleta	210	40.5	565	24.2	13.2	1 213 137	2 147	55 333	15.5	41 653	8.3	91.7	31.7	7.3	329	4.6
Baca	1 503	15.6	2 040	62.6	872.6	1 133 718	556	153 448	125.3	170 012	63.0	37.0	48.3	28.9	15 510	87.9
Bent	726	-17.3	2 620	31.5	107.1	1 219 368	465	156 993	70.8	255 574	17.9	82.1	55.6	27.8	2 945	58.8

Table B. States and Counties — Water Use, Wholesale Trade, Retail Trade, and Real Estate

STATE County	Water use, 2010		Wholesale trade,[1] 2012				Retail trade,[2] 2012				Real estate and rental and leasing,[2] 2012			
	Total water withdrawn (mil gal/day)	Gallons withdrawn per person per day	Number of establishments	Number of employees	Sales (mil dol)	Annual payroll (mil dol)	Number of establishments	Number of employees	Sales (mil dol)	Annual payroll (mil dol)	Number of establishments	Number of employees	Receipts (mil dol)	Annual payroll (mil dol)
	133	134	135	136	137	138	139	140	141	142	143	144	145	146
CALIFORNIA	37 962.2	1 019	52 664	723 526	666 652.2	48 408.7	106 419	1 540 055	481 800.5	43 361.0	49 276	273 511	78 740.2	13 467.5
Alameda	254.9	169	2 366	44 934	37 580.6	3 133.2	4 213	61 372	20 901.0	1 826.9	1 920	9 602	2 575.5	460.9
Alpine	4.5	3 804	NA	NA	NA	NA	4	8	0.6	0.1	2	D	D	D
Amador	32.4	850	20	D	D	D	121	1 489	321.5	35.7	38	100	17.3	3.5
Butte	715.3	3 252	148	D	D	D	725	9 231	2 576.9	240.4	234	1 160	147.6	28.3
Calaveras	23.4	513	18	D	D	D	133	1 044	252.3	27.2	44	170	23.2	3.5
Colusa	835.0	38 985	27	338	428.7	18.7	59	434	127.9	10.6	19	40	7.8	1.2
Contra Costa	302.7	289	753	6 570	6 887.2	417.8	2 490	41 494	11 847.9	1 181.4	1 306	6 491	1 779.2	334.1
Del Norte	13.7	478	6	D	D	D	60	1 012	192.8	22.5	33	96	14.7	2.8
El Dorado	55.7	308	107	553	316.7	28.7	530	5 841	1 597.8	155.8	242	856	176.1	27.6
Fresno	2 813.2	3 024	819	12 981	9 266.3	663.0	2 421	32 954	9 117.8	836.0	769	4 299	715.1	139.6
Glenn	606.6	21 571	17	224	160.1	11.8	73	688	191.2	16.3	20	41	5.4	1.4
Humboldt	114.0	847	105	1 028	361.9	41.5	578	6 600	1 759.2	170.3	174	536	89.9	15.2
Imperial	1 169.2	6 699	197	1 801	1 599.1	72.5	446	7 322	1 676.9	160.3	119	574	92.6	15.9
Inyo	111.6	6 016	20	D	D	D	87	836	229.0	22.4	23	82	6.7	1.7
Kern	2 159.9	2 572	582	7 990	6 987.9	447.4	1 867	27 918	8 640.6	700.7	634	3 492	733.6	141.3
Kings	1 298.9	8 490	69	684	746.6	36.3	285	3 961	1 032.0	92.2	97	371	71.0	9.9
Lake	50.9	786	24	D	D	D	167	2 041	522.3	49.8	59	160	24.5	4.1
Lassen	202.6	5 806	9	D	D	D	79	784	215.8	19.7	23	44	19.3	3.2
Los Angeles	3 064.0	312	21 270	237 644	199 804.8	12 881.4	28 427	385 441	121 389.4	10 699.7	13 874	82 043	29 586.3	4 476.1
Madera	748.7	4 963	76	815	508.9	37.8	326	3 455	1 012.9	84.3	75	336	38.4	8.5
Marin	42.9	170	359	2 780	1 864.6	180.8	1 053	14 698	5 087.5	544.8	589	2 455	1 458.6	168.7
Mariposa	5.3	291	6	22	18.9	0.7	64	419	102.5	9.7	26	82	8.3	2.7
Mendocino	81.5	928	67	679	407.6	28.3	462	4 551	1 095.2	117.1	130	494	61.6	12.8
Merced	1 494.7	5 843	112	1 635	2 260.2	71.2	528	7 497	1 959.5	173.3	152	532	79.1	14.6
Modoc	261.5	27 001	7	D	D	D	30	203	45.7	4.9	7	15	1.3	0.2
Mono	229.7	16 174	7	D	D	D	72	653	139.8	15.2	62	312	31.1	8.0
Monterey	545.5	1 314	346	4 574	5 775.2	278.9	1 316	16 335	4 457.4	437.2	444	1 873	436.3	69.6
Napa	96.9	710	167	D	D	D	524	6 318	1 699.0	184.2	207	1 026	160.4	38.2
Nevada	48.7	493	75	D	D	D	400	3 965	1 012.3	110.2	157	747	204.6	36.7
Orange	765.4	254	6 434	79 685	97 796.0	5 200.7	9 390	143 012	45 193.6	4 135.3	5 320	38 952	9 259.7	1 921.2
Placer	191.2	549	311	4 317	4 474.4	239.9	1 231	20 999	6 437.9	592.9	661	3 544	620.1	146.9
Plumas	118.7	5 934	7	D	D	D	86	577	139.3	13.6	34	83	14.4	2.6
Riverside	1 099.3	502	1 568	21 800	18 716.8	1 071.9	4 996	81 017	25 058.9	2 128.9	2 038	8 466	1 684.9	303.8
Sacramento	681.1	480	1 096	14 448	18 746.3	816.5	3 512	55 910	15 227.3	1 484.7	1 650	8 879	1 621.2	364.9
San Benito	85.4	1 546	39	638	275.4	41.6	105	1 276	345.2	34.9	53	116	25.7	4.1
San Bernardino	659.4	324	2 493	33 768	30 996.2	1 574.6	4 748	79 792	24 380.5	2 013.4	1 570	7 788	1 622.3	316.3
San Diego	2 818.2	910	3 883	59 227	35 937.4	4 055.0	9 219	138 929	39 786.1	3 787.5	5 401	28 321	7 895.7	1 308.8
San Francisco	93.5	116	1 066	12 056	11 121.7	850.7	3 573	43 378	14 632.7	1 455.0	1 828	15 000	6 000.9	1 071.1
San Joaquin	1 753.4	2 559	515	9 279	11 713.5	495.7	1 602	24 097	7 059.5	616.4	572	2 655	464.7	97.2
San Luis Obispo	2 579.1	9 565	289	D	D	D	1 177	13 992	3 624.0	361.5	430	1 552	278.4	52.2
San Mateo	93.1	130	1 050	15 030	15 969.7	1 249.1	2 041	34 069	11 330.6	1 062.8	1 142	7 018	2 227.1	348.4
Santa Barbara	264.3	623	406	5 325	3 475.6	397.1	1 509	18 781	4 853.8	501.5	691	3 047	570.7	113.7
Santa Clara	298.2	167	2 310	84 304	91 859.0	10 822.2	4 927	84 158	40 336.7	3 212.4	2 426	12 827	4 458.9	763.7
Santa Cruz	66.4	253	266	5 614	5 898.2	297.2	887	11 120	4 368.0	294.7	363	1 271	264.1	41.8
Shasta	239.0	1 349	158	1 437	1 023.9	59.8	647	8 980	2 507.1	241.4	207	765	121.4	22.1
Sierra	39.0	12 046	1	D	D	D	9	31	5.1	0.6	1	D	D	D
Siskiyou	411.1	9 155	28	266	165.2	9.0	179	1 563	426.7	36.0	53	114	10.8	2.4
Solano	452.8	1 095	249	4 165	2 803.7	215.6	1 060	17 610	5 106.6	469.9	381	1 629	389.2	59.2
Sonoma	259.5	536	593	8 047	4 443.2	557.8	1 768	23 032	6 016.3	655.8	679	2 824	631.1	103.4
Stanislaus	1 642.7	3 193	405	6 087	5 295.1	313.6	1 374	20 970	5 933.6	527.1	433	2 141	387.9	73.2
Sutter	722.0	7 621	70	1 658	1 197.3	99.6	287	4 188	1 069.5	101.8	89	436	50.5	11.1
Tehama	825.6	13 009	25	190	88.8	6.4	151	1 696	654.6	45.5	48	152	25.7	4.6
Trinity	22.5	1 634	2	D	D	D	53	333	72.7	7.3	7	D	D	D
Tulare	2 600.3	5 881	325	4 564	3 890.5	191.8	1 044	14 210	3 903.5	340.6	306	1 421	249.0	40.9
Tuolumne	35.8	646	31	D	D	D	173	2 219	573.3	54.5	82	174	32.6	4.4
Ventura	719.5	874	985	D	D	D	2 562	37 012	11 194.2	1 011.0	1 008	4 568	983.6	196.5
Yolo	780.2	3 885	254	4 938	6 762.1	269.9	442	7 171	1 968.8	190.3	279	1 604	265.1	59.4
Yuba	261.7	3 627	26	D	D	D	127	1 369	390.2	34.7	45	123	18.0	3.3
COLORADO	10 994.2	2 186	5 733	75 717	77 035.0	4 762.1	18 474	245 704	67 815.2	6 508.6	9 295	38 706	8 482.5	1 569.6
Adams	230.9	523	608	13 547	12 918.6	760.9	1 044	16 769	5 548.7	487.2	434	2 611	522.7	91.5
Alamosa	152.4	9 868	18	166	78.8	6.0	85	1 091	280.7	27.7	18	83	11.1	2.6
Arapahoe	187.0	327	668	8 515	17 863.9	604.2	1 866	30 885	9 404.7	875.8	1 073	4 537	1 313.9	204.3
Archuleta	59.3	4 905	6	32	9.3	0.8	88	506	130.8	12.6	34	97	11.7	2.2
Baca	98.5	26 006	23	57	86.1	2.0	16	128	38.4	3.1	3	D	D	D
Bent	152.4	23 454	NA	NA	NA	NA	12	73	17.4	1.3	NA	NA	NA	NA

1. Merchant wholesalers, except manufacturers' sales branches and offices. 2. Employer establishments.

Table B. States and Counties — Professional Services, Manufacturing, and Accommodation and Food Services

STATE County	Professional, scientific, and technical services, 2012				Manufacturing, 2012				Accommodation and food services, 2012			
	Number of establish-ments	Number of employees	Receipts (mil dol)	Annual payroll (mil dol)	Number of establish-ments	Number of employees	Receipts (mil dol)	Annual payroll (mil dol)	Number of establish-ments	Number of employees	Sales (mil dol)	Annual payroll (mil dol)
	147	148	149	150	151	152	153	154	155	156	157	158
CALIFORNIA	114 321	1 303 232	234 371.2	90 437.3	38 741	1 163 341	512 303.2	69 316.8	78 560	1 394 984	90 830.4	25 147.8
Alameda	5 387	60 272	13 550.3	5 414.1	1 846	63 679	D	4 502.1	3 631	51 283	3 192.4	884.9
Alpine	3	D	D	D	NA	NA	NA	NA	9	D	D	D
Amador	80	277	29.1	9.8	38	599	139.6	31.6	100	2 088	242.0	53.1
Butte	424	2 394	388.0	97.2	177	4 126	1 341.1	168.3	397	7 091	350.5	96.4
Calaveras	63	187	18.1	7.1	33	358	D	11.7	99	1 105	69.6	16.6
Colusa	18	51	4.0	1.4	25	716	474.5	33.3	41	931	97.8	21.5
Contra Costa	3 347	27 079	5 926.1	2 112.6	540	15 118	33 681.2	1 090.7	1 805	27 719	1 660.0	455.8
Del Norte	30	D	D	D	9	D	D	41.2	68	611	32.3	7.8
El Dorado	515	D	D	D	162	2 415	517.4	130.9	424	5 565	319.8	86.7
Fresno	1 522	10 531	1 367.8	474.3	585	25 269	8 658.3	1 052.9	1 450	24 100	1 226.2	333.9
Glenn	33	278	45.0	21.2	26	636	D	24.4	55	598	33.2	8.4
Humboldt	244	1 996	164.6	62.4	134	2 149	D	80.9	374	4 746	257.5	70.0
Imperial	179	787	79.1	30.4	50	2 218	1 466.0	95.4	258	3 516	182.6	47.9
Inyo	35	D	D	D	13	161	D	7.4	91	1 525	99.6	26.7
Kern	1 204	11 757	1 641.3	637.3	391	12 257	6 890.7	558.2	1 278	19 829	1 092.2	284.0
Kings	85	461	51.0	18.4	60	4 380	2 904.0	180.5	172	2 824	378.6	42.6
Lake	66	243	22.2	7.6	32	265	80.5	11.1	130	1 460	88.8	24.9
Lassen	26	121	13.5	6.4	NA	NA	NA	NA	46	619	36.0	10.6
Los Angeles	31 324	521 067	66 261.5	26 244.3	12 760	359 532	163 829.6	19 852.8	20 298	355 736	22 965.1	6 390.6
Madera	116	493	66.9	21.6	92	3 298	1 441.1	168.0	193	2 461	150.1	37.1
Marin	1 744	9 095	2 037.3	698.0	219	1 935	D	92.7	751	11 578	729.7	225.6
Mariposa	19	D	D	D	14	78	D	3.5	56	1 473	157.9	32.3
Mendocino	206	729	68.1	22.9	123	2 066	453.4	82.1	339	3 369	182.6	50.8
Merced	142	791	67.1	26.2	116	9 973	4 435.6	405.4	298	4 585	232.9	60.2
Modoc	12	60	5.3	1.5	3	D	D	D	21	149	8.3	1.9
Mono	23	80	10.5	3.4	7	39	D	1.2	141	3 450	246.9	67.4
Monterey	806	7 448	847.3	338.0	263	6 078	2 258.9	252.3	979	17 786	1 328.8	378.0
Napa	395	1 801	280.5	101.5	431	10 837	4 623.5	622.5	375	10 466	774.1	247.7
Nevada	346	1 415	227.0	89.1	140	1 381	319.7	72.4	245	5 007	231.2	69.9
Orange	14 120	112 581	24 110.2	8 899.6	4 701	150 020	47 299.4	8 879.0	7 141	143 519	9 050.6	2 599.9
Placer	1 180	D	D	D	261	4 246	932.9	216.9	823	18 063	1 452.0	327.3
Plumas	51	D	D	D	17	444	D	19.8	100	D	D	D
Riverside	3 182	16 261	2 149.0	811.3	1 447	41 519	15 137.0	1 930.4	3 350	75 061	5 230.9	1 376.8
Sacramento	3 754	32 572	5 743.4	2 153.4	758	19 902	6 960.7	1 161.8	2 560	44 722	2 422.7	671.9
San Benito	70	213	26.4	8.9	62	2 222	591.1	95.6	80	925	49.9	13.5
San Bernardino	2 489	16 890	2 201.9	776.5	1 814	46 822	17 591.6	2 112.8	3 126	53 047	2 858.0	773.6
San Diego	12 528	134 334	24 111.3	9 099.2	2 891	97 346	33 320.5	6 196.1	6 880	147 457	10 403.8	2 857.4
San Francisco	6 295	84 841	29 389.5	9 033.5	693	7 506	D	327.6	4 059	73 417	6 142.7	1 841.6
San Joaquin	780	4 463	491.1	190.0	517	18 703	9 212.4	879.0	997	15 422	808.6	211.0
San Luis Obispo	868	4 914	673.1	269.5	382	6 107	2 854.0	285.7	865	14 254	824.8	229.5
San Mateo	2 999	32 982	8 831.3	3 659.8	633	22 708	D	2 299.6	1 910	33 203	2 552.9	710.9
Santa Barbara	1 347	9 785	1 751.7	654.0	458	13 896	4 157.6	851.5	1 087	20 623	1 428.9	400.1
Santa Clara	8 395	125 395	30 138.9	13 549.8	2 385	100 981	41 450.6	9 169.2	4 407	72 491	4 809.2	1 336.2
Santa Cruz	880	4 268	603.0	249.2	293	4 479	1 213.4	219.2	678	10 032	586.0	168.6
Shasta	358	D	D	D	147	1 990	511.9	93.7	376	5 421	285.5	76.7
Sierra	1	D	D	D	3	D	D	D	14	D	D	D
Siskiyou	96	362	38.8	12.0	31	667	203.4	28.2	135	1 317	71.5	19.7
Solano	547	3 258	415.3	150.6	259	9 266	11 412.2	558.9	711	11 129	625.6	163.2
Sonoma	1 514	9 140	1 244.4	524.0	821	19 324	6 131.7	1 085.2	1 192	17 606	1 058.7	301.8
Stanislaus	649	5 111	507.5	196.0	395	19 963	11 703.6	1 007.8	813	13 611	705.7	192.6
Sutter	120	568	57.8	22.1	61	1 551	543.5	78.0	142	2 263	116.6	30.1
Tehama	61	211	27.9	8.6	38	1 648	449.5	70.1	121	1 367	65.1	16.6
Trinity	19	74	7.0	2.5	14	194	D	7.9	46	205	13.4	3.3
Tulare	407	D	D	D	237	11 412	8 362.4	538.0	568	8 540	451.9	118.1
Tuolumne	88	456	57.6	23.1	59	818	173.1	38.4	161	1 611	92.8	25.9
Ventura	2 634	22 377	3 185.4	2 063.2	867	23 166	8 334.0	1 295.4	1 598	27 725	1 597.4	442.6
Yolo	411	3 207	484.6	184.3	167	6 236	2 538.4	311.3	414	8 216	656.6	177.5
Yuba	84	410	60.6	24.1	39	540	107.2	20.9	82	1 111	54.8	14.8
COLORADO	23 872	180 064	33 740.7	12 932.1	4 898	114 632	50 447.1	6 230.1	12 744	240 484	13 617.7	3 994.6
Adams	740	4 696	984.2	266.5	375	9 555	7 311.4	481.8	695	12 606	705.8	189.3
Alamosa	43	169	16.8	6.4	14	108	13.8	3.5	44	790	35.4	9.7
Arapahoe	2 748	21 416	3 778.7	1 553.6	392	7 527	1 672.6	412.7	1 226	22 577	1 235.6	366.0
Archuleta	45	120	13.1	4.2	11	63	5.0	1.6	58	744	64.9	15.8
Baca	5	D	D	D	NA	NA	NA	NA	7	D	D	D
Bent	3	5	0.7	0.1	NA	NA	NA	NA	6	50	1.9	0.5

1. Establishment subject to federal tax.

Table B. States and Counties — **Health Care and Social Assistance, Other Services, Nonemployer Businesses, and Residential Construction**

STATE County	Health care and social assistance, 2012				Other services, 2012				Nonemployer businesses, 2015		Value of residential construction authorized by building permits, 2016	
	Number of establishments	Number of employees	Receipts (mil dol)	Annual payroll (mil dol)	Number of establishments	Number of employees	Receipts (mil dol)	Annual payroll (mil dol)	Number	Receipts (mil dol)	New Construction ($1,000)	Number of housing units
	159	160	161	162	163	164	165	166	167	168	169	170
CALIFORNIA	103 207	1 776 440	248 953.6	91 139.9	57 009	395 836	50 439.2	12 251.2	3 206 958	169 373.0	24 045 190	102 350
Alameda	4 273	82 510	12 949.1	4 762.2	2 761	19 955	2 642.5	739.4	139 261	6 943.1	1 460 018	5 692
Alpine	4	D	D	D	2	D	D	D	92	3.2	430	2
Amador	99	1 353	147.7	55.2	51	169	19.4	5.1	2 696	119.4	7 139	41
Butte	716	12 868	1 434.5	560.2	321	2 158	190.0	56.0	13 528	626.5	95 201	697
Calaveras	97	985	108.9	41.7	60	265	20.4	5.6	3 574	160.4	48 934	182
Colusa	28	448	41.2	16.6	20	D	D	D	1 026	55.8	10 707	47
Contra Costa	2 877	50 689	8 262.6	3 051.1	1 515	10 368	1 238.8	338.4	91 637	5 164.4	749 612	2 921
Del Norte	68	1 214	121.3	44.7	21	D	D	D	1 226	47.2	5 236	22
El Dorado	461	6 504	680.9	276.7	289	1 393	129.6	38.2	16 363	820.4	293 506	762
Fresno	2 204	42 281	5 325.6	1 997.0	1 000	7 367	747.6	200.1	50 405	2 577.2	729 163	2 904
Glenn	42	546	52.0	22.2	24	70	12.7	1.8	1 341	67.1	12 629	57
Humboldt	442	7 111	695.5	263.6	225	1 257	136.4	34.1	11 630	460.7	30 029	229
Imperial	268	4 536	511.1	182.9	142	608	53.4	16.5	9 817	338.8	44 156	215
Inyo	55	1 106	121.6	44.8	40	172	17.1	4.6	1 304	49.5	2 590	15
Kern	1 550	27 833	3 675.0	1 265.4	835	5 099	567.8	153.6	45 226	2 186.4	488 500	2 256
Kings	231	4 770	587.8	203.5	94	382	37.4	9.9	4 378	196.1	126 276	605
Lake	154	2 345	256.6	98.1	67	213	22.2	5.6	3 910	154.2	135 719	242
Lassen	59	838	84.1	31.0	29	D	D	D	1 113	40.7	2 883	13
Los Angeles	29 822	498 944	67 261.3	24 116.1	15 843	110 674	13 562.1	3 278.3	1 022 938	54 198.1	4 910 545	20 591
Madera	204	5 871	761.0	321.0	112	489	45.2	11.8	7 161	350.2	52 021	300
Marin	1 117	15 860	2 102.3	848.3	643	4 539	583.8	160.1	37 822	2 795.9	75 963	112
Mariposa	33	D	D	D	18	D	D	D	1 318	52.7	9 518	34
Mendocino	265	4 296	427.2	174.9	158	642	78.5	17.9	8 461	342.7	21 920	163
Merced	427	6 718	788.1	302.8	183	895	72.4	26.3	10 850	545.0	114 818	720
Modoc	17	477	33.9	13.4	12	D	D	D	570	25.5	640	6
Mono	27	386	69.4	23.7	54	230	19.5	5.2	1 391	73.1	12 009	39
Monterey	994	14 898	2 151.0	838.2	560	3 765	457.6	111.7	24 701	1 366.2	148 744	627
Napa	404	10 222	1 360.7	553.3	241	1 359	127.7	40.0	11 921	730.9	69 137	212
Nevada	339	4 649	525.9	214.7	177	888	101.8	27.9	12 245	584.0	55 075	252
Orange	10 873	152 659	20 682.2	7 379.9	4 980	35 537	3 782.2	1 039.3	300 969	17 595.1	2 445 261	11 523
Placer	1 089	18 349	3 125.4	1 093.3	575	4 671	529.7	133.6	31 508	1 780.5	746 262	2 419
Plumas	49	900	85.2	32.9	39	124	12.9	3.3	1 570	71.2	7 996	47
Riverside	4 199	66 036	8 412.1	3 037.7	2 444	14 761	1 331.7	372.9	161 369	7 221.7	1 625 972	6 996
Sacramento	3 303	77 506	12 358.7	4 694.3	2 163	16 184	1 973.8	553.2	101 015	4 775.4	808 876	3 350
San Benito	96	1 309	143.2	61.4	68	249	22.4	5.3	3 455	177.4	118 772	458
San Bernardino	3 784	81 285	11 199.3	4 102.6	2 244	15 260	1 344.6	415.7	141 417	6 045.0	821 694	3 925
San Diego	8 522	151 783	21 337.8	7 872.6	5 193	41 437	4 080.6	1 179.4	268 900	13 549.9	2 223 118	10 791
San Francisco	3 119	62 075	10 175.8	3 926.9	2 411	20 361	4 964.1	840.0	98 890	6 047.3	1 144 467	4 087
San Joaquin	1 361	27 052	3 447.7	1 264.8	841	5 038	445.0	135.0	36 951	1 944.5	548 046	1 998
San Luis Obispo	1 010	14 086	1 580.5	650.0	430	2 668	216.9	60.5	24 586	1 308.5	228 688	853
San Mateo	2 279	33 776	5 167.0	1 928.7	1 390	11 134	3 296.9	458.0	70 022	4 495.3	627 093	1 975
Santa Barbara	1 360	20 279	2 637.3	949.2	725	4 544	933.5	142.1	33 871	1 940.5	199 502	842
Santa Clara	5 410	99 127	17 021.0	6 095.5	3 008	20 859	3 493.8	728.5	139 245	8 316.8	1 176 448	5 709
Santa Cruz	893	12 989	1 689.9	622.3	451	2 973	328.1	98.5	25 004	1 275.9	83 703	489
Shasta	634	10 525	1 324.6	469.3	296	1 658	162.7	48.2	11 869	557.8	74 158	400
Sierra	8	D	D	D	NA	NA	NA	NA	225	7.0	1 594	8
Siskiyou	115	1 630	174.1	72.8	72	242	17.3	5.0	3 341	131.8	16 775	67
Solano	861	21 490	3 241.8	1 204.0	552	3 228	326.8	102.6	23 834	990.2	251 034	944
Sonoma	1 462	23 222	3 156.2	1 198.4	853	4 845	494.1	146.9	46 138	2 542.0	188 186	919
Stanislaus	1 075	24 257	3 635.0	1 274.8	604	3 817	371.6	118.9	27 111	1 418.2	116 156	573
Sutter	249	3 369	392.4	147.2	108	571	53.1	16.5	5 473	373.2	20 305	74
Tehama	141	1 951	179.5	73.0	68	436	43.9	13.8	3 237	148.0	17 499	92
Trinity	24	315	27.9	11.8	12	34	3.4	0.9	964	39.6	3 327	27
Tulare	836	15 488	1 610.2	632.1	383	2 114	219.4	60.0	20 102	979.6	266 646	1 316
Tuolumne	170	2 692	345.6	131.5	79	355	35.5	11.3	4 179	174.3	8 798	41
Ventura	2 557	32 438	3 987.6	1 434.5	1 176	7 150	763.3	188.6	67 736	3 653.3	340 979	1 609
Yolo	371	6 923	847.0	333.6	300	2 124	256.0	72.3	12 683	615.9	178 272	673
Yuba	80	2 197	396.9	106.0	47	153	14.0	4.3	3 389	121.8	42 445	187
COLORADO	14 869	257 898	29 488.2	11 877.0	10 246	64 398	8 519.0	2 100.1	480 847	23 001.6	8 928 897	38 974
Adams	659	14 707	1 732.1	715.9	651	4 571	456.1	138.6	31 136	1 397.3	663 994	2 657
Alamosa	64	D	D	D	39	178	11.8	3.2	1 089	44.8	4 616	75
Arapahoe	1 885	27 029	2 888.9	1 245.0	1 114	7 534	1 008.0	267.0	54 789	2 821.7	849 658	4 660
Archuleta	35	248	15.8	6.6	18	102	8.6	2.8	1 906	93.5	29 828	131
Baca	6	D	D	D	8	D	D	D	372	15.3	209	1
Bent	7	43	2.8	1.4	3	D	D	D	222	9.3	1 312	3

Table B. States and Counties — **Government Employment and Payroll, and Local Government Finances**

STATE County	Government employment and payroll, 2012		March payroll (percent of total)							Local government finances, 2012				
										General revenue			Taxes	
													Per capita[1] (dollars)	
	Full-time equivalent employees	March payroll (dollars)	Administration, judicial, and legal	Police and Corrections	Fire Protection	Highways and transportation	Health and Welfare	Natural resources and utilities	Education and libraries	Total (mil dol)	Inter-governmental (mil dol)	Total (mil dol)	Total	Property
	171	172	173	174	175	176	177	178	179	180	181	182	183	184
CALIFORNIA	X	X	X	X	X	X	X	X	X	X	X	X	X	X
Alameda	56 184	365 163 607	5.7	11.5	5.1	11.1	17.4	11.1	35.4	11 581.0	4 300.9	3 665.4	2 358	1 599
Alpine	214	872 045	11.7	13.5	1.0	7.4	8.2	7.0	43.1	24.5	12.2	8.3	7 356	6 651
Amador	1 266	6 168 436	11.2	19.0	1.9	5.8	6.8	6.0	39.5	128.1	55.8	50.2	1 356	1 204
Butte	8 734	37 694 370	6.4	9.6	2.6	2.0	12.6	5.9	58.9	1 079.1	643.7	243.0	1 097	878
Calaveras	1 448	6 209 937	7.6	9.6	4.4	4.6	11.0	10.4	49.5	186.0	75.8	74.1	1 657	1 522
Colusa	1 069	4 506 211	9.2	12.0	1.8	3.7	9.6	7.3	55.3	146.1	73.1	36.5	1 707	1 430
Contra Costa	31 030	175 288 765	5.0	11.0	4.7	3.1	16.5	6.7	49.7	5 884.2	1 770.2	2 008.9	1 861	1 450
Del Norte	840	3 504 433	11.7	12.1	0.5	4.3	15.7	4.5	48.9	153.3	93.2	23.2	819	669
El Dorado	6 061	31 562 790	7.6	11.3	7.2	4.8	7.4	6.9	49.3	878.4	352.8	300.6	1 665	1 450
Fresno	34 954	165 436 346	4.1	10.3	2.1	3.3	9.7	4.5	65.0	5 127.4	3 047.2	1 071.6	1 131	789
Glenn	1 427	5 989 936	3.6	9.7	0.6	3.0	13.1	9.7	56.4	178.6	102.2	29.6	1 057	878
Humboldt	5 913	25 492 898	6.6	10.3	1.9	3.5	17.6	6.2	50.4	699.2	403.7	159.8	1 185	901
Imperial	10 122	49 143 599	4.2	6.0	1.7	1.1	19.5	16.2	45.5	1 293.3	740.8	180.2	1 019	733
Inyo	1 429	7 084 588	6.7	10.0	0.3	4.1	40.9	3.3	30.9	203.7	66.4	52.2	2 825	2 089
Kern	32 191	158 787 344	5.1	10.1	4.5	2.2	16.0	4.2	56.8	6 098.2	2 797.6	1 169.0	1 365	1 151
Kings	4 882	22 137 016	6.6	11.1	2.5	1.2	11.7	3.6	60.7	623.0	383.4	130.2	860	727
Lake	2 729	12 022 755	11.2	10.5	3.8	2.4	16.8	9.3	43.1	271.7	144.5	78.7	1 231	1 043
Lassen	1 280	5 212 652	7.9	9.0	1.2	3.2	10.4	8.7	58.1	128.4	89.5	24.8	738	648
Los Angeles	386 456	2 230 095 495	9.6	12.3	4.7	5.7	13.7	9.3	42.7	62 878.6	29 034.6	18 834.7	1 891	1 234
Madera	4 578	20 019 402	8.1	8.1	0.2	2.2	10.1	5.2	64.4	627.3	366.3	154.2	1 013	706
Marin	8 544	51 753 682	10.8	11.2	8.5	4.2	8.9	10.4	44.3	1 521.9	327.6	825.0	3 222	2 533
Mariposa	919	3 214 468	8.2	10.8	0.6	5.1	32.1	3.0	35.0	106.5	45.5	33.4	1 867	1 123
Mendocino	3 596	16 441 501	8.4	10.8	1.7	3.8	21.2	5.0	47.9	1 037.3	251.8	144.5	1 653	1 355
Merced	10 959	49 202 192	6.5	7.6	1.6	1.1	10.0	6.7	63.4	1 305.5	840.8	219.3	836	680
Modoc	586	2 160 529	8.3	8.7	1.4	11.9	22.7	4.7	40.8	67.3	46.4	10.6	1 140	1 021
Mono	1 012	5 526 104	7.8	11.4	5.1	6.0	35.5	9.2	22.9	195.2	38.3	79.1	5 511	4 023
Monterey	16 674	95 953 296	5.6	9.2	2.7	3.8	28.8	5.1	41.4	3 062.0	1 376.2	682.3	1 599	1 199
Napa	5 012	27 819 123	11.8	13.2	3.0	2.1	9.4	6.0	49.6	811.6	274.6	367.8	2 645	2 138
Nevada	3 125	16 593 333	8.7	9.9	4.8	4.6	26.3	10.1	30.7	498.3	165.7	159.3	1 620	1 417
Orange	85 251	527 595 855	5.4	11.0	4.8	3.1	7.4	5.7	58.4	14 543.9	5 867.6	5 580.4	1 806	1 406
Placer	12 015	67 291 627	7.1	9.6	4.2	2.3	5.5	9.5	58.5	1 867.4	613.0	730.0	2 018	1 673
Plumas	1 484	5 779 631	5.2	6.8	2.3	4.1	39.9	3.6	35.0	189.6	75.9	44.6	2 300	2 099
Riverside	68 997	380 597 495	8.6	11.0	1.9	2.3	12.6	7.6	54.4	10 975.4	5 598.2	3 090.1	1 362	1 054
Sacramento	50 509	274 337 834	5.2	13.3	5.5	4.2	8.8	13.3	46.1	7 904.0	3 980.4	1 968.0	1 357	948
San Benito	2 079	11 695 733	4.3	7.2	1.9	1.9	29.7	5.0	47.9	317.3	147.3	81.2	1 428	1 245
San Bernardino	68 989	370 218 367	5.5	10.6	4.1	2.1	13.3	5.1	56.9	11 897.3	6 945.9	2 679.6	1 287	987
San Diego	97 178	529 647 292	9.3	10.8	3.9	3.4	11.1	7.0	52.0	16 495.7	6 780.5	5 691.2	1 791	1 381
San Francisco	38 712	274 384 267	11.0	13.8	5.8	19.9	21.2	9.0	18.6	8 696.0	2 927.1	3 303.9	4 001	2 234
San Joaquin	23 911	123 453 125	6.5	12.7	3.3	2.6	14.7	5.0	53.3	3 894.7	2 276.8	855.2	1 217	851
San Luis Obispo	8 194	48 094 004	7.2	11.4	2.8	2.5	6.9	6.4	57.6	1 189.7	435.4	547.8	1 994	1 615
San Mateo	20 873	132 351 507	8.3	12.6	5.3	5.4	14.1	7.1	44.7	4 326.2	1 099.6	2 039.6	2 759	2 118
Santa Barbara	15 712	89 085 924	7.3	11.4	5.3	3.7	14.4	7.2	48.4	2 761.9	960.5	877.6	2 035	1 531
Santa Clara	59 919	402 121 133	7.6	10.2	5.0	5.0	20.4	6.5	42.7	12 701.2	3 946.9	4 816.5	2 621	1 963
Santa Cruz	9 292	50 504 116	8.1	10.1	3.9	7.3	13.5	7.9	47.1	1 432.9	632.4	483.8	1 813	1 441
Shasta	6 528	30 533 939	6.7	8.7	2.8	3.4	15.6	9.0	52.2	922.9	498.8	217.9	1 220	1 000
Sierra	204	851 638	16.3	12.9	0.1	11.6	17.0	3.1	35.4	28.6	16.9	7.5	2 443	2 207
Siskiyou	2 067	8 289 776	11.3	10.4	0.5	6.1	10.7	5.7	53.1	242.6	147.2	54.2	1 228	1 028
Solano	14 386	72 410 858	7.6	13.9	3.4	2.8	9.9	7.1	53.4	1 896.3	937.5	594.6	1 413	1 051
Sonoma	16 072	90 178 192	9.5	12.6	3.9	2.6	12.9	7.2	47.9	2 545.8	918.8	972.6	1 978	1 555
Stanislaus	19 446	94 702 481	5.9	8.3	2.5	1.6	11.8	9.4	55.0	2 696.4	1 547.9	554.1	1 062	825
Sutter	3 010	14 970 086	9.1	8.0	3.7	3.1	14.1	4.9	55.0	556.7	302.3	112.6	1 185	908
Tehama	2 320	9 999 317	7.1	9.2	1.1	3.3	13.4	2.6	61.2	246.2	160.2	57.2	902	755
Trinity	1 131	4 471 095	2.7	3.4	0.7	7.0	27.1	7.4	48.8	140.6	56.9	13.9	1 024	919
Tulare	21 502	97 324 423	4.7	7.2	1.7	1.1	30.4	3.5	50.1	3 132.9	1 499.7	450.9	998	665
Tuolumne	1 609	7 837 540	9.3	11.4	1.9	4.0	9.2	5.7	53.0	206.6	92.6	69.5	1 287	1 105
Ventura	27 714	159 457 912	10.1	10.8	4.6	3.0	13.0	7.6	49.2	4 630.9	2 005.3	1 379.1	1 650	1 378
Yolo	6 203	32 178 923	11.0	12.7	5.3	1.8	9.0	7.7	48.4	954.1	449.2	304.9	1 494	1 014
Yuba	3 659	17 894 536	5.9	8.6	0.7	1.5	7.2	2.0	71.6	385.0	230.2	77.0	1 056	932
COLORADO	X	X	X	X	X	X	X	X	X	X	X	X	X	X
Adams	14 341	67 598 280	8.2	13.6	4.3	2.6	4.0	12.3	52.8	1 856.9	785.2	806.6	1 755	1 137
Alamosa	647	1 959 302	10.3	10.3	0.7	4.6	18.5	7.3	47.7	73.8	42.5	23.1	1 428	843
Arapahoe	21 249	96 139 327	5.9	11.9	9.5	2.0	4.3	8.1	56.7	2 508.7	756.4	1 211.5	2 034	1 426
Archuleta	516	2 016 002	9.3	6.9	2.2	5.2	24.8	8.6	30.1	79.3	24.7	31.1	2 580	1 862
Baca	511	1 703 710	8.5	7.0	0.0	11.1	42.4	7.3	21.4	31.5	11.2	5.7	1 519	1 381
Bent	294	918 613	7.0	10.4	0.0	4.8	21.4	18.4	36.0	56.2	15.6	20.3	3 509	2 068

1. Based on the resident population estimated as of July 1 of the year shown.

STATE County	Total (mil dol)	Per capita[1] (dollars)	Education	Health and hospitals	Police protection	Public welfare	Highways	Total (mil dol)	Per capita[1] (dollars)	Federal civilian	Federal military	State and local	Number of returns	Mean adjusted gross income	Mean income tax
	185	186	187	188	189	190	191	192	193	194	195	196	197	198	199
CALIFORNIA	X	X	X	X	X	X	X	X	X	245 204	204 096	2 235 940	17 410 120	74 012	11 026
Alameda	12 422.0	7 990	22.9	13.4	5.2	5.4	2.3	24 528.0	15 776	9 237	3 883	104 237	762 590	85 140	12 983
Alpine	26.0	23 015	19.6	7.3	10.1	5.8	8.6	23.6	20 861	11	D	263	450	53 222	6 147
Amador	133.4	3 602	30.1	6.7	9.8	7.2	5.6	61.9	1 670	92	51	4 300	16 140	57 771	6 536
Butte	1 098.2	4 957	46.2	6.8	4.4	11.8	3.6	480.5	2 169	543	335	15 445	90 320	51 866	5 720
Calaveras	179.1	4 002	37.4	6.3	5.0	8.1	5.2	135.0	3 017	121	67	2 217	19 580	57 753	6 528
Colusa	142.2	6 642	35.7	6.2	5.7	4.9	6.5	51.5	2 404	69	32	2 106	9 500	58 856	7 571
Contra Costa	6 294.4	5 830	33.6	19.1	6.3	5.7	4.7	7 234.2	6 701	4 742	1 767	42 493	526 040	97 426	15 636
Del Norte	142.9	5 052	31.7	5.8	3.7	12.4	2.6	70.4	2 488	149	49	3 651	9 400	45 305	4 356
El Dorado	940.2	5 207	36.4	3.7	4.8	5.2	6.4	905.2	5 013	715	302	9 612	85 760	78 047	10 961
Fresno	5 031.5	5 308	44.7	7.0	5.6	10.3	3.4	3 847.5	4 059	9 673	1 680	58 293	384 300	49 762	5 490
Glenn	186.6	6 665	40.1	6.9	4.5	11.9	5.2	33.9	1 212	224	90	1 814	11 780	47 921	5 088
Humboldt	731.8	5 428	44.2	7.8	4.7	10.6	4.7	396.3	2 939	774	370	12 425	55 980	46 747	4 754
Imperial	1 172.3	6 625	40.7	23.6	4.1	7.5	2.9	1 408.8	7 962	2 228	374	15 783	77 590	38 477	3 234
Inyo	199.3	10 776	23.8	41.6	4.6	3.3	3.2	72.4	3 915	302	27	2 772	8 440	54 001	5 990
Kern	5 683.5	6 638	55.4	8.5	3.6	6.7	3.0	3 571.0	4 171	9 995	3 854	51 324	334 400	51 787	5 479
Kings	602.9	3 983	45.9	6.6	4.9	9.6	2.9	261.9	1 730	1 131	5 146	13 478	53 220	46 540	4 375
Lake	267.3	4 177	39.4	7.1	5.3	13.9	3.9	107.2	1 675	147	96	3 915	24 670	42 230	3 951
Lassen	133.2	3 956	45.5	7.1	5.0	10.9	6.5	58.3	1 734	1 874	38	4 175	9 740	52 217	5 012
Los Angeles	60 312.8	6 054	35.0	11.1	7.8	8.7	3.1	84 320.3	8 464	47 869	17 435	527 278	4 563 010	68 056	10 365
Madera	649.2	4 265	45.6	3.7	3.9	8.8	6.2	475.5	3 124	309	223	9 137	57 880	44 872	4 422
Marin	1 569.1	6 127	34.5	6.9	6.2	4.1	3.1	2 304.2	8 998	752	548	14 689	131 730	158 753	32 441
Mariposa	101.6	5 675	21.1	24.5	6.6	10.1	6.4	22.6	1 262	699	25	1 101	7 660	48 800	4 775
Mendocino	1 025.1	11 725	70.9	7.3	2.3	5.1	2.4	577.0	6 600	270	159	6 548	38 510	46 519	4 856
Merced	1 403.1	5 349	48.6	3.6	4.1	10.0	2.7	901.0	3 435	763	396	17 406	98 680	43 482	3 975
Modoc	67.1	7 198	38.4	16.9	4.0	6.8	8.8	4.6	497	239	13	881	3 450	42 077	4 077
Mono	192.0	13 383	15.1	34.5	6.6	4.9	8.7	76.3	5 321	224	240	1 290	6 430	51 526	5 843
Monterey	2 904.3	6 806	36.5	22.7	4.6	5.4	2.6	1 444.4	3 385	5 186	5 622	26 560	194 370	58 507	6 994
Napa	821.7	5 909	37.5	5.9	7.5	4.2	4.0	746.0	5 365	207	208	10 216	67 710	81 667	12 460
Nevada	537.0	5 464	23.8	31.3	4.9	5.6	4.7	392.6	3 994	369	148	5 596	48 400	63 248	7 981
Orange	13 915.7	4 503	41.4	2.9	7.7	7.3	4.5	22 316.3	7 222	11 271	5 151	140 943	1 473 110	79 585	12 299
Placer	1 896.3	5 243	41.7	2.8	5.8	5.9	6.0	2 500.4	6 913	669	581	17 190	172 500	79 662	10 825
Plumas	177.2	9 133	26.8	34.8	4.1	4.9	5.8	57.6	2 967	395	27	1 950	8 550	50 346	4 863
Riverside	11 682.2	5 149	39.3	8.1	6.7	7.1	4.3	13 164.6	5 802	6 918	3 852	118 424	944 370	51 541	5 170
Sacramento	7 966.3	5 494	34.4	6.0	4.9	8.6	5.8	16 350.5	11 275	8 915	2 987	174 697	654 660	57 127	6 593
San Benito	327.5	5 757	32.1	32.0	3.9	5.6	3.2	125.8	2 211	142	88	2 680	26 290	60 140	6 761
San Bernardino	11 798.5	5 669	38.7	15.6	6.0	7.5	5.5	11 574.3	5 561	13 527	17 838	105 502	865 800	48 656	4 655
San Diego	16 846.0	5 302	37.0	9.8	5.3	6.9	2.9	27 732.0	8 729	46 442	98 828	190 043	1 531 220	70 203	9 808
San Francisco	7 412.4	8 975	16.3	24.7	5.1	6.5	3.4	17 985.0	21 777	14 081	1 586	89 598	469 980	130 680	26 092
San Joaquin	3 717.2	5 291	40.5	9.2	5.9	8.8	3.5	3 309.2	4 710	3 066	1 146	37 456	293 270	53 299	5 823
San Luis Obispo	1 206.8	4 391	38.5	5.9	6.2	8.2	3.9	850.7	3 096	538	533	20 699	126 600	64 331	8 291
San Mateo	4 256.2	5 757	34.0	11.6	7.7	4.4	3.8	4 651.4	6 292	3 784	1 278	28 011	380 730	152 911	30 423
Santa Barbara	2 786.6	6 462	32.4	18.7	5.7	6.7	3.0	1 346.9	3 123	3 618	3 123	31 536	200 020	70 510	10 208
Santa Clara	11 865.9	6 458	32.5	21.8	5.2	5.2	2.2	17 898.2	9 740	9 949	3 363	79 609	898 250	135 133	24 732
Santa Cruz	1 415.2	5 305	36.6	6.6	6.3	8.5	2.3	1 074.8	4 029	531	397	18 204	129 940	73 672	10 667
Shasta	906.1	5 074	43.3	8.1	5.8	10.6	4.0	544.3	3 048	1 312	309	11 696	75 780	50 859	5 338
Sierra	29.0	9 401	28.7	10.0	10.3	10.1	12.9	6.1	1 986	48	D	317	1 210	48 698	4 631
Siskiyou	251.0	5 684	48.4	6.3	5.8	7.4	5.5	80.4	1 822	841	65	3 150	18 430	42 917	4 149
Solano	1 873.8	4 454	35.1	6.1	9.3	7.8	4.2	1 624.0	3 860	3 765	6 808	20 558	199 140	60 907	6 714
Sonoma	2 601.9	5 290	35.4	10.3	6.3	6.4	5.0	2 547.1	5 179	1 372	1 407	27 275	243 170	68 320	9 157
Stanislaus	2 792.3	5 352	50.1	6.9	4.9	10.2	3.4	4 496.8	8 619	830	809	27 104	216 690	50 888	5 402
Sutter	526.6	5 542	44.9	7.7	4.4	6.1	1.8	241.8	2 545	92	147	4 464	38 910	50 077	5 176
Tehama	244.9	3 862	49.8	6.6	5.9	14.9	4.0	28.9	456	220	94	3 532	24 480	46 276	4 027
Trinity	128.3	9 486	22.7	15.7	2.1	6.0	7.0	47.2	3 487	240	19	813	4 680	42 245	3 953
Tulare	3 186.6	7 050	39.0	24.4	3.2	8.0	4.7	1 380.8	3 055	1 055	690	30 131	173 730	42 428	4 129
Tuolumne	214.2	3 966	35.6	9.8	6.8	8.2	4.3	66.5	1 230	497	76	4 977	23 480	53 391	5 595
Ventura	4 471.8	5 349	38.6	13.1	7.5	4.6	3.5	3 011.8	3 603	7 173	5 059	37 115	401 040	72 570	10 045
Yolo	951.1	4 659	30.3	3.8	6.2	8.0	5.9	944.3	4 626	3 518	326	34 376	86 210	67 999	8 806
Yuba	436.2	5 982	54.3	2.1	4.1	10.8	4.0	399.0	5 472	1 481	4 325	4 885	27 320	43 909	3 492
COLORADO	X	X	X	X	X	X	X	X	X	53 453	53 609	371 628	2 553 140	70 412	10 030
Adams	1 860.3	4 048	42.2	0.3	5.7	9.9	5.6	2 579.2	5 612	1 357	1 671	38 486	221 440	52 538	5 466
Alamosa	68.0	4 210	38.8	5.3	7.5	20.9	5.9	38.4	2 379	145	40	2 200	6 470	43 542	4 080
Arapahoe	2 593.0	4 354	41.7	1.1	7.2	3.0	5.0	6 000.2	10 075	3 434	3 214	34 070	302 690	75 485	11 388
Archuleta	68.6	5 681	20.6	27.4	2.8	7.3	11.0	57.7	4 780	46	32	725	5 760	53 409	6 584
Baca	31.8	8 484	29.7	35.6	3.0	11.3	8.9	2.1	559	36	D	652	1 570	36 796	3 435
Bent	42.9	7 437	18.7	2.0	8.7	5.5	17.8	8.1	1 402	37	12	451	1 570	41 352	3 290

1. Based on the resident population estimated as of July 1 of the year shown.

Table B. States and Counties — **Land Area and Population**

STATE/ County code	CBSA code[1]	County type[2]	STATE County	Land area,[3] (sq mi) 2016	Total persons 2016	Rank	Per square mile	White	Black	American Indian, Alaska Native	Asian and Pacific Islander	Percent Hispanic or Latino[4]	Under 5 years	5 to 17 years	18 to 24 years	25 to 34 years	35 to 44 years	45 to 54 years
				1	**2**	**3**	**4**	**5**	**6**	**7**	**8**	**9**	**10**	**11**	**12**	**13**	**14**	**15**
			COLORADO—Cont'd															
08 013	14500	2	Boulder	726.3	322 226	213	443.7	80.3	1.5	0.9	5.9	13.8	4.7	14.9	15.2	13.6	12.5	13.1
08 014	19740	1	Broomfield	33.0	66 529	797	2 016.0	79.7	1.8	1.0	7.6	12.2	5.7	18.1	7.5	14.7	15.1	14.3
08 015	...	7	Chaffee	1 013.4	19 058	1 871	18.8	86.2	1.9	1.7	1.2	10.4	3.9	11.6	6.6	12.2	11.8	12.7
08 017	...	9	Cheyenne	1 778.3	1 848	3 065	1.0	85.3	1.0	1.3	0.8	12.5	8.3	18.1	6.2	9.8	11.1	12.3
08 019	19740	1	Clear Creek	395.2	9 436	2 470	23.9	90.9	1.3	1.7	1.4	6.4	3.6	12.0	5.7	10.0	13.2	16.1
08 021	...	9	Conejos	1 287.4	8 129	2 588	6.3	45.3	0.8	1.4	0.7	53.1	7.1	19.7	8.8	10.0	10.0	12.0
08 023	...	9	Costilla	1 227.6	3 721	2 920	3.0	34.9	1.0	2.0	1.5	61.8	4.6	15.2	7.1	8.9	8.4	11.4
08 025	...	8	Crowley	787.4	5 694	2 782	7.2	54.9	10.6	2.2	1.9	31.6	3.4	9.5	10.0	20.0	17.0	16.3
08 027	...	8	Custer	738.6	4 602	2 855	6.2	91.6	1.5	1.7	0.8	5.8	3.1	11.1	5.3	6.7	8.1	11.5
08 029	...	6	Delta	1 142.1	30 442	1 421	26.7	82.6	1.0	1.4	1.2	15.2	5.1	15.2	7.0	9.6	10.1	11.7
08 031	19740	1	Denver	153.3	693 060	92	4 520.9	56.1	10.1	1.2	4.8	30.2	6.4	13.9	8.4	22.6	15.6	11.7
08 033	...	9	Dolores	1 067.2	2 056	3 044	1.9	90.6	0.9	3.9	0.8	6.1	5.0	16.0	6.8	8.0	11.5	11.9
08 035	19740	1	Douglas	840.3	328 632	208	391.1	85.3	1.8	0.7	6.0	8.5	6.0	21.2	7.4	10.5	15.2	16.5
08 037	20780	5	Eagle	1 684.5	53 989	930	32.1	67.9	1.2	0.6	1.5	29.7	5.8	16.9	7.8	16.3	15.8	15.3
08 039	19740	1	Elbert	1 850.8	25 231	1 600	13.6	90.6	1.3	1.2	1.8	6.8	4.2	17.1	7.4	8.6	11.0	17.4
08 041	17820	2	El Paso	2 126.8	688 284	95	323.6	73.3	7.7	1.5	4.9	16.7	6.9	17.7	11.3	15.4	12.4	12.4
08 043	15860	4	Fremont	1 533.1	47 446	1 029	30.9	80.6	4.1	2.3	1.5	13.0	4.1	12.2	7.0	14.1	12.9	13.8
08 045	24060	5	Garfield	2 947.5	58 887	878	20.0	69.9	0.9	1.2	1.3	28.2	6.9	18.6	8.4	13.7	13.8	13.4
08 047	19740	1	Gilpin	149.9	5 931	2 760	39.6	89.4	1.4	1.8	2.4	6.9	3.4	12.9	5.1	9.6	14.5	17.8
08 049	...	7	Grand	1 846.4	15 008	2 095	8.1	89.5	1.1	1.1	1.5	8.4	4.1	13.8	7.0	13.8	12.6	14.5
08 051	...	7	Gunnison	3 239.1	16 408	2 012	5.1	88.9	1.0	1.4	1.3	8.9	4.3	12.9	19.0	14.4	12.8	11.9
08 053	...	9	Hinsdale	1 117.2	788	3 120	0.7	93.1	1.3	2.2	1.9	4.3	6.3	13.8	6.7	8.2	9.5	10.7
08 055	...	6	Huerfano	1 591.0	6 677	2 698	4.2	63.7	1.1	2.3	1.2	33.7	4.0	11.8	5.5	8.1	8.1	11.5
08 057	...	9	Jackson	1 613.7	1 357	3 089	0.8	86.8	0.5	1.3	0.7	11.6	4.2	12.3	6.4	11.6	12.9	12.4
08 059	19740	1	Jefferson	764.2	571 837	114	748.3	80.3	1.5	1.1	3.8	15.2	5.3	15.0	8.1	14.3	13.0	14.0
08 061	...	9	Kiowa	1 767.8	1 373	3 087	0.8	91.6	0.9	0.8	0.4	7.3	5.8	15.4	7.9	8.9	9.2	11.4
08 063	...	7	Kit Carson	2 160.8	8 195	2 580	3.8	75.2	3.3	1.3	1.2	20.2	6.0	16.5	8.4	13.9	12.9	12.2
08 065	...	6	Lake	376.9	7 618	2 622	20.2	61.4	0.9	1.5	1.0	36.6	5.7	16.2	9.8	15.8	13.7	13.1
08 067	20420	4	La Plata	1 689.8	55 623	909	32.9	80.3	0.8	6.7	1.2	12.7	5.3	14.0	10.0	13.9	12.9	12.8
08 069	22660	2	Larimer	2 596.2	339 993	201	131.0	85.0	1.5	1.1	3.3	11.2	5.3	14.7	14.8	14.2	12.1	11.4
08 071	...	7	Las Animas	4 772.9	14 103	2 156	3.0	53.8	1.9	1.9	1.5	42.2	4.5	14.3	8.7	11.0	10.5	11.8
08 073	...	8	Lincoln	2 577.7	5 643	2 789	2.2	79.2	5.8	1.5	1.4	13.6	5.3	14.4	8.7	15.7	12.2	14.1
08 075	44540	7	Logan	1 838.6	21 919	1 732	11.9	79.0	3.9	1.4	1.3	15.5	5.4	13.2	11.8	15.3	12.1	12.2
08 077	24300	3	Mesa	3 328.9	150 083	437	45.1	83.2	1.2	1.4	1.6	14.4	5.9	16.1	9.8	13.1	11.6	11.6
08 079	...	9	Mineral	875.8	732	3 125	0.8	92.3	1.1	1.1	0.5	5.9	3.8	10.7	4.0	12.6	7.8	12.3
08 081	18780	7	Moffat	4 743.2	13 109	2 223	2.8	81.9	1.3	1.6	1.2	15.6	7.2	18.4	7.9	13.3	11.6	13.0
08 083	...	6	Montezuma	2 029.3	26 999	1 528	13.3	73.6	0.8	14.0	1.3	12.4	6.2	16.8	7.3	10.8	10.6	12.0
08 085	33940	4	Montrose	2 240.9	41 471	1 140	18.5	77.5	0.8	1.4	1.4	20.4	5.8	16.2	7.3	10.3	10.6	12.2
08 087	22820	6	Morgan	1 280.5	28 274	1 480	22.1	60.2	3.4	0.8	1.0	35.7	7.5	18.9	9.0	13.0	11.3	11.9
08 089	...	6	Otero	1 262.0	18 295	1 900	14.5	55.9	1.2	1.4	1.3	41.6	6.0	17.8	9.2	11.2	10.7	11.5
08 091	...	9	Ouray	541.6	4 857	2 842	9.0	92.4	0.7	1.1	1.2	6.2	3.3	12.7	5.1	7.3	10.6	13.5
08 093	19740	1	Park	2 193.9	17 166	1 972	7.8	91.2	1.1	1.9	1.8	6.0	3.4	12.9	5.4	8.7	11.5	16.8
08 095	...	9	Phillips	687.9	4 288	2 876	6.2	77.3	0.9	0.7	0.9	20.9	6.3	17.6	8.3	9.8	10.1	11.8
08 097	24060	7	Pitkin	970.7	17 752	1 931	18.3	87.1	1.5	0.7	2.1	9.9	3.5	11.7	7.2	14.7	13.5	15.4
08 099	...	7	Prowers	1 638.4	11 922	2 300	7.3	61.0	1.0	1.2	0.7	37.3	7.0	18.5	10.2	11.1	11.3	11.0
08 101	39380	3	Pueblo	2 386.1	165 123	388	69.2	53.7	2.3	1.4	1.3	42.8	6.0	17.1	9.3	12.7	11.6	12.3
08 103	...	9	Rio Blanco	3 221.0	6 545	2 710	2.0	86.5	2.1	2.3	1.7	9.8	5.9	17.8	10.2	13.1	11.8	11.7
08 105	...	7	Rio Grande	912.0	11 479	2 325	12.6	53.8	0.8	1.7	0.9	44.0	6.2	17.1	8.5	11.5	10.9	11.4
08 107	44460	7	Routt	2 362.0	24 648	1 620	10.4	90.9	1.1	0.8	1.4	7.1	4.4	14.2	8.4	14.8	14.0	14.3
08 109	...	9	Saguache	3 168.6	6 389	2 724	2.0	60.1	1.4	2.6	1.3	36.8	5.4	17.0	6.2	7.6	11.0	13.0
08 111	...	9	San Juan	387.5	694	3 128	1.8	84.9	1.2	1.3	1.7	13.3	2.4	9.4	6.1	11.7	14.4	13.1
08 113	...	9	San Miguel	1 286.7	8 017	2 598	6.2	87.2	0.9	1.1	1.5	10.7	4.1	14.8	6.2	15.1	14.8	16.3
08 115	...	9	Sedgwick	548.0	2 407	3 014	4.4	82.3	1.2	0.8	1.2	15.6	5.2	14.9	6.6	10.8	10.9	10.7
08 117	14720	5	Summit	608.3	30 374	1 425	49.9	83.6	1.2	0.6	1.7	13.9	4.5	11.6	8.1	20.1	15.3	14.2
08 119	17820	2	Teller	557.0	24 043	1 641	43.2	90.8	1.2	1.8	1.6	6.5	4.1	13.7	6.6	8.8	10.2	15.6
08 121	...	9	Washington	2 518.1	4 908	2 839	1.9	89.3	1.3	0.9	0.8	9.1	5.2	17.4	7.9	11.0	10.5	12.1
08 123	24540	2	Weld	3 987.2	294 932	232	74.0	67.7	1.5	1.1	2.2	29.1	7.2	19.3	9.6	14.8	13.3	12.4
08 125	...	7	Yuma	2 364.4	10 103	2 428	4.3	76.8	0.7	0.7	0.4	22.1	6.9	19.3	8.3	11.4	11.0	12.0
09 000	...	0	CONNECTICUT	4 842.7	3 576 452	X	738.5	69.2	11.0	0.6	5.3	15.7	5.2	15.9	9.8	12.4	11.8	14.7
09 001	14860	2	Fairfield	625.0	944 177	51	1 510.7	63.8	11.6	0.4	6.3	19.4	5.6	17.5	9.2	11.5	12.6	15.3
09 003	25540	1	Hartford	735.1	892 389	61	1 214.0	63.6	14.1	0.6	5.9	17.6	5.4	16.0	9.2	13.2	12.1	14.2
09 005	45860	4	Litchfield	920.5	182 571	356	198.3	90.5	2.0	0.6	2.4	5.9	4.1	14.7	7.5	10.1	10.5	16.1
09 007	25540	1	Middlesex	369.3	163 329	394	442.3	85.8	5.6	0.6	3.8	6.1	4.3	14.2	8.8	11.2	10.8	15.8
09 009	35300	2	New Haven	604.5	856 875	66	1 417.5	65.2	13.6	0.6	4.8	17.6	5.2	15.4	10.1	13.3	11.7	14.1
09 011	35980	2	New London	665.1	269 801	252	405.7	78.3	7.3	1.8	5.5	10.4	5.1	14.8	10.3	13.0	11.0	14.2

1. CBSA = Core Based Statistical Area. See Appendix A for explanation. See Appendix B for list of metropolitan areas with component counties.   2. County type code from the Economic Research Service of USDA Rural-Urban Continuum Codes. See Appendix A for definition.   3. Dry land or land partially or temporarily covered by water.   4. May be of any race.

Table B. States and Counties — Population and Households

STATE County	Age (percent) (cont.) 55 to 64 years	65 to 74 years	75 years and over	Percent female	Population change and components of change, 2000–2016 — Total persons 2000	2010	Percent change 2000–2010	2010–2016	Components of change, 2010–2016 Births	Deaths	Net migration	Households, 2011–2015 Number	Persons per house-hold	Percent Family house-holds	Female family house-holder[1]	One per-son
	16	17	18	19	20	21	22	23	24	25	26	27	28	29	30	31

COLORADO—Cont'd

STATE County	16	17	18	19	20	21	22	23	24	25	26	27	28	29	30	31
Boulder	12.7	8.1	5.1	49.7	269 814	294 571	9.2	9.4	18 373	10 443	19 518	122 516	2.45	59.1	7.7	27.7
Broomfield	11.7	7.8	5.1	50.4	38 272	55 866	46.0	19.1	4 339	2 131	8 363	23 531	2.57	68.2	7.8	25.9
Chaffee	17.4	14.9	8.9	46.8	16 242	17 809	9.6	7.0	868	1 051	1 459	7 756	2.21	67.0	7.9	27.8
Cheyenne	14.7	9.8	9.6	49.5	2 231	1 836	-17.7	0.7	173	115	-36	743	2.63	61.4	3.1	35.4
Clear Creek	20.4	13.5	5.5	47.5	9 322	9 075	-2.6	4.0	406	353	267	4 231	2.13	60.1	6.3	33.1
Conejos	14.0	10.6	7.8	50.1	8 400	8 256	-1.7	-1.5	737	497	-391	2 948	2.78	69.8	10.1	29.2
Costilla	17.3	16.8	10.2	47.1	3 663	3 524	-3.8	5.6	183	216	238	1 457	2.46	58.2	8.9	38.7
Crowley	11.2	7.5	5.1	27.8	5 518	5 823	5.5	-2.2	229	222	-174	1 169	3.78	67.8	16.5	22.5
Custer	23.2	21.5	9.5	49.0	3 503	4 255	21.5	8.2	143	205	453	1 996	2.15	64.9	3.8	31.6
Delta	16.7	14.3	10.2	50.0	27 834	30 952	11.2	-1.6	1 927	2 232	-233	12 058	2.41	67.0	9.3	27.8
Denver	10.3	6.7	4.5	49.9	554 636	599 864	8.2	15.5	59 359	26 928	59 606	275 795	2.30	48.4	10.3	39.4
Dolores	17.6	14.1	9.2	47.8	1 844	2 064	11.9	-0.4	118	95	-29	706	2.64	65.6	12.5	29.7
Douglas	12.1	7.2	3.8	50.2	175 766	285 465	62.4	15.1	21 790	6 856	27 703	111 113	2.76	77.7	7.4	17.3
Eagle	12.8	7.0	2.4	46.9	41 659	52 197	25.3	3.4	4 122	629	-1 698	17 840	2.94	64.7	7.0	24.1
Elbert	18.7	11.0	4.6	49.7	19 872	23 086	16.2	9.3	1 122	763	1 721	8 417	2.82	76.3	3.8	18.6
El Paso	11.7	7.5	4.7	49.5	516 929	622 261	20.4	10.6	58 057	25 021	32 215	245 287	2.60	68.5	11.3	25.5
Fremont	14.8	12.6	8.7	42.3	46 145	46 824	1.5	1.3	2 323	3 335	1 523	16 342	2.21	65.1	9.8	29.5
Garfield	13.5	7.6	4.2	49.0	43 791	56 389	28.8	4.4	5 068	1 884	-702	20 622	2.72	72.0	9.6	22.1
Gilpin	21.7	11.4	3.6	47.2	4 757	5 441	14.4	9.0	254	157	388	2 576	2.14	55.1	4.6	39.5
Grand	18.9	11.3	4.1	46.9	12 442	14 843	19.3	1.1	696	370	-153	5 250	2.69	65.8	5.9	27.1
Gunnison	12.8	8.3	3.6	45.9	13 956	15 324	9.8	7.1	919	423	587	6 287	2.34	54.5	8.4	30.0
Hinsdale	18.5	17.5	8.6	49.0	790	843	6.7	-6.5	43	27	-75	397	2.18	70.3	0.5	25.9
Huerfano	19.6	18.5	13.0	48.9	7 862	6 711	-14.6	-0.5	298	598	262	3 024	2.08	56.9	9.1	37.5
Jackson	18.4	12.5	9.4	47.8	1 577	1 394	-11.6	-2.7	65	62	-47	616	2.15	58.4	2.3	36.4
Jefferson	14.8	9.5	6.1	50.3	525 507	534 760	1.8	6.9	35 923	25 610	26 550	222 892	2.44	64.8	9.8	27.6
Kiowa	16.8	12.4	12.2	51.1	1 622	1 398	-13.8	-1.8	92	117	-28	583	2.45	64.2	5.0	35.8
Kit Carson	13.2	8.9	8.1	43.6	8 011	8 270	3.2	-0.9	613	477	-230	3 003	2.35	66.9	7.9	31.1
Lake	13.8	7.8	4.0	46.2	7 812	7 310	-6.4	4.2	527	227	5	3 025	2.38	60.1	4.9	34.3
La Plata	15.7	10.4	5.1	49.5	43 941	51 335	16.8	8.4	3 458	1 994	2 817	21 513	2.38	60.1	7.3	29.7
Larimer	12.8	9.1	5.7	50.1	251 494	299 629	19.1	13.5	21 461	12 580	30 319	125 138	2.47	62.5	7.9	24.7
Las Animas	15.9	14.1	9.2	48.0	15 207	15 507	2.0	-9.1	833	1 063	-1 186	5 826	2.36	65.1	10.2	30.5
Lincoln	12.2	8.5	8.8	41.6	6 087	5 469	-10.2	3.2	375	316	110	1 677	2.24	66.0	13.0	30.7
Logan	13.2	8.8	8.0	44.4	20 504	22 709	10.8	-3.5	1 429	1 211	-1 033	7 966	2.61	63.5	11.4	30.7
Mesa	13.9	10.4	7.5	50.4	116 255	146 717	26.2	2.3	11 423	8 697	383	59 215	2.43	65.4	11.3	27.3
Mineral	20.2	17.9	10.8	48.5	831	712	-14.3	2.8	28	28	21	368	1.91	62.5	1.1	33.2
Moffat	14.8	8.7	5.1	48.3	13 184	13 795	4.6	-5.0	1 143	586	-1 250	4 986	2.60	63.2	5.4	30.6
Montezuma	16.0	12.5	7.8	50.6	23 830	25 541	7.2	5.7	1 983	1 623	1 082	10 417	2.44	63.1	8.7	30.3
Montrose	15.3	12.9	9.4	50.7	33 432	41 278	23.5	0.5	2 862	2 596	-112	16 768	2.40	68.1	10.1	26.9
Morgan	12.4	8.2	7.7	50.0	27 171	28 159	3.6	0.4	2 746	1 563	-1 161	10 421	2.67	73.5	12.6	22.3
Otero	13.8	10.7	9.2	50.5	20 311	18 831	-7.3	-2.8	1 353	1 468	-408	7 454	2.42	67.8	12.4	29.8
Ouray	21.5	18.4	7.6	49.8	3 742	4 434	18.5	9.5	179	184	427	1 980	2.31	63.5	4.4	25.1
Park	23.6	13.5	4.1	47.0	14 523	16 201	11.6	6.0	661	519	918	7 319	2.20	61.5	4.5	31.7
Phillips	13.9	10.2	12.1	51.5	4 480	4 442	-0.8	-3.5	343	309	-196	1 711	2.52	66.8	5.4	30.5
Pitkin	16.8	11.8	5.4	47.7	14 872	17 148	15.3	3.5	837	300	97	7 570	2.28	46.7	5.4	37.8
Prowers	14.3	9.5	7.1	49.8	14 483	12 551	-13.3	-5.0	1 006	730	-927	4 856	2.44	68.5	11.0	26.7
Pueblo	13.5	10.3	7.4	50.7	141 472	159 063	12.4	3.8	11 877	10 407	4 322	62 888	2.49	64.7	14.2	29.6
Rio Blanco	14.5	8.5	6.3	48.8	5 986	6 669	11.4	-1.9	501	298	-308	2 482	2.48	68.6	6.3	26.1
Rio Grande	14.4	11.8	8.1	50.6	12 413	11 982	-3.5	-4.2	882	750	-650	4 617	2.49	67.4	11.7	28.3
Routt	16.4	9.4	4.1	48.0	19 690	23 506	19.4	4.9	1 349	610	411	9 431	2.46	60.5	5.9	29.1
Saguache	19.2	14.3	6.4	49.5	5 917	6 108	3.2	4.6	448	251	80	2 598	2.39	58.1	10.4	36.1
San Juan	19.7	18.7	4.5	42.8	558	699	25.3	-0.7	26	27	-5	282	2.15	48.9	5.7	45.4
San Miguel	16.3	9.6	2.7	46.5	6 594	7 359	11.6	8.9	431	141	360	3 310	2.31	51.2	6.3	36.9
Sedgwick	16.2	13.0	11.9	49.8	2 747	2 379	-13.4	1.2	146	238	125	951	2.44	63.2	9.6	31.1
Summit	14.4	9.0	3.0	46.1	23 548	27 994	18.9	8.5	1 761	341	970	10 143	2.82	59.2	6.3	28.3
Teller	21.3	14.8	5.0	49.2	20 555	23 350	13.6	3.0	1 168	961	596	9 581	2.42	71.4	8.3	25.0
Washington	14.6	11.1	10.1	47.7	4 926	4 814	-2.3	2.0	264	287	92	1 963	2.30	69.0	7.0	28.8
Weld	11.6	7.3	4.4	49.6	180 926	252 831	39.7	16.7	24 362	9 904	26 711	94 294	2.80	72.4	10.1	21.2
Yuma	12.4	9.7	9.0	50.6	9 841	10 043	2.1	0.6	885	604	-244	3 865	2.60	59.1	5.9	37.1
CONNECTICUT	14.1	9.1	7.1	51.2	3 405 565	3 574 114	4.9	0.1	228 277	185 383	-34 774	1 352 583	2.57	66.2	13.0	28.0
Fairfield	13.6	8.1	6.7	51.3	882 567	916 846	3.9	3.0	63 616	40 998	6 322	334 320	2.76	69.7	12.3	25.1
Hartford	13.8	9.0	7.3	51.4	857 183	894 041	4.3	-0.2	59 230	49 328	-10 214	346 362	2.51	65.3	14.7	28.8
Litchfield	17.3	11.6	8.1	50.6	182 193	189 926	4.2	-3.9	9 149	10 956	-5 046	74 518	2.46	66.6	9.1	27.2
Middlesex	16.1	10.8	8.1	51.1	155 071	165 676	6.8	-1.4	8 844	9 152	-1 661	66 117	2.40	65.2	9.0	28.2
New Haven	13.8	9.1	7.1	51.8	824 008	862 462	4.7	-0.6	56 078	47 891	-12 690	326 028	2.56	63.6	14.2	30.6
New London	14.6	9.8	7.2	49.9	259 088	274 049	5.8	-1.6	17 033	14 674	-6 043	106 495	2.45	65.2	12.2	28.7

1. No spouse present.

Table B. States and Counties — **Population, Vital Statistics, Health, and Crime**

STATE County	Persons in group quarters, 2016	Daytime population, 2011–2015 Number	Employ-ment/resi-dence ratio	Births, 2016 Total	Rate[1]	Deaths, 2016 Number	Rate[1]	Persons under 65 with no health insurance, 2015 Number	Percent	Medicare, 2015 Total Beneficiaries	Enrolled in Original Medicare	Enrolled in Medicare Advantage	Serious crimes known to police,[2] 2014 Total Number	Rate[3]
	32	33	34	35	36	37	38	39	40	41	42	43	44	45
COLORADO—Cont'd														
Boulder	11 247	337 746	1.17	2 911	9.0	1 860	5.8	19 657	7.3	46 352	26 420	19 932	6 581	2 617
Broomfield	282	66 477	1.19	735	11.0	369	5.5	2 739	4.8	9 929	4 630	5 299	1 071	1 765
Chaffee	1 447	18 519	1.03	144	7.6	171	9.0	1 306	10.1	4 645	3 746	899	.286	1 522
Cheyenne	42	2 242	1.26	28	15.2	15	8.1	230	15.8	303	286	17	2	104
Clear Creek	84	7 556	0.68	55	5.8	58	6.1	475	6.3	967	632	335	201	2 287
Conejos	36	7 249	0.66	119	14.6	74	9.1	748	11.4	1 526	1 002	524	14	168
Costilla	0	3 351	0.81	26	7.0	23	6.2	405	15.8	1 102	754	348	28	792
Crowley	2 604	5 628	1.05	31	5.4	32	5.6	223	9.5	716	592	124	7	134
Custer	150	4 126	0.87	24	5.2	37	8.0	396	13.5	1 317	1 053	264	40	928
Delta	702	29 043	0.89	280	9.2	370	12.2	2 509	11.4	7 993	5 895	2 098	577	2 036
Denver	16 374	797 682	1.43	10 082	14.5	4 825	7.0	72 028	12.1	80 417	36 626	43 791	26 648	4 005
Dolores	0	1 730	0.83	20	9.7	6	2.9	189	12.5	481	423	58	20	984
Douglas	647	265 277	0.74	3 453	10.5	1 311	4.0	10 253	3.5	20 639	11 715	8 924	3 617	1 157
Eagle	79	51 171	0.95	656	12.2	108	2.0	6 799	14.0	4 081	3 747	334	1 007	1 905
Elbert	73	17 108	0.45	207	8.2	131	5.2	1 606	7.6	3 786	2 525	1 261	20	85
El Paso	18 336	655 116	1.00	9 619	14.0	4 429	6.4	46 640	8.1	88 335	59 148	29 187	22 224	3 336
Fremont	8 175	46 789	1.00	388	8.2	547	11.5	2 774	9.6	10 984	7 414	3 570	907	1 946
Garfield	883	55 259	0.94	794	13.5	352	6.0	8 124	16.0	7 342	6 431	911	1 082	1 867
Gilpin	49	8 145	1.81	35	5.9	25	4.2	217	4.4	659	383	276	360	6 353
Grand	223	14 136	0.97	108	7.2	61	4.1	1 147	9.2	2 048	1 725	323	140	1 088
Gunnison	1 058	16 397	1.08	147	9.0	68	4.1	1 565	11.7	1 820	1 691	129	231	1 478
Hinsdale	56	843	0.93	8	10.2	5	6.3	67	11.8	212	191	21	4	494
Huerfano	165	6 504	1.00	46	6.9	91	13.6	447	10.1	1 991	1 574	417	139	2 132
Jackson	2	1 348	1.02	10	7.4	9	6.6	175	16.7	301	288	13	2	146
Jefferson	8 178	499 583	0.82	5 981	10.5	4 460	7.8	33 312	7.0	87 125	35 914	51 211	16 525	2 955
Kiowa	14	1 457	0.99	15	10.9	14	10.2	131	12.2	D	303	D	NA	NA
Kit Carson	1 030	8 281	1.09	105	12.8	79	9.6	837	14.3	1 385	1 319	66	127	1 724
Lake	146	6 410	0.77	84	11.0	24	3.2	760	11.7	845	757	88	95	1 291
La Plata	1 914	53 979	1.03	582	10.5	355	6.4	4 588	10.2	8 687	7 637	1 050	833	1 541
Larimer	9 367	310 623	0.95	3 591	10.6	2 182	6.4	19 543	7.0	49 169	34 161	15 008	7 548	2 345
Las Animas	867	14 900	1.07	119	8.4	161	11.4	1 098	10.9	3 595	2 897	698	388	2 714
Lincoln	1 018	6 191	1.48	63	11.2	50	8.9	324	9.0	925	858	67	26	477
Logan	3 278	21 573	0.97	228	10.4	191	8.7	1 684	11.1	3 669	3 197	472	604	2 685
Mesa	4 437	145 372	0.96	1 787	11.9	1 455	9.7	12 847	10.8	28 355	17 255	11 100	4 393	2 955
Mineral	0	717	0.95	4	5.5	2	2.7	59	11.1	226	192	34	2	274
Moffat	102	12 339	0.88	182	13.9	80	6.1	1 168	10.5	1 913	1 731	182	246	1 891
Montezuma	243	24 888	0.93	338	12.5	263	9.7	3 074	14.8	5 428	4 718	710	530	2 053
Montrose	542	39 723	0.93	459	11.1	447	10.8	4 160	13.2	9 599	7 250	2 349	1 058	2 711
Morgan	564	28 223	0.99	447	15.8	248	8.8	2 940	12.6	4 383	3 890	493	487	1 756
Otero	457	18 403	0.98	196	10.7	219	12.0	1 764	12.4	4 445	3 645	800	428	2 335
Ouray	0	4 616	1.02	23	4.7	29	6.0	365	10.4	931	786	145	15	408
Park	92	11 389	0.45	102	5.9	103	6.0	1 199	8.8	2 539	1 788	751	67	414
Phillips	59	4 581	1.11	61	14.2	56	13.1	490	14.6	948	927	21	34	781
Pitkin	72	24 073	1.67	127	7.2	41	2.3	1 665	11.2	2 068	1 972	96	396	2 258
Prowers	342	12 140	0.98	163	13.7	112	9.4	1 325	13.8	2 230	2 156	74	234	1 904
Pueblo	4 149	159 596	0.97	1 926	11.7	1 765	10.7	11 907	9.1	33 300	20 738	12 562	9 275	5 695
Rio Blanco	296	7 063	1.11	77	11.8	39	6.0	533	9.9	928	751	177	79	1 147
Rio Grande	198	10 951	0.84	139	12.1	124	10.8	1 178	12.9	2 514	1 835	679	200	1 692
Routt	349	24 591	1.07	220	8.9	115	4.7	1 684	8.1	2 948	2 651	297	421	1 847
Saguache	18	5 965	0.89	66	10.3	55	8.6	960	19.5	1 306	937	369	84	1 341
San Juan	0	568	0.89	4	5.8	4	5.8	67	12.2	142	128	14	18	2 601
San Miguel	9	8 379	1.16	65	8.1	19	2.4	752	10.9	815	716	99	100	1 281
Sedgwick	35	2 266	0.90	18	7.5	39	16.2	200	11.2	621	581	40	30	1 266
Summit	273	30 919	1.11	295	9.7	60	2.0	3 177	11.9	2 749	2 402	347	777	2 683
Teller	132	20 613	0.76	194	8.1	172	7.2	1 469	7.8	4 856	3 097	1 759	360	1 541
Washington	184	4 272	0.75	47	9.6	49	10.0	386	10.6	903	866	37	47	973
Weld	4 944	251 288	0.85	4 106	13.9	1 725	5.8	20 906	8.4	33 383	22 250	11 133	6 203	2 261
Yuma	262	10 421	1.05	128	12.7	95	9.4	997	12.3	1 754	1 698	56	45	439
CONNECTICUT	114 956	3 576 033	0.99	35 848	10.0	30 638	8.6	201 842	6.9	592 422	421 531	170 891	77 592	2 157
Fairfield	19 530	954 607	1.03	10 050	10.6	6 800	7.2	73 657	9.2	135 618	101 362	34 256	17 221	1 857
Hartford	27 001	969 828	1.17	9 349	10.5	8 201	9.2	42 454	5.8	153 254	102 554	50 700	22 951	2 621
Litchfield	2 604	160 125	0.73	1 423	7.8	1 780	9.7	8 373	5.6	36 435	27 832	8 603	NA	NA
Middlesex	4 643	150 108	0.83	1 356	8.3	1 483	9.1	5 886	4.5	30 731	22 108	8 623	NA	NA
New Haven	29 511	838 627	0.94	8 781	10.2	7 924	9.2	49 152	7.0	144 634	98 063	46 571	24 314	3 009
New London	11 503	274 560	1.01	2 676	9.9	2 465	9.1	11 860	5.5	48 825	38 704	10 121	NA	NA

1. Per 1,000 estimated resident population.   2. Data for serious crimes have not been adjusted for underreporting; this may affect comparability between geographic areas and over time.
3. Per 100,000 population estimated by the FBI.

Table B. States and Counties — Crime, Education, Money Income, and Poverty

STATE County	Serious crimes known to police, 2014 (cont.)[1] Rate[2] Violent	Property	School enrollment and attainment, 2011–2015 Enrollment[3] Total	Percent private	Attainment[4] (percent) High school graduate or less	Bachelor's degree or more	Local government expenditures,[5] 2013–2014 Total current spending (mil dol)	Current spending per student (dollars)	Money income, 2011–2015 Per capita income[6] (dollars)	Median income (dollars)	Households Percent with income of less than $50,000	with income of $200,000 or more	Income and poverty, 2015 Median house-hold income (dollars)	Percent below poverty level All persons	Children under 18 years	Children 5 to 17 years in families
	46	47	48	49	50	51	52	53	54	55	56	57	58	59	60	61
COLORADO—Cont'd																
Boulder	246	2 372	95 913	12.4	18.6	58.9	571.5	9 409	39 074	70 961	36.9	9.8	72 392	12.3	10.9	9.2
Broomfield	51	1 714	17 007	16.2	19.0	51.9	NA	NA	40 135	81 898	28.4	8.8	86 548	4.9	5.8	5.1
Chaffee	80	1 442	3 058	12.8	35.6	34.1	21.7	10 138	28 064	51 092	48.3	2.0	50 947	11.7	17.5	16.2
Cheyenne	104	0	543	11.0	42.6	22.5	4.6	15 532	23 553	52 554	46.3	2.2	50 620	11.7	17.3	17.3
Clear Creek	569	1 718	1 580	12.2	25.2	41.5	10.2	10 957	42 812	67 710	37.3	5.8	67 262	9.6	14.3	12.5
Conejos	12	156	2 210	3.8	48.1	19.5	16.0	9 930	18 844	36 652	61.1	0.6	37 102	20.2	29.9	27.7
Costilla	226	566	703	9.1	51.5	17.9	5.9	12 787	21 809	31 321	74.2	2.1	27 944	28.2	43.3	39.4
Crowley	38	96	1 454	6.1	55.7	11.1	4.4	9 857	10 742	31 151	66.7	0.1	35 405	44.3	38.5	37.8
Custer	93	835	764	23.0	25.2	35.5	3.9	9 523	22 661	35 000	61.4	1.9	43 995	15.1	32.8	28.7
Delta	67	1 969	5 954	12.6	48.6	20.0	40.5	8 001	24 417	42 452	57.6	2.8	42 586	15.8	23.7	22.1
Denver	601	3 404	153 247	19.7	31.5	45.0	979.1	10 144	35 218	53 637	46.5	6.7	57 886	15.7	23.1	23.7
Dolores	98	886	349	1.4	48.5	21.0	3.2	10 823	20 199	31 875	67.3	2.8	44 829	14.9	22.4	19.0
Douglas	85	1 072	91 474	15.6	15.2	56.6	541.9	8 182	45 500	102 964	18.8	14.0	109 926	3.4	3.3	2.8
Eagle	163	1 743	12 760	16.1	28.7	46.7	64.4	9 870	38 193	72 214	31.3	9.5	75 191	7.6	10.6	9.4
Elbert	4	81	6 084	16.5	31.1	30.6	25.1	7 915	38 021	84 963	26.5	9.7	90 270	5.9	8.0	6.6
El Paso	385	2 951	190 467	13.1	27.2	35.9	973.0	8 332	29 659	58 206	42.3	4.5	60 050	11.0	14.9	13.4
Fremont	225	1 721	8 675	11.9	52.4	15.2	43.5	8 186	18 619	40 423	60.7	1.9	41 967	17.2	24.8	23.0
Garfield	171	1 697	14 752	12.2	40.2	29.7	102.5	8 918	27 574	56 590	42.5	3.6	64 487	10.3	14.6	13.9
Gilpin	335	6 017	1 116	5.5	28.6	32.1	5.0	11 805	38 361	65 670	32.8	2.5	67 389	8.0	12.0	8.6
Grand	101	987	2 647	9.7	31.0	36.4	17.3	10 173	31 432	63 628	40.2	4.9	59 885	8.3	13.5	11.8
Gunnison	186	1 293	4 846	12.5	21.9	54.4	17.1	8 828	25 584	48 071	51.9	1.7	47 619	12.5	14.3	13.0
Hinsdale	0	494	117	28.2	26.4	40.4	1.4	17 138	33 816	57 083	40.8	3.8	58 613	10.9	30.8	27.8
Huerfano	353	1 779	1 069	7.4	38.6	27.1	7.6	10 772	23 467	31 715	68.3	2.7	33 098	23.2	41.6	37.7
Jackson	0	146	238	2.9	53.9	18.1	2.7	12 812	27 938	46 014	55.5	1.0	46 905	13.9	25.3	22.0
Jefferson	233	2 723	133 888	13.8	27.3	41.6	747.0	8 685	37 065	70 164	35.2	6.9	71 209	7.9	9.7	8.5
Kiowa	NA	NA	400	7.8	43.3	20.3	3.4	13 253	22 731	40 304	62.8	2.7	42 108	13.9	22.1	22.8
Kit Carson	204	1 520	1 612	5.3	55.0	13.3	14.1	9 725	21 769	40 603	58.7	2.1	44 090	12.2	20.0	18.8
Lake	245	1 046	1 598	10.7	43.5	27.4	14.7	13 220	24 399	45 367	52.9	0.0	45 913	15.7	25.5	24.0
La Plata	165	1 376	13 210	11.6	24.8	43.3	70.9	10 469	31 822	60 278	40.5	3.9	60 732	9.4	11.5	10.8
Larimer	190	2 156	95 341	9.9	23.7	44.3	395.4	8 644	31 304	59 805	42.6	4.9	64 935	12.2	10.7	9.7
Las Animas	147	2 567	3 160	9.3	44.0	17.0	21.2	9 599	22 935	45 067	55.9	1.3	38 858	19.3	28.1	26.7
Lincoln	73	404	1 007	10.3	62.5	15.1	12.8	17 031	15 203	39 005	59.3	2.6	43 188	19.4	25.0	25.2
Logan	307	2 379	5 083	4.2	44.5	15.8	27.8	9 203	23 916	42 319	55.9	3.0	46 306	15.5	17.9	16.9
Mesa	346	2 609	36 513	10.6	39.2	26.3	181.6	8 069	26 569	49 322	50.6	2.8	51 449	14.1	17.8	16.4
Mineral	137	137	59	0.0	23.5	42.3	1.6	20 263	32 271	48 125	51.6	1.9	50 481	9.4	19.0	19.1
Moffat	146	1 745	3 102	11.3	50.3	15.3	20.4	9 102	24 624	51 387	48.2	1.2	59 173	11.7	17.4	15.7
Montezuma	186	1 867	5 655	8.5	39.2	26.2	32.7	8 126	23 470	43 553	56.3	1.9	42 975	19.3	28.7	27.4
Montrose	164	2 547	8 828	16.0	44.2	24.5	52.2	8 083	23 144	43 999	55.7	1.3	46 860	17.7	25.2	21.7
Morgan	216	1 540	7 192	3.8	51.9	14.9	45.6	8 205	22 101	48 450	52.1	1.9	49 087	12.1	16.9	15.8
Otero	125	2 209	4 997	7.2	44.1	15.6	33.2	10 278	19 228	32 311	66.7	0.9	34 970	20.6	30.6	29.3
Ouray	82	327	710	22.4	21.3	52.0	8.0	14 878	33 392	61 624	39.5	4.6	60 402	9.4	15.2	12.9
Park	117	297	2 925	15.3	29.8	29.2	16.3	10 032	31 734	56 969	42.8	1.9	63 319	9.2	14.7	12.5
Phillips	161	620	997	7.3	41.0	21.2	12.4	13 887	24 967	43 639	56.1	3.6	48 562	11.1	16.7	16.2
Pitkin	63	2 195	3 510	24.7	16.3	59.1	25.3	14 619	55 519	71 196	34.5	10.4	76 663	7.0	7.6	6.6
Prowers	57	1 847	3 272	5.5	46.5	13.5	21.6	9 036	20 087	40 179	62.0	0.7	41 348	19.6	27.9	24.9
Pueblo	577	5 119	42 186	8.5	41.1	21.6	214.5	7 866	22 191	41 286	57.7	1.5	40 540	19.8	27.1	25.2
Rio Blanco	102	1 045	1 678	10.7	42.6	22.0	13.4	10 579	27 274	61 842	41.5	2.4	61 426	9.7	11.2	10.3
Rio Grande	152	1 540	2 828	8.6	46.2	22.0	18.5	9 186	22 269	39 672	59.7	1.7	40 259	17.2	28.7	28.6
Routt	140	1 707	5 030	10.1	23.6	50.4	40.1	12 447	36 472	64 963	40.5	7.0	70 989	8.9	10.9	9.7
Saguache	128	1 213	1 301	5.3	46.0	27.0	12.3	12 519	21 711	33 393	65.4	2.0	34 209	29.6	49.3	44.6
San Juan	145	2 457	47	0.0	41.1	29.1	1.3	20 734	23 143	36 324	64.9	0.0	43 489	15.6	33.7	28.4
San Miguel	115	1 166	1 291	19.1	23.5	53.9	13.5	12 146	40 149	56 047	45.6	7.7	62 793	11.0	13.3	12.3
Sedgwick	338	928	466	2.1	44.4	20.6	7.6	7 126	22 857	44 191	55.3	2.3	40 325	13.6	23.8	22.3
Summit	135	2 548	5 513	13.3	22.4	48.8	36.5	11 110	35 753	67 983	36.9	5.7	69 633	8.7	10.3	9.2
Teller	304	1 237	4 649	9.9	31.8	31.8	26.7	9 003	32 707	62 372	40.4	3.0	66 191	8.8	15.3	13.6
Washington	124	849	1 127	9.2	44.2	16.3	11.8	13 280	24 817	45 541	55.1	2.8	47 592	11.4	15.6	13.6
Weld	285	1 976	78 053	9.8	40.2	26.1	337.3	8 515	26 751	60 572	41.2	3.7	69 434	11.3	13.5	12.4
Yuma	10	430	2 534	10.3	43.3	21.5	18.6	10 381	23 246	43 105	57.6	2.3	48 934	14.1	18.6	17.4
CONNECTICUT	237	1 920	939 333	20.4	37.5	37.6	9 178.5	17 204	38 803	70 331	36.5	9.7	71 333	10.6	14.6	13.6
Fairfield	246	1 611	254 747	24.2	32.9	45.8	2 617.7	17 962	50 137	84 233	31.6	18.1	86 297	9.0	11.2	10.1
Hartford	276	2 345	232 127	17.1	38.3	36.3	2 369.8	17 708	35 611	66 395	38.6	7.8	69 260	11.1	15.7	14.9
Litchfield	NA	NA	41 868	18.9	37.9	33.6	425.1	17 793	38 530	72 061	34.1	6.6	70 847	7.4	9.4	8.1
Middlesex	NA	NA	39 630	22.4	33.0	40.6	387.9	12 021	41 277	79 893	30.5	9.6	82 878	6.7	7.4	6.7
New Haven	333	2 676	225 516	23.8	41.1	34.0	2 123.0	17 186	32 852	61 640	41.3	6.6	61 758	13.6	20.0	18.8
New London	NA	NA	65 992	18.5	39.9	32.1	637.2	17 040	34 208	66 233	37.0	5.5	65 602	11.1	17.4	16.6

1. Data for serious crimes have not been adjusted for underreporting; this may affect comparability between geographic areas and over time.   2. Per 100,000 population estimated by the FBI.
3. All persons 3 years old and over enrolled in nursery school through college.   4. Persons 25 years old and over.   5. Elementary and secondary education expenditures.
6. Based on population estimated by the American Community Survey, 2011–2015.

Table B. States and Counties — **Personal Income**

STATE County	Personal income, 2015										Earnings, 2015		
	Total (mil dol)	Percent change, 2014–2015	Per capita[1] Dollars	Per capita[1] Rank	Wages and salaries (mil dol)	Supplements to wages and salaries; employer contributions (mil dol) Pension and insurance	Supplements to wages and salaries; employer contributions (mil dol) Government social insurance	Proprietors' income (mil dol)	Dividends, interest, and rent (mil dol)	Personal transfer receipts (mil dol)	Total (mil dol)	Contributions for government social insurance (mil dol) From employee and self-employed	Contributions for government social insurance (mil dol) From employer
	62	63	64	65	66	67	68	69	70	71	72	73	74
COLORADO—Cont'd													
Boulder	19 233	4.0	60 220	147	11 431	1 299	787	1 403	5 241	1 778	14 920	819	787
Broomfield	4 757	4.3	73 107	36	3 068	279	194	181	605	341	3 721	221	194
Chaffee	715	5.0	38 330	1 879	271	41	19	60	221	165	391	24	19
Cheyenne	98	7.0	53 361	339	33	6	2	30	22	14	71	2	2
Clear Creek	481	5.3	51 710	157	169	22	12	37	108	59	240	14	12
Conejos	250	4.0	30 716	2 791	48	9	3	31	38	83	92	6	3
Costilla	111	7.2	31 030	2 861	26	5	2	11	20	43	43	3	2
Crowley	145	11.6	26 039	3 091	46	8	3	27	21	39	84	3	3
Custer	195	8.5	43 887	1 273	31	5	2	38	56	45	75	5	2
Delta	950	2.1	31 685	2 123	306	51	22	70	222	280	449	29	22
Denver	46 617	2.8	68 299	102	33 391	3 754	2 309	11 165	9 487	4 605	50 620	2 703	2 309
Dolores	84	2.8	42 715	992	45	5	3	2	15	18	56	3	3
Douglas	21 277	4.6	65 999	120	7 360	710	502	1 602	3 461	1 462	10 174	581	502
Eagle	3 298	6.3	61 522	159	1 485	139	115	441	1 131	190	2 181	117	115
Elbert	1 223	5.5	49 450	507	149	20	11	68	189	140	249	16	11
El Paso	29 262	4.2	43 385	955	15 175	2 438	1 211	1 557	5 960	5 072	20 381	1 079	1 211
Fremont	1 444	5.0	30 921	2 800	551	108	38	109	273	457	805	49	38
Garfield	2 937	4.1	50 556	503	1 285	165	96	218	1 090	328	1 764	95	96
Gilpin	237	5.9	40 702	732	236	17	18	20	47	33	291	17	18
Grand	599	5.8	40 963	1 371	273	35	20	60	173	80	388	21	20
Gunnison	682	6.0	42 452	1 375	313	46	22	69	223	79	450	23	22
Hinsdale	35	4.8	44 647	1 090	9	2	1	4	15	6	15	1	1
Huerfano	235	4.5	36 232	1 999	54	10	4	13	59	93	81	6	4
Jackson	60	7.6	43 880	1 105	19	3	1	11	15	10	34	2	1
Jefferson	30 975	5.2	54 773	321	13 002	1 624	956	2 391	6 049	4 024	17 973	1 044	956
Kiowa	68	-2.7	47 936	287	23	4	1	14	15	14	42	1	1
Kit Carson	278	-3.4	35 894	1 663	118	17	8	38	61	61	182	9	8
Lake	241	5.4	32 175	2 694	86	15	6	21	47	45	128	7	6
La Plata	2 815	-2.9	51 475	488	1 238	156	86	480	776	338	1 960	103	86
Larimer	15 117	5.0	45 318	794	7 541	1 008	521	971	3 334	2 122	10 041	557	521
Las Animas	516	0.3	36 692	1 543	205	34	15	18	95	185	272	17	15
Lincoln	189	-0.8	33 968	2 209	87	16	5	13	42	43	121	6	5
Logan	1 074	6.7	48 755	1 074	347	56	25	343	178	173	771	37	25
Mesa	5 772	1.6	38 863	1 445	2 708	355	205	399	1 140	1 215	3 667	222	205
Mineral	40	6.7	55 167	268	17	2	1	4	18	8	24	1	1
Moffat	503	0.7	38 875	926	236	39	17	43	81	98	335	18	17
Montezuma	1 005	3.0	38 393	1 797	343	56	25	92	223	236	516	31	25
Montrose	1 415	4.0	34 559	2 150	569	86	42	110	313	363	807	49	42
Morgan	1 135	1.5	40 020	1 183	520	73	38	151	163	218	782	39	38
Otero	634	4.0	34 590	2 264	232	39	18	52	107	221	340	20	18
Ouray	248	8.4	52 906	593	67	9	5	44	84	35	125	7	5
Park	643	5.7	38 916	1 617	93	15	6	43	146	112	158	11	6
Phillips	178	-3.6	40 924	1 283	67	12	4	28	38	39	111	5	4
Pitkin	2 244	3.0	126 137	5	858	77	64	145	1 376	89	1 144	63	64
Prowers	466	7.2	38 998	1 437	163	27	11	90	88	118	291	13	11
Pueblo	5 698	4.7	34 831	2 164	2 589	367	201	243	940	1 729	3 401	212	201
Rio Blanco	274	-0.1	41 723	1 039	161	27	11	23	53	45	221	11	11
Rio Grande	457	9.0	39 633	1 495	152	24	12	62	92	134	250	14	12
Routt	1 586	1.7	65 734	97	678	75	50	156	634	123	960	52	50
Saguache	210	9.9	33 601	2 752	61	11	4	29	42	46	105	5	4
San Juan	30	-2.0	43 409	2 448	8	1	1	9	8	5	19	1	1
San Miguel	580	9.5	73 572	128	229	24	18	94	262	31	365	19	18
Sedgwick	102	-7.0	42 608	510	31	6	2	20	22	26	58	2	2
Summit	1 652	7.1	54 615	347	836	86	63	203	564	111	1 188	64	63
Teller	1 057	5.4	45 219	880	285	38	21	81	217	203	425	27	21
Washington	189	-9.4	38 770	562	56	10	4	34	36	37	104	5	4
Weld	12 202	8.1	42 787	1 368	5 114	633	374	1 789	1 672	1 734	7 910	418	374
Yuma	522	2.9	51 405	558	176	25	12	176	87	83	389	14	12
CONNECTICUT	246 709	2.9	68 822	X	112 327	17 037	7 708	27 871	52 179	31 690	164 942	8 666	7 708
Fairfield	100 856	2.1	106 382	6	38 548	4 754	2 323	15 075	27 096	7 521	60 699	3 117	2 323
Hartford	53 070	3.5	59 240	181	35 300	5 357	2 477	5 165	8 570	8 457	48 300	2 549	2 477
Litchfield	10 771	3.4	58 665	219	2 913	533	231	1 349	2 251	1 523	5 025	274	231
Middlesex	10 237	3.0	62 394	146	3 824	672	287	1 008	1 784	1 323	5 791	307	287
New Haven	44 551	3.4	51 835	370	20 990	3 432	1 602	3 437	7 708	8 364	29 461	1 603	1 602
New London	14 272	3.5	52 498	369	6 985	1 410	515	972	2 742	2 415	9 881	508	515

1. Based on the resident population estimated as of July 1 of the year shown.

STATE County	Farm	Mining	Construction	Manu-facturing	Infor-mation: professional, scientific, technical services	Retail trade	Finance, insur-ance, real estate and leasing	Health care and social assistance	Govern-ment	Social Security beneficiaries, December 2015 — Number	Rate[1]	Supple-mental Security Income recipients, December 2015	Housing units, 2016 — Total	Percent change, 2010–2016
	75	76	77	78	79	80	81	82	83	84	85	86	87	88
COLORADO—Cont'd														
Boulder	0.1	0.4	2.9	12.1	31.6	4.5	5.7	9.8	15.0	42 510	133	2 426	133 773	5.3
Broomfield	0.0	D	3.8	16.3	37.3	4.5	5.9	2.8	2.6	8 625	133	423	27 087	19.7
Chaffee	0.6	D	13.0	2.6	7.8	10.6	5.6	6.5	27.5	4 900	263	225	10 574	5.5
Cheyenne	33.1	7.1	D	D	D	3.3	D	D	17.9	330	182	11	979	0.4
Clear Creek	0.0	D	4.3	D	D	3.6	D	D	16.6	1 730	185	82	5 691	0.2
Conejos	19.0	2.5	9.6	2.6	D	6.0	D	11.9	24.1	1 895	233	353	4 305	0.4
Costilla	17.6	D	D	D	D	4.4	D	7.8	30.5	1 210	340	235	2 738	4.7
Crowley	30.8	0.1	3.2	0.2	0.6	4.0	D	4.5	35.4	855	152	159	1 554	-0.3
Custer	3.4	2.4	34.0	6.5	5.7	7.5	2.0	D	15.0	1 485	336	44	4 244	7.3
Delta	4.9	7.7	7.2	4.8	5.3	9.5	4.7	10.0	28.0	8 560	286	546	14 482	-0.6
Denver	0.0	13.1	3.8	3.2	16.3	2.5	8.8	6.6	11.5	84 175	124	14 515	311 462	9.0
Dolores	0.8	D	D	D	D	3.2	D	D	16.3	555	280	25	1 458	-0.6
Douglas	0.0	4.4	7.3	1.8	24.1	6.6	12.5	8.0	7.4	36 460	113	1 011	124 755	16.7
Eagle	0.1	1.1	13.2	1.0	7.3	8.1	9.7	11.0	9.2	4 580	86	111	31 889	1.8
Elbert	0.5	D	27.6	2.8	11.2	6.3	4.2	2.7	17.0	3 965	161	97	9 442	5.6
El Paso	0.0	0.1	6.3	4.3	15.9	6.2	6.2	9.7	32.9	99 805	148	8 998	272 568	7.8
Fremont	0.3	0.8	7.5	6.2	3.2	7.3	3.2	12.4	44.5	12 125	260	1 133	19 324	0.4
Garfield	0.1	9.6	16.5	1.6	7.3	7.2	5.8	10.9	17.4	7 550	131	371	23 556	1.1
Gilpin	0.0	0.0	2.7	D	D	0.4	D	D	10.0	885	152	27	3 600	1.1
Grand	1.7	0.5	16.2	2.0	D	6.7	6.6	2.1	20.6	2 170	149	69	16 412	2.2
Gunnison	1.0	D	11.7	1.3	8.3	7.0	5.3	3.5	24.5	2 080	129	70	11 695	2.5
Hinsdale	2.3	D	19.7	2.1	D	D	D	D	26.9	230	299	0	1 409	1.5
Huerfano	0.7	D	10.2	2.2	4.1	9.9	2.3	D	25.1	2 285	354	275	5 162	1.7
Jackson	21.2	D	10.3	3.9	D	6.0	D	4.9	23.5	320	237	11	1 288	0.2
Jefferson	0.0	0.4	8.0	11.7	16.8	6.6	5.9	11.2	14.9	93 810	166	5 547	237 206	3.1
Kiowa	41.6	D	1.4	0.7	D	3.4	2.7	D	24.2	330	233	20	806	0.1
Kit Carson	16.2	D	5.2	4.5	2.9	4.8	6.3	3.5	18.4	1 475	179	103	3 500	-0.8
Lake	0.0	D	16.8	D	2.4	5.1	0.8	5.9	28.1	960	129	68	4 290	0.4
La Plata	0.0	6.6	10.9	1.8	10.6	5.8	7.4	11.6	18.6	9 175	168	401	27 113	4.8
Larimer	0.4	0.4	8.1	13.6	13.2	6.8	5.6	8.7	22.1	53 095	159	2 537	143 268	7.9
Las Animas	2.0	13.0	6.5	0.7	4.1	7.0	3.5	14.5	28.1	3 865	275	586	8 295	1.0
Lincoln	1.8	D	4.8	1.0	D	7.7	4.6	5.9	46.0	1 005	181	71	2 438	0.7
Logan	8.4	6.1	3.9	21.6	1.2	6.9	3.5	7.8	16.9	3 910	178	353	8 958	-0.3
Mesa	0.6	7.7	8.7	4.4	6.4	7.4	6.9	16.0	16.9	30 805	208	2 505	65 240	4.1
Mineral	2.7	D	8.3	D	D	D	D	D	16.3	260	359	0	1 239	3.2
Moffat	2.2	14.6	6.4	1.3	D	7.5	2.6	D	19.1	2 260	175	178	6 153	-0.7
Montezuma	0.9	5.1	13.2	3.3	4.1	9.3	3.4	14.1	25.4	6 215	238	456	12 012	-0.7
Montrose	3.0	0.9	8.6	8.0	5.9	9.4	5.0	12.2	23.3	10 260	251	609	18 474	1.2
Morgan	14.0	5.0	5.9	21.7	3.6	4.6	3.0	8.1	13.2	4 840	171	411	11 531	0.4
Otero	9.1	D	4.3	8.4	4.9	6.3	3.8	D	24.5	4 380	240	813	8 880	-1.0
Ouray	1.5	D	14.1	6.1	9.5	7.1	6.2	3.4	15.5	1 180	253	20	3 191	3.5
Park	-0.8	D	19.4	2.3	D	5.3	3.9	1.6	25.0	3 285	198	141	14 304	2.6
Phillips	12.1	D	6.0	1.9	3.6	4.3	D	D	25.7	875	202	48	2 098	0.5
Pitkin	0.1	D	5.9	0.8	10.2	6.2	12.9	3.2	14.3	2 455	138	21	13 206	2.0
Prowers	23.0	2.1	7.3	4.4	3.1	7.7	5.0	6.2	23.2	2 395	200	346	5 866	-1.3
Pueblo	0.2	0.2	8.0	9.4	6.4	8.1	3.4	20.5	21.5	35 720	219	6 254	70 281	1.1
Rio Blanco	3.6	29.7	10.9	1.8	1.5	2.5	2.0	0.9	29.7	1 060	162	33	3 357	1.4
Rio Grande	15.6	0.1	6.5	2.2	2.4	4.2	4.3	7.4	19.5	3 155	275	476	6 607	-0.3
Routt	1.0	5.1	10.3	D	11.5	6.8	10.9	10.0	11.1	3 165	130	77	16 548	1.5
Saguache	27.5	D	5.2	3.2	D	4.3	1.6	2.7	22.2	1 170	188	87	3 970	3.3
San Juan	0.0	2.1	D	D	D	12.8	D	D	19.1	155	223	0	759	0.4
San Miguel	0.5	D	13.4	3.2	10.6	5.0	10.8	3.2	12.7	905	115	27	6 773	2.0
Sedgwick	34.2	0.5	D	2.8	D	4.2	D	D	25.6	650	273	38	1 404	-0.8
Summit	0.1	D	11.9	D	8.3	9.1	10.6	7.9	12.2	2 860	96	28	30 714	2.9
Teller	-0.4	D	6.4	D	8.8	7.2	3.6	5.5	16.3	5 700	244	239	12 990	2.7
Washington	27.3	D	2.2	1.6	2.2	7.2	3.3	1.2	20.3	975	201	66	2 413	-0.9
Weld	5.6	11.0	14.8	11.5	4.0	5.9	5.0	6.9	11.1	39 210	138	3 410	105 474	9.5
Yuma	32.9	4.8	3.5	7.9	1.6	4.5	5.8	D	13.1	1 860	184	87	4 436	-0.7
CONNECTICUT	0.1	0.0	5.3	11.8	11.7	5.6	16.5	11.0	13.2	659 238	184	63 736	1 499 116	0.8
Fairfield	0.0	-0.1	4.1	12.1	13.5	5.5	23.5	8.0	7.1	148 805	158	12 213	367 985	1.9
Hartford	0.1	0.0	4.4	11.3	12.5	4.3	21.0	11.5	14.1	169 935	190	20 962	375 120	0.2
Litchfield	0.1	0.2	D	15.0	6.5	9.1	D	11.5	13.3	40 940	223	1 759	87 345	-0.2
Middlesex	0.2	D	9.9	15.9	8.5	6.7	4.7	14.0	17.3	34 095	208	1 627	75 530	0.9
New Haven	0.1	0.1	6.0	8.8	10.5	6.3	6.3	15.3	15.3	161 755	188	19 858	363 122	0.3
New London	0.5	0.0	5.2	18.1	7.7	6.0	3.0	11.3	27.8	54 575	202	4 176	121 923	0.8

1. Per 1,000 resident population estimated as of July 1 of the year shown.

Table B. States and Counties — Housing, Labor Force, and Employment

STATE County	Housing units, 2011–2015 Occupied units Total	Percent	Owner-occupied Median value[1]	Median owner cost as a percent of income With a mortgage	Without a mortgage[2]	Renter-occupied Median rent[3]	Median rent as a percent of income[2]	Sub-standard units[4] (percent)	Civilian labor force, 2016 Total	Percent change, 2015–2016	Unemployment Total	Rate[5]	Civilian employment,[6] 2011–2015 Total	Percent Management, business, science and arts	Construction, production, and maintenance occupations
	89	90	91	92	93	94	95	96	97	98	99	100	101	102	103
COLORADO—Cont'd															
Boulder	122 516	62.2	368 800	21.3	10.0	1 187	34.7	2.2	180 909	2.1	4 892	2.7	166 701	52.3	11.6
Broomfield	23 531	68.4	295 500	21.2	10.0	1 336	27.4	2.3	36 455	2.3	1 071	2.9	31 807	51.4	13.0
Chaffee	7 756	75.5	274 200	25.3	10.1	802	29.5	1.0	8 779	3.1	237	2.7	8 170	36.1	20.0
Cheyenne	743	75.2	82 300	23.8	10.0	636	17.7	1.9	1 068	5.4	25	2.3	932	38.8	30.4
Clear Creek	4 231	78.7	283 900	23.2	10.0	813	27.4	1.2	5 681	2.2	182	3.2	5 114	36.8	21.1
Conejos	2 948	79.4	107 100	24.4	10.0	498	29.7	3.4	3 783	4.8	186	4.9	3 021	29.6	30.5
Costilla	1 457	76.0	102 300	27.0	11.1	502	35.0	4.7	1 707	4.9	84	4.9	1 240	23.3	32.1
Crowley	1 169	80.5	76 100	25.8	13.6	595	31.6	3.6	1 385	2.1	50	3.6	1 457	24.4	24.1
Custer	1 996	79.7	220 400	31.8	10.0	726	33.8	4.0	1 993	0.0	63	3.2	1 390	24.2	30.7
Delta	12 058	71.3	193 000	25.9	11.9	829	32.4	3.6	13 868	2.9	696	5.0	11 362	32.2	28.3
Denver	275 795	49.4	271 300	22.1	10.0	962	29.5	3.7	384 331	2.0	12 103	3.1	348 382	44.6	15.5
Dolores	706	77.1	119 100	24.9	12.4	759	30.0	5.2	1 055	-20.5	42	4.0	801	30.5	23.1
Douglas	111 113	79.4	354 700	21.3	10.0	1 399	26.4	1.2	176 472	2.2	4 758	2.7	159 911	53.0	9.4
Eagle	17 840	67.1	419 400	26.7	11.1	1 272	29.6	4.0	33 651	2.5	935	2.8	31 793	34.6	18.6
Elbert	8 417	88.7	337 400	24.3	10.0	1 083	28.3	2.5	13 714	3.1	364	2.7	12 373	38.9	22.0
El Paso	245 287	62.5	218 300	22.8	10.0	976	30.4	2.8	314 872	2.1	11 924	3.8	290 448	40.5	16.5
Fremont	16 342	70.9	158 500	25.1	11.1	712	29.6	1.4	14 595	0.4	768	5.3	13 983	26.6	18.3
Garfield	20 622	64.6	287 500	28.6	10.6	1 140	31.2	6.3	30 819	0.9	1 097	3.6	29 078	30.4	28.8
Gilpin	2 576	76.7	252 800	26.6	10.0	1 029	27.4	3.8	3 471	1.9	85	2.4	3 159	40.5	19.7
Grand	5 250	72.7	282 000	24.8	10.1	1 024	24.5	3.5	9 105	0.3	248	2.7	8 274	33.9	27.5
Gunnison	6 287	59.3	319 200	26.7	10.1	903	32.6	3.9	10 088	2.8	233	2.3	9 016	33.3	23.9
Hinsdale	397	76.1	276 000	26.4	10.0	692	23.3	5.3	442	0.2	10	2.3	451	40.6	21.7
Huerfano	3 024	73.0	147 600	28.0	12.0	597	38.6	1.4	2 489	4.8	160	6.4	2 211	33.2	21.5
Jackson	616	67.9	158 000	25.0	10.0	721	27.0	0.3	885	5.9	24	2.7	764	32.7	37.7
Jefferson	222 892	69.9	279 500	21.9	10.0	1 052	29.6	1.6	316 062	2.1	9 443	3.0	294 390	44.0	15.6
Kiowa	583	75.8	83 600	20.2	12.0	582	19.4	1.9	858	8.2	18	2.1	723	40.5	23.0
Kit Carson	3 003	68.1	122 300	21.6	14.5	672	28.1	2.0	4 471	3.2	96	2.1	3 421	31.4	27.8
Lake	3 025	56.5	168 500	24.1	11.1	850	26.6	3.5	4 572	-0.2	132	2.9	4 126	27.2	28.7
La Plata	21 513	67.0	332 700	23.5	10.0	984	30.2	2.1	30 743	2.7	901	2.9	27 965	39.2	18.8
Larimer	125 138	64.1	263 400	22.3	10.0	1 035	34.0	1.8	187 235	3.4	5 306	2.8	164 011	42.6	16.7
Las Animas	5 826	68.8	150 600	25.6	10.2	755	29.9	1.4	6 155	0.1	317	5.2	5 903	28.3	28.7
Lincoln	1 677	65.8	118 300	23.2	13.5	705	30.3	0.8	2 268	4.3	59	2.6	1 488	34.3	15.8
Logan	7 966	66.2	124 700	19.6	11.6	673	28.6	2.4	10 992	0.3	334	3.0	10 407	25.4	26.7
Mesa	59 215	69.1	199 000	23.4	10.0	837	32.5	2.3	71 959	-0.1	3 882	5.4	67 956	32.4	24.6
Mineral	368	88.3	277 100	24.6	10.0	761	30.3	0.3	463	3.8	10	2.2	309	34.6	28.5
Moffat	4 986	69.9	175 800	22.5	11.0	721	28.4	2.5	7 156	0.4	289	4.0	6 343	23.4	32.3
Montezuma	10 417	70.4	180 400	24.8	10.0	775	29.4	4.2	12 638	2.1	636	5.0	11 075	34.1	22.0
Montrose	16 768	70.1	190 900	26.9	11.4	814	30.8	3.2	19 984	3.1	842	4.2	16 832	30.3	28.4
Morgan	10 421	64.7	145 500	22.4	11.3	726	26.5	4.8	14 975	1.8	530	3.5	13 264	24.0	36.4
Otero	7 454	63.8	91 900	22.0	12.2	655	33.3	3.2	8 124	2.8	388	4.8	7 314	32.6	21.0
Ouray	1 980	71.7	388 600	29.0	10.0	1 026	24.9	1.2	2 134	-1.2	82	3.8	2 261	48.0	17.5
Park	7 319	82.3	244 800	26.5	10.7	1 088	34.0	2.4	9 590	2.1	272	2.8	8 822	34.4	24.9
Phillips	1 711	70.3	132 500	21.1	12.4	589	23.1	5.6	2 488	5.3	51	2.0	1 984	35.0	27.6
Pitkin	7 570	65.2	620 700	28.4	13.2	1 278	27.0	2.4	10 837	0.7	367	3.4	10 290	40.4	11.0
Prowers	4 856	67.2	87 400	19.0	11.9	582	31.4	1.8	6 053	3.8	198	3.3	5 488	30.1	23.1
Pueblo	62 888	64.2	138 600	23.8	12.1	774	33.6	2.5	72 966	1.5	3 543	4.9	65 300	30.1	21.5
Rio Blanco	2 482	66.7	204 800	18.8	10.0	764	19.4	3.7	2 723	-3.2	140	5.1	3 389	27.8	34.9
Rio Grande	4 617	66.7	133 700	21.5	11.8	575	22.7	3.6	5 147	5.5	260	5.1	5 093	29.0	28.1
Routt	9 431	69.1	394 600	27.4	10.0	1 137	31.5	1.8	14 802	3.4	395	2.7	14 060	33.0	19.7
Saguache	2 598	69.8	146 700	26.7	11.3	663	29.4	5.8	3 210	4.0	158	4.9	2 452	30.8	39.4
San Juan	282	64.5	223 200	34.9	12.2	886	33.2	3.2	474	0.6	18	3.8	337	28.8	25.2
San Miguel	3 310	60.5	512 800	33.4	12.1	1 143	32.2	4.7	5 136	1.0	170	3.3	4 482	37.1	20.7
Sedgwick	951	74.1	86 800	20.2	10.0	543	23.6	2.2	1 174	2.2	28	2.4	1 028	34.4	26.4
Summit	10 143	66.3	478 800	28.5	10.0	1 200	28.9	4.8	21 068	2.2	445	2.1	18 171	32.0	21.6
Teller	9 581	80.7	239 000	23.2	10.0	985	34.0	1.9	11 655	1.9	441	3.8	11 501	38.6	18.6
Washington	1 963	73.9	113 200	19.8	11.3	617	22.1	1.9	2 900	3.9	63	2.2	2 196	35.5	31.3
Weld	94 294	69.4	210 100	22.7	10.0	904	30.4	3.7	149 365	0.8	5 135	3.4	129 395	33.1	26.8
Yuma	3 865	62.9	136 400	23.1	10.0	639	27.5	2.7	5 448	5.9	119	2.2	4 878	28.2	34.6
CONNECTICUT	1 352 583	67.0	270 500	24.6	16.2	1 075	31.7	2.2	1 891 790	0.1	96 272	5.1	1 781 417	41.7	17.0
Fairfield	334 320	68.3	416 000	25.8	17.8	1 348	32.5	3.0	482 418	0.4	23 180	4.8	463 610	44.1	14.5
Hartford	346 362	64.7	236 400	23.7	15.4	992	30.4	2.3	473 144	0.0	25 304	5.3	439 719	42.6	16.5
Litchfield	74 518	77.0	254 600	24.9	15.9	955	29.4	1.1	104 907	-0.3	4 866	4.6	98 294	40.1	20.5
Middlesex	66 117	75.1	285 100	23.7	15.5	1 095	29.5	0.9	92 081	0.2	4 030	4.4	87 871	45.7	16.0
New Haven	326 028	62.8	245 200	25.3	17.3	1 061	33.9	2.1	454 896	-0.1	24 872	5.5	419 901	40.0	18.3
New London	106 495	66.5	244 000	24.0	14.3	1 022	30.1	1.6	136 592	0.0	6 878	5.0	132 990	38.4	16.9

1. Specified owner-occupied units. 2. A value of 10.0 represents 10 percent or less; a value of 50.0 represents 50 percent or more. 3. Specified renter-occupied units.
4. Overcrowded or lacking complete plumbing facilities. 5. Percent of civilian labor force. 6. Civilian employed persons 16 years old and over.

Table B. States and Counties — Nonfarm Employment and Agriculture

| STATE County | Private nonfarm establishments, employment and payroll, 2015 | | | | | | | | | Agriculture, 2012 | | | |
| | Number of establishments | Employment | | | | | | Annual payroll | | Farms | | Percent with: | |
		Total	Health care and social assistance	Manufacturing	Retail trade	Finance and insurance	Professional, scientific, and technical services	Total (mil dol)	Average per employee (dollars)	Number	Fewer than 50 acres	500 acres or more	Farm operators whose principal occupation is farming (percent)
	104	105	106	107	108	109	110	111	112	113	114	115	116
COLORADO—Cont'd													
Boulder	12 073	150 110	19 934	13 645	17 570	3 544	29 655	9 668	64 407	855	72.0	4.3	44.9
Broomfield	1 938	41 171	2 042	2 840	4 837	3 669	4 183	2 678	65 049	25	60.0	20.0	44.0
Chaffee	888	5 631	839	152	1 057	235	241	183	32 531	223	33.2	17.0	52.9
Cheyenne	64	723	D	D	59	D	4	35	48 645	345	5.5	70.4	67.5
Clear Creek	335	2 640	99	42	287	16	74	109	41 408	25	60.0	12.0	24.0
Conejos	111	696	221	32	182	D	25	25	35 819	605	26.1	19.8	47.4
Costilla	41	253	40	D	48	D	NA	6	24 071	251	34.3	15.1	65.3
Crowley	32	497	79	NA	85	13	D	17	34 223	228	11.8	50.4	58.3
Custer	138	552	28	39	152	13	27	17	29 982	198	20.7	27.8	47.0
Delta	833	6 764	1 518	424	1 251	255	158	209	30 914	1 250	58.9	5.9	56.4
Denver	24 292	430 587	53 482	16 850	31 552	25 604	42 577	25 927	60 213	10	100.0	0.0	40.0
Dolores	49	213	36	D	34	D	D	8	35 291	283	21.9	27.2	48.8
Douglas	8 677	108 115	11 599	7 553	19 330	7 415	8 981	6 566	60 736	1 116	64.3	6.3	51.1
Eagle	3 356	31 734	2 213	308	4 143	798	1 318	1 169	36 850	165	38.2	21.2	41.2
Elbert	592	2 603	141	117	448	70	204	93	35 618	1 330	32.6	21.3	42.3
El Paso	16 522	226 876	35 772	11 380	31 386	10 409	20 219	9 974	43 964	1 206	45.4	17.2	49.5
Fremont	834	7 612	2 024	339	1 696	230	167	227	29 827	809	68.0	12.0	40.8
Garfield	2 413	19 633	2 694	254	3 195	675	1 008	924	47 076	625	52.2	13.8	48.3
Gilpin	120	4 809	44	33	19	D	34	184	38 207	24	33.3	4.2	45.8
Grand	815	8 068	356	173	660	98	837	242	30 052	205	29.3	30.7	52.2
Gunnison	1 083	6 375	527	87	956	138	352	203	31 813	244	32.4	20.9	47.5
Hinsdale	71	147	D	NA	30	D	D	4	30 293	26	3.8	30.8	38.5
Huerfano	146	1 079	434	D	195	21	51	32	29 580	407	22.9	34.6	54.8
Jackson	67	260	7	D	54	D	13	9	31 200	105	14.3	63.8	63.8
Jefferson	16 826	184 909	27 566	8 783	29 373	9 125	20 154	8 490	45 912	521	72.6	5.6	41.8
Kiowa	36	217	D	D	35	D	D	7	34 327	395	2.5	64.8	58.0
Kit Carson	274	2 119	243	192	321	115	38	68	32 310	704	8.9	57.4	55.5
Lake	211	1 202	124	D	166	23	28	31	25 644	23	17.4	30.4	52.2
La Plata	2 341	20 961	3 100	574	3 429	525	1 184	854	40 751	1 124	44.3	11.3	45.7
Larimer	10 291	120 470	18 944	11 520	18 928	3 769	10 001	5 575	46 274	1 625	60.7	8.5	46.5
Las Animas	373	3 324	764	17	640	124	91	106	31 980	602	17.6	49.5	47.3
Lincoln	133	1 272	272	D	314	69	30	44	34 895	464	8.2	69.8	57.3
Logan	577	5 492	1 000	338	1 190	193	97	180	32 798	891	12.3	47.3	53.6
Mesa	4 404	51 843	9 843	2 576	8 451	1 918	2 379	2 057	39 669	2 264	75.4	5.4	48.6
Mineral	66	201	D	D	50	D	6	8	39 512	14	21.4	14.3	57.1
Moffat	412	3 382	497	54	719	88	89	150	44 446	492	29.1	31.9	37.2
Montezuma	750	6 716	1 384	294	1 263	158	290	243	36 210	1 138	49.4	9.6	45.3
Montrose	1 264	11 965	2 673	1 246	2 197	312	604	426	35 639	1 128	52.7	10.6	48.4
Morgan	669	9 342	1 244	2 809	1 062	246	176	349	37 403	754	20.2	34.9	56.5
Otero	417	4 166	1 194	499	698	165	107	129	31 060	541	29.6	25.0	48.6
Ouray	264	1 055	39	65	161	54	78	34	32 437	108	38.0	15.7	73.1
Park	448	1 378	120	84	224	21	89	45	32 556	209	23.4	26.3	41.6
Phillips	139	1 108	316	24	196	52	17	38	34 042	319	11.0	60.5	69.0
Pitkin	1 595	17 141	761	141	1 482	254	673	667	38 935	82	36.6	18.3	46.3
Prowers	350	2 917	660	185	717	183	87	89	30 499	553	19.5	46.5	52.8
Pueblo	3 020	48 828	12 944	4 370	7 954	1 151	1 999	1 827	37 423	894	38.9	21.3	52.3
Rio Blanco	222	1 920	213	D	216	45	35	117	60 914	313	31.0	36.7	53.7
Rio Grande	322	2 536	467	79	401	93	72	79	31 186	377	27.1	24.9	54.1
Routt	1 626	15 589	1 436	107	1 707	238	563	637	40 884	799	43.7	20.9	41.3
Saguache	123	845	79	89	134	D	10	26	30 275	277	14.1	44.4	59.6
San Juan	73	180	24	D	27	NA	3	5	26 806	0	0.0	0.0	0.0
San Miguel	608	4 700	142	118	489	71	182	149	31 760	135	40.0	23.7	48.9
Sedgwick	72	465	D	29	86	24	8	15	31 572	226	13.7	51.3	72.1
Summit	2 205	20 489	1 022	194	3 450	228	642	602	29 396	38	26.3	21.1	26.3
Teller	699	5 415	420	62	837	154	259	189	34 889	123	45.5	21.1	39.0
Washington	112	514	44	82	88	37	18	18	35 021	824	11.5	47.7	48.4
Weld	5 830	85 157	8 443	13 025	9 914	3 289	2 736	4 019	47 195	3 525	35.5	19.6	49.8
Yuma	378	2 580	605	80	487	149	91	95	36 757	834	12.8	56.7	61.4
CONNECTICUT	89 232	1 503 102	277 966	149 359	184 465	122 420	108 017	92 555	61 576	5 977	69.8	1.8	46.3
Fairfield	27 190	421 295	65 971	33 818	49 732	47 425	36 802	35 200	83 551	439	82.2	1.6	57.9
Hartford	22 703	440 169	83 846	45 436	49 775	51 705	27 493	26 352	59 867	899	71.2	1.3	49.6
Litchfield	4 806	51 957	9 636	8 684	8 759	1 370	1 704	2 180	41 963	1 207	67.9	2.5	41.5
Middlesex	4 202	60 899	13 953	9 326	8 870	1 741	2 741	2 923	47 995	518	78.2	1.2	48.6
New Haven	19 566	335 845	73 797	30 833	42 242	12 252	15 056	16 945	50 455	695	77.3	1.2	43.0
New London	5 805	102 909	17 185	12 546	14 605	2 111	7 863	5 096	49 524	949	64.0	1.3	48.6

STATE County	Acreage (1,000) [117]	Percent change, 2007–2012 [118]	Average size of farm [119]	Total irrigated (1,000) [120]	Total cropland (1,000) [121]	Average per farm [122]	Average per acre [123]	Value of machinery and equipment, average per farm (dollars) [124]	Total (mil dol) [125]	Average per farm (dollars) [126]	Crops [127]	Live-stock and poultry products [128]	$10,000 or more [129]	$100,000 or more [130]	Total ($1,000) [131]	Percent of farms [132]
COLORADO—Cont'd																
Boulder	133	-3.4	155	30.1	39.2	888 591	5 715	49 384	33.9	39 629	D	D	22.8	5.8	474	12.0
Broomfield	11	78.5	446	1.1	11.1	874 920	1 960	90 840	1.5	61 480	90.9	9.1	28.0	20.0	37	24.0
Chaffee	78	-2.2	348	13.5	15.9	1 053 157	3 024	75 278	9.6	43 130	30.5	69.5	30.9	9.9	74	7.6
Cheyenne	977	8.6	2 832	26.6	536.6	2 203 649	778	216 333	87.1	252 417	68.1	31.9	64.3	40.6	6 203	78.3
Clear Creek	8	-33.4	332	D	0.3	910 680	2 744	41 080	0.3	13 720	D	D	32.0	0.0	0	0.0
Conejos	258	12.7	426	100.1	112.6	646 739	1 518	97 661	42.7	70 650	61.8	38.2	47.8	16.0	1 240	28.9
Costilla	376	-6.2	1 499	34.3	49.9	1 646 637	1 099	126 490	29.0	115 398	84.7	15.3	39.8	11.2	475	28.3
Crowley	500	10.8	2 193	5.9	45.3	750 031	342	73 939	161.5	708 268	1.0	99.0	47.4	23.2	2 044	61.4
Custer	189	37.0	953	12.3	20.3	1 451 495	1 523	76 455	8.2	41 379	27.2	72.8	38.9	13.1	301	23.7
Delta	251	-0.7	201	59.2	60.7	665 865	3 319	63 422	55.6	44 511	42.4	57.6	36.3	8.2	728	9.5
Denver	0	-76.5	14	0.0	0.0	775 500	54 231	93 200	D	D	D	D	60.0	20.0	0	0.0
Dolores	160	-8.0	565	7.4	73.1	815 583	1 443	71 901	10.1	35 629	62.9	37.1	28.6	9.9	1 153	63.3
Douglas	200	5.7	179	1.7	23.3	900 148	5 022	53 598	13.7	12 234	33.5	66.5	19.5	1.3	502	4.4
Eagle	129	4.4	785	12.7	14.9	3 090 273	3 939	91 448	7.9	48 109	42.2	57.8	30.9	8.5	68	4.8
Elbert	1 043	-8.0	784	8.4	180.5	879 390	1 121	60 820	45.0	33 805	19.9	80.1	28.9	8.1	2 328	17.4
El Paso	649	5.3	538	7.9	53.7	650 029	1 208	45 053	43.9	36 403	47.1	52.9	24.5	5.1	1 232	10.3
Fremont	290	-1.8	359	8.4	17.7	839 582	2 339	42 611	21.2	26 214	20.2	79.8	19.0	2.8	313	7.0
Garfield	311	-7.3	497	32.3	46.2	1 380 994	2 777	72 635	22.7	36 272	24.9	75.1	30.2	8.8	604	12.6
Gilpin	6	-56.7	240	D	0.4	679 792	2 832	30 250	0.2	6 875	D	D	25.0	0.0	D	20.8
Grand	227	8.8	1 107	27.5	34.9	2 530 395	2 286	94 561	13.5	65 883	15.6	84.4	40.5	13.2	91	6.8
Gunnison	190	9.5	780	42.2	41.6	2 197 246	2 818	95 365	13.0	53 221	13.8	86.2	37.7	13.5	52	4.9
Hinsdale	10	73.5	394	2.4	1.1	2 083 538	5 293	91 308	0.7	27 385	15.4	84.6	38.5	3.8	0	0.0
Huerfano	581	12.0	1 427	11.7	25.1	1 233 226	864	48 887	11.3	27 656	13.1	86.9	26.8	4.7	675	13.0
Jackson	342	-11.5	3 261	59.6	65.5	3 397 571	1 042	187 457	23.6	224 771	19.8	80.1	61.9	35.2	34	11.4
Jefferson	68	-26.8	131	2.3	10.1	719 981	5 493	39 426	9.1	17 465	81.0	19.0	15.7	3.5	41	4.0
Kiowa	1 113	16.2	2 818	3.1	713.3	1 924 033	683	177 504	96.1	243 205	38.5	61.5	54.4	28.6	7 743	86.8
Kit Carson	1 377	1.8	1 956	110.2	872.3	2 214 455	1 132	320 912	499.8	709 908	28.1	71.9	58.8	37.5	12 129	75.6
Lake	12	-17.9	530	3.6	0.8	1 544 261	2 916	26 957	0.9	37 478	8.9	91.0	43.5	13.0	0	0.0
La Plata	590	3.6	525	61.7	85.9	975 981	1 858	66 034	25.0	22 234	33.4	66.6	29.5	4.3	752	9.8
Larimer	450	-8.0	277	52.5	106.4	854 599	3 083	72 401	128.6	79 167	44.6	55.4	28.8	7.6	1 061	11.2
Las Animas	2 141	-1.8	3 556	11.3	71.1	1 441 724	405	60 860	28.4	47 228	11.1	88.9	39.4	14.1	3 371	28.1
Lincoln	1 473	5.2	3 175	4.8	581.6	1 514 664	477	163 039	75.6	162 860	53.5	46.5	61.6	33.4	7 741	70.0
Logan	1 099	-2.9	1 234	94.0	516.0	1 071 964	869	167 899	566.9	636 255	20.8	79.2	63.0	34.9	9 526	76.1
Mesa	387	3.9	171	75.3	71.4	575 360	3 367	51 431	84.6	37 360	48.1	51.9	25.7	6.1	821	7.1
Mineral	7	-25.2	473	D	0.5	2 055 643	4 342	34 286	0.1	34 857	16.9	83.1	14.3	0.0	0	0.0
Moffat	930	11.2	1 890	23.5	119.6	1 380 283	730	77 575	27.0	54 866	13.0	87.0	28.9	10.6	1 866	33.9
Montezuma	691	-1.9	607	62.6	97.4	672 749	1 108	67 594	46.4	40 748	64.7	35.3	30.8	6.6	1 387	15.6
Montrose	330	2.7	292	70.4	70.0	838 902	2 871	74 786	103.2	91 508	32.6	67.4	39.5	12.9	930	17.7
Morgan	647	-11.1	858	100.9	303.6	1 224 219	1 426	198 156	615.3	816 073	17.3	82.7	59.7	32.9	6 315	66.7
Otero	707	13.2	1 306	43.6	74.3	852 516	653	124 166	144.2	266 608	20.8	79.2	53.6	22.7	2 473	54.5
Ouray	81	-13.3	753	9.8	10.1	2 138 602	2 840	88 769	4.3	39 574	16.5	83.5	40.7	13.0	24	6.5
Park	180	-44.4	861	3.8	10.2	1 146 282	1 331	64 617	7.7	37 057	9.2	90.8	22.5	2.9	140	7.7
Phillips	436	1.2	1 368	72.9	370.8	2 477 361	1 810	329 323	208.0	652 056	56.5	43.5	70.5	51.7	6 831	82.8
Pitkin	32	12.5	391	7.5	4.8	2 190 561	5 597	95 427	3.0	36 122	13.3	86.7	28.0	7.3	149	12.2
Prowers	1 022	-1.5	1 848	79.9	480.5	1 270 078	687	180 617	318.2	575 496	20.4	79.6	53.2	27.8	6 892	62.6
Pueblo	895	-1.7	1 001	18.6	88.5	735 098	734	62 169	51.1	57 149	35.4	64.6	27.2	8.1	2 223	20.6
Rio Blanco	507	31.2	1 621	25.6	42.7	2 154 358	1 329	101 540	24.4	77 994	16.2	83.8	39.3	18.8	786	15.0
Rio Grande	185	3.7	492	93.6	105.4	1 163 151	2 364	237 934	106.5	282 470	88.9	11.1	57.8	37.7	1 003	29.2
Routt	613	14.9	767	46.6	117.3	1 700 572	2 218	75 899	46.5	58 148	16.8	83.2	29.8	10.1	847	14.1
Saguache	311	8.4	1 124	90.5	115.3	1 670 177	1 486	284 354	110.0	397 069	84.2	15.8	54.5	32.9	1 298	31.0
San Juan	0	0.0	0	0.0	0.0	0	0	0	0.0	0	0.0	0.0	0.0	0.0	0	0.0
San Miguel	127	-16.2	937	12.7	14.6	1 366 578	1 458	66 570	4.7	35 089	11.3	88.7	30.4	9.6	209	14.8
Sedgwick	336	13.2	1 487	38.1	207.2	1 889 363	1 271	249 558	101.3	448 066	56.8	43.2	70.8	46.0	3 427	80.5
Summit	25	-47.0	668	4.2	5.8	2 218 579	3 324	63 553	D	D	D	D	23.7	10.5	D	2.6
Teller	71	-3.2	577	0.4	3.4	1 156 211	2 006	33 358	1.3	10 195	12.6	87.4	17.9	2.4	102	8.9
Washington	1 216	-11.6	1 476	47.0	699.7	1 441 458	977	177 691	220.7	267 856	44.6	55.4	54.0	29.2	11 607	76.5
Weld	1 956	-6.3	555	299.9	850.2	1 098 289	1 979	146 652	1 860.7	527 863	20.1	79.9	42.8	20.2	15 649	39.7
Yuma	1 353	1.4	1 623	233.0	607.2	2 223 818	1 370	298 933	1 150.3	1 379 309	27.1	72.9	60.0	43.5	12 866	73.5
CONNECTICUT	437	7.6	73	9.3	151.1	809 375	11 082	58 958	550.6	92 123	70.7	29.3	30.0	7.7	4 841	8.7
Fairfield	54	36.4	123	0.3	5.0	1 492 513	12 145	68 132	34.8	79 317	60.1	39.9	35.3	7.5	160	5.5
Hartford	54	1.0	60	4.9	25.7	760 429	12 645	63 402	113.9	126 692	94.1	5.9	36.9	12.0	583	8.8
Litchfield	91	4.1	75	0.4	37.2	859 063	11 399	52 797	46.3	38 344	60.5	39.5	26.3	5.3	1 209	10.8
Middlesex	24	44.8	46	0.6	7.7	654 002	14 074	59 284	53.5	103 257	94.5	5.5	27.0	4.6	167	5.4
New Haven	42	-7.4	61	1.3	14.1	764 679	12 561	56 881	84.6	121 755	91.7	8.3	31.9	10.1	383	7.3
New London	65	2.8	69	0.8	22.8	709 299	10 330	47 891	118.3	124 690	43.2	56.8	26.9	6.7	537	9.2

Table B. States and Counties — **Water Use, Wholesale Trade, Retail Trade, and Real Estate**

STATE County	Water use, 2010		Wholesale trade,[1] 2012				Retail trade,[2] 2012				Real estate and rental and leasing,[2] 2012			
	Total water withdrawn (mil gal/day)	Gallons withdrawn per person per day	Number of establish-ments	Number of employees	Sales (mil dol)	Annual payroll (mil dol)	Number of establish-ments	Number of employees	Sales (mil dol)	Annual payroll (mil dol)	Number of establish-ments	Number of employees	Receipts (mil dol)	Annual payroll (mil dol)
	133	134	135	136	137	138	139	140	141	142	143	144	145	146
COLORADO—Cont'd														
Boulder	231.6	786	392	D	D	D	1 174	16 623	4 498.3	478.9	648	1 954	434.3	74.5
Broomfield	6.4	115	52	D	D	D	261	4 606	1 000.2	101.7	96	313	77.1	11.4
Chaffee	101.9	5 719	19	95	41.4	2.9	134	1 049	249.3	25.4	78	132	17.4	3.2
Cheyenne	37.9	20 632	3	D	D	D	13	73	18.5	1.3	2	D	D	D
Clear Creek	1.8	200	12	D	D	D	46	265	75.3	5.1	17	24	3.1	0.6
Conejos	382.5	46 330	4	19	4.6	0.9	18	203	35.9	4.3	4	11	0.4	0.1
Costilla	139.9	39 702	1	D	D	D	10	33	11.7	0.6	NA	NA	NA	NA
Crowley	13.7	2 358	1	D	D	D	8	89	17.0	2.3	1	D	D	D
Custer	27.2	6 402	3	2	0.4	0.0	25	164	48.6	3.4	10	9	1.9	0.3
Delta	359.5	11 615	28	174	47.2	6.7	116	1 158	309.8	27.6	36	254	16.5	4.6
Denver	150.5	251	1 175	17 997	14 625.8	1 090.1	2 282	26 469	7 111.4	725.7	1 451	9 373	2 723.8	488.3
Dolores	5.6	2 708	5	D	D	D	5	39	10.0	0.7	NA	NA	NA	NA
Douglas	51.6	181	241	2 398	2 701.7	205.2	851	15 688	4 308.8	398.1	476	1 154	283.5	48.3
Eagle	137.9	2 642	68	D	D	D	455	3 621	806.0	102.1	362	1 880	280.9	63.5
Elbert	13.8	598	14	D	D	D	38	406	105.7	8.7	16	19	3.7	0.7
El Paso	116.1	187	430	4 395	2 563.3	247.4	1 955	28 743	7 929.3	757.3	1 031	3 344	657.4	119.9
Fremont	146.2	3 123	27	D	D	D	130	1 594	334.9	34.9	39	159	15.9	3.2
Garfield	261.5	4 637	62	D	D	D	285	2 982	950.0	92.1	158	794	213.2	38.1
Gilpin	3.4	618	2	D	D	D	8	20	6.4	0.6	4	7	0.5	0.2
Grand	186.5	12 567	7	17	4.7	0.5	107	628	156.1	15.7	68	583	45.0	13.3
Gunnison	562.7	36 723	9	15	3.5	0.4	133	907	190.0	20.4	89	189	23.8	5.2
Hinsdale	30.4	36 074	NA	NA	NA	NA	17	27	9.0	0.9	4	3	1.2	0.1
Huerfano	38.3	5 701	4	D	D	D	31	215	62.9	4.7	7	15	2.3	0.3
Jackson	347.9	249 541	2	D	D	D	10	63	16.5	1.6	NA	NA	NA	NA
Jefferson	78.3	146	529	4 575	3 082.1	289.5	1 866	28 060	7 465.0	724.2	866	2 800	527.7	113.3
Kiowa	5.6	3 977	8	30	20.1	0.8	6	35	10.2	0.6	NA	NA	NA	NA
Kit Carson	130.5	15 780	20	184	271.9	8.5	41	312	115.0	7.6	7	24	2.9	0.7
Lake	14.7	2 005	4	D	D	D	30	199	37.4	4.5	13	51	2.9	0.9
La Plata	336.6	6 558	55	508	222.3	22.8	314	3 128	756.9	83.4	139	454	69.9	14.9
Larimer	412.9	1 378	295	4 294	5 143.6	368.5	1 244	17 307	4 341.3	414.2	526	2 112	307.0	71.4
Las Animas	73.7	4 755	9	D	D	D	60	679	178.9	16.7	22	66	8.6	2.5
Lincoln	4.5	821	1	D	D	D	31	330	183.9	7.1	3	5	0.3	0.0
Logan	164.4	7 239	24	D	D	D	100	1 124	320.0	26.3	15	40	7.1	1.3
Mesa	754.7	5 144	219	2 076	876.5	96.2	604	7 966	2 173.3	202.6	263	889	170.7	33.7
Mineral	18.5	25 955	NA	NA	NA	NA	13	60	13.5	1.4	3	3	0.4	0.1
Moffat	170.1	12 332	23	D	D	D	72	714	201.9	21.3	9	13	3.3	0.3
Montezuma	255.1	9 989	19	164	72.6	7.2	99	1 159	349.9	32.3	29	91	20.4	3.2
Montrose	702.9	17 028	47	313	156.2	11.7	180	2 152	583.8	55.9	53	125	18.0	3.6
Morgan	186.0	6 606	32	D	D	D	92	953	256.9	21.8	26	49	5.5	1.2
Otero	436.8	23 195	24	158	94.8	5.5	75	775	213.8	17.1	14	82	8.2	1.8
Ouray	111.0	25 020	1	D	D	D	38	145	22.6	2.5	9	16	1.8	0.5
Park	24.4	1 506	10	D	D	D	40	170	49.7	4.1	22	26	5.2	1.1
Phillips	58.9	13 267	10	D	D	D	21	158	46.1	4.0	3	3	0.1	0.2
Pitkin	123.4	7 194	11	D	D	D	235	1 504	344.4	46.4	203	959	167.3	38.7
Prowers	152.3	12 131	16	115	97.5	4.0	56	656	162.3	13.1	15	D	D	D
Pueblo	288.9	1 816	85	D	D	D	508	7 551	1 952.8	183.4	143	585	105.1	17.7
Rio Blanco	267.2	40 078	4	D	D	D	35	246	54.8	4.6	9	24	7.0	1.6
Rio Grande	579.2	48 339	25	313	238.4	13.2	48	369	99.8	9.5	18	52	4.8	1.2
Routt	204.0	8 678	35	250	131.2	12.7	215	1 616	360.9	41.4	131	530	57.0	14.3
Saguache	270.9	44 355	10	265	108.1	9.8	16	118	23.3	2.1	1	D	D	D
San Juan	1.6	2 232	NA	NA	NA	NA	14	29	6.8	0.6	2	D	D	D
San Miguel	37.9	5 156	5	15	4.0	0.9	72	478	79.7	10.5	78	196	32.5	7.1
Sedgwick	61.4	25 818	4	27	20.6	1.1	13	92	28.1	2.1	1	D	D	D
Summit	68.7	2 454	30	D	D	D	346	3 041	627.2	68.0	245	932	117.6	26.3
Teller	7.6	325	12	36	13.3	1.2	70	762	207.8	17.6	43	83	11.7	2.3
Washington	73.4	15 247	7	62	209.8	4.7	14	89	31.6	1.9	1	D	D	D
Weld	462.1	1 828	246	3 166	5 349.2	157.4	620	8 154	2 707.6	228.7	212	870	149.0	31.5
Yuma	220.8	21 986	29	215	855.5	10.0	63	456	125.6	9.6	12	17	1.9	0.4
CONNECTICUT	3 311.0	926	3 675	58 814	161 962.2	3 934.4	12 597	182 528	51 632.5	4 974.5	3 219	19 778	5 349.5	958.4
Fairfield	494.3	539	1 190	18 611	130 674.8	1 622.4	3 459	49 401	15 166.5	1 553.9	1 077	6 971	1 808.6	418.1
Hartford	200.7	225	970	19 033	15 797.2	1 086.7	3 134	49 862	13 762.4	1 257.3	868	5 027	1 087.0	230.9
Litchfield	68.4	360	162	D	D	D	692	8 669	2 655.0	241.2	137	388	60.3	13.6
Middlesex	133.6	807	167	2 288	1 537.6	146.7	659	8 548	2 202.6	215.5	124	809	126.4	30.3
New Haven	113.5	132	922	14 185	11 237.2	821.2	2 901	41 925	11 567.5	1 100.7	673	5 378	2 008.0	220.2
New London	2 249.8	8 209	150	D	D	D	1 023	14 372	3 679.3	364.3	204	765	182.6	32.0

1. Merchant wholesalers, except manufacturers' sales branches and offices.   2. Employer establishments.

Table B. States and Counties — Professional Services, Manufacturing, and Accommodation and Food Services

STATE County	Professional, scientific, and technical services, 2012				Manufacturing, 2012				Accommodation and food services, 2012			
	Number of establishments	Number of employees	Receipts (mil dol)	Annual payroll (mil dol)	Number of establishments	Number of employees	Receipts (mil dol)	Annual payroll (mil dol)	Number of establishments	Number of employees	Sales (mil dol)	Annual payroll (mil dol)
	147	148	149	150	151	152	153	154	155	156	157	158
COLORADO—Cont'd												
Boulder	2 679	27 395	4 767.9	2 011.5	536	14 305	5 061.5	998.4	866	15 855	842.2	252.2
Broomfield	325	6 060	1 252.4	496.8	82	3 087	3 918.4	188.5	143	2 944	169.6	54.7
Chaffee	96	223	24.1	7.6	29	199	25.3	6.0	108	1 172	58.9	19.7
Cheyenne	4	5	0.3	0.1	NA	NA	NA	NA	4	28	1.1	0.2
Clear Creek	48	78	11.7	3.9	8	D	D	D	42	540	30.3	8.8
Conejos	5	9	0.8	0.2	5	53	D	2.6	11	38	3.9	1.0
Costilla	NA	NA	NA	NA	NA	NA	NA	NA	6	D	D	D
Crowley	3	D	D	D	NA	NA	NA	NA	3	12	0.8	0.0
Custer	16	21	3.8	0.8	7	32	D	1.3	12	56	3.2	0.7
Delta	76	D	D	D	50	619	168.1	27.4	76	623	27.2	8.0
Denver	4 291	42 123	9 140.6	3 409.8	759	17 032	5 343.9	761.4	1 982	42 906	2 884.9	823.2
Dolores	4	2	0.3	0.1	NA	NA	NA	NA	8	39	2.5	1.0
Douglas	1 623	10 273	2 561.7	798.6	133	2 169	460.4	119.3	522	10 295	541.8	167.0
Eagle	401	1 289	183.9	65.7	50	238	73.8	11.2	259	7 998	477.8	175.3
Elbert	87	176	22.0	8.5	21	143	D	6.5	26	190	9.3	2.5
El Paso	2 417	19 740	2 983.8	1 258.0	465	10 425	3 375.9	560.5	1 300	26 734	1 443.2	389.2
Fremont	64	178	14.1	4.3	34	409	116.8	20.5	85	878	39.2	11.2
Garfield	300	1 004	137.6	55.1	46	246	41.1	9.4	201	2 727	161.3	49.1
Gilpin	23	34	5.7	1.8	4	D	D	D	10	2 408	404.7	81.0
Grand	81	247	75.4	42.1	14	136	18.6	3.7	136	1 826	84.3	29.4
Gunnison	125	312	28.7	10.0	25	80	9.5	2.2	121	1 339	87.0	16.1
Hinsdale	1	D	D	D	NA	NA	NA	NA	17	75	4.1	1.3
Huerfano	14	35	2.7	1.2	3	26	D	1.4	26	172	9.0	2.4
Jackson	5	10	0.6	0.1	NA	NA	NA	NA	11	51	2.9	0.7
Jefferson	2 985	23 587	4 908.0	1 823.0	448	12 913	6 119.0	907.3	1 160	20 616	1 069.2	318.1
Kiowa	2	D	D	D	NA	NA	NA	NA	2	D	D	D
Kit Carson	18	41	3.8	1.2	8	165	D	4.6	23	261	12.8	3.4
Lake	11	40	3.6	1.6	4	36	D	D	37	268	13.1	3.7
La Plata	326	1 100	139.8	55.3	57	518	84.9	21.1	206	4 226	209.2	68.4
Larimer	1 493	8 727	1 031.1	450.9	403	10 163	4 275.7	642.6	847	14 821	756.5	218.0
Las Animas	24	93	7.2	2.8	6	56	9.0	2.6	50	656	30.9	8.4
Lincoln	10	25	2.2	0.6	NA	NA	NA	NA	19	222	9.6	2.3
Logan	30	101	10.9	3.4	20	308	213.0	11.9	46	595	26.2	7.5
Mesa	561	2 529	289.0	119.8	159	2 388	520.6	95.1	300	6 052	282.6	88.8
Mineral	3	4	0.3	0.1	NA	NA	NA	NA	19	66	7.9	2.5
Moffat	31	129	10.1	4.0	11	50	D	1.6	33	454	20.7	5.9
Montezuma	80	281	30.1	11.8	32	264	49.9	9.2	85	1 263	83.2	22.8
Montrose	110	438	46.3	20.6	66	1 167	210.7	39.2	78	1 007	49.6	15.4
Morgan	36	120	10.4	3.1	42	3 147	2 444.1	105.4	57	693	29.5	8.4
Otero	32	105	7.3	2.4	15	465	75.9	18.2	52	603	22.9	6.4
Ouray	47	78	10.4	3.7	11	36	4.9	1.2	47	280	21.5	6.3
Park	57	86	10.2	3.3	15	55	D	1.7	40	230	18.4	3.8
Phillips	10	18	2.2	0.5	3	16	4.1	0.7	15	76	2.6	0.8
Pitkin	224	636	154.3	43.7	17	104	16.7	4.5	160	5 089	305.3	118.2
Prowers	28	95	11.2	3.5	14	150	31.5	5.4	35	414	17.6	4.2
Pueblo	238	1 744	435.3	157.3	90	4 221	2 333.3	216.8	356	5 698	236.0	67.8
Rio Blanco	15	51	4.8	1.6	3	10	D	D	30	200	11.5	3.1
Rio Grande	28	72	6.1	2.1	10	59	10.5	2.4	32	278	12.8	3.9
Routt	193	531	81.9	25.5	24	118	17.4	4.8	146	5 159	241.4	80.0
Saguache	9	13	1.1	0.5	5	45	D	2.0	5	30	1.1	0.3
San Juan	6	D	D	D	3	8	D	0.4	24	86	6.2	1.5
San Miguel	75	129	19.7	5.6	14	84	10.9	4.9	72	1 439	77.2	29.2
Sedgwick	5	17	1.0	0.3	3	29	D	0.7	4	53	1.4	0.5
Summit	258	575	89.3	30.4	26	166	40.6	7.9	250	6 201	311.3	101.3
Teller	88	411	57.8	22.6	14	46	6.5	1.7	71	1 649	110.8	38.1
Washington	7	18	1.7	0.4	6	100	D	D	6	27	1.0	0.3
Weld	533	2 362	311.5	113.7	284	11 102	5 991.4	485.8	400	5 794	273.9	76.2
Yuma	27	62	6.6	2.0	11	78	164.8	2.8	26	231	8.5	2.5
CONNECTICUT	9 220	97 578	17 993.7	8 364.1	4 350	163 847	55 160.1	10 546.2	8 263	134 546	9 542.1	2 590.8
Fairfield	3 481	40 694	8 738.6	3 975.9	837	35 507	13 412.5	2 338.2	2 266	30 574	2 153.3	604.6
Hartford	2 238	26 427	5 239.4	1 968.7	1 261	57 332	16 965.5	3 899.3	2 043	32 877	1 905.3	549.8
Litchfield	372	D	D	D	382	9 062	2 615.3	463.3	411	4 426	265.2	75.3
Middlesex	374	2 735	425.1	166.9	243	8 920	3 605.4	543.1	421	5 434	329.5	99.3
New Haven	1 907	16 222	2 461.1	1 216.8	1 151	31 792	10 818.1	1 879.2	1 969	26 342	1 487.2	411.3
New London	529	8 100	666.1	862.0	172	12 435	4 693.7	950.2	698	28 347	3 023.8	748.7

1. Establishment subject to federal tax.

STATE County	Health care and social assistance, 2012				Other services, 2012				Nonemployer businesses, 2015		Value of residential construction authorized by building permits, 2016	
	Number of establishments	Number of employees	Receipts (mil dol)	Annual payroll (mil dol)	Number of establishments	Number of employees	Receipts (mil dol)	Annual payroll (mil dol)	Number	Receipts (mil dol)	New Construction ($1,000)	Number of housing units
	159	160	161	162	163	164	165	166	167	168	169	170
COLORADO—Cont'd												
Boulder	1 332	18 386	2 129.6	841.9	717	4 415	670.1	176.7	38 414	1 972.3	380 649	1 849
Broomfield	145	1 611	172.9	64.4	109	704	141.8	23.7	5 513	241.1	178 540	546
Chaffee	66	791	76.3	31.3	40	175	11.7	3.7	2 362	89.4	32 308	126
Cheyenne	1	D	D	D	4	6	1.0	0.2	196	7.0	225	3
Clear Creek	19	67	5.8	2.2	10	27	1.8	0.5	988	50.6	3 946	12
Conejos	11	254	17.1	6.9	4	D	D	D	605	26.6	3 871	20
Costilla	7	37	1.7	0.9	3	D	D	D	277	11.4	10 045	44
Crowley	3	D	D	D	1	D	D	D	178	4.8	515	4
Custer	2	D	D	D	10	120	5.3	2.6	649	28.0	15 358	57
Delta	89	1 716	115.7	48.9	50	185	15.2	4.1	2 774	119.0	2 321	15
Denver	2 093	54 161	7 316.9	3 008.8	1 607	13 247	1 868.2	472.2	66 449	3 542.0	1 260 086	7 842
Dolores	5	D	D	D	NA	NA	NA	NA	151	5.5	0	0
Douglas	743	8 339	1 137.4	412.4	508	3 075	270.0	80.6	30 353	1 582.1	755 158	3 332
Eagle	168	2 052	384.1	115.8	189	1 278	119.3	37.3	7 226	449.1	160 503	346
Elbert	25	132	8.2	3.9	42	118	11.9	3.2	2 770	138.5	29 688	120
El Paso	1 897	D	D	D	1 086	8 419	1 805.3	323.0	48 394	1 927.3	1 657 343	5 034
Fremont	93	1 982	128.3	60.6	46	214	13.1	4.4	2 797	103.3	18 452	85
Garfield	161	D	D	D	152	692	91.3	20.8	6 108	304.6	38 876	156
Gilpin	6	43	4.0	1.5	3	7	0.4	0.1	561	20.3	12 799	31
Grand	36	324	35.9	13.3	46	103	12.0	2.6	1 889	97.0	53 726	161
Gunnison	64	494	50.3	18.0	64	221	27.3	5.7	2 307	95.1	28 966	103
Hinsdale	1	D	D	D	6	D	D	D	145	6.6	1 703	7
Huerfano	18	424	31.2	15.3	7	D	D	D	601	23.0	5 662	31
Jackson	3	7	0.5	0.2	1	D	D	D	176	7.0	1 222	7
Jefferson	1 565	24 678	2 717.4	1 084.2	1 121	6 073	628.1	172.8	54 185	2 433.9	569 138	2 610
Kiowa	2	D	D	D	4	4	0.5	0.1	148	5.8	0	0
Kit Carson	26	284	22.2	9.0	13	D	D	D	685	29.4	0	0
Lake	14	195	18.3	6.8	12	32	2.1	0.5	649	25.0	6 640	32
La Plata	237	2 737	335.0	125.2	143	612	53.9	16.6	6 396	298.4	100 446	260
Larimer	1 021	18 142	1 988.2	783.2	658	3 536	374.1	96.2	30 473	1 392.6	680 813	3 532
Las Animas	36	D	D	D	36	129	11.0	3.0	955	34.7	774	4
Lincoln	7	245	21.3	8.4	11	41	3.4	0.9	386	13.8	1 940	10
Logan	65	1 027	88.3	33.5	53	203	21.5	5.2	1 232	61.4	2 705	14
Mesa	426	10 176	1 029.0	427.2	293	1 883	182.6	47.8	11 373	489.7	125 709	597
Mineral	2	D	D	D	3	D	D	D	159	12.7	2 438	14
Moffat	40	440	50.3	19.1	37	219	18.5	6.7	984	39.3	1 448	10
Montezuma	90	1 422	109.3	45.2	47	173	15.7	3.6	2 305	88.6	5 586	23
Montrose	172	2 338	221.5	83.5	86	368	36.5	9.4	3 602	150.6	19 622	114
Morgan	57	1 186	118.5	46.1	40	139	14.1	3.2	1 871	92.5	7 654	34
Otero	57	921	50.8	24.8	27	81	7.1	1.8	1 037	32.0	555	3
Ouray	18	52	3.9	1.6	8	35	2.6	0.8	945	49.8	15 009	49
Park	23	96	4.6	2.1	24	76	9.1	2.4	1 804	76.2	20 266	137
Phillips	9	298	21.2	8.8	12	24	3.2	0.7	390	20.6	226	1
Pitkin	74	D	D	D	115	913	122.3	36.8	3 677	282.4	126 115	54
Prowers	30	625	48.8	20.7	23	87	10.5	2.1	809	37.0	1 768	6
Pueblo	419	11 404	1 063.1	458.0	238	1 222	93.1	28.2	8 177	323.3	47 774	282
Rio Blanco	10	176	19.0	8.8	12	25	3.0	0.8	552	22.4	1 252	6
Rio Grande	34	420	28.7	11.9	24	94	12.6	2.9	1 048	37.4	1 406	5
Routt	118	1 170	141.6	51.0	86	438	37.7	10.9	3 709	185.0	73 719	163
Saguache	6	D	D	D	8	D	D	D	610	21.3	3 319	54
San Juan	3	D	D	D	3	17	0.7	0.4	117	4.4	2 559	8
San Miguel	28	132	10.0	4.2	44	270	29.1	7.8	1 745	99.1	53 359	35
Sedgwick	5	D	D	D	5	10	1.6	0.2	184	8.2	351	3
Summit	104	852	134.8	39.9	121	420	60.5	12.3	4 424	258.6	156 624	306
Teller	58	D	D	D	42	129	11.5	3.1	2 542	101.3	31 406	132
Washington	8	32	1.7	0.5	8	D	D	D	368	17.2	1 053	6
Weld	435	7 951	893.1	325.4	329	1 537	175.9	44.5	20 948	980.3	665 176	3 009
Yuma	26	584	53.7	22.6	22	D	D	D	961	43.4	468	3
CONNECTICUT	10 296	271 272	29 573.1	12 533.5	7 282	43 384	4 904.0	1 382.4	272 809	16 122.8	1 196 936	5 504
Fairfield	2 827	63 963	8 087.6	3 291.8	2 103	13 041	1 654.3	420.8	91 902	6 611.0	621 925	1 903
Hartford	2 771	79 917	8 536.4	3 723.3	1 935	12 855	1 454.4	450.4	58 242	3 174.9	193 675	1 461
Litchfield	515	9 500	929.2	374.9	359	1 621	163.1	46.6	17 074	956.7	32 625	157
Middlesex	470	13 869	1 411.2	645.8	339	1 650	163.1	49.9	13 359	728.6	48 502	220
New Haven	2 408	73 162	7 788.2	3 238.4	1 717	9 881	977.8	297.8	59 574	3 112.0	147 953	918
New London	734	17 357	1 728.0	751.2	459	2 498	274.7	61.9	16 548	788.9	75 891	330

Government Employment and Payroll, and Local Government Finances

STATE County	Government employment and payroll, 2012									Local government finances, 2012				
			March payroll (percent of total)							General revenue				
												Taxes		
													Per capita[1] (dollars)	
	Full-time equivalent employees	March payroll (dollars)	Administration, judicial, and legal	Police and Corrections	Fire Protection	Highways and transportation	Health and Welfare	Natural resources and utilities	Education and libraries	Total (mil dol)	Inter-governmental (mil dol)	Total (mil dol)	Total	Property
	171	172	173	174	175	176	177	178	179	180	181	182	183	184
COLORADO—Cont'd														
Boulder	11 666	48 102 144	8.2	10.8	5.0	2.7	5.3	10.3	53.3	1 374.3	334.5	816.3	2 674	1 840
Broomfield	687	3 465 698	16.4	35.0	0.0	2.4	10.3	27.3	3.9	167.6	16.5	123.6	2 120	775
Chaffee	981	3 205 729	12.3	6.1	0.6	3.3	43.6	2.3	30.5	122.6	43.2	31.0	1 707	1 041
Cheyenne	186	506 783	7.0	5.9	0.0	7.9	25.6	3.5	46.1	11.6	3.9	4.8	2 562	2 163
Clear Creek	426	1 607 157	17.1	24.4	1.0	10.4	10.2	4.5	29.9	55.5	7.7	41.0	4 539	4 152
Conejos	417	1 165 848	8.0	8.9	0.0	4.9	9.9	3.0	62.1	35.4	24.9	8.0	965	500
Costilla	216	594 990	12.8	7.1	0.6	14.3	13.6	6.0	39.9	21.5	11.8	7.4	2 049	1 959
Crowley	149	372 979	13.1	7.4	0.2	7.6	12.0	7.9	49.2	13.0	9.3	3.0	554	412
Custer	188	561 207	16.3	10.1	0.7	9.8	17.6	3.0	41.1	14.0	3.5	7.4	1 741	1 402
Delta	1 667	6 363 576	6.3	7.6	0.1	3.4	39.9	9.2	32.0	159.9	41.2	32.5	1 067	738
Denver	31 444	153 513 001	5.5	11.6	4.4	12.7	23.1	10.5	30.8	5 569.5	1 334.4	2 071.4	3 266	1 406
Dolores	125	332 266	21.5	7.7	0.0	17.4	6.7	1.6	42.7	5.7	2.5	2.8	1 418	1 324
Douglas	8 978	36 551 403	6.0	11.8	1.8	3.0	0.7	5.6	68.6	1 187.6	326.8	623.8	2 092	1 621
Eagle	1 753	9 241 964	10.1	13.6	8.4	9.4	9.0	14.1	30.0	388.1	36.2	240.3	4 632	3 109
Elbert	793	2 420 569	5.3	13.3	4.8	6.6	3.6	3.3	61.8	68.8	28.9	26.5	1 132	853
El Paso	24 223	94 407 600	4.8	9.4	3.9	2.0	15.6	15.5	46.2	2 544.0	807.4	804.8	1 248	728
Fremont	1 361	4 257 494	6.5	12.3	3.9	5.6	7.8	6.9	53.3	113.3	43.1	39.2	837	567
Garfield	2 715	10 773 217	7.9	10.4	4.9	3.5	18.8	8.7	43.3	377.7	79.3	217.3	3 815	3 060
Gilpin	323	1 493 439	17.4	31.0	11.0	10.9	2.8	6.6	15.7	64.3	18.7	33.2	6 047	1 928
Grand	899	3 399 937	11.0	8.9	1.9	8.6	29.9	12.4	25.0	112.4	11.3	66.9	4 715	3 643
Gunnison	938	4 262 174	12.1	9.1	1.5	9.8	23.1	10.8	16.9	118.1	21.2	51.6	3 335	2 295
Hinsdale	78	213 518	22.4	6.9	0.0	16.9	17.4	4.9	28.8	6.8	1.9	3.5	4 346	3 385
Huerfano	683	2 657 574	9.1	15.2	0.3	8.0	42.0	6.2	18.4	59.2	16.3	13.5	2 049	1 649
Jackson	109	283 034	16.2	7.4	0.3	12.1	6.1	7.8	43.4	7.5	4.3	2.3	1 700	1 447
Jefferson	16 292	67 925 819	8.0	14.5	6.3	2.7	4.7	8.0	53.4	1 796.8	529.1	959.0	1 758	1 296
Kiowa	195	518 331	6.2	3.4	0.1	6.2	53.7	0.0	26.7	13.7	4.6	3.5	2 400	2 321
Kit Carson	599	1 765 320	8.1	7.1	2.1	6.4	30.3	7.6	36.2	45.5	15.1	12.7	1 565	1 397
Lake	1 036	3 786 124	2.2	2.4	4.0	1.7	9.4	2.1	76.3	123.9	28.5	61.1	8 331	7 915
La Plata	2 067	7 718 347	12.2	16.8	4.4	5.9	9.2	7.1	41.1	215.9	60.0	121.8	2 324	1 552
Larimer	10 782	47 317 101	8.8	11.5	1.1	2.8	7.5	18.4	46.2	1 178.8	292.6	577.8	1 861	1 211
Las Animas	790	3 154 143	13.1	10.3	5.0	7.2	4.0	23.0	36.5	67.9	34.0	24.1	1 610	1 155
Lincoln	433	1 393 504	11.8	4.7	0.0	8.0	44.9	2.8	25.9	42.3	17.3	9.6	1 763	1 199
Logan	1 057	3 288 524	7.3	7.7	3.0	24.9	6.5	4.7	43.0	98.6	25.5	33.4	1 475	969
Mesa	5 197	18 735 519	8.2	13.3	5.0	4.1	7.0	9.6	48.8	498.4	180.8	228.0	1 542	966
Mineral	54	178 882	27.1	10.8	0.0	16.4	3.6	2.1	40.0	2.9	0.6	1.5	2 123	1 523
Moffat	596	2 538 838	9.9	13.4	0.2	10.3	6.2	10.3	44.2	92.8	17.6	36.4	2 760	2 173
Montezuma	1 215	5 805 045	11.6	22.2	1.0	7.2	7.7	14.6	27.4	95.8	39.0	40.1	1 577	1 113
Montrose	2 104	7 665 788	7.4	9.0	2.9	5.0	34.2	6.0	34.1	212.1	63.1	64.1	1 574	943
Morgan	1 340	3 811 946	7.6	9.5	0.4	4.0	9.8	9.7	57.0	108.9	39.6	44.8	1 573	1 252
Otero	1 005	2 762 692	7.5	7.2	2.0	3.8	7.9	18.7	51.8	77.3	47.6	18.6	995	589
Ouray	217	778 899	20.7	8.6	4.2	8.7	4.3	7.5	43.5	24.2	6.0	13.1	2 889	2 250
Park	565	1 709 266	7.9	11.7	9.4	8.8	7.9	2.6	45.3	79.9	43.2	27.9	1 739	1 620
Phillips	387	1 231 524	5.8	2.8	0.0	4.9	50.9	5.0	28.5	41.2	11.7	7.9	1 819	1 329
Pitkin	1 617	8 457 732	10.5	7.7	1.5	20.9	24.6	13.9	14.7	334.3	32.9	154.4	8 946	4 437
Prowers	976	3 070 921	6.7	5.7	0.9	3.5	37.0	8.6	32.8	89.1	35.2	16.6	1 340	781
Pueblo	5 698	21 434 409	5.8	12.3	11.0	3.0	6.6	9.0	49.7	552.8	247.0	223.3	1 388	895
Rio Blanco	743	2 764 159	6.3	7.4	0.2	5.5	52.7	8.3	15.4	118.7	16.4	59.8	8 716	7 064
Rio Grande	594	2 555 313	11.1	23.0	0.0	5.2	6.7	1.8	52.0	64.6	42.5	16.8	1 408	981
Routt	1 184	5 565 786	14.7	11.9	5.9	17.1	2.2	12.5	30.0	144.8	31.4	79.2	3 394	2 136
Saguache	347	1 034 643	14.8	8.6	0.3	8.8	6.1	10.3	48.3	55.6	45.0	6.6	1 042	909
San Juan	40	161 715	24.7	12.1	0.0	15.7	7.6	8.1	30.7	9.6	6.5	2.6	3 820	2 945
San Miguel	502	2 269 390	18.4	15.3	2.9	13.4	5.4	10.0	33.5	93.6	14.2	55.2	7 283	5 078
Sedgwick	255	812 165	5.4	2.7	1.9	4.4	48.8	7.8	27.6	22.9	7.9	4.8	2 001	1 581
Summit	1 631	6 095 822	12.4	10.1	11.6	10.3	3.7	14.3	28.7	206.4	13.5	141.5	5 044	2 991
Teller	955	3 818 256	16.1	19.9	2.6	7.0	8.6	7.5	33.5	87.9	28.6	45.4	1 942	1 236
Washington	385	1 126 606	13.3	11.8	0.0	8.2	7.0	2.5	56.0	43.4	28.9	10.2	2 145	1 945
Weld	8 663	35 763 495	8.2	17.4	4.0	5.2	6.6	11.0	45.5	919.9	308.8	411.9	1 562	1 194
Yuma	749	2 253 233	4.4	5.3	0.0	6.1	43.0	5.1	34.4	88.3	21.8	23.8	2 349	2 036
CONNECTICUT	X	X	X	X	X	X	X	X	X	X	X	X	X	X
Fairfield	32 029	179 963 079	3.5	9.1	5.1	3.1	3.2	3.7	70.6	4 597.7	963.2	3 193.1	3 419	3 370
Hartford	31 675	164 755 032	3.0	8.6	3.8	2.4	3.4	4.9	72.4	4 279.2	1 571.4	2 306.6	2 571	2 541
Litchfield	5 578	26 405 841	4.3	6.4	1.8	5.2	1.9	2.5	76.6	698.9	167.1	476.8	2 542	2 521
Middlesex	5 503	26 698 181	4.2	7.4	4.5	3.5	3.5	3.2	71.4	656.2	154.4	441.0	2 663	2 643
New Haven	28 448	140 929 161	3.5	10.1	6.3	2.6	2.7	5.4	68.7	3 790.8	1 443.5	2 034.2	2 358	2 333
New London	8 967	42 369 410	4.4	7.7	3.8	3.8	2.3	8.0	68.3	1 101.6	386.5	598.5	2 183	2 159

1. Based on the resident population estimated as of July 1 of the year shown.

Local Government Finances, Government Employment, and Income Taxes

	Local government finances, 2012 (cont.)									Government employment, 2015			Individual income tax returns, 2014		
	Direct general expenditure							Debt outstanding							
			Percent of total for:												
STATE County	Total (mil dol)	Per capita[1] (dollars)	Educa-tion	Health and hospitals	Police protec-tion	Public welfare	High-ways	Total (mil dol)	Per capita[1] (dollars)	Federal civilian	Federal military	State and local	Number of returns	Mean adjusted gross income	Mean income tax
	185	186	187	188	189	190	191	192	193	194	195	196	197	198	199
COLORADO—Cont'd															
Boulder	1 414.6	4 633	43.6	2.5	8.2	2.3	4.6	1 940.0	6 354	1 995	890	31 577	155 670	88 774	14 569
Broomfield	144.5	2 479	0.0	1.3	11.0	7.9	6.3	650.9	11 165	165	170	1 339	31 170	84 917	12 428
Chaffee	126.2	6 953	33.9	30.5	2.8	4.5	3.0	96.2	5 298	77	45	1 833	8 650	53 907	6 310
Cheyenne	10.0	5 359	50.3	1.1	4.3	21.9	4.7	4.3	2 284	12	D	275	820	54 348	7 383
Clear Creek	50.3	5 569	22.6	4.4	10.8	5.5	14.8	19.7	2 186	34	24	641	4 590	73 015	10 375
Conejos	32.7	3 950	48.7	4.8	3.1	18.2	5.7	7.1	857	42	21	544	2 890	37 358	2 729
Costilla	19.3	5 383	36.1	8.6	3.1	5.2	18.0	10.6	2 962	D	D	358	1 290	34 569	2 843
Crowley	12.3	2 296	34.8	0.9	4.5	16.8	7.5	5.3	989	D	D	508	1 100	36 349	2 896
Custer	14.0	3 302	29.4	21.6	5.5	3.1	12.9	5.3	1 249	15	11	239	1 910	56 306	6 930
Delta	164.5	5 405	28.7	38.1	3.5	2.1	6.4	79.3	2 607	174	77	2 190	12 630	45 673	4 372
Denver	4 720.3	7 442	20.3	15.1	4.8	3.6	3.3	12 146.9	19 151	14 334	2 426	54 755	338 820	74 868	12 228
Dolores	8.4	4 230	38.7	1.5	9.3	1.7	28.9	3.1	1 535	10	D	212	800	44 080	4 323
Douglas	1 073.0	3 598	46.7	0.7	5.5	1.9	8.1	1 832.6	6 145	408	845	12 412	145 380	111 515	18 353
Eagle	360.2	6 944	19.9	3.1	5.6	0.9	7.0	691.4	13 329	122	142	3 082	28 020	81 886	13 132
Elbert	66.6	2 849	52.4	1.1	2.8	6.7	8.4	163.8	7 006	31	65	888	11 300	80 024	10 850
El Paso	2 502.2	3 880	37.1	21.9	6.0	2.0	8.1	4 398.1	6 819	12 621	38 461	36 529	304 520	58 595	6 821
Fremont	111.0	2 373	42.2	0.5	8.6	5.0	5.7	106.8	2 282	1 078	101	4 148	17 180	44 592	4 320
Garfield	343.8	6 036	29.4	12.6	5.3	5.4	6.2	453.7	7 965	263	150	5 063	26 350	70 776	11 200
Gilpin	50.9	9 270	11.0	2.3	12.0	3.9	11.8	57.5	10 467	D	15	429	2 580	61 056	7 326
Grand	101.5	7 151	19.1	14.0	6.2	1.0	9.3	159.5	11 235	127	38	1 253	7 170	59 424	8 046
Gunnison	122.5	7 917	13.3	24.8	4.1	3.0	11.9	140.6	9 086	168	40	1 899	7 710	54 179	6 337
Hinsdale	7.9	9 716	19.4	25.6	3.8	0.3	8.5	0.7	895	D	D	86	370	55 830	6 149
Huerfano	56.4	8 549	15.8	41.7	1.6	2.4	10.2	12.0	1 821	13	17	461	2 630	40 495	3 680
Jackson	7.0	5 173	38.5	4.4	6.1	2.3	23.7	0.7	487	36	D	128	620	46 098	4 129
Jefferson	1 793.4	3 289	42.8	1.2	9.3	2.3	4.8	1 397.5	2 563	8 596	1 532	27 696	287 040	75 550	10 792
Kiowa	14.6	10 098	23.1	43.2	3.7	4.8	11.6	4.6	3 195	22	D	217	610	47 759	5 480
Kit Carson	45.0	5 561	31.8	27.5	3.7	5.2	8.8	19.9	2 455	40	19	754	3 310	52 308	7 032
Lake	135.4	18 454	79.4	5.5	1.1	1.4	2.2	36.4	4 957	51	19	717	3 320	44 053	3 993
La Plata	202.8	3 869	35.0	1.1	7.0	2.7	5.9	291.6	5 566	332	139	5 348	26 350	76 966	11 419
Larimer	1 080.2	3 479	37.9	4.5	6.4	3.0	9.0	1 388.6	4 472	2 463	879	32 873	159 430	69 012	9 658
Las Animas	67.0	4 482	36.8	3.7	4.8	14.4	8.4	26.1	1 744	71	35	1 537	5 830	43 198	4 436
Lincoln	47.4	8 698	36.7	27.0	2.8	5.8	9.1	9.7	1 786	21	12	1 003	2 070	47 133	4 907
Logan	73.2	3 236	40.5	1.4	5.0	4.8	10.0	99.6	4 400	64	49	2 387	8 580	59 153	8 292
Mesa	517.8	3 502	35.4	1.7	13.1	5.6	9.4	476.5	3 223	1 470	396	8 337	67 630	56 379	6 712
Mineral	2.9	4 056	57.4	0.8	5.3	0.0	15.9	1.2	1 746	D	D	86	430	55 819	6 156
Moffat	93.2	7 060	24.3	30.6	5.6	6.2	10.7	40.3	3 050	150	34	975	5 750	55 012	5 824
Montezuma	95.7	3 762	36.0	3.0	10.1	11.6	6.2	60.5	2 379	337	68	2 366	11 340	51 180	6 016
Montrose	215.1	5 283	25.1	29.4	6.1	3.0	9.2	127.2	3 123	304	106	2 773	17 980	47 882	4 794
Morgan	102.1	3 585	44.8	1.5	4.7	4.6	7.3	72.8	2 556	115	73	2 055	12 650	48 195	5 010
Otero	73.8	3 949	48.8	9.4	2.9	2.4	5.4	37.0	1 981	114	47	1 735	7 480	39 611	3 313
Ouray	18.2	4 027	38.4	1.5	6.2	7.7	14.2	11.3	2 485	12	12	376	2 420	68 181	9 615
Park	79.6	4 968	50.7	2.8	3.8	4.7	6.8	28.9	1 800	50	43	791	7 000	61 178	7 116
Phillips	43.4	9 946	35.1	40.0	2.6	1.2	5.0	19.5	4 468	22	11	586	2 000	54 707	6 652
Pitkin	271.6	15 734	9.3	32.7	4.0	1.8	4.6	380.2	22 024	84	47	2 134	10 200	147 271	30 308
Prowers	85.2	6 880	36.9	27.3	5.4	4.4	4.5	184.4	14 887	38	30	1 346	4 840	42 021	3 903
Pueblo	566.4	3 521	40.3	1.5	6.6	5.3	3.7	456.3	2 837	1 098	436	11 341	68 330	47 110	4 778
Rio Blanco	94.0	13 703	15.7	31.1	5.7	2.8	9.7	113.7	16 584	71	16	1 155	2 820	60 376	6 288
Rio Grande	62.5	5 236	64.5	2.5	4.3	3.9	5.0	22.1	1 851	109	30	817	5 680	42 888	4 182
Routt	151.7	6 501	26.1	0.5	3.9	3.9	7.2	168.4	7 217	103	62	1 799	12 840	80 028	13 426
Saguache	54.4	8 636	66.9	1.8	1.8	8.1	6.5	14.0	2 225	45	16	492	1 820	34 558	3 147
San Juan	9.9	14 307	73.7	1.8	5.2	0.9	5.5	1.8	2 645	D	D	71	330	34 833	4 521
San Miguel	78.7	10 376	17.1	8.1	5.4	1.7	11.2	104.6	13 797	39	21	740	4 180	86 039	16 005
Sedgwick	21.9	9 187	35.7	36.4	2.6	2.8	4.4	1.7	700	17	D	344	1 080	44 400	4 599
Summit	193.3	6 894	18.6	1.3	5.5	1.0	7.9	128.1	4 569	50	79	2 582	16 710	70 314	10 338
Teller	84.7	3 621	35.6	6.2	7.8	2.8	8.5	55.5	2 371	59	61	1 347	11 180	61 264	6 796
Washington	40.7	8 539	68.2	2.8	2.6	6.4	6.5	14.9	3 135	50	12	447	1 990	46 187	4 381
Weld	839.9	3 185	42.6	1.2	7.3	4.0	6.6	868.6	3 294	596	736	16 010	122 060	63 749	8 183
Yuma	77.9	7 698	25.5	39.3	3.2	4.7	6.7	65.7	6 497	43	26	958	4 340	54 777	6 908
CONNECTICUT	X	X	X	X	X	X	X	X	X	17 781	13 712	228 224	1 749 380	93 862	16 307
Fairfield	4 616.9	4 944	50.9	1.2	6.6	1.0	3.1	4 013.1	4 297	2 764	1 899	45 274	457 540	158 253	34 778
Hartford	4 219.6	4 703	56.1	0.9	6.3	0.8	4.1	2 673.7	2 980	5 537	1 804	68 138	443 880	73 080	10 401
Litchfield	765.4	4 081	66.1	1.3	3.5	0.2	6.7	390.3	2 081	426	367	7 987	94 430	73 881	10 122
Middlesex	673.0	4 064	63.2	0.8	4.2	0.4	4.0	355.1	2 144	378	323	10 157	83 730	80 234	11 506
New Haven	4 427.8	5 132	58.4	0.6	4.3	0.3	2.5	3 649.0	4 229	5 414	1 912	44 806	412 580	68 822	9 416
New London	1 142.0	4 165	60.1	0.7	5.5	0.6	6.1	911.5	3 324	2 728	6 859	28 499	134 330	66 909	8 660

1. Based on the resident population estimated as of July 1 of the year shown.

Table B. States and Counties — **Land Area and Population**

STATE/ County code	CBSA code[1]	County type[2]	STATE County	Population, 2016				Population and population characteristics, 2016										
								Race alone or in combination, not Hispanic or Latino (percent)					Age (percent)					
				Land area,[3] (sq mi) 2016	Total persons 2016	Rank	Per square mile	White	Black	American Indian, Alaska Native	Asian and Pacific Islander	Percent Hispanic or Latino[4]	Under 5 years	5 to 17 years	18 to 24 years	25 to 34 years	35 to 44 years	45 to 54 years
				1	2	3	4	5	6	7	8	9	10	11	12	13	14	15
			CONNECTICUT—Cont'd															
09 013	25540	1	Tolland	410.3	151 118	434	368.3	86.5	3.9	0.6	5.3	5.4	4.0	13.8	19.1	10.5	10.2	13.9
09 015	49340	2	Windham	512.9	116 192	528	226.5	84.7	2.6	1.1	1.9	11.5	4.9	15.3	9.9	12.8	11.9	14.7
10 000	...	0	DELAWARE	1 948.7	952 065	X	488.6	64.8	23.0	0.9	4.6	9.2	5.8	15.7	9.0	13.4	11.5	13.4
10 001	20100	3	Kent	586.3	174 827	372	298.2	65.0	26.8	1.4	3.3	6.9	6.3	16.8	10.3	13.5	11.5	12.9
10 003	37980	1	New Castle	426.3	556 987	118	1 306.6	60.0	25.6	0.7	6.2	9.8	5.8	16.0	9.6	14.5	12.2	14.0
10 005	41540	2	Sussex	936.1	220 251	301	235.3	76.6	13.4	1.0	1.6	9.3	5.2	14.0	6.5	10.4	9.7	12.4
11 000	...	0	DISTRICT OF COLUMBIA ..	61.1	681 170	X	11 148.4	38.1	47.5	0.8	5.1	10.9	6.4	11.4	11.8	22.8	14.5	11.4
11 001	47900	1	District of Columbia	61.1	681 170	97	11 148.4	38.1	47.5	0.8	5.1	10.9	6.4	11.4	11.8	22.8	14.5	11.4
12 000	...	0	FLORIDA	53 638.9	20 612 439	X	384.3	56.3	16.4	0.6	3.5	24.9	5.5	14.7	8.4	13.0	12.0	13.4
12 001	23540	2	Alachua	875.1	263 496	257	301.1	64.1	21.3	0.6	7.1	9.4	5.5	12.7	21.1	15.6	10.5	10.1
12 003	27260	1	Baker	585.2	27 937	1 491	47.7	82.7	14.4	1.0	0.9	2.5	6.3	18.3	8.0	14.8	12.9	13.6
12 005	37460	3	Bay	758.5	183 974	353	242.5	79.5	12.1	1.5	3.6	6.3	6.3	15.2	8.2	14.5	11.9	13.5
12 007	...	6	Bradford	294.0	26 926	1 530	91.6	75.9	19.9	1.0	1.1	4.0	5.5	14.4	7.7	14.7	12.6	13.2
12 009	37340	2	Brevard	1 015.4	579 130	113	570.3	77.2	11.1	0.9	3.4	9.9	4.8	13.7	7.3	11.0	10.1	13.7
12 011	33100	1	Broward	1 207.0	1 909 632	18	1 582.1	38.9	29.1	0.5	4.6	28.7	5.8	15.5	8.1	13.6	13.2	14.6
12 013	...	6	Calhoun	567.3	14 423	2 134	25.4	79.5	13.6	2.2	1.1	5.8	5.2	15.5	7.2	14.5	12.8	13.8
12 015	39460	3	Charlotte	681.1	178 465	365	262.0	85.8	6.2	0.7	1.9	6.9	3.1	9.4	5.2	7.8	7.4	11.2
12 017	26140	3	Citrus	581.9	143 621	448	246.8	89.8	3.4	0.9	2.0	5.4	3.8	10.9	5.5	8.1	7.7	11.6
12 019	27260	1	Clay	604.8	208 311	316	344.4	76.2	11.6	1.0	4.4	9.6	5.6	18.1	8.1	12.4	12.7	14.5
12 021	34940	2	Collier	1 998.8	365 136	189	182.7	64.6	7.2	0.4	1.8	27.0	4.6	13.0	6.6	9.7	9.8	11.9
12 023	29380	4	Columbia	797.5	69 299	772	86.9	74.5	18.8	1.1	1.4	6.0	6.1	15.9	8.7	13.1	11.6	12.8
12 027	11580	6	DeSoto	637.1	35 800	1 281	56.2	55.6	12.8	0.5	0.9	31.1	5.1	14.7	9.1	13.8	12.0	12.6
12 029	...	6	Dixie	705.1	16 300	2 025	23.1	85.3	10.2	1.2	0.6	4.2	4.7	14.1	6.5	12.0	11.7	13.4
12 031	27260	1	Duval	762.6	926 255	57	1 214.6	56.0	30.6	0.8	6.0	9.2	6.7	15.9	9.2	16.4	12.5	13.1
12 033	37860	2	Escambia	656.9	315 187	218	479.8	67.4	23.9	1.7	4.7	5.6	6.0	14.8	12.3	14.4	10.7	12.1
12 035	19660	2	Flagler	485.5	108 310	555	223.1	76.7	11.1	0.7	3.0	10.3	4.1	13.4	6.3	9.0	9.8	12.2
12 037	...	6	Franklin	545.1	11 901	2 303	21.8	80.1	14.9	1.1	0.7	5.3	4.5	11.7	7.1	15.6	11.8	12.9
12 039	45220	2	Gadsden	516.3	46 006	1 048	89.1	33.5	55.8	0.6	0.9	10.2	5.9	16.2	8.3	12.2	12.7	13.7
12 041	23540	2	Gilchrist	349.7	17 212	1 967	49.2	88.8	5.2	1.0	0.8	5.6	5.7	15.2	9.9	10.7	10.4	13.1
12 043	...	6	Glades	806.7	13 970	2 167	17.3	61.1	12.7	4.7	0.8	21.4	3.2	12.8	6.6	13.0	12.0	12.4
12 045	37460	3	Gulf	553.6	15 990	2 039	28.9	76.2	18.9	1.1	0.8	4.7	4.1	11.4	7.3	15.0	13.5	14.8
12 047	...	6	Hamilton	513.8	14 361	2 141	28.0	56.3	34.0	1.1	1.1	9.1	5.0	14.2	12.0	13.5	11.8	13.2
12 049	48100	6	Hardee	637.8	27 360	1 518	42.9	48.2	7.5	0.6	1.4	43.4	7.3	19.1	10.2	13.4	11.8	12.1
12 051	17500	6	Hendry	1 156.3	39 290	1 190	34.0	34.1	11.8	1.7	1.2	52.0	7.5	19.6	9.2	14.6	12.3	12.7
12 053	45300	1	Hernando	472.8	182 835	355	386.7	80.9	5.8	0.8	1.8	12.4	4.5	14.1	6.6	9.9	9.9	12.6
12 055	42700	3	Highlands	1 016.6	100 917	593	99.3	69.3	10.3	0.9	1.8	19.1	4.6	12.8	6.3	9.5	8.5	10.4
12 057	45300	1	Hillsborough	1 020.3	1 376 238	28	1 348.9	52.0	17.0	0.6	4.9	27.6	6.4	16.6	9.1	15.2	13.4	13.7
12 059	...	6	Holmes	478.8	19 487	1 849	40.7	89.0	7.3	2.0	1.1	2.8	5.2	15.0	8.4	12.7	11.9	13.4
12 061	42680	3	Indian River	502.8	151 563	433	301.4	77.1	9.6	0.6	2.0	12.0	4.3	12.6	6.4	9.1	8.9	11.8
12 063	...	6	Jackson	918.2	48 229	1 015	52.5	67.4	27.3	1.2	1.1	4.8	5.1	13.7	8.4	13.3	13.8	13.4
12 065	45220	2	Jefferson	598.1	13 906	2 174	23.3	60.6	34.8	0.9	0.9	4.2	4.6	13.2	6.2	11.8	11.5	14.6
12 067	...	9	Lafayette	543.4	8 617	2 540	15.9	72.4	15.2	0.7	0.6	12.5	4.2	16.2	10.5	14.7	14.9	13.5
12 069	36740	1	Lake	940.9	335 396	205	356.5	72.5	10.7	0.8	2.8	14.7	5.1	14.6	6.7	10.6	10.7	12.5
12 071	15980	2	Lee	784.1	722 336	89	921.2	69.5	8.8	0.5	2.1	20.5	4.8	13.4	6.9	10.9	10.3	12.1
12 073	45220	2	Leon	666.9	287 822	239	431.6	58.7	32.1	0.8	4.4	6.2	5.2	13.5	22.2	14.5	10.6	10.6
12 075	...	6	Levy	1 118.2	39 961	1 176	35.7	81.6	9.6	1.2	0.9	8.3	5.2	14.7	6.7	10.7	9.9	13.2
12 077	...	8	Liberty	835.6	8 202	2 579	9.8	73.2	19.7	1.3	0.5	6.8	4.7	14.0	8.6	17.0	16.0	15.1
12 079	...	6	Madison	696.1	18 224	1 904	26.2	55.8	38.9	1.0	0.7	4.9	5.4	14.0	7.6	13.8	11.9	13.6
12 081	35840	2	Manatee	743.2	375 888	183	505.8	73.0	9.3	0.6	2.5	16.1	5.0	14.0	6.8	10.6	10.3	12.5
12 083	36100	2	Marion	1 588.0	349 020	197	219.8	72.8	13.3	0.8	2.2	12.5	5.1	13.7	6.8	10.7	9.7	11.9
12 085	38940	2	Martin	543.7	158 701	408	291.9	80.0	5.7	0.5	1.8	13.2	4.1	12.5	6.3	9.1	9.2	13.1
12 086	33100	1	Miami-Dade	1 898.7	2 712 945	7	1 428.8	14.3	16.6	0.2	1.9	67.7	5.8	14.5	8.6	14.4	13.9	14.8
12 087	28580	4	Monroe	983.0	79 077	707	80.4	69.0	6.6	0.9	1.9	23.0	4.6	10.4	7.2	13.0	12.0	14.8
12 089	27260	1	Nassau	648.6	80 622	696	124.3	88.5	6.4	0.8	1.5	4.2	5.1	14.9	6.7	11.3	11.3	13.8
12 091	18880	3	Okaloosa	930.3	201 170	329	216.2	77.7	11.1	1.3	5.2	8.7	6.7	15.4	9.2	16.1	11.5	12.4
12 093	36380	4	Okeechobee	768.9	40 314	1 167	52.4	64.1	8.9	1.2	1.3	25.5	6.3	16.1	8.1	13.1	12.6	12.9
12 095	36740	1	Orange	903.3	1 314 367	30	1 455.1	43.1	21.4	0.6	6.4	30.5	6.3	16.2	10.8	16.8	14.0	13.4
12 097	36740	1	Osceola	1 327.7	336 015	204	253.1	34.8	10.4	0.5	3.3	52.3	6.4	18.3	9.3	14.3	14.2	13.4
12 099	33100	1	Palm Beach	1 969.9	1 443 810	27	732.9	57.0	19.1	0.4	3.4	21.5	5.2	14.2	7.6	11.9	11.4	13.3
12 101	45300	1	Pasco	747.6	512 368	134	685.4	77.7	6.0	0.7	3.1	14.3	5.2	15.1	7.0	10.9	12.0	13.7
12 103	45300	1	Pinellas	273.8	960 730	49	3 508.9	76.5	11.3	0.7	4.2	9.3	4.5	12.2	6.8	11.9	10.9	14.1
12 105	29460	2	Polk	1 796.8	666 149	100	370.7	62.0	15.5	0.7	2.4	21.1	5.9	16.6	8.4	12.7	11.7	12.3

1. CBSA = Core Based Statistical Area. See Appendix A for explanation. See Appendix B for list of metropolitan areas with component counties. 2. County type code from the Economic Research Service of USDA Rural-Urban Continuum Codes. See Appendix A for definition. 3. Dry land or land partially or temporarily covered by water. 4. May be of any race.

Table B. States and Counties — **Population and Households**

STATE County	55 to 64 years	65 to 74 years	75 years and over	Percent female	2000	2010	2000–2010	2010–2016	Births	Deaths	Net migration	Number	Persons per household	Family households	Female family householder[1]	One person
	16	17	18	19	20	21	22	23	24	25	26	27	28	29	30	31
CONNECTICUT—Cont'd																
Tolland.............................	13.7	8.7	6.0	49.8	136 364	152 680	12.0	-1.0	7 209	6 189	-2 337	54 467	2.49	67.0	9.8	24.9
Windham	14.9	9.3	6.4	50.4	109 091	118 434	8.6	-1.9	7 118	6 195	-3 105	44 276	2.53	67.0	12.6	26.6
DELAWARE	13.7	10.5	7.0	51.6	783 600	897 936	14.6	6.0	68 977	51 096	35 621	344 022	2.62	66.9	13.8	26.7
Kent...................................	12.4	9.8	6.6	51.8	126 697	162 349	28.1	7.7	13 743	9 272	7 638	60 571	2.71	69.8	14.8	23.8
New Castle........................	13.2	8.5	6.1	51.6	500 265	538 477	7.6	3.4	41 201	27 634	5 644	202 268	2.63	65.7	14.2	27.6
Sussex...............................	16.1	16.1	9.7	51.6	156 638	197 110	25.8	11.7	14 033	14 190	22 339	81 183	2.52	67.8	12.3	26.4
DISTRICT OF COLUMBIA..	10.3	6.7	4.9	52.5	572 059	601 766	5.2	13.2	58 893	30 473	50 470	273 390	2.22	43.4	15.7	43.8
District of Columbia..............	10.3	6.7	4.9	52.5	572 059	601 766	5.2	13.2	58 893	30 473	50 470	273 390	2.22	43.4	15.7	43.8
FLORIDA...........................	13.2	11.0	8.8	51.1	15 982 378	18 804 592	17.7	9.6	1 353 262	1 150 096	1 562 390	7 300 494	2.63	64.4	13.3	29.0
Alachua	11.1	8.0	5.4	51.7	217 955	247 335	13.5	6.5	18 044	11 284	9 071	96 703	2.46	54.1	11.2	32.2
Baker..................................	12.5	8.1	5.3	47.5	22 259	27 115	21.8	3.0	2 165	1 447	103	8 205	3.00	73.9	13.3	20.7
Bay.....................................	13.6	9.8	7.0	50.2	148 217	168 852	13.9	9.0	14 159	11 053	11 477	67 922	2.54	64.0	12.0	29.3
Bradford	13.4	10.3	8.1	45.7	26 088	28 520	9.3	-5.6	1 911	1 822	-1 775	8 770	2.72	65.8	15.4	29.9
Brevard	16.0	12.6	10.6	51.2	476 230	543 378	14.1	6.6	32 066	40 945	42 960	222 791	2.46	63.6	12.0	30.3
Broward	13.1	8.9	7.1	51.3	1 623 018	1 748 146	7.7	9.2	134 898	92 016	118 960	670 284	2.73	63.5	15.6	29.6
Calhoun	13.2	10.0	7.9	45.7	13 017	14 625	12.4	-1.4	891	939	-188	4 784	2.64	66.7	12.9	28.3
Charlotte............................	17.1	21.3	17.6	51.1	141 627	159 968	13.0	11.6	6 366	15 034	26 312	71 856	2.26	65.2	8.0	29.3
Citrus.................................	16.4	19.7	16.2	51.7	118 085	141 236	19.6	1.7	6 439	15 211	10 611	61 012	2.25	63.9	9.0	30.7
Clay....................................	13.4	9.5	5.6	50.8	140 814	190 865	35.5	9.1	13 189	9 877	13 822	69 053	2.84	74.8	13.4	20.2
Collier	13.4	16.0	14.9	50.9	251 377	321 520	27.9	13.6	20 150	19 195	41 092	129 888	2.59	67.5	9.3	27.4
Columbia	13.8	10.6	7.3	48.1	56 513	67 532	19.5	2.6	5 008	4 824	1 599	23 708	2.66	63.9	13.7	32.1
DeSoto...............................	12.1	11.2	9.3	43.3	32 209	34 862	8.2	2.7	2 383	1 839	382	11 238	2.78	65.7	13.5	27.5
Dixie..................................	15.2	13.7	8.7	44.8	13 827	16 422	18.8	-0.7	965	1 311	270	6 051	2.41	64.3	10.8	29.3
Duval..................................	12.6	8.2	5.3	51.6	778 879	864 263	11.0	7.2	78 485	47 683	30 351	337 900	2.58	62.1	15.9	31.1
Escambia............................	13.3	9.6	6.9	50.3	294 410	297 619	1.1	5.9	24 165	20 037	13 072	113 660	2.53	60.2	13.5	32.6
Flagler	15.5	17.6	12.1	51.9	49 832	95 697	92.0	13.2	5 099	7 244	14 211	36 950	2.71	70.8	8.9	23.4
Franklin..............................	14.4	14.1	7.9	42.9	11 057	11 549	4.4	3.0	652	802	507	4 338	2.24	65.5	11.4	28.6
Gadsden	14.3	10.0	6.6	52.5	45 087	47 746	5.9	-3.6	3 490	2 884	-2 328	16 964	2.53	66.9	22.6	28.7
Gilchrist	14.7	11.8	8.5	49.3	14 437	16 939	17.3	1.6	1 168	1 126	213	6 187	2.54	67.6	11.4	28.9
Glades	12.2	14.6	13.2	44.2	10 576	12 884	21.8	8.4	429	666	1 072	3 920	3.04	66.5	9.6	27.7
Gulf....................................	14.6	11.9	7.4	40.5	13 332	15 863	19.0	0.8	764	1 048	342	5 349	2.52	70.9	13.0	25.6
Hamilton	13.6	10.2	6.4	42.0	13 327	14 799	11.0	-3.0	968	816	-613	4 688	2.35	69.9	19.8	25.9
Hardee...............................	10.7	8.7	6.8	46.8	26 938	27 731	2.9	-1.3	2 478	1 252	-1 631	7 618	3.33	75.4	15.6	20.0
Hendry	10.9	7.5	5.7	47.8	36 210	39 140	8.1	0.4	3 715	1 727	-1 967	11 345	3.18	72.1	16.9	23.1
Hernando	14.4	15.2	12.6	51.9	130 802	172 775	32.1	5.8	9 347	15 850	15 782	70 452	2.45	67.6	12.2	27.7
Highlands	13.5	17.1	17.4	51.3	87 366	98 786	13.1	2.2	5 670	9 113	5 346	40 397	2.39	64.0	9.4	31.4
Hillsborough	11.9	8.1	5.6	51.3	998 948	1 229 224	23.1	12.0	104 433	61 989	102 179	486 078	2.64	63.8	14.4	28.7
Holmes	13.8	11.1	8.4	46.7	18 564	19 927	7.3	-2.2	1 228	1 587	-40	6 828	2.60	68.8	10.6	28.4
Indian River.......................	15.2	16.6	15.1	52.0	112 947	138 028	22.2	9.8	7 902	11 720	16 530	57 825	2.44	62.7	9.3	32.1
Jackson..............................	13.5	10.6	8.2	44.9	46 755	49 761	6.4	-3.1	3 072	3 569	-905	16 309	2.52	64.6	14.1	31.7
Jefferson............................	16.4	13.4	8.3	48.1	12 902	14 761	14.4	-5.8	804	926	-712	5 411	2.17	65.8	15.3	31.6
Lafayette............................	11.2	8.0	6.6	40.7	7 022	8 870	26.3	-2.9	473	438	-273	2 493	2.81	69.8	14.6	26.2
Lake....................................	13.4	14.4	12.0	51.6	210 528	297 047	41.1	12.9	19 404	22 833	40 493	119 251	2.57	69.2	9.9	25.4
Lee.....................................	14.1	15.6	11.8	51.1	440 888	618 754	40.3	16.7	40 165	40 337	100 863	252 287	2.59	65.7	10.6	28.2
Leon...................................	11.0	7.7	4.8	52.5	239 452	275 480	15.0	4.5	18 998	10 938	3 947	110 834	2.43	55.0	13.1	30.5
Levy....................................	15.8	14.4	9.4	51.0	34 450	40 801	18.4	-2.1	2 464	3 288	-26	15 516	2.53	65.3	13.6	30.3
Liberty	12.2	7.5	4.9	38.3	7 021	8 365	19.1	-1.9	503	380	-285	2 433	2.77	65.8	8.2	29.7
Madison	14.4	11.5	7.8	47.3	18 733	19 226	2.6	-5.2	1 280	1 374	-926	6 614	2.52	64.6	13.2	33.2
Manatee	14.6	14.5	11.7	51.7	264 002	322 833	22.3	16.4	21 464	22 685	52 370	134 725	2.52	65.6	10.9	28.1
Marion	13.7	15.9	12.6	52.0	258 916	331 303	28.0	5.3	21 139	28 809	24 049	132 287	2.48	65.1	11.7	29.1
Martin	15.5	15.2	15.0	50.7	126 731	146 850	15.9	8.1	7 555	11 362	15 038	61 952	2.39	62.3	8.0	32.6
Miami-Dade........................	12.0	8.5	7.4	51.5	2 253 362	2 498 018	10.9	8.6	195 783	119 755	137 932	842 153	3.08	68.0	18.2	26.4
Monroe	16.4	13.5	8.2	47.3	79 589	73 090	-8.2	8.2	4 547	4 312	5 774	28 910	2.55	57.0	7.1	32.4
Nassau...............................	15.5	13.5	7.9	50.8	57 663	73 314	27.1	10.0	4 754	4 610	6 812	28 306	2.66	72.1	11.0	23.9
Okaloosa............................	13.0	9.2	6.6	49.2	170 498	180 822	6.1	11.3	16 989	10 260	13 248	74 884	2.50	66.2	12.3	27.9
Okeechobee.......................	12.7	10.2	8.1	46.1	35 910	39 996	11.4	0.8	3 336	2 533	-654	13 046	2.77	70.1	14.8	24.8
Orange	11.1	6.8	4.5	50.9	896 344	1 145 951	27.8	14.7	99 349	45 670	114 173	434 319	2.75	64.4	15.4	26.7
Osceola	10.8	8.0	5.2	50.8	172 493	268 683	55.8	25.1	24 836	11 978	53 351	92 338	3.23	74.5	17.4	19.8
Palm Beach........................	13.0	11.4	11.9	51.7	1 131 184	1 320 134	16.7	9.4	88 668	86 631	117 814	534 605	2.54	62.2	12.1	31.1
Pasco.................................	13.3	12.8	10.1	51.3	344 765	464 703	34.8	10.3	30 152	35 615	51 153	186 318	2.53	65.9	10.9	28.2
Pinellas..............................	15.8	12.8	11.0	52.1	921 482	916 812	-0.5	4.8	53 037	72 579	61 493	402 653	2.27	55.1	11.2	37.7
Polk	12.4	11.5	8.5	51.0	483 924	602 095	24.4	10.6	46 080	39 039	55 293	221 381	2.77	69.2	14.1	25.6

1. No spouse present.

Table B. States and Counties — Population, Vital Statistics, Health, and Crime

STATE County	Persons in group quarters, 2016	Daytime population, 2011–2015 Number	Employment/ residence ratio	Births, 2016 Total	Rate[1]	Deaths, 2016 Number	Rate[1]	Persons under 65 with no health insurance, 2015 Number	Percent	Medicare, 2015 Total Beneficiaries	Enrolled in Original Medicare	Enrolled in Medicare Advantage	Serious crimes known to police,[2] 2014 Total Number	Rate[3]
	32	33	34	35	36	37	38	39	40	41	42	43	44	45
CONNECTICUT—Cont'd														
Tolland	15 383	125 001	0.65	1 158	7.7	990	6.6	4 776	4.2	22 057	15 273	6 784	NA	NA
Windham	4 781	103 177	0.75	1 055	9.1	995	8.6	5 684	6.0	20 868	15 635	5 233	NA	NA
DELAWARE	25 059	925 254	1.00	10 922	11.5	8 945	9.4	52 951	6.9	175 581	158 685	16 896	32 476	3 471
Kent	4 719	160 674	0.88	2 147	12.3	1 651	9.4	9 821	6.9	31 093	28 287	2 806	5 424	3 160
New Castle	17 411	565 245	1.06	6 492	11.7	4 732	8.5	28 078	6.1	85 952	75 789	10 163	19 718	3 557
Sussex	2 929	199 335	0.91	2 283	10.4	2 562	11.6	15 052	9.4	58 536	54 609	3 927	7 334	3 499
DISTRICT OF COLUMBIA	39 769	1 129 464	2.44	9 779	14.4	5 455	8.0	24 198	4.3	74 279	61 173	13 106	42 346	6 427
District of Columbia	39 769	1 129 464	2.44	9 779	14.4	5 455	8.0	24 198	4.3	74 279	61 173	13 106	42 346	6 427
FLORIDA	433 717	19 598 614	0.99	222 793	10.8	201 485	9.8	2 602 192	16.3	3 960 935	2 253 545	1 707 390	786 967	3 956
Alachua	13 900	269 646	1.13	2 937	11.1	1 964	7.5	27 103	12.6	39 597	31 176	8 421	9 091	3 552
Baker	2 632	23 659	0.65	344	12.3	243	8.7	2 533	11.8	4 224	3 044	1 180	454	1 668
Bay	3 985	177 009	1.02	2 346	12.8	1 913	10.4	20 566	13.8	36 622	28 809	7 813	8 060	4 532
Bradford	3 262	24 325	0.69	288	10.7	331	12.3	2 523	13.3	4 626	3 493	1 133	425	1 623
Brevard	6 570	545 204	0.96	5 317	9.2	7 040	12.2	58 601	13.5	138 722	85 688	53 034	17 253	3 098
Broward	16 914	1 767 733	0.91	22 170	11.6	15 864	8.3	261 839	16.5	279 598	117 988	161 610	64 848	3 457
Calhoun	1 841	13 171	0.69	139	9.6	145	10.1	1 653	16.3	2 571	1 799	772	139	938
Charlotte	3 227	159 627	0.89	1 044	5.8	2 658	14.9	17 535	16.8	54 788	36 946	17 842	3 208	1 918
Citrus	2 250	133 413	0.85	1 017	7.1	2 577	17.9	13 320	14.9	47 793	31 532	16 261	2 868	2 096
Clay	1 250	160 810	0.57	2 163	10.4	1 755	8.4	20 675	11.9	30 629	22 621	8 008	4 649	2 333
Collier	4 545	349 923	1.06	3 270	9.0	3 490	9.6	57 233	23.2	85 461	66 303	19 158	5 985	1 726
Columbia	5 032	68 188	1.02	815	11.8	799	11.5	6 479	12.5	14 341	11 102	3 239	2 513	3 692
DeSoto	3 744	35 100	1.01	372	10.4	312	8.7	6 464	25.7	6 403	4 688	1 715	1 109	3 197
Dixie	1 721	15 322	0.84	151	9.3	207	12.7	1 571	14.3	3 674	2 723	951	479	3 003
Duval	20 988	968 868	1.19	12 763	13.8	8 379	9.0	102 384	13.2	142 409	93 739	48 670	41 884	4 664
Escambia	19 670	322 114	1.11	3 847	12.2	3 478	11.0	30 908	12.7	62 830	43 506	19 324	14 468	4 663
Flagler	684	89 899	0.70	828	7.6	1 231	11.4	11 735	15.8	30 719	18 107	12 612	2 053	2 017
Franklin	1 793	11 851	1.05	98	8.2	108	9.1	1 275	17.1	2 497	1 772	725	212	1 811
Gadsden	3 498	41 539	0.71	532	11.6	496	10.8	5 900	16.5	8 975	4 246	4 729	1 127	2 474
Gilchrist	792	14 672	0.62	183	10.6	185	10.7	2 425	18.6	3 509	2 639	870	222	1 302
Glades	1 481	12 445	0.77	69	4.9	132	9.4	2 207	26.2	1 352	970	382	165	1 217
Gulf	3 334	14 865	0.83	116	7.3	168	10.5	1 379	14.3	3 572	2 837	735	341	2 137
Hamilton	2 705	13 938	0.88	152	10.6	117	8.1	1 378	14.7	2 765	2 138	627	466	3 238
Hardee	1 931	26 674	0.92	397	14.5	181	6.6	4 681	21.8	4 034	2 950	1 084	730	2 626
Hendry	694	38 424	1.00	600	15.3	300	7.6	8 688	26.0	5 386	3 826	1 560	1 477	3 950
Hernando	1 790	161 304	0.76	1 547	8.5	2 713	14.8	19 907	15.6	56 018	26 231	29 787	4 456	2 529
Highlands	1 734	97 300	0.97	931	9.2	1 485	14.7	11 807	18.3	31 095	21 335	9 760	2 841	3 182
Hillsborough	23 019	1 360 486	1.10	17 345	12.6	11 179	8.1	169 320	14.7	203 571	100 730	102 841	31 923	2 424
Holmes	1 805	17 154	0.59	204	10.5	242	12.4	2 318	16.7	4 344	3 494	850	341	1 719
Indian River	1 324	142 796	1.00	1 284	8.5	2 050	13.5	19 588	19.4	44 665	33 683	10 982	3 579	2 484
Jackson	8 098	48 443	0.97	494	10.2	623	12.9	4 377	13.7	11 330	9 054	2 276	956	2 057
Jefferson	1 175	11 942	0.54	123	8.8	149	10.7	1 399	14.1	3 022	1 589	1 433	321	2 265
Lafayette	1 708	8 092	0.73	65	7.5	69	8.0	1 256	22.0	1 007	823	184	70	784
Lake	3 634	280 547	0.75	3 279	9.8	4 130	12.3	34 254	14.4	135 755	90 293	45 462	7 955	2 624
Lee	8 473	648 791	0.94	6 666	9.2	7 324	10.1	100 793	19.9	163 550	109 102	54 448	15 855	2 342
Leon	14 838	301 852	1.14	3 070	10.7	1 838	6.4	27 385	11.4	35 608	18 404	17 204	14 204	4 974
Levy	334	35 208	0.67	399	10.0	545	13.6	5 258	17.4	9 477	6 816	2 661	NA	NA
Liberty	2 014	7 999	0.89	84	10.2	61	7.4	768	14.5	1 229	742	487	54	641
Madison	1 927	17 493	0.79	192	10.5	226	12.4	2 065	15.7	3 988	2 879	1 109	556	2 966
Manatee	4 813	322 361	0.85	3 590	10.6	4 001	10.6	48 161	18.1	77 185	48 713	28 472	11 798	3 374
Marion	8 967	328 992	0.93	3 509	10.1	4 824	13.8	39 320	16.6	103 609	60 874	42 735	8 346	2 444
Martin	4 206	153 684	1.04	1 279	8.1	1 966	12.4	17 862	16.7	41 450	30 489	10 961	3 025	1 968
Miami-Dade	41 977	2 709 203	1.06	31 772	11.7	21 405	7.9	473 278	21.2	418 594	137 534	281 060	122 865	4 606
Monroe	3 236	79 418	1.09	748	9.5	778	9.8	12 000	20.0	15 289	13 312	1 977	3 140	4 037
Nassau	543	64 749	0.64	779	9.7	862	10.7	7 472	12.1	17 117	12 349	4 768	1 321	1 718
Okaloosa	4 618	200 917	1.09	2 843	14.1	1 870	9.3	20 675	12.6	36 623	30 868	5 755	5 536	2 796
Okeechobee	2 905	38 459	0.94	538	13.3	403	10.0	7 081	23.9	8 539	5 324	3 215	1 369	3 469
Orange	34 839	1 378 207	1.25	16 721	12.7	8 198	6.2	175 327	15.7	161 520	83 569	77 951	57 567	4 586
Osceola	3 265	266 378	0.73	4 296	12.8	2 191	6.5	48 838	17.6	55 739	23 288	32 451	9 492	3 075
Palm Beach	21 197	1 396 266	1.03	14 696	10.2	15 207	10.5	185 701	17.2	290 947	176 775	114 172	47 324	3 391
Pasco	5 904	419 960	0.68	5 026	9.8	6 099	11.9	53 530	14.0	113 436	51 510	61 926	12 892	2 676
Pinellas	19 766	943 328	1.03	8 674	9.0	12 517	13.0	102 762	14.3	220 584	112 179	108 405	39 202	4 172
Polk	13 208	602 947	0.90	7 678	11.5	6 786	10.2	78 735	15.4	128 042	63 733	64 309	19 500	3 080

1. Per 1,000 estimated resident population.   2. Data for serious crimes have not been adjusted for underreporting; this may affect comparability between geographic areas and over time.
3. Per 100,000 population estimated by the FBI.

Table B. States and Counties — Crime, Education, Money Income, and Poverty

STATE County	Serious crimes known to police, 2014 (cont.)[1] Rate[2] Violent	Property	Education — School enrollment and attainment, 2011–2015 Enrollment[3] Total	Percent private	Attainment[4] (percent) High school graduate or less	Bachelor's degree or more	Local government expenditures,[5] 2013–2014 Total current spending (mil dol)	Current spending per student (dollars)	Money income, 2011–2015 Per capita income[6] (dollars)	Households Median income (dollars)	Percent with income of less than $50,000	Percent with income of $200,000 or more	Income and poverty, 2015 Median household income (dollars)	Percent below poverty level All persons	Children under 18 years	Children 5 to 17 years in families
	46	47	48	49	50	51	52	53	54	55	56	57	58	59	60	61
CONNECTICUT—Cont'd																
Tolland	NA	NA	49 567	10.1	33.9	38.0	349.0	16 849	35 446	79 626	30.2	7.8	81 616	7.1	7.2	6.4
Windham	NA	NA	29 886	9.9	46.0	23.1	268.8	16 641	28 140	59 392	42.2	2.5	61 303	10.9	16.8	15.6
DELAWARE	489	2 982	234 505	18.6	42.7	30.0	1 804.3	13 701	30 554	60 509	41.3	5.1	61 327	12.6	19.1	17.9
Kent	422	2 737	47 000	16.6	47.2	22.5	329.8	12 828	25 404	54 976	45.2	2.5	55 678	14.2	21.3	19.0
New Castle	532	3 025	146 996	21.4	38.5	35.0	1 085.3	14 169	32 894	65 476	38.2	6.4	66 179	12.1	17.6	16.7
Sussex	426	3 073	40 509	10.9	49.8	23.2	389.2	13 246	28 558	53 751	46.1	3.6	54 309	12.3	21.4	20.5
DISTRICT OF COLUMBIA..	1 244	5 182	162 835	43.2	28.7	54.6	1 510.3	19 651	47 675	70 848	38.1	13.5	73 115	17.7	28.3	29.3
District of Columbia	1 244	5 182	162 835	43.2	28.7	54.6	1 510.3	19 651	47 675	70 848	38.1	13.5	73 115	17.7	28.3	29.3
FLORIDA	540	3 415	4 684 695	17.4	42.6	27.3	23 729.9	8 717	26 829	47 507	52.1	4.1	49 416	15.8	23.4	22.0
Alachua	567	2 985	91 648	9.7	29.0	41.6	249.4	8 510	25 498	43 073	54.9	4.3	47 023	21.1	21.6	21.4
Baker	503	1 165	6 684	13.8	62.2	11.5	41.3	8 290	20 471	47 121	51.3	2.8	50 883	16.8	24.2	23.1
Bay	508	4 024	40 162	12.4	42.6	22.2	220.0	8 134	25 246	47 368	52.5	2.8	47 745	16.5	25.8	23.9
Bradford	420	1 203	5 495	14.7	60.5	10.9	30.3	9 349	19 739	41 606	55.9	1.9	40 879	21.3	31.0	30.6
Brevard	493	2 605	120 142	17.4	38.1	27.3	575.6	8 080	27 571	48 925	51.0	3.0	50 352	13.4	21.3	20.0
Broward	409	3 048	473 849	21.2	39.4	30.8	2 266.7	8 580	28 381	51 968	48.1	4.9	53 624	14.0	20.3	18.7
Calhoun	135	803	3 190	7.1	62.2	10.5	20.4	8 973	16 536	34 510	65.8	1.7	36 062	22.2	32.8	30.0
Charlotte	176	1 741	24 664	15.6	45.6	20.8	148.0	9 102	26 984	44 244	56.0	2.0	45 495	12.4	23.3	21.5
Citrus	355	1 741	22 642	13.0	51.5	16.9	132.1	8 764	23 979	38 312	62.1	1.9	39 982	17.5	31.4	28.8
Clay	269	2 064	54 159	13.2	40.3	23.8	284.3	8 004	26 464	58 290	41.9	3.3	59 244	11.6	15.7	14.1
Collier	260	1 466	63 308	15.3	40.7	33.2	455.0	10 244	38 297	57 452	42.8	8.9	62 385	13.6	22.9	20.8
Columbia	598	3 094	15 177	16.2	50.5	15.1	81.7	8 059	20 563	41 926	57.9	1.7	43 303	19.7	30.4	30.0
DeSoto	424	2 773	6 806	6.4	70.1	9.7	45.8	9 755	16 441	35 165	66.8	1.0	34 380	30.5	41.3	38.3
Dixie	451	2 551	2 984	9.0	62.2	7.9	18.3	8 795	17 850	36 292	67.7	1.2	35 749	29.3	38.2	37.0
Duval	687	3 977	226 913	20.7	40.0	27.3	1 127.3	8 831	26 543	47 690	51.9	3.5	49 565	16.0	25.4	24.4
Escambia	690	3 974	77 085	20.4	39.3	24.5	342.8	8 410	24 161	45 390	54.7	2.0	45 735	15.4	27.4	26.3
Flagler	246	1 772	20 112	13.7	43.8	23.0	105.2	8 248	24 360	47 866	52.4	2.1	50 347	11.7	20.9	19.4
Franklin	299	1 512	1 920	8.1	56.5	15.5	13.4	10 465	20 868	40 401	59.7	2.3	38 220	23.7	38.5	36.1
Gadsden	439	2 035	11 372	15.5	56.5	17.0	57.5	9 569	17 834	35 567	64.1	0.4	36 637	24.5	38.4	37.2
Gilchrist	323	979	3 390	7.7	55.9	11.4	25.7	9 876	21 436	40 623	60.4	1.9	39 342	19.2	29.5	28.3
Glades	258	959	2 381	14.2	67.6	8.4	14.4	9 404	17 879	34 877	67.4	1.8	40 215	22.1	33.1	28.3
Gulf	407	1 729	2 924	16.6	52.7	16.0	17.8	9 631	19 631	41 788	58.1	1.9	41 320	21.9	29.2	28.2
Hamilton	410	2 828	2 669	12.1	63.8	9.9	16.9	10 007	14 742	35 048	65.6	0.7	33 497	31.8	44.6	44.5
Hardee	245	2 381	6 346	5.5	71.8	10.7	46.5	9 037	16 298	35 457	65.3	1.7	35 850	25.9	36.5	35.0
Hendry	735	3 215	10 304	8.2	69.2	9.8	61.7	8 939	16 980	36 771	61.8	1.9	39 320	25.8	36.4	34.8
Hernando	255	2 274	35 791	13.8	50.5	15.6	184.5	8 360	21 586	40 945	60.7	1.2	43 103	14.3	24.5	23.4
Highlands	308	2 874	16 579	10.2	53.8	16.7	109.5	8 977	21 117	35 093	66.4	1.3	34 691	22.9	38.1	37.6
Hillsborough	325	2 099	346 206	16.7	39.9	30.6	1 766.9	8 685	27 764	50 579	49.4	4.7	51 710	15.8	21.4	19.8
Holmes	292	1 427	4 373	6.9	61.1	11.3	30.2	9 052	16 468	35 020	66.8	0.5	35 202	25.9	34.9	31.3
Indian River	282	2 202	26 847	15.3	42.0	26.8	153.5	8 498	31 882	45 798	53.8	5.5	49 887	13.0	22.5	21.4
Jackson	385	1 672	11 002	14.1	57.2	13.7	61.2	8 939	17 196	35 098	66.5	1.1	36 751	22.5	31.8	28.8
Jefferson	981	1 284	2 599	25.3	51.6	18.5	12.0	12 493	21 080	43 355	54.2	1.7	42 210	19.4	30.9	29.0
Lafayette	246	538	1 900	12.8	61.3	11.6	10.3	8 380	19 404	35 864	61.2	1.7	40 345	23.8	29.5	26.6
Lake	308	2 316	63 401	15.5	46.1	21.5	327.5	7 835	24 236	46 403	53.3	2.1	49 711	12.8	20.9	20.1
Lee	340	2 002	136 374	12.5	44.6	26.0	772.0	8 830	28 010	48 537	51.3	4.0	50 713	15.9	25.2	23.9
Leon	747	4 226	108 069	10.9	26.7	45.0	291.7	7 968	26 522	46 745	53.0	4.0	46 405	21.8	22.3	21.2
Levy	NA	NA	8 493	12.3	59.4	10.9	50.4	9 159	20 299	35 782	66.0	1.0	36 005	22.1	35.3	32.8
Liberty	83	558	1 619	6.5	66.2	11.2	15.0	10 416	16 972	39 406	57.9	1.5	39 623	22.6	29.9	28.8
Madison	800	2 166	3 966	10.8	57.0	11.3	25.8	10 196	16 274	32 164	68.1	0.8	34 360	27.0	36.9	35.8
Manatee	563	2 810	70 083	15.6	42.8	27.7	375.7	8 045	27 958	49 675	50.3	3.9	50 728	14.8	24.2	22.8
Marion	415	2 028	66 606	17.5	50.6	17.8	349.9	8 309	21 675	39 459	60.7	1.6	40 053	18.7	31.9	29.9
Martin	247	1 721	29 175	15.7	36.3	31.6	161.6	8 600	34 742	51 593	48.6	6.8	53 459	11.2	18.1	16.7
Miami-Dade	633	3 973	664 758	20.9	48.4	26.9	3 243.7	9 106	23 850	43 129	55.8	4.7	43 687	20.0	27.3	26.5
Monroe	505	3 532	13 106	17.8	37.0	31.3	90.9	10 706	36 208	57 290	43.3	7.1	58 332	11.3	18.8	19.0
Nassau	116	1 603	16 498	13.5	46.0	23.0	93.2	8 353	28 670	54 116	44.8	3.4	55 707	10.8	16.0	14.8
Okaloosa	394	2 402	47 047	11.4	34.9	28.8	260.2	8 611	28 902	55 880	44.3	3.8	55 391	11.3	18.7	18.4
Okeechobee	385	3 084	8 698	12.0	66.7	10.6	55.7	8 705	16 931	35 405	66.6	1.4	35 787	23.2	34.6	32.0
Orange	682	3 905	351 855	18.4	38.5	31.1	1 632.6	8 467	25 411	47 943	51.8	4.2	50 593	15.6	22.6	21.3
Osceola	411	2 664	81 370	14.0	49.1	18.0	477.9	8 211	19 165	44 254	56.5	1.7	45 127	18.5	27.5	26.0
Palm Beach	452	2 939	312 921	19.7	37.7	33.6	1 737.4	9 380	33 650	53 363	47.1	6.6	56 638	13.5	20.8	19.5
Pasco	280	2 395	104 107	14.2	45.7	21.4	553.4	8 125	24 455	45 064	54.8	2.3	46 080	14.6	19.5	17.4
Pinellas	506	3 666	183 971	18.9	39.5	28.9	938.9	9 080	30 170	45 819	53.6	3.9	47 591	13.6	20.6	18.5
Polk	349	2 732	148 577	15.5	52.7	18.9	843.3	8 610	21 196	43 162	56.2	1.8	44 024	17.3	26.7	25.1

1. Data for serious crimes have not been adjusted for underreporting; this may affect comparability between geographic areas and over time.   2. Per 100,000 population estimated by the FBI.
3. All persons 3 years old and over enrolled in nursery school through college.   4. Persons 25 years old and over.   5. Elementary and secondary education expenditures.
6. Based on population estimated by the American Community Survey, 2011–2015.

Table B. States and Counties — **Personal Income**

STATE County	Personal income, 2015										Earnings, 2015		
	Total (mil dol)	Percent change, 2014–2015	Per capita[1]		Wages and salaries (mil dol)	Supplements to wages and salaries; employer contributions (mil dol)		Proprietors' income (mil dol)	Dividends, interest, and rent (mil dol)	Personal transfer receipts (mil dol)	Total (mil dol)	Contributions for government social insurance (mil dol)	
			Dollars	Rank		Pension and insurance	Government social insurance					From employee and self-employed	From employer
	62	63	64	65	66	67	68	69	70	71	72	73	74
CONNECTICUT—Cont'd													
Tolland	7 921	3.2	52 311	405	2 021	508	139	548	1 252	1 031	3 216	164	139
Windham	5 032	4.6	43 167	1 111	1 747	370	135	317	776	1 055	2 569	143	135
DELAWARE	45 058	6.3	47 727	X	24 498	4 231	1 816	3 728	7 987	9 007	34 272	2 048	1 816
Kent	6 625	4.7	38 178	1 440	3 020	702	240	377	1 062	1 656	4 339	254	240
New Castle	28 780	7.2	51 690	346	18 468	2 960	1 337	2 182	5 082	4 778	24 947	1 470	1 337
Sussex	9 653	4.7	44 767	976	3 009	569	239	1 169	1 844	2 574	4 986	324	239
DISTRICT OF COLUMBIA	49 276	6.1	73 505	X	67 557	13 061	4 992	6 328	9 145	6 256	91 938	4 777	4 992
District of Columbia	49 276	6.1	73 302	59	67 557	13 061	4 992	6 328	9 145	6 256	91 938	4 777	4 992
FLORIDA	900 636	5.5	44 487	X	403 927	60 349	28 187	52 390	235 263	180 329	544 853	35 096	28 187
Alachua	10 450	5.3	40 199	1 332	6 007	1 272	418	356	2 106	1 913	8 053	460	418
Baker	784	4.9	28 588	2 974	253	60	18	33	98	217	363	23	18
Bay	7 214	5.4	39 717	1 396	3 460	634	263	382	1 502	1 651	4 739	291	263
Bradford	757	4.6	28 119	2 959	260	53	18	28	112	242	360	25	18
Brevard	23 014	5.4	40 511	1 334	10 109	1 590	720	944	4 890	5 781	13 362	899	720
Broward	85 167	6.1	44 909	817	42 101	5 804	2 909	5 158	18 994	13 896	55 971	3 485	2 909
Calhoun	352	3.5	24 333	3 093	99	24	7	14	51	124	144	11	7
Charlotte	6 534	6.2	37 745	1 714	1 809	288	129	339	1 882	2 194	2 565	218	129
Citrus	4 983	4.2	35 323	2 082	1 288	221	92	235	1 200	1 924	1 837	170	92
Clay	7 973	5.7	39 090	1 555	1 943	323	139	289	1 389	1 697	2 694	188	139
Collier	28 039	4.2	78 473	45	6 817	871	464	1 585	15 357	3 194	9 736	663	464
Columbia	2 212	5.9	32 366	2 652	942	196	69	164	320	655	1 371	86	69
DeSoto	834	5.9	23 522	3 105	349	68	25	85	157	283	527	33	25
Dixie	412	4.7	25 400	3 063	94	23	7	18	80	164	142	12	7
Duval	37 743	5.2	41 339	1 025	27 607	4 088	1 999	1 941	7 069	7 475	35 636	2 118	1 999
Escambia	11 945	4.3	38 408	1 662	6 523	1 223	497	538	2 559	2 905	8 781	526	497
Flagler	4 230	6.6	40 140	1 638	803	148	57	204	1 085	1 184	1 212	109	57
Franklin	400	2.6	33 973	2 382	117	25	8	28	115	106	178	13	8
Gadsden	1 396	3.8	30 334	2 831	464	107	32	67	230	424	670	45	32
Gilchrist	539	4.4	31 356	2 466	116	26	8	57	66	156	208	12	8
Glades	302	7.7	22 121	3 107	76	17	5	42	53	93	140	8	5
Gulf	478	4.4	30 125	2 946	144	32	10	21	105	140	206	15	10
Hamilton	355	7.2	24 824	3 077	143	34	10	15	46	127	202	13	10
Hardee	704	4.9	25 591	3 076	273	58	20	100	106	197	452	24	20
Hendry	1 167	8.4	29 822	2 923	500	89	37	192	145	299	817	36	37
Hernando	6 007	5.4	33 666	2 402	1 520	266	110	221	1 111	2 177	2 116	189	110
Highlands	3 179	5.2	31 949	2 634	986	177	72	179	668	1 213	1 413	109	72
Hillsborough	58 596	6.7	43 435	960	36 925	5 323	2 566	4 399	9 784	10 511	49 212	2 965	2 566
Holmes	526	4.6	27 220	3 011	113	30	8	33	79	197	184	15	8
Indian River	10 055	4.9	67 978	100	2 225	320	157	573	4 701	1 672	3 274	240	157
Jackson	1 468	3.8	30 210	2 881	531	126	38	94	238	493	790	53	38
Jefferson	515	3.6	36 596	1 869	89	20	6	39	99	140	154	11	6
Lafayette	199	0.0	23 012	3 101	49	13	3	38	29	49	104	5	3
Lake	12 285	7.1	37 698	1 809	3 583	600	256	485	2 275	3 511	4 925	380	256
Lee	31 296	5.3	44 583	931	11 112	1 721	780	2 437	11 014	6 686	16 050	1 114	780
Leon	11 356	3.9	39 670	1 421	6 723	1 408	462	608	2 205	1 885	9 201	524	462
Levy	1 293	4.9	32 457	2 646	297	63	22	71	226	426	451	36	22
Liberty	212	2.2	25 492	3 065	71	18	5	7	33	56	102	7	5
Madison	548	4.1	29 757	2 904	155	38	11	43	97	178	246	17	11
Manatee	15 669	7.5	43 121	1 073	5 134	761	360	974	4 610	3 466	7 230	506	360
Marion	11 602	4.7	33 800	2 356	3 912	663	280	434	2 614	3 987	5 289	424	280
Martin	11 127	4.4	71 197	83	2 849	419	199	580	5 097	1 580	4 046	276	199
Miami-Dade	116 553	5.0	43 278	963	61 605	8 782	4 219	10 112	26 235	23 160	84 718	5 351	4 219
Monroe	5 765	4.2	74 409	61	1 866	285	133	304	2 844	627	2 588	161	133
Nassau	3 897	5.1	49 675	518	906	146	64	174	1 043	724	1 289	94	64
Okaloosa	8 984	4.0	45 222	705	4 877	1 007	400	284	2 538	1 715	6 569	361	400
Okeechobee	1 172	5.3	29 695	2 875	431	77	31	126	168	377	666	41	31
Orange	50 998	6.9	39 591	1 453	39 710	5 228	2 713	3 206	8 100	8 798	50 856	3 012	2 713
Osceola	9 691	9.3	29 911	2 908	3 451	528	245	505	1 124	2 435	4 729	323	245
Palm Beach	97 807	5.0	68 743	73	32 874	4 289	2 200	4 816	43 280	12 784	44 179	2 858	2 200
Pasco	18 018	6.5	36 187	2 119	4 478	751	321	798	2 699	4 937	6 348	505	321
Pinellas	45 337	5.2	47 731	603	21 291	3 129	1 471	1 818	10 964	9 859	27 710	1 822	1 471
Polk	21 923	4.7	33 723	2 346	9 146	1 488	640	1 164	4 143	5 978	12 438	854	640

1. Based on the resident population estimated as of July 1 of the year shown.

Table B. States and Counties — Earnings, Social Security, and Housing

STATE County	Earnings, 2015 (cont.) Percent by selected industries									Social Security beneficiaries, December 2015		Supplemental Security Income recipients, December 2015	Housing units, 2016	
	Farm	Mining	Construction	Manufacturing	Information: professional, scientific, technical services	Retail trade	Finance, insurance, real estate and leasing	Health care and social assistance	Government	Number	Rate[1]		Total	Percent change, 2010–2016
	75	76	77	78	79	80	81	82	83	84	85	86	87	88
CONNECTICUT—Cont'd														
Tolland	0.5	D	9.2	6.9	6.6	7.2	3.5	10.5	37.8	25 665	169	1 072	58 920	1.7
Windham	0.3	D	D	18.2	5.3	8.2	D	14.3	20.9	23 470	201	2 069	49 171	0.2
DELAWARE	1.0	D	5.7	6.7	13.3	5.8	17.6	13.2	15.4	196 651	208	16 880	426 149	5.0
Kent	2.3	D	4.6	D	4.7	7.4	5.5	12.3	37.9	35 740	206	3 472	69 761	6.7
New Castle	0.1	0.0	4.9	D	16.4	4.9	21.2	13.0	12.2	97 780	176	10 147	222 967	2.5
Sussex	4.8	0.0	10.7	10.7	5.0	9.4	10.0	15.4	11.8	63 130	293	3 261	133 421	8.4
DISTRICT OF COLUMBIA	0.0	-0.1	1.5	0.2	26.6	1.0	4.7	5.7	39.0	80 546	120	26 886	313 718	5.7
District of Columbia	0.0	-0.1	1.5	0.2	26.6	1.0	4.7	5.7	39.0	80 546	120	26 886	313 718	5.7
FLORIDA	0.6	0.0	5.7	4.8	12.6	7.9	9.2	12.8	15.4	4 334 337	214	571 293	9 301 642	3.5
Alachua	0.4	D	3.3	3.8	7.8	5.5	5.4	17.6	39.0	42 280	163	6 509	115 541	2.5
Baker	4.2	0.0	5.0	1.5	2.5	8.0	1.9	D	40.5	5 115	187	631	9 622	-0.7
Bay	0.0	0.0	5.1	5.6	8.5	8.7	6.1	13.5	26.3	39 410	217	4 783	101 363	1.7
Bradford	1.9	D	3.0	4.9	2.9	9.1	2.9	14.6	30.0	5 990	222	832	10 828	-1.7
Brevard	0.2	0.0	5.0	16.2	11.2	7.6	4.3	13.9	16.9	154 590	272	11 846	274 540	1.7
Broward	0.0	0.0	6.1	3.6	14.2	8.5	9.5	10.2	14.2	308 190	163	44 876	822 931	1.5
Calhoun	1.5	0.0	D	D	D	7.1	2.9	20.4	35.9	3 040	210	568	5 896	-1.7
Charlotte	2.3	0.1	7.6	1.8	7.9	12.3	6.4	22.2	15.3	64 695	374	2 681	102 704	2.1
Citrus	0.1	0.2	9.2	1.4	7.2	11.8	4.1	22.7	13.9	57 725	409	3 326	77 900	-0.2
Clay	0.1	D	9.9	3.0	12.2	10.2	5.5	18.1	16.9	39 725	195	2 847	78 989	4.7
Collier	1.4	-0.3	10.7	3.1	12.6	9.0	11.1	11.6	9.9	88 625	249	4 061	210 128	6.5
Columbia	4.4	D	4.4	9.3	3.5	9.4	3.4	12.8	27.2	16 105	236	2 613	28 249	-1.4
DeSoto	11.4	D	4.9	4.3	D	5.6	2.7	D	20.6	7 300	206	1 015	14 853	1.8
Dixie	6.8	0.0	1.7	15.9	D	6.2	D	3.7	37.4	4 465	276	770	9 115	-2.2
Duval	0.0	0.0	5.2	5.7	11.4	5.9	14.7	13.2	14.9	157 530	173	24 961	402 313	3.6
Escambia	0.1	0.0	4.9	5.0	8.7	7.0	8.1	15.8	28.3	70 515	227	10 052	140 173	2.5
Flagler	0.4	D	6.9	5.6	10.6	10.5	6.1	12.5	18.3	35 165	334	1 735	50 566	4.1
Franklin	0.0	0.0	6.6	D	6.9	7.2	8.3	D	30.6	2 890	246	348	8 586	-0.8
Gadsden	5.3	2.0	10.2	8.0	2.0	5.4	1.1	3.9	36.2	10 680	232	2 559	19 355	-0.8
Gilchrist	25.4	0.0	4.0	1.1	1.8	3.5	1.3	D	28.7	4 110	239	496	7 234	-1.0
Glades	29.1	0.0	4.6	7.1	1.0	D	1.0	D	19.6	2 530	186	179	6 787	-2.8
Gulf	0.0	0.0	5.3	2.6	8.5	7.5	5.8	D	33.2	3 795	239	383	9 321	2.4
Hamilton	4.0	0.0	D	D	D	4.4	0.9	D	31.1	3 085	216	630	5 686	-1.6
Hardee	21.0	D	2.7	3.3	D	5.6	3.6	D	21.2	4 685	172	810	9 586	-1.4
Hendry	31.8	D	3.5	3.5	5.7	4.7	2.1	3.5	16.0	6 085	156	1 473	14 370	-1.3
Hernando	0.1	0.1	6.9	5.6	5.5	11.8	3.5	22.2	18.2	60 470	339	4 263	85 051	0.6
Highlands	9.1	0.0	3.9	2.4	3.8	10.6	3.7	22.5	16.8	33 525	337	2 838	54 834	-1.0
Hillsborough	0.4	0.0	5.4	3.9	17.0	7.3	12.6	11.1	13.6	228 795	170	41 198	568 839	6.1
Holmes	5.6	0.6	7.8	2.4	D	7.6	3.2	D	41.2	5 405	280	889	8 549	-1.1
Indian River	1.6	D	5.6	4.1	13.2	9.6	8.1	16.9	10.6	48 065	325	2 505	78 628	3.0
Jackson	2.6	0.6	7.4	8.1	D	7.8	3.0	8.1	38.8	12 340	254	2 029	20 740	-1.3
Jefferson	14.1	0.0	7.4	0.6	D	5.6	D	D	25.2	3 575	254	578	6 584	-0.7
Lafayette	36.2	D	2.7	2.2	D	4.5	D	D	34.2	1 195	139	148	3 295	-1.0
Lake	1.2	0.2	9.5	4.2	6.5	11.7	5.3	19.7	16.6	97 265	299	7 118	151 051	4.2
Lee	0.3	0.1	7.7	2.6	10.6	10.0	6.8	11.4	18.1	179 170	256	12 789	385 070	3.8
Leon	0.0	0.0	2.9	1.2	15.4	6.1	5.8	13.0	38.6	42 045	147	6 123	128 072	3.2
Levy	7.2	0.4	11.5	7.4	3.7	9.6	4.4	6.2	22.4	12 090	305	1 401	19 773	-1.7
Liberty	-0.4	0.0	3.2	19.0	D	2.7	D	13.3	41.8	1 460	175	272	3 319	-1.1
Madison	8.4	D	3.4	11.3	2.7	6.5	3.5	9.7	30.0	4 530	246	925	8 424	-0.7
Manatee	2.2	0.0	7.6	7.9	9.0	9.2	6.8	13.9	11.9	92 885	256	6 129	185 272	7.3
Marion	-0.2	0.1	6.8	9.1	6.3	11.1	5.2	19.8	16.1	112 580	328	9 610	164 416	0.2
Martin	1.7	D	7.6	6.2	11.5	9.8	7.7	18.7	9.7	44 420	285	1 629	79 518	1.5
Miami-Dade	0.3	0.0	4.7	3.0	14.9	7.3	9.7	11.5	13.9	414 805	154	162 767	1 021 527	3.2
Monroe	0.0	0.1	6.2	1.2	7.8	9.4	6.3	6.8	22.5	16 920	215	1 308	53 122	0.7
Nassau	0.3	0.0	5.0	8.6	9.8	7.3	3.3	9.4	20.3	19 445	248	1 135	37 453	7.0
Okaloosa	0.0	0.0	3.0	4.0	12.2	6.6	4.9	7.5	43.7	39 715	200	3 193	96 046	3.9
Okeechobee	14.4	D	5.0	3.9	D	8.1	3.2	D	19.8	8 750	222	1 081	18 149	-1.9
Orange	0.2	0.0	5.1	5.1	13.6	6.1	8.8	10.6	10.7	182 755	142	35 155	525 243	7.7
Osceola	1.2	0.0	6.9	1.6	4.3	10.3	5.0	15.4	17.2	57 710	179	10 646	143 514	12.0
Palm Beach	0.7	-0.2	5.5	3.6	14.7	7.4	11.5	13.3	11.4	307 975	217	24 189	683 521	2.8
Pasco	0.6	0.1	8.0	3.4	7.1	14.0	4.2	20.2	16.7	130 865	263	11 885	236 464	3.3
Pinellas	0.0	0.0	4.6	9.2	13.5	7.9	9.3	15.4	11.9	240 625	254	21 723	507 425	0.8
Polk	0.9	0.6	6.0	9.4	5.6	8.0	7.5	14.1	13.6	152 835	235	21 247	286 515	1.9

1. Per 1,000 resident population estimated as of July 1 of the year shown.

Table B. States and Counties — **Housing, Labor Force, and Employment**

STATE County	Housing units, 2011–2015								Civilian labor force, 2016				Civilian employment,[6] 2011–2015		
	Occupied units										Unemployment			Percent	
			Owner-occupied			Renter-occupied									
				Median owner cost as a percent of income											Con-struction, produc-tion, and mainte-nance occu-pations
				With a mort-gage	Without a mort-gage[2]	Median rent[3]	Median rent as a per-cent of income[2]	Sub-stand-ard units[4] (percent)		Percent change, 2015–2016				Manage-ment, business, science and arts	
	Total	Percent	Median value[1]						Total		Total	Rate[5]	Total		
	89	90	91	92	93	94	95	96	97	98	99	100	101	102	103

CONNECTICUT—Cont'd															
Tolland....................	54 467	73.2	247 700	23.1	13.7	1 040	30.2	1.0	84 865	0.0	3 712	4.4	80 190	41.8	18.9
Windham...................	44 276	70.4	197 500	24.6	15.1	847	31.1	2.0	62 887	0.1	3 430	5.5	58 842	32.1	23.7
DELAWARE	344 022	71.2	231 500	22.9	11.0	1 018	29.9	2.1	472 677	1.2	20 704	4.4	433 816	38.4	19.0
Kent.........................	60 571	69.6	200 500	23.5	11.3	985	32.2	2.0	77 541	1.2	3 681	4.7	75 246	32.7	24.1
New Castle................	202 268	69.1	242 400	22.3	10.6	1 038	29.5	2.0	295 092	0.9	12 645	4.3	268 331	42.6	15.6
Sussex.....................	81 183	77.6	228 500	24.0	11.5	974	29.4	2.4	100 044	2.0	4 378	4.4	90 239	30.5	25.0
DISTRICT OF COLUMBIA..	273 390	41.2	475 800	22.2	10.2	1 327	29.5	3.7	392 448	1.5	23 602	6.0	337 815	60.9	6.5
District of Columbia..............	273 390	41.2	475 800	22.2	10.2	1 327	29.5	3.7	392 448	1.5	23 602	6.0	337 815	60.9	6.5
FLORIDA...................	7 300 494	65.3	159 000	25.6	12.9	1 002	34.4	3.1	9 838 942	2.3	480 368	4.9	8 541 291	34.1	18.0
Alachua....................	96 703	53.2	164 000	22.0	11.0	871	35.9	2.1	132 316	2.3	5 638	4.3	116 659	46.4	10.8
Baker........................	8 205	78.1	114 300	22.0	10.0	691	32.7	4.0	11 393	2.1	557	4.9	10 174	29.6	26.0
Bay...........................	67 922	61.4	157 800	23.7	11.4	922	31.4	1.9	87 996	0.6	4 305	4.9	77 894	32.3	20.3
Bradford....................	8 770	73.9	89 200	19.6	10.0	705	34.4	2.0	10 944	2.0	466	4.3	9 225	32.8	21.8
Brevard.....................	222 791	71.7	142 200	24.0	11.7	909	32.1	1.6	262 026	2.3	13 574	5.2	229 693	36.6	17.6
Broward.....................	670 284	63.5	185 900	28.4	16.1	1 191	36.1	3.9	1 004 123	1.7	46 241	4.6	890 997	35.4	16.3
Calhoun....................	4 784	81.0	75 500	23.4	10.0	659	33.6	5.0	4 956	0.4	281	5.7	4 735	25.4	25.3
Charlotte...................	71 856	78.0	145 700	27.8	12.8	886	32.9	1.7	69 152	2.3	3 687	5.3	56 730	28.1	19.1
Citrus.......................	61 012	81.2	112 300	23.8	12.1	767	33.8	2.1	47 754	0.0	3 238	6.8	43 486	28.8	22.0
Clay..........................	69 053	74.8	153 000	22.6	10.0	1 014	28.7	2.3	100 545	2.3	4 546	4.5	86 374	33.5	21.6
Collier......................	129 888	72.2	272 800	27.7	13.0	1 063	32.6	4.1	167 737	2.6	7 987	4.8	141 106	29.7	20.2
Columbia..................	23 708	71.4	103 500	23.0	10.7	780	27.1	3.9	29 826	3.1	1 436	4.8	25 226	30.6	22.9
DeSoto......................	11 238	70.4	80 400	23.8	10.8	665	31.3	7.0	13 513	1.1	701	5.2	12 279	15.7	42.9
Dixie........................	6 051	78.8	73 800	26.5	10.8	646	31.1	3.1	5 610	0.6	311	5.5	4 910	23.9	34.1
Duval........................	337 900	59.2	142 300	24.0	11.9	943	32.9	2.3	468 907	1.9	23 601	5.0	409 421	35.5	18.2
Escambia..................	113 660	61.3	120 200	22.6	11.5	892	31.0	1.5	140 893	2.1	6 973	4.9	130 402	32.2	18.3
Flagler......................	36 950	77.5	164 100	27.7	12.3	1 053	29.7	1.7	44 984	3.2	2 492	5.5	36 923	30.0	18.0
Franklin....................	4 338	72.5	122 600	28.2	12.1	711	24.8	3.7	4 778	0.3	206	4.3	4 331	28.7	27.8
Gadsden...................	16 964	70.7	108 400	24.8	11.3	682	33.8	6.2	18 340	0.9	1 149	6.3	16 733	28.9	22.3
Gilchrist....................	6 187	80.9	99 900	23.5	12.3	658	29.6	2.3	6 652	2.5	342	5.1	6 260	27.6	29.2
Glades......................	3 920	74.2	84 500	25.2	11.3	681	33.4	3.6	4 816	2.4	299	6.2	3 701	23.2	26.1
Gulf.........................	5 349	73.3	142 700	26.4	12.5	800	30.4	3.7	5 995	0.1	272	4.5	5 604	26.9	25.6
Hamilton...................	4 688	73.0	69 500	23.6	10.6	608	33.2	3.1	4 644	2.9	262	5.6	3 966	27.4	29.0
Hardee.....................	7 618	69.6	80 700	24.9	11.6	631	29.3	8.7	9 389	-6.8	626	6.7	9 517	20.1	41.7
Hendry.....................	11 345	68.8	72 400	24.0	10.7	709	27.9	8.6	15 480	2.7	1 402	9.1	14 732	22.0	47.6
Hernando..................	70 452	77.8	109 300	25.5	12.0	884	33.5	1.7	67 466	2.2	4 122	6.1	58 359	29.1	21.2
Highlands	40 397	75.9	85 200	24.4	11.6	710	33.4	3.2	36 071	2.2	2 376	6.6	31 131	27.7	21.7
Hillsborough	486 078	58.5	159 200	23.5	11.3	965	32.4	3.6	706 028	2.6	31 675	4.5	608 977	37.4	17.1
Holmes.....................	6 828	79.4	85 100	23.4	11.5	644	34.1	2.5	6 741	0.9	364	5.4	6 118	25.7	27.3
Indian River..............	57 825	74.7	157 800	24.7	12.5	860	34.4	1.9	62 248	1.8	3 829	6.2	53 211	32.3	18.9
Jackson....................	16 309	72.0	92 100	24.2	12.8	601	30.1	3.1	17 361	0.4	916	5.3	15 621	28.3	20.6
Jefferson..................	5 411	76.7	135 200	24.2	12.6	716	33.9	1.5	5 426	1.1	289	5.3	4 946	41.1	17.1
Lafayette..................	2 493	80.3	109 800	24.0	11.6	548	27.6	4.1	3 066	-4.2	125	4.1	2 685	29.8	26.6
Lake.........................	119 251	74.8	140 100	23.9	12.3	936	33.4	2.8	144 463	2.7	7 031	4.9	121 642	31.0	19.9
Lee	252 287	69.0	157 400	25.8	13.1	951	31.9	2.9	328 512	3.0	15 077	4.6	263 079	30.2	19.2
Leon.........................	110 834	52.3	180 900	22.7	10.2	925	37.3	2.5	149 890	1.7	6 846	4.6	140 338	44.3	10.7
Levy.........................	15 516	76.7	88 600	24.7	11.4	671	30.9	2.8	16 626	1.2	862	5.2	14 392	25.1	29.3
Liberty.....................	2 433	74.0	74 000	19.1	10.0	573	21.2	4.2	2 649	0.5	141	5.3	2 748	32.3	25.0
Madison....................	6 614	78.4	78 500	24.0	14.5	599	39.0	3.9	7 412	-0.8	393	5.3	6 141	30.1	30.5
Manatee...................	134 725	69.8	169 000	24.7	12.8	954	33.2	2.7	168 742	2.5	7 693	4.6	140 416	33.2	19.1
Marion......................	132 287	75.6	111 000	25.1	12.1	803	32.7	2.0	132 670	2.1	7 731	5.8	115 459	27.4	20.4
Martin.......................	61 952	75.5	200 200	26.3	13.6	971	32.4	2.0	71 307	2.7	3 465	4.9	61 157	36.7	16.6
Miami-Dade..............	842 153	53.8	203 300	30.4	15.0	1 112	39.4	6.2	1 341 510	1.8	72 494	5.4	1 204 871	31.5	19.4
Monroe.....................	28 910	61.1	386 400	32.9	13.7	1 385	35.6	3.0	46 308	1.3	1 463	3.2	38 504	32.1	18.5
Nassau.....................	28 306	76.2	177 100	24.4	10.2	1 046	31.3	1.8	37 328	2.2	1 706	4.6	31 605	31.3	26.0
Okaloosa..................	74 884	63.5	186 300	23.5	10.8	1 024	30.9	1.9	93 827	2.4	3 767	4.0	84 899	34.0	18.3
Okeechobee..............	13 046	70.7	93 800	25.1	11.5	694	31.5	5.7	17 591	2.1	956	5.4	13 227	21.2	34.5
Orange.....................	434 319	55.0	163 800	25.4	12.5	1 033	34.6	2.8	705 333	2.9	31 043	4.4	603 683	35.0	15.8
Osceola....................	92 338	60.9	132 100	28.1	13.6	1 049	36.1	3.6	161 498	2.8	8 141	5.0	131 450	24.4	20.7
Palm Beach...............	534 605	69.1	204 700	27.3	15.0	1 170	36.0	3.3	710 513	3.0	34 228	4.8	617 902	35.6	16.1
Pasco.......................	186 318	73.8	117 800	24.5	12.1	930	32.6	2.2	220 407	2.5	11 466	5.2	187 556	35.5	17.3
Pinellas....................	402 653	64.8	150 200	25.4	14.3	952	32.7	1.8	481 914	2.5	21 081	4.4	423 351	37.4	15.7
Polk.........................	221 381	68.8	107 300	24.1	12.1	870	31.9	3.7	284 936	1.9	16 069	5.6	245 853	29.5	23.8

1. Specified owner-occupied units.   2. A value of 10.0 represents 10 percent or less; a value of 50.0 represents 50 percent or more.   3. Specified renter-occupied units.
4. Overcrowded or lacking complete plumbing facilities.   5. Percent of civilian labor force.   6. Civilian employed persons 16 years old and over.

Table B. States and Counties — Nonfarm Employment and Agriculture

STATE County	Number of establish- ments	Total	Health care and social assistance	Manufac- turing	Retail trade	Finance and insurance	Professional, scientific, and technical services	Total (mil dol)	Average per employee (dollars)	Number	Fewer than 50 acres	500 acres or more	Farm operators whose principal occu- pation is farming (percent)
	104	105	106	107	108	109	110	111	112	113	114	115	116
CONNECTICUT—Cont'd													
Tolland	2 433	32 903	6 039	3 233	5 164	590	1 226	1 164	35 365	578	64.5	2.4	34.3
Windham	2 048	30 354	7 123	5 483	5 266	692	556	1 178	38 805	692	62.0	3.0	51.3
DELAWARE	24 852	397 385	66 496	26 420	55 070	42 783	31 486	21 305	53 614	2 451	56.5	9.8	63.9
Kent	3 323	51 662	10 568	4 609	9 216	1 453	2 404	1 954	37 832	863	54.5	9.0	56.8
New Castle	15 749	275 123	44 015	11 607	32 697	38 445	26 072	16 720	60 772	374	64.7	9.4	57.8
Sussex	5 509	65 247	11 780	10 204	13 150	1 929	1 711	2 335	35 781	1 214	55.4	10.5	70.8
DISTRICT OF COLUMBIA..	22 553	513 002	66 439	1 013	21 999	17 156	100 443	38 446	74 943	NA	NA	NA	NA
District of Columbia	22 553	513 002	66 439	1 013	21 999	17 156	100 443	38 446	74 943	NA	NA	NA	NA
FLORIDA	532 830	7 777 990	1 049 304	298 117	1 070 533	344 804	487 877	337 075	43 337	47 740	68.6	5.6	48.0
Alachua	6 068	90 590	24 364	3 715	13 844	4 107	5 519	3 501	38 647	1 662	69.7	4.9	42.3
Baker	390	5 389	1 861	149	853	136	109	178	33 051	381	74.8	3.4	35.7
Bay	4 578	63 167	9 381	4 371	11 650	1 503	4 245	2 262	35 811	115	71.3	2.6	42.6
Bradford	420	4 080	818	176	998	133	100	124	30 400	470	68.3	1.9	46.0
Brevard	13 648	169 860	29 105	18 282	28 570	4 861	13 435	7 288	42 905	513	80.3	5.1	38.8
Broward	59 516	675 441	91 245	23 515	110 125	30 361	52 079	30 839	45 657	615	93.7	1.3	50.1
Calhoun	184	1 778	689	43	323	50	12	48	26 894	218	51.8	8.3	31.2
Charlotte	3 815	37 485	8 238	516	9 117	1 076	1 452	1 236	32 980	284	61.3	12.0	51.1
Citrus	2 715	27 791	9 121	282	5 742	666	844	938	33 764	559	73.9	3.4	49.7
Clay	3 708	38 638	8 165	983	8 629	1 049	3 148	1 278	33 071	403	75.9	2.0	44.7
Collier	11 293	118 795	17 249	3 102	21 075	3 843	5 267	4 918	41 395	319	74.0	10.3	43.9
Columbia	1 321	18 673	4 552	740	3 209	464	484	699	37 413	945	65.4	4.6	46.5
DeSoto	450	5 140	1 068	375	1 011	146	129	172	33 558	836	63.0	9.4	48.4
Dixie	179	1 609	290	466	298	38	29	45	27 909	204	60.3	6.4	30.9
Duval	24 599	417 943	56 614	21 377	51 733	45 461	25 984	20 169	48 258	352	76.4	3.1	59.9
Escambia	6 754	102 315	21 199	4 589	15 872	7 075	6 935	4 013	39 221	729	68.2	4.5	43.2
Flagler	2 000	17 877	3 110	1 072	3 678	626	634	569	31 814	118	46.6	14.4	54.2
Franklin	323	2 258	294	D	464	74	74	63	27 815	20	65.0	0.0	40.0
Gadsden	647	8 756	2 537	940	1 230	149	120	317	36 254	402	56.5	5.2	39.6
Gilchrist	217	1 544	585	94	185	41	45	52	33 586	581	66.3	5.3	44.8
Glades	107	802	122	110	34	18	7	28	34 401	331	53.5	15.7	39.3
Gulf	290	2 662	562	47	400	89	101	82	30 878	34	41.2	5.9	52.9
Hamilton	166	1 904	264	D	439	29	40	83	43 635	292	36.0	9.6	64.4
Hardee	383	4 050	1 213	264	678	240	62	122	30 091	982	57.3	9.4	50.2
Hendry	553	5 816	1 048	822	1 218	201	368	201	34 500	406	49.8	22.7	51.2
Hernando	3 065	32 189	8 024	1 856	7 648	736	1 276	1 008	31 307	799	76.0	3.3	51.2
Highlands	1 876	19 861	5 558	747	4 521	513	653	614	30 897	969	64.3	11.0	49.3
Hillsborough	35 038	581 249	77 841	21 354	68 778	50 500	59 335	27 870	47 948	2 466	80.3	2.1	51.7
Holmes	260	1 891	531	105	400	61	64	49	25 998	801	41.7	4.2	52.6
Indian River	4 156	42 560	8 992	1 813	9 075	1 287	1 681	1 569	36 862	461	73.1	7.2	49.0
Jackson	768	9 040	1 766	650	1 986	334	237	288	31 858	1 160	39.0	8.7	42.1
Jefferson	242	1 580	228	16	370	101	58	48	30 477	617	56.1	6.6	37.0
Lafayette	93	687	149	54	77	54	17	18	26 408	221	29.9	13.6	59.7
Lake	6 877	77 497	17 278	3 340	15 459	1 866	2 762	2 584	33 349	1 784	76.7	3.3	43.9
Lee	17 459	201 523	34 908	4 754	38 959	5 713	11 139	7 656	37 991	844	79.5	4.5	48.1
Leon	7 474	96 315	17 901	1 483	16 823	4 464	10 369	3 845	39 923	284	63.4	4.6	38.4
Levy	693	5 547	629	504	1 447	214	169	161	29 064	1 053	64.7	4.4	49.9
Liberty	81	1 251	466	381	146	10	12	38	30 591	80	30.0	5.0	30.0
Madison	312	2 932	648	459	596	68	60	84	28 818	669	36.2	10.3	38.6
Manatee	8 480	94 811	15 059	8 009	19 086	2 427	3 758	3 435	36 231	689	62.6	9.6	43.4
Marion	6 912	80 011	16 190	6 651	16 145	1 958	3 840	2 735	34 185	3 870	76.7	2.2	49.5
Martin	5 336	54 361	10 150	2 604	10 024	1 807	3 542	2 114	38 879	587	74.3	9.7	54.7
Miami-Dade	82 293	949 355	135 368	33 055	143 426	47 858	67 300	44 835	47 226	2 954	92.8	1.2	56.5
Monroe	3 740	31 647	2 490	320	6 057	701	959	1 046	33 049	28	92.9	0.0	25.0
Nassau	1 742	16 679	2 354	1 343	3 140	393	595	585	35 097	444	74.1	2.9	45.0
Okaloosa	5 206	59 151	8 622	1 795	12 337	2 297	6 195	2 180	36 862	477	52.0	4.8	37.9
Okeechobee	775	6 813	1 346	420	1 713	183	178	221	32 496	678	47.9	25.1	56.6
Orange	35 327	678 721	69 664	25 785	84 395	20 670	47 652	29 466	43 413	662	80.5	4.1	51.8
Osceola	5 635	71 589	11 195	1 616	15 360	1 241	1 737	2 286	31 927	365	58.1	15.9	58.9
Palm Beach	46 570	497 353	80 302	12 611	78 648	20 996	40 524	23 636	47 524	1 409	90.0	3.5	56.7
Pasco	9 125	93 206	20 327	3 217	21 976	2 461	4 863	3 175	34 060	1 065	75.1	5.3	52.1
Pinellas	27 498	373 627	69 507	28 371	52 965	23 766	28 551	16 046	42 948	118	91.5	0.0	45.8
Polk	11 218	174 572	27 735	14 558	26 277	10 929	5 973	6 858	39 285	2 415	64.4	7.2	45.3

Table B. States and Counties — **Agriculture**

	Agriculture, 2012 (cont.)														
STATE County	Land in farms					Value of land and buildings (dollars)		Value of machinery and equipment, average per farm (dollars)	Value of products sold				Percent of farms with sales of:		Government payments	
			Acres								Percent from:					
	Acreage (1,000)	Percent change, 2007–2012	Average size of farm	Total irrigated (1,000)	Total cropland (1,000)	Average per farm	Average per acre		Total (mil dol)	Average per farm (dollars)	Crops	Live-stock and poultry products	$10,000 or more	$100,000 or more	Total ($1,000)	Percent of farms
	117	118	119	120	121	122	123	124	125	126	127	128	129	130	131	132
·CONNECTICUT—Cont'd																
Tolland	48	21.4	83	0.5	18.5	820 254	9 926	78 550	55.0	95 107	64.9	35.1	26.8	8.0	544	7.8
Windham	58	-3.1	84	0.5	20.1	642 272	7 628	58 766	44.2	63 890	40.8	59.2	31.8	7.1	1 259	10.8
DELAWARE	509	-0.3	208	127.3	439.2	1 694 584	8 166	161 559	1 274.0	519 794	33.7	66.3	64.6	41.7	9 677	37.4
Kent	172	-0.9	200	31.8	147.4	1 596 656	7 999	121 074	277.7	321 816	D	D	53.3	29.8	2 550	37.2
New Castle	64	-4.2	172	4.6	56.1	1 704 668	9 935	138 596	75.2	200 957	D	D	51.6	18.7	1 802	31.0
Sussex	272	1.0	224	90.8	235.7	1 761 092	7 853	197 414	921.1	758 755	27.1	72.9	76.7	57.2	5 325	39.5
DISTRICT OF COLUMBIA..	NA	NA	NA	NA	NA	NA	NA	NA	NA	NA	NA	NA	NA	NA	NA	NA
District of Columbia	NA	NA	NA	NA	NA	NA	NA	NA	NA	NA	NA	NA	NA	NA	NA	NA
FLORIDA	9 548	3.4	200	1 493.3	2 744.1	1 040 259	5 201	60 838	7 701.5	161 322	77.5	22.5	34.3	10.9	40 164	8.3
Alachua	188	8.8	113	10.7	58.7	608 861	5 383	50 010	101.2	60 865	68.5	31.5	31.5	6.3	654	6.2
Baker	33	23.2	86	0.3	4.4	560 165	6 483	29 995	15.8	41 491	14.9	85.1	20.7	2.1	103	4.2
Bay	10	-15.9	91	D	2.7	473 730	5 193	36 009	2.7	23 635	83.6	16.4	20.0	0.9	65	7.0
Bradford	35	18.4	75	0.7	9.2	312 011	4 181	34 200	13.1	27 962	18.7	81.3	19.1	2.6	52	4.5
Brevard	146	-12.3	286	13.4	19.3	1 545 698	5 414	45 433	46.0	89 651	77.2	22.8	36.8	6.6	142	2.1
Broward	14	65.9	24	1.8	4.3	540 185	22 916	31 886	47.4	77 099	91.2	8.8	41.0	8.6	246	2.9
Calhoun	43	9.6	197	1.6	18.9	417 583	2 124	60 647	19.9	91 096	83.4	16.6	27.5	7.8	332	22.9
Charlotte	217	30.8	765	13.7	18.4	3 875 556	5 067	65 965	103.4	364 088	91.8	8.2	38.0	13.0	92	1.8
Citrus	41	1.3	73	0.7	7.3	480 195	6 621	29 451	14.1	25 190	54.9	45.1	17.7	3.4	146	3.6
Clay	52	24.2	128	0.6	5.2	450 531	3 520	28 380	9.3	22 970	62.8	37.2	17.1	2.2	24	3.2
Collier	124	12.4	387	26.4	66.9	1 736 727	4 482	151 806	202.8	635 583	98.1	1.9	36.4	14.7	207	2.8
Columbia	101	18.0	107	6.1	33.4	486 956	4 536	73 098	108.6	114 893	17.4	82.6	18.0	5.0	709	10.4
DeSoto	303	16.4	362	47.7	62.4	1 701 201	4 696	60 083	198.3	237 166	82.2	17.8	39.4	14.4	196	1.3
Dixie	45	7.6	222	3.4	10.6	873 338	3 943	72 917	19.1	93 686	D	D	20.6	2.9	124	5.4
Duval	28	5.6	80	1.1	5.5	557 054	6 935	32 875	16.2	45 903	75.9	24.1	21.3	2.6	141	5.1
Escambia	75	-9.0	102	4.6	40.1	499 244	4 880	59 298	42.6	58 375	89.4	10.6	18.7	6.0	1 426	24.1
Flagler	44	-25.3	369	3.9	5.5	1 566 102	4 239	60 636	16.9	143 602	91.9	8.1	33.1	11.0	D	2.5
Franklin	2	251.6	90	0.0	0.8	174 150	1 943	48 400	0.6	28 500	44.7	55.4	40.0	10.0	63	30.0
Gadsden	51	7.9	126	2.7	13.1	559 923	4 430	38 505	54.4	135 388	97.7	2.3	23.1	4.5	255	18.2
Gilchrist	84	18.0	144	12.6	43.7	481 217	3 332	62 892	88.7	152 732	31.6	68.4	27.4	7.4	746	12.0
Glades	443	10.0	1 338	88.5	56.5	4 087 441	3 056	84 066	106.5	321 807	73.2	26.8	32.3	14.8	383	7.9
Gulf	5	-3.1	135	D	0.5	565 500	4 184	39 588	0.9	27 147	4.8	95.2	14.7	5.9	D	8.8
Hamilton	72	11.0	246	9.5	28.4	710 452	2 886	87 274	45.5	155 771	80.2	19.8	31.8	9.2	234	31.8
Hardee	274	-2.1	279	36.0	51.8	1 150 569	4 125	52 140	218.4	222 378	66.4	33.6	48.1	20.0	345	2.4
Hendry	496	6.6	1 221	193.1	262.4	4 953 187	4 057	206 352	499.9	1 231 345	95.8	4.2	53.4	31.8	527	5.9
Hernando	62	10.1	78	2.7	15.5	650 753	8 394	38 645	28.4	35 492	56.1	43.9	24.8	6.1	441	1.8
Highlands	490	2.9	506	61.8	84.0	1 484 852	2 937	82 911	273.4	282 121	72.6	27.4	41.4	21.4	609	2.2
Hillsborough	215	-2.2	87	26.1	75.8	788 988	9 052	54 052	378.1	153 316	84.2	15.8	32.5	10.5	865	2.5
Holmes	106	-30.5	132	1.1	34.4	371 996	2 823	42 097	28.9	36 105	46.0	54.0	25.1	7.7	754	26.7
Indian River	162	3.3	352	57.6	54.8	1 359 020	3 856	54 672	144.9	314 419	92.2	7.8	49.7	18.4	809	4.1
Jackson	262	-15.8	226	21.5	117.6	761 272	3 367	65 673	92.7	79 907	81.4	18.6	34.0	11.0	3 805	41.3
Jefferson	130	-12.1	210	2.4	24.6	884 258	4 212	53 783	48.3	78 292	43.6	56.4	25.6	4.7	425	19.0
Lafayette	91	12.3	413	10.7	22.3	1 703 208	4 124	114 973	87.6	396 217	13.0	87.0	39.8	24.0	914	32.6
Lake	152	25.3	85	15.2	36.0	642 919	7 559	34 263	142.1	79 631	94.0	6.0	32.7	9.9	255	1.2
Lee	87	1.6	103	13.6	22.8	979 161	9 485	53 895	105.9	125 478	95.8	4.2	32.8	7.3	61	1.7
Leon	81	-10.4	286	2.0	6.6	1 574 884	5 501	37 673	3.8	13 493	72.7	27.3	22.5	3.5	42	5.6
Levy	167	-3.9	159	13.7	59.8	949 232	5 972	62 627	80.4	76 335	52.4	47.6	32.5	10.8	1 244	8.0
Liberty	14	-40.0	177	D	1.2	479 600	2 705	34 450	1.5	18 750	2.9	97.1	22.5	5.0	39	8.8
Madison	143	-4.0	214	8.1	38.5	719 737	3 367	49 706	51.8	77 463	30.4	69.6	28.4	8.4	520	26.3
Manatee	186	-17.2	271	50.1	70.4	1 512 093	5 590	115 546	298.4	433 160	91.4	8.6	42.4	13.2	11	0.9
Marion	321	20.6	83	13.2	69.8	776 909	9 353	37 481	188.2	48 624	23.3	76.7	27.8	8.2	483	2.1
Martin	139	7.7	237	34.8	43.8	1 561 876	6 581	64 925	165.5	281 862	68.1	31.9	39.0	11.6	398	4.8
Miami-Dade	81	21.3	28	45.2	64.9	699 727	25 423	47 644	604.2	204 549	98.0	2.0	58.5	16.0	6 944	8.5
Monroe	0	154.5	17	0.0	0.1	322 607	18 977	60 036	10.8	386 964	6.0	94.0	50.0	21.4	0	0.0
Nassau	39	25.8	89	0.1	4.9	424 045	4 786	37 444	6.5	14 739	18.7	81.3	14.6	1.1	D	0.9
Okaloosa	61	-6.7	129	0.2	18.6	467 688	3 628	51 556	10.3	21 562	81.1	18.9	21.0	4.4	983	30.8
Okeechobee	442	30.6	652	19.4	52.1	2 992 147	4 592	82 420	256.9	378 876	19.7	80.3	45.0	21.4	2 120	18.1
Orange	132	-2.7	200	9.5	13.8	1 673 992	8 365	56 754	261.6	395 193	96.2	3.8	51.5	26.1	11	0.6
Osceola	547	-15.4	1 499	29.2	29.7	5 917 241	3 948	89 249	108.6	297 660	63.4	36.6	38.9	16.4	326	4.4
Palm Beach	514	-2.2	365	362.7	440.7	2 586 187	7 090	182 476	999.0	709 041	98.3	1.7	43.2	16.2	1 536	6.0
Pasco	171	14.1	161	6.6	24.7	1 086 574	6 763	41 420	73.9	69 351	40.4	59.6	31.2	7.1	355	2.4
Pinellas	1	1.6	13	0.1	0.6	377 805	30 143	43 763	2.6	22 415	72.9	27.1	39.0	4.2	9	5.1
Polk	521	-5.1	216	79.9	125.1	1 182 091	5 480	64 954	350.3	145 042	90.2	9.8	48.1	18.3	419	1.4

Table B. States and Counties — **Water Use, Wholesale Trade, Retail Trade, and Real Estate**

STATE County	Water use, 2010 Total water withdrawn (mil gal/day)	Gallons withdrawn per person per day	Wholesale trade,[1] 2012 Number of establishments	Number of employees	Sales (mil dol)	Annual payroll (mil dol)	Retail trade,[2] 2012 Number of establishments	Number of employees	Sales (mil dol)	Annual payroll (mil dol)	Real estate and rental and leasing,[2] 2012 Number of establishments	Number of employees	Receipts (mil dol)	Annual payroll (mil dol)
	133	134	135	136	137	138	139	140	141	142	143	144	145	146
CONNECTICUT—Cont'd														
Tolland	15.9	104	55	516	230.0	27.9	373	4 932	1 303.1	120.4	90	312	55.7	9.5
Windham	34.6	292	59	1 048	289.3	48.4	356	4 819	1 296.2	121.2	46	128	20.9	3.7
DELAWARE	717.5	799	835	7 653	5 628.9	385.9	3 616	51 711	14 456.0	1 270.1	1 111	5 402	5 471.2	264.9
Kent	43.3	267	94	D	D	D	561	8 856	2 690.8	214.1	127	459	92.2	17.0
New Castle	404.7	752	589	D	D	D	1 948	30 756	8 623.2	768.5	717	3 548	5 144.4	199.0
Sussex	269.5	1 367	152	1 203	783.4	52.6	1 107	12 099	3 142.1	287.6	267	1 395	234.6	48.9
DISTRICT OF COLUMBIA	0.1	0	335	3 415	2 591.9	260.6	1 710	19 780	4 439.9	525.2	1 112	10 103	3 213.9	673.7
District of Columbia	0.1	0	335	3 415	2 591.9	260.6	1 710	19 780	4 439.9	525.2	1 112	10 103	3 213.9	673.7
FLORIDA	14 936.0	794	27 109	252 418	252 626.6	12 867.6	71 189	947 877	273 867.1	24 033.5	29 845	139 955	30 560.1	5 337.4
Alachua	53.8	218	197	1 852	1 297.5	90.7	929	13 067	3 208.7	283.3	319	1 714	231.1	51.9
Baker	5.2	191	12	D	D	D	69	764	217.3	16.7	12	D	D	D
Bay	301.4	1 785	157	1 460	514.8	63.4	818	10 295	2 728.2	249.7	276	1 402	207.0	39.1
Bradford	4.3	151	15	D	D	D	82	830	241.2	20.2	22	155	9.8	2.1
Brevard	251.4	463	451	3 962	1 846.5	195.7	1 955	24 885	6 527.5	606.1	642	2 056	340.7	66.7
Broward	1 279.1	732	3 902	33 141	33 606.6	1 781.8	7 070	97 344	32 042.9	2 675.4	3 237	17 682	3 934.9	701.7
Calhoun	4.1	281	6	19	4.7	0.6	39	318	70.1	6.7	4	7	0.8	0.1
Charlotte	58.8	367	94	D	D	D	558	8 000	2 091.3	185.9	232	680	113.1	19.1
Citrus	1 201.2	8 505	80	D	D	D	455	5 122	1 421.0	121.8	172	415	54.4	10.4
Clay	23.3	122	105	897	329.7	35.0	580	8 009	1 909.5	182.3	181	584	117.2	18.1
Collier	256.9	799	306	2 417	2 306.5	163.1	1 418	18 924	5 304.1	511.0	907	2 610	546.6	109.8
Columbia	13.7	203	60	760	508.6	33.0	250	2 791	815.9	69.0	51	262	32.0	6.9
DeSoto	97.4	2 793	17	D	D	D	72	1 003	255.4	23.8	22	95	11.8	2.2
Dixie	4.6	280	3	7	6.0	0.1	39	251	56.9	6.0	4	3	0.4	0.0
Duval	758.1	877	1 126	19 090	19 018.9	1 081.3	3 231	45 707	12 985.3	1 164.5	1 204	7 127	1 839.1	321.6
Escambia	311.7	1 047	273	2 534	1 396.3	108.7	1 120	14 671	4 096.3	360.1	339	1 445	287.0	47.8
Flagler	23.4	245	54	239	70.5	10.0	235	3 094	773.3	73.3	137	355	75.7	13.2
Franklin	2.3	198	11	D	D	D	67	403	97.9	8.6	17	117	12.0	4.2
Gadsden	17.8	383	34	787	404.7	27.4	132	1 114	347.3	25.6	19	46	6.6	1.2
Gilchrist	9.1	538	8	44	58.4	2.0	29	178	52.5	3.5	6	13	1.4	0.4
Glades	162.3	12 599	3	D	D	D	13	38	11.7	0.7	2	D	D	D
Gulf	2.3	142	6	12	7.3	0.5	39	341	76.9	7.2	15	58	6.3	1.7
Hamilton	37.5	2 533	4	D	D	D	38	280	78.3	5.0	3	22	0.9	0.3
Hardee	52.4	1 891	19	282	176.8	9.6	76	667	172.1	14.3	21	58	6.1	1.4
Hendry	424.1	10 834	25	D	D	D	101	991	258.1	23.2	24	70	13.0	2.7
Hernando	38.8	225	92	367	149.2	14.4	431	6 620	1 749.4	155.2	138	394	50.4	9.1
Highlands	107.8	1 091	57	D	D	D	316	4 292	1 112.5	100.2	87	264	51.2	7.5
Hillsborough	1 960.7	1 595	1 727	25 316	21 082.8	1 237.1	4 389	63 643	18 274.2	1 670.9	1 848	9 476	2 483.5	414.7
Holmes	4.5	226	11	D	D	D	54	384	104.1	7.7	5	12	0.9	0.2
Indian River	154.5	1 119	125	D	D	D	659	7 958	1 881.3	189.1	231	1 213	162.3	36.9
Jackson	62.8	1 263	22	D	D	D	170	1 799	574.0	40.6	32	82	10.7	1.9
Jefferson	7.3	495	11	D	D	D	42	284	67.3	5.9	8	17	1.3	0.4
Lafayette	6.4	722	7	D	D	D	17	125	46.6	3.3	2	D	D	D
Lake	104.9	353	217	1 208	498.0	42.8	978	13 430	3 761.0	329.6	391	1 476	262.5	45.2
Lee	746.6	1 207	585	5 144	2 481.0	232.6	2 517	34 453	9 445.3	850.6	1 218	3 992	856.4	135.9
Leon	37.6	136	230	2 339	1 763.1	169.7	991	15 309	3 482.4	334.4	395	2 024	283.9	60.1
Levy	32.5	797	30	D	D	D	141	1 342	360.8	31.4	29	67	7.5	1.3
Liberty	1.5	181	2	D	D	D	15	111	30.2	2.3	1	D	D	D
Madison	14.0	730	8	D	D	D	62	447	171.2	9.5	11	19	2.3	0.5
Manatee	126.5	392	304	2 479	1 628.8	122.9	1 136	15 943	4 191.1	378.1	487	1 935	402.6	63.6
Marion	65.4	197	277	3 157	1 719.3	143.3	1 152	14 430	4 263.6	353.9	338	1 382	211.8	41.3
Martin	101.1	691	167	D	D	D	748	9 540	2 553.3	239.1	259	1 581	252.2	57.7
Miami-Dade	461.0	185	8 242	61 377	78 985.4	3 003.6	10 389	123 883	38 361.2	3 252.7	4 776	19 563	4 936.4	811.9
Monroe	1.2	16	88	276	259.4	12.3	639	5 576	1 467.1	149.1	317	948	193.1	30.5
Nassau	50.3	686	41	D	D	D	249	2 663	703.8	63.2	88	D	D	D
Okaloosa	26.3	145	137	1 029	429.7	52.2	850	11 135	2 886.5	266.9	342	1 385	252.9	54.9
Okeechobee	61.9	1 548	29	D	D	D	157	1 518	508.1	38.7	36	94	15.3	2.9
Orange	238.3	208	1 614	19 479	18 498.9	1 016.9	4 677	74 266	23 076.7	1 791.8	2 147	18 232	5 603.4	750.0
Osceola	97.6	363	134	1 288	2 461.0	57.6	845	12 399	3 236.2	272.3	448	4 095	433.7	119.5
Palm Beach	706.5	535	1 933	15 255	12 157.3	888.7	5 236	69 625	19 700.1	1 904.6	2 462	11 445	2 133.8	482.9
Pasco	1 658.8	3 570	303	1 725	709.2	72.5	1 385	18 940	5 278.2	450.4	438	1 432	234.6	41.9
Pinellas	493.0	538	1 122	13 166	12 411.5	703.1	3 562	47 381	14 578.2	1 253.7	1 517	5 979	1 035.5	206.6
Polk	298.7	496	544	8 056	10 601.3	394.0	1 756	22 988	6 495.3	558.8	651	2 928	510.6	93.1

1. Merchant wholesalers, except manufacturers' sales branches and offices. 2. Employer establishments.

Professional Services, Manufacturing, and Accommodation and Food Services

STATE County	Professional, scientific, and technical services, 2012				Manufacturing, 2012				Accommodation and food services, 2012			
	Number of establish-ments	Number of employees	Receipts (mil dol)	Annual payroll (mil dol)	Number of establish-ments	Number of employees	Receipts (mil dol)	Annual payroll (mil dol)	Number of establish-ments	Number of employees	Sales (mil dol)	Annual payroll (mil dol)
	147	148	149	150	151	152	153	154	155	156	157	158
CONNECTICUT—Cont'd												
Tolland	189	1 152	166.2	65.5	134	3 251	903.6	179.2	221	3 719	219.1	57.1
Windham	130	D	D	D	170	5 549	2 146.1	293.6	234	2 827	158.6	44.6
DELAWARE	2 543	D	D	D	573	26 355	22 597.4	1 393.2	1 987	35 609	2 148.4	566.7
Kent	278	D	D	D	74	4 797	1 930.8	218.9	272	6 183	475.8	101.1
New Castle	1 912	D	D	D	364	12 721	17 046.7	856.3	1 102	20 628	1 128.3	312.6
Sussex	353	D	D	D	135	8 837	3 619.9	318.0	613	8 798	544.3	152.9
DISTRICT OF COLUMBIA..	5 061	97 555	31 866.3	11 196.4	113	1 361	309.8	61.5	2 371	60 370	5 101.6	1 504.8
District of Columbia	5 061	97 555	31 866.3	11 196.4	113	1 361	309.8	61.5	2 371	60 370	5 101.6	1 504.8
FLORIDA	70 785	440 858	70 175.6	27 100.4	12 890	277 089	96 924.1	14 270.0	37 118	786 082	49 817.9	13 598.2
Alachua	819	4 648	547.7	219.4	149	3 166	D	167.8	569	D	D	D
Baker	20	100	8.6	3.1	4	126	D	D	35	581	23.7	6.4
Bay	407	3 335	466.0	177.0	100	3 840	1 473.8	195.3	465	9 994	565.2	161.3
Bradford	32	94	7.1	2.6	11	137	D	5.5	38	531	28.1	6.7
Brevard	1 669	13 893	2 433.6	981.2	407	19 152	5 441.9	1 311.3	1 042	18 994	902.6	257.7
Broward	9 583	46 815	8 286.6	2 833.0	1 454	21 057	6 010.6	1 054.7	3 685	72 428	5 129.2	1 322.2
Calhoun	8	32	2.1	1.3	7	51	D	1.6	14	D	D	D
Charlotte	381	1 295	138.5	50.5	69	402	90.4	14.6	261	4 804	219.2	61.7
Citrus	254	891	106.3	35.8	44	203	35.8	7.2	191	2 362	114.6	32.2
Clay	394	D	D	D	73	927	D	D	271	5 095	238.5	67.4
Collier	1 342	4 810	784.7	270.4	197	2 722	607.5	130.0	763	19 624	1 406.5	404.2
Columbia	113	433	43.7	14.4	42	608	249.0	26.7	116	2 331	106.6	29.5
DeSoto	32	114	15.1	3.7	8	235	D	11.4	31	402	19.6	5.2
Dixie	9	D	D	D	7	418	D	14.9	18	145	7.3	1.7
Duval	3 166	29 737	5 572.2	2 176.5	598	21 699	10 158.2	1 256.0	1 930	37 804	2 016.5	558.9
Escambia	774	7 159	939.6	359.4	174	4 026	2 427.8	242.5	558	11 548	598.4	162.5
Flagler	206	462	74.0	20.1	45	591	D	26.7	155	4 248	238.7	80.8
Franklin	27	52	7.8	2.3	NA	NA	NA	NA	45	555	28.8	9.0
Gadsden	36	D	D	D	31	840	178.6	31.9	53	559	28.8	7.7
Gilchrist	22	65	5.5	1.7	9	104	D	2.0	9	D	D	D
Glades	7	D	D	D	5	103	D	5.6	10	103	4.7	1.1
Gulf	27	130	27.8	7.2	10	64	8.6	2.2	32	324	16.5	4.4
Hamilton	9	22	1.9	0.5	5	D	D	D	16	165	6.1	1.7
Hardee	24	71	4.4	1.5	8	253	D	7.6	28	364	17.2	4.2
Hendry	40	D	D	D	20	887	D	44.0	65	760	37.4	9.3
Hernando	280	1 144	102.8	34.6	85	1 490	326.4	59.4	248	3 936	193.1	54.7
Highlands	132	602	57.5	18.4	44	570	214.0	22.7	147	2 331	110.6	30.7
Hillsborough	5 216	52 511	8 442.1	3 624.5	786	19 144	9 341.8	914.9	2 329	49 344	3 410.9	839.4
Holmes	17	87	14.8	3.3	14	103	14.6	3.9	16	203	9.4	2.4
Indian River	454	1 601	229.1	84.3	84	1 487	D	68.7	250	4 351	225.1	66.2
Jackson	43	233	22.7	9.5	16	459	D	18.0	70	1 044	52.2	11.9
Jefferson	17	49	5.4	1.6	4	D	D	D	17	D	D	D
Lafayette	8	D	D	D	4	62	D	2.1	7	D	D	D
Lake	622	2 090	238.2	87.7	145	2 439	D	99.3	451	8 045	394.9	109.9
Lee	1 893	12 312	2 202.7	844.3	366	4 010	812.8	165.1	1 189	25 851	1 346.6	402.6
Leon	1 363	11 176	1 519.5	766.3	97	1 462	400.0	72.0	644	13 783	629.0	170.3
Levy	42	149	15.8	4.8	20	385	D	13.9	66	661	28.8	7.9
Liberty	5	D	D	D	4	271	138.7	11.8	4	47	2.0	0.5
Madison	19	65	5.8	2.4	12	367	181.0	16.6	22	276	13.9	4.3
Manatee	928	12 131	728.3	402.2	283	8 121	2 338.0	403.9	593	9 987	532.9	155.6
Marion	669	3 676	415.5	157.2	178	4 806	1 471.2	212.9	437	7 369	375.2	102.5
Martin	697	3 071	403.4	149.0	162	2 869	1 103.3	151.9	334	6 215	312.7	91.6
Miami-Dade	12 008	58 711	11 734.8	4 018.8	2 070	30 387	7 192.9	1 318.2	5 052	104 467	7 696.6	2 078.4
Monroe	360	1 064	165.2	53.0	49	177	26.5	6.2	511	11 414	1 002.8	275.8
Nassau	184	559	80.2	28.5	37	1 239	929.1	80.9	158	3 378	203.3	71.5
Okaloosa	613	6 033	918.6	391.1	86	2 719	D	135.1	462	10 900	566.3	167.5
Okeechobee	45	164	15.4	4.9	17	197	D	6.8	56	912	40.1	10.3
Orange	4 882	44 689	6 856.9	3 044.6	747	23 702	8 280.9	1 531.7	2 715	102 733	8 326.4	2 131.0
Osceola	428	1 862	237.0	82.6	87	1 078	D	41.5	542	13 348	866.9	237.9
Palm Beach	7 364	36 924	6 189.1	2 368.7	928	11 731	3 550.4	614.2	2 665	57 739	3 467.3	1 044.3
Pasco	978	4 249	511.1	176.0	223	2 839	743.9	130.7	608	10 473	503.4	145.1
Pinellas	3 973	27 841	3 846.9	1 490.2	1 027	28 305	8 411.6	1 478.1	2 090	36 887	2 193.1	607.3
Polk	1 036	6 724	768.7	300.4	401	14 200	9 822.2	681.0	788	15 188	797.9	220.1

1. Establishment subject to federal tax.

Table B. States and Counties — Health Care and Social Assistance, Other Services, Nonemployer Businesses, and Residential Construction

STATE County	Health care and social assistance, 2012				Other services, 2012				Nonemployer businesses, 2015		Value of residential construction authorized by building permits, 2016	
	Number of establish-ments	Number of employees	Receipts (mil dol)	Annual payroll (mil dol)	Number of establish-ments	Number of employees	Receipts (mil dol)	Annual payroll (mil dol)	Number	Receipts (mil dol)	New Construction ($1,000)	Number of housing units
	159	160	161	162	163	164	165	166	167	168	169	170
CONNECTICUT—Cont'd												
Tolland	302	5 920	501.9	227.1	188	1 110	141.8	37.2	9 357	443.6	54 678	384
Windham	269	7 584	590.7	280.9	182	728	74.7	17.8	6 753	307.1	21 686	131
DELAWARE	2 524	61 897	7 003.3	2 995.9	1 513	9 841	974.7	290.1	60 734	3 698.0	721 546	5 804
Kent	398	9 405	990.6	379.5	233	1 325	105.5	32.0	9 585	574.1	183 853	1 276
New Castle	1 603	41 861	4 843.5	2 154.2	931	6 651	703.0	207.5	35 511	2 305.8	147 335	1 730
Sussex	523	10 631	1 169.2	462.2	349	1 865	166.2	50.6	15 638	818.2	390 359	2 798
DISTRICT OF COLUMBIA	2 065	67 742	8 964.0	3 596.5	3 357	58 982	19 773.5	4 238.6	56 359	2 777.6	510 518	4 690
District of Columbia	2 065	67 742	8 964.0	3 596.5	3 357	58 982	19 773.5	4 238.6	56 359	2 777.6	510 518	4 690
FLORIDA	56 659	991 254	124 061.4	44 435.6	34 843	195 176	20 798.9	5 414.5	2 040 339	89 088.7	25 863 502	116 240
Alachua	736	21 940	2 707.5	1 027.7	384	2 650	463.7	92.8	18 043	695.9	142 747	1 060
Baker	38	1 783	117.8	66.7	32	D	D	D	1 306	41.4	12 028	70
Bay	490	9 575	1 034.4	396.1	305	1 892	157.5	42.5	13 670	669.5	217 009	898
Bradford	39	831	80.0	25.6	24	86	7.2	2.0	1 208	42.2	3 920	30
Brevard	1 522	31 218	3 727.6	1 387.7	958	4 563	372.7	117.7	42 420	1 698.9	840 332	2 915
Broward	6 273	89 756	12 193.7	4 272.6	4 124	21 448	2 245.9	602.5	252 153	10 592.5	846 723	4 105
Calhoun	29	475	40.6	14.1	7	37	3.6	0.8	732	28.5	1 665	12
Charlotte	485	8 927	1 119.6	401.0	297	1 326	113.0	33.0	12 899	602.0	52 064	665
Citrus	390	7 932	819.7	307.1	212	744	53.2	15.5	8 892	346.1	88 490	516
Clay	448	7 152	825.0	300.2	280	D	D	D	12 882	496.6	224 931	1 190
Collier	995	16 310	2 089.4	772.0	850	5 209	474.4	138.1	38 777	2 323.8	1 093 119	3 829
Columbia	175	4 387	567.3	215.6	70	299	27.1	6.3	3 950	177.5	15 463	104
DeSoto	44	1 009	96.8	38.3	25	78	4.4	1.5	1 603	60.6	11 938	71
Dixie	14	136	9.1	3.3	14	46	4.9	0.8	798	30.3	3 790	30
Duval	2 513	55 950	7 324.9	2 580.2	1 612	D	D	D	67 189	2 646.7	969 645	5 751
Escambia	758	20 561	2 476.2	948.2	439	2 685	260.9	73.5	20 822	870.4	218 294	1 456
Flagler	196	2 629	336.2	106.8	136	533	40.6	10.7	8 789	402.8	233 405	796
Franklin	21	303	22.2	8.1	15	59	4.1	1.4	1 312	54.4	14 238	65
Gadsden	54	2 437	155.6	99.5	32	111	9.1	2.6	2 977	87.2	8 935	41
Gilchrist	21	497	45.1	15.8	8	14	1.5	0.4	960	37.9	7 397	50
Glades	7	D	D	D	6	D	D	D	583	20.7	3 362	58
Gulf	25	476	43.8	16.4	16	44	3.0	0.9	1 156	51.9	32 488	157
Hamilton	17	D	D	D	13	41	3.8	1.1	584	23.4	0	0
Hardee	57	1 123	82.0	35.7	29	60	4.3	1.1	1 298	58.4	3 347	21
Hendry	69	1 081	85.1	35.8	46	172	13.0	3.7	2 902	105.2	10 419	64
Hernando	507	7 744	984.0	302.9	212	1 008	71.4	21.5	11 018	410.7	132 553	787
Highlands	325	5 021	576.5	194.8	134	504	37.4	9.1	5 802	238.2	32 541	128
Hillsborough	3 703	72 572	10 416.0	3 584.0	2 080	14 640	1 646.3	432.3	116 379	5 151.9	2 670 056	10 662
Holmes	33	511	36.0	12.2	14	49	3.1	1.1	1 081	37.8	3 589	18
Indian River	466	7 828	886.2	333.8	280	1 395	124.5	34.6	13 700	760.1	381 844	1 018
Jackson	83	1 796	157.4	64.3	53	225	22.9	6.0	2 717	93.8	6 988	48
Jefferson	26	238	12.0	5.1	12	31	2.0	0.5	1 039	35.1	3 800	23
Lafayette	11	135	7.7	3.4	3	D	D	D	340	14.4	1 255	7
Lake	825	15 150	1 648.7	639.5	449	2 246	194.7	57.9	24 235	973.1	1 061 061	3 966
Lee	1 488	26 009	3 362.1	1 226.1	1 209	6 696	580.1	164.2	63 927	3 068.8	1 260 040	5 417
Leon	745	16 817	1 893.7	744.3	615	4 445	666.4	170.7	20 385	810.6	177 022	1 380
Levy	62	566	35.3	14.5	48	111	13.2	2.3	2 775	128.0	14 076	143
Liberty	10	D	D	D	3	13	2.2	0.5	423	11.6	2 120	18
Madison	39	648	42.5	17.2	17	D	D	D	1 002	40.0	6 126	30
Manatee	877	14 956	1 512.5	582.0	534	2 743	196.5	59.5	29 731	1 413.4	817 248	4 168
Marion	878	15 494	1 874.0	674.9	455	2 315	196.6	54.0	24 391	1 017.0	238 690	1 428
Martin	536	8 591	946.3	388.8	399	2 032	181.9	54.8	15 824	899.5	232 955	427
Miami-Dade	9 030	132 886	17 547.4	6 100.1	4 903	28 561	3 116.7	758.0	462 297	19 337.4	2 088 260	9 317
Monroe	225	2 464	323.1	109.9	252	1 060	106.9	32.0	12 494	751.2	65 475	220
Nassau	168	2 337	230.5	89.6	123	D	D	D	5 798	268.5	290 893	1 025
Okaloosa	545	8 715	1 111.1	373.8	348	1 683	146.0	44.2	15 792	797.8	236 876	837
Okeechobee	99	1 305	162.4	52.9	54	225	17.6	5.0	2 248	95.0	14 416	41
Orange	3 056	66 554	8 920.9	3 080.9	2 033	15 498	1 676.9	435.9	125 651	5 091.3	2 374 812	11 952
Osceola	540	10 184	1 301.7	460.0	330	1 364	155.8	30.6	30 038	1 045.0	1 042 091	4 297
Palm Beach	5 319	75 097	9 756.7	3 371.0	3 204	18 011	1 831.0	493.9	171 074	8 594.5	1 272 494	5 320
Pasco	1 160	17 932	2 142.5	771.5	640	2 765	231.7	66.4	34 613	1 404.4	678 391	3 905
Pinellas	3 215	64 140	7 744.4	2 913.0	1 924	10 377	1 033.2	292.6	82 176	3 813.3	478 582	2 398
Polk	1 048	27 066	3 015.2	1 109.8	673	3 366	328.5	94.6	41 872	1 618.1	752 640	4 567

Table B. States and Counties — Government Employment and Payroll, and Local Government Finances

STATE County	Government employment and payroll, 2012									Local government finances, 2012				
			March payroll (percent of total)							General revenue				
												Taxes		
													Per capita[1] (dollars)	
	Full-time equivalent employees	March payroll (dollars)	Administration, judicial, and legal	Police and Corrections	Fire Protection	Highways and transportation	Health and Welfare	Natural resources and utilities	Education and libraries	Total (mil dol)	Inter-governmental (mil dol)	Total (mil dol)	Total	Property
	171	172	173	174	175	176	177	178	179	180	181	182	183	184
CONNECTICUT—Cont'd														
Tolland	4 711	21 137 708	4.8	2.7	1.1	3.4	2.1	2.9	81.0	531.4	189.3	302.4	1 996	1 971
Windham	3 899	15 623 446	4.2	2.5	1.2	4.0	0.5	3.9	82.0	430.6	207.6	189.4	1 611	1 586
DELAWARE	X	X	X	X	X	X	X	X	X	X	X	X	X	X
Kent	4 210	17 226 252	4.7	6.0	0.1	0.6	1.6	5.6	79.4	494.8	323.1	88.0	525	459
New Castle	13 350	61 131 759	5.7	9.5	1.4	3.2	2.2	5.4	70.9	1 685.7	768.1	591.4	1 083	883
Sussex	5 143	20 898 662	5.1	4.6	0.0	1.2	3.3	4.3	80.0	633.4	356.0	169.5	833	671
DISTRICT OF COLUMBIA	X	X	X	X	X	X	X	X	X	X	X	X	X	X
District of Columbia	44 423	263 772 974	11.1	14.2	4.3	27.8	12.5	5.9	19.0	11 142.1	3 474.2	5 933.8	9 384	2 970
FLORIDA	X	X	X	X	X	X	X	X	X	X	X	X	X	X
Alachua	9 411	34 346 743	10.1	15.9	4.6	4.8	3.1	12.0	45.8	854.0	266.5	363.0	1 444	1 113
Baker	867	2 564 944	5.5	3.7	1.2	2.9	5.4	3.6	77.0	73.2	44.3	18.9	699	507
Bay	8 014	30 150 146	3.2	6.0	2.6	3.8	35.9	4.9	42.5	823.2	190.5	261.0	1 518	1 060
Bradford	881	2 067 161	5.4	1.3	0.4	2.7	7.1	1.3	75.8	71.8	37.9	23.1	853	598
Brevard	19 755	66 076 682	7.5	12.3	7.0	4.4	7.8	7.9	52.0	1 764.4	557.0	634.8	1 160	923
Broward	73 864	331 154 408	5.1	13.2	6.2	3.7	29.6	6.0	33.6	9 918.0	2 186.8	3 161.3	1 742	1 392
Calhoun	510	1 309 655	4.9	3.6	0.2	5.5	0.9	3.7	80.8	46.1	34.0	8.6	581	443
Charlotte	4 654	16 650 878	13.2	15.5	8.9	5.6	2.0	7.8	45.5	559.2	101.1	264.1	1 626	1 290
Citrus	3 890	11 674 757	8.6	11.3	0.1	3.6	5.4	3.4	65.1	322.4	98.7	162.1	1 163	1 064
Clay	6 995	21 858 185	5.6	10.0	3.5	1.9	1.2	5.5	71.3	556.6	210.2	185.3	953	696
Collier	9 918	41 162 175	6.9	15.7	6.7	3.5	4.2	9.1	52.0	1 300.6	231.7	737.4	2 218	2 006
Columbia	2 446	7 323 140	6.4	8.1	2.5	3.8	3.8	3.8	69.3	195.9	99.6	58.8	865	641
DeSoto	1 506	4 657 631	3.9	13.7	4.7	2.2	25.3	4.7	44.3	123.0	39.7	31.6	911	665
Dixie	584	1 731 414	9.6	25.5	0.3	3.8	8.6	2.7	49.0	42.4	22.0	12.7	789	669
Duval	26 681	104 173 723	5.7	15.6	6.2	2.1	1.2	7.3	52.4	3 353.2	1 044.0	1 351.0	1 536	1 039
Escambia	10 348	32 971 310	5.4	14.5	2.6	2.7	4.7	8.0	59.2	937.6	348.0	338.3	1 118	772
Flagler	2 869	10 004 315	13.0	9.5	8.0	1.8	3.2	8.7	53.9	286.1	72.0	141.3	1 437	1 235
Franklin	399	1 124 749	9.6	10.0	1.7	7.1	5.5	9.5	54.3	60.6	21.8	24.9	2 130	1 812
Gadsden	1 850	4 901 351	12.9	12.9	1.7	6.4	3.2	4.9	56.6	109.5	61.3	33.5	721	528
Gilchrist	624	1 705 173	8.0	8.7	0.9	3.7	4.8	1.4	69.5	43.8	24.4	13.1	781	660
Glades	401	1 250 845	13.0	0.2	0.5	3.3	5.2	7.6	67.4	65.1	17.5	12.8	974	884
Gulf	661	1 888 717	10.9	17.7	0.2	5.5	8.9	6.1	46.3	58.3	19.3	27.3	1 735	1 504
Hamilton	602	1 883 338	4.3	14.6	0.6	4.0	4.1	19.8	50.0	60.4	31.4	21.4	1 452	1 298
Hardee	1 238	3 660 532	9.3	12.4	2.4	3.4	4.4	4.8	59.9	83.9	40.3	30.3	1 103	950
Hendry	1 671	5 341 045	10.9	8.7	1.0	3.6	17.8	12.2	43.4	156.7	60.3	45.0	1 201	842
Hernando	5 261	17 523 253	4.9	11.1	6.5	1.8	0.9	20.4	52.8	557.9	169.7	301.2	1 737	1 597
Highlands	3 358	10 445 615	8.2	12.8	2.4	5.5	3.7	6.4	56.9	264.2	111.3	100.2	1 021	799
Hillsborough	45 811	168 419 971	6.8	14.7	5.5	5.2	2.8	7.1	56.0	4 882.0	2 046.8	1 736.7	1 359	996
Holmes	889	2 422 344	5.2	5.1	0.0	3.5	20.9	5.0	58.1	71.8	52.9	10.8	548	332
Indian River	4 188	14 858 891	4.7	16.3	4.8	5.0	5.1	12.6	48.7	445.1	88.8	266.5	1 896	1 553
Jackson	2 760	8 398 373	4.9	6.0	2.2	2.8	34.8	2.6	46.1	203.4	76.8	40.3	823	456
Jefferson	365	927 774	7.8	2.9	2.0	7.8	9.8	3.9	63.2	30.2	13.1	12.4	871	675
Lafayette	373	1 167 432	11.8	22.1	0.0	1.9	8.3	6.2	48.5	18.5	10.9	4.9	555	451
Lake	10 347	30 892 756	6.4	14.3	6.8	2.9	1.5	7.4	57.3	851.0	286.9	352.0	1 161	905
Lee	29 739	118 190 826	4.0	7.9	5.4	3.4	39.4	4.7	33.6	3 672.5	586.2	1 065.4	1 651	1 448
Leon	11 335	40 616 545	8.8	12.0	3.5	5.4	3.6	15.1	47.5	1 138.8	359.2	388.1	1 368	952
Levy	1 489	4 220 044	6.6	13.3	0.6	4.8	6.8	4.6	61.2	107.5	52.0	38.2	954	772
Liberty	390	1 120 616	1.3	0.1	28.3	3.3	4.3	2.5	59.6	26.9	19.5	5.1	613	482
Madison	949	2 696 175	4.6	8.3	1.1	3.0	18.6	2.7	58.5	73.1	37.0	16.5	874	617
Manatee	11 893	40 190 709	10.2	12.9	5.6	2.7	2.6	5.6	58.7	1 162.4	346.0	503.0	1 507	1 276
Marion	10 760	33 096 942	6.2	11.8	9.0	0.5	2.5	5.9	63.0	875.9	312.2	296.0	883	746
Martin	4 603	17 106 522	8.9	17.9	12.8	2.6	1.6	5.7	48.8	500.0	104.9	304.6	2 047	1 811
Miami-Dade	102 308	498 941 928	4.9	14.9	6.0	5.9	20.8	6.6	32.3	14 058.6	3 695.7	5 524.1	2 132	1 564
Monroe	3 585	14 624 150	5.7	22.6	8.9	2.9	3.9	19.5	34.7	567.8	118.5	263.2	3 519	2 437
Nassau	1 980	6 570 847	4.2	2.9	11.2	4.6	1.0	4.9	66.5	222.9	55.5	123.9	1 660	1 424
Okaloosa	6 391	22 546 268	5.1	9.5	4.5	3.0	2.3	7.4	65.4	596.0	213.5	239.6	1 260	1 023
Okeechobee	1 527	4 441 541	4.9	15.8	5.3	1.7	1.2	7.3	62.2	123.6	58.3	42.0	1 065	682
Orange	45 111	168 174 502	6.0	14.3	7.4	5.4	6.3	9.8	48.0	5 410.1	1 451.5	2 181.6	1 815	1 273
Osceola	10 876	36 955 599	7.4	13.0	6.2	2.3	1.1	9.5	58.0	1 052.2	358.1	406.0	1 412	1 006
Palm Beach	46 198	195 497 482	7.6	16.4	10.2	2.6	5.1	13.1	41.6	6 353.4	1 180.9	3 449.0	2 542	2 211
Pasco	14 918	46 238 730	6.6	11.6	5.0	1.2	1.2	4.8	67.1	1 276.0	533.4	417.6	888	715
Pinellas	32 162	118 407 394	7.7	19.5	5.8	3.8	3.8	10.1	45.5	3 227.6	836.8	1 470.9	1 597	1 224
Polk	22 910	75 047 946	7.9	12.5	4.2	2.1	2.6	10.6	56.6	1 844.2	710.5	644.8	1 047	726

1. Based on the resident population estimated as of July 1 of the year shown.

Table B. States and Counties — Local Government Finances, Government Employment, and Income Taxes

STATE County	Local government finances, 2012 (cont.) Direct general expenditure Total (mil dol)	Per capita[1] (dollars)	Education	Health and hospitals	Police protec-tion	Public welfare	High-ways	Debt outstanding Total (mil dol)	Per capita[1] (dollars)	Government employment, 2015 Federal civilian	Federal military	State and local	Individual income tax returns, 2014 Number of returns	Mean adjusted gross income	Mean income tax
	185	186	187	188	189	190	191	192	193	194	195	196	197	198	199
CONNECTICUT—Cont'd															
Tolland	554.3	3 658	66.0	0.7	2.3	0.3	5.5	321.3	2 121	262	322	15 483	68 660	76 955	10 329
Windham	416.8	3 544	69.2	0.6	2.8	0.4	4.7	176.2	1 498	272	226	7 880	54 280	55 144	5 905
DELAWARE	X	X	X	X	X	X	X	X	X	5 668	8 566	60 333	443 820	61 998	7 786
Kent	527.3	3 145	73.4	1.1	4.4	0.0	1.5	478.7	2 856	1 742	4 164	17 468	78 250	49 048	4 846
New Castle	1 812.2	3 319	59.7	0.8	7.5	0.0	2.5	1 735.3	3 178	3 367	3 138	34 601	264 010	68 656	9 179
Sussex	613.0	3 014	69.2	2.1	4.3	0.1	1.7	515.0	2 532	559	1 264	8 264	101 570	54 661	6 428
DISTRICT OF COLUMBIA	X	X	X	X	X	X	X	X	X	193 919	14 422	40 286	336 950	88 430	15 015
District of Columbia	10 765.0	17 025	22.0	6.3	5.2	26.6	4.9	13 246.6	20 949	193 919	14 422	40 286	336 950	88 430	15 015
FLORIDA	X	X	X	X	X	X	X	X	X	134 252	94 025	937 309	9 398 170	60 691	9 104
Alachua	900.5	3 582	38.5	3.8	8.3	1.7	4.6	1 948.7	7 751	4 586	543	38 125	110 240	55 868	7 453
Baker	88.4	3 262	47.4	4.9	5.7	1.3	10.3	18.5	682	58	46	2 572	10 220	45 083	3 904
Bay	927.6	5 396	32.4	24.5	6.6	0.0	4.4	885.7	5 152	3 771	4 227	9 087	86 640	49 839	6 246
Bradford	72.8	2 691	44.9	6.1	6.5	0.0	6.2	13.5	501	34	50	1 972	9 600	42 534	3 971
Brevard	1 830.9	3 345	36.4	11.6	7.9	0.4	4.3	1 872.2	3 421	6 275	2 829	21 865	269 250	55 029	7 117
Broward	10 214.0	5 627	24.6	26.3	10.2	1.2	1.4	8 639.5	4 760	6 879	3 952	94 919	922 370	59 572	8 966
Calhoun	49.3	3 348	43.9	2.4	5.2	0.1	28.4	3.8	256	24	23	942	4 880	40 366	3 592
Charlotte	563.6	3 470	33.1	3.8	11.0	1.5	11.1	628.4	3 868	334	314	5 549	78 270	53 047	6 385
Citrus	362.7	2 602	47.4	5.5	9.1	2.5	6.6	493.5	3 541	217	256	4 096	62 370	45 989	5 084
Clay	560.4	2 884	52.3	0.7	8.2	0.5	6.0	488.9	2 515	336	375	6 716	93 250	55 768	6 128
Collier	1 313.8	3 952	37.5	3.0	12.1	0.6	6.0	2 257.5	6 791	643	648	12 222	173 430	125 170	26 098
Columbia	210.8	3 101	53.8	3.7	6.1	0.1	6.0	94.4	1 389	1 361	117	4 242	26 540	42 245	4 207
DeSoto	129.0	3 717	35.1	28.2	5.2	0.4	2.7	71.9	2 070	61	58	1 737	11 820	37 325	3 354
Dixie	42.5	2 637	45.4	10.3	7.8	0.0	6.5	11.2	694	10	27	999	5 090	37 563	3 356
Duval	3 336.4	3 793	39.0	1.9	9.4	1.4	4.4	11 704.3	13 306	15 742	13 584	38 033	437 570	54 086	7 032
Escambia	1 097.8	3 627	40.4	3.3	6.7	0.2	4.3	1 910.8	6 312	5 841	11 729	15 382	141 080	49 325	5 807
Flagler	307.1	3 122	38.2	1.4	7.1	0.2	6.7	437.4	4 447	133	192	3 423	48 410	54 038	7 315
Franklin	62.9	5 386	27.2	14.8	10.5	0.2	5.5	56.4	4 826	15	18	992	4 440	50 201	7 288
Gadsden	120.4	2 588	50.5	4.7	7.8	0.8	7.5	55.7	1 197	91	78	4 426	19 900	38 432	3 371
Gilchrist	44.2	2 629	55.7	5.0	6.8	0.4	8.4	4.7	282	32	30	1 084	6 440	41 564	3 726
Glades	69.5	5 305	21.6	4.0	6.8	0.1	6.4	202.1	15 417	11	22	463	3 900	48 576	5 829
Gulf	59.6	3 791	32.4	9.7	5.8	0.4	7.6	52.0	3 310	14	23	1 203	5 700	52 446	5 945
Hamilton	59.7	4 061	31.9	3.6	5.9	0.1	5.3	3.7	253	26	21	1 128	4 700	36 700	2 989
Hardee	86.6	3 149	54.2	4.1	11.3	0.2	5.3	9.9	360	48	47	1 609	9 910	38 315	3 224
Hendry	180.1	4 810	32.7	25.6	7.7	0.4	3.5	74.6	1 991	71	71	2 031	16 090	37 434	3 574
Hernando	566.7	3 268	33.0	2.6	5.9	0.1	3.9	365.6	2 108	322	325	5 471	75 660	42 562	4 172
Highlands	276.6	2 818	46.6	3.7	7.8	0.6	6.0	143.0	1 457	262	180	3 736	40 520	39 928	3 883
Hillsborough	5 230.4	4 093	38.8	3.2	7.5	2.6	3.9	6 006.8	4 701	14 620	8 062	66 026	618 330	59 485	8 485
Holmes	71.5	3 610	38.8	22.5	3.3	0.1	8.7	33.4	1 686	64	33	1 339	6 630	37 185	3 004
Indian River	470.0	3 343	38.2	4.8	9.4	0.8	8.2	436.2	3 103	330	269	4 673	70 520	94 952	17 433
Jackson	226.5	4 626	38.1	33.8	3.4	0.0	8.3	82.2	1 680	484	74	4 777	18 210	41 998	4 342
Jefferson	31.4	2 204	37.8	7.2	14.4	0.5	9.5	3.9	274	34	23	685	5 860	47 037	4 894
Lafayette	19.1	2 172	55.0	7.9	4.8	0.6	8.7	1.7	189	14	13	630	2 430	41 288	3 352
Lake	925.8	3 054	40.3	3.7	8.1	0.5	5.1	1 090.4	3 596	569	592	12 759	148 780	49 854	5 684
Lee	3 730.8	5 782	25.4	32.3	4.8	0.5	3.9	5 119.6	7 934	2 563	1 333	37 394	318 780	67 501	10 238
Leon	1 138.4	4 012	38.2	0.6	7.6	0.0	7.4	4 257.0	15 002	1 751	549	51 836	125 560	56 410	7 535
Levy	112.3	2 806	46.8	5.0	8.6	0.8	9.0	30.9	772	66	101	1 826	16 530	36 655	3 376
Liberty	27.8	3 361	51.9	8.1	3.7	0.3	10.1	4.7	568	37	11	765	2 620	42 445	3 534
Madison	78.8	4 166	48.6	15.6	5.2	0.4	9.1	16.3	861	43	30	1 356	7 030	39 474	3 525
Manatee	1 227.1	3 675	40.6	2.5	8.5	0.7	4.4	1 359.0	4 070	918	690	11 311	165 040	63 646	9 405
Marion	879.1	2 623	48.9	2.0	7.6	0.7	6.3	732.6	2 186	670	617	13 660	151 600	44 870	5 320
Martin	526.0	3 534	36.8	8.1	9.7	2.3	3.4	296.9	1 995	265	281	5 533	74 490	101 334	18 621
Miami-Dade	14 468.1	5 584	25.8	12.2	7.5	3.5	2.2	23 549.3	9 089	19 917	7 407	118 473	1 267 780	55 737	9 194
Monroe	536.4	7 170	22.9	4.6	11.0	0.5	2.3	1 453.0	19 423	1 205	1 414	4 551	45 230	89 839	16 743
Nassau	230.5	3 089	41.0	5.2	7.0	0.2	6.7	231.3	3 100	551	143	2 739	37 200	72 989	10 700
Okaloosa	687.4	3 616	51.5	2.4	6.6	0.3	2.9	368.2	1 937	8 410	15 861	8 014	99 040	56 279	7 250
Okeechobee	121.9	3 087	49.3	2.5	8.0	0.7	4.0	78.4	1 987	71	68	2 125	14 730	41 633	4 136
Orange	5 320.5	4 426	36.8	4.6	7.1	0.7	4.0	9 996.1	8 315	11 112	2 646	63 079	607 460	52 854	7 397
Osceola	1 153.9	4 015	42.2	1.2	7.2	1.7	8.7	2 678.5	9 319	395	589	11 972	146 760	38 136	3 400
Palm Beach	6 575.2	4 847	27.6	4.7	9.3	2.5	2.5	7 440.3	5 485	6 761	2 729	55 375	692 560	91 812	17 726
Pasco	1 277.5	2 716	49.4	2.0	7.9	0.8	5.8	1 324.5	2 816	765	905	16 102	214 620	49 497	5 516
Pinellas	3 402.6	3 693	34.6	4.2	11.2	3.0	4.2	3 555.7	3 859	7 037	2 772	36 713	463 560	60 135	8 868
Polk	1 992.7	3 234	48.6	3.2	8.2	1.6	5.5	2 776.3	4 506	1 065	1 238	26 233	275 310	46 114	4 850

1. Based on the resident population estimated as of July 1 of the year shown.

Table B. States and Counties — **Land Area and Population**

STATE/ County code	CBSA code[1]	County type[2]	STATE County	Land area[3] (sq mi) 2016	Total persons 2016	Rank	Per square mile	White	Black	American Indian, Alaska Native	Asian and Pacific Islander	Percent Hispanic or Latino[4]	Under 5 years	5 to 17 years	18 to 24 years	25 to 34 years	35 to 44 years	45 to 54 years
				1	2	3	4	5	6	7	8	9	10	11	12	13	14	15
			FLORIDA—Cont'd															
12 107	37260	4	Putnam	727.9	72 277	750	99.3	73.1	16.6	1.0	0.9	9.8	5.7	15.9	7.3	11.0	10.1	12.6
12 109	27260	1	St. Johns	600.7	235 087	281	391.4	85.0	5.9	0.6	3.7	6.6	5.1	16.8	7.1	10.1	12.6	14.6
12 111	38940	2	St. Lucie	571.7	306 507	224	536.1	59.9	20.4	0.6	2.5	18.3	5.3	14.9	7.4	11.3	10.9	12.9
12 113	37860	2	Santa Rosa	1 011.8	170 497	378	168.5	85.2	7.1	1.6	3.6	5.4	5.7	16.6	7.9	13.8	12.8	14.5
12 115	35840	2	Sarasota	555.8	412 569	169	742.3	84.8	5.0	0.5	2.1	8.9	3.6	10.9	5.8	8.3	8.6	11.9
12 117	36740	1	Seminole	309.5	455 479	151	1 471.7	63.7	12.1	0.7	5.3	20.4	5.2	15.9	8.4	14.4	13.3	14.4
12 119	45540	3	Sumter	547.6	123 996	506	226.4	86.0	7.5	0.7	1.2	5.5	2.0	5.1	3.1	5.8	5.9	6.9
12 121	...	6	Suwannee	688.6	43 794	1 096	63.6	76.9	13.6	1.0	0.9	9.1	5.4	15.6	7.8	13.1	11.6	12.8
12 123	...	6	Taylor	1 043.3	22 175	1 720	21.3	74.3	20.4	1.6	1.2	4.2	5.5	14.1	7.8	14.6	12.2	13.1
12 125	...	6	Union	243.6	15 142	2 086	62.2	70.7	23.3	0.8	0.9	5.8	5.2	13.9	8.7	15.8	13.6	14.4
12 127	19660	2	Volusia	1 101.2	529 364	129	480.7	74.3	11.2	0.8	2.4	13.0	4.7	13.0	8.2	11.5	10.4	13.0
12 129	45220	2	Wakulla	606.4	31 893	1 381	52.6	80.9	14.8	1.3	1.1	3.8	5.4	15.9	7.1	14.3	14.3	15.1
12 131	18880	3	Walton	1 037.7	65 889	806	63.5	86.6	6.0	1.8	1.9	6.1	5.9	14.4	6.3	12.6	12.1	13.8
12 133	...	6	Washington	584.2	24 569	1 622	42.1	79.3	16.1	2.1	1.1	3.6	5.1	14.9	8.6	13.3	13.0	14.2
13 000	...	0	**GEORGIA**	57 594.8	10 310 371	X	179.0	54.9	32.2	0.7	4.7	9.4	6.4	17.9	9.8	13.8	13.2	13.7
13 001	...	7	Appling	507.1	18 428	1 895	36.3	70.5	19.5	0.5	1.0	9.6	7.1	17.9	8.2	11.9	11.9	12.8
13 003	...	9	Atkinson	339.3	8 273	2 568	24.4	57.4	17.2	0.8	0.6	25.2	8.0	20.2	8.9	12.2	13.2	13.3
13 005	...	7	Bacon	284.0	11 372	2 337	40.0	74.5	17.2	0.3	0.8	8.7	6.9	18.9	8.7	12.6	13.6	12.0
13 007	10500	3	Baker	341.9	3 150	2 958	9.2	48.1	45.6	0.8	1.2	5.6	4.7	15.3	7.1	11.5	11.3	14.0
13 009	33300	4	Baldwin	258.6	45 144	1 072	174.6	53.6	42.7	0.5	2.1	2.2	5.0	14.2	19.0	11.6	10.4	12.1
13 011	...	8	Banks	232.1	18 397	1 896	79.3	89.1	3.2	0.8	1.6	6.7	5.5	17.3	7.9	11.2	13.1	14.4
13 013	12060	1	Barrow	160.4	77 126	716	480.8	74.3	12.3	0.7	4.1	10.3	7.1	19.5	8.0	14.7	14.1	13.5
13 015	12060	1	Bartow	459.5	103 807	579	225.9	79.6	11.5	0.8	1.3	8.5	6.4	18.2	8.4	13.2	12.9	14.7
13 017	22340	7	Ben Hill	250.1	17 243	1 963	68.9	57.6	35.8	0.7	1.0	6.1	7.0	19.0	8.0	12.6	11.4	12.5
13 019	...	6	Berrien	451.9	18 993	1 872	42.0	83.3	10.9	0.6	1.2	5.1	6.3	18.2	7.6	12.2	11.8	13.9
13 021	31420	3	Bibb	249.3	152 760	428	612.8	39.9	55.3	0.6	2.5	3.2	7.0	17.9	10.3	13.4	11.6	12.2
13 023	...	6	Bleckley	215.9	12 970	2 229	60.1	69.3	27.1	0.4	1.4	2.8	5.4	15.2	15.2	11.2	10.8	13.1
13 025	15260	3	Brantley	442.4	18 355	1 897	41.5	94.0	3.9	1.2	0.4	2.1	6.1	17.9	8.2	11.7	12.5	14.6
13 027	46660	3	Brooks	493.1	15 687	2 060	31.8	58.1	35.2	0.9	1.1	5.9	6.2	15.9	7.7	12.3	10.8	13.7
13 029	42340	2	Bryan	436.4	36 230	1 269	83.0	76.4	15.5	0.9	2.9	7.1	7.4	21.8	7.5	14.0	15.3	12.9
13 031	44340	4	Bulloch	673.0	74 722	739	111.0	65.1	29.9	0.7	2.1	3.7	5.6	14.2	24.4	14.1	10.5	10.4
13 033	12260	3	Burke	827.0	22 688	1 697	27.4	48.6	48.1	0.8	0.7	3.1	7.0	19.2	8.6	11.8	11.4	13.0
13 035	12060	1	Butts	183.8	23 817	1 646	129.6	68.0	28.5	0.7	0.8	3.2	5.8	15.0	9.3	14.4	13.1	14.4
13 037	...	8	Calhoun	280.4	6 324	2 730	22.6	33.4	61.6	0.7	0.9	4.7	4.6	13.6	9.1	15.2	15.7	14.5
13 039	41220	4	Camden	613.2	53 008	947	86.4	72.5	20.1	1.2	2.5	6.5	7.3	16.8	13.2	16.4	10.9	11.8
13 043	...	7	Candler	243.1	10 910	2 363	44.9	63.2	25.1	0.5	0.9	11.3	6.3	18.6	8.0	12.0	11.6	13.0
13 045	12060	1	Carroll	499.0	116 261	527	233.0	72.9	20.1	0.7	1.3	6.9	6.3	17.9	13.2	13.3	12.2	12.7
13 047	16860	2	Catoosa	162.2	66 398	804	409.4	92.6	3.4	0.9	1.8	2.9	5.6	17.7	7.8	11.9	13.2	14.3
13 049	...	6	Charlton	773.6	12 497	2 259	16.2	64.2	31.8	1.1	1.0	3.7	5.0	14.1	9.3	16.1	14.0	14.6
13 051	42340	2	Chatham	429.1	289 082	236	673.7	50.6	40.8	0.7	3.7	6.3	6.6	15.4	11.3	16.7	12.1	11.7
13 053	17980	2	Chattahoochee	248.7	10 922	2 361	43.9	61.8	20.6	1.7	4.6	14.4	7.6	11.9	33.4	24.1	9.7	5.0
13 055	44900	6	Chattooga	313.3	24 824	1 616	79.2	84.3	10.8	0.7	0.8	5.0	5.9	16.4	8.4	12.6	12.7	13.4
13 057	12060	1	Cherokee	421.1	241 689	276	573.9	81.4	7.1	0.7	2.6	10.0	6.1	19.2	7.9	11.9	14.2	15.4
13 059	12020	3	Clarke	119.2	124 707	501	1 046.2	56.9	28.5	0.5	5.2	10.8	5.4	12.1	26.7	16.6	11.1	9.0
13 061	...	9	Clay	195.4	3 020	2 967	15.5	37.7	60.5	0.7	0.7	1.5	5.9	15.5	6.7	10.7	9.8	10.3
13 063	12060	1	Clayton	141.6	279 462	244	1 973.6	12.2	70.3	0.7	5.7	13.1	7.6	20.7	10.0	15.1	13.4	13.4
13 065	...	6	Clinch	800.2	6 829	2 690	8.5	66.9	28.0	1.0	0.6	5.3	7.0	18.8	8.8	12.6	12.1	12.2
13 067	12060	1	Cobb	339.7	748 150	84	2 202.4	54.5	28.2	0.7	6.1	12.9	6.4	17.9	9.1	14.3	14.4	14.5
13 069	20060	7	Coffee	575.4	43 012	1 112	74.8	59.4	28.5	0.5	1.1	11.6	6.8	17.8	10.1	14.5	13.0	13.4
13 071	34220	6	Colquitt	547.0	45 708	1 056	83.6	56.7	23.1	0.6	1.0	19.6	7.1	19.7	8.9	13.0	12.8	12.7
13 073	12260	2	Columbia	290.1	147 450	442	508.3	72.0	17.8	0.8	5.6	6.6	6.3	19.3	8.1	14.1	13.9	13.6
13 075	...	6	Cook	227.2	17 167	1 971	75.6	66.4	27.3	0.6	1.0	5.9	6.7	20.0	8.3	11.9	12.8	12.9
13 077	12060	1	Coweta	440.9	140 526	458	318.7	73.2	18.5	0.7	2.6	6.8	6.2	19.0	8.2	12.1	13.6	15.2
13 079	31420	3	Crawford	324.9	12 322	2 270	37.9	75.1	21.1	1.0	0.9	3.1	4.9	15.9	7.2	11.5	11.0	15.4
13 081	18380	3	Crisp	272.6	22 721	1 692	83.3	51.1	44.6	0.5	1.5	3.3	6.5	18.1	8.3	11.9	11.5	12.6
13 083	16860	2	Dade	174.0	16 257	2 026	93.4	95.0	1.6	1.0	1.3	2.3	5.0	14.3	12.2	11.4	11.4	12.9
13 085	12060	1	Dawson	210.8	23 604	1 656	112.0	94.1	1.2	0.9	0.9	4.2	5.1	15.6	7.5	11.5	11.5	14.8
13 087	12460	6	Decatur	597.1	26 822	1 536	44.9	51.7	42.1	0.6	0.7	5.9	6.6	18.1	9.0	12.1	11.8	13.3
13 089	12060	1	DeKalb	267.6	740 321	87	2 766.5	30.5	55.1	0.7	7.1	8.5	7.2	16.5	8.7	16.8	14.4	13.5
13 091	...	6	Dodge	495.9	20 563	1 795	41.5	66.5	29.9	0.5	0.7	3.6	5.5	14.8	8.8	13.1	13.0	15.2
13 093	...	6	Dooly	391.9	13 763	2 183	35.1	43.2	48.7	0.5	0.9	7.7	3.8	14.6	8.0	13.3	13.7	14.0
13 095	10500	3	Dougherty	328.6	90 017	644	273.9	26.4	70.3	0.5	1.2	2.7	6.8	17.9	11.6	13.4	11.5	11.7
13 097	12060	1	Douglas	200.1	142 224	452	710.8	43.8	46.0	0.9	2.2	9.4	6.4	20.0	9.2	12.4	14.1	15.3
13 099	...	6	Early	512.6	10 339	2 402	20.2	46.8	50.3	0.7	0.8	2.2	6.6	18.5	8.2	10.5	11.3	12.9
13 101	46660	3	Echols	414.9	3 962	2 903	9.5	63.9	5.0	2.1	1.1	29.6	7.6	19.4	8.6	15.0	14.2	12.5

1. CBSA = Core Based Statistical Area. See Appendix A for explanation. See Appendix B for list of metropolitan areas with component counties. 2. County type code from the Economic Research Service of USDA Rural-Urban Continuum Codes. See Appendix A for definition. 3. Dry land or land partially or temporarily covered by water. 4. May be of any race.

STATE County	55 to 64 years	65 to 74 years	75 years and over	Percent female	2000	2010	2000–2010	2010–2016	Births	Deaths	Net migration	Number	Persons per house-hold	Family house-holds	Female family house-holder[1]	One per-son
	16	17	18	19	20	21	22	23	24	25	26	27	28	29	30	31
FLORIDA—Cont'd																
Putnam	15.5	12.9	9.1	50.7	70 423	74 364	5.6	-2.8	5 213	5 951	-1 141	27 683	2.57	62.4	14.3	31.5
St. Johns	14.3	11.9	7.4	51.2	123 135	190 038	54.3	23.7	12 469	10 456	41 721	79 242	2.62	69.4	9.0	24.5
St. Lucie	13.8	12.9	10.6	51.2	192 695	277 257	43.9	10.5	18 834	18 374	27 509	107 898	2.64	66.6	12.3	27.6
Santa Rosa	13.4	9.4	5.8	48.8	117 743	151 372	28.6	12.6	11 503	8 086	15 259	58 654	2.65	73.0	10.8	20.6
Sarasota	15.5	18.3	17.1	52.3	325 957	379 435	16.4	8.7	18 081	32 782	45 958	175 185	2.21	60.8	8.4	32.8
Seminole	13.1	8.9	6.3	51.8	365 196	422 718	15.8	7.8	27 906	19 609	23 448	152 260	2.85	66.5	12.4	27.4
Sumter	14.9	34.8	21.5	50.0	53 345	93 420	75.1	32.7	2 925	9 004	35 174	48 039	2.05	68.5	5.0	27.3
Suwannee	13.9	11.6	8.8	47.7	34 844	41 551	19.2	5.4	2 868	3 344	2 634	15 649	2.69	69.2	14.4	25.2
Taylor	13.6	11.5	7.7	44.3	19 256	22 568	17.2	-1.7	1 480	1 449	-428	7 605	2.44	68.4	14.7	25.5
Union	15.4	8.5	4.5	34.3	13 442	15 535	15.6	-2.5	1 033	1 273	-174	3 883	2.58	71.5	18.0	24.7
Volusia	15.3	13.5	10.6	51.3	443 343	494 597	11.6	7.0	29 563	40 738	44 593	200 180	2.46	61.5	11.1	31.6
Wakulla	13.7	9.4	4.9	45.1	22 863	30 783	34.6	3.6	2 015	1 523	587	10 691	2.57	71.6	15.0	22.4
Walton	15.5	12.3	7.2	49.5	40 601	55 043	35.6	19.7	4 409	3 521	9 578	23 490	2.45	64.3	9.7	30.8
Washington	13.4	10.8	7.0	45.6	20 973	24 896	18.7	-1.3	1 484	1 724	-72	8 246	2.66	67.4	11.0	29.0
GEORGIA	12.0	8.1	5.0	51.3	8 186 453	9 688 680	18.4	6.4	817 366	468 825	263 358	3 574 362	2.73	67.8	15.3	26.8
Appling	13.6	10.0	6.5	50.1	17 419	18 236	4.7	1.1	1 621	1 211	-203	6 812	2.63	69.5	14.3	27.3
Atkinson	11.7	7.8	4.7	49.9	7 609	8 382	10.2	-1.3	823	415	-537	2 772	2.98	67.1	13.0	29.1
Bacon	12.4	9.0	5.9	50.7	10 103	11 096	9.8	2.5	930	775	143	3 951	2.71	68.3	11.4	26.6
Baker	16.9	11.6	7.6	51.4	4 074	3 451	-15.3	-8.7	200	147	-328	1 291	2.55	66.9	16.2	30.7
Baldwin	12.6	9.0	5.9	49.4	44 700	45 835	2.5	-1.5	2 920	2 543	-1 059	15 978	2.62	57.6	17.5	32.6
Banks	13.6	11.0	5.9	49.0	14 422	18 395	27.5	0.0	1 220	925	-322	6 553	2.80	75.9	11.0	21.2
Barrow	11.2	7.7	4.2	50.9	46 144	69 367	50.3	11.2	6 587	3 354	4 377	23 560	3.05	75.5	14.2	19.2
Bartow	12.6	8.6	4.9	50.7	76 019	100 155	31.7	3.6	8 095	5 272	772	35 732	2.81	72.7	13.0	21.0
Ben Hill	13.4	9.7	6.5	52.1	17 484	17 634	0.9	-2.2	1 485	1 344	-533	6 413	2.68	66.4	20.3	30.8
Berrien	13.3	10.0	6.8	50.6	16 235	19 286	18.8	-1.5	1 474	1 213	-556	6 958	2.71	69.5	14.7	27.0
Bibb	12.7	8.6	6.2	53.0	153 887	155 514	1.1	-1.8	14 022	10 221	-6 492	57 111	2.59	62.3	20.9	33.0
Bleckley	12.1	9.3	7.8	52.1	11 666	13 063	12.0	-0.7	824	875	-68	4 113	2.71	66.1	13.7	30.1
Brantley	13.6	9.9	5.5	50.6	14 629	18 410	25.8	-0.3	1 286	1 128	-186	6 581	2.79	75.0	11.8	22.0
Brooks	14.5	11.7	7.1	50.9	16 450	16 322	-0.8	-3.9	1 261	1 187	-737	6 577	2.37	61.6	13.5	33.3
Bryan	10.3	6.7	4.0	50.7	23 417	30 213	29.0	19.9	3 121	1 423	4 237	11 441	2.89	80.0	13.1	16.3
Bulloch	10.1	6.6	4.1	50.8	55 983	70 251	25.5	6.4	5 336	3 103	2 118	26 128	2.54	60.3	15.6	22.4
Burke	14.0	9.4	5.5	52.1	22 243	23 316	4.8	-2.7	1 980	1 536	-1 113	8 102	2.81	69.8	21.6	25.4
Butts	12.6	9.5	5.9	46.8	19 522	23 655	21.2	0.7	1 685	1 534	-1	7 774	2.70	72.5	12.3	23.9
Calhoun	13.7	7.8	5.8	39.6	6 320	6 694	5.9	-5.5	359	360	-414	1 836	2.13	60.5	19.3	34.6
Camden	11.2	8.2	4.1	48.1	43 664	50 513	15.7	4.9	4 982	1 947	-643	18 638	2.68	75.2	12.5	19.2
Candler	13.1	10.7	6.6	51.0	9 577	10 995	14.8	-0.8	898	774	-228	3 909	2.75	70.5	15.6	24.3
Carroll	11.3	8.0	5.0	51.1	87 268	110 591	26.7	5.1	9 236	6 117	2 504	40 074	2.72	67.9	14.4	25.5
Catoosa	12.7	10.1	6.7	51.5	53 282	63 936	20.0	3.9	4 597	3 493	1 180	23 943	2.71	71.9	10.6	24.5
Charlton	12.5	8.5	5.8	41.2	10 282	12 171	18.4	2.7	788	619	51	3 524	3.32	73.4	11.4	23.3
Chatham	11.9	8.6	5.7	51.8	232 048	265 128	14.3	9.0	24 671	14 394	13 334	104 912	2.55	61.1	16.1	31.3
Chattahoochee	3.7	2.7	2.0	31.5	14 882	11 267	-24.3	-3.1	1 508	191	-1 731	2 599	3.24	76.6	7.6	15.0
Chattooga	13.7	10.1	6.8	49.0	25 470	26 015	2.1	-4.6	1 786	1 919	-1 016	9 364	2.49	67.3	14.3	28.9
Cherokee	12.3	8.7	4.3	50.7	141 903	214 346	51.1	12.8	17 444	8 142	17 652	79 133	2.84	74.8	11.1	20.6
Clarke	8.9	6.1	4.1	52.3	101 489	116 707	15.0	6.9	8 744	4 390	3 445	43 356	2.55	48.0	13.0	34.6
Clay	15.9	14.9	10.3	52.6	3 357	3 183	-5.2	-5.1	215	232	-139	1 183	2.57	58.2	19.1	37.3
Clayton	10.9	6.0	2.9	53.0	236 517	259 470	9.7	7.7	26 181	9 618	3 419	88 793	2.97	66.5	24.0	28.3
Clinch	12.7	10.5	5.2	50.8	6 878	6 798	-1.2	0.5	629	439	-170	2 581	2.49	65.1	19.7	31.0
Cobb	11.9	7.3	4.1	51.8	607 751	688 070	13.2	8.7	59 214	24 860	25 933	268 616	2.64	68.2	13.2	25.1
Coffee	11.5	8.1	4.9	48.8	37 413	42 356	13.2	1.5	3 682	2 376	-716	14 321	2.73	65.8	15.5	30.3
Colquitt	11.3	8.9	5.7	50.4	42 053	45 497	8.2	0.5	4 276	2 855	-1 202	15 737	2.86	72.3	16.5	24.4
Columbia	12.2	7.9	4.6	51.1	89 288	124 059	38.9	18.9	10 402	5 158	17 707	45 488	2.98	78.5	11.9	18.4
Cook	11.8	9.3	6.2	51.8	15 771	17 212	9.1	-0.3	1 394	1 204	-241	6 157	2.74	74.2	17.6	21.5
Coweta	12.5	8.4	4.7	51.3	89 215	127 317	42.7	10.4	10 287	5 729	8 354	48 777	2.73	74.7	12.3	21.5
Crawford	15.9	11.9	6.3	49.7	12 495	12 630	1.1	-2.4	817	721	-409	4 538	2.72	72.2	14.7	24.3
Crisp	13.9	10.2	7.0	52.8	21 996	23 439	6.6	-3.1	1 886	1 502	-1 050	8 659	2.64	70.3	21.5	26.3
Dade	14.6	11.0	7.1	50.9	15 154	16 633	9.8	-2.3	1 028	1 053	-330	6 150	2.47	75.3	8.3	19.8
Dawson	14.4	13.1	6.3	50.0	15 999	22 339	39.6	5.7	1 473	1 111	800	8 213	2.74	75.3	9.7	20.4
Decatur	12.7	9.4	7.1	51.6	28 240	27 842	-1.4	-3.7	2 254	1 930	-1 371	10 614	2.46	65.5	20.3	32.0
DeKalb	11.7	7.0	4.1	52.6	665 865	691 992	3.9	7.0	68 639	27 222	7 366	267 396	2.63	58.5	17.3	33.5
Dodge	13.7	9.5	6.3	47.9	19 171	21 797	13.7	-5.7	1 498	1 398	-1 353	8 064	2.35	68.9	16.6	28.6
Dooly	15.7	10.6	6.4	45.7	11 525	14 918	29.4	-7.7	696	752	-1 110	5 004	2.52	65.6	17.4	31.1
Dougherty	12.4	8.5	6.1	53.8	96 065	94 565	-1.6	-4.8	8 498	5 595	-7 516	35 455	2.52	62.2	24.6	32.7
Douglas	11.6	7.2	3.8	52.4	92 174	132 339	43.6	7.5	10 951	5 545	4 375	47 079	2.87	73.3	18.7	22.6
Early	12.8	11.1	8.2	53.1	12 354	11 004	-10.9	-6.0	885	834	-747	3 981	2.62	67.6	21.3	29.6
Echols	11.0	6.6	5.2	49.4	3 754	4 034	7.5	-1.8	389	159	-313	1 416	2.86	72.0	14.4	23.9

1. No spouse present.

Table B. States and Counties — Population, Vital Statistics, Health, and Crime

STATE County	Persons in group quarters, 2016	Daytime population, 2011–2015 Number	Employment/residence ratio	Births, 2016 Total	Rate[1]	Deaths, 2016 Number	Rate[1]	Persons under 65 with no health insurance, 2015 Number	Percent	Medicare, 2015 Total Beneficiaries	Enrolled in Original Medicare	Enrolled in Medicare Advantage	Serious crimes known to police,[2] 2014 Total Number	Rate[3]
	32	33	34	35	36	37	38	39	40	41	42	43	44	45
FLORIDA—Cont'd														
Putnam	1 396	68 752	0.83	804	11.1	951	13.2	9 514	17.2	16 976	11 825	5 151	2 566	3 527
St. Johns	2 815	188 368	0.77	2 199	9.4	1 898	8.1	18 427	10.1	46 039	34 412	11 627	4 419	2 044
St. Lucie	3 049	264 539	0.79	3 078	10.0	3 281	10.7	41 404	18.2	65 880	39 894	25 986	7 045	2 419
Santa Rosa	6 556	132 899	0.60	1 883	11.0	1 445	8.5	15 901	11.7	29 049	20 469	8 580	2 072	1 259
Sarasota	5 789	409 515	1.11	2 955	7.2	5 771	14.0	41 835	15.9	139 862	101 738	38 124	10 018	2 528
Seminole	3 516	408 465	0.86	4 553	10.0	3 532	7.8	45 214	11.9	62 860	36 254	26 606	11 502	2 597
Sumter	8 203	112 646	1.19	501	4.0	1 742	14.0	5 463	12.0	20 255	12 511	7 744	1 302	1 178
Suwannee	3 227	41 348	0.85	425	9.7	566	12.9	5 571	17.5	9 898	7 723	2 175	883	1 987
Taylor	2 983	23 092	1.06	227	10.2	244	11.0	2 225	14.7	4 320	3 362	958	503	2 176
Union	4 925	15 875	1.18	144	9.5	218	14.4	950	10.9	1 974	1 537	437	161	1 062
Volusia	13 659	482 538	0.89	4 886	9.2	6 920	13.1	59 477	15.5	132 676	69 010	63 666	17 894	3 546
Wakulla	3 296	24 385	0.47	333	10.4	233	7.3	2 655	11.1	5 626	2 669	2 957	697	2 226
Walton	1 985	60 085	1.02	775	11.8	585	8.9	8 639	17.4	10 317	7 975	2 342	1 734	2 820
Washington	2 558	23 412	0.85	240	9.8	285	11.6	2 625	14.9	4 773	3 832	941	411	1 658
GEORGIA	256 905	10 005 327	1.00	130 862	12.7	81 525	7.9	1 366 843	15.8	1 474 898	958 395	516 503	369 413	3 659
Appling	407	18 893	1.07	250	13.6	214	11.6	2 893	19.2	3 278	2 316	962	211	1 139
Atkinson	21	7 184	0.67	149	18.0	61	7.4	1 857	25.6	1 427	978	449	NA	NA
Bacon	325	11 088	0.97	144	12.7	109	9.6	1 889	20.2	1 776	1 219	557	NA	NA
Baker	0	2 713	0.54	32	10.2	27	8.6	369	14.3	122	84	38	31	932
Baldwin	5 715	46 469	1.04	442	9.8	452	10.0	4 915	14.5	8 149	4 394	3 755	1 649	3 561
Banks	0	15 124	0.58	216	11.7	154	8.4	2 868	18.5	2 306	1 564	742	450	2 436
Barrow	288	58 122	0.56	1 074	13.9	588	7.6	11 393	17.1	11 816	7 572	4 244	2 253	3 123
Bartow	968	94 531	0.85	1 298	12.5	882	8.5	14 345	16.2	15 933	10 916	5 017	5 407	5 342
Ben Hill	296	17 572	1.02	236	13.7	224	13.0	2 412	16.8	3 621	2 373	1 248	757	4 316
Berrien	188	16 420	0.60	263	13.8	216	11.4	2 994	19.1	3 618	2 528	1 090	472	2 479
Bibb	6 108	177 390	1.38	2 248	14.7	1 742	11.4	19 389	15.4	32 517	20 680	11 837	NA	NA
Bleckley	1 376	11 196	0.64	129	9.9	132	10.2	1 374	14.4	996	779	217	504	3 955
Brantley	58	14 717	0.44	208	11.3	197	10.7	2 908	18.6	2 823	2 042	781	597	3 261
Brooks	176	13 259	0.56	177	11.3	201	12.8	2 418	19.4	2 681	1 844	837	479	3 252
Bryan	98	25 192	0.47	545	15.0	240	6.6	4 048	12.9	4 930	3 303	1 627	567	1 668
Bulloch	5 352	70 473	0.94	894	12.0	531	7.1	10 658	17.9	9 004	6 516	2 488	1 964	2 766
Burke	246	23 769	1.09	298	13.1	247	10.9	3 047	15.9	3 634	2 132	1 502	936	4 147
Butts	2 662	21 735	0.80	259	10.9	249	10.5	2 897	16.4	4 854	2 910	1 944	492	2 108
Calhoun	1 642	6 496	1.00	55	8.7	45	7.1	839	21.1	1 557	992	565	730	12 352
Camden	2 420	48 514	0.88	767	14.5	323	6.1	5 535	12.5	6 887	5 258	1 629	1 551	3 071
Candler	264	10 054	0.76	131	12.0	137	12.6	1 871	21.2	1 903	1 247	656	NA	NA
Carroll	3 933	107 845	0.90	1 512	13.0	1 046	9.0	15 870	16.5	21 485	14 109	7 376	4 057	3 586
Catoosa	502	51 935	0.55	707	10.6	656	9.9	7 371	13.4	8 717	5 981	2 736	2 528	3 839
Charlton	2 492	11 242	0.59	118	9.4	81	6.5	1 214	14.5	1 875	1 388	487	203	1 513
Chatham	13 823	305 825	1.21	4 059	14.0	2 479	8.6	35 990	15.4	44 454	28 424	16 030	11 517	4 076
Chattahoochee	3 277	20 344	2.29	199	18.2	25	2.3	836	11.0	549	354	195	8	60
Chattooga	1 332	23 426	0.79	305	12.3	286	11.5	3 511	17.9	5 751	3 760	1 991	614	2 507
Cherokee	1 657	181 500	0.59	2 763	11.4	1 465	6.1	28 283	13.8	18 359	11 790	6 569	3 420	1 497
Clarke	10 212	138 849	1.34	1 387	11.1	771	6.2	18 404	18.4	16 682	11 643	5 039	4 702	3 833
Clay	55	2 809	0.65	31	10.3	35	11.6	395	17.2	589	365	224	NA	NA
Clayton	4 301	252 181	0.86	3 976	14.2	1 676	6.0	46 247	18.9	37 913	21 022	16 891	13 362	5 020
Clinch	139	6 823	1.01	101	14.8	58	8.5	1 037	18.0	1 356	927	429	279	4 091
Cobb	9 361	698 208	0.94	9 713	13.0	4 469	6.0	95 190	14.6	106 394	67 971	38 423	19 613	2 699
Coffee	3 112	44 174	1.08	576	13.4	396	9.2	6 999	20.3	6 690	4 554	2 136	2 151	5 086
Colquitt	926	44 601	0.92	623	13.6	453	9.9	9 275	24.1	8 010	5 522	2 488	NA	NA
Columbia	688	105 050	0.50	1 710	11.6	907	6.2	14 586	11.5	15 393	10 870	4 523	2 221	1 602
Cook	142	14 972	0.70	220	12.8	210	12.2	2 707	18.8	3 125	2 152	973	411	2 533
Coweta	499	111 283	0.64	1 680	12.0	992	7.1	15 141	12.6	19 459	12 395	7 064	2 832	2 098
Crawford	135	9 456	0.36	101	8.2	116	9.4	1 683	16.6	1 120	668	452	325	2 822
Crisp	412	24 004	1.08	292	12.9	267	11.8	2 801	15.0	4 448	2 800	1 648	1 140	4 873
Dade	974	13 712	0.64	159	9.8	182	11.2	1 817	14.5	3 617	2 452	1 165	252	1 524
Dawson	139	20 864	0.81	255	10.8	196	8.3	3 159	16.8	4 595	3 200	1 395	460	2 013
Decatur	961	26 713	0.93	351	13.1	332	12.4	4 013	18.4	5 060	3 537	1 523	2 247	8 221
DeKalb	11 804	682 829	0.90	11 028	14.9	4 645	6.3	108 525	16.9	83 470	46 710	36 760	45 768	6 348
Dodge	1 755	19 238	0.75	214	10.4	236	11.5	2 600	16.2	4 944	3 472	1 472	861	4 562
Dooly	1 869	13 537	0.84	94	6.8	110	8.0	1 967	19.9	1 965	1 250	715	NA	NA
Dougherty	4 062	106 578	1.40	1 234	13.7	949	10.5	12 617	16.8	17 800	12 218	5 582	5 512	5 936
Douglas	1 327	119 976	0.73	1 771	12.5	1 019	7.2	18 999	15.2	16 659	10 322	6 337	4 384	3 182
Early	107	10 500	0.98	133	12.9	135	13.1	1 283	15.2	2 197	1 420	777	506	4 944
Echols	0	2 751	0.22	39	9.8	17	4.3	973	27.6	151	120	31	30	736

1. Per 1,000 estimated resident population.   2. Data for serious crimes have not been adjusted for underreporting; this may affect comparability between geographic areas and over time.
3. Per 100,000 population estimated by the FBI.

Table B. States and Counties — Crime, Education, Money Income, and Poverty

STATE County	Serious crimes known to police, 2014 (cont.)[1] Rate[2] Violent	Property	Education School enrollment and attainment, 2011–2015 Enrollment[3] Total	Percent private	High school graduate or less	Bachelor's degree or more	Local government expenditures,[5] 2013–2014 Total current spending (mil dol)	Current spending per student (dollars)	Money income, 2011–2015 Per capita income[6] (dollars)	Median income (dollars)	Households Percent with income of less than $50,000	with income of $200,000 or more	Income and poverty, 2015 Median household income (dollars)	Percent below poverty level All persons	Children under 18 years	Children 5 to 17 years in families
	46	47	48	49	50	51	52	53	54	55	56	57	58	59	60	61
FLORIDA—Cont'd																
Putnam	561	2 967	14 936	10.3	60.4	11.8	103.2	9 286	18 082	31 715	67.9	1.0	32 351	27.3	41.1	39.0
St. Johns	258	1 786	54 076	22.0	27.4	42.1	277.5	8 120	37 581	66 194	37.4	9.0	71 896	9.8	10.1	8.9
St. Lucie	327	2 093	67 568	13.4	47.9	19.9	338.9	8 585	23 657	43 459	56.4	2.5	45 918	16.4	25.3	24.1
Santa Rosa	151	1 109	40 722	11.6	37.6	26.6	203.6	7 864	27 892	58 923	41.2	4.2	59 289	12.3	16.9	15.2
Sarasota	260	2 269	65 384	15.0	37.8	32.4	433.2	10 465	34 479	51 766	48.2	5.0	55 882	9.7	17.6	16.6
Seminole	341	2 256	120 797	16.7	31.0	35.3	523.6	8 074	29 162	57 010	43.8	5.2	57 357	11.5	16.1	14.6
Sumter	188	990	9 476	14.0	41.1	28.0	72.8	8 788	30 145	50 350	49.7	2.7	54 592	10.1	30.6	29.2
Suwannee	481	1 505	8 960	14.9	62.0	11.6	51.2	8 561	18 573	36 289	62.3	1.3	37 368	23.6	35.2	34.0
Taylor	679	1 497	4 351	13.6	62.9	9.0	27.4	9 065	15 811	36 181	67.4	0.4	39 116	21.2	30.0	29.0
Union	303	759	2 731	7.8	63.3	7.8	20.9	8 827	12 291	39 163	63.6	0.6	41 078	26.2	26.4	24.6
Volusia	434	3 112	109 749	18.4	45.1	21.6	502.7	8 209	24 026	41 117	59.1	2.2	42 334	16.3	25.1	23.4
Wakulla	275	1 951	6 781	9.0	50.5	16.1	41.2	8 131	20 823	50 340	49.7	1.2	48 703	16.5	21.3	19.1
Walton	382	2 438	11 529	10.4	42.9	25.9	76.7	9 510	27 393	44 966	55.5	4.7	47 875	14.8	26.1	24.7
Washington	202	1 456	5 318	8.4	60.9	11.1	33.6	9 989	18 164	38 970	62.0	1.3	36 328	24.8	34.2	32.1
GEORGIA	377	3 281	2 771 331	14.6	43.0	28.8	15 773.1	9 150	25 737	49 620	50.3	4.3	51 225	17.2	24.7	23.6
Appling	65	1 074	4 039	4.6	66.6	13.1	35.5	9 777	19 178	37 135	63.3	0.6	39 588	22.5	34.2	33.0
Atkinson	NA	NA	2 281	4.7	69.7	7.8	16.3	9 274	17 022	30 933	67.2	1.0	32 398	26.9	40.5	40.4
Bacon	NA	NA	2 644	3.2	63.0	12.8	18.7	8 941	18 349	37 162	60.8	0.8	35 431	23.9	36.8	33.3
Baker	120	812	784	11.1	61.9	8.6	4.9	15 420	20 959	44 297	57.5	1.8	34 455	28.7	41.9	40.0
Baldwin	562	3 000	14 428	13.0	56.5	17.7	48.5	8 375	18 611	32 460	64.2	1.0	38 015	26.0	35.5	35.4
Banks	76	2 360	4 294	5.8	67.4	11.2	26.6	9 312	19 211	41 472	57.7	0.8	44 146	15.8	24.4	21.8
Barrow	466	2 657	19 790	12.8	53.1	16.5	112.0	8 508	21 411	52 012	48.1	1.5	53 789	15.6	21.3	22.1
Bartow	506	4 836	24 940	10.2	53.3	17.8	170.0	9 236	22 592	48 893	50.9	1.7	50 900	13.6	21.5	20.8
Ben Hill	319	3 997	4 062	4.5	62.0	10.9	30.0	9 088	15 316	29 994	72.4	0.3	30 776	32.5	46.9	47.7
Berrien	215	2 264	4 713	6.6	56.7	12.5	27.4	8 518	16 523	31 835	66.9	0.3	35 518	25.5	36.9	33.7
Bibb	NA	NA	42 512	21.2	49.4	23.8	230.3	9 478	21 591	36 519	61.0	3.0	38 870	26.7	41.6	39.9
Bleckley	369	3 586	4 114	6.7	60.7	16.5	21.4	8 828	19 503	38 991	59.4	1.1	42 716	19.3	31.7	30.7
Brantley	180	3 080	4 699	4.9	66.6	8.4	31.0	8 735	17 276	37 206	64.0	0.6	37 709	21.6	34.3	30.9
Brooks	455	2 797	3 773	8.6	60.0	11.7	23.2	10 544	19 744	32 663	68.4	1.2	36 820	25.4	38.9	39.7
Bryan	174	1 494	10 106	15.1	38.0	31.1	59.7	7 232	26 934	63 327	39.2	3.5	69 650	13.1	16.2	15.2
Bulloch	180	2 586	30 309	6.3	41.2	29.0	95.1	9 371	18 719	36 032	61.8	1.8	36 544	29.9	31.3	30.0
Burke	611	3 535	5 989	12.0	62.3	9.6	55.4	12 581	17 546	33 641	65.6	0.5	36 977	25.1	37.9	36.3
Butts	197	1 911	5 274	12.0	67.7	10.1	29.3	8 495	19 433	41 667	55.8	1.4	44 166	19.0	26.9	26.5
Calhoun	2 809	9 543	1 511	12.4	65.8	9.9	11.2	10 358	14 242	25 513	72.3	3.2	30 972	37.5	42.4	39.1
Camden	400	2 671	12 933	11.0	40.1	21.1	83.1	9 049	23 856	52 473	47.1	2.3	52 706	13.6	20.4	21.3
Candler	NA	NA	2 880	5.1	61.1	15.4	19.4	8 913	16 897	30 185	67.2	1.3	32 806	28.1	43.3	39.9
Carroll	293	3 294	33 871	8.1	55.4	17.9	167.0	8 586	21 320	43 586	56.6	1.7	45 453	20.4	26.4	26.4
Catoosa	284	3 555	15 895	16.2	47.4	18.6	101.6	9 360	22 642	50 876	48.6	1.1	50 979	13.1	19.6	18.6
Charlton	194	1 320	2 707	5.4	67.2	10.0	15.2	9 100	18 036	42 778	57.5	0.3	37 037	32.5	37.7	36.5
Chatham	412	3 664	78 334	24.9	36.6	32.6	357.1	9 537	25 690	47 218	52.4	4.0	48 885	17.8	25.3	24.9
Chattahoochee	0	60	3 330	9.3	35.2	25.7	9.8	10 332	19 487	43 378	58.3	0.5	41 066	21.0	24.5	28.9
Chattooga	155	2 352	5 277	7.9	69.0	8.8	36.9	8 739	16 333	32 913	70.0	1.1	38 063	20.4	28.8	26.3
Cherokee	90	1 407	61 660	16.2	35.4	34.7	341.7	8 363	30 595	68 926	34.8	5.6	74 885	9.4	12.3	11.5
Clarke	368	3 465	50 979	7.9	35.5	40.2	152.0	11 852	19 276	32 162	65.8	2.8	33 302	38.1	41.6	44.9
Clay	NA	NA	574	9.6	65.1	7.8	3.9	11 105	12 790	20 438	80.3	0.0	25 941	34.3	52.0	52.5
Clayton	588	4 432	80 554	13.2	49.5	18.3	433.7	8 256	18 107	40 938	59.8	0.8	41 731	23.3	35.4	33.9
Clinch	543	3 548	1 533	3.8	62.2	13.5	13.3	9 482	17 127	24 015	69.0	0.9	31 848	28.2	39.6	38.7
Cobb	255	2 445	203 134	17.0	28.5	44.1	1 054.4	8 870	33 778	65 873	38.5	7.7	70 097	11.4	16.4	15.6
Coffee	392	4 693	11 266	5.5	61.7	13.7	73.1	9 356	17 540	33 965	68.4	2.2	34 775	22.6	34.0	32.2
Colquitt	NA	NA	11 805	2.9	64.0	13.1	85.2	8 810	17 353	32 409	67.2	1.4	34 151	24.1	35.5	35.5
Columbia	51	1 551	37 817	12.6	32.0	35.3	201.0	8 069	30 603	71 021	31.3	5.7	75 232	9.3	11.3	10.7
Cook	160	2 372	4 507	6.4	64.3	12.9	29.5	8 831	18 790	35 683	60.8	1.7	34 505	24.1	35.7	33.1
Coweta	224	1 875	34 518	13.1	43.2	27.6	266.6	7 325	28 106	62 461	40.0	3.4	67 268	10.9	16.4	15.4
Crawford	104	2 718	3 105	14.1	57.3	12.8	16.2	8 857	20 904	41 825	60.2	0.6	43 559	20.6	28.9	26.8
Crisp	351	4 523	6 449	9.0	57.5	14.6	43.4	10 099	19 439	31 615	66.7	2.1	31 095	32.3	47.4	45.3
Dade	659	865	4 218	33.7	55.2	14.1	20.4	9 149	21 547	46 434	53.5	1.2	43 632	16.2	21.8	21.5
Dawson	92	1 921	5 312	11.0	43.2	27.6	35.1	9 955	28 832	56 943	41.2	5.9	60 195	12.1	18.0	16.6
Decatur	955	7 266	6 598	7.5	55.1	15.8	48.7	8 941	18 310	31 284	69.3	2.4	37 661	27.3	39.9	39.2
DeKalb	679	5 669	193 365	23.8	32.7	41.1	934.3	8 917	29 486	51 376	48.6	6.1	53 994	17.8	27.7	27.4
Dodge	419	4 143	4 346	7.3	61.1	14.7	34.0	10 285	17 887	34 271	65.3	0.5	34 611	24.8	38.1	39.4
Dooly	NA	NA	3 176	10.8	68.5	9.2	14.2	9 924	14 295	28 696	73.5	0.3	32 323	33.8	45.4	42.9
Dougherty	867	5 069	30 487	8.4	48.4	18.9	163.6	10 447	18 999	32 084	67.2	1.7	34 799	29.4	42.1	42.3
Douglas	288	2 894	41 794	15.8	43.5	26.0	224.8	8 789	23 158	53 881	46.4	2.2	58 443	14.1	21.6	20.1
Early	1 036	3 908	2 836	6.7	59.0	15.2	21.5	9 810	18 116	31 680	67.6	1.0	31 935	26.5	41.6	37.3
Echols	98	638	1 203	5.7	64.7	8.3	8.0	9 708	16 954	32 959	66.3	1.6	34 414	25.9	39.3	38.6

1. Data for serious crimes have not been adjusted for underreporting; this may affect comparability between geographic areas and over time.   2. Per 100,000 population estimated by the FBI.
3. All persons 3 years old and over enrolled in nursery school through college.   4. Persons 25 years old and over.   5. Elementary and secondary education expenditures.
6. Based on population estimated by the American Community Survey, 2011–2015.

Table B. States and Counties — **Personal Income**

STATE County	Personal income, 2015										Earnings, 2015		
	Total (mil dol)	Percent change, 2014–2015	Per capita[1]		Wages and salaries (mil dol)	Supplements to wages and salaries; employer contributions (mil dol)		Proprietors' income (mil dol)	Dividends, interest, and rent (mil dol)	Personal transfer receipts (mil dol)	Total (mil dol)	Contributions for government social insurance (mil dol)	
			Dollars	Rank		Pension and insurance	Government social insurance					From employee and self-employed	From employer
	62	63	64	65	66	67	68	69	70	71	72	73	74
FLORIDA—Cont'd													
Putnam	2 053	3.8	28 501	2 978	651	132	46	81	320	803	911	70	46
St. Johns	13 698	6.3	60 441	151	3 055	457	213	542	3 556	1 771	4 267	291	213
St. Lucie	10 636	6.6	35 625	2 092	3 043	535	216	460	2 270	2 951	4 255	319	216
Santa Rosa	6 722	6.1	40 240	1 508	1 516	287	114	331	1 236	1 334	2 248	155	114
Sarasota	22 884	4.8	56 426	229	7 732	1 071	534	1 249	9 718	4 560	10 586	757	534
Seminole	19 246	6.0	42 851	971	8 720	1 216	611	668	3 262	3 158	11 216	706	611
Sumter	4 638	7.2	39 012	1 517	1 103	203	81	156	1 304	2 024	1 543	166	81
Suwannee	1 332	6.4	30 449	2 877	396	84	28	189	181	440	697	43	28
Taylor	683	4.9	30 354	2 922	303	57	21	46	98	199	427	28	21
Union	278	4.4	18 255	3 112	136	41	9	11	43	94	197	12	9
Volusia	19 577	5.5	37 802	1 776	6 750	1 084	485	878	4 357	5 382	9 197	675	485
Wakulla	990	4.9	31 405	2 776	200	48	14	44	137	220	306	23	14
Walton	3 165	5.3	49 839	615	906	138	64	352	949	502	1 460	98	64
Washington	669	4.7	27 096	3 039	211	49	15	28	96	228	304	22	15
GEORGIA	411 721	5.0	40 367	X	224 339	33 993	15 533	30 914	68 783	72 940	304 778	17 878	15 533
Appling	547	3.1	29 629	2 814	311	71	21	52	66	158	455	25	21
Atkinson	220	4.3	26 140	3 013	75	15	5	26	25	64	121	7	5
Bacon	327	3.2	28 971	2 804	140	29	10	38	36	102	217	12	10
Baker	105	3.3	33 167	2 809	21	4	1	20	16	31	47	2	1
Baldwin	1 314	1.8	28 910	2 841	566	129	37	49	207	444	780	48	37
Banks	588	4.1	31 775	2 295	112	21	8	79	67	141	219	13	8
Barrow	2 455	6.6	32 570	2 558	713	122	49	166	274	497	1 050	68	49
Bartow	3 479	5.1	33 856	2 199	1 584	266	114	256	434	771	2 220	135	114
Ben Hill	476	2.3	27 364	2 944	203	40	16	27	79	172	286	19	16
Berrien	538	6.2	28 392	2 930	130	30	9	19	86	166	189	13	9
Bibb	5 900	3.7	38 379	1 569	3 827	595	270	496	1 068	1 509	5 188	313	270
Bleckley	391	1.4	31 964	2 475	86	23	6	7	71	114	122	9	6
Brantley	449	5.7	24 315	3 097	70	18	5	27	50	147	120	10	5
Brooks	505	2.6	32 246	2 538	113	22	8	43	84	150	185	12	8
Bryan	1 667	7.4	47 448	624	286	54	19	74	230	242	433	28	19
Bulloch	2 126	4.6	29 258	2 914	910	196	62	108	348	489	1 277	73	62
Burke	717	3.4	31 527	2 660	422	91	28	46	86	212	588	33	28
Butts	692	4.2	29 320	2 822	225	46	15	24	95	197	311	21	15
Calhoun	161	3.7	24 838	3 059	38	10	2	22	24	52	73	4	2
Camden	1 707	4.4	32 754	2 485	1 055	233	87	27	355	365	1 403	74	87
Candler	296	2.6	27 213	2 936	92	20	6	16	40	105	133	9	6
Carroll	3 856	4.6	33 662	2 369	1 743	306	121	224	597	887	2 395	144	121
Catoosa	2 137	4.8	32 358	2 522	565	98	41	137	241	515	840	59	41
Charlton	322	6.0	24 840	3 087	79	15	6	17	35	89	116	8	6
Chatham	12 085	4.9	42 115	1 077	7 480	1 222	546	781	2 403	2 260	10 028	574	546
Chattahoochee	403	4.6	35 448	2 436	1 111	330	117	3	239	35	1 562	54	117
Chattooga	705	4.0	28 274	2 938	220	47	16	41	87	235	324	23	16
Cherokee	10 351	6.9	43 878	1 024	2 382	357	164	716	1 225	1 387	3 620	233	164
Clarke	3 636	5.0	29 343	2 845	3 194	663	207	175	801	766	4 239	223	207
Clay	89	4.2	28 185	2 920	18	4	1	1	15	36	25	2	1
Clayton	7 130	5.8	26 025	3 022	6 310	1 115	425	305	847	1 848	8 154	459	425
Clinch	201	3.3	29 132	2 932	90	17	7	25	21	74	140	8	7
Cobb	36 400	5.8	49 101	413	20 795	2 532	1 417	2 039	5 793	4 205	26 783	1 567	1 417
Coffee	1 226	3.4	28 445	2 916	582	109	42	92	176	355	825	49	42
Colquitt	1 357	3.9	29 603	2 832	502	103	34	103	197	405	741	44	34
Columbia	6 374	7.0	44 250	857	1 294	216	91	324	969	944	1 924	123	91
Cook	458	4.0	26 724	3 032	120	28	8	27	66	151	183	12	8
Coweta	5 593	6.3	40 402	1 301	1 582	264	113	195	750	872	2 154	137	113
Crawford	385	3.4	31 046	2 362	52	10	4	29	50	104	94	7	4
Crisp	621	4.4	27 120	3 016	305	54	21	32	99	209	413	26	21
Dade	489	3.7	30 047	2 871	125	22	9	42	64	134	198	14	9
Dawson	883	5.6	37 879	1 632	249	41	18	81	138	167	388	25	18
Decatur	912	4.4	33 563	2 270	303	64	20	94	161	254	480	27	20
DeKalb	31 467	5.2	42 819	735	17 292	2 424	1 213	1 378	5 644	4 732	22 307	1 309	1 213
Dodge	564	2.0	27 009	3 004	168	43	11	29	88	174	251	16	11
Dooly	325	9.0	23 185	3 108	121	27	8	33	51	102	190	12	8
Dougherty	2 985	1.1	32 682	2 453	2 034	374	145	177	544	923	2 730	160	145
Douglas	4 516	5.7	32 089	2 473	1 616	258	113	104	504	922	2 091	131	113
Early	379	6.2	35 826	1 959	200	39	13	37	52	112	289	16	13
Echols	96	1.9	23 721	3 064	20	4	1	7	13	23	32	2	1

1. Based on the resident population estimated as of July 1 of the year shown.

Table B. States and Counties — **Earnings, Social Security, and Housing**

STATE County	Farm	Mining	Construction	Manu-facturing	Information: professional, scientific, technical services	Retail trade	Finance, insurance, real estate and leasing	Health care and social assistance	Government	Number	Rate[1]	Supplemental Security Income recipients, December 2015	Total	Percent change, 2010–2016
	75	76	77	78	79	80	81	82	83	84	85	86	87	88
FLORIDA—Cont'd														
Putnam	1.9	0.4	4.6	13.2	D	8.9	2.9	14.3	27.4	20 240	281	2 963	36 399	-2.5
St. Johns	0.6	0.0	6.5	6.2	10.1	8.7	9.0	11.8	14.6	48 160	212	2 472	102 280	13.9
St. Lucie	0.8	0.0	6.3	4.3	6.6	10.0	4.0	16.3	20.8	76 185	255	6 945	139 039	1.6
Santa Rosa	0.6	0.5	7.3	2.3	10.2	8.3	5.6	12.5	25.9	33 655	202	2 507	69 662	7.6
Sarasota	0.1	0.1	8.2	5.2	13.9	9.1	9.7	17.1	10.0	131 890	326	4 615	235 695	3.2
Seminole	0.1	D	8.5	4.0	14.4	10.0	11.0	10.4	9.8	78 085	174	7 195	187 713	3.5
Sumter	1.3	0.2	10.9	4.3	D	8.8	6.6	13.3	22.7	64 785	545	1 623	68 199	28.6
Suwannee	19.7	0.2	5.8	12.1	2.2	7.6	1.6	8.1	21.1	11 805	270	1 427	18 763	-2.1
Taylor	0.6	D	6.3	28.5	D	7.0	1.5	D	20.0	5 250	234	778	10 853	-1.4
Union	0.9	D	4.0	4.5	D	D	0.8	D	59.2	2 355	155	385	4 464	-1.0
Volusia	0.4	0.0	5.4	7.5	8.4	10.2	5.9	18.6	14.6	145 420	281	12 191	257 946	1.5
Wakulla	0.0	0.0	9.0	16.1	7.9	7.3	2.3	5.2	32.5	5 995	190	590	12 981	1.4
Walton	1.2	0.2	10.4	1.5	6.8	14.5	8.6	9.7	13.5	13 860	218	930	49 950	10.7
Washington	1.1	D	7.8	3.2	D	6.7	2.3	D	39.1	6 110	248	915	10 648	-1.4
GEORGIA	0.8	0.2	5.0	9.2	14.9	6.2	8.0	9.8	16.5	1 714 145	168	258 401	4 218 776	3.2
Appling	8.8	0.0	5.2	8.0	1.5	6.9	1.8	D	15.1	4 050	220	665	8 381	-1.5
Atkinson	16.1	D	D	36.3	D	4.1	2.9	D	16.3	1 550	186	338	3 429	-2.7
Bacon	14.0	D	1.8	21.7	D	4.1	D	D	13.9	2 305	204	408	4 715	-1.8
Baker	39.7	0.9	D	D	D	3.3	D	4.0	11.0	785	248	154	1 620	-1.9
Baldwin	0.0	D	3.9	15.9	D	9.1	3.7	16.0	34.9	9 165	202	1 503	20 277	0.5
Banks	23.2	0.5	7.9	8.2	D	7.7	D	3.6	18.7	3 875	210	336	7 527	-0.9
Barrow	1.8	D	10.4	11.7	D	11.9	4.1	7.4	16.5	12 885	172	1 825	27 602	4.6
Bartow	1.8	0.4	8.7	28.2	4.8	6.1	3.8	7.5	13.3	19 220	187	2 301	40 196	0.9
Ben Hill	2.0	0.0	2.3	24.8	D	8.1	3.8	D	18.5	3 960	228	919	7 860	-1.0
Berrien	3.9	D	4.3	27.7	D	8.5	4.8	D	26.3	4 105	216	822	8 598	-1.3
Bibb	0.0	D	2.9	7.3	9.2	7.9	14.3	21.3	11.6	32 375	211	8 098	70 259	0.9
Bleckley	-1.3	0.1	6.6	1.7	2.2	11.5	D	4.9	46.8	2 695	211	427	5 257	-0.9
Brantley	0.1	D	13.7	10.0	D	4.4	1.4	4.3	34.3	3 580	194	524	7 875	-2.6
Brooks	19.2	0.0	2.3	6.3	1.6	5.0	4.2	8.3	18.3	3 810	243	763	7 638	-0.9
Bryan	1.1	0.1	9.4	6.7	D	7.6	7.3	D	26.0	5 395	154	645	13 640	15.3
Bulloch	0.7	D	5.6	7.5	4.2	7.9	5.2	12.9	32.9	10 370	142	1 649	30 393	5.5
Burke	4.6	0.0	1.6	6.7	4.5	4.1	1.9	D	13.7	4 930	217	1 088	9 830	-0.4
Butts	0.6	0.0	D	14.0	D	9.0	4.0	D	27.2	5 130	218	722	9 281	-0.8
Calhoun	27.4	D	D	D	D	4.1	D	D	32.8	1 240	192	316	2 365	-1.8
Camden	0.2	0.0	D	5.1	20.0	4.9	2.5	4.2	49.7	8 450	161	805	21 563	2.1
Candler	1.1	0.1	9.0	4.6	8.7	10.5	D	D	26.8	2 470	226	472	4 672	-1.8
Carroll	2.4	D	7.6	16.5	D	8.2	3.4	15.8	18.1	22 265	194	3 407	44 772	0.3
Catoosa	1.7	D	7.3	14.1	2.7	12.0	5.0	12.9	16.9	13 985	212	888	27 071	1.8
Charlton	5.8	D	6.4	13.0	D	4.2	D	3.0	21.6	2 235	172	360	4 392	-1.9
Chatham	0.0	D	4.1	17.4	5.5	6.4	5.3	13.7	17.7	49 325	172	6 935	124 384	4.2
Chattahoochee	0.1	0.0	0.3	D	D	0.2	D	0.2	91.1	670	58	160	3 327	-1.5
Chattooga	3.5	0.0	4.3	39.3	D	6.4	2.5	D	21.1	6 370	256	1 038	10 850	-1.2
Cherokee	0.4	0.1	13.9	7.3	12.2	9.0	6.0	10.0	14.4	36 625	155	2 236	89 351	8.5
Clarke	0.1	D	2.3	10.8	4.5	6.4	6.5	16.2	34.7	16 765	136	3 103	52 765	3.3
Clay	-1.6	0.3	D	1.5	0.2	5.5	D	12.1	44.7	835	271	166	2 074	-1.3
Clayton	0.0	D	3.2	3.8	1.7	5.1	2.3	6.3	11.8	36 700	134	8 595	104 996	0.3
Clinch	10.0	0.2	1.9	38.1	D	3.7	D	3.6	16.7	1 610	234	427	2 946	-2.0
Cobb	0.0	0.1	9.0	6.9	17.4	6.9	8.3	9.3	8.7	97 725	132	9 482	297 399	3.8
Coffee	4.8	0.2	5.7	17.3	3.0	9.4	4.1	D	16.3	7 845	182	1 664	16 844	-1.3
Colquitt	9.0	0.0	4.3	13.6	D	8.4	4.5	D	25.5	9 470	207	1 954	18 283	-0.1
Columbia	0.2	D	10.2	10.2	7.9	11.5	8.4	11.6	17.5	21 770	151	1 585	55 897	14.9
Cook	7.6	D	9.4	12.1	3.4	7.1	3.1	D	31.3	3 735	219	718	7 250	-0.5
Coweta	0.2	D	6.7	14.2	6.2	9.3	3.8	17.0	15.3	22 655	164	2 086	53 552	6.7
Crawford	25.5	D	9.9	2.3	D	3.4	D	6.1	21.7	2 810	226	284	5 244	-0.9
Crisp	2.6	0.0	2.4	11.9	D	8.3	4.9	D	17.7	4 775	209	1 118	10 676	-0.5
Dade	4.6	0.2	D	18.4	5.2	5.3	4.2	8.3	13.0	3 875	239	406	7 248	-0.8
Dawson	4.4	0.0	6.8	9.0	D	24.0	5.2	7.3	14.8	4 670	201	428	10 897	4.4
Decatur	14.7	D	4.9	7.2	3.5	8.4	5.6	D	26.8	6 045	222	1 344	12 104	-0.2
DeKalb	0.0	D	3.9	4.5	13.8	6.8	7.7	12.2	14.3	99 615	136	18 800	310 214	1.7
Dodge	3.3	D	3.2	10.1	2.0	8.6	3.7	D	39.8	4 330	208	850	9 688	-1.7
Dooly	7.8	0.2	D	D	0.5	4.9	3.7	D	21.0	2 605	187	775	6 176	-2.4
Dougherty	0.6	0.0	4.4	9.6	7.1	6.2	4.9	19.6	23.5	18 690	205	5 202	40 711	-0.2
Douglas	0.0	D	5.7	11.0	3.7	11.2	5.3	11.6	16.7	21 190	151	2 890	52 194	1.0
Early	10.9	0.0	3.0	24.1	D	5.7	3.0	D	23.7	2 590	247	635	4 897	-1.5
Echols	10.7	0.0	9.0	2.9	D	D	D	D	26.9	550	136	45	1 528	-1.9

1. Per 1,000 resident population estimated as of July 1 of the year shown.

Table B. States and Counties — **Housing, Labor Force, and Employment**

STATE County	Housing units, 2011–2015								Civilian labor force, 2016				Civilian employment,[6] 2011–2015		
	Occupied units										Unemployment			Percent	
			Owner-occupied			Renter-occupied									
				Median owner cost as a percent of income											Construction, production, and maintenance occupations
	Total	Percent	Median value[1]	With a mortgage	Without a mortgage[2]	Median rent[3]	Median rent as a percent of income[2]	Substandard units[4] (percent)	Total	Percent change, 2015–2016	Total	Rate[5]	Total	Management, business, science and arts	
	89	90	91	92	93	94	95	96	97	98	99	100	101	102	103

FLORIDA—Cont'd

Putnam	27 683	73.6	85 500	25.8	11.0	665	35.0	2.9	27 387	0.6	1 724	6.3	24 209	23.3	29.4
St. Johns	79 242	75.5	244 400	23.8	10.3	1 119	31.3	1.2	116 071	2.5	4 303	3.7	96 436	45.1	12.6
St. Lucie	107 898	72.8	125 600	26.6	13.5	993	38.6	2.4	134 319	2.4	7 601	5.7	112 310	28.3	20.0
Santa Rosa	58 654	72.6	161 400	22.6	10.9	1 031	29.2	2.4	75 638	2.4	3 435	4.5	67 510	37.1	20.8
Sarasota	175 185	73.0	181 400	25.4	12.8	1 023	31.6	1.3	182 217	2.6	8 327	4.6	155 023	34.2	16.1
Seminole	152 260	67.6	176 100	24.4	11.4	1 077	32.5	1.3	243 532	3.0	10 541	4.3	210 450	42.6	12.9
Sumter	48 039	90.2	213 900	24.1	10.8	787	31.6	1.4	29 239	2.3	2 052	7.0	22 298	29.3	20.3
Suwannee	15 649	68.7	92 600	23.8	10.6	677	29.4	3.6	18 247	1.9	901	4.9	15 676	24.0	28.2
Taylor	7 605	77.1	83 700	24.2	11.6	632	26.0	1.6	8 904	-0.7	491	5.5	7 155	26.9	26.8
Union	3 883	65.6	87 500	25.6	10.0	640	23.3	4.6	4 786	1.2	212	4.4	3 955	23.7	23.0
Volusia	200 180	70.0	131 600	26.6	13.1	918	36.9	2.1	245 626	3.1	12 528	5.1	199 287	31.0	20.3
Wakulla	10 691	74.8	122 200	22.6	10.5	827	29.1	2.4	14 172	1.6	586	4.1	12 899	29.5	21.3
Walton	23 490	71.8	169 800	27.3	10.2	971	32.4	5.3	28 461	2.4	1 217	4.3	25 377	32.0	19.5
Washington	8 246	78.2	82 900	22.5	11.7	641	34.0	2.8	9 731	1.4	509	5.2	8 307	28.8	24.8
GEORGIA	3 574 362	63.3	148 100	22.6	11.3	879	31.3	2.8	4 920 469	2.8	264 211	5.4	4 388 274	35.9	22.3
Appling	6 812	69.8	72 300	21.7	10.1	499	23.1	3.0	9 245	6.6	594	6.4	7 071	25.5	42.0
Atkinson	2 772	71.6	74 400	22.0	12.4	460	25.8	3.8	4 021	4.0	211	5.2	3 389	18.6	44.0
Bacon	3 951	68.9	62 800	16.7	10.7	587	28.8	1.9	4 918	0.5	262	5.3	4 598	28.7	38.6
Baker	1 291	75.1	78 500	22.4	11.7	408	36.0	5.4	1 182	5.3	91	7.7	1 282	27.8	30.9
Baldwin	15 978	54.4	101 700	23.8	11.2	673	40.6	2.0	17 915	1.0	1 221	6.8	16 387	29.9	22.3
Banks	6 553	77.3	121 600	25.5	12.4	713	33.3	3.0	8 820	7.3	428	4.9	7 801	24.5	37.5
Barrow	23 560	73.2	119 700	22.9	10.0	913	29.2	2.6	37 322	3.4	1 768	4.7	32 137	27.3	28.5
Bartow	35 732	65.0	123 800	22.8	10.3	822	27.7	3.1	48 309	3.1	2 473	5.1	44 594	29.0	30.5
Ben Hill	6 413	63.9	80 900	24.1	12.6	613	31.3	2.6	5 662	3.4	457	8.1	6 019	26.9	33.1
Berrien	6 958	72.9	84 300	24.7	12.0	547	33.4	2.7	7 176	1.9	446	6.2	6 457	26.0	31.1
Bibb	57 111	53.0	118 700	23.2	11.7	743	36.3	2.4	68 856	1.4	4 118	6.0	60 115	34.6	17.6
Bleckley	4 113	74.3	87 100	19.5	15.9	606	29.9	1.8	4 411	0.9	316	7.2	4 365	29.5	25.8
Brantley	6 581	79.9	67 400	23.2	11.8	530	26.2	2.6	7 189	4.1	482	6.7	6 702	27.4	32.2
Brooks	6 577	69.2	94 900	26.0	14.2	609	33.2	6.4	7 063	2.6	368	5.2	5 703	24.8	34.4
Bryan	11 441	68.3	195 600	22.3	10.0	1 071	29.6	1.8	16 582	2.7	819	4.9	14 224	34.7	23.5
Bulloch	26 128	49.6	129 700	20.4	10.0	773	39.0	2.5	35 793	3.1	2 045	5.7	31 144	32.3	21.8
Burke	8 102	70.6	81 000	20.6	14.6	546	31.5	3.3	9 366	2.6	716	7.6	8 676	27.1	33.4
Butts	7 774	71.7	113 900	24.2	11.3	775	36.6	2.9	10 413	2.9	587	5.6	8 700	25.8	32.6
Calhoun	1 836	65.5	56 600	28.1	15.4	501	27.9	0.5	2 205	3.6	128	5.8	2 036	21.6	28.6
Camden	18 638	61.1	151 100	24.0	10.0	921	27.9	2.1	20 402	-8.5	1 166	5.7	20 674	33.1	21.8
Candler	3 909	60.6	89 000	25.0	11.1	541	34.1	4.4	5 021	1.1	245	4.9	4 168	27.0	30.6
Carroll	40 074	62.8	112 100	21.8	10.7	796	31.7	2.4	53 418	3.2	3 201	6.0	47 372	26.3	33.0
Catoosa	23 943	75.0	129 800	20.8	10.1	730	26.5	2.1	32 216	2.7	1 558	4.8	30 069	32.3	25.5
Charlton	3 524	78.8	82 000	21.8	10.0	687	29.6	0.8	4 786	0.4	276	5.8	4 705	28.1	35.9
Chatham	104 912	54.6	171 500	24.2	12.9	951	32.5	2.2	136 309	2.3	7 124	5.2	124 627	35.1	20.2
Chattahoochee	2 599	27.4	64 800	16.6	15.5	1 236	32.1	4.3	2 119	0.4	178	8.4	2 204	28.6	31.1
Chattooga	9 364	66.3	63 900	23.0	12.8	584	27.8	8.5	10 719	1.6	665	6.2	8 976	23.8	41.9
Cherokee	79 133	77.4	190 500	21.7	10.0	1 010	29.1	2.4	124 452	3.4	5 289	4.2	110 111	38.0	18.4
Clarke	43 356	40.5	150 300	22.3	12.0	790	38.3	2.6	58 904	3.1	3 323	5.6	53 922	39.4	16.8
Clay	1 183	59.2	69 400	28.7	15.6	375	32.0	5.9	885	3.0	93	10.5	848	23.1	39.4
Clayton	88 793	52.7	85 200	24.2	11.8	881	35.1	4.8	129 852	2.8	8 574	6.6	114 144	23.5	28.2
Clinch	2 581	69.0	58 000	22.1	13.5	417	24.8	2.2	2 804	1.2	173	6.2	2 309	30.0	38.3
Cobb	268 616	64.2	197 400	20.8	10.0	1 006	29.6	2.3	411 452	3.3	18 755	4.6	366 793	44.3	15.6
Coffee	14 321	66.7	83 400	25.3	11.1	545	29.4	2.3	18 118	4.8	1 062	5.9	15 358	31.6	30.9
Colquitt	15 737	64.8	79 600	23.1	12.1	598	34.1	6.0	21 191	5.7	1 118	5.3	18 354	25.2	39.6
Columbia	45 488	78.3	170 800	20.9	10.0	1 094	27.0	1.1	70 254	2.4	3 277	4.7	60 928	42.9	17.8
Cook	6 157	68.1	86 000	23.1	12.7	688	30.0	3.0	7 516	3.2	408	5.4	7 043	25.4	33.6
Coweta	48 777	72.8	181 000	21.6	10.7	933	29.3	1.9	70 241	3.5	3 489	5.0	62 298	34.0	25.4
Crawford	4 538	79.5	85 800	24.8	12.3	701	30.9	2.5	5 691	2.1	337	5.9	4 843	29.2	33.4
Crisp	8 659	59.0	98 200	21.3	13.3	597	38.9	3.8	9 253	-1.8	563	6.1	8 633	29.9	25.0
Dade	6 150	77.9	118 300	21.7	10.2	677	29.6	3.4	8 077	2.9	410	5.1	7 848	27.2	29.5
Dawson	8 213	75.4	188 300	23.8	10.0	976	29.3	1.2	11 332	3.6	530	4.7	9 787	32.2	27.9
Decatur	10 614	59.4	114 400	24.1	13.5	633	31.9	7.1	11 631	2.1	775	6.7	9 892	29.3	30.0
DeKalb	267 396	55.3	163 000	23.7	11.6	991	32.3	3.2	384 723	3.1	20 658	5.4	344 876	42.7	16.5
Dodge	8 064	65.6	67 900	22.2	10.4	574	27.6	3.6	6 967	0.2	517	7.4	7 871	34.4	29.8
Dooly	5 004	64.3	73 000	23.8	12.6	499	33.2	4.8	5 010	5.3	292	5.8	4 895	21.7	40.2
Dougherty	35 455	45.7	101 400	22.6	13.7	689	33.5	3.4	38 261	1.0	2 628	6.9	34 097	30.3	25.3
Douglas	47 079	67.3	121 300	23.4	10.6	949	30.8	2.5	70 359	3.0	3 887	5.5	61 844	33.3	24.5
Early	3 981	66.3	81 600	22.5	14.0	585	29.4	5.4	4 428	1.6	309	7.0	3 742	27.7	32.7
Echols	1 416	65.8	67 600	19.5	13.4	612	24.0	5.0	1 937	3.8	83	4.3	1 675	21.7	46.0

1. Specified owner-occupied units.   2. A value of 10.0 represents 10 percent or less; a value of 50.0 represents 50 percent or more.   3. Specified renter-occupied units.
4. Overcrowded or lacking complete plumbing facilities.   5. Percent of civilian labor force.   6. Civilian employed persons 16 years old and over.

Table B. States and Counties — Nonfarm Employment and Agriculture

STATE County	Number of establishments	Total	Health care and social assistance	Manufacturing	Retail trade	Finance and insurance	Professional, scientific, and technical services	Total (mil dol)	Average per employee (dollars)	Number	Fewer than 50 acres	500 acres or more	Farm operators whose principal occupation is farming (percent)
	104	105	106	107	108	109	110	111	112	113	114	115	116
FLORIDA—Cont'd													
Putnam	1 223	12 135	2 492	1 840	2 667	322	289	418	34 457	430	64.0	7.9	44.7
St. Johns	5 759	56 179	7 736	1 640	10 258	1 796	3 559	2 034	36 206	188	67.0	12.2	47.3
St. Lucie	5 345	57 491	11 225	2 592	13 224	1 201	2 430	1 971	34 281	406	50.7	18.0	53.0
Santa Rosa	2 585	24 185	3 698	502	5 095	856	1 834	842	34 823	666	59.6	6.9	41.3
Sarasota	13 405	137 827	27 649	7 250	23 601	5 068	9 751	5 548	40 250	283	72.1	7.1	44.5
Seminole	13 042	164 140	18 724	6 094	27 831	14 112	11 382	6 942	42 293	312	84.6	2.2	49.4
Sumter	1 383	20 144	4 088	1 185	3 528	650	541	717	35 590	1 367	70.1	4.0	34.7
Suwannee	682	8 011	1 507	1 775	1 536	135	173	242	30 262	1 266	50.6	5.5	54.2
Taylor	407	4 746	672	1 561	1 017	73	78	182	38 308	181	44.8	7.2	57.5
Union	137	2 253	690	D	162	18	D	85	37 909	291	58.4	4.1	41.2
Volusia	12 380	140 144	27 104	8 109	25 735	4 539	6 727	4 929	35 174	1 363	81.6	2.5	55.1
Wakulla	425	3 371	212	D	900	69	158	104	30 905	171	70.2	5.3	49.7
Walton	2 037	18 895	2 162	205	4 260	259	540	637	33 726	670	43.0	6.4	44.8
Washington	382	3 702	892	272	706	132	215	115	31 119	406	41.9	5.7	36.0
GEORGIA	224 593	3 692 490	478 276	365 088	468 517	173 080	252 351	174 839	47 350	42 257	39.9	10.4	47.0
Appling	366	5 919	1 032	642	992	147	32	270	45 610	475	38.5	13.9	43.2
Atkinson	88	1 373	D	675	173	67	D	46	33 686	194	28.4	20.6	70.1
Bacon	219	2 873	521	913	293	138	57	94	32 772	268	35.1	12.7	48.1
Baker	25	226	D	NA	32	5	D	9	38 111	150	17.3	32.7	72.7
Baldwin	795	12 537	3 674	1 544	2 328	384	204	436	34 752	124	38.7	7.3	42.7
Banks	273	3 097	157	301	819	36	39	82	26 339	519	40.7	1.9	59.5
Barrow	1 122	15 944	1 434	3 013	2 613	273	936	514	32 231	304	52.3	3.3	35.9
Bartow	1 934	30 841	2 855	7 930	4 071	662	551	1 252	40 580	458	53.1	5.0	50.7
Ben Hill	323	4 880	596	1 926	737	186	55	156	32 016	209	38.8	13.9	44.0
Berrien	252	3 883	256	D	484	137	15	124	31 942	380	28.4	25.3	64.2
Bibb	4 107	71 546	15 429	4 807	10 141	8 691	2 470	2 802	39 166	113	38.1	1.8	50.4
Bleckley	168	1 536	214	35	463	80	22	42	27 514	219	31.5	15.5	39.3
Brantley	181	1 255	119	159	299	36	27	37	29 313	215	49.3	2.8	49.8
Brooks	204	2 033	520	184	364	65	54	64	31 255	364	39.3	19.5	51.9
Bryan	631	5 757	643	322	1 174	167	231	171	29 783	60	65.0	11.7	58.3
Bulloch	1 412	17 385	3 146	1 664	3 524	526	558	502	28 850	544	28.9	18.6	42.1
Burke	301	8 694	451	569	740	140	D	597	68 634	393	29.3	20.4	43.3
Butts	354	4 234	570	779	801	97	87	135	31 984	140	44.3	5.0	58.6
Calhoun	72	622	74	NA	78	31	D	22	35 273	151	25.2	37.1	48.3
Camden	800	8 180	892	160	2 425	278	470	239	29 228	69	60.9	10.1	44.9
Candler	206	2 245	579	173	418	96	64	63	28 190	238	29.4	11.3	47.5
Carroll	2 010	33 794	4 895	7 971	4 963	675	563	1 326	39 232	909	45.5	1.8	50.8
Catoosa	914	11 714	1 846	1 475	2 750	383	602	365	31 189	269	50.2	1.1	43.9
Charlton	149	1 857	261	274	218	32	57	59	32 022	84	48.8	8.3	51.2
Chatham	7 559	133 952	20 037	15 668	17 982	2 828	5 157	5 511	41 143	35	37.1	5.7	57.1
Chattahoochee	107	1 497	78	D	148	20	403	65	43 112	13	15.4	15.4	30.8
Chattooga	307	4 675	347	2 241	674	132	81	132	28 314	292	31.8	7.5	39.0
Cherokee	5 089	48 418	5 982	4 531	9 724	1 407	2 930	1 713	35 372	430	69.5	1.9	49.1
Clarke	2 989	46 038	9 512	5 615	7 239	1 081	1 564	1 716	37 269	90	64.4	3.3	23.3
Clay	38	288	40	NA	57	D	D	8	27 865	70	17.1	21.4	45.7
Clayton	3 746	70 709	8 140	3 936	10 740	1 629	897	2 689	38 027	23	87.0	0.0	69.6
Clinch	130	1 743	191	D	148	35	31	55	31 386	80	35.0	16.3	55.0
Cobb	19 689	326 060	32 297	17 765	38 449	17 296	28 162	17 714	54 328	110	81.8	0.0	55.5
Coffee	831	12 744	1 991	2 836	1 955	310	233	416	32 630	587	29.1	15.2	43.8
Colquitt	897	10 830	2 197	2 785	1 846	302	162	342	31 578	484	30.2	19.2	60.5
Columbia	2 177	27 466	3 595	2 627	5 623	787	1 346	948	34 513	145	57.2	2.8	45.5
Cook	305	2 796	445	650	563	124	59	83	29 820	234	41.0	18.4	41.0
Coweta	2 289	30 782	4 990	4 592	5 764	682	854	1 135	36 864	357	52.1	4.5	44.5
Crawford	112	542	50	54	92	12	7	18	33 803	155	38.7	8.4	53.5
Crisp	503	6 743	1 194	1 046	1 418	205	141	220	32 685	244	30.3	23.4	51.2
Dade	212	2 646	240	498	482	93	47	99	37 337	192	38.5	3.1	38.5
Dawson	594	6 367	387	893	2 808	112	139	159	24 897	182	64.3	1.6	41.2
Decatur	597	6 620	921	1 439	1 421	248	170	222	33 536	358	27.7	25.7	55.0
DeKalb	16 558	269 019	41 922	11 499	33 665	8 950	19 718	13 944	51 832	25	84.0	4.0	36.0
Dodge	329	3 206	890	357	699	129	84	88	27 435	401	26.4	8.7	53.4
Dooly	153	2 191	60	1 015	313	62	9	78	35 601	290	27.2	21.0	58.6
Dougherty	2 291	37 280	8 721	2 738	6 538	931	2 487	1 355	36 354	121	45.5	18.2	51.2
Douglas	2 479	36 427	4 789	3 160	7 982	768	967	1 202	32 997	117	67.5	2.6	43.6
Early	210	2 809	325	836	377	113	72	127	45 342	334	25.1	27.8	47.3
Echols	27	126	D	D	6	D	NA	4	30 119	40	17.5	17.5	40.0

Table B. States and Counties — Agriculture

	Agriculture, 2012 (cont.)														
	Land in farms					Value of land and buildings (dollars)			Value of products sold				Percent of farms with sales of:		Government payments	
			Acres					Value of machinery and equipment, average per farm (dollars)			Percent from:					
STATE County	Acreage (1,000)	Percent change, 2007–2012	Average size of farm	Total irrigated (1,000)	Total cropland (1,000)	Average per farm	Average per acre		Total (mil dol)	Average per farm (dollars)	Crops	Live-stock and poultry products	$10,000 or more	$100,000 or more	Total ($1,000)	Percent of farms
	117	118	119	120	121	122	123	124	125	126	127	128	129	130	131	132
FLORIDA—Cont'd																
Putnam	70	-5.5	164	5.5	10.3	904 658	5 529	50 742	44.2	102 761	85.0	15.0	31.9	9.5	153	5.3
St. Johns	34	0.3	179	11.7	18.5	1 172 793	6 556	259 819	69.7	370 527	98.7	1.3	38.8	16.5	162	5.9
St. Lucie	195	27.1	481	59.2	66.6	2 287 172	4 758	82 488	168.1	413 975	87.5	12.5	48.3	25.1	872	6.7
Santa Rosa	98	39.1	147	2.4	69.6	518 886	3 539	87 569	62.8	94 249	94.9	5.1	31.7	13.2	2 545	31.5
Sarasota	80	31.3	283	2.0	4.7	1 363 223	4 814	44 753	25.0	88 456	60.0	40.0	28.6	10.6	384	2.5
Seminole	22	-39.0	70	1.2	2.4	547 465	7 872	35 391	27.5	88 042	95.1	4.9	34.0	9.3	40	2.2
Sumter	183	14.7	134	3.1	20.7	717 143	5 350	45 931	42.1	30 773	58.9	41.1	19.3	5.3	164	2.9
Suwannee	193	15.5	153	27.8	84.1	613 355	4 014	92 742	296.3	234 060	29.2	70.8	35.8	13.3	1 332	12.1
Taylor	37	11.7	207	D	2.3	787 271	3 805	39 011	5.8	32 160	58.7	41.3	26.0	4.4	19	5.5
Union	46	-0.7	159	1.0	7.3	567 890	3 574	39 282	7.4	25 495	75.8	24.2	25.4	3.4	111	4.8
Volusia	106	27.3	78	9.0	23.4	477 479	6 137	44 275	111.5	81 802	89.7	10.3	35.2	9.5	1 427	8.0
Wakulla	31	9.1	181	0.2	2.0	632 977	3 502	31 655	2.3	13 322	D	D	31.0	2.3	39	7.6
Walton	148	16.6	221	1.3	30.7	634 997	2 876	47 294	28.6	42 633	37.5	62.5	22.8	6.0	819	25.2
Washington	58	-21.1	144	1.1	18.4	412 480	2 874	59 667	13.5	33 370	69.3	30.7	25.9	4.4	450	30.0
GEORGIA	9 621	-5.2	228	1 125.4	4 190.9	702 282	3 085	93 143	9 255.1	219 020	39.7	60.3	37.4	17.3	142 322	34.4
Appling	123	21.0	259	7.5	73.8	605 707	2 341	143 872	139.6	293 888	45.8	54.2	48.8	28.8	2 049	44.8
Atkinson	87	12.5	448	6.6	35.1	1 195 005	2 669	136 820	70.0	360 840	43.0	57.0	60.3	36.6	961	49.5
Bacon	58	-8.7	215	4.4	30.3	624 134	2 896	108 507	65.2	243 127	48.6	51.4	56.0	23.5	624	34.3
Baker	146	8.4	977	30.5	60.6	2 680 720	2 745	266 427	84.4	562 620	74.0	26.0	56.7	38.7	3 011	74.7
Baldwin	19	-37.7	151	0.0	4.5	368 589	2 448	60 427	1.2	9 936	42.4	57.6	26.6	0.8	10	7.3
Banks	60	27.8	115	0.1	14.3	631 780	5 494	70 378	179.5	345 890	1.0	99.0	56.1	40.1	247	16.8
Barrow	30	-12.0	98	0.1	6.5	538 576	5 493	46 885	39.9	131 306	1.4	98.6	29.9	10.9	123	10.5
Bartow	64	-1.9	140	2.2	25.6	618 074	4 430	68 517	95.4	208 210	15.5	84.5	35.2	17.0	1 141	21.2
Ben Hill	57	-23.3	274	6.9	26.5	695 507	2 536	93 340	27.0	129 029	86.7	13.3	32.5	13.4	762	58.9
Berrien	143	20.7	377	21.6	76.4	1 001 384	2 653	184 247	101.6	267 384	80.0	20.0	55.3	29.7	2 653	56.6
Bibb	15	2.2	130	0.3	6.2	425 690	3 267	48 389	11.4	100 770	11.3	88.7	28.3	10.6	86	17.7
Bleckley	66	-25.1	301	13.0	33.3	701 356	2 328	91 685	24.6	112 502	93.9	6.1	32.0	16.9	1 049	66.7
Brantley	23	-7.6	109	0.8	7.5	315 219	2 893	50 674	7.7	35 967	52.0	48.0	37.2	5.1	143	22.3
Brooks	148	-21.6	407	19.7	77.0	1 344 739	3 303	144 365	112.1	308 014	66.7	33.3	38.7	17.9	3 095	53.8
Bryan	15	-25.0	254	D	4.4	743 867	2 932	105 567	D	D	D	D	20.0	6.7	D	25.0
Bulloch	180	-8.5	331	7.8	108.9	802 399	2 421	124 037	105.3	193 612	84.7	15.3	40.1	20.0	3 610	68.4
Burke	161	-15.9	411	27.5	88.7	924 547	2 252	159 715	106.4	270 817	67.0	33.0	39.2	19.3	3 146	52.2
Butts	21	-16.9	151	0.0	4.9	526 171	3 484	47 029	2.4	17 143	51.2	48.9	35.0	3.6	21	14.3
Calhoun	108	-12.3	712	21.1	61.4	1 560 185	2 191	279 291	93.2	617 053	72.4	27.6	53.6	32.5	2 817	78.8
Camden	16	17.4	228	0.0	1.0	497 348	2 180	32 899	0.5	6 594	71.0	29.0	14.5	1.4	102	15.9
Candler	54	-27.6	225	3.0	23.4	536 151	2 383	64 819	22.4	94 277	60.6	39.4	34.0	14.3	832	49.2
Carroll	86	-10.7	95	D	19.4	419 188	4 435	51 799	192.1	211 382	4.7	95.3	29.9	13.0	513	9.9
Catoosa	21	0.3	77	0.3	7.3	434 822	5 669	62 424	43.4	161 260	10.1	89.9	31.6	14.5	77	9.7
Charlton	13	-34.5	159	0.1	1.5	324 679	2 040	56 214	8.8	105 214	6.2	93.8	23.8	4.4	25	10.7
Chatham	4	-10.8	110	0.0	1.5	565 600	5 162	52 943	4.1	118 029	93.1	6.9	31.4	11.4	4	11.4
Chattahoochee	4	-4.3	314	0.0	0.3	652 846	2 080	42 462	0.0	3 154	D	D	7.7	0.0	13	46.2
Chattooga	50	-5.6	172	0.2	13.0	528 260	3 079	54 678	23.8	81 565	7.7	92.3	34.2	6.5	152	23.3
Cherokee	25	7.5	59	0.1	5.0	555 347	9 486	39 460	44.0	102 426	14.6	85.4	27.7	9.8	16	3.0
Clarke	9	-15.0	99	0.1	2.1	557 689	5 648	38 556	41.1	457 111	D	D	34.4	6.7	68	25.6
Clay	40	-10.2	571	6.8	18.7	945 343	1 654	150 500	17.8	254 800	96.3	3.7	27.1	22.9	718	81.4
Clayton	1	-50.9	36	D	0.2	202 348	5 574	23 609	0.1	4 130	34.7	65.3	13.0	0.0	0	0.0
Clinch	27	41.0	333	2.9	5.4	903 375	2 710	152 763	23.5	293 513	91.7	8.3	67.5	41.3	68	25.0
Cobb	5	-39.5	47	0.0	1.4	572 027	12 235	30 482	3.4	31 227	88.6	11.4	20.0	3.6	20	14.5
Coffee	168	-9.2	286	22.8	87.0	753 704	2 633	133 838	200.2	341 043	44.3	55.7	47.2	29.8	3 049	56.0
Colquitt	189	-4.1	390	47.5	106.6	1 144 308	2 938	154 525	251.6	519 804	65.2	34.8	50.8	28.3	4 920	60.5
Columbia	13	-30.5	90	0.1	2.0	443 579	4 910	51 034	3.0	20 538	65.0	35.0	23.4	3.4	10	2.8
Cook	68	5.1	293	14.8	44.2	804 987	2 751	158 726	87.0	371 714	64.5	35.5	50.4	23.9	1 661	55.6
Coweta	55	-25.8	155	0.4	11.4	766 835	4 942	50 751	11.5	32 140	51.9	48.1	19.6	3.1	161	7.6
Crawford	34	-9.9	219	4.7	14.0	675 006	3 084	92 968	52.2	336 626	50.9	49.1	38.7	20.0	125	24.5
Crisp	117	40.8	481	22.3	81.9	1 004 480	2 090	216 049	77.1	315 783	90.0	10.0	42.2	27.0	2 312	62.7
Dade	32	-7.9	169	0.0	7.2	535 115	3 163	50 755	29.4	153 193	1.8	98.2	27.1	8.9	195	9.9
Dawson	13	-24.8	70	0.0	2.3	543 434	7 782	82 945	54.3	298 418	1.2	98.8	32.4	20.9	21	6.6
Decatur	199	10.6	556	54.7	123.6	1 545 198	2 780	229 341	209.4	584 919	90.7	9.3	40.2	29.1	4 158	72.9
DeKalb	3	205.2	118	0.0	0.3	335 920	2 857	32 920	0.6	25 800	84.5	15.5	44.0	12.0	22	20.0
Dodge	90	-29.3	225	7.9	27.7	494 833	2 202	61 095	35.6	88 838	52.9	47.1	26.2	6.7	1 142	61.3
Dooly	127	-18.5	437	28.0	86.6	1 025 624	2 345	215 472	80.9	279 052	86.4	13.6	41.0	24.1	3 688	77.9
Dougherty	65	-25.5	541	13.0	19.7	1 771 504	3 277	134 256	33.6	277 562	94.2	5.8	24.8	12.4	408	42.1
Douglas	8	17.3	71	D	2.2	469 940	6 591	30 325	1.2	9 974	69.8	30.2	17.1	2.6	55	9.4
Early	169	-4.6	507	32.7	93.8	1 089 147	2 148	143 674	86.5	258 934	91.2	8.8	43.1	26.3	4 347	72.8
Echols	13	-7.1	333	2.3	4.8	878 025	2 638	152 050	8.3	208 125	88.8	11.2	42.5	20.0	80	47.5

Table B. States and Counties — Water Use, Wholesale Trade, Retail Trade, and Real Estate

STATE County	Water use, 2010		Wholesale trade,[1] 2012				Retail trade,[2] 2012				Real estate and rental and leasing,[2] 2012			
	Total water withdrawn (mil gal/day)	Gallons withdrawn per person per day	Number of establishments	Number of employees	Sales (mil dol)	Annual payroll (mil dol)	Number of establishments	Number of employees	Sales (mil dol)	Annual payroll (mil dol)	Number of establishments	Number of employees	Receipts (mil dol)	Annual payroll (mil dol)
	133	134	135	136	137	138	139	140	141	142	143	144	145	146
FLORIDA—Cont'd														
Putnam	74.7	1 004	24	D	D	D	239	2 429	633.5	56.8	52	136	16.2	3.3
St. Johns	43.9	231	163	1 429	1 426.3	81.2	760	9 003	2 502.6	205.6	302	1 076	199.0	34.0
St. Lucie	1 201.3	4 325	185	1 473	686.0	61.8	690	12 368	3 709.5	361.3	260	752	134.5	22.9
Santa Rosa	26.2	173	57	419	323.2	16.0	357	4 644	1 259.9	108.4	150	336	53.3	9.0
Sarasota	31.3	82	447	3 613	1 868.1	160.1	1 696	21 356	5 751.7	548.8	814	2 753	666.0	116.9
Seminole	69.1	164	617	6 435	2 813.7	295.8	1 666	24 591	6 972.0	608.4	705	3 850	609.2	131.7
Sumter	32.0	342	45	D	D	D	217	2 840	908.8	62.1	79	176	25.6	5.7
Suwannee	138.2	3 325	31	D	D	D	128	1 347	343.1	32.5	28	106	10.8	2.4
Taylor	42.9	1 901	20	D	D	D	87	816	205.2	17.5	12	27	2.8	0.7
Union	2.7	172	5	D	D	D	29	158	44.8	3.8	4	8	1.0	0.2
Volusia	228.3	462	420	2 983	1 655.1	144.8	1 869	23 642	6 168.3	569.3	655	2 511	402.4	75.0
Wakulla	5.3	173	10	D	D	D	62	738	176.1	16.1	16	25	3.3	0.5
Walton	13.9	252	47	595	454.1	27.0	344	3 638	817.4	79.6	186	915	151.9	31.4
Washington	3.7	148	11	D	D	D	67	736	174.7	15.7	12	22	2.7	0.6
GEORGIA	4 718.8	487	10 637	150 168	143 645.3	8 476.3	33 426	433 840	119 801.5	10 290.1	10 484	55 551	14 232.4	2 703.7
Appling	60.9	3 341	23	137	86.1	4.7	76	699	211.3	15.4	10	31	2.9	0.6
Atkinson	2.6	313	5	94	46.5	2.6	29	141	43.8	3.1	1	D	D	D
Bacon	2.3	203	16	230	160.9	6.9	40	280	72.7	5.4	2	D	D	D
Baker	36.5	10 568	2	D	D	D	5	25	4.7	0.4	2	D	D	D
Baldwin	6.9	151	23	D	D	D	182	2 187	554.5	46.6	34	D	D	D
Banks	3.7	200	13	158	110.3	7.1	58	795	213.7	16.9	5	D	D	D
Barrow	6.5	94	61	732	1 189.7	34.5	181	2 350	671.6	56.5	36	90	10.1	1.8
Bartow	109.2	1 090	103	995	861.5	44.9	302	3 590	1 264.9	87.7	92	301	40.0	8.2
Ben Hill	6.0	339	10	D	D	D	78	724	200.3	14.6	10	31	3.2	0.6
Berrien	4.9	256	18	68	58.5	2.8	67	465	127.1	10.8	6	8	2.0	0.2
Bibb	41.9	270	192	2 433	1 522.4	117.0	815	10 199	2 597.5	232.7	194	906	170.4	30.8
Bleckley	8.3	634	5	33	22.8	1.9	45	340	88.4	7.1	5	D	D	D
Brantley	1.7	95	4	D	D	D	40	299	74.0	5.2	3	6	0.3	0.1
Brooks	8.7	536	8	D	D	D	46	309	83.9	6.9	3	D	D	D
Bryan	3.3	107	20	D	D	D	96	1 051	352.3	23.8	28	D	D	D
Bulloch	9.0	128	44	273	311.2	11.2	266	3 203	796.8	67.6	72	304	48.8	7.7
Burke	74.6	3 201	18	248	210.7	9.2	54	712	196.7	17.2	8	D	D	D
Butts	3.0	127	10	187	534.9	8.1	79	681	333.8	13.9	16	28	3.7	0.6
Calhoun	27.8	4 154	8	70	26.4	2.2	15	100	19.6	2.0	1	D	D	D
Camden	6.4	127	10	D	D	D	158	2 314	600.1	50.2	43	173	23.1	3.7
Candler	2.2	200	7	D	D	D	51	401	120.0	9.2	6	13	0.7	0.2
Carroll	15.0	136	79	601	436.0	24.4	364	4 474	1 310.4	104.7	80	304	46.7	7.9
Catoosa	6.9	109	41	470	244.2	19.8	174	2 500	687.4	56.9	39	139	23.6	4.3
Charlton	1.3	104	9	97	51.5	2.7	32	224	58.8	3.8	3	D	D	D
Chatham	278.2	1 049	317	3 925	5 812.9	197.6	1 204	15 767	4 256.4	375.3	388	1 837	383.3	60.4
Chattahoochee	0.9	78	1	D	D	D	18	126	22.7	1.9	NA	NA	NA	NA
Chattooga	10.8	416	10	D	D	D	74	657	158.0	13.5	6	19	2.8	0.5
Cherokee	24.4	114	220	1 639	711.9	83.8	544	8 254	2 271.6	196.1	207	527	95.8	18.0
Clarke	15.1	130	99	1 801	1 947.0	85.0	516	6 963	1 684.2	145.6	190	926	140.6	27.0
Clay	4.8	1 508	2	D	D	D	13	76	12.5	1.1	1	D	D	D
Clayton	7.7	30	240	6 102	4 341.7	257.4	733	10 921	3 229.6	270.5	199	900	210.0	34.9
Clinch	3.4	496	5	67	13.1	1.8	22	176	44.7	3.3	3	D	D	D
Cobb	55.0	80	1 090	16 264	18 591.4	968.9	2 222	35 733	10 368.7	905.9	1 045	5 639	1 390.1	303.0
Coffee	9.4	223	45	447	487.9	19.7	191	1 784	487.5	38.7	29	99	11.4	2.4
Colquitt	24.2	531	48	501	513.5	19.9	184	1 784	460.0	40.0	37	89	14.1	2.4
Columbia	19.1	154	64	882	382.2	44.6	298	5 383	1 580.6	140.9	95	409	71.7	12.3
Cook	8.6	501	16	139	40.3	5.2	60	486	136.6	9.7	8	27	4.6	0.6
Coweta	53.1	417	73	830	1 518.7	38.1	329	5 166	1 479.5	120.0	120	300	61.3	11.3
Crawford	3.5	276	1	D	D	D	24	115	23.1	2.3	NA	NA	NA	NA
Crisp	21.0	897	32	D	D	D	119	1 365	303.5	24.7	27	188	13.4	3.8
Dade	2.3	137	3	D	D	D	61	455	184.6	8.5	3	7	0.5	0.1
Dawson	2.5	110	18	87	23.5	3.3	191	2 520	523.9	47.5	18	60	28.4	1.9
Decatur	73.5	2 641	29	D	D	D	136	1 333	324.7	28.8	22	D	D	D
DeKalb	2.7	4	756	9 390	5 554.7	488.9	2 217	30 430	7 956.5	738.7	890	6 039	1 710.5	263.3
Dodge	13.5	620	12	41	24.9	1.0	72	713	152.3	12.6	15	57	6.7	1.4
Dooly	29.3	1 962	11	79	67.5	3.1	39	250	147.1	6.1	1	D	D	D
Dougherty	82.3	871	120	1 451	841.3	65.1	494	6 397	1 529.9	135.0	141	537	98.4	17.1
Douglas	23.0	174	97	1 387	1 224.2	64.3	427	7 174	1 955.8	171.8	114	560	107.1	17.3
Early	146.4	13 299	12	58	85.6	2.5	51	388	86.1	6.8	5	21	2.9	0.8
Echols	1.5	374	1	D	D	D	3	D	D	D	1	D	D	D

1. Merchant wholesalers, except manufacturers' sales branches and offices. 2. Employer establishments.

Table B. States and Counties — Professional Services, Manufacturing, and Accommodation and Food Services

STATE County	Professional, scientific, and technical services, 2012				Manufacturing, 2012				Accommodation and food services, 2012			
	Number of establishments	Number of employees	Receipts (mil dol)	Annual payroll (mil dol)	Number of establishments	Number of employees	Receipts (mil dol)	Annual payroll (mil dol)	Number of establishments	Number of employees	Sales (mil dol)	Annual payroll (mil dol)
	147	148	149	150	151	152	153	154	155	156	157	158
FLORIDA—Cont'd												
Putnam	101	286	25.2	8.2	35	1 678	865.8	89.8	94	1 218	56.9	15.1
St. Johns	759	D	D	D	91	1 449	409.8	59.3	455	8 680	517.9	149.3
St. Lucie	514	2 173	281.6	97.3	134	2 015	605.7	85.4	390	6 652	329.3	91.3
Santa Rosa	289	1 851	295.2	126.7	55	407	124.1	19.7	189	3 219	145.7	41.4
Sarasota	1 775	8 573	1 216.7	439.1	308	5 559	1 200.1	267.0	853	16 450	896.2	263.7
Seminole	1 884	10 221	1 479.7	542.0	358	5 741	1 567.5	244.9	776	14 747	761.1	216.2
Sumter	128	500	53.9	21.0	36	942	461.9	40.7	106	2 464	117.2	35.9
Suwannee	49	204	18.8	5.3	19	D	D	46.9	53	679	34.1	8.2
Taylor	29	109	8.1	3.1	18	1 458	691.7	84.2	38	427	19.9	5.3
Union	8	D	D	D	4	D	D	D	9	82	3.6	0.9
Volusia	1 304	6 854	812.3	281.4	335	7 633	D	340.7	1 001	18 628	895.8	260.7
Wakulla	38	D	D	D	9	D	D	D	41	429	19.7	5.2
Walton	198	452	57.3	16.6	27	113	D	4.5	204	5 140	373.8	110.8
Washington	32	214	27.1	10.2	6	D	D	12.5	38	434	21.9	5.1
GEORGIA	28 112	D	D	D	7 456	333 837	155 836.8	15 316.6	18 815	353 638	18 976.6	5 173.4
Appling	20	55	5.7	1.7	25	529	407.3	23.1	29	410	18.8	5.0
Atkinson	2	D	D	D	10	468	144.8	15.3	7	52	2.4	0.5
Bacon	12	46	3.8	1.4	12	496	D	16.2	16	181	9.0	2.2
Baker	2	D	D	D	NA	NA	NA	NA	NA	NA	NA	NA
Baldwin	51	D	D	D	20	D	D	D	92	D	D	D
Banks	12	D	D	D	9	208	D	8.3	43	912	47.5	13.0
Barrow	101	3 525	137.7	87.7	69	1 940	889.2	76.1	81	D	D	D
Bartow	141	486	78.1	20.2	106	7 133	4 341.9	348.0	163	2 977	140.6	40.7
Ben Hill	12	66	5.1	1.4	28	1 408	512.4	51.6	35	361	17.7	3.9
Berrien	13	15	1.3	0.5	14	1 583	453.4	63.1	21	270	10.2	3.0
Bibb	382	2 581	340.7	118.9	119	4 441	1 573.5	213.4	403	7 905	352.5	98.9
Bleckley	11	52	2.7	1.7	8	303	D	12.3	14	202	10.2	2.5
Brantley	7	19	2.5	0.8	10	110	D	4.0	10	138	4.2	1.2
Brooks	12	53	5.8	2.1	10	187	D	7.4	16	D	D	D
Bryan	66	230	30.2	12.1	13	291	D	14.8	74	968	36.7	9.4
Bulloch	116	497	57.1	19.0	39	1 442	416.8	52.4	136	2 757	114.0	30.9
Burke	16	D	D	D	14	677	197.0	25.9	26	D	D	D
Butts	22	78	6.1	2.1	11	589	259.6	19.7	34	536	24.2	7.0
Calhoun	2	D	D	D	NA	NA	NA	NA	5	18	0.8	0.3
Camden	66	D	D	D	7	111	D	6.3	107	1 950	80.5	23.4
Candler	20	63	7.4	2.2	10	156	D	6.5	24	D	D	D
Carroll	147	716	74.8	23.5	112	7 174	6 237.8	299.1	198	3 261	157.7	42.4
Catoosa	64	300	26.4	10.4	43	1 537	D	71.1	89	1 733	87.5	23.4
Charlton	9	44	1.8	0.8	5	237	D	6.9	15	178	7.3	1.9
Chatham	708	5 871	640.2	253.4	175	13 829	D	1 015.1	897	18 046	1 024.7	277.3
Chattahoochee	28	232	26.4	11.4	NA	NA	NA	NA	9	42	2.0	0.5
Chattooga	13	58	7.1	2.2	14	2 156	403.9	56.9	31	318	17.4	3.8
Cherokee	740	2 735	421.6	133.0	144	3 813	1 027.8	145.6	323	6 256	281.7	81.2
Clarke	303	1 697	190.6	68.5	78	5 115	2 004.8	229.5	342	6 927	307.6	83.9
Clay	1	D	D	D	NA	NA	NA	NA	2	D	D	D
Clayton	221	982	119.9	39.9	100	3 676	1 873.4	165.7	388	8 178	450.9	129.9
Clinch	11	D	D	D	9	D	D	D	11	D	D	D
Cobb	3 387	33 011	5 509.8	2 097.4	460	19 738	8 587.2	1 180.3	1 451	27 543	1 516.1	418.6
Coffee	60	219	22.1	8.2	35	2 338	670.4	79.8	61	1 178	54.7	14.4
Colquitt	57	173	17.8	4.9	42	2 811	760.1	78.7	59	D	D	D
Columbia	208	1 348	626.9	70.9	55	2 978	2 023.7	168.7	182	3 389	153.2	41.0
Cook	15	44	3.7	1.9	25	517	201.8	17.9	29	D	D	D
Coweta	195	894	89.1	35.1	86	4 315	1 908.9	192.7	166	3 647	168.5	48.2
Crawford	3	D	D	D	7	D	D	D	4	33	1.4	0.3
Crisp	24	76	4.8	2.1	22	1 024	426.9	45.7	44	D	D	D
Dade	7	D	D	D	13	538	D	22.0	22	D	D	D
Dawson	54	135	19.6	5.4	21	1 161	263.5	37.0	40	697	39.9	10.9
Decatur	38	147	15.4	5.5	32	1 260	D	54.0	41	D	D	D
DeKalb	2 872	17 884	3 291.8	1 107.2	412	10 958	3 630.8	511.5	1 413	23 641	1 358.1	362.0
Dodge	21	90	6.7	2.3	18	639	193.9	27.3	25	360	15.3	4.4
Dooly	10	17	2.6	0.8	9	877	176.9	25.4	17	123	5.7	1.5
Dougherty	220	D	D	D	65	3 262	3 184.1	185.6	217	4 149	185.3	48.8
Douglas	226	1 000	102.4	37.2	88	2 512	690.3	101.7	202	4 276	210.1	56.6
Early	15	77	6.0	1.9	9	776	D	57.4	21	156	7.6	2.0
Echols	NA	NA	NA	NA	NA	NA	NA	NA	1	D	D	D

1. Establishment subject to federal tax.

Table B. States and Counties — Health Care and Social Assistance, Other Services, Nonemployer Businesses, and Residential Construction

STATE County	Health care and social assistance, 2012				Other services, 2012				Nonemployer businesses, 2015		Value of residential construction authorized by building permits, 2016	
	Number of establish-ments	Number of employees	Receipts (mil dol)	Annual payroll (mil dol)	Number of establish-ments	Number of employees	Receipts (mil dol)	Annual payroll (mil dol)	Number	Receipts (mil dol)	New Construction ($1,000)	Number of housing units
	159	160	161	162	163	164	165	166	167	168	169	170
FLORIDA—Cont'd												
Putnam	170	2 503	234.6	77.7	86	401	28.2	8.4	3 986	129.0	10 910	80
St. Johns	518	7 502	740.5	278.5	322	2 269	1 094.9	119.1	19 947	963.6	996 965	3 732
St. Lucie	655	10 230	1 342.1	441.1	362	1 779	148.2	42.0	24 217	911.1	276 367	1 510
Santa Rosa	261	3 479	429.1	143.2	155	732	46.8	15.0	11 232	489.5	212 627	1 417
Sarasota	1 516	25 814	2 976.0	1 087.1	914	4 738	451.7	117.4	41 455	2 162.4	997 207	3 936
Seminole	1 305	16 947	1 937.9	704.4	780	4 186	378.4	110.8	41 797	1 706.0	491 468	3 039
Sumter	146	2 956	381.2	123.8	64	304	22.2	6.7	6 006	251.6	308 368	1 072
Suwannee	65	1 342	104.8	38.7	37	186	20.1	5.5	2 413	91.4	10 582	71
Taylor	41	838	70.7	29.0	25	131	8.9	2.3	907	32.3	5 520	49
Union	15	D	D	D	5	D	D	D	561	21.9	294	27
Volusia	1 346	25 561	2 776.3	1 051.0	1 014	4 984	543.9	175.7	40 090	1 648.5	505 735	1 900
Wakulla	26	164	13.1	4.1	33	114	9.9	2.1	2 007	71.4	26 596	169
Walton	113	2 560	266.9	100.3	87	462	52.0	12.3	7 519	475.8	621 716	1 692
Washington	47	796	65.8	25.3	24	172	7.4	2.7	1 475	48.9	6 506	45
GEORGIA	22 734	448 460	51 800.6	19 515.2	13 828	89 302	10 617.1	2 703.1	870 897	34 826.0	9 380 677	51 675
Appling	36	D	D	D	28	99	8.6	2.2	1 121	43.4	333	3
Atkinson	3	D	D	D	2	D	D	D	534	22.0	0	0
Bacon	18	D	D	D	16	D	D	D	622	25.0	0	0
Baker	3	D	D	D	2	D	D	D	213	6.9	0	0
Baldwin	111	D	D	D	50	283	19.2	6.0	3 007	92.0	10 993	59
Banks	13	113	12.5	3.7	13	D	D	D	1 263	48.8	4 061	29
Barrow	91	1 292	117.4	44.6	79	322	34.7	9.0	5 775	240.5	55 112	388
Bartow	177	2 803	324.2	123.9	120	805	108.5	25.0	8 013	345.6	84 787	514
Ben Hill	31	698	49.9	18.9	22	D	D	D	1 071	34.7	741	7
Berrien	32	316	19.3	8.2	10	22	2.8	0.5	1 087	43.1	3 392	20
Bibb	540	14 875	1 757.6	642.6	256	1 605	183.0	51.2	12 700	417.0	14 938	89
Bleckley	20	291	19.7	8.0	10	33	3.8	0.9	844	25.3	1 480	12
Brantley	15	121	7.8	3.3	15	24	2.8	0.5	1 034	34.6	430	2
Brooks	17	D	D	D	18	D	D	D	901	34.9	4 215	23
Bryan	52	D	D	D	43	D	D	D	2 479	108.8	97 769	433
Bulloch	183	2 747	318.0	109.8	96	446	39.7	9.9	4 581	188.4	47 988	345
Burke	30	D	D	D	18	D	D	D	1 430	50.4	8 950	50
Butts	29	529	39.8	14.2	27	D	D	D	1 540	55.4	7 628	50
Calhoun	8	252	17.0	6.8	2	D	D	D	314	10.4	470	3
Camden	103	672	63.9	24.5	59	219	19.7	5.1	2 494	80.9	54 764	215
Candler	15	545	35.7	14.5	7	34	2.2	0.6	813	33.6	0	0
Carroll	214	4 784	634.3	238.3	122	D	D	D	8 285	307.0	61 380	290
Catoosa	100	D	D	D	40	272	18.5	5.2	4 088	178.8	28 518	172
Charlton	11	260	17.6	7.2	5	13	1.5	0.4	486	14.7	2 149	20
Chatham	721	18 354	2 327.4	860.8	414	D	D	D	20 662	924.3	207 778	958
Chattahoochee	5	20	2.6	1.0	5	D	D	D	238	4.8	367	2
Chattooga	28	382	27.7	10.9	17	65	11.5	2.0	1 479	70.4	200	2
Cherokee	447	5 141	471.4	208.8	324	1 402	118.2	35.1	22 671	1 025.7	664 756	2 494
Clarke	439	8 443	1 124.3	446.3	192	1 261	184.9	38.6	8 420	298.6	22 649	119
Clay	5	D	D	D	2	D	D	D	179	3.7	960	6
Clayton	400	7 024	810.1	306.3	270	1 349	144.9	36.5	27 839	642.2	126 783	560
Clinch	12	159	13.9	4.7	6	11	1.0	0.2	413	14.8	1 002	5
Cobb	1 803	28 679	3 519.7	1 393.8	1 237	9 389	847.7	295.9	76 224	3 351.9	726 623	4 017
Coffee	103	1 877	210.2	72.2	49	218	17.0	5.3	2 987	114.8	9 671	64
Colquitt	92	2 148	192.2	73.9	48	193	17.9	4.3	2 888	113.4	10 084	60
Columbia	215	3 078	254.4	102.3	134	794	69.6	22.5	9 502	414.7	231 016	1 280
Cook	31	D	D	D	12	50	3.7	1.1	1 050	43.7	3 666	27
Coweta	228	3 415	373.4	152.0	144	653	57.4	16.3	11 108	382.0	303 250	972
Crawford	7	D	D	D	7	51	5.0	1.9	826	24.7	3 874	17
Crisp	73	1 235	130.4	39.5	30	148	20.9	4.5	1 664	51.7	2 666	20
Dade	18	D	D	D	18	87	6.9	2.1	1 030	39.3	85	1
Dawson	41	D	D	D	35	161	11.0	2.9	2 127	109.3	70 070	492
Decatur	56	D	D	D	42	157	12.4	3.2	1 837	63.9	1 945	13
DeKalb	1 782	39 802	4 808.8	1 748.3	1 075	6 406	806.5	217.5	76 127	2 557.4	455 385	2 319
Dodge	51	893	65.8	27.5	17	124	6.0	1.7	1 487	44.6	2 119	11
Dooly	11	123	6.3	3.1	11	D	D	D	710	31.5	0	0
Dougherty	306	8 924	875.1	336.1	152	994	90.1	24.5	7 229	207.2	9 737	86
Douglas	266	4 639	498.1	185.7	183	796	87.3	22.3	12 251	380.5	84 871	382
Early	16	346	32.1	11.7	14	35	2.7	0.8	678	23.2	1 639	10
Echols	4	D	D	D	1	D	D	D	175	6.3	435	3

Table B. States and Counties — Government Employment and Payroll, and Local Government Finances

STATE County	Government employment and payroll, 2012									Local government finances, 2012				
			March payroll (percent of total)							General revenue				
												Taxes		
													Per capita[1] (dollars)	
	Full-time equivalent employees	March payroll (dollars)	Adminis-tration, judicial, and legal	Police and Corrections	Fire Protection	Highways and transpor-tation	Health and Welfare	Natural resources and utilities	Education and libraries	Total (mil dol)	Inter-govern-mental (mil dol)	Total (mil dol)	Total	Property
	171	172	173	174	175	176	177	178	179	180	181	182	183	184
FLORIDA—Cont'd														
Putnam	3 846	14 358 652	7.4	13.9	0.8	1.5	2.5	26.1	46.6	395.8	157.9	190.3	2 597	2 417
St. Johns	6 382	21 674 061	7.3	12.2	6.8	2.0	1.9	5.0	59.5	671.6	162.3	311.6	1 541	1 380
St. Lucie	10 618	40 360 120	6.2	13.8	7.0	2.1	1.9	6.5	59.0	1 062.2	343.2	409.9	1 444	1 184
Santa Rosa	4 424	14 124 230	11.2	10.2	1.2	2.6	1.4	3.0	69.2	350.7	153.5	129.3	816	709
Sarasota	15 008	61 458 391	6.0	10.2	6.3	3.8	31.5	5.2	34.0	2 009.8	280.1	709.8	1 838	1 447
Seminole	13 257	48 666 111	6.8	14.5	7.5	2.5	1.1	6.0	60.1	1 274.8	440.7	579.9	1 346	977
Sumter	1 509	4 669 736	4.3	3.1	1.1	6.4	1.4	4.3	72.3	251.5	43.7	105.9	1 042	834
Suwannee	1 250	3 665 519	1.8	2.1	4.9	6.0	1.5	1.5	76.2	111.4	59.1	33.8	773	579
Taylor	786	2 148 026	10.9	14.9	3.3	3.6	2.4	3.5	59.2	67.3	33.3	26.1	1 148	904
Union	487	1 232 008	5.4	0.2	0.0	3.3	7.6	4.3	78.2	32.6	21.2	6.6	433	280
Volusia	20 784	73 359 257	5.4	11.5	4.2	2.1	24.3	6.2	44.1	2 117.9	503.9	753.8	1 517	1 158
Wakulla	827	2 245 238	3.1	0.4	1.1	0.0	4.2	3.1	87.4	79.8	43.2	24.2	784	664
Walton	2 328	7 662 784	10.7	15.8	12.5	4.9	2.3	2.2	47.4	217.6	48.3	141.1	2 450	1 824
Washington	925	2 765 292	6.8	13.6	0.1	3.5	2.8	2.9	69.5	77.2	44.1	22.4	901	681
GEORGIA	X	X	X	X	X	X	X	X	X	X	X	X	X	X
Appling	1 166	3 357 745	5.4	4.9	0.2	3.4	40.2	2.3	42.9	101.3	23.2	31.5	1 717	1 055
Atkinson	477	2 010 541	3.8	3.1	0.0	1.5	3.3	1.4	85.2	27.4	15.3	7.7	927	571
Bacon	457	1 275 084	6.8	7.3	3.9	3.1	3.3	3.9	70.6	31.3	15.9	11.6	1 032	637
Baker	109	265 135	10.3	11.8	0.0	4.2	6.9	0.3	66.0	7.6	2.8	4.1	1 214	935
Baldwin	2 074	6 857 034	4.5	7.7	2.8	1.2	39.8	4.6	38.7	195.7	44.2	53.0	1 143	638
Banks	669	1 937 141	7.1	10.1	4.9	1.5	0.8	3.5	69.3	49.3	16.9	23.2	1 267	661
Barrow	2 271	8 023 913	5.3	11.2	6.0	1.9	0.4	3.2	70.8	183.6	75.3	79.2	1 129	694
Bartow	3 986	13 981 683	6.0	7.9	4.2	1.8	11.2	5.6	61.8	329.5	108.9	176.5	1 753	972
Ben Hill	1 147	3 286 219	4.4	6.3	2.0	2.8	28.8	5.8	44.8	73.5	21.8	20.5	1 168	664
Berrien	719	2 060 957	6.9	9.8	0.2	4.4	3.1	4.2	71.1	50.3	26.7	17.3	911	561
Bibb	6 298	22 932 839	6.6	10.3	5.2	2.3	5.6	6.2	62.4	582.3	249.1	239.3	1 530	1 004
Bleckley	611	1 809 213	5.2	7.5	1.5	2.9	15.6	2.6	64.0	43.0	19.1	12.4	960	647
Brantley	674	1 858 203	5.0	7.6	1.1	3.5	4.4	0.6	76.4	47.4	24.7	17.9	963	714
Brooks	547	1 728 938	6.4	10.4	2.7	2.7	0.2	3.5	70.4	39.5	17.4	16.6	1 079	809
Bryan	1 408	4 117 520	6.2	9.0	3.9	3.1	0.9	1.8	72.5	105.5	39.0	54.1	1 679	990
Bulloch	2 932	8 670 844	4.4	9.3	1.3	2.3	13.2	5.4	62.9	203.4	80.5	82.0	1 128	580
Burke	1 329	4 107 904	4.5	7.8	10.8	4.1	1.0	2.7	66.7	98.4	35.0	53.8	2 324	1 816
Butts	841	2 814 107	8.3	12.6	6.9	3.6	1.8	7.2	58.7	67.2	18.6	39.3	1 671	1 021
Calhoun	366	979 335	10.2	7.4	0.7	2.9	40.9	1.9	35.5	30.9	10.8	7.0	1 076	732
Camden	2 030	7 548 391	6.8	8.0	6.1	2.8	1.4	3.1	70.2	151.8	54.9	73.4	1 428	963
Candler	567	1 831 024	5.7	4.7	0.3	2.6	32.8	2.7	50.3	45.3	16.5	11.4	1 029	561
Carroll	4 120	14 298 798	4.5	9.2	3.6	1.3	0.9	5.5	74.6	321.7	126.8	135.2	1 212	693
Catoosa	521	1 425 530	21.0	30.9	13.0	7.3	4.0	13.5	1.6	366.0	65.6	70.0	1 077	575
Charlton	616	1 655 066	4.2	6.4	0.0	3.2	24.8	3.3	57.2	42.4	11.9	18.8	1 412	1 079
Chatham	10 068	34 099 398	11.9	16.1	3.9	3.9	4.3	8.5	48.0	1 650.2	303.7	617.1	2 233	1 331
Chattahoochee	245	688 357	6.1	3.3	0.0	3.3	1.1	3.7	81.0	12.5	8.2	2.8	217	112
Chattooga	892	2 643 680	6.6	8.6	0.4	3.0	1.5	9.6	68.8	64.8	29.2	23.2	901	517
Cherokee	7 029	24 643 064	5.0	7.9	5.8	1.4	0.4	4.0	73.8	584.3	192.5	290.4	1 312	942
Clarke	4 598	14 811 444	7.4	13.2	5.1	3.9	6.5	8.9	52.4	786.3	118.3	156.8	1 304	951
Clay	153	338 738	12.0	11.6	0.0	5.9	10.5	4.9	53.7	11.6	5.8	4.5	1 443	1 081
Clayton	10 173	35 407 764	8.8	11.0	2.0	2.2	3.2	6.1	63.2	920.8	359.2	426.5	1 604	962
Clinch	408	1 264 709	7.4	6.1	2.4	2.4	26.1	1.7	53.7	37.6	11.7	10.4	1 552	1 170
Cobb	21 811	86 644 451	7.5	8.4	4.5	1.1	2.0	6.1	69.0	2 213.0	659.3	1 157.2	1 636	1 103
Coffee	1 488	4 411 069	6.7	9.4	3.0	2.6	0.9	5.5	70.9	107.8	47.8	44.0	1 020	537
Colquitt	2 449	7 687 804	4.2	6.3	1.7	2.0	30.8	3.3	49.7	222.7	74.9	47.4	1 028	553
Columbia	3 933	13 876 194	6.0	9.6	0.3	1.7	1.1	3.8	75.8	345.5	122.6	173.7	1 319	749
Cook	873	2 387 884	12.7	9.3	2.3	3.3	2.5	4.1	61.5	46.6	20.7	17.3	1 025	578
Coweta	4 492	16 492 046	4.9	10.2	4.8	1.9	0.7	3.7	71.5	348.5	120.9	183.0	1 397	887
Crawford	409	1 190 596	12.1	7.9	0.3	4.3	0.0	2.2	71.6	30.1	16.0	10.8	855	645
Crisp	1 725	5 432 319	3.5	6.3	2.7	2.0	36.6	9.1	38.4	77.9	34.1	32.8	1 391	767
Dade	530	1 479 400	6.8	9.6	0.2	3.2	0.6	3.0	72.4	34.2	13.9	16.9	1 027	529
Dawson	883	2 870 993	9.9	10.6	5.7	1.7	1.3	5.5	64.0	77.9	18.2	53.2	2 374	1 408
Decatur	1 769	5 577 746	4.6	10.6	0.9	2.4	30.0	3.0	47.3	136.5	40.7	37.7	1 372	723
DeKalb	26 888	103 868 526	7.1	8.8	3.1	0.8	23.2	3.6	52.3	2 945.3	639.0	1 074.5	1 520	1 096
Dodge	906	3 199 644	3.3	4.7	0.8	1.5	30.4	2.0	56.5	119.4	31.6	18.8	881	486
Dooly	464	1 464 602	8.7	18.6	0.6	3.5	5.3	4.9	57.6	43.0	17.6	16.5	1 150	731
Dougherty	4 532	14 341 822	8.6	11.0	5.2	3.2	6.8	9.3	52.1	390.9	181.4	135.1	1 429	878
Douglas	4 786	16 883 097	6.3	9.7	3.9	1.7	1.1	5.1	70.7	416.9	160.6	203.6	1 520	907
Early	569	1 743 416	4.9	3.4	2.7	3.8	5.9	5.5	72.8	41.8	16.7	18.3	1 726	1 066
Echols	193	553 759	4.6	9.7	0.0	4.1	4.2	1.7	75.0	10.7	5.7	4.4	1 110	953

1. Based on the resident population estimated as of July 1 of the year shown.

STATE County	Total (mil dol) 185	Per capita¹ (dollars) 186	Education 187	Health and hospitals 188	Police protection 189	Public welfare 190	Highways 191	Total (mil dol) 192	Per capita¹ (dollars) 193	Federal civilian 194	Federal military 195	State and local 196	Number of returns 197	Mean adjusted gross income 198	Mean income tax 199
FLORIDA—Cont'd															
Putnam	399.5	5 452	34.5	1.8	5.6	0.6	3.0	210.9	2 879	112	130	3 759	28 170	36 917	3 112
St. Johns	735.8	3 639	40.2	2.2	9.5	1.0	5.3	1 504.0	7 439	613	415	8 764	103 850	95 324	16 566
St. Lucie	1 134.8	3 998	41.4	1.0	7.9	0.9	6.3	2 450.5	8 632	735	616	12 128	133 920	46 879	5 206
Santa Rosa	415.0	2 618	54.4	1.5	8.3	0.0	4.4	1 574.0	9 930	769	1 461	5 730	71 780	58 446	7 107
Sarasota	2 019.2	5 229	26.3	30.5	5.5	0.1	4.4	1 927.4	4 991	999	789	13 372	200 310	78 782	13 205
Seminole	1 294.2	3 004	46.2	1.0	8.8	0.8	9.2	890.7	2 067	892	819	15 761	214 700	60 569	8 324
Sumter	263.4	2 592	27.3	1.6	6.0	0.5	7.8	594.1	5 846	1 611	203	2 962	52 270	72 195	10 493
Suwannee	116.7	2 674	46.6	3.1	7.6	0.8	7.6	34.0	778	95	74	2 377	15 990	39 219	3 664
Taylor	68.5	3 013	44.4	2.4	9.4	0.2	11.3	16.9	741	31	35	1 555	8 070	42 716	4 165
Union	34.6	2 273	56.6	4.9	7.0	1.2	3.9	2.9	192	16	19	2 148	4 500	42 175	3 751
Volusia	2 177.8	4 382	29.7	25.3	7.3	0.4	3.5	2 589.6	5 211	1 198	995	18 125	239 680	47 912	5 744
Wakulla	81.9	2 657	52.0	3.7	9.6	0.2	3.4	16.7	542	87	52	1 708	12 800	47 084	4 367
Walton	219.9	3 819	35.9	5.8	9.3	0.1	9.2	133.4	2 316	143	142	2 985	28 440	70 559	13 584
Washington	78.4	3 150	61.0	1.7	5.4	0.1	8.3	30.5	1 226	37	40	1 965	9 010	38 852	3 191
GEORGIA	X	X	X	X	X	X	X	X	X	99 029	94 611	572 337	4 377 430	57 932	7 401
Appling	103.6	5 642	37.2	40.4	3.0	1.1	5.8	23.1	1 257	45	51	1 350	7 060	40 926	3 488
Atkinson	26.9	3 242	60.6	0.2	3.6	0.4	3.5	11.0	1 324	18	23	414	3 090	29 451	2 163
Bacon	33.2	2 969	55.2	3.2	4.9	1.2	7.9	46.1	4 115	22	31	587	4 180	38 052	3 210
Baker	7.5	2 220	56.9	5.0	7.4	0.6	8.6	0.8	252	D	D	113	1 180	38 114	3 764
Baldwin	184.3	3 974	29.8	43.5	4.6	0.1	2.8	85.5	1 843	66	131	5 155	16 870	42 533	3 937
Banks	40.1	2 192	68.6	0.3	5.3	0.4	2.2	21.8	1 192	15	52	856	6 970	41 208	3 325
Barrow	186.4	2 657	60.5	0.7	6.9	0.3	2.8	222.6	3 172	166	210	2 788	31 810	46 841	4 548
Bartow	347.5	3 452	58.9	1.4	8.8	0.2	4.1	306.7	3 047	195	285	4 725	42 880	47 621	4 820
Ben Hill	81.8	4 663	37.3	32.7	4.5	0.4	3.3	18.0	1 027	25	48	1 045	6 650	37 450	2 734
Berrien	45.9	2 409	60.4	2.4	5.6	0.4	7.6	17.9	939	32	53	950	6 710	36 418	3 158
Bibb	601.4	3 844	44.1	7.1	6.5	0.3	1.9	510.5	3 262	1 049	413	8 934	65 940	48 454	5 694
Bleckley	45.7	3 536	52.6	19.3	4.9	1.0	4.6	14.9	1 152	28	33	1 243	4 710	44 186	3 944
Brantley	50.2	2 701	61.4	2.5	3.2	0.6	11.1	13.3	715	27	76	819	6 390	36 826	2 631
Brooks	42.2	2 737	55.7	1.6	6.5	0.4	4.6	12.1	786	24	43	662	6 230	37 288	3 834
Bryan	99.9	3 100	63.6	2.1	7.7	0.9	3.7	45.2	1 404	215	98	1 675	15 910	60 029	6 444
Bulloch	216.1	2 973	48.2	11.2	5.7	0.0	4.0	302.9	4 167	134	202	7 773	25 860	44 993	4 772
Burke	98.6	4 264	55.4	3.2	4.7	0.4	6.1	14.9	643	38	63	1 447	9 250	40 423	3 663
Butts	62.8	2 668	49.4	2.9	7.3	0.3	5.2	43.9	1 866	48	59	1 558	9 210	44 975	4 131
Calhoun	30.5	4 684	35.5	34.1	3.8	0.3	3.0	4.2	644	20	13	520	1 980	33 424	2 490
Camden	144.7	2 816	55.4	4.1	7.1	0.2	4.1	84.7	1 648	2 229	4 277	2 283	21 570	46 275	3 977
Candler	48.2	4 334	45.1	28.6	3.5	0.0	4.0	21.3	1 913	20	30	704	4 070	36 767	2 978
Carroll	329.8	2 956	58.0	0.6	6.4	0.2	2.6	335.3	3 005	205	311	7 574	47 460	48 523	5 091
Catoosa	277.3	4 263	51.2	31.2	2.8	0.4	2.1	143.9	2 212	75	184	2 519	26 370	47 827	4 423
Charlton	40.5	3 046	38.8	25.3	5.1	0.3	7.6	12.6	947	42	28	455	3 500	39 009	2 946
Chatham	1 559.0	5 640	26.6	30.7	10.1	0.3	2.2	741.4	2 682	2 606	5 886	15 987	127 110	55 134	6 832
Chattahoochee	16.1	1 234	73.5	1.4	3.7	4.7	3.0	4.9	376	101	17 559	265	3 260	34 433	1 939
Chattooga	68.3	2 655	56.6	0.3	5.8	0.3	4.1	31.8	1 237	34	66	1 301	9 310	37 365	2 711
Cherokee	581.9	2 629	63.6	3.8	4.8	0.4	2.5	701.9	3 172	297	658	7 695	105 320	66 988	8 227
Clarke	854.7	7 107	20.1	50.3	3.2	0.1	1.3	564.4	4 693	969	392	23 055	46 040	47 037	5 308
Clay	11.5	3 685	36.6	23.2	6.0	0.7	6.5	1.6	517	41	D	162	1 180	26 649	1 983
Clayton	908.8	3 418	54.3	3.7	8.1	0.7	2.7	457.9	1 722	1 393	804	14 282	123 450	31 661	2 124
Clinch	33.2	4 943	44.6	27.7	3.7	0.3	5.5	16.1	2 403	14	19	510	2 540	35 811	3 061
Cobb	2 261.5	3 197	56.3	1.0	7.2	0.7	7.3	3 722.8	5 262	2 462	2 379	32 275	345 240	73 314	10 546
Coffee	114.8	2 659	57.4	0.3	6.5	0.2	5.8	18.7	434	107	112	2 592	15 810	37 370	3 847
Colquitt	216.3	4 688	39.4	34.4	3.5	0.1	4.0	54.2	1 175	112	126	3 441	17 360	36 560	3 176
Columbia	330.5	2 511	64.3	0.9	6.4	0.3	6.0	242.1	1 840	285	402	5 089	60 650	68 275	8 122
Cook	49.1	2 900	54.5	1.3	8.1	0.5	6.5	18.8	1 112	27	48	1 222	6 470	36 521	3 265
Coweta	343.0	2 620	61.2	1.1	6.1	0.1	4.2	213.3	1 629	224	386	5 021	61 190	60 189	6 748
Crawford	30.2	2 394	59.2	1.1	4.7	0.3	5.5	12.0	952	D	34	428	4 930	40 025	3 047
Crisp	83.6	3 542	57.8	1.1	7.1	0.3	5.0	31.7	1 343	54	63	1 337	8 430	38 450	3 333
Dade	36.5	2 215	63.4	1.1	8.9	0.2	6.0	9.7	586	22	43	572	6 050	43 708	3 899
Dawson	84.8	3 783	48.5	2.7	4.7	0.9	3.3	124.1	5 535	39	65	1 082	9 960	55 096	6 502
Decatur	143.5	5 218	34.0	27.4	5.0	0.1	3.7	45.5	1 655	47	73	2 538	11 100	40 353	3 565
DeKalb	2 937.7	4 155	37.1	33.5	4.6	0.5	1.6	2 476.3	3 502	10 602	2 137	31 816	345 390	59 964	8 163
Dodge	77.8	3 646	46.0	31.2	3.4	1.0	3.8	21.4	1 005	40	53	1 953	7 260	35 210	2 878
Dooly	37.4	2 615	43.0	10.8	9.8	0.5	6.6	10.1	704	54	34	750	3 920	37 294	3 240
Dougherty	400.6	4 239	40.5	13.1	5.7	0.1	2.1	219.4	2 322	2 617	572	6 990	38 070	39 308	3 843
Douglas	492.1	3 674	53.7	0.9	4.5	0.4	2.1	632.2	4 719	167	392	5 420	61 190	46 451	4 379
Early	43.1	4 068	53.5	7.9	10.2	0.0	3.3	13.2	1 250	32	29	1 363	4 140	38 304	3 165
Echols	10.8	2 706	74.2	0.3	4.4	0.4	3.7	19.9	4 981	D	11	209	1 380	29 722	2 690

1. Based on the resident population estimated as of July 1 of the year shown.

Table B. States and Counties — Land Area and Population

STATE/ County code	CBSA code[1]	County type[2]	STATE County	Land area,[3] (sq mi) 2016	Total persons 2016	Rank	Per square mile	White	Black	American Indian, Alaska Native	Asian and Pacific Islander	Percent Hispanic or Latino[4]	Under 5 years	5 to 17 years	18 to 24 years	25 to 34 years	35 to 44 years	45 to 54 years
				1	2	3	4	5	6	7	8	9	10	11	12	13	14	15
			GEORGIA—Cont'd															
13 103	42340	2	Effingham	477.7	58 712	880	122.9	80.6	14.5	0.9	1.7	4.1	7.0	19.6	8.2	13.8	13.9	14.2
13 105	...	6	Elbert	351.1	19 143	1 865	54.5	64.9	29.0	0.5	1.0	5.6	5.9	16.1	7.7	11.6	11.0	13.3
13 107	...	7	Emanuel	680.6	22 635	1 704	33.3	60.6	34.5	0.4	0.8	4.6	6.8	18.1	8.6	13.3	12.1	12.1
13 109	...	6	Evans	182.9	10 670	2 378	58.3	57.8	29.8	0.6	1.0	11.8	7.4	19.1	7.6	13.0	12.2	12.3
13 111	...	8	Fannin	387.1	24 900	1 611	64.3	96.1	1.0	1.1	0.8	2.2	4.3	13.0	6.2	8.9	9.8	12.7
13 113	12060	1	Fayette	194.4	111 627	545	574.2	65.0	23.5	0.7	5.6	7.1	4.4	18.9	9.1	8.4	11.1	15.7
13 115	40660	3	Floyd	509.9	96 560	615	189.4	73.1	15.2	0.7	1.8	10.8	6.1	17.4	10.0	12.6	12.1	12.9
13 117	12060	1	Forsyth	224.1	221 009	299	986.2	75.0	3.9	0.6	12.7	9.3	6.1	22.0	7.0	9.8	16.0	16.8
13 119	...	8	Franklin	261.5	22 320	1 714	85.4	85.0	9.8	0.7	1.3	4.6	5.8	16.0	9.3	11.8	10.9	13.3
13 121	12060	1	Fulton	526.7	1 023 336	43	1 942.9	41.5	44.8	0.7	7.8	7.3	6.2	16.5	10.2	16.5	14.5	14.1
13 123	...	6	Gilmer	426.3	29 733	1 438	69.7	86.8	0.9	1.0	0.7	11.7	5.3	14.7	7.0	9.9	11.1	12.9
13 125	...	9	Glascock	143.7	3 006	2 970	20.9	88.7	9.8	1.0	0.5	1.5	4.7	18.4	7.8	10.3	12.6	14.7
13 127	15260	3	Glynn	419.8	84 502	673	201.3	65.2	27.0	0.7	2.1	6.9	5.9	16.9	8.2	12.0	11.5	13.0
13 129	15660	4	Gordon	355.8	56 904	898	159.9	79.0	4.7	0.6	1.3	15.5	6.2	18.7	8.5	12.6	13.3	14.4
13 131	...	6	Grady	454.5	24 808	1 617	54.6	59.6	28.9	1.1	0.7	10.8	6.8	18.4	7.6	12.1	11.5	13.1
13 133	...	6	Greene	387.4	17 003	1 980	43.9	58.1	34.8	0.7	1.2	6.3	5.3	13.6	6.1	9.7	10.2	11.3
13 135	12060	1	Gwinnett	430.4	907 135	60	2 107.7	40.3	27.8	0.7	12.7	20.8	6.7	20.7	9.1	13.2	14.8	15.0
13 137	18460	6	Habersham	276.7	44 246	1 085	159.9	79.3	4.1	0.8	2.7	14.4	5.8	16.8	9.4	12.3	12.0	13.1
13 139	23580	3	Hall	392.8	196 637	335	500.6	62.5	8.0	0.6	2.3	28.0	6.6	19.4	9.0	12.9	12.8	13.7
13 141	33300	7	Hancock	471.1	8 640	2 538	18.3	24.8	71.9	0.6	1.1	2.2	4.1	12.2	8.3	13.9	11.3	13.7
13 143	12060	1	Haralson	282.2	29 042	1 453	102.9	92.5	5.5	0.9	1.0	1.7	6.2	17.8	7.9	12.6	12.0	14.8
13 145	17980	2	Harris	463.9	33 652	1 337	72.5	78.6	17.3	0.8	1.6	3.3	4.6	17.2	7.9	10.0	12.0	15.5
13 147	...	6	Hart	232.4	25 553	1 582	110.0	76.3	19.7	0.4	1.2	3.7	5.3	15.9	7.5	11.1	11.0	13.8
13 149	12060	1	Heard	296.0	11 487	2 323	38.8	86.4	10.8	0.9	0.9	2.7	5.6	17.3	8.5	11.6	12.0	14.5
13 151	12060	1	Henry	318.6	221 768	297	696.1	47.1	43.8	0.8	4.1	6.6	5.9	20.5	9.4	11.8	14.1	15.6
13 153	47580	3	Houston	375.6	152 122	430	405.0	59.4	31.8	0.9	4.0	6.6	6.8	19.0	9.0	14.7	12.9	13.4
13 155	...	7	Irwin	354.4	9 422	2 471	26.6	68.2	27.7	0.4	1.0	3.7	4.8	16.8	8.6	13.0	12.9	13.6
13 157	27600	4	Jackson	339.7	64 615	819	190.2	83.6	7.7	0.7	2.3	7.3	6.7	18.9	7.7	12.7	13.9	14.4
13 159	12060	1	Jasper	368.2	13 654	2 191	37.1	75.4	20.8	0.8	0.5	3.9	6.0	17.9	7.6	11.4	11.8	14.2
13 161	...	7	Jeff Davis	330.8	14 877	2 110	45.0	72.5	15.3	0.5	0.9	11.9	7.1	20.2	8.0	12.1	12.8	13.1
13 163	...	6	Jefferson	526.5	15 916	2 045	30.2	42.7	53.2	0.4	0.8	3.7	6.2	17.4	8.1	12.3	11.4	13.0
13 165	...	6	Jenkins	347.3	8 849	2 519	25.5	52.0	42.2	0.5	0.7	5.5	5.6	15.7	9.6	14.2	12.5	13.1
13 167	20140	7	Johnson	303.0	9 505	2 467	31.4	63.0	34.5	0.4	0.5	2.4	4.4	14.2	8.0	13.5	14.1	15.1
13 169	31420	3	Jones	393.9	28 623	1 469	72.7	72.6	25.5	0.6	0.9	1.5	5.1	18.4	8.0	11.3	12.6	14.5
13 171	12060	1	Lamar	183.5	18 469	1 891	100.6	66.5	31.0	0.7	1.0	2.5	5.5	15.0	14.0	12.1	11.0	12.7
13 173	46660	3	Lanier	185.3	10 399	2 397	56.1	70.9	22.7	1.2	2.1	5.7	7.4	18.1	7.8	16.2	13.2	12.5
13 175	20140	5	Laurens	807.3	47 516	1 026	58.9	59.7	37.0	0.5	1.3	2.7	6.6	18.0	8.2	11.9	12.0	12.9
13 177	10500	3	Lee	355.9	29 337	1 449	82.4	73.5	21.1	0.6	3.1	3.0	6.5	20.0	8.0	12.8	14.6	13.7
13 179	25980	3	Liberty	516.3	62 570	844	121.2	43.2	43.7	1.2	3.9	12.3	9.9	18.2	14.8	19.4	10.7	9.4
13 181	12260	2	Lincoln	210.4	7 828	2 609	37.2	66.7	31.4	1.0	0.9	1.5	5.1	14.6	7.5	10.9	9.7	13.0
13 183	25980	3	Long	400.4	18 437	1 894	46.0	60.9	26.9	1.2	2.7	11.9	8.0	20.6	8.8	17.2	14.2	12.5
13 185	46660	3	Lowndes	496.1	114 628	536	231.1	55.7	37.3	0.7	2.7	5.6	6.9	17.0	17.5	14.9	11.1	10.9
13 187	...	6	Lumpkin	282.9	31 445	1 398	111.2	92.3	2.1	1.4	1.3	4.6	4.5	13.6	18.4	10.8	10.5	11.6
13 189	12260	2	McDuffie	257.5	21 490	1 753	83.5	55.3	41.8	0.7	0.9	2.9	6.8	18.8	8.1	11.9	10.9	13.2
13 191	15260	3	McIntosh	424.3	13 927	2 169	32.8	63.1	34.7	0.8	0.8	2.1	4.3	13.2	7.2	9.9	10.2	14.0
13 193	...	6	Macon	400.6	13 450	2 198	33.6	34.4	59.9	0.5	1.9	4.1	5.1	14.5	9.6	15.0	12.3	13.4
13 195	12020	3	Madison	283.2	28 824	1 465	102.1	83.9	7.7	0.7	2.0	5.2	6.1	16.9	8.2	11.8	12.3	14.4
13 197	17980	2	Marion	366.0	8 524	2 548	23.3	60.5	30.9	1.2	1.5	7.4	5.1	16.6	7.8	10.9	10.7	14.6
13 199	12060	1	Meriwether	501.2	21 074	1 771	42.0	57.8	39.8	0.8	0.9	2.1	5.9	15.9	8.1	11.5	10.9	13.6
13 201	...	8	Miller	282.4	5 926	2 761	21.0	70.1	26.7	0.7	0.9	2.7	5.9	17.2	7.7	11.2	10.8	13.5
13 205	...	6	Mitchell	512.1	22 459	1 711	43.9	47.3	47.9	0.6	0.8	4.3	5.9	17.3	8.6	13.1	12.6	13.3
13 207	31420	3	Monroe	396.1	27 306	1 520	68.9	73.5	23.6	0.6	1.2	2.3	5.0	15.5	8.4	11.3	12.0	14.3
13 209	47080	9	Montgomery	239.5	9 060	2 504	37.8	67.5	26.0	0.5	0.7	6.5	5.3	15.8	11.3	12.8	11.7	13.2
13 211	12060	1	Morgan	347.4	18 170	1 906	52.3	72.9	23.4	0.7	1.0	3.3	5.3	17.4	7.8	10.2	11.4	14.1
13 213	19140	3	Murray	344.5	39 315	1 189	114.1	83.9	1.2	0.7	0.6	14.6	6.1	18.8	8.5	12.5	13.0	14.7
13 215	17980	2	Muscogee	216.4	197 485	334	912.6	43.2	47.4	0.9	3.8	7.6	7.4	17.2	10.8	16.0	12.5	11.8
13 217	12060	1	Newton	272.2	106 999	560	393.1	49.1	45.2	0.7	1.6	5.3	6.5	20.1	9.5	12.3	13.3	14.3
13 219	12020	3	Oconee	184.3	36 838	1 254	199.9	85.9	5.5	0.4	4.6	4.9	5.5	21.2	8.0	9.0	13.6	15.1
13 221	12020	3	Oglethorpe	439.0	14 921	2 102	34.0	77.5	17.8	0.8	1.6	4.3	5.5	15.9	7.8	11.9	11.8	14.5
13 223	12060	1	Paulding	312.3	155 825	416	499.0	73.9	19.6	0.8	1.7	6.1	6.4	20.5	8.6	12.9	14.8	15.7
13 225	47580	3	Peach	150.3	26 655	1 539	177.3	47.3	45.0	0.8	1.6	7.2	6.0	16.0	13.5	12.7	11.1	12.8
13 227	12060	1	Pickens	232.1	30 832	1 413	132.8	94.6	1.6	1.0	1.0	3.1	4.9	15.5	7.2	10.8	11.1	13.9
13 229	48180	6	Pierce	340.2	19 171	1 864	56.4	84.8	9.3	0.9	1.2	5.2	6.3	18.8	8.0	11.6	13.1	13.7
13 231	12060	1	Pike	216.1	17 941	1 923	83.0	88.1	10.1	0.8	0.8	1.6	4.9	18.8	8.5	10.9	12.9	15.6
13 233	16340	4	Polk	310.3	41 776	1 133	134.6	73.4	13.5	0.6	1.0	13.0	6.8	18.9	8.4	13.5	12.0	12.9
13 235	47580	3	Pulaski	249.1	11 251	2 341	45.2	63.2	32.6	0.5	1.3	3.5	4.3	14.7	8.1	12.2	12.1	14.3

1. CBSA = Core Based Statistical Area. See Appendix A for explanation. See Appendix B for list of metropolitan areas with component counties. 2. County type code from the Economic Research Service of USDA Rural-Urban Continuum Codes. See Appendix A for definition. 3. Dry land or land partially or temporarily covered by water. 4. May be of any race.

Table B. States and Counties — Population and Households

STATE County	55 to 64 years	65 to 74 years	75 years and over	Percent female	2000	2010	2000–2010	2010–2016	Births	Deaths	Net migration	Number	Persons per household	Family households	Female family householder[1]	One person
	16	17	18	19	20	21	22	23	24	25	26	27	28	29	30	31
GEORGIA—Cont'd																
Effingham	11.9	7.4	3.9	50.1	37 535	52 257	39.2	12.4	4 485	2 361	4 204	18 432	2.95	76.7	11.7	18.3
Elbert	14.3	11.3	8.7	51.9	20 511	20 166	-1.7	-5.1	1 425	1 576	-862	7 744	2.49	68.6	16.6	28.3
Emanuel	12.6	9.7	6.7	50.7	21 837	22 594	3.5	0.2	2 003	1 719	-298	8 156	2.68	66.2	20.0	29.9
Evans	12.6	9.1	6.7	51.5	10 495	11 001	4.8	-3.0	993	694	-660	3 982	2.60	69.6	17.5	25.5
Fannin	17.9	17.1	10.0	51.3	19 798	23 696	19.7	5.1	1 267	1 882	1 752	9 510	2.48	66.4	10.6	28.9
Fayette	15.0	10.8	6.6	51.5	91 263	106 566	16.8	4.7	5 227	5 004	4 697	38 535	2.80	78.1	9.4	20.5
Floyd	12.6	9.3	6.9	51.6	90 565	96 317	6.4	0.3	7 439	6 434	-749	34 874	2.64	67.4	14.1	27.2
Forsyth	10.5	7.5	4.3	50.3	98 407	175 511	78.4	25.9	14 028	6 236	36 617	62 295	3.14	81.2	8.5	15.4
Franklin	13.6	11.4	7.9	50.9	20 285	22 084	8.9	1.1	1 664	1 733	301	8 433	2.54	69.3	12.1	25.9
Fulton	11.1	6.7	4.3	51.6	816 006	920 547	12.8	11.2	79 854	38 194	60 303	379 957	2.50	54.6	14.5	38.0
Gilmer	15.6	15.0	8.5	50.1	23 456	28 281	20.6	5.1	1 950	1 647	1 045	10 985	2.58	70.1	8.0	25.9
Glascock	13.5	10.3	7.7	50.6	2 556	3 082	20.6	-2.5	173	231	-29	1 121	2.67	70.9	10.6	25.8
Glynn	13.9	11.5	7.3	52.7	67 568	79 626	17.8	6.1	6 220	5 080	3 563	32 311	2.49	67.3	16.7	28.1
Gordon	12.2	8.7	5.3	50.4	44 104	55 186	25.1	3.1	4 382	3 031	363	19 539	2.83	73.7	12.8	21.8
Grady	13.4	10.4	6.9	51.5	23 659	25 012	5.7	-0.8	2 174	1 535	-842	9 270	2.70	70.2	15.0	26.0
Greene	15.5	18.6	9.7	51.5	14 406	15 996	11.0	6.3	1 043	1 203	1 120	6 707	2.40	70.1	16.4	26.0
Gwinnett	11.1	6.1	3.2	51.1	588 448	805 305	36.9	12.6	72 273	23 951	53 265	274 017	3.12	76.4	14.7	19.1
Habersham	12.6	10.5	7.5	52.5	35 902	43 041	19.9	2.8	3 112	2 581	623	14 864	2.74	72.0	9.3	24.5
Hall	11.3	8.6	5.8	50.3	139 277	179 684	29.0	9.4	15 990	8 412	9 028	61 992	3.00	73.9	12.2	21.6
Hancock	15.5	12.8	8.2	45.1	10 076	9 402	-6.7	-8.1	489	578	-689	2 815	2.49	56.7	18.8	39.4
Haralson	12.4	9.9	6.5	51.4	25 690	28 780	12.0	0.9	2 183	2 149	201	10 733	2.63	72.9	12.3	23.6
Harris	15.1	11.7	6.0	50.1	23 695	32 026	35.2	5.1	1 804	1 553	1 385	11 570	2.79	77.4	9.8	20.1
Hart	14.1	12.4	8.9	50.5	22 997	25 213	9.6	1.3	1 699	1 750	334	9 955	2.48	68.5	13.8	26.0
Heard	14.5	10.3	5.8	50.3	11 012	11 834	7.5	-2.9	773	758	-362	4 336	2.65	68.5	12.2	26.4
Henry	11.6	7.2	3.9	52.4	119 341	203 879	70.8	8.8	15 246	8 304	10 736	70 281	3.00	77.4	17.4	19.2
Houston	11.8	7.4	5.0	51.4	110 765	139 909	26.3	8.7	12 655	6 688	5 975	53 771	2.72	70.4	15.1	25.5
Irwin	12.0	10.2	8.1	48.5	9 931	9 532	-4.0	-1.2	627	594	-186	3 262	2.71	65.7	13.4	29.7
Jackson	12.0	8.8	5.0	50.6	41 589	60 485	45.4	6.8	4 912	3 333	2 291	21 048	2.88	76.7	11.8	19.0
Jasper	14.8	10.5	5.8	51.1	11 426	13 900	21.7	-1.8	1 066	816	-539	5 162	2.61	71.6	11.6	22.5
Jeff Davis	12.2	9.0	5.6	50.9	12 684	15 068	18.8	-1.3	1 305	950	-514	5 404	2.75	73.0	12.9	22.5
Jefferson	13.6	10.6	7.4	51.5	17 266	16 930	-1.9	-6.0	1 315	1 400	-981	6 057	2.61	65.5	21.5	31.6
Jenkins	12.7	10.1	6.6	46.7	8 575	8 336	-2.8	6.2	634	636	446	3 495	2.53	64.4	22.1	31.3
Johnson	14.3	9.9	6.5	43.5	8 560	9 984	16.6	-4.8	538	553	-485	3 299	2.80	69.7	15.8	28.0
Jones	13.4	10.4	6.3	51.6	23 639	28 669	21.3	-0.2	1 851	1 605	-386	10 326	2.76	76.1	15.7	20.7
Lamar	13.0	10.4	6.4	51.9	15 912	18 317	15.1	0.8	1 220	1 251	133	6 431	2.62	69.1	15.8	27.8
Lanier	12.0	7.8	5.0	49.3	7 241	10 074	39.1	3.2	834	530	-3	3 712	2.72	70.5	16.7	28.2
Laurens	12.9	9.9	7.5	52.7	44 874	48 434	7.9	-1.9	4 005	3 395	-1 572	17 640	2.65	67.3	17.8	29.2
Lee	12.4	8.1	3.9	49.8	24 757	28 298	14.3	3.7	2 232	1 204	-67	10 015	2.76	79.4	12.6	16.7
Liberty	9.0	5.8	2.8	48.7	61 610	63 472	3.0	-1.4	8 913	2 020	-8 113	22 943	2.72	72.6	16.2	21.7
Lincoln	17.4	13.8	8.1	51.3	8 348	7 996	-4.2	-2.1	457	522	-94	3 425	2.23	62.8	15.3	34.5
Long	10.7	4.9	3.0	50.2	10 304	14 443	40.2	27.7	1 505	564	2 976	5 017	3.27	74.0	17.7	22.7
Lowndes	10.0	7.0	4.7	51.2	92 115	109 233	18.6	4.9	10 303	5 206	30	39 328	2.78	62.5	16.6	28.0
Lumpkin	13.8	10.9	5.9	50.3	21 016	29 966	42.6	4.9	1 903	1 529	984	11 086	2.66	64.9	9.2	26.2
McDuffie	13.3	10.5	6.5	53.3	21 231	21 869	3.0	-1.7	1 846	1 483	-766	8 131	2.61	74.0	21.0	22.7
McIntosh	17.8	14.2	9.1	51.0	10 847	14 332	32.1	-2.8	754	736	-420	5 296	2.63	68.7	16.9	27.8
Macon	14.5	10.1	5.4	45.2	14 074	14 740	4.7	-8.8	857	926	-1 190	4 684	2.62	65.3	20.8	31.8
Madison	14.1	10.2	6.2	50.7	25 730	28 120	9.3	2.5	2 115	1 739	342	10 195	2.75	69.5	10.1	26.2
Marion	15.4	11.8	7.0	50.2	7 144	8 742	22.4	-2.5	570	470	-329	3 055	2.83	62.9	13.4	33.7
Meriwether	14.6	12.0	7.4	52.0	22 534	21 992	-2.4	-4.2	1 562	1 593	-877	7 943	2.65	71.0	18.3	25.3
Miller	13.1	10.6	10.1	52.1	6 383	6 129	-4.0	-3.3	433	490	-160	2 376	2.42	68.9	20.9	27.5
Mitchell	12.8	9.3	7.0	48.0	23 932	23 498	-1.8	-4.4	1 740	1 489	-1 374	8 140	2.55	64.7	20.5	32.4
Monroe	15.5	10.8	7.2	50.3	21 757	26 457	21.6	3.2	1 686	1 629	675	9 581	2.68	74.7	14.7	22.0
Montgomery	13.0	10.2	6.7	48.5	8 270	9 176	11.0	-1.3	629	514	-261	3 140	2.62	65.9	13.8	29.6
Morgan	14.5	11.5	7.8	51.7	15 457	17 866	15.6	1.7	1 175	1 082	217	6 418	2.76	76.3	14.6	20.8
Murray	12.3	9.1	5.0	50.5	36 506	39 628	8.6	-0.8	3 085	2 239	-1 186	14 236	2.75	73.6	12.5	22.4
Muscogee	11.6	7.4	5.4	51.1	186 291	190 545	2.3	3.6	19 553	11 280	-1 669	72 760	2.61	63.8	19.6	31.4
Newton	11.3	8.1	4.6	52.6	62 001	99 958	61.2	7.0	8 321	5 024	3 616	34 641	2.92	71.7	18.9	23.8
Oconee	13.1	9.0	5.4	50.9	26 225	32 815	25.1	12.3	2 051	1 339	3 266	11 880	2.88	80.2	9.4	17.0
Oglethorpe	14.2	11.0	7.4	50.7	12 635	14 899	17.9	0.1	988	839	-169	5 542	2.63	71.9	12.5	24.3
Paulding	10.8	6.8	3.6	51.2	81 678	142 324	74.3	9.5	11 630	5 107	6 709	49 110	2.99	79.6	13.4	17.3
Peach	13.5	8.9	5.6	52.1	23 668	27 695	17.0	-3.8	1 943	1 466	-1 564	9 941	2.50	69.1	18.8	26.3
Pickens	15.3	14.0	7.4	50.6	22 983	29 421	28.0	4.8	1 896	1 904	1 347	11 286	2.61	76.2	7.9	19.6
Pierce	12.3	9.9	6.3	50.4	15 636	18 758	20.0	2.2	1 481	1 200	148	6 890	2.72	75.8	16.7	21.0
Pike	13.2	9.4	6.0	50.9	13 688	17 869	30.5	0.4	995	981	34	6 017	2.92	79.9	12.0	18.5
Polk	12.3	9.4	6.0	50.7	38 127	41 475	8.8	0.7	3 518	2 898	-310	14 694	2.78	70.9	13.5	26.7
Pulaski	14.1	11.8	8.4	56.5	9 588	12 001	25.2	-6.2	571	656	-664	3 947	2.55	68.6	18.3	27.5

1. No spouse present.

Table B. States and Counties — Population, Vital Statistics, Health, and Crime

STATE County	Persons in group quarters, 2016	Daytime population, 2011–2015 Number	Employment/residence ratio	Births, 2016 Total	Rate[1]	Deaths, 2016 Number	Rate[1]	Persons under 65 with no health insurance, 2015 Number	Percent	Medicare, 2015 Total Beneficiaries	Enrolled in Original Medicare	Enrolled in Medicare Advantage	Serious crimes known to police,[2] 2014 Total Number	Rate[3]
	32	33	34	35	36	37	38	39	40	41	42	43	44	45
GEORGIA—Cont'd														
Effingham	590	40 692	0.45	757	12.9	416	7.1	6 332	12.5	6 703	4 691	2 012	505	916
Elbert	269	19 107	0.94	213	11.1	260	13.6	2 765	18.0	4 790	3 233	1 557	734	3 757
Emanuel	1 035	22 086	0.92	306	13.5	269	11.9	2 875	15.8	4 596	2 963	1 633	642	2 917
Evans	389	11 071	1.07	137	12.8	128	12.0	1 705	19.7	1 997	1 292	705	119	1 208
Fannin	160	22 814	0.89	216	8.7	310	12.4	3 583	20.1	7 035	5 268	1 767	427	1 790
Fayette	502	104 887	0.92	915	8.2	876	7.8	10 067	11.0	18 789	12 870	5 919	1 663	1 525
Floyd	3 830	100 793	1.12	1 170	12.1	1 097	11.4	13 654	17.6	19 506	14 182	5 324	4 392	4 576
Forsyth	696	178 858	0.81	2 288	10.4	1 201	5.4	19 860	10.5	18 238	11 647	6 591	2 020	1 005
Franklin	773	22 478	1.05	263	11.8	275	12.3	3 219	18.5	5 497	3 909	1 588	341	1 692
Fulton	32 634	1 357 520	1.80	13 237	12.9	7 157	7.0	121 648	14.0	105 193	61 585	43 608	55 136	5 499
Gilmer	187	26 347	0.78	312	10.5	330	11.1	5 056	22.4	6 860	5 111	1 749	599	2 084
Glascock	84	2 316	0.42	27	9.0	27	9.0	313	12.4	658	450	208	9	368
Glynn	1 303	87 374	1.16	986	11.7	871	10.3	11 692	17.3	16 823	12 295	4 528	4 247	5 166
Gordon	641	55 954	1.00	709	12.5	526	9.2	9 327	19.4	9 428	7 166	2 262	1 547	2 797
Grady	167	22 079	0.66	313	12.6	245	9.9	4 611	22.3	4 313	2 852	1 461	739	2 907
Greene	157	16 749	1.07	164	9.6	209	12.3	2 356	19.7	4 730	3 312	1 418	368	2 236
Gwinnett	4 847	812 706	0.88	11 630	12.8	4 382	4.8	143 838	17.8	75 653	45 194	30 459	21 401	2 445
Habersham	2 507	42 792	0.96	494	11.2	441	10.0	6 858	20.3	8 960	6 029	2 931	1 088	2 502
Hall	2 879	189 382	1.02	2 622	13.3	1 533	7.8	34 845	21.3	29 871	20 230	9 641	4 071	2 139
Hancock	1 302	7 941	0.56	67	7.8	122	14.1	796	14.2	1 958	1 025	933	119	1 355
Haralson	318	26 555	0.81	360	12.4	354	12.2	3 578	14.9	5 740	3 813	1 927	1 249	4 380
Harris	457	23 801	0.39	287	8.5	318	9.4	2 817	10.4	4 700	3 149	1 551	357	1 120
Hart	669	23 006	0.74	263	10.3	304	11.9	3 303	16.8	4 516	3 348	1 168	866	3 473
Heard	124	9 260	0.46	102	8.9	118	10.3	1 475	15.3	1 708	1 088	620	155	1 345
Henry	864	181 590	0.67	2 597	11.7	1 535	6.9	24 801	12.8	26 736	16 032	10 704	6 209	2 911
Houston	1 515	148 738	1.02	1 939	12.7	1 210	8.0	16 425	12.6	21 035	16 890	4 145	6 774	4 518
Irwin	981	8 515	0.71	93	9.9	95	10.1	1 040	15.1	1 482	1 014	468	260	2 761
Jackson	685	57 034	0.83	830	12.8	582	9.0	8 570	15.8	13 928	9 455	4 473	1 163	1 956
Jasper	91	10 997	0.52	148	10.8	120	8.8	2 023	17.8	2 148	1 362	786	241	1 776
Jeff Davis	111	14 271	0.87	213	14.3	159	10.7	2 435	19.3	2 537	1 859	678	462	3 074
Jefferson	597	16 068	0.94	202	12.7	241	15.1	2 429	19.1	3 541	2 276	1 265	606	3 898
Jenkins	1 189	8 030	0.70	93	10.5	102	11.5	1 097	17.3	1 552	954	598	NA	NA
Johnson	1 732	8 258	0.60	76	8.0	93	9.8	1 017	15.7	1 663	1 117	546	175	1 868
Jones	302	21 456	0.39	247	8.6	272	9.5	3 115	13.1	3 055	1 789	1 266	1 190	4 224
Lamar	1 237	15 904	0.67	200	10.8	213	11.5	2 044	14.5	3 394	2 019	1 375	1 583	9 124
Lanier	180	8 436	0.46	134	12.9	100	9.6	1 494	17.0	1 161	840	321	243	2 309
Laurens	996	49 305	1.09	605	12.7	538	11.3	5 773	14.8	9 987	6 720	3 267	1 566	3 430
Lee	867	20 806	0.37	328	11.2	215	7.3	3 060	12.2	3 346	2 452	894	841	3 265
Liberty	2 442	71 774	1.26	1 350	21.6	338	5.4	6 911	12.6	5 826	4 224	1 602	2 127	3 286
Lincoln	59	6 058	0.46	83	10.6	88	11.2	985	16.5	1 729	1 126	603	221	2 864
Long	321	11 672	0.24	262	14.2	111	6.0	2 724	17.0	1 016	760	256	286	1 661
Lowndes	6 383	120 884	1.16	1 616	14.1	896	7.8	15 875	16.8	17 105	12 884	4 221	4 790	4 198
Lumpkin	2 366	26 217	0.67	271	8.6	281	8.9	4 528	19.0	4 635	3 361	1 274	351	1 126
McDuffie	267	20 891	0.92	281	13.1	256	11.9	2 774	15.6	4 168	2 363	1 805	NA	NA
McIntosh	70	11 922	0.59	113	8.1	124	8.9	1 774	16.5	2 628	1 658	970	307	2 533
Macon	1 914	13 458	0.86	127	9.4	154	11.4	1 879	19.3	2 171	1 257	914	456	3 394
Madison	248	21 377	0.40	346	12.0	251	8.7	4 467	18.8	5 581	3 747	1 834	657	2 435
Marion	74	7 801	0.70	84	9.9	80	9.4	1 264	17.8	1 005	622	383	NA	NA
Meriwether	245	19 439	0.75	244	11.6	261	12.4	2 891	17.0	4 211	2 449	1 762	740	3 641
Miller	127	5 307	0.73	64	10.8	85	14.3	795	17.3	1 237	864	373	167	2 832
Mitchell	2 222	23 870	1.12	252	11.2	245	10.9	3 037	17.9	4 007	2 544	1 463	616	2 721
Monroe	1 071	24 138	0.74	249	9.1	299	10.9	3 146	14.7	3 992	2 718	1 274	737	2 709
Montgomery	692	7 212	0.47	87	9.6	84	9.3	1 190	17.5	1 601	1 053	548	NA	NA
Morgan	140	19 512	1.22	196	10.8	154	8.5	2 212	15.1	3 766	2 380	1 386	450	2 642
Murray	176	34 520	0.69	465	11.8	383	9.7	6 727	19.9	6 460	5 260	1 200	926	2 355
Muscogee	7 020	226 848	1.31	3 003	15.2	1 887	9.6	22 660	13.5	34 043	22 974	11 069	14 548	7 038
Newton	1 492	87 505	0.64	1 341	12.5	855	8.0	13 743	15.1	17 045	10 179	6 866	3 006	2 908
Oconee	126	30 701	0.77	333	9.0	213	5.8	3 510	11.4	5 151	3 635	1 516	546	1 587
Oglethorpe	170	10 862	0.39	160	10.7	155	10.4	2 067	17.1	1 762	1 225	537	399	2 750
Paulding	460	106 736	0.41	1 770	11.4	949	6.1	17 336	12.6	12 346	7 781	4 565	3 470	2 337
Peach	1 052	24 978	0.81	341	12.8	252	9.5	3 890	17.6	6 130	4 296	1 834	951	3 534
Pickens	349	27 844	0.85	309	10.0	332	10.8	3 903	16.4	7 529	5 281	2 248	530	2 039
Pierce	180	16 416	0.65	238	12.4	196	10.2	2 817	17.7	3 970	2 872	1 098	262	1 377
Pike	213	13 563	0.41	159	8.9	170	9.5	2 340	15.5	3 214	2 054	1 160	235	1 346
Polk	612	38 202	0.81	555	13.3	490	11.7	6 380	18.3	8 823	6 114	2 709	4 409	10 694
Pulaski	1 197	11 547	0.99	88	7.8	129	11.5	1 404	17.5	2 081	1 543	538	NA	NA

1. Per 1,000 estimated resident population.   2. Data for serious crimes have not been adjusted for underreporting; this may affect comparability between geographic areas and over time.
3. Per 100,000 population estimated by the FBI.

STATE County	Serious crimes known to police, 2014 (cont.)[1] Rate[2] Violent	Property	Education — School enrollment and attainment, 2011–2015 — Enrollment[3] Total	Per-cent private	Attainment[4] (percent) High school grad-uate or less	Bach-elor's degree or more	Local government expenditures,[5] 2013–2014 Total current spending (mil dol)	Current spend-ing per student (dollars)	Money income, 2011–2015 Per capita income[6] (dollars)	Median income (dollars)	Households Percent with income of less than $50,000	with income of $200,000 or more	Income and poverty, 2015 Median house-hold income (dollars)	Percent below poverty level All per-sons	Children under 18 years	Children 5 to 17 years in families
	46	47	48	49	50	51	52	53	54	55	56	57	58	59	60	61
GEORGIA—Cont'd																
Effingham	76	839	15 187	11.3	52.3	16.9	96.6	8 372	25 123	63 100	37.8	2.3	63 255	11.4	15.3	13.3
Elbert	312	3 445	4 363	8.4	68.8	10.6	31.2	10 078	19 841	35 388	66.3	1.7	35 814	23.7	35.3	34.8
Emanuel	227	2 690	5 631	4.8	63.7	10.8	39.6	9 048	17 096	32 229	69.7	1.4	31 772	27.0	40.2	39.3
Evans	122	1 086	2 703	16.2	63.5	15.4	17.0	9 143	19 625	37 865	61.2	2.4	34 085	27.4	41.8	41.2
Fannin	126	1 664	4 552	9.7	57.9	16.2	32.5	10 994	20 534	37 049	62.5	0.5	39 796	17.4	29.8	28.5
Fayette	76	1 449	31 033	16.4	27.5	43.8	174.7	8 668	36 362	79 066	30.5	9.5	80 588	7.0	10.0	8.5
Floyd	349	4 227	24 575	21.7	52.0	18.6	159.0	9 665	21 218	41 549	57.3	2.0	41 130	19.6	28.7	28.0
Forsyth	56	949	58 898	17.0	27.3	45.6	323.3	7 946	35 696	88 816	27.0	10.9	97 886	6.3	6.9	5.9
Franklin	114	1 578	4 908	14.6	63.7	12.6	30.4	8 306	17 743	33 816	65.9	0.3	40 156	21.9	31.3	29.1
Fulton	791	4 707	280 669	21.9	27.1	49.3	1 587.6	10 700	37 926	57 207	44.4	10.5	59 911	16.0	23.8	23.0
Gilmer	292	1 792	5 587	9.5	57.4	16.7	44.0	10 223	21 766	40 228	61.0	2.0	43 907	16.9	30.6	28.8
Glascock	41	327	757	2.4	65.3	8.1	6.2	9 868	18 921	40 759	61.0	0.4	40 732	17.8	24.4	21.1
Glynn	522	4 645	19 464	12.1	40.9	27.3	122.1	9 525	26 541	45 918	53.7	4.0	46 377	18.2	30.0	28.8
Gordon	284	2 513	13 977	7.4	59.7	13.7	92.4	8 679	19 707	41 612	59.8	1.9	44 580	18.1	26.4	25.9
Grady	209	2 699	6 363	5.0	61.2	13.3	38.7	8 326	16 953	34 187	67.4	1.0	36 486	29.3	41.1	37.5
Greene	201	2 035	2 858	9.6	53.7	24.7	31.7	13 884	28 209	42 408	57.1	5.4	43 326	21.2	37.9	36.8
Gwinnett	195	2 250	258 707	12.9	36.2	34.7	1 630.7	9 240	25 831	60 289	41.1	4.5	61 797	12.6	17.9	17.0
Habersham	189	2 313	10 272	12.3	55.8	17.5	65.4	9 403	19 026	40 907	58.8	1.6	44 400	16.6	23.5	22.5
Hall	173	1 965	50 510	9.9	50.1	22.7	295.5	8 539	24 292	51 202	48.5	3.9	54 578	16.9	24.3	22.8
Hancock	125	1 230	1 597	7.6	68.0	10.3	14.5	14 579	12 358	24 925	77.9	0.4	28 328	34.7	43.7	43.3
Haralson	698	3 682	7 006	8.5	59.3	14.1	52.3	9 130	20 740	41 910	55.8	0.8	41 167	19.2	27.0	24.9
Harris	72	1 048	8 077	9.9	37.9	26.6	45.9	8 831	30 386	63 824	40.0	5.4	65 887	9.9	13.6	12.1
Hart	329	3 144	5 391	13.3	57.4	13.6	31.8	9 075	20 733	37 653	61.4	1.3	39 567	18.6	28.7	28.1
Heard	191	1 154	2 767	8.3	66.7	10.1	19.4	9 526	19 222	41 525	59.7	0.2	41 514	19.1	30.7	28.1
Henry	175	2 736	66 360	16.1	40.9	27.0	334.8	8 222	24 996	60 424	39.9	2.8	65 437	9.9	15.8	14.9
Houston	289	4 229	43 533	10.3	40.4	23.5	258.3	9 242	24 368	53 270	47.0	2.2	55 860	15.2	22.6	22.3
Irwin	276	2 485	2 214	4.4	59.1	10.6	16.6	9 184	17 576	34 156	65.4	2.8	35 284	24.7	37.1	36.1
Jackson	153	1 803	15 919	8.9	51.6	19.2	103.7	8 741	23 504	53 379	46.0	2.3	56 102	13.0	17.8	16.7
Jasper	302	1 474	3 224	14.3	61.5	11.9	19.7	8 500	20 570	42 368	59.2	1.1	46 398	17.4	28.9	27.5
Jeff Davis	413	2 662	4 163	2.7	61.4	9.7	24.8	7 947	18 446	36 385	64.7	1.1	36 186	21.7	34.1	32.6
Jefferson	592	3 306	3 881	5.7	68.3	10.1	27.0	9 634	16 048	26 557	72.7	0.9	32 023	27.7	39.7	38.8
Jenkins	NA	NA	2 598	9.7	65.6	12.2	14.4	10 578	17 366	24 604	74.8	1.9	29 924	35.9	47.3	44.2
Johnson	374	1 495	2 337	7.4	63.6	8.9	11.3	9 871	16 954	34 438	65.2	0.0	30 794	30.2	37.1	32.4
Jones	99	4 125	7 263	9.3	50.6	19.7	49.9	9 101	26 005	51 857	48.0	2.8	52 777	14.2	20.7	18.5
Lamar	697	8 427	5 407	11.5	53.2	17.1	25.2	9 596	19 217	40 344	60.4	1.7	42 177	21.0	29.3	28.9
Lanier	333	1 977	2 739	7.4	54.1	12.7	16.7	9 186	16 688	37 605	62.6	0.2	37 616	21.8	35.9	35.5
Laurens	263	3 167	11 540	7.7	62.5	15.1	81.5	9 033	19 194	32 356	65.7	1.8	36 960	25.5	36.0	34.3
Lee	198	3 067	8 824	10.9	41.8	23.2	50.6	7 933	27 999	61 537	38.7	4.1	68 636	10.7	16.1	15.0
Liberty	399	2 888	17 984	10.8	41.5	18.7	95.5	9 356	19 785	42 201	58.5	1.0	39 612	20.3	27.3	29.6
Lincoln	389	2 475	1 547	4.1	60.9	12.1	12.1	10 063	22 373	34 243	67.5	1.2	39 089	21.4	31.9	30.9
Long	99	1 562	4 650	8.5	51.7	15.0	25.3	8 033	18 166	48 863	51.3	0.3	42 542	19.1	27.7	26.6
Lowndes	278	3 920	37 603	8.1	44.5	23.5	160.2	8 646	19 173	36 834	62.7	1.9	37 699	26.5	32.4	30.6
Lumpkin	42	1 084	9 121	7.2	43.6	28.1	35.1	9 263	21 963	43 804	55.8	2.9	48 101	16.5	22.4	21.9
McDuffie	NA	NA	5 557	5.5	61.7	14.2	41.6	9 579	19 065	36 656	62.5	0.9	36 346	27.4	40.5	37.5
McIntosh	91	2 443	2 826	6.7	54.4	13.1	16.5	9 958	23 887	42 988	57.6	1.5	38 770	24.0	39.3	36.7
Macon	365	3 030	3 155	8.3	66.1	7.9	17.4	10 606	13 431	28 684	74.6	0.4	30 696	33.5	43.6	41.1
Madison	174	2 261	6 632	11.0	58.3	15.6	47.3	9 895	20 857	41 912	57.1	1.9	40 735	15.1	23.0	20.8
Marion	NA	NA	2 021	6.1	61.9	12.2	13.5	9 837	19 077	36 242	65.0	2.2	35 265	25.5	40.1	37.8
Meriwether	276	3 365	4 687	11.4	65.4	9.3	31.5	10 096	18 059	35 832	63.5	1.2	37 866	22.1	33.7	32.1
Miller	271	2 561	1 281	14.0	60.7	12.8	10.5	9 523	18 904	33 983	64.7	1.4	35 357	25.1	37.8	35.9
Mitchell	278	2 443	5 560	11.2	65.7	11.4	36.4	9 234	15 297	31 915	67.5	0.3	34 139	28.0	38.1	35.3
Monroe	217	2 492	6 351	21.6	53.7	21.3	41.0	10 182	25 539	48 744	51.1	2.7	53 070	14.2	19.5	18.5
Montgomery	NA	NA	2 203	22.4	61.8	14.6	10.5	6 681	17 402	34 672	67.5	1.4	36 821	24.3	32.2	30.8
Morgan	176	2 466	4 400	9.5	52.4	22.1	29.5	8 978	24 435	51 820	48.3	2.7	51 081	14.3	22.8	20.7
Murray	221	2 134	9 403	6.6	66.8	10.3	61.7	8 097	17 043	35 539	63.2	0.5	43 142	17.8	26.7	25.5
Muscogee	533	6 505	57 557	11.7	41.3	24.1	321.3	10 001	23 318	42 306	56.3	2.9	41 828	22.2	31.1	31.2
Newton	370	2 537	30 145	13.7	47.7	20.2	166.2	8 515	21 717	49 179	51.0	1.7	51 177	14.9	23.3	22.2
Oconee	110	1 476	10 477	14.6	28.1	44.9	59.3	8 750	33 528	72 182	33.4	7.8	76 371	6.8	8.6	7.3
Oglethorpe	407	2 344	3 407	9.3	56.9	17.2	21.9	9 677	21 848	44 226	54.5	1.3	43 428	16.9	25.2	24.6
Paulding	153	2 184	44 225	13.6	46.0	23.8	229.8	8 084	24 930	60 109	39.6	2.1	62 658	8.8	12.7	11.7
Peach	524	3 010	8 799	10.4	45.0	20.9	34.9	9 264	20 689	41 588	55.8	0.7	41 725	22.0	33.4	32.1
Pickens	215	1 823	6 242	10.3	47.4	25.1	44.7	10 288	27 720	54 123	46.9	3.8	56 289	12.6	22.2	21.0
Pierce	173	1 203	4 457	7.4	59.4	14.2	31.7	8 503	21 619	40 247	58.2	1.3	39 648	22.1	31.1	29.8
Pike	120	1 226	4 974	14.9	52.3	16.0	26.7	7 826	23 150	51 338	48.6	1.8	56 233	11.7	16.9	15.1
Polk	832	9 862	10 297	13.1	62.8	13.1	64.1	8 315	20 293	37 853	60.2	1.5	39 402	20.8	32.3	31.1
Pulaski	NA	NA	2 302	12.2	62.7	12.1	13.6	9 702	17 656	38 750	61.3	0.3	39 209	24.4	34.5	31.4

1. Data for serious crimes have not been adjusted for underreporting; this may affect comparability between geographic areas and over time.   2. Per 100,000 population estimated by the FBI.
3. All persons 3 years old and over enrolled in nursery school through college.   4. Persons 25 years old and over.   5. Elementary and secondary education expenditures.
6. Based on population estimated by the American Community Survey, 2011–2015.

Table B. States and Counties — **Personal Income**

STATE County	Personal income, 2015										Earnings, 2015		
			Per capita[1]			Supplements to wages and salaries; employer contributions (mil dol)						Contributions for government social insurance (mil dol)	
	Total (mil dol)	Percent change, 2014–2015	Dollars	Rank	Wages and salaries (mil dol)	Pension and insurance	Government social insurance	Proprietors' income (mil dol)	Dividends, interest, and rent (mil dol)	Personal transfer receipts (mil dol)	Total (mil dol)	From employee and self-employed	From employer
	62	63	64	65	66	67	68	69	70	71	72	73	74
GEORGIA—Cont'd													
Effingham	2 142	6.6	37 507	1 762	423	83	27	59	199	359	593	39	27
Elbert	610	1.6	31 519	2 490	203	43	14	60	102	199	320	22	14
Emanuel	632	2.9	27 824	2 957	233	52	16	33	82	234	334	23	16
Evans	335	3.5	31 036	2 730	155	30	10	33	48	91	228	14	10
Fannin	749	5.9	30 816	2 709	196	36	14	70	141	266	315	25	14
Fayette	6 019	5.2	54 361	253	1 875	274	131	229	1 080	795	2 508	158	131
Floyd	3 383	3.6	35 054	2 159	1 701	284	120	291	509	912	2 397	149	120
Forsyth	11 571	7.5	54 466	445	3 799	488	254	1 016	1 312	936	5 556	332	254
Franklin	758	4.3	33 976	2 115	283	49	21	130	104	213	482	27	21
Fulton	70 716	4.3	69 977	91	62 313	7 352	4 119	10 514	15 868	6 121	84 298	4 795	4 119
Gilmer	905	4.9	30 769	2 679	242	48	17	129	150	287	437	28	17
Glascock	86	3.5	27 955	2 981	12	3	1	4	11	27	20	2	1
Glynn	3 328	5.5	39 814	1 413	1 627	293	114	176	851	720	2 209	134	114
Gordon	1 780	4.5	31 463	2 606	884	141	64	163	200	422	1 251	74	64
Grady	778	4.8	30 885	2 750	219	43	15	99	109	203	377	25	15
Greene	756	4.5	45 219	712	217	35	15	67	250	195	333	23	15
Gwinnett	33 240	6.5	37 106	1 885	19 587	2 478	1 330	2 534	4 045	4 325	25 928	1 513	1 330
Habersham	1 302	2.7	29 603	2 812	525	116	37	105	215	356	782	48	37
Hall	7 083	5.9	36 597	1 858	3 877	589	253	515	1 092	1 371	5 235	316	253
Hancock	219	2.1	25 607	3 012	59	15	4	4	33	91	82	7	4
Haralson	919	4.5	31 840	2 582	272	51	19	59	113	265	402	28	19
Harris	1 399	4.5	41 900	691	151	32	10	56	262	250	250	20	10
Hart	831	2.4	32 528	2 525	243	47	18	98	136	242	406	26	18
Heard	327	2.5	28 363	2 970	106	25	7	23	35	95	161	10	7
Henry	7 549	5.6	34 671	2 151	2 198	381	157	269	891	1 372	3 005	192	157
Houston	5 881	3.6	39 199	1 342	2 947	736	229	177	1 071	1 144	4 088	222	229
Irwin	256	6.1	27 651	2 963	70	16	5	11	44	89	101	7	5
Jackson	2 225	5.2	35 110	1 940	940	152	66	112	270	466	1 270	78	66
Jasper	446	3.1	32 701	2 456	71	16	5	38	59	116	130	10	5
Jeff Davis	432	2.7	28 961	2 651	169	33	12	30	63	127	245	16	12
Jefferson	488	2.8	30 327	2 768	173	36	12	40	67	171	261	17	12
Jenkins	235	2.0	26 195	3 072	48	12	3	11	36	82	74	6	3
Johnson	227	2.4	23 464	3 100	58	14	4	11	28	85	87	7	4
Jones	959	2.5	33 643	2 292	166	33	12	32	121	229	243	19	12
Lamar	541	2.7	29 742	2 807	136	30	9	35	68	169	211	14	9
Lanier	246	2.2	23 847	3 089	50	13	3	5	32	80	70	5	3
Laurens	1 550	4.0	32 477	2 455	705	143	51	71	246	459	970	62	51
Lee	1 216	1.6	41 626	1 088	214	41	15	58	157	195	329	20	15
Liberty	2 092	2.0	33 488	2 380	1 773	513	167	39	517	440	2 492	104	167
Lincoln	251	4.4	32 682	2 323	46	10	3	12	41	75	71	6	3
Long	399	7.4	22 525	3 102	35	11	2	13	52	99	61	4	2
Lowndes	3 745	3.3	33 182	2 267	2 066	439	154	174	679	864	2 834	155	154
Lumpkin	981	3.7	31 232	2 665	267	60	18	60	155	257	405	26	18
McDuffie	691	2.9	32 096	2 428	246	46	18	32	97	207	341	22	18
McIntosh	365	4.5	26 097	3 073	61	15	4	15	66	116	95	8	4
Macon	391	1.4	28 672	2 856	115	23	7	72	57	113	217	11	7
Madison	910	3.3	31 988	2 418	112	26	8	94	113	243	240	17	8
Marion	213	4.0	24 273	3 067	43	10	3	14	31	70	70	5	3
Meriwether	666	3.4	31 438	2 609	181	39	13	28	94	216	261	19	13
Miller	211	4.7	36 029	2 195	62	15	4	16	38	59	97	6	4
Mitchell	745	8.6	32 983	2 688	258	55	18	138	99	204	468	25	18
Monroe	1 085	4.0	40 025	1 465	305	69	20	68	165	224	462	28	20
Montgomery	245	5.8	27 392	3 043	63	12	4	9	32	73	89	7	4
Morgan	753	3.6	41 708	957	250	42	18	53	152	158	362	22	18
Murray	1 063	3.2	26 855	3 028	336	61	26	60	104	307	483	33	26
Muscogee	7 702	3.5	38 401	1 406	4 682	866	336	279	1 842	1 817	6 163	350	336
Newton	3 179	5.5	30 144	2 838	1 020	190	71	116	363	757	1 397	92	71
Oconee	1 986	5.6	55 216	348	423	69	29	164	393	218	685	42	29
Oglethorpe	498	2.6	33 480	2 378	58	13	4	83	63	118	158	8	4
Paulding	5 026	7.1	33 011	2 491	860	152	59	181	472	819	1 251	86	59
Peach	936	4.9	35 027	2 322	364	71	28	59	152	249	522	31	28
Pickens	1 225	4.5	40 420	1 218	348	54	23	71	229	308	496	36	23
Pierce	599	5.9	31 369	2 619	152	29	10	27	79	180	219	16	10
Pike	616	5.0	34 324	2 310	102	22	7	30	79	136	161	12	7
Polk	1 213	5.6	29 216	2 888	446	80	32	51	147	387	609	42	32
Pulaski	303	2.5	26 551	3 042	110	21	7	14	59	88	153	9	7

1. Based on the resident population estimated as of July 1 of the year shown.

Table B. States and Counties — Earnings, Social Security, and Housing

STATE County	Earnings, 2015 (cont.)									Social Security beneficiaries, December 2015			Housing units, 2016	
	Percent by selected industries											Supplemental Security Income recipients, December 2015		Percent change, 2010–2016
	Farm	Mining	Construction	Manufacturing	Information: professional, scientific, technical services	Retail trade	Finance, insurance, real estate and leasing	Health care and social assistance	Government	Number	Rate[1]		Total	
	75	76	77	78	79	80	81	82	83	84	85	86	87	88
GEORGIA—Cont'd														
Effingham	0.2	D	6.0	20.2	6.2	6.9	3.1	D	27.7	8 960	157	854	21 922	10.2
Elbert	5.8	3.4	3.7	27.4	2.0	6.1	4.7	5.5	21.0	5 440	282	869	9 473	-1.1
Emanuel	0.4	D	3.4	21.9	3.0	7.1	3.6	D	29.6	5 305	234	1 119	9 829	-1.4
Evans	5.8	0.2	7.1	37.3	D	5.9	D	D	14.8	2 255	210	452	4 634	-0.7
Fannin	1.5	0.0	D	3.6	5.1	14.1	5.9	D	16.2	8 085	333	714	16 883	4.1
Fayette	0.1	D	9.4	10.8	8.7	8.2	5.2	15.6	13.9	21 305	193	1 002	42 108	3.2
Floyd	1.0	D	2.6	16.9	D	7.0	4.2	24.2	13.5	21 860	227	3 340	40 414	-0.3
Forsyth	0.2	0.1	9.9	11.0	19.5	5.6	5.0	8.7	8.5	24 835	117	884	77 444	20.9
Franklin	18.9	0.0	4.1	17.2	D	6.0	3.6	D	11.6	5 870	263	897	10 445	-1.0
Fulton	0.0	0.1	2.5	3.7	29.5	4.2	12.7	7.7	10.4	127 115	126	27 072	464 473	6.3
Gilmer	15.4	D	7.8	13.7	D	9.1	4.0	7.4	15.2	8 280	282	636	16 761	1.2
Glascock	5.9	D	D	1.0	D	D	D	D	37.0	680	224	99	1 497	-1.4
Glynn	0.0	D	3.8	6.8	5.7	7.8	4.7	8.1	31.4	18 835	225	1 959	42 419	4.2
Gordon	5.2	0.0	5.8	35.8	2.1	5.5	3.0	8.6	12.8	11 140	198	1 542	22 301	0.1
Grady	7.5	0.0	6.0	8.9	2.5	6.4	D	7.0	17.6	5 455	217	1 096	10 660	-0.9
Greene	6.4	0.8	11.9	8.2	5.4	8.3	8.8	10.7	13.1	5 440	325	594	9 379	7.9
Gwinnett	0.0	D	8.4	9.0	15.9	7.9	8.6	6.8	9.0	98 070	110	11 446	305 436	4.8
Habersham	5.7	D	4.3	28.1	D	7.1	3.4	5.4	20.4	10 025	228	940	18 055	-0.5
Hall	0.4	D	5.4	21.1	4.5	6.8	5.0	16.9	11.5	35 060	181	3 135	70 954	3.1
Hancock	1.9	D	D	D	D	3.6	D	D	44.4	2 435	284	456	5 266	-1.3
Haralson	3.5	0.0	9.0	25.8	3.8	5.7	3.4	8.3	21.0	6 915	240	1 002	12 233	-0.4
Harris	0.2	0.0	13.1	16.7	D	2.2	6.3	D	24.6	6 710	202	408	13 883	3.6
Hart	12.8	0.5	5.8	24.9	3.8	6.8	2.8	D	15.0	6 695	262	575	12 937	-0.5
Heard	5.8	D	10.6	19.9	D	1.5	1.3	1.9	20.5	2 495	217	346	5 092	-1.1
Henry	0.0	0.3	5.3	8.0	4.5	10.6	5.0	13.2	20.9	33 330	154	4 024	79 628	4.1
Houston	0.0	D	2.4	7.6	7.6	5.1	2.4	6.2	57.5	24 280	162	3 575	61 877	6.1
Irwin	5.4	0.2	4.9	8.8	D	6.6	D	5.5	32.9	2 205	239	378	4 008	-0.6
Jackson	4.3	D	4.2	25.3	D	7.6	5.3	4.0	12.1	12 765	202	1 794	24 263	2.2
Jasper	6.0	0.1	D	16.1	D	3.7	3.3	D	23.4	3 075	226	334	6 300	2.2
Jeff Davis	0.6	0.0	2.2	26.3	D	10.6	4.6	3.2	17.0	3 185	213	501	6 386	-1.6
Jefferson	8.2	D	5.5	16.6	D	6.6	3.5	D	19.7	4 130	257	949	7 197	-1.4
Jenkins	6.9	D	3.2	1.1	D	5.0	2.0	6.1	35.9	1 890	211	470	4 159	-1.4
Johnson	1.5	0.1	6.9	6.1	1.0	4.9	D	16.5	32.9	2 110	220	589	4 047	-1.8
Jones	1.4	D	13.4	0.9	D	4.9	4.7	D	25.2	6 005	210	374	11 626	-0.5
Lamar	7.8	D	3.9	18.7	1.7	5.9	4.9	5.6	29.5	4 195	230	524	7 519	0.6
Lanier	1.2	0.1	3.6	8.5	D	4.9	D	2.5	46.0	1 740	169	337	4 308	1.4
Laurens	-0.5	0.0	5.4	14.4	D	8.3	3.7	D	30.2	11 355	238	2 202	21 224	-0.7
Lee	10.8	D	13.5	3.8	D	6.9	3.2	D	23.1	4 815	164	457	10 921	6.3
Liberty	0.1	0.0	D	6.3	D	2.4	1.5	1.8	76.7	7 415	119	1 218	27 599	3.1
Lincoln	1.4	0.0	24.0	4.2	2.0	5.5	6.3	2.6	26.0	2 195	286	250	4 779	-0.1
Long	5.4	D	8.5	D	0.8	2.7	1.6	2.0	54.3	1 725	97	242	6 571	9.0
Lowndes	0.4	D	5.9	8.5	6.3	7.4	4.0	9.6	35.9	18 795	165	3 899	46 385	5.6
Lumpkin	1.9	D	8.3	9.5	D	7.6	2.3	8.6	35.4	6 340	203	498	13 306	2.9
McDuffie	6.0	0.2	4.6	23.7	4.0	9.1	3.5	D	20.7	4 970	231	970	9 227	-1.0
McIntosh	3.1	D	4.8	D	D	8.9	1.2	2.0	33.9	3 125	224	413	9 286	0.7
Macon	27.9	D	5.8	20.9	D	3.5	1.5	D	18.9	2 455	180	442	6 013	-2.0
Madison	23.1	0.9	11.6	4.5	D	4.9	3.6	D	25.7	6 700	236	1 010	11 780	0.0
Marion	11.3	D	5.4	19.0	D	4.9	D	6.1	24.9	1 755	203	284	4 091	-1.6
Meriwether	2.5	0.0	10.8	13.8	D	5.0	3.3	D	26.4	5 295	250	920	9 902	-0.6
Miller	6.0	0.3	6.9	1.6	D	8.2	8.4	D	41.8	1 450	248	310	2 738	-1.9
Mitchell	17.8	0.0	1.4	30.6	D	5.0	2.7	D	16.3	4 810	214	1 091	8 961	-0.4
Monroe	4.1	D	7.0	2.0	D	4.1	3.8	D	29.9	6 010	222	536	11 041	3.0
Montgomery	0.9	0.0	7.7	7.8	0.5	4.9	D	D	20.8	1 940	216	339	3 896	-1.1
Morgan	9.0	0.0	6.7	19.3	D	7.0	4.9	3.2	16.0	4 525	251	433	7 562	1.2
Murray	4.3	D	2.7	40.3	D	7.2	2.7	D	15.9	8 245	209	1 167	15 711	-1.7
Muscogee	0.0	D	3.0	7.4	7.6	6.0	17.7	13.0	26.4	37 005	185	7 477	84 736	2.5
Newton	0.1	D	8.2	25.4	D	6.8	2.6	8.9	19.3	18 815	179	3 024	38 655	0.8
Oconee	3.7	D	6.6	4.0	9.9	6.2	13.1	12.0	12.7	6 240	174	368	13 790	11.3
Oglethorpe	43.3	2.7	9.5	4.0	D	2.4	3.3	D	17.2	3 245	217	293	6 502	0.3
Paulding	0.4	D	14.4	4.8	5.0	10.9	4.2	9.6	24.5	20 740	136	1 491	54 840	5.2
Peach	4.9	0.0	6.6	32.9	D	7.2	3.4	5.0	21.8	5 480	206	1 204	11 425	3.4
Pickens	3.1	D	8.1	9.9	5.0	7.4	5.1	25.5	14.6	8 890	293	602	13 737	0.4
Pierce	3.6	0.0	8.8	9.5	D	7.2	3.4	D	20.0	4 195	219	730	7 986	0.0
Pike	1.2	D	14.8	11.8	D	5.4	4.0	D	23.6	3 780	211	402	6 848	0.4
Polk	1.7	D	5.9	31.4	D	10.2	2.5	7.5	16.1	9 585	231	1 632	16 898	-0.1
Pulaski	8.2	0.1	D	D	D	6.1	D	D	21.5	2 215	195	379	5 137	-0.2

1. Per 1,000 resident population estimated as of July 1 of the year shown.

Table B. States and Counties — Housing, Labor Force, and Employment

	Housing units, 2011–2015								Civilian labor force, 2016				Civilian employment,[6] 2011–2015		
	Occupied units										Unemployment		Percent		
		Owner-occupied				Renter-occupied									
STATE County	Total	Percent	Median value[1]	Median owner cost as a percent of income — With a mortgage	Without a mortgage[2]	Median rent[3]	Median rent as a percent of income[2]	Sub-standard units[4] (percent)	Total	Percent change, 2015–2016	Total	Rate[5]	Total	Management, business, science and arts	Construction, production, and maintenance occupations
	89	90	91	92	93	94	95	96	97	98	99	100	101	102	103
GEORGIA—Cont'd															
Effingham	18 432	76.5	152 600	20.9	10.3	914	27.4	2.9	27 904	2.7	1 356	4.9	25 352	30.2	32.9
Elbert	7 744	68.2	82 400	21.7	12.5	609	31.7	3.1	7 735	1.6	506	6.5	7 210	22.6	40.6
Emanuel	8 156	66.7	67 800	23.4	13.3	563	30.1	4.6	8 468	1.9	660	7.8	8 300	21.8	36.2
Evans	3 982	63.6	87 900	21.9	13.4	614	29.2	4.2	4 836	3.7	240	5.0	3 979	31.5	38.6
Fannin	9 510	78.0	164 600	24.7	13.5	664	32.1	1.4	10 745	6.3	573	5.3	8 669	25.4	30.2
Fayette	38 535	81.3	229 500	21.3	10.0	1 096	27.9	1.5	55 982	3.4	2 646	4.7	49 795	43.3	18.5
Floyd	34 874	60.7	117 100	21.2	12.1	674	30.6	2.7	43 531	1.3	2 628	6.0	39 669	28.3	28.8
Forsyth	62 295	84.1	267 300	20.7	10.0	1 172	27.9	1.0	108 078	3.5	4 517	4.2	92 504	48.4	13.3
Franklin	8 433	69.6	102 700	25.0	13.4	607	30.7	2.2	9 728	4.8	514	5.3	8 038	28.9	35.0
Fulton	379 957	51.7	241 300	22.4	11.5	1 001	30.2	2.3	531 176	3.2	28 521	5.4	471 816	49.4	11.5
Gilmer	10 985	76.4	139 600	26.0	10.7	688	33.3	3.3	11 880	1.4	668	5.6	10 938	27.0	28.0
Glascock	1 121	74.0	66 300	24.2	10.0	473	21.6	3.0	1 275	3.4	78	6.1	1 344	29.0	38.7
Glynn	32 311	61.0	159 200	23.2	10.0	828	29.6	2.6	39 072	3.7	2 071	5.3	36 375	31.9	20.0
Gordon	19 539	65.4	113 000	22.1	10.4	654	29.4	2.7	25 105	-4.0	1 421	5.7	23 587	23.4	39.7
Grady	9 270	57.8	115 100	24.4	13.3	727	34.5	2.9	10 301	-1.1	571	5.5	9 291	28.7	32.3
Greene	6 707	71.9	169 300	24.5	14.0	636	34.0	2.7	6 910	1.2	399	5.8	5 952	24.1	26.7
Gwinnett	274 017	66.4	167 700	23.2	10.2	1 043	32.1	3.3	467 706	3.4	22 141	4.7	410 562	37.6	19.8
Habersham	14 864	74.9	131 500	23.5	13.0	687	30.1	4.5	19 368	3.0	1 021	5.3	16 970	24.6	32.7
Hall	61 992	66.8	159 700	23.4	10.2	858	29.9	5.5	96 105	3.6	4 300	4.5	84 198	28.3	32.3
Hancock	2 815	78.3	66 700	36.6	18.8	630	34.1	1.5	2 527	1.6	213	8.4	2 159	25.1	27.1
Haralson	10 733	70.4	103 500	20.8	12.7	670	30.5	2.6	12 238	3.1	713	5.8	11 136	28.2	33.3
Harris	11 570	83.7	201 100	22.6	13.2	868	30.6	1.6	15 758	0.4	781	5.0	15 071	36.6	24.2
Hart	9 955	73.3	116 600	24.8	12.2	592	30.6	1.7	10 913	4.9	596	5.5	9 660	27.5	34.6
Heard	4 336	72.7	88 200	24.4	13.6	757	34.8	2.3	5 080	3.5	298	5.9	4 547	25.2	40.8
Henry	70 281	72.9	140 300	23.0	10.5	1 056	30.0	1.7	108 313	3.1	5 950	5.5	92 993	32.9	23.1
Houston	53 771	65.3	132 400	19.4	10.4	850	29.5	2.7	67 338	2.5	3 611	5.4	64 013	35.3	24.1
Irwin	3 262	75.1	80 000	20.2	13.5	571	31.5	0.9	3 218	2.7	249	7.7	3 158	30.9	32.3
Jackson	21 048	77.0	155 700	23.0	11.7	777	29.2	1.7	33 204	8.0	1 410	4.2	26 679	31.5	26.5
Jasper	5 162	73.0	111 200	24.3	12.5	782	34.8	3.3	6 654	3.3	318	4.8	5 520	23.3	39.1
Jeff Davis	5 404	75.8	71 800	21.7	11.7	486	25.2	4.0	6 239	-1.6	394	6.3	5 606	23.7	32.1
Jefferson	6 057	64.8	64 800	24.3	15.9	534	35.5	3.8	6 594	3.6	492	7.5	5 097	24.4	38.9
Jenkins	3 495	65.9	54 700	26.8	14.2	508	43.9	5.5	3 161	1.8	240	7.6	3 035	27.1	38.5
Johnson	3 299	71.0	67 600	22.8	13.0	515	30.8	2.8	3 949	2.0	243	6.2	3 909	23.6	38.2
Jones	10 326	80.8	129 300	22.5	12.5	819	31.0	1.6	13 692	1.6	665	4.9	12 176	31.9	26.0
Lamar	6 431	69.9	124 300	23.5	12.9	650	31.8	1.3	7 880	2.6	514	6.5	6 860	30.8	27.9
Lanier	3 712	63.7	100 900	24.3	11.2	634	30.0	4.5	3 834	1.4	219	5.7	3 476	28.4	24.4
Laurens	17 640	63.6	84 100	22.0	11.6	594	35.1	2.4	18 964	1.8	1 278	6.7	16 926	30.7	25.4
Lee	10 015	71.6	157 100	19.4	11.3	931	29.2	1.2	14 328	1.4	684	4.8	12 990	39.6	19.6
Liberty	22 943	47.5	122 400	24.5	12.3	958	30.8	1.6	25 248	1.1	1 456	5.8	23 102	28.6	24.5
Lincoln	3 425	75.4	113 800	26.9	18.9	571	28.6	0.8	3 448	2.5	204	5.9	3 121	19.6	36.6
Long	5 017	64.0	103 300	20.5	10.0	724	29.4	3.5	7 217	1.9	394	5.5	5 728	27.1	27.7
Lowndes	39 328	51.3	135 000	23.3	10.6	758	32.9	3.2	51 048	1.4	2 657	5.2	45 595	29.2	21.5
Lumpkin	11 086	64.9	167 400	24.0	10.0	840	35.7	2.0	15 815	3.3	777	4.9	14 185	31.5	23.2
McDuffie	8 131	63.4	102 300	24.4	11.3	597	35.2	3.3	8 919	1.5	644	7.2	8 314	25.7	34.2
McIntosh	5 296	77.6	108 400	26.5	13.3	600	29.6	1.5	6 065	4.3	350	5.8	5 410	22.8	30.0
Macon	4 684	61.4	68 100	23.4	16.0	560	34.9	2.5	4 680	1.4	388	8.3	4 461	20.5	39.6
Madison	10 195	72.2	122 700	21.2	10.1	710	28.0	3.6	13 013	3.1	651	5.0	11 393	30.6	31.3
Marion	3 055	72.2	93 300	26.0	13.9	492	24.7	3.0	3 437	-0.2	255	7.4	3 219	26.0	42.0
Meriwether	7 943	66.6	89 800	23.6	16.8	756	37.5	4.1	8 912	2.8	609	6.8	7 730	19.9	44.4
Miller	2 376	65.7	92 500	23.7	13.6	595	30.2	7.6	2 768	3.6	151	5.5	2 373	27.4	30.2
Mitchell	8 140	66.0	76 700	26.7	13.9	589	29.7	3.8	8 588	-1.4	569	6.6	7 956	28.4	33.2
Monroe	9 581	75.7	153 300	22.6	10.1	729	35.5	3.3	12 889	1.8	675	5.2	10 914	35.2	23.0
Montgomery	3 140	70.4	75 200	25.8	12.0	558	28.1	4.0	3 661	-1.3	277	7.6	3 394	25.2	33.9
Morgan	6 418	77.7	182 900	26.9	12.3	853	26.6	1.5	8 741	3.8	439	5.0	7 624	31.3	28.6
Murray	14 236	67.6	89 800	22.4	11.5	636	31.9	4.7	16 328	1.6	1 119	6.9	16 079	19.5	42.1
Muscogee	72 760	49.8	134 500	23.3	11.3	830	31.0	2.3	78 724	-0.2	5 407	6.9	78 531	32.9	19.3
Newton	34 641	70.2	115 500	24.1	10.8	889	32.5	2.2	49 904	3.1	2 974	6.0	43 639	29.9	27.3
Oconee	11 880	79.6	235 700	20.9	10.1	883	24.6	1.0	18 177	3.4	750	4.1	16 227	51.3	14.2
Oglethorpe	5 542	75.2	121 200	22.9	10.9	745	30.1	1.1	6 948	3.3	340	4.9	6 355	31.3	35.5
Paulding	49 110	79.0	133 500	21.9	11.1	1 018	31.2	1.8	78 820	3.3	3 642	4.6	70 001	33.6	23.6
Peach	9 941	65.5	124 600	23.0	10.0	687	30.7	2.2	11 556	2.4	803	6.9	11 481	27.6	31.5
Pickens	11 286	77.0	175 000	22.3	12.1	833	29.3	1.5	14 344	3.4	700	4.9	12 678	30.8	26.1
Pierce	6 890	74.7	98 000	22.6	12.4	569	29.0	2.2	8 369	4.1	453	5.4	7 262	32.0	32.2
Pike	6 017	83.7	155 200	23.8	13.4	796	28.5	1.8	8 507	3.4	440	5.2	7 323	33.2	29.2
Polk	14 694	67.2	102 600	24.6	12.6	670	28.9	3.6	18 154	0.1	1 107	6.1	16 190	23.6	36.7
Pulaski	3 947	60.7	100 700	21.5	10.0	625	31.4	4.4	4 126	2.9	243	5.9	3 949	32.6	27.5

1. Specified owner-occupied units.   2. A value of 10.0 represents 10 percent or less; a value of 50.0 represents 50 percent or more.   3. Specified renter-occupied units.
4. Overcrowded or lacking complete plumbing facilities.   5. Percent of civilian labor force.   6. Civilian employed persons 16 years old and over.

Table B. States and Counties — Nonfarm Employment and Agriculture

STATE County	Private nonfarm establishments, employment and payroll, 2015									Agriculture, 2012			
	Number of establishments	Employment						Annual payroll		Farms			Farm operators whose principal occupation is farming (percent)
		Total	Health care and social assistance	Manufacturing	Retail trade	Finance and insurance	Professional, scientific, and technical services	Total (mil dol)	Average per employee (dollars)	Number	Percent with:		
											Fewer than 50 acres	500 acres or more	
	104	105	106	107	108	109	110	111	112	113	114	115	116

STATE County	104	105	106	107	108	109	110	111	112	113	114	115	116
GEORGIA—Cont'd													
Effingham	694	7 419	958	1 710	1 388	147	259	295	39 740	186	48.9	9.1	35.5
Elbert	425	4 473	504	1 930	605	190	49	137	30 549	411	35.3	4.6	55.2
Emanuel	382	5 005	779	1 935	812	162	119	150	30 034	438	24.9	19.6	39.3
Evans	222	3 887	424	1 849	498	87	72	123	31 693	202	32.2	8.4	45.5
Fannin	586	5 099	906	428	1 223	147	233	140	27 383	198	62.6	1.0	41.4
Fayette	3 285	38 356	6 101	2 718	6 879	1 110	2 231	1 545	40 275	126	50.8	3.2	52.4
Floyd	1 940	34 336	7 640	6 082	4 580	759	715	1 270	36 993	559	44.4	3.6	36.5
Forsyth	5 996	71 758	7 361	7 947	9 961	1 952	5 761	3 354	46 739	311	68.8	0.0	53.7
Franklin	417	6 061	604	1 546	843	139	132	194	32 080	775	44.6	1.8	52.3
Fulton	35 391	763 933	82 088	19 325	52 842	61 056	95 852	52 543	68 780	187	66.3	2.1	56.7
Gilmer	534	5 767	721	1 345	1 125	112	152	164	28 373	296	43.9	0.7	66.2
Glascock	25	216	D	D	21	D	D	5	23 574	96	30.2	17.7	47.9
Glynn	2 498	30 339	4 405	2 164	5 231	706	940	1 075	35 425	53	77.4	1.9	45.3
Gordon	1 002	18 950	1 731	7 002	2 379	277	213	734	38 725	671	47.5	4.2	53.1
Grady	405	4 371	466	1 002	739	136	114	142	32 452	471	34.2	13.2	35.2
Greene	416	4 552	493	424	763	207	114	150	33 027	193	34.7	11.9	58.5
Gwinnett	22 575	318 822	26 897	21 814	45 183	15 187	26 692	15 760	49 431	179	67.6	1.1	37.4
Habersham	816	11 920	1 211	4 558	1 847	394	237	424	35 543	422	58.5	2.4	53.8
Hall	4 100	72 187	12 736	19 376	8 354	2 219	1 789	3 163	43 818	622	59.0	2.3	51.3
Hancock	65	628	132	D	94	D	D	20	31 150	133	30.8	11.3	40.6
Haralson	428	5 303	839	1 568	974	127	128	200	37 727	299	48.5	1.7	38.5
Harris	401	4 450	256	1 127	286	395	69	109	24 522	252	42.5	4.0	50.0
Hart	389	5 575	348	2 326	937	106	121	199	35 613	584	42.8	4.1	58.9
Heard	125	1 307	78	658	90	28	20	50	38 011	168	38.1	6.0	39.9
Henry	3 527	47 981	6 731	3 201	9 741	1 193	1 410	1 614	33 638	254	56.7	2.8	47.6
Houston	2 497	37 539	6 559	4 310	7 225	1 073	3 813	1 233	32 845	226	52.7	13.3	38.9
Irwin	118	1 605	604	D	163	32	32	53	33 298	373	23.6	22.3	50.7
Jackson	1 224	18 368	1 083	5 751	3 046	264	542	690	37 542	774	53.0	3.2	47.5
Jasper	153	1 511	229	417	221	59	16	42	27 643	239	39.3	7.1	51.0
Jeff Davis	234	3 757	327	1 649	675	74	41	114	30 476	192	32.8	24.0	46.4
Jefferson	300	3 850	498	931	598	158	39	138	35 893	358	23.7	20.7	40.5
Jenkins	105	948	169	19	160	34	D	28	29 672	224	24.6	23.2	41.5
Johnson	121	979	225	115	166	30	13	30	30 949	255	22.0	10.2	31.8
Jones	319	2 457	410	51	458	60	75	80	32 759	175	37.1	2.9	41.1
Lamar	234	2 915	305	583	449	105	46	89	30 696	252	44.4	4.4	33.3
Lanier	96	632	49	114	155	71	20	17	26 731	86	38.4	26.7	41.9
Laurens	1 062	15 059	3 076	2 729	2 597	485	263	527	34 977	694	26.2	12.1	32.1
Lee	378	4 047	281	237	703	185	301	151	37 301	192	28.1	19.3	46.4
Liberty	806	12 622	2 016	2 039	1 944	357	766	478	37 907	46	47.8	10.9	34.8
Lincoln	130	816	22	76	149	39	66	23	28 483	150	44.0	6.7	37.3
Long	66	276	19	D	71	20	D	7	24 076	67	34.3	4.5	46.3
Lowndes	2 723	40 229	7 378	3 411	6 536	1 063	1 229	1 256	31 223	411	50.6	5.4	46.0
Lumpkin	503	4 815	676	710	1 032	160	174	142	29 531	220	63.6	0.9	53.6
McDuffie	425	6 729	889	1 835	1 131	125	145	213	31 590	208	44.2	11.1	35.1
McIntosh	176	1 307	37	19	336	79	31	30	23 050	56	62.5	8.9	42.9
Macon	180	1 887	384	391	244	44	14	79	42 113	279	26.5	17.2	60.2
Madison	357	1 996	228	196	438	58	71	60	29 961	745	46.3	0.9	46.4
Marion	83	1 314	124	221	111	19	D	34	26 138	203	24.1	12.3	42.4
Meriwether	315	3 327	1 028	674	522	120	45	115	34 417	295	32.9	8.1	44.7
Miller	122	1 032	335	D	188	47	26	33	31 873	183	20.8	30.1	56.3
Mitchell	369	5 640	576	2 704	696	150	139	161	28 610	443	30.5	25.5	47.9
Monroe	501	6 406	1 274	662	883	171	177	233	36 444	183	41.0	8.7	38.8
Montgomery	107	927	D	153	184	26	36	31	33 149	229	30.6	13.1	36.2
Morgan	465	5 596	461	1 357	965	169	285	186	33 181	572	35.1	6.1	45.5
Murray	385	7 831	413	4 598	770	97	54	254	32 413	320	48.4	3.8	39.1
Muscogee	4 291	77 624	14 471	6 279	11 671	12 045	2 439	3 127	40 290	22	40.9	13.6	45.5
Newton	1 349	18 109	2 210	3 949	3 131	500	489	731	40 390	285	50.2	6.0	53.3
Oconee	1 072	10 646	1 480	615	2 108	427	804	381	35 744	375	44.8	5.1	43.2
Oglethorpe	174	1 252	99	86	139	29	42	43	34 081	406	34.7	8.1	50.2
Paulding	1 815	17 160	2 449	796	4 542	353	619	533	31 074	142	66.2	0.7	35.2
Peach	459	6 125	692	2 284	873	129	117	227	37 042	190	58.9	8.9	36.8
Pickens	663	6 023	1 162	717	1 199	227	157	207	34 313	262	63.0	1.1	48.5
Pierce	336	3 157	207	391	466	95	75	97	30 842	356	46.3	11.8	52.8
Pike	244	1 588	213	159	190	140	67	50	31 766	296	44.6	5.7	35.1
Polk	604	10 108	1 018	3 741	1 519	179	119	333	32 966	353	45.0	2.8	41.4
Pulaski	174	1 912	761	D	340	66	44	70	36 505	176	37.5	18.2	52.8

178 GA(Effingham)—GA(Pulaski)

Table B. States and Counties — **Agriculture**

STATE County	Land in farms Acreage (1,000)	Land in farms Percent change, 2007–2012	Acres Average size of farm	Acres Total irrigated (1,000)	Acres Total cropland (1,000)	Value of land and buildings (dollars) Average per farm	Value of land and buildings (dollars) Average per acre	Value of machinery and equipment, average per farm (dollars)	Value of products sold Total (mil dol)	Value of products sold Average per farm (dollars)	Percent from: Crops	Percent from: Livestock and poultry products	Percent of farms with sales of: $10,000 or more	Percent of farms with sales of: $100,000 or more	Government payments Total ($1,000)	Government payments Percent of farms
	117	118	119	120	121	122	123	124	125	126	127	128	129	130	131	132
GEORGIA—Cont'd																
Effingham	40	0.0	217	1.1	17.4	604 253	2 779	106 022	13.8	74 038	90.5	9.5	36.0	10.2	255	28.5
Elbert	57	-9.4	139	0.1	13.6	490 494	3 537	53 966	79.2	192 749	3.7	96.3	37.2	17.3	362	32.6
Emanuel	152	9.5	346	3.7	65.1	738 584	2 132	92 105	57.3	130 845	92.8	7.2	37.4	17.1	2 136	58.2
Evans	36	-31.7	178	3.0	14.7	461 465	2 587	75 366	39.8	197 055	40.8	59.2	39.1	17.8	429	33.7
Fannin	14	-26.3	70	0.2	3.7	455 722	6 505	47 121	16.1	81 293	8.0	92.0	23.7	7.1	16	5.6
Fayette	11	-6.8	91	0.1	2.7	557 341	6 110	48 786	4.0	31 635	90.4	9.6	21.4	4.0	9	6.3
Floyd	70	-17.1	126	0.8	19.6	489 283	3 898	54 420	77.0	137 828	6.9	93.1	29.3	8.6	616	19.7
Forsyth	16	-18.8	52	0.1	3.3	568 206	10 995	41 273	31.7	101 897	8.2	91.8	24.8	10.9	30	4.5
Franklin	77	-5.0	100	0.3	19.7	539 779	5 412	76 230	367.1	473 618	1.2	98.8	52.8	36.4	328	14.3
Fulton	14	-9.3	75	0.8	3.0	511 385	6 780	35 460	4.6	24 460	71.8	28.2	29.4	3.2	44	9.6
Gilmer	26	-30.1	86	0.1	5.3	530 159	6 141	88 270	213.9	722 466	1.0	99.0	56.1	44.3	140	8.4
Glascock	24	13.1	250	0.3	6.4	461 958	1 847	50 208	3.4	35 135	77.8	22.2	33.3	5.2	160	25.0
Glynn	4	-38.3	68	0.0	0.3	266 472	3 923	116 453	0.4	6 943	60.3	39.7	22.6	0.0	16	15.1
Gordon	85	7.3	127	1.8	32.8	607 225	4 797	66 523	261.2	389 270	4.9	95.1	45.5	23.1	1 200	16.5
Grady	130	9.5	277	9.2	54.4	850 864	3 077	104 682	99.2	210 690	64.1	35.9	43.1	17.4	2 083	52.4
Greene	49	-12.2	252	0.2	8.3	811 705	3 225	67 798	47.8	247 829	4.5	95.5	43.0	16.1	215	13.5
Gwinnett	10	25.4	58	0.1	2.1	604 374	10 335	53 011	12.1	67 425	92.5	7.5	27.4	4.5	33	10.1
Habersham	38	29.5	90	0.0	9.6	516 374	5 746	66 038	125.8	298 085	1.3	98.7	48.1	31.3	142	9.2
Hall	52	-9.3	84	0.1	12.3	686 416	8 212	68 188	166.3	267 434	2.1	97.9	34.9	19.8	115	8.2
Hancock	32	-15.9	240	0.2	4.8	822 805	3 424	61 669	4.5	34 008	35.8	64.2	33.1	6.8	165	18.0
Haralson	27	-22.0	90	0.0	5.4	377 763	4 212	46 033	42.6	142 539	0.8	99.2	23.4	7.7	172	9.7
Harris	32	-46.7	129	0.2	6.9	618 067	4 802	39 357	2.3	9 183	62.8	37.2	18.7	0.8	42	5.2
Hart	68	-3.0	117	1.6	21.7	605 507	5 181	79 663	208.1	356 355	3.7	96.3	46.9	26.2	793	22.8
Heard	27	14.7	161	D	3.4	559 560	3 473	58 190	36.1	215 137	2.4	97.6	38.7	17.3	70	6.5
Henry	22	-7.9	85	0.1	5.6	489 512	5 735	26 445	3.3	12 917	58.6	41.4	24.0	2.0	70	9.8
Houston	47	1.7	210	9.0	23.1	650 288	3 097	94 969	22.5	99 668	69.3	30.7	31.0	10.2	756	25.7
Irwin	148	2.1	398	31.6	95.7	1 012 070	2 542	182 375	117.5	314 944	86.3	13.7	52.5	33.0	4 677	71.0
Jackson	77	-8.8	100	0.3	17.7	553 712	5 539	69 008	189.4	244 758	2.9	97.1	39.7	20.8	502	14.7
Jasper	44	-22.3	183	0.4	8.1	634 649	3 462	64 134	25.2	105 586	13.7	86.3	28.0	4.2	114	9.2
Jeff Davis	79	35.7	411	9.8	44.5	1 364 479	3 321	119 953	51.9	270 260	78.6	21.4	43.8	26.0	1 115	49.0
Jefferson	146	33.7	407	22.3	74.7	812 567	1 998	116 911	72.9	203 567	72.7	27.3	43.0	22.6	2 695	65.4
Jenkins	91	7.9	408	14.2	44.1	766 795	1 879	141 826	37.5	167 295	90.5	9.5	37.5	20.5	1 808	68.3
Johnson	57	-14.2	224	1.7	15.1	401 690	1 796	53 239	6.7	26 443	78.9	21.2	28.2	3.9	405	45.9
Jones	23	-28.9	132	0.0	6.3	417 766	3 176	68 857	10.4	59 269	5.3	94.7	23.4	5.1	156	9.1
Lamar	35	-0.6	141	1.7	12.0	540 194	3 837	77 290	54.4	215 821	19.7	80.3	34.9	14.3	268	21.4
Lanier	42	-21.7	484	6.9	19.7	1 649 140	3 408	207 430	21.2	246 209	98.1	1.9	39.5	25.6	824	58.1
Laurens	184	11.7	265	10.3	60.7	544 447	2 051	74 219	35.9	51 713	84.5	15.5	31.0	7.8	2 023	61.1
Lee	105	-16.5	549	16.9	52.7	1 579 948	2 877	164 563	72.5	377 734	D	D	39.6	19.3	1 529	59.9
Liberty	6	-33.7	135	0.0	0.6	285 370	2 111	33 000	0.3	6 761	47.9	52.1	28.3	0.0	23	17.4
Lincoln	24	-14.5	157	0.0	3.6	436 273	2 772	62 560	4.1	27 020	12.9	87.1	22.7	3.3	127	20.7
Long	10	-21.9	153	D	2.8	377 328	2 463	58 806	11.5	172 179	6.1	93.9	35.8	11.9	120	40.3
Lowndes	65	-4.4	158	8.0	25.4	559 107	3 538	72 920	31.1	75 786	79.1	20.9	30.4	7.8	464	40.1
Lumpkin	17	-21.1	79	0.1	3.0	710 636	8 994	47 768	52.5	238 436	3.8	96.2	37.7	18.6	71	6.8
McDuffie	38	5.2	183	0.3	8.2	523 361	2 866	40 394	27.8	133 582	D	D	26.0	4.3	251	14.4
McIntosh	17	87.3	305	0.3	1.0	786 375	2 581	88 643	3.5	62 732	63.5	36.5	37.5	12.5	5	5.4
Macon	101	-17.4	362	29.3	53.9	928 871	2 563	145 670	172.5	618 305	21.0	79.0	51.3	33.7	2 301	58.4
Madison	71	-6.9	96	0.2	19.5	536 699	5 616	54 460	213.3	286 311	1.4	98.6	43.4	21.9	611	16.8
Marion	47	1.6	233	2.1	13.2	524 025	2 246	69 227	27.4	134 818	20.9	79.1	33.5	9.9	367	41.9
Meriwether	62	-23.8	210	0.9	16.0	666 929	3 171	63 573	12.4	42 003	46.0	54.0	28.1	5.8	287	16.6
Miller	96	-5.9	523	31.7	61.0	1 289 738	2 465	233 066	69.8	381 339	91.7	8.3	63.4	36.6	2 746	67.2
Mitchell	191	-6.5	431	67.2	117.4	1 233 991	2 860	189 664	277.8	627 196	51.4	48.6	54.2	34.5	4 902	57.8
Monroe	34	-12.2	189	0.0	5.3	642 836	3 410	79 377	37.3	203 885	2.2	97.8	27.9	9.8	354	18.0
Montgomery	58	11.9	252	5.0	18.1	435 651	1 728	75 183	14.3	62 358	85.3	14.7	25.8	8.7	795	61.6
Morgan	95	2.3	165	1.4	30.0	722 206	4 371	118 593	103.0	180 004	6.9	93.1	37.6	16.1	858	32.9
Murray	47	17.6	147	0.6	18.8	629 225	4 288	81 572	78.7	246 072	14.2	85.8	40.0	17.5	273	16.6
Muscogee	4	-44.5	194	0.0	2.0	997 818	5 137	43 500	0.1	2 273	34.0	66.0	0.0	0.0	6	22.7
Newton	41	5.7	143	0.1	8.8	603 568	4 224	46 418	D	D	D	D	27.4	2.5	81	12.3
Oconee	45	-7.2	121	2.1	12.7	872 227	7 223	56 709	73.7	196 496	32.0	68.0	34.7	13.9	336	30.4
Oglethorpe	81	-6.7	199	0.7	17.2	644 724	3 239	78 283	180.7	445 118	4.6	95.4	43.3	27.3	697	24.4
Paulding	8	-26.7	59	0.0	2.4	385 641	6 544	37 458	13.9	97 789	3.6	96.4	23.9	4.9	8	8.5
Peach	35	-11.7	186	4.7	22.2	743 532	3 999	102 589	31.0	163 116	94.4	5.6	26.3	8.9	307	19.5
Pickens	17	-29.1	64	0.0	4.0	431 542	6 715	42 969	72.6	277 233	1.4	98.6	29.4	15.6	22	2.3
Pierce	78	9.0	220	10.8	44.9	523 298	2 381	125 357	64.4	180 787	61.1	38.9	42.7	16.9	2 363	46.3
Pike	38	-17.4	129	0.6	9.0	469 351	3 650	40 432	11.1	37 419	22.3	77.7	22.0	2.7	248	22.0
Polk	45	2.5	127	0.0	13.7	459 448	3 606	51 759	35.1	99 442	8.6	91.4	27.8	6.8	437	18.7
Pulaski	63	9.8	355	19.5	43.7	929 739	2 617	236 636	76.2	433 119	64.8	35.2	35.2	27.3	1 512	60.8

Table B. States and Counties — **Water Use, Wholesale Trade, Retail Trade, and Real Estate**

STATE County	Water use, 2010 Total water withdrawn (mil gal/day)	Gallons withdrawn per person per day	Wholesale trade,[1] 2012 Number of establish-ments	Number of employees	Sales (mil dol)	Annual payroll (mil dol)	Retail trade,[2] 2012 Number of establish-ments	Number of employees	Sales (mil dol)	Annual payroll (mil dol)	Real estate and rental and leasing,[2] 2012 Number of establish-ments	Number of employees	Receipts (mil dol)	Annual payroll (mil dol)
	133	134	135	136	137	138	139	140	141	142	143	144	145	146
GEORGIA—Cont'd														
Effingham	122.8	2 350	11	D	D	D	107	1 290	358.5	28.6	29	D	D	D
Elbert	3.5	172	41	309	61.8	8.3	79	611	142.0	13.1	3	D	D	D
Emanuel	6.6	292	18	143	89.1	4.2	82	778	203.3	16.4	15	D	D	D
Evans	5.0	455	5	33	4.4	0.6	56	453	178.8	12.5	3	11	1.6	0.2
Fannin	9.3	391	18	73	21.1	2.5	104	943	256.6	20.3	29	55	11.2	1.4
Fayette	12.9	121	168	1 664	1 205.2	90.0	407	6 588	1 453.7	139.4	176	565	79.3	17.3
Floyd	474.7	4 928	74	812	691.5	33.8	386	3 986	1 022.4	89.3	76	252	41.7	8.2
Forsyth	27.4	156	384	5 014	3 722.6	349.7	581	8 463	2 366.8	230.9	232	507	105.3	21.6
Franklin	4.7	214	23	257	105.8	7.1	91	881	270.7	17.3	9	12	2.0	0.3
Fulton	208.5	227	1 496	27 530	29 149.1	1 970.4	3 368	49 050	13 382.7	1 292.8	2 068	17 597	5 968.3	1 241.3
Gilmer	6.8	240	23	134	63.5	4.3	91	1 103	291.8	23.6	32	53	8.6	1.4
Glascock	0.4	130	NA	NA	NA	NA	5	14	5.7	0.3	NA	NA	NA	NA
Glynn	64.6	811	66	446	270.0	19.9	452	4 567	1 407.1	111.2	143	512	70.6	16.4
Gordon	13.5	245	65	D	D	D	240	2 311	627.5	48.5	42	125	26.5	3.5
Grady	9.8	392	27	408	364.4	16.8	79	754	184.7	16.0	20	46	4.4	1.2
Greene	4.5	280	15	65	38.6	3.8	72	695	206.0	16.1	21	42	5.5	1.7
Gwinnett	10.6	13	1 718	30 603	30 301.0	2 002.5	2 759	41 508	12 673.4	1 068.5	976	4 554	1 286.3	214.0
Habersham	12.2	283	35	179	99.2	6.3	158	1 795	462.1	41.2	22	50	6.8	0.9
Hall	100.2	558	235	3 265	9 022.6	173.1	579	7 640	2 231.9	193.5	164	450	116.5	17.1
Hancock	2.3	246	1	D	D	D	21	99	24.8	2.1	2	D	D	D
Haralson	3.9	136	20	142	52.6	7.4	84	851	321.2	23.5	8	D	D	D
Harris	7.1	222	9	D	D	D	43	260	70.2	4.9	13	D	D	D
Hart	4.2	168	15	154	33.9	6.0	75	849	173.6	15.9	10	D	D	D
Heard	50.5	4 267	NA	NA	NA	NA	18	84	22.8	2.3	4	D	D	D
Henry	43.0	211	98	1 182	833.8	74.2	550	9 005	2 402.5	200.7	164	590	112.3	19.0
Houston	34.2	245	48	377	220.6	13.3	442	6 625	1 762.8	150.4	124	447	68.8	12.0
Irwin	8.8	924	9	136	79.6	4.1	30	149	32.3	2.9	2	D	D	D
Jackson	13.5	224	53	953	574.8	36.2	232	2 594	1 482.5	54.3	44	75	15.9	2.1
Jasper	2.9	208	2	D	D	D	26	213	47.6	4.0	4	2	0.3	0.0
Jeff Davis	4.7	309	10	131	64.4	4.3	67	726	251.9	17.8	5	D	D	D
Jefferson	17.1	1 007	16	259	217.8	6.3	70	640	142.8	12.3	8	42	1.9	1.0
Jenkins	2.7	320	3	D	D	D	23	154	40.5	2.9	1	D	D	D
Johnson	2.0	196	6	29	19.2	0.9	24	148	37.1	3.0	NA	NA	NA	NA
Jones	10.3	358	7	D	D	D	51	423	97.0	8.4	13	D	D	D
Lamar	3.8	209	5	84	20.6	2.6	43	421	107.2	9.1	4	D	D	D
Lanier	2.0	199	4	D	D	D	21	D	D	D	1	D	D	D
Laurens	27.7	571	36	396	306.0	16.5	248	2 647	700.5	53.5	38	129	15.0	3.2
Lee	43.1	1 523	15	259	566.2	30.7	61	589	155.0	13.8	17	45	8.8	1.7
Liberty	16.6	262	11	D	D	D	171	1 938	564.1	40.9	48	183	24.6	5.5
Lincoln	1.8	229	7	33	11.1	0.8	22	160	38.8	3.2	4	D	D	D
Long	2.2	149	1	D	D	D	12	52	16.2	1.1	3	4	0.4	0.1
Lowndes	29.1	266	115	1 069	1 227.0	41.2	493	5 974	1 748.5	132.2	137	1 447	104.7	26.2
Lumpkin	3.3	110	6	38	12.7	1.1	81	767	192.3	18.3	24	D	D	D
McDuffie	7.0	318	9	29	21.9	1.3	103	1 027	295.0	23.9	15	54	5.4	1.3
McIntosh	1.6	110	4	D	D	D	58	433	98.1	7.4	5	8	1.0	0.1
Macon	30.8	2 088	12	76	265.1	4.4	43	227	43.5	4.6	3	4	0.6	0.1
Madison	3.3	116	13	D	D	D	57	403	135.7	8.7	13	D	D	D
Marion	3.0	347	2	D	D	D	22	104	35.3	2.2	NA	NA	NA	NA
Meriwether	1.7	79	6	19	16.8	0.8	90	622	116.1	11.8	5	D	D	D
Miller	46.8	7 639	5	63	54.6	2.4	33	237	77.4	5.0	5	7	0.3	0.1
Mitchell	67.4	2 870	22	394	172.9	10.2	96	735	156.8	14.6	9	21	1.6	0.5
Monroe	68.9	2 607	21	198	112.6	8.8	74	783	186.9	16.4	17	43	6.8	1.3
Montgomery	2.5	270	6	49	17.9	1.8	28	190	46.7	3.6	3	4	0.5	0.1
Morgan	5.4	299	15	190	117.0	6.6	69	893	309.2	19.5	18	31	4.2	1.0
Murray	3.9	97	26	399	123.5	17.1	90	711	198.1	16.0	12	D	D	D
Muscogee	44.1	232	157	1 843	1 550.1	80.6	796	11 371	2 847.8	250.2	237	1 461	258.1	55.7
Newton	14.3	143	53	518	278.2	20.9	210	2 778	747.3	60.7	52	182	36.8	6.6
Oconee	7.3	222	28	257	90.7	11.6	103	1 630	397.2	38.2	58	246	79.0	14.1
Oglethorpe	2.2	148	8	D	D	D	22	145	40.6	3.1	1	D	D	D
Paulding	2.1	15	62	254	161.7	12.2	253	4 075	1 174.4	96.7	51	284	55.7	15.5
Peach	10.4	376	23	D	D	D	102	806	296.1	19.0	21	60	11.6	2.3
Pickens	4.1	138	18	87	56.6	2.7	97	1 177	327.4	26.9	34	D	D	D
Pierce	4.1	219	16	D	D	D	65	414	114.4	8.9	9	17	7.9	0.6
Pike	8.1	453	11	D	D	D	31	165	36.2	3.1	5	D	D	D
Polk	7.8	187	15	D	D	D	131	1 399	326.5	30.8	18	85	8.2	1.9
Pulaski	18.0	1 495	2	D	D	D	37	358	87.6	9.6	6	12	0.7	0.2

1. Merchant wholesalers, except manufacturers' sales branches and offices. 2. Employer establishments.

Table B. States and Counties — Professional Services, Manufacturing, and Accommodation and Food Services

STATE County	Professional, scientific, and technical services, 2012				Manufacturing, 2012				Accommodation and food services, 2012			
	Number of establish-ments	Number of employees	Receipts (mil dol)	Annual payroll (mil dol)	Number of establish-ments	Number of employees	Receipts (mil dol)	Annual payroll (mil dol)	Number of establish-ments	Number of employees	Sales (mil dol)	Annual payroll (mil dol)
	147	148	149	150	151	152	153	154	155	156	157	158
GEORGIA—Cont'd												
Effingham	59	259	22.0	9.3	20	1 743	D	108.9	62	727	36.5	9.6
Elbert	21	50	4.1	1.2	89	2 028	379.6	70.7	24	325	13.7	4.0
Emanuel	26	D	D	D	29	1 694	706.3	50.5	32	416	17.4	4.2
Evans	11	54	3.9	1.6	14	1 769	D	45.0	14	D	D	D
Fannin	47	201	17.0	5.8	23	311	39.8	9.4	57	683	40.8	9.4
Fayette	422	2 127	275.0	130.8	92	2 230	853.7	112.5	217	4 857	211.5	64.6
Floyd	186	809	104.1	35.0	100	5 567	3 615.6	265.3	183	3 593	163.4	46.9
Forsyth	1 066	4 442	841.2	307.1	223	6 998	2 364.3	311.6	297	5 679	257.6	74.5
Franklin	25	109	8.1	2.7	30	1 204	434.5	49.5	43	643	29.4	7.9
Fulton	6 943	93 363	19 604.0	7 831.0	590	17 925	8 987.2	929.6	2 941	70 043	4 627.8	1 273.8
Gilmer	46	168	14.0	5.0	28	1 507	369.4	40.2	52	712	33.5	8.7
Glascock	2	D	D	D	NA	NA	NA	NA	1	D	D	D
Glynn	267	870	116.3	39.6	52	2 059	975.6	126.1	259	6 502	387.5	119.8
Gordon	62	337	66.0	23.5	104	6 492	2 499.1	260.5	92	1 371	70.9	18.0
Grady	19	61	7.3	1.9	19	511	141.2	21.4	28	310	14.2	3.2
Greene	39	92	12.0	4.0	11	414	557.6	19.3	29	887	56.7	19.0
Gwinnett	3 177	D	D	D	700	19 358	6 847.7	984.4	1 597	25 387	1 355.5	366.5
Habersham	63	257	36.1	8.6	52	4 122	1 219.0	137.8	75	1 145	53.5	13.7
Hall	402	D	D	D	225	17 020	7 629.2	647.1	283	4 742	298.3	67.4
Hancock	1	D	D	D	4	D	D	D	9	D	D	D
Haralson	33	86	8.3	2.2	33	1 364	834.1	55.2	38	D	D	D
Harris	30	D	D	D	18	D	D	D	28	523	25.0	6.7
Hart	38	104	11.9	3.6	28	2 115	602.1	91.1	29	D	D	D
Heard	4	D	D	D	10	419	D	17.4	8	D	D	D
Henry	294	1 380	198.3	57.5	69	2 872	2 035.1	137.2	340	5 783	281.5	73.1
Houston	271	3 288	437.6	169.5	54	3 105	2 051.0	129.1	270	5 726	259.0	69.1
Irwin	9	106	5.4	2.2	5	106	D	4.6	6	28	2.1	0.5
Jackson	99	468	75.5	21.3	70	4 420	1 924.1	183.9	68	1 015	46.9	13.3
Jasper	11	D	D	D	15	308	84.0	13.1	12	103	5.8	1.4
Jeff Davis	15	43	3.5	1.6	23	994	304.0	35.4	16	269	10.8	2.8
Jefferson	10	38	2.4	0.8	27	981	251.4	39.3	22	258	11.4	2.7
Jenkins	2	D	D	D	5	12	D	0.4	10	D	D	D
Johnson	6	16	0.8	0.2	5	167	14.9	3.5	9	54	2.7	0.6
Jones	20	68	5.1	1.8	12	68	D	3.2	20	D	D	D
Lamar	16	54	3.8	1.2	12	436	230.4	19.4	24	324	13.2	3.3
Lanier	4	17	0.8	0.2	4	124	D	3.4	12	103	4.6	1.4
Laurens	65	293	30.2	12.4	41	2 533	640.0	99.0	99	1 727	77.8	20.3
Lee	28	102	10.4	3.3	12	203	D	5.7	21	279	11.9	3.3
Liberty	74	D	D	D	18	D	D	D	99	D	D	D
Lincoln	10	D	D	D	4	93	10.7	2.8	15	D	D	D
Long	2	D	D	D	NA	NA	NA	NA	6	D	D	D
Lowndes	223	1 165	137.6	49.0	89	2 953	2 600.3	131.5	293	5 705	245.8	66.0
Lumpkin	59	159	15.4	5.5	25	569	100.0	22.3	59	974	46.7	12.3
McDuffie	24	D	D	D	32	1 627	554.4	63.2	38	515	24.7	5.9
McIntosh	18	23	2.6	0.7	7	28	D	0.9	29	402	17.9	4.3
Macon	6	13	1.1	0.3	16	547	478.5	31.9	14	D	D	D
Madison	25	75	5.9	1.9	24	210	21.4	7.3	20	D	D	D
Marion	4	D	D	D	3	D	D	D	6	16	1.3	0.2
Meriwether	13	43	3.6	1.3	14	688	320.5	27.6	29	D	D	D
Miller	8	22	1.7	0.6	NA	NA	NA	NA	10	78	3.1	0.7
Mitchell	20	253	17.4	7.8	16	2 928	D	80.3	29	354	18.6	5.1
Monroe	57	176	17.0	7.2	15	489	116.2	15.8	40	590	25.2	6.5
Montgomery	4	12	1.1	0.3	6	61	D	2.8	8	52	2.5	0.6
Morgan	44	479	56.9	19.3	26	1 097	314.1	50.0	52	830	35.4	10.3
Murray	19	D	D	D	65	3 656	1 306.6	122.5	41	D	D	D
Muscogee	350	2 520	301.3	113.9	122	6 977	1 937.2	297.0	442	10 453	519.3	149.2
Newton	103	392	43.9	12.8	77	3 759	1 854.8	186.1	108	1 718	112.9	23.6
Oconee	147	738	93.8	31.6	25	566	D	20.3	57	D	D	D
Oglethorpe	15	D	D	D	11	58	D	2.2	4	D	D	D
Paulding	165	565	65.6	22.3	48	775	191.0	31.9	129	2 645	121.1	33.8
Peach	27	101	7.6	2.7	28	D	D	D	55	764	40.8	9.4
Pickens	81	328	20.7	7.3	40	757	144.6	28.4	45	672	33.5	9.4
Pierce	15	73	4.7	1.6	14	380	D	13.6	21	239	11.2	2.9
Pike	18	D	D	D	8	160	D	6.0	9	D	D	D
Polk	36	113	9.5	2.8	31	3 234	D	132.0	65	903	40.6	10.9
Pulaski	14	56	4.9	2.1	3	D	D	D	18	229	10.5	2.3

1. Establishment subject to federal tax.

Table B. States and Counties — Health Care and Social Assistance, Other Services, Nonemployer Businesses, and Residential Construction

STATE County	Health care and social assistance, 2012				Other services, 2012				Nonemployer businesses, 2015		Value of residential construction authorized by building permits, 2016	
	Number of establishments	Number of employees	Receipts (mil dol)	Annual payroll (mil dol)	Number of establishments	Number of employees	Receipts (mil dol)	Annual payroll (mil dol)	Number	Receipts (mil dol)	New Construction ($1,000)	Number of housing units
	159	160	161	162	163	164	165	166	167	168	169	170
GEORGIA—Cont'd												
Effingham	57	D	D	D	41	D	D	D	3 491	136.3	142 667	580
Elbert	33	D	D	D	19	55	6.1	1.2	1 470	56.4	3 258	21
Emanuel	50	875	69.5	26.3	26	87	9.5	2.1	1 817	71.0	558	9
Evans	19	482	38.8	14.8	14	69	5.6	2.0	705	23.1	1 819	14
Fannin	66	1 039	115.7	39.3	29	106	9.7	2.4	2 736	127.1	52 708	261
Fayette	369	5 006	692.1	256.5	226	1 441	123.1	37.0	10 518	457.8	116 968	437
Floyd	281	8 058	1 049.2	412.6	104	831	64.9	19.5	6 891	252.9	30 055	226
Forsyth	463	6 830	704.5	283.8	307	1 541	188.7	50.8	19 752	1 041.9	437 059	3 515
Franklin	42	711	67.5	27.8	27	172	41.0	5.3	1 617	63.2	6 145	40
Fulton	3 542	71 584	9 875.8	3 610.7	2 108	21 451	3 833.9	763.1	106 684	5 440.4	1 918 886	11 411
Gilmer	46	577	46.2	20.2	37	169	16.4	4.8	2 563	102.2	29 518	128
Glascock	5	D	D	D	3	4	0.3	0.0	181	7.5	NA	NA
Glynn	262	5 031	645.8	235.5	141	746	84.3	17.9	6 633	298.6	145 812	483
Gordon	66	1 518	207.6	64.2	44	D	D	D	3 524	167.5	15 991	103
Grady	33	447	43.4	12.9	25	81	10.3	2.1	1 453	49.1	5 147	27
Greene	49	568	48.2	19.2	23	105	8.9	3.3	1 494	72.6	83 936	188
Gwinnett	1 834	25 079	2 700.3	1 067.6	1 382	8 424	840.6	245.4	99 862	4 118.1	613 000	3 977
Habersham	85	1 360	108.1	48.2	47	187	13.7	4.2	2 991	110.3	19 040	96
Hall	443	9 275	1 297.8	493.4	246	1 193	123.8	32.4	14 989	667.9	250 634	1 578
Hancock	6	D	D	D	7	D	D	D	547	12.2	2 528	19
Haralson	39	699	64.2	24.3	36	D	D	D	2 106	81.9	9 390	43
Harris	24	231	16.5	6.2	14	D	D	D	2 376	109.4	42 575	180
Hart	33	567	45.5	17.4	27	115	10.4	2.2	1 814	63.4	10 389	64
Heard	5	D	D	D	8	D	D	D	745	27.4	3 867	22
Henry	396	6 223	782.2	239.1	226	996	79.7	23.1	19 378	666.9	286 848	1 454
Houston	289	5 917	553.9	220.3	143	799	63.9	18.2	9 580	289.7	152 556	775
Irwin	20	758	42.8	20.1	7	25	3.5	0.8	601	21.0	1 655	19
Jackson	84	1 182	80.2	34.7	74	521	48.8	19.4	5 095	206.5	179 578	873
Jasper	14	D	D	D	7	29	1.5	0.5	1 041	42.8	8 306	62
Jeff Davis	18	316	24.0	9.5	10	19	1.6	0.3	874	31.7	145	2
Jefferson	22	430	32.2	16.4	14	D	D	D	1 196	38.5	80	1
Jenkins	8	393	14.6	9.7	6	14	1.8	0.4	528	20.0	1 300	13
Johnson	11	314	21.2	8.9	8	D	D	D	562	20.2	0	0
Jones	33	D	D	D	20	71	16.5	2.2	1 925	74.1	3 437	23
Lamar	22	D	D	D	13	216	14.4	7.2	1 182	34.2	5 333	45
Lanier	10	D	D	D	4	D	D	D	545	21.3	1 756	16
Laurens	142	4 233	600.0	214.6	64	D	D	D	3 983	152.1	1 065	17
Lee	32	360	21.7	10.8	27	D	D	D	2 188	80.4	14 975	121
Liberty	76	2 026	249.2	101.0	66	D	D	D	2 848	83.9	62 839	276
Lincoln	6	D	D	D	10	D	D	D	534	20.6	5 160	24
Long	5	29	1.9	0.6	2	D	D	D	594	17.4	23 829	141
Lowndes	369	D	D	D	151	881	60.2	17.1	6 945	350.8	166 326	976
Lumpkin	52	612	54.6	23.0	28	75	7.0	1.7	2 494	94.0	30 159	173
McDuffie	51	970	76.8	24.9	28	114	16.0	3.6	1 390	47.1	3 277	23
McIntosh	14	54	3.6	1.6	13	36	2.5	0.7	944	39.1	8 945	41
Macon	18	425	33.8	11.5	8	D	D	D	824	21.3	766	4
Madison	25	D	D	D	15	D	D	D	2 155	81.3	1 745	8
Marion	7	D	D	D	2	D	D	D	410	14.4	1 165	13
Meriwether	28	948	63.0	29.4	16	39	3.6	0.7	1 555	46.1	7 893	36
Miller	12	318	24.5	10.7	6	23	2.4	0.5	330	10.9	250	1
Mitchell	25	472	36.4	14.8	29	117	8.3	2.5	1 423	45.2	1 611	11
Monroe	55	D	D	D	29	D	D	D	2 095	87.4	23 522	106
Montgomery	4	24	1.2	0.5	3	4	0.2	0.1	560	19.6	1 939	14
Morgan	34	456	33.1	13.9	32	128	13.4	3.2	1 973	92.9	22 999	105
Murray	33	469	42.8	17.3	24	103	8.5	2.9	1 890	79.2	9 478	42
Muscogee	590	14 823	1 454.8	578.6	322	2 293	223.3	62.4	12 982	427.3	75 763	384
Newton	122	2 039	189.0	77.1	79	336	25.9	7.4	9 366	288.3	74 966	333
Oconee	126	1 525	127.0	56.1	53	380	44.3	11.8	3 795	210.4	100 576	418
Oglethorpe	12	D	D	D	11	D	D	D	1 002	34.6	585	39
Paulding	143	2 000	184.6	69.1	124	455	38.3	11.0	11 842	411.4	141 497	1 339
Peach	42	618	39.3	16.8	30	171	14.6	4.4	1 924	71.0	9 348	56
Pickens	64	1 186	118.7	48.4	39	D	D	D	3 049	140.4	30 277	116
Pierce	22	263	13.8	6.6	24	66	4.7	1.2	1 197	42.6	3 612	34
Pike	17	D	D	D	17	D	D	D	1 525	64.6	12 913	76
Polk	52	781	57.6	25.9	40	395	40.3	10.9	2 664	84.7	15 932	106
Pulaski	20	715	60.9	27.3	8	13	1.0	0.3	691	18.2	1 157	8

Table B. States and Counties — Government Employment and Payroll, and Local Government Finances

	Government employment and payroll, 2012									Local government finances, 2012				
			March payroll (percent of total)							General revenue				
												Taxes		
													Per capita[1] (dollars)	
STATE County	Full-time equivalent employees	March payroll (dollars)	Administration, judicial, and legal	Police and Corrections	Fire Protection	Highways and transportation	Health and Welfare	Natural resources and utilities	Education and libraries	Total (mil dol)	Inter-governmental (mil dol)	Total (mil dol)	Total	Property
	171	172	173	174	175	176	177	178	179	180	181	182	183	184
GEORGIA—Cont'd														
Effingham	2 486	7 934 109	4.0	6.9	1.7	0.8	16.1	2.9	65.1	191.3	66.5	72.8	1 366	843
Elbert	1 023	2 910 130	6.0	7.4	1.7	2.3	20.0	5.2	54.4	74.4	24.4	21.3	1 084	728
Emanuel	1 380	4 099 290	4.7	6.6	1.2	3.3	32.4	1.6	49.5	134.4	38.4	25.2	1 102	650
Evans	411	1 161 088	7.5	7.5	1.2	2.3	0.9	7.4	72.6	32.8	16.8	10.9	1 022	548
Fannin	760	2 415 781	6.9	7.2	1.6	5.7	4.3	5.2	68.0	63.1	21.3	34.9	1 484	927
Fayette	4 677	16 227 469	6.0	9.6	6.9	2.0	0.0	3.4	70.7	331.0	78.7	204.0	1 897	1 391
Floyd	3 631	12 476 709	5.7	9.3	4.2	4.2	1.7	5.5	67.7	620.3	284.0	151.4	1 574	957
Forsyth	5 440	15 768 647	8.4	9.3	5.1	2.1	0.8	5.4	66.7	548.8	158.2	323.5	1 721	1 160
Franklin	907	2 573 274	6.9	12.5	0.0	2.6	4.2	5.9	64.4	64.2	24.6	29.2	1 334	759
Fulton	43 801	165 333 873	9.4	12.0	4.7	15.4	3.4	6.1	47.6	5 335.6	1 131.9	2 739.7	2 802	1 941
Gilmer	920	2 851 278	9.0	12.0	2.0	3.3	4.8	1.4	67.0	76.9	24.5	43.0	1 524	1 036
Glascock	129	342 830	4.9	4.2	0.0	3.5	1.7	4.2	80.7	8.3	4.5	3.0	970	705
Glynn	4 919	18 972 711	4.6	6.1	2.8	0.9	46.3	3.8	35.3	515.4	78.5	158.8	1 960	1 234
Gordon	2 032	7 129 189	6.2	7.7	4.0	2.9	0.3	5.2	71.1	172.1	62.6	78.3	1 404	810
Grady	1 132	2 874 976	6.5	7.8	2.0	1.9	2.7	6.1	69.6	66.6	29.6	25.7	1 009	623
Greene	269	680 713	19.0	33.4	1.8	17.6	6.5	14.2	0.0	58.7	12.0	38.3	2 379	1 693
Gwinnett	27 778	103 170 776	5.7	8.0	3.3	0.8	1.5	3.8	75.9	2 774.6	950.1	1 287.6	1 529	1 100
Habersham	3 305	10 231 305	4.4	3.6	1.2	1.1	19.8	2.2	67.1	181.0	64.5	53.3	1 225	714
Hall	6 523	22 620 107	6.4	9.1	7.3	1.6	4.4	4.9	65.4	563.5	217.3	266.2	1 436	890
Hancock	382	962 206	6.0	11.2	0.0	2.9	5.0	4.4	68.0	28.6	10.2	16.3	1 811	1 568
Haralson	1 277	3 955 709	6.4	9.3	4.8	2.9	2.1	6.3	67.7	88.2	38.2	39.1	1 375	852
Harris	1 034	3 285 198	4.4	8.8	0.1	2.2	4.9	3.4	74.7	80.5	24.1	43.3	1 331	974
Hart	900	2 651 269	5.4	6.4	1.0	2.6	1.4	3.1	73.5	59.3	20.8	30.8	1 208	771
Heard	504	1 507 476	3.9	8.3	9.3	3.8	1.5	6.9	62.5	42.2	12.2	27.6	2 376	938
Henry	7 960	25 579 364	7.4	7.5	4.5	1.4	1.0	5.6	71.5	718.9	328.0	305.3	1 460	969
Houston	5 500	18 181 428	5.3	9.1	2.9	2.2	2.3	3.3	73.1	461.3	189.3	203.0	1 389	803
Irwin	623	2 698 793	4.3	21.9	4.3	7.8	23.1	6.2	32.3	40.3	14.0	9.7	1 013	702
Jackson	2 530	7 918 962	6.3	11.0	0.4	1.4	3.5	4.7	71.2	198.5	64.2	107.0	1 767	1 201
Jasper	596	1 714 273	5.5	6.8	0.6	0.7	23.1	3.8	56.7	44.3	14.2	16.0	1 176	880
Jeff Davis	671	2 209 748	5.1	5.1	1.9	1.6	22.2	2.5	60.6	64.7	22.7	14.5	959	451
Jefferson	926	2 709 948	7.4	10.5	1.1	0.9	22.0	2.9	53.3	61.2	24.1	20.9	1 273	787
Jenkins	429	1 431 503	7.7	9.7	1.7	6.7	21.4	3.0	48.9	28.0	15.0	8.5	923	581
Johnson	327	789 670	7.1	8.8	1.3	2.1	5.8	3.8	70.5	20.2	10.3	7.8	788	516
Jones	1 142	2 976 385	4.8	7.6	0.3	3.1	1.4	2.8	79.5	77.2	38.1	33.3	1 165	839
Lamar	637	1 432 522	7.9	19.7	2.3	3.0	3.1	7.3	55.8	44.4	15.3	19.3	1 069	698
Lanier	309	907 306	5.1	6.3	0.4	4.9	0.6	0.8	81.4	22.8	12.3	8.7	840	599
Laurens	2 333	6 680 665	4.4	7.5	2.2	2.2	14.7	4.0	62.8	168.6	86.7	55.3	1 151	626
Lee	1 281	3 572 458	6.0	9.8	3.1	2.1	3.3	1.7	73.1	83.1	33.8	38.4	1 337	897
Liberty	2 620	8 517 567	5.5	9.7	1.7	0.8	17.6	1.9	58.9	231.2	86.6	70.0	1 070	640
Lincoln	343	943 673	7.0	8.3	0.1	4.6	4.7	4.1	70.2	24.9	9.7	11.6	1 495	1 126
Long	484	1 237 309	6.2	6.7	0.0	3.9	0.5	1.1	81.0	41.0	26.8	10.9	678	497
Lowndes	6 045	19 639 563	3.1	7.2	1.9	1.4	42.6	2.7	39.9	581.5	129.5	139.2	1 215	637
Lumpkin	914	2 710 822	6.9	9.8	4.9	4.4	1.3	4.6	66.2	65.6	21.0	35.6	1 164	771
McDuffie	1 115	3 376 988	4.5	5.8	1.9	1.8	17.5	5.3	60.7	89.6	43.8	29.4	1 357	750
McIntosh	543	1 451 916	10.8	16.2	0.3	3.5	4.5	2.5	58.6	37.8	12.8	19.7	1 422	1 061
Macon	468	1 330 912	6.2	9.8	1.1	3.9	3.2	8.0	66.6	35.4	15.4	15.7	1 103	778
Madison	1 012	3 107 942	5.4	7.1	0.0	1.8	4.3	1.4	78.7	69.1	34.5	27.9	998	714
Marion	276	887 260	6.5	7.1	0.0	4.2	3.2	3.5	74.6	27.1	16.3	8.1	933	664
Meriwether	1 203	3 245 971	5.5	9.3	0.8	1.8	22.0	3.1	55.0	84.2	30.1	25.7	1 210	867
Miller	558	1 697 352	5.4	6.0	0.2	1.6	45.2	3.2	35.5	39.7	21.9	7.8	1 308	873
Mitchell	1 021	2 901 088	6.0	10.9	2.5	2.8	3.0	6.3	61.9	77.9	28.7	31.6	1 366	899
Monroe	1 172	3 579 175	4.2	11.4	1.2	4.4	12.1	3.3	61.1	93.8	21.4	53.1	1 992	1 362
Montgomery	230	587 331	8.4	7.4	0.5	6.6	3.1	1.4	72.5	17.7	8.0	7.4	835	546
Morgan	953	3 020 860	6.6	5.9	0.9	3.0	17.7	3.8	59.5	58.7	20.9	31.5	1 763	1 132
Murray	1 247	3 919 836	4.1	6.6	2.6	2.5	1.1	1.8	77.8	92.6	46.9	36.7	932	519
Muscogee	9 038	29 241 738	4.1	12.0	4.8	2.6	7.5	7.2	60.0	741.6	293.1	273.0	1 376	1 010
Newton	4 446	13 949 576	4.8	7.6	3.4	1.7	14.6	4.6	61.7	372.2	178.8	121.8	1 200	823
Oconee	1 252	3 915 501	7.1	6.7	0.4	2.2	1.3	3.9	74.9	100.2	32.7	57.1	1 698	1 106
Oglethorpe	532	1 614 557	5.6	5.6	0.8	1.8	3.5	1.4	81.2	31.8	13.7	15.1	1 034	808
Paulding	5 393	14 332 833	3.2	7.3	2.8	1.5	0.5	2.6	80.1	356.7	171.7	150.3	1 038	665
Peach	1 087	3 443 843	6.7	12.0	3.0	1.1	15.5	2.4	56.5	102.9	28.0	38.7	1 399	851
Pickens	1 155	3 419 594	7.3	9.4	3.0	2.8	3.9	5.3	64.6	83.1	24.1	47.4	1 618	1 120
Pierce	624	2 237 998	1.9	4.1	0.0	2.0	2.7	2.2	84.6	46.0	24.2	18.2	963	622
Pike	638	1 686 429	6.9	9.0	0.0	3.2	0.0	2.0	78.9	39.8	18.6	17.9	1 005	826
Polk	1 548	4 904 910	5.6	10.2	2.6	2.4	1.4	4.0	66.8	116.2	53.1	48.3	1 172	717
Pulaski	358	909 842	9.2	11.0	3.6	4.3	1.3	4.5	64.6	27.3	12.1	11.6	990	649

1. Based on the resident population estimated as of July 1 of the year shown.

Table B. States and Counties — Local Government Finances, Government Employment, and Income Taxes

STATE County	Local government finances, 2012 (cont.)									Government employment, 2015			Individual income tax returns, 2014		
	Direct general expenditure							Debt outstanding							
			Percent of total for:												
	Total (mil dol)	Per capita¹ (dollars)	Education	Health and hospitals	Police protection	Public welfare	Highways	Total (mil dol)	Per capita¹ (dollars)	Federal civilian	Federal military	State and local	Number of returns	Mean adjusted gross income	Mean income tax
	185	186	187	188	189	190	191	192	193	194	195	196	197	198	199

GEORGIA—Cont'd

STATE County	185	186	187	188	189	190	191	192	193	194	195	196	197	198	199
Effingham	215.1	4 037	47.5	28.2	3.7	0.3	2.7	102.6	1 925	66	159	2 873	24 030	53 071	4 980
Elbert	78.1	3 967	39.3	26.1	4.2	0.7	4.5	17.7	901	118	53	1 116	8 030	37 781	3 000
Emanuel	128.4	5 609	29.9	50.2	2.4	0.2	2.9	34.5	1 507	62	61	1 997	8 860	34 400	2 457
Evans	39.2	3 664	67.4	1.1	4.4	0.0	3.4	8.1	760	38	29	639	4 290	38 770	3 014
Fannin	65.9	2 803	54.6	3.5	4.0	0.5	11.3	12.3	524	47	68	894	9 810	41 097	4 180
Fayette	360.7	3 354	57.2	1.1	6.8	0.2	4.4	279.1	2 596	494	350	4 468	52 000	82 985	11 816
Floyd	658.4	6 846	27.4	47.2	2.2	0.1	2.6	238.0	2 474	207	261	5 521	39 980	48 567	5 057
Forsyth	529.3	2 816	59.8	0.4	6.1	0.5	4.9	349.8	1 861	180	594	6 911	87 630	93 455	13 871
Franklin	58.5	2 670	56.1	3.0	9.3	0.4	6.3	16.0	730	48	60	1 069	8 820	39 814	3 335
Fulton	4 905.9	5 017	36.2	1.9	6.5	2.3	2.4	20 181.5	20 640	24 511	2 964	78 071	457 280	98 695	18 569
Gilmer	71.0	2 520	60.5	0.4	6.0	0.2	2.7	75.3	2 672	84	82	1 163	11 930	43 249	4 244
Glascock	8.8	2 789	73.4	1.9	3.4	1.5	6.9	0.4	113	D	D	184	1 070	39 874	2 923
Glynn	522.7	6 452	28.7	45.8	4.4	0.1	1.6	353.6	4 364	1 743	271	6 939	37 020	55 921	7 265
Gordon	172.7	3 096	59.5	1.2	6.0	0.4	3.7	114.7	2 057	87	156	2 667	22 580	43 731	4 058
Grady	73.3	2 881	53.7	1.8	4.8	0.0	6.5	41.6	1 635	77	70	1 129	10 000	38 162	3 152
Greene	66.3	4 122	48.1	0.3	8.8	1.2	6.7	33.3	2 068	42	46	765	7 310	80 616	12 721
Gwinnett	2 810.6	3 338	58.1	1.5	5.7	0.1	4.5	3 709.8	4 406	2 427	2 602	33 124	400 000	55 313	6 357
Habersham	168.2	3 865	41.0	30.6	3.5	0.3	3.1	147.2	3 382	106	116	2 837	17 270	45 636	4 292
Hall	566.0	3 053	55.8	6.1	4.5	0.8	2.5	1 522.9	8 213	467	535	10 076	82 640	55 230	6 595
Hancock	25.7	2 852	59.1	3.1	5.4	1.7	5.0	11.1	1 235	15	20	767	3 170	33 291	2 528
Haralson	90.4	3 182	64.8	1.4	5.5	0.3	2.9	42.6	1 502	43	80	1 531	11 120	43 908	3 676
Harris	77.2	2 371	65.4	3.4	5.0	0.0	4.2	45.3	1 392	57	92	1 190	13 940	64 424	7 237
Hart	58.4	2 289	53.1	3.2	5.6	0.4	4.4	16.0	628	81	70	1 065	10 020	42 960	4 252
Heard	36.5	3 133	56.5	4.4	5.1	2.9	4.3	21.9	1 878	13	32	621	4 160	41 089	3 419
Henry	565.4	2 705	60.8	0.4	5.5	0.9	6.1	704.9	3 372	915	609	7 991	95 730	50 677	5 054
Houston	446.8	3 057	57.5	4.7	6.4	0.0	5.5	209.8	1 435	14 779	3 785	9 461	67 290	51 121	4 971
Irwin	42.7	4 450	40.9	35.7	4.1	0.2	7.1	10.1	1 048	23	24	678	3 560	39 098	3 344
Jackson	211.8	3 497	53.3	2.4	5.8	0.3	7.5	505.9	8 352	142	175	2 787	26 780	50 682	4 952
Jasper	43.8	3 215	45.0	24.5	4.1	0.6	6.1	15.0	1 099	18	38	639	5 490	43 857	3 902
Jeff Davis	60.0	3 960	38.1	36.0	3.5	0.2	7.6	20.3	1 337	28	42	803	5 500	42 891	4 809
Jefferson	64.9	3 950	43.6	21.7	4.9	1.0	3.6	24.3	1 480	44	43	1 005	6 900	35 377	2 750
Jenkins	26.9	2 917	51.4	4.2	4.4	0.8	9.3	4.9	533	20	22	549	2 980	33 498	2 370
Johnson	19.4	1 960	61.3	3.0	5.3	0.3	6.1	0.9	88	16	22	631	2 890	35 562	2 520
Jones	72.0	2 520	65.4	0.6	5.4	0.6	6.1	11.5	403	32	79	1 148	11 780	48 707	4 383
Lamar	47.0	2 605	52.2	0.8	7.4	0.7	3.3	56.0	3 100	38	48	1 100	7 090	40 284	3 216
Lanier	22.1	2 125	69.1	0.5	7.1	0.4	6.2	11.4	1 096	16	28	600	3 330	34 603	2 291
Laurens	182.6	3 801	47.1	15.1	4.8	0.3	4.0	54.7	1 138	1 468	132	2 795	19 890	42 402	3 912
Lee	84.5	2 939	66.3	3.3	5.2	0.0	3.2	70.7	2 459	44	79	1 500	13 190	59 431	6 381
Liberty	250.0	3 818	53.4	19.3	4.8	0.0	2.3	82.6	1 262	3 890	16 241	3 177	26 430	37 766	2 543
Lincoln	23.8	3 082	54.0	3.7	3.6	2.7	6.6	35.4	4 577	14	21	396	3 200	43 436	3 783
Long	36.7	2 284	68.5	0.5	5.4	1.5	8.2	6.7	417	11	49	683	5 150	37 416	2 182
Lowndes	649.1	5 667	24.9	53.1	3.9	0.7	2.3	369.8	3 228	1 124	4 538	10 255	45 130	43 522	4 564
Lumpkin	67.2	2 197	60.3	1.9	7.6	0.1	3.6	75.2	2 455	73	127	2 475	11 600	48 316	4 819
McDuffie	90.0	4 153	49.0	21.0	4.1	1.3	2.2	31.7	1 464	27	140	1 244	9 220	39 962	3 296
McIntosh	35.7	2 581	47.5	2.9	9.5	0.0	4.1	3.4	246	25	39	627	4 860	41 099	3 810
Macon	36.4	2 549	51.7	1.7	6.1	0.5	5.1	4.5	314	24	33	836	4 550	33 091	2 419
Madison	72.1	2 583	67.3	2.6	3.1	0.5	4.4	51.6	1 850	43	79	1 156	11 550	43 553	3 702
Marion	31.7	3 643	77.5	1.8	2.4	2.2	1.7	21.1	2 425	24	24	340	2 790	37 909	3 384
Meriwether	85.0	3 997	44.3	21.9	5.5	0.2	2.8	60.8	2 859	47	59	1 345	9 030	38 252	3 009
Miller	38.7	6 487	24.8	50.2	3.2	0.1	3.5	25.7	4 303	18	16	752	2 270	39 276	3 952
Mitchell	87.6	3 783	42.9	4.0	5.8	0.0	7.0	58.1	2 509	78	57	1 497	8 360	36 019	2 791
Monroe	92.6	3 477	43.8	14.7	6.5	0.1	5.1	33.5	1 257	33	73	2 534	11 360	60 483	7 472
Montgomery	17.6	1 979	59.5	3.0	4.8	1.0	4.3	1.9	217	14	23	379	3 120	40 570	3 604
Morgan	72.8	4 070	44.7	20.5	4.7	0.9	5.4	29.9	1 674	36	50	1 101	8 300	55 453	6 832
Murray	90.2	2 289	67.5	2.4	4.0	0.9	5.5	39.4	1 001	94	110	1 311	14 940	38 641	3 021
Muscogee	832.5	4 196	45.9	7.7	5.9	2.3	4.4	677.3	3 413	6 617	4 109	13 047	87 690	47 221	5 125
Newton	383.8	3 782	52.5	20.5	4.2	0.0	2.1	387.3	3 816	215	291	4 301	44 460	42 600	3 617
Oconee	98.9	2 943	63.3	1.2	4.1	0.6	5.9	108.6	3 230	101	100	1 413	15 760	95 444	15 784
Oglethorpe	32.9	2 254	68.3	2.8	3.0	1.0	3.7	24.2	1 653	15	41	559	5 790	42 895	3 545
Paulding	341.1	2 355	68.6	0.9	5.0	0.1	7.3	260.6	1 800	123	426	4 869	62 780	52 263	4 872
Peach	89.7	3 247	45.2	13.6	6.8	0.2	2.5	47.6	1 722	104	77	1 956	11 340	43 478	4 018
Pickens	82.3	2 812	55.3	3.3	6.4	0.2	4.6	22.2	758	54	84	1 216	13 780	56 570	6 194
Pierce	44.8	2 375	64.8	2.3	3.1	0.8	6.5	18.5	982	48	53	715	7 570	43 189	4 039
Pike	37.6	2 114	69.3	2.4	7.0	0.2	3.7	11.8	662	28	50	724	7 400	52 241	5 071
Polk	111.7	2 712	59.9	1.2	7.3	0.3	4.7	44.4	1 079	67	115	1 566	16 230	38 958	2 892
Pulaski	35.2	3 007	42.6	2.6	5.9	0.2	5.4	5.9	508	18	29	676	3 680	41 489	4 088

1. Based on the resident population estimated as of July 1 of the year shown.

Table B. States and Counties — **Land Area and Population**

STATE/ County code	CBSA code[1]	County type[2]	STATE County	Land area,[3] (sq mi) 2016	Total persons 2016	Rank	Per square mile	White	Black	American Indian, Alaska Native	Asian and Pacific Islander	Percent Hispanic or Latino[4]	Under 5 years	5 to 17 years	18 to 24 years	25 to 34 years	35 to 44 years	45 to 54 years
				1	2	3	4	5	6	7	8	9	10	11	12	13	14	15
			GEORGIA—Cont'd															
13 237	...	6	Putnam	344.6	21 477	1 755	62.3	66.2	27.0	0.5	0.9	6.6	5.5	15.2	6.7	11.5	9.9	13.0
13 239	21640	9	Quitman	151.2	2 335	3 020	15.4	50.1	48.2	0.7	0.5	1.8	4.1	13.8	5.9	9.4	8.4	12.4
13 241	...	7	Rabun	370.1	16 559	2 005	44.7	89.0	1.9	1.1	1.2	8.2	4.5	13.2	7.1	10.2	10.6	12.6
13 243	...	6	Randolph	428.2	7 177	2 653	16.8	35.8	61.3	0.3	0.7	2.6	5.9	15.0	10.5	10.7	9.2	11.6
13 245	12260	2	Richmond	324.3	201 647	327	621.8	37.0	57.0	0.8	2.8	4.9	6.9	16.5	11.5	16.4	11.3	11.7
13 247	12060	1	Rockdale	129.8	89 355	649	688.4	34.7	53.9	0.7	2.5	10.3	5.9	19.4	9.1	11.5	12.4	14.8
13 249	11140	8	Schley	166.9	5 098	2 826	30.5	73.3	21.3	0.5	0.9	5.2	4.9	21.1	7.8	10.5	12.5	15.3
13 251	...	6	Screven	645.1	14 044	2 159	21.8	55.9	41.8	0.6	0.8	2.1	5.9	15.7	8.6	12.4	11.2	13.3
13 253	...	6	Seminole	235.2	8 468	2 555	36.0	62.2	34.4	0.6	0.9	3.1	5.6	15.8	8.1	9.9	10.7	13.0
13 255	12060	1	Spalding	195.9	64 806	816	330.8	60.6	34.3	0.7	1.4	4.6	6.3	17.6	8.3	13.1	12.0	12.7
13 257	45740	7	Stephens	179.1	25 751	1 573	143.8	84.6	12.4	0.8	1.2	3.2	6.3	16.1	9.9	11.2	10.9	13.0
13 259	...	8	Stewart	458.7	5 705	2 780	12.4	26.4	44.1	0.7	2.0	27.8	3.9	10.0	12.9	20.0	13.9	12.2
13 261	11140	8	Sumter	482.7	30 389	1 423	63.0	40.4	53.0	0.6	1.5	5.4	6.2	17.3	13.6	12.0	10.7	12.2
13 263	...	8	Talbot	391.4	6 171	2 738	15.8	41.5	55.9	0.8	0.5	2.6	4.3	14.1	7.0	9.8	10.0	15.3
13 265	...	8	Taliaferro	194.6	1 593	3 075	8.2	39.0	56.9	0.7	0.8	4.3	4.9	12.7	7.0	11.0	10.3	13.7
13 267	...	6	Tattnall	479.5	25 092	1 606	52.3	59.2	29.4	0.5	0.8	11.1	5.6	15.5	9.8	16.0	14.3	14.3
13 269	...	8	Taylor	376.7	8 232	2 577	21.9	58.3	38.8	0.5	0.9	2.5	5.1	15.2	8.6	11.1	11.5	14.2
13 271	...	7	Telfair	437.3	15 965	2 041	36.5	50.0	35.3	0.3	1.0	14.3	4.0	13.8	7.5	15.3	15.6	14.0
13 273	10500	3	Terrell	335.4	8 967	2 512	26.7	36.5	60.5	0.5	0.7	2.8	6.2	17.1	8.4	12.6	9.9	12.3
13 275	45620	4	Thomas	544.6	45 248	1 067	83.1	58.5	37.0	0.8	1.3	3.7	6.4	17.6	7.8	12.1	11.7	13.3
13 277	45700	5	Tift	260.9	40 828	1 158	156.5	57.2	29.9	0.5	1.7	11.8	7.1	17.6	11.4	13.1	12.2	12.2
13 279	47080	7	Toombs	364.0	27 196	1 523	74.7	61.9	26.2	0.5	1.2	11.5	7.3	19.7	8.4	12.4	11.9	12.3
13 281	...	9	Towns	166.5	11 391	2 333	68.4	95.3	1.4	0.7	0.9	2.5	3.5	9.8	13.1	7.3	7.6	10.3
13 283	...	7	Treutlen	199.4	6 637	2 701	33.3	64.8	32.6	0.5	0.5	2.5	6.0	18.1	9.2	13.2	11.9	12.4
13 285	29300	4	Troup	414.0	70 005	768	169.1	58.3	36.7	0.5	2.4	3.6	6.5	18.5	10.0	13.3	12.1	12.9
13 287	...	6	Turner	285.4	8 030	2 595	28.1	55.4	39.3	0.6	1.1	4.6	6.8	17.4	8.8	12.5	10.4	12.3
13 289	31420	3	Twiggs	358.4	8 171	2 582	22.8	55.7	41.8	0.7	0.6	2.3	5.1	14.5	6.8	11.1	10.0	14.2
13 291	...	9	Union	322.0	22 928	1 684	71.2	95.1	1.0	1.0	1.0	3.1	3.6	12.4	6.0	7.9	8.6	12.0
13 293	45580	6	Upson	323.4	26 335	1 548	81.4	68.5	28.8	0.7	1.0	2.4	6.2	16.2	8.4	11.4	11.5	13.7
13 295	16860	2	Walker	446.4	67 896	784	152.1	92.6	5.2	0.8	0.8	2.1	5.6	16.7	7.8	11.9	13.0	13.8
13 297	12060	1	Walton	325.7	90 184	642	276.9	76.8	17.9	0.7	1.9	4.2	6.3	19.0	8.4	11.9	12.6	14.8
13 299	48180	5	Ware	892.9	35 738	1 283	40.0	65.1	30.4	0.7	1.3	4.0	6.7	17.2	8.6	13.5	11.8	12.6
13 301	...	8	Warren	284.3	5 442	2 806	19.1	38.8	59.5	0.5	0.7	1.5	5.4	15.6	7.8	10.5	9.7	13.5
13 303	...	7	Washington	678.5	20 457	1 803	30.2	44.1	53.5	0.3	0.8	2.3	5.9	16.4	8.8	12.6	11.7	13.7
13 305	27700	6	Wayne	641.8	30 104	1 430	46.9	73.1	20.6	0.8	1.0	6.3	6.7	17.9	7.8	13.5	12.8	13.4
13 307	...	8	Webster	209.1	2 599	2 997	12.4	53.4	42.8	0.6	0.8	3.9	4.7	15.7	7.7	9.3	10.6	15.3
13 309	...	9	Wheeler	295.5	7 978	2 600	27.0	57.2	37.9	0.4	0.4	5.3	4.2	12.7	10.0	18.1	15.3	14.9
13 311	...	6	White	240.7	28 884	1 461	120.0	93.7	2.7	1.1	0.8	3.2	4.8	15.7	8.9	10.2	11.0	13.4
13 313	19140	8	Whitfield	290.5	104 589	572	360.0	60.2	4.3	0.6	1.8	34.4	6.8	20.0	9.3	13.3	12.9	13.5
13 315	...	8	Wilcox	377.7	8 761	2 527	23.2	59.9	35.1	0.8	0.9	4.7	5.2	14.1	8.8	15.1	14.0	14.0
13 317	...	6	Wilkes	469.5	9 805	2 447	20.9	53.0	42.8	0.5	1.0	4.5	5.5	16.0	7.4	10.2	10.5	13.4
13 319	...	8	Wilkinson	447.3	9 104	2 498	20.4	57.8	39.4	0.6	0.8	2.6	5.5	17.5	7.5	11.1	10.6	14.1
13 321	10500	3	Worth	570.7	20 748	1 787	36.4	68.6	28.7	0.7	0.9	2.3	6.0	17.0	7.8	12.3	11.0	13.5
15 000	...	0	**HAWAII**	6 422.5	1 428 557	X	222.4	36.3	3.0	1.7	75.1	10.4	6.4	15.2	9.0	14.6	12.4	12.5
15 001	25900	5	Hawaii	4 028.5	198 449	332	49.3	47.9	1.7	2.5	68.2	12.6	6.2	15.6	7.6	12.2	11.5	12.0
15 003	46520	2	Honolulu	600.6	992 605	46	1 652.7	32.1	3.6	1.5	78.2	9.7	6.5	14.9	9.7	15.5	12.5	12.3
15 005	27980	3	Kalawao	12.0	88	3 142	7.3	39.8	6.8	3.4	64.8	1.1	0.0	0.0	0.0		10.2	20.5
15 007	28180	5	Kauai	619.9	72 029	755	116.2	44.5	1.4	1.8	68.2	11.0	6.3	16.0	7.1	12.2	12.1	12.9
15 009	27980	3	Maui	1 161.5	165 386	387	142.4	44.1	1.4	1.8	67.6	11.1	6.1	16.0	7.3	12.8	13.0	13.8
16 000	...	0	**IDAHO**	82 642.4	1 683 140	X	20.4	84.2	1.1	1.9	2.5	12.3	6.8	19.1	9.3	13.2	12.2	11.8
16 001	14260	2	Ada	1 052.5	444 028	158	421.9	87.3	1.7	1.1	4.3	8.1	6.0	18.4	8.5	14.5	13.8	13.1
16 003	...	9	Adams	1 362.8	3 900	2 910	2.9	94.6	0.7	2.3	1.1	3.5	4.2	12.8	4.9	9.1	11.3	
16 005	38540	3	Bannock	1 112.5	84 377	676	75.8	86.3	1.3	3.6	2.3	8.4	7.3	19.2	10.0	15.4	12.2	10.5
16 007	...	9	Bear Lake	975.0	5 945	2 755	6.1	94.4	0.4	1.1	0.8	4.2	6.9	19.8	7.2	10.8	11.1	10.0
16 009	...	6	Benewah	776.9	9 092	2 499	11.7	88.4	0.8	10.1	1.0	3.3	6.0	16.5	5.9	9.5	10.3	12.5
16 011	13940	3	Bingham	2 093.9	45 201	1 069	21.6	75.2	0.5	6.3	1.5	17.8	8.0	23.4	8.6	11.8	11.8	11.0
16 013	25200	7	Blaine	2 637.6	21 791	1 738	8.3	76.8	0.5	0.7	1.3	21.7	5.4	17.6	6.8	10.6	12.6	13.7
16 015	14260	2	Boise	1 899.6	7 124	2 662	3.8	93.3	0.8	2.3	1.6	4.1	3.4	13.8	5.8	7.2	9.6	13.9
16 017	41760	6	Bonner	1 733.0	42 536	1 120	24.5	95.4	0.5	1.9	1.2	2.9	5.0	14.8	6.1	9.5	10.7	12.6
16 019	26820	3	Bonneville	1 865.9	112 232	544	60.1	85.0	1.0	1.2	1.7	12.8	8.6	22.5	8.4	13.9	12.4	10.6
16 021	...	7	Boundary	1 268.7	11 681	2 311	9.2	91.9	0.8	2.8	1.3	5.0	6.3	17.0	7.3	9.4	11.1	11.7
16 023	26820	9	Butte	2 236.3	2 501	3 005	1.1	93.2	0.8	2.0	1.1	5.0	5.5	19.6	7.3	8.9	10.4	10.7
16 025	25200	9	Camas	1 074.2	1 072	3 106	1.0	89.8	1.4	3.5	1.0	7.8	4.7	18.5	5.0	8.1	14.3	13.8
16 027	14260	2	Canyon	587.4	211 698	310	360.4	72.6	0.9	1.5	1.9	25.0	7.8	21.6	9.4	13.2	12.7	11.6

1. CBSA = Core Based Statistical Area. See Appendix A for explanation. See Appendix B for list of metropolitan areas with component counties.   2. County type code from the Economic Research Service of USDA Rural-Urban Continuum Codes. See Appendix A for definition.   3. Dry land or land partially or temporarily covered by water.   4. May be of any race.

Table B. States and Counties — **Population and Households**

STATE County	Population, 2016 (cont.) Age (percent) (cont.) 55 to 64 years	65 to 74 years	75 years and over	Percent female	Population change and components of change, 2000–2016 Total persons 2000	2010	Percent change 2000–2010	2010–2016	Components of change, 2010–2016 Births	Deaths	Net migration	Households, 2011–2015 Number	Persons per house-hold	Family house-holds	Percent Female family house-holder[1]	One per-son
	16	17	18	19	20	21	22	23	24	25	26	27	28	29	30	31
GEORGIA—Cont'd																
Putnam	15.7	14.5	8.1	51.4	18 812	21 218	12.8	1.2	1 480	1 472	275	8 462	2.49	73.4	12.7	16.8
Quitman	16.2	18.3	11.3	51.5	2 598	2 513	-3.3	-7.1	151	172	-150	1 015	2.29	62.0	19.6	35.3
Rabun	15.3	16.2	10.3	50.8	15 050	16 276	8.1	1.7	938	1 221	530	6 789	2.34	64.6	8.3	30.2
Randolph	15.2	12.0	9.9	53.9	7 791	7 719	-0.9	-7.0	528	546	-509	2 794	2.54	67.0	25.3	27.3
Richmond	12.5	7.9	5.3	51.6	199 775	200 549	0.4	0.5	18 597	12 076	-5 242	71 724	2.68	60.7	22.0	34.1
Rockdale	13.2	8.8	4.9	52.7	70 111	85 174	21.5	4.9	6 249	3 881	1 810	29 623	2.91	72.5	19.2	23.5
Schley	12.4	9.7	5.8	52.0	3 766	5 010	33.0	1.8	312	212	-5	1 879	2.70	71.9	13.4	26.1
Screven	15.2	10.9	6.8	50.8	15 374	14 593	-5.1	-3.8	1 156	1 099	-626	5 290	2.61	66.2	16.3	30.0
Seminole	14.7	13.2	9.2	52.1	9 369	8 729	-6.8	-3.0	637	691	-200	3 301	2.62	70.9	16.4	26.3
Spalding	12.8	10.5	6.6	51.6	58 417	64 073	9.7	1.1	5 222	4 471	-149	22 717	2.76	71.0	20.8	25.3
Stephens	13.8	11.5	7.4	52.0	25 435	26 172	2.9	-1.6	1 970	2 089	-340	9 198	2.70	72.5	12.2	25.3
Stewart	11.5	8.7	6.9	37.5	5 252	6 058	15.3	-5.8	294	418	-271	1 731	2.48	57.3	29.9	38.6
Sumter	12.1	9.7	6.3	52.5	33 200	32 817	-1.2	-7.4	2 473	2 114	-2 836	11 403	2.58	65.2	21.3	32.0
Talbot	18.9	12.8	7.7	52.8	6 498	6 863	5.6	-10.1	353	468	-582	2 665	2.43	66.8	18.1	30.1
Taliaferro	16.8	13.6	10.1	50.3	2 077	1 717	-17.3	-7.2	93	150	-66	707	2.42	58.0	14.6	35.2
Tattnall	11.7	7.9	4.9	42.5	22 305	25 517	14.4	-1.7	1 871	1 438	-867	7 880	2.46	70.0	16.1	26.6
Taylor	15.1	11.4	7.7	52.0	8 815	8 906	1.0	-7.6	543	603	-694	3 405	2.39	70.9	23.9	27.2
Telfair	13.2	9.0	7.5	41.5	11 794	16 500	39.9	-3.2	838	896	-508	5 289	2.37	65.1	16.3	32.0
Terrell	14.4	11.2	7.8	52.5	10 970	9 507	-13.3	-5.7	775	619	-699	3 312	2.68	69.1	25.2	27.6
Thomas	13.3	10.2	7.4	52.6	42 737	44 719	4.6	1.2	3 667	3 121	-37	17 385	2.53	66.3	17.3	30.1
Tift	12.0	8.4	6.0	51.6	38 407	40 131	4.5	1.7	3 607	2 398	-582	14 127	2.76	67.5	19.3	27.4
Toombs	12.2	9.2	6.6	52.6	26 067	27 174	4.2	0.1	2 534	1 892	-639	10 681	2.50	67.9	14.8	28.8
Towns	13.9	18.9	15.5	52.4	9 319	10 471	12.4	8.8	500	992	1 338	4 268	2.34	65.7	5.7	30.3
Treutlen	13.4	9.5	6.4	49.5	6 854	6 881	0.4	-3.5	485	404	-302	2 627	2.38	64.1	17.6	33.3
Troup	12.3	8.6	5.8	51.9	58 779	67 044	14.1	4.4	5 712	4 184	1 461	24 645	2.73	68.9	21.4	27.0
Turner	12.2	11.1	8.3	51.0	9 504	8 930	-6.0	-10.1	718	669	-980	3 013	2.63	70.3	21.7	27.4
Twiggs	17.5	13.1	7.7	50.7	10 590	9 023	-14.8	-9.4	581	698	-752	3 022	2.79	69.7	15.9	28.8
Union	16.6	19.7	13.1	51.5	17 289	21 359	23.5	7.3	1 013	1 838	2 256	8 357	2.54	69.8	7.7	27.7
Upson	14.1	11.0	7.4	52.3	27 597	27 153	-1.6	-3.0	2 047	2 272	-611	10 159	2.55	68.0	14.5	28.8
Walker	13.9	10.4	6.9	50.7	61 053	68 756	12.6	-1.3	4 622	4 483	-863	25 860	2.59	71.1	14.5	24.7
Walton	12.0	9.3	5.7	51.4	60 687	83 768	38.0	7.7	6 731	4 744	4 280	29 667	2.88	80.4	13.5	17.0
Ware	12.9	9.4	7.3	50.4	35 483	36 306	2.3	-1.6	3 028	2 769	-907	13 901	2.39	69.6	16.8	27.1
Warren	16.0	12.8	8.7	52.5	6 336	5 834	-7.9	-6.7	364	460	-302	2 125	2.58	59.1	17.6	39.2
Washington	13.9	9.9	7.0	49.5	21 176	21 187	0.1	-3.4	1 500	1 358	-926	7 230	2.64	70.5	21.9	27.3
Wayne	12.3	9.3	6.1	48.5	26 565	30 099	13.3	0.0	2 538	1 977	-608	10 066	2.77	71.0	15.4	25.0
Webster	15.6	11.6	9.5	50.4	2 390	2 801	17.2	-7.2	127	101	-252	1 062	2.56	66.7	16.3	30.2
Wheeler	11.1	8.6	5.0	35.1	6 179	7 421	20.1	7.5	380	377	517	2 012	2.16	67.9	14.0	31.6
White	14.5	13.2	8.3	50.9	19 944	27 144	36.1	6.4	1 637	1 643	1 656	11 316	2.42	71.2	7.8	25.3
Whitfield	11.0	7.8	5.5	50.3	83 525	102 599	22.8	1.9	8 807	4 891	-1 844	34 575	2.96	73.5	13.1	21.6
Wilcox	12.4	9.0	7.4	40.6	8 577	9 255	7.9	-5.3	570	668	-437	2 742	2.52	64.9	14.0	33.7
Wilkes	14.8	13.0	9.3	51.9	10 687	10 593	-0.9	-7.4	699	847	-674	4 006	2.45	62.1	16.1	34.5
Wilkinson	14.9	10.7	8.1	51.9	10 220	9 563	-6.4	-4.8	700	728	-436	3 313	2.80	68.2	17.0	29.7
Worth	14.2	11.0	7.2	51.9	21 967	21 679	-1.3	-4.3	1 572	1 354	-1 158	7 924	2.65	69.4	15.5	27.4
HAWAII	12.9	9.7	7.3	49.8	1 211 537	1 360 301	12.3	5.0	117 502	68 045	20 050	450 572	3.02	69.6	12.2	23.6
Hawaii	15.8	12.1	7.0	50.2	148 677	185 079	24.5	7.2	15 202	10 071	8 054	65 048	2.90	66.6	12.2	25.7
Honolulu	11.9	9.0	7.6	49.6	876 156	953 207	8.8	4.1	84 327	47 150	3 708	309 602	3.06	70.4	12.3	23.1
Kalawao	23.9	10.2	27.3	53.4	147	90	-38.8	-2.2	0	2	0	54	1.37	20.4	0.0	61.1
Kauai	14.7	11.3	7.3	50.2	58 463	67 090	14.8	7.4	5 505	3 589	2 974	22 405	3.07	69.9	10.0	22.3
Maui	14.4	10.3	6.3	50.1	128 094	154 835	20.9	6.8	12 468	7 233	5 314	53 463	2.96	68.6	12.4	23.9
IDAHO	12.4	9.1	6.0	49.9	1 293 953	1 567 650	21.2	7.4	142 224	76 045	47 053	589 320	2.69	68.9	9.5	25.1
Ada	12.1	8.3	5.2	49.9	300 904	392 377	30.4	13.2	31 848	16 410	35 186	157 286	2.61	66.5	9.0	26.4
Adams	22.4	17.5	9.4	48.1	3 476	3 978	14.4	-2.0	173	186	-21	1 592	2.39	66.4	9.6	29.4
Bannock	11.8	8.2	5.3	50.1	75 565	82 839	9.6	1.9	8 202	4 144	-2 486	30 394	2.67	66.0	10.8	26.6
Bear Lake	13.6	12.1	8.5	50.4	6 411	5 986	-6.6	-0.7	503	388	-149	2 346	2.51	74.0	7.1	23.9
Benewah	16.9	14.3	8.1	49.5	9 171	9 283	1.2	-2.1	686	725	-164	3 668	2.45	64.0	9.5	30.2
Bingham	12.0	7.8	5.7	49.9	41 735	45 607	9.3	-0.9	4 599	2 065	-2 872	14 698	3.07	76.5	9.3	20.4
Blaine	15.6	11.9	6.0	49.4	18 991	21 378	12.6	1.9	1 402	634	-374	8 924	2.35	64.1	8.6	30.8
Boise	22.4	17.1	6.8	48.1	6 670	7 028	5.4	1.4	244	321	191	2 970	2.29	61.9	5.5	32.4
Bonner	18.1	14.7	8.5	50.1	36 835	40 877	11.0	4.1	2 480	2 524	1 521	17 193	2.36	65.7	8.8	27.9
Bonneville	10.9	7.5	5.3	50.3	82 522	104 298	26.4	7.6	12 051	4 845	587	36 686	2.90	73.4	11.1	22.6
Boundary	16.3	13.1	7.8	49.9	9 871	10 972	11.2	6.5	805	679	567	4 265	2.55	66.1	6.0	28.2
Butte	16.6	12.0	9.1	49.4	2 899	2 893	-0.2	-13.5	182	145	-433	1 009	2.59	66.1	8.1	30.0
Camas	14.4	13.2	8.0	48.6	991	1 117	12.7	-4.0	63	29	-94	435	2.42	60.9	3.7	33.1
Canyon	10.6	8.1	5.0	50.4	131 441	188 911	43.7	12.1	19 650	8 352	11 016	65 807	2.98	72.2	12.0	23.2

1. No spouse present.

Table B. States and Counties — **Population, Vital Statistics, Health, and Crime**

STATE County	Persons in group quarters, 2016	Daytime population, 2011–2015 Number	Daytime population, 2011–2015 Employ-ment/resi-dence ratio	Births, 2016 Total	Births, 2016 Rate[1]	Deaths, 2016 Number	Deaths, 2016 Rate[1]	Persons under 65 with no health insurance, 2015 Number	Persons under 65 with no health insurance, 2015 Percent	Medicare, 2015 Total Beneficiaries	Medicare, 2015 Enrolled in Original Medicare	Medicare, 2015 Enrolled in Medicare Advantage	Serious crimes known to police,[2] 2014 Total Number	Serious crimes known to police,[2] 2014 Total Rate[3]
	32	33	34	35	36	37	38	39	40	41	42	43	44	45
GEORGIA—Cont'd														
Putnam	171	18 799	0.73	218	10.2	266	12.4	2 794	17.0	4 723	3 295	1 428	814	3 789
Quitman	0	1 978	0.53	23	9.9	17	7.3	316	19.4	187	126	61	4	171
Rabun	406	16 527	1.04	159	9.6	221	13.3	2 578	21.8	4 488	3 475	1 013	401	2 463
Randolph	415	7 265	0.98	75	10.5	72	10.0	863	16.2	1 513	929	584	135	1 900
Richmond	10 967	242 155	1.51	2 993	14.8	2 046	10.1	23 774	14.4	36 878	22 992	13 886	3 478	1 714
Rockdale	819	87 377	1.01	1 021	11.4	661	7.4	12 308	16.1	12 715	7 298	5 417	2 955	3 374
Schley	0	4 275	0.58	47	9.2	37	7.3	776	17.7	719	444	275	52	1 015
Screven	442	13 081	0.79	167	11.9	174	12.4	1 830	16.2	2 856	1 893	963	349	2 556
Seminole	99	8 539	0.92	96	11.3	105	12.4	1 063	15.9	2 140	1 501	639	163	1 806
Spalding	1 217	61 913	0.91	790	12.2	754	11.6	8 150	15.5	13 335	8 169	5 166	3 354	5 243
Stephens	598	25 189	0.96	342	13.3	334	13.0	3 108	15.3	7 537	5 335	2 202	876	3 416
Stewart	1 523	5 735	0.91	43	7.5	65	11.4	652	19.5	986	549	437	6	136
Sumter	1 649	32 418	1.09	350	11.5	342	11.3	3 976	16.3	5 698	3 571	2 127	1 824	6 003
Talbot	0	4 741	0.29	47	7.6	85	13.8	902	17.8	1 464	855	609	84	1 396
Taliaferro	7	1 456	0.53	10	6.3	32	20.1	248	19.9	449	258	191	NA	NA
Tattnall	4 549	24 182	0.84	279	11.1	253	10.1	3 461	19.7	3 858	2 441	1 417	379	1 694
Taylor	160	7 655	0.73	79	9.6	83	10.1	1 170	17.6	1 946	1 217	729	117	1 390
Telfair	3 229	16 908	1.11	133	8.3	162	10.1	1 620	15.8	2 520	1 686	834	NA	NA
Terrell	269	8 466	0.76	110	12.3	104	11.6	1 254	17.4	2 014	1 197	817	214	2 384
Thomas	847	46 600	1.11	592	13.1	507	11.2	5 891	16.0	10 970	7 362	3 608	2 014	4 494
Tift	1 518	45 844	1.32	623	15.3	388	9.5	6 522	19.5	7 838	5 277	2 561	1 953	4 831
Toombs	405	29 273	1.19	416	15.3	325	12.0	4 368	19.2	6 020	4 334	1 686	1 007	4 385
Towns	1 035	10 675	0.97	84	7.4	165	14.5	1 129	17.3	4 324	3 098	1 226	178	1 638
Treutlen	363	5 667	0.58	74	11.1	67	10.1	868	16.0	1 198	742	456	NA	NA
Troup	2 328	78 171	1.34	948	13.5	736	10.5	8 441	14.5	12 538	8 626	3 912	2 914	4 177
Turner	383	7 719	0.78	126	15.7	95	11.8	1 210	19.1	2 001	1 200	801	1 266	17 319
Twiggs	89	7 642	0.66	86	10.5	144	17.6	1 058	16.1	1 688	1 028	660	154	1 835
Union	250	22 147	1.06	168	7.3	289	12.6	2 551	17.1	7 128	5 201	1 927	336	1 549
Upson	364	25 525	0.89	333	12.6	390	14.8	3 444	16.2	5 640	3 363	2 277	881	3 321
Walker	1 262	56 366	0.57	753	11.1	783	11.5	8 018	14.4	15 414	10 403	5 011	5 661	8 295
Walton	653	72 028	0.61	1 136	12.6	842	9.3	10 551	14.0	17 278	10 815	6 463	3 590	4 152
Ware	2 349	39 297	1.28	467	13.1	427	11.9	4 790	17.3	8 924	6 418	2 506	1 849	5 185
Warren	89	4 978	0.70	49	9.0	66	12.1	706	16.5	1 223	730	493	96	1 739
Washington	1 603	20 966	1.02	239	11.7	228	11.1	2 277	14.5	3 891	2 182	1 709	566	2 777
Wayne	2 057	29 644	0.96	406	13.5	320	10.6	3 799	16.1	5 396	3 765	1 631	1 737	5 759
Webster	0	2 204	0.54	22	8.5	12	4.6	339	16.2	379	221	158	14	516
Wheeler	2 567	8 088	1.10	56	7.0	68	8.5	723	16.6	1 031	685	346	51	639
White	617	25 803	0.82	270	9.3	294	10.2	3 461	15.9	6 022	4 008	2 014	778	2 776
Whitfield	1 089	114 429	1.25	1 409	13.5	822	7.9	19 941	22.3	16 385	13 323	3 062	3 185	3 157
Wilcox	1 925	8 522	0.81	81	9.2	105	12.0	937	16.9	1 701	1 140	561	81	962
Wilkes	133	9 538	0.88	110	11.2	140	14.3	1 402	18.4	2 610	1 726	884	105	1 058
Wilkinson	119	9 218	0.95	103	11.3	137	15.0	1 098	14.8	2 266	1 443	823	99	1 252
Worth	179	16 958	0.49	233	11.2	220	10.6	2 939	17.3	3 289	2 326	963	595	2 797
HAWAII	44 287	1 407 039	1.00	18 507	13.0	12 237	8.6	55 299	4.8	225 587	108 099	117 488	46 977	3 309
Hawaii	3 803	190 936	0.99	2 440	12.3	1 892	9.5	9 414	5.9	36 035	20 015	16 020	7 182	3 722
Honolulu	36 429	985 573	1.00	13 231	13.3	8 352	8.4	35 329	4.4	153 378	70 276	83 102	11 193	1 126
Kalawao	3	85	1.00	0	0.0	0	0.0	0	0.0	NA	NA	NA	NA	NA
Kauai	1 225	69 781	1.00	903	12.5	664	9.2	3 056	5.2	12 376	7 032	5 344	1 120	1 592
Maui	2 827	160 664	1.00	1 933	11.7	1 329	8.0	7 500	5.4	23 798	10 776	13 022	6 309	3 889
IDAHO	30 052	1 593 788	0.97	22 792	13.5	12 496	7.4	177 426	12.8	277 220	180 020	97 200	33 784	2 067
Ada	10 683	436 123	1.09	5 127	11.5	2 831	6.4	35 031	9.5	64 052	32 540	31 512	7 989	1 878
Adams	21	3 635	0.83	29	7.4	18	4.6	440	15.7	1 082	864	218	24	628
Bannock	2 129	81 652	0.95	1 263	15.0	653	7.7	8 107	11.5	13 694	8 782	4 912	2 131	2 540
Bear Lake	31	5 384	0.78	78	13.1	53	8.9	514	10.9	1 280	1 198	82	103	1 723
Benewah	70	9 341	1.07	108	11.9	116	12.8	1 103	15.8	2 437	1 909	528	141	1 558
Bingham	324	42 289	0.83	695	15.4	345	7.6	6 168	16.0	6 605	5 014	1 591	655	1 440
Blaine	258	22 291	1.08	212	9.7	104	4.8	3 045	16.9	3 642	2 749	893	221	1 028
Boise	34	6 104	0.71	43	6.0	54	7.6	727	13.4	1 267	671	596	102	1 610
Bonner	353	39 828	0.92	401	9.4	421	9.9	4 224	13.1	9 736	6 685	3 051	878	2 145
Bonneville	1 241	113 226	1.12	1 918	17.1	802	7.1	11 101	11.6	16 272	12 448	3 824	2 449	2 247
Boundary	73	10 592	0.90	145	12.4	120	10.3	1 488	16.8	2 655	1 811	844	129	1 184
Butte	18	4 367	2.80	27	10.8	13	5.2	258	13.1	614	575	39	10	385
Camas	0	961	0.82	6	5.6	3	2.8	184	22.0	194	145	49	2	194
Canyon	3 374	180 730	0.77	3 237	15.3	1 433	6.8	27 700	15.7	31 556	14 942	16 614	5 051	2 491

1. Per 1,000 estimated resident population.   2. Data for serious crimes have not been adjusted for underreporting; this may affect comparability between geographic areas and over time.
3. Per 100,000 population estimated by the FBI.

Table B. States and Counties — Crime, Education, Money Income, and Poverty

STATE County	Serious crimes known to police, 2014 (cont.)[1] Rate[2] Violent	Property	Education School enrollment and attainment, 2011–2015 Enrollment[3] Total	Per-cent private	Attainment[4] (percent) High school grad-uate or less	Bach-elor's degree or more	Local government expenditures,[5] 2013–2014 Total current spending (mil dol)	Current spend-ing per student (dollars)	Money income, 2011–2015 Per capita income[6] (dollars)	Median income (dollars)	Households Percent with income of less than $50,000	with income of $200,000 or more	Income and poverty, 2015 Median house-hold income (dollars)	Percent below poverty level All per-sons	Children under 18 years	Children 5 to 17 years in families
	46	47	48	49	50	51	52	53	54	55	56	57	58	59	60	61
GEORGIA—Cont'd																
Putnam	582	3 207	4 283	22.1	54.5	17.5	31.2	11 164	25 864	44 299	55.2	3.2	44 323	18.1	33.1	30.9
Quitman	85	85	444	11.5	67.6	6.7	4.6	13 717	17 334	31 487	71.6	0.4	29 921	28.9	47.9	46.9
Rabun	129	2 334	3 017	18.8	47.9	25.9	28.0	12 344	22 869	35 211	63.7	2.8	40 834	16.1	28.1	26.7
Randolph	239	1 660	1 624	17.2	62.4	14.7	12.0	10 718	26 031	28 377	74.8	2.1	30 505	26.9	44.1	44.2
Richmond	127	1 587	53 806	14.6	47.9	20.4	293.1	9 159	20 659	37 424	62.2	1.7	40 821	24.3	37.7	37.5
Rockdale	282	3 092	24 233	11.9	45.0	25.5	150.6	9 384	22 614	50 455	49.5	2.0	51 510	15.9	26.0	24.4
Schley	195	820	1 645	2.8	57.2	14.7	13.7	9 919	19 858	39 375	59.4	1.2	41 737	19.5	29.0	25.1
Screven	425	2 131	3 544	9.4	61.2	13.3	22.3	9 420	18 597	34 466	62.8	1.4	35 911	27.0	40.0	41.1
Seminole	144	1 662	1 980	6.5	57.7	15.1	15.6	9 344	19 891	34 905	66.3	0.8	31 615	25.8	42.7	41.7
Spalding	583	4 660	15 071	9.9	57.5	15.9	101.2	9 520	19 588	40 246	59.5	1.6	41 250	22.2	35.5	34.9
Stephens	281	3 135	6 343	15.0	58.3	16.2	40.7	10 112	20 001	40 315	59.4	1.4	38 503	21.2	31.0	29.1
Stewart	45	90	860	6.6	74.6	10.8	6.6	12 153	13 721	21 118	75.4	0.6	28 977	42.0	48.4	48.5
Sumter	698	5 305	9 346	6.8	54.9	19.0	48.3	9 849	17 404	32 758	66.6	1.2	33 802	30.8	48.1	52.1
Talbot	66	1 330	1 325	17.7	65.3	13.7	6.2	11 916	18 971	34 078	68.3	1.3	33 510	25.6	41.8	39.5
Taliaferro	NA	NA	211	12.8	74.9	9.9	3.2	16 020	14 805	26 306	76.9	0.0	28 952	33.5	54.4	58.0
Tattnall	49	1 645	4 977	9.4	64.4	11.0	32.4	8 797	14 957	33 980	65.6	1.8	37 163	27.5	36.1	34.4
Taylor	226	1 164	2 006	15.6	60.9	11.1	13.9	9 135	16 857	28 143	72.8	1.3	32 041	27.3	41.1	36.9
Telfair	NA	NA	2 672	3.2	75.7	9.3	15.8	9 136	12 155	26 449	78.1	0.4	31 149	34.7	42.2	37.3
Terrell	379	2 006	2 279	12.5	61.5	11.2	15.1	10 176	16 242	28 688	68.1	0.5	32 342	36.5	55.7	56.3
Thomas	290	4 204	11 576	15.5	51.6	19.2	79.9	9 299	20 471	36 641	62.6	2.0	40 449	21.7	32.4	31.7
Tift	552	4 279	11 540	7.2	53.9	16.8	72.9	9 272	20 078	37 653	61.3	2.8	39 988	27.1	39.8	37.8
Toombs	414	3 972	7 299	7.7	60.0	15.7	48.0	8 362	19 564	33 679	63.9	1.9	34 953	25.1	39.0	39.3
Towns	285	1 353	2 485	24.0	46.3	22.4	12.7	11 730	19 978	37 000	64.6	0.9	39 782	16.7	26.6	26.7
Treutlen	NA	NA	1 459	5.8	64.4	14.8	9.7	8 116	21 127	38 596	62.1	1.9	32 086	28.7	41.6	38.2
Troup	308	3 869	17 780	12.8	51.8	18.7	113.5	8 953	21 559	41 489	57.7	3.0	41 289	19.3	28.4	27.9
Turner	2 066	15 253	2 182	16.6	61.8	11.7	16.1	10 786	18 227	31 806	68.2	1.4	35 117	28.4	44.8	41.4
Twiggs	226	1 609	1 467	9.7	70.3	9.7	10.9	12 003	17 768	30 468	68.9	0.1	36 086	26.3	35.1	35.0
Union	230	1 318	3 620	16.1	45.6	21.9	28.3	10 577	21 872	40 799	57.7	0.8	42 782	14.3	26.7	24.0
Upson	381	2 940	6 028	6.3	54.8	12.1	39.7	9 106	19 069	35 774	64.7	1.2	37 864	22.7	33.7	33.6
Walker	816	7 479	15 443	13.6	57.2	14.7	94.4	8 943	21 430	41 632	59.1	1.9	42 249	18.8	26.5	25.9
Walton	365	3 787	22 802	13.5	50.3	17.9	127.7	8 290	23 625	54 453	45.9	2.9	57 312	12.7	19.3	17.5
Ware	477	4 708	8 147	6.0	59.4	12.9	61.5	10 226	18 100	34 909	66.5	1.1	35 270	28.4	45.6	43.5
Warren	217	1 522	1 128	22.7	71.2	12.5	7.4	10 919	18 174	29 176	70.1	1.0	32 350	27.7	43.9	41.4
Washington	299	2 478	4 767	11.6	63.5	12.9	32.9	10 620	18 285	37 932	61.7	1.4	36 499	26.3	36.5	33.9
Wayne	491	5 268	7 111	9.5	60.0	13.1	47.5	8 696	18 291	38 955	58.8	1.3	41 466	20.8	32.8	33.1
Webster	221	295	694	11.2	70.7	7.6	4.4	10 555	18 767	37 063	63.0	0.4	35 770	23.6	36.1	31.3
Wheeler	25	614	926	1.1	78.0	5.6	10.5	10 035	8 292	27 620	74.7	0.0	30 926	39.3	39.2	37.2
White	153	2 622	6 116	13.3	45.9	20.7	58.4	11 613	21 718	40 888	59.8	1.6	43 598	15.2	24.9	22.3
Whitfield	216	2 941	27 797	5.3	60.4	14.0	190.2	9 073	20 353	40 596	59.3	2.9	45 921	15.3	22.1	19.7
Wilcox	285	677	1 652	13.3	72.3	8.5	12.8	10 518	13 521	32 043	69.7	0.3	32 480	30.4	40.4	37.8
Wilkes	282	776	2 132	9.6	63.7	15.7	18.5	11 107	18 392	32 727	67.3	0.9	34 031	22.9	34.7	34.5
Wilkinson	164	1 088	2 052	14.3	70.0	7.4	18.1	11 543	18 037	38 485	61.3	0.4	38 103	20.9	34.2	34.2
Worth	338	2 458	5 020	9.3	66.4	9.4	30.6	8 997	18 762	37 974	63.9	1.0	39 560	21.7	34.3	33.8
HAWAII	259	3 050	337 337	23.4	36.9	30.8	2 327.5	12 458	29 822	69 515	35.3	6.3	73 097	10.7	14.5	13.4
Hawaii	237	3 486	43 058	16.8	40.6	26.8	NA	NA	24 548	52 108	48.1	2.9	54 914	18.3	28.5	26.3
Honolulu	72	1 054	243 756	25.4	35.5	32.7	2 327.5	12 458	31 041	74 460	32.0	7.2	76 544	9.2	11.5	10.6
Kalawao	NA	NA	2	0.0	41.0	34.6	NA	NA	46 769	66 250	33.3	0.0	0	0.0	0.0	0.0
Kauai	128	1 464	14 228	15.8	38.4	28.0	NA	NA	27 441	65 101	38.5	4.8	70 122	11.2	15.9	14.8
Maui	314	3 575	36 293	20.3	39.7	26.1	NA	NA	29 664	66 476	37.2	5.7	68 684	10.7	15.3	13.5
IDAHO	212	1 855	445 917	13.3	38.0	25.9	1 934.0	6 527	23 399	47 583	52.2	2.6	48 311	14.7	17.7	15.9
Ada	226	1 651	117 215	12.5	27.2	37.1	492.2	6 339	28 851	56 356	43.9	4.4	58 431	11.7	12.2	10.5
Adams	131	497	775	7.7	46.9	21.5	3.7	8 773	21 219	39 565	63.2	0.8	39 943	15.8	26.5	24.5
Bannock	223	2 317	25 953	7.1	35.0	26.4	88.6	6 247	21 598	43 779	55.8	1.4	43 298	22.3	22.2	20.3
Bear Lake	268	1 455	1 387	6.3	45.8	19.1	7.7	6 848	22 959	48 654	51.2	1.4	48 309	13.7	19.7	18.5
Benewah	276	1 282	1 903	12.7	54.8	13.3	12.6	9 378	20 937	39 863	61.8	0.9	41 368	18.0	25.5	22.6
Bingham	101	1 338	13 417	6.9	44.2	17.5	64.9	6 199	20 164	50 155	49.8	2.0	49 644	14.0	18.2	16.5
Blaine	144	884	4 287	10.4	27.7	42.9	54.4	15 791	34 208	60 088	43.8	6.2	65 272	8.9	12.0	10.1
Boise	110	1 500	1 356	12.8	33.7	25.1	8.0	9 034	27 276	44 238	54.4	1.6	52 728	14.4	23.0	19.1
Bonner	122	2 023	8 062	14.3	40.2	20.9	42.6	7 746	23 981	42 171	58.8	2.1	44 072	15.8	23.6	21.3
Bonneville	183	2 063	31 085	10.8	36.4	27.2	133.1	5 706	23 926	50 762	49.1	3.4	54 008	13.2	16.7	15.3
Boundary	73	1 111	2 152	19.5	48.3	16.0	10.5	7 027	20 795	38 961	58.6	2.3	41 803	15.8	24.3	22.1
Butte	269	115	711	10.7	46.8	15.6	3.3	7 345	21 982	37 891	61.7	2.4	43 780	15.9	20.2	16.3
Camas	0	194	220	2.7	40.8	18.3	1.8	11 865	24 588	42 614	59.8	6.9	46 203	10.7	15.4	12.0
Canyon	258	2 233	57 080	13.5	48.8	17.7	227.6	5 648	17 915	42 888	58.0	0.9	44 585	15.9	19.1	16.6

1. Data for serious crimes have not been adjusted for underreporting; this may affect comparability between geographic areas and over time.   2. Per 100,000 population estimated by the FBI.
3. All persons 3 years old and over enrolled in nursery school through college.   4. Persons 25 years old and over.   5. Elementary and secondary education expenditures.
6. Based on population estimated by the American Community Survey, 2011–2015.

Table B. States and Counties — **Personal Income**

STATE County	Personal income, 2015										Earnings, 2015		
	Total (mil dol)	Percent change, 2014–2015	Per capita¹		Wages and salaries (mil dol)	Supplements to wages and salaries; employer contributions (mil dol)		Proprietors' income (mil dol)	Dividends, interest, and rent (mil dol)	Personal transfer receipts (mil dol)	Total (mil dol)	Contributions for government social insurance (mil dol)	
			Dollars	Rank		Pension and insurance	Government social insurance					From employee and self-employed	From employer
	62	63	64	65	66	67	68	69	70	71	72	73	74
GEORGIA—Cont'd													
Putnam	694	3.0	32 497	2 116	184	40	13	28	155	207	263	19	13
Quitman	63	2.0	27 169	3 034	12	4	1	4	8	27	21	2	1
Rabun	571	4.3	35 058	2 170	155	29	11	43	163	172	238	18	11
Randolph	211	2.2	29 290	2 383	66	15	5	23	31	73	108	7	5
Richmond	6 864	4.2	34 015	2 363	5 746	1 225	436	417	1 335	1 875	7 824	414	436
Rockdale	2 866	6.0	32 259	2 535	1 663	261	115	123	377	665	2 162	131	115
Schley	142	7.0	27 488	3 035	39	10	3	11	21	34	62	4	3
Screven	388	2.1	27 371	2 919	119	25	8	23	61	136	176	12	8
Seminole	300	-3.0	34 719	2 581	85	17	6	60	43	98	169	11	6
Spalding	2 005	4.1	31 305	2 681	834	162	59	116	297	621	1 171	77	59
Stephens	867	4.4	33 902	2 097	382	67	27	71	127	262	547	35	27
Stewart	127	0.8	21 677	3 099	49	10	4	4	22	47	67	5	4
Sumter	952	4.3	30 930	2 752	392	87	27	49	178	293	554	34	27
Talbot	197	2.7	31 146	2 751	29	6	2	2	34	69	40	4	2
Taliaferro	41	-4.2	25 207	3 025	6	2	0	5	7	18	14	1	0
Tattnall	735	3.7	29 116	2 886	218	50	15	110	93	182	392	19	15
Taylor	218	4.5	26 128	3 053	64	13	5	9	36	79	91	7	5
Telfair	317	3.5	19 306	3 111	112	25	9	27	43	118	172	11	9
Terrell	348	2.0	38 174	1 420	86	17	6	25	69	96	134	9	6
Thomas	1 738	4.4	38 574	1 603	928	146	64	103	319	449	1 242	78	64
Tift	1 523	12.9	37 363	2 286	867	176	55	152	230	351	1 251	68	55
Toombs	898	4.1	32 973	2 470	446	79	33	61	122	262	619	38	33
Towns	344	5.7	30 808	2 622	108	24	8	25	86	146	165	14	8
Treutlen	175	4.8	25 810	3 056	36	8	3	10	23	64	57	4	3
Troup	2 368	3.9	33 940	2 233	1 766	267	131	103	368	584	2 267	135	131
Turner	263	3.8	32 047	2 504	76	15	5	22	35	92	118	8	5
Twiggs	294	2.5	35 057	2 568	44	10	3	32	30	95	88	8	3
Union	762	5.8	34 214	2 271	241	50	16	47	151	258	355	27	16
Upson	826	3.2	31 330	2 613	257	47	18	43	124	270	365	26	18
Walker	2 026	3.0	29 772	2 898	470	107	35	142	266	599	754	55	35
Walton	3 025	4.1	34 223	2 320	863	147	61	113	423	658	1 184	79	61
Ware	1 082	4.4	30 587	2 737	616	111	51	50	157	385	827	54	51
Warren	167	2.5	30 586	2 882	64	12	5	6	27	60	86	6	5
Washington	615	1.4	29 553	2 696	268	58	18	25	124	194	369	24	18
Wayne	935	3.1	31 651	2 698	343	72	24	59	120	281	497	32	24
Webster	70	7.5	26 327	3 006	20	4	1	7	13	19	33	2	1
Wheeler	127	2.7	16 007	3 113	43	9	3	13	17	51	68	5	3
White	874	5.5	30 871	2 802	252	44	18	82	138	248	397	27	18
Whitfield	3 472	3.5	33 317	2 381	2 489	366	185	350	605	736	3 390	199	185
Wilcox	228	5.6	25 744	3 062	41	11	3	31	34	77	85	5	3
Wilkes	290	1.9	29 350	2 772	102	22	7	36	56	107	167	10	7
Wilkinson	293	2.6	32 018	2 671	163	28	11	23	35	96	225	15	11
Worth	616	0.8	29 763	2 660	130	26	9	19	97	171	182	14	9
HAWAII	69 129	4.8	48 506	X	34 578	7 295	2 789	4 960	14 284	10 872	49 622	2 860	2 789
Hawaii	7 067	5.1	35 979	1 957	2 939	610	226	418	1 566	1 785	4 193	264	226
Honolulu	52 055	4.5	52 122	397	26 894	5 852	2 204	3 558	10 605	7 342	38 509	2 173	2 204
Kalawao	(2)	(2)	(2)	(2)	(2)	(2)	(2)	(2)	(2)	(2)	(2)	(2)	(2)
Kauai	3 018	5.0	42 070	1 149	1 389	252	106	248	650	599	1 996	124	106
Maui	(2)6 989	(2)6.1	(2)42 430	(2)1 255	(2)3 356	(2)580	(2)253	(2)734	(2)1 464	(2)1 146	(2)4 923	(2)299	(2)253
IDAHO	63 535	4.6	38 440	X	27 837	4 510	2 426	7 948	13 080	11 812	42 720	2 630	2 426
Ada	19 997	5.7	46 053	783	10 636	1 559	895	2 703	4 087	2 765	15 793	979	895
Adams	141	6.2	36 800	2 113	43	9	4	16	42	36	72	5	4
Bannock	2 792	4.4	33 344	2 431	1 261	243	116	164	455	652	1 784	117	116
Bear Lake	212	2.0	35 867	1 800	57	13	6	16	38	52	91	6	6
Benewah	291	6.6	32 134	2 468	142	27	13	20	57	90	202	14	13
Bingham	1 504	4.7	33 422	2 422	530	95	46	210	252	310	881	51	46
Blaine	1 889	3.0	87 496	23	534	69	48	175	1 045	134	826	51	48
Boise	260	7.3	36 828	1 927	42	10	4	17	60	62	73	6	4
Bonner	1 450	3.7	34 634	2 149	482	89	45	95	434	359	711	52	45
Bonneville	4 383	5.4	39 814	1 388	1 787	282	160	664	850	751	2 893	180	160
Boundary	354	2.6	31 283	2 747	129	25	12	44	80	96	210	14	12
Butte	84	1.2	33 506	2 098	664	58	50	9	17	22	781	49	50
Camas	42	0.6	39 431	2 534	22	3	2	9	10	7	35	2	2
Canyon	5 863	4.4	28 258	2 985	2 168	362	197	497	877	1 444	3 224	215	197

1. Based on the resident population estimated as of July 1 of the year shown.   2. Kalawao county is included with Maui county.

Table B. States and Counties — Earnings, Social Security, and Housing

STATE County	Earnings, 2015 (cont.) Percent by selected industries									Social Security beneficiaries, December 2015		Supplemental Security Income recipients, December 2015	Housing units, 2016	
	Farm	Mining	Construction	Manufacturing	Information: professional, scientific, technical services	Retail trade	Finance, insurance, real estate and leasing	Health care and social assistance	Government	Number	Rate[1]		Total	Percent change, 2010-2016
	75	76	77	78	79	80	81	82	83	84	85	86	87	88
GEORGIA—Cont'd														
Putnam	3.6	0.0	8.5	8.1	D	9.0	5.5	D	29.6	5 765	271	517	12 798	0.0
Quitman	12.0	0.0	D	D	D	D	D	D	33.1	775	337	156	1 992	-2.7
Rabun	2.1	D	13.4	7.5	3.5	13.2	5.6	D	19.3	5 085	313	425	12 499	1.5
Randolph	8.7	0.1	D	D	D	6.3	D	D	26.1	1 780	249	438	4 073	-1.9
Richmond	0.0	D	4.0	7.7	7.0	4.7	4.0	14.2	40.8	38 635	192	8 158	88 173	2.1
Rockdale	0.0	D	10.9	24.5	8.8	7.2	5.2	10.6	12.1	15 905	179	1 990	33 457	0.6
Schley	8.5	0.3	D	27.4	D	4.7	D	D	28.1	885	171	138	2 151	-2.6
Screven	6.5	0.0	4.0	27.3	4.4	6.4	3.4	D	26.8	3 455	245	721	6 623	-1.7
Seminole	8.0	0.0	2.1	23.1	D	4.9	4.4	11.9	13.7	2 510	292	425	4 757	-0.8
Spalding	-0.1	D	3.7	18.3	D	7.4	5.2	15.4	21.3	15 230	238	2 687	27 195	1.6
Stephens	4.4	D	D	21.2	2.6	7.4	2.6	D	16.9	7 070	277	1 214	12 477	-1.5
Stewart	3.8	0.0	D	D	D	2.4	D	23.4	33.4	1 090	189	275	2 319	-2.7
Sumter	4.1	D	2.0	12.4	2.7	7.4	3.3	15.4	25.4	6 620	215	1 342	13 791	-0.8
Talbot	-0.4	15.4	24.4	0.3	D	2.0	D	D	28.0	1 695	268	354	3 348	-1.5
Taliaferro	32.7	0.0	D	D	0.0	D	D	D	43.4	475	290	104	998	-1.7
Tattnall	26.3	0.0	4.0	2.1	2.4	4.0	3.1	D	25.7	4 330	172	950	9 818	-1.5
Taylor	5.9	D	8.4	3.7	D	6.0	2.9	15.6	23.2	1 940	233	412	4 493	-1.5
Telfair	4.2	0.6	4.2	D	3.6	4.7	4.1	4.7	22.4	2 730	166	618	7 169	-1.8
Terrell	10.0	0.0	2.6	14.4	D	8.0	6.1	D	22.3	2 390	263	559	4 140	-0.5
Thomas	0.1	D	2.8	18.1	3.5	5.7	6.8	D	14.6	10 910	242	2 256	20 375	1.0
Tift	1.6	0.2	2.8	6.1	4.0	7.8	4.4	7.3	41.3	8 220	202	1 654	16 422	-0.1
Toombs	3.7	0.0	4.9	9.1	D	9.3	2.9	D	13.2	6 120	225	1 333	12 050	-0.6
Towns	0.4	D	9.3	3.8	5.8	7.0	6.8	D	15.0	4 605	413	254	8 062	4.3
Treutlen	5.0	0.2	3.6	1.5	D	11.2	D	D	30.6	1 535	227	322	2 968	-0.8
Troup	0.1	D	4.6	36.7	3.8	7.4	4.6	8.6	9.6	13 950	200	2 403	28 356	1.1
Turner	10.1	0.0	1.3	13.5	D	7.2	4.9	4.3	24.8	2 205	274	492	3 906	1.7
Twiggs	0.7	D	D	D	D	D	D	D	17.5	2 480	299	424	4 160	-1.8
Union	1.9	D	6.3	4.4	D	8.7	4.8	D	24.5	8 200	369	469	14 415	2.6
Upson	5.2	0.1	5.8	19.2	D	7.4	5.2	18.9	19.3	7 165	273	1 157	12 067	-0.8
Walker	4.1	D	6.0	31.6	D	5.7	5.0	5.1	21.7	16 155	237	2 226	30 123	0.1
Walton	0.9	0.1	14.6	14.3	5.2	11.3	3.2	8.0	18.7	17 135	194	2 549	33 084	2.0
Ware	0.7	0.0	3.2	9.8	D	10.2	3.8	19.8	19.7	8 035	227	1 796	16 495	1.0
Warren	2.2	D	2.0	27.6	D	4.4	0.6	D	14.2	1 515	278	276	2 931	-1.8
Washington	0.5	3.8	5.0	8.9	4.9	6.0	5.0	D	28.9	4 845	233	925	9 123	0.8
Wayne	2.3	0.0	9.8	19.8	D	8.1	2.5	8.1	30.4	6 545	222	1 091	12 061	-1.1
Webster	18.4	D	D	D	0.2	6.7	1.3	0.2	19.5	570	216	85	1 501	-1.5
Wheeler	10.6	0.0	4.1	0.0	D	2.4	D	3.2	20.1	1 220	154	224	2 584	-1.6
White	7.0	D	13.9	13.1	D	9.3	3.8	D	15.3	7 260	256	578	16 003	-0.4
Whitfield	0.6	0.3	1.9	34.6	8.1	7.4	4.2	9.4	9.3	18 430	177	2 543	39 619	-0.7
Wilcox	28.2	0.0	D	D	D	3.4	D	D	32.1	1 805	204	362	3 471	-1.1
Wilkes	15.0	D	5.4	17.0	D	6.3	4.5	7.3	22.7	2 945	298	470	5 125	-0.6
Wilkinson	0.8	43.1	8.5	13.4	D	1.8	D	2.8	10.6	2 520	275	384	4 407	-1.8
Worth	5.5	0.0	6.2	10.8	D	7.0	D	D	26.1	4 450	215	715	9 146	-1.1
HAWAII	0.6	0.1	7.6	1.8	7.1	6.1	6.0	9.8	30.9	256 912	180	24 778	537 114	3.4
Hawaii	2.5	D	8.0	1.5	D	8.5	4.5	D	25.8	42 525	217	5 447	86 778	5.4
Honolulu	0.2	0.1	7.4	1.9	7.8	5.5	6.2	10.2	33.7	171 060	172	16 308	347 413	3.1
Kalawao	(2)	(2)	(2)	(2)	(2)	(2)	(2)	(2)	(2)	0	0	0	113	0.0
Kauai	1.1	D	8.6	0.9	D	8.1	6.1	D	20.3	14 640	205	967	30 672	3.0
Maui	(2)1.6	(2)D	(2)8.5	(2)1.5	(2)4.3	(2)8.2	(2)5.7	(2)7.2	(2)17.3	28 685	175	2 056	72 138	2.5
IDAHO	5.3	1.2	7.0	11.1	8.7	8.9	5.8	11.8	16.7	315 571	191	30 774	700 825	4.9
Ada	0.4	1.9	7.3	12.4	9.8	9.3	7.6	13.9	14.1	72 120	166	6 645	174 792	9.6
Adams	8.7	0.2	6.1	12.4	4.8	5.2	2.9	D	25.7	1 260	328	53	2 632	-0.2
Bannock	0.7	D	5.7	7.8	5.5	8.1	7.4	15.4	25.5	14 295	170	1 942	33 568	1.1
Bear Lake	8.9	D	2.0	3.3	D	8.2	D	4.3	35.1	1 445	245	102	4 029	3.0
Benewah	1.3	D	2.6	19.0	D	4.1	2.2	D	33.8	2 705	299	245	4 609	-0.4
Bingham	14.2	D	6.1	14.9	2.1	4.6	5.7	9.3	20.6	8 130	181	893	16 316	1.1
Blaine	1.2	D	15.1	3.8	15.0	7.0	8.5	7.8	11.4	3 945	183	110	15 225	1.2
Boise	1.6	0.4	10.5	3.7	D	5.2	D	5.7	34.1	1 995	285	101	5 396	2.0
Bonner	0.4	1.5	9.1	18.2	6.2	9.6	4.4	8.0	19.4	11 670	279	807	24 570	-0.4
Bonneville	1.5	D	6.2	7.5	7.3	17.1	3.9	16.7	12.4	18 445	168	2 221	41 655	4.8
Boundary	3.4	0.2	7.6	14.6	4.0	7.1	5.9	7.7	28.1	3 115	275	255	5 317	2.7
Butte	1.1	0.0	0.2	0.4	93.7	0.2	D	0.6	1.9	650	260	73	1 346	-0.7
Camas	14.1	D	3.6	0.2	D	2.4	D	D	16.1	225	211	11	838	0.8
Canyon	4.5	0.1	10.7	15.4	4.8	9.6	3.9	9.3	15.3	36 035	174	4 797	73 253	5.5

1. Per 1,000 resident population estimated as of July 1 of the year shown.   2. Kalawao county is included with Maui county.

Table B. States and Counties — Housing, Labor Force, and Employment

STATE County	Housing units, 2011–2015								Civilian labor force, 2016		Unemployment		Civilian employment,[6] 2011–2015		
	Occupied units												Percent		
	Owner-occupied				Renter-occupied										
				Median owner cost as a percent of income			Median rent as a percent of income[2]	Sub-standard units[4] (percent)		Percent change, 2015–2016				Manage-ment, business, science and arts	Con-struction, produc-tion, and mainte-nance occu-pations
	Total	Percent	Median value[1]	With a mort-gage	Without a mort-gage[2]	Median rent[3]			Total		Total	Rate[5]	Total		
	89	90	91	92	93	94	95	96	97	98	99	100	101	102	103
GEORGIA—Cont'd															
Putnam	8 462	73.3	155 100	22.7	12.1	660	29.8	0.7	7 930	1.7	559	7.0	9 448	29.3	24.2
Quitman	1 015	74.6	69 200	27.6	13.2	684	43.7	0.6	801	-2.0	59	7.4	753	14.5	37.7
Rabun	6 789	73.5	161 500	29.2	13.5	689	37.1	2.3	6 669	2.6	394	5.9	6 236	31.4	26.4
Randolph	2 794	61.0	68 400	31.2	13.2	592	29.8	5.6	2 472	1.9	210	8.5	2 503	26.8	33.1
Richmond	71 724	53.1	101 900	22.6	11.8	790	33.6	2.6	85 856	1.9	5 740	6.7	76 807	29.8	21.6
Rockdale	29 623	68.9	140 000	23.5	10.0	916	34.2	3.2	43 537	3.0	2 499	5.7	37 374	32.3	25.6
Schley	1 879	64.5	91 500	20.6	13.8	659	25.4	3.7	2 100	-0.4	135	6.4	1 964	28.4	34.0
Screven	5 290	70.2	80 500	24.6	12.4	548	29.6	2.4	5 245	4.1	399	7.6	5 482	27.0	31.7
Seminole	3 301	74.8	75 600	27.6	12.6	666	24.7	3.9	3 126	1.2	247	7.9	2 999	32.4	23.5
Spalding	22 717	61.4	111 500	24.5	12.4	786	35.0	3.0	27 810	2.6	1 902	6.8	23 471	26.8	29.7
Stephens	9 198	72.0	101 100	21.3	11.6	567	29.2	2.9	11 110	2.3	654	5.9	10 224	25.9	32.0
Stewart	1 731	62.2	52 500	21.4	17.7	503	38.6	1.4	2 142	1.3	142	6.6	1 485	30.0	28.6
Sumter	11 403	58.3	84 700	25.4	12.0	634	33.4	2.7	12 730	-0.8	981	7.7	11 392	33.0	26.0
Talbot	2 665	80.4	72 300	26.1	16.6	572	29.2	3.8	2 756	2.2	186	6.7	2 513	19.9	35.8
Taliaferro	707	73.7	63 100	28.3	20.2	521	22.8	2.5	599	1.0	39	6.5	574	16.0	40.2
Tattnall	7 880	69.2	80 600	25.5	12.2	545	24.2	4.1	9 374	1.1	505	5.4	7 310	29.6	26.6
Taylor	3 405	70.2	58 000	27.7	15.9	566	23.2	5.0	3 523	27.1	253	7.2	2 869	25.7	35.0
Telfair	5 289	59.6	56 400	28.1	13.7	571	26.1	3.6	4 765	-1.2	410	8.6	4 472	25.2	34.2
Terrell	3 312	58.6	83 700	23.5	13.9	594	39.4	4.4	3 675	1.2	241	6.6	3 181	24.3	31.7
Thomas	17 385	59.9	123 100	23.9	13.3	709	33.2	2.8	17 257	2.7	1 103	6.4	17 359	34.0	22.0
Tift	14 127	58.1	112 400	20.9	10.0	586	26.8	3.4	18 464	0.7	1 016	5.5	16 038	29.6	27.2
Toombs	10 681	62.0	89 900	21.8	12.0	572	30.8	5.0	11 738	-1.0	921	7.8	10 615	26.7	33.3
Towns	4 268	79.9	175 100	31.6	13.0	680	34.8	1.3	4 142	5.8	278	6.7	3 722	30.1	21.8
Treutlen	2 627	69.7	71 100	23.4	11.2	461	22.9	2.4	2 742	1.6	214	7.8	2 692	18.5	34.5
Troup	24 645	57.9	116 300	22.4	12.1	770	31.8	3.2	36 588	2.8	1 878	5.1	28 677	29.1	31.8
Turner	3 013	70.3	70 900	22.5	17.1	583	31.3	6.0	3 232	1.3	214	6.6	2 900	32.8	27.7
Twiggs	3 022	77.4	56 900	22.2	14.4	531	35.2	2.7	3 013	1.7	261	8.7	2 581	24.0	38.9
Union	8 357	78.8	184 900	22.4	12.4	625	29.4	0.6	10 333	5.1	489	4.7	7 291	28.7	24.5
Upson	10 159	63.7	85 600	23.2	12.2	673	32.6	3.1	11 175	0.4	721	6.5	9 904	24.7	33.8
Walker	25 860	71.9	105 900	21.4	11.6	648	28.6	4.6	30 209	2.8	1 684	5.6	28 164	26.6	33.5
Walton	29 667	73.2	152 900	22.8	10.7	845	32.2	1.8	43 061	3.4	2 104	4.9	37 547	29.8	25.0
Ware	13 901	64.3	78 600	20.9	12.3	635	31.1	3.5	15 034	3.8	829	5.5	13 022	30.7	30.3
Warren	2 125	68.8	62 300	22.1	15.9	569	33.4	0.8	2 701	2.4	188	7.0	1 998	20.7	37.3
Washington	7 230	69.8	80 400	21.9	11.8	558	32.9	3.7	7 203	0.1	463	6.4	7 370	30.1	25.6
Wayne	10 066	68.4	91 400	22.0	11.6	625	29.3	1.7	11 469	-0.8	766	6.7	10 495	29.7	33.2
Webster	1 062	84.1	46 000	23.1	10.0	553	19.3	2.8	963	-0.5	85	8.8	1 139	30.9	29.5
Wheeler	2 012	63.1	49 400	23.1	10.6	475	28.2	1.8	1 718	1.4	156	9.1	1 339	25.9	35.1
White	11 316	73.8	155 800	26.2	12.5	706	32.9	2.4	14 467	5.0	666	4.6	11 029	29.5	26.8
Whitfield	34 575	64.3	120 400	22.0	10.0	671	29.0	6.0	46 293	1.6	2 741	5.9	45 345	21.1	42.5
Wilcox	2 742	71.9	64 900	21.4	11.8	478	36.4	4.5	2 840	3.6	200	7.0	2 446	28.9	30.5
Wilkes	4 006	70.8	95 200	27.3	15.4	617	36.8	1.2	3 954	1.7	248	6.3	3 798	26.5	36.0
Wilkinson	3 313	77.6	71 500	20.4	12.3	571	29.7	3.4	3 674	2.0	231	6.3	3 287	20.0	35.5
Worth	7 924	73.8	70 800	21.8	11.9	627	33.0	1.4	9 008	1.9	534	5.9	8 359	24.5	34.8
HAWAII	450 572	56.9	515 300	27.9	10.0	1 438	33.4	9.6	685 380	1.6	20 689	3.0	653 284	34.0	18.4
Hawaii	65 048	66.4	301 700	27.4	10.0	1 056	33.5	9.0	90 445	2.0	3 432	3.8	82 124	31.1	19.7
Honolulu	309 602	54.4	580 200	27.4	10.0	1 569	34.1	9.3	473 947	1.4	13 357	2.8	455 481	35.8	17.9
Kalawao	54	3.7	0.0	0.0	0.0	856	16.3	0.0	NA	NA	NA	NA	64	31.3	23.4
Kauai	22 405	61.6	480 600	32.0	11.0	1 267	29.4	8.4	35 531	1.2	1 181	3.3	33 996	29.3	18.8
Maui	53 463	57.7	509 700	29.7	10.0	1 287	30.8	12.4	85 457	1.9	2 719	3.2	81 619	29.0	19.9
IDAHO	589 320	68.9	162 900	22.7	10.0	743	29.4	3.5	814 575	2.2	31 140	3.8	715 861	33.5	24.4
Ada	157 286	67.3	188 800	21.5	10.0	856	29.4	2.0	225 083	3.4	7 487	3.3	199 955	42.4	15.4
Adams	1 592	77.1	145 000	21.9	11.8	573	27.2	2.6	1 744	1.4	124	7.1	1 474	27.9	28.2
Bannock	30 394	66.8	145 300	21.5	10.1	636	30.2	2.8	42 300	0.7	1 483	3.5	37 206	34.4	22.4
Bear Lake	2 346	79.6	138 900	17.5	10.2	558	22.3	2.0	2 827	-0.3	130	4.6	2 598	25.3	31.6
Benewah	3 668	72.2	142 800	24.6	11.4	656	26.0	5.8	4 036	-0.3	251	6.2	3 600	25.3	37.9
Bingham	14 698	74.1	141 400	20.7	10.0	645	24.2	5.3	22 748	2.9	816	3.6	19 121	30.9	32.9
Blaine	8 924	65.9	374 800	28.0	11.2	941	28.0	2.4	11 797	-0.5	378	3.2	11 941	31.9	19.3
Boise	2 970	82.5	188 200	22.4	11.3	668	29.4	3.8	3 139	2.6	173	5.5	2 768	36.8	23.5
Bonner	17 193	72.7	211 300	28.9	10.0	724	30.4	4.4	18 820	1.3	1 029	5.5	16 399	27.4	27.9
Bonneville	36 686	71.6	155 600	21.0	10.0	720	29.7	2.9	52 175	2.1	1 675	3.2	47 191	34.7	22.7
Boundary	4 265	74.0	172 800	24.3	11.1	707	35.1	3.6	5 080	-0.5	270	5.3	3 888	28.4	32.3
Butte	1 009	79.8	105 800	21.8	12.0	594	30.6	0.8	1 306	2.1	54	4.1	960	34.3	30.3
Camas	435	68.0	164 500	29.1	10.0	661	28.0	3.0	657	1.1	25	3.8	500	28.4	34.2
Canyon	65 807	68.7	122 200	24.2	10.8	746	29.2	5.0	93 761	2.8	4 107	4.4	81 460	25.7	30.3

1. Specified owner-occupied units.   2. A value of 10.0 represents 10 percent or less; a value of 50.0 represents 50 percent or more.   3. Specified renter-occupied units.
4. Overcrowded or lacking complete plumbing facilities.   5. Percent of civilian labor force.   6. Civilian employed persons 16 years old and over.

Table B. States and Counties — **Nonfarm Employment and Agriculture**

STATE County	Private nonfarm establishments, employment and payroll, 2015									Agriculture, 2012			
		Employment						Annual payroll		Farms			
												Percent with:	
	Number of establish-ments	Total	Health care and social assistance	Manufac-turing	Retail trade	Finance and insurance	Professional, scientific, and technical services	Total (mil dol)	Average per employee (dollars)	Number	Fewer than 50 acres	500 acres or more	Farm operators whose principal occu-pation is farming (percent)
	104	105	106	107	108	109	110	111	112	113	114	115	116
GEORGIA—Cont'd													
Putnam	432	4 326	432	562	928	157	61	128	29 502	165	37.0	6.7	41.2
Quitman	37	239	D	D	57	13	D	6	24 402	21	19.0	23.8	23.8
Rabun	475	3 995	528	268	1 000	129	130	119	29 880	114	57.0	0.9	62.3
Randolph	125	1 353	281	D	166	38	26	46	34 001	197	11.2	27.4	45.7
Richmond	4 327	89 062	24 612	7 165	11 554	2 231	5 153	3 659	41 084	123	59.3	5.7	40.7
Rockdale	1 946	32 079	3 895	6 716	4 561	838	922	1 384	43 143	103	77.7	1.0	58.3
Schley	66	693	19	315	112	D	D	26	38 013	92	17.4	19.6	41.3
Screven	199	2 120	158	898	328	98	41	67	31 718	344	14.8	26.2	48.5
Seminole	186	1 530	353	15	352	82	66	47	31 037	149	28.2	27.5	67.1
Spalding	1 133	17 144	4 300	2 914	2 705	431	444	579	33 793	258	63.6	1.9	49.2
Stephens	519	7 645	1 359	2 147	1 178	128	124	262	34 334	218	45.0	0.9	53.7
Stewart	63	649	111	D	53	19	3	22	33 989	108	7.4	36.1	36.1
Sumter	616	8 287	2 543	1 014	1 429	211	234	260	31 410	369	19.2	19.0	38.2
Talbot	64	482	D	D	48	28	3	18	38 351	90	22.2	23.3	43.3
Taliaferro	18	53	D	D	13	D	NA	1	24 264	55	16.4	10.9	43.6
Tattnall	288	3 113	666	105	437	130	131	106	33 937	565	35.6	8.3	59.1
Taylor	118	911	201	64	123	54	D	32	35 220	224	21.0	15.2	46.9
Telfair	183	3 129	361	D	330	89	29	70	22 234	300	29.3	9.0	36.7
Terrell	172	1 766	155	428	318	81	26	55	31 211	248	21.4	24.2	44.3
Thomas	1 109	15 079	3 571	2 471	2 179	623	320	655	43 456	407	35.4	21.1	54.3
Tift	1 019	15 433	2 393	1 350	2 658	424	533	527	34 156	285	19.3	15.4	43.2
Toombs	658	9 596	2 216	1 086	1 759	296	469	324	33 741	268	36.9	12.7	29.9
Towns	270	3 031	501	39	385	66	224	79	26 104	109	58.7	0.0	49.5
Treutlen	89	716	166	94	219	25	D	18	25 031	149	31.5	11.4	27.5
Troup	1 423	34 039	3 225	11 249	3 165	1 060	574	1 462	42 950	212	48.1	7.1	50.5
Turner	153	1 442	154	372	212	65	47	44	30 384	262	34.7	20.2	40.8
Twiggs	73	1 549	134	NA	57	D	D	59	38 276	108	36.1	12.0	37.0
Union	549	5 142	1 141	313	1 146	525	160	178	34 680	249	51.8	2.8	42.6
Upson	451	5 516	1 335	1 115	1 029	201	177	189	34 319	296	43.6	5.1	39.9
Walker	670	10 384	870	4 215	1 372	301	153	356	34 240	528	40.3	6.3	53.4
Walton	1 569	16 465	1 595	2 009	2 526	415	487	610	37 029	477	50.3	3.4	54.3
Ware	865	11 810	2 815	1 403	2 489	335	225	415	35 130	280	44.3	8.9	43.9
Warren	61	720	122	292	79	12	6	27	37 650	134	26.1	13.4	38.1
Washington	336	5 410	898	496	780	151	183	222	41 010	408	22.5	13.0	36.8
Wayne	536	5 879	1 019	1 001	1 211	163	239	213	36 211	287	37.3	13.9	41.5
Webster	29	408	D	D	45	9	NA	24	59 311	102	19.6	22.5	39.2
Wheeler	64	860	63	NA	62	D	D	28	32 922	136	15.4	17.6	25.7
White	597	5 841	753	798	1 182	141	124	180	30 806	299	64.2	2.7	53.8
Whitfield	2 160	48 419	4 528	17 696	4 803	683	1 715	1 950	40 268	378	45.2	2.6	49.2
Wilcox	87	512	159	13	82	53	D	15	29 078	365	21.6	23.6	47.9
Wilkes	193	2 072	419	521	343	72	27	62	29 971	317	24.0	13.2	47.0
Wilkinson	136	2 018	169	677	163	37	32	100	49 409	114	29.8	4.4	39.5
Worth	257	2 495	421	484	529	58	54	82	32 755	487	27.3	28.5	51.1
HAWAII	31 915	523 677	69 873	12 449	71 688	18 975	22 734	22 068	42 141	7 000	88.1	2.6	52.0
Hawaii	4 002	53 713	8 262	1 328	9 518	1 191	1 508	1 957	36 426	4 282	87.6	2.3	48.2
Honolulu	21 167	355 607	52 207	9 656	48 249	16 269	17 949	15 778	44 368	999	90.6	2.1	66.3
Kalawao	1	D	NA	NA	D	NA	NA	D	D	NA	NA	NA	NA
Kauai	2 014	26 708	3 203	308	4 133	387	922	1 000	37 458	591	85.3	4.2	52.3
Maui	4 545	61 991	6 189	1 157	9 774	900	1 512	2 390	38 550	1 128	89.0	3.5	54.0
IDAHO	44 757	546 524	89 070	57 884	82 400	21 637	33 003	21 120	38 644	24 816	47.9	17.1	49.8
Ada	12 757	188 732	31 933	14 058	24 872	9 379	14 473	8 664	45 908	1 233	80.0	3.1	43.6
Adams	101	529	44	169	113	11	12	15	28 129	234	35.5	20.1	53.4
Bannock	1 987	24 406	5 065	1 426	4 479	2 253	1 582	767	31 417	819	46.6	16.1	42.6
Bear Lake	119	938	296	40	244	45	8	27	28 553	493	25.2	24.7	46.9
Benewah	226	2 114	393	D	283	52	36	79	37 377	274	35.0	16.8	45.6
Bingham	843	10 149	1 915	2 269	1 303	280	226	351	34 584	1 265	56.4	17.1	58.5
Blaine	1 396	10 731	831	383	1 466	272	703	427	39 831	186	39.2	30.1	58.6
Boise	150	574	22	16	114	D	12	14	24 244	105	43.8	12.4	57.1
Bonner	1 446	11 489	1 589	1 916	2 140	277	477	394	34 300	686	51.0	3.4	42.9
Bonneville	3 394	45 621	8 030	2 939	7 660	1 255	6 636	1 870	40 985	893	53.1	18.6	39.0
Boundary	368	2 373	532	386	473	59	87	76	32 209	370	44.3	12.2	41.4
Butte	59	864	D	D	82	11	D	59	68 649	214	21.5	31.3	71.0
Camas	31	161	8	D	21	D	NA	5	28 913	114	24.6	36.8	56.1
Canyon	3 838	49 253	6 980	8 778	8 199	984	1 417	1 596	32 398	2 331	71.3	6.0	45.6

STATE County	Land in farms — Acreage (1,000)	Percent change, 2007–2012	Average size of farm	Total irrigated (1,000)	Total cropland (1,000)	Value of land and buildings (dollars) Average per farm	Average per acre	Value of machinery and equipment, average per farm (dollars)	Value of products sold Total (mil dol)	Average per farm (dollars)	Percent from: Crops	Live-stock and poultry products	Percent of farms with sales of: $10,000 or more	$100,000 or more	Government payments Total ($1,000)	Percent of farms
	117	118	119	120	121	122	123	124	125	126	127	128	129	130	131	132
GEORGIA—Cont'd																
Putnam	28	-24.5	173	0.8	9.6	656 891	3 803	91 436	38.0	230 521	3.8	96.2	35.8	13.3	567	20.0
Quitman	9	-20.0	433	0.0	2.4	924 667	2 133	66 762	D	D	D	D	14.3	9.5	D	57.1
Rabun	8	1.7	71	D	3.6	500 658	7 078	73 737	21.3	186 719	20.8	79.2	50.9	21.9	138	11.4
Randolph	119	32.4	605	22.0	64.7	1 171 264	1 935	185 523	50.3	255 442	95.8	4.2	40.1	22.3	2 025	79.7
Richmond	14	11.1	113	0.1	3.9	299 699	2 650	58 967	2.0	16 276	45.6	54.4	28.5	6.5	42	12.2
Rockdale	5	-13.6	53	0.0	0.9	370 515	6 982	38 777	0.5	4 660	56.5	43.5	11.7	1.0	4	6.8
Schley	35	-2.3	385	0.8	7.1	875 543	2 273	56 413	18.1	196 239	11.2	88.8	34.8	15.2	284	58.7
Screven	180	1.0	525	17.9	103.0	1 119 872	2 134	170 779	66.6	193 669	92.3	7.7	37.5	18.3	2 076	75.0
Seminole	88	-14.8	592	38.9	62.0	1 600 074	2 703	268 034	74.7	501 631	90.7	9.3	63.1	35.6	1 883	65.1
Spalding	19	-28.8	73	0.0	5.1	381 438	5 229	37 888	5.2	20 298	19.2	80.8	17.4	3.9	60	12.8
Stephens	18	19.7	84	0.0	4.8	445 170	5 272	96 917	79.7	365 583	0.6	99.4	50.5	25.7	189	12.4
Stewart	59	28.6	549	4.4	19.7	1 076 824	1 963	127 593	14.6	135 417	80.6	19.4	30.6	17.6	917	68.5
Sumter	160	4.8	435	44.3	90.4	983 650	2 264	167 710	123.3	334 236	68.4	31.6	36.3	18.4	3 044	68.6
Talbot	34	-18.7	377	D	4.9	784 578	2 084	42 133	0.7	8 200	37.0	63.1	18.9	2.2	266	21.1
Taliaferro	14	-2.1	251	0.1	3.6	552 345	2 202	66 745	8.5	153 709	5.0	95.0	40.0	18.2	75	23.6
Tattnall	108	-20.7	190	13.8	49.2	528 524	2 778	97 715	236.2	418 099	36.7	63.3	49.4	27.1	1 594	36.5
Taylor	62	-29.0	275	6.0	21.7	556 027	2 025	65 634	22.7	101 505	55.5	44.5	29.0	6.7	510	51.3
Telfair	67	7.9	222	4.0	13.8	422 643	1 903	46 887	6.1	20 390	78.8	21.2	25.7	4.7	581	57.3
Terrell	121	-11.6	487	25.8	73.2	1 150 536	2 364	163 758	68.2	274 843	96.7	3.3	33.9	26.2	3 795	81.5
Thomas	173	-15.2	426	11.5	81.6	1 423 002	3 344	159 329	83.5	205 061	77.8	22.2	43.7	22.6	2 676	56.3
Tift	84	-36.4	296	20.6	50.0	941 074	3 176	135 681	70.6	247 653	94.0	6.0	43.5	23.5	1 695	50.5
Toombs	73	-18.5	273	9.9	30.6	647 821	2 371	84 123	58.9	219 746	78.3	21.7	31.3	11.2	745	48.5
Towns	8	12.3	77	0.0	2.1	456 587	5 913	50 862	3.2	29 367	36.6	63.4	30.3	8.3	35	4.6
Treutlen	35	16.7	236	D	9.7	423 060	1 794	64 107	8.3	55 376	95.0	5.0	20.1	3.4	259	60.4
Troup	32	-14.4	153	0.2	5.2	608 769	3 981	52 245	4.2	19 660	23.6	76.3	25.9	2.4	94	8.1
Turner	87	-25.0	332	19.1	47.5	791 313	2 384	141 511	58.4	223 050	86.8	13.2	39.7	19.8	2 000	72.1
Twiggs	39	-13.9	358	5.1	14.3	895 907	2 501	93 389	9.3	85 685	93.5	6.5	23.1	7.4	738	30.6
Union	21	-1.2	83	0.0	6.1	500 076	6 015	65 426	19.4	77 751	23.5	76.5	39.8	5.6	221	15.7
Upson	45	-6.1	151	D	8.2	478 044	3 160	51 111	23.0	77 770	8.5	91.5	20.9	5.7	193	14.5
Walker	80	12.0	151	0.3	28.5	589 797	3 907	71 972	108.2	204 932	8.1	91.9	42.8	13.6	1 049	16.3
Walton	52	-2.3	110	0.9	14.3	590 239	5 367	39 698	29.4	61 660	21.2	78.8	32.1	7.5	371	21.0
Ware	57	12.8	203	4.9	18.5	499 896	2 468	72 825	30.6	109 114	65.6	34.4	40.4	10.4	339	32.9
Warren	34	-7.5	257	0.1	9.2	518 627	2 019	54 731	5.6	41 694	58.0	42.0	27.6	8.2	225	23.1
Washington	100	-9.3	245	7.8	42.8	506 213	2 067	88 184	27.5	67 507	73.8	26.2	32.8	9.8	1 104	52.0
Wayne	62	9.6	217	6.6	35.6	595 854	2 746	115 289	44.3	154 456	59.8	40.2	42.5	19.5	748	42.5
Webster	48	-12.1	471	4.8	22.2	834 667	1 772	59 471	17.2	168 471	88.7	11.3	32.4	16.7	619	74.5
Wheeler	51	-11.4	372	2.5	11.6	556 206	1 493	60 529	8.1	59 706	95.5	4.5	28.7	6.6	473	66.9
White	23	11.8	79	0.1	5.9	539 097	6 866	50 181	77.4	258 957	2.9	97.1	45.2	27.1	129	9.7
Whitfield	39	-8.5	103	0.0	10.6	501 405	4 846	66 577	144.2	381 362	1.2	98.8	36.0	17.2	85	7.4
Wilcox	115	14.5	316	28.4	75.2	771 348	2 439	146 175	104.9	287 512	64.5	35.5	41.9	26.3	2 491	80.3
Wilkes	94	4.4	296	0.1	19.7	820 962	2 777	62 407	58.7	185 306	5.6	94.4	45.1	16.7	662	33.1
Wilkinson	16	-46.8	140	0.5	4.8		2 134	40 939	4.5	39 614	29.3	70.7	24.6	8.8	42	23.7
Worth	229	19.1	471	47.2	137.4	1 216 889	2 584	177 600	153.5	315 187	90.6	9.4	42.5	28.7	5 342	67.8
HAWAII	1 129	0.7	161	81.8	174.0	1 461 342	9 058	43 999	661.3	94 478	81.5	18.5	41.6	7.2	5 228	9.0
Hawaii	687	0.4	160	7.0	72.0	1 280 898	7 985	36 698	247.2	57 741	63.3	36.7	40.6	6.1	4 153	8.2
Honolulu	69	14.5	69	10.8	22.2	1 396 597	20 171	56 908	161.5	161 650	90.0	10.0	54.6	12.7	283	6.1
Kalawao	NA	NA	NA	NA	NA	NA	NA	NA	NA	NA	NA	NA	NA	NA	NA	NA
Kauai	144	-4.9	244	22.5	30.2	1 853 486	7 600	57 464	64.5	109 161	86.3	13.7	35.2	6.6	234	16.2
Maui	229	1.6	203	41.5	49.6	1 998 207	9 836	53 229	188.1	166 755	96.5	3.5	37.1	7.1	558	10.5
IDAHO	11 760	2.3	474	3 365.3	5 793.3	1 052 941	2 222	143 835	7 801.4	314 372	44.1	55.9	44.3	20.5	99 789	37.7
Ada	144	-24.8	117	55.3	53.4	616 596	5 278	70 942	221.0	179 229	20.2	79.8	26.8	7.9	704	10.2
Adams	136	-8.6	582	19.0	19.8	885 517	1 521	67 226	13.5	57 902	25.1	74.9	41.9	11.5	104	16.7
Bannock	295	-8.3	360	52.6	164.1	651 077	1 807	83 179	54.3	66 267	66.6	33.4	29.4	9.2	3 067	37.0
Bear Lake	258	10.6	523	54.5	112.5	743 225	1 421	101 310	29.5	59 850	35.4	64.6	52.7	15.8	1 316	47.1
Benewah	147	-4.5	535	0.9	81.7	849 000	1 587	106 938	23.9	87 058	96.9	3.1	29.6	10.9	1 516	45.6
Bingham	870	-4.7	687	333.4	369.5	1 536 482	2 235	194 538	453.3	358 314	82.7	17.3	46.5	23.7	5 568	33.9
Blaine	179	-6.7	963	41.9	47.6	2 752 371	2 858	165 301	38.6	207 376	72.2	27.8	62.9	32.8	415	40.3
Boise	D	D	D	2.4	3.0	667 895	D	34 914	3.1	29 133	39.8	60.3	29.5	6.7	D	6.7
Bonner	81	-14.6	118	1.2	26.1	513 108	4 366	43 496	10.2	14 940	60.1	39.9	24.2	1.9	96	4.7
Bonneville	409	-9.7	458	133.6	278.8	1 061 908	2 317	134 569	204.2	228 641	71.8	28.2	39.9	17.9	5 044	43.2
Boundary	75	2.3	203	2.1	46.7	694 997	3 420	72 922	27.8	75 203	84.1	15.8	41.1	15.7	785	23.5
Butte	125	3.3	585	58.7	68.6	901 136	1 540	148 860	39.3	183 640	82.4	17.6	71.0	38.8	1 539	67.3
Camas	168	21.1	1 471	20.4	82.7	2 182 649	1 484	176 982	21.6	189 500	83.5	16.5	51.8	26.3	406	55.3
Canyon	304	16.7	130	225.3	217.8	694 984	5 332	109 214	513.7	220 387	53.0	47.0	38.9	15.6	2 241	20.6

STATE County	Water use, 2010		Wholesale trade,[1] 2012				Retail trade,[2] 2012				Real estate and rental and leasing,[2] 2012			
	Total water withdrawn (mil gal/day)	Gallons withdrawn per person per day	Number of establishments	Number of employees	Sales (mil dol)	Annual payroll (mil dol)	Number of establishments	Number of employees	Sales (mil dol)	Annual payroll (mil dol)	Number of establishments	Number of employees	Receipts (mil dol)	Annual payroll (mil dol)
	133	134	135	136	137	138	139	140	141	142	143	144	145	146
GEORGIA—Cont'd														
Putnam	957.6	45 130	16	68	57.9	2.7	75	668	157.4	14.1	12	225	9.7	3.9
Quitman	0.5	183	1	D	D	D	10	55	12.1	0.9	1	D	D	D
Rabun	3.2	194	4	6	0.5	0.1	76	902	247.7	22.3	19	D	D	D
Randolph	25.2	3 263	5	40	70.8	1.7	27	191	47.6	4.2	5	5	1.8	0.1
Richmond	114.4	571	182	1 856	864.7	81.5	812	10 830	2 627.3	229.5	201	1 069	248.9	37.9
Rockdale	13.6	160	80	636	525.7	34.1	293	4 625	1 239.6	116.2	77	327	83.0	14.9
Schley	1.0	202	4	56	44.4	2.1	14	76	19.3	1.6	NA	NA	NA	NA
Screven	7.1	488	8	D	D	D	49	360	74.5	6.9	4	7	0.7	0.2
Seminole	45.6	5 224	13	76	109.1	4.2	52	331	73.0	6.4	4	7	1.4	0.1
Spalding	6.3	98	39	428	467.1	17.9	224	2 669	638.8	59.4	48	185	29.9	5.7
Stephens	5.9	225	19	D	D	D	99	1 113	262.5	24.5	14	46	6.2	1.2
Stewart	1.6	262	2	D	D	D	15	42	17.1	1.0	1	D	D	D
Sumter	42.1	1 282	35	425	305.9	13.2	137	1 382	311.0	29.1	22	57	8.1	1.3
Talbot	2.9	415	3	11	8.8	0.2	12	65	11.7	0.8	NA	NA	NA	NA
Taliaferro	0.1	76	NA	NA	NA	NA	5	10	2.3	0.1	1	D	D	D
Tattnall	9.0	351	21	459	212.9	18.1	64	444	103.0	8.0	6	17	2.0	0.3
Taylor	6.0	671	4	D	D	D	29	152	36.9	2.6	3	8	0.7	0.1
Telfair	6.2	378	11	48	35.7	1.4	43	290	59.8	4.8	1	D	D	D
Terrell	26.1	2 798	7	162	250.1	4.0	45	316	68.0	6.0	4	D	D	D
Thomas	11.1	249	60	441	406.8	18.4	218	2 154	564.6	48.0	42	123	82.2	4.6
Tift	17.3	432	67	1 041	634.1	42.8	221	2 405	805.6	54.4	36	136	21.8	4.5
Toombs	10.8	396	28	566	996.3	20.8	149	1 640	406.4	35.5	24	59	7.6	1.3
Towns	4.5	429	8	19	2.9	0.4	57	344	87.1	6.9	15	22	7.0	0.8
Treutlen	2.2	312	2	D	D	D	22	140	29.9	2.6	1	D	D	D
Troup	12.0	179	58	D	D	D	258	3 072	911.1	73.7	61	272	41.3	7.5
Turner	9.4	1 053	13	148	81.6	5.3	32	179	66.7	4.0	2	D	D	D
Twiggs	6.6	729	3	D	D	D	16	68	27.9	1.1	1	D	D	D
Union	8.0	375	9	57	26.8	1.9	93	1 007	242.9	22.0	32	71	9.9	2.1
Upson	6.3	231	7	D	D	D	93	970	207.9	20.6	11	26	3.4	0.6
Walker	8.6	125	34	D	D	D	151	1 441	355.1	28.1	16	29	4.4	1.0
Walton	6.8	81	74	620	295.0	28.5	196	2 403	744.5	57.9	65	149	23.0	5.0
Ware	5.8	159	33	D	D	D	204	2 356	627.4	52.4	26	85	10.2	2.2
Warren	1.8	300	1	D	D	D	14	86	14.5	1.7	3	10	0.5	0.2
Washington	24.4	1 151	12	105	133.5	4.1	72	766	187.0	17.3	14	117	9.2	3.2
Wayne	62.0	2 059	12	99	71.0	2.9	120	1 201	293.1	25.4	16	57	5.3	1.3
Webster	9.3	3 323	3	D	D	D	5	38	9.0	1.1	NA	NA	NA	NA
Wheeler	2.9	385	3	5	6.5	0.3	14	70	21.2	1.2	2	D	D	D
White	2.9	106	15	79	30.7	2.1	119	1 097	279.7	23.0	18	59	6.1	1.0
Whitfield	22.6	220	191	2 604	1 196.6	103.0	435	4 690	1 302.4	107.7	63	D	D	D
Wilcox	8.9	966	7	38	34.3	1.5	19	90	23.4	1.6	NA	NA	NA	NA
Wilkes	1.9	180	9	81	24.1	3.2	48	406	70.4	7.4	4	11	0.9	0.3
Wilkinson	15.1	1 578	8	35	8.4	1.1	24	150	32.5	2.4	1	D	D	D
Worth	19.0	876	22	D	D	D	56	430	117.1	10.9	9	D	D	D
HAWAII	1 273.8	936	1 561	16 686	9 608.0	724.5	4 643	68 360	18 901.7	1 835.0	1 919	11 369	3 411.2	483.9
Hawaii	134.7	728	178	D	D	D	648	9 084	2 390.8	241.3	245	1 172	226.5	39.1
Honolulu	799.2	838	1 167	13 446	8 052.8	596.9	2 889	46 165	13 036.4	1 233.1	1 219	7 213	2 553.5	340.7
Kalawao	0.0	111	NA	NA	NA	NA	1	D	D	D	NA	NA	NA	NA
Kauai	61.8	921	76	D	D	D	347	3 937	1 013.5	102.4	149	962	176.9	33.3
Maui	278.1	1 796	140	1 141	714.6	50.4	758	D	D	D	306	2 022	454.4	70.8
IDAHO	17 230.5	10 992	1 739	21 470	17 906.0	960.8	5 815	72 980	20 444.3	1 794.0	2 033	6 268	1 039.9	184.2
Ada	832.2	2 121	550	8 141	7 352.5	419.6	1 410	20 428	5 766.7	538.7	712	2 578	456.9	85.2
Adams	78.2	19 663	1	D	D	D	12	D	D	D	7	4	0.4	0.1
Bannock	168.1	2 029	80	D	D	D	299	4 330	1 155.3	95.7	80	221	31.5	5.2
Bear Lake	177.0	29 571	5	54	13.8	1.4	26	232	58.8	4.0	5	14	1.1	0.2
Benewah	2.5	265	4	D	D	D	34	286	76.5	7.3	6	9	1.2	0.2
Bingham	956.8	20 979	50	1 047	635.9	33.6	111	1 132	256.2	23.6	19	37	5.7	1.1
Blaine	109.2	5 107	31	D	D	D	183	1 348	298.6	38.7	92	D	D	D
Boise	6.8	966	1	D	D	D	15	107	20.0	1.5	5	11	1.4	0.2
Bonner	20.1	491	28	157	45.5	5.5	199	1 960	438.0	45.4	68	220	30.9	6.9
Bonneville	716.8	6 877	169	2 021	3 049.6	90.5	477	6 757	1 956.5	157.1	134	460	80.6	13.8
Boundary	100.8	9 191	7	D	D	D	47	386	100.1	9.0	7	5	0.8	0.1
Butte	160.7	55 597	3	D	D	D	13	86	21.8	1.6	2	D	D	D
Camas	164.7	147 449	NA	NA	NA	NA	3	D	D	D	NA	NA	NA	NA
Canyon	746.5	3 951	148	1 600	1 089.0	71.7	485	7 102	2 149.4	182.5	149	434	49.0	10.6

1. Merchant wholesalers, except manufacturers' sales branches and offices.   2. Employer establishments.

Table B. States and Counties — Professional Services, Manufacturing, and Accommodation and Food Services

STATE County	Professional, scientific, and technical services, 2012				Manufacturing, 2012				Accommodation and food services, 2012			
	Number of establish-ments	Number of employees	Receipts (mil dol)	Annual payroll (mil dol)	Number of establish-ments	Number of employees	Receipts (mil dol)	Annual payroll (mil dol)	Number of establish-ments	Number of employees	Sales (mil dol)	Annual payroll (mil dol)
	147	148	149	150	151	152	153	154	155	156	157	158
GEORGIA—Cont'd												
Putnam	32	66	8.6	1.7	21	612	127.2	18.6	23	399	16.4	4.7
Quitman	1	D	D	D	NA	NA	NA	NA	1	D	D	D
Rabun	36	122	10.2	3.7	21	336	D	11.8	62	736	47.2	12.7
Randolph	8	28	2.5	0.6	4	D	D	D	11	66	2.7	0.7
Richmond	478	4 251	569.6	213.8	111	7 884	5 452.2	451.0	424	9 448	447.0	125.6
Rockdale	181	952	100.6	43.4	84	4 746	2 292.2	252.3	175	3 708	179.0	51.3
Schley	2	D	D	D	7	416	123.7	18.7	4	15	0.9	0.2
Screven	13	37	2.3	0.8	13	829	173.4	36.5	17	D	D	D
Seminole	8	D	D	D	3	6	D	D	15	D	D	D
Spalding	85	374	47.2	14.5	56	3 005	2 404.7	152.9	111	1 718	86.9	23.9
Stephens	39	205	28.1	15.2	54	1 807	511.6	73.5	42	595	24.9	6.4
Stewart	2	D	D	D	NA	NA	NA	NA	6	25	1.3	0.2
Sumter	39	D	D	D	25	1 103	492.5	37.8	59	882	37.2	10.2
Talbot	3	7	0.3	0.1	3	9	D	D	2	D	D	D
Taliaferro	NA	NA	NA	NA	NA	NA	NA	NA	1	D	D	D
Tattnall	20	76	5.4	1.7	9	59	7.3	1.5	15	D	D	D
Taylor	3	D	D	D	6	74	D	2.1	6	20	1.2	0.3
Telfair	10	37	2.7	1.0	8	D	D	D	15	D	D	D
Terrell	9	D	D	D	6	493	D	13.4	13	D	D	D
Thomas	74	331	41.1	12.2	41	2 677	674.9	109.0	82	1 240	59.3	15.0
Tift	81	533	47.6	23.0	39	1 289	528.1	51.5	98	2 175	100.8	26.9
Toombs	48	402	26.4	10.4	34	1 558	D	44.8	63	1 032	49.5	12.1
Towns	19	61	6.4	2.3	9	41	D	1.3	30	621	32.4	9.2
Treutlen	2	D	D	D	4	79	D	1.4	3	37	1.4	0.6
Troup	96	965	66.2	29.0	88	10 356	12 011.1	522.6	122	2 187	96.7	26.8
Turner	8	29	2.9	0.9	10	300	92.8	11.5	19	208	8.8	1.9
Twiggs	5	D	D	D	NA	NA	NA	NA	3	D	D	D
Union	43	165	15.3	5.5	27	260	54.0	10.2	46	547	28.4	7.1
Upson	30	126	15.3	3.8	19	1 252	D	51.1	39	512	25.3	6.6
Walker	51	497	16.1	7.1	55	3 652	1 753.7	129.3	49	D	D	D
Walton	158	516	65.3	18.8	56	1 800	777.9	84.4	103	1 603	72.9	19.9
Ware	61	252	23.2	6.9	31	1 118	D	35.1	66	1 317	59.3	14.8
Warren	4	6	0.7	0.2	NA	NA	NA	NA	3	7	0.4	0.1
Washington	24	170	14.2	7.8	17	565	157.5	21.4	27	409	18.3	5.0
Wayne	32	141	9.7	8.2	20	1 161	D	69.7	51	690	34.5	8.2
Webster	NA	NA	NA	NA	NA	NA	NA	NA	NA	NA	NA	NA
Wheeler	1	D	D	D	NA	NA	NA	NA	5	17	1.0	0.1
White	41	95	11.9	3.4	29	715	122.9	31.9	88	956	63.9	14.4
Whitfield	169	D	D	D	265	14 310	5 805.3	546.3	172	D	D	D
Wilcox	1	D	D	D	NA	NA	NA	NA	4	11	0.6	0.2
Wilkes	11	30	2.3	0.7	16	549	175.7	21.1	16	184	6.7	1.8
Wilkinson	5	38	2.9	0.9	12	763	D	52.9	6	25	1.0	0.2
Worth	16	55	5.4	1.7	11	256	D	10.2	14	D	D	D
HAWAII	3 226	21 629	3 334.1	1 265.6	796	11 440	D	465.0	3 518	98 364	9 536.7	2 536.0
Hawaii	294	1 502	193.3	72.1	112	1 182	283.3	46.4	430	12 297	1 124.5	324.7
Honolulu	2 399	18 234	2 895.1	1 105.4	544	9 076	D	370.8	2 355	57 486	5 273.2	1 333.0
Kalawao	NA	NA	NA	NA	NA	NA	NA	NA	NA	NA	NA	NA
Kauai	143	512	59.3	21.1	41	185	D	6.8	234	8 638	831.5	252.5
Maui	390	1 381	186.4	67.0	99	997	D	41.1	499	19 943	2 307.5	625.7
IDAHO	4 198	32 076	4 273.6	1 728.0	1 759	52 084	20 201.4	2 445.5	3 564	54 257	2 680.2	726.1
Ada	1 634	12 378	1 827.8	721.2	373	14 538	D	931.7	947	16 660	763.1	220.7
Adams	8	D	D	D	7	98	D	3.4	14	D	D	D
Bannock	165	1 277	84.2	40.3	44	1 633	916.3	67.7	197	3 199	135.5	37.2
Bear Lake	5	5	0.7	0.2	3	25	6.7	1.2	14	117	4.9	1.4
Benewah	9	D	D	D	11	548	D	D	23	D	D	D
Bingham	51	197	16.3	5.7	41	2 384	768.9	91.5	46	2 628	138.2	49.2
Blaine	154	652	91.7	45.5	45	298	57.8	12.8	111	D	D	D
Boise	9	8	0.6	0.1	4	13	4.2	0.7	23	D	D	D
Bonner	139	D	D	D	79	1 647	369.4	77.9	113	1 816	65.0	20.2
Bonneville	377	8 397	1 371.6	583.9	134	2 447	631.0	90.6	235	4 462	198.3	57.1
Boundary	23	90	6.0	2.2	24	293	D	11.6	23	D	D	D
Butte	2	D	D	D	NA	NA	NA	NA	11	D	D	D
Camas	NA	NA	NA	NA	NA	NA	NA	NA	7	32	1.4	0.2
Canyon	255	1 212	113.0	48.5	189	7 267	D	273.4	254	4 257	180.1	49.5

1. Establishment subject to federal tax.

STATE County	Health care and social assistance, 2012				Other services, 2012				Nonemployer businesses, 2015		Value of residential construction authorized by building permits, 2016	
	Number of establish-ments	Number of employees	Receipts (mil dol)	Annual payroll (mil dol)	Number of establish-ments	Number of employees	Receipts (mil dol)	Annual payroll (mil dol)	Number	Receipts (mil dol)	New Construction ($1,000)	Number of housing units
	159	160	161	162	163	164	165	166	167	168	169	170
GEORGIA—Cont'd												
Putnam	30	476	36.2	14.9	21	165	5.9	5.1	1 858	77.9	16 842	62
Quitman	3	D	D	D	2	D	D	D	142	3.6	100	1
Rabun	34	532	41.8	18.5	36	113	13.3	3.2	1 803	73.7	20 930	55
Randolph	8	D	D	D	8	18	2.8	0.4	450	12.3	750	3
Richmond	645	24 184	3 260.4	1 241.3	275	1 816	196.3	53.1	12 412	388.8	67 975	598
Rockdale	242	3 648	392.9	138.9	135	804	89.1	22.6	8 507	277.4	45 799	200
Schley	4	D	D	D	5	D	D	D	318	9.8	1 277	6
Screven	14	222	11.5	5.2	23	91	7.3	1.5	953	29.0	6 820	32
Seminole	22	D	D	D	11	D	D	D	629	27.9	645	4
Spalding	132	4 459	351.5	122.9	76	415	32.4	9.5	5 089	158.8	23 914	195
Stephens	52	1 390	110.8	47.2	29	222	12.1	3.9	1 646	63.9	6 479	32
Stewart	9	171	13.0	4.4	7	54	3.3	0.9	247	5.7	0	0
Sumter	80	D	D	D	45	D	D	D	1 908	58.7	2 451	16
Talbot	3	D	D	D	6	13	1.1	0.3	450	12.9	450	5
Taliaferro	1	D	D	D	4	D	D	D	88	3.4	NA	NA
Tattnall	27	720	99.8	26.5	15	D	D	D	1 239	52.5	3 138	24
Taylor	16	198	10.2	4.2	7	D	D	D	599	18.6	1 688	12
Telfair	18	476	25.2	12.3	14	51	6.4	1.4	708	27.4	3 916	49
Terrell	15	D	D	D	14	D	D	D	749	23.7	802	6
Thomas	146	3 668	404.9	149.3	63	483	52.9	11.5	3 211	143.5	33 969	239
Tift	110	3 122	399.3	149.5	56	290	26.7	7.8	3 100	133.0	16 159	159
Toombs	106	1 982	197.9	78.5	40	215	22.9	6.1	1 915	82.4	1 597	20
Towns	25	548	34.2	14.7	10	17	1.5	0.4	1 168	50.5	25 208	128
Treutlen	9	131	7.3	3.1	7	25	1.5	0.5	443	12.5	0	0
Troup	131	3 139	300.6	128.6	81	636	66.4	18.2	5 536	167.6	33 313	148
Turner	8	170	7.2	3.3	7	D	D	D	666	21.0	1 020	6
Twiggs	7	D	D	D	6	D	D	D	600	15.0	205	1
Union	66	1 110	97.3	39.7	28	168	20.5	4.3	2 224	84.3	39 570	155
Upson	65	1 433	130.3	53.2	40	D	D	D	1 705	51.1	2 893	18
Walker	53	957	64.0	26.6	39	258	22.2	7.7	4 121	157.5	21 296	144
Walton	133	1 554	176.9	57.5	113	346	33.7	8.0	7 927	295.7	67 761	513
Ware	119	2 883	284.9	112.7	53	261	25.1	7.1	1 886	70.9	14 109	114
Warren	5	134	6.5	3.2	4	D	D	D	344	10.6	0	0
Washington	33	1 001	56.1	27.1	29	71	6.4	1.7	1 248	40.2	7 671	71
Wayne	65	1 036	102.4	35.3	31	160	16.3	3.7	1 745	58.1	4 535	31
Webster	1	D	D	D	1	D	D	D	157	6.1	498	6
Wheeler	5	D	D	D	3	3	0.4	0.1	373	14.6	0	0
White	34	418	26.6	11.1	41	168	13.5	3.4	2 503	98.1	13 828	70
Whitfield	192	4 275	482.4	180.7	117	855	76.7	25.8	5 998	296.0	19 271	131
Wilcox	12	D	D	D	7	D	D	D	559	17.4	NA	NA
Wilkes	24	547	32.2	13.1	10	37	3.5	0.7	646	22.1	350	5
Wilkinson	15	D	D	D	10	29	2.2	0.6	627	17.9	1 042	9
Worth	26	D	D	D	27	64	7.4	1.8	1 266	45.1	3 165	17
HAWAII	3 559	66 772	8 136.9	3 290.6	2 808	19 348	2 004.8	538.7	104 707	5 039.0	1 266 133	3 369
Hawaii	469	7 503	781.2	356.4	288	1 387	166.1	41.0	17 400	759.9	365 774	978
Honolulu	2 520	50 049	6 302.6	2 481.0	2 012	14 967	1 522.4	411.8	64 258	3 187.6	641 470	1 658
Kalawao	NA	NA	NA	NA	NA	NA	NA	NA	NA	NA	NA	NA
Kauai	177	3 082	311.6	145.0	125	809	78.2	23.9	6 875	303.0	107 781	166
Maui	393	6 138	741.5	308.2	383	2 185	238.1	62.0	16 174	788.5	151 108	567
IDAHO	4 865	83 505	7 895.6	3 171.2	2 553	12 188	1 118.2	311.4	122 221	5 332.7	2 367 554	12 165
Ada	1 387	29 953	3 174.3	1 355.9	768	4 121	377.4	112.2	35 880	1 675.9	1 056 832	4 697
Adams	5	D	D	D	3	D	D	D	375	13.2	5 053	9
Bannock	335	3 819	314.1	115.4	120	591	61.6	15.7	5 007	198.7	26 237	202
Bear Lake	13	314	24.7	10.4	5	D	D	D	445	15.2	10 350	34
Benewah	16	391	28.2	12.2	14	D	D	D	541	23.0	1 685	14
Bingham	96	1 817	155.9	67.8	51	279	33.8	8.4	2 792	124.6	14 283	130
Blaine	72	687	73.4	31.9	89	299	46.6	11.2	3 504	207.7	90 987	85
Boise	5	18	1.3	0.5	8	D	D	D	612	19.6	14 021	57
Bonner	141	1 640	130.6	53.4	79	322	22.6	6.5	3 983	152.5	17 887	130
Bonneville	537	7 680	846.0	289.1	174	852	87.1	22.0	8 231	374.0	104 673	707
Boundary	28	536	30.2	14.8	18	40	3.4	0.9	931	36.9	12 193	51
Butte	7	D	D	D	6	D	D	D	208	6.2	808	5
Camas	4	13	0.4	0.2	NA	NA	NA	NA	105	2.9	645	5
Canyon	374	6 754	530.8	216.1	206	1 039	93.0	26.7	12 342	509.1	250 655	1 882

Table B. States and Counties — Government Employment and Payroll, and Local Government Finances

STATE County	Full-time equivalent employees	March payroll (dollars)	Adminis-tration, judicial, and legal	Police and Corrections	Fire Protection	Highways and transportation	Health and Welfare	Natural resources and utilities	Education and libraries	Total (mil dol)	Inter-govern-mental (mil dol)	Total (mil dol)	Total (per capita, dollars)	Property (per capita, dollars)
	171	172	173	174	175	176	177	178	179	180	181	182	183	184
GEORGIA—Cont'd														
Putnam	984	3 113 107	7.0	8.5	2.1	1.9	21.4	3.9	53.4	77.1	16.7	40.8	1 927	1 196
Quitman	121	315 487	9.9	7.4	0.2	4.3	8.7	2.9	65.7	8.3	4.1	3.2	1 332	1 155
Rabun	712	2 242 761	6.8	10.9	2.2	4.4	7.2	5.6	61.5	63.4	12.6	43.0	2 638	1 882
Randolph	534	1 324 386	4.1	6.0	1.2	2.8	42.1	4.5	38.3	42.9	11.1	14.3	1 951	1 486
Richmond	7 950	24 545 151	7.9	10.6	4.4	2.7	3.5	7.3	62.0	723.6	324.4	222.4	1 098	673
Rockdale	3 955	12 355 812	6.2	9.9	4.2	1.3	0.7	4.5	71.2	266.8	93.9	129.0	1 503	1 071
Schley	221	708 164	2.4	6.6	0.0	3.3	4.8	4.1	78.8	16.0	8.4	5.0	1 011	733
Screven	656	1 803 310	6.3	10.5	2.8	3.9	4.8	5.5	64.2	45.6	23.1	16.0	1 128	780
Seminole	372	1 424 704	4.2	9.3	2.0	3.8	4.4	1.3	74.5	27.2	10.7	13.1	1 463	928
Spalding	2 703	8 758 007	4.7	13.1	5.5	2.0	7.8	7.1	56.8	223.0	90.1	90.6	1 418	906
Stephens	894	2 549 588	7.6	10.7	2.8	2.5	1.9	9.9	61.7	120.9	28.0	31.7	1 223	823
Stewart	231	632 898	9.4	19.7	2.8	4.9	5.1	4.7	52.5	14.0	5.9	5.5	915	668
Sumter	1 492	4 667 090	4.8	12.0	4.4	1.8	14.0	4.3	55.3	123.8	56.0	47.3	1 498	959
Talbot	263	648 950	15.0	7.1	0.0	6.9	4.5	5.3	60.1	16.0	5.2	8.8	1 350	1 039
Taliaferro	95	252 316	11.8	15.2	0.0	6.8	1.6	0.9	60.8	6.4	2.1	3.2	1 880	1 613
Tattnall	764	2 267 688	6.8	7.3	0.0	4.7	3.0	3.2	73.4	51.7	24.6	20.6	810	496
Taylor	402	1 087 805	6.6	7.8	0.7	2.6	1.3	2.5	76.3	24.2	12.5	8.6	1 017	618
Telfair	434	1 158 142	7.7	9.9	4.9	3.3	2.8	4.0	66.4	30.4	12.8	13.3	813	533
Terrell	443	1 230 523	6.4	14.1	3.6	2.3	4.9	4.0	64.2	29.7	13.0	12.4	1 376	912
Thomas	2 420	7 648 981	5.7	7.9	3.2	3.4	8.3	6.5	59.1	194.9	58.8	64.1	1 432	870
Tift	3 242	12 909 421	2.9	4.3	0.8	1.6	59.8	2.1	26.8	404.4	50.3	64.4	1 568	788
Toombs	1 085	3 290 743	4.9	9.0	1.7	1.4	3.9	3.2	74.9	191.8	42.5	32.2	1 177	561
Towns	518	1 438 233	4.8	7.4	0.8	3.1	0.3	24.8	49.8	26.3	6.4	15.9	1 518	962
Treutlen	241	645 937	7.5	7.8	0.4	3.2	1.3	4.5	74.0	28.8	21.1	5.0	740	446
Troup	3 339	10 586 640	4.7	11.9	4.4	1.8	9.1	6.2	59.3	240.0	99.8	101.3	1 480	879
Turner	509	1 317 091	10.3	7.4	1.7	4.5	3.8	5.8	62.7	31.0	13.3	10.2	1 209	826
Twiggs	296	826 420	11.0	20.1	0.5	4.9	0.4	1.5	60.0	20.2	6.9	10.5	1 247	910
Union	1 493	4 119 774	3.0	5.1	1.6	1.3	48.9	4.1	35.5	56.7	15.8	34.2	1 593	1 016
Upson	965	2 830 552	6.4	11.2	2.1	2.0	0.7	3.7	72.7	154.8	37.1	28.6	1 073	730
Walker	2 622	7 660 154	5.8	5.5	2.5	2.1	10.7	4.8	66.0	172.5	90.6	54.3	798	474
Walton	3 007	10 183 150	6.0	8.9	3.5	2.6	2.5	5.6	68.5	253.5	88.7	125.8	1 487	1 043
Ware	1 747	5 214 214	5.1	10.2	4.2	3.4	17.2	1.0	56.2	150.2	74.1	48.2	1 345	705
Warren	197	551 517	8.8	6.8	0.0	4.0	6.1	5.3	64.2	16.7	6.7	7.4	1 320	928
Washington	1 131	3 414 908	4.5	6.7	0.9	3.9	35.1	4.5	42.2	125.1	24.7	31.9	1 530	951
Wayne	1 486	4 440 469	3.8	6.1	0.9	3.2	35.1	2.4	45.9	139.5	38.9	37.7	1 243	759
Webster	104	294 610	7.7	5.3	0.0	3.0	2.2	1.0	80.8	9.5	3.7	4.2	1 493	1 310
Wheeler	259	643 558	10.3	8.6	0.0	6.2	1.6	4.0	68.1	17.9	10.2	6.1	772	542
White	868	2 678 650	6.8	11.0	0.9	2.2	1.2	3.4	72.6	77.2	27.9	40.3	1 464	942
Whitfield	4 096	14 180 499	3.9	6.7	4.0	3.4	7.2	11.9	61.8	347.4	152.6	112.5	1 088	733
Wilcox	281	825 846	7.4	8.9	0.0	5.0	0.3	1.5	76.4	20.6	10.9	7.4	819	578
Wilkes	700	2 101 724	4.1	4.7	2.3	3.1	36.0	3.8	45.3	48.7	11.7	15.5	1 540	1 102
Wilkinson	479	1 156 738	10.2	14.5	0.0	4.8	0.4	1.9	66.2	39.7	18.0	19.1	1 997	1 336
Worth	797	2 247 660	7.4	8.5	3.1	4.5	0.1	4.6	69.5	50.7	23.4	19.6	900	588
HAWAII	X	X	X	X	X	X	X	X	X	X	X	X	X	X
Hawaii	2 415	11 250 002	15.2	26.6	22.6	11.1	5.5	17.0	0.0	375.6	91.7	253.3	1 339	1 101
Honolulu	9 304	47 881 176	14.1	35.4	14.0	2.6	6.8	20.8	0.0	2 232.4	331.8	1 316.4	1 348	833
Kalawao	NA	NA	NA	NA	NA	NA	NA	NA	NA	NA	NA	NA	NA	NA
Kauai	1 232	5 830 608	20.2	19.2	15.5	10.5	6.2	20.4	0.0	188.8	66.9	100.2	1 465	1 179
Maui	2 328	11 762 934	19.0	23.7	16.4	6.9	6.2	25.4	0.0	252.6	23.1	224.7	1 420	1 317
IDAHO	X	X	X	X	X	X	X	X	X	X	X	X	X	X
Ada	12 112	39 983 613	9.7	14.3	6.3	4.1	3.0	5.8	55.5	1 138.5	454.6	413.3	1 010	956
Adams	147	443 031	15.8	17.4	0.0	11.4	1.6	4.6	45.7	11.9	6.2	4.4	1 132	952
Bannock	2 618	8 746 568	9.9	14.1	5.7	4.5	6.0	6.6	51.4	238.0	114.9	73.0	871	828
Bear Lake	229	654 192	13.1	9.9	0.2	7.8	3.3	5.5	57.6	22.6	13.4	2.6	441	419
Benewah	501	1 444 872	5.0	6.6	1.0	3.3	36.5	3.9	43.4	44.1	19.2	5.9	652	616
Bingham	1 565	4 338 272	6.4	11.2	2.5	4.1	0.9	3.8	70.0	101.5	63.5	23.4	514	501
Blaine	959	4 228 217	10.2	10.1	5.2	3.3	0.5	6.4	61.6	114.6	26.2	66.7	3 152	3 047
Boise	251	737 278	24.2	12.1	0.6	8.0	2.0	2.2	50.8	23.1	11.0	7.0	1 022	1 015
Bonner	1 368	4 223 862	11.1	13.5	5.6	4.8	4.5	6.4	51.1	107.8	42.8	46.9	1 158	1 112
Bonneville	3 464	10 839 917	6.9	10.9	5.5	3.6	4.1	8.8	57.9	271.5	135.2	82.8	776	747
Boundary	529	1 491 650	6.9	7.2	0.6	4.2	37.3	5.6	37.2	38.9	14.5	7.6	707	698
Butte	218	969 719	3.5	4.5	0.0	4.1	61.6	0.6	25.3	15.1	4.0	3.5	1 273	1 204
Camas	63	187 878	16.7	9.7	0.0	19.8	0.0	1.9	52.0	4.7	2.8	1.5	1 353	1 312
Canyon	5 895	18 424 410	6.4	13.6	4.1	2.0	2.4	5.1	63.5	487.9	253.1	149.0	768	705

1. Based on the resident population estimated as of July 1 of the year shown.

Table B. States and Counties — Local Government Finances, Government Employment, and Income Taxes

STATE County	Direct general expenditure — Total (mil dol)	Direct general expenditure — Per capita¹ (dollars)	Percent of total for: Education	Percent of total for: Health and hospitals	Percent of total for: Police protection	Percent of total for: Public welfare	Percent of total for: Highways	Debt outstanding — Total (mil dol)	Debt outstanding — Per capita¹ (dollars)	Government employment 2015 — Federal civilian	Government employment 2015 — Federal military	Government employment 2015 — State and local	Income tax returns 2014 — Number of returns	Income tax returns 2014 — Mean adjusted gross income	Income tax returns 2014 — Mean income tax
	185	186	187	188	189	190	191	192	193	194	195	196	197	198	199
GEORGIA—Cont'd															
Putnam	72.9	3 441	44.6	23.5	6.0	0.8	3.3	32.9	1 552	63	59	1 472	9 180	49 237	5 564
Quitman	8.2	3 406	52.3	7.2	6.2	1.8	4.5	6.3	2 614	D	D	145	850	32 032	2 032
Rabun	76.9	4 718	60.5	4.4	4.4	0.2	5.2	64.1	3 932	57	45	751	7 110	47 029	4 343
Randolph	40.0	5 457	32.6	34.8	3.1	0.0	2.6	8.5	1 166	20	19	615	2 640	33 030	2 386
Richmond	773.0	3 816	44.0	5.8	5.2	0.1	2.9	1 078.9	5 326	7 570	11 704	22 997	86 870	40 222	3 789
Rockdale	265.4	3 093	63.2	1.2	6.2	0.4	1.5	131.0	1 526	103	249	4 348	38 790	45 202	4 130
Schley	15.2	3 050	68.7	0.6	3.4	0.2	3.0	10.5	2 102	D	14	326	1 720	41 533	2 986
Screven	51.6	3 634	47.5	4.3	4.4	0.5	7.2	16.6	1 168	40	38	938	5 650	37 921	3 050
Seminole	28.0	3 127	58.5	3.1	7.8	0.0	6.4	2.0	222	21	24	457	3 460	40 883	4 102
Spalding	220.8	3 457	49.2	9.1	6.7	0.1	2.5	97.8	1 531	128	176	4 665	26 430	40 949	3 654
Stephens	131.2	5 068	39.4	38.7	2.9	0.3	1.2	65.0	2 510	67	70	1 718	10 010	43 348	4 580
Stewart	14.4	2 389	48.8	0.7	7.9	0.1	8.9	2.2	358	90	12	261	1 620	33 093	2 334
Sumter	189.6	6 009	27.5	40.2	3.7	0.1	1.5	43.4	1 374	121	82	2 767	12 110	38 699	3 457
Talbot	16.6	2 545	46.5	5.7	6.5	0.7	8.6	6.3	967	12	18	241	2 660	34 714	2 655
Taliaferro	6.4	3 816	48.9	2.7	14.8	2.5	5.5	0.7	438	D	D	140	640	31 852	2 319
Tattnall	52.9	2 082	60.1	2.7	5.1	0.1	7.0	17.8	701	49	58	2 064	8 000	39 136	3 425
Taylor	23.7	2 820	66.0	2.8	6.0	0.4	4.5	3.3	389	19	23	415	3 170	37 088	2 686
Telfair	30.5	1 866	55.4	3.3	8.2	0.4	6.3	11.0	675	28	36	803	3 890	33 155	2 419
Terrell	29.3	3 236	51.1	4.8	7.0	0.1	4.1	9.0	992	69	25	509	4 020	40 924	4 007
Thomas	190.8	4 266	41.2	9.8	5.5	0.1	5.3	245.9	5 499	190	124	3 105	18 750	51 661	6 492
Tift	381.3	9 285	20.1	64.4	1.5	0.1	1.9	195.8	4 767	201	110	5 484	17 060	43 067	4 398
Toombs	186.3	6 822	31.2	50.6	2.8	0.0	1.5	76.6	2 805	67	75	1 583	11 100	41 541	3 916
Towns	27.3	2 598	47.1	4.4	6.0	2.9	4.7	28.4	2 702	25	28	501	4 860	46 399	4 814
Treutlen	32.8	4 842	80.8	1.3	2.9	0.7	1.9	13.3	1 965	13	18	334	2 360	34 917	2 406
Troup	264.2	3 858	45.4	7.1	6.4	0.4	8.6	84.1	1 228	138	189	3 825	29 730	44 974	4 414
Turner	30.7	3 654	53.3	4.1	8.0	0.8	7.1	13.4	1 596	29	22	554	3 400	33 348	2 576
Twiggs	20.6	2 444	54.2	2.1	10.0	1.2	8.4	10.3	1 223	10	23	330	3 670	35 847	2 552
Union	54.6	2 546	54.2	3.2	5.7	0.9	3.8	28.4	1 326	48	62	1 689	9 300	45 304	4 568
Upson	143.4	5 384	30.0	51.3	2.2	0.0	1.4	37.4	1 403	39	73	1 314	10 610	39 569	3 308
Walker	177.3	2 604	57.4	15.8	4.9	0.8	3.6	84.0	1 233	103	187	3 275	25 510	41 857	3 664
Walton	248.4	2 937	56.6	1.1	6.4	1.4	4.9	295.1	3 490	143	246	3 485	36 830	53 995	5 389
Ware	150.8	4 210	40.9	26.4	5.2	0.2	4.1	43.3	1 209	100	94	3 023	13 630	40 232	3 709
Warren	15.9	2 855	53.9	0.2	11.9	1.1	8.2	9.0	1 620	17	15	266	2 250	33 865	2 332
Washington	93.4	4 474	37.1	33.1	4.7	0.1	6.2	65.8	3 153	49	53	2 284	8 010	42 046	3 909
Wayne	133.6	4 408	40.5	35.6	3.7	0.5	4.6	47.0	1 550	407	78	2 125	10 860	43 099	3 746
Webster	9.9	3 552	48.2	4.4	3.0	0.6	5.2	2.9	1 037	D	D	133	930	32 574	2 285
Wheeler	20.1	2 548	57.2	2.6	5.1	0.0	4.0	7.1	901	11	15	288	1 800	31 672	2 279
White	82.8	3 003	62.2	1.4	5.2	0.4	3.1	24.2	879	47	78	1 034	11 000	43 434	3 956
Whitfield	397.4	3 845	52.0	10.1	3.9	0.2	4.6	103.9	1 005	138	289	5 426	42 040	46 497	4 948
Wilcox	20.2	2 223	65.8	2.8	6.4	1.0	7.1	1.1	120	22	19	583	2 730	34 354	2 448
Wilkes	56.9	5 644	29.5	36.5	4.0	0.5	3.2	51.2	5 077	35	27	745	4 090	37 393	3 282
Wilkinson	52.8	5 509	73.3	2.0	4.8	0.6	3.6	25.9	2 707	19	25	489	3 980	38 793	2 987
Worth	55.0	2 532	54.0	1.3	8.3	0.1	10.1	14.9	684	36	58	872	8 550	37 798	2 965
HAWAII	X	X	X	X	X	X	X	X	X	33 088	58 274	94 002	681 790	58 211	6 748
Hawaii	354.9	1 876	0.0	0.0	13.4	1.9	13.5	415.5	2 196	1 340	1 365	11 833	85 110	48 554	5 239
Honolulu	1 596.7	1 635	0.0	1.5	15.2	0.0	7.8	5 300.0	5 428	30 403	55 136	68 941	483 720	60 995	7 170
Kalawao	NA	NA	NA	NA	NA	NA	NA	NA	NA	(2)	(2)	(2)	NA	NA	NA
Kauai	196.1	2 865	0.0	0.0	13.7	5.8	8.0	246.2	3 598	532	618	4 146	34 430	53 493	6 080
Maui	264.1	1 669	0.0	0.0	15.8	6.0	2.7	281.6	1 780	(2)813	(2)1 155	(2)9 082	78 530	53 599	6 078
IDAHO	X	X	X	X	X	X	X	X	X	12 630	8 772	106 892	701 960	52 763	5 920
Ada	1 060.4	2 592	40.6	0.3	10.7	0.9	7.6	516.6	1 263	5 510	1 527	28 112	193 620	65 199	8 753
Adams	10.4	2 645	37.6	0.0	12.3	0.0	13.2	4.7	1 205	112	13	208	1 620	41 730	3 885
Bannock	221.0	2 637	41.2	2.7	8.1	1.0	5.5	54.8	654	549	280	7 751	33 960	47 062	4 309
Bear Lake	24.3	4 106	33.5	22.5	2.2	0.4	1.3	2.5	424	48	20	612	2 490	44 708	3 921
Benewah	38.9	4 264	35.2	40.0	2.3	0.7	4.2	11.6	1 277	53	31	1 272	3 840	40 720	3 321
Bingham	100.2	2 204	61.5	0.3	7.5	0.7	6.2	46.6	1 024	218	152	3 727	18 200	48 199	4 450
Blaine	113.0	5 346	53.5	2.2	8.7	3.0	3.7	69.4	3 281	100	73	1 360	11 660	91 978	15 594
Boise	17.6	2 582	45.9	0.8	0.9	0.9	9.6	15.5	2 261	132	24	331	3 000	53 377	5 698
Bonner	109.1	2 696	37.9	3.6	6.5	0.6	9.0	31.1	769	180	141	2 189	18 660	49 719	5 587
Bonneville	269.6	2 527	46.0	1.3	7.4	0.3	4.9	252.9	2 370	772	374	5 451	45 370	57 455	6 601
Boundary	40.5	3 751	26.8	27.6	9.8	1.0	7.6	14.5	1 345	158	38	944	4 790	41 903	3 609
Butte	12.7	4 635	28.6	45.0	2.1	0.8	3.4	2.7	1 003	66	25	150	1 040	43 865	3 540
Camas	4.6	4 281	41.0	0.3	12.3	0.2	19.9	3.6	3 301	23	D	86	450	49 940	5 498
Canyon	467.4	2 411	45.9	1.7	8.3	1.0	4.9	465.5	2 401	353	697	8 838	80 440	42 685	3 547

1. Based on the resident population estimated as of July 1 of the year shown.   2. Kalawao county is included with Maui county.

Table B. States and Counties — **Land Area and Population**

STATE/ County code	CBSA code[1]	County type[2]	STATE County	Land area[3] (sq mi) 2016	Total persons 2016	Rank	Per square mile	White	Black	American Indian, Alaska Native	Asian and Pacific Islander	Percent Hispanic or Latino[4]	Under 5 years	5 to 17 years	18 to 24 years	25 to 34 years	35 to 44 years	45 to 54 years
				1	2	3	4	5	6	7	8	9	10	11	12	13	14	15
			IDAHO—Cont'd															
16 029	...	6	Caribou	1 764.1	6 887	2 682	3.9	93.3	0.4	1.2	1.0	5.5	7.0	21.3	6.7	11.2	12.3	10.5
16 031	15420	7	Cassia	2 565.6	23 504	1 658	9.2	71.0	0.5	1.1	1.2	27.4	8.3	23.9	9.0	11.8	11.7	10.0
16 033	...	9	Clark	1 763.2	860	3 113	0.5	54.4	1.2	1.5	1.3	43.1	6.2	21.0	7.4	14.2	11.5	12.7
16 035	...	6	Clearwater	2 457.2	8 497	2 552	3.5	92.3	1.0	3.2	1.3	4.3	3.8	12.6	6.3	10.4	10.3	13.4
16 037	...	8	Custer	4 922.6	4 096	2 896	0.8	93.9	0.8	1.8	1.0	4.4	4.4	12.4	5.5	9.2	10.1	12.0
16 039	34300	6	Elmore	3 075.0	26 018	1 563	8.5	76.1	3.7	2.0	5.0	16.4	8.2	17.3	12.4	16.0	11.2	11.0
16 041	30860	3	Franklin	663.2	13 406	2 203	20.2	92.2	0.5	1.2	0.5	6.8	7.6	25.4	8.5	10.5	12.5	10.4
16 043	39940	6	Fremont	1 863.8	12 943	2 230	6.9	86.3	0.5	1.4	0.7	12.3	6.7	20.3	8.8	10.8	11.7	11.8
16 045	14260	2	Gem	559.8	17 184	1 970	30.7	89.5	0.5	1.8	1.8	8.4	5.9	17.4	7.1	10.1	10.3	12.5
16 047	...	7	Gooding	729.3	15 185	2 083	20.8	69.0	0.5	1.5	1.2	29.3	6.7	20.7	8.9	11.1	11.9	11.5
16 049	...	6	Idaho	8 477.3	16 156	2 030	1.9	92.9	0.7	4.0	1.1	3.3	5.0	14.8	6.9	8.9	9.4	11.6
16 051	26820	3	Jefferson	1 093.8	27 839	1 495	25.5	87.9	0.4	1.2	1.2	10.6	8.9	25.4	7.9	12.0	13.1	10.3
16 053	46300	7	Jerome	597.2	22 994	1 680	38.5	64.4	0.4	1.1	0.8	34.3	8.8	22.4	8.9	13.1	11.5	11.3
16 055	17660	3	Kootenai	1 237.6	154 311	422	124.7	92.9	0.7	2.3	2.0	4.4	6.1	17.2	7.8	12.7	11.7	12.6
16 057	34140	4	Latah	1 075.9	39 196	1 196	36.4	91.6	1.5	1.5	3.6	4.3	5.5	13.1	24.4	14.2	9.8	9.5
16 059	...	7	Lemhi	4 563.4	7 723	2 615	1.7	95.3	0.8	1.9	1.0	3.1	4.5	13.9	5.4	9.2	9.0	11.0
16 061	...	8	Lewis	478.9	3 853	2 916	8.0	88.5	1.1	8.0	1.7	4.4	5.9	17.2	5.9	9.0	8.9	10.8
16 063	25200	9	Lincoln	1 201.4	5 271	2 814	4.4	68.5	0.7	1.2	0.9	30.1	6.6	23.8	8.3	11.4	13.6	11.5
16 065	39940	4	Madison	469.3	39 048	1 206	83.2	90.2	0.8	0.8	2.4	7.4	10.0	17.3	30.4	15.7	7.7	6.3
16 067	15420	7	Minidoka	757.2	20 616	1 792	27.2	63.6	0.6	1.4	0.8	34.8	8.1	20.6	9.2	11.7	11.3	10.8
16 069	30300	3	Nez Perce	848.3	40 369	1 166	47.6	89.2	0.9	6.7	1.8	3.8	6.2	15.3	8.9	13.0	11.2	12.1
16 071	...	8	Oneida	1 198.8	4 343	2 873	3.6	94.2	0.5	0.8	0.9	4.4	6.2	22.3	7.0	9.0	11.0	10.8
16 073	14260	2	Owyhee	7 666.0	11 389	2 334	1.5	69.4	0.7	3.9	1.0	26.7	6.4	19.8	8.6	10.3	11.6	12.6
16 075	36620	6	Payette	406.9	23 026	1 678	56.6	80.2	0.6	2.1	1.7	17.5	6.9	20.1	7.8	11.1	11.5	12.6
16 077	...	6	Power	1 403.8	7 654	2 619	5.5	62.6	0.7	3.0	1.0	34.3	8.8	22.9	8.2	11.9	10.4	11.1
16 079	...	6	Shoshone	2 637.6	12 452	2 263	4.7	93.7	0.7	3.1	1.2	3.5	5.9	14.0	6.9	10.2	10.1	13.0
16 081	27220	9	Teton	449.2	10 960	2 358	24.4	81.8	0.4	0.6	0.8	17.0	7.4	19.5	6.6	13.1	17.2	14.7
16 083	46300	5	Twin Falls	1 921.8	83 514	678	43.5	81.3	0.9	1.3	2.2	15.9	7.7	20.1	8.5	14.0	12.2	10.9
16 085	...	8	Valley	3 665.2	10 496	2 390	2.9	93.9	0.5	1.4	1.0	4.7	4.7	13.5	5.3	9.9	11.8	12.4
16 087	...	6	Washington	1 452.9	10 172	2 419	7.0	80.4	0.5	1.9	1.3	17.5	5.7	17.6	7.2	8.8	10.2	11.7
17 000	...	0	**ILLINOIS**	55 517.1	12 801 539	X	230.6	63.1	14.9	0.5	6.1	17.0	6.0	16.8	9.5	13.9	12.9	13.4
17 001	39500	5	Adams	855.2	66 578	794	77.9	93.7	5.0	0.5	1.1	1.5	6.1	16.5	8.1	12.3	11.2	12.6
17 003	16020	3	Alexander	235.5	6 478	2 715	27.5	64.1	34.5	1.0	0.6	2.0	7.3	16.4	6.7	9.8	10.6	13.1
17 005	41180	1	Bond	380.3	16 824	1 992	44.2	88.6	7.2	0.8	1.0	3.7	4.7	14.5	8.5	13.6	13.3	13.6
17 007	40420	2	Boone	280.7	53 503	940	190.6	75.1	2.8	0.6	1.7	21.2	5.7	19.9	8.9	10.5	12.7	14.9
17 009	...	7	Brown	305.6	6 762	2 692	22.1	74.1	19.3	0.4	0.4	6.3	4.2	11.0	11.2	19.4	15.7	13.7
17 011	36860	7	Bureau	869.0	33 359	1 346	38.4	89.2	1.3	0.6	1.1	9.0	5.1	16.5	7.6	10.7	11.1	13.3
17 013	41180	1	Calhoun	253.8	4 894	2 841	19.3	98.0	0.6	0.4	0.3	1.1	5.0	15.6	7.2	9.2	10.6	13.9
17 015	...	7	Carroll	445.1	14 539	2 129	32.7	94.4	1.6	0.7	1.0	3.6	4.7	14.7	7.1	10.1	10.5	12.6
17 017	...	6	Cass	375.8	12 676	2 250	33.7	77.2	4.2	0.4	0.6	18.4	6.3	17.6	8.3	11.9	13.2	
17 019	16580	3	Champaign	996.2	208 419	315	209.2	70.5	14.0	0.5	11.9	5.8	5.6	13.3	23.2	14.7	10.8	9.9
17 021	45380	6	Christian	709.4	33 309	1 347	47.0	96.0	2.1	0.5	0.9	1.5	5.0	15.5	7.8	12.1	11.9	13.9
17 023	...	6	Clark	501.4	15 938	2 043	31.8	97.4	0.9	0.6	0.6	1.5	5.8	16.9	7.3	11.3	11.5	13.7
17 025	...	7	Clay	468.3	13 300	2 213	28.4	97.1	0.9	0.6	1.0	1.3	5.9	16.7	7.2	11.3	11.2	13.3
17 027	41180	1	Clinton	474.1	37 729	1 229	79.6	92.5	4.1	0.5	0.9	3.1	5.6	15.6	8.2	13.2	12.5	14.2
17 029	16660	5	Coles	508.3	52 343	955	103.0	92.2	4.8	0.5	1.4	2.5	4.7	13.3	18.3	13.6	10.4	11.0
17 031	16980	1	Cook	945.0	5 203 499	2	5 506.3	43.7	24.1	0.5	8.0	25.3	6.3	16.0	9.2	16.3	13.5	12.9
17 033	...	7	Crawford	443.6	19 308	1 857	43.5	91.9	5.4	0.5	0.9	2.3	5.3	14.6	7.6	13.6	12.5	13.5
17 035	16660	9	Cumberland	346.0	10 858	2 366	31.4	97.4	0.8	0.6	1.0	1.1	5.8	16.8	7.1	11.2	12.0	13.5
17 037	16980	1	DeKalb	631.4	104 528	573	165.5	78.7	8.2	0.5	3.3	11.1	5.8	15.8	20.1	13.3	11.0	11.3
17 039	14010	3	De Witt	397.5	16 226	2 028	40.8	95.8	1.4	0.6	0.8	2.6	5.4	16.3	7.2	11.2	12.4	13.8
17 041	...	6	Douglas	416.7	19 630	1 845	47.1	91.1	1.1	0.6	0.9	7.4	6.3	18.7	7.8	12.6	11.8	12.3
17 043	16980	1	DuPage	327.5	929 368	56	2 837.8	68.9	5.5	0.4	12.7	14.3	5.9	17.1	8.9	12.6	12.8	14.4
17 045	...	6	Edgar	623.4	17 566	1 943	28.2	97.7	0.9	0.5	0.5	1.2	5.2	15.5	7.4	10.8	11.7	12.8
17 047	...	9	Edwards	222.4	6 523	2 712	29.3	97.6	1.1	0.5	0.6	1.3	5.9	16.6	7.1	10.3	11.8	13.3
17 049	20820	7	Effingham	478.8	34 386	1 313	71.8	96.8	0.8	0.3	0.9	1.9	6.4	17.0	8.2	13.0	11.1	12.8
17 051	...	6	Fayette	716.5	21 789	1 739	30.4	92.7	5.5	0.6	0.6	1.7	5.6	15.6	8.7	12.9	12.9	13.4
17 053	16580	3	Ford	485.6	13 575	2 192	28.0	95.2	1.3	0.6	0.9	3.2	5.6	17.3	7.4	10.7	11.6	12.5
17 055	...	4	Franklin	408.9	39 156	1 200	95.8	97.2	1.1	0.8	0.7	1.5	5.9	16.3	7.4	11.2	12.1	13.2
17 057	15900	6	Fulton	865.6	35 536	1 290	41.1	92.9	4.1	0.6	0.5	2.8	4.9	15.1	7.9	12.2	12.7	13.3
17 059	...	8	Gallatin	323.1	5 212	2 818	16.1	96.9	1.4	1.0	0.4	1.7	5.6	15.2	6.5	10.5	12.1	12.9
17 061	...	6	Greene	543.0	13 093	2 225	24.1	97.2	1.5	0.5	0.4	1.2	5.3	16.1	7.9	10.8	13.7	14.2
17 063	16980	1	Grundy	418.1	50 437	980	120.6	87.9	1.8	0.4	1.2	9.7	6.2	19.3	8.0	12.6	13.7	14.1
17 065	...	7	Hamilton	434.7	8 061	2 590	18.5	97.1	1.1	0.4	0.6	1.7	5.1	17.1	7.2	11.0	11.7	12.8
17 067	22800	7	Hancock	793.7	18 508	1 890	23.3	97.4	1.0	0.6	0.7	1.4	5.2	15.6	6.9	10.1	10.6	12.6

1. CBSA = Core Based Statistical Area. See Appendix A for explanation. See Appendix B for list of metropolitan areas with component counties. 2. County type code from the Economic Research Service of USDA Rural-Urban Continuum Codes. See Appendix A for definition. 3. Dry land or land partially or temporarily covered by water. 4. May be of any race.

Table B. States and Counties — Population and Households

STATE County	55 to 64 years	65 to 74 years	75 years and over	Percent female	Total persons 2000	Total persons 2010	2000–2010	2010–2016	Births	Deaths	Net migration	Number	Persons per house-hold	Family house-holds	Female family house-holder[1]	One per-son
	16	17	18	19	20	21	22	23	24	25	26	27	28	29	30	31
IDAHO—Cont'd																
Caribou	13.5	9.8	7.7	49.3	7 304	6 963	-4.7	-1.1	560	383	-240	2 606	2.57	71.9	3.7	24.1
Cassia	11.3	7.8	6.3	49.1	21 416	22 958	7.2	2.4	2 373	1 210	-587	7 732	2.96	73.6	7.9	22.6
Clark	12.2	7.4	7.3	47.4	1 022	982	-3.9	-12.4	64	45	-141	274	3.22	76.3	15.3	20.8
Clearwater	16.9	15.5	10.8	44.9	8 930	8 761	-1.9	-3.0	388	673	27	3 648	2.05	65.0	6.9	26.8
Custer	19.6	17.2	9.6	49.0	4 342	4 366	0.6	-6.2	237	244	-268	1 767	2.33	68.6	5.7	27.0
Elmore	11.1	7.6	5.2	47.7	29 130	27 038	-7.2	-3.8	2 941	1 067	-2 985	9 785	2.60	70.2	7.9	23.9
Franklin	11.2	7.8	6.1	49.0	11 329	12 786	12.9	4.8	1 230	587	-17	4 236	3.03	80.7	7.2	16.8
Fremont	13.2	9.9	6.8	48.0	11 819	13 238	12.0	-2.2	1 212	664	-854	4 477	2.75	78.4	6.0	19.4
Gem	14.8	12.6	9.3	50.0	15 181	16 719	10.1	2.8	1 227	1 200	433	6 311	2.63	68.2	12.5	26.4
Gooding	12.3	9.2	7.6	48.7	14 155	15 464	9.2	-1.8	1 294	874	-675	5 327	2.84	71.9	8.2	20.7
Idaho	17.8	15.2	10.4	47.6	15 511	16 267	4.9	-0.7	991	1 098	23	6 583	2.38	67.8	6.8	27.7
Jefferson	10.9	7.0	4.4	49.5	19 155	26 142	36.5	6.5	3 006	902	-383	8 102	3.30	81.6	7.3	15.9
Jerome	11.5	7.3	5.1	49.3	18 342	22 374	22.0	2.8	2 512	963	-923	7 624	2.95	74.2	9.8	21.0
Kootenai	13.7	11.1	7.1	50.7	108 685	138 464	27.4	11.4	10 965	7 885	12 327	56 421	2.54	68.6	10.3	24.7
Latah	10.6	7.6	5.1	48.7	34 935	37 242	6.6	5.2	2 811	1 405	570	15 080	2.33	54.9	6.2	27.2
Lemhi	17.8	17.2	12.0	49.2	7 806	7 936	1.7	-2.7	451	607	-51	3 721	2.03	58.5	4.3	37.2
Lewis	16.7	13.9	11.8	50.0	3 747	3 821	2.0	0.8	249	218	13	1 625	2.31	63.2	7.4	31.3
Lincoln	11.3	8.3	5.2	48.7	4 044	5 206	28.7	1.2	471	236	-167	1 624	3.21	76.5	7.4	18.3
Madison	6.2	3.7	2.6	49.6	27 467	37 549	36.7	4.0	6 809	797	-4 569	10 305	3.60	78.7	5.5	13.3
Minidoka	12.4	8.8	7.1	49.6	20 174	20 063	-0.6	2.8	2 056	1 070	-425	7 148	2.83	76.7	8.7	21.2
Nez Perce	13.9	10.4	9.0	50.5	37 410	39 267	5.0	2.8	2 974	3 076	1 236	16 096	2.40	64.1	11.2	29.5
Oneida	14.2	10.5	9.0	49.8	4 125	4 286	3.9	1.3	312	232	-13	1 582	2.66	70.5	6.0	28.7
Owyhee	13.6	10.4	6.8	49.2	10 644	11 526	8.3	-1.2	868	566	-430	3 929	2.85	70.5	10.3	25.7
Payette	12.5	10.3	7.4	50.2	20 578	22 623	9.9	1.8	1 932	1 235	-300	8 147	2.77	70.7	9.3	25.0
Power	12.5	8.5	5.7	49.6	7 538	7 817	3.7	-2.1	850	369	-638	2 563	2.99	76.2	14.6	20.2
Shoshone	17.1	13.6	9.1	49.8	13 771	12 795	-7.1	-2.7	845	1 116	-71	5 712	2.16	60.8	5.9	34.6
Teton	12.2	6.6	2.8	47.9	5 999	10 165	69.4	7.8	965	229	68	3 605	2.85	66.4	7.3	24.3
Twin Falls	11.5	8.6	6.5	50.0	64 284	77 230	20.1	8.1	7 543	4 502	3 156	29 017	2.71	71.2	11.1	24.1
Valley	19.3	15.7	7.5	48.5	7 651	9 860	28.9	6.5	543	408	461	3 188	2.99	66.1	7.4	30.8
Washington	14.7	13.8	10.4	50.0	9 977	10 198	2.2	-0.3	657	737	1	3 812	2.59	64.7	9.5	30.5
ILLINOIS	12.9	8.4	6.2	50.9	12 419 293	12 831 574	3.3	-0.2	992 140	649 058	-361 646	4 786 388	2.63	65.3	12.6	28.9
Adams	13.8	10.2	9.2	51.1	68 277	67 103	-1.7	-0.8	5 098	4 899	-794	26 883	2.44	64.2	9.9	30.6
Alexander	16.0	11.5	8.6	51.8	9 590	8 238	-14.1	-21.4	643	613	-1 769	2 644	2.65	62.2	21.0	35.0
Bond	14.3	9.6	7.7	47.4	17 633	17 768	0.8	-5.3	1 024	1 041	-937	6 148	2.57	66.0	9.3	29.5
Boone	12.5	9.0	5.9	50.1	41 786	54 167	29.6	-1.2	3 699	2 358	-1 976	18 129	2.95	76.0	11.5	19.1
Brown	11.3	7.2	6.4	35.2	6 950	6 937	-0.2	-2.5	332	336	-159	2 140	2.43	61.9	6.7	33.1
Bureau	14.7	11.0	9.9	50.9	35 503	34 978	-1.5	-4.6	2 093	2 338	-1 318	14 023	2.40	66.9	9.7	29.1
Calhoun	15.2	12.2	11.0	50.2	5 084	5 089	0.1	-3.8	315	342	-173	2 063	2.37	72.7	5.3	25.0
Carroll	16.0	13.8	10.4	50.1	16 674	15 388	-7.7	-5.5	872	1 165	-515	6 617	2.22	63.9	9.5	31.7
Cass	13.3	9.2	7.9	49.5	13 695	13 638	-0.4	-7.1	1 080	908	-1 151	5 200	2.51	66.2	11.3	29.3
Champaign	10.7	6.8	5.0	50.0	179 669	201 081	11.9	3.6	14 973	7 849	325	79 912	2.38	53.1	10.2	34.0
Christian	14.5	10.2	9.2	49.1	35 372	34 800	-1.6	-4.3	2 124	2 517	-1 080	14 013	2.31	64.5	10.6	30.1
Clark	14.2	10.5	8.8	50.6	17 008	16 335	-4.0	-2.4	1 204	1 314	-272	6 647	2.40	69.1	10.9	25.5
Clay	14.9	10.8	8.6	50.6	14 560	13 815	-5.1	-3.7	1 003	1 049	-426	5 525	2.39	70.2	10.8	27.5
Clinton	14.1	9.0	7.6	48.2	35 535	37 762	6.3	-0.1	2 603	2 129	-536	13 866	2.59	68.8	7.7	26.4
Coles	12.9	8.6	7.2	51.5	53 196	53 873	1.3	-2.8	3 152	3 109	-1 465	21 063	2.31	58.4	11.2	31.8
Cook	12.3	7.7	5.8	51.4	5 376 741	5 195 075	-3.4	0.2	436 610	250 020	-169 830	1 942 959	2.65	61.0	15.0	32.3
Crawford	14.1	10.1	8.7	48.1	20 452	19 817	-3.1	-2.6	1 327	1 469	-365	7 620	2.37	66.2	7.2	29.9
Cumberland	15.1	10.4	8.0	49.8	11 253	11 048	-1.8	-1.7	751	685	-257	4 310	2.51	68.3	9.5	28.9
DeKalb	10.8	6.8	5.1	50.4	88 969	105 160	18.2	-0.6	7 560	4 366	-3 893	37 269	2.65	60.8	11.5	28.0
De Witt	14.9	10.8	8.0	50.4	16 798	16 561	-1.4	-2.0	1 118	1 145	-288	6 840	2.36	65.5	7.8	30.5
Douglas	13.6	9.0	7.8	50.4	19 922	19 982	0.3	-1.8	1 565	1 182	-681	7 618	2.58	68.9	8.1	25.9
DuPage	13.9	8.5	5.9	50.9	904 161	916 889	1.4	1.4	66 650	37 696	-15 078	338 083	2.72	70.9	9.2	24.6
Edgar	15.7	11.3	9.6	51.2	19 704	18 576	-5.7	-5.4	1 149	1 488	-652	7 716	2.29	70.3	12.0	26.3
Edwards	14.8	11.0	9.2	50.8	6 971	6 721	-3.6	-2.9	477	448	-216	2 785	2.37	64.9	8.4	31.1
Effingham	14.1	9.4	8.1	50.2	34 264	34 242	-0.1	0.4	2 747	2 196	-464	13 330	2.54	67.2	8.6	28.3
Fayette	13.5	9.3	8.1	46.7	21 802	22 142	1.6	-1.6	1 537	1 330	-604	7 761	2.63	69.1	8.3	27.5
Ford	15.0	9.7	10.2	51.1	14 241	14 081	-1.1	-3.6	907	1 228	-226	5 626	2.39	64.0	8.9	30.8
Franklin	14.0	11.4	8.7	50.6	39 018	39 989	2.5	-2.1	2 953	3 323	-406	16 257	2.41	62.8	11.5	33.1
Fulton	14.1	10.8	9.0	48.1	38 250	37 069	-3.1	-4.1	2 200	2 790	-928	14 375	2.37	65.6	10.2	29.0
Gallatin	13.9	13.8	9.6	51.6	6 445	5 589	-13.3	-6.7	377	521	-219	2 408	2.23	65.9	13.0	30.8
Greene	14.9	10.2	8.6	49.4	14 761	13 886	-5.9	-5.7	862	934	-706	5 458	2.43	66.0	10.4	28.9
Grundy	12.5	8.1	5.4	50.0	37 535	50 063	33.4	0.7	3 882	2 408	-1 125	18 492	2.70	72.9	11.7	23.2
Hamilton	15.1	10.7	9.4	51.0	8 621	8 457	-1.9	-4.7	514	699	-191	3 473	2.36	66.9	6.9	27.8
Hancock	15.2	12.8	11.0	50.4	20 121	19 104	-5.1	-3.1	1 189	1 308	-545	7 862	2.35	68.7	8.3	27.7

1. No spouse present.

Table B. States and Counties — **Population, Vital Statistics, Health, and Crime**

STATE County	Persons in group quarters, 2016	Daytime population, 2011–2015 Number	Employ-ment/resi-dence ratio	Births, 2016 Total	Rate[1]	Deaths, 2016 Number	Rate[1]	Persons under 65 with no health insurance, 2015 Number	Percent	Medicare, 2015 Total Beneficiaries	Enrolled in Original Medicare	Enrolled in Medicare Advantage	Serious crimes known to police,[2] 2014 Total Number	Rate[3]
	32	33	34	35	36	37	38	39	40	41	42	43	44	45
IDAHO—Cont'd														
Caribou	79	7 392	1.19	81	11.8	60	8.7	589	10.6	1 265	1 041	224	48	704
Cassia	286	24 342	1.10	358	15.2	189	8.0	3 627	18.3	3 489	2 691	798	530	2 249
Clark	2	828	0.83	11	12.8	2	2.3	199	26.9	119	88	31	13	1 535
Clearwater	626	8 761	1.07	57	6.7	102	12.0	736	12.9	2 282	2 164	118	205	2 377
Custer	21	4 133	0.94	35	8.5	33	8.1	407	13.5	1 032	971	61	29	682
Elmore	606	25 602	0.95	449	17.3	179	6.9	2 952	13.5	3 673	2 951	722	371	1 420
Franklin	102	11 140	0.66	183	13.7	81	6.0	1 516	13.6	1 963	1 730	233	142	1 095
Fremont	460	11 191	0.66	187	14.4	105	8.1	1 628	15.9	2 203	1 773	430	118	912
Gem	151	14 907	0.68	201	11.7	189	11.0	1 919	14.8	3 937	2 090	1 847	131	779
Gooding	52	14 560	0.90	204	13.4	110	7.2	2 743	21.9	2 644	1 979	665	194	1 286
Idaho	498	15 934	0.94	163	10.1	168	10.4	1 734	14.8	3 659	3 484	175	198	1 223
Jefferson	111	22 561	0.61	454	16.3	152	5.5	3 085	12.9	3 446	2 607	839	208	762
Jerome	106	22 153	0.95	389	16.9	148	6.4	4 146	21.1	3 122	2 065	1 057	434	1 913
Kootenai	1 489	137 430	0.88	1 834	11.9	1 354	8.8	14 296	11.6	31 622	21 428	10 194	4 328	2 951
Latah	3 206	35 421	0.84	453	11.6	213	5.4	3 131	10.1	5 297	4 322	975	926	2 402
Lemhi	80	7 693	0.97	77	10.0	102	13.2	786	14.3	2 309	2 248	61	87	1 128
Lewis	74	3 838	1.02	39	10.1	28	7.3	448	16.1	1 737	1 634	103	73	1 848
Lincoln	37	4 510	0.66	72	13.7	37	7.0	861	19.0	732	575	157	28	520
Madison	633	38 941	1.07	1 107	28.3	122	3.1	3 177	9.1	2 581	1 972	609	353	937
Minidoka	82	19 282	0.89	327	15.9	163	7.9	3 302	19.4	3 559	2 577	982	393	1 918
Nez Perce	1 055	43 072	1.18	477	11.8	470	11.6	3 569	11.2	9 741	7 395	2 346	1 295	3 209
Oneida	50	3 801	0.74	49	11.3	36	8.3	404	11.8	888	714	174	26	605
Owyhee	160	10 476	0.79	145	12.7	89	7.8	2 246	24.4	1 817	1 049	768	178	1 541
Payette	94	19 830	0.69	306	13.3	208	9.0	2 826	15.1	4 471	2 658	1 813	358	1 573
Power	47	8 307	1.18	140	18.3	57	7.4	1 196	18.5	1 039	804	235	110	1 421
Shoshone	160	12 757	1.04	157	12.6	162	13.0	1 242	13.0	3 282	2 596	686	397	3 108
Teton	7	8 474	0.66	154	14.1	37	3.4	1 873	19.5	1 056	963	93	53	511
Twin Falls	984	80 663	1.02	1 201	14.4	757	9.1	10 325	15.0	14 412	9 908	4 504	1 993	2 456
Valley	66	9 983	1.06	90	8.6	81	7.7	1 057	13.5	2 236	1 589	647	206	2 139
Washington	119	9 283	0.79	103	10.1	96	9.4	1 316	17.5	2 521	1 621	900	165	1 658
ILLINOIS	300 819	12 861 738	1.00	155 238	12.1	108 040	8.4	885 019	8.2	1 965 613	1 451 929	513 684	315 048	2 466
Adams	2 230	69 982	1.09	814	12.2	819	12.3	2 963	5.6	14 450	12 514	1 936	1 769	2 666
Alexander	132	6 772	0.75	90	13.9	95	14.7	369	6.8	1 663	1 486	177	315	4 209
Bond	1 891	15 650	0.78	157	9.3	169	10.0	744	6.0	3 323	2 820	503	148	876
Boone	310	46 669	0.71	603	11.3	354	6.6	3 609	7.9	7 991	5 811	2 180	772	1 433
Brown	2 107	8 369	1.55	54	8.0	61	9.0	182	4.7	946	779	167	NA	NA
Bureau	457	31 276	0.82	314	9.4	377	11.3	1 714	6.4	7 385	6 296	1 089	415	1 304
Calhoun	90	3 892	0.49	49	10.0	66	13.5	217	5.8	1 158	967	191	NA	NA
Carroll	223	13 277	0.76	132	9.1	189	13.0	719	6.5	4 020	3 102	918	132	1 074
Cass	184	12 871	0.94	170	13.4	140	11.0	892	8.4	2 459	2 045	414	175	1 322
Champaign	16 226	215 125	1.09	2 413	11.6	1 345	6.5	11 185	6.6	25 718	12 894	12 824	6 201	3 034
Christian	1 608	30 592	0.76	300	9.0	389	11.7	1 462	5.6	7 278	5 562	1 716	417	1 266
Clark	221	14 155	0.72	181	11.4	210	13.2	706	5.5	3 536	2 826	710	83	679
Clay	305	13 078	0.92	160	12.0	179	13.5	664	6.2	2 972	2 760	212	168	1 245
Clinton	2 072	31 274	0.65	420	11.1	383	10.2	1 420	4.7	5 883	5 142	741	375	1 097
Coles	3 952	55 053	1.08	507	9.7	484	9.2	2 532	6.2	8 879	6 671	2 208	729	1 360
Cook	90 942	5 408 293	1.07	68 049	13.1	42 297	8.1	475 088	10.6	703 256	489 387	213 869	163 003	3 158
Crawford	1 495	19 670	1.02	218	11.3	248	12.8	797	5.5	4 024	3 642	382	NA	NA
Cumberland	117	8 602	0.51	112	10.3	103	9.5	536	6.0	2 062	1 658	404	82	752
DeKalb	6 068	95 773	0.83	1 182	11.3	716	6.8	6 088	7.0	14 076	10 977	3 099	2 192	2 127
De Witt	249	14 964	0.82	178	11.0	217	13.4	632	4.8	3 305	2 393	912	182	1 269
Douglas	168	18 724	0.88	239	12.2	168	8.6	1 487	9.0	3 010	1 818	1 192	137	831
DuPage	12 877	1 030 016	1.21	10 582	11.4	6 452	6.9	47 224	5.9	134 503	105 819	28 684	12 508	1 338
Edgar	249	17 987	1.00	174	9.9	229	13.0	919	6.6	3 891	3 236	655	307	1 858
Edwards	52	6 539	0.96	74	11.3	67	10.3	316	6.1	1 386	1 279	107	32	555
Effingham	440	38 568	1.25	432	12.6	342	9.9	1 337	4.7	7 465	6 674	791	629	1 834
Fayette	1 914	20 550	0.82	250	11.5	208	9.5	1 271	7.7	4 063	3 568	495	299	1 424
Ford	410	13 089	0.88	151	11.1	196	14.4	689	6.3	2 605	1 913	692	229	1 767
Franklin	517	34 824	0.68	475	12.1	518	13.2	2 303	7.3	9 732	7 843	1 889	605	1 732
Fulton	2 698	30 666	0.63	353	9.9	463	13.0	1 727	6.5	7 939	5 781	2 158	471	1 506
Gallatin	25	4 794	0.73	65	12.5	83	15.9	283	7.0	1 396	1 251	145	63	1 390
Greene	280	11 163	0.59	123	9.4	165	12.6	677	6.4	3 007	2 647	360	130	959
Grundy	254	45 363	0.79	605	12.0	401	8.0	2 147	4.9	7 794	6 919	875	720	1 463
Hamilton	117	7 083	0.65	74	9.2	115	14.3	403	6.2	1 795	1 580	215	NA	NA
Hancock	223	15 083	0.57	189	10.2	217	11.7	816	5.8	4 414	3 838	576	NA	NA

1. Per 1,000 estimated resident population.   2. Data for serious crimes have not been adjusted for underreporting; this may affect comparability between geographic areas and over time.
3. Per 100,000 population estimated by the FBI.

Table B. States and Counties — Crime, Education, Money Income, and Poverty

STATE County	Serious crimes known to police, 2014 (cont.)[1] Rate[2] Violent	Property	Education — School enrollment and attainment, 2011-2015 Enrollment[3] Total	Percent private	Attainment[4] (percent) High school graduate or less	Bachelor's degree or more	Local government expenditures,[5] 2013-2014 Total current spending (mil dol)	Current spending per student (dollars)	Money income, 2011-2015 Per capita income[6] (dollars)	Median income (dollars)	Households Percent with income of less than $50,000	with income of $200,000 or more	Income and poverty, 2015 Median household income (dollars)	Percent below poverty level All persons	Children under 18 years	Children 5 to 17 years in families
	46	47	48	49	50	51	52	53	54	55	56	57	58	59	60	61
IDAHO—Cont'd																
Caribou	15	690	1 806	4.9	44.1	19.3	11.8	7 562	25 172	58 021	44.2	1.9	57 017	10.8	14.0	12.7
Cassia	170	2 079	6 422	5.5	47.0	17.8	32.0	5 871	18 227	45 695	54.5	1.1	47 932	16.7	20.5	18.4
Clark	118	1 417	189	0.0	61.2	15.0	1.8	11 466	15 151	33 672	67.2	0.0	40 098	15.3	16.5	13.5
Clearwater	244	2 134	1 358	16.2	47.6	16.9	11.2	10 935	20 079	38 837	63.6	1.5	42 630	15.3	24.0	21.1
Custer	47	635	766	9.1	44.0	27.1	5.3	8 758	22 861	39 457	59.8	0.3	45 801	14.0	19.5	18.3
Elmore	222	1 198	6 815	11.8	42.2	16.6	30.3	6 073	21 326	43 848	55.9	1.5	44 509	15.0	21.7	21.2
Franklin	31	1 064	3 762	8.3	43.1	18.4	17.5	5 367	18 855	48 133	51.3	0.4	53 901	9.7	13.0	11.0
Fremont	77	834	3 571	11.6	45.0	20.5	15.7	6 799	20 302	47 988	51.8	0.7	49 555	15.0	24.1	22.1
Gem	107	672	3 710	10.1	50.9	16.0	19.0	7 471	19 726	40 828	60.9	0.7	44 017	15.8	24.2	22.2
Gooding	172	1 113	4 064	10.7	57.3	14.3	22.4	6 743	19 688	39 930	58.6	1.7	48 950	13.9	21.3	19.6
Idaho	105	1 118	3 315	22.7	48.0	19.3	17.1	9 778	19 611	38 191	63.6	0.4	41 157	16.3	23.0	20.9
Jefferson	26	737	8 281	11.2	42.9	20.2	34.4	7 587	19 501	51 171	48.3	2.0	53 555	10.5	13.9	12.4
Jerome	238	1 675	6 440	7.9	55.9	14.0	26.9	5 827	17 708	41 630	60.8	1.5	47 034	15.8	21.7	20.9
Kootenai	279	2 672	35 045	13.3	36.2	23.3	140.1	6 163	25 744	49 403	50.6	3.1	48 864	14.7	19.2	17.4
Latah	83	2 319	15 078	11.0	24.3	45.6	43.1	8 417	22 766	42 439	56.8	1.7	46 360	19.6	14.5	12.0
Lemhi	259	869	1 190	18.0	42.3	21.5	8.0	8 073	22 134	34 329	64.5	1.2	40 087	17.6	26.8	23.4
Lewis	101	1 746	791	12.6	45.7	15.2	8.8	10 652	21 152	36 505	63.6	0.9	41 688	16.3	26.8	24.2
Lincoln	242	279	1 481	4.5	59.7	11.6	8.1	8 073	17 204	43 273	58.3	0.6	46 168	14.5	23.6	20.6
Madison	45	892	19 143	54.9	20.4	34.8	38.4	5 498	14 653	32 233	66.0	1.4	38 065	28.1	18.6	19.3
Minidoka	156	1 762	5 210	6.9	52.5	12.9	26.3	5 949	20 674	44 853	55.9	2.5	45 429	17.0	20.7	18.9
Nez Perce	156	3 053	9 294	13.0	39.3	23.4	47.4	8 253	25 177	48 160	51.8	1.3	50 939	13.5	18.5	17.4
Oneida	23	581	1 090	6.9	44.9	14.1	5.3	5 728	20 089	41 338	62.2	0.6	47 037	12.2	18.1	15.8
Owyhee	138	1 402	2 911	11.7	62.3	8.9	17.2	7 082	16 854	33 440	66.9	1.2	39 738	19.9	30.2	28.6
Payette	228	1 344	5 521	7.9	46.9	15.7	25.5	5 735	20 689	44 257	57.5	1.2	44 499	15.7	22.0	20.5
Power	90	1 331	2 102	11.0	61.7	13.0	14.2	8 445	18 877	44 779	57.7	0.9	44 004	14.1	20.8	22.2
Shoshone	344	2 764	2 379	9.3	50.0	14.1	18.8	9 825	21 254	37 665	64.2	0.6	37 497	21.1	30.3	27.4
Teton	116	395	2 307	12.8	30.0	39.8	11.8	6 683	24 118	53 474	46.4	2.4	58 013	9.8	15.9	14.8
Twin Falls	242	2 214	21 934	8.7	43.5	17.7	97.1	6 337	21 553	44 048	56.0	2.2	45 799	14.6	19.3	18.1
Valley	374	1 765	2 058	15.7	35.2	29.8	14.4	11 031	23 962	48 384	51.7	1.7	51 774	10.7	18.1	16.5
Washington	60	1 597	2 281	10.0	51.6	13.9	13.3	7 075	18 343	34 775	67.1	1.0	38 592	17.1	25.0	21.8
ILLINOIS	370	2 076	3 429 755	18.7	38.9	32.3	27 060.7	13 088	30 494	57 574	43.8	5.8	59 590	13.6	19.1	17.9
Adams	335	2 331	15 263	18.6	44.8	21.2	96.7	9 973	24 380	45 965	53.9	1.7	47 264	13.4	18.9	17.6
Alexander	1 416	2 793	1 668	5.3	58.1	8.0	13.0	11 959	14 729	27 265	73.8	0.4	32 922	28.6	52.2	51.8
Bond	41	835	4 291	18.1	52.9	17.6	22.5	9 492	22 867	47 946	51.9	1.8	50 206	14.8	19.1	17.2
Boone	154	1 279	14 628	19.7	49.2	20.2	104.9	10 524	26 170	58 248	40.7	4.0	62 382	10.3	14.5	12.2
Brown	NA	NA	1 379	7.2	56.1	14.0	7.2	9 367	21 065	50 739	49.0	2.1	53 516	16.7	15.8	15.1
Bureau	129	1 175	7 724	10.9	49.3	17.9	64.0	11 953	27 304	50 423	49.5	2.6	51 275	12.6	19.3	17.9
Calhoun	NA	NA	1 112	34.1	52.1	15.6	7.0	12 545	26 407	53 869	45.3	2.4	51 109	11.6	15.5	14.5
Carroll	16	1 057	2 954	10.4	52.8	16.2	27.8	11 417	26 493	48 631	51.1	2.1	50 432	10.7	19.3	17.7
Cass	484	839	3 158	8.2	61.0	13.9	21.8	9 185	24 262	47 434	51.9	2.1	46 647	12.2	18.1	15.4
Champaign	480	2 554	81 206	7.5	28.5	43.4	304.2	12 290	26 078	46 495	52.3	4.1	50 813	20.1	18.3	16.9
Christian	206	1 059	7 443	9.8	56.0	14.2	66.7	11 198	23 263	45 334	53.6	1.6	49 041	12.7	19.2	17.6
Clark	204	474	3 723	8.2	48.1	18.1	24.3	8 917	25 744	50 517	49.3	2.3	50 700	13.8	21.5	19.8
Clay	44	1 201	2 965	3.9	50.6	14.8	21.0	8 704	22 797	44 209	56.1	1.1	43 577	14.5	21.1	19.8
Clinton	111	986	8 749	16.1	43.1	20.8	51.7	9 700	28 839	63 236	38.8	3.4	64 030	8.5	12.0	10.1
Coles	220	1 140	17 700	5.4	41.9	24.1	82.1	12 547	23 525	39 588	59.5	2.1	42 613	21.8	24.5	22.6
Cook	558	2 600	1 372 757	23.4	38.7	35.8	11 340.3	14 579	31 013	55 251	45.7	6.5	56 841	16.2	23.5	22.7
Crawford	NA	NA	4 258	10.4	44.6	18.8	29.5	9 997	26 351	47 468	51.9	3.4	49 856	13.4	20.2	19.5
Cumberland	147	605	2 419	4.2	49.0	13.6	15.8	9 030	22 596	46 061	53.8	1.0	51 505	12.0	17.5	16.1
DeKalb	250	1 877	37 863	9.6	34.2	30.0	230.6	13 583	24 025	54 101	46.5	2.0	56 874	16.2	16.3	15.6
De Witt	188	1 081	3 591	10.0	46.2	19.2	28.7	10 306	29 100	53 959	44.9	2.5	54 796	11.6	19.3	17.5
Douglas	200	631	4 487	16.1	52.3	17.8	32.3	10 026	25 455	51 810	48.1	2.6	53 213	10.2	16.3	14.9
DuPage	83	1 255	250 379	22.2	26.6	46.7	2 369.8	15 041	39 336	79 658	30.5	11.0	81 616	7.1	9.2	8.4
Edgar	327	1 531	3 821	2.7	51.8	18.1	30.8	10 043	25 389	45 691	53.8	1.7	50 306	13.9	22.6	19.8
Edwards	104	451	1 429	7.3	48.5	11.0	9.1	9 400	22 885	44 497	57.7	1.4	48 329	11.3	15.9	14.8
Effingham	201	1 633	8 251	15.3	45.2	20.9	51.5	9 718	26 775	52 224	47.8	3.2	53 077	9.8	14.1	13.1
Fayette	129	1 296	4 926	14.1	57.3	13.2	29.3	10 041	21 472	43 944	56.6	1.9	41 838	18.5	29.8	27.2
Ford	216	1 551	3 120	8.7	49.7	16.6	34.2	11 777	26 010	49 947	50.1	3.4	53 151	11.3	18.1	16.4
Franklin	166	1 566	8 669	6.8	46.8	14.8	72.4	11 009	21 625	39 512	59.4	1.0	43 428	18.7	28.2	26.5
Fulton	131	1 375	8 125	5.9	48.3	16.0	50.6	10 210	22 651	46 083	53.8	1.1	44 649	14.9	21.0	19.7
Gallatin	132	1 257	1 098	4.0	55.4	9.5	7.7	9 991	22 125	39 636	62.7	0.4	40 817	17.9	27.7	24.7
Greene	170	789	2 907	13.1	55.3	11.9	19.7	9 651	22 105	42 565	57.5	1.0	43 943	16.6	23.4	22.5
Grundy	89	1 374	13 419	12.2	45.1	20.8	149.1	11 562	29 622	65 887	36.8	3.4	71 928	7.7	10.2	9.3
Hamilton	NA	NA	1 676	9.2	47.5	14.0	12.5	9 977	24 110	44 159	52.7	1.2	45 926	13.0	22.4	20.6
Hancock	NA	NA	3 788	7.2	45.6	20.3	32.9	10 644	25 085	47 699	51.8	2.1	48 213	12.7	19.0	17.5

1. Data for serious crimes have not been adjusted for underreporting; this may affect comparability between geographic areas and over time.   2. Per 100,000 population estimated by the FBI.
3. All persons 3 years old and over enrolled in nursery school through college.   4. Persons 25 years old and over.   5. Elementary and secondary education expenditures.
6. Based on population estimated by the American Community Survey, 2011-2015.

Table B. States and Counties — **Personal Income**

STATE County	Personal income, 2015										Earnings, 2015		
			Per capita[1]			Supplements to wages and salaries; employer contributions (mil dol)						Contributions for government social insurance (mil dol)	
	Total (mil dol)	Percent change, 2014–2015	Dollars	Rank	Wages and salaries (mil dol)	Pension and insurance	Government social insurance	Proprietors' income (mil dol)	Dividends, interest, and rent (mil dol)	Personal transfer receipts (mil dol)	Total (mil dol)	From employee and self-employed	From employer
	62	63	64	65	66	67	68	69	70	71	72	73	74
DAHO—Cont'd													
Caribou	263	2.6	38 795	1 392	176	33	15	22	50	50	246	14	15
Cassia	1 007	1.6	42 823	1 010	391	62	34	335	140	153	822	34	34
Clark	23	1.6	26 480	3 084	17	3	1	3	6	4	23	1	1
Clearwater	288	4.8	33 885	2 374	109	24	10	18	62	92	160	12	10
Custer	177	6.0	43 399	829	51	11	4	20	51	37	86	5	4
Elmore	902	2.6	34 851	2 128	419	108	41	86	228	182	654	30	41
Franklin	419	4.0	32 057	2 724	106	22	9	63	61	77	201	11	9
Fremont	446	7.0	34 828	2 441	108	22	9	92	90	91	232	12	9
Gem	555	4.7	32 963	2 595	119	22	11	39	131	156	192	16	11
Gooding	845	-3.0	55 281	168	218	34	18	378	96	111	647	17	18
Idaho	500	0.7	30 711	2 469	171	35	15	40	130	131	261	19	15
Jefferson	826	3.1	30 407	2 700	206	37	19	99	122	151	361	22	19
Jerome	854	0.8	37 418	1 571	332	51	29	261	106	143	674	28	29
Kootenai	5 804	5.5	38 605	1 656	2 184	371	198	447	1 248	1 216	3 201	218	198
Latah	1 412	4.3	36 425	2 072	521	127	44	103	324	230	795	48	44
Lemhi	285	3.0	36 860	1 743	80	18	7	26	90	79	131	9	7
Lewis	170	2.1	44 969	932	55	11	5	19	29	65	90	7	5
Lincoln	191	-0.8	36 100	1 492	54	11	5	62	26	33	130	4	5
Madison	898	7.0	23 456	3 104	478	87	43	105	133	220	712	41	43
Minidoka	770	5.6	37 614	2 147	287	47	25	144	139	135	503	27	25
Nez Perce	1 576	4.6	39 358	1 639	884	145	76	137	304	358	1 242	82	76
Oneida	137	6.1	32 056	2 615	33	8	3	9	24	35	52	4	3
Owyhee	372	-0.8	32 867	2 482	95	16	7	85	68	80	203	9	7
Payette	802	2.0	35 045	2 146	246	41	22	127	143	183	436	27	22
Power	275	5.5	36 019	2 345	144	25	12	57	44	52	238	11	12
Shoshone	438	6.6	35 229	2 165	212	32	19	11	84	133	274	20	19
Teton	328	7.4	31 023	2 851	107	16	10	31	95	48	165	10	10
Twin Falls	2 890	2.5	35 079	2 015	1 290	205	116	403	516	613	2 014	123	116
Valley	464	7.7	45 902	913	154	27	14	43	169	82	238	16	14
Washington	356	5.6	35 649	2 136	93	19	9	44	68	92	165	11	9
ILLINOIS	646 789	3.5	50 377	X	350 206	54 742	23 901	48 801	122 541	99 401	477 651	26 416	23 901
Adams	2 772	0.9	41 369	1 284	1 433	259	102	197	522	591	1 991	117	102
Alexander	210	-1.3	31 012	2 855	76	21	4	10	30	93	112	6	4
Bond	568	-0.9	33 534	2 285	208	50	15	35	99	143	307	19	15
Boone	2 217	3.5	41 376	1 267	863	154	66	73	319	361	1 157	68	66
Brown	184	-0.8	26 990	3 002	184	33	12	9	34	40	238	13	12
Bureau	1 291	1.5	38 446	1 381	493	96	35	39	247	285	664	42	35
Calhoun	176	0.6	36 000	1 824	26	7	2	5	32	45	40	3	2
Carroll	602	0.1	41 212	1 242	167	37	12	36	123	151	252	17	12
Cass	482	-2.3	37 483	1 606	236	48	19	38	70	108	341	19	19
Champaign	8 823	3.1	42 243	1 448	4 760	1 180	293	1 086	1 622	1 146	7 319	343	293
Christian	1 223	-2.0	36 363	1 681	420	88	31	76	219	318	615	38	31
Clark	593	-3.2	37 098	1 275	187	44	13	31	106	143	275	17	13
Clay	461	-2.3	34 341	1 707	203	48	15	1	81	146	266	18	15
Clinton	1 561	-1.0	41 300	1 005	426	92	31	108	256	292	657	37	31
Coles	1 908	1.8	36 325	2 096	1 034	236	71	102	367	427	1 442	75	71
Cook	286 603	4.2	54 714	320	173 513	24 706	11 707	27 130	59 569	43 632	237 056	13 019	11 707
Crawford	813	-3.3	41 872	1 303	380	108	26	116	133	167	630	34	26
Cumberland	402	-1.9	36 864	1 280	101	21	7	20	64	87	150	10	7
DeKalb	3 754	3.4	35 970	1 986	1 754	420	115	136	655	635	2 425	124	115
De Witt	674	-1.4	41 486	983	278	58	19	43	108	143	398	23	19
Douglas	877	-2.1	44 244	800	370	69	28	122	142	152	589	33	28
DuPage	59 814	5.1	64 059	122	40 686	5 274	2 837	4 712	11 195	5 787	53 509	2 935	2 837
Edgar	659	-2.1	37 330	1 314	282	59	21	7	112	177	370	23	21
Edwards	225	-1.6	34 496	2 305	101	21	7	17	45	55	147	9	7
Effingham	1 466	-2.8	42 657	799	811	139	60	121	303	267	1 132	65	60
Fayette	649	-0.3	29 446	2 739	189	44	13	36	121	188	282	18	13
Ford	665	-1.1	48 382	493	201	41	14	143	99	120	398	22	14
Franklin	1 319	1.5	33 417	2 330	331	74	25	71	202	423	501	35	25
Fulton	1 195	-0.4	33 461	2 246	313	78	21	24	198	334	435	31	21
Gallatin	206	-3.8	39 041	877	45	10	3	30	37	59	87	5	3
Greene	450	-4.2	33 953	2 021	88	21	6	25	69	128	140	10	6
Grundy	2 422	-5.6	47 930	862	1 109	202	76	322	300	321	1 709	95	76
Hamilton	328	-3.5	39 959	1 072	97	20	7	36	57	83	160	9	7
Hancock	730	-2.4	39 374	1 028	147	36	10	56	122	170	249	17	10

1. Based on the resident population estimated as of July 1 of the year shown.

Table B. States and Counties — Earnings, Social Security, and Housing

STATE County	Earnings, 2015 (cont.) Percent by selected industries									Social Security beneficiaries, December 2015			Housing units, 2016	
	Farm	Mining	Construction	Manufacturing	Information: professional, scientific, technical services	Retail trade	Finance, insurance, real estate and leasing	Health care and social assistance	Government	Number	Rate[1]	Supplemental Security Income recipients, December 2015	Total	Percent change 2010–2016
	75	76	77	78	79	80	81	82	83	84	85	86	87	88
IDAHO—Cont'd														
Caribou	9.1	D	D	D	D	3.0	D	D	13.8	1 405	208	62	3 216	-0.3
Cassia	34.6	0.8	4.4	9.5	D	6.5	4.0	7.7	9.0	4 130	176	404	8 530	1.9
Clark	11.1	0.0	D	D	D	D	D	D	26.5	125	143	7	537	1.1
Clearwater	-0.6	D	5.6	6.0	2.6	5.7	2.6	D	35.3	2 880	340	253	4 484	0.7
Custer	15.1	10.5	6.2	0.8	5.7	5.2	D	D	26.8	1 260	308	57	3 076	-0.8
Elmore	11.4	0.0	2.5	3.6	D	4.7	1.7	5.3	56.8	4 400	171	548	12 239	0.6
Franklin	19.3	D	8.5	6.6	4.3	8.7	4.6	D	20.2	2 265	174	176	4 714	4.1
Fremont	28.7	D	9.8	2.5	D	3.9	4.0	D	23.1	2 580	201	159	8 730	2.4
Gem	4.6	D	13.1	2.9	2.9	7.8	3.9	16.9	23.4	4 690	277	466	7 137	0.5
Gooding	63.3	D	1.8	7.7	D	1.8	D	D	8.0	3 055	201	286	6 050	-0.7
Idaho	2.8	1.6	9.4	7.7	4.7	9.6	3.7	9.9	29.6	4 205	259	339	8 603	-1.6
Jefferson	11.8	0.0	10.8	12.9	2.2	6.6	7.3	D	14.2	4 115	152	290	9 039	3.6
Jerome	36.1	0.1	4.0	12.2	2.1	5.5	1.7	4.0	7.4	3 610	159	385	8 312	2.6
Kootenai	0.1	0.7	9.0	8.7	7.1	10.6	7.0	12.5	21.0	35 530	236	2 682	68 281	8.1
Latah	-0.4	D	5.3	2.7	7.4	8.8	3.9	10.0	44.4	5 995	155	508	16 477	3.1
Lemhi	9.7	D	9.7	3.4	5.8	8.6	2.2	D	36.6	2 595	335	198	4 754	0.5
Lewis	11.3	D	5.1	15.1	3.4	6.5	4.6	4.2	22.8	2 030	535	239	1 874	-0.3
Lincoln	50.9	0.0	D	D	D	1.8	D	4.3	18.0	870	164	75	1 949	-1.3
Madison	3.4	D	5.3	5.6	5.6	7.7	4.1	6.7	14.6	2 940	77	275	13 561	20.1
Minidoka	20.4	0.1	4.3	17.1	3.3	5.0	2.4	D	13.2	3 955	194	388	7 844	2.3
Nez Perce	-0.1	D	5.7	21.5	4.6	8.5	8.1	16.3	17.9	10 140	253	964	17 493	0.3
Oneida	11.3	D	1.4	2.2	D	D	7.9	4.2	32.8	1 030	240	58	1 960	2.8
Owyhee	44.4	D	5.5	4.4	D	3.7	D	D	14.3	2 395	212	243	4 774	-0.1
Payette	15.2	D	4.6	13.2	D	3.7	7.6	D	11.4	5 465	239	574	9 169	2.5
Power	25.0	0.1	2.0	29.0	D	2.7	D	D	12.1	1 425	187	106	2 926	-0.6
Shoshone	-0.1	28.7	4.7	2.3	4.6	19.8	2.4	7.9	17.4	3 870	311	471	6 971	-1.4
Teton	3.2	0.0	12.9	3.0	11.7	6.5	5.7	8.6	15.1	1 260	119	60	5 598	2.2
Twin Falls	7.9	D	4.6	12.7	6.4	9.3	5.1	17.7	11.6	15 800	192	1 858	32 384	4.2
Valley	1.1	D	11.4	1.5	6.2	9.0	6.8	D	25.6	2 570	255	115	12 048	2.2
Washington	19.3	0.1	4.8	13.5	7.9	5.9	3.1	D	21.8	2 945	295	273	4 549	0.4
ILLINOIS	0.1	0.3	4.9	11.1	13.9	5.3	10.7	10.2	14.1	2 174 883	169	274 621	5 326 970	0.6
Adams	-0.3	0.8	5.8	18.1	4.5	8.3	7.8	17.8	12.0	15 370	229	1 347	30 016	0.6
Alexander	3.4	D	D	7.9	D	2.6	D	D	46.2	1 780	263	454	3 937	-1.7
Bond	2.1	0.1	5.5	23.4	2.9	3.1	2.7	D	24.8	3 665	217	322	7 179	1.3
Boone	-0.2	D	7.1	50.6	2.6	4.4	2.1	3.7	12.3	9 915	185	534	19 924	-0.2
Brown	-0.5	D	6.4	1.2	D	D	D	D	13.3	1 105	162	99	2 437	-1.0
Bureau	-2.3	0.4	6.2	16.2	D	5.4	4.3	D	20.7	8 010	239	416	15 654	-0.4
Calhoun	-1.0	D	10.4	3.2	D	8.6	D	D	36.2	1 340	274	83	2 840	0.2
Carroll	0.5	D	7.4	20.8	D	6.4	6.3	D	19.1	4 220	288	233	8 402	-0.4
Cass	5.9	0.0	3.4	33.6	D	3.7	4.3	D	14.8	2 600	202	235	5 762	-1.3
Champaign	0.2	D	4.0	6.4	7.8	12.7	4.9	12.6	36.4	26 920	130	3 125	91 519	4.5
Christian	1.0	0.6	5.4	15.8	5.3	7.6	4.2	14.7	18.1	8 210	245	677	15 508	-0.4
Clark	1.6	3.6	8.1	31.5	D	4.9	3.8	5.3	17.8	3 860	242	270	7 742	-0.4
Clay	-11.4	3.9	3.5	39.2	D	6.1	4.0	D	22.8	3 375	252	315	6 349	-0.9
Clinton	5.5	D	13.3	8.7	3.0	8.7	D	11.0	23.0	7 195	190	295	15 646	2.2
Coles	0.2	0.3	4.8	13.4	D	5.9	4.6	16.8	28.0	9 760	186	1 117	23 385	-0.2
Cook	0.0	0.1	3.9	6.8	18.7	4.1	14.2	9.6	12.3	789 600	151	155 373	2 181 535	0.1
Crawford	1.1	2.6	8.4	41.9	D	3.7	3.2	D	16.0	4 570	235	333	8 637	-0.3
Cumberland	4.0	D	4.2	20.0	D	9.4	D	D	19.2	2 450	226	173	4 835	-0.8
DeKalb	-1.7	D	11.8	10.8	3.4	6.6	4.0	D	33.2	14 795	142	926	41 019	-0.1
De Witt	2.3	D	12.5	8.4	D	5.8	2.6	D	14.9	3 630	223	251	7 514	-0.1
Douglas	4.2	D	8.4	44.2	1.2	5.4	3.1	3.0	10.2	4 010	203	231	8 381	-0.1
DuPage	0.0	0.1	5.4	9.2	15.9	5.0	9.8	9.5	7.9	141 850	152	7 960	359 103	0.8
Edgar	-2.1	0.0	3.8	38.9	2.9	4.7	10.0	D	16.8	4 505	255	438	8 807	0.0
Edwards	1.6	2.3	D	D	D	3.7	D	1.9	9.9	1 640	252	72	3 152	-1.1
Effingham	0.1	0.2	7.7	14.0	D	8.6	5.7	19.7	10.1	7 380	215	499	14 773	1.4
Fayette	1.2	2.7	6.3	7.5	3.3	8.3	5.3	D	24.8	4 910	223	462	9 196	-1.2
Ford	7.2	D	3.9	9.1	1.9	5.0	2.3	D	11.1	3 050	222	200	6 324	0.7
Franklin	0.3	1.8	9.6	6.6	D	8.8	3.7	9.5	26.6	10 455	265	1 352	18 472	-1.2
Fulton	-5.5	D	7.8	3.6	2.9	8.6	5.7	19.7	33.1	8 605	241	721	16 189	0.0
Gallatin	25.5	D	6.4	4.5	D	3.7	D	D	16.6	1 565	297	213	2 724	-0.8
Greene	1.0	D	11.1	3.7	2.7	8.9	D	D	27.1	3 260	245	402	6 386	0.0
Grundy	-0.4	D	12.3	18.9	D	8.0	3.2	8.1	10.7	8 900	176	374	20 633	3.2
Hamilton	8.4	D	6.9	3.4	D	3.6	6.2	4.6	19.9	1 915	234	188	4 061	-1.0
Hancock	6.0	D	8.0	8.2	7.1	4.7	7.6	D	22.9	4 885	263	313	9 208	-0.7

1. Per 1,000 resident population estimated as of July 1 of the year shown.

Table B. States and Counties — **Housing, Labor Force, and Employment**

STATE County	Housing units, 2011–2015								Civilian labor force, 2016				Civilian employment,[6] 2011–2015		
	Occupied units										Unemployment		Percent		
	Owner-occupied					Renter-occupied									
				Median owner cost as a percent of income											
	Total	Percent	Median value[1]	With a mortgage	Without a mortgage[2]	Median rent[3]	Median rent as a percent of income[2]	Sub-standard units[4] (percent)	Total	Percent change, 2015–2016	Total	Rate[5]	Total	Management, business, science and arts	Construction, production, and maintenance occupations
	89	90	91	92	93	94	95	96	97	98	99	100	101	102	103
DAHO—Cont'd															
Caribou	2 606	81.3	126 600	17.6	10.0	542	15.9	1.5	3 753	-0.5	138	3.7	3 121	32.8	32.9
Cassia	7 732	70.7	131 500	21.2	10.0	589	26.0	4.9	11 601	1.0	352	3.0	9 771	24.5	38.2
Clark	274	62.4	97 300	36.4	13.1	528	13.0	9.5	399	0.8	14	3.5	442	22.9	44.6
Clearwater	3 648	78.5	126 200	24.3	12.6	635	23.9	1.7	3 063	-1.0	229	7.5	2 877	30.0	34.6
Custer	1 767	78.6	161 500	22.8	10.0	590	32.2	1.8	2 139	0.2	112	5.2	1 784	29.8	31.3
Elmore	9 785	58.8	135 300	21.5	10.1	757	27.1	4.0	10 878	1.0	462	4.2	9 981	28.5	32.4
Franklin	4 236	79.1	160 900	23.9	12.3	691	24.3	2.9	6 569	1.6	204	3.1	5 401	23.5	38.0
Fremont	4 477	82.3	152 100	22.6	10.0	663	28.4	4.9	7 392	2.8	250	3.4	5 305	28.9	33.0
Gem	6 311	70.2	140 200	23.6	10.3	787	30.9	1.5	7 741	2.5	365	4.7	5 789	30.8	24.4
Gooding	5 327	67.4	127 700	23.0	10.9	750	29.0	8.7	8 003	-0.2	252	3.1	6 844	27.5	42.2
Idaho	6 583	80.2	153 700	25.9	11.1	606	23.0	4.4	6 425	0.2	368	5.7	6 526	25.6	33.2
Jefferson	8 102	82.2	156 000	23.3	10.0	648	23.0	3.9	12 718	1.8	399	3.1	11 157	33.7	31.6
Jerome	7 624	63.8	135 800	24.6	10.9	711	28.5	8.1	11 581	0.8	361	3.1	9 641	24.7	40.6
Kootenai	56 421	70.2	185 700	23.9	10.3	837	29.9	3.1	73 499	2.4	3 501	4.8	65 216	31.0	23.4
Latah	15 080	54.0	191 100	20.7	10.0	658	35.2	2.3	19 801	1.4	650	3.3	18 842	41.7	18.0
Lemhi	3 721	71.1	172 700	24.3	10.8	556	32.6	4.1	3 396	0.3	214	6.3	3 165	31.2	26.6
Lewis	1 625	72.4	115 300	22.4	12.2	599	28.6	3.2	1 615	1.3	105	6.5	1 547	29.5	27.1
Lincoln	1 624	71.1	121 000	23.0	11.0	733	27.0	7.3	2 654	0.3	119	4.5	2 212	20.8	41.2
Madison	10 305	47.6	177 700	22.6	10.0	641	44.8	9.7	20 449	3.2	505	2.5	16 153	37.4	18.1
Minidoka	7 148	74.1	111 000	19.3	10.0	559	22.0	4.2	10 821	1.0	353	3.3	9 136	21.7	41.9
Nez Perce	16 096	70.0	167 900	22.6	10.5	664	26.9	2.5	20 884	1.1	700	3.4	18 668	31.0	25.5
Oneida	1 582	79.6	132 500	28.5	12.7	530	27.8	3.7	2 169	1.8	81	3.7	1 749	28.3	37.7
Owyhee	3 929	67.1	122 400	25.3	11.0	557	24.8	6.4	5 395	3.2	244	4.5	4 304	22.7	45.3
Payette	8 147	76.0	129 300	24.6	10.4	668	28.5	4.1	11 239	1.0	532	4.7	9 393	26.3	27.5
Power	2 563	71.2	125 500	23.3	10.0	711	21.5	6.0	3 905	0.5	164	4.2	3 184	19.9	43.8
Shoshone	5 712	68.3	119 600	20.7	12.4	621	27.9	3.1	5 080	-1.2	372	7.3	4 992	27.9	27.8
Teton	3 605	71.8	222 900	28.4	11.3	844	26.9	2.7	5 996	2.7	193	3.2	5 342	32.3	27.1
Twin Falls	29 017	66.2	147 900	23.6	10.0	704	28.4	3.8	40 466	1.9	1 368	3.4	36 316	28.4	28.8
Valley	3 188	72.6	221 500	29.6	10.0	762	30.9	3.8	4 914	2.3	273	5.6	4 292	31.8	23.8
Washington	3 812	73.2	127 400	26.4	10.4	675	40.8	3.8	4 557	-0.4	258	5.7	3 650	26.1	35.2
ILLINOIS	4 786 388	66.4	173 800	23.5	13.3	907	30.3	2.9	6 539 021	0.5	384 145	5.9	6 086 226	36.8	21.2
Adams	26 883	70.7	110 000	19.2	10.3	572	28.7	1.2	32 390	-0.5	1 558	4.8	32 400	29.6	25.4
Alexander	2 644	67.2	50 200	26.0	14.1	358	22.8	4.2	2 303	0.4	213	9.2	2 400	20.7	26.1
Bond	6 148	76.8	106 900	21.0	12.7	608	25.2	2.2	7 901	1.5	406	5.1	7 563	26.4	26.2
Boone	18 129	81.1	143 700	23.7	12.8	722	26.8	2.6	26 317	-0.2	1 671	6.3	24 714	29.6	32.6
Brown	2 140	74.2	85 800	17.3	11.3	569	21.8	2.8	2 865	3.0	97	3.4	2 772	26.8	36.6
Bureau	14 023	75.3	105 600	20.1	12.2	640	27.5	1.4	17 353	1.3	1 050	6.1	16 206	27.4	30.9
Calhoun	2 063	79.4	121 400	24.5	11.4	590	26.9	2.8	2 367	0.9	148	6.3	2 231	26.9	34.3
Carroll	6 617	76.8	95 700	20.3	12.1	601	27.2	1.6	7 850	-1.2	444	5.7	6 866	28.5	36.7
Cass	5 200	72.8	77 000	18.8	10.3	594	24.4	2.9	6 228	-3.5	350	5.6	6 183	24.7	38.9
Champaign	79 912	54.9	150 200	20.3	11.1	814	34.6	2.5	105 140	0.4	5 367	5.1	101 720	44.8	15.1
Christian	14 013	74.6	83 800	18.6	11.4	598	27.2	1.5	15 349	-0.8	972	6.3	15 151	26.7	29.4
Clark	6 647	74.5	86 200	18.9	12.8	638	24.6	1.7	8 104	0.2	476	5.9	7 425	29.4	33.0
Clay	5 525	79.5	77 000	19.6	11.8	508	20.1	3.9	6 697	1.1	458	6.8	6 270	25.3	38.5
Clinton	13 866	83.1	134 500	19.3	11.7	779	23.4	1.2	20 394	1.5	913	4.5	19 250	31.8	27.5
Coles	21 063	62.1	91 800	19.7	12.0	626	34.1	0.8	24 390	1.2	1 442	5.9	24 939	28.9	24.5
Cook	1 942 959	57.0	218 700	26.2	15.4	980	31.3	4.1	2 666 307	0.8	163 990	6.2	2 463 655	38.3	19.1
Crawford	7 620	79.7	81 000	17.5	10.5	561	27.0	1.9	9 014	-6.5	563	6.2	8 369	28.1	34.8
Cumberland	4 310	80.7	93 400	19.0	11.8	515	23.5	2.7	5 940	0.4	311	5.2	4 932	28.9	34.7
DeKalb	37 269	58.5	165 200	23.8	14.0	860	33.0	2.9	54 759	0.2	2 931	5.4	51 637	33.4	22.4
De Witt	6 840	78.3	105 300	18.8	10.2	577	23.8	1.3	7 846	-1.2	451	5.7	8 066	27.2	28.6
Douglas	7 618	75.1	100 500	19.9	10.0	653	24.1	2.3	10 244	1.5	484	4.7	9 415	26.3	33.1
DuPage	338 083	73.5	278 500	24.2	14.2	1 143	28.7	2.6	516 049	0.9	24 722	4.8	479 592	44.8	16.0
Edgar	7 716	74.1	76 700	18.7	10.7	604	31.2	1.3	9 668	2.4	580	6.0	7 807	27.0	33.9
Edwards	2 785	84.4	69 300	19.5	10.0	471	26.4	0.8	2 967	0.7	173	5.8	2 968	23.6	41.5
Effingham	13 330	79.1	128 200	19.7	11.1	581	23.9	1.4	18 647	1.1	884	4.7	17 382	29.2	28.0
Fayette	7 761	81.3	82 400	19.3	10.8	578	27.2	2.3	9 636	-0.7	645	6.7	8 943	24.5	32.0
Ford	5 626	74.8	93 100	20.0	11.0	611	23.9	2.0	6 584	1.0	360	5.5	6 179	29.9	32.5
Franklin	16 257	73.9	66 300	19.5	10.8	590	27.9	1.8	16 568	0.4	1 350	8.1	15 510	26.9	30.5
Fulton	14 375	75.3	81 500	18.4	12.5	607	27.5	1.5	15 774	-0.3	1 170	7.4	15 565	28.7	30.7
Gallatin	2 408	77.1	65 700	17.7	11.1	383	26.4	2.3	2 512	1.7	192	7.6	2 280	29.5	32.3
Greene	5 458	76.2	76 000	19.4	12.0	607	25.6	2.0	6 034	-0.3	353	5.9	5 944	27.5	32.7
Grundy	18 492	75.0	182 400	23.1	12.4	929	28.4	3.2	25 665	0.8	1 755	6.8	23 887	28.9	29.5
Hamilton	3 473	78.0	84 700	17.6	10.2	577	27.3	1.1	4 224	-3.6	266	6.3	3 618	25.7	36.3
Hancock	7 862	79.3	83 400	18.8	10.8	565	22.7	1.2	8 790	-1.5	576	6.6	8 595	29.3	29.7

1. Specified owner-occupied units.   2. A value of 10.0 represents 10 percent or less; a value of 50.0 represents 50 percent or more.   3. Specified renter-occupied units.
4. Overcrowded or lacking complete plumbing facilities.   5. Percent of civilian labor force.   6. Civilian employed persons 16 years old and over.

Table B. States and Counties — Nonfarm Employment and Agriculture

STATE County	Number of establishments	Total	Health care and social assistance	Manufacturing	Retail trade	Finance and insurance	Professional, scientific, and technical services	Total (mil dol)	Average per employee (dollars)	Number	Fewer than 50 acres	500 acres or more	Farm operators whose principal occupation is farming (percent)
	104	105	106	107	108	109	110	111	112	113	114	115	116
IDAHO—Cont'd													
Caribou	187	2 553	250	762	244	48	33	167	65 497	436	19.3	40.4	55.3
Cassia	645	7 783	1 203	1 325	1 564	220	171	253	32 507	668	42.7	27.1	56.1
Clark	14	81	NA	D	40	D	D	2	29 284	72	12.5	41.7	61.1
Clearwater	231	1 848	491	307	234	39	43	66	35 833	256	35.5	11.7	34.8
Custer	162	717	67	30	164	18	24	26	36 611	272	36.4	23.9	52.9
Elmore	442	4 105	800	466	1 063	146	97	113	27 423	349	53.9	21.2	47.6
Franklin	295	2 151	356	323	547	62	61	65	30 151	834	19.2	43.5	43.5
Fremont	285	1 632	212	56	230	39	33	50	30 942	601	33.8	22.1	52.2
Gem	364	2 429	735	138	460	58	66	67	27 769	830	68.1	7.3	48.3
Gooding	359	2 819	523	536	413	71	72	95	33 747	596	53.4	14.1	52.0
Idaho	457	3 439	704	574	476	166	187	127	36 945	731	24.5	33.0	51.8
Jefferson	467	4 099	365	834	578	67	77	127	30 980	776	53.5	16.8	43.9
Jerome	535	6 265	494	1 399	914	105	91	231	36 945	560	46.3	15.4	63.2
Kootenai	4 513	47 532	9 300	5 019	8 390	2 094	2 148	1 781	37 466	824	58.4	6.7	48.1
Latah	905	8 432	1 241	393	1 869	214	532	245	29 007	1 053	30.6	15.9	43.3
Lemhi	288	1 757	510	D	408	33	65	49	27 732	350	46.6	20.0	48.6
Lewis	123	795	61	152	180	23	5	22	28 063	216	13.9	44.9	54.6
Lincoln	85	599	92	D	77	D	14	19	31 489	310	27.1	23.5	57.7
Madison	811	14 972	1 313	982	1 905	248	315	366	24 422	472	48.3	19.7	46.2
Minidoka	403	4 607	535	965	473	92	120	175	38 089	622	51.1	14.0	56.6
Nez Perce	1 132	17 164	3 137	3 916	2 472	1 168	470	656	38 213	430	41.4	30.0	52.1
Oneida	88	737	205	59	170	D	6	22	29 190	503	28.2	27.8	45.5
Owyhee	187	1 699	200	157	190	31	44	50	29 223	578	41.0	26.6	67.6
Payette	487	4 639	612	1 230	487	223	142	157	33 775	655	65.8	6.6	52.1
Power	164	2 222	165	808	164	50	56	87	39 114	308	24.4	50.3	63.3
Shoshone	351	4 160	525	140	1 037	67	177	189	45 400	36	61.1	0.0	33.3
Teton	451	2 117	308	106	277	44	116	86	40 629	291	30.2	21.3	42.3
Twin Falls	2 522	30 422	6 012	3 319	5 117	892	1 576	966	31 762	1 294	42.9	13.4	55.3
Valley	592	3 293	478	87	501	74	89	100	30 418	117	35.9	22.2	47.0
Washington	209	1 993	339	603	284	39	59	52	26 183	559	42.4	20.9	54.4
ILLINOIS	318 266	5 427 549	796 016	540 999	626 903	334 298	403 049	289 184	53 281	75 087	34.1	20.4	50.4
Adams	1 793	30 966	5 639	5 269	4 901	1 624	788	1 212	39 130	1 298	28.2	18.3	44.5
Alexander	93	1 020	227	166	112	18	37	41	39 740	144	25.0	19.4	56.9
Bond	312	3 726	510	807	360	114	69	127	34 216	661	39.2	16.5	46.1
Boone	850	15 438	955	8 628	1 340	239	590	849	54 984	479	49.9	15.7	53.0
Brown	113	3 282	208	167	116	46	27	143	43 592	413	23.2	16.7	41.2
Bureau	753	9 518	2 118	1 552	1 041	327	308	385	40 414	1 056	26.1	26.1	55.8
Calhoun	90	560	91	12	94	68	7	13	22 334	478	30.5	10.0	39.3
Carroll	393	3 699	431	1 117	473	192	47	124	33 479	643	26.7	22.4	56.9
Cass	232	4 668	367	D	443	161	67	167	35 778	446	29.6	24.2	48.2
Champaign	4 189	68 872	12 564	7 093	10 386	2 944	2 751	2 776	40 300	1 312	29.3	30.6	57.7
Christian	702	8 754	1 656	967	1 374	325	455	287	32 810	816	34.1	27.2	51.6
Clark	340	3 977	368	1 144	477	157	128	138	34 737	677	34.0	21.4	47.6
Clay	377	4 813	574	2 174	452	156	96	176	36 481	774	35.4	18.7	49.6
Clinton	871	8 999	1 837	811	1 675	295	174	283	31 394	915	31.0	16.3	47.9
Coles	1 179	18 287	4 624	2 701	2 714	584	410	673	36 807	704	37.2	23.2	56.7
Cook	132 237	2 361 405	366 297	178 127	240 254	189 367	224 326	142 226	60 230	127	81.1	3.9	44.1
Crawford	420	6 361	877	1 759	699	223	170	288	45 246	599	32.4	18.9	51.3
Cumberland	188	2 059	562	492	195	110	17	58	28 197	733	40.5	13.5	38.5
DeKalb	1 990	26 727	5 309	3 693	4 464	913	661	1 020	38 182	880	32.7	26.9	61.1
De Witt	371	4 885	591	811	690	104	272	236	48 268	511	32.4	24.7	55.4
Douglas	582	6 458	289	2 531	1 176	187	81	269	41 666	735	40.7	21.1	54.8
DuPage	33 696	604 592	68 156	54 354	63 400	33 213	45 316	35 028	57 937	74	82.4	2.7	35.1
Edgar	353	6 183	870	2 588	634	211	99	257	41 522	673	27.3	31.1	54.4
Edwards	141	2 115	98	D	191	66	21	87	41 214	365	41.4	16.4	39.7
Effingham	1 200	24 529	2 735	2 983	2 884	461	317	923	37 624	1 302	37.6	12.5	47.2
Fayette	474	4 693	897	316	885	219	133	135	28 860	1 240	39.2	12.6	42.7
Ford	372	4 233	1 087	727	533	134	110	159	37 678	546	26.4	35.7	53.5
Franklin	730	6 436	919	389	1 466	275	225	213	33 131	711	42.9	10.4	38.8
Fulton	652	6 275	1 811	193	1 371	323	193	183	29 105	970	29.7	20.2	53.1
Gallatin	96	832	110	11	63	24	23	35	41 975	203	24.1	36.0	56.2
Greene	235	1 754	333	118	376	140	63	58	33 161	689	30.2	22.9	52.8
Grundy	1 100	16 288	2 235	1 245	1 913	384	766	943	57 865	431	23.2	29.5	63.8
Hamilton	213	1 723	417	69	167	48	57	78	45 113	695	37.6	12.5	25.6
Hancock	386	2 829	497	362	428	193	152	103	36 303	1 090	28.4	21.5	50.0

Table B. States and Counties — **Agriculture**

STATE County	Land in farms — Acreage (1,000)	Percent change, 2007–2012	Acres — Average size of farm	Total irrigated (1,000)	Total cropland (1,000)	Value of land and buildings (dollars) — Average per farm	Average per acre	Value of machinery and equipment, average per farm (dollars)	Value of products sold — Total (mil dol)	Average per farm (dollars)	Percent from: Crops	Live-stock and poultry products	Percent of farms with sales of: $10,000 or more	$100,000 or more	Government payments — Total ($1,000)	Percent of farms
	117	118	119	120	121	122	123	124	125	126	127	128	129	130	131	132
IDAHO—Cont'd																
Caribou	395	-6.4	905	66.0	215.4	1 267 638	1 401	196 009	88.0	201 934	76.8	23.2	51.6	27.3	4 068	62.8
Cassia	611	-5.2	915	237.8	333.8	2 143 115	2 343	350 045	953.7	1 427 737	27.0	73.0	58.5	37.3	5 934	43.9
Clark	151	-4.2	2 101	29.2	52.5	3 059 583	1 456	304 333	35.2	488 792	75.1	24.9	66.7	38.9	572	56.9
Clearwater	73	4.4	284	0.2	28.9	534 063	1 883	59 699	9.7	38 078	74.6	25.4	25.8	6.3	797	43.0
Custer	143	15.0	525	51.6	44.4	1 208 224	2 302	107 033	26.2	96 471	33.6	66.4	50.4	22.8	588	23.2
Elmore	345	-0.5	988	89.9	117.9	2 021 562	2 046	204 605	350.6	1 004 536	26.9	73.1	41.0	21.5	838	20.9
Franklin	263	16.8	315	61.2	140.8	632 061	2 007	117 307	106.1	127 228	23.1	76.9	45.1	18.5	3 420	48.7
Fremont	316	9.8	526	124.8	207.8	1 175 121	2 233	216 087	158.6	263 942	89.5	10.5	47.4	24.0	3 473	52.1
Gem	179	-6.2	216	34.2	31.7	595 434	2 761	57 441	42.4	51 031	39.1	60.9	34.5	9.3	517	19.9
Gooding	240	7.4	402	142.0	150.7	1 539 908	3 830	272 973	942.8	1 581 904	10.7	89.3	59.9	33.7	1 873	29.0
Idaho	639	8.2	874	5.0	209.8	1 219 897	1 395	99 766	80.8	110 564	77.4	22.6	47.2	23.1	5 658	50.5
Jefferson	323	-0.8	416	175.3	191.1	1 089 749	2 620	162 642	257.2	331 387	57.8	42.2	51.3	25.4	2 332	41.0
Jerome	188	-0.4	336	149.0	148.9	1 289 525	3 840	304 766	617.1	1 101 943	23.5	76.5	65.9	36.4	1 880	47.3
Kootenai	124	-5.1	151	13.8	64.3	624 138	4 139	57 726	23.7	28 750	83.8	16.2	19.5	4.1	1 075	20.1
Latah	416	20.9	396	0.5	254.2	713 039	1 803	102 611	87.9	83 435	94.5	5.5	26.7	12.6	8 001	69.0
Lemhi	187	-1.2	535	56.7	49.7	1 189 800	2 222	89 217	32.2	91 863	15.1	84.9	44.6	20.0	533	12.6
Lewis	221	-10.0	1 024	D	158.7	1 437 389	1 403	201 764	62.5	289 292	95.4	4.6	57.4	40.7	3 763	80.6
Lincoln	130	10.5	418	71.4	72.6	1 098 352	2 625	208 332	175.6	566 510	21.8	78.2	64.2	33.2	1 703	44.2
Madison	201	-4.4	427	122.3	167.4	1 413 886	3 314	232 362	131.1	277 674	94.2	5.8	54.0	26.9	2 678	49.4
Minidoka	244	7.9	392	204.5	217.4	1 360 826	3 468	253 349	368.9	593 125	72.6	27.4	57.2	33.9	2 782	52.6
Nez Perce	322	-8.8	749	0.8	181.4	1 261 165	1 683	150 307	81.2	188 777	89.0	11.0	46.0	26.3	5 030	56.0
Oneida	329	4.7	653	34.1	175.7	775 891	1 187	106 209	32.5	64 545	58.1	41.9	42.5	12.1	3 972	66.4
Owyhee	749	31.5	1 295	133.5	140.7	1 590 689	1 228	183 332	291.6	504 424	32.2	67.8	66.8	36.7	2 041	40.1
Payette	157	-5.5	240	56.9	51.6	724 612	3 021	117 252	236.2	360 676	21.3	78.7	43.4	16.9	652	22.1
Power	467	3.5	1 517	120.9	361.7	2 293 497	1 512	378 549	238.3	773 747	85.4	14.6	48.7	31.5	6 836	67.9
Shoshone	D	D	D	D	0.8	387 167	D	43 778	0.1	3 944	32.4	66.9	11.1	0.0	D	2.8
Teton	133	8.8	458	56.4	87.6	1 506 742	3 292	137 058	35.8	123 086	83.9	16.1	44.0	18.6	1 206	44.0
Twin Falls	484	10.1	374	257.0	275.1	1 155 801	3 090	159 620	599.6	463 355	36.0	64.0	63.3	36.9	3 657	48.1
Valley	61	-1.3	524	26.2	8.8	1 294 667	2 473	72 564	6.6	56 675	18.2	81.8	36.8	11.1	62	12.8
Washington	426	2.3	763	42.7	79.5	762 163	999	96 005	75.3	134 664	49.1	50.9	48.3	20.4	1 036	39.9
ILLINOIS	26 938	0.6	359	522.5	23 752.8	2 261 778	6 305	203 184	17 187.1	228 895	82.3	17.7	54.5	33.0	553 300	75.0
Adams	389	3.9	299	2.3	294.2	1 479 562	4 940	147 340	174.0	134 044	74.9	25.1	55.5	27.4	7 898	73.2
Alexander	62	31.1	434	5.0	51.8	1 433 333	3 306	145 569	25.7	178 771	97.9	2.1	39.6	20.8	778	66.0
Bond	198	-11.8	300	0.0	176.7	1 941 345	6 470	174 467	66.0	99 800	82.0	18.0	46.3	24.5	3 940	74.7
Boone	135	-1.8	281	0.9	126.9	1 926 883	6 849	204 127	99.0	206 676	89.1	10.9	56.8	35.5	3 391	51.4
Brown	138	-9.0	333	0.4	85.5	1 327 644	3 987	105 603	42.0	101 717	79.4	20.6	40.2	20.1	3 102	87.9
Bureau	450	-5.9	426	10.6	410.8	3 125 461	7 332	246 925	420.2	397 908	89.9	10.1	68.7	49.0	8 943	80.8
Calhoun	88	-0.2	184	0.0	48.5	697 808	3 801	80 816	23.7	49 513	83.1	16.9	35.8	11.1	2 053	76.4
Carroll	256	-3.4	398	11.3	218.8	2 723 697	6 838	250 918	270.7	421 009	69.6	30.4	57.5	43.7	6 884	81.3
Cass	183	5.3	410	21.3	151.1	2 290 363	5 592	209 209	123.7	277 296	77.8	22.2	53.1	29.8	3 866	80.5
Champaign	616	12.0	470	17.9	591.1	3 740 816	7 961	294 914	424.2	323 295	94.5	5.5	73.5	50.7	11 068	84.7
Christian	374	-16.9	458	D	352.7	3 469 135	7 576	240 299	288.7	353 750	90.6	9.4	60.2	44.2	5 962	79.0
Clark	267	11.8	394	6.6	230.3	1 935 795	4 912	234 895	130.8	193 163	69.9	30.1	47.1	25.1	6 033	79.8
Clay	270	28.8	349	0.1	235.2	1 663 978	4 764	148 499	66.7	86 142	81.2	18.8	38.6	19.3	6 246	85.5
Clinton	285	6.4	312	1.9	259.6	1 824 631	5 848	228 694	206.0	225 184	42.9	57.1	62.4	33.1	5 669	81.5
Coles	267	4.7	379	0.0	245.9	2 671 436	7 050	235 723	136.0	193 229	96.3	3.7	54.5	34.8	4 927	77.6
Cook	8	3.7	67	0.4	7.5	700 701	10 471	76 598	10.7	84 150	79.4	20.6	51.2	18.1	104	15.0
Crawford	215	4.7	359	8.3	186.7	1 793 496	4 997	228 519	65.9	110 018	86.3	13.7	43.4	22.7	6 248	85.1
Cumberland	170	17.4	232	0.1	143.5	1 262 847	5 440	150 681	89.1	121 583	68.5	31.5	41.9	21.4	4 423	84.2
DeKalb	398	7.3	452	3.3	383.5	3 549 751	7 853	289 255	474.9	539 667	70.8	29.2	70.2	55.3	11 835	76.1
De Witt	196	-1.6	383	0.1	182.6	2 749 990	7 188	228 883	154.9	303 139	89.0	11.0	53.8	36.6	3 265	73.6
Douglas	263	0.5	358	0.3	247.8	2 721 101	7 609	214 850	166.7	226 789	85.4	14.6	61.6	40.5	4 948	63.8
DuPage	7	-8.8	98	0.1	5.9	680 851	6 947	82 162	10.0	135 514	95.3	4.7	37.8	14.9	80	14.9
Edgar	352	-0.2	523	D	326.3	3 432 028	6 568	287 382	205.1	304 807	D	D	62.3	42.9	6 450	83.2
Edwards	107	-8.5	292	D	88.1	1 176 600	4 024	173 096	33.7	92 282	85.7	14.3	39.7	18.4	2 276	80.8
Effingham	287	18.6	220	1.7	241.9	1 277 618	5 796	157 144	165.8	127 337	50.5	49.5	49.9	27.3	6 722	80.2
Fayette	303	0.0	244	0.3	248.2	1 089 291	4 456	131 927	97.4	78 521	86.1	13.9	40.0	18.8	5 615	73.7
Ford	308	13.8	564	0.8	298.0	4 278 846	7 581	312 397	191.7	351 125	82.5	17.5	74.4	50.0	5 740	85.3
Franklin	181	-12.8	255	0.1	152.7	946 098	3 709	113 533	55.8	78 457	73.0	27.0	27.3	12.8	3 330	66.5
Fulton	355	-7.9	366	2.1	266.4	1 921 065	5 249	166 037	212.1	218 637	71.7	28.3	53.8	28.9	6 943	67.1
Gallatin	186	0.3	917	25.9	170.3	4 030 990	4 394	455 074	90.1	443 606	98.8	1.2	69.5	40.9	2 545	83.3
Greene	290	6.2	421	8.8	233.4	2 373 734	5 637	220 164	186.2	270 305	77.0	23.0	55.7	32.4	6 005	74.0
Grundy	217	0.7	504	0.0	206.0	3 835 093	7 617	315 223	128.9	298 993	96.7	3.3	74.9	54.1	3 667	80.0
Hamilton	223	1.6	321	0.0	195.3	1 163 304	3 620	146 839	55.7	80 098	98.0	2.0	26.9	14.5	4 621	84.7
Hancock	386	-1.7	354	2.6	315.7	2 029 171	5 726	194 508	317.2	290 977	66.7	33.3	57.7	35.0	8 365	78.3

STATE County	Water use, 2010 Total water withdrawn (mil gal/day)	Gallons withdrawn per person per day	Wholesale trade,[1] 2012 Number of establishments	Number of employees	Sales (mil dol)	Annual payroll (mil dol)	Retail trade,[2] 2012 Number of establishments	Number of employees	Sales (mil dol)	Annual payroll (mil dol)	Real estate and rental and leasing,[2] 2012 Number of establishments	Number of employees	Receipts (mil dol)	Annual payroll (mil dol)
	133	134	135	136	137	138	139	140	141	142	143	144	145	146
IDAHO—Cont'd														
Caribou	307.9	44 221	12	88	134.6	3.5	33	279	79.2	7.4	4	5	0.7	0.1
Cassia	812.7	35 410	30	360	702.9	15.6	116	1 301	323.9	29.8	23	38	6.0	0.8
Clark	96.9	98 625	1	D	D	D	4	D	D	D	1	D	D	D
Clearwater	68.9	7 859	4	94	54.1	5.5	36	279	55.5	6.4	6	10	0.5	0.1
Custer	678.7	155 389	NA	NA	NA	NA	29	212	39.4	3.5	6	D	D	D
Elmore	362.8	13 418	13	83	36.5	3.0	76	974	256.3	22.2	13	28	3.7	0.5
Franklin	224.1	17 523	10	D	D	D	45	511	116.4	9.7	9	D	D	D
Fremont	358.7	27 087	8	195	114.5	5.8	33	241	73.4	6.8	6	7	1.2	0.2
Gem	468.3	28 011	12	D	D	D	43	412	93.6	8.8	9	23	2.6	0.4
Gooding	1 284.6	83 072	21	178	217.6	6.4	44	355	91.5	7.1	7	D	D	D
Idaho	24.4	1 500	11	101	54.1	4.0	57	455	94.8	11.1	10	17	2.1	0.4
Jefferson	1 405.3	53 760	25	D	D	D	44	464	116.4	10.0	11	D	D	D
Jerome	1 437.6	64 252	36	308	217.3	14.1	71	845	277.0	20.3	22	73	8.0	1.9
Kootenai	56.5	408	132	D	D	D	574	7 996	2 501.7	207.0	201	623	122.6	19.1
Latah	10.5	282	21	D	D	D	139	1 874	356.1	37.2	44	159	19.3	3.5
Lemhi	268.8	33 875	5	D	D	D	42	335	98.4	8.0	16	33	2.5	0.7
Lewis	1.5	390	5	D	D	D	23	133	26.5	2.5	5	13	1.2	0.2
Lincoln	281.4	54 038	NA	NA	NA	NA	12	D	D	D	3	D	D	D
Madison	481.2	12 820	37	533	221.2	15.5	118	1 607	370.7	34.2	56	174	25.1	3.2
Minidoka	629.2	31 352	46	661	430.9	27.8	62	418	157.9	9.3	12	37	6.1	1.2
Nez Perce	128.3	3 268	42	D	D	D	200	2 249	682.9	56.9	39	137	25.5	4.5
Oneida	177.0	41 295	1	D	D	D	18	142	30.4	2.3	4	15	1.0	0.1
Owyhee	811.3	70 386	6	D	D	D	24	169	42.6	3.9	4	9	0.2	0.0
Payette	242.0	10 697	21	203	113.5	6.0	61	483	136.4	10.7	21	26	3.8	0.6
Power	452.0	57 827	13	212	221.7	7.3	16	164	29.6	3.1	7	D	D	D
Shoshone	3.0	231	11	D	D	D	61	846	518.2	31.2	13	35	4.4	0.4
Teton	180.3	17 731	9	D	D	D	38	299	66.1	6.3	34	51	7.6	1.5
Twin Falls	1 462.0	18 930	111	1 096	492.8	42.6	380	4 789	1 233.5	112.8	112	313	49.7	8.5
Valley	71.3	7 228	10	65	20.0	2.2	69	462	105.9	10.3	38	58	10.0	1.4
Washington	203.2	19 924	9	194	26.4	3.6	33	276	83.7	6.5	11	27	2.3	0.4
ILLINOIS	13 091.3	1 020	16 036	255 531	295 457.0	15 973.3	39 947	592 942	166 634.5	14 576.1	12 035	76 794	23 649.1	3 816.1
Adams	19.4	289	120	D	D	D	299	4 790	1 066.5	101.4	61	D	D	D
Alexander	2.2	271	5	16	8.0	0.5	23	135	24.2	2.3	3	8	0.8	0.2
Bond	2.0	113	21	247	182.4	11.2	46	363	124.2	6.5	8	D	D	D
Boone	6.0	110	31	239	202.6	12.4	108	1 369	395.4	31.6	24	61	9.9	1.6
Brown	0.5	75	10	D	D	D	20	149	32.8	3.0	NA	NA	NA	NA
Bureau	6.0	173	53	896	1 472.5	39.3	97	1 166	299.8	23.2	16	D	D	D
Calhoun	0.5	104	5	D	D	D	15	116	27.3	2.5	1	D	D	D
Carroll	6.5	422	28	243	285.8	9.1	50	427	95.5	8.8	7	21	1.5	0.2
Cass	5.6	411	18	179	501.0	8.7	48	491	119.8	10.3	5	16	2.0	0.4
Champaign	32.3	161	176	2 872	2 589.6	126.5	626	10 256	2 472.7	220.2	201	2 986	557.4	117.9
Christian	838.9	24 107	45	605	845.6	30.5	111	1 377	410.3	31.4	20	94	12.9	2.7
Clark	5.6	345	19	191	257.9	6.0	51	445	141.7	10.9	5	22	4.4	0.7
Clay	1.3	94	26	196	172.8	6.8	46	464	113.3	8.9	7	49	3.9	0.9
Clinton	11.9	315	48	541	451.0	20.9	141	1 561	425.9	40.3	21	181	14.7	8.9
Coles	5.0	94	50	553	627.4	25.3	198	2 645	701.3	59.5	50	166	29.4	4.8
Cook	1 672.7	322	6 130	94 754	100 829.6	6 169.4	15 225	222 918	62 767.4	5 733.8	5 629	40 439	12 377.8	2 244.4
Crawford	69.2	3 493	19	181	179.3	6.2	61	796	187.1	16.2	14	D	D	D
Cumberland	1.4	125	16	153	188.2	5.0	24	188	38.6	2.9	1	D	D	D
DeKalb	10.4	99	60	586	353.2	27.1	280	4 404	1 052.7	91.7	69	447	100.2	14.2
De Witt	767.1	46 317	30	352	603.6	23.8	52	677	220.6	17.3	9	30	2.5	0.4
Douglas	3.0	150	30	329	478.1	16.6	120	1 173	218.7	19.1	12	38	8.3	1.0
DuPage	16.6	18	2 322	45 595	65 510.4	3 110.6	3 336	59 068	17 758.8	1 543.7	1 310	11 880	6 433.2	673.0
Edgar	4.3	232	13	148	227.4	9.4	51	623	157.0	13.6	9	30	4.6	0.9
Edwards	0.7	103	15	D	D	D	28	202	55.0	3.9	2	D	D	D
Effingham	4.5	130	62	D	D	D	203	2 977	934.7	66.1	43	214	32.0	7.0
Fayette	3.9	176	25	321	398.4	13.1	85	929	256.4	19.5	12	25	3.1	0.7
Ford	3.9	280	34	354	566.7	19.9	51	537	119.1	10.1	8	D	D	D
Franklin	15.3	388	34	265	126.3	13.3	143	1 549	408.1	35.0	15	69	6.4	1.6
Fulton	283.6	7 650	22	247	184.1	11.7	115	1 378	316.6	27.8	15	49	6.7	1.1
Gallatin	28.2	5 038	4	43	25.0	1.5	13	76	16.1	1.7	1	D	D	D
Greene	1.9	136	18	152	321.5	5.9	49	408	125.6	9.1	3	2	0.1	0.0
Grundy	501.9	10 026	47	490	738.0	27.1	144	1 744	524.7	38.1	28	71	15.7	2.4
Hamilton	0.7	84	8	81	64.5	3.2	34	161	45.4	3.4	7	15	1.3	0.3
Hancock	2.9	152	31	233	361.4	9.8	67	474	97.0	9.0	4	10	1.2	0.2

1. Merchant wholesalers, except manufacturers' sales branches and offices.   2. Employer establishments.

Table B. States and Counties — Professional Services, Manufacturing, and Accommodation and Food Services

STATE County	Professional, scientific, and technical services, 2012				Manufacturing, 2012				Accommodation and food services, 2012			
	Number of establishments	Number of employees	Receipts (mil dol)	Annual payroll (mil dol)	Number of establishments	Number of employees	Receipts (mil dol)	Annual payroll (mil dol)	Number of establishments	Number of employees	Sales (mil dol)	Annual payroll (mil dol)
	147	148	149	150	151	152	153	154	155	156	157	158
IDAHO—Cont'd												
Caribou	10	D	D	D	9	761	D	52.8	18	119	3.9	1.1
Cassia	49	146	12.1	4.1	31	1 345	917.1	53.3	51	D	D	D
Clark	2	D	D	D	3	D	D	0.3	1	D	D	D
Clearwater	11	46	2.4	1.1	21	251	D	8.5	27	175	6.5	2.1
Custer	8	D	D	D	5	D	D	D	31	D	D	D
Elmore	19	82	8.1	2.6	11	343	D	9.7	54	613	28.9	7.6
Franklin	17	51	6.2	1.5	19	247	39.9	8.7	16	204	5.6	1.6
Fremont	14	41	3.9	0.9	13	33	5.7	0.8	30	140	10.7	2.3
Gem	23	50	4.4	1.4	16	68	D	1.7	28	D	D	D
Gooding	21	D	D	D	23	405	D	20.5	30	183	7.3	1.9
Idaho	24	D	D	D	37	519	161.3	21.5	51	273	12.0	3.3
Jefferson	27	D	D	D	22	D	214.8	26.5	34	D	D	D
Jerome	25	113	13.4	3.8	24	1 301	D	52.9	30	329	16.7	4.0
Kootenai	442	D	D	D	241	4 011	D	170.2	362	D	D	D
Latah	80	D	D	D	26	277	D	12.3	121	D	D	D
Lemhi	19	62	3.1	1.2	9	60	12.2	1.5	35	223	10.3	2.5
Lewis	2	D	D	D	5	142	45.8	4.8	15	114	4.9	1.4
Lincoln	5	12	1.1	0.6	3	D	D	D	4	28	1.2	0.3
Madison	67	734	44.6	20.0	29	878	184.6	26.1	52	901	32.3	9.1
Minidoka	26	D	D	D	23	935	649.7	42.3	29	D	D	D
Nez Perce	80	D	D	D	35	2 791	1 124.5	133.9	99	2 096	108.5	30.1
Oneida	3	D	D	D	5	32	D	1.9	10	90	2.8	0.7
Owyhee	7	25	1.7	0.7	7	146	D	4.7	25	D	D	D
Payette	34	124	12.7	3.6	28	1 101	D	30.8	34	237	8.0	2.1
Power	8	D	D	D	7	D	D	D	12	52	2.2	0.5
Shoshone	27	D	D	D	16	182	D	7.4	42	D	D	D
Teton	39	103	11.1	3.8	9	76	D	2.6	37	257	15.0	5.0
Twin Falls	223	1 079	99.4	37.2	96	2 876	D	113.3	173	2 721	132.5	34.7
Valley	36	89	9.5	3.3	16	36	4.0	1.0	76	774	40.1	13.7
Washington	19	56	4.1	1.5	12	453	D	12.6	19	138	5.4	1.5
ILLINOIS	38 673	364 336	70 263.2	28 314.9	13 868	542 004	281 037.8	28 413.7	27 117	469 870	27 937.4	7 707.1
Adams	132	D	D	D	88	4 749	D	242.0	147	2 278	103.2	29.2
Alexander	7	37	1.7	0.8	4	145	D	6.2	14	61	2.2	0.7
Bond	25	D	D	D	16	838	419.8	37.4	33	332	14.9	3.8
Boone	59	639	57.0	29.4	78	7 619	5 906.2	404.0	69	796	41.8	10.6
Brown	6	26	2.0	0.7	5	138	36.3	5.9	11	D	D	D
Bureau	48	330	20.4	6.9	37	1 358	D	62.2	81	818	33.4	9.0
Calhoun	4	D	D	D	4	13	2.0	0.5	19	D	D	D
Carroll	24	62	6.6	1.6	26	784	293.1	31.4	39	317	15.0	3.7
Cass	11	54	6.0	1.7	13	2 297	D	83.4	28	D	D	D
Champaign	439	2 767	362.4	137.4	132	7 063	3 024.6	313.9	517	9 809	437.5	120.4
Christian	47	471	20.8	8.3	21	1 059	D	49.1	68	887	34.0	9.9
Clark	16	90	11.9	5.6	16	1 004	539.2	46.5	43	446	19.9	5.3
Clay	16	127	7.0	2.7	17	1 772	763.1	74.3	29	292	12.5	3.2
Clinton	46	208	18.6	7.1	33	732	D	26.3	98	1 090	41.4	10.8
Coles	67	405	40.7	13.1	40	2 615	D	109.0	130	2 232	84.7	24.1
Cook	19 017	217 861	48 255.4	18 955.5	5 120	181 315	79 527.0	9 622.8	11 329	207 364	14 553.1	4 023.7
Crawford	29	165	18.2	7.5	16	1 878	D	131.4	34	367	17.2	4.7
Cumberland	7	32	2.2	0.8	12	443	D	11.8	7	D	D	D
DeKalb	151	683	64.4	24.5	110	3 499	1 339.4	154.6	214	3 161	135.9	35.7
De Witt	23	90	9.1	2.7	14	513	181.4	20.7	38	489	19.8	5.7
Douglas	28	89	6.4	2.0	82	2 146	841.3	106.5	50	656	28.1	7.2
DuPage	5 117	46 480	8 120.0	3 347.2	1 680	53 913	18 896.7	2 921.6	2 132	40 549	2 424.3	690.5
Edgar	25	99	8.3	2.5	20	1 751	714.8	76.0	30	D	D	D
Edwards	7	22	1.7	0.5	9	D	D	D	11	103	2.8	0.8
Effingham	56	310	39.4	11.9	60	2 913	697.9	123.5	106	2 111	97.5	26.7
Fayette	21	134	9.9	4.2	13	439	113.9	15.6	45	506	21.0	6.0
Ford	18	104	10.2	3.1	17	562	D	24.7	31	D	D	D
Franklin	43	253	25.3	8.1	39	783	199.1	31.3	77	972	38.2	10.5
Fulton	38	187	17.6	7.7	19	218	47.5	6.8	72	856	28.7	8.1
Gallatin	7	22	1.5	0.7	4	7	1.0	0.2	8	29	1.4	0.3
Greene	16	65	6.6	2.6	12	167	D	6.0	28	D	D	D
Grundy	94	781	86.9	37.0	47	1 306	2 113.8	97.8	100	1 380	59.7	15.8
Hamilton	12	40	2.9	1.1	7	72	D	2.4	12	123	4.6	1.3
Hancock	21	173	32.3	7.4	24	1 217	D	D	32	227	10.5	2.8

1. Establishment subject to federal tax.

Table B. States and Counties — Health Care and Social Assistance, Other Services, Nonemployer Businesses, and Residential Construction

STATE County	Health care and social assistance, 2012				Other services, 2012				Nonemployer businesses, 2015		Value of residential construction authorized by building permits, 2016	
	Number of establishments	Number of employees	Receipts (mil dol)	Annual payroll (mil dol)	Number of establishments	Number of employees	Receipts (mil dol)	Annual payroll (mil dol)	Number	Receipts (mil dol)	New Construction ($1,000)	Number of housing units
	159	160	161	162	163	164	165	166	167	168	169	170
IDAHO—Cont'd												
Caribou	21	226	18.2	6.9	15	D	D	D	445	15.5	2 289	11
Cassia	83	1 246	95.1	34.2	37	D	D	D	1 498	78.2	12 657	74
Clark	1	D	D	D	NA	NA	NA	NA	64	1.3	0	0
Clearwater	24	515	40.4	19.1	14	D	D	D	489	19.1	3 098	29
Custer	8	D	D	D	5	6	0.5	0.1	448	13.6	0	0
Elmore	51	723	56.4	22.1	34	125	7.0	2.2	1 237	44.2	12 891	58
Franklin	25	325	25.1	9.1	19	D	D	D	1 044	43.3	9 787	60
Fremont	17	222	12.8	5.2	16	D	D	D	1 157	52.9	15 987	103
Gem	46	733	46.0	18.8	23	D	D	D	1 220	40.9	10 619	97
Gooding	35	496	39.5	15.0	23	D	D	D	883	31.5	3 376	19
Idaho	32	700	48.8	23.3	21	D	D	D	1 260	48.2	111	1
Jefferson	33	D	D	D	14	D	D	D	2 127	100.8	30 228	169
Jerome	36	502	35.3	17.7	48	162	17.0	4.1	1 169	55.0	10 542	73
Kootenai	509	8 630	806.2	308.4	236	D	D	D	11 983	520.3	315 990	1 666
Latah	85	1 360	115.0	49.3	52	D	D	D	2 541	90.1	26 410	127
Lemhi	27	366	28.2	10.7	22	75	7.7	1.5	716	25.2	5 023	41
Lewis	13	D	D	D	3	D	D	D	319	9.9	750	20
Lincoln	8	99	4.7	2.1	3	6	0.7	0.1	291	10.7	104	1
Madison	92	1 390	131.8	42.0	33	D	D	D	2 713	108.7	58 556	411
Minidoka	40	519	34.4	15.2	26	D	D	D	1 187	49.6	48 083	240
Nez Perce	138	3 029	341.2	123.0	85	D	D	D	2 151	85.0	16 663	76
Oneida	8	D	D	D	3	D	D	D	338	13.3	1 421	8
Owyhee	17	142	6.9	3.0	5	D	D	D	644	27.2	4 135	25
Payette	42	535	34.8	15.2	27	80	6.8	2.1	1 413	57.6	10 693	90
Power	12	190	11.5	5.4	11	58	6.6	1.4	381	17.4	3 587	15
Shoshone	33	488	35.7	13.6	17	58	5.0	1.6	774	22.3	2 362	13
Teton	29	250	21.1	9.0	20	61	6.0	1.8	1 432	55.5	43 314	116
Twin Falls	325	5 626	497.8	192.1	155	850	75.4	21.4	5 477	254.6	76 258	443
Valley	29	393	32.7	16.6	31	186	12.1	3.8	1 230	59.5	33 711	149
Washington	26	401	28.2	11.1	14	72	5.0	1.3	634	21.5	2 600	22
ILLINOIS	33 055	770 484	83 431.8	32 574.0	23 334	165 366	21 355.5	5 826.6	968 330	41 719.8	4 388 478	22 603
Adams	142	5 586	691.3	238.4	158	D	D	D	3 911	149.6	10 314	66
Alexander	8	237	12.2	6.6	6	10	0.8	0.2	343	8.3	0	0
Bond	30	593	47.3	21.9	21	99	8.8	2.6	990	28.3	2 276	13
Boone	73	1 077	80.1	30.0	67	372	30.0	9.4	3 100	123.9	3 518	19
Brown	9	D	D	D	12	D	D	D	338	8.4	0	0
Bureau	80	2 114	171.6	75.8	78	D	D	D	1 937	76.3	3 920	20
Calhoun	5	D	D	D	5	14	1.1	0.3	325	12.5	718	5
Carroll	26	616	23.8	9.5	32	191	13.4	4.0	1 014	36.1	4 555	16
Cass	17	379	15.7	7.3	25	D	D	D	721	22.3	2 251	9
Champaign	364	D	D	D	271	2 173	403.7	66.3	11 898	459.0	165 237	974
Christian	64	1 721	119.7	48.2	62	292	19.8	5.1	1 939	67.9	4 120	22
Clark	22	375	20.4	8.9	20	63	5.4	1.2	1 095	37.3	947	17
Clay	41	650	42.4	18.8	31	95	8.6	1.7	968	34.7	606	13
Clinton	84	1 624	128.7	52.6	66	284	25.0	6.1	2 335	83.1	18 329	81
Coles	155	3 981	367.2	149.0	96	465	35.2	11.2	2 689	96.6	2 058	12
Cook	14 637	358 374	39 639.9	15 523.6	9 887	78 562	12 262.7	3 166.7	475 448	20 649.1	1 909 931	10 956
Crawford	42	975	73.2	28.7	41	170	15.7	3.5	1 235	44.7	400	2
Cumberland	14	260	14.4	6.1	16	100	7.4	3.3	754	24.7	100	2
DeKalb	229	4 786	503.1	179.1	147	994	67.3	17.8	6 075	224.2	15 461	74
De Witt	28	581	38.5	17.1	27	98	9.5	2.5	873	30.5	2 043	11
Douglas	30	356	20.6	8.8	31	111	8.8	2.5	1 573	65.3	4 351	25
DuPage	3 215	62 644	7 846.5	3 116.4	2 047	17 768	2 184.8	676.0	81 992	4 371.9	410 312	1 386
Edgar	30	752	65.5	25.4	24	96	9.9	2.4	1 010	33.3	740	3
Edwards	14	120	5.9	3.2	14	D	D	D	473	14.9	NA	NA
Effingham	124	2 778	320.0	109.8	94	989	65.7	28.0	2 727	121.4	7 525	39
Fayette	42	987	48.3	20.2	33	157	14.7	3.6	1 299	49.9	160	1
Ford	35	1 053	88.1	37.9	28	D	D	D	972	37.2	1 421	10
Franklin	73	1 229	75.4	28.5	55	186	24.0	3.9	2 190	72.5	1 599	19
Fulton	70	2 037	171.7	66.2	50	260	14.2	4.2	1 702	53.0	6 339	56
Gallatin	7	109	5.3	2.0	11	D	D	D	299	12.5	NA	NA
Greene	22	378	22.9	11.7	15	D	D	D	794	29.1	511	3
Grundy	124	D	D	D	85	487	55.3	13.1	2 864	126.4	22 409	208
Hamilton	19	447	25.3	10.1	17	55	5.8	1.4	500	16.2	NA	NA
Hancock	28	493	34.1	15.0	29	70	5.7	1.5	1 306	48.9	1 240	7

Table B. States and Counties — Government Employment and Payroll, and Local Government Finances

	Government employment and payroll, 2012									Local government finances, 2012				
			March payroll (percent of total)							General revenue				
												Taxes		
													Per capita[1] (dollars)	
STATE County	Full-time equivalent employees	March payroll (dollars)	Adminis-tration, judicial, and legal	Police and Corrections	Fire Protection	Highways and transpor-tation	Health and Welfare	Natural resources and utilities	Education and libraries	Total (mil dol)	Inter-govern-mental (mil dol)	Total (mil dol)	Total	Property
	171	172	173	174	175	176	177	178	179	180	181	182	183	184
IDAHO—Cont'd														
Caribou	536	1 743 847	5.7	7.1	0.0	5.1	23.6	2.6	54.8	30.0	15.1	9.8	1 451	1 424
Cassia	841	2 609 053	6.9	10.2	1.3	4.4	1.0	7.7	66.0	72.2	36.8	15.3	658	460
Clark	64	182 907	15.4	10.5	0.0	12.5	0.0	3.3	58.1	5.0	3.3	1.2	1 353	1 265
Clearwater	338	951 830	12.2	14.7	0.3	8.5	5.3	6.8	50.6	26.1	13.8	8.4	974	934
Custer	193	546 688	12.5	6.7	0.1	16.9	1.2	5.5	56.7	15.9	9.6	3.8	876	845
Elmore	1 019	3 030 975	6.9	10.0	0.6	5.4	25.3	5.0	45.8	85.0	33.0	18.8	717	631
Franklin	560	1 720 585	5.4	4.8	0.0	3.4	34.4	1.8	50.0	29.4	21.3	5.3	417	394
Fremont	515	1 419 098	11.6	16.1	2.7	6.1	2.9	5.3	54.6	35.8	16.2	14.1	1 086	1 034
Gem	557	1 566 566	7.1	9.6	1.2	2.9	21.3	5.1	50.7	48.1	18.9	14.1	844	831
Gooding	579	1 442 650	8.1	9.0	1.3	5.5	3.6	3.7	66.2	56.3	24.7	15.8	1 036	1 004
Idaho	626	1 781 949	5.1	6.7	0.0	7.5	28.5	2.9	44.8	45.1	21.7	8.0	491	490
Jefferson	872	2 231 238	5.7	8.4	1.8	4.0	1.4	0.9	76.4	54.6	35.5	14.4	541	538
Jerome	672	1 876 675	11.2	10.1	3.4	5.6	0.5	5.4	62.3	54.6	29.4	15.7	697	673
Kootenai	6 580	25 436 541	6.0	8.3	3.6	2.4	37.6	3.3	38.1	678.7	158.8	148.1	1 040	972
Latah	1 001	3 595 367	11.4	10.5	0.8	5.9	0.5	6.2	63.7	82.9	35.0	31.3	819	745
Lemhi	403	1 235 515	7.2	7.5	0.2	3.9	46.4	3.5	30.0	38.3	15.0	4.0	511	478
Lewis	228	620 176	8.8	8.6	0.0	7.6	0.3	4.4	69.1	19.4	10.6	6.1	1 560	1 538
Lincoln	225	639 708	10.8	7.0	0.8	6.1	0.7	4.7	69.2	12.7	7.9	3.6	675	614
Madison	1 018	2 964 631	10.1	13.1	1.9	4.4	1.9	2.7	63.6	142.6	48.3	21.2	565	517
Minidoka	971	2 994 496	5.6	6.8	1.4	1.2	25.7	9.8	49.0	70.9	29.8	11.3	562	530
Nez Perce	1 348	5 048 001	7.1	13.3	6.7	5.6	4.0	8.5	50.0	119.0	49.4	44.7	1 132	1 075
Oneida	180	488 815	12.4	9.4	0.2	6.7	2.2	3.2	65.1	13.7	7.2	3.0	709	690
Owyhee	420	1 130 203	5.4	8.3	0.9	4.7	0.4	2.7	73.7	36.6	20.4	12.9	1 130	780
Payette	742	2 179 486	8.8	11.0	1.4	4.1	2.9	4.4	66.6	54.2	28.9	16.9	747	643
Power	430	1 383 820	5.4	5.9	0.3	7.0	26.0	3.4	51.1	39.7	13.4	10.9	1 398	1 360
Shoshone	609	1 865 396	6.7	7.4	2.8	7.1	21.4	5.7	48.1	52.0	20.0	14.5	1 140	1 102
Teton	450	1 567 917	7.7	3.7	5.3	2.4	33.2	1.8	43.6	55.4	16.6	14.5	1 445	1 299
Twin Falls	3 114	9 543 688	6.8	11.2	2.7	2.8	5.5	3.6	66.3	357.5	212.6	68.8	876	846
Valley	517	1 760 053	11.5	14.1	6.6	9.0	7.9	8.9	39.9	49.2	15.8	24.3	2 542	2 475
Washington	545	1 653 304	6.7	8.4	0.8	4.2	28.1	6.1	43.6	48.8	16.8	12.1	1 202	1 131
ILLINOIS	X	X	X	X	X	X	X	X	X	X	X	X	X	X
Adams	2 703	8 715 868	5.5	10.4	4.2	4.1	5.0	6.1	62.7	223.4	108.4	76.6	1 140	966
Alexander	313	970 447	7.7	9.2	0.0	10.6	2.3	10.0	57.2	30.3	20.7	4.6	595	522
Bond	553	1 740 375	8.4	8.6	0.2	5.4	9.2	6.9	61.0	47.8	21.7	14.3	811	782
Boone	1 665	6 568 081	5.5	11.2	2.8	2.0	1.2	4.1	72.4	168.6	64.4	88.0	1 632	1 512
Brown	202	635 285	9.5	7.4	0.4	13.0	4.1	3.1	62.1	17.3	8.3	5.3	772	738
Bureau	1 639	5 498 491	7.7	6.6	1.2	2.6	22.0	6.1	53.1	152.9	48.9	47.1	1 371	1 315
Calhoun	170	503 707	8.6	7.8	0.2	10.3	6.6	2.8	63.7	12.8	6.7	4.6	917	910
Carroll	571	1 922 747	6.7	10.1	1.2	4.6	1.4	4.6	70.2	50.2	17.9	26.2	1 744	1 700
Cass	549	1 630 366	5.5	5.1	0.7	5.7	1.6	4.6	73.9	47.1	27.4	13.9	1 039	967
Champaign	7 295	27 910 700	5.6	8.8	3.9	7.8	5.7	5.8	60.6	779.8	297.9	355.6	1 749	1 502
Christian	1 070	3 699 842	8.2	9.1	2.1	5.7	2.0	6.3	66.0	97.0	49.7	35.0	1 009	963
Clark	656	1 941 162	6.3	7.0	1.4	5.2	2.5	7.5	65.2	49.9	25.6	16.5	1 017	965
Clay	731	2 318 318	7.1	5.7	0.1	3.7	25.1	6.3	51.0	65.8	22.2	11.1	807	758
Clinton	1 065	3 651 290	8.0	9.9	0.0	4.7	3.6	5.9	67.0	83.0	32.3	37.3	980	957
Coles	2 055	7 515 260	6.6	9.1	4.4	3.1	2.6	3.4	70.1	193.9	95.6	62.8	1 170	1 079
Cook	198 590	1 055 085 174	5.5	19.7	3.8	8.4	5.0	6.1	49.9	30 214.0	10 506.2	14 465.1	2 765	2 126
Crawford	1 004	3 546 258	3.9	4.8	1.2	4.9	40.2	1.7	42.6	92.3	22.6	23.8	1 214	1 192
Cumberland	489	1 701 831	5.1	5.3	0.6	4.4	1.3	6.8	75.7	24.9	13.2	8.4	765	749
DeKalb	3 677	13 579 842	6.4	11.5	5.3	3.7	5.7	4.9	61.7	427.7	136.1	235.3	2 247	1 839
De Witt	856	2 898 838	6.6	7.9	0.9	3.4	26.5	4.6	49.0	74.5	16.6	32.1	1 956	1 907
Douglas	604	1 931 336	13.2	8.9	0.8	4.9	0.1	2.9	68.4	57.7	23.4	26.8	1 352	1 325
DuPage	34 627	161 978 004	4.8	10.0	5.2	2.3	1.4	8.6	66.4	4 380.5	931.7	2 785.7	3 002	2 700
Edgar	762	2 449 135	5.9	7.4	2.5	12.8	1.9	5.1	63.4	53.8	26.7	21.4	1 175	1 081
Edwards	230	593 869	6.7	6.9	0.5	3.2	1.4	6.8	74.3	13.3	7.7	3.8	573	568
Effingham	1 139	4 092 064	7.6	10.0	2.5	4.1	2.3	4.6	67.2	103.7	48.7	39.5	1 151	1 088
Fayette	798	2 298 002	8.1	12.9	0.0	4.6	5.0	3.9	65.2	56.1	29.6	16.6	754	737
Ford	495	1 697 539	6.4	9.3	0.0	5.1	0.0	3.3	75.1	45.2	18.3	21.4	1 530	1 465
Franklin	1 582	5 056 096	5.7	8.6	1.7	3.6	12.7	9.1	58.0	140.8	72.3	25.5	646	571
Fulton	1 688	5 342 718	6.0	7.3	2.2	3.1	5.4	5.4	70.1	131.1	60.0	46.1	1 259	1 214
Gallatin	190	667 273	12.7	6.1	0.2	4.8	0.2	7.6	67.8	16.8	10.0	3.8	699	636
Greene	546	1 577 821	8.0	6.8	0.3	8.5	4.3	8.2	63.4	36.4	17.9	12.3	908	861
Grundy	1 993	7 671 944	5.9	9.9	3.1	2.7	1.3	1.8	74.1	223.4	53.5	147.8	2 939	2 877
Hamilton	413	1 340 057	6.2	3.3	0.0	3.7	34.5	5.5	46.3	33.7	13.2	5.1	604	603
Hancock	809	2 296 267	7.2	7.5	0.4	6.0	1.8	4.7	71.8	55.0	25.2	21.7	1 147	1 101

1. Based on the resident population estimated as of July 1 of the year shown.

STATE County	Local government finances, 2012 (cont.)									Government employment, 2015			Individual income tax returns, 2014		
	Direct general expenditure							Debt outstanding							
			Percent of total for:												
	Total (mil dol)	Per capita¹ (dollars)	Education	Health and hospitals	Police protection	Public welfare	Highways	Total (mil dol)	Per capita¹ (dollars)	Federal civilian	Federal military	State and local	Number of returns	Mean adjusted gross income	Mean income tax
	185	186	187	188	189	190	191	192	193	194	195	196	197	198	199
IDAHO—Cont'd															
Caribou	29.0	4 268	41.5	0.2	10.7	0.5	13.5	1.0	151	43	23	628	2 720	57 238	5 115
Cassia	58.1	2 497	57.1	0.4	5.3	0.8	5.6	30.3	1 303	125	79	1 503	9 260	45 627	4 491
Clark	5.2	6 037	40.8	0.2	6.5	0.5	26.7	4.2	4 807	28	D	105	320	31 719	2 003
Clearwater	26.0	3 028	39.9	2.2	7.1	1.3	13.0	2.0	229	164	27	791	3 390	43 782	3 780
Custer	16.4	3 790	37.4	7.3	4.7	0.5	14.1	0.2	42	148	14	288	1 860	46 670	4 798
Elmore	76.8	2 930	37.5	27.0	6.8	0.0	7.2	27.5	1 049	842	3 192	1 023	11 240	41 380	3 611
Franklin	28.7	2 243	61.1	1.8	7.2	0.4	7.4	5.0	394	34	44	971	4 950	46 375	3 510
Fremont	39.0	3 014	39.0	1.3	7.0	0.8	11.9	29.5	2 277	74	42	916	5 320	40 870	2 916
Gem	41.4	2 481	43.1	21.4	5.8	0.6	5.5	23.5	1 409	78	57	800	7 050	41 463	3 483
Gooding	85.0	5 557	26.2	51.3	2.6	0.7	3.7	49.5	3 236	65	52	1 099	6 370	35 946	3 934
Idaho	41.4	2 537	44.3	2.9	4.7	1.4	20.3	6.4	391	319	54	911	6 300	43 835	3 950
Jefferson	64.3	2 411	54.0	0.0	6.7	0.2	4.6	89.0	3 335	54	92	1 196	10 260	48 417	4 245
Jerome	53.8	2 393	44.7	0.3	5.9	1.1	9.0	39.2	1 743	51	77	1 004	9 330	33 716	3 372
Kootenai	637.0	4 475	29.8	40.2	5.8	0.4	3.9	121.1	851	596	507	10 065	69 710	51 389	5 560
Latah	87.4	2 290	48.2	0.3	11.6	1.1	4.1	40.7	1 065	166	141	6 261	15 700	51 786	5 315
Lemhi	34.8	4 485	25.3	39.2	3.9	0.7	4.9	15.4	1 987	208	26	588	3 520	42 767	4 877
Lewis	21.4	5 498	42.3	0.7	5.0	0.7	11.4	4.3	1 109	53	13	381	1 780	43 023	3 933
Lincoln	12.3	2 332	69.2	0.0	4.6	0.1	9.2	6.3	1 194	80	18	367	2 020	40 609	3 133
Madison	144.7	3 862	27.9	37.4	3.3	0.2	4.1	137.2	3 662	58	128	2 003	12 280	40 810	3 050
Minidoka	75.3	3 760	38.1	24.8	4.2	0.5	5.7	46.9	2 341	86	69	1 352	8 680	43 975	3 844
Nez Perce	119.5	3 023	41.4	0.7	8.3	0.2	7.5	25.2	637	201	135	3 901	18 350	50 220	5 131
Oneida	14.2	3 368	42.9	22.5	6.2	0.3	7.9	2.7	633	19	14	413	1 750	38 022	3 053
Owyhee	32.2	2 814	58.3	0.0	6.5	0.9	6.7	21.0	1 836	45	38	633	4 460	36 255	3 384
Payette	52.4	2 315	48.3	3.5	7.4	1.5	7.7	25.3	1 117	30	78	1 027	9 460	49 524	5 236
Power	34.2	4 401	40.1	20.7	3.4	0.6	11.8	11.5	1 480	22	26	595	3 200	40 871	3 696
Shoshone	52.1	4 102	38.6	21.3	5.0	0.8	10.7	38.7	3 043	67	42	878	5 260	43 390	4 115
Teton	51.0	5 069	26.2	24.7	2.1	0.1	4.7	22.8	2 269	40	36	410	4 490	50 476	5 266
Twin Falls	356.9	4 541	65.8	1.8	3.6	0.9	4.2	190.1	2 418	365	278	4 324	35 060	45 181	4 534
Valley	50.0	5 243	33.1	0.0	8.0	0.2	14.2	52.4	5 495	244	34	728	4 830	52 476	5 658
Washington	43.6	4 322	34.4	33.0	5.6	1.2	5.7	9.6	952	51	34	700	4 070	39 358	3 153
ILLINOIS	X	X	X	X	X	X	X	X	X	80 035	42 385	753 594	6 130 850	69 200	10 038
Adams	201.0	2 991	56.5	3.5	5.7	0.2	5.8	99.6	1 482	235	132	3 912	32 170	53 448	6 081
Alexander	30.3	3 916	49.2	1.4	5.2	0.5	5.8	3.3	426	22	13	584	2 590	37 061	2 891
Bond	45.6	2 583	46.2	7.7	7.5	0.1	9.0	52.0	2 948	336	31	732	7 000	49 130	4 685
Boone	156.0	2 893	62.0	1.2	6.0	0.1	5.4	126.3	2 341	67	108	2 092	25 350	58 940	6 839
Brown	16.0	2 312	46.9	4.0	5.1	0.0	14.3	5.3	774	43	10	377	2 370	47 442	4 716
Bureau	156.2	4 551	37.8	25.0	3.8	0.0	9.0	77.1	2 245	117	67	2 190	16 630	53 267	6 201
Calhoun	11.5	2 294	52.1	0.5	3.8	0.1	22.6	8.5	1 693	20	10	240	2 160	50 717	5 185
Carroll	49.2	3 280	55.2	1.4	4.9	0.0	10.6	31.3	2 088	67	29	780	7 560	50 857	5 439
Cass	48.5	3 633	48.0	10.6	5.0	0.1	5.9	32.3	2 418	54	26	828	6 410	45 468	4 064
Champaign	826.4	4 066	48.3	2.5	5.1	1.9	5.6	670.9	3 301	1 284	422	35 614	85 580	59 898	7 437
Christian	110.2	3 182	62.3	1.4	5.2	0.2	6.9	48.6	1 404	74	65	1 786	15 470	50 068	5 207
Clark	50.6	3 123	49.6	1.9	5.8	0.2	12.5	27.6	1 705	51	32	836	7 580	49 812	5 100
Clay	65.1	4 732	32.8	32.8	3.4	0.1	5.2	24.2	1 756	43	27	935	6 270	44 621	3 975
Clinton	81.6	2 145	54.7	2.6	8.5	0.0	9.4	57.5	1 510	100	72	2 244	17 510	57 075	6 116
Coles	224.0	4 175	60.6	1.0	4.9	0.1	7.5	97.1	1 809	140	102	5 852	21 340	52 363	6 322
Cook	29 791.5	5 695	39.4	4.1	7.7	1.3	4.1	59 701.4	11 412	38 104	10 922	285 828	2 536 230	71 593	11 269
Crawford	103.4	5 277	28.7	46.8	2.5	0.1	5.6	46.4	2 366	57	36	1 823	8 770	53 982	6 220
Cumberland	25.4	2 316	59.2	2.1	4.8	0.2	11.9	9.6	878	30	22	462	4 870	48 083	4 293
DeKalb	465.9	4 450	45.9	1.7	5.4	3.0	4.9	394.6	3 769	187	201	12 926	45 890	54 783	5 903
De Witt	72.0	4 384	38.0	25.7	5.5	0.1	7.2	34.3	2 088	48	32	983	7 710	55 046	6 284
Douglas	56.1	2 825	47.8	1.8	6.3	0.3	11.0	34.9	1 760	56	40	1 041	10 000	51 195	5 216
DuPage	4 276.8	4 609	55.0	0.8	6.9	1.6	4.5	4 424.5	4 768	4 937	1 922	46 856	472 040	89 707	14 599
Edgar	59.4	3 263	54.0	3.0	5.0	0.0	11.2	50.5	2 777	50	35	952	8 080	48 919	5 131
Edwards	13.2	1 968	61.7	1.1	4.8	0.1	7.8	6.7	1 005	22	13	282	2 900	50 232	4 488
Effingham	107.8	3 137	47.2	2.6	6.9	0.7	10.6	58.0	1 688	149	70	1 636	17 670	56 261	6 802
Fayette	56.3	2 557	53.8	6.6	7.2	0.0	7.1	24.9	1 130	57	41	1 035	9 160	45 147	4 311
Ford	49.5	3 535	64.3	0.7	5.7	0.0	8.3	21.0	1 501	48	27	770	6 540	51 303	5 271
Franklin	143.4	3 639	47.5	12.4	7.3	0.3	5.1	32.0	811	195	79	1 824	16 720	44 062	4 019
Fulton	132.3	3 611	54.8	3.6	4.8	2.2	7.8	85.5	2 332	96	67	2 243	15 830	46 202	4 472
Gallatin	16.0	2 938	50.0	0.8	2.9	0.3	11.8	8.2	1 509	25	11	248	2 300	53 312	6 145
Greene	37.1	2 735	54.1	5.0	5.5	0.4	12.8	12.2	901	46	27	673	5 840	43 952	3 861
Grundy	239.2	4 757	60.5	1.0	4.2	0.0	7.5	311.7	6 199	105	102	2 685	24 590	64 025	7 584
Hamilton	35.0	4 183	33.6	40.5	2.7	0.1	8.6	25.1	3 002	35	16	501	3 630	50 347	5 267
Hancock	59.2	3 132	56.6	5.9	3.8	1.1	11.6	21.0	1 109	72	37	1 100	8 740	48 259	4 571

1. Based on the resident population estimated as of July 1 of the year shown.

Table B. States and Counties — **Land Area and Population**

STATE/County code	CBSA code[1]	County type[2]	STATE County	Land area[3] (sq mi) 2016	Total persons 2016	Rank	Per square mile	White	Black	American Indian, Alaska Native	Asian and Pacific Islander	Percent Hispanic or Latino[4]	Under 5 years	5 to 17 years	18 to 24 years	25 to 34 years	35 to 44 years	45 to 54 years
				1	2	3	4	5	6	7	8	9	10	11	12	13	14	15
			ILLINOIS—Cont'd															
17 069	...	9	Hardin	177.5	4 024	2 900	22.7	94.7	2.6	1.0	0.9	2.0	3.5	14.5	6.8	9.4	11.3	14.6
17 071	15460	9	Henderson	378.9	6 869	2 686	18.1	97.4	0.8	0.6	0.7	1.6	5.0	13.9	6.8	9.6	9.7	13.7
17 073	19340	2	Henry	823.0	49 280	995	59.9	91.9	2.4	0.5	0.8	5.7	5.4	17.0	7.7	10.7	12.0	13.2
17 075	...	6	Iroquois	1 117.3	28 334	1 476	25.4	91.4	1.6	0.6	0.9	6.7	5.2	16.6	7.5	10.4	11.2	13.0
17 077	16060	3	Jackson	584.1	58 870	879	100.8	77.0	15.9	1.0	4.8	4.2	5.5	12.7	22.2	14.2	9.9	10.1
17 079	...	7	Jasper	494.5	9 536	2 466	19.3	97.8	0.5	0.4	0.5	1.5	5.7	17.1	7.0	11.1	11.4	14.0
17 081	34500	7	Jefferson	571.2	38 460	1 213	67.3	87.2	9.8	0.5	1.6	2.5	6.5	15.7	7.8	12.7	12.4	13.0
17 083	41180	1	Jersey	369.3	22 025	1 727	59.6	96.9	1.2	0.7	1.0	1.4	4.9	15.9	9.3	11.0	11.0	14.3
17 085	...	6	Jo Daviess	600.9	21 770	1 741	36.2	95.6	1.1	0.4	0.8	3.0	4.4	15.0	6.5	9.0	10.0	12.9
17 087	...	8	Johnson	343.9	12 902	2 234	37.5	86.8	9.7	0.6	0.5	3.4	4.3	14.0	8.8	13.6	12.4	13.7
17 089	16980	1	Kane	520.2	531 715	126	1 022.1	58.7	6.0	0.4	4.6	31.8	6.5	19.9	9.0	12.0	13.6	14.4
17 091	28100	3	Kankakee	676.6	110 008	550	162.6	73.4	16.0	0.5	1.4	10.4	5.9	17.7	10.2	12.1	12.1	13.0
17 093	16980	1	Kendall	320.3	124 695	502	389.3	72.0	7.5	0.4	3.8	18.0	7.1	22.1	8.1	12.8	16.5	14.1
17 095	23060	4	Knox	716.4	50 938	974	71.1	85.6	9.1	0.6	1.4	5.6	5.3	14.3	9.7	11.9	11.5	12.5
17 097	16980	1	Lake	443.9	703 047	90	1 583.8	63.8	7.6	0.5	8.5	21.5	5.8	18.9	10.5	10.9	12.6	14.8
17 099	36860	4	LaSalle	1 135.1	110 642	546	97.5	86.8	3.1	0.5	1.2	9.5	5.3	16.3	8.1	12.0	11.6	13.6
17 101	...	7	Lawrence	372.2	16 377	2 015	44.0	85.4	10.6	0.5	0.5	3.8	5.4	13.6	9.3	14.8	14.0	13.1
17 103	19940	6	Lee	724.9	34 251	1 318	47.2	87.9	5.8	0.5	1.1	5.9	5.1	14.8	8.0	12.3	11.9	14.2
17 105	38700	4	Livingston	1 044.2	36 526	1 264	35.0	90.1	5.2	0.5	1.0	4.5	5.2	16.0	8.6	12.5	11.6	13.4
17 107	30660	6	Logan	618.1	29 527	1 444	47.8	87.4	8.8	0.5	1.2	3.4	5.2	14.1	10.6	13.9	12.6	12.7
17 109	31380	5	McDonough	589.4	30 996	1 409	52.6	89.6	6.1	0.6	2.5	2.7	4.5	12.3	23.5	12.9	9.2	10.0
17 111	16980	1	McHenry	603.2	307 004	223	509.0	82.7	1.8	0.4	3.5	12.9	5.5	18.7	8.6	11.0	12.7	16.1
17 113	14010	3	McLean	1 183.4	172 418	376	145.7	81.9	8.8	0.5	6.1	4.8	5.9	15.9	17.8	13.0	12.0	11.9
17 115	19500	3	Macon	580.7	106 550	563	183.5	79.1	19.1	0.6	1.7	2.2	6.0	16.3	9.0	11.7	11.5	12.3
17 117	41180	1	Macoupin	862.9	45 908	1 051	53.2	97.1	1.3	0.7	0.6	1.2	5.0	16.3	7.7	11.0	11.8	13.4
17 119	41180	1	Madison	715.7	265 759	255	371.3	87.1	9.5	0.6	1.5	3.2	5.8	16.2	8.2	13.7	12.0	13.5
17 121	16460	4	Marion	572.4	38 140	1 220	66.6	93.0	5.3	0.5	1.0	2.0	6.4	16.5	7.8	11.7	11.1	12.9
17 123	37900	2	Marshall	386.8	11 939	2 298	30.9	95.6	0.9	0.5	0.7	3.1	5.3	14.9	7.5	10.1	10.8	13.3
17 125	...	6	Mason	539.2	13 507	2 195	25.1	97.6	1.1	0.8	0.7	1.1	4.8	16.2	7.4	10.1	11.9	14.0
17 127	37140	7	Massac	237.2	14 658	2 122	61.8	90.5	7.0	0.9	0.9	2.9	5.4	16.7	7.0	10.2	11.7	13.3
17 129	44100	3	Menard	314.4	12 516	2 258	39.8	97.0	1.5	0.7	0.6	1.5	5.1	16.9	7.3	10.6	12.0	14.0
17 131	19340	2	Mercer	561.2	15 730	2 058	28.0	96.4	1.0	0.5	0.6	2.3	5.0	16.4	7.0	10.0	11.3	14.0
17 133	41180	1	Monroe	385.0	34 068	1 324	88.5	97.3	0.6	0.5	0.9	1.5	5.5	17.1	7.2	10.7	12.3	14.7
17 135	...	6	Montgomery	703.7	28 952	1 457	41.1	94.0	3.9	0.4	0.7	1.8	4.9	15.2	8.0	12.6	11.9	13.7
17 137	27300	4	Morgan	568.8	34 277	1 316	60.3	90.6	7.3	0.5	0.9	2.4	5.1	14.4	9.8	12.7	11.5	12.9
17 139	...	6	Moultrie	335.9	14 827	2 113	44.1	97.8	0.8	0.4	0.5	1.2	6.4	18.5	7.4	11.6	11.5	12.1
17 141	40300	4	Ogle	758.6	51 273	971	67.6	88.2	1.6	0.5	0.8	10.0	5.3	17.4	7.8	11.0	11.6	14.3
17 143	37900	2	Peoria	619.2	185 006	351	298.8	72.8	20.0	0.6	4.7	4.7	7.1	16.9	9.0	14.0	12.1	12.2
17 145	...	6	Perry	441.8	21 357	1 758	48.3	87.7	9.4	0.5	0.9	3.0	4.8	14.7	9.4	13.6	12.9	13.3
17 147	16580	3	Piatt	439.2	16 560	2 004	37.7	97.3	1.0	0.5	0.8	1.4	5.9	16.8	7.2	10.9	11.9	13.4
17 149	...	7	Pike	831.4	15 950	2 042	19.2	96.3	2.3	0.6	0.5	1.3	5.8	16.3	7.5	11.6	11.3	12.8
17 151	...	8	Pope	368.8	4 157	2 887	11.3	90.1	7.3	1.1	0.7	2.0	3.1	10.6	11.4	9.3	9.9	14.1
17 153	...	8	Pulaski	199.2	5 619	2 791	28.2	65.9	32.2	1.2	0.8	2.3	5.3	16.8	7.0	10.9	11.2	11.2
17 155	36860	8	Putnam	160.2	5 611	2 792	35.0	93.2	1.1	0.5	0.6	5.5	4.7	15.1	7.2	10.1	10.8	14.0
17 157	...	6	Randolph	575.5	32 621	1 366	56.7	85.5	11.2	0.5	0.7	3.2	5.1	14.0	7.8	14.1	13.2	13.7
17 159	...	7	Richland	360.0	15 930	2 044	44.3	96.5	1.2	0.7	1.2	1.7	6.4	16.1	7.1	11.7	11.3	12.8
17 161	19340	2	Rock Island	427.5	144 784	445	338.7	74.7	11.4	0.7	3.0	12.7	6.2	16.0	8.8	12.5	11.8	12.3
17 163	41180	1	St. Clair	657.8	262 759	258	399.5	64.0	31.4	0.7	2.3	4.0	6.3	17.5	8.6	13.1	12.7	13.5
17 165	...	6	Saline	379.8	24 307	1 631	64.0	93.2	4.9	1.0	1.0	1.8	6.1	15.5	7.8	12.0	11.3	13.6
17 167	44100	3	Sangamon	868.3	197 499	333	227.5	82.9	14.2	0.6	2.5	2.2	5.7	16.9	8.2	12.8	12.1	13.5
17 169	...	7	Schuyler	437.3	6 923	2 679	15.8	94.1	3.6	0.4	0.3	2.0	4.1	14.9	6.5	10.6	12.9	14.9
17 171	27300	9	Scott	250.9	5 053	2 831	20.1	97.9	0.9	0.6	0.3	1.2	4.7	16.4	7.6	10.0	11.9	14.7
17 173	...	6	Shelby	758.5	21 717	1 744	28.6	98.0	0.8	0.5	0.6	1.0	5.6	15.6	7.2	10.7	11.0	13.4
17 175	37900	2	Stark	288.1	5 776	2 770	20.0	97.2	1.3	0.6	0.8	1.4	5.2	15.7	7.3	9.3	10.6	12.5
17 177	23300	4	Stephenson	564.5	45 624	1 059	80.8	85.6	11.8	0.5	1.1	3.8	5.6	16.1	7.5	10.5	10.2	13.3
17 179	37900	2	Tazewell	646.9	134 385	472	207.7	95.4	1.8	0.6	1.2	2.3	5.9	16.9	7.3	12.3	12.9	13.1
17 181	...	6	Union	413.5	17 212	1 967	41.6	92.8	1.8	0.8	1.0	5.1	5.2	15.5	7.1	11.5	11.5	13.4
17 183	19180	3	Vermilion	898.4	78 111	709	86.9	80.5	14.8	0.6	1.2	5.0	6.3	17.5	8.1	12.0	11.6	12.6
17 185	...	7	Wabash	223.3	11 492	2 322	51.5	95.8	1.3	0.6	1.5	2.1	6.0	16.2	7.4	11.9	11.4	12.3
17 187	...	6	Warren	542.4	17 378	1 951	32.0	85.6	3.4	0.6	2.5	9.5	5.8	16.1	12.1	10.0	11.1	11.7
17 189	...	6	Washington	562.6	14 154	2 153	25.2	97.2	1.4	0.4	0.8	1.3	5.4	15.6	7.2	11.5	11.9	13.7
17 191	...	7	Wayne	713.8	16 396	2 013	23.0	97.0	1.0	0.6	0.9	1.6	6.3	16.4	7.3	11.3	11.5	12.7
17 193	...	6	White	494.8	14 292	2 147	28.9	97.3	0.9	0.6	0.6	1.5	5.9	16.0	6.5	11.4	10.8	12.7
17 195	44580	4	Whiteside	684.3	56 536	903	82.6	85.9	2.3	0.5	0.7	11.9	5.6	16.7	7.8	11.0	11.1	13.2
17 197	16980	1	Will	836.9	689 529	94	823.9	65.7	12.2	0.4	6.3	17.0	5.9	19.8	9.2	11.6	13.9	15.4
17 199	16060	3	Williamson	420.2	67 560	786	160.8	91.4	5.4	0.7	1.5	2.6	5.9	16.0	7.2	13.3	12.9	13.1

1. CBSA = Core Based Statistical Area. See Appendix A for explanation. See Appendix B for list of metropolitan areas with component counties.   2. County type code from the Economic Research Service of USDA Rural-Urban Continuum Codes. See Appendix A for definition.   3. Dry land or land partially or temporarily covered by water.   4. May be of any race.

Table B. States and Counties — **Population and Households**

| | Population, 2016 (cont.) | | | | Population change and components of change, 2000–2016 | | | | | | | Households, 2011–2015 | | | | |
| | Age (percent) (cont.) | | | | Total persons | | Percent change | | Components of change, 2010–2016 | | | | | | Percent | | |
STATE County	55 to 64 years	65 to 74 years	75 years and over	Percent female	2000	2010	2000–2010	2010–2016	Births	Deaths	Net migration	Number	Persons per household	Family households	Female family householder[1]	One person
	16	17	18	19	20	21	22	23	24	25	26	27	28	29	30	31
ILLINOIS—Cont'd																
Hardin	16.2	14.7	9.1	47.9	4 800	4 320	-10.0	-6.9	191	370	-90	1 677	2.49	64.2	8.9	32.2
Henderson	17.4	13.3	10.7	50.7	8 213	7 328	-10.8	-6.3	416	522	-340	3 094	2.26	68.0	10.7	27.9
Henry	14.8	10.8	8.5	50.0	51 020	50 485	-1.0	-2.4	3 331	3 260	-1 208	20 170	2.44	68.1	9.0	27.1
Iroquois	15.0	11.2	9.9	51.0	31 334	29 718	-5.2	-4.7	1 875	2 263	-970	11 829	2.42	67.5	10.0	27.2
Jackson	11.2	8.1	6.0	49.9	59 612	60 218	1.0	-2.2	4 294	2 887	-2 768	23 390	2.36	51.3	9.5	36.8
Jasper	15.0	9.9	8.8	49.6	10 117	9 698	-4.1	-1.7	702	626	-214	3 781	2.53	69.8	6.4	27.2
Jefferson	13.5	10.6	7.8	48.5	40 045	38 825	-3.0	-0.9	3 020	2 811	-549	15 277	2.39	63.9	10.3	31.7
Jersey	15.1	10.1	8.4	51.2	21 668	22 985	6.1	-4.2	1 312	1 469	-813	8 830	2.45	72.8	12.4	23.9
Jo Daviess	16.2	15.3	10.7	49.9	22 289	22 677	1.7	-4.0	1 159	1 524	-457	9 542	2.33	67.7	7.6	27.3
Johnson	13.8	11.8	7.7	43.2	12 878	12 582	-2.3	2.5	696	751	413	4 407	2.48	66.9	7.7	29.8
Kane	12.2	7.7	5.0	50.3	404 119	515 258	27.5	3.2	42 995	19 022	-8 087	172 479	3.01	74.7	10.7	20.9
Kankakee	13.2	9.0	6.8	50.9	103 833	113 449	9.3	-3.0	8 355	6 770	-5 018	40 880	2.61	67.5	15.2	26.8
Kendall	9.7	6.2	3.5	50.5	54 544	114 792	110.5	8.6	10 522	3 282	2 656	38 516	3.11	78.8	8.2	17.2
Knox	14.3	11.2	9.3	49.5	55 836	52 919	-5.2	-3.7	3 401	4 142	-1 202	21 301	2.25	58.2	11.2	35.5
Lake	13.4	7.8	5.3	50.0	644 356	703 404	9.2	-0.1	49 858	27 050	-23 228	242 426	2.83	74.0	10.7	22.1
LaSalle	14.9	9.8	8.4	49.5	111 509	113 915	2.2	-2.9	7 415	7 974	-2 640	44 242	2.48	65.4	10.8	29.1
Lawrence	13.0	8.9	8.0	43.8	15 452	16 903	9.4	-3.1	1 098	1 273	-332	5 015	2.22	67.0	12.6	31.2
Lee	15.2	10.4	8.1	47.1	36 062	36 031	-0.1	-4.9	2 173	2 258	-1 603	13 517	2.37	65.0	9.0	28.4
Livingston	14.4	9.7	8.6	49.5	39 678	38 950	-1.8	-6.2	2 521	2 571	-2 374	14 464	2.32	66.9	10.4	28.9
Logan	13.3	9.3	8.4	49.2	31 183	30 305	-2.8	-2.6	1 929	2 000	-722	10 711	2.17	65.8	10.9	28.6
McDonough	11.8	8.6	7.1	50.5	32 913	32 612	-0.9	-5.0	1 837	1 844	-1 651	12 129	2.29	55.7	9.4	34.5
McHenry	14.1	8.3	4.9	50.2	260 077	308 820	18.7	-0.6	20 513	12 251	-10 205	109 491	2.79	75.2	9.6	20.0
McLean	11.3	7.0	5.2	51.4	150 433	169 572	12.7	1.7	12 975	7 121	-2 904	65 346	2.53	62.0	9.0	28.0
Macon	14.4	10.4	8.4	52.0	114 706	110 768	-3.4	-3.8	8 446	7 475	-5 016	44 915	2.35	61.6	13.2	33.3
Macoupin	15.1	10.9	8.7	50.6	49 019	47 765	-2.6	-3.9	2 860	3 510	-1 225	18 982	2.42	68.1	10.1	27.2
Madison	14.2	9.2	7.1	51.2	258 941	269 328	4.0	-1.3	19 522	17 229	-5 604	107 111	2.45	65.6	12.1	28.1
Marion	14.5	10.4	8.7	51.2	41 691	39 437	-5.4	-3.3	3 102	3 058	-1 371	15 783	2.40	66.0	13.0	29.8
Marshall	15.5	12.1	10.4	50.3	13 180	12 640	-4.1	-5.5	756	960	-491	4 993	2.38	64.8	7.4	31.0
Mason	15.1	11.3	9.3	50.5	16 038	14 666	-8.6	-7.9	850	1 166	-950	6 116	2.27	63.5	10.2	31.9
Massac	14.3	11.4	10.0	52.2	15 161	15 429	1.8	-5.0	1 016	1 291	-517	5 987	2.45	62.9	10.9	33.5
Menard	15.0	10.9	8.1	51.3	12 486	12 705	1.8	-1.5	764	824	-125	5 144	2.42	67.9	7.4	26.4
Mercer	15.0	12.0	9.3	50.1	16 957	16 434	-3.1	-4.3	954	1 118	-536	6 607	2.40	70.3	8.1	25.7
Monroe	15.5	9.1	7.9	50.5	27 619	32 957	19.3	3.4	2 071	1 778	754	12 699	2.62	76.1	7.5	21.1
Montgomery	14.4	9.9	9.4	47.5	30 652	30 104	-1.8	-3.8	1 775	2 231	-706	10 985	2.17	70.8	10.3	26.1
Morgan	14.3	10.5	8.8	49.5	36 616	35 551	-2.9	-3.6	2 320	2 404	-1 139	13 825	2.29	64.8	11.5	30.3
Moultrie	13.3	9.9	9.3	51.1	14 287	14 846	3.9	-0.1	1 148	1 151	-56	5 799	2.51	69.6	9.7	25.3
Ogle	14.5	10.1	7.9	50.3	51 032	53 497	4.8	-4.2	3 309	3 057	-2 444	20 731	2.50	66.9	8.9	27.4
Peoria	12.9	8.9	6.8	51.5	183 433	186 494	1.7	-0.8	16 665	11 085	-6 731	76 133	2.39	61.2	13.9	32.8
Perry	13.5	10.2	7.7	45.4	23 094	22 350	-3.2	-4.4	1 279	1 488	-767	8 025	2.46	62.0	11.1	33.3
Piatt	15.3	10.6	8.1	50.5	16 365	16 727	2.2	-1.0	1 098	1 102	-158	6 645	2.47	73.2	7.6	23.4
Pike	14.4	10.6	9.6	49.4	17 384	16 430	-5.5	-2.9	1 108	1 248	-329	6 677	2.34	64.7	7.6	31.1
Pope	19.0	13.3	9.4	47.5	4 413	4 470	1.3	-7.0	199	276	-216	1 593	2.52	64.4	7.4	34.1
Pulaski	16.4	11.4	9.7	51.8	7 348	6 161	-16.2	-8.8	385	484	-425	2 334	2.50	58.1	11.2	39.2
Putnam	17.1	12.8	8.1	48.9	6 086	6 006	-1.3	-6.6	303	339	-309	2 453	2.37	68.0	7.7	26.1
Randolph	14.2	9.6	8.2	44.4	33 893	33 476	-1.2	-2.6	2 139	2 304	-682	11 895	2.49	66.1	11.2	29.9
Richland	14.3	9.9	10.4	50.6	16 144	16 233	0.5	-1.9	1 244	1 241	-271	6 503	2.43	62.6	8.2	31.7
Rock Island	14.0	10.1	8.2	50.7	149 374	147 546	-1.2	-1.9	11 512	9 471	-4 593	60 391	2.36	61.9	12.8	33.5
St. Clair	13.7	8.3	6.3	51.7	256 082	270 063	5.5	-2.7	21 209	15 728	-12 633	102 267	2.57	65.8	16.9	30.1
Saline	13.9	11.0	8.8	50.7	26 733	24 913	-6.8	-2.4	1 985	2 182	-380	9 955	2.43	66.7	14.4	30.0
Sangamon	14.1	9.7	7.0	51.9	188 951	197 465	4.5	0.0	14 382	12 019	-2 100	82 885	2.35	61.4	12.7	32.0
Schuyler	15.7	11.1	9.4	47.2	7 189	7 544	4.9	-8.2	388	506	-438	3 000	2.20	66.4	7.5	28.8
Scott	15.1	10.0	9.6	51.1	5 537	5 355	-3.3	-5.6	293	357	-215	2 124	2.42	66.2	11.3	27.4
Shelby	14.9	12.0	9.6	50.4	22 893	22 363	-2.3	-2.9	1 536	1 470	-646	9 044	2.42	70.6	7.9	25.2
Stark	14.6	12.9	11.9	50.3	6 332	5 994	-5.3	-3.6	369	512	-45	2 391	2.41	67.1	6.1	29.2
Stephenson	15.3	11.3	10.3	51.5	48 979	47 711	-2.6	-4.4	3 109	3 342	-1 825	19 299	2.37	64.1	11.8	30.6
Tazewell	13.7	9.9	8.0	50.7	128 485	135 394	5.4	-0.7	9 995	8 669	-2 349	54 288	2.45	68.2	9.8	27.3
Union	14.9	11.6	9.3	50.3	18 293	17 808	-2.7	-3.3	1 134	1 417	-316	6 712	2.53	68.3	10.2	28.9
Vermilion	13.9	10.1	7.9	50.2	83 919	81 625	-2.7	-4.3	6 364	5 936	-3 803	31 531	2.47	64.0	14.2	31.0
Wabash	15.4	10.4	9.2	50.2	12 937	11 947	-7.7	-3.8	855	863	-402	4 871	2.37	66.0	8.8	30.9
Warren	13.9	10.6	8.7	50.8	18 735	17 710	-5.5	-1.9	1 275	1 139	-466	6 829	2.42	65.7	10.2	29.6
Washington	15.6	10.0	9.2	49.9	15 148	14 716	-2.9	-3.8	930	928	-562	5 777	2.46	67.0	7.3	29.4
Wayne	14.2	11.2	9.1	50.4	17 151	16 760	-2.3	-2.2	1 260	1 329	-230	7 043	2.34	68.3	9.1	29.4
White	14.7	11.2	10.8	51.0	15 371	14 665	-4.6	-2.5	1 047	1 392	-55	6 171	2.28	65.8	8.2	29.5
Whiteside	14.8	10.8	9.0	50.5	60 653	58 498	-3.6	-3.4	3 946	3 969	-1 825	23 548	2.40	65.3	9.8	30.4
Will	12.1	7.4	4.6	50.3	502 266	677 544	34.9	1.8	49 834	25 586	-12 637	223 640	3.02	76.3	11.0	20.1
Williamson	13.5	10.5	7.7	50.0	61 296	66 362	8.3	1.8	4 915	4 698	1 046	26 796	2.43	67.7	12.3	28.1

1. No spouse present.

Table B. States and Counties — **Population, Vital Statistics, Health, and Crime**

STATE County	Persons in group quarters, 2016	Daytime population, 2011–2015 Number	Employment/ residence ratio	Births, 2016 Total	Rate[1]	Deaths, 2016 Number	Rate[1]	Persons under 65 with no health insurance, 2015 Number	Percent	Medicare, 2015 Total Beneficiaries	Enrolled in Original Medicare	Enrolled in Medicare Advantage	Serious crimes known to police,[2] 2014 Total Number	Rate[3]
	32	33	34	35	36	37	38	39	40	41	42	43	44	45
ILLINOIS—Cont'd														
Hardin	110	3 887	0.77	20	5.0	61	15.2	218	7.1	1 047	903	144	56	1 350
Henderson	51	5 207	0.44	72	10.5	89	13.0	342	6.4	1 560	1 322	238	NA	NA
Henry	724	41 722	0.65	510	10.3	547	11.1	2 282	5.8	9 986	8 214	1 772	758	1 702
Iroquois	468	25 920	0.77	293	10.3	346	12.2	1 690	7.5	6 788	5 742	1 046	465	1 652
Jackson	3 851	63 118	1.14	718	12.2	457	7.8	3 535	7.4	9 899	7 636	2 263	1 967	3 332
Jasper	54	8 270	0.70	103	10.8	89	9.3	512	6.5	1 879	1 652	227	87	911
Jefferson	2 207	43 257	1.29	517	13.4	441	11.5	1 665	5.7	8 149	7 101	1 048	1 400	3 630
Jersey	817	18 145	0.56	191	8.7	203	9.2	883	4.9	3 851	3 230	621	397	1 762
Jo Daviess	167	20 104	0.79	176	8.1	248	11.4	1 017	6.2	5 697	3 430	2 267	221	1 006
Johnson	1 798	11 638	0.71	106	8.2	133	10.3	470	5.5	2 986	2 315	671	111	957
Kane	6 805	493 743	0.88	6 776	12.7	3 365	6.3	46 378	10.0	71 357	52 704	18 653	7 563	1 475
Kankakee	5 160	108 646	0.93	1 278	11.6	1 140	10.4	6 396	7.1	20 056	15 855	4 201	2 999	3 053
Kendall	208	91 700	0.53	1 605	12.9	533	4.3	5 402	4.8	9 170	7 201	1 969	1 536	1 277
Knox	3 964	51 966	0.99	546	10.7	596	11.7	2 257	6.0	11 970	7 984	3 986	1 392	3 137
Lake	18 544	718 366	1.04	7 773	11.1	4 589	6.5	48 591	8.1	91 702	77 213	14 489	12 035	1 722
LaSalle	3 553	108 409	0.92	1 200	10.8	1 235	11.2	5 778	6.5	22 403	19 363	3 040	2 067	1 904
Lawrence	2 584	17 092	1.10	184	11.2	227	13.9	668	5.9	3 115	2 846	269	133	951
Lee	2 962	34 050	0.94	325	9.5	394	11.5	1 417	5.5	7 121	5 804	1 317	385	1 145
Livingston	2 716	37 455	0.98	357	9.8	365	10.0	1 596	5.7	6 587	5 043	1 544	617	1 624
Logan	4 327	28 835	0.90	321	10.9	314	10.6	979	4.8	5 559	3 881	1 678	590	2 094
McDonough	3 837	33 248	1.09	281	9.1	284	9.2	1 574	6.8	5 349	3 886	1 463	546	1 685
McHenry	1 648	259 466	0.69	3 280	10.7	1 995	6.5	15 936	6.0	49 143	42 735	6 408	3 510	1 166
McLean	10 602	178 032	1.05	1 957	11.4	1 198	6.9	6 718	4.7	23 468	15 867	7 601	3 598	2 072
Macon	4 215	115 007	1.12	1 317	12.4	1 171	11.0	4 965	5.9	23 218	18 166	5 052	3 039	2 793
Macoupin	836	37 964	0.57	451	9.8	586	12.8	2 223	6.1	10 812	9 338	1 474	666	1 521
Madison	3 828	250 019	0.86	3 032	11.4	2 814	10.6	12 404	5.6	50 483	34 137	16 346	5 136	2 246
Marion	758	37 896	0.95	503	13.2	414	10.9	1 963	6.4	9 893	8 744	1 149	1 041	2 802
Marshall	255	10 592	0.72	127	10.6	139	11.6	492	5.3	2 624	2 118	506	110	1 036
Mason	206	12 660	0.76	121	9.0	173	12.8	711	6.6	3 682	3 033	649	NA	NA
Massac	292	13 368	0.71	156	10.6	178	12.1	719	6.2	3 312	2 813	499	374	2 497
Menard	154	8 855	0.39	119	9.5	145	11.6	488	4.8	2 449	1 628	821	50	483
Mercer	185	12 152	0.47	153	9.7	179	11.4	634	5.1	3 375	2 592	783	NA	NA
Monroe	343	25 647	0.53	349	10.2	313	9.2	1 107	3.9	5 738	3 670	2 068	193	575
Montgomery	2 469	29 151	0.98	248	8.6	386	13.3	1 256	5.8	6 727	5 838	889	395	1 355
Morgan	2 920	35 611	1.03	366	10.7	368	10.7	1 381	5.3	7 090	5 608	1 482	653	1 960
Moultrie	395	13 789	0.84	187	12.6	160	10.8	861	7.2	3 353	2 789	564	NA	NA
Ogle	525	45 736	0.73	529	10.3	481	9.4	2 672	6.3	9 466	7 024	2 442	297	747
Peoria	4 884	209 974	1.27	2 679	14.5	1 782	9.6	8 887	5.8	33 870	21 972	11 898	6 989	3 702
Perry	2 418	19 992	0.78	191	8.9	225	10.5	880	5.7	4 223	3 452	771	185	875
Piatt	72	12 623	0.54	187	11.3	172	10.4	643	4.8	3 534	2 128	1 406	124	827
Pike	627	14 523	0.77	182	11.4	186	11.7	848	6.9	3 631	3 170	461	178	1 108
Pope	371	3 969	0.75	37	8.9	25	6.0	225	7.3	969	798	171	NA	NA
Pulaski	21	6 318	1.24	59	10.5	71	12.6	322	7.2	1 387	1 198	189	50	1 033
Putnam	2	4 977	0.69	44	7.8	61	10.9	259	5.8	1 298	1 102	196	28	637
Randolph	4 523	33 857	1.06	331	10.1	390	12.0	1 230	5.3	6 735	5 400	1 335	357	1 177
Richland	364	15 914	0.97	194	12.2	190	11.9	728	5.7	3 765	3 358	407	384	2 376
Rock Island	4 643	159 038	1.18	1 798	12.4	1 464	10.1	7 436	6.4	29 505	22 520	6 985	3 955	2 702
St. Clair	4 686	253 731	0.89	3 282	12.5	2 678	10.2	14 005	6.3	44 033	29 375	14 658	7 551	2 930
Saline	886	25 196	1.04	329	13.5	329	13.5	1 176	6.1	6 338	5 420	918	502	2 158
Sangamon	3 914	213 418	1.15	2 192	11.1	2 111	10.7	8 245	5.0	37 304	22 281	15 023	8 784	4 600
Schuyler	463	6 389	0.69	57	8.2	70	10.1	393	7.0	1 503	1 249	254	70	944
Scott	43	4 310	0.61	47	9.3	47	9.3	227	5.5	1 002	834	168	NA	NA
Shelby	205	18 888	0.67	257	11.8	249	11.5	1 033	6.0	4 848	4 379	469	86	495
Stark	92	5 010	0.66	51	8.8	87	15.1	262	6.0	1 370	1 036	334	NA	NA
Stephenson	836	45 222	0.93	497	10.9	550	12.1	2 114	5.9	11 373	7 318	4 055	856	1 871
Tazewell	2 736	128 137	0.88	1 536	11.4	1 443	10.7	4 773	4.4	26 929	19 242	7 687	2 370	1 846
Union	580	15 651	0.74	174	10.1	230	13.4	982	7.1	4 020	3 087	933	343	1 958
Vermilion	2 925	79 308	0.97	918	11.8	940	12.0	3 869	6.2	17 126	9 995	7 131	3 240	4 120
Wabash	88	10 157	0.72	137	11.9	126	11.0	543	5.8	2 439	2 207	232	201	1 735
Warren	1 013	16 981	0.91	187	10.8	186	10.7	1 024	7.7	3 464	2 703	761	296	1 671
Washington	246	14 743	1.04	145	10.2	140	9.9	601	5.2	2 688	2 325	363	246	1 712
Wayne	76	15 211	0.82	205	12.5	205	12.5	837	6.4	3 601	3 299	302	242	1 557
White	391	14 029	0.93	174	12.2	217	15.2	650	5.9	3 721	3 284	437	NA	NA
Whiteside	1 011	53 897	0.86	602	10.6	624	11.0	2 918	6.4	13 565	11 300	2 265	986	1 765
Will	9 190	605 023	0.76	7 829	11.4	4 483	6.5	36 123	6.0	79 720	61 777	17 943	9 998	1 478
Williamson	2 132	66 968	0.99	792	11.7	783	11.6	2 960	5.5	13 108	10 660	2 448	950	1 497

1. Per 1,000 estimated resident population. 2. Data for serious crimes have not been adjusted for underreporting; this may affect comparability between geographic areas and over time.
3. Per 100,000 population estimated by the FBI.

Table B. States and Counties — Crime, Education, Money Income, and Poverty

STATE County	Serious crimes known to police, 2014 (cont.)[1] Rate[2] Violent	Property	Education — School enrollment and attainment, 2011–2015 Enrollment[3] Total	Per cent private	Attainment[4] (percent) High school graduate or less	Bachelor's degree or more	Local government expenditures,[5] 2013–2014 Total current spending (mil dol)	Current spending per student (dollars)	Money income, 2011–2015 Per capita income[6] (dollars)	Median income (dollars)	Households Percent with income of less than $50,000	with income of $200,000 or more	Income and poverty, 2015 Median household income (dollars)	Percent below poverty level All persons	Children under 18 years	Children 5 to 17 years in families
	46	47	48	49	50	51	52	53	54	55	56	57	58	59	60	61
ILLINOIS—Cont'd																
Hardin	265	1 085	906	4.1	50.9	11.8	5.3	8 188	21 415	38 838	62.1	2.1	39 128	20.6	35.6	32.1
Henderson	NA	NA	1 294	10.2	56.0	13.9	9.3	9 956	26 603	47 672	51.7	0.6	47 354	11.5	18.8	18.0
Henry	128	1 574	11 427	10.3	45.6	20.6	90.7	9 718	27 402	53 480	46.4	2.4	58 983	10.7	14.7	13.2
Iroquois	121	1 531	6 506	9.5	52.4	15.3	57.8	12 486	25 565	47 834	51.8	2.6	49 836	13.3	20.1	19.1
Jackson	425	2 907	23 372	5.1	33.3	35.3	96.4	13 089	21 147	33 871	64.5	2.0	36 613	23.5	29.7	30.1
Jasper	42	869	2 068	13.2	49.5	17.6	19.5	13 547	25 303	54 209	44.8	1.1	52 608	12.0	16.7	15.8
Jefferson	570	3 059	8 737	13.1	46.8	16.3	63.9	10 410	22 975	43 247	56.4	1.9	46 460	16.7	26.5	25.6
Jersey	102	1 659	5 872	28.0	46.8	17.4	26.9	9 734	25 901	53 271	45.0	1.8	53 864	11.4	16.4	15.2
Jo Daviess	109	897	4 642	12.9	46.0	23.6	42.1	12 581	29 362	53 221	46.2	2.5	51 201	9.4	13.5	12.3
Johnson	233	724	2 611	5.0	47.3	16.7	18.9	9 534	20 014	42 287	57.1	1.6	46 838	14.3	19.5	17.3
Kane	159	1 316	150 365	15.7	40.8	31.6	1 431.3	11 609	31 056	70 696	34.6	7.4	70 502	10.8	16.1	15.4
Kankakee	329	2 724	30 469	21.0	46.4	18.8	211.6	11 118	24 449	52 110	47.5	2.1	53 227	15.2	22.3	21.3
Kendall	95	1 182	36 899	12.3	31.0	34.8	292.6	11 093	31 053	84 385	25.0	5.8	88 773	4.8	6.6	6.1
Knox	338	2 799	12 118	17.7	49.4	17.7	79.5	10 213	22 241	39 976	59.9	1.4	43 796	17.2	26.8	24.5
Lake	148	1 574	197 928	16.1	31.9	43.2	2 046.8	14 912	39 299	78 026	31.8	12.6	82 160	9.0	12.3	11.4
LaSalle	118	1 786	26 686	11.6	49.2	16.2	212.6	12 589	25 755	50 633	49.4	2.2	52 316	12.9	19.6	17.7
Lawrence	93	858	3 601	15.8	57.2	9.4	21.2	9 174	14 468	40 841	59.5	1.1	43 268	17.7	23.4	21.6
Lee	92	1 053	7 777	13.3	49.7	17.3	50.7	11 649	25 363	52 379	47.5	2.3	52 581	12.7	18.1	15.7
Livingston	190	1 435	8 675	8.5	52.9	15.2	79.0	12 330	25 769	54 254	45.5	2.2	55 474	12.8	18.2	16.9
Logan	302	1 792	7 485	17.1	47.3	17.2	38.3	11 318	21 786	50 539	49.4	2.2	58 191	13.7	20.1	19.2
McDonough	231	1 454	12 280	7.1	36.9	34.1	47.8	13 691	21 664	40 314	58.0	1.6	44 221	22.8	26.0	23.5
McHenry	91	1 075	85 204	15.2	34.1	32.5	626.6	12 214	33 735	77 222	30.1	6.9	80 513	8.1	10.7	9.3
McLean	279	1 794	57 604	12.5	30.7	44.0	285.1	10 909	31 305	62 211	40.9	5.3	65 766	11.7	11.6	11.1
Macon	364	2 429	25 795	20.3	45.6	22.9	215.8	13 117	26 895	47 176	52.7	2.9	48 302	18.2	27.7	25.1
Macoupin	144	1 377	11 389	12.2	47.5	18.1	79.7	9 084	25 962	51 206	48.9	2.0	50 460	13.7	21.1	18.8
Madison	196	2 050	68 756	15.6	40.3	25.3	424.0	10 164	28 337	53 431	46.3	3.2	52 969	12.9	17.7	16.4
Marion	280	2 522	8 650	11.2	47.8	14.5	82.1	11 783	22 808	42 238	57.2	1.2	43 018	18.0	29.5	26.0
Marshall	188	848	2 565	10.1	48.6	16.8	15.3	11 281	27 739	53 423	45.8	2.3	53 610	10.6	16.3	14.4
Mason	NA	NA	3 029	5.3	54.0	14.1	29.9	10 511	24 173	41 567	57.2	1.4	43 743	13.9	23.3	21.4
Massac	307	2 190	3 490	5.3	49.5	14.7	24.4	9 880	22 927	40 977	60.0	2.0	41 548	16.8	26.5	24.9
Menard	77	406	2 854	8.9	44.8	23.1	22.4	9 260	30 578	60 486	41.5	4.6	64 706	10.3	16.6	15.0
Mercer	NA	NA	3 638	7.0	50.2	15.7	27.2	9 166	26 823	54 757	45.9	2.4	57 934	10.1	13.8	12.2
Monroe	39	536	8 170	19.0	39.7	27.5	49.5	9 373	32 889	70 859	33.6	5.4	79 686	5.0	5.5	4.6
Montgomery	158	1 197	6 387	6.7	56.1	13.0	40.7	8 808	19 866	46 966	52.4	1.6	46 006	16.6	24.2	22.4
Morgan	93	1 867	9 201	29.5	50.9	22.3	55.9	11 325	24 586	45 978	53.3	2.2	45 259	14.8	22.3	21.9
Moultrie	NA	NA	3 507	12.5	52.5	15.7	15.7	9 296	25 053	49 681	50.2	1.8	58 975	8.6	15.6	14.4
Ogle	78	669	13 237	9.8	45.5	19.8	119.7	12 819	27 451	54 849	45.8	2.2	57 268	10.4	14.5	12.2
Peoria	472	3 229	48 043	26.2	38.4	29.2	337.0	11 528	28 610	51 147	48.7	3.8	53 781	15.6	23.0	21.5
Perry	109	766	4 726	6.7	52.5	13.4	28.8	10 311	21 720	42 478	56.4	1.4	46 598	16.8	23.6	22.9
Piatt	147	680	4 057	10.5	40.3	27.6	31.9	10 058	32 724	66 261	36.6	4.5	65 122	6.5	9.2	8.4
Pike	93	1 014	3 630	9.4	55.5	15.2	26.7	10 144	21 594	40 588	59.2	0.9	45 106	15.0	22.9	21.0
Pope	NA	NA	745	6.7	46.6	15.1	5.1	9 083	21 131	39 223	58.8	1.3	41 150	18.1	30.6	29.0
Pulaski	351	682	1 407	8.7	55.0	11.6	13.2	13 434	18 923	31 980	68.2	0.8	35 135	24.7	39.9	35.7
Putnam	0	637	1 331	8.3	52.5	12.5	10.7	11 540	29 918	56 358	45.9	4.4	60 590	8.8	16.0	14.0
Randolph	115	1 062	6 631	14.3	57.7	12.0	47.4	11 429	22 895	48 158	51.5	2.0	50 129	14.3	19.7	18.0
Richland	278	2 098	3 790	13.6	45.0	20.9	23.3	9 370	23 498	44 127	56.3	2.3	43 332	14.9	20.3	19.1
Rock Island	327	2 376	36 158	19.1	43.7	22.0	251.4	11 347	26 391	48 817	51.1	2.5	50 419	13.2	20.8	20.1
St. Clair	618	2 313	73 792	15.2	37.8	26.0	472.0	11 255	26 738	49 895	50.1	3.0	50 416	16.4	25.6	23.2
Saline	288	1 870	5 109	4.3	47.4	14.0	40.4	9 437	21 175	38 258	60.2	1.4	40 873	23.2	35.2	33.1
Sangamon	835	3 764	50 461	15.6	36.0	33.4	352.1	11 768	31 024	56 167	44.8	4.0	57 591	15.3	22.8	20.7
Schuyler	135	809	1 475	4.5	51.4	15.9	11.4	9 442	24 077	47 723	53.4	1.2	50 720	12.9	19.6	17.6
Scott	NA	NA	1 234	10.5	58.6	11.9	9.4	10 185	24 978	47 222	53.0	2.3	50 474	11.3	18.0	15.5
Shelby	52	444	4 724	9.3	53.7	14.9	23.6	9 794	23 697	47 850	52.5	1.2	49 633	11.6	17.1	15.8
Stark	NA	NA	1 235	13.1	50.3	17.6	10.7	11 294	27 148	50 085	49.9	4.7	50 083	12.7	17.7	16.7
Stephenson	116	1 756	11 121	12.4	44.8	18.1	82.8	12 221	24 253	45 331	55.7	1.3	46 430	13.0	22.5	20.7
Tazewell	188	1 659	32 583	17.2	40.4	25.0	214.3	10 584	29 718	58 194	42.6	3.2	57 747	8.4	12.2	11.2
Union	205	1 752	3 914	7.9	46.3	21.6	28.1	9 815	23 140	42 606	56.8	2.3	44 221	15.3	25.6	23.4
Vermilion	598	3 523	17 738	7.3	53.8	13.8	148.2	11 198	22 233	42 977	56.5	1.5	44 705	18.4	29.1	26.6
Wabash	181	1 553	2 761	13.6	42.9	15.6	15.4	8 693	24 155	47 491	51.7	1.1	51 224	12.2	19.6	17.8
Warren	209	1 462	4 969	30.2	47.2	20.9	24.3	8 921	22 876	43 699	56.6	2.0	48 381	14.3	20.8	17.8
Washington	397	1 315	3 180	19.7	43.7	20.9	19.6	10 076	28 683	53 202	47.4	2.1	57 019	8.8	13.7	12.5
Wayne	283	1 274	3 699	10.8	47.8	13.8	25.8	10 000	23 869	44 993	56.0	1.6	47 995	12.8	21.7	20.6
White	NA	NA	2 881	4.7	47.4	13.6	33.5	13 286	25 534	44 648	54.4	2.3	46 588	14.9	23.0	22.1
Whiteside	175	1 589	13 392	12.1	46.9	16.9	104.7	10 963	25 490	47 401	51.8	1.7	45 463	12.8	19.6	17.9
Will	162	1 316	200 709	16.3	36.5	33.0	1 388.0	11 845	31 310	76 101	30.8	6.9	76 293	8.0	11.3	10.4
Williamson	63	1 434	14 892	7.3	40.7	21.0	104.7	10 104	24 669	44 453	54.9	2.0	47 678	16.2	25.0	23.0

1. Data for serious crimes have not been adjusted for underreporting; this may affect comparability between geographic areas and over time.   2. Per 100,000 population estimated by the FBI.
3. All persons 3 years old and over enrolled in nursery school through college.   4. Persons 25 years old and over.   5. Elementary and secondary education expenditures.
6. Based on population estimated by the American Community Survey, 2011–2015.

Table B. States and Counties — **Personal Income**

STATE County	Personal income, 2015										Earnings, 2015		
	Total (mil dol)	Percent change, 2014–2015	Per capita[1]		Wages and salaries (mil dol)	Supplements to wages and salaries; employer contributions (mil dol)		Proprietors' income (mil dol)	Dividends, interest, and rent (mil dol)	Personal transfer receipts (mil dol)	Total (mil dol)	Contributions for government social insurance (mil dol)	
			Dollars	Rank		Pension and insurance	Government social insurance					From employee and self-employed	From employer
	62	63	64	65	66	67	68	69	70	71	72	73	74
ILLINOIS—Cont'd													
Hardin	139	-4.0	33 690	2 208	32	8	2	14	20	53	55	4	2
Henderson	256	-3.0	36 661	1 416	39	11	3	13	48	63	65	5	3
Henry	2 079	-0.2	42 010	949	570	127	40	134	383	394	871	54	40
Iroquois	1 127	-2.3	39 320	1 138	297	64	21	80	214	277	462	29	21
Jackson	1 980	2.9	33 363	2 340	1 173	335	70	114	390	454	1 693	78	70
Jasper	365	-7.8	38 022	943	86	21	6	51	72	81	163	9	6
Jefferson	1 400	1.3	36 493	1 620	875	155	64	61	234	361	1 156	67	64
Jersey	821	1.1	36 696	1 841	187	44	13	19	129	192	262	18	13
Jo Daviess	1 018	1.3	46 080	747	303	64	22	72	261	197	461	30	22
Johnson	333	1.8	26 081	2 991	87	26	5	13	55	107	131	9	5
Kane	23 971	4.6	45 156	862	10 585	1 850	752	1 217	3 489	3 060	14 403	779	752
Kankakee	4 108	3.1	37 049	1 830	1 894	370	137	153	554	985	2 554	147	137
Kendall	5 417	6.1	43 910	1 067	1 186	237	81	231	559	542	1 736	96	81
Knox	1 942	1.4	37 748	1 727	834	163	75	90	330	548	1 161	75	75
Lake	49 152	3.5	69 827	85	26 927	3 917	1 678	3 119	11 472	4 264	35 640	1 927	1 678
LaSalle	4 407	2.1	39 582	1 386	2 010	380	144	154	740	936	2 687	160	144
Lawrence	598	-3.7	36 249	2 253	181	43	13	90	101	153	326	20	13
Lee	1 311	0.3	37 895	1 422	548	106	38	58	221	299	750	45	38
Livingston	1 464	-4.0	39 910	1 367	659	131	44	173	234	296	1 007	55	44
Logan	995	-2.4	33 746	2 094	370	77	25	70	174	243	542	31	25
McDonough	1 063	-2.7	33 934	2 122	516	152	31	44	209	235	742	35	31
McHenry	15 200	5.0	49 457	543	4 654	831	333	575	2 293	1 807	6 393	364	333
McLean	7 735	2.0	44 670	826	5 007	818	316	476	1 196	975	6 617	354	316
Macon	4 762	1.9	44 383	802	2 710	455	199	363	780	1 041	3 727	216	199
Macoupin	1 664	-0.5	36 145	1 866	404	88	28	39	284	423	559	41	28
Madison	11 173	3.9	41 970	1 187	4 574	876	333	531	1 773	2 284	6 313	368	333
Marion	1 482	1.2	38 643	1 626	564	116	44	92	235	444	816	50	44
Marshall	484	-2.4	40 408	1 137	126	26	10	18	88	113	181	12	10
Mason	487	-4.8	35 580	1 644	128	33	8	25	87	140	194	13	8
Massac	514	2.3	34 828	2 127	196	38	13	19	82	161	266	17	13
Menard	499	-1.9	40 081	1 186	69	19	4	23	85	97	116	8	4
Mercer	642	-0.8	40 487	1 007	116	27	8	23	121	139	174	13	8
Monroe	1 737	3.7	51 277	378	318	63	22	95	290	236	498	31	22
Montgomery	961	-3.5	33 254	2 241	351	75	24	70	182	271	520	32	24
Morgan	1 245	-1.1	35 757	1 873	598	121	43	64	236	319	825	49	43
Moultrie	722	-12.1	48 373	972	166	32	12	185	92	124	395	24	12
Ogle	2 102	1.5	40 698	1 197	794	165	54	48	346	407	1 061	65	54
Peoria	8 767	1.9	47 076	634	5 608	858	404	339	1 563	1 523	7 209	407	404
Perry	738	-3.9	34 243	2 616	194	51	13	108	117	184	366	22	13
Piatt	756	-2.6	46 140	502	131	31	8	32	122	130	202	13	8
Pike	568	-5.2	35 553	1 544	161	35	11	63	100	147	271	16	11
Pope	135	4.7	31 926	2 738	23	7	2	12	22	38	44	3	2
Pulaski	193	0.1	33 973	2 081	78	22	5	3	27	76	109	6	5
Putnam	296	3.5	52 533	977	82	15	6	72	51	46	175	10	6
Randolph	1 088	0.5	33 105	2 437	484	112	33	42	199	281	671	38	33
Richland	605	-1.9	37 767	1 518	238	50	17	63	111	158	368	21	17
Rock Island	5 894	1.8	40 332	1 198	4 340	753	298	280	1 148	1 213	5 671	320	298
St. Clair	10 750	3.3	40 711	1 361	4 672	992	363	494	1 902	2 376	6 520	362	363
Saline	899	-0.5	36 633	1 670	369	80	27	68	138	284	544	33	27
Sangamon	8 706	2.4	43 810	921	4 986	969	338	494	1 664	1 592	6 787	362	338
Schuyler	306	-5.4	43 570	710	106	24	7	29	42	59	165	9	7
Scott	172	-7.1	33 852	1 932	43	11	3	8	29	39	65	4	3
Shelby	767	-4.5	35 244	1 844	172	38	12	60	133	188	282	19	12
Stark	204	-5.9	35 185	1 661	56	13	4	7	42	50	80	5	4
Stephenson	1 774	0.0	38 766	1 545	765	141	56	111	337	430	1 073	67	56
Tazewell	5 759	1.2	42 719	982	3 589	538	245	172	1 010	1 063	4 543	263	245
Union	619	2.2	35 578	2 145	165	42	11	37	100	200	255	17	11
Vermilion	2 825	-0.1	35 630	1 935	1 250	269	92	164	432	773	1 776	106	92
Wabash	472	-1.3	40 897	1 022	129	33	8	25	90	106	196	12	8
Warren	600	-4.2	34 228	2 020	233	46	17	30	110	140	325	20	17
Washington	682	-2.6	47 808	539	292	61	21	100	115	118	474	25	21
Wayne	616	-4.2	37 484	1 339	161	39	12	105	105	153	317	17	12
White	616	-4.1	43 014	616	185	38	14	82	114	151	318	19	14
Whiteside	2 254	1.2	39 483	1 299	868	201	60	86	417	552	1 215	72	60
Will	32 180	5.1	46 823	772	11 334	1 983	815	1 316	4 084	4 064	15 448	858	815
Williamson	2 723	2.8	40 359	1 325	1 192	263	87	158	419	601	1 700	98	87

1. Based on the resident population estimated as of July 1 of the year shown.

Items 62—74

STATE County	Farm	Mining	Construction	Manufacturing	Information: professional, scientific, technical services	Retail trade	Finance, insurance, real estate and leasing	Health care and social assistance	Government	Number	Rate[1]	Supplemental Security Income recipients, December 2015	Total	Percent change, 2010–2016
	75	76	77	78	79	80	81	82	83	84	85	86	87	88
ILLINOIS—Cont'd														
Hardin	0.2	D	D	D	D	3.4	D	19.3	22.6	1 335	325	179	2 450	-1.5
Henderson	7.6	D	5.3	D	D	4.1	7.3	9.3	28.2	1 800	258	109	3 818	-0.2
Henry	-0.7	D	11.2	17.0	D	7.2	5.6	9.7	23.3	11 370	230	636	22 085	-0.3
Iroquois	6.4	0.2	9.6	7.9	D	8.0	5.0	D	18.6	7 220	252	573	13 420	-0.2
Jackson	0.3	D	4.9	2.7	4.2	6.1	2.9	16.6	45.7	9 600	162	1 583	28 694	0.4
Jasper	16.0	4.3	5.7	5.7	3.8	4.4	D	D	17.4	2 260	236	142	4 326	-0.4
Jefferson	-0.8	1.3	2.6	24.9	4.1	6.3	5.8	D	14.4	8 640	225	1 003	16 793	-0.9
Jersey	-4.4	0.0	9.2	2.8	D	10.7	4.7	D	30.7	5 290	237	348	10 042	2.0
Jo Daviess	4.1	D	9.0	15.5	4.0	6.4	5.3	D	18.2	6 230	283	198	13 598	0.2
Johnson	-1.5	D	6.4	1.9	3.6	4.5	D	10.6	53.0	3 200	249	264	5 545	-0.9
Kane	-0.1	0.1	7.5	16.8	8.7	5.3	5.8	10.6	17.6	72 370	137	5 031	185 947	2.1
Kankakee	0.4	D	4.3	19.0	D	6.8	5.4	18.0	16.6	22 380	202	2 658	45 181	-0.1
Kendall	0.4	D	9.2	15.4	5.5	8.1	5.0	6.4	23.0	15 010	122	727	41 509	2.9
Knox	0.6	D	3.8	6.0	D	9.3	3.8	D	19.0	12 165	237	1 288	23 818	-1.1
Lake	0.0	D	3.7	23.4	9.9	7.1	6.6	6.3	12.6	101 765	145	8 134	262 603	0.9
LaSalle	-1.5	3.2	6.7	20.7	4.2	7.6	4.6	9.6	15.8	25 070	225	1 647	49 848	-0.3
Lawrence	-0.9	32.3	4.2	16.3	1.5	3.8	8.0	7.8	16.6	3 490	211	303	7 020	1.2
Lee	-0.3	1.0	3.8	26.6	2.9	6.4	4.2	17.8	17.9	7 980	232	488	15 011	-0.2
Livingston	4.2	D	6.0	19.0	D	12.0	3.9	8.3	17.5	8 030	219	520	15 797	-0.6
Logan	5.1	D	3.7	18.7	3.4	6.2	5.0	11.2	18.5	6 220	211	411	11 995	-0.9
McDonough	0.1	D	4.5	12.6	2.9	6.1	3.8	D	50.9	5 660	181	555	14 369	-0.3
McHenry	-0.4	0.1	10.0	17.5	6.2	8.0	4.0	10.6	16.6	49 070	160	2 005	117 966	1.6
McLean	0.3	0.0	3.5	4.8	4.8	5.4	36.9	9.4	15.4	25 405	147	1 737	71 760	3.0
Macon	0.6	0.0	7.3	30.8	4.7	5.0	4.2	12.5	10.7	24 915	232	3 276	50 241	-0.5
Macoupin	-5.6	D	8.5	8.7	D	9.6	5.0	D	24.1	11 470	249	1 010	21 552	-0.1
Madison	0.2	0.2	8.2	17.2	7.5	6.9	4.6	11.4	17.2	55 540	209	5 869	118 637	1.3
Marion	2.4	2.4	7.0	18.7	D	5.3	4.4	16.2	17.0	9 350	244	1 200	18 068	-1.2
Marshall	-1.3	0.8	8.4	34.0	3.0	3.5	D	6.1	16.3	3 095	258	141	5 882	-0.5
Mason	1.4	D	5.2	2.1	2.7	6.2	4.7	6.5	35.2	3 690	270	281	7 004	-1.0
Massac	2.5	0.0	D	20.6	1.3	3.5	2.5	5.9	24.0	4 035	274	479	7 051	-0.9
Menard	1.3	D	13.1	1.5	D	6.4	6.7	D	31.7	2 760	222	156	5 683	0.5
Mercer	-0.3	0.0	7.1	14.1	2.4	7.6	5.7	13.4	25.6	4 125	260	170	7 389	0.4
Monroe	0.7	D	9.4	4.9	14.9	8.8	9.5	6.9	17.7	6 435	190	165	13 969	4.3
Montgomery	3.5	3.6	6.1	6.8	3.6	9.6	5.8	16.2	20.0	7 050	241	664	13 046	-0.3
Morgan	-0.6	0.0	4.8	17.9	5.0	7.4	6.8	13.2	20.1	8 070	233	876	15 373	-0.9
Moultrie	2.3	D	8.6	45.7	D	2.8	D	D	7.8	3 160	212	162	6 419	2.5
Ogle	-2.4	D	6.4	22.2	D	5.1	6.6	D	17.4	11 025	213	562	22 543	-0.1
Peoria	-0.2	D	4.6	11.0	17.2	4.8	6.6	20.5	11.3	36 820	198	5 027	83 504	0.6
Perry	2.2	D	4.8	21.9	D	5.0	8.2	D	28.0	4 840	226	436	9 500	0.8
Piatt	0.7	D	7.9	6.3	D	7.1	6.7	11.7	26.9	3 505	214	109	7 353	1.2
Pike	10.8	D	7.0	2.1	D	9.6	8.5	D	19.8	3 770	236	354	7 923	-0.4
Pope	17.0	D	3.3	D	D	D	D	D	40.1	1 040	247	99	2 463	-1.1
Pulaski	-1.0	0.0	3.2	4.5	D	3.5	D	D	54.2	1 605	283	286	3 117	-1.2
Putnam	4.0	D	D	29.3	D	6.3	4.4	1.6	9.0	1 435	255	43	3 133	1.9
Randolph	-0.4	3.1	7.2	20.4	D	7.4	3.7	7.9	27.0	7 075	215	514	13 786	0.6
Richland	4.9	6.2	3.6	7.7	2.6	6.1	5.5	15.3	16.8	3 925	245	448	7 470	-0.6
Rock Island	0.2	0.2	4.5	13.2	6.5	5.0	5.1	10.2	20.2	31 175	214	2 761	65 902	0.2
St. Clair	0.1	D	5.3	6.1	8.8	6.6	4.1	12.8	31.6	48 705	184	8 116	119 195	2.5
Saline	1.0	D	9.0	3.4	4.6	7.7	5.4	13.6	20.8	6 500	265	1 091	11 592	-0.9
Sangamon	-0.2	D	5.5	3.3	9.3	6.2	8.7	19.6	25.5	41 245	208	4 586	90 965	1.2
Schuyler	10.2	D	6.2	2.5	1.1	3.8	2.5	3.6	26.7	1 635	232	85	3 431	-0.8
Scott	3.2	0.0	D	D	D	3.6	D	D	24.6	1 035	202	66	2 438	-0.9
Shelby	6.9	D	6.0	16.1	D	6.4	9.5	8.2	16.0	5 370	246	334	10 484	0.8
Stark	-3.5	0.1	11.8	22.6	D	7.8	D	5.9	23.5	1 380	239	83	2 657	-0.6
Stephenson	0.8	0.2	10.5	25.3	3.9	5.1	6.8	14.8	15.4	11 825	258	1 141	21 845	-1.1
Tazewell	-0.1	0.0	5.3	44.4	3.1	5.3	3.8	5.2	10.7	29 040	216	1 820	58 759	2.2
Union	3.5	D	6.0	6.0	2.9	8.0	4.4	D	31.1	4 640	267	640	7 904	-0.3
Vermilion	0.7	D	3.2	21.9	2.3	6.7	5.0	9.7	22.5	18 715	237	2 789	35 888	-1.2
Wabash	-1.6	11.7	9.2	7.3	5.9	7.9	4.3	D	32.6	2 725	236	192	5 512	-1.3
Warren	-0.8	D	4.6	35.0	D	5.7	4.9	D	13.3	3 560	203	289	7 647	-0.5
Washington	8.0	2.3	4.4	20.0	D	10.1	3.8	D	10.5	3 070	215	147	6 568	0.5
Wayne	17.0	8.8	5.0	7.8	2.7	6.8	3.4	D	17.0	4 045	246	287	7 871	-1.3
White	4.3	23.2	5.7	4.8	2.5	9.7	5.2	D	14.6	3 935	274	406	7 115	-0.9
Whiteside	-1.0	D	4.0	24.2	4.2	6.3	4.5	6.3	26.9	14 290	251	1 120	25 707	-0.2
Will	0.0	0.2	7.7	11.8	7.4	6.6	3.8	10.7	16.2	99 170	144	6 644	241 802	1.8
Williamson	0.0	D	5.2	10.4	D	7.3	6.5	17.5	26.7	15 275	226	1 642	30 916	1.8

1. Per 1,000 resident population estimated as of July 1 of the year shown.

Table B. States and Counties — Housing, Labor Force, and Employment

STATE County	Housing units, 2011–2015								Civilian labor force, 2016				Civilian employment,[6] 2011–2015		
	Total	Occupied units									Unemployment			Percent	
		Percent	Owner-occupied			Renter-occupied									
			Median value[1]	Median owner cost as a percent of income		Median rent[3]	Median rent as a percent of income[2]	Sub-standard units[4] (percent)	Total	Percent change, 2015–2016	Total	Rate[5]	Total	Manage-ment, business, science and arts	Con-struction, produc-tion, and mainte-nance occu-pations
				With a mort-gage	Without a mort-gage[2]										
	89	90	91	92	93	94	95	96	97	98	99	100	101	102	103
ILLINOIS—Cont'd															
Hardin	1 677	82.9	68 800	19.3	12.2	356	29.2	1.3	1 397	-8.6	137	9.8	1 493	26.9	35.2
Henderson	3 094	78.7	87 100	18.7	10.0	582	22.7	1.8	3 711	-1.1	229	6.2	3 350	25.5	34.4
Henry	20 170	78.6	110 800	19.0	11.9	596	24.4	0.7	25 066	-0.1	1 522	6.1	23 544	30.9	29.0
Iroquois	11 829	76.2	95 900	21.2	11.8	610	28.6	3.5	14 800	-0.1	817	5.5	13 533	28.5	32.8
Jackson	23 390	52.3	103 000	19.8	12.0	667	40.5	1.5	28 710	0.2	1 556	5.4	25 623	38.0	16.5
Jasper	3 781	84.1	94 500	19.3	10.0	537	34.2	0.8	4 599	-1.0	292	6.3	4 691	29.2	31.7
Jefferson	15 277	73.0	87 300	19.4	12.3	590	28.8	2.7	17 304	0.7	1 123	6.5	16 528	26.6	30.1
Jersey	8 830	81.3	124 300	20.5	11.9	675	26.8	1.2	11 179	0.8	651	5.8	10 587	31.5	24.4
Jo Daviess	9 542	78.9	138 900	22.5	12.8	616	23.3	0.8	11 353	-1.0	614	5.4	10 991	26.6	29.7
Johnson	4 407	82.5	93 100	20.0	14.1	624	25.5	1.7	4 177	1.0	361	8.6	4 244	30.6	24.0
Kane	172 479	73.6	213 200	24.6	13.8	1 011	31.2	4.8	268 147	0.1	14 874	5.5	255 530	33.7	24.5
Kankakee	40 880	69.2	138 700	23.3	13.2	820	29.0	1.7	54 834	0.0	3 534	6.4	49 815	30.1	28.2
Kendall	38 516	82.5	200 200	24.9	14.6	1 305	27.7	2.3	66 843	1.0	3 487	5.2	61 270	39.7	20.4
Knox	21 301	66.7	80 400	19.2	11.8	576	28.7	1.9	23 190	-0.2	1 415	6.1	21 475	30.0	26.9
Lake	242 426	74.2	245 300	24.4	14.5	1 069	30.3	2.8	371 411	0.8	19 439	5.2	338 959	41.9	17.2
LaSalle	44 242	73.1	123 100	21.3	12.2	700	28.9	1.4	57 245	-0.3	3 861	6.7	51 452	26.4	29.9
Lawrence	5 015	76.9	66 700	17.5	10.0	544	25.3	3.6	6 168	0.3	460	7.5	4 197	30.4	25.1
Lee	13 517	74.1	113 600	20.6	12.2	672	24.6	1.5	17 948	0.5	924	5.1	15 539	29.2	28.1
Livingston	14 464	73.1	107 200	19.6	12.5	626	25.9	1.2	16 778	-2.8	918	5.5	15 994	26.4	32.9
Logan	10 711	67.8	98 900	17.8	11.1	624	26.8	0.8	13 083	0.4	696	5.3	10 856	31.1	23.0
McDonough	12 129	63.7	89 900	18.3	10.1	630	37.6	1.8	13 955	-0.1	877	6.3	14 279	34.1	19.9
McHenry	109 491	80.6	208 200	24.4	14.6	1 074	29.8	1.8	167 068	0.8	8 915	5.3	157 226	37.0	20.7
McLean	65 346	65.7	160 500	19.5	11.1	780	28.7	1.5	89 679	-1.4	4 571	5.1	90 810	42.2	14.5
Macon	44 915	69.0	94 900	18.6	11.6	656	28.9	1.8	50 325	-0.6	3 328	6.6	48 783	31.9	25.2
Macoupin	18 982	77.6	94 300	18.9	10.5	618	29.9	2.2	23 324	1.1	1 391	6.0	21 098	31.1	28.9
Madison	107 111	70.9	126 500	20.3	12.0	778	29.7	1.2	134 759	1.2	7 935	5.9	125 030	33.9	23.8
Marion	15 783	74.6	68 600	19.6	11.9	623	30.9	2.5	17 907	-1.1	1 154	6.4	17 066	27.1	31.2
Marshall	4 993	83.2	104 600	19.9	10.8	646	27.7	1.2	5 691	-0.9	375	6.6	5 651	28.2	32.4
Mason	6 116	76.9	81 300	19.6	12.4	608	27.8	1.0	6 450	-2.7	460	7.1	6 190	28.9	32.0
Massac	5 987	72.9	83 900	22.0	12.4	693	29.7	1.7	6 059	-0.9	427	7.0	5 821	28.8	28.9
Menard	5 144	77.7	127 900	18.6	10.6	647	24.1	2.5	6 816	1.0	315	4.6	6 252	35.4	22.0
Mercer	6 607	78.1	98 000	18.7	11.6	566	23.6	0.9	8 204	0.7	510	6.2	7 568	29.6	33.2
Monroe	12 699	82.1	191 200	21.6	13.0	830	26.8	1.3	18 307	1.1	746	4.1	17 120	37.2	20.5
Montgomery	10 985	77.8	78 300	17.6	11.9	595	26.3	1.3	12 103	0.5	855	7.1	9 604	32.4	23.2
Morgan	13 825	69.3	98 500	19.2	10.2	603	27.7	0.9	17 052	0.3	844	4.9	16 089	32.0	26.0
Moultrie	5 799	76.2	100 900	19.2	10.0	622	25.8	2.9	7 413	0.5	339	4.6	6 963	28.1	33.1
Ogle	20 731	75.9	140 000	20.9	13.9	674	26.0	2.0	25 819	-0.5	1 526	5.9	24 989	31.3	31.7
Peoria	76 133	64.7	126 600	20.1	11.5	713	28.2	2.0	89 339	-1.4	6 078	6.8	85 639	38.1	18.7
Perry	8 025	75.9	78 400	20.1	11.3	479	29.4	1.4	8 666	-2.3	617	7.1	8 312	24.7	35.4
Piatt	6 645	83.5	123 600	18.3	10.3	745	23.2	0.4	8 416	0.7	424	5.0	8 451	35.9	25.0
Pike	6 677	77.5	75 300	19.4	11.6	517	25.7	1.7	7 544	-1.0	385	5.1	7 197	25.6	34.0
Pope	1 593	83.4	102 000	19.4	14.2	455	27.2	1.9	1 765	-0.2	123	7.0	1 469	21.7	34.6
Pulaski	2 334	74.7	57 600	19.6	14.2	490	33.2	2.6	2 093	0.1	185	8.8	1 935	25.9	27.1
Putnam	2 453	80.1	121 300	19.4	10.0	605	24.1	1.6	3 115	2.3	174	5.6	2 827	28.8	33.9
Randolph	11 895	77.4	96 700	19.0	10.8	623	26.8	1.2	14 528	1.5	731	5.0	13 698	24.6	35.7
Richland	6 503	71.9	83 800	18.3	10.6	533	26.5	2.8	7 511	0.5	449	6.0	7 317	27.7	32.5
Rock Island	60 391	69.5	113 800	20.8	11.8	678	28.8	2.4	72 000	-0.4	4 522	6.3	68 438	29.5	27.8
St. Clair	102 257	66.3	120 400	21.1	12.4	796	31.7	1.8	127 263	0.8	7 721	6.1	116 537	34.7	21.1
Saline	9 955	71.5	69 400	19.0	11.6	575	29.4	2.4	9 978	-3.7	859	8.6	9 841	23.1	29.4
Sangamon	82 885	69.6	130 900	19.3	10.6	743	30.1	1.7	106 214	0.7	5 168	4.9	96 155	41.2	15.6
Schuyler	3 000	81.5	78 100	18.4	11.5	523	19.3	0.8	3 338	-4.2	192	5.8	3 062	27.5	28.2
Scott	2 124	75.7	84 300	18.4	11.6	548	24.5	1.8	2 545	-0.5	143	5.6	2 370	27.9	33.6
Shelby	9 044	81.6	85 300	19.3	10.8	554	23.2	1.1	10 336	0.9	597	5.8	9 895	27.6	33.9
Stark	2 391	82.2	85 100	19.0	11.0	571	24.1	1.5	2 780	0.0	201	7.2	2 556	35.5	26.1
Stephenson	19 299	70.7	98 900	20.6	12.6	610	31.3	0.9	21 507	-0.3	1 258	5.8	21 853	29.1	30.3
Tazewell	54 288	76.5	134 900	19.4	11.1	682	25.9	1.3	66 508	-1.2	4 219	6.3	64 883	35.5	23.6
Union	6 712	78.6	93 900	20.2	12.7	489	25.9	2.5	7 498	1.9	556	7.4	7 339	31.6	28.7
Vermilion	31 531	69.0	75 800	19.1	11.2	638	28.3	1.7	34 974	-1.5	2 528	7.2	32 514	25.7	32.4
Wabash	4 871	73.5	81 100	19.4	10.3	561	25.6	1.3	5 639	0.2	362	6.4	5 501	26.5	36.1
Warren	6 829	75.6	81 900	19.6	12.1	554	25.2	3.1	8 589	0.2	456	5.3	8 068	29.4	29.7
Washington	5 777	78.8	106 600	21.0	10.9	615	25.3	1.6	9 602	2.5	365	3.8	7 194	31.6	33.7
Wayne	7 043	80.2	77 800	18.5	10.7	552	28.5	2.4	7 269	-3.2	622	8.6	7 523	26.6	36.9
White	6 171	74.6	70 900	17.7	11.0	542	23.5	1.9	6 834	-1.5	452	6.6	6 095	25.6	34.7
Whiteside	23 548	75.3	99 200	19.9	12.2	639	28.8	1.4	28 622	0.3	1 668	5.8	26 336	26.9	30.9
Will	223 640	81.5	209 800	24.6	13.8	1 039	31.5	2.1	359 565	0.8	21 849	6.1	333 433	36.4	22.5
Williamson	26 796	72.5	99 200	19.5	12.1	649	28.6	1.2	32 053	0.3	1 985	6.2	29 214	31.1	21.7

1. Specified owner-occupied units. 2. A value of 10.0 represents 10 percent or less; a value of 50.0 represents 50 percent or more. 3. Specified renter-occupied units.
4. Overcrowded or lacking complete plumbing facilities. 5. Percent of civilian labor force. 6. Civilian employed persons 16 years old and over.

Table B. States and Counties — Nonfarm Employment and Agriculture

| | Private nonfarm establishments, employment and payroll, 2015 | | | | | | | | | Agriculture, 2012 | | | |
| | Employment | | | | | | Annual payroll | | Farms | | | |
STATE County	Number of establishments	Total	Health care and social assistance	Manufacturing	Retail trade	Finance and insurance	Professional, scientific, and technical services	Total (mil dol)	Average per employee (dollars)	Number	Fewer than 50 acres	500 acres or more	Farm operators whose principal occupation is farming (percent)
	104	105	106	107	108	109	110	111	112	113	114	115	116
ILLINOIS—Cont'd													
Hardin	68	700	345	NA	70	13	D	24	33 859	150	22.0	6.7	34.0
Henderson	118	667	136	D	94	82	39	19	28 226	396	24.2	28.8	68.7
Henry	1 069	13 423	1 545	4 403	1 835	541	295	466	34 734	1 373	30.6	21.5	56.6
Iroquois	691	6 134	1 629	634	1 020	331	108	210	34 310	1 470	25.4	29.2	55.0
Jackson	1 323	16 969	4 185	914	3 723	593	712	553	32 581	783	34.7	10.9	42.1
Jasper	215	1 467	125	181	260	110	51	48	32 684	910	34.5	19.6	41.2
Jefferson	967	18 381	3 545	3 974	2 446	439	654	706	38 392	1 063	38.4	8.8	33.1
Jersey	423	4 794	1 227	102	927	190	130	132	27 550	509	37.9	17.5	47.0
Jo Daviess	721	6 890	716	1 055	932	209	179	244	35 397	935	26.4	13.6	50.6
Johnson	166	1 280	278	34	219	69	165	26	20 406	558	33.0	5.7	30.1
Kane	12 528	182 936	21 871	31 457	24 047	8 136	9 352	7 946	43 437	590	51.4	16.1	66.3
Kankakee	2 339	36 979	7 466	5 807	5 949	1 387	790	1 367	36 967	818	33.7	24.4	56.8
Kendall	2 104	22 867	1 911	2 425	5 662	645	721	775	33 885	364	35.2	21.2	61.5
Knox	1 044	15 792	3 570	1 204	3 480	420	280	471	29 816	856	29.7	22.1	56.9
Lake	19 572	322 271	35 153	37 024	38 499	14 116	34 666	23 644	73 368	349	79.7	4.3	56.2
LaSalle	2 685	39 080	5 702	4 892	6 398	1 339	1 492	1 556	39 828	1 583	29.1	24.1	58.8
Lawrence	264	3 454	543	1 019	424	115	49	121	34 898	379	36.4	26.4	58.8
Lee	710	10 399	2 160	3 233	1 400	307	249	431	41 484	835	28.0	26.7	55.2
Livingston	872	11 301	1 655	3 158	1 654	390	216	438	38 719	1 349	25.2	31.9	62.9
Logan	581	7 422	1 471	1 125	1 063	292	194	240	32 345	779	32.6	31.2	54.8
McDonough	678	9 021	1 847	1 406	1 675	307	229	273	30 312	740	26.9	23.9	58.4
McHenry	7 901	85 603	11 127	14 604	16 143	2 119	3 412	3 714	43 382	911	52.3	13.0	62.5
McLean	3 635	77 458	8 531	3 960	10 031	21 363	2 578	3 945	50 933	1 489	30.2	29.0	55.6
Macon	2 461	45 585	8 070	6 635	5 915	1 525	1 167	1 948	42 738	674	35.9	29.5	59.1
Macoupin	884	8 369	1 632	556	1 338	446	115	279	33 333	1 190	29.9	19.6	48.7
Madison	5 805	85 945	14 451	11 803	12 631	2 905	3 748	3 579	41 648	1 110	45.2	15.1	41.9
Marion	917	11 435	2 724	3 038	1 295	394	282	405	35 447	1 152	36.4	11.8	44.1
Marshall	270	2 795	473	899	304	107	22	101	36 045	440	20.9	29.3	58.0
Mason	284	2 333	470	70	442	134	22	86	36 674	490	25.5	33.9	58.4
Massac	229	3 563	862	452	305	102	D	144	40 275	412	39.8	11.7	40.5
Menard	210	1 282	75	37	281	110	87	40	31 340	369	37.4	26.8	56.9
Mercer	275	2 184	318	506	351	129	30	71	32 499	715	32.2	21.1	59.3
Monroe	781	8 354	931	348	1 382	336	624	278	33 245	563	39.6	20.2	43.9
Montgomery	700	6 868	1 319	647	1 487	394	184	223	32 534	1 021	31.5	22.8	48.1
Morgan	841	12 983	2 485	1 931	1 861	1 112	654	460	35 421	757	31.0	26.0	62.1
Moultrie	324	4 881	720	2 143	349	114	121	185	37 994	553	45.8	20.3	55.3
Ogle	1 049	13 125	1 431	3 388	1 457	518	356	582	44 381	1 148	36.8	19.5	52.3
Peoria	4 475	108 901	22 523	5 949	10 742	3 654	4 955	6 419	58 944	917	35.2	16.5	49.9
Perry	412	4 260	868	373	730	166	83	149	34 899	560	30.7	19.5	43.0
Piatt	339	2 294	383	187	407	152	118	77	33 779	483	28.6	35.2	58.2
Pike	378	3 104	621	173	613	211	83	97	31 127	970	24.8	23.1	55.6
Pope	46	237	71	D	48	11	5	6	23 376	349	20.9	9.7	35.5
Pulaski	93	810	148	D	119	49	D	31	37 894	230	30.4	20.0	34.8
Putnam	133	1 159	D	396	127	40	16	65	55 694	183	25.7	16.4	46.4
Randolph	676	10 694	2 188	2 922	1 277	293	275	389	36 361	793	27.9	17.7	47.7
Richland	451	5 204	1 055	462	643	191	99	181	34 806	554	41.5	19.3	37.9
Rock Island	3 169	61 913	9 621	7 774	8 031	2 727	3 237	3 188	51 488	666	41.3	11.9	50.3
St. Clair	5 257	77 883	14 492	4 730	13 427	2 316	4 966	2 893	37 140	732	38.4	21.2	47.4
Saline	572	7 614	2 061	422	1 301	296	162	282	37 012	483	40.4	14.9	37.5
Sangamon	4 993	85 180	23 275	2 703	12 636	5 787	4 232	3 450	40 501	1 092	41.4	20.0	50.5
Schuyler	150	1 147	356	68	213	63	21	35	30 568	542	24.0	16.6	35.2
Scott	79	603	17	D	78	56	9	25	41 295	356	29.5	23.0	43.8
Shelby	418	4 167	677	1 145	589	202	238	142	34 162	1 282	32.9	19.9	51.6
Stark	124	973	121	228	153	74	68	38	39 275	348	29.0	33.0	62.4
Stephenson	1 078	14 537	2 387	3 064	1 995	733	457	593	40 809	1 087	36.0	17.7	56.9
Tazewell	2 796	43 662	5 429	7 111	7 436	1 845	1 475	1 726	39 542	942	36.5	22.7	49.8
Union	350	3 586	1 327	257	651	147	73	96	26 843	623	35.8	6.9	37.4
Vermilion	1 426	24 983	5 453	4 913	3 855	1 155	430	969	38 775	956	36.6	29.5	54.5
Wabash	261	2 692	797	164	313	97	122	103	38 318	213	29.6	25.4	52.1
Warren	352	5 420	586	1 971	594	201	108	179	33 057	605	25.8	32.2	59.2
Washington	386	4 853	375	1 481	556	167	99	195	40 241	777	27.0	26.9	50.7
Wayne	387	3 282	882	411	611	125	73	87	26 635	1 187	34.5	13.6	34.5
White	382	3 551	645	302	520	153	69	131	36 926	582	35.6	19.6	38.3
Whiteside	1 241	17 356	3 151	3 647	2 801	567	321	632	36 425	1 110	33.4	20.4	50.5
Will	14 752	211 243	26 228	18 236	31 649	4 635	9 855	9 227	43 679	882	55.8	15.4	54.8
Williamson	1 630	23 789	6 344	2 753	3 913	1 323	637	860	36 148	702	44.7	6.1	39.6

Table B. States and Counties — **Agriculture**

STATE County	Land in farms — Acreage (1,000) [117]	Land in farms — Percent change, 2007–2012 [118]	Land in farms — Average size of farm [119]	Land in farms — Acres — Total irrigated (1,000) [120]	Land in farms — Acres — Total cropland (1,000) [121]	Value of land and buildings (dollars) — Average per farm [122]	Value of land and buildings (dollars) — Average per acre [123]	Value of machinery and equipment, average per farm (dollars) [124]	Value of products sold — Total (mil dol) [125]	Value of products sold — Average per farm (dollars) [126]	Percent from: Crops [127]	Percent from: Livestock and poultry products [128]	Percent of farms with sales of: $10,000 or more [129]	Percent of farms with sales of: $100,000 or more [130]	Government payments — Total ($1,000) [131]	Government payments — Percent of farms [132]
ILLINOIS—Cont'd																
Hardin	33	-4.4	221	0.0	16.8	782 720	3 536	68 840	4.0	26 513	D	D	27.3	5.3	288	48.7
Henderson	172	0.7	433	10.9	141.7	2 681 811	6 190	237 106	138.4	349 467	84.8	15.2	70.2	51.5	3 974	81.8
Henry	479	-2.2	349	8.7	436.8	2 384 519	6 831	226 993	397.9	289 824	79.6	20.4	62.6	42.4	11 930	78.6
Iroquois	669	-1.3	455	3.1	638.2	3 096 555	6 801	256 896	493.5	335 710	86.4	13.6	72.0	50.5	15 428	87.8
Jackson	214	-4.6	274	1.5	172.9	1 077 216	3 938	144 249	67.4	86 087	87.9	12.1	34.6	13.9	2 883	59.9
Jasper	251	3.0	276	D	218.2	1 396 085	5 066	154 589	159.3	175 074	46.9	53.1	51.3	27.3	11 040	87.4
Jefferson	214	-8.0	201	0.3	172.5	725 120	3 604	102 292	60.2	56 591	81.3	18.7	34.2	11.9	3 775	69.3
Jersey	155	-17.9	305	0.0	126.1	1 800 929	5 896	165 061	69.2	135 959	94.7	5.3	50.5	27.7	2 589	73.5
Jo Daviess	272	-3.4	291	0.1	190.2	1 411 296	4 855	151 134	154.1	164 857	54.0	46.0	50.8	27.4	8 935	79.9
Johnson	90	-10.7	161	0.1	48.2	485 810	3 022	71 670	12.1	21 685	70.6	29.4	23.8	4.3	1 747	52.7
Kane	169	-12.4	286	1.8	154.3	2 535 083	8 874	199 881	196.2	332 464	84.1	15.9	60.7	37.1	4 322	45.3
Kankakee	343	-11.2	419	14.6	327.9	2 769 373	6 612	264 800	287.5	351 460	90.2	9.8	71.8	48.5	5 827	76.5
Kendall	130	-22.3	356	D	123.6	3 094 407	8 682	229 712	103.0	283 091	83.8	16.2	70.6	42.0	1 986	69.2
Knox	348	-4.2	406	0.0	288.7	2 788 956	6 868	193 379	293.1	342 459	80.2	19.8	56.2	34.7	8 091	74.6
Lake	30	-13.0	86	0.5	22.0	894 759	10 396	88 287	35.4	101 544	72.6	27.4	43.0	14.6	272	9.2
LaSalle	602	-6.4	380	5.0	569.0	2 790 132	7 890	247 122	459.3	290 132	94.7	5.3	71.4	48.3	10 769	78.8
Lawrence	184	-5.1	486	13.6	169.3	2 378 997	4 897	257 005	101.5	267 902	71.6	28.4	53.3	34.3	4 542	76.5
Lee	369	-6.7	442	25.4	348.9	3 344 959	7 568	293 399	361.0	432 352	86.7	13.3	67.9	51.7	8 885	81.8
Livingston	656	4.4	486	0.4	632.1	3 496 319	7 187	280 713	409.6	303 664	81.4	18.6	76.6	52.2	11 676	85.5
Logan	363	13.4	466	1.1	343.0	3 349 367	7 182	250 374	240.0	308 109	91.0	9.0	62.3	43.9	8 215	85.5
McDonough	292	-5.1	395	0.1	253.5	2 773 084	7 027	210 159	209.2	282 639	88.7	11.3	60.7	38.9	6 739	76.5
McHenry	234	8.6	257	11.2	212.6	2 074 731	8 070	177 105	182.4	200 256	83.6	16.4	51.0	27.6	4 732	38.1
McLean	692	2.4	465	1.6	653.9	3 803 046	8 180	297 883	501.0	336 465	88.6	11.4	69.4	47.8	13 140	81.7
Macon	337	15.8	499	0.0	321.7	3 911 432	7 833	294 921	211.3	313 540	95.7	4.3	66.0	42.7	5 762	80.1
Macoupin	439	11.3	369	0.0	371.0	2 291 757	6 218	186 864	221.8	186 369	81.3	18.7	53.4	31.9	8 416	79.0
Madison	307	-1.9	277	2.4	276.5	1 765 512	6 381	184 861	141.7	127 692	87.3	12.7	54.8	23.8	4 518	60.8
Marion	267	2.4	232	0.2	216.9	972 948	4 201	103 237	68.8	59 693	75.6	24.4	28.0	12.7	5 884	82.6
Marshall	209	2.2	475	2.2	183.7	3 290 455	6 924	274 420	136.1	309 418	96.2	3.8	71.8	51.4	4 416	85.7
Mason	290	6.0	592	102.3	265.5	3 458 004	5 846	344 157	201.2	410 545	88.7	11.3	63.9	43.9	5 881	84.1
Massac	102	14.0	248	6.1	83.3	887 687	3 577	115 689	39.5	95 782	81.8	18.2	37.6	15.3	2 256	66.7
Menard	158	-6.4	428	4.3	139.9	2 703 653	6 324	240 477	84.6	229 138	94.3	5.7	52.0	35.2	2 978	77.8
Mercer	252	-17.7	352	7.9	212.3	2 139 906	6 072	196 516	216.9	303 290	82.2	17.8	55.5	38.0	6 391	78.2
Monroe	193	8.5	343	3.8	167.7	1 777 323	5 179	209 716	111.7	198 455	81.0	19.0	50.1	31.3	2 792	68.0
Montgomery	382	10.0	375	D	346.7	2 230 784	5 956	197 314	227.3	222 582	78.6	21.4	54.9	34.3	7 252	80.6
Morgan	309	-3.5	408	3.8	272.3	2 729 232	6 683	232 711	201.9	266 663	86.0	14.0	60.2	38.8	5 870	78.1
Moultrie	205	22.2	371	0.0	194.2	2 849 613	7 687	206 665	130.7	236 318	94.8	5.2	58.8	34.7	3 550	59.1
Ogle	376	2.7	328	1.1	335.9	2 273 063	6 932	209 389	323.7	281 925	76.4	23.6	58.5	37.7	9 746	69.3
Peoria	250	-3.4	273	3.2	211.1	1 888 508	6 920	163 937	187.4	204 315	87.3	12.7	60.5	32.5	4 738	64.6
Perry	181	-9.8	323	0.2	143.9	1 313 157	4 071	168 170	45.4	81 054	88.6	11.4	43.6	22.5	2 310	78.9
Piatt	259	-3.1	608	1.0	251.4	5 262 390	8 654	359 110	187.0	438 925	98.2	1.8	70.9	50.9	4 294	81.9
Pike	411	5.6	424	1.7	310.2	2 085 246	4 916	160 991	232.2	239 381	65.5	34.5	51.5	26.9	9 067	79.0
Pope	78	28.3	223	0.3	43.6	582 077	2 605	67 040	12.7	36 364	81.0	19.0	25.5	8.0	1 251	66.2
Pulaski	82	-18.8	357	1.2	64.7	1 384 774	4 022	155 809	28.3	123 191	95.4	4.6	30.9	17.0	1 604	72.2
Putnam	60	-4.1	329	1.0	52.3	2 068 290	6 294	239 754	81.7	446 224	97.1	2.9	61.2	41.5	1 727	84.7
Randolph	279	10.1	351	1.1	228.0	1 566 426	4 459	174 168	104.4	131 629	89.1	10.9	53.0	26.6	4 034	73.4
Richland	189	-6.9	341	D	167.3	1 498 597	4 395	160 653	81.4	146 910	53.9	46.1	42.8	20.0	5 909	82.1
Rock Island	149	-16.5	224	4.0	119.6	1 396 574	6 235	141 845	101.4	152 303	88.7	11.3	50.6	28.4	3 369	66.8
St. Clair	252	-17.8	344	0.5	227.4	2 173 104	6 314	225 559	119.2	162 816	89.3	10.7	56.8	33.1	4 174	69.4
Saline	140	19.3	290	0.0	117.7	1 221 402	4 218	137 004	58.7	121 449	65.7	34.3	35.0	17.8	1 878	68.1
Sangamon	514	-0.8	471	1.0	475.8	3 468 062	7 367	270 515	358.4	328 162	93.9	6.1	50.6	34.0	9 359	72.4
Schuyler	182	-12.2	336	1.7	124.6	1 470 393	4 377	119 697	78.4	144 705	67.2	32.8	43.4	19.2	3 899	85.2
Scott	148	8.7	414	7.0	122.8	2 412 295	5 821	232 750	89.2	250 511	85.6	14.4	57.0	30.9	2 904	79.5
Shelby	406	4.8	317	0.0	362.7	1 910 895	6 037	175 446	214.3	167 165	82.0	18.0	54.7	29.4	8 301	76.5
Stark	168	-1.0	483	D	159.5	3 592 802	7 437	309 853	133.0	382 089	94.4	5.6	68.1	53.2	3 634	85.1
Stephenson	352	4.3	324	0.0	315.8	2 205 409	6 801	208 247	313.2	288 094	57.7	42.3	58.5	36.4	9 449	73.2
Tazewell	337	2.5	358	38.5	304.0	2 664 259	7 439	207 022	263.7	279 942	88.7	11.3	59.3	41.7	6 853	77.5
Union	121	-1.0	194	0.8	79.3	689 525	3 545	81 409	33.9	54 413	91.2	8.8	30.2	6.3	2 516	58.4
Vermilion	434	-5.0	454	0.2	409.5	3 200 276	7 043	259 283	283.6	296 653	95.7	4.3	60.4	41.8	7 122	76.2
Wabash	106	-6.9	500	1.1	94.4	2 653 826	5 311	244 742	43.5	204 188	95.3	4.7	49.3	33.3	1 690	77.9
Warren	338	14.8	559	8.0	306.0	3 871 392	6 921	290 898	274.6	453 820	87.1	12.9	74.9	51.7	6 194	77.4
Washington	355	0.3	457	0.6	325.7	2 366 162	5 180	263 172	144.8	186 342	65.5	34.5	62.9	35.8	6 187	85.5
Wayne	369	10.6	310	2.9	318.7	1 387 644	4 470	115 500	150.3	126 600	70.1	29.9	32.3	17.0	7 260	85.2
White	311	4.7	534	15.2	275.1	2 394 223	4 482	260 127	130.9	224 912	94.5	5.5	41.4	23.9	4 491	79.7
Whiteside	403	-0.5	363	57.4	370.0	2 485 254	6 841	238 705	435.7	392 487	77.4	22.6	62.8	42.4	11 400	78.3
Will	234	6.1	266	1.5	221.2	2 080 146	7 832	185 451	169.1	191 723	94.2	5.8	54.6	29.3	3 639	53.4
Williamson	103	9.9	147	0.0	72.1	649 405	4 408	74 148	22.5	32 031	74.2	25.8	24.6	6.1	1 392	46.7

Table B. States and Counties — Water Use, Wholesale Trade, Retail Trade, and Real Estate

STATE County	Water use, 2010		Wholesale trade,[1] 2012				Retail trade,[2] 2012				Real estate and rental and leasing,[2] 2012			
	Total water withdrawn (mil gal/day)	Gallons withdrawn per person per day	Number of establishments	Number of employees	Sales (mil dol)	Annual payroll (mil dol)	Number of establishments	Number of employees	Sales (mil dol)	Annual payroll (mil dol)	Number of establishments	Number of employees	Receipts (mil dol)	Annual payroll (mil dol)
	133	134	135	136	137	138	139	140	141	142	143	144	145	146
ILLINOIS—Cont'd														
Hardin	1.3	306	NA	NA	NA	NA	8	57	14.5	1.0	2	D	D	D
Henderson	9.1	1 240	12	61	303.0	3.4	15	105	39.4	2.2	1	D	D	D
Henry	7.8	155	64	656	1 229.5	29.1	156	1 792	500.1	41.6	20	31	5.5	0.7
Iroquois	5.7	191	56	590	822.4	26.8	87	1 074	287.4	21.3	18	50	7.9	1.3
Jackson	70.3	1 167	26	239	187.6	9.7	225	3 684	1 008.3	76.4	77	350	49.9	7.4
Jasper	660.1	68 062	18	108	211.5	4.6	31	288	73.3	6.0	2	D	D	D
Jefferson	1.3	34	56	D	D	D	180	2 295	709.5	55.0	21	68	12.1	2.0
Jersey	4.0	174	24	D	D	D	69	909	230.6	21.3	10	16	3.0	0.5
Jo Daviess	7.7	341	21	135	94.8	5.3	118	880	293.7	21.2	18	27	6.7	1.3
Johnson	1.6	130	4	7	3.1	0.3	27	240	88.6	5.6	4	1	0.1	0.0
Kane	65.8	128	741	9 371	9 628.8	571.7	1 487	22 836	5 681.1	508.2	439	2 045	583.8	83.7
Kankakee	26.8	236	119	2 196	1 443.3	95.0	370	5 548	1 463.3	120.0	95	371	70.9	10.6
Kendall	12.5	109	75	1 327	2 125.6	64.4	237	4 777	1 151.5	106.6	60	139	21.8	4.0
Knox	1.9	36	48	680	502.4	29.0	193	3 463	791.3	75.6	35	123	18.6	2.7
Lake	657.3	934	1 106	27 371	26 255.5	2 227.7	2 309	37 702	14 900.5	1 112.0	745	3 386	994.6	193.0
LaSalle	110.6	971	124	1 719	2 344.1	78.3	420	6 168	1 689.5	142.3	86	533	63.6	16.9
Lawrence	16.9	1 003	14	233	113.8	7.5	38	406	117.3	9.0	7	14	1.4	0.3
Lee	15.8	439	28	D	D	D	100	1 264	379.9	30.1	21	112	13.8	2.6
Livingston	7.6	196	60	692	1 011.2	36.9	135	1 610	479.4	36.9	16	69	6.9	1.9
Logan	13.5	446	45	552	858.7	32.1	88	1 082	292.3	24.7	25	86	9.9	2.1
McDonough	3.9	120	29	D	D	D	121	1 554	340.8	32.9	26	110	16.3	2.1
McHenry	35.2	114	411	5 284	2 932.5	264.5	941	15 021	3 664.4	337.2	219	745	113.4	24.1
McLean	14.5	85	166	2 515	9 130.9	161.3	580	9 434	2 441.6	201.1	143	718	149.0	22.7
Macon	39.4	356	112	D	D	D	395	5 724	1 494.2	133.7	88	471	105.2	13.8
Macoupin	6.2	129	47	680	885.2	29.6	133	1 375	392.0	30.0	21	54	5.9	1.5
Madison	404.8	1 503	226	2 822	2 764.2	147.4	832	12 506	3 230.2	292.4	230	974	171.4	31.4
Marion	4.1	104	39	336	334.8	11.8	150	1 349	353.7	30.6	23	101	10.3	2.6
Marshall	3.3	259	16	D	D	D	42	384	85.7	6.7	6	D	D	D
Mason	98.6	6 722	27	306	664.8	14.7	45	445	130.5	8.9	5	11	1.2	0.2
Massac	665.5	43 134	8	D	D	D	37	319	84.9	7.5	5	36	3.0	0.6
Menard	2.0	158	10	87	153.4	4.7	31	319	76.8	5.9	4	7	0.9	0.2
Mercer	3.2	195	14	148	435.0	6.5	41	351	72.6	6.7	6	10	1.1	0.2
Monroe	3.3	100	21	284	182.7	13.4	96	1 393	481.7	41.7	28	151	18.8	5.4
Montgomery	478.7	15 901	47	314	372.9	13.3	128	1 518	432.5	34.1	15	53	6.5	1.2
Morgan	109.6	3 084	42	D	D	D	151	1 845	454.5	37.9	27	D	D	D
Moultrie	1.8	119	11	95	245.4	4.4	42	363	109.4	7.3	5	15	0.7	0.1
Ogle	66.2	1 237	53	D	D	D	138	1 466	408.1	29.2	36	104	11.3	1.9
Peoria	535.9	2 873	202	3 235	1 782.0	153.6	726	10 839	2 576.7	249.2	198	987	181.7	33.1
Perry	2.1	93	13	D	D	D	59	718	189.5	16.1	5	11	1.3	0.4
Piatt	5.8	344	25	275	429.7	15.4	47	446	143.4	10.6	4	D	D	D
Pike	14.6	890	24	193	340.6	9.4	53	566	174.3	12.2	7	16	7.6	0.3
Pope	0.1	16	NA	NA	NA	NA	11	52	11.5	0.8	2	D	D	D
Pulaski	0.7	117	6	D	D	D	18	85	35.0	2.2	NA	NA	NA	NA
Putnam	200.4	33 370	9	59	224.7	2.2	16	135	29.2	2.5	1	D	D	D
Randolph	37.1	1 109	33	429	406.4	20.0	100	1 440	373.4	32.9	9	21	3.8	0.6
Richland	3.0	184	25	329	566.0	12.1	62	720	176.4	15.2	6	20	1.6	0.4
Rock Island	1 140.0	7 726	152	2 826	3 164.9	182.9	479	7 931	1 859.1	186.9	119	526	108.1	14.3
St. Clair	20.7	77	177	1 846	2 643.8	85.8	910	13 296	3 234.2	305.3	230	1 005	171.6	31.4
Saline	2.6	103	14	104	51.3	3.5	111	1 245	353.6	31.5	9	39	10.1	1.3
Sangamon	323.6	1 639	196	3 346	3 372.0	151.3	754	11 950	3 128.6	277.1	211	842	153.5	25.5
Schuyler	1.5	192	7	67	68.6	3.1	28	207	39.0	4.6	3	D	D	D
Scott	7.9	1 466	3	D	D	D	9	98	39.1	2.4	1	D	D	D
Shelby	4.0	177	26	226	239.8	7.8	71	603	155.0	11.4	9	D	D	D
Stark	0.8	140	8	D	D	D	21	168	68.1	5.4	3	D	D	D
Stephenson	8.3	174	49	D	D	D	157	2 026	521.6	45.8	29	92	10.8	2.5
Tazewell	98.9	731	131	2 089	1 929.2	98.6	406	6 864	1 942.3	169.6	88	306	78.9	9.8
Union	4.0	224	12	130	40.2	3.8	64	649	167.1	15.3	11	34	3.8	0.8
Vermilion	14.0	171	77	1 788	3 136.5	84.3	255	3 401	850.3	74.3	45	158	28.7	4.5
Wabash	4.5	379	13	D	D	D	42	345	81.1	8.3	11	18	2.7	0.5
Warren	3.4	189	29	240	516.2	10.2	54	552	143.2	11.1	9	18	2.0	0.3
Washington	4.0	273	30	586	415.7	25.9	64	584	200.8	15.3	14	24	1.7	0.2
Wayne	7.0	415	22	196	214.0	8.6	68	602	157.6	13.7	7	13	1.5	0.4
White	23.4	1 594	25	218	161.9	7.4	58	510	142.9	11.2	10	52	14.2	2.1
Whiteside	24.3	415	61	597	689.1	24.7	190	2 676	578.0	57.9	38	111	15.1	2.5
Will	2 363.1	3 488	735	11 420	14 925.1	680.5	1 606	27 615	7 862.1	657.3	467	2 311	458.3	97.1
Williamson	216.9	3 269	60	723	255.2	28.5	271	3 783	1 116.3	93.8	51	187	29.2	5.3

1. Merchant wholesalers, except manufacturers' sales branches and offices.   2. Employer establishments.

Table B. States and Counties — Professional Services, Manufacturing, and Accommodation and Food Services

STATE County	Professional, scientific, and technical services, 2012				Manufacturing, 2012				Accommodation and food services, 2012			
	Number of establishments	Number of employees	Receipts (mil dol)	Annual payroll (mil dol)	Number of establishments	Number of employees	Receipts (mil dol)	Annual payroll (mil dol)	Number of establishments	Number of employees	Sales (mil dol)	Annual payroll (mil dol)
	147	148	149	150	151	152	153	154	155	156	157	158
ILLINOIS—Cont'd												
Hardin	4	D	D	D	NA	NA	NA	NA	9	D	D	D
Henderson	6	29	2.3	0.7	NA	NA	NA	NA	11	D	D	D
Henry	69	289	21.2	7.2	55	4 230	D	155.3	85	D	D	D
Iroquois	33	206	12.6	4.4	30	642	515.2	21.9	60	537	22.5	6.6
Jackson	108	689	68.5	27.1	39	673	178.3	25.8	140	2 927	111.5	31.4
Jasper	10	22	1.9	0.5	12	288	101.6	10.7	15	122	4.4	1.2
Jefferson	76	523	48.4	20.2	32	2 998	D	144.3	81	1 647	71.1	20.9
Jersey	20	146	13.5	6.7	14	62	D	2.2	44	644	26.3	7.4
Jo Daviess	56	250	36.1	12.2	37	1 018	480.2	45.1	108	1 656	73.6	22.5
Johnson	13	259	5.4	2.5	9	36	D	1.7	17	D	D	D
Kane	1 539	9 323	1 603.3	573.6	799	30 327	10 338.7	1 548.3	850	15 058	720.3	207.4
Kankakee	152	735	64.1	24.5	100	4 889	4 842.8	269.7	219	3 675	160.3	47.4
Kendall	199	D	D	D	79	2 298	719.2	108.9	163	2 865	139.4	38.1
Knox	64	307	27.7	11.0	38	D	321.4	36.3	124	1 715	76.3	21.3
Lake	3 052	26 120	3 483.8	2 220.4	846	35 174	12 046.0	1 950.0	1 498	24 702	1 399.2	405.5
LaSalle	166	1 098	120.8	43.7	143	4 665	2 345.6	246.9	318	4 213	188.6	52.3
Lawrence	13	45	4.8	1.2	11	541	D	20.7	22	D	D	D
Lee	38	256	32.0	13.0	36	2 775	1 193.6	117.0	82	722	38.9	8.8
Livingston	55	229	27.4	9.1	60	3 376	1 210.5	166.3	76	855	36.2	9.2
Logan	34	180	16.6	6.4	18	1 034	555.3	46.3	63	853	31.0	9.5
McDonough	44	258	20.2	8.5	20	1 538	420.9	68.9	96	1 599	71.6	17.9
McHenry	898	D	D	D	491	15 508	5 163.2	820.7	558	9 074	435.7	125.5
McLean	363	2 852	280.7	125.2	92	3 881	1 590.2	199.5	379	8 136	393.0	108.7
Macon	157	1 216	142.7	54.0	109	8 240	13 379.3	435.3	225	4 331	189.8	55.6
Macoupin	40	149	15.3	4.3	33	567	D	24.6	89	D	D	D
Madison	549	3 711	748.1	216.0	193	12 308	19 140.5	841.4	582	9 920	431.2	124.6
Marion	60	250	18.1	8.2	42	2 567	710.6	101.5	77	848	38.2	11.1
Marshall	12	24	2.2	0.7	12	888	D	37.1	30	281	7.4	2.4
Mason	9	23	2.5	0.7	12	80	24.6	3.5	41	D	D	D
Massac	9	D	D	D	10	522	D	29.5	28	D	D	D
Menard	15	79	7.2	2.5	5	24	D	1.1	21	231	5.5	1.5
Mercer	11	28	2.5	0.7	12	669	D	25.8	22	D	D	D
Monroe	81	596	89.9	40.9	23	264	D	11.3	63	1 134	43.0	12.7
Montgomery	35	198	17.2	6.6	23	679	313.6	29.4	63	875	37.3	10.8
Morgan	39	642	60.3	29.9	30	1 867	D	82.1	90	1 353	63.7	15.9
Moultrie	16	67	5.9	3.1	36	1 621	533.4	65.0	26	D	D	D
Ogle	68	210	16.0	7.5	62	3 356	1 530.9	146.0	110	1 063	52.9	12.0
Peoria	429	5 236	719.2	311.0	157	7 747	6 197.5	466.3	470	8 372	383.5	109.8
Perry	19	52	4.9	1.4	19	412	D	19.0	37	492	15.5	4.8
Piatt	28	96	8.5	3.7	13	183	D	7.0	31	D	D	D
Pike	17	73	8.0	2.2	19	143	62.4	6.2	37	350	14.0	3.6
Pope	5	D	D	D	NA	NA	NA	NA	5	9	0.6	0.1
Pulaski	1	D	D	D	NA	NA	NA	NA	6	D	D	D
Putnam	5	20	1.7	0.6	8	440	D	16.8	14	69	2.5	0.5
Randolph	36	227	24.2	8.3	28	2 902	609.3	77.6	64	806	29.6	8.5
Richland	25	135	50.1	9.9	28	438	143.5	17.2	36	D	D	D
Rock Island	291	2 847	667.4	163.6	153	8 245	6 845.4	451.8	342	5 592	344.4	75.6
St. Clair	511	5 662	870.2	364.7	158	4 922	2 779.9	241.6	561	10 416	589.3	155.9
Saline	39	160	16.3	5.5	24	348	D	11.5	47	776	37.2	8.3
Sangamon	527	4 381	549.2	224.9	109	2 834	D	139.1	523	9 447	439.2	129.0
Schuyler	7	23	2.4	0.7	6	95	D	2.4	12	D	D	D
Scott	3	9	1.1	0.3	4	163	D	6.8	11	56	2.7	0.6
Shelby	21	184	21.6	8.5	21	1 042	D	45.2	41	375	14.2	4.0
Stark	8	66	5.0	1.9	7	248	D	11.5	3	6	0.3	0.1
Stephenson	81	454	55.4	19.6	62	3 037	1 145.2	155.4	89	1 033	47.6	12.0
Tazewell	180	1 187	118.5	52.8	110	8 215	5 850.3	443.8	306	6 143	358.5	92.3
Union	19	80	6.7	2.9	12	164	D	5.4	30	D	D	D
Vermilion	84	428	46.7	16.6	96	5 168	2 353.2	256.1	143	2 161	86.0	25.4
Wabash	22	140	14.2	5.7	9	188	43.3	8.9	21	296	11.8	3.5
Warren	20	85	8.1	2.2	17	1 803	632.7	71.2	36	481	20.6	5.4
Washington	22	105	12.2	3.9	14	D	445.6	D	30	D	D	D
Wayne	21	58	4.2	1.4	16	607	D	24.6	22	D	D	D
White	19	71	6.0	1.8	12	304	D	10.6	26	D	D	D
Whiteside	81	341	36.1	12.6	88	3 955	1 453.2	198.3	124	1 589	66.5	18.6
Will	1 586	D	D	D	588	20 377	20 627.2	1 191.0	1 108	20 582	1 313.5	320.8
Williamson	121	636	65.4	21.4	42	1 748	793.0	78.5	148	2 724	123.7	35.4

1. Establishment subject to federal tax.

Table B. States and Counties — Health Care and Social Assistance, Other Services, Nonemployer Businesses, and Residential Construction

STATE County	Health care and social assistance, 2012 Number of establishments	Number of employees	Receipts (mil dol)	Annual payroll (mil dol)	Other services, 2012 Number of establishments	Number of employees	Receipts (mil dol)	Annual payroll (mil dol)	Nonemployer businesses, 2015 Number	Receipts (mil dol)	Value of residential construction authorized by building permits, 2016 New Construction ($1,000)	Number of housing units
	159	160	161	162	163	164	165	166	167	168	169	170
ILLINOIS—Cont'd												
Hardin	12	252	18.3	7.9	3	3	0.3	0.1	220	5.2	0	0
Henderson	8	153	7.3	3.4	7	D	D	D	393	16.2	1 210	13
Henry	88	1 640	123.4	49.0	97	380	31.0	8.7	2 781	93.0	7 007	35
Iroquois	66	1 588	105.2	44.6	48	148	19.7	3.2	1 980	70.8	4 050	24
Jackson	167	3 463	517.9	159.6	93	396	41.7	8.4	3 224	110.3	3 580	23
Jasper	14	143	6.6	2.2	19	61	5.6	1.0	813	27.4	0	0
Jefferson	146	3 518	391.1	145.4	82	416	43.0	11.2	2 275	87.7	1 111	10
Jersey	48	D	D	D	35	109	8.5	2.3	1 256	38.8	4 990	32
Jo Daviess	41	656	43.1	17.8	57	247	22.8	6.0	1 958	76.6	10 780	50
Johnson	19	209	12.6	4.7	10	D	D	D	765	23.7	0	0
Kane	1 153	21 559	2 406.9	968.7	821	5 885	596.9	169.7	33 140	1 449.5	278 326	1 596
Kankakee	311	7 349	753.9	294.5	180	956	100.3	25.1	6 193	214.8	18 964	86
Kendall	177	D	D	D	164	795	73.6	21.5	8 000	306.9	47 323	274
Knox	122	3 696	338.7	125.8	77	562	125.9	15.1	2 330	71.1	2 914	16
Lake	1 949	33 669	4 026.3	1 549.4	1 276	7 626	728.2	224.2	53 924	3 000.8	252 425	842
LaSalle	284	5 993	448.1	188.7	237	1 205	109.6	31.7	5 888	199.6	17 189	74
Lawrence	23	617	30.3	13.5	22	111	11.0	3.5	806	27.9	7 935	46
Lee	80	2 137	166.8	72.1	60	345	33.1	9.5	1 893	66.0	5 630	31
Livingston	74	2 090	144.5	62.4	66	334	29.3	8.3	1 900	60.1	2 151	17
Logan	58	1 330	111.3	41.5	54	206	15.9	4.2	1 405	46.5	965	7
McDonough	71	1 768	138.8	58.5	65	D	D	D	1 494	49.6	99	1
McHenry	718	D	D	D	634	3 300	260.3	77.6	22 100	957.8	88 620	466
McLean	371	8 547	969.7	368.4	259	2 311	212.2	74.8	9 529	395.8	42 597	331
Macon	291	8 193	886.2	332.1	176	1 170	239.1	37.3	5 713	183.7	12 547	56
Macoupin	91	1 920	115.8	48.0	85	318	25.5	6.3	2 574	93.1	10 755	53
Madison	677	13 914	1 194.9	486.2	456	2 888	272.1	79.6	14 373	550.9	119 687	487
Marion	113	3 009	249.3	94.0	73	268	21.7	5.6	2 150	71.5	806	4
Marshall	19	468	22.1	9.5	15	D	D	D	616	22.7	1 525	6
Mason	26	506	36.7	16.5	27	90	6.8	1.6	710	27.7	1 671	8
Massac	26	755	53.8	24.4	21	65	7.9	1.8	843	25.7	65	1
Menard	12	75	6.3	2.1	16	64	5.6	1.3	785	23.7	4 182	20
Mercer	24	344	23.5	9.3	16	64	5.9	1.6	903	29.5	2 080	12
Monroe	79	846	57.1	24.2	71	407	25.0	9.6	2 135	86.2	34 777	142
Montgomery	73	D	D	D	57	233	20.8	5.6	1 580	51.0	4 960	27
Morgan	121	D	D	D	64	260	18.4	4.8	1 949	69.5	1 043	6
Moultrie	32	735	36.2	16.8	17	D	D	D	1 032	35.9	4 203	49
Ogle	82	1 505	103.9	41.0	75	343	36.6	10.3	3 352	117.0	7 916	42
Peoria	516	22 518	2 665.0	1 057.0	304	4 714	449.2	206.3	9 715	367.7	28 961	105
Perry	45	890	63.7	25.9	46	161	11.9	3.1	1 059	28.8	10 027	48
Piatt	21	D	D	D	18	D	D	D	1 145	41.9	6 632	27
Pike	25	586	49.0	18.0	26	109	12.8	3.2	1 073	40.7	1 334	16
Pope	11	D	D	D	3	D	D	D	226	6.3	0	0
Pulaski	14	151	6.8	2.6	14	43	3.6	0.9	302	9.0	800	8
Putnam	4	18	1.5	0.6	4	D	D	D	368	15.6	2 308	16
Randolph	73	2 170	260.4	123.7	61	266	28.4	8.6	1 436	44.9	5 515	26
Richland	50	1 014	71.7	31.3	40	162	17.2	4.0	1 159	40.1	750	3
Rock Island	416	8 883	802.3	345.0	265	1 600	138.9	43.0	6 816	264.8	19 945	107
St. Clair	595	15 933	1 363.8	594.9	387	2 528	213.0	73.6	14 301	467.3	105 128	436
Saline	78	1 808	143.9	60.3	47	172	22.0	4.0	1 542	58.7	0	0
Sangamon	445	20 510	2 559.6	892.3	474	3 319	416.7	124.8	12 205	472.0	83 627	406
Schuyler	14	323	28.2	10.7	12	D	D	D	478	14.4	0	0
Scott	4	D	D	D	4	10	1.4	0.3	304	8.1	NA	NA
Shelby	33	674	42.3	18.7	32	93	11.9	2.5	1 311	42.4	7 175	35
Stark	8	167	8.9	3.7	4	D	D	D	335	14.0	453	4
Stephenson	104	2 545	329.3	92.9	95	642	46.2	16.0	2 866	96.7	1 910	10
Tazewell	246	5 435	388.8	155.2	242	1 270	113.7	37.2	6 471	239.7	42 580	168
Union	52	1 215	72.6	30.4	22	80	7.1	2.1	1 066	38.2	1 362	13
Vermilion	143	4 736	514.4	235.4	121	540	47.4	13.3	4 239	136.9	1 406	10
Wabash	26	832	62.0	22.6	22	94	6.5	1.5	799	27.7	0	0
Warren	37	694	48.6	19.5	31	115	11.8	2.2	892	31.3	1 774	10
Washington	26	616	39.9	15.4	27	61	7.0	1.3	938	34.1	4 629	22
Wayne	32	799	53.9	22.2	27	113	14.4	3.2	1 232	45.8	50	1
White	43	638	36.5	14.9	33	160	16.2	4.7	1 109	45.9	418	2
Whiteside	99	3 068	261.2	99.1	109	608	54.1	13.5	2 810	102.1	3 503	18
Will	1 406	24 364	2 467.6	967.5	1 053	6 884	681.5	195.1	46 617	2 042.4	394 802	1 782
Williamson	204	5 977	677.0	251.1	93	519	52.4	14.1	4 230	155.0	15 910	113

Table B. States and Counties — Government Employment and Payroll, and Local Government Finances

	Government employment and payroll, 2012									Local government finances, 2012				
				March payroll (percent of total)							General revenue			
													Taxes	
													Per capita[1] (dollars)	
STATE County	Full-time equivalent employees	March payroll (dollars)	Adminis- tration, judicial, and legal	Police and Corrections	Fire Protection	Highways and transpor- tation	Health and Welfare	Natural resources and utilities	Education and libraries	Total (mil dol)	Inter- govern- mental (mil dol)	Total (mil dol)	Total	Property
	171	172	173	174	175	176	177	178	179	180	181	182	183	184
ILLINOIS—Cont'd														
Hardin	285	791 768	2.8	3.0	0.0	56.6	0.9	4.7	31.7	16.6	13.4	1.6	384	331
Henderson	266	806 748	8.3	7.3	0.3	7.4	10.9	2.4	62.8	21.4	9.7	7.4	1 047	1 030
Henry	1 997	6 801 070	4.9	8.8	1.9	3.9	16.2	5.8	57.8	199.6	66.8	68.8	1 372	1 289
Iroquois	1 017	3 877 441	5.9	6.3	0.5	4.2	0.4	1.9	79.8	90.3	38.3	39.1	1 337	1 242
Jackson	2 101	6 263 626	8.2	10.9	3.5	4.0	8.7	8.4	55.9	187.5	83.7	70.9	1 181	879
Jasper	379	1 198 050	10.1	7.5	0.4	7.8	10.7	3.7	59.8	34.3	16.7	13.8	1 437	1 424
Jefferson	1 638	5 345 187	5.0	7.6	2.9	4.0	1.2	3.6	74.9	147.2	83.4	43.3	1 119	882
Jersey	837	3 076 248	4.5	7.9	0.3	2.8	30.8	3.6	48.9	78.3	24.9	21.1	926	828
Jo Daviess	997	3 300 597	8.1	8.4	0.4	5.4	17.9	2.0	56.6	94.9	21.9	52.5	2 329	2 191
Johnson	372	1 081 737	6.4	5.0	0.0	5.0	0.2	4.9	77.4	26.5	15.8	7.0	547	545
Kane	21 805	101 252 430	5.2	10.1	5.2	2.0	0.9	6.8	68.3	2 745.0	798.1	1 591.7	3 046	2 837
Kankakee	4 413	16 356 166	7.8	13.5	3.6	3.7	1.5	3.4	65.4	441.9	208.0	169.2	1 496	1 433
Kendall	3 451	14 665 867	5.1	10.4	5.3	1.3	0.8	4.9	71.6	446.4	125.8	268.8	2 276	2 192
Knox	2 362	8 240 583	5.2	9.0	3.0	3.3	7.4	6.1	64.9	191.6	87.1	68.2	1 306	1 155
Lake	27 930	134 406 176	5.8	8.4	4.0	2.3	3.7	6.6	68.5	3 687.1	912.8	2 300.4	3 276	3 089
LaSalle	4 146	16 025 437	6.1	10.7	2.6	3.3	2.5	3.9	69.6	433.1	147.6	217.8	1 928	1 756
Lawrence	525	1 443 702	5.9	7.2	0.3	7.5	2.8	3.7	71.9	44.1	29.2	8.7	523	515
Lee	1 249	4 093 940	7.1	9.2	4.8	4.5	2.0	3.9	68.0	116.7	37.8	58.8	1 677	1 531
Livingston	1 564	5 591 107	6.4	8.8	1.4	4.2	3.1	3.6	72.0	146.1	52.6	67.2	1 738	1 641
Logan	897	2 996 965	7.7	10.0	3.8	5.0	4.3	2.9	65.3	74.1	29.9	31.4	1 045	1 003
McDonough	1 625	5 796 187	4.2	7.7	1.7	2.8	51.0	3.4	28.6	163.5	47.6	32.0	983	944
McHenry	11 260	47 454 823	5.9	10.6	5.0	2.9	2.6	5.6	65.8	1 313.1	295.8	821.5	2 666	2 473
McLean	6 296	24 583 518	6.5	10.3	4.7	4.3	5.2	5.3	61.6	657.7	182.2	354.7	2 059	1 702
Macon	4 204	17 133 160	5.9	11.8	4.5	3.0	2.0	8.2	63.3	407.1	180.7	163.9	1 488	1 260
Macoupin	1 579	5 464 855	7.7	8.5	0.5	3.9	2.1	5.6	71.2	159.2	103.8	40.1	850	818
Madison	8 550	34 777 691	7.6	11.4	3.9	3.8	1.5	6.9	63.4	966.9	418.8	400.7	1 496	1 338
Marion	1 941	6 738 024	6.0	6.5	2.0	6.9	1.1	4.0	73.0	188.6	94.3	42.9	1 104	1 038
Marshall	389	1 147 988	11.1	7.9	0.1	5.9	0.0	3.3	70.7	32.3	9.0	19.1	1 547	1 484
Mason	923	2 905 218	5.6	6.6	1.1	4.1	31.2	2.1	49.0	70.8	24.6	21.1	1 473	1 402
Massac	642	2 312 058	4.9	5.8	3.7	5.1	27.2	5.6	47.5	66.0	26.3	12.5	822	786
Menard	629	1 816 714	5.1	6.6	0.0	3.4	18.6	6.4	58.9	48.9	20.5	18.4	1 447	1 400
Mercer	808	2 500 408	4.4	7.5	0.1	4.2	27.9	2.7	52.0	60.4	20.7	22.0	1 356	1 324
Monroe	1 183	4 219 452	6.0	6.8	0.1	3.0	9.8	5.0	68.2	102.0	27.3	50.1	1 503	1 423
Montgomery	1 039	3 506 922	6.9	10.8	2.5	5.7	5.0	6.3	61.4	82.3	39.4	28.5	963	919
Morgan	1 212	4 876 454	5.8	9.2	2.8	3.7	1.9	5.1	70.1	101.9	48.0	40.0	1 135	1 038
Moultrie	521	1 796 777	7.8	7.6	2.7	4.3	1.3	9.1	66.3	36.7	14.6	17.0	1 135	1 079
Ogle	2 397	8 623 161	5.6	8.6	3.0	3.7	0.9	6.5	71.3	242.2	66.1	126.2	2 388	2 325
Peoria	6 795	26 829 973	7.0	12.3	5.0	5.9	4.2	8.9	54.4	819.7	356.0	319.4	1 706	1 383
Perry	777	2 700 659	4.7	8.5	1.5	3.8	27.6	5.4	47.3	84.4	42.3	13.8	627	594
Piatt	763	2 418 221	6.8	10.0	0.5	5.3	14.9	3.4	57.7	66.5	26.6	26.9	1 631	1 599
Pike	558	1 854 503	4.9	7.2	0.0	8.0	4.7	8.8	66.1	46.6	23.4	15.2	932	910
Pope	138	448 003	20.0	12.1	0.0	2.4	0.2	11.1	54.2	9.3	5.8	2.3	545	536
Pulaski	327	899 884	7.1	8.9	0.0	20.1	0.0	3.3	59.6	25.7	17.3	2.4	395	366
Putnam	225	602 290	16.8	7.7	4.2	6.1	0.0	5.9	58.5	21.9	11.9	8.0	1 357	1 315
Randolph	1 307	4 546 917	4.9	6.9	0.2	2.7	38.8	4.6	41.3	133.8	44.5	27.5	833	774
Richland	975	3 144 076	4.3	4.3	0.6	2.4	0.2	3.1	84.3	57.1	27.3	13.0	807	742
Rock Island	5 596	23 551 782	5.9	9.4	3.6	6.1	4.6	7.6	61.4	620.9	245.3	250.9	1 701	1 489
St. Clair	9 810	39 541 919	4.8	9.2	1.9	2.6	2.2	3.8	73.7	1 194.0	627.0	382.0	1 421	1 216
Saline	1 108	4 428 993	4.7	6.7	0.9	2.6	0.3	6.0	77.8	90.8	50.3	23.2	930	837
Sangamon	8 380	36 468 884	5.0	9.4	3.8	4.6	1.2	19.7	56.0	774.9	316.2	329.5	1 654	1 429
Schuyler	476	1 475 450	5.3	4.7	0.2	4.4	42.6	3.1	38.9	44.3	11.9	8.0	1 069	1 046
Scott	279	678 856	8.7	3.5	0.5	4.1	18.9	5.6	57.3	16.8	8.0	4.6	873	829
Shelby	598	1 947 657	9.5	8.9	1.8	7.6	2.8	6.4	62.1	47.8	23.5	17.9	808	790
Stark	247	745 997	7.9	3.6	5.2	4.9	5.8	1.4	71.0	24.8	11.5	10.9	1 837	1 825
Stephenson	2 084	7 077 197	4.5	9.2	3.6	2.9	5.4	4.5	68.9	190.9	85.0	73.4	1 563	1 449
Tazewell	4 864	18 067 473	5.1	9.0	3.1	2.4	2.6	4.8	70.8	521.3	190.4	225.1	1 655	1 450
Union	758	2 771 148	9.5	6.1	0.8	5.1	0.0	5.2	72.8	60.0	30.9	17.9	1 015	992
Vermilion	3 642	12 242 579	7.0	7.8	2.7	3.5	3.6	4.2	67.9	289.5	151.8	91.4	1 132	940
Wabash	629	2 227 140	2.9	4.6	1.3	1.8	48.4	3.1	37.5	63.3	16.1	9.7	830	795
Warren	522	1 914 920	7.4	10.5	4.1	3.6	0.2	4.0	69.9	49.1	22.4	18.5	1 044	1 001
Washington	568	1 952 729	6.8	5.6	0.6	5.3	31.1	4.1	46.3	61.8	13.6	15.4	1 056	1 044
Wayne	680	1 956 742	7.1	7.6	1.1	3.6	2.2	8.9	66.5	46.0	28.5	12.0	724	652
White	705	2 274 585	7.3	7.6	0.6	4.7	1.6	8.1	69.3	49.9	30.9	10.9	747	707
Whiteside	3 387	13 850 341	3.2	4.6	1.2	1.9	52.6	3.0	32.7	404.5	88.0	74.4	1 287	1 222
Will	22 376	101 738 743	4.7	11.4	5.8	2.2	2.7	5.6	66.5	2 654.5	767.6	1 489.2	2 182	2 004
Williamson	2 123	8 108 041	5.1	8.0	3.0	3.7	0.5	5.2	72.9	224.1	117.2	75.8	1 137	974

1. Based on the resident population estimated as of July 1 of the year shown.

Table B. States and Counties — Local Government Finances, Government Employment, and Income Taxes

STATE County	Local government finances, 2012 (cont.)									Government employment, 2015			Individual income tax returns, 2014		
	Direct general expenditure							Debt outstanding							
			Percent of total for:												
	Total (mil dol)	Per capita¹ (dollars)	Education	Health and hospitals	Police protection	Public welfare	Highways	Total (mil dol)	Per capita¹ (dollars)	Federal civilian	Federal military	State and local	Number of returns	Mean adjusted gross income	Mean income tax
	185	186	187	188	189	190	191	192	193	194	195	196	197	198	199
ILLINOIS—Cont'd															
Hardin	9.4	2 219	53.6	4.3	2.9	0.3	6.9	3.9	917	D	D	203	1 570	49 500	5 876
Henderson	23.7	3 370	36.9	8.9	3.5	0.0	12.3	3.3	465	35	14	370	3 300	48 612	5 048
Henry	218.5	4 357	39.3	20.6	5.2	2.4	5.6	98.2	1 957	120	99	3 574	24 000	60 456	7 307
Iroquois	91.6	3 132	53.4	3.1	3.5	0.1	7.9	32.1	1 098	96	57	1 661	13 800	50 054	5 308
Jackson	186.2	3 100	49.6	4.1	7.0	4.9	4.5	96.1	1 600	160	125	11 954	23 460	47 549	5 355
Jasper	35.9	3 739	55.0	4.2	2.9	0.1	13.9	9.9	1 031	35	19	482	4 660	50 420	4 955
Jefferson	141.2	3 647	60.3	0.7	5.4	0.0	6.2	65.0	1 679	143	74	2 380	16 670	49 137	5 162
Jersey	88.3	3 885	32.7	37.7	3.8	0.1	7.5	73.1	3 212	44	44	1 128	10 190	52 890	5 423
Jo Daviess	84.9	3 767	44.0	15.8	6.1	0.0	11.0	34.5	1 528	65	44	1 349	12 690	49 288	5 586
Johnson	27.3	2 141	60.1	1.3	4.1	0.1	8.6	19.6	1 535	77	22	798	4 910	49 365	4 546
Kane	2 646.1	5 064	55.1	0.4	6.5	0.1	5.6	4 427.4	8 474	1 642	1 064	29 724	242 440	69 061	8 985
Kankakee	442.3	3 912	52.1	0.7	6.1	0.1	5.9	327.2	2 894	237	214	6 062	50 580	50 795	5 195
Kendall	434.1	3 676	60.8	0.5	5.2	0.9	3.7	902.1	7 638	116	250	5 776	55 570	69 188	7 750
Knox	198.6	3 801	51.6	1.5	5.0	4.2	8.6	156.9	3 002	168	96	3 306	23 220	49 917	5 468
Lake	3 519.2	5 012	56.6	2.1	5.9	0.6	4.2	3 079.5	4 386	5 417	12 736	37 029	341 720	104 583	19 151
LaSalle	473.9	4 195	57.8	1.3	5.1	1.1	6.6	284.6	2 520	356	220	6 101	54 090	53 161	6 011
Lawrence	51.2	3 083	63.6	1.4	3.9	0.1	9.0	34.7	2 091	48	28	808	6 370	48 743	5 152
Lee	113.4	3 238	58.0	1.7	5.2	0.1	7.1	71.5	2 040	85	65	1 883	16 260	53 372	5 944
Livingston	169.3	4 381	47.9	3.0	3.8	0.2	5.0	65.3	1 689	106	69	2 305	17 260	54 653	6 071
Logan	71.3	2 376	51.1	5.0	5.4	0.1	7.6	26.9	895	101	51	1 400	12 580	52 444	5 485
McDonough	169.8	5 218	27.4	39.5	3.7	3.4	9.6	21.4	657	95	60	5 461	12 390	49 120	5 236
McHenry	1 256.5	4 078	49.3	2.2	6.5	1.2	7.2	1 209.9	3 926	467	620	14 848	153 260	70 674	9 127
McLean	663.9	3 853	46.3	1.2	4.8	1.3	5.4	781.5	4 536	462	336	14 803	77 770	68 662	9 035
Macon	452.8	4 112	52.8	2.0	7.8	0.1	8.1	462.5	4 200	318	219	5 457	49 350	55 564	6 655
Macoupin	129.5	2 741	63.8	2.0	7.1	0.2	7.8	66.0	1 397	118	92	2 245	21 070	50 317	5 091
Madison	939.6	3 507	50.9	0.8	6.8	1.6	6.8	839.9	3 135	571	537	15 629	125 100	57 550	6 678
Marion	186.5	4 794	59.6	11.4	3.2	0.2	3.5	110.6	2 844	109	76	2 080	17 880	45 216	4 393
Marshall	33.3	2 658	45.3	2.0	5.5	0.1	16.2	9.4	759	36	24	481	5 980	53 881	5 950
Mason	72.0	5 027	41.2	33.1	3.0	0.0	4.5	27.4	1 914	60	27	1 071	6 430	49 493	5 300
Massac	63.9	4 197	33.1	34.0	4.6	0.0	6.8	35.3	2 315	47	29	927	6 420	44 593	4 114
Menard	46.5	3 652	52.7	4.5	4.3	13.7	7.4	27.0	2 121	31	25	708	6 110	61 450	6 833
Mercer	59.7	3 679	42.8	21.8	3.5	0.1	6.2	15.9	978	54	32	780	7 770	56 992	6 201
Monroe	99.7	2 990	44.6	3.1	5.8	10.1	10.9	136.3	4 085	68	68	1 452	16 830	72 133	9 272
Montgomery	84.4	2 851	51.5	3.4	7.1	0.1	10.4	52.7	1 779	98	54	1 495	12 600	51 289	5 298
Morgan	103.7	2 940	52.8	1.6	5.8	3.3	9.0	36.7	1 040	82	64	2 318	15 820	50 693	5 459
Moultrie	39.7	2 658	46.1	1.8	4.8	0.0	9.9	11.4	763	28	29	496	6 730	56 074	6 846
Ogle	280.5	5 307	64.6	0.8	3.1	0.0	5.5	269.6	5 101	113	104	2 842	25 370	55 367	5 983
Peoria	776.9	4 149	41.7	1.1	6.6	3.2	6.5	850.1	4 540	1 634	441	9 401	89 470	65 554	8 998
Perry	91.6	4 151	51.3	22.3	3.7	0.2	4.4	32.0	1 453	46	39	1 320	8 820	46 179	4 215
Piatt	65.0	3 940	47.2	2.6	3.6	12.4	9.9	36.4	2 205	35	33	978	8 030	63 204	7 520
Pike	48.7	2 986	53.6	6.0	6.0	0.3	9.7	27.7	1 701	57	31	881	7 010	43 861	4 422
Pope	9.6	2 241	48.1	0.0	2.7	0.0	16.4	0.3	64	70	D	197	1 600	43 411	3 826
Pulaski	23.9	3 981	59.8	1.8	6.4	0.3	6.2	12.7	2 118	66	11	823	2 360	39 464	3 039
Putnam	21.7	3 688	43.8	2.5	4.8	0.3	13.3	3.0	508	14	11	315	2 900	57 975	6 463
Randolph	140.7	4 269	35.0	36.0	4.5	2.8	6.9	54.6	1 657	88	58	2 480	13 770	50 717	5 188
Richland	75.7	4 677	78.3	0.4	3.6	0.1	5.2	28.2	1 746	49	32	969	7 550	46 790	4 509
Rock Island	636.7	4 318	45.3	1.1	6.6	3.0	5.2	418.1	2 835	4 947	737	7 689	71 090	52 101	5 812
St. Clair	1 159.8	4 314	54.3	1.3	5.1	0.1	4.2	908.3	3 378	6 059	4 870	13 047	121 790	53 940	5 967
Saline	95.1	3 814	54.7	1.0	5.6	0.6	5.5	54.8	2 197	99	48	1 861	10 380	49 255	5 182
Sangamon	823.4	4 132	52.9	1.4	7.6	0.2	4.4	2 513.3	12 612	1 759	440	18 669	99 980	63 384	8 289
Schuyler	47.2	6 325	29.5	48.7	2.2	0.1	10.2	10.5	1 403	24	13	674	3 170	48 173	4 729
Scott	17.4	3 281	46.2	2.2	3.3	13.9	8.8	6.2	1 174	15	10	325	2 430	50 603	5 007
Shelby	50.5	2 273	53.6	3.0	5.5	0.1	12.8	14.9	670	99	44	797	10 230	48 924	4 662
Stark	18.9	3 183	55.8	0.5	5.0	0.5	11.8	11.4	1 922	25	12	321	2 650	55 029	6 323
Stephenson	184.9	3 937	57.2	2.4	4.7	3.3	6.3	98.3	2 092	125	91	2 704	22 290	47 178	4 659
Tazewell	547.5	4 028	52.3	1.6	5.5	0.1	6.4	349.0	2 567	517	268	7 337	64 450	61 325	7 225
Union	60.8	3 445	72.9	2.7	4.1	0.0	5.3	53.7	3 042	60	34	1 151	7 770	46 699	4 452
Vermilion	308.3	3 819	56.4	0.7	6.4	3.5	6.3	102.1	1 265	1 510	155	4 250	34 250	45 174	4 421
Wabash	60.5	5 156	29.5	47.7	4.0	0.5	5.0	14.7	1 254	24	23	1 054	5 320	56 034	6 597
Warren	53.0	2 987	53.6	0.4	5.3	0.0	6.7	45.8	2 584	66	34	842	8 010	48 317	4 928
Washington	72.8	4 985	42.5	34.2	2.5	0.1	6.1	55.0	3 766	49	28	827	7 220	54 959	6 071
Wayne	47.3	2 854	59.1	1.9	4.8	0.1	9.4	21.3	1 285	54	33	927	7 350	48 260	4 511
White	56.9	3 908	63.4	1.7	4.0	0.1	9.2	23.5	1 610	45	28	806	6 420	55 413	6 322
Whiteside	392.0	6 777	27.5	52.5	2.6	0.2	2.3	129.8	2 244	153	114	4 664	27 940	50 580	5 369
Will	2 568.4	3 763	52.2	1.6	6.9	0.8	5.1	3 781.8	5 541	958	1 390	33 754	326 950	69 982	8 898
Williamson	279.8	4 196	65.4	0.0	3.9	0.1	4.9	229.8	3 447	1 713	133	4 199	29 930	51 419	5 655

1. Based on the resident population estimated as of July 1 of the year shown.

Table B. States and Counties — **Land Area and Population**

STATE/ County code	CBSA code[1]	County type[2]	STATE County	Land area,[3] (sq mi) 2016	Total persons 2016	Rank	Per square mile	White	Black	American Indian, Alaska Native	Asian and Pacific Islander	Percent Hispanic or Latino[4]	Under 5 years	5 to 17 years	18 to 24 years	25 to 34 years	35 to 44 years	45 to 54 years
				1	2	3	4	5	6	7	8	9	10	11	12	13	14	15
			ILLINOIS—Cont'd															
17 201	40420	2	Winnebago	513.4	285 873	241	556.8	71.9	13.9	0.6	3.4	12.5	6.2	17.5	8.4	12.5	11.9	13.5
17 203	37900	2	Woodford	527.8	39 140	1 202	74.2	96.6	1.2	0.5	1.1	1.8	5.9	18.5	8.5	10.8	11.9	13.1
18 000	...	0	INDIANA	35 826.6	6 633 053	X	185.1	81.3	10.4	0.7	2.7	6.8	6.4	17.4	10.0	13.0	12.3	13.1
18 001	19540	6	Adams	339.0	35 232	1 297	103.9	94.5	0.8	0.5	0.5	4.5	9.5	21.9	8.6	11.3	10.6	11.5
18 003	23060	2	Allen	657.3	370 404	187	563.5	76.8	13.4	0.8	4.5	7.3	7.1	18.9	9.2	13.6	12.3	12.6
18 005	18020	3	Bartholomew	406.9	81 402	691	200.1	84.4	2.9	0.6	7.1	6.5	6.7	17.2	8.3	14.4	12.6	12.9
18 007	29200	3	Benton	406.4	8 650	2 535	21.3	93.4	1.4	0.5	0.4	5.4	6.7	18.8	7.9	11.1	11.0	13.6
18 009	...	6	Blackford	165.1	12 149	2 283	73.6	96.9	1.4	0.9	0.8	1.6	6.0	16.1	7.6	10.8	10.8	13.2
18 011	26900	1	Boone	422.9	64 653	818	152.9	92.8	2.3	0.6	3.1	2.8	6.9	19.8	7.7	11.8	13.6	14.7
18 013	26900	1	Brown	312.0	14 912	2 105	47.8	97.0	0.9	1.0	0.7	1.7	3.9	14.7	6.9	9.0	10.4	14.9
18 015	29200	3	Carroll	372.2	19 970	1 830	53.7	95.1	1.0	0.6	0.3	4.0	5.7	17.1	7.5	10.8	12.0	13.5
18 017	30900	4	Cass	412.2	37 946	1 225	92.1	81.5	2.1	0.6	1.9	15.0	6.4	17.2	8.5	11.3	12.3	13.6
18 019	31140	1	Clark	372.8	116 031	530	311.2	85.9	8.9	0.7	1.5	5.3	6.4	16.5	7.8	13.8	13.6	13.7
18 021	45460	3	Clay	357.6	26 309	1 549	73.6	97.4	1.1	0.7	0.5	1.4	6.0	16.7	7.9	11.8	12.3	13.3
18 023	23140	6	Clinton	405.1	32 457	1 371	80.1	83.5	0.9	0.5	0.4	15.4	6.9	19.2	7.9	11.9	11.7	12.7
18 025	...	8	Crawford	305.6	10 539	2 386	34.5	97.5	0.9	1.0	0.5	1.4	5.6	16.6	7.2	10.6	12.1	13.8
18 027	47780	7	Daviess	429.5	32 969	1 355	76.8	92.8	2.2	0.5	0.6	4.8	8.2	21.1	8.5	12.5	10.9	11.9
18 029	17140	1	Dearborn	305.0	49 331	993	161.7	97.3	1.1	0.6	0.7	1.3	5.3	17.7	8.0	10.8	12.2	14.8
18 031	24700	6	Decatur	372.6	26 598	1 542	71.4	96.1	0.8	0.5	1.5	2.0	6.4	18.3	8.1	12.1	12.1	13.3
18 033	12140	4	DeKalb	362.8	42 746	1 116	117.8	96.0	0.9	0.5	0.8	2.8	6.3	18.4	8.3	11.9	12.1	13.8
18 035	34620	3	Delaware	392.1	115 603	531	294.8	89.0	8.3	0.7	1.9	2.3	5.2	13.5	19.6	11.3	10.1	11.7
18 037	27540	5	Dubois	427.3	42 552	1 118	99.6	91.4	0.8	0.4	0.7	7.3	6.6	17.3	8.4	11.0	11.6	14.0
18 039	21140	2	Elkhart	463.2	203 781	322	439.9	77.4	7.0	0.7	1.5	15.5	7.6	20.3	8.9	12.7	12.2	12.6
18 041	18220	6	Fayette	215.0	23 331	1 663	108.5	96.9	2.1	0.6	0.6	1.0	5.2	17.0	7.7	10.2	12.5	13.7
18 043	31140	1	Floyd	148.0	76 990	719	520.2	90.1	6.6	0.7	1.6	3.1	5.9	16.9	8.4	12.5	12.3	14.1
18 045	...	6	Fountain	395.7	16 486	2 008	41.7	96.4	0.8	0.8	0.6	2.5	5.6	16.6	8.0	10.9	10.9	14.1
18 047	...	6	Franklin	384.4	22 715	1 693	59.1	97.7	0.6	0.5	0.9	1.0	5.7	18.2	8.0	10.1	12.0	14.2
18 049	...	7	Fulton	368.4	20 139	1 823	54.7	93.1	1.3	0.8	0.8	5.2	6.4	17.7	7.4	11.1	11.9	12.6
18 051	...	6	Gibson	487.5	33 703	1 335	69.1	95.7	3.1	0.6	0.8	1.5	6.4	17.1	8.3	11.8	11.7	13.5
18 053	31980	4	Grant	414.1	66 937	790	161.6	87.4	8.6	0.8	1.3	4.2	5.5	15.3	13.1	10.6	10.5	12.7
18 055	...	6	Greene	542.5	32 211	1 376	59.4	97.7	0.6	0.8	0.6	1.3	5.4	16.6	7.6	11.0	11.8	14.5
18 057	26900	1	Hamilton	394.3	316 373	217	802.4	85.9	4.8	0.4	6.9	3.9	6.8	21.0	7.5	11.9	15.1	14.9
18 059	26900	1	Hancock	306.0	73 717	743	240.9	94.1	3.1	0.6	1.3	2.3	5.6	17.9	7.9	11.8	12.9	14.8
18 061	31140	1	Harrison	484.5	39 826	1 181	82.2	96.9	1.0	0.7	0.8	1.8	5.9	16.9	7.2	11.8	12.3	14.5
18 063	26900	1	Hendricks	406.9	160 610	402	394.7	87.0	7.3	0.5	3.2	3.8	6.1	19.5	7.8	12.6	14.4	14.3
18 065	35220	4	Henry	391.9	48 521	1 012	123.8	95.1	3.2	0.6	0.7	1.6	5.1	15.6	8.0	11.9	12.5	14.3
18 067	29020	3	Howard	293.0	82 568	683	281.8	88.0	8.8	0.9	1.7	3.3	6.1	16.6	8.1	11.7	11.5	13.2
18 069	26540	6	Huntington	382.6	36 400	1 266	95.1	96.1	1.1	0.8	0.9	2.2	5.7	16.2	9.9	11.9	11.8	13.3
18 071	42980	4	Jackson	509.3	44 013	1 092	86.4	90.1	1.5	0.7	2.4	6.4	6.8	17.7	7.8	12.4	13.0	13.5
18 073	16980	1	Jasper	559.6	33 433	1 344	59.7	92.4	1.2	0.6	0.7	6.1	5.9	17.9	9.7	11.0	12.4	12.9
18 075	...	6	Jay	383.9	21 046	1 772	54.8	95.8	0.8	0.6	0.7	3.0	7.4	18.8	8.3	10.9	11.2	13.5
18 077	31500	6	Jefferson	360.6	32 418	1 373	89.9	94.4	2.7	0.7	1.2	2.6	5.6	15.4	10.1	11.7	12.1	13.7
18 079	35860	6	Jennings	376.6	27 758	1 500	73.7	96.5	1.2	0.7	0.4	2.3	6.4	17.2	8.7	11.4	12.1	15.0
18 081	26900	1	Johnson	320.4	151 982	431	474.4	91.5	2.7	0.6	3.4	3.5	6.4	18.5	8.6	13.1	13.5	13.5
18 083	47180	5	Knox	516.0	37 744	1 228	73.1	90.3	3.8	0.6	1.2	1.9	6.1	15.2	13.8	11.5	10.5	12.1
18 085	47700	4	Kosciusko	531.4	79 092	706	148.8	89.6	1.5	0.6	1.6	7.9	6.7	17.7	9.3	12.6	11.4	13.0
18 087	...	6	LaGrange	379.6	39 110	1 204	103.0	94.8	0.7	0.5	0.8	4.0	9.1	24.0	8.9	12.0	11.1	10.9
18 089	16980	1	Lake	498.9	485 846	143	973.8	55.7	24.7	0.6	1.9	18.7	6.2	17.8	8.9	12.2	12.5	13.1
18 091	33140	3	LaPorte	598.3	110 015	549	183.9	81.5	12.4	0.7	1.0	6.5	6.0	15.8	8.5	13.0	12.2	13.6
18 093	13260	6	Lawrence	449.2	45 518	1 065	101.3	96.8	0.8	0.9	1.0	1.6	5.4	16.6	7.5	11.2	11.8	13.9
18 095	26900	1	Madison	451.9	129 296	488	286.1	86.8	9.4	0.6	0.9	4.0	5.6	16.2	8.6	12.6	12.4	13.6
18 097	26900	1	Marion	396.4	941 229	52	2 374.4	58.5	29.5	0.8	3.7	10.2	7.4	17.5	9.5	16.7	12.7	12.3
18 099	38500	6	Marshall	443.6	46 556	1 039	105.0	88.9	1.1	0.6	0.9	9.7	6.2	18.9	8.5	11.0	11.6	13.2
18 101	...	7	Martin	335.8	10 171	2 420	30.3	98.0	0.8	0.7	0.6	1.0	6.7	16.0	7.9	10.9	11.7	13.4
18 103	37940	6	Miami	373.8	35 883	1 276	96.0	90.8	5.7	1.5	0.8	3.1	5.3	16.5	8.4	12.7	13.3	14.1
18 105	14020	3	Monroe	394.5	145 496	444	368.8	86.0	4.4	0.7	7.9	3.4	4.5	11.4	26.9	15.0	10.2	9.8
18 107	18820	6	Montgomery	504.6	38 074	1 224	75.5	93.4	1.5	0.7	1.0	4.7	6.1	16.8	9.7	11.5	11.2	13.7
18 109	26900	1	Morgan	404.0	69 698	770	172.5	97.2	0.8	0.7	0.8	1.5	5.4	17.6	7.9	11.1	11.9	15.0
18 111	16980	1	Newton	401.8	13 924	2 170	34.7	92.2	1.0	0.8	0.6	6.3	5.0	16.5	7.6	11.1	11.8	14.2
18 113	28340	6	Noble	410.8	47 638	1 024	116.0	88.4	1.0	0.6	0.8	10.3	6.5	18.6	8.5	11.7	12.2	13.5
18 115	17140	1	Ohio	86.1	5 932	2 759	68.9	97.5	1.0	0.7	0.6	1.3	4.6	14.3	6.3	10.8	11.4	14.7
18 117	...	6	Orange	398.4	19 335	1 856	48.5	96.4	1.6	0.9	0.7	1.6	5.8	17.1	7.8	10.8	11.6	13.7
18 119	14020	3	Owen	385.3	20 840	1 781	54.1	97.5	0.9	0.9	0.7	1.2	5.4	16.3	7.3	10.7	11.3	14.7
18 121	...	6	Parke	444.7	16 800	1 993	37.8	95.5	2.9	0.6	0.3	1.5	5.8	15.8	7.7	12.9	11.4	13.7
18 123	...	6	Perry	381.7	18 966	1 874	49.7	95.3	2.9	0.6	0.7	1.4	5.1	15.7	8.0	12.8	12.5	13.3

1. CBSA = Core Based Statistical Area. See Appendix A for explanation. See Appendix B for list of metropolitan areas with component counties. 2. County type code from the Economic Research Service of USDA Rural-Urban Continuum Codes. See Appendix A for definition. 3. Dry land or land partially or temporarily covered by water. 4. May be of any race.

STATE County	55 to 64 years	65 to 74 years	75 years and over	Percent female	2000	2010	2000–2010	2010–2016	Births	Deaths	Net migration	Number	Persons per household	Family households	Female family householder[1]	One person
	Age (percent)				Total persons		Percent change		Components of change, 2010–2016			Households, 2011–2015		Percent		
	16	17	18	19	20	21	22	23	24	25	26	27	28	29	30	31
ILLINOIS—Cont'd																
Winnebago	13.7	9.5	7.0	51.1	278 418	295 264	6.1	-3.2	22 587	17 167	-14 629	113 912	2.51	65.7	14.3	29.2
Woodford	14.2	9.2	8.0	50.3	35 469	38 664	9.0	1.2	2 724	2 315	-3	14 350	2.65	74.1	8.4	23.6
INDIANA	13.0	8.7	6.3	50.7	6 080 485	6 484 136	6.6	2.3	521 319	372 748	4 511	2 501 937	2.55	66.2	12.3	28.0
Adams	11.8	7.9	6.9	50.3	33 625	34 387	2.3	2.5	4 218	1 852	-1 469	12 183	2.80	70.4	8.7	26.9
Allen	12.5	8.1	5.7	51.1	331 849	355 327	7.1	4.2	32 656	18 644	1 478	140 536	2.55	65.4	13.6	29.0
Bartholomew	12.4	8.9	6.5	49.9	71 435	76 786	7.5	6.0	6 543	4 495	2 668	30 518	2.57	67.5	10.2	27.2
Benton	14.2	9.3	7.4	50.2	9 421	8 836	-6.2	-2.1	661	522	-274	3 429	2.52	65.3	9.3	29.2
Blackford	14.5	11.8	9.1	50.7	14 048	12 766	-9.1	-4.8	868	960	-530	5 228	2.35	68.4	11.6	28.0
Boone	12.6	7.7	5.4	50.4	46 107	56 638	22.8	14.2	4 674	3 009	6 211	22 924	2.61	73.9	9.9	22.2
Brown	17.9	14.8	7.6	50.4	14 957	15 245	1.9	-2.2	689	928	-80	6 095	2.44	68.8	9.9	25.2
Carroll	15.0	10.7	7.8	50.1	20 165	20 159	0.0	-0.9	1 361	1 099	-388	7 793	2.55	69.1	7.3	26.3
Cass	13.7	9.3	7.6	49.8	40 930	38 966	-4.8	-2.6	3 120	2 424	-1 681	14 555	2.57	67.1	9.7	29.1
Clark	13.4	9.2	5.8	51.2	96 472	110 234	14.3	5.3	9 129	6 869	3 505	42 974	2.59	65.6	12.6	28.6
Clay	14.4	10.0	7.6	50.7	26 556	26 887	1.2	-2.1	1 937	1 835	-707	10 345	2.54	72.2	10.6	23.8
Clinton	13.3	8.7	7.7	50.4	33 866	33 219	-1.9	-2.3	2 780	2 157	-1 376	11 643	2.76	70.0	10.8	25.2
Crawford	16.0	11.3	6.8	49.4	10 743	10 713	-0.3	-1.6	741	710	-199	4 101	2.56	68.0	12.5	27.6
Daviess	12.0	8.3	6.5	49.9	29 820	31 654	6.2	4.2	3 324	2 084	122	11 452	2.78	72.3	8.6	25.4
Dearborn	15.1	9.8	6.4	50.2	46 109	50 047	8.5	-1.4	3 229	2 735	-1 185	18 634	2.63	71.7	8.7	23.9
Decatur	13.7	8.8	7.2	50.3	24 555	25 740	4.8	3.3	2 062	1 603	423	10 074	2.57	69.9	10.9	25.6
DeKalb	13.7	9.2	6.3	50.2	40 285	42 223	4.8	1.2	3 338	2 457	-348	16 247	2.58	69.1	11.7	27.0
Delaware	12.0	9.2	7.3	51.7	118 769	117 671	-0.9	-1.8	7 785	7 496	-2 218	45 761	2.40	60.3	12.6	28.8
Dubois	14.4	9.1	7.6	50.2	39 674	41 889	5.6	1.6	3 371	2 474	-293	16 190	2.55	70.7	7.9	25.8
Elkhart	11.8	7.9	6.0	50.5	182 791	197 561	8.1	3.1	19 060	10 009	-2 626	70 439	2.80	71.8	12.9	23.2
Fayette	14.3	11.1	8.3	50.5	25 588	24 302	-5.0	-4.0	1 522	1 906	-543	9 336	2.50	68.1	13.2	26.2
Floyd	14.3	9.3	6.2	51.5	70 823	74 578	5.3	3.2	5 594	4 558	1 339	29 088	2.57	67.9	13.3	27.4
Fountain	13.9	10.7	9.2	50.1	17 954	17 238	-4.0	-4.4	1 172	1 207	-689	6 951	2.40	67.4	9.7	26.8
Franklin	14.9	9.4	7.0	49.8	22 151	23 087	4.2	-1.6	1 549	1 305	-580	8 848	2.57	76.7	7.6	18.9
Fulton	14.4	10.5	7.9	50.3	20 511	20 836	1.6	-3.3	1 622	1 465	-780	7 963	2.55	67.5	7.2	28.9
Gibson	14.2	9.4	7.5	50.2	32 500	33 503	3.1	0.6	2 642	2 243	-156	13 102	2.51	69.5	9.8	25.3
Grant	13.9	10.3	8.2	52.2	73 403	70 063	-4.6	-4.5	4 760	5 040	-2 747	26 477	2.39	65.3	13.8	29.6
Greene	14.4	10.9	7.9	49.9	33 157	33 164	0.0	-2.9	2 150	2 401	-668	12 798	2.54	68.1	9.0	28.6
Hamilton	11.4	7.0	4.4	51.2	182 740	274 569	50.3	15.2	24 029	9 184	26 220	108 253	2.73	74.0	8.3	21.7
Hancock	13.5	9.5	6.2	50.8	55 391	70 045	26.5	5.2	4 726	3 734	2 701	26 340	2.68	72.5	10.2	23.2
Harrison	14.6	10.4	6.5	49.9	34 325	39 364	14.7	1.2	2 648	2 334	168	14 604	2.67	69.9	10.2	25.1
Hendricks	12.3	7.9	5.2	50.1	104 093	145 412	39.7	10.5	10 958	6 383	10 241	54 652	2.76	75.0	9.9	21.5
Henry	13.9	10.6	8.0	48.0	48 508	49 462	2.0	-1.9	2 983	3 526	-445	18 010	2.54	66.9	11.1	28.5
Howard	13.9	10.7	8.1	51.5	84 964	82 752	-2.6	-0.2	6 203	5 777	-575	34 413	2.37	64.7	11.6	30.6
Huntington	14.7	9.0	7.6	50.8	38 075	37 124	-2.5	-2.0	2 634	2 517	-879	14 480	2.44	67.6	9.1	25.8
Jackson	13.0	9.0	6.8	50.1	41 335	42 380	2.5	3.9	3 664	2 807	777	16 614	2.57	70.4	10.3	25.1
Jasper	13.8	9.7	6.8	50.2	30 043	33 478	11.4	-0.1	2 400	2 006	-396	11 996	2.71	74.4	9.0	21.7
Jay	13.2	9.6	7.2	50.5	21 806	21 253	-2.5	-1.0	1 963	1 439	-694	8 117	2.58	67.3	10.0	27.8
Jefferson	14.3	10.3	6.8	51.8	31 705	32 428	2.3	0.0	2 286	2 294	29	12 694	2.37	69.3	13.5	26.6
Jennings	13.6	9.7	5.8	49.7	27 554	28 525	3.5	-2.7	2 185	1 770	-1 135	10 607	2.62	68.1	11.3	26.0
Johnson	12.0	8.4	6.0	50.7	115 209	139 866	21.4	8.7	11 425	7 637	8 082	53 270	2.69	73.2	10.8	21.5
Knox	13.7	9.4	7.6	49.4	39 256	38 440	-2.1	-1.8	2 982	2 745	-856	14 779	2.40	63.3	10.6	31.7
Kosciusko	13.5	9.3	6.5	50.4	74 057	77 356	4.5	2.2	6 491	4 276	-300	29 586	2.58	71.6	8.5	23.6
LaGrange	10.8	7.9	5.3	49.6	34 909	37 130	6.4	5.3	4 592	1 613	-955	11 719	3.22	79.1	7.9	18.0
Lake	13.8	8.8	6.6	51.6	484 564	496 050	2.4	-2.1	37 924	29 445	-17 984	183 314	2.65	67.2	17.1	28.1
LaPorte	14.2	9.9	6.7	48.5	110 106	111 467	1.2	-1.3	8 207	7 209	-2 294	43 004	2.38	65.4	12.8	28.4
Lawrence	14.5	10.1	7.9	50.4	45 922	46 129	0.5	-1.3	2 985	3 425	-118	18 494	2.44	70.3	11.2	25.4
Madison	13.4	10.1	7.4	50.2	133 358	131 636	-1.3	-1.8	9 301	9 206	-2 210	51 274	2.41	65.1	13.2	30.1
Marion	12.1	6.9	4.9	51.8	860 454	903 389	5.0	4.2	90 491	48 303	-2 877	363 558	2.50	57.7	16.5	34.9
Marshall	13.6	9.3	7.6	50.2	45 128	47 047	4.3	-1.0	3 588	2 843	-1 223	17 324	2.67	69.1	9.5	26.8
Martin	15.5	10.5	7.4	49.4	10 369	10 378	0.1	-2.0	815	650	-345	4 201	2.42	62.2	9.9	33.1
Miami	13.4	9.6	6.7	46.5	36 082	36 903	2.3	-2.8	2 326	2 186	-1 105	13 164	2.60	69.2	10.9	27.0
Monroe	10.4	6.9	5.0	50.2	120 563	137 959	14.4	5.5	8 123	5 444	4 954	54 165	2.36	51.3	9.4	33.1
Montgomery	13.8	9.4	7.8	49.6	37 629	38 126	1.3	-0.1	2 839	2 401	-441	14 637	2.52	67.8	9.2	26.3
Morgan	14.8	10.0	6.2	50.5	66 689	68 937	3.4	1.1	4 730	4 019	76	25 609	2.68	73.2	11.1	21.1
Newton	15.4	10.9	7.5	49.1	14 566	14 244	-2.2	-2.2	842	968	-193	5 401	2.56	69.2	11.0	25.8
Noble	13.7	9.2	6.1	49.9	46 275	47 536	2.7	0.2	3 753	2 794	-897	18 101	2.58	72.4	10.9	24.7
Ohio	17.1	12.4	8.4	49.8	5 623	6 128	9.0	-3.2	327	390	-146	2 389	2.50	67.6	8.2	29.1
Orange	14.8	11.0	7.4	50.3	19 306	19 840	2.8	-2.5	1 396	1 324	-536	7 648	2.54	68.3	10.0	27.4
Owen	16.2	11.4	6.6	49.8	21 786	21 583	-0.9	-3.4	1 383	1 427	-711	8 553	2.46	70.0	10.6	25.4
Parke	14.7	10.9	7.1	52.6	17 241	17 354	0.7	-3.2	1 186	1 035	-676	5 995	2.58	69.9	8.6	24.7
Perry	14.6	10.3	7.6	47.0	18 899	19 338	2.3	-1.9	1 205	1 257	-314	7 282	2.42	69.2	9.2	26.3

1. No spouse present.

Table B. States and Counties — **Population, Vital Statistics, Health, and Crime**

STATE County	Persons in group quarters, 2016	Daytime population, 2011–2015 Number	Daytime population, 2011–2015 Employ-ment/resi-dence ratio	Births, 2016 Total	Births, 2016 Rate[1]	Deaths, 2016 Number	Deaths, 2016 Rate[1]	Persons under 65 with no health insurance, 2015 Number	Persons under 65 with no health insurance, 2015 Percent	Medicare, 2015 Total Beneficiaries	Medicare, 2015 Enrolled in Original Medicare	Medicare, 2015 Enrolled in Medicare Advantage	Serious crimes known to police,[2] 2014 Total Number	Serious crimes known to police,[2] 2014 Total Rate[3]
	32	33	34	35	36	37	38	39	40	41	42	43	44	45
ILLINOIS—Cont'd														
Winnebago....................	4 718	295 959	1.04	3 576	12.5	2 747	9.6	17 162	7.2	54 014	36 896	17 118	11 199	3 890
Woodford.......................	1 022	31 816	0.61	413	10.6	408	10.4	1 366	4.2	6 082	4 841	1 241	327	946
INDIANA.......................	187 052	6 515 413	0.98	83 267	12.6	60 909	9.2	621 372	11.3	1 132 898	841 591	291 307	198 875	3 015
Adams...........................	421	34 066	0.96	683	19.4	254	7.2	3 862	13.1	5 416	3 445	1 971	NA	NA
Allen.............................	6 112	376 281	1.08	5 259	14.2	3 089	8.3	37 602	12.0	58 386	31 742	26 644	10 470	2 868
Bartholomew................	1 147	89 392	1.26	1 064	13.1	711	8.7	6 974	10.2	15 485	12 455	3 030	2 664	3 316
Benton..........................	92	7 295	0.63	116	13.4	82	9.5	888	12.3	1 756	1 467	289	NA	NA
Blackford.......................	163	11 190	0.75	131	10.8	169	13.9	1 006	10.4	3 014	2 345	669	250	2 036
Boone...........................	574	54 266	0.79	827	12.8	480	7.4	4 070	7.4	8 452	6 230	2 222	NA	NA
Brown...........................	163	11 415	0.48	102	6.8	142	9.5	1 473	12.7	2 002	1 466	536	122	814
Carroll..........................	106	16 486	0.61	221	11.1	188	9.4	1 890	11.7	3 147	2 474	673	NA	NA
Cass.............................	1 043	37 047	0.92	502	13.2	413	10.9	4 568	14.7	7 164	5 593	1 571	1 044	2 722
Clark............................	1 327	106 132	0.87	1 472	12.7	1 142	9.8	10 404	10.7	21 200	16 211	4 989	4 415	3 886
Clay..............................	341	22 557	0.64	304	11.6	290	11.0	2 153	9.9	5 995	5 023	972	NA	NA
Clinton..........................	831	30 129	0.81	453	14.0	325	10.0	3 476	12.9	6 066	4 912	1 154	1 067	3 246
Crawford.......................	62	8 641	0.54	128	12.1	112	10.6	1 027	12.0	2 525	2 065	460	115	1 084
Daviess.........................	581	30 809	0.89	524	15.9	332	10.1	4 644	16.8	4 943	4 455	488	762	2 337
Dearborn.......................	530	41 284	0.65	507	10.3	444	9.0	3 515	8.5	9 213	6 911	2 302	NA	NA
Decatur.........................	377	28 466	1.18	334	12.6	271	10.2	2 169	9.8	4 961	3 754	1 207	NA	NA
DeKalb..........................	615	43 936	1.08	548	12.8	399	9.3	3 634	10.1	8 369	4 593	3 776	NA	NA
Delaware.......................	8 414	119 405	1.04	1 215	10.5	1 198	10.4	9 907	11.0	23 216	18 879	4 337	3 820	3 250
Dubois..........................	894	47 646	1.25	574	13.5	406	9.5	3 494	9.9	7 468	6 678	790	NA	NA
Elkhart..........................	3 797	225 034	1.27	3 128	15.3	1 622	8.0	27 967	16.2	31 610	22 074	9 536	5 051	2 507
Fayette.........................	392	21 770	0.78	246	10.5	287	12.3	2 287	12.2	5 761	4 790	971	NA	NA
Floyd............................	1 330	70 323	0.85	923	12.0	750	9.7	5 680	8.8	14 538	11 598	2 940	2 640	3 590
Fountain.......................	172	15 314	0.79	179	10.9	188	11.4	1 436	10.8	4 230	3 494	736	NA	NA
Franklin........................	187	17 256	0.48	248	10.9	200	8.8	2 082	10.9	3 472	2 400	1 072	134	630
Fulton...........................	224	18 507	0.77	275	13.7	206	10.2	2 277	13.8	4 080	2 444	1 636	NA	NA
Gibson..........................	738	38 317	1.30	427	12.7	389	11.5	2 376	8.6	6 474	4 763	1 711	NA	NA
Grant............................	4 930	70 653	1.06	735	11.0	814	12.2	5 412	10.6	15 416	11 960	3 456	1 967	2 852
Greene..........................	281	26 852	0.57	342	10.6	413	12.8	3 176	12.1	6 660	5 848	812	467	1 530
Hamilton.......................	1 634	272 462	0.84	3 839	12.1	1 667	5.3	17 689	6.4	32 529	23 183	9 346	NA	NA
Hancock........................	649	58 188	0.62	738	10.0	602	8.2	4 617	7.6	12 442	8 561	3 881	750	1 042
Harrison........................	461	32 557	0.63	451	11.3	348	8.7	3 176	9.7	7 577	6 084	1 493	446	1 139
Hendricks.....................	3 886	135 822	0.77	1 785	11.1	1 046	6.5	10 269	7.6	20 219	14 087	6 132	3 164	2 027
Henry............................	3 610	43 444	0.70	479	9.9	565	11.6	3 935	10.7	10 521	8 037	2 484	NA	NA
Howard.........................	1 280	87 620	1.14	987	12.0	942	11.4	6 451	9.7	19 261	16 361	2 900	2 466	3 017
Huntington....................	1 336	34 840	0.88	419	11.5	394	10.8	3 202	10.8	8 165	4 362	3 803	NA	NA
Jackson.........................	595	45 203	1.09	613	13.9	444	10.1	4 151	11.3	8 544	6 059	2 485	1 514	3 463
Jasper..........................	929	31 139	0.85	375	11.2	326	9.8	2 848	10.4	6 536	5 519	1 017	NA	NA
Jay...............................	243	20 496	0.92	336	16.0	227	10.8	1 968	11.3	4 308	3 102	1 206	263	1 373
Jefferson......................	1 952	31 707	0.95	390	12.0	349	10.8	2 656	10.6	7 389	6 366	1 023	NA	NA
Jennings.......................	298	24 229	0.68	354	12.8	303	10.9	2 519	10.8	5 004	3 815	1 189	470	1 666
Johnson........................	2 558	124 677	0.70	1 821	12.0	1 285	8.5	12 030	9.5	24 322	17 363	6 959	4 371	3 000
Knox.............................	2 564	39 044	1.06	486	12.9	406	10.8	3 146	10.8	8 263	7 439	824	NA	NA
Kosciusko.....................	1 803	78 251	1.01	1 078	13.6	694	8.8	8 238	12.6	12 873	7 326	5 547	1 157	1 480
LaGrange......................	325	37 291	0.95	699	17.9	257	6.6	8 734	26.0	5 245	3 337	1 908	218	570
Lake.............................	6 488	480 661	0.95	5 918	12.2	4 908	10.1	47 220	11.6	85 089	70 325	14 764	16 973	3 689
LaPorte........................	6 280	106 671	0.90	1 293	11.8	1 195	10.9	9 456	10.9	20 843	18 083	2 760	2 473	2 427
Lawrence......................	653	40 954	0.76	474	10.4	535	11.8	4 389	12.0	9 961	8 115	1 846	884	2 130
Madison........................	5 927	119 971	0.81	1 405	10.9	1 438	11.1	10 804	10.6	29 368	21 723	7 645	3 375	2 641
Marion..........................	17 294	1 051 765	1.29	14 433	15.3	8 015	8.5	111 205	13.7	135 781	95 507	40 274	54 433	6 133
Marshall.......................	671	45 440	0.93	565	12.1	471	10.1	5 260	13.6	8 318	5 117	3 201	NA	NA
Martin..........................	134	13 689	1.74	129	12.7	97	9.5	943	11.4	2 238	2 018	220	NA	NA
Miami...........................	3 288	31 698	0.69	375	10.5	359	10.0	3 185	11.9	7 047	5 651	1 396	627	1 741
Monroe.........................	15 076	150 873	1.12	1 305	9.0	894	6.1	13 956	12.3	19 059	15 320	3 739	4 166	2 916
Montgomery..................	1 174	37 326	0.95	446	11.7	385	10.1	4 002	13.0	7 991	5 757	2 234	1 111	2 906
Morgan.........................	592	54 710	0.54	754	10.8	656	9.4	5 756	9.9	12 874	9 564	3 310	NA	NA
Newton.........................	169	11 525	0.58	126	9.0	144	10.3	1 393	12.3	2 273	1 938	335	99	704
Noble............................	820	45 463	0.90	633	13.3	452	9.5	4 778	11.9	7 674	4 337	3 337	488	1 077
Ohio.............................	52	4 839	0.58	47	7.9	78	13.1	461	9.8	1 117	875	242	NA	NA
Orange..........................	258	19 076	0.92	211	10.9	211	10.9	1 804	11.4	4 162	3 355	807	NA	NA
Owen............................	197	17 602	0.61	208	10.0	238	11.4	2 075	12.2	3 863	2 975	888	NA	NA
Parke............................	1 467	14 496	0.60	183	10.9	173	10.3	1 585	12.9	3 073	2 547	526	64	372
Perry............................	1 359	18 655	0.91	180	9.5	176	9.3	1 375	9.5	3 763	3 342	421	NA	NA

1. Per 1,000 estimated resident population.   2. Data for serious crimes have not been adjusted for underreporting; this may affect comparability between geographic areas and over time.
3. Per 100,000 population estimated by the FBI.

Table B. States and Counties — **Crime, Education, Money Income, and Poverty**

STATE County	Serious crimes known to police, 2014 (cont.)[1] — Rate[2] Violent	Property	Education — School enrollment and attainment, 2011–2015 — Enrollment[3] Total	Percent private	Attainment[4] (percent) High school graduate or less	Bachelor's degree or more	Local government expenditures,[5] 2013–2014 Total current spending (mil dol)	Current spending per student (dollars)	Money income, 2011–2015 Per capita income[6] (dollars)	Median income (dollars)	Households Percent with income of less than $50,000	with income of $200,000 or more	Income and poverty, 2015 Median household income (dollars)	Percent below poverty level All persons	Children under 18 years	Children 5 to 17 years in families
	46	47	48	49	50	51	52	53	54	55	56	57	58	59	60	61
ILLINOIS—Cont'd																
Winnebago	764	3 127	72 755	19.9	46.1	21.9	571.6	12 294	25 198	48 225	51.5	2.7	50 024	14.7	22.5	19.8
Woodford	78	868	10 473	15.0	38.9	28.4	87.0	10 897	30 804	65 852	36.5	4.1	68 233	7.0	9.0	7.9
INDIANA	365	2 649	1 732 471	16.3	46.8	24.1	9 907.7	9 475	25 346	49 255	50.7	2.8	50 510	14.4	20.4	18.8
Adams	NA	NA	8 623	30.8	58.9	15.0	45.2	10 264	21 274	48 188	51.4	2.1	49 251	12.8	25.3	24.8
Allen	257	2 610	101 079	21.8	40.1	27.0	513.6	9 498	25 770	49 092	50.8	3.0	50 017	14.6	20.8	20.2
Bartholomew	110	3 206	19 397	15.3	44.0	29.4	115.0	9 146	27 987	55 050	45.4	3.4	55 580	11.9	15.5	15.1
Benton	NA	NA	2 011	12.2	56.2	16.9	19.1	10 083	22 526	47 046	53.3	0.5	50 754	11.1	18.2	16.7
Blackford	41	1 995	2 671	6.5	64.0	10.1	16.7	9 241	20 534	38 190	63.7	1.0	39 611	14.5	24.0	23.1
Boone	NA	NA	15 852	12.4	33.4	42.7	107.1	9 262	38 038	67 552	36.3	9.9	75 163	6.0	7.4	6.4
Brown	67	747	3 205	7.4	48.1	22.3	23.6	11 082	29 903	54 615	44.9	2.9	53 801	11.4	19.9	18.3
Carroll	NA	NA	4 745	13.9	53.3	17.0	23.1	8 787	25 365	52 005	47.5	2.0	52 550	9.4	13.7	12.0
Cass	70	2 651	9 423	8.9	57.9	14.2	68.0	10 289	22 125	42 290	57.1	1.9	45 575	13.1	20.0	18.0
Clark	393	3 492	26 913	15.7	46.8	20.1	151.8	8 880	25 470	51 699	48.2	1.9	51 614	10.4	16.2	15.3
Clay	NA	NA	6 221	8.5	57.6	15.1	39.9	9 145	21 856	47 602	52.8	1.2	48 947	12.9	20.4	18.7
Clinton	113	3 134	7 861	7.3	59.3	15.1	56.2	8 959	22 337	48 478	51.7	1.6	50 342	11.9	18.5	16.4
Crawford	236	849	2 315	5.7	67.3	9.7	15.8	10 023	18 835	38 695	63.5	0.0	41 331	18.7	28.5	25.3
Daviess	175	2 162	7 240	22.3	62.3	13.7	42.2	9 330	21 101	47 342	52.9	1.6	47 019	14.6	21.9	20.0
Dearborn	NA	NA	12 485	14.4	49.2	19.5	76.8	8 764	27 907	58 680	41.7	3.4	64 093	8.9	12.7	11.5
Decatur	NA	NA	6 297	13.2	56.7	16.2	40.8	9 204	23 346	49 799	50.2	1.4	51 625	13.0	18.6	16.7
DeKalb	NA	NA	10 763	15.4	52.5	17.0	91.3	12 539	24 016	48 341	51.5	2.0	52 382	10.5	14.9	13.0
Delaware	281	2 970	37 732	5.6	46.8	23.2	158.9	9 851	21 179	38 830	61.6	1.6	40 633	23.0	31.2	25.6
Dubois	NA	NA	10 284	8.9	54.0	18.7	69.0	9 371	25 972	53 513	45.7	2.1	57 336	7.6	9.0	8.4
Elkhart	357	2 149	51 244	14.5	56.1	18.1	340.2	9 409	21 817	47 913	52.1	1.9	50 117	14.0	19.4	17.0
Fayette	NA	NA	5 354	7.3	62.4	9.8	40.1	10 673	20 508	39 379	62.7	1.5	42 538	16.2	23.8	22.3
Floyd	126	3 464	19 142	16.0	42.9	25.8	110.1	9 303	28 116	54 914	45.5	3.6	57 367	11.3	17.5	15.5
Fountain	NA	NA	3 697	5.0	56.5	13.6	26.7	8 945	24 619	46 760	53.0	1.5	51 108	12.1	18.9	18.1
Franklin	33	597	5 612	16.3	55.7	19.3	43.1	8 694	24 032	51 748	47.9	1.8	53 263	9.9	13.7	12.3
Fulton	NA	NA	4 784	10.8	58.4	13.2	22.6	8 560	22 807	45 332	54.3	0.8	51 660	11.7	19.7	18.5
Gibson	NA	NA	8 049	15.6	50.5	15.1	47.4	9 445	24 682	48 303	52.2	2.1	53 483	11.0	14.6	13.5
Grant	218	2 635	18 626	32.9	55.2	17.3	110.4	9 956	20 440	40 294	61.0	1.1	39 984	18.0	26.9	25.7
Greene	36	1 494	7 018	9.5	55.6	13.7	50.9	9 775	22 767	45 397	53.9	1.1	47 952	14.7	21.6	19.6
Hamilton	NA	NA	86 979	17.3	19.8	55.9	503.0	8 832	41 316	86 222	26.4	11.6	91 844	4.7	5.2	4.7
Hancock	78	964	19 072	16.2	39.3	28.3	104.7	8 310	29 058	66 606	36.6	3.3	70 277	6.0	8.1	7.0
Harrison	77	1 063	8 708	14.6	54.1	16.0	55.5	9 223	24 460	52 128	47.8	2.0	53 719	11.2	15.3	14.0
Hendricks	210	1 818	41 131	14.8	35.2	33.4	229.2	8 145	30 364	70 163	33.3	4.1	73 478	5.5	6.7	6.0
Henry	NA	NA	11 379	9.0	57.0	15.6	73.0	9 585	21 286	41 855	58.6	1.5	47 954	14.7	20.6	19.2
Howard	225	2 792	20 185	10.8	48.3	18.9	129.9	9 199	24 297	44 226	54.9	1.8	47 390	16.9	24.8	20.7
Huntington	NA	NA	9 192	23.2	53.6	18.0	49.7	8 885	22 606	46 945	52.9	1.0	49 103	10.9	16.2	15.2
Jackson	208	3 255	10 167	17.4	60.6	15.0	61.1	9 051	22 421	47 000	52.8	0.9	45 504	12.1	16.8	16.1
Jasper	NA	NA	8 580	17.9	54.9	15.3	42.4	8 130	24 614	55 374	44.1	1.7	60 195	9.3	13.2	11.7
Jay	99	1 274	5 038	10.9	64.4	10.1	36.5	10 531	19 591	41 021	59.1	1.0	42 646	15.2	24.9	23.4
Jefferson	NA	NA	7 460	23.7	52.8	17.6	43.4	9 732	22 139	45 718	54.8	0.5	47 841	13.4	20.2	18.4
Jennings	298	1 368	6 862	13.8	63.6	10.4	47.2	10 039	21 434	44 736	54.9	1.3	46 047	13.1	21.1	19.2
Johnson	256	2 744	38 646	15.2	41.8	28.5	229.0	8 947	28 889	62 147	39.4	4.1	68 256	8.0	10.7	9.6
Knox	NA	NA	10 372	9.3	49.8	15.2	48.7	9 365	21 928	42 725	56.0	1.8	42 818	19.1	24.1	24.0
Kosciusko	133	1 347	18 684	16.5	52.3	20.7	134.1	9 713	26 011	52 821	46.4	3.1	54 147	10.0	13.8	13.0
LaGrange	97	473	8 630	29.9	70.1	9.8	57.6	9 803	20 413	49 964	50.1	2.5	56 662	8.6	13.6	13.1
Lake	447	3 241	129 061	15.3	48.2	20.4	834.8	9 864	24 756	50 135	49.9	2.5	50 613	16.6	26.5	26.0
LaPorte	143	2 283	26 322	14.2	52.6	17.2	179.0	9 931	23 499	46 872	52.5	2.3	47 401	15.7	24.7	23.8
Lawrence	275	1 855	10 172	13.9	55.6	13.8	66.8	9 702	23 404	45 875	54.0	1.6	46 890	13.9	21.0	19.3
Madison	181	2 460	29 907	19.3	51.9	17.5	170.8	8 954	22 236	44 195	56.2	1.3	45 065	16.7	25.2	23.0
Marion	1 226	4 907	245 834	18.9	43.4	28.3	1 534.7	10 067	24 330	42 168	57.1	2.5	41 407	20.6	31.0	28.9
Marshall	NA	NA	11 485	15.8	55.9	18.3	71.8	9 341	22 895	48 485	51.5	1.7	49 714	10.6	15.0	13.6
Martin	NA	NA	2 441	10.7	60.0	12.1	14.5	9 450	22 939	44 589	55.5	0.4	47 717	13.8	19.5	18.3
Miami	164	1 577	8 778	4.9	58.0	11.9	46.0	8 470	21 745	45 184	54.3	0.9	46 968	14.8	22.6	20.9
Monroe	281	2 636	60 494	7.9	30.0	45.0	130.3	9 326	24 266	42 404	56.4	3.5	45 341	23.5	18.2	17.1
Montgomery	837	2 069	9 117	16.8	55.8	16.0	59.9	10 012	22 911	48 213	51.7	1.7	49 425	12.3	18.7	17.9
Morgan	NA	NA	16 892	13.3	53.3	15.7	100.1	8 619	26 175	55 432	44.4	1.9	58 376	11.4	16.2	14.4
Newton	64	640	3 184	8.4	63.5	9.7	22.9	9 830	23 154	46 895	51.6	1.9	48 316	12.2	17.6	15.8
Noble	97	980	11 696	15.4	56.8	14.3	67.6	8 974	23 477	49 331	50.7	1.6	51 876	9.8	14.2	12.9
Ohio	NA	NA	1 195	11.1	62.0	12.9	8.1	9 656	23 848	48 780	50.9	0.0	53 177	10.2	15.6	13.9
Orange	NA	NA	4 342	9.2	63.5	11.4	37.4	11 190	19 660	39 812	61.6	0.6	40 918	15.7	24.3	23.6
Owen	NA	NA	4 543	17.0	60.4	10.5	25.9	9 490	21 842	43 948	55.9	0.9	43 731	15.8	24.8	22.6
Parke	64	308	3 677	6.4	55.1	13.5	22.7	10 288	20 592	40 781	58.6	1.0	43 637	17.2	25.0	23.5
Perry	NA	NA	3 809	5.4	65.5	11.5	28.4	9 687	20 964	47 470	52.3	1.1	47 192	13.2	18.0	16.1

1. Data for serious crimes have not been adjusted for underreporting; this may affect comparability between geographic areas and over time.   2. Per 100,000 population estimated by the FBI.
3. All persons 3 years old and over enrolled in nursery school through college.   4. Persons 25 years old and over.   5. Elementary and secondary education expenditures.
6. Based on population estimated by the American Community Survey, 2011–2015.

STATE County	Personal income, 2015										Earnings, 2015		
	Total (mil dol)	Percent change, 2014–2015	Per capita[1] Dollars	Per capita[1] Rank	Wages and salaries (mil dol)	Supplements to wages and salaries; employer contributions (mil dol) Pension and insurance	Supplements... Government social insurance	Proprietors' income (mil dol)	Dividends, interest, and rent (mil dol)	Personal transfer receipts (mil dol)	Total (mil dol)	Contributions for government social insurance (mil dol) From employee and self-employed	From employer
	62	63	64	65	66	67	68	69	70	71	72	73	74
ILLINOIS—Cont'd													
Winnebago	11 298	3.8	39 357	1 451	6 187	1 079	447	501	1 731	2 455	8 213	474	447
Woodford	1 848	0.7	47 111	626	467	88	33	112	347	271	700	41	33
INDIANA	277 629	4.0	41 984	X	138 591	22 301	10 381	26 078	42 212	54 532	197 351	11 917	10 381
Adams	1 220	0.9	34 885	2 211	518	96	40	216	172	240	870	50	40
Allen	15 301	5.2	41 528	1 223	8 617	1 316	656	1 280	2 538	2 928	11 869	723	656
Bartholomew	3 699	3.8	45 575	751	2 718	408	201	214	597	624	3 541	212	201
Benton	307	-7.3	35 402	891	94	18	7	23	52	70	142	9	7
Blackford	436	2.0	35 447	1 967	122	23	9	18	65	136	172	13	9
Boone	3 966	4.4	62 603	98	1 191	175	91	277	702	384	1 734	103	91
Brown	620	4.4	41 406	1 236	89	19	7	53	104	144	168	13	7
Carroll	768	-1.5	38 695	1 233	195	35	14	69	118	156	313	20	14
Cass	1 326	0.2	34 916	2 071	551	105	41	63	191	380	761	50	41
Clark	4 699	4.3	40 732	1 508	2 187	374	169	406	569	989	3 136	192	169
Clay	909	0.9	34 300	2 057	278	56	22	48	128	248	404	28	22
Clinton	1 131	-0.6	34 675	2 099	455	81	33	34	174	271	604	40	33
Crawford	338	3.9	32 287	2 636	68	15	5	16	38	108	105	8	5
Daviess	1 256	2.4	38 167	1 614	429	74	32	192	200	263	727	41	32
Dearborn	2 075	3.8	41 953	949	579	104	44	91	294	416	817	55	44
Decatur	1 010	0.3	38 095	1 398	598	99	45	71	148	220	812	50	45
DeKalb	1 616	3.2	37 945	1 598	1 023	158	80	100	233	349	1 361	85	80
Delaware	3 844	3.2	32 896	2 444	1 897	354	144	174	614	1 133	2 569	166	144
Dubois	2 163	2.7	50 943	382	1 230	181	92	232	537	325	1 735	100	92
Elkhart	8 115	5.3	39 882	1 548	5 850	934	461	800	1 211	1 479	8 045	471	461
Fayette	831	2.5	35 453	2 112	241	44	19	40	117	287	345	26	19
Floyd	3 748	5.2	48 815	642	1 259	217	94	177	748	679	1 747	110	94
Fountain	578	-2.3	34 857	1 627	164	35	13	24	86	155	235	17	13
Franklin	955	3.8	41 749	1 307	156	33	12	70	158	196	271	20	12
Fulton	761	1.6	37 464	1 791	254	46	19	47	131	181	366	25	19
Gibson	1 357	1.5	40 172	952	1 062	168	80	116	196	286	1 426	84	80
Grant	2 496	2.9	36 715	1 847	1 141	198	90	161	347	775	1 590	105	90
Greene	1 162	1.5	35 806	1 931	234	47	18	72	174	309	371	26	18
Hamilton	20 023	4.8	64 654	99	7 524	963	542	1 472	3 551	1 522	10 501	616	542
Hancock	3 187	3.7	43 941	773	995	151	73	160	465	545	1 380	91	73
Harrison	1 511	5.2	38 166	1 766	386	68	29	72	207	326	555	39	29
Hendricks	6 857	4.3	43 345	851	2 492	387	191	329	832	928	3 399	211	191
Henry	1 645	2.0	33 589	2 312	458	87	35	65	234	500	644	49	35
Howard	3 084	3.2	37 356	1 816	1 961	302	152	117	453	861	2 532	165	152
Huntington	1 364	2.5	37 225	1 686	554	103	43	55	223	319	754	50	43
Jackson	1 747	3.9	39 645	1 360	909	167	70	116	232	355	1 262	75	70
Jasper	1 395	4.4	41 677	1 154	478	83	36	189	189	271	786	46	36
Jay	838	4.9	39 662	1 430	276	54	21	196	88	186	547	28	21
Jefferson	1 249	5.0	38 536	1 634	520	102	39	77	185	327	738	47	39
Jennings	969	3.4	34 730	2 358	291	51	23	43	101	309	408	28	23
Johnson	6 458	4.4	43 161	961	1 996	316	155	381	920	1 047	2 848	181	155
Knox	1 564	-0.7	41 234	1 008	710	144	52	138	233	416	1 044	61	52
Kosciusko	3 527	10.3	44 864	1 122	2 194	425	147	244	526	580	3 009	174	147
LaGrange	1 325	5.2	34 150	2 575	563	100	44	264	169	211	971	52	44
Lake	19 464	4.7	39 896	1 407	9 283	1 457	691	1 036	2 676	4 494	12 466	785	691
LaPorte	4 194	3.8	37 827	1 795	1 711	288	133	276	633	969	2 407	154	133
Lawrence	1 640	3.9	36 058	2 043	516	87	40	73	229	449	716	51	40
Madison	4 583	5.4	35 328	2 358	1 558	255	118	397	600	1 316	2 328	161	118
Marion	44 611	5.1	47 508	1 166	33 885	4 958	2 475	9 532	6 162	7 882	50 850	2 855	2 475
Marshall	1 732	2.3	36 958	1 813	743	129	58	82	269	370	1 011	65	58
Martin	397	2.7	38 788	1 417	486	133	41	40	69	91	700	37	41
Miami	1 115	0.6	31 097	2 672	376	82	31	46	181	305	536	36	31
Monroe	5 113	4.8	35 335	2 119	2 808	623	204	212	1 103	888	3 847	223	204
Montgomery	1 456	1.7	38 092	1 928	689	114	52	156	199	326	1 011	63	52
Morgan	2 737	2.4	39 299	1 604	603	104	46	168	330	588	922	65	46
Newton	524	0.0	37 437	1 540	138	24	10	49	68	117	221	13	10
Noble	1 698	3.9	35 578	2 261	752	134	59	145	212	355	1 091	67	59
Ohio	216	2.9	36 368	2 026	45	8	4	17	26	50	74	5	4
Orange	653	0.2	33 308	2 296	266	42	22	35	90	199	365	25	22
Owen	716	4.2	34 287	2 477	194	47	14	44	95	205	299	21	14
Parke	531	0.4	31 434	2 706	106	24	8	48	84	156	186	13	8
Perry	684	3.1	35 344	2 153	271	52	20	52	100	166	395	25	20

1. Based on the resident population estimated as of July 1 of the year shown.

STATE County	Farm	Mining	Construction	Manu-facturing	Information: professional, scientific, technical services	Retail trade	Finance, insurance, real estate and leasing	Health care and social assistance	Government	Number	Rate[1]	Supplemental Security Income recipients, December 2015	Total	Percent change, 2010–2016
					Earnings, 2015 (cont.) — Percent by selected industries					Social Security beneficiaries, December 2015			Housing units, 2016	
	75	76	77	78	79	80	81	82	83	84	85	86	87	88
ILLINOIS—Cont'd														
Winnebago	-0.1	0.0	4.0	23.4	4.9	6.9	6.0	17.0	13.0	60 335	210	7 283	125 353	-0.5
Woodford	4.2	D	15.2	19.5	3.6	6.6	3.5	7.9	16.0	7 620	195	230	15 469	2.1
INDIANA	0.7	0.3	5.9	20.9	6.9	6.1	8.6	12.3	12.7	1 301 948	197	128 781	2 854 546	2.1
Adams	3.7	D	16.4	34.3	D	6.2	3.5	4.3	12.3	6 220	178	359	13 188	1.3
Allen	-0.1	0.1	6.7	17.3	6.8	6.3	8.3	18.9	9.6	67 840	184	8 055	156 236	2.7
Bartholomew	0.3	D	3.7	48.5	5.0	4.0	3.9	7.1	9.2	16 305	201	1 255	33 886	2.4
Benton	8.2	D	5.5	16.3	D	5.2	8.9	D	19.5	2 005	231	148	3 905	-0.6
Blackford	0.0	D	2.6	37.1	D	5.0	4.4	9.9	14.4	3 525	287	254	5 973	-1.3
Boone	0.1	D	10.1	7.5	9.5	17.2	6.5	6.9	12.1	9 895	156	462	26 079	14.6
Brown	0.4	0.0	11.3	4.6	8.2	8.8	3.7	D	21.4	4 230	284	179	8 573	3.5
Carroll	10.8	D	7.9	D	2.3	5.1	4.4	D	12.8	4 620	232	188	9 493	0.2
Cass	-0.3	D	6.1	29.9	2.5	8.3	3.9	D	22.8	8 465	222	800	16 273	-1.2
Clark	0.1	D	6.4	18.6	2.9	9.9	6.0	9.8	13.2	24 325	211	2 349	49 768	4.2
Clay	1.3	D	4.2	41.2	D	7.0	3.1	D	14.9	6 370	241	653	11 676	-0.2
Clinton	0.6	0.0	5.5	39.7	D	4.8	4.8	8.7	14.0	6 825	210	547	13 236	-0.6
Crawford	-1.2	D	D	D	1.1	5.0	D	5.0	22.1	2 825	269	356	5 445	-1.4
Daviess	6.4	D	18.8	17.1	4.1	8.9	3.8	5.8	13.6	5 765	176	530	12 461	-0.1
Dearborn	-0.1	D	9.0	15.6	4.0	8.5	4.3	8.5	21.6	11 030	223	641	20 301	0.6
Decatur	1.4	D	3.8	44.5	D	4.5	3.5	4.0	11.1	5 760	218	441	11 276	0.6
DeKalb	0.2	0.4	3.6	46.0	3.0	3.7	2.7	5.9	7.9	9 190	216	690	17 723	0.9
Delaware	-0.3	D	4.5	11.0	5.8	8.1	6.3	19.1	22.8	25 860	223	3 086	52 425	0.1
Dubois	5.0	D	3.9	37.4	2.8	6.6	3.4	12.2	6.4	8 730	206	376	17 722	1.9
Elkhart	1.0	D	3.5	49.1	2.6	4.2	2.9	7.8	6.0	35 415	174	3 058	78 179	0.5
Fayette	1.1	D	4.1	24.8	3.9	8.5	4.3	19.0	15.9	6 805	290	888	10 791	-1.0
Floyd	0.0	D	7.0	23.8	6.4	5.6	4.6	11.9	21.7	15 835	206	1 513	32 539	1.8
Fountain	-2.7	0.0	5.2	40.7	2.9	6.7	5.1	D	16.5	4 320	261	316	7 787	-1.0
Franklin	1.9	0.3	11.1	20.7	D	8.3	4.8	7.8	17.7	5 955	260	418	9 599	-1.0
Fulton	-1.3	D	12.4	28.2	2.8	6.9	5.4	4.8	20.9	4 935	243	373	9 636	-0.7
Gibson	2.9	9.1	1.9	47.0	D	3.7	1.5	D	4.9	7 215	214	506	14 918	1.9
Grant	-0.3	D	3.4	24.7	2.7	6.5	3.8	16.2	14.5	17 310	256	2 079	30 292	-0.5
Greene	6.6	1.1	9.7	8.8	4.9	7.5	4.3	D	24.7	7 880	243	748	15 025	-1.2
Hamilton	0.0	0.2	5.9	4.8	13.4	6.9	18.9	10.8	7.5	40 175	130	1 481	123 950	16.1
Hancock	-0.1	0.0	10.0	16.5	D	6.2	3.7	6.5	15.8	14 680	203	638	29 543	5.0
Harrison	1.3	1.3	6.1	16.7	3.0	7.5	4.7	D	20.6	8 855	223	616	16 761	1.4
Hendricks	0.3	D	6.7	8.3	3.7	11.8	3.5	7.3	14.9	24 735	156	853	60 273	8.7
Henry	0.1	D	7.0	19.4	2.9	8.4	5.2	8.0	25.4	12 380	253	1 072	21 090	-0.9
Howard	-0.3	D	3.0	47.7	2.5	6.0	3.7	12.2	9.9	21 310	258	2 199	39 106	1.1
Huntington	1.4	D	5.9	31.3	D	5.2	5.1	9.5	10.2	8 525	233	579	15 903	0.6
Jackson	4.7	D	4.0	38.5	1.8	5.8	2.7	4.9	14.3	9 730	221	871	18 794	3.3
Jasper	6.0	D	7.6	21.7	2.5	5.8	3.5	D	11.1	7 400	221	455	13 412	1.9
Jay	18.9	D	6.6	37.1	2.1	3.4	2.3	3.9	12.5	4 940	234	394	9 188	-0.4
Jefferson	-0.3	0.0	4.9	27.8	D	9.2	2.7	14.0	15.9	7 770	239	783	14 329	0.1
Jennings	2.6	D	11.9	26.5	1.7	5.5	2.8	7.8	16.2	6 550	235	702	12 076	0.1
Johnson	0.1	D	7.4	14.0	5.1	9.4	5.0	12.8	15.1	27 565	185	1 575	59 836	5.6
Knox	3.9	9.4	4.7	11.1	2.6	5.8	3.2	11.5	24.8	8 640	228	946	16 963	-0.4
Kosciusko	3.2	D	2.9	54.9	2.0	4.2	2.7	5.3	5.4	15 845	201	907	37 902	2.3
LaGrange	9.7	D	5.1	47.3	1.6	6.0	2.7	D	7.0	5 915	153	313	14 561	3.3
Lake	-0.1	0.1	8.6	20.8	4.6	6.6	3.9	15.9	11.3	97 500	200	13 044	211 463	1.3
LaPorte	1.1	D	8.6	20.8	3.3	6.7	4.2	13.9	15.1	24 230	219	2 214	48 837	0.8
Lawrence	1.1	1.7	6.8	24.7	6.5	8.5	4.9	D	14.3	11 410	251	1 038	20 920	-0.7
Madison	0.0	0.2	5.9	22.0	3.7	6.3	4.5	15.3	14.5	32 040	247	3 377	58 706	-0.6
Marion	0.0	0.0	4.6	12.1	11.2	5.2	17.5	13.2	11.3	153 880	164	26 400	420 871	0.7
Marshall	-0.1	D	4.8	39.8	D	6.8	4.8	8.3	11.0	9 925	212	659	20 021	0.9
Martin	3.7	0.0	0.9	3.5	9.7	1.2	0.6	0.8	74.5	2 445	240	218	4 744	-0.9
Miami	0.8	0.6	6.2	20.6	2.2	5.3	4.6	D	29.4	7 450	208	796	15 261	-1.4
Monroe	0.0	0.3	4.9	12.7	7.3	5.8	4.7	12.2	34.6	20 995	146	1 815	60 796	2.9
Montgomery	0.2	D	3.3	36.7	D	7.2	2.9	D	9.7	8 520	223	596	16 544	0.0
Morgan	1.8	0.3	12.6	17.7	D	8.9	4.9	10.6	14.4	15 625	224	952	28 081	1.1
Newton	18.2	D	6.8	16.8	D	3.1	D	5.0	15.0	3 115	222	205	6 039	0.1
Noble	1.7	D	3.8	55.4	D	4.6	2.5	5.1	9.0	9 705	203	685	20 278	0.8
Ohio	0.8	0.0	5.2	D	D	3.0	D	3.7	21.5	1 380	232	73	2 807	0.8
Orange	3.0	D	12.3	16.6	D	5.2	2.3	D	12.8	4 950	254	498	9 071	-1.1
Owen	1.4	0.0	6.8	45.6	D	4.6	3.4	D	12.3	5 330	256	397	9 970	-1.2
Parke	0.6	D	12.7	15.6	D	6.9	5.6	D	26.5	3 815	226	245	8 081	-0.1
Perry	1.0	0.3	4.7	40.5	2.6	5.1	6.7	D	19.7	4 500	233	332	8 599	1.2

1. Per 1,000 resident population estimated as of July 1 of the year shown.

Table B. States and Counties — **Housing, Labor Force, and Employment**

STATE County	Housing units, 2011–2015								Civilian labor force, 2016				Civilian employment,[6] 2011–2015		
	Occupied units							Sub-stand-ard units[4] (percent)			Unemployment			Percent	
	Owner-occupied					Renter-occupied									
				Median owner cost as a percent of income											
	Total	Percent	Median value[1]	With a mort-gage	Without a mort-gage[2]	Median rent[3]	Median rent as a per-cent of income[2]		Total	Percent change, 2015–2016	Total	Rate[5]	Total	Manage-ment, business, science and arts	Con-struction, produc-tion, and mainte-nance occu-pations
	89	90	91	92	93	94	95	96	97	98	99	100	101	102	103
ILLINOIS—Cont'd															
Winnebago	113 912	66.3	117 700	22.5	12.8	748	29.8	2.3	141 635	-0.5	9 400	6.6	131 172	30.3	27.7
Woodford	14 350	81.3	158 200	20.7	10.5	737	26.6	1.1	19 545	-0.8	1 057	5.4	18 798	37.1	22.8
INDIANA	2 501 937	69.0	124 200	19.8	10.7	745	29.8	2.1	3 326 905	1.7	147 091	4.4	3 038 762	32.4	27.3
Adams	12 183	78.4	116 900	20.2	10.0	545	27.0	9.6	17 007	0.5	609	3.6	14 982	26.5	38.8
Allen	140 536	68.9	114 600	18.9	10.0	682	28.1	2.1	180 637	1.3	7 686	4.3	170 294	34.4	25.1
Bartholomew	30 518	70.7	136 000	19.6	11.4	818	24.6	2.6	44 457	1.9	1 502	3.4	38 666	39.0	26.0
Benton	3 429	70.7	83 800	18.9	10.0	680	28.5	2.2	4 657	1.6	194	4.2	4 096	26.6	37.5
Blackford	5 228	74.2	67 500	19.3	12.2	593	30.7	1.2	5 309	1.1	287	5.4	5 199	21.0	42.4
Boone	22 924	75.9	187 600	19.3	11.6	796	29.1	1.5	34 418	2.6	1 166	3.4	30 471	45.1	20.2
Brown	6 095	79.4	162 300	21.5	15.8	932	35.3	3.0	7 610	2.1	303	4.0	7 039	33.5	26.7
Carroll	7 793	80.5	112 100	19.6	10.2	667	27.5	2.7	10 227	1.9	429	4.2	9 224	24.9	36.3
Cass	14 555	75.4	82 400	20.4	10.6	617	27.3	3.6	17 983	1.1	839	4.7	17 342	25.1	37.8
Clark	42 974	71.1	129 000	20.1	11.3	755	28.2	1.6	60 672	2.9	2 505	4.1	54 754	29.6	27.2
Clay	10 345	75.2	95 000	19.5	11.7	653	29.6	2.3	12 423	0.3	586	4.7	11 766	26.7	32.5
Clinton	11 643	72.4	98 100	19.4	10.0	680	25.9	1.7	17 163	1.3	667	3.9	15 003	22.8	44.9
Crawford	4 101	79.2	86 300	20.4	13.1	533	31.1	2.3	5 018	1.9	282	5.6	4 273	22.9	37.8
Daviess	11 452	72.4	110 200	19.1	10.0	609	25.1	2.3	15 951	1.5	567	3.6	14 319	24.5	42.2
Dearborn	18 634	78.6	159 100	20.6	12.0	747	27.6	1.5	25 719	1.9	1 204	4.7	24 159	29.6	29.4
Decatur	10 074	70.2	115 100	19.1	10.3	739	25.8	2.2	14 473	1.1	517	3.6	12 601	27.8	39.4
DeKalb	16 247	76.9	110 100	20.1	10.0	657	26.7	1.4	22 168	1.6	874	3.9	19 542	26.8	37.6
Delaware	45 761	63.8	87 700	19.0	11.8	691	37.3	0.9	54 851	0.6	2 863	5.2	51 781	30.8	22.6
Dubois	16 190	75.7	137 700	19.1	10.2	605	24.1	3.1	23 391	3.0	730	3.1	21 742	29.6	34.3
Elkhart	70 439	78.3	124 000	19.6	10.0	719	28.4	2.7	107 999	3.0	3 768	3.5	91 085	24.2	38.8
Fayette	9 336	68.9	81 900	21.1	13.3	648	33.6	1.9	9 292	3.2	538	5.8	9 245	24.0	31.6
Floyd	29 088	72.4	156 300	19.8	10.4	723	30.0	1.8	41 205	3.0	1 680	4.1	37 064	34.5	23.6
Fountain	6 951	74.7	87 500	18.2	11.0	639	23.2	2.1	7 962	-1.2	462	5.8	7 533	26.6	40.5
Franklin	8 848	79.9	147 600	21.8	10.5	649	26.3	2.3	11 488	0.7	498	4.3	11 103	31.7	33.2
Fulton	7 963	76.9	95 400	18.9	12.8	616	29.2	0.8	9 814	-0.6	464	4.7	9 122	24.9	43.9
Gibson	13 102	77.3	103 000	18.2	10.7	658	26.2	2.2	19 196	1.6	701	3.7	16 013	26.0	40.0
Grant	26 477	69.7	82 800	20.0	10.4	650	28.4	1.5	32 112	-1.4	1 599	5.0	29 151	28.4	26.1
Greene	12 798	79.1	90 500	18.6	11.5	582	26.1	4.2	13 721	-0.4	903	6.6	14 187	27.7	32.5
Hamilton	108 253	78.3	222 900	19.0	10.0	1 016	25.3	0.9	172 142	2.8	5 495	3.2	154 190	51.8	11.2
Hancock	26 340	78.2	156 300	19.5	10.6	832	26.7	0.7	38 359	2.5	1 456	3.8	35 339	37.7	22.2
Harrison	14 604	81.5	129 300	19.4	10.1	669	29.4	1.9	19 992	2.8	837	4.2	18 294	29.3	30.7
Hendricks	54 652	80.2	162 400	19.2	10.7	958	27.1	1.3	85 157	2.6	2 965	3.5	76 792	40.0	20.4
Henry	18 010	73.5	91 600	20.2	11.1	626	30.1	0.9	22 147	2.1	1 029	4.6	19 488	28.7	30.4
Howard	34 413	69.0	95 700	18.3	10.0	646	31.4	1.0	38 176	3.1	1 780	4.7	35 740	29.3	29.3
Huntington	14 480	75.8	99 900	20.0	11.7	672	28.4	1.7	18 739	0.4	761	4.1	17 909	27.8	35.3
Jackson	16 614	74.2	112 200	19.6	10.7	700	29.0	2.7	22 209	1.8	816	3.7	19 885	27.1	35.6
Jasper	11 996	77.6	148 300	19.3	10.0	733	28.3	2.1	16 540	1.0	882	5.3	15 197	27.1	38.2
Jay	8 117	74.8	79 400	19.9	11.2	576	28.5	3.9	9 930	-0.3	452	4.6	9 495	22.1	45.4
Jefferson	12 694	71.8	112 100	20.0	10.5	680	29.2	2.9	15 282	-0.4	718	4.7	14 381	27.3	35.6
Jennings	10 607	75.8	95 400	21.2	13.1	696	23.7	2.8	13 210	0.2	636	4.8	12 285	23.6	38.1
Johnson	53 270	70.8	145 400	19.5	10.0	849	29.2	2.3	79 639	2.5	2 897	3.6	70 667	37.4	22.1
Knox	14 779	66.0	84 700	18.3	10.7	623	28.4	1.4	19 076	0.1	835	4.4	17 864	27.5	31.2
Kosciusko	29 586	76.5	132 900	19.4	10.2	714	24.3	2.0	41 310	1.5	1 544	3.7	37 483	27.4	37.9
LaGrange	11 719	81.2	162 200	23.0	10.0	665	23.7	5.1	19 279	1.1	659	3.4	15 663	19.5	52.7
Lake	183 314	68.9	136 100	21.6	11.8	819	31.6	2.5	232 458	1.1	14 696	6.3	212 423	29.9	27.0
LaPorte	43 004	70.6	123 300	20.0	10.8	702	30.5	2.0	48 521	-0.1	2 875	5.9	46 864	26.9	31.0
Lawrence	18 494	77.0	100 500	20.6	11.6	637	26.6	2.4	20 570	1.3	1 171	5.7	20 669	29.5	31.4
Madison	51 274	69.1	90 400	19.7	11.2	702	30.5	2.0	59 596	2.2	2 975	5.0	54 576	28.1	25.0
Marion	363 558	54.3	118 300	20.6	11.5	788	32.3	2.7	483 993	2.3	21 480	4.4	436 687	33.7	22.2
Marshall	17 324	76.9	123 100	20.3	11.3	674	27.3	3.7	24 337	1.2	916	3.8	21 470	26.9	38.5
Martin	4 201	77.9	91 800	19.6	10.0	521	24.3	1.9	5 155	2.0	214	4.2	4 716	30.4	34.5
Miami	13 164	73.0	85 500	18.7	11.8	651	26.3	2.1	16 033	1.7	760	4.7	14 752	24.7	37.0
Monroe	54 165	53.6	160 400	19.9	10.0	836	39.7	1.3	68 167	1.0	3 155	4.6	69 887	42.8	16.0
Montgomery	14 637	71.0	110 600	19.2	10.1	654	27.3	1.7	19 063	-1.2	737	3.9	17 497	24.0	37.1
Morgan	25 609	76.4	143 700	20.6	10.0	754	27.7	1.7	36 279	2.4	1 528	4.2	32 732	28.6	32.2
Newton	5 401	75.2	113 400	20.0	12.1	699	23.4	1.0	7 059	1.3	395	5.6	6 146	18.9	43.2
Noble	18 101	75.1	113 000	19.7	10.2	640	26.8	3.6	23 363	-1.4	949	4.1	21 795	24.0	43.6
Ohio	2 389	78.7	141 000	21.9	13.9	671	27.7	1.0	3 235	1.6	157	4.9	2 909	21.5	36.3
Orange	7 648	76.3	89 400	21.0	11.8	580	27.3	3.4	8 863	1.4	453	5.1	8 330	24.8	33.9
Owen	8 553	79.6	110 200	22.6	13.0	678	24.6	3.3	9 343	0.5	515	5.5	9 276	24.6	38.9
Parke	5 995	79.8	88 200	20.5	11.4	579	27.8	3.0	7 241	2.5	381	5.3	6 730	21.4	37.1
Perry	7 282	79.6	100 800	19.4	10.3	608	27.0	1.0	9 475	2.5	438	4.6	8 399	19.8	41.4

1. Specified owner-occupied units.   2. A value of 10.0 represents 10 percent or less; a value of 50.0 represents 50 percent or more.   3. Specified renter-occupied units.
4. Overcrowded or lacking complete plumbing facilities.   5. Percent of civilian labor force.   6. Civilian employed persons 16 years old and over.

Table B. States and Counties — Nonfarm Employment and Agriculture

	Private nonfarm establishments, employment and payroll, 2015									Agriculture, 2012			
		Employment						Annual payroll		Farms			
											Percent with:		
STATE County	Number of establishments	Total	Health care and social assistance	Manufacturing	Retail trade	Finance and insurance	Professional, scientific, and technical services	Total (mil dol)	Average per employee (dollars)	Number	Fewer than 50 acres	500 acres or more	Farm operators whose principal occupation is farming (percent)
	104	105	106	107	108	109	110	111	112	113	114	115	116
ILLINOIS—Cont'd													
Winnebago	6 492	118 528	20 887	25 037	14 682	3 552	4 467	4 976	41 985	807	46.0	12.4	44.2
Woodford	757	8 867	1 401	1 934	1 011	232	208	329	37 059	958	32.7	20.5	52.8
INDIANA	145 116	2 660 503	418 733	489 137	317 863	98 502	111 959	113 315	42 592	58 695	46.6	12.8	43.7
Adams	722	11 619	1 514	4 939	1 470	218	241	408	35 072	1 476	61.9	6.8	32.4
Allen	9 084	170 038	32 855	25 527	21 316	8 505	5 735	7 046	41 439	1 725	57.7	7.8	43.4
Bartholomew	1 821	46 808	4 732	12 257	4 663	1 068	3 098	2 238	47 810	623	44.1	14.4	44.8
Benton	177	1 403	54	372	175	94	44	49	34 634	381	26.0	36.7	63.5
Blackford	244	2 786	407	1 029	295	78	118	98	35 017	263	43.7	16.3	46.8
Boone	1 459	20 475	2 546	1 914	2 969	347	821	800	39 051	607	49.6	21.4	47.3
Brown	352	2 070	392	167	329	36	92	51	24 704	173	54.9	2.3	24.9
Carroll	379	4 513	261	D	380	80	105	156	34 604	491	35.6	23.2	50.7
Cass	714	13 338	2 634	4 243	1 563	295	198	452	33 875	688	42.7	16.9	42.9
Clark	2 419	47 286	6 055	7 873	6 935	1 884	1 133	1 762	37 257	515	49.3	7.4	41.6
Clay	472	5 816	635	2 212	984	119	62	191	32 804	579	44.9	16.1	39.4
Clinton	596	9 662	1 226	3 946	1 060	195	125	348	36 034	597	43.4	22.8	50.9
Crawford	134	1 401	159	D	191	35	12	44	31 197	338	27.8	3.6	29.9
Daviess	880	10 400	1 446	2 051	1 459	258	346	345	33 178	1 325	60.1	7.0	28.6
Dearborn	895	12 591	2 668	1 712	1 957	353	249	445	35 353	561	39.9	1.6	39.8
Decatur	616	11 788	1 268	4 182	1 291	267	113	455	38 640	610	31.1	19.0	49.0
DeKalb	982	19 684	1 717	9 016	1 491	331	482	858	43 581	924	49.9	8.5	28.2
Delaware	2 393	39 382	9 861	4 538	6 191	2 877	1 503	1 396	35 454	610	49.5	13.3	54.8
Dubois	1 295	27 095	3 421	10 730	3 055	529	351	1 119	41 314	720	34.2	12.4	40.3
Elkhart	4 866	123 927	10 868	63 752	9 233	2 094	1 959	5 353	43 192	1 724	62.8	3.9	38.3
Fayette	458	5 655	1 634	1 155	958	160	193	201	35 563	347	40.9	12.4	44.4
Floyd	1 757	26 021	5 507	5 997	3 226	762	1 117	1 010	38 797	277	67.9	2.9	48.0
Fountain	309	3 666	391	1 639	599	154	77	123	33 452	460	34.6	22.8	48.0
Franklin	422	5 321	695	624	671	192	39	132	24 754	727	32.2	7.7	47.9
Fulton	458	5 233	773	1 798	929	166	125	178	34 011	653	40.9	13.9	49.0
Gibson	703	18 575	1 624	7 782	1 625	165	318	908	48 898	589	36.8	23.6	52.3
Grant	1 301	29 167	5 942	5 080	2 984	615	381	974	33 380	500	37.6	22.2	53.6
Greene	574	5 020	989	653	992	134	314	148	29 533	810	41.0	8.5	42.0
Hamilton	8 442	126 155	18 381	5 963	16 376	14 666	11 234	6 534	51 794	598	62.2	11.5	40.1
Hancock	1 386	17 789	2 580	3 261	2 107	336	1 521	701	39 415	604	60.1	15.1	41.6
Harrison	660	9 147	1 436	1 642	1 364	234	158	282	30 876	967	48.5	4.7	43.3
Hendricks	3 119	53 932	7 713	3 133	9 491	802	1 398	1 983	36 761	694	55.9	15.6	54.3
Henry	838	10 522	3 008	1 871	1 501	382	171	352	33 429	702	50.4	13.0	42.3
Howard	1 751	32 084	5 291	9 943	4 978	737	675	1 410	43 951	476	40.8	15.5	57.4
Huntington	854	13 002	1 858	3 927	1 312	337	186	399	30 693	695	47.5	16.3	44.9
Jackson	997	20 031	2 429	7 273	2 297	442	269	793	39 606	744	37.0	13.2	39.5
Jasper	747	9 651	1 357	1 567	1 525	294	173	348	36 086	615	38.7	24.7	47.2
Jay	390	6 898	873	3 539	616	147	97	228	33 008	836	50.6	11.2	38.9
Jefferson	660	11 806	2 085	3 270	1 673	194	217	431	36 477	615	42.4	5.9	38.2
Jennings	422	6 472	879	1 993	795	93	95	231	35 766	528	47.2	11.0	39.2
Johnson	3 069	45 326	7 189	5 956	9 048	1 094	1 455	1 637	36 107	562	57.8	14.9	45.0
Knox	906	14 085	3 537	1 689	2 013	295	224	507	35 990	496	30.2	31.5	61.3
Kosciusko	1 919	37 175	4 154	14 302	3 860	807	496	1 932	51 963	1 247	54.2	10.2	39.9
LaGrange	792	12 390	934	6 872	1 205	206	173	515	41 580	2 419	58.7	2.3	43.3
Lake	9 925	167 326	32 871	24 077	24 814	3 954	5 691	7 268	43 437	430	57.2	15.1	47.0
LaPorte	2 303	34 473	6 041	7 413	5 951	729	768	1 307	37 911	731	43.8	17.1	51.4
Lawrence	874	11 328	2 732	2 177	1 977	344	632	391	34 516	800	42.0	6.5	39.5
Madison	2 246	35 819	6 911	3 616	4 816	849	1 457	1 224	34 159	737	52.6	16.1	54.5
Marion	23 103	516 593	86 892	38 762	47 289	25 392	40 459	25 739	49 824	231	79.7	4.8	36.4
Marshall	1 057	17 623	1 886	6 552	2 093	508	305	641	36 351	878	46.8	12.3	40.7
Martin	187	2 442	125	370	308	47	947	103	42 117	283	44.9	9.5	35.3
Miami	581	6 971	1 123	1 891	875	344	119	235	33 742	666	45.0	14.6	44.4
Monroe	3 010	49 259	10 240	7 230	6 817	1 669	1 982	1 904	38 643	462	48.3	3.7	37.7
Montgomery	846	13 467	1 269	5 293	1 673	259	180	536	39 802	732	44.3	20.8	48.9
Morgan	1 179	12 379	1 839	2 128	2 284	385	333	436	35 193	583	55.6	11.1	42.5
Newton	248	2 460	252	628	285	110	92	81	32 933	348	29.6	32.2	54.9
Noble	870	15 862	1 375	8 788	1 615	240	171	591	37 264	1 163	52.8	8.0	38.5
Ohio	84	1 044	92	18	77	19	11	25	23 807	171	38.0	2.9	33.9
Orange	399	5 586	767	1 288	659	105	65	176	31 430	478	33.7	9.4	36.8
Owen	295	2 945	518	945	444	104	79	106	36 107	549	39.5	7.1	40.3
Parke	248	2 111	250	531	295	68	71	67	31 645	574	38.0	13.4	43.4
Perry	370	5 849	865	2 498	694	121	122	212	36 264	413	26.6	5.1	39.2

Table B. States and Counties — **Agriculture**

STATE County	Acreage (1,000) [117]	Percent change, 2007–2012 [118]	Average size of farm [119]	Total irrigated (1,000) [120]	Total cropland (1,000) [121]	Average per farm [122]	Average per acre [123]	Value of machinery and equipment, average per farm (dollars) [124]	Total (mil dol) [125]	Average per farm (dollars) [126]	Crops [127]	Live-stock and poultry products [128]	$10,000 or more [129]	$100,000 or more [130]	Total ($1,000) [131]	Percent of farms [132]
ILLINOIS—Cont'd																
Winnebago	183	-0.4	227	0.5	159.6	1 434 529	6 329	127 939	106.4	131 822	79.1	20.9	43.2	23.4	5 109	61.6
Woodford	323	12.0	337	0.5	291.6	2 612 922	7 750	210 760	240.6	251 196	78.5	21.5	62.3	40.6	6 107	79.2
INDIANA	14 720	-0.4	251	437.4	12 590.6	1 342 826	5 354	143 235	11 210.8	191 001	67.2	32.8	48.3	24.4	267 287	54.7
Adams	210	15.2	142	0.1	186.0	825 272	5 794	92 331	250.3	169 571	48.1	51.9	55.8	25.1	3 765	37.6
Allen	271	6.6	157	0.4	241.5	969 217	6 174	87 928	187.6	108 776	79.6	20.4	48.8	20.6	6 302	52.5
Bartholomew	172	3.2	275	13.5	153.4	1 619 191	5 878	151 406	95.6	153 387	89.5	10.5	54.9	27.1	4 647	63.7
Benton	254	-6.1	667	D	247.4	4 308 843	6 457	328 864	210.9	553 499	80.8	19.2	73.5	59.8	4 782	85.0
Blackford	88	4.0	335	D	81.2	1 414 730	4 228	176 620	71.5	271 764	D	D	56.3	28.9	1 380	66.2
Boone	222	-0.5	365	0.9	210.3	2 253 794	6 171	194 476	146.0	240 486	88.5	11.5	52.9	32.6	3 428	54.7
Brown	15	-14.0	84	0.1	6.6	337 468	4 002	37 514	4.2	24 486	D	D	16.8	2.9	156	28.3
Carroll	204	6.1	416	0.4	189.5	2 837 483	6 826	234 244	221.4	450 982	61.5	38.5	65.4	46.4	3 497	63.7
Cass	200	-12.2	291	1.9	181.6	1 575 185	5 412	185 317	158.4	230 281	78.2	21.8	55.8	30.5	4 080	73.3
Clark	79	-9.4	153	0.4	54.2	644 767	4 228	83 882	32.1	62 418	82.4	17.6	37.9	11.5	1 034	48.2
Clay	163	3.4	281	0.2	137.4	1 226 095	4 358	143 682	60.3	104 079	92.2	7.8	42.8	22.3	2 433	76.0
Clinton	223	-12.5	374	D	211.6	2 497 002	6 672	245 072	251.5	421 293	71.0	29.0	61.1	40.7	4 216	69.5
Crawford	46	2.2	137	0.0	16.2	351 639	2 561	40 038	7.2	21 323	D	D	17.2	2.4	288	29.6
Daviess	225	12.9	170	5.8	189.4	1 100 902	6 479	108 929	190.1	143 498	41.9	58.1	44.5	17.1	3 949	24.0
Dearborn	57	-14.1	101	0.1	26.8	410 578	4 071	46 287	12.4	22 191	74.9	25.1	27.3	6.1	650	33.9
Decatur	187	-8.9	306	0.0	162.6	1 627 090	5 321	166 746	159.4	261 293	58.0	42.0	62.8	37.0	3 721	74.1
DeKalb	161	0.1	174	0.8	136.8	771 247	4 429	92 135	106.9	115 738	65.5	34.5	35.8	16.6	4 689	73.6
Delaware	175	13.5	287	0.0	160.4	1 522 762	5 300	152 951	125.6	205 836	93.2	6.8	52.1	26.9	3 980	67.4
Dubois	175	-4.0	243	0.2	130.0	1 086 538	4 473	142 382	241.0	334 742	21.8	78.2	55.7	25.1	3 256	63.5
Elkhart	173	5.8	100	25.5	140.2	808 782	8 067	83 012	296.8	172 178	28.0	72.0	51.8	27.4	2 785	20.1
Fayette	78	-15.4	225	D	63.8	1 047 712	4 647	117 945	40.1	115 651	82.7	17.3	49.3	25.1	1 421	61.1
Floyd	21	-10.6	77	0.0	12.2	413 040	5 331	53 170	4.6	16 621	78.7	21.4	17.3	3.2	299	23.8
Fountain	214	13.6	466	D	190.5	2 236 072	4 797	218 709	116.7	253 644	D	D	52.4	30.9	3 690	68.9
Franklin	125	-1.1	172	0.1	85.1	786 644	4 577	92 254	54.0	74 304	78.8	21.2	47.3	17.6	2 101	61.9
Fulton	188	1.9	289	22.9	169.4	1 449 573	5 024	178 933	140.7	215 464	84.9	15.1	57.7	31.1	3 180	61.1
Gibson	268	16.0	455	4.8	250.3	2 426 261	5 329	255 418	146.4	248 542	87.7	12.3	63.2	35.5	4 803	70.6
Grant	183	-9.3	367	D	171.5	2 046 020	5 579	209 740	138.0	275 964	90.4	9.6	60.0	36.8	3 298	68.4
Greene	181	6.7	224	2.2	132.9	881 351	3 942	108 274	97.4	120 212	55.7	44.3	37.9	12.3	2 470	40.7
Hamilton	131	5.9	219	3.7	120.9	1 406 630	6 428	132 154	116.2	194 256	97.1	2.9	45.8	21.7	1 833	44.1
Hancock	166	-3.4	275	0.2	156.6	1 570 192	5 718	148 467	110.4	182 821	83.7	16.3	47.2	24.8	3 001	50.8
Harrison	135	-12.9	140	0.0	85.0	513 898	3 681	71 044	58.0	59 968	47.1	52.9	29.2	8.0	1 556	38.8
Hendricks	218	27.2	315	0.1	200.9	1 835 824	5 834	163 981	89.4	128 772	92.0	8.0	42.9	20.7	3 783	48.4
Henry	176	1.2	251	0.0	158.4	1 244 617	4 952	157 963	115.5	164 479	74.6	25.4	49.1	23.8	3 282	58.4
Howard	144	-11.1	303	D	134.5	1 924 391	6 353	182 880	140.4	294 874	81.1	18.9	68.1	37.2	2 993	67.0
Huntington	189	-5.1	272	0.7	172.6	1 481 458	5 452	216 573	174.8	251 550	65.7	34.3	50.5	28.2	4 185	71.7
Jackson	184	-12.1	247	2.9	139.9	1 132 552	4 582	174 212	184.4	247 907	42.2	57.8	50.8	24.5	3 876	66.7
Jasper	283	-16.9	460	21.1	256.7	2 819 873	6 132	250 876	357.4	581 142	58.3	41.7	61.3	40.0	4 736	72.8
Jay	176	-10.9	210	D	156.3	1 380 341	6 565	137 579	282.0	337 292	35.2	64.8	53.7	29.3	3 621	64.6
Jefferson	95	-6.9	155	0.0	61.7	549 182	3 540	72 820	40.4	65 737	76.7	23.3	32.4	8.8	1 907	53.3
Jennings	123	-10.8	234	0.1	87.7	910 475	3 896	126 716	79.7	150 917	57.8	42.2	37.5	16.9	3 214	57.4
Johnson	145	1.7	257	3.1	131.6	1 567 699	6 091	140 655	70.6	125 575	87.1	12.9	42.7	23.5	2 779	50.5
Knox	329	0.6	664	34.9	304.0	3 748 448	5 646	405 986	218.1	439 627	83.4	16.6	70.8	45.8	5 837	72.6
Kosciusko	255	1.4	204	18.0	219.6	1 198 890	5 866	110 144	282.1	226 226	47.0	53.0	42.4	20.8	4 140	51.7
LaGrange	204	26.2	84	25.6	147.4	628 366	7 448	56 611	262.6	108 542	26.1	73.9	55.2	23.1	2 276	12.5
Lake	133	3.6	309	8.1	124.2	1 755 500	5 673	178 735	100.8	234 374	98.1	1.9	44.4	30.0	2 419	49.1
LaPorte	228	-11.0	312	54.4	209.3	1 896 432	6 084	188 253	223.1	305 215	80.5	19.5	55.7	33.8	4 036	58.4
Lawrence	135	0.0	168	D	70.8	534 073	3 172	64 313	33.2	41 486	68.1	31.9	31.5	5.3	2 091	48.1
Madison	205	-5.6	278	0.9	191.5	1 677 897	6 028	169 689	164.4	223 026	91.7	8.3	53.5	29.0	3 565	58.8
Marion	20	16.5	87	0.2	16.0	558 134	6 422	60 861	27.3	117 991	D	D	29.4	10.8	220	16.5
Marshall	206	15.2	235	13.4	181.8	1 222 325	5 202	140 648	147.6	168 141	73.5	26.5	49.7	26.9	3 430	49.2
Martin	63	2.0	221	0.4	39.0	892 177	4 037	105 095	54.3	191 735	24.9	75.1	36.7	13.4	701	33.2
Miami	175	-1.5	263	3.1	158.1	1 333 943	5 069	145 643	156.9	235 605	67.1	32.9	55.0	32.6	3 696	68.8
Monroe	53	-1.4	114	0.1	27.6	551 762	4 831	55 294	13.0	28 134	66.7	33.3	28.4	5.6	754	29.0
Montgomery	287	-4.8	392	1.0	264.6	2 189 187	5 585	199 959	175.4	239 638	83.9	16.1	53.4	30.6	6 178	68.6
Morgan	137	20.2	235	0.0	114.2	1 158 144	4 922	130 446	51.8	88 768	87.9	12.1	36.4	14.8	2 146	46.0
Newton	192	0.8	552	6.3	174.3	3 131 055	5 674	315 417	242.6	697 187	53.1	46.9	66.1	46.3	3 086	79.6
Noble	181	13.5	156	13.7	150.1	754 298	4 834	95 800	143.7	123 588	57.4	42.6	44.3	18.4	4 236	52.5
Ohio	21	-0.2	126	0.2	10.5	446 731	3 560	57 649	4.2	24 462	74.7	25.3	28.7	4.1	368	34.5
Orange	98	0.9	206	0.0	56.9	717 036	3 488	102 278	64.0	133 902	22.4	77.6	30.3	8.6	1 599	47.9
Owen	96	8.8	174	0.1	62.5	590 885	3 396	76 073	23.5	42 805	82.7	17.3	29.0	8.0	1 537	49.7
Parke	177	-0.4	308	2.7	120.9	1 282 422	4 169	131 817	64.2	111 779	81.9	18.1	43.7	22.1	2 785	50.7
Perry	66	-5.9	160	0.0	30.7	481 276	2 999	62 182	20.3	49 208	47.4	52.6	35.1	7.5	605	42.4

Table B. States and Counties — Water Use, Wholesale Trade, Retail Trade, and Real Estate

STATE County	Water use, 2010		Wholesale trade,[1] 2012				Retail trade,[2] 2012				Real estate and rental and leasing,[2] 2012			
	Total water withdrawn (mil gal/day)	Gallons withdrawn per person per day	Number of establishments	Number of employees	Sales (mil dol)	Annual payroll (mil dol)	Number of establishments	Number of employees	Sales (mil dol)	Annual payroll (mil dol)	Number of establishments	Number of employees	Receipts (mil dol)	Annual payroll (mil dol)
	133	134	135	136	137	138	139	140	141	142	143	144	145	146
ILLINOIS—Cont'd														
Winnebago	35.6	120	333	4 123	2 700.4	207.0	986	14 298	3 752.1	326.5	212	1 512	169.0	43.7
Woodford	9.6	248	44	578	608.0	31.7	95	956	337.8	25.6	17	30	2.6	0.5
INDIANA	8 643.0	1 333	6 460	91 474	81 173.4	4 650.5	21 601	309 552	85 858.0	7 078.7	5 729	31 715	6 547.9	1 171.7
Adams	7.8	226	35	267	240.0	9.9	133	1 500	377.2	33.3	19	D	D	D
Allen	48.6	137	506	7 683	9 187.6	368.3	1 273	19 912	5 197.7	467.2	382	1 863	361.6	66.5
Bartholomew	18.2	237	77	998	774.4	52.7	306	4 701	1 113.1	99.4	72	303	57.0	9.4
Benton	0.9	101	15	201	203.4	8.0	31	199	53.3	3.8	3	2	0.3	0.1
Blackford	2.0	155	10	D	D	D	38	406	96.7	9.0	12	33	3.5	0.5
Boone	4.4	78	58	901	1 684.0	45.1	160	2 238	1 137.9	72.0	52	170	35.1	5.4
Brown	0.3	21	5	46	2.6	0.6	77	343	58.4	6.4	11	76	5.4	1.5
Carroll	5.1	255	18	161	302.4	7.1	51	395	99.8	8.0	11	38	5.1	1.3
Cass	28.8	738	39	434	570.0	19.0	118	1 502	341.6	33.5	17	59	8.2	1.3
Clark	25.7	233	95	1 011	1 024.5	52.3	426	6 966	1 814.3	158.5	79	502	87.5	17.1
Clay	1.2	43	13	D	D	D	84	878	312.7	19.0	15	24	5.2	0.6
Clinton	6.2	185	24	D	D	D	102	992	239.1	21.3	11	38	4.8	0.8
Crawford	2.8	262	5	80	42.5	2.5	24	201	89.9	3.8	3	D	D	D
Daviess	8.6	271	31	336	227.3	14.3	122	1 502	485.9	37.9	18	58	6.9	1.1
Dearborn	601.2	12 013	31	207	311.2	9.3	140	1 962	576.5	48.7	36	103	14.2	2.7
Decatur	5.3	204	32	391	455.7	17.2	110	1 259	357.2	27.8	17	45	8.1	1.2
DeKalb	8.8	208	41	D	D	D	125	1 469	383.3	32.2	25	118	14.5	4.9
Delaware	15.6	132	92	894	805.8	32.1	428	6 189	1 519.9	131.9	95	447	90.7	16.5
Dubois	7.6	182	74	1 053	637.0	50.3	217	3 332	919.2	79.8	31	D	D	D
Elkhart	33.0	167	340	5 803	3 329.9	249.5	678	8 754	2 440.4	206.9	157	768	134.5	25.4
Fayette	2.9	117	14	114	110.9	5.5	75	1 070	234.4	23.6	20	68	7.1	1.3
Floyd	254.6	3 414	69	579	323.3	23.3	206	3 146	772.3	69.6	69	205	34.4	5.9
Fountain	2.2	129	12	77	127.3	3.6	64	572	148.3	10.8	5	12	1.1	0.3
Franklin	3.9	169	7	33	14.8	1.3	68	662	170.2	13.4	8	14	1.6	0.3
Fulton	7.7	368	18	141	98.2	5.6	79	913	214.0	19.3	15	39	4.3	0.9
Gibson	59.8	1 785	20	267	188.5	11.3	120	1 643	557.6	37.8	17	47	11.8	1.4
Grant	11.8	169	37	367	251.0	15.6	244	3 113	793.3	65.7	43	154	17.7	3.8
Greene	5.5	166	17	130	107.2	4.5	103	1 054	252.4	20.2	19	59	5.2	1.3
Hamilton	72.7	265	357	4 138	3 403.7	291.1	865	15 746	4 338.4	397.7	395	2 349	1 394.5	144.2
Hancock	7.0	100	42	624	737.6	27.2	162	2 102	600.8	48.3	45	167	32.4	4.6
Harrison	3.7	95	20	D	D	D	114	1 423	470.2	30.7	18	36	5.8	0.8
Hendricks	8.6	59	101	2 980	2 723.4	141.5	441	8 760	2 561.4	201.3	108	506	82.6	16.7
Henry	5.1	103	31	D	D	D	152	1 551	466.2	33.1	25	73	7.5	1.7
Howard	17.5	212	62	559	512.7	31.6	328	4 927	1 193.3	104.0	71	311	50.4	8.9
Huntington	4.7	125	36	D	D	D	135	1 347	318.1	26.9	30	73	12.2	1.6
Jackson	9.9	233	35	D	D	D	183	2 225	592.7	49.9	45	115	17.7	2.5
Jasper	55.6	1 662	33	251	529.3	14.7	123	1 449	572.1	31.3	20	89	23.1	2.2
Jay	4.2	195	15	185	230.3	7.3	66	650	136.9	14.1	6	9	2.2	0.3
Jefferson	1 249.1	38 519	19	D	D	D	128	1 550	390.9	35.3	30	70	11.6	2.1
Jennings	3.1	107	15	D	D	D	66	751	196.9	16.9	10	32	3.2	0.8
Johnson	13.6	97	103	1 981	1 174.7	114.6	494	8 639	2 324.6	192.1	117	356	84.5	10.3
Knox	47.1	1 224	54	588	463.0	23.6	161	2 062	459.1	40.1	38	197	21.5	4.2
Kosciusko	24.4	315	89	D	D	D	298	3 566	921.5	82.7	72	162	24.7	3.8
LaGrange	19.9	536	33	313	182.4	10.4	151	1 127	284.4	24.7	26	47	7.4	1.2
Lake	1 696.0	3 419	413	4 472	4 599.1	219.2	1 513	23 986	7 495.3	551.0	373	2 090	371.9	74.3
LaPorte	44.0	395	100	1 161	694.9	46.8	457	5 845	1 367.8	116.2	84	367	95.2	10.6
Lawrence	8.2	177	22	D	D	D	160	1 897	519.2	42.6	21	68	8.1	1.8
Madison	19.1	145	73	974	1 301.2	50.0	346	4 944	1 378.7	107.9	81	348	58.2	10.3
Marion	283.5	314	1 295	23 766	18 700.3	1 359.0	2 952	46 739	14 421.7	1 155.9	1 244	11 355	2 105.2	465.9
Marshall	7.3	154	53	523	430.5	21.5	172	1 993	568.6	45.0	30	86	10.9	2.1
Martin	1.5	149	4	D	D	D	34	350	150.1	7.8	3	10	0.2	0.1
Miami	21.2	575	29	D	D	D	94	900	226.2	18.1	17	44	4.9	0.8
Monroe	18.3	133	82	D	D	D	458	7 390	1 661.3	145.2	163	865	152.5	27.7
Montgomery	6.1	160	41	343	365.7	16.0	129	1 651	446.6	34.4	29	63	12.0	1.9
Morgan	183.8	2 668	33	275	139.3	13.8	196	2 374	638.0	49.7	44	97	15.6	2.8
Newton	6.0	422	19	178	214.9	7.2	40	336	88.0	6.4	5	13	0.6	0.2
Noble	11.2	235	39	507	450.7	22.7	139	1 543	392.9	33.4	34	87	12.2	2.2
Ohio	1.0	162	4	D	D	D	13	88	15.3	1.3	3	D	D	D
Orange	1.5	77	12	74	63.7	2.9	61	668	156.0	13.6	11	35	2.3	0.6
Owen	2.5	115	10	D	D	D	38	424	111.9	9.3	7	7	1.5	0.2
Parke	2.8	163	7	97	47.6	2.8	43	304	70.1	5.7	11	66	6.2	2.2
Perry	2.5	131	9	66	13.3	1.9	65	718	157.2	13.2	11	33	4.3	0.7

1. Merchant wholesalers, except manufacturers' sales branches and offices.   2. Employer establishments.

Table B. States and Counties — **Professional Services, Manufacturing, and Accommodation and Food Services**

STATE County	Professional, scientific, and technical services, 2012				Manufacturing, 2012				Accommodation and food services, 2012			
	Number of establish-ments	Number of employees	Receipts (mil dol)	Annual payroll (mil dol)	Number of establish-ments	Number of employees	Receipts (mil dol)	Annual payroll (mil dol)	Number of establish-ments	Number of employees	Sales (mil dol)	Annual payroll (mil dol)
	147	148	149	150	151	152	153	154	155	156	157	158
ILLINOIS—Cont'd												
Winnebago	608	3 779	660.0	191.5	600	25 024	8 145.6	1 491.8	566	10 168	490.0	137.0
Woodford	47	205	20.5	8.5	45	2 464	1 363.6	122.9	61	830	28.5	8.2
INDIANA	12 829	99 962	14 702.0	5 490.6	8 141	452 513	242 763.8	23 041.3	13 057	255 223	13 076.6	3 432.7
Adams	45	215	19.0	8.0	63	4 246	2 200.6	172.8	55	800	27.7	7.3
Allen	874	5 326	720.8	254.0	501	24 975	16 200.1	1 336.5	712	15 250	643.1	190.1
Bartholomew	159	3 550	299.0	234.7	142	11 663	5 636.4	553.6	201	4 243	198.6	54.2
Benton	8	31	3.5	0.8	15	341	D	13.3	9	51	1.8	0.4
Blackford	11	97	13.3	3.5	24	1 056	255.6	43.8	20	221	7.7	2.2
Boone	166	645	120.2	33.5	69	1 759	D	70.7	117	1 686	71.4	20.3
Brown	32	80	9.5	4.0	15	111	D	2.7	33	D	D	D
Carroll	23	90	7.0	2.2	25	1 963	D	76.1	32	407	19.4	5.6
Cass	44	224	17.7	5.9	50	4 197	1 768.1	144.2	79	1 062	40.8	11.0
Clark	177	1 021	126.2	37.9	143	7 708	2 376.6	340.7	219	D	D	D
Clay	23	D	D	D	33	2 198	520.4	82.3	45	531	21.4	5.7
Clinton	44	144	12.6	4.1	37	3 035	3 192.7	143.0	52	680	27.5	7.9
Crawford	4	12	0.4	0.1	5	D	D	D	21	D	D	D
Daviess	42	554	125.3	42.0	73	1 726	848.1	56.0	56	981	35.3	9.4
Dearborn	69	320	24.6	9.3	46	1 460	385.1	64.9	69	D	D	D
Decatur	31	131	12.6	4.2	56	4 722	4 663.4	208.9	51	953	38.1	10.8
DeKalb	71	449	40.5	14.5	111	8 128	4 742.1	414.3	81	1 387	53.1	14.7
Delaware	163	1 522	240.5	63.4	130	4 205	1 591.3	191.2	211	4 417	172.7	49.6
Dubois	83	355	34.8	12.1	103	9 834	D	363.1	100	1 727	65.8	18.1
Elkhart	313	2 004	220.2	81.0	795	53 705	14 833.3	2 288.0	348	6 500	280.7	75.8
Fayette	28	214	10.5	4.1	30	1 195	489.7	60.2	43	D	D	D
Floyd	195	1 068	151.9	45.7	108	5 421	1 726.9	264.2	130	D	D	D
Fountain	17	75	4.8	1.5	21	2 368	615.1	96.6	38	370	13.0	3.7
Franklin	17	52	9.1	1.3	18	551	258.0	26.2	40	589	27.1	7.3
Fulton	32	142	43.4	4.5	43	1 751	513.9	75.7	45	488	18.9	4.8
Gibson	48	281	29.9	16.3	41	6 144	6 041.4	368.0	68	1 192	45.9	13.2
Grant	75	359	31.6	10.8	68	4 770	2 013.0	278.8	129	2 061	89.8	24.7
Greene	47	253	25.7	9.6	23	449	118.7	23.9	54	702	22.1	6.5
Hamilton	1 260	6 790	1 168.3	472.1	196	5 171	1 641.7	242.7	579	11 974	588.2	166.1
Hancock	124	4 210	274.6	186.2	56	2 998	1 183.9	124.7	98	1 872	80.7	23.3
Harrison	40	159	11.1	4.6	41	1 613	473.0	64.4	61	2 442	349.8	49.6
Hendricks	285	1 105	127.4	44.7	96	3 336	2 660.1	148.1	298	6 387	292.8	82.5
Henry	50	209	17.5	5.4	42	1 845	579.9	78.3	64	921	42.8	11.5
Howard	114	631	61.2	22.6	70	7 671	D	593.4	186	3 866	159.9	46.1
Huntington	43	180	15.6	5.4	64	3 417	1 740.6	170.7	87	1 207	47.3	13.3
Jackson	54	294	25.9	8.4	64	5 395	2 307.5	268.1	86	1 536	65.4	18.3
Jasper	49	203	16.0	4.9	35	1 426	650.4	65.8	64	868	34.5	9.5
Jay	22	83	4.7	1.7	34	3 042	1 059.2	119.1	33	545	19.9	5.4
Jefferson	42	242	15.3	7.4	43	2 754	1 548.4	132.8	83	1 408	50.6	14.6
Jennings	19	88	11.1	3.3	37	1 712	425.6	68.3	31	453	17.8	4.9
Johnson	270	1 332	166.6	51.7	123	4 932	2 024.1	237.4	282	6 135	263.6	75.4
Knox	46	216	18.9	6.1	40	1 789	464.0	66.8	84	1 508	63.5	16.8
Kosciusko	138	475	44.8	14.4	173	13 247	7 235.4	750.6	167	2 452	113.3	31.3
LaGrange	39	178	10.8	4.3	134	5 141	1 416.3	234.2	68	907	39.6	11.2
Lake	886	6 003	709.3	261.6	349	23 122	30 831.9	1 746.0	983	18 097	1 167.0	265.5
LaPorte	158	1 069	85.0	40.4	172	7 589	2 644.0	350.5	235	4 992	357.0	78.7
Lawrence	66	784	87.5	34.2	60	2 008	437.3	100.3	69	1 177	52.2	13.6
Madison	182	769	70.8	23.0	94	2 701	1 391.1	129.3	229	3 885	165.5	47.6
Marion	2 747	32 947	5 954.4	2 344.4	881	42 808	28 049.4	2 579.2	2 130	47 455	2 645.5	734.8
Marshall	62	334	24.4	8.9	130	5 712	1 816.5	240.3	90	1 343	56.6	16.7
Martin	20	1 107	163.2	64.4	10	324	64.2	15.9	25	243	8.8	2.7
Miami	31	111	8.6	3.1	38	1 542	D	68.7	55	796	31.2	8.7
Monroe	289	2 014	240.8	98.8	94	6 578	1 548.5	283.0	368	7 805	335.9	92.3
Montgomery	53	187	15.3	5.1	64	4 658	2 719.5	230.0	91	1 150	49.5	12.6
Morgan	94	323	31.4	10.1	64	1 847	649.4	86.0	71	D	D	D
Newton	17	61	5.8	1.9	24	663	156.2	24.9	28	209	8.7	2.2
Noble	46	165	16.6	5.0	123	8 351	2 937.7	337.5	74	1 046	38.5	10.5
Ohio	4	D	D	D	4	16	D	D	12	D	D	D
Orange	18	75	4.5	1.8	24	1 216	208.9	43.5	39	1 921	148.8	37.4
Owen	22	68	5.3	1.9	27	1 117	169.4	48.8	18	363	12.3	3.4
Parke	10	62	4.0	1.4	13	402	D	20.2	24	211	9.1	2.3
Perry	24	78	10.4	2.9	29	1 883	945.5	102.1	40	500	23.7	6.1

1. Establishment subject to federal tax.

Table B. States and Counties — Health Care and Social Assistance, Other Services, Nonemployer Businesses, and Residential Construction

STATE County	Health care and social assistance, 2012				Other services, 2012				Nonemployer businesses, 2015		Value of residential construction authorized by building permits, 2016	
	Number of establishments	Number of employees	Receipts (mil dol)	Annual payroll (mil dol)	Number of establishments	Number of employees	Receipts (mil dol)	Annual payroll (mil dol)	Number	Receipts (mil dol)	New Construction ($1,000)	Number of housing units
	159	160	161	162	163	164	165	166	167	168	169	170
ILLINOIS—Cont'd												
Winnebago	665	19 871	2 398.9	923.1	534	3 186	306.6	82.3	18 120	642.5	24 503	194
Woodford	51	2 063	112.3	60.6	48	213	24.0	6.6	2 495	90.4	15 506	67
INDIANA	15 156	396 923	42 493.1	16 208.7	10 777	72 937	8 909.7	2 106.7	403 546	16 458.7	3 875 847	18 713
Adams	53	1 475	100.3	47.7	76	392	31.2	7.6	3 132	169.9	2 683	24
Allen	947	28 368	2 803.4	1 195.5	661	4 571	441.6	133.1	23 179	947.1	258 232	1 338
Bartholomew	221	4 824	512.8	203.1	111	692	82.5	19.7	4 184	169.7	52 293	300
Benton	13	67	4.0	2.2	10	29	3.5	0.8	609	22.1	1 269	9
Blackford	22	385	27.6	10.6	21	65	7.0	1.5	625	21.7	311	4
Boone	120	2 318	207.4	87.6	98	606	44.7	11.8	5 192	264.8	130 132	433
Brown	22	311	18.8	8.2	18	97	7.2	2.5	1 448	53.6	11 412	45
Carroll	26	255	18.4	7.9	26	85	6.8	1.8	1 307	56.1	8 750	57
Cass	65	2 332	180.8	88.4	59	328	22.5	5.1	1 786	62.9	2 283	17
Clark	239	5 916	591.2	239.0	173	1 192	138.5	33.2	6 718	302.4	93 958	537
Clay	44	574	59.5	17.3	40	360	23.0	6.4	1 420	50.3	877	6
Clinton	50	1 162	79.5	34.0	48	303	26.9	7.6	1 680	61.3	2 711	26
Crawford	14	D	D	D	8	D	D	D	625	24.3	0	0
Daviess	75	1 452	99.5	42.3	69	325	81.7	12.4	2 144	90.0	400	4
Dearborn	117	D	D	D	71	328	29.3	8.1	3 000	126.0	22 181	120
Decatur	59	1 064	99.7	42.2	40	242	22.8	4.7	1 557	61.1	9 714	47
DeKalb	87	1 613	126.8	53.2	70	353	26.5	6.2	2 527	103.9	31 240	151
Delaware	313	9 158	873.1	318.7	174	1 043	105.9	26.2	5 649	206.4	20 048	124
Dubois	124	3 358	314.6	124.1	82	462	58.1	13.4	2 751	107.5	18 530	65
Elkhart	362	10 105	1 160.8	413.6	336	2 069	261.0	61.1	12 754	562.7	74 728	354
Fayette	61	1 773	127.7	57.0	39	171	13.6	3.8	1 042	36.7	498	5
Floyd	238	5 715	577.4	218.7	127	864	81.9	18.4	5 174	226.7	73 938	258
Fountain	24	511	36.2	11.8	33	82	7.4	1.7	977	35.0	3 390	47
Franklin	52	833	55.8	19.3	38	107	10.4	2.6	1 598	66.8	8 083	38
Fulton	45	847	78.6	26.9	38	126	14.1	3.0	1 303	53.0	2 398	10
Gibson	77	1 923	150.9	61.2	53	246	21.9	6.2	1 652	58.6	22 318	149
Grant	192	5 281	508.2	211.7	106	475	50.7	13.4	3 308	112.1	8 958	46
Greene	66	1 049	75.4	27.6	50	176	14.2	3.2	1 821	54.5	NA	NA
Hamilton	897	16 978	2 311.3	740.4	498	3 201	249.8	74.1	27 498	1 409.9	793 129	2 553
Hancock	136	2 511	256.0	93.5	94	391	36.8	9.4	5 045	199.2	88 539	487
Harrison	68	1 346	103.6	39.4	39	127	13.8	3.4	2 553	90.9	26 329	132
Hendricks	296	7 036	763.3	293.4	206	1 574	114.9	37.1	10 736	442.3	232 782	1 232
Henry	90	2 718	194.9	82.2	66	323	31.9	6.7	2 407	85.8	7 350	51
Howard	221	5 417	456.4	182.6	129	922	68.2	18.9	4 225	150.6	34 057	318
Huntington	66	1 812	141.2	53.9	75	369	23.1	6.4	1 827	64.6	15 620	71
Jackson	106	2 528	237.0	87.4	75	435	38.5	9.3	2 139	83.7	20 924	191
Jasper	47	1 400	85.1	40.8	55	D	D	D	1 791	75.7	16 168	79
Jay	28	819	62.4	25.5	35	99	10.6	1.8	1 347	59.3	3 799	21
Jefferson	74	1 963	187.1	80.7	53	257	19.9	4.8	1 818	73.7	5 515	33
Jennings	74	933	70.5	30.0	24	84	6.5	1.7	1 444	53.2	5 132	37
Johnson	331	7 291	632.2	272.9	222	1 587	160.0	49.9	9 886	453.4	157 468	688
Knox	110	3 345	327.7	129.2	69	347	36.4	9.9	1 866	68.8	8 164	45
Kosciusko	149	3 711	321.4	118.8	145	934	108.8	24.1	5 019	192.4	47 547	281
LaGrange	46	807	69.7	25.4	44	197	20.3	5.8	3 653	162.0	24 462	128
Lake	1 254	31 946	3 812.7	1 353.0	876	6 336	638.4	185.0	28 274	1 056.4	252 055	1 122
LaPorte	228	5 626	611.2	208.3	194	1 090	79.0	22.5	5 858	206.4	21 719	108
Lawrence	94	2 646	202.8	80.1	73	361	30.7	8.6	2 577	92.2	3 145	18
Madison	251	6 498	697.3	262.5	199	1 088	77.1	21.6	6 670	235.0	21 562	98
Marion	2 414	83 226	10 235.0	4 151.7	1 625	17 182	3 477.5	665.9	61 844	2 452.5	365 995	1 995
Marshall	72	1 809	156.9	50.9	84	501	50.6	14.3	2 818	114.1	19 858	85
Martin	9	D	D	D	12	63	6.2	2.2	618	21.6	0	0
Miami	40	1 148	98.7	36.7	44	349	34.5	9.2	1 668	62.7	3 164	17
Monroe	329	8 906	927.6	356.4	204	1 905	265.5	55.8	9 182	348.7	87 449	465
Montgomery	84	1 332	106.2	43.3	83	304	24.1	5.8	2 084	81.8	8 501	46
Morgan	109	2 069	235.0	74.2	97	452	42.8	11.5	4 482	181.4	24 101	112
Newton	13	253	13.1	6.2	18	D	D	D	736	30.1	3 373	16
Noble	73	1 347	132.7	43.6	81	280	42.4	7.7	2 553	94.0	20 056	111
Ohio	8	D	D	D	6	D	D	D	343	12.1	1 682	11
Orange	42	862	69.7	25.6	31	138	11.1	2.3	1 153	44.9	330	3
Owen	23	422	22.9	10.0	27	68	4.8	1.1	1 374	51.8	6 227	36
Parke	19	D	D	D	29	71	8.0	1.6	1 082	60.7	6 090	41
Perry	36	846	80.3	26.4	26	83	6.8	1.8	882	35.3	5 055	30

Table B. States and Counties — Government Employment and Payroll, and Local Government Finances

	Government employment and payroll, 2012									Local government finances, 2012				
			March payroll (percent of total)							General revenue				
												Taxes		
													Per capita[1] (dollars)	
STATE County	Full-time equivalent employees	March payroll (dollars)	Administration, judicial, and legal	Police and Corrections	Fire Protection	Highways and transportation	Health and Welfare	Natural resources and utilities	Education and libraries	Total (mil dol)	Inter-governmental (mil dol)	Total (mil dol)	Total	Property
	171	172	173	174	175	176	177	178	179	180	181	182	183	184
ILLINOIS—Cont'd														
Winnebago	10 237	41 731 581	5.0	11.9	6.0	3.7	3.9	7.5	61.2	1 183.6	493.6	527.0	1 804	1 627
Woodford	1 508	5 339 422	4.9	6.4	1.3	4.5	0.9	2.8	78.6	119.7	45.6	61.2	1 570	1 555
INDIANA	X	X	X	X	X	X	X	X	X	X	X	X	X	X
Adams	1 561	4 888 145	4.7	5.9	0.8	2.1	44.7	3.1	37.8	145.4	46.1	31.4	914	779
Allen	10 511	40 339 187	6.4	12.9	4.3	4.7	1.4	5.9	62.8	1 115.0	515.1	426.4	1 183	960
Bartholomew	4 371	15 688 309	3.2	6.6	2.9	1.3	44.5	3.1	37.7	469.7	111.3	106.7	1 348	1 076
Benton	555	1 313 464	8.3	7.4	0.0	6.3	5.5	2.3	69.0	40.6	19.2	16.2	1 838	1 489
Blackford	419	1 328 279	7.1	13.0	1.8	3.7	2.2	4.2	65.8	39.7	21.9	11.2	898	707
Boone	2 618	9 699 681	4.3	6.4	4.6	1.8	30.1	1.6	50.8	311.1	88.4	80.6	1 367	1 089
Brown	487	1 429 248	8.6	9.6	0.0	3.1	3.6	3.8	70.3	49.6	24.3	20.7	1 373	893
Carroll	613	1 723 537	7.5	7.8	0.0	5.1	6.1	5.3	66.8	54.7	26.6	20.7	1 030	776
Cass	2 403	7 224 020	3.1	5.7	1.4	1.6	31.7	7.4	48.9	182.8	62.7	46.0	1 192	797
Clark	4 732	18 084 071	3.7	7.9	2.7	2.4	38.3	3.7	41.0	466.1	142.4	134.5	1 201	884
Clay	1 049	2 619 145	6.8	6.9	1.9	3.0	1.0	5.5	72.4	75.7	42.8	22.3	831	529
Clinton	1 323	4 321 114	6.4	5.1	2.9	2.8	0.7	8.5	67.5	112.5	54.4	40.9	1 238	878
Crawford	416	1 229 568	6.6	5.4	0.0	4.7	3.2	1.7	77.0	32.3	18.4	8.3	783	640
Daviess	1 354	4 234 993	5.9	7.5	1.3	3.1	36.1	7.1	38.5	148.6	57.8	30.0	937	730
Dearborn	2 410	9 132 488	4.4	7.5	0.7	1.6	40.1	3.6	41.5	318.7	143.7	50.2	1 007	864
Decatur	1 237	4 252 343	4.4	5.2	2.3	2.0	40.2	2.9	42.7	119.2	37.5	26.3	1 009	794
DeKalb	1 614	5 058 353	9.1	8.5	2.6	3.0	1.3	8.0	66.9	153.8	68.7	51.5	1 216	955
Delaware	3 335	10 832 587	6.2	9.0	3.6	4.7	3.7	4.2	64.9	345.4	171.1	109.1	930	778
Dubois	1 643	4 804 962	7.3	8.1	0.8	5.6	2.5	16.6	59.1	155.2	64.9	49.7	1 180	905
Elkhart	6 985	24 411 992	5.4	8.4	4.1	2.5	1.6	3.6	73.6	630.5	315.1	218.4	1 094	907
Fayette	815	2 807 530	4.2	10.7	4.2	2.9	3.8	5.1	67.2	77.2	42.2	24.8	1 032	701
Floyd	4 128	15 144 305	3.0	3.9	2.2	0.8	54.1	2.1	33.3	467.4	119.9	81.4	1 081	846
Fountain	702	1 835 852	6.6	8.5	1.6	5.5	6.2	3.5	67.3	53.7	31.0	15.9	930	767
Franklin	568	1 607 664	8.0	8.8	0.0	4.5	1.5	2.6	73.5	47.8	26.1	16.2	704	477
Fulton	976	3 541 251	3.8	5.5	1.3	2.2	47.4	1.8	37.3	96.4	27.9	20.7	1 000	751
Gibson	1 093	3 390 759	8.4	7.1	3.0	3.7	4.8	4.6	68.3	107.6	54.3	38.1	1 140	1 012
Grant	2 226	7 247 230	7.6	13.8	3.6	3.3	0.8	2.9	67.7	198.6	103.6	70.9	1 023	759
Greene	1 299	4 191 866	4.9	6.2	1.0	2.4	23.5	4.2	56.9	123.7	53.8	24.9	756	573
Hamilton	9 749	38 707 131	4.7	8.4	7.3	2.0	14.0	2.7	59.9	1 219.3	387.4	488.6	1 688	1 330
Hancock	2 896	9 851 360	4.6	8.2	3.9	1.7	31.8	2.5	45.9	327.9	103.5	93.6	1 319	977
Harrison	1 349	4 713 395	5.2	4.9	0.0	2.6	36.7	2.0	47.0	155.4	72.7	26.9	689	469
Hendricks	6 025	22 075 204	3.7	5.6	5.8	1.4	30.4	2.6	50.1	681.2	209.2	213.8	1 421	1 074
Henry	2 369	7 555 604	4.3	5.2	1.2	2.3	32.1	3.4	50.6	241.5	75.8	42.1	853	643
Howard	4 091	15 459 399	5.0	6.2	3.5	2.0	35.8	3.0	42.2	435.8	136.7	118.7	1 433	1 170
Huntington	1 237	3 734 687	5.5	8.0	4.3	3.5	1.1	5.4	69.0	101.2	49.3	39.0	1 055	770
Jackson	2 118	8 012 413	3.8	6.5	2.3	1.6	47.5	1.4	36.3	212.1	54.8	30.5	707	506
Jasper	1 433	4 507 418	5.5	8.1	0.3	2.6	29.7	5.3	47.8	131.9	42.0	40.9	1 224	719
Jay	1 099	3 415 778	5.2	6.1	1.4	1.7	36.1	3.1	45.2	123.7	55.6	25.5	1 196	860
Jefferson	902	3 038 763	7.5	7.5	0.7	2.5	2.6	4.5	74.2	89.4	47.0	26.9	826	757
Jennings	908	2 922 410	4.4	7.4	0.6	3.0	2.6	5.4	75.0	78.7	47.6	22.3	793	611
Johnson	4 964	16 948 881	4.8	8.7	2.9	1.9	18.6	2.7	59.4	506.1	198.1	162.0	1 131	885
Knox	2 489	8 335 443	2.7	4.6	1.9	1.6	60.2	2.8	25.4	286.7	52.9	33.9	890	737
Kosciusko	2 569	8 158 465	6.1	8.0	0.4	2.3	0.9	3.7	77.8	243.0	119.1	85.5	1 101	909
LaGrange	1 149	3 367 799	4.8	6.5	0.3	3.1	0.6	2.5	80.6	95.5	51.4	32.4	865	663
Lake	18 892	64 877 066	9.2	9.9	4.1	4.4	2.1	8.2	60.1	2 367.0	1 042.1	989.0	2 003	1 956
LaPorte	4 264	12 639 630	5.9	11.9	4.3	3.5	3.5	6.6	63.1	369.8	180.5	137.0	1 231	1 055
Lawrence	1 833	6 258 969	4.2	7.1	2.2	2.7	24.3	3.4	55.6	143.8	73.1	50.7	1 100	799
Madison	3 695	12 894 572	8.1	13.7	4.5	3.9	1.5	11.3	55.4	411.1	191.4	142.7	1 095	811
Marion	34 223	145 267 021	3.8	7.6	6.1	1.6	14.0	18.4	48.0	4 321.3	1 815.1	1 329.5	1 447	1 014
Marshall	1 390	4 686 571	6.2	10.5	1.5	4.0	1.4	5.1	69.8	140.9	76.1	48.0	1 020	856
Martin	313	962 585	8.0	8.2	0.0	3.8	2.8	1.5	67.8	29.8	16.1	7.1	689	541
Miami	1 311	4 091 188	4.5	6.1	2.6	3.8	0.7	6.7	70.0	119.6	65.2	34.0	931	637
Monroe	3 589	12 483 781	10.4	10.4	5.5	5.0	2.7	8.7	56.9	339.2	139.6	147.6	1 046	827
Montgomery	1 366	4 441 185	3.7	7.5	4.2	3.9	1.0	10.2	68.9	131.4	58.1	56.2	1 468	1 078
Morgan	2 356	7 692 514	4.7	7.9	3.4	3.0	18.5	1.3	60.5	238.5	98.7	72.4	1 044	538
Newton	607	1 789 217	10.0	9.0	0.0	3.9	4.7	2.6	67.9	61.2	25.8	18.1	1 291	1 109
Noble	1 526	4 688 687	7.9	9.1	1.0	3.1	0.3	4.9	73.3	132.6	63.7	46.2	972	770
Ohio	248	804 741	9.9	6.7	0.0	5.5	3.4	20.4	52.3	29.4	20.3	4.8	786	579
Orange	656	2 087 602	7.2	6.3	0.2	4.7	1.4	5.5	73.3	74.2	49.7	16.5	838	620
Owen	478	1 467 231	7.6	11.8	0.0	5.3	4.5	1.2	68.4	51.9	27.2	15.9	742	538
Parke	550	1 469 526	6.3	9.1	0.8	4.5	3.5	4.2	69.9	47.3	28.5	14.7	862	531
Perry	892	2 938 269	4.0	4.8	0.4	4.2	35.8	7.7	42.5	92.9	30.5	18.1	929	744

1. Based on the resident population estimated as of July 1 of the year shown.

STATE County	Total (mil dol) [185]	Per capita[1] (dollars) [186]	Education [187]	Health and hospitals [188]	Police protection [189]	Public welfare [190]	Highways [191]	Total (mil dol) [192]	Per capita[1] (dollars) [193]	Federal civilian [194]	Federal military [195]	State and local [196]	Number of returns [197]	Mean adjusted gross income [198]	Mean income tax [199]
ILLINOIS—Cont'd															
Winnebago	1 135.0	3 886	50.2	1.7	8.1	3.0	5.4	750.7	2 570	818	597	14 230	136 220	50 766	5 531
Woodford	116.2	2 982	68.7	1.1	3.9	0.0	7.1	40.0	1 026	69	78	1 835	18 220	73 409	9 523
INDIANA	X	X	X	X	X	X	X	X	X	36 696	20 861	385 558	3 078 600	54 204	6 413
Adams	133.8	3 893	35.3	41.5	1.9	0.6	3.0	120.4	3 505	58	107	2 042	15 000	48 453	5 102
Allen	969.6	2 690	50.6	0.7	6.5	0.4	3.3	1 061.3	2 945	1 908	1 150	17 169	174 050	54 498	6 729
Bartholomew	465.6	5 883	32.7	40.9	1.8	0.5	0.9	364.3	4 603	168	247	6 143	39 650	59 621	7 060
Benton	35.9	4 079	50.7	2.9	2.6	0.5	7.6	27.8	3 163	25	27	590	4 120	43 955	4 301
Blackford	31.6	2 526	55.3	0.6	5.0	0.9	4.4	22.9	1 830	23	38	541	5 840	40 448	3 524
Boone	254.2	4 312	38.4	34.0	3.4	0.2	3.0	422.2	7 162	96	194	3 362	29 790	94 184	16 038
Brown	46.1	3 056	59.2	0.2	2.0	0.2	4.2	23.3	1 545	14	46	827	7 560	51 680	5 788
Carroll	44.9	2 233	56.6	1.7	3.2	1.1	6.3	15.9	791	65	61	813	9 500	50 096	5 042
Cass	169.3	4 387	43.5	32.2	4.5	0.2	2.9	80.8	2 094	93	114	3 067	18 050	43 010	3 912
Clark	456.8	4 081	34.1	34.1	3.8	0.2	1.1	411.3	3 674	1 403	354	5 585	55 920	48 031	4 675
Clay	70.5	2 627	57.4	1.1	2.7	0.5	3.4	38.3	1 426	73	81	1 217	12 080	44 311	3 909
Clinton	106.0	3 210	57.5	0.5	2.8	0.7	3.5	96.4	2 919	59	98	1 633	15 350	45 071	4 042
Crawford	28.5	2 676	60.9	2.8	2.1	0.1	4.3	20.9	1 955	21	32	548	4 590	38 617	2 992
Daviess	136.7	4 263	34.6	34.7	1.9	0.2	4.2	136.4	4 253	71	100	1 743	14 370	47 815	4 991
Dearborn	292.4	5 869	28.3	29.1	2.1	0.0	1.6	199.3	3 999	102	151	2 884	24 610	54 548	5 768
Decatur	123.9	4 759	32.1	32.1	1.8	0.1	1.8	144.4	5 545	61	81	1 480	12 760	47 134	4 530
DeKalb	141.5	3 344	61.2	0.3	3.3	0.3	3.6	92.5	2 185	80	130	1 979	20 370	47 840	4 785
Delaware	323.3	2 755	48.4	0.8	3.9	0.5	2.7	191.9	1 635	283	338	10 601	49 030	44 690	4 665
Dubois	122.5	2 913	62.4	0.6	3.1	0.1	4.8	195.3	4 641	105	128	2 100	22 180	62 647	8 677
Elkhart	609.8	3 055	58.2	1.0	3.9	0.2	3.5	758.8	3 801	260	617	8 464	93 840	52 688	6 184
Fayette	72.1	3 001	59.5	1.8	4.9	0.2	5.4	37.9	1 577	45	71	1 025	10 050	40 420	3 540
Floyd	441.6	5 865	25.8	49.3	1.8	0.0	1.1	309.6	4 113	215	233	6 071	37 690	63 777	8 806
Fountain	45.0	2 632	61.9	2.3	2.9	0.3	7.1	40.9	2 387	60	51	764	7 920	43 910	3 970
Franklin	38.8	1 688	69.0	0.1	2.0	0.3	4.9	26.8	1 166	43	70	953	10 760	53 397	5 758
Fulton	83.1	4 008	31.5	45.7	2.8	0.1	2.5	22.8	1 097	46	62	1 349	9 530	46 288	4 563
Gibson	99.3	2 969	54.6	1.5	3.1	0.1	6.2	186.7	5 581	89	102	1 326	16 120	51 432	5 348
Grant	175.3	2 529	54.4	0.3	7.8	0.2	3.4	108.6	1 566	1 011	195	2 879	29 800	41 784	3 813
Greene	110.5	3 356	48.9	22.9	1.7	0.1	3.4	52.3	1 587	75	99	1 735	14 480	44 873	4 118
Hamilton	1 098.2	3 794	43.5	16.9	3.8	0.1	2.9	2 131.8	7 364	383	952	12 808	142 530	100 883	16 915
Hancock	259.1	3 652	38.3	36.3	2.5	0.1	3.7	430.2	6 065	107	222	3 702	35 210	60 559	6 863
Harrison	142.1	3 631	38.8	32.2	0.5	0.1	1.6	105.0	2 682	95	121	2 049	18 310	48 558	4 686
Hendricks	586.7	3 900	37.8	29.3	2.6	0.1	1.7	985.7	6 552	283	477	7 889	73 900	64 346	7 372
Henry	226.4	4 588	34.1	40.7	1.5	0.1	1.6	118.3	2 397	90	140	2 899	21 660	43 768	4 149
Howard	406.5	4 907	32.7	36.7	3.9	0.3	1.8	200.3	2 417	197	252	4 975	40 210	48 103	4 971
Huntington	90.3	2 442	58.2	0.3	3.7	0.1	4.3	59.5	1 608	85	109	1 419	17 790	46 227	4 332
Jackson	185.0	4 294	31.0	55.4	1.0	0.1	1.1	103.4	2 400	90	134	2 921	21 570	47 193	4 551
Jasper	124.9	3 732	37.4	35.2	2.1	0.1	2.1	207.7	6 207	89	101	1 722	15 380	53 237	5 568
Jay	94.3	4 414	38.3	35.4	2.3	0.6	3.7	67.3	3 148	44	65	1 308	9 540	39 485	3 410
Jefferson	77.9	2 394	64.1	1.2	3.5	0.2	4.5	52.1	1 600	78	94	2 374	14 760	47 736	4 923
Jennings	82.7	2 935	66.8	0.7	2.7	0.2	2.8	49.5	1 758	74	85	1 194	12 840	40 499	3 424
Johnson	466.1	3 255	49.3	17.5	3.5	0.1	2.7	489.4	3 417	391	751	6 638	70 680	63 199	7 854
Knox	274.0	7 186	18.6	63.3	1.2	0.1	2.8	128.9	3 381	163	109	4 862	16 700	48 178	5 123
Kosciusko	216.4	2 788	61.0	1.0	3.8	0.1	4.8	226.2	2 915	163	238	3 011	38 300	54 960	6 394
LaGrange	85.5	2 278	67.1	0.1	1.4	0.1	3.8	71.2	1 896	59	119	1 293	16 810	48 009	4 440
Lake	1 850.2	3 748	45.8	0.6	5.4	1.1	1.8	1 929.7	3 909	1 355	1 489	24 284	227 750	52 198	5 821
LaPorte	330.9	2 974	53.0	1.0	4.1	0.3	2.3	311.4	2 799	171	341	6 649	51 490	49 230	5 332
Lawrence	114.9	2 494	59.2	0.4	4.2	0.2	6.0	97.1	2 107	114	139	2 000	20 790	43 458	3 975
Madison	322.0	2 470	48.2	0.7	5.0	0.2	3.7	497.2	3 814	247	383	5 988	59 370	43 723	4 167
Marion	4 896.8	5 329	31.1	23.0	4.5	0.2	0.9	11 765.5	12 803	14 766	3 134	65 677	456 270	49 236	5 880
Marshall	129.3	2 749	63.4	1.7	4.8	0.2	5.4	98.6	2 098	97	164	2 082	22 100	48 082	4 912
Martin	26.7	2 598	58.5	0.8	2.4	0.3	8.0	14.6	1 421	4 184	76	457	4 710	45 446	4 175
Miami	111.4	3 054	57.5	0.2	2.1	0.2	4.7	101.3	2 777	632	114	1 979	15 380	43 320	3 969
Monroe	289.9	2 055	45.2	1.2	4.9	0.4	4.3	383.5	2 719	304	442	21 841	57 090	55 726	6 955
Montgomery	110.0	2 875	52.3	0.3	3.9	0.5	5.8	103.4	2 703	78	115	1 807	18 210	46 183	4 402
Morgan	210.4	3 033	48.5	21.5	2.5	0.1	2.6	96.0	1 385	92	213	2 607	33 420	52 324	5 356
Newton	55.2	3 932	46.4	2.3	2.3	0.2	6.4	34.2	2 435	24	43	713	6 610	48 307	4 530
Noble	113.5	2 385	60.5	0.3	5.9	0.1	4.5	94.3	1 982	77	145	1 850	22 060	45 907	4 253
Ohio	23.6	3 888	36.5	0.1	3.4	0.1	3.1	15.6	2 573	14	18	332	2 780	46 304	4 382
Orange	63.7	3 235	54.0	0.2	0.9	0.1	3.8	72.0	3 654	40	60	943	8 640	38 302	3 062
Owen	40.1	1 878	63.7	0.0	2.5	0.2	4.4	41.4	1 939	33	64	765	9 500	41 874	3 421
Parke	44.2	2 588	55.1	0.9	2.6	0.1	6.9	39.4	2 308	49	47	1 046	6 850	44 721	4 264
Perry	80.3	4 126	33.1	41.5	1.7	0.0	3.6	65.0	3 340	73	55	1 410	8 630	45 453	4 276

1. Based on the resident population estimated as of July 1 of the year shown.

Table B. States and Counties — **Land Area and Population**

				Population, 2016				Population and population characteristics, 2016									
								Race alone or in combination, not Hispanic or Latino (percent)					Age (percent)					
STATE/ County code	CBSA code[1]	County type[2]	STATE County	Land area,[3] (sq mi) 2016	Total persons 2016	Rank	Per square mile	White	Black	American Indian, Alaska Native	Asian and Pacific Islander	Percent Hispanic or Latino[4]	Under 5 years	5 to 17 years	18 to 24 years	25 to 34 years	35 to 44 years	45 to 54 years
				1	2	3	4	5	6	7	8	9	10	11	12	13	14	15
			INDIANA—Cont'd															
18 125	27540	8	Pike	334.2	12 431	2 266	37.2	97.3	1.0	0.6	0.5	1.4	5.7	16.2	6.9	10.7	11.7	14.0
18 127	16980	1	Porter	418.1	167 791	382	401.3	84.9	4.1	0.6	1.9	9.8	5.5	16.9	9.1	12.3	12.9	13.5
18 129	21780	2	Posey	409.6	25 476	1 586	62.2	97.1	1.7	0.5	0.8	1.2	5.8	16.6	7.9	11.1	11.5	13.8
18 131	...	6	Pulaski	433.6	12 660	2 251	29.2	95.5	1.2	0.9	0.6	2.9	5.3	16.9	7.8	10.5	11.8	13.8
18 133	26900	1	Putnam	480.5	37 436	1 237	77.9	93.1	4.2	0.6	1.5	1.8	4.9	14.6	14.4	11.9	11.2	13.8
18 135	...	6	Randolph	452.4	25 082	1 607	55.4	95.4	1.2	0.7	0.6	3.2	6.1	17.2	7.7	10.2	11.9	13.3
18 137	...	6	Ripley	446.4	28 846	1 464	64.6	96.6	0.8	0.7	1.1	1.9	5.7	18.0	8.2	10.5	11.8	13.9
18 139	...	6	Rush	408.1	16 649	2 001	40.8	96.9	1.5	0.5	0.5	1.6	5.8	17.1	8.1	10.9	11.4	14.3
18 141	43780	2	St. Joseph	457.9	269 141	253	587.8	75.7	14.6	0.9	3.0	8.6	6.5	17.4	11.0	13.1	11.7	12.3
18 143	31140	1	Scott	190.4	23 730	1 649	124.6	96.6	0.8	0.5	0.8	2.1	5.9	16.5	8.1	11.9	12.4	14.6
18 145	26900	1	Shelby	411.2	44 324	1 083	107.8	93.6	1.6	0.6	1.1	4.2	5.7	17.3	7.8	11.7	12.1	14.3
18 147	...	8	Spencer	396.8	20 648	1 790	52.0	95.9	1.2	0.5	0.5	2.8	5.6	17.0	7.4	10.2	11.5	14.1
18 149	...	6	Starke	309.1	23 009	1 679	74.4	95.4	0.8	0.8	0.4	3.6	5.8	17.0	7.7	11.4	11.8	13.5
18 151	11420	7	Steuben	308.8	34 116	1 323	110.5	94.7	1.1	0.6	1.1	3.6	5.5	15.0	10.6	10.7	10.7	13.7
18 153	45460	3	Sullivan	447.1	20 802	1 783	46.5	93.3	4.9	0.7	0.5	1.7	5.7	14.5	8.4	14.0	13.4	14.0
18 155	...	8	Switzerland	220.7	10 527	2 388	47.7	96.6	1.1	0.6	0.6	2.2	6.5	18.4	7.2	11.4	11.8	14.4
18 157	29200	3	Tippecanoe	499.8	188 059	345	376.3	78.3	6.0	0.6	8.9	8.2	6.2	14.7	24.0	14.2	10.5	10.0
18 159	...	6	Tipton	260.5	15 182	2 084	58.3	95.9	1.0	0.5	0.8	2.8	4.9	16.0	8.0	9.9	11.3	14.6
18 161	17140	1	Union	161.2	7 212	2 651	44.7	96.9	1.3	0.8	0.7	1.7	5.3	16.1	8.5	10.2	11.6	15.1
18 163	21780	2	Vanderburgh	233.7	181 721	358	777.6	86.3	11.0	0.6	1.9	2.6	6.1	15.7	10.1	14.5	11.5	12.3
18 165	45460	3	Vermillion	256.9	15 645	2 062	60.9	97.8	0.8	0.5	0.7	1.2	5.3	16.8	7.5	10.7	12.0	13.3
18 167	45460	3	Vigo	403.5	107 931	556	267.5	87.9	8.5	0.8	2.6	2.6	5.8	14.8	15.2	12.8	11.5	12.0
18 169	47340	6	Wabash	412.4	31 762	1 384	77.0	95.5	1.1	1.1	0.7	2.6	5.2	15.8	10.0	10.6	11.0	12.6
18 171	...	8	Warren	364.7	8 166	2 584	22.4	97.3	0.7	0.5	0.9	1.5	5.7	16.3	7.0	9.9	11.2	14.8
18 173	21780	2	Warrick	384.8	62 498	845	162.4	93.9	2.2	0.5	2.9	1.8	5.7	18.6	7.6	10.7	12.9	13.7
18 175	31140	1	Washington	513.7	27 670	1 505	53.9	97.7	0.8	0.6	0.5	1.3	5.7	17.2	7.8	11.4	12.5	14.7
18 177	39980	5	Wayne	401.7	66 568	795	165.7	91.0	6.6	0.8	1.5	2.8	5.7	16.4	9.0	11.4	11.8	13.3
18 179	23060	2	Wells	368.1	27 949	1 490	75.9	95.5	1.1	0.6	0.9	2.9	6.4	17.8	8.1	11.1	11.4	12.9
18 181	...	6	White	505.1	23 999	1 643	47.5	90.7	0.9	0.9	0.8	7.9	6.0	17.1	7.7	10.0	11.3	13.0
18 183	23060	2	Whitley	335.6	33 449	1 343	99.7	96.9	0.8	0.7	0.7	1.9	5.9	17.2	7.7	11.5	12.1	13.2
19 000	...	0	IOWA	55 856.5	3 134 693	X	56.1	87.7	4.4	0.7	3.0	5.8	6.4	16.9	10.3	12.6	11.7	12.4
19 001	...	8	Adair	569.3	7 092	2 663	12.5	97.2	0.8	0.5	0.6	1.7	5.1	16.2	6.4	10.5	10.3	13.0
19 003	...	9	Adams	423.4	3 693	2 924	8.7	97.1	0.4	0.7	0.9	1.5	6.6	15.3	6.4	10.5	10.2	12.2
19 005	...	6	Allamakee	639.1	13 884	2 176	21.7	91.6	1.9	0.5	0.6	6.0	6.4	16.2	7.1	9.9	9.9	12.4
19 007	...	7	Appanoose	497.3	12 462	2 261	25.1	96.8	1.1	0.8	0.8	1.8	6.0	16.2	7.0	10.4	10.6	12.7
19 009	...	8	Audubon	443.0	5 678	2 786	12.8	97.7	0.7	0.5	0.7	1.3	5.3	14.7	7.4	9.0	9.4	13.3
19 011	16300	2	Benton	716.3	25 699	1 576	35.9	97.4	1.0	0.5	0.5	1.5	5.8	17.8	7.7	10.0	11.9	14.6
19 013	47940	3	Black Hawk	565.8	132 904	475	234.9	84.0	10.3	0.5	3.0	4.3	6.5	15.1	15.5	13.0	10.9	11.0
19 015	14340	6	Boone	571.6	26 532	1 544	46.4	95.3	1.6	0.6	0.9	2.6	5.5	16.5	7.5	12.3	12.1	13.0
19 017	47940	3	Bremer	435.5	24 798	1 618	56.9	96.3	1.5	0.4	1.3	1.6	5.7	16.4	11.9	10.7	11.5	11.9
19 019	...	6	Buchanan	571.0	20 992	1 776	36.8	97.4	1.0	0.5	0.7	1.4	6.9	19.5	7.2	11.6	11.6	12.5
19 021	44740	7	Buena Vista	574.9	20 332	1 815	35.4	61.8	3.3	0.5	10.4	25.2	7.7	17.6	12.1	12.3	10.5	11.4
19 023	...	8	Butler	580.1	14 791	2 118	25.5	97.5	0.8	0.4	0.9	1.3	5.4	17.5	6.5	10.4	11.2	12.3
19 025	...	9	Calhoun	569.8	9 846	2 443	17.3	95.3	2.4	0.7	0.4	2.1	6.2	15.1	8.0	10.8	10.4	11.6
19 027	16140	7	Carroll	569.4	20 437	1 808	35.9	96.1	1.4	0.5	0.7	2.3	6.7	17.5	7.9	10.5	10.5	12.6
19 029	...	6	Cass	564.3	13 157	2 219	23.3	96.2	0.8	0.4	0.8	2.5	5.7	17.2	6.9	10.2	11.0	12.1
19 031	...	6	Cedar	579.4	18 454	1 892	31.9	96.7	1.0	0.6	1.0	1.9	5.1	17.3	7.1	10.4	12.2	13.8
19 033	32380	5	Cerro Gordo	568.3	43 070	1 110	75.8	92.3	2.4	0.6	1.6	4.7	5.6	15.3	8.0	11.4	10.7	12.7
19 035	...	6	Cherokee	576.9	11 508	2 319	19.9	94.7	1.4	0.7	0.8	3.5	5.9	15.0	6.6	10.2	9.8	12.2
19 037	...	6	Chickasaw	504.4	12 023	2 292	23.8	96.9	0.9	0.3	0.4	2.1	5.9	17.6	7.5	9.9	10.5	12.7
19 039	...	6	Clarke	431.2	9 309	2 482	21.6	84.7	1.2	0.6	0.9	13.5	7.1	18.2	7.3	11.6	10.8	12.3
19 041	43980	7	Clay	567.2	16 333	2 020	28.8	94.6	1.3	0.6	1.0	3.6	6.3	16.4	7.5	11.3	11.5	11.9
19 043	...	8	Clayton	778.5	17 590	1 941	22.6	97.0	1.1	0.4	0.6	1.8	5.7	16.2	7.0	9.6	10.0	12.6
19 045	17540	4	Clinton	694.9	47 309	1 030	68.1	93.1	4.1	0.7	0.9	3.1	6.0	17.0	7.8	10.9	11.1	13.4
19 047	...	7	Crawford	714.2	16 940	1 982	23.7	67.2	3.1	0.4	2.2	27.6	7.0	18.4	9.3	11.2	11.7	12.2
19 049	19780	2	Dallas	588.4	84 516	672	143.6	87.2	2.4	0.5	5.2	6.0	8.1	20.1	6.8	14.7	15.5	12.9
19 051	36900	9	Davis	502.2	8 860	2 516	17.6	97.9	0.4	0.6	0.6	1.4	8.4	20.4	7.9	10.8	10.7	11.5
19 053	...	9	Decatur	531.9	8 141	2 586	15.3	94.0	2.3	1.0	1.3	2.7	6.1	15.6	17.9	9.3	9.0	10.2
19 055	...	6	Delaware	577.8	17 327	1 954	30.0	97.5	1.0	0.3	0.5	1.4	6.2	17.5	7.8	9.7	10.7	13.6
19 057	15460	5	Des Moines	416.1	39 739	1 183	95.5	90.0	7.2	0.7	1.3	3.2	6.0	16.6	7.4	11.6	11.5	12.7
19 059	44020	7	Dickinson	380.6	17 243	1 963	45.3	96.9	0.7	0.4	1.0	1.9	5.0	14.3	6.3	10.1	10.5	12.2
19 061	20220	3	Dubuque	608.3	97 003	611	159.5	92.7	3.9	0.5	2.1	2.3	6.3	16.7	10.2	12.8	10.8	12.8
19 063	...	7	Emmet	395.9	9 658	2 455	24.4	88.6	1.3	0.8	0.8	9.4	5.5	16.0	8.7	10.9	10.9	11.6
19 065	...	6	Fayette	730.8	20 054	1 825	27.4	95.2	1.9	0.5	1.3	2.3	5.3	15.7	10.0	10.6	9.8	12.7
19 067	...	7	Floyd	500.6	15 873	2 049	31.7	93.4	2.8	0.4	1.7	2.7	5.9	17.1	7.8	10.4	10.5	12.7

1. CBSA = Core Based Statistical Area. See Appendix A for explanation. See Appendix B for list of metropolitan areas with component counties. 2. County type code from the Economic Research Service of USDA Rural-Urban Continuum Codes. See Appendix A for definition. 3. Dry land or land partially or temporarily covered by water. 4. May be of any race.

Table B. States and Counties — **Population and Households**

STATE County	55 to 64 years	65 to 74 years	75 years and over	Percent female	Total persons 2000	2010	Percent change 2000–2010	2010–2016	Births	Deaths	Net migration	Number	Persons per household	Family households	Female family householder[1]	One person
	16	17	18	19	20	21	22	23	24	25	26	27	28	29	30	31
INDIANA—Cont'd																
Pike	15.5	11.1	8.3	49.7	12 837	12 770	-0.5	-2.7	846	844	-324	4 994	2.49	70.8	8.4	26.0
Porter	14.3	9.5	6.0	50.6	146 798	164 347	12.0	2.1	11 089	8 828	1 270	62 103	2.62	71.4	12.4	23.6
Posey	16.3	10.1	6.9	50.2	27 061	25 910	-4.3	-1.7	1 701	1 481	-586	10 098	2.51	72.2	8.5	24.2
Pulaski	14.9	10.5	8.4	49.0	13 755	13 402	-2.6	-5.5	867	931	-678	5 184	2.48	68.6	8.8	28.0
Putnam	13.2	8.9	7.1	47.4	36 019	37 952	5.4	-1.4	2 190	2 131	-570	12 649	2.52	71.2	12.1	23.9
Randolph	14.1	10.8	8.7	50.9	27 401	26 171	-4.5	-4.2	1 880	1 789	-1 163	10 529	2.39	65.0	9.2	29.3
Ripley	13.6	10.6	7.8	50.9	26 523	28 818	8.7	0.1	2 084	1 919	-218	10 921	2.58	72.5	10.7	24.0
Rush	14.6	9.8	8.1	51.0	18 261	17 392	-4.8	-4.3	1 156	1 174	-683	6 942	2.42	70.7	12.1	24.4
St. Joseph	12.9	8.4	6.5	51.4	265 559	266 929	0.5	0.8	21 909	15 774	-3 382	102 005	2.50	63.8	13.1	30.1
Scott	14.0	10.3	6.3	50.5	22 960	24 181	5.3	-1.9	1 729	1 877	-332	8 962	2.61	69.6	11.9	25.8
Shelby	14.6	9.3	7.1	50.4	43 445	44 393	2.2	-0.2	3 206	2 741	-475	17 193	2.54	67.5	11.6	26.5
Spencer	15.2	11.2	7.8	49.5	20 391	20 952	2.8	-1.5	1 458	1 237	-596	7 964	2.58	73.6	6.6	22.7
Starke	15.2	10.6	7.0	50.0	23 556	23 363	-0.8	-1.5	1 620	1 723	-249	8 789	2.62	70.3	11.1	25.5
Steuben	15.4	11.4	7.1	49.0	33 214	34 183	2.9	-0.2	2 303	1 904	-404	13 485	2.44	69.5	9.8	25.4
Sullivan	13.2	10.1	6.8	45.7	21 751	21 475	-1.3	-3.1	1 494	1 454	-707	7 639	2.47	71.9	11.1	23.4
Switzerland	13.4	10.4	6.5	48.9	9 065	10 613	17.1	-0.8	791	649	-214	4 071	2.55	73.0	11.4	22.0
Tippecanoe	9.7	6.2	4.5	48.9	148 955	172 803	16.0	8.8	14 218	6 986	8 167	67 756	2.46	55.8	10.2	30.3
Tipton	15.0	11.7	8.5	50.0	16 577	15 936	-3.9	-4.7	938	1 081	-578	6 394	2.40	70.4	11.5	26.0
Union	14.8	11.2	7.3	50.4	7 349	7 516	2.3	-4.0	471	426	-384	2 963	2.44	64.2	7.0	31.7
Vanderburgh	14.0	8.7	7.1	51.6	171 922	179 703	4.5	1.1	14 175	11 829	-12	74 217	2.35	60.7	12.9	33.4
Vermillion	14.7	11.6	8.1	50.2	16 788	16 212	-3.4	-3.5	985	1 321	-233	6 538	2.39	63.4	10.8	31.7
Vigo	12.3	8.9	6.7	49.1	105 848	107 848	1.9	0.1	8 097	7 152	-1 055	40 315	2.45	61.1	12.3	31.4
Wabash	14.4	10.6	9.8	51.4	34 960	32 888	-5.9	-3.4	2 129	2 583	-759	12 901	2.36	68.6	10.2	27.6
Warren	15.3	11.0	8.7	50.3	8 419	8 508	1.1	-4.0	576	468	-476	3 305	2.50	74.1	8.4	22.4
Warrick	13.8	10.3	6.8	50.7	52 383	59 689	13.9	4.7	4 079	3 340	1 973	22 883	2.63	74.3	8.6	22.3
Washington	14.4	9.9	6.5	50.3	27 223	28 262	3.8	-2.1	1 931	1 829	-684	10 542	2.62	69.6	12.3	26.4
Wayne	13.9	10.3	8.3	51.6	71 097	69 003	-2.9	-3.5	4 884	5 215	-2 025	27 168	2.40	65.4	14.4	29.6
Wells	14.6	9.8	7.9	50.5	27 600	27 636	0.1	1.1	2 130	1 652	-177	10 831	2.52	70.8	9.3	26.7
White	15.0	11.4	8.4	50.3	25 267	24 643	-2.5	-2.6	1 783	1 676	-744	9 513	2.53	70.0	7.6	25.8
Whitley	15.5	9.9	6.9	50.1	30 707	33 291	8.4	0.5	2 453	1 879	-343	13 152	2.50	72.6	9.9	23.7
IOWA	13.3	9.0	7.4	50.3	2 926 324	3 046 869	4.1	2.9	243 461	178 416	24 643	1 236 409	2.42	64.5	9.3	28.9
Adair	15.6	10.7	12.1	50.6	8 243	7 682	-6.8	-7.7	429	674	-357	3 229	2.25	63.5	7.7	30.6
Adams	16.7	11.3	10.6	50.0	4 482	4 029	-10.1	-8.3	290	305	-289	1 718	2.18	68.2	4.7	26.8
Allamakee	15.7	12.4	10.0	49.0	14 675	14 328	-2.4	-3.1	1 103	1 012	-521	6 048	2.26	65.4	5.3	28.4
Appanoose	15.2	12.0	9.9	50.6	13 721	12 887	-6.1	-3.3	919	1 083	-250	5 481	2.28	61.0	6.6	34.4
Audubon	16.2	11.6	13.1	51.1	6 830	6 119	-10.4	-7.2	390	486	-322	2 659	2.15	64.5	8.6	31.3
Benton	14.4	9.7	8.0	50.3	25 308	26 076	3.0	-1.4	1 795	1 437	-745	10 154	2.51	70.9	7.3	24.8
Black Hawk	12.5	8.6	6.9	51.0	128 012	131 090	2.4	1.4	10 756	7 381	-1 306	52 410	2.42	59.1	10.1	32.0
Boone	15.6	9.7	7.8	49.5	26 224	26 306	0.3	0.9	1 856	1 847	223	10 759	2.37	64.3	7.1	30.2
Bremer	12.8	10.1	9.1	50.7	23 325	24 276	4.1	2.2	1 595	1 305	236	9 365	2.45	68.9	6.0	26.8
Buchanan	13.6	9.4	7.7	50.3	21 093	20 958	-0.6	0.2	1 789	1 264	-459	8 268	2.50	67.7	7.9	27.1
Buena Vista	13.0	7.6	7.8	49.5	20 411	20 260	-0.7	0.4	2 007	1 162	-724	7 635	2.55	67.2	9.0	28.3
Butler	14.6	11.8	10.2	50.1	15 305	14 867	-2.9	-0.5	979	1 121	66	6 207	2.37	69.3	5.8	26.1
Calhoun	15.6	11.0	11.4	48.2	11 115	10 177	-8.4	-3.3	692	888	-100	4 261	2.19	64.5	8.4	31.8
Carroll	14.7	9.3	10.4	51.0	21 421	20 816	-2.8	-1.8	1 626	1 526	-490	8 547	2.36	64.4	7.5	33.5
Cass	15.0	11.4	10.5	50.3	14 684	13 956	-5.0	-5.7	909	1 199	-513	6 080	2.18	62.7	8.5	33.2
Cedar	15.2	10.1	8.8	50.3	18 187	18 495	1.7	-0.2	1 157	1 105	-57	7 620	2.37	67.8	7.1	27.1
Cerro Gordo	15.7	10.8	9.8	51.0	46 447	44 151	-4.9	-2.4	2 958	3 086	-929	19 519	2.17	60.6	9.1	34.3
Cherokee	16.5	11.3	12.6	50.0	13 035	12 072	-7.4	-4.7	797	990	-376	5 334	2.14	61.1	9.5	34.2
Chickasaw	15.9	10.8	9.0	49.6	13 095	12 439	-5.0	-3.3	869	835	-355	5 312	2.27	66.7	7.1	28.2
Clarke	14.0	10.3	8.4	49.9	9 133	9 286	1.7	0.2	775	661	-103	3 744	2.43	63.2	7.5	31.6
Clay	15.2	9.8	10.1	50.7	17 372	16 667	-4.1	-2.0	1 249	1 215	-347	7 146	2.27	63.6	8.8	29.4
Clayton	17.0	11.5	10.4	49.7	18 678	18 129	-2.9	-3.0	1 208	1 207	-509	7 608	2.30	65.9	7.6	28.9
Clinton	14.9	10.3	8.8	50.9	50 149	49 116	-2.1	-3.7	3 597	3 398	-1 993	20 067	2.36	64.2	10.4	29.4
Crawford	13.1	9.1	8.0	48.5	16 942	17 096	0.9	-0.9	1 480	990	-574	6 355	2.64	70.0	11.2	26.8
Dallas	10.1	6.7	5.1	50.8	40 750	66 137	62.3	27.8	7 381	2 437	13 105	27 593	2.69	72.0	8.2	22.7
Davis	12.9	9.1	8.2	50.2	8 541	8 753	2.5	1.2	852	522	-244	3 165	2.73	71.3	7.3	24.9
Decatur	13.0	9.5	9.4	49.6	8 689	8 457	-2.7	-3.7	583	590	-315	3 144	2.38	64.9	9.9	30.3
Delaware	15.7	9.7	9.1	49.8	18 404	17 764	-3.5	-2.5	1 291	1 079	-650	6 973	2.48	71.7	7.7	24.2
Des Moines	14.3	10.9	9.0	51.1	42 351	40 325	-4.8	-1.5	2 934	2 884	-606	16 741	2.36	64.2	12.9	31.7
Dickinson	16.7	13.6	11.4	50.1	16 424	16 667	1.5	3.5	1 041	1 222	784	7 804	2.14	66.1	4.9	29.4
Dubuque	13.5	9.0	7.9	50.6	89 143	93 653	5.1	3.6	7 542	5 554	1 389	37 891	2.41	65.5	9.2	28.1
Emmet	15.4	10.6	10.3	49.7	11 027	10 302	-6.6	-6.3	687	767	-581	4 145	2.23	62.6	8.9	31.3
Fayette	15.1	10.8	10.2	49.8	22 008	20 880	-5.1	-4.0	1 330	1 548	-573	8 556	2.31	63.7	8.7	30.9
Floyd	14.2	11.0	10.4	50.7	16 900	16 303	-3.5	-2.6	1 183	1 214	-408	6 901	2.28	65.4	11.7	30.9

1. No spouse present.

Table B. States and Counties — **Population, Vital Statistics, Health, and Crime**

STATE County	Persons in group quarters, 2016	Daytime population, 2011–2015 Number	Daytime population, 2011–2015 Employment/residence ratio	Births, 2016 Total	Births, 2016 Rate[1]	Deaths, 2016 Number	Deaths, 2016 Rate[1]	Persons under 65 with no health insurance, 2015 Number	Persons under 65 with no health insurance, 2015 Percent	Medicare, 2015 Total Beneficiaries	Medicare, 2015 Enrolled in Original Medicare	Medicare, 2015 Enrolled in Medicare Advantage	Serious crimes known to police,[2] 2014 Total Number	Serious crimes known to police,[2] 2014 Total Rate[3]
	32	33	34	35	36	37	38	39	40	41	42	43	44	45
INDIANA—Cont'd														
Pike	213	10 751	0.67	118	9.5	143	11.5	983	9.8	2 643	2 082	561	125	1 214
Porter	3 416	152 306	0.81	1 763	10.5	1 575	9.4	12 221	8.7	27 200	22 348	4 852	2 330	1 456
Posey	242	22 920	0.78	259	10.2	245	9.6	1 578	7.4	4 368	3 263	1 105	591	2 326
Pulaski	193	12 413	0.89	137	10.8	138	10.9	1 266	12.2	2 849	2 350	499	NA	NA
Putnam	4 964	36 018	0.89	348	9.3	340	9.1	2 620	9.8	6 115	4 447	1 668	NA	NA
Randolph	329	22 664	0.74	288	11.5	268	10.7	2 391	11.9	5 675	4 733	942	NA	NA
Ripley	449	26 941	0.87	329	11.4	306	10.6	2 382	10.1	6 408	4 981	1 427	289	1 230
Rush	178	14 533	0.68	201	12.1	187	11.2	1 645	12.1	3 259	2 621	638	NA	NA
St. Joseph	11 386	270 027	1.02	3 458	12.8	2 471	9.2	25 111	11.5	46 740	31 351	15 389	9 184	3 449
Scott	312	21 081	0.72	267	11.3	306	12.9	2 244	11.4	5 455	4 367	1 088	520	2 636
Shelby	683	41 987	0.88	516	11.6	436	9.8	3 927	10.6	7 593	5 652	1 941	1 102	2 457
Spencer	368	18 576	0.77	245	11.9	236	11.4	1 764	10.5	4 073	3 339	734	NA	NA
Starke	16	18 901	0.55	249	10.8	283	12.3	2 362	12.5	4 795	3 947	848	149	763
Steuben	1 304	32 811	0.91	366	10.7	322	9.4	3 127	11.6	7 117	4 004	3 113	801	2 326
Sullivan	2 176	19 843	0.84	243	11.7	204	9.8	1 734	11.3	4 054	3 436	618	166	978
Switzerland	107	8 693	0.58	125	11.9	111	10.5	1 151	13.3	1 659	1 391	268	NA	NA
Tippecanoe	14 476	191 745	1.13	2 356	12.5	1 138	6.1	19 274	12.6	22 335	17 960	4 375	5 132	2 852
Tipton	205	14 196	0.81	156	10.3	165	10.9	1 248	10.3	2 996	2 476	520	123	788
Union	67	5 489	0.46	79	11.0	67	9.3	654	11.1	1 532	1 221	311	NA	NA
Vanderburgh	7 549	202 122	1.24	2 188	12.0	1 887	10.4	14 519	9.8	35 760	25 806	9 954	8 382	4 607
Vermillion	209	14 255	0.76	146	9.3	200	12.8	1 232	9.8	3 438	2 975	463	NA	NA
Vigo	9 510	116 898	1.19	1 291	12.0	1 160	10.7	9 178	11.1	20 564	17 556	3 008	4 424	4 164
Wabash	1 841	31 698	0.95	318	10.0	411	12.9	2 546	10.4	7 383	4 345	3 038	NA	NA
Warren	84	6 728	0.58	86	10.5	85	10.4	671	10.1	1 181	1 028	153	NA	NA
Warrick	727	48 588	0.58	671	10.7	609	9.7	3 961	7.7	10 797	8 042	2 755	945	1 539
Washington	261	22 710	0.55	308	11.1	293	10.6	3 120	13.5	5 190	3 792	1 398	NA	NA
Wayne	2 706	69 665	1.06	734	11.0	889	13.4	6 546	12.4	15 637	13 665	1 972	NA	NA
Wells	472	25 658	0.84	331	11.8	247	8.8	2 087	9.1	4 913	2 874	2 039	478	1 715
White	307	22 795	0.86	278	11.6	293	12.2	2 390	12.3	5 782	4 760	1 022	37	151
Whitley	436	29 546	0.77	411	12.3	298	8.9	2 715	9.8	6 676	3 160	3 516	NA	NA
IOWA	100 516	3 096 371	1.00	39 349	12.6	28 739	9.2	149 178	5.9	563 423	471 906	91 517	73 553	2 367
Adair	154	6 689	0.80	68	9.6	99	14.0	309	5.6	1 414	1 307	107	60	807
Adams	84	3 513	0.81	41	11.1	44	11.9	226	7.7	897	864	33	42	1 085
Allamakee	300	12 616	0.79	176	12.7	180	13.0	840	7.9	3 208	2 832	376	7	49
Appanoose	126	12 306	0.94	137	11.0	187	15.0	677	7.0	3 145	2 691	454	358	2 825
Audubon	117	5 196	0.77	66	11.6	64	11.3	304	7.0	1 412	1 357	55	35	601
Benton	297	19 392	0.50	300	11.7	239	9.3	1 103	5.2	4 500	3 603	897	64	276
Black Hawk	5 506	141 957	1.14	1 768	13.3	1 189	8.9	6 995	6.4	24 135	20 738	3 397	4 559	3 424
Boone	721	23 715	0.79	279	10.5	304	11.5	1 039	4.8	4 763	4 100	663	406	1 536
Bremer	1 610	23 779	0.94	274	11.0	226	9.1	758	4.1	5 036	4 581	455	241	973
Buchanan	326	18 320	0.74	288	13.7	186	8.9	933	5.4	4 021	3 446	575	41	195
Buena Vista	970	21 726	1.12	319	15.7	167	8.2	1 821	11.1	3 441	3 244	197	322	1 558
Butler	190	12 056	0.60	145	9.8	171	11.6	591	5.1	3 522	3 156	366	13	86
Calhoun	730	8 627	0.71	116	11.8	142	14.4	452	6.4	2 355	2 246	109	74	748
Carroll	461	21 594	1.09	258	12.6	258	12.6	803	4.9	4 842	4 462	380	144	700
Cass	249	13 595	1.00	137	10.4	178	13.5	669	6.4	3 355	3 051	304	206	1 521
Cedar	316	14 613	0.61	191	10.4	183	9.9	729	4.9	3 238	2 607	631	170	924
Cerro Gordo	1 047	45 958	1.11	469	10.9	497	11.5	1 628	4.8	10 552	10 178	374	1 350	3 101
Cherokee	372	11 353	0.92	127	11.0	169	14.7	525	6.0	2 754	2 460	294	109	914
Chickasaw	99	11 219	0.83	131	10.9	114	9.5	674	6.9	2 434	2 342	92	76	617
Clarke	155	9 232	0.99	123	13.2	96	10.3	510	6.8	1 663	1 524	139	160	1 711
Clay	254	17 102	1.07	199	12.2	185	11.3	716	5.4	3 935	3 886	49	325	1 971
Clayton	276	16 625	0.87	192	10.9	185	10.5	884	6.4	4 169	3 411	758	48	271
Clinton	634	48 523	1.01	574	12.1	527	11.1	1 808	4.7	9 890	8 326	1 564	1 673	3 460
Crawford	530	17 061	0.98	224	13.2	155	9.1	1 734	12.3	3 160	2 862	298	62	353
Dallas	700	64 869	0.75	1 268	15.0	433	5.1	2 989	4.2	7 050	5 803	1 247	1 262	1 640
Davis	91	7 951	0.79	145	16.4	85	9.6	793	11.1	1 617	1 461	156	25	284
Decatur	758	7 749	0.86	97	11.9	80	9.8	453	7.6	1 637	1 447	190	2	25
Delaware	219	15 669	0.80	222	12.8	176	10.2	795	5.6	3 102	2 522	580	204	1 165
Des Moines	598	43 509	1.18	469	11.8	431	10.8	1 717	5.4	9 327	8 578	749	1 493	3 676
Dickinson	203	17 346	1.04	174	10.1	177	10.3	639	5.0	4 438	4 228	210	144	844
Dubuque	4 343	104 221	1.17	1 237	12.8	900	9.3	3 629	4.7	19 085	10 957	8 128	1 908	1 980
Emmet	452	9 316	0.88	107	11.1	109	11.3	647	8.6	2 185	2 115	70	155	1 558
Fayette	914	19 719	0.91	213	10.6	238	11.9	971	6.3	4 377	3 879	498	263	1 286
Floyd	306	14 880	0.85	192	12.1	197	12.4	800	6.4	3 501	3 289	212	161	1 002

1. Per 1,000 estimated resident population.   2. Data for serious crimes have not been adjusted for underreporting; this may affect comparability between geographic areas and over time.
3. Per 100,000 population estimated by the FBI.

Table B. States and Counties — Crime, Education, Money Income, and Poverty

STATE County	Serious crimes known to police, 2014 (cont.)[1] Rate[2] Violent	Property	School enrollment and attainment, 2011–2015 Enrollment[3] Total	Percent private	Attainment[4] (percent) High school graduate or less	Bachelor's degree or more	Local government expenditures,[5] 2013–2014 Total current spending (mil dol)	Current spending per student (dollars)	Per capita income[6] (dollars)	Median income (dollars)	Households Percent with income of less than $50,000	with income of $200,000 or more	Median household income (dollars)	Percent below poverty level All persons	Children under 18 years	Children 5 to 17 years in families
	46	47	48	49	50	51	52	53	54	55	56	57	58	59	60	61
INDIANA—Cont'd																
Pike	58	1 156	2 741	9.7	60.4	11.6	20.8	10 636	23 169	44 399	55.1	0.7	47 324	11.1	16.2	14.9
Porter	96	1 360	43 537	19.0	43.2	26.4	234.8	8 509	29 922	63 926	39.2	3.7	66 070	11.6	14.8	13.4
Posey	232	2 094	5 896	18.2	46.1	20.6	39.2	10 892	29 821	58 101	42.0	2.8	58 298	9.7	12.9	11.5
Pulaski	NA	NA	3 001	10.2	60.1	11.4	22.4	10 545	22 798	43 836	58.3	1.7	47 455	14.2	21.1	19.3
Putnam	NA	NA	9 759	30.7	54.8	15.2	59.0	9 838	22 983	51 355	48.8	2.2	53 910	13.6	17.6	16.3
Randolph	NA	NA	5 840	3.8	58.5	12.3	42.1	9 771	23 000	40 810	60.3	1.3	41 315	18.0	27.1	25.6
Ripley	30	1 200	6 892	14.5	57.7	16.4	36.9	11 487	23 534	51 170	48.2	1.6	51 553	10.6	15.4	14.5
Rush	NA	NA	3 910	8.8	61.6	14.9	23.9	9 588	23 186	45 121	54.5	1.3	48 970	13.9	20.4	19.6
St. Joseph	344	3 106	75 748	30.8	43.2	27.9	379.1	9 713	24 395	45 471	54.4	3.1	46 881	16.7	24.5	23.8
Scott	243	2 393	5 572	14.7	59.6	12.2	36.0	9 087	21 385	44 442	56.0	0.5	43 104	15.6	24.0	22.4
Shelby	499	1 958	10 621	9.8	56.9	14.8	64.4	8 672	24 645	53 584	46.2	1.4	54 639	11.9	17.2	15.6
Spencer	NA	NA	4 764	7.1	54.6	15.0	29.1	8 708	24 936	55 247	45.3	1.6	56 451	9.4	12.0	10.9
Starke	97	666	5 281	11.1	60.0	11.6	39.4	10 478	20 899	42 208	57.5	0.9	48 106	14.8	23.0	20.8
Steuben	46	2 279	8 574	23.0	48.6	20.0	36.4	9 134	24 576	48 472	51.4	2.2	53 191	10.1	16.0	14.6
Sullivan	147	830	3 922	11.2	56.5	13.2	30.0	9 410	19 715	45 023	54.4	0.9	44 939	16.4	20.9	18.4
Switzerland	NA	NA	2 458	7.1	62.3	9.1	14.5	9 650	19 516	44 061	58.2	1.0	46 344	15.9	28.3	26.0
Tippecanoe	228	2 623	70 283	9.9	36.3	35.2	210.1	9 396	23 529	45 932	53.5	2.7	50 170	18.9	17.8	15.8
Tipton	90	698	3 373	9.5	52.1	19.4	21.1	8 160	25 868	51 613	48.4	1.7	56 292	8.7	12.9	11.0
Union	NA	NA	1 778	5.1	54.6	18.6	16.0	10 876	21 487	44 277	54.4	0.0	45 050	12.4	20.3	17.8
Vanderburgh	368	4 239	42 974	18.3	44.5	24.2	236.0	10 139	24 961	43 046	56.4	2.3	43 823	17.2	24.8	22.9
Vermillion	NA	NA	3 721	7.0	55.0	13.5	25.1	9 841	22 022	43 600	57.9	0.8	44 376	12.9	18.5	17.2
Vigo	264	3 900	31 166	13.9	46.3	22.5	143.9	9 237	21 626	40 313	59.4	2.1	39 635	20.4	25.2	23.6
Wabash	NA	NA	8 018	19.6	54.3	18.8	54.8	10 347	22 674	45 649	55.3	1.6	48 223	12.0	18.1	16.5
Warren	NA	NA	1 750	12.1	55.0	18.6	10.9	9 626	27 731	56 042	43.3	3.7	57 768	10.2	16.3	14.7
Warrick	192	1 347	15 509	16.4	40.6	27.0	87.1	8 712	30 507	62 185	38.9	4.5	66 461	7.5	9.8	8.7
Washington	NA	NA	6 459	8.3	61.8	12.4	40.1	9 228	20 483	41 289	58.3	1.1	43 498	14.4	22.9	21.3
Wayne	NA	NA	16 203	17.7	54.6	17.4	96.0	8 867	22 093	38 494	61.7	1.9	41 849	18.0	28.4	26.3
Wells	14	1 701	6 684	15.2	51.1	17.6	41.1	8 655	24 253	51 101	48.4	1.2	55 987	9.5	13.8	12.9
White	16	135	5 214	5.7	54.8	15.5	44.8	9 380	24 944	52 154	48.5	1.5	50 370	10.9	17.9	16.9
Whitley	NA	NA	8 146	16.5	51.5	18.4	40.8	8 492	26 383	54 389	43.8	1.8	56 142	7.9	11.3	10.3
IOWA	273	2 094	812 755	16.0	40.7	26.7	5 352.7	10 645	27 950	53 183	46.9	3.2	54 843	12.1	14.9	13.7
Adair	67	740	1 596	4.7	52.2	15.3	9.4	10 412	25 990	46 526	54.2	2.4	51 531	11.9	16.5	14.0
Adams	129	956	782	8.4	46.4	15.1	6.8	12 660	26 428	48 043	51.0	2.0	48 162	12.5	20.2	20.3
Allamakee	0	49	2 984	14.4	53.7	16.3	22.5	9 813	26 077	45 890	53.4	2.4	47 756	10.8	17.0	16.1
Appanoose	221	2 604	2 630	11.7	47.6	17.6	19.7	9 490	23 653	41 394	59.5	1.9	41 018	16.5	25.2	24.0
Audubon	34	566	1 259	9.1	52.3	14.3	8.2	10 154	29 882	46 979	52.3	3.5	50 948	10.3	15.3	13.8
Benton	17	259	6 420	14.0	43.7	21.6	36.4	9 454	29 990	60 606	40.9	2.7	65 127	8.3	10.3	9.2
Black Hawk	558	2 866	38 358	10.3	42.2	27.0	235.9	12 528	25 382	48 369	51.4	2.1	50 335	14.2	16.8	16.0
Boone	310	1 225	6 569	11.2	40.9	23.2	38.2	9 761	26 935	52 985	46.7	2.0	58 010	8.8	11.4	10.4
Bremer	250	723	7 153	28.7	38.7	28.6	48.8	9 626	30 504	62 163	39.6	4.0	65 295	7.8	7.1	6.3
Buchanan	10	185	5 155	15.9	50.6	16.8	30.2	9 823	29 045	56 150	43.9	3.3	55 848	10.3	14.4	13.2
Buena Vista	295	1 263	5 513	14.9	52.1	18.9	42.6	10 233	24 511	48 195	52.0	2.5	51 991	13.7	19.1	18.3
Butler	7	80	3 333	6.2	48.6	15.2	11.8	6 064	26 498	52 360	46.6	2.1	54 947	9.2	11.8	10.4
Calhoun	40	708	2 006	4.5	44.6	18.4	17.5	10 056	26 524	44 921	54.5	3.1	49 206	12.5	16.5	16.0
Carroll	87	612	4 868	26.8	48.3	20.1	25.8	10 044	27 100	50 559	49.7	2.3	58 575	8.7	10.5	9.7
Cass	222	1 299	2 827	5.1	52.5	19.9	30.4	11 621	25 868	43 750	58.1	2.6	45 915	13.9	19.7	17.5
Cedar	60	864	4 430	6.3	44.4	21.5	33.7	9 677	27 879	59 047	38.4	2.8	60 120	7.3	9.7	8.3
Cerro Gordo	115	2 986	9 253	13.3	38.2	22.2	64.0	10 250	28 270	46 122	54.1	2.8	50 208	12.3	14.7	13.5
Cherokee	143	772	2 454	9.3	45.0	18.8	17.0	9 706	27 934	48 599	51.0	3.1	52 879	10.3	14.2	13.4
Chickasaw	195	422	2 893	17.4	53.5	15.0	20.5	10 107	26 981	47 040	53.4	2.6	57 559	8.5	13.6	12.4
Clarke	128	1 583	2 056	7.3	55.9	13.9	16.4	8 899	22 586	43 327	57.5	0.7	49 424	11.8	18.2	17.2
Clay	164	1 807	3 783	12.6	43.6	19.3	24.5	9 896	27 138	50 389	49.5	1.6	52 584	11.6	15.7	13.9
Clayton	79	192	3 844	8.7	52.7	16.8	47.7	19 706	26 124	48 007	52.4	1.8	48 598	11.2	16.6	15.2
Clinton	416	3 045	11 782	12.9	44.8	19.6	82.0	10 340	27 255	50 498	49.6	2.5	52 945	13.4	18.2	16.0
Crawford	51	302	4 246	9.1	58.3	13.5	37.9	10 000	23 344	48 084	51.8	2.3	51 834	15.1	18.4	16.4
Dallas	187	1 453	20 151	21.4	26.1	44.2	147.6	9 361	37 669	76 320	30.7	9.0	81 381	5.3	6.0	5.6
Davis	114	170	1 818	27.1	51.6	16.8	12.1	9 777	23 867	48 888	51.5	2.8	49 851	12.7	21.0	20.7
Decatur	0	25	2 362	37.2	51.5	19.8	11.9	10 879	19 493	38 560	61.8	1.5	39 424	21.7	27.1	24.3
Delaware	154	1 011	4 085	15.3	54.2	14.8	22.0	9 667	27 563	58 274	41.8	2.6	59 260	10.2	12.9	11.9
Des Moines	460	3 215	9 058	11.1	44.2	20.0	65.8	9 973	24 614	44 423	56.4	2.0	50 125	14.7	22.6	20.5
Dickinson	70	774	3 262	5.3	34.8	27.4	25.5	9 993	34 218	57 265	43.2	4.6	56 869	8.6	10.7	9.4
Dubuque	177	1 803	25 419	34.5	43.3	28.7	154.8	10 616	27 096	54 605	46.2	2.7	57 862	12.0	13.9	12.3
Emmet	392	1 166	2 570	4.7	45.3	16.2	17.4	9 930	27 707	47 795	53.0	2.8	46 092	13.8	19.0	17.0
Fayette	308	978	4 894	21.1	50.0	18.5	38.2	10 360	24 513	44 928	55.7	1.9	47 615	12.9	18.1	16.8
Floyd	180	822	3 524	12.8	47.5	18.2	21.6	10 310	25 918	44 797	53.9	1.8	49 111	14.5	18.1	16.7

1. Data for serious crimes have not been adjusted for underreporting; this may affect comparability between geographic areas and over time.   2. Per 100,000 population estimated by the FBI.
3. All persons 3 years old and over enrolled in nursery school through college.   4. Persons 25 years old and over.   5. Elementary and secondary education expenditures.
6. Based on population estimated by the American Community Survey, 2011–2015.

Table B. States and Counties — Personal Income

	Personal income, 2015										Earnings, 2015		
			Per capita[1]			Supplements to wages and salaries; employer contributions (mil dol)						Contributions for government social insurance (mil dol)	
STATE County	Total (mil dol)	Percent change, 2014–2015	Dollars	Rank	Wages and salaries (mil dol)	Pension and insurance	Government social insurance	Proprietors' income (mil dol)	Dividends, interest, and rent (mil dol)	Personal transfer receipts (mil dol)	Total (mil dol)	From employee and self-employed	From employer
	62	63	64	65	66	67	68	69	70	71	72	73	74
INDIANA—Cont'd													
Pike	449	1.1	35 617	1 669	157	30	11	28	59	121	227	15	11
Porter	7 798	5.1	46 501	716	2 749	422	207	401	1 124	1 303	3 780	241	207
Posey	1 140	0.7	44 674	695	482	100	34	97	189	213	712	42	34
Pulaski	499	-1.3	38 707	1 395	189	35	14	36	95	119	274	17	14
Putnam	1 250	1.9	33 264	2 520	485	85	38	82	175	287	689	45	38
Randolph	896	0.2	35 614	1 443	293	53	22	58	134	246	426	29	22
Ripley	1 133	0.0	39 492	1 305	565	98	41	45	172	221	749	47	41
Rush	658	-0.4	39 475	1 355	203	39	15	71	96	153	328	20	15
St. Joseph	11 554	5.4	43 040	1 126	5 614	875	429	1 394	1 858	2 198	8 312	497	429
Scott	818	4.9	34 442	2 507	275	50	21	37	92	243	383	27	21
Shelby	1 713	-1.0	38 511	1 522	793	128	60	95	252	387	1 075	68	60
Spencer	858	2.4	41 437	1 211	281	52	21	65	112	167	420	26	21
Starke	705	1.9	30 693	2 670	152	32	12	48	84	240	243	19	12
Steuben	1 294	3.6	37 638	1 780	571	102	45	63	232	288	781	51	45
Sullivan	660	-0.3	31 546	2 526	251	54	18	19	93	194	342	23	18
Switzerland	305	3.2	28 951	2 986	79	12	6	20	37	76	117	8	6
Tippecanoe	6 453	3.7	34 725	2 234	4 018	765	297	420	1 113	1 063	5 499	316	297
Tipton	615	0.0	40 280	1 168	185	32	14	31	107	141	261	18	14
Union	242	-0.5	33 714	2 290	47	10	4	20	34	62	81	6	4
Vanderburgh	7 434	2.6	40 875	1 153	5 015	753	382	541	1 351	1 666	6 691	409	382
Vermillion	545	-1.2	34 742	1 857	209	38	15	18	78	162	280	19	15
Vigo	3 768	2.6	34 922	2 181	2 046	369	159	241	637	1 035	2 816	175	159
Wabash	1 268	2.2	39 447	1 173	453	81	35	122	206	344	691	44	35
Warren	335	-5.0	40 483	980	75	13	6	44	44	71	138	8	6
Warrick	3 008	4.1	48 593	629	762	121	56	227	463	480	1 166	75	56
Washington	991	4.0	35 615	2 219	220	42	17	108	119	253	387	24	17
Wayne	2 445	2.1	36 494	1 968	1 183	206	90	156	364	731	1 636	106	90
Wells	1 058	0.4	37 823	1 290	421	73	32	66	172	225	593	39	32
White	936	-0.3	38 545	1 528	364	64	28	60	155	225	517	33	28
Whitley	1 308	2.4	39 145	1 585	513	93	38	58	186	259	702	46	38
IOWA	143 394	3.8	45 930	X	70 124	11 705	5 255	16 396	25 827	24 677	103 479	6 249	5 255
Adair	334	0.9	46 184	576	102	18	8	56	61	59	185	10	8
Adams	227	9.8	59 850	119	50	10	4	88	35	37	153	9	4
Allamakee	577	1.4	41 538	1 003	176	37	13	99	113	118	325	20	13
Appanoose	448	2.1	35 778	1 820	167	32	13	35	74	129	248	18	13
Audubon	302	-0.2	52 381	205	60	12	4	77	58	56	152	7	4
Benton	1 242	3.8	48 422	564	221	44	16	162	208	198	444	29	16
Black Hawk	5 375	2.1	40 273	1 213	3 393	556	250	306	935	1 114	4 505	282	250
Boone	1 229	3.7	46 124	719	397	78	33	104	215	264	612	39	33
Bremer	1 103	1.7	44 610	731	415	77	31	87	215	188	610	39	31
Buchanan	901	0.1	42 757	946	241	47	18	105	182	166	410	25	18
Buena Vista	976	2.5	47 617	396	394	74	29	268	153	152	766	37	29
Butler	648	-1.0	43 467	531	138	28	10	92	117	136	269	16	10
Calhoun	470	-1.3	47 888	401	103	21	8	106	85	91	238	12	8
Carroll	1 023	0.1	49 914	342	442	74	32	216	192	183	764	43	32
Cass	597	3.7	44 488	708	224	45	17	86	124	138	372	22	17
Cedar	855	1.7	46 629	587	213	38	16	90	172	129	358	23	16
Cerro Gordo	2 438	9.5	56 676	566	1 010	157	78	679	401	422	1 924	126	78
Cherokee	714	12.8	61 661	278	179	34	13	309	105	104	536	31	13
Chickasaw	611	5.2	50 531	224	187	32	15	142	117	101	376	22	15
Clarke	336	2.0	36 327	1 515	160	29	12	39	48	87	240	14	12
Clay	816	7.5	49 426	591	358	63	26	183	153	138	630	34	26
Clayton	816	2.4	46 227	682	256	48	21	132	174	159	456	27	21
Clinton	1 918	2.4	40 161	1 294	882	152	70	104	321	467	1 207	81	70
Crawford	687	-4.8	40 186	915	297	54	21	109	127	127	482	27	21
Dallas	4 760	5.8	59 405	202	2 138	271	151	333	824	392	2 893	179	151
Davis	316	-2.0	36 029	1 890	70	15	5	69	47	66	159	11	5
Decatur	272	1.2	33 059	2 273	76	17	6	34	40	70	133	8	6
Delaware	781	1.6	44 894	470	273	53	21	133	158	127	479	27	21
Des Moines	1 953	8.0	48 760	448	948	156	78	378	327	396	1 560	103	78
Dickinson	927	8.7	54 156	352	366	68	30	122	242	155	587	37	30
Dubuque	4 273	2.8	43 997	828	2 548	385	191	272	865	768	3 396	218	191
Emmet	434	6.8	44 457	978	151	29	11	82	67	89	273	15	11
Fayette	816	1.4	40 294	1 269	255	47	20	119	155	210	442	26	20
Floyd	682	5.2	42 748	939	246	49	18	84	128	156	398	24	18

1. Based on the resident population estimated as of July 1 of the year shown.

Table B. States and Counties — Earnings, Social Security, and Housing

STATE County	Earnings, 2015 (cont.) — Percent by selected industries									Social Security beneficiaries, December 2015		Supplemental Security Income recipients, December 2015	Housing units, 2016	
	Farm	Mining	Construction	Manu-facturing	Information: professional, scientific, technical services	Retail trade	Finance, insurance, real estate and leasing	Health care and social assistance	Govern-ment	Number	Rate¹		Total	Percent change, 2010–2016
	75	76	77	78	79	80	81	82	83	84	85	86	87	88
INDIANA—Cont'd														
Pike	5.6	5.0	11.6	5.6	D	2.9	D	5.1	12.6	3 240	260	238	5 726	0.4
Porter	-0.1	D	8.8	22.5	6.0	6.6	4.7	13.7	9.8	33 155	198	1 958	67 871	2.6
Posey	4.1	1.7	6.0	45.0	4.0	6.3	2.2	D	8.3	5 625	221	342	11 390	1.6
Pulaski	8.3	D	3.7	33.7	D	5.2	4.3	D	20.3	3 255	253	262	6 039	-0.3
Putnam	1.0	0.7	6.1	23.7	3.3	4.9	3.4	D	17.5	7 650	203	442	14 880	1.2
Randolph	1.5	D	9.7	31.4	4.5	3.7	2.6	D	13.2	6 440	256	523	11 616	-1.1
Ripley	0.8	0.2	5.0	18.6	4.7	4.1	5.6	D	8.8	5 795	202	337	12 201	2.1
Rush	8.5	D	8.3	24.2	2.9	6.6	4.4	D	16.9	4 010	240	307	7 456	-0.7
St. Joseph	0.0	D	5.1	15.4	9.3	5.8	5.2	14.9	9.2	51 295	191	5 957	115 988	1.0
Scott	-0.4	D	4.6	34.6	2.5	7.8	3.2	D	15.3	6 220	262	881	10 462	0.2
Shelby	1.0	0.4	8.2	33.0	2.5	5.0	2.7	6.9	13.6	9 480	213	685	19 154	0.4
Spencer	4.1	0.1	6.1	21.4	D	3.5	2.8	4.9	11.2	4 735	228	255	8 968	1.1
Starke	5.6	0.0	6.4	20.9	2.7	8.1	2.7	D	19.9	6 205	270	564	11 019	0.5
Steuben	0.7	0.0	4.9	37.8	2.9	7.5	2.5	D	9.1	8 025	234	443	19 645	1.4
Sullivan	-1.6	D	3.8	11.6	4.0	5.1	2.7	3.9	27.1	4 740	227	381	8 841	-1.1
Switzerland	1.8	D	D	D	D	2.7	D	D	20.3	1 975	188	199	5 163	3.9
Tippecanoe	-0.1	D	4.7	22.9	5.2	5.4	5.1	13.3	27.0	25 035	135	2 274	75 124	5.7
Tipton	1.9	0.0	12.0	29.2	5.0	7.1	4.4	D	14.1	3 745	245	148	6 946	-0.7
Union	-2.1	0.0	9.8	18.8	2.2	7.7	D	D	25.2	1 640	228	124	3 212	-0.8
Vanderburgh	0.1	0.2	8.9	16.4	6.9	6.4	4.6	18.5	9.2	38 835	213	4 580	83 708	0.8
Vermillion	0.4	D	17.9	25.2	D	7.1	D	10.3	11.5	4 110	263	332	7 441	-0.6
Vigo	0.3	0.4	6.0	16.3	4.1	7.0	5.6	18.6	18.2	22 740	211	3 173	46 752	1.6
Wabash	6.3	D	5.8	30.7	3.0	6.3	4.4	D	11.1	8 690	271	592	14 070	-0.7
Warren	12.5	D	5.1	22.0	D	4.0	D	11.9	12.3	1 990	240	92	3 693	0.4
Warrick	0.1	3.3	9.0	20.0	5.8	5.1	6.3	22.8	9.9	12 740	206	673	25 382	4.9
Washington	14.4	D	8.9	23.8	2.9	7.2	3.4	8.4	15.5	6 570	237	642	12 189	-0.3
Wayne	0.5	D	4.2	21.2	3.2	7.8	4.7	20.5	14.0	17 335	259	2 163	31 179	-0.2
Wells	1.4	D	5.6	29.3	D	5.1	5.6	11.2	10.6	6 145	220	315	11 734	0.6
White	5.0	D	8.3	29.6	D	7.7	3.9	6.9	12.1	5 975	247	337	12 964	0.0
Whitley	-0.3	0.0	7.5	46.0	2.0	5.2	3.9	6.2	10.3	7 270	218	366	14 552	1.9
IOWA	5.7	0.2	7.2	16.8	6.2	5.7	9.6	10.0	15.9	622 906	200	51 059	1 380 162	3.3
Adair	22.9	D	7.1	16.3	D	4.8	4.4	D	13.5	1 715	238	95	3 659	-1.1
Adams	20.2	D	3.3	27.7	3.5	2.6	D	D	8.1	1 025	273	66	1 999	-0.5
Allamakee	15.0	0.2	8.2	15.0	1.8	8.2	3.5	7.6	17.4	3 580	258	180	7 677	0.8
Appanoose	2.8	D	5.2	23.4	2.9	8.1	3.4	D	13.9	1 585	276	75	3 010	1.3
Audubon	40.2	0.0	4.8	7.5	1.6	3.4	4.2	D	15.4					
Benton	11.1	D	9.5	17.5	3.1	7.6	5.7	D	19.5	5 465	213	302	11 080	-0.1
Black Hawk	0.7	D	4.6	25.2	5.4	6.6	6.4	13.1	15.9	26 360	197	3 154	57 295	2.5
Boone	8.7	D	8.4	5.6	D	5.9	D	8.4	24.6	5 750	216	319	11 833	0.7
Bremer	5.1	D	6.0	19.4	3.2	5.8	15.2	D	18.7	5 340	216	187	10 275	3.6
Buchanan	12.3	D	11.1	17.8	2.4	6.7	5.2	6.1	20.3	4 350	206	297	9 013	0.5
Buena Vista	24.4	0.0	3.6	22.2	D	5.1	4.0	D	13.0	3 610	178	258	8 276	0.5
Butler	25.8	D	3.8	17.5	3.1	5.0	3.9	6.6	15.1	3 805	255	168	6 743	0.9
Calhoun	36.1	0.0	5.4	2.5	1.7	4.6	4.0	D	14.9	2 610	266	154	5 094	-0.3
Carroll	15.1	D	6.6	10.3	3.1	6.8	9.7	D	8.9	4 750	232	264	9 443	0.7
Cass	13.5	D	8.2	11.7	D	6.5	4.9	8.4	22.7	3 680	276	301	6 558	-0.5
Cedar	8.5	0.0	8.4	12.8	6.4	5.3	3.7	D	15.7	3 955	215	161	8 145	1.0
Cerro Gordo	2.4	D	4.5	31.4	4.7	5.7	5.1	18.8	8.9	11 195	260	827	22 309	0.7
Cherokee	16.2	D	4.3	36.6	2.9	3.7	D	D	10.8	2 990	258	127	5 759	-0.3
Chickasaw	15.8	D	6.4	28.5	2.5	5.2	3.7	D	9.1	2 890	239	129	5 661	-0.3
Clarke	10.8	D	D	30.1	1.1	6.4	2.4	6.6	18.4	2 085	226	142	4 170	2.1
Clay	18.6	D	5.5	9.4	D	10.7	3.7	9.0	16.2	3 990	242	232	8 178	1.4
Clayton	18.4	D	13.8	12.9	2.6	5.2	3.7	D	16.3	4 650	263	218	9 030	0.3
Clinton	0.7	D	7.1	28.0	3.6	6.5	4.8	14.9	11.8	11 115	233	1 133	21 840	0.5
Crawford	16.6	0.0	4.3	28.3	2.0	5.2	4.3	5.5	16.7	3 550	209	202	7 036	1.3
Dallas	0.9	D	5.6	4.2	5.2	6.9	45.4	7.7	7.7	10 610	131	433	34 535	26.7
Davis	7.4	D	13.9	13.5	6.0	6.0	3.4	D	20.5	1 800	205	130	3 578	-0.6
Decatur	14.4	D	D	D	3.4	5.0	D	D	22.1	1 795	219	187	3 843	0.2
Delaware	17.4	0.0	7.9	25.4	2.4	4.2	3.7	D	15.8	3 645	209	199	8 024	0.0
Des Moines	0.3	D	5.8	39.0	3.8	5.9	3.2	13.2	9.8	9 695	242	1 000	18 461	-0.4
Dickinson	6.7	D	13.4	23.9	3.4	9.0	5.3	6.3	12.0	4 965	290	188	13 474	4.9
Dubuque	1.8	D	6.2	20.0	8.2	6.1	10.4	14.0	8.4	20 540	212	1 583	40 880	5.0
Emmet	21.1	0.0	7.2	15.7	3.3	5.1	3.5	D	16.0	2 345	241	129	4 805	1.0
Fayette	18.5	D	7.2	6.6	2.5	5.7	3.8	D	14.3	5 075	251	493	9 522	-0.4
Floyd	12.5	0.0	7.0	26.6	2.9	6.0	6.1	D	14.7	4 080	256	338	7 567	0.5

1. Per 1,000 resident population estimated as of July 1 of the year shown.

Table B. States and Counties — **Housing, Labor Force, and Employment**

STATE County	Total (89)	Percent (90)	Median value[1] (91)	With a mortgage (92)	Without a mortgage[2] (93)	Median rent[3] (94)	Median rent as a percent of income[2] (95)	Substandard units[4] (percent) (96)	Total (97)	Percent change, 2015–2016 (98)	Unemployment Total (99)	Rate[5] (100)	Total (101)	Management, business, science and arts (102)	Construction, production, and maintenance occupations (103)
INDIANA—Cont'd															
Pike	4 994	82.0	88 400	18.4	11.9	620	26.2	1.5	6 299	1.6	277	4.4	5 902	23.6	41.7
Porter	62 103	77.0	165 500	19.5	10.4	862	28.2	1.6	85 964	1.4	4 417	5.1	78 219	35.3	26.4
Posey	10 098	83.1	133 800	18.4	10.1	666	31.9	2.7	13 460	1.1	534	4.0	12 101	31.0	33.3
Pulaski	5 184	76.6	93 000	21.2	11.2	681	27.8	1.2	6 351	1.1	289	4.6	5 831	27.2	41.6
Putnam	12 649	73.7	122 800	21.4	11.4	693	21.3	2.2	16 788	2.2	749	4.5	15 518	28.2	31.0
Randolph	10 529	73.7	78 200	19.3	12.1	580	26.9	1.1	12 608	-0.8	570	4.5	11 319	27.1	36.4
Ripley	10 921	77.3	129 800	20.2	11.6	678	25.3	2.0	13 995	2.5	642	4.6	13 088	27.5	33.1
Rush	6 942	71.4	100 700	19.5	11.2	630	25.9	0.9	8 930	0.9	339	3.8	7 787	28.8	35.6
St. Joseph	102 005	68.5	114 800	19.4	10.0	719	29.9	1.6	133 809	2.5	6 061	4.5	123 170	34.6	23.2
Scott	8 962	72.5	98 700	22.1	11.9	735	27.4	0.7	10 568	2.6	511	4.8	9 803	21.2	41.5
Shelby	17 193	72.3	120 800	19.7	11.1	711	26.4	1.9	23 208	2.4	921	4.0	21 379	25.2	37.0
Spencer	7 964	82.2	116 100	19.6	10.0	587	23.3	1.6	10 987	0.0	452	4.1	10 060	28.1	35.7
Starke	8 789	81.0	96 900	22.4	11.3	679	24.4	2.5	10 881	3.0	590	5.4	9 583	24.8	38.4
Steuben	13 485	77.5	128 800	20.8	11.0	674	26.2	1.2	19 970	-0.2	744	3.7	16 375	26.5	33.5
Sullivan	7 639	73.2	78 200	18.5	10.8	661	34.9	3.9	8 713	0.5	514	5.9	8 203	25.5	36.0
Switzerland	4 071	71.5	119 100	25.5	16.4	785	26.0	3.0	4 984	2.5	243	4.9	4 314	17.4	37.7
Tippecanoe	67 756	52.8	135 200	19.0	10.0	795	34.1	2.1	95 085	2.0	3 800	4.0	86 629	37.9	22.9
Tipton	6 394	77.8	111 500	19.5	10.3	696	28.9	1.0	8 514	1.4	331	3.9	7 195	31.1	32.6
Union	2 963	72.0	102 500	21.5	11.7	650	30.8	1.1	3 630	1.8	147	4.0	3 384	25.9	26.4
Vanderburgh	74 217	63.3	115 500	20.4	11.3	716	31.0	2.2	93 215	0.9	3 828	4.1	86 077	30.8	25.3
Vermillion	6 538	76.2	75 000	19.4	11.5	555	24.5	0.9	7 258	0.3	477	6.6	6 686	23.1	36.5
Vigo	40 315	60.8	91 200	18.6	11.7	688	32.5	2.3	49 137	0.2	2 663	5.4	47 334	31.2	25.6
Wabash	12 901	74.1	95 100	18.8	10.7	640	27.8	1.3	15 484	0.5	665	4.3	14 892	30.0	30.6
Warren	3 305	80.5	107 200	18.4	10.0	753	24.9	2.9	4 109	0.1	200	4.9	4 031	27.4	40.7
Warrick	22 883	81.7	148 400	19.8	10.5	771	29.2	2.2	32 150	1.1	1 307	4.1	29 930	36.3	23.4
Washington	10 542	76.7	102 900	22.3	10.6	622	28.6	2.2	13 861	2.3	629	4.5	11 783	25.6	40.3
Wayne	27 168	68.4	92 200	21.2	11.8	623	30.8	1.9	30 909	0.7	1 484	4.8	28 437	29.3	27.8
Wells	10 831	81.2	115 200	18.2	10.0	621	29.3	1.0	14 233	1.3	508	3.6	13 510	25.7	34.6
White	9 513	77.4	105 500	18.2	11.1	681	25.2	1.9	13 659	0.2	546	4.0	11 433	22.9	38.3
Whitley	13 152	82.4	130 400	20.6	10.0	624	23.6	1.7	17 285	1.4	673	3.9	16 503	26.2	37.2
IOWA	1 236 409	71.5	129 200	19.6	11.5	697	27.5	1.9	1 700 696	-0.1	62 404	3.7	1 573 510	34.5	25.6
Adair	3 229	76.9	89 600	21.1	12.1	553	22.9	0.9	4 242	0.3	129	3.0	3 776	27.1	36.4
Adams	1 718	73.0	87 800	20.1	11.6	538	19.8	1.3	2 258	-1.5	60	2.7	1 994	36.3	32.1
Allamakee	6 048	77.4	110 900	19.1	13.3	554	22.5	2.7	7 717	0.1	388	5.0	6 904	29.8	35.5
Appanoose	5 481	72.5	78 200	19.4	13.4	536	26.6	1.5	6 204	-0.4	298	4.8	5 799	27.2	34.0
Audubon	2 659	82.4	65 000	17.9	10.2	547	21.6	0.7	3 319	2.4	110	3.3	3 008	30.5	29.7
Benton	10 154	81.2	140 600	20.3	10.7	593	26.0	1.0	13 695	-0.7	499	3.6	13 080	32.5	29.9
Black Hawk	52 410	67.5	130 200	19.4	11.0	700	30.5	1.7	69 678	-1.3	3 280	4.7	67 141	32.0	25.4
Boone	10 759	75.4	119 600	20.2	12.5	644	26.1	2.3	15 264	-0.4	432	2.8	13 403	32.8	27.0
Bremer	9 365	80.0	151 600	19.6	10.4	591	25.0	0.6	13 890	-0.7	508	3.7	12 843	35.0	25.0
Buchanan	8 268	79.5	126 600	19.3	11.1	629	25.5	2.5	11 271	-0.5	471	4.2	10 375	29.6	34.4
Buena Vista	7 635	68.9	103 900	20.2	10.0	593	23.8	6.5	11 611	0.1	416	3.6	10 725	25.8	38.4
Butler	6 207	79.9	107 400	18.4	11.8	566	20.5	1.3	8 102	-2.3	357	4.4	7 419	27.9	33.1
Calhoun	4 261	76.8	76 100	18.5	10.3	517	29.3	1.1	4 518	1.3	175	3.9	4 614	32.8	27.2
Carroll	8 547	74.7	113 200	18.1	10.0	542	28.1	0.9	11 359	0.4	297	2.6	10 722	29.4	30.4
Cass	6 080	71.2	89 500	19.9	11.5	569	25.7	0.9	7 334	-1.8	245	3.3	6 712	28.4	31.0
Cedar	7 620	79.8	134 700	19.4	12.8	670	22.0	1.3	10 918	-0.7	368	3.4	9 763	33.9	27.6
Cerro Gordo	19 519	71.0	115 200	19.6	11.9	617	27.5	0.7	23 150	0.5	846	3.7	22 601	30.2	27.3
Cherokee	5 334	73.8	84 200	16.8	10.0	516	19.7	1.0	6 351	0.0	234	3.7	6 018	27.8	33.3
Chickasaw	5 312	78.0	103 400	18.3	12.0	556	25.3	0.8	6 442	-0.4	288	4.5	6 148	27.9	36.7
Clarke	3 744	69.8	91 200	21.6	14.2	678	30.3	2.4	4 855	1.7	167	3.4	4 504	27.0	34.7
Clay	7 146	74.5	110 500	19.0	11.1	594	24.5	1.8	8 749	-1.3	345	3.9	8 504	28.4	32.5
Clayton	7 608	78.4	106 700	21.3	12.5	574	23.9	1.7	10 391	0.8	448	4.3	8 996	27.9	33.0
Clinton	20 067	73.7	110 100	19.2	12.4	620	29.1	0.9	23 914	-2.2	1 202	5.0	23 564	27.8	31.0
Crawford	6 355	75.1	90 200	18.7	10.0	541	25.3	3.7	8 484	-3.2	472	5.6	8 192	25.7	39.6
Dallas	27 593	76.6	190 700	19.5	10.8	910	24.8	1.5	44 232	1.1	1 195	2.7	40 388	47.5	15.0
Davis	3 165	79.3	99 900	20.9	11.2	582	26.2	5.9	4 306	2.9	187	4.3	3 821	28.3	36.4
Decatur	3 144	67.0	81 500	21.1	13.6	462	27.7	5.2	4 448	0.3	146	3.3	3 660	32.8	26.7
Delaware	6 973	80.0	123 300	20.4	10.5	602	25.5	1.3	10 795	0.9	381	3.5	9 442	28.7	36.3
Des Moines	16 741	73.7	98 200	20.2	13.1	637	28.7	2.3	20 222	-1.6	1 009	5.0	18 798	28.1	29.2
Dickinson	7 804	75.5	167 800	21.5	10.0	643	25.4	0.7	10 359	1.3	451	4.4	8 899	34.3	28.5
Dubuque	37 891	72.4	149 400	19.9	11.5	696	29.8	1.3	55 049	-1.3	1 991	3.6	50 102	33.7	23.6
Emmet	4 145	76.9	84 100	18.8	11.4	608	26.7	2.0	5 611	-1.1	244	4.3	4 955	27.8	35.2
Fayette	8 556	75.3	88 200	18.9	12.4	553	27.9	1.1	10 767	-0.6	486	4.5	10 050	31.4	31.3
Floyd	6 901	72.0	98 200	19.1	10.5	556	26.6	1.1	8 724	0.1	325	3.7	7 998	32.3	30.4

1. Specified owner-occupied units.   2. A value of 10.0 represents 10 percent or less; a value of 50.0 represents 50 percent or more.   3. Specified renter-occupied units.
4. Overcrowded or lacking complete plumbing facilities.   5. Percent of civilian labor force.   6. Civilian employed persons 16 years old and over.

Items 89—103

Table B. States and Counties — Nonfarm Employment and Agriculture

| | Private nonfarm establishments, employment and payroll, 2015 | | | | | | | | | Agriculture, 2012 | | | |
| | | | | | | | | | | | | | |

| STATE County | Number of establish-ments | Employment | | | | | | Annual payroll | | Farms | | | |
| | | Total | Health care and social assistance | Manufac-turing | Retail trade | Finance and insurance | Professional, scientific, and technical services | Total (mil dol) | Average per employee (dollars) | Number | Fewer than 50 acres | 500 acres or more | Farm operators whose principal occu-pation is farming (percent) |
	104	105	106	107	108	109	110	111	112	113	114	115	116
INDIANA—Cont'd													
Pike	197	2 198	388	164	248	38	27	102	46 558	321	34.0	11.2	32.1
Porter	3 504	54 945	9 222	10 389	7 591	1 011	1 814	2 312	42 080	481	53.4	15.2	48.0
Posey	506	8 328	400	2 627	660	114	289	486	58 348	408	31.6	31.6	60.5
Pulaski	314	3 412	582	1 310	404	129	58	131	38 526	536	38.6	20.7	46.6
Putnam	691	11 192	1 803	2 567	1 281	252	187	364	32 536	847	49.6	11.9	41.0
Randolph	495	6 253	698	2 070	653	159	108	222	35 546	772	40.7	18.3	52.7
Ripley	627	9 789	1 365	2 184	828	235	136	468	47 768	876	41.3	10.0	43.8
Rush	363	3 484	541	684	407	98	118	116	33 152	601	32.6	20.6	54.2
St. Joseph	5 746	119 428	19 065	15 372	15 725	3 693	4 706	4 749	39 764	691	54.7	11.7	45.0
Scott	393	6 285	1 159	1 851	861	99	141	199	31 730	321	51.4	5.9	35.5
Shelby	935	15 221	1 741	5 571	1 531	188	243	621	40 770	569	39.4	24.4	56.8
Spencer	409	5 007	291	1 300	750	165	236	213	42 556	597	32.8	15.1	38.5
Starke	297	2 621	263	763	584	65	58	88	33 676	511	50.7	13.3	33.9
Steuben	954	14 251	1 359	5 138	2 126	219	173	461	32 382	562	39.0	8.5	38.3
Sullivan	338	4 176	573	570	543	98	90	165	39 434	433	32.3	23.8	55.2
Switzerland	124	1 528	149	88	125	26	15	49	32 176	383	41.0	3.1	39.9
Tippecanoe	3 486	63 798	10 504	14 524	9 575	1 499	2 500	2 625	41 149	702	56.7	15.2	39.3
Tipton	306	3 257	541	723	520	103	73	122	37 306	377	35.3	23.3	53.8
Union	105	894	66	335	199	20	20	28	30 845	242	31.0	19.8	49.6
Vanderburgh	4 956	100 952	19 455	11 329	12 639	4 675	3 849	4 302	42 610	275	46.5	16.4	42.5
Vermillion	264	3 175	515	690	613	61	53	149	46 983	270	37.8	23.7	48.1
Vigo	2 440	43 628	9 454	6 892	6 615	1 179	1 042	1 532	35 121	450	56.2	14.2	44.7
Wabash	730	10 837	2 013	2 808	1 332	291	207	364	33 607	745	44.8	13.4	44.4
Warren	128	1 415	250	555	111	31	21	48	33 696	413	43.1	22.0	46.2
Warrick	1 125	14 131	3 590	2 553	1 580	499	437	670	47 421	379	47.8	16.1	44.9
Washington	447	4 529	731	1 520	651	120	136	139	30 673	831	40.7	9.7	49.8
Wayne	1 492	25 840	5 507	5 531	3 810	797	402	921	35 633	805	41.5	8.9	44.7
Wells	623	10 515	1 796	2 946	995	175	194	368	35 022	636	40.1	17.5	49.2
White	602	7 072	799	2 556	1 168	185	108	249	35 228	631	39.9	25.0	53.2
Whitley	670	11 192	1 142	4 913	1 359	231	206	432	38 614	710	51.7	8.5	34.4
IOWA	80 952	1 338 418	219 531	211 610	184 663	93 674	55 059	55 080	41 153	88 637	30.9	22.4	54.1
Adair	188	1 686	316	D	260	71	54	56	33 251	726	25.4	28.5	55.2
Adams	113	1 107	420	204	95	34	21	45	40 555	467	24.4	27.4	53.3
Allamakee	401	4 310	972	1 167	568	186	77	135	31 425	1 011	25.4	17.5	41.5
Appanoose	310	3 662	637	1 082	620	92	80	118	32 298	744	30.1	13.4	46.1
Audubon	189	1 092	281	100	189	54	28	37	33 440	622	33.1	28.1	61.1
Benton	566	4 459	827	686	777	195	75	158	35 352	1 215	30.1	24.1	54.3
Black Hawk	3 228	69 426	15 655	12 801	9 210	2 385	3 744	2 570	37 017	924	33.0	21.4	55.6
Boone	565	7 139	1 728	516	1 071	177	168	253	35 411	938	42.6	19.9	49.7
Bremer	600	9 240	1 852	1 667	1 225	1 058	203	369	39 958	982	34.7	16.6	49.1
Buchanan	484	5 395	1 282	967	859	228	90	197	36 524	1 075	30.6	19.7	57.6
Buena Vista	559	9 442	1 392	3 505	1 119	562	212	333	35 307	858	27.9	32.5	65.3
Butler	334	2 773	510	925	396	140	63	94	33 970	1 096	37.2	19.9	51.3
Calhoun	282	2 194	672	97	333	108	39	68	30 855	826	29.5	31.1	52.7
Carroll	867	10 111	2 060	1 364	1 634	706	203	362	35 827	1 065	29.1	21.6	57.0
Cass	479	4 721	1 150	515	893	215	120	153	32 495	703	25.3	29.2	50.2
Cedar	459	4 196	605	615	606	144	86	144	34 296	955	37.6	21.3	51.8
Cerro Gordo	1 400	19 856	4 132	2 860	3 672	1 031	643	767	38 627	780	35.1	27.4	59.0
Cherokee	340	3 797	894	353	615	161	100	131	34 408	805	22.0	28.6	64.0
Chickasaw	401	3 957	610	1 422	428	162	59	152	38 413	1 036	34.0	18.8	55.5
Clarke	186	3 199	560	915	555	88	41	107	33 452	627	27.1	15.3	35.9
Clay	603	7 296	1 547	687	1 424	271	169	258	35 385	720	26.1	32.1	57.6
Clayton	525	5 285	1 129	979	669	184	102	184	34 843	1 577	29.2	13.9	50.3
Clinton	1 148	19 028	3 385	4 493	2 835	708	305	683	35 917	1 244	30.9	23.4	63.1
Crawford	435	6 477	1 019	2 556	778	210	89	230	35 475	900	26.6	30.6	61.7
Dallas	1 839	36 988	3 551	1 785	5 916	12 406	1 446	1 847	49 938	1 001	43.6	17.5	43.7
Davis	172	1 450	386	125	284	56	54	50	34 352	917	28.9	10.9	44.1
Decatur	138	1 753	313	59	216	43	30	40	22 891	711	27.3	18.3	44.6
Delaware	478	5 841	1 133	1 908	673	247	113	218	37 297	1 382	29.7	16.2	60.2
Des Moines	1 102	20 084	3 632	4 798	3 190	530	334	761	37 874	663	37.4	17.3	46.5
Dickinson	757	7 154	989	1 625	1 093	238	161	284	39 641	441	29.5	32.0	58.0
Dubuque	2 762	55 142	7 879	9 172	7 261	3 680	2 475	2 269	41 147	1 462	28.3	10.3	52.5
Emmet	315	3 282	746	838	482	128	82	107	32 634	475	25.9	37.3	64.0
Fayette	554	6 318	1 346	626	844	186	118	187	29 553	1 286	30.4	18.2	56.2
Floyd	399	4 500	1 206	603	791	194	106	171	38 098	944	35.1	22.9	51.8

Table B. States and Counties — **Agriculture**

STATE County	Land in farms Acreage (1,000)	Percent change, 2007–2012	Acres Average size of farm	Total irrigated (1,000)	Total cropland (1,000)	Value of land and buildings (dollars) Average per farm	Average per acre	Value of machinery and equipment, average per farm (dollars)	Value of products sold Total (mil dol)	Average per farm (dollars)	Percent from: Crops	Live-stock and poultry products	Percent of farms with sales of: $10,000 or more	$100,000 or more	Government payments Total ($1,000)	Percent of farms
	117	118	119	120	121	122	123	124	125	126	127	128	129	130	131	132
INDIANA—Cont'd																
Pike	80	8.7	249	D	65.0	1 064 710	4 271	115 533	50.8	158 343	57.1	42.9	39.6	20.9	1 395	71.3
Porter	121	4.8	251	10.0	109.4	1 502 112	5 993	176 526	106.8	222 133	93.2	6.8	48.6	31.0	2 268	55.5
Posey	229	12.1	561	16.4	215.7	2 689 417	4 797	375 517	139.7	342 500	87.5	12.5	69.4	44.4	3 332	75.2
Pulaski	217	-6.8	404	18.5	197.1	2 080 849	5 152	192 328	185.3	345 784	67.9	32.1	53.9	34.9	4 080	79.7
Putnam	198	17.3	233	0.1	156.0	979 574	4 198	116 544	76.1	89 791	80.9	19.1	33.6	14.0	3 467	50.6
Randolph	241	4.0	312	0.2	216.6	1 588 816	5 088	181 580	227.0	294 035	56.6	43.4	60.4	34.7	4 656	66.8
Ripley	167	4.8	190	0.1	124.1	776 272	4 079	98 368	94.0	107 283	80.6	19.4	47.7	20.2	2 604	66.4
Rush	208	-4.3	345	0.5	188.7	2 103 171	6 089	216 255	162.5	270 401	60.6	39.4	68.1	42.1	4 158	67.1
St. Joseph	152	-14.9	220	27.6	136.3	1 350 298	6 140	142 120	123.5	178 734	86.6	13.4	48.3	24.6	2 468	54.7
Scott	51	-17.0	160	D	38.4	575 841	3 591	96 140	24.0	74 903	97.3	2.7	25.5	9.0	877	45.5
Shelby	233	13.4	410	4.3	220.6	2 508 759	6 125	238 496	128.9	226 522	86.5	13.5	65.7	38.7	4 519	63.4
Spencer	170	13.4	285	0.2	132.5	1 104 744	3 870	158 107	91.9	153 982	65.6	34.4	52.8	22.9	2 593	66.3
Starke	133	-13.1	261	25.6	115.4	1 144 699	4 383	156 188	69.8	136 528	95.0	5.0	32.9	19.0	3 463	82.0
Steuben	105	-1.7	186	2.1	84.6	834 635	4 486	109 486	61.8	109 888	65.9	34.1	36.7	14.6	1 868	72.6
Sullivan	170	-4.0	393	6.0	150.0	1 642 543	4 178	216 111	91.5	211 358	79.0	21.0	56.4	31.2	2 788	71.6
Switzerland	51	6.4	132	0.1	25.9	465 300	3 528	56 084	12.3	32 180	D	D	28.2	5.2	940	50.7
Tippecanoe	220	0.9	314	4.3	201.7	2 111 205	6 731	195 491	150.6	214 583	88.0	12.0	43.2	24.2	4 159	53.1
Tipton	145	-12.5	385	1.2	138.7	2 812 836	7 304	249 233	159.9	424 141	82.5	17.5	74.5	46.9	2 774	80.9
Union	74	1.7	308	D	63.9	1 525 157	4 955	172 099	41.7	172 190	88.3	11.7	61.6	33.1	1 200	69.4
Vanderburgh	77	6.4	278	D	70.6	1 177 945	4 231	157 189	36.1	131 247	90.2	9.8	52.4	28.4	1 078	64.0
Vermillion	118	-10.5	438	D	100.3	2 083 200	4 751	218 111	62.2	230 389	74.1	25.9	45.6	28.9	2 502	67.8
Vigo	118	-3.2	261	1.1	101.3	1 012 440	3 876	123 420	47.4	105 222	97.7	2.3	40.2	17.8	1 437	55.1
Wabash	198	-1.5	265	2.1	172.9	1 370 395	5 167	177 270	227.2	305 032	51.3	48.7	52.5	29.9	4 325	67.8
Warren	176	-10.2	426	2.1	156.5	2 509 559	5 890	222 634	111.7	270 574	94.8	5.2	43.3	29.3	3 349	66.3
Warrick	100	-9.4	263	D	88.6	1 276 810	4 856	164 979	39.7	104 873	93.1	6.9	37.7	22.4	2 192	63.6
Washington	200	-0.2	240	0.1	142.8	797 445	3 321	105 395	129.2	155 489	43.2	56.8	40.7	17.1	3 448	42.5
Wayne	156	-5.0	194	0.7	124.6	1 002 708	5 177	111 768	91.9	114 170	73.6	26.4	49.6	23.7	3 828	59.6
Wells	200	2.9	315	0.0	189.0	1 993 800	6 330	195 305	210.2	330 434	67.1	32.9	64.6	39.5	3 322	73.6
White	288	-9.4	457	4.2	267.7	3 122 778	6 837	265 100	297.4	471 342	57.0	43.0	59.1	40.1	4 960	71.2
Whitley	140	2.2	197	2.2	120.3	1 013 832	5 138	132 938	100.2	141 182	75.9	24.1	48.6	21.3	2 465	60.7
IOWA	30 623	-0.4	345	171.7	26 256.3	2 207 220	6 389	213 849	30 821.5	347 728	56.3	43.7	62.8	41.0	782 290	78.4
Adair	324	3.8	446	0.0	251.5	2 085 152	4 679	214 081	188.2	259 185	65.6	34.4	64.0	38.0	5 695	76.0
Adams	229	1.9	491	D	165.9	2 107 058	4 292	208 206	120.3	257 557	64.8	35.2	61.2	36.2	4 107	79.4
Allamakee	289	5.2	286	0.0	185.8	1 217 119	4 255	144 265	220.6	218 199	41.4	58.6	51.8	29.8	7 526	82.7
Appanoose	188	-5.1	252	D	111.8	749 059	2 969	84 641	38.4	51 620	55.5	44.5	43.5	10.2	3 704	69.1
Audubon	280	0.5	451	0.0	251.9	3 003 379	6 663	236 170	287.9	462 814	48.9	51.1	62.7	43.4	7 006	82.0
Benton	422	5.3	347	0.1	381.8	2 508 267	7 219	235 523	381.4	313 927	72.2	27.8	67.1	47.0	10 826	78.0
Black Hawk	297	5.2	321	0.1	273.8	2 559 448	7 969	245 895	287.2	310 850	65.4	34.6	68.2	44.2	7 606	81.4
Boone	313	-5.6	334	0.1	283.3	2 520 885	7 546	180 946	301.8	321 707	74.9	25.1	54.6	34.2	6 378	75.8
Bremer	272	11.7	276	0.7	242.5	2 132 518	7 713	222 672	271.7	276 729	63.2	36.8	62.9	41.1	7 929	81.6
Buchanan	342	-5.1	318	0.0	318.5	2 331 990	7 332	246 866	390.7	363 461	63.2	36.8	71.5	47.6	10 788	71.9
Buena Vista	361	-0.5	421	0.7	334.0	3 070 632	7 301	290 162	577.1	672 564	44.5	55.5	73.5	60.1	8 715	83.4
Butler	363	-3.5	331	0.4	330.9	2 260 181	6 829	206 931	358.2	326 838	55.1	44.9	59.7	38.0	9 333	81.2
Calhoun	358	-0.3	434	0.3	337.4	3 332 812	7 685	276 166	366.3	443 500	57.8	42.2	68.3	51.9	7 928	88.7
Carroll	359	0.2	337	D	328.1	2 535 277	7 524	243 800	540.6	507 578	35.6	64.4	75.6	53.0	8 377	81.3
Cass	290	-8.8	412	0.3	240.7	2 253 533	5 464	220 265	228.3	324 761	57.7	42.3	63.4	41.8	5 974	78.1
Cedar	312	-7.3	327	0.4	275.6	2 346 182	7 171	250 577	315.9	330 800	69.4	30.6	58.2	42.2	8 363	75.2
Cerro Gordo	327	-2.9	419	D	306.3	2 778 794	6 631	282 482	245.0	314 089	80.4	19.6	60.1	42.3	8 384	82.3
Cherokee	337	7.1	419	0.0	290.4	3 110 383	7 422	272 880	407.5	506 183	56.5	43.5	84.8	65.0	6 226	82.7
Chickasaw	299	3.5	289	0.3	271.3	2 067 023	7 158	208 558	336.2	324 558	52.2	47.8	64.0	41.3	11 550	82.2
Clarke	169	-11.4	269	0.0	98.9	910 281	3 378	87 847	93.4	148 973	29.5	70.5	43.7	15.3	4 294	67.3
Clay	319	-2.9	443	0.3	292.5	3 269 768	7 385	292 085	403.5	560 428	58.5	41.5	71.5	54.6	7 683	83.6
Clayton	398	-2.7	252	0.2	291.7	1 207 906	4 786	149 960	402.6	255 286	47.8	52.2	54.4	32.4	15 965	80.9
Clinton	417	5.5	335	0.0	372.1	2 381 902	7 103	228 046	381.3	306 518	70.4	29.6	68.2	46.8	10 432	78.9
Crawford	451	4.3	501	1.0	404.7	3 465 877	6 918	324 907	417.6	463 991	63.3	36.7	74.3	49.4	7 985	77.0
Dallas	306	3.1	306	0.4	270.7	2 059 497	6 728	168 490	237.2	236 924	73.6	26.4	51.0	29.8	6 868	65.7
Davis	214	-2.1	233	0.1	135.2	686 799	2 943	94 828	90.8	99 061	32.3	67.7	49.8	15.2	4 670	59.2
Decatur	232	1.3	326	D	127.0	972 918	2 988	121 181	92.4	130 018	34.7	65.3	47.5	19.3	5 905	66.4
Delaware	366	9.5	265	0.1	321.2	1 906 151	7 206	228 110	495.1	358 221	41.9	58.1	70.2	49.6	14 190	85.2
Des Moines	173	-6.6	260	3.1	137.6	1 451 878	5 574	166 958	118.7	179 054	82.3	17.7	54.1	30.6	4 631	82.8
Dickinson	187	-17.2	425	0.9	173.6	2 999 796	7 061	278 673	192.3	435 941	67.6	32.4	67.1	52.6	3 868	80.7
Dubuque	291	-6.2	199	0.0	224.3	1 214 544	6 093	172 274	387.8	265 260	31.0	69.0	67.5	39.7	11 080	81.2
Emmet	219	-12.3	461	0.4	201.9	3 356 078	7 280	322 318	292.2	615 097	53.7	46.3	71.8	57.3	4 456	82.3
Fayette	388	-6.9	302	0.3	333.3	2 077 995	6 879	214 755	432.2	336 045	54.0	46.0	61.5	44.3	13 738	87.1
Floyd	318	6.4	337	2.1	291.1	2 154 441	6 401	225 738	280.4	297 050	65.8	34.2	58.3	41.2	8 273	80.8

Table B. States and Counties — Water Use, Wholesale Trade, Retail Trade, and Real Estate

STATE County	Water use, 2010		Wholesale trade,[1] 2012				Retail trade,[2] 2012				Real estate and rental and leasing,[2] 2012			
	Total water withdrawn (mil gal/day)	Gallons withdrawn per person per day	Number of establishments	Number of employees	Sales (mil dol)	Annual payroll (mil dol)	Number of establishments	Number of employees	Sales (mil dol)	Annual payroll (mil dol)	Number of establishments	Number of employees	Receipts (mil dol)	Annual payroll (mil dol)
	133	134	135	136	137	138	139	140	141	142	143	144	145	146
INDIANA—Cont'd														
Pike	595.1	46 329	7	D	D	D	31	266	72.5	4.8	6	D	D	D
Porter	599.5	3 648	147	1 860	1 574.9	94.2	449	6 931	2 035.4	159.7	150	648	101.3	19.6
Posey	18.9	731	22	329	506.8	15.8	67	692	307.6	18.3	10	27	3.2	0.6
Pulaski	9.2	687	25	272	480.8	10.8	60	438	134.3	9.4	5	7	0.8	0.1
Putnam	8.7	228	16	141	48.5	6.3	106	1 211	349.0	25.4	24	69	7.4	1.5
Randolph	5.1	193	15	161	127.5	6.4	71	600	443.4	12.9	10	26	2.1	0.4
Ripley	3.3	116	17	D	D	D	102	844	222.9	19.9	19	D	D	D
Rush	2.8	163	23	516	527.1	32.5	49	420	108.1	9.0	12	15	2.6	0.3
St. Joseph	45.6	171	307	4 366	3 131.0	213.3	911	14 702	3 775.3	343.9	218	1 233	205.3	41.5
Scott	3.6	147	10	D	D	D	79	828	240.2	18.1	19	41	6.3	1.0
Shelby	9.3	210	37	676	370.9	25.8	118	1 392	502.4	37.0	41	126	18.5	3.6
Spencer	33.5	1 600	17	D	D	D	66	708	130.1	19.2	12	22	1.5	0.2
Starke	6.1	262	14	83	95.9	3.6	59	625	170.7	14.8	13	24	2.5	0.4
Steuben	4.9	144	37	279	185.1	10.7	185	2 028	613.8	41.1	44	102	16.9	3.0
Sullivan	423.9	19 741	18	162	164.4	6.9	54	553	138.2	11.7	8	16	1.2	0.4
Switzerland	2.2	209	3	7	2.3	0.4	15	108	20.2	1.6	2	D	D	D
Tippecanoe	33.9	196	109	1 275	751.1	54.5	529	8 815	2 225.7	189.2	167	852	142.9	28.6
Tipton	1.9	116	13	126	108.6	5.7	57	499	180.6	12.8	9	17	1.1	0.3
Union	0.7	96	4	D	D	D	21	191	32.9	3.4	1	D	D	D
Vanderburgh	31.3	174	259	4 815	2 679.5	295.9	791	12 637	3 141.7	290.9	208	1 500	247.1	45.5
Vermillion	623.2	38 441	13	D	D	D	52	591	194.1	12.8	4	6	0.7	0.2
Vigo	334.3	3 100	91	1 163	506.6	48.6	445	6 676	1 588.3	137.4	89	524	86.4	17.7
Wabash	7.0	212	31	275	348.5	12.0	130	1 332	324.5	29.8	15	95	8.9	2.7
Warren	1.5	181	9	146	206.2	6.7	14	86	22.1	1.5	2	D	D	D
Warrick	761.3	12 754	40	D	D	D	126	1 630	391.1	33.7	27	152	23.5	3.4
Washington	4.7	166	12	36	9.2	1.2	79	691	215.4	14.6	9	29	3.3	0.6
Wayne	11.1	160	55	678	868.2	27.3	267	3 664	950.8	80.7	53	190	37.5	5.9
Wells	7.2	259	26	D	D	D	84	982	231.5	21.6	23	66	6.8	1.5
White	5.9	239	34	324	339.4	16.7	97	1 099	302.9	25.5	17	53	5.9	0.9
Whitley	4.4	132	24	D	D	D	108	1 415	343.4	31.4	23	76	16.8	2.5
IOWA	3 070.5	1 008	4 302	58 872	62 318.3	2 841.8	12 046	174 556	44 905.6	3 865.3	2 742	12 031	2 268.3	425.9
Adair	2.3	301	10	132	183.2	5.2	30	252	63.0	4.3	5	D	D	D
Adams	1.8	454	5	46	36.3	1.5	19	101	21.3	2.1	2	D	D	D
Allamakee	123.3	8 602	33	443	275.9	16.0	59	563	144.6	11.2	13	36	2.5	0.5
Appanoose	11.1	864	9	64	40.4	1.9	58	636	138.8	13.0	8	D	D	D
Audubon	2.1	346	16	125	203.5	5.1	18	186	40.3	2.9	1	D	D	D
Benton	3.3	126	30	319	295.3	11.4	87	744	197.2	15.7	11	D	D	D
Black Hawk	37.0	282	151	2 687	1 980.4	126.8	509	8 793	2 110.5	191.0	138	617	118.1	17.5
Boone	3.6	136	23	D	D	D	69	978	217.2	22.9	15	26	2.3	0.6
Bremer	3.9	162	27	283	299.5	14.3	86	1 246	361.8	27.1	18	D	D	D
Buchanan	4.3	207	29	329	337.0	15.6	79	901	247.4	19.5	11	D	D	D
Buena Vista	8.2	402	25	256	514.6	12.7	94	1 149	281.0	24.8	18	71	8.9	2.6
Butler	5.9	397	29	225	407.7	8.6	58	372	104.9	7.0	7	4	1.0	0.1
Calhoun	2.9	295	20	235	353.0	11.6	48	340	127.0	8.3	4	23	3.1	0.9
Carroll	6.8	326	55	1 543	1 888.5	69.9	144	1 596	360.0	36.7	20	121	25.2	4.6
Cass	3.0	212	24	207	260.4	9.1	75	875	195.9	18.0	14	55	10.9	2.3
Cedar	4.8	261	28	384	387.3	15.0	59	611	208.1	12.2	13	18	2.7	0.4
Cerro Gordo	9.9	224	83	932	1 320.8	45.1	226	3 784	956.5	81.2	60	146	27.0	4.1
Cherokee	6.6	544	19	137	201.0	5.8	59	658	145.6	13.3	4	D	D	D
Chickasaw	4.0	318	33	292	469.7	14.8	51	437	116.9	9.3	5	9	1.2	0.2
Clarke	2.2	235	4	29	30.9	1.2	36	560	151.1	10.8	6	7	0.6	0.1
Clay	4.2	254	49	D	D	D	111	1 460	313.0	34.6	25	98	16.8	2.9
Clayton	6.5	360	26	310	917.2	15.2	82	654	211.6	13.4	9	16	2.8	0.5
Clinton	106.9	2 176	47	391	396.2	18.0	193	2 708	652.1	56.4	35	119	22.5	3.6
Crawford	7.0	408	19	208	318.8	10.4	72	853	184.4	15.8	7	8	1.1	0.2
Dallas	5.3	80	52	501	412.8	28.7	256	5 292	1 270.5	105.0	68	519	111.8	35.0
Davis	1.6	184	6	51	31.3	1.5	31	274	62.2	5.3	3	D	D	D
Decatur	1.6	184	7	82	34.8	1.6	24	210	35.6	3.1	4	6	0.7	0.1
Delaware	8.4	472	29	327	360.6	14.0	62	674	188.1	15.0	9	21	3.9	0.6
Des Moines	77.3	1 916	48	621	1 096.2	27.7	203	3 064	684.2	66.2	37	654	117.8	25.6
Dickinson	7.3	440	20	D	D	D	111	1 083	292.9	26.0	44	87	15.0	2.2
Dubuque	40.5	432	158	2 353	2 083.1	107.4	442	7 157	1 659.1	149.1	110	381	72.4	12.2
Emmet	3.3	320	17	107	222.5	4.1	50	467	90.0	8.6	6	13	0.7	0.1
Fayette	4.5	217	40	415	696.5	19.9	88	760	178.0	16.2	12	36	8.3	0.9
Floyd	4.1	252	20	380	295.8	20.4	62	723	188.8	14.0	10	35	3.3	0.7

1. Merchant wholesalers, except manufacturers' sales branches and offices.   2. Employer establishments.

Table B. States and Counties — Professional Services, Manufacturing, and Accommodation and Food Services

STATE County	Professional, scientific, and technical services, 2012				Manufacturing, 2012				Accommodation and food services, 2012			
	Number of establishments	Number of employees	Receipts (mil dol)	Annual payroll (mil dol)	Number of establishments	Number of employees	Receipts (mil dol)	Annual payroll (mil dol)	Number of establishments	Number of employees	Sales (mil dol)	Annual payroll (mil dol)
	147	148	149	150	151	152	153	154	155	156	157	158
INDIANA—Cont'd												
Pike	9	28	2.1	0.7	7	247	D	11.7	17	138	5.2	1.4
Porter	350	2 035	273.7	101.0	137	9 239	9 469.9	695.2	319	5 925	270.6	72.2
Posey	37	518	44.5	21.6	26	2 689	6 454.3	235.2	35	463	18.8	5.8
Pulaski	24	58	4.9	1.1	21	1 274	498.6	65.4	21	166	8.0	2.0
Putnam	50	187	13.9	5.4	30	2 001	745.6	82.7	69	1 216	51.4	13.3
Randolph	34	100	10.5	2.8	49	2 045	847.6	93.2	40	512	18.8	5.2
Ripley	37	145	8.6	4.7	43	2 444	864.9	98.9	41	D	D	D
Rush	34	136	17.0	4.0	28	616	D	21.5	23	328	14.7	3.8
St. Joseph	516	4 882	1 359.4	273.9	365	13 831	6 508.6	733.1	559	10 899	485.6	139.1
Scott	28	178	14.5	5.3	21	1 594	866.1	72.8	39	D	D	D
Shelby	66	225	23.3	8.3	80	4 770	2 700.7	235.3	77	1 495	62.6	17.6
Spencer	20	84	7.2	2.0	24	1 399	1 634.2	64.3	27	335	19.4	4.4
Starke	19	51	4.4	1.3	20	853	253.1	30.2	30	326	14.2	3.7
Steuben	55	171	13.0	4.1	95	4 044	1 279.2	161.0	93	1 397	60.1	16.8
Sullivan	21	103	6.6	2.5	14	712	D	29.5	31	409	15.4	4.3
Switzerland	10	15	0.8	0.3	8	D	D	D	16	D	D	D
Tippecanoe	300	2 297	334.4	105.9	121	14 295	11 875.0	846.1	405	8 035	362.1	98.9
Tipton	19	56	4.4	1.4	17	777	236.3	33.9	26	295	12.9	3.3
Union	8	D	D	D	5	36	D	D	8	86	3.8	1.0
Vanderburgh	434	3 727	471.4	178.0	248	10 623	3 972.5	494.1	465	11 293	566.5	150.0
Vermillion	13	D	D	D	15	676	D	54.3	33	443	24.5	5.8
Vigo	200	1 162	120.3	44.0	112	8 872	3 512.9	438.4	276	5 439	230.1	66.6
Wabash	52	375	30.8	8.2	62	2 623	1 312.0	121.0	68	1 049	40.2	11.5
Warren	6	15	2.0	0.3	13	635	165.3	20.9	8	D	D	D
Warrick	98	389	44.3	14.7	48	2 631	1 853.2	174.2	71	1 087	44.1	13.0
Washington	27	111	11.9	3.2	36	1 395	339.0	55.5	30	D	D	D
Wayne	90	433	30.5	12.2	105	4 875	2 155.1	214.3	154	2 812	120.3	34.6
Wells	39	216	22.3	7.4	51	2 536	1 126.5	101.9	41	587	20.5	5.8
White	31	102	7.5	2.5	35	2 144	926.4	91.2	61	540	23.2	6.3
Whitley	37	179	14.4	4.7	69	4 541	2 199.7	220.0	64	851	39.5	8.7
IOWA	6 204	48 521	6 420.6	2 466.8	3 598	203 722	116 668.8	10 021.2	7 047	115 134	5 468.7	1 466.6
Adair	13	36	2.9	0.9	3	D	D	D	14	D	D	D
Adams	9	25	2.9	0.7	8	155	D	6.7	6	D	D	D
Allamakee	19	102	11.5	3.0	27	1 208	262.1	36.0	33	235	9.7	2.3
Appanoose	22	64	5.6	1.9	17	599	303.3	24.6	29	422	16.5	5.4
Audubon	9	16	1.9	0.3	7	172	D	8.0	6	D	D	D
Benton	30	76	7.2	2.4	29	717	166.5	24.6	33	D	D	D
Black Hawk	232	3 781	288.1	203.8	164	13 067	9 665.5	655.2	304	6 630	318.4	84.6
Boone	38	145	15.4	5.5	28	416	97.7	19.6	46	499	16.9	4.2
Bremer	36	180	17.7	5.5	36	1 714	883.7	86.3	46	562	20.0	5.5
Buchanan	22	83	10.3	2.9	41	1 124	677.4	45.2	33	399	12.2	3.1
Buena Vista	36	182	20.3	8.5	30	3 507	2 233.5	121.1	45	738	23.2	6.9
Butler	19	68	5.5	1.4	28	836	463.6	35.4	16	D	D	D
Calhoun	16	43	3.6	0.9	14	82	D	2.9	15	D	D	D
Carroll	46	197	27.4	6.9	38	1 286	904.3	60.2	59	687	22.5	6.4
Cass	27	115	12.3	4.8	21	513	157.5	20.5	36	371	14.4	3.8
Cedar	23	93	10.1	2.9	34	643	255.0	27.8	38	D	D	D
Cerro Gordo	95	613	73.7	29.9	52	2 687	1 361.7	122.5	129	D	D	D
Cherokee	18	77	10.4	2.0	23	1 109	653.3	38.9	28	344	11.6	3.3
Chickasaw	18	59	6.2	1.5	48	1 242	712.4	52.0	24	284	8.5	2.1
Clarke	13	45	3.3	1.0	13	887	D	34.8	22	571	67.5	8.7
Clay	39	179	18.9	6.4	27	999	320.1	44.5	55	645	24.9	6.4
Clayton	26	149	21.0	5.7	31	899	217.8	33.5	58	D	D	D
Clinton	60	295	35.6	10.2	53	4 405	4 731.1	228.3	108	1 664	103.5	22.7
Crawford	21	92	8.7	2.9	21	2 471	1 657.9	98.6	44	419	14.9	4.3
Dallas	184	1 361	229.7	70.2	39	2 067	740.2	77.8	149	2 911	148.0	44.0
Davis	14	52	5.3	1.5	8	145	D	5.5	15	100	3.2	0.9
Decatur	6	20	1.6	0.3	5	76	D	2.9	12	D	D	D
Delaware	27	105	11.2	4.6	37	1 831	872.7	78.1	29	246	8.4	2.3
Des Moines	60	317	31.9	11.6	52	4 367	1 626.7	194.1	97	D	D	D
Dickinson	46	148	15.2	5.2	37	1 491	719.8	55.8	94	978	56.8	16.6
Dubuque	166	2 956	450.9	147.7	144	8 498	6 036.4	434.6	242	4 456	169.5	49.8
Emmet	19	80	8.5	3.1	21	931	357.0	38.9	22	291	9.6	2.9
Fayette	34	112	8.6	3.4	25	530	D	21.5	45	570	18.4	4.8
Floyd	26	90	5.2	2.0	20	947	593.4	51.9	36	344	13.3	3.1

1. Establishment subject to federal tax.

Table B. States and Counties — Health Care and Social Assistance, Other Services, Nonemployer Businesses, and Residential Construction

STATE County	Health care and social assistance, 2012				Other services, 2012				Nonemployer businesses, 2015		Value of residential construction authorized by building permits, 2016	
	Number of establish-ments	Number of employees	Receipts (mil dol)	Annual payroll (mil dol)	Number of establish-ments	Number of employees	Receipts (mil dol)	Annual payroll (mil dol)	Number	Receipts (mil dol)	New Construction ($1,000)	Number of housing units
	159	160	161	162	163	164	165	166	167	168	169	170
INDIANA—Cont'd												
Pike	17	376	19.0	7.3	21	70	8.5	2.9	562	18.0	3 645	20
Porter	377	7 837	775.3	316.8	282	2 002	150.3	49.5	9 687	419.5	139 756	612
Posey	36	550	29.4	11.7	40	134	14.7	3.4	1 436	44.2	7 767	36
Pulaski	25	573	40.6	18.2	21	80	7.5	1.7	810	29.0	2 076	15
Putnam	71	1 649	110.7	46.2	66	278	18.9	5.5	2 040	80.7	13 966	58
Randolph	38	645	51.8	19.6	43	169	13.7	2.9	1 408	52.2	3 219	20
Ripley	67	1 404	130.5	53.0	49	178	17.3	4.0	1 770	69.1	18 497	109
Rush	31	555	50.8	17.7	28	88	8.9	1.7	1 122	43.6	2 037	11
St. Joseph	644	17 762	2 160.5	722.0	459	D	D	D	15 738	629.5	64 011	291
Scott	53	865	65.9	25.4	23	105	8.1	2.2	1 109	39.3	3 672	22
Shelby	77	2 008	194.2	70.0	69	452	41.0	10.7	2 812	119.1	13 682	72
Spencer	24	D	D	D	32	86	7.5	1.9	1 166	41.4	9 024	53
Starke	23	460	35.9	12.3	31	131	10.8	2.5	1 220	46.1	10 028	49
Steuben	84	1 384	97.2	36.3	76	424	53.0	12.3	2 165	104.2	32 625	133
Sullivan	31	647	50.7	20.5	21	113	6.9	1.7	940	29.5	210	2
Switzerland	15	D	D	D	13	39	4.1	0.9	577	23.0	3 321	57
Tippecanoe	385	10 859	1 194.7	423.0	240	1 793	208.1	46.8	9 125	400.0	111 744	561
Tipton	26	614	63.4	26.0	20	102	10.4	2.4	1 010	39.0	1 284	7
Union	11	D	D	D	12	D	D	D	506	22.4	3 802	12
Vanderburgh	554	18 044	2 025.2	775.4	360	2 889	300.6	86.0	9 565	390.9	55 033	426
Vermillion	23	534	61.6	19.5	23	54	5.4	0.9	749	23.8	0	0
Vigo	360	8 910	1 138.1	352.1	178	1 150	109.0	30.3	4 802	185.9	27 753	406
Wabash	76	2 143	141.7	52.9	60	303	25.0	5.5	1 699	54.8	5 082	28
Warren	10	D	D	D	6	D	D	D	524	22.6	4 387	21
Warrick	125	3 119	369.6	124.9	86	431	49.5	12.6	3 711	162.3	81 067	439
Washington	45	765	52.8	21.0	25	148	10.2	3.5	1 710	64.5	5 401	33
Wayne	205	5 350	523.3	204.3	117	509	47.0	10.5	3 705	144.7	12 728	107
Wells	57	1 641	128.3	51.5	61	280	21.2	5.7	1 658	62.2	12 439	62
White	36	852	63.3	25.2	33	121	12.6	2.7	1 454	61.8	7 464	40
Whitley	65	1 120	103.5	35.8	69	344	28.9	8.4	2 152	81.2	21 449	136
IOWA	8 131	206 906	18 583.8	7 894.4	5 866	30 672	3 343.2	847.7	207 167	9 137.9	2 660 753	14 317
Adair	16	336	21.7	8.4	15	D	D	D	641	25.6	6 572	50
Adams	17	327	27.3	9.5	9	32	1.9	0.5	344	13.6	808	4
Allamakee	48	1 022	51.1	24.2	33	90	12.2	2.5	1 152	55.5	5 298	33
Appanoose	37	714	52.5	21.7	25	71	7.5	1.5	900	38.3	5 377	59
Audubon	15	321	21.6	8.8	18	52	5.2	1.4	480	21.7	25	1
Benton	45	775	50.7	21.4	51	148	15.6	3.9	1 830	65.4	5 795	29
Black Hawk	362	10 530	990.2	416.7	225	1 484	137.5	36.7	7 342	339.4	68 677	422
Boone	53	1 623	110.8	48.8	48	171	19.1	5.0	1 712	68.8	11 072	68
Bremer	58	1 672	119.4	51.6	64	D	D	D	1 663	69.2	24 650	121
Buchanan	41	1 025	71.1	32.3	20	D	D	D	1 468	67.3	5 193	29
Buena Vista	46	1 341	90.4	41.8	32	129	13.0	2.9	1 306	59.0	1 136	5
Butler	28	513	24.4	11.6	22	D	D	D	1 111	39.4	6 266	34
Calhoun	33	685	51.2	20.8	14	D	D	D	734	32.6	5 839	21
Carroll	110	2 188	172.5	68.7	58	200	19.7	4.2	1 879	92.3	12 422	49
Cass	46	1 154	80.9	34.9	39	154	20.8	3.7	1 193	48.1	1 250	7
Cedar	51	617	29.3	13.6	33	D	D	D	1 280	50.4	8 867	35
Cerro Gordo	141	4 853	541.7	217.7	110	D	D	D	2 950	117.6	12 928	38
Cherokee	36	915	64.1	31.7	27	78	9.6	2.2	823	36.1	4 100	14
Chickasaw	36	561	50.0	16.7	31	98	14.3	1.9	978	34.8	3 030	9
Clarke	28	617	39.3	15.4	18	D	D	D	578	22.0	2 767	31
Clay	60	1 480	139.3	60.9	37	202	18.3	4.7	1 311	67.5	9 115	85
Clayton	57	999	54.8	24.3	35	D	D	D	1 388	52.4	7 250	46
Clinton	131	3 554	248.0	107.2	92	331	28.8	7.8	2 710	104.3	16 766	80
Crawford	37	1 008	67.8	28.2	38	D	D	D	938	41.2	2 376	9
Dallas	169	3 175	271.9	123.9	88	731	72.0	35.2	6 131	330.8	260 031	1 180
Davis	21	418	33.6	14.2	11	31	2.9	0.6	751	53.4	233	3
Decatur	20	335	21.0	10.2	5	D	D	D	596	23.0	0	0
Delaware	38	969	65.8	30.0	42	149	14.3	2.8	1 319	67.1	3 117	29
Des Moines	143	3 273	323.7	123.0	93	447	37.9	10.8	2 410	92.9	6 185	32
Dickinson	56	647	34.5	15.1	39	169	14.2	3.8	1 759	81.8	70 570	362
Dubuque	271	7 806	702.0	318.7	201	1 157	109.4	28.1	6 335	278.9	79 185	368
Emmet	35	941	72.2	28.6	26	76	6.4	1.7	666	28.1	1 755	8
Fayette	56	1 290	80.7	36.4	49	197	22.5	5.3	1 366	54.5	5 885	29
Floyd	49	969	62.3	28.7	36	119	8.8	2.2	1 195	40.9	3 580	20

Table B. States and Counties — Government Employment and Payroll, and Local Government Finances

	Government employment and payroll, 2012									Local government finances, 2012				
			March payroll (percent of total)							General revenue				
												Taxes		
													Per capita[1] (dollars)	
STATE County	Full-time equivalent employees	March payroll (dollars)	Administration, judicial, and legal	Police and Corrections	Fire Protection	Highways and transportation	Health and Welfare	Natural resources and utilities	Education and libraries	Total (mil dol)	Intergovernmental (mil dol)	Total (mil dol)	Total	Property
	171	172	173	174	175	176	177	178	179	180	181	182	183	184
INDIANA—Cont'd														
Pike	517	1 538 013	6.0	5.7	0.0	2.8	2.9	3.1	78.9	37.9	19.2	13.1	1 029	1 017
Porter	4 682	15 472 739	6.2	11.3	4.3	3.7	2.1	4.6	66.6	488.1	210.9	195.5	1 180	1 059
Posey	911	2 762 902	6.5	6.5	1.9	5.2	4.2	4.8	69.9	91.5	46.7	35.1	1 370	1 173
Pulaski	708	2 273 852	6.2	7.1	0.1	2.4	37.6	1.9	44.1	67.8	28.8	13.4	1 019	724
Putnam	1 642	4 711 936	4.0	5.6	1.1	2.5	24.9	2.7	57.3	152.8	52.1	46.2	1 223	1 010
Randolph	1 040	2 903 572	6.2	8.7	2.2	3.1	2.3	2.6	74.3	87.0	51.7	23.2	898	698
Ripley	1 010	3 272 378	6.6	6.7	0.8	3.3	2.0	5.4	74.4	92.3	48.8	27.6	967	752
Rush	863	2 783 719	5.3	5.5	1.8	3.6	34.1	2.2	47.2	62.7	23.4	13.5	788	596
St. Joseph	9 537	31 853 965	4.7	12.0	7.2	4.2	1.2	7.1	62.0	1 039.1	434.1	391.0	1 468	1 064
Scott	984	3 352 561	6.3	6.5	0.1	1.7	23.7	3.5	56.0	87.7	37.4	20.6	865	696
Shelby	1 997	6 919 558	3.0	7.4	2.7	1.5	36.5	2.1	46.2	272.2	100.9	54.8	1 233	968
Spencer	769	2 237 381	7.1	8.1	0.1	3.7	2.1	4.2	74.1	70.8	38.9	21.7	1 042	882
Starke	708	2 237 301	6.6	4.8	2.5	3.1	0.7	1.7	75.9	73.3	44.3	20.2	868	715
Steuben	1 096	3 394 672	9.6	9.3	2.3	3.8	4.4	6.2	63.6	108.5	47.5	40.3	1 182	873
Sullivan	911	2 516 743	6.1	5.1	1.0	4.1	30.7	3.5	49.0	93.6	35.3	20.1	951	859
Switzerland	398	1 091 343	11.4	6.6	0.0	5.1	2.6	5.1	68.7	40.0	28.0	6.9	658	486
Tippecanoe	4 468	15 188 885	7.3	12.7	5.8	5.8	2.2	5.7	59.5	457.5	213.5	170.7	962	767
Tipton	903	3 143 238	4.0	4.5	1.9	2.0	42.8	4.2	38.9	44.9	22.7	15.5	989	726
Union	448	1 183 280	9.6	3.8	1.0	2.9	1.2	2.3	78.6	26.8	13.9	8.2	1 116	890
Vanderburgh	5 583	20 513 638	6.9	13.0	6.2	3.9	1.5	8.7	57.8	578.5	275.8	204.6	1 131	901
Vermillion	614	1 596 357	7.0	7.2	0.5	4.5	1.0	2.1	76.9	49.4	28.3	15.4	963	931
Vigo	3 145	11 398 778	8.5	10.1	5.8	4.8	0.9	6.3	62.4	343.5	178.1	110.8	1 022	808
Wabash	1 443	4 610 578	4.1	7.2	4.2	2.4	29.9	2.5	49.7	143.9	51.1	32.9	1 017	612
Warren	295	823 372	8.8	8.6	0.0	7.3	2.3	2.0	70.9	26.8	11.8	11.6	1 393	1 027
Warrick	1 757	5 629 245	7.9	6.7	0.8	2.6	1.7	3.6	76.2	168.5	76.5	59.4	982	827
Washington	845	2 699 186	6.9	6.0	1.0	3.5	1.8	2.8	76.4	72.6	43.4	21.5	769	601
Wayne	2 355	8 196 624	6.3	10.4	3.9	3.3	3.6	11.9	58.9	225.2	109.7	75.5	1 104	906
Wells	917	2 758 659	6.4	11.3	1.0	3.1	1.4	4.9	70.3	82.1	43.3	25.6	927	656
White	1 059	3 072 979	5.9	7.0	4.5	4.1	1.4	4.8	71.6	119.7	51.9	36.9	1 509	1 286
Whitley	1 054	3 089 365	6.7	13.1	0.0	4.8	0.9	1.6	71.8	89.8	43.2	27.3	820	609
IOWA	X	X	X	X	X	X	X	X	X	X	X	X	X	X
Adair	361	1 122 671	8.0	6.1	0.0	8.8	28.8	3.4	44.3	37.5	13.2	12.9	1 725	1 407
Adams	179	522 990	8.9	6.5	0.0	10.7	6.7	3.3	62.4	16.9	7.2	7.4	1 901	1 634
Allamakee	647	2 079 591	5.0	5.7	0.1	6.8	25.3	3.2	53.2	65.4	22.8	22.7	1 596	1 243
Appanoose	443	1 437 537	5.8	7.1	0.8	6.8	1.1	3.0	74.6	41.7	21.0	16.6	1 308	1 005
Audubon	328	1 089 236	5.8	5.2	0.0	7.5	33.7	1.3	45.9	32.8	8.6	11.6	1 971	1 623
Benton	846	2 776 401	7.0	6.1	0.1	7.7	1.3	7.5	70.0	87.3	37.6	37.9	1 468	1 188
Black Hawk	4 471	16 944 268	4.8	10.2	4.6	4.7	6.0	11.4	55.6	566.6	249.4	219.9	1 668	1 325
Boone	1 271	4 353 230	3.6	5.2	1.3	4.7	29.4	4.3	50.3	126.6	35.0	39.6	1 510	1 205
Bremer	952	3 191 387	7.1	7.5	0.0	5.7	7.0	3.2	66.5	149.1	41.3	41.6	1 698	1 343
Buchanan	834	2 711 732	5.2	6.6	0.5	5.4	22.7	8.0	51.3	79.4	27.4	29.1	1 389	1 115
Buena Vista	1 236	4 037 429	5.3	5.7	0.3	4.3	36.7	2.1	45.6	128.8	34.8	37.1	1 802	1 417
Butler	352	1 075 176	10.9	10.2	0.1	14.2	6.9	7.8	48.7	80.8	53.4	20.5	1 365	1 136
Calhoun	506	1 374 475	7.1	6.8	0.0	9.4	7.0	3.4	64.2	42.3	15.6	21.9	2 208	1 889
Carroll	828	2 504 489	5.6	6.3	0.2	7.0	5.5	7.6	66.7	87.4	32.6	36.2	1 753	1 373
Cass	903	2 917 219	3.3	2.3	0.2	3.9	43.1	0.9	45.0	91.1	26.3	27.8	2 024	1 557
Cedar	668	1 997 014	6.7	9.8	0.1	8.4	4.5	4.8	63.2	67.2	27.0	32.7	1 774	1 427
Cerro Gordo	1 766	6 541 728	4.4	8.2	2.8	8.5	5.2	5.1	64.4	203.2	74.2	86.1	1 967	1 505
Cherokee	418	1 242 156	8.2	6.7	0.6	9.2	1.4	5.2	66.5	40.1	14.5	20.3	1 703	1 336
Chickasaw	502	1 552 970	6.1	5.4	0.0	7.3	4.9	6.3	69.5	40.9	17.3	18.5	1 511	1 176
Clarke	529	1 675 579	5.4	5.8	0.0	5.3	31.8	3.4	47.7	54.9	15.5	16.8	1 795	1 452
Clay	1 187	4 281 441	3.5	4.2	0.5	6.0	45.8	8.0	29.0	143.1	24.9	30.2	1 822	1 405
Clayton	718	2 326 866	6.3	6.5	0.1	7.1	14.8	3.5	61.2	88.3	36.5	28.8	1 614	1 312
Clinton	1 731	6 177 764	5.4	9.5	3.6	5.4	2.6	5.5	66.4	199.4	80.5	85.7	1 760	1 345
Crawford	917	3 208 303	4.3	4.0	0.1	5.6	29.6	4.8	49.8	89.7	30.6	26.4	1 524	1 243
Dallas	2 341	8 457 626	5.2	4.5	0.6	2.8	6.9	2.8	76.8	257.1	92.3	126.9	1 764	1 534
Davis	419	1 521 730	4.6	4.0	0.1	5.6	40.7	2.5	42.4	45.3	13.6	10.3	1 184	967
Decatur	476	1 395 435	5.0	5.3	0.0	7.8	24.8	1.6	54.5	38.0	14.7	12.4	1 498	1 205
Delaware	974	3 412 646	4.0	3.6	0.0	4.3	41.3	2.0	44.6	99.6	31.6	29.8	1 695	1 409
Des Moines	1 756	6 340 038	4.4	7.5	3.3	4.2	1.8	4.4	73.0	171.7	72.6	68.2	1 691	1 253
Dickinson	844	3 005 898	7.0	6.0	0.0	4.6	29.5	6.9	45.5	102.7	15.7	50.1	2 950	2 520
Dubuque	3 261	12 486 456	6.7	9.6	3.9	7.2	5.0	6.0	60.6	400.9	169.8	165.8	1 743	1 320
Emmet	840	2 701 635	4.3	4.2	0.0	4.0	1.6	3.9	81.5	71.8	26.5	22.1	2 185	1 847
Fayette	775	2 536 072	6.6	8.5	0.5	8.6	2.3	3.9	69.1	78.2	37.2	31.6	1 519	1 194
Floyd	655	2 381 344	4.8	5.4	1.3	6.9	31.5	3.8	44.8	76.5	22.6	24.9	1 552	1 207

1. Based on the resident population estimated as of July 1 of the year shown.

Table B. States and Counties — **Local Government Finances, Government Employment, and Income Taxes**

STATE County	Total (mil dol)	Per capita[1] (dollars)	Education	Health and hospitals	Police protection	Public welfare	Highways	Total (mil dol)	Per capita[1] (dollars)	Federal civilian	Federal military	State and local	Number of returns	Mean adjusted gross income	Mean income tax
	185	186	187	188	189	190	191	192	193	194	195	196	197	198	199
INDIANA—Cont'd															
Pike	34.3	2 684	63.8	1.9	2.6	0.2	4.1	28.8	2 253	31	38	568	5 730	48 493	4 638
Porter	434.6	2 623	59.0	1.1	3.4	0.2	3.6	510.5	3 081	453	508	6 459	80 660	66 106	8 605
Posey	70.6	2 759	61.6	1.8	2.5	0.3	4.9	54.0	2 108	66	78	1 097	12 260	61 539	7 414
Pulaski	61.0	4 646	39.3	31.3	2.5	0.3	4.3	30.0	2 286	38	39	1 037	6 000	47 588	4 849
Putnam	123.0	3 258	52.6	25.9	2.2	0.1	3.9	99.5	2 636	77	100	2 372	15 780	47 234	4 518
Randolph	72.4	2 803	61.3	1.1	3.3	0.3	5.5	45.1	1 749	62	77	1 191	11 750	41 895	3 835
Ripley	77.1	2 698	69.6	0.9	2.4	0.1	3.5	73.8	2 582	73	87	1 309	13 260	49 288	5 123
Rush	60.9	3 561	39.7	33.6	2.8	0.2	6.5	41.7	2 438	43	51	1 046	7 970	44 957	4 126
St. Joseph	848.7	3 186	49.9	0.6	4.9	0.4	3.0	856.7	3 216	866	940	12 681	124 860	52 764	6 316
Scott	82.2	3 453	49.0	26.1	3.2	0.1	2.3	53.4	2 245	76	72	1 069	10 430	41 257	3 509
Shelby	217.7	4 896	31.6	43.4	3.2	0.1	2.2	156.3	3 515	128	135	2 382	21 510	48 330	4 801
Spencer	60.9	2 923	50.0	0.5	2.5	0.2	3.3	52.3	2 510	69	63	967	9 760	49 784	4 827
Starke	57.6	2 481	62.7	1.4	2.4	0.1	5.1	49.3	2 124	42	71	984	10 330	41 536	3 618
Steuben	88.6	2 597	53.3	1.0	3.4	0.2	3.8	103.6	3 037	61	102	1 476	16 370	49 274	5 591
Sullivan	83.4	3 936	37.2	35.1	0.9	0.2	3.7	81.5	3 848	49	58	1 765	8 740	45 905	4 266
Switzerland	38.7	3 712	40.1	0.3	1.1	0.2	3.1	17.5	1 683	20	32	451	4 090	39 884	3 282
Tippecanoe	406.1	2 288	50.8	0.2	6.3	0.6	5.9	369.7	2 083	450	581	23 586	74 030	54 928	6 530
Tipton	40.8	2 597	56.2	0.2	3.5	0.2	6.7	38.3	2 442	35	47	759	7 570	54 511	6 055
Union	23.2	3 150	73.7	0.1	2.6	0.0	4.3	25.2	3 429	13	22	418	3 290	43 634	3 832
Vanderburgh	605.3	3 347	39.0	0.7	7.5	0.3	2.7	673.3	3 723	1 001	545	9 596	85 510	53 022	6 388
Vermillion	47.0	2 933	53.2	0.4	2.5	0.4	5.1	23.9	1 493	31	48	668	7 230	44 415	3 938
Vigo	303.7	2 801	52.3	0.6	4.1	0.6	2.7	415.8	3 835	1 124	326	7 495	46 400	48 443	5 448
Wabash	128.9	3 983	46.9	29.1	2.8	0.1	3.3	49.4	1 525	73	94	1 540	15 070	48 995	5 417
Warren	25.3	3 032	48.5	1.2	1.6	1.1	6.3	5.8	698	15	25	344	3 980	51 365	5 511
Warrick	150.3	2 485	55.3	0.5	3.2	0.1	2.8	121.4	2 008	102	189	2 131	29 080	69 433	9 558
Washington	72.9	2 611	64.1	0.6	1.7	0.2	4.2	47.7	1 710	57	85	1 171	12 330	40 738	3 409
Wayne	192.9	2 822	52.8	1.7	4.5	0.3	3.0	101.7	1 489	158	199	4 658	30 470	43 065	4 341
Wells	73.2	2 646	66.0	0.6	4.1	0.1	4.5	54.7	1 977	60	85	1 233	13 110	51 016	5 135
White	92.9	3 804	53.9	0.2	2.1	0.1	3.9	122.7	5 024	57	74	1 366	12 130	46 883	4 817
Whitley	83.9	2 515	50.7	0.4	3.1	0.1	5.2	89.8	2 693	73	102	1 355	16 500	52 620	5 696
IOWA	X	X	X	X	X	X	X	X	X	17 555	11 706	237 829	1 445 500	59 636	7 026
Adair	35.9	4 797	29.3	28.1	3.8	0.1	14.9	30.8	4 112	28	27	436	3 500	46 900	4 274
Adams	18.9	4 842	43.4	5.1	6.6	0.8	17.5	25.1	6 408	28	14	215	1 900	44 619	4 456
Allamakee	60.7	4 262	38.8	26.8	3.5	0.2	12.3	42.3	2 969	74	51	1 064	6 710	44 310	4 025
Appanoose	38.5	3 030	55.1	4.8	8.0	0.2	13.4	8.5	670	50	47	628	5 500	40 544	3 301
Audubon	32.4	5 481	33.4	34.9	4.0	0.2	13.4	10.0	1 694	26	21	352	2 840	57 387	7 237
Benton	81.0	3 135	52.4	3.2	3.8	0.1	11.3	122.8	4 756	66	96	1 453	12 040	60 861	6 588
Black Hawk	637.5	4 836	53.7	3.2	4.6	0.3	7.4	430.8	3 268	535	507	11 461	60 270	56 298	6 354
Boone	124.1	4 739	36.1	35.5	3.3	0.4	7.7	248.4	9 484	112	98	2 334	12 620	58 581	6 279
Bremer	157.5	6 436	38.3	35.9	2.7	0.2	6.4	95.8	3 915	61	87	1 902	11 030	65 440	7 407
Buchanan	82.2	3 927	41.5	24.9	4.2	0.1	11.1	83.7	3 995	42	78	1 397	9 440	55 073	5 672
Buena Vista	124.9	6 065	34.7	32.6	3.3	0.1	7.7	93.1	4 522	95	74	1 611	9 710	50 836	5 244
Butler	80.9	5 400	24.9	40.1	2.8	0.3	13.2	30.8	2 054	43	56	770	6 850	53 671	5 055
Calhoun	44.1	4 453	58.6	8.7	3.3	0.5	11.4	14.8	1 490	38	34	624	4 530	52 467	5 366
Carroll	82.7	4 011	45.1	5.7	3.3	4.3	11.5	57.3	2 780	80	76	1 206	10 240	58 196	6 950
Cass	117.4	8 552	29.2	40.3	2.1	0.2	6.2	80.0	5 832	69	50	1 316	6 440	49 625	5 061
Cedar	69.5	3 774	57.4	5.4	4.1	0.0	10.6	54.8	2 977	82	68	972	8 770	58 997	6 147
Cerro Gordo	204.6	4 672	54.1	4.7	5.2	0.6	6.3	164.2	3 750	153	159	2 649	21 010	56 813	6 848
Cherokee	39.0	3 267	46.5	3.5	4.6	0.1	19.0	23.5	1 969	44	42	951	5 720	56 015	6 247
Chickasaw	44.7	3 641	56.0	3.0	4.0	0.2	13.2	29.3	2 390	53	45	579	5 860	59 520	7 387
Clarke	51.9	5 544	32.9	36.7	3.5	0.4	8.8	35.1	3 750	36	34	752	4 260	44 619	3 689
Clay	129.8	7 817	21.1	46.9	2.7	0.2	5.4	102.7	6 185	59	62	1 581	8 200	57 164	6 697
Clayton	98.8	5 538	51.9	15.0	3.1	0.4	9.5	56.2	3 150	73	66	1 252	8 370	49 235	5 165
Clinton	230.7	4 735	45.9	4.9	4.2	0.3	8.2	231.1	4 743	111	178	2 446	22 680	50 414	5 035
Crawford	93.1	5 378	36.5	33.2	2.6	0.1	10.1	85.1	4 916	69	63	1 260	7 880	49 552	4 831
Dallas	257.2	3 574	65.5	8.1	2.9	0.2	6.0	404.2	5 617	98	307	3 633	36 470	92 380	13 886
Davis	44.2	5 085	27.2	43.8	2.8	0.2	9.8	35.8	4 115	33	33	508	3 450	46 495	4 137
Decatur	44.9	5 439	33.8	43.0	3.1	1.0	8.7	35.6	4 310	31	28	549	3 180	40 014	3 332
Delaware	94.8	5 392	30.9	40.4	2.9	0.2	10.4	55.0	3 130	41	65	1 221	8 430	51 951	5 127
Des Moines	184.0	4 560	60.7	3.6	4.8	0.2	4.9	138.1	3 424	140	151	2 440	19 400	50 996	5 519
Dickinson	103.1	6 073	27.9	30.2	3.5	0.3	13.2	137.6	8 106	72	64	1 144	8 850	69 714	9 562
Dubuque	405.9	4 268	37.6	4.5	4.7	2.0	7.0	372.4	3 916	259	368	4 482	47 230	58 936	7 178
Emmet	70.6	6 975	75.4	3.2	3.2	0.1	6.0	24.8	2 448	37	35	774	4 550	49 317	4 997
Fayette	72.6	3 494	51.6	4.0	5.1	0.2	16.4	32.0	1 541	73	73	1 134	9 110	47 735	4 606
Floyd	71.8	4 475	33.5	31.9	2.8	0.9	9.2	26.4	1 647	37	59	983	7 370	52 678	5 566

1. Based on the resident population estimated as of July 1 of the year shown.

Table B. States and Counties — Land Area and Population

STATE/ County code	CBSA code[1]	County type[2]	STATE County	Land area,[3] (sq mi) 2016	Total persons 2016	Rank	Per square mile	White	Black	American Indian, Alaska Native	Asian and Pacific Islander	Percent Hispanic or Latino[4]	Under 5 years	5 to 17 years	18 to 24 years	25 to 34 years	35 to 44 years	45 to 54 years
				1	2	3	4	5	6	7	8	9	10	11	12	13	14	15
			IOWA—Cont'd															
19 069	...	7	Franklin	582.0	10 170	2 421	17.5	85.9	1.0	0.5	0.7	12.9	5.7	17.4	7.5	10.0	10.7	12.3
19 071	...	8	Fremont	511.1	6 950	2 676	13.6	96.2	0.8	0.8	0.6	2.6	5.3	16.8	7.0	9.6	10.6	12.7
19 073	...	6	Greene	569.6	9 011	2 509	15.8	95.9	0.8	0.8	0.9	2.7	5.7	17.2	7.2	9.9	10.1	12.8
19 075	47940	3	Grundy	501.9	12 313	2 271	24.5	97.8	0.9	0.4	0.6	1.3	5.4	18.0	6.7	10.9	11.5	12.5
19 077	19780	2	Guthrie	590.6	10 625	2 381	18.0	96.2	0.8	0.7	0.7	2.6	5.6	17.0	7.0	9.1	10.7	13.4
19 079	...	6	Hamilton	576.8	15 076	2 092	26.1	90.6	1.3	0.7	2.7	6.0	6.3	16.9	7.1	11.0	11.1	13.0
19 081	...	7	Hancock	571.0	10 835	2 368	19.0	94.5	1.0	0.5	0.8	4.1	5.3	17.1	7.4	10.1	10.8	12.5
19 083	...	6	Hardin	569.3	17 226	1 965	30.3	93.4	1.9	0.7	1.1	4.2	5.3	15.4	8.8	10.5	10.9	12.5
19 085	36540	2	Harrison	696.8	14 149	2 154	20.3	97.3	0.7	0.8	0.5	1.7	5.7	17.0	7.2	10.2	11.0	13.4
19 087	...	6	Henry	434.3	19 773	1 841	45.5	90.2	3.0	0.7	3.0	4.7	5.6	16.3	9.2	11.7	11.7	13.0
19 089	...	6	Howard	473.2	9 332	2 478	19.7	97.4	0.9	0.3	0.5	1.6	6.6	18.2	6.8	10.7	10.6	12.5
19 091	...	7	Humboldt	434.4	9 487	2 468	21.8	95.2	0.9	0.5	0.6	3.8	5.8	17.2	7.0	11.1	10.4	12.2
19 093	...	8	Ida	431.5	6 985	2 672	16.2	96.4	0.8	0.5	0.8	2.4	5.6	17.9	7.3	10.3	10.2	11.2
19 095	...	6	Iowa	586.5	16 311	2 023	27.8	96.1	0.9	0.4	0.7	2.7	6.1	16.9	7.6	10.2	11.5	13.6
19 097	...	6	Jackson	636.0	19 472	1 850	30.6	96.7	1.3	0.6	1.2	1.3	5.6	16.5	7.6	10.0	10.2	14.0
19 099	35500	6	Jasper	730.4	36 708	1 259	50.3	94.9	2.4	0.7	1.0	2.1	5.8	16.4	7.4	11.8	12.1	13.6
19 101	21840	7	Jefferson	435.5	18 090	1 914	41.5	82.2	2.4	0.8	13.2	2.9	4.3	11.7	13.0	14.2	10.2	10.1
19 103	26980	3	Johnson	614.0	146 547	443	238.7	81.1	7.5	0.6	7.5	5.5	6.1	14.1	21.2	15.8	11.7	10.2
19 105	16300	2	Jones	575.6	20 439	1 806	35.5	94.8	2.8	0.4	0.8	1.9	5.4	16.5	7.1	11.4	12.0	13.6
19 107	...	8	Keokuk	579.2	10 119	2 427	17.5	97.4	1.0	0.4	0.3	1.6	6.3	16.9	7.3	10.4	10.6	12.5
19 109	...	7	Kossuth	972.7	15 114	2 089	15.5	95.9	1.4	0.4	0.8	2.5	5.7	16.4	7.7	10.0	9.5	12.0
19 111	22800	5	Lee	517.5	34 615	1 309	66.9	92.7	3.9	0.7	1.0	3.5	6.0	15.3	7.7	11.6	11.1	13.3
19 113	16300	2	Linn	716.9	221 661	298	309.2	89.0	6.5	0.7	3.1	3.2	6.5	17.2	9.2	13.7	12.7	13.1
19 115	...	8	Louisa	401.8	11 142	2 345	27.7	79.5	1.3	0.6	3.9	15.8	6.3	16.6	8.2	11.1	12.3	14.0
19 117	...	6	Lucas	430.6	8 647	2 536	20.1	97.5	0.6	0.5	0.5	1.7	5.6	17.2	7.7	9.1	10.4	13.0
19 119	...	8	Lyon	587.7	11 754	2 308	20.0	96.5	0.5	0.5	0.6	2.6	7.2	21.2	7.3	10.5	12.2	11.3
19 121	19780	2	Madison	561.0	15 848	2 051	28.2	96.8	0.8	0.7	0.9	1.9	5.8	19.4	7.0	9.6	12.7	14.7
19 123	36820	7	Mahaska	570.9	22 181	1 718	38.9	95.0	2.2	0.5	1.4	2.1	6.5	17.6	9.3	11.5	11.7	11.9
19 125	37800	5	Marion	554.5	33 189	1 351	59.9	95.6	1.3	0.5	1.8	1.9	5.9	18.2	10.7	10.7	11.4	12.6
19 127	32260	4	Marshall	572.5	40 312	1 168	70.4	73.1	2.5	0.7	4.0	21.1	6.9	18.3	8.6	11.8	10.6	12.1
19 129	36540	2	Mills	437.4	14 972	2 097	34.2	95.4	1.1	0.9	0.9	3.0	5.9	18.0	7.3	9.4	12.2	14.4
19 131	...	7	Mitchell	469.1	10 763	2 375	22.9	97.1	1.0	0.4	0.8	1.4	6.0	17.9	7.5	9.9	9.8	12.7
19 133	...	6	Monona	694.1	8 898	2 514	12.8	96.2	1.1	1.4	0.7	1.8	5.2	16.0	7.6	9.1	9.7	11.9
19 135	...	7	Monroe	433.7	7 870	2 607	18.1	95.3	1.6	0.4	0.8	2.8	5.5	17.9	7.5	10.4	11.1	13.3
19 137	...	6	Montgomery	424.1	10 225	2 412	24.1	95.1	0.9	0.7	0.7	3.6	5.9	16.6	7.3	9.4	10.7	13.0
19 139	34700	4	Muscatine	437.4	42 940	1 114	98.2	78.8	2.7	0.6	1.5	17.5	6.6	18.8	8.3	12.3	11.8	12.9
19 141	...	7	O'Brien	573.0	14 020	2 161	24.5	93.4	1.1	0.4	1.3	4.7	6.0	17.5	7.5	10.7	10.6	11.9
19 143	...	7	Osceola	398.7	6 064	2 745	15.2	90.8	0.9	0.6	1.1	7.6	6.5	17.0	7.0	10.0	10.0	12.6
19 145	...	6	Page	534.9	15 391	2 072	28.8	92.6	3.2	1.1	1.5	3.1	5.2	14.7	7.8	11.4	12.3	12.1
19 147	...	7	Palo Alto	563.9	9 047	2 505	16.0	94.9	1.6	0.7	1.4	2.5	5.9	17.0	8.2	11.1	10.4	11.3
19 149	43580	3	Plymouth	862.8	25 200	1 603	29.2	93.4	1.3	0.6	1.1	4.7	6.4	18.4	8.0	10.1	11.7	12.9
19 151	...	9	Pocahontas	577.2	6 886	2 683	11.9	94.2	1.6	0.7	0.8	4.1	5.7	17.1	7.0	9.4	9.1	12.4
19 153	19780	2	Polk	573.7	474 045	145	826.3	80.2	7.8	0.6	5.4	8.2	7.4	17.8	8.8	15.6	13.4	12.9
19 155	36540	2	Pottawattamie	950.6	93 582	627	98.4	89.6	2.4	0.9	1.3	7.5	6.3	17.3	8.8	12.3	11.9	12.9
19 157	...	7	Poweshiek	584.9	18 533	1 889	31.7	92.9	2.1	0.6	2.6	3.3	5.0	15.2	14.5	9.9	9.6	11.6
19 159	...	9	Ringgold	535.5	5 068	2 828	9.5	96.1	0.8	0.5	0.8	2.5	5.4	18.2	6.5	10.1	9.5	11.6
19 161	...	9	Sac	575.0	9 876	2 441	17.2	96.3	0.9	0.5	0.5	2.9	6.1	16.4	6.8	9.6	9.6	12.5
19 163	19340	2	Scott	458.1	172 474	375	376.5	83.0	9.1	0.8	3.4	6.6	6.6	17.4	8.4	13.5	12.6	13.0
19 165	...	6	Shelby	590.8	11 800	2 306	20.0	94.9	0.9	0.7	0.7	3.7	5.5	16.9	7.4	8.5	9.9	14.3
19 167	...	7	Sioux	767.9	34 898	1 307	45.4	87.9	0.8	0.3	1.2	10.5	7.3	19.8	13.6	11.1	10.8	10.6
19 169	11180	3	Story	572.7	97 090	610	169.5	85.6	3.4	0.5	9.0	3.3	4.6	12.1	31.8	13.1	9.3	8.6
19 171	...	6	Tama	721.0	17 319	1 955	24.0	83.3	1.0	7.6	1.0	9.0	6.5	17.6	7.7	10.1	10.4	13.6
19 173	...	9	Taylor	531.9	6 216	2 735	11.7	91.5	0.8	0.5	0.6	7.6	6.6	16.9	7.2	11.2	10.6	12.0
19 175	...	6	Union	423.6	12 420	2 267	29.3	95.0	1.4	0.5	0.9	3.1	5.4	17.0	9.2	11.0	11.2	12.2
19 177	...	9	Van Buren	484.8	7 271	2 647	15.0	97.5	0.7	0.6	0.8	1.5	6.1	17.1	6.7	9.8	10.6	12.7
19 179	36900	5	Wapello	431.8	34 982	1 305	81.0	84.3	4.1	0.7	1.5	10.7	6.1	16.4	9.2	12.7	11.7	12.6
19 181	19780	2	Warren	569.8	49 691	989	87.2	95.4	1.3	0.5	1.3	2.6	6.1	18.8	9.5	11.1	12.6	13.5
19 183	26980	3	Washington	568.9	22 281	1 716	39.2	92.4	1.4	0.5	0.9	5.9	7.2	17.9	7.5	11.1	10.9	12.7
19 185	...	9	Wayne	525.5	6 452	2 718	12.3	97.2	1.1	0.6	0.7	1.6	6.7	18.4	7.3	10.5	9.8	11.3
19 187	22700	5	Webster	715.6	36 769	1 256	51.4	89.5	5.6	0.7	1.6	4.5	5.9	15.6	11.6	12.2	10.5	12.0
19 189	...	6	Winnebago	400.5	10 631	2 380	26.5	93.2	1.9	0.5	1.4	4.3	5.8	16.2	9.7	10.3	10.3	11.7
19 191	...	7	Winneshiek	689.9	20 561	1 797	29.8	95.9	1.1	0.3	1.3	2.2	4.2	14.1	16.6	9.3	9.6	12.0
19 193	43580	3	Woodbury	872.9	102 779	587	117.7	76.3	4.5	2.2	3.6	16.0	7.3	19.0	10.0	13.0	11.9	12.2
19 195	32380	9	Worth	400.1	7 572	2 627	18.9	95.6	1.3	0.5	1.0	2.8	5.4	15.4	8.4	10.2	10.8	12.2
19 197	...	7	Wright	580.4	12 779	2 243	22.0	87.3	1.1	0.6	0.8	11.3	6.0	17.8	6.9	9.9	10.4	11.4

1. CBSA = Core Based Statistical Area. See Appendix A for explanation. See Appendix B for list of metropolitan areas with component counties.   2. County type code from the Economic Research Service of USDA Rural-Urban Continuum Codes. See Appendix A for definition.   3. Dry land or land partially or temporarily covered by water.   4. May be of any race.

Table B. States and Counties — Population and Households

STATE County	Age (percent) (cont.) 55 to 64 years	65 to 74 years	75 years and over	Percent female	Total persons 2000	2010	Percent change 2000–2010	2010–2016	Components of change, 2010–2016 Births	Deaths	Net migration	Households, 2011–2015 Number	Persons per household	Percent Family households	Female family householder[1]	One person
	16	17	18	19	20	21	22	23	24	25	26	27	28	29	30	31
IOWA—Cont'd																
Franklin	15.8	10.2	10.3	49.5	10 704	10 680	-0.2	-4.8	764	714	-543	4 258	2.42	69.1	9.8	25.1
Fremont	16.3	11.6	10.1	50.1	8 010	7 441	-7.1	-6.6	471	557	-357	2 954	2.36	68.7	8.1	26.7
Greene	15.5	10.7	10.9	50.7	10 366	9 337	-9.9	-3.5	638	741	-203	3 927	2.30	67.8	8.7	28.9
Grundy	14.5	10.4	10.1	50.7	12 369	12 453	0.7	-1.1	820	787	-160	5 183	2.37	68.8	5.9	26.9
Guthrie	15.5	11.6	10.0	49.9	11 353	10 954	-3.5	-3.0	678	787	-158	4 514	2.34	67.5	8.5	28.5
Hamilton	14.7	10.3	9.7	50.4	16 438	15 673	-4.7	-3.8	1 135	1 067	-691	6 384	2.36	66.3	8.2	30.4
Hancock	15.8	10.8	10.3	49.7	12 100	11 341	-6.3	-4.5	699	788	-373	4 673	2.33	66.0	6.2	29.7
Hardin	15.3	10.3	10.9	50.2	18 812	17 534	-6.8	-1.8	1 177	1 374	-61	6 973	2.37	63.0	5.3	33.4
Harrison	15.5	10.7	9.3	50.3	15 666	14 937	-4.7	-5.3	968	1 143	-617	5 973	2.37	65.9	8.8	28.6
Henry	13.5	10.4	8.5	48.7	20 336	20 145	-0.9	-1.8	1 427	1 346	-472	7 623	2.43	67.2	9.0	27.4
Howard	14.2	10.4	10.0	50.0	9 932	9 566	-3.7	-2.4	738	667	-296	3 867	2.39	62.8	6.7	31.5
Humboldt	15.6	10.1	10.6	50.4	10 381	9 814	-5.5	-3.3	651	733	-242	4 190	2.28	66.8	9.5	28.2
Ida	15.2	10.9	11.4	49.9	7 837	7 089	-9.5	-1.5	488	581	-35	3 101	2.24	66.8	6.4	29.2
Iowa	15.4	9.0	9.8	50.4	15 671	16 355	4.4	-0.3	1 180	1 116	-125	6 819	2.34	71.1	7.3	24.2
Jackson	15.5	11.1	9.4	50.1	20 296	19 848	-2.2	-1.9	1 283	1 439	-244	8 433	2.29	67.6	8.5	27.4
Jasper	14.4	10.0	8.5	48.8	37 213	36 842	-1.0	-0.4	2 593	2 323	-363	14 437	2.41	67.6	8.3	26.4
Jefferson	16.0	13.2	7.3	45.1	16 181	16 843	4.1	7.4	932	983	1 323	6 913	2.24	60.0	7.3	33.0
Johnson	10.1	6.5	4.3	50.4	111 006	130 882	17.9	12.0	11 214	4 154	8 481	55 426	2.37	55.2	8.6	29.7
Jones	14.9	10.4	9.0	48.0	20 221	20 636	2.1	-1.0	1 330	1 275	-202	8 171	2.34	69.6	8.8	25.1
Keokuk	15.5	10.6	9.9	49.2	11 400	10 511	-7.8	-3.7	772	681	-476	4 347	2.33	64.1	6.9	30.3
Kossuth	16.1	10.4	12.2	49.8	17 163	15 543	-9.4	-2.8	1 033	1 151	-258	6 723	2.23	64.5	6.2	32.3
Lee	15.2	11.4	8.3	49.8	38 052	35 862	-5.8	-3.5	2 546	2 685	-1 063	14 412	2.40	64.3	10.6	30.3
Linn	12.6	8.4	6.5	50.6	191 701	211 229	10.2	4.9	17 283	10 410	3 776	87 318	2.42	62.6	9.7	29.4
Louisa	14.4	9.6	7.5	49.1	12 183	11 387	-6.5	-2.2	854	650	-444	4 311	2.58	70.6	9.9	25.0
Lucas	15.6	11.2	10.2	49.6	9 422	8 898	-5.6	-2.8	612	667	-219	3 678	2.34	64.1	9.2	31.6
Lyon	13.0	8.5	8.8	49.2	11 763	11 581	-1.5	1.5	1 054	695	-154	4 496	2.57	72.0	5.5	25.0
Madison	13.9	9.4	7.5	49.8	14 019	15 679	11.8	1.1	1 033	928	49	6 225	2.48	67.7	5.0	25.4
Mahaska	14.1	9.2	8.2	49.4	22 335	22 381	0.2	-0.9	1 786	1 394	-570	9 023	2.41	64.7	9.8	29.9
Marion	13.4	9.4	7.8	50.1	32 052	33 309	3.9	-0.4	2 287	2 092	-324	12 978	2.43	68.3	5.9	28.2
Marshall	13.6	9.8	8.3	49.5	39 311	40 648	3.4	-0.8	3 396	2 986	-731	15 297	2.60	68.6	9.8	26.2
Mills	16.0	10.4	6.4	49.7	14 547	15 059	3.5	-0.6	967	828	-191	5 399	2.63	73.9	7.6	23.6
Mitchell	14.5	10.0	11.7	50.7	10 874	10 772	-0.9	-0.1	790	823	25	4 358	2.41	67.1	6.7	29.3
Monona	15.4	12.0	13.1	50.7	10 020	9 242	-7.8	-3.7	534	909	18	4 043	2.19	59.8	6.3	35.4
Monroe	14.6	10.6	8.9	50.2	8 016	7 970	-0.6	-1.3	555	616	-16	3 326	2.37	64.5	9.5	28.9
Montgomery	15.7	11.0	10.4	51.2	11 771	10 740	-8.8	-4.8	728	934	-310	4 610	2.22	67.9	13.3	27.8
Muscatine	13.3	9.3	6.7	50.1	41 722	42 749	2.5	0.4	3 426	2 405	-795	16 345	2.59	69.9	9.6	25.8
O'Brien	15.1	9.6	11.0	49.9	15 102	14 398	-4.7	-2.6	1 036	1 149	-275	6 004	2.28	65.2	5.1	31.0
Osceola	16.2	9.7	10.9	49.0	7 003	6 462	-7.7	-6.2	448	431	-412	2 670	2.28	64.9	4.6	30.3
Page	15.2	10.9	10.2	47.5	16 976	15 943	-6.1	-3.5	1 086	1 285	-311	6 294	2.34	63.1	6.0	31.9
Palo Alto	14.5	10.2	11.5	50.2	10 147	9 421	-7.2	-4.0	641	782	-231	3 977	2.23	63.5	8.2	31.6
Plymouth	14.4	9.8	8.4	50.4	24 849	24 981	0.5	0.9	1 791	1 489	-23	9 995	2.45	69.6	8.6	26.4
Pocahontas	16.4	11.3	11.6	50.3	8 662	7 310	-15.6	-5.8	477	576	-301	3 197	2.18	59.4	5.8	35.8
Polk	11.8	7.3	5.0	50.8	374 601	430 635	15.0	10.1	42 359	20 337	21 075	177 049	2.50	64.6	11.3	28.2
Pottawattamie	14.2	9.3	7.0	50.7	87 704	93 149	6.2	0.5	7 493	5 556	-1 300	36 683	2.48	66.6	12.8	27.7
Poweshiek	14.1	10.3	9.9	51.3	18 815	18 914	0.5	-2.0	1 123	1 390	-109	7 351	2.31	63.0	9.1	32.1
Ringgold	13.9	11.7	13.0	50.7	5 469	5 131	-6.2	-1.2	328	471	86	2 030	2.40	65.6	5.6	29.8
Sac	16.4	10.7	12.0	50.9	11 529	10 350	-10.2	-4.6	694	864	-273	4 406	2.25	64.4	6.7	32.2
Scott	13.3	8.8	6.4	50.9	158 668	165 224	4.1	4.4	13 940	8 952	2 482	67 709	2.46	63.0	10.8	30.4
Shelby	15.2	10.6	11.8	50.6	13 173	12 167	-7.6	-3.0	761	899	-224	5 066	2.32	62.1	5.9	33.5
Sioux	11.7	7.4	7.7	49.8	31 589	33 704	6.7	3.5	3 199	1 567	-415	11 765	2.73	75.2	5.5	21.3
Story	9.4	6.1	5.0	47.8	79 981	89 542	12.0	8.4	5 828	3 022	4 858	35 901	2.35	52.6	5.7	27.0
Tama	14.5	10.0	9.6	50.3	18 103	17 767	-1.9	-2.5	1 400	1 302	-539	6 790	2.51	71.4	9.9	25.1
Taylor	14.1	11.3	10.2	49.8	6 958	6 317	-9.2	-1.6	483	457	-128	2 744	2.23	67.6	9.3	26.2
Union	13.9	10.5	9.4	51.2	12 309	12 534	1.8	-0.9	844	918	-28	5 337	2.30	61.0	7.9	32.3
Van Buren	15.9	11.5	9.5	49.4	7 809	7 570	-3.1	-3.9	561	550	-296	2 944	2.49	69.7	5.1	27.3
Wapello	14.2	9.4	7.8	50.5	36 051	35 625	-1.2	-1.8	2 712	2 530	-746	14 493	2.38	65.3	11.4	29.6
Warren	12.8	8.9	6.6	50.7	40 671	46 228	13.7	7.5	3 348	2 394	2 492	18 009	2.54	73.3	9.6	23.2
Washington	13.8	10.0	8.9	50.5	20 670	21 704	5.0	2.7	1 871	1 499	190	8 938	2.43	66.6	8.1	27.5
Wayne	14.5	10.4	11.1	51.1	6 730	6 403	-4.9	0.8	539	535	30	2 596	2.41	64.0	8.4	33.7
Webster	14.4	9.6	8.2	48.2	40 235	38 013	-5.5	-3.3	2 776	2 806	-1 152	15 155	2.27	60.1	12.1	33.8
Winnebago	15.5	10.0	10.7	51.0	11 723	10 866	-7.3	-2.2	736	795	-193	4 580	2.20	63.4	4.5	33.9
Winneshiek	15.0	9.8	9.4	50.4	21 310	21 058	-1.2	-2.4	1 061	1 100	-413	8 248	2.24	65.9	6.0	29.1
Woodbury	12.3	8.1	6.1	50.4	103 877	102 177	-1.6	0.6	9 623	5 795	-2 975	38 656	2.58	66.1	12.9	28.2
Worth	15.7	10.6	9.7	50.1	7 909	7 598	-3.9	-0.3	480	525	33	3 180	2.35	67.7	8.8	28.2
Wright	15.6	10.6	11.4	49.6	14 334	13 229	-7.7	-3.4	932	1 017	-345	5 495	2.31	61.7	8.1	33.6

1. No spouse present.

Table B. States and Counties — **Population, Vital Statistics, Health, and Crime**

STATE County	Persons in group quarters, 2016	Daytime population, 2011–2015 Number	Employment/residence ratio	Births, 2016 Total	Rate[1]	Deaths, 2016 Number	Rate[1]	Persons under 65 with no health insurance, 2015 Number	Percent	Medicare, 2015 Total Beneficiaries	Enrolled in Original Medicare	Enrolled in Medicare Advantage	Serious crimes known to police,[2] 2014 Total Number	Rate[3]
	32	33	34	35	36	37	38	39	40	41	42	43	44	45
IOWA—Cont'd														
Franklin	193	10 181	0.94	126	12.4	99	9.7	717	8.8	1 956	1 904	52	13	123
Fremont	134	6 294	0.76	78	11.2	84	12.1	286	5.3	1 654	1 483	171	4	57
Greene	80	8 777	0.91	98	10.9	121	13.4	423	6.0	2 152	1 870	282	64	703
Grundy	151	10 417	0.67	122	9.9	122	9.9	432	4.3	2 493	2 196	297	91	739
Guthrie	145	9 125	0.69	116	10.9	130	12.2	516	6.2	2 590	2 186	404	52	488
Hamilton	201	14 588	0.90	209	13.9	169	11.2	663	5.5	3 174	2 854	320	251	1 644
Hancock	134	10 922	0.97	120	11.1	129	11.9	506	5.8	2 244	2 195	49	54	488
Hardin	755	17 155	0.97	201	11.7	235	13.6	782	6.0	4 147	3 853	294	231	1 567
Harrison	279	11 778	0.63	156	11.0	182	12.9	703	6.2	3 139	2 783	356	57	397
Henry	1 374	20 002	0.99	227	11.5	198	10.0	849	5.6	4 102	3 685	417	389	2 116
Howard	201	9 218	0.94	118	12.6	113	12.1	537	7.2	2 101	2 043	58	132	1 384
Humboldt	119	9 161	0.89	98	10.3	112	11.8	448	5.9	2 024	1 926	98	69	713
Ida	105	7 724	1.19	74	10.6	99	14.2	332	6.1	1 537	1 385	152	95	1 324
Iowa	284	16 517	1.02	187	11.5	197	12.1	633	4.7	3 155	2 626	529	113	690
Jackson	195	16 750	0.71	211	10.8	228	11.7	1 031	6.7	4 254	3 221	1 033	207	1 058
Jasper	1 754	31 716	0.70	407	11.1	384	10.5	1 429	5.0	7 175	6 128	1 047	881	2 402
Jefferson	1 731	18 377	1.14	155	8.6	170	9.4	947	7.5	3 467	3 041	426	395	2 344
Johnson	8 529	148 960	1.12	1 800	12.3	727	5.0	7 824	6.4	15 259	12 862	2 397	3 186	2 252
Jones	1 199	17 826	0.72	211	10.3	208	10.2	847	5.5	3 877	3 073	804	137	664
Keokuk	130	8 533	0.64	115	11.4	100	9.9	521	6.5	2 383	2 001	382	53	640
Kossuth	240	15 437	1.02	166	11.0	170	11.2	626	5.4	3 444	3 361	83	93	608
Lee	1 328	37 772	1.15	395	11.4	423	12.2	1 482	5.4	7 569	6 720	849	937	2 624
Linn	5 056	227 956	1.10	2 815	12.7	1 753	7.9	8 478	4.6	36 721	26 185	10 536	6 585	3 025
Louisa	118	9 733	0.72	150	13.5	115	10.3	756	8.2	2 045	1 747	298	67	594
Lucas	76	8 408	0.92	97	11.2	101	11.7	483	7.1	1 938	1 677	261	205	2 349
Lyon	165	10 517	0.80	170	14.5	100	8.5	564	5.8	2 051	1 887	164	113	1 234
Madison	189	12 012	0.52	162	10.2	160	10.1	696	5.3	2 671	2 195	476	155	1 006
Mahaska	663	20 363	0.81	295	13.3	221	10.0	962	5.3	4 073	3 515	558	465	2 070
Marion	1 342	34 346	1.07	359	10.8	332	10.0	1 065	4.0	6 281	5 636	645	NA	NA
Marshall	1 305	40 885	1.00	515	12.8	484	12.0	2 839	8.7	8 687	7 447	1 240	1 033	2 510
Mills	566	12 244	0.62	162	10.8	120	8.0	573	4.8	2 836	2 445	391	269	1 808
Mitchell	242	10 375	0.93	125	11.6	126	11.7	636	7.5	2 542	2 509	33	60	627
Monona	205	8 171	0.78	91	10.2	142	16.0	451	6.7	2 214	1 820	394	111	1 218
Monroe	110	7 970	0.99	90	11.4	80	10.2	450	7.0	1 635	1 464	171	71	884
Montgomery	197	10 558	1.02	123	12.0	130	12.7	530	6.6	2 475	2 285	190	175	1 686
Muscatine	536	44 556	1.08	544	12.7	364	8.5	2 378	6.6	7 473	5 704	1 769	782	1 821
O'Brien	385	13 705	0.95	174	12.4	190	13.6	669	6.1	3 204	3 052	152	205	1 466
Osceola	94	5 542	0.79	77	12.7	73	12.0	387	8.0	1 297	1 229	68	13	211
Page	1 455	16 298	1.09	171	11.1	193	12.5	738	6.7	3 564	3 247	317	225	1 434
Palo Alto	299	8 753	0.90	111	12.3	114	12.6	417	6.0	2 200	2 149	51	116	1 268
Plymouth	313	23 350	0.88	300	11.0	228	9.0	1 009	5.0	4 288	3 600	688	316	1 264
Pocahontas	110	7 007	0.97	76	11.0	88	12.8	329	6.1	1 794	1 709	85	38	533
Polk	9 690	494 372	1.18	6 986	14.7	3 466	7.3	23 124	5.7	66 976	53 373	13 603	14 919	3 260
Pottawattamie	2 216	86 751	0.86	1 160	12.4	928	9.9	4 563	5.9	17 874	13 438	4 436	5 184	5 589
Poweshiek	1 648	20 074	1.14	177	9.6	209	11.3	781	5.8	3 776	3 325	451	301	1 621
Ringgold	174	4 699	0.83	53	10.5	65	12.8	324	8.5	1 192	1 107	85	29	572
Sac	200	9 020	0.79	110	11.1	128	13.0	489	6.3	2 455	2 349	106	47	469
Scott	3 426	173 907	1.05	2 229	12.9	1 454	8.4	7 262	5.0	29 667	22 802	6 865	5 650	3 309
Shelby	205	12 174	1.03	120	10.2	144	12.2	504	5.5	2 768	2 531	237	NA	NA
Sioux	2 313	36 864	1.13	506	14.5	255	7.3	2 111	7.6	5 215	4 842	373	139	399
Story	11 836	96 168	1.05	886	9.1	502	5.2	3 751	5.0	11 896	10 436	1 460	1 647	1 903
Tama	293	15 101	0.71	238	13.7	197	11.4	1 136	8.2	3 677	3 142	535	199	1 350
Taylor	80	5 449	0.75	80	12.9	57	9.2	417	8.5	1 527	1 504	23	26	424
Union	457	13 406	1.13	123	9.9	138	11.1	620	6.4	3 507	3 235	272	207	1 639
Van Buren	53	6 806	0.81	83	11.4	92	12.7	453	7.9	1 859	1 641	218	86	1 159
Wapello	877	36 610	1.08	441	12.6	389	11.1	2 460	8.6	8 090	7 295	795	1 298	3 667
Warren	1 636	34 874	0.48	549	11.0	415	8.4	1 500	3.8	7 610	6 172	1 438	844	1 770
Washington	314	19 594	0.78	324	14.5	234	10.5	1 182	6.6	4 494	3 896	598	204	921
Wayne	95	6 081	0.89	82	12.7	94	14.6	404	8.2	1 460	1 255	205	46	717
Webster	2 666	38 982	1.10	450	12.2	427	11.6	1 641	5.8	8 094	7 257	837	1 604	4 345
Winnebago	415	11 068	1.09	117	11.0	122	11.5	440	5.4	2 511	2 383	128	77	733
Winneshiek	2 269	21 320	1.04	166	8.1	171	8.3	657	4.4	4 152	3 494	658	108	514
Woodbury	2 553	101 558	0.98	1 514	14.7	927	9.0	7 156	8.3	18 005	13 659	4 346	3 752	3 668
Worth	89	6 317	0.67	80	10.6	75	9.9	352	5.9	1 536	1 429	107	69	914
Wright	216	13 201	1.05	152	11.9	165	12.9	746	7.5	3 037	2 890	147	76	587

1. Per 1,000 estimated resident population.   2. Data for serious crimes have not been adjusted for underreporting; this may affect comparability between geographic areas and over time.
3. Per 100,000 population estimated by the FBI.

Table B. States and Counties — Crime, Education, Money Income, and Poverty

	Serious crimes known to police, 2014 (cont.)[1]		Education						Money income, 2011–2015				Income and poverty, 2015		
	Rate[2]		School enrollment and attainment, 2011–2015				Local government expenditures,[5] 2013–2014			Households			Percent below poverty level		
			Enrollment[3]		Attainment[4] (percent)						Percent					
STATE County					High school graduate or less	Bachelor's degree or more	Total current spending (mil dol)	Current spending per student (dollars)	Per capita income[6] (dollars)	Median income (dollars)	with income of less than $50,000	with income of $200,000 or more	Median household income (dollars)	All persons	Children under 18 years	Children 5 to 17 years in families
	Violent	Property	Total	Percent private												
	46	47	48	49	50	51	52	53	54	55	56	57	58	59	60	61
IOWA—Cont'd																
Franklin	9	114	2 388	5.1	50.0	16.7	16.9	10 694	25 417	48 605	52.3	2.2	52 975	11.9	17.3	16.1
Fremont	43	14	1 596	4.4	44.2	21.5	10.1	11 888	29 060	53 324	44.9	4.1	55 421	12.1	17.0	15.6
Greene	77	626	2 120	7.1	44.1	18.6	14.0	8 768	26 918	46 898	53.0	2.8	51 002	11.1	16.5	14.9
Grundy	98	642	2 880	9.4	40.5	22.7	27.2	9 844	31 076	56 750	43.7	3.9	62 423	6.3	8.6	8.1
Guthrie	66	423	2 484	5.6	47.3	19.2	24.4	9 342	28 946	51 013	48.6	3.6	54 719	10.4	13.6	12.6
Hamilton	242	1 402	3 707	7.5	42.2	19.9	28.8	10 572	26 001	49 813	50.1	2.0	54 042	11.0	15.6	14.8
Hancock	117	371	2 433	6.6	44.3	18.1	16.9	10 603	26 846	52 981	47.2	2.5	56 746	9.2	12.2	11.0
Hardin	88	1 479	4 195	9.7	44.1	18.2	33.4	10 438	26 256	51 019	48.5	2.2	50 947	9.6	16.5	14.9
Harrison	21	377	3 295	8.6	47.3	17.4	28.8	10 053	26 910	53 567	46.6	1.7	57 244	9.9	13.2	11.7
Henry	299	1 817	4 567	15.4	45.5	18.8	35.2	10 197	23 439	49 321	50.7	1.6	50 241	12.0	16.4	14.5
Howard	94	1 290	2 057	17.6	55.5	12.8	16.8	9 988	25 804	49 869	50.1	2.3	50 602	11.0	15.7	14.6
Humboldt	83	630	2 253	16.0	45.2	17.6	15.6	9 923	27 814	47 252	51.8	1.9	52 702	10.8	14.5	12.9
Ida	167	1 157	1 553	6.4	48.5	19.3	12.3	10 152	28 398	46 993	52.8	3.6	53 804	10.6	13.1	12.6
Iowa	98	593	3 845	12.2	45.6	20.7	26.7	9 862	29 022	59 375	44.2	2.4	63 185	6.9	8.2	7.5
Jackson	61	997	4 486	11.5	54.2	15.3	29.8	9 670	25 546	49 028	50.9	1.6	49 956	12.9	17.6	16.3
Jasper	248	2 154	8 411	10.6	47.3	18.2	56.7	9 612	26 138	55 033	45.6	1.8	53 765	9.3	12.9	11.8
Jefferson	59	2 285	5 047	47.9	36.1	31.9	25.1	10 675	25 209	42 899	55.7	2.1	43 495	15.3	20.0	18.4
Johnson	254	1 998	51 629	8.6	22.3	51.3	173.5	10 166	31 271	55 700	45.5	5.7	57 706	18.3	12.7	11.6
Jones	82	582	4 689	14.8	47.5	16.6	31.1	9 626	26 937	55 060	44.3	2.9	55 789	11.1	14.3	12.8
Keokuk	145	495	2 297	6.8	52.3	15.5	11.8	9 586	23 076	43 838	55.2	1.0	50 054	12.1	18.1	17.1
Kossuth	157	451	3 451	18.5	44.1	19.1	23.4	11 729	28 952	51 496	48.3	3.0	52 433	11.6	15.1	13.3
Lee	498	2 126	7 725	11.3	50.2	15.5	51.5	10 117	22 746	43 312	55.5	1.0	45 428	15.9	22.9	22.1
Linn	222	2 803	58 257	18.1	32.7	31.5	422.8	11 526	30 829	59 322	41.9	3.7	58 142	11.0	12.2	11.2
Louisa	106	488	2 657	4.8	54.8	13.2	26.9	10 200	26 176	51 144	48.9	1.9	53 197	10.8	15.8	14.3
Lucas	172	2 177	1 875	6.9	54.1	14.9	14.0	9 990	23 512	43 962	55.2	1.5	46 933	14.7	24.1	22.3
Lyon	153	1 081	2 902	23.0	46.6	20.8	19.7	9 154	26 777	57 130	41.5	3.3	64 057	7.4	9.1	8.4
Madison	117	889	3 813	8.3	44.9	21.7	31.2	9 028	28 922	60 060	40.9	3.2	65 294	8.2	10.3	8.8
Mahaska	249	1 820	6 147	28.3	46.2	22.7	29.6	9 668	25 228	48 726	51.2	2.0	50 335	14.4	16.7	15.8
Marion	NA	NA	8 940	31.3	43.7	24.8	55.0	9 867	26 280	54 693	43.7	2.2	57 411	9.2	10.6	9.5
Marshall	420	2 090	9 385	7.4	49.4	19.7	69.9	9 798	24 648	53 351	44.8	2.0	53 980	11.3	17.3	16.8
Mills	249	1 559	3 849	11.7	42.8	23.8	29.8	9 521	28 280	63 979	38.9	2.3	62 507	10.3	13.5	11.5
Mitchell	31	596	2 366	13.5	53.4	14.9	15.4	9 433	25 706	49 488	50.6	2.8	61 352	9.3	14.7	13.3
Monona	143	1 076	1 837	6.4	51.7	14.5	17.1	10 785	24 730	40 302	60.0	1.7	43 991	13.2	18.0	16.4
Monroe	50	834	1 905	5.1	55.8	17.2	11.9	9 597	25 753	46 304	53.2	1.2	48 181	12.1	16.0	14.6
Montgomery	173	1 513	2 163	5.9	49.3	14.9	19.3	10 761	23 445	42 418	57.3	1.4	43 210	13.4	19.6	18.7
Muscatine	405	1 416	10 920	7.6	48.8	18.8	73.3	9 446	25 503	53 676	46.4	1.8	53 401	11.5	16.2	15.6
O'Brien	250	1 216	3 307	17.1	45.6	18.8	24.5	10 079	30 600	55 227	45.9	4.3	53 907	9.2	12.3	11.2
Osceola	65	146	1 411	10.1	51.8	17.4	8.0	9 989	25 306	49 448	50.6	2.2	54 415	9.6	14.7	14.2
Page	134	1 300	3 498	14.2	46.5	20.0	25.6	10 604	23 617	43 912	55.0	1.9	46 870	15.7	24.0	21.9
Palo Alto	350	918	2 205	12.8	38.1	20.0	17.5	10 209	26 154	47 113	53.1	1.3	48 992	11.6	15.6	14.5
Plymouth	132	1 132	6 380	17.4	43.5	20.5	41.1	10 033	27 991	57 130	42.9	1.9	61 929	8.3	10.2	9.5
Pocahontas	98	434	1 441	13.2	46.2	17.4	34.5	31 533	26 406	45 069	54.3	2.5	47 872	13.1	20.8	19.8
Polk	361	2 900	118 538	19.9	33.5	35.8	837.0	11 125	31 291	60 061	41.4	4.6	60 436	11.9	14.7	13.8
Pottawattamie	491	5 099	23 211	10.7	45.7	20.2	188.1	11 963	27 057	51 976	47.9	2.9	52 927	13.5	18.7	17.5
Poweshiek	199	1 422	5 217	37.4	43.9	24.6	28.0	9 724	26 018	51 006	48.9	2.4	52 861	10.9	12.6	11.5
Ringgold	79	493	1 115	7.5	45.7	20.8	8.5	11 237	26 557	47 042	54.0	3.8	45 870	14.1	24.9	22.2
Sac	30	439	2 165	10.0	47.4	19.7	18.4	10 521	26 991	49 572	50.6	2.0	52 506	10.9	14.3	12.9
Scott	468	2 840	43 641	18.6	35.7	32.1	313.7	10 968	29 391	55 114	45.0	3.8	58 160	12.4	16.7	15.9
Shelby	NA	NA	2 771	12.9	45.1	21.3	18.8	11 126	27 695	50 952	48.8	2.2	54 614	9.2	11.3	10.2
Sioux	29	370	10 547	50.1	42.7	25.5	45.7	9 468	26 029	61 627	38.8	4.0	62 875	7.6	8.0	7.3
Story	127	1 776	41 420	4.1	22.9	48.3	110.0	9 830	25 589	50 438	49.5	3.4	51 706	18.6	9.5	8.4
Tama	353	997	4 096	9.4	50.1	15.7	23.8	9 981	26 432	55 203	43.5	2.1	59 226	11.2	16.5	14.7
Taylor	33	391	1 385	4.7	50.7	14.5	10.8	10 781	23 821	44 246	55.3	1.5	46 466	14.7	20.3	19.4
Union	174	1 465	3 065	13.3	47.3	14.7	20.8	9 849	24 022	44 351	56.0	1.9	45 010	14.3	19.6	18.4
Van Buren	135	1 024	1 534	18.2	54.5	12.7	10.6	10 429	23 268	45 111	55.7	1.3	43 653	15.8	24.7	23.0
Wapello	271	3 396	8 188	8.7	50.5	16.8	81.4	12 809	22 716	42 095	57.6	1.4	44 738	16.0	22.1	20.2
Warren	306	1 464	13 119	20.6	37.0	28.2	85.2	9 214	30 086	64 447	37.2	2.6	67 728	7.8	8.9	7.3
Washington	298	623	5 173	11.0	45.5	20.9	38.3	9 978	27 228	56 390	45.0	1.7	55 283	10.9	14.9	13.8
Wayne	140	577	1 337	24.2	54.0	13.9	10.7	9 652	23 009	43 358	55.5	1.9	44 381	16.4	26.2	25.5
Webster	496	3 849	9 791	13.5	42.2	18.8	50.6	9 821	23 718	42 408	56.7	2.2	44 922	14.6	19.6	18.6
Winnebago	114	619	2 645	24.7	42.9	20.6	24.9	10 718	25 021	47 668	52.4	1.2	48 408	10.8	15.0	14.1
Winneshiek	10	504	6 258	44.3	41.0	27.7	31.9	11 431	26 211	54 429	45.0	2.0	59 096	9.5	9.5	8.3
Woodbury	317	3 352	27 385	15.4	48.6	21.1	211.8	11 486	23 630	46 720	52.6	2.1	50 774	14.0	19.6	18.6
Worth	146	769	1 662	10.1	44.1	15.4	14.0	9 438	24 734	48 459	51.7	1.8	50 761	10.9	15.1	13.9
Wright	70	518	2 789	2.3	47.6	17.0	28.0	10 027	26 316	43 698	55.1	2.7	49 882	12.6	18.2	17.2

1. Data for serious crimes have not been adjusted for underreporting; this may affect comparability between geographic areas and over time.   2. Per 100,000 population estimated by the FBI.
3. All persons 3 years old and over enrolled in nursery school through college.   4. Persons 25 years old and over.   5. Elementary and secondary education expenditures.
6. Based on population estimated by the American Community Survey, 2011–2015.

STATE County	Personal income, 2015										Earnings, 2015		
			Per capita[1]			Supplements to wages and salaries; employer contributions (mil dol)						Contributions for government social insurance (mil dol)	
	Total (mil dol)	Percent change, 2014–2015	Dollars	Rank	Wages and salaries (mil dol)	Pension and insurance	Government social insurance	Proprietors' income (mil dol)	Dividends, interest, and rent (mil dol)	Personal transfer receipts (mil dol)	Total (mil dol)	From employee and self-employed	From employer
	62	63	64	65	66	67	68	69	70	71	72	73	74
IOWA—Cont'd													
Franklin	530	-0.9	51 495	233	167	32	12	125	114	86	336	16	12
Fremont	317	0.4	45 925	584	120	21	9	44	53	73	193	11	9
Greene	447	-0.2	49 533	415	136	28	10	83	90	88	257	14	10
Grundy	599	0.6	48 180	372	170	29	13	56	141	97	269	17	13
Guthrie	569	6.3	53 340	467	125	25	9	154	96	100	313	18	9
Hamilton	840	4.8	55 316	270	220	41	16	268	134	132	545	30	16
Hancock	593	5.3	54 069	240	295	53	23	123	95	91	494	24	23
Hardin	838	1.7	48 245	460	277	55	21	180	172	156	533	28	21
Harrison	591	3.4	41 425	934	162	31	12	43	96	136	248	17	12
Henry	752	0.7	37 705	1 356	369	66	29	48	143	168	512	33	29
Howard	432	5.0	45 956	687	150	30	12	100	88	75	292	15	12
Humboldt	454	4.5	47 547	305	156	31	11	77	88	81	275	15	11
Ida	339	3.6	48 232	435	153	26	11	58	75	62	249	14	11
Iowa	836	2.7	50 955	304	371	83	32	94	192	125	580	33	32
Jackson	800	2.7	41 123	1 251	211	40	16	76	155	171	344	23	16
Jasper	1 438	1.5	39 044	1 335	426	82	33	110	249	297	651	44	33
Jefferson	704	1.8	40 079	1 342	284	58	22	74	211	140	438	27	22
Johnson	6 770	4.3	46 933	657	4 067	1 009	300	479	1 392	747	5 854	323	300
Jones	829	4.1	40 524	1 159	245	47	19	70	164	165	381	25	19
Keokuk	451	-2.5	44 374	539	85	18	6	84	83	88	193	11	6
Kossuth	807	6.3	53 198	259	286	48	21	196	156	134	551	28	21
Lee	1 388	4.9	39 570	1 508	825	133	69	73	247	339	1 100	71	69
Linn	10 557	3.6	48 003	525	6 785	989	507	533	1 860	1 652	8 813	548	507
Louisa	414	0.2	37 021	1 526	143	28	10	40	66	83	222	14	10
Lucas	344	1.7	39 618	1 314	133	23	10	34	63	82	201	13	10
Lyon	671	1.5	57 116	132	169	30	12	225	107	74	436	17	12
Madison	698	3.2	44 301	815	139	27	11	62	113	112	239	16	11
Mahaska	863	1.2	38 653	1 346	304	62	24	91	160	182	480	29	24
Marion	1 389	3.4	41 716	1 221	755	124	57	82	282	250	1 017	64	57
Marshall	1 609	3.4	39 478	1 414	780	137	59	106	289	385	1 082	69	59
Mills	731	4.5	49 265	481	168	37	12	62	103	203	280	18	12
Mitchell	511	7.0	47 161	301	135	27	10	149	101	84	321	18	10
Monona	389	1.0	43 315	768	99	18	8	63	77	90	189	11	8
Monroe	307	-0.2	38 444	1 318	164	29	12	32	56	68	238	14	12
Montgomery	423	2.4	41 304	1 259	161	32	12	49	75	108	255	16	12
Muscatine	1 861	2.4	43 264	613	1 109	170	85	139	328	342	1 502	94	85
O'Brien	772	3.7	55 180	243	256	45	19	162	145	126	481	24	19
Osceola	398	12.5	64 641	365	86	15	6	179	52	48	287	14	6
Page	616	0.7	39 682	1 147	226	46	17	62	126	153	350	22	17
Palo Alto	545	11.1	59 715	440	136	28	10	228	76	81	402	21	10
Plymouth	1 356	3.7	54 663	200	491	80	38	279	242	176	886	45	38
Pocahontas	371	1.4	52 972	299	119	21	9	102	61	64	250	11	9
Polk	22 593	4.3	48 306	456	15 902	2 183	1 159	1 600	3 840	3 189	20 844	1 274	1 159
Pottawattamie	3 917	9.3	41 819	1 260	1 603	259	126	411	603	854	2 400	156	126
Poweshiek	833	3.0	44 915	697	418	67	32	134	157	141	650	36	32
Ringgold	222	-0.9	43 718	669	54	11	4	45	48	50	114	6	4
Sac	512	0.2	51 092	217	124	23	9	124	107	91	281	13	9
Scott	8 424	2.9	48 943	491	4 006	596	304	571	1 539	1 526	5 478	347	304
Shelby	612	0.7	51 332	312	227	44	17	116	121	115	404	23	17
Sioux	1 719	5.6	49 200	516	799	139	59	487	301	214	1 484	72	59
Story	3 764	5.6	39 204	1 455	2 182	515	158	378	833	500	3 233	186	158
Tama	747	2.5	43 114	929	196	40	14	79	141	145	330	21	14
Taylor	268	1.4	43 265	825	71	14	5	64	41	57	155	8	5
Union	469	-2.1	37 606	1 410	236	48	18	53	79	114	356	22	18
Van Buren	283	-1.1	38 509	1 659	65	16	5	48	53	69	133	8	5
Wapello	1 274	1.7	36 211	1 854	650	115	50	61	194	344	875	58	50
Warren	2 159	4.1	44 410	921	411	76	32	144	325	320	663	47	32
Washington	1 109	-0.6	49 859	494	298	57	23	242	194	180	619	36	23
Wayne	254	-1.0	39 783	1 288	70	18	5	52	46	59	145	9	5
Webster	1 606	5.1	43 327	932	831	144	64	216	275	343	1 256	77	64
Winnebago	438	6.1	41 329	1 364	158	30	12	86	86	93	285	15	12
Winneshiek	913	3.0	44 103	838	402	77	31	133	190	160	642	37	31
Woodbury	4 172	5.9	40 591	1 446	2 300	363	182	403	632	825	3 248	202	182
Worth	383	9.8	50 642	1 254	83	15	7	135	55	58	239	15	7
Wright	712	8.3	55 745	483	241	46	18	220	112	128	526	26	18

1. Based on the resident population estimated as of July 1 of the year shown.

STATE County	Farm	Mining	Construction	Manufacturing	Information: professional, scientific, technical services	Retail trade	Finance, insurance, real estate and leasing	Health care and social assistance	Government	Social Security beneficiaries, December 2015 Number	Rate[1]	Supplemental Security Income recipients, December 2015	Housing units, 2016 Total	Percent change, 2010–2016
	75	76	77	78	79	80	81	82	83	84	85	86	87	88
IOWA—Cont'd														
Franklin	31.7	D	6.2	18.4	1.9	3.1	3.7	3.7	12.6	2 435	236	111	4 841	-1.1
Fremont	16.0	0.0	3.9	33.4	D	8.7	3.3	D	11.9	1 840	267	136	3 440	0.3
Greene	22.8	D	4.5	18.1	3.2	4.9	6.6	5.2	17.4	2 445	273	155	4 525	-0.5
Grundy	13.1	0.0	18.4	7.7	D	4.1	D	D	13.0	2 900	234	83	5 560	0.5
Guthrie	21.8	0.1	8.7	21.7	3.7	2.7	7.9	4.9	15.4	2 900	272	128	5 746	-0.2
Hamilton	22.1	D	4.0	26.5	3.7	3.5	5.8	D	12.0	3 575	235	208	7 169	-0.7
Hancock	23.2	D	1.6	43.3	D	1.9	1.7	D	7.6	2 575	234	95	5 315	-0.3
Hardin	22.6	D	7.3	11.0	3.3	5.2	4.5	D	18.1	4 270	247	234	8 144	-1.0
Harrison	6.8	D	6.5	9.4	4.1	8.3	5.1	D	18.7	3 335	234	241	6 757	0.4
Henry	3.5	D	5.8	23.8	D	5.8	4.1	D	20.4	4 545	228	339	8 283	0.0
Howard	24.8	0.0	7.5	24.5	1.6	5.3	3.9	D	13.3	2 240	239	113	4 353	-0.3
Humboldt	18.3	D	6.6	23.0	3.0	5.0	D	D	13.4	2 320	243	145	4 724	0.9
Ida	14.2	0.0	5.7	36.2	D	4.5	6.4	8.9	7.7	1 745	249	58	3 425	0.0
Iowa	8.1	D	5.7	47.0	2.4	6.0	1.9	4.2	10.0	3 610	220	163	7 286	0.4
Jackson	11.3	0.0	7.1	13.8	3.7	8.2	8.4	8.2	16.6	4 855	250	360	9 482	0.7
Jasper	7.5	D	7.6	17.6	D	6.7	4.4	7.4	22.1	8 540	233	545	16 152	-0.2
Jefferson	5.9	D	4.3	13.2	8.0	7.3	17.9	4.9	15.5	3 935	220	325	7 543	-0.7
Johnson	0.6	0.1	4.5	6.4	6.4	5.3	5.0	7.4	45.9	17 820	123	1 646	61 822	10.5
Jones	9.3	D	10.3	13.6	3.5	8.8	4.4	D	20.5	4 630	227	272	8 914	0.0
Keokuk	25.9	D	5.9	4.9	2.3	4.5	3.6	5.0	15.1	2 520	249	208	4 869	-1.3
Kossuth	25.7	0.0	5.5	15.4	4.3	4.8	9.4	D	11.0	4 125	272	174	7 522	0.5
Lee	1.6	D	19.3	29.4	2.6	5.3	2.8	9.7	12.4	8 630	246	979	16 140	-0.4
Linn	0.3	0.1	6.9	21.7	9.4	5.2	10.2	11.0	10.5	40 740	185	3 712	96 271	4.4
Louisa	10.1	D	4.0	32.8	D	4.1	3.2	D	17.5	2 340	208	179	5 000	0.0
Lucas	6.9	0.0	5.0	5.5	2.3	5.6	D	D	19.6	2 190	252	224	4 196	-1.0
Lyon	43.2	D	6.4	9.7	5.3	2.7	3.7	2.9	7.7	2 200	187	50	4 998	3.1
Madison	10.2	1.1	14.8	6.5	5.0	7.8	6.0	6.1	22.8	3 200	203	152	6 857	4.6
Mahaska	11.1	D	6.0	21.8	3.9	6.4	3.6	5.2	19.6	4 830	217	443	9 809	0.4
Marion	2.2	D	4.5	46.5	2.9	4.2	4.1	10.6	9.6	7 050	213	405	14 093	1.3
Marshall	3.6	D	7.3	29.0	3.9	5.8	3.0	10.6	19.3	8 970	221	708	16 691	-0.8
Mills	6.4	D	5.0	12.6	D	3.9	4.1	D	35.8	3 245	219	234	6 082	-0.4
Mitchell	22.7	D	6.1	24.0	3.2	4.6	3.7	D	12.3	2 575	239	120	4 935	1.8
Monona	25.0	0.0	4.1	2.8	2.2	5.9	D	17.7	14.9	2 530	282	140	4 704	0.2
Monroe	8.6	D	6.0	42.6	D	3.4	2.2	D	13.7	1 865	235	119	3 957	1.9
Montgomery	9.7	D	6.4	16.9	7.0	5.5	5.0	D	22.0	2 730	267	240	5 203	-0.7
Muscatine	0.7	0.2	4.6	41.4	6.3	4.3	2.7	6.5	10.9	8 695	202	827	18 013	0.6
O'Brien	26.9	D	9.8	8.5	3.3	4.4	4.4	11.5	11.2	3 385	242	204	6 647	0.0
Osceola	29.6	D	3.4	31.9	1.8	1.7	D	D	5.6	1 475	241	60	2 959	-1.0
Page	8.9	D	5.0	18.0	D	6.2	4.1	D	23.6	4 045	261	335	7 163	-0.3
Palo Alto	24.8	0.2	2.6	30.9	2.2	3.3	2.6	D	12.6	2 175	238	134	4 594	-0.7
Plymouth	23.3	D	5.1	20.9	D	4.0	3.9	4.1	9.9	5 150	207	204	10 711	1.6
Pocahontas	35.2	D	9.9	9.9	D	4.6	D	D	12.4	1 855	265	111	3 758	-0.9
Polk	0.1	0.1	6.9	5.8	10.8	5.4	19.6	10.8	13.3	72 615	156	7 893	196 673	7.9
Pottawattamie	3.6	D	9.8	17.3	4.7	7.7	3.7	12.6	15.1	19 120	204	2 233	39 646	0.8
Poweshiek	14.5	D	8.3	14.5	D	3.8	10.6	D	7.7	4 180	226	213	9 072	1.4
Ringgold	31.7	D	11.8	D	D	4.6	D	6.2	22.4	1 335	264	100	2 598	-0.6
Sac	35.7	D	3.7	11.6	2.3	3.1	D	7.7	11.2	2 570	257	91	5 384	-0.8
Scott	0.4	0.0	9.4	17.5	5.5	7.4	6.0	13.6	10.6	32 630	190	3 973	73 635	2.5
Shelby	17.2	0.0	6.1	8.9	6.9	6.7	5.4	D	15.0	3 120	262	195	5 564	0.4
Sioux	22.9	0.2	6.7	24.5	3.2	3.6	5.1	5.5	8.1	5 715	164	185	12 763	3.9
Story	0.9	D	6.3	14.0	7.6	4.7	4.0	7.4	38.9	12 375	128	623	39 126	6.4
Tama	14.2	0.0	7.6	14.0	D	4.3	4.3	6.1	29.8	4 145	239	215	7 740	-0.3
Taylor	32.5	0.0	5.0	18.6	D	2.7	3.2	D	12.6	1 590	255	111	3 084	-0.7
Union	6.3	D	5.3	23.2	D	6.7	4.1	5.8	22.9	3 015	242	266	5 911	-0.4
Van Buren	20.2	D	D	18.9	1.6	5.2	4.5	D	21.8	1 970	269	131	3 617	-1.4
Wapello	0.7	D	5.6	28.2	2.2	7.9	4.2	13.6	17.6	8 150	231	1 092	15 980	-0.7
Warren	2.1	0.0	15.0	5.9	5.9	8.8	6.4	10.7	20.8	8 860	182	396	19 550	6.4
Washington	15.1	D	11.8	10.3	5.3	5.3	3.8	5.5	14.1	4 980	224	334	9 625	1.1
Wayne	17.6	0.0	D	21.2	D	3.9	D	4.0	24.1	1 650	258	128	3 177	-1.1
Webster	5.5	D	7.1	21.5	4.4	5.9	3.1	12.7	14.1	8 585	232	870	17 010	-0.1
Winnebago	25.0	D	7.0	14.5	3.8	6.9	5.0	D	13.9	2 615	247	132	5 170	-0.5
Winneshiek	11.1	D	7.6	15.0	4.0	6.1	4.0	D	18.1	4 490	216	186	8 873	1.7
Woodbury	2.5	D	17.4	10.9	4.1	7.9	4.5	14.8	14.1	19 135	187	2 001	41 989	1.2
Worth	9.8	0.8	5.1	43.9	D	2.4	D	2.5	8.5	1 745	231	71	3 516	-0.9
Wright	26.5	D	3.3	24.9	3.5	2.7	4.8	3.9	16.7	3 215	251	177	6 483	-0.7

1. Per 1,000 resident population estimated as of July 1 of the year shown.

Table B. States and Counties — Housing, Labor Force, and Employment

STATE County	Housing units, 2011–2015								Civilian labor force, 2016		Unemployment		Civilian employment,[6] 2011–2015		
	Occupied units													Percent	
	Owner-occupied				Renter-occupied										
				Median owner cost as a percent of income											
	Total	Percent	Median value[1]	With a mort-gage	Without a mort-gage[2]	Median rent[3]	Median rent as a per-cent of income[2]	Sub-stand-ard units[4] (percent)	Total	Percent change, 2015–2016	Total	Rate[5]	Total	Manage-ment, business, science and arts	Con-struction, produc-tion, and mainte-nance occu-pations
	89	90	91	92	93	94	95	96	97	98	99	100	101	102	103
IOWA—Cont'd															
Franklin	4 258	74.2	85 900	19.4	10.1	574	21.3	1.1	5 985	0.3	212	3.5	5 012	30.4	34.2
Fremont	2 954	75.8	100 100	18.0	10.1	608	26.7	1.4	4 018	-3.3	134	3.3	3 463	34.8	29.3
Greene	3 927	75.9	85 300	20.6	11.2	588	26.3	1.0	5 704	2.3	181	3.2	4 452	33.8	27.8
Grundy	5 183	80.5	125 700	18.9	11.3	567	26.3	1.3	6 713	-0.4	235	3.5	6 164	34.1	29.5
Guthrie	4 514	80.5	103 700	19.7	11.9	601	26.0	1.5	5 739	1.9	207	3.6	5 312	32.3	28.1
Hamilton	6 384	69.9	93 600	19.4	11.3	638	25.8	1.6	7 172	-0.9	276	3.8	7 476	30.0	33.1
Hancock	4 673	80.1	91 600	19.2	10.0	551	25.4	0.8	6 460	1.3	177	2.7	5 640	30.9	35.9
Hardin	6 973	75.5	88 700	17.9	11.2	567	21.4	1.3	8 621	-2.3	342	4.0	8 293	29.4	33.6
Harrison	5 973	75.0	106 400	20.1	11.3	639	26.5	1.2	7 602	0.7	258	3.4	7 352	29.5	30.0
Henry	7 623	72.9	103 900	19.7	12.1	612	24.9	2.6	9 614	0.0	348	3.6	8 992	29.3	29.5
Howard	3 867	79.6	94 600	20.6	11.1	605	31.0	1.8	5 363	-0.4	196	3.7	4 666	29.0	38.8
Humboldt	4 190	72.2	89 800	18.0	10.8	576	25.4	0.4	5 437	1.6	160	2.9	4 652	29.2	33.4
Ida	3 101	75.2	80 300	16.3	10.0	414	19.4	0.2	4 040	1.9	105	2.6	3 579	33.7	32.2
Iowa	6 819	78.0	138 700	20.5	10.5	520	21.3	1.8	10 691	2.8	336	3.1	8 818	30.7	30.1
Jackson	8 433	75.0	114 300	20.0	11.7	589	26.7	0.9	11 173	-0.1	473	4.2	9 687	25.9	34.6
Jasper	14 437	73.0	117 700	19.7	11.7	685	25.8	1.5	19 302	0.9	698	3.6	17 247	30.2	30.1
Jefferson	6 913	66.5	101 000	19.2	12.4	634	26.5	1.7	9 182	0.2	339	3.7	7 751	36.1	21.5
Johnson	55 426	59.5	193 600	20.1	10.5	870	33.9	2.5	84 510	0.6	2 209	2.6	78 838	45.5	15.6
Jones	8 171	78.2	129 300	20.9	11.3	599	24.8	0.7	10 795	0.0	467	4.3	9 815	29.9	32.4
Keokuk	4 347	77.6	77 100	19.0	13.4	576	27.7	2.8	5 349	-1.5	233	4.4	4 921	32.6	31.4
Kossuth	6 723	78.7	92 300	18.4	10.0	579	24.9	0.9	8 909	0.7	239	2.7	7 788	34.0	29.7
Lee	14 412	74.4	85 400	20.1	12.0	577	26.1	1.8	17 483	-4.5	1 079	6.2	16 414	23.4	34.8
Linn	87 318	73.6	147 400	19.6	12.5	695	27.3	1.4	118 969	-1.2	4 427	3.7	114 142	38.2	21.6
Louisa	4 311	77.8	99 900	20.4	11.9	618	20.1	5.6	6 153	2.0	245	4.0	5 614	25.5	40.8
Lucas	3 678	79.3	82 400	21.4	13.4	479	26.4	3.5	4 387	-0.5	142	3.2	4 122	27.2	27.5
Lyon	4 496	82.8	111 100	18.6	11.0	595	18.2	1.3	7 111	0.6	147	2.1	5 968	36.9	27.2
Madison	6 225	74.9	160 200	21.4	12.5	818	26.1	1.4	8 343	1.2	298	3.6	7 712	37.6	26.2
Mahaska	9 023	70.3	106 200	20.7	11.0	593	24.3	1.0	11 917	0.5	449	3.8	10 859	32.3	31.4
Marion	12 978	74.0	137 300	20.1	12.0	647	26.4	1.3	17 559	0.6	539	3.1	17 020	36.1	26.0
Marshall	15 297	72.5	104 500	19.7	11.6	650	23.8	3.2	19 314	-0.8	952	4.9	19 409	27.0	34.9
Mills	5 399	80.0	153 100	20.3	11.0	701	26.2	0.7	7 437	0.0	273	3.7	7 089	33.4	26.2
Mitchell	4 358	83.7	108 700	19.8	10.9	535	22.6	2.0	5 924	5.7	159	2.7	5 319	30.0	35.6
Monona	4 043	71.4	79 400	18.5	12.1	550	26.0	0.7	4 766	-0.1	198	4.2	4 165	28.7	28.5
Monroe	3 326	74.6	96 300	19.2	13.7	590	22.7	3.3	3 970	-1.9	186	4.7	3 580	32.0	29.3
Montgomery	4 610	68.7	78 700	18.6	12.6	609	25.8	1.5	5 131	-0.9	185	3.6	4 660	32.6	29.1
Muscatine	16 345	73.9	126 900	19.8	12.0	732	27.1	2.5	22 595	1.6	873	3.9	21 210	27.9	34.9
O'Brien	6 004	74.0	102 700	17.3	10.0	584	21.1	0.9	8 424	-0.2	236	2.8	7 237	28.4	33.2
Osceola	2 670	78.3	83 600	18.4	10.0	550	21.9	2.7	3 674	3.5	100	2.7	3 282	29.1	36.5
Page	6 294	74.4	82 500	18.1	11.9	564	24.4	3.1	6 512	-1.0	332	5.1	7 075	33.5	29.3
Palo Alto	3 977	74.4	85 300	17.9	10.3	529	25.5	1.3	5 007	2.8	158	3.2	4 637	32.1	29.4
Plymouth	9 995	79.2	138 300	18.2	10.1	585	24.3	0.5	14 847	0.2	391	2.6	12 978	31.8	29.1
Pocahontas	3 197	77.3	64 700	15.9	10.3	532	20.3	1.4	4 384	1.6	126	2.9	3 483	31.6	33.8
Polk	177 049	67.6	157 200	19.9	11.8	799	28.0	2.7	258 529	1.0	9 057	3.5	238 720	39.9	18.0
Pottawattamie	36 683	69.4	125 800	21.0	12.0	755	27.6	2.2	48 943	-0.3	1 668	3.4	46 439	29.4	26.1
Poweshiek	7 351	71.2	128 700	21.5	11.5	640	26.5	0.6	10 443	-0.9	366	3.5	9 636	33.2	26.2
Ringgold	2 030	77.5	77 600	20.3	13.0	505	23.3	1.2	2 622	2.0	93	3.5	2 133	35.9	29.4
Sac	4 406	80.1	81 200	18.1	10.0	534	20.2	0.8	5 558	-1.6	170	3.1	5 151	27.3	30.6
Scott	67 709	68.1	148 200	19.4	11.8	715	28.0	1.4	86 289	-1.6	3 999	4.6	83 140	35.8	23.0
Shelby	5 066	79.3	108 800	19.9	11.6	600	26.2	0.4	6 845	-2.6	206	3.0	6 153	32.1	28.7
Sioux	11 765	78.9	140 900	19.4	10.0	622	22.3	3.3	20 808	0.1	486	2.3	18 867	32.5	29.1
Story	35 901	53.4	166 000	19.4	10.0	772	35.2	2.0	57 150	-0.6	1 348	2.4	50 519	44.8	17.1
Tama	6 790	77.0	103 000	18.6	10.6	672	25.7	2.3	9 851	1.7	417	4.2	8 283	29.4	33.4
Taylor	2 744	71.7	70 400	18.8	11.1	592	26.0	2.3	3 246	0.0	97	3.0	3 061	28.2	38.9
Union	5 337	71.2	87 200	18.5	13.7	593	26.9	0.9	6 571	-0.2	252	3.8	6 385	25.2	36.1
Van Buren	2 944	85.6	76 300	21.0	12.1	476	22.3	3.7	3 896	1.2	145	3.7	3 305	27.0	39.3
Wapello	14 493	73.2	80 400	19.5	13.1	612	31.2	3.3	17 997	-0.2	1 061	5.9	16 128	26.5	36.4
Warren	18 009	77.0	159 900	19.9	11.5	748	27.1	1.4	27 010	1.0	876	3.2	25 008	37.7	20.6
Washington	8 938	71.9	122 100	20.2	10.9	692	24.6	1.6	12 542	1.1	370	3.0	11 358	32.5	28.8
Wayne	2 596	81.3	70 600	20.2	12.7	476	26.2	3.8	2 849	-0.2	110	3.9	2 800	32.3	36.4
Webster	15 155	67.7	85 900	18.7	11.1	573	27.4	0.7	20 675	1.4	837	4.0	16 774	30.5	26.4
Winnebago	4 580	75.4	94 100	19.3	11.3	515	21.6	0.9	5 210	0.6	184	3.5	5 214	28.2	32.8
Winneshiek	8 248	77.0	157 800	21.8	12.2	588	23.6	0.5	12 095	-1.2	435	3.6	12 230	36.4	25.0
Woodbury	38 656	67.5	99 600	19.3	11.4	678	28.4	2.5	56 031	-0.4	2 027	3.6	51 599	28.3	29.2
Worth	3 180	78.4	96 400	19.3	11.5	523	27.5	1.7	4 286	1.2	150	3.5	3 800	24.7	33.9
Wright	5 495	75.3	73 400	17.6	10.2	568	30.1	1.5	6 745	-2.5	280	4.2	5 996	28.7	35.1

1. Specified owner-occupied units.   2. A value of 10.0 represents 10 percent or less; a value of 50.0 represents 50 percent or more.   3. Specified renter-occupied units.
4. Overcrowded or lacking complete plumbing facilities.   5. Percent of civilian labor force.   6. Civilian employed persons 16 years old and over.

Table B. States and Counties — **Nonfarm Employment and Agriculture**

STATE County	Number of establishments	Total	Health care and social assistance	Manufacturing	Retail trade	Finance and insurance	Professional, scientific, and technical services	Total (mil dol)	Average per employee (dollars)	Number	Fewer than 50 acres	500 acres or more	Farm operators whose principal occupation is farming (percent)
	104	105	106	107	108	109	110	111	112	113	114	115	116

IOWA—Cont'd

STATE County	104	105	106	107	108	109	110	111	112	113	114	115	116
Franklin	322	3 196	579	887	323	108	40	127	39 592	853	29.9	29.3	54.3
Fremont	182	2 043	285	618	560	74	43	68	33 090	533	27.0	32.8	62.3
Greene	269	2 932	623	439	617	119	70	103	35 060	780	31.0	30.5	60.8
Grundy	297	3 247	678	451	428	185	44	144	44 208	737	33.0	27.0	56.3
Guthrie	317	2 528	431	400	392	254	62	92	36 208	829	29.2	24.2	53.3
Hamilton	383	4 410	733	603	693	183	114	161	36 455	761	36.4	27.1	56.6
Hancock	304	3 726	487	1 270	369	76	295	139	37 352	889	32.2	28.0	65.8
Hardin	560	5 172	1 029	709	899	286	142	185	35 741	819	31.3	28.0	54.1
Harrison	367	3 192	818	273	480	138	95	110	34 372	819	28.2	32.5	57.4
Henry	519	8 258	1 215	2 545	891	165	134	294	35 576	903	31.3	16.4	47.5
Howard	269	3 076	625	1 065	405	127	43	98	31 972	883	30.2	19.3	51.4
Humboldt	310	3 473	432	1 014	528	115	73	130	37 398	574	28.6	30.1	52.4
Ida	246	2 933	493	1 091	253	163	49	127	43 154	547	30.2	30.5	55.4
Iowa	483	8 080	746	4 249	1 340	115	136	314	38 853	1 019	32.0	17.0	48.4
Jackson	529	4 576	622	831	885	265	79	148	32 271	1 255	29.6	12.7	47.4
Jasper	729	8 751	1 678	1 837	1 445	251	470	279	31 939	1 098	34.9	21.8	52.8
Jefferson	704	6 982	735	967	904	936	548	260	37 198	685	29.6	15.6	46.3
Johnson	3 216	60 913	16 559	5 011	9 186	2 325	2 769	2 544	41 769	1 342	34.7	14.7	50.2
Jones	495	4 715	858	798	894	208	197	153	32 347	1 061	28.8	20.8	53.3
Keokuk	248	1 807	368	212	259	90	35	61	33 634	982	27.2	20.0	47.5
Kossuth	557	5 881	888	1 389	874	487	213	226	38 448	1 349	25.0	33.5	67.4
Lee	895	15 119	2 109	4 206	2 046	360	2 022	596	39 416	917	32.4	16.4	42.6
Linn	5 411	120 487	15 691	16 940	15 519	10 693	6 010	5 667	47 037	1 402	37.4	15.5	58.6
Louisa	214	2 787	354	1 276	213	77	30	107	38 447	612	34.3	18.1	43.0
Lucas	169	3 074	514	143	553	94	33	115	37 335	648	25.0	14.8	37.7
Lyon	398	3 370	544	514	429	164	115	117	34 832	1 139	25.2	21.3	62.6
Madison	369	2 842	539	178	657	120	103	92	32 319	961	37.3	15.7	40.9
Mahaska	564	6 600	1 094	1 175	1 175	184	135	248	37 623	1 012	30.4	22.6	48.7
Marion	823	16 176	2 548	6 956	1 541	303	361	657	40 635	1 024	38.3	16.0	39.9
Marshall	798	14 179	2 027	5 062	2 138	317	344	579	40 824	882	34.4	25.3	60.1
Mills	303	2 181	597	34	349	114	124	72	32 928	500	32.0	30.8	61.4
Mitchell	321	3 177	602	1 054	390	117	69	111	34 883	903	29.1	24.9	65.7
Monona	232	2 159	662	D	385	124	48	66	30 442	538	19.5	39.2	65.8
Monroe	172	2 299	428	962	288	66	36	86	37 260	592	24.2	17.1	34.8
Montgomery	299	3 250	796	649	573	112	54	110	33 914	499	21.2	34.1	62.3
Muscatine	930	20 780	1 990	7 477	2 130	418	807	987	47 497	786	34.4	18.1	51.4
O'Brien	517	5 449	1 417	638	892	197	187	162	29 734	884	24.8	25.1	61.3
Osceola	195	1 581	260	329	149	87	21	56	35 257	555	22.2	33.0	71.4
Page	411	5 778	1 538	1 841	601	161	105	193	33 426	739	20.7	29.1	58.9
Palo Alto	295	2 952	773	567	340	108	46	92	31 274	874	31.5	27.0	54.6
Plymouth	709	9 749	1 327	2 543	1 010	300	205	414	42 511	1 331	24.0	28.8	67.8
Pocahontas	224	1 886	257	478	221	95	51	66	34 774	742	26.5	34.9	72.0
Polk	12 294	256 340	35 621	16 301	31 584	35 399	15 837	12 701	49 549	773	51.2	16.0	51.5
Pottawattamie	1 959	32 393	5 960	5 093	6 229	805	674	1 100	33 970	1 188	29.5	30.3	66.2
Poweshiek	534	9 445	1 089	1 552	1 254	831	107	345	36 541	852	27.6	24.8	55.4
Ringgold	148	1 056	347	39	224	46	43	33	30 807	651	20.4	24.9	46.2
Sac	338	2 569	539	447	307	131	55	90	34 896	914	32.5	28.9	53.9
Scott	4 370	81 839	12 542	11 625	12 054	2 431	2 902	3 314	40 496	759	35.4	18.7	55.3
Shelby	389	5 396	923	875	561	237	160	195	36 185	869	21.7	33.1	65.0
Sioux	1 260	18 527	2 605	5 196	1 663	577	966	675	36 435	1 618	31.4	19.2	61.0
Story	2 045	32 074	5 273	5 106	5 163	708	1 387	1 274	39 730	966	42.8	20.9	49.1
Tama	331	4 336	499	1 100	560	122	52	133	30 775	1 132	29.7	24.1	62.4
Taylor	142	1 691	249	688	132	37	26	63	37 212	639	25.2	22.1	44.4
Union	327	5 020	868	1 437	726	189	67	165	32 781	648	33.0	16.7	44.3
Van Buren	153	1 525	229	690	190	64	25	54	35 526	753	27.2	14.1	48.2
Wapello	738	14 835	2 754	4 089	2 497	421	212	525	35 380	742	31.4	15.0	45.0
Warren	810	8 357	1 257	533	1 703	275	257	256	30 689	1 334	43.4	10.0	37.3
Washington	693	6 928	1 310	1 086	1 036	209	173	219	31 681	1 139	31.3	17.3	53.8
Wayne	146	1 423	398	422	258	38	44	48	33 639	691	27.4	21.3	43.0
Webster	1 007	16 183	2 881	1 686	2 687	404	1 197	648	40 045	968	29.8	29.3	64.2
Winnebago	331	6 572	580	3 327	500	189	128	252	38 326	642	34.0	26.2	52.5
Winneshiek	624	9 889	1 450	1 404	1 229	271	224	310	31 330	1 535	33.4	15.2	49.1
Woodbury	2 668	46 054	8 775	4 886	7 631	1 170	1 073	1 619	35 151	973	28.5	28.6	58.6
Worth	180	1 799	197	459	167	57	17	59	32 730	640	33.4	28.0	54.5
Wright	376	4 317	919	1 493	484	135	114	176	40 823	775	34.2	32.8	61.3

Table B. States and Counties — **Agriculture**

STATE County	Land in farms Acreage (1,000)	Percent change, 2007–2012	Acres Average size of farm	Total irrigated (1,000)	Total cropland (1,000)	Value of land and buildings (dollars) Average per farm	Average per acre	Value of machinery and equipment, average per farm (dollars)	Value of products sold Total (mil dol)	Average per farm (dollars)	Percent from: Crops	Live-stock and poultry products	Percent of farms with sales of: $10,000 or more	$100,000 or more	Government payments Total ($1,000)	Percent of farms
	117	118	119	120	121	122	123	124	125	126	127	128	129	130	131	132
IOWA—Cont'd																
Franklin	355	-3.1	417	D	336.7	2 769 033	6 646	259 810	454.4	532 687	55.9	44.1	69.3	51.9	9 424	83.0
Fremont	287	17.2	539	8.5	253.9	3 311 917	6 141	274 623	180.4	338 409	89.6	10.4	62.7	46.5	5 009	83.1
Greene	357	0.9	458	D	325.6	3 185 444	6 962	289 094	308.1	395 058	67.7	32.3	65.3	47.9	7 356	82.3
Grundy	318	0.7	432	0.0	301.1	3 465 753	8 031	330 237	362.7	492 126	76.6	23.4	69.2	56.9	7 556	82.8
Guthrie	328	-7.7	395	D	262.2	2 291 450	5 798	193 695	257.5	310 555	52.5	47.5	55.9	31.8	8 272	81.3
Hamilton	327	-5.6	430	D	305.1	3 489 958	8 121	268 636	540.4	710 103	44.2	55.8	64.9	50.2	9 809	80.0
Hancock	353	-2.1	397	1.2	338.4	2 765 206	6 957	268 795	475.1	534 388	49.3	50.7	69.0	51.6	8 438	86.6
Hardin	332	-2.0	406	0.0	306.2	2 996 061	7 385	272 880	534.5	652 620	48.8	51.2	66.3	50.5	9 829	80.0
Harrison	394	7.8	481	29.1	343.3	2 799 425	5 824	257 150	249.2	304 277	85.9	14.1	64.2	44.1	7 528	83.9
Henry	270	12.5	299	0.0	220.7	1 471 299	4 929	145 765	171.8	190 219	70.4	29.6	45.4	27.5	8 270	82.5
Howard	300	7.6	340	0.2	273.3	2 239 316	6 593	243 708	322.3	365 058	57.3	42.7	62.7	41.0	9 932	81.9
Humboldt	235	-13.1	409	0.0	220.1	3 120 220	7 627	258 958	242.1	421 793	70.1	29.9	72.5	57.1	6 158	81.9
Ida	261	-4.3	477	D	234.1	3 237 473	6 786	276 272	272.2	497 678	60.1	39.9	72.8	53.9	7 024	83.7
Iowa	336	-2.6	330	D	275.5	1 996 335	6 053	170 894	276.9	271 734	64.8	35.2	58.5	36.3	8 803	80.0
Jackson	309	4.2	246	0.2	214.2	1 312 333	5 331	150 764	236.1	188 110	45.6	54.4	58.1	26.8	8 990	76.2
Jasper	374	-12.7	340	0.8	324.8	2 115 648	6 217	209 787	327.0	297 853	76.7	23.3	63.2	42.5	7 997	74.4
Jefferson	198	0.4	289	0.1	153.4	1 328 096	4 591	134 391	104.1	151 991	70.2	29.8	43.8	22.6	6 713	78.4
Johnson	329	2.3	245	0.2	285.1	1 682 142	6 868	154 571	258.3	192 443	67.9	32.1	58.7	34.1	8 623	67.7
Jones	314	-3.1	296	0.1	255.7	1 982 445	6 699	205 726	276.2	260 306	59.6	40.4	65.7	39.2	9 960	80.5
Keokuk	295	-7.1	301	0.0	240.6	1 499 580	4 984	164 024	230.8	234 996	57.0	43.0	54.9	33.2	12 904	85.0
Kossuth	599	-0.3	444	0.3	568.6	3 380 844	7 608	295 763	722.3	535 440	64.2	35.8	74.9	62.1	13 183	87.5
Lee	236	-0.9	257	1.1	172.3	1 098 520	4 268	114 699	130.1	141 845	70.7	29.3	49.5	23.8	5 417	72.5
Linn	339	1.2	242	0.2	292.6	1 626 668	6 722	173 044	260.8	185 998	76.1	23.9	58.3	30.0	8 202	72.7
Louisa	169	-9.4	275	9.9	139.5	1 581 547	5 743	187 708	172.5	281 889	60.8	39.2	53.8	33.5	5 560	77.8
Lucas	177	3.6	274	D	101.5	786 495	2 874	99 623	51.1	78 872	47.7	52.3	42.1	15.3	4 571	73.6
Lyon	370	14.5	325	1.5	334.0	2 677 244	8 245	275 852	836.1	734 068	30.7	69.3	87.4	65.6	7 064	79.0
Madison	276	-2.6	287	0.1	184.1	1 408 613	4 903	122 793	132.9	138 322	65.2	34.8	47.9	19.9	5 013	65.9
Mahaska	323	9.4	319	0.1	273.9	1 794 609	5 623	204 132	311.1	307 382	54.9	45.1	60.8	36.9	11 369	79.8
Marion	265	7.6	259	0.1	200.0	1 154 279	4 462	117 525	137.9	134 660	80.5	19.5	46.4	22.4	6 603	72.3
Marshall	312	-3.7	354	0.2	280.6	2 345 805	6 623	227 533	313.1	354 966	75.1	24.9	63.7	45.7	7 063	76.1
Mills	206	4.8	413	D	182.3	2 606 084	6 316	242 756	120.6	241 170	95.4	4.6	59.8	44.2	4 403	77.6
Mitchell	296	0.7	328	1.0	272.8	2 418 524	7 372	214 307	363.4	402 482	47.0	53.0	73.6	51.9	6 663	75.0
Monona	338	-14.1	629	61.1	300.6	3 451 381	5 491	370 487	221.3	411 253	86.6	13.4	73.6	51.9	5 639	82.0
Monroe	195	-3.0	330	D	111.8	1 045 139	3 171	95 228	59.0	99 581	55.3	44.7	49.3	17.2	3 873	70.9
Montgomery	245	11.1	491	0.4	207.4	2 753 371	5 610	272 595	189.4	379 615	71.3	28.7	71.1	47.9	4 831	82.8
Muscatine	215	-3.1	274	7.4	183.2	1 720 141	6 289	166 092	187.3	238 233	72.5	27.5	56.4	35.1	6 401	76.0
O'Brien	304	-11.9	344	0.9	276.5	2 940 939	8 538	244 251	533.4	603 437	43.4	56.6	84.8	66.9	5 935	81.9
Osceola	238	-5.2	429	1.3	223.3	3 021 315	7 039	277 225	410.6	739 865	42.8	57.2	81.8	66.5	5 504	86.8
Page	317	16.9	429	0.2	263.0	2 158 371	5 031	221 513	198.3	268 369	81.6	18.4	70.5	44.8	6 816	83.8
Palo Alto	359	1.5	410	4.8	340.8	3 088 190	7 523	288 436	498.6	570 531	55.0	45.0	65.7	50.2	8 245	86.3
Plymouth	542	4.7	407	2.0	479.8	2 992 740	7 352	280 373	643.1	483 173	40.8	59.2	77.9	51.8	11 860	80.5
Pocahontas	332	-8.4	448	0.6	317.5	3 416 818	7 635	309 951	406.7	548 144	64.8	35.2	76.7	61.7	9 485	90.3
Polk	198	-20.8	256	0.5	178.6	1 802 039	7 052	169 371	153.9	199 128	92.3	7.7	54.5	27.0	4 768	62.0
Pottawattamie	533	9.6	449	3.9	481.8	3 154 295	7 033	280 880	464.5	391 035	70.1	29.9	67.3	47.6	9 377	72.9
Poweshiek	334	6.9	393	0.0	286.8	2 386 670	6 080	231 304	350.4	411 247	60.1	39.9	64.9	42.3	7 393	79.3
Ringgold	270	1.8	414	D	178.8	1 417 304	3 420	149 154	116.6	179 161	41.8	58.2	58.7	26.0	6 034	76.8
Sac	357	-1.7	391	0.5	333.0	2 898 569	7 420	255 801	474.7	519 315	45.6	54.4	71.6	50.1	9 715	82.5
Scott	221	-11.3	291	0.6	201.4	2 359 184	8 118	234 090	248.2	326 949	66.5	33.5	65.9	43.1	7 134	71.5
Shelby	372	3.9	428	0.0	344.3	2 901 694	6 772	255 117	351.3	404 253	70.4	29.6	80.9	58.1	8 494	85.7
Sioux	484	1.2	299	8.5	442.4	2 726 452	9 105	277 347	1 613.1	996 964	19.7	80.3	83.9	66.1	11 514	74.1
Story	306	-13.1	317	0.4	279.4	2 482 983	7 838	205 934	292.8	303 082	79.6	20.4	60.0	37.3	6 566	73.5
Tama	403	-6.5	356	0.0	351.7	2 313 300	6 503	214 804	355.2	313 764	78.5	21.5	65.4	43.1	9 820	81.4
Taylor	279	-1.4	436	0.0	212.0	1 668 700	3 827	195 518	144.2	225 667	58.6	41.4	56.3	28.5	6 371	78.7
Union	214	-0.1	331	0.0	147.6	1 138 708	3 441	138 670	118.2	182 338	46.2	53.8	50.5	24.7	4 243	70.7
Van Buren	213	-3.7	283	0.0	140.8	984 527	3 475	101 955	110.1	146 246	52.6	47.4	43.8	17.9	5 497	68.7
Wapello	189	13.6	255	0.1	138.7	1 049 902	4 125	126 195	86.2	116 235	72.4	27.6	42.0	19.5	5 473	67.7
Warren	264	9.1	198	0.0	184.0	1 010 263	5 114	93 412	110.1	82 542	81.6	18.4	42.1	12.1	7 169	57.6
Washington	314	-3.5	276	0.2	264.6	1 685 741	6 107	175 919	526.8	462 551	31.7	68.3	59.3	39.4	12 460	75.9
Wayne	274	0.2	396	0.1	199.0	1 280 719	3 233	143 864	74.3	107 534	64.5	35.5	47.9	19.0	7 885	72.4
Webster	409	-9.9	422	D	383.6	3 106 004	7 352	252 019	353.6	365 319	82.4	17.6	65.4	48.7	11 421	85.4
Winnebago	235	-6.4	367	0.0	222.0	2 474 578	6 748	266 843	281.5	438 438	59.4	40.6	61.4	44.7	6 474	87.1
Winneshiek	376	19.9	245	0.0	305.3	1 460 745	5 959	173 344	345.9	225 362	50.0	50.0	56.7	35.2	14 181	83.2
Woodbury	446	0.0	458	5.3	384.6	2 736 038	5 974	230 038	416.5	428 025	56.6	43.4	66.9	46.5	9 174	77.6
Worth	235	1.4	367	1.1	218.4	2 255 917	6 145	240 556	188.1	293 936	86.8	13.2	60.2	43.9	6 708	86.1
Wright	360	9.8	464	0.0	344.6	3 345 938	7 209	316 590	484.9	625 738	53.0	47.0	65.5	51.7	11 670	84.3

Table B. States and Counties — Water Use, Wholesale Trade, Retail Trade, and Real Estate

STATE County	Water use, 2010 Total water withdrawn (mil gal/day)	Gallons withdrawn per person per day	Wholesale trade,[1] 2012 Number of establishments	Number of employees	Sales (mil dol)	Annual payroll (mil dol)	Retail trade,[2] 2012 Number of establishments	Number of employees	Sales (mil dol)	Annual payroll (mil dol)	Real estate and rental and leasing,[2] 2012 Number of establishments	Number of employees	Receipts (mil dol)	Annual payroll (mil dol)
	133	134	135	136	137	138	139	140	141	142	143	144	145	146
IOWA—Cont'd														
Franklin	4.1	386	23	346	697.8	14.5	40	327	79.7	6.9	11	20	3.0	0.4
Fremont	2.6	345	14	202	212.1	9.7	30	534	145.6	10.6	6	10	0.2	0.1
Greene	5.8	624	12	449	1 016.7	24.4	39	367	94.1	7.0	4	10	0.6	0.1
Grundy	2.2	178	19	240	494.8	12.9	44	406	83.4	7.0	8	D	D	D
Guthrie	3.2	294	15	119	175.2	5.1	44	378	105.7	7.1	9	D	D	D
Hamilton	4.1	264	33	828	731.6	37.2	60	660	158.6	12.3	6	D	D	D
Hancock	4.6	406	26	176	333.3	8.1	47	424	216.1	8.2	8	28	1.9	0.5
Hardin	9.2	526	38	889	2 961.5	51.1	80	819	175.9	17.3	14	30	5.1	0.8
Harrison	10.6	712	28	452	263.2	17.9	52	467	197.2	10.8	9	15	1.3	0.5
Henry	3.3	164	31	279	224.8	9.9	63	880	229.1	19.3	16	32	2.8	0.3
Howard	4.3	448	18	165	262.0	6.3	45	363	100.7	7.4	4	D	D	D
Humboldt	3.1	311	31	238	274.0	11.6	50	480	108.9	9.4	9	19	1.8	0.4
Ida	3.3	464	17	184	272.8	7.5	36	305	64.1	5.5	8	12	1.4	0.4
Iowa	3.2	196	18	139	162.0	6.4	130	1 365	234.1	20.2	4	D	D	D
Jackson	3.2	161	26	230	201.6	8.5	76	946	258.0	18.9	13	20	2.8	0.4
Jasper	7.9	213	36	342	445.1	13.7	108	1 302	355.4	27.7	24	60	6.5	1.4
Jefferson	2.2	132	38	D	D	D	86	916	171.7	18.8	26	48	6.9	1.0
Johnson	37.3	285	85	1 389	1 011.8	61.0	509	8 743	1 861.7	195.8	134	538	131.1	20.8
Jones	4.1	200	24	301	903.0	12.0	79	1 062	269.3	26.3	14	D	D	D
Keokuk	3.1	299	25	229	214.3	9.9	36	240	55.0	3.5	4	12	1.4	0.1
Kossuth	6.5	417	38	388	500.1	19.6	93	879	246.8	19.2	11	48	2.4	0.7
Lee	28.3	790	39	390	482.8	18.1	151	2 014	474.3	43.4	22	72	9.9	1.7
Linn	146.0	691	310	4 863	3 030.7	261.4	716	14 387	4 483.3	351.2	214	944	203.0	34.1
Louisa	15.7	1 378	12	175	242.2	10.7	25	210	60.7	3.9	7	8	0.7	0.1
Lucas	1.3	148	5	D	D	D	29	381	86.1	8.0	4	6	1.0	0.1
Lyon	7.4	642	26	252	461.6	10.7	52	364	106.6	7.0	8	19	1.5	0.8
Madison	2.1	135	13	227	221.0	9.5	45	493	92.5	8.4	5	D	D	D
Mahaska	4.2	189	34	D	D	D	103	1 210	242.5	24.4	10	26	4.8	0.8
Marion	4.0	121	42	459	315.8	19.2	131	1 517	363.8	33.4	26	63	10.9	1.4
Marshall	11.3	279	39	D	D	D	150	2 059	438.0	43.6	32	394	74.0	14.1
Mills	2.1	136	16	222	173.7	10.5	36	315	96.4	6.1	15	50	7.1	1.4
Mitchell	5.8	539	23	294	514.0	14.8	55	365	73.8	6.1	7	50	0.9	0.2
Monona	16.5	1 780	12	105	140.9	4.7	43	392	119.6	9.0	2	D	D	D
Monroe	2.6	324	11	173	52.0	5.8	32	302	85.9	5.7	5	4	0.7	0.1
Montgomery	2.1	198	15	119	222.4	6.2	49	529	108.4	10.1	9	46	4.4	1.2
Muscatine	235.3	5 505	50	D	D	D	141	2 070	489.0	44.1	47	199	28.1	5.7
O'Brien	6.5	451	32	358	776.7	14.7	99	930	204.5	17.5	4	18	4.4	0.5
Osceola	7.0	1 077	8	D	D	D	29	164	81.0	3.5	1	D	D	D
Page	3.3	208	18	157	146.9	6.3	72	692	153.8	12.6	8	10	1.9	0.1
Palo Alto	4.8	511	17	138	262.9	6.2	41	340	81.1	6.9	7	17	4.0	0.3
Plymouth	10.5	419	35	351	469.0	13.8	97	1 013	270.0	20.9	18	57	5.9	1.3
Pocahontas	2.2	298	12	137	303.5	5.6	33	245	50.3	4.7	1	D	D	D
Polk	58.3	135	678	11 409	9 500.5	631.6	1 518	27 663	7 616.3	689.8	549	3 095	632.1	123.1
Pottawattamie	568.5	6 102	96	1 331	1 737.8	64.7	308	5 957	1 757.6	128.5	80	351	53.4	8.8
Poweshiek	3.0	161	21	182	226.5	7.6	84	1 107	432.9	33.4	13	28	2.9	0.5
Ringgold	1.5	298	7	55	90.7	2.2	28	194	79.6	4.3	2	D	D	D
Sac	8.8	848	29	229	275.3	13.3	57	381	101.6	7.5	4	4	1.4	0.1
Scott	120.6	730	266	4 020	2 642.1	195.5	638	11 210	3 098.7	266.1	181	744	194.3	27.8
Shelby	3.5	284	28	400	255.2	13.5	56	571	175.3	10.7	5	17	1.7	0.2
Sioux	20.8	618	87	1 554	1 401.0	60.6	149	1 622	433.3	35.3	24	106	18.4	5.8
Story	12.5	140	74	D	D	D	288	4 708	1 084.2	98.5	97	465	75.5	16.1
Tama	5.8	325	22	136	204.5	5.7	64	530	122.3	11.1	5	D	D	D
Taylor	1.0	158	5	D	D	D	18	147	32.6	2.2	3	D	D	D
Union	6.1	483	18	236	552.4	10.1	49	756	174.9	16.8	11	D	D	D
Van Buren	1.2	152	8	46	39.3	1.5	29	192	40.5	3.4	3	D	D	D
Wapello	14.6	410	29	211	314.3	7.9	135	2 290	538.4	48.5	23	91	12.5	2.9
Warren	2.6	56	37	549	287.1	24.6	103	1 513	367.8	32.3	23	69	10.4	1.6
Washington	5.3	244	42	306	273.0	13.4	103	1 091	256.1	22.1	12	22	1.6	0.3
Wayne	0.8	120	5	79	55.3	2.6	31	197	70.1	4.2	1	D	D	D
Webster	16.5	433	59	D	D	D	171	2 616	595.8	54.5	39	103	20.2	2.6
Winnebago	2.8	256	22	169	280.8	7.4	56	485	131.4	9.5	5	D	D	D
Winneshiek	6.3	298	33	271	281.9	14.5	121	1 185	293.0	26.8	11	23	1.9	0.4
Woodbury	1 021.4	9 997	149	2 253	2 107.7	101.7	432	7 336	1 776.1	155.7	90	516	65.2	13.3
Worth	10.2	1 344	14	103	189.5	4.8	20	183	36.7	3.6	1	D	D	D
Wright	6.2	470	18	286	628.1	15.4	61	606	117.9	10.4	14	21	2.7	0.3

1. Merchant wholesalers, except manufacturers' sales branches and offices.   2. Employer establishments.

Table B. States and Counties — **Professional Services, Manufacturing, and Accommodation and Food Services**

STATE County	Professional, scientific, and technical services, 2012				Manufacturing, 2012				Accommodation and food services, 2012			
	Number of establish-ments	Number of employees	Receipts (mil dol)	Annual payroll (mil dol)	Number of establish-ments	Number of employees	Receipts (mil dol)	Annual payroll (mil dol)	Number of establish-ments	Number of employees	Sales (mil dol)	Annual payroll (mil dol)
	147	148	149	150	151	152	153	154	155	156	157	158
IOWA—Cont'd												
Franklin	20	76	5.6	2.2	24	719	229.3	36.4	18	154	5.6	1.6
Fremont	8	34	3.2	1.2	10	632	654.4	30.5	21	180	7.5	1.9
Greene	17	79	7.5	3.5	10	287	86.0	13.5	18	D	D	D
Grundy	12	37	4.4	1.3	13	504	153.9	20.5	20	138	4.4	1.2
Guthrie	17	68	10.2	2.5	9	354	D	15.4	18	D	D	D
Hamilton	24	99	12.1	4.1	22	639	275.3	22.3	29	286	10.1	2.7
Hancock	16	163	13.3	5.0	23	1 037	348.5	44.8	20	D	D	D
Hardin	34	164	14.1	4.7	25	535	1 272.7	24.5	34	441	14.6	3.8
Harrison	18	D	D	D	13	303	107.6	13.1	30	302	10.3	2.9
Henry	40	148	18.3	6.0	36	2 139	815.9	86.0	43	565	24.1	6.1
Howard	14	52	3.2	1.3	23	944	260.5	38.8	22	D	D	D
Humboldt	18	62	9.3	2.2	23	934	228.7	41.0	22	215	8.8	2.3
Ida	10	55	3.6	1.1	13	1 026	679.5	49.9	11	D	D	D
Iowa	26	147	26.7	15.9	27	3 254	1 475.9	168.2	41	567	21.6	6.8
Jackson	32	114	7.7	2.6	31	839	255.2	28.8	47	496	16.6	4.7
Jasper	55	469	116.8	18.6	37	1 576	306.3	53.5	59	846	33.6	9.3
Jefferson	133	697	69.8	25.1	36	1 134	266.2	50.4	46	467	19.0	5.9
Johnson	272	1 969	299.6	92.2	80	4 983	3 400.4	232.9	375	D	D	D
Jones	28	120	11.3	4.5	28	811	246.0	35.4	38	D	D	D
Keokuk	10	37	7.0	1.7	12	185	53.1	7.8	11	D	D	D
Kossuth	35	187	22.0	7.1	28	1 223	875.8	53.6	34	380	13.8	3.6
Lee	49	189	18.1	5.1	62	4 138	2 511.7	227.0	95	1 047	38.7	10.1
Linn	506	5 486	728.9	321.5	208	17 686	10 073.9	1 288.4	499	8 790	388.8	113.4
Louisa	11	33	2.6	0.8	12	1 401	D	49.0	19	99	4.1	1.0
Lucas	12	34	2.7	0.9	11	146	D	6.9	16	D	D	D
Lyon	21	120	17.2	9.7	27	589	111.8	26.8	18	D	D	D
Madison	31	102	9.7	3.3	15	162	D	6.6	23	D	D	D
Mahaska	35	136	12.5	6.2	33	1 211	969.9	60.6	38	D	D	D
Marion	58	360	32.5	11.9	43	6 128	2 031.6	378.0	68	935	30.8	8.7
Marshall	43	338	51.3	13.6	38	5 011	2 232.2	246.8	87	1 070	44.7	12.1
Mills	26	D	D	D	7	35	8.2	1.0	16	145	6.4	1.6
Mitchell	12	87	4.8	1.5	25	984	644.4	41.6	21	D	D	D
Monona	15	46	4.2	1.8	4	74	D	D	25	D	D	D
Monroe	10	40	5.0	1.2	12	426	D	14.0	21	D	D	D
Montgomery	15	68	9.5	2.5	9	417	242.8	21.1	25	254	10.0	2.9
Muscatine	59	678	71.9	36.2	63	6 623	3 982.7	339.5	88	1 129	47.1	12.6
O'Brien	27	158	21.2	5.6	25	522	D	24.1	27	D	D	D
Osceola	8	26	4.9	0.7	14	271	D	10.3	12	D	D	D
Page	19	110	6.4	2.8	17	1 355	303.3	60.0	31	369	14.4	3.9
Palo Alto	11	30	4.5	1.5	20	514	676.5	23.7	26	548	43.5	7.7
Plymouth	35	234	12.7	12.6	31	2 471	1 084.3	111.7	57	857	26.9	7.4
Pocahontas	17	52	3.2	1.2	13	342	75.3	15.3	15	D	D	D
Polk	1 398	14 140	2 345.9	878.5	337	16 660	10 472.9	834.2	1 100	20 540	1 012.6	290.6
Pottawattamie	130	686	77.2	27.1	62	4 787	3 929.2	205.4	207	5 282	412.8	90.8
Poweshiek	41	126	10.9	3.5	33	1 576	453.7	61.1	53	583	20.9	5.4
Ringgold	8	50	16.3	1.8	6	D	3.1	0.6	10	D	D	D
Sac	15	43	5.5	1.1	24	398	198.0	14.3	22	D	D	D
Scott	405	2 548	316.6	108.5	182	11 389	6 704.5	657.0	423	8 987	440.2	120.6
Shelby	20	136	13.3	4.2	19	666	176.3	27.1	25	D	D	D
Sioux	83	980	124.2	32.9	90	5 331	1 596.6	208.6	74	1 248	40.6	11.3
Story	203	1 114	118.0	53.3	77	4 821	2 787.2	256.8	229	4 269	172.6	48.0
Tama	22	61	5.2	1.5	19	280	116.9	12.7	27	D	D	D
Taylor	9	37	2.5	0.7	6	539	237.5	16.2	8	D	D	D
Union	17	63	5.0	2.1	13	1 654	284.0	61.1	28	366	14.3	3.7
Van Buren	7	25	2.1	0.7	11	901	203.7	39.9	12	D	D	D
Wapello	48	280	24.7	10.0	24	4 264	D	196.6	77	1 198	47.0	13.2
Warren	56	294	37.6	12.4	27	425	78.6	19.5	64	890	32.9	9.1
Washington	56	158	14.5	4.6	45	1 078	398.8	43.5	44	D	D	D
Wayne	8	39	4.1	1.0	9	408	102.1	14.3	11	80	2.1	0.6
Webster	71	1 053	35.7	52.8	44	1 246	1 549.8	68.0	83	1 365	61.9	16.6
Winnebago	23	168	10.4	4.7	18	2 588	734.7	109.0	23	D	D	D
Winneshiek	28	161	19.7	8.4	34	1 402	300.9	60.6	61	757	32.4	8.0
Woodbury	196	977	121.1	40.3	91	5 068	4 061.2	210.7	268	4 980	240.7	66.7
Worth	9	23	1.6	0.6	12	431	257.4	15.9	10	D	D	D
Wright	23	125	12.0	3.0	22	1 280	1 437.3	63.4	36	D	D	D

1. Establishment subject to federal tax.

Table B. States and Counties — Health Care and Social Assistance, Other Services, Nonemployer Businesses, and Residential Construction

STATE County	Health care and social assistance, 2012				Other services, 2012				Nonemployer businesses, 2015		Value of residential construction authorized by building permits, 2016	
	Number of establish-ments	Number of employees	Receipts (mil dol)	Annual payroll (mil dol)	Number of establish-ments	Number of employees	Receipts (mil dol)	Annual payroll (mil dol)	Number	Receipts (mil dol)	New Construction ($1,000)	Number of housing units
	159	160	161	162	163	164	165	166	167	168	169	170
IOWA—Cont'd												
Franklin	31	560	35.3	14.7	28	91	8.7	1.9	779	35.6	840	2
Fremont	17	415	25.6	11.0	12	D	D	D	473	19.1	2 108	9
Greene	30	588	39.3	16.5	26	88	8.6	1.7	685	30.2	1 809	11
Grundy	26	493	33.0	14.0	20	D	D	D	877	32.6	2 225	8
Guthrie	27	535	34.8	16.1	28	83	9.7	2.2	989	42.8	2 348	8
Hamilton	34	D	D	D	31	94	16.0	2.6	1 026	37.8	650	3
Hancock	18	463	30.9	12.8	26	253	26.4	10.1	849	36.2	3 464	16
Hardin	49	1 054	69.8	30.2	47	137	13.8	3.8	1 248	49.6	2 075	9
Harrison	33	858	59.3	23.9	25	63	5.4	1.2	1 039	41.6	7 104	34
Henry	54	1 141	85.2	39.3	43	137	9.5	3.3	1 305	42.4	6 988	41
Howard	22	547	28.3	11.9	16	46	4.0	1.0	792	39.2	1 225	6
Humboldt	24	472	27.1	11.1	16	49	6.1	1.2	739	32.8	6 381	16
Ida	22	503	31.8	12.6	14	D	D	D	554	24.6	900	6
Iowa	37	827	46.2	22.7	26	D	D	D	1 239	51.2	3 094	20
Jackson	41	855	51.8	23.7	49	120	17.7	2.7	1 524	59.3	6 844	38
Jasper	83	1 563	102.4	46.8	60	283	17.4	5.1	2 258	85.0	14 133	59
Jefferson	46	726	58.7	22.9	47	154	74.3	4.8	1 850	65.3	2 621	18
Johnson	383	15 739	1 967.8	768.9	217	1 519	187.4	42.4	9 296	450.4	312 821	1 874
Jones	36	842	55.1	21.8	41	108	12.6	2.4	1 378	52.3	1 863	10
Keokuk	21	374	21.0	10.5	19	D	D	D	698	31.7	0	0
Kossuth	44	829	66.4	25.6	49	126	15.2	3.0	1 444	65.6	2 685	8
Lee	108	2 268	166.4	74.7	74	232	24.8	5.6	1 909	69.2	6 579	55
Linn	582	14 939	1 451.7	615.2	377	2 610	253.6	77.3	13 207	596.4	85 869	748
Louisa	28	343	15.5	7.2	17	D	D	D	625	23.2	941	5
Lucas	25	595	33.6	15.2	13	26	3.7	0.7	629	33.6	100	1
Lyon	24	443	21.6	8.0	32	94	9.4	2.1	997	51.2	7 271	32
Madison	28	572	37.8	15.9	22	62	6.8	1.6	1 308	61.5	23 664	91
Mahaska	51	1 056	80.1	39.2	39	142	14.7	3.4	1 493	57.8	3 761	34
Marion	92	1 991	165.7	70.9	60	215	17.8	4.8	2 128	76.4	16 103	79
Marshall	82	1 930	155.4	70.4	61	284	25.3	6.0	1 870	71.0	12 321	66
Mills	37	740	32.8	17.2	24	62	6.4	1.6	967	40.3	1 290	4
Mitchell	33	590	37.3	15.3	33	73	6.9	1.7	925	38.2	4 516	20
Monona	21	698	60.5	21.2	14	49	3.4	1.1	620	22.5	1 882	9
Monroe	21	454	28.9	10.3	7	16	2.4	0.3	505	22.6	2 762	12
Montgomery	32	765	52.9	24.7	32	131	13.4	3.8	738	25.7	2 894	11
Muscatine	97	1 944	139.9	60.2	68	368	48.6	10.2	2 071	90.5	11 839	62
O'Brien	52	1 446	82.4	32.1	41	171	21.6	4.6	949	55.4	6 380	46
Osceola	14	260	16.5	6.5	11	D	D	D	420	17.0	0	0
Page	57	1 452	106.6	48.4	23	69	6.9	1.4	908	30.7	3 165	18
Palo Alto	30	705	48.2	20.4	15	D	D	D	687	32.0	1 250	8
Plymouth	56	1 139	81.9	30.9	59	277	30.5	8.1	1 732	84.3	13 329	61
Pocahontas	19	315	18.7	8.3	9	D	D	D	553	26.1	500	2
Polk	1 113	33 649	3 659.7	1 655.7	942	6 904	887.0	228.0	31 764	1 532.4	958 048	5 014
Pottawattamie	225	5 323	509.6	184.3	159	772	98.3	22.0	5 021	223.5	25 295	114
Poweshiek	55	1 098	87.2	38.0	35	112	13.2	3.0	1 292	47.7	7 420	34
Ringgold	14	399	27.5	12.2	13	40	5.3	0.9	450	19.1	100	1
Sac	28	560	32.8	15.3	16	43	4.9	1.1	859	39.5	2 490	11
Scott	482	12 086	1 132.3	490.6	306	2 165	188.8	52.9	10 384	482.2	97 659	493
Shelby	39	1 134	78.1	26.2	28	114	9.5	2.1	965	41.9	2 838	13
Sioux	78	2 437	149.6	62.7	83	306	36.2	7.4	2 689	125.8	28 642	139
Story	192	4 855	513.2	206.0	146	1 000	136.1	27.5	5 459	227.4	116 036	709
Tama	29	460	22.3	10.3	20	67	5.2	1.2	1 103	42.4	2 516	12
Taylor	15	D	D	D	11	D	D	D	559	25.2	1 023	5
Union	40	917	64.6	29.4	28	128	22.3	4.5	799	26.7	3 351	24
Van Buren	14	315	19.5	8.0	12	13	1.8	0.3	664	30.4	134	2
Wapello	92	2 615	214.4	90.0	50	249	19.9	6.7	1 675	65.6	1 521	20
Warren	77	1 232	73.9	33.0	63	227	17.4	4.6	3 603	140.7	87 511	404
Washington	67	1 252	78.5	34.9	53	148	20.3	4.0	1 734	70.3	7 768	47
Wayne	16	366	26.5	13.9	11	D	D	D	601	37.0	301	3
Webster	116	2 974	238.4	109.4	62	372	52.0	11.6	2 114	85.3	3 718	18
Winnebago	40	620	27.1	11.2	14	D	D	D	831	34.8	2 959	38
Winneshiek	61	1 422	105.8	51.0	42	D	D	D	1 886	68.7	13 048	56
Woodbury	331	8 431	820.1	310.1	181	1 331	92.1	29.0	5 753	251.1	48 918	277
Worth	12	179	8.5	3.9	12	D	D	D	554	17.8	700	5
Wright	38	924	83.8	34.0	24	57	5.3	1.1	886	37.8	2 042	11

Table B. States and Counties — Government Employment and Payroll, and Local Government Finances

	Government employment and payroll, 2012									Local government finances, 2012				
			March payroll (percent of total)							General revenue				
												Taxes		
													Per capita[1] (dollars)	
STATE County	Full-time equivalent employees	March payroll (dollars)	Administration, judicial, and legal	Police and Corrections	Fire Protection	Highways and transportation	Health and Welfare	Natural resources and utilities	Education and libraries	Total (mil dol)	Inter-governmental (mil dol)	Total (mil dol)	Total	Property
	171	172	173	174	175	176	177	178	179	180	181	182	183	184
IOWA—Cont'd														
Franklin	668	2 088 400	4.9	4.3	0.0	6.1	28.3	1.6	54.1	66.9	22.7	23.0	2 183	1 785
Fremont	347	973 340	7.5	7.8	0.0	11.0	2.0	3.1	66.2	34.7	15.8	16.0	2 243	1 866
Greene	666	2 223 582	5.3	3.9	0.1	5.8	41.2	3.9	39.3	57.4	14.6	19.1	2 082	1 727
Grundy	563	1 970 199	5.6	4.4	0.0	5.6	33.3	4.7	45.8	64.2	18.4	21.5	1 731	1 370
Guthrie	748	2 384 845	4.1	2.8	0.0	5.3	24.8	3.4	59.0	68.4	20.6	29.3	2 716	2 276
Hamilton	889	2 941 083	5.3	6.3	0.7	5.4	28.8	4.7	47.5	85.2	24.2	29.7	1 934	1 608
Hancock	533	1 678 758	4.9	4.9	1.1	7.4	29.0	1.1	50.1	52.6	15.5	18.7	1 678	1 364
Hardin	771	2 439 397	10.0	8.8	0.3	7.6	3.2	3.8	65.7	93.9	30.1	33.2	1 921	1 546
Harrison	661	2 116 699	6.1	6.5	0.0	7.4	2.6	6.5	68.9	60.2	26.0	28.5	1 960	1 608
Henry	1 101	3 801 450	6.1	5.0	0.3	3.4	27.7	5.1	50.9	103.1	34.1	30.0	1 484	1 188
Howard	610	1 837 491	3.8	4.1	0.0	6.3	32.8	4.1	48.6	53.0	15.0	18.0	1 887	1 526
Humboldt	551	1 979 695	10.2	4.3	0.1	15.7	23.2	4.8	41.3	51.5	15.8	17.9	1 843	1 479
Ida	324	944 758	6.5	5.6	0.0	8.7	0.4	3.6	73.9	24.5	9.5	11.8	1 661	1 328
Iowa	946	2 546 590	3.6	5.9	0.1	6.6	25.6	2.5	55.1	74.3	23.2	29.8	1 838	1 381
Jackson	760	2 545 154	6.2	8.0	0.2	6.2	18.9	3.4	56.7	78.0	28.3	27.5	1 395	1 119
Jasper	1 510	5 999 123	4.8	6.2	2.0	4.5	25.8	3.5	51.2	155.2	47.6	58.5	1 597	1 284
Jefferson	662	2 186 709	5.0	7.9	0.9	5.5	30.3	6.8	43.2	74.0	18.6	24.1	1 426	1 178
Johnson	2 791	12 750 946	7.7	8.1	1.5	4.7	5.9	5.3	62.3	508.5	160.5	263.7	1 934	1 579
Jones	764	2 287 665	6.5	6.6	0.0	6.9	3.4	2.6	72.1	73.5	35.1	28.3	1 369	1 067
Keokuk	574	1 571 936	7.3	3.7	0.0	8.5	14.2	3.5	62.2	51.8	19.5	19.7	1 897	1 573
Kossuth	791	2 418 144	8.4	5.5	0.2	7.0	33.0	4.1	41.0	91.7	21.6	29.7	1 937	1 582
Lee	1 300	4 660 014	5.4	7.2	3.1	4.7	4.4	9.0	64.9	121.2	55.2	48.2	1 353	989
Linn	9 095	37 187 147	3.6	5.9	2.8	6.2	2.3	4.9	72.4	1 182.6	511.6	437.3	2 031	1 562
Louisa	609	1 866 882	4.6	6.3	0.0	4.4	2.1	2.8	79.3	56.0	27.3	22.6	2 003	1 495
Lucas	520	1 767 462	3.7	2.9	0.0	5.3	32.1	16.9	38.6	45.7	14.5	12.3	1 406	1 112
Lyon	499	1 482 179	6.0	6.8	0.0	8.4	4.9	6.3	65.1	46.7	19.3	20.2	1 715	1 324
Madison	798	2 825 675	6.6	2.7	0.0	7.8	22.7	7.6	52.2	80.3	28.9	28.9	1 848	1 518
Mahaska	1 014	3 634 697	4.3	4.7	0.9	4.1	46.1	1.9	35.8	108.1	29.6	33.7	1 503	1 164
Marion	1 252	3 936 638	5.4	7.6	0.0	6.5	4.1	9.6	65.6	122.5	47.7	49.1	1 469	1 141
Marshall	1 954	7 209 585	3.6	6.6	1.9	3.7	0.6	4.3	78.3	184.2	83.4	70.1	1 715	1 332
Mills	661	1 998 540	5.5	6.9	1.4	7.4	5.2	1.1	71.4	51.3	23.3	23.3	1 569	1 336
Mitchell	526	1 692 873	5.0	4.8	0.0	5.4	33.0	2.6	47.2	57.0	14.0	18.3	1 705	1 409
Monona	396	1 218 905	10.0	7.1	0.0	11.2	2.6	8.7	59.5	37.4	15.9	15.8	1 736	1 419
Monroe	387	1 402 370	4.4	6.0	0.1	5.9	41.4	2.3	39.4	25.8	12.4	11.4	1 418	1 109
Montgomery	722	2 440 051	4.3	3.9	1.5	5.4	42.7	3.0	37.5	72.5	19.7	21.2	2 004	1 573
Muscatine	1 797	6 903 785	4.4	8.5	3.1	3.4	2.3	23.5	51.0	179.8	71.9	69.9	1 630	1 298
O'Brien	688	2 291 194	4.3	7.0	0.0	6.3	0.5	5.0	75.2	67.6	25.7	28.4	2 007	1 628
Osceola	225	737 061	10.1	8.0	0.0	13.2	1.6	6.2	60.4	21.0	8.0	9.8	1 588	1 342
Page	735	2 422 895	5.4	5.6	0.4	5.2	28.7	4.2	50.0	75.7	24.0	22.9	1 458	1 116
Palo Alto	595	1 986 443	5.8	3.7	0.8	6.9	35.4	3.3	43.7	67.2	16.0	23.3	2 512	2 103
Plymouth	1 172	4 151 413	4.7	5.6	0.3	5.4	25.2	3.7	54.8	126.6	33.5	46.1	1 850	1 539
Pocahontas	388	1 255 236	7.6	7.3	0.0	7.9	24.8	7.4	43.9	40.0	11.0	14.7	2 054	1 718
Polk	17 358	73 983 487	5.6	9.0	3.6	4.4	8.6	5.6	61.7	2 215.8	755.8	962.0	2 168	1 882
Pottawattamie	3 555	14 074 472	5.1	12.0	3.8	3.4	3.5	4.9	66.5	469.3	187.7	200.8	2 162	1 672
Poweshiek	616	2 161 055	7.6	7.8	1.1	6.4	2.2	6.6	67.8	70.4	26.8	32.7	1 745	1 368
Ringgold	380	1 133 677	4.5	3.2	0.0	9.7	40.0	2.0	40.3	38.0	10.1	11.1	2 172	1 874
Sac	370	1 168 894	8.0	8.4	0.0	9.1	4.9	9.7	53.3	38.8	16.2	16.8	1 655	1 346
Scott	6 132	26 019 745	5.1	9.3	3.9	3.8	2.4	4.0	69.8	729.6	283.5	333.3	1 974	1 565
Shelby	746	2 472 519	5.4	3.6	0.2	6.1	48.6	4.6	28.4	74.6	17.8	20.6	1 705	1 402
Sioux	1 410	5 040 852	7.0	4.6	0.0	5.6	32.1	5.9	45.0	155.5	40.9	50.2	1 466	1 159
Story	2 892	10 932 541	7.4	7.6	2.9	7.7	10.1	9.9	52.8	476.0	102.3	138.3	1 518	1 219
Tama	838	2 616 822	5.8	6.4	0.0	7.4	4.6	3.7	70.0	73.1	34.0	30.1	1 717	1 370
Taylor	283	832 177	7.3	5.5	0.0	10.1	5.8	4.1	65.8	26.1	12.6	9.8	1 572	1 285
Union	985	3 478 275	2.6	3.0	0.6	3.4	37.5	2.3	50.1	116.7	47.2	22.5	1 788	1 421
Van Buren	420	1 439 759	4.4	3.0	0.0	5.3	38.1	2.3	46.6	36.7	12.5	10.5	1 409	1 133
Wapello	1 563	6 980 218	2.5	3.5	1.9	4.5	2.0	4.5	80.0	186.1	86.6	52.4	1 482	1 084
Warren	1 608	6 242 328	5.6	5.6	1.1	3.5	2.5	5.3	75.5	156.4	71.0	65.1	1 387	1 216
Washington	1 128	3 614 174	5.4	6.2	0.4	4.7	26.2	4.4	52.3	111.8	34.7	38.8	1 771	1 403
Wayne	428	1 412 234	4.6	3.7	0.0	5.5	52.3	1.9	31.5	45.4	11.7	10.9	1 714	1 444
Webster	1 646	5 911 455	5.2	5.8	2.4	3.6	3.2	3.1	76.3	189.7	73.6	61.4	1 648	1 262
Winnebago	563	1 699 897	5.9	5.4	0.0	5.7	4.8	5.5	71.6	53.4	20.2	24.6	2 324	1 932
Winneshiek	1 453	4 847 620	2.3	3.4	0.2	3.7	28.1	2.1	59.9	162.1	45.6	40.6	1 928	1 635
Woodbury	3 937	16 380 806	4.5	9.7	4.1	5.4	2.2	5.6	67.1	475.0	216.3	177.2	1 732	1 265
Worth	353	1 078 114	9.5	7.7	0.0	8.8	3.7	3.5	65.9	35.3	14.3	16.5	2 191	1 830
Wright	944	3 639 368	3.1	3.8	0.0	4.6	48.9	2.0	37.6	120.8	27.5	28.8	2 216	1 856

1. Based on the resident population estimated as of July 1 of the year shown.

Table B. States and Counties — Local Government Finances, Government Employment, and Income Taxes

STATE County	Local government finances, 2012 (cont.)									Government employment, 2015			Individual income tax returns, 2014		
	Direct general expenditure							Debt outstanding		Federal civilian	Federal military	State and local	Number of returns	Mean adjusted gross income	Mean income tax
	Total (mil dol)	Per capita¹ (dollars)	Percent of total for:					Total (mil dol)	Per capita¹ (dollars)						
			Education	Health and hospitals	Police protection	Public welfare	High-ways								
	185	186	187	188	189	190	191	192	193	194	195	196	197	198	199
IOWA—Cont'd															
Franklin	74.7	7 078	38.7	27.4	2.8	0.1	7.5	53.7	5 092	44	38	771	4 720	54 261	6 250
Fremont	36.0	5 034	46.9	4.3	4.1	0.1	19.2	10.1	1 415	27	26	454	3 190	57 367	6 353
Greene	58.6	6 398	31.8	39.4	3.0	0.2	8.2	19.5	2 133	36	34	768	4 240	50 662	5 000
Grundy	60.9	4 889	35.4	29.1	3.1	0.1	12.1	34.5	2 773	33	47	672	5 790	67 080	7 813
Guthrie	64.7	6 005	45.4	24.0	2.4	0.1	9.0	71.3	6 614	55	40	850	5 010	56 420	6 109
Hamilton	89.3	5 820	41.9	27.7	3.4	0.2	7.1	95.4	6 215	40	57	1 168	7 190	57 674	5 733
Hancock	59.9	5 378	31.9	38.4	3.3	0.1	11.3	36.3	3 260	44	41	620	5 290	55 459	6 003
Hardin	98.1	5 668	39.4	22.8	3.6	0.1	10.4	60.0	3 470	77	62	1 785	7 910	55 104	6 221
Harrison	56.0	3 853	56.3	5.5	3.7	0.3	12.4	33.4	2 299	70	53	825	6 660	55 973	5 752
Henry	99.5	4 919	39.9	36.4	3.0	0.3	4.6	76.0	3 758	66	71	1 622	8 860	50 396	4 833
Howard	49.9	5 214	37.9	32.9	2.9	0.4	8.5	14.5	1 518	27	35	730	4 590	50 415	5 502
Humboldt	60.5	6 223	36.7	23.4	2.9	0.2	10.8	37.9	3 894	46	36	656	4 600	58 915	7 023
Ida	25.1	3 531	55.4	4.9	4.2	0.2	13.6	14.0	1 973	28	26	366	3 390	61 454	8 061
Iowa	74.5	4 600	48.3	23.2	3.7	0.4	9.2	69.2	4 275	49	61	974	7 990	58 302	6 230
Jackson	75.2	3 817	46.3	20.7	4.1	0.1	9.2	36.7	1 860	78	73	1 006	9 490	48 310	4 722
Jasper	146.8	4 011	39.1	28.3	4.3	0.3	6.0	102.6	2 802	93	133	2 210	16 660	53 390	5 271
Jefferson	72.9	4 323	28.0	30.9	3.6	0.2	10.0	71.8	4 254	63	60	1 052	7 480	54 975	5 674
Johnson	524.4	3 847	35.0	4.1	4.1	0.9	6.0	708.3	5 196	1 987	555	33 948	63 570	68 241	9 045
Jones	81.7	3 958	56.2	5.0	3.3	0.1	12.9	52.6	2 548	53	73	1 329	9 090	53 763	5 700
Keokuk	46.7	4 504	42.3	19.6	2.4	0.1	11.3	24.3	2 344	45	38	533	4 560	49 279	4 500
Kossuth	92.1	6 004	26.6	34.3	2.6	0.2	10.8	73.1	4 765	60	56	1 026	7 460	59 238	7 046
Lee	137.2	3 851	55.0	7.3	5.0	0.5	5.8	121.6	3 414	99	146	1 955	15 870	48 939	5 069
Linn	1 336.0	6 206	46.5	3.0	3.7	1.2	4.7	1 559.7	7 244	1 020	813	12 651	105 490	66 110	8 239
Louisa	54.0	4 790	58.9	3.9	3.7	0.1	10.4	92.9	8 237	58	42	650	5 090	48 660	4 406
Lucas	45.7	5 216	36.3	40.7	2.3	0.2	8.8	77.6	8 862	31	33	649	3 940	45 409	4 076
Lyon	43.5	3 701	45.1	4.4	4.6	0.1	20.2	26.6	2 260	38	44	650	5 190	60 453	6 606
Madison	80.3	5 130	45.0	29.6	2.4	0.1	8.2	120.8	7 718	40	59	915	7 060	63 496	7 138
Mahaska	103.0	4 588	32.3	43.1	3.7	0.2	7.0	35.6	1 584	56	82	1 401	9 770	54 527	5 581
Marion	110.4	3 302	53.4	5.1	4.5	0.3	11.9	105.0	3 142	134	120	1 677	14 720	60 334	6 375
Marshall	192.9	4 722	64.1	3.0	4.2	0.3	6.4	177.1	4 335	116	149	3 317	18 220	51 537	5 088
Mills	49.6	3 346	58.3	5.0	5.7	1.1	10.6	46.3	3 118	36	54	1 586	6 630	64 479	7 735
Mitchell	58.6	5 460	27.5	34.6	2.8	0.1	12.4	39.9	3 723	37	40	714	4 820	56 726	6 630
Monona	39.6	4 341	49.5	4.3	4.7	0.4	17.8	19.2	2 100	41	33	528	4 190	51 311	5 705
Monroe	25.6	3 175	52.7	6.3	5.3	0.3	19.1	18.5	2 294	37	30	519	3 490	46 596	4 656
Montgomery	75.5	7 150	27.3	38.4	8.7	0.2	5.5	34.3	3 246	39	38	936	4 790	49 165	4 855
Muscatine	169.3	3 949	47.2	3.6	5.1	0.4	6.8	78.4	1 828	83	161	2 615	20 790	54 614	5 749
O'Brien	67.2	4 738	61.1	4.1	3.9	0.2	8.1	45.7	3 226	45	52	1 066	6 700	55 923	6 649
Osceola	20.4	3 288	41.6	8.9	9.7	0.1	18.2	8.6	1 389	25	23	283	3 020	49 236	4 756
Page	86.1	5 483	33.4	39.4	2.8	0.1	7.4	65.9	4 192	69	53	1 305	6 630	50 500	5 084
Palo Alto	64.4	6 948	31.7	32.8	2.9	0.1	15.3	37.1	4 003	36	33	987	4 280	51 153	5 383
Plymouth	123.5	4 958	40.4	28.0	3.4	2.2	7.8	86.7	3 483	78	93	1 450	12 170	61 549	7 333
Pocahontas	41.8	5 851	31.5	27.7	4.1	0.5	11.0	23.7	3 313	36	26	540	3 370	51 938	5 349
Polk	2 428.8	5 474	46.0	7.6	4.5	1.5	5.2	2 789.0	6 286	5 931	1 861	29 591	221 400	67 126	8 787
Pottawattamie	475.8	5 121	56.9	3.4	5.2	0.3	4.5	433.2	4 662	213	348	5 355	42 850	53 047	5 527
Poweshiek	66.2	3 533	47.3	5.0	4.5	0.2	10.8	65.3	3 483	60	64	863	8 280	54 862	5 809
Ringgold	38.2	7 503	25.9	44.8	2.8	0.2	9.0	42.2	8 280	32	19	421	2 070	52 618	5 939
Sac	42.6	4 196	49.4	6.2	4.3	0.1	13.4	17.5	1 720	44	37	596	4 810	53 909	5 658
Scott	760.2	4 504	54.4	2.6	4.9	0.1	3.6	683.1	4 047	586	640	8 228	82 370	64 385	8 383
Shelby	87.3	7 233	22.6	50.5	1.7	0.1	7.8	52.5	4 348	46	44	1 050	5 890	56 745	6 489
Sioux	160.8	4 691	31.1	29.5	3.1	0.1	6.7	182.6	5 329	94	123	2 138	14 470	66 792	8 853
Story	440.2	4 830	30.3	42.8	3.2	0.5	3.7	391.5	4 295	958	344	19 019	36 480	64 591	7 794
Tama	71.1	4 056	60.3	5.1	3.5	0.1	12.6	36.6	2 088	62	65	1 996	8 350	49 660	4 781
Taylor	30.7	4 937	39.9	4.5	3.6	0.1	25.2	25.0	4 034	42	23	374	2 790	41 637	3 576
Union	122.3	9 707	35.7	41.6	1.4	0.1	4.0	91.1	7 230	55	46	1 289	5 560	46 519	4 171
Van Buren	35.9	4 821	31.7	41.5	2.3	0.1	11.2	9.2	1 230	35	28	553	3 180	44 616	4 211
Wapello	204.9	5 795	64.7	3.0	2.8	0.3	9.3	88.9	2 514	117	130	2 529	15 790	46 696	4 688
Warren	173.5	3 701	60.2	4.1	4.2	0.3	5.2	262.4	5 595	82	178	2 212	22 100	64 794	7 189
Washington	127.8	5 831	38.9	20.4	2.8	0.3	9.4	155.3	7 085	65	83	1 495	10 480	53 603	5 118
Wayne	43.2	6 809	20.6	52.3	2.4	0.2	7.7	24.6	3 877	36	24	573	2 730	41 686	3 463
Webster	231.6	6 213	65.0	3.5	2.6	0.2	5.7	235.4	6 314	183	130	2 812	16 750	50 691	5 274
Winnebago	54.8	5 168	50.8	4.8	4.2	0.1	18.2	51.9	4 900	47	39	718	5 100	50 446	4 915
Winneshiek	175.5	8 333	54.9	26.3	1.7	0.1	5.5	125.4	5 954	70	70	2 171	9 430	55 265	5 954
Woodbury	498.8	4 875	56.0	4.2	4.6	0.6	3.9	465.5	4 550	684	379	6 339	47 030	50 032	5 279
Worth	37.0	4 920	43.7	3.8	4.3	0.1	12.6	25.7	3 424	28	28	375	3 620	50 291	4 896
Wright	134.7	10 370	22.1	58.1	1.8	0.2	4.2	130.1	10 011	62	48	1 294	5 970	51 912	5 136

1. Based on the resident population estimated as of July 1 of the year shown.

Table B. States and Counties — **Land Area and Population**

STATE/ County code	CBSA code[1]	County type[2]	STATE County	Land area,[3] (sq mi) 2016	Total persons 2016	Rank	Per square mile	White	Black	American Indian, Alaska Native	Asian and Pacific Islander[4]	Percent Hispanic or Latino[4]	Under 5 years	5 to 17 years	18 to 24 years	25 to 34 years	35 to 44 years	45 to 54 years
				1	2	3	4	5	6	7	8	9	10	11	12	13	14	15
20 000	...	0	KANSAS	81 758.4	2 907 289	X	35.6	78.6	7.0	1.8	3.6	11.6	6.7	17.9	10.2	13.2	11.9	12.2
20 001	...	7	Allen	500.3	12 714	2 247	25.4	92.9	3.4	1.8	1.1	3.4	5.9	17.1	9.0	10.9	11.2	11.8
20 003	...	6	Anderson	579.6	7 827	2 611	13.5	96.3	1.0	1.4	0.8	1.8	6.3	18.4	7.0	10.3	10.3	12.3
20 005	11860	6	Atchison	431.2	16 380	2 014	38.0	90.6	6.4	1.5	1.0	3.0	6.1	17.2	13.9	11.2	10.2	12.0
20 007	...	9	Barber	1 134.1	4 688	2 851	4.1	93.8	1.4	1.7	0.7	4.0	6.3	16.1	7.3	11.3	9.2	11.4
20 009	24460	7	Barton	895.4	26 775	1 537	29.9	83.1	2.1	1.2	0.5	14.7	6.5	17.7	8.9	12.0	10.4	11.8
20 011	...	6	Bourbon	635.5	14 617	2 125	23.0	92.6	4.0	2.0	1.4	2.5	7.1	18.2	9.2	11.3	10.9	11.1
20 013	...	6	Brown	570.9	9 684	2 453	17.0	85.9	2.2	9.5	0.9	4.1	6.6	18.3	7.1	10.7	10.2	12.2
20 015	48620	2	Butler	1 429.9	67 025	789	46.9	91.2	2.6	1.9	1.8	4.7	6.0	19.7	8.6	12.0	12.5	13.0
20 017	...	9	Chase	773.1	2 669	2 991	3.5	93.0	1.8	1.6	1.0	4.6	5.5	15.7	8.6	10.0	10.5	11.7
20 019	...	8	Chautauqua	638.9	3 374	2 945	5.3	89.7	1.8	8.4	0.7	4.2	5.4	15.3	6.9	10.3	9.3	11.4
20 021	...	6	Cherokee	587.6	20 246	1 819	34.5	92.0	1.4	6.9	1.1	2.4	5.7	17.8	7.4	11.0	11.3	13.9
20 023	...	9	Cheyenne	1 019.9	2 661	2 992	2.6	91.1	0.5	0.5	1.9	6.8	5.5	15.5	7.4	9.2	10.3	10.0
20 025	...	9	Clark	974.6	2 072	3 042	2.1	85.9	1.3	2.5	2.2	10.8	5.2	19.4	8.3	9.4	10.6	12.3
20 027	...	6	Clay	645.3	8 143	2 585	12.6	96.1	1.1	1.4	0.8	2.2	6.5	17.2	6.5	10.3	11.4	11.8
20 029	...	7	Cloud	715.3	9 150	2 496	12.8	94.4	1.4	1.2	1.5	3.0	6.2	16.1	10.0	11.6	10.1	11.1
20 031	...	6	Coffey	626.9	8 433	2 556	13.5	94.7	1.3	1.7	1.2	2.6	5.6	16.8	7.5	10.3	11.0	13.1
20 033	...	9	Comanche	788.3	1 862	3 063	2.4	92.4	1.1	1.3	0.5	6.4	6.7	17.9	6.3	8.4	10.8	10.3
20 035	11680	4	Cowley	1 125.7	35 753	1 282	31.8	82.6	3.9	3.2	2.5	10.7	6.4	17.7	10.2	12.0	11.1	12.0
20 037	38260	4	Crawford	589.8	39 164	1 197	66.4	89.4	3.3	2.0	2.5	5.3	6.3	15.8	18.1	11.9	10.6	10.9
20 039	...	9	Decatur	893.5	2 832	2 984	3.2	96.3	1.2	1.0	0.6	2.3	6.2	13.7	6.1	9.7	7.6	11.4
20 041	...	7	Dickinson	847.1	19 064	1 870	22.5	93.1	2.1	1.4	1.1	4.5	5.9	18.1	6.9	11.4	11.3	12.8
20 043	41140	3	Doniphan	393.4	7 664	2 618	19.5	91.7	4.4	2.1	1.0	2.9	4.9	15.7	12.1	11.0	11.2	12.4
20 045	29940	3	Douglas	455.9	119 440	518	262.0	82.2	5.9	3.5	6.1	6.1	5.3	13.5	23.9	14.7	11.4	9.9
20 047	...	9	Edwards	621.9	2 938	2 977	4.7	78.2	1.0	1.3	0.6	20.4	6.2	17.3	7.1	9.0	10.4	12.9
20 049	...	8	Elk	644.3	2 547	3 002	4.0	93.3	1.2	3.0	1.3	4.4	5.2	14.6	6.4	7.7	8.7	11.4
20 051	25700	5	Ellis	899.9	28 893	1 460	32.1	91.3	1.7	0.7	2.0	5.6	5.9	15.6	17.3	13.8	10.5	10.4
20 053	...	7	Ellsworth	715.8	6 328	2 729	8.8	87.1	5.7	1.3	0.9	6.3	4.6	13.2	9.1	13.8	11.7	12.7
20 055	23780	5	Finney	1 302.0	36 722	1 258	28.2	43.2	3.1	0.8	4.6	49.5	8.8	22.1	10.7	13.9	11.5	12.1
20 057	19980	5	Ford	1 098.3	33 971	1 327	30.9	41.8	2.8	0.8	1.7	53.9	9.3	21.2	10.1	13.7	12.0	12.1
20 059	36840	6	Franklin	571.8	25 560	1 581	44.7	93.4	2.1	1.8	0.8	4.1	6.3	18.4	9.0	11.7	11.2	13.3
20 061	27920	4	Geary	384.6	35 586	1 288	92.5	61.1	20.2	2.0	6.1	16.3	11.7	18.8	15.6	21.1	11.6	6.9
20 063	...	9	Gove	1 071.7	2 589	2 998	2.4	96.1	0.8	0.6	0.7	2.7	6.6	17.7	6.6	10.2	10.2	9.8
20 065	...	9	Graham	898.5	2 564	2 999	2.9	91.8	4.6	1.8	1.4	3.4	5.7	15.3	5.7	9.5	9.2	11.9
20 067	...	7	Grant	574.8	7 646	2 620	13.3	52.1	0.8	1.0	0.5	46.7	8.1	23.6	9.8	11.5	11.9	11.0
20 069	...	9	Gray	868.9	6 034	2 748	6.9	83.3	1.1	0.6	0.5	15.3	7.3	20.0	8.2	10.6	12.3	11.7
20 071	...	9	Greeley	778.4	1 296	3 095	1.7	80.9	0.5	0.8	0.5	18.0	7.3	18.1	6.0	11.7	10.5	10.0
20 073	...	6	Greenwood	1 143.3	6 151	2 741	5.4	94.0	1.2	2.3	0.8	3.9	5.1	15.6	6.4	9.1	10.0	12.2
20 075	...	9	Hamilton	996.5	2 536	3 003	2.5	64.6	1.0	1.3	0.8	33.9	8.4	21.5	8.2	12.7	12.1	12.3
20 077	...	8	Harper	801.3	5 685	2 784	7.1	91.8	1.0	1.9	0.7	6.0	6.8	17.8	6.7	10.9	10.4	10.2
20 079	48620	2	Harvey	539.8	34 913	1 306	64.7	85.1	2.7	1.4	1.3	11.6	6.5	18.2	9.7	11.1	11.2	11.3
20 081	...	9	Haskell	577.5	4 006	2 902	6.9	67.6	0.8	1.0	1.5	30.2	7.0	21.6	10.0	10.6	12.6	11.8
20 083	...	9	Hodgeman	860.0	1 870	3 061	2.2	89.8	1.6	1.2	0.7	7.8	6.5	16.1	6.5	9.5	9.0	11.2
20 085	45820	3	Jackson	656.2	13 291	2 215	20.3	87.3	1.4	9.2	0.9	4.3	6.4	18.7	7.8	10.4	10.7	13.8
20 087	45820	3	Jefferson	532.6	18 897	1 879	35.5	95.6	1.1	2.0	0.6	2.7	5.4	17.7	7.1	10.4	10.9	14.6
20 089	...	9	Jewell	909.8	2 901	2 979	3.2	96.4	0.7	1.0	0.5	2.3	5.1	13.9	6.6	8.8	7.8	11.1
20 091	28140	1	Johnson	473.5	584 451	111	1 234.3	82.5	5.7	0.9	5.7	7.5	6.4	18.4	7.9	13.7	13.8	13.6
20 093	23780	9	Kearny	870.5	3 917	2 908	4.5	66.3	1.6	1.9	0.6	31.5	8.2	20.3	9.3	12.5	11.1	12.0
20 095	48620	2	Kingman	863.4	7 467	2 633	8.6	95.1	0.5	1.6	0.7	3.4	4.9	17.0	6.8	10.0	10.0	12.7
20 097	...	9	Kiowa	722.6	2 483	3 007	3.4	90.7	1.7	1.7	1.5	6.1	5.9	15.9	12.0	9.6	10.6	11.0
20 099	37660	7	Labette	645.3	20 444	1 805	31.7	89.0	5.5	4.0	1.0	4.4	6.3	17.1	7.6	11.8	10.6	13.3
20 101	...	9	Lane	717.4	1 636	3 074	2.3	90.3	1.8	1.8	0.7	7.6	6.7	15.9	7.1	10.3	8.9	12.7
20 103	28140	1	Leavenworth	463.1	80 204	699	173.2	81.6	10.3	1.6	2.6	6.9	6.6	17.3	8.1	13.9	14.5	13.4
20 105	...	9	Lincoln	719.4	3 073	2 962	4.3	95.4	0.9	1.1	0.6	3.0	5.4	18.6	6.5	8.0	10.0	12.0
20 107	28140	1	Linn	594.1	9 558	2 465	16.1	95.3	1.3	2.1	0.7	2.6	5.6	17.8	6.0	10.2	11.4	12.8
20 109	...	9	Logan	1 073.0	2 831	2 985	2.6	91.4	1.4	1.1	2.0	5.8	6.4	16.4	7.9	12.4	11.3	10.5
20 111	21380	4	Lyon	847.5	33 510	1 340	39.5	73.3	3.3	1.6	3.2	21.1	6.0	16.3	17.8	12.4	10.0	10.8
20 113	32700	7	McPherson	898.3	28 804	1 466	32.1	93.4	1.8	1.1	1.4	4.0	5.9	17.1	8.8	11.5	10.7	11.5
20 115	...	6	Marion	944.3	12 112	2 289	12.8	94.3	1.4	1.6	0.9	3.5	5.3	16.3	9.9	9.0	9.4	12.4
20 117	...	6	Marshall	900.2	9 836	2 445	10.9	96.3	1.0	1.0	0.9	2.4	6.3	17.2	6.6	10.3	10.3	11.5
20 119	...	9	Meade	978.1	4 216	2 881	4.3	80.6	1.4	1.5	0.8	16.9	6.9	19.0	9.2	10.1	9.3	13.3
20 121	28140	1	Miami	575.7	32 964	1 356	57.3	94.5	1.8	1.5	0.8	3.1	6.2	19.1	7.2	10.1	12.2	14.7
20 123	...	7	Mitchell	701.8	6 243	2 733	8.9	95.9	0.6	0.9	1.1	2.6	6.7	16.1	9.3	9.8	9.7	11.2
20 125	17700	5	Montgomery	643.5	32 746	1 364	50.9	84.3	6.8	6.0	1.5	6.3	6.7	17.0	8.8	11.7	10.6	12.1
20 127	...	8	Morris	695.3	5 573	2 795	8.0	93.6	1.2	1.4	1.0	4.7	5.3	15.0	6.4	10.3	9.7	12.7
20 129	...	9	Morton	729.7	2 848	2 983	3.9	72.9	1.4	1.7	1.9	23.5	6.7	18.7	7.1	9.2	12.7	12.7
20 131	...	6	Nemaha	717.4	10 241	2 410	14.3	96.7	1.1	1.0	0.7	1.7	7.5	18.6	7.8	10.4	10.0	12.1

1. CBSA = Core Based Statistical Area. See Appendix A for explanation. See Appendix B for list of metropolitan areas with component counties.   2. County type code from the Economic Research Service of USDA Rural-Urban Continuum Codes. See Appendix A for definition.   3. Dry land or land partially or temporarily covered by water.   4. May be of any race.

Table B. States and Counties — **Population and Households**

| | Population, 2016 (cont.) | | | | Population change and components of change, 2000–2016 | | | | | | | Households, 2011–2015 | | | | |
| | Age (percent) (cont.) | | | | Total persons | | Percent change | | Components of change, 2010–2016 | | | | | Percent | | |
STATE County	55 to 64 years	65 to 74 years	75 years and over	Percent female	2000	2010	2000– 2010	2010– 2016	Births	Deaths	Net migration	Number	Persons per house- hold	Family house- holds	Female family house- holder[1]	One per- son
	16	17	18	19	20	21	22	23	24	25	26	27	28	29	30	31
KANSAS	12.8	8.4	6.6	50.2	2 688 418	2 853 129	6.1	1.9	246 116	157 380	-34 632	1 113 472	2.53	65.5	10.2	28.7
Allen	14.2	10.6	9.4	51.0	14 385	13 371	-7.0	-4.9	938	1 132	-471	5 306	2.39	62.1	8.8	32.7
Anderson	14.0	11.5	9.9	50.0	8 110	8 102	-0.1	-3.4	608	579	-295	3 280	2.37	65.9	8.0	31.3
Atchison	13.0	8.8	7.6	51.4	16 774	16 924	0.9	-3.2	1 273	1 120	-696	6 033	2.53	62.7	9.3	33.9
Barber	16.9	12.4	9.1	48.4	5 307	4 861	-8.4	-3.6	395	355	-188	1 981	2.38	65.6	6.1	30.9
Barton	14.8	9.2	8.7	50.5	28 205	27 674	-1.9	-3.2	2 243	1 870	-1 250	11 306	2.38	65.3	11.3	29.9
Bourbon	13.6	10.2	8.5	50.5	15 379	15 173	-1.3	-3.7	1 337	1 132	-783	5 660	2.54	67.6	11.2	27.9
Brown	14.9	11.1	8.8	51.1	10 724	9 984	-6.9	-3.0	823	799	-333	4 102	2.38	64.3	9.4	33.4
Butler	13.5	8.3	6.3	49.8	59 482	65 880	10.8	1.7	4 745	3 879	230	24 273	2.63	71.4	9.3	24.8
Chase	14.2	13.5	10.3	49.0	3 030	2 790	-7.9	-4.3	170	198	-76	1 110	2.34	59.4	7.0	35.0
Chautauqua	15.9	12.4	13.1	48.8	4 359	3 669	-15.8	-8.0	206	327	-161	1 557	2.21	66.7	7.8	31.2
Cherokee	14.4	10.8	7.7	50.2	22 605	21 603	-4.4	-6.3	1 465	1 689	-1 093	7 988	2.59	72.3	9.7	25.4
Cheyenne	15.9	12.5	13.7	50.1	3 165	2 726	-13.9	-2.4	183	242	-6	1 262	2.09	62.4	5.9	35.3
Clark	13.2	9.3	12.3	50.8	2 390	2 215	-7.3	-6.5	137	189	-98	927	2.25	64.5	10.5	30.9
Clay	14.0	11.6	10.7	50.4	8 822	8 535	-3.3	-4.6	657	666	-396	3 377	2.45	71.4	8.3	25.8
Cloud	13.4	10.7	10.8	50.7	10 268	9 533	-7.2	-4.0	694	834	-226	3 964	2.24	60.7	10.2	35.3
Coffey	15.4	11.7	8.6	51.0	8 865	8 598	-3.0	-1.9	550	606	-95	3 569	2.33	68.2	7.3	27.7
Comanche	15.1	14.0	10.5	51.3	1 967	1 891	-3.9	-1.5	142	182	7	784	2.48	67.7	6.1	30.2
Cowley	13.1	9.5	7.9	49.9	36 291	36 311	0.1	-1.5	2 866	2 652	-778	13 688	2.48	66.7	10.2	27.6
Crawford	11.4	8.2	6.9	50.1	38 242	39 134	2.3	0.1	3 217	2 500	-679	15 065	2.49	57.9	8.4	32.5
Decatur	17.3	12.7	15.3	49.3	3 472	2 961	-14.7	-4.4	209	285	-62	1 473	1.91	52.3	6.4	42.4
Dickinson	14.2	9.5	9.6	50.0	19 344	19 754	2.1	-3.5	1 411	1 420	-670	7 822	2.45	68.4	7.9	27.4
Doniphan	14.5	10.1	8.2	50.0	8 249	7 945	-3.7	-3.5	477	455	-282	3 109	2.32	69.0	10.0	26.3
Douglas	10.0	6.7	4.5	50.1	99 962	110 826	10.9	7.8	7 675	4 004	4 926	43 729	2.43	54.4	8.3	30.9
Edwards	16.6	10.6	9.8	49.4	3 449	3 037	-11.9	-3.3	222	205	-103	1 274	2.27	65.7	6.8	30.9
Elk	16.9	14.9	14.2	50.5	3 261	2 882	-11.6	-11.6	176	254	-266	1 256	2.10	61.9	7.2	34.5
Ellis	12.0	7.5	7.0	49.7	27 507	28 452	3.4	1.5	2 274	1 552	-274	11 847	2.35	54.9	8.0	33.6
Ellsworth	14.7	10.5	9.7	43.3	6 525	6 497	-0.4	-2.6	367	483	-42	2 585	2.08	62.0	8.3	33.7
Finney	10.7	6.0	4.3	49.0	40 523	36 776	-9.2	-0.1	4 374	1 286	-3 109	12 600	2.90	72.9	13.2	23.1
Ford	10.6	5.9	5.1	48.2	32 458	33 848	4.3	0.4	4 163	1 481	-2 647	11 205	3.04	73.7	13.0	22.2
Franklin	14.1	9.3	6.7	50.1	24 784	25 996	4.9	-1.7	1 996	1 578	-861	9 830	2.56	70.5	8.5	24.8
Geary	6.0	4.6	3.6	46.9	27 947	34 362	23.0	3.6	6 503	1 279	-4 211	12 723	2.83	69.3	10.3	24.6
Gove	15.3	11.0	12.6	49.0	3 068	2 695	-12.2	-3.9	215	242	-72	1 190	2.25	70.3	5.4	27.1
Graham	17.7	10.9	14.1	50.4	2 946	2 597	-11.8	-1.3	158	191	2	1 201	2.12	62.5	6.8	34.1
Grant	11.9	7.0	5.2	49.5	7 909	7 829	-1.0	-2.3	768	299	-666	2 707	2.86	75.6	9.8	17.5
Gray	12.7	8.4	6.9	49.7	5 904	6 006	1.7	0.5	543	276	-257	2 150	2.78	76.4	6.9	20.4
Greeley	15.4	8.6	12.5	52.1	1 534	1 247	-18.7	3.9	119	96	20	487	2.46	72.5	4.7	24.2
Greenwood	17.3	13.3	11.1	49.8	7 673	6 689	-12.8	-8.0	387	555	-342	2 824	2.23	63.3	8.7	33.9
Hamilton	12.1	7.2	5.3	49.0	2 670	2 690	0.7	-5.7	265	153	-265	998	2.59	71.9	8.7	23.1
Harper	15.2	10.7	11.3	50.0	6 536	6 034	-7.7	-5.8	471	559	-246	2 433	2.34	62.5	6.4	32.5
Harvey	13.3	9.2	9.4	50.8	32 869	34 684	5.5	0.7	2 712	2 364	-157	13 581	2.47	68.9	7.9	27.0
Haskell	13.5	7.2	5.7	50.2	4 307	4 256	-1.2	-5.9	314	145	-437	1 395	2.93	76.5	8.6	20.7
Hodgeman	16.8	10.0	14.3	50.7	2 085	1 916	-8.1	-2.4	150	125	-93	811	2.36	71.0	5.1	26.8
Jackson	13.8	10.8	7.6	50.2	12 657	13 462	6.4	-1.3	1 026	824	-385	5 281	2.51	72.3	9.5	23.1
Jefferson	15.9	10.5	7.6	49.1	18 426	19 124	3.8	-1.2	1 158	1 097	-261	7 542	2.47	71.7	6.6	24.8
Jewell	17.9	14.1	14.7	48.7	3 791	3 077	-18.8	-5.7	178	258	-102	1 433	2.10	64.2	5.7	32.9
Johnson	12.5	8.1	5.5	51.0	451 086	544 179	20.6	7.4	46 103	22 646	16 229	219 735	2.56	68.1	9.1	26.4
Kearny	11.6	8.2	6.8	49.9	4 531	3 977	-12.2	-1.5	381	231	-214	1 379	2.81	77.8	6.8	19.2
Kingman	15.8	11.2	11.5	50.1	8 673	7 858	-9.4	-5.0	480	630	-246	3 006	2.54	68.4	8.3	28.1
Kiowa	14.5	10.2	10.2	50.5	3 278	2 553	-22.1	-2.7	198	167	-106	1 066	2.21	64.0	6.3	30.6
Labette	14.4	10.8	8.2	50.5	22 835	21 607	-5.4	-5.4	1 663	1 646	-1 175	8 413	2.44	58.6	10.7	28.0
Lane	15.4	11.6	11.4	50.7	2 155	1 750	-18.8	-6.5	131	146	-109	805	2.07	56.8	6.6	35.0
Leavenworth	12.8	8.2	5.3	46.7	68 691	76 227	11.0	5.2	6 038	3 522	1 531	26 747	2.70	71.5	10.5	24.7
Lincoln	17.2	11.6	10.6	49.9	3 578	3 241	-9.4	-5.2	210	224	-152	1 335	2.31	60.8	9.2	33.7
Linn	15.0	12.5	8.5	50.0	9 570	9 656	0.9	-1.0	636	712	6	4 182	2.26	67.8	7.5	30.1
Logan	15.3	9.6	10.2	49.2	3 046	2 756	-9.5	2.7	217	217	75	1 243	2.21	60.4	7.2	33.3
Lyon	12.3	7.9	6.4	51.3	35 935	33 690	-6.2	-0.5	2 595	1 734	-1 085	13 272	2.43	61.2	10.5	30.8
McPherson	14.4	10.0	10.0	51.0	29 554	29 180	-1.3	-1.3	2 093	2 331	-196	11 791	2.37	67.0	6.4	28.4
Marion	15.2	11.3	11.2	50.2	13 361	12 660	-5.2	-4.3	740	982	-292	4 808	2.40	68.4	6.8	28.8
Marshall	16.2	10.4	11.3	50.4	10 965	10 117	-7.7	-2.8	741	779	-235	4 322	2.27	66.8	6.6	29.2
Meade	13.4	8.7	10.1	49.6	4 631	4 575	-1.2	-7.8	349	276	-435	1 694	2.51	75.7	7.5	22.7
Miami	14.4	9.1	7.0	50.4	28 351	32 783	15.6	0.6	2 339	1 658	-510	12 560	2.55	70.2	10.3	25.5
Mitchell	14.0	11.4	11.9	49.0	6 932	6 373	-8.1	-2.0	502	578	-66	2 687	2.25	63.8	4.5	34.1
Montgomery	14.1	10.3	8.7	50.7	36 252	35 471	-2.2	-7.7	2 800	2 640	-2 921	13 435	2.47	64.3	11.0	31.4
Morris	16.1	12.5	12.0	50.2	6 104	5 923	-3.0	-5.9	384	454	-254	2 406	2.36	68.2	7.4	27.9
Morton	13.5	9.4	10.0	49.8	3 496	3 233	-7.5	-11.9	253	217	-422	1 189	2.53	69.6	10.4	26.1
Nemaha	13.4	8.8	11.4	49.3	10 717	10 178	-5.0	0.6	901	773	-85	4 239	2.32	66.1	5.3	29.7

1. No spouse present.

Table B. States and Counties — **Population, Vital Statistics, Health, and Crime**

STATE County	Persons in group quarters, 2016 (32)	Daytime population, 2011–2015 Number (33)	Employment/residence ratio (34)	Births, 2016 Total (35)	Rate[1] (36)	Deaths, 2016 Number (37)	Rate[1] (38)	Persons under 65 with no health insurance, 2015 Number (39)	Percent (40)	Medicare, 2015 Total Beneficiaries (41)	Enrolled in Original Medicare (42)	Enrolled in Medicare Advantage (43)	Serious crimes known to police,[2] 2014 Total Number (44)	Rate[3] (45)
KANSAS	79 042	2 905 191	1.01	38 702	13.3	25 128	8.6	253 816	10.5	473 699	402 096	71 603	89 554	3 084
Allen	382	13 835	1.13	152	12.0	171	13.4	924	9.3	2 835	2 589	246	296	2 265
Anderson	103	6 704	0.66	96	12.3	99	12.6	693	11.4	1 740	1 628	112	144	1 834
Atchison	1 382	16 339	0.96	199	12.1	171	10.4	1 110	8.9	3 026	2 799	227	493	2 948
Barber	40	4 704	0.97	56	11.9	51	10.9	415	10.8	1 024	984	40	100	2 010
Barton	672	27 193	0.98	339	12.7	307	11.5	2 799	12.8	5 175	5 069	106	1 298	4 724
Bourbon	410	14 685	0.98	220	15.1	156	10.7	1 232	10.6	3 070	2 723	347	539	3 647
Brown	116	10 290	1.09	118	12.2	122	12.6	885	11.3	2 015	1 969	46	225	2 249
Butler	2 307	55 630	0.66	743	11.1	630	9.4	4 780	8.6	10 201	8 589	1 612	1 614	2 479
Chase	145	2 369	0.70	32	12.0	13	4.9	191	9.9	562	546	16	11	410
Chautauqua	79	3 113	0.73	30	8.9	42	12.4	394	15.7	859	828	31	20	567
Cherokee	202	18 308	0.72	238	11.8	265	13.1	1 883	11.3	4 241	3 807	434	650	3 248
Cheyenne	49	2 581	0.92	31	11.6	43	16.2	264	13.6	731	694	37	40	1 488
Clark	57	1 948	0.81	16	7.7	18	8.7	205	12.5	374	360	14	42	1 915
Clay	140	8 095	0.92	108	13.3	112	13.8	498	7.7	1 868	1 759	109	162	1 935
Cloud	498	9 251	0.98	103	11.3	139	15.2	695	10.0	2 186	2 121	65	301	3 258
Coffey	130	9 074	1.15	88	10.4	80	9.5	518	7.7	1 774	1 689	85	89	1 140
Comanche	65	1 979	0.97	18	9.7	15	8.1	176	13.0	478	464	14	NA	NA
Cowley	2 006	34 729	0.91	450	12.6	408	11.4	3 097	11.1	6 522	6 121	401	1 188	3 352
Crawford	1 775	39 714	1.02	550	14.0	365	9.3	3 470	10.9	7 356	6 881	475	1 716	4 400
Decatur	81	2 687	0.84	37	13.1	37	13.1	232	11.0	804	755	49	10	342
Dickinson	307	17 959	0.83	220	11.5	209	11.0	1 487	9.6	3 768	3 653	115	357	1 824
Doniphan	427	6 885	0.74	61	8.0	70	9.1	583	9.7	1 561	1 520	41	144	1 839
Douglas	8 800	108 351	0.89	1 224	10.2	655	5.5	9 585	9.8	15 210	13 143	2 067	2 521	2 190
Edwards	35	2 713	0.81	34	11.6	25	8.5	317	13.5	634	611	23	20	685
Elk	40	2 459	0.79	29	11.4	35	13.7	248	13.5	781	751	30	13	499
Ellis	1 033	29 611	1.04	325	11.2	255	8.8	2 193	9.1	4 792	4 664	128	659	2 255
Ellsworth	979	6 372	0.99	54	8.5	71	11.2	376	8.9	1 277	1 246	31	103	1 748
Finney	547	37 337	1.01	684	18.6	208	5.7	5 721	17.5	4 107	3 948	159	1 222	3 290
Ford	708	35 630	1.06	637	18.8	231	6.8	5 683	18.9	4 264	4 126	138	1 035	2 955
Franklin	478	23 780	0.84	310	12.1	255	10.0	1 705	8.1	4 649	4 207	442	698	2 718
Geary	847	43 368	1.38	1 068	30.0	214	6.0	2 828	8.6	3 422	3 082	340	815	2 147
Gove	56	2 884	1.11	39	15.1	38	14.7	223	11.1	665	645	20	24	860
Graham	40	2 563	0.98	25	9.8	34	13.3	219	11.3	660	628	32	31	1 197
Grant	79	7 737	0.98	126	16.5	28	3.7	1 214	18.0	975	960	15	147	1 842
Gray	78	5 724	0.89	79	13.1	44	7.3	807	15.5	992	964	28	92	1 532
Greeley	26	1 301	1.13	16	12.3	12	9.3	155	14.7	D	280	D	6	462
Greenwood	90	5 659	0.74	66	10.7	72	11.7	485	10.4	1 708	1 658	50	127	1 996
Hamilton	0	2 582	1.00	38	15.0	15	5.9	485	22.7	D	379	D	10	386
Harper	129	6 015	1.06	82	14.4	97	17.1	571	12.6	1 300	1 274	26	132	2 984
Harvey	1 314	33 686	0.93	423	12.1	337	9.7	2 855	10.3	7 019	5 697	1 322	852	2 452
Haskell	33	4 157	1.01	48	12.0	17	4.2	672	19.0	D	506	D	63	1 535
Hodgeman	14	1 783	0.84	25	13.4	30	16.0	172	12.0	D	371	D	24	1 223
Jackson	133	11 274	0.67	164	12.3	135	10.2	1 055	9.7	2 623	2 395	228	175	1 380
Jefferson	235	14 070	0.47	175	9.3	150	7.9	1 327	8.6	3 609	3 194	415	367	1 958
Jewell	27	2 723	0.78	33	11.4	33	11.4	251	11.9	860	814	46	NA	NA
Johnson	5 159	587 205	1.07	7 336	12.6	3 890	6.7	30 651	6.1	78 355	54 272	24 083	9 318	1 689
Kearny	81	3 646	0.83	59	15.1	25	6.4	527	15.7	533	522	11	71	1 817
Kingman	190	7 046	0.79	72	9.6	108	14.5	591	10.0	1 597	1 560	37	112	1 521
Kiowa	149	2 689	1.12	27	10.9	26	10.5	211	10.9	526	511	15	28	1 113
Labette	480	21 677	1.07	254	12.4	234	11.4	1 706	10.2	4 535	4 165	370	577	2 778
Lane	3	1 655	0.98	21	12.8	18	11.0	168	13.1	427	411	16	35	2 038
Leavenworth	6 535	70 924	0.79	984	12.3	592	7.4	4 093	6.5	10 540	8 940	1 600	2 008	2 554
Lincoln	50	2 869	0.81	37	12.0	35	11.4	268	11.1	703	686	17	55	1 759
Linn	63	8 298	0.69	112	11.7	117	12.2	861	11.5	2 203	1 678	525	74	866
Logan	41	2 797	1.00	37	13.7	23	8.1	261	11.5	626	588	38	41	1 461
Lyon	1 447	33 093	0.98	403	12.0	266	7.9	3 707	13.5	5 657	5 318	339	536	1 644
McPherson	926	30 395	1.07	332	11.5	364	12.6	1 844	8.1	5 928	5 428	500	944	3 356
Marion	723	10 923	0.76	124	10.2	142	11.7	961	10.8	2 812	2 738	74	171	1 411
Marshall	164	10 601	1.12	116	11.8	114	11.6	688	8.9	2 357	2 211	146	153	1 533
Meade	119	4 232	0.93	52	12.3	38	9.0	466	13.4	799	776	23	45	1 051
Miami	644	25 676	0.55	407	12.3	277	8.4	1 920	7.1	4 752	3 599	1 153	638	1 943
Mitchell	246	7 103	1.26	92	14.7	98	15.7	404	8.6	1 492	1 430	62	82	1 383
Montgomery	1 114	36 008	1.13	420	12.8	365	11.4	3 086	11.8	8 060	7 652	408	NA	NA
Morris	66	5 166	0.79	60	10.8	77	13.8	435	10.2	1 558	1 505	53	97	1 701
Morton	83	3 199	1.07	38	13.3	29	10.2	334	13.8	552	538	14	41	1 313
Nemaha	259	10 607	1.09	158	15.4	86	8.4	634	7.8	2 115	2 065	50	92	905

1. Per 1,000 estimated resident population.   2. Data for serious crimes have not been adjusted for underreporting; this may affect comparability between geographic areas and over time.
3. Per 100,000 population estimated by the FBI.

Table B. States and Counties — Crime, Education, Money Income, and Poverty

STATE County	Serious crimes known to police, 2014 (cont.)[1] Rate[2] Violent	Property	Education — School enrollment and attainment, 2011–2015 — Enrollment[3] Total	Percent private	High school graduate or less	Bachelor's degree or more	Local government expenditures,[5] 2013–2014 Total current spending (mil dol)	Current spending per student (dollars)	Money income, 2011–2015 Per capita income[6] (dollars)	Median income (dollars)	Households Percent with income of less than $50,000	with income of $200,000 or more	Income and poverty, 2015 Median household income (dollars)	Percent below poverty level All persons	Children under 18 years	Children 5 to 17 years in families
	46	47	48	49	50	51	52	53	54	55	56	57	58	59	60	61
KANSAS	349	2 735	795 462	13.5	36.8	31.0	4 673.3	9 414	27 706	52 205	47.7	3.7	53 802	12.9	16.9	15.3
Allen	191	2 073	3 062	5.7	42.8	18.2	27.3	11 201	20 671	38 698	60.9	1.1	41 604	18.9	26.0	23.4
Anderson	293	1 541	1 721	11.6	48.5	16.5	13.7	10 146	21 226	40 696	59.3	0.4	47 267	14.0	19.9	18.2
Atchison	287	2 661	4 938	35.4	48.2	19.9	24.5	10 704	21 677	43 581	56.2	1.0	46 110	16.6	21.5	19.9
Barber	342	1 668	895	9.3	45.0	20.2	8.6	11 350	28 174	51 811	48.2	3.4	54 176	11.1	17.3	16.4
Barton	360	4 364	6 595	8.9	47.8	16.9	42.4	9 452	24 338	44 013	54.7	1.3	50 558	14.4	20.1	18.4
Bourbon	575	3 072	3 702	9.2	41.8	22.1	22.8	9 525	20 783	38 280	61.9	1.5	39 609	18.2	26.5	23.9
Brown	240	2 009	2 252	8.3	47.1	19.8	17.1	11 767	22 600	43 724	56.9	1.7	46 884	14.9	23.0	20.9
Butler	184	2 295	19 394	10.4	33.9	28.0	137.2	6 831	27 647	58 897	41.3	3.2	61 473	10.6	12.8	10.9
Chase	149	261	599	11.5	43.4	24.3	4.3	11 224	23 459	38 707	59.8	1.4	48 911	12.7	16.5	14.5
Chautauqua	57	510	663	11.0	50.0	17.5	6.1	11 403	23 584	37 993	61.5	2.2	42 324	16.8	25.6	23.9
Cherokee	305	2 943	5 049	6.0	47.6	17.4	41.2	11 013	19 809	41 388	58.0	0.6	39 842	18.0	27.8	25.3
Cheyenne	223	1 264	491	3.5	38.6	22.3	5.3	12 410	26 626	44 500	54.8	0.7	44 111	12.3	19.2	17.0
Clark	274	1 642	531	4.0	34.2	29.7	5.9	12 462	25 106	42 589	58.3	2.3	50 392	12.0	15.6	13.8
Clay	191	1 743	1 957	10.1	37.4	23.7	13.9	9 723	26 807	52 066	47.1	3.0	51 351	11.1	16.9	15.7
Cloud	465	2 793	2 359	9.6	43.1	17.5	19.5	11 751	22 441	39 282	62.2	1.3	42 730	12.8	18.1	16.0
Coffey	38	1 102	1 944	7.5	44.0	21.0	17.9	11 214	29 382	57 433	43.3	2.8	57 160	9.9	12.4	11.0
Comanche	NA	NA	473	4.2	36.7	24.0	4.3	11 786	23 661	45 288	54.1	1.3	43 809	11.4	15.1	13.6
Cowley	302	3 050	9 477	12.5	40.3	19.2	61.7	10 063	21 950	43 860	55.7	1.7	47 851	15.3	21.4	18.9
Crawford	295	4 105	12 863	12.3	38.2	28.6	64.2	10 421	20 346	36 534	62.2	1.6	38 139	19.1	24.5	22.0
Decatur	68	273	506	15.2	47.1	26.6	4.5	12 297	29 891	40 657	62.3	3.7	43 919	12.3	19.6	18.6
Dickinson	143	1 681	4 628	10.2	46.5	20.0	36.2	10 181	24 430	49 096	50.9	2.3	47 570	12.2	16.1	15.2
Doniphan	141	1 699	2 198	9.5	48.6	16.5	16.8	11 486	23 471	47 209	52.2	1.6	47 000	13.2	19.3	17.3
Douglas	203	1 986	44 198	10.1	25.1	49.1	143.5	9 548	27 611	50 939	49.0	3.8	52 447	19.4	13.2	11.7
Edwards	171	514	650	2.9	48.4	18.7	6.1	12 562	25 584	47 303	53.8	1.7	46 380	10.6	14.0	12.6
Elk	0	499	496	6.3	46.3	17.4	6.8	13 840	21 764	36 458	61.2	0.5	39 147	17.6	30.7	27.0
Ellis	263	1 991	9 459	9.2	34.3	32.3	38.5	10 136	26 098	45 579	53.9	2.7	49 192	12.0	12.2	11.7
Ellsworth	170	1 578	1 155	8.6	42.6	21.2	13.8	11 524	24 102	47 736	51.3	2.2	49 986	10.6	13.1	11.8
Finney	506	2 783	10 666	5.4	51.2	18.6	88.6	10 253	22 145	49 227	51.0	2.8	53 245	14.6	20.5	18.3
Ford	400	2 555	9 369	5.8	53.6	17.9	75.0	9 923	20 619	50 777	48.5	2.4	47 915	13.2	18.9	16.8
Franklin	280	2 438	6 573	15.6	43.6	21.2	47.7	10 565	24 567	51 081	48.6	1.7	51 484	11.7	17.3	15.2
Geary	414	1 733	10 632	9.3	37.4	20.4	81.7	9 937	21 450	43 992	59.4	1.5	45 590	11.9	20.1	22.5
Gove	107	752	569	6.7	44.6	21.4	7.0	13 539	25 484	46 364	53.8	2.2	46 580	9.9	14.9	13.6
Graham	116	1 081	476	5.7	39.4	26.5	4.4	10 717	28 233	43 826	55.9	2.2	45 018	12.2	16.9	15.3
Grant	263	1 579	1 998	7.0	57.3	18.2	15.6	8 691	25 195	55 432	43.6	3.1	59 218	10.2	15.8	14.2
Gray	216	1 315	1 546	11.8	49.4	19.1	16.0	11 830	26 131	61 000	37.1	2.7	64 284	8.3	11.0	9.3
Greeley	154	308	292	7.9	42.2	25.5	2.9	11 794	25 994	47 750	52.8	1.6	44 667	11.4	18.4	17.7
Greenwood	141	1 854	1 382	2.6	50.3	16.5	12.2	11 829	23 335	38 838	61.9	1.4	41 168	15.8	24.6	21.4
Hamilton	155	232	587	5.8	55.0	13.3	5.8	11 244	22 250	45 114	57.0	1.4	50 056	13.1	19.8	17.7
Harper	430	2 555	1 227	6.2	48.0	19.7	11.9	11 087	24 640	43 973	54.1	3.4	46 869	13.7	19.6	18.9
Harvey	391	2 061	9 441	19.4	39.7	26.5	57.3	9 327	24 453	51 327	49.0	1.3	55 470	9.4	13.5	12.3
Haskell	244	1 291	1 057	12.3	50.2	17.7	9.9	12 372	24 362	56 484	42.9	3.3	59 356	11.2	16.0	13.8
Hodgeman	102	1 121	351	5.1	33.3	23.7	3.7	12 059	31 547	54 856	46.2	4.2	54 513	9.6	12.2	11.8
Jackson	189	1 190	3 259	7.5	46.6	18.7	25.6	9 922	25 038	54 077	46.6	1.6	51 662	11.3	14.2	12.8
Jefferson	171	1 787	4 438	9.1	47.9	19.5	41.3	10 988	26 227	57 236	39.7	0.5	59 080	9.1	13.9	12.1
Jewell	NA	NA	571	5.8	46.0	15.4	3.8	12 494	23 002	40 553	63.0	1.4	43 201	13.5	21.6	19.4
Johnson	136	1 553	155 464	19.6	19.4	52.8	625.4	6 608	40 331	76 113	31.3	9.0	83 007	5.5	6.5	5.6
Kearny	281	1 535	1 035	3.5	45.8	17.2	10.9	11 414	23 884	50 506	49.4	3.7	59 134	11.5	16.6	15.3
Kingman	177	1 345	1 764	12.7	44.3	20.5	13.1	11 443	24 998	50 844	49.1	1.5	52 907	11.5	16.9	15.3
Kiowa	239	875	629	26.4	35.4	27.3	7.1	11 901	24 116	43 963	55.4	1.5	46 381	12.6	16.8	15.9
Labette	385	2 393	4 892	8.6	44.4	16.6	40.2	10 054	21 006	41 439	58.7	1.3	42 323	18.2	27.3	23.8
Lane	175	1 864	362	0.0	36.9	21.4	4.4	12 594	31 458	56 507	40.9	2.7	57 388	9.6	14.8	13.6
Leavenworth	440	2 114	21 771	16.1	39.5	29.0	120.4	9 083	27 138	63 726	39.8	3.4	61 465	10.7	13.1	11.8
Lincoln	32	1 727	662	11.5	38.2	20.3	7.5	11 534	24 953	44 276	53.7	1.4	42 277	12.5	19.5	17.0
Linn	129	737	2 111	2.5	49.0	15.0	21.2	10 894	26 519	46 964	53.1	1.5	46 065	14.0	21.2	17.7
Logan	107	1 354	635	14.0	43.2	18.2	6.2	11 679	28 974	46 875	52.9	3.3	48 399	9.4	13.1	11.9
Lyon	141	1 503	10 709	5.8	45.5	25.6	57.5	10 276	20 943	40 021	61.1	1.6	39 562	17.5	18.9	17.0
McPherson	146	3 210	7 082	17.5	38.2	27.4	49.4	10 133	28 396	56 128	43.6	2.5	61 356	7.6	10.0	8.3
Marion	116	1 296	2 929	19.2	47.8	22.6	23.3	11 124	23 642	45 927	53.6	1.3	51 196	10.9	14.4	12.7
Marshall	120	1 413	2 156	14.6	50.7	16.6	19.6	10 609	26 313	45 374	54.5	2.6	49 270	10.7	14.1	13.2
Meade	70	981	1 048	5.8	45.4	22.2	7.2	11 800	23 446	52 250	44.7	1.3	56 325	9.5	12.3	10.2
Miami	167	1 775	8 875	10.9	38.1	23.3	46.8	9 295	29 413	60 966	40.4	3.5	62 375	8.8	11.4	9.9
Mitchell	304	1 080	1 556	19.5	39.0	25.7	13.6	11 815	27 555	48 217	51.6	3.5	48 310	10.5	14.8	14.0
Montgomery	NA	NA	8 469	10.4	43.3	17.1	56.0	9 592	20 864	41 083	61.0	1.1	43 289	19.9	27.6	24.5
Morris	140	1 561	1 160	6.6	47.0	17.6	12.0	11 057	23 928	47 089	55.0	1.2	49 720	10.8	16.9	16.1
Morton	352	961	705	7.0	46.9	13.9	12.2	8 521	22 297	46 028	53.2	1.9	53 443	10.3	15.3	13.4
Nemaha	118	787	2 340	11.2	51.3	22.6	19.8	10 877	26 041	48 653	51.1	1.8	54 486	8.8	10.0	9.4

1. Data for serious crimes have not been adjusted for underreporting; this may affect comparability between geographic areas and over time.   2. Per 100,000 population estimated by the FBI.
3. All persons 3 years old and over enrolled in nursery school through college.   4. Persons 25 years old and over.   5. Elementary and secondary education expenditures.
6. Based on population estimated by the American Community Survey, 2011–2015.

Table B. States and Counties — Personal Income

STATE County	Personal income, 2015										Earnings, 2015		
	Total (mil dol)	Percent change, 2014–2015	Per capita[1] Dollars	Per capita[1] Rank	Wages and salaries (mil dol)	Supplements to wages and salaries; employer contributions (mil dol) Pension and insurance	Supplements to wages and salaries; employer contributions (mil dol) Government social insurance	Proprietors' income (mil dol)	Dividends, interest, and rent (mil dol)	Personal transfer receipts (mil dol)	Total (mil dol)	Contributions for government social insurance (mil dol) From employee and self-employed	Contributions for government social insurance (mil dol) From employer
	62	63	64	65	66	67	68	69	70	71	72	73	74
KANSAS	137 316	2.0	47 241	X	66 666	11 201	5 264	16 159	26 155	21 256	99 290	5 664	5 264
Allen..............................	485	0.0	38 100	1 052	204	45	17	54	78	129	319	19	17
Anderson.......................	327	4.4	41 831	858	71	15	6	81	40	74	174	10	6
Atchison........................	553	-1.4	33 694	2 014	236	43	20	23	99	135	321	21	20
Barber...........................	195	-10.7	40 437	571	64	14	5	28	52	43	111	7	5
Barton	1 306	-5.6	48 193	367	501	90	39	286	227	234	916	50	39
Bourbon........................	556	0.9	37 777	1 921	247	46	21	75	74	134	389	24	21
Brown...........................	396	-4.5	40 502	879	194	39	15	25	75	94	273	17	15
Butler...........................	2 823	3.8	42 301	824	762	168	61	254	406	459	1 244	73	61
Chase...........................	108	-10.5	40 161	37	25	6	2	15	26	22	48	3	2
Chautauqua	150	-3.2	44 173	399	26	6	2	20	27	37	55	3	2
Cherokee......................	701	0.8	34 132	1 497	244	48	20	67	93	194	379	24	20
Cheyenne......................	118	-0.7	44 191	930	31	6	2	31	22	27	71	3	2
Clark.............................	114	-1.2	54 399	343	28	7	2	33	21	20	70	3	2
Clay..............................	386	-0.7	46 249	341	106	23	8	30	73	75	167	10	8
Cloud............................	315	-1.0	34 221	1 833	115	24	9	28	60	87	175	11	9
Coffey...........................	426	-5.4	50 865	274	264	57	20	68	55	81	408	23	20
Comanche.....................	78	14.1	42 487	2 410	21	5	2	15	17	19	43	2	2
Cowley	1 338	4.2	37 381	1 369	561	111	45	196	195	318	913	55	45
Crawford........................	1 344	0.4	34 260	2 515	627	132	51	85	248	335	896	55	51
Decatur.........................	145	6.1	49 467	506	29	6	2	47	28	29	85	3	2
Dickinson......................	834	2.7	43 220	967	233	52	20	44	143	164	349	22	20
Doniphan.......................	262	-0.9	33 621	1 827	88	20	7	10	43	65	126	8	7
Douglas........................	4 567	6.3	38 686	1 649	1 975	416	153	304	849	658	2 848	163	153
Edwards........................	158	9.6	53 066	509	51	8	4	41	23	26	105	5	4
Elk.................................	116	-2.0	44 598	1 201	20	5	2	25	19	31	52	3	2
Ellis..............................	1 331	-0.8	45 843	585	626	121	48	252	218	203	1 047	57	48
Ellsworth	243	-9.2	38 241	959	88	20	7	30	44	53	146	8	7
Finney	1 493	0.1	40 227	1 287	734	129	56	270	210	213	1 189	61	56
Ford..............................	1 163	1.2	33 663	2 227	683	122	51	108	163	188	964	54	51
Franklin.........................	970	3.5	37 872	1 876	393	64	31	88	135	213	576	36	31
Geary............................	1 588	3.5	42 875	809	1 637	479	165	34	335	229	2 314	94	165
Gove.............................	183	21.9	69 469	1 152	43	9	3	97	24	24	153	7	3
Graham.........................	122	-3.2	46 910	166	37	8	3	27	21	29	74	4	3
Grant............................	367	-5.8	47 396	670	162	30	12	124	40	42	328	13	12
Gray..............................	445	-3.7	72 611	58	120	22	9	219	44	35	370	10	9
Greeley	57	-16.1	43 147	427	26	5	2	8	11	11	40	2	2
Greenwood	260	-3.4	41 643	1 128	58	13	5	38	45	68	113	7	5
Hamilton........................	149	-21.3	60 381	86	40	7	3	74	16	16	125	3	3
Harper...........................	256	0.0	44 051	774	94	21	7	50	41	54	172	10	7
Harvey...........................	1 346	3.8	38 369	764	575	100	49	126	191	287	850	54	49
Haskell..........................	253	-21.1	62 294	103	75	13	5	102	39	24	196	5	5
Hodgeman	86	-6.9	45 643	904	20	5	1	21	17	15	47	2	1
Jackson.........................	500	0.3	37 478	1 223	146	31	11	19	79	111	206	15	11
Jefferson.......................	755	2.2	39 884	1 394	148	29	12	41	104	142	230	16	12
Jewell............................	128	-3.2	43 213	577	26	7	2	27	29	30	61	3	2
Johnson.........................	37 739	6.6	65 050	110	19 945	2 468	1 510	3 716	7 352	3 364	27 638	1 609	1 510
Kearny...........................	218	-2.4	55 054	306	57	12	4	84	28	26	157	4	4
Kingman.........................	314	3.8	40 881	953	95	18	8	33	68	67	154	10	8
Kiowa............................	90	-3.1	34 937	1 324	48	9	4	3	20	22	63	4	4
Labette..........................	837	1.4	40 251	1 194	370	79	30	57	118	233	536	34	30
Lane..............................	145	3.9	86 725	51	28	6	2	77	20	17	113	2	2
Leavenworth	3 131	5.1	39 477	1 345	1 393	350	128	97	631	544	1 967	105	128
Lincoln..........................	113	-9.3	36 267	1 172	32	8	2	7	23	30	49	3	2
Linn..............................	320	3.7	33 533	2 183	99	24	8	12	49	89	142	10	8
Logan............................	132	-4.7	46 890	641	47	12	3	21	27	25	83	4	3
Lyon..............................	1 118	3.8	33 543	2 710	541	115	43	65	189	249	764	47	43
McPherson.....................	1 419	3.0	49 015	603	732	141	57	214	216	240	1 145	65	57
Marion...........................	460	3.8	37 990	1 577	121	26	10	62	69	108	218	14	10
Marshall........................	441	3.5	44 372	560	201	36	18	54	84	91	309	19	18
Meade...........................	268	1.9	61 794	325	68	14	5	93	43	31	180	6	5
Miami............................	1 412	3.2	43 387	1 177	320	59	26	86	217	240	491	32	26
Mitchell.........................	325	1.3	51 775	793	123	26	9	96	48	60	254	13	9
Montgomery	1 258	-1.9	37 751	1 562	606	120	52	116	181	326	895	55	52
Morris...........................	244	0.0	43 169	1 086	52	11	5	39	45	53	107	6	5
Morton...........................	138	3.1	45 757	1 238	47	10	3	36	21	23	96	4	3
Nemaha.........................	491	-7.0	48 019	242	210	38	16	61	121	79	325	18	16

1. Based on the resident population estimated as of July 1 of the year shown.

Table B. States and Counties — **Earnings, Social Security, and Housing**

STATE County	Earnings, 2015 (cont.) Percent by selected industries									Social Security beneficiaries, December 2015		Housing units, 2016		
	Farm	Mining	Construction	Manu-facturing	Information: professional, scientific, technical services	Retail trade	Finance, insur-ance, real estate and leasing	Health care and social assistance	Govern-ment	Number	Rate[1]	Supple-mental Security Income recipients, December 2015	Total	Percent change, 2010–2016
	75	76	77	78	79	80	81	82	83	84	85	86	87	88
KANSAS..............	2.5	2.3	5.5	13.8	9.1	5.5	8.6	10.6	17.5	528 174	182	48 360	1 259 864	2.2
Allen	3.2	D	3.2	33.5	2.3	5.8	3.9	6.7	22.5	3 275	257	349	6 262	0.6
Anderson..............	11.9	2.3	7.6	26.1	D	7.9	3.7	D	14.6	1 965	251	121	3 705	-0.4
Atchison................	0.5	D	6.4	26.0	3.7	6.2	5.1	D	14.1	3 300	201	318	6 923	-1.0
Barber...................	-5.0	20.3	7.5	13.2	D	7.8	D	D	26.1	1 210	251	65	2 737	-1.0
Barton..................	6.1	20.7	7.6	6.5	3.1	7.1	7.9	D	12.6	5 815	215	491	12 634	-0.5
Bourbon................	0.8	0.5	4.9	17.8	4.0	4.7	9.3	14.4	13.8	3 540	240	384	7 084	-1.2
Brown	1.2	D	3.8	20.1	4.2	7.8	8.4	15.2	25.1	2 350	241	213	4 736	-0.9
Butler....................	4.8	3.0	11.7	14.5	D	5.8	4.8	12.1	22.5	12 235	184	779	26 568	2.0
Chase...................	23.9	D	4.8	6.8	D	2.1	D	D	21.1	610	228	41	1 494	-0.6
Chautauqua..........	18.3	D	4.7	6.1	D	4.3	D	11.5	19.9	1 095	323	111	2 133	-0.8
Cherokee..............	4.5	D	11.8	26.3	2.4	4.6	2.9	12.7	17.8	5 050	246	621	9 793	-1.0
Cheyenne..............	31.9	D	2.7	8.0	D	2.1	D	12.9	13.7	775	288	24	1 496	-1.4
Clark	43.4	D	D	D	D	2.7	D	D	31.0	495	237	26	1 128	-0.6
Clay	10.0	D	6.0	12.6	3.2	6.6	4.2	D	25.3	2 015	242	110	4 053	0.3
Cloud	6.2	D	5.7	9.9	6.2	8.1	4.1	D	20.7	2 360	256	173	4 606	-1.1
Coffey	2.4	7.3	4.9	2.5	D	2.9	D	D	14.4	2 170	260	150	4 025	1.6
Comanche............	17.5	4.2	3.1	6.2	D	8.1	D	D	26.2	485	264	31	1 032	-1.1
Cowley..................	2.0	2.1	4.1	37.9	2.4	5.1	3.8	D	19.0	7 840	219	765	16 030	0.0
Crawford..............	-0.2	0.3	3.9	14.8	4.2	9.1	4.4	13.3	27.1	7 640	195	1 034	17 983	1.0
Decatur.................	45.0	D	D	D	D	4.9	D	9.3	11.5	860	294	47	1 800	-1.0
Dickinson..............	4.2	D	5.9	23.6	3.7	5.8	5.2	D	23.8	4 325	224	291	9 099	1.4
Doniphan..............	0.4	D	6.3	19.2	D	3.1	4.7	6.0	31.2	1 690	218	110	3 541	-1.0
Douglas................	0.5	0.4	4.7	8.5	10.2	6.5	6.0	7.3	35.0	16 125	137	1 360	49 286	5.5
Edwards	31.2	D	D	D	D	2.3	3.5	7.1	10.5	670	226	42	1 622	-0.9
Elk	23.5	19.0	8.9	D	D	2.6	D	D	25.1	910	350	55	1 750	-0.6
Ellis	1.6	13.4	6.1	6.5	6.5	7.3	6.4	17.5	17.5	5 015	173	290	13 131	2.0
Ellsworth..............	9.0	D	3.3	14.7	7.2	4.0	D	5.8	31.5	1 475	233	80	3 205	-1.0
Finney..................	8.7	3.0	6.7	17.6	2.7	7.6	5.1	9.4	14.5	4 695	127	646	13 405	1.0
Ford	4.0	0.1	6.6	30.1	3.7	6.0	3.5	D	15.8	4 335	127	456	12 141	1.1
Franklin................	1.8	2.9	6.4	9.8	2.9	6.6	3.1	D	18.8	5 615	220	524	11 083	-0.6
Geary...................	0.0	0.0	1.1	1.6	D	1.7	1.7	1.1	83.4	4 240	115	550	15 198	4.7
Gove....................	6.1	2.0	2.0	28.5	D	12.6	8.7	8.1	12.1	685	258	17	1 429	4.1
Graham................	4.8	22.3	D	D	D	3.5	D	4.9	21.8	775	299	40	1 483	-0.1
Grant	29.8	16.1	6.5	4.1	D	2.9	3.8	4.3	10.1	1 150	150	77	2 912	-1.1
Gray.....................	53.6	D	5.9	1.5	3.8	1.9	4.3	1.5	10.3	980	161	32	2 413	3.1
Greeley.................	27.2	D	2.6	0.3	D	9.1	D	D	17.8	295	224	0	634	0.8
Greenwood...........	20.5	14.2	5.0	8.9	4.4	3.3	2.0	D	17.4	1 905	305	159	4 024	-1.1
Hamilton...............	66.4	D	D	D	D	1.5	5.2	D	12.3	415	167	26	1 219	-1.4
Harper..................	0.2	17.2	3.8	15.2	D	8.4	D	D	24.0	1 445	250	95	3 160	1.4
Harvey..................	2.5	3.6	7.1	28.1	3.3	6.3	4.3	D	11.8	7 400	212	475	14 664	0.9
Haskell.................	51.4	D	4.1	4.5	D	1.3	D	D	14.5	600	148	31	1 657	-0.5
Hodgeman............	34.0	D	1.7	D	D	3.9	6.8	0.2	27.9	445	235	17	969	-0.4
Jackson	-3.1	D	8.3	6.8	3.3	6.5	5.6	D	47.3	3 185	239	186	5 815	0.6
Jefferson..............	0.9	D	28.6	4.9	D	3.5	D	D	23.3	4 075	216	239	8 265	1.3
Jewell	30.9	0.4	D	D	D	5.4	3.8	D	23.8	925	311	43	2 018	-0.7
Johnson................	0.0	0.2	4.7	5.5	18.3	5.7	16.1	10.6	7.1	85 765	148	3 913	238 219	5.1
Kearny..................	52.0	D	D	D	D	2.1	D	0.6	21.8	660	167	56	1 554	-0.1
Kingman...............	-1.0	10.1	14.0	16.1	D	4.3	9.8	10.4	15.9	1 895	248	108	3 809	-0.2
Kiowa...................	-5.4	D	25.3	D	D	D	3.6	D	23.6	570	223	57	1 226	0.5
Labette.................	1.1	D	2.6	22.1	2.3	6.1	3.2	13.0	27.5	5 195	250	745	10 017	-0.7
Lane.....................	68.6	D	D	0.1	D	D	2.8	D	9.9	440	265	10	975	-1.5
Leavenworth.........	-0.1	D	4.9	3.5	6.5	3.8	4.4	4.1	62.9	13 055	165	951	29 418	2.5
Lincoln	4.4	D	12.7	D	D	2.6	4.8	4.5	38.6	780	250	44	1 852	-0.6
Linn......................	-5.7	4.6	12.3	5.8	D	5.6	4.5	D	25.2	2 580	270	188	5 481	0.6
Logan...................	10.6	D	2.9	2.9	D	5.3	7.4	D	40.0	635	226	40	1 441	0.0
Lyon.....................	-0.1	0.5	4.2	22.4	D	6.8	4.0	8.4	28.8	5 970	180	656	15 217	-0.1
McPherson	1.8	4.5	13.0	32.1	3.2	3.7	3.9	8.0	8.3	6 395	221	302	13 086	2.9
Marion	6.8	1.2	5.5	17.5	3.6	4.9	4.2	D	18.7	3 030	250	153	5 927	-0.3
Marshall...............	10.0	D	4.1	25.7	7.2	5.7	6.5	7.5	10.6	2 425	245	134	4 921	1.1
Meade..................	41.5	1.4	4.5	3.3	D	2.3	6.2	D	15.2	880	205	33	1 993	-0.3
Miami...................	0.9	1.7	13.6	7.8	5.0	7.3	8.7	11.9	22.8	6 225	190	421	13 451	2.0
Mitchell................	10.0	D	6.2	9.7	D	6.0	D	D	19.2	1 535	243	76	3 289	-0.2
Montgomery	1.8	0.9	5.6	27.8	D	5.3	3.6	D	13.9	8 330	250	1 105	16 377	-1.2
Morris	25.1	0.2	7.2	8.0	D	4.6	4.8	D	19.4	1 495	265	81	3 187	-0.6
Morton	40.8	4.4	3.2	D	D	4.0	2.7	D	25.0	610	204	35	1 448	-1.3
Nemaha................	12.8	D	5.7	24.9	2.7	4.2	D	D	10.6	2 240	219	99	4 589	0.6

1. Per 1,000 resident population estimated as of July 1 of the year shown.

Table B. States and Counties — Housing, Labor Force, and Employment

STATE County	Housing units, 2011–2015 Occupied units		Owner-occupied			Renter-occupied		Sub-stand-ard units[4] (percent)	Civilian labor force, 2016		Unemployment		Civilian employment,[6] 2011–2015	Percent	
	Total	Percent	Median value[1]	With a mortgage	Without a mortgage[2]	Median rent[3]	Median rent as a percent of income[2]		Total	Percent change, 2015–2016	Total	Rate[5]	Total	Management, business, science and arts	Construction, production, and maintenance occupations
	89	90	91	92	93	94	95	96	97	98	99	100	101	102	103
KANSAS	1 113 472	66.7	132 000	20.5	11.8	757	27.9	2.5	1 484 012	-0.3	61 889	4.2	1 401 197	36.8	23.5
Allen	5 306	72.5	68 200	20.1	12.7	531	26.1	2.0	6 354	-3.6	377	5.9	5 863	29.6	33.3
Anderson	3 280	75.4	90 400	21.5	13.1	610	28.7	1.4	4 195	1.7	190	4.5	3 593	27.6	33.1
Atchison	6 033	72.3	88 100	22.6	12.7	586	26.6	0.6	7 153	-4.0	459	6.4	7 519	32.8	28.4
Barber	1 981	73.1	78 100	14.9	10.0	609	19.7	1.5	2 525	-4.9	103	4.1	2 350	33.8	31.9
Barton	11 306	67.4	81 200	18.4	10.8	591	24.4	2.9	14 037	-3.5	664	4.7	13 200	29.9	27.7
Bourbon	5 660	68.9	81 400	18.6	12.9	586	28.1	3.2	7 125	0.0	361	5.1	6 541	31.6	28.1
Brown	4 102	68.5	84 600	21.2	10.9	517	26.4	1.7	5 168	-3.3	199	3.9	4 606	31.7	29.4
Butler	24 273	73.2	134 500	20.4	12.6	756	28.1	1.8	31 877	-0.3	1 380	4.3	31 277	38.1	24.7
Chase	1 110	74.3	76 600	22.0	13.3	473	30.7	1.5	1 399	12.0	52	3.7	1 187	32.3	31.6
Chautauqua	1 557	78.9	48 500	21.3	14.2	608	23.5	1.0	1 520	-1.7	84	5.5	1 510	29.7	37.9
Cherokee	7 988	75.7	72 500	20.7	12.5	657	28.1	2.0	10 300	-0.8	477	4.6	9 378	31.4	30.6
Cheyenne	1 262	80.0	82 800	18.4	13.1	564	22.2	0.8	1 343	-0.8	39	2.9	1 321	35.6	24.8
Clark	927	70.1	62 200	18.8	10.0	715	26.0	4.4	1 125	-2.7	33	2.9	1 040	40.9	24.1
Clay	3 377	81.4	96 500	18.6	11.5	613	23.1	0.9	3 998	-2.6	180	4.5	4 169	33.6	24.0
Cloud	3 964	72.0	69 000	17.4	12.8	588	25.0	1.8	4 121	-4.2	186	4.5	4 514	27.7	28.6
Coffey	3 569	75.8	102 000	18.0	11.0	578	24.6	1.9	4 471	-5.5	280	6.3	4 207	33.0	27.7
Comanche	784	77.0	61 800	16.9	11.9	511	19.1	0.0	954	-3.5	32	3.4	995	38.8	23.9
Cowley	13 688	67.5	83 200	20.0	12.3	639	28.2	2.1	17 024	0.1	780	4.6	15 686	27.4	31.0
Crawford	15 065	61.1	85 900	20.4	12.7	673	34.8	4.2	18 958	0.4	941	5.0	18 643	32.1	25.3
Decatur	1 473	76.4	55 900	21.7	11.4	557	32.9	0.7	1 318	-2.2	55	4.2	1 389	37.4	26.1
Dickinson	7 822	73.0	108 200	20.4	12.9	626	28.0	0.9	9 309	-2.0	429	4.6	8 898	31.4	29.1
Doniphan	3 109	72.1	86 900	19.5	12.6	574	20.8	2.8	4 280	-0.7	175	4.1	3 790	30.8	31.9
Douglas	43 729	52.2	179 800	21.3	11.4	859	32.3	1.8	65 556	0.4	2 351	3.6	61 881	44.6	14.8
Edwards	1 274	75.4	56 400	18.1	10.0	490	18.1	2.7	1 664	-4.6	52	3.1	1 451	32.0	35.1
Elk	1 256	78.6	49 200	19.6	13.8	532	27.9	3.1	1 212	-5.0	64	5.3	1 121	38.4	27.6
Ellis	11 847	63.6	150 200	20.8	12.0	634	30.2	1.5	17 130	-2.0	544	3.2	16 045	32.1	22.1
Ellsworth	2 585	75.8	81 400	19.6	10.0	607	24.6	1.1	2 803	-4.3	118	4.2	2 787	36.0	26.6
Finney	12 600	62.1	117 000	22.3	12.0	689	22.8	6.8	20 285	1.0	648	3.2	18 612	23.5	36.9
Ford	11 205	61.2	99 500	20.6	10.8	661	25.3	6.4	18 043	0.2	593	3.3	16 237	21.5	44.4
Franklin	9 830	71.8	122 900	23.2	12.7	741	27.7	2.3	14 231	1.2	615	4.3	12 701	30.0	31.3
Geary	12 723	42.8	136 000	22.4	13.4	1 027	29.1	4.6	12 295	0.5	715	5.8	12 884	26.9	27.3
Gove	1 190	78.3	76 300	19.9	10.0	559	24.4	1.3	1 470	-0.8	38	2.6	1 367	37.5	27.2
Graham	1 201	79.7	68 600	17.7	11.5	474	25.0	0.3	1 207	-5.0	60	5.0	1 282	36.0	27.1
Grant	2 707	77.7	99 400	19.4	10.0	570	24.8	4.8	3 797	-2.4	143	3.8	3 618	27.5	36.9
Gray	2 150	72.8	107 900	18.8	10.0	640	18.7	3.7	3 422	-4.7	80	2.3	3 183	33.9	30.2
Greeley	487	71.5	84 500	20.0	13.9	810	19.0	3.9	913	-2.0	21	2.3	592	36.3	22.1
Greenwood	2 824	77.4	57 200	18.4	11.7	522	28.8	3.0	3 303	0.7	171	5.2	2 876	29.3	32.8
Hamilton	998	72.0	86 600	23.4	12.6	553	16.8	3.9	1 602	-2.8	43	2.7	1 322	29.4	37.1
Harper	2 433	76.2	66 900	19.7	11.6	601	24.4	0.9	2 849	0.0	110	3.9	2 750	33.1	27.8
Harvey	13 581	69.8	115 800	19.9	11.4	683	27.4	1.3	17 183	0.1	752	4.4	16 472	35.3	28.1
Haskell	1 395	72.4	116 000	18.4	10.0	699	19.9	5.7	2 309	-1.8	62	2.7	2 078	30.6	32.6
Hodgeman	811	73.5	82 900	17.6	10.0	567	20.5	1.0	1 030	0.6	30	2.9	1 005	44.0	26.2
Jackson	5 281	75.3	119 400	21.0	12.8	670	27.7	1.6	7 229	0.1	259	3.6	6 496	31.5	30.0
Jefferson	7 542	82.0	127 100	22.3	12.7	731	23.3	2.4	10 160	0.0	412	4.1	9 264	32.0	29.2
Jewell	1 433	80.3	53 100	18.8	11.7	516	20.0	1.6	1 347	-1.8	63	4.7	1 468	39.9	27.8
Johnson	219 735	69.5	215 600	20.2	10.2	947	26.3	1.6	325 758	0.6	10 871	3.3	302 532	49.8	12.5
Kearny	1 379	74.8	94 100	20.2	11.6	626	17.0	2.5	2 088	-2.5	69	3.3	1 930	34.3	37.7
Kingman	3 006	73.4	88 000	20.7	11.8	625	22.7	2.0	3 612	-0.8	169	4.7	3 509	31.3	34.2
Kiowa	1 066	65.0	121 300	22.7	10.0	502	25.6	0.8	1 455	0.8	42	2.9	1 315	41.4	25.1
Labette	8 413	69.3	70 200	18.9	12.6	559	29.6	4.1	10 747	0.2	609	5.7	9 572	29.9	30.4
Lane	805	76.3	66 200	15.6	10.0	504	27.3	1.1	826	-5.7	28	3.4	926	34.9	25.7
Leavenworth	26 747	66.4	167 500	21.7	11.8	883	25.7	1.8	35 390	0.6	1 572	4.4	33 513	36.6	21.8
Lincoln	1 335	79.0	66 900	19.5	12.8	532	22.1	2.8	1 746	-2.6	66	3.8	1 497	38.5	32.3
Linn	4 182	77.9	90 300	21.5	13.4	630	23.6	6.0	4 337	0.4	292	6.7	3 987	31.7	29.4
Logan	1 243	70.8	79 200	19.7	10.2	675	25.4	2.8	1 706	-2.5	47	2.8	1 399	35.5	31.0
Lyon	13 272	59.7	93 400	21.7	12.9	600	28.2	2.3	16 927	2.0	710	4.2	16 784	28.0	32.2
McPherson	11 791	76.0	132 900	19.7	10.8	641	22.5	1.4	16 446	-4.0	537	3.3	15 406	36.3	29.7
Marion	4 808	79.4	81 600	19.8	12.0	561	26.7	3.0	6 050	-1.6	258	4.3	5 820	31.7	29.8
Marshall	4 322	73.9	86 700	19.5	10.6	544	26.5	3.1	5 599	-2.1	179	3.2	4 933	29.7	33.3
Meade	1 694	71.0	86 500	18.0	10.9	655	19.4	2.2	2 381	-1.3	68	2.9	2 137	37.6	32.0
Miami	12 560	77.4	167 400	21.9	13.4	776	32.2	1.8	16 808	0.5	721	4.3	16 030	34.2	27.5
Mitchell	2 687	72.6	89 000	18.3	11.5	531	24.4	1.3	3 660	-2.8	130	3.6	3 086	39.1	29.5
Montgomery	13 435	69.5	70 600	19.2	12.8	624	28.6	2.6	15 884	-3.9	1 018	6.4	14 514	27.8	33.4
Morris	2 406	76.7	85 200	21.9	11.2	619	24.7	2.9	3 099	0.1	126	4.1	2 819	27.4	35.0
Morton	1 189	70.2	99 400	19.8	14.2	599	23.6	1.1	1 376	-3.8	57	4.1	1 408	26.1	35.5
Nemaha	4 239	76.8	109 900	19.0	11.2	532	23.7	1.8	5 931	0.1	166	2.8	5 302	33.0	29.5

1. Specified owner-occupied units.   2. A value of 10.0 represents 10 percent or less; a value of 50.0 represents 50 percent or more.   3. Specified renter-occupied units.
4. Overcrowded or lacking complete plumbing facilities.   5. Percent of civilian labor force.   6. Civilian employed persons 16 years old and over.

Table B. States and Counties — **Nonfarm Employment and Agriculture**

STATE County	Number of establishments	Total	Health care and social assistance	Manufacturing	Retail trade	Finance and insurance	Professional, scientific, and technical services	Total (mil dol)	Average per employee (dollars)	Number	Fewer than 50 acres	500 acres or more	Farm operators whose principal occupation is farming (percent)
	104	105	106	107	108	109	110	111	112	113	114	115	116
KANSAS..........................	74 526	1 189 876	193 684	167 014	150 465	61 271	64 246	51 260	43 080	61 773	19.0	31.6	48.3
Allen..............................	392	4 496	455	2 144	576	120	102	143	31 912	650	20.5	19.5	46.2
Anderson......................	211	1 501	357	189	389	93	30	47	31 383	707	20.8	25.5	47.5
Atchison........................	346	5 589	878	1 162	587	114	77	180	32 177	611	19.8	17.7	50.2
Barber..........................	206	1 476	249	D	203	57	52	52	35 425	378	10.1	50.3	54.2
Barton..........................	966	10 729	2 145	1 318	1 646	700	344	364	33 952	694	14.4	39.2	45.7
Bourbon........................	353	4 692	937	1 302	656	240	99	147	31 331	903	18.9	18.4	45.0
Brown...........................	261	3 296	757	555	400	175	83	108	32 716	510	19.8	29.2	60.6
Butler...........................	1 312	13 457	2 968	1 401	2 218	498	746	464	34 472	1 353	34.3	20.8	39.8
Chase...........................	72	564	D	188	54	16	12	19	33 151	252	15.9	45.6	54.8
Chautauqua..................	67	443	111	50	92	D	7	13	28 305	312	8.0	38.1	53.2
Cherokee.......................	343	5 402	952	1 521	543	129	76	218	40 377	729	27.8	24.8	50.2
Cheyenne......................	108	587	D	D	88	29	21	18	30 680	393	9.4	51.7	47.8
Clark............................	60	467	D	D	77	36	19	17	35 867	283	4.9	51.9	53.0
Clay.............................	263	2 349	555	378	375	95	62	74	31 373	541	15.0	37.5	53.2
Cloud...........................	309	2 949	701	251	504	117	89	97	32 782	461	14.8	35.1	46.4
Coffey..........................	236	3 123	448	127	382	110	42	204	65 460	667	19.2	26.7	38.5
Comanche.....................	76	440	155	67	67	30	7	10	22 257	234	6.8	61.1	52.1
Cowley..........................	744	11 140	2 100	3 604	1 532	364	225	379	34 009	990	19.3	24.5	48.6
Crawford.......................	899	14 054	2 882	2 622	1 860	325	314	419	29 820	846	25.5	19.1	36.9
Decatur........................	107	645	193	D	91	33	27	16	24 471	293	10.6	55.6	61.1
Dickinson......................	455	5 155	958	1 043	751	190	127	158	30 666	1 011	19.8	31.2	41.5
Doniphan......................	160	1 510	176	411	135	56	21	54	35 981	422	20.4	24.9	55.2
Douglas........................	2 698	40 240	6 103	3 558	6 179	1 324	1 656	1 197	29 741	945	38.5	9.7	35.8
Edwards........................	87	612	163	145	73	23	9	21	34 910	292	7.9	45.2	61.3
Elk..............................	71	323	D	D	42	29	16	8	23 328	315	14.9	42.5	53.0
Ellis.............................	1 146	13 434	3 363	1 139	2 204	394	339	446	33 173	645	13.2	35.0	40.2
Ellsworth.......................	172	1 648	452	279	245	88	70	57	34 830	435	11.0	34.9	48.7
Finney..........................	1 009	14 936	1 802	3 583	2 772	411	270	521	34 872	499	11.0	60.1	65.1
Ford.............................	780	14 360	1 250	5 743	1 768	287	506	505	35 187	655	12.4	43.1	51.0
Franklin........................	567	8 703	1 365	826	1 189	149	418	350	40 202	1 024	31.1	16.3	42.5
Geary...........................	561	8 427	1 586	726	1 268	242	403	265	31 409	238	28.2	27.3	45.4
Gove............................	133	1 030	234	129	182	45	16	31	30 096	395	8.6	55.4	57.7
Graham........................	101	704	214	D	104	46	9	23	32 771	431	7.4	43.2	49.2
Grant...........................	218	2 472	198	189	233	114	31	114	46 180	329	10.6	40.7	45.9
Gray............................	215	1 356	172	84	187	77	52	53	38 886	418	9.6	46.2	53.1
Greeley.........................	42	326	D	NA	67	21	7	12	36 985	262	5.0	53.8	55.7
Greenwood....................	181	1 120	218	93	221	59	31	34	30 712	551	13.2	37.4	52.5
Hamilton......................	69	583	130	D	83	57	D	20	34 158	397	4.5	54.4	53.9
Harper..........................	216	1 855	320	524	245	94	21	64	34 496	482	13.5	39.6	49.8
Harvey..........................	746	13 888	3 067	3 526	1 452	317	279	517	37 245	744	30.5	25.1	48.9
Haskell.........................	127	830	D	57	66	D	31	31	37 070	187	10.7	61.5	74.9
Hodgeman.....................	44	270	D	NA	37	D	D	9	32 237	399	3.0	56.6	57.9
Jackson........................	257	2 945	507	205	387	122	72	85	28 922	1 054	26.7	15.3	36.8
Jefferson.......................	307	2 311	369	300	302	69	59	88	37 960	996	27.9	10.9	38.2
Jewell..........................	79	462	D	D	49	35	14	13	28 602	453	9.1	50.1	66.2
Johnson........................	17 625	328 159	39 513	24 338	36 764	28 426	29 035	17 532	53 426	571	52.0	8.4	35.4
Kearny..........................	78	653	D	D	52	63	10	25	37 596	343	4.7	50.7	53.6
Kingman........................	212	2 194	319	472	186	125	329	76	34 469	808	14.2	31.7	43.8
Kiowa...........................	91	752	206	NA	54	31	D	27	35 574	403	6.5	43.7	43.4
Labette.........................	463	8 674	3 490	2 088	944	233	110	270	31 115	977	20.2	17.3	46.6
Lane............................	64	361	D	D	33	36	13	13	35 213	315	8.6	52.4	48.3
Leavenworth..................	1 251	13 916	2 953	1 201	2 098	790	1 184	503	36 144	1 133	41.0	6.6	35.4
Lincoln.........................	91	531	D	D	54	42	7	14	25 505	431	13.7	41.5	62.9
Linn.............................	186	1 253	56	138	257	74	26	59	47 028	913	18.8	16.2	38.4
Logan...........................	112	721	191	NA	125	58	19	23	31 997	325	5.2	55.7	48.6
Lyon............................	838	11 688	1 934	2 901	1 859	326	267	367	31 383	946	21.7	26.5	47.5
McPherson....................	899	13 082	2 232	4 064	1 174	652	235	569	43 470	1 147	20.2	29.9	54.7
Marion..........................	290	2 663	612	294	285	100	85	68	25 350	981	19.1	32.7	50.8
Marshall........................	372	4 132	491	1 383	703	202	97	154	37 259	796	14.8	34.3	55.8
Meade..........................	126	919	D	15	176	50	24	32	35 276	439	7.7	51.9	52.4
Miami..........................	711	6 683	2 004	463	986	248	321	245	36 724	1 305	38.4	9.7	41.5
Mitchell........................	262	2 575	558	396	407	150	43	82	31 706	415	11.1	43.4	60.5
Montgomery	810	12 470	2 359	3 360	1 592	323	220	431	34 542	1 012	23.9	14.4	41.3
Morris..........................	131	1 232	284	218	171	59	54	39	31 436	454	13.4	35.0	53.1
Morton.........................	104	830	D	D	91	40	15	31	37 931	323	3.7	49.8	50.5
Nemaha........................	373	4 759	883	1 387	498	181	116	189	39 797	903	15.2	26.7	49.3

STATE County	Land in farms		Acres			Value of land and buildings (dollars)		Value of machinery and equipment, average per farm (dollars)	Value of products sold		Percent from:		Percent of farms with sales of:		Government payments	
	Acreage (1,000)	Percent change, 2007–2012	Average size of farm	Total irrigated (1,000)	Total cropland (1,000)	Average per farm	Average per acre		Total (mil dol)	Average per farm (dollars)	Crops	Live-stock and poultry products	$10,000 or more	$100,000 or more	Total ($1,000)	Percent of farms
	117	118	119	120	121	122	123	124	125	126	127	128	129	130	131	132
KANSAS	46 137	-0.4	747	2 881.3	28 503.3	1 218 662	1 632	156 737	18 460.6	298 845	37.8	62.2	56.0	25.5	442 090	68.6
Allen	245	-8.3	377	D	129.5	526 683	1 396	93 555	38.2	58 702	58.5	41.5	46.9	13.1	2 652	62.9
Anderson	366	-0.3	518	1.4	224.0	806 658	1 557	132 429	73.4	103 812	55.7	44.3	57.9	21.8	4 436	66.3
Atchison	220	-13.3	361	0.5	144.4	777 051	2 154	134 581	56.5	92 530	76.6	23.4	64.2	21.8	2 999	60.9
Barber	591	-3.4	1 563	8.9	193.1	1 898 704	1 215	171 399	88.5	234 053	51.3	48.7	68.3	37.3	2 849	75.7
Barton	566	1.3	816	39.2	421.3	1 278 262	1 567	210 909	279.0	401 964	34.5	65.5	64.4	31.8	5 572	80.8
Bourbon	334	2.1	370	0.3	126.4	536 239	1 448	68 483	53.7	59 508	29.6	70.4	46.3	9.6	2 601	56.6
Brown	295	-15.0	578	5.0	232.3	1 891 461	3 271	223 178	140.5	275 506	85.4	14.6	67.5	36.1	3 416	72.9
Butler	768	-2.4	568	5.1	295.9	999 409	1 760	108 387	282.3	208 676	27.9	72.1	44.6	17.7	3 069	37.5
Chase	393	22.7	1 558	D	56.0	2 113 111	1 356	118 929	84.7	336 111	12.8	87.2	72.2	34.5	714	52.0
Chautauqua	310	0.7	995	D	39.7	1 148 269	1 155	73 324	35.2	112 805	D	D	61.5	18.3	626	34.9
Cherokee	308	-5.0	423	0.8	226.4	787 462	1 862	118 760	86.9	119 213	81.1	18.9	55.3	21.3	3 158	50.6
Cheyenne	547	-5.2	1 391	39.5	336.7	2 203 377	1 584	192 557	143.9	366 117	52.4	47.6	61.8	39.9	4 717	84.7
Clark	503	3.6	1 778	6.6	191.4	1 617 572	910	143 989	126.2	445 763	13.0	87.0	49.8	29.0	3 389	89.0
Clay	363	3.3	670	29.2	230.8	1 414 349	2 111	204 776	115.9	214 174	69.5	30.5	68.6	38.1	3 830	81.9
Cloud	322	-16.2	698	15.2	208.8	1 390 777	1 991	175 219	80.0	173 627	84.4	15.6	70.1	31.0	3 226	73.1
Coffey	329	1.4	494	1.2	183.4	753 148	1 526	94 421	61.7	92 496	53.0	47.0	46.6	18.3	3 527	76.6
Comanche	485	12.2	2 073	7.5	144.9	1 910 051	921	146 675	48.7	208 034	44.7	55.3	66.7	41.0	2 448	79.5
Cowley	575	-0.2	580	6.2	266.1	831 902	1 433	134 058	109.0	110 077	54.0	46.0	54.3	18.7	3 203	61.0
Crawford	323	-5.6	382	1.1	192.1	640 069	1 675	105 483	75.6	89 355	68.3	31.7	49.2	15.6	2 040	61.5
Decatur	462	-4.3	1 578	11.1	269.1	2 407 051	1 525	246 949	136.8	466 915	37.6	62.4	75.1	42.3	3 139	85.7
Dickinson	510	-5.0	505	4.3	335.4	1 017 926	2 017	139 688	157.1	155 342	52.5	47.5	55.2	26.0	5 935	79.7
Doniphan	180	-27.5	425	1.2	133.8	1 531 073	3 599	178 036	80.8	191 472	93.4	6.6	58.3	33.2	2 819	70.4
Douglas	211	-4.5	223	3.3	127.3	636 186	2 854	82 519	43.9	46 436	66.2	33.8	37.7	8.4	2 332	46.9
Edwards	394	-10.2	1 351	92.3	284.9	2 882 414	2 134	298 442	151.7	519 538	83.7	16.3	64.0	43.2	3 850	92.1
Elk	316	-0.1	1 004	D	51.4	1 274 378	1 269	84 156	42.1	133 556	16.0	84.0	56.5	23.5	694	41.3
Ellis	497	-5.6	770	1.9	253.4	1 025 119	1 332	130 081	99.6	154 462	32.7	67.3	59.8	19.1	3 503	78.9
Ellsworth	381	4.4	876	0.6	182.7	1 161 667	1 326	144 347	51.6	118 699	66.8	33.2	54.3	25.5	2 787	84.8
Finney	816	7.3	1 635	186.6	670.4	2 353 291	1 439	399 313	909.2	1 822 062	20.3	79.7	64.1	46.5	9 784	80.0
Ford	700	10.3	1 068	82.0	541.7	1 301 528	1 218	232 826	441.8	674 560	25.9	74.1	60.6	31.3	7 279	79.4
Franklin	362	15.4	353	2.2	200.8	820 041	2 321	103 643	101.3	98 951	54.6	45.4	43.5	10.8	3 448	52.6
Geary	146	-1.9	612	3.6	57.9	1 187 118	1 939	121 773	30.4	127 550	51.0	49.0	45.4	22.7	971	67.6
Gove	579	-2.5	1 465	21.1	368.9	1 883 304	1 286	227 359	196.1	496 537	34.9	65.1	68.1	42.3	6 300	83.5
Graham	483	-6.2	1 120	13.3	292.0	1 478 046	1 319	183 213	57.9	134 887	76.3	23.7	54.3	25.3	5 847	81.9
Grant	364	7.8	1 105	88.7	298.2	1 471 553	1 332	253 924	918.2	2 790 860	9.4	90.6	50.8	36.2	5 153	84.5
Gray	547	0.2	1 309	124.2	420.9	1 747 136	1 335	320 818	939.4	2 247 407	14.9	85.1	59.8	44.3	7 391	82.8
Greeley	497	0.9	1 898	23.2	458.2	2 823 103	1 487	306 420	123.1	470 031	47.9	52.1	64.5	42.7	5 269	90.8
Greenwood	701	15.1	1 272	0.2	104.0	1 792 824	1 409	96 279	89.6	162 530	19.8	80.2	59.9	21.4	1 382	45.6
Hamilton	635	4.0	1 600	30.9	486.4	1 617 219	1 011	198 665	367.2	925 033	15.1	84.9	47.4	29.0	6 441	88.9
Harper	506	5.1	1 050	3.8	329.0	1 592 678	1 517	176 824	109.6	227 477	58.8	41.2	60.4	35.1	5 601	85.5
Harvey	340	0.3	456	47.2	297.2	1 173 019	2 570	154 589	161.7	217 360	69.4	30.6	59.4	31.6	4 135	68.5
Haskell	364	-8.8	1 944	116.7	259.0	2 676 770	1 377	550 995	1 009.9	5 400 412	10.6	89.4	71.7	59.9	4 074	82.9
Hodgeman	543	3.2	1 360	30.7	328.1	1 461 356	1 075	227 945	182.1	456 386	29.2	70.8	65.4	36.6	6 590	87.7
Jackson	329	-3.0	312	0.8	136.1	549 724	1 760	78 991	57.9	54 893	40.3	59.7	45.7	11.4	2 322	50.4
Jefferson	244	-14.8	245	3.6	133.4	547 394	2 238	86 031	53.1	53 344	62.7	37.3	41.6	8.9	2 013	45.5
Jewell	464	-1.6	1 024	15.0	294.8	1 975 925	1 930	223 843	136.5	301 278	77.1	22.9	73.7	47.0	5 236	83.9
Johnson	99	-13.0	174	1.1	59.2	755 205	4 340	76 618	24.4	42 680	66.0	34.0	34.2	9.3	911	30.3
Kearny	547	5.3	1 594	70.9	423.6	2 067 618	1 297	238 297	337.4	983 639	23.9	76.1	56.9	38.2	6 069	86.6
Kingman	542	-0.8	671	33.7	329.3	958 710	1 429	139 131	103.2	127 708	74.0	26.0	56.7	25.0	5 868	84.2
Kiowa	455	3.4	1 130	49.9	233.2	1 391 826	1 232	141 444	80.6	199 943	79.4	20.6	56.3	26.6	3 852	88.6
Labette	371	-0.2	379	0.6	196.7	563 481	1 486	94 384	122.8	125 668	41.5	58.5	53.7	14.7	2 247	51.4
Lane	452	12.7	1 436	18.7	337.0	1 846 321	1 286	204 457	216.8	688 343	14.4	85.6	54.0	30.8	5 512	91.4
Leavenworth	184	-5.3	163	0.3	102.5	526 699	3 235	63 351	36.4	32 098	69.3	30.7	35.7	5.9	1 452	29.0
Lincoln	397	-8.2	922	1.4	204.7	1 377 181	1 494	166 234	63.5	147 355	68.1	31.9	65.7	31.8	3 280	87.9
Linn	355	33.7	388	0.0	167.8	683 687	1 760	75 490	39.5	43 245	62.7	37.3	41.9	8.1	2 608	54.3
Logan	566	0.0	1 743	11.1	329.4	2 057 326	1 180	197 542	78.8	242 551	74.3	25.7	70.8	41.2	4 297	83.4
Lyon	535	12.9	565	0.4	228.4	881 912	1 560	107 999	111.4	117 727	31.6	68.4	49.3	17.1	3 429	67.4
McPherson	572	0.9	498	42.3	409.1	1 124 564	2 257	171 576	208.5	181 763	61.5	38.5	66.4	32.3	8 021	77.6
Marion	596	-0.5	608	4.4	341.4	1 282 189	2 109	140 915	151.5	154 412	51.1	48.9	62.3	31.4	4 559	76.8
Marshall	438	-14.8	551	2.9	301.7	1 483 474	2 693	194 613	127.9	160 700	81.4	18.6	71.4	36.4	4 946	80.9
Meade	618	2.6	1 408	129.5	372.2	1 717 237	1 220	295 836	296.8	676 175	49.6	50.4	58.1	37.4	6 661	86.1
Miami	296	-3.7	227	1.3	166.5	709 454	3 131	71 108	51.0	39 090	66.4	33.6	36.9	7.4	1 946	36.2
Mitchell	439	-1.2	1 058	8.4	303.5	2 369 728	2 240	254 643	153.5	369 872	57.3	42.7	71.8	44.6	4 609	84.8
Montgomery	336	6.9	332	3.7	163.1	513 052	1 547	98 773	79.4	78 478	61.2	38.8	45.9	9.4	1 771	37.7
Morris	389	-5.9	857	0.5	153.9	1 259 154	1 469	134 231	116.8	257 302	28.1	71.9	68.3	27.1	2 296	72.9
Morton	457	3.4	1 414	59.5	389.3	1 197 084	846	156 164	169.7	525 477	34.4	65.6	47.4	30.0	6 208	86.4
Nemaha	383	-15.1	424	0.9	259.0	1 195 878	2 822	170 190	224.6	248 729	34.9	65.1	73.8	32.3	6 391	79.8

Table B. States and Counties — **Water Use, Wholesale Trade, Retail Trade, and Real Estate**

STATE County	Water use, 2010		Wholesale trade,[1] 2012				Retail trade,[2] 2012				Real estate and rental and leasing,[2] 2012			
	Total water withdrawn (mil gal/day)	Gallons withdrawn per person per day	Number of establishments	Number of employees	Sales (mil dol)	Annual payroll (mil dol)	Number of establishments	Number of employees	Sales (mil dol)	Annual payroll (mil dol)	Number of establishments	Number of employees	Receipts (mil dol)	Annual payroll (mil dol)
	133	134	135	136	137	138	139	140	141	142	143	144	145	146
KANSAS	4 004.8	1 404	3 790	52 168	60 226.3	3 055.4	10 548	145 480	38 276.5	3 325.0	2 999	14 256	2 743.1	507.6
Allen	3.8	284	17	D	D	D	57	544	152.8	12.7	22	42	2.8	0.5
Anderson	1.9	239	12	54	69.0	2.3	38	268	92.1	5.8	2	D	D	D
Atchison	5.4	321	18	382	206.5	15.1	49	640	126.9	12.7	9	D	D	D
Barber	5.9	1 220	11	94	89.0	5.5	32	222	76.4	4.5	5	8	1.0	0.1
Barton	36.8	1 328	65	542	389.6	27.0	128	1 651	420.4	38.0	29	105	16.3	3.8
Bourbon	3.1	203	13	D	D	D	48	611	132.7	12.1	9	35	4.6	0.9
Brown	2.5	246	15	128	244.4	5.7	32	365	74.8	7.1	4	8	0.6	0.1
Butler	15.6	237	54	440	317.5	23.2	184	2 053	620.1	46.4	52	103	17.3	2.6
Chase	1.4	516	3	D	D	D	9	64	16.0	0.9	2	D	D	D
Chautauqua	1.0	262	2	D	D	D	15	96	20.0	1.4	NA	NA	NA	NA
Cherokee	94.1	4 354	17	154	209.1	6.5	56	497	125.4	10.3	4	16	2.0	0.4
Cheyenne	42.9	15 719	11	115	113.2	4.8	22	79	17.2	1.4	3	3	0.7	0.1
Clark	5.2	2 348	1	D	D	D	9	53	9.1	1.0	NA	NA	NA	NA
Clay	9.1	1 060	15	169	135.3	8.2	38	425	94.2	7.8	4	D	D	D
Cloud	10.7	1 117	20	264	199.1	10.6	56	558	136.5	12.5	5	9	1.2	0.2
Coffey	21.1	2 451	12	72	63.7	2.4	50	408	111.4	7.8	3	D	D	D
Comanche	8.3	4 363	2	D	D	D	17	69	18.7	1.6	1	D	D	D
Cowley	8.4	230	26	D	D	D	121	1 445	337.1	32.9	19	39	6.6	1.1
Crawford	7.2	185	39	577	297.7	20.8	165	1 915	406.1	37.0	38	108	15.2	2.3
Decatur	9.4	3 168	10	79	83.7	2.1	19	89	23.6	1.6	4	10	1.4	0.2
Dickinson	5.8	292	24	282	231.1	12.8	70	768	187.5	17.0	14	D	D	D
Doniphan	0.6	70	11	98	90.0	4.0	21	141	30.9	2.5	2	D	D	D
Douglas	19.1	172	71	610	282.9	24.6	373	6 066	1 354.2	122.6	157	761	97.7	20.9
Edwards	99.3	32 697	9	124	150.2	5.0	13	82	54.5	1.4	1	D	D	D
Elk	0.9	316	2	D	D	D	10	56	23.1	0.7	1	D	D	D
Ellis	5.5	192	46	405	201.7	17.0	183	2 166	621.0	49.5	43	145	18.2	3.3
Ellsworth	2.6	405	9	73	80.9	2.8	29	238	53.6	4.0	1	D	D	D
Finney	281.3	7 650	79	D	D	D	174	2 393	577.0	53.7	36	132	33.5	5.1
Ford	96.5	2 850	62	750	633.9	36.1	126	1 805	499.5	40.9	23	60	15.5	2.7
Franklin	3.6	140	15	148	138.8	6.9	90	1 054	271.1	21.9	13	D	D	D
Geary	14.7	428	8	D	D	D	96	1 309	345.9	27.4	37	292	77.1	11.6
Gove	17.9	6 642	11	D	D	D	20	184	91.5	4.8	NA	NA	NA	NA
Graham	14.2	5 483	9	24	29.2	1.3	21	132	35.5	2.8	2	D	D	D
Grant	129.1	16 493	13	123	87.6	6.9	33	269	52.8	5.0	6	D	D	D
Gray	190.1	31 648	22	210	238.5	9.9	29	171	50.1	4.0	5	25	4.5	0.6
Greeley	17.7	14 226	3	D	D	D	6	44	11.8	1.1	NA	NA	NA	NA
Greenwood	1.8	271	9	D	D	D	32	193	49.5	4.0	2	D	D	D
Hamilton	43.5	16 186	6	58	89.5	2.6	11	95	19.1	1.9	NA	NA	NA	NA
Harper	3.7	617	15	98	151.1	5.6	36	233	62.7	5.3	2	D	D	D
Harvey	44.1	1 273	31	250	144.0	9.9	120	1 446	335.1	32.2	26	D	D	D
Haskell	198.6	46 668	15	124	147.5	5.5	13	63	21.1	1.1	1	D	D	D
Hodgeman	23.2	12 098	5	D	D	D	8	D	D	D	NA	NA	NA	NA
Jackson	2.2	162	13	85	45.3	3.1	40	379	83.2	7.6	6	18	1.9	0.6
Jefferson	3.7	196	6	20	5.7	0.4	48	318	74.0	5.4	1	D	D	D
Jewell	55.3	17 979	10	56	30.5	1.6	13	59	18.3	1.0	NA	NA	NA	NA
Johnson	18.1	33	915	18 267	27 613.7	1 397.4	1 868	35 648	10 481.4	897.6	914	4 765	1 271.2	217.1
Kearny	175.7	44 182	5	D	D	D	9	51	12.2	0.7	3	D	D	D
Kingman	22.2	2 824	25	145	100.4	5.8	26	202	45.7	3.8	6	6	1.2	0.1
Kiowa	58.5	22 902	10	104	115.6	6.2	16	85	28.3	1.8	NA	NA	NA	NA
Labette	4.5	209	15	D	D	D	89	931	198.6	19.8	12	34	4.0	0.8
Lane	15.4	8 811	9	54	52.5	1.8	12	50	9.6	0.8	NA	NA	NA	NA
Leavenworth	27.0	354	19	94	45.0	3.8	174	2 088	541.5	45.8	48	164	45.5	4.9
Lincoln	1.5	463	7	74	31.1	1.8	11	57	9.2	1.0	1	D	D	D
Linn	11.6	1 201	6	30	12.1	1.2	35	241	53.5	3.6	1	D	D	D
Logan	6.7	2 442	13	85	103.9	3.6	15	126	35.3	2.7	NA	NA	NA	NA
Lyon	7.7	227	21	426	287.8	17.2	162	1 814	493.9	36.5	38	152	14.8	3.4
McPherson	31.5	1 080	37	264	560.9	14.9	130	1 197	295.5	27.0	24	75	5.4	1.1
Marion	3.6	284	19	187	133.9	8.7	50	313	79.2	6.1	7	7	2.5	0.3
Marshall	3.5	348	25	159	229.5	7.3	70	687	234.9	13.9	6	12	0.5	0.1
Meade	153.3	33 510	12	104	198.5	5.1	22	221	32.2	3.6	NA	NA	NA	NA
Miami	4.9	149	21	65	97.6	3.1	87	981	262.4	22.7	28	D	D	D
Mitchell	13.0	2 045	23	191	109.5	7.9	43	426	127.7	10.4	5	26	2.2	0.4
Montgomery	11.7	330	30	D	D	D	131	1 536	350.3	35.2	29	89	8.7	1.6
Morris	1.7	285	4	13	11.1	0.6	28	185	44.0	3.8	NA	NA	NA	NA
Morton	47.7	14 748	10	89	127.7	4.1	13	97	21.5	2.1	NA	NA	NA	NA
Nemaha	3.3	327	21	142	141.0	5.9	74	616	156.5	11.4	1	D	D	D

1. Merchant wholesalers, except manufacturers' sales branches and offices. 2. Employer establishments.

Table B. States and Counties — Professional Services, Manufacturing, and Accommodation and Food Services

STATE County	Professional, scientific, and technical services, 2012				Manufacturing, 2012				Accommodation and food services, 2012			
	Number of establishments	Number of employees	Receipts (mil dol)	Annual payroll (mil dol)	Number of establishments	Number of employees	Receipts (mil dol)	Annual payroll (mil dol)	Number of establishments	Number of employees	Sales (mil dol)	Annual payroll (mil dol)
	147	148	149	150	151	152	153	154	155	156	157	158
KANSAS	7 110	60 989	8 716.1	3 596.2	2 875	152 423	86 076.3	7 578.3	5 943	106 850	4 873.4	1 342.9
Allen	27	97	7.1	2.6	25	1 875	470.9	65.1	25	315	13.2	3.2
Anderson	13	29	1.9	0.6	11	150	D	7.3	16	D	D	D
Atchison	21	D	D	D	19	1 333	635.0	79.6	34	D	D	D
Barber	13	54	4.1	1.5	7	119	39.6	5.9	14	110	5.3	1.0
Barton	58	332	38.4	13.9	47	D	337.4	D	62	934	41.1	11.1
Bourbon	28	116	9.4	3.6	27	980	174.9	35.9	32	386	15.2	4.1
Brown	12	68	8.5	3.4	17	530	248.8	20.4	22	289	7.9	2.4
Butler	104	838	49.7	17.5	46	1 306	D	84.7	102	1 590	74.7	18.0
Chase	6	D	D	D	4	88	D	3.6	5	D	D	D
Chautauqua	3	D	D	D	5	79	24.7	2.0	8	D	D	D
Cherokee	28	91	5.6	1.7	33	1 475	452.8	64.0	28	340	13.2	3.6
Cheyenne	7	20	1.7	0.6	3	11	D	D	6	D	D	D
Clark	6	30	3.7	0.9	NA	NA	NA	NA	5	34	0.5	0.1
Clay	15	63	5.6	1.6	10	339	D	13.3	18	162	6.9	1.9
Cloud	14	76	6.5	3.1	9	424	D	16.5	21	285	14.1	3.6
Coffey	14	D	D	D	6	131	D	4.4	22	176	7.2	2.0
Comanche	5	7	0.6	0.1	7	44	D	1.3	6	50	1.5	0.4
Cowley	64	218	21.6	5.6	39	3 333	2 043.9	161.6	62	1 008	48.0	11.7
Crawford	68	D	D	D	49	2 347	823.4	90.7	82	1 488	59.2	14.4
Decatur	6	26	2.6	0.7	NA	NA	NA	NA	7	D	D	D
Dickinson	31	160	14.4	4.1	15	1 146	280.6	42.1	41	442	17.8	4.9
Doniphan	10	D	D	D	13	375	110.8	16.6	8	D	D	D
Douglas	292	D	D	D	69	3 079	1 217.3	136.1	301	6 511	261.1	72.2
Edwards	6	13	0.7	0.2	6	133	D	4.6	5	22	0.9	0.2
Elk	7	15	0.9	0.3	NA	NA	NA	NA	7	D	D	D
Ellis	79	329	34.2	12.4	37	D	219.0	40.5	99	1 925	74.9	21.8
Ellsworth	6	69	6.9	2.7	10	296	52.4	13.7	12	132	4.4	1.3
Finney	58	263	28.5	9.9	26	3 711	D	124.1	76	1 412	74.5	18.5
Ford	45	488	50.8	23.1	23	6 272	5 948.2	220.2	73	1 032	56.1	14.4
Franklin	36	D	D	D	27	654	318.7	30.2	50	D	D	D
Geary	40	D	D	D	7	655	189.3	19.1	82	1 475	64.7	16.5
Gove	9	11	1.2	0.3	7	77	22.8	4.2	8	D	D	D
Graham	8	13	1.2	0.5	NA	NA	NA	NA	6	D	D	D
Grant	10	30	3.0	0.9	12	188	131.6	9.7	17	249	9.7	2.6
Gray	17	55	6.1	2.6	9	84	D	4.3	8	D	D	D
Greeley	4	5	0.7	0.3	NA	NA	NA	NA	2	D	D	D
Greenwood	9	24	2.2	0.7	6	68	D	4.2	12	107	3.4	0.9
Hamilton	3	10	0.5	0.1	NA	NA	NA	NA	5	D	D	D
Harper	12	20	2.1	0.5	21	424	154.1	16.3	17	191	10.7	2.5
Harvey	48	235	22.0	8.3	62	3 004	1 286.7	134.5	61	956	32.7	9.8
Haskell	8	29	2.9	1.0	3	D	D	2.3	8	D	D	D
Hodgeman	3	D	D	D	NA	NA	NA	NA	3	9	0.4	0.1
Jackson	21	78	5.0	1.4	6	214	D	7.6	21	D	D	D
Jefferson	23	54	9.8	1.7	10	282	D	10.5	23	D	D	D
Jewell	4	10	0.7	0.2	NA	NA	NA	NA	7	D	D	D
Johnson	2 669	29 498	4 846.6	2 133.2	478	20 164	7 140.8	1 058.6	1 158	25 214	1 225.3	365.9
Kearny	6	22	1.0	0.2	NA	NA	NA	NA	6	51	1.6	0.4
Kingman	11	47	4.1	1.3	9	403	D	18.2	13	168	7.2	1.5
Kiowa	3	D	D	D	NA	NA	NA	NA	6	D	D	D
Labette	22	105	9.9	3.4	40	1 908	415.1	80.8	36	481	18.7	4.9
Lane	6	14	1.3	0.6	NA	NA	NA	NA	2	D	D	D
Leavenworth	125	D	D	D	33	1 202	455.8	41.9	98	1 439	66.7	17.1
Lincoln	7	8	1.1	0.5	NA	NA	NA	NA	5	D	D	D
Linn	13	D	D	D	10	67	D	2.3	11	D	D	D
Logan	8	25	4.1	0.7	3	11	D	D	8	D	D	D
Lyon	45	D	D	D	37	2 723	2 034.0	119.9	88	1 358	50.0	15.1
McPherson	48	225	18.4	6.8	59	4 633	5 481.6	264.6	62	853	33.1	9.7
Marion	15	D	D	D	25	325	D	12.6	21	D	D	D
Marshall	22	93	13.3	3.3	16	1 391	341.7	67.1	25	221	10.6	2.6
Meade	6	26	1.3	0.4	NA	NA	NA	NA	9	D	D	D
Miami	67	D	D	D	25	447	D	26.7	44	D	D	D
Mitchell	16	53	4.6	1.3	13	574	144.2	22.9	14	D	D	D
Montgomery	49	182	15.5	5.2	52	3 468	6 105.5	196.5	85	1 265	46.3	13.0
Morris	10	53	5.1	1.6	7	171	D	7.4	13	D	D	D
Morton	5	16	1.3	0.3	3	D	D	D	7	D	D	D
Nemaha	22	80	11.4	3.1	26	1 307	413.2	59.7	25	282	8.2	2.0

1. Establishment subject to federal tax.

Health Care and Social Assistance, Other Services, Nonemployer Businesses, and Residential Construction

STATE County	Health care and social assistance, 2012				Other services, 2012				Nonemployer businesses, 2015		Value of residential construction authorized by building permits, 2016	
	Number of establishments	Number of employees	Receipts (mil dol)	Annual payroll (mil dol)	Number of establishments	Number of employees	Receipts (mil dol)	Annual payroll (mil dol)	Number	Receipts (mil dol)	New Construction ($1,000)	Number of housing units
	159	160	161	162	163	164	165	166	167	168	169	170
KANSAS	7 934	192 272	18 248.4	7 504.6	5 147	29 521	3 433.0	849.2	195 777	8 760.9	1 769 952	9 807
Allen	41	626	47.8	20.1	29	76	9.6	2.1	840	26.0	2 461	19
Anderson	21	359	24.2	9.8	11	17	1.7	0.3	618	22.1	0	0
Atchison	46	799	64.6	26.7	20	D	D	D	828	29.7	838	5
Barber	14	288	14.7	8.4	21	52	5.8	1.1	551	26.2	0	0
Barton	111	1 917	152.5	64.0	75	309	38.4	8.6	2 226	100.5	3 487	24
Bourbon	42	1 031	70.0	32.2	29	82	15.6	2.0	1 001	33.1	0	0
Brown	37	882	58.3	27.0	21	D	D	D	733	28.6	412	2
Butler	156	3 409	278.4	103.7	76	400	32.7	8.4	4 258	166.3	40 666	165
Chase	3	D	D	D	9	15	1.3	0.2	217	7.4	20	1
Chautauqua	7	138	8.1	4.0	2	D	D	D	302	11.9	0	0
Cherokee	40	984	70.6	25.8	22	118	5.8	1.5	1 053	40.2	195	2
Cheyenne	10	D	D	D	5	D	D	D	244	9.3	125	1
Clark	7	D	D	D	4	D	D	D	221	5.9	320	2
Clay	25	565	36.1	16.9	26	65	6.1	1.4	641	24.0	2 585	13
Cloud	35	744	38.1	19.1	25	78	5.9	1.6	660	22.2	0	0
Coffey	27	493	39.9	15.4	15	D	D	D	686	30.0	3 350	24
Comanche	7	166	7.1	3.2	6	9	0.7	0.2	162	5.8	0	0
Cowley	118	2 199	132.1	59.1	53	208	24.0	5.0	2 007	70.0	5 549	34
Crawford	129	3 042	233.8	97.9	63	261	20.0	5.5	2 116	71.4	10 456	59
Decatur	7	251	11.8	5.9	8	19	1.7	0.4	252	9.8	0	0
Dickinson	42	883	49.6	24.6	42	148	12.5	2.4	1 249	43.1	2 900	19
Doniphan	9	179	8.7	3.5	7	D	D	D	497	18.7	489	4
Douglas	289	6 580	545.8	211.1	181	1 423	230.7	37.2	8 004	329.5	143 555	1 395
Edwards	10	158	14.6	5.8	11	D	D	D	204	8.1	147	1
Elk	5	D	D	D	5	D	D	D	280	13.5	NA	NA
Ellis	117	3 239	319.4	128.5	85	362	40.8	8.9	2 890	117.4	16 685	77
Ellsworth	23	466	30.5	13.8	16	32	3.4	0.7	454	15.1	800	4
Finney	98	D	D	D	69	D	D	D	2 275	131.0	5 043	29
Ford	92	1 583	164.3	63.8	59	282	28.6	7.1	1 857	98.9	4 045	22
Franklin	68	1 733	93.7	42.1	43	179	14.3	4.6	1 586	64.2	4 930	23
Geary	51	1 577	153.3	58.7	55	241	18.9	5.5	1 312	43.2	2 619	17
Gove	11	237	18.0	6.9	11	D	D	D	292	17.3	1 903	22
Graham	12	237	14.1	6.1	5	D	D	D	298	12.3	0	0
Grant	17	104	7.3	2.7	15	43	5.5	1.3	512	27.2	795	6
Gray	11	149	6.5	3.1	11	D	D	D	634	31.7	1 139	6
Greeley	1	D	D	D	4	D	D	D	137	4.3	400	1
Greenwood	14	270	20.1	9.6	11	16	1.9	0.4	553	17.5	0	0
Hamilton	6	144	9.5	4.1	6	D	D	D	191	9.7	120	1
Harper	16	300	19.5	9.1	14	38	4.3	1.0	519	26.1	1 094	4
Harvey	117	2 967	251.3	102.3	56	262	26.2	7.2	2 382	81.5	9 104	46
Haskell	7	D	D	D	8	D	D	D	387	18.8	0	0
Hodgeman	7	D	D	D	5	D	D	D	179	7.8	229	2
Jackson	22	530	32.5	13.4	27	100	8.6	2.1	791	31.5	4 288	27
Jefferson	29	D	D	D	27	D	D	D	1 219	45.7	9 049	58
Jewell	4	D	D	D	6	16	1.9	0.3	255	9.5	0	0
Johnson	1 739	37 514	4 657.7	1 766.9	969	7 032	789.4	227.0	48 824	2 674.1	754 471	3 256
Kearny	5	D	D	D	4	D	D	D	311	17.1	300	4
Kingman	21	425	22.1	11.0	16	22	2.2	0.5	615	27.2	2 776	11
Kiowa	10	192	12.9	5.5	6	8	1.4	0.2	222	8.5	0	0
Labette	88	4 122	178.2	88.9	33	D	D	D	1 219	41.4	93	3
Lane	4	D	D	D	6	D	D	D	193	6.8	0	0
Leavenworth	137	2 981	288.2	114.7	99	447	36.5	11.6	3 765	133.9	52 330	298
Lincoln	7	D	D	D	7	22	0.9	0.2	232	8.0	0	0
Linn	10	D	D	D	14	71	6.7	1.4	693	22.3	3 168	42
Logan	7	D	D	D	13	23	1.9	0.4	268	12.6	0	0
Lyon	101	2 138	148.3	64.3	60	228	24.9	5.2	1 736	64.9	5 595	43
McPherson	100	2 333	128.2	58.7	84	364	36.0	9.6	2 453	92.3	21 878	189
Marion	31	608	38.3	14.8	26	88	14.9	2.3	963	28.9	3 350	13
Marshall	34	588	38.3	16.6	31	96	6.9	1.7	765	27.3	3 747	17
Meade	9	D	D	D	11	D	D	D	398	19.5	315	3
Miami	67	D	D	D	50	166	13.6	3.6	2 472	114.6	31 555	130
Mitchell	24	607	43.1	20.3	21	63	5.7	1.5	635	23.8	2 285	8
Montgomery	100	2 270	119.4	57.7	58	200	17.1	4.7	1 833	62.6	2 454	20
Morris	14	268	18.7	6.8	8	14	1.1	0.2	484	20.3	430	2
Morton	7	D	D	D	5	D	D	D	212	6.4	0	0
Nemaha	43	848	51.3	24.0	28	57	7.7	1.4	770	28.7	3 385	14

Table B. States and Counties — Government Employment and Payroll, and Local Government Finances

STATE County	Government employment and payroll, 2012									Local government finances, 2012				
			March payroll (percent of total)							General revenue				
												Taxes		
													Per capita[1] (dollars)	
	Full-time equivalent employees	March payroll (dollars)	Adminis-tration, judicial, and legal	Police and Corrections	Fire Protection	Highways and transpor-tation	Health and Welfare	Natural resources and utilities	Education and libraries	Total (mil dol)	Inter-govern-mental (mil dol)	Total (mil dol)	Total	Property
	171	172	173	174	175	176	177	178	179	180	181	182	183	184
KANSAS	X	X	X	X	X	X	X	X	X	X	X	X	X	X
Allen	895	2 577 982	5.0	6.1	3.4	3.7	4.1	8.9	67.1	63.9	30.0	21.1	1 583	1 268
Anderson	497	1 619 637	6.2	5.4	1.6	4.7	1.1	6.1	73.7	23.0	11.7	7.8	980	756
Atchison	692	1 978 776	6.6	8.4	3.3	4.3	7.8	7.0	60.5	55.0	21.3	23.4	1 390	1 002
Barber	411	1 245 913	6.3	3.3	0.1	7.0	45.0	3.3	32.0	35.8	4.2	16.4	3 382	2 951
Barton	1 660	5 166 241	4.8	6.8	2.0	3.6	6.0	4.3	70.0	122.6	44.4	49.3	1 788	1 396
Bourbon	839	2 300 103	4.1	6.3	2.0	3.3	0.0	5.1	77.6	59.7	27.2	20.2	1 354	1 059
Brown	402	1 209 798	8.3	11.3	0.2	5.2	0.6	6.9	64.8	36.4	13.4	17.7	1 790	1 406
Butler	4 199	12 617 495	2.9	6.0	1.7	2.3	2.5	2.9	79.0	296.1	116.0	108.1	1 642	1 429
Chase	138	378 267	8.3	25.9	0.5	9.7	5.3	1.8	44.0	11.2	3.5	6.0	2 181	1 999
Chautauqua	172	502 746	9.7	7.9	0.0	8.5	6.3	5.4	60.4	13.8	5.5	6.9	1 943	1 619
Cherokee	874	3 187 294	11.0	10.0	0.6	9.2	3.4	2.6	61.3	64.1	33.3	21.8	1 027	758
Cheyenne	165	389 236	10.5	5.0	0.1	7.4	2.7	8.2	64.4	12.1	4.1	6.6	2 450	2 088
Clark	347	1 038 878	4.4	3.1	0.0	2.2	61.9	2.5	24.8	28.0	3.9	8.5	3 919	3 852
Clay	803	2 480 508	2.7	3.1	1.1	3.9	30.1	7.3	50.0	45.5	12.6	13.2	1 545	1 227
Cloud	581	1 796 777	3.3	5.8	1.8	7.0	2.6	3.3	72.8	44.9	18.4	15.2	1 616	1 216
Coffey	673	2 404 634	6.2	5.9	0.0	6.6	43.0	4.7	31.1	69.1	9.0	35.4	4 162	4 031
Comanche	187	510 886	10.4	5.9	0.0	8.5	34.5	11.2	28.4	18.5	6.5	6.4	3 350	3 116
Cowley	2 458	8 016 863	4.3	5.7	2.3	2.2	22.2	5.9	56.0	203.4	66.1	46.6	1 284	1 024
Crawford	1 777	5 700 396	5.1	9.6	2.5	3.3	21.7	6.6	49.1	136.9	53.7	45.9	1 166	827
Decatur	132	423 037	12.8	5.9	0.4	9.6	3.7	7.1	54.7	9.9	2.9	5.6	1 953	1 752
Dickinson	1 141	3 857 618	5.1	5.3	1.0	3.4	29.1	5.5	49.6	105.0	33.0	29.3	1 484	1 175
Doniphan	654	1 750 518	4.8	4.1	0.0	3.2	3.0	4.0	80.3	45.4	18.2	12.9	1 635	1 413
Douglas	4 535	18 551 008	5.6	11.2	5.0	2.9	33.2	7.9	33.4	537.2	114.0	188.6	1 671	1 239
Edwards	153	450 266	16.0	7.2	0.2	14.9	6.8	4.1	50.1	13.9	5.5	7.3	2 459	2 226
Elk	292	687 044	6.7	3.5	0.3	5.8	15.5	4.5	62.3	14.4	5.9	5.3	1 934	1 803
Ellis	1 003	3 461 008	7.9	9.4	2.7	5.0	5.7	5.6	61.1	88.4	23.1	51.1	1 759	1 232
Ellsworth	296	866 464	7.5	7.6	0.0	7.7	5.7	8.2	60.7	28.4	9.8	14.2	2 194	1 862
Finney	2 267	7 504 277	5.0	10.7	1.8	2.9	2.9	4.3	70.6	186.5	73.2	74.7	2 008	1 584
Ford	1 844	5 930 863	5.1	8.2	3.9	2.6	3.3	4.3	71.6	177.3	76.6	65.8	1 894	1 286
Franklin	1 501	5 023 604	6.2	8.2	1.6	2.3	29.7	5.6	44.5	115.7	36.0	39.3	1 518	1 176
Geary	2 097	7 346 708	3.8	7.7	1.7	1.2	23.2	1.3	60.2	186.7	68.2	47.0	1 236	779
Gove	329	918 512	4.3	1.7	0.0	4.8	54.5	0.9	32.9	24.5	5.7	7.8	2 849	2 457
Graham	232	804 031	8.2	3.8	0.6	8.9	44.4	4.5	28.5	22.4	4.0	9.8	3 805	3 282
Grant	403	1 281 935	6.8	7.4	0.2	7.9	5.9	5.1	65.0	41.0	11.0	26.3	3 319	3 166
Gray	309	995 915	8.2	7.4	0.0	6.0	2.2	5.2	67.3	26.3	10.8	12.0	1 998	1 829
Greeley	53	153 774	8.6	0.0	0.0	6.4	1.7	4.3	78.3	4.0	1.5	2.0	1 555	1 519
Greenwood	339	898 356	8.5	7.0	0.4	6.6	4.3	4.5	67.1	22.5	10.0	10.4	1 605	1 400
Hamilton	163	402 085	10.0	8.0	0.1	7.1	6.4	7.9	57.3	13.4	3.7	8.9	3 358	3 144
Harper	602	1 701 546	6.8	3.5	0.1	6.1	45.7	4.3	29.4	45.9	10.6	12.9	2 179	2 024
Harvey	1 517	4 865 931	8.6	8.1	5.6	3.6	3.0	5.5	65.1	120.5	49.4	44.5	1 277	900
Haskell	378	1 272 364	6.3	6.7	0.0	7.9	37.3	0.8	40.4	39.0	3.8	22.7	5 336	5 085
Hodgeman	127	312 316	11.2	6.4	0.0	12.3	7.7	10.6	49.0	11.5	3.2	6.7	3 390	3 354
Jackson	744	2 123 015	4.8	7.4	0.0	4.1	0.8	6.6	74.7	41.1	21.8	14.9	1 107	922
Jefferson	801	2 548 797	6.5	6.7	0.0	4.8	6.2	3.9	68.5	65.4	32.7	24.4	1 288	1 179
Jewell	228	595 682	6.9	3.1	0.0	12.6	38.5	5.3	30.9	15.8	4.4	6.1	2 003	1 819
Johnson	22 393	88 446 886	6.5	10.0	4.1	3.0	4.2	7.6	63.3	2 399.0	615.6	1 250.4	2 233	1 568
Kearny	501	1 624 976	4.9	5.2	1.0	3.4	47.9	3.2	32.3	40.1	5.1	19.2	4 834	4 739
Kingman	303	939 992	10.2	7.8	0.3	9.1	3.5	5.9	62.1	29.0	9.1	16.4	2 088	1 871
Kiowa	190	513 068	15.3	8.3	1.6	10.8	2.8	6.8	50.3	18.3	5.8	10.3	4 132	3 569
Labette	1 476	4 983 554	3.5	5.4	1.3	2.4	37.6	2.9	46.0	131.2	39.2	25.9	1 215	896
Lane	185	518 931	8.0	5.3	2.8	7.3	34.7	3.4	37.1	15.3	2.4	7.9	4 633	4 497
Leavenworth	2 924	9 219 623	4.7	9.0	2.4	3.1	3.7	5.2	70.5	234.3	105.0	92.8	1 194	954
Lincoln	278	791 585	5.0	2.8	0.1	6.6	36.5	5.0	42.1	16.1	5.5	7.6	2 408	2 131
Linn	469	1 414 132	7.1	7.1	0.7	5.0	2.4	6.1	70.4	38.3	14.7	20.4	2 163	2 067
Logan	328	920 118	5.1	3.8	0.2	3.2	54.6	2.9	29.9	24.5	3.1	9.2	3 298	2 915
Lyon	2 245	7 549 055	4.5	8.4	2.7	3.3	26.6	2.6	50.3	180.6	54.8	53.5	1 586	1 073
McPherson	1 486	4 467 777	5.3	7.9	1.7	5.1	4.7	13.1	58.6	102.2	34.2	49.8	1 697	1 261
Marion	702	1 972 669	7.2	6.2	0.1	6.0	17.8	6.6	54.8	54.7	18.7	20.1	1 630	1 376
Marshall	507	1 385 386	5.8	6.0	0.0	7.1	3.5	3.5	71.8	35.7	13.7	17.7	1 764	1 524
Meade	403	1 284 083	4.9	3.3	1.1	4.4	54.9	3.4	27.0	33.8	5.5	11.9	2 711	2 487
Miami	1 386	4 167 179	7.7	8.9	1.2	4.9	3.1	3.9	68.5	96.7	33.9	47.7	1 463	1 199
Mitchell	539	1 523 148	6.6	5.9	0.1	6.8	5.3	10.9	62.8	39.3	15.8	13.9	2 189	1 626
Montgomery	1 708	5 095 652	3.7	7.7	2.9	3.7	1.3	9.3	68.3	148.4	54.4	62.4	1 812	1 449
Morris	233	667 311	10.9	7.8	0.3	7.9	1.6	3.9	64.1	17.4	6.0	9.0	1 545	1 277
Morton	433	1 384 778	4.2	3.1	0.1	4.3	50.6	2.3	32.2	39.0	7.6	14.7	4 633	4 454
Nemaha	548	1 548 782	6.0	6.7	0.0	5.8	2.1	9.9	67.8	39.4	16.0	18.2	1 794	1 515

1. Based on the resident population estimated as of July 1 of the year shown.

Table B. States and Counties — Local Government Finances, Government Employment, and Income Taxes

STATE County	Local government finances, 2012 (cont.)									Government employment, 2015			Individual income tax returns, 2014		
	Direct general expenditure							Debt outstanding							
			Percent of total for:												
	Total (mil dol)	Per capita[1] (dollars)	Education	Health and hospitals	Police protection	Public welfare	Highways	Total (mil dol)	Per capita[1] (dollars)	Federal civilian	Federal military	State and local	Number of returns	Mean adjusted gross income	Mean income tax
	185	186	187	188	189	190	191	192	193	194	195	196	197	198	199
KANSAS	X	X	X	X	X	X	X	X	X	25 049	34 937	235 232	1 336 350	62 404	8 131
Allen	63.1	4 735	58.0	4.0	3.4	0.0	6.4	50.6	3 796	57	49	1 614	5 980	42 863	3 683
Anderson	40.1	5 062	61.6	2.1	2.8	0.0	8.0	28.9	3 654	37	31	525	3 510	46 019	4 274
Atchison	59.4	3 536	45.7	1.0	4.9	4.7	7.9	33.0	1 961	46	60	893	6 950	46 200	4 312
Barber	36.3	7 477	24.0	41.7	2.6	0.0	10.3	11.4	2 336	25	19	639	2 350	56 594	7 367
Barton	120.9	4 389	60.4	2.7	3.3	0.0	7.9	58.1	2 108	73	106	2 369	12 740	54 006	6 552
Bourbon	65.3	4 385	57.0	0.9	3.2	0.0	6.3	43.5	2 920	74	57	1 127	6 240	39 475	3 345
Brown	35.1	3 553	49.9	0.9	4.2	0.0	11.2	44.1	4 465	97	39	1 511	4 400	50 035	5 299
Butler	329.4	5 004	68.1	1.1	2.9	0.0	5.2	551.1	8 372	125	257	5 807	29 000	64 100	8 008
Chase	11.4	4 131	37.7	3.0	3.4	0.0	10.4	5.1	1 857	20	10	238	1 220	44 782	4 011
Chautauqua	13.5	3 787	47.9	5.7	3.6	0.0	9.6	9.2	2 578	17	13	245	1 460	46 968	4 570
Cherokee	63.8	3 007	60.9	2.7	4.3	0.0	8.9	20.0	944	54	81	1 399	8 690	41 991	3 733
Cheyenne	11.4	4 256	50.1	5.6	3.7	0.0	9.9	0.8	296	13	11	234	1 270	48 339	5 052
Clark	28.0	12 839	20.3	57.2	4.3	0.0	4.7	5.4	2 461	11	D	434	980	51 307	4 534
Clay	46.8	5 482	29.6	33.0	3.0	0.0	7.6	34.9	4 095	33	33	894	3 970	49 819	4 667
Cloud	46.3	4 930	66.5	3.2	3.3	0.0	6.9	13.5	1 434	41	35	800	4 230	43 387	3 652
Coffey	70.3	8 270	29.8	34.4	3.0	0.0	10.8	13.0	1 531	51	33	1 111	4 070	57 832	6 651
Comanche	19.2	10 056	20.4	23.8	2.0	0.0	6.2	6.1	3 165	D	D	260	870	53 582	5 961
Cowley	191.8	5 286	45.5	21.1	3.6	0.0	3.2	166.3	4 583	99	135	3 378	15 800	47 357	4 689
Crawford	135.7	3 448	45.0	17.8	5.0	0.0	3.9	114.8	2 916	85	154	4 869	16 290	49 003	5 683
Decatur	10.3	3 573	44.7	3.6	4.6	0.0	12.8	7.9	2 755	21	11	249	1 470	45 054	4 341
Dickinson	107.2	5 425	50.6	21.7	3.1	0.0	5.6	91.6	4 637	94	76	1 686	9 190	47 110	4 345
Doniphan	45.9	5 834	72.7	2.2	2.9	0.0	6.0	12.8	1 623	38	29	914	3 370	48 418	4 861
Douglas	474.7	4 206	28.6	35.1	4.9	0.0	3.3	544.9	4 828	428	469	15 406	50 280	59 019	7 364
Edwards	14.5	4 871	42.0	3.4	4.5	0.0	14.5	1.2	396	19	12	230	1 480	53 466	6 090
Elk	14.6	5 351	44.7	2.8	2.7	13.2	10.2	3.0	1 097	13	10	318	1 200	40 284	3 840
Ellis	86.9	2 990	45.4	3.2	5.5	0.0	7.4	38.7	1 332	134	112	3 429	13 490	59 033	7 764
Ellsworth	28.5	4 390	50.2	3.3	4.0	0.0	18.7	22.2	3 424	26	21	889	2 780	51 138	5 442
Finney	182.2	4 899	60.1	1.9	6.7	0.0	4.4	162.9	4 378	125	146	3 129	17 600	52 393	6 457
Ford	201.8	5 806	49.4	1.2	3.5	1.0	2.6	336.1	9 671	229	135	2 692	15 790	44 559	3 927
Franklin	118.9	4 591	39.4	30.1	1.6	0.0	5.7	81.1	3 129	66	100	1 962	11 810	47 425	4 507
Geary	176.2	4 653	47.3	25.0	6.0	0.0	2.9	273.5	7 194	3 283	17 240	2 773	19 250	37 197	2 453
Gove	24.9	9 123	26.3	51.1	1.8	0.0	8.5	1.5	532	14	10	421	1 380	51 780	6 096
Graham	21.4	8 308	22.0	38.9	2.6	0.0	9.1	0.4	152	24	10	328	1 300	48 705	5 407
Grant	35.6	4 496	41.9	5.9	4.7	0.0	7.6	27.3	3 445	17	31	709	3 340	54 906	5 791
Gray	25.6	4 246	56.7	2.7	4.4	0.0	11.9	24.2	4 013	24	24	902	2 780	60 284	7 754
Greeley	4.0	3 089	72.8	0.0	1.1	0.0	4.3	5.0	3 847	11	D	185	650	52 038	5 528
Greenwood	21.3	3 303	53.1	3.8	5.8	0.0	13.3	21.4	3 323	41	25	475	2 860	45 480	4 473
Hamilton	11.6	4 401	48.9	2.0	5.9	0.0	10.1	4.6	1 740	D	10	327	1 090	44 203	4 387
Harper	45.6	7 720	25.8	36.2	2.0	6.9	9.7	21.2	3 581	32	23	847	2 720	58 626	8 353
Harvey	109.6	3 145	50.9	2.7	5.6	0.1	5.4	180.9	5 190	67	135	1 991	15 880	52 028	5 158
Haskell	39.1	9 192	29.1	42.9	3.2	0.0	10.1	10.5	2 463	16	16	564	1 770	43 269	6 450
Hodgeman	10.7	5 451	37.8	5.5	4.6	0.0	12.0	11.5	5 870	16	D	271	920	52 882	5 586
Jackson	41.1	3 058	62.3	0.8	5.4	0.0	10.4	21.9	1 625	52	53	1 949	6 180	48 040	4 347
Jefferson	63.2	3 338	64.8	5.4	5.1	0.0	7.4	46.3	2 446	73	75	1 096	8 540	53 998	5 377
Jewell	13.7	4 485	29.6	21.3	2.8	0.0	17.3	0.8	250	27	12	332	1 490	44 653	4 223
Johnson	2 304.6	4 116	47.4	2.5	7.7	0.9	5.7	5 877.0	10 496	2 642	2 329	28 344	281 740	95 165	15 704
Kearny	42.8	10 778	27.2	45.6	2.8	0.0	6.2	5.6	1 409	15	15	677	1 850	54 006	5 798
Kingman	29.4	3 741	43.5	3.2	4.6	0.0	13.3	19.1	2 432	32	30	562	3 590	54 241	6 203
Kiowa	16.8	6 718	43.0	3.4	4.6	0.0	10.9	3.4	1 371	14	10	370	1 140	50 418	5 322
Labette	134.7	6 331	39.7	39.0	2.6	0.0	4.0	95.8	4 500	80	81	2 814	9 680	41 402	3 865
Lane	15.6	9 127	29.8	31.7	3.9	0.0	8.7	0.5	288	15	D	252	880	56 941	6 950
Leavenworth	188.5	2 425	61.8	0.0	5.1	0.0	3.5	316.9	4 076	4 333	3 849	4 032	32 910	59 316	6 200
Lincoln	16.5	5 197	44.3	7.0	2.8	0.0	13.6	1.8	569	32	12	414	1 500	40 528	3 557
Linn	38.3	4 053	55.6	3.0	4.7	0.0	10.2	11.7	1 244	47	38	745	4 140	44 170	3 945
Logan	27.7	9 951	22.7	51.3	2.8	0.0	4.7	6.2	2 220	20	11	736	1 430	55 973	6 785
Lyon	166.1	4 920	39.3	28.9	4.3	0.0	4.3	94.4	2 798	98	127	4 218	14 650	45 545	4 317
McPherson	101.4	3 454	45.5	2.3	4.3	0.0	12.0	90.9	3 097	79	112	1 941	13 950	59 171	6 969
Marion	54.2	4 388	42.4	18.1	3.1	0.0	9.1	43.6	3 528	64	45	960	5 320	48 746	4 616
Marshall	34.8	3 472	53.8	2.9	4.3	0.0	13.1	19.2	1 915	51	39	814	5 050	52 105	5 812
Meade	34.5	7 851	21.7	41.1	2.2	3.8	7.6	13.7	3 120	18	17	606	1 980	60 967	7 937
Miami	87.9	2 695	49.6	2.9	5.9	0.0	9.2	104.9	3 215	64	127	2 099	14 920	63 458	7 835
Mitchell	42.4	6 669	50.7	7.8	3.9	0.0	12.6	15.4	2 417	31	24	1 031	3 090	50 662	5 389
Montgomery	142.0	4 121	61.6	2.3	3.8	0.0	5.5	137.7	3 996	109	129	2 545	14 350	44 081	4 066
Morris	25.5	4 361	59.2	5.3	2.7	0.0	10.7	21.0	3 594	33	22	441	2 640	47 633	4 594
Morton	37.0	11 666	31.7	47.6	0.9	0.0	2.7	4.6	1 453	21	12	486	1 470	53 281	5 571
Nemaha	36.9	3 640	57.0	1.5	3.6	0.0	11.8	35.6	3 511	52	40	753	5 000	62 514	7 577

1. Based on the resident population estimated as of July 1 of the year shown.

Table B. States and Counties — **Land Area and Population**

STATE/ County code	CBSA code[1]	County type[2]	STATE County	Land area[3] (sq mi) 2016	Total persons 2016	Rank	Per square mile	White	Black	American Indian, Alaska Native	Asian and Pacific Islander	Percent Hispanic or Latino[4]	Under 5 years	5 to 17 years	18 to 24 years	25 to 34 years	35 to 44 years	45 to 54 years
				1	2	3	4	5	6	7	8	9	10	11	12	13	14	15
			KANSAS—Cont'd															
20 133	...	7	Neosho	571.5	16 146	2 031	28.3	91.7	1.8	1.9	1.0	5.4	6.9	18.0	8.6	11.0	10.6	12.2
20 135	...	9	Ness	1 074.7	2 962	2 973	2.8	89.7	1.3	0.9	0.4	9.0	6.0	15.6	7.2	8.8	9.1	11.4
20 137	...	7	Norton	878.0	5 493	2 803	6.3	90.8	3.7	0.8	1.1	5.0	5.0	14.0	8.1	13.2	11.8	14.4
20 139	45820	3	Osage	705.5	15 843	2 052	22.5	94.8	1.4	1.6	0.9	3.3	5.5	18.0	7.4	9.7	11.1	13.4
20 141	...	9	Osborne	892.5	3 642	2 930	4.1	96.2	0.9	0.8	1.4	1.9	5.8	14.9	7.3	11.0	8.9	11.8
20 143	41460	9	Ottawa	720.7	5 920	2 762	8.2	95.4	1.8	1.0	0.5	2.7	5.0	18.3	7.7	9.3	11.4	13.8
20 145	...	7	Pawnee	754.3	6 743	2 693	8.9	85.7	6.3	1.3	0.8	7.8	4.2	13.5	8.0	12.7	12.6	13.7
20 147	...	7	Phillips	885.9	5 428	2 807	6.1	94.7	1.0	0.9	1.2	3.6	6.2	17.2	7.2	10.3	9.8	11.7
20 149	31740	3	Pottawatomie	841.0	23 661	1 652	28.1	91.6	2.0	1.4	1.7	5.3	7.6	21.4	8.4	12.9	12.5	11.4
20 151	...	7	Pratt	735.0	9 584	2 461	13.0	90.5	2.1	1.3	0.9	7.0	7.4	17.1	9.7	11.6	10.3	10.6
20 153	...	9	Rawlins	1 069.4	2 549	3 001	2.4	92.2	1.3	0.7	0.7	6.5	6.0	15.0	6.2	10.0	8.1	11.2
20 155	26740	4	Reno	1 255.3	63 220	837	50.4	86.5	4.2	1.4	0.9	9.2	5.7	17.2	8.7	12.4	11.1	12.0
20 157	...	9	Republic	717.4	4 699	2 850	6.6	96.9	1.1	0.7	0.7	1.7	5.3	14.9	6.3	8.7	8.4	11.5
20 159	...	7	Rice	726.2	9 831	2 446	13.5	85.3	2.1	1.6	1.2	11.7	6.1	17.3	11.8	11.2	10.0	11.1
20 161	31740	3	Riley	609.8	73 343	744	120.3	79.9	8.0	1.2	6.4	7.8	5.9	11.1	32.2	18.3	9.2	6.9
20 163	...	9	Rooks	890.5	5 076	2 827	5.7	95.6	1.6	0.8	1.1	2.6	6.2	16.6	7.2	11.4	10.1	11.9
20 165	...	9	Rush	717.8	3 058	2 964	4.3	94.9	1.0	1.3	0.5	3.6	4.4	15.1	6.4	10.3	9.4	12.4
20 167	...	7	Russell	886.3	6 988	2 671	7.9	93.7	2.0	1.5	0.9	3.5	6.8	15.1	6.5	11.5	9.8	12.2
20 169	41460	5	Saline	720.2	55 142	917	76.6	82.7	4.8	1.1	3.1	11.0	6.6	17.3	9.1	12.5	11.2	12.9
20 171	...	7	Scott	717.6	5 032	2 833	7.0	80.1	1.1	1.0	1.2	17.6	7.2	19.1	7.9	10.4	10.9	12.1
20 173	48620	2	Sedgwick	997.5	511 995	135	513.3	71.3	10.5	2.0	5.3	14.4	7.2	18.9	9.4	14.4	12.0	12.0
20 175	30580	5	Seward	639.3	22 709	1 695	35.5	31.8	4.6	0.9	3.2	60.8	9.4	22.2	11.1	15.2	11.8	11.6
20 177	45820	3	Shawnee	544.0	178 146	366	327.5	77.3	10.0	2.1	2.1	12.0	6.4	17.6	8.4	12.7	11.5	12.5
20 179	...	9	Sheridan	896.0	2 509	3 004	2.8	94.4	1.0	0.6	0.3	4.7	5.4	17.7	6.8	8.6	9.5	12.2
20 181	...	7	Sherman	1 056.1	5 965	2 752	5.6	86.6	1.6	0.9	0.8	11.7	6.8	16.9	8.3	12.2	10.2	11.3
20 183	...	9	Smith	895.5	3 632	2 932	4.1	96.8	1.1	1.3	0.7	2.2	4.0	15.3	6.7	8.0	9.9	12.5
20 185	...	9	Stafford	792.0	4 208	2 882	5.3	84.7	1.0	1.5	0.6	13.7	6.5	17.6	7.5	10.0	9.3	12.7
20 187	...	9	Stanton	680.4	2 062	3 043	3.0	61.1	1.5	1.7	0.5	36.9	6.8	20.7	7.4	10.6	11.8	13.1
20 189	...	7	Stevens	727.3	5 584	2 794	7.7	62.2	1.1	1.2	0.6	35.9	7.3	22.3	8.8	11.2	11.3	13.1
20 191	48620	2	Sumner	1 181.6	23 272	1 667	19.7	91.9	1.8	2.4	0.7	5.4	5.9	18.4	7.9	11.0	11.2	12.1
20 193	...	7	Thomas	1 074.7	7 892	2 606	7.3	92.4	1.3	1.0	1.3	5.4	7.2	16.0	13.4	12.7	10.6	10.1
20 195	...	9	Trego	889.5	2 872	2 982	3.2	96.2	1.2	0.9	0.9	1.9	5.5	13.2	6.7	10.6	9.5	12.7
20 197	45820	3	Wabaunsee	794.3	6 891	2 681	8.7	94.5	1.3	1.8	0.7	3.6	6.2	18.0	6.6	9.7	10.8	13.4
20 199	...	9	Wallace	913.7	1 497	3 079	1.6	91.2	1.1	0.9	0.1	7.7	6.1	18.6	7.7	9.5	9.3	11.5
20 201	...	9	Washington	894.8	5 546	2 797	6.2	95.0	0.9	0.6	1.0	3.5	6.2	16.4	7.5	9.5	10.0	12.6
20 203	...	9	Wichita	718.6	2 112	3 038	2.9	69.3	1.2	0.7	0.3	29.4	6.9	20.4	7.4	9.9	10.2	12.0
20 205	...	7	Wilson	570.4	8 723	2 529	15.3	94.4	1.3	2.8	1.1	3.1	6.2	17.3	7.1	10.1	10.9	11.6
20 207	...	9	Woodson	497.8	3 165	2 957	6.4	95.0	1.3	2.3	0.6	3.1	5.0	16.3	6.0	10.7	10.5	12.1
20 209	28140	1	Wyandotte	151.6	163 831	393	1 080.7	43.7	24.2	1.4	5.0	28.3	8.3	19.7	8.8	15.0	12.9	11.8
21 000	...	0	**KENTUCKY**	39 485.2	4 436 974	X	112.4	86.6	9.1	0.7	1.9	3.5	6.2	16.6	9.5	13.0	12.5	13.5
21 001	...	7	Adair	405.3	19 280	1 859	47.6	94.6	3.7	0.7	0.5	1.8	5.3	15.2	13.0	11.2	11.0	13.4
21 003	14540	3	Allen	344.3	20 631	1 791	59.9	96.5	1.6	0.8	0.5	1.9	6.3	17.6	7.6	12.3	12.0	14.0
21 005	23180	6	Anderson	201.8	22 158	1 722	109.8	95.5	2.8	0.7	0.9	1.6	5.9	17.8	7.7	11.6	13.3	15.3
21 007	37140	9	Ballard	246.7	8 054	2 592	32.6	94.8	4.5	1.0	0.5	1.3	5.1	16.6	7.3	10.4	12.3	13.7
21 009	23980	6	Barren	487.5	43 993	1 093	90.2	91.4	4.8	0.6	1.0	3.1	6.6	17.2	7.8	12.0	12.3	13.5
21 011	34460	8	Bath	278.8	12 327	2 269	44.2	96.4	2.1	0.6	0.4	1.8	7.0	18.4	7.7	10.7	12.4	13.8
21 013	33180	7	Bell	359.0	27 117	1 526	75.5	96.0	3.1	1.1	0.6	1.0	6.1	15.1	8.2	12.3	11.9	14.0
21 015	17140	1	Boone	246.2	128 536	490	522.1	89.7	4.0	0.5	3.3	4.2	6.8	20.1	7.9	12.4	13.9	14.6
21 017	30460	2	Bourbon	289.7	20 030	1 826	69.1	87.1	7.1	0.6	0.5	6.6	6.1	16.6	8.2	11.0	11.9	14.3
21 019	26580	2	Boyd	159.9	48 132	1 016	301.0	94.6	3.5	0.7	0.9	1.7	6.1	15.3	7.0	12.2	12.6	13.8
21 021	19220	7	Boyle	180.4	30 018	1 431	166.4	87.8	8.9	0.7	1.3	3.3	5.5	14.9	11.9	11.3	11.8	13.3
21 023	17140	1	Bracken	205.6	8 400	2 560	40.9	97.5	1.1	0.7	0.3	1.7	6.5	17.9	7.4	11.9	11.8	14.2
21 025	...	7	Breathitt	492.4	13 284	2 216	27.0	97.7	0.8	0.5	0.9	0.9	6.2	15.0	8.1	12.0	13.1	14.7
21 027	...	8	Breckinridge	567.2	19 961	1 831	35.2	96.1	2.8	0.9	0.5	1.2	5.7	17.3	7.3	10.4	11.3	14.1
21 029	31140	1	Bullitt	297.0	79 151	705	266.5	96.1	1.6	0.9	0.9	1.9	5.3	17.3	8.0	12.8	13.3	15.2
21 031	14540	3	Butler	426.1	12 845	2 239	30.1	95.8	0.8	0.7	0.3	3.5	5.9	16.6	6.5	12.3	12.7	13.7
21 033	...	7	Caldwell	344.8	12 568	2 256	36.5	92.0	6.5	0.7	0.5	1.7	6.0	16.4	7.4	11.0	11.7	13.2
21 035	34660	7	Calloway	385.0	38 437	1 214	99.8	90.8	4.8	0.6	2.5	2.7	5.1	12.9	20.4	11.8	10.2	11.4
21 037	17140	1	Campbell	151.3	92 211	635	609.5	94.0	3.9	0.6	1.4	1.9	5.9	15.4	10.0	14.7	12.0	13.3
21 039	...	9	Carlisle	189.4	4 855	2 843	25.6	95.5	2.0	1.0	0.5	2.3	6.5	15.7	6.9	11.2	11.7	12.6
21 041	...	6	Carroll	128.6	10 679	2 377	83.0	90.8	2.7	0.8	0.8	6.7	7.5	18.0	7.9	12.4	12.2	13.0
21 043	...	6	Carter	409.5	27 046	1 527	66.0	97.7	0.9	0.7	0.4	1.2	6.4	16.2	8.9	11.6	11.9	13.9
21 045	...	9	Casey	444.2	15 815	2 055	35.6	96.0	1.2	0.7	0.5	2.8	6.4	16.5	7.5	11.3	11.9	13.5
21 047	17300	2	Christian	717.5	72 351	748	100.8	68.5	23.0	1.1	2.9	7.6	9.6	17.8	15.8	16.5	10.3	9.1
21 049	30460	2	Clark	252.5	35 819	1 279	141.9	91.6	5.6	0.6	0.7	3.0	5.9	16.5	7.7	11.6	13.0	14.4

1. CBSA = Core Based Statistical Area. See Appendix A for explanation. See Appendix B for list of metropolitan areas with component counties.   2. County type code from the Economic Research Service of USDA Rural-Urban Continuum Codes. See Appendix A for definition.   3. Dry land or land partially or temporarily covered by water.   4. May be of any race.

Table B. States and Counties — **Population and Households**

STATE County	55 to 64 years	65 to 74 years	75 years and over	Percent female	Total persons 2000	Total persons 2010	Percent change 2000–2010	Percent change 2010–2016	Births	Deaths	Net migration	Households Number	Persons per house-hold	Family house-holds	Female family house-holder[1]	One per-son
	16	17	18	19	20	21	22	23	24	25	26	27	28	29	30	31

KANSAS—Cont'd

STATE County	16	17	18	19	20	21	22	23	24	25	26	27	28	29	30	31
Neosho	13.7	9.9	9.0	50.1	16 997	16 512	-2.9	-2.2	1 367	1 240	-469	6 463	2.47	68.6	12.0	28.5
Ness	17.4	11.0	13.5	50.7	3 454	3 107	-10.0	-4.7	218	279	-81	1 383	2.18	67.0	5.6	31.1
Norton	13.4	10.0	10.1	43.9	5 953	5 671	-4.7	-3.1	323	380	-126	2 119	2.24	69.1	10.2	28.2
Osage	15.9	10.9	8.2	49.9	16 712	16 295	-2.5	-2.8	1 048	1 173	-326	6 505	2.44	68.2	8.0	28.7
Osborne	15.7	11.0	13.6	49.4	4 452	3 858	-13.3	-5.6	278	330	-168	1 764	2.08	59.8	5.6	37.1
Ottawa	15.5	10.4	8.7	48.5	6 163	6 091	-1.2	-2.8	352	401	-108	2 493	2.39	68.9	6.5	28.1
Pawnee	15.4	10.0	10.0	44.2	7 233	6 973	-3.6	-3.3	404	466	-180	2 552	2.32	56.8	8.7	37.2
Phillips	15.3	11.9	10.3	49.8	6 001	5 642	-6.0	-3.8	411	444	-162	2 349	2.29	66.4	5.6	31.7
Pottawatomie	12.1	7.8	5.9	50.4	18 209	21 604	18.6	9.5	2 231	1 051	871	8 192	2.72	71.6	5.9	24.5
Pratt	14.6	9.0	9.7	50.3	9 647	9 656	0.1	-0.7	880	700	-235	3 902	2.39	65.5	10.2	31.2
Rawlins	16.6	12.2	14.8	49.4	2 966	2 519	-15.1	1.2	177	216	65	1 212	2.07	59.9	4.2	37.6
Reno	14.0	10.0	8.8	49.6	64 790	64 511	-0.4	-2.0	4 624	4 626	-1 195	25 097	2.44	65.1	9.7	30.0
Republic	17.0	13.2	14.6	51.4	5 835	4 980	-14.7	-5.6	293	538	-23	2 275	2.07	57.0	4.9	39.0
Rice	14.3	9.2	8.9	49.4	10 761	10 083	-6.3	-2.5	759	748	-244	3 881	2.42	66.8	5.9	29.0
Riley	7.6	4.9	3.8	47.0	62 843	71 131	13.2	3.1	6 787	2 073	-2 677	26 467	2.49	53.5	7.1	29.7
Rooks	15.5	10.8	10.3	51.7	5 685	5 181	-8.9	-2.0	388	410	-84	2 206	2.28	63.5	9.3	32.9
Rush	17.6	11.6	12.8	49.4	3 551	3 307	-6.9	-7.5	160	285	-117	1 486	2.10	58.7	6.2	35.0
Russell	15.3	11.7	11.0	51.1	7 370	6 970	-5.4	0.3	549	561	74	3 239	2.12	64.1	10.3	29.4
Saline	13.8	9.1	7.5	50.4	53 597	55 606	3.7	-0.8	4 777	3 240	-1 888	22 390	2.42	63.4	12.5	29.8
Scott	13.5	9.7	9.2	49.8	5 120	4 936	-3.6	1.9	419	357	19	2 196	2.21	62.8	2.7	32.7
Sedgwick	12.6	7.8	5.7	50.6	452 869	498 365	10.0	2.7	47 528	26 277	-7 339	192 961	2.59	64.6	12.3	30.4
Seward	9.4	5.2	4.1	48.5	22 510	22 952	2.0	-1.1	2 795	823	-2 210	7 480	3.05	72.5	17.1	22.2
Shawnee	13.9	9.6	7.4	51.5	169 871	177 934	4.7	0.1	14 955	10 909	-3 712	71 368	2.44	62.6	11.3	31.1
Sheridan	16.1	11.1	12.6	49.8	2 813	2 556	-9.1	-1.8	160	185	-25	1 133	2.21	66.4	7.2	32.4
Sherman	14.7	10.1	9.4	49.8	6 760	6 010	-11.1	-0.7	492	451	-98	2 786	2.14	57.2	9.0	37.0
Smith	16.9	12.1	14.7	50.4	4 536	3 853	-15.1	-5.7	186	366	-49	1 667	2.21	63.3	4.8	34.3
Stafford	15.6	9.9	10.9	48.5	4 789	4 437	-7.4	-5.2	302	337	-172	1 794	2.35	68.2	6.9	29.2
Stanton	12.8	7.7	9.1	50.0	2 406	2 235	-7.1	-7.7	175	113	-223	820	2.58	70.0	7.0	27.1
Stevens	12.1	7.2	6.6	50.7	5 463	5 724	4.8	-2.4	496	257	-355	2 007	2.84	78.8	6.7	19.1
Sumner	15.4	10.0	8.1	50.1	25 946	24 132	-7.0	-3.6	1 677	1 640	-932	9 091	2.55	67.6	8.5	29.7
Thomas	14.1	8.1	7.9	51.3	8 180	7 900	-3.4	-0.1	733	451	-287	3 174	2.39	64.0	6.5	31.7
Trego	17.3	12.7	11.8	49.4	3 319	3 001	-9.6	-4.3	201	279	-63	1 302	2.21	68.7	7.2	28.5
Wabaunsee	16.4	10.8	8.0	49.1	6 885	7 053	2.4	-2.3	506	385	-261	2 668	2.59	69.9	6.1	27.5
Wallace	15.2	10.7	11.4	51.0	1 749	1 485	-15.1	0.8	113	112	8	625	2.52	62.9	2.7	34.1
Washington	14.2	11.1	12.5	49.4	6 483	5 799	-10.6	-4.4	415	443	-211	2 442	2.27	67.8	7.3	29.2
Wichita	14.9	8.9	9.5	48.4	2 531	2 234	-11.7	-5.5	174	146	-142	781	2.79	73.5	10.8	25.9
Wilson	15.8	11.8	9.2	50.9	10 332	9 409	-8.9	-7.3	711	793	-561	3 769	2.37	66.2	11.0	28.9
Woodson	17.2	11.7	10.5	49.4	3 788	3 309	-12.6	-4.4	209	308	-30	1 531	2.08	59.2	8.8	35.7
Wyandotte	11.9	6.8	4.7	50.6	157 882	157 505	-0.2	4.0	17 129	8 607	-2 005	58 870	2.71	63.6	17.9	30.2
KENTUCKY	13.3	9.3	6.3	50.7	4 041 769	4 339 344	7.4	2.2	346 968	273 427	26 135	1 708 499	2.50	66.5	12.8	28.1
Adair	13.5	10.2	7.1	50.5	17 244	18 656	8.2	3.3	1 286	1 218	568	7 048	2.50	66.8	10.0	29.9
Allen	13.3	10.3	6.5	50.5	17 800	19 967	12.2	3.3	1 587	1 342	451	7 774	2.59	70.8	9.4	25.8
Anderson	13.2	9.3	6.0	51.3	19 111	21 417	12.1	3.5	1 526	1 228	442	8 446	2.56	71.2	10.9	23.3
Ballard	14.8	11.4	8.6	50.2	8 286	8 247	-0.5	-2.3	518	640	-61	3 288	2.48	66.3	9.5	29.9
Barren	13.5	9.8	7.4	51.6	38 033	42 173	10.9	4.3	3 452	3 003	1 305	16 979	2.48	69.2	12.0	28.5
Bath	13.5	9.6	6.9	50.2	11 085	11 585	4.5	6.4	1 027	861	570	4 297	2.76	68.7	11.7	26.6
Bell	14.3	10.9	7.1	51.0	30 060	28 691	-4.6	-5.5	2 172	2 307	-1 368	11 088	2.44	63.6	16.6	31.9
Boone	12.3	7.7	4.3	50.5	85 991	118 819	38.2	8.2	10 308	4 849	4 334	44 709	2.77	75.1	11.5	20.5
Bourbon	13.7	10.4	7.8	51.5	19 360	19 980	3.2	0.3	1 441	1 311	-43	7 867	2.51	67.1	13.7	27.0
Boyd	14.4	10.5	8.0	50.2	49 752	49 538	-0.4	-2.8	3 718	3 659	-1 343	19 383	2.41	67.9	12.0	27.4
Boyle	12.7	10.4	8.2	49.9	27 697	28 420	2.6	5.6	1 960	1 916	1 472	11 045	2.42	64.3	10.7	31.1
Bracken	14.3	9.6	6.4	50.2	8 279	8 488	2.5	-1.0	653	581	-153	3 303	2.54	65.0	10.7	29.6
Breathitt	14.7	10.2	6.1	49.8	16 100	13 876	-13.8	-4.3	1 089	1 221	-467	5 494	2.41	67.1	16.3	30.2
Breckinridge	15.3	11.6	7.0	49.8	18 648	20 042	7.5	-0.4	1 353	1 392	8	7 297	2.71	71.4	8.2	23.6
Bullitt	13.6	9.4	5.2	50.4	61 236	74 319	21.4	6.5	4 928	3 364	3 184	28 267	2.71	74.4	12.4	20.9
Butler	14.2	10.5	7.6	50.1	13 010	12 690	-2.5	1.2	945	864	71	5 176	2.44	68.9	11.1	28.1
Caldwell	14.4	11.7	8.2	51.5	13 060	12 984	-0.6	-3.2	934	1 045	-234	5 293	2.39	69.2	14.8	27.2
Calloway	11.9	9.5	6.9	51.4	34 177	37 191	8.8	3.4	2 481	2 468	1 244	14 834	2.35	57.7	9.1	34.2
Campbell	14.0	8.5	6.1	50.9	88 616	90 336	1.9	2.1	6 827	5 151	314	35 477	2.49	63.4	11.9	29.6
Carlisle	13.9	11.3	9.8	51.3	5 351	5 104	-4.6	-4.9	417	400	-260	2 059	2.39	68.2	7.5	29.0
Carroll	13.4	9.4	6.1	49.9	10 155	10 811	6.5	-1.2	996	759	-388	3 988	2.63	63.1	8.6	30.7
Carter	13.8	10.6	6.7	50.6	26 889	27 718	3.1	-2.4	2 246	1 916	-1 052	10 487	2.54	69.3	12.5	26.8
Casey	13.3	12.0	7.6	51.3	15 447	15 952	3.3	-0.9	1 233	1 195	-188	6 384	2.44	69.2	8.5	28.9
Christian	9.0	6.6	5.2	46.9	72 265	73 939	2.3	-2.1	9 718	3 736	-7 754	25 521	2.67	70.7	14.5	25.6
Clark	13.8	10.2	6.8	51.0	33 144	35 609	7.4	0.6	2 559	2 453	156	14 173	2.49	68.0	12.1	24.4

1. No spouse present.

Table B. States and Counties — **Population, Vital Statistics, Health, and Crime**

STATE County	Persons in group quarters, 2016	Daytime population, 2011–2015 Number	Daytime population, 2011–2015 Employment/residence ratio	Births, 2016 Total	Births, 2016 Rate[1]	Deaths, 2016 Number	Deaths, 2016 Rate[1]	Persons under 65 with no health insurance, 2015 Number	Persons under 65 with no health insurance, 2015 Percent	Medicare, 2015 Total Beneficiaries	Medicare, 2015 Enrolled in Original Medicare	Medicare, 2015 Enrolled in Medicare Advantage	Serious crimes known to police,[2] 2014 Total Number	Serious crimes known to police,[2] 2014 Total Rate[3]
	32	33	34	35	36	37	38	39	40	41	42	43	44	45
KANSAS—Cont'd														
Neosho	450	15 940	0.94	216	13.4	176	10.9	1 152	8.9	3 348	3 165	183	204	1 242
Ness	70	3 265	1.13	35	11.8	44	14.9	291	12.8	772	749	23	39	1 272
Norton	821	5 673	1.03	55	10.0	71	12.9	358	9.7	1 139	1 076	63	62	1 104
Osage	194	12 349	0.48	170	10.7	204	12.9	1 160	9.1	3 383	3 184	199	186	1 183
Osborne	100	3 612	0.91	49	13.5	39	10.7	347	12.7	931	902	29	49	1 285
Ottawa	98	4 742	0.56	49	8.3	65	11.0	473	9.8	1 161	1 122	39	92	1 525
Pawnee	1 028	7 568	1.22	59	8.7	74	11.0	429	9.4	767	756	11	180	2 583
Phillips	68	5 483	0.99	74	13.6	64	11.8	428	10.2	1 336	1 295	41	11	199
Pottawatomie	299	21 928	0.94	352	14.9	185	7.8	1 296	6.5	3 064	2 833	231	332	1 447
Pratt	380	10 063	1.07	149	15.5	93	9.7	812	10.6	1 787	1 757	30	305	3 068
Rawlins	40	2 512	0.97	39	15.3	22	8.6	227	12.6	678	651	27	23	881
Reno	3 118	63 486	0.98	719	11.4	702	11.1	4 921	10.0	13 529	12 638	891	2 254	3 515
Republic	103	4 629	0.93	50	10.6	66	14.0	368	10.7	1 315	1 276	39	108	2 255
Rice	649	9 519	0.90	121	12.3	100	10.2	897	11.8	1 992	1 927	65	NA	NA
Riley	9 080	73 254	0.96	1 062	14.5	352	4.8	5 319	8.8	7 264	6 767	497	1 375	1 799
Rooks	72	5 123	0.98	63	12.4	74	14.6	415	10.2	1 197	1 162	35	34	654
Rush	66	2 949	0.85	22	7.2	28	9.2	230	9.7	824	802	22	95	3 011
Russell	89	6 718	0.92	88	12.6	89	12.7	578	10.7	1 748	1 715	33	143	2 066
Saline	1 465	57 643	1.07	737	13.4	481	8.7	5 036	11.0	10 739	9 623	1 116	2 169	3 890
Scott	105	4 732	0.92	74	14.7	66	13.1	539	13.5	560	548	12	76	1 502
Sedgwick	7 287	524 156	1.07	7 278	14.2	4 407	8.6	59 098	13.5	77 361	61 578	15 783	23 243	4 583
Seward	476	24 303	1.09	431	19.0	118	5.2	3 966	19.4	2 038	2 001	37	693	2 949
Shawnee	4 399	191 751	1.16	2 290	12.9	1 801	10.1	13 432	9.2	35 374	31 833	3 541	7 867	4 430
Sheridan	33	2 483	0.96	22	8.8	21	8.4	277	14.4	D	507	D	21	822
Sherman	102	5 928	0.96	76	12.7	83	13.9	608	12.8	1 255	1 233	22	135	2 197
Smith	56	3 671	0.96	27	7.4	47	12.9	288	10.7	1 096	1 060	36	NA	NA
Stafford	69	3 952	0.82	55	13.1	45	10.7	546	16.4	1 421	1 380	41	61	1 404
Stanton	47	2 152	1.00	24	11.6	16	7.8	339	20.0	D	318	D	NA	NA
Stevens	72	5 706	0.98	64	11.5	28	5.0	808	16.1	722	706	16	NA	NA
Sumner	409	20 860	0.74	257	11.0	257	11.0	1 801	9.4	5 044	4 377	667	556	2 544
Thomas	353	8 332	1.10	135	17.1	62	7.9	575	9.0	1 307	1 258	49	211	2 653
Trego	64	2 791	0.90	39	13.6	47	16.4	229	10.4	D	662	D	31	1 041
Wabaunsee	90	5 381	0.51	65	9.4	49	7.1	432	7.7	1 317	1 263	54	92	1 304
Wallace	19	1 561	0.95	19	12.7	15	10.0	134	11.3	361	350	11	1	63
Washington	114	5 060	0.78	67	12.1	85	15.3	500	11.8	1 415	1 358	57	25	447
Wichita	26	2 371	1.16	27	12.8	18	8.5	316	17.9	D	383	D	31	1 421
Wilson	121	8 973	0.98	103	11.8	117	13.4	880	12.7	2 057	1 972	85	202	2 235
Woodson	39	2 686	0.66	35	11.1	45	14.2	301	12.6	790	739	51	97	3 029
Wyandotte	1 335	176 226	1.22	2 755	16.8	1 434	8.8	24 516	17.3	23 296	15 486	7 810	9 074	5 633
KENTUCKY	131 248	4 422 821	1.01	55 198	12.4	44 883	10.1	258 239	7.1	843 937	604 212	239 725	108 506	2 459
Adair	1 409	16 851	0.73	211	10.9	222	11.5	1 208	8.3	3 744	2 907	837	106	564
Allen	197	17 620	0.67	256	12.4	238	11.5	1 336	7.8	3 893	3 026	867	204	1 000
Anderson	108	16 180	0.47	238	10.7	195	8.8	1 059	5.7	3 882	2 405	1 477	141	643
Ballard	127	7 559	0.80	81	10.1	102	12.7	447	6.9	2 355	1 896	459	119	1 423
Barren	701	43 045	1.01	601	13.7	514	11.7	2 550	7.1	8 719	6 552	2 167	653	1 508
Bath	103	10 236	0.57	176	14.3	158	12.8	809	8.0	2 378	1 568	810	9	75
Bell	952	29 378	1.18	323	11.9	360	13.3	1 664	7.7	6 807	5 412	1 395	869	3 135
Boone	835	144 489	1.32	1 700	13.2	923	7.2	5 714	5.1	19 079	11 473	7 606	2 803	2 226
Bourbon	236	18 867	0.87	239	11.9	227	11.3	1 567	9.6	3 856	2 434	1 422	359	1 792
Boyd	2 143	57 356	1.47	575	11.9	584	12.1	2 422	6.4	10 904	8 225	2 679	1 286	2 638
Boyle	3 218	32 873	1.29	324	10.8	313	10.4	1 330	6.2	6 791	4 983	1 808	513	1 759
Bracken	41	6 498	0.44	104	12.4	102	12.1	450	6.5	1 860	1 286	574	94	1 210
Breathitt	322	12 995	0.85	175	13.2	196	14.8	893	8.0	3 320	2 551	769	33	245
Breckinridge	300	17 169	0.61	218	10.9	201	10.1	1 334	8.3	4 052	3 352	700	43	214
Bullitt	340	62 398	0.60	828	10.5	621	7.8	3 475	5.2	10 905	7 394	3 511	1 099	1 417
Butler	203	11 309	0.69	147	11.4	125	9.7	886	8.4	2 422	1 667	755	126	982
Caldwell	148	12 310	0.90	144	11.5	158	12.6	612	6.0	3 065	2 381	684	241	1 883
Calloway	3 232	39 141	1.06	407	10.6	408	10.6	2 184	7.5	7 092	5 206	1 886	928	2 455
Campbell	3 294	76 571	0.67	1 191	12.9	884	9.6	4 385	5.7	14 439	8 527	5 912	2 422	2 655
Carlisle	60	4 035	0.54	74	15.2	60	12.4	313	8.1	1 205	959	246	32	642
Carroll	325	13 762	1.70	159	14.9	125	11.7	737	8.3	2 209	1 627	582	102	927
Carter	652	24 319	0.69	350	12.9	346	12.8	1 564	7.1	4 618	3 345	1 273	182	671
Casey	478	14 103	0.68	198	12.5	212	13.4	1 150	9.3	3 216	2 594	622	88	546
Christian	5 394	97 400	1.76	1 622	22.4	617	8.5	4 173	7.0	10 643	8 343	2 300	1 790	2 435
Clark	458	33 663	0.87	388	10.8	357	10.0	1 892	6.4	7 133	4 724	2 409	1 120	3 141

1. Per 1,000 estimated resident population. 2. Data for serious crimes have not been adjusted for underreporting; this may affect comparability between geographic areas and over time.
3. Per 100,000 population estimated by the FBI.

Table B. States and Counties — **Crime, Education, Money Income, and Poverty**

STATE County	Serious crimes known to police, 2014 (cont.)[1] Rate[2] Violent	Property	School enrollment and attainment, 2011–2015 Enrollment[3] Total	Percent private	Attainment[4] (percent) High school graduate or less	Bachelor's degree or more	Local government expenditures,[5] 2013–2014 Total current spending (mil dol)	Current spending per student (dollars)	Per capita income[6] (dollars)	Households Median income (dollars)	Percent with income of less than $50,000	with income of $200,000 or more	Median household income (dollars)	Percent below poverty level All persons	Children under 18 years	Children 5 to 17 years in families
	46	47	48	49	50	51	52	53	54	55	56	57	58	59	60	61
KANSAS—Cont'd																
Neosho	152	1 090	3 969	7.7	41.9	18.6	25.3	10 141	22 354	43 195	58.0	1.9	40 744	18.9	28.1	25.2
Ness	261	1 011	635	11.7	44.9	19.8	5.8	12 467	29 968	44 904	55.0	3.0	53 456	9.4	13.6	12.0
Norton	107	997	1 162	2.8	48.3	17.4	10.3	11 185	23 702	47 852	51.3	2.6	45 096	12.7	15.2	13.9
Osage	64	1 119	3 693	8.6	49.8	19.5	30.3	10 934	24 243	49 915	50.1	1.3	48 364	12.7	17.1	14.6
Osborne	131	1 154	766	15.8	46.1	20.6	6.4	14 432	27 132	40 216	60.1	2.7	43 518	13.1	20.1	19.8
Ottawa	83	1 443	1 466	10.0	39.8	21.4	14.0	10 932	26 260	52 479	47.6	1.3	50 302	10.0	13.8	11.6
Pawnee	258	2 325	1 574	11.6	39.0	21.7	12.4	9 671	24 125	43 250	54.3	2.6	47 359	14.5	17.4	14.8
Phillips	72	127	1 268	3.9	43.1	21.6	9.6	12 044	25 072	44 170	57.0	1.9	46 984	11.1	17.0	16.2
Pottawatomie	214	1 233	6 388	18.7	35.4	32.2	40.7	10 051	25 964	60 216	40.5	2.9	60 601	8.1	10.6	9.7
Pratt	191	2 877	2 334	6.3	36.8	25.9	16.4	9 464	27 078	49 550	50.5	2.5	52 634	10.8	15.6	14.4
Rawlins	191	689	472	2.1	38.7	25.0	4.2	12 772	27 559	41 579	57.2	1.4	47 448	11.7	19.1	16.7
Reno	363	3 152	15 576	14.0	40.5	20.2	101.2	9 960	23 578	45 288	54.5	1.9	47 178	13.1	17.9	16.4
Republic	230	2 025	921	10.1	42.3	20.0	8.3	11 608	25 317	40 449	61.1	1.1	44 593	11.2	17.3	16.3
Rice	NA	NA	2 655	17.4	42.5	21.2	22.0	11 521	23 687	48 460	51.1	1.1	52 400	13.8	18.1	15.5
Riley	242	1 557	30 709	6.1	22.3	44.9	75.6	10 067	23 992	44 437	56.0	2.9	46 690	23.4	15.5	15.5
Rooks	135	520	1 095	8.8	44.9	22.0	10.4	12 235	23 891	43 558	57.4	2.0	45 309	11.7	15.5	14.4
Rush	158	2 853	623	4.0	42.6	21.7	6.6	12 551	24 843	38 854	59.4	1.6	43 895	11.5	17.1	15.1
Russell	361	1 704	1 443	4.3	43.1	24.0	9.0	10 970	26 128	41 102	57.3	1.4	42 625	13.2	20.7	19.7
Saline	373	3 517	14 565	13.4	43.7	23.4	89.2	10 424	25 641	47 801	52.9	2.9	47 052	14.3	21.7	21.4
Scott	376	1 127	1 105	16.0	48.5	20.5	9.8	10 067	30 179	51 850	46.6	1.1	56 267	7.7	12.0	11.0
Sedgwick	604	3 979	142 636	16.4	37.8	29.4	838.1	9 944	26 016	50 657	49.3	3.2	50 995	15.2	20.7	18.0
Seward	370	2 579	7 035	5.0	60.8	11.8	55.6	9 719	20 442	47 134	52.4	2.6	45 807	15.0	18.2	17.0
Shawnee	425	4 005	46 685	13.5	40.3	29.0	293.4	10 261	26 691	50 378	49.6	2.5	51 316	14.2	19.9	17.2
Sheridan	117	705	514	1.9	42.2	21.6	6.6	10 973	28 733	49 750	50.2	3.3	51 221	10.9	17.3	14.4
Sherman	293	1 904	1 407	2.1	44.0	14.1	10.3	9 489	21 786	39 029	61.3	1.1	42 491	16.5	24.4	23.4
Smith	NA	NA	773	3.6	44.6	18.1	8.5	13 244	27 315	43 848	56.8	2.6	43 872	12.2	16.5	14.9
Stafford	184	1 220	1 053	4.7	41.2	21.8	11.7	12 071	25 476	47 377	52.4	2.7	47 129	12.8	20.8	18.4
Stanton	NA	NA	608	6.9	44.7	22.2	5.5	11 965	22 690	43 780	53.2	0.2	55 341	10.9	16.6	15.3
Stevens	NA	NA	1 615	7.4	52.8	15.4	15.5	11 236	24 827	55 433	42.5	3.5	59 735	11.3	15.5	13.0
Sumner	224	2 320	6 077	8.6	43.9	19.9	41.6	10 802	24 214	50 141	49.8	1.7	51 451	11.7	17.6	15.6
Thomas	390	2 263	2 091	8.9	35.7	28.3	11.6	10 971	26 309	48 504	52.3	4.8	50 574	10.9	12.0	11.1
Trego	67	973	609	12.2	39.2	25.0	4.3	10 523	28 817	54 000	43.5	1.3	48 576	10.4	14.6	11.5
Wabaunsee	340	964	1 618	14.9	43.9	23.0	11.9	12 179	23 962	54 688	45.1	0.7	57 339	8.3	12.5	11.5
Wallace	63	0	382	8.6	41.4	25.2	4.3	14 890	28 265	47 279	50.9	4.0	48 426	12.4	15.9	14.4
Washington	72	376	1 233	10.0	48.0	17.0	9.4	11 260	23 440	45 159	55.3	1.1	46 153	10.7	13.2	11.8
Wichita	504	917	588	1.7	51.8	16.1	5.3	12 176	23 367	57 171	44.3	2.0	52 917	10.9	16.5	14.9
Wilson	266	1 970	1 924	6.1	51.1	14.7	18.5	11 475	22 538	40 306	59.8	1.6	41 461	15.6	24.0	22.0
Woodson	312	2 717	628	5.3	48.6	16.0	5.9	12 154	21 432	35 787	63.3	1.3	37 394	19.5	29.6	24.9
Wyandotte	703	4 930	42 524	10.2	54.3	15.9	319.5	10 508	18 912	40 113	60.6	0.7	41 746	21.9	32.1	29.9
KENTUCKY	212	2 247	1 093 200	14.7	49.5	22.3	6 396.7	9 443	24 063	43 740	55.4	2.6	45 178	18.3	25.3	23.8
Adair	27	538	4 874	24.7	61.4	15.9	23.1	8 542	18 277	33 362	64.8	1.0	32 007	27.2	41.0	37.5
Allen	44	956	4 720	13.2	58.5	13.6	25.5	8 528	20 702	41 326	58.0	1.4	42 287	19.8	30.2	27.1
Anderson	59	584	5 114	8.6	50.7	18.9	32.0	8 185	24 353	53 974	46.0	1.3	55 523	10.7	16.8	14.4
Ballard	24	1 399	1 879	8.1	54.4	13.6	12.7	9 013	24 056	42 244	58.1	2.1	44 352	15.1	24.5	21.6
Barren	83	1 425	10 016	8.7	60.3	15.6	52.3	8 793	20 262	38 370	62.7	1.2	40 017	19.3	28.7	26.5
Bath	8	66	2 896	9.2	63.5	12.2	17.7	8 359	18 719	33 483	68.3	1.6	35 143	24.9	37.8	35.0
Bell	137	2 998	5 932	8.1	69.4	9.8	44.8	9 209	13 701	22 443	78.8	0.5	23 966	44.7	56.8	57.3
Boone	108	2 118	34 390	18.8	36.1	30.8	182.2	8 430	29 866	66 730	35.2	4.8	68 804	8.2	10.5	9.2
Bourbon	115	1 677	4 436	12.0	53.8	16.0	33.3	9 043	23 620	45 208	55.0	1.3	46 370	14.8	24.4	23.0
Boyd	121	2 517	10 696	10.5	47.4	17.7	68.1	8 961	25 745	42 319	56.7	3.0	43 406	20.5	29.4	27.0
Boyle	154	1 605	7 758	23.9	49.4	22.7	42.3	8 982	22 368	39 704	59.9	2.3	40 459	17.2	24.9	23.4
Bracken	39	1 171	1 892	10.7	60.5	14.0	12.8	8 145	21 054	36 327	57.7	0.8	44 846	15.7	24.7	23.3
Breathitt	15	230	2 807	9.9	65.5	11.2	25.2	10 015	15 737	25 817	73.1	1.0	28 196	32.9	42.9	43.2
Breckinridge	30	184	4 452	12.0	65.8	9.5	30.2	9 139	19 185	43 479	56.1	0.6	42 347	19.0	25.6	24.6
Bullitt	86	1 331	18 560	15.8	54.5	14.3	104.2	7 803	24 458	55 975	44.4	1.3	54 755	9.6	14.5	13.3
Butler	86	896	2 622	20.5	68.2	8.7	18.4	8 053	18 502	33 536	66.6	0.2	39 545	21.6	31.3	28.9
Caldwell	172	1 711	2 640	3.5	58.0	16.4	16.8	7 852	20 840	42 537	58.7	1.2	39 355	18.8	29.4	29.2
Calloway	119	2 336	12 737	4.9	44.2	27.5	63.4	9 129	20 701	37 034	62.0	1.5	40 585	21.1	24.1	22.4
Campbell	172	2 483	24 125	21.1	41.7	29.1	112.1	9 537	28 248	54 621	45.6	3.4	51 694	14.4	17.8	16.7
Carlisle	20	622	1 039	12.1	56.1	13.3	7.5	9 094	21 499	38 829	59.0	0.2	43 144	14.8	25.2	23.6
Carroll	82	845	2 304	5.9	65.9	11.2	22.1	10 656	20 129	41 439	59.9	0.4	46 499	17.6	28.7	27.5
Carter	30	642	6 610	15.9	61.6	12.8	41.6	8 632	18 948	36 696	63.6	0.3	37 204	19.7	29.4	28.3
Casey	25	521	3 222	6.1	64.8	11.2	21.5	9 418	17 526	32 341	70.5	0.7	33 576	25.1	38.2	37.1
Christian	200	2 235	19 272	12.5	47.4	16.6	84.3	9 038	19 614	39 521	61.4	1.5	39 840	20.3	28.9	30.7
Clark	140	3 000	8 103	13.4	51.2	20.7	48.8	8 431	25 492	47 959	52.0	2.1	54 812	15.4	23.9	22.1

1. Data for serious crimes have not been adjusted for underreporting; this may affect comparability between geographic areas and over time.　2.　Per 100,000 population estimated by the FBI.
3. All persons 3 years old and over enrolled in nursery school through college.　4.　Persons 25 years old and over.　5.　Elementary and secondary education expenditures.
6. Based on population estimated by the American Community Survey, 2011–2015.

Table B. States and Counties — **Personal Income**

STATE County	Personal income, 2015										Earnings, 2015		
			Per capita[1]			Supplements to wages and salaries; employer contributions (mil dol)						Contributions for government social insurance (mil dol)	
	Total (mil dol)	Percent change, 2014–2015	Dollars	Rank	Wages and salaries (mil dol)	Pension and insurance	Government social insurance	Proprietors' income (mil dol)	Dividends, interest, and rent (mil dol)	Personal transfer receipts (mil dol)	Total (mil dol)	From employee and self-employed	From employer
	62	63	64	65	66	67	68	69	70	71	72	73	74
KANSAS—Cont'd													
Neosho	527	0.5	32 225	2 472	229	46	18	47	84	160	341	22	18
Ness	159	-7.3	53 009	194	51	11	4	39	39	28	104	5	4
Norton	218	-6.9	39 297	1 169	96	21	7	41	43	42	165	9	7
Osage	601	0.9	37 926	1 705	91	22	7	31	86	143	151	12	7
Osborne	154	-3.5	41 731	781	48	10	4	25	33	36	85	5	4
Ottawa	223	3.7	37 312	1 963	47	10	4	22	34	48	83	5	4
Pawnee	263	-6.2	38 428	1 320	117	29	8	45	46	61	199	10	8
Phillips	281	4.2	51 856	423	91	24	7	67	53	54	189	10	7
Pottawatomie	1 090	3.2	46 772	511	393	69	31	63	150	143	557	33	31
Pratt	439	-1.5	45 328	884	183	34	14	93	80	78	324	17	14
Rawlins	122	0.8	48 611	236	37	7	3	27	28	28	74	4	3
Reno	2 387	2.4	37 469	1 792	1 049	190	82	176	443	544	1 497	95	82
Republic	219	4.3	46 263	905	65	14	5	59	35	47	142	7	5
Rice	433	2.5	43 415	1 426	149	30	12	104	63	79	295	15	12
Riley	2 897	3.4	38 499	1 773	1 240	283	94	176	669	346	1 792	98	94
Rooks	217	-3.6	41 867	1 469	76	16	6	35	42	46	134	8	6
Rush	133	-6.0	42 480	1 013	41	9	3	20	26	32	74	4	3
Russell	332	-5.1	47 117	1 096	107	25	8	75	63	70	214	12	8
Saline	2 385	3.4	42 824	1 028	1 209	211	97	319	426	444	1 835	108	97
Scott	321	-0.8	64 644	328	85	14	6	144	46	40	249	7	6
Sedgwick	25 808	1.9	50 448	579	12 585	2 033	1 001	3 334	6 727	3 629	18 952	1 086	1 001
Seward	813	-1.4	35 123	1 948	446	87	33	160	88	121	726	38	33
Shawnee	7 724	3.3	43 216	1 031	4 612	790	361	520	1 262	1 627	6 283	383	361
Sheridan	131	-5.1	52 337	334	42	8	3	34	27	21	86	4	3
Sherman	251	10.2	41 887	1 569	93	19	7	50	42	57	169	8	7
Smith	155	-0.4	41 796	1 103	42	9	3	32	35	39	86	4	3
Stafford	206	-12.1	48 657	1 655	45	11	3	64	38	37	123	6	3
Stanton	123	-3.7	59 139	468	35	7	2	37	25	14	81	4	2
Stevens	235	-8.4	40 468	984	99	18	7	37	45	31	162	8	7
Sumner	857	3.3	36 407	2 061	271	52	24	71	131	186	417	27	24
Thomas	313	0.9	39 613	1 983	150	27	11	46	56	56	234	13	11
Trego	129	-4.6	44 166	864	47	11	4	26	22	30	88	5	4
Wabaunsee	325	0.5	46 762	706	45	10	4	19	88	54	77	5	4
Wallace	67	-12.4	44 412	656	21	4	2	14	14	13	41	2	2
Washington	227	-5.4	40 582	1 042	63	15	5	32	43	53	114	6	5
Wichita	164	-12.6	76 001	74	32	6	2	83	26	17	123	3	2
Wilson	356	-0.7	40 218	1 657	131	31	11	52	60	95	225	14	11
Woodson	111	-4.4	35 515	1 700	22	6	2	13	20	30	42	3	2
Wyandotte	5 814	-16.3	35 589	2 813	4 895	771	405	1 258	543	1 283	7 329	417	405
KENTUCKY	170 756	4.4	38 592	X	85 339	15 295	6 680	11 048	26 231	42 201	118 362	7 314	6 680
Adair	511	3.6	26 876	3 029	155	35	12	29	64	208	230	17	12
Allen	616	5.5	29 847	2 155	158	31	12	54	68	194	256	18	12
Anderson	810	5.1	36 834	1 861	172	37	13	23	102	174	244	18	13
Ballard	293	-0.4	35 717	1 596	121	18	9	18	41	82	167	11	9
Barren	1 541	5.8	35 361	2 269	608	112	48	189	205	427	958	62	48
Bath	356	4.9	29 076	2 906	70	16	6	17	37	127	108	9	6
Bell	794	2.7	29 042	2 925	292	64	23	25	89	391	405	30	23
Boone	5 446	4.8	42 645	988	3 854	567	301	230	627	792	4 953	296	301
Bourbon	777	6.2	38 632	1 829	294	49	23	61	144	183	426	27	23
Boyd	1 737	2.3	35 941	1 888	1 222	225	93	79	220	560	1 619	102	93
Boyle	1 033	4.1	34 660	2 253	561	101	47	61	187	282	770	50	47
Bracken	275	2.6	33 058	2 350	54	12	4	12	30	77	82	7	4
Breathitt	404	1.9	29 968	2 684	116	28	9	10	37	216	163	13	9
Breckinridge	663	3.8	33 108	2 316	125	29	9	63	105	199	226	16	9
Bullitt	2 862	6.3	36 362	1 855	827	138	67	101	268	596	1 133	79	67
Butler	415	3.7	32 054	2 549	102	24	8	30	44	138	164	11	8
Caldwell	428	2.1	33 734	2 158	141	28	12	28	62	137	208	15	12
Calloway	1 280	2.4	33 387	2 262	578	146	43	87	199	317	854	50	43
Campbell	3 974	3.5	43 164	1 032	1 254	232	94	183	609	729	1 763	112	94
Carlisle	198	-3.3	40 684	1 203	32	7	2	36	29	53	77	5	2
Carroll	474	11.0	44 329	2 016	376	57	29	109	43	110	571	35	29
Carter	814	2.9	29 976	2 836	191	40	15	31	77	310	277	23	15
Casey	445	6.9	28 153	2 972	124	29	10	26	53	188	188	14	10
Christian	2 713	2.8	37 011	1 887	3 189	866	317	209	565	595	4 581	198	317
Clark	1 332	4.5	37 244	1 127	599	102	48	65	189	342	814	53	48

1. Based on the resident population estimated as of July 1 of the year shown.

Table B. States and Counties — **Earnings, Social Security, and Housing**

STATE County	Earnings, 2015 (cont.) Percent by selected industries									Social Security beneficiaries, December 2015		Supplemental Security Income recipients, December 2015	Housing units, 2016	
	Farm	Mining	Construction	Manufacturing	Information: professional, scientific, technical services	Retail trade	Finance, insurance, real estate and leasing	Health care and social assistance	Government	Number	Rate[1]		Total	Percent change, 2010–2016
	75	76	77	78	79	80	81	82	83	84	85	86	87	88
KANSAS—Cont'd														
Neosho	2.7	6.2	4.8	17.9	D	7.5	4.9	D	27.5	3 760	230	377	7 709	2.6
Ness	14.0	26.4	4.9	3.2	D	2.6	D	0.5	20.1	785	260	20	1 727	-0.7
Norton	7.1	D	3.2	10.1	4.5	5.0	D	9.7	26.0	1 265	228	56	2 532	-0.4
Osage	1.8	D	12.1	4.8	D	6.7	5.8	9.4	33.7	3 845	242	329	7 485	-0.2
Osborne	11.3	5.8	3.9	D	D	8.1	5.8	8.2	18.3	1 020	277	46	2 178	-1.3
Ottawa	14.3	D	3.7	10.9	D	3.7	8.5	12.8	23.6	1 395	235	71	2 770	-0.3
Pawnee	16.5	D	6.1	1.4	1.6	3.7	4.7	7.2	46.3	1 475	217	73	3 153	0.0
Phillips	5.8	2.9	3.1	29.2	2.4	3.4	D	1.8	20.8	1 475	272	43	3 082	1.1
Pottawatomie	1.3	0.0	9.9	25.3	4.7	9.2	6.1	8.4	10.8	3 880	167	208	9 404	9.0
Pratt	12.1	7.8	7.8	2.9	D	9.7	6.6	D	16.2	2 030	209	119	4 471	-1.0
Rawlins	9.3	0.2	7.5	4.4	D	11.4	D	4.9	19.1	730	288	29	1 459	0.1
Reno	1.9	0.8	6.9	12.6	6.0	7.2	7.0	15.1	18.3	14 650	230	1 301	28 370	0.3
Republic	26.9	D	5.8	12.6	3.4	4.5	D	D	14.5	1 420	301	62	2 890	0.5
Rice	13.8	7.1	4.4	20.7	3.8	3.0	D	D	16.6	2 165	218	134	4 556	0.2
Riley	0.7	D	5.6	2.4	6.4	5.8	7.7	11.0	42.3	7 340	97	544	30 370	7.6
Rooks	7.8	15.0	D	D	3.0	3.4	4.0	4.3	22.8	1 320	256	60	2 758	-0.4
Rush	6.3	2.9	4.0	28.1	D	3.1	5.2	3.2	20.7	890	287	54	1 857	-0.6
Russell	7.4	27.6	5.1	14.6	3.9	3.7	3.1	D	12.7	1 880	267	133	3 877	-0.8
Saline	0.9	D	5.7	16.1	6.5	7.5	5.5	18.3	12.4	11 505	207	1 042	24 254	0.6
Scott	53.7	D	2.7	2.7	D	3.4	D	D	7.0	1 055	212	50	2 193	0.0
Sedgwick	0.1	5.4	5.5	23.0	6.6	5.7	6.3	11.0	12.1	88 840	174	10 919	216 541	2.3
Seward	3.3	5.2	D	D	D	6.3	4.0	D	17.9	2 515	109	341	8 127	0.8
Shawnee	0.1	0.2	5.5	7.0	9.6	5.0	11.4	15.2	23.4	38 105	213	4 858	79 619	0.6
Sheridan	23.8	2.6	D	D	D	3.2	D	D	18.0	585	234	14	1 260	-0.4
Sherman	23.4	D	2.6	3.8	2.9	7.1	D	D	23.6	1 360	228	119	3 111	-1.2
Smith	31.0	D	4.8	1.9	2.0	5.5	3.2	11.4	17.4	1 190	322	60	2 243	0.5
Stafford	2.8	46.6	1.8	3.7	D	1.4	3.8	D	20.7	970	229	60	2 301	-0.8
Stanton	16.8	2.1	D	D	D	4.3	D	D	20.0	350	170	11	975	-1.5
Stevens	15.2	D	12.5	10.8	D	4.2	4.6	D	22.5	820	143	38	2 287	-0.8
Sumner	6.4	2.5	4.0	17.8	4.3	6.1	5.0	D	21.1	5 110	218	366	10 860	0.0
Thomas	3.9	D	6.6	3.2	5.4	9.8	9.7	D	16.1	1 425	180	77	3 588	1.5
Trego	18.0	D	2.9	3.8	D	4.0	D	D	25.9	800	274	37	1 672	-0.6
Wabaunsee	5.2	D	14.6	12.9	D	2.0	D	D	25.9	1 545	224	83	3 266	1.2
Wallace	31.3	0.6	D	D	D	3.0	D	D	16.4	340	225	18	776	-0.6
Washington	20.1	D	5.9	10.3	D	4.2	D	5.9	24.7	1 530	275	66	2 947	-0.3
Wichita	64.7	0.8	1.8	2.7	0.2	2.0	D	0.7	11.4	425	198	18	1 041	-1.2
Wilson	1.3	1.2	7.0	40.4	3.1	3.9	3.7	8.4	19.9	2 455	277	228	4 633	-1.0
Woodson	6.3	17.9	D	D	D	6.3	D	5.2	25.9	815	261	72	2 000	-1.1
Wyandotte	0.0	0.1	5.4	26.0	5.8	3.9	2.1	15.2	15.8	25 940	159	5 317	67 700	1.4
KENTUCKY	0.7	1.0	5.8	14.9	7.0	6.0	6.8	12.2	19.6	963 497	218	184 103	1 965 556	2.0
Adair	3.4	0.3	7.3	7.3	D	8.4	5.7	D	22.1	4 605	239	964	8 503	-0.8
Allen	7.8	0.0	D	24.5	D	5.5	3.5	D	16.9	4 870	237	905	9 337	0.3
Anderson	-1.4	D	8.0	30.5	3.0	8.6	4.5	5.9	20.0	4 705	215	415	9 312	2.0
Ballard	7.8	0.0	14.5	31.5	D	3.9	1.1	3.4	12.6	2 155	262	290	3 885	0.0
Barren	2.6	0.0	3.6	20.5	D	8.4	3.4	15.0	13.2	10 715	245	1 789	19 527	1.8
Bath	3.3	0.0	15.7	D	D	3.4	2.4	7.7	26.5	3 120	254	893	5 384	-0.4
Bell	-0.1	8.0	3.2	12.4	D	10.4	4.6	17.1	22.8	7 670	281	2 994	13 086	-0.5
Boone	0.0	D	3.7	18.4	5.0	6.3	5.0	6.1	8.8	20 135	158	1 665	48 774	5.7
Bourbon	4.8	D	4.8	20.9	D	7.7	4.7	D	12.6	4 750	237	648	9 033	1.2
Boyd	-0.1	0.8	9.3	17.6	6.8	6.8	3.2	21.4	12.6	12 625	260	2 503	21 657	-0.7
Boyle	-0.2	D	3.5	16.0	D	7.9	4.3	23.5	13.3	7 100	238	1 163	12 491	1.5
Bracken	-2.1	0.0	8.1	D	D	3.0	2.4	6.5	25.5	2 015	242	320	3 829	-0.3
Breathitt	0.2	D	D	1.3	2.0	9.8	4.6	27.7	34.8	3 830	285	2 071	6 207	-0.4
Breckinridge	11.3	0.6	12.8	7.8	3.2	7.9	4.7	D	20.7	5 175	259	860	10 618	0.0
Bullitt	-0.2	D	9.5	16.5	3.1	4.4	3.0	4.7	15.0	15 970	203	1 346	30 955	5.6
Butler	7.2	D	8.1	30.0	1.2	3.2	3.7	D	19.6	3 275	255	504	5 860	-0.3
Caldwell	2.8	D	4.0	23.3	3.9	10.7	4.7	D	16.6	3 480	274	525	6 274	-0.3
Calloway	2.5	D	5.7	16.7	4.9	7.1	3.4	5.6	32.1	8 110	211	781	18 632	3.1
Campbell	0.0	0.3	D	12.1	7.6	7.4	5.3	12.4	23.8	16 710	182	1 927	40 174	1.6
Carlisle	25.8	0.0	8.2	3.2	1.9	3.8	23.8	7.4	15.6	1 385	282	164	2 438	-0.1
Carroll	0.3	0.6	D	49.1	12.8	3.9	1.9	D	7.2	2 640	246	526	4 682	-0.3
Carter	-0.9	1.7	9.0	12.2	D	17.9	4.4	D	24.8	7 225	265	1 696	12 282	-0.2
Casey	1.7	D	6.0	24.6	D	6.4	D	11.8	18.1	4 140	262	946	7 403	-1.1
Christian	0.5	D	1.6	8.2	2.5	2.1	1.7	5.0	68.8	12 055	164	2 351	29 798	1.2
Clark	-0.1	D	6.4	23.0	7.8	6.2	4.0	10.8	11.3	8 295	232	1 386	15 762	0.4

1. Per 1,000 resident population estimated as of July 1 of the year shown.

Table B. States and Counties — Housing, Labor Force, and Employment

STATE County	Housing units, 2011–2015								Civilian labor force, 2016				Civilian employment,[6] 2011–2015		
	Occupied units										Unemployment			Percent	
			Owner-occupied			Renter-occupied									
				Median owner cost as a percent of income											Construction, production, and maintenance occupations
	Total	Percent	Median value[1]	With a mort-gage	Without a mort-gage[2]	Median rent[3]	Median rent as a per-cent of income[2]	Sub-stand-ard units[4] (percent)	Total	Percent change, 2015–2016	Total	Rate[5]	Total	Manage-ment, business, science and arts	
	89	90	91	92	93	94	95	96	97	98	99	100	101	102	103
KANSAS—Cont'd															
Neosho	6 463	71.4	69 800	19.0	11.2	589	26.2	3.0	6 108	-2.3	460	7.5	7 816	30.4	30.5
Ness	1 383	78.4	67 100	18.1	10.0	575	21.1	1.9	1 415	-7.7	54	3.8	1 524	32.3	31.3
Norton	2 119	77.6	72 900	17.2	12.8	647	21.5	4.2	2 887	-1.8	75	2.6	2 650	33.5	25.0
Osage	6 505	75.5	98 300	20.7	12.6	628	26.8	2.2	8 005	-0.4	370	4.6	7 264	30.1	30.0
Osborne	1 764	74.9	57 400	18.7	10.0	455	21.7	1.5	2 078	-0.3	76	3.7	1 884	40.0	26.4
Ottawa	2 493	82.8	92 600	20.2	12.9	606	24.4	0.7	3 190	-1.0	127	4.0	3 008	35.8	29.7
Pawnee	2 552	69.5	77 400	21.1	10.2	432	26.7	0.0	3 203	-2.9	115	3.6	3 012	36.5	25.2
Phillips	2 349	77.0	72 700	19.9	11.4	510	23.5	1.0	2 876	-2.4	93	3.2	2 746	38.3	25.8
Pottawatomie	8 192	78.1	160 700	19.9	11.9	730	23.8	2.9	12 317	-1.0	432	3.5	10 795	38.8	25.5
Pratt	3 902	68.9	85 900	18.4	11.0	638	22.1	1.3	5 071	-3.9	218	4.3	4 618	34.3	27.8
Rawlins	1 212	71.6	75 600	20.6	12.6	582	25.7	0.3	1 518	-0.8	40	2.6	1 247	42.5	22.2
Reno	25 097	67.2	94 100	20.1	12.1	666	25.8	2.2	30 107	-2.1	1 372	4.6	29 564	29.7	26.0
Republic	2 275	78.5	48 900	19.8	10.8	474	22.5	1.8	2 552	-1.2	74	2.9	2 455	35.1	27.6
Rice	3 881	75.0	75 300	17.9	10.6	516	22.8	3.0	5 345	-2.2	222	4.2	4 905	30.7	31.1
Riley	26 467	41.8	181 200	21.1	11.2	884	32.6	7.4	36 884	-0.8	1 227	3.3	34 186	41.0	16.7
Rooks	2 206	74.8	67 900	20.9	10.9	525	23.6	2.2	2 683	-4.3	140	5.2	2 626	32.0	29.0
Rush	1 486	78.6	62 100	18.1	11.1	539	33.0	1.3	1 749	-2.3	74	4.2	1 577	39.0	26.1
Russell	3 239	75.0	81 000	18.6	12.5	537	27.6	2.3	3 557	-4.5	160	4.5	3 463	32.8	31.4
Saline	22 390	65.7	122 200	21.5	12.3	692	29.6	1.7	30 819	0.1	1 165	3.8	28 311	31.3	29.8
Scott	2 196	72.1	126 000	22.2	10.0	792	25.5	2.2	2 879	0.1	74	2.6	2 613	37.3	31.6
Sedgwick	192 961	64.1	126 500	20.7	11.3	731	28.2	2.4	245 673	-0.2	11 759	4.8	239 060	34.9	24.3
Seward	7 480	67.6	87 100	20.7	10.3	664	23.7	6.9	10 228	-3.5	471	4.6	11 031	20.5	49.0
Shawnee	71 368	64.3	122 200	19.7	12.0	738	29.6	2.5	91 289	0.3	3 767	4.1	84 199	36.0	19.7
Sheridan	1 133	78.3	91 400	15.2	12.3	479	18.2	0.8	1 448	-2.0	37	2.6	1 286	39.1	32.0
Sherman	2 786	58.1	77 000	20.6	12.2	643	27.6	0.4	2 952	-4.2	102	3.5	2 992	32.0	26.2
Smith	1 667	80.3	64 000	19.9	11.0	459	22.5	1.0	2 035	-2.5	72	3.5	1 836	37.4	26.4
Stafford	1 794	83.8	65 100	17.3	12.2	579	23.5	3.1	2 087	-4.2	85	4.1	2 108	36.6	24.5
Stanton	820	78.0	73 800	22.9	10.8	567	22.1	2.4	1 047	-1.0	32	3.1	1 116	32.9	31.1
Stevens	2 007	74.9	96 400	19.2	10.2	647	24.6	0.7	2 885	-9.0	127	4.4	2 696	29.3	37.6
Sumner	9 091	77.6	83 900	20.9	12.7	630	24.4	2.4	10 994	-0.5	487	4.4	10 758	30.4	32.1
Thomas	3 174	69.7	105 100	19.1	12.4	463	22.2	1.1	4 320	-1.9	126	2.9	4 376	33.0	23.9
Trego	1 302	77.1	86 900	18.0	10.0	542	25.3	0.2	1 511	0.5	63	4.2	1 684	34.0	26.0
Wabaunsee	2 668	85.9	115 300	21.0	13.5	711	24.1	2.4	3 712	-0.3	140	3.8	3 295	35.5	26.6
Wallace	625	76.0	76 300	18.0	10.0	406	17.5	0.5	864	-1.1	25	2.9	755	39.2	20.3
Washington	2 442	80.3	68 800	18.7	11.2	460	18.9	0.5	3 085	-1.1	109	3.5	2 950	29.9	35.5
Wichita	781	72.2	70 600	17.4	12.6	598	18.1	7.2	1 212	-3.1	30	2.5	1 077	32.5	38.6
Wilson	3 769	74.5	60 100	21.2	10.8	596	27.6	1.9	4 152	3.9	267	6.4	4 052	32.6	32.6
Woodson	1 531	79.6	48 300	18.4	14.0	558	28.8	4.2	1 592	-0.9	98	6.2	1 557	27.6	38.3
Wyandotte	58 870	58.7	89 200	24.3	15.8	777	31.4	4.4	76 263	0.4	4 369	5.7	70 518	22.5	32.0
KENTUCKY	1 708 499	67.2	123 200	20.6	10.8	675	29.3	2.3	1 991 981	1.3	99 701	5.0	1 891 381	32.9	26.3
Adair	7 048	73.6	82 400	20.4	10.4	505	29.4	2.5	6 738	-2.4	447	6.6	7 700	27.6	33.1
Allen	7 774	72.9	95 500	20.2	10.0	588	25.6	4.7	8 788	2.9	369	4.2	8 576	25.2	39.2
Anderson	8 446	77.0	136 800	20.7	11.0	721	26.8	1.4	11 211	0.7	445	4.0	10 646	29.0	29.5
Ballard	3 288	81.4	101 800	19.7	10.0	611	31.9	2.0	3 690	3.0	317	8.6	3 489	26.9	33.4
Barren	16 979	67.5	105 800	20.2	11.9	594	30.4	2.7	18 885	3.3	869	4.6	18 672	27.1	36.8
Bath	4 297	74.6	73 500	23.5	12.5	589	32.4	4.3	4 729	0.9	342	7.2	4 045	28.4	35.1
Bell	11 088	66.2	60 400	25.0	11.1	478	35.4	3.6	8 661	-1.2	777	9.0	8 018	23.6	31.9
Boone	44 709	73.3	175 100	20.0	10.0	905	26.5	2.0	65 523	1.4	2 480	3.8	62 624	38.8	20.7
Bourbon	7 867	61.9	139 600	20.8	10.0	690	29.2	1.2	9 826	2.3	463	4.7	8 984	29.8	29.3
Boyd	19 383	70.2	99 700	19.2	10.7	625	30.7	1.3	18 117	0.5	1 472	8.1	18 376	34.7	23.8
Boyle	11 045	65.5	132 500	21.1	10.7	637	29.8	0.8	12 157	2.0	592	4.9	12 218	33.6	25.1
Bracken	3 303	76.2	95 800	21.4	11.9	556	33.0	3.2	3 722	1.5	224	6.0	3 486	29.9	34.9
Breathitt	5 494	73.7	47 500	22.7	12.2	493	28.9	4.7	3 882	-2.1	363	9.4	4 239	28.4	25.4
Breckinridge	7 297	79.3	88 000	19.5	10.0	529	24.7	4.1	7 883	0.2	472	6.0	7 683	25.0	39.2
Bullitt	28 267	81.2	144 700	21.4	10.5	769	27.1	1.3	39 731	2.2	1 639	4.1	37 079	26.2	32.8
Butler	5 176	73.4	90 800	19.1	11.5	534	29.1	3.9	5 160	2.9	275	5.3	5 003	26.7	37.2
Caldwell	5 293	71.2	96 700	19.0	10.6	534	28.7	1.5	5 397	0.6	285	5.3	5 396	33.9	31.7
Calloway	14 834	63.1	119 900	19.8	11.8	580	35.4	1.4	18 431	1.0	827	4.5	16 904	31.7	24.3
Campbell	35 477	68.7	150 400	20.2	10.9	748	28.2	1.8	47 693	1.4	1 817	3.8	45 872	38.3	19.2
Carlisle	2 059	79.2	77 200	19.4	10.0	571	25.8	3.0	2 723	18.3	162	5.9	2 122	22.9	33.6
Carroll	3 988	60.8	99 200	19.0	10.2	645	26.9	5.5	5 083	3.1	252	5.0	4 263	20.6	41.6
Carter	10 487	78.0	77 100	20.1	12.1	559	27.7	2.8	10 066	-0.7	1 023	10.2	10 039	25.4	33.9
Casey	6 384	79.7	76 500	23.8	12.1	479	24.7	2.6	6 831	2.7	314	4.6	5 926	28.4	35.2
Christian	25 521	47.7	108 500	20.5	10.0	754	29.9	2.5	24 725	0.7	1 489	6.0	23 856	29.2	30.4
Clark	14 173	64.2	142 700	20.0	11.4	698	28.6	2.3	16 862	1.4	797	4.7	15 950	33.2	26.7

1. Specified owner-occupied units.   2. A value of 10.0 represents 10 percent or less; a value of 50.0 represents 50 percent or more.   3. Specified renter-occupied units.
4. Overcrowded or lacking complete plumbing facilities.   5. Percent of civilian labor force.   6. Civilian employed persons 16 years old and over.

STATE County	Number of establish-ments	Total	Health care and social assistance	Manufac-turing	Retail trade	Finance and insurance	Professional, scientific, and technical services	Total (mil dol)	Average per employee (dollars)	Number	Fewer than 50 acres	500 acres or more	Farm operators whose principal occu-pation is farming (percent)
	104	105	106	107	108	109	110	111	112	113	114	115	116
KANSAS—Cont'd													
Neosho	439	5 186	1 147	918	791	199	133	176	33 856	702	23.4	19.8	43.2
Ness	148	1 030	255	35	86	54	19	37	35 697	557	8.3	45.6	44.0
Norton	175	1 755	462	241	206	82	40	64	36 560	367	12.3	48.2	59.7
Osage	249	1 672	493	D	358	126	57	41	24 635	1 014	22.9	21.0	43.0
Osborne	147	1 139	293	102	203	59	51	35	30 665	343	10.2	50.1	65.0
Ottawa	135	889	290	58	113	66	29	25	27 983	525	12.0	35.4	49.9
Pawnee	158	1 972	1 076	D	224	67	84	73	37 054	401	13.7	45.4	53.1
Phillips	234	1 614	260	194	212	116	101	60	37 387	441	17.7	46.3	58.3
Pottawatomie	581	8 488	1 312	1 603	1 612	193	181	331	38 938	890	22.5	23.7	42.9
Pratt	402	3 724	684	115	747	155	129	133	35 807	543	7.6	37.9	45.1
Rawlins	104	616	166	37	89	34	14	23	36 644	307	6.2	67.1	63.2
Reno	1 619	23 223	4 440	3 943	3 377	875	612	814	35 061	1 633	20.6	23.6	49.0
Republic	189	1 440	386	169	191	56	34	38	26 597	575	13.0	60.7	60.7
Rice	269	2 799	372	492	263	143	187	92	32 961	532	15.0	38.9	54.5
Riley	1 608	20 770	3 471	724	4 379	859	1 163	623	30 014	493	24.3	22.7	44.6
Rooks	191	1 550	261	96	215	79	40	53	34 066	440	10.9	50.0	48.2
Rush	102	1 109	156	367	69	36	20	37	33 587	528	12.3	40.7	47.0
Russell	265	1 931	299	116	266	78	43	59	30 366	504	11.1	36.5	48.2
Saline	1 538	27 576	4 801	5 302	4 034	855	1 115	933	33 817	674	19.7	30.1	46.7
Scott	204	1 410	386	49	284	99	48	45	31 596	269	14.5	51.7	64.3
Sedgwick	11 941	231 175	33 375	47 415	29 376	7 740	10 557	10 508	45 453	1 344	36.5	19.0	46.1
Seward	554	9 513	1 114	D	1 291	208	158	345	36 263	363	8.8	39.7	44.6
Shawnee	4 199	77 775	18 270	6 454	9 842	5 453	4 486	3 263	41 958	826	39.8	11.3	39.3
Sheridan	108	682	D	D	95	59	20	25	36 296	384	6.0	60.4	67.7
Sherman	256	1 971	397	71	374	97	72	61	30 850	416	6.3	51.2	58.7
Smith	142	939	257	81	164	59	17	22	23 580	497	12.3	47.3	62.2
Stafford	133	667	209	D	105	64	9	21	31 171	536	9.0	45.0	51.3
Stanton	68	481	D	D	61	53	25	19	38 913	278	0.7	54.0	52.5
Stevens	141	2 206	D	156	161	62	19	82	36 956	315	6.0	41.0	38.4
Sumner	484	4 414	974	837	636	224	68	146	33 081	1 096	17.5	33.2	51.8
Thomas	353	2 901	396	85	721	134	63	97	33 391	460	10.0	51.5	58.5
Trego	130	968	D	43	138	33	21	32	32 949	384	9.9	47.9	50.3
Wabaunsee	123	801	111	130	98	45	2	23	29 037	617	18.2	27.9	43.9
Wallace	59	350	D	D	42	20	D	13	37 760	294	6.1	57.5	54.1
Washington	208	1 476	360	177	193	68	26	39	26 204	732	15.6	37.6	52.3
Wichita	82	479	D	61	59	26	4	19	39 190	265	7.9	60.0	62.6
Wilson	222	3 843	683	1 078	264	96	48	161	41 786	423	13.0	33.1	52.2
Woodson	89	463	150	D	59	59	10	12	25 266	315	14.0	41.9	53.0
Wyandotte	3 172	69 618	14 030	10 174	7 924	1 132	2 547	3 339	47 966	164	70.7	1.8	39.6
KENTUCKY	91 845	1 579 477	253 185	232 007	207 315	73 587	72 731	63 741	40 356	77 064	36.5	6.2	41.7
Adair	306	4 117	715	407	690	180	57	107	25 869	1 243	33.8	3.8	38.5
Allen	242	2 961	467	408	402	137	79	92	31 118	1 080	35.7	4.6	48.0
Anderson	322	3 459	353	1 008	788	111	86	117	33 958	676	38.2	3.4	40.4
Ballard	123	1 665	109	659	150	20	95	90	54 073	408	36.5	11.3	46.1
Barren	876	14 527	2 254	3 861	2 391	371	302	460	31 661	1 869	39.5	4.4	51.1
Bath	136	1 204	228	D	164	61	27	44	36 710	690	23.9	8.4	47.4
Bell	482	6 825	1 455	1 048	1 499	263	135	205	30 006	81	56.8	3.7	48.1
Boone	3 076	77 322	4 623	14 094	9 189	3 797	2 134	3 308	42 786	608	53.5	3.5	40.3
Bourbon	391	5 235	747	1 452	863	212	231	216	41 235	907	38.4	11.4	53.3
Boyd	1 361	22 814	5 865	2 063	3 958	592	786	1 051	46 088	214	37.9	1.4	35.5
Boyle	716	14 627	2 927	2 282	1 587	319	308	465	31 777	620	38.7	8.5	39.0
Bracken	92	842	78	D	133	35	11	27	32 641	587	28.4	3.7	42.2
Breathitt	245	2 953	929	46	481	116	61	85	28 905	120	34.2	10.0	26.7
Breckinridge	299	2 435	496	264	552	163	69	75	30 789	1 304	27.2	7.6	37.3
Bullitt	1 093	18 342	1 289	2 718	1 891	294	365	611	33 306	488	54.5	1.8	43.9
Butler	195	2 037	354	721	232	64	28	60	29 420	697	23.4	8.3	36.4
Caldwell	290	3 805	518	1 007	667	117	55	93	24 471	538	32.5	8.0	34.6
Calloway	818	14 064	2 274	2 649	1 824	418	319	415	29 475	821	40.4	9.4	38.4
Campbell	1 654	23 889	3 166	2 420	4 122	499	1 029	838	35 088	504	48.0	1.6	42.1
Carlisle	96	621	83	96	100	66	14	17	27 733	325	41.2	14.2	39.7
Carroll	236	5 904	384	2 666	593	70	97	330	55 886	278	20.1	5.4	37.4
Carter	433	5 063	533	730	912	187	108	130	25 586	786	30.8	3.7	31.3
Casey	231	3 272	543	1 514	365	85	D	86	26 427	1 118	27.4	4.1	52.6
Christian	1 312	24 234	3 132	6 297	3 091	662	725	859	35 436	1 179	27.1	10.7	45.9
Clark	734	12 275	1 481	2 723	1 509	284	390	465	37 879	883	42.7	7.1	39.2

Table B. States and Counties — **Agriculture**

	Agriculture, 2012 (cont.)															
	Land in farms				Value of land and buildings (dollars)			Value of products sold					Percent of farms with sales of:		Government payments	
			Acres								Percent from:					
STATE County	Acreage (1,000)	Percent change, 2007–2012	Average size of farm	Total irrigated (1,000)	Total cropland (1,000)	Average per farm	Average per acre	Value of machinery and equipment, average per farm (dollars)	Total (mil dol)	Average per farm (dollars)	Crops	Live-stock and poultry products	$10,000 or more	$100,000 or more	Total ($1,000)	Percent of farms
	117	118	119	120	121	122	123	124	125	126	127	128	129	130	131	132
KANSAS—Cont'd																
Neosho	308	-4.2	439	0.1	175.4	657 053	1 497	105 855	68.0	96 806	60.8	39.2	50.1	15.1	2 284	57.0
Ness	678	9.4	1 218	4.8	412.3	1 267 795	1 041	143 088	63.5	114 077	71.7	28.3	55.1	28.4	7 435	90.7
Norton	502	-5.5	1 368	14.5	270.6	1 812 496	1 325	210 428	146.1	397 976	34.9	65.1	66.5	32.7	3 716	85.3
Osage	442	16.3	436	0.0	251.4	709 350	1 626	105 941	71.0	70 021	52.4	47.6	43.3	14.9	4 728	64.1
Osborne	440	4.7	1 283	6.7	232.5	1 758 099	1 370	162 679	69.6	202 854	67.6	32.4	70.0	42.3	3 088	85.1
Ottawa	420	-4.0	800	4.2	239.0	1 505 440	1 883	167 135	99.0	188 631	60.6	39.4	64.4	28.0	3 509	82.3
Pawnee	480	-1.4	1 198	78.5	398.5	2 184 032	1 823	247 526	362.3	903 614	25.4	74.6	61.3	35.4	5 993	90.3
Phillips	495	0.0	1 123	7.5	232.2	1 404 333	1 251	170 676	100.4	227 633	48.7	51.3	63.7	34.9	3 275	76.9
Pottawatomie	410	-4.4	460	21.9	164.9	878 335	1 908	101 524	117.0	131 421	44.8	55.2	53.9	17.9	2 860	57.2
Pratt	465	-3.3	855	86.2	356.8	1 368 877	1 600	188 613	273.4	503 547	46.0	54.0	53.6	33.0	7 049	86.6
Rawlins	609	3.1	1 984	17.7	354.9	3 461 316	1 744	266 081	91.4	297 700	75.7	24.3	85.7	54.1	4 191	87.9
Reno	790	1.1	483	58.4	591.7	868 492	1 796	138 632	267.3	163 698	56.7	43.3	50.6	22.3	9 785	73.1
Republic	361	-11.2	628	46.5	258.5	1 664 624	2 651	228 520	197.3	343 073	58.8	41.2	71.7	37.7	4 144	78.6
Rice	458	6.8	860	28.6	360.9	1 373 859	1 597	238 983	258.2	485 303	38.3	61.7	62.8	37.8	5 201	79.3
Riley	218	-5.9	443	4.1	99.4	809 619	1 829	107 047	54.4	110 404	66.7	33.3	54.6	22.7	1 265	64.9
Rooks	551	-1.8	1 253	6.9	316.9	1 644 650	1 312	187 098	85.3	193 841	66.6	33.4	58.2	35.7	3 975	85.2
Rush	453	11.6	858	13.2	321.9	1 112 680	1 297	166 716	66.8	126 566	71.4	28.6	55.7	25.9	5 200	86.7
Russell	436	-1.8	864	0.5	234.9	986 889	1 142	129 329	56.8	112 649	64.6	35.4	56.0	22.8	4 283	83.9
Saline	364	-15.5	541	4.8	236.2	1 068 445	1 976	155 677	84.4	125 258	70.5	29.5	58.6	25.4	3 461	77.0
Scott	453	0.0	1 686	36.5	363.4	2 556 929	1 517	344 584	979.8	3 642 543	6.6	93.4	71.7	46.5	4 947	76.6
Sedgwick	487	-4.6	362	45.4	396.0	860 281	2 376	133 063	148.5	110 479	87.7	12.3	52.8	20.4	4 973	58.3
Seward	402	1.5	1 107	101.0	307.7	1 274 033	1 151	214 950	465.3	1 281 838	20.6	79.4	46.3	26.4	4 481	77.4
Shawnee	194	-5.8	235	19.0	117.7	585 475	2 489	78 510	50.3	60 844	83.0	17.0	39.5	10.4	2 350	40.8
Sheridan	562	7.6	1 463	79.3	363.5	2 808 255	1 919	288 505	328.7	855 951	33.3	66.7	79.7	51.0	5 406	83.6
Sherman	595	-9.6	1 430	87.0	498.7	2 441 558	1 707	280 512	170.2	409 043	77.2	22.8	63.5	41.8	7 341	86.8
Smith	500	9.4	1 007	7.3	334.4	1 633 296	1 622	212 620	111.0	223 270	67.2	32.8	71.6	38.6	5 354	84.3
Stafford	499	-0.7	931	103.4	396.5	1 644 125	1 767	234 315	197.6	368 696	60.8	39.2	55.6	36.4	6 769	85.6
Stanton	429	3.6	1 544	76.7	390.6	1 708 899	1 107	304 309	163.7	588 986	48.6	51.4	54.7	36.3	6 864	91.4
Stevens	456	-9.5	1 446	145.2	354.3	1 982 368	1 371	373 492	328.5	1 042 711	44.0	56.0	47.3	31.4	5 414	84.4
Sumner	720	1.4	657	16.1	592.9	1 177 329	1 793	178 303	168.7	153 935	88.8	11.2	62.9	28.2	7 384	77.0
Thomas	675	2.7	1 468	90.0	576.5	3 128 313	2 132	332 954	253.4	550 976	57.6	42.4	73.3	47.0	8 819	80.7
Trego	447	4.0	1 163	6.7	258.7	1 525 997	1 312	157 602	58.9	153 425	60.8	39.2	62.8	28.4	3 651	89.6
Wabaunsee	396	-15.8	642	7.0	107.6	944 000	1 470	92 042	58.3	94 561	36.9	63.1	53.3	21.1	1 959	56.7
Wallace	488	13.6	1 660	58.0	353.3	2 093 398	1 261	233 490	97.2	330 708	66.2	33.8	64.3	40.5	6 452	85.0
Washington	490	-10.6	669	9.7	298.2	1 562 583	2 334	197 657	187.1	255 668	53.2	46.8	69.5	36.9	5 492	79.5
Wichita	464	-10.8	1 750	67.5	351.2	2 375 008	1 357	320 019	624.8	2 357 736	D	D	72.1	49.1	5 701	87.2
Wilson	255	-23.6	602	2.2	142.4	865 076	1 437	129 043	55.4	131 021	84.4	15.6	62.4	23.6	1 636	65.0
Woodson	295	12.6	935	0.0	153.9	1 286 667	1 376	140 746	54.6	173 343	49.5	50.5	60.0	28.9	1 856	69.5
Wyandotte	12	-33.7	73	D	7.3	352 140	4 809	42 561	3.3	20 067	82.2	17.8	22.6	3.0	106	9.8
KENTUCKY	13 049	-6.7	169	73.6	6 336.2	512 033	3 024	70 188	5 067.3	65 755	45.0	55.0	36.5	8.2	169 821	43.3
Adair	170	-9.5	137	0.1	66.6	350 537	2 560	49 813	53.4	42 936	25.9	74.1	37.4	7.1	2 392	54.9
Allen	146	-12.6	135	0.3	52.3	398 629	2 955	51 991	53.2	49 291	26.5	73.5	39.4	6.9	2 086	44.4
Anderson	81	-7.5	120	0.2	29.4	373 490	3 116	48 127	12.7	18 857	33.7	66.3	29.6	3.3	625	22.9
Ballard	107	-2.7	263	0.4	85.2	893 627	3 402	150 120	57.6	141 206	54.7	45.3	42.6	14.7	1 937	65.9
Barren	249	-6.1	133	0.2	130.0	391 780	2 945	68 049	113.0	60 474	33.4	66.6	45.2	8.2	4 232	40.6
Bath	142	10.2	206	0.0	47.9	402 174	1 951	58 223	19.3	27 915	46.7	53.3	42.6	5.8	1 041	41.6
Bell	8	-20.9	100	0.0	1.8	193 704	1 945	25 827	0.5	6 037	D	D	21.0	0.0	7	7.4
Boone	67	-10.1	111	0.2	28.3	682 016	6 170	64 265	12.4	20 467	66.2	33.8	26.3	4.6	450	26.2
Bourbon	184	-0.3	203	0.4	74.8	862 352	4 256	90 714	108.4	119 568	34.5	65.5	50.3	13.2	1 916	39.6
Boyd	22	-24.1	102	0.0	4.8	237 617	2 333	53 234	1.9	8 813	27.0	73.0	13.6	0.9	22	6.5
Boyle	102	7.8	164	0.2	41.9	557 629	3 405	64 198	31.0	49 953	22.9	77.1	41.5	9.8	687	33.5
Bracken	87	-13.8	148	0.2	29.0	309 826	2 095	53 532	10.9	18 547	62.5	37.5	31.9	3.4	837	39.0
Breathitt	22	-49.0	185	0.0	4.8	264 842	1 430	58 558	1.7	14 267	43.0	57.0	14.2	3.3	192	39.2
Breckinridge	260	-5.4	199	0.0	116.6	477 849	2 399	64 376	79.5	60 995	42.8	57.2	40.3	8.2	3 246	58.2
Bullitt	46	-9.8	95	D	20.2	344 717	3 645	48 629	7.7	15 873	59.6	40.4	21.5	2.7	369	23.0
Butler	153	-12.3	219	0.2	62.8	442 750	2 023	59 912	42.4	60 822	54.7	45.3	29.6	7.9	2 052	48.6
Caldwell	133	-6.5	248	D	85.5	678 645	2 735	83 006	38.5	71 561	86.7	13.3	33.1	7.4	2 270	60.4
Calloway	176	11.6	214	3.8	131.9	636 456	2 968	109 851	109.7	133 619	57.3	42.7	35.8	16.2	5 573	68.7
Campbell	42	-10.9	84	0.1	15.0	367 526	4 393	49 331	6.9	13 718	45.7	54.3	24.4	3.2	179	16.3
Carlisle	99	3.0	303	0.6	79.6	858 588	2 829	151 486	73.1	224 939	46.6	53.4	38.2	20.0	2 245	74.2
Carroll	54	-15.9	193	0.1	21.7	508 050	2 637	55 694	6.4	23 169	69.9	30.1	36.0	2.5	354	41.7
Carter	106	-15.7	135	0.1	22.6	236 774	1 758	40 621	9.5	12 080	32.7	67.3	21.5	1.7	400	23.9
Casey	179	-6.5	160	0.1	60.6	325 356	2 031	49 997	29.6	26 471	47.1	52.9	38.2	5.1	1 559	47.5
Christian	360	4.0	306	3.3	252.3	1 055 497	3 454	121 645	185.8	157 625	80.2	19.8	48.3	20.6	7 302	56.4
Clark	137	-7.9	156	0.2	50.5	510 663	3 282	63 019	34.8	39 361	31.7	68.3	40.1	8.3	790	25.3

Table B. States and Counties — Water Use, Wholesale Trade, Retail Trade, and Real Estate

STATE County	Water use, 2010		Wholesale trade,[1] 2012				Retail trade,[2] 2012				Real estate and rental and leasing,[2] 2012			
	Total water withdrawn (mil gal/day)	Gallons withdrawn per person per day	Number of establishments	Number of employees	Sales (mil dol)	Annual payroll (mil dol)	Number of establishments	Number of employees	Sales (mil dol)	Annual payroll (mil dol)	Number of establishments	Number of employees	Receipts (mil dol)	Annual payroll (mil dol)
	133	134	135	136	137	138	139	140	141	142	143	144	145	146
KANSAS—Cont'd														
Neosho	2.8	170	28	223	96.2	8.2	86	800	197.7	18.8	11	18	2.0	0.4
Ness	4.1	1 304	16	D	D	D	19	98	15.4	1.6	1	D	D	D
Norton	13.8	2 437	8	68	38.3	2.5	27	183	51.2	3.9	1	D	D	D
Osage	2.3	144	15	73	48.6	2.9	42	360	74.0	5.8	5	D	D	D
Osborne	2.0	513	14	136	157.7	5.9	31	212	46.6	3.2	NA	NA	NA	NA
Ottawa	2.8	458	10	D	D	D	14	79	16.2	1.3	3	2	1.3	0.1
Pawnee	71.5	10 260	9	100	130.3	5.0	28	224	50.1	4.7	4	16	1.9	0.3
Phillips	18.3	3 251	13	63	69.7	2.8	35	227	51.5	4.1	1	D	D	D
Pottawatomie	40.7	1 883	30	549	224.8	23.5	81	1 819	338.9	48.4	18	D	D	D
Pratt	89.1	9 225	25	190	230.6	9.2	54	734	173.3	16.4	13	36	2.7	0.6
Rawlins	14.1	5 613	9	109	108.6	6.4	15	103	25.1	1.8	1	D	D	D
Reno	70.9	1 098	84	D	D	D	265	3 345	818.1	74.6	67	167	26.8	4.6
Republic	17.7	3 544	15	120	181.0	3.9	39	237	48.2	4.2	2	D	D	D
Rice	24.3	2 409	18	113	113.7	4.9	39	280	50.0	4.7	3	5	0.5	0.1
Riley	5.3	75	26	176	82.3	7.3	272	4 389	903.9	81.6	111	D	D	D
Rooks	11.1	2 142	17	159	178.2	6.9	28	200	69.2	3.8	2	D	D	D
Rush	8.9	2 703	14	74	58.6	2.9	10	65	29.1	1.8	NA	NA	NA	NA
Russell	1.3	182	14	114	101.2	4.3	39	267	76.5	4.7	8	25	3.1	0.6
Saline	10.4	188	95	1 195	996.5	54.7	250	3 989	1 120.4	87.4	64	208	52.5	6.4
Scott	43.7	8 857	19	126	192.1	6.1	33	223	56.8	3.9	4	3	0.5	0.1
Sedgwick	94.0	189	589	8 367	8 308.4	478.6	1 720	27 362	7 201.5	646.4	554	3 997	582.4	133.0
Seward	157.4	6 857	36	407	264.4	19.7	91	1 262	317.1	28.5	20	54	10.3	2.1
Shawnee	36.0	202	154	1 992	1 376.1	100.0	653	9 678	2 364.3	212.6	202	903	134.7	26.3
Sheridan	72.3	28 290	14	124	160.6	7.1	19	89	21.0	1.6	NA	NA	NA	NA
Sherman	99.1	16 491	23	225	341.0	9.3	34	409	132.3	8.9	4	D	D	D
Smith	2.2	563	10	134	128.2	4.8	24	169	67.4	3.4	2	D	D	D
Stafford	88.5	19 950	8	D	D	D	17	125	34.8	2.3	1	D	D	D
Stanton	113.5	50 774	9	D	D	D	5	D	D	D	1	D	D	D
Stevens	197.6	34 521	11	95	128.0	4.2	14	144	37.0	3.3	2	D	D	D
Sumner	9.4	391	28	167	157.4	7.0	65	592	159.8	11.1	12	D	D	D
Thomas	82.4	10 433	28	296	388.2	16.2	63	666	233.5	14.3	8	34	8.5	0.8
Trego	6.1	2 029	11	78	104.2	2.7	24	154	47.7	3.1	3	D	D	D
Wabaunsee	3.7	519	4	34	20.5	1.5	18	88	36.7	1.7	4	D	D	D
Wallace	45.3	30 478	5	D	D	D	7	42	7.6	1.0	2	D	D	D
Washington	5.7	988	21	183	264.8	6.3	36	215	45.6	4.1	6	9	0.4	0.0
Wichita	53.9	24 105	11	93	111.4	3.8	14	70	19.8	1.5	NA	NA	NA	NA
Wilson	2.6	281	5	20	31.7	0.7	43	234	57.7	4.5	3	3	0.2	0.0
Woodson	1.2	369	5	44	25.9	1.7	17	69	22.0	1.7	3	D	D	D
Wyandotte	287.0	1 822	225	5 758	5 611.1	302.2	452	6 929	1 769.4	172.6	136	593	112.2	20.2
KENTUCKY	4 326.5	997	3 690	57 630	71 745.9	3 090.3	15 224	202 615	54 870.0	4 619.2	3 534	18 250	4 845.5	637.3
Adair	3.4	184	15	72	42.1	1.6	64	691	204.3	16.2	5	D	D	D
Allen	2.3	114	9	D	D	D	59	410	111.3	8.4	9	23	2.4	0.6
Anderson	4.1	190	6	33	10.1	1.4	51	738	188.9	15.4	14	49	4.3	1.0
Ballard	31.7	3 837	4	D	D	D	26	162	57.6	3.6	3	D	D	D
Barren	10.4	246	39	D	D	D	188	2 193	562.8	49.5	23	71	9.9	1.6
Bath	6.0	515	3	D	D	D	31	182	47.8	3.8	8	D	D	D
Bell	4.4	152	18	189	212.9	5.9	128	1 515	365.1	31.2	19	71	9.2	1.6
Boone	11.1	94	170	6 614	21 688.2	542.7	470	9 132	2 564.6	208.6	102	719	175.3	25.2
Bourbon	3.2	162	4	D	D	D	65	876	248.2	21.8	10	16	4.0	0.5
Boyd	44.1	890	65	904	1 288.6	39.3	239	3 719	1 010.4	78.8	45	408	52.6	14.6
Boyle	6.8	240	20	140	114.1	5.7	134	1 717	431.4	39.6	23	66	8.7	1.5
Bracken	1.7	203	2	D	D	D	18	131	25.6	2.2	2	D	D	D
Breathitt	10.3	744	1	D	D	D	45	499	118.3	10.4	8	21	2.6	0.5
Breckinridge	2.6	132	8	72	36.0	2.3	55	543	148.2	12.2	9	23	2.2	0.8
Bullitt	6.9	92	28	564	519.7	22.0	144	1 550	586.4	36.0	31	118	19.6	4.0
Butler	1.7	134	6	D	D	D	33	232	49.9	4.3	4	5	0.3	0.1
Caldwell	1.4	108	9	D	D	D	57	687	159.9	15.0	6	9	1.7	0.3
Calloway	6.4	172	39	D	D	D	153	1 987	523.8	41.4	37	188	20.8	4.5
Campbell	29.9	330	60	1 036	835.3	60.6	265	4 285	1 105.2	94.3	62	544	93.9	26.4
Carlisle	0.7	141	4	20	4.2	0.5	12	81	19.9	1.6	7	8	2.3	0.2
Carroll	42.9	3 965	8	53	17.0	1.8	49	629	187.8	13.7	3	D	D	D
Carter	5.1	184	11	289	209.6	7.6	96	881	272.8	17.6	13	D	D	D
Casey	1.8	115	12	136	33.7	3.1	56	375	83.1	6.7	4	11	0.5	0.1
Christian	17.4	235	67	886	1 060.4	33.1	249	3 239	1 019.9	77.6	58	D	D	D
Clark	94.0	2 638	34	623	873.0	27.9	127	1 623	471.5	37.0	28	71	12.0	1.7

1. Merchant wholesalers, except manufacturers' sales branches and offices. 2. Employer establishments.

Table B. States and Counties — Professional Services, Manufacturing, and Accommodation and Food Services

STATE County	Professional, scientific, and technical services, 2012				Manufacturing, 2012				Accommodation and food services, 2012			
	Number of establishments	Number of employees	Receipts (mil dol)	Annual payroll (mil dol)	Number of establishments	Number of employees	Receipts (mil dol)	Annual payroll (mil dol)	Number of establishments	Number of employees	Sales (mil dol)	Annual payroll (mil dol)
	147	148	149	150	151	152	153	154	155	156	157	158
KANSAS—Cont'd												
Neosho	33	123	42.9	5.5	31	922	223.1	39.6	27	D	D	D
Ness	5	20	1.7	0.5	4	23	7.5	1.0	7	D	D	D
Norton	14	46	3.8	0.8	5	D	D	D	13	140	6.1	1.8
Osage	17	54	6.0	1.6	3	D	D	D	20	D	D	D
Osborne	7	42	12.6	1.6	6	113	D	4.5	12	D	D	D
Ottawa	14	D	D	D	8	84	D	2.2	10	41	1.2	0.3
Pawnee	16	74	8.1	2.2	NA	NA	NA	NA	16	153	5.5	1.5
Phillips	16	97	11.6	4.0	10	178	D	11.1	14	140	4.3	1.0
Pottawatomie	52	198	15.5	5.8	30	1 368	377.5	74.6	35	422	17.7	4.5
Pratt	28	115	11.7	4.7	9	78	42.6	3.4	32	438	25.0	5.1
Rawlins	11	16	1.3	0.3	7	31	9.4	1.2	5	25	0.5	0.1
Reno	102	642	61.8	24.5	87	3 752	1 232.8	168.4	117	2 141	91.6	26.3
Republic	13	25	3.4	0.6	10	168	D	6.3	11	D	D	D
Rice	16	143	9.4	2.6	14	328	291.2	14.9	22	D	D	D
Riley	146	D	D	D	30	480	94.5	18.9	166	3 903	146.8	42.1
Rooks	13	43	4.9	1.9	6	130	D	4.1	17	88	3.1	0.8
Rush	6	14	1.4	0.7	6	320	D	11.3	7	36	1.5	0.3
Russell	12	44	4.7	1.2	7	114	D	5.1	18	283	11.6	3.3
Saline	112	D	D	D	75	5 497	D	237.2	137	3 047	119.6	31.8
Scott	19	52	7.7	1.6	6	20	D	1.0	14	D	D	D
Sedgwick	1 155	10 100	1 586.7	570.9	533	40 629	15 547.1	2 316.4	1 102	22 151	1 029.8	287.6
Seward	22	139	12.0	5.0	7	D	D	D	45	789	40.4	10.4
Shawnee	449	D	D	D	105	5 291	2 588.3	244.4	362	D	D	D
Sheridan	3	16	1.0	0.3	3	6	D	D	6	D	D	D
Sherman	22	79	6.6	1.9	5	46	D	2.1	25	D	D	D
Smith	8	21	2.6	0.4	6	107	D	3.3	8	D	D	D
Stafford	6	11	2.0	0.7	NA	NA	NA	NA	10	D	D	D
Stanton	5	16	1.2	0.4	NA	NA	NA	NA	4	D	D	D
Stevens	11	40	3.3	0.9	4	22	D	1.9	12	144	5.0	1.3
Sumner	32	114	13.9	5.6	37	827	D	35.6	42	458	19.3	5.0
Thomas	28	65	7.2	2.1	9	45	D	1.8	31	464	21.8	6.2
Trego	8	24	1.4	0.4	6	41	D	1.4	11	119	4.8	1.2
Wabaunsee	7	8	1.2	0.3	7	D	D	D	8	30	1.3	0.2
Wallace	3	D	D	D	NA	NA	NA	NA	3	D	D	D
Washington	10	24	3.4	0.8	8	174	35.1	5.4	12	110	3.2	0.8
Wichita	4	6	0.3	0.1	4	62	D	2.3	4	D	D	D
Wilson	13	34	4.1	1.1	19	888	181.5	35.0	20	D	D	D
Woodson	5	D	D	D	3	13	D	0.5	8	D	D	D
Wyandotte	191	2 703	305.9	93.5	174	10 537	11 105.9	666.4	265	5 206	284.6	75.1
KENTUCKY	8 101	62 851	7 782.5	2 816.7	3 782	213 545	129 284.4	10 140.1	7 678	156 965	7 500.1	2 083.5
Adair	17	D	D	D	25	323	153.1	10.9	19	D	D	D
Allen	7	84	3.4	1.7	10	D	D	D	16	D	D	D
Anderson	29	96	11.1	3.1	26	1 130	746.5	70.8	30	403	20.4	5.5
Ballard	10	D	D	D	11	678	D	49.0	10	D	D	D
Barren	47	265	22.5	7.9	45	3 480	929.5	139.8	86	1 554	71.9	18.6
Bath	10	D	D	D	8	D	D	4.8	12	D	D	D
Bell	29	104	9.2	3.3	19	1 075	304.4	34.6	44	855	36.7	9.5
Boone	224	2 184	228.4	72.6	188	12 910	5 069.7	653.0	286	D	D	D
Bourbon	32	321	35.0	14.7	24	1 731	1 066.6	78.2	27	D	D	D
Boyd	96	720	73.9	33.4	34	2 798	D	218.5	120	2 704	129.4	35.0
Boyle	55	275	34.6	10.2	22	1 881	673.6	77.7	61	1 325	59.6	17.2
Bracken	4	12	0.6	0.3	NA	NA	NA	NA	8	D	D	D
Breathitt	10	D	D	D	5	25	D	1.0	10	D	D	D
Breckinridge	19	77	6.0	2.0	13	248	29.7	9.4	15	195	8.7	2.4
Bullitt	77	336	31.4	11.4	42	2 117	811.5	85.7	90	1 930	82.9	22.4
Butler	10	31	1.6	0.7	13	573	185.8	24.0	13	D	D	D
Caldwell	18	45	3.5	0.8	12	864	391.2	31.8	25	393	13.2	3.5
Calloway	65	357	29.6	12.5	30	2 548	828.7	93.4	87	1 679	60.4	16.1
Campbell	146	950	125.1	41.8	78	2 651	994.7	123.9	208	D	D	D
Carlisle	2	D	D	D	4	80	10.4	1.8	6	31	1.3	0.3
Carroll	16	93	10.0	4.6	13	2 452	D	177.2	28	D	D	D
Carter	28	111	6.9	2.6	15	791	253.5	23.6	32	636	28.1	7.3
Casey	10	D	D	D	31	1 266	237.7	28.4	12	192	7.6	2.6
Christian	111	958	100.0	41.0	72	4 647	1 894.8	207.8	113	D	D	D
Clark	55	293	31.4	13.5	40	2 378	1 016.0	108.4	58	1 148	56.5	15.6

1. Establishment subject to federal tax.

Table B. States and Counties — Health Care and Social Assistance, Other Services, Nonemployer Businesses, and Residential Construction

STATE County	Health care and social assistance, 2012				Other services, 2012				Nonemployer businesses, 2015		Value of residential construction authorized by building permits, 2016	
	Number of establishments	Number of employees	Receipts (mil dol)	Annual payroll (mil dol)	Number of establishments	Number of employees	Receipts (mil dol)	Annual payroll (mil dol)	Number	Receipts (mil dol)	New Construction ($1,000)	Number of housing units
	159	160	161	162	163	164	165	166	167	168	169	170
KANSAS—Cont'd												
Neosho	52	1 148	94.8	36.3	31	102	8.7	1.7	1 098	41.8	679	5
Ness	9	257	15.5	7.4	14	D	D	D	316	11.4	0	0
Norton	22	497	26.3	13.1	11	D	D	D	432	12.8	1 530	8
Osage	27	1 648	40.6	25.0	18	D	D	D	1 035	41.1	4 391	29
Osborne	13	334	16.2	8.1	10	33	4.5	0.9	353	10.4	0	0
Ottawa	12	D	D	D	11	D	D	D	500	18.3	361	3
Pawnee	16	1 210	87.4	43.8	14	30	2.7	0.5	431	22.2	200	1
Phillips	19	346	21.3	10.5	25	84	11.0	1.6	489	16.1	195	2
Pottawatomie	50	1 048	78.1	29.6	53	152	14.6	3.8	1 756	79.5	42 185	164
Pratt	36	713	64.2	27.4	34	107	9.5	2.3	806	35.3	294	1
Rawlins	9	210	12.3	5.8	7	11	1.2	0.2	265	9.2	529	2
Reno	176	4 895	441.4	176.7	115	514	46.5	12.0	3 896	136.5	9 941	53
Republic	15	296	16.8	8.1	15	42	4.0	0.8	420	15.0	0	0
Rice	20	400	22.1	11.7	19	62	8.2	1.7	649	19.2	3 740	19
Riley	180	3 201	313.2	112.9	119	1 100	208.7	44.9	3 366	144.5	94 097	798
Rooks	12	245	17.8	7.2	10	39	3.5	0.7	568	21.5	175	1
Rush	7	163	9.1	3.7	5	D	D	D	280	9.8	0	0
Russell	13	132	8.1	3.6	18	71	7.4	1.7	828	38.9	1 118	6
Saline	181	D	D	D	113	D	D	D	3 459	143.2	10 542	53
Scott	11	341	19.6	10.4	17	42	6.5	1.0	475	17.9	2 575	16
Sedgwick	1 358	34 266	3 501.4	1 450.6	796	5 733	677.1	172.7	31 576	1 463.2	311 133	1 857
Seward	74	1 079	91.4	35.5	44	166	23.0	4.5	1 290	76.1	3 489	25
Shawnee	523	16 404	1 706.2	740.6	371	3 580	322.3	102.6	9 505	414.2	53 663	264
Sheridan	7	D	D	D	10	58	1.8	0.3	285	12.0	NA	NA
Sherman	38	353	23.9	11.7	20	71	7.4	1.7	453	17.5	0	0
Smith	7	D	D	D	13	D	D	D	327	9.5	0	0
Stafford	15	168	10.1	4.7	13	21	1.7	0.3	391	15.7	1 635	9
Stanton	3	D	D	D	5	D	D	D	197	8.8	0	0
Stevens	6	D	D	D	8	D	D	D	360	19.5	590	3
Sumner	58	947	58.2	25.4	39	116	9.9	2.6	1 474	53.7	2 180	19
Thomas	34	407	33.1	13.4	29	121	10.8	2.9	838	29.3	2 506	12
Trego	6	D	D	D	9	22	1.7	0.5	332	12.8	325	2
Wabaunsee	8	D	D	D	6	D	D	D	501	19.2	2 533	10
Wallace	4	D	D	D	6	D	D	D	169	4.8	0	0
Washington	25	317	16.3	7.6	19	D	D	D	462	17.8	0	0
Wichita	6	D	D	D	8	D	D	D	197	9.9	0	0
Wilson	33	695	46.6	18.8	17	35	3.8	0.8	630	23.1	60	1
Woodson	10	126	5.7	2.1	5	D	D	D	290	12.1	750	7
Wyandotte	320	13 552	1 568.6	707.1	222	1 320	270.7	42.0	7 442	291.3	50 603	272
KENTUCKY	11 425	251 878	26 264.7	10 184.1	5 849	38 364	4 071.4	1 090.0	280 835	11 996.9	1 727 013	12 714
Adair	36	739	48.8	20.2	14	D	D	D	1 568	61.8	347	7
Allen	23	D	D	D	17	D	D	D	1 448	61.6	900	10
Anderson	34	329	19.1	8.4	30	84	8.6	2.3	1 447	49.3	15 809	77
Ballard	6	D	D	D	5	D	D	D	474	16.0	NA	NA
Barren	105	D	D	D	59	223	14.9	4.7	3 223	121.5	10 827	61
Bath	9	296	10.1	4.3	8	D	D	D	791	22.6	300	1
Bell	78	D	D	D	35	154	11.2	2.9	1 393	40.0	2 606	26
Boone	243	4 772	446.2	181.8	180	D	D	D	7 374	322.3	74 945	556
Bourbon	47	714	59.3	22.2	21	D	D	D	1 364	60.9	7 233	38
Boyd	245	7 292	993.0	372.3	96	D	D	D	2 545	107.0	0	0
Boyle	132	2 917	297.4	130.9	53	208	16.8	4.2	2 031	76.8	6 688	35
Bracken	8	D	D	D	5	D	D	D	587	19.2	NA	NA
Breathitt	48	1 277	97.7	42.7	10	34	5.2	1.3	584	18.4	0	0
Breckinridge	31	589	39.9	13.5	19	38	3.7	0.8	1 247	55.3	90	1
Bullitt	108	1 386	95.1	39.7	90	1 584	46.3	42.7	4 335	176.4	86 069	429
Butler	20	352	19.9	9.7	18	D	D	D	841	34.1	0	0
Caldwell	34	570	44.7	16.4	17	D	D	D	723	28.3	0	0
Calloway	110	2 119	190.7	73.4	47	182	13.1	3.8	2 446	107.9	10 688	119
Campbell	158	3 490	334.3	130.9	126	D	D	D	5 476	213.3	67 833	447
Carlisle	6	D	D	D	5	10	1.1	0.2	436	16.4	NA	NA
Carroll	20	373	32.0	13.9	14	D	D	D	574	25.8	0	0
Carter	44	519	38.8	14.9	30	D	D	D	1 765	63.9	515	6
Casey	21	527	35.4	16.0	8	34	3.0	0.7	1 140	53.4	0	0
Christian	157	3 130	300.4	106.2	87	D	D	D	3 258	136.2	10 223	138
Clark	126	1 518	139.2	51.2	45	181	15.1	4.4	2 179	85.7	15 872	117

Table B. States and Counties — Government Employment and Payroll, and Local Government Finances

	Government employment and payroll, 2012									Local government finances, 2012				
			March payroll (percent of total)							General revenue				
												Taxes		
													Per capita[1] (dollars)	
STATE County	Full-time equivalent employees	March payroll (dollars)	Administration, judicial, and legal	Police and Corrections	Fire Protection	Highways and transportation	Health and Welfare	Natural resources and utilities	Education and libraries	Total (mil dol)	Inter-governmental (mil dol)	Total (mil dol)	Total	Property
	171	172	173	174	175	176	177	178	179	180	181	182	183	184
KANSAS—Cont'd														
Neosho	1 176	4 053 546	4.7	4.8	1.4	3.1	33.7	7.7	43.8	111.1	29.1	28.8	1 755	1 392
Ness	342	928 162	3.6	3.8	0.3	7.5	55.5	2.1	25.8	27.2	3.0	10.5	3 412	3 238
Norton	415	1 296 107	5.9	8.5	0.2	5.3	36.1	4.9	38.5	21.8	9.5	8.3	1 476	1 235
Osage	664	1 848 318	7.4	9.1	0.0	4.8	2.0	8.1	66.8	51.8	25.1	19.9	1 231	1 069
Osborne	160	407 550	12.5	11.0	0.0	10.3	6.0	16.5	39.9	12.2	3.9	6.3	1 668	1 374
Ottawa	333	902 710	6.3	6.6	0.0	8.3	3.0	8.5	63.2	26.0	12.4	11.0	1 813	1 494
Pawnee	440	1 250 370	6.8	9.0	0.2	6.2	4.7	6.2	62.4	27.5	10.2	13.2	1 900	1 520
Phillips	269	733 417	9.3	5.4	0.0	11.5	9.3	7.3	56.3	24.1	8.0	10.9	1 969	1 705
Pottawatomie	900	2 555 697	7.0	7.4	0.4	6.4	5.6	4.0	68.4	81.2	25.0	45.4	2 033	1 711
Pratt	620	2 089 279	5.5	7.1	0.6	5.9	5.9	8.3	64.6	48.5	14.6	24.6	2 526	2 145
Rawlins	120	323 307	14.0	8.7	0.1	13.4	2.7	5.2	54.9	9.2	3.2	4.8	1 855	1 554
Reno	3 036	10 310 558	4.2	9.4	4.3	3.9	2.4	5.3	68.8	260.0	97.6	109.2	1 695	1 318
Republic	280	743 094	10.6	6.2	0.0	10.1	3.1	14.2	51.3	22.0	7.1	12.0	2 465	2 116
Rice	740	2 211 947	5.2	5.5	0.1	4.7	28.7	3.7	50.7	54.4	18.2	18.8	1 885	1 542
Riley	2 188	7 227 365	9.0	12.5	5.2	5.3	2.9	8.2	55.4	194.7	54.3	101.1	1 339	930
Rooks	433	1 169 894	7.0	5.2	0.1	6.4	36.2	3.6	40.2	44.1	11.5	14.8	2 837	2 597
Rush	240	677 611	5.6	5.2	0.0	9.2	28.1	6.5	42.1	19.8	4.2	7.4	2 306	2 203
Russell	400	1 117 489	12.4	9.0	1.7	7.9	3.8	13.6	49.3	31.8	7.8	19.4	2 790	2 354
Saline	2 537	8 460 384	4.0	12.5	4.8	4.8	1.1	5.4	63.9	204.8	71.4	88.3	1 578	1 104
Scott	243	604 532	5.5	5.8	0.4	5.4	1.4	5.5	73.4	23.7	6.5	15.0	3 033	2 531
Sedgwick	17 666	64 762 573	6.4	12.0	4.9	3.5	5.0	4.5	61.8	1 873.6	724.4	682.0	1 354	1 041
Seward	1 811	5 549 695	5.2	6.6	1.4	2.3	29.2	3.6	49.3	146.4	48.8	38.4	1 629	1 116
Shawnee	8 380	28 121 726	3.6	11.0	4.3	2.8	2.6	4.9	70.3	768.6	263.0	299.3	1 672	1 189
Sheridan	256	590 482	3.7	3.2	0.0	5.6	53.2	2.1	27.9	10.1	2.5	6.2	2 430	2 074
Sherman	464	1 377 731	5.7	6.0	0.9	6.3	39.8	6.9	32.6	30.8	10.9	12.2	1 999	1 467
Smith	252	661 334	7.3	6.7	0.0	9.5	8.4	7.9	57.9	20.6	8.5	9.3	2 464	2 115
Stafford	276	853 136	9.9	5.7	0.8	9.4	3.5	6.5	62.0	24.1	7.5	12.6	2 881	2 680
Stanton	212	627 118	5.8	6.3	0.0	9.1	35.1	3.1	40.4	19.3	3.0	11.2	5 142	4 980
Stevens	518	1 610 255	4.2	4.8	0.3	4.7	38.6	4.1	41.0	50.0	6.3	27.4	4 762	4 526
Sumner	1 279	3 843 881	5.5	7.0	2.2	5.1	19.6	5.9	51.4	100.9	37.4	33.6	1 421	1 151
Thomas	600	1 667 889	4.5	6.5	1.4	4.8	3.5	6.7	70.3	44.9	12.3	19.0	2 396	1 891
Trego	344	1 000 545	5.7	4.2	0.2	6.3	56.4	2.5	22.3	13.1	3.4	7.5	2 518	2 196
Wabaunsee	308	821 494	10.9	7.3	0.0	6.3	2.4	6.6	65.2	27.8	12.1	10.7	1 521	1 395
Wallace	110	277 969	12.4	3.3	0.0	9.0	2.3	2.0	66.6	8.8	2.7	5.1	3 337	3 267
Washington	376	1 063 217	7.0	4.3	0.0	6.6	18.3	6.1	55.7	29.9	10.0	12.3	2 144	1 966
Wichita	216	654 420	4.5	3.3	0.1	4.9	41.8	2.5	39.5	16.5	3.9	5.9	2 609	2 207
Wilson	601	1 662 594	4.6	6.7	0.8	4.2	19.9	9.3	49.8	43.5	17.0	11.6	1 274	1 131
Woodson	181	419 389	10.5	9.6	3.3	11.4	2.2	8.1	52.8	13.3	5.4	6.7	2 052	1 782
Wyandotte	8 144	34 012 450	5.6	11.1	6.6	2.6	2.4	14.3	54.4	766.0	289.0	302.6	1 901	1 204
KENTUCKY	X	X	X	X	X	X	X	X	X	X	X	X	X	X
Adair	919	2 441 497	2.9	3.7	0.0	1.1	35.9	4.2	51.1	55.9	21.6	8.0	427	308
Allen	767	1 841 667	2.0	8.2	0.2	1.6	4.0	4.1	78.7	41.3	23.7	11.2	555	342
Anderson	809	2 162 986	6.1	5.8	0.3	3.2	5.0	4.0	75.1	51.0	24.5	18.4	846	649
Ballard	248	590 155	9.9	12.4	0.0	2.7	9.1	4.7	61.1	23.3	12.4	8.2	986	597
Barren	1 664	5 001 627	2.5	3.2	0.0	0.8	0.2	25.7	67.1	124.1	60.3	35.4	831	508
Bath	406	1 111 046	4.3	4.3	0.9	1.2	4.3	5.5	79.0	26.0	18.6	5.0	425	253
Bell	1 171	3 090 979	2.7	6.2	2.6	2.0	1.9	1.6	81.4	75.8	50.5	15.0	534	291
Boone	3 843	13 434 279	1.9	8.5	6.9	1.7	0.4	3.4	75.6	360.0	112.7	201.9	1 637	990
Bourbon	965	3 068 260	6.3	8.4	5.9	2.9	15.6	4.1	55.9	56.7	29.4	20.5	1 028	562
Boyd	2 063	6 328 157	3.3	7.1	4.8	2.9	12.1	6.5	61.5	147.1	62.5	56.2	1 143	583
Boyle	1 287	4 095 739	3.9	9.0	16.6	1.6	5.9	2.0	59.3	83.9	32.8	34.1	1 190	651
Bracken	356	894 119	6.9	4.0	0.0	2.5	7.4	5.6	73.1	19.7	12.1	5.3	621	450
Breathitt	629	1 632 815	3.0	3.4	0.6	2.7	1.6	1.3	86.6	44.7	30.3	8.4	615	272
Breckinridge	636	1 726 384	4.2	7.6	0.0	2.7	3.3	0.7	81.4	49.9	26.8	10.3	513	381
Bullitt	2 379	7 126 688	1.5	7.4	2.5	1.5	4.1	1.8	80.6	162.7	71.4	70.4	927	693
Butler	426	1 274 899	3.6	4.6	0.0	4.2	0.0	5.4	82.2	27.2	19.3	5.9	459	211
Caldwell	534	1 550 863	4.7	6.1	2.3	3.5	12.5	10.7	58.9	23.5	15.7	6.2	481	274
Calloway	2 147	6 749 443	2.1	4.3	1.7	1.6	54.4	1.7	34.0	317.2	34.5	23.7	628	447
Campbell	2 562	8 812 479	5.0	13.2	6.5	2.9	0.4	2.0	69.5	232.7	71.5	119.3	1 312	806
Carlisle	229	547 363	15.5	2.7	0.0	3.0	7.2	0.5	71.2	13.3	8.5	2.9	573	399
Carroll	523	1 513 204	6.2	11.6	1.6	2.3	2.6	4.1	71.1	176.6	16.1	13.1	1 202	549
Carter	1 152	2 867 307	1.7	3.7	0.0	1.6	9.7	2.9	78.0	60.6	42.8	11.2	410	234
Casey	760	1 971 527	2.7	6.8	0.5	1.5	27.9	2.2	58.2	51.9	25.0	6.6	412	269
Christian	1 972	5 973 027	3.9	11.1	5.4	1.2	2.6	9.3	61.0	153.9	80.7	50.3	666	318
Clark	1 289	3 897 749	3.3	8.0	8.0	1.8	7.1	3.9	65.0	104.2	43.5	36.8	1 029	594

1. Based on the resident population estimated as of July 1 of the year shown.

STATE County	Total (mil dol)	Per capita[1] (dollars)	Education	Health and hospitals	Police protection	Public welfare	Highways	Total (mil dol)	Per capita[1] (dollars)	Federal civilian	Federal military	State and local	Number of returns	Mean adjusted gross income	Mean income tax
	185	186	187	188	189	190	191	192	193	194	195	196	197	198	199
KANSAS—Cont'd															
Neosho	113.5	6 916	38.0	33.2	2.1	0.0	7.7	154.6	9 423	57	63	1 741	7 100	45 277	4 347
Ness	25.4	8 281	22.4	50.3	3.1	0.0	8.6	2.1	688	27	12	427	1 520	60 923	7 843
Norton	22.4	3 997	48.1	6.0	4.3	0.0	6.6	10.5	1 866	26	19	814	2 400	48 075	4 932
Osage	52.1	3 229	56.9	1.1	5.3	0.0	9.4	54.0	3 346	73	63	1 153	7 410	45 848	3 998
Osborne	12.6	3 304	32.2	8.6	8.0	0.0	13.4	3.3	875	26	14	329	1 900	45 077	4 498
Ottawa	26.4	4 347	50.1	4.7	3.2	0.0	13.3	17.8	2 933	23	23	443	2 840	47 577	4 307
Pawnee	26.1	3 762	43.8	6.6	5.2	0.0	13.5	27.5	3 968	37	23	1 707	2 930	48 315	4 917
Phillips	25.4	4 596	38.5	5.1	3.7	0.0	12.6	4.9	881	39	21	904	2 650	46 287	4 532
Pottawatomie	89.9	4 029	54.4	5.8	3.3	0.0	7.9	77.1	3 455	54	94	1 217	10 570	57 754	5 961
Pratt	49.1	5 044	57.5	3.6	5.0	0.0	9.2	35.4	3 643	33	37	1 087	4 590	57 075	6 827
Rawlins	10.8	4 225	35.7	5.3	4.3	0.0	11.1	4.4	1 700	18	10	314	1 270	54 962	7 262
Reno	245.7	3 812	58.1	2.1	5.1	0.0	4.6	208.5	3 236	168	242	5 297	28 940	50 639	5 406
Republic	23.3	4 788	35.1	4.3	3.0	0.0	14.7	7.7	1 591	31	18	479	2 410	47 358	4 846
Rice	56.5	5 654	43.4	25.1	2.5	0.0	7.7	50.8	5 088	41	37	1 067	4 290	52 828	5 386
Riley	230.8	3 057	51.3	0.7	7.0	0.0	6.1	524.1	6 941	425	299	11 488	27 620	52 828	6 051
Rooks	50.5	9 668	22.1	22.3	3.3	5.5	5.9	39.4	7 551	33	20	638	2 540	45 634	4 919
Rush	21.5	6 668	27.9	26.9	0.9	0.0	10.6	8.4	2 621	26	12	340	1 550	46 882	4 481
Russell	31.0	4 458	38.8	4.9	4.7	0.0	12.1	17.1	2 459	31	28	674	3 330	49 091	5 162
Saline	211.2	3 772	45.1	1.4	5.3	0.0	7.8	251.6	4 493	253	218	4 111	27 130	54 311	6 634
Scott	22.4	4 533	43.6	4.5	6.5	2.3	7.7	37.8	7 650	22	19	347	2 420	60 451	7 171
Sedgwick	1 940.5	3 851	46.8	4.2	5.7	0.1	5.3	5 893.5	11 696	4 586	4 772	26 458	234 450	63 269	8 386
Seward	172.9	7 343	40.9	33.7	2.9	0.0	2.5	86.1	3 658	94	91	2 386	10 600	44 781	3 830
Shawnee	739.9	4 134	52.9	2.2	6.5	0.2	2.7	1 291.7	7 217	3 437	802	19 168	84 930	53 509	6 081
Sheridan	9.9	3 891	38.8	11.7	2.2	0.0	16.8	0.6	238	16	10	333	1 290	55 458	8 669
Sherman	28.9	4 724	57.7	3.1	3.6	0.0	7.8	18.3	2 989	51	23	715	2 800	44 910	4 375
Smith	21.3	5 645	40.2	5.3	2.0	0.0	17.3	2.0	535	33	15	339	1 920	43 325	4 027
Stafford	24.7	5 668	48.8	4.4	4.1	0.0	14.9	2.2	513	42	17	606	1 980	51 522	6 131
Stanton	28.2	12 976	20.1	52.9	1.2	0.0	8.9	15.2	6 985	D	D	326	980	57 578	6 415
Stevens	55.6	9 664	30.0	27.7	3.3	0.0	8.1	24.5	4 259	25	23	716	2 430	60 028	6 636
Sumner	97.3	4 110	41.6	20.7	4.1	0.0	7.7	85.1	3 595	70	92	1 774	10 630	51 027	5 067
Thomas	47.7	6 010	55.4	1.6	2.9	0.0	9.6	33.5	4 224	27	30	891	3 850	51 937	6 340
Trego	13.1	4 381	37.4	4.9	2.1	0.6	14.1	16.4	5 487	16	11	484	1 550	53 640	6 666
Wabaunsee	25.0	3 546	48.3	1.1	3.9	0.0	12.8	27.4	3 889	22	27	479	3 170	51 362	4 904
Wallace	9.8	6 453	40.5	2.8	3.1	2.3	13.0	5.2	3 412	11	D	160	730	56 540	6 219
Washington	29.5	5 125	44.0	14.4	0.8	0.0	17.0	3.2	559	46	22	677	2 880	44 973	4 488
Wichita	16.8	7 467	32.0	38.6	3.0	0.0	8.8	7.0	3 099	17	D	290	1 090	56 361	6 678
Wilson	43.9	4 825	41.2	25.8	5.1	0.0	6.6	43.5	4 772	37	35	895	3 970	46 858	5 009
Woodson	12.5	3 824	43.4	1.9	6.1	0.0	13.6	2.8	845	14	12	280	1 470	53 680	5 497
Wyandotte	733.0	4 606	51.2	1.5	7.1	0.0	1.3	2 162.3	13 588	1 341	648	16 417	70 720	38 634	3 075
KENTUCKY	X	X	X	X	X	X	X	X	X	36 648	48 037	273 056	1 891 680	52 017	5 876
Adair	60.0	3 213	34.8	41.3	2.1	0.0	3.2	137.2	7 348	46	56	917	6 900	34 329	2 612
Allen	49.2	2 435	63.1	7.8	3.4	0.1	4.2	71.1	3 516	43	64	787	7 810	38 548	2 999
Anderson	51.5	2 370	63.4	5.7	3.7	0.0	3.5	69.4	3 192	39	68	902	10 250	49 363	4 511
Ballard	29.1	3 486	40.4	3.5	3.4	0.0	6.5	122.6	14 712	29	25	383	3 430	49 614	5 076
Barren	120.1	2 816	69.4	1.0	3.9	0.7	2.6	241.8	5 673	101	134	2 194	18 230	42 276	4 052
Bath	23.4	1 987	68.5	4.7	2.1	0.0	5.2	23.4	1 980	27	38	512	4 520	36 554	2 687
Bell	70.9	2 517	61.7	2.1	3.4	0.0	2.6	42.0	1 492	126	82	1 630	8 920	33 819	2 492
Boone	317.2	2 573	54.9	0.6	4.8	1.9	8.0	852.8	6 915	1 179	397	5 284	58 830	64 282	7 595
Bourbon	58.2	2 912	60.5	5.7	3.8	0.1	3.2	52.5	2 629	36	62	955	9 070	42 251	4 824
Boyd	151.0	3 072	52.9	5.0	3.7	0.0	4.0	303.6	6 176	426	144	3 053	19 540	50 647	5 506
Boyle	80.8	2 820	48.5	3.9	4.6	0.3	3.0	210.1	7 332	64	83	1 793	11 980	49 828	5 322
Bracken	19.5	2 296	59.4	6.5	3.2	0.0	7.7	14.9	1 758	18	26	428	3 620	42 760	3 355
Breathitt	41.9	3 073	57.4	8.4	3.1	0.0	7.9	24.9	1 827	58	41	904	4 520	37 641	2 909
Breckinridge	54.2	2 698	52.5	2.3	2.2	0.1	4.0	265.6	13 235	60	62	852	7 830	43 571	3 785
Bullitt	164.4	2 166	55.3	3.4	4.5	0.0	2.2	188.8	2 488	69	245	2 752	36 580	49 318	4 496
Butler	27.0	2 105	61.6	0.3	3.5	0.1	7.5	53.2	4 145	25	40	631	5 120	39 583	2 877
Caldwell	28.0	2 163	70.3	2.5	2.0	0.1	6.9	20.0	1 544	37	39	659	5 500	41 817	3 683
Calloway	176.1	4 676	22.2	62.3	2.8	0.0	1.6	108.2	2 874	69	109	5 069	14 850	45 148	4 361
Campbell	217.1	2 389	52.4	0.5	8.0	0.4	4.4	506.2	5 568	364	277	5 884	42 940	60 690	7 415
Carlisle	16.7	3 315	59.4	5.5	1.6	0.0	10.4	23.2	4 601	15	15	236	2 140	50 601	5 640
Carroll	170.1	15 605	12.4	0.6	0.8	0.0	1.2	3 066.5	281 328	37	32	710	4 770	44 465	3 882
Carter	66.1	2 418	70.9	4.9	3.9	0.0	3.5	99.7	3 647	60	83	1 258	10 340	41 322	3 416
Casey	49.1	3 053	40.2	33.9	1.5	0.0	4.4	63.3	3 935	28	48	681	5 740	33 653	2 537
Christian	164.3	2 178	52.4	3.1	7.2	0.2	3.3	420.2	5 571	3 793	29 347	3 638	30 530	40 612	3 729
Clark	108.6	3 033	59.0	5.7	3.5	0.1	2.7	125.2	3 499	98	110	1 422	15 930	47 464	4 566

1. Based on the resident population estimated as of July 1 of the year shown.

Table B. States and Counties — **Land Area and Population**

STATE/ County code	CBSA code[1]	County type[2]	STATE County	Land area,[3] (sq mi) 2016	Total persons 2016	Rank	Per square mile	White	Black	American Indian, Alaska Native	Asian and Pacific Islander	Percent Hispanic or Latino[4]	Under 5 years	5 to 17 years	18 to 24 years	25 to 34 years	35 to 44 years	45 to 54 years
					Population, 2016			Population and population characteristics, 2016											
								Race alone or in combination, not Hispanic or Latino (percent)					Age (percent)					
				1	2	3	4	5	6	7	8	9	10	11	12	13	14	15
			KENTUCKY—Cont'd															
21 051	...	7	Clay	469.2	20 766	1 785	44.3	93.6	4.5	0.6	0.3	2.0	6.3	15.2	7.6	15.1	13.9	14.5
21 053	...	9	Clinton	197.2	10 177	2 418	51.6	96.3	0.9	0.8	0.5	2.8	6.1	17.1	7.2	11.3	11.5	14.2
21 055	...	7	Crittenden	360.0	9 188	2 493	25.5	97.4	1.4	0.8	0.5	1.0	6.1	17.1	6.9	11.0	11.8	13.3
21 057	...	9	Cumberland	305.2	6 738	2 695	22.1	95.7	3.9	0.5	0.4	1.3	6.1	15.5	6.8	10.6	10.2	14.0
21 059	36980	3	Daviess	458.4	99 674	596	217.4	90.7	6.3	0.4	1.7	2.9	6.8	17.6	8.2	12.7	11.9	13.0
21 061	14540	3	Edmonson	302.9	12 114	2 288	40.0	96.4	2.3	1.0	0.5	1.1	4.7	14.3	8.7	11.3	12.4	13.6
21 063	...	9	Elliott	234.3	7 588	2 626	32.4	95.0	3.8	0.4	0.4	1.1	4.6	13.5	7.5	13.7	13.9	14.0
21 065	...	6	Estill	253.1	14 307	2 145	56.5	98.3	0.6	0.6	0.2	1.0	5.6	16.1	7.3	11.2	12.3	15.3
21 067	30460	2	Fayette	283.6	318 449	214	1 122.9	74.1	16.1	0.7	4.7	6.9	6.2	14.8	14.4	15.7	13.0	12.0
21 069	...	7	Fleming	348.5	14 507	2 130	41.6	96.9	2.0	0.5	0.4	1.3	6.6	18.0	7.6	10.9	12.3	14.1
21 071	...	7	Floyd	393.3	37 110	1 249	94.4	97.8	1.2	0.5	0.3	0.8	6.1	15.6	7.9	11.8	12.8	13.8
21 073	23180	4	Franklin	207.8	50 560	979	243.3	84.0	12.3	0.7	2.2	3.0	5.7	15.3	9.5	12.4	12.3	13.8
21 075	46460	9	Fulton	205.9	6 179	2 736	30.0	73.1	25.2	1.0	1.2	1.7	6.1	15.0	7.9	13.1	10.7	12.6
21 077	17140	1	Gallatin	98.3	8 609	2 541	87.6	92.6	2.3	0.7	0.7	5.4	5.9	18.7	8.4	12.5	12.1	15.6
21 079	...	6	Garrard	230.1	17 292	1 957	75.1	95.3	2.6	0.5	0.4	2.3	5.5	16.5	7.0	11.0	12.3	15.2
21 081	17140	1	Grant	258.0	24 923	1 609	96.6	95.5	1.5	0.6	0.8	2.8	7.4	19.8	8.2	12.3	12.7	14.2
21 083	32460	7	Graves	551.8	37 182	1 247	67.4	88.9	5.6	0.7	0.6	6.1	6.6	17.6	7.7	11.5	11.9	13.5
21 085	...	6	Grayson	498.6	26 184	1 553	52.5	97.0	1.6	0.7	0.5	1.3	6.5	17.2	7.8	11.9	12.5	13.1
21 087	...	8	Green	286.0	11 060	2 349	38.7	95.5	2.9	0.8	0.5	1.7	5.2	16.0	6.8	10.1	12.0	14.7
21 089	26580	2	Greenup	344.5	35 893	1 275	104.2	97.4	1.2	0.8	0.7	1.1	5.4	16.4	7.2	10.8	12.3	13.6
21 091	36980	3	Hancock	187.7	8 810	2 522	46.9	96.7	1.9	0.6	0.5	1.5	6.9	18.7	7.6	10.7	12.3	14.0
21 093	21060	3	Hardin	623.3	107 316	559	172.2	79.5	14.0	1.0	3.7	5.4	6.7	18.0	9.5	13.4	12.6	13.7
21 095	...	7	Harlan	465.8	27 168	1 524	58.3	96.3	2.7	0.6	0.6	0.9	6.5	15.8	7.3	12.3	11.9	13.6
21 097	...	6	Harrison	306.4	18 646	1 886	60.9	94.9	2.8	0.6	0.5	2.4	5.8	17.2	7.8	10.7	11.9	14.6
21 099	...	8	Hart	412.5	18 627	1 887	45.2	92.8	5.6	0.7	0.6	1.9	6.7	17.2	7.9	11.3	11.5	14.2
21 101	21780	2	Henderson	436.5	46 253	1 043	106.0	89.0	9.3	0.5	0.8	2.4	6.1	17.2	7.5	12.7	12.2	13.2
21 103	31140	1	Henry	286.3	15 818	2 054	55.2	93.3	3.8	1.0	0.5	3.2	5.6	18.1	7.4	11.2	11.9	14.4
21 105	...	9	Hickman	242.3	4 627	2 854	19.1	88.3	10.1	0.8	0.6	1.6	4.9	15.0	6.9	10.3	10.8	13.9
21 107	31580	5	Hopkins	542.0	45 904	1 052	84.7	90.6	7.9	0.7	1.0	1.9	6.1	16.9	7.5	12.0	12.1	13.2
21 109	...	9	Jackson	345.2	13 368	2 208	38.7	98.6	0.5	0.5	0.2	0.8	6.0	16.5	7.3	11.5	13.5	14.2
21 111	31140	1	Jefferson	380.5	765 352	82	2 011.4	70.3	22.9	0.7	3.4	5.1	6.4	16.1	8.6	14.7	12.5	13.0
21 113	30460	2	Jessamine	172.1	52 357	954	304.2	91.0	5.1	0.8	1.8	3.3	6.7	17.9	9.7	12.5	12.7	13.5
21 115	...	7	Johnson	262.0	22 978	1 682	87.7	98.3	0.7	0.6	0.6	0.7	6.1	16.4	7.6	11.6	12.8	14.2
21 117	17140	1	Kenton	160.3	164 945	389	1 029.0	90.6	6.0	0.5	1.8	3.1	6.7	17.4	8.0	14.8	12.9	13.5
21 119	...	9	Knott	351.5	15 544	2 070	44.2	97.9	1.2	0.6	0.3	1.0	5.8	15.0	10.3	10.5	11.8	14.3
21 121	30940	7	Knox	386.3	31 687	1 389	82.0	96.9	1.8	0.8	0.6	1.2	6.5	17.0	8.8	12.3	11.9	13.3
21 123	21060	3	Larue	261.5	14 096	2 157	53.9	93.1	3.8	1.0	0.6	3.2	5.5	16.4	7.6	12.2	12.0	14.0
21 125	30940	5	Laurel	434.0	60 250	866	138.8	96.9	1.1	0.9	0.8	1.5	6.1	17.1	7.8	12.7	13.0	14.1
21 127	...	6	Lawrence	415.6	15 863	2 050	38.2	98.3	1.0	0.8	0.5	1.0	6.7	17.2	7.2	11.8	12.5	13.7
21 129	...	9	Lee	208.9	6 580	2 703	31.5	97.7	1.3	1.0	0.4	0.8	5.5	14.9	7.1	11.5	11.2	16.6
21 131	...	9	Leslie	400.8	10 538	2 387	26.3	98.8	0.7	0.6	0.3	0.6	6.1	15.6	6.7	12.4	12.4	14.3
21 133	...	9	Letcher	337.9	22 773	1 687	67.4	98.3	0.8	0.5	0.3	0.7	5.9	15.9	6.9	11.8	12.4	14.0
21 135	...	8	Lewis	482.8	13 442	2 200	27.8	98.5	0.8	0.7	0.1	0.7	5.6	16.3	7.7	11.3	12.5	14.3
21 137	19220	7	Lincoln	332.7	24 372	1 629	73.3	95.8	3.0	0.8	0.4	1.6	6.2	16.9	7.7	11.5	12.1	14.5
21 139	37140	9	Livingston	313.1	9 269	2 485	29.6	97.0	0.9	0.9	0.8	1.6	5.6	14.7	6.7	10.2	11.0	14.5
21 141	...	6	Logan	552.1	26 593	1 543	48.2	90.4	7.5	0.7	0.5	2.8	6.3	17.3	7.6	12.0	11.5	13.6
21 143	...	9	Lyon	213.8	8 069	2 589	37.7	92.6	5.6	1.0	0.7	1.6	3.2	11.5	6.6	11.1	12.0	14.2
21 145	37140	5	McCracken	248.7	65 162	812	262.0	85.7	12.1	0.8	1.3	2.4	5.9	16.0	7.4	12.1	12.1	13.0
21 147	...	9	McCreary	426.8	17 511	1 945	41.0	90.9	6.0	1.6	0.5	2.6	6.0	15.8	8.1	14.0	14.6	14.2
21 149	36980	3	McLean	252.5	9 475	2 469	37.5	97.3	1.3	0.7	0.3	1.5	5.9	18.0	6.9	10.4	11.6	14.0
21 151	40080	4	Madison	437.3	89 547	647	204.8	91.7	5.6	0.8	1.6	2.3	5.7	15.3	17.7	12.2	12.2	12.4
21 153	...	9	Magoffin	308.4	12 684	2 249	41.1	98.3	0.5	0.7	0.2	1.1	6.0	16.7	7.3	11.5	12.9	14.8
21 155	...	7	Marion	343.0	19 205	1 863	56.0	89.7	8.2	0.5	0.9	2.5	6.5	18.1	8.3	11.3	12.4	14.1
21 157	...	7	Marshall	301.3	31 365	1 400	104.1	97.6	0.7	0.7	0.6	1.5	5.4	15.5	6.7	10.9	11.7	13.6
21 159	...	9	Martin	229.6	12 002	2 297	52.3	89.3	7.0	0.7	0.3	3.5	4.9	15.2	7.4	16.6	14.2	13.8
21 161	32500	6	Mason	240.1	17 190	1 969	71.6	91.2	7.4	0.7	0.9	1.7	6.1	17.4	8.0	11.5	11.6	13.8
21 163	21060	3	Meade	305.4	28 126	1 485	92.1	91.3	4.2	1.3	1.6	3.9	5.0	18.2	8.3	12.9	13.5	14.8
21 165	34460	9	Menifee	203.6	6 408	2 723	31.5	95.8	3.2	0.7	0.3	1.2	5.3	14.3	9.1	10.8	12.1	13.8
21 167	...	6	Mercer	248.8	21 477	1 755	86.3	93.0	4.6	0.7	1.0	2.7	5.9	16.3	7.8	10.7	11.1	14.7
21 169	23980	9	Metcalfe	289.6	10 018	2 433	34.6	96.1	2.2	0.6	0.4	1.8	6.3	17.2	7.2	11.4	11.4	13.9
21 171	...	8	Monroe	329.4	10 588	2 384	32.1	94.8	2.5	0.5	0.4	2.9	6.3	16.4	7.5	11.0	11.7	13.9
21 173	34460	6	Montgomery	197.4	27 771	1 498	140.7	94.0	3.4	0.6	0.6	2.6	6.6	17.3	7.7	12.4	13.6	14.3
21 175	...	9	Morgan	381.1	13 298	2 214	34.9	93.6	4.7	0.7	0.9	1.0	5.1	13.9	7.8	15.1	14.4	14.1
21 177	16420	6	Muhlenberg	467.1	31 028	1 408	66.4	93.1	5.5	0.6	0.5	1.5	5.3	15.4	8.9	12.6	12.6	13.6
21 179	12680	6	Nelson	417.5	45 559	1 063	109.1	92.0	6.1	0.5	0.9	2.1	6.4	17.9	8.2	12.3	12.6	14.4
21 181	...	8	Nicholas	195.2	7 084	2 664	36.3	96.8	1.0	0.5	0.3	2.1	6.1	17.5	7.9	10.7	12.1	14.6

1. CBSA = Core Based Statistical Area. See Appendix A for explanation. See Appendix B for list of metropolitan areas with component counties.   2. County type code from the Economic Research Service of USDA Rural-Urban Continuum Codes. See Appendix A for definition.   3. Dry land or land partially or temporarily covered by water.   4. May be of any race.

Table B. States and Counties — Population and Households

	Population, 2016 (cont.) Age (percent) (cont.)				Population change and components of change, 2000-2016							Households, 2011-2015				
STATE County	55 to 64 years	65 to 74 years	75 years and over	Percent female	Total persons 2000	Total persons 2010	Percent change 2000-2010	Percent change 2010-2016	Births	Deaths	Net migration	Number	Persons per house-hold	Family house-holds	Female family house-holder[1]	One per-son
	16	17	18	19	20	21	22	23	24	25	26	27	28	29	30	31
KENTUCKY—Cont'd																
Clay	12.8	9.1	5.5	47.4	24 556	21 730	-11.5	-4.4	1 786	1 623	-1 140	7 707	2.53	69.8	16.3	28.5
Clinton	14.4	11.0	7.3	50.4	9 634	10 267	6.6	-0.9	760	783	-37	3 858	2.60	66.6	9.2	32.1
Crittenden	14.2	11.3	8.3	49.6	9 384	9 315	-0.7	-1.4	660	749	-7	3 755	2.40	66.7	8.7	29.8
Cumberland	15.6	11.9	9.3	51.6	7 147	6 856	-4.1	-1.7	494	636	19	2 743	2.45	69.9	12.7	27.6
Daviess	13.4	9.2	7.2	51.3	91 545	96 658	5.6	3.1	8 328	6 265	998	38 536	2.48	67.5	12.0	27.5
Edmonson	14.6	12.5	7.9	49.7	11 644	12 161	4.4	-0.4	662	819	86	4 659	2.51	71.9	9.6	24.4
Elliott	13.4	11.3	8.1	43.5	6 748	7 852	16.4	-3.4	408	453	-239	2 750	2.44	71.5	13.9	22.4
Estill	14.2	11.1	6.8	50.6	15 307	14 672	-4.1	-2.5	995	1 137	-195	5 750	2.49	69.6	17.1	26.6
Fayette	11.6	7.3	5.0	50.9	260 512	295 805	13.5	7.7	25 403	13 531	11 081	125 752	2.35	57.6	12.4	32.2
Fleming	13.4	10.6	6.5	50.6	13 792	14 355	4.1	1.1	1 202	1 065	20	5 636	2.57	70.7	11.5	26.1
Floyd	14.7	10.8	6.6	51.2	42 441	39 451	-7.0	-5.9	3 111	3 258	-2 260	15 418	2.45	69.0	14.3	27.9
Franklin	13.8	10.3	6.9	51.7	47 687	49 283	3.3	2.6	3 616	3 158	777	21 033	2.28	60.8	13.1	33.9
Fulton	14.9	11.4	8.3	50.6	7 752	6 813	-12.1	-9.3	501	669	-485	2 568	2.33	62.1	13.5	35.6
Gallatin	15.5	8.5	4.1	49.6	7 870	8 589	9.1	0.2	656	542	-113	3 097	2.73	67.8	12.7	28.2
Garrard	15.5	10.3	6.7	50.8	14 792	16 912	14.3	2.2	1 081	1 015	319	6 594	2.55	77.0	13.3	20.7
Grant	12.1	8.4	4.9	50.1	22 384	24 662	10.2	1.1	2 206	1 346	-617	8 325	2.91	76.2	13.4	19.1
Graves	13.3	10.3	7.7	51.1	37 028	37 121	0.3	0.2	3 125	2 734	-284	14 390	2.56	68.7	11.6	28.9
Grayson	13.9	10.3	6.8	49.8	24 053	25 746	7.0	1.7	2 101	1 944	334	9 840	2.60	70.2	9.4	27.1
Green	14.8	11.6	8.8	50.4	11 518	11 260	-2.2	-1.8	712	821	-87	4 477	2.46	69.0	10.7	28.0
Greenup	14.3	11.7	8.2	51.3	36 891	36 914	0.1	-2.8	2 424	2 804	-586	14 200	2.54	72.3	10.6	23.7
Hancock	12.8	10.5	6.5	48.4	8 392	8 565	2.1	2.9	716	518	52	3 265	2.62	75.8	13.8	22.4
Hardin	12.6	7.9	5.5	50.1	94 174	105 537	12.1	1.7	9 952	5 494	-2 878	40 376	2.58	69.3	13.5	26.7
Harlan	14.8	10.9	6.8	51.7	33 202	29 278	-11.8	-7.2	2 376	2 579	-1 925	11 406	2.43	69.3	14.3	27.7
Harrison	15.0	9.9	7.1	51.1	17 983	18 849	4.8	-1.1	1 300	1 374	-130	7 120	2.57	65.3	13.0	30.1
Hart	14.6	9.8	6.7	50.4	17 445	18 199	4.3	2.4	1 551	1 270	155	7 294	2.49	71.7	12.2	24.8
Henderson	14.5	9.7	6.8	51.6	44 829	46 250	3.2	0.0	3 519	3 108	-306	18 742	2.41	66.7	13.1	29.5
Henry	14.5	10.5	6.4	50.6	15 060	15 414	2.4	2.6	1 034	1 031	433	5 992	2.57	72.0	13.4	24.4
Hickman	14.0	13.0	11.3	52.6	5 262	4 902	-6.8	-5.6	254	414	-112	1 973	2.29	64.4	13.1	30.2
Hopkins	14.5	10.2	7.5	51.2	46 519	46 920	0.9	-2.2	3 469	3 584	-860	18 622	2.45	68.0	13.6	28.4
Jackson	14.7	10.2	6.0	50.3	13 495	13 494	0.0	-0.9	990	1 004	-96	5 546	2.39	75.2	14.1	22.1
Jefferson	13.6	8.8	6.4	51.7	693 604	741 106	6.8	3.3	62 681	46 131	9 209	306 915	2.41	60.5	14.8	32.9
Jessamine	12.9	8.3	5.8	51.3	39 041	48 584	24.4	7.8	4 226	2 514	1 937	18 312	2.65	76.0	13.6	19.2
Johnson	14.0	10.8	6.6	50.9	23 445	23 358	-0.4	-1.6	1 877	1 843	-375	9 035	2.53	70.6	9.2	26.0
Kenton	13.1	8.2	5.4	50.5	151 464	159 713	5.4	3.3	14 204	8 673	-27	62 225	2.58	64.8	13.9	28.7
Knott	15.3	10.6	6.5	50.4	17 649	16 346	-7.4	-4.9	1 169	1 253	-690	5 984	2.57	68.9	13.4	26.9
Knox	12.5	10.4	7.2	51.3	31 795	31 883	0.3	-0.6	2 544	2 487	-333	12 467	2.50	65.3	14.2	31.5
Larue	14.6	9.9	7.9	50.8	13 373	14 193	6.1	-0.7	914	1 028	15	5 328	2.60	70.3	13.2	24.9
Laurel	13.4	9.6	6.3	51.2	52 715	58 849	11.6	2.4	4 554	3 622	474	23 164	2.54	69.9	12.9	25.5
Lawrence	14.4	10.4	6.1	49.9	15 569	15 858	1.9	0.0	1 306	1 286	-96	6 033	2.60	72.9	11.6	24.4
Lee	15.3	11.6	6.3	49.5	7 916	7 889	-0.3	-16.6	450	630	-1 148	2 859	2.20	57.8	10.7	38.5
Leslie	14.9	10.5	7.1	50.6	12 401	11 310	-8.8	-6.8	883	1 034	-671	4 150	2.59	69.2	14.6	27.9
Letcher	15.2	11.2	6.8	51.0	25 277	24 519	-3.0	-7.1	1 776	1 987	-1 552	9 592	2.44	69.8	13.6	27.2
Lewis	14.8	10.4	7.1	50.2	14 092	13 872	-1.6	-3.1	898	938	-361	5 373	2.54	72.1	12.1	24.7
Lincoln	13.4	10.5	7.2	50.8	23 361	24 754	6.0	-1.5	1 964	1 725	-612	9 770	2.48	73.2	14.5	23.7
Livingston	16.2	12.9	8.2	50.7	9 804	9 519	-2.9	-2.6	635	789	-93	3 826	2.44	72.4	10.3	23.6
Logan	13.9	10.4	7.4	50.9	26 573	26 835	1.0	-0.9	2 123	1 855	-496	10 870	2.44	66.4	12.0	29.2
Lyon	16.3	15.3	9.8	44.7	8 080	8 319	3.0	-3.0	348	700	100	3 230	2.19	60.7	7.8	33.9
McCracken	14.5	10.8	8.2	52.0	65 514	65 565	0.1	-0.6	4 756	5 042	-41	27 514	2.33	61.9	13.4	33.5
McCreary	12.5	9.4	5.4	45.8	17 080	18 306	7.2	-4.3	1 405	1 194	-977	6 277	2.56	72.4	12.0	25.7
McLean	13.8	11.5	8.0	50.5	9 938	9 531	-4.1	-0.6	715	753	-30	3 759	2.50	72.1	8.3	24.6
Madison	11.3	8.1	5.2	51.5	70 872	82 916	17.0	8.0	6 242	4 349	4 583	32 064	2.49	63.3	11.7	27.9
Magoffin	14.8	9.9	6.1	50.0	13 332	13 333	0.0	-4.9	972	930	-694	4 996	2.57	69.7	13.2	28.7
Marion	13.2	9.5	6.6	50.5	18 212	19 820	8.8	-3.1	1 543	1 285	-932	7 395	2.51	66.3	11.5	29.5
Marshall	14.8	12.5	8.9	50.9	30 125	31 448	4.4	-0.3	1 993	2 604	576	12 602	2.43	70.8	8.9	25.8
Martin	12.8	9.2	5.7	44.8	12 578	12 929	2.8	-7.2	849	872	-912	4 320	2.57	71.9	13.1	24.3
Mason	14.2	10.4	7.1	51.9	16 800	17 490	4.1	-1.7	1 310	1 263	-338	6 736	2.52	70.6	13.9	26.2
Meade	13.7	8.4	5.1	49.8	26 349	28 621	8.6	-1.7	1 667	1 372	-858	10 574	2.73	75.7	10.0	19.7
Menifee	15.6	11.6	7.6	49.3	6 556	6 306	-3.8	1.6	433	447	112	2 427	2.56	71.2	14.3	24.9
Mercer	14.6	11.3	7.5	51.1	20 817	21 335	2.5	0.7	1 543	1 581	209	8 824	2.40	70.0	11.9	25.7
Metcalfe	14.3	10.2	8.1	50.5	10 037	10 099	0.6	-0.8	812	783	-123	3 936	2.51	68.4	8.1	27.4
Monroe	14.3	11.3	7.6	50.1	11 756	10 963	-6.7	-3.4	801	936	-229	4 443	2.39	66.6	10.3	28.1
Montgomery	12.6	9.4	6.0	51.1	22 554	26 507	17.5	4.8	2 453	1 638	447	10 248	2.61	66.9	13.9	26.7
Morgan	14.5	9.2	6.1	43.6	13 948	13 923	-0.2	-4.5	836	920	-547	4 808	2.45	73.7	12.6	23.1
Muhlenberg	13.6	10.8	7.7	49.0	31 839	31 499	-1.1	-1.5	2 123	2 431	-127	11 539	2.60	72.2	12.4	25.3
Nelson	13.7	9.1	5.4	50.6	37 477	43 437	15.9	4.9	3 704	2 294	721	16 817	2.62	75.0	13.1	23.4
Nicholas	13.7	10.5	6.9	50.6	6 813	7 128	4.6	-0.6	534	640	68	2 824	2.47	68.3	12.3	26.3

1. No spouse present.

Table B. States and Counties — Population, Vital Statistics, Health, and Crime

STATE County	Persons in group quarters, 2016	Daytime population, 2011–2015 Number	Employment/ residence ratio	Births, 2016 Total	Births, 2016 Rate[1]	Deaths, 2016 Number	Deaths, 2016 Rate[1]	Persons under 65 with no health insurance, 2015 Number	Percent	Medicare, 2015 Total Beneficiaries	Enrolled in Original Medicare	Enrolled in Medicare Advantage	Serious crimes known to police,[2] 2014 Total Number	Rate[3]
	32	33	34	35	36	37	38	39	40	41	42	43	44	45
KENTUCKY—Cont'd														
Clay	1 869	19 951	0.75	267	12.9	244	11.7	1 401	8.7	4 393	3 472	921	113	530
Clinton	136	10 817	1.18	128	12.6	103	10.1	750	9.2	2 437	1 969	468	6	59
Crittenden	210	8 248	0.73	115	12.5	106	11.5	537	7.4	1 969	1 571	398	74	800
Cumberland	86	6 468	0.86	74	11.0	120	17.8	433	8.1	1 681	1 291	390	38	560
Daviess	2 579	100 249	1.05	1 353	13.6	1 043	10.5	4 740	5.8	20 849	16 326	4 523	2 874	2 911
Edmonson	354	9 328	0.40	107	8.8	142	11.7	851	8.9	1 971	1 511	460	62	515
Elliott	1 061	7 001	0.64	72	9.5	72	9.5	383	7.3	2 773	1 836	937	1	13
Estill	118	12 053	0.48	154	10.8	174	12.2	981	8.4	3 442	2 545	897	56	387
Fayette	13 900	338 546	1.20	4 107	12.9	2 231	7.0	21 391	8.1	42 509	27 990	14 519	13 919	4 463
Fleming	22	12 466	0.64	186	12.8	174	12.0	1 159	9.5	3 277	2 389	888	65	447
Floyd	670	38 170	0.96	437	11.8	560	15.1	2 426	7.8	10 492	7 633	2 859	117	306
Franklin	1 906	60 314	1.47	585	11.6	507	10.0	2 786	6.9	13 605	8 458	5 147	1 431	2 873
Fulton	445	6 773	1.16	80	12.9	102	16.5	323	7.0	1 887	1 591	296	NA	NA
Gallatin	85	7 230	0.64	92	10.7	66	7.7	577	7.7	1 324	898	426	76	899
Garrard	109	12 524	0.36	164	9.5	175	10.1	1 214	8.5	3 429	2 485	944	158	933
Grant	456	20 234	0.55	353	14.2	223	8.9	1 480	7.0	4 912	3 013	1 899	243	980
Graves	463	34 263	0.79	485	13.0	411	11.1	2 494	8.2	8 737	6 499	2 238	548	1 484
Grayson	768	24 054	0.81	334	12.8	292	11.2	1 642	7.8	6 060	4 828	1 232	390	1 531
Green	113	8 879	0.49	116	10.5	129	11.7	737	8.4	2 423	1 894	529	37	331
Greenup	454	31 750	0.64	381	10.6	460	12.8	1 917	6.7	10 396	7 673	2 723	161	441
Hancock	90	9 744	1.30	128	14.5	81	9.2	379	5.3	1 784	1 470	314	24	275
Hardin	3 257	113 163	1.11	1 442	13.4	938	8.7	5 325	6.0	19 504	16 168	3 336	1 948	1 793
Harlan	627	28 527	1.02	340	12.5	392	14.4	1 972	8.7	7 203	5 676	1 527	150	529
Harrison	275	16 381	0.68	215	11.5	205	11.0	1 102	7.1	3 820	2 789	1 031	427	2 312
Hart	227	17 057	0.80	257	13.8	194	10.4	1 325	8.7	3 578	2 842	736	53	284
Henderson	1 165	45 460	0.95	561	12.1	535	11.6	2 495	6.5	9 443	6 589	2 854	1 292	2 783
Henry	80	12 026	0.51	146	9.2	159	10.1	996	7.7	3 476	2 225	1 251	35	252
Hickman	212	4 615	0.94	45	9.7	72	15.6	261	7.7	928	758	170	37	784
Hopkins	1 086	46 016	0.97	566	12.3	543	11.8	2 596	6.9	10 449	7 882	2 567	802	1 720
Jackson	110	11 855	0.62	155	11.6	153	11.4	882	7.9	2 836	2 224	612	59	439
Jefferson	15 195	838 074	1.23	9 918	13.0	7 513	9.8	43 109	6.8	136 339	91 733	44 606	35 527	4 670
Jessamine	1 723	46 058	0.81	681	13.0	400	7.6	3 279	7.6	7 672	5 137	2 535	1 458	2 880
Johnson	531	22 366	0.86	283	12.3	297	12.9	1 447	7.7	5 689	4 171	1 518	144	613
Kenton	2 508	148 781	0.82	2 357	14.3	1 460	8.9	8 731	6.2	23 932	14 620	9 312	3 954	2 408
Knott	792	14 611	0.70	191	12.3	192	12.4	1 021	8.2	3 131	2 239	892	22	150
Knox	692	31 188	0.93	385	12.2	450	14.2	2 036	8.0	5 529	4 427	1 102	198	622
Larue	313	11 903	0.60	138	9.8	162	11.5	925	8.0	2 960	2 297	663	43	306
Laurel	698	62 229	1.12	719	11.9	649	10.8	4 045	8.1	11 036	8 451	2 585	651	1 089
Lawrence	108	14 393	0.72	200	12.6	210	13.2	952	7.3	3 709	2 907	802	83	523
Lee	179	6 972	0.91	72	10.9	105	16.0	376	7.0	1 576	1 205	371	10	140
Leslie	227	10 126	0.68	131	12.4	167	15.8	702	8.1	2 567	1 902	665	11	104
Letcher	243	22 605	0.85	266	11.7	298	13.1	1 439	7.6	5 797	4 289	1 508	82	350
Lewis	139	11 935	0.59	137	10.2	149	11.1	868	7.7	2 856	2 201	655	45	326
Lincoln	219	20 389	0.54	291	11.9	272	11.2	1 613	8.1	5 793	4 248	1 545	52	226
Livingston	69	8 335	0.71	100	10.8	124	13.4	527	7.2	2 455	1 977	478	78	836
Logan	277	25 223	0.84	302	11.4	280	10.5	1 758	8.0	5 851	4 652	1 199	408	1 516
Lyon	1 019	7 772	0.76	53	6.6	129	16.0	384	7.4	2 149	1 565	584	61	718
McCracken	1 190	76 832	1.40	728	11.2	848	13.0	3 472	6.7	14 921	11 712	3 209	1 849	2 827
McCreary	1 991	16 628	0.68	195	11.1	169	9.7	1 187	8.8	3 565	2 798	767	85	474
McLean	82	8 038	0.62	102	10.8	114	12.0	602	7.9	2 323	1 681	642	58	610
Madison	6 285	83 516	0.94	1 013	11.3	716	8.0	4 568	6.5	14 716	9 912	4 804	2 177	2 522
Magoffin	127	11 732	0.65	145	11.4	153	12.1	1 016	9.5	2 875	2 087	788	19	148
Marion	502	20 515	1.11	260	13.5	196	10.2	1 061	6.6	3 825	3 015	810	168	847
Marshall	464	29 919	0.90	335	10.7	430	13.7	1 624	6.7	7 833	6 069	1 764	421	1 355
Martin	1 508	12 897	1.11	110	9.2	160	13.3	729	8.1	2 533	1 876	657	100	793
Mason	298	19 092	1.25	197	11.5	192	11.2	982	7.1	3 864	2 881	983	447	2 592
Meade	212	22 656	0.45	241	8.6	215	7.6	1 578	6.6	3 755	2 952	803	182	619
Menifee	272	5 433	0.57	63	9.8	89	13.9	493	9.6	1 904	1 175	729	45	717
Mercer	128	19 559	0.81	238	11.1	267	12.4	1 125	6.5	4 777	3 400	1 377	336	1 646
Metcalfe	121	8 891	0.72	120	12.0	137	13.7	642	8.0	2 459	1 673	786	60	602
Monroe	143	10 089	0.83	133	12.6	152	14.4	753	8.8	2 739	2 121	618	1	10
Montgomery	355	27 812	1.06	385	13.9	281	10.1	1 732	7.5	5 315	3 554	1 761	832	3 029
Morgan	1 808	12 835	0.83	130	9.8	157	11.8	789	8.3	2 616	1 729	887	NA	NA
Muhlenberg	2 096	29 119	0.81	333	10.7	434	14.0	1 993	8.3	7 084	5 539	1 545	163	524
Nelson	496	40 654	0.80	582	12.8	390	8.6	2 385	6.2	8 601	6 590	2 011	545	1 216
Nicholas	95	5 609	0.48	78	11.0	115	16.2	486	8.3	1 560	1 172	388	47	669

1. Per 1,000 estimated resident population.   2. Data for serious crimes have not been adjusted for underreporting; this may affect comparability between geographic areas and over time.
3. Per 100,000 population estimated by the FBI.

Table B. States and Counties — Crime, Education, Money Income, and Poverty

STATE County	Serious crimes known to police, 2014 (cont.)[1] Rate[2] Violent	Property	School enrollment and attainment, 2011–2015 Enrollment[3] Total	Percent private	Attainment[4] (percent) High school graduate or less	Bachelor's degree or more	Local government expenditures,[5] 2013–2014 Total current spending (mil dol)	Current spending per student (dollars)	Money income, 2011–2015 Per capita income[6] (dollars)	Median income (dollars)	Households Percent with income of less than $50,000	with income of $200,000 or more	Income and poverty, 2015 Median household income (dollars)	Percent below poverty level All persons	Children under 18 years	Children 5 to 17 years in families
	46	47	48	49	50	51	52	53	54	55	56	57	58	59	60	61
KENTUCKY—Cont'd																
Clay	47	483	4 336	6.4	73.2	9.6	35.3	10 307	13 802	21 549	77.4	0.3	24 001	46.8	53.0	55.1
Clinton	10	49	2 288	12.4	66.6	9.6	17.2	9 524	16 712	28 025	71.9	1.5	29 178	26.4	39.6	37.0
Crittenden	65	735	1 766	8.3	58.0	11.4	11.3	8 491	21 248	35 316	60.2	1.4	40 202	19.2	31.3	28.1
Cumberland	0	560	1 542	11.3	62.0	13.4	9.6	9 775	17 571	32 019	75.0	1.7	30 989	24.8	36.2	34.3
Daviess	147	2 764	24 695	17.0	49.8	20.3	149.2	9 021	23 952	45 989	53.2	2.6	48 724	14.9	20.9	18.9
Edmonson	83	432	2 521	4.4	63.3	13.3	17.3	8 777	20 304	41 710	59.1	1.2	38 673	20.0	28.6	26.8
Elliott	0	13	1 421	7.8	67.2	7.5	10.0	9 437	15 319	28 224	71.2	1.0	30 299	34.4	40.3	36.0
Estill	28	360	2 989	4.1	74.3	7.8	22.8	8 929	16 446	29 770	70.1	0.6	32 541	28.2	38.8	35.3
Fayette	344	4 119	91 115	15.1	30.8	41.2	436.6	10 894	30 031	49 778	50.2	4.8	51 963	19.1	22.6	20.7
Fleming	21	426	3 200	11.4	60.6	12.8	20.4	8 741	21 453	35 469	61.6	2.5	47 030	20.0	31.8	30.1
Floyd	31	274	7 930	8.2	59.6	12.8	60.0	9 463	18 173	30 096	68.5	0.8	30 888	29.5	43.1	41.1
Franklin	233	2 640	11 466	11.2	45.0	27.0	62.8	8 773	26 778	47 964	51.6	1.9	50 471	13.7	22.5	20.9
Fulton	NA	NA	1 353	6.9	59.4	13.1	11.7	11 941	18 082	28 359	70.3	0.2	30 798	30.4	47.6	48.3
Gallatin	35	864	1 916	8.8	62.0	10.1	15.3	8 912	21 634	48 370	51.7	1.3	47 679	15.0	23.8	22.0
Garrard	77	856	3 776	7.3	59.2	15.1	23.2	8 675	22 567	44 243	55.7	1.0	45 018	17.0	24.3	21.5
Grant	60	919	6 507	8.3	62.3	12.4	41.2	8 356	19 667	44 824	55.9	0.6	45 307	16.4	27.0	26.7
Graves	84	1 400	9 184	8.9	54.1	17.3	54.9	8 391	20 805	39 530	60.5	1.4	39 515	16.3	27.4	25.5
Grayson	79	1 453	6 020	7.7	65.1	9.1	36.6	8 692	19 902	35 030	65.4	1.3	37 057	22.9	32.5	31.1
Green	18	313	2 375	13.6	67.6	10.2	16.3	9 461	19 563	34 982	65.2	1.6	36 226	20.5	29.1	26.5
Greenup	25	417	8 111	8.3	51.6	16.9	53.0	8 627	23 649	45 370	54.3	2.2	45 690	16.8	23.5	23.0
Hancock	23	252	2 082	7.0	58.7	11.2	15.9	9 274	22 330	50 476	49.2	1.1	52 929	13.8	20.0	18.0
Hardin	110	1 683	29 390	14.1	43.0	23.2	151.0	8 738	24 845	50 765	49.3	1.9	49 637	15.0	21.6	18.4
Harlan	46	483	6 329	6.4	63.9	11.7	43.8	8 474	15 840	25 814	75.1	0.5	27 425	35.5	47.7	47.5
Harrison	103	2 209	4 188	8.8	61.1	14.0	25.6	8 235	20 490	35 681	62.7	1.2	47 040	16.2	24.4	22.9
Hart	21	262	4 138	13.5	68.6	10.3	23.3	9 517	18 993	34 774	67.2	1.0	34 764	22.0	31.1	28.7
Henderson	162	2 621	10 789	12.3	56.0	16.8	73.0	9 645	22 628	41 036	57.7	2.0	45 718	17.0	24.2	22.4
Henry	14	237	3 623	9.3	63.3	11.2	24.7	8 517	21 806	46 495	53.5	1.3	47 802	17.7	26.5	24.5
Hickman	64	721	1 095	8.1	60.4	9.2	8.1	9 456	19 597	41 218	64.6	0.5	40 890	17.6	29.9	24.9
Hopkins	88	1 632	10 049	8.5	55.0	15.3	69.3	8 902	22 517	42 346	56.8	1.1	44 750	18.4	26.6	24.2
Jackson	15	424	2 786	4.6	71.3	9.7	22.6	9 568	16 405	29 826	71.8	0.7	30 565	31.2	41.0	38.2
Jefferson	549	4 121	189 423	23.4	38.6	31.5	1 141.6	11 307	28 822	48 695	51.0	4.3	51 230	15.4	22.4	21.4
Jessamine	130	2 750	13 536	27.4	43.8	29.0	69.9	8 621	26 230	50 558	49.5	4.7	49 839	18.3	23.8	23.4
Johnson	51	562	5 204	8.5	60.2	10.8	43.3	9 422	18 436	35 570	65.4	1.0	36 051	25.9	34.4	32.6
Kenton	184	2 224	41 465	19.7	40.2	28.9	209.2	8 965	27 847	54 296	46.3	3.9	52 631	12.8	18.2	17.0
Knott	0	150	3 515	17.0	64.5	12.3	25.4	10 111	17 939	30 411	66.4	0.2	30 138	33.8	46.4	43.2
Knox	35	588	7 584	6.8	70.4	11.0	51.4	9 980	15 599	26 599	76.4	0.6	28 578	32.0	45.2	42.7
Larue	43	263	3 187	9.3	60.1	10.3	21.4	8 773	20 570	38 578	61.2	2.0	40 202	18.1	27.7	26.5
Laurel	54	1 035	13 315	8.4	61.8	12.3	80.9	8 137	18 795	36 020	64.3	1.3	37 737	23.0	33.1	31.4
Lawrence	50	473	3 413	5.2	64.0	11.9	22.5	8 911	18 890	35 935	62.6	0.7	36 276	25.0	34.3	31.3
Lee	0	140	1 554	4.1	71.1	7.9	9.7	9 248	13 688	22 698	78.4	0.3	26 201	34.7	50.2	47.2
Leslie	9	94	2 312	5.9	68.7	8.6	18.6	9 817	15 558	25 872	71.5	0.7	28 722	33.7	39.4	38.0
Letcher	9	342	4 788	3.0	62.6	11.8	36.2	9 542	17 194	30 333	69.8	0.4	31 079	33.2	41.9	39.3
Lewis	22	304	3 137	6.7	68.5	10.9	20.9	8 854	16 662	28 630	69.8	0.5	33 867	24.7	35.6	34.4
Lincoln	4	221	5 280	7.8	66.4	10.6	36.6	8 985	18 564	37 139	64.8	0.9	37 220	21.2	31.4	28.8
Livingston	64	772	1 993	17.5	63.9	10.4	12.6	9 828	23 079	42 171	56.7	1.1	44 551	15.3	25.0	23.4
Logan	137	1 378	6 090	4.7	62.0	13.2	41.3	8 909	19 126	38 570	61.9	0.8	43 795	15.5	24.3	23.4
Lyon	0	718	1 255	7.9	51.4	17.8	8.2	8 871	24 723	46 931	53.9	2.4	48 189	16.9	22.4	20.3
McCracken	188	2 639	14 914	12.1	43.4	23.0	90.3	9 169	28 577	44 067	55.1	3.2	47 184	15.2	24.6	23.5
McCreary	22	452	4 063	7.1	68.1	7.0	28.8	9 394	10 880	19 328	80.3	0.1	25 655	41.5	51.9	48.6
McLean	42	568	2 147	11.7	58.3	10.9	14.7	9 066	20 910	40 770	58.3	0.9	44 007	17.3	26.0	24.4
Madison	155	2 367	27 734	14.5	43.6	28.6	101.6	7 966	21 977	42 390	56.0	1.9	46 342	18.2	20.1	18.1
Magoffin	8	140	2 988	2.8	68.9	8.5	21.6	30 225	16 046	28 500	71.4	0.2	29 921	32.6	45.1	41.6
Marion	76	771	4 615	9.2	63.2	13.4	29.2	9 080	19 347	38 826	61.7	1.1	41 189	20.5	27.6	24.9
Marshall	61	1 294	6 268	8.5	54.8	15.8	41.9	8 678	23 707	45 212	55.0	1.5	49 771	12.1	19.5	17.6
Martin	56	738	2 399	3.8	67.7	6.5	21.0	9 526	14 179	25 795	74.9	0.7	29 198	40.0	45.3	42.6
Mason	128	2 465	4 071	7.7	55.1	16.0	25.1	8 593	23 773	38 824	60.9	3.0	37 071	19.5	29.3	28.0
Meade	71	548	7 476	6.5	53.3	14.8	40.6	7 862	23 473	49 884	50.1	1.4	51 111	13.5	20.3	18.3
Menifee	0	717	1 404	4.7	65.3	10.7	10.2	9 681	16 768	31 503	67.9	0.3	34 299	26.8	43.5	40.1
Mercer	83	1 563	4 867	15.6	54.2	18.8	30.9	8 975	22 658	42 083	56.0	1.5	46 346	15.1	21.9	21.2
Metcalfe	10	592	2 142	17.4	65.1	11.6	16.4	10 055	17 608	32 294	70.7	0.6	32 654	22.9	38.4	37.3
Monroe	0	10	2 327	6.3	67.1	14.1	19.1	9 965	17 635	31 045	68.9	0.6	31 603	25.3	37.8	36.2
Montgomery	109	2 920	6 297	6.1	56.7	17.1	41.9	8 531	20 850	39 275	61.5	1.8	42 468	21.5	29.9	30.1
Morgan	NA	NA	2 485	4.7	63.6	11.8	19.1	9 027	16 007	29 707	70.4	0.4	31 489	31.3	40.9	37.5
Muhlenberg	64	460	6 846	4.2	64.5	10.4	53.9	10 449	19 609	38 961	60.8	0.7	40 272	19.4	26.2	24.2
Nelson	83	1 133	10 817	17.1	54.8	16.2	65.7	8 737	24 699	49 298	50.7	2.3	51 843	12.5	18.8	17.1
Nicholas	43	626	1 572	10.4	61.5	11.2	9.6	9 210	20 039	36 097	63.9	0.9	37 267	21.5	34.3	33.8

1. Data for serious crimes have not been adjusted for underreporting; this may affect comparability between geographic areas and over time.   2. Per 100,000 population estimated by the FBI.
3. All persons 3 years old and over enrolled in nursery school through college.   4. Persons 25 years old and over.   5. Elementary and secondary education expenditures.
6. Based on population estimated by the American Community Survey, 2011–2015.

STATE County	Personal income, 2015										Earnings, 2015		
			Per capita[1]			Supplements to wages and salaries; employer contributions (mil dol)						Contributions for government social insurance (mil dol)	
	Total (mil dol)	Percent change, 2014–2015	Dollars	Rank	Wages and salaries (mil dol)	Pension and insurance	Government social insurance	Proprietors' income (mil dol)	Dividends, interest, and rent (mil dol)	Personal transfer receipts (mil dol)	Total (mil dol)	From employee and self-employed	From employer
	62	63	64	65	66	67	68	69	70	71	72	73	74
KENTUCKY—Cont'd													
Clay	559	4.8	26 608	3 060	150	39	12	27	52	304	227	18	12
Clinton	293	3.1	28 825	2 892	116	26	9	26	31	137	178	12	9
Crittenden	318	-1.1	34 585	2 030	58	14	5	19	41	100	96	7	5
Cumberland	209	6.3	30 967	2 793	60	13	5	15	24	101	92	7	5
Daviess	3 973	3.9	40 032	1 271	1 862	320	143	248	677	981	2 573	163	143
Edmonson	355	4.4	29 588	2 893	53	15	4	16	39	125	87	8	4
Elliott	166	9.7	21 745	3 110	30	10	2	5	18	80	47	4	2
Estill	438	4.9	30 484	2 891	87	19	7	13	46	177	126	11	7
Fayette	14 227	5.3	45 238	734	9 341	1 717	700	1 097	2 736	2 342	12 855	721	700
Fleming	434	3.5	29 663	2 860	107	26	8	44	53	148	186	13	8
Floyd	1 231	2.1	32 592	2 378	440	88	34	105	134	564	667	52	34
Franklin	1 979	4.9	39 290	1 473	1 389	364	96	102	325	536	1 951	107	96
Fulton	195	-1.7	31 244	2 338	75	17	6	12	33	84	110	7	6
Gallatin	253	4.2	29 322	2 782	122	22	9	9	22	70	161	10	9
Garrard	522	5.6	30 309	2 742	87	19	7	32	70	154	144	12	7
Grant	795	4.2	32 114	2 567	191	38	15	34	80	230	278	21	15
Graves	1 317	1.0	35 204	2 007	404	81	31	175	164	401	692	42	31
Grayson	831	5.4	31 693	2 702	260	58	22	59	113	267	398	28	22
Green	369	4.0	33 484	2 513	58	16	4	28	46	134	106	8	4
Greenup	1 342	2.4	37 195	1 903	359	64	33	67	148	426	523	42	33
Hancock	333	9.2	38 284	1 331	306	44	23	40	33	76	413	25	23
Hardin	4 148	1.5	38 972	1 377	2 404	566	205	259	740	963	3 434	186	205
Harlan	773	1.6	27 920	2 958	236	54	18	23	88	412	332	26	18
Harrison	631	5.1	33 604	2 367	199	41	15	36	82	166	291	20	15
Hart	599	5.6	32 465	2 865	178	36	14	81	75	185	310	21	14
Henderson	1 706	3.4	36 766	1 988	818	147	64	121	235	445	1 150	73	64
Henry	549	5.2	35 170	2 129	105	24	8	28	76	145	166	13	8
Hickman	174	-10.9	37 788	994	33	8	3	47	24	59	91	4	3
Hopkins	1 688	1.2	36 518	1 830	764	140	60	98	241	474	1 063	68	60
Jackson	337	4.1	25 214	3 079	61	18	5	11	34	147	95	9	5
Jefferson	35 476	5.4	46 457	636	24 664	3 556	1 882	2 510	6 314	6 834	32 611	1 974	1 882
Jessamine	1 987	4.7	38 243	1 599	650	112	52	128	308	363	942	60	52
Johnson	745	2.3	32 127	2 562	197	44	15	32	90	303	288	23	15
Kenton	8 164	4.0	49 475	588	3 351	559	252	640	1 851	1 246	4 803	293	252
Knott	450	1.3	28 652	2 921	89	21	7	17	43	225	134	12	7
Knox	854	1.7	26 907	2 918	260	59	21	50	87	409	390	30	21
Larue	473	5.6	33 232	2 421	89	20	7	18	72	137	135	11	7
Laurel	1 938	5.2	32 254	2 598	936	165	79	110	196	626	1 290	86	79
Lawrence	459	4.3	29 138	2 945	125	25	10	20	46	204	180	15	10
Lee	199	4.1	29 455	3 069	55	12	5	11	22	103	83	7	5
Leslie	322	3.1	30 047	2 755	64	16	5	8	27	168	93	8	5
Letcher	707	2.5	30 562	2 780	167	36	13	46	60	341	262	21	13
Lewis	388	3.8	28 324	2 996	68	17	5	27	35	149	117	10	5
Lincoln	714	4.3	29 204	2 954	144	32	11	38	95	253	225	19	11
Livingston	329	4.4	35 284	2 277	123	23	10	18	43	104	174	12	10
Logan	930	5.0	34 555	2 202	351	65	27	89	130	265	533	34	27
Lyon	248	3.6	29 914	2 872	71	20	5	11	43	89	108	8	5
McCracken	2 889	4.0	44 428	896	1 705	283	135	246	544	687	2 369	148	135
McCreary	411	5.2	23 016	3 103	98	28	8	17	46	234	152	13	8
McLean	352	-3.8	37 007	1 389	68	14	5	52	39	100	139	8	5
Madison	2 968	5.5	33 800	2 386	1 355	291	107	124	397	708	1 878	114	107
Magoffin	321	2.4	25 070	3 066	60	16	5	11	33	188	92	9	5
Marion	661	5.6	34 122	2 604	319	58	27	37	85	184	441	28	27
Marshall	1 181	4.0	37 972	1 531	572	101	45	66	181	328	783	52	45
Martin	333	-2.1	27 056	2 955	116	27	9	2	43	168	155	13	9
Mason	630	3.5	36 840	1 873	383	71	31	41	107	169	526	33	31
Meade	974	1.3	34 894	2 229	165	38	13	49	155	222	264	19	13
Menifee	186	6.1	29 196	2 937	30	8	2	6	20	79	46	5	2
Mercer	731	3.6	34 165	2 196	302	53	23	37	102	206	415	28	23
Metcalfe	295	3.7	29 794	2 940	67	16	5	27	31	114	115	8	5
Monroe	357	5.0	33 435	2 618	103	22	8	51	39	135	185	12	8
Montgomery	925	6.0	33 507	2 509	422	78	34	53	111	251	588	38	34
Morgan	322	3.5	24 281	3 088	101	28	8	9	35	147	147	11	8
Muhlenberg	981	1.7	31 472	2 591	404	81	32	60	133	331	578	39	32
Nelson	1 711	6.6	37 908	1 507	607	109	48	77	220	374	842	56	48
Nicholas	234	6.1	32 780	2 447	29	8	2	18	26	79	57	5	2

1. Based on the resident population estimated as of July 1 of the year shown.

Table B. States and Counties — Earnings, Social Security, and Housing

STATE County	Earnings, 2015 (cont.) Percent by selected industries									Social Security beneficiaries, December 2015		Supplemental Security Income recipients, December 2015	Housing units, 2016	
	Farm	Mining	Construction	Manu-facturing	Infor-mation: professional, scientific, technical services	Retail trade	Finance, insur-ance, real estate and leasing	Health care and social assistance	Govern-ment	Number	Rate[1]		Total	Percent change, 2010–2016
	75	76	77	78	79	80	81	82	83	84	85	86	87	88
KENTUCKY—Cont'd														
Clay	-0.6	D	D	1.7	3.2	8.6	2.6	D	42.2	5 410	257	3 245	8 866	-0.1
Clinton	4.1	D	4.7	32.9	1.3	6.0	2.2	15.7	17.4	2 790	275	847	5 229	-1.5
Crittenden	6.4	D	D	15.8	3.5	5.7	5.4	D	20.9	2 470	269	290	4 549	-0.4
Cumberland	3.6	0.0	D	10.3	D	5.6	3.7	33.1	18.8	1 915	283	464	3 650	-1.1
Daviess	1.4	0.5	4.3	16.2	D	7.6	8.8	19.6	12.8	23 165	233	3 606	42 955	3.6
Edmonson	-2.7	0.1	16.3	D	D	4.0	D	D	44.0	3 200	266	416	6 455	-0.2
Elliott	1.0	0.0	4.0	1.1	D	2.9	D	10.8	60.8	1 765	231	481	3 363	-0.2
Estill	-1.9	1.8	7.1	D	D	7.4	2.9	17.2	28.2	3 735	260	1 295	6 843	-0.3
Fayette	0.2	0.3	6.5	8.4	11.1	5.7	5.8	12.1	25.0	46 940	149	6 694	140 976	4.3
Fleming	4.6	D	9.7	12.9	2.4	7.6	4.7	D	24.6	3 895	267	753	6 601	-0.4
Floyd	0.0	D	6.9	3.3	8.2	6.9	2.7	17.9	19.5	12 225	324	4 048	18 182	0.0
Franklin	-0.2	D	3.4	8.8	5.4	4.3	4.0	D	49.7	13 510	269	1 531	23 253	0.4
Fulton	7.0	D	4.1	17.7	D	10.1	4.4	D	24.4	1 865	298	503	3 354	-0.5
Gallatin	-0.2	D	3.8	D	D	3.4	1.2	3.9	14.6	1 320	154	217	3 834	1.3
Garrard	2.7	0.0	20.7	6.4	5.4	3.5	3.0	D	23.8	4 185	244	642	7 462	0.0
Grant	-0.4	0.0	6.2	14.8	6.2	11.0	3.3	D	23.7	5 710	231	876	10 006	0.6
Graves	15.0	D	5.9	12.0	D	7.7	4.1	10.8	16.3	9 440	253	1 600	16 742	-0.2
Grayson	2.3	D	10.1	26.0	D	6.9	2.5	D	22.1	6 780	258	1 411	13 493	-0.5
Green	7.3	0.1	D	4.3	D	9.0	6.9	10.4	33.6	3 095	281	596	5 275	-0.9
Greenup	-0.5	D	3.8	12.2	4.4	6.2	3.1	24.2	15.6	9 135	254	1 441	16 259	-0.4
Hancock	0.7	D	15.4	65.0	D	0.9	D	D	5.9	2 200	253	277	3 710	-0.6
Hardin	0.1	D	3.0	14.5	6.2	5.9	3.8	6.1	45.1	20 195	190	3 288	46 153	6.7
Harlan	-0.1	15.6	3.5	1.1	3.6	7.5	2.7	20.0	28.0	8 495	308	2 759	13 469	-0.3
Harrison	1.4	D	8.8	32.4	2.2	5.9	2.0	D	15.6	4 430	237	785	8 221	0.1
Hart	2.5	D	10.1	41.0	1.3	4.5	1.6	D	14.4	4 440	240	947	8 885	3.8
Henderson	1.4	0.6	5.8	29.9	3.1	6.3	3.7	11.8	13.5	10 800	233	1 720	20 559	1.2
Henry	1.9	D	7.8	18.3	D	4.6	D	D	26.8	3 705	238	531	6 695	0.8
Hickman	46.7	0.0	D	D	D	2.9	5.1	D	14.3	1 410	304	183	2 339	-0.1
Hopkins	2.2	10.0	5.7	15.2	D	7.3	3.4	16.3	16.8	11 515	249	2 007	21 336	0.7
Jackson	-4.6	D	D	4.3	4.6	5.0	3.3	D	36.8	3 430	257	1 365	6 518	-0.1
Jefferson	0.0	0.0	5.1	12.8	10.1	5.0	12.4	13.0	11.5	148 645	195	25 547	344 657	2.1
Jessamine	0.5	D	10.8	17.4	D	11.8	2.5	6.4	14.7	9 235	178	1 291	20 237	4.7
Johnson	-0.3	D	5.5	1.3	7.2	14.2	4.4	D	27.8	6 815	294	2 036	10 533	-0.9
Kenton	-0.1	D	7.0	8.7	7.6	4.8	12.0	14.8	15.4	28 415	173	3 925	69 812	1.2
Knott	-0.5	D	D	D	7.9	8.0	D	D	29.7	4 260	271	1 553	7 448	-0.2
Knox	-0.4	1.0	4.7	6.7	11.4	9.5	3.0	D	23.0	8 165	258	3 347	14 460	-0.2
Larue	-0.2	0.0	14.9	16.5	D	5.0	D	10.6	24.9	3 555	250	522	6 328	2.5
Laurel	-0.1	2.2	4.8	17.7	6.4	8.9	4.1	12.4	12.8	14 575	243	3 195	25 453	0.0
Lawrence	-0.7	D	9.8	D	D	9.5	2.6	24.2	19.6	4 315	272	1 440	7 273	-0.2
Lee	-0.8	4.7	D	D	D	8.5	D	19.9	25.2	1 970	292	841	3 433	-0.1
Leslie	-0.1	D	D	D	D	5.7	D	D	30.3	3 315	310	1 144	5 271	-0.1
Letcher	0.0	7.7	3.3	2.4	4.1	8.9	2.9	D	22.6	7 150	310	2 123	11 585	-0.1
Lewis	1.0	0.0	D	15.6	2.6	4.1	D	9.5	26.5	3 210	236	997	6 475	-0.1
Lincoln	0.1	0.0	12.1	13.0	D	8.4	3.0	10.2	23.6	6 300	258	1 567	10 878	0.5
Livingston	1.6	D	20.8	3.7	D	3.7	1.0	9.4	16.7	2 775	298	333	4 819	-0.1
Logan	5.5	D	6.1	38.9	2.8	5.7	2.8	5.7	12.4	6 565	246	972	12 313	-0.2
Lyon	-1.5	0.1	8.7	D	4.3	5.2	1.4	9.5	45.4	2 430	293	167	4 820	0.6
McCracken	0.2	D	5.2	5.3	9.8	8.8	4.8	21.5	11.8	16 485	254	2 272	31 976	2.9
McCreary	-0.6	D	D	D	D	5.9	3.4	7.7	54.6	4 325	242	1 840	7 405	-1.4
McLean	29.7	D	4.4	7.2	D	6.3	D	D	17.5	2 645	279	342	4 250	-0.3
Madison	0.1	D	5.9	19.8	8.3	7.0	2.8	10.1	26.6	16 640	188	3 069	36 277	3.5
Magoffin	-1.8	D	7.1	D	D	6.2	D	13.0	34.4	3 620	283	1 677	5 933	-0.3
Marion	0.7	D	3.9	48.1	D	4.7	2.6	11.3	10.9	4 355	226	979	8 222	0.5
Marshall	1.0	D	20.7	34.2	3.2	5.7	3.9	D	12.2	9 095	292	822	16 006	1.6
Martin	-0.6	16.3	D	D	D	7.5	D	7.9	44.0	3 350	271	1 329	5 156	-0.2
Mason	1.3	D	14.7	17.1	D	8.6	2.8	D	12.8	4 270	250	724	8 138	0.4
Meade	2.5	2.8	13.9	13.1	5.4	8.1	4.5	D	21.9	5 695	204	589	12 281	4.3
Menifee	-1.2	D	D	13.6	D	5.1	D	D	40.1	1 860	292	550	3 755	0.3
Mercer	0.8	D	7.2	43.7	D	5.6	2.3	D	11.8	5 495	256	685	10 143	2.0
Metcalfe	8.6	D	D	30.8	D	5.0	2.6	3.4	22.4	2 765	279	652	4 674	-0.1
Monroe	14.5	0.1	8.0	14.3	D	7.0	4.5	11.9	16.4	2 990	281	704	5 205	0.0
Montgomery	0.1	D	4.9	39.8	D	8.9	4.1	D	12.3	6 395	231	1 264	11 793	0.8
Morgan	-2.0	D	11.2	11.5	D	6.8	D	8.1	35.4	3 240	244	996	5 893	1.1
Muhlenberg	3.8	D	10.3	7.4	D	6.1	2.3	11.0	28.0	8 380	269	1 392	13 644	-0.4
Nelson	0.3	D	9.5	32.5	2.9	7.1	4.3	10.0	12.5	10 020	222	1 308	18 823	4.1
Nicholas	12.7	0.1	13.3	5.2	D	3.9	D	11.0	28.6	1 850	261	313	3 244	-0.4

1. Per 1,000 resident population estimated as of July 1 of the year shown.

Items 75—88

STATE County	Housing units, 2011–2015								Civilian labor force, 2016				Civilian employment,[6] 2011–2015		
	Occupied units										Unemployment		Percent		
			Owner-occupied			Renter-occupied									
				Median owner cost as a percent of income				Sub-stand-ard units[4] (percent)							Con-struction, produc-tion, and mainte-nance occu-pations
	Total	Percent	Median value[1]	With a mort-gage	Without a mort-gage[2]	Median rent[3]	Median rent as a per-cent of income[2]		Total	Percent change, 2015–2016	Total	Rate[5]	Total	Manage-ment, business, science and arts	
	89	90	91	92	93	94	95	96	97	98	99	100	101	102	103

STATE County	89	90	91	92	93	94	95	96	97	98	99	100	101	102	103
KENTUCKY—Cont'd															
Clay	7 707	74.1	56 300	22.6	12.8	473	37.2	3.0	5 635	4.5	542	9.6	5 459	25.2	32.7
Clinton	3 858	75.0	65 300	21.6	12.3	528	26.8	1.7	3 732	-2.3	274	7.3	3 555	24.7	37.7
Crittenden	3 755	77.9	76 000	19.9	10.0	492	22.7	3.1	4 081	7.4	204	5.0	3 645	26.7	37.8
Cumberland	2 743	71.8	63 500	27.8	12.5	454	23.6	1.3	2 900	0.4	160	5.5	2 449	30.7	32.3
Daviess	38 536	69.1	115 400	19.2	10.0	644	29.5	2.5	45 469	1.3	2 036	4.5	43 941	29.6	27.9
Edmonson	4 659	81.6	88 800	24.3	10.2	602	27.8	0.4	4 734	2.6	290	6.1	4 730	24.7	33.4
Elliott	2 750	79.2	66 100	23.0	12.5	445	34.2	2.6	2 160	2.4	235	10.9	2 088	23.7	41.5
Estill	5 750	69.8	71 400	23.9	11.9	545	32.0	4.9	5 312	1.1	302	5.7	4 855	20.6	43.2
Fayette	125 752	54.2	168 100	19.8	10.0	778	30.4	2.3	168 079	1.5	5 875	3.5	157 198	42.5	15.1
Fleming	5 636	75.6	86 700	21.1	11.2	497	26.7	4.3	6 035	-2.7	358	5.9	5 897	27.3	35.9
Floyd	15 418	69.7	70 600	21.1	10.8	543	32.6	2.4	11 684	-1.4	1 268	10.9	11 922	29.4	26.2
Franklin	21 033	63.0	137 500	20.7	10.0	687	29.5	1.9	24 023	0.6	966	4.0	22 601	36.4	24.0
Fulton	2 568	60.1	61 000	20.8	13.1	479	32.7	1.1	2 067	-0.1	140	6.8	2 274	29.1	30.3
Gallatin	3 097	68.8	107 500	21.3	12.6	669	20.9	3.4	3 838	1.5	184	4.8	3 821	21.3	38.4
Garrard	6 594	76.6	128 500	22.2	11.0	630	31.1	3.5	7 570	0.1	358	4.7	7 138	28.5	32.9
Grant	8 325	70.4	124 900	22.7	13.1	715	27.7	3.7	11 056	1.3	539	4.9	10 215	22.2	36.0
Graves	14 390	74.3	92 900	21.0	10.8	575	31.7	2.9	15 461	1.0	924	6.0	15 840	27.9	30.6
Grayson	9 840	72.2	95 500	22.4	10.7	528	29.4	1.4	10 876	2.5	701	6.4	10 342	28.0	40.1
Green	4 477	79.3	74 200	21.3	10.6	524	32.0	1.6	5 033	0.9	220	4.4	4 459	21.9	37.5
Greenup	14 200	77.3	97 700	20.5	10.0	629	28.5	2.2	13 577	0.3	1 174	8.6	13 500	34.5	25.3
Hancock	3 265	76.9	104 200	16.5	10.0	539	21.3	1.8	3 900	1.9	211	5.4	3 647	23.4	43.0
Hardin	40 376	62.5	143 100	20.1	10.0	762	26.6	1.8	47 349	2.1	2 084	4.4	46 001	33.8	24.4
Harlan	11 406	69.8	52 000	20.9	11.0	456	28.2	3.2	7 208	-3.0	874	12.1	8 189	28.2	29.0
Harrison	7 120	67.3	113 000	22.0	12.6	597	32.8	1.5	8 474	1.5	389	4.6	7 303	23.8	35.4
Hart	7 294	72.3	83 600	21.8	10.5	498	29.6	2.7	7 942	2.8	364	4.6	6 958	21.2	42.0
Henderson	18 742	63.3	105 500	20.1	10.8	612	30.3	1.8	21 180	0.4	1 003	4.7	20 337	28.7	29.5
Henry	5 992	70.0	121 300	22.2	11.1	700	30.5	2.6	7 712	2.1	313	4.1	7 099	26.4	33.8
Hickman	1 973	74.5	68 400	22.4	11.8	531	26.0	4.0	2 010	-0.8	112	5.6	1 742	24.2	36.5
Hopkins	18 622	71.5	89 500	18.2	10.8	592	27.1	1.6	20 017	2.5	1 100	5.5	19 388	30.7	30.3
Jackson	5 546	76.4	65 900	23.7	12.8	523	30.0	4.7	4 262	-0.8	319	7.5	3 993	29.5	36.8
Jefferson	306 915	61.9	150 400	20.6	11.4	749	29.0	1.9	380 367	2.2	16 621	4.4	361 510	37.0	21.8
Jessamine	18 312	63.8	160 400	22.6	10.6	771	29.9	2.9	25 279	1.5	973	3.8	23 096	34.5	24.3
Johnson	9 035	74.9	79 200	19.7	12.5	543	31.4	3.6	7 360	-3.0	704	9.6	7 136	30.4	26.6
Kenton	62 225	65.8	145 200	20.3	10.4	747	27.6	2.1	83 093	1.4	3 394	4.1	79 447	35.8	22.1
Knott	5 984	77.6	57 900	19.9	10.0	479	28.2	3.5	4 603	-3.9	517	11.2	4 755	31.4	26.7
Knox	12 467	62.6	78 400	22.0	11.6	545	31.9	2.8	9 816	1.0	772	7.9	9 477	25.8	30.3
Larue	5 328	73.1	110 100	21.3	10.0	657	31.6	1.9	5 941	2.0	266	4.5	5 771	22.0	43.3
Laurel	23 164	69.5	94 400	22.2	11.7	579	28.8	2.5	23 625	1.2	1 436	6.1	22 079	25.5	30.0
Lawrence	6 033	78.0	81 400	20.2	11.2	519	30.6	2.8	5 140	0.8	534	10.4	5 366	23.7	33.0
Lee	2 859	76.3	67 700	25.5	16.0	435	48.4	3.6	1 991	-3.3	184	9.2	1 694	29.8	31.8
Leslie	4 150	77.1	45 500	20.7	10.0	438	24.6	6.0	2 831	-2.9	369	13.0	2 816	28.8	33.0
Letcher	9 592	74.1	56 300	21.1	10.0	531	35.0	3.3	6 562	-3.8	780	11.9	7 281	34.1	27.4
Lewis	5 373	76.6	67 100	21.7	11.2	438	27.7	4.0	4 970	-1.1	456	9.2	4 643	26.2	42.0
Lincoln	9 770	73.6	93 600	20.0	11.9	569	32.1	3.1	9 126	1.9	543	6.0	9 202	25.5	36.6
Livingston	3 826	79.2	86 900	20.4	10.6	607	28.3	3.9	3 692	0.8	259	7.0	3 840	21.0	43.4
Logan	10 870	67.7	94 600	21.2	12.5	588	30.9	1.8	11 829	1.9	502	4.2	10 471	23.9	39.3
Lyon	3 230	81.9	141 000	22.7	10.0	419	28.3	1.2	3 039	3.4	171	5.6	2 655	29.1	25.1
McCracken	27 514	67.3	124 400	19.5	10.0	604	27.4	1.4	28 851	0.8	1 632	5.7	29 043	32.2	23.6
McCreary	6 277	69.4	62 300	24.8	14.9	556	41.8	2.6	4 748	-1.2	366	7.7	4 377	20.7	33.4
McLean	3 759	80.5	91 700	18.4	10.0	490	26.8	2.3	4 253	1.5	204	4.8	3 938	30.5	34.6
Madison	32 064	59.2	144 800	20.5	10.9	647	30.7	1.2	44 105	-0.4	1 808	4.1	39 435	36.2	20.2
Magoffin	4 996	72.6	53 100	20.5	11.7	478	34.8	4.0	3 237	-7.2	608	18.8	3 663	28.1	36.8
Marion	7 395	74.4	98 200	22.3	11.0	554	29.8	3.4	9 486	3.6	390	4.1	7 818	25.3	38.4
Marshall	12 602	77.9	111 600	21.2	10.1	596	27.6	1.7	14 843	0.6	837	5.6	13 051	30.2	31.0
Martin	4 320	71.4	68 200	34.1	10.3	420	34.3	4.8	3 094	-3.9	314	10.1	2 445	27.2	35.7
Mason	6 736	67.0	101 100	21.5	10.0	547	26.8	1.2	7 216	-2.6	442	6.1	7 127	30.9	29.8
Meade	10 574	71.5	126 100	20.2	10.0	772	27.9	3.0	11 982	2.2	604	5.0	11 311	27.3	35.0
Menifee	2 427	77.4	78 100	23.2	11.1	511	38.9	2.4	2 383	1.0	201	8.4	2 200	21.5	38.9
Mercer	8 824	71.4	133 600	20.1	11.0	580	31.2	3.0	9 910	1.9	467	4.7	9 331	29.1	33.3
Metcalfe	3 936	77.2	82 600	22.7	10.0	504	28.1	2.5	4 106	3.0	183	4.5	4 014	24.5	38.0
Monroe	4 443	72.7	70 600	23.8	11.4	520	30.6	3.4	4 699	2.5	190	4.0	3 943	29.9	38.0
Montgomery	10 248	64.6	114 000	20.4	11.2	646	27.1	2.0	11 832	0.9	740	6.3	10 948	28.0	35.2
Morgan	4 808	74.4	75 500	22.7	11.9	504	32.5	1.5	4 518	1.0	351	7.8	3 744	28.4	34.1
Muhlenberg	11 539	79.5	77 800	19.4	10.7	531	27.8	1.8	11 581	-0.2	811	7.0	11 534	24.5	39.2
Nelson	16 817	76.1	133 600	21.2	10.0	702	32.9	3.3	21 541	2.5	960	4.5	20 232	26.3	36.1
Nicholas	2 824	71.4	83 900	19.4	11.8	487	28.7	3.7	3 337	0.9	180	5.4	2 877	26.0	35.8

1. Specified owner-occupied units.   2. A value of 10.0 represents 10 percent or less; a value of 50.0 represents 50 percent or more.   3. Specified renter-occupied units.
4. Overcrowded or lacking complete plumbing facilities.   5. Percent of civilian labor force.   6. Civilian employed persons 16 years old and over.

Table B. States and Counties — Nonfarm Employment and Agriculture

	Private nonfarm establishments, employment and payroll, 2015									Agriculture, 2012			
		Employment						Annual payroll		Farms			
												Percent with:	
STATE County	Number of establishments	Total	Health care and social assistance	Manufacturing	Retail trade	Finance and insurance	Professional, scientific, and technical services	Total (mil dol)	Average per employee (dollars)	Number	Fewer than 50 acres	500 acres or more	Farm operators whose principal occupation is farming (percent)
	104	105	106	107	108	109	110	111	112	113	114	115	116
KENTUCKY—Cont'd													
Clay	243	2 801	917	275	634	73	50	73	25 892	243	31.7	4.5	33.3
Clinton	193	3 063	486	1 649	287	78	20	82	26 892	508	33.9	6.5	43.7
Crittenden	160	2 116	396	313	255	80	240	64	30 231	592	27.4	10.3	33.4
Cumberland	111	1 111	391	226	168	57	21	33	29 427	371	31.8	7.5	49.1
Daviess	2 317	42 110	7 874	5 127	6 174	3 139	1 789	1 561	37 081	837	46.5	12.7	48.7
Edmonson	121	853	256	D	160	67	16	22	26 227	638	33.1	4.2	32.0
Elliott	51	338	161	NA	60	14	NA	9	25 154	389	26.5	4.1	38.8
Estill	189	1 496	389	189	315	70	41	43	28 583	380	27.1	4.5	39.2
Fayette	8 638	156 925	31 244	8 497	20 673	4 860	13 301	6 628	42 238	718	47.4	7.4	57.0
Fleming	234	2 166	630	379	456	104	44	66	30 409	1 087	26.9	5.7	47.7
Floyd	818	8 877	2 095	208	1 479	245	273	319	35 886	87	54.0	3.4	29.9
Franklin	1 164	16 351	2 219	2 572	2 551	956	876	641	39 199	579	35.8	5.5	37.1
Fulton	121	1 487	305	415	213	75	18	46	30 612	178	33.7	23.6	51.1
Gallatin	93	894	302	D	183	29	22	22	24 331	185	34.1	5.9	47.6
Garrard	224	1 451	229	254	161	51	51	42	28 758	805	35.5	6.7	44.5
Grant	366	3 605	460	701	930	94	79	119	33 047	812	36.5	3.1	46.1
Graves	680	9 275	1 406	2 572	1 330	320	630	309	33 309	1 442	41.7	8.5	45.5
Grayson	490	5 977	999	1 632	997	218	84	182	30 503	1 407	30.9	4.3	32.8
Green	160	1 285	555	57	245	50	31	34	26 228	1 050	32.0	3.5	41.2
Greenup	497	4 961	1 181	612	690	246	154	179	35 993	604	30.6	3.6	40.2
Hancock	127	3 360	123	2 490	121	69	42	231	68 649	350	33.4	4.0	26.6
Hardin	2 326	35 028	7 445	5 890	5 766	1 256	1 254	1 273	36 352	1 357	45.8	6.1	40.8
Harlan	420	4 684	1 306	114	966	128	167	157	33 587	34	58.8	11.8	29.4
Harrison	278	4 038	918	1 255	615	79	95	160	39 527	1 064	29.9	6.6	44.1
Hart	289	4 030	451	2 382	425	78	51	121	29 933	1 372	35.9	3.4	38.5
Henderson	996	16 771	2 381	5 645	2 169	415	441	644	38 406	465	41.9	14.8	44.7
Henry	212	2 188	489	452	337	92	46	63	28 801	869	33.9	4.1	48.3
Hickman	73	993	138	D	274	64	5	32	31 861	298	32.2	16.4	53.0
Hopkins	1 035	15 131	3 259	2 054	2 397	427	497	654	43 231	731	33.2	9.8	40.5
Jackson	92	1 325	241	509	160	48	D	35	26 393	588	32.1	4.1	30.8
Jefferson	19 664	415 722	65 058	42 819	43 931	29 039	23 164	20 024	48 166	382	69.6	1.0	44.0
Jessamine	1 065	15 275	1 173	2 749	2 462	224	641	534	34 979	668	49.6	4.0	38.6
Johnson	410	4 066	715	53	1 446	181	147	127	31 133	196	31.6	1.5	31.6
Kenton	3 091	52 170	10 140	3 670	5 632	5 082	3 273	2 466	47 261	459	51.4	1.5	34.9
Knott	174	1 534	418	D	300	42	42	46	29 695	42	31.0	9.5	19.0
Knox	447	8 039	1 135	988	1 229	200	1 056	216	26 810	243	32.5	4.9	40.3
Larue	231	1 810	359	547	223	190	59	57	31 501	720	40.1	4.9	46.5
Laurel	1 149	23 433	2 581	3 702	3 183	893	708	729	31 131	1 006	44.3	1.6	37.0
Lawrence	215	2 531	763	8	662	84	58	85	33 537	291	26.5	5.5	35.4
Lee	100	1 549	831	D	201	18	20	32	20 432	142	38.0	3.5	30.3
Leslie	112	1 372	288	D	194	78	50	40	29 415	15	40.0	6.7	26.7
Letcher	338	3 752	1 037	D	657	122	118	123	32 780	54	57.4	0.0	24.1
Lewis	124	1 326	375	307	279	95	15	41	31 237	676	25.3	6.8	39.1
Lincoln	308	2 593	442	448	571	114	77	84	32 300	1 202	40.8	7.2	45.8
Livingston	141	1 926	363	99	186	35	31	83	42 887	403	15.9	15.9	32.0
Logan	497	6 917	747	3 220	955	180	180	295	42 598	1 060	29.3	9.2	43.4
Lyon	153	1 196	262	D	191	15	49	34	28 105	219	27.4	4.6	32.0
McCracken	2 079	34 665	6 964	2 847	6 068	1 245	1 252	1 397	40 314	447	51.5	5.8	31.5
McCreary	180	1 502	307	308	298	97	114	37	24 791	155	45.2	3.9	36.8
McLean	168	1 169	161	105	217	87	19	43	36 430	413	38.5	16.7	56.9
Madison	1 648	22 798	3 438	4 685	4 035	596	657	806	35 348	1 219	36.8	8.2	45.9
Magoffin	166	1 221	205	D	225	57	129	32	26 032	361	31.0	2.2	34.1
Marion	368	7 796	1 138	4 464	641	107	131	275	35 315	1 016	33.4	6.7	40.1
Marshall	645	8 935	919	2 365	1 181	311	226	445	49 764	719	46.3	4.5	27.8
Martin	158	1 832	229	D	396	75	20	75	40 930	20	40.0	15.0	45.0
Mason	428	7 358	1 417	1 088	1 403	248	93	253	34 317	634	26.7	8.4	43.7
Meade	375	3 453	332	D	595	121	313	122	35 197	754	44.6	4.9	49.3
Menifee	62	504	198	87	98	D	11	15	29 133	294	31.0	5.1	38.8
Mercer	351	5 481	646	2 464	649	118	53	248	45 276	1 067	42.3	4.6	40.9
Metcalfe	119	1 180	109	633	164	43	15	35	29 585	924	32.9	4.5	48.4
Monroe	203	2 390	481	579	549	77	27	71	29 857	858	26.8	9.0	49.3
Montgomery	562	10 062	1 086	3 832	1 519	325	153	341	33 934	609	35.1	4.9	42.0
Morgan	159	1 971	322	355	359	117	69	60	30 665	694	23.1	7.1	35.0
Muhlenberg	563	6 097	1 199	738	1 196	200	160	205	33 644	630	33.0	7.8	39.8
Nelson	957	14 816	1 397	4 346	1 765	336	248	553	37 298	1 326	47.5	5.1	43.1
Nicholas	79	472	151	53	108	18	28	12	26 144	570	23.3	6.0	49.3

Table B. States and Counties — Agriculture

STATE County	Acreage (1,000)	Percent change, 2007–2012	Average size of farm	Total irrigated (1,000)	Total cropland (1,000)	Average per farm	Average per acre	Value of machinery and equipment, average per farm (dollars)	Total (mil dol)	Average per farm (dollars)	Crops	Live-stock and poultry products	$10,000 or more	$100,000 or more	Total ($1,000)	Percent of farms
				Acres		Value of land and buildings (dollars)			Value of products sold		Percent from:		Percent of farms with sales of:		Government payments	
	117	118	119	120	121	122	123	124	125	126	127	128	129	130	131	132
KENTUCKY—Cont'd																
Clay	35	-31.4	145	0.2	9.9	230 173	1 592	48 691	4.7	19 169	70.5	29.5	25.1	7.0	239	33.3
Clinton	74	-18.7	146	0.3	26.0	378 150	2 594	53 791	29.8	58 632	12.7	87.3	43.5	6.9	551	44.7
Crittenden	149	-7.1	251	1.1	83.0	541 215	2 153	75 215	31.6	53 311	63.0	37.0	34.0	5.9	2 672	50.7
Cumberland	65	-36.7	176	D	17.7	301 164	1 707	42 027	12.8	34 596	25.0	75.0	29.6	3.0	346	42.9
Daviess	237	-7.7	283	9.6	190.2	1 100 748	3 884	144 342	176.4	210 760	65.6	34.4	43.0	18.5	3 286	54.4
Edmonson	85	-12.1	133	0.0	34.9	316 882	2 379	44 666	20.2	31 699	33.5	66.5	28.4	4.5	1 960	44.8
Elliott	56	-15.7	145	0.1	13.5	196 622	1 358	39 936	3.2	8 321	42.9	57.1	26.7	0.0	479	30.3
Estill	52	-19.3	138	0.0	14.1	254 342	1 848	37 968	4.4	11 655	51.2	48.7	26.6	2.1	337	41.3
Fayette	115	-15.5	160	1.1	40.4	1 457 641	9 112	96 464	176.2	245 461	7.7	92.3	46.9	14.8	1 263	28.7
Fleming	183	0.9	169	0.2	73.1	353 267	2 096	62 407	52.7	48 516	34.1	65.9	50.6	9.1	1 630	63.6
Floyd	8	4.8	94	0.0	1.2	138 034	1 472	22 207	0.6	6 644	74.4	25.6	11.5	1.1	D	2.3
Franklin	79	2.9	136	0.3	30.1	499 653	3 684	55 269	19.4	33 463	41.9	58.1	35.4	4.7	546	31.3
Fulton	83	-8.8	468	2.5	74.3	1 635 017	3 490	183 713	46.6	261 562	72.4	27.6	48.3	31.5	2 716	77.0
Gallatin	28	-17.8	150	0.0	10.8	454 384	3 026	67 178	5.7	30 546	80.0	20.0	31.9	6.5	232	38.9
Garrard	127	4.6	158	0.2	43.7	390 569	2 471	61 070	38.5	47 794	27.2	72.8	43.4	9.2	805	37.6
Grant	98	-14.4	121	0.1	33.0	370 686	3 060	53 784	11.7	14 408	56.4	43.6	28.7	2.2	729	30.7
Graves	292	5.0	202	4.5	221.9	656 060	3 242	105 221	337.7	234 209	25.7	74.3	36.4	18.5	7 722	69.1
Grayson	201	-7.2	143	0.1	87.1	324 133	2 270	54 270	45.7	32 454	40.1	59.9	33.1	5.0	2 928	51.0
Green	153	4.8	145	0.1	67.4	329 032	2 265	59 282	39.2	37 304	56.1	43.9	42.5	6.4	2 908	61.1
Greenup	79	-14.4	130	0.1	17.5	230 462	1 770	45 828	5.0	8 333	56.1	43.9	20.0	0.3	311	33.3
Hancock	52	-17.2	149	0.5	23.4	419 334	2 812	81 900	14.0	40 037	72.6	27.4	30.9	3.7	515	50.3
Hardin	203	-8.7	150	0.7	114.4	524 307	3 505	74 682	57.9	42 704	70.2	29.8	35.9	6.9	2 030	40.5
Harlan	6	106.5	184	D	0.3	243 765	1 323	34 529	0.3	8 294	53.9	46.1	14.7	2.9	D	2.9
Harrison	164	1.7	155	2.0	64.2	422 032	2 730	61 867	36.0	33 848	54.0	46.0	39.4	7.3	1 123	34.7
Hart	182	-4.5	133	0.2	76.1	295 020	2 219	53 891	33.5	24 409	42.5	57.5	35.1	5.2	4 176	54.4
Henderson	176	-10.1	378	6.0	150.0	1 381 355	3 651	193 890	78.6	169 024	93.2	6.8	47.1	17.6	3 464	67.1
Henry	129	-12.2	148	0.8	58.2	494 348	3 343	59 478	30.7	35 292	60.0	40.0	42.8	6.6	1 549	47.6
Hickman	141	8.8	474	6.1	119.7	1 647 913	3 480	199 456	159.2	534 356	35.7	64.3	48.0	29.9	2 918	76.8
Hopkins	163	2.3	223	0.2	94.2	646 970	2 902	81 895	107.7	147 369	32.6	67.4	26.7	9.2	2 662	46.5
Jackson	78	-5.8	132	0.0	23.0	240 571	1 818	43 282	9.9	16 774	26.4	73.6	27.9	3.2	588	44.0
Jefferson	23	-28.5	60	0.2	11.0	521 759	8 633	43 777	7.8	20 343	79.4	20.6	22.8	3.9	288	18.1
Jessamine	84	4.4	125	0.2	33.6	685 317	5 473	49 979	25.0	37 446	21.1	78.9	35.9	7.0	863	36.4
Johnson	24	-12.5	124	D	4.9	216 969	1 750	44 179	1.3	6 561	35.8	64.3	15.8	0.5	81	20.9
Kenton	38	-10.3	83	0.1	15.1	362 353	4 360	48 092	5.3	11 475	43.2	56.8	20.5	3.3	324	29.4
Knott	7	-2.8	161	0.0	1.8	217 095	1 352	61 881	0.4	8 524	17.6	82.4	23.8	2.4	D	2.4
Knox	34	-34.4	138	0.1	9.6	241 292	1 749	50 700	2.3	9 358	60.6	39.4	19.3	0.8	206	21.4
Larue	112	-10.7	156	0.1	66.9	532 196	3 422	82 204	41.9	58 163	74.3	25.7	39.9	7.8	1 295	43.2
Laurel	96	-6.3	95	0.1	35.0	329 341	3 449	43 809	15.3	15 187	41.5	58.5	27.4	2.1	536	29.3
Lawrence	42	-30.8	143	0.0	6.5	202 818	1 416	41 120	1.6	5 375	53.4	46.6	15.8	0.0	31	12.4
Lee	22	-24.5	156	0.0	5.4	297 641	1 902	40 134	1.0	6 852	47.2	52.8	19.0	1.4	86	30.3
Leslie	D	D	D	0.0	0.2	412 867	D	33 533	0.0	267	D	D	0.0	0.0	3	20.0
Letcher	3	-20.5	53	D	0.4	123 185	2 313	43 722	0.1	2 463	64.7	34.6	3.7	0.0	0	0.0
Lewis	118	-19.6	174	0.0	32.8	256 246	1 469	49 519	12.8	18 944	70.8	29.2	27.4	4.0	968	49.6
Lincoln	181	1.4	150	0.3	72.6	374 358	2 489	59 559	57.4	47 729	30.6	69.4	42.3	9.7	1 680	43.5
Livingston	123	5.3	306	0.0	62.5	650 496	2 128	90 191	21.3	52 898	50.3	49.7	40.4	10.7	1 651	54.8
Logan	276	-4.9	260	2.7	192.4	871 373	3 349	105 848	134.9	127 283	71.8	28.2	42.8	15.2	6 034	59.8
Lyon	42	-23.1	190	D	23.6	384 995	2 025	67 187	6.8	30 968	78.0	22.0	37.0	6.4	561	52.5
McCracken	67	-10.8	150	0.3	49.7	462 497	3 077	66 349	22.2	49 738	73.3	26.7	28.6	8.1	947	53.0
McCreary	18	20.2	117	0.0	3.3	208 974	1 790	42 200	1.0	6 671	35.4	64.6	21.3	0.0	11	5.8
McLean	124	-13.7	301	1.2	96.5	1 132 448	3 760	162 719	179.7	435 218	32.1	67.9	55.9	32.0	2 451	71.7
Madison	233	6.7	191	0.2	73.0	576 284	3 018	65 868	60.5	49 656	14.2	85.8	43.3	9.5	783	43.3
Magoffin	44	-27.9	123	D	7.9	182 543	1 482	33 341	1.3	3 479	53.7	46.3	8.9	0.0	235	32.7
Marion	166	3.6	164	0.3	70.2	441 025	2 693	65 181	56.5	55 601	40.2	59.8	46.8	11.1	1 357	56.6
Marshall	95	-2.9	132	0.1	54.8	403 344	3 057	61 174	45.3	63 042	31.7	68.3	25.0	6.1	1 902	52.9
Martin	D	D	D	0.0	0.3	1 783 100	D	35 100	0.1	4 750	D	D	10.0	0.0	0	0.0
Mason	127	-9.4	200	0.0	57.9	515 345	2 578	69 967	30.9	48 784	59.5	40.5	48.3	12.1	1 693	52.8
Meade	119	-1.6	158	0.0	63.7	514 138	3 244	78 910	36.6	48 503	51.7	48.3	35.7	7.6	1 424	52.0
Menifee	41	-5.0	139	D	10.0	248 966	1 787	41 129	3.8	13 082	44.1	55.9	22.8	2.7	177	29.3
Mercer	144	2.0	135	0.0	59.4	456 854	3 379	67 196	50.7	47 495	18.6	81.4	42.4	9.3	1 472	31.8
Metcalfe	125	-16.2	136	0.1	49.7	305 962	2 256	56 923	35.0	37 899	30.1	69.9	43.5	8.4	2 185	45.0
Monroe	172	-2.0	201	0.1	62.0	473 586	2 359	68 647	77.2	90 021	23.5	76.5	51.6	11.2	1 603	48.0
Montgomery	99	-7.0	163	0.0	40.0	447 880	2 743	58 650	19.0	31 209	31.1	68.9	42.2	6.4	539	36.1
Morgan	119	-12.8	171	0.0	24.0	218 340	1 276	50 761	6.9	9 938	42.0	58.0	26.4	0.4	579	37.3
Muhlenberg	129	-8.6	204	0.2	67.1	474 975	2 324	78 500	68.9	109 373	35.6	64.4	31.0	9.5	2 162	44.6
Nelson	188	-4.3	142	0.7	97.2	476 235	3 363	65 611	64.4	48 597	53.3	46.7	34.9	8.1	2 129	35.2
Nicholas	102	-7.3	179	0.1	40.9	387 086	2 159	59 526	20.7	36 384	50.6	49.4	45.4	7.5	712	36.0

Table B. States and Counties — Water Use, Wholesale Trade, Retail Trade, and Real Estate

STATE County	Water use, 2010		Wholesale trade,[1] 2012				Retail trade,[2] 2012				Real estate and rental and leasing,[2] 2012			
	Total water withdrawn (mil gal/day)	Gallons withdrawn per person per day	Number of establishments	Number of employees	Sales (mil dol)	Annual payroll (mil dol)	Number of establishments	Number of employees	Sales (mil dol)	Annual payroll (mil dol)	Number of establishments	Number of employees	Receipts (mil dol)	Annual payroll (mil dol)
	133	134	135	136	137	138	139	140	141	142	143	144	145	146
KENTUCKY—Cont'd														
Clay	4.5	205	5	D	D	D	63	543	138.8	11.6	7	D	D	D
Clinton	4.0	393	11	64	87.1	2.3	39	296	59.4	4.4	7	19	3.0	0.4
Crittenden	1.4	151	5	118	11.8	2.5	31	273	58.8	5.1	6	13	1.7	0.3
Cumberland	1.0	144	NA	NA	NA	NA	30	181	46.0	3.4	3	7	0.3	0.1
Daviess	268.9	2 782	97	1 266	1 105.8	55.6	411	5 906	1 443.4	134.3	80	578	99.7	19.2
Edmonson	2.2	180	NA	NA	NA	NA	31	177	39.2	3.0	NA	NA	NA	NA
Elliott	0.6	74	NA	NA	NA	NA	12	D	D	D	NA	NA	NA	NA
Estill	1.6	111	3	D	D	D	42	299	75.3	5.9	5	D	D	D
Fayette	52.3	177	352	7 283	4 517.8	527.7	1 192	19 820	4 994.8	466.9	431	2 128	442.3	76.6
Fleming	2.3	162	10	D	D	D	61	455	134.8	11.2	10	15	1.9	0.2
Floyd	5.4	136	39	475	395.4	19.0	164	1 506	448.3	34.4	30	131	18.2	5.3
Franklin	10.2	206	28	282	372.8	15.5	178	2 477	654.2	54.0	38	191	22.2	4.6
Fulton	1.3	194	7	53	377.2	4.8	26	184	44.0	3.2	4	7	0.6	0.2
Gallatin	2.4	274	1	D	D	D	21	241	128.0	4.6	7	D	D	D
Garrard	2.4	141	6	23	7.4	0.8	35	167	59.1	3.3	7	10	2.0	0.2
Grant	2.3	95	8	D	D	D	74	943	284.4	21.2	17	38	4.0	1.0
Graves	10.2	273	38	613	767.9	25.6	123	1 374	403.7	32.0	34	70	10.9	1.5
Grayson	3.4	133	11	D	D	D	104	1 069	258.6	22.2	12	141	7.1	3.7
Green	2.7	239	6	29	15.1	0.9	32	246	62.1	5.2	3	D	D	D
Greenup	14.1	382	9	D	D	D	86	837	211.7	18.0	16	57	8.1	1.3
Hancock	306.8	35 820	3	D	D	D	17	138	43.5	2.6	5	13	2.5	0.3
Hardin	16.8	159	57	422	245.7	18.3	408	5 754	1 639.1	137.8	109	490	62.4	11.7
Harlan	5.4	185	25	204	177.3	9.5	101	1 043	205.4	21.2	14	46	4.8	0.9
Harrison	3.9	207	10	44	30.0	1.3	46	566	134.5	11.7	7	32	2.9	0.6
Hart	5.2	285	9	39	12.7	1.5	65	406	157.9	8.1	7	16	1.5	0.7
Henderson	14.8	320	45	D	D	D	170	2 174	729.9	53.7	44	275	23.4	5.2
Henry	1.3	84	13	D	D	D	36	342	171.4	6.3	4	D	D	D
Hickman	5.6	1 144	6	31	67.8	0.9	20	267	76.1	6.2	3	5	0.3	0.0
Hopkins	12.8	273	44	414	240.3	20.6	182	2 325	692.4	55.5	41	114	15.2	3.3
Jackson	2.1	156	NA	NA	NA	NA	25	187	45.7	2.7	5	14	1.4	0.4
Jefferson	687.0	927	1 006	15 867	13 048.4	836.7	2 659	41 294	10 964.4	1 004.0	926	7 168	2 895.1	289.1
Jessamine	7.0	144	40	D	D	D	158	2 638	920.3	71.1	31	124	14.0	3.3
Johnson	3.0	129	17	110	57.2	4.0	91	1 333	383.0	31.1	16	41	4.5	0.9
Kenton	0.5	3	119	1 888	886.0	92.5	394	5 422	1 331.7	120.4	129	656	161.3	27.0
Knott	2.2	136	NA	NA	NA	NA	39	297	72.5	5.4	3	D	D	D
Knox	1.0	31	11	70	39.9	2.0	106	1 194	343.1	26.2	11	51	4.8	1.0
Larue	1.1	80	7	D	D	D	30	255	63.9	4.6	3	3	0.1	0.1
Laurel	9.7	165	61	732	597.3	29.0	228	3 348	1 015.1	78.2	46	166	27.6	4.6
Lawrence	12.0	757	11	229	136.5	9.0	52	645	161.5	12.5	9	36	4.0	0.7
Lee	0.8	105	4	17	4.8	0.5	22	236	63.9	4.9	4	D	D	D
Leslie	1.8	156	NA	NA	NA	NA	26	220	55.6	3.7	NA	NA	NA	NA
Letcher	3.7	152	11	D	D	D	59	678	151.2	15.1	11	18	3.9	0.6
Lewis	1.6	118	3	D	D	D	32	252	70.5	4.1	2	D	D	D
Lincoln	3.3	135	14	D	D	D	61	623	145.9	10.9	6	10	1.1	0.2
Livingston	4.2	443	9	D	D	D	25	181	47.1	3.7	4	D	D	D
Logan	2.4	88	22	192	156.6	6.8	98	926	264.9	22.1	11	18	3.4	0.5
Lyon	3.1	368	3	D	D	D	20	190	65.1	4.0	3	4	0.9	0.1
McCracken	779.8	11 893	104	D	D	D	411	6 163	1 638.5	140.7	79	330	60.9	9.8
McCreary	2.1	114	2	D	D	D	42	378	81.9	7.5	8	13	0.8	0.4
McLean	1.9	200	8	D	D	D	28	185	61.0	4.1	NA	NA	NA	NA
Madison	11.9	144	38	308	262.0	9.6	299	4 171	1 080.7	85.1	68	D	D	D
Magoffin	1.3	97	2	D	D	D	34	241	61.1	4.8	2	D	D	D
Marion	5.9	298	11	68	34.4	2.1	65	649	171.0	14.0	9	19	3.1	0.8
Marshall	18.7	594	27	228	99.3	9.2	103	1 081	392.3	27.7	15	29	4.7	0.7
Martin	5.0	386	4	D	D	D	40	364	93.8	7.9	3	D	D	D
Mason	22.9	1 306	15	358	79.8	14.0	93	1 385	363.8	29.8	13	34	6.2	1.0
Meade	9.7	338	10	77	49.2	2.8	63	609	197.3	12.5	17	50	5.6	1.1
Menifee	1.3	198	NA	NA	NA	NA	15	123	23.2	1.4	3	D	D	D
Mercer	9.5	445	8	32	14.7	0.7	62	705	169.7	15.4	11	21	2.8	0.5
Metcalfe	0.8	82	2	D	D	D	27	233	49.6	4.7	3	4	0.9	0.1
Monroe	3.0	275	7	47	26.9	1.5	42	449	104.1	9.8	6	18	1.3	0.3
Montgomery	3.7	141	17	D	D	D	114	1 501	457.8	34.0	19	35	5.1	0.8
Morgan	1.7	121	NA	NA	NA	NA	45	390	93.9	7.9	2	D	D	D
Muhlenberg	1 236.8	39 263	13	151	33.9	6.2	115	1 291	304.1	27.5	15	58	6.8	1.4
Nelson	8.5	196	30	292	147.4	9.4	159	1 826	535.2	42.7	28	63	11.6	2.1
Nicholas	1.9	262	1	D	D	D	16	139	27.4	2.8	1	D	D	D

1. Merchant wholesalers, except manufacturers' sales branches and offices. 2. Employer establishments.

Table B. States and Counties — **Professional Services, Manufacturing, and Accommodation and Food Services**

STATE County	Professional, scientific, and technical services, 2012				Manufacturing, 2012				Accommodation and food services, 2012			
	Number of establishments	Number of employees	Receipts (mil dol)	Annual payroll (mil dol)	Number of establishments	Number of employees	Receipts (mil dol)	Annual payroll (mil dol)	Number of establishments	Number of employees	Sales (mil dol)	Annual payroll (mil dol)
	147	148	149	150	151	152	153	154	155	156	157	158
KENTUCKY—Cont'd												
Clay	19	62	5.1	1.4	8	236	D	4.0	20	D	D	D
Clinton	15	33	2.6	1.0	12	D	D	D	15	D	D	D
Crittenden	12	224	11.0	5.6	12	170	D	5.0	12	202	5.3	1.7
Cumberland	9	D	D	D	7	189	30.8	6.4	14	D	D	D
Daviess	155	1 499	100.4	42.9	104	5 092	3 773.5	238.6	173	D	D	D
Edmonson	5	13	1.1	0.3	3	D	D	D	13	D	D	D
Elliott	NA	NA	NA	NA	NA	NA	NA	NA	5	D	D	D
Estill	9	41	1.8	0.5	8	180	D	4.0	20	D	D	D
Fayette	1 072	10 073	1 441.2	561.1	224	8 005	2 922.0	351.1	772	17 490	939.4	270.7
Fleming	15	36	3.5	1.0	20	350	82.9	11.4	7	D	D	D
Floyd	69	D	D	D	13	145	30.7	5.0	49	851	36.3	9.1
Franklin	127	777	88.9	33.5	41	2 383	1 748.1	110.1	106	1 948	98.3	26.3
Fulton	7	19	1.3	0.5	9	366	240.7	14.0	13	170	7.2	1.9
Gallatin	10	37	10.3	1.2	4	D	D	D	10	D	D	D
Garrard	15	34	3.2	1.0	15	240	39.2	7.3	11	D	D	D
Grant	24	67	4.8	1.9	15	588	860.2	24.3	43	D	D	D
Graves	47	370	17.4	7.3	48	2 128	480.8	75.8	51	808	29.6	7.7
Grayson	27	77	5.5	1.8	28	1 507	441.0	52.9	30	D	D	D
Green	12	27	2.4	0.9	9	58	D	1.3	9	174	6.4	1.7
Greenup	31	208	13.3	5.0	17	557	D	27.2	36	676	30.4	9.1
Hancock	6	45	3.5	1.5	12	1 720	D	114.2	6	D	D	D
Hardin	217	1 492	168.9	63.4	68	4 931	2 078.1	230.9	182	4 504	192.0	54.4
Harlan	37	257	17.5	9.6	10	74	D	3.3	33	334	13.1	3.3
Harrison	16	90	6.8	3.5	19	1 182	559.7	66.4	22	D	D	D
Hart	16	62	4.2	1.5	18	2 113	D	75.1	24	D	D	D
Henderson	71	416	39.9	13.8	76	4 930	2 857.6	215.1	85	1 411	65.4	16.8
Henry	18	52	3.4	1.1	4	396	D	17.7	15	D	D	D
Hickman	4	D	D	D	3	D	D	D	4	D	D	D
Hopkins	60	380	38.7	14.3	46	2 270	964.5	127.5	73	1 415	54.3	15.0
Jackson	6	13	1.0	0.4	9	181	D	8.4	7	44	2.2	0.6
Jefferson	2 197	22 198	3 274.3	1 139.3	718	40 666	28 642.1	2 159.3	1 651	39 711	2 006.3	572.1
Jessamine	85	548	81.4	20.4	69	2 550	681.4	93.4	73	D	D	D
Johnson	30	141	23.9	6.1	6	53	D	1.4	40	D	D	D
Kenton	355	2 723	313.0	130.5	90	3 891	1 674.8	219.8	307	D	D	D
Knott	11	45	8.3	2.1	NA	NA	NA	NA	8	81	5.3	1.3
Knox	40	1 133	57.5	27.4	14	1 021	191.2	35.0	43	715	37.5	9.7
Larue	20	48	4.4	1.3	14	498	D	D	17	121	5.2	1.5
Laurel	93	467	40.0	15.7	54	3 237	924.1	129.5	94	2 181	101.9	28.3
Lawrence	12	66	5.1	2.3	3	7	D	0.3	20	D	D	D
Lee	5	17	0.9	0.4	NA	NA	NA	NA	5	D	D	D
Leslie	7	50	6.6	1.6	NA	NA	NA	NA	4	D	D	D
Letcher	19	177	10.0	5.6	8	21	D	0.7	23	D	D	D
Lewis	4	D	D	D	14	385	94.8	12.1	8	D	D	D
Lincoln	22	76	5.9	1.9	13	726	188.1	24.4	18	397	12.6	3.4
Livingston	7	D	D	D	6	73	D	3.5	10	D	D	D
Logan	29	148	11.8	5.0	39	2 271	2 571.5	118.6	34	D	D	D
Lyon	10	39	3.2	1.5	NA	NA	NA	NA	22	D	D	D
McCracken	203	1 194	219.4	56.2	58	3 077	2 308.6	164.2	213	4 111	181.7	52.4
McCreary	6	72	3.4	0.9	10	373	D	7.2	17	273	7.9	2.3
McLean	8	19	1.4	0.4	9	126	D	4.6	14	91	3.6	0.9
Madison	137	679	71.4	25.1	65	3 597	D	162.6	159	3 495	164.5	43.5
Magoffin	16	105	14.2	4.1	NA	NA	NA	NA	10	154	6.4	1.8
Marion	28	101	8.3	3.1	31	3 586	895.0	135.8	34	D	D	D
Marshall	36	197	20.6	9.3	36	2 172	3 212.2	171.1	79	1 224	45.9	12.6
Martin	11	23	2.7	0.8	3	27	D	0.6	12	152	6.3	1.6
Mason	25	110	9.3	3.5	11	1 249	D	57.1	40	774	35.6	10.1
Meade	33	269	11.2	4.4	6	250	D	D	30	409	23.1	5.9
Menifee	2	D	D	D	5	D	D	3.4	2	D	D	D
Mercer	23	58	4.7	1.4	12	2 096	2 130.5	131.8	38	D	D	D
Metcalfe	5	11	0.8	0.2	8	716	311.6	22.4	10	89	3.8	1.0
Monroe	8	16	0.8	0.3	18	547	85.9	17.4	16	D	D	D
Montgomery	35	149	14.0	4.5	35	3 919	1 040.4	140.0	35	D	D	D
Morgan	13	75	3.8	1.7	5	409	47.4	8.2	11	D	D	D
Muhlenberg	34	148	16.8	3.9	26	793	218.7	26.1	49	D	D	D
Nelson	68	243	18.9	5.2	53	3 434	1 820.0	164.9	59	1 198	48.3	13.3
Nicholas	6	11	1.1	0.4	4	39	4.5	1.2	6	30	1.2	0.2

1. Establishment subject to federal tax.

Table B. States and Counties — Health Care and Social Assistance, Other Services, Nonemployer Businesses, and Residential Construction

STATE County	Health care and social assistance, 2012				Other services, 2012				Nonemployer businesses, 2015		Value of residential construction authorized by building permits, 2016	
	Number of establish-ments	Number of employees	Receipts (mil dol)	Annual payroll (mil dol)	Number of establish-ments	Number of employees	Receipts (mil dol)	Annual payroll (mil dol)	Number	Receipts (mil dol)	New Construction ($1,000)	Number of housing units
	159	160	161	162	163	164	165	166	167	168	169	170
KENTUCKY—Cont'd												
Clay	36	943	106.1	37.7	10	34	3.9	0.9	1 066	35.0	0	0
Clinton	24	322	28.5	11.4	5	D	D	D	773	29.6	0	0
Crittenden	17	407	26.9	12.5	14	D	D	D	662	25.7	48	1
Cumberland	14	456	37.2	15.8	9	27	2.9	0.6	600	22.5	0	0
Daviess	324	7 657	744.6	296.5	150	D	D	D	5 583	245.3	33 007	370
Edmonson	18	D	D	D	8	D	D	D	859	35.8	NA	NA
Elliott	10	130	7.6	3.9	2	D	D	D	304	9.8	NA	NA
Estill	28	442	36.8	15.8	7	24	2.6	0.6	812	19.4	0	0
Fayette	1 048	29 625	3 726.0	1 437.5	553	4 405	738.6	141.8	22 407	1 113.5	165 709	1 365
Fleming	21	561	48.2	18.4	16	D	D	D	1 277	53.6	0	0
Floyd	131	1 939	198.7	75.6	43	298	34.9	9.8	2 264	93.1	375	2
Franklin	156	1 800	210.2	60.8	128	749	87.8	25.3	3 239	125.0	9 658	58
Fulton	15	D	D	D	6	D	D	D	311	10.3	0	0
Gallatin	9	D	D	D	5	D	D	D	382	13.6	2 623	14
Garrard	24	231	13.0	6.0	10	D	D	D	1 257	41.0	0	0
Grant	32	D	D	D	24	D	D	D	1 337	59.1	5 334	33
Graves	97	D	D	D	33	217	28.9	8.0	2 628	116.8	0	0
Grayson	58	1 131	86.6	34.8	29	D	D	D	1 850	94.4	2 606	21
Green	24	572	39.7	17.5	16	47	4.9	0.9	936	39.6	0	0
Greenup	104	D	D	D	25	D	D	D	1 902	61.2	5 174	15
Hancock	14	102	6.4	2.1	5	D	D	D	431	13.1	1 021	5
Hardin	341	7 473	697.5	304.9	145	D	D	D	5 376	220.5	43 787	363
Harlan	52	1 332	137.9	50.6	24	86	8.7	2.0	1 363	39.1	0	0
Harrison	46	909	84.0	30.6	21	D	D	D	1 033	42.1	7 555	37
Hart	27	470	32.1	14.9	16	46	4.4	1.1	1 642	85.9	11 578	109
Henderson	137	2 500	233.7	87.1	62	534	76.6	19.5	2 360	97.5	8 354	46
Henry	19	257	15.2	7.0	16	D	D	D	1 096	45.4	6 286	36
Hickman	10	179	12.6	5.7	2	D	D	D	332	11.3	NA	NA
Hopkins	122	3 143	289.1	117.6	68	498	56.4	15.7	2 291	91.5	8 187	57
Jackson	9	219	15.1	6.2	4	12	1.6	0.3	880	27.0	0	0
Jefferson	2 390	65 785	7 401.3	2 838.2	1 307	11 226	1 278.7	353.7	52 540	2 455.3	338 062	2 852
Jessamine	112	1 026	64.9	31.7	68	235	26.2	5.7	4 199	190.9	54 259	196
Johnson	56	828	84.6	29.5	30	D	D	D	1 404	49.3	1 299	3
Kenton	344	10 407	1 298.0	519.8	232	D	D	D	9 628	440.1	63 378	349
Knott	17	220	21.0	6.6	9	D	D	D	811	28.4	NA	NA
Knox	71	1 357	93.3	38.0	19	D	D	D	2 009	74.8	0	0
Larue	19	284	11.9	6.1	14	46	4.5	1.1	1 034	38.1	4 983	23
Laurel	136	2 528	320.2	128.2	67	D	D	D	3 903	177.1	641	9
Lawrence	30	702	69.8	25.8	18	D	D	D	822	27.8	NA	NA
Lee	19	612	21.3	10.6	1	D	D	D	406	13.6	NA	NA
Leslie	16	328	26.3	10.8	4	26	2.7	0.7	519	19.5	NA	NA
Letcher	45	937	96.7	36.6	13	D	D	D	1 193	35.0	0	0
Lewis	12	298	20.4	8.7	9	26	1.8	0.3	866	32.8	142	2
Lincoln	39	710	51.7	20.4	22	D	D	D	1 591	54.6	5 663	28
Livingston	20	D	D	D	9	D	D	D	556	18.7	NA	NA
Logan	48	677	68.6	19.4	34	105	9.5	2.9	1 751	81.1	2 220	20
Lyon	14	204	12.3	5.1	7	D	D	D	523	18.7	2 276	14
McCracken	276	6 441	782.5	281.4	129	D	D	D	4 299	184.7	43 523	239
McCreary	25	320	18.3	8.3	4	D	D	D	859	35.7	0	0
McLean	10	132	8.3	3.1	12	D	D	D	514	16.6	150	2
Madison	254	3 580	283.6	115.7	96	515	53.7	13.4	5 547	220.3	24 193	343
Magoffin	17	278	20.2	7.3	11	29	4.4	0.6	616	16.0	NA	NA
Marion	44	1 333	86.5	33.5	17	D	D	D	1 161	45.1	1 549	15
Marshall	64	986	59.3	25.8	38	174	15.1	4.3	2 235	83.9	15 737	86
Martin	23	237	18.3	6.8	7	24	2.9	0.9	426	10.7	NA	NA
Mason	65	1 200	109.4	40.9	42	160	10.7	2.9	1 136	45.4	4 119	26
Meade	38	363	19.3	8.6	23	D	D	D	1 508	59.3	11 602	81
Menifee	10	185	12.5	5.6	2	D	D	D	423	12.1	NA	NA
Mercer	42	696	60.8	24.2	29	D	D	D	1 462	64.5	5 643	34
Metcalfe	17	D	D	D	8	16	1.1	0.2	806	27.2	NA	NA
Monroe	29	494	34.3	14.7	9	44	5.3	0.9	919	36.6	NA	NA
Montgomery	73	913	83.4	30.2	29	D	D	D	1 840	61.4	5 743	59
Morgan	16	297	28.1	10.5	11	D	D	D	748	24.5	1 500	20
Muhlenberg	58	1 318	87.0	37.2	41	163	15.6	4.1	1 621	54.2	638	7
Nelson	97	1 577	126.8	49.4	46	182	15.5	4.0	2 980	118.7	26 423	159
Nicholas	13	269	15.2	7.2	4	23	1.7	0.5	485	14.9	0	0

	Government employment and payroll, 2012								Local government finances, 2012				
			March payroll (percent of total)						General revenue				
												Taxes	
													Per capita[1] (dollars)
STATE County	Full-time equivalent employees	March payroll (dollars)	Administration, judicial, and legal	Police and Corrections	Fire Protection	Highways and transportation	Health and Welfare	Natural resources and utilities	Education and libraries	Total (mil dol)	Inter-governmental (mil dol)	Total (mil dol)	Total	Property
	171	172	173	174	175	176	177	178	179	180	181	182	183	184
KENTUCKY—Cont'd														
Clay	994	2 631 167	3.1	5.8	0.0	2.7	3.9	4.3	79.7	47.7	34.9	7.4	345	209
Clinton	443	1 162 284	4.8	3.5	0.0	2.1	6.0	0.7	82.6	24.4	16.8	5.6	548	258
Crittenden	318	847 790	5.5	13.8	0.0	2.2	0.0	6.6	71.2	21.9	15.1	4.5	482	288
Cumberland	454	1 348 734	2.8	4.3	0.1	1.8	42.8	3.6	43.6	42.0	9.9	4.0	592	292
Daviess	4 233	13 420 532	3.9	7.2	3.3	2.8	7.4	14.6	60.1	320.6	123.3	99.0	1 012	595
Edmonson	508	1 172 078	2.9	4.0	0.4	1.8	3.8	6.2	80.7	24.3	16.3	5.3	442	332
Elliott	264	668 556	3.5	2.6	0.0	3.1	11.5	2.5	75.8	15.4	11.7	2.1	276	169
Estill	575	2 082 079	1.7	13.1	7.0	4.2	11.0	3.5	58.3	35.1	24.2	6.6	452	275
Fayette	9 962	37 856 745	4.3	13.5	7.8	2.1	6.3	4.9	58.5	920.0	203.8	539.7	1 767	835
Fleming	697	2 194 909	3.1	2.3	0.7	1.3	36.8	2.2	53.4	87.7	20.7	8.0	553	322
Floyd	1 386	3 755 718	2.5	3.5	2.7	1.3	3.7	4.8	81.3	96.9	62.9	22.7	584	472
Franklin	1 716	6 237 758	4.5	8.7	9.2	2.6	1.1	8.1	54.8	158.6	42.6	66.3	1 332	688
Fulton	418	1 044 790	3.3	7.0	5.9	10.5	0.4	9.6	58.4	26.4	17.0	5.5	847	491
Gallatin	332	954 873	7.1	3.3	0.0	2.1	2.1	3.8	81.6	30.0	13.7	8.5	1 007	632
Garrard	526	1 692 901	3.4	1.7	0.1	1.9	5.2	1.5	86.1	39.9	19.9	12.9	761	479
Grant	998	2 854 787	5.3	7.3	1.9	1.5	1.5	5.4	77.4	59.9	37.6	15.0	611	477
Graves	1 308	3 544 113	2.9	8.2	3.0	2.3	0.0	2.8	79.5	77.1	43.4	23.1	614	366
Grayson	956	2 669 148	4.8	14.5	0.3	2.2	2.1	3.6	70.5	66.8	40.3	15.8	608	317
Green	635	2 084 431	5.8	8.4	4.2	2.1	27.5	9.5	41.8	40.4	15.6	5.1	451	288
Greenup	1 220	4 273 541	2.1	6.9	1.4	1.9	0.4	3.3	82.5	86.3	43.9	29.1	793	654
Hancock	406	1 128 193	8.8	3.1	0.0	3.6	5.5	3.0	73.5	70.5	13.2	9.1	1 052	490
Hardin	5 176	17 598 804	1.2	3.7	1.8	1.2	45.7	3.6	41.7	459.3	132.4	90.3	844	479
Harlan	1 193	3 057 085	2.8	6.7	0.2	2.7	1.0	4.6	81.1	96.7	61.1	16.0	562	404
Harrison	635	1 973 639	6.3	9.3	3.0	3.0	0.0	2.3	76.0	38.3	20.2	14.4	771	361
Hart	599	1 691 514	2.9	6.7	0.1	2.1	4.8	5.2	76.9	36.5	22.7	9.6	522	293
Henderson	2 096	5 804 471	5.3	9.5	3.7	4.2	1.2	14.4	60.1	156.8	64.1	42.2	908	550
Henry	640	1 779 003	8.8	3.5	0.0	1.4	1.9	5.1	79.3	35.5	21.0	10.1	661	488
Hickman	198	524 720	7.5	5.4	0.0	2.2	2.3	1.0	80.8	11.7	7.7	3.0	622	421
Hopkins	1 879	5 461 945	4.2	9.4	3.9	3.0	5.6	7.9	65.5	126.7	65.8	37.0	791	444
Jackson	523	1 629 435	2.4	2.5	0.0	2.9	0.5	0.3	90.4	29.9	23.5	5.0	377	231
Jefferson	25 957	96 919 915	3.8	11.0	4.8	4.5	4.7	8.9	60.3	2 308.9	694.0	1 084.7	1 445	808
Jessamine	1 836	5 035 213	4.3	7.1	3.4	1.5	7.8	4.8	68.6	116.9	46.1	57.3	1 153	712
Johnson	862	2 638 353	2.4	1.8	1.1	1.5	0.7	2.6	86.7	69.4	42.9	14.0	598	338
Kenton	5 823	21 356 962	2.4	8.9	5.6	14.3	2.9	9.7	54.0	710.4	161.7	228.8	1 415	873
Knott	613	1 519 486	4.8	3.6	0.0	2.3	3.8	6.9	78.6	39.0	27.2	8.8	546	448
Knox	1 187	3 283 773	1.7	2.6	0.1	1.9	10.4	2.7	80.2	87.2	55.9	18.9	597	369
Larue	547	1 474 160	4.8	6.4	0.0	1.7	3.2	2.6	80.9	31.5	21.6	7.0	497	357
Laurel	2 042	5 388 170	2.8	6.5	0.3	2.5	3.9	3.5	79.3	125.4	73.3	38.1	641	329
Lawrence	604	1 562 126	4.8	3.3	1.1	2.4	4.5	4.0	78.6	54.7	23.2	8.2	517	381
Lee	279	772 061	4.6	4.7	0.0	3.4	11.0	4.8	71.3	19.3	12.6	4.2	539	364
Leslie	447	1 317 537	5.5	3.0	0.0	2.8	0.0	4.1	79.4	32.5	23.5	7.5	668	472
Letcher	1 021	2 457 149	1.7	4.3	0.4	2.2	3.8	4.0	81.9	57.9	40.2	11.8	493	377
Lewis	560	1 776 699	3.4	5.5	0.0	2.3	1.5	4.2	82.9	29.1	20.7	6.3	457	316
Lincoln	879	2 396 927	2.4	4.3	0.3	1.9	3.1	3.5	84.1	50.5	35.4	11.5	471	295
Livingston	346	854 563	7.6	3.0	8.2	3.7	4.9	4.1	68.4	22.0	13.3	6.5	688	436
Logan	972	2 732 295	5.2	7.8	1.4	1.6	0.3	3.8	78.6	68.7	39.7	21.0	787	379
Lyon	237	841 257	5.7	3.3	0.2	3.5	5.4	4.3	50.3	18.0	7.4	7.1	847	615
McCracken	2 541	8 688 735	3.1	9.6	3.2	4.7	11.0	11.5	55.4	229.1	82.8	78.2	1 193	632
McCreary	751	1 960 007	1.9	4.5	0.0	1.6	6.3	4.0	80.7	47.9	30.0	16.4	907	789
McLean	404	945 835	4.5	1.7	0.0	2.1	0.7	5.7	75.6	30.6	17.9	7.4	778	382
Madison	2 628	7 891 742	2.5	5.2	3.8	2.3	9.6	4.2	68.4	199.0	81.8	79.3	935	482
Magoffin	510	1 498 254	4.1	2.3	0.8	3.5	6.7	3.0	79.4	38.5	29.7	6.1	470	216
Marion	789	2 206 926	2.6	13.7	0.3	6.2	3.0	6.0	67.3	49.3	25.1	15.3	763	452
Marshall	1 233	3 676 388	2.4	4.3	0.0	2.0	23.4	5.4	61.5	138.8	34.7	36.4	1 160	589
Martin	565	1 560 146	7.3	3.2	0.0	2.3	6.6	3.2	77.0	32.7	22.1	7.2	566	272
Mason	917	2 257 527	7.8	11.9	3.1	2.4	6.1	5.7	59.4	62.2	21.7	18.3	1 043	494
Meade	931	2 688 037	3.4	5.7	0.1	1.5	3.2	3.3	81.9	56.8	35.1	14.8	508	380
Menifee	255	589 112	3.9	0.5	0.0	2.1	3.1	2.7	87.6	17.2	10.7	4.3	691	525
Mercer	736	2 237 637	6.9	9.4	2.9	5.4	2.8	4.1	67.1	50.4	24.0	20.1	944	596
Metcalfe	377	953 969	2.6	3.0	0.0	3.1	0.6	4.9	85.9	23.2	15.8	5.4	544	294
Monroe	585	1 493 674	4.7	6.7	0.0	1.6	5.1	5.9	75.8	28.4	19.3	6.0	550	323
Montgomery	853	2 642 340	1.3	2.9	6.2	0.8	6.6	1.1	80.9	69.6	34.6	22.4	832	434
Morgan	486	1 237 685	4.6	5.7	0.0	1.9	4.7	5.7	76.6	34.6	23.0	6.2	453	241
Muhlenberg	1 235	3 174 925	4.8	7.6	1.4	3.6	3.9	4.0	74.3	72.9	47.9	14.7	471	350
Nelson	1 501	4 602 823	4.7	5.8	0.7	1.6	4.5	4.2	76.6	108.2	44.4	36.8	829	669
Nicholas	219	557 957	7.9	3.1	0.4	3.0	1.0	7.7	75.2	15.4	10.3	3.1	437	281

1. Based on the resident population estimated as of July 1 of the year shown.

Local Government Finances, Government Employment, and Income Taxes

	Local government finances, 2012 (cont.)									Government employment, 2015			Individual income tax returns, 2014		
	Direct general expenditure							Debt outstanding							
			Percent of total for:												
STATE County	Total (mil dol)	Per capita¹ (dollars)	Education	Health and hospitals	Police protection	Public welfare	Highways	Total (mil dol)	Per capita¹ (dollars)	Federal civilian	Federal military	State and local	Number of returns	Mean adjusted gross income	Mean income tax
	185	186	187	188	189	190	191	192	193	194	195	196	197	198	199
KENTUCKY—Cont'd															
Clay	48.2	2 236	66.0	2.1	3.1	0.0	7.1	33.2	1 542	363	59	1 173	6 390	34 088	2 455
Clinton	23.1	2 250	70.0	3.9	2.9	0.0	4.7	18.9	1 842	50	31	589	3 700	31 796	1 983
Crittenden	20.2	2 174	49.6	0.3	3.2	0.0	6.6	34.3	3 698	18	28	415	3 610	43 168	3 635
Cumberland	47.8	7 014	21.3	57.7	1.5	0.0	3.3	40.3	5 903	D	21	327	2 560	32 911	2 470
Daviess	344.4	3 519	39.4	6.6	4.3	0.1	2.9	1 124.1	11 488	254	325	5 547	45 050	51 786	5 537
Edmonson	23.8	1 975	69.3	5.0	2.8	0.0	5.3	36.6	3 036	213	36	505	4 670	38 138	2 833
Elliott	14.7	1 891	60.4	9.7	1.5	1.2	7.3	16.4	2 107	D	21	548	2 080	37 719	2 483
Estill	39.4	2 719	67.4	7.2	1.3	0.0	3.6	33.1	2 286	20	45	697	5 390	36 594	2 750
Fayette	871.4	2 852	47.8	1.8	5.5	1.0	1.3	1 402.6	4 591	4 147	1 002	37 628	141 210	59 539	7 882
Fleming	60.2	4 132	42.2	39.1	1.6	0.0	3.5	101.3	6 957	45	46	816	5 960	38 870	2 974
Floyd	95.8	2 460	58.7	3.2	3.0	0.0	4.7	77.1	1 979	123	116	2 328	13 020	41 777	4 014
Franklin	148.7	2 986	38.2	6.9	4.7	0.1	3.3	147.3	2 957	504	171	13 816	24 440	49 636	5 131
Fulton	26.8	4 114	37.8	0.2	5.2	0.0	5.6	13.8	2 107	27	35	499	2 350	36 200	3 161
Gallatin	31.5	3 721	44.7	3.1	3.1	0.0	2.2	306.7	36 176	33	27	416	3 510	41 437	3 338
Garrard	36.7	2 171	53.0	18.0	3.1	0.0	3.4	63.2	3 736	25	53	647	6 720	43 855	3 693
Grant	60.7	2 479	63.9	0.5	3.4	0.1	3.7	87.4	3 568	45	76	1 173	10 340	43 550	3 680
Graves	76.9	2 049	62.2	0.3	2.9	0.2	4.8	208.0	5 539	201	115	1 747	15 130	43 938	3 984
Grayson	62.1	2 391	54.7	1.0	2.5	0.6	4.1	106.8	4 113	95	79	1 567	10 070	41 114	3 708
Green	39.0	3 443	35.6	43.0	2.1	0.0	3.4	34.9	3 088	19	34	721	4 340	35 153	2 485
Greenup	85.0	2 315	62.5	3.4	4.2	0.0	4.8	61.8	1 684	57	111	1 421	14 790	51 968	5 431
Hancock	79.0	9 101	19.3	0.8	0.8	0.1	2.2	714.6	82 360	21	27	428	3 750	50 160	4 454
Hardin	430.7	4 025	34.9	44.6	2.8	0.0	2.0	304.8	2 848	5 919	5 318	7 100	46 840	48 780	4 749
Harlan	95.7	3 353	47.6	20.0	2.5	1.4	4.6	87.7	3 072	75	85	1 731	9 090	34 594	2 959
Harrison	37.7	2 026	62.3	1.1	5.4	0.2	9.1	17.8	956	37	58	791	7 730	44 760	3 947
Hart	35.3	1 923	58.3	4.8	2.9	0.1	5.4	51.6	2 807	40	57	789	7 280	35 621	2 640
Henderson	158.7	3 411	41.1	0.2	3.9	0.4	4.8	595.8	12 809	116	141	2 681	20 060	51 424	5 562
Henry	38.5	2 513	68.2	3.6	3.2	0.0	4.4	41.2	2 690	95	49	709	6 990	44 905	3 974
Hickman	12.5	2 633	61.6	0.0	3.3	0.0	8.4	15.6	3 280	23	14	231	1 890	43 004	3 892
Hopkins	127.9	2 738	50.6	2.9	4.8	0.7	5.6	336.3	7 198	169	141	3 215	19 200	50 523	5 446
Jackson	37.2	2 791	73.7	0.3	0.9	0.0	5.1	39.0	2 924	32	41	680	4 400	35 485	2 299
Jefferson	2 460.2	3 277	46.7	1.4	4.8	0.5	3.0	4 784.1	6 372	6 524	2 579	41 920	370 770	58 145	7 449
Jessamine	118.6	2 390	54.7	4.5	6.5	0.1	5.6	197.1	3 971	76	157	2 330	21 590	59 550	7 564
Johnson	63.4	2 719	62.6	7.2	2.4	0.0	4.6	48.3	2 065	42	71	1 434	8 040	44 307	4 022
Kenton	844.4	5 222	24.0	2.1	3.6	0.0	2.7	2 312.8	14 302	3 856	547	7 034	77 650	75 705	11 424
Knott	35.4	2 196	66.3	0.1	2.3	0.2	6.1	25.7	1 594	38	47	717	4 940	39 586	3 321
Knox	85.5	2 695	53.4	8.3	1.8	0.0	3.5	96.3	3 036	150	97	1 404	11 050	35 025	2 623
Larue	29.1	2 055	63.2	2.5	2.5	0.0	4.3	46.0	3 247	45	43	570	6 120	41 187	3 447
Laurel	122.8	2 066	64.1	2.4	3.8	0.9	3.4	206.4	3 470	249	185	2 583	23 420	42 664	4 096
Lawrence	56.4	3 560	42.6	2.7	1.4	0.0	5.0	323.0	20 378	30	49	679	5 510	43 288	3 642
Lee	18.2	2 364	53.5	6.3	4.4	0.1	10.1	9.1	1 180	11	21	422	2 190	33 750	2 542
Leslie	38.3	3 427	60.6	0.3	1.6	0.0	6.1	45.7	4 093	13	33	535	3 450	38 970	3 019
Letcher	57.7	2 407	65.1	0.2	2.3	0.0	4.0	48.6	2 030	48	71	1 085	7 600	40 699	3 554
Lewis	32.1	2 322	56.5	3.9	2.6	0.0	6.9	85.2	6 155	20	42	620	4 760	38 107	2 630
Lincoln	57.7	2 358	64.0	2.6	1.3	0.1	4.4	51.0	2 086	59	76	956	9 370	38 098	2 948
Livingston	21.9	2 329	53.2	2.8	2.6	0.0	6.2	29.9	3 170	84	29	461	3 990	44 537	4 043
Logan	70.1	2 633	53.7	15.9	4.9	0.0	4.2	64.5	2 421	63	83	1 225	11 350	44 263	4 105
Lyon	19.0	2 270	40.7	6.1	4.4	0.8	10.5	27.6	3 304	31	22	908	3 260	47 950	4 728
McCracken	222.0	3 387	53.7	0.1	3.1	0.1	3.3	760.9	11 608	586	226	3 750	30 020	56 721	7 097
McCreary	46.4	2 568	59.4	1.1	0.7	0.0	4.6	41.3	2 284	474	49	719	4 860	29 909	1 911
McLean	31.1	3 277	41.5	3.3	0.7	0.6	9.6	42.6	4 483	31	29	488	3 940	46 201	4 179
Madison	191.9	2 263	56.3	9.2	4.2	0.1	3.1	375.9	4 434	1 068	278	7 268	34 720	49 912	5 064
Magoffin	33.9	2 601	61.0	4.8	2.9	0.0	5.3	40.5	3 109	12	40	625	4 050	38 097	2 727
Marion	48.7	2 426	52.2	2.0	3.7	0.0	4.4	59.9	2 983	43	59	866	8 250	41 202	3 579
Marshall	146.0	4 657	26.1	18.0	3.9	0.3	2.3	483.2	15 417	88	96	1 639	13 830	50 727	5 045
Martin	33.5	2 633	63.8	9.1	1.1	0.0	5.6	13.4	1 048	400	33	567	3 210	40 364	3 355
Mason	67.9	3 879	34.1	4.5	4.5	0.0	7.5	293.2	16 743	53	52	1 432	7 280	48 653	4 906
Meade	55.3	1 892	66.3	2.2	2.1	0.0	3.0	96.2	3 291	32	86	1 081	12 110	47 866	4 223
Menifee	19.5	3 133	66.1	3.5	3.4	0.2	4.2	20.7	3 323	46	19	333	2 240	33 789	2 240
Mercer	48.2	2 267	58.2	3.7	3.9	0.0	4.4	86.2	4 054	42	66	875	9 560	44 817	4 012
Metcalfe	34.7	3 479	78.8	1.8	2.2	0.0	4.0	60.2	6 042	18	31	491	3 920	32 282	2 193
Monroe	27.3	2 526	64.8	9.0	3.4	0.0	4.9	27.3	2 518	25	33	600	4 260	36 129	3 054
Montgomery	73.1	2 716	63.0	9.0	4.6	0.0	2.4	73.0	2 713	67	85	1 218	11 370	44 119	4 248
Morgan	36.5	2 671	54.2	4.4	1.9	6.8	7.3	55.1	4 035	32	36	987	4 140	38 257	3 023
Muhlenberg	94.2	3 022	66.4	2.4	2.2	0.1	4.0	83.6	2 681	490	91	1 743	12 090	45 582	4 105
Nelson	117.2	2 645	59.2	2.1	3.0	0.2	2.8	245.4	5 537	78	139	1 721	21 200	48 510	4 840
Nicholas	15.9	2 269	62.2	1.2	3.9	0.5	10.0	17.4	2 481	15	22	309	2 910	36 938	3 004

1. Based on the resident population estimated as of July 1 of the year shown.

STATE/ County code	CBSA code[1]	County type[2]	STATE County	Land area,[3] (sq mi) 2016	Total persons 2016	Rank	Per square mile	White	Black	American Indian, Alaska Native	Asian and Pacific Islander	Percent Hispanic or Latino[4]	Under 5 years	5 to 17 years	18 to 24 years	25 to 34 years	35 to 44 years	45 to 54 years
								Race alone or in combination, not Hispanic or Latino (percent)					Age (percent)					
				1	2	3	4	5	6	7	8	9	10	11	12	13	14	15
			KENTUCKY—Cont'd															
21 183	...	6	Ohio	587.3	24 378	1 627	41.5	94.6	1.5	0.5	0.4	3.9	5.8	18.5	8.1	11.8	12.5	12.8
21 185	31140	1	Oldham	187.2	65 560	809	350.2	89.7	5.0	0.7	2.2	3.9	5.1	20.4	8.2	10.2	14.6	16.6
21 187	...	8	Owen	351.1	10 642	2 379	30.3	95.9	1.6	0.8	0.3	2.6	5.0	17.6	7.2	10.8	12.6	14.0
21 189	...	9	Owsley	197.4	4 491	2 862	22.8	97.6	0.9	0.6	0.4	1.4	5.9	16.0	6.8	12.6	11.4	14.2
21 191	17140	1	Pendleton	277.2	14 560	2 128	52.5	97.7	1.1	0.7	0.5	1.2	6.0	16.9	7.9	11.7	11.9	15.5
21 193	...	7	Perry	339.7	27 343	1 519	80.5	96.7	2.2	0.6	0.7	1.0	6.7	15.5	7.2	12.5	12.7	13.9
21 195	...	7	Pike	786.8	60 555	863	77.0	97.7	1.1	0.4	0.7	0.8	5.5	15.2	8.3	11.9	14.1	14.1
21 197	...	6	Powell	179.0	12 308	2 272	68.8	97.2	1.3	0.7	0.4	1.5	6.7	17.4	8.0	12.2	13.0	14.0
21 199	43700	5	Pulaski	658.4	63 956	827	97.1	95.4	1.6	0.7	0.9	2.4	5.7	16.6	7.3	11.7	12.3	14.0
21 201	...	8	Robertson	99.9	2 155	3 035	21.6	98.1	0.8	0.7	0.3	1.3	5.3	14.4	7.9	8.9	11.5	15.0
21 203	40080	7	Rockcastle	316.5	16 850	1 988	53.2	98.3	0.6	0.9	0.3	0.8	5.4	16.4	7.8	11.4	12.0	15.3
21 205	...	7	Rowan	279.8	24 451	1 624	87.4	95.4	2.3	0.5	1.0	1.8	5.4	13.5	23.4	11.7	10.1	11.4
21 207	...	9	Russell	253.7	17 722	1 932	69.9	94.9	1.3	0.7	0.6	3.6	6.2	16.4	7.3	10.7	11.6	14.0
21 209	30460	2	Scott	281.8	53 972	931	191.5	88.8	6.5	0.5	1.6	4.3	6.5	18.8	10.4	13.0	14.4	14.1
21 211	31140	1	Shelby	379.6	46 408	1 040	122.3	82.3	8.4	0.7	1.6	9.1	6.7	17.3	8.5	12.3	13.2	14.4
21 213	...	6	Simpson	234.2	18 083	1 915	77.2	86.8	10.7	0.8	1.3	2.4	6.3	18.0	8.2	12.3	12.1	13.5
21 215	31140	1	Spencer	186.7	18 274	1 902	97.9	95.5	2.3	0.7	0.7	2.1	5.7	17.8	7.3	10.4	14.1	16.8
21 217	15820	7	Taylor	266.3	25 397	1 590	95.4	91.5	6.3	0.6	1.1	2.3	6.3	16.0	11.9	12.2	10.4	12.4
21 219	...	8	Todd	374.5	12 295	2 273	32.8	87.7	8.9	0.8	0.5	3.8	7.0	19.7	7.9	12.1	11.8	13.2
21 221	17300	2	Trigg	441.4	14 264	2 148	32.3	89.9	8.2	0.9	0.8	2.1	5.2	16.3	6.6	9.8	10.8	14.1
21 223	31140	1	Trimble	151.6	8 620	2 539	56.9	95.7	1.1	0.8	1.0	2.9	5.6	16.8	8.2	10.9	12.5	15.5
21 225	...	6	Union	342.8	14 880	2 109	43.4	83.5	14.5	0.6	1.1	1.9	5.4	13.9	16.4	11.2	11.6	12.1
21 227	14540	3	Warren	541.6	125 532	500	231.8	81.8	10.4	0.6	4.2	5.2	6.4	16.2	16.6	13.3	12.2	11.8
21 229	...	9	Washington	297.3	12 189	2 280	41.0	89.1	6.7	0.5	0.9	4.2	6.2	16.9	9.5	10.6	11.7	14.1
21 231	...	7	Wayne	458.2	20 453	1 804	44.6	94.7	2.3	0.6	0.6	3.0	5.5	15.5	7.6	11.5	12.2	13.8
21 233	...	8	Webster	331.9	13 316	2 212	40.1	90.0	4.7	0.7	0.8	5.3	6.4	17.0	7.6	11.8	12.6	13.1
21 235	30940	7	Whitley	437.8	36 096	1 272	82.4	97.2	1.2	0.8	0.7	1.2	7.5	17.3	11.2	11.8	11.6	12.7
21 237	...	9	Wolfe	222.2	7 159	2 656	32.2	98.2	0.7	0.7	0.3	1.0	5.8	17.5	6.7	11.0	12.3	13.6
21 239	30460	2	Woodford	188.8	26 124	1 557	138.4	87.5	5.8	0.5	1.0	6.6	5.7	16.7	8.0	10.6	12.1	14.4
22 000	...	0	**LOUISIANA**	43 206.7	4 681 666	X	108.4	60.2	32.9	1.1	2.2	5.0	6.6	17.2	9.5	14.6	12.3	12.6
22 001	29180	2	Acadia	655.1	62 645	841	95.6	78.9	18.9	0.6	0.6	2.4	7.0	19.3	8.4	13.5	11.7	12.9
22 003	...	6	Allen	761.8	25 684	1 578	33.7	72.7	23.2	2.8	0.9	2.0	6.4	16.4	8.1	15.9	13.8	13.5
22 005	12940	2	Ascension	290.0	121 587	514	419.3	70.0	23.4	0.7	1.9	5.2	7.3	20.2	8.1	14.1	14.0	14.0
22 007	...	6	Assumption	338.7	22 695	1 696	67.0	66.5	30.1	0.9	0.5	2.9	5.6	16.5	8.6	12.6	11.7	14.0
22 009	...	6	Avoyelles	832.4	41 117	1 151	49.4	66.4	30.6	1.8	1.1	1.8	6.7	17.2	8.2	13.7	12.2	12.9
22 011	19760	6	Beauregard	1 157.3	36 927	1 253	31.9	82.0	13.4	1.9	1.2	3.7	6.7	18.1	8.6	13.5	12.6	12.8
22 013	...	6	Bienville	811.3	13 865	2 177	17.1	55.8	42.3	1.0	0.5	1.8	6.5	16.4	8.1	12.0	13.3	13.2
22 015	43340	2	Bossier	840.2	126 057	498	150.0	69.1	22.8	1.0	2.8	6.6	7.1	18.1	9.1	15.5	13.1	11.9
22 017	43340	2	Caddo	878.5	248 851	270	283.3	46.4	49.7	0.9	1.7	2.8	7.0	17.2	8.7	14.2	11.9	11.9
22 019	29340	3	Calcasieu	1 064.3	200 601	330	188.5	69.5	26.3	1.1	1.7	3.3	6.9	17.9	8.9	14.8	12.0	12.3
22 021	...	8	Caldwell	529.4	10 087	2 429	19.1	80.0	16.9	0.8	0.4	2.9	6.5	16.9	8.1	13.1	12.4	13.0
22 023	29340	3	Cameron	1 284.9	6 882	2 684	5.4	91.7	4.5	1.0	0.4	3.5	5.1	17.1	8.5	12.5	11.5	14.5
22 025	...	9	Catahoula	708.0	9 921	2 437	14.0	67.3	31.2	0.8	0.3	1.6	5.7	16.1	8.6	14.7	12.0	11.9
22 027	...	6	Claiborne	754.9	16 132	2 032	21.4	46.3	51.8	0.9	0.8	1.5	5.3	13.3	8.2	15.4	12.5	13.7
22 029	35020	7	Concordia	697.0	19 920	1 833	28.6	57.8	40.4	0.7	0.6	1.5	6.4	17.7	8.8	13.6	11.5	12.0
22 031	43340	2	De Soto	876.4	27 149	1 525	31.0	59.5	37.0	1.4	0.6	2.8	6.2	17.8	7.9	12.1	12.0	13.0
22 033	12940	2	East Baton Rouge	455.3	447 037	156	981.9	46.1	46.8	0.6	3.8	4.0	6.6	16.1	14.2	14.9	11.6	11.4
22 035	...	7	East Carroll	420.7	7 271	2 647	17.3	28.5	68.5	0.7	0.8	2.5	7.7	17.4	10.1	14.5	11.8	12.0
22 037	12940	2	East Feliciana	453.4	19 683	1 843	43.4	53.9	44.3	0.9	0.5	1.7	5.1	14.0	8.4	12.9	12.2	14.3
22 039	...	6	Evangeline	662.4	33 709	1 334	50.9	67.9	28.3	0.6	0.6	3.7	7.2	18.5	9.8	13.4	11.4	12.8
22 041	...	7	Franklin	624.6	20 330	1 816	32.5	66.1	32.2	0.5	0.6	1.5	6.7	18.7	8.1	12.5	11.3	12.1
22 043	10780	3	Grant	643.0	22 365	1 713	34.8	78.2	16.1	1.7	0.6	4.9	5.9	15.6	7.9	17.0	14.5	12.9
22 045	29180	2	Iberia	574.1	73 273	745	127.6	60.4	33.1	0.8	3.3	4.1	7.3	19.3	8.8	13.1	11.3	12.9
22 047	12940	2	Iberville	618.6	32 920	1 358	53.2	48.5	48.8	0.5	0.5	2.6	6.0	15.2	8.9	15.0	12.8	14.2
22 049	...	6	Jackson	569.2	15 808	2 056	27.8	68.7	29.7	0.9	0.7	1.6	5.6	16.3	8.0	13.2	11.8	12.8
22 051	35380	1	Jefferson	295.6	436 523	161	1 476.7	54.5	27.0	0.8	4.7	14.5	6.3	15.6	7.9	14.8	12.4	13.1
22 053	27660	6	Jefferson Davis	651.4	31 413	1 399	48.2	80.0	17.9	1.1	0.6	2.4	7.1	18.6	8.4	12.6	11.6	12.7
22 055	29180	2	Lafayette	268.7	241 398	277	898.4	67.3	26.7	0.7	2.2	4.6	6.9	16.9	9.6	17.1	12.9	12.3
22 057	26380	3	Lafourche	1 068.3	98 305	603	92.0	78.3	14.3	3.5	1.2	4.4	6.4	17.0	9.0	14.5	12.1	13.8
22 059	...	6	La Salle	624.7	15 052	2 094	24.1	83.8	12.5	1.7	0.3	2.7	6.1	17.2	8.7	14.3	12.7	12.2
22 061	40820	4	Lincoln	471.7	47 745	1 023	101.2	54.4	41.3	0.7	1.9	2.9	5.7	14.3	25.7	12.8	9.4	9.4
22 063	12940	2	Livingston	648.2	140 138	459	216.2	89.1	6.7	0.8	1.0	3.6	6.9	19.2	8.0	14.7	13.8	13.3
22 065	...	7	Madison	624.4	11 528	2 317	18.5	34.8	62.9	0.7	0.4	2.1	7.6	17.1	9.5	16.3	11.5	12.4
22 067	12820	6	Morehouse	794.9	26 071	1 560	32.8	50.4	48.0	0.6	0.8	1.3	6.8	17.3	8.1	12.3	11.3	12.3
22 069	35060	6	Natchitoches	1 252.3	39 162	1 199	31.3	54.8	42.1	1.9	1.0	2.3	6.5	17.1	16.5	11.5	10.1	10.8

1. CBSA = Core Based Statistical Area. See Appendix A for explanation. See Appendix B for list of metropolitan areas with component counties. 2. County type code from the Economic Research Service of USDA Rural-Urban Continuum Codes. See Appendix A for definition. 3. Dry land or land partially or temporarily covered by water. 4. May be of any race.

Table B. States and Counties — Population and Households

STATE County	55 to 64 years	65 to 74 years	75 years and over	Percent female	2000	2010	2000–2010	2010–2016	Births	Deaths	Net migration	Number	Persons per household	Family households	Female family householder[1]	One person
	16	17	18	19	20	21	22	23	24	25	26	27	28	29	30	31
KENTUCKY—Cont'd																
Ohio	13.3	10.1	7.1	50.0	22 916	23 842	4.0	2.2	1 796	1 679	475	8 813	2.70	73.4	11.2	23.0
Oldham	12.5	8.4	4.1	47.0	46 178	60 329	30.6	8.7	3 321	2 317	4 238	19 706	2.98	81.2	9.1	16.1
Owen	15.6	10.6	6.5	50.2	10 547	10 835	2.7	-1.8	650	656	-145	4 123	2.59	69.8	10.2	26.9
Owsley	14.9	10.8	7.5	51.5	4 858	4 755	-2.1	-5.6	315	463	-104	1 773	2.56	67.2	16.9	32.0
Pendleton	14.9	9.4	5.7	49.3	14 390	14 876	3.4	-2.1	1 035	913	-421	5 356	2.67	70.2	9.2	24.6
Perry	14.8	10.3	6.4	50.8	29 390	28 712	-2.3	-4.8	2 475	2 617	-1 272	11 080	2.47	70.5	14.1	25.1
Pike	15.1	10.7	6.7	50.9	68 736	65 024	-5.4	-6.9	4 426	5 128	-3 712	26 124	2.38	68.5	11.9	27.6
Powell	13.5	9.4	5.8	50.5	13 237	12 613	-4.7	-2.4	1 018	978	-318	4 767	2.56	64.1	14.7	31.5
Pulaski	14.0	11.1	7.4	51.0	56 217	63 063	12.2	1.4	4 600	4 857	1 164	25 593	2.45	67.5	14.6	27.5
Robertson	14.8	12.3	9.9	48.9	2 266	2 282	0.7	-5.6	151	203	-79	930	2.31	66.3	11.0	31.1
Rockcastle	14.1	10.9	6.7	51.0	16 582	17 056	2.9	-1.2	1 110	1 285	-18	6 621	2.51	70.2	13.3	26.3
Rowan	11.0	7.7	5.8	51.3	22 094	23 333	5.6	4.8	1 726	1 369	734	8 542	2.44	60.5	10.8	31.6
Russell	14.4	11.1	8.2	51.0	16 315	17 568	7.7	0.9	1 342	1 394	259	7 050	2.48	63.8	12.3	32.8
Scott	11.6	7.2	4.1	50.9	33 061	47 183	42.7	14.4	4 007	2 038	4 689	18 421	2.65	73.7	12.7	21.8
Shelby	13.2	9.2	5.3	51.5	33 337	42 056	26.2	10.3	3 882	2 077	2 561	15 888	2.67	74.4	11.2	21.7
Simpson	13.2	9.9	6.6	51.1	16 405	17 327	5.6	4.4	1 411	1 136	503	6 793	2.56	67.4	11.4	27.9
Spencer	14.8	8.9	4.3	49.5	11 766	17 058	45.0	7.1	1 243	813	773	6 418	2.72	80.6	9.5	15.9
Taylor	13.2	10.0	7.7	51.5	22 927	24 512	6.9	3.6	2 022	1 836	671	9 715	2.46	65.5	14.9	30.2
Todd	12.4	9.5	6.5	50.5	11 971	12 460	4.1	-1.3	1 058	822	-433	4 567	2.70	71.9	12.2	25.4
Trigg	15.3	13.5	8.5	50.8	12 597	14 334	13.8	-0.5	874	1 088	167	6 014	2.35	69.6	12.7	24.6
Trimble	13.9	10.4	6.1	49.5	8 125	8 809	8.4	-2.1	618	525	-274	3 548	2.46	68.5	8.0	26.4
Union	13.7	9.6	6.2	47.5	15 637	15 007	-4.0	-0.8	1 109	1 032	-207	5 562	2.43	66.9	12.8	29.2
Warren	11.0	7.5	5.0	50.9	92 522	113 781	23.0	10.3	9 706	5 696	7 700	45 387	2.48	65.0	12.3	27.8
Washington	13.5	10.1	7.5	50.8	10 916	11 717	7.3	4.0	846	830	451	4 495	2.56	70.5	13.2	25.8
Wayne	15.0	11.6	7.3	50.5	19 923	20 813	4.5	-1.7	1 413	1 365	-323	7 917	2.57	65.7	11.5	31.4
Webster	14.5	9.9	7.1	50.6	14 120	13 621	-3.5	-2.2	1 046	1 050	-281	5 129	2.54	70.8	9.5	25.9
Whitley	12.4	9.4	6.1	50.5	35 865	35 637	-0.6	1.3	3 466	2 832	-280	13 110	2.60	73.0	14.7	23.0
Wolfe	14.4	11.8	6.8	50.7	7 065	7 355	4.1	-2.7	555	628	-133	2 918	2.45	61.8	12.4	33.1
Woodford	15.4	10.8	6.4	51.7	23 208	24 941	7.5	4.7	1 738	1 364	774	9 802	2.55	69.3	9.4	25.5
LOUISIANA	12.9	8.6	5.8	51.1	4 468 976	4 533 479	1.4	3.3	393 453	267 075	21 958	1 727 919	2.60	65.3	16.6	29.4
Acadia	12.8	8.2	6.0	51.4	58 861	61 770	4.9	1.4	5 520	4 060	-563	22 599	2.70	67.4	15.3	27.9
Allen	11.9	8.2	5.8	43.1	25 440	25 764	1.3	-0.3	2 069	1 559	-552	8 027	2.66	64.8	12.8	32.9
Ascension	11.4	7.1	3.8	50.5	76 627	107 194	39.9	13.4	10 463	4 499	8 211	40 110	2.84	75.8	14.1	20.4
Assumption	14.5	9.8	6.6	51.3	23 388	23 421	0.1	-3.1	1 612	1 379	-922	8 660	2.64	70.5	13.6	25.3
Avoyelles	12.9	9.4	6.9	49.6	41 481	42 073	1.4	-2.3	3 448	3 073	-1 348	14 943	2.52	67.1	16.9	29.0
Beauregard	12.8	9.1	5.9	48.9	32 986	35 654	8.1	3.6	3 076	2 212	409	13 152	2.69	73.5	12.5	23.2
Bienville	14.0	10.5	9.1	52.2	15 752	14 353	-8.9	-3.4	1 138	1 300	-354	5 814	2.35	64.5	18.9	32.0
Bossier	11.7	7.8	5.7	50.5	98 310	116 979	19.0	7.8	11 300	6 105	3 811	47 125	2.57	66.3	14.8	29.6
Caddo	13.2	9.1	6.7	52.6	252 161	254 969	1.1	-2.4	23 387	16 960	-12 287	97 991	2.55	62.6	20.1	33.1
Calcasieu	12.9	8.4	5.8	51.2	183 577	192 770	5.0	4.1	16 979	12 082	3 220	75 325	2.55	67.3	15.5	27.8
Caldwell	13.2	10.1	6.8	48.5	10 560	10 132	-4.1	-0.4	830	769	-103	3 838	2.48	65.0	12.9	32.1
Cameron	15.2	9.2	6.4	50.2	9 991	6 859	-31.3	0.3	407	297	-101	2 608	2.57	77.0	7.5	19.3
Catahoula	14.3	9.7	7.0	46.9	10 920	10 407	-4.7	-4.7	758	821	-422	3 748	2.48	70.7	13.0	27.7
Claiborne	13.7	9.7	8.2	43.5	16 851	17 195	2.0	-6.2	1 076	1 158	-971	5 852	2.51	64.8	19.3	32.7
Concordia	13.6	9.4	6.9	49.1	20 247	20 822	2.8	-4.3	1 664	1 478	-1 080	7 896	2.33	66.4	21.7	30.4
De Soto	13.9	10.2	6.7	51.5	25 494	26 656	4.6	1.8	2 140	1 799	187	10 244	2.61	67.8	17.4	28.1
East Baton Rouge	12.0	8.0	5.2	52.2	412 852	440 178	6.6	1.6	37 850	23 035	-7 312	169 120	2.57	61.0	17.1	31.1
East Carroll	12.7	7.5	6.1	46.0	9 421	7 759	-17.6	-6.3	765	477	-769	2 678	2.26	62.7	29.2	35.5
East Feliciana	15.8	10.9	6.4	45.9	21 360	20 263	-5.1	-2.9	1 339	1 468	-517	6 937	2.43	71.9	18.5	25.6
Evangeline	12.4	8.4	6.2	48.9	35 434	33 984	-4.1	-0.8	3 033	2 316	-961	11 954	2.65	67.8	19.0	28.6
Franklin	13.2	9.7	7.8	51.5	21 263	20 767	-2.3	-2.1	1 730	1 668	-463	7 469	2.54	65.5	18.8	32.0
Grant	11.9	8.8	5.6	43.9	18 698	22 309	19.3	0.3	1 614	1 294	-222	7 197	2.63	66.6	11.9	29.1
Iberia	13.3	8.3	5.8	51.2	73 266	73 240	0.0	0.0	6 752	4 455	-2 232	26 345	2.77	71.8	19.3	24.9
Iberville	13.3	8.7	5.9	49.1	33 320	33 407	0.3	-1.5	2 573	1 922	-1 086	11 191	2.61	68.3	18.4	28.1
Jackson	13.2	10.8	8.2	48.7	15 397	16 274	5.7	-2.9	1 123	1 171	-372	6 038	2.49	71.2	16.8	24.3
Jefferson	13.9	9.4	6.6	51.4	455 466	432 552	-5.0	0.9	35 850	25 662	-5 571	168 104	2.57	63.2	16.2	31.4
Jefferson Davis	13.1	8.8	7.1	51.2	31 435	31 594	0.5	-0.6	2 725	2 304	-613	11 652	2.65	68.5	16.4	27.7
Lafayette	12.3	7.2	4.8	51.1	190 503	221 594	16.3	8.9	20 852	10 622	9 426	88 995	2.55	62.5	14.3	30.2
Lafourche	12.8	8.4	6.0	50.8	89 974	96 596	7.4	1.8	7 691	5 362	-510	35 592	2.68	70.7	14.3	23.7
La Salle	12.5	9.2	7.1	48.4	14 282	14 890	4.3	1.1	1 093	1 042	130	5 551	2.46	71.8	13.9	22.6
Lincoln	9.6	7.4	5.6	51.1	42 509	46 735	9.9	2.2	3 571	2 326	-254	17 169	2.56	58.9	16.1	29.0
Livingston	11.7	7.9	4.5	50.7	91 814	128 040	39.5	9.4	11 449	6 350	6 823	47 608	2.79	73.5	13.2	22.0
Madison	12.0	8.1	5.5	50.3	13 728	12 099	-11.9	-4.7	1 122	830	-879	4 060	2.55	62.5	24.3	34.3
Morehouse	14.1	10.3	7.6	51.8	31 021	27 979	-9.8	-6.8	2 302	2 362	-1 853	10 447	2.50	63.0	17.8	32.8
Natchitoches	11.4	9.3	6.8	52.0	39 080	39 566	1.2	-1.0	3 278	2 431	-1 281	14 456	2.66	61.5	16.9	30.6

1. No spouse present.

Table B. States and Counties — Population, Vital Statistics, Health, and Crime

STATE County	Persons in group quarters, 2016	Daytime population, 2011–2015 Number	Employ-ment/resi-dence ratio	Births, 2016 Total	Rate[1]	Deaths, 2016 Number	Rate[1]	Persons under 65 with no health insurance, 2015 Number	Percent	Medicare, 2015 Total Beneficiaries	Enrolled in Original Medicare	Enrolled in Medicare Advantage	Serious crimes known to police,[2] 2014 Total Number	Rate[3]
	32	33	34	35	36	37	38	39	40	41	42	43	44	45
KENTUCKY—Cont'd														
Ohio	307	23 574	0.94	257	10.5	262	10.7	1 482	7.5	5 103	3 795	1 308	194	806
Oldham	5 113	50 366	0.56	565	8.6	390	5.9	2 218	4.2	7 343	4 946	2 397	586	931
Owen	0	9 064	0.61	96	9.0	106	10.0	576	6.5	1 545	1 013	532	34	320
Owsley	90	4 305	0.73	53	11.8	60	13.4	304	8.4	1 114	886	228	5	110
Pendleton	215	11 257	0.49	180	12.4	152	10.4	770	6.3	2 678	1 683	995	121	870
Perry	611	30 776	1.30	387	14.2	440	16.1	1 824	8.0	7 459	5 793	1 666	400	1 435
Pike	1 615	66 453	1.15	623	10.3	831	13.7	4 232	8.4	16 001	11 786	4 215	666	1 056
Powell	188	10 945	0.63	164	13.3	141	11.5	845	8.2	2 674	1 865	809	160	1 283
Pulaski	962	65 550	1.08	716	11.2	795	12.4	4 170	8.1	16 294	11 743	4 551	1 506	2 357
Robertson	57	1 851	0.55	24	11.1	31	14.4	133	8.1	453	327	126	2	103
Rockcastle	341	15 245	0.71	174	10.3	242	14.4	996	7.2	3 364	2 610	754	68	440
Rowan	3 179	25 390	1.18	266	10.9	204	8.3	1 314	7.2	4 239	2 655	1 584	287	1 216
Russell	177	18 036	1.06	202	11.4	220	12.4	1 309	9.2	4 162	3 169	993	133	746
Scott	1 651	53 762	1.14	653	12.1	384	7.1	2 666	5.9	6 794	4 214	2 580	1 215	2 398
Shelby	1 832	40 414	0.81	628	13.5	308	6.6	3 357	8.8	6 520	4 420	2 100	796	1 781
Simpson	327	18 638	1.13	220	12.2	157	8.7	891	6.0	3 464	2 720	744	439	2 448
Spencer	113	10 954	0.22	219	12.0	150	8.2	924	5.9	2 665	1 844	821	115	646
Taylor	1 378	26 574	1.16	319	12.6	321	12.6	1 435	7.2	6 579	5 181	1 398	592	2 396
Todd	195	10 621	0.59	146	11.9	134	10.9	906	8.8	2 112	1 713	399	134	1 069
Trigg	78	12 733	0.73	131	9.2	172	12.1	888	8.0	3 547	2 581	966	176	1 231
Trimble	41	6 871	0.45	96	11.1	101	11.7	486	6.6	1 657	1 215	442	4	45
Union	1 663	15 569	1.07	188	12.6	178	12.0	975	7.7	2 957	2 236	721	155	1 035
Warren	6 453	126 564	1.14	1 636	13.0	929	7.4	8 151	8.0	20 279	15 395	4 884	3 726	3 115
Washington	426	10 509	0.73	129	10.6	129	10.6	864	8.9	2 327	1 783	544	46	386
Wayne	331	19 610	0.84	221	10.8	197	9.6	1 349	8.3	4 466	3 276	1 190	175	847
Webster	393	12 454	0.82	184	13.8	152	11.4	928	8.7	2 989	2 139	850	51	430
Whitley	1 739	36 010	1.02	571	15.8	442	12.2	2 062	7.1	12 018	9 643	2 375	509	1 420
Wolfe	132	6 737	0.72	82	11.5	103	14.4	487	8.3	1 949	1 383	566	60	830
Woodford	327	22 914	0.81	282	10.8	226	8.7	1 559	7.4	4 705	2 909	1 796	471	1 856
LOUISIANA	128 612	4 637 841	1.01	63 570	13.6	45 030	9.6	538 466	13.8	771 398	513 995	257 403	184 758	3 974
Acadia	1 050	53 717	0.65	875	14.0	668	10.7	8 181	15.3	10 244	8 897	1 347	1 715	2 818
Allen	4 180	25 657	1.00	319	12.4	240	9.3	2 573	14.1	3 955	3 410	545	NA	NA
Ascension	790	101 314	0.75	1 765	14.5	842	6.9	9 839	9.3	14 288	6 045	8 243	3 834	3 300
Assumption	199	17 611	0.41	249	11.0	222	9.8	2 506	13.1	3 964	2 774	1 190	388	1 675
Avoyelles	3 343	37 933	0.76	535	13.0	457	11.1	5 047	15.9	8 024	6 857	1 167	1 401	3 591
Beauregard	1 295	31 968	0.70	498	13.5	378	10.2	4 381	14.6	7 018	6 154	864	650	1 792
Bienville	319	13 547	0.91	188	13.6	204	14.7	1 523	13.8	3 139	2 562	577	267	1 920
Bossier	2 567	116 035	0.88	1 814	14.4	1 050	8.3	12 950	12.1	17 301	13 982	3 319	4 369	3 481
Caddo	6 259	270 220	1.14	3 506	14.1	2 731	11.0	27 764	13.3	45 644	35 411	10 233	11 618	4 625
Calcasieu	3 801	201 227	1.06	2 775	13.8	1 997	10.0	21 744	13.0	34 969	28 886	6 083	9 984	5 095
Caldwell	584	8 962	0.74	154	15.3	125	12.4	1 204	15.4	2 122	1 633	489	263	2 640
Cameron	20	8 118	1.46	66	9.6	62	9.0	757	13.2	534	426	108	150	2 227
Catahoula	866	9 106	0.69	107	10.8	119	12.0	1 249	16.2	2 210	1 834	376	216	2 227
Claiborne	2 913	15 623	0.81	175	10.8	191	11.8	1 676	15.7	2 917	2 408	509	NA	NA
Concordia	1 485	19 812	0.91	267	13.4	247	12.4	2 470	15.9	3 808	3 109	699	833	4 092
De Soto	215	25 242	0.83	330	12.2	284	10.5	3 321	14.9	5 228	4 378	850	851	3 130
East Baton Rouge	11 154	500 281	1.26	6 034	13.5	3 880	8.7	45 105	11.9	66 848	35 337	31 511	20 851	4 669
East Carroll	1 067	7 513	1.01	117	16.1	73	10.0	727	13.9	1 256	966	290	106	1 417
East Feliciana	2 405	17 435	0.65	208	10.6	229	11.6	1 740	12.2	3 876	2 289	1 587	208	1 060
Evangeline	1 380	31 300	0.77	495	14.7	383	11.4	4 296	15.5	6 283	5 691	592	611	2 329
Franklin	732	19 428	0.84	259	12.7	275	13.5	2 751	16.7	3 993	3 179	814	159	812
Grant	2 951	18 344	0.42	268	12.0	180	8.0	2 189	13.4	3 761	3 018	743	191	869
Iberia	944	74 959	1.03	1 113	15.2	770	10.5	9 899	15.7	13 102	11 681	1 421	1 509	2 202
Iberville	3 991	36 714	1.27	406	12.3	292	8.9	3 215	13.0	5 744	2 771	2 973	1 281	3 837
Jackson	1 038	14 085	0.61	178	11.3	210	13.3	1 616	13.4	3 495	2 710	785	NA	NA
Jefferson	3 315	427 641	0.96	5 796	13.3	4 301	9.9	56 690	15.5	78 841	31 506	47 335	17 691	4 062
Jefferson Davis	567	28 062	0.73	456	14.5	399	12.7	3 750	14.2	5 446	4 916	530	509	1 891
Lafayette	5 171	259 528	1.24	3 477	14.4	1 870	7.7	28 105	13.5	32 664	27 715	4 949	10 965	4 921
Lafourche	1 630	94 735	0.93	1 245	12.7	863	8.8	13 335	16.1	15 147	11 243	3 904	2 453	2 520
La Salle	1 243	14 422	0.91	180	12.0	177	11.8	1 578	13.8	2 675	2 260	415	70	474
Lincoln	4 936	47 963	1.03	565	11.8	413	8.7	5 937	16.0	6 870	5 461	1 409	1 512	3 556
Livingston	1 192	101 393	0.46	1 864	13.3	1 115	8.0	14 497	12.1	18 708	8 414	10 294	4 467	3 308
Madison	1 596	11 404	0.88	181	15.7	158	13.7	1 253	14.8	1 673	1 434	239	460	3 958
Morehouse	768	24 197	0.71	367	14.1	367	14.1	3 039	14.3	6 113	4 418	1 695	1 697	6 315
Natchitoches	2 205	38 868	0.97	494	12.6	403	10.3	4 439	14.2	6 980	5 847	1 133	2 051	5 249

1. Per 1,000 estimated resident population.   2. Data for serious crimes have not been adjusted for underreporting; this may affect comparability between geographic areas and over time.
3. Per 100,000 population estimated by the FBI.

Table B. States and Counties — Crime, Education, Money Income, and Poverty

STATE County	Serious crimes known to police, 2014 (cont.)[1] Rate[2] Violent	Property	Education — Enrollment[3] Total	Percent private	High school graduate or less	Bachelor's degree or more	Local government expenditures,[5] 2013–2014 Total current spending (mil dol)	Current spending per student (dollars)	Money income, 2011–2015 Per capita income[6] (dollars)	Households Median income (dollars)	Percent with income of less than $50,000	with income of $200,000 or more	Income and poverty, 2015 Median household income (dollars)	Percent below poverty level All persons	Children under 18 years	Children 5 to 17 years in families
	46	47	48	49	50	51	52	53	54	55	56	57	58	59	60	61
KENTUCKY—Cont'd																
Ohio	83	723	5 424	9.4	64.4	9.7	35.0	8 218	19 254	40 189	62.8	1.3	40 661	19.9	27.5	25.4
Oldham	49	882	18 301	17.7	30.9	39.4	99.6	8 116	34 423	85 452	26.7	10.2	84 415	6.2	6.7	5.5
Owen	0	320	2 489	11.5	63.1	12.2	15.8	8 199	22 878	41 934	58.5	1.9	43 686	16.9	25.4	22.4
Owsley	0	110	1 012	6.4	66.6	16.6	9.6	11 816	15 158	20 985	68.5	0.1	23 341	42.4	61.6	60.0
Pendleton	14	856	3 248	12.2	64.0	10.8	21.9	8 796	23 725	48 353	51.0	1.6	49 345	16.4	23.5	21.4
Perry	57	1 377	6 120	5.7	59.1	14.0	48.8	9 354	18 910	32 667	64.4	1.2	31 740	28.5	37.2	38.8
Pike	17	1 039	13 681	10.0	62.9	13.3	102.2	34 388	20 061	33 183	66.3	1.7	34 315	25.0	32.0	30.0
Powell	56	1 227	2 792	12.2	66.6	13.0	22.4	8 886	17 241	29 736	64.8	1.0	34 510	26.0	39.3	38.6
Pulaski	106	2 251	14 088	7.2	60.2	14.4	87.5	7 916	20 215	34 790	65.4	1.6	40 702	23.0	31.7	29.6
Robertson	0	103	409	5.1	61.5	16.0	3.5	9 529	19 246	31 741	67.4	0.0	40 027	22.5	36.7	29.9
Rockcastle	78	363	3 907	7.0	67.3	9.8	26.2	8 891	16 963	31 555	69.0	1.1	33 293	22.9	32.4	29.9
Rowan	25	1 190	8 126	5.7	49.0	26.9	28.4	8 927	18 185	36 860	62.9	0.6	36 597	27.2	32.4	30.2
Russell	62	684	3 674	9.2	61.8	12.4	26.9	8 630	17 010	30 720	71.6	0.6	31 968	24.6	35.8	34.6
Scott	150	2 248	13 634	23.4	41.6	27.8	70.7	8 058	28 232	63 027	40.3	3.3	63 775	13.1	18.1	17.2
Shelby	114	1 667	10 956	17.1	45.6	23.8	64.1	9 032	27 631	60 324	42.7	4.9	60 189	11.5	17.1	16.1
Simpson	139	2 309	4 066	14.4	58.1	15.1	26.1	8 715	19 397	39 679	59.8	0.8	45 496	16.0	26.2	25.0
Spencer	34	613	4 441	22.4	47.7	18.5	23.2	7 938	27 016	63 000	34.3	2.3	68 147	9.0	11.9	10.4
Taylor	125	2 271	6 104	21.7	58.0	15.8	33.7	8 898	18 120	33 340	67.0	0.9	35 700	23.0	33.8	35.2
Todd	56	1 013	2 967	15.7	64.6	10.8	18.8	8 652	19 042	40 497	59.7	1.1	40 963	19.3	28.1	26.9
Trigg	70	1 161	3 222	9.2	47.5	17.6	19.2	9 012	26 001	44 083	54.7	2.1	45 106	15.1	26.5	24.4
Trimble	0	45	2 049	14.2	63.2	10.3	13.4	9 783	23 465	47 409	52.7	0.3	48 392	15.7	22.3	19.8
Union	120	914	3 857	21.1	57.0	11.3	22.6	9 553	20 164	40 120	60.6	1.4	45 239	20.7	20.7	19.1
Warren	198	2 917	36 780	6.6	43.5	28.1	152.7	8 212	23 823	44 911	53.8	2.4	45 964	18.0	22.9	22.6
Washington	25	361	3 031	23.8	61.5	14.5	15.0	8 956	19 793	40 976	59.9	1.0	45 143	17.1	23.6	22.5
Wayne	58	789	4 257	5.4	65.9	10.0	31.3	9 109	15 475	28 573	75.0	0.5	29 826	28.0	40.3	36.8
Webster	42	388	2 831	10.2	63.7	9.2	18.9	8 248	19 891	38 917	60.9	0.7	44 245	18.1	24.9	24.4
Whitley	98	1 323	9 029	18.1	61.3	15.9	73.8	8 868	16 748	31 014	69.4	1.4	31 903	29.2	38.9	40.0
Wolfe	69	760	1 567	10.4	71.1	11.9	13.4	9 940	13 901	20 504	77.7	1.0	27 196	30.7	50.4	48.0
Woodford	55	1 801	6 579	16.8	39.8	32.9	36.0	8 755	30 490	58 750	43.9	4.8	57 862	11.6	17.0	15.5
LOUISIANA	515	3 459	1 183 921	18.9	50.5	22.5	7 665.2	10 774	24 981	45 047	54.0	3.5	45 829	19.5	28.1	26.7
Acadia	414	2 404	15 169	20.2	65.5	10.5	92.5	9 166	20 552	37 649	60.1	1.8	42 033	23.7	32.5	30.4
Allen	NA	NA	5 546	9.0	64.6	11.6	46.6	10 737	19 868	40 948	59.4	1.4	42 120	20.4	24.3	23.7
Ascension	334	2 966	31 602	18.0	46.5	26.0	221.3	10 356	29 269	70 551	36.1	4.0	74 852	10.7	14.8	13.9
Assumption	263	1 412	5 344	17.8	66.7	10.7	43.7	11 326	23 886	49 167	50.9	2.2	48 516	16.8	25.2	23.3
Avoyelles	643	2 948	9 377	15.2	68.8	9.5	62.0	9 421	18 967	33 739	63.9	1.6	34 803	25.3	34.7	32.6
Beauregard	116	1 676	8 186	9.9	58.8	15.1	63.8	10 615	22 961	45 969	52.4	2.5	48 206	19.5	24.8	22.7
Bienville	316	1 604	3 205	6.1	60.7	11.2	32.7	14 559	20 464	32 876	64.6	0.6	34 565	25.4	37.4	34.4
Bossier	409	3 071	31 462	11.9	41.1	25.7	213.6	9 780	27 572	52 892	47.1	3.4	55 403	14.5	20.4	19.9
Caddo	603	4 022	63 766	13.3	47.0	23.8	448.6	10 826	24 876	41 234	57.4	3.5	41 081	22.2	34.8	33.3
Calcasieu	555	4 541	50 466	14.0	50.0	20.7	345.5	10 360	25 005	45 312	53.5	3.2	46 523	17.5	26.0	25.9
Caldwell	231	2 409	2 363	9.1	68.1	10.2	18.1	11 085	21 493	33 294	65.1	1.7	38 564	22.9	32.8	31.9
Cameron	223	2 004	1 531	5.6	55.6	15.8	26.5	20 694	29 679	64 231	37.2	5.5	56 259	12.7	17.6	15.9
Catahoula	289	1 938	2 020	9.5	67.4	12.3	17.6	12 038	21 851	34 904	61.6	3.4	33 958	27.2	37.0	36.0
Claiborne	NA	NA	3 305	14.8	64.4	12.8	19.3	11 194	17 547	32 072	66.8	1.2	33 740	30.9	37.1	32.3
Concordia	845	3 247	4 589	10.5	64.8	11.6	40.3	10 322	17 498	29 654	66.3	0.7	33 068	29.5	41.6	39.4
De Soto	382	2 747	6 431	9.5	60.7	12.1	78.0	15 334	22 513	41 468	58.3	2.2	41 691	24.9	38.7	38.4
East Baton Rouge	565	4 103	131 364	19.9	37.3	34.1	708.9	11 758	27 944	49 285	50.6	4.7	50 389	18.5	26.5	25.1
East Carroll	535	882	1 827	10.5	69.7	8.8	13.1	11 785	11 313	21 099	81.5	0.6	26 325	43.5	56.1	57.8
East Feliciana	331	728	4 042	18.1	61.6	12.3	22.9	11 535	21 348	45 520	54.5	1.9	43 105	21.8	27.6	27.1
Evangeline	213	2 116	8 213	16.1	65.2	12.6	58.2	9 484	18 484	30 009	66.2	2.1	33 407	25.7	32.1	30.4
Franklin	51	761	5 020	19.1	67.0	10.8	30.7	9 800	17 324	30 275	66.5	1.3	33 845	25.4	40.7	37.7
Grant	68	801	4 651	11.9	63.8	8.6	28.6	9 098	17 987	39 914	59.6	1.4	43 437	21.3	28.1	26.2
Iberia	209	1 993	18 237	17.4	64.6	13.0	131.1	9 364	23 977	45 261	54.8	3.0	45 039	20.8	32.7	30.6
Iberville	1 072	2 765	7 505	17.6	62.0	13.1	69.9	14 982	21 428	45 117	53.5	1.7	42 000	22.3	30.7	28.9
Jackson	NA	NA	3 422	12.5	63.0	13.0	23.6	10 180	18 986	38 029	63.4	0.8	41 029	21.1	30.8	28.5
Jefferson	441	3 621	104 422	32.3	46.6	24.6	498.2	10 660	27 127	47 947	51.7	3.9	49 503	16.3	27.1	26.2
Jefferson Davis	238	1 653	7 996	9.6	62.3	14.0	61.1	10 391	22 260	39 063	59.9	2.9	43 677	20.3	27.2	26.8
Lafayette	569	4 353	61 914	22.3	42.5	29.9	317.5	10 254	30 240	51 869	47.7	6.0	52 411	17.0	20.7	19.9
Lafourche	139	2 382	24 132	17.3	64.7	15.4	153.0	10 327	25 303	51 030	49.0	3.0	53 482	14.1	20.0	19.2
La Salle	217	258	3 110	12.4	65.5	11.7	27.1	10 195	20 818	37 310	58.9	1.6	46 258	18.5	21.8	19.7
Lincoln	393	3 163	18 128	10.2	41.0	35.6	69.4	10 572	21 003	33 467	61.9	2.9	38 118	25.5	29.8	29.5
Livingston	446	2 862	34 775	9.7	56.0	18.3	222.4	8 688	25 999	58 251	43.2	2.5	58 774	13.5	17.6	17.1
Madison	585	3 373	2 521	11.0	63.9	11.4	23.2	12 641	14 205	23 854	75.5	0.6	27 225	37.6	52.7	54.7
Morehouse	554	5 761	5 671	13.1	64.4	12.7	51.8	11 523	18 209	28 003	71.6	1.6	31 777	31.1	50.0	47.0
Natchitoches	619	4 630	12 209	15.1	51.0	20.4	80.8	11 492	19 883	31 345	66.2	2.1	33 786	29.6	36.2	36.0

1. Data for serious crimes have not been adjusted for underreporting; this may affect comparability between geographic areas and over time. 2. Per 100,000 population estimated by the FBI.
3. All persons 3 years old and over enrolled in nursery school through college. 4. Persons 25 years old and over. 5. Elementary and secondary education expenditures.
6. Based on population estimated by the American Community Survey, 2011–2015.

Table B. States and Counties — **Personal Income**

STATE County	Personal income, 2015 Total (mil dol)	Percent change, 2014–2015	Per capita[1] Dollars	Rank	Wages and salaries (mil dol)	Supplements to wages and salaries; employer contributions (mil dol) Pension and insurance	Government social insurance	Proprietors' income (mil dol)	Dividends, interest, and rent (mil dol)	Personal transfer receipts (mil dol)	Earnings, 2015 Total (mil dol)	Contributions for government social insurance (mil dol) From employee and self-employed	From employer
	62	63	64	65	66	67	68	69	70	71	72	73	74
KENTUCKY—Cont'd													
Ohio	766	3.0	31 613	2 502	257	58	21	54	88	247	389	26	21
Oldham	3 482	5.9	53 671	355	665	120	50	166	587	373	1 000	63	50
Owen	371	6.9	34 589	2 375	67	17	5	23	39	103	113	9	5
Owsley	128	6.1	28 741	2 964	21	7	2	5	11	79	34	3	2
Pendleton	489	3.9	33 951	2 528	99	20	7	21	67	128	147	11	7
Perry	969	2.4	35 148	2 009	473	95	37	39	119	425	643	42	37
Pike	2 061	1.3	33 354	2 139	935	166	74	77	236	829	1 252	89	74
Powell	375	6.5	30 572	2 726	84	21	7	11	35	152	123	10	7
Pulaski	2 285	5.5	35 823	2 174	933	181	76	134	260	848	1 324	90	76
Robertson	64	0.7	30 034	2 856	8	3	1	2	7	24	14	1	1
Rockcastle	494	6.4	29 138	2 948	119	28	10	15	45	195	173	14	10
Rowan	692	4.9	28 951	2 907	352	88	27	27	84	236	494	30	27
Russell	564	3.3	31 907	2 729	171	40	14	90	79	209	315	22	14
Scott	2 066	6.4	39 415	1 483	1 386	201	108	74	225	323	1 769	106	108
Shelby	1 808	6.2	39 613	1 491	644	116	53	83	279	319	895	57	53
Simpson	615	5.0	34 139	2 252	334	58	27	57	81	168	476	30	27
Spencer	722	6.3	40 375	1 622	71	16	5	29	64	132	121	10	5
Taylor	847	5.7	33 309	2 485	390	74	32	49	114	275	545	36	32
Todd	443	0.0	35 344	2 039	84	19	7	68	57	110	177	11	7
Trigg	498	3.9	34 991	2 111	106	23	9	25	76	144	164	13	9
Trimble	295	5.2	33 644	2 529	48	12	4	6	29	82	70	6	4
Union	516	-3.7	34 286	1 907	226	40	18	22	77	152	306	21	18
Warren	4 418	5.5	35 966	2 054	2 578	467	200	354	622	962	3 599	213	200
Washington	443	6.5	36 694	1 985	131	26	10	24	62	115	192	13	10
Wayne	563	4.6	27 508	3 026	173	39	15	29	71	240	255	19	15
Webster	486	-0.8	36 870	1 677	181	35	13	59	59	133	288	17	13
Whitley	1 160	5.9	32 100	2 673	463	91	39	47	128	501	641	46	39
Wolfe	191	4.9	26 264	3 052	38	10	3	5	17	114	56	5	3
Woodford	1 166	5.4	45 213	720	421	74	32	43	233	198	570	36	32
LOUISIANA	200 594	3.2	42 963	X	97 087	16 253	6 279	21 014	33 557	40 818	140 633	7 612	6 279
Acadia	2 211	-1.6	35 335	1 170	567	106	36	178	317	548	888	53	36
Allen	764	3.6	29 735	2 714	309	73	18	41	96	208	441	22	18
Ascension	5 431	5.1	45 469	345	2 647	416	171	242	574	742	3 475	193	171
Assumption	886	1.3	38 791	1 266	190	35	12	31	105	205	269	18	12
Avoyelles	1 392	1.4	33 859	2 101	365	80	22	104	186	454	570	33	22
Beauregard	1 462	4.0	40 088	1 376	385	71	24	58	196	334	538	33	24
Bienville	448	2.7	32 500	2 027	175	36	11	15	67	163	238	15	11
Bossier	5 329	5.5	42 574	1 141	2 109	428	156	674	826	1 025	3 367	168	156
Caddo	12 342	3.2	49 080	769	5 433	940	363	2 725	2 345	2 438	9 460	491	363
Calcasieu	8 476	6.9	42 639	1 171	4 607	820	301	738	1 242	1 700	6 465	351	301
Caldwell	363	5.1	36 373	2 052	86	19	5	20	39	112	131	8	5
Cameron	312	2.4	45 776	837	572	69	33	21	62	40	695	38	33
Catahoula	292	-6.0	28 728	2 565	76	17	5	31	42	111	129	8	5
Claiborne	587	1.7	36 034	2 364	152	34	9	112	91	163	307	16	9
Concordia	631	-1.5	31 309	2 497	199	43	12	41	105	209	295	17	12
De Soto	1 017	3.9	37 595	1 580	363	66	21	42	192	265	492	30	21
East Baton Rouge	20 500	3.1	45 887	835	14 367	2 319	901	1 638	3 879	3 583	19 225	994	901
East Carroll	226	-8.8	30 938	1 998	67	15	4	13	40	93	99	5	4
East Feliciana	740	5.7	37 578	1 708	215	55	10	30	102	220	310	16	10
Evangeline	1 179	0.9	34 937	1 980	308	63	20	78	147	361	469	29	20
Franklin	618	4.3	30 266	2 555	164	38	10	52	78	238	264	16	10
Grant	660	3.5	29 548	2 765	150	39	11	31	77	190	231	15	11
Iberia	2 830	-1.0	38 194	1 229	1 625	244	102	197	474	677	2 168	123	102
Iberville	1 217	3.9	36 764	1 697	1 039	184	65	43	158	304	1 330	72	65
Jackson	540	1.3	34 050	2 084	163	34	10	46	62	163	252	15	10
Jefferson	20 471	3.1	46 922	598	10 140	1 409	661	2 287	3 782	3 757	14 496	822	661
Jefferson Davis	1 218	3.6	38 743	1 292	347	68	22	80	165	285	517	30	22
Lafayette	11 884	-1.8	49 496	307	7 284	1 001	470	1 918	2 195	1 681	10 674	567	470
Lafourche	4 513	-3.0	45 899	184	2 151	360	135	187	987	774	2 833	157	135
La Salle	533	-3.7	35 603	1 609	175	38	10	35	60	139	258	14	10
Lincoln	1 702	5.6	35 628	2 107	723	139	44	236	336	364	1 142	57	44
Livingston	5 249	5.5	38 095	1 739	1 056	189	69	287	487	959	1 601	98	69
Madison	319	-3.0	27 712	2 902	114	27	7	32	40	117	180	9	7
Morehouse	890	0.9	33 714	2 205	235	47	16	69	112	339	367	23	16
Natchitoches	1 369	4.3	34 937	1 873	499	111	29	151	194	375	790	40	29

1. Based on the resident population estimated as of July 1 of the year shown.

Table B. States and Counties — Earnings, Social Security, and Housing

STATE County	Earnings, 2015 (cont.) Percent by selected industries									Social Security beneficiaries, December 2015		Supplemental Security Income recipients, December 2015	Housing units, 2016	
	Farm	Mining	Construction	Manufacturing	Information: professional, scientific, technical services	Retail trade	Finance, insurance, real estate and leasing	Health care and social assistance	Government	Number	Rate[1]		Total	Percent change, 2010–2016
	75	76	77	78	79	80	81	82	83	84	85	86	87	88
KENTUCKY—Cont'd														
Ohio	3.9	D	6.1	33.0	D	6.2	2.0	D	21.5	6 265	259	1 091	10 264	0.4
Oldham	0.2	D	10.2	6.8	10.5	5.2	14.0	12.7	19.7	9 295	144	523	21 699	4.9
Owen	2.6	0.0	8.3	D	D	5.1	D	8.7	22.9	2 630	246	404	5 639	0.1
Owsley	-1.5	D	5.9	D	D	D	4.5	16.6	49.2	1 210	271	830	2 327	0.0
Pendleton	-0.9	D	D	16.0	D	3.3	3.3	8.0	23.3	3 275	226	522	6 310	-0.4
Perry	0.0	D	2.1	0.4	D	8.8	3.7	D	20.4	7 870	286	2 929	12 798	0.1
Pike	-0.1	14.3	3.7	3.3	5.8	9.3	4.6	23.2	14.9	18 860	305	4 867	30 339	0.1
Powell	-0.8	D	D	11.5	D	9.4	2.6	9.7	30.5	3 460	282	1 067	5 594	-0.1
Pulaski	0.3	D	5.9	15.3	4.4	8.6	4.0	21.8	15.5	18 035	283	3 878	31 124	-1.0
Robertson	-3.9	0.0	9.7	1.4	D	D	D	17.9	43.2	520	241	109	1 090	-0.5
Rockcastle	0.2	D	D	3.5	D	4.9	2.9	29.6	23.4	4 320	255	1 166	7 694	-0.1
Rowan	0.1	D	3.6	9.7	1.9	8.1	3.7	D	34.9	5 010	203	1 217	10 156	0.5
Russell	1.9	0.6	D	28.5	D	8.0	3.7	D	17.2	4 825	274	1 195	9 958	-0.4
Scott	0.6	D	3.1	50.1	3.2	3.0	1.6	5.5	7.1	8 180	156	1 019	21 240	10.0
Shelby	-0.2	D	5.0	29.8	D	7.7	4.4	7.4	14.0	8 350	183	750	17 472	5.3
Simpson	3.6	0.0	4.8	39.9	D	9.8	2.8	D	10.2	4 170	232	507	7 629	2.6
Spencer	-0.6	0.0	14.4	D	D	8.5	5.7	10.6	28.6	3 370	187	312	7 065	5.4
Taylor	1.5	0.0	D	10.5	2.2	7.8	5.0	D	20.0	6 635	260	1 277	10 970	1.0
Todd	18.2	0.5	8.5	13.8	D	6.4	4.2	D	16.4	2 665	214	376	5 292	0.1
Trigg	2.6	D	11.1	16.8	3.8	8.9	5.0	D	24.1	4 025	283	444	7 843	0.4
Trimble	-2.3	0.0	D	D	D	2.4	5.9	D	27.0	2 100	240	254	3 927	-0.1
Union	-0.8	29.4	3.8	11.5	D	5.2	4.1	D	12.9	3 495	232	454	6 221	1.3
Warren	0.7	0.2	6.3	18.2	5.0	6.7	5.5	14.1	15.8	20 795	169	3 596	51 351	8.8
Washington	2.3	0.0	12.6	34.5	D	3.7	D	D	14.1	2 890	239	449	5 139	1.9
Wayne	3.4	D	4.2	25.6	D	9.4	D	D	20.6	5 500	270	1 811	10 795	-1.3
Webster	12.5	D	12.8	5.7	D	3.6	D	4.3	12.0	3 385	256	501	5 916	-0.3
Whitley	-0.5	D	3.2	8.7	6.7	6.9	3.0	D	18.1	9 465	263	3 977	15 206	0.3
Wolfe	-2.5	D	D	2.4	D	9.0	3.6	D	38.3	2 220	307	1 222	3 655	-0.1
Woodford	2.5	0.0	5.5	23.7	7.3	5.5	2.7	D	15.8	5 580	216	399	11 095	3.6
LOUISIANA	0.4	7.6	8.8	9.4	8.5	6.4	5.7	11.5	16.0	868 017	186	178 954	2 036 975	3.7
Acadia	2.8	5.2	12.3	6.9	5.9	7.9	5.3	10.6	16.6	11 800	188	2 671	26 120	2.9
Allen	1.3	D	1.7	10.6	D	4.8	1.6	D	52.6	4 870	190	814	9 817	0.9
Ascension	0.1	D	22.0	25.3	4.3	6.0	4.1	5.1	9.1	17 175	144	2 203	45 878	12.5
Assumption	2.9	3.1	13.7	13.0	D	6.0	7.6	D	21.2	4 910	215	1 005	10 570	2.1
Avoyelles	4.9	D	8.7	2.5	6.1	9.9	5.4	D	29.2	9 445	230	2 662	18 261	1.2
Beauregard	-0.4	0.7	8.9	19.1	D	6.9	7.7	11.6	17.1	7 435	204	1 065	15 286	1.6
Bienville	1.4	5.2	3.9	24.6	D	3.5	6.2	7.9	20.1	3 455	249	829	7 724	0.1
Bossier	0.0	14.0	5.0	4.3	4.0	9.8	3.9	7.5	30.2	20 495	163	3 270	55 899	13.3
Caddo	0.0	22.2	4.3	5.5	5.5	5.9	4.4	17.3	14.5	50 255	200	13 197	113 153	1.0
Calcasieu	0.2	1.1	13.9	19.1	7.5	6.9	3.9	11.9	12.4	38 700	195	6 343	87 878	7.1
Caldwell	0.4	5.7	5.4	D	D	5.2	7.8	23.3	23.4	2 220	221	487	5 055	1.2
Cameron	1.2	2.0	70.3	6.8	D	D	0.6	0.7	6.1	1 170	172	68	3 923	9.2
Catahoula	3.9	15.0	D	D	D	6.2	D	8.7	24.1	2 335	232	597	4 919	0.9
Claiborne	10.0	31.5	4.1	3.6	D	5.3	1.6	D	21.8	3 525	217	796	7 758	0.0
Concordia	3.8	3.3	3.1	2.9	D	10.7	4.2	D	27.3	4 515	224	1 279	9 463	0.9
De Soto	-0.7	20.4	D	D	1.8	5.6	2.1	D	20.4	6 205	229	1 324	12 610	2.6
East Baton Rouge	0.0	0.3	13.7	7.2	13.0	5.7	7.0	13.1	17.5	72 085	162	14 993	193 679	3.4
East Carroll	15.3	D	0.7	6.9	D	7.4	3.5	D	29.7	1 395	191	635	2 895	-0.3
East Feliciana	1.3	1.0	3.7	7.7	D	3.4	3.7	10.4	50.1	4 170	212	852	8 264	3.1
Evangeline	4.4	1.5	4.8	12.9	2.8	7.5	4.7	D	18.1	7 365	218	2 208	14 933	1.8
Franklin	7.4	0.4	9.6	3.1	D	11.5	4.8	D	28.3	4 630	227	1 306	9 135	1.1
Grant	0.0	0.5	8.1	7.4	D	3.4	D	D	50.1	4 390	196	848	9 125	2.7
Iberia	0.3	18.7	7.5	14.3	7.1	6.6	8.1	7.2	11.2	14 810	200	3 204	30 250	1.9
Iberville	0.6	2.0	14.9	39.8	2.3	2.4	2.8	D	13.7	6 505	196	1 404	13 196	3.8
Jackson	3.2	D	D	D	2.2	5.2	2.7	D	22.3	3 635	229	719	7 789	1.4
Jefferson	0.0	2.0	8.2	4.9	9.5	7.9	9.1	14.2	10.0	85 945	197	13 351	189 307	0.1
Jefferson Davis	2.4	8.6	6.8	6.2	3.3	7.7	6.8	16.0	21.3	6 345	202	1 089	13 733	3.2
Lafayette	0.0	20.7	5.6	6.7	10.0	6.3	6.7	13.5	8.4	35 775	149	5 898	101 103	7.9
Lafourche	0.6	5.8	6.8	9.2	3.3	4.6	2.9	6.2	15.6	18 600	189	3 219	40 441	4.6
La Salle	-0.3	16.4	3.7	4.8	D	6.4	3.4	6.9	29.2	3 065	204	511	6 601	0.6
Lincoln	3.2	4.1	7.1	8.4	6.7	8.3	5.9	13.8	21.4	6 980	146	1 515	19 875	2.0
Livingston	0.0	1.0	16.2	10.6	7.0	12.1	5.4	7.0	19.7	22 395	163	2 790	55 216	10.0
Madison	10.0	0.6	0.9	8.4	1.6	7.7	3.6	D	25.0	2 090	181	740	5 019	4.5
Morehouse	8.4	D	7.4	6.6	D	8.6	4.4	18.4	17.5	6 790	257	1 755	12 535	0.9
Natchitoches	4.6	0.2	5.5	15.9	D	6.6	3.8	7.0	28.7	7 740	198	2 161	18 843	1.4

1. Per 1,000 resident population estimated as of July 1 of the year shown.

Table B. States and Counties — Housing, Labor Force, and Employment

STATE County	Housing units, 2011–2015								Civilian labor force, 2016				Civilian employment,[6] 2011–2015		
	Occupied units							Sub-stand-ard units[4] (percent)		Percent change, 2015–2016	Unemployment			Percent	
	Owner-occupied					Renter-occupied									
				Median owner cost as a percent of income										Management, business, science and arts	Con-struction, produc-tion, and mainte-nance occu-pations
	Total	Percent	Median value[1]	With a mort-gage	Without a mort-gage[2]	Median rent[3]	Median rent as a per-cent of income[2]		Total	Percent change, 2015–2016	Total	Rate[5]	Total		
	89	90	91	92	93	94	95	96	97	98	99	100	101	102	103
KENTUCKY—Cont'd															
Ohio	8 813	77.9	83 700	19.4	10.5	533	28.8	3.9	9 489	1.4	617	6.5	8 906	26.4	38.4
Oldham	19 706	85.8	247 500	20.2	10.0	833	27.0	1.1	31 146	2.1	1 054	3.4	29 304	45.3	17.6
Owen	4 123	75.5	98 000	21.6	12.0	565	26.3	4.1	5 595	2.0	230	4.1	4 351	24.5	37.8
Owsley	1 773	75.5	69 800	27.5	14.8	351	29.3	4.3	1 133	-3.8	107	9.4	1 211	33.0	23.0
Pendleton	5 356	77.5	104 800	23.1	11.2	583	24.7	1.5	6 649	1.2	321	4.8	6 507	24.2	42.0
Perry	11 080	72.0	71 200	21.3	10.0	535	25.3	3.6	8 629	-3.7	908	10.5	9 364	30.7	25.1
Pike	26 124	73.0	70 400	21.6	10.7	616	29.8	2.3	19 989	-3.8	2 155	10.8	20 861	29.2	29.2
Powell	4 767	69.8	76 600	20.1	12.3	543	31.4	4.7	4 947	1.2	346	7.0	4 360	24.9	38.7
Pulaski	25 593	69.0	106 800	21.3	11.7	598	33.7	2.2	25 367	-1.1	1 348	5.3	25 669	29.7	25.0
Robertson	930	79.0	104 000	22.9	12.2	539	32.1	1.7	810	2.3	48	5.9	806	31.4	37.8
Rockcastle	6 621	75.8	73 900	21.1	13.1	522	28.6	2.9	6 692	-0.6	397	5.9	6 015	21.8	32.5
Rowan	8 542	62.1	115 300	21.5	10.1	620	28.6	2.0	10 657	2.5	588	5.5	10 022	30.4	22.6
Russell	7 050	73.4	88 000	23.8	11.9	508	28.4	3.0	6 072	-1.0	503	8.3	6 014	28.6	34.4
Scott	18 421	70.7	164 600	18.9	10.0	760	26.2	2.6	26 986	1.7	1 011	3.7	25 105	34.6	29.5
Shelby	15 888	69.1	175 700	20.5	10.0	796	29.8	3.1	23 071	2.2	817	3.5	21 103	34.4	24.5
Simpson	6 793	62.9	116 800	19.8	10.3	641	28.6	1.3	8 316	0.4	365	4.4	7 524	25.7	33.1
Spencer	6 418	82.9	176 900	20.1	11.2	598	22.2	3.0	9 321	2.1	353	3.8	8 691	32.0	30.6
Taylor	9 715	65.4	93 700	21.4	10.0	578	35.3	1.7	11 571	4.8	591	5.1	10 395	25.3	29.6
Todd	4 567	72.0	87 300	21.5	10.9	587	26.9	1.7	5 493	1.8	232	4.2	4 648	22.8	44.9
Trigg	6 014	82.2	114 100	21.3	10.0	569	32.8	3.4	5 698	1.1	318	5.6	5 584	34.1	29.3
Trimble	3 548	75.7	112 000	21.2	10.7	744	27.3	2.1	3 878	2.3	207	5.3	3 598	23.8	41.2
Union	5 562	72.2	84 100	18.4	13.1	543	30.4	3.5	6 177	0.3	412	6.7	6 085	24.3	38.7
Warren	45 387	57.6	141 500	20.1	10.0	692	29.4	2.8	60 328	3.0	2 326	3.9	56 780	32.2	24.9
Washington	4 495	78.5	98 100	21.0	11.3	556	31.9	3.6	6 161	1.4	252	4.1	5 468	25.1	38.5
Wayne	7 917	70.6	80 300	20.6	11.8	479	36.5	3.7	7 480	3.4	544	7.3	6 681	23.3	38.5
Webster	5 129	70.7	74 600	20.5	10.0	555	25.4	2.4	5 811	-3.3	340	5.9	5 186	26.2	40.9
Whitley	13 110	66.6	77 900	23.7	11.0	573	30.0	2.0	13 241	1.0	859	6.5	12 406	27.6	25.8
Wolfe	2 918	66.3	52 700	25.8	11.9	489	50.0	2.2	1 960	0.9	191	9.7	1 967	22.0	26.4
Woodford	9 802	69.0	181 300	20.2	10.0	725	24.8	1.2	14 438	1.9	461	3.2	12 748	38.0	24.6
LOUISIANA	1 727 919	65.8	144 100	20.6	10.0	788	32.0	2.8	2 121 226	-1.8	129 105	6.1	2 016 049	32.4	24.5
Acadia	22 599	70.6	91 000	18.5	10.0	535	27.9	3.8	24 484	-5.3	1 817	7.4	24 619	28.0	30.3
Allen	8 027	74.5	81 100	19.1	10.0	522	26.6	3.8	8 909	0.8	571	6.4	8 269	27.5	29.5
Ascension	40 110	80.4	168 600	18.5	10.0	882	28.4	2.5	61 331	-0.7	3 005	4.9	55 380	36.3	24.1
Assumption	8 660	80.3	107 300	17.2	10.0	626	31.7	2.6	9 184	-6.4	779	8.5	9 407	26.5	35.2
Avoyelles	14 943	69.9	89 500	20.9	10.1	612	31.9	3.2	15 720	-1.7	1 110	7.1	14 998	27.6	26.9
Beauregard	13 152	76.4	104 100	18.2	10.0	669	29.8	3.6	15 045	-1.1	906	6.0	14 287	25.9	35.4
Bienville	5 814	70.8	69 600	18.4	10.0	482	28.9	2.4	5 675	-2.4	437	7.7	5 177	30.5	35.3
Bossier	47 125	65.1	154 100	19.7	10.0	895	29.1	3.5	56 987	-2.2	3 050	5.4	56 570	36.3	23.1
Caddo	97 991	61.3	128 100	20.4	10.0	742	32.2	2.4	107 764	-2.5	7 134	6.6	108 738	32.4	21.6
Calcasieu	75 325	68.6	124 600	19.3	10.0	758	30.1	2.4	102 869	3.5	4 909	4.8	86 840	30.3	26.7
Caldwell	3 838	74.8	64 400	17.6	10.7	513	29.2	2.3	3 989	-1.1	304	7.6	3 955	23.0	31.4
Cameron	2 608	90.8	97 400	16.1	10.0	727	35.8	3.6	3 816	3.9	168	4.4	3 077	26.4	36.4
Catahoula	3 748	74.5	71 100	19.7	10.0	473	24.8	2.6	3 441	-4.9	321	9.3	3 749	29.7	32.5
Claiborne	5 852	69.8	73 700	20.8	10.0	617	37.0	4.3	5 989	-3.4	404	6.7	5 494	24.7	33.5
Concordia	7 896	59.7	77 400	21.5	10.9	494	32.7	3.3	7 268	-3.8	606	8.3	7 078	24.7	29.9
De Soto	10 244	73.9	98 400	19.1	10.0	589	33.5	4.1	10 815	-2.6	800	7.4	10 521	25.6	32.3
East Baton Rouge	169 120	59.7	170 500	20.9	10.0	842	33.0	2.6	233 578	-0.8	12 012	5.1	215 513	37.9	18.4
East Carroll	2 678	47.7	49 300	23.2	11.9	450	35.8	4.3	2 150	-3.3	252	11.7	1 882	27.9	29.0
East Feliciana	6 937	81.6	127 100	20.3	10.0	665	29.8	4.1	8 160	-0.8	466	5.7	7 165	26.8	27.8
Evangeline	11 954	66.0	83 900	18.3	11.1	539	36.8	3.1	12 688	-2.4	945	7.4	10 978	26.4	33.1
Franklin	7 469	70.4	79 300	18.9	10.0	496	30.3	3.4	7 292	-3.3	666	9.1	7 062	28.0	30.7
Grant	7 197	74.0	83 200	18.9	10.0	729	29.0	1.6	8 379	-1.3	586	7.0	7 068	25.7	31.9
Iberia	26 345	70.5	99 600	18.7	10.0	657	28.3	3.8	30 436	-4.5	2 850	9.4	31 517	25.7	31.3
Iberville	11 191	74.6	112 700	18.7	10.0	626	30.5	4.2	14 278	-1.1	974	6.8	13 049	24.1	28.7
Jackson	6 038	68.1	77 200	19.6	10.0	510	34.1	2.8	7 029	-2.0	400	5.7	5 536	25.4	32.5
Jefferson	168 104	61.9	172 700	23.5	10.2	900	32.3	2.5	217 426	-1.1	11 504	5.3	210 346	31.9	23.9
Jefferson Davis	11 652	74.0	91 900	18.3	10.0	546	31.0	5.4	13 578	-0.3	820	6.0	12 657	28.1	30.8
Lafayette	88 995	64.4	166 700	19.2	10.0	781	28.9	2.6	113 761	-5.4	7 030	6.2	116 522	35.4	20.9
Lafourche	35 592	75.8	133 200	18.8	10.0	720	27.7	2.9	43 241	-7.4	2 734	6.3	43 542	27.6	33.4
La Salle	5 551	78.3	70 300	16.5	10.0	523	23.0	2.1	6 259	-5.4	415	6.6	5 354	30.7	30.4
Lincoln	17 169	53.8	126 100	19.4	10.0	666	39.0	2.6	20 576	2.4	1 342	6.5	20 541	37.0	19.1
Livingston	47 608	80.1	152 600	19.1	10.0	793	27.4	3.3	67 999	-0.6	3 448	5.1	61 631	30.8	29.8
Madison	4 060	52.9	61 700	22.0	11.0	517	33.3	4.7	3 820	-2.3	344	9.0	3 967	25.0	24.0
Morehouse	10 447	65.6	80 600	23.7	10.5	561	34.2	2.1	10 635	-1.9	1 038	9.8	9 888	24.6	31.4
Natchitoches	14 456	58.0	101 900	19.2	10.0	614	39.9	4.6	16 083	0.5	1 128	7.0	14 446	26.5	27.9

1. Specified owner-occupied units. 2. A value of 10.0 represents 10 percent or less; a value of 50.0 represents 50 percent or more. 3. Specified renter-occupied units.
4. Overcrowded or lacking complete plumbing facilities. 5. Percent of civilian labor force. 6. Civilian employed persons 16 years old and over.

Table B. States and Counties — Nonfarm Employment and Agriculture

STATE County	Private nonfarm establishments, employment and payroll, 2015									Agriculture, 2012			
	Number of establishments	Employment						Annual payroll		Farms			
		Total	Health care and social assistance	Manufacturing	Retail trade	Finance and insurance	Professional, scientific, and technical services	Total (mil dol)	Average per employee (dollars)	Number	Percent with:		Farm operators whose principal occupation is farming (percent)
											Fewer than 50 acres	500 acres or more	
	104	105	106	107	108	109	110	111	112	113	114	115	116
KENTUCKY—Cont'd													
Ohio	359	8 157	1 078	2 638	741	110	88	278	34 070	944	32.1	5.1	31.0
Oldham	1 231	12 191	2 638	1 067	1 160	1 394	744	470	38 532	419	53.9	7.2	40.1
Owen	119	1 486	246	D	163	47	9	50	33 400	701	23.3	7.4	40.8
Owsley	50	351	206	D	98	D	D	8	23 217	163	22.7	6.7	47.2
Pendleton	178	1 663	236	496	198	58	47	60	36 299	810	32.1	3.3	33.2
Perry	614	10 143	2 640	94	1 835	314	222	386	38 072	49	51.0	14.3	44.9
Pike	1 300	17 671	4 226	597	4 097	737	639	674	38 116	56	26.8	14.3	42.9
Powell	174	1 605	236	135	390	70	10	42	26 112	229	41.5	3.1	39.7
Pulaski	1 464	19 870	5 083	3 686	3 321	667	397	683	34 367	1 713	38.3	3.7	50.0
Robertson	18	145	D	NA	D	7	D	3	21 434	251	21.1	5.2	48.6
Rockcastle	200	2 670	988	119	297	87	52	77	28 766	677	36.8	4.1	36.2
Rowan	508	7 144	2 003	934	1 343	222	91	226	31 668	356	35.7	3.1	29.5
Russell	376	5 541	1 023	951	715	1 252	50	139	25 078	726	45.5	4.7	39.4
Scott	920	22 858	1 720	10 312	1 738	278	340	1 173	51 299	838	44.4	7.4	50.5
Shelby	941	17 398	1 356	3 822	2 484	299	272	567	32 562	1 518	50.4	4.0	40.5
Simpson	377	7 309	461	2 804	999	153	56	264	36 102	467	50.7	8.6	50.3
Spencer	204	1 112	256	28	210	50	56	30	27 413	529	44.2	4.0	41.0
Taylor	631	8 877	1 425	1 299	1 443	248	90	275	30 928	874	42.9	4.3	37.8
Todd	196	1 445	199	370	278	80	33	43	29 594	603	22.4	13.8	55.9
Trigg	240	2 288	372	574	396	78	31	67	29 406	397	30.2	10.1	41.3
Trimble	80	673	121	D	72	60	8	32	48 068	439	37.1	4.3	40.1
Union	258	4 344	852	428	769	94	53	189	43 424	310	35.5	25.2	46.1
Warren	2 981	52 061	8 803	8 576	7 629	1 547	1 866	1 997	38 358	1 648	45.9	4.7	32.9
Washington	257	2 880	415	1 001	298	71	57	99	34 427	1 011	28.7	4.3	37.1
Wayne	290	3 930	569	1 583	677	175	48	109	27 835	778	35.5	5.7	49.9
Webster	216	2 316	275	261	321	87	27	105	45 263	500	26.0	13.2	40.0
Whitley	625	10 254	2 601	861	1 574	237	917	317	30 908	496	38.7	2.6	29.8
Wolfe	81	691	252	22	169	11	7	18	25 479	297	28.6	4.7	37.7
Woodford	534	6 701	586	1 953	739	188	482	282	42 113	713	44.6	7.3	38.7
LOUISIANA	105 575	1 724 973	289 548	125 354	238 174	63 015	105 778	76 685	44 456	28 093	43.7	11.6	43.2
Acadia	1 122	12 561	2 190	1 121	2 489	426	415	402	31 997	841	50.9	14.3	47.1
Allen	308	3 413	739	553	614	121	59	105	30 855	429	48.0	9.3	35.7
Ascension	2 182	39 004	3 287	5 445	6 265	1 076	2 312	2 082	53 380	250	60.8	9.6	32.8
Assumption	248	2 918	421	315	432	105	73	119	40 920	81	37.0	42.0	66.7
Avoyelles	717	8 655	2 336	268	1 560	347	199	255	29 494	937	43.1	15.0	43.0
Beauregard	599	6 890	1 221	889	1 357	721	201	268	38 857	860	36.9	5.9	37.0
Bienville	227	3 285	495	1 038	284	148	49	119	36 375	233	33.0	6.4	54.1
Bossier	2 444	37 135	4 073	1 449	7 387	1 026	1 274	1 191	32 068	472	50.8	8.3	53.0
Caddo	6 310	103 394	25 893	5 839	13 708	2 880	4 781	4 243	41 041	614	54.4	9.6	48.2
Calcasieu	4 444	74 430	13 920	8 594	11 152	1 982	4 773	3 248	43 638	902	51.3	9.3	35.9
Caldwell	179	1 842	699	36	344	127	90	52	28 164	295	39.7	10.5	40.3
Cameron	153	1 409	85	D	119	14	218	125	88 612	342	25.7	20.5	33.9
Catahoula	189	1 485	293	D	346	119	79	41	27 591	567	25.2	18.3	34.0
Claiborne	240	2 592	749	156	360	83	36	93	35 814	295	32.5	7.8	42.0
Concordia	362	4 170	1 009	198	892	210	167	139	33 443	461	26.2	23.4	33.8
De Soto	422	5 130	594	D	853	181	125	249	48 599	669	38.1	8.5	49.6
East Baton Rouge	12 179	242 643	37 351	10 006	29 657	12 048	20 044	11 648	48 005	432	54.4	4.9	39.8
East Carroll	122	1 358	312	122	137	35	22	49	35 814	227	18.9	46.3	61.2
East Feliciana	248	3 315	1 810	285	249	129	66	125	37 605	399	36.8	12.8	32.3
Evangeline	513	6 272	2 552	951	969	283	119	198	31 607	663	45.2	10.3	36.3
Franklin	381	3 697	957	185	973	201	198	96	25 850	915	33.7	12.8	38.6
Grant	173	1 830	255	D	269	65	6	63	34 422	238	35.3	10.1	29.4
Iberia	1 678	27 787	3 534	4 546	3 512	839	859	1 263	45 446	279	57.7	16.8	57.3
Iberville	543	10 804	828	3 792	1 073	264	800	781	72 320	165	38.8	24.2	61.8
Jackson	237	2 663	563	D	505	105	42	109	40 906	196	48.0	1.0	49.5
Jefferson	11 715	183 249	30 568	7 101	29 677	8 781	11 298	8 239	44 960	57	70.2	3.5	14.0
Jefferson Davis	643	7 259	1 604	500	1 454	270	314	246	33 927	656	35.5	19.1	48.6
Lafayette	8 481	132 130	24 166	7 345	17 534	3 352	9 301	6 124	46 350	632	70.1	3.0	31.0
Lafourche	1 772	28 237	3 983	2 117	4 132	824	871	1 324	46 893	407	43.0	10.8	36.6
La Salle	364	3 620	970	43	537	140	197	124	34 145	186	35.5	2.7	31.2
Lincoln	1 050	15 136	2 858	1 360	2 410	637	718	514	33 976	346	33.2	4.6	41.9
Livingston	1 747	21 464	2 250	1 869	5 518	632	1 195	757	35 264	405	69.6	0.7	42.2
Madison	201	2 663	1 215	D	419	53	19	72	27 101	295	13.9	42.0	54.9
Morehouse	433	5 512	1 974	519	986	197	90	147	26 694	434	23.5	31.3	48.2
Natchitoches	795	11 431	2 087	2 511	1 799	358	231	380	33 230	630	31.9	15.7	39.5

Table B. States and Counties — **Agriculture**

STATE County	Acreage (1,000)	Percent change, 2007–2012	Average size of farm	Total irrigated (1,000)	Total cropland (1,000)	Value of land and buildings Average per farm	Value of land and buildings Average per acre	Value of machinery and equipment, average per farm (dollars)	Value of products sold Total (mil dol)	Value of products sold Average per farm (dollars)	Percent from: Crops	Percent from: Live-stock and poultry products	$10,000 or more	$100,000 or more	Government payments Total ($1,000)	Percent of farms
	117	118	119	120	121	122	123	124	125	126	127	128	129	130	131	132
KENTUCKY—Cont'd																
Ohio	158	-6.1	168	0.6	78.8	410 305	2 448	84 484	98.8	104 698	36.8	63.2	29.0	7.1	1 434	48.8
Oldham	60	0.5	144	0.2	24.3	899 907	6 247	68 687	14.8	35 439	61.4	38.6	41.5	5.3	296	18.4
Owen	132	-16.4	188	0.3	45.8	434 031	2 306	56 652	21.2	30 298	49.3	50.7	37.2	5.7	1 113	42.2
Owsley	28	-23.1	169	0.0	6.9	228 049	1 349	41 859	1.6	9 939	71.1	28.9	25.8	0.6	234	42.3
Pendleton	101	-19.8	125	0.9	31.7	296 179	2 368	50 151	11.5	14 167	73.6	26.4	23.6	2.5	622	26.3
Perry	11	2.7	224	D	0.9	269 490	1 206	68 408	2.1	42 082	7.3	92.7	24.5	10.2	D	2.0
Pike	13	-5.9	239	0.0	2.1	318 875	1 334	49 732	0.6	10 018	40.8	59.0	32.1	0.0	D	1.8
Powell	30	-8.3	131	0.0	7.5	208 742	1 590	42 210	2.5	10 773	63.4	36.6	22.7	1.7	133	34.9
Pulaski	228	-1.6	133	0.4	90.1	385 814	2 896	58 635	63.5	37 072	36.5	63.5	39.9	6.9	1 599	38.4
Robertson	39	-24.6	155	0.1	12.7	279 578	1 808	58 873	4.1	16 163	43.6	56.4	30.3	3.6	396	37.8
Rockcastle	91	0.5	134	0.0	30.3	272 708	2 032	49 790	12.4	18 251	53.5	46.5	29.4	3.1	557	32.6
Rowan	42	-15.4	119	0.0	15.0	253 205	2 133	47 567	5.2	14 705	48.1	51.9	18.5	2.8	262	31.2
Russell	89	-4.0	123	0.0	34.9	379 095	3 080	62 912	44.5	61 331	16.1	83.9	40.5	9.2	1 892	46.6
Scott	127	-8.3	152	0.8	48.1	695 570	4 572	63 774	38.8	46 254	34.6	65.4	36.2	10.4	1 180	31.5
Shelby	199	-2.9	131	1.3	111.3	640 994	4 881	68 175	76.8	50 596	71.4	28.6	34.1	7.6	2 489	34.3
Simpson	102	-14.8	217	0.2	78.5	905 017	4 163	107 238	73.9	158 208	60.0	40.0	43.9	12.8	2 406	57.8
Spencer	69	-5.7	131	0.4	31.2	409 495	3 134	54 915	15.6	29 516	66.0	34.0	35.9	5.3	487	42.7
Taylor	115	-3.5	131	0.1	59.5	364 644	2 782	60 556	37.9	43 362	44.5	55.5	37.4	8.1	1 458	58.7
Todd	181	-8.6	300	1.5	126.6	1 107 604	3 690	133 570	180.2	298 915	48.2	51.8	64.2	31.5	3 015	51.2
Trigg	129	-4.9	325	1.5	71.8	961 912	2 960	103 461	47.2	118 862	82.6	17.4	43.3	14.9	1 514	46.3
Trimble	56	-14.5	127	0.1	19.0	399 913	3 156	57 303	9.1	20 738	73.6	26.4	33.0	3.9	519	42.6
Union	195	-3.0	629	2.6	167.9	2 579 713	4 104	324 342	96.5	311 268	92.3	7.7	49.0	27.1	2 969	61.3
Warren	247	-6.9	150	0.4	146.2	539 892	3 606	71 369	114.7	69 603	47.9	52.1	31.9	8.1	6 190	39.2
Washington	141	-13.5	139	0.3	55.9	356 909	2 560	55 341	33.8	33 403	47.7	52.3	43.1	6.0	2 275	38.9
Wayne	129	-9.9	165	0.1	40.8	376 098	2 274	65 197	68.1	87 496	17.2	82.8	41.5	11.2	544	39.3
Webster	152	-1.7	305	0.4	107.9	973 724	3 194	135 228	102.4	204 744	43.3	56.7	33.2	16.4	4 331	73.4
Whitley	58	-20.4	118	0.0	16.9	255 401	2 168	39 494	5.4	10 851	31.4	68.6	20.6	1.6	86	14.9
Wolfe	42	-26.4	143	0.0	8.0	212 566	1 487	43 566	1.7	5 721	57.9	42.1	15.2	0.0	377	45.5
Woodford	112	-6.0	157	0.3	34.7	1 280 116	8 155	103 851	76.6	107 421	12.5	87.5	46.1	12.3	997	26.8
LOUISIANA	7 901	-2.6	281	1 092.9	4 275.6	718 179	2 554	104 418	3 809.4	135 600	73.1	26.9	33.0	11.7	138 164	33.6
Acadia	238	2.3	283	82.9	187.1	628 439	2 219	117 468	124.3	147 830	86.7	13.3	34.2	16.3	6 775	51.6
Allen	88	5.8	205	18.4	47.2	431 168	2 101	76 105	23.7	55 187	85.2	14.8	28.2	7.7	2 111	35.4
Ascension	50	11.0	202	0.0	20.3	710 252	3 519	90 016	20.5	81 968	86.4	13.6	26.4	5.6	56	3.2
Assumption	62	-2.4	768	D	56.0	2 339 247	3 048	556 259	64.8	800 235	98.6	1.4	65.4	48.1	65	8.6
Avoyelles	299	7.4	319	21.7	203.5	724 316	2 269	113 847	137.8	147 048	91.2	8.8	37.9	14.5	5 632	45.4
Beauregard	146	-18.3	170	3.1	42.6	424 519	2 497	56 241	15.7	18 269	59.7	40.3	25.1	2.7	1 523	18.3
Bienville	56	37.3	240	0.1	16.2	570 425	2 379	88 854	34.5	148 039	5.5	94.5	30.9	8.2	136	10.3
Bossier	81	-21.4	172	1.5	28.4	579 184	3 363	91 169	17.7	37 517	60.8	39.2	27.1	6.8	717	11.0
Caddo	140	-7.5	228	13.5	58.6	620 078	2 722	81 067	50.6	82 437	83.6	16.4	28.3	7.7	2 364	14.8
Calcasieu	338	-8.1	375	15.8	85.9	961 407	2 566	70 263	33.2	36 756	60.0	40.0	23.9	5.1	2 653	22.2
Caldwell	62	-7.7	211	4.1	28.8	522 678	2 476	70 064	11.5	38 929	84.1	15.9	28.5	9.2	1 762	44.4
Cameron	235	8.8	688	11.5	55.3	1 210 319	1 759	97 509	19.1	55 857	61.7	38.3	36.3	9.1	896	24.0
Catahoula	224	-3.1	395	33.7	166.2	958 256	2 427	129 684	91.9	162 157	96.0	4.0	37.0	15.7	7 435	71.4
Claiborne	57	17.8	194	D	12.5	488 681	2 518	90 197	71.2	241 434	2.7	97.3	34.2	17.6	177	15.3
Concordia	240	14.2	522	28.5	171.3	1 203 475	2 308	172 974	118.3	256 534	97.9	2.1	37.1	21.0	6 348	85.2
De Soto	164	-1.8	246	0.3	30.2	665 374	2 709	74 991	17.7	26 417	25.2	74.8	28.3	3.7	841	11.7
East Baton Rouge	58	-20.3	133	0.7	13.3	765 382	5 746	48 398	11.5	26 523	24.0	76.0	26.2	3.9	209	8.1
East Carroll	251	-3.7	1 106	125.6	214.3	3 029 084	2 739	409 366	192.3	846 934	99.6	0.4	68.3	51.1	7 976	85.5
East Feliciana	113	-12.2	282	0.2	26.0	840 722	2 981	74 306	13.5	33 802	49.6	50.4	35.8	6.3	527	15.0
Evangeline	192	11.4	289	40.1	103.9	613 686	2 121	77 027	62.6	94 450	83.6	16.4	32.0	10.6	4 088	47.7
Franklin	246	-29.1	269	88.8	162.4	613 407	2 280	106 741	143.2	156 467	96.7	3.3	35.8	17.3	7 665	80.2
Grant	48	-7.3	202	0.5	17.0	430 168	2 134	65 084	7.9	33 050	74.8	25.2	28.2	8.4	723	22.3
Iberia	107	-7.5	384	0.4	85.5	1 205 219	3 135	231 706	92.2	330 351	97.2	2.8	39.8	18.6	311	16.8
Iberville	163	90.5	990	1.0	63.0	1 785 261	1 803	395 085	67.6	409 436	96.6	3.4	52.7	20.6	223	23.6
Jackson	19	-7.3	95	0.1	3.5	268 638	2 830	49 990	30.6	155 934	1.1	98.9	27.0	9.7	48	2.6
Jefferson	8	-48.7	136	D	0.8	517 123	3 804	58 070	1.6	28 228	24.1	75.8	42.1	7.0	41	21.1
Jefferson Davis	265	-8.0	404	67.7	186.5	917 733	2 272	122 320	85.1	129 771	87.3	12.7	38.4	17.2	5 149	59.3
Lafayette	56	-17.4	88	3.2	34.8	420 315	4 770	67 704	30.5	48 180	89.2	10.8	19.0	4.0	316	11.4
Lafourche	158	49.0	389	0.4	52.4	834 602	2 148	117 747	58.0	142 462	73.7	26.3	41.0	6.6	51	2.5
La Salle	20	-3.8	105	D	4.0	269 210	2 565	56 677	1.0	5 538	34.4	65.7	13.4	0.0	186	10.8
Lincoln	56	6.4	161	0.4	9.4	536 971	3 328	65 902	101.7	293 928	1.4	98.6	37.9	18.2	387	13.6
Livingston	28	-8.1	68	0.3	5.3	391 205	5 747	46 447	4.8	11 924	25.6	74.4	20.5	1.2	103	5.7
Madison	225	-4.2	761	63.1	180.7	1 877 692	2 467	335 441	155.1	525 681	99.4	0.6	58.3	45.4	6 131	87.1
Morehouse	279	2.0	643	141.5	206.7	1 521 809	2 367	204 793	176.1	405 781	96.9	3.1	47.2	31.1	11 646	68.7
Natchitoches	201	-9.4	319	10.5	70.3	774 152	2 427	91 722	129.0	204 767	23.4	76.6	40.2	13.8	3 061	33.0

Table B. States and Counties — Water Use, Wholesale Trade, Retail Trade, and Real Estate

STATE County	Water use, 2010		Wholesale trade,[1] 2012				Retail trade,[2] 2012				Real estate and rental and leasing,[2] 2012			
	Total water withdrawn (mil gal/day)	Gallons withdrawn per person per day	Number of establishments	Number of employees	Sales (mil dol)	Annual payroll (mil dol)	Number of establishments	Number of employees	Sales (mil dol)	Annual payroll (mil dol)	Number of establishments	Number of employees	Receipts (mil dol)	Annual payroll (mil dol)
	133	134	135	136	137	138	139	140	141	142	143	144	145	146
KENTUCKY—Cont'd														
Ohio	11.3	474	7	77	22.6	2.4	67	724	190.0	14.6	11	26	2.5	0.5
Oldham	6.4	106	36	280	117.6	14.9	103	1 182	369.3	30.5	52	89	18.4	3.1
Owen	1.8	167	4	48	18.3	0.8	29	186	62.2	4.2	3	D	D	D
Owsley	0.4	90	1	D	D	D	8	100	16.1	1.6	2	D	D	D
Pendleton	2.9	198	8	D	D	D	26	202	51.5	4.1	4	D	D	D
Perry	6.7	235	29	448	254.1	24.0	146	1 950	525.1	42.1	20	96	60.5	4.0
Pike	10.9	167	50	512	483.2	26.0	281	3 734	936.2	86.0	40	164	25.7	5.2
Powell	2.2	171	5	39	10.0	1.6	41	451	100.4	7.4	5	9	1.9	0.2
Pulaski	165.0	2 616	66	D	D	D	282	3 304	864.1	76.4	51	211	22.4	5.0
Robertson	0.2	79	NA	NA	NA	NA	3	D	D	D	1	D	D	D
Rockcastle	2.9	168	9	44	13.1	1.3	50	323	95.2	6.2	3	D	D	D
Rowan	5.7	244	14	143	39.1	4.5	100	1 399	339.0	27.9	21	54	11.0	1.8
Russell	18.7	1 065	8	D	D	D	90	694	185.9	14.0	6	37	8.5	0.9
Scott	4.4	93	27	D	D	D	125	1 828	573.3	38.1	37	118	27.3	3.0
Shelby	4.4	104	33	D	D	D	126	1 654	569.1	39.3	39	155	27.2	4.3
Simpson	2.1	123	16	181	372.0	6.1	67	1 016	389.6	23.3	12	44	5.1	0.8
Spencer	0.5	30	NA	NA	NA	NA	26	233	81.1	4.8	3	D	D	D
Taylor	5.2	213	22	D	D	D	126	1 416	342.1	31.9	21	79	8.8	2.0
Todd	1.9	155	9	42	77.4	1.4	35	295	77.3	5.7	5	11	0.9	0.1
Trigg	3.2	222	3	15	5.2	0.4	46	405	95.2	7.8	8	D	D	D
Trimble	10.2	1 158	NA	NA	NA	NA	13	96	25.6	1.1	1	D	D	D
Union	4.9	327	15	214	278.4	9.9	67	703	195.9	16.7	7	D	D	D
Warren	19.8	174	131	1 800	2 822.5	83.0	489	7 103	1 692.1	154.7	125	427	84.0	12.7
Washington	2.8	237	9	D	D	D	37	285	76.0	5.4	4	D	D	D
Wayne	3.1	147	11	124	27.8	2.9	62	663	157.7	14.4	4	6	0.2	0.1
Webster	10.8	793	10	134	38.1	3.6	39	342	80.0	6.9	1	D	D	D
Whitley	6.1	170	22	351	172.0	17.7	132	1 432	442.6	32.5	23	62	9.3	1.7
Wolfe	0.5	64	2	D	D	D	29	185	58.2	3.8	2	D	D	D
Woodford	23.0	921	16	244	115.0	11.5	67	743	230.3	17.4	17	17	5.5	0.6
LOUISIANA	8 540.3	1 884	4 823	64 259	68 012.8	3 260.2	16 743	220 257	61 396.4	5 334.6	4 500	31 298	7 486.4	1 461.4
Acadia	230.9	3 738	44	709	528.8	24.4	192	2 383	602.7	55.5	34	163	20.4	5.3
Allen	24.5	951	8	24	18.8	0.6	65	623	157.6	12.2	5	14	1.3	0.3
Ascension	162.1	1 512	138	1 667	995.5	92.4	374	5 491	1 538.9	129.5	89	559	177.7	30.8
Assumption	21.2	906	11	64	79.4	1.8	42	475	121.0	10.4	5	8	3.1	0.4
Avoyelles	56.4	1 340	26	253	306.5	10.3	159	1 446	354.7	29.5	21	59	7.8	1.3
Beauregard	27.8	781	13	D	D	D	104	1 330	383.7	29.1	21	111	15.7	4.4
Bienville	13.2	918	8	68	27.6	3.1	47	344	66.5	6.0	4	D	D	D
Bossier	15.3	131	114	1 453	941.9	68.3	452	6 434	1 923.3	159.1	109	556	114.1	17.5
Caddo	147.0	576	328	5 258	5 800.1	258.1	958	13 053	4 034.9	331.3	307	2 379	445.9	94.8
Calcasieu	223.6	1 160	188	2 125	1 941.1	97.9	755	10 139	3 127.1	238.7	208	954	213.8	38.5
Caldwell	3.8	378	4	26	9.0	1.0	28	267	81.1	5.5	3	D	D	D
Cameron	26.6	3 892	11	71	29.9	4.8	17	101	28.3	2.3	8	64	21.9	2.9
Catahoula	30.0	2 883	15	89	315.8	3.5	35	268	66.6	5.4	2	D	D	D
Claiborne	2.6	152	11	152	134.7	6.4	48	362	83.7	7.9	5	D	D	D
Concordia	42.8	2 053	12	232	344.5	11.2	81	904	275.4	20.8	11	104	6.2	3.1
De Soto	36.6	1 375	11	36	13.2	1.4	68	873	251.6	20.2	13	116	25.6	5.2
East Baton Rouge	179.4	408	568	7 674	4 993.5	417.3	1 863	27 576	7 389.7	677.5	546	3 088	631.1	111.2
East Carroll	26.6	3 426	12	142	466.5	6.9	22	147	30.7	2.9	2	D	D	D
East Feliciana	3.7	183	10	D	D	D	42	276	80.3	5.9	5	12	2.8	0.4
Evangeline	203.7	5 993	15	112	72.2	3.2	108	986	213.7	18.8	24	75	9.2	1.7
Franklin	40.3	1 942	19	125	248.8	4.3	78	914	250.9	19.2	11	30	4.5	0.7
Grant	5.3	238	2	D	D	D	27	227	83.2	5.2	2	D	D	D
Iberia	31.0	423	94	1 192	560.5	57.3	285	3 524	970.7	89.3	104	2 038	915.5	192.9
Iberville	481.4	14 418	24	D	D	D	88	1 083	279.3	23.7	22	149	42.9	7.2
Jackson	4.0	245	4	D	D	D	40	547	128.1	11.2	7	12	0.7	0.2
Jefferson	816.7	1 888	719	9 641	8 453.9	518.4	1 807	27 991	8 112.3	737.5	498	3 605	896.5	141.6
Jefferson Davis	175.1	5 541	27	275	261.1	10.9	127	1 504	402.8	32.5	19	317	73.2	16.8
Lafayette	41.2	186	485	7 554	4 113.5	406.8	1 057	15 818	4 355.1	399.4	473	3 636	938.6	194.0
Lafourche	43.6	453	61	868	947.9	46.3	290	4 020	965.6	86.0	66	333	58.8	11.5
La Salle	2.4	164	10	153	257.8	5.5	51	563	142.3	11.8	10	26	3.5	0.7
Lincoln	8.2	176	34	500	197.0	15.2	166	2 243	592.6	52.9	48	235	25.7	6.2
Livingston	15.2	119	47	389	345.3	17.8	287	4 390	1 180.5	98.7	63	565	43.8	13.3
Madison	42.1	3 480	12	90	258.9	5.0	38	387	158.9	9.2	9	D	D	D
Morehouse	83.3	2 977	15	223	147.1	10.6	85	978	237.4	22.7	23	59	9.9	1.4
Natchitoches	34.3	868	24	157	77.8	5.8	145	1 676	404.8	33.6	46	223	28.7	3.6

1. Merchant wholesalers, except manufacturers' sales branches and offices.   2. Employer establishments.

Professional Services, Manufacturing, and Accommodation and Food Services

STATE County	Professional, scientific, and technical services, 2012				Manufacturing, 2012				Accommodation and food services, 2012			
	Number of establishments	Number of employees	Receipts (mil dol)	Annual payroll (mil dol)	Number of establishments	Number of employees	Receipts (mil dol)	Annual payroll (mil dol)	Number of establishments	Number of employees	Sales (mil dol)	Annual payroll (mil dol)
	147	148	149	150	151	152	153	154	155	156	157	158
KENTUCKY—Cont'd												
Ohio	23	78	6.5	2.3	27	2 667	576.2	73.3	22	D	D	D
Oldham	170	516	69.3	25.6	45	785	304.0	36.9	70	1 322	72.8	16.8
Owen	5	D	D	D	NA	NA	NA	NA	10	D	D	D
Owsley	3	6	0.7	0.3	NA	NA	NA	NA	1	D	D	D
Pendleton	9	42	2.3	1.1	16	D	D	D	10	D	D	D
Perry	52	248	25.4	9.4	10	143	20.0	6.8	49	977	46.4	12.7
Pike	105	886	99.6	40.6	24	616	219.0	28.8	89	1 845	91.8	24.3
Powell	7	8	0.6	0.2	10	194	D	6.2	19	D	D	D
Pulaski	97	390	41.2	12.6	74	3 470	1 411.6	132.3	100	1 837	88.2	23.8
Robertson	1	D	D	D	NA	NA	NA	NA	NA	NA	NA	NA
Rockcastle	17	47	2.9	1.2	12	98	D	4.2	21	292	12.7	3.7
Rowan	22	82	5.7	2.0	20	981	291.9	30.5	51	1 057	46.4	11.9
Russell	21	66	4.3	1.1	25	1 610	404.0	42.8	32	376	16.2	4.1
Scott	77	311	36.7	14.1	37	8 525	10 844.2	552.2	88	1 795	89.7	24.1
Shelby	94	317	35.4	10.7	55	3 562	1 484.5	149.2	61	D	D	D
Simpson	16	112	9.2	2.9	34	2 958	1 387.3	137.3	41	868	40.0	10.9
Spencer	18	49	4.6	1.7	7	D	D	D	12	187	7.0	2.2
Taylor	51	97	9.5	2.6	26	1 191	D	37.7	45	818	35.2	8.7
Todd	11	30	3.3	1.2	19	416	108.9	11.5	11	104	3.1	0.9
Trigg	9	33	2.3	0.7	15	536	136.6	18.4	19	D	D	D
Trimble	4	7	0.4	0.1	3	D	142.8	16.0	4	D	D	D
Union	10	50	4.3	1.5	14	440	D	D	18	D	D	D
Warren	212	2 075	179.7	63.0	113	7 962	5 110.1	405.4	260	5 737	264.1	70.6
Washington	17	51	4.2	1.2	12	858	248.3	39.2	13	D	D	D
Wayne	18	52	3.8	1.4	24	1 498	267.2	44.9	26	D	D	D
Webster	10	23	1.4	0.3	12	259	189.4	10.8	14	D	D	D
Whitley	55	910	51.1	23.0	21	888	228.0	32.8	67	1 109	53.0	15.3
Wolfe	3	7	0.6	0.2	3	21	D	D	5	D	D	D
Woodford	63	496	76.6	29.7	29	1 828	644.1	103.0	33	D	D	D
LOUISIANA	11 728	88 093	13 546.2	5 022.9	3 308	136 327	271 191.1	8 489.3	9 019	193 928	11 697.9	3 110.7
Acadia	125	378	43.2	15.9	43	1 138	D	45.5	74	1 185	52.7	13.3
Allen	23	64	7.2	1.6	11	584	D	29.7	28	D	D	D
Ascension	162	922	137.4	53.2	100	4 518	14 208.5	427.9	173	3 211	167.2	43.5
Assumption	37	88	12.3	3.8	9	375	D	19.7	12	67	3.9	0.8
Avoyelles	60	224	28.0	7.4	20	279	D	8.4	51	1 842	153.8	39.6
Beauregard	50	189	15.6	5.9	18	757	D	57.2	40	720	35.0	8.7
Bienville	12	52	5.3	2.8	11	1 165	D	30.0	17	D	D	D
Bossier	197	1 032	116.1	42.2	70	1 534	911.8	74.6	235	7 792	667.0	135.9
Caddo	620	4 278	613.6	214.6	182	6 230	4 965.5	347.6	493	12 976	766.3	200.0
Calcasieu	423	5 141	451.3	218.1	126	D	D	D	353	10 769	983.3	210.5
Caldwell	26	74	13.4	1.9	6	24	D	0.8	10	D	D	D
Cameron	9	71	28.0	4.8	NA	NA	NA	NA	5	48	1.4	0.3
Catahoula	30	74	8.1	3.1	NA	NA	NA	NA	8	D	D	D
Claiborne	11	35	4.4	1.0	11	185	D	8.2	16	D	D	D
Concordia	28	162	19.6	6.6	11	234	79.7	9.9	25	382	17.9	4.5
De Soto	24	93	6.1	2.1	13	707	D	D	32	416	23.0	4.9
East Baton Rouge	1 693	17 189	2 800.2	1 013.8	334	11 176	53 388.8	774.5	1 000	23 462	1 230.7	345.7
East Carroll	5	18	1.6	0.5	5	D	D	1.3	13	64	3.5	0.7
East Feliciana	22	75	12.8	3.4	12	236	D	13.0	14	D	D	D
Evangeline	43	119	10.7	3.5	18	704	D	24.7	25	D	D	D
Franklin	34	163	13.8	4.2	9	178	D	4.1	22	D	2.6	0.8
Grant	6	D	D	D	11	307	D	10.8	5	76	2.6	0.8
Iberia	149	820	123.7	42.5	135	4 659	D	254.8	94	1 685	78.9	20.1
Iberville	33	208	23.6	13.8	30	3 165	8 877.1	287.6	36	497	22.5	6.6
Jackson	16	50	5.9	1.3	8	D	D	D	17	D	D	D
Jefferson	1 336	10 711	1 848.1	687.2	317	11 438	2 996.9	626.6	1 037	19 493	1 056.5	303.1
Jefferson Davis	65	344	33.4	17.7	17	534	D	21.4	43	669	29.4	7.3
Lafayette	1 269	8 970	1 597.9	547.4	295	10 996	D	717.5	665	14 444	782.6	230.2
Lafourche	160	1 635	138.6	73.0	59	2 575	864.1	119.7	159	2 654	115.3	29.1
La Salle	100	150	27.3	7.2	6	55	D	2.5	14	D	D	D
Lincoln	91	669	97.6	38.6	35	1 084	421.6	59.2	93	2 015	91.0	23.9
Livingston	140	627	65.0	24.5	67	1 772	504.0	81.0	156	2 737	115.9	31.5
Madison	11	29	1.5	0.8	5	D	D	D	20	D	D	D
Morehouse	23	96	12.4	3.4	14	111	D	4.2	26	D	D	D
Natchitoches	64	251	33.1	8.3	16	2 340	1 162.1	97.2	81	1 647	70.0	17.6

1. Establishment subject to federal tax.

STATE County	Health care and social assistance, 2012				Other services, 2012				Nonemployer businesses, 2015		Value of residential construction authorized by building permits, 2016	
	Number of establishments	Number of employees	Receipts (mil dol)	Annual payroll (mil dol)	Number of establishments	Number of employees	Receipts (mil dol)	Annual payroll (mil dol)	Number	Receipts (mil dol)	New Construction ($1,000)	Number of housing units
	159	160	161	162	163	164	165	166	167	168	169	170
KENTUCKY—Cont'd												
Ohio	39	1 020	65.6	28.4	30	89	9.8	2.5	1 134	38.3	1 764	13
Oldham	142	2 410	169.5	76.5	81	D	D	D	5 154	250.1	100 281	341
Owen	10	265	23.0	8.2	10	38	2.7	0.7	739	27.4	0	4
Owsley	9	192	10.5	5.2	3	16	1.3	0.3	263	9.4	NA	NA
Pendleton	18	249	14.7	6.5	11	D	D	D	763	28.6	0	0
Perry	128	2 853	304.5	107.6	27	D	D	D	1 405	46.2	640	6
Pike	213	4 427	579.9	210.9	78	389	41.9	11.3	2 834	110.4	2 106	7
Powell	19	213	17.6	6.6	8	42	3.5	0.9	834	28.0	0	0
Pulaski	240	5 134	484.7	192.4	66	353	29.9	8.2	4 387	184.2	2 565	32
Robertson	3	D	D	D	1	D	D	D	119	2.8	NA	NA
Rockcastle	36	808	66.5	31.2	11	76	6.0	1.6	931	30.8	NA	NA
Rowan	86	1 998	198.5	79.0	24	117	6.6	1.8	1 410	46.5	2 142	24
Russell	47	1 015	86.4	30.8	17	D	D	D	1 304	53.4	1 250	16
Scott	129	1 426	119.6	46.7	68	273	24.2	6.7	3 256	131.5	94 527	931
Shelby	85	1 415	110.8	44.5	67	501	50.2	13.4	3 148	141.4	54 337	377
Simpson	35	D	D	D	23	111	10.0	2.6	1 206	56.7	16 090	162
Spencer	17	219	13.4	6.1	14	D	D	D	1 218	48.3	27 060	132
Taylor	84	D	D	D	43	D	D	D	1 698	58.9	2 045	17
Todd	17	215	14.6	5.3	9	D	D	D	823	40.4	432	5
Trigg	22	378	23.4	9.7	14	D	D	D	887	37.1	2 274	10
Trimble	6	108	10.6	4.2	3	D	D	D	493	15.2	NA	NA
Union	33	896	83.6	28.0	12	56	9.5	1.7	704	27.6	1 608	9
Warren	383	7 745	852.6	320.8	199	1 035	86.7	25.8	8 981	511.3	162 768	1 335
Washington	27	410	18.6	8.7	16	110	7.5	2.1	734	28.1	2 013	28
Wayne	32	546	35.4	16.0	16	D	D	D	1 161	44.5	0	0
Webster	19	266	14.3	7.2	11	46	6.5	1.3	632	20.6	40	5
Whitley	97	2 467	272.1	98.8	31	D	D	D	2 207	87.6	686	7
Wolfe	12	230	14.7	6.1	3	D	D	D	417	16.0	NA	NA
Woodford	62	559	45.4	18.6	37	D	D	D	2 151	95.8	16 399	85
LOUISIANA	11 999	284 979	27 951.8	10 646.9	6 293	43 500	5 408.9	1 479.2	358 223	15 250.9	2 766 650	14 503
Acadia	128	2 215	157.2	62.7	70	346	26.4	7.1	4 259	181.4	22 866	143
Allen	43	907	61.8	22.1	20	D	D	D	1 147	32.1	7 643	40
Ascension	180	3 300	255.4	105.2	150	1 260	152.0	44.6	8 055	339.8	139 089	857
Assumption	22	675	25.3	13.4	17	D	D	D	1 559	58.0	11 687	47
Avoyelles	85	2 104	131.1	49.3	42	153	13.8	3.4	2 447	88.8	7 495	50
Beauregard	64	1 086	84.1	35.7	29	121	10.8	2.7	1 935	75.3	26 703	146
Bienville	15	486	30.7	10.9	11	D	D	D	780	26.9	0	0
Bossier	216	4 289	376.0	137.9	141	846	84.5	23.3	8 439	387.5	113 296	680
Caddo	818	28 245	2 809.9	1 111.3	381	D	D	D	20 266	860.7	67 601	259
Calcasieu	519	D	D	D	240	1 605	177.0	50.8	13 412	613.5	216 471	1 512
Caldwell	25	651	49.7	20.7	13	37	3.4	0.8	623	21.6	4 289	18
Cameron	2	D	D	D	4	12	1.0	0.3	687	31.7	7 467	51
Catahoula	15	526	19.1	9.8	14	D	D	D	653	21.6	1 083	11
Claiborne	21	791	46.2	19.7	13	63	4.2	0.8	787	26.1	0	0
Concordia	46	882	62.5	24.8	26	D	D	D	1 166	44.4	2 199	10
De Soto	30	722	54.5	19.8	20	D	D	D	1 854	63.6	31 952	215
East Baton Rouge	1 403	38 136	4 112.4	1 527.3	876	8 742	1 008.1	367.9	35 766	1 475.5	322 407	1 340
East Carroll	11	328	22.1	8.8	6	9	0.6	0.1	415	16.3	0	0
East Feliciana	32	1 821	117.2	64.9	16	54	9.1	1.7	1 277	46.6	9 187	48
Evangeline	95	2 618	184.3	72.9	26	55	4.7	1.0	1 663	63.4	10 649	49
Franklin	52	1 157	75.5	34.1	22	73	6.8	1.4	1 456	55.9	4 075	14
Grant	17	255	14.9	5.4	11	50	3.4	0.9	1 004	43.7	8 576	42
Iberia	207	3 985	309.5	122.6	124	868	111.9	29.7	6 031	223.3	17 281	84
Iberville	48	D	D	D	30	136	15.8	4.8	2 126	61.6	25 762	111
Jackson	22	555	41.0	15.6	17	71	5.2	1.6	821	29.8	14 089	28
Jefferson	1 318	26 711	3 077.9	1 178.8	730	5 002	551.7	161.5	41 867	1 970.7	115 691	598
Jefferson Davis	75	1 553	121.3	49.7	35	116	18.2	3.3	1 761	66.6	14 496	85
Lafayette	1 018	22 618	2 452.2	909.5	421	3 607	491.3	120.7	22 150	1 068.1	226 558	1 190
Lafourche	194	4 123	476.7	177.9	110	686	71.7	19.8	6 922	314.9	83 719	538
La Salle	22	747	69.1	23.3	12	D	D	D	912	39.1	2 048	12
Lincoln	115	3 306	304.1	106.2	52	214	15.2	4.7	2 852	138.6	12 055	125
Livingston	150	2 060	141.1	56.9	106	487	56.7	15.2	8 740	338.6	161 266	733
Madison	36	1 145	56.4	24.7	12	26	2.1	0.4	732	19.5	11 661	76
Morehouse	76	2 087	112.7	49.9	32	137	7.3	2.0	1 703	50.1	1 349	41
Natchitoches	102	1 758	138.0	50.9	41	150	12.0	2.7	2 362	92.2	9 793	55

Table B. States and Counties — Government Employment and Payroll, and Local Government Finances

	Government employment and payroll, 2012									Local government finances, 2012				
STATE County			March payroll (percent of total)									General revenue		
												Taxes		
													Per capita[1] (dollars)	
	Full-time equivalent employees	March payroll (dollars)	Adminis-tration, judicial, and legal	Police and Corrections	Fire Protection	Highways and transpor-tation	Health and Welfare	Natural resources and utilities	Education and libraries	Total (mil dol)	Inter-govern-mental (mil dol)	Total (mil dol)	Total	Property
	171	172	173	174	175	176	177	178	179	180	181	182	183	184
KENTUCKY—Cont'd														
Ohio	1 248	3 369 261	2.7	2.9	0.0	1.3	36.2	2.8	52.4	62.2	36.1	14.2	590	347
Oldham	2 024	6 660 606	0.3	5.8	2.0	0.6	3.6	1.6	84.6	158.6	58.3	71.9	1 171	957
Owen	363	1 105 970	4.6	2.3	3.8	2.1	0.7	0.2	83.4	23.3	14.0	7.1	661	495
Owsley	278	620 892	6.0	3.8	0.0	3.9	0.3	2.8	81.2	13.2	10.6	1.4	301	184
Pendleton	588	1 671 881	4.1	2.6	1.6	2.8	15.0	6.1	67.8	38.5	22.7	9.2	631	467
Perry	1 406	4 111 977	3.0	3.4	1.5	2.6	18.7	2.8	66.7	100.4	52.4	23.0	814	540
Pike	2 126	6 896 536	3.5	4.4	1.3	2.8	7.1	1.3	78.6	183.6	110.6	49.7	775	500
Powell	571	1 479 612	5.5	7.2	0.0	1.0	5.3	5.1	75.7	31.1	21.3	6.1	493	235
Pulaski	2 626	7 286 813	4.1	5.1	1.6	1.7	17.0	5.8	64.1	151.6	74.3	49.2	773	465
Robertson	124	297 631	8.0	3.4	0.0	4.9	0.2	0.6	83.0	5.9	4.4	1.2	557	414
Rockcastle	758	1 967 231	6.5	9.5	0.0	2.3	2.6	2.4	74.7	38.4	26.7	7.6	448	184
Rowan	813	2 389 386	2.9	7.6	0.4	3.5	14.9	2.7	67.0	61.6	29.3	19.7	841	374
Russell	920	2 454 498	2.9	5.5	0.4	0.9	28.6	4.1	57.3	61.4	21.4	14.1	807	422
Scott	1 616	5 156 528	2.9	7.7	7.0	2.1	6.1	0.1	73.2	151.0	48.9	60.2	1 227	530
Shelby	1 282	4 061 414	3.4	9.9	2.6	1.9	6.5	0.8	73.8	102.9	42.5	43.5	997	724
Simpson	616	2 092 237	8.9	11.0	1.5	2.3	5.8	3.3	66.5	48.7	23.2	18.0	1 026	501
Spencer	523	1 426 278	5.8	4.0	0.7	1.4	3.1	2.3	81.4	34.5	19.5	12.1	693	525
Taylor	1 374	4 732 730	2.1	2.7	0.9	1.1	51.8	2.5	38.2	123.7	56.5	19.0	769	374
Todd	505	1 331 511	3.1	7.5	0.2	1.9	3.5	7.4	76.3	31.2	20.1	6.9	544	268
Trigg	587	1 746 830	2.8	3.6	0.1	2.4	28.3	5.6	56.1	27.8	15.3	10.2	708	456
Trimble	305	972 373	7.5	3.6	0.0	1.9	2.3	5.1	78.5	32.6	10.9	5.6	634	445
Union	599	1 762 787	11.1	6.4	2.1	5.7	0.5	5.2	67.9	38.7	23.0	11.5	777	532
Warren	4 084	12 459 019	3.2	8.5	4.4	1.8	4.7	10.4	63.3	304.6	116.1	128.4	1 096	529
Washington	407	1 176 342	5.5	5.0	0.0	4.1	9.6	4.1	69.1	26.8	14.5	8.5	718	377
Wayne	760	2 029 072	4.1	6.1	0.2	1.7	4.0	0.3	83.0	44.7	31.3	10.0	478	288
Webster	605	1 592 385	5.5	8.5	4.2	2.0	2.8	7.4	66.8	37.5	24.0	7.8	574	425
Whitley	1 867	5 263 187	2.4	4.6	3.4	1.6	6.6	7.3	73.7	112.5	68.5	23.7	669	308
Wolfe	313	774 203	3.3	1.9	0.0	1.4	0.4	3.3	85.8	23.7	18.4	2.4	336	190
Woodford	911	3 023 818	4.5	9.8	2.1	1.8	8.6	2.9	68.0	69.9	26.8	32.2	1 286	739
LOUISIANA	X	X	X	X	X	X	X	X	X	X	X	X	X	X
Acadia	1 914	5 479 946	5.7	5.4	2.7	4.1	2.9	4.6	73.3	180.8	90.9	63.9	1 033	388
Allen	973	2 882 412	11.1	8.9	0.4	3.1	19.2	2.8	54.4	94.4	48.2	28.5	1 114	473
Ascension	4 531	13 738 983	6.7	8.8	2.0	2.3	2.8	3.8	71.9	408.3	139.8	213.9	1 905	870
Assumption	1 463	4 579 903	6.7	5.0	0.6	13.3	13.8	10.4	49.4	74.9	42.1	25.4	1 102	571
Avoyelles	1 542	3 784 002	3.9	22.1	1.3	2.7	13.2	4.5	52.2	121.6	72.1	26.8	644	144
Beauregard	1 561	4 516 320	4.2	3.0	1.7	3.0	29.5	1.5	56.6	146.5	59.0	50.2	1 382	629
Bienville	604	1 849 545	7.1	11.8	0.0	5.8	0.4	1.9	72.9	72.4	15.3	51.7	3 673	2 477
Bossier	4 814	15 229 557	8.2	15.0	5.4	2.1	0.4	3.1	64.8	444.2	156.3	238.0	1 948	757
Caddo	11 080	37 545 778	5.6	16.6	7.2	2.8	2.9	5.7	57.7	1 117.9	399.7	540.3	2 102	1 067
Calcasieu	9 145	28 598 210	5.0	14.5	3.5	5.7	7.9	5.4	56.0	961.3	315.0	432.3	2 223	866
Caldwell	302	782 732	5.3	3.7	0.3	0.5	0.0	1.0	89.3	33.5	19.0	10.2	1 019	536
Cameron	525	1 990 275	6.0	0.0	0.3	7.0	7.7	4.9	74.1	94.4	45.2	42.7	6 367	6 281
Catahoula	616	1 309 075	8.8	22.3	0.4	5.1	2.5	3.4	57.4	54.6	21.6	8.9	869	412
Claiborne	847	2 308 077	5.0	2.0	2.4	2.3	47.8	2.4	38.2	69.3	34.1	15.8	939	530
Concordia	1 328	3 662 764	3.6	24.2	2.0	3.1	16.5	5.2	44.7	109.8	52.5	25.5	1 253	622
De Soto	1 141	3 608 492	7.4	7.4	0.8	6.3	2.6	3.1	71.2	213.8	37.7	149.7	5 553	2 010
East Baton Rouge	16 122	60 516 124	9.3	10.2	6.8	4.4	7.2	8.9	49.7	1 776.4	573.7	866.4	1 949	820
East Carroll	291	819 177	9.3	8.7	1.7	2.4	46.3	8.0	23.1	47.3	28.8	7.1	947	459
East Feliciana	631	1 666 825	14.0	19.9	0.0	2.6	1.1	4.2	58.2	44.3	27.0	13.4	671	245
Evangeline	1 334	3 509 390	4.9	9.7	2.3	4.2	2.0	5.9	70.6	136.3	68.0	37.5	1 111	500
Franklin	1 046	2 791 309	5.1	15.1	1.2	2.0	28.2	2.9	45.4	84.3	40.9	21.5	1 046	283
Grant	604	1 502 745	8.0	3.6	0.0	2.3	3.2	5.7	76.5	50.6	32.7	12.2	551	301
Iberia	3 450	9 630 156	4.1	12.3	3.2	2.7	20.2	5.1	51.6	320.8	141.9	101.3	1 368	514
Iberville	1 742	4 067 035	7.6	14.8	2.5	5.7	1.5	5.6	57.3	154.3	45.0	93.6	2 817	1 287
Jackson	824	2 175 796	2.6	14.3	1.3	2.9	30.0	2.2	46.2	80.9	29.0	33.0	2 033	1 323
Jefferson	16 179	70 416 195	8.0	11.6	2.9	2.3	31.2	6.3	36.3	2 140.2	681.5	696.5	1 606	721
Jefferson Davis	1 386	3 583 234	4.3	9.8	2.0	2.1	0.3	3.8	76.9	101.8	54.3	35.4	1 127	532
Lafayette	8 193	26 367 258	8.2	13.8	4.3	3.8	0.8	11.2	56.6	791.5	255.4	391.9	1 726	692
Lafourche	4 602	16 739 494	5.8	10.8	0.0	3.9	32.6	3.4	42.1	526.8	177.3	149.9	1 545	846
La Salle	890	2 469 446	4.0	15.2	0.4	1.6	31.7	2.8	44.0	119.2	60.2	20.7	1 388	759
Lincoln	1 655	6 428 631	8.8	13.7	9.5	6.9	3.8	12.8	43.0	139.1	54.9	66.4	1 414	645
Livingston	4 067	13 075 838	6.4	8.4	0.8	1.6	0.8	3.2	78.1	359.5	202.1	123.4	935	334
Madison	681	1 378 550	9.2	30.1	0.1	5.0	0.3	1.6	53.3	76.9	38.0	17.4	1 428	929
Morehouse	1 347	4 002 380	5.9	10.2	2.9	1.8	23.0	0.9	54.6	125.8	64.1	30.3	1 099	513
Natchitoches	2 176	6 441 570	5.4	11.8	1.9	2.7	29.9	5.7	41.6	198.4	86.0	59.1	1 498	518

1. Based on the resident population estimated as of July 1 of the year shown.

Local Government Finances, Government Employment, and Income Taxes

STATE County	Local government finances, 2012 (cont.)									Government employment, 2015			Individual income tax returns, 2014		
	Direct general expenditure							Debt outstanding							
			Percent of total for:												
	Total (mil dol)	Per capita¹ (dollars)	Educa-tion	Health and hospitals	Police protec-tion	Public welfare	High-ways	Total (mil dol)	Per capita¹ (dollars)	Federal civilian	Federal military	State and local	Number of returns	Mean adjusted gross income	Mean income tax
	185	186	187	188	189	190	191	192	193	194	195	196	197	198	199
KENTUCKY—Cont'd															
Ohio	54.6	2 269	56.5	1.1	4.2	0.1	4.9	203.8	8 463	85	75	1 434	9 630	43 290	3 684
Oldham	156.7	2 552	60.0	4.3	4.0	0.4	2.1	428.5	6 978	69	187	3 158	27 130	88 085	13 058
Owen	24.6	2 286	63.4	3.3	2.4	0.5	6.5	37.0	3 440	21	33	451	4 280	43 356	3 714
Owsley	13.9	2 954	73.5	0.4	2.7	0.0	7.0	5.8	1 224	D	40	305	1 290	30 840	1 864
Pendleton	38.4	2 629	51.2	14.8	3.0	0.0	6.3	59.7	4 086	28	44	634	6 120	45 700	4 053
Perry	108.4	3 839	51.5	14.3	2.9	0.0	4.1	267.3	9 465	138	84	2 532	10 180	43 788	4 386
Pike	184.3	2 872	57.9	3.3	2.1	0.2	4.9	348.9	5 437	237	189	2 986	20 610	46 891	4 897
Powell	29.2	2 335	66.0	6.6	2.1	0.0	3.4	14.4	1 150	32	38	765	4 990	34 876	2 516
Pulaski	161.3	2 537	51.9	11.8	5.1	0.1	3.7	170.4	2 679	186	197	3 937	25 410	41 851	4 168
Robertson	15.0	6 849	83.7	0.5	0.9	0.0	3.9	36.7	16 787	D	D	136	820	39 052	3 185
Rockcastle	38.2	2 248	63.7	4.5	2.8	0.0	4.0	25.4	1 494	33	52	754	6 040	36 867	2 592
Rowan	57.8	2 467	44.0	13.0	4.0	0.6	5.0	89.2	3 802	93	70	3 178	8 570	41 889	3 760
Russell	56.8	3 247	41.5	34.9	2.6	0.4	3.2	42.4	2 424	65	55	974	7 000	37 944	3 128
Scott	139.0	2 834	46.7	7.0	4.0	0.2	2.7	633.9	12 922	54	159	2 232	22 870	57 993	6 205
Shelby	102.9	2 359	54.2	6.2	3.7	0.0	2.4	238.0	5 456	74	137	2 296	20 590	57 298	6 660
Simpson	44.9	2 560	53.3	3.9	5.1	1.0	3.9	71.7	4 088	39	55	821	8 070	41 878	3 798
Spencer	29.0	1 665	65.8	2.9	4.3	0.1	5.6	48.6	2 788	24	56	609	8 000	58 296	5 717
Taylor	135.0	5 469	23.2	57.5	1.9	0.0	2.1	111.7	4 523	85	76	1 720	10 300	38 665	3 317
Todd	33.7	2 664	60.0	5.0	3.2	0.0	4.5	102.5	8 103	31	39	606	4 860	44 532	4 339
Trigg	28.2	1 952	58.5	2.4	4.6	0.1	8.2	21.2	1 469	82	44	629	6 000	43 123	3 979
Trimble	33.1	3 770	40.0	1.5	0.6	0.0	3.9	423.4	48 190	17	27	339	3 690	44 568	3 751
Union	38.1	2 567	54.2	0.6	4.9	0.4	7.4	15.5	1 046	57	42	729	5 910	51 531	5 537
Warren	300.9	2 570	45.9	4.4	6.6	0.1	3.4	970.8	8 290	366	374	9 632	52 120	50 785	5 691
Washington	29.1	2 457	61.1	3.2	3.0	0.1	7.7	78.0	6 592	30	36	497	5 220	41 436	3 566
Wayne	46.9	2 252	65.2	3.1	3.1	0.0	3.8	44.3	2 129	40	63	938	7 440	34 493	2 592
Webster	36.1	2 657	46.4	1.2	2.4	0.0	5.6	63.7	4 692	41	40	648	5 360	50 585	5 019
Whitley	116.0	3 267	65.4	7.7	3.4	0.0	3.2	141.1	3 974	79	107	2 151	13 470	38 586	3 383
Wolfe	19.1	2 667	68.4	0.1	0.9	0.0	6.6	20.2	2 819	22	22	400	2 310	32 074	2 124
Woodford	67.4	2 689	51.3	5.2	8.7	0.0	4.7	133.5	5 323	40	79	1 501	12 340	58 760	7 673
LOUISIANA	X	X	X	X	X	X	X	X	X	30 243	36 715	295 913	2 007 690	57 884	7 639
Acadia	174.4	2 817	55.1	8.1	6.4	0.3	4.6	40.6	656	92	271	2 571	25 110	52 212	5 977
Allen	95.8	3 750	51.3	17.0	5.7	0.0	5.7	24.4	955	636	95	3 650	8 780	45 233	3 917
Ascension	402.3	3 583	57.6	3.1	6.1	0.0	4.1	796.9	7 097	135	524	4 875	51 280	68 878	8 721
Assumption	72.6	3 151	65.4	0.1	5.9	0.8	2.8	12.4	536	30	100	1 012	9 710	53 780	5 821
Avoyelles	119.8	2 877	51.1	10.8	10.3	0.0	2.9	26.7	640	77	166	3 597	16 320	44 217	4 347
Beauregard	151.0	4 161	49.3	23.5	4.9	0.0	5.2	90.4	2 493	72	156	1 666	13 940	56 553	6 071
Bienville	72.3	5 139	63.9	2.2	6.1	0.2	6.3	29.9	2 123	46	59	768	5 780	44 757	3 911
Bossier	464.2	3 799	47.3	1.0	9.1	0.1	5.0	486.1	3 978	1 867	5 627	6 911	59 830	56 905	6 482
Caddo	1 081.2	4 206	48.6	1.7	7.4	0.0	2.2	1 079.9	4 201	2 870	1 117	16 186	113 190	54 398	7 326
Calcasieu	908.6	4 671	38.0	7.0	6.7	0.4	7.0	2 311.6	11 885	528	946	12 508	86 680	57 479	7 085
Caldwell	34.6	3 461	63.2	7.2	3.0	0.2	3.0	14.9	1 485	27	41	600	3 800	53 511	5 797
Cameron	87.3	13 024	42.4	9.7	4.1	0.4	4.8	20.4	3 043	15	30	752	3 060	69 725	10 592
Catahoula	65.8	6 390	33.4	42.7	3.0	0.0	2.4	37.4	3 632	46	41	565	3 720	46 789	4 547
Claiborne	68.0	4 039	33.4	28.7	3.9	0.7	3.0	18.0	1 071	44	59	1 173	5 490	47 752	4 813
Concordia	116.6	5 726	35.0	12.7	6.4	0.0	2.6	38.7	1 899	62	82	1 490	7 620	45 717	4 590
De Soto	190.9	7 081	58.1	1.3	4.0	1.7	8.4	134.5	4 987	49	118	1 576	11 630	51 755	5 526
East Baton Rouge	2 083.6	4 687	38.7	5.0	6.4	0.1	5.2	2 247.5	5 056	2 279	2 121	46 321	201 020	63 206	9 385
East Carroll	50.8	6 748	38.0	18.4	3.5	0.0	2.7	36.4	4 836	19	28	548	2 640	43 922	5 377
East Feliciana	43.2	2 161	59.7	0.7	8.1	0.0	4.6	5.3	264	26	76	2 510	8 220	51 521	5 527
Evangeline	132.8	3 939	46.5	23.7	4.1	0.0	6.4	25.6	760	52	143	1 633	12 670	47 508	4 745
Franklin	83.8	4 076	38.5	25.0	7.6	0.3	4.2	14.2	691	52	87	1 375	7 910	42 089	4 262
Grant	55.3	2 505	70.8	0.2	6.0	0.0	2.2	23.9	1 085	750	94	784	7 890	47 454	4 149
Iberia	346.8	4 686	45.5	17.9	5.9	0.2	5.6	224.6	3 035	101	323	4 143	32 890	54 569	6 902
Iberville	172.3	5 186	44.7	0.6	7.8	1.5	10.8	142.1	4 275	88	128	2 867	13 650	51 247	5 802
Jackson	80.7	4 976	35.7	20.0	10.5	0.0	5.3	72.6	4 475	30	65	1 105	6 050	48 236	4 531
Jefferson	2 141.8	4 939	30.3	30.9	4.8	2.5	3.5	1 621.8	3 740	1 423	2 433	18 429	205 850	56 469	7 631
Jefferson Davis	102.5	3 259	62.2	1.3	8.7	0.1	3.0	56.9	1 811	97	136	1 903	13 290	49 695	5 359
Lafayette	816.4	3 596	40.1	0.7	7.8	0.1	5.7	1 609.2	7 087	971	1 074	12 645	108 250	72 802	11 656
Lafourche	483.7	4 985	32.9	32.8	5.3	0.5	2.6	200.2	2 064	132	449	6 745	41 750	61 754	8 409
La Salle	118.0	7 903	25.1	37.6	3.9	0.0	1.8	23.9	1 604	46	61	1 402	5 300	62 948	7 060
Lincoln	137.7	2 933	55.0	0.5	7.2	0.6	5.1	82.8	1 764	106	199	4 238	17 870	55 557	7 191
Livingston	373.0	2 827	65.1	0.6	5.1	0.0	2.6	445.0	3 373	146	602	5 461	56 730	55 647	5 746
Madison	79.7	6 557	26.6	19.8	12.1	0.1	3.5	74.6	6 141	36	44	753	4 120	34 175	2 836
Morehouse	124.7	4 525	44.2	20.5	4.1	0.1	2.7	101.1	3 668	53	113	1 224	11 200	38 985	3 532
Natchitoches	210.4	5 335	45.1	20.9	4.9	0.5	3.0	50.5	1 281	165	167	3 823	15 340	48 011	5 206

1. Based on the resident population estimated as of July 1 of the year shown.

Table B. States and Counties — Land Area and Population

STATE/ County code	CBSA code[1]	County type[2]	STATE County	Land area,[3] (sq mi) 2016	Total persons 2016	Rank	Per square mile	White	Black	American Indian, Alaska Native	Asian and Pacific Islander	Percent Hispanic or Latino[4]	Under 5 years	5 to 17 years	18 to 24 years	25 to 34 years	35 to 44 years	45 to 54 years
				1	2	3	4	5	6	7	8	9	10	11	12	13	14	15
			LOUISIANA—Cont'd															
22 071	35380	1	Orleans	169.4	391 495	177	2 311.1	31.9	59.8	0.7	3.4	5.6	6.0	14.4	9.3	18.6	13.1	12.4
22 073	33740	3	Ouachita	610.4	156 983	413	257.2	59.2	37.9	0.6	1.3	2.2	7.1	18.3	9.9	14.2	12.3	12.1
22 075	35380	1	Plaquemines	780.3	23 464	1 661	30.1	67.2	21.3	2.5	5.0	6.8	6.8	19.7	8.4	13.4	12.9	13.7
22 077	12940	2	Pointe Coupee	557.3	22 159	1 721	39.8	61.5	36.0	0.5	0.5	2.6	6.2	16.3	8.0	11.5	13.3	13.3
22 079	10780	3	Rapides	1 318.0	132 424	480	100.5	62.7	32.7	1.5	1.9	3.1	6.8	18.3	8.8	13.2	11.9	12.6
22 081	...	8	Red River	389.1	8 550	2 547	22.0	57.3	39.9	0.7	0.4	2.5	6.7	17.2	8.1	11.9	10.9	13.6
22 083	...	6	Richland	559.3	20 430	1 809	36.5	61.2	36.4	0.6	0.6	2.2	6.6	17.8	8.3	13.0	12.2	12.2
22 085	...	6	Sabine	866.7	23 977	1 644	27.7	70.9	17.8	10.3	0.7	3.7	6.2	18.0	7.3	12.1	10.9	12.8
22 087	35380	1	St. Bernard	377.5	45 688	1 057	121.0	65.2	23.0	1.3	2.8	9.8	7.5	19.6	8.1	16.9	12.9	12.3
22 089	35380	1	St. Charles	277.7	52 923	948	190.6	66.4	26.7	0.7	1.5	6.1	6.1	18.6	8.6	13.0	12.8	14.5
22 091	12940	2	St. Helena	408.4	10 512	2 389	25.7	45.4	53.0	1.0	0.4	1.6	5.5	16.3	8.7	13.3	10.3	12.8
22 093	35380	1	St. James	241.5	21 557	1 748	89.3	48.8	49.5	0.5	0.4	1.6	6.3	17.1	8.6	13.1	10.7	13.8
22 095	35380	1	St. John the Baptist	214.3	43 631	1 099	203.6	36.8	56.4	0.6	1.4	6.0	6.5	18.5	8.7	13.2	12.2	13.7
22 097	36660	4	St. Landry	923.9	83 883	677	90.8	55.7	42.1	0.6	0.7	2.1	7.5	19.6	8.4	12.7	11.0	12.4
22 099	29180	2	St. Martin	737.7	54 007	929	73.2	65.5	30.8	0.8	1.2	3.0	7.0	17.8	8.4	13.0	11.2	13.3
22 101	34020	4	St. Mary	555.5	52 093	960	93.8	57.8	32.8	2.3	2.1	7.0	7.1	17.4	8.6	13.2	11.2	13.5
22 103	35380	1	St. Tammany	845.7	253 602	266	299.9	80.5	12.6	1.0	2.1	5.5	6.0	18.2	7.6	11.6	12.6	13.9
22 105	25220	3	Tangipahoa	791.3	130 710	484	165.2	64.6	30.7	0.8	1.1	4.2	7.3	17.3	10.2	15.0	12.0	12.0
22 107	...	9	Tensas	602.8	4 597	2 856	7.6	43.6	55.0	0.6	0.3	1.8	6.6	17.4	7.3	9.4	9.7	11.7
22 109	26380	3	Terrebonne	1 231.8	113 220	541	91.9	68.8	20.1	6.8	1.6	5.2	7.2	18.6	8.4	14.6	12.2	13.1
22 111	33740	3	Union	877.0	22 487	1 710	25.6	69.2	25.7	0.6	0.3	4.8	6.0	16.4	7.7	11.7	10.9	12.9
22 113	29180	2	Vermilion	1 173.2	60 205	867	51.3	79.4	15.1	0.7	2.6	3.5	6.8	19.3	7.6	13.2	12.4	13.2
22 115	22860	5	Vernon	1 327.9	50 569	978	38.1	72.8	15.4	2.3	3.8	9.3	8.5	17.3	13.6	17.3	12.7	10.0
22 117	14220	6	Washington	669.5	46 310	1 042	69.2	66.9	31.0	0.8	0.5	2.1	6.2	17.9	8.1	12.3	11.8	12.4
22 119	43340	2	Webster	593.2	39 710	1 185	66.9	63.2	34.6	1.0	0.7	1.8	6.2	16.5	8.1	12.3	11.2	13.0
22 121	12940	2	West Baton Rouge	192.4	25 795	1 570	134.1	57.0	39.8	0.5	0.7	3.0	6.9	17.6	8.3	16.1	12.1	13.2
22 123	...	9	West Carroll	359.6	11 114	2 347	30.9	80.4	15.7	0.8	0.5	3.6	5.8	17.4	8.3	11.4	12.3	12.7
22 125	12940	2	West Feliciana	403.2	15 344	2 074	38.1	52.6	45.6	0.5	0.4	1.7	4.2	12.2	5.9	13.8	17.9	17.9
22 127	...	6	Winn	950.1	14 376	2 139	15.1	66.1	31.3	1.4	0.7	2.0	5.6	16.1	7.8	13.7	12.7	13.7
23 000	...	0	MAINE	30 843.9	1 331 479	X	43.2	95.1	1.9	1.4	1.7	1.6	4.9	14.2	8.3	11.8	11.3	14.3
23 001	30340	3	Androscoggin	467.9	107 319	558	229.4	93.1	4.8	1.1	1.4	1.8	6.0	15.8	8.7	12.3	11.9	14.4
23 003	...	7	Aroostook	6 671.1	67 959	782	10.2	95.6	1.2	2.7	0.7	1.1	4.8	13.7	7.9	9.9	10.4	14.2
23 005	38860	2	Cumberland	835.7	292 041	235	349.5	92.5	3.5	0.9	3.0	2.0	5.0	14.2	8.9	13.3	12.0	14.5
23 007	...	6	Franklin	1 697.0	30 001	1 433	17.7	97.1	0.9	1.3	0.9	1.3	4.4	13.7	10.2	10.6	10.0	13.9
23 009	...	6	Hancock	1 587.0	54 419	925	34.3	96.1	1.2	1.1	1.5	1.4	4.5	13.2	6.8	10.7	10.5	13.9
23 011	12300	4	Kennebec	867.5	120 569	517	139.0	96.4	1.1	1.3	1.4	1.5	5.1	14.6	8.5	11.6	11.5	14.6
23 013	...	7	Knox	365.1	39 744	1 182	108.9	96.8	1.0	1.3	1.0	1.4	4.7	13.4	6.6	10.4	11.0	13.4
23 015	...	8	Lincoln	455.8	34 216	1 319	75.1	96.7	0.8	1.0	1.5	1.2	4.1	13.2	6.6	9.3	9.9	13.3
23 017	...	6	Oxford	2 076.9	57 217	895	27.5	97.0	0.8	1.3	1.1	1.3	4.5	14.5	6.8	10.2	11.2	14.7
23 019	12620	3	Penobscot	3 397.2	151 806	432	44.7	95.5	1.3	2.0	1.5	1.3	4.7	13.7	10.7	13.4	11.1	13.9
23 021	...	8	Piscataquis	3 960.9	16 843	1 989	4.3	96.6	0.8	1.3	1.2	1.4	4.1	12.9	6.1	8.9	10.2	14.0
23 023	38860	2	Sagadahoc	254.0	35 273	1 294	138.9	96.4	1.3	1.0	1.4	1.6	5.0	14.2	6.5	11.2	11.0	14.4
23 025	...	6	Somerset	3 924.4	50 915	975	13.0	97.1	0.9	1.3	1.1	1.1	4.7	14.7	7.0	10.4	11.5	15.2
23 027	...	6	Waldo	729.9	39 364	1 188	53.9	97.0	0.8	1.3	1.1	1.2	4.6	14.5	7.4	10.5	11.7	13.8
23 029	...	7	Washington	2 562.7	31 450	1 397	12.3	91.7	1.0	6.5	0.8	2.0	4.9	14.1	7.5	9.6	10.3	13.5
23 031	38860	2	York	990.8	202 343	325	204.2	96.0	1.2	1.0	1.7	1.6	4.8	14.5	7.7	11.8	11.3	14.7
24 000	...	0	MARYLAND	9 709.6	6 016 447	X	619.6	53.5	31.0	0.8	7.5	9.8	6.1	16.3	9.1	13.9	12.7	14.2
24 001	19060	3	Allegany	424.2	72 130	753	170.0	88.9	9.3	0.5	1.4	1.7	4.6	13.0	12.5	12.7	11.6	12.8
24 003	12580	1	Anne Arundel	414.9	568 346	115	1 369.8	71.4	18.0	0.8	5.2	7.5	6.2	16.2	8.9	14.2	13.0	14.4
24 005	12580	1	Baltimore	598.4	831 026	71	1 388.7	59.9	29.4	0.8	7.0	5.3	5.9	15.7	9.0	14.0	12.0	13.3
24 009	47900	1	Calvert	213.2	91 251	640	428.0	81.1	14.1	1.0	2.9	3.7	5.4	18.2	8.4	11.4	11.6	16.5
24 011	...	6	Caroline	319.4	32 850	1 360	102.8	77.9	15.0	0.7	1.2	7.2	6.0	17.5	7.8	12.5	12.0	14.1
24 013	12580	1	Carroll	447.6	167 656	383	374.6	91.1	4.2	0.5	2.5	3.4	5.1	16.7	8.7	11.2	11.0	16.4
24 015	37980	1	Cecil	346.3	102 603	588	296.3	87.3	7.8	0.8	1.9	4.3	5.6	17.4	8.2	12.4	12.0	15.3
24 017	47900	1	Charles	457.8	157 705	411	344.5	44.5	47.8	1.6	4.5	5.5	6.1	18.1	9.1	12.8	12.9	16.4
24 019	15700	6	Dorchester	540.8	32 258	1 375	59.6	65.1	29.2	0.8	1.6	5.3	5.8	16.5	7.2	12.0	10.2	13.4
24 021	47900	1	Frederick	660.4	247 591	273	374.9	76.7	10.4	0.7	5.8	9.1	5.9	17.7	8.8	12.4	12.7	15.6
24 023	...	6	Garrett	647.1	29 425	1 445	45.5	97.2	1.4	0.4	0.6	1.2	5.0	14.0	7.9	10.9	11.3	14.0
24 025	12580	1	Harford	437.1	251 032	268	574.3	78.8	14.7	0.7	4.0	4.4	5.6	16.9	8.3	12.5	12.0	15.1
24 027	12580	1	Howard	250.9	317 233	215	1 264.4	56.2	20.1	0.8	19.9	6.6	6.0	18.6	8.2	12.3	13.9	15.2
24 029	...	6	Kent	277.0	19 730	1 842	71.2	79.3	15.8	0.5	1.5	4.5	4.3	12.1	11.8	10.7	8.4	11.9
24 031	47900	1	Montgomery	493.0	1 043 863	42	2 117.4	47.0	19.4	0.6	16.8	19.1	6.4	17.0	8.0	12.9	13.7	14.3
24 033	47900	1	Prince George's	482.7	908 049	59	1 881.2	14.5	64.0	0.9	5.1	17.8	6.6	15.9	10.1	14.9	13.4	14.2
24 035	12580	1	Queen Anne's	371.7	48 929	1 000	131.6	88.4	7.3	0.7	1.8	3.6	4.9	16.8	7.4	10.4	10.8	16.3

1. CBSA = Core Based Statistical Area. See Appendix A for explanation. See Appendix B for list of metropolitan areas with component counties. 2. County type code from the Economic Research Service of USDA Rural-Urban Continuum Codes. See Appendix A for definition. 3. Dry land or land partially or temporarily covered by water. 4. May be of any race.

Table B. States and Counties — **Population and Households**

STATE County	55 to 64 years	65 to 74 years	75 years and over	Percent female	Total persons 2000	Total persons 2010	Percent change 2000–2010	Percent change 2010–2016	Births	Deaths	Net migration	Number	Persons per household	Family households	Female family householder[1]	One person
	16	17	18	19	20	21	22	23	24	25	26	27	28	29	30	31
LOUISIANA—Cont'd																
Orleans	13.2	8.0	5.0	52.4	484 674	343 829	-29.1	13.9	30 292	19 488	36 057	153 140	2.38	50.0	18.7	42.0
Ouachita	12.2	8.0	5.9	52.1	147 250	153 726	4.4	2.1	14 249	9 485	-1 489	57 690	2.55	65.2	19.5	30.6
Plaquemines	12.4	7.5	5.3	49.9	26 757	23 039	-13.9	1.8	1 917	1 105	-369	8 614	2.70	73.4	16.4	22.6
Pointe Coupee	14.9	11.3	7.9	51.8	22 763	22 802	0.2	-2.8	1 777	1 546	-855	8 726	2.56	66.6	14.5	28.3
Rapides	12.8	9.0	6.6	51.7	126 337	131 613	4.2	0.6	11 447	8 715	-1 806	47 674	2.68	66.7	16.9	29.3
Red River	14.5	10.1	7.0	51.6	9 622	9 091	-5.5	-6.0	767	649	-637	3 434	2.54	64.6	17.3	31.6
Richland	13.6	9.5	6.7	51.3	20 981	20 725	-1.2	-1.4	1 736	1 453	-554	7 619	2.59	72.1	18.7	25.3
Sabine	13.4	11.5	7.8	50.2	23 459	24 233	3.3	-1.1	1 850	1 657	-359	9 171	2.60	67.5	13.3	28.6
St. Bernard	12.2	6.6	3.9	50.7	67 229	35 897	-46.6	27.3	4 021	2 011	7 482	14 545	2.92	70.0	18.9	23.5
St. Charles	13.9	7.7	4.8	50.9	48 072	52 887	10.0	0.1	3 990	2 585	-1 405	18 383	2.83	73.7	17.1	21.4
St. Helena	14.2	10.7	8.1	51.1	10 525	11 203	6.4	-6.2	727	706	-756	4 131	2.59	67.4	21.8	31.1
St. James	14.4	9.3	6.8	51.7	21 216	22 102	4.2	-2.5	1 730	1 220	-1 099	7 964	2.69	73.8	23.1	21.7
St. John the Baptist	13.6	8.5	5.1	51.4	43 044	45 817	6.4	-4.8	3 654	2 536	-3 389	15 332	2.83	74.3	20.9	21.7
St. Landry	13.0	8.9	6.5	51.8	87 700	83 387	-4.9	0.6	8 049	5 922	-1 618	30 683	2.68	67.0	19.0	29.1
St. Martin	13.6	8.8	5.4	50.7	48 583	52 162	7.4	3.5	4 638	2 863	14	19 055	2.77	71.6	16.7	24.6
St. Mary	13.7	9.0	6.4	50.5	53 500	54 650	2.1	-4.7	4 783	3 408	-3 865	20 320	2.58	66.8	18.6	28.0
St. Tammany	14.1	10.0	6.0	51.4	191 268	233 737	22.2	8.5	17 668	13 105	14 984	89 036	2.70	73.4	13.0	22.0
Tangipahoa	12.6	8.6	5.0	51.6	100 588	121 101	20.4	7.9	11 845	7 306	4 867	45 483	2.68	68.1	17.8	26.1
Tensas	15.8	13.9	8.1	51.4	6 618	5 252	-20.6	-12.5	384	330	-709	1 915	2.48	57.4	20.8	39.7
Terrebonne	12.6	8.1	5.3	50.7	104 503	111 580	6.8	1.5	10 411	6 397	-2 381	40 086	2.78	69.9	15.3	24.5
Union	15.1	11.4	7.9	50.3	22 803	22 779	-0.1	-1.3	1 768	1 548	-447	8 517	2.60	68.6	15.1	28.0
Vermilion	13.1	8.2	6.3	51.4	53 807	57 981	7.8	3.8	5 045	3 419	609	21 796	2.69	68.9	15.0	25.6
Vernon	9.0	6.9	4.6	47.0	52 531	52 334	-0.4	-3.4	6 531	2 339	-6 052	17 842	2.82	72.4	12.0	24.1
Washington	14.1	10.4	6.7	50.5	43 926	47 171	7.4	-1.8	3 603	3 558	-858	17 604	2.54	66.9	16.9	30.2
Webster	13.6	10.5	8.5	51.3	41 831	41 207	-1.5	-3.6	3 125	3 247	-1 344	15 765	2.51	63.3	16.5	33.7
West Baton Rouge	13.1	7.4	5.2	50.5	21 601	23 788	10.1	8.4	2 188	1 201	1 030	9 179	2.61	71.0	18.5	24.1
West Carroll	13.3	10.3	8.4	49.3	12 314	11 604	-5.8	-4.2	861	870	-486	4 296	2.48	68.5	17.5	29.2
West Feliciana	14.1	8.8	5.1	34.2	15 111	15 625	3.4	-1.8	776	706	-348	3 911	3.04	74.1	13.2	23.2
Winn	13.3	10.2	6.8	46.4	16 894	15 313	-9.4	-6.1	1 042	1 052	-878	5 513	2.36	71.2	16.1	26.4
MAINE	15.8	11.4	7.9	51.0	1 274 923	1 328 364	4.2	0.2	79 584	83 138	7 753	553 284	2.34	62.8	9.6	29.2
Androscoggin	14.2	9.8	7.0	51.0	103 793	107 702	3.8	-0.4	8 025	6 471	-1 869	44 636	2.34	62.3	11.2	29.4
Aroostook	16.7	12.8	9.7	50.6	73 938	71 871	-2.8	-5.4	4 092	5 254	-2 537	30 355	2.24	63.4	8.8	31.9
Cumberland	14.6	10.2	7.2	51.4	265 612	281 673	6.0	3.7	17 614	15 797	8 349	117 135	2.37	61.5	9.6	29.6
Franklin	16.7	12.4	8.1	50.9	29 467	30 768	4.4	-2.5	1 612	1 936	-374	11 841	2.48	64.4	8.0	27.0
Hancock	17.4	14.0	8.9	51.5	51 791	54 420	5.1	0.0	2 940	3 609	794	24 371	2.18	60.3	7.7	31.6
Kennebec	16.1	10.6	7.4	51.2	117 114	122 151	4.3	-1.3	7 480	8 051	-276	51 443	2.28	62.6	11.1	29.3
Knox	17.0	13.8	9.7	50.5	39 618	39 736	0.3	0.0	2 189	2 671	539	16 999	2.27	62.7	9.9	32.0
Lincoln	17.0	16.2	10.6	50.8	33 616	34 457	2.5	-0.7	1 714	2 569	577	14 876	2.25	63.3	8.4	29.9
Oxford	17.6	12.2	8.4	50.3	54 755	57 831	5.6	-1.1	3 204	3 919	153	21 767	2.60	65.3	9.5	28.7
Penobscot	14.9	10.2	7.5	50.5	144 919	153 920	6.2	-1.4	9 058	9 467	-1 668	61 973	2.36	61.8	9.0	28.2
Piscataquis	18.8	15.6	9.4	50.4	17 235	17 535	1.7	-3.9	856	1 377	-131	7 529	2.24	63.9	10.1	28.4
Sagadahoc	16.6	12.4	8.6	51.3	35 214	35 293	0.2	-0.1	2 154	2 167	-56	15 405	2.26	63.2	9.2	29.0
Somerset	16.4	12.4	7.8	50.4	50 888	52 228	2.6	-2.5	3 014	3 460	-848	21 800	2.34	64.5	11.3	28.3
Waldo	16.7	13.3	7.6	50.8	36 280	38 786	6.9	1.5	2 251	2 404	781	16 888	2.26	63.9	9.3	28.3
Washington	16.9	13.9	9.2	50.8	33 941	32 856	-3.2	-4.3	1 885	2 595	-602	14 139	2.18	62.3	10.2	31.7
York	16.1	11.3	7.9	51.3	186 742	197 137	5.6	2.6	11 496	11 391	4 921	82 127	2.40	64.8	8.9	27.2
MARYLAND	13.2	8.6	6.0	51.6	5 296 486	5 773 786	9.0	4.2	457 026	286 739	77 875	2 166 389	2.67	66.9	14.5	27.0
Allegany	13.3	10.7	8.8	47.9	74 930	75 087	0.2	-3.9	4 264	5 675	-1 402	28 324	2.33	60.8	11.2	32.6
Anne Arundel	13.0	8.5	5.5	50.5	489 656	537 650	9.8	5.7	43 308	25 191	13 794	203 336	2.66	69.4	11.4	24.4
Baltimore	13.6	9.1	7.4	52.6	754 292	804 911	6.7	3.2	61 356	49 558	15 070	312 900	2.56	65.1	14.4	28.7
Calvert	14.4	8.5	5.5	50.6	74 563	88 736	19.0	2.8	5 750	3 990	671	31 155	2.87	74.6	12.5	20.3
Caroline	14.1	9.4	6.5	50.9	29 772	33 081	11.1	-0.7	2 442	2 047	-633	11 920	2.70	70.7	13.8	24.1
Carroll	14.6	9.5	6.7	50.6	150 897	167 138	10.8	0.3	10 027	9 179	-598	60 004	2.73	74.6	8.9	21.2
Cecil	14.3	9.3	5.4	50.3	85 951	101 108	17.6	1.5	6 983	5 547	240	36 728	2.73	71.7	11.8	23.1
Charles	12.6	7.4	4.5	51.8	120 546	146 560	21.6	7.6	11 577	6 032	5 524	53 171	2.84	73.2	16.2	22.6
Dorchester	15.3	11.9	8.7	52.5	30 674	32 618	6.3	-1.1	2 367	2 316	-373	13 265	2.41	66.9	18.4	27.6
Frederick	13.2	8.1	5.5	50.7	195 277	233 382	19.5	6.1	17 427	10 312	7 118	88 494	2.68	71.8	10.7	22.3
Garrett	15.6	12.5	8.7	50.5	29 846	30 095	0.8	-2.2	1 796	1 917	-546	11 863	2.47	69.7	9.3	27.3
Harford	14.2	9.3	6.1	51.1	218 590	244 828	12.0	2.5	16 862	12 291	1 710	91 727	2.69	73.0	12.0	22.3
Howard	12.8	8.1	5.0	51.1	247 842	287 129	15.9	10.5	21 717	9 781	18 470	108 555	2.78	74.6	10.9	20.8
Kent	15.2	14.4	11.3	52.3	19 197	20 191	5.2	-2.3	1 052	1 526	-18	7 624	2.39	62.8	10.8	32.9
Montgomery	13.1	8.3	6.3	51.8	873 341	971 952	11.3	7.4	82 196	36 788	27 683	365 235	2.76	69.4	11.5	25.1
Prince George's	12.6	7.8	4.5	51.9	801 515	863 379	7.7	5.2	75 688	34 348	4 917	305 610	2.86	66.1	20.2	21.8
Queen Anne's	15.2	11.2	7.0	50.4	40 563	47 788	17.8	2.4	2 846	2 493	850	17 522	2.75	75.4	9.1	20.2

1. No spouse present.

Table B. States and Counties — Population, Vital Statistics, Health, and Crime

STATE County	Persons in group quarters, 2016	Daytime population, 2011–2015 Number	Employment/residence ratio	Births, 2016 Total	Rate[1]	Deaths, 2016 Number	Rate[1]	Persons under 65 with no health insurance, 2015 Number	Percent	Medicare, 2015 Total Beneficiaries	Enrolled in Original Medicare	Enrolled in Medicare Advantage	Serious crimes known to police,[2] 2014 Total Number	Rate[3]
	32	33	34	35	36	37	38	39	40	41	42	43	44	45
LOUISIANA—Cont'd														
Orleans	13 424	427 582	1.30	5 102	13.0	3 418	8.7	45 856	13.9	53 835	26 103	27 732	20 564	5 312
Ouachita	5 554	161 469	1.09	2 281	14.5	1 644	10.5	17 221	13.2	25 830	19 555	6 275	11 125	7 341
Plaquemines	272	31 963	1.82	324	13.8	189	8.1	3 018	14.8	3 127	1 331	1 796	298	1 259
Pointe Coupee	116	19 717	0.68	287	13.0	248	11.2	2 476	13.8	4 187	2 222	1 965	420	1 997
Rapides	4 501	137 452	1.10	1 884	14.2	1 441	10.9	15 538	14.3	26 167	21 648	4 519	7 766	6 039
Red River	164	8 296	0.83	110	12.9	114	13.3	1 029	14.7	1 551	1 232	319	183	2 065
Richland	1 039	20 213	0.93	266	13.0	241	11.8	2 449	14.9	3 938	3 112	826	659	3 673
Sabine	438	22 691	0.81	280	11.7	229	9.6	3 461	17.9	4 911	4 117	794	241	1 082
St. Bernard	293	38 607	0.75	661	14.5	378	8.3	6 096	15.1	5 422	2 611	2 811	919	2 025
St. Charles	592	54 092	1.06	636	12.0	428	8.1	4 960	10.8	7 378	3 044	4 334	1 202	2 285
St. Helena	121	8 920	0.45	119	11.3	105	10.0	1 312	15.3	1 266	791	475	199	1 969
St. James	204	22 013	1.04	286	13.3	210	9.7	2 008	11.2	3 908	2 037	1 871	656	3 587
St. John the Baptist	471	41 777	0.88	579	13.3	421	9.6	4 984	13.3	7 040	3 241	3 799	1 379	3 183
St. Landry	1 105	77 018	0.78	1 271	15.2	1 026	12.2	10 508	14.9	18 009	15 340	2 669	3 198	4 124
St. Martin	701	44 569	0.63	801	14.8	502	9.3	6 588	14.4	8 118	6 783	1 335	796	1 692
St. Mary	868	57 735	1.21	777	14.9	547	10.5	7 794	17.6	9 852	8 156	1 696	1 960	3 676
St. Tammany	1 277	222 730	0.81	3 012	11.9	2 285	9.0	25 158	12.0	43 280	20 652	22 628	4 211	1 722
Tangipahoa	3 656	116 121	0.82	1 909	14.6	1 283	9.8	16 380	15.1	22 199	14 664	7 535	7 591	6 096
Tensas	16	4 790	0.94	54	11.7	50	10.9	620	16.6	1 018	864	154	NA	NA
Terrebonne	1 479	122 894	1.21	1 680	14.8	1 087	9.6	17 148	17.5	19 662	16 382	3 280	4 108	3 631
Union	476	19 790	0.65	277	12.3	233	10.4	2 797	15.7	5 056	3 859	1 197	387	1 739
Vermilion	536	50 845	0.66	841	14.0	582	9.7	7 770	15.2	9 835	8 910	925	1 714	2 876
Vernon	2 260	54 089	1.07	948	18.7	369	7.3	5 071	11.8	6 921	6 321	600	1 269	2 620
Washington	1 582	44 336	0.85	602	13.0	609	13.2	5 859	15.8	10 093	7 050	3 043	1 801	3 892
Webster	1 231	38 639	0.87	489	12.3	542	13.6	4 566	14.4	9 339	7 429	1 910	779	1 989
West Baton Rouge	556	24 761	1.01	365	14.2	208	8.1	2 399	11.0	3 701	1 657	2 044	760	3 071
West Carroll	434	10 310	0.70	134	12.1	153	13.8	1 507	17.1	2 469	1 961	508	305	2 665
West Feliciana	5 315	15 634	1.04	119	7.8	119	7.8	948	11.5	1 762	1 115	647	208	1 350
Winn	1 760	14 424	0.91	150	10.4	194	13.5	1 599	15.1	2 684	2 186	498	423	2 876
MAINE	35 892	1 313 863	0.98	12 542	9.4	13 842	10.4	108 771	10.3	298 007	223 261	74 746	28 121	2 114
Androscoggin	2 833	104 960	0.95	1 215	11.3	1 052	9.8	8 068	9.3	23 261	16 229	7 032	2 474	2 297
Aroostook	2 087	69 544	0.98	639	9.4	841	12.4	6 506	12.4	18 772	15 987	2 785	987	1 416
Cumberland	9 288	313 803	1.18	2 880	9.9	2 657	9.1	21 477	9.1	55 813	38 528	17 285	6 562	2 288
Franklin	1 115	29 718	0.95	247	8.2	324	10.8	2 542	11.1	6 572	4 757	1 815	443	1 454
Hancock	867	54 125	0.98	474	8.7	626	11.5	4 948	11.9	12 891	10 408	2 483	924	1 679
Kennebec	3 696	124 293	1.06	1 221	10.1	1 295	10.7	8 467	8.8	28 036	19 357	8 679	3 092	2 554
Knox	1 318	41 588	1.10	339	8.5	441	11.1	3 481	11.8	10 430	8 086	2 344	693	1 752
Lincoln	474	31 013	0.80	277	8.1	415	12.1	3 129	12.6	9 417	6 816	2 601	491	1 442
Oxford	896	51 760	0.77	483	8.4	668	11.7	5 009	11.1	13 123	10 165	2 958	1 425	2 490
Penobscot	7 476	156 087	1.04	1 380	9.1	1 577	10.4	13 784	11.5	33 833	25 971	7 862	3 585	2 337
Piscataquis	253	17 032	0.98	131	7.8	219	13.0	1 475	11.7	4 858	4 049	809	263	1 543
Sagadahoc	263	34 112	0.94	359	10.2	401	11.4	2 239	8.0	7 808	5 473	2 335	499	1 426
Somerset	723	49 155	0.89	455	8.9	535	10.5	4 483	11.1	12 135	9 993	2 142	1 450	2 808
Waldo	528	34 381	0.74	322	8.2	418	10.6	3 681	12.0	9 102	6 850	2 252	495	1 269
Washington	831	31 991	0.98	289	9.2	409	13.0	3 728	15.7	8 544	7 556	988	490	1 528
York	3 244	170 301	0.71	1 831	9.0	1 964	9.7	15 754	9.7	43 412	33 036	10 376	4 045	2 020
MARYLAND	140 535	5 662 700	0.91	73 321	12.2	50 036	8.3	374 972	7.4	856 896	767 104	89 792	176 520	2 954
Allegany	7 600	76 929	1.12	667	9.2	928	12.9	3 362	6.4	17 027	16 169	858	2 580	3 520
Anne Arundel	14 709	549 462	0.98	6 980	12.3	4 385	7.7	27 017	5.7	80 168	74 081	6 087	15 896	2 833
Baltimore	21 434	769 949	0.87	9 945	12.0	8 589	10.3	46 119	6.8	132 848	117 853	14 995	24 582	2 966
Calvert	640	68 852	0.53	916	10.0	702	7.7	3 592	4.6	12 673	12 142	531	1 665	1 829
Caroline	444	26 353	0.58	383	11.7	336	10.2	2 388	8.7	5 891	5 812	79	888	2 719
Carroll	3 360	137 714	0.66	1 658	9.9	1 557	9.3	6 018	4.4	31 497	29 820	1 677	2 593	1 544
Cecil	1 447	87 728	0.70	1 149	11.2	982	9.6	5 394	6.2	16 643	16 127	516	3 388	3 312
Charles	1 406	119 190	0.56	1 850	11.7	1 063	6.7	6 783	5.0	17 666	16 262	1 404	3 597	2 326
Dorchester	502	30 591	0.87	380	11.8	405	12.6	2 216	8.6	7 532	7 385	147	1 231	3 763
Frederick	4 312	221 235	0.84	2 815	11.4	1 752	7.1	11 898	5.7	31 312	28 902	2 410	4 340	1 781
Garrett	528	29 413	0.97	285	9.7	343	11.7	1 750	7.5	6 051	5 597	454	527	1 763
Harford	2 738	221 204	0.78	2 703	10.8	2 156	8.6	9 259	4.4	39 387	36 418	2 969	4 266	1 702
Howard	1 697	301 082	0.98	3 583	11.3	1 766	5.6	12 060	4.5	29 365	26 547	2 818	6 343	2 050
Kent	1 498	20 299	1.04	159	8.1	276	14.0	1 245	9.1	5 957	5 822	135	385	1 933
Montgomery	9 290	983 302	0.94	13 100	12.5	6 275	6.0	75 158	8.5	125 358	108 737	16 621	18 475	1 795
Prince George's	20 066	770 242	0.73	12 149	13.4	6 484	7.1	88 761	11.3	105 189	86 273	18 916	30 671	3 415
Queen Anne's	436	39 695	0.64	455	9.3	389	8.0	2 317	5.8	7 559	7 313	246	863	1 769

1. Per 1,000 estimated resident population.   2. Data for serious crimes have not been adjusted for underreporting; this may affect comparability between geographic areas and over time.
3. Per 100,000 population estimated by the FBI.

Table B. States and Counties — Crime, Education, Money Income, and Poverty

STATE County	Serious crimes known to police, 2014 (cont.)[1] Rate[2] — Violent	Property	Education — School enrollment and attainment, 2011–2015 — Enrollment[3] Total	Percent private	Attainment[4] (percent) High school graduate or less	Bachelor's degree or more	Local government expenditures,[5] 2013–2014 Total current spending (mil dol)	Current spending per student (dollars)	Money income, 2011–2015 Per capita income[6] (dollars)	Households Median income (dollars)	Percent with income of less than $50,000	with income of $200,000 or more	Income and poverty, 2015 Median household income (dollars)	Percent below poverty level All persons	Children under 18 years	Children 5 to 17 years in families
	46	47	48	49	50	51	52	53	54	55	56	57	58	59	60	61
LOUISIANA—Cont'd																
Orleans	976	4 336	98 151	32.2	38.0	35.3	598.1	12 730	27 721	36 792	60.5	4.9	38 640	24.0	38.2	36.0
Ouachita	1 399	5 942	40 294	10.1	48.5	24.0	299.1	10 401	21 770	37 754	59.7	3.4	38 453	23.0	33.1	30.9
Plaquemines	135	1 124	6 237	16.0	59.2	14.2	80.8	16 162	24 837	50 314	49.6	2.9	49 122	17.3	19.7	17.1
Pointe Coupee	594	1 403	5 318	28.6	61.2	13.4	33.5	11 609	25 024	43 825	54.1	3.2	42 919	19.3	29.2	27.9
Rapides	952	5 087	33 880	14.3	53.5	18.4	223.7	9 267	21 671	40 734	58.6	2.2	42 758	21.6	31.7	29.3
Red River	485	1 580	2 053	19.3	67.0	12.0	19.6	12 769	23 016	38 000	63.1	3.2	41 742	25.7	31.7	29.3
Richland	485	3 188	4 846	11.2	62.2	14.5	43.2	10 161	19 699	36 421	62.2	2.4	34 588	24.7	37.3	36.0
Sabine	130	952	5 397	11.0	59.6	14.1	44.9	10 229	22 605	38 828	60.1	2.8	42 196	18.1	25.9	24.8
St. Bernard	190	1 836	11 279	10.8	59.4	12.5	78.8	11 035	20 160	42 753	56.8	1.3	41 540	20.4	30.3	30.7
St. Charles	333	1 953	14 079	14.6	49.3	20.3	149.4	15 481	27 247	59 990	40.8	3.3	61 601	11.8	17.4	16.0
St. Helena	336	1 633	2 451	6.2	65.9	10.0	9.1	11 407	18 620	35 437	65.2	0.8	36 602	19.9	34.0	32.6
St. James	552	3 034	5 302	16.6	60.6	14.2	59.7	15 778	24 071	51 107	49.7	2.0	52 258	18.3	26.6	25.8
St. John the Baptist	127	3 056	12 408	26.6	54.9	16.5	78.1	13 096	22 660	50 921	48.7	1.9	50 596	20.5	29.9	29.0
St. Landry	672	3 452	19 678	17.5	68.3	12.8	135.3	9 140	19 156	32 625	64.5	2.1	33 503	27.0	37.2	36.6
St. Martin	232	1 460	13 435	23.0	63.8	13.2	78.6	9 495	22 983	42 794	55.4	2.8	45 435	18.3	27.9	27.1
St. Mary	439	3 237	11 755	14.1	68.2	11.1	102.5	10 555	21 847	40 781	59.0	2.5	40 945	19.7	28.3	26.4
St. Tammany	157	1 565	62 800	25.1	38.5	30.6	422.5	11 212	31 022	62 137	40.8	6.5	63 499	12.5	17.3	15.7
Tangipahoa	789	5 308	35 424	12.9	53.9	19.3	182.4	9 136	21 671	41 302	57.0	1.8	41 768	24.0	35.0	33.8
Tensas	NA	NA	1 102	24.2	66.3	10.3	9.2	13 871	16 912	22 940	75.2	1.2	27 077	35.1	52.6	46.6
Terrebonne	331	3 300	26 863	16.5	62.9	13.7	166.0	8 964	23 626	47 826	51.7	3.0	44 450	20.1	24.9	23.4
Union	274	1 465	4 291	11.9	61.3	11.7	31.6	10 604	19 676	34 992	63.1	1.8	38 741	21.9	34.3	33.3
Vermilion	408	2 469	14 013	14.4	64.7	12.4	92.5	9 713	23 261	45 374	54.1	2.0	46 807	18.1	23.6	21.7
Vernon	283	2 337	13 520	12.0	48.3	19.2	95.8	9 921	21 578	46 312	54.7	1.6	44 733	17.5	23.3	23.5
Washington	573	3 319	11 195	13.2	63.7	12.3	82.3	11 053	17 745	30 705	67.2	1.6	33 453	26.2	36.9	33.9
Webster	398	1 591	9 058	10.0	60.3	14.0	62.8	9 504	20 248	33 681	65.6	1.1	34 566	25.9	40.0	36.2
West Baton Rouge	364	2 707	6 069	21.0	54.3	19.7	49.4	12 606	26 118	53 703	46.4	2.2	55 074	15.1	22.1	21.0
West Carroll	245	2 421	2 519	3.3	69.0	11.1	21.3	9 720	19 353	31 926	61.9	1.4	35 484	22.7	32.1	30.5
West Feliciana	247	1 103	3 850	9.0	55.1	21.6	28.1	13 072	22 122	56 685	46.3	3.8	56 680	23.9	21.7	19.8
Winn	530	2 346	3 133	9.0	63.6	12.5	25.3	9 993	17 877	31 087	65.7	1.5	36 173	24.0	30.4	28.7
MAINE	128	1 986	299 595	16.8	41.6	29.0	2 376.7	13 005	27 655	49 331	50.6	3.0	51 419	13.2	17.5	16.0
Androscoggin	141	2 156	26 297	19.8	48.6	20.3	201.3	11 828	25 011	47 537	51.9	1.7	48 930	15.0	21.8	19.1
Aroostook	105	1 311	14 723	8.5	52.4	17.2	130.7	13 093	21 763	36 923	62.6	1.2	37 104	18.4	21.8	19.4
Cumberland	121	2 167	67 922	19.7	29.7	43.0	516.9	13 810	34 081	60 051	42.3	5.7	63 191	10.7	12.2	11.5
Franklin	92	1 362	7 021	10.4	44.7	25.6	42.6	13 594	22 980	42 811	57.5	1.8	42 859	14.6	21.4	19.9
Hancock	65	1 614	10 879	20.2	39.4	32.7	99.6	15 469	28 432	47 030	52.2	2.8	48 601	11.5	16.2	14.4
Kennebec	184	2 370	26 734	18.7	44.2	25.0	198.7	12 265	25 957	46 917	52.4	2.2	50 408	13.1	18.0	16.7
Knox	33	1 719	7 452	11.3	41.8	31.2	87.5	14 847	28 144	50 693	49.2	3.3	47 489	11.4	17.9	16.5
Lincoln	167	1 274	6 041	20.3	39.4	31.2	53.8	13 392	29 078	50 462	49.6	3.3	50 152	14.1	20.2	17.6
Oxford	126	2 365	12 472	14.1	54.5	18.1	116.6	12 750	21 280	40 630	59.0	1.0	42 674	17.0	25.6	23.0
Penobscot	77	2 260	39 806	13.2	48.2	24.5	264.8	11 992	24 149	44 271	55.2	2.2	44 647	17.1	19.1	17.6
Piscataquis	123	1 420	3 144	17.7	51.8	17.4	18.4	10 064	22 856	37 495	62.6	1.7	36 463	19.1	30.5	27.7
Sagadahoc	29	1 397	7 254	10.5	38.0	32.2	63.6	13 646	30 062	53 298	46.8	2.5	55 645	11.2	17.2	15.3
Somerset	130	2 678	11 015	11.3	53.5	15.4	99.4	12 515	21 729	40 066	60.1	1.1	40 165	18.7	25.9	23.7
Waldo	82	1 187	8 114	21.9	41.9	30.3	54.7	14 539	24 473	44 082	56.0	1.3	43 198	14.4	21.3	19.4
Washington	125	1 403	6 432	11.4	50.6	20.1	68.0	16 284	21 977	38 083	63.9	1.0	35 576	18.8	28.8	27.1
York	153	1 867	44 289	19.1	39.3	30.5	360.0	12 398	30 705	57 919	42.9	3.9	61 340	8.3	11.4	10.7
MARYLAND	446	2 508	1 572 476	19.4	36.2	37.9	12 139.4	13 994	36 897	74 551	33.2	9.2	75 784	9.9	13.9	12.8
Allegany	274	3 246	17 262	7.7	53.6	17.4	127.2	14 341	21 674	40 551	58.9	1.9	39 859	20.0	27.1	23.8
Anne Arundel	431	2 402	144 534	19.9	33.4	38.3	1 033.5	13 167	41 706	89 860	24.9	11.3	90 825	6.0	8.1	7.3
Baltimore	448	2 517	215 916	22.2	36.6	36.6	1 443.1	13 338	35 011	67 095	36.1	6.7	68 317	9.1	11.9	11.2
Calvert	144	1 685	24 915	10.7	38.3	29.1	220.3	13 578	39 011	95 828	22.5	9.7	98 937	5.9	8.1	7.1
Caroline	321	2 397	7 572	9.2	57.9	15.5	68.4	12 344	24 943	52 465	46.4	3.1	51 294	14.4	22.9	21.1
Carroll	218	1 325	44 663	19.2	38.5	33.1	349.0	13 255	36 936	85 385	28.0	7.8	84 506	6.2	7.2	6.3
Cecil	485	2 827	24 524	18.7	49.9	22.0	199.4	12 599	29 538	66 396	36.8	4.3	68 972	10.0	14.8	12.9
Charles	353	1 973	41 599	12.1	39.9	27.4	358.6	13 556	36 809	90 607	25.0	9.2	87 941	7.1	10.4	9.6
Dorchester	434	3 329	7 119	12.4	53.4	20.2	63.6	13 340	27 870	47 093	51.9	2.5	44 664	18.1	29.8	29.8
Frederick	249	1 532	66 010	18.9	32.7	39.1	521.1	12 821	37 449	83 700	27.5	8.8	83 746	7.4	9.0	8.4
Garrett	241	1 522	6 184	18.7	53.8	19.0	55.2	14 209	25 348	45 432	55.0	2.2	46 469	13.6	19.3	18.3
Harford	244	1 458	64 726	18.1	35.2	33.8	478.0	12 630	35 746	80 465	29.0	7.6	77 992	7.8	10.3	9.2
Howard	198	1 852	88 636	17.1	19.1	60.6	811.0	15 358	48 104	110 238	18.1	18.0	110 224	5.2	6.5	5.6
Kent	231	1 702	4 382	44.0	46.2	30.0	30.7	14 506	30 081	58 147	43.3	5.8	52 274	14.8	21.6	19.0
Montgomery	169	1 626	273 607	22.9	22.8	57.9	2 296.8	15 181	49 110	99 435	23.3	18.1	98 314	7.5	10.5	9.6
Prince George's	460	2 956	247 152	17.7	40.5	31.1	1 767.2	13 977	32 639	74 260	30.9	6.6	76 366	9.5	14.2	12.9
Queen Anne's	223	1 546	11 365	13.1	38.6	34.9	90.2	11 691	38 733	85 963	26.2	9.5	83 914	7.2	10.5	9.4

1. Data for serious crimes have not been adjusted for underreporting; this may affect comparability between geographic areas and over time.   2. Per 100,000 population estimated by the FBI.
3. All persons 3 years old and over enrolled in nursery school through college.   4. Persons 25 years old and over.   5. Elementary and secondary education expenditures.
6. Based on population estimated by the American Community Survey, 2011–2015.

Table B. States and Counties — Personal Income

STATE County	Personal income, 2015										Earnings, 2015		
	Total (mil dol)	Percent change, 2014–2015	Per capita¹ Dollars	Per capita¹ Rank	Wages and salaries (mil dol)	Supplements to wages and salaries; employer contributions (mil dol) Pension and insurance	Supplements to wages and salaries; employer contributions (mil dol) Government social insurance	Proprietors' income (mil dol)	Dividends, interest, and rent (mil dol)	Personal transfer receipts (mil dol)	Total (mil dol)	Contributions for government social insurance (mil dol) From employee and self-employed	Contributions for government social insurance (mil dol) From employer
	62	63	64	65	66	67	68	69	70	71	72	73	74
LOUISIANA—Cont'd													
Orleans	18 189	5.3	46 684	594	10 854	1 699	733	2 147	4 297	3 167	15 433	815	733
Ouachita	5 706	4.2	36 396	1 639	2 997	515	193	387	929	1 458	4 092	227	193
Plaquemines	1 084	2.1	46 136	575	1 025	188	65	161	157	168	1 439	74	65
Pointe Coupee	917	2.4	41 203	1 148	213	40	15	60	141	214	328	20	15
Rapides	5 645	4.5	42 716	1 145	2 476	468	163	635	916	1 575	3 742	203	163
Red River	296	5.2	34 413	2 192	109	22	7	19	49	91	157	9	7
Richland	704	3.6	34 292	2 203	228	45	15	53	80	239	342	21	15
Sabine	795	1.1	32 890	2 230	208	42	13	89	126	237	352	21	13
St. Bernard	1 329	6.3	29 279	2 873	536	127	33	67	174	333	764	41	33
St. Charles	2 395	3.3	45 347	785	1 888	360	117	136	290	374	2 501	132	117
St. Helena	409	4.5	38 748	1 431	62	14	3	16	40	130	95	7	3
St. James	920	2.7	42 678	1 023	597	126	36	53	94	190	812	44	36
St. John the Baptist	1 703	2.4	39 031	1 482	857	174	54	146	180	383	1 231	68	54
St. Landry	3 187	1.1	38 012	1 725	970	187	62	264	421	957	1 483	89	62
St. Martin	2 036	-0.7	37 820	1 583	572	95	37	172	278	457	876	53	37
St. Mary	2 020	-0.4	38 257	1 326	1 381	218	87	130	351	500	1 816	100	87
St. Tammany	14 312	7.9	57 229	272	4 244	669	265	2 419	2 393	2 046	7 598	404	265
Tangipahoa	4 641	5.9	36 043	2 083	1 613	328	100	300	548	1 291	2 340	127	100
Tensas	149	-13.6	31 383	1 520	40	8	2	9	36	54	58	4	2
Terrebonne	5 123	-1.2	44 952	861	3 166	438	205	485	711	927	4 294	240	205
Union	785	4.7	34 941	2 079	164	34	11	76	96	234	285	18	11
Vermilion	2 289	-0.8	38 226	1 434	623	113	38	204	333	492	978	55	38
Vernon	1 965	1.7	38 683	1 408	1 045	290	94	72	380	411	1 500	66	94
Washington	1 487	5.3	32 062	2 605	408	85	25	70	170	544	587	39	25
Webster	1 439	2.6	35 944	1 782	494	91	32	89	214	443	706	44	32
West Baton Rouge	1 123	5.4	44 043	970	701	117	47	99	107	195	965	52	47
West Carroll	313	-0.6	27 725	2 960	81	18	5	22	40	128	126	8	5
West Feliciana	518	4.2	33 680	2 347	295	71	15	51	93	94	432	19	15
Winn	515	1.8	35 344	2 255	184	35	13	103	58	150	335	19	13
MAINE	56 894	3.7	42 795	X	26 833	4 661	2 016	4 041	10 090	12 833	37 551	2 474	2 016
Androscoggin	3 979	3.6	37 106	1 722	2 109	340	163	179	524	1 068	2 791	187	163
Aroostook	2 520	2.4	36 717	1 803	1 049	224	79	130	367	830	1 482	102	79
Cumberland	15 165	4.0	52 298	394	9 329	1 346	691	1 041	3 001	2 420	12 407	786	691
Franklin	1 045	2.6	34 849	2 236	412	81	31	67	199	302	591	41	31
Hancock	2 470	4.2	45 190	1 140	894	154	69	380	560	527	1 497	103	69
Kennebec	4 986	2.5	41 554	1 235	2 572	539	184	297	751	1 201	3 592	221	184
Knox	1 743	4.5	43 738	1 109	685	122	52	234	433	393	1 093	75	52
Lincoln	1 541	3.4	45 358	936	413	72	32	135	399	355	652	50	32
Oxford	1 996	3.6	34 891	2 140	642	122	49	119	329	583	932	69	49
Penobscot	5 654	3.4	37 032	1 788	2 962	560	219	279	832	1 491	4 020	259	219
Piscataquis	586	2.4	34 634	2 224	196	46	15	43	103	200	300	22	15
Sagadahoc	1 606	4.3	45 702	859	822	154	63	87	338	324	1 125	73	63
Somerset	1 838	3.2	35 951	1 850	715	128	55	122	251	568	1 020	72	55
Waldo	1 442	3.2	36 833	1 936	450	75	35	118	264	391	677	51	35
Washington	1 176	4.2	37 185	1 993	393	87	30	128	189	416	637	44	30
York	9 146	4.5	45 466	853	3 190	612	249	683	1 551	1 766	4 734	318	249
MARYLAND	336 187	4.1	56 078	X	162 273	27 770	12 191	25 336	63 904	46 673	227 570	13 096	12 191
Allegany	2 699	2.8	37 214	1 785	1 239	260	104	131	474	865	1 735	114	104
Anne Arundel	34 206	3.9	60 628	140	20 053	3 855	1 569	1 977	6 764	3 915	27 454	1 519	1 569
Baltimore	45 210	2.7	54 395	238	21 554	3 502	1 618	2 274	9 289	7 165	28 948	1 739	1 618
Calvert	5 075	3.7	56 018	251	1 196	216	89	185	912	623	1 687	103	89
Caroline	1 372	2.4	42 110	1 053	398	78	31	111	203	334	618	37	31
Carroll	9 388	3.8	56 006	262	2 637	431	201	515	1 481	1 258	3 784	236	201
Cecil	4 441	4.1	43 374	995	1 537	301	119	180	686	874	2 137	133	119
Charles	8 151	4.4	52 212	353	2 047	411	160	264	1 379	1 029	2 882	170	160
Dorchester	1 346	2.4	41 553	1 179	473	103	37	108	251	389	721	45	37
Frederick	13 467	4.2	54 893	279	5 489	911	420	751	2 183	1 604	7 571	442	420
Garrett	1 216	3.3	41 262	854	446	89	36	106	241	301	676	43	36
Harford	13 168	3.8	52 612	340	5 113	1 014	406	476	2 133	1 925	7 009	415	406
Howard	21 936	4.2	69 991	71	11 802	1 440	850	1 331	3 755	1 740	15 423	893	850
Kent	1 037	2.3	52 430	362	345	63	27	72	332	237	507	34	27
Montgomery	79 946	5.4	76 863	48	35 832	5 506	2 581	11 036	17 327	6 124	54 956	3 061	2 581
Prince George's	40 807	4.3	44 866	717	18 877	3 771	1 462	1 386	6 937	5 843	25 496	1 444	1 462
Queen Anne's	2 748	3.1	56 189	247	599	110	46	201	540	392	956	60	46

1. Based on the resident population estimated as of July 1 of the year shown.

Table B. States and Counties — Earnings, Social Security, and Housing

| | Earnings, 2015 (cont.) | | | | | | | | | Social Security beneficiaries, December 2015 | | | Housing units, 2016 | |
| | Percent by selected industries | | | | | | | | | | | | | |
STATE County	Farm	Mining	Construction	Manu-facturing	Infor-mation: professional, scientific, technical services	Retail trade	Finance, insur-ance, real estate and leasing	Health care and social assistance	Govern-ment	Number	Rate[1]	Supple-mental Security Income recipients, December 2015	Total	Percent change, 2010-2016
	75	76	77	78	79	80	81	82	83	84	85	86	87	88
LOUISIANA—Cont'd														
Orleans	0.0	4.5	2.9	2.2	16.8	3.9	5.8	9.9	18.8	60 785	156	20 646	193 104	1.7
Ouachita	0.2	1.1	5.4	9.5	9.4	7.4	7.3	18.9	16.0	28 945	184	6 893	67 487	4.7
Plaquemines	0.4	17.3	6.4	15.8	D	D	4.1	D	13.4	3 630	154	591	10 014	4.4
Pointe Coupee	5.0	4.0	5.2	9.1	D	9.9	5.5	7.0	18.4	4 795	216	1 014	11 382	2.3
Rapides	0.6	1.6	7.1	8.4	5.4	10.4	4.3	20.5	20.9	28 315	214	6 907	57 517	3.3
Red River	3.7	D	4.9	12.5	3.1	4.7	0.0	D	21.2	1 695	196	487	4 131	0.1
Richland	2.2	D	8.6	10.7	D	9.3	5.1	D	16.2	4 470	218	1 154	8 885	3.1
Sabine	10.8	4.8	6.7	16.2	5.9	7.0	4.2	D	18.5	5 670	235	972	14 567	3.1
St. Bernard	0.2	D	10.6	29.6	2.2	6.3	1.9	D	17.6	6 630	146	1 745	16 920	0.8
St. Charles	0.0	D	17.1	29.6	6.5	3.0	2.0	3.0	9.1	9 010	171	1 151	20 494	2.8
St. Helena	4.4	D	5.8	16.2	1.4	5.1	D	5.7	32.7	3 290	311	1 009	5 168	0.3
St. James	0.7	D	6.2	46.4	D	2.2	3.2	1.5	11.8	4 505	209	737	8 798	4.1
St. John the Baptist	0.2	3.7	10.8	32.2	2.7	5.3	2.8	3.9	11.5	8 665	199	1 749	17 671	1.2
St. Landry	0.2	4.5	10.2	6.5	5.4	10.6	5.9	13.6	19.9	19 620	234	5 416	36 394	2.0
St. Martin	0.4	8.0	6.9	24.1	4.4	9.7	7.2	7.1	12.1	10 645	197	1 804	22 857	4.2
St. Mary	0.1	15.3	5.0	20.8	3.8	4.8	7.4	D	14.4	11 255	213	2 292	23 303	1.2
St. Tammany	0.1	22.0	8.3	3.8	7.8	7.1	5.9	11.0	12.4	48 500	194	4 874	101 268	6.1
Tangipahoa	0.3	1.1	4.9	5.6	4.8	12.6	5.0	12.2	27.2	22 955	178	5 260	53 763	7.4
Tensas	11.7	D	D	3.5	D	5.4	D	D	27.9	1 195	253	422	3 389	1.0
Terrebonne	0.1	17.4	8.1	12.4	6.7	6.4	5.5	9.7	7.5	21 765	191	4 795	45 035	2.8
Union	12.9	D	8.3	D	D	7.5	3.2	8.1	16.2	5 405	241	975	11 484	1.2
Vermilion	4.2	17.2	8.9	6.8	5.1	8.7	4.7	6.5	18.3	11 770	196	1 893	26 143	3.6
Vernon	-0.2	0.5	4.4	2.5	5.2	3.3	1.9	4.7	67.0	7 900	156	1 209	21 877	2.1
Washington	0.7	0.8	9.7	16.3	D	6.7	3.9	D	25.5	11 285	244	2 930	21 395	1.7
Webster	0.0	9.3	9.6	13.7	3.3	9.2	4.1	D	16.5	9 910	247	2 019	19 469	0.7
West Baton Rouge	-0.1	2.1	24.4	24.5	D	5.7	3.1	D	10.1	4 255	167	791	10 540	13.0
West Carroll	8.4	D	D	D	D	8.2	D	8.9	33.0	2 745	243	506	5 090	0.9
West Feliciana	1.7	D	6.9	7.8	D	4.0	2.6	D	34.6	1 925	125	319	5 347	4.9
Winn	2.5	10.4	3.1	14.1	D	3.9	7.0	17.1	11.8	3 260	224	586	7 230	-0.1
MAINE	0.3	0.0	7.1	9.5	8.1	7.8	6.8	16.2	18.3	329 559	248	37 328	730 705	1.2
Androscoggin	0.6	D	7.2	11.4	6.9	7.7	5.8	21.4	11.8	25 510	238	4 113	49 053	-0.1
Aroostook	2.1	0.0	4.6	11.5	3.4	9.0	4.4	18.3	26.2	20 530	299	2 652	39 391	-0.4
Cumberland	0.1	D	5.7	6.2	12.5	6.5	12.0	17.0	11.9	59 555	205	5 641	141 728	2.2
Franklin	0.2	0.0	7.4	18.7	D	9.5	3.6	D	19.8	7 870	262	917	21 860	0.7
Hancock	0.3	D	10.8	6.2	11.6	9.2	3.8	12.3	13.2	14 380	265	1 038	40 653	1.2
Kennebec	0.3	D	5.2	4.9	6.3	8.5	3.3	16.5	31.6	30 460	253	4 080	61 742	1.3
Knox	0.1	0.0	9.2	9.5	7.2	8.9	4.8	14.2	14.7	11 100	279	855	24 020	1.2
Lincoln	0.2	0.0	11.6	D	8.0	9.5	5.4	13.9	14.4	10 425	306	689	23 636	0.6
Oxford	0.2	0.1	9.2	18.3	2.9	9.1	2.9	13.2	18.7	15 790	276	1 962	36 364	0.9
Penobscot	0.2	D	5.9	4.7	5.3	9.4	4.4	22.3	21.4	36 880	242	5 468	74 690	1.1
Piscataquis	0.2	D	5.8	24.6	D	10.0	2.5	D	27.9	5 350	316	718	15 304	-0.2
Sagadahoc	0.2	0.0	8.0	D	6.9	5.6	2.5	5.0	11.6	8 835	251	690	18 498	1.2
Somerset	1.2	D	15.5	20.0	3.4	7.2	2.8	13.7	15.0	14 320	280	2 109	30 435	-0.4
Waldo	0.5	D	10.3	8.2	5.0	7.7	9.7	14.9	13.5	10 515	269	1 266	22 020	2.1
Washington	3.8	D	5.1	9.7	3.2	8.0	3.3	13.7	24.4	9 655	305	1 343	23 038	0.2
York	0.1	0.1	8.9	10.8	6.0	7.8	4.1	11.7	27.7	48 385	241	3 787	108 273	2.4
MARYLAND	0.1	0.1	6.6	4.3	16.5	5.3	8.9	11.2	24.6	952 251	159	120 254	2 447 127	2.9
Allegany	0.0	0.3	4.0	9.3	D	7.6	4.4	22.3	26.0	17 405	240	2 317	33 114	-0.6
Anne Arundel	0.0	0.0	5.7	5.5	13.8	4.8	4.4	7.3	36.4	88 675	157	7 646	223 290	5.0
Baltimore	0.1	0.0	7.4	4.3	12.8	6.8	12.2	13.9	18.7	154 335	186	15 823	338 183	0.8
Calvert	-0.3	D	18.0	2.6	7.8	6.3	4.2	13.9	19.5	14 410	159	954	35 056	3.8
Caroline	7.5	D	10.0	10.4	D	8.7	D	D	18.6	6 920	212	793	13 535	0.4
Carroll	0.3	D	13.3	7.9	10.9	8.4	4.8	14.1	15.3	31 030	185	1 689	63 623	1.9
Cecil	0.9	D	5.5	20.7	D	6.1	2.0	10.2	24.4	19 160	187	1 809	42 590	3.6
Charles	-0.1	D	11.2	1.5	8.1	13.1	4.2	10.2	31.9	21 080	135	2 256	59 992	9.1
Dorchester	4.3	D	D	20.0	D	4.8	3.3	11.0	23.7	8 180	253	1 265	16 681	0.8
Frederick	0.2	D	D	5.7	D	D	10.0	D	19.8	37 680	154	2 118	95 901	6.4
Garrett	1.8	4.4	10.4	8.8	6.2	10.0	D	D	16.1	7 330	249	644	19 267	2.2
Harford	0.1	0.1	6.7	5.6	13.6	6.2	4.3	9.5	35.4	45 250	181	3 270	99 710	4.3
Howard	0.0	D	6.7	4.5	31.4	5.0	7.2	8.0	9.7	38 525	123	3 312	118 070	8.0
Kent	0.9	D	8.5	11.4	9.8	D	5.6	12.8	13.6	5 655	286	380	10 691	1.4
Montgomery	0.0	0.0	5.4	3.3	24.2	4.3	14.9	8.9	21.1	130 820	126	14 055	390 559	3.9
Prince George's	0.0	D	9.9	2.3	11.8	6.2	3.6	8.0	38.9	114 240	126	14 238	332 564	1.3
Queen Anne's	1.1	D	11.0	7.5	9.4	9.7	4.3	5.9	19.1	9 835	201	376	21 032	4.4

1. Per 1,000 resident population estimated as of July 1 of the year shown.

Table B. States and Counties — **Housing, Labor Force, and Employment**

STATE County	Housing units, 2011–2015								Civilian labor force, 2016				Civilian employment,[6] 2011–2015		
	Occupied units										Unemployment			Percent	
			Owner-occupied			Renter-occupied									
				Median owner cost as a percent of income										Manage-ment, business, science and arts	Con-struction, produc-tion, and mainte-nance occu-pations
	Total	Percent	Median value[1]	With a mort-gage	Without a mort-gage[2]	Median rent[3]	Median rent as a per-cent of income[2]	Sub-stand-ard units[4] (percent)	Total	Percent change, 2015–2016	Total	Rate[5]	Total		
	89	90	91	92	93	94	95	96	97	98	99	100	101	102	103
LOUISIANA—Cont'd															
Orleans	153 140	46.3	192 400	26.0	13.8	924	37.0	2.6	179 967	-1.3	10 565	5.9	170 454	41.8	15.3
Ouachita	57 690	59.7	123 300	19.6	10.0	689	32.4	2.4	71 851	-0.8	4 371	6.1	64 578	33.8	19.9
Plaquemines	8 614	69.0	155 300	23.7	10.0	982	27.6	3.4	10 245	-1.0	547	5.3	9 777	25.1	36.1
Pointe Coupee	8 726	76.9	115 800	19.3	10.0	566	28.9	4.3	10 065	-0.8	650	6.5	9 105	25.3	31.0
Rapides	47 674	63.0	125 800	21.2	10.0	733	31.9	2.4	57 569	-1.3	3 540	6.1	52 620	30.8	22.8
Red River	3 434	74.8	83 000	19.3	10.0	571	28.1	3.5	3 800	-3.1	233	6.1	3 241	28.0	35.1
Richland	7 619	66.3	82 500	18.7	10.0	531	24.7	2.2	8 439	-2.7	624	7.4	8 038	26.5	26.1
Sabine	9 171	76.9	79 900	16.8	10.0	496	26.5	2.9	9 171	-3.4	635	6.9	8 803	29.5	37.1
St. Bernard	14 545	67.4	130 000	21.2	10.0	840	35.3	2.2	19 522	-1.2	1 191	6.1	17 494	24.5	33.0
St. Charles	18 383	81.0	184 300	20.8	10.3	896	28.6	2.2	25 389	-1.1	1 348	5.3	24 804	30.4	26.4
St. Helena	4 131	85.1	78 400	25.1	10.8	619	30.0	6.3	4 442	-2.2	339	7.6	3 619	22.1	32.6
St. James	7 964	79.0	129 200	20.0	10.0	709	28.4	3.0	9 657	-1.7	723	7.5	9 035	23.7	31.8
St. John the Baptist	15 332	76.2	150 000	22.7	10.0	869	31.7	2.2	20 144	-1.3	1 372	6.8	19 661	29.3	29.0
St. Landry	30 683	69.7	90 800	19.9	10.3	593	35.6	2.7	32 748	-3.1	2 653	8.1	31 154	26.0	28.2
St. Martin	19 055	78.5	101 700	18.9	10.0	656	26.5	4.4	22 895	-5.1	1 786	7.8	23 917	24.2	31.6
St. Mary	20 320	67.0	92 900	19.8	10.4	674	27.6	5.1	22 138	-8.9	2 085	9.4	21 161	25.3	34.0
St. Tammany	89 036	77.1	197 100	22.4	10.1	984	32.0	1.7	116 448	-1.1	5 824	5.0	110 923	38.0	19.0
Tangipahoa	45 483	67.6	137 500	21.3	10.0	752	34.4	3.2	54 225	-0.2	3 645	6.7	53 685	28.9	26.7
Tensas	1 915	60.9	54 200	20.1	12.2	434	41.7	2.5	1 643	-4.6	162	9.9	1 636	23.2	31.2
Terrebonne	40 086	71.7	137 000	19.3	10.0	860	27.5	3.7	49 199	-7.4	3 440	7.0	48 450	24.1	33.7
Union	8 517	80.1	88 000	22.0	10.0	506	37.5	4.4	9 283	-1.0	604	6.5	8 096	25.8	36.0
Vermilion	21 796	75.2	98 100	17.7	10.0	631	25.5	5.3	24 573	-5.1	1 880	7.7	25 011	25.4	32.3
Vernon	17 842	53.5	98 000	17.5	10.0	913	26.4	2.2	16 996	-2.7	1 233	7.3	17 705	31.3	25.6
Washington	17 604	72.4	79 600	22.3	11.2	571	37.0	3.9	16 986	-0.5	1 192	7.0	15 327	27.8	30.3
Webster	15 765	70.9	81 800	20.3	10.5	596	31.7	2.8	15 269	-2.2	1 309	8.6	15 313	24.1	33.5
West Baton Rouge	9 119	70.5	162 500	18.7	10.0	774	27.1	1.7	13 178	-0.8	704	5.3	11 757	30.3	27.6
West Carroll	4 296	68.9	66 800	17.4	10.0	519	23.3	1.9	4 145	0.3	494	11.9	3 917	28.4	29.7
West Feliciana	3 911	76.0	188 200	21.6	10.1	822	26.6	4.1	5 375	-0.7	275	5.1	5 021	39.1	23.2
Winn	5 513	66.2	73 100	15.9	10.1	586	32.5	2.4	5 210	-2.5	406	7.8	4 920	29.9	33.5
MAINE	553 284	71.2	173 800	23.2	13.8	777	30.9	2.1	690 624	1.2	26 615	3.9	648 687	35.4	22.1
Androscoggin	44 636	63.6	151 100	23.0	14.5	710	29.2	2.3	55 377	1.1	1 993	3.6	52 961	31.5	24.3
Aroostook	30 355	70.7	94 800	21.0	12.8	547	30.1	2.0	31 576	-0.3	1 804	5.7	30 612	30.3	27.4
Cumberland	117 135	67.5	243 800	23.7	14.3	971	30.9	1.6	160 736	1.9	4 686	2.9	152 196	43.3	15.6
Franklin	11 841	79.9	129 600	22.1	11.5	635	30.6	3.0	14 485	-0.5	638	4.4	14 386	30.2	25.7
Hancock	24 371	73.0	198 300	24.0	13.3	776	32.2	3.0	29 190	0.7	1 371	4.7	26 665	34.8	24.9
Kennebec	51 443	70.3	150 600	21.6	13.3	691	30.6	2.0	62 284	1.2	2 258	3.6	57 787	35.7	20.8
Knox	16 999	76.4	197 000	25.2	14.0	764	28.8	2.7	20 691	1.3	741	3.6	19 270	33.8	24.8
Lincoln	14 876	79.5	204 100	23.3	13.6	772	29.8	2.7	17 010	1.8	645	3.8	16 480	32.7	27.1
Oxford	21 767	79.1	135 500	23.9	14.6	624	34.0	2.4	26 597	0.2	1 266	4.8	25 041	27.1	31.9
Penobscot	61 973	67.6	137 400	21.9	13.5	734	33.2	2.4	76 955	0.3	3 362	4.4	71 852	35.2	19.7
Piscataquis	7 529	74.6	109 700	23.1	14.2	630	31.5	3.4	7 511	0.5	407	5.4	6 632	29.4	33.1
Sagadahoc	15 405	75.5	189 300	23.6	13.5	793	31.9	1.3	19 206	1.5	577	3.0	17 689	36.7	21.0
Somerset	21 800	76.6	107 300	22.7	13.0	684	36.0	4.1	23 574	-0.1	1 373	5.8	22 275	26.9	31.3
Waldo	16 888	77.5	157 800	23.9	14.4	744	30.7	2.7	20 742	1.0	873	4.2	18 381	33.8	24.2
Washington	14 139	75.2	106 900	23.9	14.2	593	28.0	2.7	14 123	0.7	875	6.2	12 954	28.1	31.8
York	82 127	73.2	229 600	24.2	14.5	899	30.8	1.4	110 567	2.0	3 746	3.4	103 506	34.1	22.5
MARYLAND	2 166 389	66.8	286 900	23.4	11.7	1 230	30.8	2.4	3 170 012	0.7	135 881	4.3	2 976 504	44.6	15.7
Allegany	28 324	68.8	120 800	20.1	13.9	624	31.1	1.6	32 427	0.2	1 963	6.1	29 810	29.5	21.5
Anne Arundel	203 336	74.0	334 100	23.0	11.0	1 497	29.0	1.8	303 850	0.8	11 168	3.7	284 092	46.0	15.0
Baltimore	312 900	66.3	246 600	22.6	11.6	1 163	30.7	2.0	448 934	0.7	20 139	4.5	412 199	43.3	15.6
Calvert	31 155	81.6	341 800	23.3	10.4	1 557	31.4	1.3	47 809	1.5	1 826	3.8	45 249	39.9	19.9
Caroline	11 920	70.5	193 300	26.6	14.6	897	32.4	2.7	17 629	0.7	820	4.7	15 306	26.0	29.7
Carroll	60 004	82.0	321 300	23.3	12.5	1 079	29.7	1.4	93 859	0.7	3 292	3.5	88 196	43.0	18.2
Cecil	36 728	73.6	242 900	23.6	13.3	996	29.6	1.4	52 581	-0.2	2 663	5.1	48 849	35.8	24.4
Charles	53 171	77.7	284 500	24.2	11.4	1 487	33.9	1.6	81 960	1.6	3 447	4.2	76 622	41.1	16.4
Dorchester	13 265	65.6	187 700	24.6	14.0	845	30.9	1.6	15 870	0.3	956	6.0	15 354	31.4	25.8
Frederick	88 494	73.9	300 100	23.1	11.0	1 285	30.7	1.8	129 440	0.5	4 853	3.7	127 105	46.1	15.7
Garrett	11 863	74.6	165 300	23.7	11.2	658	27.6	1.4	15 533	-0.9	855	5.5	13 830	31.3	28.5
Harford	91 727	78.6	278 500	22.8	11.8	1 152	29.9	1.0	137 089	0.7	5 590	4.1	127 274	42.4	17.9
Howard	108 555	73.4	429 100	22.6	10.0	1 579	28.7	2.2	178 637	0.9	5 691	3.2	163 278	60.0	9.2
Kent	7 624	71.9	247 200	25.1	14.4	822	27.6	1.5	10 308	-2.7	484	4.7	8 984	35.9	20.7
Montgomery	365 235	66.2	454 700	22.8	10.0	1 627	30.6	3.1	551 392	0.5	18 191	3.3	540 333	56.2	10.1
Prince George's	305 610	62.0	254 700	25.7	11.2	1 294	31.1	4.0	494 517	1.4	21 637	4.4	465 639	37.5	18.1
Queen Anne's	17 522	83.8	339 900	24.2	12.8	1 178	29.0	1.7	26 788	0.4	1 008	3.8	25 305	40.6	18.3

1. Specified owner-occupied units.   2. A value of 10.0 represents 10 percent or less; a value of 50.0 represents 50 percent or more.   3. Specified renter-occupied units.
4. Overcrowded or lacking complete plumbing facilities.   5. Percent of civilian labor force.   6. Civilian employed persons 16 years old and over.

Table B. States and Counties — Nonfarm Employment and Agriculture

	Private nonfarm establishments, employment and payroll, 2015								Agriculture, 2012			
		Employment					Annual payroll		Farms			
										Percent with:		
STATE County	Number of establish-ments	Total	Health care and social assistance	Manufac-turing	Retail trade	Finance and insurance	Professional, scientific, and technical services	Total (mil dol)	Average per employee (dollars)	Number	Fewer than 50 acres	500 acres or more	Farm operators whose principal occu-pation is farming (percent)
	104	105	106	107	108	109	110	111	112	113	114	115	116
LOUISIANA—Cont'd													
Orleans	9 117	173 931	22 755	3 573	14 809	6 776	13 911	8 254	47 457	14	100.0	0.0	64.3
Ouachita	4 214	63 011	14 614	4 864	9 940	3 481	2 869	2 368	37 574	450	48.2	9.1	41.1
Plaquemines	700	11 295	491	2 123	559	115	484	757	67 040	140	52.1	20.7	42.9
Pointe Coupee	348	4 276	746	366	992	182	88	165	38 494	393	39.4	18.1	47.1
Rapides	3 152	47 268	13 859	3 784	8 009	1 392	1 951	1 736	36 719	853	54.6	9.5	50.1
Red River	135	2.050	448	342	143	78	30	84	40 851	252	32.9	21.0	56.0
Richland	412	5 877	1 698	D	882	202	85	179	30 512	762	31.8	19.2	47.1
Sabine	485	4 341	810	820	984	175	187	148	34 176	392	37.5	4.3	51.3
St. Bernard	682	7 721	629	1 246	1 718	144	165	336	43 574	56	46.4	23.2	60.7
St. Charles	979	21 526	1 435	4 729	1 528	250	2 194	1 459	67 758	70	45.7	2.9	64.3
St. Helena	115	1 293	442	242	287	31	9	42	32 131	373	41.3	7.2	44.0
St. James	319	6 545	446	2 554	554	196	198	471	72 008	63	46.0	25.4	61.9
St. John the Baptist	713	15 666	966	2 375	1 674	282	376	783	49 998	23	39.1	13.0	56.5
St. Landry	1 630	21 732	5 564	1 281	3 846	688	591	836	38 458	1 338	51.0	10.6	40.3
St. Martin	956	12 798	1 503	1 860	1 743	334	334	526	41 131	340	64.1	12.1	44.4
St. Mary	1 284	21 669	1 837	4 284	2 256	539	865	1 049	48 429	128	46.9	32.0	50.8
St. Tammany	6 273	76 874	15 124	2 504	13 919	3 238	4 802	3 227	41 983	604	74.3	1.8	42.4
Tangipahoa	2 317	35 571	8 589	2 161	6 994	2 310	1 010	1 265	35 569	1 070	52.1	3.0	44.1
Tensas	79	491	68	23	92	39	D	15	31 401	251	27.1	29.1	37.8
Terrebonne	2 994	53 746	7 667	6 961	7 176	1 096	2 531	2 577	47 952	189	47.6	14.8	58.7
Union	335	3 892	772	D	576	127	54	122	31 472	413	31.0	4.1	48.2
Vermilion	1 036	10 535	1 721	444	2 162	366	357	380	36 059	1 184	43.2	10.9	53.7
Vernon	718	8 428	1 816	163	1 621	318	123	284	33 670	471	53.1	2.5	49.7
Washington	627	9 441	2 703	1 008	1 278	375	123	311	32 946	826	52.8	3.1	44.1
Webster	818	11 190	2 357	1 500	2 133	338	219	415	37 107	447	40.5	2.7	44.7
West Baton Rouge	548	11 499	453	2 279	1 113	180	264	580	50 432	106	66.0	15.1	50.9
West Carroll	183	1 723	536	D	367	71	24	50	29 115	733	28.5	9.5	25.0
West Feliciana	188	2 966	447	D	320	85	250	165	55 674	163	28.2	28.2	40.5
Winn	290	4 185	828	698	517	138	48	157	37 530	179	37.4	3.4	43.6
MAINE	40 801	500 549	109 725	50 316	82 303	27 149	22 832	20 413	40 782	8 173	43.0	6.7	48.5
Androscoggin	2 706	45 347	9 828	5 996	6 036	3 262	1 802	1 764	38 897	463	51.6	5.0	56.4
Aroostook	2 000	21 282	5 804	2 800	4 518	761	343	717	33 668	895	18.2	19.1	43.9
Cumberland	11 191	165 345	33 615	9 351	22 642	13 021	10 214	7 677	46 429	718	60.6	4.2	46.5
Franklin	814	9 464	1 762	1 274	1 651	797	116	291	30 709	388	43.6	3.9	34.3
Hancock	2 225	16 774	3 218	1 534	3 404	535	1 775	678	40 449	404	50.0	5.0	52.0
Kennebec	3 203	45 976	12 944	2 722	8 535	1 292	1 699	1 730	37 618	604	47.4	4.6	45.7
Knox	1 734	14 160	3 042	1 707	2 797	675	425	523	36 903	314	53.8	1.6	54.8
Lincoln	1 374	8 272	1 841	723	1 596	310	310	305	36 816	344	53.2	1.5	51.2
Oxford	1 306	14 138	2 845	2 370	2 233	312	315	474	33 537	551	44.5	6.4	44.8
Penobscot	4 109	57 350	14 412	3 635	11 036	1 870	1 745	2 160	37 658	677	36.9	7.7	51.7
Piscataquis	438	4 575	1 314	1 024	908	71	50	147	32 032	203	21.7	9.4	51.2
Sagadahoc	912	13 596	1 568	D	1 929	316	708	642	47 203	229	53.7	3.1	48.9
Somerset	1 164	13 549	2 643	2 887	2 306	273	384	519	38 341	579	32.5	11.4	50.3
Waldo	981	8 662	1 749	1 121	1 455	936	207	311	35 910	633	41.5	3.5	48.7
Washington	839	6 763	1 627	839	1 681	272	136	242	35 753	392	35.5	8.7	44.9
York	5 537	52 357	11 141	6 771	9 573	1 625	1 917	2 022	38 620	779	53.8	1.5	54.0
MARYLAND	137 204	2 239 817	366 774	97 575	290 304	100 070	273 594	118 497	52 905	12 256	49.2	7.6	48.9
Allegany	1 554	25 414	6 080	2 324	3 900	858	1 413	847	33 311	291	30.9	2.1	43.0
Anne Arundel	13 970	229 708	28 333	11 333	33 406	5 886	31 628	12 651	55 073	381	66.9	2.9	57.5
Baltimore	19 823	316 796	58 517	14 641	48 345	19 936	26 919	15 329	48 388	640	63.0	3.1	49.5
Calvert	1 708	18 497	3 441	434	3 067	333	1 827	810	43 789	269	49.4	5.9	45.0
Caroline	612	7 022	751	1 147	1 206	156	237	270	38 433	658	37.4	14.7	60.0
Carroll	4 220	49 067	10 106	3 380	8 427	1 061	2 621	1 923	39 196	1 092	59.3	4.9	39.7
Cecil	1 783	24 117	4 760	4 025	3 724	378	446	1 093	45 321	496	54.4	7.3	51.2
Charles	2 622	33 341	4 672	489	8 658	761	2 252	1 241	37 234	382	52.1	5.0	52.6
Dorchester	692	9 410	1 817	2 420	1 341	235	191	334	35 462	423	36.2	16.1	54.1
Frederick	6 035	86 308	11 815	6 075	12 487	5 766	8 202	4 064	47 088	1 308	49.5	6.0	47.6
Garrett	896	10 886	1 648	1 090	1 620	372	395	358	32 905	667	31.8	4.2	49.0
Harford	5 429	69 137	10 647	4 694	14 242	1 868	7 672	2 931	42 390	582	58.4	4.5	42.8
Howard	9 225	168 100	15 463	5 021	16 059	7 050	40 146	10 514	62 546	293	65.9	7.2	37.9
Kent	619	7 372	1 314	1 150	946	188	244	260	35 270	367	27.0	17.7	49.3
Montgomery	27 160	423 361	68 341	8 220	46 001	19 936	74 250	26 769	63 230	540	66.9	4.8	42.0
Prince George's	14 728	250 701	31 367	6 658	38 849	5 762	31 250	11 642	46 437	347	61.4	2.3	44.4
Queen Anne's	1 371	11 503	927	1 112	2 434	313	604	414	36 034	530	36.6	17.0	48.9

Table B. States and Counties — **Agriculture**

	Agriculture, 2012 (cont.)														
STATE County	Land in farms					Value of land and buildings (dollars)		Value of machinery and equipment, average per farm (dollars)	Value of products sold				Percent of farms with sales of:		Government payments	
			Acres								Percent from:					
	Acreage (1,000)	Percent change, 2007–2012	Average size of farm	Total irrigated (1,000)	Total cropland (1,000)	Average per farm	Average per acre		Total (mil dol)	Average per farm (dollars)	Crops	Live-stock and poultry products	$10,000 or more	$100,000 or more	Total ($1,000)	Percent of farms
	117	118	119	120	121	122	123	124	125	126	127	128	129	130	131	132
LOUISIANA—Cont'd																
Orleans	111	D	8	0.0	0.0	122 786	15 486	114 143	0.5	37 143	41.2	59.0	42.9	7.1	D	7.1
Ouachita	93	9.1	207	12.1	47.4	603 420	2 916	72 287	49.1	109 047	54.9	45.1	29.3	9.8	1 933	25.8
Plaquemines	89	-26.8	635	0.1	8.5	801 564	1 262	64 250	15.0	107 457	39.1	61.0	61.4	15.0	60	7.9
Pointe Coupee	182	-4.4	464	6.1	143.8	1 272 481	2 744	240 089	130.1	331 163	95.8	4.2	58.8	18.3	2 786	41.0
Rapides	211	19.0	247	21.1	132.1	628 930	2 543	99 732	132.2	154 972	88.3	11.7	42.3	16.4	3 644	22.2
Red River	135	31.0	537	3.0	34.3	1 049 234	1 954	129 516	38.6	153 024	33.5	66.5	41.3	15.5	1 506	34.9
Richland	279	-4.2	366	85.1	189.5	840 475	2 296	126 639	127.3	167 038	93.5	6.5	37.1	18.2	10 171	76.1
Sabine	52	2.5	132	0.1	12.0	420 495	3 180	71 528	142.1	362 612	0.9	99.1	37.8	14.0	441	11.5
St. Bernard	32	-0.5	569	0.0	4.3	946 804	1 663	68 750	5.8	103 482	2.7	97.3	32.1	12.5	19	14.3
St. Charles	16	D	232	D	1.9	501 871	2 166	57 929	1.2	16 571	12.8	87.3	44.3	0.0	D	8.6
St. Helena	53	1.4	142	1.4	17.0	476 399	3 346	62 539	25.6	68 542	8.3	91.7	28.4	7.5	298	18.2
St. James	40	-7.7	634	0.0	37.1	2 231 444	3 520	369 730	33.2	526 270	98.8	1.2	58.7	28.6	84	17.5
St. John the Baptist	11	-21.5	468	0.0	8.0	1 361 261	2 910	240 391	9.3	402 696	98.6	1.4	43.5	13.0	D	4.3
St. Landry	301	0.8	225	29.8	223.9	540 722	2 405	90 250	125.0	93 408	91.7	8.3	28.3	9.7	5 809	39.3
St. Martin	76	-3.8	223	6.7	58.2	552 229	2 473	154 956	52.8	155 250	91.0	9.0	37.1	14.1	506	17.6
St. Mary	76	4.6	594	0.0	63.0	1 490 961	2 508	392 164	65.8	513 867	98.4	1.6	43.8	27.3	173	21.1
St. Tammany	34	-25.0	56	0.4	7.9	413 126	7 315	44 215	11.3	18 685	61.1	38.9	22.2	4.0	38	2.5
Tangipahoa	107	-13.8	100	0.7	36.3	410 570	4 117	54 967	45.7	42 694	40.2	59.8	29.1	7.2	790	17.3
Tensas	197	-12.8	783	40.3	168.2	1 721 227	2 197	275 825	129.2	514 558	99.8	0.2	37.5	29.5	7 350	86.5
Terrebonne	93	-47.9	492	0.6	21.5	1 102 540	2 243	147 534	37.1	196 418	43.6	56.4	37.0	13.2	95	9.0
Union	63	-7.0	152	0.0	16.8	441 254	2 909	75 138	92.9	224 986	1.5	98.5	40.7	15.3	166	9.2
Vermilion	284	-2.3	240	59.2	171.9	622 631	2 599	100 574	141.1	119 207	69.7	30.3	36.7	10.3	6 832	57.3
Vernon	49	-3.2	104	0.0	8.9	328 764	3 160	43 987	3.2	6 794	29.0	70.9	14.0	0.6	89	4.0
Washington	81	-16.7	99	0.4	28.6	349 438	3 545	54 988	28.3	34 259	40.2	59.8	23.0	4.4	434	14.6
Webster	52	5.6	117	D	10.1	407 367	3 483	51 532	10.1	22 501	17.3	82.7	27.1	2.2	81	7.2
West Baton Rouge	30	17.4	286	0.1	25.6	1 071 953	3 750	222 868	31.4	295 934	88.7	11.3	39.6	17.9	181	33.0
West Carroll	166	-15.8	226	45.2	115.9	482 630	2 135	86 151	72.5	98 966	97.1	2.9	19.9	11.3	5 879	83.8
West Feliciana	101	51.9	621	0.0	28.9	1 639 712	2 639	99 767	18.7	114 497	76.8	23.2	41.1	8.0	273	30.7
Winn	25	16.7	139	0.0	4.1	337 184	2 418	59 615	18.0	100 575	4.0	96.0	24.6	4.5	118	14.0
MAINE	1 454	7.9	178	30.9	477.3	410 633	2 308	69 762	763.1	93 364	62.1	37.9	34.6	9.5	10 162	16.3
Androscoggin	59	16.9	128	0.8	22.0	329 181	2 564	72 955	53.8	116 266	22.1	77.9	32.8	8.0	445	15.6
Aroostook	351	-6.6	392	11.4	187.5	559 514	1 427	157 318	210.5	235 215	91.6	8.4	42.9	21.5	2 492	43.0
Cumberland	63	21.2	87	0.7	18.0	428 535	4 907	61 922	26.3	36 635	65.6	34.4	33.7	7.5	497	8.1
Franklin	49	21.3	127	0.1	9.6	276 724	2 172	47 778	D	D	D	D	22.4	5.4	595	17.8
Hancock	53	1.2	132	0.2	12.0	444 960	3 369	51 351	D	D	D	D	38.6	6.9	187	14.9
Kennebec	78	-5.3	129	0.4	32.8	370 354	2 866	69 992	49.8	82 505	28.9	71.1	36.8	8.8	711	12.3
Knox	29	-2.3	94	0.3	7.5	355 739	3 798	35 876	D	D	D	D	31.2	4.1	116	14.6
Lincoln	32	5.2	92	0.1	7.4	320 218	3 489	43 009	10.2	29 541	51.2	48.8	32.8	5.5	269	7.8
Oxford	75	9.5	137	0.4	15.7	347 443	2 543	48 483	19.2	34 880	75.4	24.6	27.0	5.3	488	12.5
Penobscot	113	-1.4	167	2.3	35.6	336 186	2 015	63 316	50.2	74 084	32.3	67.7	33.4	9.0	1 044	13.3
Piscataquis	47	37.1	230	0.2	12.4	394 502	1 715	49 310	D	D	D	D	29.1	9.4	405	22.2
Sagadahoc	20	7.9	88	0.2	5.2	331 555	3 779	39 664	D	D	D	D	30.1	5.7	139	7.4
Somerset	140	25.7	242	0.2	30.2	512 425	2 119	92 294	86.4	149 278	64.1	35.9	44.7	19.2	1 053	16.6
Waldo	131	91.5	206	0.2	24.8	384 874	1 865	39 363	D	D	D	D	29.1	6.5	837	16.6
Washington	149	-5.9	380	12.1	35.7	594 518	1 564	79 079	154.6	394 508	D	D	45.7	9.4	526	18.6
York	65	8.7	83	1.3	21.0	403 257	4 869	58 392	27.5	35 239	D	D	31.8	6.4	358	5.9
MARYLAND	2 031	-1.0	166	104.9	1 396.1	1 148 268	6 930	115 879	2 271.4	185 329	46.3	53.7	43.1	20.6	36 024	37.8
Allegany	36	-1.0	125	0.0	11.8	435 282	3 493	52 261	3.1	10 735	59.5	40.5	30.6	1.0	253	31.6
Anne Arundel	28	-3.9	74	0.3	14.7	854 354	11 579	71 680	19.7	51 627	84.0	16.0	25.7	5.8	160	10.0
Baltimore	70	-10.0	110	0.5	44.6	1 038 656	9 440	91 152	76.3	119 228	88.6	11.4	34.5	12.5	840	18.3
Calvert	33	24.4	122	0.2	21.2	921 743	7 536	72 149	11.1	41 416	95.3	4.7	37.2	9.7	523	23.8
Caroline	150	14.5	229	27.0	121.4	1 395 853	6 109	155 213	257.9	391 968	33.1	66.9	68.2	46.0	3 335	61.7
Carroll	133	-6.6	121	1.4	97.2	989 130	8 144	101 499	111.6	102 232	67.3	32.7	34.5	12.6	3 440	40.2
Cecil	77	-9.8	155	0.6	54.8	1 121 347	7 255	132 554	113.8	229 466	60.3	39.7	43.8	19.4	1 505	30.4
Charles	47	-10.5	122	0.5	25.3	788 220	6 453	70 134	11.9	31 272	89.8	10.2	26.4	6.5	508	22.8
Dorchester	126	-5.1	299	22.4	92.0	1 557 508	5 211	204 546	187.1	442 215	37.3	62.7	51.1	40.0	2 501	75.9
Frederick	182	-10.2	139	1.4	127.1	1 053 941	7 595	108 462	150.5	115 030	49.5	50.5	41.1	17.9	3 060	33.6
Garrett	95	-0.3	143	0.0	41.5	600 378	4 207	80 346	31.5	47 168	34.7	65.3	46.0	14.4	540	18.9
Harford	65	-12.9	112	0.5	40.4	929 613	8 264	89 722	46.0	79 041	68.1	31.9	33.8	12.9	894	28.5
Howard	37	27.6	128	0.2	20.9	1 401 898	10 961	84 051	31.9	108 816	86.9	13.1	32.4	11.9	309	20.8
Kent	133	3.9	363	8.3	104.6	2 472 676	6 813	197 866	112.3	305 858	69.8	30.2	61.3	33.2	2 931	77.9
Montgomery	63	-6.1	118	1.0	45.6	1 195 894	10 171	101 435	48.3	89 520	86.6	13.4	29.1	10.6	836	17.2
Prince George's	33	-11.9	94	0.8	14.4	741 326	7 889	56 916	18.0	51 873	91.3	8.7	30.0	5.2	157	11.5
Queen Anne's	157	6.8	296	15.8	129.9	2 204 232	7 444	181 240	166.9	314 821	61.9	38.1	53.2	35.1	4 242	73.6

STATE County	Water use, 2010		Wholesale trade,[1] 2012				Retail trade,[2] 2012				Real estate and rental and leasing,[2] 2012			
	Total water withdrawn (mil gal/day)	Gallons withdrawn per person per day	Number of establishments	Number of employees	Sales (mil dol)	Annual payroll (mil dol)	Number of establishments	Number of employees	Sales (mil dol)	Annual payroll (mil dol)	Number of establishments	Number of employees	Receipts (mil dol)	Annual payroll (mil dol)
	133	134	135	136	137	138	139	140	141	142	143	144	145	146
LOUISIANA—Cont'd														
Orleans	615.3	1 790	256	3 794	2 687.0	191.5	1 275	12 371	3 245.1	337.8	379	2 156	411.6	79.1
Ouachita	68.2	443	182	D	D	D	710	9 203	2 387.1	205.9	185	1 145	228.0	37.9
Plaquemines	85.1	3 694	54	982	2 228.3	57.5	66	499	134.1	13.3	41	364	116.3	23.0
Pointe Coupee	343.8	15 077	10	140	436.2	6.3	77	775	201.2	17.0	12	37	10.7	1.7
Rapides	547.9	4 163	123	D	D	D	584	7 769	2 211.5	188.3	137	D	D	D
Red River	4.4	484	7	70	22.9	2.3	18	154	37.3	2.6	3	D	D	D
Richland	30.6	1 474	21	234	529.8	13.8	65	715	250.4	16.9	16	113	8.1	2.0
Sabine	4.2	172	14	123	55.8	4.6	79	860	217.2	19.3	13	23	3.1	0.4
St. Bernard	260.7	7 263	26	D	D	D	137	1 432	392.2	35.7	19	60	8.9	2.2
St. Charles	2 475.5	46 903	73	1 944	4 939.9	105.6	112	1 184	402.9	31.0	35	172	49.9	9.3
St. Helena	1.1	96	2	D	D	D	29	345	80.0	4.4	2	D	D	D
St. James	192.4	8 703	10	D	D	D	50	490	128.6	10.7	6	14	1.8	0.3
St. John the Baptist	67.5	1 471	29	D	D	D	118	1 586	479.2	36.4	29	199	58.2	8.7
St. Landry	77.3	926	59	578	782.4	24.5	305	3 806	976.8	86.8	53	674	124.3	31.0
St. Martin	39.5	757	52	795	458.3	43.5	142	1 615	559.0	33.9	38	814	352.9	59.5
St. Mary	120.7	2 208	75	D	D	D	198	2 295	605.2	54.2	80	1 141	259.8	65.0
St. Tammany	28.6	122	244	2 224	5 060.2	125.1	915	12 433	3 550.7	301.2	215	1 112	250.7	55.5
Tangipahoa	20.1	166	86	1 701	1 300.4	68.5	438	6 290	1 769.7	144.7	94	498	86.5	18.5
Tensas	31.7	6 043	9	72	195.4	3.7	15	78	27.7	1.8	NA	NA	NA	NA
Terrebonne	5.9	52	196	2 102	996.0	113.8	503	7 070	1 929.4	170.2	167	1 690	471.5	101.9
Union	4.1	179	5	D	D	D	66	609	141.3	14.4	5	9	1.3	0.2
Vermilion	93.7	1 616	33	307	235.8	15.1	180	2 057	577.3	47.8	39	224	41.9	9.0
Vernon	8.5	162	18	90	57.3	3.3	134	1 537	426.7	34.7	31	268	70.5	11.3
Washington	34.6	733	20	118	128.3	3.5	138	1 152	297.0	26.5	15	41	4.0	0.8
Webster	7.3	177	34	394	204.7	15.4	163	2 193	549.4	47.2	33	155	34.4	6.7
West Baton Rouge	10.8	454	43	755	967.9	41.2	85	1 173	455.5	25.3	11	121	29.2	5.9
West Carroll	15.2	1 308	5	D	D	D	34	397	87.4	7.8	5	12	1.8	0.3
West Feliciana	41.6	2 664	3	D	D	D	28	283	86.6	5.7	6	D	D	D
Winn	2.3	152	10	108	65.2	3.8	48	543	113.9	11.3	8	29	3.3	0.8
MAINE	449.3	338	1 344	14 753	12 961.3	691.5	6 351	80 155	21 521.7	1 884.6	1 580	6 242	1 100.4	220.6
Androscoggin	15.3	142	102	1 236	473.9	54.6	439	6 018	1 818.1	138.5	111	376	62.9	11.6
Aroostook	23.0	320	72	503	308.9	21.8	346	4 186	1 119.4	90.0	76	252	50.4	6.5
Cumberland	64.1	228	456	5 956	5 925.3	308.3	1 448	21 738	5 751.4	522.3	516	2 787	519.6	109.3
Franklin	39.1	1 270	14	D	D	D	161	1 623	395.5	34.4	27	68	8.2	1.6
Hancock	31.2	573	59	464	244.5	14.7	379	3 471	852.6	86.4	80	185	27.2	5.5
Kennebec	12.9	105	96	1 990	1 613.7	96.4	526	8 111	2 179.3	201.2	99	429	65.5	14.1
Knox	5.0	126	49	256	165.9	9.6	257	2 656	632.9	60.7	69	151	22.2	5.5
Lincoln	2.5	74	30	D	D	D	210	1 648	421.7	39.6	49	114	15.2	3.2
Oxford	37.2	644	34	D	D	D	224	2 212	611.4	53.6	37	129	14.6	3.5
Penobscot	58.4	379	162	1 794	955.4	82.3	735	10 931	3 203.1	249.6	172	692	123.3	22.9
Piscataquis	2.5	141	8	D	D	D	91	823	212.2	19.0	12	27	3.3	0.6
Sagadahoc	2.6	74	22	108	43.5	3.8	141	1 864	465.5	42.8	32	60	8.7	1.9
Somerset	72.9	1 396	28	176	61.1	6.6	213	2 353	611.0	51.9	31	219	48.7	10.0
Waldo	4.0	103	23	D	D	D	163	1 479	365.7	34.4	29	59	7.1	2.1
Washington	31.4	956	45	230	125.4	5.2	150	1 670	433.1	37.1	20	46	4.1	1.2
York	47.3	240	144	1 163	818.2	55.2	868	9 372	2 448.7	223.0	220	648	119.4	21.0
MARYLAND	7 382.0	1 279	4 768	73 369	60 734.2	4 378.5	18 179	281 678	76 379.7	7 168.5	6 001	42 838	13 410.1	2 253.2
Allegany	42.2	562	45	D	D	D	288	3 854	822.8	81.5	52	199	29.3	5.6
Anne Arundel	341.2	635	492	8 187	7 606.5	484.5	2 005	33 052	8 758.8	831.2	566	4 232	1 254.5	203.5
Baltimore	673.3	836	749	10 796	5 548.5	609.6	2 745	47 973	12 645.7	1 235.1	855	6 432	3 201.7	344.6
Calvert	3 265.4	36 798	42	268	91.8	13.6	205	2 955	848.4	72.4	80	285	79.2	15.3
Caroline	19.7	594	21	186	118.9	8.3	86	980	476.2	28.7	15	D	D	D
Carroll	13.8	83	150	1 286	723.9	61.7	495	7 901	2 245.2	184.3	137	474	83.1	15.7
Cecil	8.4	83	60	D	D	D	264	3 895	1 146.3	87.9	72	191	27.7	5.5
Charles	1 282.1	8 748	56	435	950.4	21.1	495	8 729	2 245.0	207.7	107	394	97.3	13.3
Dorchester	21.0	643	32	276	234.2	12.2	100	1 133	288.7	25.4	37	92	8.3	2.6
Frederick	40.6	174	199	2 212	1 185.8	119.4	736	11 814	3 267.7	299.3	246	864	207.0	39.8
Garrett	7.7	257	23	D	D	D	136	1 714	517.9	39.1	34	D	D	D
Harford	19.1	78	170	1 865	2 420.7	99.4	723	13 420	3 792.9	342.6	215	751	192.9	27.9
Howard	4.1	14	478	11 707	9 266.7	784.1	854	15 811	4 867.7	427.7	379	3 356	1 025.9	181.9
Kent	5.2	257	24	172	127.1	6.9	99	848	185.9	18.6	25	57	18.0	2.0
Montgomery	737.9	759	676	9 113	10 456.8	672.7	2 702	46 240	13 706.2	1 333.7	1 324	12 342	4 534.5	829.3
Prince George's	745.3	863	536	11 108	7 639.8	651.0	2 217	36 414	9 358.1	907.2	640	6 216	1 186.5	281.3
Queen Anne's	14.0	294	70	778	353.0	37.8	210	2 305	547.5	49.1	47	155	36.1	4.8

1. Merchant wholesalers, except manufacturers' sales branches and offices. 2. Employer establishments.

Table B. States and Counties — Professional Services, Manufacturing, and Accommodation and Food Services

STATE County	Professional, scientific, and technical services, 2012				Manufacturing, 2012				Accommodation and food services, 2012			
	Number of establishments	Number of employees	Receipts (mil dol)	Annual payroll (mil dol)	Number of establishments	Number of employees	Receipts (mil dol)	Annual payroll (mil dol)	Number of establishments	Number of employees	Sales (mil dol)	Annual payroll (mil dol)
	147	148	149	150	151	152	153	154	155	156	157	158
LOUISIANA—Cont'd												
Orleans	1 450	13 212	2 613.2	971.7	144	6 049	4 352.7	335.6	1 300	35 510	2 765.4	764.7
Ouachita	435	2 696	373.8	123.8	126	D	D	D	294	D	D	D
Plaquemines	51	382	114.7	28.9	37	2 174	D	192.2	61	737	59.8	18.8
Pointe Coupee	30	99	15.8	5.4	8	385	D	16.0	37	344	18.5	3.8
Rapides	285	D	D	D	72	3 851	D	217.3	237	4 330	216.8	58.3
Red River	9	29	4.0	1.0	4	194	D	8.2	10	D	D	D
Richland	27	92	10.4	2.8	11	904	396.5	37.5	24	D	D	D
Sabine	50	185	19.8	7.6	16	753	D	36.1	25	D	D	D
St. Bernard	34	148	14.2	4.3	33	1 195	11 904.0	109.8	81	D	D	D
St. Charles	95	1 402	162.3	75.5	40	4 695	29 174.8	471.2	82	995	49.3	12.7
St. Helena	6	16	2.2	0.4	5	257	D	D	8	D	D	D
St. James	17	75	8.0	3.3	24	2 156	D	201.7	25	D	D	D
St. John the Baptist	57	335	46.3	15.3	24	2 788	D	234.5	75	1 235	58.5	14.4
St. Landry	142	553	78.8	25.3	57	1 353	3 421.2	60.8	99	1 594	76.6	21.0
St. Martin	100	325	50.6	13.5	69	1 911	D	86.0	75	1 321	63.2	15.5
St. Mary	104	614	97.7	34.5	81	4 170	1 901.2	249.1	107	2 823	201.1	55.7
St. Tammany	844	5 154	700.8	292.6	123	3 676	D	205.3	556	9 615	443.8	128.0
Tangipahoa	208	889	93.5	33.6	79	2 389	681.2	84.4	213	4 285	185.8	50.9
Tensas	2	D	D	D	3	13	D	D	6	D	D	D
Terrebonne	287	2 797	353.6	138.9	143	6 301	1 538.3	343.2	235	5 138	295.2	84.7
Union	14	41	5.3	1.4	10	D	D	D	16	D	D	D
Vermilion	118	291	33.0	11.6	40	636	D	24.9	61	928	49.4	11.3
Vernon	86	725	70.3	32.6	14	200	D	6.4	66	1 412	58.8	16.2
Washington	43	133	19.4	5.2	27	1 027	616.1	65.5	61	713	33.5	8.5
Webster	53	247	21.0	6.4	29	1 436	D	D	61	807	34.8	8.7
West Baton Rouge	26	238	22.2	8.1	36	2 300	7 272.3	151.5	56	878	49.1	10.9
West Carroll	11	D	D	D	3	D	D	D	11	186	6.3	1.8
West Feliciana	26	77	7.9	4.3	8	324	D	D	27	341	14.7	3.9
Winn	21	47	4.4	1.4	14	606	D	28.1	18	D	D	D
MAINE	3 492	22 943	3 352.6	1 238.0	1 650	49 238	16 044.5	2 424.3	3 958	49 672	2 901.3	850.8
Androscoggin	183	1 652	359.2	80.1	150	5 205	1 886.9	251.6	209	3 021	153.3	44.5
Aroostook	97	343	31.4	11.9	92	2 689	1 037.9	121.1	156	1 897	83.2	23.9
Cumberland	1 410	10 188	1 627.5	641.9	380	8 691	D	433.9	973	15 001	839.9	254.8
Franklin	43	D	D	D	25	1 454	D	72.7	92	1 114	41.4	12.8
Hancock	138	1 773	268.7	99.5	90	1 463	520.2	73.7	301	2 040	211.1	54.9
Kennebec	302	D	D	D	95	2 386	634.2	114.8	302	4 055	222.9	66.8
Knox	132	440	53.5	20.8	94	1 443	377.8	63.4	166	1 663	96.8	30.9
Lincoln	108	D	D	D	72	742	D	31.9	149	1 127	84.6	24.3
Oxford	75	307	32.8	10.9	61	2 434	860.6	138.6	133	2 562	103.8	32.5
Penobscot	328	1 831	179.4	84.5	134	3 749	977.7	164.0	315	5 639	313.9	86.7
Piscataquis	13	D	D	D	22	1 045	177.5	37.8	47	259	14.9	3.6
Sagadahoc	99	917	103.0	52.7	39	D	D	D	81	1 053	54.9	17.1
Somerset	59	332	37.1	13.4	72	3 330	1 607.3	177.8	92	846	43.8	12.8
Waldo	60	187	15.7	7.1	45	1 163	168.4	36.4	93	789	46.2	13.3
Washington	31	D	D	D	36	994	359.2	40.7	80	558	28.2	7.8
York	414	2 078	356.0	106.6	243	D	2 762.3	D	769	8 048	562.4	164.0
MARYLAND	19 714	244 710	50 024.9	20 161.2	3 096	100 079	39 533.0	5 908.9	11 344	204 222	12 516.8	3 410.5
Allegany	96	486	42.7	18.3	52	2 547	D	119.2	181	D	D	D
Anne Arundel	2 027	24 815	5 787.2	2 467.9	275	11 547	4 456.9	993.6	1 158	25 939	1 564.0	419.4
Baltimore	2 692	24 678	3 990.9	1 657.7	451	16 807	8 066.7	1 003.7	1 578	27 158	1 555.8	415.4
Calvert	215	1 286	162.5	54.7	38	455	84.1	18.8	146	D	D	D
Caroline	38	D	D	D	28	1 167	302.3	42.8	36	D	D	D
Carroll	494	2 471	324.9	125.6	124	3 402	1 019.4	178.4	262	5 810	246.8	73.1
Cecil	155	570	52.7	19.1	49	4 496	1 989.3	312.3	176	2 792	154.1	41.7
Charles	273	1 979	311.6	127.5	43	399	84.0	18.4	244	D	D	D
Dorchester	53	169	17.8	5.2	44	2 546	843.1	93.7	58	D	D	D
Frederick	845	6 686	1 098.7	427.9	163	6 026	3 236.1	354.3	441	8 452	449.6	130.0
Garrett	53	397	37.4	17.3	50	1 128	D	39.6	74	D	D	D
Harford	697	D	D	D	137	4 058	1 866.8	207.2	394	7 960	390.9	104.7
Howard	1 883	35 086	10 616.5	3 126.2	186	5 013	1 538.2	276.8	543	11 000	610.9	177.1
Kent	51	D	D	D	29	945	360.0	50.7	74	D	D	D
Montgomery	5 701	74 255	14 389.9	6 751.1	381	8 233	2 172.6	619.7	1 818	31 526	2 080.0	571.8
Prince George's	1 662	26 331	4 349.1	1 903.9	264	7 291	2 216.8	424.1	1 269	23 872	1 685.5	436.2
Queen Anne's	158	D	D	D	49	921	208.3	41.8	94	2 111	113.0	33.7

1. Establishment subject to federal tax.

STATE County	Health care and social assistance, 2012				Other services, 2012				Nonemployer businesses, 2015		Value of residential construction authorized by building permits, 2016	
	Number of establishments	Number of employees	Receipts (mil dol)	Annual payroll (mil dol)	Number of establishments	Number of employees	Receipts (mil dol)	Annual payroll (mil dol)	Number	Receipts (mil dol)	New Construction ($1,000)	Number of housing units
	159	160	161	162	163	164	165	166	167	168	169	170
LOUISIANA—Cont'd												
Orleans	861	21 761	2 667.4	964.2	578	4 297	791.8	139.5	37 229	1 549.0	131 484	608
Ouachita	629	14 085	1 354.2	483.6	229	1 533	141.0	41.4	12 655	515.3	125 311	635
Plaquemines	21	468	40.0	17.7	44	D	D	D	2 408	135.4	15 934	53
Pointe Coupee	35	709	49.3	19.3	28	D	D	D	1 526	59.9	10 707	45
Rapides	506	14 112	1 514.4	554.9	198	1 018	104.1	27.5	7 967	363.6	64 543	348
Red River	15	444	37.8	11.4	6	D	D	D	486	14.5	0	0
Richland	80	1 783	100.9	40.6	18	D	D	D	1 453	53.5	706	19
Sabine	44	846	53.5	20.5	22	79	19.5	2.2	1 324	56.0	13 127	60
St. Bernard	51	D	D	D	37	D	D	D	3 502	138.9	14 760	107
St. Charles	65	D	D	D	50	D	D	D	4 022	168.8	26 877	126
St. Helena	14	D	D	D	7	D	D	D	839	19.7	0	0
St. James	28	764	69.8	29.3	16	D	D	D	1 316	41.3	11 567	41
St. John the Baptist	70	D	D	D	39	367	57.3	16.1	3 124	90.6	6 710	42
St. Landry	289	6 071	433.5	172.0	77	361	31.7	8.9	5 723	215.5	25 145	118
St. Martin	79	1 675	79.2	37.7	44	126	20.5	4.3	4 364	154.9	31 428	159
St. Mary	115	2 094	164.1	64.7	89	523	65.0	19.2	3 865	142.9	6 587	43
St. Tammany	791	14 504	1 581.8	607.7	356	1 993	219.0	60.3	23 003	1 185.3	332 401	1 411
Tangipahoa	301	8 143	655.2	261.4	149	966	98.1	25.5	9 340	324.9	94 783	698
Tensas	9	66	5.1	2.1	2	D	D	D	372	11.5	1 017	13
Terrebonne	284	6 992	704.8	288.9	175	1 449	232.6	73.0	8 102	373.6	33 160	144
Union	32	851	53.6	20.7	14	35	3.3	0.7	1 450	58.1	6 112	35
Vermilion	101	1 764	122.8	46.2	56	252	24.6	6.2	4 386	158.2	20 391	122
Vernon	77	2 010	222.5	85.8	41	170	15.3	3.6	2 034	77.2	9 671	54
Washington	84	2 309	171.6	73.6	28	106	10.0	2.3	2 905	101.6	13 998	84
Webster	86	2 332	173.5	65.1	39	250	29.9	7.2	2 563	103.3	6 980	32
West Baton Rouge	32	443	26.4	11.3	38	263	40.4	10.7	1 570	64.8	39 731	263
West Carroll	16	549	35.9	14.9	15	60	4.2	1.1	645	22.1	1 225	6
West Feliciana	24	462	36.9	13.6	10	D	D	D	753	24.8	11 790	29
Winn	38	957	67.2	29.2	18	D	D	D	668	38.1	0	0
MAINE	4 730	109 231	10 297.0	4 393.0	2 786	13 755	1 462.8	376.3	113 012	5 075.9	11 022 421	83
Androscoggin	385	9 531	947.5	402.8	211	1 024	84.6	23.5	6 137	288.8	33 356	185
Aroostook	229	6 120	471.8	207.2	122	397	45.8	9.1	4 035	166.0	6 994	57
Cumberland	1 339	33 687	3 348.8	1 475.2	734	4 502	518.8	130.4	28 144	1 428.0	248 996	1 366
Franklin	106	1 882	156.4	74.4	44	214	19.8	4.8	2 391	82.3	12 899	67
Hancock	159	3 144	306.6	127.7	140	686	101.2	21.7	7 621	356.1	55 458	198
Kennebec	464	13 374	1 293.6	552.0	289	1 265	139.0	37.9	8 395	321.4	38 979	216
Knox	163	3 022	256.5	104.8	126	593	66.9	19.1	5 919	306.2	23 533	112
Lincoln	113	1 800	144.6	51.5	81	547	51.7	16.2	4 652	183.0	31 946	89
Oxford	125	2 777	198.2	85.1	90	335	31.1	8.4	4 401	183.4	29 606	154
Penobscot	547	14 740	1 570.2	624.9	273	1 395	142.7	36.9	9 201	361.0	49 775	271
Piscataquis	36	1 508	106.4	51.6	25	92	6.6	1.9	1 149	41.1	2 845	17
Sagadahoc	116	1 375	80.7	36.0	59	266	27.3	6.9	3 213	126.0	25 663	126
Somerset	144	2 809	208.6	96.4	88	286	26.2	6.3	3 188	115.6	7 248	58
Waldo	113	1 622	148.9	65.4	82	264	26.3	6.4	3 853	134.2	10 752	68
Washington	108	2 058	137.6	66.4	51	209	19.7	4.3	3 776	185.8	4 627	38
York	583	9 782	920.8	371.5	371	1 680	155.0	42.5	16 937	797.2	183 244	905
MARYLAND	16 000	359 734	40 821.9	16 319.9	9 978	79 391	10 879.7	2 928.5	475 518	20 715.5	3 166 845	17 044
Allegany	250	6 283	616.1	235.0	139	780	58.0	16.9	3 031	109.0	7 146	41
Anne Arundel	1 272	26 683	2 975.3	1 196.9	1 077	8 665	902.9	291.8	41 227	1 986.8	371 830	2 394
Baltimore	2 619	58 216	6 062.4	2 458.5	1 376	9 983	1 044.2	295.7	65 395	2 916.2	237 170	1 293
Calvert	181	3 475	342.2	149.7	122	773	59.6	20.1	6 447	274.2	53 572	236
Caroline	46	826	44.6	23.3	48	226	23.7	7.6	2 575	109.0	8 102	85
Carroll	459	9 821	950.3	358.3	355	2 195	180.2	57.5	12 230	536.0	66 975	294
Cecil	196	4 679	534.5	259.0	164	867	68.1	20.9	5 613	246.1	18 588	78
Charles	325	4 598	456.6	190.4	213	1 353	113.6	35.7	10 522	363.0	170 653	869
Dorchester	84	1 826	158.1	65.8	68	360	19.7	5.3	2 410	93.5	13 825	81
Frederick	613	11 380	1 206.1	516.3	426	2 837	348.7	93.7	18 267	839.1	339 606	1 906
Garrett	76	1 797	118.6	52.0	73	1 219	106.6	47.9	2 373	106.7	16 819	43
Harford	594	10 550	1 029.1	406.1	422	2 691	227.0	90.5	16 506	712.2	150 409	847
Howard	928	14 235	1 406.4	600.2	509	4 399	552.9	179.8	26 462	1 379.7	378 713	2 154
Kent	74	1 374	115.6	47.4	44	172	19.5	4.8	1 768	83.5	5 935	28
Montgomery	3 584	61 807	7 227.2	3 069.1	1 891	19 109	4 325.3	1 001.8	108 980	5 622.5	424 990	2 170
Prince George's	1 812	31 493	3 126.4	1 249.8	1 126	8 923	996.2	297.7	73 775	2 181.5	396 213	2 060
Queen Anne's	85	1 064	74.1	34.4	103	526	45.1	12.7	4 704	272.1	37 647	145

Table B. States and Counties — Government Employment and Payroll, and Local Government Finances

	Government employment and payroll, 2012		March payroll (percent of total)							Local government finances, 2012				
										General revenue				
												Taxes		
													Per capita[1] (dollars)	
STATE County	Full-time equivalent employees	March payroll (dollars)	Adminis-tration, judicial, and legal	Police and Corrections	Fire Protection	Highways and transpor-tation	Health and Welfare	Natural resources and utilities	Education and libraries	Total (mil dol)	Inter-govern-mental (mil dol)	Total (mil dol)	Total	Property
	171	172	173	174	175	176	177	178	179	180	181	182	183	184
LOUISIANA—Cont'd														
Orleans	7 189	28 500 562	12.7	30.3	9.1	2.5	3.8	25.1	9.9	1 968.9	669.4	766.2	2 075	1 020
Ouachita	7 210	21 316 630	7.2	10.3	3.6	2.2	3.7	5.2	67.2	636.4	302.9	268.8	1 730	618
Plaquemines	1 620	5 259 702	13.4	13.1	0.6	7.9	7.0	6.2	48.6	320.9	176.8	96.4	4 031	2 274
Pointe Coupee	1 063	2 905 856	7.3	13.8	0.0	1.6	21.6	5.3	50.2	93.0	34.1	31.6	1 391	766
Rapides	5 615	17 417 361	10.4	15.6	7.9	3.6	1.4	5.7	52.6	487.4	230.0	195.3	1 475	567
Red River	533	1 454 876	5.8	37.4	0.0	1.9	0.9	1.0	50.4	43.6	18.0	22.1	2 455	992
Richland	1 229	3 799 353	5.9	17.8	0.1	3.2	35.8	2.3	34.3	105.4	49.7	25.9	1 238	508
Sabine	818	2 028 527	9.4	18.3	0.0	4.8	3.6	7.0	55.7	96.4	47.5	40.6	1 668	405
St. Bernard	1 804	5 761 067	8.7	16.2	6.9	6.4	1.4	5.2	54.8	484.3	396.4	68.9	1 655	655
St. Charles	3 451	12 023 950	5.4	15.1	0.0	1.8	10.8	8.5	57.6	387.0	80.9	211.6	4 016	2 217
St. Helena	456	1 219 647	8.6	9.7	0.0	3.8	45.3	1.3	30.5	32.8	13.8	7.5	676	349
St. James	1 306	4 803 097	7.4	11.1	0.0	2.6	16.4	8.2	49.6	231.2	42.5	70.5	3 247	1 994
St. John the Baptist	1 701	5 496 602	10.6	10.0	0.0	8.8	0.1	9.7	60.5	229.3	53.3	82.6	1 845	913
St. Landry	4 416	14 852 877	5.9	10.1	3.0	2.4	26.6	3.1	48.4	409.3	165.3	100.0	1 196	372
St. Martin	1 824	5 579 531	5.5	14.8	0.1	2.7	7.9	2.9	65.6	147.8	80.2	54.1	1 026	489
St. Mary	3 043	9 174 661	6.1	12.3	1.5	2.5	10.9	8.1	57.1	251.5	102.3	102.4	1 907	1 061
St. Tammany	10 707	35 822 862	5.7	10.3	0.3	2.6	33.9	2.1	44.3	1 250.6	404.2	450.6	1 882	995
Tangipahoa	6 393	23 444 209	4.2	6.0	1.2	1.7	46.4	1.8	37.5	621.2	213.8	128.9	1 044	366
Tensas	264	627 291	16.3	4.0	0.0	4.9	1.7	3.9	68.6	27.3	17.2	7.3	1 474	872
Terrebonne	5 509	18 140 503	3.6	8.6	1.2	1.4	31.1	4.6	49.2	603.6	234.4	173.9	1 554	551
Union	834	2 308 579	6.3	18.6	0.2	2.1	11.0	6.9	53.9	62.9	32.1	20.7	923	359
Vermilion	2 406	8 239 940	6.2	8.3	1.8	3.2	23.4	6.7	50.2	227.6	95.5	73.9	1 258	572
Vernon	2 133	5 249 110	6.4	9.9	1.2	3.6	0.1	1.9	76.0	155.1	98.2	46.0	855	294
Washington	1 946	5 729 429	5.2	6.2	1.5	2.7	14.9	1.9	66.9	160.0	81.0	45.0	964	454
Webster	1 523	4 175 873	6.3	15.2	1.4	3.3	0.1	7.0	65.3	133.5	64.2	57.4	1 402	613
West Baton Rouge	1 000	3 133 887	7.9	4.1	2.2	2.9	2.9	12.2	62.7	112.9	36.3	55.4	2 296	1 199
West Carroll	438	1 121 168	6.5	2.8	0.0	4.1	3.9	2.4	79.0	46.7	23.8	13.0	1 133	428
West Feliciana	748	2 572 616	10.2	10.9	0.2	3.9	16.8	3.4	53.6	68.8	21.1	29.6	1 922	1 366
Winn	679	1 633 669	7.5	13.5	1.8	3.1	0.7	8.9	63.3	42.7	25.9	13.6	909	416
MAINE	X	X	X	X	X	X	X	X	X	X	X	X	X	X
Androscoggin	3 959	13 779 680	4.1	8.3	4.8	4.2	2.0	5.1	70.2	355.6	153.6	163.3	1 517	1 507
Aroostook	3 302	10 418 372	5.5	4.9	2.0	3.8	16.3	5.3	61.4	264.2	111.0	83.6	1 180	1 174
Cumberland	10 861	40 790 587	5.2	9.0	5.8	4.8	5.4	6.8	61.0	1 129.5	280.4	610.0	2 149	2 117
Franklin	1 043	3 602 511	5.4	8.2	1.3	4.4	1.5	4.1	73.6	80.5	29.1	43.4	1 418	1 414
Hancock	1 982	6 326 482	6.8	6.5	2.5	3.7	1.0	4.2	73.3	197.6	39.3	137.4	2 518	2 502
Kennebec	4 312	13 281 549	5.2	7.6	3.0	3.6	1.2	5.8	72.6	343.2	144.3	155.9	1 280	1 266
Knox	1 307	4 815 634	8.9	8.8	3.1	4.4	3.3	2.5	67.5	129.9	19.5	90.5	2 283	2 267
Lincoln	1 389	4 505 799	5.7	4.0	0.5	2.0	2.2	3.4	80.2	135.6	34.2	88.2	2 582	2 572
Oxford	2 319	7 212 500	4.7	5.3	2.5	4.9	0.8	2.5	78.4	186.7	69.4	103.9	1 807	1 800
Penobscot	5 352	18 128 721	5.6	7.8	5.2	7.6	1.3	6.1	64.9	466.9	185.2	205.7	1 338	1 324
Piscataquis	1 109	4 071 817	4.7	4.0	0.2	1.9	47.9	1.9	38.2	99.6	35.5	26.2	1 514	1 504
Sagadahoc	1 209	4 568 672	5.0	6.6	2.7	2.7	1.0	3.8	74.9	131.3	38.0	73.7	2 093	2 078
Somerset	2 667	8 560 527	3.4	6.5	1.2	2.5	0.5	1.6	82.6	185.9	90.8	84.4	1 626	1 622
Waldo	1 256	3 892 726	8.1	6.4	0.8	2.8	1.9	2.4	74.8	102.4	36.3	56.7	1 460	1 455
Washington	1 219	3 492 782	6.9	7.3	1.2	2.6	3.5	5.0	70.9	100.0	42.2	47.1	1 450	1 445
York	7 047	25 948 699	5.4	9.0	4.1	3.0	1.2	5.9	70.5	637.1	181.5	390.3	1 961	1 938
MARYLAND	X	X	X	X	X	X	X	X	X	X	X	X	X	X
Allegany	2 826	11 858 505	3.5	6.0	2.0	3.5	0.4	6.3	75.4	272.3	133.1	86.3	1 167	773
Anne Arundel	17 468	83 267 035	4.0	8.6	6.2	4.4	2.8	3.8	67.7	2 076.5	568.1	1 135.3	2 062	1 152
Baltimore	26 532	122 265 325	4.1	12.0	5.2	1.3	3.0	2.6	69.5	2 786.6	910.6	1 567.3	1 917	1 039
Calvert	3 256	15 584 064	4.8	7.8	0.1	1.9	2.8	4.8	74.3	388.6	117.7	224.0	2 500	1 684
Caroline	1 269	4 767 293	5.8	8.2	0.0	2.2	3.3	4.6	71.4	117.5	59.9	45.1	1 379	973
Carroll	5 844	23 979 765	5.5	5.5	0.7	1.6	1.0	2.9	80.6	641.8	205.1	366.2	2 190	1 331
Cecil	3 436	14 149 378	4.6	8.1	1.2	1.6	2.8	2.0	76.9	375.0	153.4	172.0	1 691	1 137
Charles	5 864	27 330 417	4.8	12.4	0.0	0.6	3.1	3.7	73.5	663.0	226.7	318.3	2 114	1 346
Dorchester	1 251	4 831 214	5.1	13.0	0.0	3.8	4.8	2.5	66.5	134.8	62.3	54.8	1 683	1 219
Frederick	10 553	47 827 090	4.3	6.4	4.0	1.9	4.9	3.7	73.1	1 033.9	315.3	529.5	2 210	1 385
Garrett	1 283	4 466 807	6.7	4.8	0.8	10.6	1.8	3.9	70.1	214.5	59.8	111.5	3 734	2 998
Harford	8 483	39 111 192	6.1	9.6	0.3	2.6	1.8	4.3	73.8	952.9	307.2	524.4	2 109	1 291
Howard	12 202	62 646 998	4.3	7.7	1.9	1.0	4.2	4.1	75.2	1 532.5	372.1	962.2	3 214	1 692
Kent	708	2 731 612	8.4	10.5	0.0	4.3	1.1	5.9	64.0	74.9	18.1	46.4	2 298	1 677
Montgomery	38 590	236 750 984	3.3	7.6	4.0	3.0	6.2	10.6	64.3	5 240.0	1 125.4	3 182.9	3 168	1 422
Prince George's	27 062	140 810 958	4.4	15.2	3.4	1.2	4.0	1.6	67.6	3 399.7	1 344.2	1 551.8	1 761	1 007
Queen Anne's	1 906	8 133 110	4.6	6.4	0.2	2.6	7.3	5.6	72.6	207.2	65.4	111.4	2 293	1 412

1. Based on the resident population estimated as of July 1 of the year shown.

Table B. States and Counties — Local Government Finances, Government Employment, and Income Taxes

STATE County	Local government finances, 2012 (cont.)									Government employment, 2015			Individual income tax returns, 2014		
	Direct general expenditure							Debt outstanding							
			Percent of total for:												
	Total (mil dol)	Per capita¹ (dollars)	Education	Health and hospitals	Police protection	Public welfare	Highways	Total (mil dol)	Per capita¹ (dollars)	Federal civilian	Federal military	State and local	Number of returns	Mean adjusted gross income	Mean income tax
	185	186	187	188	189	190	191	192	193	194	195	196	197	198	199
LOUISIANA—Cont'd															
Orleans	1 848.6	5 006	12.2	0.7	7.8	0.1	6.6	2 707.7	7 333	8 938	3 797	26 078	163 260	63 196	10 090
Ouachita	687.9	4 428	53.4	2.3	5.8	0.1	2.6	489.7	3 152	427	668	10 361	66 940	52 295	6 323
Plaquemines	321.2	13 429	37.8	2.1	4.1	0.5	1.0	163.7	6 844	670	452	1 688	10 300	59 457	7 481
Pointe Coupee	90.9	4 001	37.3	22.2	6.6	0.4	2.1	45.9	2 021	62	98	1 128	9 810	52 277	6 310
Rapides	504.4	3 810	49.3	0.1	8.4	0.1	5.3	504.4	3 811	2 278	565	9 707	57 700	52 174	5 992
Red River	47.2	5 251	59.8	0.0	3.7	0.0	1.4	5.0	560	28	37	503	3 350	50 872	6 417
Richland	109.4	5 231	36.1	29.1	3.4	0.1	5.6	51.6	2 464	75	86	974	8 300	46 185	4 983
Sabine	85.0	3 493	69.8	0.2	4.8	0.0	5.6	27.9	1 145	40	105	1 261	8 910	56 361	6 040
St. Bernard	516.0	12 393	31.7	3.5	2.5	0.2	1.3	186.9	4 490	43	199	2 281	17 060	37 802	3 283
St. Charles	382.3	7 256	43.1	9.6	4.8	0.3	5.3	894.4	16 978	153	230	3 299	24 160	63 091	7 818
St. Helena	32.3	2 917	31.4	38.0	4.6	0.0	8.8	5.1	457	10	46	599	5 540	40 022	3 390
St. James	156.3	7 194	43.5	11.8	3.9	0.6	2.5	1 439.8	66 281	36	94	1 432	9 990	53 320	5 757
St. John the Baptist	252.0	5 630	34.8	0.5	4.6	0.5	5.1	1 281.3	28 626	99	190	2 084	19 490	47 814	4 846
St. Landry	414.8	4 958	43.1	29.0	4.8	0.0	3.0	98.9	1 182	166	366	5 236	36 100	48 285	5 361
St. Martin	141.4	2 682	59.3	0.9	8.4	0.2	5.1	123.9	2 349	62	234	1 834	23 520	53 604	6 468
St. Mary	245.0	4 562	42.6	10.2	6.7	0.2	3.8	139.7	2 602	130	355	4 482	23 680	52 068	6 297
St. Tammany	1 244.6	5 198	37.0	28.1	5.6	0.3	4.8	977.9	4 084	477	1 098	13 586	111 590	71 529	10 640
Tangipahoa	692.4	5 610	29.5	47.0	3.7	0.0	2.7	361.5	2 929	359	553	10 122	50 900	48 861	5 413
Tensas	26.2	5 284	36.9	2.0	4.8	0.0	4.9	26.6	5 361	22	21	296	1 850	42 436	4 631
Terrebonne	620.6	5 546	29.9	28.6	4.4	0.3	2.9	301.9	2 698	262	539	5 221	49 310	69 172	10 815
Union	60.2	2 685	49.1	8.9	5.4	0.2	6.0	5.9	265	90	97	727	8 940	47 068	4 480
Vermilion	223.8	3 812	42.2	20.8	4.9	2.1	5.1	37.7	643	141	274	2 930	25 010	56 656	6 980
Vernon	159.1	2 953	69.0	0.3	5.5	0.1	5.4	78.1	1 451	2 128	8 210	2 339	20 820	46 565	4 126
Washington	160.8	3 445	54.9	14.8	4.7	0.0	5.1	63.6	1 363	102	197	2 526	16 610	41 437	3 672
Webster	135.1	3 299	55.0	0.5	6.2	0.1	4.2	123.2	3 010	102	171	2 010	16 660	47 048	4 997
West Baton Rouge	118.0	4 896	36.6	0.9	8.9	0.6	4.0	182.2	7 559	70	110	1 558	11 690	56 148	6 356
West Carroll	47.4	4 114	52.9	20.0	3.8	2.1	3.9	8.1	701	33	48	712	4 300	46 965	4 378
West Feliciana	67.9	4 410	41.6	23.6	6.1	0.1	2.4	71.0	4 612	16	44	2 369	4 520	74 581	10 885
Winn	46.7	3 110	63.7	0.5	5.9	0.0	4.7	11.5	766	56	56	761	5 050	51 537	4 704
MAINE	X	X	X	X	X	X	X	X	X	14 520	6 936	84 726	638 230	53 552	5 955
Androscoggin	348.5	3 239	53.0	0.2	4.0	0.4	5.6	353.5	3 285	259	341	5 104	48 600	46 213	4 466
Aroostook	269.7	3 805	46.4	17.9	2.8	0.3	7.2	101.0	1 426	1 182	216	4 987	30 340	42 208	3 743
Cumberland	1 113.8	3 923	43.9	0.9	4.4	2.5	5.5	1 208.5	4 257	1 921	2 233	17 915	149 290	67 761	8 979
Franklin	104.7	3 419	60.2	0.7	3.7	0.2	8.5	100.7	3 287	110	94	1 958	12 870	44 518	4 154
Hancock	188.4	3 453	54.5	0.6	3.0	0.2	9.3	154.0	2 823	323	267	2 957	26 910	52 082	5 492
Kennebec	348.6	2 861	58.7	0.5	3.4	0.3	6.1	214.9	1 764	2 151	432	14 181	57 920	49 271	5 011
Knox	129.2	3 257	48.4	1.5	4.4	0.2	9.5	77.3	1 950	110	202	2 440	19 970	52 405	5 804
Lincoln	134.0	3 920	66.7	0.7	2.9	0.4	7.8	90.9	2 659	75	133	1 548	17 500	52 614	5 622
Oxford	185.2	3 222	64.2	0.5	2.9	0.4	8.6	87.1	1 516	131	183	3 058	25 410	42 153	3 716
Penobscot	527.2	3 429	48.1	1.1	3.8	0.2	4.2	409.3	2 662	1 181	485	12 865	67 550	49 699	5 308
Piscataquis	98.3	5 686	30.4	44.3	1.9	0.2	4.5	37.9	2 194	46	54	1 343	7 180	40 923	3 654
Sagadahoc	124.2	3 528	56.8	0.2	3.5	0.3	5.7	98.8	2 807	329	130	1 469	18 170	56 345	6 146
Somerset	179.7	3 461	69.3	0.2	2.5	0.2	6.3	81.7	1 574	188	164	2 404	21 800	42 596	3 853
Waldo	97.2	2 504	58.5	1.5	3.5	0.6	10.7	48.3	1 244	83	133	1 455	18 000	44 792	4 118
Washington	103.7	3 194	54.3	2.0	2.7	0.1	8.6	31.8	979	342	159	2 337	13 860	39 365	3 375
York	629.4	3 163	57.4	0.5	5.3	0.3	6.4	355.5	1 787	6 089	1 710	8 705	102 930	55 513	6 098
MARYLAND	X	X	X	X	X	X	X	X	X	173 183	50 284	344 059	2 935 420	72 757	9 879
Allegany	267.9	3 619	60.6	0.8	3.3	0.6	4.9	173.8	2 348	511	207	5 747	29 070	45 622	4 369
Anne Arundel	2 207.3	4 010	54.8	2.4	5.2	1.0	4.4	1 723.1	3 130	42 186	17 790	33 467	280 000	81 445	11 467
Baltimore	3 004.9	3 676	56.3	1.7	6.9	0.4	2.5	3 573.5	4 372	15 406	2 628	40 848	411 330	72 857	10 074
Calvert	401.4	4 479	58.4	0.8	3.8	1.0	3.2	210.1	2 344	117	322	4 126	43 830	77 839	9 516
Caroline	111.8	3 416	59.2	0.3	4.3	0.1	4.2	60.3	1 842	69	102	1 641	15 110	45 954	4 205
Carroll	634.2	3 793	62.1	0.8	3.5	1.2	4.4	467.0	2 793	289	529	7 970	83 150	74 316	9 094
Cecil	362.9	3 569	58.9	0.9	5.1	1.4	5.0	330.6	3 251	1 801	322	4 516	46 300	59 275	6 344
Charles	647.7	4 301	63.4	0.9	8.5	0.6	1.8	442.9	2 941	2 205	1 082	7 419	76 690	70 845	8 333
Dorchester	119.9	3 683	50.4	0.7	6.1	0.1	5.4	66.4	2 040	178	102	2 123	15 150	44 641	4 448
Frederick	1 022.3	4 267	56.6	0.7	5.2	3.4	3.4	1 148.1	4 792	3 656	1 938	11 682	120 030	73 517	9 056
Garrett	204.6	6 852	39.8	0.8	9.6	0.1	12.7	131.5	4 404	66	92	1 615	13 460	47 279	4 617
Harford	983.7	3 957	58.8	0.5	6.5	0.7	5.0	907.9	3 652	11 193	2 488	9 363	123 900	70 483	8 444
Howard	1 583.8	5 289	57.3	0.6	5.3	0.9	2.7	1 520.4	5 078	627	1 147	16 682	150 240	101 668	15 875
Kent	68.7	3 405	43.8	1.6	9.3	1.4	5.8	56.0	2 776	60	58	985	9 290	66 486	8 586
Montgomery	5 475.9	5 450	50.5	1.8	5.2	3.2	3.5	5 936.8	5 909	47 465	7 988	42 359	521 920	100 378	16 752
Prince George's	3 659.3	4 153	49.8	1.7	6.7	0.8	3.4	2 724.6	3 092	26 338	7 577	65 087	480 620	53 601	5 236
Queen Anne's	220.6	4 540	56.7	1.1	3.1	1.6	2.2	152.9	3 146	88	154	2 491	23 860	75 994	9 954

1. Based on the resident population estimated as of July 1 of the year shown.

Table B. States and Counties — **Land Area and Population**

					Population, 2016			Population and population characteristics, 2016										
								Race alone or in combination, not Hispanic or Latino (percent)					Age (percent)					
STATE/ County code	CBSA code¹	County type²	STATE County	Land area,³ (sq mi) 2016	Total persons 2016	Rank	Per square mile	White	Black	American Indian, Alaska Native	Asian and Pacific Islander	Percent Hispanic or Latino⁴	Under 5 years	5 to 17 years	18 to 24 years	25 to 34 years	35 to 44 years	45 to 54 years
				1	2	3	4	5	6	7	8	9	10	11	12	13	14	15
			MARYLAND—Cont'd															
24 037	15680	3	St. Mary's	357.4	112 587	543	315.0	77.6	15.7	0.9	4.0	5.0	6.4	18.1	9.5	14.1	12.1	14.8
24 039	41540	2	Somerset	319.7	25 928	1 567	81.1	53.2	43.1	1.0	1.4	3.6	4.8	12.4	17.6	13.2	10.9	12.2
24 041	20660	6	Talbot	268.5	37 278	1 243	138.8	79.3	13.3	0.5	1.8	6.6	4.5	14.0	6.4	9.9	9.2	12.8
24 043	25180	2	Washington	457.8	150 292	435	328.3	82.1	12.7	0.6	2.5	4.7	5.8	16.4	8.1	12.9	12.4	14.7
24 045	41540	2	Wicomico	374.4	102 577	589	274.0	65.5	27.4	0.7	3.8	5.1	6.0	16.1	15.2	12.0	10.9	12.1
24 047	41540	2	Worcester	468.3	51 444	970	109.9	81.7	14.1	0.6	1.9	3.4	4.5	13.1	6.7	10.2	9.3	13.5
24 510	12580	1	Baltimore city	80.9	614 664	108	7 597.8	29.1	63.6	0.9	3.4	5.1	6.5	14.5	10.1	19.0	12.1	12.3
25 000	...	0	MASSACHUSETTS	7 801.0	6 811 779	X	873.2	74.6	7.9	0.6	7.4	11.5	5.3	14.9	10.3	14.0	12.1	14.1
25 001	12700	3	Barnstable	394.2	214 276	307	543.6	92.1	3.6	1.2	2.0	2.9	3.6	11.8	7.2	8.8	8.6	13.2
25 003	38340	3	Berkshire	926.9	126 903	496	136.9	90.9	4.1	0.6	2.1	4.3	4.2	13.1	9.7	10.4	10.2	14.0
25 005	39300	1	Bristol	553.1	558 324	117	1 009.4	85.6	5.1	0.7	2.9	7.6	5.2	15.6	9.4	12.5	12.2	15.0
25 007	47240	7	Dukes	103.3	17 246	1 961	167.0	89.7	5.4	2.4	1.7	3.7	4.6	13.5	6.7	10.8	11.3	14.4
25 009	14460	1	Essex	492.4	779 018	81	1 582.1	72.9	4.0	0.4	4.1	20.0	5.6	16.0	9.4	12.0	11.8	14.6
25 011	24640	4	Franklin	699.2	70 382	764	100.7	92.8	1.9	1.0	2.4	3.8	4.4	13.3	7.4	11.7	11.4	14.1
25 013	44140	2	Hampden	617.0	468 467	146	759.3	64.9	8.7	0.6	2.9	24.6	5.7	16.3	10.8	13.0	11.4	13.5
25 015	44140	2	Hampshire	527.2	161 816	398	306.9	85.8	3.5	0.6	6.6	5.6	3.5	11.6	23.5	10.4	9.6	12.1
25 017	14460	1	Middlesex	817.7	1 589 774	22	1 944.2	75.0	5.8	0.4	13.0	7.9	5.5	14.8	9.9	15.2	13.0	14.2
25 019	...	7	Nantucket	46.1	11 008	2 354	238.8	75.9	10.4	0.5	1.8	13.0	6.3	14.7	7.0	13.6	15.2	15.4
25 021	14460	1	Norfolk	396.1	697 181	91	1 760.1	77.7	7.3	0.4	12.0	4.4	5.3	15.9	8.8	12.5	12.4	14.9
25 023	14460	1	Plymouth	658.8	513 565	133	779.5	84.4	10.8	0.7	2.1	3.8	5.3	16.6	8.7	10.6	11.5	15.4
25 025	14460	1	Suffolk	58.2	784 230	79	13 474.7	47.5	21.8	0.7	9.7	22.5	5.4	11.7	13.9	23.1	12.8	11.4
25 027	49340	2	Worcester	1 510.6	819 589	73	542.6	79.3	5.3	0.6	5.5	11.0	5.4	16.1	10.0	12.6	12.1	15.0
26 000	...	0	MICHIGAN	56 546.7	9 928 300	X	175.6	77.4	15.0	1.3	3.7	5.0	5.8	16.3	9.8	12.6	11.7	13.6
26 001	...	9	Alcona	674.6	10 352	2 400	15.3	97.0	0.8	1.4	0.6	1.4	2.9	9.7	5.2	6.7	7.4	12.7
26 003	...	7	Alger	915.1	9 219	2 489	10.1	86.4	8.0	6.3	0.8	1.5	3.5	11.6	6.8	11.3	10.9	13.2
26 005	26090	4	Allegan	825.2	115 548	532	140.0	90.1	2.0	1.2	1.1	7.3	6.2	18.2	7.8	11.6	11.8	13.9
26 007	10980	7	Alpena	571.9	28 704	1 467	50.2	97.0	0.8	1.1	0.8	1.4	4.8	14.3	7.4	10.1	10.6	13.4
26 009	...	9	Antrim	475.7	23 144	1 671	48.7	96.3	0.7	1.9	0.5	2.1	4.5	13.9	6.7	8.7	9.1	13.3
26 011	...	8	Arenac	363.2	15 122	2 088	41.6	96.1	0.8	1.8	0.7	2.0	4.5	13.5	6.7	9.7	10.0	13.2
26 013	...	9	Baraga	898.3	8 503	2 550	9.5	76.9	8.4	16.7	0.8	1.6	4.6	14.2	8.2	11.7	11.7	14.1
26 015	24340	2	Barry	553.1	59 702	869	107.9	95.8	0.9	1.0	0.7	2.8	5.6	16.8	7.9	11.0	11.2	14.4
26 017	13020	3	Bay	442.3	104 747	569	236.8	92.0	2.6	1.2	0.9	5.2	5.0	15.6	7.8	12.2	11.3	13.5
26 019	45900	9	Benzie	319.7	17 572	1 942	55.0	94.9	1.0	2.3	0.6	2.5	4.6	13.9	6.7	9.7	9.6	13.6
26 021	35660	3	Berrien	567.8	154 010	423	271.2	77.3	16.0	1.2	2.6	5.3	5.9	16.3	8.4	11.5	11.3	13.3
26 023	17740	6	Branch	506.4	43 427	1 103	85.8	92.2	2.6	1.0	1.2	4.6	6.1	17.5	7.7	11.9	11.8	13.3
26 025	12980	3	Calhoun	706.3	134 386	471	190.3	80.9	12.8	1.4	3.0	5.0	6.2	16.9	8.9	12.1	11.6	13.1
26 027	43780	2	Cass	490.1	51 599	965	105.3	89.1	6.8	2.2	1.3	3.7	5.0	15.8	7.8	10.1	10.9	14.4
26 029	...	7	Charlevoix	416.3	26 174	1 555	62.9	95.5	0.9	2.6	0.9	1.8	4.5	15.2	6.8	10.0	9.7	13.7
26 031	...	7	Cheboygan	715.3	25 401	1 589	35.5	94.8	1.1	4.8	0.7	1.4	4.1	13.0	6.7	9.1	9.8	13.3
26 033	42300	7	Chippewa	1 558.4	37 724	1 231	24.2	74.8	7.3	19.7	1.6	1.7	4.9	13.7	12.0	13.2	12.5	13.1
26 035	...	6	Clare	564.3	30 358	1 426	53.8	96.3	1.1	1.5	0.6	2.0	5.3	14.6	6.9	10.3	10.2	13.3
26 037	29620	2	Clinton	566.4	77 888	711	137.5	91.7	2.5	0.9	2.1	4.5	5.4	17.2	8.5	11.9	11.9	14.6
26 039	...	7	Crawford	556.3	13 744	2 186	24.7	96.1	1.2	1.3	0.9	1.8	4.6	13.9	6.2	9.1	9.2	14.3
26 041	21540	5	Delta	1 171.1	36 202	1 270	30.9	95.3	0.9	4.1	0.8	1.3	5.2	15.1	6.9	9.8	10.7	13.0
26 043	27020	7	Dickinson	761.4	25 535	1 584	33.5	96.7	0.8	1.4	0.9	1.4	4.9	14.9	7.3	10.6	10.3	13.7
26 045	29620	2	Eaton	575.2	109 160	553	189.8	85.4	7.9	1.1	2.7	5.2	5.5	15.9	8.7	12.7	11.5	13.5
26 047	22420	7	Emmet	467.5	33 182	1 352	71.0	93.4	1.2	4.9	0.9	1.6	4.8	15.0	7.7	11.0	10.8	12.8
26 049	22420	2	Genesee	637.0	408 615	171	641.5	74.7	21.7	1.3	1.5	3.4	6.0	17.0	8.8	11.9	11.9	13.8
26 051	...	6	Gladwin	501.8	25 122	1 605	50.1	96.8	0.8	1.1	0.7	1.6	4.9	14.0	6.4	9.0	9.8	13.1
26 053	...	7	Gogebic	1 101.9	15 243	2 079	13.8	91.1	4.8	3.7	0.7	1.3	3.9	11.8	7.7	11.4	10.9	13.5
26 055	45900	5	Grand Traverse	464.3	92 084	636	198.3	94.1	1.7	1.9	1.2	2.8	5.3	15.2	7.7	13.0	11.7	13.4
26 057	10940	6	Gratiot	568.5	41 202	1 148	72.5	87.7	5.9	1.0	0.7	5.8	5.1	15.2	11.0	12.9	12.2	13.7
26 059	25880	6	Hillsdale	598.1	45 774	1 055	76.5	96.2	1.1	1.1	0.7	2.2	5.8	16.2	9.5	10.6	10.9	13.1
26 061	26340	5	Houghton	1 009.1	36 555	1 263	36.2	93.7	1.4	1.3	3.7	1.5	5.1	14.9	21.6	10.3	9.0	10.3
26 063	...	7	Huron	836.1	31 481	1 395	37.7	96.2	0.8	0.8	0.8	2.3	4.6	14.5	6.9	9.5	9.7	13.5
26 065	29620	2	Ingham	556.1	288 051	238	518.0	73.6	13.7	1.3	7.6	7.7	5.4	14.4	19.8	14.0	10.9	11.1
26 067	26960	4	Ionia	571.3	64 232	823	112.4	89.6	5.2	1.0	0.8	4.7	5.8	17.0	9.3	13.6	13.1	14.0
26 069	...	7	Iosco	549.1	25 327	1 594	46.1	95.8	1.2	1.7	1.0	2.0	4.6	12.3	6.0	9.1	8.5	12.7
26 071	...	7	Iron	1 166.1	11 195	2 342	9.6	96.2	0.8	1.8	0.8	1.8	4.4	12.1	5.6	8.4	8.6	12.1
26 073	34380	4	Isabella	572.7	71 282	760	124.5	88.0	3.8	4.5	2.7	3.8	4.7	12.7	28.5	12.7	9.5	10.0
26 075	27100	3	Jackson	701.7	158 460	409	225.8	87.3	9.7	1.0	1.2	3.5	5.7	16.1	8.9	12.3	11.7	14.0
26 077	28020	2	Kalamazoo	562.2	261 654	259	465.4	80.8	13.2	1.2	3.4	4.8	6.1	15.7	15.7	13.4	11.4	11.5
26 079	45900	7	Kalkaska	559.9	17 263	1 960	30.8	96.2	1.0	1.8	0.9	1.9	5.3	16.0	6.8	11.0	11.5	13.7
26 081	24340	2	Kent	847.7	642 173	103	757.5	76.5	11.1	1.0	3.5	10.4	6.9	17.8	9.5	15.6	12.2	12.7

1. CBSA = Core Based Statistical Area. See Appendix A for explanation. See Appendix B for list of metropolitan areas with component counties. 2. County type code from the Economic Research Service of USDA Rural-Urban Continuum Codes. See Appendix A for definition. 3. Dry land or land partially or temporarily covered by water. 4. May be of any race.

STATE County	Population, 2016 (cont.) Age (percent) (cont.) 55 to 64 years	65 to 74 years	75 years and over	Percent female	Population change and components of change, 2000–2016 Total persons 2000	2010	Percent change 2000– 2010	2010– 2016	Components of change, 2010–2016 Births	Deaths	Net migration	Households, 2011–2015 Number	Persons per house- hold	Percent Family house- holds	Female family house- holder[1]	One per- son
	16	17	18	19	20	21	22	23	24	25	26	27	28	29	30	31
MARYLAND—Cont'd																
St. Mary's	12.3	7.5	5.1	50.1	86 211	105 148	22.0	7.1	8 985	4 691	3 010	38 243	2.79	72.5	10.8	22.0
Somerset	13.0	9.4	6.6	46.3	24 747	26 470	7.0	-2.0	1 603	1 655	-497	8 385	2.26	59.6	17.0	32.7
Talbot	15.3	15.3	12.7	52.8	33 812	37 782	11.7	-1.3	2 088	2 738	149	16 231	2.30	67.6	12.7	27.7
Washington	13.1	9.3	7.3	49.1	131 923	147 430	11.8	1.9	10 891	9 337	1 161	56 067	2.50	67.4	12.9	26.5
Wicomico	12.7	8.9	6.2	52.5	84 644	98 733	16.6	3.9	7 696	5 733	1 830	36 989	2.62	66.9	14.6	25.2
Worcester	16.0	15.2	11.4	51.3	46 543	51 451	10.5	0.0	2 798	3 831	1 033	20 773	2.45	64.6	9.9	29.8
Baltimore city	12.6	7.6	5.3	53.0	651 154	621 139	-4.6	-1.0	55 307	39 763	-21 288	242 268	2.47	51.5	22.4	39.2
MASSACHUSETTS	13.5	9.0	6.8	51.5	6 349 097	6 547 813	3.1	4.0	452 120	341 961	163 483	2 549 721	2.53	63.6	12.6	28.7
Barnstable	17.5	16.5	12.8	52.2	222 230	215 868	-2.9	-0.7	9 771	17 790	6 338	94 417	2.24	61.5	9.0	32.9
Berkshire	16.2	12.5	9.7	51.7	134 953	131 272	-2.7	-3.3	6 891	9 057	-1 956	55 240	2.22	59.8	12.0	34.3
Bristol	13.8	9.3	7.0	51.5	534 678	548 260	2.5	1.8	35 559	31 703	6 970	212 029	2.53	65.5	14.2	28.2
Dukes	16.6	14.4	7.8	50.9	14 987	16 535	10.3	4.3	993	851	580	6 007	2.79	66.4	12.3	28.4
Essex	14.1	9.3	7.0	51.8	723 419	743 171	2.7	4.8	52 950	40 178	23 937	287 912	2.59	66.8	13.7	27.4
Franklin	17.6	12.7	7.3	51.2	71 535	71 372	-0.2	-1.4	3 852	4 223	-391	30 202	2.30	59.5	10.1	30.4
Hampden	13.6	8.9	6.9	51.7	456 228	463 625	1.6	1.0	33 308	27 117	-409	176 900	2.57	65.4	18.0	28.5
Hampshire	13.3	9.6	6.4	53.4	152 251	158 080	3.8	2.4	6 833	7 610	4 406	58 631	2.36	58.4	9.9	30.5
Middlesex	12.8	8.2	6.4	51.1	1 465 396	1 503 057	2.6	5.8	110 042	69 160	49 224	585 642	2.56	64.3	9.7	27.3
Nantucket	13.2	9.0	5.7	49.4	9 520	10 172	6.8	8.2	879	373	325	3 923	2.62	58.5	9.8	32.4
Norfolk	13.8	8.9	7.4	52.0	650 308	670 985	3.2	3.9	45 297	35 243	17 515	259 545	2.58	65.8	10.0	27.7
Plymouth	14.6	10.3	7.0	51.4	472 822	494 949	4.7	3.8	32 141	26 946	13 120	181 425	2.71	71.2	12.9	23.8
Suffolk	10.4	6.5	4.9	51.6	689 807	722 079	4.7	8.6	59 313	29 388	33 648	296 672	2.39	49.6	16.9	36.3
Worcester	13.9	8.6	6.3	50.6	750 963	798 388	6.3	2.7	54 291	42 322	10 176	301 176	2.60	66.7	12.5	26.7
MICHIGAN	14.0	9.5	6.8	50.8	9 938 444	9 884 129	-0.5	0.4	710 867	573 859	-87 519	3 841 148	2.52	65.0	12.7	29.1
Alcona	19.9	20.2	15.3	49.5	11 719	10 942	-6.6	-5.4	378	1 133	201	5 001	2.08	64.1	5.2	31.7
Alger	17.6	14.5	10.5	45.1	9 862	9 601	-2.6	-4.0	363	705	-55	3 470	2.43	63.1	6.1	32.9
Allegan	14.4	9.7	6.3	50.1	105 665	111 408	5.4	3.7	8 520	5 747	1 186	41 893	2.67	73.4	9.6	21.6
Alpena	17.0	12.2	10.2	50.8	31 314	29 598	-5.5	-3.0	1 672	2 226	-285	12 722	2.24	64.5	11.5	30.3
Antrim	17.6	15.3	11.0	50.3	23 110	23 580	2.0	-1.8	1 237	1 664	19	9 689	2.38	70.0	7.6	25.5
Arenac	18.5	13.8	10.0	49.4	17 269	15 899	-7.9	-4.9	782	1 305	-216	6 447	2.36	66.5	9.2	29.1
Baraga	15.2	12.0	8.3	44.7	8 746	8 860	1.3	-4.0	491	639	-197	2 974	2.14	60.9	10.0	35.5
Barry	15.4	10.7	7.1	49.7	56 755	59 175	4.3	0.9	3 943	3 238	-182	22 836	2.56	71.1	7.0	23.7
Bay	15.4	11.0	8.4	50.8	110 157	107 771	-2.2	-2.8	6 654	7 308	-2 288	43 565	2.42	64.0	11.5	30.1
Benzie	16.8	14.8	10.4	50.6	15 998	17 525	9.5	0.3	946	1 316	395	7 225	2.37	65.4	8.8	29.1
Berrien	14.7	10.6	8.0	50.9	162 453	156 817	-3.5	-1.8	11 516	10 473	-3 714	61 167	2.46	65.8	13.3	29.7
Branch	14.4	10.0	7.2	48.5	45 787	45 248	-1.2	-4.0	3 295	2 658	-2 416	16 022	2.58	68.5	10.7	25.9
Calhoun	14.0	9.6	7.5	51.1	137 985	136 148	-1.3	-1.3	10 355	9 055	-2 917	52 850	2.48	63.6	14.3	30.9
Cass	15.6	12.7	7.6	50.0	51 104	52 286	2.3	-1.3	3 042	3 189	-561	20 101	2.56	69.7	10.1	25.7
Charlevoix	17.6	13.5	9.0	50.6	26 090	25 949	-0.5	0.9	1 481	1 716	445	10 794	2.39	66.1	8.1	29.0
Cheboygan	18.0	15.3	10.6	50.0	26 448	26 150	-1.1	-2.9	1 254	2 004	54	11 223	2.26	67.4	9.1	28.0
Chippewa	13.5	9.9	7.1	44.8	38 543	38 673	0.3	-2.5	2 249	2 267	-979	13 997	2.46	62.9	9.2	30.8
Clare	16.8	13.7	8.9	50.1	31 252	30 926	-1.0	-1.8	2 047	2 423	-112	13 255	2.28	64.7	11.5	30.4
Clinton	14.3	9.5	6.7	50.6	64 753	75 382	16.4	3.3	4 894	3 659	1 130	28 857	2.64	69.3	8.8	23.7
Crawford	17.7	14.9	10.1	49.5	14 273	14 074	-1.4	-2.3	747	1 044	39	5 954	2.30	65.6	8.1	28.8
Delta	16.8	12.5	10.0	50.3	38 520	37 069	-3.8	-2.3	2 328	2 663	-492	15 685	2.30	63.3	9.1	31.2
Dickinson	16.9	11.3	10.0	50.1	27 472	26 168	-4.7	-2.4	1 528	1 886	-223	11 059	2.31	65.1	10.3	30.7
Eaton	14.8	10.5	6.9	51.1	103 655	107 759	4.0	1.3	7 317	6 038	227	43 632	2.45	65.1	10.9	29.5
Emmet	16.5	12.6	8.8	50.5	31 437	32 694	4.0	1.5	1 918	2 108	620	13 948	2.33	66.1	7.7	27.2
Genesee	14.2	9.5	6.9	51.8	436 141	425 790	-2.4	-4.0	31 085	27 239	-20 784	165 268	2.48	64.5	16.5	29.8
Gladwin	16.9	15.4	10.5	49.7	26 023	25 692	-1.3	-2.2	1 562	2 106	58	10 960	2.30	66.8	8.5	29.0
Gogebic	16.7	13.4	10.6	45.8	17 370	16 427	-5.4	-7.2	762	1 349	-530	6 741	2.10	57.3	9.1	36.8
Grand Traverse	15.4	10.9	7.4	50.6	77 654	86 986	12.0	5.9	5 806	5 029	4 199	35 082	2.46	64.6	8.9	28.7
Gratiot	12.8	9.2	7.9	46.9	42 285	42 476	0.5	-3.0	2 586	2 691	-1 249	14 716	2.45	67.4	10.3	27.4
Hillsdale	15.3	10.9	7.6	50.1	46 527	46 688	0.3	-2.0	3 370	2 893	-1 358	17 810	2.50	67.8	8.8	27.6
Houghton	11.8	9.5	7.3	45.9	36 016	36 628	1.7	-0.2	2 365	2 184	-293	13 765	2.51	58.4	7.5	30.7
Huron	17.0	13.3	11.0	50.6	36 079	33 118	-8.2	-4.9	1 845	2 762	-647	13 805	2.30	65.5	8.5	30.9
Ingham	11.6	7.7	4.9	51.3	279 320	280 891	0.6	2.5	20 629	12 795	-427	110 418	2.40	55.2	12.0	33.3
Ionia	13.3	8.5	5.3	46.2	61 518	63 905	3.9	0.5	4 618	3 150	-1 122	22 092	2.72	70.4	10.0	24.9
Iosco	18.2	16.4	12.1	50.1	27 339	25 887	-5.3	-2.2	1 435	2 451	516	11 343	2.20	61.8	9.2	32.9
Iron	19.6	15.8	13.6	50.4	13 138	11 817	-10.1	-5.3	559	1 163	-20	5 392	2.07	56.2	7.9	38.6
Isabella	10.6	6.7	4.9	51.4	63 351	70 311	11.0	1.4	4 174	2 866	-312	24 661	2.61	55.9	11.1	26.6
Jackson	14.4	9.8	7.0	48.9	158 422	160 248	1.2	-1.1	11 280	10 018	-2 907	60 591	2.48	65.9	12.3	28.8
Kalamazoo	12.0	8.2	6.1	51.0	238 603	250 327	4.9	4.5	19 620	12 822	4 532	100 341	2.47	60.2	11.7	29.9
Kalkaska	16.1	12.3	7.1	48.8	16 571	17 153	3.5	0.6	1 082	1 115	164	7 185	2.38	63.8	7.3	30.0
Kent	12.3	7.4	5.5	50.7	574 335	602 622	4.9	6.6	55 398	27 964	12 457	232 961	2.63	66.3	12.6	26.6

1. No spouse present.

Table B. States and Counties — Population, Vital Statistics, Health, and Crime

STATE County	Persons in group quarters, 2016	Daytime population, 2011–2015 Number	Employment/residence ratio	Births, 2016 Total	Births, 2016 Rate[1]	Deaths, 2016 Number	Deaths, 2016 Rate[1]	Persons under 65 with no health insurance, 2015 Number	Percent	Medicare, 2015 Total Beneficiaries	Enrolled in Original Medicare	Enrolled in Medicare Advantage	Serious crimes known to police,[2] 2014 Total Number	Rate[3]
	32	33	34	35	36	37	38	39	40	41	42	43	44	45
MARYLAND—Cont'd														
St. Mary's	2 809	105 967	0.93	1 479	13.1	822	7.3	4 797	5.0	14 028	13 558	470	2 474	2 232
Somerset	5 339	24 903	0.86	244	9.4	269	10.4	1 585	9.4	4 713	4 646	67	534	2 033
Talbot	372	41 807	1.23	324	8.7	469	12.6	2 244	8.2	10 053	9 731	322	901	2 370
Washington	8 235	151 957	1.04	1 741	11.6	1 538	10.2	8 202	6.9	27 479	24 688	2 791	3 715	2 471
Wicomico	4 860	101 983	1.02	1 237	12.1	1 007	9.8	6 824	8.1	17 394	17 084	310	3 884	3 823
Worcester	722	53 982	1.11	465	9.0	672	13.1	2 919	7.7	13 358	12 919	439	2 422	4 680
Baltimore city	26 091	728 861	1.40	8 654	14.1	6 871	11.2	43 064	8.2	97 748	83 218	14 530	38 656	6 200
MASSACHUSETTS	252 586	6 774 896	1.02	72 024	10.6	57 563	8.5	180 139	3.2	1 144 789	868 326	276 463	151 666	2 248
Barnstable	4 148	211 551	0.97	1 506	7.0	2 908	13.6	5 212	3.5	67 818	59 246	8 572	5 243	2 434
Berkshire	5 898	131 192	1.03	1 046	8.2	1 467	11.6	3 263	3.4	31 447	29 686	1 761	2 911	2 446
Bristol	16 363	505 979	0.82	5 625	10.1	5 198	9.3	16 732	3.7	109 099	90 117	18 982	14 496	2 610
Dukes	105	17 140	1.01	152	8.8	138	8.0	558	4.1	3 958	3 855	103	NA	NA
Essex	19 783	707 487	0.85	8 518	10.9	6 834	8.8	21 939	3.4	137 056	108 156	28 900	15 926	2 088
Franklin	1 587	64 112	0.81	589	8.4	684	9.7	1 719	3.0	14 998	11 695	3 303	1 386	2 312
Hampden	15 830	462 597	0.97	5 204	11.1	4 426	9.4	15 505	4.0	92 069	61 005	31 064	15 982	3 471
Hampshire	22 591	155 394	0.93	1 056	6.5	1 239	7.7	3 109	2.7	26 478	20 545	5 933	2 819	1 815
Middlesex	56 732	1 625 788	1.09	17 592	11.1	11 727	7.4	38 311	2.9	231 629	171 313	60 316	24 908	1 587
Nantucket	59	10 824	1.04	143	13.0	53	4.8	391	4.2	1 574	1 538	36	309	2 945
Norfolk	17 614	667 152	0.94	7 278	10.4	5 946	8.5	12 222	2.1	108 560	85 408	23 152	9 607	1 462
Plymouth	12 169	448 552	0.78	5 216	10.2	4 603	9.0	11 144	2.7	92 325	77 081	15 244	9 054	1 965
Suffolk	50 631	1 007 615	1.63	9 470	12.1	5 152	6.6	30 048	4.6	92 847	68 086	24 761	27 101	3 540
Worcester	29 076	759 513	0.87	8 629	10.5	7 188	8.8	19 986	2.9	134 931	80 595	54 336	18 697	2 322
MICHIGAN	230 466	9 862 954	0.99	113 437	11.4	94 353	9.5	590 197	7.2	1 880 854	1 172 531	708 323	244 895	2 471
Alcona	127	9 383	0.63	53	5.1	167	16.1	619	9.3	3 999	2 907	1 092	148	1 408
Alger	1 054	9 167	0.90	59	6.4	123	13.3	586	9.5	2 456	1 702	754	90	945
Allegan	955	103 625	0.82	1 394	12.1	926	8.0	6 431	6.7	17 946	9 050	8 896	1 601	1 418
Alpena	512	29 921	1.07	274	9.5	340	11.8	1 762	7.9	9 102	7 292	1 810	547	1 886
Antrim	226	20 409	0.69	201	8.7	267	11.5	1 510	8.9	6 157	4 183	1 974	432	1 850
Arenac	207	14 777	0.88	130	8.6	206	13.6	1 009	8.7	4 933	3 568	1 365	164	1 128
Baraga	1 010	9 181	1.21	76	8.9	103	12.1	586	9.8	2 068	1 468	600	NA	NA
Barry	613	46 716	0.52	638	10.7	558	9.3	3 006	6.2	9 897	5 158	4 739	674	1 190
Bay	1 438	97 377	0.79	1 011	9.7	1 168	11.2	5 598	6.6	24 340	17 056	7 284	2 436	2 283
Benzie	252	14 888	0.66	155	8.8	212	12.1	1 212	9.3	4 537	2 971	1 566	200	1 148
Berrien	3 535	155 401	1.00	1 786	11.6	1 662	10.8	10 879	8.8	36 752	23 446	13 306	3 541	2 345
Branch	1 974	41 256	0.86	516	11.9	408	9.4	2 687	7.8	8 384	5 837	2 547	715	1 651
Calhoun	4 129	141 074	1.11	1 638	12.2	1 405	10.5	8 045	7.4	28 844	19 560	9 284	4 563	3 383
Cass	611	42 280	0.56	511	9.9	542	10.5	3 327	8.1	7 430	4 815	2 615	706	1 532
Charlevoix	279	25 274	0.93	231	8.8	284	10.9	1 591	7.8	6 738	4 627	2 111	394	1 503
Cheboygan	388	23 308	0.76	209	8.2	358	14.1	1 824	9.8	6 740	4 905	1 835	397	1 547
Chippewa	4 802	38 513	1.00	362	9.6	360	9.5	2 738	10.1	7 756	5 359	2 397	567	1 462
Clare	391	28 508	0.79	336	11.1	388	12.8	2 224	9.5	8 343	6 121	2 222	695	2 279
Clinton	655	61 632	0.57	749	9.6	580	7.4	3 378	5.2	10 243	6 726	3 517	561	727
Crawford	197	13 292	0.88	125	9.1	166	12.1	792	7.7	3 143	2 315	828	266	1 916
Delta	623	36 166	0.96	380	10.5	426	11.8	2 181	7.8	10 363	6 755	3 608	802	2 174
Dickinson	453	27 899	1.17	231	9.0	306	12.0	1 301	6.4	6 570	4 383	2 187	NA	NA
Eaton	1 633	104 408	0.92	1 157	10.6	983	9.0	4 924	5.5	15 872	10 644	5 228	1 932	1 823
Emmet	505	36 208	1.21	310	9.3	316	9.5	2 128	8.1	8 829	6 291	2 538	429	1 289
Genesee	5 821	402 182	0.91	4 831	11.8	4 510	11.0	23 029	6.8	88 034	54 781	33 253	13 935	3 374
Gladwin	289	22 401	0.64	262	10.4	374	14.9	1 666	9.0	7 979	5 631	2 348	380	1 493
Gogebic	1 469	15 745	0.99	118	7.7	213	14.0	925	8.8	4 499	2 890	1 609	204	1 290
Grand Traverse	2 419	98 295	1.19	944	10.3	833	9.0	4 765	6.5	22 076	14 347	7 729	1 190	1 310
Gratiot	5 253	41 419	0.97	401	9.7	437	10.6	1 755	5.9	8 339	6 140	2 199	657	1 568
Hillsdale	1 654	43 238	0.84	518	11.3	463	10.1	2 861	7.9	9 214	6 650	2 564	571	1 241
Houghton	3 114	36 283	0.97	364	10.0	346	9.5	2 290	8.3	6 568	4 057	2 511	462	1 278
Huron	524	32 883	1.04	289	9.2	465	14.8	1 984	8.2	8 529	6 641	1 888	373	1 251
Ingham	18 479	317 231	1.26	3 381	11.7	2 184	7.6	17 982	7.7	52 403	37 617	14 786	8 162	2 886
Ionia	5 371	55 661	0.68	725	11.3	522	8.1	3 209	6.4	10 159	6 589	3 570	1 007	1 671
Iosco	400	26 208	1.09	240	9.5	392	15.5	1 424	7.9	8 671	6 362	2 309	513	2 023
Iron	355	10 949	0.87	89	7.9	190	17.0	628	7.9	3 439	2 370	1 069	216	1 886
Isabella	6 572	73 756	1.10	687	9.6	457	6.4	5 420	9.6	10 377	7 412	2 965	1 340	1 900
Jackson	8 834	155 639	0.94	1 808	11.4	1 624	10.2	7 775	6.2	32 356	23 792	8 564	4 054	2 559
Kalamazoo	8 282	263 299	1.05	3 175	12.1	2 175	8.3	14 634	6.7	43 563	23 515	20 048	8 494	3 286
Kalkaska	138	15 305	0.71	173	10.0	171	9.9	1 242	9.0	3 252	2 395	857	387	2 246
Kent	11 599	672 063	1.17	8 986	14.0	4 695	7.3	40 882	7.5	97 546	45 944	51 602	14 921	2 379

1. Per 1,000 estimated resident population.   2. Data for serious crimes have not been adjusted for underreporting; this may affect comparability between geographic areas and over time.
3. Per 100,000 population estimated by the FBI.

Table B. States and Counties — Crime, Education, Money Income, and Poverty

STATE County	Serious crimes known to police, 2014 (cont.)[1] Rate[2] Violent	Property	School enrollment and attainment, 2011–2015 Enrollment[3] Total	Percent private	Attainment[4] (percent) High school graduate or less	Bachelor's degree or more	Local government expenditures,[5] 2013–2014 Total current spending (mil dol)	Current spending per student (dollars)	Money income, 2011–2015 Per capita income[6] (dollars)	Median income (dollars)	Households Percent with income of less than $50,000	with income of $200,000 or more	Income and poverty, 2015 Median household income (dollars)	Percent below poverty level All persons	Children under 18 years	Children 5 to 17 years in families
	46	47	48	49	50	51	52	53	54	55	56	57	58	59	60	61
MARYLAND—Cont'd																
St. Mary's	237	1 995	30 309	15.7	40.0	30.6	222.3	12 463	36 668	86 987	27.3	8.4	83 148	8.7	12.7	12.0
Somerset	266	1 766	7 653	8.0	62.6	14.8	42.3	14 359	16 631	35 154	61.4	1.0	38 692	25.8	35.9	34.4
Talbot	266	2 104	7 587	20.3	39.4	33.9	54.8	12 085	38 317	58 228	43.2	7.8	62 018	10.4	15.9	14.8
Washington	319	2 152	34 987	12.6	51.5	19.9	287.3	12 771	27 066	56 228	44.8	3.2	55 270	12.0	17.8	15.9
Wicomico	446	3 377	30 576	10.1	44.0	28.5	191.3	13 255	26 241	52 278	47.5	3.2	52 153	14.7	21.7	20.1
Worcester	367	4 313	9 875	15.3	42.4	30.2	109.4	16 449	32 419	56 773	44.3	4.9	53 366	11.3	20.7	19.1
Baltimore city	1 355	4 845	161 323	24.2	47.2	28.7	1 318.7	15 490	25 707	42 241	56.3	3.4	43 192	22.7	33.9	33.7
MASSACHUSETTS	391	1 857	1 755 492	26.7	35.6	40.5	14 467.9	15 138	36 895	68 563	37.9	8.9	70 659	11.5	14.9	13.9
Barnstable	431	2 003	40 135	16.4	29.8	40.1	441.9	17 258	37 678	63 251	39.9	5.5	65 735	7.6	11.5	10.8
Berkshire	309	2 136	29 616	24.4	41.0	31.6	278.8	16 553	30 469	49 956	50.0	4.0	50 646	14.3	19.6	18.1
Bristol	543	2 068	136 975	16.9	47.4	25.9	1 080.6	13 624	29 607	56 842	44.6	4.4	59 839	12.6	17.3	15.1
Dukes	NA	NA	3 305	22.0	29.9	40.3	60.0	26 385	38 560	64 222	41.0	6.7	64 456	8.5	13.4	12.4
Essex	386	1 702	193 259	20.7	36.9	37.5	1 667.1	14 483	36 212	69 068	38.0	8.9	68 237	11.5	16.6	15.3
Franklin	424	1 888	15 499	14.0	34.9	35.2	156.9	16 230	30 584	55 221	45.3	3.0	57 325	11.8	16.9	15.4
Hampden	595	2 875	122 924	17.9	45.9	24.5	1 088.5	14 886	26 560	50 461	49.6	3.6	51 415	17.1	27.4	25.9
Hampshire	261	1 554	57 706	19.5	30.3	44.2	283.1	15 041	30 244	61 368	41.7	5.1	60 853	15.3	11.6	10.9
Middlesex	190	1 397	413 644	31.8	28.7	52.0	3 383.3	15 613	44 152	85 118	30.1	13.4	90 025	7.6	8.2	7.4
Nantucket	67	2 878	2 375	22.2	30.6	43.7	30.7	20 743	45 000	84 057	26.6	9.0	86 014	7.3	8.5	8.2
Norfolk	192	1 270	180 625	31.6	27.1	50.6	1 519.0	14 821	45 829	88 262	29.1	14.4	93 187	7.1	6.4	6.0
Plymouth	366	1 599	129 451	16.8	36.7	34.4	1 149.2	13 380	36 163	75 459	33.3	8.6	74 736	9.7	12.4	10.8
Suffolk	770	2 770	217 600	46.2	39.3	41.7	1 560.5	19 688	34 420	55 044	46.2	7.5	56 530	19.8	29.3	30.5
Worcester	431	1 891	212 378	20.6	39.1	34.4	1 768.3	13 690	32 284	65 313	39.2	6.6	65 621	12.1	15.2	14.5
MICHIGAN	427	2 044	2 604 680	13.1	40.3	26.9	16 471.5	10 912	26 607	49 576	50.4	3.5	51 063	15.7	22.2	20.8
Alcona	95	1 313	1 475	7.1	51.3	14.3	7.1	9 531	23 933	38 033	63.6	1.5	37 618	15.8	30.8	28.0
Alger	252	693	1 595	16.0	54.4	18.4	11.3	10 379	21 259	39 300	60.6	0.8	43 341	14.6	21.0	19.0
Allegan	213	1 205	27 597	13.4	48.5	21.5	176.2	9 990	25 161	54 264	54.0	2.2	55 611	11.2	15.1	13.7
Alpena	265	1 621	6 274	9.2	43.7	16.5	44.8	11 016	22 082	38 829	63.4	1.1	40 665	16.2	24.6	23.1
Antrim	146	1 704	4 594	6.6	43.6	25.3	33.4	9 599	27 155	46 845	53.3	3.6	49 118	14.2	24.1	21.3
Arenac	241	887	2 919	5.1	57.7	11.7	21.0	9 195	21 197	38 307	63.0	1.5	37 120	20.1	30.5	27.6
Baraga	NA	NA	1 353	14.4	61.7	13.1	11.9	10 369	17 461	39 803	61.9	1.7	42 389	17.3	24.3	22.1
Barry	136	1 054	13 984	10.9	45.3	19.2	82.4	8 959	25 795	55 064	45.4	1.7	57 665	9.3	14.0	12.9
Bay	284	1 999	25 151	12.4	46.3	18.3	162.7	11 191	24 445	45 583	54.1	1.8	46 256	14.5	20.8	19.8
Benzie	115	1 033	3 288	9.9	42.8	24.2	19.9	9 290	25 023	47 388	52.3	1.6	48 127	10.5	19.1	16.7
Berrien	390	1 955	39 083	21.7	41.9	26.1	276.6	10 920	25 241	44 993	54.0	2.8	46 588	17.1	26.2	25.9
Branch	282	1 369	9 844	11.3	52.8	13.5	74.6	11 344	21 263	44 373	55.5	1.7	47 146	14.9	23.7	21.7
Calhoun	548	2 835	33 691	12.1	45.6	20.1	246.4	12 173	23 150	42 520	56.8	1.9	43 864	16.1	24.0	23.3
Cass	215	1 317	12 120	9.5	48.0	16.9	68.3	10 167	24 314	46 570	53.7	2.0	49 889	14.8	22.5	20.0
Charlevoix	137	1 366	5 598	9.7	39.6	27.9	58.4	15 310	28 188	46 554	53.2	3.7	48 267	11.6	18.3	16.6
Cheboygan	121	1 426	4 738	9.7	50.3	18.1	43.6	11 926	23 631	40 219	61.4	1.7	41 036	17.1	28.4	26.3
Chippewa	273	1 188	8 870	9.4	48.8	19.1	62.2	12 504	20 396	41 993	58.2	1.1	42 473	19.7	27.4	23.8
Clare	321	1 958	6 306	8.8	55.1	11.6	54.1	12 254	19 181	33 015	69.4	0.6	33 250	24.7	38.8	38.0
Clinton	80	647	21 791	11.4	34.7	29.7	103.8	10 431	29 766	60 909	40.9	4.1	65 051	10.0	10.8	9.5
Crawford	259	1 657	2 613	8.5	47.9	17.2	15.3	9 329	22 595	41 743	57.5	0.3	40 907	17.2	31.2	29.7
Delta	160	2 014	7 723	9.6	43.2	18.9	51.7	10 835	23 061	42 031	57.6	0.9	43 020	14.8	20.8	19.5
Dickinson	NA	NA	5 293	9.2	46.7	22.4	43.3	11 624	24 880	43 779	56.6	1.9	47 616	12.3	17.8	16.7
Eaton	205	1 619	26 662	14.1	36.1	24.7	177.3	10 136	27 577	54 993	44.7	2.4	56 760	10.9	15.7	14.6
Emmet	201	1 087	7 515	11.9	32.5	33.2	50.1	9 963	31 109	51 018	48.7	4.4	49 774	11.0	15.7	14.1
Genesee	654	2 720	108 225	10.2	43.5	19.3	748.7	10 893	22 957	42 327	57.1	1.9	44 181	20.5	30.2	26.7
Gladwin	212	1 280	4 759	12.2	55.2	12.3	26.7	8 813	21 234	38 021	63.4	1.4	40 746	19.8	32.2	31.8
Gogebic	89	1 202	2 687	7.9	46.0	18.3	18.0	10 435	21 008	35 686	65.4	1.1	38 416	18.6	27.5	25.7
Grand Traverse	216	1 094	20 366	13.1	33.1	31.5	165.7	13 049	28 050	52 950	46.6	3.4	54 874	8.5	12.3	11.6
Gratiot	217	1 351	9 966	21.2	52.2	14.1	76.7	11 371	19 618	41 912	58.3	1.6	42 800	16.5	20.6	19.4
Hillsdale	183	1 058	11 283	26.0	53.4	15.5	66.9	10 700	21 291	41 961	58.3	1.3	46 786	16.6	24.6	21.9
Houghton	116	1 162	12 808	6.2	41.8	31.1	55.1	10 331	20 081	37 776	61.4	1.5	41 775	17.4	18.4	16.4
Huron	201	1 050	6 431	11.1	56.5	14.1	58.7	11 639	23 382	42 161	58.4	1.6	45 917	11.7	18.9	17.2
Ingham	580	2 306	101 584	8.2	29.8	37.2	480.9	11 587	25 436	45 679	53.8	3.3	47 470	21.0	24.1	22.5
Ionia	241	1 430	15 769	13.3	49.9	14.9	94.8	11 376	20 921	49 124	50.8	1.2	51 013	14.2	17.7	16.2
Iosco	213	1 810	4 396	10.5	51.9	16.1	40.3	10 278	23 486	37 317	65.8	1.3	39 874	16.1	32.3	32.7
Iron	148	1 737	1 959	7.7	53.8	19.3	12.7	9 666	21 725	33 663	67.1	1.0	36 570	14.6	25.5	23.7
Isabella	191	1 709	30 602	5.4	40.7	27.3	60.4	9 503	20 518	39 377	59.3	2.0	41 957	26.1	20.0	18.6
Jackson	414	2 145	39 302	15.7	45.0	20.0	267.1	11 433	23 377	46 326	53.0	2.1	50 683	16.2	25.2	24.1
Kalamazoo	500	2 786	82 087	10.2	29.9	35.1	376.3	10 943	26 416	47 476	52.0	3.5	52 252	16.0	19.0	18.5
Kalkaska	325	1 921	3 554	10.3	55.8	12.7	21.4	9 624	21 320	40 534	61.9	1.2	42 829	16.5	27.5	25.7
Kent	365	2 015	171 403	20.2	35.9	33.3	1 171.1	10 741	27 032	53 063	47.1	3.8	54 550	14.5	19.1	18.3

1. Data for serious crimes have not been adjusted for underreporting; this may affect comparability between geographic areas and over time.   2. Per 100,000 population estimated by the FBI.
3. All persons 3 years old and over enrolled in nursery school through college.   4. Persons 25 years old and over.   5. Elementary and secondary education expenditures.
6. Based on population estimated by the American Community Survey, 2011–2015.

Table B. States and Counties — Personal Income

	Personal income, 2015										Earnings, 2015		
STATE County	Total (mil dol)	Percent change, 2014–2015	Per capita[1] Dollars	Per capita[1] Rank	Wages and salaries (mil dol)	Supplements to wages and salaries; employer contributions (mil dol) Pension and insurance	Government social insurance	Proprietors' income (mil dol)	Dividends, interest, and rent (mil dol)	Personal transfer receipts (mil dol)	Total (mil dol)	Contributions for government social insurance (mil dol) From employee and self-employed	From employer
	62	63	64	65	66	67	68	69	70	71	72	73	74
MARYLAND—Cont'd													
St. Mary's	5 792	4.6	51 990	373	3 154	659	253	208	1 065	757	4 274	237	253
Somerset	765	2.4	29 684	2 792	324	86	24	68	132	256	502	28	24
Talbot	2 431	2.4	64 804	101	844	136	65	187	771	426	1 232	79	65
Washington	6 320	3.3	42 248	1 195	3 038	531	233	428	1 026	1 348	4 231	258	233
Wicomico	3 974	4.1	38 816	1 574	2 024	394	152	305	638	963	2 875	169	152
Worcester	2 724	3.9	52 847	406	885	159	75	297	743	581	1 416	89	75
Baltimore city	27 970	3.7	44 979	909	22 367	3 747	1 631	2 737	4 644	7 726	30 482	1 748	1 631
MASSACHUSETTS	425 353	5.6	62 697	X	235 282	35 746	15 459	33 933	81 907	63 029	320 420	17 109	15 459
Barnstable	13 874	4.9	64 730	133	4 496	850	327	1 366	4 003	2 634	7 039	406	327
Berkshire	6 482	4.9	50 712	501	2 848	539	205	438	1 363	1 581	4 030	228	205
Bristol	26 888	6.1	48 294	692	11 109	2 099	771	1 642	3 498	5 932	15 620	859	771
Dukes	1 362	6.5	78 745	68	441	78	33	248	495	155	799	41	33
Essex	46 811	5.9	60 320	192	18 453	3 162	1 290	3 650	8 388	7 284	26 554	1 432	1 290
Franklin	3 419	4.7	48 428	671	1 099	251	78	243	624	848	1 671	93	78
Hampden	21 754	5.4	46 216	804	10 226	2 027	714	1 115	2 846	6 301	14 082	758	714
Hampshire	7 541	4.9	46 756	901	2 992	773	189	676	1 470	1 147	4 630	216	189
Middlesex	116 135	5.3	73 265	62	72 691	9 320	4 716	8 151	25 530	11 347	94 878	5 119	4 716
Nantucket	1 173	7.9	107 341	13	401	55	31	267	467	67	754	38	31
Norfolk	56 177	5.4	80 711	43	22 332	3 285	1 552	4 471	12 617	5 150	31 640	1 688	1 552
Plymouth	30 252	6.2	59 273	187	9 776	1 840	680	2 182	4 914	4 785	14 478	772	680
Suffolk	51 414	6.3	66 074	104	60 138	8 064	3 610	6 822	9 839	8 542	78 633	4 108	3 610
Worcester	42 070	5.7	51 370	471	18 281	3 403	1 264	2 663	5 853	7 256	25 611	1 353	1 264
MICHIGAN	424 807	4.6	42 833	X	214 703	32 757	16 204	28 370	73 797	91 438	292 034	18 402	16 204
Alcona	364	3.5	35 207	2 141	63	13	5	14	83	152	95	11	5
Alger	274	3.9	29 150	2 928	98	21	8	13	55	96	139	11	8
Allegan	4 539	5.0	39 598	1 341	1 791	301	134	328	746	868	2 554	157	134
Alpena	1 050	4.2	36 467	1 893	459	90	37	51	170	376	637	44	37
Antrim	920	4.1	39 731	1 458	176	37	15	54	257	279	282	24	15
Arenac	522	4.2	34 226	2 166	161	31	13	27	83	193	233	18	13
Baraga	257	0.1	29 928	2 572	112	29	8	11	49	83	161	10	8
Barry	2 376	4.4	40 063	1 359	507	105	38	193	388	479	843	58	38
Bay	4 003	3.2	37 884	1 702	1 602	271	122	174	631	1 182	2 168	150	122
Benzie	656	4.1	37 557	1 866	144	26	12	39	171	187	221	18	12
Berrien	6 485	4.0	41 939	1 158	3 025	567	228	312	1 107	1 564	4 132	260	228
Branch	1 410	4.0	32 293	2 548	533	99	41	73	243	411	747	50	41
Calhoun	4 964	4.6	36 958	1 916	2 947	487	224	184	780	1 374	3 842	244	224
Cass	2 006	4.2	38 838	1 572	365	70	28	87	354	489	551	43	28
Charlevoix	1 207	5.3	46 000	820	450	77	36	77	332	262	640	43	36
Cheboygan	880	4.2	34 608	2 336	215	39	19	46	206	308	319	27	19
Chippewa	1 193	3.5	31 358	2 693	486	128	38	47	211	359	699	44	38
Clare	951	5.0	31 137	2 663	278	57	22	56	149	377	414	33	22
Clinton	3 130	2.7	40 446	1 212	722	111	57	158	482	527	1 047	72	57
Crawford	413	4.2	29 960	2 754	163	30	13	27	76	148	234	17	13
Delta	1 321	3.2	36 319	1 970	567	98	47	50	226	411	762	54	47
Dickinson	1 101	2.5	42 709	997	631	122	51	30	195	288	834	52	51
Eaton	4 126	4.3	37 921	1 695	1 941	317	147	172	637	896	2 578	168	147
Emmet	1 621	4.2	48 882	666	725	115	59	125	455	348	1 024	65	59
Genesee	15 042	4.5	36 612	1 954	6 269	1 008	483	769	2 149	4 592	8 530	585	483
Gladwin	817	3.3	32 450	2 635	152	30	13	34	143	316	229	23	13
Gogebic	548	4.1	35 495	2 235	202	43	16	19	124	193	281	20	16
Grand Traverse	4 021	4.7	43 876	886	2 158	348	167	481	836	793	3 154	194	167
Gratiot	1 395	3.3	33 571	2 051	546	108	43	77	201	390	774	50	43
Hillsdale	1 506	4.5	32 778	2 494	571	105	45	74	223	412	795	53	45
Houghton	1 199	3.8	32 968	2 510	491	111	38	51	246	357	691	45	38
Huron	1 380	1.2	43 271	918	450	82	35	161	310	385	728	44	35
Ingham	10 626	4.9	37 142	1 794	7 231	1 367	533	590	1 845	2 304	9 720	571	533
Ionia	2 027	5.6	31 562	2 716	642	132	50	148	242	464	972	59	50
Iosco	852	3.7	33 604	2 439	279	55	23	37	167	356	395	32	23
Iron	438	7.5	38 557	1 856	146	29	11	16	80	170	202	15	11
Isabella	2 255	3.9	31 900	2 614	1 124	257	86	120	387	635	1 586	94	86
Jackson	5 808	4.1	36 413	2 029	2 662	478	204	294	861	1 514	3 639	236	204
Kalamazoo	11 207	4.7	43 062	1 040	5 974	969	446	599	2 223	2 081	7 988	487	446
Kalkaska	562	3.8	32 581	2 630	190	31	15	56	82	177	292	21	15
Kent	30 862	5.3	48 496	550	18 355	2 635	1 399	2 732	7 389	4 588	25 121	1 503	1 399

1. Based on the resident population estimated as of July 1 of the year shown.

Table B. States and Counties — Earnings, Social Security, and Housing

STATE County	Earnings, 2015 (cont.) Percent by selected industries									Social Security beneficiaries, December 2015			Housing units, 2016	
	Farm	Mining	Construction	Manu-facturing	Infor-mation: professional, scientific, technical services	Retail trade	Finance, insur-ance, real estate and leasing	Health care and social assistance	Govern-ment	Number	Rate[1]	Supple-mental Security Income recipients, December 2015	Total	Percent change, 2010–2016
	75	76	77	78	79	80	81	82	83	84	85	86	87	88
MARYLAND—Cont'd														
St. Mary's	-0.1	D	3.9	0.7	24.3	3.8	2.0	6.3	46.7	15 520	139	1 599	44 184	7.0
Somerset	9.1	0.0	D	3.4	2.5	D	D	12.4	45.4	5 235	203	838	11 420	2.6
Talbot	0.2	D	7.0	4.9	12.6	7.2	9.6	20.5	11.6	10 770	287	561	20 246	3.4
Washington	0.6	D	5.5	11.5	5.4	9.9	11.8	14.0	15.0	31 385	210	3 536	61 525	1.2
Wicomico	1.9	D	5.9	7.5	5.8	9.5	5.7	19.6	18.4	19 855	195	2 633	42 277	2.6
Worcester	2.0	D	6.4	2.6	5.6	9.5	7.2	9.0	18.9	15 140	295	850	56 021	0.5
Baltimore city	0.0	0.0	3.5	2.7	12.8	2.0	9.1	19.4	21.0	103 815	167	37 292	297 596	0.3
MASSACHUSETTS	0.0	0.1	5.6	8.4	18.9	4.6	11.1	13.5	12.7	1 236 248	182	188 207	2 858 026	1.8
Barnstable	0.0	D	13.2	D	8.9	9.5	5.7	16.1	18.7	69 870	326	3 271	162 500	1.4
Berkshire	0.1	0.1	D	9.9	8.7	7.9	5.4	19.0	15.0	34 080	267	4 070	68 458	-0.1
Bristol	0.1	D	D	D	6.8	7.9	3.5	15.0	15.7	119 860	215	19 164	232 068	0.7
Dukes	0.2	D	D	D	D	9.2	4.6	8.9	15.6	4 165	242	134	17 713	3.1
Essex	0.0	D	7.5	16.2	11.8	6.4	6.0	15.8	13.4	146 975	189	22 919	309 644	0.9
Franklin	0.0	D	9.5	15.1	5.8	6.2	2.8	12.8	20.0	16 680	236	2 081	33 746	0.0
Hampden	0.0	0.1	6.1	10.0	5.7	6.2	9.5	20.0	19.8	100 555	214	30 498	192 079	0.0
Hampshire	0.0	0.1	5.9	4.7	6.7	6.3	3.5	12.2	32.0	29 765	185	2 868	63 087	0.8
Middlesex	0.1	0.0	4.1	11.3	29.5	3.4	5.4	9.3	9.0	244 065	154	25 394	625 409	2.2
Nantucket	0.0	0.0	26.6	1.2	D	9.5	5.8	5.6	10.3	1 645	152	32	12 075	3.9
Norfolk	0.0	0.0	8.1	7.8	16.5	6.2	11.9	12.5	10.0	119 220	172	10 431	274 987	1.7
Plymouth	0.1	0.1	11.2	5.6	8.4	7.8	6.4	13.6	19.0	102 385	201	9 182	204 122	2.0
Suffolk	0.0	D	2.6	D	21.6	2.1	25.1	15.4	11.6	97 035	125	35 059	331 329	5.0
Worcester	0.0	0.1	7.0	12.7	10.3	6.0	7.0	16.0	16.9	149 950	183	23 104	330 809	1.2
MICHIGAN	0.5	0.4	5.1	16.5	12.5	5.9	7.2	12.4	14.1	2 141 824	216	275 866	4 560 055	0.6
Alcona	1.2	0.2	7.2	13.5	D	8.9	3.5	21.4	19.5	4 700	455	311	11 045	-0.3
Alger	0.8	0.1	5.1	25.1	D	4.8	D	8.0	31.4	2 905	311	163	6 617	1.0
Allegan	4.7	1.6	8.6	36.7	3.1	5.4	2.9	4.7	11.5	23 540	205	1 629	50 291	1.8
Alpena	0.2	1.8	5.0	17.4	D	9.5	4.0	10.5	30.0	9 650	335	1 189	15 937	-0.7
Antrim	2.2	D	12.0	16.7	5.5	7.5	4.7	D	23.3	7 510	329	501	17 881	0.3
Arenac	3.5	D	4.0	15.8	D	7.1	4.2	14.7	19.4	5 240	343	618	9 740	-0.6
Baraga	0.2	D	3.2	18.0	3.1	3.9	D	D	53.5	2 185	256	164	5 254	-0.3
Barry	3.6	0.1	7.0	33.5	D	4.4	6.6	9.0	16.0	13 695	231	752	27 217	0.8
Bay	0.6	0.2	3.8	13.6	13.8	7.5	4.4	18.3	17.3	28 550	270	3 250	48 017	-0.4
Benzie	1.5	D	14.4	9.3	D	8.8	6.7	9.5	19.9	5 370	308	296	12 345	1.2
Berrien	1.2	0.2	3.8	31.9	3.8	5.3	4.4	11.2	13.6	37 235	241	4 851	76 856	-0.1
Branch	2.0	D	6.3	18.4	D	6.9	5.3	6.1	24.6	10 325	237	985	20 550	-1.4
Calhoun	0.5	D	4.0	22.3	D	4.9	2.5	13.8	20.7	32 580	242	4 943	60 541	-0.8
Cass	2.6	0.0	6.8	22.2	4.0	5.3	5.2	D	22.3	12 770	247	990	25 964	0.3
Charlevoix	0.2	D	D	27.6	D	5.0	4.5	D	16.4	7 460	285	487	17 486	1.4
Cheboygan	0.6	D	14.3	2.9	5.5	12.5	5.1	8.5	20.1	8 815	347	707	18 326	0.0
Chippewa	0.4	0.4	3.8	4.1	2.7	7.2	2.8	4.6	57.5	8 650	228	876	21 216	-0.2
Clare	0.9	D	9.1	14.3	3.8	8.5	3.0	8.9	25.5	10 130	331	1 356	23 091	-0.6
Clinton	4.6	0.4	11.1	18.3	D	8.5	6.0	6.5	13.9	14 810	191	683	31 302	2.0
Crawford	0.0	D	D	12.6	4.3	7.0	3.7	22.2	23.7	4 155	301	345	11 085	-0.1
Delta	0.6	D	8.7	20.9	D	8.2	4.6	D	17.1	11 325	311	1 012	20 202	-0.1
Dickinson	0.0	0.0	17.7	19.9	D	7.2	2.4	6.5	26.2	7 255	282	528	13 993	0.0
Eaton	0.2	0.1	5.4	21.1	5.2	6.2	15.3	5.4	14.7	24 475	225	1 725	47 125	0.2
Emmet	0.2	D	8.6	8.7	D	9.8	5.2	21.5	15.4	8 675	262	539	21 424	0.6
Genesee	0.2	0.0	5.0	12.3	8.3	9.3	6.4	18.2	16.2	98 190	239	17 112	190 970	-0.6
Gladwin	0.8	D	14.0	16.9	2.3	11.8	3.1	D	20.1	9 060	359	901	17 662	-0.1
Gogebic	0.0	0.2	4.6	15.0	2.9	7.0	3.4	14.5	32.2	4 835	313	450	10 722	-0.7
Grand Traverse	0.4	4.9	7.5	9.9	8.2	8.8	9.1	20.5	13.9	21 435	234	1 449	43 002	3.4
Gratiot	4.8	D	3.2	19.3	D	5.3	3.6	D	20.3	9 300	224	1 121	16 175	-1.0
Hillsdale	3.6	0.0	4.1	33.4	D	6.0	3.0	D	18.6	10 960	239	1 131	21 689	-0.3
Houghton	0.3	D	6.8	5.2	5.8	7.2	3.5	16.4	41.2	8 080	222	640	18 612	-0.1
Huron	16.2	D	6.9	13.2	D	5.8	5.4	D	14.1	9 670	304	723	21 157	-0.2
Ingham	0.2	0.2	3.7	8.6	8.8	4.6	7.3	15.0	31.6	49 120	172	7 874	122 641	1.1
Ionia	11.0	D	6.7	21.0	1.7	6.8	4.7	5.4	23.6	12 315	192	1 308	24 598	-0.7
Iosco	0.5	0.5	6.9	11.5	3.5	8.3	4.5	D	23.0	9 740	384	840	20 414	-0.1
Iron	0.8	0.1	8.3	8.8	D	11.2	3.5	13.0	26.2	4 155	366	302	9 266	0.8
Isabella	0.7	3.2	8.6	10.5	3.3	6.1	6.6	7.6	37.4	11 285	160	1 220	28 798	1.5
Jackson	0.2	0.2	4.8	19.7	4.6	6.3	4.3	14.8	14.6	36 490	229	4 558	68 999	-0.7
Kalamazoo	0.7	0.2	5.8	22.5	5.5	5.9	8.7	15.9	13.1	49 485	190	6 373	111 081	1.0
Kalkaska	0.6	17.0	12.6	6.5	2.3	5.0	4.8	2.7	17.7	4 910	284	368	12 148	-0.2
Kent	0.2	0.2	5.4	20.7	8.8	5.9	7.6	14.9	7.5	109 290	172	14 632	251 370	1.8

1. Per 1,000 resident population estimated as of July 1 of the year shown.

Table B. States and Counties — Housing, Labor Force, and Employment

STATE County	Housing units, 2011–2015 Occupied units — Owner-occupied Total	Percent	Median value[1]	Median owner cost as a percent of income — With a mortgage	Without a mortgage[2]	Renter-occupied Median rent[3]	Median rent as a percent of income[2]	Sub-standard units[4] (percent)	Civilian labor force, 2016 Total	Percent change, 2015–2016	Unemployment Total	Rate[5]	Civilian employment,[6] 2011–2015 Total	Percent Management, business, science and arts	Construction, production, and maintenance occupations
	89	90	91	92	93	94	95	96	97	98	99	100	101	102	103
MARYLAND—Cont'd															
St. Mary's	38 243	72.3	297 200	21.7	11.6	1 263	26.8	2.0	54 683	0.0	2 243	4.1	53 945	44.0	18.3
Somerset	8 385	64.8	149 600	26.6	16.0	703	40.3	1.4	9 234	0.3	648	7.0	8 103	26.9	23.7
Talbot	16 231	68.6	319 500	24.4	12.7	1 039	34.1	0.9	19 494	1.0	796	4.1	17 620	37.6	17.7
Washington	56 067	64.2	200 100	23.2	12.2	858	27.8	1.8	76 939	0.1	3 750	4.9	67 555	32.5	24.8
Wicomico	36 989	62.3	172 400	22.6	12.8	994	33.0	3.2	50 653	1.1	3 032	6.0	47 947	33.7	21.5
Worcester	20 773	75.3	243 100	26.2	13.9	963	31.5	1.5	25 401	0.0	2 274	9.0	22 979	36.0	17.4
Baltimore city	242 268	47.1	152 400	24.7	14.5	951	32.8	2.7	294 985	0.3	18 555	6.3	270 930	40.5	15.6
MASSACHUSETTS	2 549 721	62.1	333 100	24.1	14.6	1 102	30.3	2.2	3 588 613	0.2	132 786	3.7	3 415 975	44.2	15.7
Barnstable	94 417	78.8	363 500	27.5	15.1	1 104	33.4	1.1	110 749	-0.4	5 225	4.7	102 995	37.0	18.2
Berkshire	55 240	68.6	204 700	23.1	14.3	754	30.4	1.0	64 477	-1.5	2 773	4.3	62 596	37.3	17.6
Bristol	212 029	62.1	273 100	24.6	14.6	820	29.6	1.6	287 648	-0.2	13 474	4.7	269 391	34.4	21.8
Dukes	6 007	79.9	660 800	36.8	21.6	1 428	29.7	1.2	9 350	-0.8	469	5.0	8 849	44.2	21.1
Essex	287 912	63.0	353 100	24.5	15.0	1 076	31.4	2.5	407 474	0.2	15 477	3.8	383 882	40.8	17.3
Franklin	30 202	69.0	220 800	24.5	13.9	851	30.4	1.8	39 307	-0.1	1 312	3.3	37 218	41.1	20.7
Hampden	176 900	61.7	196 400	22.9	15.1	822	32.6	2.8	220 913	-0.6	11 152	5.0	212 742	33.5	20.3
Hampshire	58 631	65.8	265 400	23.7	13.8	965	32.6	1.4	86 767	-0.1	2 892	3.3	84 303	45.7	14.7
Middlesex	585 642	62.4	414 600	23.4	14.1	1 341	28.6	2.1	866 322	0.7	26 067	3.0	832 753	53.4	12.2
Nantucket	3 923	65.5	902 500	31.0	18.1	1 609	26.3	4.1	7 012	1.0	298	4.2	6 157	26.3	29.3
Norfolk	259 545	68.8	399 500	23.6	14.6	1 332	29.6	1.8	370 658	0.7	11 983	3.2	358 283	51.6	12.0
Plymouth	181 425	76.0	328 600	25.0	15.6	1 132	32.4	1.4	268 693	0.3	10 491	3.9	252 016	38.3	17.4
Suffolk	296 672	35.6	377 100	25.4	15.5	1 298	31.1	3.8	423 130	0.7	14 392	3.4	401 271	44.4	12.3
Worcester	301 176	64.7	252 600	23.5	14.4	934	29.7	2.4	426 113	-0.1	16 781	3.9	403 519	40.9	18.5
MICHIGAN	3 841 148	71.0	122 400	21.7	13.1	783	31.7	1.9	4 836 771	1.7	237 716	4.9	4 373 518	34.9	23.2
Alcona	5 001	89.1	97 500	23.8	13.2	609	29.3	1.5	3 842	1.0	283	7.4	3 288	22.8	32.2
Alger	3 470	85.8	116 400	23.0	12.7	595	32.1	1.7	3 244	0.6	260	8.0	3 166	29.5	27.8
Allegan	41 893	80.9	140 400	21.8	12.1	739	25.7	2.4	61 542	1.8	2 296	3.7	51 081	28.8	34.6
Alpena	12 722	76.2	93 300	21.9	12.5	564	29.6	1.2	13 705	0.7	779	5.7	12 233	29.6	25.0
Antrim	9 689	83.6	140 700	25.0	13.3	695	33.1	2.7	10 058	0.8	686	6.8	9 528	26.3	28.4
Arenac	6 447	83.0	87 500	24.5	13.8	587	30.6	1.5	6 117	-1.7	496	8.1	5 569	26.8	29.6
Baraga	2 974	84.0	88 100	23.5	13.3	516	28.8	1.6	3 249	-1.4	257	7.9	2 358	27.2	27.5
Barry	22 836	81.9	134 700	21.6	12.4	762	29.1	2.1	30 955	2.5	1 188	3.8	26 899	31.3	32.4
Bay	43 565	77.7	92 800	21.1	13.2	657	31.8	1.0	52 090	-0.2	2 731	5.2	45 913	29.7	23.9
Benzie	7 225	85.3	150 000	23.8	12.6	713	27.6	2.0	8 813	1.7	561	6.4	7 579	29.7	25.7
Berrien	61 167	70.9	132 600	21.0	12.6	674	31.1	1.7	73 901	0.7	3 548	4.8	68 463	32.9	25.3
Branch	16 022	76.4	95 200	21.5	11.9	662	29.2	3.4	19 171	0.2	890	4.6	18 328	22.8	34.3
Calhoun	52 850	69.3	96 000	21.4	13.7	682	31.0	1.5	64 544	0.6	2 978	4.6	56 687	27.7	29.4
Cass	20 101	82.6	122 800	23.4	12.4	698	29.7	2.2	24 469	1.9	1 115	4.6	22 556	28.2	34.4
Charlevoix	10 794	80.5	153 000	24.1	13.1	648	29.4	0.9	13 127	0.7	690	5.3	11 793	29.5	25.8
Cheboygan	11 223	81.4	112 400	23.2	12.3	592	29.1	1.7	10 850	1.7	979	9.0	10 029	24.8	26.2
Chippewa	13 997	70.3	106 300	20.1	12.6	608	29.5	1.3	16 491	-1.1	1 219	7.4	14 733	30.7	19.6
Clare	13 255	80.6	79 800	25.9	13.2	596	34.5	2.5	11 927	1.3	856	7.2	10 708	23.8	29.7
Clinton	28 857	80.1	154 400	20.7	11.9	779	30.2	1.0	40 510	2.0	1 444	3.6	36 177	39.3	20.6
Crawford	5 954	80.7	96 800	22.2	12.6	710	30.0	2.1	5 348	1.5	396	7.4	5 197	27.2	27.8
Delta	15 685	78.6	101 900	22.1	12.8	537	31.2	1.8	17 189	-0.2	1 088	6.3	15 510	26.9	31.2
Dickinson	11 059	81.2	86 300	21.1	13.7	676	27.3	0.9	12 577	-0.2	650	5.2	11 161	32.4	26.5
Eaton	43 632	71.2	134 500	21.1	12.7	771	28.3	1.6	57 072	2.2	2 264	4.0	51 451	33.9	22.7
Emmet	13 948	75.5	163 100	22.5	12.5	773	31.3	1.8	17 673	0.3	1 103	6.2	15 869	35.3	18.5
Genesee	165 268	69.5	88 500	22.9	13.8	715	33.9	1.5	183 107	0.8	9 938	5.4	161 750	30.5	24.9
Gladwin	10 960	83.3	98 100	24.0	13.6	574	30.9	2.7	9 837	-1.4	668	6.8	8 730	25.2	33.2
Gogebic	6 741	77.8	68 800	20.6	13.5	526	30.3	1.1	6 418	-1.1	420	6.5	5 759	28.4	29.7
Grand Traverse	35 082	76.2	167 900	23.0	13.6	859	29.2	1.4	49 359	1.9	2 043	4.1	43 804	34.9	19.6
Gratiot	14 716	73.7	88 900	22.0	12.7	607	32.7	2.0	18 254	-0.2	908	5.0	15 980	28.1	28.6
Hillsdale	17 810	77.3	98 700	22.9	12.9	654	29.7	2.8	21 331	1.5	1 037	4.9	19 316	26.4	35.6
Houghton	13 765	68.1	93 800	20.4	12.3	637	33.6	2.7	16 447	-0.7	969	5.9	15 440	39.1	18.1
Huron	13 805	81.5	92 900	22.7	12.5	606	29.8	1.4	16 107	-1.5	805	5.0	13 869	27.3	34.2
Ingham	110 418	57.8	117 400	21.6	12.9	785	33.6	1.7	148 845	2.1	6 140	4.1	133 091	39.6	17.1
Ionia	22 092	78.5	110 000	22.3	12.7	696	31.4	2.3	29 758	1.4	1 209	4.1	26 785	26.3	33.0
Iosco	11 343	80.1	85 400	22.8	12.2	581	27.8	1.6	10 052	-0.4	711	7.1	8 780	22.4	31.3
Iron	5 392	83.7	74 400	23.7	15.7	516	29.9	0.7	5 255	1.0	342	6.5	4 324	25.6	29.6
Isabella	24 661	60.2	122 500	21.6	12.0	717	41.5	2.5	35 432	0.4	1 596	4.5	33 411	29.7	19.4
Jackson	60 591	71.9	111 500	21.2	12.8	728	32.7	1.9	74 432	2.0	3 495	4.7	65 183	29.0	27.1
Kalamazoo	100 341	64.1	137 100	21.1	12.6	722	31.5	1.4	132 145	2.4	5 149	3.9	122 809	38.4	18.8
Kalkaska	7 185	80.6	98 300	24.2	12.8	709	28.3	2.4	7 744	1.6	536	6.9	6 815	20.6	33.3
Kent	232 961	68.7	139 300	20.6	12.1	767	30.0	2.2	351 974	2.8	11 843	3.4	305 508	35.2	23.8

1. Specified owner-occupied units.   2. A value of 10.0 represents 10 percent or less; a value of 50.0 represents 50 percent or more.   3. Specified renter-occupied units.
4. Overcrowded or lacking complete plumbing facilities.   5. Percent of civilian labor force.   6. Civilian employed persons 16 years old and over.

STATE County	Number of establishments	Total	Health care and social assistance	Manufacturing	Retail trade	Finance and insurance	Professional, scientific, and technical services	Total (mil dol)	Average per employee (dollars)	Number	Fewer than 50 acres	500 acres or more	Farm operators whose principal occupation is farming (percent)
	104	105	106	107	108	109	110	111	112	113	114	115	116
MARYLAND—Cont'd													
St. Mary's	1 909	28 799	4 441	292	4 597	473	8 146	1 431	49 700	632	48.3	3.3	53.6
Somerset	369	3 663	1 130	366	440	76	96	139	37 987	286	44.4	12.9	55.6
Talbot	1 452	16 767	3 216	1 096	2 700	582	1 006	661	39 425	328	34.8	22.9	46.0
Washington	3 419	60 292	10 215	6 176	9 917	6 743	1 774	2 287	37 928	860	46.3	5.3	49.8
Wicomico	2 501	37 591	8 833	3 430	6 621	1 169	1 352	1 475	39 233	510	52.4	8.0	60.2
Worcester	2 114	17 423	2 086	549	3 584	572	628	600	34 434	374	44.9	11.2	49.7
Baltimore city	12 451	295 269	75 944	11 453	17 702	16 935	21 587	17 725	60 031	NA	NA	NA	NA
MASSACHUSETTS	175 225	3 167 329	620 843	221 773	366 046	182 925	276 712	198 027	62 522	7 755	67.5	1.5	50.0
Barnstable	8 488	74 140	16 078	2 045	15 376	2 165	4 721	3 293	44 414	333	91.9	0.0	58.0
Berkshire	3 868	53 467	11 652	5 020	8 744	1 951	2 387	2 291	42 843	525	49.9	4.4	51.0
Bristol	12 686	195 213	41 606	24 627	33 744	4 508	6 360	8 522	43 655	717	74.5	0.7	49.0
Dukes	1 071	5 377	787	106	1 126	247	233	315	58 641	88	83.0	2.3	55.7
Essex	18 453	282 412	64 919	36 844	39 761	11 321	13 757	14 334	50 757	522	78.0	1.0	56.7
Franklin	1 582	20 104	3 311	3 640	3 052	466	563	812	40 411	780	49.4	3.3	56.9
Hampden	9 600	167 383	38 445	18 721	23 491	8 764	6 703	7 434	44 415	582	62.7	1.0	41.6
Hampshire	3 576	60 573	21 248	2 753	7 943	1 671	1 869	2 044	33 752	799	62.5	1.4	50.6
Middlesex	43 548	869 949	132 021	56 048	83 424	30 174	114 036	65 698	75 519	739	75.9	0.1	52.1
Nantucket	996	4 300	462	60	759	111	167	311	72 227	20	85.0	5.0	15.0
Norfolk	19 893	340 091	69 530	18 127	45 119	26 903	23 672	18 771	55 194	245	78.0	0.8	58.4
Plymouth	12 157	163 503	33 092	10 522	28 361	7 021	9 669	7 699	47 088	825	73.9	1.9	49.7
Suffolk	20 896	595 158	122 262	10 757	35 616	70 715	70 586	49 555	83 264	20	100.0	0.0	65.0
Worcester	17 812	288 933	62 733	32 503	39 485	14 901	18 630	13 966	48 337	1 560	64.4	1.0	43.4
MICHIGAN	219 627	3 725 280	601 090	566 793	465 941	151 233	263 238	174 874	46 943	52 194	43.9	8.8	48.4
Alcona	174	1 132	187	208	254	29	47	38	33 352	235	34.0	7.7	55.3
Alger	226	1 659	245	492	269	76	47	64	38 334	93	48.4	9.7	50.5
Allegan	2 304	36 120	3 068	13 220	3 761	388	1 603	1 596	44 183	1 396	51.8	7.9	48.2
Alpena	757	10 326	2 729	1 282	1 971	312	215	361	34 958	458	33.2	6.6	49.6
Antrim	550	3 798	321	784	583	123	111	121	31 850	415	41.0	5.5	56.9
Arenac	328	3 176	569	749	496	70	84	107	33 718	421	38.7	10.5	38.0
Baraga	185	1 746	303	489	268	51	10	54	31 137	57	29.8	15.8	43.9
Barry	876	10 253	1 369	3 248	1 273	735	317	386	37 599	1 031	44.5	6.7	43.5
Bay	2 193	30 703	7 328	3 933	5 582	995	1 350	1 178	38 370	766	36.9	14.6	54.4
Benzie	445	3 545	379	730	501	143	66	113	31 779	181	41.4	3.9	52.5
Berrien	3 543	53 404	8 894	9 147	6 987	1 386	1 952	2 369	44 361	1 063	57.9	7.0	51.0
Branch	816	11 522	1 605	2 687	1 796	461	364	419	36 383	1 054	41.0	10.8	46.0
Calhoun	2 614	53 395	9 209	14 145	6 107	990	2 115	2 463	46 130	1 023	35.1	10.8	45.7
Cass	727	7 386	900	2 524	862	195	174	248	33 633	798	43.4	10.0	49.0
Charlevoix	785	8 032	1 344	2 418	878	193	204	328	40 779	297	36.7	4.0	38.0
Cheboygan	735	4 312	671	274	1 117	208	103	155	35 830	313	39.0	4.8	40.6
Chippewa	809	9 021	2 053	615	1 747	270	284	269	29 804	409	25.4	11.7	39.1
Clare	560	5 894	1 253	962	1 040	145	149	211	35 761	460	40.7	5.0	50.2
Clinton	1 302	15 949	1 882	2 349	2 471	964	497	590	36 993	1 128	44.1	10.1	46.3
Crawford	304	3 695	1 317	553	542	55	66	141	38 128	49	61.2	0.0	49.0
Delta	1 042	11 774	1 905	2 115	2 229	701	356	430	36 479	283	23.3	16.3	58.3
Dickinson	851	12 442	2 714	2 066	1 935	310	317	524	42 118	162	27.2	8.0	35.2
Eaton	2 071	39 546	3 722	7 814	5 917	3 704	935	1 714	43 340	1 163	40.9	10.9	49.6
Emmet	1 474	14 608	3 232	1 199	2 730	339	425	568	38 854	287	33.1	3.5	44.9
Genesee	7 737	117 246	26 738	10 769	20 091	3 974	3 734	4 619	39 392	835	58.6	6.2	50.1
Gladwin	414	3 879	722	862	687	98	50	131	33 650	533	35.5	3.2	41.8
Gogebic	378	4 219	701	729	743	109	94	121	28 592	62	32.3	0.0	27.4
Grand Traverse	3 371	44 560	9 432	5 001	7 901	2 026	2 287	1 799	40 379	504	52.4	3.4	55.2
Gratiot	735	11 250	2 363	2 875	1 357	402	228	404	35 873	878	37.5	17.3	56.3
Hillsdale	762	10 565	1 343	4 020	1 355	264	183	382	36 147	1 530	44.2	7.8	38.4
Houghton	850	8 737	2 042	837	1 631	363	497	273	31 216	177	29.4	5.1	37.3
Huron	941	10 828	1 800	3 552	1 428	402	235	385	35 578	1 205	31.4	21.3	55.5
Ingham	6 080	105 291	22 829	7 604	13 426	8 102	5 905	4 558	43 287	944	55.3	8.5	51.5
Ionia	881	10 717	1 283	3 539	1 848	612	175	380	35 416	1 109	42.1	11.5	48.0
Iosco	619	6 451	978	1 210	1 276	231	170	213	33 076	283	40.3	5.3	45.2
Iron	350	2 517	412	321	420	116	104	83	32 830	117	30.8	6.8	49.6
Isabella	1 383	23 447	3 094	2 752	3 422	730	566	756	32 253	928	34.6	8.9	49.2
Jackson	2 892	48 974	9 622	8 901	7 341	1 259	2 760	2 193	44 769	1 073	48.7	7.7	45.4
Kalamazoo	5 549	105 691	18 843	16 694	13 381	5 452	3 974	4 870	46 081	734	56.1	8.9	48.6
Kalkaska	330	3 754	539	467	657	63	69	172	45 842	224	46.0	3.6	39.3
Kent	16 099	347 340	48 205	63 013	35 304	14 823	15 150	15 560	44 798	1 159	53.9	4.6	48.2

Table B. States and Counties — **Agriculture**

STATE County	Acreage (1,000) [117]	Percent change, 2007–2012 [118]	Average size of farm [119]	Total irrigated (1,000) [120]	Total cropland (1,000) [121]	Average per farm [122]	Average per acre [123]	Value of machinery and equipment, average per farm (dollars) [124]	Total (mil dol) [125]	Average per farm (dollars) [126]	Crops [127]	Live-stock and poultry products [128]	$10,000 or more [129]	$100,000 or more [130]	Total ($1,000) [131]	Percent of farms [132]
MARYLAND—Cont'd																
St. Mary's	67	-2.3	106	0.7	41.2	700 921	6 603	80 758	21.8	34 494	87.4	12.6	42.6	6.6	783	30.1
Somerset	65	8.2	228	0.4	36.4	1 247 458	5 471	182 073	219.0	765 559	12.2	87.8	58.0	50.0	1 653	61.9
Talbot	119	9.6	364	7.6	98.2	2 408 598	6 612	177 098	89.5	272 893	71.2	28.8	58.5	34.8	2 380	69.2
Washington	130	13.6	151	0.8	85.3	901 269	5 981	117 867	107.7	125 219	42.2	57.8	47.6	24.2	1 078	26.2
Wicomico	84	-9.8	164	9.4	56.1	1 031 771	6 284	134 363	236.3	463 375	22.7	77.3	54.9	35.5	2 360	53.7
Worcester	99	-10.4	266	5.0	71.3	1 585 529	5 971	163 979	199.3	532 794	25.8	74.2	52.7	39.6	1 733	58.6
Baltimore city	NA	NA	NA	NA	NA	NA	NA	NA	NA	NA	NA	NA	NA	NA	NA	NA
MASSACHUSETTS	524	1.1	68	23.4	160.8	704 071	10 430	53 920	492.2	63 470	77.8	22.2	32.7	9.8	8 124	10.1
Barnstable	5	-10.6	14	1.2	1.5	500 691	35 657	50 009	19.1	57 438	50.8	49.2	40.5	11.4	358	7.5
Berkshire	62	-7.1	117	0.2	18.4	824 924	7 024	51 476	22.5	42 796	45.1	54.9	29.5	6.7	268	9.3
Bristol	35	-11.2	49	1.6	11.9	709 223	14 584	51 411	37.7	52 522	79.4	20.6	36.3	8.6	1 527	12.7
Dukes	13	60.6	145	0.2	D	1 416 193	9 800	84 943	3.5	39 671	71.9	28.1	34.1	6.8	D	3.4
Essex	22	-19.5	43	0.6	9.2	893 351	20 821	56 138	25.2	48 205	71.7	28.3	31.0	8.0	207	4.0
Franklin	90	13.0	115	2.1	22.5	700 144	6 083	68 964	55.1	70 585	71.0	29.0	31.9	10.3	1 987	16.4
Hampden	39	5.1	67	0.9	11.1	488 323	7 343	45 735	23.6	40 564	73.6	26.4	26.5	6.5	480	9.1
Hampshire	54	2.3	68	0.9	21.5	544 950	8 071	53 222	49.2	61 613	75.6	24.4	30.5	10.1	682	11.9
Middlesex	28	-16.7	38	1.7	10.7	730 977	19 135	50 583	76.6	103 593	89.7	10.3	35.7	10.1	482	9.3
Nantucket	1	100.3	62	D	0.6	1 642 150	26 658	20 950	1.7	82 800	84.0	15.9	55.0	15.0	0	0.0
Norfolk	9	-18.9	39	0.6	3.4	936 188	24 277	47 890	12.5	51 012	75.8	24.2	33.5	12.7	D	6.9
Plymouth	64	29.1	78	12.0	17.3	893 370	11 510	65 783	108.1	130 986	92.2	7.8	46.9	19.2	1 306	12.4
Suffolk	0	-75.8	1	D	D	246 000	205 000	7 700	0.2	8 100	96.3	4.3	40.0	0.0	0	0.0
Worcester	102	-4.3	65	1.3	32.2	609 428	9 338	47 396	57.5	36 845	68.9	31.1	25.4	7.0	690	8.1
MICHIGAN	9 949	-0.8	191	592.2	7 669.1	766 148	4 020	122 528	8 678.1	166 265	63.5	36.5	44.0	18.0	155 919	39.5
Alcona	38	-15.6	163	0.0	23.8	394 591	2 421	78 426	11.4	48 511	40.3	59.7	31.9	9.8	263	24.3
Alger	18	-3.1	191	0.0	8.7	395 710	2 070	54 075	3.0	32 527	29.4	70.6	38.7	6.5	119	29.0
Allegan	270	-1.8	194	28.1	223.3	927 485	4 790	152 066	580.8	416 071	33.4	66.6	45.1	19.7	3 286	27.1
Alpena	69	-19.4	151	0.0	44.1	367 974	2 433	82 430	23.7	51 644	40.2	59.8	37.3	11.4	694	32.8
Antrim	64	-4.7	155	3.4	33.9	554 149	3 584	77 942	21.0	50 593	73.0	27.0	29.9	8.7	1 324	31.1
Arenac	82	-13.7	194	D	63.0	539 781	2 782	114 143	51.2	121 620	70.0	30.0	33.0	17.8	1 570	72.2
Baraga	18	-4.9	311	0.0	7.9	574 842	1 848	71 667	1.5	25 825	53.2	46.9	38.6	7.0	79	26.3
Barry	165	-1.8	160	4.3	119.4	637 736	3 980	89 944	140.1	135 859	33.9	66.1	35.3	11.2	2 853	37.1
Bay	194	4.0	253	6.3	174.5	1 015 918	4 017	198 977	165.3	215 789	95.1	4.9	58.6	31.9	2 628	68.0
Benzie	21	-2.0	114	0.3	9.8	475 486	4 169	65 177	6.4	35 337	51.9	48.1	30.9	8.8	808	20.4
Berrien	156	-7.5	147	18.1	126.1	822 736	5 591	123 913	161.5	151 968	90.3	9.7	51.6	20.6	3 303	29.4
Branch	244	-2.4	232	44.5	197.7	823 531	3 554	132 288	175.3	166 362	71.5	28.5	44.0	20.3	4 329	54.2
Calhoun	225	-1.4	220	10.7	175.6	807 980	3 676	117 543	133.0	130 044	64.6	35.4	43.4	17.5	3 618	47.7
Cass	189	-0.9	236	57.6	148.0	936 370	3 960	147 259	187.2	234 535	67.1	32.9	43.1	19.9	2 666	47.9
Charlevoix	38	-9.4	126	0.2	20.8	465 684	3 684	52 899	9.9	33 391	60.3	39.7	30.6	6.4	182	14.5
Cheboygan	46	-4.2	146	0.5	21.8	361 479	2 483	51 425	9.3	29 633	60.5	39.5	25.2	3.2	221	20.1
Chippewa	93	-6.0	227	0.1	57.4	368 870	1 622	60 252	12.6	30 724	41.7	58.3	39.6	6.8	934	31.5
Clare	63	-8.6	136	D	30.7	385 265	2 835	54 583	20.4	44 263	30.3	69.7	31.1	8.3	438	24.8
Clinton	244	-10.2	216	4.2	205.7	939 125	4 345	133 106	262.6	232 828	46.7	53.3	49.6	21.5	3 797	54.2
Crawford	3	9.2	56	0.0	0.8	185 959	3 307	54 816	0.3	5 306	26.9	73.1	14.3	0.0	0	0.0
Delta	71	-8.9	250	0.6	35.0	488 406	1 951	83 208	15.0	52 883	51.0	49.0	38.5	13.1	588	35.7
Dickinson	29	15.0	177	0.3	15.5	390 512	2 211	77 451	5.6	34 759	51.6	48.4	34.0	7.4	186	30.2
Eaton	223	0.5	192	1.5	176.1	714 449	3 722	119 525	119.0	102 364	83.8	16.2	46.9	19.8	3 008	46.6
Emmet	40	0.6	139	0.3	17.9	438 456	3 161	55 383	6.7	23 429	66.1	33.9	34.1	4.9	117	12.5
Genesee	123	-4.6	148	1.5	102.6	570 910	3 867	107 984	91.3	109 389	88.7	11.3	38.4	12.9	2 131	32.2
Gladwin	67	-0.7	126	0.5	40.1	355 311	2 820	61 334	19.3	36 300	70.6	29.4	34.5	4.7	599	38.3
Gogebic	6	55.6	98	0.0	2.4	257 194	2 624	34 226	0.5	8 016	72.8	27.2	25.8	0.0	D	3.2
Grand Traverse	55	-12.8	108	3.0	36.4	577 258	5 333	79 274	18.2	36 202	76.3	23.7	40.1	9.7	1 273	28.8
Gratiot	289	0.9	330	9.5	259.5	1 486 503	4 510	209 694	345.0	392 976	57.7	42.3	56.3	31.7	4 522	68.6
Hillsdale	262	-2.8	171	9.1	207.9	590 512	3 444	101 482	161.5	105 577	71.8	28.2	35.6	14.5	6 159	57.7
Houghton	27	15.0	154	0.1	10.8	272 254	1 772	42 633	4.0	22 678	53.0	47.0	27.7	2.3	101	18.1
Huron	452	2.6	375	2.0	406.0	1 952 800	5 202	304 740	654.6	543 207	51.1	48.9	62.5	43.8	9 479	79.6
Ingham	201	7.7	212	1.7	167.4	866 715	4 079	128 773	131.3	139 131	77.4	22.6	42.2	17.2	2 925	27.2
Ionia	248	4.2	224	6.0	203.1	934 093	4 170	154 311	406.1	366 228	31.6	68.4	50.9	25.4	4 662	51.9
Iosco	38	-20.4	134	0.0	23.7	358 890	2 673	85 230	17.1	60 364	36.4	63.6	29.3	7.8	467	30.4
Iron	23	-17.3	196	0.5	9.5	390 043	1 989	50 376	3.7	31 222	87.3	12.7	25.6	6.8	25	17.9
Isabella	188	-3.9	203	3.4	148.9	772 920	3 806	104 693	119.4	128 664	65.7	34.3	46.7	19.2	2 703	52.3
Jackson	183	0.4	171	3.9	136.0	652 247	3 822	85 794	78.2	72 866	69.2	30.8	36.4	12.0	4 210	32.1
Kalamazoo	144	-0.9	196	39.1	112.9	909 857	4 653	148 903	244.0	332 383	79.7	20.3	48.5	21.5	2 473	26.7
Kalkaska	26	10.0	115	1.6	12.9	350 875	3 044	45 339	8.8	39 299	92.1	7.9	23.2	3.1	104	17.0
Kent	157	-7.4	136	10.0	120.5	795 991	5 858	111 424	231.9	200 053	77.8	22.2	42.6	16.6	2 417	22.7

Table B. States and Counties — **Water Use, Wholesale Trade, Retail Trade, and Real Estate**

STATE County	Water use, 2010		Wholesale trade,[1] 2012				Retail trade,[2] 2012				Real estate and rental and leasing,[2] 2012			
	Total water withdrawn (mil gal/day)	Gallons withdrawn per person per day	Number of establishments	Number of employees	Sales (mil dol)	Annual payroll (mil dol)	Number of establishments	Number of employees	Sales (mil dol)	Annual payroll (mil dol)	Number of establishments	Number of employees	Receipts (mil dol)	Annual payroll (mil dol)
	133	134	135	136	137	138	139	140	141	142	143	144	145	146
MARYLAND—Cont'd														
St. Mary's	7.9	75	39	397	189.5	17.6	294	4 835	1 227.0	109.5	83	312	94.7	11.4
Somerset	3.8	145	14	D	D	D	61	434	112.2	9.5	17	42	4.8	0.7
Talbot	7.2	191	56	443	277.4	19.9	222	2 635	670.2	64.6	55	179	34.7	6.3
Washington	58.8	399	137	1 917	1 804.2	89.0	612	9 244	2 457.6	207.6	141	755	216.5	29.4
Wicomico	19.9	202	108	1 122	1 231.4	49.9	390	6 375	1 608.3	145.0	126	624	86.3	20.7
Worcester	18.2	354	47	D	D	D	401	3 370	835.6	81.9	152	467	75.3	15.1
Baltimore city	25.3	41	544	8 592	7 954.3	495.2	1 839	15 747	3 647.7	379.0	596	4 055	883.7	187.6
MASSACHUSETTS	2 995.9	458	6 619	114 195	123 904.4	8 035.1	24 311	351 598	92 915.4	9 161.7	6 485	42 788	13 628.4	2 357.9
Barnstable	60.8	282	178	1 152	563.1	57.0	1 503	14 395	3 856.9	401.4	331	1 361	260.5	53.1
Berkshire	24.3	185	105	1 242	455.0	58.0	711	8 482	1 916.5	201.7	108	715	99.5	23.1
Bristol	882.1	1 609	517	10 556	9 375.8	626.2	2 192	33 806	8 403.5	813.8	418	1 382	293.7	53.1
Dukes	3.1	186	16	D	D	D	205	1 276	373.6	43.7	63	142	41.6	6.6
Essex	420.3	566	726	11 128	15 101.2	768.2	2 585	37 792	10 037.9	995.4	602	2 734	629.9	113.9
Franklin	47.1	659	64	D	D	D	262	2 903	703.7	73.3	37	110	16.9	2.9
Hampden	148.2	320	385	6 581	6 028.9	355.0	1 573	22 637	5 753.0	540.3	364	1 839	289.2	66.0
Hampshire	28.4	180	85	1 676	1 807.0	81.2	546	7 914	1 750.0	187.6	114	435	279.8	15.5
Middlesex	431.1	287	1 760	36 339	46 631.4	3 169.0	5 156	80 738	21 344.6	2 155.0	1 567	11 979	5 087.1	616.2
Nantucket	4.5	446	7	D	D	D	155	998	317.5	35.8	53	157	59.7	7.9
Norfolk	44.1	66	890	15 930	13 702.9	1 083.4	2 548	43 010	11 801.1	1 163.3	774	6 263	1 778.1	382.1
Plymouth	619.6	1 252	488	5 947	9 622.7	353.9	1 892	26 703	6 889.6	698.5	364	1 550	341.1	69.6
Suffolk	0.2	0	630	11 314	12 840.7	809.3	2 411	31 965	8 851.0	892.5	1 093	11 366	3 821.2	826.9
Worcester	282.3	353	768	11 502	7 126.8	636.8	2 572	38 979	10 916.5	959.5	597	2 755	630.2	120.8
MICHIGAN	10 837.2	1 096	9 392	132 490	115 704.9	7 474.6	34 858	441 190	119 302.0	10 527.3	7 826	48 706	11 974.5	1 806.9
Alcona	6.3	575	4	14	3.2	0.4	35	236	52.5	4.9	3	5	0.8	0.1
Alger	5.6	582	3	D	D	D	45	272	64.6	5.6	3	4	0.7	0.1
Allegan	23.6	212	106	1 354	609.4	130.1	335	3 354	949.9	76.3	69	210	38.9	8.0
Alpena	120.3	4 065	32	409	223.9	17.6	146	1 731	448.8	41.5	18	111	7.3	2.1
Antrim	58.7	2 490	9	40	15.7	1.2	88	530	169.6	13.4	22	D	D	D
Arenac	61.1	3 842	10	D	D	D	71	459	150.8	9.6	5	D	D	D
Baraga	15.5	1 752	3	9	3.3	0.2	29	275	53.1	5.3	5	D	D	D
Barry	8.2	139	26	179	122.5	7.3	124	1 198	286.0	24.0	24	68	8.1	2.8
Bay	608.3	5 644	87	D	D	D	419	5 526	1 303.0	124.5	65	212	29.3	4.7
Benzie	2.6	146	5	D	D	D	73	535	128.0	11.2	15	33	3.3	0.7
Berrien	2 019.0	12 875	133	D	D	D	587	6 783	1 681.1	147.2	152	614	78.3	19.5
Branch	13.2	292	28	265	124.3	11.3	132	1 612	435.2	39.0	31	77	15.0	2.2
Calhoun	28.1	206	94	D	D	D	488	5 858	1 702.3	133.4	87	373	53.9	10.5
Cass	22.6	432	45	321	316.2	15.8	116	876	256.9	18.9	28	48	7.9	1.0
Charlevoix	21.3	820	15	51	9.6	1.4	116	823	196.8	18.0	29	115	18.0	3.9
Cheboygan	7.6	291	13	89	37.4	3.1	147	1 161	310.2	27.3	17	D	D	D
Chippewa	8.9	232	25	295	145.4	11.0	148	1 725	454.1	36.8	26	96	8.9	1.8
Clare	3.8	122	11	D	D	D	118	1 027	261.3	22.5	9	24	2.5	0.4
Clinton	9.7	128	52	869	659.2	39.7	170	2 090	749.2	53.0	53	204	34.7	6.8
Crawford	2.3	161	4	34	21.5	1.3	60	531	214.6	12.0	13	22	3.7	0.7
Delta	67.4	1 817	45	331	157.1	12.3	183	2 160	507.1	45.0	29	64	6.8	1.2
Dickinson	25.2	963	42	D	D	D	154	1 824	431.2	40.4	28	D	D	D
Eaton	8.9	83	71	1 474	1 076.7	65.4	330	5 619	1 453.0	129.9	79	380	78.8	12.4
Emmet	6.3	193	34	217	95.8	9.4	293	2 606	627.8	63.5	41	204	24.8	3.9
Genesee	13.4	31	272	3 969	3 673.6	218.5	1 459	19 368	5 307.9	444.9	318	1 843	255.8	57.1
Gladwin	2.3	91	7	38	11.2	1.4	82	598	141.0	11.6	13	102	6.1	2.6
Gogebic	2.3	138	9	66	74.3	2.1	79	764	159.6	15.1	14	104	7.2	1.6
Grand Traverse	14.3	165	134	1 146	454.0	52.5	560	7 184	1 767.8	174.8	151	488	96.5	17.0
Gratiot	8.4	198	27	D	D	D	135	1 339	344.2	28.2	19	60	7.5	1.3
Hillsdale	9.4	201	33	301	407.9	12.7	139	1 330	370.2	32.1	25	54	12.0	1.4
Houghton	4.0	110	21	D	D	D	149	1 638	329.4	32.7	25	D	D	D
Huron	62.5	1 887	38	518	523.6	26.4	161	1 481	361.9	29.1	9	11	2.6	0.4
Ingham	220.5	785	204	2 701	5 407.9	130.9	916	13 217	3 260.5	293.0	253	1 946	236.4	68.8
Ionia	9.7	151	26	D	D	D	143	1 589	430.4	34.8	17	45	6.9	1.1
Iosco	4.3	168	5	D	D	D	115	1 302	327.2	28.8	19	37	4.3	0.6
Iron	1.4	115	10	44	11.7	1.3	61	433	101.6	9.1	17	37	3.5	0.7
Isabella	8.2	117	51	504	362.3	19.7	215	3 322	769.9	71.5	55	1 077	70.7	27.6
Jackson	20.3	127	137	D	D	D	526	7 003	1 841.7	163.5	99	567	82.0	15.5
Kalamazoo	51.8	207	234	3 668	1 553.7	197.3	863	12 708	3 129.4	284.2	210	2 328	223.7	71.6
Kalkaska	3.4	197	18	167	75.7	7.1	54	525	155.9	12.7	9	D	D	D
Kent	27.7	46	976	22 090	17 703.0	1 235.3	2 116	31 615	8 698.6	803.1	640	3 990	698.0	143.7

1. Merchant wholesalers, except manufacturers' sales branches and offices. 2. Employer establishments.

Table B. States and Counties — Professional Services, Manufacturing, and Accommodation and Food Services

STATE County	Professional, scientific, and technical services, 2012				Manufacturing, 2012				Accommodation and food services, 2012			
	Number of establishments	Number of employees	Receipts (mil dol)	Annual payroll (mil dol)	Number of establishments	Number of employees	Receipts (mil dol)	Annual payroll (mil dol)	Number of establishments	Number of employees	Sales (mil dol)	Annual payroll (mil dol)
	147	148	149	150	151	152	153	154	155	156	157	158
MARYLAND—Cont'd												
St. Mary's	309	8 327	1 654.0	640.7	28	225	D	9.6	184	3 670	166.6	48.1
Somerset	20	D	D	D	13	340	223.2	13.2	29	272	12.8	3.1
Talbot	134	1 678	260.2	97.6	41	1 465	D	57.9	133	2 476	131.4	42.1
Washington	234	1 726	190.6	72.1	127	5 612	2 735.0	307.2	290	5 083	258.7	73.8
Wicomico	227	1 661	238.8	91.0	79	3 108	1 216.8	127.2	208	3 871	187.1	48.7
Worcester	142	642	65.5	28.7	36	604	241.7	24.6	413	6 050	552.3	153.6
Baltimore city	1 555	21 994	4 747.0	1 890.5	409	11 748	5 043.3	574.0	1 541	21 832	1 607.8	435.6
MASSACHUSETTS	21 422	255 022	60 370.0	23 826.5	6 806	234 168	81 927.8	14 395.3	16 898	273 185	17 509.0	5 019.8
Barnstable	733	4 806	932.9	341.7	187	2 157	478.6	119.4	1 143	13 117	1 000.4	291.5
Berkshire	338	2 688	397.7	162.8	151	5 275	1 288.9	310.7	522	7 006	418.7	124.2
Bristol	1 045	6 050	823.3	295.3	674	26 935	8 015.0	1 552.1	1 241	19 755	969.1	276.1
Dukes	62	221	38.5	13.6	21	108	D	4.6	138	878	120.3	36.7
Essex	2 137	15 135	2 330.9	1 075.8	869	38 451	12 747.9	2 517.9	1 797	25 502	1 536.1	431.0
Franklin	132	584	153.6	27.6	105	3 615	1 682.5	171.4	147	1 864	85.5	25.4
Hampden	854	6 893	883.2	358.6	583	20 588	6 259.4	1 100.7	928	14 276	714.2	198.4
Hampshire	360	1 834	228.2	87.6	134	2 939	1 096.3	140.0	384	5 977	264.4	78.5
Middlesex	6 817	111 444	28 751.6	11 746.3	1 652	59 454	22 760.7	4 255.8	3 662	59 109	3 940.3	1 125.1
Nantucket	56	176	35.7	11.0	18	75	D	2.0	111	849	119.4	36.6
Norfolk	2 640	20 674	4 096.5	1 498.9	628	20 613	10 798.9	1 248.1	1 596	27 505	1 613.3	463.8
Plymouth	1 245	7 134	1 125.5	426.1	487	10 374	2 493.2	521.2	1 038	18 005	909.4	272.8
Suffolk	3 188	61 414	17 726.5	6 606.9	335	8 908	3 805.2	472.0	2 469	54 643	4 551.0	1 304.5
Worcester	1 815	15 969	2 846.1	1 174.2	962	34 677	10 475.8	1 979.4	1 722	24 699	1 266.9	355.4
MICHIGAN	21 650	D	D	D	12 444	514 058	238 892.4	27 611.4	19 491	347 337	17 962.4	4 871.7
Alcona	7	29	5.0	1.6	17	175	27.5	8.0	26	102	3.9	1.1
Alger	10	17	2.3	1.1	11	471	D	24.9	40	260	16.8	3.7
Allegan	161	1 387	171.6	85.8	202	13 273	5 286.6	633.9	207	2 697	131.9	37.1
Alpena	40	193	16.8	6.9	43	1 227	480.3	56.0	72	879	35.1	10.4
Antrim	36	128	9.8	3.3	40	776	175.0	29.6	59	946	42.6	15.5
Arenac	15	83	11.1	5.4	28	694	145.7	28.0	48	457	28.2	8.0
Baraga	3	11	0.9	0.3	21	440	150.3	17.1	17	D	D	D
Barry	63	308	20.7	8.9	49	2 725	1 115.7	122.9	80	982	38.5	11.3
Bay	152	1 360	111.0	57.1	123	3 650	1 149.4	190.6	233	4 039	172.0	47.6
Benzie	31	61	5.6	1.8	21	363	D	10.8	56	1 068	50.4	16.9
Berrien	284	2 149	201.0	108.3	289	8 330	1 962.8	388.9	365	5 323	241.7	69.4
Branch	45	391	114.4	18.1	72	2 604	812.7	115.1	78	1 071	47.2	12.8
Calhoun	191	1 058	93.0	55.5	148	11 179	5 445.1	599.3	280	6 023	471.2	104.3
Cass	47	191	15.4	5.8	70	2 249	721.7	96.4	65	778	30.9	8.5
Charlevoix	61	224	23.7	8.3	47	2 266	728.4	109.2	75	1 288	61.9	18.6
Cheboygan	41	112	11.2	4.2	31	248	57.1	10.2	119	689	67.4	18.0
Chippewa	42	D	D	D	27	498	90.1	22.1	111	2 157	136.3	38.3
Clare	30	144	16.5	7.9	26	811	254.0	42.7	64	812	34.7	9.1
Clinton	132	576	82.5	26.7	60	1 868	625.5	98.0	98	1 504	55.9	16.5
Crawford	17	62	10.3	2.1	21	499	184.2	24.2	43	550	22.6	5.6
Delta	78	499	57.8	12.1	68	2 364	854.3	137.4	99	1 213	45.3	12.4
Dickinson	53	358	31.3	12.4	41	2 224	983.6	109.6	73	809	31.6	8.7
Eaton	177	883	100.9	37.8	91	7 872	10 600.6	488.1	206	4 230	169.2	50.6
Emmet	110	394	61.3	22.2	54	984	281.2	40.1	139	2 280	122.4	37.5
Genesee	639	3 544	370.3	143.2	273	10 675	9 418.1	684.4	704	13 207	563.9	157.4
Gladwin	26	51	4.5	1.2	27	771	185.0	33.5	43	476	17.8	5.1
Gogebic	18	90	7.3	3.3	19	641	90.8	22.7	59	968	42.1	11.7
Grand Traverse	369	2 118	295.2	109.2	176	4 464	1 153.9	216.1	249	5 649	343.1	93.6
Gratiot	29	142	14.2	7.0	51	2 401	809.7	116.7	72	1 009	42.5	12.4
Hillsdale	46	166	17.1	5.4	77	3 673	1 445.7	149.8	68	786	31.8	8.7
Houghton	72	455	47.8	20.3	41	552	D	D	110	1 372	51.0	14.0
Huron	48	227	22.2	10.9	65	3 285	891.7	132.1	102	885	38.0	9.8
Ingham	742	5 940	1 026.8	344.1	190	7 572	4 972.9	416.5	609	11 266	483.0	134.6
Ionia	46	159	15.0	6.6	70	3 251	1 363.0	135.5	77	976	35.5	10.2
Iosco	30	218	11.9	5.5	41	869	226.7	33.2	80	677	34.0	9.1
Iron	29	105	9.9	4.2	17	395	D	16.7	33	293	12.5	3.0
Isabella	104	677	62.2	26.0	59	2 197	616.7	95.8	125	5 523	447.4	98.9
Jackson	217	2 504	367.1	180.4	268	8 414	2 621.3	409.3	275	4 788	201.5	57.3
Kalamazoo	544	3 689	576.8	203.2	311	15 557	7 385.6	911.1	546	11 663	477.9	146.3
Kalkaska	18	38	7.6	2.1	13	430	146.4	20.5	31	345	16.6	4.6
Kent	1 635	13 433	2 016.6	777.1	1 068	57 371	17 535.6	2 899.2	1 192	25 307	1 154.4	335.4

1. Establishment subject to federal tax.

Table B. States and Counties — Health Care and Social Assistance, Other Services, Nonemployer Businesses, and Residential Construction

STATE County	Health care and social assistance, 2012				Other services, 2012				Nonemployer businesses, 2015		Value of residential construction authorized by building permits, 2016	
	Number of establishments	Number of employees	Receipts (mil dol)	Annual payroll (mil dol)	Number of establishments	Number of employees	Receipts (mil dol)	Annual payroll (mil dol)	Number	Receipts (mil dol)	New Construction ($1,000)	Number of housing units
	159	160	161	162	163	164	165	166	167	168	169	170
MARYLAND—Cont'd												
St. Mary's	179	4 110	379.9	172.2	142	865	80.7	30.1	6 732	259.4	143 497	698
Somerset	38	1 121	74.7	35.1	30	101	11.8	2.2	1 429	47.4	3 812	25
Talbot	173	3 517	387.0	147.2	118	610	74.4	17.4	4 287	217.8	17 391	50
Washington	440	10 210	1 056.4	428.4	261	1 594	136.6	38.4	8 443	366.8	49 313	200
Wicomico	361	8 798	935.1	385.7	189	1 286	99.0	31.1	6 150	269.4	23 320	171
Worcester	140	1 956	196.1	80.4	143	868	82.8	23.4	5 083	269.1	46 627	233
Baltimore city	1 471	79 915	11 349.2	4 158.7	939	8 989	1 303.0	305.5	41 109	1 454.4	184 694	943
MASSACHUSETTS	18 386	587 485	63 583.1	27 696.7	14 008	93 489	10 455.1	2 931.3	514 298	27 654.9	3 946 447	16 288
Barnstable	811	15 781	1 766.8	730.5	590	3 176	320.4	95.6	25 597	1 336.3	202 512	505
Berkshire	438	11 415	1 091.4	488.4	278	1 675	144.1	39.5	10 183	450.2	63 551	191
Bristol	1 414	39 217	3 485.9	1 573.5	1 085	5 614	479.1	138.6	31 874	1 574.2	214 477	1 338
Dukes	61	784	91.1	42.7	54	164	25.6	6.4	3 856	225.7	80 414	121
Essex	2 080	62 430	5 324.0	2 497.2	1 449	8 386	727.3	225.5	60 336	3 122.8	274 019	1 065
Franklin	194	3 671	291.8	121.8	132	578	52.4	15.2	6 168	226.8	9 999	54
Hampden	1 161	37 660	3 822.0	1 659.5	809	5 662	497.1	138.7	24 116	1 188.1	64 497	328
Hampshire	435	18 108	875.9	459.1	301	1 627	164.1	48.9	12 965	570.9	65 632	257
Middlesex	4 489	124 041	15 136.6	6 421.7	3 397	24 727	2 984.3	890.7	134 915	7 511.2	901 934	4 336
Nantucket	35	392	53.4	23.0	44	155	39.9	8.1	2 472	192.6	152 624	200
Norfolk	2 234	66 785	5 406.8	2 524.8	1 576	10 253	1 184.0	321.8	56 887	3 529.9	494 904	1 743
Plymouth	1 213	31 032	2 904.1	1 305.7	969	5 915	500.5	163.9	37 096	2 020.0	277 904	1 219
Suffolk	1 816	116 274	16 983.3	7 058.9	1 988	17 967	2 602.9	629.2	56 292	3 152.3	844 908	3 439
Worcester	2 005	59 895	6 350.0	2 790.0	1 336	7 590	733.5	209.4	51 541	2 553.8	299 072	1 492
MICHIGAN	26 231	585 530	63 018.8	25 556.5	15 919	96 150	10 407.7	2 719.9	700 254	30 144.5	12 170 323	65
Alcona	12	D	D	D	8	D	D	D	676	27.6	2 411	24
Alger	20	299	22.2	8.6	13	37	4.0	0.9	553	19.8	4 965	24
Allegan	172	3 225	265.9	111.8	172	795	92.5	22.7	7 802	342.3	91 917	349
Alpena	83	1 724	122.6	47.4	65	258	23.5	5.3	1 886	77.7	4 507	32
Antrim	54	302	15.9	7.7	39	160	13.5	3.8	2 035	89.9	9 804	49
Arenac	34	647	58.7	20.6	24	D	D	D	922	36.1	648	3
Baraga	18	324	27.2	10.4	16	36	3.5	0.7	409	14.7	1 013	7
Barry	82	1 336	123.4	50.3	83	402	42.0	11.3	3 563	153.5	32 142	171
Bay	329	7 152	682.5	261.2	190	928	70.8	21.3	5 472	199.7	14 474	71
Benzie	30	D	D	D	25	86	5.6	1.7	1 756	68.7	16 887	76
Berrien	399	9 410	816.5	329.2	251	1 199	116.0	32.2	9 842	395.1	86 878	312
Branch	100	1 497	143.0	57.1	67	276	18.4	6.8	2 430	109.2	10 733	41
Calhoun	323	9 313	966.4	421.9	208	1 173	448.4	41.7	6 424	242.1	8 825	44
Cass	60	904	66.3	30.0	58	D	D	D	3 088	127.4	33 308	114
Charlevoix	74	1 187	104.5	48.7	65	247	25.4	6.3	2 575	111.1	13 442	66
Cheboygan	54	1 025	87.3	35.4	74	208	17.6	5.1	1 959	78.6	13 999	62
Chippewa	79	1 939	170.1	68.1	53	D	D	D	1 931	53.6	5 364	50
Clare	59	1 106	86.2	28.5	38	159	14.1	3.3	1 691	72.2	2 973	23
Clinton	112	1 664	140.4	50.3	94	495	37.7	11.6	5 289	221.6	43 020	202
Crawford	32	971	111.5	41.9	21	155	16.7	5.7	857	30.7	3 317	15
Delta	104	2 016	167.7	67.1	84	392	37.7	9.2	1 992	70.5	5 591	36
Dickinson	118	D	D	D	66	249	21.5	5.6	1 461	56.9	4 607	27
Eaton	236	3 506	282.4	117.2	157	1 093	136.7	45.4	7 009	248.4	40 666	165
Emmet	185	2 962	345.5	151.9	109	651	67.7	17.6	3 543	166.1	26 574	135
Genesee	1 294	25 418	2 787.5	1 148.7	562	3 406	376.2	91.1	27 934	979.0	69 253	374
Gladwin	39	611	55.8	17.0	26	154	11.1	2.9	1 479	72.9	12 453	49
Gogebic	32	661	63.0	25.8	42	131	10.2	2.6	882	29.4	4 020	20
Grand Traverse	396	8 782	995.6	397.1	199	1 327	133.2	37.5	9 287	444.0	96 312	606
Gratiot	104	2 339	236.7	82.4	46	223	35.1	6.4	2 219	86.7	6 627	29
Hillsdale	104	D	D	D	51	D	D	D	2 833	119.6	16 174	112
Houghton	92	D	D	D	67	D	D	D	1 956	58.9	7 267	44
Huron	97	1 741	159.2	59.9	60	234	24.6	5.6	2 279	102.3	4 612	21
Ingham	807	22 354	2 566.1	999.5	566	5 094	633.8	183.6	18 835	889.3	159 019	858
Ionia	103	1 226	105.2	39.0	66	271	22.9	5.7	3 211	112.2	17 794	85
Iosco	52	814	81.5	29.8	50	176	12.6	3.1	1 539	56.3	4 720	34
Iron	18	431	52.4	19.1	24	D	D	D	762	22.7	3 923	17
Isabella	202	3 040	222.1	94.7	111	601	46.0	12.3	3 518	151.5	8 041	60
Jackson	351	9 060	936.8	409.4	210	1 361	129.7	37.1	8 894	342.6	29 927	136
Kalamazoo	653	18 751	2 261.9	865.0	427	3 007	384.4	91.0	15 943	679.5	146 948	620
Kalkaska	27	475	42.9	15.0	26	136	17.2	5.2	1 199	49.0	7 319	40
Kent	1 581	50 294	5 244.9	2 133.2	1 083	8 294	765.1	220.5	45 412	2 260.7	517 320	2 823

Table B. States and Counties — Government Employment and Payroll, and Local Government Finances

	Government employment and payroll, 2012									Local government finances, 2012				
			March payroll (percent of total)							General revenue				
												Taxes		
													Per capita[1] (dollars)	
STATE County	Full-time equivalent employees	March payroll (dollars)	Adminis- tration, judicial, and legal	Police and Corrections	Fire Protection	Highways and transpor- tation	Health and Welfare	Natural resources and utilities	Education and libraries	Total (mil dol)	Inter- govern- mental (mil dol)	Total (mil dol)	Total	Property
	171	172	173	174	175	176	177	178	179	180	181	182	183	184
MARYLAND—Cont'd														
St. Mary's	3 187	14 069 480	5.9	10.5	0.0	2.3	1.5	4.3	73.2	356.5	125.4	191.8	1 760	923
Somerset	890	3 320 415	5.7	9.8	0.0	2.6	2.1	5.5	67.9	83.1	45.3	26.3	1 002	735
Talbot	1 356	5 353 079	6.3	12.0	0.0	3.6	4.8	9.8	53.9	135.2	24.3	75.9	1 992	1 178
Washington	5 270	21 889 886	4.2	7.2	2.7	2.6	0.7	8.0	73.2	547.6	234.3	228.4	1 531	989
Wicomico	4 063	15 857 286	4.2	10.7	1.8	1.7	1.9	5.3	73.7	376.1	166.7	134.3	1 334	842
Worcester	2 609	11 789 178	8.3	14.2	2.1	3.0	6.7	9.7	51.9	340.0	56.3	227.1	4 403	3 313
Baltimore city	27 461	126 508 297	5.8	15.9	7.5	3.3	8.2	10.7	47.4	3 714.0	1 967.9	1 238.8	1 994	1 229
MASSACHUSETTS	X	X	X	X	X	X	X	X	X	X	X	X	X	X
Barnstable	7 548	35 968 725	7.2	11.5	10.0	4.2	3.5	6.4	53.6	1 003.5	207.7	645.0	2 994	2 809
Berkshire	4 790	19 230 480	4.3	8.5	3.3	5.5	1.3	4.1	71.5	506.3	218.2	246.7	1 897	1 828
Bristol	17 070	76 423 100	3.0	10.6	7.2	2.1	2.0	5.3	68.1	2 032.5	942.1	830.7	1 507	1 453
Dukes	1 048	4 632 999	7.6	11.3	1.4	6.7	6.9	4.4	59.7	141.2	27.4	88.5	5 195	4 963
Essex	25 587	123 574 109	3.4	8.7	6.1	2.3	1.3	6.5	69.6	2 861.5	1 081.5	1 475.0	1 952	1 898
Franklin	2 963	11 147 283	5.4	6.1	2.8	5.5	1.3	4.8	71.6	305.5	144.0	135.0	1 887	1 847
Hampden	18 660	82 237 236	2.8	9.5	5.8	2.3	1.5	8.2	68.6	2 010.8	1 105.6	711.6	1 527	1 484
Hampshire	5 845	24 568 656	4.7	9.8	7.3	3.2	2.8	5.3	64.6	489.0	185.2	236.2	1 478	1 434
Middlesex	51 015	257 135 128	5.3	9.1	7.3	2.5	5.9	5.3	61.9	7 258.0	1 991.8	3 798.4	2 471	2 386
Nantucket	564	3 317 115	5.0	8.7	5.6	10.9	11.3	6.7	48.7	127.3	11.0	80.2	7 784	6 281
Norfolk	21 584	108 297 457	3.8	9.0	7.0	2.5	1.4	5.7	68.8	2 684.4	649.6	1 685.1	2 471	2 399
Plymouth	17 576	78 325 658	3.7	8.5	6.3	2.3	1.5	4.3	71.8	1 886.5	696.4	1 001.7	2 004	1 943
Suffolk	22 999	131 415 091	3.4	16.9	11.5	2.0	7.1	7.2	49.6	3 908.1	1 488.3	1 972.4	2 650	2 442
Worcester	28 380	132 203 123	3.5	8.3	5.1	3.2	1.5	4.3	73.0	3 064.8	1 424.8	1 314.3	1 630	1 589
MICHIGAN	X	X	X	X	X	X	X	X	X	X	X	X	X	X
Alcona	260	869 231	18.9	12.8	2.7	13.1	5.9	0.9	43.1	26.7	8.8	13.3	1 250	1 247
Alger	293	1 015 817	13.5	7.1	0.5	18.5	0.2	4.4	52.0	30.8	13.5	10.2	1 071	1 037
Allegan	3 023	10 951 667	9.1	7.0	1.3	3.2	8.0	2.2	67.1	353.3	194.8	109.8	980	962
Alpena	2 199	8 769 942	4.0	2.3	1.9	3.0	58.9	0.8	28.5	257.0	79.4	32.4	1 109	1 087
Antrim	795	2 618 552	12.6	9.1	1.8	7.2	4.1	3.3	59.1	89.8	22.9	43.1	1 841	1 822
Arenac	446	1 462 195	13.6	6.7	0.0	5.4	0.6	3.4	66.5	44.9	24.2	14.4	928	920
Baraga	413	1 533 081	10.5	4.7	0.2	7.7	36.0	3.8	36.1	56.1	20.1	9.9	1 142	1 141
Barry	1 440	5 121 005	9.4	7.0	1.4	5.4	12.9	2.3	58.3	149.7	79.8	42.0	711	706
Bay	4 027	15 471 429	6.7	5.7	2.4	4.8	13.5	5.1	61.1	536.8	284.0	123.7	1 157	1 137
Benzie	473	1 629 367	11.3	8.6	1.6	6.8	9.1	2.1	57.3	57.9	16.6	24.9	1 423	1 407
Berrien	4 813	18 604 576	9.6	10.9	2.0	2.9	2.9	4.5	64.6	601.1	301.4	200.9	1 288	1 264
Branch	1 691	6 939 089	6.6	5.2	1.3	2.4	38.9	3.2	38.5	226.8	88.1	39.0	889	873
Calhoun	4 008	16 572 500	10.0	11.0	3.1	3.3	5.9	4.4	61.4	671.0	371.6	175.1	1 296	1 142
Cass	1 418	4 769 730	10.8	7.3	0.6	2.9	0.9	2.2	72.4	172.3	89.2	43.1	825	808
Charlevoix	1 150	4 194 441	10.6	5.9	1.3	5.8	28.6	3.6	42.0	158.1	43.7	73.2	2 813	2 799
Cheboygan	787	2 583 533	17.3	8.3	0.3	7.1	0.7	3.5	58.4	82.5	33.6	37.9	1 467	1 464
Chippewa	1 196	4 184 040	10.1	7.0	2.7	11.4	6.7	6.0	52.6	135.4	67.2	34.8	894	891
Clare	1 104	4 192 533	8.2	5.7	0.9	5.4	0.8	1.5	74.1	127.0	64.5	31.2	1 013	1 002
Clinton	1 742	6 413 165	10.6	9.9	0.7	3.5	0.4	3.2	69.3	200.2	105.1	60.4	794	775
Crawford	409	1 431 323	13.6	11.5	1.6	16.3	4.0	2.0	47.9	39.4	16.7	15.9	1 133	1 086
Delta	1 241	4 680 702	6.7	9.5	0.0	5.2	3.8	6.7	65.7	127.4	66.1	38.2	1 037	1 028
Dickinson	1 535	6 348 874	4.3	5.6	1.0	3.4	58.2	2.3	23.9	184.8	56.0	31.4	1 196	1 182
Eaton	2 554	9 735 640	10.8	10.4	3.7	4.1	3.2	4.4	60.8	310.5	152.5	99.7	923	899
Emmet	1 325	5 336 908	10.4	6.0	0.7	4.0	16.4	3.6	56.1	264.7	141.6	74.6	2 266	2 213
Genesee	15 234	64 330 939	5.5	5.9	1.4	3.5	24.1	3.5	55.1	2 005.4	1 056.8	353.2	844	786
Gladwin	706	2 311 382	11.6	6.0	5.6	5.3	0.0	6.6	61.0	64.7	29.2	22.5	882	866
Gogebic	622	2 249 336	12.5	6.4	0.2	9.6	0.9	8.4	60.0	90.5	45.8	17.4	1 082	1 078
Grand Traverse	3 921	13 601 114	7.7	6.2	1.5	4.9	19.6	4.5	54.3	484.0	209.1	154.5	1 733	1 707
Gratiot	1 175	3 955 893	11.4	7.1	0.6	5.7	0.5	4.7	67.3	148.7	93.4	35.9	853	831
Hillsdale	1 203	4 074 488	12.8	8.9	1.5	5.5	0.3	8.2	59.8	131.8	71.6	31.6	684	680
Houghton	1 000	3 212 799	11.7	7.0	0.3	9.7	5.5	5.2	58.7	146.4	70.0	29.8	815	804
Huron	1 172	3 974 661	13.7	7.4	3.0	6.1	17.1	4.5	45.7	144.4	58.3	49.0	1 508	1 483
Ingham	10 953	47 886 830	7.3	7.2	3.2	4.6	11.6	7.8	53.9	1 384.5	665.7	427.0	1 516	1 387
Ionia	1 653	5 904 984	8.9	6.9	0.5	4.2	2.6	4.1	71.7	208.2	123.1	53.2	832	780
Iosco	1 129	3 442 430	9.4	4.0	0.3	4.8	27.8	2.2	46.8	108.8	50.8	33.6	1 326	1 313
Iron	408	1 333 527	19.7	8.3	1.1	6.9	9.9	12.6	38.2	67.8	34.2	17.2	1 482	1 471
Isabella	1 686	5 798 126	10.7	6.7	1.2	7.0	29.5	4.2	39.4	236.5	148.6	46.1	653	641
Jackson	4 304	17 626 740	7.6	8.1	2.4	4.2	3.5	3.4	69.5	585.1	325.3	139.2	868	809
Kalamazoo	6 988	32 644 262	7.1	11.8	16.7	2.9	2.7	3.6	54.2	970.9	521.9	297.6	1 169	1 137
Kalkaska	695	2 106 824	12.6	6.6	0.4	8.0	43.8	2.8	23.7	84.6	15.9	18.4	1 075	1 058
Kent	16 442	72 374 352	7.5	10.6	3.2	4.8	1.8	4.9	66.1	2 471.0	1 223.4	763.8	1 243	1 084

1. Based on the resident population estimated as of July 1 of the year shown.

Table B. States and Counties — Local Government Finances, Government Employment, and Income Taxes

STATE County	Local government finances, 2012 (cont.) Direct general expenditure Total (mil dol)	Per capita¹ (dollars)	Education	Health and hospitals	Police protection	Public welfare	Highways	Debt outstanding Total (mil dol)	Per capita¹ (dollars)	Government employment, 2015 Federal civilian	Federal military	State and local	Individual income tax returns, 2014 Number of returns	Mean adjusted gross income	Mean income tax
	185	186	187	188	189	190	191	192	193	194	195	196	197	198	199
MARYLAND—Cont'd															
St. Mary's	331.8	3 045	62.8	2.2	6.2	0.9	2.7	197.3	1 810	9 518	2 521	4 681	50 850	72 300	8 533
Somerset	126.9	4 833	34.0	0.9	3.5	0.2	3.0	52.4	1 996	48	94	2 970	8 790	39 636	3 312
Talbot	130.3	3 419	40.1	3.0	8.2	0.8	5.1	87.8	2 304	214	135	1 661	19 050	81 098	12 135
Washington	564.3	3 783	59.9	0.7	4.0	0.4	4.5	391.3	2 623	581	464	8 342	67 940	54 107	5 735
Wicomico	357.2	3 549	57.8	1.0	6.3	3.1	2.6	203.7	2 024	284	313	7 673	45 180	47 933	4 990
Worcester	300.6	5 827	35.7	2.9	10.6	0.7	4.0	284.8	5 522	182	192	3 540	27 300	56 830	6 995
Baltimore city	4 080.5	6 567	34.4	2.9	9.1	0.0	5.1	2 807.8	4 519	10 101	2 039	57 071	272 490	48 890	5 957
MASSACHUSETTS	X	X	X	X	X	X	X	X	X	45 980	19 682	396 228	3 343 170	85 436	13 773
Barnstable	1 041.6	4 835	45.9	1.1	5.3	0.2	3.5	892.5	4 143	1 685	1 182	13 356	124 250	68 293	9 131
Berkshire	629.4	4 841	60.3	0.5	3.2	0.3	5.9	274.5	2 111	373	309	8 129	64 490	59 004	7 365
Bristol	1 991.8	3 614	57.9	0.9	5.0	1.0	2.5	1 318.2	2 392	1 133	1 376	27 749	267 240	60 463	7 437
Dukes	159.8	9 379	47.0	2.7	4.8	0.1	3.1	92.7	5 440	45	42	1 505	10 710	69 717	9 508
Essex	2 925.1	3 871	57.7	0.4	4.6	0.2	2.8	1 876.8	2 484	3 673	1 967	38 352	388 700	79 292	12 229
Franklin	333.5	4 661	58.8	0.4	2.7	0.4	4.8	96.2	1 344	197	171	4 915	35 390	53 676	5 813
Hampden	2 073.1	4 449	58.0	0.5	4.5	0.6	2.9	1 537.4	3 300	3 888	1 367	30 436	216 810	53 875	6 386
Hampshire	545.4	3 413	56.1	0.8	5.8	0.5	3.8	283.7	1 775	1 327	360	17 208	71 900	65 379	8 257
Middlesex	7 035.9	4 577	49.7	11.6	4.1	0.2	2.6	4 420.3	2 876	11 473	4 910	77 417	786 490	107 175	18 945
Nantucket	106.8	10 369	26.6	0.4	4.0	6.2	0.6	224.6	21 811	50	54	668	7 330	87 282	13 925
Norfolk	2 651.4	3 889	55.1	0.5	5.1	0.2	3.0	2 012.1	2 951	1 550	1 695	33 542	348 940	120 794	22 723
Plymouth	1 986.2	3 974	61.8	0.6	4.6	0.3	2.6	1 305.2	2 612	3 325	1 278	28 108	255 110	79 563	12 000
Suffolk	3 805.2	5 112	33.9	7.5	8.8	1.3	1.5	2 110.9	2 836	14 258	2 995	66 152	373 450	88 577	15 592
Worcester	3 304.7	4 099	61.5	0.4	4.0	0.2	3.4	2 495.3	3 095	3 003	1 976	48 691	392 410	68 477	9 157
MICHIGAN	X	X	X	X	X	X	X	X	X	51 545	17 943	534 668	4 685 120	56 949	7 266
Alcona	27.1	2 545	30.2	4.5	5.3	0.9	24.2	3.8	359	21	17	318	4 810	40 512	3 726
Alger	32.4	3 395	36.3	4.6	2.9	0.0	17.5	26.3	2 754	79	13	671	4 010	44 783	4 132
Allegan	347.7	3 103	55.1	7.4	3.5	3.5	7.8	410.3	3 662	169	185	4 813	54 210	54 779	6 228
Alpena	248.9	8 516	25.0	59.1	1.5	0.3	2.8	47.7	1 630	122	49	2 826	13 930	42 274	4 315
Antrim	88.3	3 774	40.2	3.4	4.7	14.5	8.8	44.8	1 913	63	37	1 077	11 360	51 458	6 053
Arenac	43.2	2 790	50.7	2.2	3.0	0.5	12.9	32.8	2 122	42	24	680	7 230	40 267	3 748
Baraga	72.9	8 401	19.5	53.3	1.1	0.2	10.4	63.4	7 303	30	12	1 548	3 510	42 146	3 366
Barry	150.3	2 547	48.0	5.6	3.7	9.3	7.8	79.7	1 352	82	95	2 198	27 590	54 996	6 022
Bay	521.5	4 877	44.7	20.6	3.3	4.5	4.2	246.5	2 305	246	231	5 568	53 070	46 817	4 876
Benzie	56.3	3 226	36.8	7.9	2.1	12.2	8.7	30.3	1 734	36	43	682	8 990	46 202	4 613
Berrien	618.7	3 965	53.9	7.1	5.5	1.4	5.2	398.2	2 551	316	265	8 967	73 360	52 461	6 340
Branch	225.6	5 114	34.9	36.1	2.4	5.3	5.0	73.0	1 664	78	67	2 708	19 100	43 744	4 153
Calhoun	680.5	5 037	45.5	17.6	4.3	2.6	5.4	473.1	3 502	2 970	273	7 828	61 870	47 322	4 882
Cass	179.5	3 436	58.6	7.1	3.5	4.6	5.4	185.2	3 544	78	83	2 011	23 340	52 360	6 369
Charlevoix	145.4	5 587	41.5	16.3	2.3	9.8	7.0	79.2	3 043	52	63	1 667	13 560	56 894	8 304
Cheboygan	82.0	3 173	52.2	1.5	4.4	1.1	11.7	35.0	1 356	49	104	908	12 300	42 859	4 306
Chippewa	142.9	3 672	42.0	7.3	3.4	0.4	14.8	140.9	3 620	473	225	6 095	15 760	41 169	3 840
Clare	130.5	4 244	66.9	0.3	2.7	0.5	8.1	36.5	1 188	85	49	1 590	13 060	37 388	3 103
Clinton	197.5	2 598	55.6	0.4	4.2	0.6	7.3	261.6	3 442	223	128	1 894	36 010	62 231	7 638
Crawford	38.5	2 750	41.0	1.0	4.9	1.1	14.9	20.3	1 451	130	22	689	6 100	39 550	3 583
Delta	137.3	3 722	63.6	3.6	2.1	0.2	6.5	110.1	2 984	193	58	1 823	17 600	46 337	4 632
Dickinson	190.3	7 257	25.2	50.0	2.2	0.1	4.5	120.1	4 580	841	61	2 065	13 090	49 517	5 441
Eaton	316.4	2 929	51.9	3.6	5.8	6.6	6.0	453.6	4 200	208	174	5 392	53 570	52 399	5 530
Emmet	280.3	8 515	27.0	38.8	1.4	4.8	4.5	162.6	4 941	99	54	2 449	17 660	57 354	7 549
Genesee	2 064.7	4 935	41.9	28.1	3.5	1.1	3.3	995.9	2 380	1 059	657	19 420	192 350	46 305	4 970
Gladwin	61.5	2 415	46.1	2.0	3.8	0.6	13.3	37.6	1 474	51	40	767	11 160	41 366	3 673
Gogebic	91.1	5 666	31.9	7.4	3.1	10.2	9.5	75.9	4 719	145	22	1 495	6 680	43 080	4 459
Grand Traverse	471.3	5 288	46.6	17.8	2.7	5.6	3.8	445.4	4 998	495	259	5 973	47 620	57 770	7 664
Gratiot	152.9	3 635	57.9	7.3	3.1	1.2	8.1	103.0	2 449	73	58	2 340	17 030	47 017	5 161
Hillsdale	131.8	2 850	51.6	0.9	3.3	14.1	8.6	74.2	1 605	96	73	2 380	19 800	43 599	3 996
Houghton	140.9	3 858	41.4	5.6	2.0	13.7	7.0	113.0	3 095	164	88	3 628	14 610	45 438	4 356
Huron	148.9	4 587	35.1	11.1	2.9	10.7	18.5	113.5	3 496	97	67	1 674	16 580	46 214	5 175
Ingham	1 371.5	4 868	44.9	13.6	4.2	3.1	3.5	1 588.9	5 640	1 490	626	40 168	123 930	54 263	6 695
Ionia	225.2	3 523	60.0	7.0	2.6	0.5	5.8	294.7	4 610	115	95	3 261	27 030	46 238	4 421
Iosco	108.1	4 265	39.8	17.8	2.4	6.7	7.8	52.0	2 052	113	62	1 508	12 100	38 536	3 428
Iron	59.7	5 151	21.7	4.9	2.7	29.2	9.9	46.6	4 026	34	18	926	5 560	39 399	3 361
Isabella	230.9	3 270	25.5	39.2	3.2	5.6	6.2	128.0	1 812	160	109	10 580	26 400	48 867	5 355
Jackson	586.0	3 655	54.4	10.1	2.6	3.6	6.4	539.6	3 366	340	244	7 316	71 280	49 531	5 312
Kalamazoo	958.5	3 765	47.3	14.6	7.5	1.0	4.4	1 168.8	4 591	700	416	13 696	119 410	60 557	7 859
Kalkaska	63.6	3 721	23.4	42.5	3.6	0.2	7.4	40.1	2 342	27	28	916	7 970	42 502	4 279
Kent	2 442.6	3 975	51.3	6.7	4.7	1.7	3.6	3 992.0	6 497	2 680	1 070	23 625	302 010	61 305	7 924

1. Based on the resident population estimated as of July 1 of the year shown.

Table B. States and Counties — **Land Area and Population**

STATE/County code	CBSA code[1]	County type[2]	STATE County	Land area[3] (sq mi) 2016	Total persons 2016	Rank	Per square mile	White	Black	American Indian, Alaska Native	Asian and Pacific Islander	Percent Hispanic or Latino[4]	Under 5 years	5 to 17 years	18 to 24 years	25 to 34 years	35 to 44 years	45 to 54 years
				1	2	3	4	5	6	7	8	9	10	11	12	13	14	15
			MICHIGAN—Cont'd															
26 083	26340	9	Keweenaw	540.1	2 199	3 030	4.1	98.1	0.4	0.7	0.3	1.4	3.5	12.3	5.0	7.4	8.4	10.9
26 085	...	9	Lake	567.5	11 496	2 321	20.3	87.2	10.0	1.9	0.7	2.8	4.3	12.4	5.7	8.5	9.3	13.5
26 087	19820	1	Lapeer	644.2	88 340	654	137.1	93.2	1.5	1.0	0.9	4.7	4.9	16.5	8.2	10.4	11.2	15.7
26 089	45900	9	Leelanau	347.2	21 765	1 742	62.7	91.9	0.8	3.8	1.0	4.0	4.2	12.1	6.5	8.3	11.8	11.9
26 091	10300	4	Lenawee	749.6	98 504	601	131.4	88.5	3.6	1.1	0.9	7.8	5.5	16.0	9.3	11.5	11.7	13.7
26 093	19820	2	Livingston	565.1	188 624	344	333.8	95.8	0.8	0.9	1.4	2.4	5.1	17.0	8.2	10.5	11.4	16.3
26 095	...	7	Luce	899.1	6 358	2 725	7.1	81.8	11.9	7.3	0.7	1.5	4.0	12.7	7.9	12.7	13.1	13.8
26 097	...	7	Mackinac	1 021.9	10 820	2 370	10.6	78.7	3.1	20.6	1.1	1.6	3.8	12.4	6.4	8.6	9.7	13.5
26 099	19820	1	Macomb	479.1	867 730	64	1 811.2	81.8	12.5	0.9	4.6	2.5	5.5	16.0	8.3	13.0	12.2	14.7
26 101	...	7	Manistee	542.2	24 373	1 628	45.0	91.0	4.0	3.3	0.7	2.9	4.0	13.4	7.4	10.4	9.9	13.0
26 103	32100	5	Marquette	1 808.5	66 435	801	36.7	94.3	2.2	3.0	1.2	1.5	4.8	13.2	15.1	11.7	10.7	11.8
26 105	31220	7	Mason	495.1	28 876	1 462	58.3	93.0	1.5	1.7	1.0	4.6	5.2	15.5	7.3	10.4	10.3	12.8
26 107	13660	6	Mecosta	555.1	43 221	1 106	77.9	93.3	3.8	1.6	1.3	2.2	4.8	13.8	19.0	10.9	9.3	11.1
26 109	31940	3	Menominee	1 044.0	23 281	1 665	22.3	94.6	0.6	3.5	0.7	1.7	4.6	14.3	6.9	9.5	10.2	14.1
26 111	33220	3	Midland	516.3	83 462	679	161.7	92.9	2.0	1.0	2.9	2.7	5.4	16.3	8.6	12.2	11.5	14.3
26 113	15620	9	Missaukee	564.7	15 102	2 091	26.7	95.6	1.0	1.5	0.8	2.7	6.5	16.7	7.6	10.9	10.0	13.4
26 115	33780	2	Monroe	549.4	149 208	439	271.6	93.2	3.1	0.9	1.0	3.5	5.3	16.6	8.0	11.5	11.7	14.6
26 117	24340	2	Montcalm	705.4	62 974	839	89.3	93.3	2.8	1.2	0.7	3.5	5.8	16.8	8.0	12.1	12.3	13.9
26 119	...	9	Montmorency	546.7	9 173	2 495	16.8	97.4	0.9	1.4	0.5	1.3	3.4	11.4	5.3	7.8	8.3	12.3
26 121	34740	3	Muskegon	500.0	173 408	373	346.8	78.7	15.6	1.6	1.1	5.6	6.2	17.3	8.6	12.8	11.9	13.1
26 123	...	6	Newaygo	815.7	47 938	1 019	58.8	92.0	1.6	1.3	0.8	5.6	5.9	16.8	7.5	11.3	10.5	14.0
26 125	19820	1	Oakland	867.5	1 243 970	33	1 434.0	74.5	15.0	0.8	8.0	3.9	5.5	16.0	8.2	12.8	12.4	14.8
26 127	...	6	Oceana	512.1	26 027	1 561	50.8	83.4	1.1	1.6	0.5	14.8	5.7	17.8	7.7	10.3	10.4	13.2
26 129	...	9	Ogemaw	563.5	20 904	1 778	37.1	96.1	0.7	1.7	0.7	2.2	4.7	13.8	6.7	9.5	9.7	12.6
26 131	...	9	Ontonagon	1 311.3	5 911	2 764	4.5	96.5	0.8	1.9	0.8	1.4	2.2	10.2	4.4	5.4	7.8	13.9
26 133	...	9	Osceola	566.4	23 110	1 674	40.8	96.5	1.7	1.4	0.6	1.7	5.9	17.1	7.3	10.8	10.8	13.1
26 135	...	9	Oscoda	565.7	8 264	2 570	14.6	97.2	0.8	1.5	0.5	1.5	5.2	13.5	6.7	8.6	8.2	11.4
26 137	...	7	Otsego	515.0	24 470	1 623	47.5	96.0	1.2	1.6	1.0	1.8	5.6	15.9	7.8	10.8	10.5	13.8
26 139	24340	2	Ottawa	563.6	282 250	243	500.8	85.8	2.3	0.7	3.4	9.5	6.4	18.0	13.5	12.0	11.6	12.4
26 141	...	7	Presque Isle	658.7	12 762	2 244	19.4	97.0	1.0	1.3	0.6	1.2	3.9	12.2	5.8	7.2	8.9	12.1
26 143	...	7	Roscommon	519.6	23 700	1 650	45.6	96.1	1.0	1.5	1.0	1.7	3.8	11.5	5.6	7.7	7.9	12.5
26 145	40980	3	Saginaw	800.5	192 326	342	240.3	71.3	19.8	0.8	1.7	8.4	5.8	15.9	9.8	12.1	10.9	13.0
26 147	19820	1	St. Clair	721.2	159 587	406	221.3	93.1	3.5	1.1	1.0	3.3	5.1	16.3	8.0	10.8	11.3	15.3
26 149	44780	4	St. Joseph	500.6	60 853	856	121.6	88.6	3.8	1.0	1.1	7.7	6.6	18.2	8.1	11.7	11.4	12.8
26 151	...	6	Sanilac	962.6	41 409	1 142	43.0	95.0	0.9	0.9	0.5	3.7	5.4	16.4	7.5	10.2	10.4	13.6
26 153	...	7	Schoolcraft	1 171.4	8 001	2 599	6.8	89.5	1.1	11.6	0.6	0.9	4.1	12.9	6.8	7.6	9.6	13.5
26 155	37020	4	Shiawassee	530.8	68 554	779	129.2	95.6	1.1	1.0	0.8	2.8	5.3	16.3	8.6	11.3	11.5	14.7
26 157	...	6	Tuscola	803.4	53 338	941	66.4	94.7	1.1	1.1	0.5	3.3	5.2	15.6	7.7	11.0	11.0	14.2
26 159	28020	2	Van Buren	607.8	75 223	733	123.8	83.5	4.7	1.6	1.0	11.5	6.2	17.6	7.9	11.0	11.5	13.5
26 161	11460	2	Washtenaw	706.0	364 709	190	516.6	73.5	13.9	1.0	10.4	4.6	5.0	13.9	19.0	14.2	11.3	12.1
26 163	19820	1	Wayne	612.0	1 749 366	19	2 858.4	51.6	40.0	1.1	4.0	5.8	6.6	17.4	9.1	13.6	12.0	13.5
26 165	15620	7	Wexford	565.0	33 163	1 353	58.7	96.3	1.2	1.5	1.0	1.8	6.1	17.4	7.5	11.4	10.9	13.3
27 000	...	0	**MINNESOTA**	79 626.7	5 519 952	X	69.3	82.6	7.1	1.7	5.6	5.2	6.4	17.0	9.2	13.6	12.3	13.2
27 001	...	8	Aitkin	1 821.7	15 583	2 069	8.6	95.0	1.0	3.3	0.8	1.4	3.8	13.1	5.4	8.0	8.3	12.0
27 003	33460	1	Anoka	423.0	345 957	198	817.9	84.6	7.0	1.4	5.4	4.4	6.2	17.9	8.0	13.1	13.1	15.0
27 005	...	6	Becker	1 315.1	33 734	1 333	25.7	89.7	1.0	9.7	0.9	1.9	6.4	17.9	7.3	10.5	10.9	11.9
27 007	13420	7	Beltrami	2 504.7	46 106	1 045	18.4	75.5	1.5	22.8	1.2	2.2	7.4	17.8	13.7	12.5	10.4	10.4
27 009	41060	3	Benton	408.3	39 992	1 175	97.9	92.7	4.2	1.0	1.8	2.2	7.1	17.6	8.1	15.2	12.9	12.7
27 011	...	9	Big Stone	499.0	5 050	2 832	10.1	97.4	0.8	0.9	0.4	1.4	5.5	15.1	6.8	9.3	9.0	11.9
27 013	31860	3	Blue Earth	747.8	66 441	800	88.8	90.3	4.6	0.6	2.9	3.4	5.5	14.1	21.9	13.7	10.3	9.9
27 015	35580	6	Brown	611.1	25 331	1 593	41.5	94.4	0.8	0.3	0.9	4.2	5.7	16.2	9.8	10.6	10.0	12.2
27 017	20260	2	Carlton	861.3	35 738	1 283	41.5	90.5	2.0	7.2	1.0	1.7	5.5	17.1	7.5	12.0	12.5	14.0
27 019	33460	1	Carver	354.2	100 262	595	283.1	90.9	2.3	0.6	3.8	4.1	6.5	20.8	8.2	10.9	14.0	16.0
27 021	14660	9	Cass	2 021.5	28 993	1 456	14.3	85.3	0.8	13.3	0.8	2.0	6.0	15.3	6.3	9.3	9.1	12.3
27 023	...	7	Chippewa	581.1	12 133	2 285	20.9	89.5	1.3	1.6	2.4	6.9	7.1	15.8	8.4	11.4	10.2	11.9
27 025	33460	1	Chisago	414.9	54 748	919	132.0	94.9	1.8	1.1	1.4	2.1	5.6	17.3	7.9	12.0	12.3	16.0
27 027	22020	3	Clay	1 045.3	62 875	840	60.2	90.1	3.5	2.2	2.0	4.5	7.1	16.8	15.3	14.0	12.1	10.7
27 029	...	8	Clearwater	999.0	8 827	2 521	8.8	88.0	1.3	11.5	0.9	1.8	6.2	18.7	6.8	10.5	11.1	12.0
27 031	...	9	Cook	1 452.4	5 286	2 813	3.6	88.2	1.4	9.3	1.3	2.1	4.4	11.1	5.9	10.0	9.8	12.5
27 033	...	7	Cottonwood	639.9	11 470	2 327	17.9	88.3	1.4	0.9	3.8	6.9	7.0	17.0	7.6	9.5	10.1	11.8
27 035	14660	4	Crow Wing	998.4	63 940	829	64.0	96.4	1.3	1.5	0.9	1.5	5.7	16.1	7.0	11.1	10.7	12.5
27 037	33460	1	Dakota	562.4	417 486	166	742.3	81.8	7.3	0.9	5.8	6.8	6.6	18.1	8.1	13.0	13.1	14.5
27 039	40340	3	Dodge	439.3	20 506	1 798	46.7	93.3	1.0	0.8	1.2	5.2	6.6	20.1	7.9	11.6	13.2	13.9
27 041	10820	6	Douglas	637.0	37 456	1 236	58.8	97.0	0.9	0.7	0.8	1.6	5.7	15.6	7.1	11.8	10.7	11.9
27 043	...	6	Faribault	712.5	13 935	2 168	19.6	92.1	0.9	0.7	0.6	6.6	6.4	16.5	7.0	9.8	10.7	11.9

1. CBSA = Core Based Statistical Area. See Appendix A for explanation. See Appendix B for list of metropolitan areas with component counties. See Appendix A for definition.   3. Dry land or land partially or temporarily covered by water.   2. County type code from the Economic Research Service of USDA Rural-Urban Continuum Codes.   4. May be of any race.

Table B. States and Counties — **Population and Households**

STATE County	55 to 64 years	65 to 74 years	75 years and over	Percent female	2000	2010	2000–2010	2010–2016	Births	Deaths	Net migration	Number	Persons per household	Family house-holds	Female family house-holder[1]	One person
	16	17	18	19	20	21	22	23	24	25	26	27	28	29	30	31
MICHIGAN—Cont'd																
Keweenaw	17.9	20.8	13.8	48.7	2 301	2 156	-6.3	2.0	111	116	12	1 040	2.10	61.1	8.7	35.2
Lake	19.9	16.3	10.2	48.9	11 333	11 539	1.8	-0.4	601	961	335	4 365	2.53	60.8	10.0	34.1
Lapeer	16.0	10.6	6.5	49.3	87 904	88 316	0.5	0.0	5 154	4 998	-153	32 682	2.64	74.3	9.3	21.9
Leelanau	18.9	16.8	13.1	50.9	21 119	21 708	2.8	0.3	1 053	1 458	351	9 234	2.31	68.7	6.7	25.8
Lenawee	14.5	10.6	7.1	49.3	98 890	99 892	1.0	-1.4	6 564	6 068	-1 802	37 964	2.46	66.2	11.0	28.7
Livingston	15.6	10.0	6.0	49.9	156 951	180 967	15.3	4.2	11 041	8 642	4 950	68 980	2.66	74.7	8.5	21.1
Luce	15.3	11.3	9.2	41.7	7 024	6 631	-5.6	-4.1	333	453	-142	2 377	2.27	63.9	9.2	31.3
Mackinac	18.2	15.9	11.6	48.9	11 943	11 113	-6.9	-2.6	519	823	5	5 209	2.07	61.9	9.0	32.1
Macomb	14.1	9.2	7.0	51.3	788 149	840 987	6.7	3.2	57 817	51 571	21 223	336 379	2.52	66.3	13.0	28.9
Manistee	17.6	14.3	10.1	48.0	24 527	24 733	0.8	-1.5	1 169	1 924	457	10 142	2.28	63.2	8.2	32.0
Marquette	14.7	10.5	7.4	49.6	64 634	67 077	3.8	-1.0	3 981	4 030	-532	26 457	2.38	59.4	7.7	31.9
Mason	16.5	12.9	9.2	50.1	28 274	28 705	1.5	0.6	1 849	2 040	426	12 248	2.30	65.9	11.1	29.6
Mecosta	13.5	10.5	7.1	49.4	40 553	42 798	5.5	1.0	2 661	2 314	103	15 478	2.61	62.3	8.2	28.7
Menominee	17.6	12.8	10.1	49.2	25 326	24 029	-5.1	-3.1	1 290	1 653	-317	10 679	2.19	61.4	9.1	34.5
Midland	14.3	9.5	7.9	50.7	82 874	83 629	0.9	-0.2	5 399	4 406	-1 133	33 617	2.45	68.6	8.9	25.7
Missaukee	15.0	12.0	8.1	49.1	14 478	14 849	2.6	1.7	1 109	1 014	175	5 866	2.52	69.3	8.9	26.5
Monroe	15.3	10.0	7.0	50.6	145 945	152 021	4.2	-1.9	9 565	8 765	-3 630	58 566	2.55	70.4	10.9	25.1
Montcalm	14.2	9.8	6.9	48.4	61 266	63 342	3.4	-0.6	4 513	3 703	-1 123	23 284	2.59	69.8	11.3	25.7
Montmorency	21.1	17.8	12.6	49.3	10 315	9 765	-5.3	-6.1	401	980	-27	4 070	2.27	64.2	9.8	30.4
Muskegon	14.3	9.4	6.5	50.2	170 200	172 188	1.2	0.7	13 168	10 455	-1 520	64 490	2.56	67.7	14.6	27.3
Newaygo	15.4	11.0	7.7	49.7	47 874	48 460	1.2	-1.1	3 439	3 037	-868	18 339	2.58	70.5	9.8	24.0
Oakland	14.3	9.4	6.5	51.2	1 194 156	1 202 362	0.7	3.5	83 694	63 570	22 936	493 489	2.47	65.3	10.6	29.3
Oceana	15.2	11.7	8.0	49.6	26 873	26 570	-1.1	-2.0	1 931	1 598	-877	9 822	2.60	72.2	9.0	23.9
Ogemaw	18.1	14.5	10.3	50.3	21 645	21 699	0.2	-3.7	1 180	1 859	-19	9 434	2.22	65.0	11.3	29.8
Ontonagon	21.5	20.2	14.3	49.3	7 818	6 780	-13.3	-12.8	185	609	-431	3 084	2.01	56.4	4.3	38.2
Osceola	15.1	11.7	8.3	49.4	23 197	23 528	1.4	-1.8	1 676	1 496	-532	8 757	2.60	67.9	11.4	26.2
Oscoda	19.5	15.8	11.1	49.2	9 418	8 640	-8.3	-4.4	525	775	-98	3 686	2.27	62.9	6.4	33.0
Otsego	15.3	11.9	8.3	50.4	23 301	24 164	3.7	1.3	1 568	1 622	360	9 956	2.38	68.1	8.7	25.2
Ottawa	12.0	8.1	5.9	50.7	238 314	263 801	10.7	7.0	21 035	11 030	8 281	96 283	2.74	73.7	8.6	20.5
Presque Isle	19.4	16.9	13.5	50.2	14 411	13 376	-7.2	-4.6	585	1 197	26	5 999	2.13	65.3	6.0	31.2
Roscommon	20.2	18.6	12.2	50.0	25 469	24 449	-4.0	-3.1	1 081	2 419	697	11 543	2.06	60.9	10.4	33.7
Saginaw	14.3	10.3	7.9	51.4	210 039	200 169	-4.7	-3.9	14 212	12 815	-8 997	77 925	2.44	63.8	14.8	31.2
St. Clair	15.5	10.4	7.2	50.3	164 235	163 040	-0.7	-2.1	9 898	10 559	-2 731	64 143	2.47	67.5	10.5	26.8
St. Joseph	14.1	9.9	7.2	50.2	62 422	61 295	-1.8	-0.7	5 119	3 828	-1 625	23 270	2.59	69.2	11.6	25.9
Sanilac	16.0	11.9	8.7	50.2	44 547	43 114	-3.2	-4.0	2 781	2 887	-1 507	16 280	2.55	65.5	8.3	29.8
Schoolcraft	19.6	14.9	11.0	50.5	8 903	8 485	-4.7	-5.7	419	687	-217	3 419	2.38	62.3	8.0	33.0
Shiawassee	15.0	10.3	7.0	50.6	71 687	70 648	-1.4	-3.0	4 429	4 374	-2 115	27 409	2.49	70.0	10.5	24.5
Tuscola	15.7	11.4	8.1	49.9	58 266	55 729	-4.4	-4.3	3 467	3 561	-2 286	21 304	2.49	70.3	9.3	25.3
Van Buren	15.3	10.4	6.6	50.2	76 263	76 265	0.0	-1.4	5 698	4 536	-2 161	28 367	2.61	68.2	11.7	25.7
Washtenaw	11.5	7.8	5.1	50.5	322 895	345 066	6.9	5.7	23 359	13 512	9 891	138 067	2.43	57.5	9.5	30.6
Wayne	13.4	8.4	6.0	51.9	2 061 162	1 820 641	-11.7	-3.9	146 578	112 285	-104 909	667 275	2.63	62.5	19.5	32.7
Wexford	15.0	10.8	7.5	50.2	30 484	32 735	7.4	1.3	2 577	2 168	49	12 673	2.56	68.0	9.7	26.0
MINNESOTA	13.4	8.6	6.5	50.2	4 919 479	5 303 924	7.8	4.1	431 430	254 314	42 028	2 124 745	2.49	64.8	9.6	28.3
Aitkin	18.4	18.4	12.7	49.5	15 301	16 202	5.9	-3.8	701	1 271	-5	7 609	2.05	64.4	6.6	30.4
Anoka	13.8	8.0	4.9	50.0	298 084	330 858	11.0	4.6	25 961	11 635	1 125	124 477	2.70	71.9	10.8	22.5
Becker	15.1	11.7	8.3	50.1	30 000	32 504	8.3	3.8	2 614	2 149	806	13 562	2.41	67.7	9.4	26.4
Beltrami	12.2	8.8	6.7	50.2	39 650	44 442	12.1	3.7	4 342	2 564	-142	16 739	2.59	65.0	14.2	28.3
Benton	11.8	7.8	6.8	49.9	34 226	38 451	12.3	4.0	3 541	2 050	-4	15 632	2.45	64.7	10.9	26.1
Big Stone	16.5	11.9	13.9	50.9	5 820	5 269	-9.5	-4.2	340	460	-104	2 282	2.18	66.5	7.0	30.8
Blue Earth	11.0	7.4	6.2	49.5	55 941	64 013	14.4	3.8	4 605	2 896	687	24 847	2.46	57.8	7.4	27.5
Brown	14.8	10.1	10.5	50.4	26 911	25 893	-3.8	-2.2	1 698	1 836	-431	10 679	2.27	63.6	6.5	30.3
Carlton	14.3	9.6	7.5	47.7	31 671	35 386	11.7	1.0	2 308	2 298	323	13 398	2.51	66.3	8.1	28.0
Carver	12.8	6.4	4.4	50.4	70 205	91 086	29.7	10.1	7 217	2 877	4 810	34 421	2.76	75.4	7.2	20.2
Cass	17.1	15.0	9.5	49.0	27 150	28 567	5.2	1.5	2 140	1 905	266	12 856	2.19	69.7	10.4	25.1
Chippewa	14.4	10.5	10.2	50.6	13 088	12 441	-4.9	-2.5	1 038	914	-426	5 036	2.36	65.8	10.3	30.7
Chisago	14.0	8.9	6.0	48.3	41 101	53 887	31.1	1.6	3 452	2 367	-291	19 808	2.63	72.0	7.4	22.2
Clay	11.1	6.8	6.1	50.6	51 229	58 999	15.2	6.6	5 118	2 846	1 601	22 674	2.51	64.8	9.2	28.1
Clearwater	14.6	11.2	8.9	49.5	8 423	8 695	3.2	1.5	671	594	74	3 486	2.48	67.4	7.2	27.5
Cook	20.1	16.7	9.4	50.2	5 168	5 176	0.2	2.1	284	271	121	2 652	1.93	64.0	8.1	29.3
Cottonwood	14.1	11.1	11.8	50.5	12 167	11 687	-3.9	-1.9	976	851	-354	4 779	2.38	64.8	7.3	31.4
Crow Wing	15.1	12.5	9.2	50.1	55 099	62 500	13.4	2.3	4 542	3 976	909	26 365	2.36	66.2	9.1	27.5
Dakota	13.5	7.9	5.3	50.8	355 904	398 581	12.0	4.7	32 587	14 444	479	156 466	2.59	69.5	10.2	24.4
Dodge	13.0	7.6	6.1	50.1	17 731	20 087	13.3	2.1	1 577	852	-277	7 556	2.67	73.9	9.5	21.8
Douglas	14.8	12.1	10.3	50.0	32 821	36 009	9.7	4.0	2 544	2 473	1 277	15 559	2.32	66.0	5.1	28.8
Faribault	15.9	11.2	11.6	50.3	16 181	14 553	-10.1	-4.2	909	1 175	-368	6 374	2.18	65.3	8.4	29.9

1. No spouse present.

Table B. States and Counties — Population, Vital Statistics, Health, and Crime

STATE County	Persons in group quarters, 2016	Daytime population, 2011–2015 Number	Employment/residence ratio	Births, 2016 Total	Rate[1]	Deaths, 2016 Number	Rate[1]	Persons under 65 with no health insurance, 2015 Number	Percent	Medicare, 2015 Total Beneficiaries	Enrolled in Original Medicare	Enrolled in Medicare Advantage	Serious crimes known to police,[2] 2014 Total Number	Rate[3]
	32	33	34	35	36	37	38	39	40	41	42	43	44	45
MICHIGAN—Cont'd														
Keweenaw	10	1 917	0.66	18	8.2	16	7.3	113	7.9	1 063	705	358	51	2 313
Lake	397	10 315	0.65	98	8.5	146	12.7	747	9.3	3 153	2 294	859	261	2 296
Lapeer	1 699	76 083	0.67	826	9.4	867	9.8	5 375	7.4	16 224	10 652	5 572	1 051	1 187
Leelanau	284	19 876	0.80	168	7.7	231	10.6	1 338	8.6	4 909	3 085	1 824	114	523
Lenawee	5 490	88 068	0.74	1 037	10.5	985	10.0	5 210	6.8	21 551	15 076	6 475	1 276	1 287
Livingston	1 385	151 715	0.64	1 798	9.5	1 502	8.0	7 412	4.7	25 784	16 204	9 580	1 707	920
Luce	1 161	6 832	1.17	53	8.3	85	13.4	390	9.8	1 520	1 070	450	136	2 097
Mackinac	95	11 195	1.03	81	7.5	133	12.3	974	12.3	3 010	2 032	978	356	3 217
Macomb	7 518	791 590	0.84	9 377	10.8	8 438	9.7	51 706	7.2	159 902	96 766	63 136	18 157	2 114
Manistee	1 423	24 159	0.96	191	7.8	305	12.5	1 520	8.7	6 733	4 820	1 913	360	1 473
Marquette	3 891	68 100	1.02	617	9.3	664	10.0	2 899	5.6	14 027	9 100	4 927	1 074	1 581
Mason	442	28 515	0.98	303	10.5	296	10.3	1 699	7.6	7 738	5 636	2 102	693	2 423
Mecosta	3 338	42 341	0.94	417	9.6	355	8.2	2 528	7.8	9 057	5 760	3 297	877	2 029
Menominee	382	21 269	0.76	222	9.5	239	10.3	1 239	6.8	5 669	3 421	2 248	448	1 885
Midland	1 272	86 679	1.08	883	10.6	734	8.8	4 044	5.9	15 648	10 296	5 352	1 148	1 366
Missaukee	194	13 369	0.73	183	12.1	163	10.8	1 095	9.2	3 004	2 207	797	234	1 547
Monroe	1 463	128 247	0.67	1 456	9.8	1 420	9.5	7 345	5.9	28 548	19 035	9 513	2 847	1 947
Montcalm	2 830	56 780	0.74	688	10.9	592	9.4	3 773	7.5	13 918	8 851	5 067	1 148	1 889
Montmorency	156	9 146	0.91	63	6.9	163	17.8	603	9.4	4 039	2 982	1 057	39	421
Muskegon	6 372	164 236	0.89	2 059	11.9	1 734	10.0	10 030	7.1	36 381	21 414	14 967	6 907	4 041
Newaygo	557	43 892	0.77	551	11.5	523	10.9	2 973	7.7	9 566	5 095	4 471	931	1 955
Oakland	13 315	1 307 510	1.13	13 486	10.8	10 789	8.7	66 479	6.4	213 992	139 377	74 615	18 943	1 528
Oceana	303	24 005	0.78	298	11.4	250	9.6	2 289	11.0	6 436	4 126	2 310	564	2 395
Ogemaw	244	21 231	1.00	186	8.9	280	13.4	1 467	9.4	6 601	5 107	1 494	391	1 906
Ontonagon	83	5 937	0.82	27	4.6	109	18.4	345	8.7	2 302	1 586	716	37	594
Osceola	455	22 201	0.88	250	10.8	231	10.0	1 694	9.3	6 221	4 359	1 862	335	1 443
Oscoda	65	8 023	0.84	93	11.3	109	13.2	646	10.7	2 175	1 684	491	163	1 957
Otsego	345	25 442	1.12	262	10.7	286	11.7	1 527	8.0	5 958	4 258	1 700	415	1 719
Ottawa	8 734	259 927	0.90	3 415	12.1	1 842	6.5	13 605	5.8	45 402	18 348	27 054	4 730	1 719
Presque Isle	230	12 229	0.82	98	7.7	183	14.3	810	9.0	4 597	3 363	1 234	87	668
Roscommon	277	23 982	0.99	166	7.0	366	15.4	1 548	9.4	9 463	6 786	2 677	494	2 065
Saginaw	7 077	208 146	1.15	2 208	11.5	2 122	11.0	10 617	6.9	43 840	29 014	14 826	5 135	2 621
St. Clair	2 000	143 096	0.75	1 569	9.8	1 705	10.7	9 052	6.9	34 745	23 569	11 176	2 895	1 809
St. Joseph	765	59 003	0.92	795	13.1	577	9.5	4 391	8.7	11 577	7 794	3 783	1 240	2 114
Sanilac	564	38 663	0.80	427	10.3	489	11.8	2 979	9.0	9 523	7 095	2 428	519	1 351
Schoolcraft	140	8 208	0.97	62	7.7	105	13.1	597	9.8	2 446	1 744	702	NA	NA
Shiawassee	821	58 662	0.64	708	10.3	706	10.3	3 910	6.9	15 570	10 326	5 244	1 125	1 668
Tuscola	1 079	46 401	0.65	569	10.7	643	12.1	2 909	6.8	13 053	9 312	3 741	618	1 186
Van Buren	877	67 903	0.76	877	11.7	788	10.5	5 651	9.1	16 829	9 894	6 935	1 471	1 952
Washtenaw	22 313	391 595	1.22	3 709	10.2	2 323	6.4	16 409	5.5	49 455	33 816	15 639	7 632	2 139
Wayne	22 889	1 838 704	1.09	23 209	13.3	18 231	10.4	125 477	8.4	312 807	174 361	138 446	75 016	4 268
Wexford	389	34 542	1.14	411	12.4	323	9.7	1 973	7.3	7 972	5 839	2 133	908	2 898
MINNESOTA	132 543	5 432 271	1.00	69 190	12.5	41 938	7.6	237 981	5.2	889 652	375 169	514 483	137 882	2 527
Aitkin	274	14 502	0.79	106	6.8	198	12.7	734	6.8	5 133	2 043	3 090	377	2 409
Anoka	2 981	280 020	0.67	4 181	12.1	1 958	5.7	13 383	4.5	42 261	14 686	27 575	8 361	2 449
Becker	458	31 533	0.90	402	11.9	380	11.3	1 786	6.7	7 071	2 938	4 133	477	1 426
Beltrami	2 064	45 796	1.02	658	14.3	426	9.2	3 186	8.6	8 444	4 577	3 867	1 639	3 562
Benton	1 049	35 342	0.80	565	14.1	322	8.1	1 454	4.3	4 482	1 653	2 829	788	1 997
Big Stone	137	4 935	0.92	48	9.5	70	13.9	215	5.8	1 403	675	728	53	1 040
Blue Earth	4 165	69 649	1.13	700	10.5	454	6.8	2 407	4.4	11 505	5 550	5 955	1 770	2 682
Brown	1 112	27 203	1.13	281	11.1	272	10.7	825	4.3	5 864	2 961	2 903	298	1 181
Carlton	2 007	33 462	0.88	366	10.2	368	10.3	1 523	5.4	7 105	3 268	3 837	851	2 395
Carver	889	84 294	0.78	1 198	11.9	513	5.1	2 754	3.1	9 613	3 310	6 303	1 027	1 061
Cass	223	27 290	0.90	346	11.9	304	10.5	1 877	8.7	7 139	3 293	3 846	1 207	4 223
Chippewa	237	11 869	0.95	188	15.5	131	10.8	624	6.5	2 453	978	1 475	213	1 771
Chisago	1 681	43 440	0.62	563	10.3	387	7.1	1 905	4.2	9 574	3 381	6 193	704	1 308
Clay	3 152	50 463	0.68	864	13.7	456	7.3	2 193	4.3	8 676	4 274	4 402	1 150	1 881
Clearwater	115	8 184	0.84	111	12.6	84	9.5	563	8.1	2 000	893	1 107	148	1 666
Cook	51	5 279	1.03	49	9.3	36	6.8	324	8.4	1 424	668	756	120	2 301
Cottonwood	244	11 933	1.06	164	14.3	144	12.6	537	6.1	2 067	1 067	1 000	128	1 102
Crow Wing	741	64 871	1.06	716	11.2	653	10.2	2 407	4.9	16 337	6 822	9 515	1 569	2 472
Dakota	2 832	369 009	0.82	5 226	12.5	2 509	6.0	14 725	4.1	39 707	15 320	24 387	8 722	2 119
Dodge	149	16 036	0.60	250	12.2	143	7.0	762	4.3	2 953	1 418	1 535	284	1 390
Douglas	522	38 145	1.08	426	11.4	430	11.5	1 201	4.2	9 889	3 439	6 450	697	1 897
Faribault	336	13 610	0.91	154	11.1	165	11.8	623	5.8	3 587	1 500	2 087	171	1 210

1. Per 1,000 estimated resident population.　　2. Data for serious crimes have not been adjusted for underreporting; this may affect comparability between geographic areas and over time.
3. Per 100,000 population estimated by the FBI.

Table B. States and Counties — **Crime, Education, Money Income, and Poverty**

STATE County	Serious crimes known to police, 2014 (cont.)[1] Rate[2] Violent	Property	Education — School enrollment and attainment, 2011–2015 Enrollment[3] Total	Percent private	Attainment[4] (percent) High school graduate or less	Bachelor's degree or more	Local government expenditures,[5] 2013–2014 Total current spending (mil dol)	Current spending per student (dollars)	Money income, 2011–2015 Per capita income[6] (dollars)	Median income (dollars)	Households Percent with income of less than $50,000	with income of $200,000 or more	Income and poverty, 2015 Median household income (dollars)	Percent below poverty level All persons	Children under 18 years	Children 5 to 17 years in families
	46	47	48	49	50	51	52	53	54	55	56	57	58	59	60	61
MICHIGAN—Cont'd																
Keweenaw	227	2 086	358	6.7	40.2	22.8	0.2	24 375	24 384	37 813	67.4	2.7	40 862	13.4	21.4	18.8
Lake	369	1 926	1 960	13.0	59.6	9.4	8.1	14 510	16 679	30 439	72.7	0.4	32 971	24.8	45.2	40.3
Lapeer	155	1 033	20 995	9.5	46.3	17.5	122.2	9 630	24 478	52 996	45.6	1.7	57 774	10.0	14.7	13.5
Leelanau	83	441	4 279	17.0	27.3	40.0	28.7	12 409	34 322	56 189	43.6	5.6	61 397	7.9	13.4	12.2
Lenawee	189	1 098	25 135	16.1	46.9	19.2	170.8	11 061	23 252	48 043	51.9	1.3	49 013	14.3	20.9	18.3
Livingston	101	820	47 701	13.3	30.5	33.6	263.4	9 621	33 619	75 204	31.3	5.5	76 934	6.5	7.8	6.8
Luce	324	1 774	1 073	7.7	56.6	12.4	6.9	9 813	18 427	37 088	61.8	0.5	41 870	19.6	29.7	27.2
Mackinac	217	3 000	1 848	6.0	48.1	18.3	14.9	10 607	23 889	38 434	63.2	1.6	40 091	16.1	26.1	24.5
Macomb	288	1 826	213 507	12.1	41.7	23.3	1 362.6	10 645	27 525	54 582	45.8	2.6	54 939	11.7	16.8	15.4
Manistee	229	1 244	4 710	17.7	47.6	19.7	36.7	10 816	22 647	41 395	60.0	1.6	41 811	15.0	25.8	23.7
Marquette	155	1 427	18 737	6.9	38.6	28.8	90.1	10 924	23 785	45 409	54.9	2.0	48 108	15.0	17.9	17.0
Mason	311	2 112	6 106	9.5	42.7	20.2	53.9	13 177	24 244	42 024	58.2	1.5	43 620	16.8	26.9	25.1
Mecosta	507	1 523	14 685	9.2	45.1	22.7	71.6	11 926	20 405	41 889	58.4	1.2	41 755	21.3	29.6	28.3
Menominee	198	1 687	4 795	12.1	51.9	15.1	38.5	10 551	23 233	40 373	59.6	1.2	42 591	16.9	26.8	25.3
Midland	125	1 241	21 226	14.7	36.1	32.5	133.3	11 114	30 172	54 059	46.3	5.6	59 248	11.5	15.0	13.9
Missaukee	205	1 342	3 268	13.6	56.2	13.1	19.7	9 100	20 530	41 098	59.9	1.2	42 836	17.5	26.2	24.1
Monroe	224	1 723	36 490	10.8	46.0	18.6	246.9	10 458	26 982	55 653	44.7	2.4	56 161	10.6	14.6	13.3
Montcalm	342	1 547	14 775	11.0	51.7	13.1	97.7	10 767	19 955	41 584	59.2	1.0	41 728	17.9	26.9	24.3
Montmorency	65	357	1 420	11.1	56.4	10.7	7.7	10 314	20 771	36 250	69.9	0.7	37 153	18.2	33.9	31.0
Muskegon	443	3 597	43 288	10.8	45.9	18.2	297.7	10 332	21 291	42 829	57.0	1.5	46 709	16.1	23.4	22.8
Newaygo	326	1 630	11 070	10.5	55.1	13.9	85.4	10 711	21 230	43 693	56.7	1.3	45 086	16.3	23.1	21.6
Oakland	174	1 353	316 857	17.0	26.8	44.4	2 129.3	11 412	37 728	67 465	37.4	8.4	70 150	9.3	11.7	10.5
Oceana	221	2 174	5 949	13.5	49.4	16.8	32.0	9 912	20 234	41 617	58.3	1.2	43 211	17.2	28.9	27.5
Ogemaw	268	1 638	4 102	8.8	55.9	11.7	18.5	9 005	20 972	36 063	65.3	1.1	37 057	19.4	34.2	32.2
Ontonagon	112	482	931	5.7	49.2	15.1	10.9	17 622	21 896	34 459	66.7	0.4	37 508	14.6	30.3	25.8
Osceola	224	1 219	5 213	9.8	56.7	13.2	37.6	9 382	19 205	38 999	62.4	0.9	41 782	18.7	29.9	28.3
Oscoda	192	1 765	1 492	19.7	56.9	9.7	8.7	9 588	19 520	33 021	68.9	0.8	36 724	20.5	32.8	30.3
Otsego	157	1 561	5 167	14.4	44.6	20.5	35.4	9 124	25 743	48 917	51.0	2.0	50 420	12.1	19.2	18.0
Ottawa	233	1 486	82 739	19.6	37.6	31.1	476.6	10 678	26 519	58 989	41.6	3.3	61 429	8.6	9.2	8.7
Presque Isle	115	553	2 247	14.3	52.5	16.9	7.7	8 971	23 550	41 213	59.9	0.9	41 658	13.6	25.0	22.9
Roscommon	284	1 780	4 038	7.7	50.7	14.4	36.2	12 479	22 513	35 133	69.2	1.2	38 516	19.2	40.3	40.3
Saginaw	659	1 962	51 503	11.3	46.1	20.2	306.3	10 740	23 139	43 042	57.1	2.0	43 344	18.6	27.7	25.8
St. Clair	286	1 523	38 128	10.7	45.7	17.4	294.1	9 772	25 429	49 730	50.2	2.1	51 183	12.8	18.9	17.4
St. Joseph	303	1 810	14 389	8.6	53.7	14.7	109.4	10 230	21 559	44 449	56.4	1.5	46 667	14.7	22.3	20.2
Sanilac	266	1 086	9 445	10.4	57.3	12.3	66.1	9 884	21 374	41 100	59.5	1.3	41 861	16.7	24.8	23.4
Schoolcraft	NA	NA	1 508	14.0	59.5	13.2	8.1	9 832	20 580	34 118	65.6	1.2	36 741	15.9	24.8	23.4
Shiawassee	239	1 429	17 130	11.7	45.7	15.7	122.2	10 353	23 582	48 233	52.4	1.4	50 807	12.4	19.6	18.3
Tuscola	217	969	12 087	14.5	53.2	13.9	91.3	11 621	21 904	43 768	56.8	1.1	45 800	15.5	25.1	23.5
Van Buren	308	1 644	18 955	8.6	47.7	19.5	181.3	11 521	22 358	46 008	53.9	1.4	47 806	15.7	22.8	22.1
Washtenaw	288	1 851	123 919	10.0	21.3	52.6	507.5	11 550	34 738	61 003	42.2	7.2	62 401	14.2	13.4	12.2
Wayne	995	3 273	476 942	12.3	45.6	22.0	3 134.0	10 969	22 897	41 210	57.4	2.7	41 585	24.8	37.0	35.4
Wexford	338	2 560	7 255	11.4	50.0	16.8	63.7	12 732	20 988	41 534	59.3	1.4	42 922	14.8	25.2	24.1
MINNESOTA	229	2 297	1 407 569	16.6	33.6	33.7	9 653.5	11 373	32 157	61 492	40.6	5.2	63 459	10.2	13.1	12.1
Aitkin	128	2 281	2 625	4.2	49.3	15.5	21.2	10 569	25 591	42 252	58.3	1.2	43 817	14.2	22.4	20.4
Anoka	125	2 324	88 426	13.7	35.1	27.8	678.3	10 692	31 775	70 873	32.8	4.1	73 276	7.1	9.2	8.3
Becker	66	1 360	7 670	11.7	41.8	22.4	48.0	10 393	26 399	52 038	47.7	2.8	54 304	11.3	16.5	14.8
Beltrami	243	3 318	13 026	7.2	35.6	26.6	110.6	13 781	22 524	44 757	54.6	2.0	46 031	16.2	23.5	22.0
Benton	147	1 850	10 054	11.3	40.6	21.5	51.4	8 616	25 341	52 178	48.4	1.7	52 513	11.4	13.5	11.4
Big Stone	39	1 001	984	2.0	52.4	17.4	10.4	12 224	27 426	47 794	52.0	2.7	47 583	11.5	15.9	15.1
Blue Earth	198	2 483	22 834	9.1	33.8	31.3	104.1	9 934	26 440	50 061	50.0	3.0	49 664	17.2	14.0	12.3
Brown	67	1 113	6 021	40.5	47.0	21.3	39.1	11 806	28 018	52 598	47.5	2.9	56 330	8.3	10.6	9.3
Carlton	158	2 238	8 749	11.2	42.2	22.8	62.1	9 647	24 584	53 227	46.3	1.5	54 945	10.8	12.2	11.0
Carver	60	1 001	27 271	18.0	26.1	45.2	158.6	9 654	40 322	86 323	26.0	11.8	93 887	4.5	4.7	3.9
Cass	280	3 943	5 505	9.1	44.1	20.2	50.1	12 001	25 720	46 531	53.7	1.9	47 645	15.0	26.0	24.8
Chippewa	141	1 630	2 676	5.7	46.4	15.9	24.2	12 097	26 372	50 858	49.1	1.6	50 896	11.1	15.3	13.6
Chisago	76	1 232	13 533	8.0	40.7	22.0	74.4	9 837	29 553	71 001	32.3	2.9	70 036	6.3	7.9	6.7
Clay	137	1 743	18 372	22.6	33.4	31.7	91.1	9 585	25 896	57 965	44.3	2.5	60 417	12.1	12.5	11.5
Clearwater	259	1 407	2 005	8.5	51.4	14.9	15.8	10 610	23 391	43 421	56.3	2.2	42 689	14.6	23.3	21.2
Cook	38	2 262	751	7.2	29.4	39.0	7.6	12 770	33 056	52 299	47.0	2.5	50 350	11.1	17.8	16.1
Cottonwood	146	956	2 639	9.7	46.7	18.5	22.0	11 496	24 978	46 750	52.4	2.7	49 448	13.7	19.1	17.3
Crow Wing	192	2 280	14 205	8.6	38.3	23.2	99.5	10 390	27 936	49 435	50.5	2.9	50 755	10.4	14.9	13.1
Dakota	118	2 001	107 476	16.2	26.9	40.3	803.5	10 885	36 171	75 567	30.7	7.0	77 576	7.1	9.1	8.0
Dodge	157	1 233	5 466	9.1	39.5	23.7	36.6	8 845	30 091	68 116	34.9	2.9	65 494	6.9	8.6	7.5
Douglas	133	1 764	8 179	10.4	35.9	24.7	51.7	9 837	29 953	54 531	45.5	3.3	56 819	8.8	11.4	10.1
Faribault	78	1 132	2 985	8.4	49.7	16.9	20.7	10 865	27 135	47 540	51.9	2.9	52 169	11.3	18.1	16.5

1. Data for serious crimes have not been adjusted for underreporting; this may affect comparability between geographic areas and over time.   2. Per 100,000 population estimated by the FBI.
3. All persons 3 years old and over enrolled in nursery school through college.   4. Persons 25 years old and over.   5. Elementary and secondary education expenditures.
6. Based on population estimated by the American Community Survey, 2011–2015.

Table B. States and Counties — **Personal Income**

STATE County	Personal income, 2015										Earnings, 2015		
			Per capita[1]			Supplements to wages and salaries; employer contributions (mil dol)						Contributions for government social insurance (mil dol)	
	Total (mil dol)	Percent change, 2014–2015	Dollars	Rank	Wages and salaries (mil dol)	Pension and insurance	Government social insurance	Proprietors' income (mil dol)	Dividends, interest, and rent (mil dol)	Personal transfer receipts (mil dol)	Total (mil dol)	From employee and self-employed	From employer
	62	63	64	65	66	67	68	69	70	71	72	73	74
MICHIGAN—Cont'd													
Keweenaw	84	2.9	38 827	1 591	12	3	1	3	22	27	19	2	1
Lake	338	5.3	29 607	2 803	56	12	5	12	65	154	84	9	5
Lapeer	3 395	5.4	38 417	1 716	845	154	66	186	455	777	1 251	90	66
Leelanau	1 306	0.5	59 396	441	242	46	19	220	436	221	528	36	19
Lenawee	3 514	4.7	35 652	2 175	1 169	212	90	127	516	899	1 598	112	90
Livingston	9 292	5.9	49 608	534	2 512	387	195	447	1 323	1 318	3 542	234	195
Luce	180	3.9	28 089	2 951	68	17	5	8	34	70	99	7	5
Mackinac	420	3.3	38 607	1 689	148	28	13	24	101	132	214	15	13
Macomb	36 191	5.7	41 847	1 196	17 515	2 511	1 350	2 209	4 967	7 333	23 585	1 507	1 350
Manistee	868	4.4	35 472	2 187	287	64	22	45	172	305	416	30	22
Marquette	2 473	1.9	36 788	1 837	1 143	218	88	89	431	659	1 538	99	88
Mason	1 066	2.6	37 046	1 643	416	79	33	55	196	330	583	40	33
Mecosta	1 278	3.7	29 673	2 817	539	123	41	49	207	390	753	50	41
Menominee	904	2.6	38 377	1 552	267	57	21	47	173	233	392	27	21
Midland	3 760	1.4	44 954	586	2 179	333	153	-216	783	730	2 449	208	153
Missaukee	464	-0.7	31 109	2 550	129	23	10	40	78	142	202	14	10
Monroe	6 238	4.8	41 707	1 285	2 059	335	153	272	805	1 305	2 819	191	153
Montcalm	1 952	5.0	31 015	2 825	620	120	48	128	257	557	916	62	48
Montmorency	313	5.8	33 848	2 482	75	15	6	13	68	137	109	11	6
Muskegon	5 979	5.1	34 604	2 306	2 677	457	208	290	849	1 724	3 633	240	208
Newaygo	1 592	4.1	33 201	2 493	494	91	38	82	240	464	705	51	38
Oakland	78 829	4.6	63 454	138	44 511	5 332	3 315	8 094	15 377	9 927	61 252	3 701	3 315
Oceana	889	3.6	34 066	2 459	258	48	20	55	159	270	381	27	20
Ogemaw	647	3.5	30 925	2 712	196	37	16	26	122	271	275	23	16
Ontonagon	205	2.8	34 124	2 275	44	11	3	8	41	90	67	6	3
Osceola	710	2.9	30 805	2 842	283	47	22	50	99	234	402	29	22
Oscoda	269	2.5	32 631	2 584	59	13	5	24	48	109	100	9	5
Otsego	851	4.6	35 102	2 148	393	65	31	76	164	236	566	38	31
Ottawa	11 931	5.4	42 619	1 278	5 619	924	427	850	2 208	1 809	7 819	470	427
Presque Isle	440	3.6	34 262	2 296	121	24	10	15	85	162	171	15	10
Roscommon	793	4.4	33 199	2 546	173	37	14	38	172	364	262	26	14
Saginaw	6 849	2.8	35 429	2 110	3 719	618	290	391	1 045	2 111	5 018	330	290
St. Clair	6 278	4.9	39 268	1 525	2 019	360	159	303	950	1 523	2 841	197	159
St. Joseph	2 088	4.7	34 215	2 417	948	167	74	103	318	547	1 292	83	74
Sanilac	1 452	4.0	35 005	2 156	418	76	34	112	251	455	639	43	34
Schoolcraft	290	2.9	35 475	2 038	109	25	8	8	53	107	151	11	8
Shiawassee	2 407	3.9	35 078	2 314	651	127	52	123	324	662	953	70	52
Tuscola	1 870	6.4	34 771	2 527	461	93	36	212	261	582	802	58	36
Van Buren	2 796	5.0	37 247	2 105	910	180	70	186	426	726	1 347	87	70
Washtenaw	18 447	5.0	51 400	461	10 893	2 138	786	983	3 799	2 378	14 801	844	786
Wayne	67 756	4.6	38 512	1 627	43 349	6 021	3 215	3 913	9 956	19 246	56 498	3 546	3 215
Wexford	1 089	4.6	32 993	2 570	514	100	41	60	167	339	714	47	41
MINNESOTA	279 263	4.2	50 938	X	153 846	21 410	11 385	22 841	50 923	44 234	209 481	12 657	11 385
Aitkin	558	-0.1	35 546	1 720	133	26	11	26	127	190	195	16	11
Anoka	15 678	5.0	45 556	803	6 324	891	487	861	1 946	2 418	8 563	539	487
Becker	1 405	3.7	42 079	974	543	92	43	131	259	349	809	53	43
Beltrami	1 659	4.1	36 329	1 929	759	142	60	105	285	481	1 065	67	60
Benton	1 543	4.4	38 845	1 054	697	104	57	106	213	301	964	60	57
Big Stone	254	3.6	50 308	469	71	14	5	31	59	64	122	8	5
Blue Earth	2 840	6.2	43 168	1 093	1 649	266	127	420	497	473	2 462	143	127
Brown	1 207	2.5	47 688	612	550	99	43	156	232	249	848	49	43
Carlton	1 347	3.4	37 872	1 637	574	108	46	56	189	342	784	51	46
Carver	6 249	5.5	63 291	131	2 100	312	154	494	952	493	3 060	184	154
Cass	1 184	4.0	41 263	927	314	67	26	68	283	386	475	36	26
Chippewa	542	1.1	44 722	376	218	41	17	77	101	118	353	19	17
Chisago	2 306	5.1	42 475	1 200	649	107	52	112	305	399	921	61	52
Clay	2 504	3.9	40 177	1 382	810	138	70	216	370	481	1 234	80	70
Clearwater	330	3.4	37 432	1 693	119	21	10	26	56	93	176	12	10
Cook	238	4.6	45 900	921	92	19	7	31	65	55	150	10	7
Cottonwood	518	1.7	44 872	527	182	35	15	112	97	123	344	19	15
Crow Wing	2 582	4.4	40 710	1 481	1 142	187	93	217	507	673	1 640	112	93
Dakota	22 273	4.6	53 710	288	10 245	1 434	780	1 384	3 395	2 769	13 842	840	780
Dodge	877	1.4	43 069	781	265	45	21	94	125	132	425	25	21
Douglas	1 739	5.9	46 902	833	767	128	59	210	335	381	1 164	78	59
Faribault	604	5.6	42 967	614	180	34	15	90	125	150	319	19	15

1. Based on the resident population estimated as of July 1 of the year shown.

Table B. States and Counties — Earnings, Social Security, and Housing

STATE County	Earnings, 2015 (cont.) Percent by selected industries									Social Security beneficiaries, December 2015		Supplemental Security Income recipients, December 2015	Housing units, 2016	
	Farm	Mining	Construction	Manufacturing	Information: professional, scientific, technical services	Retail trade	Finance, insurance, real estate and leasing	Health care and social assistance	Government	Number	Rate[1]		Total	Percent change, 2010–2016
	75	76	77	78	79	80	81	82	83	84	85	86	87	88
MICHIGAN—Cont'd														
Keweenaw	0.0	D	D	D	D	2.9	D	D	32.4	795	365	32	2 479	0.5
Lake	0.8	0.3	5.1	3.4	D	6.1	4.9	19.5	32.1	4 155	365	610	14 981	0.1
Lapeer	1.4	0.7	8.6	24.1	3.5	8.2	4.5	7.0	20.2	20 545	232	1 341	36 316	0.0
Leelanau	2.7	D	11.6	3.3	D	3.6	5.9	6.5	18.9	6 825	311	132	15 405	3.1
Lenawee	1.4	D	4.8	27.5	3.0	7.3	5.3	10.2	19.1	24 265	247	2 050	43 450	0.0
Livingston	0.3	0.1	10.0	19.3	10.0	8.0	6.1	8.7	11.5	36 850	197	1 182	75 985	4.4
Luce	1.4	0.2	3.9	4.9	D	7.7	5.7	D	53.9	1 775	276	216	4 338	-0.1
Mackinac	1.3	D	6.8	1.9	D	8.5	3.8	D	26.0	3 665	336	205	11 038	0.3
Macomb	0.1	0.0	6.9	23.5	13.6	6.7	4.3	10.3	12.9	180 235	208	20 904	363 975	2.1
Manistee	0.4	0.9	6.1	16.3	2.7	7.6	2.5	D	40.3	7 715	315	673	15 654	-0.3
Marquette	0.0	10.7	5.3	3.7	6.7	6.9	4.9	20.5	22.6	15 870	236	1 128	34 590	0.8
Mason	2.2	D	7.7	19.5	D	7.8	4.2	12.3	18.8	8 430	293	729	17 307	0.1
Mecosta	1.4	D	2.7	15.7	3.6	10.0	2.7	9.2	38.6	10 165	236	1 093	21 132	0.0
Menominee	3.5	0.1	4.0	32.5	D	4.8	3.5	D	24.5	6 760	287	492	14 170	-0.4
Midland	0.2	D	7.0	8.8	5.2	5.1	8.6	14.3	9.1	18 975	227	1 605	36 538	1.6
Missaukee	12.2	1.1	10.0	15.0	2.7	7.1	3.2	D	15.2	3 965	266	310	9 072	-0.5
Monroe	1.0	D	8.9	16.1	7.8	6.6	3.1	9.8	12.6	33 860	226	2 572	63 683	1.1
Montcalm	5.8	D	6.1	20.4	3.0	7.9	2.8	D	21.0	15 205	242	1 759	28 127	-0.3
Montmorency	0.9	D	8.0	13.5	3.5	5.9	D	5.3	20.1	4 125	445	358	9 515	-0.8
Muskegon	0.8	D	5.7	27.2	4.1	9.6	3.7	17.1	14.0	41 655	241	6 331	73 465	-0.1
Newaygo	3.2	D	7.1	22.2	6.0	9.1	8.7	8.2	19.3	12 695	265	1 327	24 973	-0.4
Oakland	0.0	0.0	4.3	10.3	23.0	5.7	13.0	11.0	5.9	237 235	191	21 801	536 801	1.8
Oceana	7.6	0.6	7.1	21.7	1.8	5.4	3.1	D	21.1	7 165	274	799	15 961	0.1
Ogemaw	3.2	0.9	7.6	5.4	2.6	14.9	4.3	D	21.7	7 470	357	791	16 037	-0.1
Ontonagon	1.1	0.1	7.0	D	D	14.1	4.7	15.0	31.5	2 615	435	151	5 648	-0.4
Osceola	2.5	D	22.6	25.2	D	4.2	2.0	10.8	14.5	6 645	288	860	13 580	-0.4
Oscoda	0.8	0.4	11.1	18.9	2.9	10.1	2.8	D	25.5	3 070	371	268	9 081	-0.4
Otsego	0.4	10.0	6.4	11.0	D	13.9	4.6	D	14.4	6 695	276	551	14 774	0.3
Ottawa	2.2	0.1	7.1	35.7	5.2	4.7	5.0	5.7	13.5	49 975	178	2 677	106 897	4.3
Presque Isle	1.8	D	5.4	4.2	2.4	7.6	4.1	D	20.2	5 050	393	384	10 388	-0.4
Roscommon	-0.1	D	8.6	10.5	D	16.4	5.2	D	27.4	10 330	434	963	24 342	-0.5
Saginaw	0.3	0.2	4.5	19.2	6.2	7.3	6.0	19.0	14.2	49 135	254	8 577	87 037	0.2
St. Clair	0.3	0.3	7.1	18.3	D	7.6	4.2	15.5	16.5	38 515	241	3 585	71 874	0.1
St. Joseph	1.9	D	5.0	45.1	D	6.3	2.0	8.3	13.0	13 995	230	1 294	27 633	-0.5
Sanilac	9.9	0.8	6.3	19.3	D	9.7	5.2	D	16.9	11 275	272	995	22 827	0.4
Schoolcraft	0.5	9.1	5.6	5.8	D	7.2	D	6.0	41.3	2 665	327	276	6 331	0.3
Shiawassee	1.3	D	7.5	12.7	D	9.5	4.1	12.6	19.8	16 860	246	1 698	29 984	-1.1
Tuscola	4.5	D	5.8	26.2	D	5.6	3.9	D	21.9	14 835	276	1 387	24 219	-0.9
Van Buren	5.0	D	7.0	10.5	9.0	6.1	2.9	6.0	24.2	17 850	238	2 208	36 718	-0.2
Washtenaw	0.1	0.0	2.7	7.9	16.9	4.3	5.1	11.2	35.1	56 060	155	5 585	149 948	1.6
Wayne	0.0	0.1	3.7	15.0	D	4.5	5.4	13.6	12.2	356 595	203	84 892	814 282	-0.9
Wexford	0.3	0.5	3.5	26.9	D	8.3	3.8	12.1	18.0	8 840	268	1 173	16 691	-0.3
MINNESOTA	1.7	0.4	5.9	12.8	10.9	5.4	10.2	12.6	13.1	979 776	179	94 146	2 409 935	2.7
Aitkin	0.5	D	8.3	9.6	D	8.9	4.7	D	23.6	4 760	304	268	16 434	2.5
Anoka	0.1	0.0	9.8	25.6	5.6	6.1	4.8	11.8	12.5	54 775	159	4 408	130 506	3.0
Becker	3.1	0.5	9.7	15.7	2.6	9.8	5.1	D	21.6	8 560	256	661	19 357	3.0
Beltrami	0.4	D	9.4	5.0	5.0	8.3	3.5	18.4	30.3	8 935	196	1 303	21 093	2.8
Benton	2.7	D	16.7	22.3	2.8	6.1	3.7	8.8	10.4	6 775	171	411	16 768	3.9
Big Stone	13.7	D	14.5	1.4	1.4	3.7	3.8	D	27.7	1 475	293	93	3 127	0.4
Blue Earth	4.5	D	6.1	15.5	7.9	8.1	5.2	19.3	14.3	10 895	166	985	27 992	6.8
Brown	9.0	D	7.9	22.5	6.7	6.1	5.2	12.6	11.5	6 300	249	289	11 638	1.3
Carlton	-0.2	D	10.4	14.8	3.4	5.9	4.4	10.0	35.7	7 760	218	577	15 829	1.1
Carver	0.9	0.1	7.2	26.3	6.6	4.0	6.4	10.7	10.3	12 255	124	512	37 532	8.6
Cass	0.4	0.0	9.9	6.9	2.4	7.1	4.5	D	40.0	9 690	338	701	25 549	2.6
Chippewa	16.4	D	5.5	19.7	4.0	5.0	5.5	5.8	19.5	2 655	219	147	5 689	-0.6
Chisago	0.8	D	10.9	22.0	2.4	6.9	2.8	21.1	16.7	10 010	184	582	21 632	2.2
Clay	1.7	D	7.0	10.4	4.3	7.1	4.2	D	21.9	9 940	160	1 052	25 978	8.4
Clearwater	6.2	0.0	17.0	20.8	D	3.3	D	D	15.4	2 210	252	223	4 756	-0.4
Cook	0.0	0.0	10.0	D	3.4	8.1	3.6	4.2	33.7	1 590	305	45	6 036	3.4
Cottonwood	22.2	D	6.5	19.3	D	5.0	3.4	D	13.3	3 050	265	219	5 400	-0.2
Crow Wing	0.2	D	11.2	8.5	7.0	10.6	7.9	15.9	18.2	17 295	273	1 161	41 512	3.3
Dakota	0.4	0.1	8.2	13.1	12.1	7.5	12.1	7.8	11.2	63 075	152	4 406	164 740	3.2
Dodge	10.3	D	12.3	25.3	2.9	3.0	3.5	2.1	15.9	3 395	167	166	8 117	2.1
Douglas	1.0	D	9.0	18.7	4.1	7.6	6.1	8.8	18.7	10 175	275	473	20 859	4.8
Faribault	19.6	0.0	6.0	22.6	D	4.1	6.3	D	14.0	3 785	269	253	7 027	-0.9

1. Per 1,000 resident population estimated as of July 1 of the year shown.

Items 75—88

Table B. States and Counties — Housing, Labor Force, and Employment

STATE County	Housing units, 2011–2015								Civilian labor force, 2016				Civilian employment,[6] 2011–2015		
	Occupied units										Unemployment			Percent	
			Owner-occupied			Renter-occupied									
				Median owner cost as a percent of income											Con-struction, produc-tion, and mainte-nance occu-pations
	Total	Percent	Median value[1]	With a mort-gage	Without a mort-gage[2]	Median rent[3]	Median rent as a per-cent of income[2]	Sub-stand-ard units[4] (percent)	Total	Percent change, 2015–2016	Total	Rate[5]	Total	Manage-ment, business, science and arts	
	89	90	91	92	93	94	95	96	97	98	99	100	101	102	103
MICHIGAN—Cont'd															
Keweenaw	1 040	88.7	102 000	23.5	15.1	563	37.0	3.8	926	-1.3	78	8.4	842	35.6	19.7
Lake	4 365	82.6	79 500	28.1	14.0	562	36.0	3.7	3 783	2.9	275	7.3	3 297	21.5	31.1
Lapeer	32 682	83.1	132 300	23.5	12.8	781	31.0	2.1	40 485	1.8	2 642	6.5	37 682	29.2	31.0
Leelanau	9 234	84.9	241 900	26.5	12.2	805	29.3	1.8	10 721	1.3	501	4.7	9 628	38.3	20.6
Lenawee	37 964	76.9	114 900	23.2	13.4	731	31.2	1.3	47 618	0.3	2 136	4.5	43 095	28.0	28.4
Livingston	68 980	84.6	192 500	21.6	11.5	917	28.5	1.0	98 727	2.3	4 128	4.2	92 068	38.5	21.3
Luce	2 377	75.5	74 200	20.3	12.3	606	29.4	2.2	2 425	-1.3	158	6.5	2 103	24.4	26.5
Mackinac	5 209	73.7	121 300	23.6	13.4	578	27.0	2.3	5 230	2.2	493	9.4	4 470	24.2	24.1
Macomb	336 379	73.3	126 000	21.4	13.5	861	31.1	1.8	431 844	2.4	22 937	5.3	401 146	33.8	23.0
Manistee	10 142	80.8	107 100	23.5	13.1	659	29.6	1.5	10 587	1.8	663	6.3	9 010	27.2	25.4
Marquette	26 457	68.6	131 400	19.6	11.9	626	30.9	1.3	33 374	0.0	1 865	5.6	29 522	31.2	22.3
Mason	12 248	75.0	119 900	24.7	13.2	680	31.0	2.3	14 298	-0.7	796	5.6	12 183	30.1	28.6
Mecosta	15 478	74.5	110 500	22.4	12.1	628	35.8	2.7	19 174	0.2	1 034	5.4	17 639	28.6	28.4
Menominee	10 679	78.6	93 400	21.6	12.3	538	28.4	2.2	11 418	-0.9	638	5.6	10 346	25.4	34.9
Midland	33 617	75.4	131 200	19.9	11.8	727	29.4	1.8	41 182	-0.6	1 870	4.5	37 406	39.3	21.1
Missaukee	5 866	82.0	103 200	23.7	13.0	718	28.8	3.1	6 994	0.2	402	5.7	6 096	23.8	37.9
Monroe	58 566	79.5	137 200	21.3	12.3	784	29.2	1.7	76 929	1.0	3 342	4.3	68 024	29.3	31.3
Montcalm	23 284	79.1	94 100	23.3	13.4	692	29.6	1.8	28 248	2.1	1 419	5.0	24 588	25.0	35.3
Montmorency	4 070	85.5	91 200	26.1	12.3	571	33.6	1.8	3 101	1.2	302	9.7	2 937	21.4	30.4
Muskegon	64 490	74.9	99 000	21.0	12.5	673	34.9	2.2	77 329	0.1	4 046	5.2	69 673	28.3	28.7
Newaygo	18 339	83.2	101 500	23.0	13.6	670	32.7	2.6	23 401	1.4	1 104	4.7	18 619	25.8	35.4
Oakland	493 489	70.5	178 900	20.9	12.8	942	28.2	1.5	648 101	2.3	27 402	4.2	606 484	47.8	13.9
Oceana	9 822	80.6	104 200	23.7	13.3	667	30.9	5.0	12 252	-1.8	867	7.1	10 360	25.5	38.2
Ogemaw	9 434	81.5	86 900	24.5	14.3	670	36.7	2.4	8 283	-1.4	625	7.5	7 661	24.8	27.6
Ontonagon	3 084	87.8	68 900	25.1	13.4	411	31.7	1.5	2 239	-2.3	186	8.3	2 048	26.3	30.6
Osceola	8 757	78.8	90 300	22.7	13.1	577	30.8	2.5	10 490	3.3	579	5.5	8 807	25.0	37.8
Oscoda	3 686	84.6	80 600	24.7	13.7	600	32.4	2.5	2 907	0.0	208	7.2	2 792	22.3	31.3
Otsego	9 956	79.1	121 700	20.4	13.0	701	31.7	1.5	11 722	2.8	672	5.7	10 733	29.0	25.0
Ottawa	96 283	77.1	155 400	20.2	11.1	792	29.1	2.3	156 239	2.6	5 037	3.2	135 496	34.1	27.9
Presque Isle	5 999	87.3	92 900	21.0	12.6	558	28.2	1.4	5 342	-0.2	491	9.2	4 490	27.6	32.0
Roscommon	11 543	82.3	91 400	26.2	12.5	631	36.8	1.4	7 928	1.6	645	8.1	7 563	24.7	28.4
Saginaw	77 925	72.2	92 900	21.9	13.0	705	32.7	1.5	88 844	0.5	4 542	5.1	81 106	30.4	22.9
St. Clair	64 143	76.1	120 800	22.4	13.5	736	31.9	1.6	74 350	2.0	4 579	6.2	69 940	27.2	30.2
St. Joseph	23 270	75.0	105 900	22.1	11.5	647	29.1	2.8	29 436	1.4	1 175	4.0	26 332	24.6	41.7
Sanilac	16 280	79.9	94 800	22.4	13.4	612	29.3	1.6	19 402	-0.5	1 165	6.0	17 147	25.8	35.1
Schoolcraft	3 419	80.1	89 000	21.4	13.2	574	36.5	1.6	3 318	-3.9	303	9.1	2 803	25.8	26.9
Shiawassee	27 409	76.1	105 100	21.9	12.5	673	29.2	1.3	33 646	1.8	1 700	5.1	29 702	28.2	30.7
Tuscola	21 304	81.4	93 700	22.9	13.1	642	31.4	1.8	24 230	-1.1	1 473	6.1	23 074	26.1	32.0
Van Buren	28 367	77.4	118 700	22.9	13.4	666	30.0	2.8	35 577	1.0	1 957	5.5	32 252	29.1	30.1
Washtenaw	138 067	59.8	208 200	21.4	12.3	953	30.3	1.7	191 860	1.9	6 586	3.4	176 383	51.3	12.5
Wayne	667 275	63.0	83 000	22.5	14.6	794	35.5	2.8	773 086	1.8	49 298	6.4	696 900	31.3	23.7
Wexford	12 673	76.7	91 800	23.3	13.0	717	29.8	2.1	14 764	1.4	831	5.6	13 441	26.5	34.4
MINNESOTA	2 124 745	71.7	186 200	21.7	11.3	848	29.2	2.4	3 001 146	0.9	117 046	3.9	2 827 195	39.5	20.9
Aitkin	7 609	82.4	166 400	26.9	13.2	633	29.7	3.4	7 013	2.8	492	7.0	6 428	27.6	26.0
Anoka	124 477	80.0	187 600	21.7	10.9	971	30.8	2.2	190 604	1.2	7 166	3.8	181 190	36.7	22.8
Becker	13 562	79.1	175 000	22.5	12.2	671	27.5	2.2	18 205	-0.3	848	4.7	15 929	32.7	29.6
Beltrami	16 739	69.1	148 800	22.8	12.0	664	28.9	3.1	23 515	0.8	1 241	5.3	20 579	31.4	21.3
Benton	15 632	70.3	156 100	22.8	11.6	648	31.1	2.5	21 540	0.5	961	4.5	20 104	29.5	31.9
Big Stone	2 282	79.0	94 900	19.2	10.9	508	27.8	2.5	2 718	2.1	132	4.9	2 406	34.3	28.3
Blue Earth	24 847	64.6	161 500	21.3	10.5	727	32.2	1.5	39 471	1.0	1 267	3.2	36 492	32.5	22.4
Brown	10 679	77.7	125 500	20.3	10.9	606	27.2	1.9	14 755	1.7	609	4.1	13 583	31.3	29.7
Carlton	13 398	78.7	156 900	22.3	12.6	691	28.3	2.9	17 409	-0.2	942	5.4	16 478	30.9	25.7
Carver	34 421	80.3	267 000	21.6	10.7	950	27.8	1.4	55 388	1.2	1 855	3.3	52 573	45.0	16.2
Cass	12 856	80.8	172 000	24.0	12.0	665	27.7	3.3	14 330	2.9	967	6.7	12 165	29.4	25.9
Chippewa	5 036	70.3	100 600	19.2	10.0	630	23.6	0.9	6 962	1.0	316	4.5	6 367	29.8	31.1
Chisago	19 808	85.0	192 300	23.4	10.5	785	30.0	1.7	28 858	1.2	1 259	4.4	27 553	33.5	26.5
Clay	22 674	70.2	159 500	20.9	11.1	723	34.6	1.4	35 544	1.0	1 233	3.5	33 104	34.4	22.5
Clearwater	3 486	78.5	116 200	22.2	12.9	558	28.0	5.3	4 697	2.2	453	9.6	3 634	26.9	36.8
Cook	2 652	73.7	242 400	24.9	10.0	655	24.6	4.8	3 056	-2.4	140	4.6	2 788	33.9	19.2
Cottonwood	4 779	78.7	87 200	19.5	10.9	607	28.5	3.1	5 524	-3.8	401	7.3	5 408	29.6	32.5
Crow Wing	26 365	75.3	178 400	23.2	11.6	730	29.6	1.1	31 636	1.2	1 627	5.1	29 263	31.7	22.3
Dakota	156 466	74.7	220 400	21.2	10.0	971	28.4	1.6	233 145	1.1	7 980	3.4	223 989	42.4	17.1
Dodge	7 556	82.9	158 700	20.1	11.6	635	25.8	1.7	11 474	0.9	431	3.8	10 890	36.7	27.6
Douglas	15 559	76.3	188 400	23.2	12.7	730	28.5	0.7	20 112	0.6	706	3.5	18 975	33.2	25.7
Faribault	6 374	76.8	85 600	19.7	11.4	538	23.8	1.6	7 310	-1.8	325	4.4	7 117	32.1	30.8

1. Specified owner-occupied units.   2. A value of 10.0 represents 10 percent or less; a value of 50.0 represents 50 percent or more.   3. Specified renter-occupied units.
4. Overcrowded or lacking complete plumbing facilities.   5. Percent of civilian labor force.   6. Civilian employed persons 16 years old and over.

Table B. States and Counties — **Nonfarm Employment and Agriculture**

STATE County	___ Private nonfarm establishments, employment and payroll, 2015									Agriculture, 2012			
	Number of establishments	Employment						Annual payroll		Farms	Percent with:		
		Total	Health care and social assistance	Manufacturing	Retail trade	Finance and insurance	Professional, scientific, and technical services	Total (mil dol)	Average per employee (dollars)	Number	Fewer than 50 acres	500 acres or more	Farm operators whose principal occupation is farming (percent)
	104	105	106	107	108	109	110	111	112	113	114	115	116
MICHIGAN—Cont'd													
Keweenaw	63	188	D	15	11	D	D	5	28 239	6	66.7	0.0	33.3
Lake	158	1 061	229	90	259	62	D	29	27 801	200	38.0	5.0	49.5
Lapeer	1 628	18 060	2 785	5 033	3 082	417	586	627	34 741	1 133	52.8	7.2	51.3
Leelanau	757	4 515	581	315	721	174	213	178	39 393	494	38.3	2.6	55.5
Lenawee	1 800	23 100	3 150	5 223	3 647	815	502	808	34 983	1 618	45.7	11.7	39.3
Livingston	4 237	50 254	5 698	9 400	9 182	3 784	2 511	1 939	38 584	734	58.3	4.6	54.8
Luce	170	1 551	388	248	281	60	13	52	33 570	43	44.2	16.3	44.2
Mackinac	436	2 075	365	106	352	83	37	108	51 979	103	30.1	11.7	57.3
Macomb	18 824	293 464	39 439	67 812	41 891	6 800	28 963	13 946	47 523	502	59.4	6.4	53.8
Manistee	554	5 617	961	773	1 154	165	95	205	36 425	324	35.2	2.5	43.8
Marquette	1 624	21 195	5 574	988	3 818	938	670	820	38 671	168	41.1	6.0	48.8
Mason	732	9 351	1 310	2 169	1 515	205	145	348	37 173	440	34.5	8.2	45.2
Mecosta	721	9 457	1 460	2 180	2 056	223	356	318	33 669	779	31.8	5.9	48.1
Menominee	448	5 534	225	2 008	629	142	150	182	32 830	398	25.6	9.8	47.5
Midland	2 167	34 633	6 111	6 003	4 043	1 091	928	2 112	60 993	555	47.9	7.0	46.7
Missaukee	292	2 329	389	398	391	51	35	70	30 142	433	38.6	10.6	48.3
Monroe	2 254	36 847	5 184	7 145	5 165	874	1 328	1 585	43 021	1 144	53.0	10.9	46.3
Montcalm	999	12 168	2 895	2 314	2 424	362	227	410	33 655	1 127	41.3	9.4	54.3
Montmorency	199	1 651	236	459	235	69	13	53	32 215	151	31.1	8.6	36.4
Muskegon	3 137	53 027	10 169	12 474	7 979	1 050	1 598	2 078	39 183	514	56.6	4.9	48.4
Newaygo	798	10 456	1 590	2 482	1 592	680	339	395	37 745	923	45.8	5.1	45.1
Oakland	38 759	679 551	104 573	52 804	75 433	34 648	96 332	39 434	58 030	537	70.9	2.0	51.6
Oceana	483	4 448	618	1 427	621	123	89	149	33 403	609	37.9	9.4	52.7
Ogemaw	554	5 528	1 429	314	1 443	125	96	171	30 931	280	24.6	11.4	49.3
Ontonagon	163	930	216	D	210	58	11	25	26 347	109	12.8	14.7	45.0
Osceola	426	6 091	952	2 043	589	118	95	251	41 203	750	34.0	4.9	35.9
Oscoda	182	1 431	133	360	224	31	21	52	35 996	145	43.4	2.1	52.4
Otsego	755	8 687	1 502	1 011	2 101	182	165	294	33 852	180	37.2	9.4	47.2
Ottawa	5 965	105 177	10 779	35 016	10 438	2 462	3 416	4 267	40 574	1 363	55.2	5.6	51.5
Presque Isle	331	2 263	292	252	350	101	40	76	33 525	323	22.9	9.9	55.1
Roscommon	539	4 611	577	D	1 309	157	58	172	37 326	58	44.8	3.4	34.5
Saginaw	4 300	79 117	17 254	11 127	12 716	2 741	2 448	3 075	38 867	1 318	44.0	12.1	48.9
St. Clair	3 079	41 911	8 051	8 934	7 239	1 113	970	1 571	37 480	1 049	46.1	7.9	56.0
St. Joseph	1 154	19 461	1 758	9 573	2 486	388	431	745	38 277	967	44.9	10.9	41.8
Sanilac	815	8 213	1 321	2 678	1 567	404	186	280	34 042	1 467	29.9	17.3	55.6
Schoolcraft	241	1 850	436	57	379	169	32	64	34 852	65	27.7	6.2	50.8
Shiawassee	1 149	13 218	2 557	2 120	2 550	339	278	433	32 776	1 033	42.1	10.6	51.2
Tuscola	836	8 709	2 378	1 380	1 623	300	239	300	34 394	1 322	40.0	12.3	48.6
Van Buren	1 273	15 912	2 508	2 864	2 721	322	1 750	642	40 329	1 113	49.5	4.4	53.2
Washtenaw	8 096	148 265	37 043	14 120	17 126	3 541	14 640	7 805	52 642	1 236	55.3	6.9	48.8
Wayne	32 034	626 743	106 162	82 116	68 696	30 310	40 407	33 378	53 256	287	77.7	1.4	59.9
Wexford	831	12 401	1 986	3 183	2 077	234	244	453	36 496	357	42.6	3.4	37.5
MINNESOTA	148 666	2 612 314	452 260	304 497	300 197	152 797	179 196	133 093	50 948	74 542	25.2	18.2	52.9
Aitkin	399	3 097	813	320	580	91	36	98	31 483	471	19.7	12.5	40.8
Anoka	7 566	117 308	16 339	20 578	16 037	2 299	3 725	6 266	53 414	396	58.3	4.5	44.7
Becker	952	10 352	2 467	1 868	2 015	249	183	364	35 154	1 107	17.3	15.4	54.9
Beltrami	1 142	14 539	3 809	942	3 102	421	418	517	35 543	573	15.5	17.6	44.9
Benton	908	16 843	3 575	3 289	2 162	202	220	630	37 425	958	29.7	7.8	51.8
Big Stone	197	1 650	746	16	184	77	37	59	35 875	400	14.8	34.0	63.0
Blue Earth	1 960	35 959	8 926	4 241	6 264	988	1 110	1 298	36 109	1 070	26.9	22.4	53.7
Brown	769	12 687	2 306	2 794	1 687	446	442	474	37 398	1 055	21.0	19.9	55.9
Carlton	710	8 295	2 081	1 338	1 404	422	165	316	38 100	501	21.6	5.8	43.7
Carver	2 479	37 985	5 433	10 601	3 676	757	2 023	2 002	52 706	789	38.3	9.6	51.3
Cass	812	6 608	1 160	340	953	181	479	198	30 025	546	20.1	12.6	54.0
Chippewa	401	5 374	1 165	1 289	650	194	83	194	36 037	674	23.7	30.4	67.1
Chisago	1 216	13 451	3 884	2 349	1 892	269	747	583	43 374	832	44.2	4.7	37.6
Clay	1 289	18 078	4 165	965	2 902	427	479	594	32 873	804	20.5	33.6	52.6
Clearwater	203	2 716	623	D	232	67	50	134	49 470	519	12.5	15.4	36.0
Cook	283	2 065	216	54	334	49	25	63	30 711	18	50.0	5.6	16.7
Cottonwood	339	4 189	684	1 588	495	93	72	132	31 537	813	23.1	31.1	66.8
Crow Wing	2 110	25 470	5 844	2 284	4 638	1 218	945	934	36 676	533	28.5	8.1	50.5
Dakota	10 391	177 727	24 646	17 412	23 991	11 926	9 008	8 673	48 799	892	42.2	13.6	56.8
Dodge	428	4 502	357	1 321	477	115	85	192	42 665	621	39.6	19.5	58.5
Douglas	1 342	17 546	3 701	3 765	3 031	429	475	690	39 298	1 091	24.6	11.2	39.4
Faribault	421	3 979	748	1 155	578	227	72	146	36 770	824	21.4	32.0	67.4

Table B. States and Counties — **Agriculture**

STATE County	Land in farms — Acreage (1,000)	Percent change, 2007–2012	Acres — Average size of farm	Acres — Total irrigated (1,000)	Acres — Total cropland (1,000)	Value of land and buildings — Average per farm	Value of land and buildings — Average per acre	Value of machinery and equipment, average per farm (dollars)	Value of products sold — Total (mil dol)	Value of products sold — Average per farm (dollars)	Percent from: Crops	Percent from: Livestock and poultry products	Percent of farms with sales of: $10,000 or more	Percent of farms with sales of: $100,000 or more	Government payments — Total ($1,000)	Government payments — Percent of farms
	117	118	119	120	121	122	123	124	125	126	127	128	129	130	131	132
MICHIGAN—Cont'd																
Keweenaw	0	-80.1	53	0.0	0.0	133 333	2 516	34 167	D	D	D	D	0.0	0.0	0	0.0
Lake	26	21.7	130	0.0	11.5	338 075	2 598	55 965	4.1	20 305	56.4	43.6	22.0	4.0	88	12.0
Lapeer	176	-0.4	155	2.1	137.1	708 546	4 572	126 049	113.4	100 049	80.6	19.4	41.8	15.3	2 214	23.1
Leelanau	59	6.7	120	2.2	33.3	810 441	6 731	96 296	20.5	41 486	86.7	13.3	43.1	9.1	2 363	31.0
Lenawee	344	-1.2	213	4.4	299.3	863 720	4 058	134 226	204.6	126 435	70.4	29.6	42.0	17.4	10 028	62.1
Livingston	86	-10.7	117	1.4	61.0	569 114	4 849	88 651	52.3	71 187	74.1	25.9	36.0	10.4	1 090	16.5
Luce	12	31.5	270	D	4.3	619 116	2 295	97 233	3.6	84 070	81.7	18.3	39.5	11.6	79	20.9
Mackinac	22	3.3	218	0.0	11.5	452 359	2 078	57 767	5.4	52 039	22.1	77.9	45.6	7.8	142	21.4
Macomb	68	9.6	135	2.5	58.4	747 673	5 523	120 797	73.2	145 900	79.7	20.3	53.4	24.7	956	23.5
Manistee	44	-3.8	137	1.3	20.1	393 093	2 875	41 111	7.6	23 543	85.1	14.9	28.4	5.9	241	13.0
Marquette	31	2.0	183	0.1	9.2	372 268	2 038	68 690	2.3	13 679	35.5	64.5	26.8	1.2	209	8.9
Mason	79	3.4	180	3.0	56.7	512 948	2 855	109 655	52.9	120 184	59.9	40.1	43.0	15.0	828	27.0
Mecosta	123	7.2	158	14.4	79.7	471 610	2 987	90 709	113.3	145 388	40.6	59.4	46.5	13.0	904	36.5
Menominee	92	-11.3	231	0.0	50.3	463 201	2 006	84 543	41.4	104 025	19.1	80.9	37.7	14.6	1 131	37.4
Midland	90	-1.2	161	1.0	69.5	580 838	3 600	98 339	70.1	126 285	67.9	32.1	39.1	14.1	2 310	44.3
Missaukee	100	12.6	230	7.5	71.7	695 275	3 025	154 582	126.0	290 998	24.8	75.2	41.6	18.7	1 568	28.6
Monroe	215	3.2	188	9.8	196.2	853 688	4 553	135 682	173.9	152 008	95.5	4.5	54.6	20.3	3 653	50.8
Montcalm	237	-2.3	211	55.9	181.1	702 214	3 336	131 319	213.9	189 831	72.1	27.9	41.1	17.9	2 577	40.6
Montmorency	24	11.6	161	D	14.6	366 252	2 272	84 497	8.1	53 854	52.8	47.2	37.7	9.9	175	25.2
Muskegon	74	-6.8	144	9.5	49.0	741 080	5 130	95 333	76.0	147 860	61.6	38.4	38.9	15.6	658	21.8
Newaygo	126	-5.8	136	7.5	83.4	484 268	3 557	91 385	113.8	123 346	39.9	60.1	39.5	13.8	1 193	20.8
Oakland	32	-2.4	59	0.7	18.8	506 358	8 572	54 261	25.9	48 244	87.5	12.5	25.1	6.9	226	6.9
Oceana	128	3.6	210	10.4	89.4	675 791	3 221	124 509	101.2	166 141	63.3	36.7	48.6	18.7	2 529	31.2
Ogemaw	68	11.8	243	0.1	40.2	645 025	2 650	129 246	46.3	165 218	29.1	70.9	42.1	18.9	927	47.1
Ontonagon	29	-5.7	267	0.0	13.9	451 716	1 694	61 257	2.2	20 220	75.1	24.9	40.4	4.6	91	12.8
Osceola	111	-9.5	147	1.4	64.7	373 809	2 536	65 007	45.7	60 912	28.5	71.5	30.0	8.5	1 124	22.8
Oscoda	17	-4.7	116	0.0	7.9	303 648	2 629	48 641	6.9	47 635	17.1	82.9	45.5	13.8	44	6.2
Otsego	32	-3.9	179	1.2	14.3	453 122	2 526	72 189	7.1	39 250	85.5	14.5	39.4	6.1	88	32.2
Ottawa	186	9.2	137	18.1	138.1	881 996	6 458	142 875	534.4	392 080	56.2	43.8	56.9	26.9	2 689	25.5
Presque Isle	82	14.7	252	1.4	45.4	541 449	2 145	82 938	22.8	70 653	76.5	23.5	39.6	10.8	684	31.0
Roscommon	7	56.2	128	0.3	2.7	336 517	2 626	56 966	D	D	D	D	24.1	0.0	D	6.9
Saginaw	310	-4.5	235	2.3	274.5	896 656	3 816	144 832	243.6	184 855	91.7	8.3	55.8	27.6	6 093	71.6
St. Clair	180	12.1	172	0.4	151.6	640 936	3 736	122 904	107.9	102 895	90.7	9.3	47.5	17.8	1 714	32.6
St. Joseph	222	2.9	229	112.4	188.2	1 090 049	4 754	158 897	238.1	246 177	80.2	19.8	48.4	25.0	4 196	46.8
Sanilac	457	9.5	311	1.8	405.5	1 365 955	4 386	217 288	421.0	286 957	66.5	33.5	61.0	36.3	7 213	60.3
Schoolcraft	19	-27.2	299	D	5.3	485 169	1 624	59 031	2.2	33 354	63.0	37.1	32.3	9.2	93	10.8
Shiawassee	223	-1.4	216	0.8	195.2	773 484	3 577	136 423	145.2	140 532	78.1	21.9	52.6	22.0	3 634	55.3
Tuscola	325	-5.1	246	5.4	284.5	1 117 802	4 542	168 867	274.4	207 599	82.4	17.6	48.9	26.2	4 778	56.9
Van Buren	175	-5.5	157	34.0	125.1	699 335	4 445	132 358	194.7	174 900	82.9	17.1	46.6	16.4	2 425	21.5
Washtenaw	170	2.0	138	3.6	133.5	701 358	5 095	92 338	87.8	71 004	77.0	23.0	42.5	14.6	3 466	31.7
Wayne	16	-9.6	55	0.3	10.9	408 840	7 442	80 902	26.5	92 456	98.2	1.8	36.9	8.4	102	9.4
Wexford	40	4.8	113	0.9	23.7	321 616	2 847	47 675	9.7	27 104	49.9	50.1	26.1	5.0	122	15.1
MINNESOTA	26 036	-3.3	349	524.0	21 597.1	1 474 057	4 220	197 702	21 280.2	285 479	65.2	34.8	60.0	33.5	467 867	70.0
Aitkin	123	-7.6	260	3.1	61.8	458 718	1 762	64 280	15.7	33 395	52.4	47.6	36.9	6.8	275	22.1
Anoka	45	-2.5	113	2.6	33.0	683 038	6 032	84 725	47.5	119 922	81.5	18.5	35.6	11.6	329	23.7
Becker	435	9.9	393	10.4	309.9	1 067 005	2 716	145 055	261.5	236 218	67.8	32.2	45.9	21.0	6 592	62.9
Beltrami	181	-14.4	315	2.6	88.2	535 471	1 699	70 642	32.4	56 518	66.0	34.0	41.2	10.3	1 146	32.6
Benton	189	1.5	197	11.5	139.9	676 684	3 435	130 284	167.5	174 846	44.1	55.9	59.5	24.5	3 168	63.9
Big Stone	249	-1.4	622	2.1	215.7	2 426 078	3 901	304 623	164.6	411 560	84.0	16.0	72.0	47.5	3 512	85.8
Blue Earth	376	-9.4	352	1.7	338.8	2 256 415	6 413	234 723	505.4	472 358	51.8	48.2	65.8	46.4	7 732	80.4
Brown	326	-8.1	309	2.4	296.4	1 705 125	5 518	216 063	382.9	362 955	57.5	42.5	76.5	51.5	7 384	88.3
Carlton	93	-5.5	185	D	42.4	345 838	1 872	55 281	11.0	21 878	49.3	50.7	39.1	2.4	D	12.2
Carver	155	-8.3	197	0.2	131.6	1 139 812	5 793	194 842	134.4	170 340	65.4	34.6	59.6	28.9	3 149	62.4
Cass	157	-7.1	288	8.8	61.3	549 962	1 910	68 947	38.2	69 877	27.5	72.5	44.3	8.1	542	23.4
Chippewa	335	-8.9	497	4.3	310.6	2 569 132	5 167	332 969	333.2	494 408	79.3	20.7	66.5	48.5	6 261	87.5
Chisago	114	-1.3	137	1.6	76.2	595 308	4 354	79 403	56.5	67 945	77.7	22.3	47.8	12.6	1 081	38.6
Clay	611	-0.5	760	9.9	555.2	2 673 295	3 519	311 899	398.1	495 118	90.3	9.7	62.3	41.3	8 241	75.7
Clearwater	167	-14.0	322	4.0	76.2	539 944	1 679	79 719	31.1	59 836	48.3	51.7	48.4	9.8	886	41.0
Cook	2	-5.4	126	0.0	0.2	598 778	4 744	28 444	0.3	14 278	90.3	9.7	27.8	5.6	D	5.6
Cottonwood	373	-2.2	459	1.4	336.4	2 519 027	5 494	312 232	374.1	460 135	62.6	37.4	70.6	53.4	7 918	83.9
Crow Wing	100	-17.9	188	2.2	44.8	485 445	2 588	75 574	24.8	46 593	58.6	41.5	36.8	8.8	546	30.6
Dakota	220	-10.6	246	50.4	192.7	1 398 640	5 675	195 370	241.0	270 188	77.8	22.2	63.9	32.5	3 892	54.4
Dodge	225	-9.2	363	D	202.5	2 231 597	6 148	237 108	288.1	463 976	61.6	38.4	63.6	40.3	4 124	68.9
Douglas	268	1.8	245	3.4	197.8	754 903	3 078	113 163	120.9	110 813	73.7	26.3	52.6	23.1	4 467	77.7
Faribault	390	-14.0	473	0.3	370.2	2 662 949	5 624	317 608	414.2	502 671	77.9	22.1	78.9	61.0	7 763	82.8

STATE County	Total water withdrawn (mil gal/day)	Gallons withdrawn per person per day	Number of establishments	Number of employees	Sales (mil dol)	Annual payroll (mil dol)	Number of establishments	Number of employees	Sales (mil dol)	Annual payroll (mil dol)	Number of establishments	Number of employees	Receipts (mil dol)	Annual payroll (mil dol)
	133	134	135	136	137	138	139	140	141	142	143	144	145	146
MICHIGAN—Cont'd														
Keweenaw	0.2	93	2	D	D	D	11	39	3.9	0.5	1	D	D	D
Lake	2.0	173	4	D	D	D	30	243	60.2	4.8	4	D	D	D
Lapeer	7.9	90	50	438	282.1	20.7	239	2 859	867.1	66.0	56	219	24.5	5.2
Leelanau	3.6	167	11	D	D	D	124	568	139.3	12.4	30	D	D	D
Lenawee	13.3	133	56	D	D	D	304	3 804	961.6	86.9	57	169	30.5	8.2
Livingston	20.0	111	198	2 435	3 092.5	144.1	599	8 695	2 410.2	205.7	124	544	95.4	18.5
Luce	1.3	201	4	D	D	D	26	256	84.2	5.9	7	36	2.4	0.6
Mackinac	10.1	908	8	48	65.3	1.9	93	366	121.9	10.3	12	D	D	D
Macomb	9.2	11	787	10 277	5 776.1	580.9	2 786	40 305	11 304.2	1 006.0	617	3 018	572.1	99.2
Manistee	42.9	1 736	13	117	225.6	6.6	107	905	231.9	19.0	18	42	5.8	0.9
Marquette	271.9	4 053	47	370	203.2	15.9	275	3 741	789.3	77.2	64	266	37.8	6.3
Mason	23.7	827	19	135	190.9	5.8	113	1 428	370.3	32.4	30	560	117.8	31.7
Mecosta	15.1	353	19	D	D	D	142	1 881	488.2	40.3	38	94	15.8	2.4
Menominee	5.8	243	18	297	144.1	11.9	68	584	155.5	11.9	16	D	D	D
Midland	10.6	127	44	297	703.7	16.7	314	4 050	1 015.7	88.4	63	257	36.8	8.4
Missaukee	3.9	263	16	111	69.6	4.5	39	332	120.0	8.9	4	5	0.5	0.1
Monroe	1 830.0	12 038	89	D	D	D	377	4 977	1 471.2	110.5	78	306	43.8	7.9
Montcalm	30.0	474	39	314	144.6	12.0	214	2 231	601.8	50.2	22	64	9.5	1.4
Montmorency	1.1	110	2	D	D	D	33	224	66.7	4.9	3	D	D	D
Muskegon	271.7	1 578	121	D	D	D	552	7 597	1 919.4	171.2	91	457	71.7	14.8
Newaygo	8.3	171	29	201	105.1	8.7	149	1 423	377.1	31.9	26	65	9.0	1.7
Oakland	50.2	42	2 048	28 521	25 910.5	1 806.5	4 880	70 570	20 886.2	1 879.2	1 644	15 464	3 085.1	678.8
Oceana	6.4	241	10	65	31.2	2.7	88	606	160.5	12.8	17	43	6.2	1.2
Ogemaw	3.2	149	21	441	155.5	17.4	119	1 574	387.6	35.3	21	58	9.0	1.6
Ontonagon	5.5	807	4	9	1.9	0.3	30	242	48.4	5.2	3	5	0.3	0.2
Osceola	5.5	234	13	116	134.7	5.2	73	601	176.1	15.4	9	9	2.3	0.4
Oscoda	1.2	142	2	D	D	D	37	241	59.5	4.6	7	14	1.8	0.2
Otsego	4.1	171	42	379	167.4	15.1	148	2 025	528.6	46.1	21	66	9.7	1.8
Ottawa	944.1	3 579	295	3 659	2 645.2	190.1	764	9 714	2 666.6	230.5	196	825	143.8	27.3
Presque Isle	23.7	1 770	5	8	2.0	0.2	64	388	110.9	8.6	7	D	D	D
Roscommon	2.7	112	10	48	12.6	1.4	111	1 220	331.4	28.7	15	63	9.7	1.6
Saginaw	22.3	111	181	1 975	1 264.9	96.7	870	12 210	2 913.3	262.8	132	602	101.1	16.3
St. Clair	1 495.2	9 171	89	924	548.7	40.4	532	6 745	1 760.6	148.7	94	272	56.4	8.2
St. Joseph	35.6	580	42	D	D	D	196	2 254	631.8	51.7	40	133	18.7	2.7
Sanilac	6.1	141	33	315	248.9	16.9	156	1 502	374.2	30.7	18	41	5.3	1.0
Schoolcraft	7.7	904	6	5	2.8	0.1	46	376	124.6	7.9	1	D	D	D
Shiawassee	7.4	104	40	457	201.1	18.2	200	2 413	713.9	58.1	35	77	11.2	2.0
Tuscola	8.9	160	39	465	404.6	23.0	157	1 581	481.9	34.8	19	75	8.7	1.4
Van Buren	167.0	2 189	53	D	D	D	252	2 285	634.6	54.1	32	102	15.3	1.9
Washtenaw	34.8	101	276	3 580	4 695.9	221.8	1 106	16 577	4 461.1	411.4	306	2 409	727.2	115.9
Wayne	1 797.3	987	1 483	23 525	25 358.3	1 417.5	6 091	65 409	17 409.4	1 539.9	1 070	6 044	4 464.6	225.3
Wexford	7.6	232	25	409	162.6	19.5	163	1 922	497.4	42.8	34	105	15.6	2.9
MINNESOTA	3 821.2	720	6 569	108 467	104 485.1	7 170.1	19 109	288 888	78 898.2	6 857.5	6 300	34 499	7 827.9	1 396.0
Aitkin	3.4	212	12	114	125.1	4.8	69	647	173.3	13.3	9	9	1.4	0.2
Anoka	126.1	381	326	12 633	7 485.0	1 617.5	884	15 209	3 982.1	355.7	345	1 149	249.9	34.9
Becker	8.6	264	37	263	150.8	10.1	132	1 731	459.7	38.9	34	77	17.8	2.5
Beltrami	6.4	144	44	D	D	D	220	3 106	702.7	66.5	30	83	14.5	2.4
Benton	21.9	568	42	1 130	911.7	58.9	119	1 800	510.3	42.9	35	80	13.5	2.4
Big Stone	1.4	270	8	74	208.2	3.9	27	209	38.2	3.7	3	3	0.3	0.1
Blue Earth	34.6	540	89	1 383	953.2	65.6	321	6 061	1 413.1	128.0	83	557	66.5	13.3
Brown	4.0	155	28	376	701.3	19.2	109	1 606	347.1	32.6	18	59	7.5	1.5
Carlton	10.7	302	17	287	226.0	11.4	107	1 344	351.8	28.3	16	51	10.5	1.1
Carver	11.2	122	127	2 247	1 699.4	200.5	210	3 484	907.8	80.6	96	603	123.4	29.1
Cass	6.0	211	14	187	87.9	10.0	131	913	255.7	19.8	37	236	13.3	5.9
Chippewa	2.1	170	19	313	532.2	15.7	54	650	198.9	13.9	14	122	6.5	2.4
Chisago	4.7	86	45	435	176.2	18.3	154	1 722	469.2	37.1	44	D	D	D
Clay	6.6	112	68	900	1 175.4	47.0	160	2 682	665.1	57.7	41	160	19.2	3.7
Clearwater	5.7	660	2	D	D	D	34	245	48.8	4.1	NA	NA	NA	NA
Cook	174.8	33 773	3	D	D	D	52	337	66.7	7.8	15	43	4.3	0.9
Cottonwood	5.4	464	25	168	287.4	9.6	51	506	102.8	9.8	6	19	3.3	0.8
Crow Wing	11.4	182	67	450	265.1	18.4	365	4 518	1 125.0	101.2	89	203	46.4	6.3
Dakota	339.7	852	524	7 768	11 786.0	484.9	1 122	21 719	6 485.6	576.6	479	2 310	439.8	83.3
Dodge	2.6	131	21	521	406.7	28.5	48	452	87.9	7.1	7	D	D	D
Douglas	5.7	159	48	997	502.2	44.5	234	3 078	743.4	65.8	43	146	36.6	4.5
Faribault	3.2	218	25	227	227.0	6.6	66	618	122.3	11.8	5	10	1.0	0.2

1. Merchant wholesalers, except manufacturers' sales branches and offices.   2. Employer establishments.

Table B. States and Counties — Professional Services, Manufacturing, and Accommodation and Food Services

STATE County	Professional, scientific, and technical services, 2012				Manufacturing, 2012				Accommodation and food services, 2012			
	Number of establishments	Number of employees	Receipts (mil dol)	Annual payroll (mil dol)	Number of establishments	Number of employees	Receipts (mil dol)	Annual payroll (mil dol)	Number of establishments	Number of employees	Sales (mil dol)	Annual payroll (mil dol)
	147	148	149	150	151	152	153	154	155	156	157	158
MICHIGAN—Cont'd												
Keweenaw	NA	NA	NA	NA	4	10	D	D	19	99	5.4	1.5
Lake	4	16	1.1	0.5	8	D	D	D	30	D	D	D
Lapeer	132	623	74.6	25.7	125	4 923	1 303.5	198.8	117	1 933	80.2	22.4
Leelanau	72	223	32.2	10.0	35	240	D	8.8	72	718	46.5	17.0
Lenawee	119	613	50.9	20.1	131	4 569	2 047.2	234.5	167	2 658	105.7	30.4
Livingston	502	2 276	402.4	129.3	248	8 508	3 252.3	420.4	264	5 085	226.3	62.0
Luce	8	12	0.9	0.4	6	171	69.2	7.7	22	180	7.0	1.9
Mackinac	16	32	3.5	1.4	19	143	D	4.6	115	749	122.1	35.2
Macomb	1 581	30 331	3 348.4	2 177.3	1 593	59 114	27 017.3	3 495.8	1 565	28 350	1 263.1	347.5
Manistee	40	108	11.6	4.1	24	816	419.5	46.5	54	1 406	155.4	25.1
Marquette	113	676	66.7	28.6	49	871	275.7	45.3	174	2 806	114.4	34.9
Mason	44	156	13.1	5.0	38	1 800	432.2	86.2	88	980	50.2	13.9
Mecosta	46	281	34.3	16.4	32	1 880	677.0	77.4	78	1 178	45.7	13.5
Menominee	28	88	6.4	2.5	47	1 665	461.7	76.7	47	575	21.8	6.0
Midland	154	785	87.9	34.9	62	6 241	3 591.1	466.1	138	2 861	136.2	40.7
Missaukee	11	18	2.0	0.7	21	363	99.4	12.7	20	168	10.0	2.6
Monroe	147	828	129.9	40.6	128	6 591	2 976.5	351.3	259	4 280	179.9	49.6
Montcalm	51	220	16.1	5.6	74	2 738	528.3	121.1	82	1 003	44.9	12.2
Montmorency	10	21	1.8	0.7	15	369	74.5	12.6	22	D	D	D
Muskegon	223	1 513	182.5	65.7	259	12 483	3 727.0	608.0	335	5 450	236.1	67.6
Newaygo	54	348	52.1	17.4	40	1 897	663.4	84.6	76	906	39.9	10.5
Oakland	6 134	82 960	13 269.4	6 209.6	1 669	47 243	18 446.3	2 707.5	2 755	51 669	2 567.3	739.9
Oceana	28	123	14.4	5.5	41	1 324	473.2	46.6	57	599	29.3	8.2
Ogemaw	31	118	9.5	3.4	30	265	79.0	8.1	65	789	38.1	11.0
Ontonagon	6	9	0.8	0.2	NA	NA	NA	NA	27	156	6.2	1.4
Osceola	25	88	8.5	2.7	41	1 898	968.5	92.5	39	543	25.4	8.0
Oscoda	9	58	2.8	1.4	17	246	70.0	8.9	23	196	8.0	2.4
Otsego	55	205	31.2	9.7	37	682	141.4	25.9	60	1 037	54.4	14.7
Ottawa	466	3 228	471.5	190.5	544	31 831	11 067.3	1 529.6	381	7 573	321.8	89.8
Presque Isle	14	32	1.9	0.6	13	166	D	7.0	43	286	10.6	3.0
Roscommon	30	160	5.4	2.1	16	602	131.7	29.2	71	987	39.8	12.2
Saginaw	318	2 226	299.2	109.3	206	11 249	4 523.3	653.2	368	7 829	373.8	97.6
St. Clair	222	982	112.8	39.8	235	8 080	4 027.0	384.7	283	4 635	191.5	53.3
St. Joseph	74	4 239	44.9	63.4	132	7 683	3 542.4	350.7	104	1 368	57.9	15.8
Sanilac	51	210	15.3	5.3	74	2 385	729.7	95.7	61	567	27.8	6.9
Schoolcraft	9	45	2.9	1.2	9	185	104.4	11.4	35	261	11.6	3.1
Shiawassee	66	308	33.5	10.8	60	1 811	466.5	71.7	109	1 491	61.7	16.8
Tuscola	50	193	19.6	7.9	44	1 216	513.6	54.5	61	753	29.3	8.0
Van Buren	77	1 348	195.0	65.4	87	2 781	1 224.1	140.8	149	1 967	97.2	26.8
Washtenaw	1 284	13 390	2 329.9	928.1	332	13 232	5 419.9	725.8	766	14 879	764.9	216.3
Wayne	2 848	46 825	7 135.0	3 444.6	1 483	71 526	56 638.5	4 413.5	3 184	61 446	4 238.8	1 050.2
Wexford	60	298	28.1	13.2	49	3 890	1 119.0	173.9	78	1 064	46.6	12.8
MINNESOTA	16 348	140 927	23 449.1	9 739.3	7 313	297 884	123 076.3	15 822.6	11 345	221 859	11 722.6	3 238.0
Aitkin	14	D	D	D	27	298	62.1	11.4	51	448	18.8	5.1
Anoka	720	3 290	511.7	176.0	611	20 086	6 716.2	1 164.4	470	9 467	434.0	123.0
Becker	53	181	24.5	7.1	43	2 240	455.7	97.3	88	1 097	57.7	14.6
Beltrami	64	359	34.3	13.6	37	732	D	25.3	94	1 711	76.2	22.1
Benton	48	217	31.1	12.6	70	2 975	681.7	124.1	59	1 072	45.0	12.6
Big Stone	11	D	D	D	5	20	1.1	0.3	18	D	D	D
Blue Earth	147	1 090	127.2	52.6	88	3 896	3 938.5	189.7	156	3 584	143.6	39.2
Brown	43	405	43.4	15.9	38	2 935	1 506.6	129.7	61	955	32.5	9.4
Carlton	45	178	15.3	5.1	27	1 397	D	85.8	67	887	34.6	9.5
Carver	319	2 820	373.5	97.0	144	9 666	3 992.3	572.5	145	D	D	D
Cass	35	131	10.9	4.6	36	300	56.4	10.2	136	2 297	144.7	38.5
Chippewa	19	77	6.9	2.9	27	1 085	358.5	47.3	29	406	14.1	3.5
Chisago	72	D	D	D	80	1 952	552.9	88.0	86	D	D	D
Clay	77	D	D	D	38	832	409.3	D	81	1 824	68.8	20.2
Clearwater	11	53	3.1	1.0	13	443	D	14.1	21	D	D	D
Cook	15	D	D	D	5	43	12.5	1.9	62	637	46.8	14.0
Cottonwood	19	72	7.4	2.2	26	1 780	1 059.6	60.6	21	272	9.7	2.6
Crow Wing	143	940	125.8	50.7	104	2 480	496.6	103.9	209	3 003	169.5	45.9
Dakota	1 385	8 495	1 552.6	595.7	432	16 946	17 442.9	921.0	688	15 357	762.1	211.9
Dodge	22	D	D	D	23	1 123	719.7	57.8	27	336	12.6	3.3
Douglas	83	508	84.5	21.4	89	3 174	920.1	157.1	117	2 023	89.8	25.7
Faribault	20	79	7.9	2.8	24	1 134	326.0	46.6	34	260	11.8	2.5

1. Establishment subject to federal tax.

STATE County	Health care and social assistance, 2012				Other services, 2012				Nonemployer businesses, 2015		Value of residential construction authorized by building permits, 2016	
	Number of establishments	Number of employees	Receipts (mil dol)	Annual payroll (mil dol)	Number of establishments	Number of employees	Receipts (mil dol)	Annual payroll (mil dol)	Number	Receipts (mil dol)	New Construction ($1,000)	Number of housing units
	159	160	161	162	163	164	165	166	167	168	169	170
MICHIGAN—Cont'd												
Keweenaw	1	D	D	D	2	D	D	D	158	3.8	1 143	8
Lake	12	248	13.8	7.4	10	23	1.9	0.3	600	20.1	1 638	57
Lapeer	201	2 532	239.7	91.1	103	420	37.5	9.3	6 565	272.1	28 030	139
Leelanau	55	D	D	D	34	84	9.3	2.3	2 789	131.9	38 073	137
Lenawee	231	3 168	274.6	112.9	146	758	50.6	14.1	5 884	222.6	21 713	110
Livingston	376	5 161	522.1	191.9	281	1 853	146.9	48.3	14 911	710.7	173 539	660
Luce	16	414	37.4	15.9	10	D	D	D	308	10.2	1 264	6
Mackinac	19	332	47.3	13.9	15	D	D	D	913	29.9	8 152	42
Macomb	2 308	37 149	4 079.6	1 683.2	1 391	7 991	736.6	223.6	62 979	2 713.5	400 845	1 747
Manistee	65	906	93.7	35.5	44	179	13.7	4.4	1 676	58.0	5 356	43
Marquette	237	5 537	592.1	252.1	131	564	52.6	13.2	3 477	104.7	20 742	95
Mason	93	1 446	124.1	56.5	57	203	16.5	4.7	2 019	66.8	12 766	50
Mecosta	84	1 528	112.8	51.6	62	336	29.4	7.1	2 238	80.7	13 948	124
Menominee	40	334	18.5	8.2	30	161	16.5	4.0	1 337	65.9	6 722	34
Midland	239	6 268	682.2	242.8	147	882	113.0	23.2	4 899	192.0	26 204	201
Missaukee	26	326	14.1	6.6	19	50	4.8	1.2	1 106	49.5	3 206	20
Monroe	282	5 347	457.9	193.6	156	727	67.6	17.0	8 299	363.4	62 555	511
Montcalm	106	3 054	276.4	110.5	88	317	32.7	7.5	3 694	141.6	15 872	90
Montmorency	12	219	15.7	6.1	13	D	D	D	563	21.4	0	0
Muskegon	369	11 494	982.3	483.8	250	1 315	120.8	29.6	9 379	357.4	45 718	233
Newaygo	76	1 706	168.0	69.7	66	211	40.0	5.2	2 763	117.1	13 657	79
Oakland	5 120	100 125	10 835.6	4 461.3	2 371	16 548	1 962.1	474.5	113 364	6 578.1	792 106	3 196
Oceana	45	628	44.7	18.8	37	93	8.7	2.0	1 706	61.5	195	2
Ogemaw	66	1 321	102.6	45.5	44	152	11.1	2.9	1 293	52.1	4 062	23
Ontonagon	18	243	17.0	6.9	12	44	7.2	0.8	363	12.8	1 105	9
Osceola	50	1 106	90.0	34.5	30	109	12.4	2.8	1 407	62.8	2 420	21
Oscoda	14	164	9.9	3.6	12	50	3.3	0.8	588	22.6	3 500	19
Otsego	83	1 420	211.2	58.3	61	238	21.0	5.8	1 931	83.7	1 296	16
Ottawa	516	9 453	895.3	314.2	436	2 569	261.1	73.9	18 807	929.9	336 546	1 633
Presque Isle	26	331	22.9	9.0	23	45	5.3	0.9	913	25.3	180	1
Roscommon	45	531	38.0	15.3	56	176	14.5	3.9	1 461	53.2	6 598	35
Saginaw	582	17 262	1 766.5	712.8	328	1 943	161.3	45.2	10 737	406.8	40 089	281
St. Clair	378	7 828	696.4	292.1	201	912	87.1	20.5	10 337	425.5	39 661	188
St. Joseph	108	2 062	187.0	74.5	97	330	31.6	9.0	3 474	141.2	13 758	64
Sanilac	90	1 317	114.8	37.9	55	153	18.0	3.9	3 115	124.2	4 382	39
Schoolcraft	22	D	D	D	14	71	5.0	1.4	383	12.7	1 073	9
Shiawassee	134	2 549	217.0	87.8	97	463	37.7	9.1	4 259	167.4	8 822	40
Tuscola	107	2 444	186.7	78.4	55	168	13.0	3.2	3 454	130.8	7 041	38
Van Buren	107	2 497	195.5	81.3	89	360	30.1	6.6	4 739	191.5	23 003	104
Washtenaw	964	36 873	4 710.2	2 219.2	537	3 891	489.6	143.2	29 232	1 273.4	114 638	438
Wayne	4 091	101 848	12 420.4	4 712.3	2 645	16 865	1 763.8	497.5	126 572	4 098.6	358 370	1 729
Wexford	96	2 022	169.8	70.1	68	254	25.5	6.6	2 215	87.2	9 854	46
MINNESOTA	15 107	440 195	40 403.6	17 514.4	10 832	72 715	7 877.3	2 017.1	397 378	18 435.2	4 593 041	21 449
Aitkin	29	720	67.2	25.3	35	127	14.7	2.1	1 096	46.8	32 157	155
Anoka	625	15 314	1 631.1	710.6	535	3 642	350.2	102.1	22 344	974.2	298 342	1 287
Becker	78	1 800	149.8	65.9	82	371	39.4	7.1	2 872	145.2	33 959	171
Beltrami	138	3 934	434.5	151.1	90	415	49.8	12.1	2 911	117.5	36 477	401
Benton	84	3 071	116.7	56.0	79	588	48.9	15.2	2 554	114.7	40 759	217
Big Stone	20	898	56.9	24.6	15	33	3.7	0.5	406	18.7	2 410	13
Blue Earth	223	9 080	671.0	323.3	130	D	D	D	4 105	178.5	51 282	285
Brown	64	2 350	172.1	74.3	70	269	35.9	7.3	1 815	75.5	9 920	52
Carlton	88	2 058	145.3	68.3	62	243	22.2	5.8	1 891	70.0	18 696	82
Carver	201	4 828	471.1	202.5	171	1 051	84.6	24.4	7 985	411.0	189 491	678
Cass	68	1 227	65.1	27.7	59	228	18.4	3.7	2 598	124.5	35 547	161
Chippewa	39	1 100	69.6	29.2	41	156	20.1	3.9	845	37.6	1 900	8
Chisago	131	4 202	313.6	152.4	95	400	29.8	8.6	3 756	156.7	36 387	214
Clay	167	3 955	186.6	87.0	105	491	38.3	10.8	3 943	147.6	81 676	576
Clearwater	16	551	22.9	12.0	13	34	3.8	0.6	646	26.4	776	6
Cook	15	233	20.9	8.1	9	D	D	D	775	29.5	7 546	38
Cottonwood	34	818	50.1	19.9	27	89	8.0	2.0	805	38.1	4 475	21
Crow Wing	231	5 938	482.6	215.6	141	694	54.5	13.7	5 061	243.0	33 228	158
Dakota	1 012	23 031	1 679.6	745.8	729	6 034	582.8	183.3	28 643	1 328.5	364 129	1 342
Dodge	31	245	15.0	6.9	41	264	29.3	7.6	1 353	76.1	17 132	87
Douglas	129	3 480	266.1	105.0	109	464	42.6	9.5	3 329	172.3	35 422	207
Faribault	38	807	56.7	23.5	32	141	14.8	3.5	1 131	53.3	1 017	4

Table B. States and Counties — Government Employment and Payroll, and Local Government Finances

	Government employment and payroll, 2012		March payroll (percent of total)							Local government finances, 2012				
STATE County										General revenue		Taxes		
													Per capita[1] (dollars)	
	Full-time equivalent employees	March payroll (dollars)	Administration, judicial, and legal	Police and Corrections	Fire Protection	Highways and transportation	Health and Welfare	Natural resources and utilities	Education and libraries	Total (mil dol)	Inter-governmental (mil dol)	Total (mil dol)	Total	Property
	171	172	173	174	175	176	177	178	179	180	181	182	183	184
MICHIGAN—Cont'd														
Keweenaw	94	226 587	43.0	12.5	0.3	32.4	0.3	5.4	3.3	7.1	2.2	2.4	1 085	1 064
Lake	335	1 121 895	29.9	22.5	0.7	15.2	0.2	4.0	24.4	41.5	20.4	15.6	1 355	1 353
Lapeer	2 193	8 102 009	9.7	7.1	0.9	3.7	6.5	3.4	67.0	261.5	141.1	64.1	727	687
Leelanau	610	2 337 768	17.9	7.8	10.1	6.0	1.3	2.0	50.2	66.0	15.8	38.3	1 774	1 747
Lenawee	2 916	10 906 000	8.3	8.7	1.9	4.7	2.7	5.5	65.8	340.2	180.3	97.9	989	958
Livingston	3 683	15 206 225	8.3	7.3	2.3	3.3	1.3	2.2	69.7	518.2	264.0	170.8	934	916
Luce	511	1 851 870	3.9	1.5	0.5	3.4	68.0	1.9	19.9	52.1	10.7	6.0	924	922
Mackinac	650	2 008 291	8.8	6.7	0.6	5.6	41.9	4.0	30.0	45.0	12.9	23.1	2 077	1 972
Macomb	20 477	98 514 743	5.7	8.9	3.4	3.3	4.1	2.4	70.5	3 154.9	1 534.9	942.2	1 112	1 087
Manistee	1 223	4 900 512	8.6	4.0	2.1	5.6	46.5	1.1	31.4	89.4	31.4	32.7	1 326	1 315
Marquette	2 307	8 582 841	9.4	7.9	1.6	8.1	17.8	11.0	40.6	242.6	106.7	75.0	1 105	1 084
Mason	951	3 483 823	12.1	7.3	0.1	7.1	0.9	4.3	66.7	123.3	40.6	57.2	1 996	1 980
Mecosta	1 566	5 890 046	7.7	5.5	1.5	4.1	36.2	3.2	40.3	182.4	76.2	42.5	980	926
Menominee	588	2 056 771	19.0	9.3	2.8	9.0	0.0	3.2	55.6	62.8	33.4	19.2	806	799
Midland	2 175	9 622 686	11.4	7.8	3.3	4.0	3.3	5.7	62.5	271.7	113.5	103.5	1 235	1 220
Missaukee	422	1 353 016	12.8	7.9	0.0	5.9	3.8	2.5	64.8	51.3	27.9	11.7	775	714
Monroe	3 882	16 268 085	7.1	8.4	1.4	3.3	1.1	4.8	72.4	475.7	225.8	166.5	1 102	1 074
Montcalm	1 898	7 424 584	9.0	5.3	0.5	3.4	5.9	1.9	72.7	230.7	138.4	56.8	901	887
Montmorency	201	694 558	20.5	8.4	2.1	11.4	4.4	2.8	43.7	25.7	7.3	10.4	1 095	1 081
Muskegon	5 428	21 789 876	7.5	7.4	2.5	3.3	9.1	3.1	65.4	721.5	413.6	168.4	989	913
Newaygo	1 567	5 734 250	9.2	6.4	0.9	3.1	12.6	1.5	64.0	180.6	100.9	46.4	967	962
Oakland	32 137	148 761 141	8.1	11.5	4.0	2.5	1.6	3.0	67.0	4 845.3	2 149.8	1 849.8	1 515	1 468
Oceana	787	2 716 638	12.5	6.8	0.6	9.1	6.1	3.2	57.2	91.5	36.3	30.4	1 156	1 142
Ogemaw	842	2 976 350	8.9	6.3	0.2	5.1	44.2	1.3	31.8	88.5	51.5	18.2	849	836
Ontonagon	240	749 123	19.9	5.8	0.6	28.7	0.1	8.1	33.5	31.1	13.6	12.2	1 900	1 897
Osceola	733	2 622 547	9.4	6.1	0.6	5.1	5.4	1.4	70.9	69.7	41.4	19.9	853	849
Oscoda	244	725 038	18.2	5.2	0.5	9.3	2.2	2.3	61.4	22.2	10.6	9.0	1 046	1 036
Otsego	766	3 112 250	10.4	4.0	0.5	8.3	0.2	1.8	71.3	77.8	31.0	34.0	1 415	1 413
Ottawa	6 822	27 516 658	8.5	6.3	1.4	2.9	4.0	6.4	67.9	866.8	436.0	302.6	1 125	1 104
Presque Isle	353	1 093 950	16.9	10.3	0.0	9.1	0.4	3.7	54.2	39.4	19.9	14.6	1 112	1 107
Roscommon	871	3 202 024	11.2	10.4	2.9	8.2	2.8	1.9	61.8	97.6	32.0	44.6	1 849	1 841
Saginaw	5 686	21 466 345	8.3	8.5	2.2	2.7	9.8	4.8	61.7	786.5	475.8	154.2	777	684
St. Clair	4 714	19 193 428	9.3	10.1	2.3	4.7	2.9	4.1	64.9	638.8	345.1	182.6	1 136	1 082
St. Joseph	2 407	8 504 558	8.9	6.1	1.5	3.5	17.3	3.9	56.9	263.0	120.1	64.5	1 061	1 051
Sanilac	1 146	3 992 557	10.8	9.0	0.7	4.8	2.5	4.3	65.5	164.8	92.6	39.4	932	918
Schoolcraft	461	1 943 689	9.8	4.5	1.3	9.9	52.0	3.2	18.6	62.6	11.5	8.5	1 020	1 018
Shiawassee	2 564	9 090 340	7.2	7.6	1.3	2.6	17.5	2.4	59.3	229.5	141.1	48.8	706	694
Tuscola	1 649	6 143 983	21.0	6.5	0.2	4.3	0.6	1.4	64.0	203.6	117.9	44.3	810	798
Van Buren	2 988	10 792 044	6.7	6.5	1.0	3.0	15.9	2.4	63.8	369.9	183.5	110.9	1 470	1 455
Washtenaw	9 997	45 620 706	8.5	10.1	3.0	4.2	5.2	5.4	62.0	1 472.6	631.4	577.8	1 646	1 596
Wayne	52 078	243 918 311	7.3	16.2	6.7	6.5	2.2	6.4	52.0	9 260.6	4 384.4	2 686.6	1 499	1 195
Wexford	861	3 131 204	9.3	8.2	2.0	8.9	0.5	6.9	62.4	121.3	63.1	38.8	1 190	1 183
MINNESOTA	X	X	X	X	X	X	X	X	X	X	X	X	X	X
Aitkin	582	2 073 612	15.2	11.2	0.4	6.7	11.2	4.6	46.4	60.1	32.6	17.4	1 089	1 074
Anoka	10 501	53 828 905	6.5	8.8	1.4	2.5	5.0	3.0	71.0	1 331.2	702.4	418.5	1 244	1 193
Becker	932	4 604 178	7.8	4.6	0.0	8.2	10.4	5.5	61.2	127.6	63.7	39.1	1 185	1 161
Beltrami	1 932	6 706 796	6.4	7.1	0.7	3.3	9.3	2.1	68.3	213.6	142.5	38.4	846	783
Benton	983	5 694 288	6.7	6.0	0.2	10.1	6.5	2.2	67.4	129.9	70.8	39.7	1 023	988
Big Stone	457	1 386 890	7.6	3.9	0.1	6.3	36.5	4.2	39.3	61.1	19.6	7.4	1 429	1 407
Blue Earth	2 214	8 872 355	7.8	8.8	1.3	4.6	6.9	5.2	63.0	311.6	161.3	79.4	1 221	1 080
Brown	1 088	4 160 686	9.0	10.8	0.0	6.2	20.5	12.8	39.2	121.7	52.1	29.1	1 145	1 070
Carlton	1 862	6 624 488	5.4	5.5	3.7	4.3	24.0	2.7	53.1	175.9	81.0	37.5	1 060	1 044
Carver	2 896	13 125 660	8.3	9.1	0.5	3.7	9.7	7.6	58.3	405.9	156.2	153.3	1 636	1 556
Cass	1 234	4 242 722	11.4	8.7	0.0	4.7	8.0	7.4	56.2	139.1	77.1	36.0	1 270	1 262
Chippewa	807	3 441 530	7.9	4.1	0.2	6.5	37.5	2.9	37.6	70.5	36.6	15.5	1 281	1 255
Chisago	1 385	5 404 860	10.1	10.6	0.1	5.4	10.2	3.2	57.7	193.7	95.4	66.1	1 237	1 214
Clay	2 229	9 153 639	5.8	9.5	2.1	3.2	9.3	7.6	60.6	275.2	152.5	52.4	871	834
Clearwater	344	1 650 939	7.5	7.1	0.0	4.2	13.2	2.5	62.5	36.7	20.9	8.5	982	979
Cook	357	1 321 609	10.7	6.6	0.1	6.3	41.6	8.6	23.6	43.3	14.6	10.6	2 035	1 721
Cottonwood	572	1 944 398	8.0	7.4	0.1	6.3	7.4	9.1	58.7	74.4	30.9	14.0	1 205	1 195
Crow Wing	2 463	11 443 269	7.2	9.3	0.8	3.7	30.0	2.2	44.6	346.9	130.2	91.9	1 461	1 378
Dakota	12 238	59 978 327	5.3	8.3	1.1	2.3	5.3	4.9	70.7	1 651.5	821.5	536.9	1 325	1 284
Dodge	717	3 409 832	6.5	6.4	0.0	3.9	12.4	1.9	67.9	88.6	44.2	22.9	1 131	1 119
Douglas	1 101	6 909 728	5.8	7.2	0.1	2.6	9.8	5.5	66.7	237.1	64.8	46.8	1 286	1 248
Faribault	667	3 058 474	6.0	6.7	0.1	5.1	34.0	6.2	39.8	90.8	34.3	16.1	1 130	1 101

1. Based on the resident population estimated as of July 1 of the year shown.

Local Government Finances, Government Employment, and Income Taxes

STATE County	Total (mil dol) 185	Per capita[1] (dollars) 186	Education 187	Health and hospitals 188	Police protection 189	Public welfare 190	Highways 191	Total (mil dol) 192	Per capita[1] (dollars) 193	Federal civilian 194	Federal military 195	State and local 196	Number of returns 197	Mean adjusted gross income 198	Mean income tax 199
MICHIGAN—Cont'd															
Keweenaw	6.9	3 101	2.6	1.3	7.4	0.3	34.9	4.3	1 951	24	D	111	1 040	45 437	4 055
Lake	31.5	2 738	24.3	2.6	4.3	1.0	15.0	21.8	1 898	53	18	403	4 440	35 748	2 889
Lapeer	274.0	3 108	46.0	7.1	3.5	8.9	6.8	238.6	2 706	140	140	4 065	42 230	52 091	5 621
Leelanau	61.1	2 829	43.8	4.2	3.6	0.7	9.8	51.6	2 388	129	35	1 728	11 810	69 492	9 932
Lenawee	351.5	3 551	55.5	5.5	3.4	4.6	6.5	276.7	2 796	190	151	4 679	45 290	48 524	4 822
Livingston	530.7	2 902	57.0	7.6	3.3	0.5	5.0	1 200.5	6 566	248	301	6 064	93 450	71 485	9 574
Luce	51.6	7 912	15.9	60.1	0.9	0.2	7.0	15.2	2 335	12	D	804	2 500	42 364	3 948
Mackinac	45.6	4 094	32.8	5.3	3.6	0.1	14.6	33.1	2 975	54	60	948	5 930	41 361	4 162
Macomb	3 200.9	3 777	51.2	8.3	6.2	1.5	3.9	3 701.0	4 368	7 830	1 823	28 442	438 670	52 827	6 028
Manistee	95.8	3 885	34.2	1.9	3.0	12.4	11.2	104.6	4 240	88	56	2 662	11 440	41 990	4 006
Marquette	235.2	3 464	37.8	1.8	6.5	6.4	9.7	135.1	1 989	282	119	5 393	30 570	51 901	5 554
Mason	115.8	4 037	56.0	0.9	2.9	9.4	8.9	57.5	2 005	95	62	1 851	14 070	45 148	4 760
Mecosta	174.1	4 018	38.9	30.3	3.2	0.8	5.0	74.8	1 726	95	64	4 623	16 840	45 068	4 642
Menominee	61.6	2 585	51.9	0.5	6.7	0.2	12.8	22.8	958	62	37	1 945	11 160	45 181	4 407
Midland	272.5	3 250	51.0	2.8	4.1	2.1	7.6	318.6	3 800	146	133	3 270	40 170	71 048	10 399
Missaukee	54.0	3 591	36.3	33.2	2.2	0.6	9.3	4.1	276	26	24	497	6 590	39 784	3 146
Monroe	515.6	3 414	53.6	6.7	3.7	0.2	9.1	557.6	3 691	228	241	5 338	73 050	56 044	6 287
Montcalm	236.5	3 748	58.8	7.6	2.3	0.4	7.4	191.1	3 029	125	97	2 918	27 010	40 656	3 532
Montmorency	24.1	2 539	34.8	1.0	4.8	1.0	13.9	10.5	1 103	17	15	391	4 320	38 555	3 301
Muskegon	746.4	4 386	51.2	13.2	3.2	3.6	4.5	688.6	4 046	338	295	7 254	77 840	44 649	4 587
Newaygo	194.0	4 046	57.6	5.7	2.5	6.5	7.1	159.0	3 316	72	77	2 195	21 150	44 343	4 234
Oakland	4 863.5	3 984	50.4	6.9	6.5	0.2	4.9	4 726.4	3 872	4 779	2 118	44 288	630 980	84 343	14 004
Oceana	89.5	3 401	42.0	4.4	3.7	17.2	11.9	48.9	1 859	152	42	1 176	12 030	43 839	4 540
Ogemaw	91.5	4 268	23.9	47.2	2.2	0.7	7.5	60.2	2 807	57	33	1 030	9 340	37 324	3 373
Ontonagon	29.7	4 631	39.8	1.3	2.4	0.1	24.2	24.8	3 875	38	10	338	2 780	39 703	3 345
Osceola	69.8	2 999	56.1	2.5	3.0	0.3	11.7	41.1	1 765	56	37	921	9 890	39 660	3 295
Oscoda	22.1	2 573	44.7	4.2	4.0	8.4	11.5	3.6	419	54	13	367	3 560	35 768	2 906
Otsego	81.5	3 391	48.3	3.2	2.7	0.6	12.1	42.7	1 777	136	40	1 018	12 040	46 111	4 833
Ottawa	885.8	3 292	57.1	5.1	3.6	0.9	6.5	1 000.3	3 717	395	501	15 609	128 950	63 948	8 161
Presque Isle	40.5	3 081	35.5	1.1	3.7	0.7	13.8	21.2	1 618	52	20	587	6 290	41 753	3 652
Roscommon	94.2	3 908	58.3	2.5	4.2	1.6	7.4	44.3	1 836	28	38	1 271	11 040	40 468	4 093
Saginaw	801.9	4 043	42.8	14.5	5.8	0.7	5.8	494.0	2 490	1 420	313	9 323	90 260	46 355	5 097
St. Clair	651.8	4 058	44.3	15.8	3.9	0.1	6.4	526.8	3 280	709	328	5 964	78 090	50 524	5 466
St. Joseph	268.7	4 420	49.4	24.1	3.0	0.3	4.3	186.9	3 074	105	98	2 744	28 270	43 542	4 124
Sanilac	165.3	3 911	47.1	12.6	4.3	6.0	11.0	127.3	3 011	104	66	1 708	19 030	42 259	4 035
Schoolcraft	58.9	7 054	15.2	41.3	2.0	13.4	8.4	36.7	4 402	42	13	1 031	3 840	44 358	4 355
Shiawassee	236.8	3 421	55.9	8.0	3.1	6.2	8.8	102.4	1 479	127	110	3 120	33 000	45 123	4 303
Tuscola	211.4	3 867	51.0	9.0	3.1	9.1	9.0	137.5	2 515	128	85	2 774	25 350	42 466	3 793
Van Buren	365.1	4 839	52.4	18.4	2.7	0.9	6.5	300.6	3 984	140	120	4 996	34 610	47 000	4 839
Washtenaw	1 495.8	4 262	46.0	12.6	6.5	0.9	4.9	2 033.3	5 794	4 073	606	69 709	163 820	75 953	11 320
Wayne	9 500.3	5 300	36.3	3.3	7.0	5.2	2.9	21 084.6	11 764	14 043	3 275	73 079	800 950	48 721	5 859
Wexford	112.1	3 437	54.4	1.5	4.1	1.5	9.9	59.5	1 825	129	54	1 894	15 170	41 203	3 812
MINNESOTA	X	X	X	X	X	X	X	X	X	31 599	19 967	370 038	2 687 660	68 533	9 144
Aitkin	64.5	4 049	33.1	1.4	4.3	8.2	22.4	16.8	1 053	43	56	792	7 220	45 581	4 234
Anoka	1 279.3	3 803	53.7	0.9	5.4	5.1	9.5	1 587.7	4 720	461	1 230	14 640	172 200	63 099	7 270
Becker	136.5	4 137	44.4	1.1	4.2	11.3	12.3	95.6	2 898	232	119	2 838	15 540	53 195	5 757
Beltrami	237.7	5 239	45.5	1.1	3.5	7.4	8.2	329.6	7 264	412	157	4 843	19 640	47 844	4 844
Benton	105.9	2 726	49.8	1.2	5.5	8.3	10.1	177.0	4 555	84	140	1 643	19 120	49 363	4 725
Big Stone	57.1	11 056	19.8	43.6	2.3	4.0	9.5	316.3	61 258	36	18	624	2 450	51 541	5 247
Blue Earth	298.5	4 586	38.2	0.6	4.8	5.4	14.5	311.4	4 785	256	246	5 232	29 930	55 148	6 542
Brown	114.6	4 507	33.1	12.3	4.8	7.0	11.5	109.7	4 315	72	87	1 621	13 240	56 331	6 352
Carlton	170.7	4 830	39.9	19.7	3.8	7.4	8.0	194.2	5 495	68	121	5 143	16 270	51 545	4 844
Carver	420.3	4 485	43.0	0.6	4.3	4.9	9.0	930.8	9 933	211	354	4 619	46 830	99 689	15 821
Cass	150.7	5 316	45.3	1.8	4.4	6.4	12.0	129.6	4 571	247	103	3 755	13 840	47 533	4 899
Chippewa	70.8	5 832	38.1	1.0	3.7	12.0	12.1	81.7	6 730	69	43	1 128	6 200	52 029	5 346
Chisago	182.5	3 415	43.9	1.5	4.9	4.7	15.5	291.7	5 458	94	190	2 468	26 270	61 430	6 798
Clay	286.2	4 758	32.4	1.9	4.5	6.9	10.4	437.1	7 267	122	212	4 318	27 920	54 974	5 658
Clearwater	40.3	4 626	44.8	0.2	5.1	9.0	18.1	19.0	2 179	36	31	487	3 770	56 001	6 770
Cook	44.8	8 644	13.1	30.8	6.2	4.2	13.3	40.0	7 721	136	19	792	2 930	47 514	4 502
Cottonwood	74.7	6 441	31.9	19.0	3.8	5.3	14.2	80.5	6 940	57	41	777	5 740	52 386	5 734
Crow Wing	333.5	5 303	34.0	22.0	4.7	6.2	6.0	491.9	7 822	201	252	4 456	30 820	51 225	5 415
Dakota	1 670.9	4 125	51.3	0.8	5.2	4.3	6.8	2 383.8	5 885	2 242	1 486	17 867	211 610	73 985	9 844
Dodge	88.6	4 380	46.8	2.3	6.2	13.6	9.3	114.3	5 648	36	73	1 178	9 810	58 559	5 987
Douglas	244.5	6 713	25.3	35.9	2.8	3.2	7.4	374.7	10 290	139	132	3 330	18 520	58 856	7 242
Faribault	106.3	7 456	21.6	34.8	2.4	1.7	14.0	77.3	5 420	58	49	890	7 050	48 097	4 714

1. Based on the resident population estimated as of July 1 of the year shown.

Table B. States and Counties — **Land Area and Population**

STATE/ County code	CBSA code[1]	County type[2]	STATE County	Land area,[3] (sq mi) 2016	Total persons 2016	Rank	Per square mile	White	Black	American Indian, Alaska Native	Asian and Pacific Islander	Percent Hispanic or Latino[4]	Under 5 years	5 to 17 years	18 to 24 years	25 to 34 years	35 to 44 years	45 to 54 years
				1	2	3	4	5	6	7	8	9	10	11	12	13	14	15
			MINNESOTA—Cont'd															
27 045	40340	3	Fillmore	861.3	21 003	1 775	24.4	97.3	0.8	0.4	0.7	1.5	6.5	17.8	7.1	9.9	10.9	12.3
27 047	10660	7	Freeborn	707.1	30 446	1 420	43.1	87.1	1.7	0.6	2.3	9.5	5.6	16.1	6.9	11.1	10.7	12.5
27 049	39860	4	Goodhue	756.9	46 676	1 037	61.7	93.6	1.8	1.7	1.2	3.3	5.7	16.7	7.4	10.9	11.4	13.4
27 051	...	9	Grant	547.8	5 956	2 754	10.9	96.4	1.0	0.8	0.9	2.4	6.3	16.5	6.1	10.7	10.8	11.4
27 053	33460	1	Hennepin	553.6	1 232 483	34	2 226.3	72.1	14.3	1.5	8.3	6.9	6.6	15.6	8.7	17.1	13.1	13.0
27 055	29100	3	Houston	552.0	18 814	1 883	34.1	97.5	1.4	0.5	0.9	1.0	5.7	15.9	7.2	10.0	10.9	13.1
27 057	...	7	Hubbard	925.9	20 718	1 789	22.4	94.8	1.1	3.2	0.9	1.9	5.6	15.7	6.1	8.7	10.0	12.7
27 059	33460	1	Isanti	435.7	39 025	1 207	89.6	95.8	1.3	1.1	1.6	1.9	5.9	18.0	7.6	12.5	12.2	14.4
27 061	24330	6	Itasca	2 667.3	45 242	1 068	17.0	94.1	1.0	5.0	0.9	1.3	5.3	15.8	7.0	9.8	10.8	12.5
27 063	...	7	Jackson	703.0	9 944	2 435	14.1	94.3	1.1	0.6	2.1	3.1	5.6	16.3	7.4	10.2	11.0	12.3
27 065	...	6	Kanabec	521.6	15 830	2 053	30.3	96.7	0.9	1.6	0.9	1.6	5.0	16.4	7.2	10.1	11.4	13.6
27 067	48820	4	Kandiyohi	797.3	42 495	1 123	53.3	82.3	4.8	0.6	1.1	12.1	6.8	17.2	8.1	12.3	11.0	11.8
27 069	...	9	Kittson	1 098.8	4 333	2 874	3.9	97.0	0.7	0.5	0.7	2.0	5.6	15.7	7.4	8.3	9.0	13.0
27 071	...	6	Koochiching	3 104.2	12 628	2 252	4.1	94.9	1.1	3.7	0.8	1.4	4.2	14.4	6.9	9.2	10.2	13.5
27 073	...	9	Lac qui Parle	765.0	6 715	2 697	8.8	96.4	1.0	0.6	1.1	2.1	4.7	15.0	7.4	8.2	9.6	11.5
27 075	...	6	Lake	2 109.3	10 625	2 381	5.0	97.0	0.7	1.4	0.7	1.5	4.8	13.5	6.1	9.5	10.1	11.9
27 077	...	9	Lake of the Woods	1 297.9	3 814	2 918	2.9	95.4	1.3	2.5	2.1	1.3	4.9	13.2	6.8	8.4	10.2	13.4
27 079	33460	1	Le Sueur	448.8	27 591	1 509	61.5	92.6	1.0	0.8	1.1	5.7	5.9	18.1	7.6	10.8	12.1	14.4
27 081	...	9	Lincoln	536.8	5 783	2 769	10.8	97.2	0.5	0.5	0.7	1.9	6.1	16.7	6.5	9.4	10.2	11.3
27 083	32140	7	Lyon	714.6	25 699	1 576	36.0	86.2	3.5	0.9	4.5	6.4	7.2	18.0	10.5	13.1	11.8	11.6
27 085	26780	6	McLeod	491.5	35 842	1 278	72.9	92.3	1.0	0.6	1.0	6.0	5.9	17.5	8.0	11.6	11.6	13.7
27 087	...	8	Mahnomen	557.9	5 465	2 805	9.8	54.1	1.3	48.4	0.7	4.1	9.1	22.2	7.2	10.2	10.2	10.9
27 089	...	8	Marshall	1 775.1	9 324	2 480	5.3	94.3	0.8	1.0	0.5	4.5	6.2	16.6	7.5	10.5	10.5	13.0
27 091	21860	7	Martin	712.3	19 829	1 838	27.8	94.3	0.9	0.6	0.9	4.2	5.5	16.1	7.4	10.3	10.1	12.1
27 093	...	6	Meeker	608.2	23 110	1 674	38.0	94.9	1.0	0.5	0.7	3.8	6.2	18.1	7.5	10.1	11.1	12.7
27 095	33460	1	Mille Lacs	572.3	25 866	1 568	45.2	90.9	1.2	6.5	0.9	2.3	6.2	17.6	7.0	11.4	11.6	13.8
27 097	...	6	Morrison	1 125.1	32 821	1 362	29.2	97.0	0.9	0.9	0.7	1.6	5.9	17.6	7.3	11.0	11.2	13.4
27 099	12380	4	Mower	711.3	39 163	1 198	55.1	81.4	4.2	0.6	4.0	11.2	6.5	18.5	8.0	12.0	11.5	12.4
27 101	...	9	Murray	704.7	8 329	2 563	11.8	94.0	0.7	0.5	1.8	3.8	5.1	16.4	6.9	9.4	9.8	11.9
27 103	31860	3	Nicollet	448.6	33 575	1 339	74.8	90.8	3.7	0.7	2.1	4.3	6.0	16.1	12.9	13.2	12.2	11.7
27 105	49380	7	Nobles	715.1	21 848	1 734	30.6	60.9	5.0	0.6	7.1	27.4	8.0	18.7	9.1	12.8	11.3	11.8
27 107	...	8	Norman	872.8	6 579	2 704	7.5	91.8	1.0	3.5	1.2	5.0	5.6	17.4	7.3	9.3	11.0	12.7
27 109	40340	3	Olmsted	653.7	153 102	427	234.2	82.9	6.6	0.6	7.2	4.8	7.1	17.6	7.7	14.7	12.7	12.5
27 111	22260	6	Otter Tail	1 972.0	58 085	888	29.5	94.0	1.7	1.2	1.0	3.4	5.9	15.8	7.2	9.7	9.7	12.2
27 113	...	6	Pennington	616.6	14 235	2 149	23.1	92.5	2.1	2.3	1.4	3.5	6.5	16.6	8.3	13.7	12.0	12.0
27 115	...	6	Pine	1 411.3	28 874	1 463	20.5	91.0	2.7	4.3	1.1	2.9	4.7	15.3	6.8	11.5	12.0	14.4
27 117	...	6	Pipestone	465.1	9 202	2 490	19.8	90.4	1.8	2.0	1.3	6.2	6.8	18.4	7.3	10.1	10.2	12.5
27 119	24220	3	Polk	1 971.1	31 660	1 391	16.1	89.3	2.5	2.5	1.4	6.3	6.7	17.1	9.3	12.4	10.8	12.2
27 121	...	8	Pope	669.6	11 049	2 351	16.5	97.2	1.0	0.7	0.8	1.3	5.8	14.9	6.6	11.1	10.1	11.7
27 123	33460	1	Ramsey	152.2	540 649	123	3 552.2	65.5	13.3	1.4	15.7	7.4	7.1	16.3	10.3	16.6	11.9	11.8
27 125	...	8	Red Lake	432.4	4 007	2 901	9.3	94.1	1.3	1.9	0.4	3.5	6.8	17.7	6.1	9.9	11.8	12.1
27 127	...	7	Redwood	878.6	15 263	2 077	17.4	89.3	0.9	5.1	3.4	3.1	5.9	18.4	7.6	10.3	10.3	12.4
27 129	...	8	Renville	982.9	14 660	2 120	14.9	90.0	0.9	1.4	1.0	7.9	6.0	16.2	7.4	10.1	10.4	12.9
27 131	22060	4	Rice	495.8	65 622	808	132.4	84.7	5.0	0.7	3.0	8.0	5.5	16.3	14.8	11.2	11.4	13.0
27 133	...	6	Rock	482.5	9 564	2 464	19.8	95.1	1.4	0.9	1.1	2.8	6.0	19.4	7.4	9.8	11.4	11.7
27 135	...	7	Roseau	1 671.6	15 626	2 065	9.3	93.6	1.0	2.3	3.4	1.3	6.1	18.2	8.3	10.4	10.9	14.7
27 137	20260	2	St. Louis	6 247.6	199 980	331	32.0	93.5	2.4	3.3	1.6	1.6	5.1	14.0	12.8	11.6	10.8	12.1
27 139	33460	1	Scott	356.3	143 680	447	403.3	84.0	4.7	1.4	7.2	5.0	7.1	21.0	7.6	12.3	14.8	15.6
27 141	33460	1	Sherburne	432.9	93 528	629	216.0	93.3	3.2	1.0	1.8	2.5	6.8	20.0	8.5	13.3	13.9	15.0
27 143	33460	1	Sibley	588.8	14 827	2 113	25.2	90.0	1.1	0.5	0.9	8.6	5.6	18.0	7.6	10.6	11.7	13.9
27 145	41060	3	Stearns	1 342.8	155 652	418	115.9	88.9	6.0	0.6	2.8	3.2	6.3	16.6	15.4	12.3	10.9	12.2
27 147	36940	5	Steele	429.6	36 805	1 255	85.7	88.0	3.7	0.5	1.4	7.6	6.5	18.7	7.7	11.8	11.6	13.3
27 149	...	7	Stevens	563.6	9 693	2 452	17.2	90.7	1.6	2.3	2.2	5.4	6.1	14.9	20.4	10.9	9.6	9.5
27 151	...	7	Swift	742.0	9 419	2 472	12.7	92.8	1.8	0.8	1.0	4.8	6.0	16.8	7.1	10.9	10.7	12.5
27 153	...	6	Todd	945.0	24 233	1 634	25.6	92.5	1.0	1.0	1.2	5.7	6.6	17.2	7.7	9.7	10.1	13.0
27 155	...	9	Traverse	573.9	3 356	2 948	5.8	91.7	1.3	5.8	0.8	2.7	5.1	15.4	7.3	8.7	9.8	12.2
27 157	40340	3	Wabasha	522.9	21 273	1 763	40.7	95.4	1.1	0.6	0.9	3.0	5.6	16.4	7.4	10.3	11.1	14.0
27 159	...	7	Wadena	536.3	13 761	2 184	25.7	96.1	1.5	1.3	0.7	1.9	6.7	17.7	7.5	10.1	10.6	11.5
27 161	...	6	Waseca	423.4	18 911	1 878	44.7	90.4	2.9	1.0	1.2	5.9	5.9	17.7	7.8	12.5	12.3	12.9
27 163	33460	1	Washington	384.4	253 117	267	658.5	85.4	5.3	0.9	6.6	4.0	6.1	18.8	8.1	11.5	12.8	14.9
27 165	...	6	Watonwan	435.0	10 908	2 364	25.1	73.9	1.0	0.6	1.2	24.1	6.9	17.1	8.7	10.4	10.9	11.7
27 167	47420	6	Wilkin	751.0	6 359	2 725	8.5	95.0	1.1	1.8	0.6	2.7	5.4	17.0	7.9	10.3	11.3	13.8
27 169	49100	4	Winona	626.1	50 948	973	81.4	92.3	2.2	0.7	3.0	2.9	4.8	13.4	20.8	11.3	9.8	11.0
27 171	33460	1	Wright	661.3	132 550	478	200.4	94.3	1.9	0.7	1.9	2.8	7.1	21.3	7.4	11.8	14.1	14.6
27 173	...	9	Yellow Medicine	759.1	9 935	2 436	13.1	91.4	0.9	4.1	0.8	4.1	6.0	17.0	8.0	11.0	9.9	12.5

1. CBSA = Core Based Statistical Area. See Appendix A for explanation. See Appendix B for list of metropolitan areas with component counties. 2. County type code from the Economic Research Service of USDA Rural-Urban Continuum Codes. See Appendix A for definition. 3. Dry land or land partially or temporarily covered by water. 4. May be of any race.

Table B. States and Counties — **Population and Households**

STATE County	Population, 2016 (cont.) Age (percent) (cont.) 55 to 64 years	65 to 74 years	75 years and over	Percent female	Population change and components of change, 2000–2016 Total persons 2000	2010	Percent change 2000–2010	2010–2016	Components of change, 2010–2016 Births	Deaths	Net migration	Households, 2011–2015 Number	Persons per house-hold	Percent Family house-holds	Female family house-holder[1]	One per-son
	16	17	18	19	20	21	22	23	24	25	26	27	28	29	30	31
MINNESOTA—Cont'd																
Fillmore	14.6	10.7	10.3	49.9	21 122	20 866	-1.2	0.7	1 580	1 452	-24	8 531	2.40	66.8	6.6	28.8
Freeborn	15.2	11.2	10.7	50.1	32 584	31 255	-4.1	-2.6	2 154	2 241	-651	12 993	2.33	63.6	9.4	30.4
Goodhue	15.2	10.4	9.0	50.1	44 127	46 182	4.7	1.1	3 238	2 969	88	18 793	2.42	66.9	9.0	27.6
Grant	14.7	12.2	11.2	50.0	6 289	6 018	-4.3	-1.0	434	441	-22	2 530	2.32	66.8	7.5	28.1
Hennepin	12.7	7.6	5.6	50.6	1 116 200	1 152 381	3.2	7.0	102 696	50 693	30 163	490 196	2.39	57.9	10.1	32.8
Houston	16.9	11.1	9.2	50.1	19 718	19 027	-3.5	-1.1	1 198	1 087	-359	7 886	2.35	68.0	7.6	27.9
Hubbard	16.6	14.6	10.0	49.3	18 376	20 428	11.2	1.4	1 387	1 223	128	8 787	2.32	69.0	6.9	25.2
Isanti	13.9	8.8	6.7	49.3	31 287	37 810	20.8	3.2	2 816	1 833	134	14 059	2.68	70.2	10.7	23.7
Itasca	16.7	12.8	9.3	49.4	43 992	45 058	2.4	0.4	2 929	3 233	560	18 965	2.33	67.9	7.8	26.6
Jackson	16.3	9.9	11.0	48.9	11 268	10 266	-8.9	-3.1	691	666	-330	4 354	2.32	65.6	7.3	29.9
Kanabec	16.5	12.0	7.9	49.4	14 996	16 239	8.3	-2.5	932	926	-382	6 191	2.55	68.3	9.1	26.0
Kandiyohi	14.8	9.7	8.3	49.8	41 203	42 239	2.5	0.6	3 615	2 387	-944	16 701	2.48	68.7	9.0	26.9
Kittson	17.4	11.5	11.9	49.9	5 285	4 552	-13.9	-4.8	301	411	-98	1 912	2.28	62.5	7.8	33.8
Koochiching	18.3	13.1	10.3	49.8	14 355	13 311	-7.3	-5.1	665	945	-380	5 844	2.18	61.8	7.5	34.6
Lac qui Parle	17.5	12.1	13.9	49.5	8 067	7 259	-10.0	-7.5	402	554	-371	3 078	2.24	65.7	6.3	30.5
Lake	18.1	13.8	12.2	49.0	11 058	10 866	-1.7	-2.2	664	875	-45	5 087	2.06	64.4	5.5	30.0
Lake of the Woods	20.3	13.2	9.7	48.5	4 522	4 045	-10.5	-5.7	207	295	-150	1 623	2.40	61.3	3.8	34.3
Le Sueur	14.4	9.7	7.0	49.6	25 426	27 703	9.0	-0.4	1 949	1 328	-677	10 839	2.52	70.1	7.3	24.8
Lincoln	14.8	11.5	13.7	49.3	6 429	5 896	-8.3	-1.9	429	489	-89	2 497	2.25	63.7	5.0	32.4
Lyon	12.7	7.7	7.3	50.0	25 425	25 857	1.7	-0.6	2 260	1 370	-1 065	9 958	2.46	63.2	9.0	30.1
McLeod	13.5	9.7	8.5	50.2	34 898	36 651	5.0	-2.2	2 640	2 050	-1 474	14 819	2.40	67.1	8.4	27.8
Mahnomen	12.9	9.8	7.6	49.5	5 190	5 413	4.3	1.0	637	370	-222	2 001	2.71	68.6	16.1	26.6
Marshall	15.4	10.2	10.1	49.2	10 155	9 439	-7.1	-1.2	677	485	-276	4 027	2.32	64.9	6.2	29.8
Martin	16.0	11.0	11.3	50.6	21 802	20 840	-4.4	-4.9	1 369	1 572	-768	8 831	2.26	63.9	8.8	32.3
Meeker	15.2	10.6	8.5	49.1	22 644	23 300	2.9	-0.8	1 719	1 338	-587	9 174	2.48	68.6	6.2	26.6
Mille Lacs	13.8	10.1	8.5	49.7	22 330	26 097	16.9	-0.9	2 017	1 779	-457	10 046	2.52	67.2	11.7	26.9
Morrison	15.2	10.0	8.3	49.5	31 712	33 198	4.7	-1.1	2 366	1 972	-722	13 352	2.43	68.2	7.8	27.1
Mower	13.1	9.1	9.0	49.8	38 603	39 163	1.5	0.0	3 137	2 316	-851	15 425	2.51	65.2	9.3	30.6
Murray	15.7	12.8	12.1	50.0	9 165	8 725	-4.8	-4.5	521	633	-291	3 737	2.24	63.2	4.6	31.8
Nicollet	12.8	8.5	6.6	49.6	29 771	32 727	9.9	2.6	2 450	1 346	-264	12 629	2.39	67.1	10.4	26.2
Nobles	12.4	7.9	8.0	48.5	20 832	21 378	2.6	2.2	2 247	1 110	-597	7 842	2.71	70.4	8.7	26.2
Norman	15.0	10.7	11.1	49.8	7 442	6 852	-7.9	-4.0	437	582	-122	2 728	2.40	65.0	7.4	30.8
Olmsted	13.1	7.9	6.8	51.1	124 277	144 260	16.1	6.1	13 572	6 011	1 085	57 899	2.52	66.5	9.6	27.5
Otter Tail	16.3	12.7	10.5	49.7	57 159	57 303	0.3	1.4	3 997	4 227	1 129	24 042	2.34	67.3	6.9	29.0
Pennington	13.8	9.1	7.9	49.9	13 584	13 930	2.5	2.2	1 163	827	-3	5 920	2.34	60.2	9.2	34.8
Pine	16.0	11.2	8.2	46.6	26 530	29 750	12.1	-2.9	1 804	1 681	-939	11 361	2.42	64.4	7.8	29.3
Pipestone	13.9	9.5	11.3	51.0	9 895	9 596	-3.0	-4.1	736	674	-457	3 980	2.30	64.5	9.0	31.4
Polk	13.9	9.2	8.3	49.6	31 369	31 600	0.7	0.2	2 510	2 140	-294	12 723	2.37	63.3	7.9	31.4
Pope	16.1	12.8	11.0	49.1	11 236	10 995	-2.1	0.5	777	795	77	4 809	2.23	66.5	5.6	29.5
Ramsey	12.4	7.8	5.9	51.2	511 035	508 639	-0.5	6.3	48 315	24 923	9 620	206 857	2.47	58.3	12.1	33.2
Red Lake	16.1	10.2	9.3	49.4	4 299	4 089	-4.9	-2.0	335	232	-202	1 661	2.43	64.5	6.4	31.2
Redwood	14.1	10.4	10.7	50.0	16 815	16 059	-4.5	-5.0	1 164	1 142	-875	6 307	2.43	63.7	7.2	33.0
Renville	16.0	10.2	10.8	49.3	17 154	15 730	-8.3	-6.8	1 087	1 194	-966	6 341	2.34	64.7	6.1	30.5
Rice	12.8	8.3	6.7	48.9	56 665	64 142	13.2	2.3	4 430	2 859	-208	22 532	2.50	68.5	9.9	26.3
Rock	13.7	10.3	10.4	50.8	9 721	9 687	-0.3	-1.3	693	748	-98	3 929	2.37	66.5	7.0	31.4
Roseau	15.0	9.0	7.5	48.6	16 338	15 629	-4.3	0.0	1 203	851	-357	6 318	2.44	69.0	8.0	26.4
St. Louis	15.4	10.4	7.8	49.8	200 528	200 226	-0.0	-0.1	12 735	12 933	441	84 545	2.26	58.9	9.6	33.4
Scott	11.5	6.2	3.9	50.1	89 498	129 910	45.2	10.6	11 859	3 668	5 452	46 805	2.90	76.3	9.0	18.5
Sherburne	11.7	6.7	4.1	48.6	64 417	88 492	37.4	5.7	7 331	2 980	637	30 574	2.89	76.5	8.6	17.4
Sibley	14.4	9.5	8.7	49.6	15 356	15 226	-0.8	-2.6	1 060	897	-563	6 014	2.46	68.5	7.0	27.2
Stearns	12.1	7.9	6.3	49.5	133 166	150 642	13.1	3.3	12 126	6 000	-937	57 265	2.52	65.1	8.5	25.0
Steele	13.5	8.9	8.0	50.3	33 680	36 576	8.6	0.6	2 973	1 846	-957	14 271	2.52	67.5	8.7	28.0
Stevens	11.5	8.2	8.8	50.2	10 053	9 726	-3.3	-0.3	732	520	-207	3 668	2.55	59.6	3.7	32.0
Swift	14.6	10.8	10.6	49.4	11 956	9 783	-18.2	-3.7	681	666	-361	4 231	2.21	64.0	7.9	32.3
Todd	15.7	11.3	8.6	48.6	24 426	24 895	1.9	-2.7	1 963	1 291	-1 349	9 889	2.45	66.7	6.2	29.9
Traverse	15.9	10.6	15.0	50.4	4 134	3 558	-13.9	-5.7	196	324	-71	1 524	2.19	65.1	4.7	31.0
Wabasha	15.5	11.3	8.4	50.1	21 610	21 664	0.2	-1.8	1 461	1 138	-690	8 953	2.36	69.2	7.5	26.1
Wadena	13.8	11.3	10.7	50.3	13 713	13 843	0.9	-0.6	1 126	1 193	0	5 673	2.35	63.3	9.9	33.0
Waseca	13.7	9.4	7.8	52.3	19 526	19 136	-2.0	-1.2	1 359	996	-591	7 325	2.43	67.9	7.1	27.3
Washington	13.8	8.4	5.6	50.6	201 130	238 128	18.4	6.3	17 754	8 936	5 902	90 932	2.67	73.0	10.1	21.8
Watonwan	14.5	9.4	10.4	50.2	11 876	11 211	-5.6	-2.7	946	759	-483	4 450	2.45	65.2	9.5	30.5
Wilkin	15.6	9.3	9.4	48.7	7 138	6 576	-7.9	-3.3	425	480	-163	2 776	2.29	62.8	7.5	34.8
Winona	13.1	8.7	7.1	50.4	49 985	51 461	3.0	-1.0	2 943	2 521	-908	19 068	2.46	59.3	7.0	31.2
Wright	11.6	7.2	4.8	49.5	89 986	124 697	38.6	6.3	11 333	4 444	894	45 265	2.82	76.4	8.8	19.4
Yellow Medicine	15.3	9.6	10.7	49.5	11 080	10 438	-5.8	-4.8	712	743	-461	4 196	2.33	68.1	7.5	27.1

1. No spouse present.

Table B. States and Counties — Population, Vital Statistics, Health, and Crime

STATE County	Persons in group quarters, 2016	Daytime population, 2011–2015 Number	Employment/residence ratio	Births, 2016 Total	Rate[1]	Deaths, 2016 Number	Rate[1]	Persons under 65 with no health insurance, 2015 Number	Percent	Medicare, 2015 Total Beneficiaries	Enrolled in Original Medicare	Enrolled in Medicare Advantage	Serious crimes known to police,[2] 2014 Total Number	Rate[3]
	32	33	34	35	36	37	38	39	40	41	42	43	44	45
MINNESOTA—Cont'd														
Fillmore	359	17 607	0.69	256	12.2	237	11.3	1 091	6.6	4 733	2 260	2 473	64	307
Freeborn	637	29 198	0.89	327	10.7	357	11.7	1 506	6.4	6 971	2 932	4 039	541	1 749
Goodhue	901	45 988	0.98	504	10.8	468	10.0	1 877	5.0	9 164	3 700	5 464	903	1 937
Grant	110	5 374	0.80	70	11.8	57	9.6	249	5.5	1 564	721	843	64	1 067
Hennepin	25 724	1 421 489	1.35	16 737	13.6	8 563	6.9	60 982	5.8	176 049	71 173	104 876	42 770	3 529
Houston	257	15 039	0.61	205	10.9	194	10.3	727	4.9	4 106	2 105	2 001	84	447
Hubbard	154	18 467	0.77	221	10.7	178	8.6	988	6.4	4 974	2 209	2 765	544	2 621
Isanti	465	30 992	0.62	430	11.0	284	7.3	1 465	4.5	5 799	2 217	3 582	781	2 037
Itasca	1 020	44 148	0.94	472	10.4	510	11.3	1 949	5.6	10 933	5 291	5 642	794	1 735
Jackson	110	10 559	1.07	109	11.0	106	10.7	341	4.3	2 444	1 468	976	103	1 003
Kanabec	246	13 337	0.63	148	9.3	159	10.0	775	6.1	3 126	1 399	1 727	269	1 685
Kandiyohi	1 057	43 495	1.05	586	13.8	353	8.3	2 236	6.5	7 922	2 973	4 949	840	1 976
Kittson	111	4 295	0.91	46	10.6	58	13.4	174	5.1	1 042	497	545	14	311
Koochiching	241	12 897	0.97	97	7.7	147	11.6	684	7.0	3 521	1 633	1 888	295	2 234
Lac qui Parle	154	6 380	0.81	55	8.2	92	13.7	260	5.1	1 644	681	963	39	558
Lake	224	10 425	0.93	92	8.7	136	12.8	349	4.4	2 689	1 395	1 294	74	687
Lake of the Woods	53	3 584	0.81	35	9.2	46	12.1	192	6.4	995	484	511	12	307
Le Sueur	270	22 204	0.61	303	11.0	224	8.1	1 195	5.2	5 883	2 292	3 591	225	807
Lincoln	135	5 095	0.76	70	12.1	81	14.0	223	5.2	1 412	844	568	7	120
Lyon	1 050	27 529	1.13	356	13.9	240	9.3	1 025	4.9	5 281	3 167	2 114	423	1 663
McLeod	476	34 773	0.93	422	11.8	333	9.3	1 377	4.7	8 268	2 980	5 288	642	1 793
Mahnomen	79	5 903	1.19	95	17.4	59	10.8	400	9.0	1 097	615	482	289	5 190
Marshall	76	7 874	0.66	105	11.3	85	9.1	429	5.7	1 987	959	1 028	0	0
Martin	348	19 992	0.96	219	11.0	237	12.0	915	5.9	5 392	2 678	2 714	370	1 818
Meeker	354	20 277	0.75	264	11.4	202	8.7	1 048	5.6	4 515	1 471	3 044	348	1 506
Mille Lacs	523	24 581	0.89	311	12.0	267	10.3	1 398	6.8	6 606	2 560	4 046	841	3 258
Morrison	527	30 103	0.82	367	11.2	342	10.4	1 543	5.8	6 995	2 538	4 457	411	1 252
Mower	632	38 396	0.96	500	12.8	365	9.3	2 079	6.6	8 648	5 104	3 544	786	1 994
Murray	163	7 826	0.83	78	9.4	95	11.4	348	5.5	2 015	1 249	766	98	1 152
Nicollet	2 858	31 586	0.92	402	12.0	243	7.2	1 058	4.0	4 644	1 959	2 685	574	1 731
Nobles	385	22 395	1.07	357	16.3	163	7.5	1 823	10.1	3 457	2 305	1 152	267	1 230
Norman	149	6 109	0.81	70	10.6	92	14.0	353	6.8	1 517	795	722	68	1 032
Olmsted	2 513	164 539	1.20	2 184	14.3	1 006	6.6	5 398	4.2	23 155	13 443	9 712	2 713	1 801
Otter Tail	1 184	54 910	0.90	670	11.5	687	11.8	2 451	5.6	14 170	5 590	8 580	907	1 571
Pennington	327	16 659	1.34	188	13.2	127	8.9	577	4.9	2 543	1 049	1 494	368	2 594
Pine	1 656	26 981	0.82	264	9.1	282	9.8	1 347	6.2	6 189	2 546	3 643	1 476	5 090
Pipestone	205	9 480	1.03	113	12.3	117	12.7	495	6.8	2 125	1 386	739	71	771
Polk	1 272	28 961	0.84	406	12.8	348	11.0	1 347	5.3	6 023	2 866	3 157	489	1 548
Pope	184	10 207	0.86	121	11.0	123	11.1	406	4.8	2 672	1 100	1 572	84	768
Ramsey	17 865	589 288	1.24	7 874	14.6	4 137	7.7	28 953	6.4	107 529	42 723	64 806	19 855	3 732
Red Lake	34	3 390	0.67	47	11.7	23	5.7	203	6.2	849	247	602	14	345
Redwood	373	15 651	0.99	187	12.3	171	11.2	838	6.9	3 415	1 619	1 796	232	1 478
Renville	342	14 312	0.88	160	10.9	185	12.6	827	6.2	3 241	1 684	1 557	156	1 035
Rice	7 273	61 218	0.89	682	10.4	454	6.9	2 904	5.9	10 106	3 885	6 221	1 103	1 688
Rock	260	8 774	0.83	110	11.5	105	11.0	384	5.1	2 175	1 211	964	169	1 779
Roseau	191	16 282	1.08	178	11.4	134	8.6	669	5.1	2 739	910	1 829	232	1 493
St. Louis	9 005	208 311	1.08	2 000	10.0	2 082	10.4	7 676	4.8	42 730	20 350	22 380	6 482	3 226
Scott	1 307	112 731	0.66	1 834	12.8	647	4.5	5 221	4.1	12 182	4 442	7 740	2 181	1 567
Sherburne	2 194	68 774	0.53	1 165	12.5	523	5.6	3 321	4.1	8 295	3 016	5 279	1 421	1 568
Sibley	230	12 409	0.66	147	9.9	134	9.0	702	5.8	2 637	1 062	1 575	0	0
Stearns	7 570	163 090	1.13	1 949	12.5	975	6.3	5 978	4.7	30 343	13 286	17 057	4 010	2 626
Steele	594	38 465	1.11	476	12.9	301	8.2	1 275	4.2	6 662	2 620	4 042	773	2 117
Stevens	1 019	10 675	1.18	119	12.3	74	7.6	328	4.5	1 704	968	736	156	1 599
Swift	150	9 281	0.95	109	11.6	101	10.7	429	5.9	2 265	1 128	1 137	99	1 041
Todd	346	21 494	0.74	297	12.3	203	8.4	1 414	7.4	4 932	1 628	3 304	356	1 465
Traverse	100	3 317	0.93	31	9.2	34	10.1	162	6.4	965	541	424	62	1 809
Wabasha	246	18 012	0.70	223	10.5	185	8.7	729	4.3	5 027	2 117	2 910	187	873
Wadena	482	14 399	1.11	194	14.1	184	13.4	636	6.0	3 609	1 390	2 219	140	1 013
Waseca	1 081	17 407	0.82	219	11.6	147	7.8	664	4.5	3 547	1 472	2 075	301	1 574
Washington	3 299	207 245	0.69	2 816	11.1	1 571	6.2	7 338	3.4	22 273	7 801	14 472	5 353	2 150
Watonwan	150	9 942	0.80	164	15.0	115	10.5	797	9.2	2 389	1 264	1 125	164	1 473
Wilkin	152	5 968	0.83	65	10.2	86	13.5	244	4.7	1 327	621	706	103	1 569
Winona	4 277	50 957	0.99	467	9.2	445	8.7	2 316	5.9	8 821	4 743	4 078	179	349
Wright	1 105	104 675	0.64	1 744	13.2	742	5.6	4 518	3.9	16 464	5 714	10 750	1 919	1 482
Yellow Medicine	290	9 685	0.92	116	11.7	114	11.5	470	6.0	2 469	1 379	1 090	104	1 031

1. Per 1,000 estimated resident population.   2. Data for serious crimes have not been adjusted for underreporting; this may affect comparability between geographic areas and over time.
3. Per 100,000 population estimated by the FBI.

Table B. States and Counties — Crime, Education, Money Income, and Poverty

STATE County	Serious crimes known to police, 2014 (cont.)[1] Rate[2] Violent	Property	School enrollment and attainment, 2011–2015 Enrollment[3] Total	Percent private	High school graduate or less	Bachelor's degree or more	Local government expenditures,[5] 2013–2014 Total current spending (mil dol)	Current spending per student (dollars)	Money income, 2011–2015 Per capita income[6] (dollars)	Median income (dollars)	Households Percent with income of less than $50,000	with income of $200,000 or more	Income and poverty, 2015 Median household income (dollars)	Percent below poverty level All persons	Children under 18 years	Children 5 to 17 years in families
	46	47	48	49	50	51	52	53	54	55	56	57	58	59	60	61
MINNESOTA—Cont'd																
Fillmore	53	254	4 849	11.7	44.8	19.5	25.4	10 186	26 348	51 665	48.5	1.9	52 170	10.8	17.1	15.4
Freeborn	113	1 636	6 758	9.7	47.7	16.1	48.0	11 834	26 494	47 105	52.6	2.1	47 418	13.4	19.7	17.3
Goodhue	109	1 828	10 961	13.2	40.2	23.4	74.6	11 095	30 236	57 062	44.6	3.1	60 285	8.9	10.8	9.7
Grant	17	1 051	1 183	10.1	40.7	18.9	11.7	10 764	27 952	50 174	49.9	2.9	50 570	10.6	15.1	14.2
Hennepin	427	3 101	307 916	18.1	25.2	47.0	2 024.7	12 471	38 724	65 834	38.6	8.4	68 902	10.9	13.9	13.6
Houston	69	378	4 309	15.3	41.5	21.4	46.4	10 105	27 626	53 809	46.2	2.1	56 276	8.2	10.2	9.3
Hubbard	120	2 501	4 020	7.8	39.1	25.0	24.2	10 120	25 725	47 486	51.9	1.9	52 841	10.6	18.3	17.5
Isanti	112	1 925	9 646	11.2	47.1	17.7	60.7	10 054	27 152	59 865	40.4	2.0	63 134	7.7	10.1	8.9
Itasca	210	1 525	9 913	9.6	39.0	21.9	76.4	11 558	25 219	47 761	52.2	1.5	52 064	12.7	17.7	16.4
Jackson	29	973	2 305	7.5	43.5	18.8	15.8	10 132	27 494	50 574	49.3	2.5	54 001	9.2	13.0	11.7
Kanabec	144	1 541	3 657	6.6	51.5	13.5	21.0	9 151	23 661	47 384	52.3	1.8	48 907	11.7	18.2	17.1
Kandiyohi	181	1 794	9 980	9.7	39.2	22.2	60.3	10 926	27 560	52 632	46.7	2.8	52 597	10.9	16.8	16.0
Kittson	22	289	900	8.6	44.8	20.9	9.5	13 712	29 279	52 326	47.9	1.8	55 545	10.2	14.1	12.9
Koochiching	182	2 053	2 593	15.4	47.1	18.4	22.5	12 317	25 398	42 919	57.3	2.0	46 807	14.3	22.0	19.6
Lac qui Parle	57	501	1 453	7.4	46.1	17.7	14.7	11 384	29 541	49 903	50.1	4.3	50 764	8.4	13.5	12.6
Lake	139	548	1 967	3.2	41.3	24.4	14.6	10 378	29 346	48 417	52.4	2.3	53 093	9.8	14.6	13.0
Lake of the Woods	77	230	682	3.2	53.4	15.5	6.2	13 400	22 543	42 263	56.7	0.1	46 128	11.7	16.2	15.0
Le Sueur	65	742	6 638	13.5	44.9	21.2	41.4	9 632	28 483	60 632	41.5	2.7	62 672	8.5	10.9	9.4
Lincoln	120	0	1 240	8.1	48.6	19.2	11.4	11 671	26 910	49 575	50.3	1.8	52 164	9.3	13.1	12.0
Lyon	134	1 529	7 136	10.8	43.0	25.8	73.5	17 004	28 010	51 600	47.7	3.4	55 051	12.2	16.7	15.1
McLeod	92	1 701	8 450	13.5	46.1	18.0	54.1	10 148	27 612	56 128	44.2	1.8	60 549	8.6	11.0	10.0
Mahnomen	413	4 777	1 354	7.6	51.4	12.9	18.2	13 588	19 743	41 118	57.9	1.2	40 849	21.5	34.3	34.8
Marshall	0	0	1 970	8.8	48.6	18.7	18.7	14 307	27 863	54 092	45.6	2.0	55 889	8.3	11.6	10.6
Martin	118	1 700	4 214	15.4	49.6	18.9	35.2	11 979	28 244	51 391	48.9	3.0	48 478	13.6	19.5	17.9
Meeker	108	1 398	5 383	9.5	46.7	18.9	25.5	10 155	27 313	55 042	43.9	2.3	58 607	7.9	10.5	9.3
Mille Lacs	155	3 103	6 183	13.1	48.7	14.7	62.1	9 736	23 603	49 094	50.7	1.6	50 633	12.4	18.5	16.7
Morrison	43	1 209	7 419	12.1	49.1	17.0	53.1	10 088	24 984	50 049	49.9	2.2	54 245	10.9	15.0	12.9
Mower	218	1 776	10 251	10.0	44.6	19.0	70.5	11 474	26 265	49 427	50.6	2.6	50 878	10.8	16.1	14.4
Murray	59	1 093	1 740	13.8	47.4	18.1	12.4	11 530	28 976	51 983	47.8	2.8	50 378	9.0	12.7	11.4
Nicollet	142	1 589	9 936	39.6	32.9	32.5	35.9	14 884	28 118	58 640	41.6	3.1	58 839	10.7	11.6	10.0
Nobles	120	1 110	5 104	6.7	55.2	13.8	41.7	10 962	23 515	50 625	49.3	2.6	50 100	12.9	17.2	16.8
Norman	15	1 017	1 446	7.9	49.8	15.1	13.0	11 984	25 314	50 377	49.6	2.1	50 775	11.7	17.6	15.5
Olmsted	157	1 643	39 133	17.4	26.8	41.3	237.4	10 246	35 267	68 023	35.9	6.5	70 063	8.9	11.1	10.6
Otter Tail	118	1 453	11 743	12.6	39.2	24.5	134.1	17 728	28 066	52 365	47.8	2.8	55 357	9.7	14.1	13.0
Pennington	155	2 439	3 299	7.2	44.9	16.1	76.4	34 598	25 500	47 127	51.9	1.4	51 341	10.4	12.0	11.2
Pine	262	4 828	6 086	11.3	53.6	13.2	39.9	10 299	22 436	44 549	55.8	1.4	46 332	13.9	18.6	16.7
Pipestone	33	738	2 006	15.3	49.5	19.0	17.0	11 064	26 842	46 990	53.0	2.7	51 939	11.0	15.7	14.1
Polk	209	1 339	7 803	9.1	40.3	23.2	53.8	10 598	26 766	53 326	46.4	2.2	54 270	11.8	16.2	14.7
Pope	101	667	2 094	7.5	39.7	22.2	15.2	12 294	30 071	52 785	46.9	2.8	53 267	8.4	13.0	12.2
Ramsey	421	3 311	144 575	25.5	32.0	40.4	1 177.4	13 642	30 333	56 104	45.0	4.7	57 299	15.1	22.5	22.2
Red Lake	25	320	863	6.0	49.1	15.4	9.9	13 209	25 183	50 332	49.6	1.1	52 244	9.7	12.0	11.0
Redwood	96	1 382	3 638	12.8	49.6	17.0	27.0	10 852	25 716	47 211	53.3	2.3	48 520	11.0	15.4	14.2
Renville	93	943	3 197	15.2	48.0	15.7	19.3	10 171	28 698	52 149	47.9	3.3	56 835	9.5	15.2	13.7
Rice	153	1 535	20 298	37.8	41.4	27.6	89.3	10 646	26 660	59 598	42.0	3.5	59 863	9.2	11.2	9.9
Rock	1 116	663	2 458	15.9	48.7	20.4	14.8	9 337	26 065	51 496	48.9	2.5	55 462	9.7	12.6	10.7
Roseau	13	1 481	3 672	5.4	45.4	19.0	30.6	10 423	26 698	53 199	46.7	2.5	54 416	9.4	12.0	11.5
St. Louis	241	2 985	50 561	12.5	36.3	27.0	276.3	11 046	27 190	48 331	51.1	2.5	50 141	13.4	15.2	12.7
Scott	93	1 473	39 542	18.4	28.7	38.2	230.1	9 810	36 180	87 794	24.3	8.7	92 898	5.1	6.0	5.5
Sherburne	93	1 475	25 240	12.9	32.9	26.5	184.4	9 316	29 923	74 170	30.0	4.1	79 495	7.5	8.1	6.9
Sibley	0	0	3 516	16.6	51.4	16.3	24.4	10 238	27 493	56 990	43.6	2.6	57 052	8.9	12.3	10.4
Stearns	187	2 440	46 513	19.6	38.4	25.9	261.7	10 551	27 135	56 336	44.0	3.1	55 244	13.5	14.3	13.0
Steele	107	2 010	9 581	14.5	43.6	25.4	61.3	9 418	28 087	57 858	43.0	2.8	60 970	9.4	13.2	12.6
Stevens	133	1 466	3 357	5.8	35.9	28.3	16.3	10 662	25 739	52 302	47.5	4.1	54 323	10.9	8.6	7.4
Swift	84	957	1 947	2.5	50.0	16.2	14.9	9 962	27 202	49 035	50.7	1.9	47 130	11.9	15.2	14.0
Todd	91	1 375	5 528	17.3	49.3	15.2	48.3	14 963	23 808	46 414	53.4	1.6	48 840	12.8	19.3	19.0
Traverse	146	1 663	704	5.0	44.6	18.0	6.0	11 976	29 120	49 186	50.9	3.2	46 764	14.4	22.7	21.0
Wabasha	98	775	4 768	13.6	45.8	21.2	41.9	9 262	30 468	56 510	43.3	3.4	57 873	6.9	9.7	9.0
Wadena	123	890	3 153	4.3	50.4	12.7	28.5	9 581	22 002	41 906	57.6	1.9	45 597	15.0	19.6	18.1
Waseca	78	1 496	4 285	10.8	43.1	20.4	35.2	9 734	26 457	53 564	45.7	2.3	54 495	9.9	13.6	12.2
Washington	85	2 065	67 471	17.5	26.0	41.6	401.7	10 144	38 461	83 706	27.0	9.5	88 329	5.1	6.0	5.2
Watonwan	144	1 329	2 452	7.7	54.7	15.8	21.0	11 504	25 973	50 604	48.7	2.0	48 044	11.3	16.7	15.1
Wilkin	122	1 448	1 513	9.8	39.1	17.5	11.6	10 662	26 862	51 476	48.2	1.7	56 583	9.8	13.2	12.0
Winona	70	279	16 217	17.1	38.0	28.2	67.5	12 602	24 660	50 547	49.5	2.6	54 367	12.7	12.7	11.4
Wright	61	1 421	35 020	11.7	34.9	27.3	256.8	9 688	30 238	73 557	30.6	3.7	76 407	5.1	6.1	5.4
Yellow Medicine	109	922	2 328	7.0	46.4	16.1	18.9	12 663	26 885	53 041	46.9	2.4	51 569	12.5	15.0	13.1

1. Data for serious crimes have not been adjusted for underreporting; this may affect comparability between geographic areas and over time.   2. Per 100,000 population estimated by the FBI.
3. All persons 3 years old and over enrolled in nursery school through college.   4. Persons 25 years old and over.   5. Elementary and secondary education expenditures.
6. Based on population estimated by the American Community Survey, 2011–2015.

Table B. States and Counties — **Personal Income**

	Personal income, 2015										Earnings, 2015		
STATE County	Total (mil dol)	Percent change, 2014–2015	Per capita[1] Dollars	Per capita[1] Rank	Wages and salaries (mil dol)	Supplements to wages and salaries; employer contributions (mil dol) Pension and insurance	Supplements to wages and salaries; employer contributions (mil dol) Government social insurance	Proprietors' income (mil dol)	Dividends, interest, and rent (mil dol)	Personal transfer receipts (mil dol)	Total (mil dol)	Contributions for government social insurance (mil dol) From employee and self-employed	Contributions for government social insurance (mil dol) From employer
	62	63	64	65	66	67	68	69	70	71	72	73	74

MINNESOTA—Cont'd

Fillmore	938	8.2	45 036	1 107	213	40	17	203	151	183	473	31	17
Freeborn	1 266	3.3	41 371	1 131	500	79	39	132	229	305	750	48	39
Goodhue	2 249	3.2	48 427	665	1 036	167	78	275	391	391	1 556	95	78
Grant	284	6.7	48 039	755	78	13	6	53	59	69	150	9	6
Hennepin	79 787	3.8	65 231	93	62 798	7 549	4 470	6 364	17 785	9 580	81 181	4 803	4 470
Houston	874	3.4	46 557	696	172	35	14	80	156	165	301	20	14
Hubbard	761	5.1	36 847	1 724	214	39	17	46	154	220	316	24	17
Isanti	1 495	4.5	38 905	1 369	446	79	35	78	193	314	638	43	35
Itasca	1 714	4.3	37 733	1 719	699	124	58	80	320	504	960	67	58
Jackson	528	5.4	52 392	422	209	40	16	109	110	92	375	19	16
Kanabec	596	6.1	37 606	1 898	144	28	12	55	84	160	239	18	12
Kandiyohi	2 087	6.0	49 060	649	892	150	71	365	356	397	1 478	90	71
Kittson	240	1.9	54 231	285	63	12	5	53	49	45	132	6	5
Koochiching	468	2.1	36 482	1 783	193	36	17	19	77	156	265	19	17
Lac qui Parle	345	-2.1	50 380	228	87	17	7	70	73	81	180	10	7
Lake	461	3.4	43 408	966	196	34	16	25	81	124	271	19	16
Lake of the Woods	173	5.5	44 007	771	53	11	4	25	33	45	93	6	4
Le Sueur	1 223	4.6	44 197	797	365	64	30	104	211	213	563	35	30
Lincoln	267	2.5	46 333	495	63	12	5	49	51	59	128	7	5
Lyon	1 176	4.0	45 806	767	640	108	47	153	215	215	949	55	47
McLeod	1 562	4.6	43 484	1 142	767	123	61	129	262	302	1 081	68	61
Mahnomen	180	-0.4	32 950	2 451	70	16	5	6	35	64	97	6	5
Marshall	445	1.0	47 256	514	104	19	8	66	80	92	197	12	8
Martin	946	2.4	47 232	661	351	57	26	139	225	219	573	33	26
Meeker	944	6.8	40 861	1 206	275	49	22	87	155	205	432	28	22
Mille Lacs	957	4.3	37 095	2 093	334	63	26	57	139	269	480	33	26
Morrison	1 264	3.1	38 561	1 538	394	76	31	163	206	311	664	40	31
Mower	1 657	2.3	42 364	1 118	811	117	55	148	297	378	1 131	69	55
Murray	460	8.0	54 719	317	112	21	9	127	84	85	269	12	9
Nicollet	1 489	3.4	44 646	894	614	112	46	136	298	246	909	53	46
Nobles	966	7.4	44 383	1 092	427	69	32	223	166	170	751	40	32
Norman	295	-0.7	44 162	654	69	12	5	54	62	72	140	7	5
Olmsted	7 702	4.5	50 858	457	5 468	690	397	426	1 232	1 077	6 982	418	397
Otter Tail	2 448	2.7	42 411	1 078	873	158	67	253	486	594	1 351	90	67
Pennington	697	3.6	49 041	443	463	74	36	52	143	128	625	37	36
Pine	960	3.5	33 026	2 521	267	59	22	50	149	289	397	28	22
Pipestone	472	1.3	50 952	351	160	30	12	137	80	87	339	17	12
Polk	1 355	-0.4	42 975	942	488	87	40	125	225	311	739	45	40
Pope	514	2.9	46 556	572	198	32	15	42	111	115	288	19	15
Ramsey	26 076	4.5	48 457	521	20 910	2 854	1 500	1 613	5 085	4 723	26 877	1 599	1 500
Red Lake	182	-2.9	44 797	622	38	8	3	31	25	35	81	4	3
Redwood	877	9.8	56 714	547	240	47	18	285	153	154	590	33	18
Renville	772	2.1	51 844	371	233	40	19	172	160	149	464	21	19
Rice	2 585	4.5	39 532	1 553	1 078	165	84	178	442	472	1 505	95	84
Rock	480	6.6	49 961	513	140	25	10	127	85	88	302	14	10
Roseau	671	3.5	42 554	619	360	68	27	41	137	123	496	29	27
St. Louis	8 580	2.3	42 805	1 006	4 473	721	350	538	1 467	2 073	6 082	390	350
Scott	7 460	5.8	52 660	447	2 305	323	180	540	946	718	3 349	206	180
Sherburne	3 804	4.6	41 482	1 258	1 137	191	91	194	437	568	1 613	103	91
Sibley	652	6.1	43 865	1 205	143	27	11	81	116	129	262	15	11
Stearns	6 512	3.5	42 092	1 144	3 877	617	303	614	1 055	1 207	5 410	320	303
Steele	1 570	1.7	42 712	920	922	141	71	101	262	300	1 235	75	71
Stevens	512	-2.2	52 226	364	224	41	17	128	118	76	409	20	17
Swift	503	15.7	53 874	867	141	28	11	175	77	101	355	20	11
Todd	892	2.2	36 759	1 447	226	43	17	128	130	245	414	27	17
Traverse	188	1.3	55 225	245	45	8	3	41	49	40	98	4	3
Wabasha	937	1.2	44 126	948	265	48	21	102	166	181	435	27	21
Wadena	493	4.0	35 497	2 313	230	43	17	54	82	167	344	23	17
Waseca	890	7.3	46 847	1 308	281	50	23	219	131	163	573	34	23
Washington	14 634	4.8	58 163	241	3 735	556	285	806	2 590	1 611	5 383	345	285
Watonwan	418	1.0	38 124	1 523	142	27	11	51	81	100	231	14	11
Wilkin	328	-0.4	51 214	595	90	14	7	77	56	63	188	12	7
Winona	2 190	1.1	43 034	986	1 025	195	78	137	535	396	1 435	84	78
Wright	5 791	4.9	44 103	985	1 744	285	140	443	699	788	2 611	165	140
Yellow Medicine	585	14.6	59 238	611	153	31	12	184	105	109	380	21	12

1. Based on the resident population estimated as of July 1 of the year shown.

STATE County	Farm	Mining	Construction	Manufacturing	Information: professional, scientific, technical services	Retail trade	Finance, insurance, real estate and leasing	Health care and social assistance	Government	Social Security beneficiaries, December 2015 Number	Rate[1]	Supplemental Security Income recipients, December 2015	Housing units, 2016 Total	Percent change, 2010–2016
	75	76	77	78	79	80	81	82	83	84	85	86	87	88
MINNESOTA—Cont'd														
Fillmore	7.8	D	7.9	33.7	2.6	5.1	4.5	D	13.2	4 875	234	180	9 878	1.5
Freeborn	8.6	D	5.7	22.5	D	8.8	6.7	16.2	11.9	8 040	263	520	14 306	0.5
Goodhue	4.0	0.0	5.6	26.0	2.7	5.0	3.2	11.0	15.1	10 190	219	482	20 364	0.1
Grant	21.9	0.0	12.4	6.4	3.4	3.7	4.9	D	13.4	1 725	293	77	3 293	-0.9
Hennepin	0.0	0.1	3.6	8.7	17.8	4.5	16.2	9.7	9.3	181 660	149	27 007	528 445	3.7
Houston	10.6	D	11.3	10.1	6.8	5.0	2.9	9.2	20.0	4 455	237	221	8 674	0.8
Hubbard	2.3	D	9.8	15.7	2.8	8.4	4.2	D	21.9	6 015	291	357	14 609	-0.1
Isanti	0.5	0.0	7.4	16.8	D	8.8	3.9	D	18.3	7 560	197	423	15 695	2.5
Itasca	0.0	6.7	11.5	7.5	2.8	7.3	4.3	15.2	20.8	12 760	281	920	27 346	1.0
Jackson	19.4	0.1	3.3	30.6	D	2.1	2.2	D	10.4	2 385	237	109	5 042	1.0
Kanabec	-0.7	0.5	22.5	9.9	2.3	7.2	5.0	D	30.3	4 170	264	231	7 800	-0.6
Kandiyohi	6.5	D	7.6	21.4	4.0	6.8	4.4	D	16.7	9 270	218	720	19 699	1.1
Kittson	30.2	0.0	6.4	7.2	D	3.6	D	D	15.7	1 135	258	56	2 602	-0.1
Koochiching	0.8	0.0	6.8	25.5	2.4	6.7	4.2	D	24.1	3 825	298	289	7 847	-0.7
Lac qui Parle	22.8	-0.4	11.9	5.6	D	5.6	6.1	8.1	20.4	1 890	276	81	3 673	-0.5
Lake	0.0	D	D	13.4	1.9	4.7	3.3	D	19.0	3 065	288	120	7 875	2.5
Lake of the Woods	0.4	0.0	D	D	1.2	5.7	D	9.1	18.7	1 125	288	35	3 680	0.2
Le Sueur	7.4	D	8.2	33.9	2.9	4.7	5.8	4.1	12.2	5 230	189	242	12 547	1.1
Lincoln	27.5	D	12.1	3.9	2.9	4.0	2.8	D	11.1	1 470	255	57	3 114	0.2
Lyon	5.7	0.1	5.8	16.8	D	6.4	10.6	7.5	19.0	4 870	190	410	11 193	0.9
McLeod	1.9	D	5.6	37.9	2.7	5.7	3.7	13.5	10.2	7 795	217	368	15 724	-0.2
Mahnomen	0.3	0.0	4.8	D	D	3.5	D	D	59.5	960	177	147	2 767	-0.7
Marshall	13.5	D	8.9	20.0	2.5	3.7	D	6.2	17.6	2 190	233	95	4 792	-0.4
Martin	17.6	0.0	5.3	12.1	D	6.3	6.4	14.9	11.6	5 595	280	373	9 937	-0.7
Meeker	9.1	0.1	11.5	19.7	D	5.2	4.9	7.9	14.6	5 155	223	220	10 749	0.7
Mille Lacs	0.4	D	9.6	9.0	3.6	6.1	4.0	D	36.4	6 445	250	444	12 732	-0.1
Morrison	16.3	0.2	7.9	9.3	5.4	6.8	3.5	D	21.5	7 720	236	576	15 983	1.6
Mower	5.7	0.0	3.9	17.4	D	4.1	3.0	D	13.7	8 955	228	718	16 974	-0.3
Murray	37.2	0.5	7.8	8.6	2.5	4.5	D	D	12.6	2 215	263	90	4 607	1.1
Nicollet	7.0	D	3.5	24.9	D	4.2	4.5	D	20.9	5 720	171	344	13 358	3.8
Nobles	15.7	0.1	4.5	28.9	3.6	6.2	3.8	D	10.9	4 050	186	302	8 581	0.5
Norman	31.6	0.0	5.7	0.5	6.3	3.9	D	12.0	15.8	1 740	261	122	3 407	-0.4
Olmsted	0.5	0.0	4.5	9.4	4.3	5.2	3.1	52.3	8.6	25 765	170	2 167	63 793	5.4
Otter Tail	5.8	0.1	10.0	17.2	4.4	7.0	3.8	13.5	15.9	15 720	272	811	35 743	0.4
Pennington	3.8	0.0	3.5	9.9	D	4.6	2.1	D	12.8	2 870	201	198	6 436	2.2
Pine	2.2	D	9.5	2.8	D	6.5	3.4	9.0	42.7	6 915	238	504	17 243	-0.2
Pipestone	24.5	D	8.9	6.9	6.5	5.0	D	D	14.5	2 070	223	143	4 466	-0.4
Polk	8.6	0.2	8.2	14.9	3.4	6.3	4.1	D	20.6	6 790	216	589	14 737	0.9
Pope	7.6	0.0	6.4	19.0	2.2	5.9	4.5	D	17.5	2 690	244	128	6 586	2.3
Ramsey	0.0	0.0	4.6	10.7	9.6	4.2	8.3	12.9	17.4	85 115	159	16 874	218 997	0.8
Red Lake	25.7	0.0	6.7	D	D	3.9	D	3.2	18.3	910	225	38	1 932	-0.8
Redwood	15.2	D	3.2	31.4	1.9	3.3	4.8	D	15.6	3 640	235	202	7 273	0.0
Renville	33.5	D	4.9	14.1	3.3	2.5	D	D	13.9	3 575	241	222	7 297	-0.8
Rice	2.6	0.2	7.7	20.2	3.6	5.4	3.7	10.2	14.7	11 490	176	780	24 703	1.0
Rock	35.1	D	4.7	6.7	3.3	4.0	11.8	8.7	11.6	2 305	240	95	4 276	0.3
Roseau	4.2	0.0	1.6	52.8	1.6	4.0	3.6	D	12.8	3 215	205	147	7 497	0.4
St. Louis	0.1	7.3	6.1	5.1	6.7	7.0	5.1	24.4	17.5	46 585	233	5 162	103 839	0.8
Scott	0.5	0.2	12.4	18.5	8.4	5.4	3.2	7.9	17.9	16 685	118	1 257	50 407	7.0
Sherburne	0.3	D	13.4	14.4	3.6	7.3	3.1	10.4	17.4	13 340	146	995	33 399	3.2
Sibley	21.5	0.0	12.0	8.2	2.4	2.5	3.1	D	15.1	3 150	212	154	6 550	-0.5
Stearns	3.1	D	8.4	12.8	6.0	7.3	6.3	18.5	14.7	26 675	172	2 373	63 702	2.8
Steele	3.1	D	3.4	29.0	D	7.1	15.4	9.5	10.7	7 485	204	502	15 456	0.7
Stevens	18.8	D	4.9	23.1	3.8	4.4	3.9	8.4	17.6	1 720	176	116	4 160	0.0
Swift	13.6	D	5.2	34.7	2.3	3.6	3.0	D	13.3	2 290	245	162	4 809	-0.5
Todd	14.4	D	5.8	26.7	2.1	4.3	3.3	D	17.6	5 945	245	396	13 008	0.7
Traverse	39.5	0.0	2.9	2.7	D	4.6	D	7.7	15.8	985	290	75	2 072	0.0
Wabasha	11.6	D	7.7	21.8	2.7	4.7	4.4	D	14.1	4 875	229	210	10 093	1.0
Wadena	4.7	0.0	6.4	9.4	2.8	5.6	3.4	D	20.2	3 860	279	398	7 018	1.7
Waseca	10.9	D	5.5	40.8	D	3.5	3.5	6.7	14.7	4 195	221	238	7 907	0.1
Washington	0.4	0.1	7.2	12.5	8.0	8.0	8.3	13.8	13.8	40 155	160	2 040	97 048	5.1
Watonwan	14.2	D	6.7	23.1	2.0	4.5	4.5	9.2	17.0	2 340	214	132	5 019	-0.6
Wilkin	9.1	D	3.8	2.4	D	3.4	D	10.8	11.7	1 415	221	94	3 072	-0.2
Winona	4.5	D	3.7	29.1	D	5.3	4.0	9.0	15.4	9 470	186	623	21 013	1.2
Wright	0.9	D	16.2	15.5	3.1	7.7	4.1	11.2	13.7	19 435	148	900	50 779	3.6
Yellow Medicine	16.1	D	6.4	22.8	2.4	3.1	4.2	D	18.0	2 485	251	150	4 741	-0.4

1. Per 1,000 resident population estimated as of July 1 of the year shown.

Table B. States and Counties — Housing, Labor Force, and Employment

STATE County	Housing units, 2011–2015								Civilian labor force, 2016		Unemployment		Civilian employment,[6] 2011–2015		
	Occupied units												Percent		
			Owner-occupied			Renter-occupied									
				Median owner cost as a percent of income											Construction, production, and maintenance occupations
	Total	Percent	Median value[1]	With a mortgage	Without a mortgage[2]	Median rent[3]	Median rent as a percent of income[2]	Substandard units[4] (percent)	Total	Percent change, 2015–2016	Total	Rate[5]	Total	Management, business, science and arts	
	89	90	91	92	93	94	95	96	97	98	99	100	101	102	103
MINNESOTA—Cont'd															
Fillmore	8 531	78.3	140 100	22.2	11.8	595	28.1	2.6	11 398	0.7	464	4.1	10 595	34.7	28.4
Freeborn	12 993	76.4	104 800	20.3	11.1	598	27.0	1.9	16 158	-0.4	627	3.9	15 322	27.4	32.0
Goodhue	18 793	75.8	179 200	22.6	12.7	705	29.2	1.6	26 702	0.1	1 002	3.8	23 662	34.5	28.2
Grant	2 530	80.3	101 500	20.6	12.3	512	28.1	1.3	3 270	-1.6	155	4.7	2 943	34.7	27.5
Hennepin	490 196	62.7	229 200	21.8	12.0	951	29.2	2.9	679 285	1.1	22 859	3.4	650 324	47.7	13.5
Houston	7 886	80.7	159 000	22.5	12.2	634	29.5	1.6	10 481	0.7	418	4.0	9 795	33.9	29.0
Hubbard	8 787	81.4	174 300	24.8	12.8	673	26.7	2.6	9 789	3.2	635	6.5	9 475	30.3	27.2
Isanti	14 059	80.9	164 900	23.8	12.4	843	29.9	2.1	20 333	1.4	963	4.7	19 504	28.4	29.8
Itasca	18 965	79.5	155 500	23.6	11.8	642	28.9	2.7	21 851	-1.3	1 892	8.7	19 970	31.2	26.9
Jackson	4 354	76.5	104 100	18.1	10.5	540	23.8	1.5	6 088	-2.4	277	4.5	5 392	34.7	30.7
Kanabec	6 191	80.3	137 300	24.8	14.3	764	30.9	2.8	8 951	2.1	587	6.6	7 287	27.4	32.0
Kandiyohi	16 701	72.6	160 800	22.0	11.7	666	30.6	1.9	24 065	0.8	925	3.8	21 757	32.8	29.6
Kittson	1 912	80.8	72 600	18.3	10.0	504	21.8	1.6	2 396	-2.4	112	4.7	2 182	33.9	34.3
Koochiching	5 844	78.2	101 400	19.6	11.6	559	34.0	1.4	6 159	-0.8	525	8.5	5 877	27.5	30.6
Lac qui Parle	3 078	80.6	83 000	19.3	10.0	554	26.7	1.1	3 628	-2.9	157	4.3	3 506	36.3	27.5
Lake	5 087	79.9	157 700	23.8	10.4	680	29.4	3.1	5 373	-3.5	347	6.5	4 870	30.5	27.8
Lake of the Woods	1 623	85.5	117 000	23.9	14.0	634	32.0	2.6	2 406	0.1	114	4.7	1 975	27.7	37.5
Le Sueur	10 839	81.5	176 500	22.9	11.6	694	28.2	1.6	15 564	0.9	761	4.9	14 456	31.9	31.9
Lincoln	2 497	79.3	92 500	21.3	10.9	528	23.4	1.0	3 371	0.1	123	3.6	2 974	32.8	30.2
Lyon	9 958	67.7	133 700	19.6	10.0	605	24.0	2.3	15 085	-0.6	537	3.6	13 788	33.2	29.7
McLeod	14 819	76.2	148 300	22.1	12.1	710	24.6	1.2	19 584	-2.3	875	4.5	18 957	30.5	31.5
Mahnomen	2 001	73.4	97 300	20.3	13.2	518	27.4	4.3	2 386	-0.1	137	5.7	2 222	26.8	23.0
Marshall	4 027	80.8	93 500	18.3	11.1	542	22.7	1.4	5 606	-1.7	413	7.4	4 726	33.3	32.0
Martin	8 831	73.8	105 400	19.3	10.0	613	27.4	1.8	10 427	0.6	433	4.2	10 273	30.9	30.7
Meeker	9 174	80.1	157 200	23.0	12.2	686	29.2	1.9	13 171	-0.5	598	4.5	11 477	32.2	33.9
Mille Lacs	10 046	73.7	140 900	23.5	14.3	734	29.1	2.4	12 667	1.2	762	6.0	11 752	28.2	31.3
Morrison	13 352	79.7	153 300	23.4	12.7	655	28.3	1.8	17 723	0.3	1 005	5.7	16 533	29.5	32.5
Mower	15 425	71.9	111 700	19.3	10.0	697	30.5	1.8	20 444	1.2	647	3.2	19 166	28.9	33.3
Murray	3 737	81.3	98 600	20.7	11.0	555	22.3	0.9	4 955	-1.4	237	4.8	4 244	36.9	29.5
Nicollet	12 629	73.0	170 400	22.1	10.0	757	27.1	1.5	20 337	0.9	578	2.8	18 672	38.5	21.1
Nobles	7 842	72.1	106 900	20.4	10.4	627	26.1	6.1	11 364	-0.7	433	3.8	10 431	24.6	40.8
Norman	2 728	80.7	83 200	19.0	11.5	527	28.5	2.9	3 435	0.6	167	4.9	3 105	33.5	28.6
Olmsted	57 899	73.7	173 000	20.2	10.0	827	28.9	1.9	84 313	1.3	2 533	3.0	80 162	48.1	15.8
Otter Tail	24 042	78.5	164 900	21.3	11.4	656	28.7	1.7	31 146	0.9	1 368	4.4	27 662	34.5	29.1
Pennington	5 920	74.0	115 200	19.8	11.8	604	26.9	1.6	9 031	0.2	523	5.8	7 636	28.4	28.1
Pine	11 361	78.1	141 200	25.4	13.5	711	29.5	3.8	14 760	0.6	868	5.9	12 645	25.0	30.5
Pipestone	3 980	74.4	92 300	20.1	10.4	546	26.1	2.7	4 874	-1.3	188	3.9	4 572	28.7	32.2
Polk	12 723	72.4	136 700	19.6	11.6	626	29.0	1.6	17 158	0.7	747	4.4	15 978	34.8	25.8
Pope	4 809	80.1	150 900	22.6	11.6	652	24.9	1.3	6 261	-1.2	225	3.6	5 406	35.2	27.2
Ramsey	206 857	59.0	193 700	22.0	11.5	865	30.6	4.6	280 628	1.1	10 190	3.6	266 709	43.1	16.8
Red Lake	1 661	82.4	97 800	19.0	11.5	484	24.8	1.7	2 329	0.7	167	7.2	2 079	29.0	31.2
Redwood	6 307	78.5	92 600	19.8	11.2	572	24.9	1.6	8 306	1.2	342	4.1	7 577	33.6	28.4
Renville	6 341	79.5	95 700	19.7	10.8	578	24.8	1.3	8 432	-1.1	446	5.3	7 573	32.5	34.3
Rice	22 532	73.9	185 200	23.6	11.6	722	28.4	2.1	35 888	2.1	1 265	3.5	33 503	35.9	25.3
Rock	3 929	75.3	128 300	20.6	11.6	619	28.4	1.5	5 874	0.3	137	2.3	4 716	31.5	27.8
Roseau	6 318	78.6	113 200	21.1	11.0	646	26.8	2.6	8 284	-3.0	425	5.1	8 447	28.7	41.4
St. Louis	84 545	71.1	139 900	21.1	11.5	685	31.5	2.0	101 358	0.2	5 888	5.8	96 700	33.6	21.5
Scott	46 805	83.1	247 600	21.5	10.2	1 024	28.3	1.5	79 453	1.1	2 583	3.3	74 498	41.1	20.5
Sherburne	30 574	80.9	190 600	22.1	10.4	925	31.5	2.0	49 647	1.1	2 055	4.1	47 444	34.0	26.5
Sibley	6 014	78.7	131 300	21.5	11.9	630	25.3	1.4	8 495	0.6	364	4.3	7 867	30.7	36.3
Stearns	57 265	70.0	166 400	21.3	11.3	742	28.9	2.4	88 054	0.7	3 358	3.8	83 520	31.9	25.1
Steele	14 271	76.4	150 500	20.9	11.5	731	31.2	1.7	21 166	0.6	757	3.6	18 434	31.7	26.9
Stevens	3 668	67.2	131 500	17.9	10.0	587	36.8	0.9	5 647	-0.3	172	3.0	5 058	33.3	24.9
Swift	4 231	73.4	92 400	18.3	11.1	579	25.3	1.4	5 100	-0.6	271	5.3	4 865	32.8	31.7
Todd	9 839	81.6	131 400	24.1	12.9	567	26.8	4.1	12 885	-0.2	609	4.7	11 437	28.4	37.3
Traverse	1 524	80.7	70 900	18.9	10.0	530	25.2	0.9	1 805	-0.9	67	3.7	1 623	42.0	20.8
Wabasha	8 953	81.4	159 500	22.6	11.5	699	28.0	1.3	11 986	0.7	445	3.7	11 221	33.2	28.9
Wadena	5 673	76.9	114 300	23.7	13.4	569	28.9	1.8	6 244	-0.6	373	6.0	5 859	24.7	35.1
Waseca	7 325	77.4	141 800	20.0	11.3	571	25.3	2.4	9 470	-2.1	407	4.3	9 630	31.7	31.0
Washington	90 932	80.1	243 600	21.3	10.0	1 144	28.5	1.5	137 771	1.2	4 646	3.4	130 036	45.2	16.2
Watonwan	4 450	74.3	93 400	18.3	10.2	566	23.6	1.6	6 409	3.3	321	5.0	5 676	28.1	40.1
Wilkin	2 776	75.5	114 800	19.8	10.0	437	23.9	1.2	3 693	0.9	122	3.3	3 312	32.6	30.4
Winona	19 068	69.9	153 900	21.9	10.5	608	29.1	1.7	29 217	-0.1	1 040	3.6	28 307	32.8	26.0
Wright	45 265	82.8	193 100	22.1	10.5	899	28.7	2.0	72 305	1.2	2 817	3.9	67 669	35.1	26.4
Yellow Medicine	4 196	78.8	96 800	19.8	10.2	578	28.2	1.4	5 439	-1.7	211	3.9	5 147	33.6	29.5

1. Specified owner-occupied units.   2. A value of 10.0 represents 10 percent or less; a value of 50.0 represents 50 percent or more.   3. Specified renter-occupied units.
4. Overcrowded or lacking complete plumbing facilities.   5. Percent of civilian labor force.   6. Civilian employed persons 16 years old and over.

STATE County	Private nonfarm establishments, employment and payroll, 2015									Agriculture, 2012			
	Number of establishments	Employment						Annual payroll		Farms			Farm operators whose principal occupation is farming (percent)
		Total	Health care and social assistance	Manufacturing	Retail trade	Finance and insurance	Professional, scientific, and technical services	Total (mil dol)	Average per employee (dollars)	Number	Percent with:		
											Fewer than 50 acres	500 acres or more	
	104	105	106	107	108	109	110	111	112	113	114	115	116

MINNESOTA—Cont'd

STATE County	104	105	106	107	108	109	110	111	112	113	114	115	116
Fillmore	596	4 637	879	848	699	221	133	151	32 604	1 553	24.8	14.8	50.4
Freeborn	785	11 522	2 568	2 755	1 928	506	193	426	36 990	1 122	33.9	23.4	54.0
Goodhue	1 325	21 324	3 673	5 373	2 575	440	473	915	42 921	1 536	34.2	11.4	47.7
Grant	197	1 444	369	116	240	68	31	52	35 918	542	23.4	25.1	42.3
Hennepin	39 905	884 589	131 535	72 509	76 196	78 269	83 729	54 094	61 152	627	60.3	6.2	65.1
Houston	426	3 976	1 046	484	595	93	102	121	30 475	920	14.9	11.3	48.5
Hubbard	589	4 596	822	874	1 030	158	99	158	34 476	406	18.7	11.1	51.5
Isanti	830	8 882	1 978	1 414	1 827	322	201	319	35 905	844	43.4	7.8	44.1
Itasca	1 133	14 402	3 485	1 264	2 382	423	650	591	41 017	401	23.2	8.0	45.6
Jackson	312	4 975	1 313	1 209	334	89	63	179	35 891	826	21.3	30.0	59.9
Kanabec	292	2 874	887	534	507	107	85	108	37 568	648	23.1	8.6	50.8
Kandiyohi	1 389	19 228	5 521	2 595	3 094	545	559	683	35 497	1 310	27.0	14.8	44.7
Kittson	147	1 272	363	171	296	58	23	43	33 470	544	10.8	36.2	43.0
Koochiching	392	3 714	620	D	777	144	53	133	35 828	187	9.1	17.6	43.9
Lac qui Parle	207	1 763	590	139	300	101	17	52	29 301	852	18.7	35.2	57.4
Lake	301	3 006	507	531	354	103	40	112	37 203	44	50.0	2.3	29.5
Lake of the Woods	157	1 350	D	D	228	31	17	41	30 094	196	15.3	19.9	36.2
Le Sueur	703	7 343	863	2 776	732	207	174	300	40 879	1 051	35.8	11.4	40.6
Lincoln	205	1 516	529	16	238	50	37	47	30 705	699	17.6	24.5	54.6
Lyon	826	13 178	2 335	2 096	1 957	1 098	400	519	39 389	904	17.7	30.6	64.8
McLeod	962	16 413	3 074	5 870	2 154	404	390	681	41 482	966	32.6	16.6	62.6
Mahnomen	106	1 777	335	D	119	55	18	53	30 014	310	15.8	37.1	52.6
Marshall	264	1 707	288	293	244	118	42	73	42 998	1 148	8.1	33.0	44.9
Martin	628	8 094	1 938	1 457	1 317	329	185	303	37 426	897	20.3	33.2	67.8
Meeker	569	6 417	1 289	1 872	908	186	107	222	34 629	1 147	31.8	13.1	49.4
Mille Lacs	682	8 180	1 763	1 076	1 198	223	230	255	31 179	731	31.5	7.4	43.2
Morrison	883	8 145	1 655	1 447	1 451	245	190	274	33 643	1 957	18.3	8.7	50.3
Mower	850	14 293	2 727	3 757	1 801	307	257	648	45 329	1 053	30.7	22.5	64.1
Murray	307	2 553	478	531	328	146	69	82	32 121	895	20.7	31.1	59.1
Nicollet	627	12 689	2 339	3 722	964	207	435	497	39 156	764	23.6	20.9	62.6
Nobles	607	8 931	1 412	3 002	1 461	239	197	319	35 722	995	22.7	26.1	65.7
Norman	190	1 266	416	D	205	83	31	49	38 571	610	7.9	43.9	64.6
Olmsted	3 582	93 708	19 354	4 293	10 988	1 752	D	5 306	56 621	1 150	35.6	11.6	50.3
Otter Tail	1 663	18 818	4 013	4 093	2 880	553	378	650	34 530	3 033	17.0	13.9	46.6
Pennington	395	9 530	1 302	1 015	1 099	131	334	363	38 079	515	12.6	25.2	37.5
Pine	612	7 089	1 392	348	1 035	181	114	183	25 771	870	16.6	10.6	47.2
Pipestone	323	3 135	482	434	547	111	101	101	32 145	637	25.1	25.0	57.1
Polk	785	9 567	2 298	1 941	1 478	246	242	335	34 968	1 322	11.6	37.3	56.1
Pope	366	3 746	604	765	367	114	256	153	40 868	931	21.6	16.6	37.1
Ramsey	13 401	304 874	60 437	23 188	27 754	19 113	14 842	16 794	55 087	97	96.9	0.0	83.5
Red Lake	101	617	114	D	147	58	22	20	32 976	322	8.4	29.8	57.1
Redwood	517	5 692	891	877	791	334	70	190	33 384	1 163	19.9	31.2	68.5
Renville	460	4 616	923	1 284	555	162	174	172	37 192	1 061	20.2	32.9	63.4
Rice	1 520	24 419	3 415	4 045	2 739	445	431	865	35 405	1 304	40.9	7.7	45.6
Rock	274	2 893	873	300	398	298	93	89	30 923	689	26.6	23.9	62.1
Roseau	419	7 237	787	4 214	821	173	87	265	36 580	977	9.6	27.2	41.2
St. Louis	5 329	87 679	24 453	4 222	12 560	3 340	3 521	3 619	41 274	685	26.1	6.6	38.4
Scott	3 285	42 817	4 823	6 579	5 011	662	2 399	2 230	52 086	847	41.0	6.8	51.6
Sherburne	1 993	22 237	4 064	3 447	2 930	373	590	922	41 457	455	41.1	12.5	42.2
Sibley	348	3 549	624	1 135	362	125	63	121	34 033	949	25.7	20.9	63.8
Stearns	4 341	80 548	16 345	12 070	11 131	4 103	2 608	3 474	43 123	3 501	23.0	8.4	55.4
Steele	1 020	18 979	2 637	4 862	2 759	2 150	227	835	43 979	796	38.4	14.2	55.5
Stevens	320	4 571	1 470	942	547	110	101	165	36 068	560	25.2	31.1	56.3
Swift	310	3 140	634	691	381	99	64	103	32 666	801	22.2	26.0	55.2
Todd	546	5 741	1 604	1 723	791	214	77	202	35 164	1 931	18.4	6.8	52.9
Traverse	122	834	294	41	186	38	3	23	28 169	458	22.7	36.7	62.7
Wabasha	566	5 672	977	1 272	735	159	102	188	33 147	909	24.1	14.2	58.7
Wadena	398	4 059	989	312	737	162	100	136	33 418	643	15.7	6.4	42.8
Waseca	465	5 328	952	1 770	670	175	145	222	41 702	805	31.3	18.8	55.8
Washington	5 738	76 210	12 126	7 802	13 162	5 756	3 706	3 206	42 063	602	54.0	6.5	57.3
Watonwan	283	3 529	525	1 265	436	146	29	109	30 786	503	25.0	27.4	60.2
Wilkin	161	1 805	486	D	195	62	D	61	33 844	391	14.8	49.9	68.3
Winona	1 164	22 429	3 380	4 961	2 792	549	475	789	35 170	1 115	22.6	11.9	52.6
Wright	3 265	36 431	6 155	5 545	7 066	702	985	1 475	40 499	1 463	39.2	8.3	48.8
Yellow Medicine	325	3 875	911	219	380	114	50	169	43 672	885	22.7	32.3	60.8

Table B. States and Counties — **Agriculture**

STATE County	| Agriculture, 2012 (cont.)															
	Land in farms				Value of land and buildings (dollars)		Value of machinery and equipment, average per farm (dollars)	Value of products sold				Percent of farms with sales of:		Government payments	
		Acres								Percent from:					
	Acreage (1,000)	Percent change, 2007– 2012	Average size of farm	Total irrigated (1,000)	Total cropland (1,000)	Average per farm	Average per acre		Total (mil dol)	Average per farm (dollars)	Crops	Live-stock and poultry products	$10,000 or more	$100,000 or more	Total ($1,000)	Percent of farms
	117	118	119	120	121	122	123	124	125	126	127	128	129	130	131	132
MINNESOTA—Cont'd																
Fillmore	422	-5.3	272	0.2	316.8	1 248 138	4 588	164 626	342.2	220 351	60.6	39.4	62.8	33.5	8 809	70.3
Freeborn	382	-1.7	340	2.4	356.7	1 857 024	5 454	222 874	416.0	370 784	68.8	31.2	64.0	42.7	8 422	76.1
Goodhue	398	0.4	259	4.5	330.0	1 404 395	5 418	191 857	435.7	283 650	60.9	39.1	64.1	36.1	7 646	66.3
Grant	303	-5.8	559	5.0	279.6	2 020 910	3 616	233 819	213.5	393 849	95.2	4.8	46.1	33.0	6 952	92.4
Hennepin	69	3.5	110	0.6	54.3	904 309	8 235	109 024	64.5	102 821	82.7	17.3	44.0	15.8	1 002	33.2
Houston	229	-6.2	249	0.1	129.4	860 452	3 453	133 811	146.3	158 974	51.1	48.9	59.1	28.3	4 864	78.9
Hubbard	117	-7.3	288	19.6	68.9	649 106	2 254	92 340	46.1	113 475	90.7	9.3	40.4	7.1	362	26.8
Isanti	142	12.9	169	3.1	98.9	628 475	3 724	101 475	61.0	72 306	78.5	21.5	40.9	12.0	1 812	45.9
Itasca	84	-9.9	210	D	40.1	395 067	1 884	63 691	11.2	27 870	58.4	41.6	42.1	4.7	286	13.5
Jackson	358	-10.7	433	0.1	330.0	2 646 869	6 110	298 615	376.4	455 643	66.9	33.1	77.2	54.8	6 712	82.9
Kanabec	129	-9.2	199	D	65.9	456 122	2 295	77 170	32.0	49 326	61.5	38.5	39.8	11.1	785	35.5
Kandiyohi	415	-0.5	317	21.0	354.1	1 522 722	4 806	206 989	495.4	378 160	57.4	42.6	48.7	28.6	9 979	82.8
Kittson	470	-13.2	865	D	391.1	1 516 086	1 754	285 081	180.6	331 914	94.5	5.5	44.1	30.9	8 938	86.4
Koochiching	53	-3.1	286	D	24.7	335 963	1 176	73 214	9.1	48 604	56.7	43.3	45.5	7.5	256	19.3
Lac qui Parle	446	8.4	524	4.2	407.9	2 298 670	4 386	298 212	311.8	365 912	81.1	18.9	67.3	50.1	8 663	89.2
Lake	4	9.0	85	0.0	1.5	279 023	3 285	45 000	0.4	8 841	83.5	16.5	20.5	0.0	D	2.3
Lake of the Woods	90	-6.9	461	D	56.2	686 286	1 490	112 276	19.1	97 541	92.4	7.6	45.4	15.3	962	57.7
Le Sueur	242	-3.5	230	0.9	207.5	1 276 799	5 548	158 177	224.3	213 423	63.3	36.7	55.5	26.9	5 726	78.9
Lincoln	291	1.6	416	0.4	256.6	1 614 046	3 878	224 119	198.6	284 117	68.1	31.9	66.1	41.6	7 282	89.0
Lyon	413	-3.7	457	0.0	379.7	2 373 903	5 197	279 675	403.0	445 815	59.9	40.1	73.9	54.8	8 729	83.5
McLeod	264	8.2	273	0.1	237.0	1 471 040	5 385	207 760	234.5	242 789	76.3	23.7	64.9	38.1	7 031	78.3
Mahnomen	216	13.1	696	D	178.5	1 417 135	2 035	281 677	96.0	309 745	93.8	6.2	61.0	40.0	3 698	85.5
Marshall	820	-9.9	714	1.0	740.4	1 506 519	2 109	258 963	322.3	280 777	97.7	2.3	48.3	30.4	15 614	89.4
Martin	429	-4.7	478	0.8	405.6	2 931 235	6 134	300 925	619.6	690 708	53.3	46.7	80.9	61.8	9 526	85.8
Meeker	304	-5.6	265	8.5	259.9	1 101 923	4 160	177 291	291.7	254 347	59.0	41.0	53.0	29.1	6 376	77.8
Mille Lacs	128	2.3	175	0.2	78.9	481 513	2 753	77 425	53.0	72 476	58.8	41.2	47.5	13.7	1 131	44.7
Morrison	437	1.2	223	20.3	256.1	618 675	2 774	154 393	429.9	219 691	26.0	74.0	66.8	27.6	5 626	64.3
Mower	450	7.1	427	3.2	422.9	2 557 820	5 988	260 886	475.8	451 853	68.6	31.4	70.8	46.6	8 929	78.3
Murray	408	-4.9	456	D	374.9	2 572 509	5 644	305 709	365.5	408 348	63.6	36.4	70.9	50.3	9 673	87.5
Nicollet	274	0.1	359	0.0	250.0	2 329 018	6 489	288 609	386.6	506 060	46.1	53.9	78.4	54.3	6 050	84.4
Nobles	381	-9.9	382	D	351.0	2 263 207	5 917	291 514	477.6	480 017	50.8	49.2	79.7	57.8	8 290	83.1
Norman	532	3.8	873	0.9	492.5	2 611 572	2 992	359 020	281.2	461 039	93.6	6.4	69.3	48.5	7 950	85.6
Olmsted	264	-10.7	230	0.2	209.4	1 258 339	5 473	166 763	250.1	217 472	65.8	34.2	58.4	29.4	5 524	70.8
Otter Tail	882	-1.8	291	59.0	623.3	728 692	2 505	127 789	504.3	166 272	64.2	35.8	50.4	20.6	13 475	76.7
Pennington	272	-16.5	528	0.0	225.5	958 184	1 816	167 614	82.4	160 095	90.2	9.8	50.5	24.7	5 827	87.0
Pine	204	-1.9	234	0.5	103.8	472 323	2 018	83 011	65.4	75 223	46.7	53.3	48.2	10.7	1 176	37.1
Pipestone	242	-1.1	380	2.9	206.0	1 994 403	5 250	245 870	307.9	483 356	38.1	61.9	77.7	49.5	4 263	78.6
Polk	1 095	-0.4	828	9.4	991.4	2 403 190	2 902	415 046	594.5	449 722	96.3	3.7	59.2	39.1	17 706	85.2
Pope	334	-7.3	359	28.9	267.5	1 314 806	3 666	183 074	237.7	255 321	72.5	27.5	47.5	29.4	6 786	84.1
Ramsey	1	-23.2	7	0.1	0.4	68 392	9 176	26 876	2.9	30 330	84.3	15.7	29.9	7.2	0	0.0
Red Lake	199	-11.1	617	D	167.7	1 079 854	1 750	181 960	74.8	232 242	87.8	12.2	59.3	32.3	3 215	84.5
Redwood	521	-5.9	448	0.0	489.6	2 835 987	6 325	301 476	518.4	445 711	70.4	29.6	78.3	60.4	10 261	86.1
Renville	622	0.3	586	0.3	589.1	3 547 517	6 055	357 959	710.3	669 506	76.8	23.2	76.5	61.9	10 308	83.4
Rice	237	-6.5	181	0.9	197.3	1 039 649	5 731	131 569	231.6	177 599	63.5	36.5	51.4	21.9	5 113	69.3
Rock	281	0.5	407	1.9	252.7	2 862 247	7 030	286 846	398.4	578 213	44.7	55.3	85.8	62.6	4 542	75.3
Roseau	556	-6.0	569	0.0	445.4	676 111	1 188	161 546	158.4	162 140	86.1	13.9	45.5	22.5	9 192	80.1
St. Louis	127	-14.4	186	D	60.4	349 235	1 880	49 045	17.1	24 904	59.9	40.1	36.9	3.5	245	5.0
Scott	141	20.1	167	0.2	111.6	1 038 302	6 227	115 534	112.2	132 462	61.8	38.2	56.0	22.0	2 679	53.6
Sherburne	112	5.9	247	29.7	88.7	1 062 160	4 301	153 305	88.5	194 532	77.9	22.1	40.7	17.4	1 589	46.6
Sibley	346	0.2	365	0.1	318.6	2 187 458	5 994	250 711	377.0	397 289	63.0	37.0	76.5	49.2	6 433	77.6
Stearns	758	7.0	216	52.0	582.8	844 095	3 901	175 663	808.5	230 933	32.3	67.7	68.1	38.2	16 012	74.0
Steele	238	-10.6	299	0.6	217.9	1 793 508	5 999	217 629	293.1	368 157	66.9	33.1	57.9	36.7	5 456	79.4
Stevens	319	-6.2	570	19.1	297.3	2 547 307	4 467	347 489	441.3	788 107	53.9	46.1	62.5	47.0	5 149	84.1
Swift	361	-7.1	451	27.1	326.6	2 305 811	5 116	259 010	339.2	423 437	71.0	29.0	59.4	40.1	7 598	87.1
Todd	394	4.0	204	14.1	248.1	482 272	2 364	92 717	241.0	124 812	39.3	60.7	60.7	19.4	4 869	62.6
Traverse	348	6.3	761	0.3	335.0	3 384 218	4 448	355 653	264.5	577 596	95.3	4.7	61.6	47.6	7 019	91.7
Wabasha	246	-6.3	270	1.4	177.8	1 269 843	4 698	210 095	231.2	254 341	49.7	50.3	69.3	41.0	5 237	74.4
Wadena	149	-1.5	232	20.0	83.5	412 974	1 784	74 162	57.5	89 401	62.3	37.7	49.6	14.2	1 954	61.7
Waseca	232	-9.0	288	D	213.6	1 692 842	5 881	207 745	303.9	377 523	59.1	40.9	69.6	45.1	5 979	83.5
Washington	81	-0.4	134	3.5	58.5	1 107 086	8 238	108 400	86.4	143 586	90.6	9.4	46.8	17.9	1 090	33.1
Watonwan	237	-11.9	471	3.2	223.3	2 880 443	6 111	300 348	281.0	558 740	64.3	35.7	69.6	52.1	5 266	86.7
Wilkin	444	4.6	1 136	1.9	428.8	4 434 734	3 903	532 286	303.9	777 363	99.0	1.0	71.6	57.5	7 125	86.7
Winona	277	-9.2	249	0.1	180.0	1 165 445	4 686	177 996	282.0	252 939	38.0	62.0	69.4	33.8	5 695	66.8
Wright	288	8.6	197	3.7	231.8	1 055 837	5 361	139 010	227.5	155 519	65.2	34.8	56.0	22.3	4 703	58.9
Yellow Medicine	395	-3.5	446	0.4	364.5	2 043 238	4 578	287 805	322.8	364 741	73.7	26.3	68.6	50.7	9 119	87.5

STATE County	Water use, 2010		Wholesale trade,[1] 2012				Retail trade,[2] 2012				Real estate and rental and leasing,[2] 2012			
	Total water withdrawn (mil gal/day)	Gallons withdrawn per person per day	Number of establishments	Number of employees	Sales (mil dol)	Annual payroll (mil dol)	Number of establishments	Number of employees	Sales (mil dol)	Annual payroll (mil dol)	Number of establishments	Number of employees	Receipts (mil dol)	Annual payroll (mil dol)
	133	134	135	136	137	138	139	140	141	142	143	144	145	146
MINNESOTA—Cont'd														
Fillmore	13.9	668	24	256	362.7	12.1	90	653	189.5	14.2	6	D	D	D
Freeborn	5.7	183	43	516	479.1	24.3	137	1 806	559.8	43.7	22	73	10.2	1.6
Goodhue	617.6	13 372	42	566	582.2	25.8	222	2 356	737.9	55.5	39	109	21.1	3.5
Grant	1.5	253	10	131	957.4	7.9	32	202	60.9	4.4	2	D	D	D
Hennepin	182.2	158	2 046	36 257	32 265.1	2 340.4	4 184	74 958	23 926.9	2 033.8	2 218	17 614	4 192.5	829.4
Houston	2.4	127	16	132	108.0	4.4	70	624	136.2	12.1	4	10	2.4	0.3
Hubbard	11.3	554	3	D	D	D	103	947	216.1	19.3	14	D	D	D
Isanti	4.1	108	24	172	79.9	6.5	97	1 522	482.8	36.8	29	D	D	D
Itasca	196.9	4 370	31	234	133.0	11.1	198	2 347	568.6	50.9	30	82	12.9	2.1
Jackson	2.7	267	14	270	297.2	10.5	43	327	85.2	5.8	7	D	D	D
Kanabec	1.5	95	6	27	9.0	0.8	44	527	130.7	10.1	2	D	D	D
Kandiyohi	11.1	263	70	D	D	D	224	2 988	666.4	61.3	47	130	15.5	2.7
Kittson	1.6	341	15	77	191.2	4.3	31	268	128.4	4.9	2	D	D	D
Koochiching	45.9	3 448	11	50	15.2	1.8	78	749	189.5	16.0	13	33	4.5	0.9
Lac qui Parle	3.5	478	12	122	235.9	5.3	38	309	67.5	5.2	3	7	0.4	0.1
Lake	124.7	11 474	2	D	D	D	43	358	136.0	9.8	9	D	D	D
Lake of the Woods	1.0	237	4	20	18.2	0.7	27	204	53.2	3.7	4	7	0.6	0.1
Le Sueur	23.8	860	28	246	268.8	10.7	86	783	210.7	14.5	23	32	5.6	0.8
Lincoln	2.3	383	6	61	106.9	3.5	38	242	66.9	4.7	4	9	1.3	0.1
Lyon	7.3	282	36	D	D	D	134	2 020	458.9	41.4	29	119	10.3	4.6
McLeod	7.2	197	32	504	260.1	27.3	156	2 113	501.4	42.3	35	92	15.4	2.4
Mahnomen	0.6	115	6	D	D	D	20	161	26.8	2.8	3	D	D	D
Marshall	1.1	114	20	227	431.5	11.2	36	271	123.0	7.2	2	D	D	D
Martin	10.2	487	40	712	1 166.5	44.7	96	1 242	294.5	27.5	17	37	17.3	0.9
Meeker	4.8	204	20	206	224.9	8.8	83	809	250.0	19.3	12	26	5.9	0.9
Mille Lacs	2.6	101	26	238	180.0	7.9	99	1 141	252.6	21.2	26	71	7.8	1.3
Morrison	14.5	437	26	337	238.0	10.6	135	1 487	419.9	32.3	16	49	5.5	0.8
Mower	10.1	259	28	D	D	D	132	1 826	370.0	35.4	21	126	20.1	1.8
Murray	2.1	241	11	131	354.5	6.2	42	266	46.8	4.4	6	26	1.7	0.6
Nicollet	6.6	200	34	415	372.2	19.5	74	869	232.6	23.1	21	135	9.0	3.6
Nobles	6.0	280	35	D	D	D	111	1 471	328.0	30.1	13	46	3.2	0.5
Norman	0.8	115	16	148	171.2	5.6	28	214	47.0	4.3	4	6	0.7	0.1
Olmsted	27.0	187	102	1 210	715.3	58.1	598	10 457	2 447.2	232.4	173	749	143.4	23.0
Otter Tail	104.3	1 820	56	385	738.6	16.8	253	2 903	776.5	64.3	57	95	24.1	2.7
Pennington	2.5	179	20	D	D	D	76	1 028	233.5	20.3	12	D	D	D
Pine	3.1	105	15	60	12.9	1.3	96	1 030	262.9	20.7	15	50	6.0	0.9
Pipestone	3.5	361	20	237	573.1	8.5	52	478	135.5	9.7	3	D	D	D
Polk	13.1	416	44	469	960.5	20.0	109	1 377	331.6	28.5	9	50	3.1	1.2
Pope	16.0	1 458	56	D	D	D	41	311	138.5	7.7	6	7	1.6	0.2
Ramsey	194.9	383	617	10 538	8 499.7	647.1	1 639	26 639	6 557.0	643.7	684	3 885	1 421.2	176.0
Red Lake	2.3	562	5	D	D	D	19	151	61.8	3.5	1	D	D	D
Redwood	3.1	192	30	430	287.2	22.3	72	735	169.6	15.9	15	26	3.1	0.3
Renville	3.5	219	27	261	559.4	13.4	67	514	120.6	9.0	4	8	1.7	0.4
Rice	8.5	133	62	1 013	2 093.8	55.6	202	2 664	683.4	59.6	50	185	48.5	4.0
Rock	3.7	385	17	220	726.3	8.8	40	391	104.0	8.1	10	23	3.0	0.5
Roseau	1.8	115	7	D	D	D	88	876	271.2	16.7	11	32	2.3	0.5
St. Louis	358.3	1 789	206	2 363	1 301.6	114.0	911	11 842	3 008.1	263.3	207	937	154.8	26.9
Scott	18.4	142	152	2 134	2 117.5	132.7	318	4 704	1 337.1	104.4	143	332	72.6	10.9
Sherburne	71.4	807	65	497	353.4	23.2	186	2 778	795.5	65.2	74	162	27.9	4.5
Sibley	3.7	243	17	D	D	D	54	363	75.9	5.7	11	D	D	D
Stearns	36.2	240	183	3 672	2 063.4	161.2	671	10 874	2 917.9	244.9	161	820	132.8	22.7
Steele	6.2	169	44	598	531.4	31.4	178	2 699	568.1	55.5	27	292	18.3	5.4
Stevens	6.2	632	19	99	522.7	4.8	50	545	210.1	12.8	7	18	1.2	0.3
Swift	9.2	936	13	D	D	D	45	373	93.7	7.4	5	73	2.8	1.4
Todd	8.6	346	14	132	178.2	5.1	94	722	156.8	13.0	22	D	D	D
Traverse	0.4	118	11	103	130.5	5.2	23	182	46.7	3.1	2	D	D	D
Wabasha	4.8	221	24	250	191.1	9.7	87	867	223.9	17.7	8	24	2.3	0.3
Wadena	7.0	507	17	391	246.9	17.1	74	750	164.3	17.9	6	D	D	D
Waseca	4.4	231	24	185	180.0	10.0	61	682	180.6	19.1	12	23	2.5	0.4
Washington	391.7	1 645	176	1 817	4 760.1	103.6	699	12 623	2 976.4	267.4	284	1 069	184.9	38.9
Watonwan	3.3	293	14	104	190.1	3.9	40	392	64.3	6.5	5	23	1.1	0.5
Wilkin	0.7	103	13	188	315.2	10.6	26	188	68.4	4.8	6	5	2.7	0.5
Winona	11.7	228	56	D	D	D	164	2 742	681.9	58.1	41	129	21.2	3.0
Wright	365.4	2 930	100	1 135	636.9	61.6	428	6 934	1 713.5	142.5	93	179	48.6	5.5
Yellow Medicine	2.8	265	15	200	647.8	8.3	48	377	100.0	7.0	4	D	D	D

1. Merchant wholesalers, except manufacturers' sales branches and offices.   2. Employer establishments.

Professional Services, Manufacturing, and Accommodation and Food Services

STATE County	Professional, scientific, and technical services, 2012				Manufacturing, 2012				Accommodation and food services, 2012			
	Number of establish-ments	Number of employees	Receipts (mil dol)	Annual payroll (mil dol)	Number of establish-ments	Number of employees	Receipts (mil dol)	Annual payroll (mil dol)	Number of establish-ments	Number of employees	Sales (mil dol)	Annual payroll (mil dol)
	147	148	149	150	151	152	153	154	155	156	157	158
MINNESOTA—Cont'd												
Fillmore	36	D	D	D	47	800	332.9	31.9	72	437	16.5	4.4
Freeborn	37	235	24.3	9.5	54	2 572	806.5	106.0	73	1 000	36.7	10.4
Goodhue	74	401	53.9	21.9	87	4 839	1 869.4	223.3	111	3 145	246.2	62.6
Grant	12	D	D	D	14	98	16.7	3.0	14	D	D	D
Hennepin	6 831	74 416	14 339.4	5 730.4	1 675	72 307	22 020.7	4 518.2	2 735	66 296	3 791.2	1 108.5
Houston	24	94	7.7	2.5	22	287	54.9	11.3	35	192	8.3	2.2
Hubbard	32	77	6.2	2.1	35	933	325.8	37.7	83	646	30.3	7.3
Isanti	60	D	D	D	70	1 518	394.8	80.0	53	D	D	D
Itasca	78	D	D	D	44	1 231	471.9	63.9	108	1 294	58.9	16.4
Jackson	16	67	7.5	2.0	14	1 359	D	75.3	21	258	8.7	2.2
Kanabec	18	90	6.6	2.1	17	622	116.0	22.5	27	269	11.1	2.6
Kandiyohi	95	538	60.4	21.5	73	2 916	1 140.0	115.0	91	1 427	55.4	15.4
Kittson	7	D	D	D	6	129	D	5.2	8	D	D	D
Koochiching	17	67	4.5	1.7	18	1 021	D	59.8	47	479	24.2	5.8
Lac qui Parle	9	D	D	D	12	283	D	12.1	13	D	D	D
Lake	13	34	3.9	1.5	18	553	167.8	27.4	66	681	36.6	11.0
Lake of the Woods	6	9	0.5	0.2	5	120	D	7.1	38	487	27.7	6.7
Le Sueur	36	D	D	D	52	2 130	883.4	101.4	48	466	18.2	4.9
Lincoln	7	D	D	D	5	15	D	0.5	12	D	D	D
Lyon	49	360	29.8	20.1	36	1 882	1 131.2	76.3	66	1 194	40.1	11.9
McLeod	64	392	32.3	15.5	80	5 465	1 882.5	277.2	64	1 043	39.6	11.2
Mahnomen	3	D	D	D	NA	NA	NA	NA	13	D	D	D
Marshall	11	30	6.9	1.5	17	251	59.7	11.0	23	D	D	D
Martin	39	193	21.3	7.9	39	1 313	1 576.5	59.8	38	749	26.9	7.3
Meeker	33	115	10.8	3.8	55	1 753	828.4	75.9	38	450	14.6	3.9
Mille Lacs	29	D	D	D	40	852	400.9	37.2	67	D	D	D
Morrison	35	195	18.2	8.2	51	1 319	397.7	50.4	89	911	35.5	9.5
Mower	44	D	D	D	36	3 752	D	151.6	71	1 052	44.0	11.3
Murray	15	D	D	D	8	387	D	9.5	24	D	D	D
Nicollet	42	450	46.7	25.0	50	3 678	965.1	131.9	52	759	26.5	7.6
Nobles	34	D	D	D	25	2 856	1 585.0	123.2	42	616	27.9	6.9
Norman	12	D	D	D	NA	NA	NA	NA	14	50	2.1	0.5
Olmsted	278	10 867	1 070.1	668.3	90	9 046	3 209.0	591.8	331	7 596	391.7	111.1
Otter Tail	95	482	48.6	19.3	83	3 875	1 464.5	156.1	149	1 471	69.7	19.7
Pennington	16	D	D	D	17	884	D	38.2	37	1 023	53.8	16.3
Pine	28	D	D	D	26	276	44.3	9.2	65	2 524	232.7	48.8
Pipestone	14	58	13.0	1.5	13	385	92.1	11.3	24	394	10.8	3.1
Polk	48	D	D	D	34	1 526	1 187.8	63.8	61	1 171	48.7	14.9
Pope	23	D	D	D	23	616	113.4	25.8	28	283	11.7	2.7
Ramsey	1 724	13 007	2 300.4	893.6	591	22 817	6 172.0	1 343.7	1 102	21 792	1 080.4	320.4
Red Lake	4	D	D	D	3	D	D	D	14	D	D	D
Redwood	19	58	8.3	2.7	31	1 021	371.8	34.9	39	1 122	98.0	20.8
Renville	24	123	17.8	6.4	23	1 028	559.3	49.6	31	265	8.5	1.9
Rice	137	642	54.3	22.5	77	3 907	1 741.9	189.7	124	2 082	82.6	24.4
Rock	16	85	10.5	4.3	13	267	86.4	9.8	16	205	7.5	1.8
Roseau	24	85	7.8	2.4	24	3 941	2 082.2	147.1	36	533	28.2	7.5
St. Louis	393	D	D	D	213	4 380	D	210.9	530	9 670	525.9	125.7
Scott	426	2 207	229.3	381.8	182	5 671	2 301.5	330.9	193	6 476	581.2	139.3
Sherburne	157	582	60.7	22.1	149	3 078	857.7	157.6	116	2 114	86.3	23.5
Sibley	26	D	D	D	23	1 028	1 018.4	44.3	21	D	D	D
Stearns	311	D	D	D	248	11 231	3 539.4	480.1	360	6 378	266.7	72.2
Steele	59	D	D	D	63	4 535	1 539.8	209.2	84	1 614	61.5	17.4
Stevens	16	99	11.4	4.5	16	776	D	36.1	25	413	16.5	3.9
Swift	16	69	7.7	2.4	16	814	D	46.5	28	252	8.8	2.2
Todd	27	96	6.3	2.6	43	1 509	885.9	63.1	45	384	18.3	4.8
Traverse	3	D	D	D	7	22	5.4	0.9	8	D	D	D
Wabasha	32	D	D	D	34	1 506	523.1	60.1	63	594	20.6	5.6
Wadena	19	54	7.8	2.8	18	342	43.1	10.6	30	322	11.2	2.9
Waseca	31	149	10.1	3.8	28	2 263	1 061.5	99.8	34	351	12.5	3.0
Washington	783	3 673	535.3	207.7	188	6 928	5 767.1	427.3	399	8 618	399.0	115.3
Watonwan	9	36	4.3	1.1	19	1 231	343.2	39.5	23	D	D	D
Wilkin	7	D	D	D	5	11	D	D	13	152	4.3	1.3
Winona	79	360	32.1	11.5	102	4 996	1 567.9	232.0	125	2 124	76.4	20.2
Wright	305	881	98.2	31.7	196	4 776	1 184.9	234.7	190	3 095	123.8	34.0
Yellow Medicine	16	D	D	D	21	261	177.9	11.5	25	605	41.5	10.3

1. Establishment subject to federal tax.

STATE County	Health care and social assistance, 2012				Other services, 2012				Nonemployer businesses, 2015		Value of residential construction authorized by building permits, 2016	
	Number of establish-ments	Number of employees	Receipts (mil dol)	Annual payroll (mil dol)	Number of establish-ments	Number of employees	Receipts (mil dol)	Annual payroll (mil dol)	Number	Receipts (mil dol)	New Construction ($1,000)	Number of housing units
	159	160	161	162	163	164	165	166	167	168	169	170
MINNESOTA—Cont'd												
Fillmore	49	D	D	D	44	147	12.5	2.5	1 757	73.9	5 207	43
Freeborn	71	2 569	208.3	94.6	66	369	20.1	5.2	1 817	81.2	5 095	27
Goodhue	141	3 780	254.3	123.6	103	483	41.6	10.5	3 016	136.8	25 484	150
Grant	20	511	32.7	16.4	15	39	3.8	0.5	524	22.6	0	0
Hennepin	3 899	128 451	14 036.0	6 012.9	2 651	22 081	2 761.6	721.7	103 278	5 344.4	1 294 844	5 364
Houston	45	1 047	35.7	18.7	41	106	9.8	2.0	1 452	69.0	5 201	25
Hubbard	52	917	85.4	37.0	38	187	14.0	3.0	1 708	66.5	6 189	55
Isanti	78	2 198	217.6	91.0	61	D	D	D	2 653	113.5	34 672	204
Itasca	151	3 495	248.9	112.8	85	387	56.8	9.9	2 969	112.9	31 389	177
Jackson	31	1 421	49.5	23.6	24	95	8.9	1.4	802	35.6	2 298	11
Kanabec	32	938	79.3	32.3	26	85	6.8	1.7	975	45.8	3 549	24
Kandiyohi	179	5 189	303.2	164.6	98	599	52.4	10.8	3 085	139.9	23 028	102
Kittson	11	359	19.0	8.7	10	50	4.0	0.7	337	13.2	385	3
Koochiching	41	668	49.7	19.1	27	109	9.4	1.7	830	25.4	2 453	13
Lac qui Parle	15	585	31.6	15.4	15	60	9.0	1.1	620	24.5	1 552	4
Lake	29	473	28.5	11.9	20	177	13.6	4.1	827	32.2	10 672	52
Lake of the Woods	8	D	D	D	10	54	5.3	0.9	371	13.2	5 049	21
Le Sueur	57	844	46.3	19.8	63	D	D	D	1 989	94.0	10 310	59
Lincoln	16	535	32.7	14.1	14	87	10.5	2.0	478	17.0	1 925	9
Lyon	82	2 006	164.5	63.0	51	D	D	D	1 726	77.0	7 787	38
McLeod	113	2 714	223.3	93.4	79	500	38.0	9.3	2 303	108.9	10 794	52
Mahnomen	8	176	12.8	5.0	7	48	4.9	0.9	306	13.1	0	0
Marshall	17	283	13.1	7.1	23	D	D	D	642	25.0	579	2
Martin	64	2 030	139.3	57.1	52	156	14.5	3.0	1 558	66.6	3 135	12
Meeker	57	1 240	81.2	32.4	42	181	14.7	2.6	1 652	68.9	11 966	50
Mille Lacs	71	1 845	104.2	45.5	54	D	D	D	1 798	69.0	10 595	50
Morrison	83	1 749	134.0	54.5	86	341	40.4	7.1	2 400	114.1	11 167	94
Mower	86	2 920	201.5	93.2	91	537	46.7	10.0	1 846	82.2	7 673	39
Murray	17	455	32.6	13.7	22	67	11.2	1.6	731	36.4	3 689	15
Nicollet	78	2 303	152.6	93.6	56	D	D	D	2 137	90.1	22 126	119
Nobles	63	1 298	66.4	31.0	51	294	24.5	5.7	1 251	59.2	8 999	61
Norman	15	401	22.6	11.1	12	38	3.0	0.5	476	23.0	1 910	8
Olmsted	412	20 014	2 408.0	854.4	240	1 846	155.2	46.2	9 714	437.4	284 016	1 563
Otter Tail	172	4 540	285.9	126.7	130	517	46.0	10.3	4 752	209.7	25 794	197
Pennington	40	1 255	108.3	42.5	45	260	15.4	3.9	871	32.4	5 657	66
Pine	76	1 035	73.6	26.3	42	186	22.5	3.8	1 682	71.2	9 162	63
Pipestone	28	738	49.6	19.0	22	71	6.8	1.5	757	39.2	3 305	13
Polk	90	2 512	154.4	71.4	56	301	23.2	5.4	2 206	91.3	17 997	104
Pope	25	666	43.0	20.7	25	75	7.1	1.5	980	41.8	7 164	28
Ramsey	1 850	57 676	5 557.3	2 429.7	1 090	9 996	1 273.8	320.8	37 078	1 574.1	218 702	1 498
Red Lake	6	D	D	D	5	D	D	D	240	11.2	200	1
Redwood	38	865	62.8	23.7	53	237	18.9	4.7	1 038	43.0	5 620	22
Renville	33	1 020	48.1	21.9	33	D	D	D	1 046	50.7	3 193	11
Rice	159	3 193	215.8	101.4	129	606	48.6	12.3	4 240	173.8	33 352	157
Rock	15	634	29.9	11.9	20	75	4.8	1.2	743	35.6	3 099	18
Roseau	30	841	60.8	21.9	36	129	13.1	1.8	1 084	42.9	3 942	18
St. Louis	729	24 700	2 210.0	1 048.0	386	2 505	239.0	58.7	11 479	449.5	82 425	426
Scott	238	4 719	395.9	170.5	221	1 260	108.5	31.7	10 572	526.6	179 046	588
Sherburne	146	4 147	216.9	112.8	147	727	71.0	21.0	6 526	279.7	83 060	401
Sibley	23	568	28.5	13.4	25	D	D	D	1 055	44.7	3 918	17
Stearns	413	14 979	1 619.6	743.1	359	2 344	237.3	58.0	10 356	513.1	148 286	890
Steele	125	2 486	218.1	92.0	89	525	55.0	12.6	2 364	98.9	16 000	65
Stevens	37	1 392	77.0	37.9	22	106	9.8	2.1	653	31.4	5 946	71
Swift	24	674	40.8	16.0	28	114	13.7	2.7	659	25.6	847	4
Todd	58	1 546	121.8	63.8	44	129	13.8	2.2	1 601	76.0	13 941	105
Traverse	11	294	14.5	5.8	8	D	D	D	264	10.7	1 356	9
Wabasha	57	D	D	D	43	149	11.3	2.8	1 568	69.1	9 868	44
Wadena	46	1 073	92.7	34.5	27	117	9.9	1.8	995	43.8	3 638	31
Waseca	50	975	56.4	22.0	33	114	10.1	2.2	1 148	56.0	1 981	9
Washington	580	10 469	1 052.7	428.2	397	2 671	194.9	63.4	17 999	850.0	320 449	1 181
Watonwan	20	484	41.4	15.7	27	115	13.5	2.0	656	25.0	965	6
Wilkin	20	743	61.1	23.4	12	D	D	D	461	43.0	2 045	12
Winona	122	3 195	220.1	90.3	84	429	44.4	10.5	2 892	117.0	13 586	68
Wright	266	6 437	397.7	187.1	225	1 238	90.3	24.3	9 743	409.2	179 599	708
Yellow Medicine	28	1 122	67.3	31.0	22	52	5.8	1.3	778	31.1	2 431	9

Table B. States and Counties — Government Employment and Payroll, and Local Government Finances

	Government employment and payroll, 2012									Local government finances, 2012				
			March payroll (percent of total)							General revenue				
												Taxes		
													Per capita[1] (dollars)	
STATE County	Full-time equivalent employees	March payroll (dollars)	Adminis-tration, judicial, and legal	Police and Corrections	Fire Protection	Highways and transpor-tation	Health and Welfare	Natural resources and utilities	Education and libraries	Total (mil dol)	Inter-govern-mental (mil dol)	Total (mil dol)	Total	Property
	171	172	173	174	175	176	177	178	179	180	181	182	183	184
MINNESOTA—Cont'd														
Fillmore	743	2 541 608	12.4	9.9	0.0	8.7	11.1	6.0	50.3	79.4	42.2	20.8	999	988
Freeborn	1 073	4 355 329	8.3	11.4	1.9	7.2	10.0	5.7	54.1	127.7	69.2	36.7	1 183	1 110
Goodhue	1 720	6 840 668	9.9	13.6	2.1	4.3	9.2	6.0	53.4	204.8	92.0	69.5	1 500	1 468
Grant	273	953 527	13.2	7.0	0.0	7.4	8.2	5.8	57.5	34.1	18.5	9.7	1 624	1 620
Hennepin	35 312	195 123 070	8.9	12.4	2.0	3.7	9.4	8.3	54.2	6 392.6	2 496.9	2 262.3	1 910	1 724
Houston	731	2 758 225	7.6	7.3	0.3	4.4	7.9	2.9	66.7	81.1	51.4	19.2	1 022	1 012
Hubbard	660	2 206 385	9.8	10.0	0.0	6.0	8.6	2.6	59.7	84.9	48.1	26.6	1 305	1 278
Isanti	1 257	4 796 343	6.7	9.3	0.1	4.0	7.5	2.3	68.0	131.8	76.3	35.3	924	904
Itasca	1 538	7 554 704	6.6	8.1	0.4	8.7	15.2	3.8	55.3	301.4	126.6	54.1	1 196	1 185
Jackson	515	1 776 829	11.8	7.0	0.2	8.4	20.7	6.0	44.4	50.6	24.7	15.9	1 544	1 531
Kanabec	867	2 925 087	5.0	6.1	0.0	4.3	35.1	1.6	43.5	90.0	33.3	14.7	920	889
Kandiyohi	2 286	9 769 471	6.3	8.2	0.4	2.9	40.7	4.1	36.3	282.7	84.2	49.6	1 170	1 089
Kittson	282	1 417 262	8.1	3.9	0.0	6.1	5.8	4.7	69.0	29.6	16.1	6.4	1 432	1 411
Koochiching	528	2 114 323	5.7	6.7	1.6	5.8	7.4	7.8	61.4	61.1	35.8	8.3	632	626
Lac qui Parle	625	1 888 050	6.9	3.8	0.0	5.1	33.9	3.0	45.7	46.7	21.4	8.4	1 176	1 141
Lake	361	1 980 601	12.9	10.1	0.3	9.4	6.4	8.7	48.8	64.0	33.4	15.7	1 454	1 414
Lake of the Woods	143	726 420	14.0	7.3	0.0	9.2	10.2	5.3	51.7	20.3	13.0	5.1	1 272	1 255
Le Sueur	871	2 940 497	8.0	8.1	0.0	4.7	11.3	5.1	60.6	96.7	50.3	31.2	1 128	1 088
Lincoln	199	603 609	18.2	11.9	0.1	15.9	1.7	6.8	38.3	21.7	9.6	8.1	1 392	1 384
Lyon	1 012	3 496 744	7.5	9.5	0.1	6.3	1.3	11.7	60.6	145.6	71.4	30.6	1 199	1 151
McLeod	1 516	6 615 440	5.8	6.3	0.2	3.2	37.7	10.6	34.8	212.6	66.7	39.1	1 084	1 063
Mahnomen	413	1 411 273	11.1	5.4	0.0	2.8	22.1	3.6	50.5	40.8	24.5	6.0	1 085	1 083
Marshall	459	1 668 424	9.8	5.5	0.5	7.6	16.1	9.7	49.9	55.9	36.6	9.4	991	982
Martin	655	3 114 449	10.3	9.8	0.1	7.4	3.2	9.6	56.8	92.7	49.5	24.0	1 170	1 158
Meeker	1 226	4 903 007	5.1	5.4	0.1	2.7	21.6	3.2	60.7	139.5	63.7	28.6	1 239	1 222
Mille Lacs	1 239	4 213 762	8.0	10.1	0.2	3.3	6.5	3.4	67.4	113.5	71.6	30.4	1 182	1 162
Morrison	1 124	4 203 099	7.6	8.2	0.9	5.8	10.1	2.5	63.7	118.8	71.3	29.8	903	875
Mower	1 542	6 255 175	7.7	8.0	0.8	4.4	8.9	12.3	56.6	166.8	93.6	36.0	915	853
Murray	420	2 070 204	5.7	4.9	0.0	4.6	33.5	2.7	42.5	54.5	22.6	10.9	1 273	1 259
Nicollet	835	3 375 650	8.8	10.9	0.1	6.1	20.8	7.8	43.0	108.0	39.0	29.6	899	839
Nobles	747	5 019 216	4.9	6.5	0.1	3.1	5.4	4.5	73.5	104.9	59.6	21.9	1 019	964
Norman	410	1 309 952	11.1	4.4	0.2	8.7	6.0	6.0	61.5	40.3	26.4	8.4	1 266	1 263
Olmsted	4 101	28 521 111	5.6	8.4	2.3	3.1	9.3	7.4	60.7	672.3	289.4	201.9	1 373	1 242
Otter Tail	2 164	8 240 552	8.0	7.4	0.2	4.7	21.9	3.4	52.3	298.8	109.1	62.1	1 083	1 068
Pennington	640	2 304 729	5.4	8.5	1.6	4.2	7.5	11.0	56.5	114.3	37.7	13.8	984	963
Pine	879	3 660 809	9.4	7.3	0.3	7.0	4.0	1.4	67.8	103.3	61.8	27.4	938	920
Pipestone	661	2 186 364	6.7	4.4	0.1	5.7	33.1	2.8	46.0	72.9	31.8	11.0	1 175	1 146
Polk	1 733	5 824 889	5.7	5.8	1.5	3.5	29.5	8.1	43.7	191.1	112.8	36.5	1 161	1 082
Pope	553	2 333 307	3.9	5.8	0.0	8.4	42.6	1.9	32.2	48.8	23.1	14.2	1 302	1 287
Ramsey	16 492	141 646 187	5.1	8.3	2.7	4.8	6.3	4.1	67.7	2 881.4	1 248.1	805.8	1 549	1 417
Red Lake	258	709 610	7.9	6.0	0.0	6.6	6.3	5.2	67.6	24.0	15.3	4.3	1 044	1 038
Redwood	739	3 232 367	9.3	5.7	0.2	4.8	7.0	5.7	65.2	101.1	39.6	20.4	1 287	1 261
Renville	704	2 316 532	18.7	8.2	0.0	9.5	12.1	4.4	43.1	88.9	34.9	21.9	1 424	1 401
Rice	2 519	10 254 560	4.8	6.6	0.7	2.9	41.2	2.9	39.9	352.9	102.9	62.2	959	916
Rock	396	1 387 361	10.8	6.2	0.1	8.3	1.0	11.6	59.9	45.4	21.6	11.5	1 203	1 152
Roseau	687	2 591 371	8.0	6.4	0.0	5.4	6.6	3.1	69.0	74.6	50.8	14.1	909	899
St. Louis	7 560	37 760 893	7.0	10.6	2.8	7.2	13.4	8.3	44.2	1 073.0	545.0	233.2	1 164	1 026
Scott	3 486	17 619 282	8.6	9.3	0.5	3.5	6.2	5.2	64.4	500.4	232.5	180.8	1 338	1 287
Sherburne	3 233	14 013 536	5.6	10.8	0.4	2.4	4.7	3.2	71.3	366.7	185.3	126.0	1 408	1 391
Sibley	636	2 194 050	9.3	7.3	0.3	6.5	27.2	1.9	46.6	76.3	33.5	18.9	1 250	1 235
Stearns	4 907	24 879 439	7.5	10.1	1.5	2.8	14.9	4.1	56.2	676.6	322.4	196.7	1 297	1 129
Steele	1 297	5 726 547	5.5	10.8	0.9	4.1	6.2	10.3	60.3	147.4	81.6	42.4	1 167	1 112
Stevens	479	1 791 149	11.2	17.4	0.6	6.2	9.0	11.6	40.3	43.2	23.3	12.2	1 258	1 229
Swift	748	2 235 013	8.5	5.5	0.0	5.7	37.9	3.6	34.8	82.8	25.2	13.2	1 379	1 363
Todd	994	3 435 036	8.2	8.5	0.0	4.5	12.5	2.3	58.8	94.8	59.3	21.3	869	840
Traverse	251	735 078	9.6	10.4	0.1	13.3	21.2	2.5	41.3	26.6	9.8	7.7	2 242	2 236
Wabasha	717	2 663 637	12.2	9.5	0.1	4.8	7.6	8.0	55.6	95.1	50.4	27.4	1 278	1 244
Wadena	723	2 230 614	6.7	2.7	0.1	5.3	11.7	4.2	66.3	67.0	41.7	12.2	887	870
Waseca	839	2 685 918	9.1	9.2	1.4	6.3	7.1	5.6	60.1	83.8	42.3	21.8	1 133	1 094
Washington	6 573	28 742 198	7.5	9.9	1.5	2.6	4.9	4.1	68.0	850.9	369.3	318.3	1 304	1 251
Watonwan	544	1 961 440	9.4	7.3	0.3	6.3	9.4	7.3	57.7	52.1	29.2	12.3	1 097	1 083
Wilkin	308	1 120 394	10.9	8.0	0.0	10.2	10.2	7.3	51.6	36.4	21.4	9.3	1 417	1 407
Winona	1 299	5 244 944	8.6	10.3	2.2	4.6	9.2	8.7	54.4	161.3	88.3	44.7	866	816
Wright	4 086	18 042 110	5.5	7.7	0.2	3.1	16.3	2.4	60.5	548.1	243.1	150.9	1 185	1 154
Yellow Medicine	412	1 492 491	12.8	9.7	0.0	10.5	8.7	6.7	48.7	72.8	27.5	13.9	1 364	1 345

1. Based on the resident population estimated as of July 1 of the year shown.

Table B. States and Counties — Local Government Finances, Government Employment, and Income Taxes

STATE County	Local government finances, 2012 (cont.) Direct general expenditure — Total (mil dol)	Per capita¹ (dollars)	Percent of total for: Education	Health and hospitals	Police protection	Public welfare	Highways	Debt outstanding Total (mil dol)	Per capita¹ (dollars)	Government employment, 2015 Federal civilian	Federal military	State and local	Individual income tax returns, 2014 Number of returns	Mean adjusted gross income	Mean income tax
	185	186	187	188	189	190	191	192	193	194	195	196	197	198	199
MINNESOTA—Cont'd															
Fillmore	76.1	3 651	36.6	4.1	4.6	4.1	17.1	66.9	3 213	75	74	1 204	9 770	51 700	5 257
Freeborn	125.1	4 028	42.5	2.8	6.6	6.1	15.4	132.0	4 249	85	108	1 422	15 200	51 051	5 591
Goodhue	204.0	4 403	43.7	3.7	6.0	4.9	10.8	184.3	3 977	123	164	3 909	23 360	60 457	6 829
Grant	31.2	5 248	38.6	0.9	4.1	11.4	16.0	31.1	5 236	26	21	341	2 930	55 648	6 337
Hennepin	7 135.3	6 024	29.8	13.2	5.5	5.6	5.3	9 944.8	8 395	12 991	4 711	83 955	624 350	86 819	13 915
Houston	81.7	4 339	53.8	2.6	5.0	5.5	10.5	57.5	3 052	71	67	1 110	9 470	53 931	5 769
Hubbard	78.2	3 842	35.6	0.3	3.6	14.6	18.2	83.3	4 093	38	74	1 184	9 330	49 232	4 726
Isanti	136.1	3 558	50.4	3.4	6.9	7.7	11.0	169.3	4 426	75	137	1 976	18 260	53 020	5 243
Itasca	350.2	7 744	24.1	20.6	2.5	8.1	14.2	319.0	7 054	163	160	3 298	20 700	52 346	5 333
Jackson	50.2	4 887	33.0	4.1	3.8	7.8	19.0	50.8	4 943	30	36	762	5 240	56 531	6 401
Kanabec	84.8	5 300	27.0	37.5	2.3	6.2	8.2	63.2	3 950	37	56	1 208	7 210	48 889	4 954
Kandiyohi	300.9	7 100	20.9	38.3	5.5	4.8	6.1	333.7	7 875	148	149	3 883	21 270	55 363	6 336
Kittson	33.3	7 415	39.2	0.7	3.3	4.6	22.4	21.5	4 785	52	16	294	2 180	52 897	5 423
Koochiching	70.6	5 344	34.8	3.6	4.7	13.7	11.0	39.7	3 002	182	45	863	6 180	47 342	4 736
Lac qui Parle	48.9	6 880	33.1	26.2	3.0	4.0	16.2	28.8	4 046	39	24	708	3 490	55 536	6 284
Lake	63.2	5 838	24.4	5.5	5.8	10.5	17.5	119.8	11 076	22	38	860	5 260	53 096	5 548
Lake of the Woods	20.1	5 071	32.1	0.5	4.1	7.7	23.1	304.4	76 625	30	14	293	2 030	44 323	3 695
Le Sueur	119.9	4 333	53.4	2.4	3.8	5.4	10.2	161.8	5 845	75	99	1 314	13 860	57 578	6 193
Lincoln	25.1	4 309	25.1	0.5	6.1	11.4	20.4	39.0	6 710	30	20	258	2 690	49 816	4 827
Lyon	146.3	5 727	52.4	0.4	7.1	3.1	11.6	165.7	6 486	116	89	2 815	12 190	56 889	6 423
McLeod	206.8	5 737	26.6	34.0	4.4	4.9	10.2	191.4	5 309	82	128	1 813	18 390	54 340	5 762
Mahnomen	39.5	7 142	44.6	20.1	5.7	5.9	9.3	26.1	4 718	27	19	1 315	2 270	41 133	3 446
Marshall	64.2	6 790	36.8	0.4	2.9	5.0	21.2	37.9	4 006	50	34	558	4 610	55 409	5 971
Martin	94.4	4 613	46.0	0.5	6.6	4.8	14.2	96.9	4 732	61	71	1 262	10 440	52 224	5 900
Meeker	131.9	5 719	44.6	17.9	4.5	5.3	7.4	173.9	7 539	71	82	1 190	11 020	54 378	5 661
Mille Lacs	118.0	4 583	57.3	0.6	3.7	6.4	6.8	133.7	5 195	62	91	3 457	12 050	46 584	4 372
Morrison	121.6	3 680	48.7	1.8	3.7	7.1	14.7	122.4	3 704	435	116	1 930	15 590	45 613	4 023
Mower	168.0	4 268	46.1	1.1	4.6	8.4	11.8	1 198.8	30 447	135	139	2 491	18 650	54 355	6 321
Murray	54.4	6 337	23.7	28.8	4.7	2.0	15.6	37.9	4 418	42	30	587	4 230	55 323	5 849
Nicollet	111.3	3 380	30.7	17.7	4.8	6.8	10.6	144.3	4 383	28	110	2 864	15 630	67 139	10 198
Nobles	104.2	4 852	42.9	3.4	7.6	7.3	10.8	69.0	3 210	89	77	1 411	10 440	47 837	4 501
Norman	40.7	6 134	33.4	1.1	3.5	8.1	19.4	17.3	2 601	35	24	424	3 180	49 830	4 823
Olmsted	687.5	4 675	34.2	1.9	4.8	7.4	9.9	2 857.8	19 432	826	540	7 705	75 470	70 678	9 205
Otter Tail	312.8	5 461	45.3	8.8	3.2	5.1	10.5	310.4	5 419	209	204	3 501	28 190	52 408	5 522
Pennington	122.4	8 695	70.1	0.0	2.8	3.6	4.7	105.6	7 504	64	50	1 591	7 130	53 871	5 873
Pine	95.3	3 262	45.6	1.9	5.8	7.4	12.1	136.2	4 662	310	98	3 139	12 660	44 341	3 780
Pipestone	70.7	7 570	36.9	25.0	2.8	5.3	9.6	31.4	3 359	49	33	936	4 550	49 422	4 976
Polk	182.0	5 792	29.6	1.4	3.7	10.5	14.8	169.8	5 406	97	109	2 620	14 870	52 983	5 419
Pope	48.7	4 470	30.5	12.3	9.7	6.5	14.2	36.7	3 368	38	39	773	5 530	56 382	6 697
Ramsey	2 823.6	5 428	39.6	2.3	6.4	6.6	5.2	4 373.6	8 408	3 302	1 949	55 950	262 240	62 382	8 066
Red Lake	25.7	6 285	56.4	0.3	4.3	4.4	15.8	18.7	4 565	22	14	280	1 920	50 245	4 449
Redwood	94.9	5 987	30.0	25.7	4.1	7.3	11.4	93.1	5 876	60	54	1 954	7 780	54 138	5 940
Renville	96.1	6 251	25.3	21.0	3.3	5.9	14.5	80.0	5 207	62	52	1 101	7 670	56 389	6 553
Rice	342.7	5 285	25.9	37.7	3.6	2.9	5.8	303.1	4 673	133	210	3 349	28 960	58 268	6 451
Rock	42.6	4 461	42.5	0.6	4.4	8.4	12.8	74.6	7 811	30	34	673	4 430	55 364	5 618
Roseau	80.9	5 225	41.7	0.5	3.6	5.4	18.9	44.4	2 870	101	56	985	7 910	58 748	7 488
St. Louis	1 223.1	6 106	33.5	5.6	5.4	6.8	9.4	959.9	4 792	1 427	817	15 045	93 770	56 224	6 435
Scott	487.6	3 608	45.0	0.4	4.6	4.1	15.6	1 025.8	7 590	121	506	9 501	66 930	85 241	12 193
Sherburne	342.7	3 831	57.6	0.7	4.6	4.0	8.4	655.5	7 328	122	323	4 180	42 270	63 223	6 895
Sibley	82.9	5 484	34.0	16.4	4.2	4.8	14.5	70.1	4 636	40	53	736	7 440	51 574	4 947
Stearns	692.0	4 565	39.7	8.6	5.0	4.9	11.1	994.2	6 558	2 220	534	9 617	71 720	57 930	6 944
Steele	144.4	3 975	47.3	1.6	5.1	5.6	14.0	145.9	4 016	73	130	2 116	18 420	54 989	5 723
Stevens	43.9	4 548	36.6	0.3	5.8	5.7	19.8	77.2	7 986	79	32	1 304	4 410	70 461	8 778
Swift	86.6	9 024	19.1	41.7	2.8	4.8	8.8	45.2	4 715	49	33	882	4 670	51 447	5 373
Todd	111.4	4 544	53.4	2.6	3.5	6.4	11.8	81.6	3 330	83	86	1 349	10 730	42 218	3 474
Traverse	29.5	8 562	21.2	13.2	3.7	4.8	17.5	15.5	4 502	25	12	308	1 660	55 413	6 885
Wabasha	100.8	4 696	37.3	2.8	5.5	4.0	15.3	103.1	4 800	59	76	1 008	10 960	54 366	5 619
Wadena	92.1	6 693	61.5	1.4	3.3	12.6	6.8	28.2	2 051	48	48	1 341	6 270	42 653	3 758
Waseca	84.8	4 408	42.7	2.1	5.7	11.6	9.7	75.0	3 897	264	64	1 102	8 920	50 459	4 862
Washington	872.4	3 574	51.1	1.8	5.9	3.6	8.8	1 195.5	4 898	408	893	10 728	124 720	86 069	12 505
Watonwan	57.4	5 127	43.4	1.2	4.2	7.5	11.1	64.3	5 747	51	39	737	5 360	47 886	4 456
Wilkin	36.2	5 494	38.6	2.9	5.1	6.0	20.9	19.1	2 900	19	23	395	3 210	58 517	6 671
Winona	157.7	3 054	44.7	2.6	5.6	6.4	13.8	84.9	1 645	137	168	3 589	22 420	54 932	6 267
Wright	554.0	4 351	45.4	11.5	4.5	3.5	7.8	1 170.5	9 192	192	471	5 706	61 340	64 311	7 371
Yellow Medicine	83.2	8 190	26.8	22.5	2.0	9.0	12.3	76.0	7 477	42	35	1 437	4 920	53 028	5 611

1. Based on the resident population estimated as of July 1 of the year shown.

Table B. States and Counties — **Land Area and Population**

STATE/ County code	CBSA code[1]	County type[2]	STATE County	Land area,[3] (sq mi) 2016	Total persons 2016	Rank	Per square mile	White	Black	American Indian, Alaska Native	Asian and Pacific Islander	Percent Hispanic or Latino[4]	Under 5 years	5 to 17 years	18 to 24 years	25 to 34 years	35 to 44 years	45 to 54 years
								Race alone or in combination, not Hispanic or Latino (percent)					Age (percent)					
				1	2	3	4	5	6	7	8	9	10	11	12	13	14	15
28 000	...	0	MISSISSIPPI	46 923.0	2 988 726	X	63.7	57.8	38.0	0.8	1.4	3.1	6.3	17.8	9.9	13.2	12.2	12.7
28 001	35020	5	Adams	462.3	31 248	1 403	67.6	37.7	53.7	0.6	0.8	8.3	5.8	15.3	8.1	13.0	12.3	12.5
28 003	18420	7	Alcorn	400.0	37 304	1 241	93.3	83.7	12.8	0.6	0.6	3.4	5.9	17.6	7.9	12.5	12.6	13.4
28 005	32620	8	Amite	730.1	12 458	2 262	17.1	58.5	40.1	0.5	0.3	1.3	5.6	15.3	7.1	10.4	10.0	12.7
28 007	...	6	Attala	735.0	18 934	1 877	25.8	54.8	42.8	0.5	0.5	2.1	6.4	18.8	7.7	11.0	10.8	12.6
28 009	32820	1	Benton	406.6	8 264	2 570	20.3	61.4	36.1	0.9	0.3	2.4	5.4	16.5	8.1	11.4	11.8	14.5
28 011	17380	7	Bolivar	876.6	32 737	1 365	37.3	33.2	63.9	0.4	1.1	2.1	7.0	17.7	11.1	14.1	11.2	11.6
28 013	...	9	Calhoun	586.6	14 610	2 126	24.9	66.8	28.7	0.6	0.3	5.6	6.1	17.9	7.8	11.2	11.4	13.6
28 015	24900	9	Carroll	628.2	10 255	2 406	16.3	65.1	33.4	0.6	0.4	1.4	4.7	15.1	7.3	11.1	11.4	13.0
28 017	...	7	Chickasaw	501.8	17 246	1 961	34.4	50.9	44.4	0.5	0.6	4.5	7.0	17.8	9.3	12.7	11.4	12.8
28 019	...	9	Choctaw	418.2	8 242	2 574	19.7	68.1	29.9	0.6	0.6	1.8	5.7	17.0	7.4	11.2	11.2	12.8
28 021	46980	8	Claiborne	487.4	9 139	2 497	18.8	12.4	85.6	0.4	0.9	1.5	6.5	15.5	19.6	10.8	10.2	9.8
28 023	32940	9	Clarke	691.6	15 888	2 048	23.0	64.0	34.6	0.6	0.3	1.1	5.5	16.9	7.9	11.8	11.2	12.8
28 025	48500	7	Clay	410.1	19 850	1 837	48.4	39.8	58.7	0.4	0.4	1.4	5.4	17.7	8.8	12.8	11.5	12.3
28 027	17260	7	Coahoma	552.5	23 809	1 647	43.1	21.9	76.3	0.3	0.6	1.5	7.9	19.3	10.7	12.5	11.0	11.6
28 029	27140	2	Copiah	777.2	28 482	1 470	36.6	45.0	51.8	0.5	0.6	3.0	6.1	17.5	10.5	11.9	11.3	12.3
28 031	...	8	Covington	413.8	19 569	1 847	47.3	61.6	36.0	0.5	0.5	2.4	6.8	17.9	8.3	12.9	11.4	12.7
28 033	32820	1	DeSoto	476.3	175 611	370	368.7	66.9	27.3	0.6	1.9	4.7	6.2	20.0	8.7	12.8	14.5	14.1
28 035	25620	3	Forrest	466.0	75 979	726	163.0	58.1	38.1	0.6	1.6	2.9	6.4	16.5	15.0	15.2	11.5	11.2
28 037	...	9	Franklin	563.7	7 782	2 612	13.8	63.9	35.1	0.6	0.4	1.1	5.6	18.6	7.3	10.6	11.0	12.8
28 039	...	6	George	478.7	23 695	1 651	49.5	88.6	8.3	0.8	0.8	2.5	7.4	19.0	8.4	13.0	12.3	13.1
28 041	...	8	Greene	712.8	13 408	2 202	18.8	73.6	25.1	0.7	0.3	1.1	4.8	15.7	9.2	15.8	14.4	14.1
28 043	24980	7	Grenada	422.1	21 275	1 762	50.4	55.5	42.9	0.5	0.6	1.3	6.3	17.3	8.7	11.8	11.8	13.2
28 045	25060	2	Hancock	474.0	46 791	1 036	98.7	86.5	8.8	1.4	1.4	3.8	5.4	16.3	7.4	11.8	11.4	14.1
28 047	25060	2	Harrison	574.0	203 234	323	354.1	66.5	25.8	1.0	3.8	5.4	6.8	17.6	9.8	14.2	12.3	12.7
28 049	27140	2	Hinds	869.8	241 229	278	277.3	25.5	72.5	0.4	1.0	1.6	6.6	18.1	11.3	14.6	11.9	12.0
28 051	...	6	Holmes	756.7	17 999	1 921	23.8	16.2	82.6	0.3	0.4	1.1	6.9	19.6	12.0	12.4	10.4	11.7
28 053	...	6	Humphreys	418.5	8 513	2 549	20.3	22.0	74.8	0.4	0.5	3.1	6.7	20.7	8.5	12.4	10.4	12.0
28 055	...	8	Issaquena	413.0	1 294	3 396	3.1	34.3	63.3	0.5	0.7	1.5	3.2	10.0	12.8	16.5	12.3	14.8
28 057	46180	7	Itawamba	532.8	23 529	1 657	44.2	90.8	7.3	0.5	0.5	1.6	5.7	16.3	10.7	12.0	12.1	13.4
28 059	25060	2	Jackson	722.8	141 241	456	195.4	69.5	22.3	0.9	2.9	6.2	5.8	18.1	8.1	13.4	12.6	13.6
28 061	29860	9	Jasper	676.2	16 578	2 003	24.5	45.7	53.1	0.4	0.3	1.2	6.4	16.7	8.5	11.4	11.0	12.7
28 063	...	8	Jefferson	519.9	7 297	2 645	14.0	13.7	85.3	0.5	0.2	0.8	7.0	15.8	9.4	13.2	12.2	12.3
28 065	...	8	Jefferson Davis	408.4	11 385	2 335	27.9	39.0	59.3	0.5	0.4	1.4	5.3	14.9	8.5	11.3	11.5	13.0
28 067	29860	4	Jones	694.8	67 953	783	97.8	65.4	29.5	0.7	0.7	4.4	6.9	18.6	8.7	12.7	11.7	12.2
28 069	32940	9	Kemper	766.2	9 896	2 440	12.9	34.5	61.1	3.7	0.4	1.1	4.7	15.2	12.3	11.9	11.4	12.4
28 071	37060	4	Lafayette	631.7	53 796	936	85.2	71.4	24.1	0.5	2.6	2.4	5.1	13.0	24.1	14.5	11.2	10.0
28 073	25620	3	Lamar	497.1	60 914	854	122.5	75.3	21.1	0.6	1.8	2.5	6.4	18.8	9.0	15.4	14.0	12.8
28 075	32940	5	Lauderdale	703.7	77 755	713	110.5	53.4	43.7	0.5	1.2	2.2	6.3	17.6	9.3	13.1	11.9	12.6
28 077	...	8	Lawrence	430.7	12 749	2 245	29.6	65.4	32.2	0.5	0.5	2.0	6.3	18.3	8.1	11.7	11.6	13.0
28 079	...	6	Leake	583.0	22 620	1 705	38.8	48.1	42.0	6.0	0.5	4.3	6.6	19.8	8.5	12.8	12.2	12.2
28 081	46180	5	Lee	450.0	85 381	669	189.7	67.1	30.0	0.5	1.2	2.5	6.7	18.8	8.1	13.3	12.9	13.3
28 083	24900	5	Leflore	593.4	29 856	1 435	50.3	23.1	73.8	0.4	0.8	2.5	7.5	19.9	11.7	12.9	11.4	11.1
28 085	15020	6	Lincoln	586.1	34 523	1 312	58.9	67.8	30.9	0.5	0.6	1.1	6.5	17.8	8.2	11.9	12.8	13.0
28 087	18060	5	Lowndes	505.4	59 602	871	117.9	52.8	44.5	0.5	1.3	2.0	6.4	17.2	9.8	14.1	11.6	12.6
28 089	27140	2	Madison	714.3	105 114	566	147.2	56.3	38.6	0.4	2.8	2.8	6.4	18.8	8.8	13.1	13.4	13.6
28 091	...	6	Marion	542.4	25 251	1 599	46.6	66.1	32.3	0.5	0.7	1.4	5.9	17.7	8.0	12.5	12.1	12.7
28 093	32820	1	Marshall	706.2	35 801	1 280	50.7	48.2	48.2	0.5	0.5	3.5	6.0	15.8	9.7	12.1	11.8	13.7
28 095	...	7	Monroe	765.1	35 873	1 277	46.9	67.5	31.2	0.6	0.4	1.2	5.9	17.4	7.9	11.9	11.8	13.2
28 097	...	7	Montgomery	407.0	10 187	2 417	25.0	52.6	45.7	0.6	0.5	1.4	6.1	16.7	7.9	11.1	10.5	13.2
28 099	...	7	Neshoba	570.1	29 403	1 447	51.6	59.8	22.2	16.9	0.9	2.0	7.1	21.4	8.2	12.0	11.9	12.0
28 101	...	7	Newton	577.9	21 558	1 747	37.3	62.3	30.9	5.3	0.7	1.9	6.5	18.7	9.7	11.8	12.1	12.5
28 103	...	7	Noxubee	695.2	11 038	2 352	15.9	26.7	71.6	0.6	0.4	1.4	7.2	18.0	9.8	12.5	11.0	11.7
28 105	44260	5	Oktibbeha	458.2	49 833	987	108.8	57.4	37.7	0.5	3.8	1.8	5.1	12.7	31.2	14.1	8.9	8.3
28 107	...	6	Panola	685.1	34 164	1 321	49.9	48.0	50.5	0.5	0.5	1.6	6.9	18.5	9.0	12.6	11.7	13.1
28 109	38100	6	Pearl River	810.9	55 310	915	68.2	83.3	13.3	1.3	0.9	3.0	5.8	17.1	9.1	11.6	11.4	13.3
28 111	25620	3	Perry	647.2	12 245	2 276	18.9	78.9	19.8	0.9	0.3	1.5	6.0	17.3	8.3	11.2	12.2	12.9
28 113	32620	6	Pike	409.0	39 667	1 186	97.0	44.5	53.5	0.6	0.7	1.5	6.8	19.8	9.1	11.5	11.7	11.9
28 115	46180	7	Pontotoc	497.7	31 550	1 394	63.4	78.1	15.6	0.6	0.6	6.3	7.1	19.6	8.1	13.2	12.3	13.3
28 117	...	7	Prentiss	415.0	25 256	1 598	60.9	83.8	15.1	0.4	0.5	1.3	5.8	16.9	10.2	12.6	11.6	13.2
28 119	...	6	Quitman	405.0	7 349	2 639	18.1	27.6	71.1	0.7	0.5	1.4	6.2	18.1	8.8	11.7	11.3	13.7
28 121	27140	2	Rankin	775.4	150 228	436	193.7	75.5	21.0	0.5	1.6	2.6	6.2	17.7	7.6	14.5	14.2	13.4
28 123	...	6	Scott	609.2	28 207	1 481	46.3	50.2	38.6	0.5	0.6	11.1	7.6	19.0	8.5	12.9	12.3	12.5
28 125	...	8	Sharkey	431.7	4 552	2 858	10.5	27.4	70.2	0.2	0.8	1.9	6.5	18.5	8.1	10.5	10.9	12.3
28 127	27140	2	Simpson	589.2	26 912	1 532	45.7	62.2	35.8	0.4	0.7	1.8	5.6	18.9	8.2	12.4	11.8	12.8
28 129	...	8	Smith	636.3	15 909	2 047	25.0	74.8	23.6	0.3	0.2	1.8	5.7	17.9	8.0	11.4	11.5	13.4
28 131	...	6	Stone	445.5	18 012	1 920	40.4	77.3	20.3	1.0	0.7	1.9	5.8	16.2	12.1	12.1	12.0	13.3

1. CBSA = Core Based Statistical Area. See Appendix A for explanation. See Appendix B for list of metropolitan areas with component counties. 2. County type code from the Economic Research Service of USDA Rural-Urban Continuum Codes. See Appendix A for definition. 3. Dry land or land partially or temporarily covered by water. 4. May be of any race.

STATE County	55 to 64 years	65 to 74 years	75 years and over	Percent female	2000	2010	2000–2010	2010–2016	Births	Deaths	Net migration	Number	Persons per house-hold	Family house-holds	Female family house-holder[1]	One per-son
	16	17	18	19	20	21	22	23	24	25	26	27	28	29	30	31
MISSISSIPPI	12.7	8.9	6.2	51.5	2 844 658	2 968 103	4.3	0.7	241 975	187 223	-35 013	1 096 593	2.64	68.3	18.6	27.5
Adams	15.3	9.9	7.8	49.4	34 340	32 297	-5.9	-3.2	2 357	2 570	-818	11 854	2.50	63.5	23.6	34.3
Alcorn	12.8	10.3	7.1	51.2	34 558	37 057	7.2	0.7	2 688	2 791	413	14 806	2.49	67.8	12.9	27.9
Amite	16.7	12.6	9.6	51.6	13 599	13 128	-3.5	-5.1	861	893	-632	4 985	2.55	58.8	12.2	39.7
Attala	12.9	10.8	9.0	52.7	19 661	19 564	-0.5	-3.2	1 547	1 706	-447	7 451	2.52	69.5	21.8	28.7
Benton	13.6	11.1	7.6	50.7	8 026	8 730	8.8	-5.3	573	604	-431	2 964	2.83	69.1	15.0	29.1
Bolivar	12.3	9.4	5.6	53.3	40 633	34 148	-16.0	-4.1	3 242	2 576	-2 080	12 382	2.60	62.9	28.0	31.7
Calhoun	13.8	9.9	8.2	52.2	15 069	14 962	-0.7	-2.4	1 115	1 119	-313	5 922	2.46	67.1	17.3	30.5
Carroll	15.5	13.2	8.7	49.4	10 769	10 597	-1.6	-3.2	587	670	-292	3 694	2.75	75.2	13.2	24.2
Chickasaw	12.8	9.3	7.0	51.2	19 440	17 392	-10.5	-0.8	1 589	1 083	-608	6 484	2.63	69.1	20.3	28.0
Choctaw	14.3	11.8	8.5	51.3	9 758	8 548	-12.4	-3.6	583	547	-357	3 303	2.49	63.3	15.6	34.9
Claiborne	12.7	8.3	6.6	52.6	11 831	9 598	-18.9	-4.8	765	599	-646	3 192	2.74	63.4	30.1	34.1
Clarke	14.6	11.3	7.9	53.1	17 955	16 732	-6.8	-5.0	1 154	1 232	-740	6 486	2.51	68.5	18.0	28.9
Clay	13.9	10.2	7.5	52.9	21 979	20 634	-6.1	-3.8	1 367	1 443	-718	7 795	2.57	72.4	24.7	25.8
Coahoma	12.9	8.1	6.1	54.0	30 622	26 145	-14.6	-8.9	2 659	1 897	-3 073	9 360	2.62	66.8	31.3	30.1
Copiah	14.1	9.6	6.6	52.0	28 757	29 449	2.4	-3.3	2 296	1 974	-1 287	9 840	2.82	70.5	19.1	27.4
Covington	12.5	9.9	7.7	51.4	19 407	19 571	0.8	0.0	1 669	1 555	-101	6 969	2.76	67.6	18.2	28.8
DeSoto	11.4	7.7	4.7	51.7	107 199	161 264	50.4	8.9	12 929	7 631	8 879	60 010	2.80	73.7	14.9	22.1
Forrest	10.8	7.6	5.8	52.5	72 604	74 932	3.2	1.4	6 658	4 520	-1 180	27 983	2.58	62.8	19.2	28.4
Franklin	15.4	10.1	8.6	50.8	8 448	8 118	-3.9	-4.1	556	607	-276	3 291	2.36	74.5	15.5	25.1
George	11.9	9.5	5.3	49.6	19 144	22 579	17.9	4.9	2 235	1 531	386	7 471	3.02	74.0	12.2	24.9
Greene	12.1	8.4	5.5	42.9	13 299	14 395	8.2	-6.9	817	774	-1 044	4 180	2.59	66.8	10.3	30.6
Grenada	13.5	10.2	7.1	52.4	23 263	21 906	-5.8	-2.9	1 678	1 771	-566	7 429	2.86	65.2	18.6	32.5
Hancock	15.3	11.2	7.0	50.8	42 967	44 014	2.4	6.3	3 095	2 774	2 428	18 591	2.43	69.0	13.2	26.1
Harrison	12.6	8.4	5.7	50.8	189 601	187 105	-1.3	8.6	17 507	11 419	9 611	75 882	2.52	65.6	18.3	28.2
Hinds	12.4	7.6	5.3	53.3	250 800	245 365	-2.2	-1.7	20 848	12 896	-12 036	88 762	2.68	65.0	24.8	30.3
Holmes	12.6	8.0	6.4	52.5	21 609	19 478	-9.9	-7.6	1 734	1 367	-1 814	6 420	2.82	68.0	34.5	30.7
Humphreys	13.9	9.0	6.5	53.2	11 206	9 375	-16.3	-9.2	777	628	-1 011	3 057	2.91	60.4	28.2	35.7
Issaquena	15.5	7.4	7.4	42.0	2 274	1 406	-38.2	-8.0	74	72	-120	436	2.33	64.2	17.0	26.6
Itawamba	12.2	10.0	7.6	50.7	22 770	23 401	2.8	0.5	1 661	1 648	49	8 835	2.54	69.6	11.6	28.5
Jackson	13.4	9.1	5.9	50.8	131 420	139 668	6.3	1.1	10 165	8 175	-299	50 242	2.78	67.7	14.6	26.8
Jasper	14.4	10.8	8.2	51.3	18 149	17 062	-6.0	-2.8	1 402	1 174	-719	6 873	2.40	73.1	21.4	26.0
Jefferson	14.9	8.4	6.9	50.6	9 740	7 732	-20.6	-5.6	680	488	-638	2 545	2.81	64.6	29.9	34.5
Jefferson Davis	14.5	12.8	8.3	52.2	13 962	12 480	-10.6	-8.8	854	937	-968	5 019	2.35	62.7	22.0	34.6
Jones	13.1	9.3	6.7	51.3	64 958	67 761	4.3	0.3	6 060	4 569	-1 118	24 561	2.71	70.5	15.5	25.8
Kemper	13.4	10.3	8.3	50.1	10 453	10 461	0.1	-5.4	571	624	-519	3 665	2.53	60.9	21.6	34.9
Lafayette	10.3	7.3	4.6	51.3	38 744	47 359	22.2	13.6	3 419	2 331	5 073	17 334	2.65	59.7	13.5	29.7
Lamar	11.4	7.4	4.8	52.0	39 070	55 675	42.5	9.4	4 756	2 430	2 859	21 865	2.68	72.3	15.7	21.9
Lauderdale	12.9	9.0	7.3	51.6	78 161	80 261	2.7	-3.1	6 457	5 342	-3 504	29 701	2.56	65.6	19.4	30.2
Lawrence	14.5	9.6	6.8	50.8	13 258	12 929	-2.5	-1.4	1 009	864	-325	4 780	2.63	72.3	17.0	26.1
Leake	12.4	9.0	6.4	48.6	20 940	23 803	13.7	-5.0	1 880	1 649	-1 441	8 314	2.67	71.7	21.2	25.9
Lee	12.1	8.7	6.2	52.1	75 755	82 910	9.4	3.0	7 242	5 798	839	32 311	2.60	69.2	16.5	26.8
Leflore	12.0	7.7	6.0	53.1	37 947	32 382	-14.7	-7.8	3 042	2 257	-3 370	10 824	2.76	63.6	30.6	34.6
Lincoln	13.5	9.6	6.8	52.3	33 166	34 869	5.1	-1.0	2 882	2 482	-702	12 993	2.62	73.4	19.2	23.8
Lowndes	13.0	8.9	6.4	52.4	61 586	59 779	-2.9	-0.3	4 852	3 613	-1 376	23 270	2.50	67.0	16.8	28.8
Madison	12.7	8.2	5.1	52.2	74 674	95 203	27.5	10.4	8 070	6 416	7 949	37 107	2.65	72.1	15.8	25.1
Marion	13.3	10.1	7.6	51.5	25 595	27 081	5.8	-6.8	2 009	2 155	-1 711	9 814	2.58	72.0	17.2	24.3
Marshall	14.7	10.0	6.2	50.6	34 993	37 139	6.1	-3.6	2 809	2 613	-1 532	13 106	2.63	71.3	19.7	24.1
Monroe	13.7	10.5	7.7	52.1	38 014	36 989	-2.7	-3.0	2 672	2 544	-1 201	13 936	2.57	69.3	15.4	27.9
Montgomery	14.7	11.4	8.5	52.4	12 189	10 925	-10.4	-6.8	789	895	-627	4 261	2.43	70.5	21.3	27.8
Neshoba	12.2	8.8	6.4	52.3	28 684	29 673	3.4	-0.9	2 663	2 180	-740	10 738	2.71	70.2	20.4	27.2
Newton	11.8	9.7	7.3	52.1	21 838	21 720	-0.5	-0.7	1 791	1 745	-264	8 011	2.61	74.1	20.8	24.8
Noxubee	13.7	9.3	6.8	52.4	12 548	11 545	-8.0	-4.4	1 000	771	-793	4 067	2.69	68.5	26.1	26.8
Oktibbeha	9.0	5.9	4.8	49.9	42 902	47 671	11.1	4.5	3 489	1 876	470	17 483	2.51	53.3	14.4	33.7
Panola	13.1	9.1	6.0	51.8	34 274	34 699	1.2	-1.5	3 167	2 521	-1 175	12 133	2.81	64.9	18.7	33.0
Pearl River	13.6	11.2	6.9	50.5	48 621	55 747	14.7	-0.8	4 004	3 809	-637	20 606	2.61	70.3	14.6	26.2
Perry	14.0	10.6	7.4	51.2	12 138	12 250	0.9	0.0	908	823	-153	4 392	2.75	70.0	17.0	27.7
Pike	12.7	9.6	6.9	52.7	38 940	40 407	3.8	-1.8	3 489	3 092	-1 130	14 769	2.65	64.9	19.5	30.9
Pontotoc	12.0	8.3	6.1	50.7	26 726	29 957	12.1	5.3	2 758	1 741	571	10 542	2.87	71.2	14.2	25.8
Prentiss	12.5	9.6	7.7	51.0	25 556	25 276	-1.1	-0.1	1 944	1 662	-255	9 728	2.50	71.7	16.4	24.9
Quitman	14.1	9.1	6.8	52.5	10 117	8 223	-18.7	-10.6	622	638	-903	3 053	2.49	64.1	24.1	32.7
Rankin	12.3	8.6	5.5	51.7	115 327	142 061	23.2	5.7	11 814	6 713	3 229	53 800	2.62	72.9	14.4	23.0
Scott	12.7	8.4	5.9	51.3	28 423	28 260	-0.6	-0.2	2 849	1 775	-1 056	9 827	2.85	70.6	21.4	26.4
Sharkey	15.7	10.0	7.6	52.7	6 580	4 916	-25.3	-7.4	423	372	-430	1 769	2.64	63.2	25.3	33.7
Simpson	13.9	9.6	7.0	51.4	27 639	27 502	-0.5	-2.1	2 032	1 824	-766	9 619	2.77	70.2	16.1	26.8
Smith	14.2	10.3	7.6	51.8	16 182	16 493	1.9	-3.5	1 207	1 014	-733	6 085	2.65	74.4	16.5	24.0
Stone	13.1	9.8	5.5	49.5	13 622	17 786	30.6	1.3	1 330	1 076	-72	5 764	3.00	77.9	17.2	18.3

1. No spouse present.

Table B. States and Counties — **Population, Vital Statistics, Health, and Crime**

STATE County	Daytime population, 2011–2015			Births, 2016		Deaths, 2016		Persons under 65 with no health insurance, 2015		Medicare, 2015			Serious crimes known to police,[2] 2014 Total	
	Persons in group quarters, 2016	Number	Employ-ment/ resi-dence ratio	Total	Rate[1]	Number	Rate[1]	Number	Percent	Total Beneficiaries	Enrolled in Original Medicare	Enrolled in Medicare Advantage	Number	Rate[3]
	32	33	34	35	36	37	38	39	40	41	42	43	44	45
MISSISSIPPI	93 060	2 936 996	0.96	37 880	12.7	31 006	10.4	365 919	14.8	555 273	461 622	93 651	95 800	3 200
Adams..............	2 396	32 853	1.08	369	11.8	418	13.4	3 739	15.9	7 122	5 916	1 206	1 436	4 496
Alcorn..............	741	37 751	1.03	409	11.0	449	12.0	4 646	15.3	8 859	8 522	337	NA	NA
Amite...............	116	10 599	0.50	141	11.3	154	12.4	1 842	18.8	2 704	2 372	332	NA	NA
Attala..............	341	17 543	0.75	232	12.3	264	13.9	2 445	16.1	4 534	3 762	772	NA	NA
Benton.............	79	6 633	0.37	87	10.5	89	10.8	1 070	16.2	2 004	1 723	281	NA	NA
Bolivar.............	1 756	33 911	1.01	452	13.8	429	13.1	3 941	14.7	7 173	6 343	830	NA	NA
Calhoun............	211	13 402	0.74	178	12.2	185	12.7	2 266	18.9	3 197	2 905	292	NA	NA
Carroll.............	377	7 720	0.29	102	9.9	118	11.5	1 364	17.7	2 155	2 034	121	NA	NA
Chickasaw..........	496	17 057	0.95	255	14.8	199	11.5	2 556	18.0	4 260	3 698	562	NA	NA
Choctaw............	122	7 491	0.69	94	11.4	108	13.1	910	13.8	1 580	1 425	155	78	938
Claiborne..........	1 112	9 756	1.19	130	14.2	102	11.2	975	14.5	1 676	1 308	368	151	1 954
Clarke.............	52	14 048	0.63	186	11.7	201	12.7	1 990	15.4	3 946	3 432	514	NA	NA
Clay...............	303	18 886	0.81	196	9.9	238	12.0	2 547	15.6	3 996	3 491	505	378	1 857
Coahoma...........	706	25 777	1.06	384	16.1	293	12.3	3 058	14.7	4 776	4 329	447	NA	NA
Copiah.............	999	26 245	0.73	337	11.8	318	11.2	3 638	15.4	6 249	4 596	1 653	NA	NA
Covington..........	222	18 049	0.78	266	13.6	210	10.7	2 763	17.2	4 108	3 319	789	NA	NA
DeSoto.............	609	140 888	0.66	2 111	12.0	1 335	7.6	16 189	10.7	23 265	18 917	4 348	NA	NA
Forrest.............	3 255	85 324	1.28	1 022	13.5	757	10.0	9 815	15.5	17 531	14 045	3 486	NA	NA
Franklin............	67	6 708	0.62	89	11.4	74	9.5	951	15.1	1 652	1 494	158	NA	NA
George.............	559	19 866	0.60	350	14.8	241	10.2	2 937	15.1	4 981	3 860	1 121	73	361
Greene.............	2 397	12 342	0.53	133	9.9	132	9.8	1 434	15.3	1 811	1 586	225	72	523
Grenada............	247	22 948	1.17	259	12.2	251	11.8	2 567	14.5	5 349	4 655	694	NA	NA
Hancock............	548	44 882	0.96	524	11.2	441	9.4	6 373	16.7	8 000	5 554	2 446	NA	NA
Harrison............	5 068	207 952	1.13	2 850	14.0	1 845	9.1	28 395	16.8	36 345	29 172	7 173	8 916	4 490
Hinds..............	9 008	264 168	1.18	3 209	13.3	2 107	8.7	26 305	12.9	39 370	27 844	11 526	13 113	6 091
Holmes.............	897	17 181	0.69	266	14.8	249	13.8	2 282	15.3	4 002	3 337	665	NA	NA
Humphreys	83	8 474	0.80	104	12.2	118	13.9	1 240	16.9	1 792	1 539	253	NA	NA
Issaquena	281	1 258	0.89	8	6.2	6	4.6	159	18.3	163	141	22	NA	NA
Itawamba	994	20 437	0.67	273	11.6	250	10.6	2 809	15.0	3 935	3 699	236	352	1 503
Jackson............	1 252	137 804	0.95	1 642	11.6	1 379	9.8	17 382	14.5	23 235	17 409	5 826	4 528	3 570
Jasper.............	87	14 848	0.72	218	13.1	182	11.0	2 117	15.8	3 757	3 169	588	NA	NA
Jefferson...........	382	7 386	0.89	101	13.8	77	10.6	951	15.7	1 440	1 202	238	36	604
Jefferson Davis......	111	10 144	0.55	116	10.2	148	13.0	1 644	17.7	2 385	2 113	272	NA	NA
Jones..............	1 881	70 637	1.09	947	13.9	803	11.8	9 167	16.3	13 862	11 656	2 206	1 686	2 642
Kemper.............	954	10 371	1.05	95	9.6	103	10.4	1 450	19.9	1 838	1 560	278	86	942
Lafayette	6 125	52 341	1.05	559	10.4	400	7.4	5 847	14.2	5 856	5 330	526	NA	NA
Lamar.............	311	52 373	0.76	732	12.0	376	6.2	7 015	13.2	5 684	4 440	1 244	1 024	1 792
Lauderdale..........	3 719	84 360	1.14	1 000	12.9	851	10.9	8 722	13.9	15 108	13 186	1 922	2 741	3 419
Lawrence...........	0	11 297	0.72	164	12.9	139	10.9	1 508	14.3	3 704	3 235	469	NA	NA
Leake..............	1 596	20 792	0.71	283	12.5	290	12.8	3 709	20.9	4 477	3 617	860	NA	NA
Lee................	1 058	98 759	1.37	1 130	13.2	1 047	12.3	9 940	13.8	18 041	16 599	1 442	NA	NA
Leflore............	1 409	34 936	1.37	464	15.5	367	12.3	4 104	16.4	6 227	5 903	324	NA	NA
Lincoln............	700	33 360	0.89	460	13.3	399	11.6	4 550	15.8	6 845	5 864	981	NA	NA
Lowndes...........	1 375	62 385	1.11	745	12.5	585	9.8	7 281	14.7	12 006	10 654	1 352	NA	NA
Madison...........	1 751	105 324	1.11	1 346	12.8	1 188	11.3	9 622	10.9	14 336	11 247	3 089	1 526	1 729
Marion.............	716	26 151	1.00	297	11.8	338	13.4	3 569	17.3	5 431	4 446	985	513	1 978
Marshall...........	1 852	30 482	0.57	437	12.2	447	12.5	4 453	15.6	8 004	6 373	1 631	531	1 461
Monroe............	405	33 133	0.78	423	11.8	393	11.0	4 588	15.7	7 522	6 822	700	NA	NA
Montgomery........	99	9 836	0.82	123	12.1	121	11.9	1 289	15.8	2 869	2 728	141	NA	NA
Neshoba...........	394	29 660	1.01	417	14.2	359	12.2	4 499	18.1	4 567	4 058	509	NA	NA
Newton............	552	19 352	0.72	282	13.1	311	14.4	2 832	16.0	5 897	5 123	774	NA	NA
Noxubee...........	159	10 738	0.89	172	15.6	146	13.2	1 749	19.2	2 376	2 260	116	NA	NA
Oktibbeha..........	4 709	50 021	1.05	560	11.2	369	7.4	6 517	16.3	6 800	6 119	681	1 393	2 823
Panola.............	315	33 081	0.90	498	14.6	431	12.6	4 522	15.6	6 877	5 736	1 141	1 450	4 480
Pearl River.........	1 329	47 397	0.61	613	11.1	643	11.6	7 298	16.5	11 643	8 612	3 031	NA	NA
Perry..............	101	10 752	0.64	131	10.7	124	10.1	1 735	17.2	2 339	2 033	306	NA	NA
Pike...............	847	41 207	1.08	535	13.5	528	13.3	5 089	15.5	8 994	7 219	1 775	NA	NA
Pontotoc...........	236	27 851	0.80	460	14.6	258	8.2	4 189	15.9	5 231	4 694	537	NA	NA
Prentiss............	877	23 104	0.76	268	10.6	215	8.5	3 260	16.0	6 459	6 103	356	NA	NA
Quitman...........	137	6 860	0.60	93	12.7	104	14.2	1 059	17.1	1 641	1 485	156	NA	NA
Rankin.............	5 104	138 350	0.88	1 826	12.2	1 181	7.9	14 148	11.4	22 037	17 318	4 719	1 246	894
Scott..............	227	29 477	1.11	468	16.6	313	11.1	4 968	20.6	6 245	5 011	1 234	NA	NA
Sharkey............	106	4 679	0.92	61	13.4	49	10.8	648	17.1	1 006	878	128	NA	NA
Simpson...........	625	24 503	0.70	287	10.7	301	11.2	3 780	16.8	5 333	4 306	1 027	138	553
Smith..............	104	13 900	0.62	186	11.7	179	11.3	2 032	15.4	2 530	2 084	446	NA	NA
Stone..............	1 410	16 128	0.73	217	12.0	175	9.7	1 975	14.0	3 871	2 949	922	292	1 620

1. Per 1,000 estimated resident population.   2. Data for serious crimes have not been adjusted for underreporting; this may affect comparability between geographic areas and over time.
3. Per 100,000 population estimated by the FBI.

STATE County	Serious crimes known to police, 2014 (cont.)[1] Rate[2] Violent	Property	Education School enrollment and attainment, 2011–2015 Enrollment[3] Total	Percent private	Attainment[4] (percent) High school graduate or less	Bachelor's degree or more	Local government expenditures,[5] 2013–2014 Total current spending (mil dol)	Current spending per student (dollars)	Money income, 2011–2015 Per capita income[6] (dollars)	Households Median income (dollars)	Percent with income of less than $50,000	with income of $200,000 or more	Income and poverty, 2015 Median household income (dollars)	Percent below poverty level All persons	Children under 18 years	Children 5 to 17 years in families
	46	47	48	49	50	51	52	53	54	55	56	57	58	59	60	61
MISSISSIPPI	278	2 921	809 972	13.0	47.9	20.7	4 075.5	8 268	21 057	39 665	59.6	2.2	40 630	22.1	31.5	30.1
Adams	288	4 208	7 560	11.0	55.2	17.8	33.2	9 074	17 669	28 869	70.7	1.9	32 673	29.6	43.8	42.0
Alcorn	NA	NA	8 810	10.6	55.5	16.2	46.0	7 633	19 467	36 163	65.4	1.2	41 383	19.6	29.5	27.8
Amite	NA	NA	3 002	35.0	61.9	12.1	11.3	10 664	17 635	30 704	69.2	0.7	37 085	22.2	33.7	33.2
Attala	NA	NA	4 644	9.8	54.6	14.9	28.6	8 240	20 604	32 886	66.9	1.7	32 988	22.9	34.1	33.2
Benton	NA	NA	2 078	6.2	61.3	10.6	11.0	8 897	19 935	33 141	67.0	1.6	32 467	25.3	38.3	36.6
Bolivar	NA	NA	10 450	7.3	51.4	21.1	59.2	9 006	15 751	27 585	71.2	0.8	30 311	36.1	47.8	45.3
Calhoun	NA	NA	3 448	8.1	61.3	11.2	19.8	7 676	17 434	31 098	69.3	0.9	33 906	23.0	33.7	33.0
Carroll	NA	NA	2 308	30.8	58.4	13.6	8.3	8 222	20 627	37 289	59.8	2.1	39 439	19.0	27.1	24.8
Chickasaw	NA	NA	4 066	6.5	65.1	10.7	25.0	8 226	17 538	30 926	70.5	1.4	31 937	26.6	38.8	36.7
Choctaw	48	890	2 204	8.5	54.4	13.5	14.2	9 992	17 464	30 692	67.5	0.2	35 370	24.5	36.7	33.7
Claiborne	272	1 683	3 008	6.9	51.7	15.6	15.9	9 803	12 229	23 259	77.2	0.4	26 959	46.3	54.0	55.5
Clarke	NA	NA	3 976	5.9	54.7	13.9	24.7	8 139	20 071	35 993	63.7	0.6	38 362	21.8	33.4	30.6
Clay	319	1 538	5 850	17.0	54.3	17.8	28.8	8 467	18 405	31 669	66.3	1.2	32 360	27.6	42.1	39.3
Coahoma	NA	NA	7 748	11.6	50.5	17.6	45.7	9 351	15 393	28 851	72.3	0.8	25 948	35.0	49.3	52.3
Copiah	NA	NA	7 912	11.4	52.1	14.1	34.2	7 568	17 762	35 130	65.2	1.8	34 723	26.1	39.1	38.0
Covington	NA	NA	4 489	11.9	58.3	15.3	24.3	8 215	16 245	31 631	68.5	0.2	36 206	22.4	35.0	34.0
DeSoto	NA	NA	47 972	12.5	41.3	22.4	220.5	6 671	26 085	58 278	41.7	2.5	60 610	10.0	13.0	12.2
Forrest	NA	NA	24 717	15.2	43.4	26.7	107.4	9 263	19 897	36 416	62.1	1.7	35 198	26.6	32.2	32.0
Franklin	NA	NA	1 886	10.4	55.0	17.9	13.1	9 061	22 098	38 170	58.1	1.3	36 391	20.6	30.8	27.1
George	59	301	5 596	11.3	60.8	12.0	29.5	7 144	21 413	44 258	55.0	1.8	48 212	17.1	24.6	23.4
Greene	109	414	2 836	5.7	62.4	8.2	17.2	8 170	15 728	40 176	60.8	1.6	42 699	22.6	26.4	23.9
Grenada	NA	NA	5 542	13.5	53.3	15.6	32.7	7 595	19 138	31 779	65.4	1.5	35 163	21.3	32.4	32.6
Hancock	NA	NA	10 063	14.0	44.9	21.0	54.2	8 344	22 286	43 355	55.4	1.4	45 911	20.8	30.1	28.2
Harrison	220	4 271	48 847	14.1	43.3	21.3	260.5	8 369	22 120	41 722	57.7	1.7	42 370	22.0	33.6	33.5
Hinds	770	5 321	76 973	17.3	39.1	27.7	339.7	8 355	20 598	37 324	61.5	2.2	39 158	27.1	38.7	36.7
Holmes	NA	NA	5 600	9.1	65.0	12.3	30.1	8 518	11 972	20 732	81.9	0.2	24 065	43.3	53.6	53.2
Humphreys	NA	NA	2 423	10.5	64.3	12.1	14.2	8 069	13 503	23 216	80.4	1.9	25 625	41.5	60.2	56.6
Issaquena	NA	NA	170	24.1	74.4	7.2	NA	NA	12 423	23 491	80.3	0.5	28 859	40.4	46.0	43.3
Itawamba	107	1 396	6 159	5.5	52.0	13.2	26.7	7 557	19 483	35 004	63.6	0.8	39 296	18.1	25.4	24.8
Jackson	243	3 327	37 547	12.3	43.9	20.1	217.6	8 845	24 001	48 406	52.0	2.9	46 339	16.1	23.0	21.5
Jasper	NA	NA	3 851	12.9	57.4	13.4	22.0	9 051	18 260	31 578	71.1	1.7	35 092	22.8	31.8	31.0
Jefferson	235	369	2 014	1.1	59.8	16.5	12.2	9 235	12 601	20 743	78.5	0.4	26 405	39.3	44.6	44.5
Jefferson Davis	NA	NA	2 669	10.5	59.2	14.2	16.0	10 166	15 682	26 279	76.9	0.5	28 845	30.5	44.2	44.2
Jones	199	2 443	16 981	13.5	48.7	18.4	92.8	7 968	20 465	37 143	62.8	2.4	36 413	23.2	32.3	31.1
Kemper	99	843	2 823	7.4	54.2	11.5	12.1	10 405	14 516	30 056	76.5	0.8	30 381	31.9	43.1	39.8
Lafayette	NA	NA	20 562	5.3	31.7	38.3	58.5	8 749	23 227	44 643	55.1	4.8	43 435	21.0	20.2	19.9
Lamar	58	1 734	17 686	12.3	32.8	35.9	80.8	7 921	26 403	52 035	47.0	4.0	53 205	16.4	21.3	20.8
Lauderdale	349	3 070	21 325	10.1	45.2	18.7	108.0	8 336	21 525	38 132	61.6	2.2	38 334	22.0	33.2	33.5
Lawrence	NA	NA	3 014	9.1	56.1	12.1	17.4	7 910	19 844	35 634	64.6	1.3	39 460	20.9	31.8	30.0
Leake	NA	NA	5 942	12.9	59.7	11.8	22.8	7 745	17 696	33 452	65.5	3.2	35 804	24.3	38.9	38.3
Lee	NA	NA	21 654	10.8	43.7	21.8	131.7	8 552	22 282	42 784	56.6	2.5	43 098	17.4	25.2	24.3
Leflore	NA	NA	9 407	9.5	57.5	17.5	50.8	9 009	14 563	24 233	73.6	0.7	26 520	42.3	55.3	53.3
Lincoln	NA	NA	8 433	10.1	51.4	15.2	46.3	7 388	18 844	36 473	63.0	0.9	40 627	20.0	27.8	27.5
Lowndes	NA	NA	16 292	12.0	46.0	21.8	81.3	8 257	21 410	40 239	59.3	1.8	41 880	23.5	36.3	37.4
Madison	155	1 573	28 963	24.2	26.2	46.0	130.5	8 192	34 478	64 376	39.4	8.5	67 482	12.7	18.5	16.8
Marion	208	1 770	6 253	18.2	59.8	13.0	36.7	9 280	19 491	30 668	66.0	1.6	34 742	24.2	36.5	34.7
Marshall	338	1 123	8 168	15.9	60.2	13.4	38.9	7 953	19 047	37 419	61.8	1.1	38 006	23.3	37.3	35.8
Monroe	NA	NA	8 177	5.6	56.7	14.6	54.4	7 991	19 215	36 783	62.7	1.1	38 893	20.7	30.6	28.5
Montgomery	NA	NA	2 323	18.8	58.9	15.8	13.8	9 379	17 674	30 146	68.7	0.6	34 264	25.8	38.3	37.2
Neshoba	NA	NA	8 178	8.3	54.9	13.5	33.4	7 319	18 572	35 645	64.0	1.9	38 068	25.5	34.7	31.9
Newton	NA	NA	5 953	7.6	47.6	15.8	32.0	8 235	20 413	37 045	62.3	1.6	36 991	22.7	31.4	31.3
Noxubee	NA	NA	2 827	17.6	65.2	11.9	16.8	9 323	14 450	26 677	73.4	0.5	28 041	34.3	46.9	45.3
Oktibbeha	158	2 665	23 304	8.5	33.1	43.0	48.1	9 362	20 091	32 485	64.6	2.5	38 011	27.1	30.8	30.8
Panola	513	3 967	8 768	13.2	56.2	14.9	52.4	8 567	19 525	36 555	62.8	1.5	35 517	24.8	38.5	37.4
Pearl River	NA	NA	13 842	12.4	49.4	13.9	71.5	8 296	19 786	40 976	58.9	0.7	43 420	21.0	30.6	28.5
Perry	NA	NA	2 887	6.9	59.4	8.3	16.1	8 400	17 928	34 045	64.0	1.2	37 777	21.0	32.8	31.3
Pike	NA	NA	10 778	14.6	54.0	16.3	60.5	8 637	17 777	31 677	67.3	1.3	31 976	30.1	43.1	39.2
Pontotoc	NA	NA	7 699	5.8	57.2	13.0	43.9	7 482	19 695	40 645	57.8	1.3	39 977	15.6	25.6	21.9
Prentiss	NA	NA	6 434	3.4	57.8	11.9	29.8	8 126	17 644	32 945	69.1	0.9	38 550	19.5	28.2	27.9
Quitman	NA	NA	1 984	14.0	61.7	12.9	11.8	9 678	14 503	24 583	74.1	0.6	26 467	38.2	56.8	56.6
Rankin	60	834	37 576	20.1	37.2	29.0	184.2	7 855	27 389	58 801	42.7	3.6	58 426	9.7	14.2	12.7
Scott	NA	NA	6 973	9.9	63.4	11.2	40.8	7 253	17 256	32 935	67.7	1.2	34 469	21.7	31.5	31.0
Sharkey	NA	NA	1 275	15.3	53.1	20.0	9.2	9 984	15 993	30 525	69.3	0.5	27 589	34.3	53.7	51.6
Simpson	32	521	7 296	17.4	59.3	12.7	33.5	8 101	17 412	35 375	68.5	1.3	37 742	24.5	35.3	32.4
Smith	NA	NA	3 797	13.2	60.7	13.0	24.0	8 530	21 050	32 951	61.5	2.4	40 637	19.5	27.1	25.2
Stone	122	1 498	4 616	13.8	50.8	13.4	21.6	7 987	19 484	45 025	55.3	1.1	42 295	20.5	30.0	27.9

1. Data for serious crimes have not been adjusted for underreporting; this may affect comparability between geographic areas and over time.   2. Per 100,000 population estimated by the FBI.
3. All persons 3 years old and over enrolled in nursery school through college.   4. Persons 25 years old and over.   5. Elementary and secondary education expenditures.
6. Based on population estimated by the American Community Survey, 2011–2015.

STATE County	Personal income, 2015										Earnings, 2015		
	Total (mil dol)	Percent change, 2014–2015	Per capita[1] Dollars	Per capita[1] Rank	Wages and salaries (mil dol)	Supplements to wages and salaries; employer contributions (mil dol) Pension and insurance	Supplements to wages and salaries; employer contributions (mil dol) Government social insurance	Proprietors' income (mil dol)	Dividends, interest, and rent (mil dol)	Personal transfer receipts (mil dol)	Total (mil dol)	Contributions for government social insurance (mil dol) From employee and self-employed	Contributions for government social insurance (mil dol) From employer
	62	63	64	65	66	67	68	69	70	71	72	73	74
MISSISSIPPI..................	104 045	1.8	34 805	X	46 433	7 597	3 511	8 582	15 664	27 334	66 123	4 422	3 511
Adams........................	1 090	0.1	34 860	1 952	422	60	31	138	195	341	650	47	31
Alcorn.......................	1 145	4.0	30 633	2 810	531	83	40	70	160	393	724	53	40
Amite........................	389	1.5	30 950	2 321	71	12	5	35	45	133	123	10	5
Attala.......................	567	1.5	29 754	2 779	158	28	12	59	71	199	257	20	12
Benton.......................	225	2.1	27 483	3 030	36	7	3	11	23	85	57	6	3
Bolivar......................	1 144	-0.6	34 322	2 215	452	78	34	57	174	392	621	44	34
Calhoun......................	426	3.8	28 948	2 878	114	20	9	39	49	156	182	13	9
Carroll......................	336	4.1	32 788	2 683	43	8	3	17	46	108	72	8	3
Chickasaw....................	559	2.3	32 248	2 508	184	30	15	63	82	177	291	21	15
Choctaw......................	241	6.1	28 982	2 840	94	19	7	18	29	83	137	10	7
Claiborne....................	279	6.3	30 516	2 818	190	41	14	12	30	124	257	16	14
Clarke.......................	573	-2.1	35 778	1 749	110	19	8	28	59	183	165	14	8
Clay.........................	692	0.8	34 522	1 950	213	31	16	96	104	201	357	22	16
Coahoma......................	739	0.0	30 030	2 708	310	49	23	27	114	316	409	30	23
Copiah.......................	897	0.8	31 186	2 563	268	52	21	64	96	288	405	29	21
Covington....................	622	-0.9	31 802	2 231	184	33	14	77	74	190	307	20	14
DeSoto.......................	6 305	4.6	36 375	1 736	2 091	283	158	366	630	1 066	2 898	200	158
Forrest......................	2 678	3.3	35 269	1 934	1 728	294	129	319	510	709	2 470	155	129
Franklin.....................	245	3.3	31 604	2 719	69	14	5	18	29	88	106	8	5
George.......................	716	0.4	30 653	2 669	185	33	14	24	81	191	255	20	14
Greene.......................	328	-1.1	24 222	3 078	70	15	5	17	34	115	107	9	5
Grenada......................	751	3.3	34 819	2 180	377	64	29	50	93	246	520	36	29
Hancock......................	1 537	0.8	33 108	2 013	747	135	60	72	314	393	1 014	67	60
Harrison.....................	6 914	2.5	34 327	1 972	3 860	688	308	424	1 398	1 700	5 280	327	308
Hinds........................	9 312	1.1	38 337	1 412	6 069	1 012	445	1 175	1 722	2 170	8 701	543	445
Holmes.......................	490	0.3	26 706	3 018	128	24	10	7	53	249	169	15	10
Humphreys....................	255	-4.6	29 437	2 466	75	13	6	14	44	105	109	9	6
Issaquena....................	25	-21.4	18 019	3 046	7	1	1	-9	8	9	0	1	1
Itawamba.....................	754	4.3	31 954	2 623	241	39	18	47	85	237	345	27	18
Jackson......................	4 864	0.7	34 394	2 019	2 607	490	198	230	787	1 133	3 525	229	198
Jasper.......................	570	-0.8	34 409	1 902	155	27	12	51	68	175	245	17	12
Jefferson....................	228	-0.9	30 438	2 690	43	11	3	6	21	92	62	5	3
Jefferson Davis..............	341	0.0	29 262	2 687	65	12	5	21	36	128	103	9	5
Jones	2 544	0.9	37 299	1 630	1 264	220	90	259	362	741	1 833	118	90
Kemper.......................	275	-2.0	27 575	2 853	173	28	13	17	32	107	231	15	13
Lafayette....................	1 879	5.0	35 342	1 983	928	162	67	167	374	372	1 323	83	67
Lamar........................	2 122	5.7	35 014	2 556	632	90	48	255	299	381	1 025	69	48
Lauderdale...................	2 746	-0.1	34 964	2 012	1 398	230	110	208	448	739	1 946	128	110
Lawrence.....................	413	1.9	32 698	2 316	126	20	9	45	40	147	200	14	9
Leake........................	621	-5.8	27 283	2 864	173	29	14	85	63	209	302	20	14
Lee..........................	3 192	4.6	37 426	1 871	2 182	295	166	285	498	711	2 928	192	166
Leflore......................	947	-1.0	30 562	2 445	525	95	40	49	175	345	708	47	40
Lincoln......................	1 242	1.5	35 834	1 942	464	68	34	99	136	339	665	47	34
Lowndes......................	2 197	1.0	36 793	1 654	1 195	198	94	114	377	533	1 601	103	94
Madison......................	5 997	3.2	57 964	148	2 607	331	190	726	1 215	698	3 855	246	190
Marion.......................	785	0.8	30 723	2 398	320	47	24	40	111	280	430	32	24
Marshall.....................	1 068	2.5	29 738	2 917	281	40	21	72	105	338	414	33	21
Monroe.......................	1 163	2.8	32 455	2 565	420	69	33	81	161	356	603	45	33
Montgomery...................	331	0.5	32 623	2 499	87	15	7	16	44	127	126	11	7
Neshoba......................	1 003	-2.0	34 051	1 383	460	77	33	128	130	289	698	42	33
Newton.......................	689	-2.0	31 690	2 409	205	39	15	56	82	233	316	22	15
Noxubee......................	336	-3.3	30 459	2 540	86	17	7	52	39	132	162	10	7
Oktibbeha....................	1 516	3.2	30 445	2 771	792	162	58	89	263	336	1 101	68	58
Panola.......................	1 036	2.1	30 321	2 774	425	68	32	88	126	334	613	44	32
Pearl River..................	1 864	3.9	33 778	2 289	376	66	28	92	233	545	562	48	28
Perry........................	345	3.7	28 100	3 001	108	16	7	18	35	125	149	12	7
Pike.........................	1 216	1.2	30 433	2 749	515	89	39	111	159	417	754	53	39
Pontotoc.....................	926	4.3	29 950	2 806	447	63	37	66	98	243	613	44	37
Prentiss.....................	725	2.6	28 483	2 966	253	43	20	35	89	243	350	27	20
Quitman......................	197	-5.3	26 311	2 927	43	8	3	-5	30	93	50	6	3
Rankin.......................	6 357	3.5	42 652	1 176	2 671	375	197	707	811	1 152	3 950	259	197
Scott........................	823	-2.4	29 133	2 777	451	75	37	81	76	267	645	40	37
Sharkey......................	136	-3.7	29 737	2 648	40	7	3	-1	26	61	49	4	3
Simpson......................	927	-1.6	34 068	1 982	227	39	17	96	90	308	379	26	17
Smith........................	515	-6.0	32 043	2 309	118	21	9	89	50	153	237	14	9
Stone........................	538	1.7	29 777	2 839	149	26	11	21	66	184	207	16	11

1. Based on the resident population estimated as of July 1 of the year shown.

STATE County	Farm	Mining	Construction	Manu-facturing	Information: professional, scientific, technical services	Retail trade	Finance, insurance, real estate and leasing	Health care and social assistance	Govern-ment	Number	Rate[1]	Supplemental Security Income recipients, December 2015	Total	Percent change, 2010–2016
	75	76	77	78	79	80	81	82	83	84	85	86	87	88
MISSISSIPPI	1.7	1.8	6.1	13.2	5.7	7.7	5.2	11.3	22.6	647 420	217	123 207	1 307 441	2.6
Adams	1.0	12.5	4.8	4.6	4.7	12.9	5.5	D	11.8	7 985	255	1 904	14 637	-0.1
Alcorn	0.4	0.1	4.5	20.2	2.5	10.8	4.2	11.2	21.1	10 195	273	1 662	17 131	0.3
Amite	15.4	2.4	3.5	10.2	D	5.4	2.1	D	16.0	3 430	273	581	6 646	0.2
Attala	2.6	0.7	17.7	12.0	D	11.7	3.8	D	20.7	4 935	260	973	9 140	0.2
Benton	6.1	0.1	6.6	12.0	D	D	1.5	D	35.7	2 185	268	435	4 207	0.5
Bolivar	0.2	0.2	5.2	16.3	D	12.1	4.3	14.3	19.9	8 130	244	3 074	14 337	1.9
Calhoun	14.8	0.1	3.4	20.0	2.8	7.2	3.8	D	20.9	4 030	274	675	6 935	0.3
Carroll	-2.8	D	17.4	9.9	D	4.0	D	D	22.3	2 965	290	505	5 073	0.4
Chickasaw	9.6	0.2	4.2	37.8	2.2	9.1	3.0	D	14.2	4 570	263	1 009	7 520	0.1
Choctaw	3.5	D	3.8	10.2	D	3.5	D	D	24.4	2 000	241	351	4 160	0.2
Claiborne	3.2	0.1	6.4	3.3	1.2	2.0	D	D	32.2	2 190	239	683	4 230	0.2
Clarke	6.0	9.4	6.9	12.1	2.6	6.6	D	D	21.5	4 580	286	762	7 884	0.1
Clay	20.1	D	5.0	12.8	2.9	8.3	3.0	D	12.3	4 970	248	965	9 208	0.3
Coahoma	-1.5	0.1	3.0	7.4	4.7	7.2	9.7	D	23.3	5 690	232	2 115	10 742	-0.4
Copiah	4.5	2.7	3.9	30.1	D	6.3	2.3	D	18.5	6 785	236	1 559	12 127	-0.5
Covington	16.7	1.2	5.9	17.3	D	6.5	3.2	6.0	20.0	4 700	240	993	8 532	0.4
DeSoto	0.1	D	8.4	8.4	3.1	10.6	4.0	11.9	13.1	28 890	167	2 786	65 826	6.8
Forrest	0.1	1.5	5.5	7.6	3.9	9.7	4.3	16.0	28.8	14 745	194	2 756	32 888	1.9
Franklin	5.5	D	4.4	3.0	D	8.5	3.9	D	32.7	2 145	276	427	4 167	0.3
George	1.3	D	10.3	7.2	3.9	11.4	4.1	6.3	30.9	4 990	213	772	9 382	0.5
Greene	7.1	0.5	D	D	D	4.7	1.6	D	43.3	2 800	208	439	5 135	0.3
Grenada	0.8	0.0	2.4	28.6	D	10.6	4.5	D	20.0	6 055	282	1 389	10 207	0.5
Hancock	-0.1	0.7	6.7	8.1	11.6	4.4	1.8	4.2	38.6	9 700	209	1 220	24 605	12.5
Harrison	0.0	D	5.9	4.9	5.5	7.3	4.4	8.3	34.7	39 760	198	6 434	91 454	7.4
Hinds	0.2	4.8	3.1	2.9	8.6	5.9	6.9	15.4	31.1	45 665	188	11 088	104 642	1.2
Holmes	-5.7	D	4.1	14.7	D	8.7	7.4	D	34.2	4 565	249	2 007	8 433	0.2
Humphreys	2.0	0.7	5.3	17.6	D	6.5	12.9	D	19.2	2 170	251	1 058	3 823	-0.8
Issaquena	2 942.2	0.0	D	0.0	D	D	D	D	-1 368.5	190	143	62	559	-0.2
Itawamba	1.8	D	11.8	34.6	1.4	6.8	2.7	6.7	16.9	6 395	270	854	10 188	0.6
Jackson	-0.1	0.2	6.9	38.0	6.4	4.4	2.7	7.0	18.3	29 900	212	3 247	61 641	2.6
Jasper	13.1	3.1	2.2	27.9	4.9	5.6	D	D	18.3	4 480	271	866	8 237	0.3
Jefferson	5.9	D	1.3	D	D	4.5	D	13.8	46.6	1 915	256	692	3 686	0.3
Jefferson Davis	12.0	D	19.1	3.5	2.7	6.9	D	D	28.2	2 970	256	630	5 892	0.3
Jones	3.1	11.1	8.5	19.9	D	5.4	3.5	5.0	18.7	15 560	228	2 641	28 715	1.0
Kemper	5.1	D	D	5.2	D	1.5	D	D	14.2	2 265	228	521	4 745	0.5
Lafayette	0.2	D	3.7	8.4	10.9	6.5	4.8	14.5	35.3	7 735	146	931	25 112	10.5
Lamar	1.1	1.3	6.7	1.2	D	15.2	8.9	20.7	11.2	9 915	164	1 535	24 358	1.2
Lauderdale	0.1	D	4.1	8.0	4.7	9.2	5.6	19.6	21.2	16 515	210	3 175	35 091	1.1
Lawrence	13.7	0.9	11.2	31.5	D	3.7	D	4.3	16.1	3 650	289	591	6 051	0.5
Leake	19.2	0.4	D	D	D	7.7	D	D	13.3	5 115	225	1 043	9 436	0.2
Lee	0.2	0.1	3.2	19.9	6.7	9.2	6.3	19.5	9.9	19 010	223	3 018	36 411	1.5
Leflore	1.4	D	5.5	11.2	5.0	7.4	5.0	9.5	31.7	6 815	225	2 612	13 157	-0.3
Lincoln	3.8	2.0	7.5	8.6	4.0	9.7	4.1	14.7	12.7	8 240	238	1 331	15 304	0.3
Lowndes	0.1	0.6	6.0	19.8	3.5	7.1	5.0	12.7	23.2	12 835	215	2 461	27 130	2.2
Madison	0.0	4.3	5.3	16.2	15.3	8.3	10.0	8.3	6.8	17 060	165	2 084	42 536	10.3
Marion	7.0	7.5	13.0	4.8	D	9.7	4.2	D	15.9	6 525	256	1 240	11 854	0.2
Marshall	-0.2	0.0	14.8	10.3	D	7.2	5.1	D	15.7	8 390	234	1 786	15 239	2.4
Monroe	1.6	1.1	12.7	31.2	D	5.7	2.5	D	13.2	9 535	267	1 370	16 458	0.0
Montgomery	1.6	0.1	6.9	3.0	4.4	8.8	D	D	23.5	3 020	297	728	5 583	7.5
Neshoba	10.6	D	14.2	4.5	2.0	7.0	2.7	D	40.4	6 615	225	1 284	12 373	0.1
Newton	10.9	D	6.8	15.0	1.7	5.6	2.2	D	29.6	5 280	244	714	9 386	0.1
Noxubee	21.1	D	3.9	19.2	0.6	11.5	2.4	D	24.2	2 790	252	946	5 156	-0.3
Oktibbeha	0.3	0.1	2.7	7.9	4.7	7.2	3.3	6.3	50.8	7 040	142	1 475	21 796	4.1
Panola	1.4	0.2	6.4	15.1	7.8	9.7	5.4	D	18.1	8 260	242	2 115	14 761	0.5
Pearl River	0.3	0.3	11.0	6.8	D	12.6	5.6	D	29.1	14 395	261	1 861	24 863	3.9
Perry	1.6	0.9	3.4	32.3	D	4.7	D	9.6	15.9	3 040	249	519	5 533	0.3
Pike	1.4	1.1	3.5	13.6	3.8	12.7	5.6	8.8	25.3	9 605	240	2 325	18 087	1.3
Pontotoc	0.2	0.0	3.5	49.1	D	6.1	2.4	D	10.4	6 975	226	899	12 625	1.5
Prentiss	0.6	0.0	7.9	21.5	D	7.5	4.4	D	21.9	6 400	253	748	11 104	0.5
Quitman	-19.4	D	D	D	1.6	D	8.9	D	40.0	1 875	250	659	3 585	-0.1
Rankin	0.9	1.1	12.4	6.3	4.6	10.1	8.5	11.1	13.0	28 025	188	2 689	59 246	4.9
Scott	8.8	0.1	6.1	44.9	D	5.5	2.2	6.1	11.2	6 350	225	1 369	11 502	0.3
Sharkey	-8.8	D	2.3	0.3	D	9.4	7.2	D	39.4	1 245	271	409	2 121	1.0
Simpson	14.3	0.7	5.9	1.8	D	7.6	5.0	D	19.6	6 395	236	1 361	11 966	0.3
Smith	29.7	D	4.8	23.7	D	2.4	D	4.4	11.9	3 860	240	540	7 260	0.3
Stone	1.7	D	5.2	12.8	3.6	9.1	3.4	D	27.9	4 020	223	638	7 322	2.2

1. Per 1,000 resident population estimated as of July 1 of the year shown.

Table B. States and Counties — Housing, Labor Force, and Employment

STATE County	Total (89)	Percent (90)	Median value[1] (91)	With a mortgage (92)	Without a mortgage[2] (93)	Median rent[3] (94)	Median rent as a percent of income[2] (95)	Sub-standard units[4] (percent) (96)	Total (97)	Percent change, 2015–2016 (98)	Total (99)	Rate[5] (100)	Total (101)	Management, business, science and arts (102)	Construction, production, and maintenance occupations (103)
MISSISSIPPI	1 096 593	68.4	103 100	22.2	11.7	717	31.7	3.3	1 280 438	0.8	74 660	5.8	1 203 914	31.1	27.5
Adams	11 854	65.2	85 600	25.2	12.6	588	34.5	3.1	11 264	-1.8	935	8.3	10 730	27.4	26.5
Alcorn	14 806	68.7	84 800	22.3	10.9	604	27.1	3.6	15 899	0.6	824	5.2	14 784	29.2	30.4
Amite	4 985	84.3	71 600	26.4	13.6	620	29.1	2.2	4 525	-0.2	334	7.4	4 562	22.8	38.4
Attala	7 451	72.2	73 600	21.1	11.3	562	27.8	4.2	7 013	-0.1	473	6.7	6 643	27.1	35.7
Benton	2 964	87.3	72 800	30.3	11.5	578	33.8	2.7	3 027	0.9	203	6.7	2 994	19.8	41.3
Bolivar	12 382	55.9	85 100	22.5	12.5	564	33.2	4.1	13 426	-0.2	981	7.3	11 834	32.0	23.4
Calhoun	5 922	72.4	61 300	21.1	12.1	516	31.7	2.9	6 212	0.7	336	5.4	5 580	23.8	41.8
Carroll	3 694	84.2	80 800	17.3	13.9	530	25.0	2.1	3 458	-0.5	260	7.5	3 705	34.1	31.8
Chickasaw	6 484	73.6	63 400	25.7	10.7	533	36.9	3.1	7 115	-1.0	472	6.6	6 554	18.6	45.0
Choctaw	3 303	71.9	70 300	24.2	12.9	537	28.1	3.9	3 743	0.4	212	5.7	2 921	29.0	37.0
Claiborne	3 192	69.9	53 800	25.1	15.5	569	38.9	6.7	3 081	-1.7	352	11.4	2 411	20.7	27.7
Clarke	6 486	82.2	65 300	22.7	11.7	586	27.3	2.6	6 080	-0.4	415	6.8	6 363	28.6	35.3
Clay	7 795	69.7	80 900	27.1	13.2	662	40.0	2.5	8 053	0.0	655	8.1	7 524	25.7	33.2
Coahoma	9 360	52.2	61 900	22.1	14.1	567	30.7	3.6	9 270	-2.4	819	8.8	8 706	30.2	23.4
Copiah	9 840	77.3	84 500	23.8	12.1	647	29.5	4.4	11 448	1.2	741	6.5	10 280	27.2	31.0
Covington	6 969	80.5	71 800	24.1	12.4	659	32.1	3.4	8 116	1.4	445	5.5	6 628	22.4	38.1
DeSoto	60 010	73.4	152 700	21.0	10.0	958	28.8	2.7	86 427	1.7	3 656	4.2	82 634	33.6	25.9
Forrest	27 983	54.8	110 600	20.6	12.0	728	35.5	2.7	33 488	1.5	1 914	5.7	32 647	32.2	23.0
Franklin	3 291	75.6	73 200	19.4	10.0	523	30.1	2.4	2 857	-3.2	205	7.2	3 102	26.9	42.9
George	7 471	85.5	101 300	20.0	10.0	742	32.9	2.5	8 809	-1.0	652	7.4	8 260	30.5	37.0
Greene	4 180	81.0	86 200	20.8	12.1	576	33.2	4.8	4 302	-1.1	315	7.3	3 955	28.5	37.8
Grenada	7 429	73.4	92 600	26.4	12.5	593	30.4	2.9	9 613	0.9	502	5.2	8 169	25.4	35.1
Hancock	18 591	71.4	133 000	24.2	12.0	758	29.8	3.3	18 873	0.6	1 146	6.1	18 482	28.8	28.1
Harrison	75 882	57.2	137 700	24.4	11.1	837	32.2	3.3	86 666	0.7	4 775	5.5	82 911	27.9	23.4
Hinds	88 762	59.4	107 100	22.8	11.1	771	36.2	3.7	111 304	1.4	6 014	5.4	105 504	32.5	21.2
Holmes	6 420	63.4	51 500	32.7	16.3	496	33.2	4.3	6 011	-2.2	661	11.0	5 301	23.2	38.2
Humphreys	3 057	54.2	60 500	33.7	15.3	522	31.3	5.9	2 383	-3.9	272	11.4	2 678	24.7	40.5
Issaquena	436	56.4	57 000	33.6	16.5	378	30.7	3.2	398	-5.5	57	14.3	305	19.0	38.0
Itawamba	8 835	77.8	83 700	23.2	12.1	630	27.7	2.7	10 521	2.6	529	5.0	9 428	26.8	41.7
Jackson	50 242	70.6	121 200	22.1	10.7	816	29.9	2.2	59 651	0.7	3 893	6.5	58 824	30.7	27.0
Jasper	6 873	82.0	69 900	24.4	13.5	708	28.6	4.0	6 179	-3.4	477	7.7	6 257	24.4	39.6
Jefferson	2 545	60.8	60 500	26.5	15.9	389	36.5	5.5	2 235	-2.3	334	14.9	1 861	23.5	36.1
Jefferson Davis	5 019	76.4	82 300	28.5	17.3	697	44.8	3.1	4 194	1.1	350	8.3	4 094	21.9	37.0
Jones	24 561	73.4	87 500	21.8	12.1	614	29.7	3.7	25 850	-3.1	1 586	6.1	26 436	29.7	32.9
Kemper	3 665	76.3	66 000	27.0	12.7	486	33.6	4.0	3 555	-1.0	311	8.7	3 537	20.1	41.2
Lafayette	17 334	59.7	159 200	20.1	10.0	800	41.4	2.5	26 222	6.7	1 268	4.8	22 584	38.2	19.1
Lamar	21 865	66.5	168 100	21.5	10.8	835	31.0	2.9	29 576	1.8	1 345	4.5	26 952	38.7	21.1
Lauderdale	29 701	65.2	87 600	22.8	11.3	688	28.8	3.2	31 861	0.2	1 887	5.9	32 747	31.5	23.2
Lawrence	4 780	78.2	86 800	19.9	13.6	642	33.0	2.0	4 691	-1.6	334	7.1	4 638	27.3	38.3
Leake	8 314	73.4	76 000	19.4	13.3	593	27.9	5.9	7 792	-1.7	474	6.1	8 537	24.5	36.8
Lee	32 311	68.3	117 000	21.6	10.9	664	30.0	3.5	41 100	2.6	1 983	4.8	37 654	30.8	28.8
Leflore	10 824	51.5	70 000	26.6	14.1	551	39.2	5.1	10 401	-1.3	966	9.3	9 422	31.5	25.9
Lincoln	12 993	74.6	85 300	22.8	11.8	638	35.9	4.0	14 441	1.0	826	5.7	13 182	29.0	32.1
Lowndes	23 270	61.5	115 700	22.6	10.0	722	33.0	2.0	25 555	1.2	1 573	6.2	24 232	29.4	27.1
Madison	37 107	71.9	206 200	19.8	10.0	898	27.8	3.2	52 816	1.8	2 281	4.3	48 562	46.0	15.9
Marion	9 814	76.3	78 400	23.5	12.2	612	39.0	4.4	10 294	2.4	680	6.6	9 272	27.9	33.1
Marshall	13 106	78.3	84 800	24.2	14.2	676	29.0	3.8	14 645	0.9	879	6.0	14 066	22.9	36.3
Monroe	13 936	74.7	79 100	21.3	11.9	571	27.2	2.9	15 694	0.9	989	6.3	14 217	25.5	34.4
Montgomery	4 261	76.2	75 200	22.8	13.8	540	41.4	3.5	4 224	0.1	272	6.4	3 608	29.4	32.6
Neshoba	10 738	71.8	77 800	23.1	12.2	602	26.0	5.7	10 711	0.3	616	5.8	12 268	30.4	25.6
Newton	8 011	77.2	76 600	22.3	12.1	620	27.4	2.7	8 668	-1.1	516	6.0	8 319	33.2	30.0
Noxubee	4 067	71.9	61 300	27.1	14.5	534	30.3	1.3	3 989	0.4	330	8.3	3 841	22.9	40.0
Oktibbeha	17 483	52.7	142 100	21.1	11.2	716	41.1	2.3	22 997	1.7	1 259	5.5	19 381	43.9	17.0
Panola	12 133	74.2	77 900	20.7	13.1	657	29.8	4.6	13 202	-2.2	973	7.4	12 826	29.7	32.0
Pearl River	20 606	76.2	114 100	23.6	12.3	787	31.3	2.8	23 290	1.4	1 392	6.0	20 219	30.0	29.2
Perry	4 392	85.7	78 000	23.6	12.8	553	30.0	3.6	4 382	1.1	311	7.1	4 131	25.9	33.6
Pike	14 769	66.3	83 300	22.9	12.3	620	31.8	2.9	14 692	-0.5	1 001	6.8	14 477	26.3	32.9
Pontotoc	10 542	76.7	81 500	20.5	11.5	622	22.5	4.1	14 266	2.3	681	4.8	13 476	22.8	40.8
Prentiss	9 728	73.2	78 100	23.0	11.8	547	27.3	1.4	11 082	0.3	608	5.5	9 559	23.5	35.3
Quitman	3 053	65.4	54 100	28.5	14.2	610	34.8	3.8	2 651	-1.8	257	9.7	2 324	30.1	26.0
Rankin	53 800	74.2	153 300	19.6	10.0	891	27.1	2.1	74 754	1.9	2 961	4.0	69 233	41.0	19.5
Scott	9 827	73.2	68 000	22.7	13.5	629	30.9	6.5	13 361	2.4	615	4.6	10 867	23.4	39.7
Sharkey	1 769	60.4	62 000	23.4	10.0	513	31.4	5.0	1 718	-1.0	153	8.9	1 678	36.4	14.8
Simpson	9 619	78.4	78 800	24.5	12.9	618	30.7	7.5	11 110	1.5	599	5.4	9 821	26.8	37.9
Smith	6 085	80.7	79 700	20.6	11.4	593	27.5	5.1	6 787	0.0	359	5.3	6 433	25.1	37.1
Stone	5 764	79.4	111 800	22.3	10.6	734	28.7	5.0	6 531	1.4	440	6.7	6 920	22.2	30.5

1. Specified owner-occupied units.   2. A value of 10.0 represents 10 percent or less; a value of 50.0 represents 50 percent or more.   3. Specified renter-occupied units.
4. Overcrowded or lacking complete plumbing facilities.   5. Percent of civilian labor force.   6. Civilian employed persons 16 years old and over.

Table B. States and Counties — **Nonfarm Employment and Agriculture**

STATE County	Private nonfarm establishments, employment and payroll, 2015									Agriculture, 2012			
	Number of establishments	Employment						Annual payroll		Farms			
		Total	Health care and social assistance	Manufacturing	Retail trade	Finance and insurance	Professional, scientific, and technical services	Total (mil dol)	Average per employee (dollars)	Number	Percent with:		Farm operators whose principal occupation is farming (percent)
											Fewer than 50 acres	500 acres or more	
	104	105	106	107	108	109	110	111	112	113	114	115	116
MISSISSIPPI	58 662	926 391	162 749	141 189	142 817	33 059	30 736	33 948	36 646	38 076	28.1	11.8	43.0
Adams	805	10 483	1 761	470	2 208	359	213	340	32 410	189	33.9	10.6	45.0
Alcorn	788	11 869	2 540	2 455	2 181	298	434	394	33 210	505	27.3	5.3	30.9
Amite	174	1 171	164	225	155	33	27	40	33 811	590	27.1	8.6	46.8
Attala	331	4 155	509	629	730	129	64	139	33 448	456	20.4	10.3	34.2
Benton	56	933	142	180	111	11	D	27	28 748	312	16.3	9.0	36.9
Bolivar	708	9 142	1 710	1 982	1 508	259	167	292	31 983	419	23.4	45.8	57.0
Calhoun	252	2 583	501	818	451	51	28	80	30 882	621	20.3	11.9	33.3
Carroll	103	617	117	D	81	22	11	17	28 326	503	18.1	17.7	33.6
Chickasaw	327	5 242	445	3 075	657	112	56	154	29 462	575	20.7	12.2	34.4
Choctaw	115	1 139	82	266	147	23	20	53	46 917	254	15.0	11.4	42.9
Claiborne	106	1 920	310	97	163	38	D	136	71 026	249	16.9	17.7	48.6
Clarke	219	2 655	431	522	355	89	43	90	33 879	329	32.5	4.9	47.4
Clay	356	4 215	641	616	784	116	243	151	35 916	420	20.5	12.1	45.7
Coahoma	539	6 243	1 705	663	1 039	233	213	217	34 693	273	22.0	44.3	63.0
Copiah	441	5 625	750	1 864	855	169	73	158	28 115	506	26.3	8.9	44.5
Covington	326	3 948	490	1 429	531	123	57	122	30 900	493	27.8	6.9	45.8
DeSoto	2 742	48 768	5 770	3 689	8 623	1 019	939	1 626	33 342	433	44.3	9.7	50.1
Forrest	1 850	32 185	8 424	3 351	4 459	1 002	867	1 264	39 265	359	49.0	3.9	36.5
Franklin	120	1 225	355	62	157	54	42	42	34 256	189	19.6	13.2	34.4
George	303	3 768	769	305	1 187	73	118	122	32 404	573	52.5	1.9	51.5
Greene	116	765	20	D	222	D	20	26	33 714	395	33.2	7.3	37.7
Grenada	545	7 624	717	2 681	1 392	205	198	257	33 723	316	17.4	14.9	41.8
Hancock	704	9 479	1 006	761	1 530	208	1 830	382	40 322	248	46.4	2.0	42.3
Harrison	4 184	71 941	14 064	3 738	11 778	2 542	2 316	2 616	36 365	331	66.2	1.5	36.0
Hinds	5 336	98 259	30 619	3 614	11 144	4 910	5 270	4 355	44 325	1 047	32.5	11.3	39.3
Holmes	236	2 148	426	462	474	81	42	55	25 664	531	18.1	19.0	28.2
Humphreys	146	1 629	183	D	311	55	7	46	28 276	262	21.4	35.9	50.8
Issaquena	10	63	D	NA	NA	D	NA	2	28 222	97	11.3	42.3	53.6
Itawamba	358	5 345	542	2 211	676	212	29	180	33 589	443	15.8	7.0	40.4
Jackson	2 244	45 739	5 369	15 497	5 168	1 000	1 687	2 130	46 570	409	62.3	2.4	41.6
Jasper	210	2 950	325	1 204	362	100	58	112	37 924	445	22.0	8.1	47.4
Jefferson	55	628	243	D	85	D	NA	23	36 175	277	22.4	15.5	51.6
Jefferson Davis	154	1 080	87	57	246	37	14	45	41 709	337	23.7	6.5	57.3
Jones	1 323	25 470	3 059	6 718	3 039	510	459	1 019	39 989	927	38.2	2.9	49.6
Kemper	118	1 479	306	223	134	50	22	75	50 937	378	15.9	12.7	41.8
Lafayette	1 152	15 791	2 487	1 684	2 695	495	1 011	560	35 466	449	17.8	8.9	40.3
Lamar	1 297	16 307	3 102	146	4 939	560	737	484	29 704	424	42.0	4.5	34.2
Lauderdale	1 918	30 132	7 248	2 242	5 337	1 527	906	1 058	35 115	373	34.9	6.2	41.8
Lawrence	170	1 811	224	677	320	60	17	85	46 921	397	28.5	6.0	42.3
Leake	289	4 346	626	D	808	129	55	116	26 800	637	25.0	6.4	44.0
Lee	2 425	46 238	7 860	8 845	7 011	2 280	1 155	1 656	35 805	525	34.3	7.8	48.4
Leflore	708	12 464	2 905	2 300	1 930	400	285	397	31 879	300	14.0	43.7	54.7
Lincoln	794	10 676	1 731	1 105	1 936	332	298	365	34 169	595	30.4	5.9	39.7
Lowndes	1 489	21 443	3 038	3 898	3 714	512	530	896	41 800	413	27.4	15.7	30.3
Madison	3 022	49 231	3 844	7 810	7 289	3 148	3 469	2 056	41 764	685	32.4	14.5	32.7
Marion	578	6 474	926	569	1 274	293	179	220	34 003	552	32.2	5.8	48.7
Marshall	415	6 841	1 423	825	872	299	69	209	30 557	573	25.7	15.4	39.4
Monroe	629	7 686	1 480	2 384	1 011	199	85	304	39 549	726	25.1	13.2	40.8
Montgomery	204	2 472	703	244	483	102	30	66	26 665	345	15.7	14.8	42.3
Neshoba	504	8 065	811	476	1 292	281	380	349	43 268	677	29.1	5.0	52.1
Newton	326	3 783	822	938	649	127	51	123	32 471	562	30.1	7.7	52.3
Noxubee	173	1 708	318	511	350	65	8	53	31 045	565	21.6	20.4	42.3
Oktibbeha	857	11 954	1 744	1 398	2 231	408	448	340	28 406	402	24.6	12.7	42.8
Panola	595	8 178	1 580	1 636	1 592	320	113	268	32 831	745	14.6	16.4	37.7
Pearl River	803	7 869	1 080	588	2 109	310	387	268	34 018	813	47.6	5.3	42.6
Perry	147	1 630	263	629	260	39	26	78	47 592	310	40.3	3.5	50.3
Pike	950	12 786	2 401	2 538	2 560	411	271	378	29 598	531	35.8	4.0	48.2
Pontotoc	493	11 509	862	7 329	1 050	204	110	344	29 893	889	29.9	6.6	26.4
Prentiss	480	5 836	703	1 803	883	170	183	163	27 908	504	24.8	6.5	32.1
Quitman	109	717	261	D	129	51	13	19	26 075	347	18.7	27.7	39.2
Rankin	3 523	53 705	7 868	4 283	9 720	2 516	1 357	2 011	37 442	670	43.4	8.7	43.1
Scott	474	9 951	656	5 432	1 226	179	93	320	32 128	716	31.6	6.4	51.5
Sharkey	122	747	197	NA	161	D	14	23	30 886	128	16.4	50.8	61.7
Simpson	419	5 755	2 156	360	1 023	488	95	161	27 975	606	29.4	5.3	54.1
Smith	178	2 173	209	894	246	66	83	81	37 495	637	27.6	4.9	62.0
Stone	275	2 838	484	499	676	123	101	86	30 163	271	43.9	5.9	42.1

Table B. States and Counties — Agriculture

STATE County	Land in farms		Acres			Value of land and buildings (dollars)		Value of machinery and equipment, average per farm (dollars)	Value of products sold		Percent from:		Percent of farms with sales of:		Government payments	
	Acreage (1,000)	Percent change, 2007–2012	Average size of farm	Total irrigated (1,000)	Total cropland (1,000)	Average per farm	Average per acre		Total (mil dol)	Average per farm (dollars)	Crops	Live-stock and poultry products	$10,000 or more	$100,000 or more	Total ($1,000)	Percent of farms
	117	118	119	120	121	122	123	124	125	126	127	128	129	130	131	132
MISSISSIPPI	10 931	-4.6	287	1 652.0	5 075.6	652 593	2 273	91 910	6 441.0	169 162	46.2	53.8	33.0	12.4	181 205	43.3
Adams	66	-5.6	349	D	20.3	757 720	2 170	73 026	9.9	52 228	85.4	14.6	18.5	4.2	1 107	38.1
Alcorn	94	-0.3	185	D	43.3	345 842	1 866	59 352	20.9	41 461	84.6	15.4	25.1	3.6	795	50.7
Amite	121	10.2	205	0.1	23.0	690 939	3 365	66 768	68.4	115 958	5.6	94.4	32.4	8.8	1 025	43.4
Attala	125	-8.6	275	0.4	29.1	495 542	1 801	48 726	23.1	50 686	54.8	45.2	22.4	4.2	1 359	52.0
Benton	82	-4.3	264	D	29.2	421 772	1 596	49 298	14.5	46 596	72.8	27.2	19.6	6.7	740	56.4
Bolivar	390	-8.8	932	247.8	362.0	2 254 100	2 419	463 976	277.0	661 122	99.9	0.1	70.9	50.1	12 645	85.0
Calhoun	175	-13.3	282	1.2	80.1	520 758	1 844	98 725	78.5	126 446	92.9	7.1	34.5	12.1	3 146	73.4
Carroll	169	-11.1	336	12.3	57.8	631 318	1 879	75 996	36.5	72 620	86.9	13.1	30.0	8.3	2 451	46.1
Chickasaw	166	-7.0	289	3.0	67.2	533 009	1 847	69 757	60.9	105 897	49.6	50.4	34.6	10.3	2 924	65.0
Choctaw	63	-12.0	250	1.0	9.0	492 768	1 973	41 854	11.4	44 945	11.1	88.9	18.9	4.3	444	49.2
Claiborne	83	-11.5	334	D	22.0	671 028	2 011	54 072	11.4	45 864	77.2	22.8	25.3	3.6	1 125	55.0
Clarke	56	-12.9	171	0.4	13.9	404 097	2 358	59 161	33.5	101 763	4.5	95.5	24.9	5.2	160	17.6
Clay	130	-8.6	310	30.8	30.8	507 521	1 639	66 540	92.3	219 655	7.8	92.2	33.3	8.3	1 554	48.6
Coahoma	261	-13.8	956	138.0	226.8	2 411 634	2 523	406 249	179.6	657 799	96.1	3.9	62.3	50.2	10 498	86.4
Copiah	116	-11.8	229	0.2	18.4	523 654	2 286	58 763	61.4	121 336	10.4	89.6	29.1	6.7	527	32.8
Covington	106	-9.0	215	0.6	24.6	631 521	2 941	97 406	203.5	412 838	3.1	96.9	46.5	22.1	617	26.4
DeSoto	119	-16.2	274	17.2	81.2	723 771	2 641	84 483	50.0	115 386	90.2	9.8	24.5	9.0	1 866	25.4
Forrest	43	-6.1	119	0.8	9.8	406 844	3 416	65 822	20.8	58 075	22.8	77.2	27.9	5.8	598	24.2
Franklin	50	6.8	266	0.0	8.8	680 487	2 562	74 143	10.5	55 667	21.7	78.3	27.5	6.3	254	39.7
George	61	-10.6	106	0.5	19.3	357 428	3 361	75 084	22.7	39 620	84.8	15.2	27.2	4.4	421	16.6
Greene	69	34.8	174	0.2	16.2	379 203	2 175	91 420	32.8	83 139	30.5	69.5	26.6	6.8	300	13.2
Grenada	88	-20.8	280	1.1	25.8	511 345	1 828	51 522	11.6	36 775	59.4	40.6	26.9	4.7	1 414	63.6
Hancock	25	-40.2	102	0.1	4.8	403 952	3 964	38 907	2.7	10 988	D	D	27.4	1.6	175	14.1
Harrison	24	12.6	73	0.1	5.6	452 586	6 199	37 532	3.4	10 417	45.8	54.2	19.6	2.1	63	6.9
Hinds	251	-3.5	240	0.5	61.8	549 542	2 292	58 127	73.4	70 106	34.0	66.0	22.0	3.2	3 055	41.2
Holmes	238	4.2	447	51.1	119.8	938 991	2 098	99 501	93.4	175 972	97.7	2.3	25.4	9.8	5 781	66.9
Humphreys	194	-0.5	740	82.7	161.4	1 633 874	2 209	292 195	132.7	506 458	87.2	12.8	55.7	42.4	5 952	84.0
Issaquena	124	2.7	1 282	19.7	75.2	2 458 216	1 917	298 340	53.3	549 691	D	D	52.6	36.1	2 396	88.7
Itawamba	95	1.7	214	0.0	30.2	429 835	2 007	59 011	17.6	39 623	67.5	32.5	29.3	5.9	786	48.8
Jackson	38	-9.3	92	0.2	14.3	347 257	3 778	60 181	14.4	35 164	87.3	12.7	22.0	3.2	277	8.8
Jasper	97	7.1	218	0.0	14.1	436 222	1 998	73 629	97.2	218 366	1.6	98.4	36.2	16.0	545	27.0
Jefferson	86	-14.7	310	0.6	29.9	655 975	2 119	67 863	31.7	114 484	46.7	53.3	32.1	10.8	815	37.5
Jefferson Davis	59	-13.2	175	0.3	10.6	347 445	1 985	54 522	36.0	106 831	4.9	95.1	30.3	7.7	460	36.5
Jones	126	14.7	136	0.4	25.5	433 357	3 189	62 438	217.0	234 063	2.2	97.8	37.6	19.2	1 212	21.6
Kemper	124	-9.1	328	0.1	18.0	569 079	1 738	52 138	20.5	54 119	9.1	90.9	31.2	4.5	619	28.6
Lafayette	109	-4.8	242	0.6	26.9	543 419	2 242	56 581	8.9	19 904	73.3	26.7	22.7	3.1	1 120	50.3
Lamar	64	-12.3	151	0.2	13.2	544 656	3 602	64 014	25.0	59 033	13.8	86.2	36.3	6.4	565	25.0
Lauderdale	69	-17.4	185	0.1	14.6	441 753	2 387	46 413	5.4	14 453	50.1	49.9	21.4	2.8	252	17.2
Lawrence	73	-9.1	183	D	18.2	492 441	2 689	75 239	79.4	199 970	7.3	92.7	40.8	10.3	804	35.5
Leake	106	-16.7	167	0.1	22.6	446 077	2 678	58 912	283.3	444 706	0.9	99.1	38.9	21.4	711	34.5
Lee	133	-9.2	253	0.4	84.7	484 651	1 913	65 162	45.0	85 766	89.3	10.7	31.0	6.9	880	39.2
Leflore	293	-6.9	977	164.1	235.8	1 970 613	2 017	381 793	241.9	806 193	78.3	21.7	55.0	41.0	7 438	81.3
Lincoln	109	-12.8	183	0.2	20.1	547 086	2 997	65 555	69.9	117 405	4.6	95.4	37.3	9.2	615	25.7
Lowndes	119	-8.3	289	4.8	57.3	613 637	2 122	89 651	43.1	104 276	62.2	37.8	33.9	12.1	1 478	47.7
Madison	203	-8.8	296	0.1	68.6	776 399	2 619	67 238	33.3	48 600	82.6	17.4	19.9	6.7	3 611	45.5
Marion	82	-11.3	148	D	18.2	438 998	2 966	75 457	97.3	176 281	2.1	97.9	28.4	13.0	1 259	37.9
Marshall	203	5.3	355	3.5	70.0	699 567	1 972	81 276	32.7	57 079	84.1	15.9	30.7	7.7	1 667	47.3
Monroe	228	14.8	314	0.5	99.6	549 209	1 749	77 127	55.2	76 070	82.2	17.8	28.0	9.6	2 655	54.8
Montgomery	97	-0.1	282	0.7	26.8	501 565	1 779	64 942	20.1	58 339	54.5	45.5	26.4	7.2	1 257	52.2
Neshoba	101	-16.0	150	0.0	20.6	461 393	3 081	79 096	246.5	364 069	0.9	99.1	43.7	21.9	249	16.2
Newton	109	-9.4	194	0.6	22.6	404 137	2 083	65 811	102.4	182 242	4.2	95.8	37.0	15.5	659	22.1
Noxubee	213	-3.8	377	17.3	105.9	815 425	2 161	147 076	140.3	248 235	48.3	51.7	49.7	31.5	2 547	59.6
Oktibbeha	105	3.3	260	0.3	21.7	573 619	2 203	56 042	15.1	37 674	15.0	85.0	24.9	4.7	912	37.8
Panola	273	1.1	366	30.4	134.8	704 463	1 924	87 615	71.9	96 451	91.6	8.4	31.3	9.8	5 745	61.9
Pearl River	118	-12.8	146	1.0	23.0	465 647	3 200	48 637	17.6	21 654	45.7	54.3	28.2	3.4	735	14.8
Perry	44	5.8	140	0.5	12.1	401 719	2 862	68 168	21.8	70 442	23.7	76.3	31.6	7.4	513	23.9
Pike	72	-1.9	136	0.1	14.6	481 913	3 552	55 004	74.4	140 021	2.3	97.7	32.8	7.7	984	38.4
Pontotoc	153	4.7	172	D	64.2	312 294	1 819	55 052	24.7	27 747	76.8	23.2	24.9	5.2	2 249	64.2
Prentiss	93	-8.1	185	0.0	38.4	290 214	1 569	45 899	15.5	30 835	83.6	16.4	23.6	5.6	966	69.4
Quitman	209	-5.3	601	68.7	155.8	1 210 934	2 014	188 674	85.1	245 130	D	D	38.6	24.5	8 654	91.4
Rankin	126	-10.3	188	0.0	28.5	561 387	2 990	65 404	111.2	165 990	8.2	91.8	32.4	12.2	829	20.4
Scott	115	-9.2	161	0.1	27.8	406 497	2 528	85 180	270.8	378 270	1.7	98.3	41.3	16.9	476	20.3
Sharkey	155	-13.5	1 214	61.0	135.2	2 782 797	2 292	455 836	108.2	844 969	96.1	3.9	61.7	45.3	3 767	88.3
Simpson	110	-6.9	181	1.2	28.2	495 135	2 739	80 403	202.4	334 068	3.4	96.6	44.2	21.5	396	16.7
Smith	108	-1.3	170	0.1	26.2	502 821	2 956	74 466	251.1	394 133	3.0	97.0	49.1	25.9	427	11.8
Stone	46	-11.9	169	0.1	7.5	615 882	3 655	58 841	10.7	39 410	D	D	32.5	2.6	298	18.1

Table B. States and Counties — Water Use, Wholesale Trade, Retail Trade, and Real Estate

STATE County	Water use, 2010		Wholesale trade,[1] 2012				Retail trade,[2] 2012				Real estate and rental and leasing,[2] 2012			
	Total water withdrawn (mil gal/day)	Gallons withdrawn per person per day	Number of establishments	Number of employees	Sales (mil dol)	Annual payroll (mil dol)	Number of establishments	Number of employees	Sales (mil dol)	Annual payroll (mil dol)	Number of establishments	Number of employees	Receipts (mil dol)	Annual payroll (mil dol)
	133	134	135	136	137	138	139	140	141	142	143	144	145	146
MISSISSIPPI	3 933.0	1 325	2 484	30 351	28 303.0	1 373.6	11 594	136 032	37 053.2	2 968.4	2 374	10 235	1 709.3	334.1
Adams	7.5	233	35	265	169.6	10.0	176	2 119	488.7	47.6	36	135	17.6	3.9
Alcorn	6.7	182	35	D	D	D	172	2 119	538.0	49.0	23	225	12.2	3.8
Amite	2.2	165	7	62	14.0	1.5	30	162	39.2	3.5	3	4	0.5	0.1
Attala	4.5	231	13	D	D	D	78	807	192.5	15.5	10	29	3.8	0.8
Benton	2.5	290	NA	NA	NA	NA	16	112	24.4	2.5	NA	NA	NA	NA
Bolivar	440.8	12 910	29	329	763.8	15.0	161	1 535	371.2	31.5	45	126	18.6	3.2
Calhoun	2.8	188	14	175	81.1	5.2	58	401	95.2	8.1	4	10	0.7	0.3
Carroll	8.0	757	4	D	D	D	15	87	22.1	1.5	1	D	D	D
Chickasaw	9.7	558	15	90	69.8	3.1	83	687	153.4	11.7	8	17	2.6	0.5
Choctaw	15.0	1 755	2	D	D	D	27	152	25.1	2.7	1	D	D	D
Claiborne	35.9	3 742	1	D	D	D	24	152	35.3	3.4	NA	NA	NA	NA
Clarke	2.8	166	4	D	D	D	51	322	63.6	5.5	2	D	D	D
Clay	4.2	203	12	119	158.4	5.8	78	792	165.4	15.2	8	20	3.5	0.6
Coahoma	164.0	6 271	28	D	D	D	117	1 043	295.4	24.6	42	255	23.4	5.0
Copiah	10.2	347	15	87	46.3	2.8	83	834	181.5	15.7	8	75	5.0	1.6
Covington	6.3	319	12	68	116.9	2.4	68	522	188.3	12.1	8	27	3.2	0.5
DeSoto	35.7	221	120	2 840	3 232.4	127.2	495	7 957	2 320.9	193.3	97	331	83.8	11.6
Forrest	18.4	245	86	857	574.3	32.9	367	4 470	3 680.2	107.7	92	377	66.1	12.8
Franklin	1.3	158	4	D	D	D	17	113	29.0	2.4	4	30	1.1	0.8
George	3.5	154	11	75	54.2	2.5	77	900	229.5	17.2	6	D	D	D
Greene	8.3	575	3	D	D	D	26	211	48.3	3.9	3	11	0.6	0.1
Grenada	11.9	545	28	D	D	D	120	1 305	415.1	32.2	17	61	13.0	2.4
Hancock	8.2	187	15	64	10.3	3.3	126	1 328	346.2	30.2	28	90	10.0	2.3
Harrison	158.3	846	161	1 537	664.4	65.1	805	10 872	2 859.1	243.0	249	1 100	210.9	35.5
Hinds	60.5	247	270	3 476	2 274.4	166.5	869	11 093	3 072.3	276.4	278	1 544	319.8	66.3
Holmes	36.1	1 880	8	26	32.7	1.0	66	467	98.1	8.9	13	29	2.8	0.4
Humphreys	105.1	11 214	4	D	D	D	34	288	100.4	6.9	2	D	D	D
Issaquena	34.3	24 403	2	D	D	D	NA	NA	NA	NA	NA	NA	NA	NA
Itawamba	11.4	485	8	138	41.9	4.6	70	614	157.1	13.2	4	10	0.7	0.2
Jackson	520.3	3 725	60	564	236.3	22.5	426	4 828	1 220.5	109.0	98	424	49.4	12.7
Jasper	11.1	650	5	D	D	D	39	360	73.0	7.8	5	47	5.2	1.2
Jefferson	1.2	155	NA	NA	NA	NA	14	108	22.0	1.5	1	D	D	D
Jefferson Davis	5.7	460	2	D	D	D	39	207	61.6	4.4	2	D	D	D
Jones	16.4	241	75	D	D	D	241	3 000	796.4	61.7	54	228	64.8	13.0
Kemper	2.3	218	3	D	D	D	25	156	37.8	2.8	4	D	D	D
Lafayette	5.6	118	31	249	161.2	9.1	211	2 576	548.8	53.2	43	97	24.5	3.3
Lamar	12.1	218	36	D	D	D	282	4 802	1 041.4	86.7	61	D	D	D
Lauderdale	11.9	148	78	1 649	1 701.4	74.1	406	5 061	1 488.2	113.4	75	266	58.2	7.9
Lawrence	37.7	2 914	1	D	D	D	36	342	62.5	6.1	1	D	D	D
Leake	5.9	249	6	60	16.9	1.8	78	776	173.0	15.9	4	6	0.2	0.1
Lee	5.2	63	153	1 526	1 049.1	63.6	510	7 242	1 628.1	154.7	96	413	76.0	12.7
Leflore	200.8	6 214	31	D	D	D	154	1 637	465.6	36.2	42	D	D	D
Lincoln	7.4	211	31	D	D	D	159	1 783	540.6	40.8	26	86	13.8	2.9
Lowndes	41.0	685	80	D	D	D	311	3 578	736.5	73.2	63	186	26.3	4.8
Madison	15.1	159	135	2 220	4 549.4	118.2	497	6 698	1 616.9	148.1	139	909	133.7	32.4
Marion	5.1	187	16	163	121.6	5.1	134	1 182	280.1	25.6	25	110	18.3	3.6
Marshall	4.7	126	17	180	96.9	9.5	95	881	185.4	16.8	9	16	1.8	0.3
Monroe	25.0	675	18	182	150.2	8.0	136	1 213	259.2	22.9	14	51	6.0	1.6
Montgomery	1.9	170	3	D	D	D	51	478	144.4	9.0	4	18	1.7	0.4
Neshoba	4.6	156	20	277	448.0	13.2	110	1 180	288.5	25.0	11	256	9.3	6.8
Newton	4.2	194	8	39	8.0	1.1	70	707	137.4	14.2	5	12	1.9	0.2
Noxubee	22.3	1 931	10	80	58.4	1.8	43	320	93.5	7.0	NA	NA	NA	NA
Oktibbeha	6.1	128	15	436	187.3	17.5	163	1 924	472.0	38.3	59	178	30.5	4.8
Panola	36.4	1 049	31	536	576.6	24.2	170	1 555	471.8	33.0	15	66	10.0	2.1
Pearl River	7.2	129	25	D	D	D	172	1 793	477.3	43.4	19	52	7.7	1.1
Perry	22.6	1 842	4	D	D	D	34	250	62.4	4.4	3	D	D	D
Pike	9.4	232	52	383	206.4	13.9	223	2 458	603.8	51.1	39	140	27.1	3.6
Pontotoc	4.1	137	16	148	65.2	3.9	88	950	259.3	19.6	8	18	1.9	0.3
Prentiss	3.7	148	15	72	11.5	1.2	103	948	189.1	17.1	32	61	7.6	1.2
Quitman	135.1	16 431	4	D	D	D	23	128	28.6	2.3	6	D	D	D
Rankin	19.8	140	224	3 551	2 354.5	186.9	509	8 324	2 361.2	190.2	167	818	143.3	28.9
Scott	10.6	374	17	72	56.4	2.3	126	1 188	243.8	23.6	9	35	4.0	1.0
Sharkey	69.6	14 164	9	82	86.7	3.4	24	174	31.5	3.1	13	24	2.7	0.4
Simpson	5.8	210	13	79	27.0	2.6	90	1 020	234.7	20.5	12	41	5.8	1.0
Smith	4.9	298	5	42	15.5	1.2	35	210	47.2	4.0	NA	NA	NA	NA
Stone	4.8	269	10	29	10.9	1.0	54	582	166.6	13.4	8	22	1.5	0.3

1. Merchant wholesalers, except manufacturers' sales branches and offices. 2. Employer establishments.

Professional Services, Manufacturing, and Accommodation and Food Services

STATE County	Professional, scientific, and technical services, 2012				Manufacturing, 2012				Accommodation and food services, 2012			
	Number of establish-ments	Number of employees	Receipts (mil dol)	Annual payroll (mil dol)	Number of establish-ments	Number of employees	Receipts (mil dol)	Annual payroll (mil dol)	Number of establish-ments	Number of employees	Sales (mil dol)	Annual payroll (mil dol)
	147	148	149	150	151	152	153	154	155	156	157	158
MISSISSIPPI	4 747	30 205	4 023.3	1 449.9	2 252	132 789	66 441.6	5 919.1	5 177	116 238	6 999.2	1 765.0
Adams	52	225	24.8	8.8	18	650	155.0	27.4	89	1 698	89.3	24.0
Alcorn	51	358	27.0	11.2	41	2 118	1 092.7	89.7	69	1 200	55.3	17.0
Amite	9	23	1.6	0.5	6	177	48.3	7.8	3	24	1.4	0.4
Attala	28	62	7.0	2.3	18	656	175.6	20.3	23	D	D	D
Benton	2	D	D	D	6	151	D	5.4	NA	NA	NA	NA
Bolivar	44	173	20.6	7.3	18	1 458	405.8	65.4	53	911	39.4	9.4
Calhoun	18	26	2.3	0.7	18	883	271.1	29.0	10	D	D	D
Carroll	8	16	2.4	0.7	NA	NA	NA	NA	3	16	0.3	0.1
Chickasaw	15	63	4.5	1.7	44	2 817	483.8	87.7	20	D	D	D
Choctaw	8	16	1.5	0.6	6	205	56.8	7.8	8	D	D	D
Claiborne	7	13	1.3	0.3	4	83	D	3.3	11	153	7.7	1.7
Clarke	11	D	D	D	16	494	D	16.1	13	D	D	D
Clay	22	247	20.3	9.7	20	704	656.6	37.9	37	499	22.6	5.9
Coahoma	41	202	31.5	9.9	19	757	288.4	28.5	46	1 244	82.3	20.3
Copiah	28	103	12.1	3.3	20	2 106	626.8	67.6	34	436	16.8	4.1
Covington	18	87	4.3	1.8	11	1 337	432.0	35.0	31	D	D	D
DeSoto	183	989	99.0	27.1	102	3 453	1 269.5	157.5	292	6 498	311.3	80.7
Forrest	187	998	116.5	42.2	64	3 248	942.4	123.6	186	4 332	181.0	50.5
Franklin	9	37	2.6	1.5	3	D	D	D	5	17	0.5	0.1
George	17	100	8.7	2.7	15	300	D	22.1	26	378	15.4	3.6
Greene	4	9	1.0	0.5	4	12	D	0.4	7	D	D	D
Grenada	30	182	21.0	9.4	28	2 239	717.9	90.9	59	940	42.0	10.1
Hancock	96	2 163	316.6	135.0	31	819	D	58.5	86	D	D	D
Harrison	388	2 313	296.4	103.5	109	3 179	1 989.8	163.3	447	18 209	1 537.7	378.0
Hinds	657	5 244	815.6	320.2	131	3 730	1 374.4	183.1	473	9 261	475.6	126.7
Holmes	14	40	7.6	1.8	4	436	D	11.7	16	122	5.5	1.5
Humphreys	5	8	1.2	0.2	4	D	D	D	9	116	4.3	1.0
Issaquena	NA	NA	NA	NA	NA	NA	NA	NA	NA	NA	NA	NA
Itawamba	12	30	3.8	0.9	42	1 542	930.6	50.7	27	404	17.2	4.7
Jackson	208	1 545	179.8	74.1	75	15 152	D	1 119.9	256	D	D	D
Jasper	17	85	9.2	3.4	16	1 599	327.7	52.4	9	25	0.9	0.3
Jefferson	NA	NA	NA	NA	NA	NA	NA	NA	5	111	4.7	1.1
Jefferson Davis	13	22	2.5	0.8	4	13	D	D	10	D	D	D
Jones	95	456	57.2	17.4	61	6 427	1 656.1	245.6	101	D	D	D
Kemper	5	D	D	D	8	415	D	11.2	12	D	D	D
Lafayette	115	924	167.9	52.6	20	1 248	167.6	59.8	128	2 797	135.6	36.9
Lamar	115	740	94.0	35.9	20	177	D	5.8	121	2 475	118.1	31.9
Lauderdale	141	1 063	98.7	40.7	58	2 141	779.4	82.0	175	3 628	174.0	45.7
Lawrence	10	13	1.8	0.4	8	646	D	49.1	11	102	4.0	1.0
Leake	15	40	4.2	1.2	7	D	D	D	22	D	D	D
Lee	187	1 105	109.8	46.2	134	9 087	3 414.0	372.8	205	4 596	199.3	55.5
Leflore	45	317	46.2	13.1	29	D	D	D	73	1 285	63.4	16.6
Lincoln	57	265	42.5	13.1	33	1 189	D	53.2	61	984	43.6	10.8
Lowndes	102	514	54.5	26.2	66	4 223	3 543.9	231.2	121	2 163	98.5	26.6
Madison	367	2 907	546.2	180.0	63	5 749	4 568.0	338.7	239	4 681	230.1	60.9
Marion	46	236	22.2	9.1	18	508	75.1	17.3	45	507	22.4	5.5
Marshall	13	D	D	D	27	543	182.5	23.5	31	383	16.3	4.0
Monroe	33	94	11.5	2.5	51	2 356	1 592.6	104.8	47	D	D	D
Montgomery	9	32	3.2	0.7	9	268	D	10.1	21	D	D	D
Neshoba	28	168	22.4	9.1	12	529	175.3	21.6	42	640	27.1	6.6
Newton	21	38	3.9	1.5	15	1 077	D	43.3	26	D	D	D
Noxubee	5	21	1.2	0.2	19	475	139.0	15.6	9	148	6.1	1.7
Oktibbeha	76	441	46.1	15.1	23	1 210	569.1	55.3	108	2 744	125.2	32.8
Panola	31	139	21.1	4.2	31	1 579	631.5	70.7	53	901	42.7	11.2
Pearl River	56	347	28.3	12.9	42	562	224.1	26.2	86	1 158	49.0	13.4
Perry	7	39	4.4	2.1	7	645	D	41.3	6	43	1.9	0.5
Pike	69	291	27.5	11.9	29	2 287	514.9	69.1	76	1 478	68.5	16.2
Pontotoc	24	100	9.8	3.4	71	6 199	1 469.9	185.6	33	492	20.3	5.1
Prentiss	38	165	22.6	5.8	34	1 818	814.2	61.7	28	435	21.8	4.9
Quitman	4	D	D	D	NA	NA	NA	NA	6	D	D	D
Rankin	311	1 356	176.7	54.7	118	3 655	1 553.2	165.9	286	5 399	278.5	71.4
Scott	30	104	6.4	2.4	22	4 883	D	164.6	37	551	26.4	6.2
Sharkey	7	17	1.1	0.3	NA	NA	NA	NA	6	D	D	D
Simpson	27	106	10.0	3.6	11	249	D	8.8	39	599	31.7	6.7
Smith	12	126	11.5	1.7	14	886	321.1	37.3	7	D	D	D
Stone	23	91	6.6	2.4	12	593	251.9	25.3	32	440	21.0	5.2

1. Establishment subject to federal tax.

STATE County	Health care and social assistance, 2012				Other services, 2012				Nonemployer businesses, 2015		Value of residential construction authorized by building permits, 2016	
	Number of establishments	Number of employees	Receipts (mil dol)	Annual payroll (mil dol)	Number of establishments	Number of employees	Receipts (mil dol)	Annual payroll (mil dol)	Number	Receipts (mil dol)	New Construction ($1,000)	Number of housing units
	159	160	161	162	163	164	165	166	167	168	169	170
MISSISSIPPI	6 211	157 620	16 630.6	6 544.7	3 540	19 232	1 951.9	548.9	211 955	8 425.7	1 125 912	6 886
Adams	89	1 903	223.0	80.8	43	196	16.1	4.6	2 417	97.9	3 508	33
Alcorn	103	2 447	271.4	79.4	41	167	13.1	3.5	2 573	122.4	1 755	10
Amite	10	166	12.5	4.5	8	38	4.9	0.8	842	35.0	58	1
Attala	24	D	D	D	22	D	D	D	1 265	47.8	435	5
Benton	8	152	9.5	3.9	5	D	D	D	583	21.9	0	0
Bolivar	90	1 919	149.1	62.5	52	194	15.5	3.8	1 938	69.6	3 013	26
Calhoun	23	468	32.0	13.6	14	D	D	D	923	35.8	300	2
Carroll	5	88	5.5	2.1	7	11	0.9	0.2	662	26.3	NA	NA
Chickasaw	21	391	31.9	15.0	20	D	D	D	1 140	41.7	380	4
Choctaw	8	203	16.5	6.2	8	D	D	D	589	18.8	0	0
Claiborne	13	301	19.2	7.4	6	11	1.1	0.2	369	11.5	0	0
Clarke	18	421	32.9	13.0	17	D	D	D	1 002	36.3	280	2
Clay	27	696	62.2	25.8	26	113	9.0	2.5	1 298	47.7	1 899	12
Coahoma	82	1 733	184.7	66.0	34	131	8.0	2.2	1 770	57.1	2 614	16
Copiah	34	701	48.0	20.5	25	D	D	D	1 715	50.9	1 505	7
Covington	30	582	48.1	20.7	24	108	9.3	2.4	1 496	58.1	150	2
DeSoto	266	5 597	637.8	225.0	167	893	88.1	23.2	12 842	567.9	177 145	1 174
Forrest	202	7 779	873.5	421.1	100	648	54.6	15.5	5 334	224.5	13 542	165
Franklin	8	D	D	D	3	D	D	D	490	14.5	0	0
George	36	821	74.9	31.3	17	53	6.3	1.4	1 367	46.8	84	1
Greene	7	D	D	D	7	D	D	D	658	19.4	0	0
Grenada	74	1 323	115.4	45.4	27	103	10.8	2.5	1 337	50.1	1 335	8
Hancock	52	D	D	D	40	291	26.0	9.0	3 379	128.2	68 623	478
Harrison	460	12 318	1 560.5	648.9	271	1 604	155.7	42.7	14 263	577.8	145 382	915
Hinds	742	27 244	3 150.9	1 279.8	405	2 731	299.2	94.4	20 766	763.2	37 532	194
Holmes	35	395	26.9	10.8	12	191	6.2	2.1	1 190	32.4	796	9
Humphreys	20	242	19.7	7.7	11	36	2.0	0.6	599	18.8	0	0
Issaquena	1	D	D	D	NA	NA	NA	NA	73	2.0	NA	NA
Itawamba	29	D	D	D	19	D	D	D	1 301	55.3	495	4
Jackson	277	D	D	D	151	768	65.8	21.6	9 013	334.7	62 953	383
Jasper	12	299	20.5	8.9	11	D	D	D	1 000	30.2	0	0
Jefferson	14	305	19.6	9.1	5	D	D	D	559	12.0	0	0
Jefferson Davis	12	D	D	D	8	D	D	D	887	21.3	0	0
Jones	108	3 252	283.3	128.7	81	D	D	D	4 302	170.2	3 623	26
Kemper	10	249	14.5	6.9	3	D	D	D	563	12.7	NA	NA
Lafayette	126	2 671	363.2	110.3	63	397	87.9	19.1	4 084	225.0	62 915	410
Lamar	147	3 066	344.9	133.1	61	262	25.9	6.2	4 394	230.2	849	9
Lauderdale	222	7 919	883.6	347.0	131	663	63.0	16.1	5 070	173.0	13 628	67
Lawrence	20	192	14.0	4.8	7	27	3.8	1.0	769	26.4	35	1
Leake	25	598	36.8	16.0	11	40	3.5	1.1	1 192	40.8	0	0
Lee	284	7 976	1 089.4	387.2	128	1 144	105.3	41.5	6 062	265.5	27 435	226
Leflore	81	2 882	245.8	104.8	44	163	12.4	2.8	1 587	68.7	2 862	13
Lincoln	70	1 784	181.2	61.2	48	290	24.6	8.9	2 429	94.0	3 313	12
Lowndes	158	2 949	323.8	111.7	87	462	42.4	11.5	3 875	134.6	12 808	125
Madison	262	4 940	339.3	129.9	156	1 298	151.4	48.5	10 623	624.5	182 743	714
Marion	45	940	63.9	25.3	26	113	10.6	2.8	1 937	64.4	1 348	12
Marshall	28	1 405	90.8	30.3	29	193	19.3	5.5	2 725	108.4	18 741	149
Monroe	78	1 773	153.8	58.3	42	102	11.3	2.6	1 953	78.5	395	3
Montgomery	20	D	D	D	18	70	5.7	1.4	599	19.6	2 029	75
Neshoba	40	1 070	102.3	43.5	36	146	13.4	3.2	1 803	58.4	141	1
Newton	25	702	57.3	19.6	19	57	4.3	1.0	1 256	44.2	0	0
Noxubee	13	293	22.5	9.9	10	19	1.9	0.4	1 004	28.1	0	0
Oktibbeha	90	1 733	158.0	63.7	64	325	65.7	6.4	3 005	111.0	16 595	87
Panola	67	1 416	136.4	48.9	22	72	7.7	1.7	2 775	90.0	1 480	11
Pearl River	101	1 041	73.9	32.7	49	328	20.7	8.3	4 052	150.4	25 758	220
Perry	19	263	19.3	7.8	7	33	2.6	0.8	737	29.9	0	0
Pike	125	2 758	280.6	119.4	56	299	22.0	6.2	3 154	99.9	16 871	190
Pontotoc	39	D	D	D	32	D	D	D	1 956	85.2	2 751	45
Prentiss	42	858	65.4	25.7	29	101	9.8	2.1	1 569	51.4	1 206	17
Quitman	14	283	15.7	7.5	9	D	D	D	545	13.4	204	1
Rankin	316	8 559	1 023.6	371.7	214	1 114	125.0	35.2	12 224	557.9	160 854	719
Scott	34	D	D	D	39	95	9.7	2.4	1 564	51.5	1 115	7
Sharkey	12	219	18.9	8.0	11	59	7.0	1.1	394	12.4	800	2
Simpson	51	2 448	150.8	64.9	26	D	D	D	1 888	77.0	5 436	28
Smith	8	221	10.8	4.8	8	22	2.3	0.5	968	33.7	263	3
Stone	22	498	42.5	16.7	9	D	D	D	1 179	46.9	6 918	52

Table B. States and Counties — Government Employment and Payroll, and Local Government Finances

STATE County	Full-time equivalent employees	March payroll (dollars)	Administration, judicial, and legal	Police and Corrections	Fire Protection	Highways and transportation	Health and Welfare	Natural resources and utilities	Education and libraries	Total (mil dol)	Intergovernmental (mil dol)	Total (mil dol)	Per capita[1] (dollars) Total	Per capita[1] (dollars) Property
	171	172	173	174	175	176	177	178	179	180	181	182	183	184
MISSISSIPPI	X	X	X	X	X	X	X	X	X	X	X	X	X	X
Adams	1 489	4 260 491	9.2	8.0	2.4	5.1	26.3	5.5	41.4	139.6	46.8	32.7	1 016	894
Alcorn	2 243	7 489 226	3.0	3.6	1.7	1.3	54.6	4.0	31.8	263.0	70.9	24.2	650	610
Amite	299	736 289	14.3	7.8	0.1	5.8	2.2	1.8	66.9	23.6	11.3	6.5	502	498
Attala	932	2 477 820	6.6	4.7	2.3	3.4	21.1	4.4	56.3	69.8	32.7	16.3	850	818
Benton	295	719 394	10.6	6.4	0.0	3.6	0.4	1.7	76.1	18.5	13.0	3.5	406	392
Bolivar	1 582	4 628 258	5.5	13.0	0.3	4.9	0.3	3.0	72.0	119.8	63.2	35.1	1 036	985
Calhoun	797	2 771 233	3.3	2.8	0.0	1.3	49.8	1.3	39.9	46.2	18.3	8.5	575	564
Carroll	314	861 917	13.2	17.2	0.2	6.8	1.7	0.3	60.4	21.1	8.8	6.4	617	604
Chickasaw	881	2 154 461	7.6	9.3	1.7	3.6	8.8	5.2	62.6	53.0	32.3	11.7	673	613
Choctaw	408	952 647	11.6	4.1	0.2	1.9	1.6	2.0	76.1	22.8	12.4	4.5	537	521
Claiborne	496	1 465 091	5.5	6.2	1.5	4.2	22.1	1.6	57.8	34.3	20.9	6.0	640	605
Clarke	690	1 711 804	10.0	5.8	0.8	4.0	1.9	7.4	68.8	41.5	20.7	15.2	917	894
Clay	763	1 943 802	4.0	6.9	4.0	3.4	11.5	2.8	66.9	50.0	29.0	16.2	791	775
Coahoma	1 488	4 098 825	5.5	7.7	3.1	2.8	0.4	13.9	66.3	114.9	75.2	21.5	837	778
Copiah	1 481	4 154 517	5.1	5.7	0.7	2.2	11.5	2.3	72.0	103.1	56.6	17.6	609	584
Covington	1 021	2 828 948	4.9	4.0	0.1	11.3	32.9	1.7	44.1	78.2	25.0	13.0	663	643
DeSoto	5 452	16 140 720	6.4	11.9	7.2	2.5	2.2	3.5	65.3	471.9	208.5	194.3	1 169	1 065
Forrest	6 510	21 206 976	3.1	4.5	2.3	1.8	60.8	2.2	24.8	662.3	117.6	91.2	1 187	1 057
Franklin	363	888 524	9.6	4.0	0.0	5.2	1.8	1.0	78.1	35.6	14.5	5.9	746	704
George	1 085	2 865 559	4.2	7.1	0.4	2.7	30.9	0.7	53.5	89.3	31.9	12.7	553	528
Greene	532	1 305 598	6.9	3.9	0.0	3.1	15.5	1.6	67.6	37.4	20.6	9.4	654	637
Grenada	1 382	4 096 902	5.7	4.4	2.9	2.1	40.8	1.9	40.3	116.3	39.5	20.6	949	909
Hancock	1 924	6 676 661	5.8	6.9	3.4	2.2	23.0	4.5	52.3	287.9	169.1	47.6	1 052	1 011
Harrison	8 736	32 935 719	4.4	8.9	5.2	4.2	30.6	3.3	42.1	1 243.7	542.0	244.1	1 258	1 055
Hinds	10 525	28 655 948	5.9	10.5	4.8	2.2	1.5	4.8	70.4	878.7	450.7	268.0	1 078	1 017
Holmes	1 272	3 625 794	5.9	6.2	0.7	2.4	0.9	1.6	81.9	86.9	59.2	11.7	625	598
Humphreys	384	897 846	4.1	7.0	1.7	2.5	13.2	3.0	68.3	30.0	17.0	9.1	991	961
Issaquena	19	50 080	41.5	24.8	0.0	24.5	6.1	1.7	0.0	5.7	0.8	1.6	1 159	1 141
Itawamba	1 223	4 512 156	2.7	2.6	0.2	1.5	0.6	1.9	90.4	109.5	57.9	13.4	576	538
Jackson	7 975	28 632 767	3.0	5.8	2.5	2.0	45.3	2.4	38.2	857.2	237.3	174.7	1 245	1 188
Jasper	861	2 242 650	7.4	4.2	0.0	4.5	26.0	3.0	54.5	55.7	24.4	18.0	1 092	1 057
Jefferson	478	1 235 476	6.8	10.4	0.0	2.4	29.1	1.1	48.4	43.5	13.0	6.2	816	767
Jefferson Davis	567	1 467 224	8.3	4.6	0.9	4.0	30.4	1.6	49.8	39.7	17.1	8.1	672	658
Jones	4 753	12 100 544	2.7	3.7	2.3	2.1	35.5	1.9	50.3	341.0	127.5	54.3	791	752
Kemper	712	2 430 022	3.8	6.4	0.1	2.1	1.0	0.6	85.7	67.6	39.0	6.3	610	594
Lafayette	1 452	4 109 506	5.9	10.5	4.9	4.1	3.5	5.7	63.4	177.9	50.8	51.3	1 036	964
Lamar	2 053	4 821 922	4.0	6.2	0.6	4.8	0.9	0.5	81.5	123.2	59.9	53.4	924	906
Lauderdale	3 227	9 470 298	9.1	5.9	3.6	6.1	0.0	4.9	68.9	246.0	129.7	76.1	949	901
Lawrence	479	1 248 756	9.0	6.6	0.7	3.8	1.7	1.5	76.3	29.2	16.0	11.0	873	858
Leake	684	1 880 375	16.5	12.0	1.7	3.7	1.5	2.2	61.0	53.2	27.1	11.1	478	447
Lee	4 000	11 007 645	6.2	9.1	3.5	3.3	2.8	6.2	68.2	257.6	136.9	85.3	1 003	974
Leflore	2 494	8 995 576	3.1	4.0	1.8	1.7	57.3	2.3	29.6	240.0	68.2	28.3	913	861
Lincoln	1 177	3 186 542	7.5	6.9	3.7	3.9	0.6	2.4	74.6	84.1	45.5	26.5	760	721
Lowndes	2 233	7 025 354	8.5	12.2	3.9	4.4	1.2	8.3	59.4	183.3	105.0	53.8	901	845
Madison	2 936	9 496 425	7.8	11.0	5.2	3.3	1.3	2.9	67.0	279.8	105.3	131.7	1 337	1 266
Marion	1 327	2 909 454	6.2	11.0	1.8	3.7	1.7	1.0	73.2	79.0	36.5	17.5	662	635
Marshall	1 090	3 348 828	7.9	14.8	1.8	9.2	0.0	8.4	56.4	69.4	40.2	23.0	629	608
Monroe	1 425	3 622 413	13.2	8.0	3.4	7.1	1.1	4.6	60.5	97.7	48.7	27.8	764	733
Montgomery	546	1 639 820	6.9	4.5	1.6	3.8	37.3	2.7	42.6	35.2	16.1	7.1	672	642
Neshoba	938	2 330 410	5.2	9.8	3.5	4.9	0.8	6.3	69.2	84.7	35.9	14.6	489	471
Newton	1 105	3 232 369	4.5	4.7	0.6	1.9	0.9	5.5	81.6	80.7	53.7	13.3	616	581
Noxubee	657	1 978 193	6.6	1.5	0.5	2.2	28.3	0.4	59.1	39.8	18.4	8.4	752	729
Oktibbeha	1 842	5 582 328	2.8	4.7	3.1	1.1	47.2	4.4	36.2	155.8	47.9	35.8	744	726
Panola	1 433	4 200 779	4.8	10.0	2.0	2.8	2.1	3.6	74.4	97.6	58.1	28.7	832	760
Pearl River	2 574	7 161 607	5.5	5.4	1.8	2.1	8.1	3.0	73.4	183.3	100.0	38.8	702	666
Perry	466	1 122 268	9.5	5.9	0.4	5.6	1.3	2.1	74.8	33.9	18.6	9.5	788	759
Pike	2 872	9 325 024	3.8	4.6	1.6	1.6	46.9	2.2	38.5	249.1	83.4	32.7	816	780
Pontotoc	982	3 251 798	6.3	8.7	2.5	3.4	1.2	4.1	73.1	74.0	42.6	18.2	594	546
Prentiss	1 158	3 605 727	3.3	4.8	2.1	1.8	1.3	1.1	85.6	87.2	54.3	15.2	598	572
Quitman	519	1 364 995	6.8	5.4	0.1	5.5	31.8	1.2	49.1	23.7	13.9	7.2	919	878
Rankin	4 244	12 845 764	5.1	11.8	6.8	3.4	0.1	3.9	68.2	344.6	160.2	130.8	901	859
Scott	1 071	2 578 316	6.0	10.4	1.4	2.8	0.9	4.7	73.7	65.2	39.7	17.6	624	583
Sharkey	279	713 380	12.1	7.5	0.1	4.4	1.2	10.7	63.5	17.4	9.5	5.1	1 064	1 028
Simpson	898	2 221 618	6.8	8.7	0.2	5.6	1.2	1.8	73.3	56.8	33.6	17.5	639	614
Smith	568	1 449 509	9.4	8.8	0.0	4.1	1.0	2.8	73.8	37.3	21.8	10.9	667	654
Stone	1 427	5 071 678	2.8	2.3	0.5	0.8	0.4	0.4	92.7	126.2	75.9	12.5	691	645

1. Based on the resident population estimated as of July 1 of the year shown.

Table B. States and Counties — Local Government Finances, Government Employment, and Income Taxes

STATE County	Total (mil dol)	Per capita[1] (dollars)	Education	Health and hospitals	Police protection	Public welfare	Highways	Total (mil dol)	Per capita[1] (dollars)	Federal civilian	Federal military	State and local	Number of returns	Mean adjusted gross income	Mean income tax
	185	186	187	188	189	190	191	192	193	194	195	196	197	198	199
MISSISSIPPI	X	X	X	X	X	X	X	X	X	25 295	27 515	221 679	1 243 270	46 825	4 935
Adams	139.6	4 345	30.8	31.5	5.2	0.2	5.9	55.9	1 739	110	174	1 419	12 770	47 301	5 541
Alcorn	255.2	6 866	20.1	53.1	2.1	0.1	2.6	317.3	8 537	92	220	2 969	13 680	43 274	4 267
Amite	19.7	1 524	56.2	1.8	6.7	0.0	13.8	0.3	25	31	75	401	4 930	46 140	4 543
Attala	75.3	3 933	38.1	28.5	2.8	0.2	5.1	32.6	1 702	55	112	1 101	7 460	40 642	3 391
Benton	19.4	2 227	67.1	0.9	4.4	0.2	12.1	3.9	444	44	49	334	3 150	33 022	2 192
Bolivar	121.4	3 582	53.7	4.8	5.9	0.2	8.4	52.7	1 553	72	190	2 672	13 760	41 314	3 973
Calhoun	49.9	3 364	39.2	32.8	3.2	0.1	5.9	14.4	971	34	87	814	5 670	35 527	2 649
Carroll	20.6	1 974	43.6	0.9	2.8	0.0	14.4	13.5	1 292	20	59	347	4 180	46 315	4 476
Chickasaw	52.1	2 994	52.7	1.8	5.1	8.9	7.0	31.3	1 795	43	101	886	7 480	34 761	2 783
Choctaw	30.5	3 651	50.2	10.5	5.3	0.1	10.2	32.0	3 838	34	49	697	3 370	37 289	2 527
Claiborne	35.4	3 783	50.8	3.0	3.9	0.2	5.8	129.3	13 835	27	48	1 698	3 560	31 454	2 270
Clarke	40.6	2 452	65.6	0.9	5.4	0.1	8.0	10.9	661	33	96	788	6 630	45 956	4 245
Clay	52.7	2 577	56.9	0.6	7.8	0.6	8.0	34.3	1 677	57	119	871	8 400	39 040	4 006
Coahoma	119.1	4 634	63.3	0.9	4.4	0.0	4.0	151.1	5 877	59	144	1 930	10 150	36 442	3 678
Copiah	112.0	3 869	65.2	13.0	4.2	0.0	7.0	26.9	930	72	167	1 595	11 700	37 768	2 942
Covington	69.3	3 537	37.9	38.8	3.9	0.1	7.3	13.5	688	66	116	1 257	8 070	39 655	3 443
DeSoto	452.7	2 723	48.5	1.1	8.4	0.0	5.1	539.6	3 246	213	1 039	6 515	77 470	52 345	5 248
Forrest	657.8	8 555	16.6	64.3	2.3	0.0	3.0	378.3	4 920	739	845	10 985	32 020	48 698	6 098
Franklin	33.3	4 206	42.1	31.8	4.6	0.0	7.5	3.6	454	55	46	612	3 140	45 413	4 211
George	87.3	3 806	33.7	44.6	2.8	0.1	6.5	28.7	1 250	42	137	1 419	8 880	49 072	4 222
Greene	39.0	2 727	52.3	0.8	6.9	16.0	9.3	7.5	522	14	67	1 104	4 300	47 880	3 817
Grenada	114.7	5 290	29.2	42.6	4.9	0.0	4.5	98.3	4 534	233	128	1 683	9 480	41 485	3 946
Hancock	284.4	6 285	23.0	16.2	2.7	0.1	4.9	96.7	2 137	1 951	763	2 017	18 200	46 891	4 887
Harrison	1 263.3	6 511	21.1	29.5	4.6	0.2	4.8	919.9	4 741	5 668	7 792	13 218	87 110	44 471	4 595
Hinds	892.8	3 591	57.8	0.8	5.7	0.3	4.2	1 035.1	4 163	4 820	1 472	35 487	108 400	45 013	5 066
Holmes	104.3	5 551	78.5	1.3	3.6	0.2	4.5	35.2	1 870	52	105	1 241	7 550	28 147	1 571
Humphreys	30.1	3 277	50.7	1.4	6.0	0.1	15.6	10.5	1 144	19	52	491	3 470	34 702	3 905
Issaquena	5.9	4 234	0.9	5.4	10.5	0.0	13.4	1.8	1 275	D	D	91	460	37 372	2 996
Itawamba	111.8	4 790	82.2	0.5	2.0	0.0	3.7	48.6	2 082	43	136	1 094	9 340	41 715	3 371
Jackson	885.7	6 313	30.2	41.1	3.1	0.1	3.7	521.2	3 715	1 103	1 023	8 670	61 280	50 189	5 226
Jasper	52.0	3 145	47.2	13.8	3.9	0.1	13.0	21.9	1 327	50	99	905	7 080	41 924	3 822
Jefferson	38.6	5 053	32.5	24.2	4.3	10.8	4.1	5.0	653	18	46	684	3 250	31 718	2 001
Jefferson Davis	43.5	3 615	47.4	27.4	3.9	0.0	7.0	9.1	759	25	69	633	4 990	36 194	2 795
Jones	365.6	5 326	40.2	37.4	2.4	0.8	3.6	230.8	3 362	217	399	7 071	27 870	47 281	4 930
Kemper	67.4	6 517	80.0	0.6	1.8	0.1	3.5	9.1	878	32	54	645	3 740	32 919	2 260
Lafayette	126.1	2 548	52.3	0.9	7.5	0.0	9.3	146.9	2 968	326	303	7 605	19 160	60 954	8 201
Lamar	128.5	2 224	68.5	0.7	6.9	0.2	7.3	76.2	1 319	45	363	2 338	24 260	62 185	7 986
Lauderdale	232.7	2 900	60.0	3.5	5.9	0.0	5.1	138.1	1 722	830	1 360	5 194	32 130	48 924	5 625
Lawrence	30.1	2 396	64.4	1.7	4.0	0.4	8.9	8.0	634	40	76	689	4 930	47 385	4 150
Leake	54.6	2 344	49.9	15.0	4.7	0.0	8.2	21.7	931	60	127	778	8 540	40 032	3 230
Lee	265.1	3 118	54.1	0.9	7.2	0.2	8.9	210.0	2 470	452	507	5 011	37 090	51 754	6 144
Leflore	246.7	7 972	21.8	53.9	3.5	0.0	2.9	171.6	5 546	108	173	4 123	12 270	38 027	4 324
Lincoln	82.3	2 359	58.3	1.7	7.0	0.0	9.8	29.6	848	94	204	1 716	13 690	49 558	4 902
Lowndes	180.6	3 026	47.7	0.8	6.3	0.1	7.7	210.1	3 521	816	1 652	3 410	25 160	48 959	5 301
Madison	302.7	3 074	49.9	0.4	6.9	0.1	12.3	478.1	4 855	215	612	4 570	47 630	78 563	12 441
Marion	79.2	2 994	45.6	21.5	5.3	0.0	4.2	27.0	1 020	47	149	1 372	9 890	45 980	4 482
Marshall	73.1	1 995	56.1	1.7	6.9	0.1	12.7	20.0	545	74	205	1 190	15 310	36 077	2 843
Monroe	96.6	2 653	58.9	1.2	7.3	0.4	7.6	47.3	1 299	128	213	1 414	14 670	41 243	3 677
Montgomery	37.1	3 497	42.0	24.7	4.2	0.3	9.9	11.3	1 062	26	60	592	4 210	38 564	3 053
Neshoba	87.8	2 947	41.8	32.2	3.5	0.0	5.2	30.9	1 037	84	175	6 178	11 670	41 663	3 773
Newton	81.2	3 757	66.9	1.0	5.1	0.0	5.2	11.7	539	73	127	2 030	8 880	41 090	3 242
Noxubee	40.0	3 569	46.0	25.3	3.7	0.1	6.1	6.0	537	38	65	730	4 760	29 644	1 900
Oktibbeha	178.0	3 694	32.7	38.4	3.7	0.0	4.9	104.4	2 167	248	282	9 886	17 960	48 094	5 198
Panola	102.7	2 980	56.0	1.3	6.9	0.2	7.0	38.1	1 104	108	204	2 181	14 330	38 095	3 605
Pearl River	195.3	3 533	60.8	8.4	3.0	0.1	6.4	65.6	1 186	120	324	3 107	21 090	45 996	4 318
Perry	35.3	2 921	48.4	1.5	4.7	0.1	17.1	88.9	7 358	19	73	564	4 660	41 374	3 257
Pike	242.6	6 051	34.8	43.8	2.9	0.0	2.6	84.1	2 098	112	235	3 455	16 500	40 737	3 751
Pontotoc	80.2	2 621	56.4	1.0	4.0	0.1	6.4	30.1	983	49	184	1 204	12 760	40 449	3 172
Prentiss	89.5	3 525	81.0	0.8	4.2	0.0	3.0	31.5	1 242	44	174	1 484	9 680	39 010	3 137
Quitman	33.0	4 231	64.9	0.9	4.1	0.0	8.6	7.5	959	23	44	334	2 830	30 245	2 518
Rankin	365.9	2 521	50.1	0.9	7.2	0.1	9.8	417.1	2 873	637	867	9 140	64 950	57 496	6 305
Scott	65.3	2 311	62.2	1.9	5.4	0.0	7.7	22.0	779	194	169	1 242	12 030	36 410	2 731
Sharkey	21.1	4 406	71.8	0.6	4.2	0.0	8.3	5.6	1 159	26	27	386	1 870	34 076	3 058
Simpson	63.8	2 330	55.8	1.6	3.8	2.0	6.9	28.1	1 027	42	160	1 608	10 610	41 575	3 582
Smith	36.8	2 253	63.0	1.0	5.3	0.0	13.3	9.9	606	24	96	604	6 050	44 579	4 153
Stone	142.2	7 887	79.3	0.5	3.6	0.0	2.5	30.7	1 701	60	100	1 109	6 680	42 770	3 649

1. Based on the resident population estimated as of July 1 of the year shown.

Table B. States and Counties — Land Area and Population

STATE/ County code	CBSA code[1]	County type[2]	STATE County	Population, 2016				Race alone or in combination, not Hispanic or Latino (percent)					Age (percent)					
				Land area,[3] (sq mi) 2016	Total persons 2016	Rank	Per square mile	White	Black	American Indian, Alaska Native	Asian and Pacific Islander	Percent Hispanic or Latino[4]	Under 5 years	5 to 17 years	18 to 24 years	25 to 34 years	35 to 44 years	45 to 54 years
				1	2	3	4	5	6	7	8	9	10	11	12	13	14	15
			MISSISSIPPI—Cont'd															
28 133	26940	7	Sunflower	697.8	26 407	1 546	37.8	24.5	73.3	0.4	0.5	1.8	5.8	17.4	10.3	16.2	12.5	13.0
28 135	...	7	Tallahatchie	645.2	14 394	2 137	22.3	36.3	56.2	0.6	1.2	6.6	5.2	14.8	10.8	16.7	13.8	12.7
28 137	32820	1	Tate	404.8	28 201	1 482	69.7	65.6	31.8	0.7	0.6	2.5	5.5	17.9	11.5	11.8	11.6	13.1
28 139	...	6	Tippah	457.8	22 190	1 717	48.5	78.4	17.4	0.5	0.4	4.7	6.2	18.4	9.1	11.7	12.1	13.4
28 141	...	8	Tishomingo	424.3	19 491	1 848	45.9	94.2	3.0	0.5	0.3	2.8	5.4	16.7	7.9	11.0	11.2	14.0
28 143	32820	1	Tunica	454.7	10 234	2 411	22.5	20.5	76.3	0.6	1.2	2.4	8.9	20.7	9.0	14.1	12.6	11.8
28 145	...	6	Union	415.6	28 311	1 477	68.1	79.4	15.9	0.6	1.3	4.3	6.5	18.6	8.1	12.5	13.2	13.1
28 147	...	9	Walthall	403.9	14 599	2 127	36.1	53.4	44.2	0.8	0.8	2.0	6.0	17.7	8.5	11.3	12.1	12.2
28 149	46980	4	Warren	588.5	47 140	1 033	80.1	47.9	49.1	0.5	1.1	2.2	6.3	18.0	8.4	12.4	12.2	12.8
28 151	24740	5	Washington	724.7	47 231	1 032	65.2	25.7	72.3	0.3	0.9	1.5	7.8	18.5	9.6	12.3	11.2	12.2
28 153	...	7	Wayne	810.7	20 480	1 800	25.3	58.2	40.1	0.6	0.4	1.6	6.5	18.1	8.4	12.8	11.6	12.6
28 155	...	9	Webster	420.9	9 767	2 450	23.2	79.0	19.7	0.5	0.3	1.6	6.0	17.4	7.8	12.3	11.4	13.7
28 157	...	8	Wilkinson	678.1	9 047	2 505	13.3	28.4	70.6	0.4	0.3	1.0	5.8	15.9	8.5	12.5	11.5	12.3
28 159	...	7	Winston	607.2	18 160	1 907	29.9	51.0	46.8	1.4	0.5	1.2	5.3	18.5	7.4	11.8	12.1	12.6
28 161	...	7	Yalobusha	467.1	12 471	2 260	26.7	58.8	39.8	0.5	0.4	1.5	6.3	16.7	7.8	11.2	11.7	12.4
28 163	27140	2	Yazoo	922.2	27 264	1 522	29.6	36.2	57.8	0.6	0.8	5.6	6.5	17.7	8.6	16.2	14.3	12.1
29 000	...	0	MISSOURI	68 746.5	6 093 000	X	88.6	81.6	12.6	1.1	2.6	4.1	6.1	16.6	9.5	13.3	12.0	13.0
29 001	28860	7	Adair	567.3	25 359	1 591	44.7	92.0	3.3	0.7	3.2	2.7	4.8	13.7	28.1	9.9	8.5	10.0
29 003	41140	3	Andrew	432.7	17 350	1 952	40.1	96.2	1.2	0.9	0.7	2.3	5.7	17.2	7.7	11.0	12.2	13.5
29 005	...	9	Atchison	547.3	5 293	2 812	9.7	97.6	0.8	0.8	0.5	1.3	5.2	14.9	6.7	10.1	10.6	13.2
29 007	33020	6	Audrain	692.2	26 021	1 562	37.6	88.9	8.1	0.8	0.9	3.1	6.4	16.6	8.4	13.5	12.4	12.5
29 009	...	6	Barry	778.3	35 732	1 285	45.9	87.7	0.8	2.0	1.9	9.2	5.8	16.6	7.7	10.7	10.6	13.3
29 011	...	6	Barton	591.9	11 908	2 301	20.1	94.9	1.2	2.9	1.1	2.5	6.0	18.1	8.0	10.4	11.0	12.5
29 013	28140	1	Bates	836.7	16 417	2 011	19.6	95.7	1.6	1.6	0.6	2.2	6.0	17.8	7.5	11.1	11.1	12.9
29 015	...	7	Benton	704.0	18 839	1 881	26.8	96.2	0.8	1.7	0.6	2.1	4.1	13.2	5.4	7.9	8.6	13.1
29 017	16020	3	Bollinger	617.9	12 052	2 291	19.5	97.5	0.7	1.3	0.4	1.2	5.4	17.0	7.0	10.7	11.7	14.4
29 019	17860	3	Boone	685.6	176 594	369	257.6	82.1	10.9	1.0	5.7	3.3	5.9	14.3	19.9	15.4	11.4	10.8
29 021	41140	3	Buchanan	408.0	88 938	651	218.0	85.9	7.0	1.0	2.0	6.4	6.4	16.4	9.4	14.5	12.1	12.9
29 023	38740	5	Butler	694.7	42 739	1 117	61.5	90.9	6.7	1.6	1.1	2.1	6.4	17.2	7.8	12.3	11.8	12.8
29 025	28140	1	Caldwell	426.4	9 062	2 503	21.3	96.3	1.2	1.5	0.7	2.1	5.3	18.6	7.7	10.1	11.5	13.6
29 027	27620	3	Callaway	834.6	45 078	1 073	54.0	92.0	5.5	1.3	1.1	2.1	5.6	15.6	11.1	13.5	12.3	13.7
29 029	...	7	Camden	656.0	44 497	1 081	67.8	95.3	1.0	1.1	1.0	2.7	4.8	13.5	6.0	9.5	9.4	12.9
29 031	16020	3	Cape Girardeau	578.5	78 913	708	136.4	88.1	8.8	0.8	2.0	2.3	5.8	15.6	14.3	12.5	11.1	11.7
29 033	...	6	Carroll	694.6	8 913	2 513	12.8	96.0	2.6	0.7	0.5	1.5	5.8	16.8	7.6	10.1	11.2	12.9
29 035	...	9	Carter	507.4	6 168	2 739	12.2	96.0	0.7	1.9	0.5	2.4	5.8	17.7	7.5	10.1	11.9	13.3
29 037	28140	1	Cass	696.6	102 845	585	147.6	90.5	4.7	1.4	1.5	4.3	6.0	18.5	7.8	11.7	12.6	13.7
29 039	...	6	Cedar	474.5	14 016	2 162	29.5	96.4	0.6	1.6	0.7	2.1	6.5	17.1	6.9	9.5	9.9	12.5
29 041	...	9	Chariton	751.2	7 516	2 631	10.0	96.2	3.1	0.7	0.4	0.9	6.2	16.8	6.6	9.7	10.1	11.9
29 043	44180	2	Christian	562.6	84 401	675	150.0	95.1	1.3	1.3	1.1	2.9	6.4	19.4	7.3	12.9	13.5	13.0
29 045	22800	9	Clark	504.7	6 723	2 696	13.3	98.1	0.8	0.8	0.5	1.0	5.6	17.3	7.0	10.3	11.1	13.3
29 047	28140	1	Clay	397.6	239 085	279	601.3	83.8	7.3	1.2	3.4	6.7	6.6	18.0	8.1	14.3	13.7	13.6
29 049	28140	1	Clinton	419.0	20 610	1 793	49.2	95.5	2.2	1.4	0.8	2.0	5.7	18.0	7.4	11.1	11.7	13.9
29 051	27620	3	Cole	391.5	76 631	720	195.7	83.5	13.0	0.8	1.8	2.9	6.0	16.6	8.8	13.7	12.8	13.6
29 053	...	6	Cooper	564.8	17 712	1 934	31.4	90.3	7.8	1.0	0.9	1.8	5.5	16.4	9.9	13.4	11.7	12.5
29 055	...	6	Crawford	742.5	24 302	1 632	32.7	96.6	0.8	1.3	0.6	1.9	6.0	17.4	7.3	11.4	11.2	13.4
29 057	...	8	Dade	490.0	7 631	2 621	15.6	96.1	0.9	2.5	0.7	2.2	4.7	16.2	7.0	9.0	10.7	13.1
29 059	44180	2	Dallas	540.8	16 448	2 010	30.4	96.4	0.8	2.1	0.6	2.1	6.2	17.2	7.1	10.3	10.7	12.8
29 061	...	8	Daviess	563.2	8 209	2 578	14.6	97.1	1.0	1.0	0.8	1.6	6.6	19.6	7.7	9.9	10.8	12.0
29 063	41140	3	DeKalb	421.4	12 613	2 254	29.9	85.0	12.0	0.8	0.7	2.4	4.2	12.5	8.1	16.1	15.2	15.0
29 065	...	7	Dent	752.8	15 387	2 073	20.4	96.0	0.9	2.0	1.0	1.8	6.0	16.5	6.7	10.8	10.6	13.1
29 067	...	6	Douglas	813.6	13 358	2 209	16.4	97.0	0.8	1.9	0.7	1.5	5.6	15.8	6.3	10.0	9.6	12.7
29 069	28380	7	Dunklin	541.1	30 535	1 417	56.4	82.8	11.1	0.8	0.6	6.4	7.0	18.5	8.0	11.0	11.6	12.6
29 071	41180	1	Franklin	922.7	102 838	586	111.5	96.5	1.4	0.8	0.8	1.7	6.1	17.2	7.9	12.2	11.3	14.2
29 073	...	6	Gasconade	519.0	14 808	2 115	28.5	97.2	1.0	0.8	0.8	1.4	5.1	15.9	6.9	10.4	10.2	13.4
29 075	...	8	Gentry	491.4	6 661	2 699	13.6	97.2	1.2	0.8	0.7	1.6	7.2	17.7	7.4	11.6	9.9	12.8
29 077	44180	2	Greene	675.3	288 690	237	427.5	90.5	4.3	1.5	2.7	3.6	6.0	14.9	13.8	14.0	11.6	11.7
29 079	...	7	Grundy	435.3	10 165	2 422	23.4	95.6	1.2	1.1	1.2	2.1	7.5	16.4	8.5	12.1	9.5	11.9
29 081	...	7	Harrison	722.5	8 556	2 546	11.8	96.5	0.8	0.9	0.8	2.2	6.5	18.2	6.8	10.5	10.6	11.8
29 083	...	6	Henry	696.9	21 594	1 745	31.0	95.3	1.8	1.5	0.8	2.3	5.9	16.3	6.6	11.0	11.1	12.9
29 085	...	8	Hickory	398.8	9 269	2 485	23.2	96.7	0.9	2.2	0.5	1.5	4.4	13.0	5.2	7.6	8.3	12.6
29 087	...	8	Holt	462.7	4 448	2 868	9.6	96.8	0.5	1.5	0.6	1.4	5.0	15.2	5.8	10.2	10.7	14.2
29 089	...	6	Howard	463.8	10 058	2 430	21.7	90.8	6.0	1.2	0.6	1.5	5.9	16.0	12.6	11.2	10.0	12.1
29 091	48460	7	Howell	927.2	40 210	1 171	43.4	96.1	0.8	1.8	1.1	2.1	6.3	17.6	7.8	12.0	11.4	12.4
29 093	...	7	Iron	550.3	10 022	2 432	18.2	95.8	2.0	1.5	0.5	1.9	4.7	16.4	7.1	10.2	11.9	13.9
29 095	28140	1	Jackson	604.6	691 801	93	1 144.2	64.9	25.0	1.3	2.7	9.0	6.8	17.2	8.4	15.4	12.4	12.8

1. CBSA = Core Based Statistical Area. See Appendix A for explanation. See Appendix B for list of metropolitan areas with component counties. 2. County type code from the Economic Research Service of USDA Rural-Urban Continuum Codes. See Appendix A for definition. 3. Dry land or land partially or temporarily covered by water. 4. May be of any race.

STATE County	55 to 64 years	65 to 74 years	75 years and over	Percent female	2000	2010	2000–2010	2010–2016	Births	Deaths	Net migration	Number	Persons per household	Family households	Female family householder[1]	One person
	16	17	18	19	20	21	22	23	24	25	26	27	28	29	30	31
MISSISSIPPI—Cont'd																
Sunflower	12.2	7.6	5.1	47.5	34 369	29 385	-14.5	-10.1	2 105	1 830	-3 326	8 508	2.81	69.6	29.9	27.6
Tallahatchie	11.7	8.0	6.1	44.2	14 903	15 383	3.2	-6.4	1 013	968	-1 026	4 386	2.40	66.1	24.7	31.4
Tate	12.9	9.7	6.0	51.9	25 370	28 882	13.8	-2.4	2 068	1 725	-1 007	10 004	2.67	72.2	18.8	24.0
Tippah	12.8	9.7	6.5	50.9	20 826	22 232	6.8	-0.2	1 712	1 609	-145	8 349	2.61	74.6	13.7	21.9
Tishomingo	13.8	11.8	8.2	51.4	19 163	19 596	2.3	-0.5	1 219	1 762	414	7 652	2.52	74.8	15.2	23.5
Tunica	11.5	7.0	4.4	53.1	9 227	10 778	16.8	-5.0	1 215	610	-1 151	3 989	2.60	66.4	26.9	30.5
Union	11.9	9.5	6.6	51.2	25 362	27 134	7.0	4.3	2 211	1 692	702	10 345	2.66	71.4	15.2	24.9
Walthall	13.6	10.4	8.3	52.0	15 156	15 443	1.9	-5.5	1 149	1 134	-860	5 761	2.58	64.2	15.1	33.5
Warren	14.3	9.3	6.3	52.5	49 644	48 773	-1.8	-3.3	3 869	3 125	-2 261	18 415	2.58	67.3	19.1	29.1
Washington	13.7	8.9	5.8	53.5	62 977	51 135	-18.8	-7.6	4 918	3 779	-5 041	18 193	2.69	66.3	28.7	30.0
Wayne	13.5	9.6	6.9	51.8	21 216	20 747	-2.2	-1.3	1 765	1 316	-727	7 630	2.67	71.5	16.8	26.0
Webster	13.8	10.4	7.2	50.9	10 294	10 252	-0.4	-4.7	750	896	-375	4 044	2.45	72.0	17.1	26.0
Wilkinson	14.1	9.2	7.4	47.0	10 312	9 878	-4.2	-8.4	712	719	-848	3 209	2.60	65.1	23.2	32.5
Winston	14.1	10.3	7.9	51.1	20 160	19 198	-4.8	-5.4	1 240	1 395	-882	7 664	2.38	69.5	23.7	28.8
Yalobusha	14.8	11.4	7.6	52.0	13 051	12 678	-2.9	-1.6	979	1 039	-141	5 101	2.39	68.9	18.1	27.9
Yazoo	11.5	7.1	5.9	45.0	28 149	28 065	-0.3	-2.9	2 319	1 739	-1 348	8 602	2.82	66.9	26.0	29.5
MISSOURI	13.4	9.2	6.9	50.9	5 595 211	5 988 928	7.0	1.7	470 801	356 501	-6 804	2 364 688	2.48	64.7	12.1	29.2
Adair	10.4	8.1	6.5	52.1	24 977	25 607	2.5	-1.0	1 604	1 322	-532	9 635	2.36	53.4	7.4	35.6
Andrew	15.1	10.1	7.5	50.4	16 492	17 291	4.8	0.3	1 136	1 022	-29	6 808	2.51	71.7	5.8	22.6
Atchison	14.6	13.7	11.1	50.8	6 430	5 685	-11.6	-6.9	339	474	-260	2 501	2.13	58.3	6.2	34.3
Audrain	13.2	9.3	7.7	54.6	25 853	25 529	-1.3	1.9	2 146	1 821	192	9 273	2.58	63.2	9.8	30.2
Barry	14.5	12.0	8.8	49.8	34 010	35 597	4.7	0.4	2 600	2 523	123	13 246	2.67	70.7	9.2	25.0
Barton	14.6	10.5	8.8	50.5	12 541	12 402	-1.1	-4.0	894	876	-514	4 988	2.41	72.7	8.8	24.2
Bates	14.5	10.0	9.0	50.7	16 653	17 049	2.4	-3.7	1 187	1 301	-518	6 690	2.44	66.0	9.8	29.7
Benton	18.1	17.6	12.0	49.9	17 180	19 056	10.9	-1.1	977	1 766	644	8 149	2.28	66.2	7.9	29.5
Bollinger	15.4	11.1	7.4	50.2	12 029	12 363	2.8	-2.5	851	815	-242	4 753	2.56	70.7	11.7	25.3
Boone	10.8	6.7	4.6	51.5	135 454	162 645	20.1	8.6	13 231	6 358	6 951	66 980	2.41	57.1	9.5	29.5
Buchanan	13.0	8.7	6.7	49.5	85 998	89 201	3.7	-0.3	7 339	5 956	-1 555	33 176	2.58	62.9	13.6	30.4
Butler	13.5	10.2	8.0	51.4	40 867	42 794	4.7	-0.1	3 465	3 538	147	16 730	2.51	67.1	13.4	27.5
Caldwell	14.1	10.9	8.3	49.5	8 969	9 424	5.1	-3.8	576	611	-340	3 715	2.39	68.3	8.4	27.8
Callaway	13.3	9.0	6.0	48.8	40 766	44 330	8.7	1.7	3 197	2 320	-49	16 150	2.52	65.2	11.6	30.8
Camden	18.1	16.6	9.1	50.4	37 051	44 001	18.8	1.1	2 578	2 874	850	16 748	2.60	71.2	7.9	24.5
Cape Girardeau	12.7	8.8	7.4	51.5	68 693	75 674	10.2	4.3	5 722	4 592	2 000	29 795	2.49	63.7	9.7	27.3
Carroll	14.0	12.1	9.5	51.0	10 285	9 295	-9.6	-4.1	661	755	-295	3 624	2.48	67.1	10.6	29.9
Carter	14.6	11.5	7.5	51.4	5 941	6 265	5.5	-1.5	472	466	-96	2 453	2.54	57.9	11.0	36.8
Cass	13.5	9.1	7.1	51.2	82 092	99 494	21.2	3.4	7 468	5 562	1 326	37 945	2.63	73.3	10.2	22.1
Cedar	13.6	13.3	10.6	50.0	13 733	13 982	1.8	0.2	1 058	1 254	324	5 904	2.33	63.6	10.1	32.0
Chariton	15.8	11.4	11.6	50.0	8 438	7 827	-7.2	-4.0	539	585	-247	2 947	2.52	65.7	6.4	31.6
Christian	12.5	9.2	5.8	51.1	54 285	77 417	42.6	9.0	6 325	3 623	4 089	29 889	2.69	76.0	10.6	20.0
Clark	15.2	11.1	9.0	49.6	7 416	7 129	-3.9	-5.7	489	526	-360	2 833	2.42	66.3	5.9	29.4
Clay	12.3	8.1	5.3	50.9	184 006	221 950	20.6	7.7	19 179	10 293	8 296	87 676	2.60	67.4	11.3	25.8
Clinton	14.4	10.1	7.8	49.8	18 979	20 743	9.3	-0.6	1 412	1 537	-41	8 076	2.48	73.1	10.0	22.4
Cole	13.3	8.9	6.3	49.4	71 397	75 983	6.4	0.9	5 784	3 892	-1 171	29 448	2.44	64.7	12.7	29.4
Cooper	13.4	9.5	7.8	47.6	16 670	17 601	5.6	0.6	1 208	1 155	41	6 488	2.47	66.9	10.2	28.6
Crawford	14.6	11.0	7.8	50.3	22 804	24 696	8.3	-1.6	1 810	1 791	-412	9 309	2.61	67.0	10.0	28.4
Dade	16.1	12.9	10.2	49.3	7 923	7 883	-0.5	-3.2	413	638	-28	3 195	2.34	67.4	10.8	27.6
Dallas	15.8	11.6	8.4	50.2	15 661	16 777	7.1	-2.0	1 240	1 157	-400	6 252	2.62	74.6	10.7	20.1
Daviess	14.1	11.6	7.8	49.4	8 016	8 433	5.2	-2.7	732	543	-398	3 047	2.65	69.6	6.1	25.4
DeKalb	12.6	8.2	8.1	37.1	11 597	12 892	11.2	-2.2	663	715	-272	3 756	2.48	65.7	6.9	30.6
Dent	15.1	11.5	9.7	50.1	14 927	15 654	4.9	-1.7	1 118	1 191	-186	5 920	2.60	68.4	11.3	27.0
Douglas	16.6	13.5	10.0	50.2	13 084	13 686	4.6	-2.4	923	985	-280	5 277	2.54	69.5	8.2	28.0
Dunklin	13.3	9.9	8.0	52.1	33 155	31 953	-3.6	-4.4	2 819	2 716	-1 491	12 623	2.44	63.1	15.7	32.9
Franklin	14.7	9.5	6.8	50.3	93 807	101 491	8.2	1.3	7 719	6 109	-323	39 915	2.53	70.4	10.0	25.3
Gasconade	15.9	11.9	10.3	50.1	15 342	15 221	-0.8	-2.7	964	1 259	-94	6 246	2.35	66.9	8.4	28.9
Gentry	13.7	9.0	10.8	51.9	6 861	6 738	-1.8	-1.1	579	527	-120	2 748	2.38	66.4	7.8	29.9
Greene	11.9	8.9	7.1	51.2	240 391	275 178	14.5	4.9	22 260	16 518	7 393	117 732	2.31	59.2	10.4	31.4
Grundy	12.9	10.8	10.5	51.9	10 432	10 261	-1.6	-0.9	929	860	-168	4 057	2.45	64.7	10.6	31.0
Harrison	14.1	10.9	10.5	50.8	8 850	8 957	1.2	-4.5	688	705	-397	3 574	2.37	67.0	7.3	28.5
Henry	14.9	12.1	9.2	50.9	21 997	22 272	1.3	-3.0	1 610	1 961	-287	9 518	2.29	63.9	8.9	29.8
Hickory	17.0	19.2	12.7	50.9	8 940	9 627	7.7	-3.7	471	904	57	4 105	2.25	66.7	6.9	28.7
Holt	15.5	12.0	11.4	50.7	5 351	4 912	-8.2	-9.4	316	395	-369	2 130	2.11	66.9	8.9	29.3
Howard	14.6	9.8	7.9	50.3	10 212	10 148	-0.6	-0.9	747	593	-210	3 729	2.53	67.1	9.7	28.6
Howell	13.4	10.8	8.4	51.2	37 238	40 400	8.5	-0.5	3 222	3 133	-264	16 263	2.45	67.2	12.2	28.5
Iron	15.9	11.7	8.2	50.1	10 697	10 628	-0.6	-5.7	652	875	-450	4 046	2.46	67.3	11.9	27.5
Jackson	12.9	8.1	6.0	51.6	654 880	674 135	2.9	2.6	59 588	38 557	-2 126	274 485	2.44	59.3	15.2	33.7

1. No spouse present.

Table B. States and Counties — Population, Vital Statistics, Health, and Crime

STATE County	Daytime population, 2011–2015			Births, 2016		Deaths, 2016		Persons under 65 with no health insurance, 2015		Medicare, 2015			Serious crimes known to police,[2] 2014 Total	
	Persons in group quarters, 2016	Number	Employment/residence ratio	Total	Rate[1]	Number	Rate[1]	Number	Percent	Total Beneficiaries	Enrolled in Original Medicare	Enrolled in Medicare Advantage	Number	Rate[3]
	32	33	34	35	36	37	38	39	40	41	42	43	44	45
MISSISSIPPI—Cont'd														
Sunflower	3 926	27 552	0.96	311	11.8	285	10.8	3 179	16.0	4 232	3 829	403	NA	NA
Tallahatchie	2 450	14 374	0.85	165	11.5	158	11.0	1 664	16.4	2 504	2 307	197	NA	NA
Tate	1 308	24 201	0.62	330	11.7	302	10.7	3 635	15.9	5 221	4 242	979	NA	NA
Tippah	314	20 775	0.84	283	12.8	235	10.6	3 096	16.9	5 525	5 122	403	3	18
Tishomingo	276	17 867	0.78	186	9.5	285	14.6	2 596	16.7	5 579	5 361	218	87	446
Tunica	104	16 208	2.38	185	18.1	94	9.2	1 144	12.6	1 691	1 351	340	526	5 009
Union	277	27 745	0.99	342	12.1	251	8.9	4 152	17.5	5 398	4 959	439	NA	NA
Walthall	122	12 594	0.54	179	12.3	177	12.1	2 258	19.0	2 723	2 327	396	NA	NA
Warren	525	50 433	1.12	607	12.9	518	11.0	5 078	12.7	9 137	7 548	1 589	2 170	4 518
Washington	726	49 834	1.02	731	15.5	664	14.1	6 775	16.7	10 181	8 376	1 805	3 162	6 772
Wayne	137	18 852	0.78	267	13.0	201	9.8	2 855	16.6	3 359	2 912	447	NA	NA
Webster	57	8 786	0.65	108	11.1	149	15.3	1 229	15.0	2 489	2 331	158	NA	NA
Wilkinson	1 055	8 979	0.87	100	11.1	130	14.4	965	14.5	1 812	1 517	295	NA	NA
Winston	444	17 589	0.84	193	10.6	225	12.4	2 516	17.3	3 905	3 434	471	50	268
Yalobusha	155	10 653	0.65	163	13.1	173	13.9	1 419	14.1	3 968	3 546	422	NA	NA
Yazoo	4 127	26 626	0.84	358	13.1	259	9.5	2 944	14.8	4 541	3 901	640	NA	NA
MISSOURI	175 397	6 084 593	1.01	74 423	12.2	58 723	9.6	574 373	11.5	1 111 675	767 306	344 369	203 093	3 349
Adair	2 908	26 458	1.08	260	10.3	194	7.7	2 554	13.4	4 187	3 882	305	772	3 016
Andrew	192	11 592	0.32	189	10.9	164	9.5	1 417	10.0	2 332	2 147	185	268	1 533
Atchison	98	4 941	0.81	53	10.0	77	14.5	497	12.4	1 389	1 293	96	41	759
Audrain	2 485	25 575	0.98	348	13.4	278	10.7	2 451	12.5	4 864	3 923	941	631	2 451
Barry	296	37 594	1.13	406	11.4	403	11.3	4 987	17.8	8 381	5 356	3 025	941	2 646
Barton	90	11 181	0.80	144	12.1	138	11.6	1 420	14.9	2 496	1 992	504	295	2 406
Bates	311	14 237	0.65	183	11.1	191	11.6	1 884	14.4	3 513	2 743	770	520	3 162
Benton	244	17 021	0.71	165	8.8	287	15.2	1 952	15.0	6 332	4 852	1 480	433	2 290
Bollinger	163	9 606	0.44	130	10.8	127	10.5	1 520	15.4	2 545	2 157	388	139	1 108
Boone	9 019	175 985	1.06	2 119	12.0	1 064	6.0	14 185	9.6	22 689	18 936	3 753	5 735	3 316
Buchanan	4 485	98 776	1.22	1 113	12.5	892	10.0	8 332	11.6	17 128	15 406	1 722	4 958	5 516
Butler	874	46 379	1.20	528	12.4	575	13.5	4 624	13.4	10 162	8 861	1 301	2 230	5 162
Caldwell	214	7 275	0.52	98	10.8	86	9.5	980	13.8	2 005	1 683	322	116	1 286
Callaway	4 026	39 980	0.77	507	11.2	394	8.7	3 751	10.8	7 580	6 211	1 369	1 206	2 715
Camden	774	45 038	1.07	417	9.4	486	10.9	5 320	16.4	9 826	8 156	1 670	911	2 077
Cape Girardeau	3 836	83 487	1.16	906	11.5	730	9.3	6 644	10.5	14 715	13 239	1 476	2 602	3 345
Carroll	88	8 082	0.74	92	10.3	118	13.2	878	12.4	2 257	1 910	347	136	1 494
Carter	40	5 940	0.86	69	11.2	89	14.4	849	16.8	1 624	1 376	248	95	1 509
Cass	1 045	79 774	0.56	1 169	11.4	909	8.8	7 792	9.2	14 768	8 893	5 875	2 271	2 249
Cedar	156	12 800	0.78	178	12.7	216	15.4	1 711	16.4	3 681	2 397	1 284	347	2 494
Chariton	213	6 553	0.67	84	11.2	104	13.8	807	14.0	1 614	1 432	182	131	1 728
Christian	582	62 043	0.49	1 035	12.3	641	7.6	7 670	10.8	14 051	7 663	6 388	1 438	1 759
Clark	90	5 619	0.59	76	11.3	74	11.0	754	13.9	1 441	1 311	130	28	408
Clay	2 652	208 323	0.81	3 070	12.8	1 753	7.3	18 981	9.3	36 613	27 361	9 252	10 081	4 332
Clinton	447	15 743	0.50	237	11.5	241	11.7	1 734	10.3	4 269	3 690	579	358	1 742
Cole	4 950	90 144	1.38	908	11.8	654	8.5	5 947	9.8	14 247	12 255	1 992	1 852	2 407
Cooper	1 528	15 886	0.78	185	10.4	179	10.1	1 517	11.5	3 309	2 687	622	428	2 420
Crawford	332	22 080	0.72	290	11.9	287	11.8	3 014	15.2	4 419	3 113	1 306	704	2 867
Dade	133	6 718	0.71	66	8.6	106	13.9	893	15.3	1 879	1 151	728	112	1 691
Dallas	199	13 392	0.46	199	12.1	202	12.3	2 173	16.8	3 476	1 920	1 556	309	1 872
Daviess	152	7 009	0.62	129	15.7	88	10.7	1 156	17.9	1 628	1 453	175	79	956
DeKalb	3 502	12 556	0.95	106	8.4	93	7.4	848	11.6	1 595	1 442	153	186	1 448
Dent	201	14 569	0.82	190	12.3	202	13.1	1 981	16.2	3 693	3 292	401	306	1 943
Douglas	123	11 937	0.67	145	10.9	162	12.1	1 707	16.9	2 848	1 495	1 353	206	1 526
Dunklin	671	30 100	0.87	418	13.7	438	14.3	3 769	15.1	7 554	6 424	1 130	1 507	4 755
Franklin	858	93 496	0.83	1 215	11.8	1 018	9.9	9 578	11.2	21 320	11 179	10 141	2 545	2 495
Gasconade	250	14 654	0.95	149	10.1	205	13.8	1 550	13.4	3 889	2 800	1 089	191	1 287
Gentry	177	6 401	0.87	95	14.3	79	11.9	735	13.8	1 434	1 338	96	33	486
Greene	11 263	318 494	1.27	3 590	12.4	2 753	9.5	31 086	13.3	54 848	30 905	23 943	16 612	5 801
Grundy	350	10 431	1.04	151	14.9	137	13.5	1 051	13.6	2 336	2 177	159	164	1 578
Harrison	145	8 486	0.94	104	12.2	119	13.9	1 119	16.7	2 135	2 000	135	118	1 356
Henry	233	21 362	0.93	236	10.9	305	14.1	2 222	13.0	6 030	4 558	1 472	830	3 766
Hickory	75	8 469	0.71	86	9.3	140	15.1	1 065	17.4	2 698	1 693	1 005	115	1 245
Holt	101	4 215	0.82	46	10.3	62	13.9	451	13.2	1 120	1 021	99	83	1 847
Howard	717	8 421	0.60	116	11.5	76	7.6	948	12.2	1 791	1 465	326	140	1 359
Howell	608	42 006	1.11	506	12.6	511	12.7	4 435	13.8	10 531	8 153	2 378	1 327	3 286
Iron	276	10 169	0.96	96	9.6	158	15.8	1 170	14.8	2 831	2 474	357	160	1 554
Jackson	11 041	739 750	1.18	9 423	13.6	6 473	9.4	73 433	12.6	115 012	70 037	44 975	32 865	4 819

1. Per 1,000 estimated resident population.   2. Data for serious crimes have not been adjusted for underreporting; this may affect comparability between geographic areas and over time.
3. Per 100,000 population estimated by the FBI.

Items 32—45

Table B. States and Counties — **Crime, Education, Money Income, and Poverty**

STATE County	Serious crimes known to police, 2014 (cont.)[1] Rate[2]		School enrollment and attainment, 2011–2015				Local government expenditures,[5] 2013–2014		Money income, 2011–2015				Income and poverty, 2015		
			Enrollment[3]		Attainment[4] (percent)						Households			Percent below poverty level		
					High school graduate or less	Bachelor's degree or more			Per capita income[6] (dollars)	Median income (dollars)	Percent		Median household income (dollars)	All persons	Children under 18 years	Children 5 to 17 years in families
	Violent	Property	Total	Percent private			Total current spending (mil dol)	Current spending per student (dollars)			with income of less than $50,000	with income of $200,000 or more				
	46	47	48	49	50	51	52	53	54	55	56	57	58	59	60	61
MISSISSIPPI—Cont'd																
Sunflower	NA	NA	7 343	14.4	56.8	14.4	39.5	9 411	13 718	27 384	71.5	1.8	28 184	39.3	50.6	49.1
Tallahatchie	NA	NA	2 329	27.2	68.1	8.5	18.3	9 094	13 819	29 731	68.2	0.1	29 474	32.9	45.2	45.5
Tate	NA	NA	8 366	13.5	49.7	16.7	33.7	7 150	21 547	42 880	55.7	3.6	43 376	19.2	29.1	27.6
Tippah	0	18	5 304	8.1	56.9	12.9	33.3	7 884	20 012	35 609	63.0	1.3	38 297	18.2	27.2	26.3
Tishomingo	26	421	4 207	6.3	61.3	11.2	27.8	8 661	18 881	35 143	67.9	1.2	37 740	17.1	24.9	23.7
Tunica	524	4 485	2 973	10.4	54.4	17.3	23.8	9 937	17 246	31 211	73.0	0.4	30 970	28.9	46.2	45.6
Union	NA	NA	7 118	4.4	57.1	13.8	39.0	7 756	18 889	35 865	64.2	1.6	42 120	17.0	25.1	26.1
Walthall	NA	NA	4 063	10.1	62.7	11.0	19.3	8 956	17 872	31 384	66.9	1.7	31 202	27.6	42.1	38.7
Warren	364	4 154	12 678	10.7	44.1	24.4	72.2	8 573	22 417	41 121	57.4	2.4	40 465	21.6	32.8	31.6
Washington	283	6 489	13 581	12.4	53.4	18.8	87.3	9 261	17 160	29 144	70.1	2.2	27 539	36.2	51.4	49.3
Wayne	NA	NA	5 427	6.0	59.8	13.6	30.3	8 767	20 231	32 557	62.1	1.9	35 989	24.5	35.8	34.8
Webster	NA	NA	2 460	12.1	51.8	17.2	15.0	7 915	19 938	34 448	63.9	2.6	40 214	20.5	30.2	28.8
Wilkinson	NA	NA	1 923	21.9	65.3	14.5	11.8	9 207	15 307	29 931	68.5	0.7	28 535	34.5	42.4	41.9
Winston	86	182	4 350	16.0	53.8	16.5	24.4	8 447	19 199	33 202	65.8	1.3	35 216	26.6	38.9	34.8
Yalobusha	NA	NA	2 721	13.6	60.1	12.4	15.3	8 423	19 679	36 502	62.9	1.3	36 062	22.4	33.4	32.9
Yazoo	NA	NA	6 521	21.1	60.6	13.3	34.1	8 143	14 934	28 961	71.4	1.0	34 218	34.2	43.4	40.0
MISSOURI	443	2 906	1 543 176	19.0	42.9	27.1	9 050.3	9 856	26 259	48 173	51.5	3.2	50 200	14.8	20.4	18.9
Adair	293	2 723	10 048	9.6	45.3	30.0	27.6	8 931	19 671	37 516	61.3	1.1	40 222	21.9	23.3	21.1
Andrew	143	1 390	3 821	10.7	50.0	23.3	23.8	8 279	26 778	55 613	46.9	2.7	58 675	9.5	12.9	11.4
Atchison	130	629	980	9.6	52.2	22.7	9.9	12 565	26 069	43 933	55.5	2.4	46 339	13.0	17.3	15.2
Audrain	202	2 249	5 555	11.4	62.9	11.5	29.7	9 017	18 934	41 310	59.7	0.9	42 480	18.7	26.9	24.6
Barry	281	2 365	8 221	14.9	59.7	14.0	57.5	8 714	19 313	39 033	61.4	0.9	37 467	20.7	29.7	27.9
Barton	212	2 194	2 849	8.6	52.6	16.7	18.6	9 118	20 780	37 467	61.6	1.8	39 633	18.0	26.9	23.1
Bates	486	2 675	3 950	11.8	58.3	13.1	24.1	9 116	21 715	41 060	59.4	1.0	45 887	14.1	22.5	21.1
Benton	370	1 920	3 436	14.6	60.0	11.3	21.1	8 106	19 122	33 042	68.8	0.4	34 156	18.7	31.8	28.1
Bollinger	136	973	2 826	12.5	66.3	10.0	15.2	8 048	19 605	39 707	63.4	1.7	41 623	18.3	27.0	25.8
Boone	342	2 974	61 916	13.0	26.7	47.3	228.1	9 806	27 150	49 899	50.1	3.6	50 865	17.7	14.6	13.0
Buchanan	412	5 105	21 800	14.2	49.5	19.5	116.9	9 045	22 218	46 315	53.2	1.7	48 294	17.3	23.7	23.2
Butler	498	4 664	10 359	7.2	55.5	14.6	53.0	7 751	19 473	35 738	64.3	1.3	35 509	23.4	36.7	33.3
Caldwell	111	1 175	2 182	5.9	55.4	17.4	16.1	10 010	23 082	43 691	54.9	1.1	44 470	12.7	19.7	17.4
Callaway	335	2 380	11 377	19.8	52.7	20.4	42.4	8 534	22 520	47 744	52.4	1.6	50 514	13.9	21.2	18.8
Camden	244	1 833	8 425	10.0	48.3	21.0	52.4	9 735	23 996	44 816	55.3	2.7	49 393	14.9	26.1	24.3
Cape Girardeau	345	3 001	22 352	13.7	42.9	28.7	86.0	8 469	24 479	46 050	53.8	2.0	49 615	16.4	19.4	16.2
Carroll	198	1 296	2 054	4.9	61.0	16.7	15.3	10 261	23 403	42 415	56.8	2.2	43 638	15.7	22.7	21.2
Carter	270	1 239	1 603	9.1	52.9	11.4	11.1	8 694	20 318	33 034	68.4	4.2	32 269	21.4	36.3	35.4
Cass	167	2 081	26 171	16.2	42.5	24.7	158.3	8 581	28 398	61 584	39.1	2.9	62 996	9.2	12.3	11.4
Cedar	295	2 200	3 219	17.1	58.8	14.3	18.7	8 248	18 255	31 532	69.9	1.0	37 654	19.9	33.7	31.3
Chariton	673	1 055	1 571	20.8	63.7	15.0	11.7	11 179	20 953	40 642	60.9	0.6	46 230	13.3	18.8	18.2
Christian	147	1 612	21 032	12.6	40.3	26.0	119.0	8 120	24 730	53 270	46.6	2.7	54 044	10.4	14.3	13.0
Clark	58	350	1 487	11.8	56.3	12.8	9.1	8 214	23 463	43 883	56.0	0.8	43 225	14.7	22.5	20.7
Clay	758	3 573	59 618	16.0	36.9	31.0	388.8	9 588	29 793	62 099	39.4	3.4	65 106	7.8	9.7	8.5
Clinton	569	1 173	4 761	8.8	46.7	17.6	39.0	9 240	25 500	54 773	45.2	1.4	59 655	10.4	15.1	13.4
Cole	218	2 189	18 890	23.8	39.7	31.6	100.2	7 520	26 014	53 088	46.2	2.0	56 393	11.9	16.2	15.1
Cooper	113	2 307	4 030	10.7	53.4	19.5	22.6	9 100	23 252	44 549	53.8	1.4	46 632	14.4	19.9	18.4
Crawford	171	2 696	5 421	9.5	61.4	12.2	27.4	7 920	19 017	36 743	62.9	0.6	38 491	19.4	28.6	26.7
Dade	181	1 510	1 616	8.6	55.5	15.3	10.8	9 747	20 828	37 035	63.0	1.4	38 516	17.5	27.6	24.6
Dallas	400	1 472	3 248	15.9	60.0	14.7	22.3	8 985	17 444	38 062	62.7	0.9	37 780	18.1	29.4	27.1
Daviess	121	835	1 773	19.5	57.5	15.8	12.9	9 958	19 208	41 642	60.2	0.8	43 135	15.3	27.6	25.6
DeKalb	280	1 168	2 484	10.1	63.4	11.5	10.7	10 071	17 125	41 406	57.8	1.8	44 429	20.0	18.5	16.9
Dent	76	1 866	3 201	8.7	61.5	13.0	17.5	8 018	19 747	36 831	64.7	1.4	36 808	21.5	31.0	28.4
Douglas	170	1 356	2 680	9.0	63.2	9.2	13.2	8 522	17 343	30 508	74.1	0.8	32 979	23.1	35.5	32.9
Dunklin	470	4 285	7 423	5.4	65.6	11.8	48.3	8 138	18 009	31 077	71.5	1.3	31 920	27.6	39.0	37.8
Franklin	179	2 316	23 478	19.7	47.7	18.6	150.7	9 161	25 241	48 480	51.3	2.5	50 438	11.4	16.3	14.9
Gasconade	94	1 193	3 095	12.5	58.7	15.0	24.3	8 412	22 845	42 826	56.6	0.8	47 717	12.1	19.2	17.3
Gentry	15	471	1 413	9.2	54.6	18.6	11.9	10 204	20 687	41 912	59.9	1.0	43 811	14.9	21.4	21.2
Greene	716	5 085	76 955	15.8	37.4	29.5	326.7	8 573	24 097	41 227	58.2	2.4	43 885	17.7	21.4	20.4
Grundy	67	1 511	2 498	7.8	52.7	17.2	14.8	8 917	19 365	37 656	62.9	1.4	38 763	19.1	27.8	26.5
Harrison	69	1 287	1 797	6.3	65.1	12.3	14.2	9 474	19 906	39 301	61.6	1.0	38 005	18.0	26.9	25.3
Henry	250	3 516	4 869	8.7	53.5	15.4	26.3	8 698	23 961	42 181	57.4	2.1	42 455	18.8	26.7	25.3
Hickory	22	1 224	1 675	13.3	59.6	10.3	8.6	9 426	18 153	32 122	72.6	0.5	31 320	23.8	39.3	36.3
Holt	245	1 602	780	2.8	54.2	19.2	7.3	12 120	25 319	42 500	55.0	1.7	42 845	13.7	20.3	18.9
Howard	87	1 272	2 939	34.1	48.8	24.2	12.0	8 298	22 158	44 820	55.2	2.1	44 634	15.9	20.9	19.2
Howell	218	3 068	9 486	8.2	54.7	14.9	46.4	8 314	18 817	32 784	67.7	1.9	36 604	19.9	30.0	28.9
Iron	359	1 195	2 027	2.4	59.8	12.0	18.1	9 680	19 559	36 239	64.4	0.8	33 415	22.9	34.4	31.8
Jackson	702	4 117	170 132	18.3	40.0	28.8	1 122.5	10 588	26 629	46 869	52.5	3.0	48 364	17.6	25.0	23.3

1. Data for serious crimes have not been adjusted for underreporting; this may affect comparability between geographic areas and over time.   2. Per 100,000 population estimated by the FBI.
3. All persons 3 years old and over enrolled in nursery school through college.   4. Persons 25 years old and over.   5. Elementary and secondary education expenditures.
6. Based on population estimated by the American Community Survey, 2011–2015.

Table B. States and Counties — Personal Income

STATE County	Personal income, 2015										Earnings, 2015		
	Total (mil dol)	Percent change, 2014–2015	Per capita[1] Dollars	Per capita[1] Rank	Wages and salaries (mil dol)	Supplements to wages and salaries; employer contributions (mil dol) Pension and insurance	Government social insurance	Proprietors' income (mil dol)	Dividends, interest, and rent (mil dol)	Personal transfer receipts (mil dol)	Total (mil dol)	Contributions for government social insurance (mil dol) From employee and self-employed	From employer
	62	63	64	65	66	67	68	69	70	71	72	73	74

STATE County	62	63	64	65	66	67	68	69	70	71	72	73	74
MISSISSIPPI—Cont'd													
Sunflower	733	-1.7	27 136	2 990	299	57	22	23	111	283	401	28	22
Tallahatchie	400	-6.1	27 405	2 799	118	18	9	30	51	137	176	13	9
Tate	905	3.0	31 984	2 516	203	36	15	49	97	260	304	24	15
Tippah	671	3.2	30 317	2 811	234	40	18	40	76	227	332	26	18
Tishomingo	565	5.3	28 920	2 943	207	35	16	30	70	204	288	23	16
Tunica	311	-4.2	30 052	2 516	315	33	25	16	48	101	390	25	25
Union	874	3.7	30 729	2 705	438	63	33	66	113	239	600	43	33
Walthall	411	-0.6	28 046	2 867	90	16	7	46	49	155	159	12	7
Warren	1 707	1.7	35 951	1 664	930	171	74	31	288	445	1 206	81	74
Washington	1 605	-0.4	33 356	2 377	665	109	51	125	234	542	949	67	51
Wayne	670	-4.6	32 564	2 300	196	32	15	108	96	195	351	22	15
Webster	314	4.0	31 690	2 718	70	12	5	17	38	122	104	10	5
Wilkinson	251	3.3	27 487	3 019	61	11	5	13	39	98	90	7	5
Winston	581	-0.4	31 746	2 503	180	28	13	49	84	198	271	20	13
Yalobusha	378	3.1	30 360	2 733	106	20	8	28	47	156	163	14	8
Yazoo	760	0.9	27 763	2 949	281	58	21	29	118	260	390	28	21
MISSOURI	257 338	3.2	42 352	X	134 523	22 533	9 765	19 532	45 673	51 659	186 353	11 189	9 765
Adair	766	1.4	30 188	2 594	345	76	25	52	152	211	498	30	25
Andrew	680	-0.7	39 302	1 075	87	20	6	24	103	127	137	11	6
Atchison	217	-19.4	40 921	388	56	12	4	25	43	52	97	6	4
Audrain	950	-1.9	36 391	1 549	352	79	25	168	141	218	625	37	25
Barry	1 173	2.6	32 752	2 223	549	99	41	140	213	326	829	50	41
Barton	390	-5.3	32 845	1 805	104	24	8	47	62	116	183	11	8
Bates	555	2.1	33 722	1 822	131	30	9	32	91	162	203	15	9
Benton	641	4.1	34 320	2 358	116	27	9	79	103	245	231	19	9
Bollinger	358	0.8	29 349	2 720	57	13	4	17	55	122	91	8	4
Boone	7 402	4.3	42 302	1 017	4 184	942	284	471	1 310	1 137	5 880	311	284
Buchanan	3 266	2.5	36 650	1 757	2 149	383	157	190	504	824	2 879	171	157
Butler	1 426	-0.1	33 212	2 049	687	142	53	78	208	509	960	63	53
Caldwell	296	-3.9	32 835	1 747	57	14	4	23	41	74	98	7	4
Callaway	1 557	2.1	34 718	1 965	611	146	43	57	227	358	858	52	43
Camden	1 537	3.8	34 740	1 904	548	94	43	128	342	455	814	57	43
Cape Girardeau	3 145	3.4	40 031	1 240	1 688	302	123	320	517	634	2 433	144	123
Carroll	399	-5.6	44 402	480	87	18	7	52	69	89	164	11	7
Carter	187	4.6	29 929	2 912	43	11	4	16	27	70	73	6	4
Cass	4 230	4.6	41 636	1 216	941	176	70	233	574	787	1 419	94	70
Cedar	430	2.1	30 852	2 628	92	22	7	38	68	159	158	12	7
Chariton	309	-13.5	40 679	374	65	14	5	37	61	76	121	7	5
Christian	2 971	6.0	35 675	1 960	586	117	44	198	388	579	946	66	44
Clark	221	-5.2	32 425	1 666	43	11	3	8	34	60	66	5	3
Clay	10 440	6.0	44 304	860	5 231	807	390	804	1 218	1 588	7 232	429	390
Clinton	790	0.1	38 313	1 480	147	32	11	25	123	163	214	15	11
Cole	3 290	2.9	42 884	973	2 276	541	154	248	555	597	3 219	170	154
Cooper	589	-0.3	33 380	2 046	186	38	14	18	93	147	255	18	14
Crawford	800	5.7	32 611	2 017	259	49	20	68	117	243	396	28	20
Dade	244	-2.2	32 080	2 294	57	13	4	29	40	75	103	7	4
Dallas	489	2.0	29 822	2 643	76	17	6	51	68	160	150	12	6
Daviess	281	-9.5	34 087	1 475	48	12	3	39	48	73	102	7	3
DeKalb	308	-2.5	24 284	3 061	114	30	8	6	47	81	157	10	8
Dent	484	3.8	31 040	2 648	126	29	9	33	75	168	198	14	9
Douglas	318	1.6	23 759	2 962	74	17	6	22	48	126	120	10	6
Dunklin	983	0.4	31 831	2 450	297	62	23	54	125	397	436	32	23
Franklin	3 965	3.9	38 714	1 418	1 582	293	120	183	591	858	2 177	140	120
Gasconade	548	3.4	36 901	1 691	174	38	13	32	104	147	257	18	13
Gentry	257	-11.0	38 352	750	83	16	6	32	42	72	136	8	6
Greene	11 220	5.2	38 947	1 441	7 162	1 214	528	1 053	1 967	2 401	9 958	595	528
Grundy	331	-2.8	32 753	2 032	128	29	9	25	54	105	191	13	9
Harrison	296	-4.7	34 346	1 567	80	19	6	30	56	87	135	9	6
Henry	854	-1.8	39 266	1 317	313	67	22	72	143	253	474	31	22
Hickory	243	4.8	26 392	3 040	37	9	3	15	41	113	64	7	3
Holt	164	-19.3	36 660	597	47	10	3	9	34	45	70	6	3
Howard	356	-0.8	35 119	1 681	89	19	7	11	62	98	126	9	7
Howell	1 271	3.3	31 677	2 579	549	110	42	89	195	418	791	53	42
Iron	318	3.1	31 407	2 696	145	29	10	14	39	137	199	14	10
Jackson	28 568	4.3	41 545	991	21 218	3 293	1 535	2 267	4 314	5 794	28 313	1 663	1 535

1. Based on the resident population estimated as of July 1 of the year shown.

Table B. States and Counties — Earnings, Social Security, and Housing

STATE County	Earnings, 2015 (cont.) — Percent by selected industries									Social Security beneficiaries, December 2015		Supplemental Security Income recipients, December 2015	Housing units, 2016	
	Farm	Mining	Construction	Manu-facturing	Information: professional, scientific, technical services	Retail trade	Finance, insurance, real estate and leasing	Health care and social assistance	Govern-ment	Number	Rate[1]		Total	Percent change, 2010–2016
	75	76	77	78	79	80	81	82	83	84	85	86	87	88
MISSISSIPPI—Cont'd														
Sunflower	1.2	0.0	3.4	3.7	2.1	5.6	4.1	6.5	42.7	5 640	209	2 018	9 699	0.1
Tallahatchie	7.9	0.4	1.8	1.6	D	7.4	3.5	D	26.8	3 130	214	1 080	5 548	0.3
Tate	1.5	D	5.9	7.4	7.5	10.0	4.8	D	27.2	6 290	222	947	11 265	2.9
Tippah	2.1	D	5.6	29.7	D	7.2	3.4	D	16.2	6 095	276	1 076	9 737	0.4
Tishomingo	0.7	0.0	11.2	34.6	1.9	7.0	3.1	D	15.1	5 785	297	732	10 332	0.3
Tunica	4.1	0.0	2.4	5.2	D	2.6	3.0	2.2	10.3	2 130	206	783	4 845	0.9
Union	1.2	0.0	4.9	38.3	D	5.6	2.6	D	10.6	6 965	246	808	11 823	2.6
Walthall	12.9	1.1	7.1	13.9	D	7.1	4.3	D	19.2	3 680	252	715	7 154	0.3
Warren	0.0	D	3.7	15.2	6.8	6.6	3.5	11.9	30.9	10 225	215	2 101	21 889	0.0
Washington	0.6	D	3.8	8.9	5.4	8.4	5.5	11.0	24.8	11 585	241	4 472	21 604	-0.5
Wayne	15.8	6.0	6.6	8.1	2.4	8.0	5.7	D	18.0	4 705	229	937	9 231	0.2
Webster	2.4	D	7.2	10.4	D	6.6	1.9	D	19.3	3 240	328	672	4 811	0.2
Wilkinson	4.1	D	1.5	8.8	D	6.9	6.3	D	30.0	2 230	245	698	5 050	0.3
Winston	8.9	D	5.4	19.6	2.9	9.3	3.1	D	14.0	4 970	272	880	8 831	1.0
Yalobusha	0.4	D	10.8	30.8	D	5.6	3.4	2.3	25.4	4 195	337	930	6 402	0.9
Yazoo	-0.5	D	4.2	11.9	D	4.9	5.4	D	37.7	5 525	202	1 767	10 080	0.1
MISSOURI	0.4	0.2	5.6	11.0	11.3	6.2	8.5	12.2	15.7	1 258 256	207	140 271	2 760 084	1.7
Adair	0.7	0.0	4.4	7.7	4.3	9.2	4.2	D	26.2	4 810	189	684	11 385	1.1
Andrew	-3.8	D	14.4	1.9	D	8.8	5.0	D	26.0	3 375	195	178	7 276	-0.4
Atchison	3.9	0.0	6.4	0.7	6.2	6.1	10.0	12.2	18.5	1 475	278	86	2 950	-1.2
Audrain	1.1	0.8	3.6	34.2	2.8	7.9	4.3	D	20.4	5 745	220	594	10 787	-0.6
Barry	8.9	0.2	4.6	29.3	16.1	6.0	5.1	5.7	9.6	9 125	255	976	17 364	-0.9
Barton	10.9	D	9.9	9.1	D	8.4	6.0	4.7	24.8	3 215	271	346	5 559	-0.7
Bates	-2.8	D	10.4	2.5	8.6	11.2	7.1	9.0	29.7	4 210	257	396	7 796	-0.6
Benton	2.4	0.0	8.1	5.4	2.1	8.4	9.0	D	23.5	6 990	374	595	13 976	-1.2
Bollinger	-2.5	D	11.9	6.8	3.0	8.2	3.4	11.0	24.5	3 285	270	432	5 809	-1.2
Boone	0.1	0.0	4.5	4.5	7.8	7.0	6.9	11.2	36.3	25 230	145	2 692	75 719	8.9
Buchanan	0.1	D	7.3	26.3	5.3	6.2	5.3	15.0	13.7	18 310	206	2 453	38 543	0.3
Butler	-2.2	0.0	3.9	13.1	5.8	10.4	6.4	D	22.6	11 425	267	2 319	19 678	-0.3
Caldwell	6.1	D	13.2	1.6	4.8	12.5	4.5	4.9	28.9	2 145	238	160	4 607	0.0
Callaway	0.8	0.4	5.6	13.6	4.1	4.6	2.7	D	23.4	9 500	212	884	18 597	0.4
Camden	0.0	D	9.8	4.1	4.7	14.5	8.8	17.5	12.2	12 735	287	697	41 424	0.6
Cape Girardeau	0.2	0.1	5.4	12.8	6.4	8.4	6.5	24.6	13.8	16 085	205	1 651	33 287	2.1
Carroll	-0.1	0.0	13.3	15.2	D	6.4	5.5	D	17.5	2 390	267	216	4 601	-0.6
Carter	-0.4	D	14.6	11.6	D	6.5	D	8.2	29.8	1 860	298	327	3 217	-0.9
Cass	0.8	0.3	12.4	6.8	4.3	9.1	5.7	8.9	20.0	19 715	194	1 003	40 986	2.4
Cedar	3.3	D	14.0	6.6	2.8	9.3	4.1	10.4	25.1	4 380	314	437	7 165	-0.8
Chariton	15.0	0.1	9.4	5.4	1.8	6.7	8.4	6.5	17.6	1 930	254	151	4 137	-0.7
Christian	0.4	D	14.5	7.5	7.7	8.9	6.6	7.0	18.1	16 420	197	1 085	33 374	5.7
Clark	-8.6	D	D	9.6	D	13.3	D	6.5	32.0	1 725	253	123	3 447	-0.7
Clay	0.0	0.1	4.7	17.8	14.3	10.9	4.2	7.5	14.8	40 335	171	2 587	96 482	2.7
Clinton	-2.6	0.0	7.9	5.6	D	5.9	6.7	22.0	27.1	4 230	205	355	8 898	0.2
Cole	0.1	D	5.5	4.6	9.5	6.4	6.1	10.9	38.5	15 910	207	1 257	33 048	2.4
Cooper	-2.7	D	11.3	8.1	D	8.5	6.9	9.0	25.6	3 955	225	324	7 435	-0.4
Crawford	-0.3	D	6.0	28.3	2.4	12.7	3.9	D	11.9	6 520	266	715	11 922	-0.3
Dade	11.0	0.4	8.8	11.3	D	4.5	D	2.1	22.3	2 170	286	190	3 924	-1.0
Dallas	2.0	D	D	5.1	2.3	10.8	6.7	D	21.6	4 520	275	540	7 560	-1.3
Daviess	11.8	0.1	16.6	D	D	8.5	3.5	D	22.7	2 020	245	137	4 176	-0.5
DeKalb	-4.1	0.0	6.9	D	1.2	9.0	9.6	D	42.0	2 280	180	117	4 296	-0.8
Dent	0.4	D	4.8	11.1	2.5	9.5	6.7	D	25.5	4 270	273	590	7 223	-0.8
Douglas	2.3	D	6.0	21.6	D	9.8	3.1	D	20.1	3 840	287	393	6 435	-1.3
Dunklin	-0.6	0.0	4.6	6.9	3.0	10.7	6.9	D	19.5	8 480	275	2 336	14 320	-0.7
Franklin	0.4	0.2	7.6	27.6	5.4	6.9	5.3	11.5	11.9	23 165	226	1 840	44 361	2.2
Gasconade	-0.8	D	6.1	29.9	D	7.3	4.9	D	20.6	4 190	283	300	8 107	-1.2
Gentry	18.0	0.1	D	D	D	5.7	D	20.7	15.7	1 680	251	168	3 194	-0.5
Greene	0.0	D	4.3	8.6	9.9	7.7	6.6	19.2	12.7	58 940	205	6 579	131 905	5.2
Grundy	0.4	D	6.8	23.2	D	6.6	4.1	13.9	24.5	2 525	251	257	4 997	-0.5
Harrison	1.2	D	3.5	1.8	D	24.2	5.9	7.1	30.2	2 290	266	234	4 382	-0.6
Henry	1.2	D	13.0	17.4	3.1	8.6	5.5	9.5	22.4	6 615	304	713	10 863	-0.2
Hickory	1.8	D	11.0	1.4	D	12.0	D	10.1	25.5	3 475	378	233	6 706	-1.9
Holt	-24.5	D	6.7	27.2	D	13.3	6.8	7.6	20.7	1 205	270	76	2 773	-1.2
Howard	-7.8	D	7.4	13.3	D	8.2	5.5	D	17.7	2 290	226	233	4 534	-1.1
Howell	0.6	0.2	3.5	15.4	5.8	7.3	5.1	19.7	15.2	11 530	287	1 663	18 036	0.1
Iron	0.3	D	D	14.4	0.9	6.6	2.0	10.2	19.5	3 085	305	615	5 259	-1.3
Jackson	0.0	0.0	6.4	6.1	18.3	4.5	11.8	11.9	16.0	127 045	185	17 281	319 794	2.5

1. Per 1,000 resident population estimated as of July 1 of the year shown.

Table B. States and Counties — Housing, Labor Force, and Employment

STATE County	Housing units, 2011–2015								Civilian labor force, 2016				Civilian employment,[6] 2011–2015		
	Occupied units										Unemployment		Percent		
		Owner-occupied				Renter-occupied									
				Median owner cost as a percent of income											Con-struction, produc-tion, and mainte-nance occu-pations
	Total	Percent	Median value[1]	With a mort-gage	Without a mort-gage[2]	Median rent[3]	Median rent as a per-cent of income[2]	Sub-stand-ard units[4] (percent)	Total	Percent change, 2015–2016	Total	Rate[5]	Total	Manage-ment, business, science and arts	
	89	90	91	92	93	94	95	96	97	98	99	100	101	102	103
MISSISSIPPI—Cont'd															
Sunflower	8 508	57.6	70 000	26.0	12.6	573	32.8	5.1	8 295	-2.6	784	9.5	8 382	28.2	29.3
Tallahatchie	4 386	74.9	58 100	21.9	13.1	559	28.6	3.3	5 765	-1.3	392	6.8	3 806	33.2	27.2
Tate	10 004	73.9	110 200	22.3	10.0	713	31.5	4.2	12 157	0.9	708	5.8	11 418	28.9	30.5
Tippah	8 349	76.8	77 800	23.8	10.6	552	27.2	2.1	9 425	-0.6	522	5.5	8 428	25.2	41.9
Tishomingo	7 652	76.6	76 600	22.4	10.0	526	27.0	2.0	8 322	3.4	456	5.5	7 885	22.0	39.1
Tunica	3 989	41.1	80 000	22.1	10.2	683	32.3	8.8	4 670	-0.2	331	7.1	4 191	23.9	18.0
Union	10 345	71.0	83 200	22.6	10.0	671	26.8	4.6	13 719	3.3	608	4.4	10 949	21.9	39.3
Walthall	5 761	85.3	93 200	26.5	13.0	475	31.1	4.0	5 054	-2.3	390	7.7	5 382	28.5	36.8
Warren	18 415	64.8	100 800	20.9	11.2	675	32.9	2.5	20 845	-0.6	1 327	6.4	19 554	36.6	22.1
Washington	18 193	55.0	73 900	23.1	13.1	632	37.1	3.2	17 892	-1.3	1 618	9.0	17 034	33.1	23.5
Wayne	7 630	85.0	74 300	18.9	12.9	508	33.7	3.1	7 561	-1.2	555	7.3	7 906	21.8	41.6
Webster	4 044	75.6	78 500	22.9	10.5	469	33.4	4.4	3 933	-0.7	246	6.3	3 544	35.8	31.4
Wilkinson	3 209	78.7	59 600	26.8	14.2	513	29.6	2.6	2 850	-1.6	290	10.2	2 914	25.3	31.4
Winston	7 664	69.1	78 600	21.7	13.0	599	32.4	3.6	7 145	0.4	505	7.1	7 034	31.8	33.5
Yalobusha	5 101	74.9	74 600	24.8	11.5	470	28.8	2.9	4 921	-0.6	306	6.2	5 055	21.8	40.3
Yazoo	8 602	61.2	68 500	24.3	12.8	575	38.0	3.7	9 335	0.9	688	7.4	8 382	26.6	30.5
MISSOURI	2 364 688	67.2	138 400	21.0	11.7	746	29.4	2.0	3 111 525	0.5	140 817	4.5	2 807 996	35.2	22.1
Adair	9 635	58.5	108 000	18.8	10.5	594	37.4	2.0	10 519	0.1	597	5.7	11 096	34.9	21.3
Andrew	6 808	78.3	127 200	21.3	10.0	726	26.1	2.5	10 018	0.3	376	3.8	8 583	31.9	25.6
Atchison	2 501	68.4	82 300	21.1	12.5	547	22.3	0.6	2 863	0.4	131	4.6	2 691	34.8	26.9
Audrain	9 273	70.3	91 900	20.0	11.4	613	25.3	2.0	11 280	-0.9	479	4.2	10 600	27.3	31.2
Barry	13 246	75.3	113 000	21.2	12.3	570	26.7	3.0	15 262	1.7	688	4.5	14 259	25.6	39.4
Barton	4 988	73.3	93 500	22.5	14.0	528	28.6	3.0	5 379	0.3	279	5.2	5 075	28.9	32.0
Bates	6 690	72.5	103 700	21.7	12.7	608	29.8	2.3	8 333	1.6	438	5.3	7 186	28.0	31.2
Benton	8 149	81.6	111 200	23.8	12.5	593	33.6	2.3	7 337	1.4	444	6.1	6 442	28.8	30.2
Bollinger	4 753	81.4	97 700	21.8	10.3	566	26.5	3.0	5 584	-0.1	286	5.1	5 064	22.5	41.0
Boone	66 980	56.0	169 400	19.8	10.0	795	33.9	1.5	99 372	-0.2	3 227	3.2	90 949	46.4	13.1
Buchanan	33 176	63.6	109 700	19.9	11.7	704	29.8	2.0	46 817	-0.0	1 917	4.1	42 029	26.7	28.1
Butler	16 730	65.1	93 300	19.9	12.5	632	29.4	1.5	19 009	-0.5	1 083	5.7	17 340	29.5	26.4
Caldwell	3 715	74.7	97 000	21.3	13.2	640	29.1	3.1	4 536	2.5	207	4.6	3 889	30.3	30.9
Callaway	16 150	73.7	124 200	21.3	10.3	650	26.2	2.7	21 942	0.6	898	4.1	19 844	31.0	25.7
Camden	16 748	78.7	169 700	23.2	11.1	665	28.7	2.2	18 999	0.7	1 088	5.7	17 403	29.0	23.3
Cape Girardeau	29 795	64.3	142 300	19.8	10.7	682	29.4	2.1	41 121	0.0	1 779	4.3	37 661	33.3	21.1
Carroll	3 624	75.0	76 400	18.7	11.6	522	27.6	2.5	4 831	-0.4	261	5.4	4 010	28.1	30.7
Carter	2 453	71.3	89 200	26.9	10.0	533	29.2	4.1	2 566	1.6	180	7.0	2 402	31.0	28.1
Cass	37 945	76.0	159 600	21.5	12.4	910	28.5	2.3	55 014	1.4	2 261	4.1	48 122	35.2	25.2
Cedar	5 904	69.7	88 900	23.9	13.8	591	32.5	2.5	5 864	-1.1	293	5.0	5 029	29.5	29.7
Chariton	2 947	77.1	75 400	18.9	12.0	504	26.0	1.8	3 889	0.3	168	4.3	3 323	26.9	32.1
Christian	29 889	73.1	143 100	21.1	11.3	769	29.5	2.6	43 591	0.6	1 699	3.9	37 578	35.4	20.2
Clark	2 833	76.4	84 000	20.0	11.4	497	20.5	2.7	3 424	-0.9	250	7.3	3 210	25.2	42.6
Clay	87 676	69.9	154 900	20.4	12.0	828	26.5	1.5	134 971	1.4	5 229	3.9	118 111	36.8	20.9
Clinton	8 076	73.8	135 500	19.8	13.0	768	24.8	1.9	11 242	1.6	468	4.2	9 653	25.7	29.3
Cole	29 448	67.6	149 200	19.6	10.0	611	24.5	1.5	39 899	0.7	1 417	3.6	35 978	39.7	18.7
Cooper	6 488	71.3	124 000	19.6	11.4	639	27.4	1.9	7 546	-1.5	369	4.9	7 916	27.5	26.7
Crawford	9 309	72.7	111 600	21.6	13.8	603	30.4	3.1	10 964	-0.1	582	5.3	9 393	25.6	35.4
Dade	3 195	78.6	79 900	22.0	12.3	594	30.9	2.6	3 631	1.0	161	4.4	3 307	33.3	29.7
Dallas	6 252	76.0	94 600	22.5	10.7	601	23.7	3.4	7 059	0.5	385	5.5	5 943	26.8	31.2
Daviess	3 047	77.6	102 500	23.5	12.5	566	25.5	4.4	4 176	1.5	159	3.8	3 420	27.6	32.1
DeKalb	3 756	62.7	110 700	19.2	12.6	497	24.5	1.5	5 123	0.8	225	4.4	4 285	30.5	30.6
Dent	5 920	71.1	88 700	23.1	11.2	511	27.8	3.3	6 278	-1.0	340	5.4	5 882	25.7	31.6
Douglas	5 277	74.7	101 200	24.1	12.4	560	30.8	3.0	5 152	1.6	313	6.1	4 897	20.4	39.2
Dunklin	12 623	63.1	67 500	19.5	12.7	489	30.5	2.5	13 058	-1.1	1 070	8.2	11 646	26.7	30.8
Franklin	39 915	73.6	149 400	22.2	11.4	696	27.0	2.0	52 985	0.2	2 313	4.4	48 336	28.1	32.7
Gasconade	6 246	74.6	120 000	21.1	10.8	580	32.7	3.6	7 794	0.8	335	4.3	6 567	26.3	36.0
Gentry	2 748	73.3	83 400	19.3	13.5	531	25.0	3.8	3 634	-0.1	134	3.7	2 989	33.2	28.8
Greene	117 732	58.5	129 400	20.5	10.1	701	30.8	1.6	151 069	0.5	5 668	3.8	135 307	35.0	19.2
Grundy	4 057	70.2	79 800	19.8	12.2	566	29.0	4.1	4 948	0.1	227	4.6	4 272	29.9	29.6
Harrison	3 574	73.4	74 300	21.1	13.1	588	26.5	4.2	4 025	0.3	169	4.2	3 755	29.7	28.1
Henry	9 518	74.8	91 100	21.8	12.7	669	28.8	4.0	9 991	-1.8	495	5.0	9 359	28.4	31.7
Hickory	4 105	81.2	94 800	25.3	13.3	558	35.7	2.9	3 732	-0.4	209	5.6	3 020	29.2	31.2
Holt	2 130	71.2	86 200	21.0	11.2	476	25.0	2.6	2 718	-0.3	89	3.3	2 238	32.4	30.7
Howard	3 729	74.3	97 900	21.0	10.0	663	28.8	2.2	5 101	0.4	225	4.4	4 533	34.0	27.1
Howell	16 263	67.0	102 800	22.1	11.3	561	30.0	2.5	16 265	-1.1	1 027	6.3	16 205	26.1	30.1
Iron	4 046	69.8	82 600	21.0	11.3	539	27.3	2.7	3 745	-3.4	267	7.1	3 878	22.5	31.4
Jackson	274 485	59.3	125 500	21.7	12.9	807	30.7	1.8	369 804	1.2	18 712	5.1	326 275	36.1	19.5

1. Specified owner-occupied units. 2. A value of 10.0 represents 10 percent or less; a value of 50.0 represents 50 percent or more. 3. Specified renter-occupied units.
4. Overcrowded or lacking complete plumbing facilities. 5. Percent of civilian labor force. 6. Civilian employed persons 16 years old and over.

Table B. States and Counties — Nonfarm Employment and Agriculture

	Private nonfarm establishments, employment and payroll, 2015									Agriculture, 2012			
		Employment						Annual payroll		Farms			
												Percent with:		Farm operators whose principal occupation is farming (percent)
STATE County	Number of establishments	Total	Health care and social assistance	Manufacturing	Retail trade	Finance and insurance	Professional, scientific, and technical services	Total (mil dol)	Average per employee (dollars)	Number	Fewer than 50 acres	500 acres or more	
	104	105	106	107	108	109	110	111	112	113	114	115	116
MISSISSIPPI—Cont'd													
Sunflower	451	5 179	1 056	331	1 002	220	57	168	32 403	350	22.6	44.0	59.7
Tallahatchie	176	1 830	425	D	258	38	44	60	32 833	509	13.6	28.7	38.9
Tate	365	3 690	595	490	803	177	93	116	31 499	569	25.3	14.1	38.8
Tippah	352	4 997	628	1 811	644	137	80	150	29 977	691	25.2	5.4	32.0
Tishomingo	364	4 485	638	1 878	584	115	86	142	31 570	287	22.0	3.8	36.2
Tunica	207	7 538	195	453	377	81	17	219	29 090	108	7.4	62.0	64.8
Union	502	9 111	1 073	3 612	1 152	219	82	340	37 291	688	29.1	6.4	25.3
Walthall	215	1 915	248	379	361	70	19	58	30 192	684	30.7	4.8	49.9
Warren	1 027	19 042	3 897	3 016	2 537	360	584	686	36 037	238	18.5	19.7	39.9
Washington	1 140	14 648	2 982	1 136	2 915	339	347	453	30 895	284	18.7	47.5	71.1
Wayne	380	4 421	613	877	976	196	117	153	34 536	508	34.4	5.5	48.0
Webster	165	1 515	428	287	225	46	68	51	33 972	362	20.7	11.0	32.9
Wilkinson	134	1 410	335	147	273	37	11	39	27 790	198	17.7	23.7	41.4
Winston	369	4 940	584	1 433	914	91	86	168	34 071	506	27.1	9.5	40.9
Yalobusha	186	2 354	343	901	312	98	35	78	33 160	364	21.2	13.7	50.5
Yazoo	387	4 102	921	573	758	137	160	140	34 186	672	14.3	25.9	49.9
MISSOURI	158 191	2 442 316	411 306	259 969	315 657	128 444	157 455	109 136	44 685	99 171	25.5	13.7	44.0
Adair	617	8 215	2 059	575	1 539	216	590	229	27 892	822	19.6	16.7	44.0
Andrew	317	1 701	347	30	308	62	49	51	29 929	826	29.5	12.8	42.1
Atchison	204	1 298	260	29	311	81	27	36	27 455	395	12.9	36.5	66.6
Audrain	548	6 921	1 198	1 829	1 136	262	121	221	31 967	1 015	18.6	25.1	55.8
Barry	747	14 152	1 845	4 956	1 556	285	D	539	38 084	1 427	31.1	8.4	43.5
Barton	255	2 679	472	378	547	149	108	79	29 592	940	24.0	22.8	45.7
Bates	358	2 827	764	88	672	214	79	83	29 187	1 169	23.4	18.1	46.6
Benton	366	2 278	436	181	692	130	61	55	24 205	800	18.5	13.1	52.8
Bollinger	205	1 405	352	155	322	48	35	37	26 282	788	16.9	12.8	42.4
Boone	4 649	75 408	17 295	4 115	13 056	6 843	3 956	2 813	37 299	1 171	39.5	8.6	38.3
Buchanan	2 301	43 243	8 251	10 399	5 547	1 687	971	1 784	41 251	727	29.4	13.1	44.4
Butler	1 288	15 204	4 321	2 348	2 869	574	370	486	31 960	509	23.8	24.6	47.9
Caldwell	148	943	100	38	330	55	19	30	32 330	1 035	24.3	10.6	41.0
Callaway	750	11 902	2 320	1 752	1 277	291	323	452	37 976	1 417	28.4	9.7	35.5
Camden	1 401	12 468	2 301	440	3 010	427	883	409	32 805	533	16.3	12.0	42.2
Cape Girardeau	2 466	37 627	10 194	3 718	6 222	1 235	1 169	1 388	36 879	1 139	29.5	10.2	47.8
Carroll	225	1 811	377	205	295	105	44	59	32 689	1 112	18.4	18.2	39.8
Carter	169	946	265	192	155	42	29	20	21 052	196	23.5	17.9	45.4
Cass	1 918	20 100	3 105	2 504	4 121	626	448	627	31 210	1 495	41.1	9.2	46.3
Cedar	288	2 411	626	322	455	82	49	62	25 876	819	19.9	10.4	45.2
Chariton	210	1 313	284	D	258	82	29	38	29 023	1 120	17.1	21.3	47.8
Christian	1 721	14 265	1 705	1 529	2 793	513	978	417	29 237	1 177	36.4	5.6	43.8
Clark	140	959	133	104	243	65	11	23	24 103	673	13.5	20.8	40.9
Clay	4 997	97 919	13 468	13 732	12 005	2 345	14 475	5 031	51 383	578	48.8	10.2	42.6
Clinton	377	2 908	986	137	501	138	80	92	31 602	758	35.1	8.8	38.5
Cole	2 265	34 652	6 428	2 252	5 503	1 934	1 616	1 313	37 887	1 055	24.1	5.4	38.2
Cooper	393	3 847	853	209	763	140	75	109	28 370	928	16.4	17.3	42.8
Crawford	498	5 464	829	1 882	657	155	142	186	34 127	679	20.2	12.8	40.4
Dade	141	1 191	41	306	180	34	12	36	29 873	734	21.5	16.5	47.0
Dallas	298	2 414	950	218	478	116	46	46	19 108	1 188	31.7	7.6	46.8
Daviess	147	902	91	231	204	55	11	25	27 619	1 199	23.4	12.9	36.8
DeKalb	218	1 895	400	35	481	221	17	60	31 925	863	22.7	12.6	40.3
Dent	416	3 653	773	593	529	176	53	126	34 394	673	21.0	13.5	35.7
Douglas	198	2 095	303	642	442	59	30	49	23 275	984	18.6	10.9	43.2
Dunklin	828	8 920	3 179	589	1 443	295	671	197	22 041	345	22.6	42.6	63.5
Franklin	2 619	35 105	4 197	9 176	4 897	1 089	906	1 311	37 349	1 841	33.6	5.1	32.6
Gasconade	413	4 712	937	1 324	671	176	98	125	26 549	859	14.6	10.0	39.1
Gentry	194	1 845	864	D	292	61	15	47	25 262	708	20.2	16.2	40.8
Greene	8 632	150 135	28 017	13 101	19 655	7 387	6 987	5 891	39 238	1 752	48.8	4.5	43.9
Grundy	249	2 664	591	761	471	83	31	87	32 526	689	23.1	12.0	42.7
Harrison	203	1 953	482	42	662	117	25	49	24 845	1 051	18.5	17.4	42.7
Henry	588	6 889	1 779	1 311	1 132	230	125	246	35 689	894	21.8	21.5	54.7
Hickory	155	722	188	18	242	40	20	17	23 791	487	14.4	18.1	56.5
Holt	150	1 009	204	156	159	55	D	31	30 559	408	20.3	26.7	49.3
Howard	207	2 126	559	235	265	84	55	58	27 374	765	17.0	19.0	36.6
Howell	1 146	13 070	3 514	2 520	2 238	379	302	399	30 556	1 535	24.8	10.1	41.3
Iron	237	2 000	701	80	302	64	17	65	32 490	273	15.4	13.6	46.2
Jackson	18 574	332 113	55 488	24 618	36 103	24 310	27 955	16 772	50 502	701	57.5	5.6	38.7

Table B. States and Counties — Agriculture

	Agriculture, 2012 (cont.)														
	Land in farms				Value of land and buildings (dollars)			Value of products sold					Percent of farms with sales of:		Government payments	
			Acres				Value of machinery and equipment, average per farm (dollars)			Percent from:					
STATE County	Acreage (1,000)	Percent change, 2007–2012	Average size of farm	Total irrigated (1,000)	Total cropland (1,000)	Average per farm	Average per acre		Total (mil dol)	Average per farm (dollars)	Crops	Live- stock and poultry products	$10,000 or more	$100,000 or more	Total ($1,000)	Percent of farms
	117	118	119	120	121	122	123	124	125	126	127	128	129	130	131	132
MISSISSIPPI—Cont'd																
Sunflower	373	-1.3	1 065	216.7	323.8	2 077 580	1 951	360 220	273.8	782 283	89.3	10.7	66.9	50.3	10 155	85.1
Tallahatchie	341	7.9	669	112.4	254.8	1 505 411	2 249	200 244	165.0	324 202	99.2	0.8	45.2	22.6	9 164	76.8
Tate	153	-2.5	269	2.2	69.6	540 237	2 008	73 946	44.4	78 025	68.7	31.3	31.1	9.3	2 745	43.8
Tippah	124	-9.9	179	0.3	37.9	291 781	1 628	51 965	22.1	31 961	66.3	33.7	20.0	2.5	932	57.3
Tishomingo	50	-12.7	173	0.7	16.6	319 711	1 852	47 373	6.1	21 167	85.7	14.3	21.6	3.8	420	52.3
Tunica	212	5.3	1 959	101.4	194.5	5 291 852	2 701	598 713	130.1	1 204 222	D	D	73.1	58.3	7 006	89.8
Union	121	-10.4	176	0.1	43.7	364 727	2 073	44 686	17.1	24 785	75.7	24.3	22.7	3.8	1 531	57.8
Walthall	118	-7.8	173	0.1	32.2	516 697	2 992	55 263	79.8	116 722	5.8	94.2	31.9	11.3	1 773	53.7
Warren	125	11.5	524	4.9	43.8	983 702	1 877	103 592	30.6	128 723	98.9	1.1	26.5	10.9	1 648	54.6
Washington	342	2.7	1 206	220.9	313.0	2 563 155	2 126	548 342	271.4	955 764	96.4	3.6	78.9	58.5	9 036	77.1
Wayne	93	8.3	184	0.5	24.0	535 941	2 914	76 234	194.0	381 982	3.5	96.5	45.9	24.6	200	13.8
Webster	81	-3.9	223	0.7	25.8	401 997	1 806	50 633	20.3	56 180	69.6	30.4	25.1	6.9	1 899	68.5
Wilkinson	103	-8.9	521	0.5	15.0	1 170 980	2 248	70 000	7.2	36 182	42.0	58.0	26.3	5.6	829	52.0
Winston	98	2.4	193	0.0	18.8	419 709	2 172	59 943	74.7	147 630	4.5	95.5	27.9	7.1	455	31.4
Yalobusha	95	-4.8	260	1.3	33.4	472 665	1 820	61 310	18.3	50 379	86.4	13.6	25.3	6.6	1 492	56.6
Yazoo	351	-1.3	522	44.8	195.4	1 096 741	2 100	118 775	151.3	225 109	92.5	7.5	34.1	16.4	9 095	74.7
MISSOURI	28 266	-2.6	285	1 180.9	15 259.3	795 444	2 791	88 960	9 164.9	92 415	49.8	50.2	46.8	12.5	323 953	41.7
Adair	273	-2.4	332	0.1	134.0	815 103	2 453	79 223	35.8	43 539	56.3	43.7	44.5	9.9	3 054	50.5
Andrew	199	-16.8	240	D	138.0	855 310	3 558	90 700	57.7	69 831	80.1	19.9	48.9	14.9	3 587	66.8
Atchison	263	-13.5	666	12.2	228.6	3 238 514	4 862	297 134	170.0	430 256	86.5	13.5	73.9	49.9	3 963	84.3
Audrain	436	2.7	430	15.1	354.0	1 643 676	3 822	172 912	151.2	148 960	59.3	40.7	62.2	26.4	5 605	66.0
Barry	268	-7.4	188	0.4	73.6	476 843	2 538	56 169	357.8	250 751	1.8	98.2	51.4	18.3	876	13.0
Barton	332	-4.9	353	11.1	224.0	743 856	2 105	126 076	120.1	127 807	61.0	39.0	56.4	23.0	4 742	59.7
Bates	448	-5.4	383	2.2	278.2	869 524	2 268	113 850	104.1	89 087	61.5	38.6	53.8	14.7	4 369	57.5
Benton	241	8.3	301	0.7	87.2	628 791	2 090	70 250	62.7	78 371	20.8	79.2	52.4	10.3	1 013	29.1
Bollinger	200	-3.7	254	6.8	79.3	511 848	2 014	58 244	31.6	40 128	52.1	47.9	44.8	7.0	1 313	42.0
Boone	241	-7.0	206	5.3	144.4	749 119	3 644	69 631	52.2	44 565	66.0	34.0	34.9	8.1	1 837	31.0
Buchanan	189	-4.5	260	D	136.1	895 721	3 451	91 761	67.5	92 891	89.6	10.4	53.1	15.4	3 153	69.1
Butler	234	-6.6	460	123.6	186.2	1 464 493	3 184	181 733	126.3	248 189	97.4	2.6	52.7	25.0	6 090	52.1
Caldwell	245	-2.2	236	D	153.0	537 488	2 275	54 284	38.9	37 541	62.4	37.6	37.4	6.6	5 312	71.0
Callaway	316	-2.1	223	5.4	160.9	728 630	3 267	79 792	84.9	59 929	40.1	59.9	40.0	8.2	2 756	40.8
Camden	139	-4.0	260	0.1	24.4	566 041	2 177	44 377	17.6	32 951	11.0	89.0	43.7	4.5	100	5.4
Cape Girardeau	253	-16.4	222	11.6	157.3	695 755	3 133	80 699	77.7	68 175	67.2	32.8	45.8	11.8	3 397	54.9
Carroll	432	7.5	388	3.5	320.9	1 216 926	3 134	121 291	130.5	117 322	85.3	14.7	48.6	16.7	7 522	80.2
Carter	74	16.3	376	D	9.6	624 724	1 663	49 066	4.6	23 520	22.7	77.3	31.6	6.1	123	12.8
Cass	319	-2.2	214	2.8	202.4	708 608	3 318	73 090	86.2	57 682	69.8	30.2	36.3	7.5	2 726	34.4
Cedar	190	-0.4	232	D	63.3	422 039	1 822	57 703	23.6	28 797	28.9	71.1	49.7	4.5	639	17.7
Chariton	406	5.7	363	3.9	282.6	1 078 481	2 973	126 969	123.8	110 555	72.1	27.9	53.2	19.3	5 823	73.5
Christian	179	-5.1	152	0.1	53.3	476 400	3 124	48 936	24.3	20 622	14.3	85.7	38.9	3.8	240	7.1
Clark	241	-8.3	358	3.2	150.9	950 793	2 654	103 065	72.1	107 064	71.9	28.1	46.5	17.7	4 399	80.8
Clay	111	-23.1	191	D	57.2	819 787	4 282	92 087	50.4	87 118	38.6	61.4	40.0	11.8	1 079	24.7
Clinton	192	-19.3	253	D	126.9	866 280	3 427	84 827	56.4	74 431	68.5	31.5	39.7	10.3	2 589	48.2
Cole	176	-2.5	167	0.9	67.5	486 792	2 913	62 366	38.4	36 372	27.4	72.6	48.5	5.5	980	30.0
Cooper	307	1.6	331	0.7	190.3	940 300	2 841	108 986	78.3	84 363	57.5	42.5	58.6	16.9	4 120	64.7
Crawford	194	3.9	286	0.0	47.6	595 339	2 080	51 605	15.2	22 392	20.5	79.5	40.4	4.6	344	12.4
Dade	246	-11.1	335	6.5	113.4	733 312	2 192	86 000	69.5	94 661	47.9	52.1	56.1	13.6	1 656	27.9
Dallas	218	-2.2	183	0.2	60.1	426 668	2 326	44 228	47.7	40 160	11.5	88.5	43.7	7.2	612	9.5
Daviess	315	-4.8	263	0.1	210.5	731 193	2 784	71 812	96.6	80 591	40.0	60.0	36.0	9.4	8 392	71.9
DeKalb	243	-6.8	281	0.0	168.3	792 630	2 817	89 886	59.9	69 447	60.8	39.2	48.0	12.4	4 479	66.9
Dent	188	6.5	279	0.4	32.1	447 679	1 602	48 750	17.3	25 779	10.7	89.3	46.2	5.1	307	9.7
Douglas	254	-0.1	258	0.4	45.2	419 160	1 624	41 030	33.3	33 851	8.8	91.2	45.3	6.8	542	8.9
Dunklin	280	-13.9	811	155.8	266.2	3 056 875	3 770	425 835	199.0	576 846	98.9	1.1	69.6	48.7	8 186	75.9
Franklin	292	-2.7	158	1.3	128.9	589 536	3 722	57 212	64.1	34 794	43.1	56.9	34.9	4.9	1 483	26.9
Gasconade	209	-1.7	243	0.4	63.7	596 109	2 451	60 327	25.9	30 207	35.7	64.3	45.4	6.2	853	39.6
Gentry	253	-8.2	358	0.0	160.4	943 222	2 636	84 585	126.6	178 880	28.1	71.9	42.4	13.3	4 831	74.0
Greene	211	-9.2	120	0.3	68.2	442 679	3 683	42 410	41.5	23 669	17.4	82.6	32.9	3.4	609	9.0
Grundy	204	-12.1	296	0.5	139.8	681 840	2 303	67 837	44.7	64 835	63.4	36.6	37.7	9.9	4 432	65.7
Harrison	401	3.2	381	0.1	264.1	951 168	2 494	96 657	76.0	72 288	77.4	22.6	41.9	12.1	8 648	77.3
Henry	358	3.6	400	D	200.2	849 449	2 124	107 462	69.9	78 166	50.1	49.9	56.6	16.2	3 752	48.2
Hickory	182	24.0	374	D	57.3	725 201	1 941	50 281	25.8	52 959	16.3	83.7	47.0	8.0	757	33.7
Holt	200	-15.4	491	19.0	166.5	1 865 299	3 799	204 819	94.9	232 583	95.9	4.1	63.5	33.3	3 139	82.8
Howard	243	-12.0	318	2.8	139.9	807 152	2 537	97 344	47.8	62 455	77.5	22.5	49.2	14.9	3 553	66.1
Howell	354	-8.2	230	0.1	58.5	433 877	1 883	51 521	53.9	35 139	4.5	95.5	41.2	5.9	829	9.6
Iron	71	1.0	258	0.5	17.3	415 751	1 610	44 161	6.0	21 967	14.8	85.2	41.0	4.0	66	5.1
Jackson	111	-20.3	158	0.3	75.1	638 655	4 037	72 385	32.5	46 408	78.2	21.8	35.1	8.8	1 036	29.7

STATE County	Water use, 2010		Wholesale trade,[1] 2012				Retail trade,[2] 2012				Real estate and rental and leasing,[2] 2012			
	Total water withdrawn (mil gal/day)	Gallons withdrawn per person per day	Number of establish-ments	Number of employees	Sales (mil dol)	Annual payroll (mil dol)	Number of establish-ments	Number of employees	Sales (mil dol)	Annual payroll (mil dol)	Number of establish-ments	Number of employees	Receipts (mil dol)	Annual payroll (mil dol)
	133	134	135	136	137	138	139	140	141	142	143	144	145	146
MISSISSIPPI—Cont'd														
Sunflower	366.4	12 441	15	330	443.3	13.5	100	922	244.1	18.8	10	20	3.5	0.5
Tallahatchie	126.0	8 193	7	76	67.2	2.7	40	262	54.1	7.0	5	8	0.8	0.1
Tate	7.4	257	13	44	16.9	1.9	73	799	191.9	17.9	8	17	3.7	0.5
Tippah	4.6	208	15	143	247.8	6.4	77	628	133.8	11.8	6	37	2.7	1.2
Tishomingo	3.2	161	18	166	59.7	4.3	81	597	114.3	12.3	12	20	2.0	0.5
Tunica	155.8	14 454	6	62	84.2	3.2	68	511	107.4	9.0	11	27	10.0	0.9
Union	3.2	118	17	166	200.6	6.7	101	1 039	297.2	22.1	16	37	4.1	0.8
Walthall	3.7	238	4	D	D	D	41	364	111.3	7.4	5	17	2.2	0.6
Warren	217.4	4 458	41	D	D	D	207	2 588	606.9	53.5	43	186	33.5	6.5
Washington	458.9	8 974	70	638	1 152.7	32.8	232	2 937	656.6	56.4	47	159	21.4	4.8
Wayne	6.0	289	21	153	205.9	9.9	83	863	183.9	17.4	9	D	D	D
Webster	1.7	165	4	9	1.8	0.2	43	225	52.6	4.4	NA	NA	NA	NA
Wilkinson	3.5	352	10	48	46.8	1.6	32	283	54.4	6.0	4	D	D	D
Winston	3.1	160	15	247	198.6	9.0	87	870	209.6	18.4	13	116	5.0	2.7
Yalobusha	3.7	288	4	D	D	D	45	354	72.0	6.3	3	26	2.1	0.2
Yazoo	44.9	1 600	19	245	282.1	13.2	94	707	177.4	14.7	18	47	4.7	1.2
MISSOURI	8 568.5	1 431	6 557	96 683	91 916.4	4 978.9	21 456	302 568	90 546.6	7 278.2	6 165	33 447	6 730.0	1 297.9
Adair	3.2	124	21	D	D	D	121	1 538	336.2	30.3	22	78	14.2	2.5
Andrew	19.7	1 140	14	D	D	D	41	332	103.8	6.9	10	D	D	D
Atchison	6.3	1 108	14	133	228.9	5.1	41	316	109.8	7.7	3	5	0.3	0.1
Audrain	13.7	537	20	D	D	D	102	1 108	253.7	21.9	13	37	5.4	0.9
Barry	19.4	545	25	419	321.4	22.5	133	1 439	379.2	29.2	27	80	11.3	1.9
Barton	14.4	1 159	12	191	192.1	6.8	44	501	146.1	9.6	4	8	1.0	0.2
Bates	3.5	207	10	124	90.3	5.2	60	650	171.7	14.2	5	9	0.6	0.2
Benton	4.8	251	10	71	25.8	1.9	67	662	183.0	13.8	9	16	2.9	0.3
Bollinger	14.0	1 129	14	99	66.5	6.5	30	316	73.3	6.6	4	9	0.4	0.1
Boone	18.7	115	135	1 461	631.4	73.2	627	11 563	3 741.0	287.7	227	920	160.6	28.8
Buchanan	78.2	877	102	1 711	1 506.6	76.6	339	5 467	1 369.3	120.6	100	329	59.6	9.9
Butler	339.5	7 933	49	371	193.1	11.7	203	2 610	758.1	56.4	41	181	21.8	6.5
Caldwell	1.2	126	6	62	46.3	2.2	24	208	47.8	3.8	4	D	D	D
Callaway	31.0	700	22	244	100.9	8.7	126	1 259	377.6	25.2	28	83	7.3	1.9
Camden	13.7	310	45	349	169.4	11.6	302	3 072	648.1	67.0	83	232	40.2	6.4
Cape Girardeau	36.5	483	128	1 450	861.4	58.4	415	5 855	1 611.4	131.1	110	340	55.2	9.4
Carroll	5.2	562	12	140	448.8	5.7	40	285	83.3	5.8	7	D	D	D
Carter	0.8	129	7	D	D	D	23	181	31.1	2.5	3	3	0.3	0.1
Cass	5.5	55	59	562	333.5	23.8	252	3 658	984.7	85.0	66	162	35.2	5.2
Cedar	2.0	144	7	58	29.3	1.3	48	483	104.9	9.2	5	22	1.6	0.6
Chariton	1.6	198	14	155	222.3	5.9	43	269	103.7	6.1	12	23	1.1	0.3
Christian	9.4	122	65	550	200.2	23.0	237	2 764	696.8	59.1	67	144	33.4	4.1
Clark	2.4	331	11	154	88.9	5.5	36	258	117.2	4.8	3	5	0.3	0.1
Clay	148.4	669	280	4 156	4 129.6	235.5	582	11 592	3 862.1	299.5	245	1 166	197.5	39.5
Clinton	2.6	124	10	84	132.0	3.0	57	449	158.0	10.8	13	42	4.3	1.0
Cole	9.3	122	77	2 154	974.4	62.8	301	5 114	1 257.9	115.0	62	247	45.8	7.2
Cooper	5.1	291	15	86	102.7	2.8	61	757	301.2	15.8	16	50	6.5	1.0
Crawford	3.2	128	14	110	47.6	5.6	76	636	205.0	14.1	22	71	10.7	2.1
Dade	7.9	1 006	8	506	254.4	15.6	28	181	37.7	2.6	3	4	0.3	0.1
Dallas	2.4	144	9	61	75.0	1.2	47	476	134.8	9.5	7	11	1.9	0.1
Daviess	2.1	251	9	58	31.1	1.8	36	186	70.9	3.8	4	3	0.3	0.1
DeKalb	1.0	75	6	D	D	D	39	529	123.6	10.7	12	D	D	D
Dent	32.5	2 076	6	D	D	D	55	538	127.7	11.2	14	51	2.9	0.7
Douglas	39.6	2 893	8	36	5.3	0.8	40	460	96.9	8.7	4	4	0.4	0.0
Dunklin	111.4	3 485	33	355	218.5	14.0	140	1 495	427.6	32.9	26	529	26.6	9.9
Franklin	1 018.9	10 039	99	981	574.7	36.9	378	4 653	1 396.4	107.9	89	288	28.4	7.8
Gasconade	2.2	146	21	204	86.7	6.7	66	657	171.4	14.4	9	13	1.1	0.3
Gentry	1.9	275	10	56	53.3	2.4	39	283	78.1	6.0	4	131	1.9	0.8
Greene	228.2	829	398	7 106	5 120.2	315.7	1 143	18 649	4 984.2	434.1	406	2 373	329.9	68.8
Grundy	4.2	409	8	88	107.3	3.1	43	413	89.6	8.0	8	24	2.5	0.4
Harrison	1.7	194	14	117	62.9	3.5	47	558	166.0	12.1	7	14	2.3	0.3
Henry	410.1	18 413	22	199	129.1	7.7	117	1 170	275.0	25.7	19	68	9.2	2.0
Hickory	1.4	149	4	15	3.8	0.3	29	236	59.9	4.7	2	D	D	D
Holt	17.0	3 453	9	103	117.3	3.7	22	146	46.4	3.0	2	D	D	D
Howard	9.7	955	9	D	D	D	34	245	53.4	3.5	3	D	D	D
Howell	8.2	203	41	398	229.2	13.2	232	2 085	561.3	45.6	41	131	14.8	3.3
Iron	6.9	648	3	D	D	D	38	262	70.8	4.9	7	19	2.4	0.7
Jackson	644.8	956	832	11 496	10 325.8	676.6	2 228	34 276	9 164.9	846.3	819	5 036	1 232.2	235.8

1. Merchant wholesalers, except manufacturers' sales branches and offices.   2. Employer establishments.

Table B. States and Counties — Professional Services, Manufacturing, and Accommodation and Food Services

STATE County	Professional, scientific, and technical services, 2012				Manufacturing, 2012				Accommodation and food services, 2012			
	Number of establish-ments	Number of employees	Receipts (mil dol)	Annual payroll (mil dol)	Number of establish-ments	Number of employees	Receipts (mil dol)	Annual payroll (mil dol)	Number of establish-ments	Number of employees	Sales (mil dol)	Annual payroll (mil dol)
	147	148	149	150	151	152	153	154	155	156	157	158
MISSISSIPPI—Cont'd												
Sunflower	23	71	6.6	2.1	14	293	137.8	9.3	33	358	18.3	4.8
Tallahatchie	10	42	3.7	1.0	4	50	D	1.5	10	90	3.4	0.8
Tate	22	D	D	D	14	784	303.8	30.9	28	403	17.5	4.7
Tippah	15	72	5.6	2.6	27	1 286	400.3	46.5	22	D	D	D
Tishomingo	21	103	5.1	1.5	29	1 345	298.8	49.6	33	D	D	D
Tunica	10	D	D	D	5	319	D	9.8	35	8 231	873.2	204.4
Union	27	84	7.9	3.1	37	3 660	2 379.3	136.5	38	536	26.2	7.1
Walthall	10	22	2.4	0.7	16	469	D	17.0	15	172	8.1	1.6
Warren	96	845	159.4	41.2	37	2 699	D	116.0	111	4 091	345.5	79.0
Washington	80	358	33.5	13.6	34	1 050	711.3	46.6	88	1 868	121.9	29.5
Wayne	40	110	13.7	3.6	11	1 057	279.9	35.6	28	D	D	D
Webster	10	66	4.9	1.5	11	352	D	10.2	10	140	5.7	1.4
Wilkinson	6	D	D	D	5	115	D	4.9	4	D	D	D
Winston	21	95	15.0	2.6	15	1 450	328.9	52.7	30	444	20.8	5.0
Yalobusha	8	45	2.6	0.9	7	857	D	30.9	11	64	4.3	1.0
Yazoo	22	160	11.5	4.3	12	497	D	29.7	25	331	18.2	4.0
MISSOURI	13 279	137 981	24 292.6	8 614.9	6 097	243 208	111 535.4	11 920.8	12 459	239 264	12 430.3	3 409.2
Adair	42	D	D	D	15	638	282.2	24.1	58	D	D	D
Andrew	13	58	3.1	2.0	4	13	2.3	0.5	15	112	4.5	1.1
Atchison	10	D	D	D	5	D	D	0.4	13	132	5.3	1.5
Audrain	22	147	9.1	4.6	36	1 702	1 124.1	68.5	40	441	17.2	4.6
Barry	43	D	D	D	39	4 713	1 391.4	158.8	57	776	33.0	9.0
Barton	13	119	10.6	5.7	17	411	101.9	15.6	17	D	D	D
Bates	21	D	D	D	14	99	D	3.2	28	D	D	D
Benton	23	D	D	D	20	167	D	4.5	47	D	D	D
Bollinger	7	D	D	D	14	154	23.6	5.0	10	110	4.4	1.1
Boone	414	3 570	424.0	156.7	99	3 994	2 042.1	173.3	419	9 006	373.2	104.7
Buchanan	153	D	D	D	89	12 338	D	474.4	183	4 062	180.1	48.6
Butler	48	386	38.3	14.4	46	2 178	545.4	66.9	80	1 678	67.4	18.7
Caldwell	8	D	D	D	6	37	D	0.8	9	D	D	D
Callaway	35	268	33.8	9.5	34	1 605	506.6	69.1	72	910	37.1	10.3
Camden	90	397	51.2	18.1	45	604	131.2	23.2	157	2 633	142.9	40.4
Cape Girardeau	158	1 137	109.6	38.5	95	3 700	2 884.5	181.9	168	4 167	171.0	48.7
Carroll	16	40	3.2	0.8	12	160	D	6.2	13	D	D	D
Carter	5	34	1.4	0.7	18	92	36.1	4.0	12	139	4.3	1.2
Cass	157	D	D	D	59	1 901	557.3	74.0	131	2 133	89.4	25.7
Cedar	14	38	3.1	0.8	20	301	149.1	12.8	32	302	11.0	3.0
Chariton	11	D	D	D	4	78	D	D	16	85	3.0	0.8
Christian	141	D	D	D	100	1 295	274.9	46.1	111	1 774	73.4	23.5
Clark	7	10	0.6	0.2	6	176	D	D	11	102	4.4	1.4
Clay	499	9 242	2 515.1	805.3	195	10 152	8 645.4	579.9	409	9 827	756.4	161.0
Clinton	24	D	D	D	13	105	D	3.1	20	303	13.2	3.7
Cole	231	1 587	238.9	81.4	56	2 293	1 877.5	101.3	166	3 172	132.4	39.4
Cooper	24	80	4.9	2.1	13	374	D	14.0	38	D	D	D
Crawford	26	148	7.4	3.2	47	1 922	345.0	57.9	58	484	23.9	6.7
Dade	3	D	D	D	12	205	64.6	7.2	13	80	2.6	0.8
Dallas	15	D	D	D	15	105	D	2.9	25	254	9.9	2.5
Daviess	5	D	D	D	8	231	D	D	13	82	2.8	0.8
DeKalb	8	20	1.8	0.7	4	23	D	1.3	17	159	7.9	2.0
Dent	16	51	3.5	1.3	21	615	D	30.4	26	D	D	D
Douglas	11	33	3.0	0.8	11	712	D	15.8	16	D	D	D
Dunklin	31	463	11.7	4.4	11	500	D	18.2	44	647	29.6	7.4
Franklin	185	1 174	144.2	42.6	221	9 002	2 617.3	382.3	184	3 157	126.4	38.1
Gasconade	29	117	7.0	2.5	40	1 161	193.2	41.2	46	449	19.4	5.5
Gentry	9	D	D	D	7	228	D	D	13	78	2.2	0.7
Greene	801	5 862	830.7	281.9	295	11 900	4 623.8	521.5	723	14 502	628.1	185.1
Grundy	14	47	2.9	0.9	8	707	D	32.3	13	217	6.9	2.0
Harrison	11	29	1.5	0.6	5	32	D	1.0	21	281	11.4	2.8
Henry	35	141	12.0	3.3	25	1 164	694.8	52.5	56	770	29.7	8.3
Hickory	8	D	D	D	5	D	D	D	17	75	3.1	0.8
Holt	2	D	D	D	7	210	D	6.7	14	112	4.1	1.0
Howard	16	45	4.2	1.4	10	245	57.5	10.2	14	171	5.2	1.7
Howell	64	306	24.9	10.3	69	2 483	672.0	78.5	89	1 241	54.1	14.3
Iron	8	D	D	D	15	88	D	2.2	22	107	4.7	1.3
Jackson	2 044	24 922	5 811.2	1 804.1	634	25 870	10 193.5	1 396.4	1 453	30 594	1 649.0	485.7

1. Establishment subject to federal tax.

Table B. States and Counties — Health Care and Social Assistance, Other Services, Nonemployer Businesses, and Residential Construction

STATE County	Health care and social assistance, 2012				Other services, 2012				Nonemployer businesses, 2015		Value of residential construction authorized by building permits, 2016	
	Number of establishments	Number of employees	Receipts (mil dol)	Annual payroll (mil dol)	Number of establishments	Number of employees	Receipts (mil dol)	Annual payroll (mil dol)	Number	Receipts (mil dol)	New Construction ($1,000)	Number of housing units
	159	160	161	162	163	164	165	166	167	168	169	170
MISSISSIPPI—Cont'd												
Sunflower	63	1 199	104.8	39.0	34	164	13.2	3.7	1 732	51.4	1 219	9
Tallahatchie	15	362	29.6	12.0	14	44	6.4	1.0	826	22.1	48	1
Tate	37	544	51.5	21.3	17	101	7.7	2.7	2 060	73.6	14 324	91
Tippah	31	628	44.5	17.6	10	42	2.5	0.7	1 406	61.2	442	7
Tishomingo	32	D	D	D	22	D	D	D	1 111	38.8	250	3
Tunica	16	190	12.3	4.8	8	D	D	D	719	23.7	1 606	20
Union	51	1 223	111.7	40.7	18	D	D	D	1 980	85.5	2 098	14
Walthall	21	285	14.0	5.4	14	D	D	D	1 128	37.5	0	0
Warren	114	2 997	293.1	108.1	58	307	29.8	7.9	3 073	112.3	173	2
Washington	164	3 083	249.4	99.9	80	556	57.1	16.3	3 473	128.3	5 774	27
Wayne	22	607	45.0	21.8	20	D	D	D	1 384	49.6	875	7
Webster	12	D	D	D	7	D	D	D	826	30.7	165	3
Wilkinson	14	350	29.1	11.5	7	D	D	D	647	18.1	0	0
Winston	28	393	34.8	12.4	17	D	D	D	1 305	57.3	633	3
Yalobusha	16	328	23.3	11.0	6	D	D	D	856	29.7	365	12
Yazoo	41	872	73.8	27.5	27	D	D	D	1 552	50.5	1 045	11
MISSOURI	17 766	399 940	40 089.3	15 746.9	10 357	62 825	6 979.9	1 834.9	402 091	17 718.5	3 282 703	18 997
Adair	101	1 929	159.3	63.3	61	D	D	D	1 485	49.0	10 358	64
Andrew	28	D	D	D	19	D	D	D	1 241	49.4	1 345	9
Atchison	14	270	16.9	6.7	15	D	D	D	422	16.5	0	0
Audrain	71	1 414	99.4	40.4	45	249	18.8	7.4	1 370	60.2	4 936	35
Barry	71	1 788	99.2	42.8	65	222	15.6	3.9	2 217	79.5	3 104	18
Barton	25	457	30.0	13.2	18	48	4.9	1.3	908	37.4	0	0
Bates	36	D	D	D	21	D	D	D	1 210	48.0	330	2
Benton	34	400	21.4	9.7	32	91	8.3	1.6	1 446	65.3	3 000	36
Bollinger	20	312	15.2	6.0	16	56	5.3	1.1	751	31.1	0	0
Boone	602	16 725	2 033.5	699.4	327	1 985	187.4	53.2	11 463	561.3	261 329	1 304
Buchanan	315	7 704	852.1	346.6	172	D	D	D	4 064	158.9	16 174	82
Butler	209	4 378	527.8	163.1	65	296	24.0	5.9	2 539	124.8	55	1
Caldwell	14	D	D	D	15	D	D	D	614	23.9	8 180	32
Callaway	64	2 368	128.3	64.9	66	229	19.6	5.5	2 398	87.3	6 616	54
Camden	121	2 143	262.5	84.9	102	358	30.7	8.1	3 817	187.8	35 051	149
Cape Girardeau	317	10 920	1 149.2	455.5	159	798	78.1	19.9	5 245	228.3	33 128	172
Carroll	22	375	24.9	7.9	18	D	D	D	636	22.5	55	1
Carter	39	237	8.5	3.9	4	9	1.7	0.3	523	30.2	0	0
Cass	159	3 056	250.2	98.6	140	522	41.2	12.2	6 823	274.6	118 800	601
Cedar	30	646	32.0	15.1	19	34	3.4	0.7	1 144	46.7	404	7
Chariton	14	261	10.8	4.5	14	36	5.9	1.2	616	19.2	0	0
Christian	115	1 434	89.7	37.4	119	429	31.5	9.0	6 617	280.2	78 517	617
Clark	13	60	4.0	1.6	11	37	4.5	0.7	417	18.3	249	5
Clay	553	12 953	1 393.1	591.2	329	1 826	171.1	54.5	14 900	610.1	92 968	721
Clinton	47	D	D	D	33	102	6.7	1.9	1 336	49.5	8 919	51
Cole	252	6 480	711.7	280.5	227	1 441	173.3	52.7	4 700	223.4	19 333	217
Cooper	52	773	45.3	18.7	28	106	8.5	2.2	1 088	41.8	1 300	12
Crawford	60	955	77.2	33.2	28	117	8.4	2.1	1 549	58.1	1 302	11
Dade	10	D	D	D	10	18	2.2	0.6	525	18.4	750	1
Dallas	30	1 021	26.9	13.1	20	D	D	D	1 320	51.3	508	2
Daviess	16	78	6.0	2.2	8	D	D	D	807	38.5	200	1
DeKalb	28	D	D	D	10	D	D	D	643	27.7	300	6
Dent	55	712	42.7	17.8	20	45	3.9	0.9	909	33.0	169	1
Douglas	20	313	16.1	7.0	14	41	4.5	0.8	1 037	37.9	300	3
Dunklin	87	3 270	167.8	57.4	39	136	13.0	2.6	1 821	114.3	3 117	17
Franklin	262	3 747	322.4	153.2	185	869	81.7	23.3	6 627	273.4	68 348	402
Gasconade	34	701	40.7	17.3	33	D	D	D	1 215	50.0	339	3
Gentry	34	777	38.0	17.2	11	26	2.5	0.7	511	17.7	250	2
Greene	820	28 578	3 027.6	1 240.2	599	4 433	401.4	117.0	20 267	986.6	191 823	1 258
Grundy	34	656	48.5	18.8	27	61	5.0	1.2	695	28.5	379	4
Harrison	24	488	29.4	12.1	21	D	D	D	685	28.7	383	2
Henry	55	1 569	122.3	55.1	42	163	10.4	3.2	1 456	53.9	4 021	37
Hickory	9	98	5.4	2.1	11	22	1.9	0.4	721	26.8	NA	NA
Holt	9	D	D	D	9	D	D	D	405	16.9	93	3
Howard	24	493	16.4	8.3	13	D	D	D	685	24.1	690	5
Howell	156	3 669	294.1	127.4	66	381	38.9	8.4	3 083	121.7	2 086	27
Iron	93	656	34.8	15.3	27	D	D	D	513	16.0	190	3
Jackson	2 040	54 553	6 169.9	2 405.2	1 236	9 447	1 762.1	312.8	43 683	1 909.5	667 931	4 507

Table B. States and Counties — Government Employment and Payroll, and Local Government Finances

	Government employment and payroll, 2012									Local government finances, 2012				
			March payroll (percent of total)							General revenue				
												Taxes		
													Per capita[1] (dollars)	
STATE County	Full-time equivalent employees	March payroll (dollars)	Adminis- tration, judicial, and legal	Police and Corrections	Fire Protection	Highways and transpor- tation	Health and Welfare	Natural resources and utilities	Education and libraries	Total (mil dol)	Inter- govern- mental (mil dol)	Total (mil dol)	Total	Property
	171	172	173	174	175	176	177	178	179	180	181	182	183	184
MISSISSIPPI—Cont'd														
Sunflower	2 017	5 682 629	3.7	5.0	1.7	2.5	30.7	1.5	53.7	155.8	63.4	20.6	724	694
Tallahatchie	772	1 986 175	8.5	7.5	0.2	4.7	29.5	0.9	48.6	34.1	21.3	8.2	542	517
Tate	1 430	4 623 219	2.1	2.6	1.1	1.1	0.9	1.2	90.6	106.6	62.4	20.6	724	690
Tippah	915	2 435 046	6.8	3.3	0.2	2.1	22.7	2.8	61.0	68.1	38.2	11.3	512	467
Tishomingo	694	1 807 779	8.5	7.3	1.2	2.3	1.2	4.4	73.2	46.2	29.7	10.1	515	495
Tunica	738	1 778 465	10.4	23.6	0.0	4.7	6.1	9.7	45.3	86.8	57.0	21.4	2 043	1 507
Union	1 025	2 626 662	4.5	7.6	2.0	3.0	1.3	10.2	71.3	61.0	37.8	16.4	596	576
Walthall	518	1 141 649	3.1	5.7	0.2	3.0	2.1	0.6	83.4	45.4	21.5	8.4	559	539
Warren	1 819	5 138 472	4.6	6.1	7.5	3.0	0.3	7.0	69.2	170.1	68.3	68.7	1 429	1 171
Washington	3 566	9 118 481	5.7	7.2	2.5	3.0	32.4	4.6	43.1	298.0	98.6	52.7	1 060	977
Wayne	1 112	3 158 182	4.3	5.0	0.4	2.8	39.5	1.7	44.9	88.7	32.9	10.5	508	496
Webster	496	1 240 223	6.4	4.4	0.1	3.7	24.5	1.5	58.9	36.7	19.1	6.3	623	599
Wilkinson	427	1 032 081	12.7	10.5	0.3	7.1	2.1	3.0	61.9	56.6	14.2	5.9	630	607
Winston	620	1 506 689	8.7	16.0	2.1	4.3	1.9	2.4	64.2	46.2	24.1	11.5	602	576
Yalobusha	708	1 878 214	6.3	4.5	1.3	4.5	39.0	4.3	40.1	42.2	18.6	8.6	691	675
Yazoo	1 019	2 766 051	5.8	9.4	4.3	6.7	2.3	10.2	60.9	70.1	40.4	21.3	755	728
MISSOURI	X	X	X	X	X	X	X	X	X	X	X	X	X	X
Adair	916	2 496 611	7.3	5.8	2.8	3.2	13.2	5.6	59.0	68.7	23.1	26.9	1 051	570
Andrew	515	1 433 245	5.1	4.2	0.9	3.0	4.0	5.7	76.7	48.4	17.6	23.4	1 345	1 199
Atchison	319	829 091	7.7	5.0	0.1	22.0	10.0	5.1	49.6	22.0	10.2	9.7	1 755	1 294
Audrain	1 347	4 107 516	4.1	5.9	0.2	2.5	49.7	3.5	33.4	133.2	34.7	34.4	1 343	940
Barry	1 307	3 855 776	4.7	5.7	1.8	2.3	1.6	5.6	77.7	94.7	45.3	37.8	1 063	636
Barton	723	2 240 324	3.5	2.9	0.7	1.9	43.2	5.8	41.8	83.5	14.1	10.7	866	674
Bates	840	2 585 067	4.7	5.8	0.3	2.0	37.0	4.7	45.0	43.7	19.9	13.4	805	577
Benton	748	1 949 137	5.2	5.4	0.1	2.8	27.9	2.2	53.8	41.5	16.6	13.2	696	514
Bollinger	361	902 476	5.5	5.4	0.3	4.6	0.0	1.6	82.4	21.6	12.4	7.2	585	414
Boone	6 008	20 052 275	7.9	5.3	3.3	2.8	2.7	11.3	63.5	497.3	161.0	228.2	1 354	805
Buchanan	3 079	9 642 143	5.9	9.4	5.3	3.7	2.5	5.0	66.6	296.5	114.1	129.1	1 439	812
Butler	1 617	4 243 462	2.3	5.6	2.5	3.4	0.0	4.2	79.9	124.9	58.1	43.7	1 015	498
Caldwell	485	1 279 896	6.3	9.6	0.0	2.5	7.8	5.3	68.5	29.5	14.3	7.8	847	648
Callaway	1 265	3 154 685	6.9	9.5	2.6	4.3	5.4	8.0	63.0	88.2	36.4	34.7	782	576
Camden	1 451	4 272 326	7.8	13.4	5.1	5.6	4.2	2.2	60.3	116.5	32.4	68.3	1 557	990
Cape Girardeau	2 602	6 797 882	6.6	9.1	5.9	6.5	1.2	10.3	58.6	207.7	74.1	101.6	1 320	702
Carroll	390	1 096 814	9.3	3.7	1.4	4.2	4.3	6.6	70.1	26.7	11.7	10.0	1 101	852
Carter	278	723 988	1.6	5.8	0.0	2.9	3.2	2.5	72.4	15.4	9.6	3.9	625	446
Cass	4 195	14 748 324	5.3	6.9	4.3	2.7	12.2	4.5	63.7	380.9	126.2	139.6	1 391	927
Cedar	643	1 585 692	4.7	5.5	0.2	3.0	25.1	6.6	54.3	50.4	15.5	11.7	850	590
Chariton	295	762 719	8.8	6.7	0.2	3.7	5.8	6.0	68.4	20.7	8.4	9.5	1 240	969
Christian	2 200	6 653 224	5.3	7.1	2.0	1.8	0.2	4.7	77.8	188.4	89.3	71.0	890	611
Clark	372	840 780	6.1	5.8	0.0	4.4	21.9	7.3	53.6	21.0	7.2	6.3	911	738
Clay	12 186	43 650 964	3.1	4.3	2.0	0.8	42.4	2.3	44.6	1 333.0	239.3	340.1	1 495	1 078
Clinton	670	2 036 971	7.0	9.3	0.4	4.7	2.3	8.2	67.6	52.6	24.6	20.4	993	788
Cole	2 439	7 947 888	7.8	8.8	4.1	4.5	3.5	5.9	65.1	213.9	62.0	116.3	1 523	890
Cooper	744	2 121 619	5.8	7.9	1.4	3.1	23.2	4.8	52.9	62.0	16.7	23.7	1 353	687
Crawford	756	1 998 530	5.7	8.1	0.0	3.7	7.3	5.6	68.1	45.1	21.5	17.0	683	512
Dade	452	949 754	5.1	2.9	0.0	1.2	37.3	2.9	50.6	20.8	9.6	6.2	824	608
Dallas	463	1 037 873	7.3	5.8	0.3	5.2	0.8	2.2	78.1	31.3	18.2	10.5	627	394
Daviess	341	863 936	7.8	3.3	0.0	3.1	2.5	7.8	74.9	20.0	9.8	7.4	895	719
DeKalb	227	666 095	6.8	3.3	0.0	4.5	3.8	6.9	74.5	18.0	7.8	6.8	522	356
Dent	677	1 899 125	6.9	2.7	0.2	3.0	33.8	4.1	48.4	46.0	16.0	9.7	622	406
Douglas	383	1 073 499	10.7	2.4	0.0	4.9	5.0	5.3	70.1	32.6	12.6	16.6	1 225	824
Dunklin	1 473	3 567 888	5.4	6.8	1.4	3.0	1.6	10.3	68.2	82.8	44.0	27.3	859	614
Franklin	3 292	11 002 286	4.9	8.8	2.3	3.4	4.3	2.7	72.9	276.7	102.6	133.5	1 317	868
Gasconade	880	2 347 282	3.9	4.6	0.0	3.4	28.6	4.8	53.1	70.3	15.8	18.8	1 257	905
Gentry	345	893 935	12.0	4.7	0.4	7.4	4.6	5.3	65.1	20.8	9.7	7.8	1 144	911
Greene	10 039	36 380 689	4.7	8.2	3.7	4.6	1.4	13.2	55.1	880.5	308.6	410.2	1 462	763
Grundy	761	1 960 447	2.6	5.1	1.0	3.5	14.2	6.8	64.8	55.4	22.3	10.8	1 048	654
Harrison	594	1 570 497	5.2	2.6	0.2	3.0	37.3	7.0	42.9	43.2	13.0	10.7	1 229	806
Henry	1 267	4 585 264	3.2	3.7	1.3	1.0	61.3	2.7	26.7	117.2	50.1	23.1	1 045	588
Hickory	326	851 720	6.0	4.2	0.0	2.3	0.0	2.3	84.9	21.9	12.6	6.7	714	572
Holt	184	461 150	11.3	6.1	0.0	5.3	1.7	7.2	68.0	16.0	6.1	7.4	1 595	1 143
Howard	396	983 070	7.8	7.5	0.4	5.0	4.3	9.4	64.8	23.9	8.7	11.5	1 135	911
Howell	1 537	3 973 191	5.5	5.3	1.4	3.4	4.8	7.9	71.2	100.7	49.7	31.7	781	439
Iron	459	1 303 360	4.7	4.4	0.6	6.5	6.1	1.8	75.7	26.1	13.0	10.3	991	765
Jackson	27 447	101 433 064	7.4	14.7	9.5	6.2	0.7	5.5	54.6	3 343.9	905.1	1 696.2	2 504	1 116

1. Based on the resident population estimated as of July 1 of the year shown.

Table B. States and Counties — Local Government Finances, Government Employment, and Income Taxes

STATE County	Local government finances, 2012 (cont.)									Government employment, 2015			Individual income tax returns, 2014		
	Direct general expenditure							Debt outstanding							
			Percent of total for:												
	Total (mil dol)	Per capita¹ (dollars)	Education	Health and hospitals	Police protection	Public welfare	Highways	Total (mil dol)	Per capita¹ (dollars)	Federal civilian	Federal military	State and local	Number of returns	Mean adjusted gross income	Mean income tax
	185	186	187	188	189	190	191	192	193	194	195	196	197	198	199
MISSISSIPPI—Cont'd															
Sunflower	160.1	5 631	46.7	34.5	2.9	0.1	5.4	30.8	1 085	53	138	3 550	9 950	33 752	2 978
Tallahatchie	39.2	2 596	54.2	1.1	5.0	0.0	7.9	12.7	843	39	73	972	5 120	32 829	2 479
Tate	144.1	5 057	68.2	0.5	2.9	0.0	3.0	96.6	3 389	82	162	1 594	11 640	42 974	3 860
Tippah	68.2	3 095	49.3	23.7	3.2	0.2	8.8	13.9	629	57	131	1 183	8 700	38 552	3 060
Tishomingo	53.8	2 746	50.8	1.1	4.8	0.0	7.0	25.8	1 315	61	116	851	7 370	40 488	3 188
Tunica	103.7	9 896	24.0	1.9	8.0	0.7	5.8	114.9	10 965	20	62	829	4 760	38 416	4 200
Union	59.7	2 178	65.6	1.4	6.1	0.0	5.6	32.4	1 180	44	169	1 197	11 350	41 916	3 512
Walthall	45.0	2 981	52.1	26.1	4.3	0.2	4.8	1.9	128	28	87	644	5 570	40 313	3 337
Warren	169.5	3 526	45.5	1.1	6.6	0.2	7.1	264.3	5 496	2 204	327	2 354	21 310	46 353	4 689
Washington	305.6	6 143	28.7	43.2	3.9	0.1	4.1	140.1	2 816	421	305	3 661	20 380	37 644	3 618
Wayne	70.5	3 414	47.5	34.9	3.4	0.1	5.6	14.5	700	37	123	1 219	8 340	48 523	5 116
Webster	31.4	3 130	63.8	1.3	4.6	0.0	7.8	7.1	706	31	59	432	3 950	40 289	3 168
Wilkinson	55.4	5 871	26.6	28.9	2.5	0.1	3.6	35.9	3 804	D	48	522	3 590	38 049	3 070
Winston	45.6	2 397	54.2	1.3	6.9	0.1	7.3	5.2	272	37	107	773	7 570	40 308	3 646
Yalobusha	40.4	3 257	39.3	27.4	4.0	0.0	10.5	17.9	1 447	62	74	823	5 260	35 931	2 729
Yazoo	75.1	2 663	51.5	1.3	5.5	0.3	5.8	42.6	1 510	803	140	1 487	9 480	38 821	3 497
MISSOURI	X	X	X	X	X	X	X	X	X	57 526	35 505	378 008	2 767 190	56 723	7 076
Adair	66.2	2 589	44.3	3.2	5.6	7.5	7.7	43.5	1 700	81	81	2 392	9 510	43 566	4 213
Andrew	36.8	2 114	65.6	3.0	5.9	1.0	6.2	25.6	1 468	35	59	715	8 170	54 825	5 856
Atchison	22.0	3 990	52.6	2.6	2.8	0.0	17.0	6.5	1 173	32	18	341	2 510	52 959	5 675
Audrain	139.4	5 440	36.1	40.4	2.1	3.8	3.0	68.4	2 669	87	81	2 312	10 660	42 103	3 765
Barry	100.1	2 815	59.9	3.2	4.9	0.0	15.0	67.2	1 892	106	124	1 449	13 880	41 011	3 857
Barton	83.6	6 780	22.2	65.7	1.4	0.0	2.7	35.3	2 861	39	40	863	5 120	41 109	3 640
Bates	44.5	2 660	58.6	0.1	9.7	6.8	7.3	46.0	2 754	56	55	1 096	7 070	43 676	3 983
Benton	41.9	2 209	51.5	5.5	3.4	22.2	5.5	22.9	1 210	98	63	962	7 730	36 746	2 912
Bollinger	21.1	1 700	73.8	1.0	4.3	0.0	7.9	3.1	248	25	41	438	4 730	37 918	2 673
Boone	580.4	3 444	44.8	3.1	4.3	0.2	6.2	2 592.5	15 382	2 515	596	28 535	77 110	57 855	7 272
Buchanan	261.5	2 915	51.6	2.2	9.4	0.7	5.3	599.9	6 688	503	313	6 533	39 310	47 721	5 075
Butler	122.1	2 837	60.0	0.0	6.4	0.0	5.4	48.6	1 129	735	144	2 829	17 550	40 099	3 941
Caldwell	28.6	3 124	59.8	1.8	3.5	5.7	7.6	9.9	1 087	40	30	616	3 830	45 462	3 757
Callaway	85.8	1 936	53.8	4.3	8.4	0.0	6.7	57.3	1 293	123	142	3 747	19 440	45 903	4 250
Camden	113.7	2 593	47.6	3.7	9.0	0.0	11.7	112.7	2 570	81	149	1 847	19 750	48 099	5 328
Cape Girardeau	211.7	2 751	54.0	0.3	5.4	0.0	9.9	197.3	2 564	373	284	5 789	35 130	55 283	6 619
Carroll	27.9	3 076	59.3	3.2	3.9	0.0	11.1	12.4	1 360	45	31	561	4 200	46 661	4 634
Carter	15.8	2 520	74.5	2.8	1.9	0.0	3.9	29.2	4 657	84	21	361	2 400	33 473	2 557
Cass	400.2	3 987	50.4	13.7	3.1	0.3	5.8	468.7	4 669	261	345	4 818	47 250	62 563	7 362
Cedar	37.7	2 733	50.1	29.0	5.1	0.0	2.8	32.6	2 361	69	47	721	5 450	35 399	2 718
Chariton	22.7	2 968	52.9	4.1	2.8	0.0	14.2	3.5	456	40	25	452	3 460	46 151	4 304
Christian	179.8	2 252	67.4	0.5	4.7	1.0	5.5	246.9	3 093	108	284	2 989	36 040	52 596	5 434
Clark	23.6	3 386	46.2	6.2	1.8	17.9	8.0	8.6	1 234	36	23	463	2 950	41 691	3 644
Clay	1 296.4	5 696	31.9	48.7	2.3	0.0	1.9	934.2	4 105	1 290	865	14 394	113 140	59 369	6 799
Clinton	50.6	2 467	62.4	1.9	7.3	0.0	8.9	42.6	2 078	77	69	1 021	9 590	52 774	5 450
Cole	222.3	2 911	50.1	2.6	10.7	0.0	10.0	194.9	2 552	628	264	19 148	36 150	55 371	6 342
Cooper	65.2	3 719	36.8	19.0	3.7	4.9	5.9	51.2	2 925	48	55	1 255	7 440	43 015	3 760
Crawford	44.2	1 780	63.0	8.1	3.6	0.0	5.8	29.0	1 169	32	83	903	10 180	40 039	3 854
Dade	20.9	2 758	51.9	1.1	3.6	23.8	6.9	4.0	526	27	26	513	3 090	40 804	3 077
Dallas	39.6	2 358	42.6	3.7	4.9	0.0	39.8	4.3	254	38	56	590	6 560	36 290	2 754
Daviess	19.9	2 419	62.2	3.1	3.1	0.1	12.4	10.1	1 231	33	28	483	3 490	38 865	3 363
DeKalb	17.0	1 315	62.4	3.4	4.1	0.0	6.0	6.2	478	31	31	1 259	4 030	43 614	3 770
Dent	47.9	3 058	43.1	38.7	4.1	0.0	4.2	2.6	166	56	53	917	5 830	39 499	3 526
Douglas	34.6	2 550	64.0	1.9	3.6	0.0	13.6	7.5	553	48	45	397	4 880	33 015	2 238
Dunklin	76.5	2 405	65.8	1.0	6.7	0.0	5.4	33.5	1 052	93	104	1 562	11 660	37 813	3 357
Franklin	286.0	2 820	58.5	2.0	6.4	0.0	9.3	497.8	4 909	218	349	4 390	49 180	52 293	5 826
Gasconade	55.7	3 719	45.7	31.4	2.9	0.5	4.5	60.7	4 054	46	50	1 039	7 070	40 838	3 484
Gentry	20.3	2 997	59.9	3.6	3.3	0.0	10.5	8.2	1 217	36	22	417	2 830	42 129	3 629
Greene	855.2	3 047	50.1	1.1	8.7	0.2	6.0	1 601.3	5 706	2 133	969	18 680	129 320	53 087	6 633
Grundy	48.8	4 722	61.4	3.0	2.3	10.7	6.0	28.4	2 746	61	33	968	4 250	41 222	3 613
Harrison	40.5	4 640	35.7	40.6	3.2	0.0	7.4	11.6	1 333	43	29	779	3 720	36 660	2 840
Henry	113.3	5 114	25.1	59.5	2.3	0.1	3.3	36.1	1 629	78	74	1 627	9 490	45 283	4 345
Hickory	21.4	2 275	79.2	1.5	2.4	0.0	5.9	11.7	1 244	41	31	295	3 420	33 422	2 408
Holt	15.2	3 273	49.5	0.6	2.4	0.0	13.7	0.8	182	31	15	295	2 120	48 065	5 175
Howard	22.1	2 174	53.2	3.8	5.5	0.3	6.2	33.3	3 276	37	32	462	4 360	45 139	4 138
Howell	94.2	2 317	67.7	2.1	5.1	0.0	5.1	39.4	970	121	136	2 181	15 920	39 992	3 775
Iron	27.4	2 641	71.9	1.5	3.9	0.0	5.6	10.9	1 046	14	64	661	3 910	36 139	2 671
Jackson	3 093.9	4 567	37.7	2.6	9.6	0.3	7.4	6 245.9	9 221	16 146	2 497	42 351	325 640	53 420	6 284

1. Based on the resident population estimated as of July 1 of the year shown.

STATE/ County code	CBSA code[1]	County type[2]	STATE County	Land area,[3] (sq mi) 2016	Total persons 2016	Rank	Per square mile	White	Black	American Indian, Alaska Native	Asian and Pacific Islander	Percent Hispanic or Latino[4]	Under 5 years	5 to 17 years	18 to 24 years	25 to 34 years	35 to 44 years	45 to 54 years
				1	2	3	4	5	6	7	8	9	10	11	12	13	14	15
			MISSOURI—Cont'd															
29 097	27900	3	Jasper	638.5	119 111	519	186.5	87.1	3.0	2.9	1.9	8.0	7.0	18.3	9.3	14.1	12.6	12.1
29 099	41180	1	Jefferson	656.7	224 226	294	341.4	96.0	1.6	0.8	1.1	1.9	6.0	17.6	7.5	13.0	12.9	14.4
29 101	47660	4	Johnson	829.3	53 942	932	65.0	88.5	5.9	1.4	3.0	4.2	6.3	15.2	20.5	14.6	10.2	10.3
29 103	...	9	Knox	504.0	3 934	2 907	7.8	97.7	1.1	1.0	0.8	1.0	6.3	17.6	7.4	10.0	9.2	12.9
29 105	30060	6	Laclede	764.7	35 490	1 292	46.4	95.5	1.4	1.7	1.0	2.4	6.6	18.1	7.6	11.7	11.7	13.5
29 107	28140	1	Lafayette	628.4	32 618	1 367	51.9	93.8	3.1	1.3	0.9	2.8	5.8	17.2	8.0	11.3	11.2	13.7
29 109	...	6	Lawrence	611.7	38 381	1 215	62.7	91.1	0.8	1.8	0.7	7.2	6.4	18.8	7.9	10.9	11.8	13.0
29 111	39500	9	Lewis	505.0	10 134	2 425	20.1	94.2	4.1	1.0	0.7	1.8	5.7	16.7	12.6	10.8	10.3	12.5
29 113	41180	1	Lincoln	626.6	55 267	916	88.2	94.8	2.7	0.9	0.9	2.4	6.7	19.0	8.2	13.0	12.4	14.2
29 115	...	7	Linn	615.6	12 164	2 282	19.8	96.4	1.6	0.6	0.4	2.2	6.2	17.5	7.9	10.3	10.7	11.8
29 117	...	6	Livingston	532.3	15 235	2 080	28.6	93.8	4.2	0.9	0.8	1.7	5.5	15.5	7.5	13.7	13.1	12.8
29 119	22220	6	McDonald	539.5	22 620	1 705	41.9	80.7	2.4	4.7	3.5	11.7	6.7	19.4	8.2	11.6	12.3	14.1
29 121	...	7	Macon	801.2	15 170	2 085	18.9	95.6	3.2	0.9	0.8	1.2	5.9	17.6	7.0	10.0	10.8	12.7
29 123	...	6	Madison	494.4	12 443	2 265	25.2	95.5	0.9	1.0	1.3	2.6	5.9	17.1	7.2	11.6	11.6	13.1
29 125	...	8	Maries	527.0	8 858	2 518	16.8	96.8	1.1	1.6	0.8	1.3	4.8	16.4	7.4	10.2	11.1	14.3
29 127	25300	5	Marion	436.9	28 894	1 459	66.1	92.3	6.3	0.8	1.2	1.6	6.3	17.0	9.1	12.3	11.3	12.7
29 129	...	9	Mercer	453.8	3 699	2 922	8.2	96.4	0.6	1.1	0.9	2.0	5.9	17.7	7.5	8.7	10.4	12.2
29 131	...	6	Miller	592.6	25 206	1 602	42.5	96.5	1.0	1.5	0.8	1.9	6.2	17.5	7.5	11.6	11.1	13.3
29 133	...	6	Mississippi	411.6	13 799	2 181	33.5	72.8	25.3	0.7	0.4	2.0	5.3	16.1	8.1	14.1	12.8	14.1
29 135	27620	6	Moniteau	415.0	16 018	2 037	38.6	90.6	4.3	1.0	0.6	4.6	6.7	18.1	7.9	13.3	13.4	13.5
29 137	...	9	Monroe	647.7	8 558	2 544	13.2	94.5	3.7	1.0	0.7	1.8	5.3	16.6	6.9	10.1	10.5	12.7
29 139	...	6	Montgomery	535.0	11 620	2 312	21.7	95.7	2.2	0.9	0.8	1.8	5.7	16.7	6.6	11.0	10.7	13.4
29 141	...	8	Morgan	597.6	20 213	1 820	33.8	95.8	1.2	1.6	0.8	2.1	6.3	16.1	6.5	10.1	9.4	12.3
29 143	...	7	New Madrid	674.8	17 915	1 925	26.5	81.7	16.8	0.8	0.7	1.8	6.3	16.8	7.7	11.5	12.0	13.0
29 145	27900	3	Newton	624.8	58 694	881	93.9	89.4	1.6	4.1	2.7	5.2	6.2	18.0	8.3	11.7	11.3	13.2
29 147	32340	6	Nodaway	877.0	22 670	1 698	25.8	93.6	3.2	0.6	2.1	1.6	4.6	11.8	28.7	10.8	8.9	9.9
29 149	...	9	Oregon	789.8	10 789	2 373	13.7	95.9	0.8	2.9	0.7	1.9	6.4	16.8	7.0	9.4	9.7	12.8
29 151	27620	3	Osage	606.6	13 664	2 190	22.5	98.3	0.7	0.5	0.3	0.8	5.5	17.4	8.8	11.0	11.7	14.3
29 153	...	9	Ozark	745.0	9 237	2 488	12.4	96.8	0.7	1.8	0.6	1.8	4.6	14.5	5.6	8.7	9.5	12.2
29 155	...	7	Pemiscot	492.5	17 073	1 975	34.7	70.4	27.5	0.8	0.5	2.5	7.5	18.8	8.4	12.1	11.3	12.6
29 157	...	6	Perry	474.4	19 285	1 858	40.7	96.4	0.9	0.8	0.8	2.2	5.9	17.9	8.0	11.4	11.9	13.4
29 159	42740	4	Pettis	682.2	42 213	1 125	61.9	86.9	4.1	0.9	1.3	8.9	6.9	18.0	8.5	13.5	11.4	12.6
29 161	40620	5	Phelps	671.8	44 608	1 109	66.4	90.9	3.2	1.6	4.2	2.5	5.7	15.4	16.8	12.2	10.4	11.6
29 163	...	6	Pike	670.4	18 438	1 893	27.5	89.4	8.6	0.6	0.6	2.2	6.0	16.1	8.5	13.6	12.3	13.6
29 165	28140	1	Platte	420.2	98 309	602	234.0	83.7	7.5	1.1	4.1	6.0	6.1	17.7	8.2	13.2	13.9	14.1
29 167	44180	2	Polk	635.5	31 285	1 402	49.2	95.2	1.4	1.4	1.1	2.5	5.9	17.2	13.1	10.6	10.8	12.4
29 169	22780	5	Pulaski	547.1	52 654	952	96.2	72.9	13.4	2.0	5.3	10.8	6.8	15.4	22.7	18.4	11.7	9.0
29 171	...	9	Putnam	517.3	4 853	2 844	9.4	97.0	0.7	0.6	1.1	1.8	6.2	16.1	6.7	9.9	10.0	12.5
29 173	25300	9	Ralls	469.8	10 224	2 413	21.8	96.7	1.9	0.7	0.5	1.3	4.9	16.7	7.0	10.1	11.6	13.8
29 175	33620	6	Randolph	482.7	24 989	1 608	51.8	91.0	7.1	1.1	1.1	2.1	5.5	16.3	9.3	13.9	12.8	14.0
29 177	28140	1	Ray	568.8	22 754	1 688	40.0	95.2	2.0	1.2	0.6	2.5	5.5	17.1	7.7	10.8	11.8	14.3
29 179	...	9	Reynolds	808.5	6 455	2 717	8.0	96.4	1.6	2.4	0.6	1.4	4.5	15.3	6.6	9.9	11.1	13.4
29 181	...	9	Ripley	629.5	13 817	2 179	21.9	96.7	1.1	1.8	0.6	1.4	6.6	16.5	6.8	11.4	11.6	12.8
29 183	41180	1	St. Charles	560.4	390 918	178	697.6	89.2	5.7	0.6	3.2	3.2	6.1	17.7	8.6	13.1	13.2	13.9
29 185	...	8	St. Clair	675.0	9 272	2 484	13.7	96.0	1.1	1.8	0.6	2.3	4.8	14.6	6.3	9.7	9.3	12.9
29 186	...	6	Ste. Genevieve	499.2	18 030	1 919	36.1	95.2	1.3	0.9	2.7	1.1	5.9	16.6	7.6	10.9	11.3	13.7
29 187	22100	4	St. Francois	451.9	66 627	793	147.4	93.1	4.9	0.9	0.7	1.5	5.5	15.8	8.3	14.7	13.4	13.8
29 189	41180	1	St. Louis	507.8	998 581	45	1 966.5	68.4	25.3	0.7	5.0	2.8	5.8	16.4	8.8	12.7	11.7	13.2
29 195	32180	6	Saline	755.5	22 980	1 681	30.4	83.0	6.4	1.0	2.2	9.8	6.3	16.8	11.4	11.8	11.3	11.8
29 197	28860	9	Schuyler	307.3	4 394	2 870	14.3	98.0	0.7	0.5	0.5	1.2	7.4	18.7	8.5	10.4	10.9	12.4
29 199	...	9	Scotland	436.7	4 932	2 838	11.3	98.3	0.6	0.7	0.3	1.0	8.4	20.2	8.4	10.9	10.3	11.7
29 201	43460	4	Scott	420.0	38 745	1 209	92.3	85.3	12.5	0.9	0.7	2.2	6.4	17.5	8.2	12.6	11.7	13.1
29 203	...	9	Shannon	1 003.8	8 168	2 583	8.1	96.4	0.8	2.8	0.6	1.7	5.0	16.9	7.2	10.5	9.9	13.8
29 205	...	9	Shelby	500.9	6 082	2 744	12.1	96.6	1.7	0.6	0.4	2.0	6.2	17.7	7.2	10.4	10.9	12.1
29 207	...	6	Stoddard	823.2	29 588	1 441	35.9	96.6	1.5	0.8	0.5	1.7	6.0	16.3	7.5	11.9	11.8	13.4
29 209	14700	6	Stone	464.0	31 047	1 407	66.9	96.3	0.8	1.5	0.6	2.2	4.1	13.0	6.1	8.1	9.1	12.8
29 211	...	9	Sullivan	648.0	6 262	2 732	9.7	78.4	3.0	0.9	0.6	18.0	6.2	16.6	7.2	10.6	12.3	14.5
29 213	14700	6	Taney	632.4	54 735	921	86.6	91.2	1.9	1.8	1.4	5.6	5.7	15.6	10.0	11.2	11.0	12.3
29 215	...	9	Texas	1 177.3	25 775	1 571	21.9	93.1	4.1	2.1	0.7	2.0	5.6	16.1	7.7	11.9	11.3	13.2
29 217	...	7	Vernon	826.4	20 723	1 788	25.1	95.5	1.3	1.7	1.0	2.3	6.3	17.8	9.0	10.8	11.3	13.0
29 219	41180	1	Warren	428.6	33 802	1 330	78.9	93.6	3.3	0.9	0.8	3.3	6.4	17.8	7.3	11.9	11.4	13.7
29 221	...	6	Washington	759.9	24 839	1 615	32.7	95.7	2.8	1.1	0.5	1.3	5.8	17.1	7.4	12.1	12.7	14.5
29 223	...	9	Wayne	759.2	13 139	2 220	17.3	96.8	1.0	1.6	0.5	1.8	5.4	15.1	6.3	10.5	9.8	14.2
29 225	44180	2	Webster	592.6	38 106	1 221	64.3	96.9	1.5	1.6	0.6	2.0	7.3	19.7	8.0	12.0	12.0	13.5
29 227	...	9	Worth	266.6	2 024	3 046	7.6	97.2	1.1	0.6	0.4	1.3	5.6	14.7	6.9	9.9	9.2	13.1
29 229	...	6	Wright	681.8	18 286	1 901	26.8	96.6	1.0	1.5	0.6	1.8	6.9	18.5	7.0	10.9	10.4	12.7

1. CBSA = Core Based Statistical Area. See Appendix A for explanation. See Appendix B for list of metropolitan areas with component counties. 2. County type code from the Economic Research Service of USDA Rural-Urban Continuum Codes. See Appendix A for definition. 3. Dry land or land partially or temporarily covered by water. 4. May be of any race.

Table B. States and Counties — **Population and Households**

| STATE County | Population, 2016 (cont.) Age (percent) (cont.) | | | | Population change and components of change, 2000–2016 | | | | | | | Households, 2011–2015 | | | | |
| | 55 to 64 years | 65 to 74 years | 75 years and over | Percent female | Total persons 2000 | Total persons 2010 | Percent change 2000–2010 | Percent change 2010–2016 | Births | Deaths | Net migration | Number | Persons per household | Family households | Female family householder[1] | One person |
	16	17	18	19	20	21	22	23	24	25	26	27	28	29	30	31
MISSOURI—Cont'd																
Jasper	12.2	8.2	6.2	51.3	104 686	117 404	12.1	1.5	10 607	7 171	-1 855	45 519	2.52	65.2	11.7	28.0
Jefferson	14.2	9.0	5.3	50.3	198 099	218 729	10.4	2.5	16 430	11 828	594	81 990	2.68	73.0	11.7	21.5
Johnson	10.5	7.2	5.2	48.4	48 258	52 595	9.0	2.6	4 509	2 454	-719	19 971	2.49	65.5	8.5	23.0
Knox	14.9	11.8	9.8	49.8	4 361	4 131	-5.3	-4.8	311	308	-188	1 689	2.34	68.5	9.9	28.5
Laclede	13.3	10.3	7.2	50.8	32 513	35 571	9.4	-0.2	2 917	2 359	-629	13 545	2.60	70.7	12.6	24.0
Lafayette	14.3	9.9	8.5	50.4	32 960	33 381	1.3	-2.3	2 357	2 274	-851	13 188	2.44	69.2	9.9	27.4
Lawrence	13.1	9.8	8.3	50.4	35 204	38 634	9.7	-0.7	3 052	2 710	-617	14 483	2.60	69.9	9.2	25.5
Lewis	13.2	9.7	8.4	49.9	10 494	10 209	-2.7	-0.7	712	665	-116	3 846	2.45	65.0	6.7	28.2
Lincoln	13.5	7.9	5.2	49.9	38 944	52 560	35.0	5.2	4 506	2 684	871	18 498	2.87	74.2	11.4	21.5
Linn	15.1	11.0	9.4	51.6	13 754	12 761	-7.2	-4.7	900	1 057	-421	4 828	2.53	66.3	9.2	29.6
Livingston	12.4	10.1	9.4	56.3	14 558	15 195	4.4	0.3	1 005	1 205	219	5 708	2.39	67.7	9.5	27.8
McDonald	13.1	8.9	5.6	49.3	21 681	23 083	6.5	-2.0	1 917	1 336	-1 002	8 318	2.71	70.5	13.3	26.3
Macon	13.8	12.0	10.1	50.8	15 762	15 566	-1.2	-2.5	1 088	1 208	-273	6 243	2.43	61.9	8.7	34.6
Madison	14.2	10.8	8.6	51.0	11 800	12 226	3.6	1.8	863	1 022	328	4 650	2.63	70.2	10.5	25.5
Maries	15.4	11.6	8.9	50.0	8 903	9 178	3.1	-3.5	528	620	-238	3 686	2.44	66.1	8.4	27.9
Marion	13.7	9.6	8.0	51.4	28 289	28 781	1.7	0.4	2 322	1 987	-211	11 213	2.43	65.4	13.9	28.9
Mercer	15.7	10.9	11.0	49.7	3 757	3 785	0.7	-2.3	260	264	-85	1 503	2.43	63.5	9.3	33.9
Miller	14.1	10.9	7.9	50.1	23 564	24 747	5.0	1.9	1 860	1 736	374	9 452	2.61	68.0	9.7	29.5
Mississippi	12.1	10.0	7.3	46.0	13 427	14 358	6.9	-3.9	1 018	1 112	-485	5 185	2.41	65.7	18.8	30.8
Moniteau	11.8	8.4	6.9	46.8	14 827	15 607	5.3	2.6	1 284	887	10	5 533	2.62	70.1	8.6	25.3
Monroe	16.2	12.2	9.6	49.4	9 311	8 840	-5.1	-3.2	564	563	-252	3 513	2.43	65.7	8.9	29.5
Montgomery	15.2	11.4	9.4	49.9	12 136	12 234	0.8	-5.0	865	982	-490	4 874	2.37	67.3	9.5	28.3
Morgan	15.4	13.9	10.1	49.6	19 309	20 565	6.5	-1.7	1 607	1 829	-77	7 812	2.55	63.2	8.9	29.6
New Madrid	14.5	10.5	7.7	52.1	19 760	18 960	-4.0	-5.5	1 438	1 477	-990	7 247	2.49	68.4	17.9	26.6
Newton	13.3	10.4	7.6	50.3	52 636	58 112	10.4	1.0	4 553	3 814	-163	22 096	2.62	71.5	9.3	24.0
Nodaway	10.5	7.4	7.3	50.0	21 912	23 370	6.7	-3.0	1 433	1 190	-961	8 659	2.28	56.4	7.7	29.3
Oregon	15.5	12.8	9.6	50.8	10 344	10 881	5.2	-0.8	830	864	-89	4 367	2.48	62.9	8.0	33.1
Osage	13.8	9.6	8.0	48.1	13 062	13 885	6.3	-1.6	914	791	-353	5 143	2.62	70.6	6.9	24.5
Ozark	17.3	16.1	11.7	50.0	9 542	9 719	1.9	-5.0	532	772	-224	4 233	2.22	69.6	10.8	26.7
Pemiscot	13.4	8.8	7.1	52.6	20 047	18 296	-8.7	-6.7	1 749	1 449	-1 472	6 975	2.53	62.9	20.1	32.8
Perry	14.1	9.4	8.0	50.3	18 132	18 971	4.6	1.7	1 368	1 238	150	7 395	2.54	72.6	10.1	24.1
Pettis	13.4	8.5	7.3	50.6	39 403	42 201	7.1	0.0	3 669	2 611	-922	16 131	2.56	67.5	10.7	27.3
Phelps	12.6	8.7	6.7	47.6	39 825	45 154	13.4	-1.2	3 318	2 673	-1 077	16 672	2.52	62.8	10.1	29.1
Pike	13.4	9.4	7.3	44.8	18 351	18 516	0.9	-0.4	1 371	1 221	-184	6 567	2.47	66.5	10.6	27.9
Platte	13.1	8.4	5.2	50.5	73 781	89 318	21.1	10.1	7 156	3 813	5 727	37 556	2.46	66.6	9.9	27.8
Polk	12.4	9.8	7.8	51.0	26 992	31 137	15.4	0.5	2 362	2 146	-3	11 752	2.52	68.7	7.7	24.4
Pulaski	7.8	4.8	3.2	43.0	41 165	52 274	27.0	0.7	5 179	1 803	-3 019	15 435	2.84	66.0	10.7	26.5
Putnam	14.8	13.3	10.5	49.6	5 223	4 979	-4.7	-2.5	354	373	-84	2 196	2.20	63.8	9.5	32.4
Ralls	15.7	12.7	7.5	49.2	9 626	10 167	5.6	0.6	605	580	46	4 021	2.53	75.0	9.8	20.9
Randolph	12.5	8.9	6.8	47.5	24 663	25 414	3.0	-1.7	1 753	1 669	-523	8 450	2.72	65.9	10.1	29.0
Ray	14.8	10.4	7.5	50.2	23 354	23 494	0.6	-3.1	1 537	1 523	-757	8 646	2.63	71.3	11.5	24.2
Reynolds	15.9	12.6	10.6	48.2	6 689	6 694	0.1	-3.6	370	547	-104	2 661	2.40	65.9	9.1	30.2
Ripley	14.3	11.1	8.9	51.0	13 509	14 100	4.4	-2.0	1 113	1 196	-179	5 423	2.57	69.1	10.4	25.8
St. Charles	13.2	8.4	5.8	50.8	283 883	360 495	27.0	8.4	28 387	15 505	17 013	138 958	2.65	72.5	9.4	23.2
St. Clair	15.9	14.7	11.8	49.5	9 652	9 805	1.6	-5.4	581	905	-232	4 015	2.31	64.5	8.3	30.7
Ste. Genevieve	16.2	10.3	7.6	49.3	17 842	18 139	1.7	-0.6	1 114	1 196	50	7 137	2.48	70.7	7.7	27.3
St. Francois	12.7	9.1	6.8	46.6	55 641	65 371	17.5	1.9	4 609	4 738	1 311	24 936	2.33	64.5	11.0	28.7
St. Louis	14.2	9.5	7.8	52.5	1 016 315	998 868	-1.7	0.0	72 781	59 633	-11 963	401 839	2.44	65.1	14.3	29.9
Saline	13.1	9.5	8.0	50.2	23 756	23 370	-1.6	-1.7	1 866	1 546	-667	8 844	2.48	65.4	13.3	29.3
Schuyler	13.6	9.7	8.4	50.5	4 170	4 431	6.3	-0.8	387	319	-57	1 722	2.52	69.4	9.8	26.4
Scotland	12.0	9.5	8.6	50.1	4 983	4 853	-2.6	1.6	481	365	-39	1 851	2.58	65.0	10.4	27.5
Scott	13.4	9.9	7.3	51.3	40 422	39 187	-3.1	-1.1	3 178	2 639	-928	15 247	2.52	69.0	15.6	25.6
Shannon	16.2	12.4	8.1	50.3	8 324	8 441	1.4	-3.2	566	546	-250	3 277	2.50	66.5	9.5	28.6
Shelby	15.0	11.1	9.5	50.3	6 799	6 373	-6.3	-4.6	457	506	-243	2 499	2.37	63.5	6.6	32.7
Stoddard	13.7	10.6	8.9	50.9	29 705	29 968	0.9	-1.3	2 278	2 395	-209	12 045	2.43	64.1	9.2	30.5
Stone	18.2	17.9	10.8	51.1	28 658	32 208	12.4	-3.6	1 565	2 295	-219	12 836	2.42	71.0	6.6	24.0
Sullivan	14.0	10.4	8.2	48.5	7 219	6 714	-7.0	-6.7	513	472	-461	2 512	2.56	63.9	10.0	31.4
Taney	13.4	12.2	8.5	51.5	39 703	51 674	30.2	5.9	3 920	3 280	2 374	21 300	2.43	66.1	12.4	27.5
Texas	14.4	11.0	8.8	47.8	23 003	26 008	13.1	-0.9	1 829	1 811	-168	9 134	2.67	66.0	9.4	29.8
Vernon	13.6	10.3	7.8	51.0	20 454	21 159	3.4	-2.1	1 608	1 561	-453	8 040	2.50	68.0	11.8	26.7
Warren	14.5	10.0	7.0	49.9	24 525	32 518	32.6	3.9	2 549	1 716	507	11 951	2.74	73.6	10.7	22.7
Washington	14.1	9.9	6.3	48.6	23 344	25 196	7.9	-1.4	1 836	1 674	-493	8 982	2.67	70.4	11.9	23.4
Wayne	16.2	13.1	9.4	50.7	13 259	13 523	2.0	-2.8	879	1 232	-21	5 453	2.43	67.0	12.9	28.1
Webster	12.6	9.0	6.0	49.1	31 045	36 202	16.6	5.3	3 303	1 980	595	12 885	2.78	75.1	9.8	21.2
Worth	17.0	11.0	12.5	51.0	2 382	2 171	-8.9	-6.8	141	182	-110	900	2.25	65.6	6.6	28.2
Wright	14.4	10.5	8.7	50.9	17 955	18 815	4.8	-2.8	1 491	1 376	-615	7 351	2.48	67.0	11.6	28.8

1. No spouse present.

Table B. States and Counties — Population, Vital Statistics, Health, and Crime

STATE County	Persons in group quarters, 2016	Daytime population, 2011–2015 Number	Daytime population Employment/residence ratio	Births, 2016 Total	Births, 2016 Rate[1]	Deaths, 2016 Number	Deaths, 2016 Rate[1]	Persons under 65 with no health insurance, 2015 Number	Percent	Medicare, 2015 Total Beneficiaries	Enrolled in Original Medicare	Enrolled in Medicare Advantage	Serious crimes known to police,[2] 2014 Total Number	Rate[3]
	32	33	34	35	36	37	38	39	40	41	42	43	44	45
MISSOURI—Cont'd														
Jasper	2 484	123 239	1.11	1 667	14.0	1 094	9.2	14 442	14.5	24 887	18 631	6 256	6 022	5 183
Jefferson	1 984	167 196	0.48	2 529	11.3	2 045	9.1	20 736	10.8	36 098	20 166	15 932	4 211	1 895
Johnson	3 855	51 384	0.89	709	13.1	405	7.5	4 672	10.6	7 062	5 614	1 448	1 360	2 468
Knox	87	3 721	0.81	47	11.9	40	10.2	539	17.9	919	858	61	39	961
Laclede	345	35 630	1.01	480	13.5	383	10.8	4 172	14.4	8 445	4 713	3 732	948	2 655
Lafayette	724	28 631	0.71	373	11.4	365	11.2	3 081	11.7	6 959	5 072	1 887	419	1 283
Lawrence	559	32 981	0.66	484	12.6	426	11.1	4 737	15.3	7 287	4 371	2 916	1 235	3 239
Lewis	785	8 592	0.67	119	11.7	112	11.1	1 014	13.0	2 188	1 978	210	80	788
Lincoln	632	42 658	0.52	721	13.0	455	8.2	5 806	12.3	8 282	5 391	2 891	730	1 346
Linn	152	12 360	0.99	158	13.0	169	13.9	1 302	13.4	3 155	2 824	331	284	2 311
Livingston	1 875	15 739	1.11	148	9.7	191	12.5	1 362	12.7	3 452	3 093	359	230	1 552
McDonald	157	20 298	0.74	305	13.5	217	9.6	4 017	21.1	3 665	2 481	1 184	573	2 551
Macon	286	14 443	0.84	166	10.9	182	12.0	1 667	14.0	3 632	3 303	329	273	1 756
Madison	164	11 392	0.79	138	11.1	176	14.1	1 446	14.7	2 967	2 545	422	297	2 376
Maries	67	6 924	0.40	86	9.7	95	10.7	1 083	15.3	1 540	1 292	248	109	1 213
Marion	1 370	31 253	1.19	375	13.0	307	10.6	2 745	11.9	6 905	6 016	889	1 180	4 074
Mercer	51	3 889	1.11	43	11.6	35	9.5	447	15.6	771	704	67	24	652
Miller	271	21 614	0.69	307	12.2	280	11.1	2 922	14.4	5 931	4 787	1 144	647	2 566
Mississippi	1 873	13 681	0.89	136	9.9	168	12.2	1 480	15.1	2 939	2 684	255	392	2 744
Moniteau	1 373	13 620	0.67	195	12.2	152	9.5	1 941	15.8	2 607	2 187	420	129	817
Monroe	129	7 187	0.61	90	10.5	92	10.8	894	13.4	2 239	1 997	242	78	888
Montgomery	394	10 196	0.65	125	10.8	145	12.5	1 257	13.8	2 870	2 247	623	176	1 478
Morgan	302	19 044	0.82	270	13.4	284	14.1	2 778	18.4	5 445	4 544	901	456	2 256
New Madrid	332	18 825	1.06	216	12.1	228	12.7	1 988	13.6	3 502	3 097	405	322	1 765
Newton	880	57 404	0.95	707	12.0	611	10.4	6 865	14.4	8 199	6 128	2 071	2 051	3 471
Nodaway	3 624	23 383	1.02	223	9.8	182	8.0	1 718	10.6	3 788	3 554	234	310	1 333
Oregon	121	10 093	0.78	137	12.7	148	13.7	1 279	15.3	2 699	2 206	493	97	880
Osage	405	11 709	0.69	140	10.2	127	9.3	1 153	10.5	2 272	1 975	297	115	842
Ozark	123	8 486	0.66	76	8.2	128	13.9	1 210	17.8	2 742	1 914	828	108	1 134
Pemiscot	202	17 336	0.92	264	15.5	244	14.3	1 886	13.0	3 646	2 857	789	827	4 784
Perry	286	19 497	1.04	209	10.8	214	11.1	1 644	10.4	3 608	3 225	383	265	1 386
Pettis	851	43 637	1.08	585	13.9	397	9.4	5 627	16.1	8 550	7 179	1 371	1 803	4 268
Phelps	3 011	46 335	1.07	502	11.3	436	9.8	4 991	14.1	8 882	7 575	1 307	1 441	3 221
Pike	2 293	18 392	0.98	219	11.9	193	10.5	1 718	12.9	3 517	2 916	601	225	1 201
Platte	869	89 773	0.93	1 155	11.7	629	6.4	6 560	7.9	12 619	9 488	3 131	3 588	3 803
Polk	1 510	28 749	0.81	375	12.0	371	11.9	3 424	13.9	6 886	3 779	3 107	1 020	3 294
Pulaski	10 010	57 611	1.15	780	14.8	271	5.1	4 275	10.9	6 046	5 210	836	1 048	1 940
Putnam	57	4 387	0.76	64	13.2	55	11.3	593	16.1	1 254	1 151	103	34	700
Ralls	54	8 665	0.67	90	8.8	86	8.4	926	11.4	1 584	1 364	220	111	1 087
Randolph	2 456	25 363	1.02	276	11.0	253	10.1	2 220	11.8	5 285	4 270	1 015	538	2 165
Ray	311	17 791	0.47	248	10.9	266	11.7	2 121	11.4	3 913	3 249	664	526	2 291
Reynolds	101	7 070	1.21	51	7.9	90	13.9	784	16.2	1 494	1 304	190	73	1 109
Ripley	63	12 187	0.66	171	12.4	213	15.4	1 763	16.1	3 352	2 938	414	433	3 230
St. Charles	5 444	318 511	0.71	4 538	11.6	2 718	7.0	23 114	7.0	58 296	33 737	24 559	6 064	1 609
St. Clair	207	8 770	0.77	94	10.1	150	16.2	1 129	16.6	2 475	1 823	652	232	2 464
Ste. Genevieve	277	15 936	0.74	184	10.2	183	10.1	1 837	12.5	3 431	2 845	586	273	1 541
St. Francois	7 011	65 724	0.99	715	10.7	766	11.5	6 150	12.4	14 560	11 746	2 814	2 045	3 077
St. Louis	19 414	1 096 830	1.20	11 591	11.6	10 027	10.0	67 284	8.2	184 451	110 877	73 574	26 121	2 604
Saline	1 277	23 148	0.98	278	12.1	232	10.1	2 432	13.4	4 471	3 646	825	511	2 199
Schuyler	47	3 560	0.54	66	15.0	47	10.7	619	17.3	1 183	1 074	109	45	1 036
Scotland	76	4 446	0.80	75	15.2	53	10.7	739	19.0	898	839	59	46	929
Scott	559	39 014	1.00	480	12.4	431	11.1	3 988	12.5	9 667	8 478	1 189	1 778	4 519
Shannon	80	7 435	0.73	80	9.8	76	9.3	1 082	16.6	1 678	1 362	316	103	1 245
Shelby	198	5 688	0.83	75	12.3	65	10.7	711	14.9	1 524	1 400	124	36	587
Stoddard	690	28 061	0.85	365	12.3	401	13.6	3 159	13.2	7 221	5 956	1 265	508	1 707
Stone	300	27 358	0.66	235	7.6	353	11.4	3 620	16.4	8 375	5 116	3 259	696	2 235
Sullivan	108	6 657	1.05	74	11.8	67	10.7	884	17.2	1 415	1 288	127	93	1 455
Taney	1 751	57 688	1.18	648	11.8	544	9.9	7 577	18.1	12 511	7 833	4 678	1 909	3 531
Texas	1 897	24 440	0.86	289	11.2	281	10.9	2 957	15.8	5 617	4 894	723	547	2 139
Vernon	759	20 893	1.00	263	12.7	243	11.7	2 308	14.1	4 789	3 883	906	946	4 521
Warren	317	26 399	0.55	408	12.1	302	8.9	3 304	12.0	5 889	3 325	2 564	840	2 534
Washington	1 087	22 018	0.66	279	11.2	281	11.3	2 757	14.0	5 038	3 793	1 245	524	2 079
Wayne	133	12 313	0.77	131	10.0	203	15.5	1 633	15.9	4 148	3 431	717	292	2 180
Webster	956	30 529	0.57	566	14.9	354	9.3	4 570	14.8	8 081	3 973	4 108	750	2 052
Worth	52	1 798	0.71	20	9.9	24	11.9	210	13.6	549	521	28	48	2 311
Wright	195	17 100	0.79	238	13.0	214	11.7	2 624	18.0	4 925	3 024	1 901	347	1 886

1. Per 1,000 estimated resident population. 2. Data for serious crimes have not been adjusted for underreporting; this may affect comparability between geographic areas and over time.
3. Per 100,000 population estimated by the FBI.

Table B. States and Counties — Crime, Education, Money Income, and Poverty

STATE County	Serious crimes known to police, 2014 (cont.)[1] Rate[2] Violent	Property	Education School enrollment and attainment, 2011–2015 Enrollment[3] Total	Percent private	Attainment[4] (percent) High school graduate or less	Bachelor's degree or more	Local government expenditures,[5] 2013–2014 Total current spending (mil dol)	Current spending per student (dollars)	Money income, 2011–2015 Per capita income[6] (dollars)	Households Median income (dollars)	Percent with income of less than $50,000	with income of $200,000 or more	Income and poverty, 2015 Median household income (dollars)	Percent below poverty level All persons	Children under 18 years	Children 5 to 17 years in families
	46	47	48	49	50	51	52	53	54	55	56	57	58	59	60	61
MISSOURI—Cont'd																
Jasper	411	4 772	30 101	13.9	49.2	22.0	170.5	7 907	22 431	41 811	57.5	1.8	43 724	16.0	22.6	21.6
Jefferson	218	1 677	54 330	16.4	46.0	18.2	326.4	9 222	25 247	55 348	44.2	1.8	58 747	10.5	13.6	12.4
Johnson	169	2 299	18 036	7.6	39.7	26.5	66.9	8 954	22 722	49 792	50.2	1.5	44 109	16.3	17.2	16.4
Knox	0	961	851	23.9	58.1	15.2	5.3	10 590	22 397	38 289	63.1	1.1	40 356	18.7	30.4	29.1
Laclede	255	2 400	8 377	13.0	57.5	13.9	48.2	7 880	19 567	39 712	61.6	0.9	40 741	17.4	25.9	24.2
Lafayette	104	1 179	7 763	15.6	53.3	18.3	48.5	9 199	24 266	50 723	49.3	1.2	50 325	12.2	18.0	16.4
Lawrence	448	2 790	9 287	13.0	54.8	16.8	48.4	8 148	19 508	40 597	61.7	1.3	41 619	18.3	27.3	26.2
Lewis	128	660	2 671	31.9	60.1	13.5	13.4	8 810	20 042	43 909	55.9	0.4	45 592	16.3	24.7	22.1
Lincoln	219	1 127	13 764	13.3	57.1	14.8	75.5	8 471	22 232	53 718	45.6	1.5	54 584	11.3	15.4	14.2
Linn	399	1 912	2 844	8.1	61.8	14.2	22.2	9 426	19 889	37 997	63.7	0.9	39 618	17.4	26.6	24.4
Livingston	169	1 383	3 031	10.6	56.3	20.0	20.1	9 358	22 557	43 350	56.1	2.2	40 808	18.8	26.2	24.5
McDonald	619	1 932	5 769	10.1	56.6	12.4	30.7	8 032	18 498	38 368	63.2	1.3	37 939	20.1	31.0	28.4
Macon	264	1 492	3 470	12.1	56.2	15.5	21.5	9 328	19 738	36 976	63.7	1.2	41 080	14.6	23.2	21.5
Madison	424	1 952	2 872	7.9	60.0	11.2	17.0	8 104	17 179	35 097	67.3	0.5	35 745	19.3	29.6	27.2
Maries	134	1 079	1 994	13.6	59.5	15.0	11.0	7 928	20 731	39 700	60.4	1.0	43 970	15.4	24.4	21.0
Marion	255	3 819	6 906	23.0	54.1	19.4	43.4	8 477	21 614	40 814	59.5	1.5	41 297	17.7	23.4	21.4
Mercer	82	571	796	15.6	61.9	13.9	6.3	9 906	20 404	40 768	61.2	0.0	43 244	14.2	21.9	19.9
Miller	337	2 229	6 068	10.1	56.3	16.4	44.8	8 854	21 268	38 094	62.7	2.5	40 077	18.7	27.3	24.6
Mississippi	497	2 247	2 881	6.5	67.6	10.8	17.7	7 913	16 515	28 347	70.8	1.0	33 283	26.6	38.0	37.0
Moniteau	177	639	3 710	19.5	60.4	18.1	19.9	8 317	20 901	47 725	52.5	1.0	50 525	14.7	20.4	18.2
Monroe	23	866	1 929	15.0	58.2	14.1	13.8	9 379	20 921	43 138	58.6	0.4	44 048	14.0	22.8	20.9
Montgomery	185	1 293	2 566	10.5	59.9	12.5	14.7	8 988	20 710	39 830	60.4	1.1	41 470	17.0	26.2	25.5
Morgan	188	2 068	3 922	23.3	62.2	13.4	16.5	7 850	18 431	33 525	64.4	0.4	39 219	23.1	33.1	31.4
New Madrid	296	1 469	3 973	5.9	65.0	11.6	26.7	9 664	19 918	33 630	63.2	1.0	36 386	23.9	36.9	33.3
Newton	169	3 301	14 570	13.1	47.3	18.8	69.2	8 014	22 735	43 290	57.8	2.5	46 125	14.5	20.7	19.0
Nodaway	120	1 212	8 960	7.2	49.8	23.9	29.0	10 448	18 307	35 854	64.2	1.0	44 119	22.9	16.8	15.0
Oregon	145	734	2 292	5.1	58.1	11.0	15.7	8 741	17 070	29 851	71.5	0.7	33 573	24.7	39.8	36.9
Osage	81	761	3 495	19.4	57.4	17.5	13.8	8 343	23 918	52 693	46.8	0.5	55 962	9.6	11.4	10.1
Ozark	126	1 008	1 699	10.4	60.7	12.9	14.9	9 448	16 959	31 399	70.8	0.0	31 838	27.7	41.3	38.7
Pemiscot	839	3 945	4 451	2.7	64.1	11.7	37.3	10 334	16 902	29 238	70.7	0.5	29 621	28.0	41.3	40.5
Perry	235	1 151	4 642	29.8	58.1	15.9	21.8	8 995	23 695	51 499	48.5	1.6	47 226	11.1	15.7	14.2
Pettis	372	3 896	10 576	13.2	49.2	17.5	54.1	8 005	20 494	39 928	60.4	1.2	42 137	15.1	22.5	21.6
Phelps	422	2 799	14 589	9.5	46.0	27.8	57.9	8 826	21 611	41 618	58.8	2.1	40 676	19.1	25.1	23.0
Pike	133	1 067	3 481	9.7	64.7	12.7	23.3	9 158	19 005	41 750	58.5	0.8	43 007	18.2	25.6	24.3
Platte	668	3 136	25 208	21.3	27.1	40.4	167.1	10 642	35 666	68 254	36.5	6.1	72 548	7.6	9.5	8.0
Polk	368	2 926	8 675	24.4	51.8	18.8	47.2	8 934	19 908	41 130	60.7	1.3	41 326	17.5	26.0	23.0
Pulaski	298	1 642	16 039	12.9	41.5	24.1	86.1	9 344	19 568	47 931	52.6	0.5	46 756	16.2	17.5	16.6
Putnam	0	700	970	10.2	54.2	18.1	6.8	9 358	20 203	36 346	66.9	0.6	37 286	18.0	27.8	25.1
Ralls	69	1 019	1 941	15.7	61.2	12.3	5.7	7 529	23 442	47 345	52.9	1.2	51 015	11.5	16.1	14.2
Randolph	121	2 045	6 333	17.1	53.2	13.7	36.4	9 444	18 151	37 832	61.0	1.7	39 976	20.0	26.5	25.2
Ray	261	2 030	5 654	10.6	58.6	13.8	27.9	8 137	24 101	52 526	47.3	1.1	54 361	11.1	16.1	14.4
Reynolds	228	881	1 312	3.9	67.5	8.1	13.4	12 293	20 082	35 648	65.2	0.5	34 076	21.5	34.3	31.2
Ripley	298	2 932	3 019	7.8	61.8	11.1	18.5	8 238	17 315	32 444	69.5	0.3	34 069	25.4	39.3	38.6
St. Charles	123	1 486	102 924	26.7	32.0	35.5	580.6	9 684	32 946	72 415	31.9	5.4	74 009	6.3	7.8	6.9
St. Clair	414	2 050	1 628	16.3	64.3	10.8	12.5	8 926	18 840	32 046	69.1	0.6	35 128	22.6	36.2	33.5
Ste. Genevieve	361	1 180	4 463	20.5	55.3	13.3	21.8	11 632	23 772	47 014	53.2	0.8	52 806	10.9	16.6	15.3
St. Francois	280	2 797	14 697	10.5	53.1	14.1	89.5	8 339	19 315	39 741	61.6	0.9	41 222	18.2	25.4	23.3
St. Louis	307	2 296	263 244	28.4	29.2	41.6	1 845.0	12 835	35 570	59 755	42.1	7.4	61 569	10.3	14.0	13.1
Saline	176	2 022	6 219	23.4	54.0	18.8	32.2	8 781	20 339	40 101	61.3	1.0	41 958	16.5	22.4	21.6
Schuyler	161	875	1 032	10.8	60.0	12.4	5.4	8 829	19 650	37 500	64.5	1.3	37 851	18.3	31.6	28.3
Scotland	61	869	1 050	21.2	60.7	14.8	6.2	10 213	20 859	39 772	63.6	2.9	41 324	15.8	25.0	23.5
Scott	1 047	3 472	8 749	12.7	60.4	13.2	54.2	7 963	20 542	39 162	62.5	1.3	40 285	18.1	25.8	24.8
Shannon	254	991	1 853	10.1	56.5	15.1	17.5	8 844	19 658	32 404	66.8	0.9	28 171	23.9	42.6	38.5
Shelby	16	570	1 359	19.4	55.9	13.1	10.1	9 365	20 569	39 087	61.3	0.7	41 696	16.8	24.4	22.8
Stoddard	134	1 573	6 309	9.0	55.3	13.7	41.9	8 318	21 797	38 203	62.8	1.5	38 773	19.0	26.4	24.4
Stone	466	1 769	5 752	13.6	54.0	16.3	39.7	9 522	22 473	40 510	59.5	1.4	42 186	14.8	25.8	23.7
Sullivan	203	1 252	1 412	3.3	63.3	12.9	10.5	10 228	19 930	40 197	61.3	1.1	41 405	17.4	23.2	21.0
Taney	314	3 217	12 451	25.2	48.6	18.3	71.3	8 818	20 520	38 357	64.7	1.2	39 320	16.0	25.0	23.7
Texas	125	2 014	5 635	11.3	61.1	13.0	32.4	8 181	17 741	35 088	65.4	0.9	34 935	23.3	33.4	31.4
Vernon	545	3 976	4 970	18.1	53.4	16.3	28.1	8 806	20 479	40 693	60.3	1.9	40 186	18.5	28.1	26.4
Warren	410	2 124	7 462	19.6	52.5	15.8	41.2	8 726	24 033	51 133	49.1	2.1	51 933	12.3	18.8	17.8
Washington	302	1 778	5 717	7.3	66.8	7.1	32.9	8 965	17 762	35 305	66.2	0.9	37 986	20.7	32.6	30.2
Wayne	224	1 956	2 484	5.4	61.7	10.7	14.8	7 907	18 748	33 750	68.9	0.4	32 566	24.3	37.7	36.1
Webster	200	1 852	8 877	19.7	54.8	15.8	55.2	7 790	19 956	44 451	55.6	1.5	43 418	19.2	30.1	27.4
Worth	96	2 215	430	8.1	54.2	17.5	3.0	9 558	23 815	45 952	54.7	1.9	43 443	15.9	25.3	24.4
Wright	266	1 619	4 255	16.5	63.1	12.4	27.5	7 805	18 481	29 778	70.4	3.4	32 634	24.1	37.5	34.7

1. Data for serious crimes have not been adjusted for underreporting; this may affect comparability between geographic areas and over time.   2. Per 100,000 population estimated by the FBI.
3. All persons 3 years old and over enrolled in nursery school through college.   4. Persons 25 years old and over.   5. Elementary and secondary education expenditures.
6. Based on population estimated by the American Community Survey, 2011–2015.

Table B. States and Counties — Personal Income

STATE County	Personal income, 2015										Earnings, 2015		
	Total (mil dol)	Percent change, 2014–2015	Per capita[1] Dollars	Rank	Wages and salaries (mil dol)	Supplements to wages and salaries; employer contributions (mil dol) Pension and insurance	Government social insurance	Proprietors' income (mil dol)	Dividends, interest, and rent (mil dol)	Personal transfer receipts (mil dol)	Total (mil dol)	Contributions for government social insurance (mil dol) From employee and self-employed	From employer
	62	63	64	65	66	67	68	69	70	71	72	73	74
MISSOURI—Cont'd													
Jasper	4 284	4.9	36 119	2 063	2 361	423	173	373	627	997	3 330	200	173
Jefferson	8 458	4.9	37 740	1 607	1 883	348	144	377	916	1 745	2 753	193	144
Johnson	1 765	2.2	32 718	2 302	787	226	66	87	320	383	1 166	59	66
Knox	136	-22.3	34 827	590	33	8	2	14	28	36	57	4	2
Laclede	1 140	2.8	32 131	2 578	454	99	37	107	183	341	698	45	37
Lafayette	1 196	0.2	36 573	1 673	306	67	23	67	178	325	463	32	23
Lawrence	1 199	3.5	31 401	2 678	326	70	24	105	177	340	524	35	24
Lewis	317	-9.4	31 103	2 144	88	19	7	20	49	85	133	9	7
Lincoln	1 930	4.8	35 292	2 154	458	89	34	92	209	430	673	46	34
Linn	454	-1.6	36 902	1 547	158	30	14	48	83	130	250	17	14
Livingston	511	-1.5	33 976	1 892	227	47	17	59	95	142	350	21	17
McDonald	611	2.0	26 988	2 998	237	48	17	63	74	166	365	22	17
Macon	556	6.9	36 229	1 914	173	42	12	87	86	156	314	20	12
Madison	412	3.4	33 217	2 460	114	26	8	25	54	155	174	12	8
Maries	299	1.4	33 410	1 530	42	10	3	19	49	83	74	6	3
Marion	1 053	-0.1	36 477	1 566	518	95	40	64	154	304	716	45	40
Mercer	122	-14.7	33 003	1 463	34	7	2	30	20	30	73	3	2
Miller	755	2.5	30 066	2 727	227	48	18	92	115	224	384	23	18
Mississippi	389	-6.8	27 708	2 593	135	30	10	8	62	143	182	13	10
Moniteau	529	-0.7	33 153	2 333	137	32	10	61	81	110	241	14	10
Monroe	326	-9.5	38 014	897	73	18	5	37	50	84	133	8	5
Montgomery	387	-3.2	33 031	2 084	103	22	8	16	66	116	149	11	8
Morgan	796	2.3	39 448	1 493	134	29	10	100	235	227	273	18	10
New Madrid	563	-3.4	30 946	2 395	320	58	24	-1	75	193	401	27	24
Newton	2 103	3.0	35 871	2 004	839	153	61	190	314	481	1 243	75	61
Nodaway	652	-6.8	28 586	2 656	284	70	20	45	124	150	420	25	20
Oregon	289	2.6	26 343	3 015	86	18	9	28	42	121	141	11	9
Osage	594	4.1	43 583	1 399	134	29	10	129	84	97	302	17	10
Ozark	258	0.8	27 385	3 036	44	11	3	25	43	107	83	8	3
Pemiscot	547	-2.3	31 302	2 250	204	48	15	14	75	211	281	19	15
Perry	680	1.8	35 465	1 908	370	70	27	44	89	166	511	31	27
Pettis	1 491	0.9	35 292	1 957	717	140	55	145	219	400	1 057	63	55
Phelps	1 496	3.9	33 403	2 408	718	168	50	92	261	402	1 028	59	50
Pike	572	-3.6	31 168	2 454	210	48	16	34	113	156	308	20	16
Platte	4 983	5.9	51 855	425	2 128	314	157	354	710	600	2 953	175	157
Polk	948	1.5	30 365	2 743	300	71	22	72	142	292	465	30	22
Pulaski	2 079	2.5	39 057	1 353	1 137	340	109	46	409	368	1 632	71	109
Putnam	168	-9.0	34 654	1 432	41	10	3	28	30	52	82	4	3
Ralls	364	-5.8	35 733	1 458	156	29	11	25	56	89	221	15	11
Randolph	910	3.3	36 247	1 696	377	81	29	92	119	256	579	36	29
Ray	843	2.0	36 947	1 384	164	40	12	45	105	206	261	19	12
Reynolds	184	1.6	28 566	2 976	72	15	5	9	34	77	102	7	5
Ripley	396	1.5	28 696	2 815	77	19	6	25	48	169	127	11	6
St. Charles	18 154	5.2	47 082	623	6 699	1 048	495	750	2 212	2 509	8 992	553	495
St. Clair	297	-1.3	31 512	2 372	52	12	4	22	50	109	90	8	4
Ste. Genevieve	652	1.1	36 385	1 756	252	43	19	18	100	161	332	22	19
St. Francois	2 027	4.3	30 471	2 741	791	176	59	71	278	676	1 097	73	59
St. Louis	62 403	3.4	62 194	125	36 841	5 007	2 584	4 670	16 606	8 321	49 101	2 909	2 584
Saline	854	-6.4	36 705	1 087	324	68	23	111	133	237	525	30	23
Schuyler	117	-5.7	26 321	2 953	20	6	1	6	21	37	34	3	1
Scotland	158	-17.5	32 468	1 121	39	12	3	25	31	40	79	4	3
Scott	1 430	0.4	36 669	1 402	599	111	47	118	208	431	874	57	47
Shannon	201	3.5	24 297	3 083	39	10	3	21	32	81	73	6	3
Shelby	232	-14.1	37 937	689	54	14	4	30	43	58	101	6	4
Stoddard	1 035	0.9	34 654	2 042	369	72	30	90	148	313	561	39	30
Stone	1 042	2.2	33 669	1 658	214	39	17	63	218	328	333	29	17
Sullivan	233	-15.8	36 670	678	108	20	7	43	31	64	179	9	7
Taney	1 767	3.2	32 363	2 654	933	145	75	216	291	495	1 370	88	75
Texas	654	-1.0	25 463	3 023	187	50	13	27	118	231	278	20	13
Vernon	690	-4.1	33 129	1 929	270	66	19	90	102	209	445	25	19
Warren	1 197	3.2	35 729	1 978	276	54	21	49	162	277	400	29	21
Washington	684	4.0	27 603	3 017	163	42	12	25	67	258	241	18	12
Wayne	367	4.8	27 410	2 997	75	19	6	21	56	161	122	11	6
Webster	1 181	5.3	31 503	2 829	242	54	18	104	149	292	418	30	18
Worth	76	-17.3	37 185	746	12	4	1	18	13	18	34	2	1
Wright	487	-0.8	26 671	3 038	137	32	10	41	80	195	220	17	10

1. Based on the resident population estimated as of July 1 of the year shown.

Table B. States and Counties — Earnings, Social Security, and Housing

STATE County	Earnings, 2015 (cont.) Percent by selected industries									Social Security beneficiaries, December 2015		Supplemental Security Income recipients, December 2015	Housing units, 2016	
	Farm	Mining	Construction	Manufacturing	Information: professional, scientific, technical services	Retail trade	Finance, insurance, real estate and leasing	Health care and social assistance	Government	Number	Rate[1]		Total	Percent change, 2010–2016
	75	76	77	78	79	80	81	82	83	84	85	86	87	88
MISSOURI—Cont'd														
Jasper	0.7	0.2	4.2	23.0	3.9	8.0	4.7	10.2	11.2	24 555	207	3 596	52 026	2.7
Jefferson	0.0	0.5	12.2	10.7	4.0	8.4	5.7	11.3	19.2	45 095	201	2 940	89 434	2.1
Johnson	0.5	D	4.4	5.9	2.2	4.5	3.7	4.6	59.8	8 335	155	698	22 045	2.4
Knox	7.8	D	8.1	13.5	6.0	4.5	6.0	3.7	21.7	1 025	263	97	2 265	-1.0
Laclede	0.9	0.0	4.8	35.9	D	10.8	4.1	8.8	12.0	9 250	261	1 216	15 741	-0.2
Lafayette	0.4	0.0	10.2	10.4	6.5	8.5	5.2	D	23.9	7 740	237	601	14 659	-0.4
Lawrence	7.0	D	8.6	15.5	3.7	8.5	5.0	D	21.5	9 510	249	874	16 520	-0.8
Lewis	0.0	D	5.4	5.6	2.1	8.9	4.4	D	21.0	2 285	224	169	4 486	-1.1
Lincoln	-0.3	1.0	13.6	16.4	D	7.8	5.7	7.3	19.4	10 615	194	903	21 185	0.8
Linn	0.0	0.3	D	21.5	5.8	6.4	6.4	9.3	15.8	3 235	263	348	6 371	-0.9
Livingston	3.1	D	6.8	8.9	2.6	9.3	5.4	D	20.8	3 610	241	348	6 735	0.1
McDonald	8.6	D	6.7	36.3	2.0	7.4	2.2	2.9	14.5	4 525	200	589	9 788	-1.4
Macon	-1.4	1.4	5.2	23.3	8.0	6.1	4.8	D	27.2	4 215	275	302	7 593	-0.9
Madison	2.9	D	8.6	11.2	D	9.8	D	9.8	24.9	3 630	293	551	5 926	-0.7
Maries	5.3	0.1	D	18.4	D	7.0	10.4	D	20.5	2 360	263	141	4 552	-1.3
Marion	0.1	D	7.6	9.1	D	9.0	5.7	D	14.5	6 860	238	1 012	12 928	0.8
Mercer	31.4	D	3.7	5.4	D	3.9	3.3	4.6	17.1	945	255	68	2 109	-1.2
Miller	10.5	D	9.9	8.9	2.7	11.1	5.1	D	19.8	5 875	234	557	12 800	0.3
Mississippi	-5.7	0.0	2.9	5.9	D	8.4	6.9	D	29.3	3 425	244	738	5 700	-0.2
Moniteau	13.9	D	13.5	14.5	2.8	5.9	3.8	D	22.0	3 140	197	211	6 123	-0.9
Monroe	18.8	D	4.0	12.1	2.3	2.4	D	4.7	24.3	2 350	275	176	4 790	-0.2
Montgomery	-3.8	1.0	12.2	21.8	2.4	7.1	5.3	7.5	23.0	3 080	263	279	6 158	0.5
Morgan	16.5	D	10.5	8.3	D	13.7	5.1	D	16.2	6 420	318	583	15 385	-0.9
New Madrid	-4.9	0.0	2.7	33.3	D	10.7	2.1	D	12.9	4 370	241	916	8 530	0.0
Newton	5.8	D	6.1	12.8	2.4	7.2	3.0	29.4	11.4	13 015	222	991	24 406	0.4
Nodaway	-2.6	D	5.0	19.2	3.1	8.4	5.2	12.4	30.2	3 925	172	257	9 701	1.9
Oregon	5.8	D	3.3	7.6	D	9.5	2.8	D	17.6	3 095	283	600	5 412	-1.3
Osage	7.3	1.1	8.5	40.5	D	4.1	3.1	3.7	12.5	2 795	205	145	6 533	-0.9
Ozark	1.7	0.3	7.3	10.0	D	7.4	7.8	5.4	24.7	3 280	349	310	5 609	-0.7
Pemiscot	-5.4	D	D	D	D	8.9	5.1	10.2	28.6	4 465	256	1 360	8 095	-0.8
Perry	1.3	D	11.1	31.8	D	6.6	4.6	D	13.1	4 390	229	362	8 624	0.7
Pettis	1.4	D	5.1	24.7	6.4	7.5	3.9	8.5	17.3	9 040	214	1 206	18 164	-0.5
Phelps	-0.2	0.1	4.1	6.7	3.1	8.1	4.5	14.4	38.3	9 160	205	1 194	19 961	2.2
Pike	-0.3	D	10.8	7.2	4.8	13.5	3.2	6.7	28.3	4 055	221	405	7 826	-0.6
Platte	-0.2	D	7.4	12.3	6.4	6.9	5.8	6.5	11.0	15 220	158	717	41 179	5.0
Polk	2.7	D	6.8	2.7	D	7.3	3.9	10.7	32.2	6 910	222	920	13 409	0.8
Pulaski	0.0	D	1.6	D	1.6	3.2	1.9	2.4	80.1	6 625	125	860	18 833	5.2
Putnam	25.5	0.0	D	D	D	6.6	6.4	2.0	29.3	1 365	281	129	2 960	-0.7
Ralls	-0.9	0.1	D	56.8	D	2.8	2.6	D	8.9	2 520	248	117	5 123	-1.2
Randolph	0.1	D	3.4	8.9	D	14.1	6.0	11.8	19.1	5 385	215	849	10 644	-0.7
Ray	-1.9	D	8.7	12.6	2.9	8.1	5.5	D	27.6	5 200	228	315	9 961	-0.2
Reynolds	-0.6	D	2.2	13.6	D	3.8	4.0	12.6	18.2	1 925	300	259	3 991	-1.0
Ripley	-1.1	0.0	5.5	14.3	2.0	11.4	4.0	13.2	26.9	3 995	289	778	6 520	-1.2
St. Charles	0.1	D	7.3	14.6	11.7	8.3	8.9	9.5	11.7	66 020	171	2 711	151 728	7.6
St. Clair	5.9	D	6.6	4.1	D	10.1	3.9	9.6	28.3	2 930	310	284	5 554	-1.5
Ste. Genevieve	0.0	5.6	9.0	12.6	D	5.5	4.0	D	18.2	4 215	236	310	8 623	-0.1
St. Francois	-0.1	0.6	7.6	8.6	3.2	8.6	6.6	15.3	27.6	16 110	242	2 602	29 525	3.7
St. Louis	0.0	0.2	4.7	9.6	13.6	5.7	11.1	12.3	8.1	200 690	200	18 095	439 909	0.4
Saline	9.2	0.1	3.1	22.4	D	6.1	4.0	D	17.4	5 040	218	616	10 122	0.0
Schuyler	-10.8	0.0	14.7	9.5	D	8.1	3.4	4.3	38.3	975	220	118	2 073	-1.4
Scotland	11.0	D	6.3	4.5	D	7.7	D	D	40.6	985	203	66	2 341	-1.2
Scott	0.5	D	6.0	15.1	6.7	5.2	6.4	16.7	14.4	10 400	267	1 799	17 083	0.6
Shannon	-0.7	D	D	26.8	D	4.9	3.9	D	20.8	2 255	274	349	4 114	-1.2
Shelby	8.8	D	5.9	11.1	4.2	8.7	4.4	D	24.1	1 550	253	126	3 169	-1.2
Stoddard	-0.5	0.2	7.4	25.9	D	7.8	9.0	D	13.7	8 260	277	1 173	13 607	0.0
Stone	1.4	D	13.8	1.8	3.7	8.3	4.3	D	17.5	10 125	328	562	20 677	1.5
Sullivan	25.6	D	2.7	D	3.0	2.9	3.4	2.9	13.2	1 580	250	203	3 325	-1.0
Taney	0.1	D	5.3	2.3	3.9	10.6	5.8	D	10.1	14 365	264	1 137	30 202	3.2
Texas	0.6	D	6.8	14.8	3.1	8.1	4.5	6.3	35.9	6 335	247	809	11 556	-1.1
Vernon	10.0	0.6	4.1	21.2	2.8	5.8	6.6	D	20.4	4 950	238	663	9 470	-0.3
Warren	-0.9	D	12.3	24.6	3.5	6.5	4.9	D	17.8	7 300	218	539	15 021	2.3
Washington	0.0	1.9	5.0	12.4	D	6.2	D	D	36.8	6 020	243	1 178	10 813	-1.9
Wayne	-0.4	D	4.6	11.5	D	8.4	4.0	13.5	24.1	4 170	312	794	7 950	-1.7
Webster	2.1	0.3	10.5	15.5	D	9.2	4.1	D	18.4	8 385	223	806	14 543	0.9
Worth	28.2	D	D	D	D	6.4	2.8	2.9	23.1	555	271	35	1 267	-1.1
Wright	1.5	D	7.3	10.6	D	13.1	4.7	D	19.8	5 430	297	857	8 596	-1.2

1. Per 1,000 resident population estimated as of July 1 of the year shown.

Table B. States and Counties — **Housing, Labor Force, and Employment**

STATE County	Housing units, 2011–2015								Civilian labor force, 2016				Civilian employment,[6] 2011–2015		
	Occupied units										Unemployment			Percent	
		Owner-occupied				Renter-occupied									
				Median owner cost as a percent of income											
	Total	Percent	Median value[1]	With a mortgage	Without a mortgage[2]	Median rent[3]	Median rent as a percent of income[2]	Sub-stand-ard units[4] (percent)	Total	Percent change, 2015–2016	Total	Rate[5]	Total	Manage-ment, business, science and arts	Con-struction, produc-tion, and mainte-nance occu-pations
	89	90	91	92	93	94	95	96	97	98	99	100	101	102	103
MISSOURI—Cont'd															
Jasper	45 519	64.1	106 300	19.7	12.3	710	29.3	2.8	58 433	0.0	2 404	4.1	55 374	29.6	26.7
Jefferson	81 990	81.0	149 900	21.9	11.8	783	28.0	1.8	118 729	0.2	5 083	4.3	106 972	29.2	26.7
Johnson	19 971	60.4	141 400	20.6	10.7	728	30.6	2.7	23 508	1.1	1 146	4.9	23 900	30.0	26.6
Knox	1 689	78.0	71 300	21.3	12.3	509	21.4	2.8	2 009	1.7	71	3.5	1 709	30.8	31.1
Laclede	13 545	70.1	103 400	21.0	11.2	598	31.1	3.7	16 201	1.0	885	5.5	14 708	25.7	33.9
Lafayette	13 188	75.7	117 400	19.9	11.7	634	28.8	1.2	17 600	1.8	751	4.3	15 021	30.1	29.6
Lawrence	14 483	71.2	98 100	22.0	12.6	613	25.6	3.3	17 937	-0.4	778	4.3	15 804	28.5	31.6
Lewis	3 846	73.7	83 800	18.7	11.8	484	20.7	2.9	5 203	-0.8	236	4.5	4 918	23.3	35.5
Lincoln	18 498	77.4	144 500	21.5	10.4	804	31.5	1.8	27 222	0.3	1 227	4.5	23 857	25.9	34.1
Linn	4 828	74.6	75 900	19.4	12.6	517	27.6	1.7	5 302	0.5	359	6.8	5 125	27.3	32.3
Livingston	5 708	69.9	102 500	18.8	11.2	598	24.8	1.9	7 393	0.5	289	3.9	6 641	30.4	27.7
McDonald	8 318	70.3	88 400	20.8	11.4	581	26.3	8.0	10 786	2.9	460	4.3	9 544	21.2	38.8
Macon	6 243	74.3	88 000	20.2	12.8	494	27.5	2.1	7 680	2.1	369	4.8	6 541	28.7	29.5
Madison	4 650	75.5	89 200	24.0	10.4	590	32.2	0.5	5 520	-0.6	303	5.5	4 854	19.3	32.9
Maries	3 686	73.2	118 000	24.0	10.0	534	26.1	2.3	3 964	0.0	200	5.0	3 551	24.1	36.9
Marion	11 213	64.9	103 700	19.2	11.5	606	27.3	1.2	14 708	-0.9	627	4.3	12 851	30.3	30.6
Mercer	1 503	75.9	77 500	18.1	11.2	496	23.8	4.7	1 944	2.3	89	4.6	1 657	30.2	34.8
Miller	9 452	77.6	120 800	22.6	10.1	639	29.9	2.9	12 031	2.6	620	5.2	10 832	25.4	25.2
Mississippi	5 185	59.8	67 700	20.9	13.1	595	30.2	6.4	6 285	-0.6	413	6.6	4 945	23.6	28.8
Moniteau	5 533	72.7	116 500	18.9	10.0	533	26.7	3.1	7 524	1.0	324	4.3	6 712	28.1	30.0
Monroe	3 513	74.3	90 800	22.0	11.0	558	23.9	1.9	4 208	-0.7	203	4.8	3 845	25.8	34.0
Montgomery	4 874	72.4	105 900	21.8	12.8	620	31.7	1.4	5 824	1.4	266	4.6	5 126	27.8	33.3
Morgan	7 812	76.3	109 300	24.9	12.6	632	31.0	1.7	8 078	-0.6	472	5.8	6 875	22.8	28.6
New Madrid	7 247	61.3	73 100	18.5	13.7	542	28.6	1.5	8 374	-3.0	778	9.3	7 298	25.3	33.3
Newton	22 096	71.9	111 700	20.9	11.8	629	27.8	1.8	28 643	0.1	1 240	4.3	26 122	29.1	28.3
Nodaway	8 659	53.9	114 500	21.5	11.6	624	32.6	1.8	11 026	-0.5	511	4.6	11 209	28.3	28.8
Oregon	4 367	75.3	79 400	23.1	11.9	473	34.7	2.1	4 177	-0.3	253	6.1	4 083	23.4	35.7
Osage	5 143	82.1	131 900	19.8	10.0	495	20.6	1.6	7 284	1.1	246	3.4	6 752	27.4	32.5
Ozark	4 233	77.1	86 600	22.7	11.2	523	33.9	6.2	3 692	0.6	270	7.3	3 112	25.2	38.2
Pemiscot	6 975	53.7	65 200	20.3	13.6	558	30.7	3.4	7 131	0.6	634	8.9	6 423	26.6	31.8
Perry	7 395	78.6	123 400	19.8	10.5	653	27.7	1.1	10 218	-0.6	361	3.5	9 292	28.2	35.9
Pettis	16 131	68.0	101 400	20.9	11.2	682	31.1	3.5	20 948	-0.5	1 026	4.9	18 740	27.0	33.3
Phelps	16 672	61.1	114 500	20.3	10.0	662	29.9	1.9	19 701	0.0	935	4.7	19 451	37.9	19.7
Pike	6 567	72.3	95 000	21.2	12.0	630	25.0	2.1	8 158	-0.1	366	4.5	7 300	27.4	33.2
Platte	37 556	64.6	190 300	20.1	11.0	880	26.8	1.7	56 664	1.5	2 051	3.6	49 463	42.4	16.9
Polk	11 752	66.9	114 600	20.7	10.0	646	31.4	3.2	14 453	0.7	698	4.8	12 978	31.2	25.9
Pulaski	15 435	48.6	129 800	21.3	10.0	969	26.5	3.2	14 664	-2.2	798	5.4	15 279	32.8	24.3
Putnam	2 196	74.2	82 800	23.7	16.4	478	30.7	1.5	2 479	-1.5	112	4.5	2 097	32.4	35.3
Ralls	4 021	80.4	112 100	20.2	11.8	655	27.1	2.4	5 665	-0.8	226	4.0	4 821	24.9	34.7
Randolph	8 450	72.5	85 500	20.7	12.3	659	29.7	1.9	10 602	0.3	555	5.2	9 519	26.8	28.3
Ray	8 646	76.5	120 200	20.5	11.4	728	28.5	2.0	11 412	1.6	554	4.9	10 147	26.2	34.0
Reynolds	2 661	78.2	85 600	22.2	10.0	521	31.1	2.6	2 710	-0.7	175	6.5	2 404	24.2	39.6
Ripley	5 423	75.2	80 800	23.5	11.2	510	30.5	3.2	5 384	0.5	379	7.0	5 480	25.5	31.3
St. Charles	138 958	79.2	188 200	20.0	11.5	931	26.6	1.0	220 324	0.6	7 764	3.5	198 960	41.4	17.1
St. Clair	4 015	75.8	79 600	24.7	13.0	446	28.7	6.7	3 993	-0.2	251	6.3	3 408	26.2	29.9
Ste. Genevieve	7 137	80.7	131 000	20.9	11.8	596	29.2	1.4	9 107	-0.2	422	4.6	8 313	20.6	41.1
St. Francois	24 936	66.3	103 500	20.8	11.1	616	28.9	3.3	26 446	-0.5	1 458	5.5	25 384	26.9	27.1
St. Louis	401 839	70.2	173 400	21.1	12.1	882	29.7	1.3	539 419	0.4	22 604	4.2	492 220	43.7	14.2
Saline	8 844	67.8	89 700	21.7	12.3	616	26.7	2.9	10 935	-1.7	509	4.7	10 642	29.7	30.9
Schuyler	1 722	74.0	86 000	20.0	14.8	498	19.5	3.5	1 948	1.5	122	6.3	1 891	30.5	33.1
Scotland	1 851	74.2	75 100	24.4	11.2	449	22.5	4.4	2 485	0.7	102	4.1	2 193	29.6	33.9
Scott	15 247	68.1	94 300	19.0	11.1	583	28.4	3.2	20 208	0.1	1 155	5.7	17 280	26.7	30.6
Shannon	3 277	77.7	89 400	22.6	10.4	502	29.5	5.6	3 364	0.1	248	7.4	3 361	26.3	45.6
Shelby	2 499	71.2	72 600	21.0	11.0	454	23.1	2.9	3 111	0.4	129	4.1	2 888	27.1	35.8
Stoddard	12 045	70.6	90 500	20.1	11.1	540	26.5	2.0	13 513	1.5	864	6.4	12 334	27.4	33.8
Stone	12 836	79.1	153 100	22.2	11.8	688	30.9	1.5	13 547	0.7	943	7.0	12 009	26.9	25.9
Sullivan	2 512	71.8	78 800	24.2	13.2	538	21.0	3.2	2 809	0.4	163	5.8	2 794	25.8	42.0
Taney	21 300	59.9	121 700	24.6	11.6	694	28.6	2.1	26 583	0.9	1 956	7.4	23 414	24.6	17.1
Texas	9 134	74.7	99 300	20.9	10.9	521	33.3	2.4	9 413	-0.6	585	6.2	9 142	23.1	31.3
Vernon	8 040	67.3	90 800	19.6	10.9	626	28.2	3.0	9 740	-1.5	470	4.8	9 449	30.0	27.1
Warren	11 951	79.1	152 800	21.3	11.8	713	29.4	3.6	17 525	0.4	735	4.2	14 863	24.6	34.2
Washington	8 982	79.6	79 700	21.1	11.4	513	28.2	3.5	10 476	-1.1	658	6.3	9 124	20.0	38.5
Wayne	5 453	77.4	70 000	21.3	10.0	566	31.8	2.9	5 738	-0.3	307	5.4	4 712	25.0	33.1
Webster	12 885	73.9	118 700	20.8	10.0	596	27.8	6.0	16 938	1.0	835	4.9	14 583	26.6	33.9
Worth	900	74.7	57 800	17.7	10.0	406	18.7	1.9	1 234	0.7	37	3.0	973	37.8	30.2
Wright	7 351	69.3	88 200	23.0	10.2	522	27.1	3.4	7 685	-0.1	454	5.9	6 583	24.8	35.0

1. Specified owner-occupied units.   2. A value of 10.0 represents 10 percent or less; a value of 50.0 represents 50 percent or more.   3. Specified renter-occupied units.
4. Overcrowded or lacking complete plumbing facilities.   5. Percent of civilian labor force.   6. Civilian employed persons 16 years old and over.

Table B. States and Counties — Nonfarm Employment and Agriculture

	Private nonfarm establishments, employment and payroll, 2015									Agriculture, 2012			
		Employment						Annual payroll		Farms			
											Percent with:		
STATE County	Number of establishments	Total	Health care and social assistance	Manufacturing	Retail trade	Finance and insurance	Professional, scientific, and technical services	Total (mil dol)	Average per employee (dollars)	Number	Fewer than 50 acres	500 acres or more	Farm operators whose principal occupation is farming (percent)
	104	105	106	107	108	109	110	111	112	113	114	115	116

MISSOURI—Cont'd

Jasper	2 772	47 920	6 104	9 515	7 901	1 140	1 005	1 794	37 444	1 299	34.9	7.4	39.9
Jefferson	4 079	40 284	6 689	3 947	7 173	1 333	1 057	1 407	34 923	705	41.3	5.4	49.1
Johnson	924	10 088	2 398	1 365	1 735	339	385	295	29 270	1 657	28.5	10.6	40.4
Knox	91	705	37	D	114	48	29	18	25 312	695	15.4	21.7	51.9
Laclede	774	11 093	1 321	4 414	1 943	369	166	352	31 722	1 398	29.2	12.1	41.3
Lafayette	692	6 174	1 151	841	972	251	188	186	30 084	1 174	32.1	14.6	49.2
Lawrence	723	6 972	1 407	1 244	1 415	170	133	227	32 615	1 849	40.1	7.4	41.4
Lewis	190	2 088	292	128	312	90	42	53	25 542	729	19.9	21.3	44.3
Lincoln	915	8 418	1 200	1 256	1 557	318	181	309	36 710	1 162	33.0	13.6	46.3
Linn	294	3 198	519	946	521	146	92	101	31 584	1 039	18.2	17.5	41.0
Livingston	424	4 914	919	504	1 244	191	113	155	31 556	847	20.2	16.1	42.3
McDonald	308	5 519	277	2 791	982	120	30	169	30 577	926	27.3	6.8	53.6
Macon	347	3 623	557	515	683	166	274	108	29 925	1 291	20.4	14.5	36.9
Madison	320	3 286	1 117	274	590	75	65	85	25 740	373	19.6	14.2	44.2
Maries	136	1 065	158	163	237	100	13	30	27 904	836	16.6	14.5	46.7
Marion	819	12 180	2 967	1 888	1 869	366	266	413	33 875	704	21.2	14.8	44.0
Mercer	70	396	66	D	102	31	D	10	25 371	567	11.8	21.2	40.9
Miller	671	5 990	509	649	1 698	248	178	179	29 912	1 013	17.1	10.4	42.7
Mississippi	249	2 191	368	77	430	133	74	67	30 540	205	16.6	47.3	70.7
Moniteau	327	2 704	343	614	444	119	54	87	32 079	1 089	20.4	9.5	45.5
Monroe	197	1 606	228	533	253	72	20	43	26 552	1 061	18.2	14.8	39.7
Montgomery	261	2 115	377	435	329	106	23	69	32 686	795	18.9	21.1	49.4
Morgan	489	3 375	324	704	858	116	65	89	26 448	922	24.8	8.6	47.5
New Madrid	472	6 016	906	1 430	1 274	172	69	232	38 529	317	11.7	56.8	74.8
Newton	1 206	22 078	6 693	2 735	2 043	562	930	762	34 529	1 578	36.8	5.1	39.4
Nodaway	467	6 053	1 094	1 476	1 136	168	137	184	30 446	1 252	23.2	18.7	46.2
Oregon	226	1 911	571	150	474	53	26	41	21 593	752	19.5	15.4	50.1
Osage	281	3 177	329	1 241	473	116	26	102	32 012	1 115	17.9	10.9	40.8
Ozark	179	952	103	103	232	74	39	21	21 644	639	13.5	20.2	52.7
Pemiscot	441	4 317	1 399	D	722	136	48	138	32 022	227	16.3	53.3	61.2
Perry	493	10 043	1 131	4 029	1 145	254	164	338	33 696	951	23.1	11.0	34.8
Pettis	1 004	17 207	2 941	4 111	2 548	388	1 481	575	33 412	1 311	28.1	17.5	45.9
Phelps	1 115	13 429	3 463	1 040	2 402	428	321	432	32 189	718	25.5	9.1	39.3
Pike	406	4 506	778	644	682	143	594	145	32 144	1 003	17.7	18.1	39.8
Platte	2 362	38 107	3 368	2 994	6 472	1 421	1 211	1 570	41 197	599	33.1	11.2	44.4
Polk	595	7 186	1 961	524	1 087	217	710	278	38 696	1 505	30.0	9.4	47.0
Pulaski	712	8 538	1 713	171	1 803	407	419	255	29 861	520	19.2	11.3	39.8
Putnam	89	671	187	86	186	59	24	20	29 374	649	12.2	21.1	45.6
Ralls	195	2 515	173	1 418	161	43	15	126	49 969	723	22.0	20.5	36.9
Randolph	574	7 595	1 291	1 078	1 239	518	84	268	35 240	818	23.0	10.9	40.3
Ray	368	3 062	620	467	576	109	95	97	31 525	1 162	27.1	9.8	50.9
Reynolds	149	1 302	215	303	120	34	D	55	42 441	363	19.0	11.8	41.6
Ripley	506	2 613	1 007	502	472	75	17	51	19 381	439	17.3	15.9	42.8
St. Charles	8 340	129 568	16 225	13 967	20 036	9 881	7 635	5 394	41 631	566	34.5	15.7	51.9
St. Clair	185	1 289	461	67	313	60	29	33	25 495	728	20.1	19.0	51.6
Ste. Genevieve	414	5 022	903	1 519	486	183	71	193	38 499	608	22.0	13.2	37.2
St. Francois	1 570	18 654	5 278	1 656	3 209	1 012	353	565	30 280	627	30.1	5.1	45.3
St. Louis	32 839	578 954	90 743	41 374	68 798	32 214	46 962	31 456	54 333	217	53.5	7.8	49.3
Saline	497	7 990	1 518	2 506	1 019	250	97	236	29 480	959	20.9	26.2	49.9
Schuyler	66	314	18	48	94	17	D	9	29 398	516	22.7	16.3	42.2
Scotland	137	926	D	99	172	48	20	25	27 455	674	19.1	19.1	46.9
Scott	1 082	14 615	3 488	2 819	1 524	451	354	491	33 616	484	32.6	20.2	49.6
Shannon	180	1 197	174	576	167	66	7	25	20 576	452	23.9	13.7	46.7
Shelby	166	967	98	170	220	50	52	27	27 866	709	18.6	26.4	43.2
Stoddard	712	8 436	1 704	2 538	1 306	410	164	290	34 397	907	29.4	23.3	49.1
Stone	672	3 899	472	115	820	147	84	114	29 324	601	26.1	7.8	42.3
Sullivan	106	1 950	233	D	163	50	13	70	36 018	798	12.5	25.2	46.4
Taney	1 774	23 809	2 221	509	4 949	487	427	689	28 959	414	21.5	14.0	47.8
Texas	519	4 085	911	807	731	178	64	113	27 548	1 296	18.7	14.7	51.2
Vernon	578	5 870	1 496	1 100	951	405	135	180	30 704	1 356	26.6	13.7	43.8
Warren	564	5 945	662	1 224	909	214	133	206	34 615	621	33.8	11.1	40.3
Washington	375	3 303	797	482	546	126	40	93	28 188	531	21.7	9.0	43.9
Wayne	264	1 576	361	363	347	61	33	36	22 654	411	12.4	13.9	44.8
Webster	658	5 168	547	841	1 148	209	205	159	30 676	1 837	35.6	5.7	44.3
Worth	47	207	15	34	79	13	3	5	23 671	384	15.6	16.7	40.9
Wright	407	3 460	500	459	912	180	54	93	26 991	1 246	23.0	11.9	50.2

Table B. States and Counties — Agriculture

STATE County	Acreage (1,000) [117]	Percent change, 2007–2012 [118]	Average size of farm [119]	Total irrigated (1,000) [120]	Total cropland (1,000) [121]	Average per farm [122]	Average per acre [123]	Value of machinery and equipment, average per farm (dollars) [124]	Total (mil dol) [125]	Average per farm (dollars) [126]	Crops [127]	Live-stock and poultry products [128]	$10,000 or more [129]	$100,000 or more [130]	Total ($1,000) [131]	Percent of farms [132]

Agriculture, 2012 (cont.) — Land in farms (Acres); Value of land and buildings (dollars); Value of products sold (Percent from:); Percent of farms with sales of:; Government payments

MISSOURI—Cont'd

STATE County	117	118	119	120	121	122	123	124	125	126	127	128	129	130	131	132
Jasper	247	-4.7	190	3.5	127.7	443 779	2 337	62 487	100.5	77 336	32.5	67.5	41.6	8.9	2 322	37.0
Jefferson	98	5.7	138	0.3	36.3	471 186	3 407	53 340	13.6	19 325	51.0	49.0	28.9	3.3	255	12.3
Johnson	391	-7.9	236	1.9	219.9	624 016	2 645	95 386	119.9	72 340	38.5	61.5	47.1	9.3	2 968	40.3
Knox	281	10.8	404	D	193.3	1 205 037	2 981	147 283	76.3	109 799	49.5	50.5	53.8	21.2	5 347	73.4
Laclede	320	10.9	229	0.2	89.6	503 814	2 200	50 168	50.4	36 045	15.1	84.9	46.4	7.4	526	10.8
Lafayette	327	-7.4	278	1.8	244.5	1 176 566	4 225	133 569	143.2	122 010	80.6	19.4	57.8	20.8	4 495	57.0
Lawrence	311	-3.6	168	2.3	118.1	431 114	2 562	62 340	204.9	110 819	7.4	92.6	45.3	10.8	1 959	18.6
Lewis	284	8.8	390	2.0	201.3	1 128 680	2 894	139 615	81.2	111 418	64.0	36.0	51.7	19.3	4 159	71.1
Lincoln	281	13.0	242	1.3	191.8	943 589	3 900	91 473	85.6	73 707	55.9	44.1	44.8	12.0	3 161	55.4
Linn	336	1.7	323	0.3	209.0	780 366	2 416	78 069	66.6	64 131	59.0	41.0	48.7	15.5	6 639	67.9
Livingston	284	-8.2	335	0.4	200.5	976 103	2 916	104 609	72.5	85 636	68.9	31.1	49.8	15.6	6 044	70.0
McDonald	187	-6.6	202	0.3	49.5	466 203	2 314	79 172	175.8	189 865	2.1	97.9	44.0	10.9	630	9.9
Macon	386	-2.1	299	0.3	214.7	740 631	2 477	78 400	66.8	51 777	53.6	46.4	41.6	10.1	6 172	58.1
Madison	107	9.0	287	D	24.1	528 405	1 840	54 603	18.4	49 201	9.8	90.2	41.8	6.7	102	13.1
Maries	241	0.4	289	0.2	59.4	563 396	1 951	60 886	35.3	42 176	13.0	87.0	53.8	6.8	435	16.1
Marion	221	-6.6	315	3.0	157.5	1 120 118	3 561	118 102	87.1	123 751	61.6	38.4	48.0	18.2	3 060	71.2
Mercer	227	12.6	400	D	119.4	887 578	2 219	93 078	102.7	181 146	18.6	81.4	40.9	12.5	3 303	67.4
Miller	248	1.2	245	1.4	62.0	544 853	2 221	58 525	103.0	101 659	4.7	95.3	51.2	11.1	549	13.7
Mississippi	245	-5.2	1 195	86.5	232.3	4 962 234	4 153	473 244	157.0	766 000	97.9	2.1	81.5	55.6	3 759	87.8
Moniteau	235	-3.2	216	0.2	99.9	582 663	2 698	67 761	173.5	159 302	9.4	90.6	57.0	13.5	2 018	37.6
Monroe	356	23.4	335	1.1	237.9	1 047 572	3 125	121 686	86.2	81 207	58.0	42.0	40.8	13.2	7 034	75.6
Montgomery	279	12.5	351	3.2	194.0	1 212 507	3 453	132 268	64.0	80 541	73.9	26.1	50.9	20.5	4 635	65.9
Morgan	198	-8.5	215	0.2	77.6	569 115	2 646	63 366	144.8	157 103	8.6	91.4	56.6	21.3	768	17.5
New Madrid	345	-9.5	1 087	196.5	332.5	4 819 981	4 435	524 943	217.1	684 994	99.9	0.1	84.2	65.6	8 243	90.9
Newton	248	0.8	157	0.3	93.4	404 596	2 577	60 035	251.5	159 393	6.0	94.0	44.3	9.5	1 034	17.3
Nodaway	424	-22.0	338	0.3	293.3	1 100 251	3 251	116 792	141.6	113 082	81.0	19.0	58.3	21.6	7 586	72.6
Oregon	254	6.0	338	0.4	35.9	525 161	1 556	53 593	34.5	45 934	3.4	96.6	45.3	6.8	955	26.7
Osage	283	-4.8	254	2.3	82.4	520 062	2 047	73 506	78.7	70 544	17.7	82.3	55.0	9.7	1 003	30.9
Ozark	229	-7.6	358	0.1	29.1	581 482	1 624	60 313	39.2	61 365	5.3	94.7	54.0	10.6	597	8.6
Pemiscot	305	-1.7	1 344	122.7	287.5	4 861 687	3 618	516 802	186.1	819 758	99.9	0.1	79.3	61.7	7 220	80.6
Perry	226	-5.2	238	D	122.0	636 469	2 673	82 989	63.4	66 614	50.1	49.9	52.2	13.4	2 226	64.9
Pettis	420	2.6	320	0.4	263.2	876 005	2 736	116 004	177.0	135 019	30.8	69.2	52.6	19.0	5 117	51.0
Phelps	157	-10.5	219	0.1	27.2	504 223	2 301	51 199	11.7	16 320	15.8	84.2	34.1	2.6	225	12.0
Pike	362	-3.1	361	3.7	226.0	1 247 567	3 461	127 424	87.4	87 094	62.9	37.1	51.7	15.3	4 506	65.7
Platte	153	-14.4	255	1.7	100.7	992 603	3 888	94 775	44.9	74 917	83.7	16.3	41.9	12.0	1 720	48.2
Polk	336	-4.0	223	1.3	102.6	461 553	2 066	49 912	85.2	56 613	10.6	89.4	49.2	10.0	859	15.3
Pulaski	112	-8.6	216	0.1	20.9	421 379	1 948	50 873	12.9	24 752	15.6	84.4	42.1	4.2	110	6.5
Putnam	293	7.3	451	D	124.7	930 538	2 063	91 116	86.1	132 669	19.3	80.7	49.3	18.3	3 373	59.5
Ralls	283	15.5	392	1.1	196.9	1 258 679	3 210	138 203	54.8	75 806	76.5	23.5	39.0	16.7	4 168	76.3
Randolph	209	-5.5	256	1.1	109.1	673 561	2 630	65 106	36.7	44 873	58.5	41.5	35.5	6.2	2 820	54.8
Ray	273	-6.4	235	7.7	174.7	641 818	2 730	86 155	74.5	64 122	71.7	28.3	41.8	10.1	3 721	53.8
Reynolds	97	-9.5	268	0.0	16.5	391 482	1 463	44 970	4.8	13 284	25.3	74.7	35.5	1.1	79	7.4
Ripley	138	0.4	314	12.1	45.1	563 134	1 794	65 385	19.1	43 583	55.8	44.2	40.5	7.3	777	26.7
St. Charles	158	1.3	279	1.1	121.0	1 184 827	4 240	119 919	62.5	110 417	84.8	15.2	53.0	20.7	1 607	55.5
St. Clair	239	-10.0	328	0.5	99.3	542 646	1 656	69 935	33.8	46 482	42.4	57.6	50.7	9.9	1 115	36.4
Ste. Genevieve	163	-13.9	267	0.2	72.3	616 641	2 305	76 181	26.6	43 755	58.6	41.4	46.9	8.7	1 492	46.4
St. Francois	116	3.4	186	0.1	32.0	466 490	2 513	46 496	14.0	22 332	32.9	67.1	36.8	2.6	343	13.1
St. Louis	30	-8.0	137	0.5	15.4	565 189	4 128	69 313	19.1	87 807	97.3	2.7	37.3	11.1	279	20.7
Saline	461	2.6	481	3.5	362.9	1 934 485	4 023	199 556	212.0	221 075	73.3	26.7	66.1	28.7	5 961	79.7
Schuyler	159	4.6	309	D	83.8	687 409	2 226	76 853	30.4	58 917	48.8	51.2	50.2	12.4	2 272	61.8
Scotland	244	5.4	362	D	158.4	1 063 616	2 936	106 022	82.2	121 938	44.7	55.3	53.9	21.5	4 627	70.0
Scott	223	-2.4	461	72.4	192.8	1 878 114	4 077	237 058	188.8	390 035	69.0	31.0	48.6	26.9	4 263	63.8
Shannon	124	11.8	274	0.0	23.0	458 142	1 670	50 407	10.5	23 197	11.5	88.5	37.4	5.8	171	6.6
Shelby	299	3.5	422	1.6	211.0	1 499 536	3 552	149 536	83.0	117 100	71.2	28.8	59.0	24.0	5 033	75.6
Stoddard	448	-2.8	494	226.7	396.3	2 169 982	4 392	245 480	315.0	347 277	81.3	18.7	49.9	26.1	11 137	73.4
Stone	118	-3.1	196	0.1	32.1	465 231	2 369	50 319	34.5	57 393	10.6	89.4	45.3	7.0	368	10.0
Sullivan	323	-3.3	405	D	158.8	751 872	1 858	87 835	149.6	187 526	12.2	87.8	46.5	14.7	5 745	61.3
Taney	116	8.8	280	0.1	18.8	549 092	1 961	49 271	11.7	28 259	10.8	89.2	38.2	4.3	209	10.1
Texas	392	10.4	303	0.1	68.0	496 529	1 641	48 862	42.0	32 416	8.8	91.2	47.4	7.5	565	10.3
Vernon	419	-8.2	309	5.4	244.4	665 520	2 156	99 091	209.0	154 128	29.8	70.2	51.6	13.6	4 561	44.8
Warren	136	-7.3	219	1.1	85.3	850 634	3 880	94 071	31.4	50 589	78.6	21.4	43.3	11.6	1 941	51.2
Washington	124	-9.7	233	0.0	24.3	447 979	1 919	44 347	11.1	20 846	20.8	79.2	37.9	4.7	106	3.6
Wayne	117	10.0	284	D	28.0	433 238	1 527	59 358	7.8	18 949	20.0	80.0	33.8	2.9	356	24.3
Webster	272	0.3	148	0.2	82.9	386 911	2 612	45 690	76.1	41 450	8.4	91.6	45.5	9.0	1 345	8.9
Worth	125	-17.6	326	D	70.0	733 870	2 254	84 737	37.1	96 646	37.1	62.9	43.2	14.1	2 824	84.1
Wright	294	3.4	236	0.2	67.2	424 095	1 797	48 860	47.2	37 913	6.9	93.1	45.8	8.7	1 041	14.4

STATE County	Water use, 2010		Wholesale trade,[1] 2012				Retail trade,[2] 2012				Real estate and rental and leasing,[2] 2012			
	Total water withdrawn (mil gal/day)	Gallons withdrawn per person per day	Number of establishments	Number of employees	Sales (mil dol)	Annual payroll (mil dol)	Number of establishments	Number of employees	Sales (mil dol)	Annual payroll (mil dol)	Number of establishments	Number of employees	Receipts (mil dol)	Annual payroll (mil dol)
	133	134	135	136	137	138	139	140	141	142	143	144	145	146
MISSOURI—Cont'd														
Jasper	30.8	262	143	1 695	972.5	70.6	514	7 769	1 987.5	166.1	114	506	75.5	13.2
Jefferson	829.3	3 791	132	1 302	798.0	65.5	484	6 756	1 952.6	162.7	143	465	62.2	14.1
Johnson	9.1	174	20	108	45.6	4.0	148	1 827	508.2	40.2	36	129	25.1	3.4
Knox	1.5	363	8	42	61.2	0.8	16	113	38.1	2.1	NA	NA	NA	NA
Laclede	17.8	500	27	305	196.2	11.3	174	1 813	502.4	42.1	28	72	10.9	1.6
Lafayette	5.7	170	34	319	184.0	11.6	106	1 055	375.5	20.5	16	D	D	D
Lawrence	10.7	276	26	239	92.5	7.1	122	1 320	449.0	31.3	20	48	4.2	0.8
Lewis	2.4	237	8	D	D	D	32	288	85.7	6.1	3	D	D	D
Lincoln	7.2	138	34	245	91.1	9.8	144	1 473	447.8	34.5	28	71	9.0	1.3
Linn	4.8	378	8	50	51.1	1.9	56	535	150.0	11.8	9	D	D	D
Livingston	2.5	163	22	272	126.7	11.4	76	1 167	359.1	26.5	11	37	9.8	0.7
McDonald	6.6	288	10	D	D	D	65	933	221.2	18.6	8	9	2.0	0.3
Macon	3.2	208	14	111	65.7	5.2	67	631	146.5	11.5	12	38	3.5	0.7
Madison	1.4	112	11	185	28.7	6.1	38	505	138.0	11.8	6	23	1.1	0.4
Maries	1.6	177	8	D	D	D	25	222	50.1	3.4	2	D	D	D
Marion	7.7	268	26	321	479.7	14.1	143	1 797	508.5	38.3	27	D	D	D
Mercer	2.2	568	1	D	D	D	13	64	25.0	1.1	1	D	D	D
Miller	4.0	160	13	167	94.6	5.7	119	1 651	377.4	38.8	51	203	30.1	5.3
Mississippi	82.6	5 753	18	191	256.2	6.9	52	474	182.1	9.5	2	D	D	D
Moniteau	3.4	218	10	173	69.8	5.0	55	457	136.2	8.5	5	8	0.5	0.1
Monroe	8.2	931	9	67	78.7	2.2	35	277	80.0	4.8	3	10	1.3	0.2
Montgomery	2.5	202	19	135	110.7	4.8	36	315	98.1	6.1	8	10	1.7	0.2
Morgan	6.5	315	17	56	22.2	1.9	91	762	195.1	16.3	19	39	4.8	0.8
New Madrid	984.5	51 936	32	428	436.0	18.3	77	1 319	495.7	28.0	9	21	3.2	0.5
Newton	9.7	167	41	1 200	1 674.4	48.3	196	2 090	853.8	49.2	29	77	10.5	1.7
Nodaway	3.3	139	17	221	181.4	8.9	72	1 122	260.0	21.2	20	35	5.7	0.6
Oregon	2.0	186	6	D	D	D	44	419	98.8	8.3	7	14	1.5	0.2
Osage	60.8	4 377	6	24	9.3	0.8	49	423	152.5	10.3	5	6	0.5	0.1
Ozark	14.2	1 460	6	32	17.3	0.7	33	214	49.6	3.4	9	16	1.0	0.2
Pemiscot	110.5	6 038	21	233	550.6	10.3	70	688	274.3	13.2	10	D	D	D
Perry	4.7	245	12	348	174.5	15.2	75	978	270.2	23.0	12	19	5.0	0.4
Pettis	9.2	217	35	350	175.4	15.7	174	2 323	615.1	54.4	44	358	37.0	9.4
Phelps	10.4	229	36	365	108.9	13.7	190	2 401	689.2	53.0	40	146	20.0	4.0
Pike	7.4	401	25	314	312.7	11.7	66	686	191.0	15.0	3	8	0.6	0.1
Platte	459.5	5 144	103	1 288	4 053.0	85.4	313	6 054	1 986.7	144.3	126	1 164	178.1	41.4
Polk	5.2	167	23	531	63.0	9.3	110	1 099	299.5	26.3	14	69	6.2	1.3
Pulaski	6.8	129	6	D	D	D	138	1 655	455.2	36.4	46	167	40.6	4.1
Putnam	1.8	364	3	D	D	D	24	176	50.3	3.1	4	14	0.8	0.2
Ralls	1.7	166	16	168	153.4	7.2	34	185	52.4	3.8	2	D	D	D
Randolph	740.2	29 127	17	D	D	D	97	1 118	296.7	25.3	19	63	9.9	1.6
Ray	6.3	266	9	114	186.2	5.7	56	607	138.7	12.6	9	21	1.7	0.4
Reynolds	5.7	851	4	D	D	D	20	122	29.6	2.0	4	9	0.4	0.1
Ripley	31.0	2 201	5	D	D	D	43	435	120.2	8.1	11	136	4.6	1.8
St. Charles	505.1	1 401	336	4 305	9 006.9	246.4	1 085	18 318	4 971.7	437.2	350	1 398	438.4	53.2
St. Clair	1.6	159	4	9	0.6	0.1	33	317	87.9	5.8	3	4	0.2	0.0
Ste. Genevieve	8.1	449	12	133	137.0	6.1	49	462	103.4	10.1	9	27	3.5	0.6
St. Francois	8.2	125	32	657	285.0	24.2	229	3 421	882.8	84.5	61	229	24.4	5.4
St. Louis	535.5	536	1 587	30 594	32 424.2	1 822.0	3 826	67 577	25 262.7	1 882.4	1 309	10 461	2 048.1	504.3
Saline	5.7	243	31	358	382.5	16.0	97	981	253.0	19.1	12	D	D	D
Schuyler	0.4	86	2	D	D	D	24	165	48.4	2.7	NA	NA	NA	NA
Scotland	0.9	176	6	D	D	D	28	162	39.8	3.0	2	D	D	D
Scott	104.6	2 670	53	823	717.9	30.8	181	1 555	415.7	33.2	40	141	17.5	4.0
Shannon	1.3	153	7	D	D	D	19	125	28.4	2.0	7	D	D	D
Shelby	1.8	282	15	97	69.7	3.5	35	223	58.9	4.4	4	5	0.5	0.1
Stoddard	333.0	11 112	37	366	428.5	13.4	118	1 277	424.0	29.6	26	51	6.7	1.2
Stone	4.6	144	17	D	D	D	99	795	216.8	18.9	38	164	19.0	5.8
Sullivan	3.6	539	2	D	D	D	27	184	50.4	3.4	5	4	0.5	0.1
Taney	33.7	651	32	D	D	D	414	4 936	939.9	88.7	116	1 023	152.0	35.8
Texas	3.8	148	22	102	36.7	2.8	83	742	172.5	14.3	10	33	2.7	0.7
Vernon	12.7	599	18	180	80.3	5.7	85	897	238.6	19.1	12	37	6.3	0.8
Warren	3.6	109	25	279	153.3	14.6	88	879	298.0	18.8	25	74	13.8	1.7
Washington	8.3	329	15	46	15.2	1.3	49	510	122.3	9.9	7	16	1.9	0.5
Wayne	1.4	104	11	D	D	D	36	319	72.3	6.3	3	3	0.4	0.0
Webster	4.5	123	32	134	69.6	5.0	109	1 123	376.7	23.8	26	50	4.0	0.9
Worth	0.3	134	4	D	D	D	12	68	18.2	1.2	2	D	D	D
Wright	2.9	156	17	223	89.9	6.9	83	952	245.6	20.0	15	41	3.6	0.6

1. Merchant wholesalers, except manufacturers' sales branches and offices.   2. Employer establishments.

Table B. States and Counties — Professional Services, Manufacturing, and Accommodation and Food Services

STATE County	Professional, scientific, and technical services, 2012				Manufacturing, 2012				Accommodation and food services, 2012			
	Number of establish-ments	Number of employees	Receipts (mil dol)	Annual payroll (mil dol)	Number of establish-ments	Number of employees	Receipts (mil dol)	Annual payroll (mil dol)	Number of establish-ments	Number of employees	Sales (mil dol)	Annual payroll (mil dol)
	147	148	149	150	151	152	153	154	155	156	157	158
MISSOURI—Cont'd												
Jasper	180	D	D	D	171	9 161	3 558.8	397.3	261	4 960	214.4	60.2
Jefferson	245	941	88.6	32.7	173	4 369	1 420.5	224.6	279	5 461	228.4	66.2
Johnson	66	D	D	D	30	1 252	D	43.0	100	1 672	66.3	16.4
Knox	4	D	D	D	NA	NA	NA	NA	6	D	D	D
Laclede	41	169	14.0	4.6	59	4 120	1 327.5	139.4	79	1 099	47.9	12.7
Lafayette	47	D	D	D	40	793	D	28.5	61	696	24.2	6.4
Lawrence	44	123	10.7	3.3	47	1 357	629.9	53.6	50	676	24.9	7.2
Lewis	13	D	D	D	6	104	D	3.9	14	113	4.1	1.2
Lincoln	51	184	15.4	5.5	49	981	387.2	51.3	58	D	D	D
Linn	22	98	9.7	3.1	15	1 003	207.5	27.4	20	226	7.8	2.2
Livingston	31	133	10.5	3.4	16	554	152.7	21.4	25	D	D	D
McDonald	13	44	2.6	0.9	23	2 974	611.6	81.9	33	264	13.3	3.3
Macon	23	D	D	D	9	472	D	15.9	32	366	18.4	5.2
Madison	13	74	5.2	1.5	14	281	D	10.2	22	D	D	D
Maries	6	D	D	D	9	165	D	8.4	11	41	1.5	0.4
Marion	45	258	24.9	8.6	39	1 475	1 488.5	72.2	74	1 115	47.0	12.7
Mercer	3	D	D	D	NA	NA	NA	NA	7	D	D	D
Miller	38	274	20.9	10.3	21	488	D	14.5	54	634	31.9	10.0
Mississippi	9	71	7.7	4.3	6	126	D	6.2	20	267	11.5	3.0
Moniteau	15	65	4.8	1.7	28	677	D	28.1	21	D	D	D
Monroe	10	D	D	D	9	218	D	D	18	141	4.7	1.3
Montgomery	8	D	D	D	19	499	154.8	17.1	21	194	6.7	1.9
Morgan	27	86	6.4	2.0	21	609	D	18.1	53	453	19.0	5.3
New Madrid	15	63	5.0	1.9	15	1 561	883.0	89.5	34	474	26.8	5.5
Newton	70	375	38.0	14.8	72	2 499	724.0	89.2	97	1 684	82.8	21.3
Nodaway	27	124	13.3	4.1	22	1 675	D	69.5	45	1 074	36.7	10.5
Oregon	10	D	D	D	11	137	24.0	3.6	14	171	5.8	1.5
Osage	9	17	1.7	0.4	29	988	D	40.1	20	D	D	D
Ozark	9	D	D	D	8	70	D	1.9	22	187	7.5	2.3
Pemiscot	11	44	3.5	0.9	12	825	D	37.0	29	311	15.1	3.3
Perry	27	118	8.8	4.2	37	3 627	1 142.3	115.6	39	618	20.9	5.8
Pettis	67	1 532	101.8	40.6	49	3 955	1 522.4	152.5	80	1 475	59.4	16.6
Phelps	77	327	35.9	11.5	50	912	484.4	43.1	114	1 810	78.1	21.6
Pike	18	522	43.8	11.5	21	555	324.3	22.8	25	D	D	D
Platte	260	D	D	D	49	2 644	1 870.0	127.4	202	5 779	394.3	101.0
Polk	43	D	D	D	22	343	D	12.1	44	780	27.0	7.3
Pulaski	58	639	99.0	45.5	15	123	24.5	D	99	2 280	91.8	39.3
Putnam	3	D	D	D	5	72	D	2.2	4	D	D	D
Ralls	5	19	1.9	0.5	15	1 272	1 405.4	66.2	11	87	3.0	1.0
Randolph	25	106	5.4	1.7	30	1 128	219.0	40.9	51	582	26.5	6.6
Ray	30	D	D	D	14	305	D	16.7	21	229	9.0	2.2
Reynolds	4	D	D	D	26	259	44.2	8.0	15	D	D	D
Ripley	10	D	D	D	30	446	D	11.6	15	195	7.7	1.9
St. Charles	765	6 210	720.9	239.7	256	10 982	6 851.7	614.3	712	16 108	918.4	227.3
St. Clair	9	25	3.3	1.0	8	28	4.9	1.2	16	78	5.4	0.8
Ste. Genevieve	23	81	6.1	2.5	30	1 467	400.4	74.7	29	D	D	D
St. Francois	79	300	33.6	8.7	49	1 474	272.2	55.7	115	1 802	76.3	21.6
St. Louis	3 618	46 440	8 274.0	3 139.6	950	35 884	15 922.9	2 621.7	2 219	47 895	2 628.8	713.8
Saline	29	D	D	D	21	1 948	747.5	68.9	43	522	17.5	5.3
Schuyler	1	D	D	D	3	9	2.9	0.4	3	D	D	D
Scotland	8	D	D	D	9	49	D	1.5	10	60	1.9	0.6
Scott	66	360	47.3	21.5	54	2 412	847.7	94.9	69	1 189	52.8	15.7
Shannon	4	D	D	D	24	372	51.1	8.9	15	64	3.4	0.8
Shelby	11	45	4.7	1.1	8	239	D	8.9	12	85	2.3	0.7
Stoddard	30	157	17.4	5.5	36	2 506	1 242.8	111.5	42	585	24.5	6.9
Stone	34	76	5.6	1.7	22	108	11.6	3.4	92	584	48.9	10.0
Sullivan	4	D	D	D	4	D	D	D	6	D	D	D
Taney	101	413	31.2	12.3	40	360	84.2	14.8	302	7 039	553.0	144.2
Texas	25	80	5.4	1.8	45	698	157.8	24.1	41	D	D	D
Vernon	34	120	11.1	2.9	20	894	D	46.8	36	456	22.3	4.8
Warren	38	145	14.4	4.9	34	1 383	453.2	58.7	49	D	D	D
Washington	13	35	2.0	0.7	19	533	290.1	17.6	22	D	D	D
Wayne	9	D	D	D	25	335	63.1	11.7	20	166	8.9	2.9
Webster	42	D	D	D	45	696	206.2	24.9	35	526	23.5	5.9
Worth	4	D	D	D	3	D	D	0.4	3	D	D	D
Wright	21	51	5.4	1.2	26	381	D	13.8	23	307	10.8	3.0

1. Establishment subject to federal tax.

Table B. States and Counties — Health Care and Social Assistance, Other Services, Nonemployer Businesses, and Residential Construction

STATE County	Health care and social assistance, 2012				Other services, 2012				Nonemployer businesses, 2015		Value of residential construction authorized by building permits, 2016	
	Number of establishments	Number of employees	Receipts (mil dol)	Annual payroll (mil dol)	Number of establishments	Number of employees	Receipts (mil dol)	Annual payroll (mil dol)	Number	Receipts (mil dol)	New Construction ($1,000)	Number of housing units
	159	160	161	162	163	164	165	166	167	168	169	170
MISSOURI—Cont'd												
Jasper	333	6 521	629.5	315.1	225	1 277	99.9	29.8	6 614	265.7	46 870	383
Jefferson	381	6 119	478.7	186.3	334	1 558	143.2	42.4	12 864	509.1	88 270	602
Johnson	100	2 309	200.4	78.6	62	D	D	D	2 903	106.9	6 632	56
Knox	8	38	2.3	0.8	9	D	D	D	340	15.8	125	1
Laclede	78	1 475	135.0	55.4	49	D	D	D	2 593	119.4	3 354	15
Lafayette	62	D	D	D	46	135	11.3	3.0	2 055	88.2	8 532	36
Lawrence	71	1 279	99.0	46.0	38	109	9.2	2.8	2 629	101.1	1 563	9
Lewis	24	311	12.4	5.9	12	D	D	D	606	27.0	120	3
Lincoln	73	D	D	D	61	D	D	D	3 310	127.5	32 903	174
Linn	24	523	37.9	15.2	27	90	9.6	1.9	921	35.3	0	0
Livingston	43	861	74.4	27.8	22	D	D	D	946	40.3	6 346	37
McDonald	26	296	16.7	7.3	17	D	D	D	1 357	53.9	364	1
Macon	31	550	40.5	15.4	26	D	D	D	1 088	41.9	254	1
Madison	29	886	38.9	20.7	16	43	3.4	0.8	700	24.0	190	3
Maries	12	138	8.6	3.0	4	15	2.0	0.2	573	22.3	209	1
Marion	136	2 858	286.2	109.4	57	332	18.2	5.2	1 649	65.6	12 725	68
Mercer	7	D	D	D	8	D	D	D	270	10.3	0	0
Miller	37	495	33.0	13.3	41	D	D	D	1 686	73.5	4 682	17
Mississippi	25	409	19.9	8.0	19	56	4.3	1.1	614	32.8	928	11
Moniteau	32	D	D	D	18	53	3.2	0.8	944	35.7	80	1
Monroe	29	D	D	D	13	D	D	D	593	26.1	0	0
Montgomery	17	382	19.7	8.2	17	D	D	D	860	37.9	4 473	26
Morgan	28	256	13.9	5.2	29	D	D	D	1 602	64.7	82	2
New Madrid	52	886	48.4	17.6	22	58	5.7	1.0	758	25.0	319	4
Newton	141	6 401	607.1	273.5	63	219	19.1	5.1	3 730	168.2	4 912	39
Nodaway	51	1 239	94.2	39.5	40	163	10.6	3.1	1 404	45.8	4 995	27
Oregon	38	458	18.1	8.9	15	D	D	D	726	25.5	0	0
Osage	22	D	D	D	14	37	4.2	0.6	971	36.9	6 453	50
Ozark	10	100	5.8	2.4	13	42	2.7	0.6	738	23.5	68	5
Pemiscot	75	1 276	74.9	32.8	14	45	3.9	1.1	825	26.5	356	9
Perry	51	1 164	86.5	31.9	38	570	17.9	22.3	1 239	47.4	8 745	84
Pettis	136	3 111	229.9	97.5	91	482	34.5	11.2	2 666	112.0	2 115	15
Phelps	148	3 820	343.0	120.7	71	323	24.2	8.3	2 620	97.0	23 341	229
Pike	52	802	49.6	21.5	21	39	5.2	1.2	1 155	50.5	1 295	15
Platte	201	3 319	354.3	139.8	163	877	94.7	27.0	7 371	361.5	77 944	367
Polk	74	1 924	159.2	63.7	42	218	9.8	2.5	2 391	93.8	2 990	21
Pulaski	62	1 773	158.5	62.7	58	248	19.2	5.9	1 926	68.9	7 421	49
Putnam	10	94	10.1	3.1	6	17	2.0	0.4	417	18.6	50	1
Ralls	13	162	10.0	4.5	12	52	4.9	1.2	723	27.1	170	2
Randolph	72	1 504	128.3	48.0	45	140	10.6	2.5	1 321	55.1	2 531	18
Ray	36	D	D	D	24	D	D	D	1 209	44.6	8 520	74
Reynolds	29	158	7.0	3.0	6	D	D	D	458	18.6	0	0
Ripley	69	796	36.3	16.8	16	46	4.2	0.8	823	34.4	0	0
St. Charles	939	15 694	1 482.9	576.5	592	3 967	336.9	102.9	24 960	1 088.1	527 393	2 341
St. Clair	28	486	22.3	10.4	13	44	4.7	1.0	681	26.4	150	1
Ste. Genevieve	46	815	59.5	23.8	34	138	9.8	2.4	1 129	34.2	1 756	8
St. Francois	244	5 279	379.4	164.4	99	441	32.0	8.9	3 127	120.4	22 914	235
St. Louis	4 190	86 410	9 445.2	3 803.8	1 961	15 935	1 682.2	529.5	74 431	3 874.6	478 129	1 635
Saline	73	1 618	110.8	47.6	35	152	16.8	4.1	1 192	41.9	2 725	16
Schuyler	3	20	1.2	0.7	7	D	D	D	341	17.4	639	3
Scotland	7	D	D	D	15	D	D	D	520	31.5	40	1
Scott	139	2 990	200.0	90.4	61	322	25.5	6.9	2 211	95.9	5 240	44
Shannon	19	215	13.0	4.7	6	15	1.7	0.4	745	29.9	0	0
Shelby	7	102	5.1	2.1	15	38	4.8	0.9	493	18.1	475	3
Stoddard	90	1 499	84.2	36.2	41	137	9.7	3.0	1 998	105.4	1 893	18
Stone	45	458	39.5	12.1	52	273	21.8	6.5	2 727	120.3	33 354	142
Sullivan	10	254	13.9	6.1	10	21	2.8	0.5	376	12.2	65	1
Taney	125	2 363	247.5	91.8	101	556	49.6	12.9	4 336	178.7	25 499	135
Texas	52	968	70.6	28.2	34	69	6.5	1.4	1 719	67.3	1 026	20
Vernon	71	1 468	91.0	38.0	34	122	7.5	1.8	1 363	58.7	2 161	59
Warren	56	D	D	D	36	D	D	D	2 060	75.3	48 491	238
Washington	76	776	66.3	22.9	16	56	4.2	1.1	1 013	35.0	160	1
Wayne	40	379	18.1	7.5	10	48	2.1	0.6	683	27.7	0	0
Webster	56	500	26.9	12.2	35	D	D	D	3 017	114.6	7 973	79
Worth	2	D	D	D	5	D	D	D	198	6.7	0	0
Wright	43	492	30.5	11.7	23	77	6.4	1.5	1 329	56.9	1 013	6

Table B. States and Counties — Government Employment and Payroll, and Local Government Finances

STATE County	Government employment and payroll, 2012		March payroll (percent of total)							Local government finances, 2012		General revenue	Taxes	
													Per capita[1] (dollars)	
	Full-time equivalent employees	March payroll (dollars)	Administration, judicial, and legal	Police and Corrections	Fire Protection	Highways and transportation	Health and Welfare	Natural resources and utilities	Education and libraries	Total (mil dol)	Intergovernmental (mil dol)	Total (mil dol)	Total	Property
	171	172	173	174	175	176	177	178	179	180	181	182	183	184
MISSOURI—Cont'd														
Jasper	4 406	12 579 406	4.8	9.9	4.0	3.6	1.3	3.8	71.5	389.2	139.5	146.6	1 272	589
Jefferson	6 669	24 871 942	2.8	6.2	4.1	2.5	3.8	3.1	76.7	560.9	238.8	255.4	1 160	796
Johnson	2 208	7 565 488	3.1	4.7	2.1	2.3	37.3	2.7	47.4	195.3	49.7	52.6	967	584
Knox	221	492 621	7.9	5.4	0.0	7.2	22.0	5.2	52.2	12.1	5.9	4.4	1 068	756
Laclede	1 413	3 701 221	5.5	5.9	1.6	12.4	1.2	6.8	65.2	72.4	35.3	26.3	742	477
Lafayette	1 188	3 488 934	7.8	8.3	0.6	3.5	2.3	9.3	67.9	88.1	38.4	34.2	1 034	710
Lawrence	1 155	3 231 901	5.5	6.1	0.7	2.7	6.5	2.7	75.5	76.5	38.1	27.2	706	425
Lewis	450	1 137 169	6.6	5.6	0.1	4.4	19.6	4.3	58.6	29.3	13.4	9.1	892	661
Lincoln	1 917	6 064 837	5.5	7.0	1.3	2.6	24.9	0.7	57.6	159.5	58.6	49.5	928	677
Linn	590	1 568 941	6.7	5.1	0.0	4.8	4.2	7.5	69.7	39.5	19.0	13.4	1 074	641
Livingston	654	1 837 354	4.6	6.8	5.3	2.6	13.9	14.2	51.7	49.5	19.1	16.1	1 073	702
McDonald	606	1 598 982	8.5	7.8	0.1	4.5	1.5	6.0	70.3	51.8	29.8	17.6	770	427
Macon	1 039	2 633 830	3.7	3.4	0.8	3.2	42.4	2.9	43.4	92.8	45.8	29.8	1 914	1 610
Madison	682	1 827 224	2.1	3.5	0.1	2.1	44.4	2.8	42.9	25.4	13.9	8.3	667	425
Maries	323	761 125	7.6	6.0	0.0	6.9	9.4	3.4	66.1	18.2	8.6	7.6	847	638
Marion	1 348	3 816 108	4.3	7.2	3.7	3.7	10.5	8.5	58.2	94.9	33.0	39.1	1 361	752
Mercer	176	501 591	15.9	5.2	0.1	7.0	6.8	4.3	59.8	9.5	4.4	3.9	1 038	887
Miller	1 205	3 202 179	4.4	4.5	1.6	2.3	11.6	1.8	73.2	80.0	30.4	36.5	1 472	1 081
Mississippi	496	1 277 944	12.1	11.0	0.1	3.6	4.4	7.4	61.1	39.2	20.9	12.9	904	600
Moniteau	498	1 342 360	7.0	4.0	0.2	3.3	8.9	4.9	70.4	34.2	15.0	12.7	813	528
Monroe	490	1 220 603	5.4	5.4	0.3	4.2	22.2	8.5	53.6	28.8	12.5	9.7	1 109	878
Montgomery	414	1 189 713	7.9	12.4	0.0	5.3	4.0	3.0	66.0	27.1	9.4	13.0	1 088	730
Morgan	588	1 595 566	8.3	9.3	0.7	4.5	8.1	2.2	61.6	37.0	13.2	17.9	892	558
New Madrid	720	1 973 525	9.1	7.8	0.4	5.1	5.0	6.0	65.2	48.9	21.7	21.3	1 153	837
Newton	1 886	5 757 934	4.6	4.8	2.8	1.7	3.3	2.2	80.6	121.7	59.7	39.0	661	405
Nodaway	726	2 001 480	9.5	5.9	0.8	3.6	4.2	6.4	68.6	62.2	22.3	27.8	1 186	755
Oregon	416	986 254	6.1	4.7	0.0	3.9	0.0	4.8	79.9	22.3	13.8	6.1	554	379
Osage	364	958 029	5.9	4.6	2.7	4.1	8.7	5.2	68.3	23.3	8.9	9.6	696	471
Ozark	375	902 737	3.5	3.0	0.0	3.7	2.8	1.2	83.1	20.2	12.4	5.9	612	453
Pemiscot	869	2 608 472	5.8	7.8	0.7	1.4	2.9	7.8	73.3	61.3	38.4	13.9	770	506
Perry	569	1 561 790	6.3	12.2	0.0	3.8	5.0	9.4	63.2	42.8	15.7	20.2	1 064	628
Pettis	2 440	8 051 066	2.4	3.6	1.7	1.5	41.8	2.5	45.8	222.9	54.6	51.1	1 207	624
Phelps	2 804	9 025 924	2.3	3.7	1.2	1.5	51.9	4.5	33.4	301.2	46.2	39.1	869	478
Pike	681	2 031 713	2.7	3.7	0.2	0.7	28.4	3.3	60.9	45.8	18.4	20.6	1 109	754
Platte	2 626	11 215 330	4.0	6.6	2.9	2.1	4.0	1.9	78.0	290.1	82.7	172.3	1 871	1 274
Polk	1 882	6 311 305	2.0	2.0	0.1	1.6	60.7	1.1	32.3	164.9	36.7	18.1	584	439
Pulaski	1 731	5 423 451	3.5	3.9	1.1	2.3	7.4	5.5	75.3	125.6	76.5	29.6	556	371
Putnam	314	940 189	4.5	2.1	0.0	2.4	55.0	5.9	29.6	17.4	5.2	7.7	1 554	1 199
Ralls	284	692 452	21.1	12.6	0.0	13.9	2.2	4.0	41.7	13.1	5.3	6.2	600	404
Randolph	1 211	3 641 751	3.9	5.9	1.9	2.1	2.9	4.9	77.8	104.1	32.8	33.6	1 328	821
Ray	1 243	21 423 521	0.8	0.5	0.3	0.3	89.8	0.8	7.3	87.1	25.3	21.5	933	704
Reynolds	325	775 935	7.0	5.6	0.0	5.7	4.1	1.6	75.1	20.4	10.7	7.5	1 131	997
Ripley	665	1 587 309	4.3	3.8	0.5	1.9	28.8	2.6	58.2	27.1	17.6	6.3	449	337
St. Charles	12 474	44 955 774	5.7	9.4	5.0	2.8	3.2	4.3	66.6	1 191.7	344.4	666.4	1 808	1 183
St. Clair	558	1 434 103	4.2	10.9	0.0	2.8	35.5	3.2	42.1	48.9	23.1	6.2	654	535
Ste. Genevieve	472	1 571 579	6.8	13.6	0.1	3.5	5.8	7.1	62.2	37.1	12.7	20.0	1 125	724
St. Francois	2 385	7 190 551	2.7	4.3	0.6	1.6	5.1	5.1	80.0	178.1	78.4	65.4	993	571
St. Louis	35 141	147 062 201	4.5	10.0	7.3	2.5	1.6	2.8	69.6	3 629.3	1 051.6	2 133.5	2 133	1 497
Saline	749	2 090 138	7.0	10.8	3.2	5.2	6.6	26.6	39.7	61.0	25.6	21.0	898	647
Schuyler	276	469 325	6.5	3.5	0.0	3.7	25.1	6.2	54.3	12.0	5.3	3.2	735	541
Scotland	479	1 508 783	7.5	3.0	0.0	5.6	60.2	4.1	19.3	31.5	5.9	4.5	918	718
Scott	1 609	5 229 887	4.1	7.7	1.4	1.8	4.2	23.8	53.9	108.4	50.7	38.1	973	559
Shannon	529	555 611	8.1	5.1	0.0	7.2	7.0	5.1	67.1	13.2	8.0	2.9	343	223
Shelby	432	1 223 611	12.6	7.4	0.3	6.2	25.9	5.7	38.5	23.5	9.7	6.6	1 064	756
Stoddard	1 139	2 920 419	5.2	6.2	0.8	8.7	6.5	5.3	66.9	72.2	30.2	21.0	704	560
Stone	846	2 351 044	6.0	5.6	1.1	2.7	0.1	2.1	82.4	74.2	35.5	30.6	969	612
Sullivan	370	985 283	6.2	4.1	0.2	3.8	27.9	5.8	50.1	23.6	9.0	6.6	1 012	748
Taney	1 787	5 327 466	7.7	9.1	3.9	4.1	8.3	6.6	58.2	198.6	59.2	103.3	1 952	978
Texas	1 227	3 278 813	3.7	3.2	0.1	3.2	31.5	5.3	50.4	84.8	28.4	20.4	791	654
Vernon	1 038	3 438 287	4.3	4.0	1.4	1.5	36.6	4.4	47.6	48.3	21.1	19.4	934	559
Warren	943	2 742 942	5.8	9.6	2.2	1.6	5.8	4.1	68.2	70.7	27.9	32.8	1 001	734
Washington	953	2 869 920	3.5	2.5	0.3	2.7	34.5	4.9	50.7	69.6	27.6	13.6	541	368
Wayne	459	1 011 584	9.4	3.6	0.0	7.6	5.0	3.2	71.2	25.2	14.3	7.7	573	378
Webster	946	2 669 213	5.5	5.0	0.3	2.8	11.0	3.5	71.2	63.4	29.0	20.2	556	309
Worth	134	294 433	8.2	2.8	0.0	3.4	21.0	5.8	57.6	6.8	2.2	2.2	1 037	834
Wright	792	2 007 501	4.3	3.8	0.3	2.7	11.1	4.2	73.0	47.2	25.3	12.2	656	392

1. Based on the resident population estimated as of July 1 of the year shown.

Table B. States and Counties — Local Government Finances, Government Employment, and Income Taxes

STATE County	Local government finances, 2012 (cont.)									Government employment, 2015			Individual income tax returns, 2014		
	Direct general expenditure							Debt outstanding							
			Percent of total for:												
	Total (mil dol)	Per capita¹ (dollars)	Education	Health and hospitals	Police protection	Public welfare	Highways	Total (mil dol)	Per capita¹ (dollars)	Federal civilian	Federal military	State and local	Number of returns	Mean adjusted gross income	Mean income tax
	185	186	187	188	189	190	191	192	193	194	195	196	197	198	199
MISSOURI—Cont'd															
Jasper	396.9	3 443	54.1	10.7	5.4	0.1	5.6	243.6	2 113	292	430	6 522	51 140	44 770	4 524
Jefferson	583.0	2 648	64.1	2.8	6.2	0.0	7.7	577.7	2 623	291	763	8 195	105 400	51 396	5 084
Johnson	233.9	4 299	31.0	47.8	3.5	0.0	4.6	246.2	4 525	1 282	3 840	5 821	22 230	46 719	4 166
Knox	10.9	2 667	49.1	8.8	4.0	18.8	5.9	0.6	147	27	13	268	1 670	33 795	2 817
Laclede	68.0	1 919	74.1	0.0	4.7	0.0	6.3	34.1	962	85	121	1 515	15 020	38 965	3 401
Lafayette	87.7	2 650	57.3	1.7	5.6	0.1	7.0	105.1	3 177	112	115	2 110	14 880	46 655	4 204
Lawrence	78.1	2 031	67.8	0.8	3.9	5.7	6.5	98.6	2 562	243	129	1 767	15 830	41 020	3 594
Lewis	26.7	2 624	50.7	1.4	3.7	15.5	8.9	11.0	1 085	48	32	577	4 250	42 047	3 565
Lincoln	153.2	2 871	47.7	26.4	4.4	0.0	4.4	139.5	2 615	110	186	2 147	24 660	48 563	4 528
Linn	37.6	3 014	60.3	3.0	4.4	0.0	11.3	26.2	2 102	57	42	769	5 460	43 253	4 078
Livingston	59.6	3 966	50.2	2.8	4.8	8.2	7.4	28.8	1 918	74	46	1 330	6 270	44 972	4 616
McDonald	44.0	1 922	69.8	0.0	4.1	0.0	8.0	31.9	1 393	86	77	890	9 000	36 227	2 592
Macon	48.3	3 102	46.4	1.1	3.5	22.2	8.9	21.2	1 363	69	52	1 561	6 890	40 685	3 568
Madison	30.2	2 426	68.9	0.0	6.2	0.0	6.2	3.9	310	32	42	853	4 950	40 219	3 658
Maries	18.1	2 013	61.7	4.7	4.0	0.0	9.9	10.7	1 187	10	31	339	3 700	40 181	3 191
Marion	99.0	3 444	54.3	3.1	3.7	6.3	4.7	133.0	4 628	103	94	1 863	12 740	46 369	4 664
Mercer	9.9	2 650	69.6	5.6	1.5	0.0	12.0	8.6	2 310	29	13	230	1 510	38 252	3 175
Miller	78.5	3 161	59.5	4.2	3.5	6.0	5.7	46.2	1 860	48	85	1 453	10 330	37 795	3 100
Mississippi	35.3	2 466	49.4	5.6	5.4	0.6	6.5	20.3	1 418	16	42	1 045	5 080	40 632	4 020
Moniteau	32.1	2 054	63.0	5.8	3.2	0.0	6.8	31.2	1 994	46	50	1 047	6 520	43 666	3 645
Monroe	28.8	3 309	49.1	3.2	3.9	16.0	10.7	54.4	6 255	71	29	623	3 860	42 637	3 863
Montgomery	28.9	2 411	56.1	3.6	5.3	0.0	7.9	11.0	913	50	39	634	5 190	41 527	3 488
Morgan	40.7	2 025	46.7	0.1	7.7	7.9	8.7	22.0	1 093	41	68	965	8 390	36 771	2 851
New Madrid	46.5	2 517	59.4	2.4	6.4	0.0	7.6	18.4	995	49	61	946	7 170	42 633	4 170
Newton	127.6	2 161	69.8	3.0	3.0	0.5	3.4	106.0	1 794	142	198	2 531	24 410	48 416	5 218
Nodaway	59.7	2 551	52.7	3.7	4.8	0.0	11.8	64.8	2 766	87	66	2 528	8 650	47 000	4 507
Oregon	21.9	1 990	73.6	1.6	2.2	0.0	5.3	3.9	358	32	37	509	3 830	34 188	2 590
Osage	23.1	1 669	59.8	6.0	2.4	0.0	5.6	11.0	794	32	45	808	6 040	46 310	3 905
Ozark	20.7	2 155	78.4	2.7	3.2	0.1	6.5	0.7	69	13	32	438	3 590	33 712	2 753
Pemiscot	61.8	3 411	67.4	1.6	4.6	0.0	5.4	11.3	624	51	59	1 523	6 700	39 942	3 845
Perry	43.0	2 261	53.4	1.8	6.3	0.0	8.0	19.0	1 001	47	65	1 194	8 940	45 628	4 077
Pettis	213.3	5 041	37.6	44.8	2.5	0.0	4.2	106.8	2 524	136	144	3 155	18 510	42 745	3 828
Phelps	295.8	6 576	23.7	59.1	2.1	0.3	2.9	165.9	3 688	344	226	5 992	17 670	46 172	4 704
Pike	43.7	2 354	53.0	1.6	7.4	0.0	9.9	24.3	1 308	63	56	1 698	7 310	42 759	3 737
Platte	285.1	3 097	65.5	0.9	4.8	0.2	5.0	434.8	4 724	730	364	3 754	46 500	75 953	10 804
Polk	168.1	5 419	28.7	60.0	1.0	0.0	3.1	55.0	1 774	64	102	2 334	11 850	41 298	3 540
Pulaski	139.6	2 621	69.4	2.9	2.8	0.0	4.4	141.0	2 648	3 622	10 557	2 199	18 690	42 707	3 184
Putnam	17.9	3 623	40.9	1.9	1.7	18.6	8.7	7.6	1 551	20	16	484	2 080	37 000	2 912
Ralls	12.4	1 207	50.3	3.6	5.3	0.0	17.2	14.9	1 451	28	35	348	4 640	48 574	4 676
Randolph	103.6	4 090	59.4	15.6	4.7	0.0	3.9	94.5	3 731	70	78	2 130	10 330	44 376	4 424
Ray	82.9	3 594	35.4	24.2	3.6	15.3	8.2	32.9	1 426	49	77	1 397	10 290	49 370	4 598
Reynolds	20.8	3 118	70.7	4.1	2.1	0.5	3.4	4.8	719	16	22	395	2 400	37 426	3 074
Ripley	26.6	1 894	72.9	5.2	4.9	0.0	4.4	1.2	88	54	47	597	5 100	33 534	2 590
St. Charles	1 188.4	3 223	54.5	2.1	6.5	0.1	9.4	1 722.2	4 671	733	1 310	15 521	187 880	68 224	8 582
St. Clair	44.1	4 651	28.5	34.9	1.9	0.0	5.3	16.1	1 703	41	32	477	3 660	36 525	2 999
Ste. Genevieve	38.8	2 184	67.5	3.0	6.6	0.0	7.8	28.1	1 581	29	61	942	8 310	48 124	4 409
St. Francois	177.6	2 694	64.6	4.1	6.8	0.1	6.3	112.4	1 705	134	204	5 697	25 540	42 470	3 916
St. Louis	3 854.3	3 853	55.7	1.6	7.0	0.9	5.2	4 175.7	4 174	5 631	3 443	49 333	505 860	83 159	13 656
Saline	61.1	2 617	55.2	5.4	6.9	0.3	7.5	7.5	323	81	75	1 801	9 840	43 762	4 168
Schuyler	11.1	2 542	46.7	3.1	1.3	22.3	14.5	7.8	1 793	31	15	299	1 740	32 516	2 495
Scotland	35.5	7 289	17.7	58.8	1.2	11.4	5.9	18.8	3 848	21	16	590	2 100	39 691	3 350
Scott	109.3	2 794	52.1	2.0	13.1	0.0	3.9	182.4	4 661	100	132	2 091	17 530	47 601	5 109
Shannon	12.9	1 551	60.4	0.2	2.3	0.0	12.2	2.7	326	18	28	319	3 040	31 335	2 368
Shelby	24.1	3 872	42.9	4.0	2.6	27.1	7.7	6.0	969	32	20	590	2 920	40 328	3 431
Stoddard	67.4	2 263	63.7	5.5	2.6	0.0	6.1	41.2	1 384	151	100	1 326	12 460	44 168	4 710
Stone	68.6	2 173	57.5	0.0	4.0	0.0	7.1	49.4	1 566	38	105	1 109	13 750	43 983	4 333
Sullivan	22.7	3 475	48.2	30.8	2.2	0.1	5.6	9.1	1 389	45	21	430	2 780	34 750	2 617
Taney	188.6	3 561	41.8	3.4	3.9	0.0	6.1	593.9	11 215	176	181	2 209	24 040	35 933	3 437
Texas	72.4	2 804	46.8	37.3	2.0	0.1	3.4	30.6	1 185	65	82	1 893	9 220	35 106	2 617
Vernon	45.8	2 207	64.9	3.0	3.5	0.0	7.3	60.2	2 903	96	69	1 657	8 440	39 569	3 320
Warren	69.9	2 135	57.6	4.6	6.2	0.0	5.1	59.4	1 815	46	115	1 273	15 260	49 370	4 789
Washington	67.9	2 707	49.1	31.2	3.2	0.0	3.5	32.5	1 294	55	81	1 506	8 690	35 290	2 519
Wayne	23.2	1 734	66.5	1.8	4.6	0.0	10.8	24.4	1 824	72	46	533	4 560	31 543	2 053
Webster	62.8	1 727	65.3	0.3	4.1	0.0	6.4	23.5	648	81	126	1 405	14 760	46 212	4 845
Worth	7.6	3 657	53.1	2.9	3.3	20.3	3.2	1.0	466	24	D	158	910	39 220	3 077
Wright	48.4	2 598	61.6	0.2	2.3	10.5	5.3	14.9	799	44	62	865	6 950	32 977	2 478

1. Based on the resident population estimated as of July 1 of the year shown.

Table B. States and Counties — Land Area and Population

STATE/ County code	CBSA code[1]	County type[2]	STATE County	Land area,[3] (sq mi) 2016	Total persons 2016	Rank	Per square mile	White	Black	American Indian, Alaska Native	Asian and Pacific Islander	Percent Hispanic or Latino[4]	Under 5 years	5 to 17 years	18 to 24 years	25 to 34 years	35 to 44 years	45 to 54 years
				Population, 2016				Race alone or in combination, not Hispanic or Latino (percent)					Age (percent)					
				1	2	3	4	5	6	7	8	9	10	11	12	13	14	15
			MISSOURI—Cont'd															
29 510	41180	1	St. Louis city	62.0	311 404	219	5 022.6	45.4	48.1	0.9	4.0	4.0	6.6	13.3	9.9	19.8	13.1	12.2
30 000	...	0	MONTANA	145 547.0	1 042 520	X	7.2	88.8	1.0	7.7	1.5	3.6	6.0	15.8	9.5	12.8	11.5	12.1
30 001	...	7	Beaverhead	5 542.7	9 401	2 474	1.7	93.1	0.7	2.7	1.5	4.1	4.9	12.8	15.3	10.2	9.5	10.8
30 003	...	6	Big Horn	4 997.1	13 343	2 210	2.7	29.9	0.8	65.7	0.9	5.5	10.0	24.3	8.9	12.7	9.8	11.2
30 005	...	9	Blaine	4 227.1	6 601	2 702	1.6	49.0	0.6	49.7	0.7	2.6	8.5	21.7	8.8	12.0	10.9	10.9
30 007	...	9	Broadwater	1 192.3	5 747	2 773	4.8	95.0	0.6	2.5	0.7	2.8	4.5	15.7	6.5	8.6	10.8	14.5
30 009	13740	3	Carbon	2 048.0	10 460	2 391	5.1	95.3	0.7	1.9	0.6	2.6	3.7	14.1	6.2	8.8	11.3	13.5
30 011	...	9	Carter	3 340.5	1 203	3 099	0.4	97.9	0.1	2.1	0.2	0.9	6.3	12.6	6.2	10.6	7.1	12.4
30 013	24500	3	Cascade	2 698.2	81 755	687	30.3	88.9	2.3	6.3	2.0	4.3	6.7	15.7	9.8	13.9	10.7	11.6
30 015	...	8	Chouteau	3 972.5	5 759	2 772	1.4	77.9	0.5	20.0	0.9	2.4	4.7	18.6	7.8	12.0	10.8	11.2
30 017	...	7	Custer	3 783.3	11 924	2 299	3.2	93.9	0.8	3.1	1.0	3.1	6.2	15.3	8.2	12.5	11.0	12.7
30 019	...	9	Daniels	1 426.0	1 755	3 070	1.2	94.5	1.0	3.5	0.4	2.6	6.3	15.6	6.1	9.5	9.9	10.7
30 021	...	7	Dawson	2 372.2	9 327	2 479	3.9	94.0	0.9	3.1	0.7	3.1	6.5	16.2	8.6	13.3	10.9	11.8
30 023	...	7	Deer Lodge	736.7	9 085	2 500	12.3	92.6	0.9	4.7	1.0	3.0	3.5	11.5	8.8	10.6	11.6	13.7
30 025	...	9	Fallon	1 620.6	3 120	2 961	1.9	96.4	0.5	1.4	1.1	2.0	8.7	18.0	7.1	12.2	11.3	10.6
30 027	...	7	Fergus	4 339.3	11 413	2 331	2.6	95.8	0.5	2.5	0.7	2.3	5.5	15.4	6.4	10.5	10.9	11.8
30 029	28060	5	Flathead	5 087.2	98 082	606	19.3	95.1	0.6	2.4	1.4	2.6	5.9	16.1	7.1	11.9	11.9	12.7
30 031	14580	5	Gallatin	2 604.7	104 502	574	40.1	93.9	0.7	1.7	2.2	3.4	6.0	14.3	16.1	16.1	13.1	10.8
30 033	...	9	Garfield	4 676.6	1 310	3 094	0.3	97.9	0.5	1.0	0.3	1.3	6.4	15.7	6.3	10.8	12.8	10.3
30 035	...	7	Glacier	2 994.9	13 694	2 189	4.6	34.1	0.5	64.7	0.8	2.9	9.3	21.9	9.1	13.7	10.9	11.3
30 037	13740	3	Golden Valley	1 174.4	831	3 114	0.7	94.1	0.7	2.5	1.4	4.0	4.1	15.5	7.0	7.3	8.8	12.5
30 039	...	8	Granite	1 727.2	3 368	2 947	1.9	95.9	1.0	2.0	0.6	2.3	3.9	12.1	5.4	7.9	9.7	11.6
30 041	...	7	Hill	2 899.4	16 542	2 007	5.7	73.4	0.8	24.1	1.4	3.5	9.1	18.4	9.5	13.9	10.8	10.6
30 043	25740	9	Jefferson	1 656.9	11 853	2 305	7.2	95.1	0.6	3.3	0.9	2.4	3.9	16.3	6.4	8.5	10.7	14.8
30 045	...	8	Judith Basin	1 869.7	1 940	3 054	1.0	97.4	0.2	1.4	0.4	1.6	4.4	14.2	6.6	7.9	9.5	13.2
30 047	...	6	Lake	1 490.5	29 758	1 436	20.0	71.8	0.7	29.0	1.2	4.2	6.5	17.8	7.6	10.4	10.2	11.3
30 049	25740	5	Lewis and Clark	3 458.5	67 282	787	19.5	93.6	0.8	3.4	1.3	3.2	5.8	15.8	8.2	12.4	11.6	12.9
30 051	...	9	Liberty	1 430.0	2 409	3 013	1.7	97.6	0.5	1.7	0.5	1.1	6.0	15.9	7.8	11.5	10.5	12.9
30 053	...	7	Lincoln	3 612.7	19 259	1 860	5.3	95.1	0.6	2.9	1.0	2.8	4.7	13.7	5.1	8.2	9.5	12.5
30 055	...	9	McCone	2 642.2	1 700	3 073	0.6	96.4	0.7	2.3	0.8	1.6	5.4	15.2	7.5	9.5	9.5	12.0
30 057	...	9	Madison	3 588.2	7 924	2 604	2.2	95.4	0.6	1.8	0.8	3.0	3.9	11.8	5.6	9.1	9.6	11.7
30 059	...	9	Meagher	2 391.9	1 827	3 067	0.8	96.4	0.2	1.8	0.9	2.1	5.5	12.4	6.8	9.1	9.1	10.9
30 061	...	8	Mineral	1 219.6	4 184	2 883	3.4	93.8	1.0	3.6	1.0	3.1	4.3	13.4	5.2	8.6	8.5	12.3
30 063	33540	3	Missoula	2 593.1	116 130	529	44.8	92.2	1.0	4.0	2.5	3.1	5.4	13.9	14.5	15.4	12.2	11.4
30 065	...	8	Musselshell	1 869.0	4 589	2 857	2.5	93.7	0.8	2.9	1.3	3.1	4.5	15.4	5.7	8.5	10.1	12.9
30 067	...	7	Park	2 802.8	16 114	2 033	5.7	95.2	0.6	2.2	1.0	2.9	4.7	14.1	5.8	10.7	12.5	13.8
30 069	...	9	Petroleum	1 655.6	489	3 136	0.3	97.8	0.0	1.6	0.2	1.2	4.3	14.3	8.8	7.0	8.0	16.8
30 071	...	9	Phillips	5 140.5	4 133	2 890	0.8	88.5	1.0	11.7	0.7	2.2	7.0	16.1	7.5	9.3	9.6	12.5
30 073	...	7	Pondera	1 624.6	6 084	2 743	3.7	84.0	1.0	14.7	0.6	1.9	6.5	17.1	7.6	11.4	9.7	11.9
30 075	...	9	Powder River	3 298.2	1 746	3 071	0.5	95.8	0.7	3.0	0.9	2.0	3.6	13.6	8.0	9.3	8.0	13.3
30 077	...	6	Powell	2 326.1	6 858	2 687	2.9	91.3	1.6	5.6	0.8	2.3	3.8	11.7	8.5	12.1	13.3	15.4
30 079	...	9	Prairie	1 736.6	1 182	3 101	0.7	95.0	1.4	3.3	1.9	2.9	6.1	13.9	4.8	9.1	10.2	9.5
30 081	...	6	Ravalli	2 391.0	42 088	1 127	17.6	94.6	0.5	2.1	1.1	3.4	4.8	14.8	6.6	9.0	10.4	13.1
30 083	...	7	Richland	2 084.3	11 482	2 324	5.5	91.1	1.1	3.7	1.0	5.7	7.5	18.4	8.3	13.5	12.4	12.4
30 085	...	7	Roosevelt	2 354.4	11 305	2 339	4.8	38.7	0.7	59.7	1.0	3.5	10.5	22.8	8.7	14.0	10.9	10.3
30 087	...	9	Rosebud	5 008.6	9 287	2 483	1.9	58.3	0.7	37.4	1.3	5.0	8.5	21.1	8.5	11.2	10.4	12.0
30 089	...	8	Sanders	2 760.4	11 534	2 316	4.2	92.6	0.6	5.8	0.8	2.9	5.0	15.0	5.9	8.1	8.8	11.4
30 091	...	9	Sheridan	1 675.8	3 648	2 929	2.2	94.6	1.0	3.1	0.9	2.7	6.1	15.0	7.5	10.9	10.5	11.3
30 093	15580	5	Silver Bow	718.0	34 553	1 311	48.1	92.3	0.9	3.1	1.2	4.2	5.9	14.6	11.1	12.1	10.8	12.3
30 095	...	8	Stillwater	1 796.6	9 406	2 473	5.2	94.7	0.6	1.9	0.9	3.7	4.8	16.6	6.4	8.5	10.7	13.8
30 097	...	9	Sweet Grass	1 855.5	3 623	2 933	2.0	96.3	0.8	1.6	0.9	2.1	4.5	16.2	7.0	8.7	10.2	12.7
30 099	...	8	Teton	2 271.6	6 056	2 747	2.7	96.3	0.7	3.2	0.7	1.6	7.1	16.6	7.3	9.8	10.1	12.2
30 101	...	7	Toole	1 915.0	4 977	2 836	2.6	89.9	1.5	5.9	1.2	3.9	5.4	13.4	8.3	13.7	13.1	13.0
30 103	...	8	Treasure	977.8	692	3 129	0.7	93.4	0.4	3.2	1.7	3.0	6.2	12.1	5.5	10.5	7.2	11.1
30 105	...	7	Valley	4 926.1	7 539	2 629	1.5	86.9	0.8	10.7	1.3	2.6	6.1	16.4	7.1	10.4	10.3	11.8
30 107	...	9	Wheatland	1 422.5	2 117	3 037	1.5	95.9	1.2	2.8	1.1	2.2	6.4	16.6	6.5	8.6	10.0	10.5
30 109	...	9	Wibaux	888.6	1 093	3 104	1.2	95.0	0.5	1.2	0.7	3.7	6.1	15.5	7.4	8.7	8.7	12.5
30 111	13740	3	Yellowstone	2 633.5	158 437	410	60.2	89.2	1.4	5.4	1.4	5.5	6.5	17.0	8.2	14.0	12.2	12.3
31 000	...	0	NEBRASKA	76 823.8	1 907 116	X	24.8	81.2	5.6	1.4	3.0	10.7	7.0	17.9	10.1	13.3	12.1	12.0
31 001	25580	4	Adams	563.3	31 684	1 390	56.2	87.7	1.3	0.8	1.9	9.4	6.6	17.1	11.4	11.7	10.6	11.8
31 003	...	9	Antelope	857.2	6 329	2 728	7.4	95.5	0.6	0.6	0.6	3.4	6.7	16.9	7.3	9.2	9.6	11.6
31 005	...	9	Arthur	715.4	469	3 138	0.7	94.9	0.6	0.9	0.2	4.5	5.1	21.7	7.9	9.0	14.7	9.4
31 007	42420	9	Banner	746.2	798	3 117	1.1	93.0	1.4	0.6	0.1	5.5	5.1	15.3	6.0	9.0	8.0	9.5

1. CBSA = Core Based Statistical Area. See Appendix A for explanation. See Appendix B for list of metropolitan areas with component counties.　2. County type code from the Economic Research Service of USDA Rural-Urban Continuum Codes. See Appendix A for definition.　3. Dry land or land partially or temporarily covered by water.　4. May be of any race.

Table B. States and Counties — **Population and Households**

STATE County	55 to 64 years	65 to 74 years	75 years and over	Percent female	2000	2010	2000–2010	2010–2016	Births	Deaths	Net migration	Number	Persons per house-hold	Family house-holds	Female family house-holder[1]	One per-son
	16	17	18	19	20	21	22	23	24	25	26	27	28	29	30	31
MISSOURI—Cont'd																
St. Louis city	13.2	7.0	4.9	51.6	348 189	319 381	-8.3	-2.5	29 496	18 669	-18 141	139 555	2.20	46.4	17.9	44.4
MONTANA	14.6	10.6	7.2	49.7	902 195	989 414	9.7	5.4	76 644	58 129	33 673	409 394	2.41	62.4	8.7	30.5
Beaverhead	15.6	12.1	8.9	48.9	9 202	9 246	0.5	1.7	561	492	79	4 080	2.15	56.7	4.9	35.7
Big Horn	11.4	7.3	4.4	50.5	12 671	12 865	1.5	3.7	1 718	807	-438	3 576	3.63	80.2	22.0	17.6
Blaine	12.8	8.1	6.3	50.9	7 009	6 491	-7.4	1.7	687	421	-145	2 238	2.87	67.2	17.5	26.9
Broadwater	17.3	14.1	8.1	49.1	4 385	5 612	28.0	2.4	302	313	160	2 427	2.32	70.3	7.1	24.3
Carbon	18.5	15.2	8.7	49.1	9 552	10 078	5.5	3.8	471	583	513	4 480	2.27	61.4	6.1	34.8
Carter	19.3	12.1	13.5	50.0	1 360	1 160	-14.7	3.7	88	78	38	504	2.38	69.8	6.2	28.2
Cascade	13.6	9.9	8.0	49.4	80 357	81 324	1.2	0.5	7 312	5 070	-1 784	33 784	2.35	62.7	10.5	31.7
Chouteau	15.9	10.7	8.3	50.2	5 970	5 813	-2.6	-0.9	301	365	26	2 288	2.50	68.0	9.4	29.8
Custer	14.9	10.2	9.1	49.7	11 696	11 699	0.0	1.9	970	902	173	4 827	2.38	64.3	9.2	31.7
Daniels	16.4	12.1	13.4	49.3	2 017	1 751	-13.2	0.2	126	142	23	866	1.99	56.6	3.1	40.4
Dawson	15.0	9.5	8.3	48.1	9 059	8 963	-1.1	4.1	757	616	250	3 974	2.24	66.9	7.4	26.4
Deer Lodge	18.1	13.4	8.8	46.7	9 417	9 292	-1.3	-2.2	448	777	99	3 851	2.13	56.8	6.0	39.4
Fallon	15.4	8.7	7.9	48.7	2 837	2 890	1.9	8.0	321	184	97	1 221	2.47	68.5	9.6	29.7
Fergus	15.8	12.9	10.8	49.0	11 893	11 586	-2.6	-1.5	745	994	83	4 879	2.25	65.9	7.3	32.0
Flathead	16.0	11.4	6.9	50.1	74 471	90 928	22.1	7.9	6 939	5 131	5 171	37 106	2.48	65.6	7.1	28.8
Gallatin	11.7	7.4	4.5	48.3	67 831	89 513	32.0	16.7	7 134	3 256	10 815	38 292	2.39	59.2	5.9	27.6
Garfield	14.4	13.7	9.5	48.9	1 279	1 209	-5.5	8.4	81	76	83	437	2.39	69.6	4.8	26.3
Glacier	12.3	6.8	4.8	51.1	13 247	13 399	1.1	2.2	1 543	890	-360	4 222	3.07	64.9	17.4	31.3
Golden Valley	17.7	15.8	11.3	48.9	1 042	884	-15.2	-6.0	44	56	-40	320	2.29	70.6	10.3	24.1
Granite	19.8	16.7	12.7	49.1	2 830	3 079	8.8	9.4	130	197	341	1 421	2.19	66.6	4.1	29.5
Hill	13.1	8.3	6.2	49.4	16 673	16 096	-3.5	2.8	1 864	914	-483	6 092	2.63	67.1	11.7	26.7
Jefferson	18.8	14.3	6.3	49.5	10 049	11 403	13.5	3.9	525	640	544	4 473	2.51	70.9	6.7	24.5
Judith Basin	20.0	13.4	10.6	47.6	2 329	2 072	-11.0	-6.4	96	111	-111	913	2.18	67.3	5.0	28.0
Lake	15.5	12.5	8.1	50.6	26 507	28 746	8.4	3.5	2 285	1 776	487	11 978	2.38	65.8	11.6	29.3
Lewis and Clark	15.4	10.8	6.9	50.5	55 716	63 395	13.8	6.1	4 745	3 550	2 614	26 753	2.38	62.5	8.9	30.3
Liberty	15.7	8.3	11.5	51.8	2 158	2 339	8.4	3.0	145	146	73	864	2.52	64.2	4.9	33.9
Lincoln	19.6	16.8	9.9	49.3	18 837	19 687	4.5	-2.2	1 100	1 471	-87	8 645	2.21	59.2	5.7	34.9
McCone	19.0	11.2	10.8	49.6	1 977	1 734	-12.3	-2.0	97	105	-25	737	2.31	68.1	2.4	29.3
Madison	19.6	18.5	10.1	48.2	6 851	7 691	12.3	3.0	361	439	286	3 369	2.23	59.1	3.9	37.6
Meagher	18.8	17.4	10.1	48.8	1 932	1 891	-2.1	-3.4	114	169	-14	757	2.47	65.4	9.5	28.1
Mineral	19.1	17.6	11.1	48.6	3 884	4 223	8.7	-0.9	280	310	-23	1 563	2.67	56.4	7.4	37.9
Missoula	12.6	9.1	5.5	49.7	95 802	109 299	14.1	6.2	7 706	5 143	4 182	46 624	2.33	57.2	9.3	30.7
Musselshell	19.8	14.6	8.5	50.1	4 497	4 538	0.9	1.1	263	326	123	1 951	2.43	64.9	5.2	31.5
Park	17.4	13.1	8.1	49.8	15 694	15 636	-0.4	3.1	925	919	469	6 793	2.28	57.4	5.8	37.2
Petroleum	17.4	11.5	12.1	46.0	493	494	0.2	-1.0	17	21	-7	192	2.31	66.1	6.3	30.7
Phillips	16.7	11.3	10.0	49.6	4 601	4 253	-7.6	-2.8	324	327	-100	1 808	2.26	66.6	7.0	31.0
Pondera	15.2	10.8	9.7	51.0	6 424	6 155	-4.2	-1.2	453	403	-121	2 296	2.52	64.0	9.3	32.1
Powder River	19.4	13.2	11.6	50.2	1 858	1 743	-6.2	0.2	71	127	49	756	2.19	62.4	9.1	33.5
Powell	15.4	11.6	8.1	38.1	7 180	7 027	-2.1	-2.4	328	456	-41	2 380	2.25	59.8	6.2	34.1
Prairie	16.7	17.6	12.3	48.9	1 199	1 179	-1.7	0.3	84	106	23	547	2.46	66.0	4.8	29.4
Ravalli	16.8	15.1	9.5	50.6	36 070	40 212	11.5	4.7	2 394	2 634	1 979	16 649	2.43	63.3	8.2	31.4
Richland	14.3	7.8	5.5	48.3	9 667	9 746	0.8	17.8	1 006	564	1 312	4 421	2.51	65.2	7.5	30.3
Roosevelt	11.7	6.7	4.5	49.9	10 620	10 425	-1.8	8.4	1 478	869	256	3 063	3.54	62.6	15.8	33.3
Rosebud	13.7	9.5	5.1	49.2	9 383	9 235	-1.6	0.6	1 028	531	-446	3 295	2.81	67.7	10.1	28.0
Sanders	19.4	17.7	10.7	48.6	10 227	11 413	11.6	1.1	670	826	265	5 038	2.21	64.7	6.4	29.7
Sheridan	17.2	10.9	10.6	48.9	4 105	3 384	-17.6	7.8	251	353	352	1 639	2.16	64.0	6.7	32.8
Silver Bow	15.0	10.2	8.0	49.6	34 606	34 209	-1.1	1.0	2 492	2 562	395	15 144	2.22	55.3	11.7	36.6
Stillwater	17.8	13.4	8.1	48.9	8 195	9 117	11.3	3.2	530	534	272	3 742	2.44	71.3	3.9	26.4
Sweet Grass	16.0	13.5	11.2	49.0	3 609	3 651	1.2	-0.8	189	251	44	1 410	2.55	70.1	4.5	28.9
Teton	14.5	11.6	11.0	50.5	6 445	6 071	-5.8	-0.2	487	394	-102	2 314	2.50	66.0	5.2	30.8
Toole	16.2	10.0	6.9	43.0	5 267	5 324	1.1	-6.5	341	281	-410	1 972	2.24	68.5	9.8	28.0
Treasure	19.5	15.2	12.6	49.0	861	718	-16.6	-3.6	51	51	-26	353	2.30	68.8	6.8	30.6
Valley	15.6	11.5	11.0	49.7	7 675	7 369	-4.0	2.3	527	493	148	3 295	2.26	66.4	7.8	30.5
Wheatland	16.4	14.5	10.5	49.4	2 259	2 168	-4.0	-2.4	143	140	-59	885	2.34	60.0	2.4	37.7
Wibaux	15.7	11.7	13.6	49.5	1 068	1 017	-4.8	7.5	70	95	85	448	2.15	64.3	7.6	33.0
Yellowstone	13.7	9.3	7.0	50.8	129 352	147 972	14.4	7.1	12 526	8 742	6 586	61 442	2.44	62.8	10.1	30.0
NEBRASKA	12.6	8.4	6.7	50.2	1 711 263	1 826 334	6.7	4.4	163 686	96 895	14 572	736 613	2.47	64.7	9.9	28.9
Adams	13.7	9.4	7.7	50.0	31 151	31 367	0.7	1.0	2 563	1 908	-328	12 670	2.35	61.2	6.9	32.4
Antelope	16.1	11.2	11.4	49.9	7 452	6 685	-10.3	-5.3	518	443	-416	2 821	2.27	70.8	6.6	26.1
Arthur	11.1	11.5	9.6	50.3	444	460	3.6	2.0	28	26	8	180	2.49	60.6	7.2	35.6
Banner	15.7	17.3	14.0	50.1	819	690	-15.8	15.7	37	28	56	339	2.42	76.1	4.7	20.4

1. No spouse present.

Table B. States and Counties — **Population, Vital Statistics, Health, and Crime**

STATE County	Persons in group quarters, 2016	Daytime population, 2011–2015 Number	Daytime population, Employment/residence ratio	Births, 2016 Total	Births, 2016 Rate[1]	Deaths, 2016 Number	Deaths, 2016 Rate[1]	Persons under 65 with no health insurance, 2015 Number	Persons under 65 with no health insurance, 2015 Percent	Medicare, 2015 Total Beneficiaries	Medicare, 2015 Enrolled in Original Medicare	Medicare, 2015 Enrolled in Medicare Advantage	Serious crimes known to police,[2] 2014 Total Number	Serious crimes known to police,[2] 2014 Total Rate[3]
	32	33	34	35	36	37	38	39	40	41	42	43	44	45
MISSOURI—Cont'd														
St. Louis city	11 871	427 165	1.76	4 547	14.6	3 070	9.9	36 858	13.7	45 315	27 663	17 652	25 913	8 134
MONTANA	28 872	1 011 854	0.99	12 431	11.9	9 597	9.2	118 357	14.2	196 663	157 436	39 227	28 625	2 797
Beaverhead	443	9 115	0.96	86	9.1	87	9.3	1 084	15.6	2 032	1 755	277	71	757
Big Horn	137	13 608	1.10	283	21.2	157	11.8	2 632	23.2	1 563	1 406	157	NA	NA
Blaine	220	6 502	0.96	110	16.7	68	10.3	1 234	22.5	968	867	101	11	203
Broadwater	52	4 908	0.70	41	7.1	49	8.5	667	15.1	1 491	1 202	289	46	805
Carbon	52	8 628	0.67	63	6.0	84	8.0	1 198	15.0	2 366	1 815	551	104	997
Carter	11	1 155	0.88	18	15.0	11	9.1	166	18.8	267	243	24	0	0
Cascade	2 463	82 237	1.00	1 124	13.7	813	9.9	8 918	13.5	16 570	12 376	4 194	2 942	3 554
Chouteau	135	5 366	0.80	54	9.4	56	9.7	1 022	22.1	1 070	878	192	NA	NA
Custer	413	11 879	0.99	163	13.7	158	13.3	1 169	12.2	2 461	2 260	201	269	2 234
Daniels	41	1 775	1.02	20	11.4	13	7.4	186	14.0	D	429	D	7	387
Dawson	498	9 162	0.96	131	14.0	93	10.0	865	11.3	1 650	1 574	76	277	2 886
Deer Lodge	842	9 082	0.97	72	7.9	125	13.8	914	13.9	2 338	2 052	286	241	2 576
Fallon	34	3 184	1.08	59	18.9	30	9.6	262	9.7	494	480	14	21	670
Fergus	465	11 379	0.98	122	10.7	152	13.3	1 233	14.4	2 817	2 203	614	159	1 382
Flathead	992	92 817	0.99	1 129	11.5	867	8.8	10 554	13.5	20 831	15 807	5 024	2 878	3 068
Gallatin	3 265	94 941	0.99	1 224	11.7	544	5.2	9 692	11.2	12 510	9 788	2 722	2 192	2 324
Garfield	0	1 031	0.97	14	10.7	13	9.9	170	16.7	259	242	17	7	530
Glacier	690	13 939	1.06	239	17.5	155	11.3	2 978	25.5	1 561	1 488	73	206	1 488
Golden Valley	89	676	0.77	8	9.6	4	4.8	107	17.8	251	194	57	9	1 051
Granite	40	2 941	0.81	24	7.1	31	9.2	430	19.0	709	617	92	54	1 708
Hill	593	17 051	1.07	305	18.4	157	9.5	2 252	16.3	2 769	2 495	274	572	3 423
Jefferson	230	9 253	0.56	81	6.8	124	10.5	1 031	11.1	2 435	1 909	526	126	1 090
Judith Basin	0	1 829	0.82	14	7.2	6	3.1	205	14.0	458	333	125	10	498
Lake	585	28 031	0.90	357	12.0	324	10.9	5 355	23.3	5 535	4 485	1 050	804	2 760
Lewis and Clark	1 950	68 179	1.09	763	11.3	608	9.0	5 740	10.6	12 338	9 649	2 689	1 816	2 755
Liberty	403	2 424	1.06	24	10.0	25	10.4	292	15.2	576	538	38	NA	NA
Lincoln	209	19 257	0.99	162	8.4	249	12.9	2 471	17.8	5 981	4 209	1 772	321	1 651
McCone	19	1 628	0.89	18	10.6	12	7.1	282	22.0	D	328	D	13	762
Madison	163	7 630	0.96	57	7.2	70	8.8	857	15.0	1 939	1 705	234	48	621
Meagher	174	1 898	1.00	14	7.7	24	13.1	225	17.0	509	481	28	35	1 792
Mineral	22	4 022	0.86	41	9.8	56	13.4	487	16.0	1 396	1 122	274	7	163
Missoula	3 638	115 398	1.06	1 234	10.6	856	7.4	11 512	12.1	18 790	15 168	3 622	3 636	3 228
Musselshell	52	4 757	0.98	43	9.4	55	12.0	528	15.1	1 156	969	187	90	1 932
Park	108	14 918	0.90	156	9.7	159	9.9	1 853	14.7	3 443	2 750	693	116	737
Petroleum	0	421	0.91	0	0.0	0	0.0	73	19.9	90	76	14	3	587
Phillips	127	4 023	0.91	61	14.8	37	9.0	629	19.4	926	872	54	73	1 752
Pondera	645	5 953	0.90	74	12.2	57	9.4	978	20.1	1 240	1 025	215	67	1 075
Powder River	35	1 737	1.04	13	7.4	18	10.3	192	14.3	326	273	53	NA	NA
Powell	1 549	7 137	1.06	53	7.7	71	10.4	634	15.6	1 389	1 198	191	169	2 414
Prairie	21	1 276	0.82	15	12.7	10	8.5	126	15.7	349	314	35	5	424
Ravalli	479	37 344	0.79	377	9.0	435	10.3	6 015	19.3	10 939	8 356	2 583	458	1 142
Richland	34	11 581	1.08	190	16.5	83	7.2	1 363	12.9	1 683	1 651	32	153	1 314
Roosevelt	186	11 609	1.15	255	22.6	164	14.5	2 466	24.7	1 432	1 396	36	198	1 792
Rosebud	65	10 001	1.16	166	17.9	101	10.9	1 402	17.6	1 437	1 265	172	64	684
Sanders	188	11 218	0.97	122	10.6	127	11.0	1 767	22.1	3 456	2 790	666	166	1 459
Sheridan	85	3 797	1.09	49	13.4	49	13.4	356	12.2	879	836	43	92	2 451
Silver Bow	998	34 517	1.00	408	11.8	430	12.4	3 475	12.5	7 252	6 092	1 160	1 643	4 740
Stillwater	112	8 783	0.88	79	8.4	85	9.0	875	11.6	2 089	1 593	496	115	1 225
Sweet Grass	45	3 809	1.11	27	7.5	31	8.6	358	13.1	820	697	123	5	136
Teton	461	5 764	0.88	84	13.9	55	9.1	767	16.3	1 352	905	447	71	1 169
Toole	796	5 386	1.11	49	9.8	42	8.4	570	15.7	553	503	50	127	2 491
Treasure	0	765	0.87	10	14.5	5	7.2	96	19.0	203	184	19	NA	NA
Valley	126	7 415	0.96	88	11.7	66	8.8	958	16.1	1 839	1 770	69	113	1 465
Wheatland	147	2 056	0.93	21	9.9	21	9.9	367	23.4	513	447	66	2	94
Wibaux	24	921	0.86	12	11.0	16	14.6	162	19.2	D	231	D	2	173
Yellowstone	3 721	155 741	1.03	2 025	12.8	1 459	9.2	16 157	12.4	27 358	21 145	6 213	6 266	4 018
NEBRASKA	52 354	1 887 908	1.02	26 553	13.9	15 355	8.1	148 165	9.4	303 681	262 157	41 524	52 754	2 804
Adams	1 479	31 265	0.99	426	13.4	308	9.7	2 417	9.7	5 524	5 237	287	1 113	3 508
Antelope	61	6 063	0.87	85	13.4	67	10.6	511	10.4	D	1 321	D	22	450
Arthur	0	417	0.83	4	8.5	4	8.5	56	15.7	D	102	D	0	0
Banner	0	677	0.68	7	8.8	2	2.5	67	12.4	D	79	D	NA	NA

1. Per 1,000 estimated resident population.   2. Data for serious crimes have not been adjusted for underreporting; this may affect comparability between geographic areas and over time.
3. Per 100,000 population estimated by the FBI.

Items 32—45

Table B. States and Counties — **Crime, Education, Money Income, and Poverty**

STATE County	Serious crimes known to police, 2014 (cont.)[1] Rate[2] Violent	Property	Education — School enrollment and attainment, 2011–2015 — Enrollment[3] Total	Percent private	Attainment[4] (percent) High school graduate or less	Bachelor's degree or more	Local government expenditures,[5] 2013–2014 Total current spending (mil dol)	Current spending per student (dollars)	Money income, 2011–2015 Per capita income[6] (dollars)	Households Median income (dollars)	Percent with income of less than $50,000	with income of $200,000 or more	Income and poverty, 2015 Median household income (dollars)	Percent below poverty level All persons	Children under 18 years	Children 5 to 17 years in families
	46	47	48	49	50	51	52	53	54	55	56	57	58	59	60	61
MISSOURI—Cont'd																
St. Louis city	1 706	6 428	80 864	32.3	39.5	31.9	438.0	12 113	23 945	35 599	63.2	2.3	37 948	25.5	39.3	39.8
MONTANA	324	2 473	237 409	12.3	37.4	29.5	1 586.9	11 010	26 381	47 169	52.4	2.9	49 650	14.4	18.8	16.8
Beaverhead	149	607	2 604	4.2	36.7	30.3	13.5	11 601	26 763	41 512	56.6	2.4	41 083	17.0	20.7	18.7
Big Horn	NA	NA	3 648	3.8	49.1	15.6	36.8	15 403	16 244	41 622	57.9	1.4	41 008	31.0	39.5	34.6
Blaine	92	111	1 697	8.2	39.0	20.3	18.3	14 341	17 442	36 744	64.2	1.5	34 667	29.6	40.4	39.7
Broadwater	385	420	1 089	17.4	46.3	23.9	6.3	9 862	29 188	50 115	49.9	3.7	51 360	10.8	15.8	13.7
Carbon	211	786	1 739	6.2	35.4	29.2	17.2	12 520	28 153	49 767	50.2	2.1	49 389	11.7	15.0	13.7
Carter	0	0	237	39.7	45.3	15.6	2.3	19 256	29 391	45 000	54.8	4.2	46 398	13.9	23.1	25.8
Cascade	249	3 305	18 391	11.1	40.5	25.5	112.4	9 660	25 870	45 205	54.3	2.6	45 597	14.4	19.2	17.8
Chouteau	NA	NA	1 479	8.4	42.1	23.3	10.6	15 805	22 032	38 521	61.3	1.8	40 280	17.6	22.9	17.3
Custer	191	2 043	2 501	11.7	37.9	20.0	16.3	9 814	25 506	48 750	50.5	2.1	47 510	12.2	16.2	14.6
Daniels	55	332	286	12.9	37.4	22.2	3.3	12 333	33 140	49 239	50.8	3.9	43 918	10.2	9.6	8.6
Dawson	240	2 647	1 989	8.2	43.6	18.8	15.3	11 408	27 878	52 738	48.3	3.0	56 648	11.0	12.4	11.3
Deer Lodge	374	2 202	1 665	13.3	47.9	16.8	11.3	10 787	23 156	39 399	62.7	1.8	37 979	18.1	23.2	21.1
Fallon	223	447	636	8.5	43.3	16.1	10.2	18 922	32 755	53 266	47.3	3.8	59 928	7.7	9.9	9.3
Fergus	365	1 017	2 226	8.7	41.8	28.2	21.6	13 542	26 111	40 881	59.2	2.8	43 823	13.6	18.0	16.2
Flathead	295	2 773	19 566	12.8	35.6	29.1	132.0	9 599	26 388	47 851	52.0	3.0	48 063	14.0	18.8	16.7
Gallatin	189	2 135	28 258	12.5	23.3	48.0	117.9	9 756	30 293	55 553	45.3	4.3	57 358	10.9	9.9	8.8
Garfield	0	530	153	2.6	52.2	14.8	2.5	12 651	26 142	39 732	57.9	3.2	45 987	14.2	18.5	15.8
Glacier	166	1 322	4 194	8.6	49.3	17.7	38.0	13 528	16 892	29 640	68.1	1.6	31 666	28.1	37.5	36.0
Golden Valley	234	818	133	21.8	49.9	20.3	2.6	22 638	21 562	40 938	63.4	0.0	37 883	20.2	31.3	30.1
Granite	127	1 582	529	6.2	47.1	25.8	4.9	13 378	27 136	48 512	50.9	1.8	43 470	14.1	24.0	20.0
Hill	395	3 028	4 410	6.9	37.9	23.2	40.3	12 889	20 869	44 633	55.3	0.7	44 178	21.2	24.8	25.4
Jefferson	285	804	2 386	16.7	33.9	32.6	16.0	10 074	30 886	60 842	42.1	4.9	62 508	9.8	13.1	10.6
Judith Basin	249	249	352	5.4	43.4	29.9	4.9	18 115	26 595	44 602	55.2	2.1	45 472	13.8	14.2	11.0
Lake	439	2 320	6 499	12.7	40.6	24.4	48.6	10 951	22 278	38 732	60.4	2.3	39 383	20.8	29.2	26.1
Lewis and Clark	375	2 380	14 908	23.4	29.2	38.0	96.1	10 037	28 476	56 197	43.8	2.3	56 755	12.2	15.1	13.0
Liberty	NA	NA	395	20.8	43.2	21.6	3.4	14 382	23 587	47 768	52.9	3.7	40 052	17.0	20.8	18.1
Lincoln	195	1 455	3 803	15.5	44.5	19.4	27.1	11 334	22 856	35 275	65.3	2.4	37 281	20.3	32.2	29.6
McCone	0	762	268	6.3	52.5	17.5	3.2	12 291	28 654	40 750	58.3	4.7	44 387	13.9	16.6	13.8
Madison	78	543	1 289	16.9	41.8	26.4	12.8	14 681	29 700	46 250	53.3	4.3	49 872	11.4	17.1	14.5
Meagher	102	1 690	336	9.5	46.7	23.3	3.0	15 208	20 736	41 641	61.3	0.7	41 391	17.3	31.8	30.5
Mineral	93	70	593	10.1	52.4	13.1	9.1	14 930	20 691	36 031	63.8	1.8	39 584	16.4	26.6	24.6
Missoula	274	2 954	31 212	9.4	27.3	40.7	143.1	10 635	26 779	46 164	53.1	3.3	44 998	15.8	16.8	15.4
Musselshell	429	1 502	1 004	10.5	49.2	16.8	8.3	11 594	23 545	39 517	56.4	1.3	41 791	17.7	27.7	25.5
Park	127	610	2 965	19.7	37.3	35.0	22.5	11 573	27 045	43 932	55.7	2.7	45 642	12.7	16.9	14.8
Petroleum	196	391	66	0.0	55.7	20.6	1.4	16 035	25 378	43 750	54.7	1.6	42 919	15.4	23.3	16.0
Phillips	216	1 536	817	10.4	46.0	19.3	10.9	16 160	22 139	36 071	62.2	1.2	38 105	16.4	21.4	19.9
Pondera	96	978	1 488	11.9	43.7	22.1	14.0	14 651	22 797	42 264	55.4	2.1	41 168	20.1	29.3	26.6
Powder River	NA	NA	312	15.7	35.6	24.4	4.6	17 734	29 902	46 346	52.5	2.4	50 491	10.7	14.3	11.3
Powell	528	1 885	1 126	20.0	48.1	19.3	10.5	14 425	21 536	40 000	61.2	2.8	42 755	18.1	20.1	18.8
Prairie	170	254	232	14.2	56.0	15.7	2.1	14 190	23 285	42 383	58.5	1.3	42 187	12.5	18.8	18.1
Ravalli	182	960	8 670	11.9	42.0	24.4	54.5	9 791	22 482	39 480	59.3	1.2	48 468	14.9	22.9	20.2
Richland	180	1 134	2 222	4.8	46.1	16.5	25.5	13 312	32 900	65 084	38.4	6.2	68 196	7.0	10.2	9.3
Roosevelt	443	1 348	2 825	3.4	55.4	13.5	38.4	15 468	16 182	32 974	62.5	1.8	39 147	24.3	32.7	30.5
Rosebud	192	491	2 254	9.9	45.3	19.8	27.2	16 448	23 238	51 159	49.2	2.3	51 732	18.8	25.0	23.6
Sanders	211	1 248	1 908	20.1	53.5	16.4	19.4	14 192	20 169	32 257	68.4	0.9	36 564	18.7	28.3	27.0
Sheridan	453	1 998	701	8.6	39.0	21.3	9.4	16 665	30 814	50 664	49.5	4.3	50 857	9.4	10.3	8.9
Silver Bow	355	4 385	8 099	11.8	44.0	24.6	44.3	9 991	24 383	37 749	61.6	2.2	42 658	16.7	21.9	20.2
Stillwater	149	1 076	1 978	16.1	43.2	23.7	17.4	12 241	29 217	58 259	43.2	2.9	60 052	9.1	10.3	8.2
Sweet Grass	54	81	782	10.4	45.7	25.2	6.7	13 015	25 522	50 588	49.7	2.4	48 361	10.7	14.2	11.6
Teton	132	1 037	1 264	14.7	41.8	23.3	13.7	12 642	24 443	46 360	53.5	0.7	47 598	12.4	19.9	17.8
Toole	510	1 981	927	13.4	52.0	13.4	9.7	14 691	22 101	44 804	55.0	1.9	43 879	17.0	19.6	16.9
Treasure	NA	NA	185	3.2	45.3	18.9	1.6	20 727	20 758	41 103	63.2	0.8	49 679	11.8	19.7	19.0
Valley	78	1 387	1 542	8.8	45.0	19.4	17.5	13 904	26 337	49 141	50.8	2.6	46 698	12.1	17.1	15.3
Wheatland	0	94	380	5.5	59.2	18.0	4.7	14 899	19 385	32 723	66.7	0.3	35 665	20.1	33.3	32.8
Wibaux	0	173	175	6.3	52.0	20.0	2.8	17 417	23 875	38 553	63.4	0.0	49 533	10.1	14.0	12.8
Yellowstone	335	3 682	36 016	13.7	38.6	28.5	218.8	9 485	29 576	52 802	47.0	4.0	57 326	10.4	14.1	12.0
NEBRASKA	280	2 523	511 862	16.4	36.9	29.3	3 604.5	11 715	27 882	52 997	46.9	3.5	55 073	12.2	15.9	14.4
Adams	249	3 259	9 241	21.5	41.3	23.0	65.1	12 939	27 690	50 635	49.4	3.5	48 579	12.7	16.3	15.4
Antelope	41	409	1 402	9.6	42.2	17.7	23.8	21 871	26 763	45 609	55.1	2.8	48 546	12.2	16.7	15.6
Arthur	0	0	126	8.7	27.6	32.7	2.0	20 608	22 035	39 375	64.4	3.3	50 753	13.2	18.0	15.2
Banner	NA	NA	138	18.1	34.8	17.4	3.1	21 611	31 735	48 897	52.2	6.2	54 115	11.9	21.1	17.8

1. Data for serious crimes have not been adjusted for underreporting; this may affect comparability between geographic areas and over time.   2. Per 100,000 population estimated by the FBI.
3. All persons 3 years old and over enrolled in nursery school through college.   4. Persons 25 years old and over.   5. Elementary and secondary education expenditures.
6. Based on population estimated by the American Community Survey, 2011–2015.

Table B. States and Counties — Personal Income

STATE County	Personal income, 2015										Earnings, 2015		
	Total (mil dol)	Percent change, 2014–2015	Per capita[1] Dollars	Per capita[1] Rank	Wages and salaries (mil dol)	Supplements to wages and salaries; employer contributions (mil dol) — Pension and insurance	Supplements to wages and salaries; employer contributions (mil dol) — Government social insurance	Proprietors' income (mil dol)	Dividends, interest, and rent (mil dol)	Personal transfer receipts (mil dol)	Total (mil dol)	Contributions for government social insurance (mil dol) — From employee and self-employed	Contributions for government social insurance (mil dol) — From employer
	62	63	64	65	66	67	68	69	70	71	72	73	74

STATE County	62	63	64	65	66	67	68	69	70	71	72	73	74
MISSOURI—Cont'd													
St. Louis city	13 143	4.0	41 632	1 276	14 361	2 299	1 038	1 852	1 989	3 074	19 549	1 109	1 038
MONTANA	43 187	4.0	41 845	X	19 271	3 112	1 749	4 608	9 797	8 088	28 740	1 845	1 749
Beaverhead	394	7.1	42 330	1 423	141	27	12	67	98	83	247	13	12
Big Horn	388	3.7	29 276	2 950	200	41	17	26	67	109	284	17	17
Blaine	178	-1.1	27 000	2 924	55	13	5	13	47	53	86	5	5
Broadwater	206	3.9	36 233	1 774	52	9	5	12	44	47	77	6	5
Carbon	448	4.4	43 012	1 101	92	16	8	41	118	84	157	12	8
Carter	63	3.8	53 182	214	12	2	1	26	12	8	42	1	1
Cascade	3 460	3.4	42 053	1 044	1 621	290	151	263	759	706	2 324	147	151
Chouteau	189	4.1	32 859	2 576	47	9	4	21	56	40	81	5	4
Custer	497	0.5	40 927	1 156	221	35	20	68	93	95	344	22	20
Daniels	76	13.0	43 357	2 543	28	5	2	14	18	15	49	3	2
Dawson	397	-3.0	41 234	1 035	190	27	19	23	68	68	260	18	19
Deer Lodge	328	4.4	35 857	2 070	119	22	11	14	63	93	166	12	11
Fallon	148	-7.6	46 333	452	89	12	7	27	25	20	135	8	7
Fergus	438	2.4	38 287	1 442	163	29	15	51	111	99	258	17	15
Flathead	3 886	6.4	40 407	1 321	1 697	240	163	401	941	773	2 502	171	163
Gallatin	4 668	7.7	46 337	919	2 198	331	199	668	1 191	512	3 396	207	199
Garfield	56	4.2	42 703	1 347	11	2	1	21	14	9	35	1	1
Glacier	439	3.4	32 148	2 461	166	38	15	39	85	121	258	14	15
Golden Valley	44	8.3	53 667	874	7	2	1	12	12	9	21	1	1
Granite	117	6.5	36 181	1 373	29	5	3	11	35	28	49	3	3
Hill	647	1.5	39 061	1 411	309	54	32	30	155	142	426	28	32
Jefferson	505	4.2	43 394	683	107	19	9	38	100	91	174	12	9
Judith Basin	101	4.6	52 234	359	20	4	2	35	26	15	61	2	2
Lake	956	3.6	32 464	2 532	303	58	27	63	251	281	450	33	27
Lewis and Clark	2 933	4.0	44 153	989	1 609	293	139	205	659	514	2 246	139	139
Liberty	81	-0.2	33 569	1 649	21	4	2	14	31	15	40	2	2
Lincoln	615	3.1	32 259	2 584	189	36	18	42	139	218	285	24	18
McCone	92	5.6	54 654	660	26	5	2	28	20	10	61	3	2
Madison	371	13.0	46 825	728	153	19	15	41	108	69	229	14	15
Meagher	85	6.0	46 327	969	18	3	2	24	20	20	47	2	2
Mineral	139	4.1	32 668	2 244	35	8	3	9	23	47	55	5	3
Missoula	4 659	5.4	40 803	1 404	2 388	378	219	405	1 170	805	3 390	218	219
Musselshell	183	3.9	39 906	1 532	67	11	5	17	42	49	101	7	5
Park	704	5.3	44 106	1 106	201	30	19	65	214	130	315	22	19
Petroleum	27	1.4	57 122	198	4	1	0	12	5	3	18	0	0
Phillips	150	1.3	36 095	1 778	48	10	4	19	37	36	81	5	4
Pondera	242	-0.4	39 187	1 048	66	11	6	25	72	56	108	7	6
Powder River	69	6.6	39 139	1 576	18	4	2	18	16	11	42	2	2
Powell	250	6.0	36 607	2 266	97	22	8	22	70	56	150	9	8
Prairie	49	9.2	41 881	1 629	13	3	1	10	12	11	27	2	1
Ravalli	1 548	4.8	37 413	1 730	408	70	38	106	413	391	621	49	38
Richland	715	-6.2	59 756	111	375	49	32	128	131	64	584	35	32
Roosevelt	406	-4.6	35 358	1 618	145	29	13	25	70	102	210	13	13
Rosebud	350	5.4	37 193	1 812	219	43	20	19	51	78	301	18	20
Sanders	366	8.1	32 258	2 816	91	19	9	42	82	129	160	13	9
Sheridan	189	-4.2	51 250	332	68	11	6	35	45	29	120	7	6
Silver Bow	1 536	-3.0	44 355	686	669	113	60	259	276	310	1 100	71	60
Stillwater	418	4.6	44 068	843	191	29	15	36	84	72	271	17	15
Sweet Grass	162	3.4	44 619	1 000	77	12	6	9	56	28	103	7	6
Teton	282	4.5	46 200	676	68	13	6	64	67	52	151	8	6
Toole	188	-5.9	36 859	779	93	18	8	16	60	33	136	8	8
Treasure	40	-1.9	57 013	141	7	1	1	11	7	6	21	1	1
Valley	326	2.4	42 622	998	142	24	15	20	82	70	200	14	15
Wheatland	81	9.2	38 570	1 631	21	4	2	22	21	19	48	2	2
Wibaux	48	-1.3	42 081	1 539	12	3	1	13	8	9	29	2	1
Yellowstone	7 258	3.6	46 213	878	3 854	546	346	864	1 316	1 146	5 610	358	346
NEBRASKA	92 048	1.2	48 606	X	45 743	7 137	3 450	13 809	16 831	13 452	70 138	3 990	3 450
Adams	1 402	4.8	44 381	940	627	104	47	186	306	261	964	56	47
Antelope	321	-2.9	49 974	79	88	15	6	91	59	57	199	8	6
Arthur	22	-17.6	49 018	113	6	1	0	7	4	4	14	0	0
Banner	54	-8.7	68 652	57	10	1	1	30	6	6	42	1	1

1. Based on the resident population estimated as of July 1 of the year shown.

Items 62—74

Table B. States and Counties — Earnings, Social Security, and Housing

STATE County	Farm	Mining	Construction	Manu- facturing	Infor- mation: professional, scientific, technical services	Retail trade	Finance, insur- ance, real estate and leasing	Health care and social assistance	Govern- ment	Number	Rate[1]	Supple- mental Security Income recipients, December 2015	Total	Percent change, 2010– 2016
	75	76	77	78	79	80	81	82	83	84	85	86	87	88
MISSOURI—Cont'd														
St. Louis city	0.0	D	D	9.6	15.8	1.6	9.7	15.4	14.6	54 150	172	16 534	175 702	-0.2
MONTANA	2.5	4.1	8.6	4.2	8.0	8.0	6.6	13.6	19.7	217 758	211	18 312	497 756	3.1
Beaverhead	21.1	D	5.6	0.8	3.8	8.1	5.5	11.6	24.0	2 215	239	129	5 232	-0.8
Big Horn	7.4	21.9	D	D	1.9	3.9	1.8	D	41.9	2 080	157	335	4 642	-1.2
Blaine	10.8	0.9	3.7	0.9	D	9.2	D	D	45.1	1 210	184	197	2 799	-1.5
Broadwater	7.6	D	6.2	19.9	D	6.1	5.1	7.3	18.8	1 430	252	66	2 681	-0.5
Carbon	4.8	5.9	13.5	1.6	6.4	5.5	6.1	8.6	20.1	2 655	256	112	6 439	0.0
Carter	65.3	0.0	D	0.0	D	4.5	D	D	11.9	300	256	8	804	-0.7
Cascade	0.8	0.1	7.4	3.6	6.3	9.0	7.1	17.0	26.9	18 060	220	1 862	38 062	2.1
Chouteau	25.9	0.0	3.9	1.4	D	6.5	5.2	D	24.9	1 205	209	62	2 855	-0.8
Custer	6.3	D	6.5	1.1	3.8	11.1	6.7	D	19.3	2 600	214	244	5 596	0.6
Daniels	2.8	D	7.9	D	D	D	D	12.1	12.2	455	258	13	1 108	-0.3
Dawson	-0.6	8.7	4.2	1.2	5.0	9.4	4.1	D	15.0	1 670	174	97	4 372	3.3
Deer Lodge	0.8	0.0	6.6	0.2	6.9	5.5	2.3	29.0	30.6	2 600	284	292	5 113	-0.2
Fallon	5.8	25.3	12.0	0.7	2.7	4.0	3.0	6.6	12.4	580	182	12	1 572	6.9
Fergus	7.0	D	15.3	5.8	3.5	8.0	4.6	D	20.7	3 045	267	202	5 773	-1.1
Flathead	0.1	0.9	10.3	7.0	6.9	8.6	8.6	17.7	12.8	21 935	228	1 327	47 659	1.5
Gallatin	1.2	0.5	13.9	5.0	12.7	11.3	7.0	9.4	16.1	13 855	138	613	47 345	12.0
Garfield	55.3	0.0	D	D	D	8.1	D	D	18.3	285	217	14	842	-0.2
Glacier	10.1	4.1	3.1	0.4	2.1	6.8	1.2	D	48.8	2 075	152	598	5 301	-0.9
Golden Valley	27.7	D	D	D	D	D	D	D	14.3	300	361	22	476	0.0
Granite	14.3	0.8	4.2	4.3	D	5.2	D	D	25.9	975	301	45	2 772	-1.8
Hill	2.3	0.1	4.5	0.4	7.3	8.2	4.7	D	28.7	2 700	163	431	7 215	-0.5
Jefferson	5.1	14.1	11.5	6.3	D	2.9	4.6	8.5	26.1	2 825	242	162	5 019	-0.7
Judith Basin	57.9	0.0	D	D	D	2.3	D	D	13.4	535	277	27	1 326	-0.7
Lake	1.2	0.6	8.7	5.1	6.2	8.3	3.7	13.8	34.3	7 145	242	732	16 567	-0.1
Lewis and Clark	0.7	0.8	5.1	2.3	10.5	6.7	8.7	12.4	36.0	14 375	216	1 108	30 946	2.5
Liberty	30.5	D	D	D	D	D	6.1	D	15.7	395	165	46	1 025	-1.7
Lincoln	-0.3	0.9	10.4	2.6	5.1	9.9	3.5	D	28.6	6 530	343	564	11 423	0.1
McCone	22.1	0.0	5.7	0.5	D	8.5	D	D	10.9	345	205	0	1 001	-0.8
Madison	10.5	3.0	8.7	1.8	3.9	3.4	3.6	4.3	12.0	2 285	289	67	6 893	-0.6
Meagher	33.1	D	D	D	D	5.1	D	D	14.3	565	311	48	1 419	-0.7
Mineral	-0.6	0.2	11.7	D	D	11.4	D	10.8	32.0	1 395	329	150	2 434	-0.9
Missoula	-0.1	0.1	6.7	3.0	9.6	8.6	7.0	18.3	19.4	20 575	181	2 129	52 321	4.4
Musselshell	6.7	42.9	6.0	0.5	2.9	3.3	D	7.5	12.7	1 345	294	102	2 642	-0.5
Park	3.5	0.2	9.8	7.1	7.2	6.7	6.1	11.3	13.6	3 630	227	234	9 382	0.1
Petroleum	63.6	D	D	0.0	D	D	D	0.0	13.4	110	233	6	325	0.3
Phillips	11.8	D	6.2	1.4	D	7.4	6.9	D	26.1	1 020	245	86	2 308	-1.2
Pondera	13.3	1.3	11.4	1.6	3.7	9.2	D	11.4	17.6	1 335	217	183	2 627	-1.2
Powder River	33.2	D	D	D	D	D	11.1	D	0.5	385	216	0	1 007	-1.5
Powell	5.7	D	D	D	2.2	3.6	2.6	8.4	47.0	1 580	231	119	3 117	0.4
Prairie	20.6	0.0	D	D	D	10.5	D	D	38.4	365	314	17	665	-1.2
Ravalli	0.0	0.2	11.1	6.1	9.9	6.9	7.1	12.9	19.9	12 295	298	745	19 502	-0.4
Richland	3.4	19.0	13.4	4.4	4.0	5.3	6.8	D	8.0	1 820	152	103	5 157	13.3
Roosevelt	-0.3	3.7	4.1	0.4	D	8.4	2.4	D	43.2	1 745	152	398	4 074	0.3
Rosebud	5.3	17.5	D	D	D	2.9	1.4	D	30.3	1 745	186	235	4 084	0.6
Sanders	1.0	2.8	16.9	5.4	3.4	6.0	3.7	11.6	23.4	4 025	356	305	6 625	-0.8
Sheridan	21.1	6.7	D	D	3.6	5.3	D	D	16.8	925	251	35	2 130	2.0
Silver Bow	0.1	16.9	3.6	4.0	5.1	6.4	6.2	16.4	15.7	8 095	234	983	16 847	0.8
Stillwater	6.3	D	D	5.0	3.7	2.7	1.7	D	9.3	2 265	239	83	4 791	-0.2
Sweet Grass	0.8	D	9.1	2.9	1.7	4.2	3.0	0.8	15.3	915	252	21	2 869	-0.8
Teton	22.8	D	10.1	1.7	D	5.0	5.5	5.7	15.8	1 505	247	115	2 125	-1.1
Toole	4.1	10.5	D	D	D	5.0	3.7	3.9	31.2	870	171	97	2 336	0.0
Treasure	57.8	0.0	D	0.0	D	D	D	D	11.3	210	302	0	419	-0.7
Valley	2.1	D	7.4	1.0	5.6	6.1	5.4	D	22.4	1 850	243	137	4 826	-1.1
Wheatland	34.2	D	D	D	D	6.3	1.6	D	15.2	515	245	51	1 183	-1.2
Wibaux	18.6	D	D	D	D	12.6	1.5	D	22.5	255	227	8	543	0.9
Yellowstone	0.8	4.8	9.2	5.8	9.7	7.7	7.9	16.2	11.2	29 755	190	2 513	69 140	8.1
NEBRASKA	7.0	0.2	6.3	9.8	7.6	5.3	8.1	10.4	15.7	330 309	174	27 909	827 156	3.8
Adams	9.8	0.0	6.5	16.2	3.5	5.9	5.5	D	14.3	6 670	211	543	13 780	3.2
Antelope	38.6	D	7.9	3.9	1.1	4.5	6.2	7.3	11.5	1 535	240	83	3 278	-0.2
Arthur	52.6	0.0	D	D	D	D	0.5	D	16.1	105	230	0	254	0.0
Banner	70.2	0.0	D	2.1	0.1	0.4	D	D	7.6	230	289	0	364	-1.4

1. Per 1,000 resident population estimated as of July 1 of the year shown.

Table B. States and Counties — Housing, Labor Force, and Employment

STATE County	Housing units, 2011–2015								Civilian labor force, 2016		Unemployment		Civilian employment,[6] 2011–2015		
	Occupied units													Percent	
			Owner-occupied			Renter-occupied									
				Median owner cost as a percent of income											
	Total	Percent	Median value[1]	With a mortgage	Without a mortgage[2]	Median rent[3]	Median rent as a percent of income[2]	Substandard units[4] (percent)	Total	Percent change, 2015–2016	Total	Rate[5]	Total	Management, business, science and arts	Construction, production, and maintenance occupations
	89	90	91	92	93	94	95	96	97	98	99	100	101	102	103

STATE County	89	90	91	92	93	94	95	96	97	98	99	100	101	102	103
MISSOURI—Cont'd															
St. Louis city	139 555	43.9	120 400	22.4	14.1	748	32.5	2.6	161 050	0.2	8 686	5.4	147 194	39.1	15.0
MONTANA	409 394	67.2	193 500	23.0	11.2	711	28.6	2.6	526 407	1.3	21 830	4.1	485 446	35.9	22.2
Beaverhead	4 080	63.8	168 800	19.8	10.0	596	31.8	1.5	5 106	2.1	170	3.3	4 615	35.2	24.2
Big Horn	3 576	61.4	88 500	19.1	10.0	617	26.9	14.5	5 573	0.0	403	7.2	4 663	32.6	21.3
Blaine	2 238	62.4	82 500	26.7	11.3	483	23.5	4.2	2 382	-1.0	110	4.6	2 574	38.0	26.9
Broadwater	2 427	77.9	184 600	22.2	10.0	655	25.0	3.6	2 570	3.0	126	4.9	2 759	31.7	35.0
Carbon	4 480	76.2	217 500	22.1	12.7	744	28.3	2.8	5 497	0.9	216	3.9	5 126	34.3	26.4
Carter	504	84.9	87 500	22.7	11.8	450	25.0	2.0	700	1.7	20	2.9	606	52.0	27.9
Cascade	33 784	63.5	162 100	21.5	10.9	639	26.9	2.5	38 358	-0.2	1 524	4.0	37 069	33.9	21.1
Chouteau	2 288	60.4	123 800	24.0	11.0	424	19.2	2.2	2 554	0.8	96	3.8	2 510	40.5	19.6
Custer	4 827	69.1	137 300	18.6	11.3	612	25.4	1.9	6 336	-1.2	224	3.5	6 196	32.6	21.4
Daniels	866	77.3	112 600	18.9	12.5	640	32.6	1.6	948	0.0	25	2.6	916	43.8	17.0
Dawson	3 974	69.3	156 500	17.3	10.0	554	23.3	2.8	4 695	-3.0	181	3.9	4 694	36.0	29.6
Deer Lodge	3 851	71.3	130 100	20.3	10.0	506	28.1	3.1	5 354	1.9	203	3.8	3 834	28.3	28.1
Fallon	1 221	70.7	143 000	17.7	10.0	592	27.1	1.9	1 845	-6.7	67	3.6	1 632	30.2	34.4
Fergus	4 879	70.5	121 700	21.4	12.5	686	27.1	4.2	5 851	2.2	229	3.9	5 579	39.6	24.7
Flathead	37 106	70.9	231 500	27.0	11.5	788	29.9	2.1	46 127	2.5	2 580	5.6	43 907	33.3	22.9
Gallatin	38 292	61.5	271 500	24.7	11.2	876	29.9	1.9	62 403	4.6	1 741	2.8	52 450	39.6	20.0
Garfield	437	74.6	150 000	21.8	11.6	497	17.5	3.0	776	1.4	22	2.8	555	50.5	21.6
Glacier	4 222	58.4	91 300	15.3	10.3	502	26.8	8.1	5 838	-0.7	504	8.6	4 515	37.3	22.6
Golden Valley	320	74.4	95 000	22.5	12.4	750	21.7	4.1	384	0.8	17	4.4	357	35.3	36.1
Granite	1 421	74.8	216 300	21.7	11.5	539	18.8	2.7	1 636	4.5	96	5.9	1 265	37.7	25.8
Hill	6 092	68.3	128 800	20.5	11.4	542	26.1	1.8	7 873	0.6	342	4.3	7 364	33.9	26.2
Jefferson	4 473	84.0	242 300	21.7	10.0	711	25.2	1.0	5 698	1.7	262	4.6	5 295	43.1	22.3
Judith Basin	913	75.9	122 000	19.2	11.8	513	20.1	0.7	945	-5.3	32	3.4	943	46.8	25.9
Lake	11 978	69.5	220 200	28.2	11.9	626	26.4	3.9	13 161	3.3	623	4.7	11 798	34.1	24.5
Lewis and Clark	26 753	69.4	208 600	22.3	10.1	783	27.3	1.9	35 542	1.1	1 170	3.3	33 126	44.6	15.0
Liberty	864	66.0	103 800	21.3	10.0	517	19.2	3.0	999	1.0	31	3.1	950	40.8	24.4
Lincoln	8 645	78.5	164 400	27.1	12.8	602	28.8	3.5	7 994	2.0	719	9.0	6 844	30.0	24.5
McCone	737	81.8	112 400	19.7	11.9	550	18.0	2.0	1 047	-1.8	21	2.0	920	52.4	18.7
Madison	3 369	74.6	237 800	27.0	11.1	691	23.6	2.0	4 442	3.2	168	3.8	3 880	34.5	29.1
Meagher	757	72.9	139 500	26.5	13.1	625	25.5	0.3	920	-2.1	37	4.0	891	35.5	25.5
Mineral	1 563	72.6	169 600	28.3	13.2	535	31.3	0.9	1 695	-2.3	129	7.6	1 527	28.0	25.1
Missoula	46 624	58.4	239 700	23.9	12.4	769	32.5	2.3	61 742	1.6	2 310	3.7	59 103	39.1	16.9
Musselshell	1 951	73.5	133 800	20.0	11.3	524	29.5	3.9	2 318	-4.1	118	5.1	1 967	26.4	37.9
Park	6 793	73.8	216 900	26.1	13.5	666	28.6	0.8	8 446	1.4	362	4.3	7 782	37.2	23.5
Petroleum	192	74.5	78 600	28.1	10.3	675	32.5	1.6	273	-4.2	13	4.8	254	43.7	26.4
Phillips	1 808	72.3	121 800	21.1	11.4	490	24.0	2.3	1 952	-1.6	104	5.3	1 767	33.7	23.3
Pondera	2 296	69.1	111 900	21.2	12.0	545	23.8	3.9	2 916	1.4	122	4.2	2 738	37.1	24.2
Powder River	756	69.6	107 800	22.6	10.4	553	23.5	1.5	1 094	3.2	25	2.3	965	43.0	25.8
Powell	2 380	69.1	119 500	19.3	11.4	525	22.0	2.0	2 898	-2.5	146	5.0	2 629	35.5	24.3
Prairie	547	91.8	80 900	21.5	10.0	614	31.3	0.0	529	-0.4	18	3.4	543	40.0	28.5
Ravalli	16 649	69.5	239 000	27.0	12.8	702	29.9	2.5	19 677	2.0	936	4.8	17 159	33.4	25.9
Richland	4 421	64.1	179 700	16.1	10.0	807	21.2	2.0	6 332	-8.3	316	5.0	5 904	28.7	35.5
Roosevelt	3 063	58.6	102 700	17.9	10.0	369	18.8	4.4	4 732	0.5	253	5.3	3 575	33.0	24.8
Rosebud	3 295	68.5	127 900	18.4	10.0	545	20.2	5.3	4 142	-1.2	228	5.5	4 002	34.6	29.4
Sanders	5 038	73.8	180 800	31.8	12.7	618	29.3	4.1	4 748	0.6	371	7.8	4 091	27.0	31.9
Sheridan	1 639	75.8	143 700	19.7	11.8	618	26.2	1.0	1 988	-4.6	65	3.3	1 904	36.6	18.9
Silver Bow	15 144	64.6	128 100	20.3	11.0	601	31.9	1.6	17 365	1.0	746	4.3	16 497	34.5	21.2
Stillwater	3 742	80.2	202 000	20.9	12.6	667	20.0	4.0	4 863	-1.7	194	4.0	4 487	28.9	34.3
Sweet Grass	1 410	72.6	191 800	23.1	11.6	655	21.7	2.3	1 810	0.8	56	3.1	1 613	31.2	35.3
Teton	2 314	74.0	143 800	22.5	10.9	582	25.9	4.5	2 869	-1.1	105	3.7	2 720	38.5	24.4
Toole	1 972	60.4	122 600	19.9	10.0	554	20.5	1.9	2 263	-1.9	79	3.5	2 308	29.7	25.9
Treasure	353	63.7	86 100	19.4	14.0	556	18.5	4.5	358	-0.3	16	4.5	379	31.1	37.7
Valley	3 295	68.2	122 000	16.7	10.0	532	24.8	1.0	4 454	1.0	152	3.4	3 753	39.5	23.9
Wheatland	885	67.0	83 300	23.5	12.9	551	23.8	5.0	810	2.4	41	5.1	917	40.2	26.6
Wibaux	448	70.3	106 100	17.7	12.6	665	24.2	0.7	526	-4.0	20	3.8	457	37.9	31.3
Yellowstone	61 442	68.3	192 500	21.9	11.1	762	28.6	2.5	82 053	1.2	2 946	3.6	78 572	33.1	22.8
NEBRASKA	736 613	66.2	133 200	20.3	11.9	726	27.0	2.3	1 011 051	0.3	32 478	3.2	968 134	35.6	23.6
Adams	12 670	69.5	104 300	18.5	11.2	623	24.8	0.8	16 673	0.3	548	3.3	15 783	33.7	26.0
Antelope	2 821	75.6	78 100	19.4	11.4	484	25.3	1.1	3 628	0.8	99	2.7	3 288	37.3	28.4
Arthur	180	58.9	100 000	19.4	13.6	683	32.5	0.6	226	0.4	14	6.2	193	54.9	30.1
Banner	339	67.3	122 100	21.6	12.9	588	26.1	2.4	418	-5.0	16	3.8	455	44.6	22.9

1. Specified owner-occupied units.   2. A value of 10.0 represents 10 percent or less; a value of 50.0 represents 50 percent or more.   3. Specified renter-occupied units.
4. Overcrowded or lacking complete plumbing facilities.   5. Percent of civilian labor force.   6. Civilian employed persons 16 years old and over.

	Private nonfarm establishments, employment and payroll, 2015								Agriculture, 2012			
	Employment						Annual payroll		Farms			
										Percent with:		
STATE County	Number of establishments	Total	Health care and social assistance	Manufacturing	Retail trade	Finance and insurance	Professional, scientific, and technical services	Total (mil dol)	Average per employee (dollars)	Number	Fewer than 50 acres	500 acres or more	Farm operators whose principal occupation is farming (percent)
	104	105	106	107	108	109	110	111	112	113	114	115	116
MISSOURI—Cont'd													
St. Louis city	12 143	226 479	37 387	17 008	9 869	12 740	18 268	12 597	55 621	NA	NA	NA	NA
MONTANA	37 270	375 041	67 806	17 937	59 901	16 728	19 801	14 227	37 935	28 008	28.1	42.2	55.1
Beaverhead	377	2 417	478	57	468	98	107	77	31 928	430	32.3	41.4	56.5
Big Horn	206	2 449	567	D	342	70	36	127	51 809	527	23.3	45.2	50.5
Blaine	143	1 119	263	27	189	40	33	43	38 099	546	9.0	66.7	67.2
Broadwater	140	854	119	D	143	36	33	26	30 101	287	21.6	39.7	54.4
Carbon	415	2 211	270	50	287	63	100	60	27 009	726	24.4	32.6	57.0
Carter	32	141	D	D	36	NA	5	4	28 943	327	6.4	83.2	76.5
Cascade	2 433	30 802	6 753	1 345	5 118	1 460	1 105	1 068	34 658	1 105	36.0	29.3	47.8
Chouteau	153	728	255	35	108	38	15	21	28 721	774	5.6	75.6	69.6
Custer	425	4 500	925	91	967	254	120	155	34 373	423	24.8	48.0	60.0
Daniels	70	614	114	D	94	42	11	26	42 383	338	3.8	71.3	53.8
Dawson	338	2 855	607	40	626	101	78	106	37 103	485	12.8	61.4	57.1
Deer Lodge	236	2 758	1 352	99	320	65	123	103	37 179	93	31.2	32.3	34.4
Fallon	149	1 208	135	D	143	47	16	64	53 144	295	14.6	62.4	60.3
Fergus	437	3 297	767	403	504	132	83	112	34 075	790	20.1	53.9	62.9
Flathead	4 015	36 507	6 200	2 620	6 071	1 864	1 547	1 353	37 055	1 035	60.4	6.3	49.9
Gallatin	5 275	43 091	5 218	2 852	7 682	1 482	2 847	1 617	37 516	1 163	47.7	18.6	45.0
Garfield	26	138	D	D	47	D	D	5	33 899	297	8.8	83.2	76.8
Glacier	242	2 164	475	15	537	44	39	79	36 414	602	12.8	48.5	58.6
Golden Valley	14	86	D	D	D	D	D	2	22 709	157	8.9	61.1	59.2
Granite	107	552	D	29	96	D	8	18	33 293	163	15.3	52.8	56.4
Hill	533	5 407	1 370	32	1 114	227	152	171	31 704	802	8.7	59.0	53.6
Jefferson	278	1 769	249	255	163	36	54	67	38 031	401	40.4	20.7	40.6
Judith Basin	60	189	10	NA	32	D	D	6	31 757	324	12.7	65.4	66.4
Lake	784	5 402	1 180	200	1 191	215	382	170	31 387	1 156	54.8	9.3	45.4
Lewis and Clark	2 195	25 198	5 913	603	3 963	1 685	1 783	956	37 935	703	59.2	17.2	36.6
Liberty	76	347	D	NA	49	23	9	9	25 524	304	3.9	80.6	74.3
Lincoln	596	3 954	924	210	781	119	115	115	29 071	325	49.8	5.8	38.2
McCone	53	368	D	D	85	24	D	13	35 918	489	3.3	73.4	68.3
Madison	361	2 348	148	81	243	63	50	76	32 363	571	28.5	37.5	48.7
Meagher	66	289	D	D	64	19	D	8	27 536	136	22.8	60.3	64.7
Mineral	118	849	165	D	218	17	23	22	25 359	95	50.5	9.5	30.5
Missoula	4 296	49 149	9 621	1 806	8 286	1 958	2 929	1 725	35 092	637	58.4	10.0	38.3
Musselshell	116	937	209	7	121	26	19	47	50 687	356	13.5	43.3	58.1
Park	795	4 961	813	403	766	175	194	161	32 455	564	36.0	36.2	55.1
Petroleum	11	34	D	NA	D	NA	D	1	14 794	100	6.0	78.0	78.0
Phillips	141	862	199	17	235	47	28	22	25 716	507	13.0	64.1	64.5
Pondera	177	1 334	258	71	225	67	28	45	33 756	505	14.1	59.2	62.2
Powder River	73	322	D	D	87	D	15	10	29 724	328	14.2	74.7	64.9
Powell	161	1 119	213	D	167	39	32	34	30 685	263	31.2	38.8	57.8
Prairie	36	139	D	D	24	14	5	4	27 000	186	11.3	69.4	71.5
Ravalli	1 441	9 062	1 602	818	1 541	378	475	279	30 809	1 438	69.6	5.7	47.0
Richland	554	6 562	673	396	632	158	158	406	61 941	544	12.7	67.3	64.2
Roosevelt	225	2 105	D	D	526	89	27	67	31 956	606	5.9	63.2	55.6
Rosebud	189	2 404	222	D	292	61	14	127	52 961	437	18.1	53.5	57.9
Sanders	359	2 080	519	220	331	47	40	59	28 561	492	31.1	16.3	41.3
Sheridan	170	987	306	D	183	71	35	31	30 908	527	2.3	67.6	66.4
Silver Bow	1 141	12 956	2 965	620	2 199	326	534	468	36 092	140	24.3	22.9	43.6
Stillwater	272	2 810	244	454	257	63	63	183	64 977	593	21.8	43.7	56.5
Sweet Grass	168	1 106	20	61	143	44	34	63	56 693	332	18.1	50.6	53.9
Teton	211	1 179	245	7	208	81	33	34	29 081	742	17.0	43.8	58.8
Toole	189	1 645	289	D	226	55	26	58	35 210	423	5.2	75.4	60.0
Treasure	20	55	D	NA	D	D	D	1	25 636	109	11.9	66.1	75.2
Valley	273	2 295	569	24	454	99	57	79	34 434	654	8.7	62.7	66.1
Wheatland	64	364	D	D	63	20	D	11	30 220	154	11.7	65.6	65.6
Wibaux	39	168	D	D	25	8	9	6	34 673	172	7.6	66.9	73.3
Yellowstone	5 565	69 990	13 254	3 214	11 205	4 320	3 465	2 982	42 607	1 330	48.0	21.8	46.9
NEBRASKA	53 719	870 279	125 501	93 149	112 829	62 428	98 940	36 968	42 428	49 969	23.3	37.7	59.7
Adams	971	13 219	2 643	2 540	2 015	379	264	464	35 076	567	25.9	38.8	65.1
Antelope	230	1 487	283	111	266	92	23	49	33 252	767	17.7	39.5	61.0
Arthur	9	62	NA	NA	D	D	D	2	28 226	85	10.6	81.2	71.8
Banner	9	36	NA	NA	NA	D	NA	2	44 444	193	5.2	63.7	62.7

Table B. States and Counties — **Agriculture**

STATE County	Land in farms					Value of land and buildings (dollars)		Value of machinery and equipment, average per farm (dollars)	Value of products sold				Percent of farms with sales of:		Government payments	
			Acres								Percent from:					
	Acreage (1,000)	Percent change, 2007–2012	Average size of farm	Total irrigated (1,000)	Total cropland (1,000)	Average per farm	Average per acre		Total (mil dol)	Average per farm (dollars)	Crops	Live-stock and poultry products	$10,000 or more	$100,000 or more	Total ($1,000)	Percent of farms
	117	118	119	120	121	122	123	124	125	126	127	128	129	130	131	132
MISSOURI—Cont'd																
St. Louis city	NA	NA	NA	NA	NA	NA	NA	NA	NA	NA	NA	NA	NA	NA	209 846	NA
MONTANA	59 759	-2.7	2 134	1 903.0	17 022.2	1 674 568	785	137 611	4 230.1	151 031	53.3	46.7	50.4	26.2	209 846	44.4
Beaverhead	1 381	11.4	3 211	238.5	178.6	3 580 193	1 115	151 598	142.9	332 270	21.8	78.2	57.9	32.3	368	15.1
Big Horn	3 149	8.6	5 975	46.3	268.1	2 633 651	441	151 454	108.7	206 351	48.8	51.2	53.7	28.8	2 505	32.6
Blaine	2 204	-5.4	4 037	50.5	626.8	2 408 179	597	202 203	113.8	208 509	62.9	37.1	68.9	39.7	8 869	67.2
Broadwater	477	0.4	1 661	39.6	151.3	1 901 303	1 144	166 115	38.1	132 909	56.2	43.8	52.6	27.2	1 700	47.0
Carbon	791	-0.3	1 090	72.8	136.7	1 283 405	1 178	115 977	76.9	105 871	33.8	66.2	52.2	20.4	1 696	35.3
Carter	1 778	4.7	5 437	1.4	234.8	2 923 162	538	205 480	83.2	254 431	14.9	85.1	83.2	51.7	2 009	58.1
Cascade	1 255	-9.1	1 136	33.4	427.7	1 197 706	1 055	96 719	111.1	100 568	48.2	51.8	40.9	16.2	5 952	51.5
Chouteau	2 072	-9.0	2 677	10.4	1 260.3	2 146 671	802	225 031	186.1	240 424	85.5	14.5	66.5	50.4	16 813	81.9
Custer	2 190	3.0	5 177	30.3	139.3	2 082 525	402	132 858	109.2	258 158	19.4	80.6	59.6	35.7	1 847	40.7
Daniels	768	-10.7	2 273	4.1	536.0	1 171 905	516	259 464	95.0	281 074	91.6	8.4	55.6	37.3	5 520	85.8
Dawson	1 258	-8.7	2 594	17.2	399.4	1 163 130	448	171 186	80.4	165 701	69.0	31.0	65.4	36.9	6 390	70.9
Deer Lodge	67	-16.1	716	10.8	11.2	1 154 925	1 613	74 237	5.5	59 613	33.5	66.5	35.5	15.1	60	16.1
Fallon	980	0.1	3 321	0.9	172.1	1 456 376	439	201 753	56.4	191 095	21.4	78.6	65.1	38.0	2 136	74.2
Fergus	1 961	-19.8	2 482	12.4	592.4	2 147 954	865	155 286	145.7	184 456	49.2	50.8	64.3	39.4	6 716	55.1
Flathead	170	-32.5	164	18.2	71.3	819 700	4 994	55 080	34.7	33 504	79.6	20.4	24.2	6.9	707	16.6
Gallatin	703	-9.5	604	79.1	225.1	1 596 942	2 643	97 028	106.0	91 118	55.5	44.5	38.9	15.4	2 741	21.6
Garfield	2 191	-8.4	7 376	1.5	386.1	3 642 283	494	210 761	72.9	245 549	37.1	62.9	78.5	51.2	3 399	60.6
Glacier	1 570	-7.6	2 609	34.1	525.6	1 781 623	683	172 369	105.6	175 380	64.6	35.4	53.5	25.6	6 940	51.3
Golden Valley	708	5.4	4 511	7.0	135.4	2 545 656	564	118 675	21.4	136 242	34.9	65.1	51.0	30.6	2 347	67.5
Granite	285	-5.8	1 751	28.5	27.4	2 233 558	1 276	92 485	19.2	117 497	17.5	82.5	58.3	32.5	152	16.0
Hill	1 598	-5.8	1 992	9.4	1 168.9	1 288 555	647	196 585	164.0	204 451	84.5	15.5	56.0	37.7	17 713	74.4
Jefferson	371	-5.1	926	29.2	50.3	1 049 736	1 134	48 180	22.4	55 920	19.5	80.5	33.2	10.0	519	11.2
Judith Basin	1 034	23.4	3 193	14.0	343.2	2 852 596	893	209 031	92.6	285 664	30.8	69.2	76.2	42.6	2 905	64.5
Lake	556	-12.8	481	80.7	80.7	767 869	1 597	58 202	56.6	48 930	42.9	57.1	42.0	10.6	783	20.2
Lewis and Clark	843	-13.2	1 199	47.5	92.4	1 816 522	1 515	56 963	46.6	66 228	39.5	60.5	27.3	8.4	1 192	14.5
Liberty	898	-0.7	2 954	5.9	604.4	1 795 457	608	271 908	84.7	278 500	81.4	18.6	70.7	51.6	9 709	92.4
Lincoln	47	-8.9	145	3.5	9.8	545 972	3 753	40 302	3.5	10 665	29.1	70.9	18.8	1.8	55	3.4
McCone	1 372	-9.0	2 806	14.2	604.9	1 347 873	480	197 613	102.2	209 053	76.1	23.9	70.3	44.2	7 765	83.6
Madison	1 085	2.3	1 901	111.9	144.9	2 382 159	1 253	124 492	81.3	142 301	33.6	66.4	49.0	23.5	856	15.6
Meagher	812	0.0	5 973	36.1	69.6	5 741 787	961	168 647	39.0	286 809	24.3	75.7	61.8	40.4	533	36.8
Mineral	17	-24.7	179	0.9	4.0	798 084	4 447	32 147	1.1	11 653	23.5	76.6	10.5	2.1	23	13.7
Missoula	247	-12.3	388	16.8	19.9	1 074 215	2 769	40 830	13.6	21 355	29.8	70.2	22.1	4.6	395	9.4
Musselshell	1 018	-10.2	2 859	11.4	124.2	1 412 604	494	87 795	38.1	107 006	27.3	72.7	36.5	18.3	1 854	32.0
Park	774	1.5	1 372	57.1	110.1	3 502 195	2 552	96 943	38.5	68 239	34.1	65.9	47.3	17.4	754	17.7
Petroleum	690	7.7	6 898	11.2	158.3	3 025 110	439	211 460	31.6	316 040	39.0	61.0	77.0	52.0	1 194	69.0
Phillips	2 067	3.0	4 076	33.2	702.0	2 344 404	575	148 256	95.8	188 955	61.0	39.0	63.9	35.9	7 362	68.8
Pondera	957	1.3	1 894	65.8	568.2	1 536 014	811	209 016	113.8	225 259	73.9	26.1	67.3	41.8	8 483	76.4
Powder River	1 589	-1.9	4 843	9.9	171.7	2 666 905	551	151 963	62.4	190 296	13.0	87.0	75.9	48.2	1 530	38.7
Powell	589	-12.1	2 240	53.3	53.5	2 120 281	946	112 894	34.2	130 114	22.3	77.7	48.7	23.6	264	15.6
Prairie	769	0.2	4 135	9.2	119.3	2 331 349	564	147 817	31.2	167 710	47.9	52.1	69.4	41.9	1 749	70.4
Ravalli	235	-10.7	163	61.6	51.3	792 834	4 856	42 915	34.7	24 148	30.2	69.8	25.4	5.4	549	8.6
Richland	1 293	1.1	2 377	62.7	556.5	1 418 388	597	263 978	139.2	255 820	89.4	10.6	58.1	34.5	7 701	79.0
Roosevelt	1 240	-14.6	2 046	16.6	729.0	1 292 137	632	213 368	126.4	208 579	28.1	71.9	56.5	27.7	2 043	31.6
Rosebud	3 142	15.8	7 189	35.9	238.9	2 970 357	413	141 041	91.7	209 929	28.1	71.9	56.5	27.7	2 043	31.6
Sanders	339	-0.9	688	17.5	34.4	817 530	1 187	47 451	14.2	28 917	38.8	61.2	29.9	6.3	501	10.8
Sheridan	1 042	-2.2	1 977	9.2	696.0	1 172 598	593	315 522	129.8	246 207	88.5	11.5	62.2	44.4	7 618	88.0
Silver Bow	70	-31.0	498	4.6	4.4	781 493	1 569	76 293	4.2	30 043	18.4	81.6	30.7	7.1	5	2.9
Stillwater	809	-5.6	1 365	21.6	187.3	1 905 005	1 396	84 403	56.9	95 933	22.8	77.2	48.6	18.7	2 997	42.5
Sweet Grass	856	5.3	2 577	35.8	78.7	2 771 482	1 075	105 373	33.5	100 892	12.8	87.2	49.7	20.8	689	25.0
Teton	975	-15.4	1 314	114.8	548.9	1 381 036	1 051	159 619	140.1	188 811	58.6	41.4	56.5	32.6	8 825	73.3
Toole	1 129	1.2	2 668	6.3	747.3	1 912 251	717	212 683	102.7	242 745	79.8	20.2	65.2	46.1	11 090	85.6
Treasure	618	33.7	5 666	21.9	44.2	2 847 431	503	329 853	46.6	427 202	48.1	51.9	80.7	48.6	548	56.0
Valley	1 635	-20.7	2 499	40.4	788.4	1 240 586	496	243 817	151.5	231 596	78.6	21.4	62.7	38.2	9 013	80.0
Wheatland	874	6.3	5 675	21.7	124.4	2 906 149	512	153 864	46.8	304 071	22.7	77.3	64.9	39.0	1 520	55.2
Wibaux	545	10.7	3 171	1.5	135.7	1 483 262	468	201 831	29.3	170 174	54.3	45.7	75.0	44.8	2 282	85.5
Yellowstone	1 668	3.3	1 254	73.2	351.1	957 953	764	95 176	216.8	163 019	28.0	72.0	38.0	15.5	3 843	30.2
NEBRASKA	45 332	-0.3	907	8 296.6	21 597.4	2 159 268	2 380	230 212	23 068.8	461 661	49.3	50.7	68.5	43.0	392 428	68.7
Adams	341	11.2	601	215.3	284.3	3 170 141	5 278	359 032	418.0	737 136	62.7	37.3	69.5	53.4	5 673	67.4
Antelope	475	-8.0	619	249.7	343.9	2 634 722	4 254	283 301	535.1	697 674	47.9	52.1	74.7	55.9	8 424	73.8
Arthur	453	-0.2	5 327	12.4	29.3	2 247 882	422	174 412	31.5	370 412	29.2	70.8	90.6	57.6	308	24.7
Banner	422	6.9	2 188	15.2	191.6	1 685 534	770	178 580	113.0	585 622	21.3	78.7	68.4	36.3	3 220	77.7

Table B. States and Counties — Water Use, Wholesale Trade, Retail Trade, and Real Estate

STATE County	Water use, 2010		Wholesale trade,[1] 2012				Retail trade,[2] 2012				Real estate and rental and leasing,[2] 2012			
	Total water withdrawn (mil gal/day)	Gallons withdrawn per person per day	Number of establishments	Number of employees	Sales (mil dol)	Annual payroll (mil dol)	Number of establishments	Number of employees	Sales (mil dol)	Annual payroll (mil dol)	Number of establishments	Number of employees	Receipts (mil dol)	Annual payroll (mil dol)
	133	134	135	136	137	138	139	140	141	142	143	144	145	146
MISSOURI—Cont'd														
St. Louis city	91.5	286	452	7 692	5 916.4	423.3	923	9 422	2 471.9	231.1	411	2 432	1 003.0	102.5
MONTANA	7 645.2	7 727	1 288	13 034	12 645.8	577.1	4 831	55 418	15 623.6	1 346.5	1 726	5 207	835.4	162.3
Beaverhead	483.0	52 234	6	D	D	D	49	423	124.5	9.6	15	72	8.7	2.4
Big Horn	268.1	20 838	6	26	20.8	1.1	47	341	101.4	7.7	8	18	1.8	0.4
Blaine	236.4	36 426	11	53	197.2	1.6	21	165	46.9	3.3	2	D	D	D
Broadwater	192.4	34 284	7	28	17.7	1.3	15	131	77.7	3.1	1	D	D	D
Carbon	400.2	39 709	15	D	D	D	50	D	D	D	24	30	2.5	0.5
Carter	1.6	1 379	NA	NA	NA	NA	6	34	14.7	0.8	3	D	D	D
Cascade	166.9	2 052	112	D	D	D	352	4 859	1 359.7	117.4	121	349	62.1	9.8
Chouteau	42.1	7 242	15	79	195.8	3.0	22	114	46.8	2.5	4	3	0.5	0.0
Custer	151.5	12 950	19	161	64.3	5.3	54	806	256.7	21.1	16	23	3.3	0.5
Daniels	3.9	2 204	5	16	38.4	0.7	16	96	51.4	2.5	NA	NA	NA	NA
Dawson	79.0	8 810	17	181	323.9	6.9	47	493	151.8	11.9	12	41	11.3	3.2
Deer Lodge	39.6	4 259	1	D	D	D	28	290	75.2	6.2	8	14	1.0	0.3
Fallon	7.0	2 419	6	D	D	D	15	137	34.7	3.0	5	2	0.3	0.1
Fergus	50.0	4 316	15	D	D	D	65	464	150.3	11.0	21	53	6.0	1.1
Flathead	61.7	679	103	958	1 283.5	38.6	473	5 317	1 515.9	138.3	223	791	86.9	21.0
Gallatin	333.2	3 722	127	1 025	600.7	40.2	582	6 760	1 710.3	166.7	332	824	152.6	25.9
Garfield	4.5	3 706	NA	NA	NA	NA	6	78	13.1	1.0	NA	NA	NA	NA
Glacier	128.1	9 561	8	52	108.7	2.2	44	448	128.7	11.2	7	5	1.0	0.1
Golden Valley	39.6	44 830	1	D	D	D	1	D	D	D	NA	NA	NA	NA
Granite	72.0	23 368	3	16	5.8	0.7	19	101	24.3	1.9	3	D	D	D
Hill	10.8	673	26	221	367.1	9.3	88	1 029	286.4	23.9	24	64	7.1	1.4
Jefferson	91.0	7 979	8	30	13.6	1.3	28	185	51.7	3.5	7	13	0.7	0.2
Judith Basin	16.8	8 127	5	25	13.0	0.9	6	20	5.6	0.3	2	D	D	D
Lake	390.6	13 587	20	59	21.8	1.5	122	1 069	268.3	26.4	37	39	6.0	0.9
Lewis and Clark	154.1	2 430	63	516	332.7	21.3	276	3 735	998.6	91.5	98	315	68.3	11.9
Liberty	29.0	12 407	7	49	59.3	1.9	10	44	12.8	1.3	2	D	D	D
Lincoln	18.2	924	11	47	35.4	1.1	83	693	172.6	15.2	24	51	5.7	0.8
McCone	25.6	14 758	3	D	D	D	10	73	24.8	1.6	1	D	D	D
Madison	434.4	56 479	3	D	D	D	44	225	59.5	4.1	25	D	D	D
Meagher	217.2	114 839	1	D	D	D	13	64	14.3	1.0	2	D	D	D
Mineral	5.2	1 238	2	D	D	D	16	215	49.3	4.1	2	D	D	D
Missoula	85.6	783	151	1 838	1 220.7	81.5	570	7 931	2 044.0	180.0	206	918	130.6	29.7
Musselshell	73.5	16 197	4	14	6.7	0.5	19	186	42.0	3.2	3	D	D	D
Park	193.5	12 373	8	18	6.0	0.6	100	669	205.4	17.6	33	41	5.8	1.1
Petroleum	49.5	100 142	NA	NA	NA	NA	2	D	D	D	1	D	D	D
Phillips	244.2	57 409	4	44	98.9	1.8	26	212	39.2	4.0	3	2	1.0	0.1
Pondera	243.5	39 574	13	133	244.5	7.3	25	227	55.9	4.7	2	D	D	D
Powder River	31.4	18 038	1	D	D	D	12	107	24.6	1.9	2	D	D	D
Powell	138.4	19 695	2	D	D	D	18	181	46.0	5.1	4	7	1.1	0.2
Prairie	72.2	61 213	NA	NA	NA	NA	5	24	6.5	0.3	1	D	D	D
Ravalli	168.9	4 200	42	151	182.9	5.6	166	1 482	330.6	31.3	44	90	8.6	1.7
Richland	259.7	26 649	24	238	470.5	9.8	57	652	215.8	17.1	23	184	54.7	11.7
Roosevelt	86.4	8 289	10	D	D	D	41	530	159.2	11.0	10	23	1.0	0.2
Rosebud	195.7	21 190	1	D	D	D	28	240	56.4	4.4	7	26	8.1	0.7
Sanders	62.2	5 446	9	52	9.6	0.9	53	325	78.0	6.4	10	20	1.2	0.2
Sheridan	20.2	5 954	5	D	D	D	27	193	61.1	4.0	1	D	D	D
Silver Bow	40.7	1 191	37	348	189.3	14.3	172	2 203	610.1	51.7	47	137	15.1	3.2
Stillwater	87.0	9 540	5	14	74.9	0.9	33	243	103.2	4.7	4	8	1.0	0.1
Sweet Grass	154.1	42 205	4	22	2.9	0.5	21	139	39.5	2.8	6	9	1.4	0.2
Teton	427.0	70 308	11	48	114.0	1.8	27	190	69.7	4.9	5	D	D	D
Toole	8.6	1 619	9	50	222.3	3.0	24	221	83.5	5.2	8	15	1.6	0.2
Treasure	90.1	125 501	1	D	D	D	3	D	D	D	NA	NA	NA	NA
Valley	191.6	25 999	14	203	248.0	9.6	47	366	158.7	8.7	6	17	1.6	0.5
Wheatland	126.9	58 552	1	D	D	D	9	71	16.7	1.2	NA	NA	NA	NA
Wibaux	3.5	3 412	NA	NA	NA	NA	4	22	6.3	0.4	NA	NA	NA	NA
Yellowstone	437.5	2 956	306	4 690	3 193.3	231.3	734	10 298	3 272.2	277.7	271	914	164.3	30.2
NEBRASKA	8 036.3	4 400	2 720	34 409	42 619.0	1 675.4	7 279	105 953	30 470.7	2 440.4	2 001	10 068	1 732.0	388.5
Adams	128.1	4 083	63	703	949.4	32.0	144	1 876	453.3	42.7	60	131	24.2	2.9
Antelope	83.1	12 432	22	225	535.0	9.7	37	275	70.2	4.7	4	2	0.5	0.1
Arthur	5.5	11 935	NA	NA	NA	NA	2	D	D	D	NA	NA	NA	NA
Banner	17.5	25 333	NA	NA	NA	NA	NA	NA	NA	NA	NA	NA	NA	NA

1. Merchant wholesalers, except manufacturers' sales branches and offices. 2. Employer establishments.

Table B. States and Counties — Professional Services, Manufacturing, and Accommodation and Food Services

STATE County	Professional, scientific, and technical services, 2012				Manufacturing, 2012				Accommodation and food services, 2012			
	Number of establishments	Number of employees	Receipts (mil dol)	Annual payroll (mil dol)	Number of establishments	Number of employees	Receipts (mil dol)	Annual payroll (mil dol)	Number of establishments	Number of employees	Sales (mil dol)	Annual payroll (mil dol)
	147	148	149	150	151	152	153	154	155	156	157	158
MISSOURI—Cont'd												
St. Louis city	1 009	17 461	3 015.1	1 200.0	484	17 422	10 737.0	975.2	1 036	22 069	1 255.7	371.4
MONTANA	3 545	16 660	2 191.9	798.8	1 237	15 729	11 535.2	714.5	3 458	46 251	2 420.5	649.5
Beaverhead	25	72	5.3	1.5	13	37	6.8	1.2	48	425	18.3	5.0
Big Horn	15	39	3.0	1.2	3	15	D	D	27	234	17.2	3.5
Blaine	13	26	4.8	1.6	5	13	3.4	0.5	12	56	2.6	0.6
Broadwater	9	28	2.5	0.7	6	159	D	6.8	21	118	5.4	1.4
Carbon	28	D	D	D	10	D	D	D	51	490	24.8	7.4
Carter	5	9	0.6	0.1	NA	NA	NA	NA	2	D	D	D
Cascade	202	1 159	131.8	50.3	62	964	955.3	45.0	240	3 887	194.7	51.5
Chouteau	9	27	2.2	0.6	7	17	5.9	0.7	18	D	D	D
Custer	28	99	7.9	3.1	13	79	D	2.2	39	543	28.5	6.8
Daniels	3	D	D	D	NA	NA	NA	NA	9	D	D	D
Dawson	24	71	6.5	2.3	4	37	D	1.6	34	502	25.7	6.4
Deer Lodge	26	112	15.6	4.9	4	87	D	D	30	275	10.9	2.6
Fallon	9	16	2.3	0.5	3	9	D	D	18	104	6.9	1.4
Fergus	34	82	7.8	2.0	26	273	60.6	11.9	47	413	18.5	4.9
Flathead	375	1 347	184.6	56.1	182	2 367	620.8	105.3	363	4 362	247.9	67.7
Gallatin	655	2 415	298.0	113.5	188	2 363	491.0	99.5	410	7 193	348.1	96.5
Garfield	NA	NA	NA	NA	NA	NA	NA	NA	5	28	1.1	0.2
Glacier	11	64	6.8	1.8	4	20	2.3	0.5	51	335	38.3	8.7
Golden Valley	1	D	D	D	NA	NA	NA	NA	4	13	0.5	0.1
Granite	5	3	0.7	0.2	5	15	2.2	0.5	16	101	8.3	2.9
Hill	30	206	20.6	10.4	7	18	2.9	0.7	56	758	35.0	9.2
Jefferson	25	36	5.2	1.7	12	234	D	14.6	21	191	7.1	2.1
Judith Basin	4	11	2.1	0.3	NA	NA	NA	NA	10	27	1.4	0.3
Lake	52	352	71.8	20.2	35	497	72.4	15.4	76	630	33.5	8.6
Lewis and Clark	250	1 661	209.8	84.0	58	525	D	22.1	198	3 083	142.0	39.6
Liberty	4	10	0.6	0.2	NA	NA	NA	NA	5	32	0.7	0.2
Lincoln	35	84	8.2	2.5	24	137	16.8	4.0	64	488	26.4	7.3
McCone	1	D	D	D	NA	NA	NA	NA	5	18	0.6	0.1
Madison	28	60	5.5	1.9	11	69	D	1.8	55	220	15.8	4.0
Meagher	3	3	0.2	0.1	NA	NA	NA	NA	15	52	2.2	0.5
Mineral	6	37	2.7	1.1	7	200	D	7.6	19	120	4.8	1.4
Missoula	501	2 865	325.4	137.2	102	1 351	310.6	49.1	342	6 106	317.4	84.0
Musselshell	8	15	1.5	0.5	3	6	1.7	0.3	13	D	D	D
Park	74	181	23.7	7.6	29	338	58.9	14.1	118	1 130	75.2	22.3
Petroleum	1	D	D	D	NA	NA	NA	NA	2	D	D	D
Phillips	9	28	2.4	0.7	5	13	1.9	0.5	16	109	4.7	1.2
Pondera	10	36	3.0	1.2	8	89	D	3.1	16	141	4.8	1.2
Powder River	4	D	D	D	NA	NA	NA	NA	12	57	2.9	0.6
Powell	9	32	3.3	0.9	8	185	D	D	22	D	D	D
Prairie	4	5	0.8	0.3	NA	NA	NA	NA	6	19	0.6	0.1
Ravalli	122	514	27.3	25.5	84	703	132.4	25.7	96	841	38.4	11.6
Richland	40	228	46.6	13.6	12	371	D	14.6	44	569	38.4	8.9
Roosevelt	11	21	2.0	0.8	NA	NA	NA	NA	24	256	13.7	3.1
Rosebud	5	15	1.4	0.3	3	7	D	D	33	247	10.8	2.6
Sanders	24	35	3.5	0.9	20	185	37.6	6.4	39	320	12.5	3.6
Sheridan	11	28	3.3	1.1	NA	NA	NA	NA	15	137	6.9	1.7
Silver Bow	107	654	73.9	30.8	35	492	D	31.5	147	2 244	102.4	28.7
Stillwater	24	55	6.0	1.7	11	441	D	25.6	25	174	11.0	2.6
Sweet Grass	12	28	4.4	1.0	10	53	D	2.0	16	140	6.4	2.0
Teton	10	36	3.7	1.0	7	15	3.0	0.5	19	107	5.2	1.2
Toole	12	36	5.0	1.5	4	30	7.0	1.3	27	202	12.0	2.7
Treasure	2	D	D	D	NA	NA	NA	NA	4	13	0.4	0.1
Valley	19	75	6.5	2.5	6	39	D	1.0	34	367	16.4	4.4
Wheatland	3	7	1.4	0.2	NA	NA	NA	NA	11	54	3.5	0.6
Wibaux	4	8	0.8	0.4	NA	NA	NA	NA	4	37	1.5	0.5
Yellowstone	604	3 578	618.7	198.5	183	3 185	6 880.3	185.8	404	7 935	452.2	121.3
NEBRASKA	4 448	74 514	5 726.7	3 639.3	1 844	92 409	57 499.2	4 002.8	4 326	70 128	3 094.5	855.4
Adams	62	306	31.4	12.2	57	2 448	1 858.9	101.8	81	1 354	53.0	13.7
Antelope	12	29	4.6	1.1	9	85	D	4.1	15	D	D	D
Arthur	1	D	D	D	NA	NA	NA	NA	1	D	D	D
Banner	NA	NA	NA	NA	NA	NA	NA	NA	NA	NA	NA	NA

1. Establishment subject to federal tax.

Table B. States and Counties — Health Care and Social Assistance, Other Services, Nonemployer Businesses, and Residential Construction

STATE County	Health care and social assistance, 2012				Other services, 2012				Nonemployer businesses, 2015		Value of residential construction authorized by building permits, 2016	
	Number of establish-ments	Number of employees	Receipts (mil dol)	Annual payroll (mil dol)	Number of establish-ments	Number of employees	Receipts (mil dol)	Annual payroll (mil dol)	Number	Receipts (mil dol)	New Construction ($1,000)	Number of housing units
	159	160	161	162	163	164	165	166	167	168	169	170
MISSOURI—Cont'd												
St. Louis city	1 219	35 572	4 162.1	1 389.0	629	4 529	647.7	151.1	21 107	817.2	103 352	1 070
MONTANA	3 512	65 657	6 469.5	2 555.4	2 278	10 917	1 222.0	302.8	86 969	3 933.1	0	0
Beaverhead	40	487	41.1	19.0	21	58	4.0	1.0	878	35.8	391	3
Big Horn	21	D	D	D	9	22	2.3	0.6	509	18.5	355	2
Blaine	15	366	31.1	12.7	10	D	D	D	329	8.6	0	0
Broadwater	7	106	7.0	3.0	9	D	D	D	500	24.3	0	0
Carbon	32	D	D	D	20	D	D	D	1 126	48.6	1 413	8
Carter	2	D	D	D	2	D	D	D	114	6.0	23	1
Cascade	262	6 363	711.9	269.1	155	871	76.6	21.7	4 680	199.2	49 503	242
Chouteau	11	130	9.5	4.9	6	9	0.3	0.1	356	14.3	2 672	10
Custer	49	978	67.2	31.3	27	123	14.2	3.2	867	39.9	0	0
Daniels	4	D	D	D	5	D	D	D	145	6.9	0	0
Dawson	29	631	45.0	20.7	30	97	9.4	2.3	628	25.4	127	1
Deer Lodge	52	1 278	110.6	51.7	12	45	5.0	1.3	462	17.2	1 408	17
Fallon	5	D	D	D	9	21	3.6	0.7	347	14.4	3 810	35
Fergus	47	855	52.9	25.3	32	122	11.1	2.1	993	40.3	239	1
Flathead	339	5 537	572.5	232.6	227	937	87.1	22.7	10 306	495.9	60 951	316
Gallatin	385	4 387	437.5	173.1	269	1 314	155.9	40.3	12 078	586.0	334 198	1 550
Garfield	1	D	D	D	2	D	D	D	132	5.2	0	0
Glacier	18	962	55.3	22.5	17	85	28.6	2.7	740	27.2	0	0
Golden Valley	2	D	D	D	1	D	D	D	81	4.3	NA	NA
Granite	4	D	D	D	3	6	0.3	0.1	323	11.8	NA	NA
Hill	58	1 374	102.1	44.4	37	173	18.3	3.9	938	29.2	785	4
Jefferson	22	225	13.9	5.3	10	34	4.1	1.3	1 024	42.1	1 439	5
Judith Basin	3	6	0.1	0.0	1	D	D	D	182	7.4	NA	NA
Lake	77	1 182	98.1	43.7	50	141	11.0	2.9	2 321	89.3	8 209	44
Lewis and Clark	271	5 376	610.0	219.5	200	1 156	126.8	41.6	5 409	248.4	28 211	176
Liberty	3	D	D	D	3	D	D	D	143	5.2	NA	NA
Lincoln	56	866	60.1	27.3	36	114	10.5	2.5	1 565	60.8	745	8
McCone	3	D	D	D	2	D	D	D	170	5.8	0	0
Madison	19	141	12.3	5.2	15	D	D	D	997	39.5	1 851	7
Meagher	7	D	D	D	2	D	D	D	190	7.4	NA	NA
Mineral	13	145	8.7	4.9	7	4	1.4	0.3	325	9.8	274	1
Missoula	489	9 292	965.9	351.1	287	1 889	258.2	56.0	9 848	453.1	90 195	930
Musselshell	9	178	11.1	3.8	8	17	1.7	0.3	340	14.0	200	1
Park	55	850	60.0	27.7	49	181	16.3	4.8	2 115	84.1	7 150	44
Petroleum	1	D	D	D	1	D	D	D	38	1.6	NA	NA
Phillips	9	184	9.5	4.8	13	37	3.9	0.9	354	11.6	148	2
Pondera	18	317	20.9	9.1	12	28	3.1	0.5	447	15.3	250	1
Powder River	1	D	D	D	7	D	D	D	178	6.2	NA	NA
Powell	16	184	14.7	5.6	5	18	1.9	0.5	496	19.9	8 572	32
Prairie	3	D	D	D	2	D	D	D	81	3.1	NA	NA
Ravalli	133	1 459	103.3	46.0	81	246	22.3	5.2	4 324	184.2	2 629	20
Richland	32	676	59.1	21.2	30	117	12.6	3.4	917	48.0	5 713	16
Roosevelt	12	D	D	D	11	58	3.1	0.6	538	21.5	288	1
Rosebud	17	300	13.0	6.1	14	77	5.3	1.9	492	14.8	57	1
Sanders	39	407	28.1	12.0	14	60	5.4	1.2	1 065	42.4	0	0
Sheridan	12	366	18.0	7.9	9	20	3.2	0.6	333	14.7	575	2
Silver Bow	159	3 303	287.5	127.1	72	289	34.1	7.2	2 138	93.1	9 097	86
Stillwater	24	259	14.5	5.4	10	18	3.0	0.5	806	38.0	0	0
Sweet Grass	6	24	1.1	0.3	10	28	2.1	0.5	453	20.5	188	1
Teton	18	238	11.8	5.6	11	14	2.8	0.6	574	25.2	158	1
Toole	12	D	D	D	11	25	2.2	0.4	319	13.4	240	2
Treasure	1	D	D	D	1	D	D	D	53	1.2	0	0
Valley	24	603	43.1	19.5	20	63	6.9	1.5	522	18.6	787	4
Wheatland	4	D	D	D	3	5	0.3	0.1	163	5.5	NA	NA
Wibaux	3	D	D	D	NA	NA	NA	NA	76	2.8	1 099	8
Yellowstone	558	12 676	1 527.6	583.0	368	2 134	234.8	58.7	11 441	605.6	136 242	1 198
NEBRASKA	5 410	125 469	12 869.4	4 907.3	3 989	21 832	2 841.3	612.5	131 518	5 743.9	1 306 195	8 078
Adams	116	2 495	247.7	103.7	55	307	33.0	6.8	2 135	93.5	16 117	71
Antelope	15	305	22.9	8.8	20	40	4.5	0.8	654	25.7	100	1
Arthur	NA	NA	NA	NA	2	D	D	D	45	3.6	NA	NA
Banner	NA	NA	NA	NA	1	D	D	D	41	1.6	NA	NA

Table B. States and Counties — Government Employment and Payroll, and Local Government Finances

	Government employment and payroll, 2012									Local government finances, 2012				
			March payroll (percent of total)							General revenue				
												Taxes		
													Per capita[1] (dollars)	
STATE County	Full-time equivalent employees	March payroll (dollars)	Administration, judicial, and legal	Police and Corrections	Fire Protection	Highways and transportation	Health and Welfare	Natural resources and utilities	Education and libraries	Total (mil dol)	Inter-governmental (mil dol)	Total (mil dol)	Total	Property
	171	172	173	174	175	176	177	178	179	180	181	182	183	184
MISSOURI—Cont'd														
St. Louis city	15 033	62 103 817	5.6	17.2	5.7	20.6	1.5	12.9	34.1	2 385.3	762.8	924.8	2 907	1 228
MONTANA	X	X	X	X	X	X	X	X	X	X	X	X	X	X
Beaverhead	518	1 862 160	5.1	4.6	0.4	2.9	54.8	1.7	29.5	66.4	12.9	10.3	1 104	1 099
Big Horn	748	2 839 698	3.5	4.0	0.0	3.4	4.1	1.1	82.8	62.2	38.7	13.7	1 049	1 040
Blaine	358	1 163 514	11.3	3.8	0.0	6.0	0.6	3.7	73.6	31.5	20.8	7.2	1 083	1 053
Broadwater	160	477 725	12.8	12.5	0.0	5.0	4.9	1.1	62.3	14.4	6.3	5.4	935	924
Carbon	377	1 229 196	11.7	8.3	1.5	6.6	1.7	4.4	62.9	33.2	13.2	15.7	1 547	1 457
Carter	67	178 052	5.5	6.2	0.0	11.1	1.6	2.3	58.2	7.1	3.5	2.6	2 229	2 201
Cascade	2 704	9 771 107	6.8	13.0	3.8	5.6	3.7	6.9	59.0	238.3	103.2	77.2	944	913
Chouteau	318	956 267	6.0	6.6	0.0	4.7	29.2	2.6	49.0	26.4	10.3	9.2	1 565	1 560
Custer	539	1 661 688	7.8	7.4	3.4	4.8	3.2	3.6	68.6	42.2	19.5	9.9	832	817
Daniels	99	271 126	13.7	7.5	0.1	5.3	5.9	3.5	61.2	10.7	3.8	5.1	2 865	1 845
Dawson	486	1 501 541	7.2	15.3	1.5	5.5	7.5	3.6	57.4	42.3	16.8	12.8	1 387	1 374
Deer Lodge	264	898 579	8.3	14.8	4.3	3.9	1.1	6.9	59.7	28.1	15.5	7.9	855	847
Fallon	190	709 670	11.6	5.6	3.4	9.5	5.9	6.1	55.5	33.9	25.4	5.0	1 645	1 614
Fergus	520	1 621 405	6.8	8.4	2.1	15.7	1.2	2.9	61.6	43.5	22.6	14.7	1 286	1 268
Flathead	2 820	10 913 778	6.6	7.4	3.2	3.5	3.5	3.7	70.8	292.8	116.8	111.5	1 216	1 179
Gallatin	2 434	9 405 208	8.1	11.0	3.8	2.9	5.0	5.6	60.7	253.4	77.2	121.2	1 309	1 215
Garfield	115	230 472	8.7	3.3	2.9	6.0	24.2	7.0	41.9	7.0	2.6	2.3	1 862	1 861
Glacier	700	2 311 773	4.2	4.6	0.0	3.2	3.2	2.5	81.1	52.7	34.1	13.8	1 008	1 004
Golden Valley	58	147 171	10.6	3.5	0.0	4.0	0.0	0.3	80.9	4.9	2.7	1.9	2 302	2 299
Granite	179	573 451	9.2	4.8	0.0	3.8	33.5	2.9	44.5	15.4	5.5	4.2	1 364	1 358
Hill	793	2 599 436	4.3	6.6	2.9	3.9	3.3	3.7	74.5	62.6	35.3	17.8	1 085	1 070
Jefferson	303	957 909	14.8	9.2	0.0	4.0	5.0	1.6	64.0	29.3	15.5	10.6	927	924
Judith Basin	121	355 407	6.9	3.6	0.0	13.7	0.1	1.1	72.7	9.7	4.7	3.9	1 915	1 915
Lake	962	3 993 744	4.2	5.9	0.2	1.6	3.5	2.9	80.7	85.3	44.4	27.2	940	933
Lewis and Clark	1 872	7 755 463	7.5	9.0	2.6	3.9	8.6	5.4	59.9	213.1	82.3	69.8	1 076	1 054
Liberty	111	316 696	12.4	8.7	0.0	7.1	6.6	4.8	58.9	8.2	3.8	3.3	1 372	1 372
Lincoln	599	1 992 630	12.4	7.4	0.5	3.8	2.7	4.3	65.2	57.6	31.7	14.9	766	754
McCone	168	326 681	15.1	4.8	0.1	1.2	1.9	4.1	42.3	8.6	3.2	4.3	2 540	2 486
Madison	459	1 488 288	7.5	4.1	0.2	3.8	40.5	2.0	39.5	41.8	10.9	17.1	2 205	2 194
Meagher	122	326 266	10.3	7.3	0.0	3.7	0.0	4.5	46.8	8.8	3.1	3.4	1 746	1 742
Mineral	297	957 709	7.9	6.9	0.3	1.9	33.5	1.3	47.5	23.2	8.6	6.0	1 442	1 403
Missoula	3 035	11 623 602	8.8	11.6	6.2	6.3	5.7	3.6	55.2	333.0	140.7	131.9	1 189	1 156
Musselshell	259	845 308	4.5	3.3	0.0	3.2	25.2	1.6	61.7	22.2	9.1	7.4	1 596	1 532
Park	528	1 727 963	10.9	8.8	4.3	3.4	4.6	4.7	62.0	50.7	22.2	18.0	1 154	1 123
Petroleum	36	121 984	11.4	0.0	0.0	5.5	0.0	6.6	74.9	4.7	3.4	0.9	1 705	1 703
Phillips	229	653 111	10.8	5.9	0.1	6.4	3.3	8.6	61.5	21.3	11.3	6.4	1 542	1 503
Pondera	212	607 909	10.4	10.1	0.2	5.9	1.8	7.3	62.5	34.1	12.3	7.0	1 132	1 127
Powder River	137	334 388	14.5	7.2	0.0	8.8	27.7	1.7	37.3	12.1	5.0	3.7	2 074	1 968
Powell	199	625 409	10.4	7.0	0.5	5.1	2.6	2.8	69.0	21.5	10.6	6.4	906	902
Prairie	95	225 508	8.2	3.7	0.0	5.1	32.5	1.7	42.7	7.5	2.4	1.9	1 617	1 608
Ravalli	1 130	3 297 468	9.0	9.9	0.2	2.5	1.0	3.9	72.3	96.2	49.5	36.0	885	874
Richland	560	1 708 186	7.9	8.6	0.2	7.8	4.4	8.1	58.4	72.7	47.2	9.4	866	853
Roosevelt	704	2 186 188	5.4	5.6	0.2	3.3	10.8	2.9	70.0	63.5	42.5	12.7	1 161	1 154
Rosebud	641	1 932 124	5.8	8.0	0.0	6.1	4.9	5.7	68.6	65.9	31.0	16.0	1 705	1 689
Sanders	390	1 112 745	8.1	9.8	0.3	5.2	3.6	1.9	69.3	33.6	16.5	12.8	1 123	1 122
Sheridan	333	1 098 598	7.7	3.6	1.6	5.2	44.9	1.5	34.4	19.8	10.2	5.6	1 551	1 542
Silver Bow	995	3 780 881	7.3	11.3	8.8	7.4	1.2	11.1	51.5	120.3	54.8	39.2	1 139	1 112
Stillwater	340	1 123 218	10.5	6.8	1.0	7.0	2.4	1.8	70.1	29.0	12.6	12.5	1 360	1 350
Sweet Grass	197	563 456	9.7	3.8	0.0	3.5	28.6	2.5	49.1	22.0	6.9	6.1	1 698	1 696
Teton	434	1 416 652	5.6	3.0	0.1	2.9	31.7	6.4	49.4	34.6	11.1	9.4	1 552	1 512
Toole	386	1 266 882	7.5	5.0	0.0	3.8	44.2	2.8	34.4	36.1	9.0	7.8	1 492	1 473
Treasure	44	114 460	17.8	4.4	0.0	4.5	6.2	7.2	53.1	3.7	1.5	1.7	2 261	2 258
Valley	402	1 205 227	6.6	9.6	0.0	6.9	3.9	4.9	66.3	36.1	17.0	11.6	1 551	1 486
Wheatland	160	440 257	19.4	6.3	0.0	12.1	3.4	4.6	49.3	9.4	4.2	4.2	1 974	1 965
Wibaux	61	199 748	22.1	5.7	0.0	16.7	2.2	0.8	52.4	6.8	4.9	1.2	1 174	1 124
Yellowstone	4 840	19 590 185	5.0	8.6	4.7	4.9	8.9	6.0	55.1	469.5	175.3	161.7	1 065	989
NEBRASKA	X	X	X	X	X	X	X	X	X	X	X	X	X	X
Adams	2 340	8 844 524	2.4	3.7	1.5	2.0	0.5	13.9	70.2	174.2	49.6	89.6	2 849	2 506
Antelope	558	1 836 977	2.9	2.2	0.0	3.6	29.5	1.6	60.0	30.0	8.2	17.8	2 718	2 366
Arthur	35	130 066	6.4	2.0	0.0	4.7	0.0	27.0	59.3	5.8	0.9	4.6	9 488	9 335
Banner	61	179 960	9.3	1.7	0.0	7.8	0.0	0.0	79.6	4.4	1.3	2.8	3 726	3 499

1. Based on the resident population estimated as of July 1 of the year shown.

Table B. States and Counties — Local Government Finances, Government Employment, and Income Taxes

STATE County	Local government finances, 2012 (cont.) Direct general expenditure Total (mil dol)	Per capita[1] (dollars)	Education	Health and hospitals	Police protection	Public welfare	High-ways	Debt outstanding Total (mil dol)	Per capita[1] (dollars)	Government employment, 2015 Federal civilian	Federal military	State and local	Individual income tax returns, 2014 Number of returns	Mean adjusted gross income	Mean income tax
	185	186	187	188	189	190	191	192	193	194	195	196	197	198	199
MISSOURI—Cont'd															
St. Louis city	2 326.2	7 311	33.4	1.7	10.8	0.0	1.1	3 993.6	12 552	13 933	1 572	21 084	147 330	44 252	5 399
MONTANA	X	X	X	X	X	X	X	X	X	13 055	7 857	74 814	491 930	55 162	6 641
Beaverhead	83.3	8 915	24.9	55.9	2.2	0.0	3.8	91.0	9 739	193	41	846	4 370	47 345	5 063
Big Horn	70.6	5 404	65.3	1.6	3.9	0.0	4.8	34.0	2 603	386	61	1 994	4 670	40 308	3 401
Blaine	33.0	4 932	63.3	2.3	5.1	0.0	8.2	3.4	513	175	29	480	2 650	36 683	3 437
Broadwater	14.1	2 447	49.7	2.6	9.1	0.2	5.3	4.7	809	43	26	199	2 500	52 638	5 210
Carbon	34.2	3 380	55.4	0.7	7.0	0.2	11.0	23.7	2 339	72	48	507	4 960	55 427	6 700
Carter	7.6	6 469	34.7	9.5	5.5	0.1	25.5	0.4	371	13	D	97	560	50 313	4 073
Cascade	242.5	2 968	53.0	1.0	9.7	1.4	5.2	90.0	1 101	1 639	3 466	4 070	40 090	49 525	5 350
Chouteau	26.7	4 530	44.1	21.5	3.3	0.0	8.4	4.1	697	36	26	424	2 280	46 536	4 291
Custer	40.6	3 415	62.2	2.4	7.6	0.1	8.1	9.5	801	197	54	855	5 730	55 933	7 330
Daniels	9.9	5 552	39.1	7.1	5.2	0.0	8.9	3.2	1 792	14	D	117	890	53 038	5 740
Dawson	38.5	4 159	54.9	3.1	5.4	1.0	7.1	8.2	884	32	42	691	4 640	59 592	7 886
Deer Lodge	30.1	3 259	41.6	2.0	6.6	2.8	4.8	4.9	531	81	38	911	4 180	43 700	4 029
Fallon	38.0	12 574	45.8	4.0	2.8	0.0	17.5	0.2	57	13	15	281	1 520	81 834	11 973
Fergus	44.0	3 847	53.6	2.3	4.8	0.0	11.5	9.5	831	142	51	879	5 670	51 522	5 755
Flathead	299.8	3 272	56.2	3.9	5.8	1.2	5.0	178.9	1 952	746	441	4 182	46 770	53 138	6 340
Gallatin	262.4	2 834	48.1	1.3	10.1	4.2	4.1	247.8	2 676	578	462	9 104	50 960	63 478	8 697
Garfield	7.3	5 772	36.8	2.4	2.5	23.3	14.2	0.6	450	23	D	119	540	49 889	4 507
Glacier	51.7	3 768	77.0	2.8	4.0	0.1	4.7	22.4	1 630	430	60	1 905	5 210	35 414	2 890
Golden Valley	4.5	5 323	65.4	0.9	4.3	0.5	4.7	0.0	5	D	D	70	460	45 274	4 450
Granite	15.6	5 012	35.1	0.6	6.3	26.8	7.6	2.0	654	35	15	214	1 340	49 183	5 484
Hill	62.8	3 840	76.1	0.8	4.8	0.0	3.2	16.7	1 020	158	74	2 016	7 680	47 420	4 759
Jefferson	31.9	2 799	57.0	3.8	8.3	0.0	5.0	4.6	400	41	53	726	5 380	61 768	7 057
Judith Basin	9.6	4 741	53.8	0.9	3.4	0.0	18.1	3.4	1 658	33	D	148	940	49 296	5 062
Lake	86.4	2 980	61.8	0.9	5.2	0.3	4.0	23.2	799	111	134	2 838	12 310	43 728	4 356
Lewis and Clark	212.2	3 270	47.9	4.1	8.6	3.1	5.3	156.7	2 415	1 945	312	8 980	33 070	57 586	6 477
Liberty	7.9	3 293	47.0	5.3	10.3	0.0	12.1	1.8	772	19	D	121	970	42 243	3 898
Lincoln	58.1	2 979	51.4	6.8	7.7	0.1	7.8	18.2	932	423	87	724	7 900	43 563	4 140
McCone	8.6	5 082	52.1	3.7	4.1	0.8	13.0	2.4	1 422	19	D	135	900	37 739	3 572
Madison	42.1	5 447	35.2	13.7	4.0	18.5	7.6	7.0	907	60	36	487	3 710	58 728	7 748
Meagher	10.9	5 666	29.5	3.3	0.7	0.0	6.7	0.3	179	29	D	113	810	44 106	3 836
Mineral	24.9	5 975	42.3	33.5	3.9	0.0	3.9	5.6	1 346	53	20	282	1 890	40 313	3 687
Missoula	338.7	3 052	44.0	5.5	7.0	0.8	5.2	188.8	1 701	1 349	520	9 354	55 820	58 631	7 528
Musselshell	23.0	4 926	37.1	29.7	2.1	0.0	4.3	1.8	390	14	21	267	1 990	48 796	5 425
Park	60.3	3 873	58.7	2.2	5.8	0.5	3.5	26.2	1 681	70	74	676	8 500	47 907	5 409
Petroleum	4.6	8 926	53.5	1.5	1.5	0.0	8.0	0.4	812	D	D	52	200	41 315	3 825
Phillips	22.5	5 449	53.5	1.7	4.2	0.0	11.5	7.9	1 903	81	19	303	1 980	42 013	3 808
Pondera	34.1	5 531	42.2	35.4	3.5	1.5	3.2	14.5	2 348	33	26	372	3 010	39 384	3 563
Powder River	12.1	6 877	33.4	1.6	5.0	22.2	16.5	0.1	69	11	D	190	840	51 660	5 451
Powell	23.3	3 289	58.1	0.9	6.4	0.4	8.2	1.7	234	79	25	1 022	2 740	42 345	3 789
Prairie	7.4	6 390	28.9	2.4	3.9	29.4	8.6	2.0	1 732	36	D	140	540	50 522	4 929
Ravalli	99.9	2 460	64.0	1.1	7.3	0.5	5.0	31.4	773	529	190	1 391	19 180	50 017	5 660
Richland	76.0	7 032	41.5	1.4	4.3	0.9	22.5	6.1	568	75	55	713	6 300	85 238	13 960
Roosevelt	58.9	5 389	63.9	10.7	5.5	0.5	4.5	9.1	836	171	52	1 542	4 360	49 729	5 791
Rosebud	68.3	7 269	51.2	7.9	4.8	0.3	4.7	257.2	27 372	237	43	1 452	4 010	52 054	5 286
Sanders	36.1	3 162	60.5	4.1	6.1	0.0	8.2	4.9	428	135	52	503	4 850	39 302	3 853
Sheridan	21.8	6 087	50.6	2.2	6.1	1.6	16.8	1.9	517	67	17	262	2 030	61 932	8 002
Silver Bow	113.4	3 297	39.5	4.4	5.9	0.1	4.1	60.4	1 757	215	194	2 258	16 430	49 743	5 534
Stillwater	30.5	3 315	64.5	0.6	4.5	0.1	6.8	2.6	287	34	43	453	4 350	60 873	6 720
Sweet Grass	22.6	6 259	30.6	0.8	5.2	32.8	6.0	1.4	398	32	17	311	1 710	51 473	4 709
Teton	35.3	5 826	43.7	23.0	0.8	4.8	5.1	8.3	1 372	57	26	462	3 030	45 699	4 517
Toole	36.4	6 970	29.7	40.6	6.4	0.0	6.6	14.4	2 766	154	20	482	2 360	46 971	5 215
Treasure	3.8	5 182	44.6	5.5	3.4	0.1	10.4	0.5	679	D	D	52	380	49 729	4 624
Valley	35.4	4 717	51.9	2.2	5.0	0.1	10.3	8.7	1 160	158	35	619	3 780	52 014	6 119
Wheatland	8.9	4 252	54.8	5.6	6.4	0.1	6.6	3.2	1 505	15	D	130	890	46 264	4 257
Wibaux	6.5	6 114	36.4	10.7	5.5	0.0	16.1	1.2	1 157	D	D	145	480	53 015	5 146
Yellowstone	506.3	3 333	47.8	7.1	5.8	0.2	6.1	224.5	1 478	1 740	749	7 148	76 850	62 553	8 150
NEBRASKA	X	X	X	X	X	X	X	X	X	16 697	12 491	145 267	889 030	61 734	7 722
Adams	180.4	5 735	72.7	0.4	3.1	0.2	6.2	136.0	4 322	106	107	2 272	14 580	57 284	6 974
Antelope	34.5	5 275	71.6	0.0	2.2	0.0	12.9	7.4	1 136	29	23	452	2 970	55 026	6 712
Arthur	4.1	8 356	45.4	0.2	0.8	0.0	11.7	0.0	0	D	D	53	190	45 958	3 653
Banner	4.4	5 725	68.1	0.3	1.3	0.0	14.7	0.0	0	D	D	67	300	45 013	3 583

1. Based on the resident population estimated as of July 1 of the year shown.

STATE/ County code	CBSA code[1]	County type[2]	STATE County	Population, 2016				Population and population characteristics, 2016										
								Race alone or in combination, not Hispanic or Latino (percent)					Age (percent)					
				Land area,[3] (sq mi) 2016	Total persons 2016	Rank	Per square mile	White	Black	American Indian, Alaska Native	Asian and Pacific Islander	Percent Hispanic or Latino[4]	Under 5 years	5 to 17 years	18 to 24 years	25 to 34 years	35 to 44 years	45 to 54 years
				1	2	3	4	5	6	7	8	9	10	11	12	13	14	15
			NEBRASKA—Cont'd															
31 009	...	9	Blaine	710.7	484	3 137	0.7	97.9	1.2	0.8	0.0	1.7	5.8	14.9	8.1	8.3	8.1	12.8
31 011	...	9	Boone	686.6	5 332	2 810	7.8	97.0	0.8	0.5	0.2	2.0	6.2	17.2	7.9	10.3	9.5	11.7
31 013	...	7	Box Butte	1 075.3	11 194	2 343	10.4	83.6	1.4	3.7	0.9	12.3	7.5	18.0	7.7	11.5	11.5	10.2
31 015	...	9	Boyd	539.9	1 982	3 049	3.7	95.8	0.2	1.5	0.9	2.2	4.2	15.7	7.8	6.4	9.3	10.6
31 017	...	9	Brown	1 221.4	2 960	2 974	2.4	97.3	0.7	1.4	0.4	1.5	5.0	16.4	7.3	8.8	9.9	12.4
31 019	28260	4	Buffalo	968.1	49 383	992	51.0	88.0	1.5	0.6	2.0	9.0	7.1	16.4	15.8	13.7	11.4	10.5
31 021	...	8	Burt	491.6	6 546	2 709	13.3	94.8	0.8	2.3	0.7	2.6	5.6	16.3	6.7	10.0	9.4	12.6
31 023	...	6	Butler	584.9	8 052	2 593	13.8	95.6	0.7	0.6	0.6	3.2	5.7	17.6	7.5	9.5	10.6	13.2
31 025	36540	2	Cass	557.4	25 767	1 572	46.2	95.4	1.0	1.1	0.9	3.0	5.9	18.3	7.3	10.2	12.2	13.9
31 027	...	9	Cedar	740.3	8 671	2 534	11.7	97.5	0.4	0.8	0.4	1.9	6.8	18.2	7.8	9.0	9.5	11.9
31 029	...	9	Chase	894.4	3 937	2 906	4.4	86.5	0.4	0.3	0.4	13.0	5.6	19.3	6.4	10.3	10.7	11.6
31 031	...	7	Cherry	5 960.5	5 832	2 766	1.0	91.4	0.9	7.0	0.9	2.9	7.0	15.6	7.5	10.3	11.4	11.7
31 033	...	7	Cheyenne	1 196.3	10 051	2 431	8.4	90.9	0.8	1.4	1.5	6.6	6.3	17.6	7.1	13.5	11.8	13.1
31 035	...	8	Clay	572.3	6 163	2 740	10.8	89.8	0.7	0.8	0.5	9.2	6.5	17.9	7.5	10.1	10.3	12.3
31 037	...	7	Colfax	411.6	10 414	2 395	25.3	51.0	3.3	0.6	0.7	45.0	8.5	22.1	8.5	12.7	11.5	11.7
31 039	...	7	Cuming	570.6	9 016	2 508	15.8	89.0	0.6	0.7	0.6	10.2	6.3	18.2	7.6	10.1	9.6	12.4
31 041	...	7	Custer	2 575.6	10 807	2 371	4.2	95.8	0.9	0.9	0.4	3.1	6.5	17.0	7.1	10.4	10.4	12.3
31 043	43580	3	Dakota	264.3	20 465	1 802	77.4	51.1	4.6	3.1	4.0	38.8	8.6	20.2	9.7	12.6	11.5	12.1
31 045	...	7	Dawes	1 396.5	8 979	2 510	6.4	87.6	2.3	4.5	2.9	5.1	5.1	13.0	23.8	9.4	9.1	9.6
31 047	30420	7	Dawson	1 013.1	23 640	1 655	23.3	60.9	4.9	0.8	1.2	33.0	8.0	19.6	8.4	12.5	11.6	11.7
31 049	...	9	Deuel	439.9	1 873	3 060	4.3	92.5	0.3	1.7	0.5	5.9	5.1	15.8	6.0	9.2	9.0	13.8
31 051	43580	3	Dixon	476.2	5 762	2 771	12.1	86.1	0.7	0.7	0.4	12.8	6.6	18.3	7.9	9.6	10.8	11.6
31 053	23340	4	Dodge	528.7	36 757	1 257	69.5	85.8	1.3	0.8	1.0	12.1	6.7	17.0	9.2	10.9	11.5	12.2
31 055	36540	2	Douglas	328.5	554 995	121	1 689.5	72.0	12.4	1.1	4.5	12.4	7.7	18.2	9.2	15.7	13.1	12.3
31 057	...	9	Dundy	919.7	1 831	3 066	2.0	89.7	1.2	0.9	0.8	9.0	4.2	15.5	8.4	8.0	10.4	11.9
31 059	...	8	Fillmore	575.4	5 720	2 778	9.9	94.3	0.7	0.8	0.9	3.9	5.2	14.6	7.2	10.7	9.6	12.9
31 061	...	9	Franklin	575.8	3 014	2 969	5.2	96.9	0.6	0.9	0.4	2.4	4.5	14.5	7.2	9.1	9.2	11.5
31 063	...	9	Frontier	974.6	2 621	2 996	2.7	97.0	0.5	0.9	0.5	2.2	5.1	14.8	11.4	10.1	9.8	10.6
31 065	...	9	Furnas	719.1	4 787	2 848	6.7	94.5	0.8	0.8	0.6	4.2	5.5	16.7	7.3	9.0	9.6	11.8
31 067	13100	6	Gage	851.5	21 799	1 736	25.6	96.0	1.0	1.1	0.8	2.3	5.8	16.4	7.3	10.3	11.0	13.1
31 069	...	9	Garden	1 704.3	1 930	3 055	1.1	93.0	0.7	1.6	0.7	5.5	5.1	13.8	5.3	9.9	8.3	11.9
31 071	...	9	Garfield	569.8	2 011	3 047	3.5	98.0	0.4	0.2	0.1	1.6	4.8	14.1	7.4	8.2	8.8	10.5
31 073	30420	9	Gosper	458.2	1 971	3 050	4.3	93.2	1.4	0.9	0.6	5.4	5.1	17.4	6.2	10.3	9.6	13.2
31 075	...	9	Grant	776.2	641	3 131	0.8	98.1	0.3	0.8	0.6	1.2	5.9	15.8	5.3	12.5	8.6	13.1
31 077	...	8	Greeley	569.8	2 399	3 015	4.2	96.8	1.3	0.3	0.4	2.0	5.8	17.5	6.6	9.1	9.3	11.7
31 079	24260	3	Hall	546.3	61 705	849	113.0	68.7	2.9	0.7	1.6	27.1	7.6	19.6	8.7	12.9	12.3	12.2
31 081	24260	3	Hamilton	541.9	9 186	2 494	17.0	95.5	0.6	0.6	0.5	3.6	5.9	18.3	8.0	10.7	11.1	13.1
31 083	...	9	Harlan	553.5	3 473	2 941	6.3	96.7	0.7	0.7	0.4	2.3	5.3	16.6	6.4	8.2	9.2	11.7
31 085	...	9	Hayes	713.1	897	3 112	1.3	95.2	0.3	0.3	0.7	3.8	5.8	12.9	7.0	10.1	7.7	9.5
31 087	...	9	Hitchcock	709.9	2 825	2 986	4.0	95.2	0.6	0.9	0.7	3.8	6.1	16.7	5.7	8.8	11.0	11.3
31 089	...	7	Holt	2 412.4	10 250	2 408	4.2	94.0	0.5	0.7	0.7	4.8	7.2	17.6	7.0	9.2	9.6	11.6
31 091	...	9	Hooker	721.2	708	3 127	1.0	96.3	0.1	0.8	0.3	3.1	6.2	16.1	5.6	7.3	10.2	7.8
31 093	24260	3	Howard	569.3	6 429	2 721	11.3	96.5	0.7	0.7	0.5	2.5	6.9	17.3	6.6	9.9	11.5	12.9
31 095	...	7	Jefferson	570.2	7 177	2 653	12.6	95.4	0.8	0.9	0.5	3.5	5.2	16.4	6.4	10.1	10.2	11.8
31 097	...	8	Johnson	376.1	5 171	2 820	13.7	81.0	6.3	1.5	1.5	10.4	4.5	15.3	7.8	13.6	13.2	14.4
31 099	28260	7	Kearney	516.2	6 552	2 708	12.7	92.9	0.5	0.5	0.5	6.2	6.2	18.1	7.3	10.9	11.4	12.6
31 101	...	7	Keith	1 061.6	8 018	2 597	7.6	91.6	1.0	1.2	0.9	6.8	5.3	15.2	7.0	10.0	9.7	12.4
31 103	...	9	Keya Paha	773.1	791	3 118	1.0	98.4	0.1	0.9	0.4	0.6	4.6	15.2	6.1	7.7	10.0	10.4
31 105	...	8	Kimball	951.8	3 679	2 925	3.9	88.5	0.9	2.5	1.5	8.7	5.8	16.5	7.1	10.2	9.5	12.2
31 107	...	7	Knox	1 108.4	8 571	2 543	7.7	87.7	0.8	9.8	0.7	2.7	6.7	17.8	6.9	8.4	9.3	11.5
31 109	30700	2	Lancaster	837.5	309 637	220	369.7	84.1	5.2	1.1	5.3	6.8	6.5	16.5	15.3	14.0	12.1	11.1
31 111	35820	5	Lincoln	2 564.1	35 550	1 289	13.9	89.2	1.3	1.0	1.3	8.4	6.1	17.8	7.7	11.4	12.2	12.2
31 113	35820	9	Logan	570.7	772	3 122	1.4	96.5	0.6	1.7	0.8	1.6	7.1	20.3	6.5	9.1	13.2	10.6
31 115	...	9	Loup	568.3	591	3 134	1.0	95.9	0.5	0.2	0.3	3.0	5.2	13.7	7.3	8.6	8.1	11.0
31 117	35820	9	McPherson	859.0	493	3 135	0.6	97.2	2.0	0.0	0.0	2.4	3.4	19.5	7.7	7.1	9.1	15.4
31 119	35740	5	Madison	572.7	35 015	1 303	61.1	81.7	2.0	1.5	1.7	14.6	7.2	17.5	9.6	12.9	11.2	11.7
31 121	24260	3	Merrick	485.9	7 828	2 609	16.1	93.6	0.8	1.1	1.4	4.2	6.3	16.9	7.7	11.0	11.4	13.0
31 123	...	9	Morrill	1 423.8	4 787	2 848	3.4	82.5	0.6	1.3	0.8	15.8	6.2	18.3	6.9	10.5	12.0	12.7
31 125	...	8	Nance	441.6	3 576	2 937	8.1	97.0	0.6	0.8	0.2	2.2	5.5	17.4	7.2	9.8	10.9	12.0
31 127	...	7	Nemaha	407.4	6 971	2 674	17.1	95.0	1.6	0.8	0.8	3.0	5.9	15.6	12.8	11.7	10.1	11.1
31 129	...	9	Nuckolls	575.2	4 265	2 879	7.4	96.1	0.4	0.7	0.7	3.0	4.6	15.6	7.0	8.7	10.0	11.0
31 131	...	6	Otoe	615.6	16 081	2 034	26.1	90.4	1.2	0.8	1.0	7.7	6.5	17.0	7.6	10.6	11.3	12.8
31 133	...	9	Pawnee	431.1	2 652	2 994	6.2	97.1	1.2	0.8	0.7	1.8	6.0	16.0	7.1	8.3	8.7	11.7
31 135	...	9	Perkins	883.3	2 898	2 980	3.3	94.9	0.6	0.3	0.3	4.3	7.1	17.9	5.9	9.9	11.2	10.2
31 137	...	7	Phelps	539.8	9 266	2 487	17.2	93.2	0.7	0.7	0.7	5.6	6.2	18.1	8.1	10.9	10.5	12.6
31 139	35740	9	Pierce	573.2	7 159	2 656	12.5	97.1	0.7	0.7	0.5	1.8	6.0	18.6	7.4	10.4	11.1	13.3

1. CBSA = Core Based Statistical Area. See Appendix A for explanation. See Appendix B for list of metropolitan areas with component counties. 2. County type code from the Economic Research Service of USDA Rural-Urban Continuum Codes. See Appendix A for definition. 3. Dry land or land partially or temporarily covered by water. 4. May be of any race.

STATE County	Age (percent) (cont.) 55 to 64 years	65 to 74 years	75 years and over	Percent female	Total persons 2000	2010	Percent change 2000–2010	2010–2016	Components of change, 2010–2016 Births	Deaths	Net migration	Households, 2011–2015 Number	Persons per household	Family households	Female family householder[1]	One person
	16	17	18	19	20	21	22	23	24	25	26	27	28	29	30	31
NEBRASKA—Cont'd																
Blaine	16.3	14.5	11.4	48.1	583	478	-18.0	1.3	35	29	-11	231	2.39	70.6	5.2	23.8
Boone	16.0	10.0	11.2	49.8	6 259	5 505	-12.0	-3.1	389	401	-134	2 227	2.37	69.1	6.8	28.4
Box Butte	16.3	9.9	7.4	50.2	12 158	11 308	-7.0	-1.0	977	701	-370	4 805	2.31	66.4	6.8	29.5
Boyd	16.3	15.7	13.9	50.6	2 438	2 099	-13.9	-5.6	107	177	-45	935	2.15	59.9	3.2	38.4
Brown	16.3	11.4	12.5	51.7	3 525	3 143	-10.8	-5.8	169	240	-96	1 511	2.00	63.7	9.6	32.8
Buffalo	11.4	7.6	6.0	50.1	42 259	46 102	9.1	7.1	4 391	2 124	960	18 352	2.49	63.0	8.9	26.4
Burt	15.8	11.1	12.5	50.6	7 791	6 858	-12.0	-4.5	437	600	-163	2 801	2.33	67.0	6.0	29.1
Butler	15.0	10.9	10.1	49.8	8 767	8 395	-4.2	-4.1	559	619	-270	3 577	2.26	69.0	7.0	27.0
Cass	15.3	10.2	6.8	49.7	24 334	25 241	3.7	2.1	1 784	1 472	244	9 756	2.57	71.8	7.1	24.3
Cedar	15.3	10.1	11.3	49.6	9 615	8 852	-7.9	-2.0	670	628	-230	3 575	2.39	68.5	4.7	28.3
Chase	15.5	9.7	10.9	50.9	4 068	3 966	-2.5	-0.7	285	319	13	1 701	2.25	68.3	5.1	27.1
Cherry	15.4	10.9	10.2	49.6	6 148	5 713	-7.1	2.1	459	375	21	2 639	2.14	67.2	2.5	26.6
Cheyenne	13.9	8.6	8.2	49.8	9 830	9 998	1.7	0.5	789	556	-187	4 393	2.27	61.1	9.2	35.9
Clay	15.5	11.2	8.9	48.9	7 039	6 539	-7.1	-5.8	490	451	-395	2 617	2.40	69.2	6.8	26.3
Colfax	11.8	6.8	6.3	48.3	10 441	10 515	0.7	-1.0	1 119	488	-720	3 634	2.87	70.1	8.8	25.3
Cuming	14.1	10.1	11.7	49.8	10 203	9 139	-10.4	-1.3	709	610	-224	3 699	2.41	67.6	5.8	30.3
Custer	14.7	11.2	10.3	50.4	11 793	10 943	-7.2	-1.2	789	839	-96	4 745	2.25	67.0	8.0	28.7
Dakota	11.6	7.9	5.8	49.8	20 253	21 006	3.7	-2.6	2 298	946	-1 945	7 290	2.81	75.2	13.1	18.6
Dawes	12.2	8.8	9.0	50.2	9 060	9 182	1.3	-2.2	610	511	-325	3 611	2.22	62.0	9.5	30.2
Dawson	12.2	8.9	7.1	48.9	24 365	24 326	-0.2	-2.8	2 444	1 326	-1 780	8 755	2.71	70.3	10.7	25.5
Deuel	16.6	12.9	11.7	50.9	2 098	1 941	-7.5	-3.5	104	135	-26	822	2.34	61.8	5.8	34.2
Dixon	15.0	11.1	9.1	49.1	6 339	6 000	-5.3	-4.0	471	388	-320	2 305	2.51	68.0	8.6	29.2
Dodge	13.1	9.7	9.6	50.6	36 160	36 685	1.5	0.2	3 052	2 700	-312	15 110	2.37	66.6	8.8	27.9
Douglas	11.7	7.2	5.0	50.7	463 585	517 116	11.5	7.3	52 908	24 119	10 067	208 541	2.52	61.9	12.5	30.9
Dundy	15.9	12.8	13.0	50.1	2 292	2 008	-12.4	-8.8	97	175	-95	900	2.18	66.8	6.1	29.3
Fillmore	16.2	11.3	12.2	50.2	6 634	5 890	-11.2	-2.9	357	527	-13	2 464	2.22	63.4	7.2	32.8
Franklin	17.5	13.1	13.4	50.0	3 574	3 225	-9.8	-6.5	167	226	-145	1 409	2.15	67.6	7.0	28.5
Frontier	16.5	11.0	10.8	49.1	3 099	2 756	-11.1	-4.9	155	109	-166	1 084	2.25	66.6	5.7	28.6
Furnas	15.8	10.0	11.2	50.6	5 324	4 959	-6.9	-3.5	309	434	-29	2 276	2.11	60.2	6.1	37.8
Gage	15.3	10.3	10.5	50.3	22 993	22 311	-3.0	-2.3	1 484	1 731	-272	9 240	2.30	64.5	7.4	30.4
Garden	17.4	13.1	15.2	48.3	2 292	2 057	-10.3	-6.2	124	181	-71	845	2.10	64.3	4.1	32.1
Garfield	17.7	13.7	14.8	49.7	1 902	2 049	7.7	-1.9	101	190	49	903	2.10	59.5	7.3	38.0
Gosper	16.9	11.5	9.7	48.1	2 143	2 044	-4.6	-3.6	134	145	-75	789	2.46	72.2	7.2	23.2
Grant	18.7	11.1	9.0	48.2	747	614	-17.8	4.4	55	33	-2	299	2.42	64.2	4.7	34.8
Greeley	14.9	11.5	13.7	50.0	2 714	2 538	-6.5	-5.5	185	173	-149	995	2.46	65.7	5.1	32.9
Hall	11.9	8.1	6.7	49.6	53 534	58 607	9.5	5.3	5 960	3 267	379	22 433	2.67	66.1	12.6	27.1
Hamilton	14.5	10.0	8.4	50.1	9 403	9 114	-3.1	0.8	602	499	-19	3 649	2.45	72.5	7.3	22.7
Harlan	17.2	14.2	11.2	48.5	3 786	3 423	-9.6	1.5	240	251	65	1 555	2.19	63.4	6.0	32.9
Hayes	20.2	12.7	14.0	48.5	1 068	960	-10.1	-6.6	69	27	-110	482	2.25	73.4	2.5	23.9
Hitchcock	16.1	12.7	11.6	49.7	3 111	2 908	-6.5	-2.9	208	234	-63	1 342	2.12	59.1	6.0	37.0
Holt	16.4	10.9	10.6	50.6	11 551	10 435	-9.7	-1.8	861	755	-301	4 520	2.25	65.8	5.0	28.7
Hooker	17.1	13.6	16.1	51.4	783	736	-6.0	-3.8	47	72	3	312	1.97	65.4	1.9	31.1
Howard	14.2	10.7	9.9	49.2	6 567	6 274	-4.5	2.5	483	379	63	2 560	2.47	65.1	6.4	30.2
Jefferson	16.3	12.2	11.3	50.0	8 333	7 547	-9.4	-4.9	468	667	-179	3 359	2.18	62.1	7.9	33.8
Johnson	14.0	8.9	8.3	40.9	4 488	5 217	16.2	-0.9	280	348	23	1 886	2.13	65.6	10.8	31.5
Kearney	14.6	9.6	9.3	50.2	6 882	6 489	-5.7	1.0	499	452	18	2 767	2.34	65.7	6.3	28.8
Keith	16.3	13.9	10.0	49.8	8 875	8 368	-5.7	-4.2	478	572	-249	3 905	2.06	62.5	7.6	31.3
Keya Paha	18.2	13.4	14.5	50.9	983	824	-16.2	-4.0	45	45	-32	343	2.07	66.8	5.5	29.7
Kimball	15.4	12.0	11.4	50.0	4 089	3 821	-6.6	-3.7	262	289	-102	1 574	2.33	63.9	8.2	34.3
Knox	15.2	11.8	12.4	51.1	9 374	8 701	-7.2	-1.5	648	725	-64	3 716	2.24	64.0	6.4	31.6
Lancaster	11.5	7.7	5.3	49.9	250 291	285 407	14.0	8.5	25 429	12 365	10 875	117 667	2.42	60.0	9.7	30.3
Lincoln	14.3	10.0	8.1	50.5	34 632	36 288	4.8	-2.0	2 644	2 219	-1 189	15 010	2.34	63.6	9.8	31.5
Logan	15.8	9.5	7.9	47.5	774	763	-1.4	1.2	70	34	-31	365	2.33	65.2	3.6	31.0
Loup	20.1	16.2	9.6	48.4	712	628	-11.8	-5.9	37	28	-49	258	2.12	75.6	8.1	19.0
McPherson	18.3	9.1	10.3	51.5	533	539	1.1	-8.5	19	17	-48	197	2.18	69.5	2.5	27.9
Madison	13.9	8.2	7.8	50.5	35 226	34 876	-1.0	0.4	3 246	2 168	-958	14 007	2.43	65.3	10.5	28.5
Merrick	14.6	10.0	9.2	49.9	8 204	7 855	-4.3	-0.3	580	522	-70	3 325	2.28	69.4	8.4	23.0
Morrill	15.2	9.2	9.0	49.4	5 440	5 042	-7.3	-5.1	340	351	-283	1 981	2.38	68.1	12.0	28.8
Nance	16.9	9.8	10.4	50.3	4 038	3 735	-7.5	-4.3	258	286	-133	1 548	2.25	65.2	7.3	32.2
Nemaha	13.8	10.5	8.5	50.5	7 576	7 248	-4.3	-3.8	466	511	-215	2 877	2.31	62.8	7.6	30.7
Nuckolls	16.9	12.6	13.6	50.2	5 057	4 500	-11.0	-5.2	265	363	-118	2 068	2.08	62.5	5.3	33.9
Otoe	14.2	10.2	10.0	50.5	15 396	15 740	2.2	2.2	1 223	1 170	271	6 447	2.41	66.0	9.3	30.2
Pawnee	16.1	12.5	13.5	50.4	3 087	2 773	-10.2	-4.4	173	219	-53	1 261	2.13	59.2	3.6	36.4
Perkins	15.2	11.4	11.1	49.0	3 200	2 970	-7.2	-2.4	246	192	-111	1 243	2.32	65.9	1.9	30.6
Phelps	13.4	9.6	10.6	49.9	9 747	9 188	-5.7	0.8	721	700	39	3 728	2.40	66.6	4.9	30.0
Pierce	14.4	9.8	8.9	49.4	7 857	7 266	-7.5	-1.5	523	435	-184	2 940	2.40	69.0	6.4	28.5

1. No spouse present.

Table B. States and Counties — Population, Vital Statistics, Health, and Crime

STATE County	Persons in group quarters, 2016	Daytime population, 2011–2015 Number	Daytime population Employment/residence ratio	Births, 2016 Total	Births, 2016 Rate[1]	Deaths, 2016 Number	Deaths, 2016 Rate[1]	Persons under 65 with no health insurance, 2015 Number	Persons under 65 with no health insurance, 2015 Percent	Medicare, 2015 Total Beneficiaries	Medicare, 2015 Enrolled in Original Medicare	Medicare, 2015 Enrolled in Medicare Advantage	Serious crimes known to police,[2] 2014 Total Number	Serious crimes known to police,[2] 2014 Total Rate[3]
	32	33	34	35	36	37	38	39	40	41	42	43	44	45
NEBRASKA—Cont'd														
Blaine	0	497	0.81	8	16.5	6	12.4	48	12.9	D	111	D	NA	NA
Boone	94	5 429	1.02	66	12.4	68	12.8	394	9.5	1 227	1 167	60	NA	NA
Box Butte	177	11 702	1.07	173	15.5	101	9.0	848	9.0	2 104	1 982	122	206	1 819
Boyd	31	1 963	0.92	15	7.6	22	11.1	160	11.3	D	626	D	NA	NA
Brown	38	3 105	1.02	25	8.4	29	9.8	290	13.0	D	778	D	33	1 146
Buffalo	2 083	49 046	1.04	729	14.8	358	7.2	3 817	9.4	6 904	6 209	695	960	1 983
Burt	126	5 960	0.77	68	10.4	95	14.5	474	9.5	1 655	1 495	160	NA	NA
Butler	166	7 088	0.72	82	10.2	96	11.9	571	9.0	1 712	1 605	107	51	614
Cass	295	18 924	0.50	281	10.9	235	9.1	1 426	6.7	4 414	3 732	682	315	1 239
Cedar	148	7 821	0.81	120	13.8	103	11.9	609	9.1	1 696	1 347	349	25	287
Chase	67	4 032	1.07	45	11.4	50	12.7	457	14.6	D	846	D	36	897
Cherry	45	6 024	1.08	87	14.9	59	10.1	544	11.9	D	1 244	D	44	757
Cheyenne	95	10 934	1.15	123	12.2	70	7.0	572	6.7	1 760	1 648	112	243	2 396
Clay	91	5 737	0.79	81	13.1	80	13.0	603	12.0	1 448	1 434	14	NA	NA
Colfax	80	10 721	1.04	190	18.2	68	6.5	1 551	17.2	2 038	1 944	94	NA	NA
Cuming	131	8 869	0.95	126	14.0	86	9.5	810	11.4	1 800	1 679	121	28	312
Custer	127	10 685	0.98	140	13.0	129	11.9	912	10.8	2 425	2 400	25	99	918
Dakota	251	22 674	1.19	359	17.5	133	6.5	2 851	16.2	1 857	1 338	519	586	2 841
Dawes	1 150	9 154	1.00	90	10.0	90	10.0	768	11.7	1 633	1 400	233	141	1 553
Dawson	296	23 850	0.98	412	17.4	199	8.4	3 126	15.8	3 737	3 245	492	495	2 045
Deuel	18	1 715	0.77	19	10.1	20	10.7	172	11.9	D	479	D	10	515
Dixon	79	4 775	0.62	78	13.5	59	10.2	563	12.3	2 114	1 627	487	90	1 653
Dodge	1 214	36 015	0.96	516	14.0	422	11.5	2 998	10.4	7 677	6 713	964	834	2 283
Douglas	12 644	590 307	1.19	8 660	15.6	3 893	7.0	44 666	9.4	75 866	56 254	19 612	23 058	4 254
Dundy	33	2 061	1.05	16	8.7	21	11.5	191	14.1	D	424	D	NA	NA
Fillmore	213	5 602	0.97	69	12.1	79	13.8	344	8.2	D	1 346	D	NA	NA
Franklin	56	2 660	0.71	26	8.6	28	9.3	220	10.0	841	828	13	13	426
Frontier	113	2 467	0.92	23	8.8	13	5.0	199	10.3	524	501	23	NA	NA
Furnas	80	4 854	0.99	59	12.3	60	12.5	398	10.8	1 341	1 318	23	4	82
Gage	516	20 503	0.88	233	10.7	268	12.3	1 463	8.5	4 842	4 416	426	621	3 049
Garden	31	1 770	0.94	22	11.4	27	14.0	154	11.3	671	644	27	NA	NA
Garfield	60	1 994	1.06	23	11.4	22	10.9	171	11.7	586	567	19	NA	NA
Gosper	40	1 626	0.67	20	10.1	20	10.1	134	8.7	525	453	72	14	715
Grant	3	739	0.93	9	14.0	3	4.7	54	10.4	D	184	D	NA	NA
Greeley	57	2 242	0.79	30	12.5	31	12.9	305	16.8	D	579	D	NA	NA
Hall	1 132	65 429	1.15	998	16.2	540	8.8	7 269	14.0	10 624	9 792	832	2 619	4 272
Hamilton	91	8 396	0.85	88	9.6	75	8.2	560	7.5	1 739	1 648	91	86	943
Harlan	47	3 122	0.80	37	10.7	38	10.9	257	10.0	D	762	D	NA	NA
Hayes	0	979	0.80	9	10.0	2	2.2	144	20.6	D	95	D	NA	NA
Hitchcock	32	2 475	0.70	32	11.3	43	15.2	224	10.4	D	780	D	29	1 010
Holt	154	10 514	1.02	132	12.9	123	12.0	826	10.3	2 294	2 281	13	32	306
Hooker	22	774	1.28	8	11.3	15	21.2	45	8.8	D	227	D	0	0
Howard	68	4 992	0.58	86	13.4	59	9.2	444	8.8	1 329	1 308	21	NA	NA
Jefferson	96	7 574	1.04	69	9.6	82	11.4	503	9.1	1 844	1 690	154	NA	NA
Johnson	1 027	5 108	0.97	44	8.5	50	9.7	363	11.1	964	922	42	19	370
Kearney	83	6 370	0.95	80	12.2	71	10.8	416	7.9	1 167	1 105	62	115	1 750
Keith	42	8 172	1.01	76	9.5	77	9.6	571	9.3	1 955	1 787	168	137	1 694
Keya Paha	0	635	0.83	8	10.1	4	5.1	80	14.0	D	179	D	2	255
Kimball	47	3 738	1.01	43	11.7	37	10.1	335	11.9	883	872	11	39	1 060
Knox	229	7 966	0.86	114	13.3	102	11.9	855	13.3	2 162	1 923	239	28	327
Lancaster	14 898	306 150	1.05	4 065	13.1	2 031	6.6	21 682	8.5	41 755	37 035	4 720	10 455	3 481
Lincoln	592	36 751	1.05	400	11.3	366	10.3	2 633	9.1	7 542	6 056	1 486	1 205	3 342
Logan	0	763	0.80	12	15.5	6	7.8	87	13.5	197	175	22	NA	NA
Loup	0	489	0.79	8	13.5	2	3.4	54	12.4	D	90	D	NA	NA
McPherson	0	346	0.60	4	8.1	2	4.1	28	7.3	93	81	12	NA	NA
Madison	1 058	38 207	1.17	512	14.6	353	10.1	3 326	11.6	6 967	5 977	990	755	2 132
Merrick	196	6 886	0.78	100	12.8	76	9.7	640	10.3	1 479	1 386	93	58	743
Morrill	78	4 572	0.87	59	12.3	43	9.0	473	12.1	1 051	967	84	23	618
Nance	143	3 218	0.76	41	11.5	32	8.9	293	10.5	748	718	30	NA	NA
Nemaha	493	7 467	1.09	66	9.5	67	9.6	428	8.1	1 374	1 357	17	53	742
Nuckolls	50	4 048	0.84	45	10.6	56	13.1	294	9.3	1 173	1 133	40	NA	NA
Otoe	317	14 743	0.86	206	12.8	169	10.5	1 089	8.6	2 921	2 645	276	NA	NA
Pawnee	35	2 602	0.90	27	10.2	27	10.2	233	11.9	D	700	D	45	1 668
Perkins	35	3 073	1.10	45	15.5	21	7.2	264	11.4	602	582	20	11	378
Phelps	253	9 640	1.09	113	12.2	102	11.0	615	8.4	1 905	1 885	20	166	1 798
Pierce	96	5 913	0.65	86	12.0	70	9.8	430	7.3	1 255	1 228	27	NA	NA

1. Per 1,000 estimated resident population.   2. Data for serious crimes have not been adjusted for underreporting; this may affect comparability between geographic areas and over time.
3. Per 100,000 population estimated by the FBI.

Table B. States and Counties — Crime, Education, Money Income, and Poverty

STATE County	Serious crimes known to police, 2014 (cont.)[1] Rate[2]		Education						Money income, 2011–2015				Income and poverty, 2015			
			School enrollment and attainment, 2011–2015				Local government expenditures,[5] 2013–2014			Households				Percent below poverty level		
			Enrollment[3]		Attainment[4] (percent)							Percent					
	Violent	Property	Total	Percent private	High school graduate or less	Bachelor's degree or more	Total current spending (mil dol)	Current spending per student (dollars)	Per capita income[6] (dollars)	Median income (dollars)	with income of less than $50,000	with income of $200,000 or more	Median household income (dollars)	All persons	Children under 18 years	Children 5 to 17 years in families
	46	47	48	49	50	51	52	53	54	55	56	57	58	59	60	61
NEBRASKA—Cont'd																
Blaine	NA	NA	131	3.1	41.5	18.3	2.3	22 762	21 854	48 875	51.9	2.2	44 824	16.6	27.3	26.5
Boone	NA	NA	1 280	21.0	48.9	16.6	13.5	15 839	27 799	50 306	49.5	4.5	54 070	9.2	12.7	11.5
Box Butte	238	1 580	2 662	11.0	43.2	15.9	22.7	11 546	25 897	51 691	48.3	2.4	54 652	11.6	15.7	14.5
Boyd	NA	NA	413	3.1	47.9	18.1	6.1	18 041	24 085	40 224	61.7	1.3	42 539	12.2	19.8	17.2
Brown	0	1 146	637	10.5	52.6	16.3	10.4	21 703	26 390	36 078	63.8	2.4	46 856	12.6	19.5	17.0
Buffalo	205	1 779	15 093	7.6	32.1	32.7	89.7	11 595	26 846	53 624	46.9	2.9	55 813	13.0	12.0	10.9
Burt	NA	NA	1 444	6.0	48.5	17.0	16.3	12 746	24 332	47 429	52.2	1.0	49 792	11.6	16.6	15.7
Butler	60	554	1 911	25.4	49.2	15.2	14.0	13 786	29 457	51 027	48.8	2.9	55 542	8.1	10.4	8.7
Cass	130	1 109	6 424	12.8	37.4	25.1	43.7	11 515	30 694	65 619	36.9	3.5	66 519	7.1	9.8	8.4
Cedar	46	241	2 056	19.5	47.5	17.7	18.0	16 322	27 774	52 250	47.6	3.7	56 092	9.4	12.4	10.8
Chase	199	697	838	2.6	44.2	18.2	10.6	12 727	29 905	52 422	47.3	2.4	55 319	8.2	11.0	9.4
Cherry	172	585	1 059	12.8	40.1	19.7	12.1	15 751	26 229	48 750	51.8	2.2	54 564	11.7	18.0	16.3
Cheyenne	375	2 022	2 385	3.5	33.0	23.4	20.5	11 831	30 339	53 814	45.4	2.8	57 255	9.0	11.1	10.1
Clay	NA	NA	1 458	5.7	43.4	19.0	19.6	13 350	26 324	51 470	48.3	2.5	51 431	10.2	14.7	13.0
Colfax	NA	NA	2 731	8.9	61.2	13.4	29.1	11 457	22 857	51 367	47.9	2.6	50 744	10.9	14.7	13.4
Cuming	22	290	2 136	22.0	50.9	18.8	20.8	12 976	25 318	50 013	50.0	2.3	56 995	9.9	13.0	10.7
Custer	121	798	2 335	9.9	40.9	21.0	26.4	14 932	29 406	46 468	53.4	2.8	51 014	11.6	16.1	14.9
Dakota	165	2 676	5 570	13.7	61.3	11.2	49.2	11 326	20 543	49 786	50.2	1.5	49 093	14.6	20.7	18.3
Dawes	143	1 409	2 879	6.0	34.8	33.2	14.2	12 074	22 176	41 038	58.6	1.4	44 135	17.8	20.5	17.2
Dawson	145	1 900	6 352	3.2	57.5	14.9	62.7	11 719	22 098	48 329	52.5	1.7	47 991	12.6	16.7	15.2
Deuel	0	515	453	3.3	45.7	17.3	7.4	16 947	27 439	50 962	48.2	2.7	47 641	11.1	18.7	17.0
Dixon	0	1 653	1 506	2.9	50.9	18.3	15.2	14 972	24 286	51 223	49.0	2.5	52 152	9.3	12.2	10.6
Dodge	186	2 097	8 581	21.2	49.1	18.9	69.4	11 691	25 112	49 068	51.1	2.1	48 969	11.6	15.1	13.9
Douglas	483	3 771	152 870	21.1	32.3	37.1	1 024.0	10 951	29 842	54 659	45.7	4.8	58 405	14.5	20.0	18.4
Dundy	NA	NA	392	12.5	39.2	19.6	5.8	15 768	28 870	42 500	58.0	5.1	45 745	13.2	19.2	16.7
Fillmore	NA	NA	1 226	13.1	46.2	18.5	14.1	14 839	27 875	52 316	47.4	2.6	54 086	9.8	12.8	11.4
Franklin	0	426	590	2.7	44.9	18.7	4.9	15 120	28 426	45 905	52.9	4.5	44 911	13.3	19.7	18.1
Frontier	NA	NA	689	6.8	39.9	18.3	9.5	16 404	25 837	49 634	50.6	2.4	50 700	12.6	19.0	16.8
Furnas	21	62	1 122	13.5	45.8	17.3	15.2	13 893	22 769	39 934	61.7	1.1	40 032	13.4	18.4	16.6
Gage	496	2 553	4 716	12.5	45.2	19.7	40.9	12 694	26 207	50 010	50.0	1.9	50 746	10.2	15.0	13.4
Garden	NA	NA	297	7.4	38.4	23.5	4.0	16 887	30 790	45 845	54.6	3.7	42 186	14.8	27.3	24.2
Garfield	NA	NA	367	5.4	45.4	16.2	4.6	12 763	23 612	43 179	60.5	1.1	44 643	11.9	15.5	13.1
Gosper	51	664	471	6.2	40.1	19.4	3.2	13 961	27 402	54 375	44.2	1.3	56 882	9.1	16.5	15.3
Grant	NA	NA	199	9.5	45.1	20.4	2.6	16 465	21 782	44 750	60.2	1.0	56 646	9.2	6.7	7.1
Greeley	NA	NA	557	14.7	47.4	14.4	7.3	17 655	23 333	42 904	59.2	2.5	44 920	12.2	20.1	17.5
Hall	243	4 029	15 532	10.1	49.7	18.3	142.8	11 559	23 995	49 252	50.9	2.1	50 093	13.5	19.5	18.5
Hamilton	143	800	2 237	14.0	38.0	25.2	19.8	12 486	30 424	59 311	39.5	4.6	65 103	7.3	8.9	7.8
Harlan	NA	NA	665	6.0	46.7	16.1	4.3	14 885	26 139	46 766	54.4	1.6	47 844	12.0	17.4	17.2
Hayes	NA	NA	225	6.7	37.6	19.7	2.6	22 632	26 221	44 500	53.1	4.6	50 516	14.7	23.8	23.0
Hitchcock	70	940	593	9.8	44.1	15.1	6.1	21 051	23 152	39 231	61.7	0.6	43 054	14.1	20.4	18.9
Holt	96	210	2 298	13.4	41.9	20.9	23.5	14 758	25 672	46 728	53.1	1.9	50 434	11.9	15.9	15.7
Hooker	0	0	92	7.6	40.7	23.1	2.9	17 720	22 949	37 317	65.1	1.6	42 989	8.1	11.5	11.8
Howard	NA	NA	1 493	11.9	49.7	19.2	9.5	12 589	26 658	50 030	50.0	1.7	52 464	10.4	13.6	12.5
Jefferson	NA	NA	1 583	3.5	53.0	13.7	20.3	13 406	25 469	43 008	56.9	2.6	46 812	12.3	17.1	15.4
Johnson	117	253	978	12.3	52.9	14.7	9.7	12 557	21 488	45 429	54.4	2.9	47 382	13.2	14.1	12.3
Kearney	137	1 613	1 486	8.0	39.5	24.1	17.1	13 569	27 360	51 934	48.2	2.6	50 645	8.6	11.9	10.6
Keith	49	1 645	1 617	14.1	42.5	20.7	20.5	18 251	26 422	41 781	57.6	1.1	46 888	10.9	19.0	16.1
Keya Paha	0	255	140	2.9	50.3	15.5	2.2	22 440	26 666	38 625	63.3	2.6	45 886	15.1	20.8	20.2
Kimball	326	734	778	4.5	46.2	17.4	6.6	12 315	24 255	40 242	56.6	1.7	45 769	12.7	19.1	17.3
Knox	82	245	1 876	11.3	46.2	19.1	23.4	15 286	26 560	45 411	53.5	2.3	45 566	13.7	20.1	18.7
Lancaster	315	3 166	90 771	15.8	29.1	36.7	451.3	10 486	27 764	51 830	47.9	3.4	54 422	13.5	14.1	12.5
Lincoln	258	3 084	9 093	15.2	39.8	20.0	59.5	10 383	27 056	50 194	49.8	2.3	53 856	12.3	16.3	14.4
Logan	NA	NA	191	11.5	37.1	22.0	2.9	15 550	25 920	48 281	51.5	1.9	51 098	8.9	13.3	12.1
Loup	NA	NA	95	5.3	45.6	18.6	1.9	24 974	27 794	55 417	46.5	3.1	52 862	15.3	24.3	19.4
McPherson	NA	NA	67	7.5	33.6	24.5	1.9	20 032	27 364	54 306	46.7	1.5	57 175	12.1	20.0	16.3
Madison	141	1 991	9 033	21.2	41.0	20.2	61.7	10 996	26 083	50 218	49.8	3.4	51 330	13.8	17.6	16.0
Merrick	26	718	1 753	11.1	42.3	16.8	12.0	12 530	26 136	51 012	47.6	2.3	51 219	10.4	15.1	13.8
Morrill	27	591	1 123	7.3	45.0	17.8	12.9	14 231	24 869	45 910	54.5	3.1	49 082	13.5	20.1	17.1
Nance	NA	NA	750	6.9	48.7	16.5	10.6	13 594	25 479	42 500	56.4	2.1	46 958	13.2	16.5	14.6
Nemaha	56	686	2 088	6.4	40.1	27.8	19.3	16 098	27 087	49 656	50.2	3.0	52 034	13.1	15.1	14.2
Nuckolls	NA	NA	853	6.3	48.5	17.3	6.2	12 666	24 447	40 488	57.8	1.7	41 956	12.5	19.4	16.8
Otoe	NA	NA	3 464	12.8	46.7	21.5	29.0	11 242	26 032	50 275	49.7	1.6	53 015	10.6	14.3	13.1
Pawnee	0	1 668	540	9.3	52.6	16.3	7.4	15 257	29 030	41 161	58.4	2.6	43 646	13.2	22.1	21.6
Perkins	69	309	599	16.4	41.2	22.0	6.5	16 251	29 171	55 893	40.9	4.0	58 066	10.1	13.4	12.4
Phelps	87	1 711	2 035	12.0	40.4	22.7	23.4	14 837	26 697	50 404	49.4	2.3	55 566	10.4	13.8	12.8
Pierce	NA	NA	1 767	17.9	42.1	20.5	15.7	12 677	26 668	54 482	44.2	2.2	56 744	9.4	11.6	9.8

1. Data for serious crimes have not been adjusted for underreporting; this may affect comparability between geographic areas and over time.   2. Per 100,000 population estimated by the FBI.
3. All persons 3 years old and over enrolled in nursery school through college.   4. Persons 25 years old and over.   5. Elementary and secondary education expenditures.
6. Based on population estimated by the American Community Survey, 2011–2015.

Table B. States and Counties — Personal Income

STATE County	Personal income, 2015										Earnings, 2015		
	Total (mil dol)	Percent change, 2014–2015	Per capita[1] Dollars	Per capita[1] Rank	Wages and salaries (mil dol)	Supplements to wages and salaries; employer contributions (mil dol) Pension and insurance	Supplements to wages and salaries; employer contributions (mil dol) Government social insurance	Proprietors' income (mil dol)	Dividends, interest, and rent (mil dol)	Personal transfer receipts (mil dol)	Total (mil dol)	Contributions for government social insurance (mil dol) From employee and self-employed	Contributions for government social insurance (mil dol) From employer
	62	63	64	65	66	67	68	69	70	71	72	73	74
NEBRASKA—Cont'd													
Blaine	31	-10.3	64 585	63	6	1	0	14	7	4	21	0	0
Boone	310	-8.7	58 283	88	88	16	6	112	58	42	223	8	6
Box Butte	465	-8.4	41 045	653	262	37	33	44	74	102	376	26	33
Boyd	102	3.1	50 673	383	18	4	1	37	16	23	61	2	1
Brown	165	-3.3	55 904	126	45	9	3	66	25	29	123	4	3
Buffalo	2 250	2.9	46 051	548	1 114	182	81	211	570	305	1 588	92	81
Burt	323	8.1	49 086	475	76	14	5	77	47	65	173	8	5
Butler	376	4.0	46 298	620	116	20	8	70	66	64	215	11	8
Cass	1 168	3.6	45 775	599	220	39	16	107	201	190	383	23	16
Cedar	429	-0.7	50 053	267	106	20	8	142	73	59	276	11	8
Chase	185	-20.5	46 817	137	74	12	5	41	41	32	132	6	5
Cherry	309	-9.6	52 841	121	85	15	6	112	57	45	217	8	6
Cheyenne	534	-5.7	52 537	152	325	44	22	64	88	73	455	26	22
Clay	282	-7.4	44 694	409	110	21	8	45	53	52	183	9	8
Colfax	437	-1.8	41 562	729	204	34	14	98	63	58	350	16	14
Cuming	684	0.7	74 971	19	156	25	11	350	81	72	542	15	11
Custer	562	-1.4	52 048	237	177	33	13	174	88	91	397	16	13
Dakota	747	4.8	35 931	1 920	526	84	38	68	85	136	716	43	38
Dawes	302	-6.9	33 366	1 624	123	26	10	40	58	68	200	12	10
Dawson	922	-0.1	38 590	1 289	439	78	32	174	136	166	723	37	32
Deuel	79	-12.9	41 360	789	20	4	1	9	20	18	35	2	1
Dixon	267	3.2	46 080	551	64	12	5	62	41	37	143	6	5
Dodge	1 537	4.6	41 875	1 118	672	113	50	189	276	314	1 024	62	50
Douglas	30 920	0.1	56 212	276	18 479	2 492	1 378	5 022	6 139	3 601	27 371	1 624	1 378
Dundy	115	-14.2	63 828	49	28	5	2	29	32	20	64	3	2
Fillmore	317	-0.8	56 450	176	95	17	6	69	63	55	188	9	6
Franklin	135	1.2	45 289	567	29	6	2	18	36	32	54	3	2
Frontier	138	-2.8	52 431	232	34	7	3	51	18	19	93	3	3
Furnas	240	-3.0	49 294	297	78	15	6	57	40	51	155	7	6
Gage	995	0.5	45 448	482	346	66	26	117	167	238	554	34	26
Garden	89	-15.2	46 254	173	23	4	2	18	20	22	46	2	2
Garfield	93	-1.7	45 711	359	29	5	2	25	21	18	61	3	2
Gosper	96	-5.9	48 840	255	20	3	1	19	21	17	44	2	1
Grant	33	-10.1	51 003	199	7	1	1	13	8	6	21	1	1
Greeley	107	-3.2	43 946	546	24	5	2	31	23	21	62	3	2
Hall	2 348	1.7	38 072	1 384	1 417	231	104	173	440	431	1 925	116	104
Hamilton	454	2.4	49 351	428	156	25	11	73	84	69	266	14	11
Harlan	166	3.9	47 994	541	32	6	2	52	27	31	92	4	2
Hayes	64	-13.0	68 543	30	10	2	1	31	9	6	43	1	1
Hitchcock	114	-3.9	39 677	801	34	8	2	16	23	30	60	4	2
Holt	538	-3.0	52 141	386	179	30	13	166	86	98	388	20	13
Hooker	36	-8.9	49 324	354	10	2	1	14	5	7	27	1	1
Howard	275	0.3	42 984	698	61	12	4	54	41	50	132	6	4
Jefferson	336	-5.5	46 303	465	132	22	11	53	70	70	218	13	11
Johnson	188	-3.3	36 361	1 167	65	16	5	33	28	34	118	6	5
Kearney	718	29.8	108 975	129	90	16	6	476	65	58	588	26	6
Keith	347	-4.6	43 093	610	127	21	9	58	64	73	215	13	9
Keya Paha	56	-8.6	69 831	52	7	1	0	30	10	7	38	1	0
Kimball	158	-13.4	42 922	402	68	12	5	10	33	35	95	6	5
Knox	397	-2.0	46 483	578	103	20	7	117	65	77	247	11	7
Lancaster	13 502	3.9	44 057	815	7 795	1 319	583	849	2 598	1 932	10 545	632	583
Lincoln	1 705	2.3	47 816	581	773	113	80	362	226	337	1 328	80	80
Logan	38	1.5	48 979	1 051	7	1	0	14	4	6	23	1	0
Loup	36	-15.2	61 809	39	4	1	0	14	5	5	19	0	0
McPherson	28	-29.8	59 379	28	4	1	0	14	5	3	19	0	0
Madison	1 574	2.6	44 915	756	885	148	64	219	270	275	1 316	75	64
Merrick	382	5.8	49 110	741	97	16	7	120	53	66	240	12	7
Morrill	242	-9.9	49 947	127	67	12	5	76	36	42	159	6	5
Nance	154	-5.7	42 957	446	46	8	3	22	24	30	80	4	3
Nemaha	302	-2.4	42 872	745	161	32	11	30	54	64	234	13	11
Nuckolls	175	-9.4	40 370	582	50	10	4	28	35	46	92	6	4
Otoe	680	0.2	42 541	832	250	44	19	76	119	131	389	23	19
Pawnee	123	-10.5	46 405	403	31	7	2	36	20	23	77	3	2
Perkins	148	-22.0	50 369	76	56	10	4	41	29	23	111	5	4
Phelps	539	0.8	57 981	161	207	37	15	184	81	81	444	17	15
Pierce	462	18.5	64 100	529	81	15	6	201	53	50	303	14	6

1. Based on the resident population estimated as of July 1 of the year shown.

Table B. States and Counties — Earnings, Social Security, and Housing

STATE County	Earnings, 2015 (cont.) Percent by selected industries									Social Security beneficiaries, December 2015		Housing units, 2016		
	Farm	Mining	Construction	Manu-facturing	Infor-mation: professional, scientific, technical services	Retail trade	Finance, insur-ance, real estate and leasing	Health care and social assistance	Govern-ment	Number	Rate[1]	Supple-mental Security Income recipients, December 2015	Total	Percent change, 2010–2016
	75	76	77	78	79	80	81	82	83	84	85	86	87	88
NEBRASKA—Cont'd														
Blaine	70.5	0.0	D	0.0	0.0	D	D	D	17.9	115	234	5	322	-1.2
Boone	47.1	0.0	3.9	6.0	1.0	3.3	4.5	3.9	15.4	1 220	230	47	2 628	-0.8
Box Butte	7.2	0.0	2.9	5.5	3.0	3.9	2.8	D	15.7	1 830	162	182	5 417	-1.1
Boyd	50.7	D	2.5	1.2	D	2.2	4.2	3.5	16.7	630	313	33	1 368	-1.6
Brown	50.1	0.0	4.9	3.7	D	4.7	2.4	1.9	19.2	800	272	51	1 835	-1.5
Buffalo	4.7	0.1	6.5	13.9	D	7.6	4.8	16.7	15.5	7 670	157	447	20 180	5.9
Burt	40.1	0.0	4.6	6.0	D	3.0	D	4.3	15.9	1 815	276	114	3 457	-0.3
Butler	27.6	D	4.7	20.0	D	2.1	D	D	16.9	1 850	228	90	4 058	0.1
Cass	16.6	4.0	6.5	9.9	3.2	6.3	5.1	4.6	19.5	4 925	193	209	11 376	2.3
Cedar	39.9	D	6.0	6.7	2.2	3.2	7.3	3.2	13.4	1 845	215	54	4 132	-0.4
Chase	26.0	D	6.1	1.7	3.8	8.3	6.0	1.7	19.1	865	217	39	1 931	-0.8
Cherry	45.7	D	5.7	1.1	3.1	5.6	1.7	4.3	14.5	1 320	226	71	3 206	1.6
Cheyenne	6.8	0.2	3.3	4.5	2.1	7.1	2.6	7.4	9.7	1 965	193	121	4 988	2.0
Clay	20.7	D	8.4	11.8	D	3.8	5.1	3.8	23.9	1 475	234	64	2 990	-0.3
Colfax	24.3	D	D	D	1.5	2.3	1.8	D	10.6	1 450	138	71	4 146	1.2
Cuming	57.7	D	2.9	9.1	1.9	2.0	3.6	D	7.0	2 125	233	63	4 218	0.3
Custer	39.0	0.0	7.1	10.9	2.3	3.6	4.1	D	11.7	2 510	232	129	5 591	0.2
Dakota	2.5	D	4.7	39.1	D	4.2	9.0	3.7	10.0	3 480	168	276	7 762	1.7
Dawes	10.9	D	4.7	D	3.0	11.2	3.6	11.5	32.6	1 765	195	85	4 204	-1.1
Dawson	20.0	D	3.3	22.4	2.9	5.4	4.7	D	18.5	4 300	180	314	10 182	0.6
Deuel	5.7	0.0	D	6.5	D	7.6	D	5.4	26.2	510	265	23	1 027	-1.6
Dixon	41.4	0.0	6.8	D	D	0.7	2.1	2.2	12.7	1 135	196	49	2 703	0.6
Dodge	6.9	0.1	4.7	20.7	4.1	8.5	4.8	D	18.3	8 370	228	570	16 645	0.4
Douglas	0.0	D	7.3	5.4	11.5	4.6	10.8	11.9	10.7	82 200	150	10 278	231 442	5.4
Dundy	37.9	0.0	2.2	1.4	D	3.9	1.6	3.2	20.7	490	272	22	1 112	-1.2
Fillmore	25.3	0.0	9.1	8.8	D	3.6	8.2	4.0	19.2	1 530	272	48	2 918	0.2
Franklin	23.7	0.0	D	D	D	5.7	D	D	28.2	905	300	52	1 723	-0.6
Frontier	47.8	D	5.9	D	D	1.7	6.6	0.6	17.1	545	208	25	1 561	-0.8
Furnas	30.7	0.0	3.3	7.1	6.2	4.1	D	8.7	16.6	1 365	282	90	2 706	-0.6
Gage	9.7	D	4.3	23.7	2.5	6.1	3.0	D	20.4	5 455	250	387	10 409	-0.4
Garden	34.1	0.0	D	D	D	8.2	D	11.8	16.7	625	324	31	1 295	-1.4
Garfield	29.6	D	D	D	D	5.5	D	D	13.5	510	252	21	1 184	0.5
Gosper	37.4	0.0	D	D	D	1.2	D	D	17.1	520	264	15	1 289	1.7
Grant	52.7	0.0	3.1	0.0	D	6.1	1.4	D	14.4	180	283	0	383	-2.0
Greeley	41.0	0.0	3.0	2.1	D	D	6.5	0.6	17.9	605	249	27	1 292	-0.6
Hall	1.8	0.1	6.5	20.1	3.6	8.7	6.1	11.8	16.8	10 585	172	921	24 512	4.1
Hamilton	19.8	0.0	5.6	13.4	6.3	5.1	3.6	D	11.4	2 075	226	63	4 071	2.7
Harlan	48.1	D	2.9	2.6	D	3.7	D	D	15.9	890	258	43	2 362	-0.5
Hayes	69.5	D	D	D	D	D	D	0.3	8.8	175	189	8	509	0.2
Hitchcock	10.7	7.2	11.6	20.9	D	3.1	1.2	0.5	23.4	795	276	46	1 719	-2.5
Holt	16.8	0.1	3.9	4.6	1.8	18.0	7.5	D	10.8	2 620	254	143	5 230	0.3
Hooker	33.4	0.0	D	D	D	3.3	D	D	14.3	225	307	0	437	1.4
Howard	36.8	D	4.3	2.0	2.0	4.3	3.7	4.2	25.8	1 460	228	59	3 046	3.2
Jefferson	16.0	0.4	7.5	16.2	3.3	7.2	3.8	8.9	13.5	1 935	267	157	3 894	-0.6
Johnson	21.4	0.0	6.0	D	D	3.8	2.6	4.6	42.9	925	178	46	2 165	-1.2
Kearney	12.5	0.6	1.7	63.8	D	2.1	D	D	4.3	1 205	183	79	2 940	1.9
Keith	15.5	D	8.3	6.5	3.6	9.4	5.5	9.1	13.6	2 210	274	105	5 366	-1.1
Keya Paha	71.0	0.0	D	D	D	D	D	D	7.5	250	311	11	542	-1.3
Kimball	1.4	11.4	4.5	12.3	D	5.3	D	D	21.0	975	262	45	1 938	-1.3
Knox	38.7	0.0	5.1	3.4	D	4.5	3.4	D	20.5	2 260	265	136	4 892	2.2
Lancaster	0.6	D	5.7	8.4	9.2	5.9	9.7	13.2	22.2	45 395	148	4 829	128 756	6.5
Lincoln	11.5	D	4.3	8.2	3.1	6.2	4.1	13.9	14.1	6 500	182	724	16 651	0.4
Logan	39.1	0.0	D	D	D	D	D	0.8	15.7	165	213	0	395	-0.6
Loup	74.1	0.0	0.0	1.6	0.0	D	D	D	13.3	160	275	9	447	5.2
McPherson	72.6	0.0	0.0	D	D	D	D	D	10.8	85	178	0	280	-1.1
Madison	7.4	D	5.2	15.3	3.8	7.9	7.7	14.9	16.3	7 050	201	540	15 178	1.1
Merrick	19.6	D	26.1	13.3	1.8	3.3	4.2	D	12.8	1 845	237	154	3 782	2.2
Morrill	42.5	D	2.2	4.3	D	3.4	4.4	D	19.1	1 025	212	95	2 417	-1.0
Nance	25.0	D	D	D	1.3	3.4	4.2	6.5	23.9	740	206	53	1 852	2.8
Nemaha	6.4	0.0	2.3	7.8	D	2.8	D	4.9	59.3	1 585	226	118	3 493	-0.1
Nuckolls	17.9	0.0	4.1	D	D	6.4	5.3	16.9	18.9	1 265	292	65	2 446	-0.8
Otoe	11.1	0.0	5.3	20.6	D	6.5	4.0	D	22.5	3 440	216	198	7 089	0.9
Pawnee	38.9	D	D	11.0	0.5	3.0	D	2.8	19.4	655	248	38	1 602	0.9
Perkins	27.2	0.0	10.3	5.1	D	2.8	D	2.4	18.6	670	228	18	1 440	-0.7
Phelps	38.6	D	D	D	2.2	4.1	3.7	D	9.8	2 095	226	120	4 226	1.2
Pierce	15.8	D	4.4	44.2	D	2.4	2.6	4.5	6.7	1 420	197	59	3 243	0.7

1. Per 1,000 resident population estimated as of July 1 of the year shown.

Table B. States and Counties — **Housing, Labor Force, and Employment**

	Housing units, 2011–2015								Civilian labor force, 2016				Civilian employment,[6] 2011–2015		
	Occupied units										Unemployment			Percent	
		Owner-occupied				Renter-occupied									
				Median owner cost as a percent of income			Median rent as a per-cent of income[3]	Sub-stand-ard units[4] (percent)		Percent change, 2015–2016				Manage-ment, business, science and arts	Con-struction, produc-tion, and mainte-nance occu-pations
STATE County	Total	Percent	Median value[1]	With a mort-gage	Without a mort-gage[2]	Median rent[3]			Total		Total	Rate[5]	Total		
	89	90	91	92	93	94	95	96	97	98	99	100	101	102	103

	89	90	91	92	93	94	95	96	97	98	99	100	101	102	103
NEBRASKA—Cont'd															
Blaine	231	53.2	72 500	22.9	10.0	608	16.3	4.3	268	0.0	12	4.5	287	40.1	38.0
Boone	2 227	78.7	97 700	19.9	11.0	557	19.0	1.5	3 005	-0.3	83	2.8	2 777	35.6	28.3
Box Butte	4 805	66.2	92 000	17.6	10.0	543	26.3	2.5	5 678	0.2	215	3.8	5 606	29.9	37.4
Boyd	935	80.5	51 700	20.9	12.0	466	30.5	2.0	1 108	1.7	35	3.2	964	41.2	29.9
Brown	1 511	69.3	70 500	16.8	14.2	451	19.8	0.6	1 369	-1.9	53	3.9	1 585	41.3	21.4
Buffalo	18 352	63.3	151 300	20.2	10.8	722	27.5	1.3	27 174	0.1	712	2.6	27 263	31.7	23.8
Burt	2 801	79.5	88 700	20.1	14.0	594	23.4	1.6	3 576	-1.0	137	3.8	3 046	32.1	28.2
Butler	3 577	78.2	100 200	21.4	10.4	650	26.1	3.7	4 659	-1.8	156	3.3	4 299	29.4	38.3
Cass	9 756	80.8	155 900	21.7	14.1	736	25.7	2.3	13 138	0.4	462	3.5	13 103	32.6	25.9
Cedar	3 575	81.6	101 400	18.7	10.9	559	23.3	1.5	4 570	-1.6	123	2.7	4 588	33.9	28.4
Chase	1 701	78.0	91 200	19.6	11.6	583	15.2	0.5	2 321	-0.8	50	2.2	2 073	39.2	27.0
Cherry	2 639	65.9	114 200	21.6	10.0	579	21.8	1.3	3 474	0.6	84	2.4	3 271	36.3	25.4
Cheyenne	4 393	68.8	113 700	17.7	11.4	600	23.4	1.9	5 434	-5.5	162	3.0	5 681	35.7	21.3
Clay	2 617	77.6	81 100	18.9	10.4	562	22.6	1.8	3 341	-1.1	110	3.3	3 171	33.0	33.9
Colfax	3 634	74.0	88 300	19.1	10.6	596	21.1	5.9	5 559	0.1	165	3.0	5 224	20.6	48.9
Cuming	3 699	70.3	102 500	18.5	11.2	588	23.5	1.4	4 740	-2.1	144	3.0	4 562	32.1	32.4
Custer	4 745	72.8	86 700	19.3	12.9	576	23.9	1.6	6 367	1.3	157	2.5	5 694	32.6	30.5
Dakota	7 290	65.3	111 400	21.1	12.7	686	23.5	6.7	11 091	0.8	479	4.3	10 025	21.6	40.0
Dawes	3 611	66.0	104 600	19.8	14.4	564	36.6	2.1	5 240	-0.3	163	3.1	4 613	37.2	19.3
Dawson	8 755	67.7	88 800	19.4	12.5	653	24.8	5.3	13 035	-0.3	407	3.1	12 312	23.1	44.2
Deuel	822	75.1	69 400	18.5	10.0	607	18.8	1.6	1 080	0.5	30	2.8	1 023	29.5	26.7
Dixon	2 305	76.0	80 900	18.8	11.6	605	24.4	2.0	3 090	0.2	107	3.5	2 916	29.5	35.2
Dodge	15 110	66.6	114 000	19.3	13.1	691	24.9	1.6	19 095	-0.1	619	3.2	18 447	26.4	29.1
Douglas	208 541	61.8	145 900	21.2	12.7	812	29.1	2.7	288 244	0.4	9 971	3.5	277 349	39.5	17.8
Dundy	900	65.1	71 900	16.4	10.5	454	17.7	0.6	1 196	-0.1	27	2.3	932	41.3	33.2
Fillmore	2 464	75.8	75 700	17.5	10.5	578	20.0	0.8	3 154	-1.8	92	2.9	2 969	32.5	30.3
Franklin	1 409	83.6	59 900	18.1	10.4	600	25.3	1.6	1 510	-0.1	47	3.1	1 575	32.3	32.9
Frontier	1 084	74.2	87 400	18.9	11.8	580	20.1	0.8	1 577	2.9	47	3.0	1 294	34.9	27.5
Furnas	2 276	70.5	62 300	23.3	12.5	527	20.3	2.8	2 733	0.1	80	2.9	2 323	36.5	28.6
Gage	9 240	71.1	108 300	19.5	11.8	627	23.9	0.9	11 062	0.1	382	3.5	11 077	33.1	28.5
Garden	845	82.8	75 000	22.1	10.9	511	22.9	1.8	1 190	-0.6	41	3.4	939	33.4	26.4
Garfield	903	75.9	89 100	23.3	10.7	337	26.3	0.7	1 160	-2.8	32	2.8	992	30.4	30.2
Gosper	789	71.6	108 500	20.7	10.0	667	17.0	0.6	1 069	-0.7	29	2.7	1 091	27.4	30.4
Grant	299	69.9	50 800	29.7	10.2	618	16.3	0.0	452	3.7	11	2.4	418	40.2	31.8
Greeley	995	81.0	59 600	22.0	12.3	500	20.2	1.7	1 224	-2.0	40	3.3	1 127	30.9	30.7
Hall	22 433	62.0	122 500	20.7	12.3	661	25.4	4.3	31 498	-0.4	1 206	3.8	31 168	25.7	33.6
Hamilton	3 649	80.0	111 600	18.8	10.4	686	28.3	1.0	4 668	-0.2	137	2.9	4 723	33.1	27.5
Harlan	1 555	78.7	78 200	19.1	12.5	553	20.3	1.1	1 752	-2.0	46	2.6	1 687	31.2	30.5
Hayes	482	67.2	73 500	22.7	12.8	440	16.7	0.4	594	-3.6	15	2.5	549	43.5	33.7
Hitchcock	1 342	72.5	59 100	17.9	13.4	632	30.3	2.8	1 312	-0.8	50	3.8	1 358	28.9	32.8
Holt	4 520	72.4	95 600	19.5	12.1	598	23.6	0.9	5 881	0.2	155	2.6	5 529	33.5	27.1
Hooker	312	76.3	70 000	21.3	12.8	638	29.6	1.0	396	-2.2	15	3.8	331	38.4	24.8
Howard	2 560	78.4	109 200	21.1	14.1	553	26.1	0.7	3 300	-0.4	115	3.5	3 287	34.9	29.6
Jefferson	3 359	76.0	71 000	18.7	12.6	495	22.0	0.1	4 239	-0.9	107	2.5	3 734	29.4	29.1
Johnson	1 886	73.6	76 800	19.4	12.8	585	22.1	0.9	2 086	-1.9	69	3.3	2 053	31.9	26.9
Kearney	2 767	68.1	109 900	18.7	11.8	703	23.3	1.0	3 752	-1.1	93	2.5	3 478	27.3	35.7
Keith	3 905	66.6	99 700	18.9	14.1	603	25.5	0.2	4 634	-1.1	142	3.1	4 116	30.3	26.6
Keya Paha	343	70.8	74 400	22.8	13.0	609	16.3	2.3	667	0.9	14	2.1	440	50.0	25.2
Kimball	1 574	64.8	80 100	22.3	14.9	632	24.5	1.1	1 964	-4.3	84	4.3	1 658	31.7	32.3
Knox	3 716	73.5	81 200	19.1	12.0	501	21.3	2.6	4 690	-0.7	151	3.2	4 277	34.8	27.0
Lancaster	117 667	59.4	152 900	20.3	10.9	729	29.7	2.1	169 126	0.9	4 882	2.9	160 866	38.5	19.6
Lincoln	15 010	66.4	114 200	20.4	13.5	631	25.1	2.0	18 757	1.1	604	3.2	17 360	27.1	31.5
Logan	365	69.0	114 300	25.7	10.2	541	17.5	2.5	483	-2.0	14	2.9	449	29.0	31.6
Loup	258	77.1	96 300	25.0	10.0	492	17.1	0.0	391	3.2	14	3.6	297	42.1	26.3
McPherson	197	65.0	133 300	22.2	11.3	648	14.1	3.6	458	-0.7	11	2.4	222	33.8	27.9
Madison	14 007	64.9	118 300	18.9	12.1	616	25.2	2.8	19 186	-0.2	557	2.9	18 727	28.8	30.3
Merrick	3 325	73.2	85 600	19.0	11.5	584	23.4	0.3	4 026	-0.1	153	3.8	4 177	30.2	28.0
Morrill	1 981	69.2	80 600	19.5	10.7	638	28.6	2.2	2 671	0.7	90	3.4	2 451	25.9	34.0
Nance	1 548	75.7	78 400	19.7	10.6	534	26.3	0.5	2 009	-2.8	57	2.8	1 784	35.5	28.8
Nemaha	2 877	71.0	102 200	18.5	12.9	583	24.2	2.0	3 661	-0.9	139	3.8	3 481	31.0	26.8
Nuckolls	2 068	74.0	54 500	17.7	11.0	501	23.9	2.0	2 374	-0.4	73	3.1	2 219	36.0	26.0
Otoe	6 447	73.3	115 800	20.0	12.3	642	25.8	1.1	8 334	1.6	294	3.5	8 225	28.9	29.3
Pawnee	1 261	77.7	63 800	17.8	12.6	467	23.9	1.8	1 674	0.1	40	2.4	1 265	44.7	26.2
Perkins	1 243	77.2	97 700	17.3	11.3	650	24.1	0.1	1 838	0.1	42	2.3	1 499	41.8	28.0
Phelps	3 728	72.0	110 000	19.5	11.3	591	24.7	0.5	4 944	-1.0	130	2.6	4 641	29.9	32.6
Pierce	2 940	76.7	98 500	19.3	11.3	574	19.1	1.4	4 153	-0.4	115	2.8	3 663	34.5	30.5

1. Specified owner-occupied units.   2. A value of 10.0 represents 10 percent or less; a value of 50.0 represents 50 percent or more.   3. Specified renter-occupied units.
4. Overcrowded or lacking complete plumbing facilities.   5. Percent of civilian labor force.   6. Civilian employed persons 16 years old and over.

STATE County	Number of establish-ments	Total	Health care and social assistance	Manufac-turing	Retail trade	Finance and insurance	Professional, scientific, and technical services	Total (mil dol)	Average per employee (dollars)	Number	Fewer than 50 acres	500 acres or more	Farm operators whose principal occu-pation is farming (percent)
	104	105	106	107	108	109	110	111	112	113	114	115	116
NEBRASKA—Cont'd													
Blaine	7	10	NA	NA	D	D	NA	0	29 600	117	14.5	66.7	76.1
Boone	203	1 430	324	121	236	72	32	49	33 987	646	12.7	42.4	68.3
Box Butte	309	2 839	582	338	416	115	100	94	32 999	466	17.8	48.7	59.9
Boyd	74	370	101	21	59	41	D	10	27 922	266	14.7	56.0	59.4
Brown	131	924	181	D	284	43	19	27	29 613	328	24.1	51.2	68.3
Buffalo	1 617	23 059	4 037	3 315	4 305	700	798	786	34 106	1 046	29.4	31.4	53.2
Burt	203	1 173	209	43	186	62	70	43	36 531	560	22.9	35.0	63.0
Butler	206	2 189	394	783	265	123	38	82	37 615	840	23.8	32.5	58.2
Cass	542	3 668	391	487	597	231	143	139	37 847	731	34.1	31.1	54.2
Cedar	307	1 957	173	254	333	128	79	64	32 783	939	20.8	29.9	58.7
Chase	159	1 113	134	18	322	68	21	38	33 698	342	11.7	54.1	64.9
Cherry	231	1 619	290	40	411	57	73	41	25 550	566	14.8	70.8	80.4
Cheyenne	298	4 704	513	315	915	145	106	247	52 445	555	10.6	54.1	58.9
Clay	190	1 191	126	78	200	83	32	40	33 837	457	25.2	42.5	67.0
Colfax	254	3 718	256	D	343	92	64	134	36 144	554	22.6	30.3	66.1
Cuming	351	2 614	363	351	349	199	113	92	35 342	918	26.1	25.1	61.2
Custer	397	2 952	608	D	596	175	105	99	33 585	1 352	21.1	43.3	62.9
Dakota	430	11 253	511	5 123	966	658	97	436	38 760	243	35.0	28.0	42.4
Dawes	274	2 180	527	16	634	84	64	63	28 918	493	11.8	52.7	53.5
Dawson	706	9 685	1 192	3 389	1 736	268	191	321	33 123	806	24.9	39.0	64.6
Deuel	60	346	64	NA	96	27	D	9	25 910	237	14.3	51.1	58.2
Dixon	109	1 237	95	D	64	42	D	32	25 907	570	24.9	31.1	60.5
Dodge	1 021	15 384	2 592	3 191	2 789	443	194	531	34 494	767	29.6	28.3	68.3
Douglas	15 333	311 615	47 294	20 681	36 645	36 155	19 373	15 560	49 933	396	58.3	13.6	44.4
Dundy	61	312	94	23	28	13	23	13	41 468	251	8.0	59.0	55.0
Fillmore	224	1 734	317	263	232	135	24	61	35 371	472	13.1	48.5	72.5
Franklin	74	418	119	NA	107	44	20	12	29 292	338	11.2	47.9	67.8
Frontier	72	413	40	D	80	48	14	14	33 346	317	15.8	51.1	60.6
Furnas	162	1 281	319	130	192	67	13	47	36 391	389	16.7	48.3	67.1
Gage	675	7 487	1 773	1 509	1 149	228	139	240	32 028	1 263	26.6	27.4	49.6
Garden	51	297	D	D	55	20	D	5	18 424	261	20.3	51.7	69.7
Garfield	95	606	117	109	122	20	23	16	26 878	226	16.8	41.2	58.0
Gosper	65	219	13	D	23	29	12	7	31 854	260	13.1	55.0	63.1
Grant	30	103	NA	D	19	D	D	2	22 990	80	13.8	65.0	75.0
Greeley	67	309	7	15	99	39	NA	9	29 395	389	9.0	47.8	68.9
Hall	1 844	30 377	4 236	6 936	5 189	1 229	640	1 100	36 223	593	29.3	34.2	59.9
Hamilton	325	2 804	331	630	313	119	87	109	38 769	572	22.7	40.2	72.0
Harlan	108	625	154	D	94	47	33	19	29 734	360	19.7	40.6	60.6
Hayes	20	49	D	D	D	D	D	2	34 327	235	8.1	60.0	67.7
Hitchcock	65	393	D	D	73	28	D	17	42 878	299	10.4	50.8	59.5
Holt	426	3 512	834	191	609	177	79	113	32 156	1 279	14.3	49.4	64.4
Hooker	29	107	D	D	29	D	D	4	34 748	82	11.0	76.8	54.9
Howard	166	1 057	347	22	205	102	39	31	29 470	682	26.1	29.0	59.1
Jefferson	239	2 690	448	647	403	88	69	89	33 098	627	21.9	33.2	55.5
Johnson	115	875	249	D	156	46	13	27	31 049	587	22.7	25.0	49.1
Kearney	172	1 826	568	299	177	77	20	59	32 360	344	15.1	56.1	78.5
Keith	346	2 643	270	244	666	176	113	80	30 227	388	14.7	46.4	72.2
Keya Paha	23	57	NA	NA	15	D	3	1	22 526	244	11.9	66.0	73.0
Kimball	127	1 181	D	330	174	D	11	41	34 610	402	9.0	52.5	52.5
Knox	269	1 767	342	39	371	175	64	44	25 102	1 080	17.5	38.1	68.3
Lancaster	8 299	133 714	23 950	12 429	18 684	10 967	8 470	5 371	40 165	1 836	51.1	14.9	34.2
Lincoln	1 065	11 856	2 874	316	2 131	478	382	403	33 984	1 168	29.8	39.2	59.2
Logan	23	80	D	NA	D	D	D	2	21 763	149	22.8	46.3	63.8
Loup	11	32	NA	NA	D	D	NA	0	10 625	138	12.3	49.3	62.3
McPherson	7	26	D	NA	D	D	NA	1	22 308	118	11.9	71.2	59.3
Madison	1 334	17 982	2 760	2 667	3 062	706	624	645	35 878	753	25.9	29.9	59.2
Merrick	235	1 728	298	228	182	96	37	71	40 805	492	27.8	33.7	57.1
Morrill	119	661	81	D	196	48	13	24	36 074	512	19.3	42.6	61.1
Nance	103	487	149	NA	99	49	17	13	26 275	355	22.8	34.9	64.2
Nemaha	183	1 513	351	D	224	106	42	45	29 426	451	16.0	33.3	57.6
Nuckolls	182	1 105	350	D	232	83	37	31	27 814	435	16.3	43.7	55.2
Otoe	460	4 981	801	1 402	816	167	78	161	32 263	897	29.8	29.7	49.3
Pawnee	64	472	119	D	79	48	D	18	37 409	540	12.4	34.1	52.0
Perkins	126	822	238	12	136	32	25	32	38 521	394	8.6	57.1	65.7
Phelps	337	3 877	829	D	424	116	93	142	36 597	405	16.3	54.1	72.3
Pierce	231	1 539	322	100	217	115	43	52	33 981	677	21.1	30.9	60.4

Table B. States and Counties — **Agriculture**

STATE County	Land in farms Acreage (1,000) [117]	Percent change, 2007–2012 [118]	Average size of farm [119]	Total irrigated (1,000) [120]	Total cropland (1,000) [121]	Value of land and buildings (dollars) Average per farm [122]	Average per acre [123]	Value of machinery and equipment, average per farm (dollars) [124]	Value of products sold Total (mil dol) [125]	Average per farm (dollars) [126]	Crops [127]	Live-stock and poultry products [128]	$10,000 or more [129]	$100,000 or more [130]	Government payments Total ($1,000) [131]	Percent of farms [132]
NEBRASKA—Cont'd																
Blaine	403	-9.2	3 440	7.0	32.6	1 760 274	512	95 709	34.7	296 214	16.3	83.7	76.9	39.3	293	32.5
Boone	434	7.2	672	184.7	326.9	2 964 181	4 408	289 596	453.4	701 850	42.9	57.1	83.4	59.0	5 870	78.8
Box Butte	675	0.7	1 449	141.6	337.5	1 547 721	1 068	292 384	299.3	642 170	56.3	43.7	65.2	43.3	4 279	68.2
Boyd	291	15.6	1 094	5.2	98.0	1 504 169	1 375	147 015	62.9	236 477	30.2	69.8	72.9	32.3	913	75.9
Brown	725	9.6	2 212	40.2	109.4	1 584 393	716	138 912	195.4	595 826	20.1	79.9	66.5	43.3	1 694	38.4
Buffalo	581	-5.2	555	240.8	342.3	2 074 083	3 737	226 212	395.1	377 751	68.9	31.1	67.5	40.6	8 102	64.9
Burt	310	12.7	553	37.6	278.5	2 886 561	5 216	245 725	226.9	405 252	66.2	33.8	72.3	50.4	4 598	77.0
Butler	370	3.9	441	110.8	306.6	2 179 969	4 948	258 019	276.4	329 043	66.9	33.1	67.0	42.9	6 657	78.6
Cass	345	22.8	472	3.5	304.3	2 732 765	5 792	210 464	149.3	204 291	93.9	6.1	60.7	41.6	4 746	66.5
Cedar	466	-1.7	497	139.0	371.7	2 189 874	4 408	211 296	388.7	413 987	42.0	58.0	75.6	45.4	6 256	73.7
Chase	541	-2.6	1 583	159.7	290.6	3 112 181	1 966	393 310	414.9	1 213 085	44.2	55.8	65.2	52.6	6 032	76.9
Cherry	3 757	-0.1	6 637	50.9	358.5	3 521 118	531	181 652	246.8	435 974	32.4	67.6	78.3	55.7	3 354	27.2
Cheyenne	703	-6.8	1 267	48.7	499.3	1 131 528	893	203 490	205.7	370 593	43.6	56.4	65.0	38.6	7 026	85.4
Clay	331	-9.5	723	191.7	259.1	3 712 295	5 133	386 182	355.1	776 978	59.6	40.4	77.9	58.4	5 141	73.7
Colfax	258	20.8	465	66.8	224.9	2 460 460	5 291	266 197	337.9	609 935	34.2	65.8	77.8	45.5	5 060	75.8
Cuming	363	0.8	395	52.4	312.6	2 120 511	5 364	285 514	1 081.3	1 177 889	12.9	87.1	79.3	49.3	6 797	76.8
Custer	1 504	-6.9	1 112	261.5	484.9	2 110 533	1 898	187 440	845.3	625 226	34.7	65.3	70.6	40.8	7 479	55.4
Dakota	158	-5.2	650	29.3	136.0	3 120 123	4 799	228 041	73.0	300 317	89.4	10.6	56.4	28.8	2 079	68.3
Dawes	824	-2.9	1 671	21.4	172.7	1 243 284	744	109 030	75.6	153 410	27.8	72.2	62.1	37.9	2 428	67.5
Dawson	630	-1.6	782	248.5	321.8	2 429 274	3 106	263 305	826.3	1 025 163	34.3	65.7	71.3	48.9	6 166	55.2
Deuel	277	-0.8	1 168	17.4	216.1	1 167 042	999	226 080	70.6	297 971	57.3	42.7	69.2	43.9	2 383	69.6
Dixon	299	20.3	525	24.0	226.3	2 176 037	4 148	211 812	169.1	296 716	42.0	58.0	63.0	35.4	4 695	73.7
Dodge	330	-2.5	430	118.0	305.0	2 414 327	5 611	281 532	326.0	425 043	60.7	39.3	72.2	48.9	5 602	74.3
Douglas	86	2.1	217	19.8	76.3	1 352 033	6 217	152 404	58.0	146 513	93.4	6.6	47.0	23.7	1 378	40.9
Dundy	521	-12.4	2 075	94.8	208.6	2 820 614	1 359	377 386	195.6	779 363	54.1	45.9	69.3	51.8	3 944	73.3
Fillmore	328	-9.3	696	211.0	296.4	3 835 816	5 513	473 146	334.8	709 335	78.0	22.0	84.1	68.9	5 465	81.4
Franklin	288	-1.3	851	85.8	166.2	2 527 118	2 969	260 417	119.1	352 447	87.0	13.0	78.4	48.2	3 802	81.1
Frontier	452	-4.9	1 426	53.3	174.7	2 093 385	1 468	232 278	124.6	393 145	53.1	46.9	70.7	41.0	3 205	74.4
Furnas	436	-2.3	1 120	66.4	282.7	2 622 414	2 341	282 820	181.6	466 720	54.2	45.8	69.9	44.2	5 719	82.3
Gage	534	-1.1	423	63.8	422.0	1 477 063	3 491	156 753	244.5	193 561	71.5	28.5	60.9	35.7	9 908	75.5
Garden	1 026	-2.1	3 932	35.7	149.4	2 403 636	611	180 276	113.6	435 341	33.3	66.7	65.5	44.1	1 714	70.1
Garfield	346	-5.4	1 531	22.5	70.7	1 517 035	991	146 903	64.8	286 597	34.9	65.1	74.3	42.9	1 373	48.7
Gosper	290	28.5	1 115	98.8	171.8	3 529 077	3 165	330 900	139.1	534 885	79.2	20.8	76.5	55.8	3 628	73.5
Grant	493	-0.4	6 167	1.7	41.0	3 407 063	552	136 288	29.0	362 063	D	D	71.3	53.8	226	8.8
Greeley	338	19.8	870	88.2	154.4	2 807 974	3 229	210 997	187.6	482 134	45.5	54.5	75.1	47.0	3 064	74.0
Hall	330	0.4	556	207.6	245.4	2 484 954	4 470	292 526	353.1	595 405	65.9	34.1	69.5	52.1	4 755	64.6
Hamilton	304	-4.6	532	235.5	273.2	3 430 491	6 446	346 014	353.2	617 547	77.1	22.9	77.4	62.4	5 705	77.6
Harlan	313	-10.9	869	93.3	211.8	2 677 533	3 082	261 208	223.5	620 828	56.6	43.4	67.8	44.2	2 989	68.1
Hayes	385	-15.1	1 639	57.1	186.1	2 121 255	1 294	253 677	163.4	695 383	44.9	55.1	70.2	50.2	4 320	92.8
Hitchcock	399	14.8	1 335	21.5	207.4	1 723 151	1 290	204 060	63.6	212 803	67.4	32.6	71.2	42.1	3 553	79.9
Holt	1 414	-7.7	1 106	280.2	600.5	2 314 973	2 093	217 735	636.4	497 540	51.7	48.3	77.2	43.2	7 584	53.2
Hooker	437	-4.4	5 327	3.1	15.7	2 361 890	443	104 793	17.3	210 500	10.9	89.1	81.7	35.4	897	34.1
Howard	312	12.0	458	115.4	182.5	1 350 003	2 949	186 560	246.3	361 128	45.5	54.5	71.7	39.9	3 603	70.1
Jefferson	352	8.2	562	92.8	270.7	2 206 616	3 928	230 150	219.6	350 234	62.2	37.8	66.3	39.4	5 179	74.8
Johnson	198	12.6	337	14.3	132.9	856 930	2 545	107 278	74.6	127 112	58.7	41.3	54.7	26.7	3 405	79.9
Kearney	294	-9.4	854	194.5	242.8	4 508 817	5 283	440 390	407.4	1 184 375	56.9	43.1	84.0	72.4	5 065	80.2
Keith	541	-6.9	1 395	115.3	253.9	2 593 289	1 859	276 216	228.3	588 492	60.7	39.3	65.7	44.3	3 371	67.0
Keya Paha	466	-3.7	1 909	20.1	98.0	1 480 037	775	148 684	107.1	438 848	27.2	72.8	77.9	43.0	733	40.6
Kimball	598	13.3	1 487	34.4	384.8	1 289 806	868	160 933	60.8	151 256	83.5	16.5	51.0	30.6	5 236	87.3
Knox	628	17.0	581	63.9	326.6	1 612 287	2 774	174 033	312.8	289 671	29.9	70.1	69.4	35.1	7 276	74.4
Lancaster	489	16.0	266	21.4	402.6	1 219 781	4 580	123 412	177.8	96 822	82.5	17.5	42.8	18.1	8 810	59.5
Lincoln	1 423	-11.1	1 219	239.8	432.3	1 749 910	1 436	196 783	782.7	670 087	33.8	66.2	62.2	33.0	5 832	45.5
Logan	330	-9.2	2 216	23.0	61.4	2 518 114	1 136	213 148	42.0	281 846	62.5	37.5	63.1	39.6	1 180	53.0
Loup	283	-20.2	2 051	8.2	29.3	1 519 891	741	106 181	32.1	232 406	24.2	75.8	68.8	37.7	772	58.7
McPherson	471	-13.2	3 990	7.1	20.2	1 789 517	449	88 102	30.1	255 144	19.5	80.5	70.3	39.8	167	18.6
Madison	352	11.6	467	122.0	291.0	2 250 416	4 817	236 368	303.7	403 263	49.2	50.8	71.8	40.2	7 057	69.5
Merrick	235	-5.2	478	167.4	200.2	1 833 841	3 838	280 335	275.2	559 394	58.6	41.4	66.1	47.8	4 182	72.6
Morrill	799	-11.4	1 561	128.6	240.5	1 440 148	923	169 750	345.2	674 223	33.1	66.9	68.9	45.1	3 595	69.7
Nance	208	-8.0	586	63.3	133.7	2 003 290	3 417	204 239	145.9	410 927	49.3	50.7	70.4	46.8	3 285	73.5
Nemaha	253	19.1	562	11.4	211.4	2 284 878	4 068	234 035	108.1	239 772	89.3	10.7	67.4	42.4	4 984	80.9
Nuckolls	350	13.9	804	65.2	230.4	3 033 191	3 773	259 074	168.4	387 140	81.8	18.2	82.8	54.7	4 756	79.3
Otoe	388	20.4	432	8.4	321.9	1 856 521	4 295	174 511	158.5	176 670	84.1	15.9	61.3	36.8	5 428	69.3
Pawnee	269	23.5	498	7.3	180.1	1 288 361	2 588	153 443	75.7	140 241	75.7	24.3	58.7	29.6	4 461	78.3
Perkins	557	-0.3	1 413	127.9	432.1	3 208 183	2 271	350 124	233.1	591 713	78.2	21.8	76.9	56.3	7 804	85.8
Phelps	331	-2.6	818	231.9	265.0	3 684 978	4 504	546 160	738.8	1 824 185	35.7	64.3	85.7	76.3	6 054	77.3
Pierce	329	3.9	486	130.0	260.6	2 102 468	4 324	270 908	261.2	385 832	56.4	43.6	72.8	41.1	5 154	70.3

Table B. States and Counties — Water Use, Wholesale Trade, Retail Trade, and Real Estate

STATE County	Water use, 2010		Wholesale trade,[1] 2012				Retail trade,[2] 2012				Real estate and rental and leasing,[2] 2012			
	Total water withdrawn (mil gal/day)	Gallons withdrawn per person per day	Number of establishments	Number of employees	Sales (mil dol)	Annual payroll (mil dol)	Number of establishments	Number of employees	Sales (mil dol)	Annual payroll (mil dol)	Number of establishments	Number of employees	Receipts (mil dol)	Annual payroll (mil dol)
	133	134	135	136	137	138	139	140	141	142	143	144	145	146
NEBRASKA—Cont'd														
Blaine	3.1	6 444	NA	NA	NA	NA	2	D	D	D	NA	NA	NA	NA
Boone	60.9	11 055	16	213	518.4	10.3	38	257	85.8	4.6	5	D	D	D
Box Butte	101.8	9 002	20	196	173.0	8.2	47	412	96.5	7.8	10	16	2.8	0.3
Boyd	9.1	4 350	3	16	8.4	0.5	11	74	14.4	1.0	1	2	D	D
Brown	51.1	16 232	4	D	D	D	31	259	68.1	5.3	2	D	D	D
Buffalo	230.8	5 007	77	902	1 254.5	43.0	236	3 677	967.0	78.9	55	156	39.0	4.4
Burt	10.6	1 550	16	180	128.0	6.2	29	179	33.8	2.5	4	5	0.3	0.0
Butler	51.2	6 100	14	129	216.5	6.9	27	298	64.2	4.8	4	3	0.3	0.1
Cass	18.4	728	17	D	D	D	70	627	177.8	13.2	20	21	3.3	0.5
Cedar	28.4	3 209	24	161	120.3	7.2	46	377	111.0	8.0	8	14	1.4	0.3
Chase	144.2	36 364	16	222	536.5	10.0	30	260	92.3	7.4	4	7	0.2	0.1
Cherry	44.7	7 826	7	102	222.5	2.3	38	422	87.3	7.6	9	7	1.4	0.2
Cheyenne	43.3	4 327	13	113	194.6	5.6	52	1 508	1 081.6	46.1	7	9	1.5	0.2
Clay	121.3	18 546	24	174	289.5	8.6	25	200	135.9	4.1	2	D	D	D
Colfax	24.1	2 294	17	131	214.2	7.6	43	342	106.0	7.6	6	14	1.4	0.2
Cuming	12.8	1 395	24	163	220.5	7.4	50	378	206.0	7.5	4	5	0.9	0.1
Custer	169.1	15 460	15	120	77.8	5.4	63	483	143.4	10.6	7	10	0.7	0.1
Dakota	7.4	350	15	249	219.1	12.3	68	897	198.7	18.5	13	D	D	D
Dawes	7.9	861	4	23	10.4	0.7	58	581	169.9	13.8	10	10	1.1	0.2
Dawson	182.7	7 511	34	433	680.1	19.5	107	1 398	423.4	34.4	19	D	D	D
Deuel	28.0	14 405	3	D	D	D	11	118	94.8	2.1	1	D	D	D
Dixon	9.6	1 597	8	35	93.3	1.7	9	61	11.7	0.8	1	D	D	D
Dodge	36.0	980	63	640	1 127.7	31.8	162	2 427	1 097.3	59.0	36	172	24.1	4.2
Douglas	386.0	746	750	10 775	12 685.1	594.8	1 749	34 754	8 586.0	839.3	713	5 700	977.6	258.1
Dundy	108.0	53 800	5	D	D	D	10	46	12.3	1.1	1	D	D	D
Fillmore	120.6	20 467	24	199	281.1	8.1	30	234	65.0	3.9	5	4	0.4	0.0
Franklin	37.5	11 622	9	68	90.2	2.2	12	102	20.4	2.0	1	D	D	D
Frontier	36.0	13 059	6	D	D	D	12	65	19.2	1.2	1	D	D	D
Furnas	32.8	6 622	10	D	D	D	33	204	52.9	3.8	1	D	D	D
Gage	24.9	1 115	36	349	369.5	15.5	112	1 036	262.4	23.0	14	23	3.7	0.6
Garden	27.9	13 578	3	D	D	D	12	65	11.9	0.9	NA	NA	NA	NA
Garfield	12.7	6 193	3	D	D	D	22	138	29.6	2.1	1	D	D	D
Gosper	57.3	28 048	6	41	101.4	1.6	5	24	3.7	0.3	4	D	D	D
Grant	2.1	3 453	3	D	D	D	4	20	3.3	0.2	NA	NA	NA	NA
Greeley	51.5	20 280	4	49	50.4	2.4	15	92	41.6	1.9	2	D	D	D
Hall	132.6	2 263	98	1 296	910.4	66.9	297	4 864	1 256.3	110.1	77	296	54.3	9.0
Hamilton	142.7	15 642	14	284	545.3	14.7	40	309	116.5	6.1	7	9	3.1	0.7
Harlan	37.2	10 876	10	46	63.2	2.0	18	97	34.4	2.0	1	D	D	D
Hayes	41.6	43 020	NA	NA	NA	NA	2	D	D	D	NA	NA	NA	NA
Hitchcock	24.6	8 473	5	D	D	D	13	71	15.8	1.4	NA	NA	NA	NA
Holt	358.2	34 327	30	374	424.0	16.2	80	615	159.9	11.2	13	17	4.2	0.4
Hooker	2.6	3 519	NA	NA	NA	NA	5	34	7.2	0.6	NA	NA	NA	NA
Howard	168.0	26 771	8	55	43.7	1.9	27	212	52.9	3.8	NA	NA	NA	NA
Jefferson	40.6	5 376	13	D	D	D	33	570	176.9	10.1	4	15	0.7	0.3
Johnson	6.9	1 326	4	D	D	D	26	144	44.8	2.9	4	23	3.6	0.3
Kearney	103.6	15 958	14	182	246.1	8.5	20	160	33.4	3.0	3	3	0.6	0.1
Keith	119.8	14 315	19	154	135.2	6.7	63	560	241.5	12.3	17	44	3.9	0.7
Keya Paha	22.1	26 796	2	D	D	D	3	9	5.0	0.2	NA	NA	NA	NA
Kimball	29.1	7 618	4	D	D	D	22	173	50.3	4.2	3	D	D	D
Knox	33.1	3 800	13	118	151.0	4.4	54	384	82.2	6.5	7	29	1.7	0.6
Lancaster	22.0	77	278	4 169	3 139.7	169.3	1 016	17 165	4 322.6	388.1	344	1 715	255.1	56.5
Lincoln	263.4	7 257	46	D	D	D	194	2 180	728.8	49.2	43	104	17.8	2.6
Logan	12.3	16 107	2	D	D	D	2	D	D	D	NA	NA	NA	NA
Loup	9.1	14 320	1	D	D	D	1	D	D	D	NA	NA	NA	NA
McPherson	6.9	12 801	NA	NA	NA	NA	2	D	D	D	NA	NA	NA	NA
Madison	40.5	1 162	64	1 730	2 252.8	78.7	212	3 061	815.2	67.6	59	172	24.8	4.2
Merrick	111.9	14 264	24	198	369.2	9.5	33	204	72.1	3.7	5	10	1.1	0.5
Morrill	213.9	42 422	12	120	71.0	5.9	20	163	37.2	2.9	3	3	0.4	0.0
Nance	36.4	9 751	5	23	52.0	0.9	16	100	25.4	2.0	1	D	D	D
Nemaha	727.0	100 304	9	57	69.5	2.5	37	235	57.7	4.6	5	10	0.8	0.1
Nuckolls	62.4	13 860	16	114	172.0	5.4	26	231	73.8	4.8	1	D	D	D
Otoe	314.8	19 998	21	171	239.4	8.0	80	833	202.5	16.9	15	63	11.9	1.9
Pawnee	4.9	1 771	1	D	D	D	10	76	15.7	1.4	NA	NA	NA	NA
Perkins	96.5	32 495	14	121	218.7	6.0	19	120	56.8	3.5	3	15	1.0	0.1
Phelps	153.9	16 748	28	378	851.6	17.3	48	404	116.5	9.3	9	13	2.7	0.2
Pierce	54.4	7 480	14	D	D	D	36	200	69.6	3.5	3	3	0.5	0.1

1. Merchant wholesalers, except manufacturers' sales branches and offices.   2. Employer establishments.

Table B. States and Counties — Professional Services, Manufacturing, and Accommodation and Food Services

STATE County	Professional, scientific, and technical services, 2012				Manufacturing, 2012				Accommodation and food services, 2012			
	Number of establishments	Number of employees	Receipts (mil dol)	Annual payroll (mil dol)	Number of establishments	Number of employees	Receipts (mil dol)	Annual payroll (mil dol)	Number of establishments	Number of employees	Sales (mil dol)	Annual payroll (mil dol)
	147	148	149	150	151	152	153	154	155	156	157	158
NEBRASKA—Cont'd												
Blaine	NA	NA	NA	NA	NA	NA	NA	NA	1	D	D	D
Boone	8	25	5.5	0.9	11	112	D	5.4	11	94	3.2	0.8
Box Butte	22	93	8.8	2.6	8	328	D	16.2	32	339	14.7	3.9
Boyd	1	D	D	D	5	16	D	0.3	6	20	0.6	0.1
Brown	6	19	1.5	0.4	3	24	D	D	10	87	2.9	0.7
Buffalo	104	630	77.1	27.0	58	3 306	1 785.0	147.3	143	3 084	121.7	33.9
Burt	8	72	20.8	3.8	8	76	22.2	2.8	15	67	2.8	0.6
Butler	9	D	D	D	10	571	D	23.9	15	D	D	D
Cass	37	127	10.3	5.2	19	381	170.5	19.2	41	D	D	D
Cedar	13	D	D	D	12	198	D	9.3	12	87	2.2	0.5
Chase	8	D	D	D	4	22	D	D	9	D	D	D
Cherry	18	62	7.4	1.7	8	23	5.1	0.9	23	300	14.0	3.8
Cheyenne	15	D	D	D	8	273	120.8	15.0	35	520	28.1	6.9
Clay	7	D	D	D	7	67	D	2.5	8	31	1.0	0.3
Colfax	11	58	8.0	1.6	3	D	D	D	19	D	D	D
Cuming	22	104	15.7	3.3	14	323	245.8	14.3	25	290	15.4	2.6
Custer	27	96	9.9	2.6	9	D	D	D	31	313	10.7	3.1
Dakota	25	D	D	D	36	D	D	D	40	526	25.1	7.2
Dawes	18	D	D	D	4	10	1.5	0.3	37	457	17.4	4.9
Dawson	57	D	D	D	26	D	D	D	61	D	D	D
Deuel	3	4	0.3	0.1	NA	NA	NA	NA	5	D	D	D
Dixon	1	D	D	D	NA	NA	NA	NA	6	17	1.1	0.1
Dodge	49	183	20.6	7.0	60	3 402	1 955.3	140.1	97	1 476	56.3	15.8
Douglas	1 742	55 558	3 260.3	2 757.2	431	20 560	10 990.1	904.0	1 258	24 758	1 170.2	342.9
Dundy	5	D	D	D	5	15	2.7	0.4	4	27	1.2	0.3
Fillmore	10	24	2.5	0.7	13	221	415.1	8.7	13	81	2.7	0.6
Franklin	4	15	1.5	0.4	NA	NA	NA	NA	6	33	1.3	0.3
Frontier	3	15	0.9	0.3	NA	NA	NA	NA	3	D	D	D
Furnas	5	18	1.2	0.4	7	98	D	4.4	12	D	D	D
Gage	33	125	10.6	3.8	40	1 252	727.0	56.1	49	628	27.4	6.7
Garden	3	D	D	D	NA	NA	NA	NA	3	32	1.0	0.2
Garfield	7	D	D	D	8	117	D	3.7	9	63	1.8	0.3
Gosper	3	D	D	D	NA	NA	NA	NA	3	D	D	D
Grant	2	D	D	D	NA	NA	NA	NA	5	12	0.1	0.0
Greeley	NA	NA	NA	NA	3	9	D	D	4	9	0.6	0.1
Hall	109	638	69.7	25.2	74	7 241	6 021.9	280.1	156	2 515	114.9	33.0
Hamilton	16	69	13.0	2.7	19	443	D	21.7	19	169	6.8	2.0
Harlan	8	D	D	D	5	37	D	D	14	91	3.6	0.8
Hayes	2	D	D	D	NA	NA	NA	NA	2	D	D	D
Hitchcock	NA	NA	NA	NA	3	85	188.0	3.6	5	17	0.6	0.1
Holt	21	63	7.7	2.8	20	190	D	6.8	41	386	12.8	3.2
Hooker	1	D	D	D	NA	NA	NA	NA	4	7	0.3	0.0
Howard	10	26	3.5	0.9	5	10	2.1	0.3	10	69	2.5	0.5
Jefferson	11	D	D	D	16	572	178.4	20.6	19	160	6.7	1.5
Johnson	4	11	0.7	0.2	4	D	D	D	10	57	2.0	0.5
Kearney	10	27	2.0	0.6	9	260	209.2	12.2	12	118	3.1	1.0
Keith	28	119	9.9	3.6	15	254	D	8.0	46	514	22.9	6.1
Keya Paha	4	5	0.2	0.0	NA	NA	NA	NA	NA	NA	NA	NA
Kimball	9	20	1.5	0.3	8	263	38.7	8.9	16	110	4.0	0.9
Knox	17	D	D	D	6	23	6.4	0.9	22	98	3.5	0.7
Lancaster	842	9 135	1 292.4	460.9	235	12 011	5 963.3	596.5	672	13 483	598.3	156.9
Lincoln	78	D	D	D	17	D	200.8	D	94	D	D	D
Logan	1	D	D	D	NA	NA	NA	NA	1	D	D	D
Loup	NA	NA	NA	NA	NA	NA	NA	NA	1	D	D	D
McPherson	NA	NA	NA	NA	NA	NA	NA	NA	1	D	D	D
Madison	88	702	51.5	20.6	55	3 092	D	132.6	101	1 644	64.6	17.8
Merrick	8	34	4.2	1.4	16	254	D	11.8	13	99	4.4	1.0
Morrill	1	D	D	D	3	36	D	1.4	18	147	4.2	1.1
Nance	5	D	D	D	NA	NA	NA	NA	14	D	D	D
Nemaha	8	36	2.1	0.7	3	D	D	D	20	253	7.0	2.5
Nuckolls	14	31	2.6	0.7	3	6	D	D	9	D	D	D
Otoe	26	85	7.3	2.1	17	1 512	D	66.9	40	398	13.9	4.4
Pawnee	4	D	D	D	5	D	D	D	5	33	0.8	0.2
Perkins	7	25	1.6	0.5	3	10	D	D	3	7	0.6	0.1
Phelps	25	89	11.2	3.6	7	D	D	D	22	316	11.3	3.1
Pierce	11	D	D	D	11	D	D	D	10	99	2.2	0.6

1. Establishment subject to federal tax.

STATE County	Health care and social assistance, 2012				Other services, 2012				Nonemployer businesses, 2015		Value of residential construction authorized by building permits, 2016	
	Number of establishments	Number of employees	Receipts (mil dol)	Annual payroll (mil dol)	Number of establishments	Number of employees	Receipts (mil dol)	Annual payroll (mil dol)	Number	Receipts (mil dol)	New Construction ($1,000)	Number of housing units
	159	160	161	162	163	164	165	166	167	168	169	170
NEBRASKA—Cont'd												
Blaine	NA	NA	NA	NA	NA	NA	NA	NA	47	1.7	NA	NA
Boone	19	244	14.0	4.7	10	26	3.1	0.8	534	20.6	0	0
Box Butte	29	607	50.5	20.0	31	105	11.7	2.3	708	26.5	930	3
Boyd	9	108	5.2	2.1	4	11	1.6	0.2	204	8.9	0	0
Brown	11	181	11.5	4.8	11	28	3.1	0.8	298	10.0	0	0
Buffalo	177	4 012	453.6	165.4	112	D	D	D	3 731	181.9	42 407	215
Burt	17	227	12.5	5.6	13	72	8.5	2.4	494	21.7	1 009	8
Butler	15	373	28.3	13.0	15	D	D	D	689	28.7	608	3
Cass	29	423	26.6	9.8	35	120	9.0	2.4	1 854	80.0	16 578	102
Cedar	13	191	10.2	4.2	25	D	D	D	756	38.4	2 398	13
Chase	10	142	11.6	5.2	12	D	D	D	435	24.8	1 265	3
Cherry	19	345	23.9	9.5	18	36	4.8	0.8	607	24.4	3 171	20
Cheyenne	19	510	45.6	16.9	23	67	6.6	1.8	682	31.2	1 316	7
Clay	16	154	5.4	2.6	8	D	D	D	540	24.9	1 050	5
Colfax	15	344	36.0	8.6	27	76	8.1	1.9	579	27.6	5 913	34
Cuming	26	385	40.9	14.6	33	132	21.1	3.8	730	36.8	3 336	15
Custer	41	713	44.0	19.8	28	59	7.2	1.2	1 120	41.7	3 770	17
Dakota	32	520	33.7	12.2	36	240	54.8	14.1	1 028	54.4	7 590	33
Dawes	33	630	44.1	21.3	19	51	3.1	0.8	650	21.8	1 967	14
Dawson	73	1 143	92.1	34.5	62	D	D	D	1 459	64.4	2 636	13
Deuel	3	19	1.0	0.4	3	D	D	D	165	8.7	0	0
Dixon	11	99	4.6	1.8	11	D	D	D	478	20.7	1 080	7
Dodge	114	2 662	231.7	85.4	92	377	36.4	8.9	2 271	101.8	14 931	54
Douglas	1 742	47 573	5 673.5	2 121.5	1 067	8 179	1 287.2	251.7	36 272	1 779.5	310 017	2 704
Dundy	8	D	D	D	3	D	D	D	169	7.3	705	4
Fillmore	14	288	20.5	8.7	22	63	9.4	1.4	501	21.0	556	3
Franklin	7	166	9.1	3.6	7	19	1.4	0.2	254	9.6	149	1
Frontier	8	40	1.0	0.5	4	D	D	D	245	12.0	1 010	4
Furnas	20	359	24.6	10.9	14	D	D	D	424	21.1	630	2
Gage	58	1 780	114.4	48.2	66	242	21.6	5.6	1 566	60.4	3 767	17
Garden	4	D	D	D	4	9	0.5	0.1	191	7.6	0	0
Garfield	7	D	D	D	8	17	1.7	0.4	225	8.8	1 217	9
Gosper	7	9	0.4	0.2	1	D	D	D	193	9.6	300	6
Grant	NA	NA	NA	NA	2	D	D	D	81	3.8	0	0
Greeley	3	10	0.1	0.1	2	D	D	D	266	12.9	259	2
Hall	185	D	D	D	145	987	92.7	21.6	3 832	170.7	33 421	313
Hamilton	19	D	D	D	23	D	D	D	837	32.4	7 165	24
Harlan	8	172	11.2	5.0	6	D	D	D	329	12.6	500	3
Hayes	1	D	D	D	NA	NA	NA	NA	80	3.4	370	3
Hitchcock	2	D	D	D	2	D	D	D	225	11.3	150	1
Holt	33	870	75.4	29.2	37	D	D	D	1 282	73.4	5 413	25
Hooker	1	D	D	D	4	4	0.5	0.1	109	4.6	400	2
Howard	10	D	D	D	12	D	D	D	517	23.4	5 455	28
Jefferson	16	411	28.1	11.9	17	D	D	D	465	18.7	770	5
Johnson	14	274	22.3	9.4	8	21	1.8	0.3	306	10.7	369	2
Kearney	14	604	27.7	13.2	13	D	D	D	485	22.3	3 706	13
Keith	23	339	32.1	10.6	24	94	8.7	2.2	745	35.4	3 151	16
Keya Paha	NA	NA	NA	NA	3	D	D	D	113	4.5	0	0
Kimball	7	97	9.1	4.0	10	D	D	D	287	12.4	0	0
Knox	19	375	24.2	9.1	12	29	3.3	0.6	659	26.3	2 859	17
Lancaster	971	23 204	2 364.8	939.4	667	4 152	578.3	130.7	20 614	817.8	361 995	2 319
Lincoln	140	D	D	D	79	398	38.3	10.1	2 272	89.7	12 416	67
Logan	1	D	D	D	3	15	0.3	0.2	74	3.2	NA	NA
Loup	NA	NA	NA	NA	1	D	D	D	78	2.2	1 068	7
McPherson	NA	NA	NA	NA	NA	NA	NA	NA	40	1.8	0	0
Madison	164	D	D	D	106	542	44.3	14.0	2 637	113.4	16 722	74
Merrick	17	343	24.3	9.1	22	48	7.3	1.2	643	27.1	3 356	21
Morrill	8	135	12.6	4.3	6	D	D	D	381	14.4	0	0
Nance	10	165	7.4	3.5	13	D	D	D	272	10.3	850	4
Nemaha	21	369	30.8	13.6	17	73	4.5	1.1	499	19.6	1 060	5
Nuckolls	15	385	28.3	11.4	23	48	4.4	0.8	345	12.4	450	3
Otoe	42	853	66.9	26.5	36	129	11.4	2.9	1 177	45.8	15 171	64
Pawnee	7	116	8.8	3.9	5	14	0.9	0.2	257	10.5	1 180	7
Perkins	7	230	16.5	6.2	10	D	D	D	300	18.6	900	3
Phelps	21	813	59.7	24.7	30	104	21.1	2.9	853	35.1	2 946	14
Pierce	17	D	D	D	13	22	2.6	0.6	647	27.0	2 537	10

Table B. States and Counties — Government Employment and Payroll, and Local Government Finances

	Government employment and payroll, 2012									Local government finances, 2012				
			March payroll (percent of total)							General revenue				
												Taxes		
													Per capita[1] (dollars)	
STATE County	Full-time equivalent employees	March payroll (dollars)	Administration, judicial, and legal	Police and Corrections	Fire Protection	Highways and transportation	Health and Welfare	Natural resources and utilities	Education and libraries	Total (mil dol)	Intergovernmental (mil dol)	Total (mil dol)	Total	Property
	171	172	173	174	175	176	177	178	179	180	181	182	183	184
NEBRASKA—Cont'd														
Blaine	38	116 097	9.8	2.6	0.0	4.4	0.0	0.8	82.3	3.5	0.8	2.4	4 720	4 449
Boone	460	1 692 880	3.4	2.8	0.0	3.1	53.1	1.6	35.2	48.2	4.1	17.4	3 205	2 668
Box Butte	797	2 934 530	5.1	4.9	0.6	2.6	34.3	4.7	46.8	73.9	15.5	21.5	1 898	1 550
Boyd	117	356 840	12.6	1.7	0.0	16.0	0.2	10.9	57.9	9.3	3.1	5.0	2 429	2 227
Brown	260	870 487	5.2	3.3	0.0	3.3	24.0	16.3	47.5	23.9	5.2	7.5	2 470	2 176
Buffalo	1 737	6 480 217	6.2	9.5	0.9	3.9	2.1	3.9	71.0	175.2	52.8	86.9	1 830	1 377
Burt	405	1 151 444	8.6	6.4	0.0	7.3	1.0	16.5	58.3	32.4	6.0	19.8	2 978	2 657
Butler	460	1 583 569	5.4	4.9	0.0	7.3	25.9	17.6	38.5	51.3	15.3	24.0	2 892	2 645
Cass	930	3 065 349	8.2	11.0	0.0	5.1	1.0	3.6	70.6	95.9	27.6	43.8	1 744	1 516
Cedar	483	1 415 097	8.1	3.5	0.0	8.8	0.8	13.3	64.8	39.6	9.7	20.9	2 385	2 173
Chase	332	1 110 424	4.3	4.0	0.0	4.7	35.2	7.8	44.0	41.9	4.1	13.9	3 412	3 043
Cherry	255	767 776	8.8	7.8	0.0	8.5	0.8	7.7	65.2	38.3	6.2	15.0	2 611	2 227
Cheyenne	473	1 711 606	5.9	6.9	0.1	6.1	2.1	17.6	59.6	50.6	16.3	25.0	3 380	3 083
Clay	462	1 297 168	6.4	2.9	0.0	4.4	10.6	4.8	67.8	36.0	7.3	21.7	2 364	1 966
Colfax	471	1 687 680	7.1	4.2	0.1	3.4	0.0	8.5	76.2	45.8	15.6	25.2	2 364	2 089
Cuming	453	1 421 997	8.3	5.2	0.0	7.6	0.8	11.8	65.0	41.8	8.7	22.9	2 521	2 184
Custer	710	2 846 682	7.1	7.6	0.6	7.7	7.1	24.5	41.2	53.1	11.4	26.7	2 483	2 199
Dakota	972	3 563 243	6.5	7.2	0.4	2.2	0.4	6.2	75.7	80.5	44.9	26.9	1 286	955
Dawes	367	1 249 160	8.1	6.9	0.0	5.6	4.6	6.3	67.5	30.8	10.5	13.6	1 487	1 140
Dawson	1 718	5 640 576	3.0	5.6	0.0	2.6	22.8	12.1	52.5	153.2	47.5	40.1	1 657	1 368
Deuel	141	507 062	13.6	7.1	0.0	10.8	0.8	3.1	63.8	13.1	2.9	7.5	3 787	3 435
Dixon	423	1 293 730	7.0	5.2	0.0	4.4	0.1	2.3	78.0	31.8	9.3	14.9	2 525	2 324
Dodge	2 164	10 158 631	3.6	5.2	1.1	2.6	42.4	7.4	36.3	221.5	79.5	60.9	1 672	1 359
Douglas	24 079	100 381 103	3.6	9.6	4.0	3.5	4.4	25.2	48.9	2 457.4	796.5	1 177.7	2 217	1 587
Dundy	208	669 425	6.4	3.2	0.0	3.8	42.5	2.5	41.3	17.3	2.2	6.8	3 356	3 043
Fillmore	362	1 220 014	6.9	3.1	0.1	6.7	29.9	2.4	49.5	43.0	5.2	18.2	3 154	2 687
Franklin	266	1 622 165	12.8	12.9	0.0	7.6	20.4	27.8	17.9	14.4	3.0	5.2	1 628	1 517
Frontier	255	1 135 230	18.7	2.7	0.0	9.6	0.0	22.2	46.4	17.7	4.4	9.4	3 436	3 195
Furnas	443	1 409 219	6.3	2.7	0.2	3.0	18.5	17.2	51.3	28.8	8.9	13.3	2 701	2 216
Gage	894	3 582 464	6.7	7.0	2.9	7.2	0.7	19.7	53.9	82.2	27.8	39.6	1 814	1 546
Garden	214	658 334	5.9	3.2	0.9	5.3	49.9	2.8	31.7	16.1	1.9	6.4	3 289	2 928
Garfield	99	296 601	11.6	3.8	0.0	6.2	0.0	8.4	68.2	7.8	2.6	4.1	2 026	1 771
Gosper	141	396 475	7.9	4.8	0.0	10.0	27.7	9.6	37.4	12.4	1.6	6.8	3 334	3 090
Grant	58	138 009	9.1	2.9	0.0	8.9	0.0	0.0	78.7	4.2	0.6	3.2	5 083	4 808
Greeley	162	445 160	7.7	2.9	0.0	5.1	0.0	6.8	77.0	13.4	3.4	7.4	3 018	2 769
Hall	2 737	10 820 863	5.4	7.6	3.9	3.5	0.6	18.3	59.8	240.9	94.1	101.1	1 675	1 264
Hamilton	408	1 264 730	9.1	7.2	0.0	7.2	3.0	5.2	67.5	39.3	8.1	21.3	2 363	2 061
Harlan	208	554 731	9.8	4.8	0.0	6.6	36.0	7.8	31.8	21.6	4.7	5.2	1 526	1 274
Hayes	59	140 504	6.9	0.0	0.0	17.5	0.0	1.1	74.5	4.9	1.1	3.3	3 501	3 306
Hitchcock	135	502 076	5.5	9.7	0.0	8.5	0.6	32.9	42.8	12.2	2.7	6.3	2 166	1 952
Holt	457	1 501 263	9.1	4.7	0.0	9.6	2.1	8.2	65.9	52.2	11.5	29.0	2 791	2 328
Hooker	94	243 859	6.4	2.5	0.0	3.0	31.7	0.0	53.1	6.6	1.1	3.3	4 499	4 234
Howard	489	1 673 314	3.0	2.5	0.0	3.5	30.8	15.6	43.1	39.6	8.7	12.1	1 910	1 679
Jefferson	388	1 330 833	4.5	5.1	0.5	4.1	1.7	10.5	71.7	34.4	8.5	21.1	2 812	2 496
Johnson	311	1 042 290	4.4	2.9	0.0	4.2	35.4	11.8	40.5	31.4	6.4	12.0	2 329	2 119
Kearney	491	1 419 422	5.9	3.6	0.2	4.7	23.6	1.7	59.6	37.0	4.9	21.7	3 345	3 061
Keith	405	1 305 826	7.9	6.0	2.7	4.6	0.5	4.9	72.0	34.2	10.9	18.9	2 304	1 808
Keya Paha	48	112 765	9.7	2.6	0.0	8.1	0.1	0.9	76.3	3.9	0.8	2.8	3 476	3 285
Kimball	327	1 077 444	7.5	4.5	0.0	4.9	31.5	6.3	43.8	23.2	8.1	9.0	2 386	2 123
Knox	455	1 410 392	6.9	5.2	0.0	6.0	0.5	11.5	69.5	39.5	15.7	18.5	2 154	1 898
Lancaster	10 733	45 755 791	5.1	7.8	4.0	4.4	4.3	11.6	61.0	979.6	313.6	469.5	1 600	1 150
Lincoln	1 720	6 235 856	4.7	7.5	3.4	4.1	1.7	7.3	69.6	279.7	58.1	71.6	1 983	1 637
Logan	59	160 033	10.8	4.2	0.0	4.3	0.0	2.4	77.5	4.8	1.4	3.0	3 927	3 676
Loup	40	120 306	13.9	4.4	0.0	11.3	0.0	1.2	68.0	3.9	1.3	2.1	3 615	3 416
McPherson	37	88 185	16.1	0.0	0.0	8.0	0.0	0.1	75.8	3.0	0.5	2.2	4 361	4 232
Madison	1 848	7 112 436	4.2	6.2	2.5	3.0	2.2	7.2	74.5	181.2	50.7	86.6	2 472	2 061
Merrick	402	1 076 825	8.5	3.7	0.0	5.6	31.5	5.5	44.2	35.9	7.1	13.5	1 732	1 569
Morrill	306	1 053 262	7.6	5.7	0.1	4.9	0.1	9.8	68.4	37.2	13.6	10.5	2 152	1 947
Nance	276	922 483	9.8	3.4	0.0	6.6	22.8	3.9	52.2	23.2	3.7	11.8	3 167	2 896
Nemaha	407	1 469 356	4.6	3.0	0.0	3.2	23.9	9.1	55.9	43.7	12.6	14.0	1 959	1 690
Nuckolls	283	687 707	10.1	4.5	0.0	6.4	0.3	41.3	36.3	18.3	8.3	7.3	1 653	1 451
Otoe	850	2 831 957	5.7	5.8	1.1	4.0	15.2	13.1	52.1	63.3	14.6	30.7	1 948	1 590
Pawnee	199	600 056	5.0	2.2	0.0	4.6	35.8	3.6	47.4	19.2	4.6	6.3	2 267	2 041
Perkins	326	1 063 703	7.6	5.6	0.0	8.0	47.1	0.7	29.4	27.8	2.7	9.8	3 327	2 981
Phelps	471	1 581 446	8.2	8.0	0.0	6.4	0.6	7.7	68.6	46.7	11.6	24.5	2 663	2 090
Pierce	446	1 313 225	5.7	3.6	0.0	4.0	19.8	2.4	64.0	35.8	6.4	16.9	2 364	2 111

1. Based on the resident population estimated as of July 1 of the year shown.

Table B. States and Counties — Local Government Finances, Government Employment, and Income Taxes

STATE County	Local government finances, 2012 (cont.) Direct general expenditure Total (mil dol)	Per capita[1] (dollars)	Education	Health and hospitals	Police protection	Public welfare	Highways	Debt outstanding Total (mil dol)	Per capita[1] (dollars)	Government employment, 2015 Federal civilian	Federal military	State and local	Individual income tax returns, 2014 Number of returns	Mean adjusted gross income	Mean income tax
	185	186	187	188	189	190	191	192	193	194	195	196	197	198	199
NEBRASKA—Cont'd															
Blaine	3.5	6 794	68.8	0.0	1.3	0.1	13.6	0.2	409	24	D	54	230	41 243	5 243
Boone	44.3	8 176	31.0	48.5	1.6	0.2	8.2	3.3	617	29	19	653	2 650	58 631	7 221
Box Butte	77.0	6 806	35.7	37.0	2.5	2.0	3.9	22.0	1 940	35	40	996	5 320	56 344	5 845
Boyd	9.7	4 699	58.5	0.6	1.5	0.2	13.1	3.5	1 709	14	D	229	890	45 954	3 907
Brown	24.8	8 204	40.4	26.1	2.3	0.3	10.6	32.9	10 893	19	10	400	1 450	42 433	4 714
Buffalo	185.9	3 916	56.3	0.0	5.0	0.1	9.3	209.9	4 423	130	166	3 943	21 930	61 020	7 511
Burt	33.4	5 018	48.1	0.0	2.4	7.6	14.7	21.0	3 159	36	23	524	3 100	52 041	5 188
Butler	46.9	5 656	32.0	32.2	1.7	0.4	12.1	67.8	8 175	44	28	610	3 870	52 076	4 981
Cass	93.1	3 704	51.2	0.3	3.0	4.3	10.9	110.7	4 404	64	90	1 362	12 210	62 797	6 990
Cedar	36.7	4 202	50.3	0.2	2.2	11.6	13.5	12.1	1 386	102	30	600	3 980	55 835	6 521
Chase	45.4	11 179	31.0	33.0	1.0	7.2	9.0	27.2	6 701	26	14	487	1 850	56 457	7 403
Cherry	38.0	6 630	32.1	37.2	1.7	0.3	10.5	8.0	1 401	53	21	539	2 800	52 394	5 732
Cheyenne	49.4	4 909	41.1	0.6	3.5	0.7	11.0	57.6	5 724	35	36	786	5 000	65 179	8 473
Clay	34.4	5 370	60.7	0.6	1.7	7.2	11.3	9.1	1 421	155	22	594	2 940	56 309	6 598
Colfax	46.8	4 390	67.4	0.0	2.2	0.1	9.4	40.1	3 760	63	37	656	5 140	48 290	4 638
Cuming	41.2	4 546	53.9	0.1	3.2	10.9	11.1	33.8	3 720	33	32	724	4 410	56 246	7 084
Custer	58.1	5 407	49.7	9.3	2.4	0.2	14.8	69.4	6 462	43	38	877	5 180	46 771	4 711
Dakota	78.7	3 764	62.6	0.2	7.4	0.1	7.6	134.6	6 433	78	73	1 078	9 810	43 197	3 793
Dawes	29.9	3 268	45.6	1.0	4.2	5.9	7.9	6.6	723	129	28	1 081	3 620	44 896	4 136
Dawson	147.3	6 083	43.0	30.0	3.4	0.3	4.0	105.3	4 347	107	84	2 173	11 340	45 450	4 171
Deuel	13.9	7 026	54.5	0.2	3.3	12.7	8.4	6.2	3 140	D	D	207	910	49 524	5 345
Dixon	37.0	6 247	66.9	0.5	2.1	6.9	10.0	11.9	2 016	36	20	391	2 740	48 253	4 997
Dodge	228.6	6 277	38.1	39.7	2.7	0.1	4.4	108.2	2 971	109	126	2 936	17 430	55 186	6 198
Douglas	2 356.0	4 435	50.4	2.4	4.8	0.7	3.5	5 801.4	10 920	5 751	2 174	34 734	262 360	73 107	10 728
Dundy	16.6	8 200	35.5	42.3	1.9	0.1	6.9	4.4	2 201	11	D	229	870	54 174	6 582
Fillmore	52.3	9 062	29.1	41.2	1.9	5.3	7.7	42.5	7 369	26	19	709	2 820	60 004	7 420
Franklin	15.0	4 719	33.2	32.0	1.8	0.8	12.7	4.5	1 407	22	11	313	1 450	48 135	4 846
Frontier	20.5	7 466	46.9	0.1	2.3	0.1	8.9	3.3	1 221	16	D	324	1 140	45 051	4 131
Furnas	28.2	5 750	56.4	1.0	2.4	0.6	7.4	29.1	5 927	36	17	540	2 270	44 480	4 510
Gage	86.9	3 984	52.5	1.0	5.5	0.3	9.7	60.4	2 770	89	76	1 948	10 310	50 244	4 897
Garden	15.6	7 995	28.9	43.5	2.2	0.1	10.1	6.3	3 250	19	D	140	930	38 378	3 805
Garfield	7.9	3 915	57.3	0.0	2.5	0.1	10.1	2.3	1 144	10	D	154	840	45 237	4 544
Gosper	10.9	5 386	31.3	0.1	3.2	25.6	12.4	14.3	7 034	D	D	165	970	58 108	6 152
Grant	3.8	6 037	69.2	0.0	2.1	0.4	9.7	0.6	886	D	D	75	340	63 432	7 709
Greeley	13.1	5 331	58.5	0.6	2.1	10.6	11.9	0.6	256	D	D	252	1 120	37 480	3 788
Hall	244.4	4 050	57.3	0.2	5.0	0.4	4.7	235.9	3 910	633	216	4 314	29 290	52 987	6 359
Hamilton	38.8	4 301	50.9	10.9	3.5	0.3	6.8	21.3	2 363	31	32	563	4 520	66 904	8 793
Harlan	18.5	5 430	23.7	38.1	1.7	0.1	10.0	8.8	2 568	31	12	262	1 550	49 961	5 149
Hayes	4.6	4 815	56.7	0.0	1.7	0.1	23.0	3.0	3 102	11	D	75	430	28 307	4 153
Hitchcock	14.2	4 921	60.3	0.0	1.9	12.2	13.1	25.6	8 853	D	10	299	1 280	47 963	4 299
Holt	51.3	4 932	45.5	0.4	1.7	4.7	17.2	22.9	2 199	43	36	814	5 040	48 711	5 670
Hooker	6.6	9 034	46.4	0.1	1.6	24.9	5.3	2.7	3 706	D	D	104	350	47 326	3 420
Howard	38.9	6 142	41.7	32.5	1.3	0.1	6.8	35.9	5 667	32	23	599	2 970	47 403	4 534
Jefferson	40.6	5 402	53.7	1.6	3.4	0.3	20.6	11.0	1 468	32	25	570	3 400	54 997	6 613
Johnson	34.2	6 653	29.7	38.9	1.2	0.3	9.9	24.3	4 729	37	15	810	2 040	45 549	3 782
Kearney	35.5	5 473	48.5	23.6	1.5	0.3	10.0	27.7	4 274	26	23	480	3 090	61 871	7 633
Keith	39.6	4 813	60.0	0.5	6.0	0.4	7.6	23.7	2 887	36	28	524	3 950	48 199	4 932
Keya Paha	3.8	4 669	59.2	0.1	1.4	0.2	21.0	0.1	63	D	D	72	400	40 958	3 193
Kimball	23.1	6 099	29.0	29.9	2.7	0.3	7.3	8.6	2 260	16	13	413	1 680	49 405	4 980
Knox	36.1	4 212	62.9	0.2	2.2	0.2	15.1	13.8	1 609	46	30	1 082	3 880	44 819	4 178
Lancaster	1 063.8	3 626	52.7	2.0	4.3	0.9	6.6	2 798.4	9 538	3 226	1 076	30 153	140 400	60 060	7 190
Lincoln	277.0	7 674	31.2	44.8	2.8	0.1	3.5	165.3	4 578	254	125	2 617	16 600	54 317	5 783
Logan	4.4	5 741	67.1	0.1	2.1	0.1	12.6	0.0	0	D	D	73	360	44 169	3 197
Loup	3.6	6 161	52.9	0.1	1.5	0.1	13.6	0.2	387	0	D	65	270	36 767	2 715
McPherson	2.7	5 281	63.8	0.0	1.7	0.0	16.4	0.2	424	D	D	42	200	59 460	4 790
Madison	170.2	4 860	59.2	2.5	5.3	4.1	7.9	156.1	4 457	178	122	3 547	16 720	54 867	6 362
Merrick	35.5	4 565	36.4	31.5	2.4	0.0	9.6	24.0	3 084	25	27	576	3 610	49 902	5 083
Morrill	33.2	6 781	39.2	26.6	3.3	9.2	5.8	13.5	2 752	22	17	548	2 190	51 616	6 571
Nance	23.3	6 270	46.3	24.6	3.0	0.1	9.3	5.5	1 467	16	12	373	1 620	38 139	3 559
Nemaha	44.9	6 283	42.5	30.4	2.7	0.2	5.5	29.2	4 079	29	23	1 596	2 980	56 483	6 301
Nuckolls	18.8	4 230	39.6	0.3	2.4	0.5	14.2	17.6	3 963	28	15	356	2 010	47 128	4 383
Otoe	67.1	4 260	45.5	16.1	3.2	0.4	12.3	89.9	5 710	60	56	1 265	7 530	55 718	5 850
Pawnee	19.3	6 965	36.0	32.5	1.5	0.2	10.3	5.3	1 916	22	D	301	1 250	42 922	3 495
Perkins	25.8	8 812	27.1	49.1	2.1	0.3	6.5	3.1	1 070	17	10	367	1 340	57 613	6 378
Phelps	43.9	4 769	54.3	0.1	2.5	4.2	9.8	37.5	4 071	59	32	732	4 460	65 023	8 225
Pierce	33.9	4 731	50.9	15.7	2.6	6.0	10.0	8.7	1 213	29	25	389	3 410	56 214	6 237

1. Based on the resident population estimated as of July 1 of the year shown.

Table B. States and Counties — Land Area and Population

STATE/ County code	CBSA code[1]	County type[2]	STATE County	Land area[3] (sq mi) 2016	Total persons 2016	Rank	Per square mile	White	Black	Amer- ican Indian, Alaska Native	Asian and Pacific Islander	Percent Hispanic or Latino[4]	Under 5 years	5 to 17 years	18 to 24 years	25 to 34 years	35 to 44 years	45 to 54 years
				1	2	3	4	5	6	7	8	9	10	11	12	13	14	15
			NEBRASKA—Cont'd															
31 141	18100	5	Platte	674.0	32 861	1 359	48.8	79.8	0.9	0.6	1.1	18.3	7.5	18.7	8.3	12.2	11.5	11.9
31 143	...	9	Polk	438.3	5 203	2 819	11.9	93.8	0.4	0.7	0.5	5.4	4.8	18.0	7.3	8.6	10.9	13.1
31 145	...	7	Red Willow	717.0	10 722	2 376	15.0	92.9	1.5	0.9	0.7	5.0	6.0	16.2	9.7	11.4	10.3	12.0
31 147	...	7	Richardson	551.8	8 060	2 591	14.6	94.3	1.0	4.0	0.9	1.9	5.7	15.3	6.9	9.9	9.6	12.6
31 149	...	9	Rock	1 008.3	1 390	3 085	1.4	97.3	0.3	0.9	0.4	1.4	4.7	15.0	5.1	9.1	10.4	10.1
31 151	...	6	Saline	574.0	14 331	2 144	25.0	71.1	1.2	0.8	3.3	24.7	6.7	17.8	13.3	11.1	11.6	12.1
31 153	36540	2	Sarpy	239.0	179 023	364	749.1	84.0	5.3	0.9	3.8	9.0	7.5	20.3	8.6	14.6	14.2	12.9
31 155	36540	2	Saunders	750.2	21 038	1 773	28.0	96.4	1.1	0.8	0.8	2.2	5.9	18.5	7.5	10.7	11.0	14.2
31 157	42420	5	Scotts Bluff	739.4	36 422	1 265	49.3	73.3	1.1	1.9	1.1	23.6	6.5	18.5	8.2	12.0	11.6	11.4
31 159	30700	2	Seward	571.4	17 284	1 958	30.2	95.7	1.0	0.9	0.8	2.7	6.2	17.4	13.1	10.2	10.8	12.2
31 161	...	9	Sheridan	2 440.9	5 234	2 816	2.1	84.6	1.1	11.6	1.3	4.9	5.9	16.4	6.6	9.0	10.5	11.4
31 163	...	8	Sherman	565.8	3 054	2 966	5.4	97.1	0.4	0.4	0.7	2.0	4.9	16.5	6.3	7.9	9.5	11.3
31 165	42420	9	Sioux	2 066.6	1 242	3 098	0.6	93.9	0.6	1.9	0.7	4.5	3.5	16.6	7.1	9.3	9.5	11.6
31 167	35740	9	Stanton	427.9	5 944	2 756	13.9	92.9	1.1	1.1	0.5	5.6	6.1	18.8	7.9	11.5	11.2	13.5
31 169	...	9	Thayer	573.8	5 101	2 825	8.9	96.2	0.9	0.9	0.6	2.7	6.0	16.5	6.9	8.9	9.4	11.7
31 171	...	9	Thomas	712.9	716	3 126	1.0	95.8	0.6	1.7	0.6	2.2	5.0	18.6	7.1	10.3	12.3	9.9
31 173	...	8	Thurston	393.6	7 127	2 661	18.1	38.3	1.0	56.7	0.8	5.3	10.4	25.7	10.0	11.7	9.4	10.1
31 175	...	9	Valley	568.0	4 184	2 883	7.4	96.5	0.8	0.6	0.5	2.7	6.3	16.6	7.0	9.2	10.2	12.4
31 177	36540	2	Washington	390.0	20 603	1 794	52.8	95.5	1.2	0.7	0.8	3.0	5.8	18.3	9.0	9.7	11.7	13.9
31 179	...	6	Wayne	442.9	9 365	2 476	21.1	90.7	2.5	0.9	1.2	6.0	5.4	14.8	23.2	10.6	9.2	10.1
31 181	...	9	Webster	574.9	3 603	2 935	6.3	94.0	1.0	1.1	1.0	4.8	5.1	16.4	8.0	9.1	9.9	12.9
31 183	...	9	Wheeler	575.2	776	3 121	1.3	97.8	0.3	1.0	0.6	1.2	5.8	15.3	8.4	8.5	9.0	12.5
31 185	...	6	York	572.5	13 794	2 182	24.1	91.7	2.1	0.9	1.3	5.2	6.5	16.8	9.7	12.0	10.1	11.5
32 000	...	0	**NEVADA**	109 780.2	2 940 058	X	26.8	52.7	9.9	1.5	11.1	28.5	6.3	16.8	8.5	14.6	13.2	13.4
32 001	21980	6	Churchill	4 930.6	24 198	1 635	4.9	76.9	2.9	5.3	5.1	13.3	6.7	16.4	8.5	12.7	10.5	12.4
32 003	29820	1	Clark	7 891.7	2 155 664	12	273.2	46.5	12.5	1.1	13.0	30.9	6.4	17.1	8.6	14.9	13.8	13.5
32 005	23820	4	Douglas	709.7	48 020	1 018	67.7	83.1	1.2	2.7	3.0	12.5	3.9	13.6	5.9	9.7	9.6	12.5
32 007	21220	5	Elko	17 169.2	52 168	958	3.0	68.3	1.5	5.5	2.0	24.6	7.1	20.6	9.0	15.1	12.7	13.2
32 009	...	9	Esmeralda	3 581.9	790	3 119	0.2	70.1	4.3	7.3	1.8	20.8	3.2	12.5	5.6	11.3	11.1	11.5
32 011	21220	9	Eureka	4 175.7	1 917	3 056	0.5	82.0	1.4	3.2	1.8	13.7	5.1	17.7	6.3	9.9	12.2	15.6
32 013	49080	7	Humboldt	9 640.8	16 842	1 990	1.7	67.4	1.6	4.7	1.8	26.8	7.8	19.9	8.2	13.8	12.2	12.9
32 015	...	7	Lander	5 490.1	5 702	2 781	1.0	70.5	1.3	4.4	1.7	23.6	7.8	18.5	7.8	13.9	10.7	13.9
32 017	...	8	Lincoln	10 633.4	5 055	2 830	0.5	86.5	3.6	2.4	1.9	8.1	4.0	18.2	8.5	10.4	11.7	12.3
32 019	22280	4	Lyon	2 001.2	53 179	944	26.6	78.1	1.8	3.6	2.8	16.7	5.5	16.3	6.8	11.8	11.0	12.6
32 021	...	7	Mineral	3 752.8	4 449	2 867	1.2	65.4	4.8	16.6	5.1	11.3	5.4	13.2	6.9	11.8	8.4	12.4
32 023	37220	4	Nye	18 181.9	43 423	1 104	2.4	79.0	3.5	2.5	3.1	14.5	4.4	12.6	6.6	9.0	8.8	12.3
32 027	...	9	Pershing	6 036.6	6 560	2 707	1.1	67.0	4.5	3.9	1.9	24.5	4.5	13.2	8.2	14.5	14.6	16.3
32 029	39900	2	Storey	262.9	4 051	2 899	15.4	86.6	2.3	2.3	2.6	7.9	2.6	9.8	5.3	7.9	9.2	13.5
32 031	39900	2	Washoe	6 302.4	453 616	153	72.0	65.9	3.0	2.0	7.9	24.2	6.0	15.9	9.1	14.8	12.0	13.1
32 033	...	7	White Pine	8 874.6	9 682	2 454	1.1	73.9	5.4	5.1	1.9	15.9	5.5	15.5	7.7	15.1	13.1	13.5
32 510	16180	3	Carson City	144.7	54 742	920	378.3	69.9	2.3	2.9	3.5	23.6	5.3	15.0	7.9	12.5	11.1	13.2
33 000	...	0	**NEW HAMPSHIRE**	8 952.7	1 334 795	X	149.1	92.3	1.8	0.7	3.2	3.5	4.8	14.7	9.6	12.0	11.4	15.1
33 001	29060	4	Belknap	401.6	60 779	859	151.3	96.3	1.0	0.8	1.5	1.7	4.5	14.3	7.2	10.4	11.0	14.3
33 003	...	6	Carroll	932.0	47 289	1 031	50.7	97.2	0.8	1.0	0.9	1.4	4.0	12.4	6.3	8.9	9.2	14.3
33 005	28300	4	Cheshire	706.7	75 774	730	107.2	95.7	1.1	0.8	1.9	1.8	4.6	13.4	12.0	12.1	10.2	13.6
33 007	13620	7	Coos	1 794.6	32 039	1 378	17.9	96.3	1.2	1.2	0.9	1.9	4.0	12.7	7.0	10.9	11.1	14.8
33 009	17200	5	Grafton	1 708.6	88 888	652	52.0	92.7	1.4	1.0	4.3	2.3	4.3	12.4	13.1	12.1	10.1	12.9
33 011	31700	2	Hillsborough	876.4	407 761	173	465.3	87.1	2.8	0.7	4.6	6.5	5.3	15.7	8.9	13.2	12.2	15.5
33 013	18180	4	Merrimack	932.8	148 582	441	159.3	94.3	1.7	0.8	2.5	2.0	4.8	14.7	9.5	11.7	11.5	14.9
33 015	14460	1	Rockingham	695.1	303 251	227	436.3	94.3	1.2	0.6	2.6	2.7	4.7	15.3	7.8	11.5	11.6	16.5
33 017	14460	1	Strafford	367.5	127 428	494	346.7	93.0	1.7	0.8	4.0	2.3	4.9	14.1	15.9	12.6	11.1	13.6
33 019	17200	7	Sullivan	537.5	43 004	1 113	80.0	96.5	1.1	1.1	1.3	1.5	4.8	14.6	6.9	11.0	11.0	14.8
34 000	...	0	**NEW JERSEY**	7 355.5	8 944 469	X	1 216.0	57.0	13.7	0.5	10.4	20.0	5.8	16.4	8.8	13.0	12.8	14.5
34 001	12100	2	Atlantic	555.6	270 991	251	487.7	57.7	15.6	0.6	9.2	18.8	5.7	16.0	9.3	12.0	11.4	14.2
34 003	35620	1	Bergen	232.8	939 151	54	4 034.2	58.3	6.0	0.3	17.5	19.4	5.3	16.2	8.2	11.6	13.2	15.2
34 005	37980	1	Burlington	798.9	449 284	155	562.4	69.8	18.0	0.7	6.2	7.9	5.1	16.0	8.7	12.4	12.3	15.1
34 007	37980	1	Camden	221.3	510 150	136	2 305.2	58.7	19.7	0.6	6.5	16.4	6.2	16.8	8.5	13.9	12.5	13.9
34 009	36140	3	Cape May	252.1	94 430	621	374.6	86.7	5.2	0.5	1.5	7.6	4.9	12.9	8.1	10.5	9.1	13.0
34 011	47220	3	Cumberland	483.5	153 797	425	318.1	48.4	20.3	1.4	1.9	30.2	6.6	17.3	8.4	14.8	13.1	13.5
34 013	35620	1	Essex	126.1	796 914	77	6 319.7	32.4	39.9	0.5	6.1	22.7	6.5	17.2	9.2	13.7	14.0	14.3
34 015	37980	1	Gloucester	322.0	292 330	234	907.9	80.5	11.2	0.5	3.7	6.0	5.4	17.0	8.9	12.3	12.4	15.0
34 017	35620	1	Hudson	46.3	677 983	98	14 643.3	29.9	11.6	0.4	16.3	43.2	6.9	13.6	8.5	21.3	15.7	12.6
34 019	35620	1	Hunterdon	427.8	124 676	503	291.4	86.9	2.7	0.3	4.9	6.4	4.0	16.2	8.7	8.6	10.6	17.6

1. CBSA = Core Based Statistical Area. See Appendix A for explanation. See Appendix B for list of metropolitan areas with component counties. 2. County type code from the Economic Research Service of USDA Rural-Urban Continuum Codes. See Appendix A for definition. 3. Dry land or land partially or temporarily covered by water. 4. May be of any race.

Table B. States and Counties — Population and Households

STATE County	55 to 64 years (16)	65 to 74 years (17)	75 years and over (18)	Percent female (19)	2000 (20)	2010 (21)	2000–2010 (22)	2010–2016 (23)	Births (24)	Deaths (25)	Net migration (26)	Number (27)	Persons per house-hold (28)	Family house-holds (29)	Female family householder[1] (30)	One per son (31)
NEBRASKA—Cont'd																
Platte	13.5	8.6	7.7	49.6	31 662	32 237	1.8	1.9	3 030	1 684	-744	12 707	2.53	66.6	7.8	29.4
Polk	16.2	11.4	9.7	50.1	5 639	5 406	-4.1	-3.8	314	387	-98	2 179	2.37	68.3	4.4	27.4
Red Willow	14.9	9.3	10.2	49.6	11 448	11 055	-3.4	-3.0	799	726	-378	4 651	2.27	62.7	4.7	31.1
Richardson	16.0	12.0	12.0	50.3	9 531	8 363	-12.3	-3.6	571	715	-127	3 761	2.14	59.3	4.5	38.5
Rock	21.1	13.6	10.9	49.1	1 756	1 528	-13.0	-9.0	82	125	-127	690	1.94	60.4	4.6	33.2
Saline	12.0	8.0	7.3	48.7	13 843	14 200	2.6	0.9	1 173	864	-155	5 104	2.61	67.7	8.8	26.2
Sarpy	10.9	6.7	4.4	50.0	122 595	158 840	29.6	12.7	16 127	5 344	9 257	61 983	2.71	74.1	10.6	21.4
Saunders	14.2	10.0	8.1	49.4	19 830	20 780	4.8	1.2	1 497	1 215	-43	8 055	2.56	69.9	6.9	25.9
Scotts Bluff	13.7	9.7	8.5	51.3	36 951	36 970	0.1	-1.5	3 068	2 570	-989	14 755	2.42	65.2	12.2	29.1
Seward	12.8	9.3	7.9	48.9	16 496	16 750	1.5	3.2	1 239	1 037	282	6 348	2.46	70.7	5.9	25.2
Sheridan	15.8	12.6	11.8	50.9	6 198	5 469	-11.8	-4.3	362	441	-132	2 259	2.29	65.6	9.0	30.3
Sherman	17.0	13.2	13.3	50.9	3 318	3 152	-5.0	-3.1	182	233	-64	1 377	2.21	64.2	7.5	31.3
Sioux	19.0	11.8	11.6	48.3	1 475	1 311	-11.1	-5.3	58	42	-82	549	2.28	70.5	5.5	27.7
Stanton	15.1	8.9	7.1	48.9	6 455	6 129	-5.1	-3.0	462	263	-392	2 323	2.61	74.1	10.2	23.7
Thayer	15.4	12.1	13.1	50.4	6 055	5 228	-13.7	-2.4	351	468	11	2 341	2.15	65.3	4.1	30.8
Thomas	15.1	12.6	9.1	48.2	729	647	-11.2	10.7	54	31	37	300	2.25	69.7	5.3	29.3
Thurston	10.6	6.6	5.5	51.0	7 171	6 940	-3.2	2.7	924	465	-277	2 084	3.30	71.0	21.0	25.7
Valley	14.0	12.5	11.9	50.5	4 647	4 260	-8.3	-1.8	328	333	-53	1 897	2.21	66.0	5.1	31.6
Washington	14.5	10.1	7.0	50.3	18 780	20 234	7.7	1.8	1 323	1 052	102	8 034	2.48	73.3	7.4	23.2
Wayne	12.2	7.2	7.3	49.5	9 851	9 595	-2.6	-2.4	623	368	-444	3 500	2.33	66.4	6.4	24.9
Webster	15.6	11.2	11.8	50.5	4 061	3 812	-6.1	-5.5	226	358	-77	1 552	2.31	61.4	5.5	35.6
Wheeler	18.7	11.5	10.3	49.6	886	818	-7.7	-5.1	47	30	-43	389	2.18	60.7	4.9	33.7
York	14.4	9.5	9.6	51.3	14 598	13 665	-6.4	0.9	1 097	899	-75	5 604	2.31	67.7	7.9	29.2
NEVADA	12.3	9.4	5.6	49.9	1 998 257	2 700 691	35.2	8.9	222 508	134 927	146 626	1 016 709	2.72	64.1	13.0	28.1
Churchill	14.0	11.5	7.3	49.4	23 982	24 877	3.7	-2.7	2 034	1 604	-1 157	9 475	2.51	66.2	10.8	27.9
Clark	11.7	8.8	5.3	50.1	1 375 765	1 951 269	41.8	10.5	166 704	91 848	125 572	724 446	2.78	64.2	13.9	28.0
Douglas	18.3	16.1	10.4	49.8	41 259	46 997	13.9	2.2	2 244	2 862	1 568	19 779	2.37	69.6	8.6	24.2
Elko	12.4	6.4	3.6	48.0	45 291	48 942	8.1	6.6	4 422	1 692	474	17 696	2.87	72.0	7.9	21.2
Esmeralda	17.0	15.2	12.7	45.3	971	784	-19.3	0.8	25	66	34	483	2.35	55.9	6.0	34.6
Eureka	17.3	9.7	6.2	46.6	1 651	1 987	20.4	-3.5	110	86	-116	767	2.17	60.2	2.2	37.0
Humboldt	13.4	7.8	4.0	47.8	16 106	16 525	2.6	1.9	1 641	730	-555	6 149	2.74	66.2	8.8	30.0
Lander	12.7	8.9	5.7	49.2	5 794	5 775	-0.3	-1.3	548	220	-404	2 114	2.79	71.6	8.0	20.9
Lincoln	13.4	13.0	8.5	46.0	4 165	5 345	28.3	-5.4	207	289	-188	1 883	2.55	71.2	8.3	27.5
Lyon	14.9	13.7	7.4	49.2	34 501	51 980	50.7	2.3	3 526	3 386	1 027	19 524	2.63	68.4	11.1	23.5
Mineral	17.0	13.9	10.9	51.1	5 071	4 771	-5.9	-6.7	307	491	-132	1 990	2.25	54.8	13.2	39.0
Nye	17.3	18.1	11.0	48.9	32 485	43 945	35.3	-1.2	2 337	4 109	1 154	17 427	2.42	65.5	9.4	27.7
Pershing	14.0	8.9	5.9	35.6	6 693	6 753	0.9	-2.9	369	296	-267	2 083	2.29	71.5	7.8	22.1
Storey	21.6	19.9	10.2	48.9	3 399	4 010	18.0	1.0	104	164	73	1 767	2.20	62.0	6.5	31.4
Washoe	13.4	9.9	5.7	49.7	339 486	421 427	24.1	7.6	33 683	22 404	20 112	166 345	2.58	61.7	11.4	29.6
White Pine	13.7	9.1	6.7	42.1	9 181	10 030	9.2	-3.5	675	565	-417	3 187	2.71	62.4	3.7	31.7
Carson City	14.6	11.6	8.7	48.9	52 457	55 274	5.4	-1.0	3 572	4 115	-152	21 594	2.43	60.3	12.8	32.6
NEW HAMPSHIRE	15.4	10.2	6.8	50.5	1 235 786	1 316 461	6.5	1.4	78 003	68 798	9 804	520 251	2.47	66.8	9.8	25.5
Belknap	17.1	13.1	8.1	50.7	56 325	60 072	6.7	1.2	3 352	4 053	1 327	24 597	2.42	67.7	10.6	24.9
Carroll	18.8	16.0	10.1	50.3	43 666	47 833	9.5	-1.1	2 255	3 185	501	21 206	2.22	66.2	7.2	27.2
Cheshire	15.6	11.0	7.5	51.1	73 825	77 117	4.5	-1.7	4 249	4 299	-1 129	30 638	2.34	63.3	9.6	27.7
Coos	16.9	13.0	9.5	47.0	33 111	33 052	-0.2	-3.1	1 581	2 637	103	14 198	2.13	63.1	10.5	31.6
Grafton	15.8	11.2	8.1	50.7	81 743	89 125	9.0	-0.3	4 748	4 924	11	35 035	2.35	61.9	8.6	30.9
Hillsborough	14.5	8.8	6.1	50.3	380 841	400 720	5.2	1.8	26 808	19 093	-457	155 208	2.55	67.0	10.7	24.9
Merrimack	15.5	10.2	7.2	50.7	136 225	146 444	7.5	1.5	8 464	8 161	1 609	56 705	2.49	66.9	9.8	26.2
Rockingham	16.2	10.1	6.3	50.5	277 359	295 214	6.4	2.7	16 296	13 708	5 802	118 095	2.51	70.1	8.9	22.8
Strafford	13.3	8.5	6.0	51.2	112 233	123 140	9.7	3.5	7 755	6 078	2 472	47 149	2.48	64.7	10.3	25.1
Sullivan	16.8	12.2	7.8	50.7	40 458	43 744	8.1	-1.7	2 495	2 660	-435	17 420	2.44	65.4	10.3	27.7
NEW JERSEY	13.4	8.7	6.7	51.2	8 414 350	8 791 953	4.5	1.7	649 061	447 845	-39 135	3 189 486	2.73	69.3	13.4	25.7
Atlantic	14.5	9.8	7.1	51.6	252 552	274 540	8.7	-1.3	20 046	16 264	-7 210	101 818	2.64	67.2	16.8	27.3
Bergen	13.9	9.0	7.5	51.5	884 118	905 117	2.4	3.8	57 998	43 888	22 172	335 550	2.73	72.0	11.3	23.9
Burlington	14.2	9.1	7.2	50.7	423 394	448 738	6.0	0.1	28 217	24 186	-2 838	164 659	2.66	69.7	11.6	25.4
Camden	13.3	8.6	6.3	51.7	508 932	513 678	0.9	-0.7	39 816	28 708	-14 053	186 101	2.71	67.4	16.5	27.4
Cape May	16.6	14.5	10.5	51.0	102 326	97 265	-4.9	-2.9	5 772	8 147	-223	40 412	2.30	64.2	9.5	31.0
Cumberland	12.0	8.3	6.1	48.8	146 438	156 628	7.0	-1.8	13 133	9 063	-6 636	50 368	2.86	69.6	19.5	24.5
Essex	12.1	7.4	5.5	51.9	793 633	784 003	-1.2	1.6	64 513	36 955	-13 871	278 085	2.77	65.2	20.2	29.9
Gloucester	13.9	9.0	6.1	51.3	254 673	288 575	13.3	1.3	19 335	15 518	-141	104 268	2.74	72.3	12.3	22.8
Hudson	10.5	6.4	4.6	50.2	608 975	634 274	4.2	6.9	63 812	24 316	4 656	249 584	2.63	61.9	17.1	28.5
Hunterdon	17.2	10.1	6.9	50.6	121 989	127 364	4.4	-2.1	5 743	5 532	-2 807	46 899	2.60	72.8	7.6	22.7

1. No spouse present.

Table B. States and Counties — Population, Vital Statistics, Health, and Crime

STATE County	Daytime population, 2011–2015 — Persons in group quarters, 2016	Number	Employment/residence ratio	Births, 2016 — Total	Rate[1]	Deaths, 2016 — Number	Rate[1]	Persons under 65 with no health insurance, 2015 — Number	Percent	Medicare, 2015 — Total Beneficiaries	Enrolled in Original Medicare	Enrolled in Medicare Advantage	Serious crimes known to police,[2] 2014 — Total Number	Rate[3]
	32	33	34	35	36	37	38	39	40	41	42	43	44	45
NEBRASKA—Cont'd														
Platte	448	34 543	1.11	493	15.0	273	8.3	2 882	10.6	5 147	4 859	288	496	1 521
Polk	105	4 380	0.68	47	9.0	50	9.6	374	9.2	993	978	15	79	1 503
Red Willow	397	11 432	1.09	134	12.5	117	10.9	740	8.8	2 282	2 254	28	288	2 615
Richardson	151	7 289	0.77	84	10.4	119	14.8	708	11.6	2 060	2 034	26	70	866
Rock	31	1 353	0.94	12	8.6	13	9.4	170	15.9	D	362	D	1	72
Saline	1 008	14 478	1.02	177	12.4	133	9.3	1 453	13.0	2 419	2 376	43	290	2 002
Sarpy	1 234	143 634	0.71	2 601	14.5	934	5.2	9 082	5.8	19 606	16 368	3 238	2 268	1 318
Saunders	336	16 599	0.59	231	11.0	206	9.8	1 221	7.1	3 713	3 251	462	237	1 130
Scotts Bluff	850	37 423	1.04	453	12.4	408	11.2	3 424	11.8	7 786	6 954	832	921	2 555
Seward	1 362	15 105	0.77	199	11.5	171	9.9	842	6.4	2 803	2 684	119	137	915
Sheridan	110	4 814	0.81	58	11.1	60	11.5	536	13.6	1 261	1 110	151	NA	NA
Sherman	55	2 633	0.70	26	8.5	41	13.4	253	11.2	715	648	67	23	742
Sioux	0	1 012	0.64	8	6.4	3	2.4	106	10.8	D	113	D	NA	NA
Stanton	1	4 912	0.62	67	11.3	32	5.4	356	7.1	555	475	80	45	732
Thayer	149	5 419	1.10	53	10.4	75	14.7	378	9.8	1 325	1 309	16	65	1 252
Thomas	2	673	0.99	8	11.2	3	4.2	53	9.9	D	137	D	NA	NA
Thurston	50	7 394	1.18	165	23.2	82	11.5	1 046	17.3	926	889	37	7	103
Valley	45	4 383	1.06	53	12.7	47	11.2	340	10.9	1 015	1 003	12	NA	NA
Washington	529	18 716	0.86	215	10.4	174	8.4	943	5.7	3 291	2 705	586	213	1 052
Wayne	1 046	9 491	1.01	90	9.6	51	5.4	671	9.6	1 245	1 101	144	NA	NA
Webster	156	3 379	0.81	34	9.4	59	16.4	283	10.4	940	926	14	26	710
Wheeler	0	866	1.04	8	10.3	3	3.9	74	12.8	D	139	D	1	134
York	787	14 901	1.15	179	13.0	136	9.9	855	8.1	2 820	2 794	26	257	1 840
NEVADA	37 920	2 802 752	1.00	36 462	12.4	23 771	8.1	341 952	14.1	429 423	269 262	160 161	92 583	3 261
Churchill	342	24 074	0.98	347	14.3	252	10.4	2 734	14.0	4 858	4 326	532	826	3 426
Clark	23 321	2 041 113	1.01	27 352	12.7	16 501	7.7	261 500	14.5	283 581	161 821	121 760	72 994	3 532
Douglas	229	46 088	0.94	363	7.6	510	10.6	4 212	11.9	9 581	8 467	1 114	837	1 759
Elko	849	49 846	0.93	763	14.6	335	6.4	6 010	13.0	5 135	4 985	150	1 482	2 755
Esmeralda	1	1 126	0.97	4	5.1	3	3.8	98	15.9	D	174	D	10	1 170
Eureka	1	5 325	5.29	18	9.4	8	4.2	142	8.4	D	261	D	42	1 984
Humboldt	183	17 211	1.02	258	15.3	103	6.1	2 131	14.2	2 318	2 249	69	251	1 416
Lander	16	6 119	1.07	90	15.8	30	5.3	608	12.0	751	737	14	167	2 714
Lincoln	259	5 138	0.97	41	8.1	50	9.9	555	14.8	2 858	2 178	680	50	950
Lyon	360	44 507	0.64	563	10.6	591	11.1	5 933	14.3	12 129	9 364	2 765	965	1 859
Mineral	52	4 673	1.06	42	9.4	101	22.7	441	13.3	1 154	1 002	152	NA	NA
Nye	1 173	41 979	0.95	367	8.5	663	15.3	4 089	13.7	14 776	7 555	7 221	883	2 087
Pershing	1 690	6 805	1.04	61	9.3	44	6.7	573	14.1	716	698	18	123	1 763
Storey	5	3 147	0.55	12	3.0	15	3.7	259	9.2	302	270	32	120	3 026
Washoe	5 300	434 111	1.00	5 489	12.1	3 820	8.4	46 279	12.3	75 223	51 409	23 814	12 055	2 735
White Pine	1 329	10 394	1.12	113	11.7	87	9.0	743	10.5	1 597	1 563	34	128	1 260
Carson City	2 810	61 096	1.28	579	10.6	658	12.0	5 645	13.7	13 973	12 203	1 770	1 035	1 906
NEW HAMPSHIRE	42 396	1 285 014	0.94	12 274	9.2	11 572	8.7	84 026	7.8	250 288	229 594	20 694	28 643	2 159
Belknap	893	55 597	0.84	507	8.3	739	12.2	4 297	9.0	15 510	14 141	1 369	1 800	2 987
Carroll	437	46 799	0.97	352	7.4	547	11.6	3 885	11.1	13 017	12 150	867	924	2 223
Cheshire	4 715	73 816	0.93	639	8.4	693	9.1	4 837	8.3	15 866	14 494	1 372	1 537	2 565
Coos	2 570	31 138	0.95	244	7.6	420	13.1	2 275	9.8	8 709	8 545	164	507	1 594
Grafton	6 621	101 619	1.28	764	8.6	781	8.8	6 440	9.7	18 778	17 322	1 456	1 782	2 096
Hillsborough	7 980	388 807	0.93	4 146	10.2	3 267	8.0	26 982	7.9	66 748	60 024	6 724	9 289	2 360
Merrimack	6 939	150 909	1.05	1 348	9.1	1 315	8.9	8 848	7.5	28 194	25 794	2 400	2 394	1 828
Rockingham	2 507	283 657	0.91	2 678	8.8	2 378	7.8	15 502	6.1	53 617	48 523	5 094	4 881	1 694
Strafford	8 969	115 972	0.85	1 212	9.5	1 006	7.9	8 207	8.2	20 776	19 731	1 045	3 321	2 655
Sullivan	765	36 700	0.69	384	8.9	426	9.9	2 753	8.0	9 073	8 870	203	716	1 873
NEW JERSEY	185 907	8 615 553	0.93	102 166	11.4	74 762	8.4	745 867	10.0	1 398 089	1 145 586	252 503	178 339	1 995
Atlantic	6 219	280 082	1.04	3 019	11.1	2 779	10.3	24 496	10.9	49 844	45 101	4 743	9 170	3 315
Bergen	10 419	904 398	0.95	9 338	9.9	7 176	7.6	74 601	9.6	145 930	121 924	24 006	10 541	1 132
Burlington	13 267	433 729	0.92	4 427	9.9	4 061	9.0	21 623	5.9	76 438	62 089	14 349	7 506	1 661
Camden	7 786	473 276	0.84	6 242	12.2	4 735	9.3	37 837	8.8	86 015	68 208	17 807	15 449	3 009
Cape May	2 613	95 453	0.99	941	10.0	1 308	13.9	7 286	10.4	25 430	22 652	2 778	3 765	3 934
Cumberland	10 782	157 405	1.01	2 053	13.3	1 443	9.4	15 749	12.7	26 997	22 864	4 133	6 931	4 397
Essex	23 409	806 501	1.04	10 134	12.7	6 307	7.9	93 037	13.6	102 657	75 456	27 201	23 449	2 960
Gloucester	4 230	255 954	0.75	3 097	10.6	2 641	9.0	16 265	6.6	44 888	36 419	8 469	6 640	2 281
Hudson	9 472	606 710	0.83	10 098	14.9	4 204	6.2	88 026	14.8	70 824	51 619	19 205	13 028	1 951
Hunterdon	3 567	118 319	0.88	921	7.4	962	7.7	4 772	4.7	20 086	18 008	2 078	870	690

1. Per 1,000 estimated resident population.   2. Data for serious crimes have not been adjusted for underreporting; this may affect comparability between geographic areas and over time.
3. Per 100,000 population estimated by the FBI.

Table B. States and Counties — Crime, Education, Money Income, and Poverty

STATE County	Serious crimes known to police, 2014 (cont.)[1] Rate[2] Violent	Property	Education School enrollment and attainment, 2011–2015 Enrollment[3] Total	Percent private	Attainment[4] (percent) High school graduate or less	Bachelor's degree or more	Local government expenditures,[5] 2013–2014 Total current spending (mil dol)	Current spending per student (dollars)	Money income, 2011–2015 Per capita income[6] (dollars)	Median income (dollars)	Households Percent with income of less than $50,000	with income of $200,000 or more	Income and poverty, 2015 Median household income (dollars)	Percent below poverty level All persons	Children under 18 years	Children 5 to 17 years in families
	46	47	48	49	50	51	52	53	54	55	56	57	58	59	60	61
NEBRASKA—Cont'd																
Platte	83	1 438	8 397	20.5	43.0	20.1	58.3	12 280	25 869	56 318	44.3	2.4	58 554	8.3	11.3	10.7
Polk	0	1 503	1 212	13.2	39.0	19.6	18.8	15 154	30 428	57 312	41.3	4.3	61 965	7.9	10.8	9.5
Red Willow	73	2 543	2 634	11.4	43.0	17.7	20.3	11 682	23 387	42 931	56.1	1.5	49 308	11.8	15.9	14.6
Richardson	0	866	1 887	9.1	48.0	20.7	17.7	14 605	25 358	42 750	57.2	1.6	44 648	13.0	19.8	18.2
Rock	0	72	237	7.2	49.3	18.0	3.4	17 005	29 205	48 456	53.0	4.1	51 447	14.2	18.3	14.7
Saline	110	1 892	4 180	19.9	50.6	14.2	33.7	11 749	21 955	51 738	48.9	1.3	55 850	10.0	13.3	12.6
Sarpy	70	1 248	51 150	15.9	27.1	36.7	270.6	10 413	30 902	70 543	33.1	4.0	73 856	5.8	7.5	6.9
Saunders	52	1 077	5 447	22.1	39.5	24.6	32.1	11 425	29 637	60 854	40.1	3.8	61 025	8.8	11.3	9.9
Scotts Bluff	164	2 391	9 432	13.3	43.3	21.5	76.0	11 597	25 064	45 992	55.1	2.1	43 428	15.1	22.8	21.3
Seward	53	861	4 971	29.7	36.5	26.1	37.3	14 462	28 124	59 662	39.8	4.1	62 455	7.5	7.6	6.7
Sheridan	NA	NA	1 245	8.0	40.9	24.5	12.0	13 772	23 734	41 985	58.4	1.6	47 005	14.3	23.4	20.0
Sherman	64	677	682	2.9	51.8	14.7	7.0	15 221	26 416	46 366	52.2	1.2	42 643	12.5	18.9	16.4
Sioux	NA	NA	256	8.6	39.8	26.6	2.6	24 491	27 216	41 215	56.1	3.1	55 606	14.0	20.5	18.8
Stanton	16	716	1 670	11.6	43.1	18.3	5.7	12 523	27 463	53 416	46.4	1.9	56 423	8.5	12.0	10.9
Thayer	212	1 040	1 015	10.0	45.3	19.3	13.8	16 879	29 120	45 741	55.3	2.4	48 947	10.2	14.9	13.6
Thomas	NA	NA	148	8.1	38.1	27.5	2.1	21 726	30 475	51 000	46.7	2.7	48 754	12.6	17.8	19.0
Thurston	29	74	2 283	4.8	48.7	13.9	29.3	16 638	18 529	41 266	59.2	2.5	42 290	25.6	35.6	32.8
Valley	NA	NA	825	7.6	49.1	19.2	9.5	13 510	25 951	44 612	54.0	3.2	49 929	12.2	16.2	14.7
Washington	74	978	5 314	16.8	35.4	29.6	36.2	10 331	31 151	65 370	37.8	3.5	68 435	6.7	8.4	7.0
Wayne	NA	NA	3 882	4.2	26.0	37.8	26.7	17 277	26 031	54 159	46.6	4.2	54 503	12.0	11.6	11.0
Webster	164	546	840	10.2	45.3	19.8	8.0	13 570	22 385	40 256	60.7	1.1	40 444	12.9	14.8	13.6
Wheeler	0	134	174	8.0	47.2	18.4	2.4	22 610	30 126	46 394	54.5	5.1	55 106	11.4	18.4	17.1
York	21	1 819	3 430	25.2	38.5	26.1	23.4	11 983	27 646	51 802	47.1	3.0	59 500	10.1	14.2	13.5
NEVADA	636	2 625	687 278	11.1	43.1	23.0	3 776.3	8 358	26 541	51 847	48.1	3.5	52 544	14.9	21.6	20.1
Churchill	236	3 190	5 841	6.5	45.4	15.9	37.6	10 224	24 202	47 415	54.0	0.9	54 134	13.1	19.3	18.5
Clark	743	2 790	501 148	11.6	44.3	22.6	2 587.9	8 074	26 048	51 575	48.3	3.5	51 624	15.4	22.6	21.1
Douglas	164	1 595	9 786	12.2	31.9	25.2	61.4	10 015	33 057	58 535	41.8	4.6	63 620	9.4	15.2	13.4
Elko	454	2 302	13 488	7.8	43.4	18.1	96.4	9 694	29 988	71 799	33.3	4.9	76 518	9.9	12.6	11.1
Esmeralda	117	1 053	187	1.6	56.2	15.7	2.1	27 013	20 984	39 271	59.4	0.0	49 057	14.7	20.7	20.6
Eureka	378	1 606	371	7.5	44.6	22.2	7.0	28 435	30 459	60 250	41.6	0.0	65 459	9.5	12.0	10.5
Humboldt	322	1 095	4 442	7.6	53.5	13.7	36.0	10 241	27 255	65 212	38.4	2.0	68 060	9.4	15.0	13.6
Lander	569	2 145	1 465	16.8	56.5	7.6	13.6	12 152	29 390	78 190	32.1	1.3	76 713	10.8	14.4	14.2
Lincoln	19	931	1 219	5.8	42.0	20.3	12.9	13 305	23 924	44 866	55.0	1.8	51 788	14.3	17.8	14.7
Lyon	277	1 581	11 417	7.7	45.2	16.6	79.9	9 858	23 173	47 255	53.0	1.5	51 934	13.8	22.6	20.3
Mineral	NA	NA	762	5.4	43.8	11.3	7.3	15 780	24 146	38 923	56.6	1.8	42 164	18.0	33.6	32.4
Nye	144	1 943	7 717	12.8	50.7	13.2	57.8	11 094	23 085	41 712	58.7	1.0	43 819	17.5	28.6	27.0
Pershing	616	1 147	1 578	5.9	57.1	12.4	10.7	15 048	17 332	45 230	56.0	0.0	54 416	18.3	19.9	18.7
Storey	706	2 320	613	7.3	37.1	21.4	6.7	16 940	35 115	64 832	38.7	2.2	61 594	7.8	13.1	11.6
Washoe	371	2 364	112 176	10.4	37.3	28.7	556.3	8 470	28 757	52 870	47.3	4.3	56 457	13.8	18.3	16.7
White Pine	305	955	2 189	8.2	50.8	13.9	17.6	13 030	24 359	57 122	43.8	1.1	54 975	14.1	19.3	18.4
Carson City	295	1 611	12 879	8.4	41.8	20.7	185.0	7 807	26 127	47 668	51.9	2.7	47 015	16.4	23.1	21.2
NEW HAMPSHIRE	196	1 963	321 106	21.8	36.5	34.9	2 658.8	14 391	34 362	66 779	37.2	6.1	70 003	8.4	11.0	9.8
Belknap	229	2 758	12 649	19.8	39.8	29.6	131.6	15 195	31 644	62 159	40.2	3.7	63 377	8.8	13.5	12.1
Carroll	202	2 021	8 510	15.5	38.3	32.1	99.8	18 796	32 612	53 306	47.0	4.0	54 351	9.6	17.7	16.1
Cheshire	194	2 371	19 449	17.4	41.6	31.6	143.6	17 374	30 181	57 782	43.1	3.6	60 339	9.9	14.0	12.6
Coos	145	1 450	6 343	10.0	51.8	17.8	64.6	16 185	24 546	42 312	57.2	2.1	40 286	16.1	23.4	20.1
Grafton	158	1 938	23 105	32.8	36.5	38.1	209.6	19 067	32 469	55 762	44.6	6.1	57 827	11.2	14.9	13.4
Hillsborough	272	2 088	99 991	25.3	36.0	35.9	738.6	13 100	35 242	71 244	34.7	7.0	73 474	8.0	10.2	9.4
Merrimack	147	1 680	35 738	25.3	35.5	34.4	324.6	13 915	32 020	65 983	37.9	4.8	68 148	8.3	10.7	9.5
Rockingham	119	1 575	69 943	18.9	32.2	38.8	632.9	13 782	40 469	81 198	28.6	8.8	87 103	5.2	6.5	5.3
Strafford	249	2 406	36 546	14.4	36.1	34.1	214.4	13 562	29 917	60 711	42.3	4.0	60 931	11.4	13.6	12.0
Sullivan	162	1 711	8 832	18.7	47.5	26.5	99.1	16 278	29 004	56 032	44.6	3.1	53 804	11.2	17.5	15.3
NEW JERSEY	261	1 734	2 278 867	19.0	40.0	36.8	24 420.0	17 845	36 582	72 093	35.7	10.1	72 337	10.8	15.5	14.6
Atlantic	384	2 931	67 528	13.4	48.3	25.1	822.8	17 934	28 005	54 461	46.2	4.6	53 296	14.1	21.9	20.2
Bergen	81	1 050	232 137	21.1	32.7	46.9	2 443.5	18 061	44 002	85 806	29.8	14.2	88 512	7.1	8.6	8.3
Burlington	167	1 493	113 475	17.2	36.9	35.7	1 251.3	17 535	37 255	78 621	30.7	8.7	74 844	7.7	10.0	9.0
Camden	465	2 544	132 704	17.3	43.4	30.2	1 475.7	18 066	30 822	62 185	41.4	5.4	63 589	13.1	19.6	17.9
Cape May	239	3 694	19 045	14.3	44.6	29.9	253.7	19 900	33 028	57 637	43.7	4.9	55 632	10.5	18.1	17.8
Cumberland	511	3 886	37 509	9.6	61.9	14.6	485.7	17 611	22 417	49 984	50.0	2.3	50 259	17.2	25.5	24.7
Essex	648	2 312	217 560	18.3	44.5	32.7	2 518.5	19 666	32 708	53 976	47.1	9.6	52 206	16.8	24.1	23.5
Gloucester	113	2 168	76 600	14.6	42.7	29.3	796.5	16 387	34 025	76 727	31.9	6.7	76 780	7.7	9.8	9.1
Hudson	360	1 592	154 191	19.1	43.2	37.5	1 536.4	17 665	33 185	59 741	43.1	7.9	60 053	17.7	27.0	29.3
Hunterdon	44	645	31 462	16.9	28.3	48.7	405.2	19 703	51 353	105 444	21.8	19.2	102 797	5.0	4.6	4.0

1. Data for serious crimes have not been adjusted for underreporting; this may affect comparability between geographic areas and over time.   2. Per 100,000 population estimated by the FBI.
3. All persons 3 years old and over enrolled in nursery school through college.   4. Persons 25 years old and over.   5. Elementary and secondary education expenditures.
6. Based on population estimated by the American Community Survey, 2011–2015.

Table B. States and Counties — **Personal Income**

STATE County	Personal income, 2015 Total (mil dol)	Percent change, 2014–2015	Per capita[1] Dollars	Rank	Wages and salaries (mil dol)	Supplements to wages and salaries; employer contributions (mil dol) Pension and insurance	Government social insurance	Proprietors' income (mil dol)	Dividends, interest, and rent (mil dol)	Personal transfer receipts (mil dol)	Earnings, 2015 Total (mil dol)	Contributions for government social insurance (mil dol) From employee and self-employed	From employer
	62	63	64	65	66	67	68	69	70	71	72	73	74
NEBRASKA—Cont'd													
Platte	1 484	2.0	45 193	625	809	147	60	248	251	219	1 264	67	60
Polk	260	2.7	49 909	333	56	11	4	81	42	41	151	6	4
Red Willow	505	-1.4	46 670	477	212	37	17	91	92	100	357	19	17
Richardson	340	-6.0	42 054	753	96	18	8	39	69	81	161	11	8
Rock	92	-10.7	66 970	29	20	4	1	43	16	8	68	2	1
Saline	544	-0.9	38 058	1 277	308	52	23	48	86	102	431	25	23
Sarpy	7 874	5.3	44 819	827	3 610	623	288	315	1 228	1 011	4 836	280	288
Saunders	967	2.3	46 035	739	212	39	15	136	154	157	402	21	15
Scotts Bluff	1 486	0.0	40 984	780	748	118	63	165	227	317	1 094	69	63
Seward	779	0.3	45 504	645	263	44	20	99	139	120	425	24	20
Sheridan	242	-12.9	46 339	264	60	12	4	52	47	45	128	6	4
Sherman	124	-0.2	40 273	1 300	28	6	2	26	21	29	62	3	2
Sioux	79	-13.5	62 599	67	10	2	1	43	11	7	55	1	1
Stanton	269	2.6	45 243	882	77	12	5	74	38	34	168	7	5
Thayer	267	-4.5	51 782	193	99	19	7	53	61	51	178	9	7
Thomas	44	-7.7	64 887	94	11	2	1	16	9	6	30	1	1
Thurston	332	-1.9	46 990	505	127	25	9	107	41	58	267	10	9
Valley	181	-2.1	43 661	647	66	13	5	40	35	40	125	6	5
Washington	1 009	4.2	49 835	489	464	75	33	87	178	145	659	38	33
Wayne	403	0.3	43 048	938	154	31	11	92	73	60	288	13	11
Webster	170	1.3	47 027	556	35	7	3	55	25	37	100	4	3
Wheeler	94	-3.5	125 171	3	11	2	1	70	8	5	84	1	1
York	670	1.5	48 511	463	317	51	23	94	134	118	486	27	23
NEVADA	121 096	5.4	41 992	X	60 874	11 181	4 550	6 033	27 094	20 713	82 638	4 734	4 550
Churchill	892	4.0	36 876	722	394	98	30	46	158	234	567	31	30
Clark	85 970	4.9	40 652	1 243	44 575	7 733	3 389	4 205	18 515	14 571	59 901	3 426	3 389
Douglas	2 860	5.4	59 953	169	838	156	64	242	1 008	436	1 300	82	64
Elko	2 274	0.8	43 791	981	1 076	207	75	126	253	269	1 484	78	75
Esmeralda	38	-5.0	45 315	390	21	5	1	-2	7	7	24	2	1
Eureka	75	-0.1	37 396	2 018	426	69	28	5	10	10	527	30	28
Humboldt	752	1.1	44 198	845	449	95	30	40	93	106	615	32	30
Lander	313	2.9	52 986	329	256	50	16	6	27	38	328	18	16
Lincoln	144	3.4	28 563	3 010	62	21	4	2	25	49	89	5	4
Lyon	1 726	6.7	32 822	2 488	470	115	34	49	257	459	668	45	34
Mineral	158	3.5	35 345	1 964	56	17	4	8	28	56	84	5	4
Nye	1 481	4.2	34 871	2 055	566	110	40	79	241	518	795	56	40
Pershing	205	0.5	30 938	2 633	101	30	5	13	25	44	149	6	5
Storey	164	8.5	41 027	1 798	258	44	23	10	34	31	335	19	23
Washoe	21 265	7.9	47 584	580	9 730	1 949	713	939	5 867	3 262	13 330	789	713
White Pine	409	3.4	41 645	1 191	228	65	13	6	54	85	312	15	13
Carson City	2 369	9.0	43 443	1 055	1 369	420	81	260	493	538	2 130	97	81
NEW HAMPSHIRE	74 388	4.4	55 926	X	34 467	5 752	2 357	6 474	14 225	10 726	49 051	2 894	2 357
Belknap	3 345	5.3	55 160	335	1 113	213	78	331	725	598	1 735	107	78
Carroll	2 538	4.5	53 682	444	746	143	54	313	760	511	1 256	80	54
Cheshire	3 715	5.8	48 942	533	1 478	289	103	325	818	664	2 194	135	103
Coos	1 286	3.7	41 203	1 231	460	110	33	72	241	397	676	45	33
Grafton	5 018	4.6	56 182	336	3 016	498	216	574	1 238	778	4 303	248	216
Hillsborough	23 254	5.1	57 180	206	12 284	1 868	831	1 852	4 083	3 026	16 836	982	831
Merrimack	7 875	0.8	53 213	433	3 925	766	269	688	1 518	1 280	5 648	324	269
Rockingham	19 440	4.5	64 417	118	8 283	1 224	558	1 718	3 467	2 149	11 783	700	558
Strafford	5 817	5.7	45 868	890	2 537	513	171	432	931	931	3 653	211	171
Sullivan	2 100	4.2	48 868	658	624	128	45	169	446	394	966	60	45
NEW JERSEY	537 026	4.1	60 101	X	250 878	38 424	18 799	49 053	96 382	76 221	357 154	21 011	18 799
Atlantic	11 982	3.7	43 695	810	6 046	1 101	496	947	2 024	2 739	8 590	520	496
Bergen	71 184	3.9	75 849	47	30 349	4 162	2 321	8 106	15 494	7 201	44 938	2 596	2 321
Burlington	24 865	4.1	55 227	246	12 138	1 971	978	1 575	4 072	3 827	16 663	989	978
Camden	24 567	3.9	48 084	530	10 804	1 835	873	1 337	3 805	5 044	14 848	916	873
Cape May	5 050	4.1	53 309	302	1 650	350	148	469	1 303	1 185	2 618	171	148
Cumberland	5 650	3.4	36 253	1 863	2 829	600	236	396	798	1 583	4 060	247	236
Essex	47 870	4.4	60 030	153	23 361	4 007	1 723	4 132	10 135	7 651	33 223	1 905	1 723
Gloucester	14 224	4.4	48 799	553	4 996	970	411	781	1 833	2 421	7 159	440	411
Hudson	36 404	6.1	53 945	381	19 225	2 880	1 351	4 269	4 748	5 238	27 724	1 589	1 351
Hunterdon	10 134	2.6	80 759	33	3 188	472	231	891	1 807	916	4 781	284	231

1. Based on the resident population estimated as of July 1 of the year shown.

Table B. States and Counties — **Earnings, Social Security, and Housing**

| | Earnings, 2015 (cont.) | | | | | | | | | Social Security beneficiaries, December 2015 | | | Housing units, 2016 | |
| | Percent by selected industries | | | | | | | | | | | | | |
STATE County	Farm	Mining	Construction	Manufacturing	Information: professional, scientific, technical services	Retail trade	Finance, insurance, real estate and leasing	Health care and social assistance	Government	Number	Rate[1]	Supplemental Security Income recipients, December 2015	Total	Percent change 2010-2016
	75	76	77	78	79	80	81	82	83	84	85	86	87	88
NEBRASKA—Cont'd														
Platte	13.1	0.0	5.6	30.5	2.7	5.6	4.5	7.5	12.9	6 320	193	304	13 694	2.4
Polk	45.9	D	3.5	1.7	D	4.3	D	4.8	17.9	1 205	232	43	2 708	-0.8
Red Willow	17.8	1.5	4.8	7.7	3.1	7.9	4.7	11.4	16.6	2 445	226	158	5 286	0.4
Richardson	9.7	0.2	7.1	13.4	4.0	5.9	4.0	D	18.0	2 225	275	144	4 409	0.4
Rock	54.1	0.0	D	D	D	1.7	4.1	0.7	14.5	205	149	13	908	-0.7
Saline	5.4	0.0	1.8	41.7	D	4.3	2.9	D	17.7	2 535	178	175	5 792	0.5
Sarpy	0.2	0.0	8.0	3.9	9.1	5.4	8.2	5.1	26.3	23 065	131	1 251	67 841	9.5
Saunders	25.1	D	9.9	6.3	4.9	5.4	4.9	D	20.5	4 090	195	169	9 519	3.2
Scotts Bluff	5.9	D	6.1	6.9	4.0	7.1	4.9	16.6	17.1	8 170	225	850	16 298	-0.7
Seward	12.6	0.0	7.5	17.7	2.6	4.3	5.1	D	15.7	3 180	186	136	7 084	3.0
Sheridan	33.5	D	2.2	7.4	1.4	7.2	D	2.0	23.6	1 350	259	74	2 893	-1.5
Sherman	21.5	0.0	3.2	9.3	D	7.1	3.7	5.0	20.2	825	267	25	1 933	-0.4
Sioux	75.7	0.0	0.3	2.3	D	D	D	D	7.4	240	190	5	819	0.5
Stanton	36.0	D	D	D	D	0.7	1.9	0.4	8.6	1 000	169	26	2 671	1.4
Thayer	25.2	D	4.6	18.4	1.0	3.0	5.5	3.9	19.7	1 360	264	90	2 744	0.5
Thomas	37.7	0.0	D	D	D	D	D	D	14.0	170	248	0	403	0.2
Thurston	33.6	0.1	1.1	5.7	D	4.0	2.2	5.5	34.2	1 115	158	226	2 417	0.4
Valley	24.1	D	4.9	5.7	D	5.4	4.0	3.3	25.9	1 085	261	68	2 279	0.3
Washington	6.6	D	11.5	18.2	4.5	9.7	4.3	D	22.9	3 875	191	153	8 528	2.7
Wayne	29.6	0.0	1.6	13.7	1.8	3.5	6.5	8.0	22.9	1 475	158	75	3 887	2.9
Webster	48.4	D	D	D	D	3.2	D	4.7	15.2	1 020	281	112	1 902	-0.5
Wheeler	87.1	0.0	D	D	0.0	D	D	0.0	3.5	150	199	0	572	-0.7
York	14.2	D	4.7	12.1	4.3	5.3	6.4	D	14.6	3 085	223	169	6 293	1.0
NEVADA	0.2	1.9	6.5	3.6	8.5	6.9	5.5	9.4	17.0	492 121	171	53 440	1 221 698	4.1
Churchill	1.0	-0.1	7.7	6.1	D	5.6	4.1	9.0	34.9	5 505	228	484	10 677	-1.4
Clark	0.0	0.0	6.1	2.5	8.4	7.2	6.8	9.3	15.7	332 650	158	41 203	881 165	4.9
Douglas	-0.1	D	10.3	9.4	8.5	5.5	7.2	7.7	13.4	13 805	290	393	23 988	1.3
Elko	2.4	14.7	10.5	0.8	3.1	6.6	2.4	6.0	18.4	6 140	119	491	20 936	7.0
Esmeralda	-8.8	D	D	D	D	D	0.0	0.0	19.6	260	322	16	819	-3.9
Eureka	0.7	D	D	0.0	D	0.2	D	D	3.0	330	163	15	1 029	-4.4
Humboldt	2.0	38.0	5.7	2.5	D	5.1	1.4	D	18.5	2 545	150	219	7 275	2.1
Lander	0.3	72.6	D	D	D	2.0	D	D	13.4	900	153	75	2 606	1.2
Lincoln	-0.7	1.0	D	D	21.1	4.9	2.1	D	49.3	1 085	215	66	2 728	-0.1
Lyon	2.0	5.8	7.1	21.0	4.2	6.2	4.2	D	21.5	13 875	265	929	22 541	0.0
Mineral	-2.0	10.8	D	D	D	D	D	D	42.0	1 310	294	142	2 773	-2.0
Nye	4.7	15.4	4.3	1.1	19.6	6.4	1.3	6.8	15.9	15 460	359	1 065	21 550	-3.6
Pershing	12.0	38.9	D	D	D	3.2	0.5	D	35.8	975	148	62	2 393	-2.9
Storey	0.0	D	11.3	20.8	D	D	D	D	5.9	1 200	302	12	1 984	-0.3
Washoe	0.1	0.1	8.1	6.7	11.1	6.8	1.6	12.0	18.1	81 450	183	7 127	191 383	3.5
White Pine	-0.5	39.1	2.1	0.3	D	3.4	1.4	D	37.2	1 755	179	138	4 415	-1.8
Carson City	0.1	D	5.3	8.6	6.7	6.4	2.8	14.0	38.3	12 875	237	1 003	23 436	-0.4
NEW HAMPSHIRE	0.1	0.1	7.3	11.6	12.3	8.2	8.8	12.4	13.2	288 891	217	19 588	625 307	1.7
Belknap	0.2	0.2	12.0	9.5	8.0	10.6	4.1	13.5	15.5	17 440	289	1 096	38 058	1.8
Carroll	-0.1	D	13.5	D	9.1	11.2	6.2	11.3	14.7	14 660	310	737	40 583	1.9
Cheshire	0.4	0.0	9.4	14.6	6.6	10.2	6.8	10.9	15.7	18 570	244	1 265	35 151	1.1
Coos	-0.3	D	D	D	2.8	9.1	3.9	18.3	28.1	10 470	324	909	21 252	-0.3
Grafton	0.4	0.1	4.8	9.6	10.4	6.5	4.7	23.5	11.1	20 445	230	1 032	52 064	1.8
Hillsborough	0.0	D	D	14.2	15.3	8.0	10.6	11.3	10.3	77 720	191	7 233	168 693	1.6
Merrimack	0.1	0.2	7.2	8.1	8.4	7.4	9.2	14.1	21.9	33 105	224	2 172	64 069	0.8
Rockingham	0.0	0.1	8.3	10.5	15.0	8.4	7.9	8.9	9.1	60 690	201	2 275	130 189	2.7
Strafford	0.1	D	D	D	7.4	7.5	13.9	13.0	22.1	24 940	197	2 049	52 899	2.3
Sullivan	0.3	D	9.7	24.1	6.8	9.5	4.8	8.0	15.5	10 850	252	820	22 349	0.0
NEW JERSEY	0.1	0.1	5.5	7.3	15.3	5.9	10.4	11.2	15.5	1 583 456	177	182 247	3 604 409	1.4
Atlantic	0.7	D	6.8	D	6.6	8.1	4.3	15.5	25.1	57 475	211	6 917	127 994	1.1
Bergen	0.0	D	5.6	6.6	15.5	6.5	9.5	13.7	9.9	161 165	172	12 250	356 474	1.2
Burlington	0.1	D	5.6	8.5	11.9	7.4	11.4	13.2	18.4	88 930	198	5 922	178 989	1.9
Camden	0.1	D	5.8	7.0	10.4	7.2	5.2	18.9	19.4	97 775	192	16 782	205 800	0.5
Cape May	0.2	D	10.7	D	5.1	9.7	7.1	10.9	27.9	28 205	297	1 814	99 235	0.9
Cumberland	1.5	0.3	6.2	14.6	D	7.3	2.9	15.5	28.5	30 570	197	5 908	56 423	1.0
Essex	0.0	0.0	3.3	4.5	13.2	3.3	13.4	10.7	22.0	118 275	149	29 218	315 496	0.8
Gloucester	0.9	0.1	9.3	9.1	D	10.7	3.7	10.3	23.1	56 185	192	4 474	113 015	2.9
Hudson	0.0	D	2.9	2.4	13.5	4.7	27.4	5.9	15.5	81 465	121	21 530	279 660	3.4
Hunterdon	0.2	0.2	10.6	4.1	18.3	7.2	11.4	10.0	15.1	23 300	186	881	50 120	1.3

1. Per 1,000 resident population estimated as of July 1 of the year shown.

Table B. States and Counties — Housing, Labor Force, and Employment

STATE County	Housing units, 2011–2015								Civilian labor force, 2016				Civilian employment,[6] 2011–2015		
	Occupied units										Unemployment		Percent		
			Owner-occupied			Renter-occupied									
				Median owner cost as a percent of income											Con-struction, produc-tion, and mainte-nance occu-pations
				With a mort-gage	Without a mort-gage[2]	Median rent[3]	Median rent as a per-cent of income[2]	Sub-stand-ard units[4] (percent)		Percent change, 2015–2016				Manage-ment, business, science and arts	
	Total	Percent	Median value[1]						Total		Total	Rate[5]	Total		
	89	90	91	92	93	94	95	96	97	98	99	100	101	102	103

STATE County	89	90	91	92	93	94	95	96	97	98	99	100	101	102	103
NEBRASKA—Cont'd															
Platte	12 707	72.8	125 200	19.3	11.1	658	21.9	3.0	16 953	-1.2	621	3.7	17 701	27.5	36.6
Polk	2 179	77.3	103 400	18.9	10.0	592	20.2	1.3	2 879	-1.1	80	2.8	2 843	35.7	31.2
Red Willow	4 651	73.0	86 100	18.7	13.2	551	26.6	1.6	5 997	-1.8	177	3.0	5 714	26.0	29.8
Richardson	3 761	74.8	72 000	18.3	12.9	468	20.9	2.2	4 235	-1.6	144	3.4	4 000	31.6	30.1
Rock	690	75.1	70 800	19.8	11.0	592	15.6	0.4	884	2.9	24	2.7	765	40.0	28.0
Saline	5 104	63.9	95 700	19.2	11.2	703	21.9	1.9	7 325	0.6	238	3.2	7 130	29.2	39.4
Sarpy	61 983	69.8	163 800	20.5	11.1	868	25.8	2.3	91 217	0.6	2 775	3.0	87 645	41.7	18.0
Saunders	8 055	78.2	150 600	21.6	12.7	729	22.1	1.0	10 958	0.2	350	3.2	10 624	36.3	23.3
Scotts Bluff	14 755	68.5	107 700	21.9	13.9	683	27.8	3.0	19 035	1.9	690	3.6	17 970	28.6	26.6
Seward	6 348	71.1	147 800	19.5	12.2	669	23.4	1.2	8 752	0.6	262	3.0	8 543	35.2	29.1
Sheridan	2 259	70.9	70 200	21.1	12.7	571	22.8	2.3	2 748	0.6	82	3.0	2 564	42.2	21.2
Sherman	1 377	77.9	86 600	22.1	11.5	520	17.9	1.2	1 724	0.9	57	3.3	1 569	37.5	31.7
Sioux	549	77.0	89 600	31.9	11.6	623	20.1	0.0	791	0.4	22	2.8	662	52.9	16.2
Stanton	2 323	84.3	103 400	20.3	11.5	639	22.3	1.4	3 451	-1.6	94	2.7	3 151	28.9	33.6
Thayer	2 341	79.2	64 700	18.3	11.5	472	20.4	1.7	2 919	-1.7	76	2.6	2 542	35.4	26.5
Thomas	300	72.3	84 300	18.4	10.0	444	16.5	0.7	446	2.3	15	3.4	385	42.3	29.1
Thurston	2 084	61.8	68 600	17.6	10.8	525	24.9	11.4	2 976	0.1	149	5.0	2 483	35.0	25.5
Valley	1 897	71.5	84 700	18.1	11.5	500	25.4	0.5	2 099	1.7	62	3.0	2 268	37.4	25.8
Washington	8 034	79.2	175 800	22.7	12.6	676	23.1	0.9	11 017	0.7	368	3.3	10 850	37.4	24.0
Wayne	3 500	61.6	116 100	17.0	10.0	532	21.9	3.9	5 610	1.2	159	2.8	5 219	35.9	21.2
Webster	1 552	78.2	77 600	22.0	12.8	444	19.8	1.3	1 719	-0.5	57	3.3	1 689	34.7	31.0
Wheeler	389	73.8	88 100	23.9	11.4	606	15.0	1.5	556	-1.2	13	2.3	494	37.2	31.8
York	5 604	68.7	117 600	19.5	10.8	617	25.7	0.6	7 314	-0.4	208	2.8	7 274	36.7	24.1
NEVADA	1 016 709	55.1	173 700	24.4	10.2	973	30.1	4.7	1 427 113	0.9	81 105	5.7	1 267 312	27.7	18.5
Churchill	9 475	61.4	151 000	22.6	10.2	851	27.9	4.2	10 674	0.5	579	5.4	9 274	29.7	28.9
Clark	724 446	52.5	170 400	24.5	10.3	999	30.6	4.8	1 048 043	0.8	60 832	5.8	923 588	26.5	17.0
Douglas	19 779	69.4	272 000	26.8	10.3	1 028	28.9	1.7	22 439	-0.3	1 259	5.6	20 371	32.1	20.7
Elko	17 696	70.3	184 600	19.2	10.0	895	21.8	4.0	26 974	0.0	1 216	4.5	25 865	25.5	32.4
Esmeralda	483	59.8	79 800	22.1	12.0	448	17.8	11.4	530	0.0	24	4.5	437	25.9	44.6
Eureka	767	71.1	93 100	16.9	10.0	692	13.8	5.2	1 045	4.2	48	4.6	853	37.5	35.2
Humboldt	6 149	73.4	159 900	18.1	10.0	818	21.9	4.2	8 309	-1.9	447	5.4	8 295	20.3	39.6
Lander	2 114	78.7	109 500	16.8	10.0	646	23.4	3.5	3 186	-3.0	198	6.2	2 644	21.4	53.7
Lincoln	1 883	67.8	128 900	22.7	10.0	592	20.6	2.7	2 028	2.8	103	5.1	1 714	35.9	17.0
Lyon	19 524	70.2	131 700	24.5	11.0	904	28.0	3.2	21 719	-0.9	1 601	7.4	19 958	24.6	30.6
Mineral	1 990	63.9	83 800	16.8	10.0	535	21.0	8.5	1 972	21.9	130	6.6	1 856	24.0	29.8
Nye	17 427	70.5	105 900	24.4	11.4	778	29.8	2.5	16 091	-0.7	1 176	7.3	14 143	23.9	25.0
Pershing	2 083	63.4	105 200	23.7	10.0	607	24.3	8.0	2 502	-0.4	148	5.9	2 101	32.4	33.6
Storey	1 767	87.5	177 000	23.1	10.1	0	21.9	0.0	1 910	1.9	121	6.3	1 777	30.6	22.9
Washoe	166 345	56.8	213 100	24.7	10.7	898	30.2	5.0	230 356	1.9	11 505	5.0	207 304	33.2	18.9
White Pine	3 187	74.9	124 900	18.6	10.0	703	23.2	2.4	4 569	-5.3	210	4.6	3 529	35.1	28.1
Carson City	21 594	56.1	186 000	24.3	11.7	817	28.4	4.1	24 766	-0.5	1 508	6.1	23 603	30.2	22.3
NEW HAMPSHIRE	520 251	71.0	237 300	24.5	16.4	1 000	29.5	1.9	748 566	0.8	21 149	2.8	698 810	39.8	20.2
Belknap	24 597	74.9	219 600	24.6	17.4	905	28.3	1.7	31 336	-0.5	871	2.8	30 396	37.9	22.4
Carroll	21 206	79.5	222 300	25.4	14.8	899	31.0	2.5	23 586	-0.6	707	3.0	22 992	32.2	21.8
Cheshire	30 638	70.9	188 800	24.5	18.0	916	31.9	2.0	41 087	-0.8	1 128	2.7	39 695	36.7	23.3
Coos	14 198	70.0	123 500	23.8	16.5	691	28.9	1.5	14 610	-1.4	575	3.9	14 644	31.1	24.7
Grafton	35 035	68.2	211 500	23.6	16.2	881	28.1	2.2	48 638	0.3	1 191	2.4	45 198	42.7	18.9
Hillsborough	155 208	66.7	245 700	24.2	15.7	1 073	29.7	2.0	231 348	1.0	6 884	3.0	215 215	40.7	19.4
Merrimack	56 705	72.1	225 200	25.0	17.1	939	29.4	1.8	81 366	0.4	2 045	2.5	76 330	39.9	19.7
Rockingham	118 095	76.5	282 500	24.8	15.6	1 123	28.5	1.3	180 714	1.4	5 389	3.0	166 354	42.4	19.0
Strafford	47 149	64.9	216 500	25.0	17.2	959	31.3	2.6	72 256	1.8	1 799	2.5	66 369	37.3	21.0
Sullivan	17 420	74.3	171 000	24.8	17.9	859	29.2	1.5	23 625	0.0	560	2.4	21 617	35.2	26.5
NEW JERSEY	3 189 486	64.5	315 900	26.9	18.1	1 192	32.1	3.6	4 524 260	-0.1	224 328	5.0	4 281 760	40.9	17.6
Atlantic	101 818	67.0	225 600	29.4	19.5	1 047	35.3	3.8	124 251	-2.7	9 198	7.4	128 151	29.9	16.2
Bergen	335 550	64.8	441 100	28.4	18.7	1 348	30.5	2.4	484 167	0.1	20 179	4.2	459 612	46.9	13.8
Burlington	164 659	76.5	245 000	25.0	16.7	1 207	31.8	1.6	233 042	0.4	10 334	4.4	221 766	42.7	16.2
Camden	186 101	67.5	196 800	25.5	18.9	978	33.2	2.2	255 629	0.3	13 989	5.5	241 708	38.8	18.0
Cape May	40 412	75.9	299 700	28.3	18.3	1 038	34.7	1.9	47 219	-2.5	4 634	9.8	42 881	35.1	18.4
Cumberland	50 368	66.3	162 400	26.0	17.5	982	35.3	3.9	67 209	-0.8	5 025	7.5	63 220	26.3	28.0
Essex	278 085	44.5	356 600	28.8	19.9	1 068	33.5	5.1	371 140	-0.9	22 334	6.0	358 229	37.3	18.7
Gloucester	104 268	79.6	214 500	24.7	17.5	1 072	34.5	1.4	150 050	0.3	7 583	5.1	141 635	41.0	18.5
Hudson	249 584	31.3	335 300	30.0	20.8	1 214	29.0	7.6	361 787	-0.1	16 883	4.7	339 606	39.4	19.3
Hunterdon	46 899	83.5	390 900	24.5	15.6	1 328	30.6	1.4	65 144	-0.5	2 451	3.8	65 918	50.8	12.5

1. Specified owner-occupied units.   2. A value of 10.0 represents 10 percent or less; a value of 50.0 represents 50 percent or more.   3. Specified renter-occupied units.
4. Overcrowded or lacking complete plumbing facilities.   5. Percent of civilian labor force.   6. Civilian employed persons 16 years old and over.

Table B. States and Counties — Nonfarm Employment and Agriculture

STATE County	Number of establishments	Employment — Total	Health care and social assistance	Manufacturing	Retail trade	Finance and insurance	Professional, scientific, and technical services	Annual payroll — Total (mil dol)	Average per employee (dollars)	Farms — Number	Percent with: Fewer than 50 acres	500 acres or more	Farm operators whose principal occupation is farming (percent)
	104	105	106	107	108	109	110	111	112	113	114	115	116
NEBRASKA—Cont'd													
Platte	1 021	15 845	1 558	5 300	2 173	499	379	619	39 060	942	24.3	31.0	64.9
Polk	152	992	252	46	134	60	81	27	27 296	466	23.2	39.7	66.1
Red Willow	406	3 811	609	326	888	229	112	122	31 944	405	26.7	39.0	47.4
Richardson	264	1 850	429	279	291	94	65	54	28 974	736	21.6	28.7	55.7
Rock	48	341	D	D	36	D	D	11	32 370	247	14.2	68.0	61.1
Saline	299	5 740	514	2 898	512	155	46	230	39 995	756	22.9	32.3	56.6
Sarpy	3 497	50 778	5 171	2 643	9 209	1 688	4 462	2 060	40 564	396	57.6	15.4	39.4
Saunders	540	4 008	696	483	649	209	121	125	31 106	1 204	30.4	25.1	55.8
Scotts Bluff	1 100	12 749	2 463	1 047	2 508	638	329	443	34 764	966	30.6	22.7	49.7
Seward	460	5 553	863	1 190	527	220	111	175	31 559	992	36.4	23.3	47.0
Sheridan	167	964	182	D	226	99	36	25	26 200	536	16.2	50.9	68.5
Sherman	89	590	161	D	131	19	10	15	25 705	414	12.1	38.9	60.9
Sioux	16	48	D	NA	D	D	D	1	31 188	354	8.2	63.6	71.2
Stanton	110	2 005	D	D	88	30	9	112	56 106	619	20.8	29.9	64.6
Thayer	213	2 096	383	D	200	116	43	76	36 202	432	15.7	44.9	63.9
Thomas	25	207	NA	D	6	D	D	8	38 995	87	14.9	70.1	66.7
Thurston	117	1 235	164	256	151	51	D	61	49 434	367	25.3	45.2	65.7
Valley	178	1 297	362	77	280	66	75	41	31 352	402	13.9	49.3	73.1
Washington	575	6 625	865	1 196	1 177	252	207	312	47 141	821	40.0	21.4	58.0
Wayne	244	3 128	490	818	360	297	155	91	29 200	518	24.7	33.0	67.0
Webster	94	672	161	NA	157	41	D	20	29 202	423	24.7	42.6	53.9
Wheeler	22	103	NA	D	D	D	NA	2	21 262	198	17.2	56.6	67.7
York	511	6 118	1 010	854	966	349	126	210	34 396	541	21.1	43.4	70.6
NEVADA	63 383	1 129 965	112 938	42 374	147 131	34 818	58 330	46 596	41 236	4 137	53.2	18.9	53.0
Churchill	492	5 178	752	397	904	149	360	182	35 208	672	63.1	7.6	54.3
Clark	43 396	824 659	79 754	19 400	108 862	25 934	43 541	33 078	40 112	252	78.6	2.0	46.8
Douglas	1 641	16 756	1 416	1 807	2 105	431	768	624	37 217	255	65.1	7.5	62.4
Elko	1 112	20 065	1 536	204	2 547	285	458	1 080	53 813	552	37.0	31.5	53.4
Esmeralda	12	210	NA	D	D	NA	NA	13	61 681	38	23.7	31.6	63.2
Eureka	40	1 741	D	D	27	D	6	139	79 976	101	8.9	49.5	68.3
Humboldt	407	6 123	570	210	1 000	79	67	331	53 989	359	36.2	38.2	54.6
Lander	90	1 373	D	D	203	14	D	82	59 473	124	37.1	47.6	62.1
Lincoln	85	619	126	D	193	31	15	17	27 086	185	35.7	20.5	43.8
Lyon	784	9 982	501	2 061	1 326	155	462	370	37 067	462	60.0	15.4	56.1
Mineral	60	995	113	D	88	D	13	41	41 603	119	67.2	1.7	27.7
Nye	658	8 680	788	79	1 539	121	D	364	41 888	198	63.6	15.2	51.0
Pershing	77	1 159	D	D	140	12	16	65	56 267	154	29.2	37.7	81.8
Storey	91	663	D	101	71	NA	23	19	28 368	6	100.0	0.0	0.0
Washoe	11 898	178 552	22 685	15 103	24 070	5 725	9 412	7 826	43 828	479	69.3	7.1	44.1
White Pine	189	2 811	267	25	370	41	23	155	55 022	160	40.6	26.3	43.8
Carson City	1 960	21 200	3 716	2 710	3 504	1 032	1 244	923	43 555	21	81.0	4.8	47.6
NEW HAMPSHIRE	37 669	576 424	90 039	67 441	98 903	27 592	30 511	28 076	48 708	4 391	55.5	3.5	48.0
Belknap	1 780	21 359	3 948	2 685	4 927	601	673	871	40 778	302	55.6	1.7	42.4
Carroll	1 849	17 023	3 009	812	3 676	338	485	558	32 789	291	53.6	3.4	52.6
Cheshire	1 900	27 494	3 635	4 369	5 741	1 275	642	1 120	40 749	407	53.6	5.7	47.4
Coos	853	8 668	2 150	619	1 793	254	121	296	34 091	293	38.2	6.5	50.2
Grafton	2 842	49 398	11 631	5 531	7 550	896	1 543	2 393	48 449	500	38.0	7.2	45.2
Hillsborough	10 938	179 115	29 400	26 169	28 664	8 883	10 665	9 593	53 558	688	64.0	1.5	50.0
Merrimack	4 011	62 229	12 109	5 729	10 378	3 434	2 779	2 930	47 080	600	55.7	3.8	49.2
Rockingham	9 623	133 465	15 806	13 946	27 133	6 766	8 982	6 491	48 637	658	69.6	0.8	48.8
Strafford	2 600	37 000	6 861	4 407	6 654	3 466	1 329	1 693	45 747	354	58.2	1.1	48.6
Sullivan	910	11 736	1 275	3 174	2 374	425	200	454	38 706	298	51.3	5.7	43.0
NEW JERSEY	230 961	3 558 619	568 289	218 549	460 856	192 320	321 642	209 072	58 751	9 071	71.2	3.1	49.5
Atlantic	6 329	103 524	18 734	1 472	16 163	2 539	4 479	3 964	38 292	402	69.4	2.2	61.4
Bergen	31 690	437 745	72 916	29 948	60 621	15 768	35 507	26 348	60 191	60	88.3	0.0	48.3
Burlington	10 456	179 646	26 825	14 470	24 645	18 089	14 398	9 437	52 531	838	69.5	5.0	56.4
Camden	11 390	172 266	40 615	11 296	24 268	4 619	12 905	8 229	47 767	175	81.1	1.1	50.3
Cape May	3 810	26 513	4 730	524	6 550	1 071	1 000	1 050	39 604	152	75.7	1.3	48.0
Cumberland	2 832	44 519	9 765	7 303	7 417	1 133	1 013	1 745	39 202	583	61.7	5.3	55.2
Essex	18 589	283 551	52 734	18 094	27 433	20 192	22 350	16 885	59 550	13	100.0	0.0	53.8
Gloucester	5 916	89 601	14 376	7 456	17 212	1 706	3 797	3 721	41 526	584	74.3	2.6	45.0
Hudson	13 191	213 451	27 869	8 262	24 135	33 910	11 780	15 037	70 446	0	0.0	0.0	0.0
Hunterdon	3 802	43 906	7 496	3 632	6 939	2 900	5 482	2 756	62 771	1 447	71.9	1.9	43.7

Table B. States and Counties — Agriculture

STATE County	Land in farms Acreage (1,000) [117]	Percent change, 2007–2012 [118]	Acres Average size of farm [119]	Total irrigated (1,000) [120]	Total cropland (1,000) [121]	Value of land and buildings (dollars) Average per farm [122]	Average per acre [123]	Value of machinery and equipment, average per farm (dollars) [124]	Value of products sold Total (mil dol) [125]	Average per farm (dollars) [126]	Percent from: Crops [127]	Live-stock and poultry products [128]	Percent of farms with sales of: $10,000 or more [129]	$100,000 or more [130]	Government payments Total ($1,000) [131]	Percent of farms [132]
NEBRASKA—Cont'd																
Platte	426	0.1	453	194.0	351.5	2 302 510	5 088	284 312	652.1	692 256	36.3	63.7	75.7	53.7	6 298	74.1
Polk	245	-8.9	526	151.0	212.2	3 128 150	5 943	329 976	326.2	700 084	51.2	48.8	80.3	64.4	3 710	79.2
Red Willow	420	-6.0	1 036	53.1	241.6	1 651 696	1 594	224 978	180.5	445 701	45.7	54.3	64.4	37.5	3 807	61.5
Richardson	319	14.3	434	4.7	245.8	1 653 332	3 812	171 026	162.0	220 139	71.0	29.0	65.4	38.2	6 434	82.2
Rock	645	2.0	2 610	36.3	146.9	2 813 632	1 078	195 603	97.8	395 903	40.2	59.8	82.6	53.8	1 332	36.0
Saline	362	21.3	479	108.1	296.7	2 306 246	4 818	261 522	208.8	276 152	82.3	17.7	65.9	41.4	5 966	80.8
Sarpy	92	-9.0	232	10.4	82.2	1 380 134	5 959	127 424	63.6	160 553	75.4	24.6	45.5	24.5	1 340	58.1
Saunders	469	9.8	390	105.6	412.0	2 054 154	5 268	198 767	380.5	316 033	59.0	41.0	65.2	37.4	7 393	72.3
Scotts Bluff	445	23.6	461	199.2	239.7	860 445	1 867	172 940	390.1	403 791	41.2	58.8	62.1	31.2	3 579	62.3
Seward	355	6.7	358	129.9	294.3	1 799 861	5 031	216 676	308.5	311 017	59.7	40.3	59.3	34.5	6 718	71.2
Sheridan	1 534	-0.4	2 863	60.7	275.5	1 983 683	693	201 590	167.5	312 541	50.0	50.0	62.5	35.1	3 179	57.3
Sherman	281	4.1	679	71.1	127.7	1 609 171	2 369	172 713	114.2	275 754	68.3	31.7	78.7	42.8	2 093	70.5
Sioux	1 224	-5.2	3 459	39.5	94.0	1 981 486	573	151 356	146.0	412 446	20.3	79.7	74.6	44.1	1 338	46.0
Stanton	254	7.9	411	28.4	195.1	1 798 275	4 375	202 628	182.1	294 158	35.1	64.9	67.7	35.4	3 656	77.9
Thayer	326	-7.1	755	135.5	254.0	3 114 514	4 123	323 176	249.4	577 278	74.7	25.3	78.7	56.9	4 259	81.5
Thomas	368	-13.5	4 225	2.9	8.0	2 125 345	503	114 736	22.4	257 770	D	D	73.6	37.9	438	18.4
Thurston	248	24.0	675	11.9	215.9	3 406 256	5 049	284 038	197.7	538 651	47.3	52.7	72.2	57.8	3 744	80.1
Valley	349	-1.9	869	93.1	150.7	1 919 602	2 209	248 953	205.1	510 179	46.5	53.5	76.9	52.2	2 783	75.1
Washington	248	14.2	302	17.3	209.8	1 820 340	6 024	180 247	163.5	199 117	62.8	37.2	54.9	32.6	4 069	59.3
Wayne	280	1.2	540	49.8	238.4	2 363 431	4 373	235 147	203.3	392 380	45.7	54.3	75.5	43.8	3 410	77.4
Webster	302	-1.1	715	55.0	177.8	2 021 950	2 830	228 965	226.9	536 404	40.4	59.6	76.8	45.2	3 545	71.6
Wheeler	357	-0.9	1 804	39.4	90.9	2 208 793	1 225	254 586	259.8	1 312 323	13.6	86.4	74.7	51.5	1 407	52.5
York	340	-1.9	628	252.4	313.1	3 534 628	5 631	429 436	415.4	767 861	72.9	27.1	81.0	65.1	6 039	74.5
NEVADA	5 914	0.8	1 429	687.8	756.9	1 324 673	927	134 626	764.1	184 710	47.9	52.1	42.0	21.2	3 253	8.2
Churchill	197	50.0	294	53.6	56.3	713 604	2 431	110 594	89.9	133 833	34.5	65.5	44.6	18.3	414	7.3
Clark	16	-82.3	62	3.7	4.4	347 790	5 611	66 325	6.8	27 083	48.2	51.8	33.7	4.4	34	3.6
Douglas	101	10.9	396	25.6	18.6	1 141 780	2 884	76 525	D	D	D	D	36.9	12.2	D	0.8
Elko	2 127	2.0	3 853	132.2	170.4	1 908 208	495	122 257	95.6	173 221	15.3	84.7	42.4	23.6	398	6.5
Esmeralda	35	38.7	911	17.5	19.2	1 631 211	1 791	350 737	13.1	345 974	98.2	1.8	60.5	60.5	0	0.0
Eureka	639	-18.5	6 325	46.7	49.1	4 087 158	646	288 782	36.0	356 634	81.2	18.8	72.3	59.4	D	3.0
Humboldt	809	6.9	2 253	137.5	165.3	2 233 571	991	271 593	135.3	376 983	75.7	24.3	48.7	37.9	703	26.7
Lander	314	-7.4	2 532	37.2	44.6	1 880 298	743	211 121	39.3	316 581	68.9	31.1	55.6	46.8	132	15.3
Lincoln	D	D	D	22.0	22.4	1 074 735	D	145 276	23.2	125 487	60.2	39.8	41.6	21.6	34	5.9
Lyon	366	40.4	792	87.7	78.3	1 738 119	2 194	137 630	133.0	287 959	43.8	56.2	44.2	21.4	485	5.8
Mineral	D	D	D	D	D	863 597	D	38 882	0.9	7 429	56.4	43.6	25.2	0.8	0	0.0
Nye	65	-28.3	329	20.0	26.4	703 429	2 139	127 217	70.5	356 035	D	D	36.9	12.6	62	6.1
Pershing	299	22.5	1 943	52.8	57.4	1 813 416	933	262 714	62.8	407 474	52.5	47.5	63.6	42.9	779	29.2
Storey	0	D	14	D	D	550 167	38 384	29 833	D	D	D	D	0.0	0.0	0	0.0
Washoe	443	-8.9	924	15.4	13.7	752 190	814	53 073	16.5	34 543	49.6	50.4	27.8	6.7	75	4.0
White Pine	193	D	1 208	32.7	24.3	987 431	817	150 775	20.7	129 069	43.9	56.1	40.6	22.5	120	7.5
Carson City	D	D	D	D	D	665 048	D	108 429	5.8	275 476	D	D	23.8	19.0	0	0.0
NEW HAMPSHIRE	474	0.5	108	2.6	98.3	449 848	4 167	56 426	190.9	43 477	52.8	47.2	26.6	6.0	3 472	10.6
Belknap	24	2.2	79	0.3	5.7	431 990	5 462	54 798	7.8	25 712	61.2	38.8	22.2	5.0	194	7.3
Carroll	29	-8.4	101	0.2	3.9	479 337	4 751	50 859	5.5	18 801	63.2	36.8	24.1	2.7	203	9.6
Cheshire	63	31.2	156	0.1	9.2	455 386	2 928	52 337	17.3	42 582	39.6	60.4	31.4	6.9	231	7.9
Coos	57	11.6	194	0.0	12.5	462 461	2 386	65 020	14.2	48 461	34.6	65.4	28.7	6.5	200	14.7
Grafton	82	-17.6	165	0.1	17.2	489 910	2 974	61 806	29.8	59 662	19.5	80.5	28.8	8.0	753	19.8
Hillsborough	48	-5.0	69	0.7	11.1	450 385	6 495	52 282	22.5	32 759	69.8	30.2	22.8	7.0	261	6.8
Merrimack	65	0.5	108	0.6	13.7	430 238	3 974	58 167	45.3	75 443	77.7	22.3	30.5	6.8	686	13.0
Rockingham	36	7.2	55	0.3	9.0	406 448	7 428	49 995	18.4	27 964	68.9	31.1	23.7	4.6	352	7.9
Strafford	31	19.2	87	0.3	7.7	425 040	4 904	61 031	12.8	36 144	47.0	53.0	30.5	3.1	295	10.7
Sullivan	39	-9.7	131	0.1	8.3	515 507	3 937	66 409	17.3	58 091	30.8	69.2	23.5	8.1	296	9.4
NEW JERSEY	715	-2.5	79	88.4	456.8	1 008 402	12 792	81 470	1 006.9	111 006	88.5	11.5	36.1	12.3	7 596	11.4
Atlantic	29	-2.9	73	11.3	18.9	903 438	12 320	135 682	125.4	312 040	98.2	1.8	51.7	25.4	247	8.2
Bergen	1	21.7	24	0.1	0.5	1 005 933	42 148	74 700	5.2	86 600	96.3	3.7	60.0	20.0	D	1.7
Burlington	96	11.8	114	13.1	52.3	1 108 438	9 686	98 032	100.9	120 390	95.4	4.6	45.3	14.4	1 939	13.4
Camden	7	-18.5	41	2.5	4.7	513 600	12 583	67 920	16.0	91 526	99.2	0.8	32.6	12.0	20	5.7
Cape May	7	-7.8	48	2.2	4.3	557 868	11 534	51 809	8.0	52 809	93.4	6.6	40.1	10.5	D	2.0
Cumberland	65	-7.1	111	19.3	49.7	889 362	8 035	130 184	170.4	292 216	97.2	2.8	50.9	22.1	520	14.9
Essex	0	-30.4	10	0.0	0.0	624 923	63 469	61 769	1.9	148 462	D	D	69.2	38.5	0	0.0
Gloucester	43	-7.3	74	9.0	32.0	882 231	11 909	93 639	87.7	150 154	93.9	6.1	33.6	15.6	700	13.0
Hudson	0	0.0	0	0.0	0.0	0	0	0	0.0	0	0.0	0.0	0.0	0.0	0	0.0
Hunterdon	96	-4.0	66	1.2	58.3	1 088 382	16 401	59 249	67.2	46 445	85.3	14.7	26.3	5.1	724	10.8

STATE County	Water use, 2010		Wholesale trade,[1] 2012				Retail trade,[2] 2012				Real estate and rental and leasing,[2] 2012			
	Total water withdrawn (mil gal/day)	Gallons withdrawn per person per day	Number of establishments	Number of employees	Sales (mil dol)	Annual payroll (mil dol)	Number of establishments	Number of employees	Sales (mil dol)	Annual payroll (mil dol)	Number of establishments	Number of employees	Receipts (mil dol)	Annual payroll (mil dol)
	133	134	135	136	137	138	139	140	141	142	143	144	145	146
NEBRASKA—Cont'd														
Platte	124.5	3 861	51	543	851.1	26.9	161	2 112	541.2	45.6	38	120	21.7	2.8
Polk	65.5	12 107	8	115	211.9	6.2	24	128	50.2	2.8	1	D	D	D
Red Willow	39.9	3 608	22	246	193.8	12.5	80	929	329.2	21.6	15	37	2.7	0.4
Richardson	2.9	343	26	137	473.1	5.0	44	331	94.1	7.2	6	16	1.7	0.5
Rock	21.6	14 174	4	D	D	D	7	44	6.8	0.7	NA	NA	NA	NA
Saline	46.1	3 245	21	175	316.6	9.1	43	536	129.2	11.1	8	18	2.6	0.3
Sarpy	35.1	221	183	2 932	4 040.2	161.1	367	7 301	2 926.4	174.8	146	580	163.2	22.0
Saunders	104.3	5 020	31	193	235.6	9.0	67	566	161.7	12.3	17	22	1.8	0.4
Scotts Bluff	518.7	14 031	56	D	D	D	178	D	D	D	46	116	19.8	3.0
Seward	51.2	3 057	27	258	528.2	14.1	47	521	105.6	10.7	9	11	2.6	0.3
Sheridan	54.4	9 947	12	206	104.3	4.8	42	236	55.7	3.8	2	D	D	D
Sherman	45.1	14 293	3	32	15.2	1.2	17	134	59.1	3.0	1	D	D	D
Sioux	99.0	75 484	1	D	D	D	3	D	D	D	NA	NA	NA	NA
Stanton	19.0	3 105	3	D	D	D	13	83	17.9	1.4	NA	NA	NA	NA
Thayer	79.1	15 132	25	215	524.6	12.3	31	173	56.1	3.4	3	D	D	D
Thomas	1.4	2 148	1	D	D	D	4	25	8.0	0.4	NA	NA	NA	NA
Thurston	5.9	853	8	99	103.3	3.5	24	219	73.0	4.7	4	D	D	D
Valley	120.0	28 174	8	76	225.5	3.3	33	267	116.5	6.0	2	D	D	D
Washington	445.8	22 032	18	D	D	D	56	1 106	747.4	42.4	15	20	2.6	0.5
Wayne	15.8	1 641	12	122	63.4	3.2	40	352	69.6	5.9	7	16	1.2	0.5
Webster	42.0	11 020	13	D	D	D	19	163	29.3	2.4	NA	NA	NA	NA
Wheeler	40.5	49 450	3	D	D	D	2	D	D	D	NA	NA	NA	NA
York	138.2	10 112	37	390	427.0	17.6	70	979	290.2	20.9	19	47	5.6	0.9
NEVADA	2 623.1	971	2 501	27 649	19 841.7	1 516.2	8 135	129 977	38 234.2	3 454.1	3 866	22 412	4 981.2	814.7
Churchill	191.8	7 708	15	78	39.1	2.9	69	966	235.1	23.4	32	113	12.5	2.6
Clark	486.6	249	1 630	16 747	11 597.1	958.8	5 712	95 369	27 971.7	2 531.6	2 794	17 855	3 700.3	647.4
Douglas	111.6	2 374	41	341	211.6	18.3	172	1 793	516.6	46.8	126	D	D	D
Elko	357.1	7 314	57	D	D	D	161	2 359	946.5	63.8	41	249	35.0	7.3
Esmeralda	25.8	32 950	1	D	D	D	1	D	D	D	NA	NA	NA	NA
Eureka	306.2	154 076	2	D	D	D	7	29	10.2	0.6	NA	NA	NA	NA
Humboldt	282.4	17 086	18	122	71.4	8.1	78	989	325.3	25.6	9	D	D	D
Lander	164.0	28 391	4	34	38.4	2.2	20	235	52.0	6.0	3	4	0.8	0.1
Lincoln	54.1	10 123	2	D	D	D	16	D	D	D	3	D	D	D
Lyon	222.1	4 274	38	749	206.4	24.6	97	1 188	465.5	29.1	33	D	D	D
Mineral	3.1	658	2	D	D	D	15	95	31.3	3.0	NA	NA	NA	NA
Nye	63.9	1 455	9	96	55.4	4.5	117	1 404	397.1	34.1	34	79	7.7	1.8
Pershing	82.8	12 261	2	D	D	D	16	131	48.4	3.3	1	D	D	D
Storey	2.0	491	NA	NA	NA	NA	20	41	6.0	0.9	1	D	D	D
Washoe	132.9	315	584	8 064	6 401.9	414.6	1 391	21 603	6 167.0	580.0	671	D	D	D
White Pine	119.8	11 943	7	64	33.7	2.2	31	408	111.0	9.6	7	D	D	D
Carson City	17.0	307	89	519	276.4	25.2	212	3 139	918.2	92.6	111	304	51.7	9.5
NEW HAMPSHIRE	1 214.6	923	1 543	21 140	18 029.2	1 307.9	6 127	95 660	26 018.2	2 403.6	1 338	7 044	1 593.1	309.7
Belknap	9.3	155	50	447	214.2	23.9	342	4 907	1 357.5	127.0	78	420	62.0	12.3
Carroll	5.0	104	39	310	99.2	14.5	363	3 558	877.7	88.9	69	237	36.1	8.6
Cheshire	7.9	103	59	1 151	637.4	47.0	368	5 839	1 692.5	150.1	60	229	45.1	8.0
Coos	13.6	411	21	295	89.3	7.5	182	1 800	566.6	45.2	25	68	11.9	2.5
Grafton	12.2	137	78	713	487.9	42.6	519	7 712	2 034.2	199.5	144	454	70.5	15.3
Hillsborough	55.1	137	537	6 822	4 749.3	470.5	1 584	26 984	7 724.7	700.9	387	2 697	565.9	123.8
Merrimack	216.2	1 476	148	3 176	2 823.3	162.5	624	10 124	2 819.7	243.0	143	848	319.9	41.4
Rockingham	871.2	2 951	487	6 804	8 203.7	455.3	1 587	26 066	6 764.5	625.5	303	1 286	316.8	55.9
Strafford	19.0	154	85	1 037	385.9	58.1	385	6 378	1 619.4	166.7	93	560	78.1	22.7
Sullivan	5.1	117	39	385	339.1	26.0	173	2 292	561.2	56.5	36	245	86.7	19.2
NEW JERSEY	5 670.7	645	12 760	208 830	288 467.8	14 976.8	31 722	436 299	133 665.7	12 676.0	8 749	53 751	17 327.6	2 813.1
Atlantic	60.1	219	188	D	D	D	1 227	16 099	4 292.7	394.9	227	1 383	351.1	52.0
Bergen	116.3	128	2 720	36 346	77 906.6	2 730.3	3 807	56 423	20 349.2	2 662.1	1 357	7 550	2 481.5	417.9
Burlington	109.5	244	492	10 202	14 927.4	618.5	1 428	23 654	6 868.6	645.4	364	3 340	886.7	201.7
Camden	57.5	112	572	8 133	4 906.7	442.3	1 730	23 577	6 445.8	593.9	398	2 660	601.1	116.3
Cape May	79.6	818	60	D	D	D	669	5 803	1 639.4	166.2	218	681	148.7	26.0
Cumberland	58.9	375	152	3 223	2 422.4	133.6	512	7 201	2 049.0	175.0	120	471	96.2	15.8
Essex	33.2	42	987	14 029	13 657.7	913.7	2 710	26 114	9 204.6	720.2	879	5 267	1 258.8	214.8
Gloucester	72.2	251	296	7 307	16 524.4	437.2	954	16 728	4 452.9	398.7	171	1 228	256.1	63.9
Hudson	209.4	330	757	15 906	26 043.1	1 009.8	2 118	23 126	6 647.6	611.5	636	3 698	1 238.8	199.0
Hunterdon	89.7	699	143	1 868	1 030.6	150.0	493	6 561	2 350.0	190.2	104	415	123.8	25.3

1. Merchant wholesalers, except manufacturers' sales branches and offices.   2. Employer establishments.

Professional Services, Manufacturing, and Accommodation and Food Services

STATE County	Professional, scientific, and technical services, 2012				Manufacturing, 2012				Accommodation and food services, 2012			
	Number of establish-ments	Number of employees	Receipts (mil dol)	Annual payroll (mil dol)	Number of establish-ments	Number of employees	Receipts (mil dol)	Annual payroll (mil dol)	Number of establish-ments	Number of employees	Sales (mil dol)	Annual payroll (mil dol)
	147	148	149	150	151	152	153	154	155	156	157	158
NEBRASKA—Cont'd												
Platte	65	465	55.7	23.1	74	5 492	4 438.5	261.6	75	968	40.9	10.5
Polk	12	18	1.9	0.4	6	53	D	1.6	6	37	1.4	0.2
Red Willow	28	123	13.9	4.4	14	293	D	14.3	30	524	21.5	6.0
Richardson	13	63	4.2	1.5	14	193	40.4	7.1	21	193	6.1	1.7
Rock	2	D	D	D	NA	NA	NA	NA	4	15	0.4	0.1
Saline	16	43	4.6	1.2	19	2 654	2 175.0	125.9	27	309	10.6	2.6
Sarpy	297	2 588	354.6	156.8	76	2 699	791.9	139.3	255	4 718	224.7	62.7
Saunders	45	119	15.0	4.9	22	288	104.6	9.5	42	D	D	D
Scotts Bluff	68	D	D	D	39	847	270.7	33.7	100	D	D	D
Seward	29	106	21.4	3.3	20	1 197	576.8	57.3	30	453	18.6	4.4
Sheridan	8	29	3.8	0.7	NA	NA	NA	NA	21	133	4.8	1.3
Sherman	6	13	0.9	0.3	3	10	D	D	8	61	2.5	0.6
Sioux	1	D	D	D	NA	NA	NA	NA	2	D	D	D
Stanton	2	D	D	D	NA	NA	NA	NA	5	60	1.7	0.4
Thayer	9	18	2.3	0.6	11	524	D	15.3	12	115	7.6	1.1
Thomas	1	D	D	D	NA	NA	NA	NA	NA	NA	NA	NA
Thurston	9	D	D	D	6	246	D	10.1	8	65	2.5	0.5
Valley	14	D	D	D	9	74	D	3.2	9	D	D	D
Washington	47	163	20.1	6.5	26	1 134	1 549.7	69.9	52	441	16.1	4.4
Wayne	16	56	10.7	2.7	12	893	217.6	28.6	23	393	11.5	2.5
Webster	2	D	D	D	NA	NA	NA	NA	4	24	0.6	0.2
Wheeler	NA	NA	NA	NA	NA	NA	NA	NA	5	8	0.2	0.1
York	29	122	14.5	4.8	28	777	359.3	34.9	39	710	32.2	8.7
NEVADA	8 102	47 934	7 758.5	2 832.1	1 706	38 123	14 719.1	1 979.3	5 815	296 762	27 481.5	8 555.6
Churchill	43	354	23.4	10.4	18	248	D	12.8	50	586	35.9	9.4
Clark	5 645	35 253	5 825.0	2 128.2	894	17 390	5 673.8	782.0	4 050	250 601	24 283.8	7 612.3
Douglas	238	786	115.6	37.2	74	1 129	713.0	55.1	126	5 326	445.8	125.1
Elko	98	666	123.7	32.7	24	D	D	D	138	5 036	442.7	121.4
Esmeralda	1	D	D	D	NA	NA	NA	NA	1	D	D	D
Eureka	4	D	D	D	NA	NA	NA	NA	5	34	1.5	0.4
Humboldt	19	96	10.3	3.6	13	241	120.0	12.0	62	1 161	84.1	15.7
Lander	1	D	D	D	NA	NA	NA	NA	14	145	6.2	1.6
Lincoln	6	20	2.4	0.6	NA	NA	NA	NA	19	D	D	D
Lyon	62	324	34.8	13.1	81	1 708	729.9	85.9	67	613	31.2	7.9
Mineral	5	22	1.5	0.6	NA	NA	NA	NA	10	D	D	D
Nye	50	155	12.5	4.3	14	60	D	1.7	81	1 401	96.5	22.5
Pershing	2	D	D	D	6	128	D	D	13	113	5.8	1.8
Storey	6	7	0.5	0.2	6	91	17.3	3.1	14	71	9.4	2.4
Washoe	1 619	9 029	1 435.4	539.9	442	13 974	6 427.4	840.4	973	28 138	1 860.8	580.8
White Pine	8	25	2.1	0.9	6	23	D	0.8	33	553	31.2	9.4
Carson City	295	1 180	170.1	60.0	122	2 798	634.0	162.7	159	2 740	133.4	41.2
NEW HAMPSHIRE	3 825	30 159	3 947.8	1 697.5	1 851	66 636	18 895.6	3 923.8	3 606	54 047	2 942.3	890.9
Belknap	147	D	D	D	86	2 483	673.3	117.2	223	2 603	157.9	50.7
Carroll	133	D	D	D	74	1 069	225.8	41.2	313	4 034	247.0	70.6
Cheshire	147	628	69.2	30.0	127	4 719	1 101.6	230.1	172	2 543	128.7	40.0
Coos	37	114	11.3	4.3	37	731	189.3	31.0	111	1 747	81.0	31.2
Grafton	254	1 537	210.1	98.4	115	5 758	1 593.9	300.2	378	5 112	296.7	92.2
Hillsborough	1 335	10 986	1 721.0	737.1	554	25 287	7 450.8	1 732.0	897	14 781	762.2	229.8
Merrimack	433	2 850	402.7	171.8	206	5 548	1 577.3	291.1	307	4 965	238.7	75.2
Rockingham	1 049	8 202	1 109.2	462.4	425	14 055	4 580.4	824.8	853	13 804	810.2	237.3
Strafford	235	1 720	217.6	95.3	137	4 428	924.4	228.1	282	3 676	182.8	52.2
Sullivan	55	180	21.1	9.0	90	2 559	578.8	128.0	70	782	37.1	11.8
NEW JERSEY	29 390	307 549	58 738.2	24 013.0	7 758	230 697	108 855.0	14 094.8	20 127	291 933	19 673.6	5 386.8
Atlantic	579	D	D	D	96	1 730	285.4	72.3	860	46 661	4 008.5	1 282.5
Bergen	4 067	37 178	6 945.7	2 557.1	1 107	33 434	12 577.6	2 133.9	2 331	28 682	2 016.7	518.2
Burlington	1 323	D	D	D	343	15 380	5 496.6	1 046.9	914	14 391	771.4	206.5
Camden	1 444	D	D	D	389	11 340	D	613.9	998	14 598	789.4	210.9
Cape May	214	D	D	D	66	615	98.2	21.5	903	5 888	593.0	160.0
Cumberland	207	D	D	D	162	8 055	2 812.0	351.2	265	3 555	173.7	43.6
Essex	2 213	28 745	6 117.7	2 678.1	720	17 556	5 942.0	921.7	1 550	20 633	1 378.7	368.3
Gloucester	514	D	D	D	235	8 056	12 683.6	440.2	483	7 832	406.6	108.0
Hudson	1 335	11 261	1 961.4	898.8	378	7 865	2 682.9	363.9	1 381	15 540	1 214.5	287.1
Hunterdon	561	4 111	888.9	350.4	141	3 485	1 400.2	198.5	312	3 518	206.3	54.9

1. Establishment subject to federal tax.

Table B. States and Counties — Health Care and Social Assistance, Other Services, Nonemployer Businesses, and Residential Construction

STATE County	Health care and social assistance, 2012 Number of establishments	Number of employees	Receipts (mil dol)	Annual payroll (mil dol)	Other services, 2012 Number of establishments	Number of employees	Receipts (mil dol)	Annual payroll (mil dol)	Nonemployer businesses, 2015 Number	Receipts (mil dol)	Value of residential construction authorized by building permits, 2016 New Construction ($1,000)	Number of housing units
	159	160	161	162	163	164	165	166	167	168	169	170
NEBRASKA—Cont'd												
Platte	82	1 551	179.9	55.9	78	360	26.7	8.4	2 205	93.9	21 123	91
Polk	9	273	17.4	7.2	9	17	2.8	0.5	446	14.6	1 563	6
Red Willow	50	604	60.9	22.5	33	90	10.1	2.4	881	35.0	4 842	24
Richardson	26	D	D	D	22	66	4.8	0.8	570	19.2	540	3
Rock	4	D	D	D	5	7	0.9	0.2	216	10.7	403	2
Saline	26	525	37.9	16.4	26	96	6.2	1.8	826	32.6	4 219	24
Sarpy	302	4 733	387.5	146.4	225	1 219	110.5	30.3	9 990	374.8	263 862	1 113
Saunders	31	672	38.8	17.6	27	D	D	D	1 796	67.7	23 508	113
Scotts Bluff	128	D	D	D	76	D	D	D	2 469	107.3	4 854	27
Seward	36	761	53.7	24.0	38	134	15.4	3.5	1 328	43.0	12 909	65
Sheridan	17	208	12.2	6.4	18	42	3.1	0.6	445	17.9	212	3
Sherman	6	D	D	D	6	11	0.9	0.1	269	10.5	175	1
Sioux	1	D	D	D	1	D	D	D	103	3.6	1 065	3
Stanton	7	D	D	D	4	23	2.7	0.4	497	21.7	1 550	6
Thayer	11	416	25.8	11.1	21	60	16.3	1.4	415	20.0	1 370	4
Thomas	NA	NA	NA	NA	1	D	D	D	87	3.5	254	1
Thurston	9	277	32.6	14.7	8	24	3.2	0.8	262	11.0	4 407	25
Valley	18	111	5.9	2.5	14	67	6.0	1.3	411	16.7	1 010	4
Washington	40	926	67.4	31.7	41	D	D	D	1 566	68.4	15 951	56
Wayne	24	458	31.7	14.2	20	D	D	D	627	26.5	4 413	38
Webster	9	189	10.7	4.7	5	17	2.1	0.3	293	8.3	490	2
Wheeler	NA	NA	NA	NA	1	D	D	D	84	4.6	20	1
York	41	1 063	79.9	35.5	57	253	20.6	5.0	1 051	41.9	6 292	27
NEVADA	6 308	108 585	13 928.5	5 094.7	3 538	25 386	2 608.9	706.5	205 980	10 838.5	2 871 930	17 952
Churchill	41	714	81.1	30.6	42	171	12.2	3.5	1 184	46.6	6 871	30
Clark	4 426	75 019	9 714.9	3 493.8	2 344	17 926	1 602.8	476.8	154 711	7 851.8	2 016 831	13 577
Douglas	121	1 310	165.9	59.1	69	514	41.2	15.1	5 187	345.8	62 643	162
Elko	125	D	D	D	70	D	D	D	2 308	104.9	25 638	174
Esmeralda	NA	NA	NA	NA	1	D	D	D	62	1.4	NA	NA
Eureka	1	D	D	D	1	D	D	D	119	5.6	NA	NA
Humboldt	37	628	55.0	22.2	36	D	D	D	840	33.3	2 068	12
Lander	9	D	D	D	4	D	D	D	265	7.3	0	0
Lincoln	6	128	7.4	3.3	2	D	D	D	285	8.7	2 705	10
Lyon	38	D	D	D	42	202	20.7	5.3	2 536	120.8	49 325	224
Mineral	6	D	D	D	4	D	D	D	150	5.4	0	0
Nye	61	821	82.6	24.3	49	203	16.8	4.4	2 170	80.9	NA	NA
Pershing	6	107	9.0	3.6	4	D	D	D	200	4.4	0	0
Storey	1	D	D	D	3	D	D	D	286	12.7	1 442	12
Washoe	1 190	D	D	D	728	D	D	D	30 391	1 779.4	669 087	3 588
White Pine	16	301	44.6	16.7	13	D	D	D	469	17.0	1 319	4
Carson City	224	3 744	510.8	182.9	126	660	62.8	19.0	4 817	412.4	34 002	159
NEW HAMPSHIRE	3 578	87 099	9 616.5	4 086.4	2 879	16 603	1 554.9	473.3	104 437	5 912.8	759 526	3 796
Belknap	137	3 536	358.6	148.0	147	626	49.1	13.8	5 609	307.3	62 811	198
Carroll	142	2 693	267.9	100.4	111	432	39.6	11.1	5 566	295.2	62 312	242
Cheshire	157	3 954	334.7	156.5	144	938	77.2	22.6	5 892	305.2	31 231	199
Coos	102	2 469	214.2	91.1	68	377	40.5	12.6	2 207	96.5	11 809	65
Grafton	273	10 236	1 482.4	659.8	207	D	D	D	8 108	441.9	72 225	249
Hillsborough	1 094	28 561	3 089.1	1 339.9	824	5 516	490.3	160.3	28 477	1 657.8	188 178	1 097
Merrimack	410	12 310	1 239.7	550.0	411	1 995	257.0	68.2	10 989	589.3	54 898	248
Rockingham	866	15 640	1 697.7	671.8	676	3 639	335.9	104.1	26 488	1 682.6	210 874	1 104
Strafford	302	6 486	834.3	327.4	204	1 192	111.9	32.9	7 920	392.8	53 841	341
Sullivan	95	1 214	97.8	41.4	87	D	D	D	3 181	144.2	11 345	53
NEW JERSEY	26 935	540 875	60 375.2	24 325.0	18 327	108 216	11 607.8	3 150.1	670 765	39 455.4	4 028 688	26 793
Atlantic	846	17 487	1 969.3	780.4	563	3 588	293.9	85.2	16 682	831.5	129 263	1 083
Bergen	3 664	70 990	9 303.0	3 642.8	2 423	12 297	1 376.8	366.9	92 417	6 364.4	656 798	3 144
Burlington	1 215	25 242	2 710.6	1 006.5	778	4 560	363.7	118.9	27 596	1 601.4	113 372	825
Camden	1 535	38 296	4 238.4	1 821.5	920	5 873	478.1	149.4	29 654	1 553.2	73 560	553
Cape May	278	4 767	443.7	186.8	296	1 237	96.3	32.4	8 066	492.5	190 565	642
Cumberland	417	8 593	872.1	338.7	240	1 253	97.1	27.3	5 918	277.7	14 350	134
Essex	2 534	53 168	6 274.3	2 462.1	1 639	12 502	1 220.6	360.6	64 781	3 405.1	241 666	2 386
Gloucester	689	13 076	1 298.2	541.2	502	2 838	223.8	66.5	15 905	775.5	78 168	727
Hudson	1 412	26 740	2 397.6	1 000.5	1 092	5 024	439.1	125.3	53 140	2 552.6	754 862	4 164
Hunterdon	363	7 216	794.4	323.9	272	1 466	120.6	38.5	11 934	802.4	46 650	355

Table B. States and Counties — Government Employment and Payroll, and Local Government Finances

STATE County	Government employment and payroll, 2012		March payroll (percent of total)							Local government finances, 2012				
										General revenue			Taxes	
													Per capita[1] (dollars)	
	Full-time equivalent employees	March payroll (dollars)	Adminis-tration, judicial, and legal	Police and Corrections	Fire Protection	Highways and transpor-tation	Health and Welfare	Natural resources and utilities	Education and libraries	Total (mil dol)	Inter-govern-mental (mil dol)	Total (mil dol)	Total	Property
	171	172	173	174	175	176	177	178	179	180	181	182	183	184
NEBRASKA—Cont'd														
Platte	3 477	20 266 212	1.3	2.8	0.3	1.8	0.3	79.5	13.4	163.8	34.4	61.8	1 892	1 373
Polk	420	1 380 326	5.6	2.1	0.0	3.0	15.0	11.8	58.7	37.3	5.7	21.1	3 974	3 451
Red Willow	459	1 542 403	5.5	7.0	2.8	3.6	3.4	14.8	59.2	39.4	13.2	18.3	1 666	1 234
Richardson	419	1 193 885	9.7	4.8	0.6	7.6	0.0	12.0	63.6	30.7	8.7	18.1	2 182	1 949
Rock	140	411 891	13.3	2.7	0.0	6.6	35.8	2.2	35.4	13.0	2.1	4.8	3 482	3 134
Saline	632	2 291 344	7.0	11.3	0.3	4.0	0.9	7.0	67.4	70.4	19.1	28.7	1 969	1 723
Sarpy	5 078	18 211 968	6.6	10.7	1.5	2.7	1.0	2.9	72.0	450.7	142.5	250.1	1 508	1 248
Saunders	810	2 374 236	6.4	9.1	0.3	4.5	15.3	6.0	56.4	83.3	19.9	36.4	1 747	1 563
Scotts Bluff	2 061	7 164 008	4.8	7.4	1.1	2.8	2.5	7.6	73.3	182.1	72.1	64.7	1 751	1 338
Seward	680	2 373 107	7.0	6.7	0.0	6.0	0.7	9.6	68.9	55.3	12.4	35.6	2 103	1 821
Sheridan	512	1 548 088	13.3	3.5	0.0	6.0	29.3	9.8	37.6	40.3	9.6	11.2	2 111	1 872
Sherman	144	428 471	12.6	3.9	0.0	9.3	0.2	2.5	70.1	13.6	4.9	7.3	2 338	2 074
Sioux	56	132 554	19.8	4.1	0.0	17.1	0.0	2.1	56.8	4.9	1.0	3.0	2 305	2 122
Stanton	142	497 786	10.8	7.3	0.0	12.3	0.9	19.3	48.7	13.2	4.4	6.8	1 111	1 047
Thayer	412	1 461 621	5.5	2.0	0.0	5.1	41.8	4.4	38.2	41.8	5.4	16.6	3 236	3 029
Thomas	60	133 894	17.6	0.2	0.0	4.3	2.3	11.2	63.8	4.0	0.7	2.8	4 143	3 988
Thurston	545	1 799 779	5.2	2.2	0.0	2.7	22.5	1.8	65.3	52.7	28.4	8.7	1 244	1 115
Valley	518	1 666 812	3.3	2.5	0.0	3.6	47.1	17.8	25.3	53.3	10.2	13.7	3 233	2 920
Washington	750	2 779 921	6.4	9.0	0.0	4.2	8.1	3.5	68.0	69.7	16.2	43.5	2 146	1 843
Wayne	341	1 199 613	9.9	5.1	0.0	9.4	0.0	6.2	69.3	36.1	12.9	18.5	1 940	1 746
Webster	258	1 370 728	10.8	2.2	0.0	8.5	14.9	37.0	25.2	25.0	5.9	8.3	2 228	1 836
Wheeler	43	129 479	13.7	4.4	0.0	13.0	0.0	0.4	68.2	4.3	0.9	3.2	3 984	3 805
York	557	2 016 974	7.4	11.4	2.9	4.0	1.6	20.2	51.6	58.5	16.3	32.4	2 356	1 736
NEVADA	X	X	X	X	X	X	X	X	X	X	X	X	X	X
Churchill	944	3 773 220	10.4	12.8	0.4	2.3	1.9	7.4	51.3	114.7	52.6	27.8	1 142	921
Clark	51 796	300 546 553	8.1	16.4	5.9	3.4	8.6	10.1	45.3	8 606.7	3 678.4	2 735.1	1 367	869
Douglas	1 543	6 734 261	11.5	13.8	10.6	2.6	1.1	9.0	47.4	190.9	73.5	79.1	1 682	1 414
Elko	1 843	7 360 751	11.7	10.6	2.2	3.0	2.9	4.9	62.8	202.1	112.9	62.5	1 220	871
Esmeralda	82	243 932	21.0	20.4	0.0	9.4	1.5	2.3	37.8	7.7	4.9	1.6	2 030	2 012
Eureka	151	777 513	15.5	14.0	0.0	9.5	5.9	8.6	42.4	52.6	15.1	33.5	16 737	16 592
Humboldt	805	3 278 576	10.2	13.2	0.3	2.8	19.5	2.9	48.7	119.3	53.7	33.6	1 972	1 745
Lander	301	1 258 391	12.7	11.1	0.0	4.5	25.4	3.4	42.8	97.8	10.8	72.9	12 271	11 925
Lincoln	324	1 339 919	8.9	8.4	0.1	6.3	17.9	11.0	44.6	43.9	32.2	5.0	930	812
Lyon	1 568	6 140 208	8.1	8.1	3.5	1.3	1.3	10.4	64.0	160.6	98.5	45.8	892	708
Mineral	326	1 115 225	7.2	7.3	1.2	2.2	44.5	6.8	29.7	44.0	21.3	4.5	977	861
Nye	1 197	5 104 254	15.1	13.0	3.6	2.6	5.5	2.8	53.7	149.5	78.9	54.1	1 259	1 117
Pershing	319	1 109 998	11.6	9.0	0.3	4.2	22.5	5.0	44.3	34.1	14.3	8.8	1 300	1 263
Storey	188	901 189	19.1	15.5	16.1	3.8	0.0	4.0	34.8	29.3	7.0	16.6	4 219	4 028
Washoe	13 423	56 391 305	10.3	14.1	5.5	4.2	4.2	8.5	50.6	1 707.2	748.2	591.5	1 376	997
White Pine	513	2 356 531	8.8	7.1	1.5	3.7	40.7	2.2	32.8	71.2	22.1	18.0	1 791	1 611
Carson City	1 396	6 652 347	9.5	13.4	7.3	4.2	3.5	6.4	53.3	189.1	96.1	54.9	1 001	717
NEW HAMPSHIRE	X	X	X	X	X	X	X	X	X	X	X	X	X	X
Belknap	2 709	10 085 919	5.6	9.4	4.9	3.9	5.2	2.9	67.2	286.0	77.2	174.6	2 894	2 867
Carroll	2 191	7 449 385	6.3	9.2	2.5	4.0	7.7	3.0	65.3	220.7	71.1	131.4	2 763	2 740
Cheshire	3 313	11 134 351	6.0	8.9	2.9	3.9	7.7	4.1	65.0	326.6	110.7	178.9	2 328	2 314
Coos	1 565	5 117 863	3.6	6.6	2.3	4.9	20.1	3.2	58.8	159.6	71.8	67.1	2 091	2 079
Grafton	4 014	15 506 186	5.7	9.6	3.8	4.9	5.6	2.9	66.7	413.3	113.5	253.8	2 845	2 823
Hillsborough	13 991	56 054 764	4.1	10.8	6.0	4.5	3.9	3.8	65.8	1 458.9	470.6	808.2	2 006	1 981
Merrimack	5 875	21 465 982	6.0	10.6	5.3	4.2	7.6	3.1	61.7	555.7	176.5	328.2	2 236	2 219
Rockingham	10 620	43 247 180	4.5	10.2	6.0	2.4	3.9	2.7	68.4	1 174.1	314.0	771.3	2 590	2 568
Strafford	4 327	16 109 116	5.0	11.0	4.3	2.9	5.3	4.6	64.6	465.8	153.2	257.6	2 076	2 027
Sullivan	1 670	6 151 956	5.3	6.7	2.1	4.8	8.2	3.5	67.8	169.0	64.2	91.6	2 126	2 114
NEW JERSEY	X	X	X	X	X	X	X	X	X	X	X	X	X	X
Atlantic	14 001	71 971 044	5.3	13.7	4.7	1.7	5.3	3.8	63.4	1 749.6	507.4	1 016.6	3 691	3 639
Bergen	32 531	187 619 946	3.6	14.1	2.2	2.4	3.4	3.1	69.8	4 811.6	664.9	3 480.7	3 788	3 728
Burlington	17 657	91 624 216	4.0	9.2	2.6	2.9	2.3	3.0	75.0	2 079.2	596.9	1 183.3	2 622	2 584
Camden	20 756	110 518 829	3.6	10.7	3.0	3.5	5.8	2.8	67.4	3 281.1	1 305.1	1 230.4	2 396	2 359
Cape May	5 885	27 086 618	8.8	13.8	3.3	3.6	9.4	7.3	49.4	701.1	152.6	449.5	4 667	4 561
Cumberland	7 697	36 180 326	5.2	9.1	0.8	1.2	4.3	5.3	72.5	886.9	544.0	234.1	1 483	1 435
Essex	27 848	164 987 769	6.6	19.3	7.5	1.4	6.3	6.8	50.7	4 140.4	1 433.6	2 242.3	2 846	2 712
Gloucester	12 453	61 264 381	3.9	10.6	0.6	1.8	6.9	3.4	70.7	1 465.5	472.5	747.5	2 581	2 536
Hudson	18 627	101 485 405	7.4	23.1	8.9	1.9	5.7	4.8	45.5	2 886.1	1 144.0	1 243.6	1 906	1 849
Hunterdon	5 140	25 927 699	5.8	5.6	0.8	4.7	2.2	2.5	77.1	623.8	82.1	477.9	3 762	3 722

1. Based on the resident population estimated as of July 1 of the year shown.

Items 171—184

Table B. States and Counties — Local Government Finances, Government Employment, and Income Taxes

STATE County	Local government finances, 2012 (cont.) Direct general expenditure Total (mil dol)	Per capita¹ (dollars)	Education	Health and hospitals	Police protection	Public welfare	Highways	Debt outstanding Total (mil dol)	Per capita¹ (dollars)	Government employment, 2015 Federal civilian	Federal military	State and local	Individual income tax returns, 2014 Number of returns	Mean adjusted gross income	Mean income tax
	185	186	187	188	189	190	191	192	193	194	195	196	197	198	199
NEBRASKA—Cont'd															
Platte	113.1	3 461	56.1	0.4	3.7	0.6	15.1	2 372.1	72 585	87	115	2 545	16 460	56 048	6 104
Polk	34.4	6 457	55.6	18.0	1.4	0.1	7.2	36.4	6 843	25	18	518	2 580	54 101	5 581
Red Willow	41.1	3 746	48.6	0.9	4.2	0.6	6.1	41.9	3 815	67	37	1 055	5 100	53 420	6 438
Richardson	30.5	3 684	56.0	0.2	3.6	0.5	13.4	14.8	1 787	34	28	569	3 800	50 470	5 407
Rock	12.2	8 902	28.5	45.3	2.3	0.2	9.0	0.5	363	D	D	207	660	46 997	4 600
Saline	69.9	4 800	47.6	15.1	3.0	5.7	7.4	56.7	3 893	57	47	1 448	6 370	49 659	4 502
Sarpy	475.3	2 866	55.1	0.8	7.4	0.2	4.2	984.0	5 933	3 132	6 253	6 686	82 790	65 484	7 385
Saunders	75.5	3 628	42.1	21.4	3.2	0.2	8.3	105.7	5 074	105	73	1 498	9 950	61 552	7 068
Scotts Bluff	188.1	5 089	58.5	0.3	4.2	1.6	3.8	124.2	3 361	162	126	3 091	16 500	49 542	5 165
Seward	66.4	3 923	62.3	0.1	3.8	0.8	11.4	73.7	4 351	48	56	1 109	7 580	63 553	7 226
Sheridan	37.7	7 085	31.7	24.7	2.1	9.8	6.1	9.5	1 782	26	18	604	2 380	42 405	4 095
Sherman	13.4	4 324	49.2	0.3	3.1	0.3	17.7	6.5	2 098	12	11	284	1 410	41 979	3 860
Sioux	4.8	3 666	52.8	0.0	2.8	0.0	23.8	0.0	0	10	D	77	570	47 879	4 574
Stanton	13.6	2 232	42.0	0.7	4.3	0.5	31.8	14.5	2 388	19	21	275	2 720	52 486	5 590
Thayer	43.3	8 429	33.8	38.7	2.7	0.2	7.2	11.5	2 243	31	18	648	2 450	58 133	7 187
Thomas	4.0	5 904	53.0	0.5	3.1	0.0	7.9	0.8	1 214	D	D	93	320	54 916	5 631
Thurston	60.1	8 565	48.8	36.6	1.1	0.1	3.6	70.6	10 050	206	25	1 476	2 700	44 630	4 630
Valley	51.9	12 276	20.8	38.7	0.9	0.1	4.8	58.0	13 716	32	15	627	1 920	36 934	4 703
Washington	65.2	3 221	57.9	0.1	4.7	0.2	11.9	202.8	10 013	48	70	1 600	9 610	70 112	8 707
Wayne	43.1	4 516	51.6	0.3	2.5	0.4	9.5	23.9	2 503	37	29	1 026	3 720	56 819	6 539
Webster	23.9	6 404	33.4	19.3	2.3	5.0	13.2	9.5	2 548	24	12	300	1 630	44 279	3 834
Wheeler	4.1	5 045	61.1	0.0	2.5	0.0	23.7	0.6	806	D	D	60	380	46 234	5 068
York	55.4	4 034	45.6	2.4	5.0	0.3	13.4	105.0	7 641	55	46	1 163	6 660	59 927	7 008
NEVADA	X	X	X	X	X	X	X	X	X	18 543	17 910	132 984	1 321 660	58 756	8 191
Churchill	117.7	4 831	40.0	0.3	7.9	1.8	3.2	48.9	2 005	603	697	1 277	10 790	46 613	4 779
Clark	9 171.7	4 584	29.1	8.3	9.6	2.7	7.2	21 727.8	10 860	12 686	15 101	84 204	957 920	56 714	7 755
Douglas	187.5	3 990	36.5	0.3	5.7	2.5	2.5	82.9	1 764	96	132	2 156	25 110	78 211	13 776
Elko	209.5	4 091	47.0	0.9	7.2	0.7	5.0	51.6	1 008	354	142	3 334	23 230	64 918	7 665
Esmeralda	8.2	10 566	34.9	3.8	14.2	0.4	10.2	1.0	1 279	D	D	95	400	48 850	5 200
Eureka	40.5	20 245	25.6	2.0	4.9	0.3	18.1	0.0	0	D	D	188	820	57 532	7 098
Humboldt	102.4	6 005	35.6	26.8	6.8	1.0	6.9	5.9	344	152	47	1 348	7 930	61 099	7 296
Lander	42.2	7 095	31.4	24.0	6.2	2.0	4.2	0.0	0	65	16	503	2 650	63 252	7 691
Lincoln	42.9	7 928	28.0	0.6	5.4	1.6	11.1	9.9	1 834	50	13	583	1 690	49 308	4 270
Lyon	173.5	3 380	52.1	0.6	14.8	3.1	4.1	198.7	3 872	67	145	2 018	24 390	43 177	4 070
Mineral	39.6	8 513	17.4	39.2	5.2	0.6	3.6	14.3	3 064	61	13	463	1 850	42 596	3 985
Nye	174.9	4 071	43.6	4.0	14.2	1.5	4.9	134.2	3 123	117	120	1 592	17 760	46 081	4 585
Pershing	35.1	5 199	33.9	28.5	4.8	1.5	1.5	18.6	2 751	16	14	712	2 050	50 670	4 963
Storey	27.2	6 900	26.2	0.0	10.5	0.8	8.2	58.6	14 880	D	11	234	1 850	57 192	6 609
Washoe	1 673.2	3 892	35.9	1.1	6.6	4.3	3.3	4 470.2	10 398	3 551	1 280	24 127	212 640	69 913	10 948
White Pine	67.7	6 746	27.2	38.8	5.4	1.6	6.0	14.1	1 407	181	24	1 219	4 100	51 721	5 430
Carson City	205.0	3 738	48.3	2.1	8.1	1.2	5.3	391.1	7 131	528	147	8 931	26 560	49 430	6 288
NEW HAMPSHIRE	X	X	X	X	X	X	X	X	X	7 544	4 616	82 278	684 980	69 498	9 614
Belknap	273.9	4 541	53.3	0.3	6.3	6.1	4.4	96.2	1 595	138	199	4 099	32 530	64 704	8 643
Carroll	240.5	5 057	57.3	1.0	4.6	7.3	6.0	161.9	3 404	127	156	2 885	25 400	72 648	11 601
Cheshire	326.5	4 248	59.3	0.8	4.3	5.5	5.6	178.9	2 328	158	238	5 416	37 210	60 615	7 570
Coos	150.6	4 691	46.4	1.2	3.9	16.3	6.1	37.2	1 158	395	99	2 635	14 990	42 371	4 107
Grafton	440.6	4 940	56.2	0.8	4.4	4.8	5.7	258.1	2 895	506	277	6 726	43 910	71 340	10 508
Hillsborough	1 496.1	3 713	52.0	0.6	6.1	3.8	4.7	1 157.0	2 872	4 018	1 372	17 505	209 830	69 487	9 556
Merrimack	608.7	4 147	55.4	0.5	5.3	7.4	4.5	341.5	2 327	800	475	15 883	74 350	66 259	8 580
Rockingham	1 129.6	3 793	60.9	0.4	6.4	4.0	3.7	523.7	1 758	1 015	1 255	13 278	164 680	80 343	11 914
Strafford	444.5	3 582	51.7	0.1	5.7	7.3	4.8	294.8	2 375	300	404	11 461	60 890	59 063	7 120
Sullivan	166.1	3 857	51.2	0.5	4.3	11.4	5.9	81.8	1 900	87	141	2 390	21 210	61 166	7 826
NEW JERSEY	X	X	X	X	X	X	X	X	X	49 288	25 185	537 355	4 342 400	81 345	12 744
Atlantic	1 718.6	6 240	52.7	0.6	6.1	2.1	1.7	1 314.6	4 773	2 631	975	20 217	135 430	51 604	5 721
Bergen	4 857.2	5 286	54.3	5.8	7.0	1.3	2.6	3 581.0	3 897	2 645	1 897	45 188	460 500	105 401	19 033
Burlington	2 064.4	4 574	62.3	1.5	4.2	2.2	3.1	2 370.1	5 251	5 102	5 956	24 209	223 760	74 012	10 094
Camden	3 129.5	6 094	51.5	4.2	4.5	3.4	4.0	3 660.4	7 128	2 346	1 067	28 929	244 100	62 186	7 758
Cape May	808.9	8 400	33.8	1.5	5.3	4.4	4.9	673.4	6 992	443	1 094	8 307	49 700	57 468	7 068
Cumberland	880.4	5 580	60.1	2.7	3.8	3.4	2.5	354.4	2 246	632	294	12 698	67 710	45 541	4 300
Essex	4 300.2	5 459	38.9	3.3	8.3	2.9	1.3	3 851.1	4 889	8 916	1 646	64 106	365 810	87 715	15 791
Gloucester	1 410.5	4 871	58.9	0.8	4.6	2.2	1.9	1 385.8	4 785	487	588	19 503	138 660	67 431	8 028
Hudson	2 833.2	4 343	33.2	3.1	8.5	2.8	1.8	3 638.2	5 577	5 676	1 497	38 595	325 010	64 318	9 443
Hunterdon	605.4	4 765	66.0	1.2	3.5	0.8	6.1	565.1	4 448	254	249	7 969	64 340	116 768	20 929

1. Based on the resident population estimated as of July 1 of the year shown.

Table B. States and Counties — Land Area and Population

STATE/ County code	CBSA code[1]	County type[2]	STATE County	Land area,[3] (sq mi) 2016	Total persons 2016	Rank	Per square mile	White	Black	American Indian, Alaska Native	Asian and Pacific Islander	Percent Hispanic or Latino[4]	Under 5 years	5 to 17 years	18 to 24 years	25 to 34 years	35 to 44 years	45 to 54 years
					Population, 2016			Race alone or in combination, not Hispanic or Latino (percent)				Population and population characteristics, 2016 / Age (percent)						
				1	2	3	4	5	6	7	8	9	10	11	12	13	14	15
			NEW JERSEY—Cont'd															
34 021	45940	2	Mercer	224.4	371 023	186	1 653.4	51.7	20.6	0.5	12.0	17.1	5.7	15.9	11.4	12.6	12.8	14.3
34 023	35620	1	Middlesex	309.3	837 073	70	2 706.3	44.8	10.1	0.5	25.4	20.7	5.8	16.0	9.5	14.0	13.7	14.0
34 025	35620	1	Monmouth	468.4	625 846	107	1 336.1	76.4	7.6	0.4	6.2	10.8	4.9	16.7	8.6	10.6	11.5	15.8
34 027	35620	1	Morris	460.6	498 423	141	1 082.1	72.9	3.7	0.3	11.4	13.3	4.9	16.8	8.6	10.8	12.2	16.3
34 029	35620	1	Ocean	628.8	592 497	109	942.3	85.7	3.5	0.3	2.4	9.1	6.9	16.7	7.4	11.0	10.1	12.3
34 031	35620	1	Passaic	186.0	507 945	137	2 730.9	42.6	11.1	0.4	6.0	41.1	6.8	17.3	9.8	13.5	12.8	13.6
34 033	37980	1	Salem	331.8	63 436	835	191.2	76.7	14.6	0.7	1.4	8.4	5.5	16.4	8.2	11.4	11.5	14.2
34 035	35620	1	Somerset	301.9	333 751	206	1 105.5	58.2	9.8	0.4	18.7	14.6	5.2	17.3	8.3	10.9	13.0	16.3
34 037	35620	1	Sussex	518.7	142 522	451	274.8	88.0	2.5	0.4	2.7	7.8	4.6	16.0	8.4	10.3	11.2	16.9
34 039	35620	1	Union	102.8	555 630	120	5 405.0	41.9	21.9	0.4	6.0	31.3	6.2	17.4	8.7	13.0	13.8	14.6
34 041	10900	2	Warren	356.5	106 617	562	299.1	83.7	4.9	0.4	3.5	8.8	4.7	15.8	8.5	11.0	11.2	16.3
35 000	...	0	**NEW MEXICO**	121 301.5	2 081 015	X	17.2	39.4	2.3	9.3	2.1	48.5	6.2	17.4	9.6	13.5	11.7	12.1
35 001	10740	2	Bernalillo	1 161.0	676 953	99	583.1	40.9	3.1	4.8	3.4	49.7	5.9	16.5	9.2	15.0	12.5	12.6
35 003	...	9	Catron	6 924.2	3 508	2 939	0.5	77.8	1.3	4.2	0.5	18.6	3.3	9.2	5.6	5.8	6.0	9.2
35 005	40740	5	Chaves	6 065.2	65 282	811	10.8	40.6	1.8	1.3	1.1	56.1	6.9	19.8	9.9	13.0	11.2	11.7
35 006	24380	6	Cibola	4 539.9	27 487	1 514	6.1	20.6	1.2	40.4	0.9	38.2	6.8	17.7	9.2	13.7	12.4	12.2
35 007	...	7	Colfax	3 758.0	12 253	2 275	3.3	47.8	1.0	2.1	0.9	49.5	5.0	13.6	7.4	10.4	9.5	12.0
35 009	17580	5	Curry	1 405.5	50 280	982	35.8	50.7	6.4	1.3	2.5	41.4	8.2	18.5	12.2	17.5	11.2	10.3
35 011	...	9	De Baca	2 323.1	1 793	3 069	0.8	57.1	0.8	2.5	0.3	41.3	4.7	17.9	7.6	8.5	9.9	11.7
35 013	29740	3	Dona Ana	3 808.2	214 207	308	56.2	28.7	1.7	1.2	1.5	68.0	6.7	18.4	14.8	12.5	10.7	10.7
35 015	16100	5	Eddy	4 176.4	57 621	892	13.8	48.9	1.6	1.6	1.0	48.1	7.6	18.9	9.2	14.1	11.6	11.8
35 017	43500	7	Grant	3 961.2	28 280	1 479	7.1	47.1	1.0	1.6	1.2	50.2	5.4	15.2	8.1	9.6	9.8	10.6
35 019	...	7	Guadalupe	3 029.8	4 376	2 871	1.4	16.3	1.7	1.9	1.5	79.3	5.1	15.4	8.5	15.1	11.4	11.8
35 021	...	9	Harding	2 125.5	665	3 130	0.3	54.9	0.5	0.6	0.0	44.5	4.4	10.2	6.2	8.0	6.9	11.4
35 023	...	9	Hidalgo	3 438.5	4 302	2 875	1.3	40.6	1.3	0.9	0.7	57.6	6.0	16.2	8.8	11.0	9.1	13.7
35 025	26020	5	Lea	4 391.4	69 749	769	15.9	37.5	4.1	1.2	0.7	57.5	8.3	22.1	9.6	14.9	12.4	11.2
35 027	40760	7	Lincoln	4 831.1	19 429	1 852	4.0	63.7	0.8	3.5	0.7	32.3	4.5	13.7	6.3	9.3	8.5	12.2
35 028	31060	6	Los Alamos	109.2	18 147	1 909	166.2	74.2	1.2	1.6	6.9	17.9	5.2	17.9	7.1	10.3	12.0	14.8
35 029	19700	6	Luna	2 965.2	24 450	1 625	8.2	31.5	1.2	1.2	0.9	66.2	7.6	18.7	9.3	11.6	9.7	10.7
35 031	23700	5	McKinley	5 450.5	74 923	737	13.7	9.7	0.9	76.3	1.2	13.6	7.9	22.4	10.1	14.5	11.6	11.5
35 033	...	9	Mora	1 927.7	4 504	2 861	2.3	18.3	0.5	0.8	0.4	80.5	4.8	13.8	7.1	9.4	9.4	13.4
35 035	10460	4	Otero	6 612.6	65 410	810	9.9	51.2	4.1	6.8	2.3	37.8	6.8	16.6	10.7	15.1	10.9	10.9
35 037	...	7	Quay	2 873.9	8 365	2 562	2.9	51.3	2.0	1.6	1.5	45.1	5.5	15.7	6.9	9.7	9.7	12.6
35 039	21580	4	Rio Arriba	5 860.9	40 040	1 172	6.8	13.3	0.5	15.5	0.6	70.8	6.8	17.4	8.2	11.5	11.2	12.6
35 041	38780	7	Roosevelt	2 446.0	19 082	1 869	7.8	54.3	2.4	1.8	1.8	41.3	7.0	17.4	18.2	13.0	10.4	10.1
35 043	10740	2	Sandoval	3 709.0	142 025	454	38.3	45.8	2.5	13.4	2.1	38.1	5.5	18.4	7.9	12.2	12.5	13.0
35 045	22140	3	San Juan	5 513.2	115 079	535	20.9	43.5	1.1	35.8	1.0	20.6	7.0	18.8	8.4	13.9	12.0	11.7
35 047	29780	6	San Miguel	4 722.1	27 760	1 499	5.9	18.4	1.8	1.5	1.2	77.9	5.2	14.2	10.6	11.5	10.4	13.1
35 049	42140	3	Santa Fe	1 908.0	148 651	440	77.9	44.2	1.1	3.1	1.8	51.0	4.5	14.3	7.5	11.1	11.3	13.0
35 051	...	6	Sierra	4 181.0	11 191	2 344	2.7	67.4	1.0	2.7	0.7	30.0	4.5	11.1	5.4	8.2	7.4	11.0
35 053	...	6	Socorro	6 646.2	17 027	1 979	2.6	36.3	1.4	12.7	1.5	49.7	6.0	16.8	11.4	11.4	10.5	11.7
35 055	45340	7	Taos	2 202.4	33 065	1 354	15.0	36.5	0.7	6.1	1.1	56.7	4.6	14.0	6.7	9.9	10.7	13.2
35 057	10740	2	Torrance	3 345.2	15 302	2 076	4.6	53.8	2.0	3.1	1.0	42.0	5.1	16.6	8.1	11.1	11.3	12.2
35 059	...	9	Union	3 823.9	4 183	2 885	1.1	54.2	2.3	2.1	0.8	41.8	4.7	13.7	8.4	14.8	12.5	12.7
35 061	10740	2	Valencia	1 065.7	75 626	731	71.0	34.3	1.3	4.3	0.9	60.3	5.7	18.3	8.9	12.2	11.5	13.0
36 000	...	0	**NEW YORK**	47 124.9	19 745 289	X	419.0	57.1	15.5	0.7	9.5	19.0	5.9	15.3	9.6	14.6	12.5	13.7
36 001	10580	2	Albany	522.8	308 846	221	590.8	74.6	13.9	0.5	7.6	5.8	5.0	13.6	15.0	13.0	11.3	12.9
36 003	...	7	Allegany	1 029.3	47 077	1 034	45.7	95.4	1.8	0.6	1.9	1.6	5.1	15.3	15.2	10.4	9.9	12.1
36 005	35620	1	Bronx	42.1	1 455 720	26	34 577.7	9.9	30.3	0.6	4.3	56.0	7.3	18.0	10.7	15.9	12.7	12.9
36 007	13780	2	Broome	705.8	195 334	339	276.8	85.8	6.5	0.7	5.4	4.1	5.3	14.3	14.4	11.1	9.9	12.5
36 009	36460	4	Cattaraugus	1 308.4	77 677	715	59.4	92.5	2.3	3.8	1.2	2.0	5.8	16.8	9.2	11.0	10.8	13.4
36 011	12180	4	Cayuga	691.6	77 861	712	112.6	92.0	5.2	0.8	1.0	2.9	5.0	15.1	8.7	12.6	11.3	14.3
36 013	27460	4	Chautauqua	1 060.2	129 504	486	122.2	89.2	3.2	0.9	1.0	7.5	5.3	15.3	10.1	11.7	10.5	13.2
36 015	21300	3	Chemung	407.4	86 322	664	211.9	89.0	7.9	0.7	2.1	3.0	5.6	16.0	8.8	12.2	11.6	13.6
36 017	...	6	Chenango	893.6	48 579	1 009	54.4	96.1	1.4	0.8	0.9	2.1	5.4	15.6	7.8	10.9	10.7	14.0
36 019	38460	5	Clinton	1 037.8	81 073	694	78.1	91.1	4.6	0.8	2.0	2.9	4.7	13.2	13.9	12.2	11.7	14.2
36 021	26460	6	Columbia	634.7	60 989	853	96.1	88.6	5.8	0.6	2.4	4.6	4.1	13.7	7.4	10.5	10.6	15.0
36 023	18660	4	Cortland	498.8	48 070	1 017	96.4	94.3	2.4	0.8	1.5	2.7	4.9	14.5	18.4	10.9	10.1	12.6
36 025	...	6	Delaware	1 442.5	45 523	1 064	31.6	93.2	2.1	0.6	1.4	3.8	4.1	13.3	10.3	9.7	9.5	13.4
36 027	35620	1	Dutchess	795.6	294 473	233	370.1	73.6	11.3	0.6	4.6	12.0	4.6	14.8	11.2	11.5	11.4	15.3
36 029	15380	1	Erie	1 042.7	921 046	58	883.3	77.3	14.0	0.9	4.2	5.3	5.4	15.1	9.6	14.0	11.0	13.5
36 031	...	6	Essex	1 794.1	38 102	1 222	21.2	92.9	3.0	0.9	1.0	3.4	3.9	12.6	7.5	11.7	11.5	14.2
36 033	31660	7	Franklin	1 629.2	50 409	981	30.9	83.2	6.0	8.0	0.9	3.4	4.7	14.8	10.0	14.1	12.3	14.3
36 035	24100	4	Fulton	495.5	53 828	934	108.6	94.2	2.6	0.6	1.1	2.9	5.0	15.2	7.8	12.0	11.6	14.8

1. CBSA = Core Based Statistical Area. See Appendix A for explanation. See Appendix B for list of metropolitan areas with component counties. 2. County type code from the Economic Research Service of USDA Rural-Urban Continuum Codes. See Appendix A for definition. 3. Dry land or land partially or temporarily covered by water. 4. May be of any race.

Table B. States and Counties — **Population and Households**

STATE County	55 to 64 years (16)	65 to 74 years (17)	75 years and over (18)	Percent female (19)	2000 (20)	2010 (21)	2000–2010 (22)	2010–2016 (23)	Births (24)	Deaths (25)	Net migration (26)	Number (27)	Persons per household (28)	Family households (29)	Female family householder[1] (30)	One person (31)
NEW JERSEY—Cont'd																
Mercer	13.0	8.1	6.3	51.1	350 761	367 517	4.8	1.0	26 395	18 011	-4 487	130 546	2.69	67.6	13.1	27.2
Middlesex	12.8	8.1	6.1	50.8	750 162	809 867	8.0	3.4	60 703	36 354	3 809	282 058	2.85	72.7	12.2	22.8
Monmouth	15.2	9.5	7.0	51.3	615 301	630 423	2.5	-0.7	37 652	33 924	-7 714	233 105	2.67	69.6	10.5	25.9
Morris	14.3	9.0	7.2	50.9	470 212	492 315	4.7	1.2	29 163	23 198	1 077	180 093	2.72	71.9	8.5	23.8
Ocean	13.2	11.9	10.3	51.8	510 916	576 548	12.8	2.8	51 101	44 201	8 939	222 494	2.59	67.3	9.8	28.6
Passaic	12.4	7.8	5.9	51.3	489 049	501 624	2.6	1.3	43 337	22 728	-13 922	161 318	3.09	72.9	18.0	23.6
Salem	14.6	10.4	7.8	51.2	64 285	66 069	2.8	-4.0	4 362	4 512	-2 519	24 347	2.61	68.5	13.7	26.4
Somerset	14.2	8.4	6.5	51.2	297 490	323 428	8.7	3.2	21 249	14 403	3 443	115 998	2.81	73.2	9.6	22.9
Sussex	16.6	10.1	5.9	50.3	144 166	148 886	3.3	-4.3	7 965	7 261	-6 778	53 941	2.67	72.9	9.0	22.4
Union	12.7	7.6	5.9	51.2	522 541	536 439	2.7	3.6	42 560	24 839	2 354	186 175	2.91	71.2	15.9	25.0
Warren	15.4	9.7	7.3	51.0	102 437	108 655	6.1	-1.9	6 189	5 837	-2 386	41 667	2.52	69.3	10.3	25.0
NEW MEXICO	13.1	9.8	6.7	50.5	1 819 046	2 059 198	13.2	1.1	165 723	106 138	-37 780	763 603	2.67	64.8	14.1	29.3
Bernalillo	13.1	9.0	6.2	51.0	556 678	662 547	19.0	2.2	51 061	32 918	-3 222	263 270	2.52	61.4	14.0	31.6
Catron	22.7	23.9	14.3	47.6	3 543	3 729	5.2	-5.9	134	215	-90	1 387	2.44	61.6	4.5	37.7
Chaves	12.2	8.4	6.7	50.1	61 382	65 651	7.0	-0.6	5 824	4 033	-2 003	23 422	2.72	70.3	16.6	26.0
Cibola	13.1	8.8	6.1	49.0	25 595	27 215	6.3	1.0	2 437	1 616	-558	8 533	2.98	68.3	18.1	28.6
Colfax	17.2	14.2	10.8	49.1	14 189	13 750	-3.1	-10.9	815	906	-1 392	5 546	2.26	59.6	12.3	36.2
Curry	10.1	6.8	5.2	48.1	45 044	48 376	7.4	3.9	5 733	2 386	-1 446	18 162	2.72	68.1	14.2	27.5
De Baca	14.8	14.4	10.4	51.0	2 240	2 022	-9.7	-11.3	100	166	-159	520	3.84	56.5	8.7	37.1
Dona Ana	11.1	8.8	6.4	50.8	174 682	209 235	19.8	2.4	19 011	9 352	-4 971	74 762	2.80	69.3	15.9	24.1
Eddy	12.7	8.0	6.2	49.5	51 658	53 829	4.2	7.0	5 268	3 459	2 068	20 638	2.66	70.3	13.5	24.8
Grant	15.0	15.3	10.9	50.7	31 002	29 514	-4.8	-4.2	1 952	2 141	-1 039	12 032	2.37	62.1	14.1	32.9
Guadalupe	13.4	9.5	9.8	43.0	4 680	4 687	0.1	-6.6	252	250	-335	1 192	3.28	62.8	19.0	33.0
Harding	20.9	16.2	15.8	47.5	810	695	-14.2	-4.3	34	50	-15	189	2.99	61.9	4.8	34.9
Hidalgo	14.1	12.0	9.1	50.0	5 932	4 895	-17.5	-12.1	336	275	-658	1 828	2.47	64.4	17.2	33.0
Lea	10.6	6.1	4.7	48.6	55 511	64 727	16.6	7.8	7 159	3 325	1 275	21 449	3.08	75.6	12.3	20.1
Lincoln	17.5	16.7	11.2	50.8	19 411	20 497	5.6	-5.2	1 172	1 222	-944	8 479	2.33	60.2	9.0	34.1
Los Alamos	15.4	9.8	7.5	49.3	18 343	17 950	-2.1	1.1	1 062	737	-151	7 615	2.34	67.7	6.3	27.8
Luna	11.6	11.3	9.6	50.0	25 016	25 095	0.3	-2.6	2 460	1 853	-1 197	9 044	2.70	60.3	13.1	34.4
McKinley	10.9	6.5	4.7	51.8	74 798	71 488	-4.4	4.8	7 376	3 483	-477	18 449	3.97	69.5	24.7	27.7
Mora	17.3	14.6	10.1	49.2	5 180	4 881	-5.8	-7.7	260	264	-366	1 654	2.81	53.4	7.5	39.9
Otero	12.2	9.5	7.3	48.4	62 298	63 799	2.4	2.5	5 561	3 556	-269	23 668	2.63	65.9	13.0	29.8
Quay	15.4	14.3	10.2	51.3	10 155	9 041	-11.0	-7.5	621	723	-600	3 347	2.59	56.6	10.8	39.9
Rio Arriba	14.5	10.6	7.2	51.1	41 190	40 244	-2.3	-0.5	3 501	2 483	-1 084	13 730	2.86	61.6	14.8	32.4
Roosevelt	10.4	7.5	6.1	49.9	18 018	19 840	10.1	-3.8	1 832	943	-1 682	7 139	2.62	64.3	13.1	27.9
Sandoval	13.8	10.5	6.0	50.9	89 908	131 578	46.3	7.9	9 254	6 100	6 797	47 931	2.83	70.0	12.2	24.5
San Juan	13.0	8.7	6.3	50.4	113 801	130 045	14.3	-11.5	11 561	5 911	-20 770	40 643	3.04	72.2	16.9	23.4
San Miguel	15.4	11.9	7.8	50.4	30 126	29 393	-2.4	-5.6	1 954	1 682	-1 884	10 788	2.51	53.3	14.4	40.5
Santa Fe	16.1	14.4	7.8	51.5	129 292	144 172	11.5	3.1	8 423	6 807	2 540	61 179	2.35	59.6	11.2	32.9
Sierra	16.8	19.8	15.8	50.1	13 270	11 994	-9.6	-6.7	627	1 444	7	5 044	2.25	57.7	9.4	38.8
Socorro	14.0	10.6	7.5	49.3	18 078	17 860	-1.2	-4.7	1 368	1 055	-1 129	4 947	3.43	57.8	17.2	36.0
Taos	16.4	15.1	9.5	51.1	29 979	32 940	9.9	0.4	1 929	1 760	-47	13 224	2.44	59.7	12.6	34.4
Torrance	16.0	12.4	7.2	47.7	16 911	16 381	-3.1	-6.6	958	907	-1 141	5 370	2.81	64.2	10.4	33.2
Union	13.4	10.9	9.0	43.0	4 174	4 554	9.1	-8.1	259	300	-324	1 559	2.39	59.8	10.2	35.9
Valencia	14.0	10.3	6.3	49.6	66 152	76 574	15.8	-1.2	5 429	3 816	-2 514	26 863	2.78	70.9	14.4	24.7
NEW YORK	13.0	8.7	6.7	51.4	18 976 457	19 378 110	2.1	1.9	1 495 760	949 141	-147 221	7 262 279	2.63	63.7	14.8	29.7
Albany	13.2	9.0	7.0	51.6	294 565	304 208	3.3	1.5	19 591	16 725	2 611	123 451	2.35	55.0	11.1	35.7
Allegany	14.3	10.2	7.6	49.2	49 927	48 919	-2.0	-3.8	3 113	2 871	-2 004	18 285	2.36	64.7	10.2	29.3
Bronx	10.7	6.7	5.1	52.8	1 332 650	1 385 107	3.9	5.1	134 732	59 125	-3 358	484 902	2.86	65.8	31.1	30.1
Broome	14.2	9.6	8.7	50.9	200 536	200 689	0.1	-2.7	13 000	13 119	-5 059	79 132	2.37	59.4	11.0	32.7
Cattaraugus	15.1	10.4	7.5	50.3	83 955	80 343	-4.3	-3.3	5 772	5 140	-3 124	31 635	2.41	63.3	11.0	29.6
Cayuga	15.2	10.1	7.6	48.7	81 963	80 003	-2.4	-2.7	4 909	4 608	-2 320	30 972	2.43	63.9	11.6	29.8
Chautauqua	15.1	10.5	8.4	50.5	139 750	134 904	-3.5	-4.0	8 788	8 894	-4 955	53 546	2.36	62.7	12.5	30.7
Chemung	14.4	9.9	7.9	50.4	91 070	88 842	-2.4	-2.8	6 200	5 817	-2 771	35 167	2.35	62.4	12.4	29.9
Chenango	15.8	11.5	8.3	49.9	51 401	50 507	-1.7	-3.8	3 301	3 424	-1 785	19 641	2.49	64.3	10.2	27.1
Clinton	14.0	9.3	6.8	48.6	79 894	82 131	2.8	-1.3	4 793	4 384	-1 456	31 898	2.32	63.5	11.4	27.5
Columbia	16.5	13.1	9.2	49.8	63 094	63 091	0.0	-3.3	3 273	4 118	-1 168	25 235	2.37	64.4	11.9	28.5
Cortland	12.8	9.2	6.7	51.2	48 599	49 285	1.4	-2.5	2 947	2 696	-1 440	17 935	2.54	60.2	9.3	32.3
Delaware	16.3	13.6	9.7	49.7	48 055	47 979	-0.2	-5.1	2 561	3 393	-1 501	19 262	2.31	60.9	9.6	33.5
Dutchess	14.7	9.4	7.1	50.2	280 150	297 448	6.2	-1.0	16 877	15 039	-4 582	106 771	2.61	67.5	11.1	26.7
Erie	14.3	9.4	7.7	51.5	950 265	919 130	-3.3	0.2	62 451	60 497	2 191	382 846	2.33	60.1	13.8	33.4
Essex	16.4	12.6	6.9	49.4	38 851	39 361	1.3	-3.2	1 951	2 476	-687	15 268	2.37	65.1	10.0	29.9
Franklin	13.9	9.3	6.5	45.0	51 134	51 606	0.9	-2.3	3 054	2 795	-1 425	19 148	2.36	63.7	11.3	29.3
Fulton	14.8	10.8	8.0	50.3	55 073	55 524	0.8	-3.1	3 357	3 774	-1 188	22 281	2.40	64.0	11.6	28.3

1. No spouse present.

Table B. States and Counties — **Population, Vital Statistics, Health, and Crime**

STATE County	Persons in group quarters, 2016	Daytime population, 2011–2015		Births, 2016		Deaths, 2016		Persons under 65 with no health insurance, 2015		Medicare, 2015			Serious crimes known to police,[2] 2014 Total	
		Number	Employ- ment/ resi- dence ratio	Total	Rate[1]	Number	Rate[1]	Number	Percent	Total Beneficiaries	Enrolled in Original Medicare	Enrolled in Medicare Advantage	Number	Rate[3]
	32	33	34	35	36	37	38	39	40	41	42	43	44	45
NEW JERSEY—Cont'd														
Mercer....................	20 531	422 832	1.30	4 193	11.3	2 974	8.0	29 873	9.9	58 920	49 261	9 659	7 866	2 117
Middlesex................	23 413	813 503	0.96	9 407	11.2	6 221	7.4	68 581	9.7	112 853	92 637	20 216	13 341	1 598
Monmouth...............	7 357	593 158	0.88	5 812	9.3	5 741	9.2	41 582	7.9	109 683	93 256	16 427	11 438	1 814
Morris.....................	8 703	534 477	1.14	4 572	9.2	3 797	7.6	25 932	6.3	76 114	66 792	9 322	4 943	985
Ocean.....................	7 177	515 296	0.72	8 359	14.1	7 108	12.0	40 307	8.8	140 783	113 493	27 290	9 739	1 663
Passaic...................	11 052	466 539	0.82	6 719	13.2	3 734	7.4	56 212	12.9	72 643	55 966	16 677	11 207	2 209
Salem.....................	1 258	60 569	0.84	681	10.7	770	12.1	4 185	8.0	12 834	11 224	1 610	1 605	2 467
Somerset.................	4 113	347 730	1.10	3 234	9.7	2 535	7.6	18 575	6.6	43 603	38 935	4 668	3 989	1 199
Sussex...................	1 743	116 001	0.60	1 236	8.7	1 241	8.7	7 414	6.1	24 151	21 572	2 579	1 421	976
Union.....................	6 825	521 677	0.90	6 699	12.1	4 097	7.4	62 335	13.0	77 350	60 107	17 243	12 303	2 230
Warren...................	1 971	91 944	0.71	984	9.2	928	8.7	7 179	8.1	20 046	18 003	2 043	1 527	1 424
NEW MEXICO...................	43 127	2 081 063	1.00	25 491	12.2	17 799	8.6	225 491	13.1	354 470	228 942	125 528	86 336	4 140
Bernalillo................	11 946	702 814	1.09	7 838	11.6	5 755	8.5	67 604	11.9	110 566	50 487	60 079	38 737	5 737
Catron....................	106	3 522	0.94	23	6.6	23	6.6	290	13.5	1 249	1 034	215	6	168
Chaves...................	1 783	63 242	0.90	912	14.0	617	9.5	7 170	13.2	11 387	9 646	1 741	3 863	5 882
Cibola....................	2 567	27 360	1.00	365	13.3	282	10.3	2 844	13.6	3 518	2 823	695	641	2 350
Colfax....................	408	13 092	1.02	125	10.2	144	11.8	952	10.5	3 151	2 565	586	329	2 549
Curry.....................	1 511	51 820	1.06	875	17.4	403	8.0	5 083	11.8	7 190	6 381	809	2 652	5 211
De Baca..................	9	1 998	0.96	14	7.8	19	10.6	286	20.8	506	451	55	8	426
Dona Ana................	4 582	207 057	0.92	2 854	13.3	1 567	7.3	24 393	13.7	35 040	22 706	12 334	7 132	3 337
Eddy......................	995	59 232	1.14	918	15.9	547	9.5	5 550	11.3	9 132	8 307	825	2 401	4 308
Grant......................	589	29 386	1.03	295	10.4	338	12.0	1 911	9.1	7 482	5 620	1 862	NA	NA
Guadalupe...............	572	4 525	1.00	37	8.5	36	8.2	327	11.0	868	693	175	112	2 486
Harding...................	0	604	1.19	6	9.0	7	10.5	47	9.7	206	182	24	NA	NA
Hidalgo...................	64	4 622	0.99	48	11.2	47	10.9	452	12.9	996	726	270	98	2 133
Lea........................	2 071	69 914	1.06	1 200	17.2	499	7.2	8 757	14.1	8 119	7 799	320	2 482	3 609
Lincoln...................	116	19 469	0.94	182	9.4	196	10.1	2 163	15.5	5 317	4 087	1 230	581	3 134
Los Alamos.............	94	25 486	1.85	172	9.5	106	5.8	457	3.1	2 835	2 584	251	NA	NA
Luna......................	551	24 807	1.00	402	16.4	286	11.7	2 919	15.5	5 970	3 772	2 198	1 090	4 451
McKinley.................	774	74 321	1.01	1 091	14.6	580	7.7	12 908	19.0	8 354	7 564	790	3 156	4 292
Mora......................	8	4 175	0.58	39	8.7	33	7.3	431	12.3	1 182	949	233	23	495
Otero.....................	2 272	65 043	0.99	892	13.6	602	9.2	7 413	14.4	10 721	8 668	2 053	1 553	2 386
Quay......................	22	8 709	1.00	84	10.0	100	12.0	644	10.1	2 295	1 917	378	237	2 772
Rio Arriba...............	425	36 605	0.78	506	12.6	443	11.1	4 818	14.9	7 643	5 342	2 301	834	2 090
Roosevelt................	1 078	18 700	0.85	285	14.9	145	7.6	2 126	13.7	2 672	2 396	276	489	2 458
Sandoval.................	761	114 946	0.62	1 469	10.3	1 051	7.4	12 688	10.9	19 609	9 580	10 029	2 804	2 053
San Juan................	1 748	125 804	1.01	1 703	14.8	1 026	8.9	16 349	16.2	17 835	17 043	792	3 155	2 518
San Miguel.............	1 299	27 267	0.86	275	9.9	278	10.0	2 334	10.8	6 346	4 878	1 468	NA	NA
Santa Fe................	2 631	149 300	1.03	1 280	8.6	1 138	7.7	17 158	14.9	32 301	21 524	10 777	4 483	3 033
Sierra....................	265	11 891	1.07	107	9.6	229	20.5	819	11.3	3 977	2 681	1 296	NA	NA
Socorro..................	580	17 348	0.97	200	11.7	156	9.2	1 965	14.4	2 969	2 148	821	693	3 965
Taos......................	470	32 898	1.00	290	8.8	309	9.3	3 830	15.3	7 817	5 986	1 831	945	2 865
Torrance.................	614	14 330	0.71	140	9.1	138	9.0	1 581	13.3	2 769	1 435	1 334	286	1 843
Union.....................	665	4 473	1.08	39	9.3	41	9.8	370	13.5	862	802	60	62	1 436
Valencia.................	1 551	66 303	0.64	825	10.9	658	8.7	8 852	14.3	13 586	6 166	7 420	3 161	4 160
NEW YORK....................	575 964	20 025 860	1.04	236 507	12.0	160 713	8.1	1 351 396	8.2	3 155 077	1 824 350	1 330 727	414 680	2 100
Albany....................	17 415	376 843	1.45	3 107	10.1	2 760	8.9	13 476	5.5	49 875	27 041	22 834	9 212	2 989
Allegany.................	4 292	45 012	0.85	495	10.5	456	9.7	2 165	6.2	9 051	5 424	3 627	644	1 342
Bronx.....................	44 245	1 255 047	0.68	21 403	14.7	10 618	7.3	139 181	11.1	176 009	65 646	110 363	(6)	(6)
Broome...................	10 784	204 541	1.07	2 084	10.7	2 152	11.0	9 823	6.4	42 905	26 230	16 675	6 402	3 248
Cattaraugus.............	2 608	76 041	0.91	898	11.6	836	10.8	4 693	7.5	17 539	9 369	8 170	1 513	1 923
Cayuga...................	4 109	71 483	0.79	764	9.8	697	9.0	4 102	6.7	14 527	10 190	4 337	1 611	2 026
Chautauqua.............	5 995	132 371	1.00	1 421	11.0	1 392	10.7	6 755	6.6	29 603	15 605	13 998	3 589	2 702
Chemung................	4 616	89 367	1.03	955	11.1	950	11.0	3 462	5.1	18 768	12 109	6 659	2 151	2 430
Chenango...............	789	47 185	0.89	545	11.2	558	11.5	2 534	6.5	11 099	6 951	4 148	938	1 900
Clinton...................	6 782	81 236	0.99	744	9.2	724	8.9	4 261	6.8	17 025	13 677	3 348	1 359	1 665
Columbia................	2 139	57 680	0.85	465	7.6	656	10.8	3 408	7.2	14 015	9 521	4 494	955	1 570
Cortland.................	3 798	47 724	0.94	465	9.7	422	8.8	1 962	5.2	8 251	5 954	2 297	678	1 384
Delaware................	2 406	46 780	0.99	382	8.4	570	12.5	2 458	7.3	10 126	7 193	2 933	795	1 746
Dutchess................	19 656	275 411	0.85	2 665	9.1	2 616	8.9	14 530	6.2	52 994	42 182	10 812	4 812	1 627
Erie.......................	28 380	950 612	1.07	10 118	11.0	9 803	10.6	40 592	5.4	178 912	69 240	109 672	28 429	3 085
Essex.....................	2 387	38 589	0.98	289	7.6	420	11.0	1 941	6.8	8 822	7 026	1 796	397	1 026
Franklin..................	6 070	51 632	1.02	434	8.6	500	9.9	2 911	7.8	8 896	6 687	2 209	847	1 635
Fulton....................	1 402	49 853	0.80	515	9.6	580	10.8	2 916	6.7	11 163	5 962	5 201	1 472	2 703

1. Per 1,000 estimated resident population.   2. Data for serious crimes have not been adjusted for underreporting; this may affect comparability between geographic areas and over time.
3. Per 100,000 population estimated by the FBI.   6. Bronx, Kings, Queens, and Richmond counties are included with New York county.

Table B. States and Counties — **Crime, Education, Money Income, and Poverty**

STATE County	Serious crimes known to police, 2014 (cont.)[1] Rate[2] Violent	Property	Education School enrollment and attainment, 2011-2015 Enrollment[3] Total	Percent private	Attainment[4] (percent) High school graduate or less	Bachelor's degree or more	Local government expenditures,[5] 2013-2014 Total current spending (mil dol)	Current spending per student (dollars)	Money income, 2011-2015 Per capita income[6] (dollars)	Households Median income (dollars)	Percent with income of less than $50,000	with income of $200,000 or more	Income and poverty, 2015 Median household income (dollars)	Percent below poverty level All persons	Children under 18 years	Children 5 to 17 years in families
	46	47	48	49	50	51	52	53	54	55	56	57	58	59	60	61
NEW JERSEY—Cont'd																
Mercer	343	1 774	102 462	24.3	38.2	39.6	1 081.6	18 723	37 680	72 804	35.0	11.6	72 172	11.2	15.2	14.3
Middlesex	155	1 443	220 330	14.8	37.6	41.0	2 012.4	16 503	34 674	79 593	31.1	9.8	78 249	8.5	10.8	10.1
Monmouth	142	1 673	162 094	21.0	32.9	42.5	1 755.4	17 380	43 469	85 242	30.2	13.8	86 722	7.5	10.0	8.9
Morris	61	924	128 449	22.1	28.7	51.0	1 367.1	17 724	49 552	100 214	22.4	18.0	101 754	5.3	5.8	5.2
Ocean	100	1 563	141 924	33.5	45.6	26.9	1 182.3	16 385	31 200	61 994	40.9	5.0	63 478	10.9	18.9	17.7
Passaic	394	1 815	135 997	14.0	52.5	26.0	1 496.4	18 001	27 643	59 739	43.6	6.6	55 723	17.3	26.3	26.0
Salem	261	2 205	15 319	12.1	52.2	20.3	201.7	17 949	29 712	61 831	41.2	3.5	63 988	11.9	18.5	17.3
Somerset	59	1 140	85 050	20.1	27.7	52.5	924.4	17 087	48 791	100 667	22.9	18.4	99 059	5.5	7.0	6.2
Sussex	51	926	36 226	18.6	37.1	33.8	446.9	20 255	38 810	86 565	26.9	8.9	84 431	5.6	7.0	6.2
Union	376	1 854	142 452	15.9	44.0	32.6	1 665.5	18 139	35 308	69 594	37.1	10.6	70 581	10.6	15.7	14.6
Warren	72	1 352	26 353	16.9	43.9	29.9	297.2	17 154	34 136	70 471	35.0	6.4	71 672	7.7	10.7	9.7
NEW MEXICO	597	3 542	564 161	10.3	42.2	26.3	3 292.3	9 705	24 012	44 963	54.4	3.0	45 524	19.8	27.2	25.6
Bernalillo	827	4 911	185 240	13.7	35.8	32.6	941.3	9 302	26 765	47 725	51.8	3.6	47 870	19.0	25.0	23.3
Catron	84	84	640	25.3	42.2	26.0	5.6	18 299	20 685	42 973	63.9	2.2	36 570	23.4	44.9	41.5
Chaves	647	5 235	18 171	10.6	48.9	18.1	112.0	9 434	20 559	40 630	58.4	1.8	39 265	21.1	28.8	27.3
Cibola	554	1 796	7 144	11.1	55.1	12.0	39.6	10 754	16 072	34 565	66.3	0.8	35 580	29.2	37.9	36.1
Colfax	232	2 317	2 754	10.6	45.3	21.5	21.5	12 045	20 534	32 380	65.9	0.6	37 269	19.7	29.8	27.8
Curry	318	4 893	14 201	8.7	42.9	20.8	85.6	8 983	21 929	41 084	58.6	1.5	41 879	21.7	29.3	29.3
De Baca	320	107	599	0.0	59.7	9.7	4.8	17 471	24 370	32 500	64.6	1.5	33 427	20.2	32.6	30.5
Dona Ana	286	3 051	68 903	4.5	43.7	27.7	399.4	9 801	20 129	38 853	60.7	2.3	39 421	25.7	38.8	36.7
Eddy	617	3 690	13 665	7.1	50.8	17.8	106.1	9 826	28 308	56 618	45.6	2.9	60 407	12.3	17.1	15.6
Grant	NA	NA	6 700	6.9	42.1	26.2	50.8	11 333	23 011	38 311	62.8	1.5	39 792	20.5	30.1	26.7
Guadalupe	666	1 820	955	15.9	65.3	13.5	10.5	14 338	16 820	30 772	71.4	0.8	31 710	23.9	31.6	28.5
Harding	NA	NA	83	3.6	50.6	25.5	3.2	38 901	22 946	33 393	69.8	2.6	39 561	14.3	20.9	20.2
Hidalgo	501	1 632	948	3.9	54.6	14.2	10.7	15 640	18 871	34 444	66.4	0.2	34 336	25.2	35.4	33.4
Lea	475	3 133	18 340	9.2	58.6	13.2	124.0	8 458	23 804	57 533	43.8	3.7	54 686	14.3	18.3	17.2
Lincoln	297	2 837	4 072	8.5	38.3	28.4	30.4	10 480	25 756	40 708	62.5	3.6	40 297	17.8	32.3	30.0
Los Alamos	NA	NA	4 508	11.8	13.8	64.2	40.1	11 388	51 148	101 934	23.7	14.4	107 126	4.0	4.1	3.5
Luna	837	3 614	6 352	9.7	62.9	12.1	54.4	10 045	15 078	27 476	74.1	0.7	27 151	30.9	41.2	39.7
McKinley	766	3 527	22 720	9.4	59.5	11.1	148.1	10 759	12 614	28 772	67.8	1.1	29 040	34.1	39.2	38.0
Mora	108	387	1 419	3.6	52.0	13.9	9.4	17 689	15 591	23 822	78.8	0.8	31 816	23.9	35.5	31.8
Otero	300	2 087	16 477	7.5	46.5	16.4	67.4	9 135	19 457	39 775	60.3	1.2	38 381	23.0	33.6	32.9
Quay	480	2 293	1 703	1.5	54.9	15.5	18.8	12 695	17 335	29 113	71.3	0.3	29 047	23.0	35.7	33.9
Rio Arriba	559	1 531	9 563	9.7	50.4	16.6	68.1	11 822	19 678	36 098	64.0	1.4	37 319	24.2	30.6	29.8
Roosevelt	141	2 317	6 794	4.5	45.1	23.1	38.1	10 884	18 187	35 546	64.6	0.6	38 053	20.4	26.6	27.6
Sandoval	215	1 838	37 988	10.3	35.4	28.5	198.8	9 123	26 742	58 982	42.3	3.8	62 833	11.2	15.7	14.4
San Juan	535	1 983	34 335	6.4	49.9	15.2	231.3	9 421	22 460	48 671	51.2	2.4	49 173	18.8	23.5	22.2
San Miguel	NA	NA	7 111	12.3	46.8	20.0	49.9	12 348	17 849	29 237	70.9	0.7	32 303	28.7	35.9	33.6
Santa Fe	267	2 766	33 940	16.8	33.7	40.1	169.1	9 134	33 044	54 315	46.2	5.9	55 247	13.1	18.6	17.1
Sierra	NA	NA	1 609	6.3	50.5	17.6	15.5	11 689	18 982	29 356	72.9	0.6	29 432	28.7	43.6	40.7
Socorro	498	3 467	5 510	6.4	56.5	17.5	25.4	11 455	18 553	34 037	65.9	2.8	33 673	23.5	40.7	37.2
Taos	430	2 434	7 019	8.4	37.9	28.6	49.9	11 874	22 358	36 582	64.1	1.4	37 092	19.9	32.0	30.0
Torrance	322	1 521	3 844	7.8	51.1	16.5	40.9	10 725	18 300	32 083	67.7	1.4	35 950	26.2	36.7	32.8
Union	93	1 343	865	14.8	55.2	17.1	8.4	13 523	21 705	36 070	65.6	2.1	36 715	17.1	26.3	23.7
Valencia	904	3 256	19 989	7.9	50.5	16.5	113.2	8 658	19 412	41 703	57.9	0.9	42 395	19.8	27.0	24.4
NEW YORK	382	1 718	4 967 141	23.6	41.1	34.2	54 094.1	19 901	33 236	59 269	43.4	7.5	60 805	15.5	22.3	21.3
Albany	339	2 650	84 463	23.6	33.7	38.6	656.6	15 914	32 779	59 887	41.7	4.8	57 312	12.6	16.4	14.7
Allegany	204	1 138	14 308	26.6	50.1	20.0	130.9	18 976	20 940	42 776	57.2	1.0	44 331	16.8	25.6	24.1
Bronx	(7)	(7)	404 350	18.1	56.7	18.9	(7)	(7)	18 456	34 299	63.9	1.8	35 102	30.3	42.6	43.1
Broome	299	2 948	54 507	8.2	42.4	27.2	479.3	17 749	25 105	46 261	53.1	2.4	46 067	17.7	23.2	22.3
Cattaraugus	208	1 714	18 417	19.4	53.1	17.8	242.9	17 924	22 336	42 601	56.7	1.4	40 933	18.0	26.1	23.6
Cayuga	245	1 781	17 541	14.6	46.4	21.4	161.0	16 813	25 786	52 082	47.9	2.0	51 925	12.7	20.3	19.4
Chautauqua	267	2 434	31 545	9.3	47.3	20.9	337.5	16 858	22 903	42 993	57.2	1.4	43 973	17.2	28.2	26.1
Chemung	186	2 243	19 797	16.0	45.9	23.4	179.0	15 173	26 262	50 320	49.7	2.8	51 285	14.9	23.2	20.9
Chenango	162	1 738	10 845	8.7	52.0	17.4	156.1	20 191	23 036	45 668	53.8	1.1	49 082	14.3	23.3	21.6
Clinton	148	1 517	19 881	9.0	49.6	22.1	214.3	19 408	24 941	49 930	50.1	2.0	46 747	17.5	22.3	20.1
Columbia	132	1 439	12 094	14.3	42.3	29.3	157.5	21 036	32 851	59 105	42.3	4.9	58 335	13.6	19.4	16.8
Cortland	102	1 282	14 902	5.9	44.9	23.6	112.0	17 158	24 228	49 514	50.4	1.8	49 894	16.2	20.0	18.5
Delaware	167	1 579	9 923	4.9	51.7	20.2	139.5	22 216	23 835	43 720	56.3	1.6	42 907	16.9	27.1	25.7
Dutchess	214	1 413	80 083	27.9	37.0	33.4	836.0	19 746	33 923	71 904	34.9	6.8	71 348	10.4	12.9	11.9
Erie	441	2 644	230 431	17.2	37.9	31.6	2 021.7	15 652	28 879	51 247	48.8	3.3	52 176	15.6	24.3	22.4
Essex	176	850	7 521	13.6	45.7	24.2	90.4	23 499	26 805	52 758	47.6	1.8	52 282	12.2	19.3	17.1
Franklin	158	1 477	10 653	14.5	51.3	17.7	149.0	19 638	22 488	47 923	52.0	1.8	45 682	18.3	26.2	24.8
Fulton	130	2 573	11 514	7.7	52.5	16.2	132.0	16 488	24 339	46 969	53.0	1.8	46 543	17.9	26.9	24.9

1. Data for serious crimes have not been adjusted for underreporting; this may affect comparability between geographic areas and over time.   2. Per 100,000 population estimated by the FBI.
3. All persons 3 years old and over enrolled in nursery school through college.   4. Persons 25 years old and over.   5. Elementary and secondary education expenditures.
6. Based on population estimated by the American Community Survey, 2011-2015.   7. Bronx, Kings, Queens, and Richmond counties are included with New York county.

Table B. States and Counties — **Personal Income**

STATE County	Personal income, 2015										Earnings, 2015		
	Total (mil dol)	Percent change, 2014–2015	Per capita[1] Dollars	Rank	Wages and salaries (mil dol)	Supplements to wages and salaries; employer contributions (mil dol) Pension and insurance	Government social insurance	Proprietors' income (mil dol)	Dividends, interest, and rent (mil dol)	Personal transfer receipts (mil dol)	Total (mil dol)	Contributions for government social insurance (mil dol) From employee and self-employed	From employer
	62	63	64	65	66	67	68	69	70	71	72	73	74
NEW JERSEY—Cont'd													
Mercer	23 490	3.2	63 247	135	15 659	2 426	1 139	1 776	4 659	3 216	21 001	1 199	1 139
Middlesex	44 961	3.3	53 467	280	27 482	4 041	2 081	3 281	6 927	6 081	36 885	2 140	2 081
Monmouth	43 639	3.9	69 410	80	14 259	2 278	1 136	3 737	8 361	5 266	21 410	1 284	1 136
Morris	43 248	3.3	86 582	25	24 784	2 992	1 716	5 012	8 141	3 529	34 504	1 966	1 716
Ocean	27 145	4.2	46 109	727	7 334	1 417	618	2 193	4 896	6 377	11 562	815	618
Passaic	24 110	5.0	47 189	787	9 208	1 629	728	2 842	3 538	4 660	14 407	864	728
Salem	2 843	3.7	44 304	866	1 252	263	97	132	418	688	1 744	109	97
Somerset	28 850	4.6	86 468	22	16 885	1 999	1 120	3 266	5 502	2 208	23 270	1 319	1 120
Sussex	7 973	3.3	55 497	273	1 840	360	150	611	1 186	1 108	2 960	191	150
Union	33 396	4.2	60 089	167	15 835	2 355	1 106	2 935	5 906	4 365	22 230	1 303	1 106
Warren	5 440	4.3	50 902	451	1 754	317	140	366	828	920	2 577	163	140
NEW MEXICO	79 104	3.5	38 025	X	37 444	6 523	3 120	4 741	14 586	19 088	51 828	3 333	3 120
Bernalillo	26 934	4.6	39 804	1 365	15 834	2 608	1 346	1 242	5 087	5 714	21 030	1 324	1 346
Catron	112	1.6	32 542	2 430	24	6	2	7	29	41	39	3	2
Chaves	2 398	-1.3	36 466	1 884	794	143	66	377	382	663	1 380	84	66
Cibola	723	5.7	26 459	3 055	312	65	26	23	102	263	425	28	26
Colfax	463	0.7	37 323	1 567	170	36	14	33	96	150	253	18	14
Curry	2 101	-3.5	41 684	847	984	209	95	245	353	456	1 533	74	95
De Baca	77	-3.5	42 078	1 151	18	4	1	16	15	26	40	3	1
Dona Ana	6 907	6.0	32 233	2 641	2 860	580	244	611	1 106	1 979	4 295	272	244
Eddy	3 087	5.5	53 609	283	1 677	261	127	483	512	515	2 549	155	127
Grant	1 025	1.0	35 824	1 789	404	88	31	30	193	379	552	39	31
Guadalupe	135	2.6	30 873	2 859	50	10	4	3	20	57	67	5	4
Harding	31	-12.3	43 749	260	7	2	1	7	8	7	16	1	1
Hidalgo	158	-1.6	35 759	1 504	66	17	5	13	28	54	101	6	5
Lea	2 491	-5.6	34 998	662	1 757	247	132	-56	306	538	2 079	158	132
Lincoln	769	2.9	39 585	1 439	216	39	18	50	232	231	323	25	18
Los Alamos	1 162	3.6	65 317	105	1 279	121	105	47	222	98	1 551	96	105
Luna	732	4.8	29 854	2 821	283	63	25	46	107	289	418	30	25
McKinley	1 890	4.5	24 640	3 085	742	180	64	85	262	699	1 072	69	64
Mora	224	12.1	48 834	2 406	25	7	2	85	27	66	119	9	2
Otero	2 192	2.2	34 058	2 166	900	212	83	78	450	568	1 273	76	83
Quay	297	1.0	35 162	1 910	99	20	8	9	54	126	136	11	8
Rio Arriba	1 273	5.7	32 254	2 589	352	75	28	32	178	464	487	36	28
Roosevelt	696	-6.6	36 417	1 476	214	48	17	79	100	184	359	18	17
Sandoval	5 281	5.3	37 885	1 767	1 365	216	113	236	777	1 082	1 931	139	113
San Juan	4 485	2.0	37 777	1 745	2 448	411	194	176	610	1 009	3 227	202	194
San Miguel	908	5.2	32 461	2 479	281	73	23	23	152	402	401	29	23
Santa Fe	7 536	3.9	50 684	464	2 905	502	226	519	2 320	1 296	4 152	273	226
Sierra	404	4.0	35 786	1 995	106	23	9	20	85	190	157	13	9
Socorro	564	2.3	32 680	2 331	211	53	16	46	87	189	326	19	16
Taos	1 136	4.7	34 535	2 279	358	64	32	73	279	376	527	40	32
Torrance	445	2.5	28 753	2 863	141	27	11	23	60	174	201	15	11
Union	138	-8.0	32 937	2 389	51	10	4	3	26	44	67	5	4
Valencia	2 328	4.4	30 733	2 788	511	103	49	76	319	757	739	59	49
NEW YORK	1 161 414	3.8	58 814	X	626 912	110 227	44 822	98 615	236 861	201 039	880 576	46 098	44 822
Albany	17 539	4.5	56 692	271	13 282	3 659	1 075	1 334	3 213	2 970	19 350	950	1 075
Allegany	1 614	2.8	34 004	2 257	536	189	46	84	216	446	855	48	46
Bronx	47 217	4.8	32 442	2 411	15 440	3 784	1 289	2 739	5 413	15 883	23 252	1 312	1 289
Broome	7 791	3.7	39 634	1 461	3 697	1 052	310	453	1 246	1 968	5 512	303	310
Cattaraugus	2 889	3.1	37 080	1 878	1 200	378	100	189	420	790	1 867	104	100
Cayuga	2 995	0.9	38 257	1 487	1 137	318	98	154	444	706	1 706	93	98
Chautauqua	4 767	3.5	36 454	2 064	1 919	533	169	348	685	1 420	2 969	168	169
Chemung	3 496	2.8	40 149	1 348	1 701	426	140	156	478	908	2 424	135	140
Chenango	1 855	2.6	37 980	1 651	797	230	67	100	262	490	1 194	67	67
Clinton	3 271	4.8	40 253	1 496	1 444	439	125	291	436	789	2 300	120	125
Columbia	3 121	3.8	50 741	607	870	241	75	327	602	656	1 513	84	75
Cortland	1 807	4.4	37 265	1 784	804	223	64	108	256	423	1 199	65	64
Delaware	1 666	0.9	36 177	1 718	640	206	55	93	303	474	994	57	55
Dutchess	14 469	3.4	48 921	517	5 851	1 340	483	680	2 512	2 656	8 354	452	483
Erie	43 164	4.1	46 786	700	22 502	5 124	1 871	2 822	6 898	9 094	32 319	1 729	1 871
Essex	1 570	1.7	40 810	1 182	580	190	50	81	308	397	902	50	50
Franklin	1 829	2.0	36 113	1 975	750	300	62	98	263	484	1 209	64	62
Fulton	2 093	4.2	38 760	1 472	665	190	58	108	285	599	1 022	62	58

1. Based on the resident population estimated as of July 1 of the year shown.

STATE County	Earnings, 2015 (cont.)									Social Security beneficiaries, December 2015		Supple-mental Security Income recipients, December 2015	Housing units, 2016	
	Percent by selected industries													
	Farm	Mining	Construction	Manu-facturing	Infor-mation: professional, scientific, technical services	Retail trade	Finance, insur-ance, real estate and leasing	Health care and social assistance	Govern-ment	Number	Rate[1]		Total	Percent change, 2010–2016
	75	76	77	78	79	80	81	82	83	84	85	86	87	88
NEW JERSEY—Cont'd														
Mercer	0.0	0.0	3.3	4.2	21.6	4.0	11.9	8.9	19.5	64 860	175	9 663	144 714	1.1
Middlesex	0.0	0.0	4.8	8.2	18.3	5.3	8.1	9.0	14.0	130 015	156	13 319	300 586	2.0
Monmouth	0.1	D	10.0	3.6	17.4	7.5	8.6	15.2	14.7	120 370	192	8 051	261 037	1.0
Morris	0.0	D	4.2	7.6	22.1	4.6	10.9	9.0	9.0	83 985	169	4 344	192 067	1.2
Ocean	0.0	0.2	10.4	3.1	8.3	10.2	5.6	18.1	21.5	155 110	263	7 461	282 152	1.5
Passaic	0.0	0.1	7.1	17.0	7.4	7.3	5.7	12.1	18.6	82 735	163	14 928	176 983	0.5
Salem	1.5	0.0	D	13.7	D	4.3	2.2	10.2	20.1	15 325	240	1 704	27 620	0.8
Somerset	0.0	0.2	3.5	15.9	21.1	4.8	9.5	6.4	7.1	51 035	153	2 866	126 268	2.6
Sussex	0.1	0.3	10.6	5.7	8.8	8.3	4.1	14.0	22.4	28 230	197	1 659	62 359	0.7
Union	0.0	D	6.8	11.1	17.7	5.1	7.0	10.4	14.0	86 310	156	11 068	201 966	1.3
Warren	1.0	D	D	11.3	6.3	8.9	2.8	13.1	18.7	22 135	207	1 488	45 451	1.2
NEW MEXICO	1.5	5.8	6.0	3.0	12.2	6.9	5.0	11.9	26.9	408 931	197	64 175	917 568	1.8
Bernalillo	0.0	0.2	6.0	4.0	17.0	6.7	6.4	13.3	25.9	122 575	182	18 101	289 833	2.0
Catron	5.1	D	6.3	1.4	D	D	D	D	48.1	1 430	413	74	3 274	-0.5
Chaves	10.0	12.2	4.3	4.7	4.8	9.3	4.3	12.4	19.4	12 910	197	2 265	26 703	0.0
Cibola	-0.1	D	1.6	0.9	D	7.4	1.8	D	40.0	5 055	185	964	11 074	-0.3
Colfax	2.0	2.5	6.4	2.0	3.3	10.6	3.7	D	34.9	3 685	297	413	10 069	0.5
Curry	14.5	D	3.5	2.7	2.6	5.2	2.5	9.4	39.8	7 470	149	1 579	20 896	4.2
De Baca	4.0	19.5	4.1	D	D	6.7	D	6.1	22.6	545	298	81	1 336	-0.6
Dona Ana	2.9	0.0	6.0	3.5	8.0	6.3	4.4	15.5	32.0	38 890	182	8 093	85 226	4.6
Eddy	1.5	37.9	7.5	5.2	3.5	4.5	3.3	6.1	11.6	10 565	183	1 300	23 895	5.8
Grant	0.6	D	3.6	0.6	2.7	6.1	2.5	9.0	35.5	8 670	304	853	14 626	-0.5
Guadalupe	2.6	0.3	2.4	D	D	10.1	D	16.1	33.1	1 100	252	259	2 379	-0.6
Harding	13.4	D	D	D	D	D	0.0	D	30.6	210	300	15	526	0.0
Hidalgo	5.3	4.2	D	D	D	4.7	D	D	56.6	1 140	258	162	2 380	-0.6
Lea	3.5	38.1	12.2	-20.4	3.5	7.3	5.7	6.1	11.7	9 380	132	1 553	25 969	4.2
Lincoln	0.4	D	9.3	0.4	D	12.3	5.3	13.2	22.9	5 900	304	371	17 746	1.3
Los Alamos	0.0	0.7	1.1	0.2	D	1.2	1.9	3.6	8.0	3 030	171	80	8 293	-0.7
Luna	3.9	1.2	5.7	9.0	D	8.5	2.2	D	37.8	6 885	281	1 445	10 915	-0.7
McKinley	-0.6	D	3.3	3.2	2.3	10.3	3.3	12.0	45.7	10 810	141	4 624	25 718	-0.3
Mora	1.6	D	D	D	D	14.1	D	D	13.4	1 500	328	305	3 216	-0.5
Otero	0.2	0.4	5.9	0.3	5.0	5.8	2.5	10.4	54.8	12 730	198	1 458	30 916	-0.3
Quay	0.2	D	4.6	D	2.6	7.9	4.9	12.4	35.1	2 620	310	415	5 545	-0.4
Rio Arriba	0.5	0.3	4.7	1.0	D	7.4	2.1	16.4	47.1	9 705	246	1 722	19 485	-0.8
Roosevelt	22.6	D	2.6	6.4	2.5	5.7	2.0	D	33.2	3 065	161	606	8 331	2.1
Sandoval	0.2	0.6	6.7	21.5	7.5	7.0	3.7	7.8	22.2	27 780	200	2 804	55 246	5.7
San Juan	0.4	21.0	8.5	2.4	D	8.2	3.3	11.9	21.2	21 405	180	3 982	49 665	0.7
San Miguel	1.0	0.2	3.5	0.8	2.6	6.5	3.2	D	51.6	7 205	258	1 887	15 489	-0.7
Santa Fe	-0.1	0.8	4.8	1.2	10.7	8.5	7.3	14.0	29.6	34 820	236	2 681	71 869	0.8
Sierra	7.8	D	7.5	1.9	2.7	7.2	2.5	D	32.6	4 415	392	593	8 248	-1.3
Socorro	12.1	D	1.2	2.4	8.5	4.2	1.4	D	46.4	3 755	218	1 085	7 966	-1.1
Taos	-0.1	1.3	6.9	1.3	8.7	9.0	4.3	16.0	22.9	9 205	280	1 177	20 422	0.8
Torrance	4.2	D	4.3	12.2	D	8.3	D	5.8	27.0	3 680	239	597	7 726	-0.9
Union	-1.5	D	D	D	D	6.3	D	12.3	27.1	960	229	114	2 299	-0.3
Valencia	0.6	0.6	8.6	4.5	3.4	9.6	3.5	9.1	31.9	15 835	209	2 517	30 287	0.7
NEW YORK	0.1	0.1	4.4	4.5	16.8	5.0	17.8	10.7	16.5	3 513 125	178	648 707	8 231 687	1.5
Albany	0.0	D	4.6	3.3	12.5	6.1	8.3	10.8	35.1	60 295	195	7 275	139 500	1.3
Allegany	1.6	0.9	6.1	17.9	2.9	5.1	1.7	7.6	36.7	11 195	236	1 376	25 943	-0.7
Bronx	0.0	D	5.7	1.7	2.7	6.2	3.5	25.8	27.6	194 940	135	106 650	525 719	2.7
Broome	0.0	0.1	5.5	11.6	6.8	6.9	4.8	16.5	27.4	47 135	240	6 773	89 607	-1.1
Cattaraugus	0.6	0.5	4.2	15.7	3.2	8.4	2.8	D	37.2	19 355	248	2 499	40 918	-0.5
Cayuga	2.6	D	6.3	14.8	5.9	8.3	2.8	12.5	29.9	17 200	220	1 758	36 449	-0.1
Chautauqua	1.7	0.3	5.1	22.9	3.5	8.0	2.5	12.7	24.9	33 415	255	4 607	66 580	-0.5
Chemung	0.0	1.8	4.7	16.5	3.8	7.2	5.5	15.6	25.0	21 295	244	3 144	38 320	-0.1
Chenango	1.2	0.0	4.9	27.8	4.7	5.5	9.0	6.3	26.7	12 875	263	1 637	25 091	1.5
Clinton	2.5	D	4.8	9.2	3.4	8.2	2.2	16.0	33.3	19 350	238	2 901	36 023	0.4
Columbia	0.9	D	7.7	5.9	6.2	7.9	3.4	15.6	24.9	15 570	253	1 413	32 982	0.6
Cortland	0.9	0.1	4.4	23.4	4.7	7.2	3.5	10.8	26.5	9 880	204	1 156	20 513	-0.2
Delaware	0.8	1.4	5.4	28.3	3.4	5.3	3.1	8.9	30.8	12 155	264	1 108	31 149	-0.2
Dutchess	0.0	0.2	6.3	13.1	6.8	7.0	3.3	15.7	24.5	59 040	200	5 377	119 293	0.6
Erie	0.1	0.5	4.5	11.3	9.1	6.5	7.9	12.4	21.4	203 630	221	27 555	422 414	0.6
Essex	0.2	1.2	6.9	8.0	3.4	7.0	2.3	11.1	39.3	9 680	252	840	25 855	1.0
Franklin	1.2	D	2.9	1.8	3.8	6.5	1.6	16.6	53.6	11 690	231	1 818	25 317	0.1
Fulton	0.1	D	3.9	9.3	4.5	12.4	3.1	17.0	28.1	14 145	262	2 067	28 630	0.3

1. Per 1,000 resident population estimated as of July 1 of the year shown.

Table B. States and Counties — Housing, Labor Force, and Employment

STATE County	Housing units, 2011–2015								Civilian labor force, 2016				Civilian employment,[6] 2011–2015		
	Occupied units										Unemployment			Percent	
			Owner-occupied			Renter-occupied									
				Median owner cost as a percent of income											Construction, production, and maintenance occupations
	Total	Percent	Median value[1]	With a mortgage	Without a mortgage[2]	Median rent[3]	Median rent as a percent of income[2]	Sub-standard units[4] (percent)	Total	Percent change, 2015–2016	Total	Rate[5]	Total	Management, business, science and arts	
	89	90	91	92	93	94	95	96	97	98	99	100	101	102	103
NEW JERSEY—Cont'd															
Mercer	130 546	64.4	276 500	25.0	15.9	1 132	31.7	2.6	199 781	0.8	8 644	4.3	177 609	43.9	14.8
Middlesex	282 058	64.3	323 300	26.3	17.2	1 299	29.6	4.2	442 447	0.6	19 499	4.4	402 766	44.2	17.4
Monmouth	233 105	74.4	385 100	26.9	16.8	1 238	34.3	1.7	331 125	0.6	14 671	4.4	307 183	43.8	15.1
Morris	180 093	75.2	423 400	25.6	16.6	1 357	27.9	1.9	260 506	-0.4	10 158	3.9	258 862	49.6	12.7
Ocean	222 494	80.4	262 700	28.1	19.1	1 322	37.8	2.4	268 849	0.3	14 080	5.2	246 680	34.5	19.6
Passaic	161 318	53.7	336 100	30.0	20.8	1 184	37.5	8.6	247 829	-0.3	15 196	6.1	229 762	32.0	25.5
Salem	24 347	72.4	187 800	23.9	18.1	974	35.7	1.6	30 616	-1.3	1 943	6.3	29 226	32.4	28.8
Somerset	115 998	76.1	399 000	25.2	15.4	1 411	28.2	1.8	173 235	-0.5	7 022	4.1	170 172	51.0	13.0
Sussex	53 941	83.3	270 600	27.0	17.6	1 205	34.7	1.2	75 959	-0.8	3 568	4.7	75 669	38.8	18.8
Union	186 175	59.1	345 500	28.4	19.2	1 174	33.2	6.3	277 389	-0.9	14 334	5.2	267 803	36.0	21.9
Warren	41 667	72.3	255 300	26.9	18.6	1 013	30.5	1.9	56 886	-0.3	2 603	4.6	53 302	35.2	21.4
NEW MEXICO	763 603	68.1	160 300	22.7	10.0	777	30.7	4.5	927 359	0.4	62 445	6.7	876 035	35.4	20.5
Bernalillo	263 270	62.2	185 500	23.1	10.0	799	32.1	3.3	324 375	1.5	18 941	5.8	307 756	40.3	16.4
Catron	1 387	92.6	166 000	26.1	10.1	540	32.5	2.4	1 180	-5.6	97	8.2	1 049	34.3	28.2
Chaves	23 422	66.7	99 700	19.6	10.0	697	29.1	4.5	27 796	1.1	1 893	6.8	26 448	29.5	27.0
Cibola	8 533	74.2	88 200	21.2	10.4	594	28.1	10.0	9 124	-0.8	754	8.3	9 625	28.4	22.0
Colfax	5 546	69.8	117 700	24.8	12.9	586	30.0	2.3	5 753	-4.0	352	6.1	4 981	33.3	20.0
Curry	18 162	58.4	125 600	20.9	10.0	786	31.5	2.7	21 716	0.0	1 109	5.1	20 599	27.8	32.2
De Baca	520	79.8	67 000	25.7	10.1	393	24.8	2.1	816	-3.0	40	4.9	619	27.5	29.2
Dona Ana	74 762	64.8	138 100	23.2	10.3	709	32.5	4.5	95 001	1.6	6 845	7.2	88 919	31.7	20.1
Eddy	20 638	73.0	124 800	17.3	10.0	764	22.5	5.2	28 304	-4.2	1 874	6.6	25 620	26.7	35.4
Grant	12 032	74.8	132 800	21.7	10.0	635	29.7	3.2	12 313	-0.5	808	6.6	10 585	33.7	22.7
Guadalupe	1 192	72.4	82 200	23.6	12.5	540	28.5	2.4	1 691	4.4	110	6.5	1 301	33.8	14.2
Harding	189	83.1	65 500	33.3	11.8	663	35.4	1.1	277	-2.1	20	7.2	205	38.5	17.1
Hidalgo	1 828	68.0	78 200	27.0	10.9	463	24.6	2.1	2 195	3.7	125	5.7	1 867	24.5	27.7
Lea	21 449	69.5	108 600	17.1	10.0	768	22.2	5.8	27 206	-8.2	2 579	9.5	29 340	24.2	38.8
Lincoln	8 479	79.0	161 900	26.3	13.2	756	29.3	6.1	8 523	-1.1	514	6.0	8 030	32.5	18.6
Los Alamos	7 615	74.2	274 200	17.6	10.0	931	23.1	1.2	8 682	3.0	367	4.2	8 916	68.3	6.6
Luna	9 044	67.4	81 900	27.5	10.7	551	27.9	4.2	10 565	-3.0	1 556	14.7	8 383	23.8	29.2
McKinley	18 449	73.1	68 300	20.4	10.0	603	25.0	21.0	24 171	0.2	2 292	9.5	22 865	28.4	24.0
Mora	1 654	80.0	84 300	16.4	13.1	640	49.1	6.0	2 226	-1.1	197	8.8	1 166	31.1	22.0
Otero	23 668	64.9	101 800	22.2	10.0	791	28.5	3.9	25 230	1.8	1 522	6.0	22 092	25.2	22.8
Quay	3 347	71.1	76 300	21.6	11.7	480	24.6	1.9	3 188	-1.6	219	6.9	2 937	31.8	26.0
Rio Arriba	13 730	77.6	155 900	22.0	10.0	634	34.7	4.3	16 560	0.7	1 241	7.5	15 272	35.2	17.8
Roosevelt	7 139	58.4	118 500	22.1	10.0	694	34.4	5.0	7 987	0.2	456	5.7	8 131	28.5	23.3
Sandoval	47 931	81.1	177 400	23.8	10.0	1 022	30.4	4.9	62 601	1.7	4 176	6.7	58 433	39.7	17.8
San Juan	40 643	73.4	145 400	20.6	10.0	744	27.9	8.3	53 752	-2.5	4 799	8.9	51 561	27.1	27.3
San Miguel	10 788	72.1	121 200	27.2	14.7	625	39.4	2.7	10 984	-0.1	850	7.7	9 751	31.8	18.7
Santa Fe	61 179	69.1	275 200	25.1	10.0	945	30.3	3.9	72 574	0.0	3 883	5.4	70 423	43.3	14.8
Sierra	5 044	72.2	98 800	22.7	11.8	575	30.8	3.0	4 044	1.2	345	8.5	3 971	28.7	22.5
Socorro	4 947	72.7	117 800	23.1	11.9	582	27.2	4.0	6 616	2.1	495	7.5	5 706	35.7	22.6
Taos	13 224	72.1	216 200	25.7	12.1	732	36.9	4.2	14 676	-0.8	1 250	8.5	14 356	35.7	17.9
Torrance	5 370	83.3	106 400	27.7	14.1	732	34.0	4.5	5 522	1.7	504	9.1	5 348	34.6	21.6
Union	1 559	64.7	87 400	19.1	13.2	646	26.0	1.4	1 888	0.5	78	4.1	1 692	39.6	22.2
Valencia	26 863	79.7	131 900	25.1	10.6	756	35.6	3.5	29 823	1.4	2 154	7.2	28 088	26.5	25.0
NEW YORK	7 262 279	53.6	283 400	24.8	14.7	1 132	32.2	5.4	9 584 458	-0.1	463 131	4.8	9 254 578	39.2	16.7
Albany	123 451	58.3	208 400	21.7	12.1	919	29.3	1.1	158 778	-0.1	6 421	4.0	155 200	43.2	13.0
Allegany	18 285	73.1	70 300	20.0	13.2	606	31.9	3.3	20 184	-1.1	1 261	6.2	20 410	32.1	27.5
Bronx	484 902	19.0	363 400	31.4	12.7	1 074	35.6	12.5	609 629	0.3	43 371	7.1	563 903	24.3	18.2
Broome	79 132	65.7	109 900	20.8	12.9	703	33.0	1.7	85 861	-1.3	4 644	5.4	88 758	36.2	19.5
Cattaraugus	31 635	71.3	84 600	20.3	13.6	617	29.2	3.4	35 029	-0.8	2 070	5.9	34 265	27.7	27.1
Cayuga	30 972	71.1	113 600	20.7	13.0	673	27.4	1.7	36 763	-1.1	1 851	5.0	37 023	32.7	25.0
Chautauqua	53 546	69.6	84 500	19.7	13.3	612	31.2	2.0	56 388	-2.4	3 255	5.8	58 012	28.9	28.7
Chemung	35 167	69.1	100 400	18.5	12.4	713	32.0	1.1	36 376	-3.2	2 060	5.7	38 219	34.4	22.1
Chenango	19 641	75.3	91 700	20.8	13.9	637	28.6	2.7	22 916	-1.0	1 155	5.0	21 652	31.2	28.1
Clinton	31 898	68.1	124 200	21.5	11.9	744	31.9	1.9	35 784	-0.7	1 914	5.3	35 522	31.2	23.2
Columbia	25 235	71.9	222 100	24.6	15.2	884	29.7	1.4	31 541	0.1	1 159	3.7	29 962	37.4	21.1
Cortland	17 935	65.7	108 200	20.2	13.7	684	27.2	1.7	23 023	-1.3	1 305	5.7	24 080	33.3	22.7
Delaware	19 262	72.7	132 400	23.6	14.2	668	31.2	3.8	19 333	-1.1	1 063	5.5	19 850	30.8	26.8
Dutchess	106 771	69.1	275 600	27.0	16.4	1 130	33.3	3.5	142 780	-0.6	5 949	4.2	143 829	40.1	17.2
Erie	382 846	65.0	130 000	20.0	13.0	739	30.0	1.3	446 601	-0.7	21 804	4.9	441 369	38.1	17.6
Essex	15 268	73.8	145 100	20.6	14.0	805	29.7	2.5	17 274	-0.5	923	5.3	17 769	32.3	21.7
Franklin	19 148	72.7	101 600	19.9	13.3	671	30.7	1.9	19 811	-1.1	1 118	5.6	20 094	31.8	20.8
Fulton	22 281	70.4	108 100	22.2	13.6	711	32.8	1.4	23 318	-0.8	1 326	5.7	24 116	27.6	26.8

1. Specified owner-occupied units.   2. A value of 10.0 represents 10 percent or less; a value of 50.0 represents 50 percent or more.   3. Specified renter-occupied units.
4. Overcrowded or lacking complete plumbing facilities.   5. Percent of civilian labor force.   6. Civilian employed persons 16 years old and over.

Table B. States and Counties — **Nonfarm Employment and Agriculture**

STATE County	Private nonfarm establishments, employment and payroll, 2015									Agriculture, 2012		
	Number of establish-ments	Employment						Annual payroll		Farms		
		Total	Health care and social assistance	Manufac-turing	Retail trade	Finance and insurance	Professional, scientific, and technical services	Total (mil dol)	Average per employee (dollars)	Number	Percent with:		Farm operators whose principal occu-pation is farming (percent)
											Fewer than 50 acres	500 acres or more	
	104	105	106	107	108	109	110	111	112	113	114	115	116
NEW JERSEY—Cont'd													
Mercer	9 664	188 908	30 894	6 284	19 849	15 418	21 524	12 428	65 788	272	71.0	2.9	46.0
Middlesex	21 671	380 921	49 120	26 765	40 398	14 883	56 909	23 848	62 607	198	73.2	5.1	43.9
Monmouth	19 113	232 880	42 917	9 344	40 603	10 476	20 335	11 372	48 831	823	82.4	2.4	57.2
Morris	16 656	290 191	36 462	13 292	30 492	19 952	40 615	22 096	76 143	366	79.0	0.8	43.4
Ocean	12 681	137 430	34 547	4 964	28 681	3 473	6 902	5 171	37 624	178	82.0	1.7	51.1
Passaic	12 022	147 166	26 825	16 675	25 940	4 553	7 766	6 846	46 521	78	92.3	0.0	48.7
Salem	1 144	17 402	2 931	2 821	1 937	447	480	941	54 101	825	60.4	6.5	53.3
Somerset	9 968	186 151	22 642	16 488	19 509	10 443	26 740	15 908	85 460	400	71.0	3.5	33.3
Sussex	3 217	32 362	7 022	2 174	5 930	836	1 257	1 281	39 595	885	69.5	1.9	47.9
Union	13 659	202 372	33 239	13 713	25 607	5 700	14 511	12 442	61 480	8	100.0	0.0	37.5
Warren	2 456	28 002	5 222	3 572	5 997	572	1 007	1 241	44 308	784	65.3	3.2	49.4
NEW MEXICO	43 793	626 284	119 731	26 145	96 659	22 777	D	25 145	40 150	24 721	51.3	25.3	50.1
Bernalillo	15 746	257 760	49 944	12 098	36 142	11 078	D	10 939	42 440	1 006	80.9	7.4	44.2
Catron	59	431	148	D	65	D	D	11	24 682	351	14.5	40.2	63.0
Chaves	1 444	17 181	3 402	878	3 335	690	912	595	34 658	595	39.7	36.1	55.3
Cibola	317	5 119	1 591	32	895	105	56	174	33 906	522	54.4	26.1	44.4
Colfax	415	3 396	491	126	621	167	82	98	28 893	290	13.4	41.4	47.9
Curry	1 063	12 819	2 855	630	2 430	464	819	396	30 905	600	16.8	49.7	45.0
De Baca	45	251	D	D	64	D	D	7	25 920	203	39.9	39.4	60.1
Dona Ana	3 570	50 155	13 655	2 129	8 274	1 671	3 656	1 508	30 057	2 184	85.6	4.5	37.7
Eddy	1 440	24 391	2 883	1 271	3 116	528	843	1 248	51 164	551	41.0	31.4	56.4
Grant	605	6 938	1 561	109	1 203	188	131	270	38 845	407	30.7	33.9	45.7
Guadalupe	97	943	75	D	199	23	5	25	26 687	372	19.9	55.9	62.4
Harding	12	36	D	NA	10	D	NA	1	21 333	202	5.4	61.4	66.8
Hidalgo	100	896	193	D	245	D	24	21	23 682	171	24.6	55.0	66.1
Lea	1 739	26 891	2 530	914	3 359	453	538	1 321	49 109	460	29.6	44.1	55.4
Lincoln	677	5 111	511	100	1 196	271	142	141	27 564	362	30.7	43.9	55.5
Los Alamos	360	12 931	956	36	544	329	9 365	1 060	81 974	9	100.0	0.0	88.9
Luna	385	4 305	1 046	333	1 032	125	82	113	26 138	190	26.3	36.8	61.6
McKinley	997	16 080	4 661	538	3 514	441	228	493	30 680	2 297	38.9	35.6	60.3
Mora	47	337	143	D	71	10	NA	8	23 433	597	31.5	19.6	61.8
Otero	941	11 931	2 380	144	2 569	320	565	348	29 140	486	49.4	22.6	48.1
Quay	226	1 918	362	50	441	102	57	48	24 949	553	13.0	53.7	52.4
Rio Arriba	558	6 306	1 920	83	1 123	215	71	221	35 114	1 892	63.4	14.3	44.2
Roosevelt	335	3 491	610	277	661	127	61	107	30 759	680	17.4	47.5	50.7
Sandoval	1 702	23 827	3 757	2 661	3 327	805	716	870	36 503	1 029	63.8	14.2	45.3
San Juan	2 721	39 736	6 819	1 751	6 389	973	1 400	1 802	45 344	2 628	61.7	20.8	54.2
San Miguel	449	6 348	3 221	54	950	165	113	160	25 211	877	19.4	39.9	53.5
Santa Fe	4 696	46 233	8 704	833	9 385	1 694	2 423	1 853	40 084	715	67.0	13.4	43.6
Sierra	218	2 318	728	83	451	60	38	60	26 039	256	35.9	36.3	67.6
Socorro	219	2 980	904	83	448	72	200	85	28 644	704	60.2	20.0	55.0
Taos	1 058	8 741	1 462	160	1 556	193	267	238	27 211	983	75.3	7.4	35.6
Torrance	231	1 946	149	139	529	38	57	77	39 383	589	16.1	40.7	53.0
Union	101	913	168	D	135	D	18	27	29 237	353	5.7	73.1	58.6
Valencia	913	10 451	1 806	578	2 374	314	330	286	27 335	1 607	87.4	2.7	43.1
NEW YORK	540 298	7 998 994	1 498 808	422 940	937 328	532 836	643 955	513 083	64 143	35 537	32.6	8.4	57.4
Albany	9 463	178 849	34 978	7 969	22 723	12 228	17 150	8 485	47 441	494	42.5	3.6	46.6
Allegany	790	11 771	1 823	2 217	1 301	199	231	378	32 089	784	23.3	6.9	51.8
Bronx	17 741	255 669	101 176	5 999	32 334	3 640	4 104	11 332	44 325	1	100.0	0.0	100.0
Broome	4 234	71 263	15 114	7 382	11 502	1 917	3 839	2 757	38 684	563	34.1	3.0	48.8
Cattaraugus	1 654	23 367	3 424	4 264	3 989	634	747	825	35 293	1 038	26.6	7.5	51.8
Cayuga	1 634	20 355	4 101	3 488	3 407	362	475	743	36 501	891	33.2	12.7	59.4
Chautauqua	2 925	41 611	8 294	9 262	6 261	850	946	1 382	33 220	1 515	35.2	4.8	54.3
Chemung	1 806	31 597	6 613	5 576	5 288	960	774	1 233	39 031	372	27.2	4.3	53.8
Chenango	928	13 558	1 909	4 154	1 708	1 177	379	598	44 077	828	22.9	8.1	56.3
Clinton	1 846	24 254	4 844	3 587	4 990	420	724	884	36 436	603	26.9	11.6	57.5
Columbia	1 743	15 760	4 486	1 365	2 891	333	533	586	37 168	494	42.1	9.7	61.5
Cortland	1 016	15 755	3 282	2 900	2 322	332	980	533	33 820	518	23.0	9.1	52.1
Delaware	1 037	10 074	1 974	3 050	1 555	319	188	432	42 899	704	27.7	9.5	62.2
Dutchess	7 486	96 612	19 485	6 093	14 409	2 883	9 867	4 523	46 815	678	44.5	7.2	54.3
Erie	22 688	416 499	74 760	43 141	53 947	29 209	29 388	18 280	43 890	1 044	45.3	5.1	57.4
Essex	1 158	10 089	2 032	772	1 870	196	225	362	35 858	261	29.5	11.1	55.6
Franklin	967	10 540	3 348	564	1 862	198	541	356	33 823	688	23.0	8.4	59.4
Fulton	1 179	14 039	3 290	2 001	2 473	299	313	492	35 021	211	37.0	6.6	57.3

STATE County	Land in farms Acreage (1,000)	Percent change, 2007–2012	Acres Average size of farm	Total irrigated (1,000)	Total cropland (1,000)	Value of land and buildings (dollars) Average per farm	Average per acre	Value of machinery and equipment, average per farm (dollars)	Value of products sold Total (mil dol)	Average per farm (dollars)	Percent from: Crops	Live-stock and poultry products	Percent of farms with sales of: $10,000 or more	$100,000 or more	Government payments Total ($1,000)	Percent of farms
	117	118	119	120	121	122	123	124	125	126	127	128	129	130	131	132
NEW JERSEY—Cont'd																
Mercer	20	-9.1	73	1.1	12.4	1 474 301	20 310	59 195	19.7	72 533	83.1	16.9	43.0	11.0	310	14.3
Middlesex	17	-7.8	87	2.7	12.3	1 716 202	19 686	104 551	29.3	147 732	98.6	1.4	46.0	20.2	130	15.2
Monmouth	39	-11.7	47	3.7	25.1	1 021 639	21 581	73 476	84.4	102 565	79.6	20.4	38.6	12.8	169	6.2
Morris	14	-15.1	40	0.7	7.2	914 418	23 148	75 101	28.4	77 560	95.8	4.2	33.6	8.5	61	2.2
Ocean	8	-19.0	45	0.7	2.9	691 534	15 446	55 247	11.6	64 888	84.3	15.7	41.0	11.2	112	5.6
Passaic	1	-26.6	19	0.1	0.2	581 667	31 204	58 385	3.4	44 051	92.5	7.5	26.9	6.4	D	1.3
Salem	102	5.5	123	18.1	81.2	974 698	7 895	107 623	112.0	135 749	84.0	16.0	37.5	17.6	1 386	22.2
Somerset	35	6.2	87	0.5	20.2	1 779 905	20 497	72 478	23.2	58 015	89.2	10.8	34.0	8.5	128	7.0
Sussex	61	-6.5	69	0.3	27.9	735 954	10 672	48 488	18.7	21 078	62.1	37.9	23.4	5.2	370	8.1
Union	0	-23.8	12	0.0	0.1	1 513 000	126 083	85 375	2.4	294 875	D	D	62.5	37.5	0	0.0
Warren	72	-3.6	92	1.7	46.4	942 751	10 230	77 084	91.2	116 333	59.9	40.1	31.9	11.4	773	17.3
NEW MEXICO	43 201	-0.1	1 748	680.3	1 976.7	755 185	432	60 316	2 550.1	103 157	24.2	75.8	24.4	7.0	70 588	22.3
Bernalillo	351	47.5	349	5.3	12.5	395 200	1 134	33 582	18.1	18 023	41.5	58.5	13.0	1.9	172	8.6
Catron	1 078	-27.3	3 070	5.4	3.1	1 311 014	427	62 142	12.7	36 302	1.3	98.7	27.4	8.8	613	13.7
Chaves	2 483	1.2	4 173	49.8	63.0	1 503 955	360	147 017	388.1	652 267	11.6	88.4	53.6	30.9	4 688	32.9
Cibola	1 559	5.4	2 987	D	3.9	930 634	312	37 464	D	D	D	D	14.8	1.3	500	26.1
Colfax	1 963	-8.8	6 769	10.3	23.9	2 682 179	396	76 979	35.7	123 255	6.0	94.0	47.2	17.9	918	23.1
Curry	881	-0.8	1 468	62.2	479.0	849 413	579	157 685	447.3	745 525	7.0	93.0	42.0	19.5	8 250	72.2
De Baca	1 068	-0.2	5 261	8.1	11.2	1 301 429	247	90 015	24.0	118 064	36.9	63.1	55.7	27.1	1 868	58.6
Dona Ana	660	12.0	302	76.3	93.8	540 877	1 790	75 238	351.0	160 729	47.5	52.5	23.9	8.1	1 453	9.5
Eddy	1 142	3.1	2 073	43.3	53.0	926 314	447	123 615	119.6	216 995	42.2	57.8	45.6	15.6	2 481	35.2
Grant	1 064	-12.3	2 615	4.0	8.4	980 442	375	52 437	14.5	35 732	14.3	85.7	33.2	5.9	1 329	15.0
Guadalupe	1 643	17.0	4 417	3.8	17.7	1 176 723	266	43 145	17.7	47 605	2.1	97.9	32.0	9.1	2 853	36.0
Harding	1 034	9.5	5 119	D	21.3	1 447 842	283	58 356	13.5	66 807	2.1	97.9	39.6	14.4	1 289	40.1
Hidalgo	930	-9.6	5 440	9.6	12.9	1 347 661	248	97 895	29.2	170 491	57.9	42.1	73.1	24.6	1 228	46.2
Lea	1 982	-16.2	4 309	51.6	117.0	1 461 422	339	136 552	188.9	410 709	21.6	78.4	48.0	23.0	5 045	37.8
Lincoln	1 553	-11.3	4 291	2.0	5.1	1 519 177	354	62 006	16.9	46 588	3.2	96.8	42.8	11.6	2 709	26.0
Los Alamos	0	88.9	2	D	D	28 889	15 294	6 556	D	D	D	D	0.0	0.0	0	0.0
Luna	550	-15.8	2 896	20.6	37.2	1 228 332	424	174 526	62.5	328 853	63.9	36.1	58.4	30.5	1 472	52.6
McKinley	3 023	-4.7	1 316	1.9	44.1	414 200	315	22 288	8.4	3 652	7.4	92.6	5.1	0.4	845	29.7
Mora	778	-14.9	1 303	7.6	13.3	723 692	555	45 174	11.6	19 469	9.9	90.1	21.1	3.2	1 839	18.8
Otero	1 224	8.6	2 518	6.0	D	1 057 944	420	53 058	14.6	30 113	55.0	45.0	30.2	5.3	1 183	12.1
Quay	1 518	1.9	2 745	7.0	216.2	919 353	335	76 897	36.8	66 526	6.4	93.6	33.5	10.8	6 471	71.1
Rio Arriba	1 433	-1.9	757	29.2	66.8	548 193	724	43 273	19.0	10 031	37.5	62.5	19.8	1.4	1 277	14.5
Roosevelt	1 349	-9.7	1 984	46.1	290.3	966 632	487	120 344	264.3	388 712	6.9	93.1	39.9	13.2	8 038	62.4
Sandoval	950	60.6	923	9.4	17.8	482 790	523	31 229	10.6	10 288	52.9	47.1	16.2	1.0	815	10.0
San Juan	2 580	58.2	982	85.9	115.6	341 496	348	41 084	71.3	27 135	88.9	11.1	13.3	1.2	1 023	14.0
San Miguel	2 350	4.9	2 680	4.6	22.4	1 010 876	377	43 104	18.6	21 244	5.1	94.9	21.4	2.7	1 639	16.5
Santa Fe	718	26.0	1 004	8.9	13.1	848 969	846	39 010	12.8	17 869	75.1	24.9	15.0	2.7	394	5.7
Sierra	1 250	-7.0	4 883	12.4	19.4	1 396 238	286	91 934	39.3	153 699	44.6	55.4	55.9	20.7	1 418	37.1
Socorro	1 271	-11.1	1 806	18.9	21.4	890 670	493	67 983	77.2	109 726	15.3	84.7	37.2	11.9	1 539	9.5
Taos	313	-31.4	319	14.5	24.6	373 969	1 173	30 988	8.4	8 561	41.0	59.0	10.8	1.6	440	9.0
Torrance	1 865	3.8	3 166	25.0	47.9	1 151 192	364	79 518	58.5	99 355	39.9	60.1	32.6	9.3	3 259	27.7
Union	1 967	-10.3	5 573	26.0	66.1	2 047 037	367	96 062	98.1	278 011	17.2	82.8	66.3	31.4	2 900	49.3
Valencia	670	32.4	417	23.1	23.4	392 418	942	48 432	55.8	34 701	23.8	76.2	13.8	2.6	641	6.3
NEW YORK	7 184	0.1	202	59.8	4 217.0	525 587	2 600	117 163	5 415.1	152 380	41.5	58.5	49.2	20.0	74 511	26.4
Albany	63	3.9	128	0.4	36.5	397 650	3 099	73 182	46.0	93 030	67.6	32.4	38.3	8.3	384	16.8
Allegany	150	-0.3	192	0.1	71.3	335 583	1 750	70 612	73.4	93 569	28.5	71.5	36.4	12.8	1 099	27.0
Bronx	D	D	D	0.0	0.0	D	D	D	D	D	D	D	100.0	0.0	0	0.0
Broome	80	-8.0	142	0.1	38.1	371 162	2 623	66 933	30.7	54 552	22.9	77.1	34.3	5.9	770	18.7
Cattaraugus	197	7.5	190	0.9	97.3	359 361	1 891	91 609	99.1	95 503	25.3	74.7	41.8	14.7	1 895	31.4
Cayuga	238	-4.4	268	0.4	181.7	860 439	3 215	216 304	293.5	329 376	33.8	66.2	59.1	29.6	2 791	35.8
Chautauqua	237	0.3	156	0.9	129.5	322 390	2 065	95 881	161.8	106 831	45.6	54.4	54.3	18.9	2 502	19.8
Chemung	58	-10.8	156	0.2	28.1	376 065	2 407	75 599	16.0	43 143	41.2	58.8	28.5	8.6	482	22.8
Chenango	167	-5.7	202	0.2	79.3	370 505	1 835	87 490	65.9	79 630	22.3	77.7	45.4	19.3	2 117	30.9
Clinton	147	-1.3	244	0.1	74.0	494 534	2 025	144 806	149.0	247 096	28.4	71.6	46.9	19.7	1 660	24.7
Columbia	95	-10.5	193	1.4	56.9	1 008 441	5 223	115 555	66.5	134 664	54.0	46.0	55.1	20.6	674	19.8
Cortland	115	-7.9	222	0.2	60.4	423 170	1 906	104 708	62.9	121 423	21.4	78.6	47.5	15.6	984	35.7
Delaware	146	-12.1	207	0.2	59.3	515 442	2 492	83 908	47.7	67 736	19.5	80.5	46.9	17.5	1 248	33.7
Dutchess	112	9.9	166	0.8	45.6	860 500	5 187	97 681	49.0	72 304	53.1	46.9	49.1	16.7	427	10.3
Erie	143	-4.5	137	1.9	93.8	404 428	2 959	112 551	133.1	127 535	46.3	53.7	42.2	16.4	1 863	23.9
Essex	55	9.2	210	0.1	20.0	443 410	2 110	75 100	11.7	44 862	47.6	52.4	34.1	8.0	209	13.0
Franklin	145	10.8	211	0.6	74.8	354 044	1 680	100 096	84.2	122 334	23.2	76.8	48.4	18.3	1 583	26.0
Fulton	32	-5.9	151	0.1	14.7	324 464	2 148	74 938	9.3	44 081	36.2	63.8	41.2	10.0	269	18.5

Table B. States and Counties — **Water Use, Wholesale Trade, Retail Trade, and Real Estate**

STATE County	Water use, 2010		Wholesale trade,[1] 2012				Retail trade,[2] 2012				Real estate and rental and leasing,[2] 2012			
	Total water withdrawn (mil gal/day)	Gallons withdrawn per person per day	Number of establish-ments	Number of employees	Sales (mil dol)	Annual payroll (mil dol)	Number of establish-ments	Number of employees	Sales (mil dol)	Annual payroll (mil dol)	Number of establish-ments	Number of employees	Receipts (mil dol)	Annual payroll (mil dol)
	133	134	135	136	137	138	139	140	141	142	143	144	145	146
NEW JERSEY—Cont'd														
Mercer	477.6	1 303	354	D	D	D	1 305	18 794	5 127.4	477.9	347	1 934	729.3	91.8
Middlesex	67.9	84	1 580	33 984	40 540.7	2 614.2	2 611	38 315	11 869.8	982.7	680	5 893	2 421.8	349.8
Monmouth	79.9	127	803	6 856	4 888.8	409.3	2 627	38 150	11 026.1	1 008.7	672	3 948	824.6	164.5
Morris	105.0	213	912	14 194	21 280.6	1 103.1	1 823	29 044	9 346.9	854.7	606	5 457	2 863.2	427.4
Ocean	574.6	997	388	2 761	1 295.7	127.9	1 869	26 568	7 695.4	724.1	546	2 525	468.2	92.8
Passaic	221.2	441	755	11 293	9 132.5	774.4	1 834	22 841	7 294.0	580.7	412	2 274	942.0	120.4
Salem	3 054.1	46 216	36	713	1 825.4	36.6	176	1 932	627.0	43.4	42	174	28.5	6.1
Somerset	13.6	42	495	12 184	25 544.7	1 040.4	1 086	18 878	5 609.3	510.5	294	1 286	442.8	62.4
Sussex	16.8	112	122	1 083	459.6	58.0	413	5 658	1 819.8	146.0	86	316	62.9	11.1
Union	147.8	276	853	15 361	14 069.6	1 380.5	1 941	24 757	7 376.3	646.2	532	3 070	1 058.3	147.7
Warren	26.1	240	95	D	D	D	389	6 076	1 573.8	143.0	58	181	43.1	6.6
NEW MEXICO	3 161.0	1 535	1 646	17 448	10 720.4	814.6	6 590	90 792	25 179.3	2 214.5	2 369	9 754	1 960.4	368.7
Bernalillo	149.0	225	791	10 150	5 620.8	495.7	2 076	33 334	9 548.2	857.5	942	4 274	818.2	150.5
Catron	20.0	5 366	1	D	D	D	13	68	10.7	0.9	NA	NA	NA	NA
Chaves	241.3	3 676	46	446	190.4	17.8	233	3 138	895.1	72.7	78	267	45.8	10.1
Cibola	11.1	408	7	D	D	D	70	864	256.7	19.1	12	36	5.8	1.1
Colfax	47.8	3 477	9	D	D	D	77	640	151.6	13.5	26	104	6.7	1.4
Curry	164.0	3 390	46	425	199.8	15.4	190	2 492	624.4	56.0	61	207	30.8	5.6
De Baca	51.8	25 628	1	D	D	D	8	54	13.0	1.1	1	D	D	D
Dona Ana	397.2	1 899	102	D	D	D	496	7 916	1 965.4	167.7	209	690	116.6	18.9
Eddy	193.5	3 594	54	558	1 075.3	23.3	191	2 674	798.7	67.0	55	283	89.5	14.7
Grant	46.5	1 576	14	109	43.3	4.1	114	1 222	257.1	25.1	40	126	15.2	2.8
Guadalupe	24.6	5 249	1	D	D	D	16	258	126.6	4.2	2	D	D	D
Harding	3.2	4 604	NA	NA	NA	NA	3	D	D	D	NA	NA	NA	NA
Hidalgo	61.6	12 585	2	D	D	D	26	237	157.7	4.8	1	D	D	D
Lea	175.5	2 711	92	D	D	D	214	2 830	919.8	71.1	91	774	247.8	53.2
Lincoln	23.3	1 135	10	D	D	D	135	1 184	279.7	26.9	60	152	22.8	3.3
Los Alamos	3.6	202	3	D	D	D	28	472	103.2	10.9	22	66	17.1	2.6
Luna	109.7	4 371	14	D	D	D	74	972	210.0	19.2	23	47	7.7	1.3
McKinley	13.8	193	44	D	D	D	227	3 271	996.7	72.6	42	158	28.4	5.4
Mora	12.7	2 600	NA	NA	NA	NA	7	D	D	D	1	D	D	D
Otero	30.1	472	24	D	D	D	186	2 185	567.7	50.6	52	151	18.7	3.5
Quay	41.6	4 597	2	D	D	D	41	461	263.9	8.7	8	13	0.9	0.4
Rio Arriba	107.1	2 660	10	55	43.7	1.0	83	1 068	254.6	27.4	24	64	7.2	1.4
Roosevelt	173.6	8 748	11	87	70.7	2.8	52	650	156.8	14.8	11	26	3.9	0.6
Sandoval	65.5	498	40	235	88.8	8.7	189	3 397	942.3	79.4	75	198	39.7	7.8
San Juan	343.7	2 643	156	1 412	663.0	73.8	450	6 210	1 801.6	157.4	107	750	205.0	36.8
San Miguel	38.5	1 309	8	D	D	D	81	921	220.9	20.5	18	49	6.3	1.2
Santa Fe	49.8	345	111	867	773.2	37.4	813	8 981	2 324.5	250.1	280	933	181.8	36.9
Sierra	42.8	3 567	2	D	D	D	43	474	102.1	9.0	9	17	2.5	0.4
Socorro	129.4	7 241	1	D	D	D	39	483	119.8	10.6	11	32	3.1	0.6
Taos	106.5	3 232	17	D	D	D	211	1 438	304.1	32.0	62	213	19.3	4.4
Torrance	55.6	3 396	9	D	D	D	43	494	154.0	9.8	2	D	D	D
Union	63.2	13 900	NA	NA	NA	NA	21	131	33.2	2.5	1	D	D	D
Valencia	163.6	2 136	18	D	D	D	140	2 212	601.3	50.0	43	D	D	D
NEW YORK	10 574.5	546	28 853	325 663	341 735.0	19 833.3	77 463	905 325	251 167.7	23 641.2	32 033	166 315	56 409.8	8 654.4
Albany	50.0	164	394	4 810	4 329.6	252.9	1 305	21 436	5 762.8	538.6	412	2 637	565.5	101.6
Allegany	5.7	116	18	131	94.9	4.5	145	1 396	271.1	26.8	19	34	6.1	1.3
Bronx	0.2	0	676	10 510	10 994.5	587.4	3 932	27 777	6 872.8	616.4	2 235	8 856	1 899.7	302.1
Broome	47.3	236	196	3 870	2 968.8	163.5	719	11 290	2 741.2	246.2	160	834	180.3	27.5
Cattaraugus	13.7	171	49	709	637.7	26.4	339	4 084	1 091.5	90.4	45	257	29.1	7.7
Cayuga	9.6	120	63	912	623.4	43.6	260	3 535	874.7	78.5	59	178	29.1	4.4
Chautauqua	436.2	3 234	109	1 405	693.2	58.8	508	6 313	1 437.9	132.3	88	560	447.5	19.9
Chemung	9.8	111	85	1 193	765.0	51.5	350	5 044	1 174.8	115.8	84	382	106.6	17.0
Chenango	7.7	153	24	D	D	D	170	1 953	512.8	41.7	24	D	D	D
Clinton	15.4	188	90	1 293	709.1	56.4	368	5 354	1 385.3	115.3	76	280	45.0	8.4
Columbia	8.5	134	53	729	306.1	30.1	267	2 770	748.8	67.9	58	181	21.7	4.2
Cortland	6.1	123	33	D	D	D	177	2 415	694.4	54.0	40	146	24.4	4.2
Delaware	455.5	9 493	30	573	256.8	29.6	183	1 784	472.7	39.1	30	75	10.7	1.8
Dutchess	77.9	262	214	1 909	4 342.1	130.8	1 046	14 155	3 792.7	349.9	325	1 324	246.3	45.7
Erie	482.8	525	998	18 454	19 343.2	1 011.2	3 343	52 423	12 106.1	1 139.3	785	5 883	862.2	190.9
Essex	22.2	564	15	169	82.5	4.9	214	2 192	514.0	49.2	31	D	D	D
Franklin	13.3	257	23	203	149.2	6.8	185	1 855	501.8	45.2	33	94	12.6	2.3
Fulton	6.4	116	50	465	244.9	21.2	205	2 382	675.3	57.4	30	118	18.2	3.6

1. Merchant wholesalers, except manufacturers' sales branches and offices.   2. Employer establishments.

474 NJ(Mercer)—NY(Fulton)

Items 133—146

Table B. States and Counties — Professional Services, Manufacturing, and Accommodation and Food Services

STATE County	Professional, scientific, and technical services, 2012				Manufacturing, 2012				Accommodation and food services, 2012			
	Number of establish-ments	Number of employees	Receipts (mil dol)	Annual payroll (mil dol)	Number of establish-ments	Number of employees	Receipts (mil dol)	Annual payroll (mil dol)	Number of establish-ments	Number of employees	Sales (mil dol)	Annual payroll (mil dol)
	147	148	149	150	151	152	153	154	155	156	157	158
NEW JERSEY—Cont'd												
Mercer	1 591	21 394	5 318.1	2 127.7	246	7 070	2 220.3	378.2	812	11 894	731.4	201.0
Middlesex	4 053	50 970	10 318.6	3 919.9	742	28 277	15 784.9	1 765.7	1 685	21 988	1 387.2	361.2
Monmouth	2 621	20 213	3 516.5	1 446.3	426	8 551	3 053.1	440.2	1 652	23 082	1 318.9	356.7
Morris	2 665	36 232	8 207.1	3 128.9	529	14 358	5 178.0	835.8	1 284	18 783	1 235.0	337.9
Ocean	1 091	5 988	839.5	301.7	278	5 069	1 400.0	231.1	1 145	12 911	801.5	203.7
Passaic	1 051	7 060	1 023.8	413.3	716	18 337	5 214.5	1 030.3	975	10 172	648.0	156.1
Salem	80	D	D	D	38	2 617	D	187.3	106	1 691	89.2	22.8
Somerset	1 827	25 815	5 063.6	2 307.5	300	12 329	4 974.7	1 007.3	798	11 509	739.9	210.9
Sussex	335	1 357	181.3	67.8	119	1 932	465.8	100.1	294	3 455	222.3	52.7
Union	1 389	16 181	1 875.4	1 171.6	619	20 790	20 139.4	1 727.9	1 134	12 856	819.1	211.9
Warren	230	D	D	D	108	3 854	2 050.3	227.0	245	2 294	122.2	32.1
NEW MEXICO	4 687	44 175	7 618.8	2 771.8	1 389	26 731	29 102.4	1 349.2	4 177	82 601	4 349.7	1 250.4
Bernalillo	2 261	18 714	3 488.9	1 101.8	575	11 976	D	569.9	1 394	31 736	1 702.6	495.5
Catron	4	D	D	D	4	13	D	0.6	12	38	1.7	0.4
Chaves	108	994	172.6	64.1	37	877	770.2	37.5	128	2 300	107.8	28.5
Cibola	17	D	D	D	6	38	D	1.1	36	584	27.5	7.7
Colfax	23	D	D	D	13	98	D	3.7	64	1 091	67.0	21.9
Curry	88	535	49.7	19.0	25	534	D	28.5	83	1 949	78.2	22.3
De Baca	1	D	D	D	NA	NA	NA	NA	5	D	D	D
Dona Ana	339	D	D	D	128	2 520	D	87.1	319	6 813	285.2	80.7
Eddy	77	593	54.1	33.5	35	1 459	D	112.1	111	2 083	118.0	31.0
Grant	47	D	D	D	14	121	D	3.6	78	862	33.1	9.6
Guadalupe	2	D	D	D	NA	NA	NA	NA	23	302	15.4	4.3
Harding	NA	NA	NA	NA	NA	NA	NA	NA	1	D	D	D
Hidalgo	4	D	D	D	NA	NA	NA	NA	16	207	9.6	2.7
Lea	82	569	82.1	30.8	37	854	D	68.0	138	2 261	132.1	30.2
Lincoln	53	D	D	D	17	67	D	2.6	99	1 185	60.5	18.0
Los Alamos	65	D	D	D	8	47	D	2.0	37	450	23.8	6.3
Luna	20	D	D	D	12	287	D	9.0	56	770	32.4	8.7
McKinley	43	D	D	D	24	383	D	26.7	143	2 508	119.4	31.5
Mora	NA	NA	NA	NA	NA	NA	NA	NA	3	D	D	D
Otero	71	D	D	D	28	190	D	5.1	108	2 422	164.7	45.1
Quay	12	D	D	D	4	24	D	1.3	33	536	22.9	6.0
Rio Arriba	35	D	D	D	22	95	D	2.9	66	1 089	70.7	20.3
Roosevelt	16	D	D	D	14	329	449.8	14.6	30	587	20.5	6.2
Sandoval	172	760	94.1	39.6	60	3 747	D	243.4	156	3 482	161.0	50.9
San Juan	256	D	D	D	85	1 318	268.6	62.8	197	4 253	201.8	56.3
San Miguel	35	D	D	D	9	48	9.1	1.5	58	719	34.4	8.9
Santa Fe	625	2 604	356.9	151.5	138	719	131.0	27.5	421	9 049	592.4	179.9
Sierra	15	D	D	D	5	121	D	3.0	39	390	15.8	4.7
Socorro	24	D	D	D	5	64	D	2.2	41	621	24.8	6.8
Taos	97	D	D	D	39	104	D	2.6	151	1 974	92.2	31.5
Torrance	13	D	D	D	11	132	D	4.5	26	D	D	D
Union	7	D	D	D	NA	NA	NA	NA	14	171	6.3	1.8
Valencia	75	D	D	D	27	523	D	23.6	91	D	D	D
NEW YORK	59 302	588 820	133 638.8	49 200.3	16 475	426 621	148 879.9	22 073.3	49 731	679 146	49 285.5	13 734.3
Albany	1 116	14 737	3 110.3	1 023.3	231	7 327	3 547.4	423.5	1 011	15 417	866.6	240.8
Allegany	49	199	20.4	7.2	46	2 433	841.8	108.8	92	1 175	50.0	12.4
Bronx	671	3 704	376.9	147.0	323	6 197	1 477.9	251.5	1 735	15 924	1 005.1	250.4
Broome	312	D	D	D	173	7 718	2 200.8	403.1	522	7 985	387.4	104.5
Cattaraugus	96	518	67.8	23.8	74	4 669	1 558.6	286.1	213	2 835	128.6	36.4
Cayuga	92	477	44.4	19.9	88	3 143	1 065.7	155.1	182	1 977	89.5	25.5
Chautauqua	194	1 108	87.5	33.3	197	9 474	5 107.5	428.6	347	4 735	208.7	57.7
Chemung	111	774	83.5	36.1	85	5 495	1 247.0	278.8	202	3 534	154.5	43.3
Chenango	64	316	26.3	8.8	74	3 443	1 661.4	165.3	94	769	34.7	10.0
Clinton	128	734	67.1	26.7	78	3 161	1 279.4	138.5	187	2 648	139.2	38.3
Columbia	175	562	73.5	27.5	73	1 290	462.6	53.7	161	1 419	72.7	20.8
Cortland	82	1 036	99.7	51.1	66	3 163	711.4	146.5	134	2 574	101.0	28.7
Delaware	75	219	21.2	5.8	36	3 593	1 557.2	195.7	124	1 060	44.6	12.4
Dutchess	775	4 010	624.7	224.1	198	8 544	2 481.9	668.2	784	9 107	499.5	136.0
Erie	2 138	28 912	3 598.2	1 656.1	1 008	42 606	15 835.4	2 250.2	2 279	41 143	1 871.9	551.5
Essex	71	D	D	D	28	782	213.1	56.6	201	2 360	150.3	47.2
Franklin	65	410	33.4	17.3	28	460	250.2	19.9	115	846	51.2	13.0
Fulton	77	300	26.2	8.9	71	1 724	712.2	66.3	131	1 209	56.1	15.8

1. Establishment subject to federal tax.

STATE County	Health care and social assistance, 2012				Other services, 2012				Nonemployer businesses, 2015		Value of residential construction authorized by building permits, 2016	
	Number of establish-ments	Number of employees	Receipts (mil dol)	Annual payroll (mil dol)	Number of establish-ments	Number of employees	Receipts (mil dol)	Annual payroll (mil dol)	Number	Receipts (mil dol)	New Construction ($1,000)	Number of housing units
	159	160	161	162	163	164	165	166	167	168	169	170
NEW JERSEY—Cont'd												
Mercer	1 165	28 970	2 981.0	1 326.6	815	6 403	1 245.5	239.1	24 347	1 353.3	81 894	711
Middlesex	2 195	46 302	5 084.5	2 039.8	1 569	10 342	1 635.7	398.2	55 578	3 209.4	243 010	2 351
Monmouth	2 382	40 905	4 809.5	1 842.3	1 477	8 532	738.0	223.9	53 781	3 584.1	307 002	1 933
Morris	1 727	34 457	4 235.4	1 784.5	1 200	7 548	802.0	232.2	42 528	3 040.9	267 673	1 695
Ocean	1 537	30 984	3 185.9	1 246.7	1 061	5 433	489.4	129.6	40 028	2 309.4	426 098	2 628
Passaic	1 431	25 884	2 516.8	1 059.9	956	4 962	443.6	118.5	38 429	1 994.6	54 493	397
Salem	165	3 312	319.9	122.3	100	386	29.1	7.5	2 799	126.0	7 773	50
Somerset	1 173	21 653	2 475.7	980.8	714	4 882	643.1	156.7	26 811	1 799.2	133 372	995
Sussex	361	6 319	551.2	232.3	300	1 285	112.4	33.1	10 927	608.4	33 168	169
Union	1 551	31 943	3 370.8	1 367.2	1 188	6 710	646.0	211.4	42 364	2 406.0	150 423	1 594
Warren	295	4 571	543.1	218.3	222	1 095	112.9	29.0	7 080	367.7	24 531	257
NEW MEXICO	4 967	116 557	11 236.6	4 588.0	2 962	17 464	1 798.6	501.4	121 279	4 788.6	91 203 142	337
Bernalillo	1 893	48 404	5 278.0	2 143.7	1 096	7 326	750.0	217.2	40 022	1 661.8	274 395	1 471
Catron	7	120	2.7	1.7	5	D	D	D	345	12.5	NA	NA
Chaves	176	3 778	331.1	133.6	79	396	33.7	9.6	2 986	135.0	22 385	218
Cibola	49	1 532	150.8	53.9	23	85	7.3	2.0	1 117	31.6	NA	NA
Colfax	39	593	52.5	25.4	28	87	8.6	2.1	769	25.6	4 065	9
Curry	118	2 829	225.6	87.1	76	468	40.0	9.4	1 942	82.3	15 261	102
De Baca	5	D	D	D	3	D	D	D	102	3.6	NA	NA
Dona Ana	496	12 122	1 010.7	418.4	234	1 124	86.4	26.3	12 253	465.5	153 181	770
Eddy	114	2 875	275.8	112.9	85	501	48.4	12.5	2 528	124.0	31 746	295
Grant	81	1 645	139.1	58.5	45	172	10.9	2.9	1 550	43.2	1 084	7
Guadalupe	9	D	D	D	9	D	D	D	161	4.6	NA	NA
Harding	1	D	D	D	NA	NA	NA	NA	56	3.4	NA	NA
Hidalgo	10	133	7.6	3.3	3	D	D	D	207	6.3	NA	NA
Lea	112	2 329	207.9	78.7	105	800	122.2	31.3	3 005	179.1	44 059	237
Lincoln	47	598	63.8	25.4	40	204	14.8	3.9	1 867	74.3	17 724	71
Los Alamos	67	1 095	102.6	41.2	24	203	11.2	2.8	1 101	37.4	1 424	4
Luna	50	855	76.3	30.1	28	83	6.6	1.6	979	30.4	2 847	17
McKinley	107	4 407	374.3	155.3	78	469	55.3	10.8	3 721	79.0	1 852	10
Mora	5	119	4.3	2.5	4	D	D	D	291	7.0	NA	NA
Otero	101	2 241	210.4	81.4	67	357	21.3	6.3	3 273	110.2	417	2
Quay	26	406	37.9	11.9	23	112	13.1	2.8	365	12.5	NA	NA
Rio Arriba	84	1 878	141.5	63.0	23	115	12.2	3.3	1 873	56.8	0	0
Roosevelt	32	752	57.3	23.2	17	69	8.1	1.7	842	32.9	2 774	17
Sandoval	201	3 058	284.8	107.2	109	583	45.2	16.1	7 865	277.2	168 456	898
San Juan	275	6 819	682.5	291.7	226	1 571	164.1	54.5	5 198	214.9	25 187	104
San Miguel	73	2 950	178.1	80.2	28	150	7.5	2.1	1 378	40.0	140	1
Santa Fe	513	8 697	961.0	384.4	335	1 892	268.6	66.4	16 363	752.4	29 198	117
Sierra	20	784	40.2	19.4	19	106	10.1	2.1	720	22.3	347	1
Socorro	29	736	48.7	24.6	12	D	D	D	754	18.9	164	1
Taos	103	1 476	120.9	53.7	57	229	18.3	5.3	3 301	108.0	8 691	78
Torrance	21	273	10.0	5.1	8	D	D	D	798	25.4	NA	NA
Union	13	D	D	D	10	34	2.9	0.6	297	7.3	NA	NA
Valencia	90	2 685	117.5	57.7	63	D	D	D	3 250	103.2	10 408	96
NEW YORK	56 734	1 468 987	155 666.1	65 180.0	45 646	271 689	39 709.2	9 395.1	1 685 636	86 950.0	6 045 261	33 711
Albany	1 017	33 297	3 522.5	1 396.7	810	5 994	691.9	220.5	17 829	944.8	130 316	740
Allegany	100	1 793	119.8	50.7	75	263	20.0	4.4	2 451	87.9	5 376	44
Bronx	2 145	98 945	10 001.3	4 584.1	1 757	8 242	782.4	224.0	114 788	3 397.5	531 101	4 003
Broome	435	14 852	1 527.8	612.6	341	1 937	151.1	43.6	10 019	418.8	18 279	239
Cattaraugus	175	3 585	324.5	123.1	123	666	53.8	13.7	3 831	146.1	9 073	62
Cayuga	198	4 036	302.4	136.8	131	518	41.1	9.8	4 243	168.8	20 720	127
Chautauqua	279	8 791	623.9	263.5	253	1 448	105.7	24.1	6 997	264.0	14 461	75
Chemung	211	6 421	621.6	294.0	128	670	57.3	15.6	3 875	141.9	17 326	41
Chenango	107	2 025	158.6	65.3	77	256	22.5	6.4	2 758	106.8	7 741	148
Clinton	239	5 147	499.7	231.6	116	560	50.1	13.0	3 942	163.2	20 480	134
Columbia	153	3 929	330.5	150.5	99	335	35.2	9.5	6 005	267.2	35 680	145
Cortland	127	3 591	231.6	106.1	93	401	35.2	9.0	2 353	94.3	5 205	43
Delaware	114	2 167	152.1	63.3	83	417	75.1	10.5	3 624	144.6	5 466	38
Dutchess	901	18 607	2 004.6	847.0	591	2 592	279.2	73.3	21 343	1 003.2	115 671	406
Erie	2 675	74 944	7 532.5	3 154.4	1 752	11 023	1 059.9	283.5	47 593	2 164.7	342 197	1 735
Essex	151	1 978	140.3	61.6	67	282	29.4	7.4	3 092	113.9	23 812	100
Franklin	170	3 276	285.0	126.0	72	225	19.5	5.0	2 781	104.5	11 689	72
Fulton	182	4 128	260.4	113.7	85	486	38.5	11.5	2 813	105.8	12 889	69

			Government employment and payroll, 2012							Local government finances, 2012				
STATE County				March payroll (percent of total)							General revenue			
													Taxes	
														Per capita[1] (dollars)
	Full-time equivalent employees	March payroll (dollars)	Administration, judicial, and legal	Police and Corrections	Fire Protection	Highways and transportation	Health and Welfare	Natural resources and utilities	Education and libraries	Total (mil dol)	Inter-governmental (mil dol)	Total (mil dol)	Total	Property
	171	172	173	174	175	176	177	178	179	180	181	182	183	184
NEW JERSEY—Cont'd														
Mercer	15 352	84 285 619	4.4	12.4	3.3	2.0	4.4	4.9	64.8	2 164.5	711.0	1 168.1	3 172	3 117
Middlesex	26 592	147 425 663	4.2	13.0	2.6	1.8	4.3	3.9	68.2	3 819.6	965.9	2 247.0	2 730	2 672
Monmouth	27 427	142 190 760	5.3	14.3	0.7	3.0	5.2	3.7	66.3	3 459.7	822.0	2 117.8	3 365	3 308
Morris	19 889	108 738 326	4.6	10.9	0.8	2.8	3.7	5.8	68.0	2 618.5	372.1	1 893.1	3 801	3 744
Ocean	20 430	99 202 051	5.5	14.5	0.4	3.0	4.9	5.2	63.9	2 394.3	580.3	1 531.1	2 638	2 603
Passaic	15 817	88 473 333	5.1	16.3	5.0	2.0	8.1	4.7	57.7	2 251.4	742.8	1 305.1	2 595	2 566
Salem	3 305	15 720 003	5.8	12.2	0.0	2.4	4.8	2.4	69.6	394.8	172.3	152.1	2 313	2 287
Somerset	13 026	68 430 732	3.9	11.5	0.6	3.4	3.0	2.1	73.5	1 611.4	277.0	1 174.0	3 583	3 530
Sussex	5 561	30 640 722	5.9	8.8	0.2	3.9	3.0	1.3	75.3	772.0	189.2	484.5	3 286	3 255
Union	23 222	130 750 946	5.8	13.4	5.4	2.2	5.9	2.3	63.3	3 230.4	1 130.6	1 723.2	3 168	3 100
Warren	4 346	20 547 388	6.3	9.9	0.9	3.6	6.8	2.0	68.4	536.8	183.8	292.4	2 716	2 688
NEW MEXICO	X	X	X	X	X	X	X	X	X	X	X	X	X	X
Bernalillo	22 833	89 838 327	6.2	16.3	6.5	6.3	5.2	6.3	51.7	2 451.4	1 173.3	882.0	1 310	743
Catron	146	386 239	12.7	8.6	0.0	7.4	4.7	1.5	64.1	15.7	10.9	2.6	698	511
Chaves	2 443	7 710 245	4.6	11.3	4.7	3.4	1.7	6.7	65.0	249.1	177.0	44.9	682	436
Cibola	909	2 491 571	7.4	11.5	1.3	2.3	1.9	3.3	70.0	97.5	46.9	12.3	451	248
Colfax	652	2 023 377	9.7	9.4	4.3	3.0	9.7	10.8	51.3	63.7	33.7	19.3	1 463	839
Curry	2 120	6 374 697	3.9	9.1	4.6	2.6	2.3	2.7	74.0	176.6	105.3	49.5	991	345
De Baca	134	371 334	8.8	11.3	0.0	8.7	3.7	10.9	56.5	13.8	7.8	2.5	1 319	841
Dona Ana	7 916	26 726 295	5.8	10.4	2.7	2.6	2.1	5.9	66.7	732.8	425.3	209.7	978	447
Eddy	2 143	8 178 370	5.4	14.2	5.2	4.3	2.1	6.4	59.3	275.0	129.3	115.7	2 126	1 225
Grant	1 747	5 905 715	4.3	7.8	1.4	2.5	44.2	2.7	35.9	187.1	80.4	29.7	1 009	473
Guadalupe	390	1 120 471	7.2	4.4	2.0	4.0	2.5	2.3	74.8	29.2	18.8	6.1	1 319	617
Harding	70	190 631	18.3	3.6	0.0	12.0	4.9	3.4	55.3	10.0	6.0	3.0	4 246	2 506
Hidalgo	293	795 504	9.1	17.5	0.0	4.5	3.0	5.4	58.2	28.3	19.6	4.7	976	778
Lea	3 191	11 349 323	4.4	10.8	3.6	2.9	15.4	4.7	55.7	413.1	170.9	153.5	2 314	1 380
Lincoln	853	2 783 245	8.5	11.0	3.3	4.9	5.2	9.6	53.8	99.8	41.5	37.7	1 857	1 135
Los Alamos	1 400	5 075 436	10.8	6.3	17.0	4.7	1.3	11.9	40.5	138.8	77.2	49.3	2 712	875
Luna	1 233	3 637 272	6.8	12.9	1.8	1.9	2.6	2.4	66.6	103.9	67.8	23.4	936	513
McKinley	3 373	9 383 425	3.6	7.5	2.2	1.6	1.9	3.4	78.5	249.0	155.9	62.8	861	271
Mora	208	516 517	10.0	3.6	0.0	4.9	0.8	0.5	79.2	16.8	10.9	2.4	506	430
Otero	1 662	5 122 202	6.3	14.5	0.3	2.5	2.3	4.7	67.9	147.4	86.7	40.4	612	307
Quay	563	1 605 317	7.9	9.3	0.4	3.2	4.0	8.7	65.3	54.3	38.6	8.0	912	461
Rio Arriba	1 378	4 062 743	9.2	7.6	1.7	2.7	5.6	3.5	67.3	133.9	69.5	50.2	1 244	819
Roosevelt	849	2 598 517	4.7	9.9	3.2	3.4	1.0	3.2	73.2	65.0	40.9	14.6	714	505
Sandoval	3 959	13 152 644	7.2	11.4	4.7	3.3	1.2	5.4	66.3	399.2	201.9	135.8	1 002	605
San Juan	5 857	21 149 302	4.2	11.0	2.6	2.0	1.9	8.4	68.4	491.8	290.9	126.9	987	702
San Miguel	1 294	3 946 008	6.9	7.5	1.7	1.8	1.8	6.1	72.8	102.3	63.7	27.0	933	408
Santa Fe	4 848	18 022 225	9.3	12.0	6.4	3.8	4.1	9.6	48.1	527.4	253.9	199.3	1 361	807
Sierra	644	2 455 286	6.7	6.0	0.0	1.9	22.5	6.1	54.0	49.9	22.0	12.6	1 060	582
Socorro	721	1 882 356	6.5	9.1	3.0	3.6	4.4	6.7	63.5	61.4	43.7	9.7	551	305
Taos	1 245	3 508 311	12.0	9.6	1.7	3.3	3.5	5.5	61.6	118.8	59.8	45.9	1 400	624
Torrance	904	2 576 995	5.9	5.6	0.5	2.0	1.4	1.7	82.4	69.5	50.0	14.8	923	704
Union	203	666 897	11.2	10.4	3.2	8.9	2.6	4.7	56.6	23.5	13.2	5.9	1 327	768
Valencia	2 378	6 663 270	5.6	7.4	1.3	1.2	2.2	2.4	79.8	195.8	120.3	56.4	736	383
NEW YORK	X	X	X	X	X	X	X	X	X	X	X	X	X	X
Albany	12 459	58 755 137	5.6	15.4	3.5	2.8	8.7	5.3	57.2	1 776.2	540.6	885.9	2 900	2 024
Allegany	2 326	8 539 230	7.1	8.0	0.7	8.2	7.3	2.7	64.1	300.9	162.2	113.9	2 356	1 929
Bronx	(3)	(3)	(3)	(3)	(3)	(3)	(3)	(3)	(3)	(3)	(3)	(3)	(3)	(3)
Broome	9 618	36 733 525	4.9	8.4	2.7	4.4	10.5	3.0	64.3	1 182.8	494.6	520.5	2 628	1 756
Cattaraugus	4 623	18 563 190	6.2	8.6	1.7	8.0	12.2	3.6	59.1	526.9	273.4	184.2	2 318	1 675
Cayuga	3 237	14 564 325	6.1	8.2	3.3	5.0	9.9	3.2	63.1	427.9	185.0	169.5	2 131	1 441
Chautauqua	6 787	27 243 053	4.8	7.7	2.9	6.8	9.0	2.9	65.0	772.7	364.8	268.8	2 013	1 539
Chemung	3 853	14 858 297	5.0	9.7	2.9	4.0	13.2	3.8	59.7	476.3	219.3	175.3	1 971	1 236
Chenango	2 731	10 005 930	6.4	7.7	1.8	9.2	7.9	1.6	64.4	295.2	157.3	105.1	2 106	1 541
Clinton	3 949	16 260 748	5.3	6.0	0.9	6.0	11.3	2.6	65.0	458.8	198.9	190.2	2 329	1 643
Columbia	3 025	13 243 189	8.0	8.1	0.4	9.6	12.9	2.0	57.7	374.6	114.6	212.1	3 394	2 596
Cortland	2 146	9 594 343	7.0	14.5	2.0	8.9	10.0	5.2	50.7	258.6	118.1	110.0	2 223	1 645
Delaware	2 262	8 403 397	8.5	6.5	0.1	11.8	10.9	1.5	59.1	286.6	118.1	136.3	2 883	2 410
Dutchess	12 054	60 953 575	5.6	9.6	3.0	3.7	5.7	1.9	69.4	1 683.1	521.2	964.5	3 244	2 611
Erie	35 259	161 616 876	3.7	12.8	3.3	2.9	5.3	5.1	65.4	5 298.2	2 255.2	2 176.7	2 368	1 547
Essex	1 990	7 313 826	9.9	6.1	1.3	9.8	14.0	4.4	53.3	255.8	76.1	132.5	3 401	2 621
Franklin	2 713	9 538 618	5.8	5.4	0.9	6.2	10.0	2.2	68.0	305.3	153.8	104.0	2 008	1 575
Fulton	2 664	9 331 227	4.7	7.9	2.7	4.8	13.2	1.3	64.4	301.1	138.4	121.2	2 207	1 595

1. Based on the resident population estimated as of July 1 of the year shown.   3. Bronx, Kings, Queens, and Richmond counties are included with New York county.

Table B. States and Counties — Local Government Finances, Government Employment, and Income Taxes

STATE County	Local government finances, 2012 (cont.) Direct general expenditure Total (mil dol)	Per capita¹ (dollars)	Percent of total for: Education	Health and hospitals	Police protection	Public welfare	Highways	Debt outstanding Total (mil dol)	Per capita¹ (dollars)	Government employment, 2015 Federal civilian	Federal military	State and local	Individual income tax returns, 2014 Number of returns	Mean adjusted gross income	Mean income tax
	185	186	187	188	189	190	191	192	193	194	195	196	197	198	199
NEW JERSEY—Cont'd															
Mercer	2 145.5	5 825	52.3	0.9	5.3	4.3	1.4	1 928.9	5 237	2 364	741	38 770	173 960	90 837	15 098
Middlesex	3 874.0	4 707	54.1	1.1	5.8	2.4	1.7	4 163.4	5 059	2 148	1 786	52 166	401 840	73 350	9 789
Monmouth	3 411.5	5 420	54.8	1.1	6.0	2.1	2.9	2 733.3	4 343	2 047	1 430	33 121	318 840	95 971	16 359
Morris	2 580.5	5 182	55.7	1.5	5.7	1.5	3.1	2 056.9	4 130	5 456	1 142	25 851	252 070	119 954	22 241
Ocean	2 437.7	4 200	51.2	0.6	6.8	3.2	3.4	2 209.0	3 805	3 085	1 367	25 092	279 800	61 451	7 211
Passaic	2 262.2	4 499	45.8	2.5	6.7	5.0	2.2	1 387.8	2 760	1 077	1 021	27 942	246 570	56 059	6 695
Salem	408.1	6 204	53.4	1.9	3.9	2.2	4.2	399.9	6 081	152	129	4 129	30 580	56 844	6 088
Somerset	1 638.3	4 999	58.6	2.0	5.3	1.0	4.6	1 441.4	4 399	1 756	673	15 990	167 600	119 135	22 258
Sussex	733.7	4 976	63.4	1.4	3.9	2.2	4.2	551.0	3 737	327	292	7 553	72 400	77 326	10 436
Union	3 281.6	6 033	53.5	2.9	6.2	1.6	1.8	2 546.6	4 681	1 525	1 127	31 449	270 510	81 943	13 133
Warren	573.8	5 330	58.0	1.8	4.0	3.5	3.9	237.2	2 203	219	214	5 571	53 270	67 089	7 984
NEW MEXICO	X	X	X	X	X	X	X	X	X	29 200	16 917	162 440	911 750	50 765	5 878
Bernalillo	2 337.5	3 471	48.0	2.0	9.0	1.6	5.0	3 333.0	4 949	13 794	5 045	54 606	306 260	53 808	6 345
Catron	17.1	4 674	36.7	2.0	4.1	0.6	7.9	9.9	2 693	99	D	202	1 350	34 410	3 275
Chaves	248.0	3 771	52.6	0.0	6.6	2.3	4.4	107.2	1 630	237	176	3 999	25 740	45 415	5 217
Cibola	102.5	3 749	38.6	30.4	2.4	3.0	2.9	41.6	1 521	320	65	2 901	9 170	37 308	2 996
Colfax	65.2	4 931	40.3	5.9	6.4	0.7	7.3	52.6	3 979	50	31	1 386	5 450	40 263	3 922
Curry	185.3	3 711	57.6	0.2	5.2	0.7	4.3	71.0	1 422	852	4 640	2 472	21 110	41 212	4 017
De Baca	13.6	7 072	35.8	17.8	4.5	0.1	4.9	5.2	2 717	10	D	183	840	41 946	3 121
Dona Ana	719.6	3 356	57.5	1.3	6.7	1.9	4.1	440.1	2 052	3 507	559	16 910	90 410	41 616	4 192
Eddy	252.5	4 640	47.2	2.8	8.5	1.6	5.2	120.4	2 213	629	148	3 281	24 750	70 909	10 569
Grant	196.6	6 690	26.5	40.7	4.6	2.8	2.6	102.5	3 489	202	73	3 212	12 470	43 009	4 109
Guadalupe	26.2	5 682	37.7	0.7	4.4	6.5	5.2	22.0	4 789	21	10	402	1 780	31 224	2 376
Harding	10.9	15 478	46.4	1.6	4.0	0.1	7.1	5.9	8 396	12	D	85	320	46 794	5 050
Hidalgo	27.3	5 693	43.1	2.0	15.9	0.6	2.6	9.5	1 987	263	11	390	1 840	37 846	3 008
Lea	416.5	6 278	45.5	12.6	5.6	1.1	7.8	219.2	3 304	86	180	3 641	29 290	62 436	8 143
Lincoln	102.5	5 048	37.3	4.2	6.6	0.5	5.9	89.0	4 382	96	50	1 080	8 890	46 331	5 352
Los Alamos	168.1	9 258	31.9	0.0	4.1	1.6	6.7	190.8	10 505	234	48	1 642	8 880	100 028	14 613
Luna	99.5	3 974	55.3	2.0	7.7	1.0	3.5	25.7	1 027	477	63	1 637	10 510	31 643	2 223
McKinley	255.3	3 497	63.0	1.1	4.0	1.8	3.8	145.8	1 997	2 448	198	5 018	32 280	32 141	2 465
Mora	17.2	3 658	55.5	0.3	2.6	0.0	3.0	10.3	2 189	40	12	253	1 960	31 191	2 311
Otero	149.2	2 258	50.7	0.5	8.4	3.1	9.6	138.3	2 094	1 745	3 892	4 579	26 230	39 450	3 412
Quay	53.7	6 124	48.7	5.9	4.7	3.6	4.1	28.0	3 197	31	22	895	3 630	32 686	2 542
Rio Arriba	130.8	3 245	54.4	0.5	4.5	1.1	2.9	101.6	2 519	305	102	4 535	16 400	39 668	3 490
Roosevelt	64.4	3 152	61.8	0.1	6.6	2.2	4.8	18.8	922	39	47	2 026	7 660	35 602	3 072
Sandoval	384.6	2 836	51.6	0.1	6.8	1.0	6.1	599.5	4 422	367	362	7 363	61 200	56 302	6 228
San Juan	551.0	4 287	55.6	3.3	6.3	1.2	4.3	2 140.3	16 652	1 491	308	9 836	51 650	52 699	5 948
San Miguel	108.9	3 769	60.5	0.3	4.2	0.7	4.8	73.4	2 539	137	70	3 585	11 480	34 834	2 848
Santa Fe	578.2	3 950	45.8	1.3	6.0	2.2	3.5	916.2	6 259	950	388	16 027	75 260	68 337	10 314
Sierra	50.5	4 245	27.8	29.9	10.1	1.0	8.1	29.4	2 475	95	29	757	4 850	32 235	2 803
Socorro	72.0	4 091	47.8	0.2	3.8	0.0	4.6	25.8	1 466	178	45	2 463	6 870	36 491	3 199
Taos	129.6	3 953	49.9	1.4	3.2	2.6	3.3	125.3	3 823	280	85	1 863	15 510	39 842	4 215
Torrance	69.7	4 348	66.8	0.8	2.8	0.8	2.9	231.1	14 425	66	39	929	5 730	35 817	3 019
Union	21.1	4 754	42.4	8.0	5.7	1.5	6.6	13.0	2 941	42	D	287	1 650	39 621	4 132
Valencia	184.9	2 413	64.8	0.5	5.8	0.6	3.4	196.9	2 570	97	194	3 995	30 330	42 424	3 727
NEW YORK	X	X	X	X	X	X	X	X	X	115 146	56 762	1 284 098	9 523 340	79 352	13 051
Albany	1 817.9	5 952	40.0	3.9	5.2	11.2	3.9	2 211.1	7 239	4 990	670	59 162	151 980	72 352	10 515
Allegany	309.4	6 398	47.0	2.5	1.8	9.8	11.7	294.0	6 080	118	68	4 010	18 880	45 380	4 310
Bronx	(3)	(3)	(3)	(3)	(3)	(3)	(3)	(3)	(3)	3 949	2 345	57 726	644 950	35 163	2 952
Broome	1 232.1	6 221	48.7	3.4	2.9	12.0	3.8	1 229.8	6 209	522	303	18 495	89 140	50 744	5 643
Cattaraugus	550.0	6 922	49.6	5.9	2.3	13.2	7.5	513.3	6 460	241	146	9 382	34 420	45 358	4 369
Cayuga	442.3	5 560	52.0	4.7	3.2	9.3	6.8	308.3	3 875	138	117	5 625	35 620	50 496	5 288
Chautauqua	806.8	6 042	50.1	3.0	2.9	12.8	6.0	665.7	4 985	300	197	8 663	57 250	45 895	4 588
Chemung	467.0	5 252	42.9	3.0	3.0	18.1	8.9	490.6	5 518	214	132	5 912	39 660	51 976	5 720
Chenango	297.2	5 953	57.1	3.1	1.6	8.2	7.3	216.1	4 329	86	76	4 114	22 780	44 509	4 126
Clinton	495.0	6 062	54.0	4.9	1.9	11.3	5.6	401.8	4 921	700	119	7 239	36 340	49 718	5 034
Columbia	381.3	6 100	48.0	4.5	2.2	13.2	9.0	225.4	3 607	157	94	4 491	29 970	64 365	8 661
Cortland	277.6	5 611	47.3	4.6	3.0	10.4	8.5	199.2	4 027	109	71	4 057	20 650	47 578	4 634
Delaware	281.8	5 961	44.9	3.5	1.5	9.4	12.5	208.3	4 406	122	70	4 386	19 870	45 586	4 456
Dutchess	1 642.8	5 525	55.5	3.6	3.3	7.6	4.0	1 417.6	4 768	1 167	438	18 488	139 970	70 634	9 238
Erie	5 644.5	6 141	44.0	10.5	3.7	9.5	3.2	5 158.7	5 613	8 190	1 689	65 435	446 800	57 838	7 237
Essex	273.6	7 022	36.7	6.8	1.3	10.7	9.0	306.9	7 877	331	57	3 997	17 850	51 163	5 807
Franklin	335.9	6 486	56.1	3.6	1.2	11.1	5.6	277.2	5 352	159	72	7 432	20 120	45 184	4 427
Fulton	288.3	5 250	49.7	2.7	2.5	16.8	5.0	192.0	3 496	77	84	3 489	24 870	45 930	4 374

1. Based on the resident population estimated as of July 1 of the year shown.   3. Bronx, Kings, Queens, and Richmond counties are included with New York county.

Table B. States and Counties — **Personal Income**

	Personal income, 2015										Earnings, 2015		
STATE County	Total (mil dol)	Percent change, 2014–2015	Per capita[1] Dollars	Rank	Wages and salaries (mil dol)	Supplements to wages and salaries; employer contributions (mil dol) Pension and insurance	Government social insurance	Proprietors' income (mil dol)	Dividends, interest, and rent (mil dol)	Personal transfer receipts (mil dol)	Total (mil dol)	Contributions for government social insurance (mil dol) From employee and self-employed	From employer
	62	63	64	65	66	67	68	69	70	71	72	73	74
NEW YORK—Cont'd													
Genesee	2 389	3.4	40 532	1 313	940	279	83	136	338	542	1 438	77	83
Greene	2 010	2.9	42 203	1 350	629	210	54	168	330	502	1 060	60	54
Hamilton	245	3.6	51 895	379	69	33	6	10	59	56	117	7	6
Herkimer	2 345	2.1	37 163	1 726	646	197	56	116	326	657	1 014	62	56
Jefferson	5 078	0.4	43 170	807	2 661	820	254	187	952	979	3 923	178	254
Kings	112 703	4.8	42 743	1 193	30 797	7 048	2 607	6 865	15 954	28 107	47 317	2 609	2 607
Lewis	1 074	-2.5	39 857	1 001	254	99	22	65	145	228	441	23	22
Livingston	2 456	3.9	37 955	1 673	769	271	67	149	335	546	1 256	69	67
Madison	2 827	2.2	39 352	1 501	861	239	75	166	443	589	1 341	75	75
Monroe	35 971	4.6	47 986	602	19 610	3 935	1 624	2 662	5 607	7 403	27 831	1 483	1 624
Montgomery	1 930	5.3	38 872	1 733	745	181	67	98	260	571	1 091	65	67
Nassau	105 861	3.0	77 762	46	37 972	7 097	3 056	8 799	24 909	12 714	56 924	2 961	3 056
New York	257 710	2.8	156 708	2	282 269	33 025	16 570	38 288	81 974	19 501	370 152	18 765	16 570
Niagara	8 794	4.1	40 355	1 310	3 050	780	265	362	1 172	2 181	4 458	262	265
Oneida	9 227	3.0	39 684	1 409	4 423	1 255	372	446	1 435	2 420	6 496	353	372
Onondaga	22 034	4.5	47 034	738	12 316	2 767	1 021	1 782	3 326	4 467	17 886	929	1 021
Ontario	5 248	4.6	47 900	605	2 785	553	204	228	820	1 001	3 770	207	204
Orange	17 566	3.8	46 513	688	6 687	1 695	569	941	2 405	3 348	9 892	515	569
Orleans	1 469	4.7	35 324	2 488	533	190	47	109	179	392	879	48	47
Oswego	4 397	4.0	36 593	2 010	1 496	464	125	132	526	1 157	2 217	127	125
Otsego	2 322	3.0	38 293	1 868	1 004	274	84	137	393	566	1 500	83	84
Putnam	5 859	3.6	59 160	185	1 345	317	113	298	933	796	2 073	116	113
Queens	98 919	5.4	42 288	1 247	33 339	7 211	2 809	7 624	13 341	24 918	50 982	2 770	2 809
Rensselaer	7 184	4.6	44 823	855	2 688	698	222	287	1 018	1 459	3 895	215	222
Richmond	23 804	5.3	50 161	508	5 536	1 278	469	1 172	3 168	5 734	8 455	488	469
Rockland	17 879	4.6	54 838	261	6 830	1 459	534	1 203	3 028	3 127	10 026	531	534
St. Lawrence	3 761	1.9	33 882	2 249	1 521	506	130	162	522	1 055	2 319	127	130
Saratoga	13 344	4.6	58 979	180	4 295	897	363	591	2 747	1 764	6 147	336	363
Schenectady	7 453	3.3	48 206	737	3 632	715	295	483	1 150	1 519	5 125	278	295
Schoharie	1 128	1.9	35 998	1 955	338	112	29	55	160	274	534	31	29
Schuyler	712	3.1	39 124	1 561	187	54	17	71	92	191	329	19	17
Seneca	1 236	3.6	35 472	1 919	536	164	45	71	190	314	815	45	45
Steuben	3 929	2.3	40 243	1 302	2 031	434	161	177	607	948	2 804	155	161
Suffolk	89 321	3.9	59 484	179	38 210	7 873	3 035	5 790	15 299	14 241	54 908	2 892	3 035
Sullivan	3 149	5.6	42 053	1 270	1 028	311	89	144	511	886	1 572	89	89
Tioga	1 980	2.7	40 033	1 405	661	156	54	105	268	454	975	58	54
Tompkins	4 312	5.2	41 095	1 498	2 621	522	226	319	838	664	3 688	187	226
Ulster	8 002	3.8	44 422	993	2 601	758	220	543	1 447	1 835	4 122	228	220
Warren	3 068	3.8	47 429	637	1 613	348	139	205	530	674	2 305	126	139
Washington	2 275	2.4	36 563	1 830	701	234	61	97	312	571	1 093	62	61
Wayne	3 797	5.0	41 524	1 464	1 207	377	104	262	458	901	1 950	109	104
Westchester	91 029	2.9	93 229	16	30 819	5 293	2 270	6 725	23 749	9 060	45 106	2 340	2 270
Wyoming	1 556	-0.5	37 941	1 587	590	202	51	119	206	345	962	49	51
Yates	911	1.9	36 371	2 282	249	74	22	100	164	229	446	25	22
NORTH CAROLINA	409 338	4.6	40 790	X	213 256	33 615	16 475	29 827	70 439	82 122	293 173	18 038	16 475
Alamance	5 673	4.6	35 839	1 968	2 406	368	191	326	889	1 310	3 291	222	191
Alexander	1 256	5.5	33 645	2 287	311	58	26	138	165	328	532	35	26
Alleghany	354	3.4	32 712	2 365	104	21	8	36	79	124	170	13	8
Anson	834	3.9	32 392	2 552	270	58	21	85	99	262	434	26	21
Ashe	852	2.9	31 519	2 554	254	46	20	89	146	282	410	30	20
Avery	548	3.3	30 958	2 625	225	41	19	43	125	161	328	22	19
Beaufort	1 800	2.7	37 773	1 710	625	115	48	130	317	541	918	65	48
Bertie	641	0.2	31 749	2 403	219	47	17	38	76	245	321	22	17
Bladen	1 122	1.5	32 681	2 325	481	90	37	120	135	377	728	44	37
Brunswick	4 457	6.0	36 307	1 894	1 239	218	100	270	926	1 409	1 827	145	100
Buncombe	10 379	5.4	40 994	1 438	5 421	866	427	927	2 293	2 216	7 642	486	427
Burke	2 795	4.4	31 458	2 457	1 132	219	91	138	424	824	1 580	110	91
Cabarrus	7 800	7.1	39 640	1 387	2 952	464	226	453	978	1 347	4 094	262	226
Caldwell	2 541	4.2	31 263	2 707	897	158	72	112	363	764	1 239	91	72
Camden	426	3.8	41 351	1 281	64	11	5	19	67	81	98	7	5
Carteret	3 044	3.5	44 199	770	815	148	64	188	715	695	1 216	85	64
Caswell	715	3.1	31 184	2 785	110	24	9	59	91	233	202	17	9
Catawba	6 243	5.5	40 265	1 641	3 659	579	296	482	1 007	1 383	5 016	316	296
Chatham	3 677	4.7	51 839	308	555	92	44	177	893	616	869	67	44
Cherokee	798	5.2	29 358	2 913	274	51	22	65	135	333	411	32	22

1. Based on the resident population estimated as of July 1 of the year shown.

Table B. States and Counties — **Earnings, Social Security, and Housing**

STATE County	Farm	Mining	Construction	Manufacturing	Information: professional, scientific, technical services	Retail trade	Finance, insurance, real estate and leasing	Health care and social assistance	Government	Social Security beneficiaries, December 2015 Number	Rate[1]	Supplemental Security Income recipients, December 2015	Housing units, 2016 Total	Percent change, 2010–2016
	75	76	77	78	79	80	81	82	83	84	85	86	87	88
NEW YORK—Cont'd														
Genesee	3.9	0.8	5.7	14.8	2.9	6.6	3.0	9.0	32.5	13 695	233	1 134	25 726	0.8
Greene	0.5	D	5.4	6.8	4.1	7.8	3.0	5.7	37.6	12 355	259	1 335	29 335	0.4
Hamilton	0.0	D	5.8	1.0	D	6.2	D	D	62.8	1 675	357	69	8 786	1.0
Herkimer	1.5	1.3	6.9	15.5	2.4	7.7	2.1	9.2	30.9	16 185	257	1 623	33 305	-0.2
Jefferson	1.1	0.1	4.0	4.5	2.6	5.9	1.9	9.7	59.3	21 570	184	2 731	59 113	2.0
Kings	0.0	0.0	5.9	2.4	8.8	7.2	6.5	20.9	22.0	330 960	126	134 269	1 031 201	3.1
Lewis	6.7	D	5.7	15.5	2.5	5.7	1.7	D	41.8	5 745	213	564	15 386	1.8
Livingston	2.1	D	7.7	10.7	2.7	6.4	2.2	8.7	38.2	13 870	215	1 266	27 362	1.2
Madison	1.5	D	6.0	13.3	4.9	7.9	3.7	D	24.5	14 635	204	1 280	31 801	0.1
Monroe	0.1	0.0	4.7	12.8	12.2	5.2	7.1	13.9	15.3	157 435	210	25 283	326 597	1.9
Montgomery	1.1	0.5	5.8	16.2	3.1	9.5	2.4	21.5	21.2	13 285	267	1 881	23 145	0.3
Nassau	0.0	0.0	5.8	3.1	12.4	8.2	10.5	17.8	17.4	255 135	188	16 914	466 904	-0.3
New York	0.0	0.0	1.4	0.8	27.5	2.7	32.2	4.9	7.9	252 295	154	70 683	875 968	3.4
Niagara	0.9	D	5.4	16.0	4.8	8.3	2.6	12.8	26.9	52 555	247	5 746	99 116	0.0
Oneida	0.3	0.1	3.6	8.8	6.5	5.7	7.6	16.6	32.5	54 805	236	8 212	103 772	-0.4
Onondaga	0.2	0.1	4.9	9.5	10.9	6.4	8.1	13.0	20.5	96 930	207	14 216	205 492	1.5
Ontario	0.8	0.1	6.3	13.0	5.5	7.9	3.3	11.2	19.0	25 725	235	1 809	50 339	4.3
Orange	0.3	0.9	5.1	6.0	7.4	9.0	3.5	14.0	31.5	64 525	171	6 760	141 135	3.0
Orleans	2.9	2.5	4.4	18.5	D	4.7	4.2	D	40.1	9 515	229	971	18 514	0.5
Oswego	0.4	0.2	6.3	11.4	D	7.4	2.4	10.7	31.2	27 095	226	3 303	53 662	0.1
Otsego	0.8	D	3.8	4.6	3.7	8.5	6.2	27.8	24.7	14 595	241	1 342	30 765	0.0
Putnam	0.1	0.0	11.6	5.7	9.2	5.0	3.9	16.2	26.0	18 315	185	799	38 332	0.2
Queens	0.0	D	12.7	2.8	4.5	5.8	6.9	14.2	20.5	327 565	141	72 337	851 525	2.0
Rensselaer	0.2	0.2	7.7	11.2	8.4	5.5	3.8	11.7	27.1	33 020	206	4 091	71 942	0.7
Richmond	0.0	0.0	10.9	0.9	6.1	7.2	5.0	22.5	22.9	88 810	187	14 917	179 411	1.6
Rockland	0.0	D	7.5	12.3	10.4	6.4	4.5	13.9	21.0	55 460	170	5 056	105 155	1.1
St. Lawrence	1.8	0.2	4.1	8.2	2.9	7.0	2.4	9.9	39.7	25 665	231	3 718	52 394	0.5
Saratoga	0.3	D	8.1	14.1	9.9	6.9	9.5	10.0	18.2	46 830	207	2 726	104 128	5.5
Schenectady	0.0	D	4.1	13.0	18.4	5.5	3.8	13.3	17.8	32 990	213	5 231	68 473	0.4
Schoharie	0.8	D	8.8	3.4	3.4	7.6	5.7	10.1	37.1	6 975	222	641	17 265	0.2
Schuyler	3.5	D	9.7	17.0	D	7.5	D	11.8	24.6	4 825	265	404	9 618	1.7
Seneca	1.9	D	4.2	26.1	D	8.0	2.3	D	33.8	8 025	230	763	16 234	1.2
Steuben	1.3	0.2	2.6	15.0	17.1	5.2	3.2	9.4	22.3	23 555	241	2 928	48 695	-0.4
Suffolk	0.2	0.2	7.8	8.3	10.3	6.7	9.6	11.7	21.6	289 755	193	20 425	570 933	0.2
Sullivan	0.6	0.5	5.3	4.5	3.6	6.1	4.1	18.9	35.7	17 715	237	2 643	49 890	1.5
Tioga	0.5	0.8	4.6	39.6	D	5.4	2.1	5.1	20.2	11 965	243	1 135	22 166	0.0
Tompkins	0.3	1.0	2.5	7.7	8.8	5.2	3.6	D	13.8	15 750	151	1 473	42 451	1.8
Ulster	0.5	0.2	6.3	6.1	5.7	8.5	3.9	12.5	32.1	40 950	228	4 111	83 920	0.3
Warren	0.1	0.5	6.6	10.6	8.5	8.9	5.7	15.4	16.5	18 015	279	1 575	39 391	1.7
Washington	3.3	0.6	8.0	19.8	D	6.3	1.6	7.3	38.9	14 525	233	1 616	29 042	0.6
Wayne	3.2	0.3	7.8	22.4	2.7	6.2	2.6	7.2	29.1	22 705	249	2 209	41 550	1.2
Westchester	0.0	D	6.9	5.5	14.5	5.1	12.4	12.9	17.0	167 035	172	17 398	369 612	-0.3
Wyoming	7.6	D	4.1	12.8	D	6.4	2.3	D	41.0	9 090	222	644	18 070	0.6
Yates	7.9	0.1	8.4	14.6	D	7.1	3.2	D	21.3	6 155	246	522	13 763	2.0
NORTH CAROLINA	1.2	0.1	5.8	11.6	10.8	6.2	8.2	10.2	19.1	1 984 962	198	235 704	4 540 498	4.9
Alamance	0.1	0.1	6.2	16.3	4.3	8.1	5.5	20.1	11.5	33 560	213	3 430	69 159	3.9
Alexander	15.0	D	4.8	30.5	D	4.4	2.8	D	19.0	9 255	248	633	16 180	0.0
Alleghany	8.0	D	7.6	14.5	D	8.3	2.7	D	18.2	3 470	321	339	8 115	0.6
Anson	14.3	D	3.3	19.0	D	4.5	1.5	D	27.4	5 910	231	1 025	11 486	-0.7
Ashe	8.7	D	14.4	9.4	D	7.9	4.5	11.5	15.0	7 930	295	830	17 544	1.5
Avery	3.0	D	9.4	1.4	D	7.5	3.8	D	23.9	4 420	251	413	14 062	1.2
Beaufort	2.0	0.0	5.0	21.0	4.7	7.6	4.9	8.4	17.1	14 015	295	1 886	25 695	4.0
Bertie	9.5	D	1.6	28.7	D	2.9	D	9.5	23.4	5 835	288	1 287	9 754	-0.7
Bladen	12.8	0.0	2.9	39.0	D	3.6	1.8	D	17.8	8 520	249	1 568	17 697	-0.1
Brunswick	1.7	D	7.8	4.6	D	8.4	5.7	11.2	16.9	40 630	331	2 306	85 161	9.9
Buncombe	0.4	0.1	5.8	10.8	8.9	7.9	5.6	20.7	14.0	58 365	231	5 767	117 677	3.8
Burke	1.2	D	3.5	27.6	2.7	5.8	3.2	17.1	24.2	22 035	248	2 028	40 645	-0.5
Cabarrus	0.7	D	7.0	8.2	4.7	9.3	3.9	7.0	21.1	33 525	171	3 172	77 422	7.6
Caldwell	0.5	D	4.9	23.7	2.8	7.4	2.1	11.7	17.3	20 450	252	1 912	37 748	0.2
Camden	4.0	0.0	8.0	3.3	D	3.9	D	D	25.3	2 025	197	132	4 193	2.2
Carteret	0.9	0.0	6.8	4.2	6.2	13.0	6.7	11.3	24.4	18 525	269	1 244	49 362	2.5
Caswell	17.4	D	9.0	7.7	D	3.7	D	7.6	31.6	6 360	276	704	10 692	0.6
Catawba	0.7	D	3.4	27.3	4.7	8.5	3.7	10.3	11.6	36 945	237	3 066	68 330	0.4
Chatham	4.6	D	5.3	13.0	10.4	7.7	2.3	13.2	16.3	17 495	247	935	31 100	8.1
Cherokee	3.5	D	9.2	10.4	7.8	9.9	5.2	D	20.1	9 675	357	852	17 933	2.4

1. Per 1,000 resident population estimated as of July 1 of the year shown.

Table B. States and Counties — **Housing, Labor Force, and Employment**

STATE County	Housing units, 2011–2015 Occupied units Owner-occupied Total	Percent	Median value[1]	Median owner cost as a percent of income With a mortgage	Without a mortgage[2]	Renter-occupied Median rent[3]	Median rent as a percent of income[2]	Sub-standard units[4] (percent)	Civilian labor force, 2016 Total	Percent change, 2015–2016	Unemployment Total	Rate[5]	Civilian employment[6] 2011–2015 Percent Total	Management, business, science and arts	Construction, production, and maintenance occupations
	89	90	91	92	93	94	95	96	97	98	99	100	101	102	103
NEW YORK—Cont'd															
Genesee	23 938	73.0	107 000	20.6	13.9	724	29.7	1.5	29 892	-1.0	1 366	4.6	29 675	30.4	28.7
Greene	17 634	75.2	177 700	25.1	14.8	837	35.8	1.6	20 613	-0.8	1 037	5.0	19 731	34.0	24.6
Hamilton	1 376	85.5	162 600	23.1	13.4	622	23.8	1.3	2 377	-2.6	154	6.5	1 887	34.0	18.9
Herkimer	26 130	71.0	96 100	20.1	13.7	623	28.1	2.1	28 173	-1.1	1 536	5.5	29 074	32.3	23.9
Jefferson	44 306	55.5	141 000	21.4	13.0	947	28.8	2.4	45 877	-1.7	2 858	6.2	44 732	32.3	21.1
Kings	931 786	29.3	570 200	32.6	15.8	1 215	32.9	11.2	1 223 044	0.4	65 084	5.3	1 167 448	38.5	15.1
Lewis	10 539	76.5	117 300	19.5	12.7	699	31.1	1.4	11 755	-0.4	787	6.7	11 966	29.3	35.0
Livingston	24 226	72.7	121 200	21.6	13.9	721	33.9	2.2	31 218	-0.4	1 531	4.9	30 099	35.2	24.9
Madison	26 288	75.1	124 900	22.0	13.4	718	27.4	1.6	32 770	-0.6	1 718	5.2	33 023	36.9	23.0
Monroe	299 764	64.2	138 600	21.4	13.4	826	33.4	1.4	363 755	-0.7	17 002	4.7	361 948	41.9	16.0
Montgomery	19 539	67.1	101 600	22.1	16.9	702	31.5	3.1	22 458	0.6	1 274	5.7	21 683	29.7	27.7
Nassau	440 640	80.3	446 400	28.6	18.8	1 578	33.7	2.7	698 999	-0.1	27 220	3.9	666 184	43.6	13.9
New York	750 419	22.9	848 700	19.2	10.0	1 519	28.5	6.0	918 498	0.7	41 629	4.5	884 457	59.2	6.2
Niagara	87 807	70.9	108 000	20.3	13.8	654	30.6	1.2	100 789	-0.6	5 818	5.8	100 718	31.7	23.1
Oneida	90 844	65.7	114 000	20.8	13.1	706	30.6	1.7	101 449	-0.9	4 915	4.8	103 944	34.9	20.8
Onondaga	184 641	65.3	135 900	20.6	13.0	787	30.1	1.8	221 090	-0.9	9 943	4.5	220 774	40.8	16.2
Ontario	44 252	72.8	145 700	20.6	13.4	809	30.6	1.4	54 880	-0.6	2 366	4.3	53 394	38.8	20.4
Orange	125 270	68.8	262 500	27.1	17.8	1 155	35.6	3.8	178 440	0.0	7 657	4.3	171 651	35.1	19.7
Orleans	16 016	75.6	91 300	23.3	17.0	639	32.8	3.7	17 825	-0.6	1 011	5.7	17 285	26.7	33.3
Oswego	45 300	72.1	94 800	21.0	13.2	721	32.2	2.4	53 521	-1.2	3 429	6.4	52 204	28.8	28.2
Otsego	23 636	73.4	142 800	22.3	13.4	776	33.2	3.5	28 320	-1.6	1 383	4.9	28 464	36.8	20.7
Putnam	34 090	82.0	354 900	26.9	17.0	1 234	33.5	2.1	50 438	-0.6	2 010	4.0	51 412	40.7	16.6
Queens	780 644	43.6	450 300	31.2	14.7	1 367	33.7	9.8	1 166 302	0.5	52 787	4.5	1 104 930	32.3	18.9
Rensselaer	63 447	65.0	179 100	22.6	13.8	875	29.6	1.7	81 666	-0.2	3 473	4.3	80 144	38.9	19.0
Richmond	165 784	68.8	439 500	28.2	15.4	1 169	32.2	4.4	221 061	0.4	11 575	5.2	209 113	39.2	17.0
Rockland	98 806	68.9	419 100	28.5	18.5	1 335	37.6	6.9	152 418	-0.1	6 355	4.2	146 049	44.0	14.0
St. Lawrence	41 449	71.4	87 600	20.5	13.4	700	32.8	3.1	43 310	-1.6	2 847	6.6	44 714	33.2	21.4
Saratoga	89 921	71.6	232 900	21.7	13.1	993	26.2	0.8	117 060	-0.1	4 441	3.8	113 884	44.1	16.4
Schenectady	56 760	66.5	165 800	22.5	13.8	845	32.5	1.4	75 813	-0.2	3 268	4.3	74 134	38.2	17.0
Schoharie	12 409	76.7	147 000	23.9	15.3	733	28.8	1.9	14 727	0.1	794	5.4	14 179	33.5	25.6
Schuyler	7 686	77.2	108 500	21.1	13.0	640	26.6	2.9	8 291	-1.0	494	6.0	8 125	32.8	26.4
Seneca	13 561	72.3	97 000	21.1	14.0	716	30.5	1.8	15 517	-1.6	735	4.7	15 385	31.6	26.6
Steuben	41 058	70.0	91 000	20.4	12.6	658	26.5	2.2	43 224	-1.4	2 505	5.8	43 199	33.5	27.1
Suffolk	493 849	79.5	375 100	28.8	19.3	1 544	35.7	2.9	777 585	-0.1	33 667	4.3	735 010	37.8	18.9
Sullivan	28 404	65.5	165 900	26.6	15.9	841	31.8	2.5	34 094	0.8	1 620	4.8	32 243	30.3	24.0
Tioga	19 872	78.4	112 600	19.3	12.9	644	28.2	1.6	23 189	-1.1	1 184	5.1	23 960	35.5	24.2
Tompkins	38 460	55.5	176 500	21.3	13.3	988	34.1	1.8	50 358	-0.4	2 079	4.1	49 291	51.8	12.6
Ulster	69 474	69.0	222 800	26.4	17.0	1 013	35.5	2.0	88 256	-0.4	3 889	4.4	85 617	38.9	19.3
Warren	26 788	70.5	189 700	23.4	13.4	862	31.9	1.7	31 981	-1.1	1 677	5.2	31 866	35.5	20.6
Washington	24 237	72.3	142 700	24.0	14.3	803	31.5	1.9	28 481	-0.9	1 322	4.6	28 744	27.4	30.8
Wayne	36 476	77.6	112 900	21.3	14.7	694	31.0	1.7	44 244	-0.4	2 189	4.9	43 117	33.0	28.4
Westchester	341 866	61.5	506 900	26.3	18.0	1 364	33.2	4.4	479 385	-0.1	20 372	4.2	465 097	46.4	12.7
Wyoming	15 787	75.2	102 000	19.8	12.1	589	27.7	1.1	18 165	-1.4	962	5.3	18 495	27.5	31.5
Yates	9 725	76.6	124 200	22.0	12.4	688	30.2	3.2	11 761	-0.1	519	4.4	11 496	31.3	26.3
NORTH CAROLINA	3 775 581	65.1	154 900	22.0	11.7	797	30.3	2.8	4 875 712	2.3	246 377	5.1	4 372 773	36.2	22.7
Alamance	61 545	65.4	138 100	21.6	11.8	745	31.5	3.2	78 973	2.2	3 737	4.7	71 156	31.7	26.2
Alexander	13 581	75.5	124 600	19.6	10.3	584	30.3	3.8	17 910	2.1	767	4.3	16 182	25.5	39.7
Alleghany	4 770	76.4	146 600	23.2	13.4	623	31.1	1.7	4 461	-0.1	248	5.6	4 365	29.8	29.9
Anson	9 511	66.0	76 900	22.6	14.7	661	31.0	3.5	10 777	-0.5	621	5.8	9 875	21.5	41.1
Ashe	11 786	75.4	151 500	25.3	10.6	628	35.4	1.2	12 559	2.0	606	4.8	11 790	26.3	33.0
Avery	6 801	78.0	137 100	25.3	10.6	671	32.7	2.7	7 650	1.6	386	5.0	6 873	26.5	25.3
Beaufort	18 516	70.8	115 100	24.5	14.4	659	30.5	2.0	20 429	1.6	1 162	5.7	18 786	29.3	29.6
Bertie	7 408	73.5	78 400	23.1	18.0	619	33.8	2.3	8 537	-0.7	568	6.7	7 158	23.9	41.5
Bladen	14 401	67.3	85 000	23.9	15.1	629	35.2	2.9	14 723	-0.1	1 020	6.9	13 040	24.9	38.8
Brunswick	49 193	76.1	182 500	25.5	12.5	846	33.9	1.7	49 758	2.5	3 158	6.3	45 213	28.8	23.7
Buncombe	101 860	63.4	192 400	22.9	11.4	829	30.8	3.0	134 843	3.4	5 183	3.8	117 252	38.8	18.9
Burke	34 180	71.3	113 100	22.1	10.3	609	29.3	3.3	40 123	2.0	1 950	4.9	36 632	28.5	31.4
Cabarrus	67 161	71.0	167 100	21.5	10.7	823	28.2	3.5	101 069	3.6	4 577	4.5	87 960	37.4	22.2
Caldwell	31 566	70.7	108 100	21.3	12.3	604	31.7	1.8	36 070	1.7	1 870	5.2	33 837	23.9	34.8
Camden	3 795	84.2	209 800	24.7	13.6	1 186	37.1	2.4	4 636	0.5	243	5.2	4 429	38.2	21.5
Carteret	29 565	71.1	196 800	23.7	12.4	794	28.6	1.9	31 737	1.3	1 637	5.2	29 496	35.5	22.6
Caswell	8 676	77.9	98 400	23.4	12.2	571	32.6	2.4	9 729	1.1	530	5.4	9 276	25.9	30.7
Catawba	58 641	69.5	132 700	20.8	10.3	672	28.6	3.3	76 722	2.1	3 640	4.7	69 954	31.4	29.8
Chatham	26 923	77.2	223 500	22.4	11.8	818	29.3	2.3	34 224	2.5	1 451	4.2	29 621	39.4	24.1
Cherokee	10 592	80.9	142 600	24.7	12.4	666	30.1	2.6	11 134	0.1	628	5.6	9 362	26.4	29.3

1. Specified owner-occupied units.   2. A value of 10.0 represents 10 percent or less; a value of 50.0 represents 50 percent or more.   3. Specified renter-occupied units.
4. Overcrowded or lacking complete plumbing facilities.   5. Percent of civilian labor force.   6. Civilian employed persons 16 years old and over.

STATE County	Number of establish-ments	Total	Health care and social assistance	Manufac-turing	Retail trade	Finance and insurance	Professional, scientific, and technical services	Total (mil dol)	Average per employee (dollars)	Number	Fewer than 50 acres	500 acres or more	Farm operators whose principal occu-pation is farming (percent)
	104	105	106	107	108	109	110	111	112	113	114	115	116
NEW YORK—Cont'd													
Genesee	1 299	16 667	2 878	3 149	2 744	377	307	588	35 280	549	35.3	12.0	56.5
Greene	1 130	10 336	1 182	873	2 096	333	207	330	31 901	273	31.9	5.9	51.3
Hamilton	192	848	41	D	178	11	D	26	30 310	26	34.6	0.0	42.3
Herkimer	1 110	12 157	2 426	2 689	2 006	294	186	413	33 956	687	21.0	7.9	59.7
Jefferson	2 435	29 527	6 232	2 393	6 837	682	872	1 057	35 813	876	20.5	17.2	57.4
Kings	56 426	578 456	189 156	21 271	75 202	15 353	20 263	23 459	40 555	10	100.0	0.0	60.0
Lewis	534	4 650	1 085	1 085	814	81	140	176	37 782	634	18.3	12.5	60.4
Livingston	1 222	13 609	2 138	2 090	2 562	251	385	454	33 397	661	34.2	14.7	55.8
Madison	1 429	17 341	3 156	2 720	2 498	462	643	610	35 169	838	27.3	10.6	58.2
Monroe	17 529	350 506	65 771	35 750	41 659	12 769	23 332	15 736	44 895	475	54.5	10.1	66.7
Montgomery	1 061	14 998	3 937	3 214	2 547	292	233	532	35 480	659	23.2	9.3	67.2
Nassau	47 911	549 909	110 024	16 070	78 602	33 411	44 424	29 476	53 602	55	90.9	1.8	47.3
New York	105 444	2 206 184	244 760	18 504	150 327	292 033	314 283	239 340	108 486	6	100.0	0.0	0.0
Niagara	4 563	60 210	11 143	8 345	11 196	1 321	1 578	2 145	35 631	760	47.2	7.0	52.9
Oneida	4 937	87 729	19 188	9 159	12 047	6 683	3 673	3 291	37 519	1 066	25.7	8.3	56.7
Onondaga	11 794	216 707	39 620	18 152	29 605	11 181	13 666	9 507	43 869	681	44.1	8.8	54.9
Ontario	2 889	46 134	8 420	6 620	9 342	819	1 478	2 325	50 393	853	40.9	10.6	58.0
Orange	9 303	115 980	21 793	7 767	23 244	2 724	6 263	4 448	38 353	658	42.1	4.6	60.6
Orleans	661	8 082	1 312	2 349	1 082	790	131	273	33 744	487	41.9	9.2	55.2
Oswego	2 129	23 952	4 697	2 982	4 467	605	1 048	998	41 686	657	32.6	5.3	54.5
Otsego	1 433	19 323	6 104	917	3 188	1 137	606	752	38 902	995	26.2	6.8	57.3
Putnam	2 872	20 773	5 221	1 227	3 117	622	1 253	923	44 410	72	72.2	4.2	50.0
Queens	48 571	552 349	133 058	21 131	63 914	22 642	15 851	25 708	46 544	6	66.7	0.0	16.7
Rensselaer	2 983	42 832	8 686	3 184	5 857	1 428	3 602	1 926	44 960	495	34.1	8.7	52.3
Richmond	9 147	97 351	31 075	1 151	15 948	2 246	3 580	3 975	40 836	8	100.0	0.0	50.0
Rockland	9 811	106 905	23 909	7 522	14 134	3 169	5 767	4 995	46 720	23	82.6	0.0	65.2
St. Lawrence	1 925	26 728	6 293	2 434	5 238	660	573	991	37 093	1 303	13.7	10.8	60.2
Saratoga	5 235	69 095	9 555	6 034	11 239	3 907	4 333	3 161	45 744	583	46.5	4.5	61.9
Schenectady	3 048	48 594	11 416	4 586	7 582	2 048	3 928	2 165	44 562	169	41.4	3.6	46.2
Schoharie	569	5 134	918	286	1 084	251	177	183	35 625	532	22.0	6.8	62.0
Schuyler	378	3 628	846	641	676	51	46	129	35 484	393	30.8	5.3	50.4
Seneca	711	8 834	1 235	1 526	2 168	160	112	304	34 371	584	30.5	9.1	69.3
Steuben	1 810	25 566	6 231	3 968	4 470	988	1 016	1 253	49 013	1 667	19.3	11.4	51.4
Suffolk	48 768	566 178	97 651	53 161	82 574	21 417	44 096	30 187	53 318	604	70.4	1.5	69.2
Sullivan	1 899	19 523	6 226	1 143	2 804	614	560	639	32 756	321	38.6	7.2	59.5
Tioga	811	7 954	1 114	1 119	1 311	224	238	261	32 848	536	22.9	8.8	54.1
Tompkins	2 369	49 525	5 709	2 600	4 922	1 105	2 239	1 830	36 957	558	43.9	6.8	50.5
Ulster	4 746	45 604	9 359	3 394	9 197	1 895	1 678	1 603	35 156	486	48.4	5.1	67.3
Warren	2 310	31 342	6 172	3 781	6 084	1 214	879	1 263	40 299	117	60.7	0.0	54.7
Washington	1 036	10 324	1 739	3 068	1 827	212	230	402	38 947	851	31.1	11.6	55.6
Wayne	1 743	20 082	3 051	6 057	3 182	553	709	802	39 927	873	38.3	8.6	62.2
Westchester	31 733	380 587	78 042	12 279	50 619	19 711	25 849	25 435	66 830	131	74.8	1.5	58.8
Wyoming	788	9 105	1 409	1 854	1 402	341	319	329	36 154	713	33.0	14.9	62.8
Yates	536	5 014	919	895	752	100	98	154	30 757	919	27.1	3.6	66.6
NORTH CAROLINA	223 209	3 670 284	568 180	423 987	481 681	177 411	211 232	164 936	44 938	50 218	48.1	6.8	48.9
Alamance	3 153	56 328	11 846	9 382	8 815	1 469	1 309	2 167	38 467	732	42.5	4.6	41.7
Alexander	556	7 238	555	3 401	885	166	197	213	29 376	603	55.4	5.0	53.2
Alleghany	244	2 106	517	445	329	67	35	61	28 850	567	43.0	4.6	49.7
Anson	382	5 090	877	1 483	730	91	102	155	30 523	429	26.8	9.3	55.7
Ashe	509	5 084	1 086	754	1 006	218	46	167	32 942	1 140	47.6	2.1	46.4
Avery	483	4 684	883	157	848	90	72	129	27 518	483	63.1	0.8	46.2
Beaufort	1 078	13 545	2 111	3 003	2 270	381	261	467	34 487	364	39.8	21.7	50.5
Bertie	315	4 882	933	2 011	384	64	34	138	28 239	325	30.8	23.1	64.0
Bladen	508	10 208	1 234	5 880	862	156	147	344	33 674	492	42.3	12.4	53.3
Brunswick	2 353	24 642	3 901	1 379	4 976	644	656	863	35 009	254	52.8	7.1	42.9
Buncombe	7 938	110 145	23 943	11 634	17 652	2 683	4 393	4 268	38 750	1 060	64.8	0.9	51.0
Burke	1 427	22 526	4 452	7 804	2 972	384	431	757	33 586	486	58.8	1.6	50.6
Cabarrus	4 117	60 437	9 441	5 897	11 918	960	1 717	2 257	37 349	589	52.0	4.2	50.1
Caldwell	1 319	18 719	3 580	6 319	2 801	360	300	619	33 092	411	56.9	1.7	44.8
Camden	117	530	27	D	111	18	26	16	29 385	60	41.7	36.7	65.0
Carteret	1 920	18 607	3 494	929	4 337	502	510	581	31 232	125	64.8	7.2	48.8
Caswell	233	1 570	365	165	304	51	40	42	26 955	543	32.2	6.6	49.9
Catawba	4 068	79 090	11 620	22 073	9 653	1 341	1 862	3 178	40 185	698	55.6	1.7	41.8
Chatham	1 361	13 637	2 725	1 936	2 249	236	520	436	31 951	1 138	47.0	1.9	45.2
Cherokee	586	6 362	1 082	1 403	1 427	172	297	191	29 947	255	54.1	3.9	54.5

Table B. States and Counties — **Agriculture**

STATE County	Acreage (1,000) 117	Percent change, 2007–2012 118	Average size of farm 119	Total irrigated (1,000) 120	Total cropland (1,000) 121	Value of land and buildings Average per farm (dollars) 122	Average per acre 123	Value of machinery and equipment, average per farm (dollars) 124	Value of products sold Total (mil dol) 125	Average per farm (dollars) 126	Percent from: Crops 127	Live-stock and poultry products 128	Percent of farms with sales of: $10,000 or more 129	$100,000 or more 130	Government payments Total ($1,000) 131	Percent of farms 132
NEW YORK—Cont'd																
Genesee	187	2.1	341	6.3	143.3	898 004	2 632	213 681	237.0	431 607	36.0	64.0	48.1	25.9	2 111	45.5
Greene	43	-3.0	157	0.7	18.7	588 198	3 736	65 901	22.4	82 022	43.5	56.5	40.3	6.2	911	23.8
Hamilton	2	361.8	80	D	0.3	145 692	1 823	28 538	0.3	13 385	D	D	19.2	7.7	0	0.0
Herkimer	140	0.2	204	0.1	76.4	393 428	1 927	92 482	70.4	102 536	25.1	74.9	57.9	21.0	1 414	32.0
Jefferson	291	10.9	332	0.3	173.5	544 535	1 640	133 429	183.6	209 551	24.7	75.3	51.6	24.1	2 974	31.5
Kings	D	D	D	0.0	D	951 000	D	15 000	2.0	199 300	D	D	60.0	40.0	0	0.0
Lewis	182	8.7	287	0.1	97.2	478 692	1 670	145 063	137.0	216 151	17.2	82.8	64.0	35.3	2 400	37.7
Livingston	195	-12.4	295	0.2	149.6	854 528	2 897	176 086	186.8	282 614	43.2	56.8	44.3	22.5	2 425	41.9
Madison	187	-0.4	224	0.8	111.0	456 792	2 042	116 047	117.7	140 489	26.4	73.6	52.0	24.7	2 231	29.2
Monroe	99	-25.8	208	0.9	79.5	737 682	3 551	142 223	90.6	190 695	89.8	10.2	46.1	19.2	1 331	21.7
Montgomery	131	5.5	199	0.2	85.9	458 426	2 299	108 599	86.8	131 701	24.8	75.2	60.8	22.8	1 523	32.0
Nassau	3	108.2	49	0.1	0.3	894 000	18 333	51 509	6.2	113 546	47.9	52.1	47.3	21.8	0	0.0
New York	D	D	D	0.0	0.0	D	D	47 000	D	D	D	D	16.7	0.0	0	0.0
Niagara	143	0.1	188	3.0	118.5	430 664	2 292	136 736	122.7	161 415	62.2	37.8	45.1	14.9	1 684	27.1
Oneida	205	6.7	192	0.2	118.7	383 145	1 991	109 238	113.2	106 181	37.3	62.7	48.2	21.7	2 155	31.5
Onondaga	150	-0.2	221	1.3	101.8	696 072	3 155	166 094	152.1	223 275	31.8	68.2	50.2	19.2	1 688	32.5
Ontario	193	-3.2	226	0.9	148.2	727 475	3 222	149 744	180.3	211 402	42.8	57.2	53.0	25.2	2 675	32.8
Orange	88	8.7	134	2.7	45.8	740 827	5 537	116 939	100.7	153 035	71.5	28.5	59.3	22.9	2 006	27.8
Orleans	135	-3.3	277	4.6	109.5	720 725	2 598	232 292	150.3	308 672	92.1	7.9	46.0	25.5	1 883	39.4
Oswego	94	-6.0	143	0.6	45.4	289 994	2 022	85 426	47.6	72 454	47.3	52.7	39.7	11.6	555	17.8
Otsego	181	2.4	182	0.2	85.5	407 769	2 245	80 409	66.8	67 096	35.6	64.4	42.7	15.8	1 391	21.8
Putnam	6	4.8	82	D	1.6	448 681	5 468	42 181	3.3	45 222	92.2	7.8	29.2	13.9	24	6.9
Queens	0	D	74	0.0	0.4	377 833	1 529	82 333	0.2	26 833	95.7	5.0	100.0	0.0	0	0.0
Rensselaer	89	4.4	179	0.6	50.6	616 113	3 436	104 002	53.1	107 204	52.9	47.1	48.3	16.0	733	30.5
Richmond	D	D	D	0.0	D	440 750	D	D	1.0	120 125	100.0	0.0	50.0	50.0	0	0.0
Rockland	1	D	23	0.1	0.2	1 980 870	86 616	71 913	1.7	75 391	96.5	3.5	56.5	21.7	0	0.0
St. Lawrence	357	2.8	274	0.6	172.1	388 063	1 417	95 682	187.4	143 794	20.7	79.3	48.3	16.7	2 569	20.7
Saratoga	79	4.2	135	0.3	43.8	647 986	4 791	109 096	80.0	137 166	24.3	75.7	43.2	12.9	613	14.2
Schenectady	20	3.9	118	0.1	9.1	406 036	3 454	77 172	4.2	24 621	70.7	29.3	36.7	5.3	101	7.1
Schoharie	98	3.0	185	0.7	55.0	421 389	2 279	86 735	39.5	74 248	39.0	61.0	49.1	13.9	1 105	31.0
Schuyler	69	4.3	176	0.2	38.0	503 155	2 857	92 982	44.5	113 160	29.1	70.9	47.6	17.6	375	16.0
Seneca	130	1.7	223	0.4	98.0	656 699	2 945	168 820	118.9	203 640	44.2	55.8	67.1	39.4	1 017	28.9
Steuben	406	9.1	243	1.2	221.7	446 421	1 834	105 887	187.2	112 301	43.4	56.6	44.6	16.4	3 112	29.8
Suffolk	36	4.6	60	11.8	23.2	696 702	11 697	138 692	239.8	397 050	85.3	14.7	63.7	32.0	790	7.1
Sullivan	54	6.8	168	0.1	22.8	617 897	3 683	74 601	27.1	84 424	15.0	85.0	44.5	13.1	274	18.1
Tioga	108	1.0	201	0.7	50.7	396 076	1 968	83 879	36.7	68 560	30.8	69.2	42.2	14.6	1 112	36.9
Tompkins	91	-16.5	163	0.3	54.4	448 507	2 757	113 717	67.4	120 772	33.7	66.3	43.7	16.1	900	25.8
Ulster	71	-5.3	147	4.2	26.1	738 835	5 042	103 237	55.9	115 019	83.0	17.0	43.0	12.6	328	10.1
Warren	10	11.4	81	0.1	1.5	325 487	3 997	58 376	D	D	D	D	28.2	11.1	0	0.9
Washington	189	-6.6	223	0.6	101.9	539 925	2 426	111 270	139.1	163 510	19.4	80.6	53.3	21.0	2 914	28.6
Wayne	179	6.3	205	1.9	126.3	508 517	2 479	166 179	205.6	235 517	72.7	27.3	60.5	31.2	2 084	27.5
Westchester	8	-9.0	59	0.1	1.5	952 855	16 102	104 863	8.8	67 176	47.6	52.4	46.6	17.6	D	2.3
Wyoming	226	3.6	317	3.4	159.5	828 938	2 617	216 229	318.5	446 711	24.5	75.5	52.7	29.3	3 057	35.1
Yates	127	0.7	138	0.6	88.1	546 444	3 956	115 875	117.0	127 336	37.6	62.4	75.1	45.8	1 081	17.1
NORTH CAROLINA	8 415	-0.7	168	174.5	4 745.0	726 944	4 338	92 882	12 588.1	250 670	34.2	65.8	37.3	16.6	120 129	28.7
Alamance	84	-4.9	114	0.9	31.8	538 171	4 715	60 452	32.9	44 986	46.8	53.2	30.3	9.2	470	17.5
Alexander	59	6.7	97	0.6	20.9	578 788	5 949	70 687	187.7	311 227	5.8	94.2	45.6	28.9	177	6.8
Alleghany	91	18.6	160	D	32.9	770 166	4 803	70 547	36.3	64 092	56.6	43.4	44.1	11.5	590	23.1
Anson	84	-7.9	195	1.1	28.3	725 956	3 725	97 247	193.9	451 900	8.7	91.3	49.4	30.3	551	36.6
Ashe	112	3.7	99	0.2	33.1	561 065	5 687	54 833	54.5	47 790	74.4	25.6	38.1	7.9	216	10.4
Avery	28	1.5	58	0.4	11.6	407 195	6 968	55 195	17.2	35 607	96.1	3.9	44.5	8.1	71	4.8
Beaufort	148	-7.5	407	2.6	129.3	1 244 750	3 056	218 201	121.6	334 074	84.7	15.3	49.2	34.6	3 011	71.7
Bertie	147	-0.4	452	4.2	95.4	1 220 674	2 703	219 246	225.2	692 822	37.4	62.6	68.9	49.2	3 200	74.8
Bladen	117	-7.7	238	4.6	52.9	784 878	3 291	106 965	308.5	627 110	19.3	80.7	46.7	26.2	1 102	38.8
Brunswick	45	3.1	179	1.2	27.4	769 642	4 302	92 492	58.2	229 197	48.0	52.0	34.3	12.6	427	24.8
Buncombe	71	-0.8	67	0.9	17.2	580 025	8 601	48 772	54.4	51 333	72.1	27.9	22.0	4.1	1 481	17.4
Burke	34	18.3	71	1.8	12.9	376 290	5 318	50 689	45.4	93 364	25.0	75.0	30.5	9.9	70	4.5
Cabarrus	66	-0.8	112	0.3	29.9	823 779	7 325	65 380	55.9	94 829	24.8	75.2	25.3	6.3	427	14.3
Caldwell	32	-1.6	78	0.4	11.8	430 625	5 521	45 667	17.8	43 294	53.7	46.3	26.0	7.3	145	6.6
Camden	49	-10.6	822	0.0	46.8	2 334 567	2 841	450 750	48.9	815 217	D	D	56.7	40.0	603	40.0
Carteret	63	13.4	503	0.2	45.5	1 653 072	3 288	92 024	29.2	233 656	98.9	1.2	33.6	15.2	363	18.4
Caswell	97	-5.1	179	1.7	24.8	514 319	2 877	64 361	34.2	63 063	51.7	48.3	29.3	8.5	946	35.4
Catawba	67	-6.7	96	0.7	29.3	519 109	5 400	59 158	67.3	96 430	29.4	70.6	32.2	9.6	447	16.0
Chatham	112	7.3	98	1.2	26.7	487 262	4 961	47 006	163.9	144 033	5.5	94.5	40.3	11.0	546	11.6
Cherokee	21	5.0	84	D	7.6	483 376	5 746	59 451	D	D	D	D	23.1	5.5	232	14.1

STATE County	Water use, 2010		Wholesale trade,[1] 2012				Retail trade,[2] 2012				Real estate and rental and leasing,[2] 2012			
	Total water withdrawn (mil gal/day)	Gallons withdrawn per person per day	Number of establishments	Number of employees	Sales (mil dol)	Annual payroll (mil dol)	Number of establishments	Number of employees	Sales (mil dol)	Annual payroll (mil dol)	Number of establishments	Number of employees	Receipts (mil dol)	Annual payroll (mil dol)
	133	134	135	136	137	138	139	140	141	142	143	144	145	146
NEW YORK—Cont'd														
Genesee	22.9	381	76	1 165	1 187.1	51.6	219	2 561	785.8	59.1	29	150	25.2	5.1
Greene	7.1	143	27	1 007	724.6	63.0	198	2 329	610.4	53.8	43	181	27.1	7.7
Hamilton	1.1	219	NA	NA	NA	NA	33	169	41.6	4.3	7	8	0.9	0.2
Herkimer	11.9	185	30	545	162.1	25.3	187	2 016	543.9	44.9	34	113	15.0	2.4
Jefferson	24.2	208	67	870	345.2	34.7	476	6 849	1 937.9	161.4	119	588	103.9	17.8
Kings	27.6	11	3 457	28 586	16 522.9	1 176.8	9 931	65 979	20 533.1	1 623.7	4 327	15 248	3 765.5	530.6
Lewis	9.2	340	7	D	D	D	74	792	258.7	19.8	12	D	D	D
Livingston	15.6	238	51	560	458.9	24.0	219	2 501	633.6	55.0	40	206	22.9	5.8
Madison	4.0	55	36	434	151.0	16.9	222	2 688	745.5	61.9	43	148	12.1	3.5
Monroe	121.9	164	788	10 459	6 131.6	562.0	2 349	40 491	9 494.1	902.0	835	6 237	1 091.2	233.4
Montgomery	10.6	211	44	D	D	D	179	2 461	673.3	55.4	22	80	10.2	1.9
Nassau	532.2	397	2 856	28 767	27 959.1	1 860.3	6 145	77 488	24 105.6	2 206.3	2 331	9 580	3 054.1	532.1
New York	29.4	19	7 678	84 273	128 760.9	6 385.0	11 691	148 493	44 040.0	5 027.8	9 627	70 399	33 323.0	4 826.9
Niagara	367.5	1 698	179	2 187	1 506.4	95.0	735	10 233	2 521.6	212.7	144	563	81.8	16.1
Oneida	36.3	155	175	2 081	1 087.5	90.9	830	11 889	3 012.2	263.6	170	686	111.9	20.0
Onondaga	109.2	234	591	10 750	17 113.3	559.0	1 682	28 932	6 916.0	639.1	588	3 756	662.3	150.5
Ontario	17.5	162	113	1 285	660.2	65.9	527	9 194	2 021.4	193.8	94	423	53.8	10.1
Orange	374.4	1 004	455	6 661	8 298.4	304.8	1 512	23 117	6 221.1	530.6	374	1 407	407.3	51.5
Orleans	7.4	171	17	281	130.4	14.3	95	1 097	252.4	22.6	20	61	9.4	1.3
Oswego	985.4	8 070	58	504	368.3	21.8	353	4 392	1 258.4	101.6	69	205	29.6	5.0
Otsego	7.4	119	46	460	308.8	19.6	290	3 373	917.0	78.7	53	215	32.7	6.9
Putnam	6.7	67	101	905	516.3	50.3	329	3 037	952.2	79.7	89	209	33.9	7.9
Queens	1 244.3	558	2 971	24 171	16 059.4	1 250.3	7 388	59 829	17 003.2	1 542.4	2 840	11 679	3 100.3	509.9
Rensselaer	22.1	139	101	1 200	2 270.2	67.3	424	5 814	1 572.2	138.4	101	464	103.0	15.5
Richmond	350.6	748	342	1 416	1 460.0	75.0	1 273	15 926	3 816.0	353.5	312	1 151	377.5	43.8
Rockland	133.3	428	504	4 697	3 892.0	282.0	1 154	14 253	4 153.7	382.2	443	1 498	281.1	55.0
St. Lawrence	23.9	214	46	446	175.0	19.9	414	5 139	1 446.6	116.3	57	167	32.7	5.0
Saratoga	39.4	179	176	3 133	2 332.0	181.5	724	10 871	2 980.0	250.5	213	975	233.2	33.5
Schenectady	40.7	263	78	774	519.3	37.3	480	7 256	1 821.1	167.3	111	510	112.4	19.5
Schoharie	169.7	5 183	19	118	54.9	4.4	95	1 049	319.0	23.9	15	46	7.2	1.5
Schuyler	20.7	1 131	3	D	D	D	59	633	141.4	12.9	5	D	D	D
Seneca	8.2	233	27	410	202.5	13.1	183	2 360	489.9	43.9	19	77	26.0	1.9
Steuben	17.7	178	40	277	122.4	9.3	326	4 238	1 074.0	95.9	51	232	32.5	8.7
Suffolk	604.0	404	2 838	37 819	32 383.0	2 260.5	6 524	79 498	23 693.4	2 182.4	1 677	6 519	1 868.5	303.8
Sullivan	102.6	1 322	43	584	363.6	21.5	291	2 673	771.5	66.5	111	398	55.5	9.6
Tioga	6.3	123	25	331	396.9	14.3	132	1 367	372.9	32.4	12	23	3.3	0.6
Tompkins	232.7	2 291	36	454	259.0	21.6	349	5 071	1 112.0	105.5	112	609	121.6	20.5
Ulster	458.2	2 511	159	1 504	810.4	71.3	733	8 606	2 324.9	211.8	195	732	116.6	22.0
Warren	54.2	824	59	575	190.4	21.0	447	6 436	1 549.1	149.5	74	240	45.0	8.9
Washington	32.6	516	30	D	D	D	186	1 759	498.8	42.4	17	46	4.8	1.0
Wayne	475.6	5 072	62	607	245.7	22.7	267	3 276	822.6	75.5	58	223	24.7	4.2
Westchester	2 044.6	2 154	1 286	16 494	20 313.9	1 493.5	3 802	48 739	14 514.2	1 395.5	1 966	8 041	2 436.5	399.2
Wyoming	18.8	447	26	219	121.9	9.8	128	1 479	376.0	33.0	18	99	11.3	2.8
Yates	76.6	3 024	10	127	41.0	3.4	92	814	208.9	17.8	22	79	10.2	2.5
NORTH CAROLINA	12 420.1	1 303	9 713	136 174	105 275.6	7 853.7	34 288	446 373	120 691.0	10 421.2	10 140	47 155	9 301.7	1 942.6
Alamance	23.9	158	143	1 642	627.2	70.0	624	8 756	2 108.4	178.0	119	607	142.0	24.4
Alexander	4.2	114	17	111	47.8	4.5	86	834	194.8	17.6	10	18	1.6	0.3
Alleghany	5.5	497	3	4	1.1	0.7	41	296	67.9	5.9	10	19	1.7	0.3
Anson	9.5	354	11	203	109.4	10.3	73	726	181.3	14.7	9	D	D	D
Ashe	17.5	641	22	214	101.9	7.0	106	1 020	273.0	22.4	24	48	7.9	1.8
Avery	19.9	1 120	18	D	D	D	82	742	195.5	15.6	32	D	D	D
Beaufort	89.9	1 882	51	477	360.7	20.7	189	2 300	548.4	51.4	36	133	16.6	2.8
Bertie	20.8	978	14	126	145.6	4.7	50	357	95.9	6.7	4	5	0.2	0.1
Bladen	93.2	2 647	22	174	226.7	6.9	91	823	199.5	15.9	14	27	5.2	0.7
Brunswick	1 384.0	12 882	69	544	237.1	21.6	371	4 423	1 125.8	100.7	128	556	85.0	20.2
Buncombe	300.6	1 261	265	2 532	1 286.7	110.6	1 135	16 104	3 884.2	381.4	393	1 287	238.0	43.0
Burke	38.9	428	48	431	226.2	17.4	260	2 541	680.5	54.9	50	128	15.0	3.0
Cabarrus	22.7	127	191	2 454	1 600.3	115.7	708	11 637	2 920.3	247.7	171	645	115.6	18.8
Caldwell	19.7	237	64	411	202.3	16.4	256	2 740	701.0	58.2	58	137	16.7	3.4
Camden	6.1	614	3	17	4.1	0.4	17	94	24.9	1.7	4	4	1.2	0.1
Carteret	10.7	160	47	272	85.7	9.8	363	3 885	972.8	89.3	118	529	63.7	13.5
Caswell	4.2	178	5	D	D	D	49	309	63.9	6.5	1	D	D	D
Catawba	1 076.7	6 975	238	5 320	4 053.8	244.5	715	9 502	2 607.3	222.3	187	534	130.5	17.0
Chatham	246.4	3 880	52	311	115.0	12.6	175	2 089	583.0	43.6	36	80	15.0	2.5
Cherokee	21.8	794	15	149	84.4	4.4	130	1 302	363.6	28.6	26	67	15.4	1.8

1. Merchant wholesalers, except manufacturers' sales branches and offices.   2. Employer establishments.

Table B. States and Counties — Professional Services, Manufacturing, and Accommodation and Food Services

STATE County	Professional, scientific, and technical services, 2012				Manufacturing, 2012				Accommodation and food services, 2012			
	Number of establishments	Number of employees	Receipts (mil dol)	Annual payroll (mil dol)	Number of establishments	Number of employees	Receipts (mil dol)	Annual payroll (mil dol)	Number of establishments	Number of employees	Sales (mil dol)	Annual payroll (mil dol)
	147	148	149	150	151	152	153	154	155	156	157	158
NEW YORK—Cont'd												
Genesee	76	322	28.3	11.5	95	2 632	983.0	125.8	144	1 910	89.9	25.2
Greene	76	258	27.5	9.9	29	735	339.8	D	191	2 675	99.2	29.4
Hamilton	2	D	D	D	3	8	D	D	57	234	22.8	4.8
Herkimer	61	184	18.3	5.9	60	2 561	666.2	119.4	168	1 469	71.3	19.9
Jefferson	142	1 092	115.9	45.4	66	2 247	770.5	102.6	335	4 117	198.8	57.0
Kings	4 346	23 391	3 467.9	1 312.8	1 756	18 296	3 644.1	731.0	4 809	34 099	2 453.4	615.5
Lewis	23	82	9.5	2.5	25	1 371	532.7	58.1	64	480	19.1	5.5
Livingston	98	374	31.7	10.9	55	2 106	635.9	91.1	142	2 123	80.4	23.4
Madison	121	681	66.5	27.7	58	2 407	885.5	109.2	164	2 024	86.4	23.8
Monroe	1 973	21 387	3 187.1	1 263.9	887	38 958	14 610.3	2 315.5	1 662	26 555	1 300.3	370.6
Montgomery	61	252	25.1	7.5	74	3 578	839.0	134.3	117	948	49.2	12.0
Nassau	6 835	43 568	6 915.5	2 542.9	1 043	16 580	5 196.7	893.7	3 483	43 996	2 938.8	818.0
New York	17 504	289 103	88 609.6	31 491.6	2 063	21 220	4 970.9	899.1	9 634	206 517	20 382.6	6 032.2
Niagara	325	1 810	234.9	86.1	273	7 987	3 134.9	463.1	521	9 841	1 055.9	183.3
Oneida	408	3 645	555.6	210.0	236	9 807	3 481.3	462.0	559	10 870	791.3	199.6
Onondaga	1 179	13 456	2 065.5	767.9	436	18 565	7 576.0	1 034.6	1 146	18 791	918.7	265.5
Ontario	239	1 469	195.5	79.9	167	6 718	2 671.0	332.4	302	4 879	237.3	72.3
Orange	872	5 909	648.5	248.4	318	7 105	2 592.4	336.9	847	9 601	575.2	150.4
Orleans	35	168	15.0	5.2	36	2 026	764.6	96.5	57	692	28.4	7.9
Oswego	135	546	55.0	19.7	85	2 669	2 131.1	139.6	290	3 599	153.2	41.2
Otsego	116	623	54.1	19.6	58	877	203.8	37.7	210	2 560	148.5	37.6
Putnam	311	1 246	208.6	74.9	87	1 478	308.6	74.3	195	1 604	100.4	26.3
Queens	3 248	13 293	1 585.1	669.1	1 294	22 240	4 438.1	972.5	4 558	40 510	3 139.1	749.9
Rensselaer	280	3 464	460.4	193.0	95	3 383	D	176.2	348	4 009	209.2	58.6
Richmond	873	3 535	663.0	169.2	136	999	285.3	44.8	770	7 805	472.6	109.8
Rockland	1 272	5 270	1 616.3	341.6	251	8 416	9 613.2	601.3	769	7 762	501.2	140.1
St. Lawrence	107	611	55.8	21.1	77	2 639	1 302.9	149.6	256	2 904	131.6	34.0
Saratoga	605	3 852	608.6	210.2	138	5 259	1 977.4	331.6	524	8 089	446.4	128.6
Schenectady	276	3 772	207.5	284.3	110	4 490	1 709.3	283.0	339	3 846	191.7	54.9
Schoharie	36	208	18.4	6.5	21	239	D	9.5	62	459	23.1	6.5
Schuyler	15	38	2.5	0.7	35	574	D	30.4	62	572	34.9	9.2
Seneca	35	139	14.4	3.8	40	1 318	674.2	68.8	72	744	35.3	11.0
Steuben	133	1 707	89.4	157.7	77	4 314	1 237.0	212.9	223	2 562	132.2	34.0
Suffolk	5 622	43 771	6 531.9	2 657.2	2 067	51 967	15 887.4	2 800.5	3 624	45 646	2 990.4	810.8
Sullivan	167	D	D	D	51	1 224	354.0	41.0	243	1 572	139.6	34.7
Tioga	55	D	D	D	44	1 228	438.2	48.6	89	829	36.2	10.6
Tompkins	274	2 312	356.6	124.1	93	2 766	861.1	150.4	334	4 408	231.7	65.4
Ulster	443	1 601	189.3	69.1	170	3 518	D	170.2	546	6 655	367.3	117.4
Warren	168	876	106.7	40.0	76	3 767	928.9	206.4	413	3 992	306.1	85.9
Washington	61	235	35.1	9.2	87	2 942	1 206.2	152.3	127	758	38.0	9.7
Wayne	105	589	116.2	26.9	137	5 702	1 656.8	241.8	165	1 732	71.7	19.1
Westchester	4 205	28 162	4 976.7	2 187.8	601	11 776	4 492.9	584.9	2 460	26 862	2 020.0	562.8
Wyoming	62	351	41.9	10.8	44	1 878	473.7	76.3	81	747	31.7	9.0
Yates	31	118	10.6	3.9	44	836	188.5	33.3	55	382	22.7	6.4
NORTH CAROLINA	22 855	196 287	31 947.9	12 940.3	8 953	403 593	202 344.6	18 191.2	19 496	358 602	18 622.3	5 040.6
Alamance	218	1 375	133.0	55.8	200	9 268	3 138.4	399.3	293	5 761	254.4	71.8
Alexander	37	123	11.5	4.2	69	3 284	591.5	107.7	38	D	D	D
Alleghany	12	40	3.1	0.9	17	444	D	15.6	22	211	10.8	3.3
Anson	27	116	10.0	3.2	20	1 428	393.3	54.5	29	401	16.8	4.7
Ashe	24	58	3.5	1.3	20	1 122	232.7	36.1	46	573	23.7	6.7
Avery	29	66	7.2	2.1	13	174	20.5	5.2	59	593	45.6	12.9
Beaufort	88	341	26.2	9.5	64	2 661	1 462.1	152.1	73	1 141	50.1	12.5
Bertie	11	51	4.9	1.5	11	D	D	42.4	15	166	6.5	1.6
Bladen	33	143	17.7	5.0	28	5 565	1 904.3	178.5	46	448	25.6	6.3
Brunswick	196	637	57.7	22.2	71	1 520	1 983.0	101.4	271	3 436	180.8	48.7
Buncombe	873	4 336	473.4	206.2	287	13 805	2 839.5	590.9	735	14 976	880.1	254.3
Burke	110	464	44.3	16.3	126	7 475	2 804.6	288.8	127	2 102	97.2	25.2
Cabarrus	338	1 505	193.8	73.3	162	5 427	1 757.9	237.4	346	8 214	428.0	113.7
Caldwell	79	324	31.9	10.5	121	6 098	1 158.1	197.1	117	D	D	D
Camden	7	28	3.0	1.5	NA	NA	NA	NA	3	28	1.5	0.4
Carteret	122	447	49.2	18.9	61	981	343.7	32.9	229	3 318	164.4	48.3
Caswell	13	37	3.5	1.4	9	172	33.3	5.6	13	D	D	D
Catawba	322	1 627	654.5	71.2	411	20 830	5 850.9	809.8	342	6 737	290.7	83.7
Chatham	145	468	59.6	22.2	72	1 538	487.4	66.7	103	1 674	91.3	25.5
Cherokee	37	250	15.7	8.3	26	1 168	317.1	41.8	61	817	41.0	11.3

1. Establishment subject to federal tax.

Table B. States and Counties — **Health Care and Social Assistance, Other Services, Nonemployer Businesses, and Residential Construction**

STATE County	Health care and social assistance, 2012				Other services, 2012				Nonemployer businesses, 2015		Value of residential construction authorized by building permits, 2016	
	Number of establish-ments	Number of employees	Receipts (mil dol)	Annual payroll (mil dol)	Number of establish-ments	Number of employees	Receipts (mil dol)	Annual payroll (mil dol)	Number	Receipts (mil dol)	New Construction ($1,000)	Number of housing units
	159	160	161	162	163	164	165	166	167	168	169	170
NEW YORK—Cont'd												
Genesee	141	3 053	221.6	98.7	100	626	51.8	15.0	2 924	126.3	9 040	39
Greene	94	1 254	88.1	38.8	83	373	32.7	8.2	3 417	139.8	20 508	87
Hamilton	6	25	1.7	0.8	7	D	D	D	479	19.9	8 239	53
Herkimer	109	2 334	184.1	70.5	94	552	32.1	8.3	3 294	133.4	21 157	71
Jefferson	277	6 183	536.8	247.5	187	912	83.3	21.0	5 164	206.7	12 454	105
Kings	6 394	184 851	16 419.6	7 123.6	4 675	18 153	1 622.5	431.4	263 777	11 593.7	619 962	4 503
Lewis	49	1 071	83.2	41.4	43	164	21.1	4.7	1 676	73.0	9 805	99
Livingston	143	2 019	140.2	61.2	88	337	39.3	8.6	3 552	147.3	11 455	112
Madison	166	3 027	272.9	110.7	98	349	30.6	7.1	4 274	167.0	20 330	105
Monroe	1 949	63 159	5 819.8	2 425.3	1 151	7 580	772.3	209.4	44 438	2 054.7	210 246	1 257
Montgomery	177	3 970	356.9	149.6	87	558	57.5	15.4	2 409	87.4	5 498	30
Nassau	5 771	111 832	13 166.2	5 522.1	4 068	21 377	2 140.6	587.0	136 547	9 394.4	321 252	741
New York	8 106	251 513	34 680.5	13 322.5	9 778	92 777	21 846.1	4 572.6	225 955	18 263.9	540 463	4 024
Niagara	512	10 096	789.4	345.9	341	1 593	109.0	31.0	9 638	378.2	48 984	229
Oneida	615	19 043	1 636.6	730.7	407	3 677	219.0	74.3	12 141	486.1	28 243	163
Onondaga	1 294	38 389	4 379.2	1 717.8	876	5 965	613.6	178.1	27 513	1 292.0	173 245	1 130
Ontario	274	8 001	685.0	340.7	211	1 252	98.6	30.5	6 872	304.9	111 266	513
Orange	961	20 593	2 176.8	957.3	749	3 963	460.3	108.4	24 613	1 149.2	166 907	1 027
Orleans	78	1 544	96.0	46.2	63	209	20.6	4.7	1 775	70.3	4 467	26
Oswego	206	4 897	347.9	156.5	183	699	57.4	13.7	5 441	189.3	25 780	135
Otsego	170	6 049	675.4	281.4	103	617	51.3	11.6	4 321	167.4	11 808	97
Putnam	261	5 055	559.1	239.5	233	1 035	118.0	32.3	9 048	454.6	14 381	50
Queens	5 047	122 646	12 103.5	5 098.2	4 645	19 428	1 863.4	500.0	243 480	9 284.7	403 536	2 849
Rensselaer	354	9 708	732.3	349.1	244	1 361	122.5	48.0	8 769	349.8	51 068	334
Richmond	1 308	30 614	2 960.7	1 274.1	869	3 779	342.3	85.5	35 265	1 602.7	147 626	901
Rockland	1 164	22 289	2 083.5	900.8	731	4 364	350.9	106.5	27 296	1 662.6	56 966	303
St. Lawrence	260	6 640	581.7	259.6	170	706	64.8	14.5	4 942	183.0	27 074	205
Saratoga	544	8 412	761.2	317.9	321	1 668	145.3	45.5	15 563	764.3	278 780	1 278
Schenectady	435	11 854	1 005.7	439.2	205	D	D	D	8 481	337.4	46 304	473
Schoharie	62	1 039	69.9	30.7	31	D	D	D	1 840	69.0	5 589	28
Schuyler	39	836	57.5	27.4	34	D	D	D	1 177	38.4	10 743	78
Seneca	63	1 335	82.0	40.4	49	233	19.1	4.6	1 810	74.8	13 177	75
Steuben	238	5 701	488.2	227.8	148	663	59.6	14.5	5 222	206.3	12 479	80
Suffolk	4 736	95 248	10 416.2	4 491.2	3 945	19 049	2 048.8	520.1	127 010	7 166.4	650 568	1 055
Sullivan	250	5 491	412.0	186.4	160	456	66.6	12.0	5 649	235.9	50 193	284
Tioga	68	1 045	54.3	26.7	65	205	20.3	4.8	2 766	105.1	12 448	99
Tompkins	271	5 283	483.0	199.8	152	966	122.9	23.9	7 389	276.1	79 641	575
Ulster	514	8 991	741.4	312.4	322	1 229	114.9	28.6	16 327	691.2	53 800	252
Warren	283	6 574	569.0	261.1	140	817	84.1	26.0	4 727	225.9	54 750	276
Washington	105	1 535	96.2	44.5	78	271	28.6	7.7	3 714	148.8	7 224	83
Wayne	151	3 061	215.0	102.9	133	434	36.2	9.0	4 759	193.5	20 804	108
Westchester	3 592	79 057	9 638.2	4 111.1	2 819	15 205	2 013.8	539.3	95 840	6 412.8	323 829	1 483
Wyoming	68	1 183	94.2	40.9	62	246	21.7	5.7	2 054	89.5	3 075	24
Yates	50	975	64.1	28.0	45	147	12.3	2.7	1 951	94.1	12 610	51
NORTH CAROLINA	22 977	529 570	55 227.5	21 757.0	13 716	80 710	9 141.5	2 321.3	722 639	30 019.8	11 091 052	60 550
Alamance	379	8 367	801.9	369.4	190	1 097	100.7	29.2	9 727	371.5	175 101	1 353
Alexander	43	559	33.5	14.6	36	139	9.8	2.1	2 254	81.3	15 106	43
Alleghany	27	517	31.1	13.8	10	D	D	D	899	36.2	6 920	29
Anson	45	826	50.7	24.7	21	D	D	D	1 252	42.3	6 115	41
Ashe	51	1 136	73.3	35.1	32	118	10.4	2.8	2 425	96.6	16 883	84
Avery	41	746	72.2	25.4	25	180	20.4	5.1	1 668	60.8	35 123	90
Beaufort	120	2 392	186.5	77.6	80	384	32.1	8.6	3 259	125.4	21 369	216
Bertie	57	1 344	63.4	28.5	18	62	5.3	1.4	890	25.2	3 894	25
Bladen	56	998	52.7	19.8	29	D	D	D	1 734	55.3	7 440	41
Brunswick	221	3 576	326.6	127.5	119	463	45.3	12.0	10 217	421.7	592 006	2 428
Buncombe	844	20 510	2 518.2	1 012.7	456	2 461	261.7	69.8	26 258	1 110.9	408 183	2 422
Burke	187	4 495	461.5	183.6	99	434	41.1	11.1	5 238	195.8	32 159	184
Cabarrus	343	6 008	568.1	244.2	266	1 435	119.0	31.6	14 505	543.7	243 113	1 918
Caldwell	132	2 924	234.4	88.5	79	397	39.0	10.9	4 961	185.9	24 627	93
Camden	5	24	1.4	0.6	7	D	D	D	671	19.8	9 906	36
Carteret	191	3 165	283.7	120.4	143	598	51.3	15.5	6 408	275.9	85 041	329
Caswell	29	467	23.7	11.6	14	D	D	D	1 081	36.0	9 141	43
Catawba	382	11 445	1 153.6	446.6	223	1 410	109.8	31.8	10 603	505.0	70 739	335
Chatham	127	2 581	179.1	67.4	83	306	36.8	8.7	5 895	265.3	201 203	707
Cherokee	76	1 217	96.7	41.9	35	103	7.6	2.2	2 227	78.9	26 454	184

Table B. States and Counties — Government Employment and Payroll, and Local Government Finances

STATE County	Full-time equivalent employees	March payroll (dollars)	Administration, judicial, and legal	Police and Corrections	Fire Protection	Highways and transportation	Health and Welfare	Natural resources and utilities	Education and libraries	Total (mil dol)	Inter-governmental (mil dol)	Total (mil dol)	Per capita Total	Per capita Property
	171	172	173	174	175	176	177	178	179	180	181	182	183	184
NEW YORK—Cont'd														
Genesee.....................	3 495	13 011 030	5.1	5.8	1.6	4.1	10.0	1.1	70.6	378.8	154.3	137.4	2 290	1 468
Greene.....................	2 313	9 425 632	7.2	6.0	0.0	7.6	11.6	1.6	64.8	291.0	101.2	151.7	3 117	2 471
Hamilton...................	511	1 883 521	13.9	3.7	0.5	18.0	10.6	5.4	45.2	54.6	10.1	40.8	8 548	7 863
Herkimer..................	3 357	17 320 913	6.2	16.3	10.9	9.4	4.5	5.4	45.2	354.3	171.8	137.0	2 124	1 648
Jefferson.................	5 239	20 682 670	6.0	6.1	2.2	6.7	6.7	3.0	66.9	631.5	312.9	217.3	1 807	1 154
Kings.....................	(3)	(3)	(3)	(3)	(3)	(3)	(3)	(3)	(3)	(3)	(3)	(3)	(3)	(3)
Lewis.....................	1 643	6 393 465	5.3	4.0	0.1	9.3	34.1	0.3	46.2	221.0	80.0	54.5	2 001	1 591
Livingston...............	2 962	11 287 932	7.2	8.2	0.0	6.5	18.2	2.0	56.7	340.1	136.2	132.2	2 039	1 556
Madison...................	2 860	10 880 867	5.6	7.3	1.1	8.0	7.4	2.2	66.8	324.2	144.9	143.1	1 977	1 638
Monroe....................	32 909	147 986 255	4.0	10.2	3.5	2.4	4.8	4.9	68.8	4 246.2	1 878.0	1 825.1	2 441	1 824
Montgomery............	2 237	9 439 506	8.2	8.8	2.4	6.9	5.7	2.1	64.3	270.8	126.1	103.0	2 062	1 500
Nassau...................	60 368	360 394 360	4.0	11.4	0.7	2.4	9.9	3.6	66.2	10 545.3	2 263.0	7 088.6	5 254	4 380
New York................	(3)411 393	(3)36 392 993	(3)3.2	(3)18.6	(3)5.3	(3)14.2	(3)17.3	(3)4.7	(3)33.2	(3)89 561.8	(3)30 794.6	(3)42 487.9	(3)5 096	(3)2 183
Niagara..................	8 942	40 897 207	4.2	9.3	3.5	3.3	5.7	3.9	65.8	1 197.2	504.4	461.1	2 144	1 505
Oneida...................	10 265	43 288 880	5.1	9.3	3.3	5.7	6.1	4.4	65.3	1 243.2	607.6	466.1	1 996	1 316
Onondaga...............	21 333	98 896 686	3.5	9.2	2.8	3.6	6.0	5.0	68.2	2 768.2	1 213.5	1 131.6	2 424	1 706
Ontario..................	5 314	22 633 286	7.3	8.2	1.0	4.3	6.4	3.2	68.2	617.9	231.6	291.0	2 682	1 907
Orange...................	15 475	79 024 558	5.0	9.7	1.3	3.8	7.6	2.1	69.2	2 388.1	851.1	1 242.0	3 316	2 623
Orleans..................	1 883	7 322 413	5.8	7.3	1.3	4.6	12.9	1.4	65.5	215.9	108.4	76.5	1 785	1 393
Oswego.................	5 833	24 108 601	4.0	4.7	1.8	4.8	6.7	1.2	74.7	720.3	332.9	266.4	2 189	1 640
Otsego..................	2 867	10 320 001	6.5	5.1	1.5	9.1	12.9	1.2	62.0	319.5	134.0	135.1	2 189	1 567
Putnam..................	3 780	21 486 132	6.3	9.6	0.0	4.8	5.6	1.1	71.4	620.4	156.8	423.9	4 256	3 653
Queens.................	(3)	(3)	(3)	(3)	(3)	(3)	(3)	(3)	(3)	(3)	(3)	(3)	(3)	(3)
Rensselaer............	7 740	35 240 411	5.4	10.0	1.8	3.0	10.0	3.2	65.6	935.0	383.9	372.9	2 333	1 782
Richmond...............	(3)	(3)	(3)	(3)	(3)	(3)	(3)	(3)	(3)	(3)	(3)	(3)	(3)	(3)
Rockland...............	12 621	72 071 900	6.2	11.8	0.2	3.4	10.5	3.3	63.3	2 081.2	511.7	1 307.8	4 116	3 491
St. Lawrence...........	5 029	19 319 273	5.7	6.1	1.0	8.5	20.0	3.1	54.2	629.7	288.6	207.1	1 845	1 390
Saratoga...............	8 393	36 185 319	5.4	6.8	1.4	6.5	7.0	2.5	68.7	1 010.7	328.4	547.9	2 467	1 874
Schenectady.........	6 336	30 200 971	4.8	10.8	2.9	3.7	8.4	3.1	64.2	840.2	334.0	398.5	2 569	1 914
Schoharie.............	1 588	6 242 263	7.0	4.8	0.1	8.7	8.1	2.1	67.7	198.0	92.7	86.5	2 696	2 164
Schuyler...............	713	2 598 532	9.7	8.4	0.0	8.0	12.3	2.8	55.9	92.6	40.4	41.0	2 213	1 616
Seneca.................	1 397	5 203 170	7.6	6.3	0.0	6.3	10.3	4.6	63.8	187.5	82.2	75.2	2 129	1 460
Steuben................	5 430	22 838 751	6.3	4.7	1.6	6.5	9.0	2.5	68.7	603.0	285.7	219.9	2 220	1 686
Suffolk.................	63 444	372 480 221	4.1	12.0	1.0	2.5	5.0	2.8	71.0	10 433.2	3 062.8	6 438.8	4 295	3 385
Sullivan................	3 903	18 183 844	6.0	6.2	4.1	7.1	11.7	2.9	59.7	571.4	182.8	285.0	3 711	3 207
Tioga...................	2 377	8 831 267	4.9	6.4	0.5	4.3	7.4	1.1	72.8	263.8	126.3	98.9	1 959	1 427
Tompkins..............	4 530	19 870 493	5.0	6.2	2.8	4.4	7.3	3.5	68.0	531.9	184.0	252.8	2 465	1 857
Ulster..................	8 282	38 442 668	5.7	7.7	1.3	4.8	8.8	1.7	68.0	1 095.2	330.4	630.3	3 467	2 848
Warren.................	3 395	12 916 351	7.7	10.3	0.3	8.0	7.0	4.0	60.4	411.0	122.0	230.3	3 513	2 589
Washington...........	3 303	11 817 292	4.2	5.9	0.6	5.8	10.6	1.3	70.1	334.5	150.3	129.8	2 063	1 703
Wayne..................	4 573	16 899 070	5.7	6.6	0.1	4.5	9.5	2.2	70.0	506.8	227.4	194.1	2 088	1 627
Westchester..........	42 725	278 687 815	4.6	13.0	4.0	2.1	14.4	4.1	55.6	8 694.6	1 905.2	4 937.7	5 135	4 223
Wyoming...............	1 997	7 253 253	6.6	6.7	0.7	6.2	29.3	3.6	45.9	224.2	78.4	71.1	1 698	1 279
Yates...................	984	3 705 476	8.7	13.4	0.2	8.3	6.2	2.9	58.0	114.7	43.0	58.3	2 300	1 770
NORTH CAROLINA.....	X	X	X	X	X	X	X	X	X	X	X	X	X	X
Alamance..............	1 005 835	17 822 770	4.1	10.8	2.8	1.7	7.8	5.8	64.0	420.3	210.4	147.7	960	694
Alexander.............	1 147	3 312 277	3.5	5.4	1.2	0.1	15.0	1.1	71.6	79.1	47.9	22.9	622	467
Alleghany.............	425	1 164 658	3.2	4.3	0.0	1.2	5.7	2.7	76.9	29.9	16.8	10.5	964	802
Anson..................	1 315	3 876 045	2.9	6.4	2.5	0.6	7.2	4.8	74.4	91.7	58.9	20.0	760	612
Ashe...................	790	2 611 411	5.6	7.1	0.0	1.1	16.3	2.1	65.4	64.2	34.4	23.7	876	672
Avery..................	815	1 974 739	6.6	9.8	1.1	1.1	14.1	2.6	59.8	51.3	22.8	24.5	1 387	1 109
Beaufort...............	2 278	5 974 850	4.5	7.2	2.1	0.6	8.3	10.0	62.5	173.8	99.8	49.9	1 050	812
Bertie..................	997	3 093 286	5.9	4.6	0.1	0.6	4.8	2.9	80.8	51.4	32.6	12.0	580	454
Bladen.................	1 399	4 935 403	2.7	6.3	0.5	0.4	11.2	2.6	74.0	133.3	64.5	29.1	834	667
Brunswick.............	3 900	12 967 182	6.8	10.3	1.5	1.3	19.2	7.5	47.9	393.3	118.2	177.6	1 582	1 215
Buncombe.............	8 896	30 002 974	4.8	8.2	3.6	1.6	11.7	7.3	59.6	751.0	306.2	322.9	1 321	936
Burke..................	3 144	9 746 027	4.9	6.5	1.0	0.9	9.1	5.9	70.6	228.4	129.8	66.9	739	594
Cabarrus...............	7 505	25 676 197	3.6	8.3	4.5	1.2	14.4	6.7	58.7	601.3	252.6	258.8	1 403	1 100
Caldwell...............	3 445	10 357 515	2.9	6.0	2.1	0.6	13.9	3.0	69.5	257.1	164.6	64.8	791	595
Camden................	352	1 014 214	1.0	5.8	0.0	0.0	0.0	4.2	71.8	30.3	17.1	11.7	1 163	952
Carteret...............	2 554	7 543 452	5.4	9.0	4.8	1.2	10.1	4.3	60.9	338.2	84.6	98.9	1 462	1 061
Caswell................	710	2 061 989	3.0	5.5	0.0	0.0	17.8	1.7	67.9	51.5	32.9	13.2	569	464
Catawba...............	7 515	27 058 433	3.4	5.6	2.5	1.6	35.0	3.0	45.2	716.3	255.5	171.8	1 113	804
Chatham...............	1 616	6 230 991	4.0	6.8	0.3	0.8	10.6	4.0	68.1	164.8	66.0	78.0	1 182	977
Cherokee..............	1 091	3 381 536	5.0	8.1	0.0	1.1	13.2	8.0	61.9	84.3	45.8	26.1	966	704

1. Based on the resident population estimated as of July 1 of the year shown. 3. Bronx, Kings, Queens, and Richmond counties are included with New York county.

Table B. States and Counties — Local Government Finances, Government Employment, and Income Taxes

STATE County	Local government finances, 2012 (cont.)									Government employment, 2015			Individual income tax returns, 2014		
	Direct general expenditure							Debt outstanding							
			Percent of total for:												
	Total (mil dol)	Per capita¹ (dollars)	Education	Health and hospitals	Police protection	Public welfare	Highways	Total (mil dol)	Per capita¹ (dollars)	Federal civilian	Federal military	State and local	Number of returns	Mean adjusted gross income	Mean income tax
	185	186	187	188	189	190	191	192	193	194	195	196	197	198	199
NEW YORK—Cont'd															
Genesee	380.9	6 350	48.2	3.3	2.6	11.4	6.0	207.2	3 454	577	91	5 230	28 260	48 685	4 749
Greene	302.4	6 212	48.5	5.4	2.1	9.8	9.4	211.7	4 350	83	70	4 280	22 050	51 945	5 608
Hamilton	53.0	11 093	36.6	5.7	1.7	2.5	16.4	24.5	5 123	14	D	880	2 610	49 362	5 052
Herkimer	352.7	5 467	56.7	3.1	1.8	9.3	8.9	252.1	3 907	105	98	4 271	27 950	45 653	4 322
Jefferson	631.0	5 247	49.6	3.4	2.6	9.2	6.9	554.7	4 612	3 168	15 779	8 370	52 390	45 482	4 274
Kings	(3)	(3)	(3)	(3)	(3)	(3)	(3)	(3)	(3)	7 619	4 376	93 336	1 202 400	53 259	7 195
Lewis	250.8	9 211	33.2	34.9	1.3	6.5	7.0	120.5	4 427	61	42	2 246	11 780	45 177	3 955
Livingston	328.9	5 074	44.9	5.5	2.8	18.2	7.8	282.5	4 359	128	93	6 087	28 160	53 013	5 532
Madison	345.6	4 774	52.0	4.3	2.3	7.4	8.1	456.5	6 307	129	106	4 234	31 400	56 424	6 732
Monroe	4 348.7	5 815	50.1	4.2	4.3	10.9	3.2	3 397.3	4 543	2 786	1 241	44 910	361 230	59 168	7 493
Montgomery	305.0	6 106	50.5	2.2	2.0	7.7	5.3	285.4	5 714	97	77	2 646	22 690	44 795	4 230
Nassau	11 105.9	8 231	48.3	7.2	8.7	5.9	3.1	9 302.1 (3)168	6 894	5 255	2 585	74 539	708 170	107 066	19 487
New York	(3)84 366.2	(3)10 120	(3)26.6	(3)10.0	(3)6.0	(3)15.1	(3)1.9	630.0	(3)20 227	22 732	2 658	245 550	887 420	210 233	48 504
Niagara	1 203.8	5 596	48.1	2.7	3.7	8.2	5.8	966.3	4 492	981	364	13 041	104 380	49 474	5 087
Oneida	1 300.4	5 568	52.4	2.6	3.1	11.0	5.5	1 381.4	5 915	2 245	403	23 497	104 560	50 030	5 381
Onondaga	3 043.0	6 518	47.4	3.2	3.3	10.4	4.6	3 160.9	6 771	4 461	844	36 465	222 590	60 376	7 683
Ontario	612.2	5 642	54.1	2.3	2.9	8.5	6.6	594.8	5 481	1 463	170	7 123	53 940	63 480	8 359
Orange	2 555.9	6 825	54.6	4.6	3.7	10.5	3.3	1 906.2	5 090	4 728	6 773	21 609	178 310	65 084	7 974
Orleans	216.3	5 050	53.5	3.8	2.2	13.7	6.1	184.0	4 295	80	61	3 779	18 560	43 700	3 835
Oswego	722.5	5 936	55.7	2.6	2.1	8.4	6.2	668.5	5 493	257	205	8 940	53 040	48 119	4 715
Otsego	326.6	5 293	47.1	2.7	1.6	14.9	9.2	292.6	4 742	125	88	4 521	26 530	51 473	5 659
Putnam	630.2	6 327	61.1	2.1	4.6	3.9	5.1	400.1	4 017	141	153	4 470	49 630	85 713	12 393
Queens	(3)	(3)	(3)	(3)	(3)	(3)	(3)	(3)	(3)	14 173	3 732	84 232	1 135 060	47 272	5 105
Rensselaer	989.2	6 189	51.6	3.4	3.1	13.0	3.7	809.6	5 065	361	260	11 210	77 610	57 016	6 373
Richmond	(3)	(3)	(3)	(3)	(3)	(3)	(3)	(3)	(3)	991	1 195	17 718	219 350	65 936	8 026
Rockland	2 333.3	7 343	45.2	11.3	4.7	6.4	4.3	1 968.4	6 195	486	505	17 849	149 040	81 656	12 435
St. Lawrence	626.2	5 579	45.3	11.0	2.3	10.4	8.4	441.9	3 937	587	262	9 785	43 380	47 556	4 575
Saratoga	1 019.1	4 588	54.8	5.8	3.1	8.2	5.3	814.5	3 667	404	2 071	11 598	115 070	92 458	14 749
Schenectady	849.4	5 476	48.9	2.4	3.7	14.9	3.5	691.5	4 458	601	243	8 964	76 070	58 894	6 669
Schoharie	201.5	6 278	47.0	3.9	1.2	7.5	15.0	132.3	4 121	72	47	2 547	13 680	48 287	4 798
Schuyler	91.9	4 963	40.6	6.3	1.9	11.2	10.5	63.1	3 409	45	28	1 085	8 720	46 889	4 610
Seneca	180.7	5 118	46.5	4.6	2.7	8.7	6.0	331.8	9 398	83	51	2 973	15 420	47 151	4 549
Steuben	616.7	6 226	58.5	3.7	1.6	11.1	8.0	529.5	5 345	1 026	153	6 775	44 090	52 703	5 847
Suffolk	11 000.9	7 338	53.4	3.5	5.3	5.4	3.3	9 786.8	6 528	11 289	2 593	92 359	773 080	82 327	12 397
Sullivan	549.1	7 150	46.8	4.4	2.6	12.2	8.2	363.9	4 739	185	112	5 720	33 510	50 122	5 348
Tioga	265.1	5 251	53.3	3.7	1.7	7.4	7.4	230.5	4 566	150	84	2 429	23 600	51 417	5 246
Tompkins	541.1	5 276	48.3	4.4	2.7	8.0	5.5	696.7	6 794	258	165	5 854	40 930	63 960	8 071
Ulster	1 119.8	6 160	51.1	2.0	2.8	12.1	5.4	695.1	3 823	465	286	12 926	86 150	58 072	6 905
Warren	406.2	6 198	44.0	4.8	3.3	10.1	9.1	365.7	5 580	197	103	4 589	33 820	56 409	7 090
Washington	349.4	5 552	55.7	4.3	1.6	11.5	6.6	209.9	3 336	122	93	4 898	28 530	46 054	4 307
Wayne	528.4	5 684	56.8	4.2	2.3	10.7	5.9	364.9	3 926	179	146	7 170	44 480	49 748	4 809
Westchester	8 708.4	9 055	42.2	12.9	4.6	6.4	1.7	6 138.8	6 383	4 521	1 504	55 799	483 430	143 711	29 946
Wyoming	218.6	5 217	34.6	26.6	2.8	7.6	9.3	135.9	3 244	87	59	4 233	18 290	48 748	4 581
Yates	112.7	4 445	44.0	5.8	4.2	8.7	10.8	161.3	6 365	59	38	1 258	11 060	47 192	4 530
NORTH CAROLINA	X	X	X	X	X	X	X	X	X	70 425	128 726	652 330	4 380 570	56 426	6 862
Alamance	427.7	2 779	50.9	3.4	8.3	5.8	1.6	182.0	1 183	224	369	6 866	68 920	48 536	4 909
Alexander	79.9	2 168	57.3	6.5	5.6	7.5	0.5	21.9	594	53	86	1 864	14 980	44 353	4 129
Alleghany	28.9	2 648	55.4	5.1	5.7	7.6	0.2	8.2	749	44	26	599	4 510	42 947	4 585
Anson	92.1	3 494	62.0	2.8	6.7	6.7	1.0	5.0	191	49	55	2 380	9 610	35 480	2 619
Ashe	66.1	2 439	50.5	2.7	5.8	13.7	1.2	26.9	992	61	64	1 103	10 810	40 872	3 836
Avery	52.4	2 970	45.9	4.8	9.0	7.8	1.8	12.6	717	43	36	1 513	6 910	39 861	3 701
Beaufort	192.0	4 042	45.1	2.4	4.2	6.6	1.0	78.5	1 653	120	113	2 839	20 320	47 269	4 752
Bertie	49.9	2 417	57.0	0.9	7.9	10.3	1.0	16.3	788	92	45	1 347	8 040	35 874	2 769
Bladen	137.6	3 942	46.1	22.2	4.7	6.1	1.2	40.6	1 164	104	81	2 316	13 010	38 819	3 325
Brunswick	396.3	3 530	32.7	9.9	9.3	4.9	1.6	543.6	4 843	431	357	4 780	54 260	55 150	6 400
Buncombe	800.5	3 274	41.8	1.9	10.0	8.4	2.1	617.7	2 527	2 931	650	12 993	121 390	54 111	6 555
Burke	231.0	2 553	56.9	2.9	7.1	6.7	0.9	69.8	771	143	207	7 071	36 960	41 470	3 600
Cabarrus	593.1	3 214	47.0	1.8	6.9	5.0	1.7	669.7	3 630	289	469	13 432	85 820	59 242	6 903
Caldwell	274.4	3 349	49.9	21.1	4.8	6.2	1.3	60.2	735	131	193	4 133	33 240	41 363	3 685
Camden	29.0	2 871	58.0	0.3	6.4	4.2	0.0	8.6	849	10	25	472	4 410	58 642	5 850
Carteret	311.1	4 600	29.2	39.1	5.8	4.1	1.4	132.7	1 963	262	393	4 538	32 150	53 454	6 127
Caswell	54.4	2 344	50.3	5.5	16.1	11.3	0.1	23.2	1 000	42	52	1 277	9 230	40 511	3 211
Catawba	685.5	4 441	36.4	32.8	4.4	5.5	1.4	324.5	2 102	333	368	9 361	70 590	53 134	6 243
Chatham	177.4	2 689	45.4	4.2	15.7	6.3	0.6	171.9	2 605	87	168	2 385	31 430	78 077	11 119
Cherokee	85.8	3 180	51.5	5.7	5.1	7.8	0.4	29.5	1 092	95	64	1 509	10 830	37 490	3 059

1. Based on the resident population estimated as of July 1 of the year shown.   3. Bronx, Kings, Queens, and Richmond counties are included with New York county.

Table B. States and Counties — Population, Vital Statistics, Health, and Crime

STATE County	Persons in group quarters, 2016	Daytime population, 2011–2015 Number	Employment/residence ratio	Births, 2016 Total	Rate[1]	Deaths, 2016 Number	Rate[1]	Persons under 65 with no health insurance, 2015 Number	Percent	Medicare, 2015 Total Beneficiaries	Enrolled in Original Medicare	Enrolled in Medicare Advantage	Serious crimes known to police,[2] 2014 Total Number	Rate[3]
	32	33	34	35	36	37	38	39	40	41	42	43	44	45
NORTH CAROLINA—Cont'd														
Chowan	251	13 665	0.82	139	9.7	207	14.4	1 524	13.9	3 696	3 252	444	337	2 285
Clay	110	9 263	0.64	80	7.3	135	12.4	1 137	15.1	3 336	2 609	727	303	2 856
Cleveland	2 094	92 745	0.89	1 068	11.0	1 242	12.8	10 339	13.2	23 327	17 411	5 916	2 059	2 228
Columbus	3 185	54 612	0.87	599	10.6	700	12.4	6 683	15.3	13 286	10 939	2 347	2 846	5 058
Craven	5 006	107 174	1.06	1 438	13.9	1 041	10.1	9 499	11.8	22 666	20 225	2 441	2 903	2 781
Cumberland	9 059	353 357	1.20	5 395	16.5	2 562	7.8	30 120	10.8	48 800	36 630	12 170	17 223	5 251
Currituck	189	19 013	0.54	264	10.2	195	7.6	2 608	12.2	4 229	3 714	515	401	1 628
Dare	145	37 004	1.12	351	9.8	302	8.4	4 204	14.7	7 400	6 584	816	1 249	3 533
Davidson	1 664	139 119	0.65	1 748	10.6	1 841	11.2	18 049	13.3	27 824	12 020	15 804	4 063	2 504
Davie	370	34 203	0.60	379	9.0	429	10.2	4 343	13.0	8 913	4 087	4 826	885	2 173
Duplin	373	56 029	0.86	745	12.6	561	9.5	10 494	21.4	9 230	7 483	1 747	1 357	2 277
Durham	12 904	343 833	1.39	4 395	14.4	2 041	6.7	35 020	13.7	38 670	26 214	12 456	14 474	4 935
Edgecombe	878	52 194	0.85	601	11.3	638	12.0	5 327	12.2	8 630	7 051	1 579	2 069	3 889
Forsyth	10 569	385 702	1.15	4 434	11.9	3 244	8.7	39 904	13.1	68 428	30 043	38 385	18 434	5 057
Franklin	1 639	50 406	0.54	692	10.7	597	9.2	7 390	14.1	9 771	6 667	3 104	1 182	1 883
Gaston	3 329	191 698	0.80	2 556	11.8	2 298	10.6	23 243	13.0	41 798	26 327	15 471	6 609	3 320
Gates	61	8 751	0.38	103	9.0	110	9.6	1 035	11.1	2 301	1 892	409	NA	NA
Graham	96	8 001	0.76	84	9.8	97	11.3	1 112	16.8	2 057	1 555	502	NA	NA
Granville	4 173	55 254	0.88	563	9.5	567	9.6	5 046	11.0	9 293	6 345	2 948	1 673	2 857
Greene	2 527	18 788	0.68	209	9.9	214	10.1	2 828	18.1	2 863	2 410	453	50	235
Guilford	17 126	554 830	1.21	6 055	11.6	4 384	8.4	56 711	13.2	86 555	40 609	45 946	17 666	3 450
Halifax	1 286	50 276	0.84	566	10.9	694	13.4	5 504	13.4	14 032	11 132	2 900	2 304	4 376
Harnett	3 478	101 245	0.54	1 901	14.5	1 023	7.8	14 421	13.1	14 152	10 848	3 304	3 755	2 941
Haywood	726	55 020	0.83	583	9.6	757	12.5	5 422	12.0	15 989	10 919	5 070	1 683	2 895
Henderson	1 306	104 369	0.88	1 103	9.7	1 448	12.7	12 274	14.6	31 163	22 742	8 421	1 966	1 780
Hertford	2 591	25 174	1.09	221	9.2	387	16.0	2 209	12.7	5 270	4 478	792	783	3 307
Hoke	833	41 107	0.50	959	18.0	334	6.3	7 849	16.6	4 330	3 096	1 234	1 275	2 431
Hyde	747	5 726	1.02	41	7.4	48	8.7	602	15.8	998	821	177	NA	NA
Iredell	1 270	162 268	0.96	1 876	10.8	1 557	9.0	16 978	11.8	29 740	19 325	10 415	4 153	2 501
Jackson	3 679	42 469	1.10	402	9.5	362	8.6	5 497	18.1	7 458	5 497	1 961	889	2 160
Johnston	1 816	149 988	0.64	2 317	12.1	1 466	7.7	22 067	13.7	24 403	18 312	6 091	3 806	2 185
Jones	87	8 270	0.51	95	9.6	138	14.0	1 138	14.7	2 387	2 004	383	NA	NA
Lee	1 008	61 484	1.08	749	12.6	573	9.6	7 869	15.8	13 546	10 283	3 263	1 735	2 905
Lenoir	1 229	62 964	1.18	652	11.4	757	13.2	6 942	14.8	14 153	12 141	2 012	2 731	4 695
Lincoln	682	68 220	0.69	814	10.0	830	10.2	9 170	13.6	15 097	10 634	4 463	1 722	2 146
McDowell	1 539	43 627	0.92	463	10.3	490	10.9	4 482	12.6	10 513	7 247	3 266	1 525	3 457
Macon	450	33 393	0.96	344	10.0	415	12.1	4 408	17.7	10 884	9 224	1 660	889	2 622
Madison	1 235	18 181	0.67	210	9.8	229	10.7	1 936	12.3	5 061	3 691	1 370	238	1 209
Martin	152	22 455	0.86	242	10.4	315	13.6	2 247	12.3	5 849	5 005	844	893	3 790
Mecklenburg	17 097	1 122 263	1.27	14 797	14.0	6 228	5.9	117 617	12.9	123 020	80 869	42 151	39 794	3 937
Mitchell	214	15 283	0.99	141	9.3	232	15.3	1 663	14.5	4 077	2 948	1 129	NA	NA
Montgomery	1 006	27 448	0.98	316	11.5	271	9.9	3 635	17.0	5 330	3 892	1 438	765	2 992
Moore	838	90 597	0.97	1 062	11.1	1 143	11.9	8 900	12.5	24 326	17 891	6 435	2 014	2 226
Nash	1 949	97 050	1.06	1 031	11.0	1 024	10.9	9 503	12.4	23 083	18 342	4 741	2 984	3 180
New Hanover	6 714	230 141	1.17	2 324	10.4	1 914	8.6	22 230	12.4	40 971	33 432	7 539	9 127	4 261
Northampton	720	19 786	0.82	171	8.6	284	14.2	1 902	12.7	5 118	4 198	920	536	3 063
Onslow	14 297	186 144	1.03	4 194	22.4	1 050	5.6	15 306	9.8	20 171	17 204	2 967	NA	NA
Orange	8 969	146 019	1.11	1 205	8.5	777	5.5	12 104	10.4	19 709	12 487	7 222	3 255	2 288
Pamlico	713	11 549	0.71	81	6.3	158	12.3	1 148	13.2	3 253	2 853	400	317	2 449
Pasquotank	2 119	40 423	1.02	515	12.9	364	9.1	3 720	11.9	8 270	7 123	1 147	1 368	3 430
Pender	1 094	45 145	0.56	640	10.8	557	9.4	6 716	14.4	11 250	9 042	2 208	1 160	2 079
Perquimans	80	11 342	0.55	111	8.3	161	12.1	1 243	14.2	3 539	3 073	466	178	1 303
Person	446	34 610	0.71	417	10.6	426	10.8	3 760	11.7	7 468	4 648	2 820	876	2 228
Pitt	6 820	175 329	1.02	2 121	12.0	1 318	7.4	18 618	12.5	26 358	21 591	4 767	6 114	3 532
Polk	353	18 022	0.72	152	7.5	254	12.5	1 974	13.6	5 818	4 541	1 277	283	1 433
Randolph	1 294	127 344	0.76	1 562	10.9	1 489	10.4	19 059	16.1	28 542	12 727	15 815	4 708	3 296
Richmond	1 133	43 684	0.86	518	11.5	568	12.6	5 623	15.2	10 490	8 757	1 733	2 600	5 598
Robeson	4 258	130 717	0.91	1 749	13.1	1 338	10.0	21 958	19.6	25 304	18 972	6 332	5 271	3 911
Rockingham	1 056	85 372	0.81	941	10.3	1 158	12.7	9 786	13.2	21 590	9 990	11 600	2 825	3 118
Rowan	4 503	132 198	0.89	1 559	11.1	1 571	11.2	15 541	13.9	26 661	15 378	11 283	3 891	2 901
Rutherford	1 259	63 001	0.84	669	10.1	845	12.7	6 946	13.2	14 920	11 615	3 305	1 696	2 709
Sampson	1 058	59 228	0.82	825	13.1	673	10.7	9 835	18.8	10 777	8 275	2 502	1 707	2 692
Scotland	2 449	37 165	1.11	435	12.3	393	11.2	3 996	14.7	7 242	5 586	1 656	1 658	4 703
Stanly	1 998	55 955	0.82	695	11.4	704	11.6	6 193	12.8	13 756	9 719	4 037	1 242	2 502
Stokes	456	36 898	0.50	405	8.8	538	11.7	4 736	12.8	9 476	3 638	5 838	1 208	2 598
Surry	944	73 191	1.00	745	10.3	884	12.3	9 242	15.9	18 486	9 062	9 424	2 423	3 318

1. Per 1,000 estimated resident population.   2. Data for serious crimes have not been adjusted for underreporting; this may affect comparability between geographic areas and over time.
3. Per 100,000 population estimated by the FBI.

Table B. States and Counties — Crime, Education, Money Income, and Poverty

STATE County	Serious crimes known to police, 2014 (cont.)[1] Rate[2] Violent	Property	Education — School enrollment and attainment, 2011–2015 — Enrollment[3] Total	Percent private	Attainment[4] (percent) High school graduate or less	Bachelor's degree or more	Local government expenditures,[5] 2013–2014 Total current spending (mil dol)	Current spending per student (dollars)	Money income, 2011–2015 Per capita income[6] (dollars)	Median income (dollars)	Households Percent with income of less than $50,000	with income of $200,000 or more	Income and poverty, 2015 Median household income (dollars)	Percent below poverty level All persons	Children under 18 years	Children 5 to 17 years in families
	46	47	48	49	50	51	52	53	54	55	56	57	58	59	60	61
NORTH CAROLINA—Cont'd																
Chowan	312	1 973	3 143	6.3	51.1	20.1	25.7	11 551	21 451	38 759	61.7	1.3	40 794	19.4	33.0	31.4
Clay	245	2 611	2 276	10.5	41.1	21.2	12.9	9 783	22 106	37 076	64.8	1.4	38 980	17.4	31.9	28.1
Cleveland	223	2 005	23 441	12.0	52.2	16.0	140.4	9 110	20 825	39 453	61.1	1.5	40 237	19.8	29.4	27.4
Columbus	473	4 585	13 071	6.5	52.1	12.1	82.3	8 828	19 814	34 949	65.1	1.3	34 478	24.0	34.1	31.3
Craven	236	2 545	24 484	13.6	40.6	22.3	116.3	8 066	24 553	47 985	52.1	2.2	47 805	15.0	24.2	24.6
Cumberland	512	4 739	94 938	15.7	36.0	23.3	419.2	8 052	22 931	44 171	55.9	1.8	42 380	18.8	27.6	26.2
Currituck	199	1 429	5 826	11.4	42.9	20.5	34.9	8 905	27 521	60 600	39.0	2.1	66 426	10.4	17.0	15.2
Dare	238	3 295	7 269	10.3	32.3	29.4	53.7	10 683	30 682	54 496	44.5	3.8	53 585	10.3	17.8	17.6
Davidson	187	2 318	39 326	10.9	51.3	18.7	195.6	7 730	23 060	43 363	55.7	1.9	46 400	14.1	21.3	19.1
Davie	155	2 018	9 539	14.2	46.6	24.4	53.7	8 397	28 141	51 527	48.8	5.2	52 525	12.3	18.4	16.6
Duplin	240	2 037	14 186	7.2	58.0	10.7	85.9	8 923	17 593	35 035	65.3	1.0	38 397	24.9	34.1	31.2
Durham	650	4 285	80 015	26.6	30.0	45.8	376.9	9 848	30 268	52 503	47.7	5.1	53 875	17.1	26.0	23.5
Edgecombe	472	3 417	12 858	7.1	58.9	10.6	62.5	8 925	17 956	32 659	66.4	1.0	32 529	27.8	42.6	41.4
Forsyth	556	4 501	94 724	19.5	38.3	32.9	477.5	8 550	26 674	45 471	53.8	4.0	47 346	18.1	28.5	27.5
Franklin	145	1 738	15 118	18.8	48.4	19.4	72.3	8 154	21 526	42 685	56.2	1.3	48 009	16.0	22.5	20.2
Gaston	374	2 947	49 195	14.3	47.2	19.0	252.8	7 565	22 828	42 429	57.4	2.0	45 031	17.3	25.0	23.3
Gates	NA	NA	2 650	14.5	52.9	13.2	17.5	10 563	22 035	49 258	50.8	0.7	46 387	16.7	23.5	21.0
Graham	NA	NA	1 985	11.4	56.5	14.3	13.4	11 262	19 372	34 805	64.2	1.4	33 827	21.0	32.6	30.7
Granville	294	2 563	14 080	14.6	49.8	17.6	70.8	8 284	23 127	50 225	49.7	2.2	50 314	16.0	21.8	18.6
Greene	28	207	5 038	9.7	56.6	10.1	32.9	10 488	18 107	35 777	64.2	1.5	35 060	25.4	34.5	32.7
Guilford	388	3 062	139 795	13.9	36.4	34.1	691.8	9 133	26 762	45 651	53.5	3.8	48 283	15.7	23.5	22.2
Halifax	458	3 919	12 832	11.0	59.2	12.7	75.6	10 142	19 709	32 245	67.0	1.3	31 952	27.9	39.1	34.6
Harnett	255	2 686	36 998	17.5	45.2	19.6	159.8	7 896	20 864	46 353	53.3	1.7	48 301	17.7	23.8	22.4
Haywood	246	2 649	11 911	9.4	41.7	23.9	65.0	8 773	25 562	42 257	56.3	2.4	43 573	17.6	27.3	24.1
Henderson	125	1 655	22 169	13.3	38.3	28.6	110.4	8 082	26 059	46 448	53.9	2.3	47 280	13.1	21.1	20.3
Hertford	325	2 982	6 296	25.6	53.1	14.0	33.3	11 014	17 280	33 008	68.0	1.0	34 453	26.9	37.6	34.0
Hoke	124	2 307	14 498	17.2	42.6	19.3	67.0	8 159	18 421	41 542	56.5	0.9	42 819	19.9	28.5	28.9
Hyde	NA	NA	1 147	4.9	55.8	10.3	10.1	17 284	19 333	42 897	57.5	1.0	37 074	23.0	30.7	29.7
Iredell	249	2 252	41 053	10.2	40.9	25.9	230.9	7 786	27 558	52 306	47.6	4.5	55 848	14.2	19.3	17.7
Jackson	204	1 956	12 527	5.0	39.4	29.5	34.3	8 912	21 517	38 015	60.5	1.5	41 537	20.9	27.3	27.2
Johnston	194	1 992	48 088	10.9	46.3	20.3	279.2	8 070	22 858	50 512	49.6	1.4	52 681	13.0	18.7	16.5
Jones	NA	NA	2 148	13.8	49.3	13.1	14.8	13 241	20 630	34 005	66.0	1.7	39 688	21.4	36.5	33.5
Lee	181	2 724	15 038	11.3	45.8	20.5	79.3	7 976	21 743	45 608	53.9	1.4	44 294	17.1	25.8	24.7
Lenoir	841	3 854	14 870	9.8	52.3	12.7	77.6	8 264	20 191	34 717	65.6	1.4	37 085	22.7	36.9	33.9
Lincoln	160	1 986	17 518	8.4	47.5	20.2	99.3	7 495	26 439	49 215	50.7	4.2	49 343	13.4	20.4	18.2
McDowell	152	3 305	9 938	10.2	55.2	13.5	56.4	8 930	18 717	35 965	64.7	0.9	37 430	18.8	26.8	26.4
Macon	127	2 495	6 470	8.5	42.7	22.5	39.4	9 110	24 060	39 133	60.8	2.1	41 395	16.9	29.4	27.2
Madison	30	1 179	4 913	24.5	50.3	21.7	22.9	9 193	21 076	37 904	61.0	1.2	37 899	20.9	29.1	27.2
Martin	552	3 238	5 503	5.9	54.9	13.7	37.3	10 115	19 032	35 080	64.8	0.9	36 543	22.5	36.3	34.1
Mecklenburg	522	3 414	268 483	18.9	29.7	42.3	1 253.1	8 264	33 169	56 854	44.2	7.2	57 029	14.3	19.1	18.5
Mitchell	NA	NA	3 506	12.0	52.6	16.8	19.4	9 967	21 429	37 391	62.5	1.4	39 955	16.7	27.5	26.4
Montgomery	227	2 765	6 069	8.0	55.1	14.5	38.8	9 359	19 331	32 500	65.3	1.5	39 096	19.9	31.3	29.3
Moore	171	2 054	19 635	13.6	36.6	32.6	112.0	8 343	29 643	50 998	48.7	4.7	52 139	13.2	21.1	18.9
Nash	449	2 731	23 930	13.8	49.9	19.2	142.5	8 278	23 082	42 713	57.6	2.4	43 450	18.1	25.9	24.3
New Hanover	465	3 797	57 272	11.4	30.4	36.9	233.7	8 963	29 880	50 088	49.9	4.3	52 456	17.3	22.1	20.9
Northampton	274	2 789	4 417	9.6	59.6	11.3	32.1	10 848	18 180	30 429	70.8	0.5	33 301	26.8	45.3	40.6
Onslow	NA	NA	46 479	14.0	38.1	19.3	202.1	8 005	21 862	46 335	54.1	1.1	46 144	15.3	21.5	23.8
Orange	148	2 140	50 650	10.8	23.5	56.6	211.4	10 502	36 380	59 290	43.6	11.3	61 570	14.3	13.1	11.6
Pamlico	270	2 179	2 458	11.8	45.3	19.3	18.8	11 052	24 176	43 444	55.9	1.9	41 004	14.6	32.3	29.4
Pasquotank	346	3 084	10 904	9.8	46.1	19.4	51.3	9 027	22 187	45 378	55.5	2.1	42 171	19.1	29.5	28.4
Pender	190	1 889	12 775	9.9	45.5	21.2	70.3	8 068	23 561	44 828	54.6	2.5	49 390	14.8	21.9	20.5
Perquimans	161	1 142	2 710	6.5	51.1	16.3	17.7	9 958	23 006	44 329	59.3	1.9	42 337	17.6	31.6	29.9
Person	186	2 042	9 298	11.3	52.4	14.7	49.3	8 677	21 148	42 105	59.5	1.2	43 917	16.3	24.0	23.0
Pitt	416	3 116	62 586	7.7	37.2	29.7	194.1	8 217	23 461	41 119	58.3	2.6	41 909	25.9	30.6	30.1
Polk	40	1 392	3 992	8.5	39.0	31.3	26.4	11 669	27 164	46 528	55.6	2.6	45 672	13.5	24.1	21.9
Randolph	155	3 142	33 279	10.5	55.3	14.5	185.7	8 069	21 175	41 947	57.6	1.0	43 216	16.4	25.0	23.1
Richmond	422	5 176	11 485	10.4	55.8	12.8	64.8	8 508	18 059	32 687	68.7	1.0	33 017	28.7	42.8	39.6
Robeson	443	3 468	35 923	4.0	58.4	12.8	203.1	8 506	15 559	30 608	69.9	1.1	32 128	30.6	41.9	38.8
Rockingham	200	2 918	20 211	10.2	56.1	13.8	114.8	8 620	20 726	38 126	62.1	0.9	40 148	18.4	26.3	24.3
Rowan	371	2 530	33 559	17.2	50.3	17.6	169.8	8 562	21 706	43 069	57.5	1.5	44 862	17.3	26.5	25.3
Rutherford	134	2 574	14 922	10.3	50.7	16.2	88.9	8 771	19 419	35 630	66.6	1.1	36 998	19.2	29.6	28.1
Sampson	213	2 479	15 645	8.0	58.0	12.4	99.6	8 591	19 063	35 490	64.3	1.2	40 660	21.4	29.5	28.6
Scotland	644	4 059	9 511	9.8	55.3	15.8	60.5	9 992	15 849	30 958	68.8	0.4	35 447	29.0	44.4	42.8
Stanly	248	2 254	13 877	16.6	51.5	16.2	73.0	8 073	20 990	40 910	58.2	1.1	44 878	17.1	25.1	24.3
Stokes	260	2 338	9 287	8.4	57.3	13.6	59.3	9 149	20 950	40 696	59.8	0.6	42 889	15.3	22.8	21.9
Surry	175	3 142	15 122	7.7	54.4	14.9	100.8	8 609	20 330	36 164	63.8	1.7	38 408	18.2	27.0	24.7

1. Data for serious crimes have not been adjusted for underreporting; this may affect comparability between geographic areas and over time. 2. Per 100,000 population estimated by the FBI.
3. All persons 3 years old and over enrolled in nursery school through college. 4. Persons 25 years old and over. 5. Elementary and secondary education expenditures.
6. Based on population estimated by the American Community Survey, 2011–2015.

Table B. States and Counties — **Personal Income**

STATE County	Personal income, 2015										Earnings, 2015		
			Per capita[1]			Supplements to wages and salaries; employer contributions (mil dol)						Contributions for government social insurance (mil dol)	
	Total (mil dol)	Percent change, 2014–2015	Dollars	Rank	Wages and salaries (mil dol)	Pension and insurance	Government social insurance	Proprietors' income (mil dol)	Dividends, interest, and rent (mil dol)	Personal transfer receipts (mil dol)	Total (mil dol)	From employee and self-employed	From employer
	62	63	64	65	66	67	68	69	70	71	72	73	74
NORTH CAROLINA— Cont'd													
Chowan	503	1.8	34 956	1 923	181	31	14	19	112	166	245	18	14
Clay	324	5.5	30 242	2 904	68	13	6	14	70	123	101	10	6
Cleveland	3 266	4.7	33 712	2 492	1 347	240	109	166	467	1 057	1 862	128	109
Columbus	1 716	0.7	30 262	2 608	579	110	45	77	251	643	810	59	45
Craven	4 195	2.3	40 555	1 256	2 222	520	192	150	945	991	3 083	174	192
Cumberland	12 180	3.4	37 611	1 513	8 542	2 126	791	458	2 779	3 039	11 916	586	791
Currituck	1 037	5.5	41 035	1 357	258	42	22	64	160	192	385	26	22
Dare	1 733	5.0	48 602	730	676	110	60	235	418	286	1 082	68	60
Davidson	5 774	4.0	35 073	1 991	1 747	287	140	326	799	1 455	2 500	183	140
Davie	1 759	4.5	42 136	1 116	437	70	36	92	308	377	634	47	36
Duplin	1 912	-1.1	32 317	1 848	686	130	54	354	248	484	1 224	62	54
Durham	13 395	5.5	44 507	868	13 761	1 851	991	1 167	2 228	2 047	17 770	1 041	991
Edgecombe	1 737	0.8	32 084	2 420	632	127	50	42	316	609	851	60	50
Forsyth	16 185	4.6	43 859	1 016	9 830	1 365	746	1 185	3 106	2 995	13 126	815	746
Franklin	2 029	4.0	31 852	2 458	511	92	39	127	245	494	768	53	39
Gaston	7 887	5.2	36 950	1 704	2 970	479	240	376	1 165	1 962	4 064	277	240
Gates	382	1.5	33 458	2 394	53	11	4	12	54	99	80	7	4
Graham	257	5.3	29 833	2 899	78	14	7	22	38	89	121	9	7
Granville	1 990	3.0	33 919	2 258	925	222	71	77	297	453	1 295	80	71
Greene	634	-1.4	30 004	2 573	147	34	11	99	78	170	292	15	11
Guilford	21 579	4.3	41 691	1 133	14 060	2 034	1 083	1 529	3 937	4 000	18 705	1 147	1 083
Halifax	1 728	2.1	32 947	2 390	576	114	45	51	250	646	786	60	45
Harnett	3 989	3.6	31 129	2 544	888	167	71	208	597	944	1 333	92	71
Haywood	2 108	4.6	35 207	2 126	642	111	51	132	388	663	935	73	51
Henderson	4 231	5.0	37 558	1 853	1 457	238	116	306	945	1 135	2 116	154	116
Hertford	721	2.2	29 808	2 854	347	65	27	48	100	247	487	31	27
Hoke	1 548	5.1	29 382	2 847	294	64	23	59	230	390	440	29	23
Hyde	186	0.7	33 724	2 280	77	15	6	37	37	45	135	7	6
Iredell	7 549	5.9	44 442	1 094	3 516	491	264	649	1 064	1 291	4 920	310	264
Jackson	1 329	5.5	32 202	2 596	613	120	47	54	274	335	834	54	47
Johnston	6 597	5.1	35 533	1 950	1 877	331	145	414	771	1 352	2 766	183	145
Jones	370	-1.4	36 906	1 329	62	12	5	35	55	110	114	7	5
Lee	2 127	4.2	35 655	1 992	1 066	183	86	100	373	550	1 435	91	86
Lenoir	2 176	1.9	37 442	1 556	1 067	206	84	162	341	649	1 519	94	84
Lincoln	3 142	4.8	38 774	1 796	869	145	70	175	416	649	1 259	86	70
McDowell	1 380	4.8	30 683	2 830	599	123	49	56	176	451	827	57	49
Macon	1 193	3.3	34 896	2 123	394	67	32	81	297	377	574	44	32
Madison	633	4.3	29 965	2 833	136	28	11	47	101	208	222	19	11
Martin	783	-0.7	33 532	2 011	279	51	21	32	108	276	382	27	21
Mecklenburg	53 905	6.8	52 129	432	44 218	5 400	3 226	6 373	8 589	6 267	59 218	3 482	3 226
Mitchell	472	2.6	30 970	2 781	179	35	15	18	74	161	247	19	15
Montgomery	915	3.0	33 198	2 400	349	64	29	73	148	245	515	32	29
Moore	4 126	3.7	43 725	999	1 377	206	107	335	1 120	961	2 025	140	107
Nash	3 661	3.0	38 982	1 524	1 738	308	137	241	565	925	2 424	154	137
New Hanover	8 922	5.5	40 487	1 165	4 878	774	375	569	2 111	1 811	6 596	424	375
Northampton	633	0.4	30 971	2 577	197	35	16	19	95	244	268	21	16
Onslow	8 189	-0.4	43 952	713	4 174	1 150	407	346	1 644	1 352	6 077	267	407
Orange	7 822	3.5	55 338	266	3 825	816	268	503	1 925	824	5 413	305	268
Pamlico	482	1.5	37 682	1 466	106	22	8	23	102	150	158	13	8
Pasquotank	1 416	3.1	35 550	2 056	687	139	55	69	233	368	950	58	55
Pender	1 898	4.2	32 937	2 542	410	73	32	139	286	499	654	47	32
Perquimans	501	3.6	37 279	1 814	75	15	6	38	90	148	134	11	6
Person	1 357	2.4	34 557	2 259	411	77	33	61	172	384	583	41	33
Pitt	6 514	3.6	37 042	1 877	3 429	676	257	429	1 109	1 396	4 791	282	257
Polk	845	3.5	41 477	1 477	169	30	14	76	234	219	289	23	14
Randolph	4 841	3.7	33 899	2 449	1 698	295	138	401	616	1 238	2 532	172	138
Richmond	1 425	3.3	31 361	2 717	521	100	45	110	178	525	776	53	45
Robeson	3 689	2.4	27 487	3 005	1 383	263	110	243	426	1 403	1 999	135	110
Rockingham	3 112	3.2	33 916	2 348	1 013	177	82	153	446	937	1 426	107	82
Rowan	4 779	5.0	34 348	2 514	2 117	377	172	279	717	1 321	2 945	195	172
Rutherford	1 935	3.1	29 142	2 884	658	125	54	112	295	674	949	72	54
Sampson	2 253	-1.1	35 357	1 802	686	122	52	369	305	600	1 229	65	52
Scotland	1 087	3.2	30 625	2 824	462	83	38	70	148	408	653	45	38
Stanly	2 068	4.5	34 063	2 356	681	123	54	140	304	569	999	70	54
Stokes	1 521	3.5	32 811	2 481	245	48	19	78	179	419	390	34	19
Surry	2 519	3.0	34 628	2 190	1 030	181	83	206	384	742	1 499	101	83

1. Based on the resident population estimated as of July 1 of the year shown.

Table B. States and Counties — Earnings, Social Security, and Housing

STATE County	Earnings, 2015 (cont.) Percent by selected industries									Social Security beneficiaries, December 2015			Housing units, 2016	
	Farm	Mining	Construction	Manufacturing	Information: professional, scientific, technical services	Retail trade	Finance, insurance, real estate and leasing	Health care and social assistance	Government	Number	Rate[1]	Supplemental Security Income recipients, December 2015	Total	Percent change, 2010–2016
	75	76	77	78	79	80	81	82	83	84	85	86	87	88
NORTH CAROLINA—Cont'd														
Chowan	2.0	0.0	3.4	9.2	6.8	8.3	4.9	D	17.7	4 255	296	578	7 245	-0.6
Clay	-2.5	0.0	14.5	D	D	13.6	3.3	D	26.5	3 785	352	291	7 268	1.7
Cleveland	2.0	D	5.9	24.2	3.0	7.5	3.0	11.6	17.1	25 720	265	3 438	43 183	-0.4
Columbus	3.2	0.0	3.8	17.8	2.8	7.9	4.9	14.0	23.1	14 820	260	3 134	26 014	-0.1
Craven	0.1	0.1	2.8	8.0	5.1	5.2	3.0	8.8	52.1	23 390	226	2 568	46 410	3.1
Cumberland	0.1	D	3.3	4.0	4.2	4.5	2.0	5.5	63.8	54 690	168	10 261	145 289	7.2
Currituck	-0.5	D	12.2	0.8	D	11.4	9.1	D	17.6	4 935	196	311	15 368	6.3
Dare	0.0	D	11.8	2.9	D	12.0	13.1	4.6	17.9	8 330	234	317	34 428	2.8
Davidson	0.7	0.1	6.6	22.3	3.2	6.7	2.7	8.5	14.3	38 125	232	3 182	73 630	1.4
Davie	0.5	0.3	9.8	21.5	D	7.5	4.2	D	13.9	10 335	248	591	18 418	1.0
Duplin	24.2	0.0	4.4	21.7	D	4.3	1.3	4.1	15.2	11 345	193	1 731	25 582	-0.4
Durham	0.1	D	2.3	19.9	18.4	2.9	7.6	18.4	9.5	42 860	143	6 291	133 488	11.0
Edgecombe	1.4	D	3.7	18.4	D	10.7	2.0	D	26.8	13 060	243	2 934	24 715	-0.5
Forsyth	0.1	0.1	3.9	10.4	8.2	6.8	10.4	17.1	9.3	71 255	194	8 520	163 289	4.1
Franklin	6.8	D	10.0	22.4	D	5.5	2.7	7.7	17.7	12 290	193	1 442	27 526	3.7
Gaston	0.0	D	5.1	24.6	4.0	8.2	4.2	16.0	13.7	46 975	220	5 573	91 547	3.2
Gates	0.1	0.0	D	D	3.3	6.2	D	D	32.9	2 600	227	315	5 241	0.7
Graham	2.3	0.0	34.0	4.6	D	4.6	3.5	4.3	21.3	2 415	280	275	5 957	0.5
Granville	1.0	D	4.3	26.9	D	3.8	1.5	D	44.4	12 095	207	1 409	23 765	4.1
Greene	31.2	-0.3	5.6	4.1	1.0	3.6	3.1	6.9	32.5	3 870	183	652	8 234	0.3
Guilford	0.2	0.0	4.7	14.4	9.1	6.1	9.5	11.9	11.3	94 980	184	11 698	226 711	4.0
Halifax	-0.4	0.0	5.2	15.9	2.4	9.4	4.0	10.2	28.7	15 270	292	3 916	25 706	-0.2
Harnett	3.3	D	11.1	6.7	5.1	10.4	3.8	7.8	23.6	20 720	162	2 824	50 615	8.3
Haywood	0.2	D	5.4	20.7	4.9	11.4	4.8	16.1	16.4	18 455	308	1 691	35 162	0.6
Henderson	0.9	D	7.9	16.1	5.0	9.0	4.6	14.5	15.5	32 485	289	1 898	56 650	3.6
Hertford	6.6	0.0	4.2	16.8	D	6.9	3.2	D	23.6	5 625	233	1 230	10 547	-0.8
Hoke	7.8	D	5.5	19.4	D	4.7	1.7	D	31.8	7 170	136	1 153	20 355	11.9
Hyde	27.0	0.0	6.0	3.5	D	4.0	D	D	25.8	1 155	210	162	3 368	0.6
Iredell	0.9	0.0	8.0	15.5	D	7.5	3.7	8.9	10.1	33 835	199	2 614	72 160	4.5
Jackson	0.4	D	5.1	1.7	D	6.4	1.7	11.8	48.0	8 645	209	687	26 949	3.9
Johnston	2.3	0.1	10.9	18.9	3.9	8.9	3.8	7.0	18.8	33 005	178	3 821	72 404	7.0
Jones	25.1	0.0	6.8	1.5	D	3.1	1.5	D	27.3	2 605	261	374	4 900	1.3
Lee	0.7	0.3	5.8	33.1	3.4	7.1	3.4	10.8	12.7	12 665	213	1 619	24 280	0.6
Lenoir	5.1	D	7.5	24.0	3.2	5.7	4.6	9.1	21.1	15 095	260	2 825	27 407	-0.2
Lincoln	2.8	D	11.1	22.1	5.4	7.9	3.4	5.0	16.7	16 520	205	1 531	34 611	3.3
McDowell	0.8	0.5	4.4	42.6	D	7.0	1.8	D	15.8	12 155	270	1 384	21 053	1.2
Macon	1.0	D	11.9	5.8	11.5	10.5	5.1	12.4	16.4	11 550	338	791	25 404	0.6
Madison	0.9	D	10.0	8.9	D	6.3	2.5	D	21.3	5 890	279	775	10 787	1.7
Martin	4.7	0.0	3.8	25.7	D	8.4	6.5	D	20.0	6 240	267	1 110	11 491	-1.8
Mecklenburg	0.1	0.0	6.4	5.0	16.0	4.8	17.7	5.8	10.4	134 115	130	18 114	435 014	9.2
Mitchell	-0.2	D	D	5.3	1.9	8.4	3.5	13.8	20.3	4 650	306	459	8 738	0.3
Montgomery	7.7	0.0	5.9	30.8	1.5	6.8	2.1	D	17.2	6 075	221	727	16 110	1.3
Moore	2.5	D	9.0	4.8	D	7.5	5.6	27.5	12.3	25 755	273	1 478	46 299	5.4
Nash	1.8	D	6.0	23.9	5.7	7.7	5.0	9.0	14.6	22 065	235	3 548	42 565	0.7
New Hanover	0.1	D	7.9	5.8	14.6	8.5	7.3	11.2	19.9	43 935	200	4 350	108 872	7.3
Northampton	0.4	D	6.8	10.1	2.1	2.9	1.3	D	21.9	5 865	287	1 195	11 511	-1.4
Onslow	1.8	D	2.9	0.8	2.1	4.5	2.2	3.1	72.2	24 595	132	3 027	77 785	14.0
Orange	0.4	0.0	2.4	2.0	10.8	4.9	4.7	6.4	54.8	19 560	139	1 479	56 957	2.6
Pamlico	3.3	0.0	5.6	4.4	4.5	11.4	3.4	D	29.2	4 020	314	257	7 630	1.3
Pasquotank	1.4	0.0	3.6	4.0	6.1	8.7	5.4	14.1	35.3	8 630	218	1 291	16 994	1.0
Pender	9.3	D	12.0	6.0	D	7.4	4.5	7.8	23.4	12 820	222	1 193	28 212	5.6
Perquimans	15.9	0.0	6.5	1.7	D	4.2	D	D	24.6	3 990	298	378	7 041	0.8
Person	3.3	0.0	7.9	17.8	3.7	7.7	3.2	10.3	17.1	9 745	249	1 103	18 235	0.2
Pitt	1.3	D	5.1	9.8	4.4	7.1	5.0	10.0	38.0	29 590	168	6 015	77 914	3.9
Polk	3.7	D	11.9	4.7	7.9	5.2	5.1	22.2	15.3	6 345	312	288	11 580	1.3
Randolph	3.7	0.1	7.8	32.1	2.8	6.2	3.2	9.0	12.9	32 250	226	3 375	61 556	0.8
Richmond	7.6	D	6.3	18.3	3.4	8.9	2.6	11.7	19.8	11 510	253	2 200	21 200	2.2
Robeson	2.6	0.0	7.1	15.2	2.4	8.3	3.2	18.6	22.9	27 755	207	7 812	52 155	-1.2
Rockingham	0.9	D	7.2	25.9	D	8.3	3.2	12.1	15.3	24 810	271	3 103	43 712	0.1
Rowan	1.4	0.4	6.0	18.5	3.4	6.6	2.7	9.6	20.2	32 225	232	2 885	60 814	1.0
Rutherford	1.1	D	6.9	16.5	7.0	9.0	3.0	13.5	18.4	17 960	270	2 017	34 104	0.7
Sampson	27.0	0.0	4.2	14.3	2.2	5.9	2.5	D	18.0	14 180	223	2 203	27 324	0.3
Scotland	2.7	0.0	3.9	20.5	2.3	8.3	3.3	17.5	19.1	9 365	264	1 841	15 191	0.0
Stanly	1.6	D	9.1	19.5	2.9	8.9	3.6	11.7	19.0	14 660	242	1 394	27 528	1.5
Stokes	4.1	0.0	8.8	12.7	D	7.3	D	12.5	24.0	11 285	243	950	21 959	0.1
Surry	4.6	0.2	14.2	12.2	D	9.4	3.9	D	16.4	19 385	267	2 142	33 719	0.0

1. Per 1,000 resident population estimated as of July 1 of the year shown.

Table B. States and Counties — Housing, Labor Force, and Employment

STATE County	Housing units, 2011–2015								Civilian labor force, 2016				Civilian employment,[6] 2011–2015		
	Occupied units										Unemployment			Percent	
	Owner-occupied					Renter-occupied									
				Median owner cost as a percent of income			Median rent as a per-cent of income[2]	Sub-stand-ard units[4] (percent)		Percent change, 2015–2016				Manage-ment, business, science and arts	Con-struction, produc-tion, and mainte-nance occu-pations
	Total	Percent	Median value[1]	With a mort-gage	Without a mort-gage[2]	Median rent[3]			Total		Total	Rate[5]	Total		
	89	90	91	92	93	94	95	96	97	98	99	100	101	102	103
NORTH CAROLINA—Cont'd															
Chowan	5 967	66.8	135 900	25.7	16.2	734	34.9	5.6	5 648	0.1	360	6.4	5 711	33.2	24.6
Clay	4 540	76.5	147 900	23.6	11.9	653	29.2	2.8	4 073	0.7	218	5.4	3 920	28.9	20.0
Cleveland	37 453	68.2	104 400	21.8	11.6	668	33.2	2.2	46 944	1.9	2 572	5.5	40 571	28.1	29.1
Columbus	22 006	70.1	83 900	25.1	13.6	596	33.3	2.3	22 778	0.7	1 458	6.4	20 746	25.9	28.8
Craven	40 131	62.6	154 500	23.2	12.1	894	29.6	2.0	41 857	1.3	2 198	5.3	40 530	32.6	24.3
Cumberland	122 643	52.6	129 300	22.6	12.0	869	30.5	2.1	127 861	1.3	8 095	6.3	118 750	33.9	20.0
Currituck	9 300	81.0	229 900	25.2	10.0	991	33.5	2.7	12 941	0.7	668	5.2	11 913	25.7	28.6
Dare	14 969	68.1	283 400	28.0	13.1	1 048	27.4	1.4	20 069	-1.1	1 353	6.7	18 579	30.2	21.7
Davidson	64 299	71.9	132 200	21.5	10.7	655	28.3	3.0	79 790	1.4	3 853	4.8	71 620	28.1	31.8
Davie	15 813	79.3	169 300	20.7	11.4	674	27.1	2.5	20 154	1.6	911	4.5	18 364	34.3	26.2
Duplin	21 946	67.9	87 900	23.4	13.8	622	30.9	5.5	26 718	0.9	1 430	5.4	24 654	25.1	40.0
Durham	115 975	53.7	183 800	20.5	10.4	895	29.9	3.1	160 846	2.7	7 230	4.5	145 135	49.5	14.9
Edgecombe	21 026	59.9	82 200	23.5	14.5	639	32.7	3.7	22 849	0.1	1 967	8.6	21 446	23.3	33.4
Forsyth	143 207	62.1	151 100	21.2	10.6	732	31.1	2.9	182 356	1.5	8 870	4.9	162 790	39.4	19.8
Franklin	23 506	74.5	129 500	23.8	14.4	729	30.5	2.7	29 641	3.2	1 526	5.1	26 738	31.7	27.1
Gaston	79 166	66.5	125 100	21.6	12.2	731	32.2	3.9	106 346	3.5	5 601	5.3	91 563	28.9	28.5
Gates	4 402	79.6	144 300	23.2	14.1	776	29.1	3.1	5 193	1.0	268	5.2	4 865	26.5	34.0
Graham	3 267	82.1	120 700	22.5	11.2	572	21.0	1.1	3 092	-3.0	273	8.8	2 947	24.7	31.6
Granville	20 223	72.5	142 600	22.2	11.6	768	28.5	3.0	29 357	2.9	1 271	4.3	24 163	33.2	28.5
Greene	7 222	69.6	87 700	23.5	14.9	602	28.3	6.3	9 573	1.0	501	5.2	8 070	24.7	35.6
Guilford	199 540	59.6	156 100	22.1	11.1	771	30.6	2.8	258 800	1.0	13 494	5.2	236 140	37.1	20.1
Halifax	21 468	63.0	86 600	22.6	15.9	662	35.8	2.2	20 806	0.2	1 655	8.0	19 726	25.6	30.6
Harnett	42 672	65.9	135 400	22.5	12.4	781	29.0	3.0	51 533	2.6	2 954	5.7	46 375	32.8	25.9
Haywood	26 111	72.9	161 300	23.0	11.1	710	32.0	2.6	28 534	3.2	1 299	4.6	24 728	32.3	26.1
Henderson	46 079	72.6	182 300	22.3	10.0	750	31.1	2.7	52 357	3.4	2 222	4.2	46 387	32.9	26.4
Hertford	8 651	65.5	83 000	23.2	14.9	635	34.1	3.4	9 388	1.8	613	6.5	8 679	28.5	26.3
Hoke	16 990	66.1	141 500	24.3	14.5	832	32.2	3.9	19 973	0.7	1 302	6.5	17 168	29.8	27.4
Hyde	2 050	77.7	90 600	18.0	12.3	822	29.0	1.2	2 137	-0.3	201	9.4	2 326	31.5	25.9
Iredell	60 893	72.9	166 300	22.0	10.0	796	28.9	2.9	84 995	3.4	4 040	4.8	76 079	33.6	27.2
Jackson	15 956	67.6	171 900	24.4	10.0	628	33.8	1.9	18 839	2.0	1 012	5.4	17 567	31.6	17.5
Johnston	61 950	70.8	145 500	22.1	11.4	774	31.9	2.8	91 112	3.4	4 219	4.6	80 656	34.5	24.7
Jones	4 136	70.6	93 900	24.6	14.0	653	33.7	1.9	4 603	1.2	242	5.3	4 029	30.8	30.5
Lee	21 206	66.7	136 900	21.9	12.4	711	28.7	3.6	26 239	0.6	1 541	5.9	25 418	28.0	29.9
Lenoir	23 335	60.4	92 500	22.8	14.3	668	30.6	2.6	27 855	0.4	1 647	5.9	23 972	26.6	31.6
Lincoln	30 088	77.1	153 200	21.0	10.5	671	28.8	2.4	41 962	3.3	1 951	4.6	36 605	29.6	31.5
McDowell	17 323	70.2	98 400	21.3	10.5	583	24.9	2.6	21 161	-0.5	1 013	4.8	17 404	25.2	32.8
Macon	15 536	72.5	165 600	23.8	10.0	731	32.2	2.8	15 281	1.1	821	5.4	13 351	29.6	21.6
Madison	8 450	73.3	159 900	25.4	10.8	629	26.9	2.2	9 757	3.0	476	4.9	8 935	31.3	27.7
Martin	9 269	68.3	85 500	24.3	15.5	596	28.7	2.6	9 889	1.8	667	6.7	9 079	29.8	31.1
Mecklenburg	379 786	57.5	184 800	20.9	11.3	938	29.2	2.6	585 312	3.6	27 415	4.7	502 455	42.4	16.2
Mitchell	6 344	76.6	141 100	24.2	10.9	558	34.1	1.6	6 225	-1.3	382	6.1	6 014	28.9	31.1
Montgomery	10 588	70.3	90 900	22.1	12.5	550	27.8	4.3	11 790	1.4	611	5.2	10 397	26.6	38.5
Moore	37 143	74.6	199 100	21.8	11.3	771	28.8	1.8	39 463	3.1	1 978	5.0	36 422	38.6	19.8
Nash	36 711	64.4	118 600	22.6	13.2	728	32.2	3.4	44 072	0.5	2 899	6.6	40 735	29.6	28.3
New Hanover	88 403	57.3	214 300	23.6	12.7	907	32.1	2.8	116 676	2.9	5 464	4.7	103 718	38.8	16.2
Northampton	8 630	68.9	82 500	24.5	14.9	644	38.0	1.4	7 925	0.8	576	7.3	7 193	27.4	32.6
Onslow	62 185	53.8	154 000	24.6	11.2	943	31.7	2.4	63 729	0.0	3 498	5.5	61 252	29.6	21.5
Orange	51 880	60.4	272 600	21.1	10.6	935	30.3	2.5	75 443	2.8	3 218	4.3	70 264	55.1	10.7
Pamlico	5 237	75.9	150 800	24.5	12.6	732	31.3	3.6	5 404	1.3	286	5.3	5 107	29.4	29.8
Pasquotank	14 448	62.5	158 800	26.1	14.1	861	34.8	4.7	17 468	0.1	1 102	6.3	17 073	31.4	25.8
Pender	20 130	76.9	153 400	24.3	14.0	818	29.5	3.3	26 687	2.6	1 409	5.3	23 242	29.2	29.3
Perquimans	5 500	77.8	165 800	26.2	14.1	728	41.3	1.8	5 165	0.2	331	6.4	4 852	33.7	28.4
Person	15 383	71.8	115 500	22.7	11.5	626	34.1	3.7	18 193	1.7	994	5.5	16 612	27.9	30.8
Pitt	67 502	52.8	135 300	21.4	12.3	736	34.6	2.1	88 381	0.8	4 885	5.5	80 392	37.2	18.4
Polk	8 701	74.8	190 700	24.6	10.0	743	25.5	2.2	8 881	2.6	413	4.7	8 270	33.0	24.7
Randolph	54 507	72.7	120 700	22.2	11.4	638	28.5	3.1	67 156	0.8	3 286	4.9	63 160	26.1	35.0
Richmond	18 461	62.7	78 600	20.8	12.7	600	34.4	2.1	16 883	-0.3	1 178	7.0	16 848	26.6	32.7
Robeson	45 773	63.1	70 200	23.0	13.3	603	31.9	4.4	50 767	-0.5	4 018	7.9	47 406	25.1	33.7
Rockingham	37 583	68.8	106 700	22.1	11.1	611	30.3	2.2	41 359	0.6	2 325	5.6	38 380	25.0	32.1
Rowan	51 612	67.4	128 300	21.6	11.8	722	29.0	2.3	65 327	3.5	3 590	5.5	56 519	28.7	30.5
Rutherford	26 426	71.4	106 600	22.0	12.0	594	29.3	2.9	24 946	-0.4	1 668	6.7	25 033	27.1	35.0
Sampson	23 280	70.8	87 600	22.1	13.8	588	31.1	4.3	29 801	0.9	1 621	5.4	26 833	24.6	38.4
Scotland	12 996	63.1	79 100	24.2	13.1	623	37.7	3.2	11 693	-1.4	1 073	9.2	11 215	31.1	25.7
Stanly	23 667	71.0	128 200	23.2	12.3	653	32.4	3.8	29 427	2.2	1 368	4.6	26 101	29.1	28.5
Stokes	18 968	77.5	117 400	21.9	11.4	614	31.9	2.3	22 110	1.4	1 056	4.8	19 972	29.8	34.1
Surry	29 267	72.1	115 500	22.6	12.0	606	28.0	3.2	33 771	1.3	1 618	4.8	30 107	27.7	31.8

1. Specified owner-occupied units.   2. A value of 10.0 represents 10 percent or less; a value of 50.0 represents 50 percent or more.   3. Specified renter-occupied units.
4. Overcrowded or lacking complete plumbing facilities.   5. Percent of civilian labor force.   6. Civilian employed persons 16 years old and over.

Table B. States and Counties — Nonfarm Employment and Agriculture

	Private nonfarm establishments, employment and payroll, 2015									Agriculture, 2012			
		Employment						Annual payroll		Farms			
											Percent with:		
STATE County	Number of establishments	Total	Health care and social assistance	Manufacturing	Retail trade	Finance and insurance	Professional, scientific, and technical services	Total (mil dol)	Average per employee (dollars)	Number	Fewer than 50 acres	500 acres or more	Farm operators whose principal occupation is farming (percent)
	104	105	106	107	108	109	110	111	112	113	114	115	116
NORTH CAROLINA—Cont'd													
Chowan	349	3 647	954	599	405	89	119	128	35 175	141	32.6	27.7	73.0
Clay	217	1 567	299	226	411	37	26	41	26 398	154	56.5	0.6	53.2
Cleveland	1 915	27 206	5 082	5 667	3 849	517	1 034	1 006	36 968	1 036	43.3	3.7	35.3
Columbus	988	10 960	2 664	1 896	2 265	802	388	388	35 401	731	41.6	11.4	48.2
Craven	2 126	27 262	6 254	3 199	4 665	838	1 837	1 043	38 246	256	45.3	14.1	59.8
Cumberland	5 620	91 672	18 898	5 965	16 728	1 942	4 961	3 132	34 169	389	41.4	10.8	45.8
Currituck	611	4 944	243	45	888	79	236	180	36 501	82	46.3	28.0	56.1
Dare	1 859	13 663	930	442	3 471	352	416	464	33 985	9	55.6	22.2	88.9
Davidson	2 749	46 822	13 812	9 049	5 106	799	1 009	1 842	39 349	1 062	54.7	1.6	45.3
Davie	785	8 481	1 220	1 343	1 381	189	216	283	33 368	640	53.4	1.9	47.2
Duplin	829	13 245	1 688	5 810	1 784	221	144	407	30 751	940	37.4	11.3	62.7
Durham	7 103	176 821	26 202	12 707	15 444	8 588	28 462	11 376	64 334	232	62.5	2.6	44.8
Edgecombe	732	12 153	2 508	2 915	1 558	155	128	389	32 015	272	34.9	19.5	52.2
Forsyth	8 366	161 704	23 566	14 987	21 101	10 468	6 644	7 870	48 671	662	65.7	1.2	50.6
Franklin	961	9 510	1 028	2 676	1 474	160	197	424	44 599	542	40.8	9.0	39.7
Gaston	3 965	63 577	11 312	14 112	9 512	1 134	1 285	2 540	39 956	520	54.8	1.0	39.8
Gates	118	713	112	D	159	41	24	19	26 842	182	33.5	14.3	44.0
Graham	163	1 543	270	125	237	44	25	53	34 340	107	54.2	0.0	39.3
Granville	847	12 408	2 299	4 064	1 351	278	212	474	38 187	589	37.0	5.4	50.6
Greene	240	2 068	637	147	301	45	53	57	27 782	260	31.9	18.8	62.7
Guilford	13 246	258 166	35 722	32 231	28 430	12 736	12 063	11 473	44 440	962	56.9	4.2	43.9
Halifax	955	12 267	2 915	1 866	2 406	309	204	383	31 197	341	28.2	27.3	49.3
Harnett	1 618	19 019	3 407	1 631	3 288	562	457	591	31 085	797	55.6	9.2	47.9
Haywood	1 356	14 477	3 088	1 755	3 030	408	423	465	32 120	597	58.8	2.5	42.2
Henderson	2 567	31 631	6 476	6 009	5 325	709	908	1 169	36 942	468	68.6	2.8	52.1
Hertford	495	7 266	1 982	996	1 191	159	124	257	35 330	162	37.7	24.7	64.8
Hoke	426	5 370	1 594	1 353	792	76	136	152	28 284	202	47.0	13.4	54.0
Hyde	160	770	105	87	142	D	16	24	31 775	158	39.9	27.8	55.1
Iredell	4 537	64 544	9 119	10 853	8 851	1 431	2 899	2 828	43 819	1 203	47.3	5.2	55.9
Jackson	951	12 290	2 233	284	1 750	192	287	427	34 780	245	59.6	0.8	44.5
Johnston	3 127	40 572	5 835	7 629	8 143	817	932	1 458	35 941	1 175	50.6	7.1	46.6
Jones	131	812	174	27	97	18	16	26	31 677	170	35.9	15.3	60.0
Lee	1 290	23 332	2 783	8 485	3 141	335	322	860	36 842	246	47.6	6.9	43.9
Lenoir	1 223	23 231	4 158	5 844	2 895	605	554	790	33 994	401	37.4	17.0	64.3
Lincoln	1 582	17 368	2 432	3 519	3 135	427	456	615	35 394	651	53.6	1.8	35.5
McDowell	718	13 003	1 681	5 818	1 647	193	157	419	32 240	334	53.6	1.5	46.1
Macon	1 062	9 134	1 319	564	1 884	373	212	292	31 944	326	62.0	0.6	42.3
Madison	302	3 042	553	311	445	48	36	74	24 398	719	49.0	1.1	38.4
Martin	437	5 115	1 115	886	1 017	143	135	142	27 755	357	22.1	23.5	61.6
Mecklenburg	30 039	588 844	67 344	26 342	59 541	69 486	49 494	35 515	60 313	237	64.1	2.5	47.7
Mitchell	375	3 884	742	606	695	85	53	125	32 151	286	62.9	0.3	37.1
Montgomery	482	6 976	1 045	2 573	798	164	69	225	32 218	250	44.0	6.0	63.6
Moore	2 235	29 471	8 910	1 608	4 496	732	1 257	1 112	37 745	718	51.9	3.3	47.9
Nash	2 013	36 449	5 935	7 913	5 067	1 452	902	1 397	38 317	430	39.8	14.9	56.5
New Hanover	7 063	90 790	16 612	4 278	15 172	2 890	6 192	3 788	41 723	50	74.0	2.0	52.0
Northampton	270	4 124	751	512	373	21	21	143	34 623	319	25.1	24.1	65.8
Onslow	2 763	35 491	5 360	888	8 758	1 002	1 856	977	27 532	347	48.4	7.2	54.2
Orange	3 235	42 675	15 838	916	6 040	1 967	2 098	1 793	42 020	645	54.0	2.6	47.8
Pamlico	260	2 694	623	90	559	50	45	75	27 699	80	40.0	31.3	68.8
Pasquotank	912	10 837	2 308	534	2 321	642	383	379	34 960	136	39.7	30.9	66.2
Pender	1 010	8 418	1 174	740	1 707	111	650	272	32 348	335	51.3	7.8	49.9
Perquimans	198	1 274	123	67	226	43	19	41	32 326	185	27.0	30.8	68.6
Person	663	7 932	1 285	1 565	1 505	181	137	282	35 554	395	36.5	12.9	50.6
Pitt	3 523	60 323	15 717	5 688	9 332	2 062	2 034	2 232	36 995	391	34.8	21.5	59.3
Polk	489	3 846	1 555	311	431	110	141	112	29 165	290	55.2	1.4	50.0
Randolph	2 508	38 392	4 789	14 890	4 310	1 032	592	1 331	34 658	1 486	46.7	2.8	48.6
Richmond	801	11 159	1 833	3 318	1 881	228	150	345	30 928	277	40.1	5.4	49.8
Robeson	1 800	30 751	7 170	7 037	5 173	1 174	569	951	30 910	941	45.2	13.2	56.3
Rockingham	1 674	21 970	3 167	5 813	3 630	450	475	752	34 210	902	44.5	3.8	46.1
Rowan	2 545	44 516	9 080	9 272	4 638	742	877	1 871	42 020	1 011	55.2	4.2	36.2
Rutherford	1 222	15 478	2 930	3 345	2 509	318	287	471	30 410	638	51.4	2.2	48.4
Sampson	989	13 730	2 420	3 533	2 234	250	294	463	33 691	1 067	36.3	13.0	55.2
Scotland	604	9 886	2 341	2 079	1 490	178	101	322	32 544	150	32.0	16.7	51.3
Stanly	1 295	15 450	2 979	3 371	2 575	331	271	515	33 350	664	54.7	4.8	44.3
Stokes	625	5 533	1 129	940	925	98	166	164	29 692	926	40.4	2.4	50.9
Surry	1 652	26 708	3 793	3 998	4 285	695	370	964	36 080	1 256	49.2	2.2	48.5

Table B. States and Counties — **Agriculture**

	Agriculture, 2012 (cont.)															
	Land in farms				Value of land and buildings (dollars)			Value of products sold					Percent of farms with sales of:		Government payments	
			Acres							Percent from:						
STATE County	Acreage (1,000)	Percent change, 2007-2012	Average size of farm	Total irrigated (1,000)	Total cropland (1,000)	Average per farm	Average per acre	Value of machinery and equipment, average per farm (dollars)	Total (mil dol)	Average per farm (dollars)	Crops	Live-stock and poultry products	$10,000 or more	$100,000 or more	Total ($1,000)	Percent of farms
	117	118	119	120	121	122	123	124	125	126	127	128	129	130	131	132
NORTH CAROLINA—Cont'd																
Chowan	58	-22.1	412	5.0	47.5	1 307 021	3 169	343 525	70.7	501 582	81.4	18.6	70.2	46.1	1 586	72.3
Clay	12	21.7	76	0.2	4.3	380 760	4 990	38 864	3.2	20 636	80.3	19.7	20.1	2.6	209	26.6
Cleveland	117	0.9	113	0.2	47.2	463 430	4 116	58 367	127.7	123 296	17.2	82.8	30.7	11.3	834	23.6
Columbus	159	4.5	218	2.4	116.3	660 404	3 032	132 025	196.5	268 835	42.1	57.9	46.5	19.7	3 374	56.0
Craven	71	-0.4	276	0.9	51.5	853 684	3 094	150 055	55.5	216 820	68.0	32.0	43.8	25.0	1 471	55.9
Cumberland	82	-6.8	212	3.4	47.7	660 437	3 121	119 159	104.8	269 383	40.3	59.7	40.1	18.0	1 021	38.8
Currituck	35	28.2	431	0.2	32.1	1 762 451	4 088	244 244	25.9	315 537	99.9	0.1	51.2	28.0	507	48.8
Dare	D	D	D	0.0	D	1 553 333	D	159 111	1.1	125 333	D	D	44.4	22.2	D	22.2
Davidson	87	-4.6	82	0.8	40.8	504 619	6 138	56 573	54.6	51 412	39.8	60.2	25.1	7.1	616	15.6
Davie	60	-14.7	93	0.1	30.0	575 472	6 178	50 453	25.4	39 625	49.7	50.3	28.0	6.3	227	11.3
Duplin	231	-6.9	246	11.7	155.0	1 001 313	4 076	159 549	1 276.4	1 357 895	10.5	89.5	69.7	53.0	3 324	41.0
Durham	21	-20.3	90	0.4	6.5	771 086	8 578	50 358	9.4	40 517	83.1	16.9	26.7	4.7	237	23.7
Edgecombe	127	-9.4	466	5.9	90.4	1 226 103	2 634	266 243	156.0	573 618	62.9	37.1	47.1	31.6	2 479	71.3
Forsyth	40	-7.2	61	0.2	19.7	507 905	8 309	46 530	16.1	24 311	89.3	10.7	20.4	3.0	254	15.4
Franklin	117	3.6	216	3.8	59.5	921 013	4 271	108 980	81.5	150 308	69.2	30.8	31.9	12.7	1 070	36.5
Gaston	42	11.6	81	0.1	15.1	488 746	6 062	41 181	17.1	32 792	30.0	70.0	23.3	5.0	186	14.2
Gates	63	-16.5	348	3.8	45.2	1 210 253	3 480	152 918	66.8	367 126	45.9	54.1	46.7	30.8	980	70.3
Graham	7	-4.8	64	0.0	1.4	385 037	6 026	55 776	1.7	15 972	32.2	67.8	32.7	1.9	94	15.0
Granville	101	-21.5	171	2.0	27.9	703 173	4 108	50 185	22.8	38 769	84.2	15.8	28.0	7.0	1 224	47.0
Greene	101	9.8	389	2.1	69.4	1 517 792	3 900	167 331	274.0	1 053 758	27.7	72.3	66.2	44.2	2 286	73.8
Guilford	91	-6.0	94	1.5	41.7	583 445	6 185	63 998	58.2	60 500	56.2	43.8	28.3	8.8	962	14.8
Halifax	196	-0.9	574	3.5	120.4	1 362 000	2 371	216 636	128.3	376 211	67.7	32.3	42.5	30.2	6 355	73.0
Harnett	120	7.2	150	2.3	77.0	803 863	5 349	95 246	190.3	238 732	38.7	61.3	35.5	19.8	3 369	38.8
Haywood	49	-12.9	82	0.4	10.1	519 586	6 334	39 461	14.1	23 660	45.5	54.5	23.8	4.5	773	23.1
Henderson	36	-5.8	76	3.4	17.4	596 389	7 807	67 859	61.8	132 139	87.6	12.4	36.8	14.1	1 427	8.8
Hertford	83	5.6	513	5.6	53.7	1 226 611	2 393	231 747	146.4	903 531	36.8	63.2	54.3	38.9	1 813	72.2
Hoke	59	-2.7	290	0.7	37.4	929 153	3 204	113 114	96.8	479 327	26.1	73.9	44.1	22.8	855	43.6
Hyde	108	30.1	681	0.5	83.1	1 674 475	2 460	333 924	133.4	844 373	D	D	47.5	29.7	1 787	79.1
Iredell	152	10.1	127	0.9	75.4	761 847	6 014	74 110	165.9	137 929	22.4	77.6	39.7	16.2	1 528	12.6
Jackson	16	21.5	66	0.1	6.2	638 514	9 656	51 196	8.2	33 502	93.6	6.4	29.4	6.1	90	11.0
Johnston	195	0.4	166	3.6	133.7	809 586	4 883	105 065	265.2	225 684	57.9	42.1	39.1	18.5	4 347	39.2
Jones	59	-14.1	349	1.1	45.3	931 588	2 668	189 171	185.6	1 091 594	16.6	83.4	55.9	38.8	2 130	57.6
Lee	39	7.9	159	1.3	15.0	663 992	4 180	71 622	34.7	141 252	49.5	50.5	32.9	12.2	569	19.5
Lenoir	122	-11.2	304	3.7	94.2	1 027 628	3 375	183 147	312.4	778 973	31.1	68.9	62.1	44.1	3 454	64.3
Lincoln	56	-6.4	85	0.2	25.6	475 570	5 571	55 046	56.5	86 731	17.2	82.8	27.6	7.5	350	18.1
McDowell	25	8.4	75	0.2	6.1	430 174	5 770	59 126	25.2	75 392	68.3	31.7	23.1	7.5	110	5.1
Macon	23	7.3	70	0.1	5.2	530 994	7 631	48 359	5.6	17 295	36.0	64.0	20.6	1.5	91	9.8
Madison	56	-15.7	78	0.2	10.2	541 449	5 414	31 459	5.7	7 861	67.5	32.5	18.1	0.8	859	34.6
Martin	127	20.6	356	0.8	88.7	1 004 266	2 819	192 616	100.3	281 070	84.3	15.7	61.3	37.8	4 684	85.4
Mecklenburg	15	-19.3	65	0.5	5.9	1 341 371	20 591	136 338	D	D	D	D	30.4	5.9	D	5.9
Mitchell	19	-15.2	68	0.0	4.3	356 112	5 271	34 846	2.5	8 703	80.4	19.6	24.1	0.3	119	13.6
Montgomery	35	-17.6	140	1.2	9.7	574 648	4 099	95 416	122.3	489 116	7.6	92.4	48.4	30.8	162	9.6
Moore	82	3.0	115	1.6	19.2	611 519	5 325	58 081	162.4	226 213	9.3	90.7	34.8	14.3	635	10.7
Nash	141	-8.4	327	6.0	91.5	1 246 505	3 812	153 670	184.4	428 723	60.8	39.2	50.5	32.6	1 705	50.5
New Hanover	3	-34.8	58	0.1	1.2	819 980	14 231	42 980	5.4	107 060	99.0	1.0	46.0	20.0	80	14.0
Northampton	163	4.6	510	3.2	109.5	1 335 680	2 618	218 533	133.0	416 821	56.9	43.1	59.2	35.4	5 226	85.6
Onslow	58	4.4	166	1.5	38.4	634 349	3 819	115 625	187.7	540 928	15.6	84.4	46.4	30.5	1 001	38.3
Orange	57	-5.6	88	0.8	21.8	587 984	6 693	53 744	30.6	47 462	50.5	49.5	31.9	6.4	611	22.6
Pamlico	47	1.4	585	2.4	39.4	1 682 463	2 877	334 763	35.8	448 100	D	D	53.8	38.8	881	63.8
Pasquotank	72	-15.6	531	D	67.7	1 678 897	3 159	307 206	69.0	507 537	99.4	0.6	58.1	40.4	969	52.2
Pender	56	-9.4	166	1.7	30.5	704 096	4 229	93 278	173.6	518 069	19.5	80.5	40.6	25.1	1 532	33.7
Perquimans	80	17.0	433	0.9	72.4	1 405 173	3 245	296 043	98.8	534 081	59.9	40.1	78.4	60.0	1 749	75.1
Person	95	-3.3	241	2.8	49.5	916 124	3 797	106 694	41.0	103 868	88.5	11.5	33.9	15.7	851	43.5
Pitt	172	0.2	439	3.6	131.7	1 397 719	3 181	233 246	215.9	552 194	51.5	48.5	60.1	38.9	3 877	57.3
Polk	24	14.8	83	0.1	7.1	609 310	7 332	49 707	D	D	D	D	20.7	5.2	56	13.1
Randolph	157	6.4	106	1.2	57.1	505 668	4 792	63 355	236.4	159 079	10.1	89.9	35.1	14.9	961	13.1
Richmond	48	16.3	172	1.5	19.4	707 336	4 119	72 953	165.2	596 390	7.1	92.9	48.7	32.5	610	27.4
Robeson	266	-0.9	282	6.5	198.6	828 756	2 937	136 951	409.6	435 310	35.2	64.8	45.7	24.4	4 522	51.1
Rockingham	112	-4.2	124	3.4	37.2	503 050	4 045	50 227	32.8	36 368	74.3	25.7	25.5	5.7	726	27.6
Rowan	121	4.5	120	1.1	65.9	677 980	5 658	79 407	84.0	83 067	60.5	39.5	29.5	8.0	458	12.6
Rutherford	60	-9.6	93	0.2	16.1	376 525	4 035	35 348	22.8	35 751	14.3	85.7	22.7	3.9	313	14.4
Sampson	292	-9.3	273	16.3	179.3	1 086 479	3 975	186 084	1 258.8	1 179 750	17.7	82.3	66.3	46.2	3 373	53.7
Scotland	69	4.8	460	2.2	33.4	1 654 193	3 600	113 933	82.2	547 833	24.5	75.5	50.7	34.7	427	44.7
Stanly	93	-11.0	140	0.5	54.5	720 660	5 141	85 458	96.5	145 354	33.8	66.2	27.1	11.0	928	26.5
Stokes	92	0.6	99	0.5	30.8	380 308	3 847	46 631	31.4	33 949	36.4	63.6	22.2	4.2	1 065	26.6
Surry	127	10.8	101	1.1	56.3	463 494	4 588	84 900	198.9	158 387	22.9	77.1	34.1	10.7	1 293	26.1

STATE County	Water use, 2010		Wholesale trade,[1] 2012				Retail trade,[2] 2012				Real estate and rental and leasing,[2] 2012			
	Total water withdrawn (mil gal/day)	Gallons withdrawn per person per day	Number of establishments	Number of employees	Sales (mil dol)	Annual payroll (mil dol)	Number of establishments	Number of employees	Sales (mil dol)	Annual payroll (mil dol)	Number of establishments	Number of employees	Receipts (mil dol)	Annual payroll (mil dol)
	133	134	135	136	137	138	139	140	141	142	143	144	145	146
NORTH CAROLINA—Cont'd														
Chowan	7.0	475	20	231	196.7	9.0	56	479	119.2	9.5	12	29	3.8	0.6
Clay	1.3	119	1	D	D	D	45	422	134.4	10.7	5	9	0.8	0.1
Cleveland	43.4	442	77	1 223	1 309.4	43.4	373	3 656	962.1	83.5	78	253	39.2	7.0
Columbus	43.1	741	37	357	295.2	17.4	217	2 125	553.1	47.2	35	85	14.3	2.1
Craven	37.3	361	75	D	D	D	394	4 358	1 213.6	103.3	99	336	43.4	9.9
Cumberland	45.7	143	164	2 628	1 028.8	103.2	1 049	15 587	4 374.2	365.3	326	D	D	D
Currituck	5.6	240	17	103	58.7	3.9	127	879	275.2	23.9	47	D	D	D
Dare	8.7	257	33	D	D	D	420	3 372	863.9	89.5	131	D	D	D
Davidson	27.2	167	148	1 904	1 032.2	77.9	466	4 824	1 301.8	108.6	91	D	D	D
Davie	6.4	155	33	349	160.1	15.9	112	1 258	360.2	28.9	29	D	D	D
Duplin	38.5	658	34	441	473.1	15.2	180	1 762	466.4	37.5	25	84	5.5	2.1
Durham	33.8	126	198	8 508	6 468.7	981.8	939	14 512	3 402.1	329.8	295	1 661	367.1	70.6
Edgecombe	15.3	270	17	359	206.0	11.2	141	1 416	372.1	29.9	39	90	24.4	3.3
Forsyth	49.5	141	380	6 070	4 220.3	285.3	1 361	19 642	5 569.4	479.4	373	1 791	313.9	65.9
Franklin	9.5	156	35	414	150.2	17.7	129	1 385	353.7	29.9	30	88	16.8	4.2
Gaston	851.7	4 133	198	2 756	2 037.7	120.2	637	9 035	2 329.5	203.3	148	742	151.2	26.1
Gates	2.9	234	7	30	23.0	1.1	26	191	43.6	3.8	1	D	D	D
Graham	39.1	4 408	2	D	D	D	33	226	44.5	4.6	3	3	0.3	0.0
Granville	8.2	137	24	D	D	D	132	1 306	350.0	29.0	34	87	11.3	1.9
Greene	7.6	357	4	D	D	D	45	303	83.5	5.3	2	D	D	D
Guilford	66.0	135	957	14 160	14 111.4	788.0	1 851	26 619	6 979.7	664.7	656	4 338	711.8	171.7
Halifax	31.7	580	25	D	D	D	236	2 448	607.0	50.9	39	138	13.6	2.7
Harnett	27.7	241	53	D	D	D	268	3 037	869.4	66.8	69	226	19.6	5.3
Haywood	101.2	1 714	36	195	109.1	10.7	254	2 768	811.0	66.3	68	170	24.1	4.2
Henderson	19.4	182	111	1 236	740.5	46.8	407	4 653	1 330.8	114.2	109	282	52.3	9.0
Hertford	10.7	432	17	96	38.7	3.2	101	1 122	254.9	22.8	12	32	5.4	0.8
Hoke	26.2	559	9	83	49.6	3.3	79	806	257.7	16.7	19	D	D	D
Hyde	1.8	312	12	89	84.8	2.4	36	166	30.4	2.8	6	53	4.5	1.5
Iredell	26.0	163	231	1 803	1 233.0	92.9	619	7 783	2 249.9	181.9	167	469	85.5	16.7
Jackson	5.1	127	16	D	D	D	157	1 519	403.7	34.0	54	184	21.5	5.4
Johnston	29.7	176	95	1 051	897.6	56.0	548	7 446	2 134.2	159.1	89	377	64.5	11.3
Jones	3.7	362	7	D	D	D	26	112	33.7	2.5	NA	NA	NA	NA
Lee	11.8	204	41	D	D	D	238	3 021	832.2	67.6	51	165	28.6	5.7
Lenoir	29.6	498	64	847	478.3	34.6	239	2 746	728.9	67.1	42	161	27.8	4.9
Lincoln	26.9	343	72	848	332.9	38.0	237	2 945	789.8	68.7	52	94	16.1	3.0
McDowell	11.1	246	30	209	393.2	9.6	125	1 597	457.8	35.9	24	54	5.5	1.2
Macon	278.1	8 198	20	94	33.8	2.8	222	1 757	432.5	43.8	56	93	14.4	2.6
Madison	2.7	132	5	21	6.8	0.3	41	408	111.5	7.6	15	17	2.2	0.6
Martin	63.6	2 594	21	163	77.3	5.6	75	914	249.1	19.9	10	28	4.8	0.7
Mecklenburg	2 804.9	3 050	1 811	28 413	21 895.9	1 802.7	3 378	52 469	14 756.9	1 291.7	1 678	9 686	2 279.5	533.3
Mitchell	4.1	265	9	28	25.0	1.1	61	679	182.1	14.4	16	42	5.3	1.4
Montgomery	6.1	220	23	185	62.7	7.9	83	719	189.8	15.7	12	18	2.3	0.3
Moore	21.1	240	61	360	224.4	16.0	352	4 380	1 094.9	97.0	97	230	32.6	7.1
Nash	20.6	215	111	2 045	2 693.9	98.1	410	5 059	1 234.5	110.3	87	374	49.0	11.3
New Hanover	42.4	209	282	2 531	1 189.4	122.7	1 027	13 512	3 871.7	336.5	378	2 111	355.7	76.9
Northampton	21.4	970	16	D	D	D	49	415	131.2	9.3	4	12	0.4	0.1
Onslow	32.3	182	50	304	139.1	11.9	545	7 716	2 213.0	177.9	187	664	127.0	20.7
Orange	24.2	181	83	678	510.4	33.2	386	5 621	1 385.3	151.1	153	558	95.7	20.0
Pamlico	3.8	286	9	D	D	D	41	412	100.1	9.3	12	40	2.7	0.8
Pasquotank	5.3	131	34	496	176.3	17.1	193	2 504	698.3	58.1	36	166	26.2	4.8
Pender	12.6	241	33	306	179.4	13.3	147	1 484	386.7	30.6	47	203	39.8	9.4
Perquimans	2.9	212	8	63	36.8	2.1	32	232	66.4	4.6	7	55	4.7	3.5
Person	1 014.8	25 714	22	320	176.0	14.5	126	1 409	378.4	29.3	19	52	7.9	1.1
Pitt	28.8	171	144	1 597	1 028.7	69.5	633	8 597	2 354.8	193.0	176	681	115.5	22.7
Polk	2.6	126	10	D	D	D	67	467	100.8	8.9	21	85	4.5	1.4
Randolph	23.4	165	148	1 753	836.6	80.9	395	4 137	1 107.9	89.7	79	235	46.2	6.7
Richmond	18.6	399	22	D	D	D	192	1 899	449.8	41.6	36	115	10.1	2.0
Robeson	37.2	277	71	1 050	604.4	34.3	390	4 921	1 395.6	117.3	60	211	27.1	4.3
Rockingham	133.4	1 424	52	769	397.6	24.6	324	3 530	866.3	77.0	56	153	15.9	3.4
Rowan	197.6	1 427	124	1 679	888.2	59.3	402	4 221	1 194.6	95.6	85	312	36.6	8.0
Rutherford	11.6	170	41	511	166.0	23.5	233	2 511	600.1	54.2	41	86	10.8	2.5
Sampson	37.9	597	43	788	450.6	35.7	191	2 219	593.0	50.2	33	94	17.0	3.0
Scotland	7.3	203	18	311	564.5	9.0	139	1 461	351.7	30.0	23	39	9.5	1.3
Stanly	9.5	157	49	328	177.7	16.4	232	2 609	618.1	55.4	36	145	22.4	4.3
Stokes	1 283.4	27 076	18	69	12.8	2.3	104	881	222.1	18.2	23	D	D	D
Surry	26.5	360	63	732	396.1	23.7	336	3 903	1 067.1	88.3	68	220	27.2	5.6

1. Merchant wholesalers, except manufacturers' sales branches and offices. 2. Employer establishments.

Table B. States and Counties — Professional Services, Manufacturing, and Accommodation and Food Services

STATE County	Professional, scientific, and technical services, 2012				Manufacturing, 2012				Accommodation and food services, 2012			
	Number of establish-ments	Number of employees	Receipts (mil dol)	Annual payroll (mil dol)	Number of establish-ments	Number of employees	Receipts (mil dol)	Annual payroll (mil dol)	Number of establish-ments	Number of employees	Sales (mil dol)	Annual payroll (mil dol)
	147	148	149	150	151	152	153	154	155	156	157	158
NORTH CAROLINA—Cont'd												
Chowan	26	138	13.5	4.5	18	493	451.2	20.5	28	430	19.1	5.1
Clay	13	40	3.4	1.4	8	156	D	5.6	18	166	8.6	2.4
Cleveland	131	747	104.7	29.5	118	5 325	1 821.2	232.2	159	2 262	109.1	28.6
Columbus	60	205	20.4	7.0	35	1 943	900.9	94.6	95	1 005	52.2	12.6
Craven	221	1 813	213.8	95.0	66	3 377	1 261.4	158.0	197	D	D	D
Cumberland	547	6 670	904.9	371.3	102	6 182	3 827.0	312.8	633	13 451	629.4	172.7
Currituck	40	115	14.2	4.9	15	43	D	1.4	70	D	D	D
Dare	130	D	D	D	36	398	47.8	13.9	325	D	D	D
Davidson	202	805	81.5	29.4	247	8 405	2 470.2	317.9	230	3 780	163.2	46.6
Davie	78	273	20.5	7.4	43	1 237	448.7	50.2	65	1 005	43.1	11.5
Duplin	53	168	15.4	5.7	32	5 482	2 056.7	169.6	63	921	44.1	10.7
Durham	1 123	32 330	5 726.0	2 810.4	171	11 001	8 955.5	782.2	709	14 103	832.5	226.9
Edgecombe	47	174	11.9	5.2	34	3 000	1 028.9	120.2	53	766	38.1	9.5
Forsyth	928	6 669	942.7	397.4	315	14 325	14 759.1	732.1	728	14 604	713.6	201.7
Franklin	69	247	30.4	12.8	53	2 327	1 047.3	126.8	51	633	27.8	7.6
Gaston	296	1 292	125.0	48.8	276	12 709	5 021.4	544.8	329	6 015	297.4	74.4
Gates	8	32	2.5	0.7	7	133	D	5.7	4	D	D	D
Graham	8	25	2.2	0.8	8	D	D	D	22	214	14.6	4.2
Granville	59	257	24.2	9.4	47	4 229	3 020.6	197.2	73	979	52.4	12.1
Greene	10	44	3.4	1.6	13	103	D	5.3	15	D	D	D
Guilford	1 439	D	D	D	641	32 428	26 932.2	1 690.3	1 143	22 863	1 158.5	319.5
Halifax	53	246	14.8	6.0	33	1 583	486.3	81.2	100	1 968	86.6	20.8
Harnett	116	437	47.8	18.4	63	1 566	358.4	58.5	135	2 305	99.1	26.0
Haywood	117	461	48.3	15.5	34	1 811	D	100.7	160	2 114	102.7	30.0
Henderson	222	821	87.6	30.9	123	5 858	2 625.0	281.7	207	2 925	170.0	48.1
Hertford	19	103	8.5	3.5	16	883	D	55.2	50	748	29.0	7.3
Hoke	30	143	7.0	2.9	13	2 011	1 654.1	66.7	24	477	16.5	4.3
Hyde	5	D	D	D	6	34	D	D	29	D	D	D
Iredell	381	2 671	438.4	124.9	280	9 940	3 628.9	459.9	345	6 011	289.6	76.9
Jackson	84	378	34.8	11.9	17	166	64.5	9.0	104	3 553	548.5	88.6
Johnston	255	845	91.4	31.6	109	6 399	3 712.6	323.3	262	4 949	243.0	61.2
Jones	6	20	1.9	0.5	5	28	D	1.2	6	D	D	D
Lee	80	304	26.5	90.5	73	8 039	2 751.5	340.9	106	1 816	84.2	23.0
Lenoir	64	498	112.4	23.8	46	3 374	D	135.8	99	1 776	78.4	20.9
Lincoln	117	471	53.2	18.2	109	3 974	1 884.9	165.4	101	1 649	75.4	20.2
McDowell	36	162	13.8	6.1	53	5 206	1 324.2	192.5	72	1 006	46.5	12.3
Macon	69	206	16.1	6.1	25	676	181.2	25.5	105	1 194	63.3	20.6
Madison	21	34	3.3	0.9	17	357	D	14.1	25	273	12.2	4.0
Martin	19	133	8.8	2.9	15	786	557.4	30.1	44	673	25.7	7.0
Mecklenburg	3 935	47 897	8 741.1	3 404.2	796	24 964	11 150.0	1 364.6	2 333	49 178	2 845.1	776.0
Mitchell	16	66	4.9	2.0	25	347	56.5	14.1	35	391	19.4	5.0
Montgomery	18	65	5.9	1.7	57	2 275	803.2	77.4	39	D	D	D
Moore	215	1 331	176.2	65.3	84	1 777	781.5	74.4	204	4 650	236.7	69.4
Nash	154	892	97.2	37.3	85	6 582	3 184.4	335.6	191	3 948	166.7	46.5
New Hanover	860	5 650	1 071.2	288.7	170	4 515	2 449.5	321.5	657	12 919	623.3	171.5
Northampton	11	29	2.2	0.8	9	444	246.4	19.2	14	123	4.6	1.3
Onslow	246	1 748	198.1	69.5	40	1 049	271.0	34.2	347	6 640	353.1	86.9
Orange	538	2 132	316.3	130.1	73	862	161.4	41.8	311	5 685	283.0	81.1
Pamlico	23	51	4.9	1.4	14	130	D	5.1	31	D	D	D
Pasquotank	63	334	35.3	13.4	27	726	D	37.4	92	1 774	76.9	19.4
Pender	77	202	19.3	6.7	37	753	191.4	28.0	89	1 032	50.5	14.0
Perquimans	13	33	1.8	0.8	5	D	D	D	13	218	8.6	2.2
Person	32	126	10.3	3.4	34	1 717	841.2	67.2	56	905	41.3	10.5
Pitt	311	1 893	247.9	84.4	87	4 905	2 160.8	248.8	362	8 055	357.6	96.7
Polk	37	135	12.4	4.2	20	304	78.2	9.3	34	352	14.4	4.4
Randolph	165	624	55.8	18.6	293	14 850	4 557.3	510.6	202	3 190	158.6	41.6
Richmond	45	171	12.8	4.0	42	2 775	794.4	87.6	66	949	42.3	10.5
Robeson	110	D	D	D	61	6 421	3 081.4	227.0	173	3 039	139.1	34.2
Rockingham	113	D	D	D	85	6 311	4 268.3	267.6	149	2 132	91.1	24.2
Rowan	177	851	87.9	29.4	186	7 529	3 856.6	327.2	219	3 619	163.2	44.5
Rutherford	78	250	21.3	7.4	71	2 639	672.5	115.4	123	1 590	71.8	19.7
Sampson	55	289	22.9	8.3	47	3 413	821.8	106.9	79	D	D	D
Scotland	27	117	9.4	3.8	30	1 662	984.2	74.8	58	923	43.8	11.3
Stanly	69	315	41.5	11.6	92	3 066	832.9	119.2	119	1 687	70.6	19.7
Stokes	39	141	11.8	4.4	25	896	489.7	33.1	52	721	35.1	9.1
Surry	96	355	33.4	11.2	93	3 511	967.8	122.4	160	2 403	105.4	28.7

1. Establishment subject to federal tax.

Table B. States and Counties — **Health Care and Social Assistance, Other Services, Nonemployer Businesses, and Residential Construction**

STATE County	Health care and social assistance, 2012				Other services, 2012				Nonemployer businesses, 2015		Value of residential construction authorized by building permits, 2016	
	Number of establishments	Number of employees	Receipts (mil dol)	Annual payroll (mil dol)	Number of establishments	Number of employees	Receipts (mil dol)	Annual payroll (mil dol)	Number	Receipts (mil dol)	New Construction ($1,000)	Number of housing units
	159	160	161	162	163	164	165	166	167	168	169	170
NORTH CAROLINA—Cont'd												
Chowan	62	1 194	94.1	39.2	16	80	5.9	1.9	1 004	33.9	4 522	19
Clay	23	270	14.9	6.5	11	D	D	D	1 062	38.2	0	0
Cleveland	227	5 245	496.8	195.7	121	607	58.8	16.3	5 414	174.7	24 113	122
Columbus	169	3 353	246.5	97.1	51	D	D	D	3 319	112.3	4 307	35
Craven	241	7 319	715.4	300.9	143	711	58.2	15.6	5 750	221.3	36 775	224
Cumberland	778	20 384	2 106.5	958.1	417	2 403	221.4	59.4	17 273	634.0	111 837	717
Currituck	27	248	18.0	7.6	43	201	22.2	5.6	2 001	91.4	78 365	255
Dare	92	D	D	D	95	404	33.6	9.7	5 242	277.1	107 383	325
Davidson	196	13 615	1 634.9	566.3	185	709	73.9	18.1	11 016	432.2	144 940	1 061
Davie	63	1 122	79.5	34.5	53	189	15.7	3.9	3 050	132.9	25 227	125
Duplin	105	1 969	133.2	60.1	52	203	17.4	5.0	3 180	127.9	7 350	49
Durham	772	25 680	3 785.0	1 271.4	433	4 298	708.8	175.8	22 742	831.8	446 272	3 097
Edgecombe	105	2 502	203.1	73.3	46	D	D	D	2 480	71.9	8 573	90
Forsyth	793	22 194	2 115.1	861.5	528	3 078	369.2	86.2	25 910	1 022.8	220 561	1 451
Franklin	81	1 162	86.9	34.7	60	219	19.9	5.2	4 107	159.0	73 864	457
Gaston	471	11 455	1 177.4	486.2	285	1 432	113.7	34.0	13 323	506.1	293 400	1 104
Gates	13	137	7.0	3.7	10	44	3.9	0.8	543	18.7	2 820	36
Graham	10	D	D	D	7	D	D	D	718	24.3	4 006	24
Granville	93	2 089	149.3	62.5	44	118	13.6	3.7	3 101	99.2	58 929	350
Greene	43	671	35.2	15.8	13	D	D	D	1 004	36.7	2 791	14
Guilford	1 289	33 134	3 512.8	1 373.9	804	5 091	830.0	155.1	39 823	1 739.6	437 303	2 204
Halifax	130	3 022	223.0	97.1	71	D	D	D	2 566	79.2	11 647	39
Harnett	175	3 533	302.4	114.4	97	383	35.6	8.8	6 594	254.0	90 381	678
Haywood	141	3 047	314.1	128.9	96	417	36.4	10.8	4 775	168.9	33 177	147
Henderson	292	6 339	581.9	236.3	174	860	84.3	24.7	9 058	362.4	110 112	555
Hertford	82	2 189	155.8	64.7	36	D	D	D	1 020	33.4	3 344	20
Hoke	65	946	49.5	20.8	24	101	7.5	1.9	2 262	60.1	50 237	236
Hyde	10	D	D	D	3	D	D	D	578	23.3	3 104	15
Iredell	455	6 805	758.7	298.5	272	1 696	149.9	39.2	13 241	620.8	344 232	1 348
Jackson	91	1 900	201.6	84.4	54	205	26.5	6.2	3 216	123.3	79 120	168
Johnston	300	5 165	457.1	177.1	200	868	74.2	21.3	12 158	549.9	340 480	2 007
Jones	15	188	47.7	9.3	5	12	1.1	0.3	586	19.8	1 662	16
Lee	160	2 732	249.7	93.8	84	393	27.9	9.2	3 520	157.3	21 291	98
Lenoir	176	4 333	305.5	133.8	81	522	45.7	13.1	3 244	114.6	13 006	112
Lincoln	137	2 343	223.5	86.8	130	491	41.6	12.3	5 535	237.2	176 591	816
McDowell	91	1 630	119.4	44.9	40	293	21.8	6.7	2 508	83.3	21 189	81
Macon	91	1 546	134.1	53.4	93	354	31.1	8.7	3 222	122.0	29 640	91
Madison	30	652	37.9	16.2	11	38	4.2	0.9	1 919	68.4	22 569	79
Martin	74	1 462	95.3	37.7	19	D	D	D	1 252	40.4	0	0
Mecklenburg	2 576	61 634	8 163.9	3 031.5	1 698	12 608	1 767.5	413.7	91 430	4 249.6	1 509 315	9 759
Mitchell	38	886	97.6	29.3	27	84	6.1	1.7	1 144	38.4	5 503	29
Montgomery	55	1 031	61.4	29.7	34	200	11.5	4.7	1 500	57.3	100	4
Moore	275	8 294	913.4	374.0	137	709	56.7	16.8	7 312	341.8	152 890	731
Nash	243	4 050	349.4	143.4	138	D	D	D	5 604	224.7	36 755	226
New Hanover	756	12 485	1 277.4	511.7	440	2 566	226.8	65.5	19 867	950.2	451 755	2 383
Northampton	32	693	26.4	12.8	17	D	D	D	877	29.1	3 701	15
Onslow	257	5 765	491.7	197.5	210	1 172	89.9	26.6	9 253	331.3	109 646	803
Orange	391	12 581	1 389.9	600.6	196	1 699	271.2	59.1	12 865	530.2	131 498	496
Pamlico	37	557	43.0	20.8	19	109	11.4	2.6	1 017	39.7	13 693	52
Pasquotank	138	2 540	225.1	97.3	62	D	D	D	2 651	82.9	18 046	106
Pender	89	1 305	97.3	38.5	55	193	17.4	5.1	4 222	168.7	95 310	564
Perquimans	16	183	8.9	4.5	11	D	D	D	949	30.4	6 372	31
Person	83	1 278	98.9	35.2	43	158	17.0	4.4	2 146	73.5	15 640	82
Pitt	510	16 075	1 880.0	681.9	183	1 104	93.9	25.1	10 307	400.6	110 418	861
Polk	58	1 457	104.4	43.8	26	D	D	D	1 904	80.3	22 646	74
Randolph	238	5 136	363.9	164.1	170	709	77.9	19.7	9 692	382.5	63 155	310
Richmond	98	2 042	177.2	73.2	56	272	16.2	4.8	1 876	65.0	8 141	205
Robeson	286	8 151	581.0	256.4	80	358	26.9	7.7	7 296	227.2	16 624	85
Rockingham	170	3 440	287.5	110.4	121	525	39.6	11.1	4 943	177.2	44 843	221
Rowan	263	8 202	837.0	406.4	142	682	58.0	18.0	8 955	331.0	104 031	320
Rutherford	132	2 951	245.8	90.6	68	377	27.7	9.1	4 109	165.7	28 515	122
Sampson	130	2 719	179.4	76.3	64	292	25.4	7.5	3 423	129.8	10 622	73
Scotland	114	2 358	236.0	97.2	32	117	10.2	2.3	1 773	53.6	3 359	9
Stanly	174	3 190	251.4	98.7	81	390	32.2	10.2	3 912	158.0	32 300	199
Stokes	51	1 156	107.1	36.4	47	D	D	D	2 861	108.2	17 131	85
Surry	171	5 086	411.6	173.2	96	487	39.4	11.2	4 768	204.5	24 973	154

Table B. States and Counties — Government Employment and Payroll, and Local Government Finances

| | Government employment and payroll, 2012 | | March payroll (percent of total) | | | | | | | Local government finances, 2012 | | | | |
STATE County	Full-time equivalent employees	March payroll (dollars)	Administration, judicial, and legal	Police and Corrections	Fire Protection	Highways and transportation	Health and Welfare	Natural resources and utilities	Education and libraries	General revenue Total (mil dol)	Inter-governmental (mil dol)	Taxes Total (mil dol)	Per capita[1] (dollars) Total	Per capita[1] (dollars) Property
	171	172	173	174	175	176	177	178	179	180	181	182	183	184
NORTH CAROLINA— Cont'd														
Chowan	470	1 457 821	1.5	4.5	1.5	0.7	1.5	4.7	79.9	47.9	24.9	15.3	1 036	830
Clay	374	1 096 838	4.9	8.6	0.1	2.1	18.6	3.2	58.6	30.3	17.7	10.0	938	759
Cleveland	5 555	17 029 077	1.4	2.7	1.1	0.6	40.8	3.7	48.8	997.0	173.6	81.7	838	665
Columbus	2 576	8 631 036	7.0	13.2	4.0	1.6	9.8	5.6	57.3	181.2	110.5	43.2	750	595
Craven	5 760	21 786 606	3.1	4.6	1.8	1.3	49.5	4.0	34.0	683.8	247.7	93.3	890	647
Cumberland	18 665	65 054 561	1.3	6.1	1.9	0.8	41.4	3.9	38.6	1 026.5	546.0	340.9	1 052	756
Currituck	1 085	3 605 883	4.2	9.0	1.4	0.2	12.9	4.4	63.7	101.1	28.3	49.2	2 044	1 156
Dare	1 891	6 914 953	10.6	12.1	4.0	0.9	18.7	6.6	40.2	195.1	51.6	121.3	3 507	2 197
Davidson	5 783	17 327 794	4.1	6.9	2.6	0.9	8.4	4.1	68.7	408.7	228.5	125.0	765	602
Davie	1 378	4 164 460	3.3	9.1	0.2	0.6	15.6	2.8	66.1	100.6	51.4	36.9	892	723
Duplin	2 596	7 169 108	4.4	6.0	0.9	1.1	11.3	3.0	71.0	166.7	96.1	42.2	702	533
Durham	9 926	33 408 797	6.2	5.0	0.4	2.0	10.8	7.2	66.1	1 014.8	394.0	460.1	1 645	1 286
Edgecombe	2 085	7 168 867	2.6	6.9	1.2	0.7	10.7	5.5	70.6	170.1	100.0	37.8	676	569
Forsyth	13 925	45 845 272	4.9	9.9	5.3	1.5	7.4	5.9	62.7	1 198.2	555.3	456.5	1 275	995
Franklin	1 848	5 584 621	4.4	7.9	0.4	0.3	14.6	2.9	65.1	141.2	69.1	51.6	840	681
Gaston	7 249	25 015 194	7.4	6.7	2.8	2.9	12.2	6.4	59.7	643.2	307.9	230.9	1 110	864
Gates	371	1 271 812	3.9	2.8	0.0	1.1	5.8	2.3	82.4	29.7	19.3	7.6	641	522
Graham	358	999 021	5.0	6.3	0.1	2.3	19.0	2.4	60.3	29.4	18.8	7.3	834	661
Granville	1 871	5 604 572	7.1	8.1	0.7	1.1	4.5	5.4	70.7	198.6	73.9	47.4	785	648
Greene	792	2 460 297	7.1	5.1	0.0	2.0	11.7	8.9	63.9	57.2	35.0	8.8	409	388
Guilford	18 710	71 857 919	4.6	10.1	4.0	2.3	6.6	6.4	63.8	1 781.8	770.6	726.5	1 450	1 146
Halifax	2 529	8 099 327	3.1	5.7	1.4	1.3	12.8	5.1	68.3	190.1	109.1	47.9	886	669
Harnett	3 872	13 569 140	4.6	12.1	0.4	1.1	9.2	4.4	66.9	288.8	164.5	83.5	684	544
Haywood	3 238	11 027 848	3.6	5.3	0.5	0.6	44.4	2.8	39.6	310.3	118.9	68.8	1 168	882
Henderson	4 495	15 113 386	3.5	6.2	0.7	0.5	37.6	2.5	46.9	628.0	121.4	105.7	976	755
Hertford	1 107	3 318 864	2.9	8.6	0.6	0.6	10.8	4.2	66.9	79.7	46.0	21.1	863	629
Hoke	1 946	6 883 544	2.2	5.4	0.2	1.0	6.2	1.3	80.3	121.2	74.9	31.7	626	463
Hyde	303	895 248	4.8	5.1	0.0	0.0	17.4	6.5	63.4	29.6	15.5	8.8	1 500	1 122
Iredell	5 871	18 788 013	4.4	8.0	3.5	0.6	9.3	4.8	66.7	482.4	216.0	188.6	1 159	907
Jackson	1 418	4 256 176	4.4	6.6	0.0	1.0	11.8	4.0	65.6	109.9	53.3	43.4	1 072	832
Johnston	7 756	24 977 350	2.3	4.6	1.2	0.6	24.0	3.4	62.5	698.3	273.2	164.7	942	743
Jones	494	1 149 556	4.9	6.6	0.0	0.2	13.5	4.3	66.8	28.8	17.3	6.8	664	556
Lee	3 038	10 911 112	3.3	6.5	2.0	1.2	5.3	3.7	57.7	206.8	113.6	67.5	1 130	854
Lenoir	2 634	8 323 127	3.5	7.1	2.0	2.2	10.0	8.6	63.7	209.1	121.6	56.5	955	735
Lincoln	2 462	7 572 141	4.1	8.7	1.3	1.3	14.4	4.8	63.7	182.3	86.5	68.9	868	682
McDowell	1 584	3 817 801	1.8	2.8	0.5	0.8	1.5	2.4	89.3	105.4	60.6	31.8	708	497
Macon	1 378	3 815 292	6.5	9.2	0.5	1.5	16.3	5.7	56.3	100.9	48.1	36.6	1 081	971
Madison	876	2 682 447	3.6	4.9	0.2	0.3	14.0	3.1	71.6	52.3	29.4	15.8	761	620
Martin	1 141	3 472 186	4.5	5.3	2.4	1.3	15.0	4.7	65.2	85.6	46.7	22.7	948	699
Mecklenburg	60 489	285 037 206	2.7	6.4	2.0	1.6	56.6	3.0	26.7	8 195.0	1 390.6	1 863.3	1 923	1 419
Mitchell	1 336	2 250 773	2.5	3.7	0.0	0.0	5.6	2.2	79.0	52.4	33.1	13.0	844	617
Montgomery	1 174	3 454 946	3.3	6.9	0.0	0.7	9.4	3.4	74.1	81.0	47.9	21.9	792	630
Moore	3 494	11 423 864	5.9	7.9	2.5	1.7	12.6	3.7	62.8	269.6	121.4	108.4	1 201	948
Nash	6 656	23 448 806	3.3	5.8	2.6	2.0	39.4	6.2	39.5	555.5	191.0	99.1	1 035	775
New Hanover	11 962	45 527 134	2.5	6.8	2.5	1.2	49.3	4.7	29.7	1 468.2	274.1	326.8	1 562	1 109
Northampton	777	2 301 803	10.7	8.8	0.0	0.6	20.3	6.4	49.8	67.1	36.8	21.0	982	870
Onslow	5 873	18 455 158	3.9	7.0	1.9	1.2	10.7	4.8	66.2	585.4	209.5	152.5	832	536
Orange	5 385	18 675 410	6.4	8.5	3.1	3.3	8.9	7.6	55.3	495.0	178.9	247.0	1 791	1 537
Pamlico	537	1 656 218	4.6	6.6	0.2	0.4	9.9	5.9	70.1	42.4	25.2	12.6	965	785
Pasquotank	3 546	11 505 340	5.8	3.9	1.2	1.0	34.4	2.5	33.1	251.3	70.2	38.8	955	676
Pender	1 621	5 227 407	6.3	8.7	1.1	0.4	9.8	2.7	65.8	149.8	76.0	58.2	1 074	864
Perquimans	396	1 289 198	8.5	2.8	0.0	0.0	8.3	6.7	68.4	34.0	18.9	10.8	795	634
Person	1 548	5 009 176	3.6	7.9	2.5	1.2	11.6	4.6	65.6	119.0	63.0	39.6	1 007	800
Pitt	6 107	20 619 861	3.8	8.9	3.2	2.0	4.2	10.9	60.2	555.7	265.7	167.7	972	677
Polk	658	2 004 992	5.0	7.0	0.0	2.3	8.7	5.2	70.0	53.2	24.8	21.2	1 045	877
Randolph	4 527	16 669 167	4.3	8.3	2.7	1.2	7.8	3.4	68.3	345.4	185.5	117.9	828	644
Richmond	2 132	5 122 800	4.4	8.9	2.0	1.6	14.1	4.9	62.7	142.5	82.7	39.5	848	648
Robeson	6 145	18 365 522	4.4	13.6	1.4	1.1	12.5	5.8	59.7	414.1	250.9	103.1	761	522
Rockingham	3 543	11 125 272	5.5	9.4	2.7	1.5	10.3	3.0	62.8	267.2	141.9	84.2	908	715
Rowan	5 594	16 509 444	3.8	6.2	1.8	1.2	7.6	4.3	71.8	395.5	204.5	128.5	930	719
Rutherford	3 135	8 814 742	3.6	6.0	1.3	1.0	9.8	3.6	57.5	200.1	101.7	53.6	796	593
Sampson	2 770	7 777 872	2.8	6.0	0.4	0.4	11.9	2.4	71.5	212.9	127.6	48.5	759	539
Scotland	1 728	5 628 337	3.5	5.7	0.4	0.9	9.5	5.0	72.9	112.7	68.9	30.4	843	662
Stanly	2 443	7 501 977	4.3	7.7	2.6	2.1	13.1	6.3	62.1	184.7	101.2	51.9	857	641
Stokes	1 636	4 531 305	4.4	6.7	2.3	0.1	12.8	2.1	70.0	122.3	78.2	33.7	720	593
Surry	3 820	12 472 258	2.4	4.5	0.8	0.5	33.1	2.1	53.9	321.4	128.8	65.4	889	603

1. Based on the resident population estimated as of July 1 of the year shown.

Table B. States and Counties — Local Government Finances, Government Employment, and Income Taxes

STATE County	Local government finances, 2012 (cont.)									Government employment, 2015			Individual income tax returns, 2014		
	Direct general expenditure							Debt outstanding							
			Percent of total for:												
	Total (mil dol)	Per capita¹ (dollars)	Education	Health and hospitals	Police protection	Public welfare	Highways	Total (mil dol)	Per capita¹ (dollars)	Federal civilian	Federal military	State and local	Number of returns	Mean adjusted gross income	Mean income tax
	185	186	187	188	189	190	191	192	193	194	195	196	197	198	199
NORTH CAROLINA—Cont'd															
Chowan	47.4	3 208	53.9	0.4	10.6	6.8	2.3	21.8	1 475	28	34	819	6 230	48 701	5 224
Clay	30.1	2 831	45.1	6.7	10.1	14.8	0.1	11.8	1 114	18	25	493	4 320	42 317	4 360
Cleveland	561.2	5 758	30.2	48.9	3.5	3.9	0.5	167.5	1 719	173	227	5 805	40 960	43 041	3 874
Columbus	177.1	3 072	58.4	4.6	6.2	8.6	0.7	63.1	1 095	123	129	3 588	21 350	39 233	3 416
Craven	658.8	6 288	21.8	54.9	3.8	3.5	0.8	179.3	1 712	5 644	8 509	6 987	45 760	50 570	5 261
Cumberland	1 088.1	3 358	50.4	3.7	7.9	6.3	1.3	508.0	1 568	14 731	48 516	22 671	141 970	43 686	4 054
Currituck	92.8	3 854	37.2	6.0	8.8	4.4	0.1	60.9	2 529	33	60	1 180	11 380	54 493	5 533
Dare	214.0	6 189	25.3	7.8	9.4	3.9	1.4	229.3	6 632	229	185	2 891	19 260	54 540	6 582
Davidson	418.5	2 563	60.4	2.9	6.7	5.2	1.1	214.7	1 315	167	390	6 421	71 410	46 869	4 543
Davie	101.9	2 459	54.9	7.3	7.9	6.1	0.9	31.0	749	61	99	1 576	18 600	59 356	7 002
Duplin	161.0	2 681	57.6	5.6	6.5	7.2	1.1	40.0	667	129	145	3 278	23 010	34 197	2 768
Durham	1 130.0	4 041	36.7	5.4	7.7	4.9	2.8	1 199.0	4 288	6 123	846	15 021	139 410	59 684	7 426
Edgecombe	174.9	3 125	52.2	4.1	6.7	12.0	1.1	31.7	567	194	128	4 094	22 590	35 862	3 028
Forsyth	1 295.8	3 618	44.3	6.0	8.5	3.9	2.2	1 426.9	3 984	1 689	901	18 628	165 300	60 947	8 116
Franklin	146.8	2 389	50.6	6.0	5.3	7.7	1.0	126.9	2 064	77	149	2 374	25 330	46 345	4 147
Gaston	705.2	3 389	45.5	9.1	9.5	5.7	2.2	453.5	2 180	337	505	9 351	92 180	49 421	5 079
Gates	29.2	2 457	67.6	0.6	4.9	6.5	0.1	8.9	752	20	27	520	4 650	45 897	3 962
Graham	26.4	3 040	48.5	6.1	10.0	8.9	1.3	9.5	1 093	33	20	481	3 270	36 666	2 939
Granville	202.2	3 345	38.7	26.8	6.4	4.7	0.7	131.9	2 182	1 492	131	6 743	24 350	49 422	4 735
Greene	57.7	2 693	65.9	4.7	3.8	7.2	0.7	25.4	1 185	36	45	1 786	7 820	36 136	2 669
Guilford	1 919.4	3 832	43.8	4.5	7.5	4.2	2.9	2 139.4	4 271	3 957	1 261	29 398	233 600	58 219	7 507
Halifax	185.9	3 442	51.7	6.0	5.5	8.7	1.6	112.0	2 073	131	122	4 027	21 550	37 717	3 295
Harnett	319.1	2 613	48.6	4.3	6.4	3.5	1.3	272.9	2 234	128	310	5 413	48 860	45 933	4 061
Haywood	325.8	5 531	28.2	47.8	4.0	5.8	1.3	100.5	1 706	110	142	2 858	26 500	44 888	4 244
Henderson	411.4	3 800	31.5	38.2	5.0	4.9	1.3	200.9	1 856	207	267	5 249	51 180	51 117	5 331
Hertford	78.3	3 203	52.5	7.5	6.9	8.5	1.0	105.4	4 314	63	52	2 110	8 530	38 754	3 411
Hoke	115.8	2 291	61.0	2.2	4.8	7.7	0.8	96.8	1 915	55	124	2 419	19 850	40 098	2 842
Hyde	31.1	5 313	35.0	17.4	4.4	5.8	0.0	21.2	3 614	38	11	637	2 100	39 997	3 590
Iredell	484.3	2 977	49.9	1.9	7.8	5.0	2.0	564.7	3 470	255	404	8 336	76 680	62 855	8 632
Jackson	117.6	2 908	51.0	4.9	4.2	6.3	0.6	47.1	1 164	55	91	7 829	16 440	44 279	4 394
Johnston	707.4	4 044	42.4	30.3	4.0	3.6	1.0	672.2	3 843	225	442	9 144	77 550	51 285	5 065
Jones	28.7	2 798	50.8	6.3	6.8	10.5	0.5	4.3	418	24	24	571	4 320	39 546	3 651
Lee	211.6	3 544	60.3	1.6	7.1	4.8	1.1	152.3	2 550	156	141	3 239	25 940	45 852	4 208
Lenoir	226.0	3 816	45.8	3.1	5.0	6.3	0.8	200.6	3 387	195	136	5 704	25 800	39 989	3 866
Lincoln	184.5	2 326	52.4	5.8	7.2	7.4	0.6	203.5	2 566	100	193	3 586	34 620	56 607	6 530
McDowell	115.5	2 567	60.9	1.8	4.8	9.3	1.1	20.1	447	72	104	2 505	18 370	39 819	3 276
Macon	106.3	3 138	46.9	3.4	10.5	5.7	2.0	49.0	1 446	164	81	1 656	15 050	49 312	5 811
Madison	53.5	2 579	46.9	5.8	7.8	10.1	0.9	10.7	515	58	48	907	8 460	38 950	3 494
Martin	89.4	3 730	50.1	10.1	7.7	7.3	1.2	36.3	1 513	48	56	1 552	10 270	36 588	3 009
Mecklenburg	7 529.3	7 770	17.3	51.9	4.4	2.3	1.8	7 935.0	8 189	5 783	2 550	71 420	480 950	72 394	11 097
Mitchell	54.4	3 537	64.7	2.0	5.5	8.9	0.2	3.0	192	39	36	1 054	6 030	38 917	3 070
Montgomery	78.0	2 820	58.5	5.5	7.0	5.5	1.1	28.8	1 042	51	64	1 707	11 090	42 148	4 031
Moore	304.5	3 372	46.2	2.7	12.1	4.3	1.8	140.3	1 553	157	237	4 444	42 250	64 095	8 091
Nash	589.1	6 155	29.3	42.9	4.8	3.1	1.6	113.0	1 181	183	221	5 968	43 260	46 602	4 691
New Hanover	1 459.0	6 973	21.3	49.4	4.8	2.5	1.1	1 476.2	7 055	929	712	19 111	100 570	62 765	8 789
Northampton	68.1	3 176	37.6	9.0	6.4	10.1	1.8	37.7	1 759	45	47	1 134	8 110	36 993	2 747
Onslow	563.2	3 073	38.6	24.7	6.7	6.5	1.0	439.4	2 398	6 779	43 028	7 945	78 430	41 522	3 302
Orange	485.2	3 518	44.0	6.5	6.9	6.2	1.4	328.7	2 383	257	354	38 957	59 990	88 687	14 133
Pamlico	43.2	3 303	51.1	3.1	4.3	7.4	0.9	13.7	1 044	28	52	881	5 480	52 123	5 705
Pasquotank	254.1	6 261	28.0	49.1	4.4	3.4	1.2	135.3	3 334	710	920	3 835	17 070	44 421	3 942
Pender	152.0	2 804	46.6	4.9	6.0	6.5	0.6	184.1	3 396	99	167	2 479	23 940	48 964	4 815
Perquimans	34.1	2 515	51.3	2.5	8.3	7.0	1.1	30.1	2 218	37	32	640	5 710	48 220	4 481
Person	126.4	3 218	53.5	5.5	6.7	8.5	0.7	200.1	5 097	53	93	1 838	16 880	44 801	3 966
Pitt	557.6	3 232	46.8	1.8	9.9	5.2	2.1	400.7	2 322	685	448	25 720	70 570	51 426	5 913
Polk	49.0	2 420	52.7	2.7	8.4	8.4	1.3	16.1	796	43	48	902	8 770	55 052	6 608
Randolph	349.0	2 450	59.5	2.6	7.6	5.8	1.4	147.2	1 033	198	339	5 925	61 450	44 664	4 341
Richmond	150.1	3 220	56.1	3.4	6.8	7.0	1.1	48.8	1 047	108	106	2 982	18 140	36 059	2 764
Robeson	429.7	3 171	54.2	4.0	5.7	7.6	1.3	103.7	765	286	312	8 413	49 500	33 922	2 464
Rockingham	263.7	2 844	53.2	2.0	6.8	7.4	2.1	167.2	1 803	146	217	3 989	39 260	43 599	4 014
Rowan	420.9	3 046	54.8	2.5	6.5	5.4	1.5	263.4	1 906	2 562	323	6 679	60 090	45 042	4 206
Rutherford	191.7	2 848	53.0	6.6	6.5	6.8	1.1	113.5	1 685	109	156	3 414	25 360	40 306	3 569
Sampson	232.7	3 639	52.4	12.4	4.0	6.9	0.7	122.1	1 909	104	150	4 031	28 140	39 431	3 527
Scotland	112.8	3 125	56.5	1.8	7.2	8.7	1.5	27.4	758	47	79	2 230	13 480	38 259	3 143
Stanly	179.1	2 956	54.3	4.3	6.6	5.6	1.2	61.7	1 019	144	141	3 425	25 540	45 725	4 349
Stokes	117.6	2 514	64.2	4.7	5.2	6.5	0.4	62.1	1 328	63	110	1 813	19 670	45 515	4 105
Surry	324.4	4 410	40.1	37.5	3.8	3.5	0.8	112.5	1 530	166	172	4 535	29 980	44 435	4 316

1. Based on the resident population estimated as of July 1 of the year shown.

Table B. States and Counties — Land Area and Population

STATE/ County code	CBSA code[1]	County type[2]	STATE County	Land area,[3] (sq mi) 2016	Total persons 2016	Rank	Per square mile	White	Black	American Indian, Alaska Native	Asian and Pacific Islander	Percent Hispanic or Latino[4]	Under 5 years	5 to 17 years	18 to 24 years	25 to 34 years	35 to 44 years	45 to 54 years
				1	2	3	4	5	6	7	8	9	10	11	12	13	14	15
			NORTH CAROLINA—Cont'd															
37 173	...	8	Swain	528.0	14 346	2 143	27.2	66.4	2.0	30.1	1.1	4.9	6.9	15.6	8.4	12.0	11.4	12.8
37 175	14820	6	Transylvania	378.5	33 482	1 342	88.5	91.8	4.6	1.0	0.9	3.3	4.3	11.8	7.9	9.4	9.7	11.7
37 177	28620	9	Tyrrell	390.8	4 141	2 888	10.6	52.5	37.9	0.7	2.5	8.3	5.1	13.5	7.8	14.2	13.0	13.0
37 179	16740	1	Union	631.7	226 606	290	358.7	74.2	12.6	0.7	3.1	11.0	5.8	21.8	8.8	9.7	14.0	16.5
37 181	25780	4	Vance	252.4	44 244	1 086	175.3	41.1	51.2	0.6	0.8	7.5	6.4	17.5	8.8	11.3	11.1	13.6
37 183	39580	1	Wake	834.8	1 046 791	41	1 253.9	62.3	21.3	0.8	7.8	10.0	6.3	18.2	9.2	14.7	15.1	14.6
37 185	...	8	Warren	429.1	19 907	1 834	46.4	39.3	51.9	5.9	0.7	3.9	4.6	14.0	7.6	10.8	10.5	12.7
37 187	...	7	Washington	346.5	12 195	2 279	35.2	46.0	48.3	0.6	0.5	5.7	5.6	15.0	7.9	9.8	9.3	13.0
37 189	14380	5	Watauga	312.4	53 922	933	172.6	93.3	2.2	0.9	1.6	3.4	3.2	9.8	29.3	11.3	9.0	10.5
37 191	24140	3	Wayne	553.9	124 150	505	224.1	55.3	32.4	0.9	1.9	11.5	6.7	17.1	9.9	13.4	11.7	12.8
37 193	35900	6	Wilkes	754.5	68 740	776	91.1	88.7	5.0	0.6	0.8	6.2	5.1	15.8	7.4	10.4	11.6	14.3
37 195	48980	4	Wilson	367.6	81 661	689	222.1	48.6	40.6	0.6	1.5	10.0	5.8	17.6	8.6	11.8	11.6	13.4
37 197	49180	2	Yadkin	334.9	37 532	1 234	112.1	85.3	3.8	0.6	0.5	11.0	5.1	16.2	8.0	10.3	11.6	15.6
37 199	...	8	Yancey	312.6	17 678	1 935	56.6	93.2	1.3	0.7	0.5	5.1	4.9	14.0	6.8	10.0	11.0	13.8
38 000	...	0	**NORTH DAKOTA**	69 001.0	757 952	X	11.0	86.8	3.4	6.1	2.1	3.6	7.3	16.0	12.0	15.0	11.4	11.3
38 001	...	9	Adams	987.6	2 305	3 022	2.3	94.8	1.1	1.7	2.4	1.8	4.7	14.7	6.3	9.7	10.0	12.5
38 003	...	6	Barnes	1 491.6	10 926	2 360	7.3	93.4	2.6	1.9	1.6	2.0	5.5	14.7	10.2	11.2	10.2	11.7
38 005	...	9	Benson	1 388.7	6 739	2 694	4.9	42.5	0.7	55.0	0.6	3.0	10.8	24.1	9.0	11.8	9.0	10.6
38 007	...	9	Billings	1 148.8	934	3 108	0.8	93.0	0.1	0.5	4.6	2.1	7.1	13.4	6.2	14.6	12.3	12.5
38 009	...	9	Bottineau	1 668.4	6 579	2 704	3.9	93.0	1.2	4.3	0.9	2.8	5.9	15.5	9.1	10.1	9.8	11.9
38 011	...	9	Bowman	1 161.9	3 241	2 956	2.8	93.0	0.6	1.7	0.3	5.4	7.0	17.4	8.0	11.2	10.5	10.6
38 013	...	9	Burke	1 103.6	2 198	3 031	2.0	94.5	1.1	2.3	0.9	2.6	8.0	17.3	6.2	12.1	10.1	12.5
38 015	13900	3	Burleigh	1 632.6	94 487	620	57.9	90.9	2.4	4.8	1.3	2.3	7.1	16.0	9.5	15.0	12.5	12.0
38 017	22020	3	Cass	1 764.9	175 249	371	99.3	87.8	5.8	1.9	3.8	2.7	7.3	15.1	15.2	17.2	12.5	10.8
38 019	...	9	Cavalier	1 488.8	3 827	2 917	2.6	96.4	0.7	2.2	0.7	1.2	5.9	14.5	6.8	9.1	8.7	11.7
38 021	...	9	Dickey	1 131.5	5 064	2 829	4.5	94.0	1.3	1.5	0.8	3.8	6.1	17.8	9.2	9.8	10.1	11.6
38 023	...	9	Divide	1 260.7	2 413	3 011	1.9	94.2	1.8	2.0	1.0	2.7	6.4	15.0	6.4	11.0	9.0	12.3
38 025	...	9	Dunn	2 008.5	4 366	2 872	2.2	83.8	1.3	10.3	1.8	4.9	7.4	15.6	8.0	14.8	11.1	13.0
38 027	...	9	Eddy	630.2	2 358	3 018	3.7	92.6	0.9	4.6	0.7	2.9	5.8	16.4	6.1	10.0	9.3	11.7
38 029	...	8	Emmons	1 510.4	3 346	2 949	2.2	97.2	0.9	1.5	0.7	0.9	4.9	15.1	8.2	7.3	8.2	13.0
38 031	...	9	Foster	635.5	3 303	2 953	5.2	96.3	0.8	1.7	0.7	1.5	6.0	15.7	7.7	10.4	10.3	12.6
38 033	...	9	Golden Valley	1 001.5	1 817	3 068	1.8	94.7	0.7	1.8	1.1	2.9	5.9	18.1	7.6	9.6	12.5	11.3
38 035	24220	3	Grand Forks	1 436.4	71 083	761	49.5	86.7	4.8	3.5	3.6	4.0	7.0	13.7	21.3	16.0	9.8	9.5
38 037	...	8	Grant	1 659.2	2 377	3 017	1.4	96.6	1.0	2.3	0.8	1.3	6.3	14.2	6.1	8.6	8.7	11.5
38 039	...	9	Griggs	708.8	2 277	3 025	3.2	97.1	0.5	0.7	0.3	1.7	4.6	13.8	7.0	7.2	9.3	11.2
38 041	...	9	Hettinger	1 132.2	2 629	2 995	2.3	93.5	1.4	3.9	0.7	2.4	5.9	16.8	6.8	11.9	9.9	11.2
38 043	...	8	Kidder	1 351.2	2 414	3 010	1.8	94.9	0.7	0.5	0.8	3.6	6.4	14.6	6.5	11.0	10.0	11.8
38 045	...	9	LaMoure	1 145.9	4 111	2 893	3.6	97.6	0.7	0.8	0.3	1.4	5.7	16.1	6.7	8.6	9.7	11.3
38 047	...	9	Logan	992.8	1 941	3 053	2.0	97.6	0.7	1.2	0.7	1.1	5.5	16.6	7.2	8.5	8.6	11.5
38 049	33500	9	McHenry	1 874.0	5 963	2 753	3.2	95.7	0.8	1.6	0.6	2.6	6.1	17.9	6.4	11.2	11.5	13.1
38 051	...	9	McIntosh	974.7	2 656	2 993	2.7	95.1	0.6	1.1	1.8	2.3	5.3	12.9	6.1	9.3	7.8	11.2
38 053	...	9	McKenzie	2 760.5	12 621	2 253	4.6	79.4	1.7	12.2	1.2	7.8	9.9	21.1	8.9	16.8	12.5	11.4
38 055	...	8	McLean	2 110.6	9 729	2 451	4.6	91.2	0.6	7.1	0.3	2.5	6.1	15.2	6.2	10.5	11.0	11.3
38 057	...	7	Mercer	1 043.0	8 694	2 532	8.3	94.0	0.9	2.9	0.8	2.8	6.6	16.1	7.2	11.3	10.6	12.9
38 059	13900	3	Morton	1 926.3	30 809	1 415	16.0	92.0	1.5	4.7	0.9	2.8	7.4	15.8	8.2	15.1	12.2	12.1
38 061	...	9	Mountrail	1 825.3	10 242	2 409	5.6	65.1	1.2	28.6	0.8	7.2	8.1	18.1	9.6	16.5	11.9	12.0
38 063	...	8	Nelson	981.8	2 960	2 974	3.0	94.3	1.6	2.3	0.3	2.9	5.0	12.8	6.2	9.2	8.3	11.1
38 065	13900	3	Oliver	722.5	1 870	3 061	2.6	94.5	1.0	3.2	0.4	2.2	6.6	18.0	5.2	10.3	10.3	12.5
38 067	...	9	Pembina	1 118.7	7 069	2 666	6.3	93.0	1.1	3.5	0.7	3.8	5.9	14.6	6.8	10.4	10.4	11.6
38 069	...	7	Pierce	1 018.6	4 267	2 878	4.2	93.4	1.0	5.2	0.2	1.5	6.2	16.0	7.8	10.1	10.3	12.1
38 071	...	7	Ramsey	1 186.9	11 547	2 315	9.7	86.9	1.1	11.5	1.0	2.5	6.9	16.4	8.9	11.9	10.2	12.2
38 073	...	8	Ransom	862.4	5 404	2 808	6.3	96.2	1.0	1.4	1.0	1.9	6.1	16.8	7.9	9.1	11.2	13.1
38 075	33500	9	Renville	877.1	2 550	3 000	2.9	96.0	1.0	1.2	0.7	2.5	6.4	16.8	6.9	12.2	9.9	12.5
38 077	47420	6	Richland	1 435.8	16 353	2 017	11.4	93.1	1.6	3.3	1.1	2.7	6.0	15.5	14.7	11.0	10.0	11.5
38 079	...	9	Rolette	903.1	14 659	2 121	16.2	21.2	0.7	78.3	0.4	2.1	9.8	24.4	9.1	12.1	10.7	11.4
38 081	...	9	Sargent	858.5	3 890	2 912	4.5	93.4	1.5	1.7	1.6	3.2	5.7	15.1	8.1	10.2	11.0	12.4
38 083	...	9	Sheridan	972.4	1 322	3 092	1.4	96.5	0.3	2.8	0.6	1.6	4.5	13.5	6.2	8.4	6.7	13.2
38 085	13900	3	Sioux	1 094.1	4 469	2 864	4.1	16.2	1.2	81.4	0.5	4.1	11.1	27.1	10.2	12.8	10.3	12.1
38 087	...	9	Slope	1 214.9	763	3 124	0.6	93.8	1.2	2.1	0.3	3.8	4.7	16.8	6.8	9.4	9.0	12.8
38 089	19860	7	Stark	1 334.8	31 199	1 404	23.4	88.5	3.3	2.1	1.8	5.9	8.5	17.5	9.1	17.5	11.8	11.5
38 091	...	8	Steele	712.2	1 962	3 051	2.8	96.0	0.5	1.8	0.4	2.0	6.0	14.2	7.5	9.6	9.0	12.8
38 093	27420	7	Stutsman	2 221.7	21 128	1 769	9.5	93.6	1.7	2.5	1.2	2.5	5.7	14.7	10.8	12.1	11.1	12.3
38 095	...	9	Towner	1 024.6	2 263	3 026	2.2	94.7	0.9	5.2	0.3	0.8	6.8	15.1	6.6	9.5	6.5	14.4
38 097	...	8	Traill	861.9	8 030	2 595	9.3	93.9	1.4	2.1	1.1	3.4	6.3	16.4	9.5	11.1	10.5	12.7
38 099	...	6	Walsh	1 281.7	10 904	2 365	8.5	85.5	0.8	2.2	1.1	11.4	6.7	16.0	7.6	10.4	10.3	12.7

1. CBSA = Core Based Statistical Area. See Appendix A for explanation. See Appendix B for list of metropolitan areas with component counties.   2. County type code from the Economic Research Service of USDA Rural-Urban Continuum Codes. See Appendix A for definition.   3. Dry land or land partially or temporarily covered by water.   4. May be of any race.

STATE County	55 to 64 years	65 to 74 years	75 years and over	Percent female	Total persons 2000	Total persons 2010	Percent change 2000–2010	Percent change 2010–2016	Births	Deaths	Net migration	Number	Persons per house-hold	Family house-holds	Female family house-holder[1]	One per-son
	16	17	18	19	20	21	22	23	24	25	26	27	28	29	30	31
NORTH CAROLINA—Cont'd																
Swain	13.3	11.6	7.8	51.7	12 968	13 981	7.8	2.6	1 259	1 144	245	5 379	2.58	65.4	11.3	31.3
Transylvania	15.8	16.1	13.3	51.6	29 334	33 090	12.8	1.2	1 699	2 436	1 163	13 667	2.31	67.9	9.1	27.9
Tyrrell	13.9	10.3	9.2	45.6	4 149	4 407	6.2	-6.0	262	252	-253	1 451	2.45	69.2	16.0	28.9
Union	11.5	7.6	4.4	50.8	123 677	201 350	62.8	12.5	14 812	7 924	17 982	70 711	2.99	79.6	10.3	16.7
Vance	13.9	10.3	7.2	53.4	42 954	45 419	5.7	-2.6	3 546	3 060	-1 678	16 589	2.65	63.1	21.2	31.5
Wake	11.2	6.6	4.0	51.4	627 846	901 037	43.5	16.2	78 613	30 306	95 334	364 669	2.61	66.9	11.6	26.2
Warren	16.9	13.6	9.3	50.1	19 972	21 037	5.3	-5.4	1 170	1 444	-874	7 817	2.48	62.5	16.1	33.8
Washington	16.5	13.3	9.7	53.3	13 723	13 218	-3.7	-7.7	784	954	-859	5 216	2.40	64.4	18.9	32.3
Watauga	11.9	9.1	5.8	49.9	42 695	51 079	19.6	5.6	2 215	2 089	2 788	19 996	2.35	53.1	7.2	28.3
Wayne	13.1	8.9	6.4	51.0	113 329	122 638	8.2	1.2	10 594	7 097	-1 834	47 530	2.56	66.5	17.6	27.9
Wilkes	14.8	11.9	8.7	50.7	65 632	69 305	5.6	-0.8	4 264	4 774	-4	27 422	2.48	69.0	10.4	27.5
Wilson	13.9	10.2	7.1	52.6	73 814	81 237	10.1	0.5	5 991	5 172	-515	32 003	2.50	66.2	18.4	28.9
Yadkin	14.2	11.0	8.1	50.4	36 348	38 406	5.7	-2.3	2 422	2 553	-706	15 369	2.45	68.9	11.0	29.1
Yancey	14.9	14.4	10.2	50.9	17 774	17 817	0.2	-0.8	1 077	1 354	190	7 416	2.35	71.0	10.3	25.6
NORTH DAKOTA	12.5	7.8	6.7	48.7	642 200	672 591	4.7	12.7	66 088	38 052	56 271	299 638	2.32	60.7	7.8	30.9
Adams	17.2	12.3	12.8	50.5	2 593	2 343	-9.6	-1.6	144	170	-32	1 067	2.14	69.4	4.5	24.6
Barnes	15.3	11.2	10.1	49.7	11 775	11 066	-6.0	-1.3	718	833	-6	5 056	2.07	60.8	5.1	31.4
Benson	12.4	7.1	5.2	48.4	6 964	6 660	-4.4	1.2	939	478	-361	2 280	2.97	71.1	19.5	26.1
Billings	15.0	10.8	8.1	45.3	888	783	-11.8	19.3	81	18	95	407	2.25	68.8	3.4	30.5
Bottineau	15.4	12.6	9.7	47.9	7 149	6 429	-10.1	2.3	452	460	172	3 035	2.09	61.5	5.2	32.5
Bowman	15.8	9.4	10.2	49.1	3 242	3 151	-2.8	2.9	275	278	113	1 377	2.28	64.3	3.6	32.1
Burke	15.9	10.6	7.3	47.1	2 242	1 968	-12.2	11.7	210	138	149	980	2.25	58.5	4.7	38.4
Burleigh	13.0	8.3	6.7	49.8	69 416	81 308	17.1	16.2	7 932	4 258	9 212	37 061	2.30	62.3	8.9	29.4
Cass	10.6	6.4	4.9	49.3	123 138	149 778	21.6	17.0	15 296	6 042	15 836	68 776	2.29	55.3	8.3	33.0
Cavalier	16.2	12.9	14.2	48.7	4 831	3 993	-17.3	-4.2	273	300	-101	1 746	2.17	65.2	2.9	32.0
Dickey	14.0	10.4	11.0	50.2	5 757	5 289	-8.1	-4.3	366	444	-162	2 132	2.30	64.6	4.4	29.4
Divide	15.9	10.8	13.3	48.9	2 283	2 071	-9.3	16.5	178	163	326	1 081	2.07	62.7	3.0	34.8
Dunn	15.6	7.4	7.1	46.4	3 600	3 536	-1.8	23.5	368	210	648	1 557	2.60	69.8	6.7	25.5
Eddy	16.9	12.1	11.7	49.7	2 757	2 385	-13.5	-1.1	167	288	90	1 060	2.15	57.9	10.5	33.6
Emmons	16.2	13.0	14.1	48.9	4 331	3 550	-18.0	-5.7	174	320	-28	1 599	2.13	61.0	4.6	34.0
Foster	15.8	9.9	11.7	50.3	3 759	3 343	-11.1	-1.2	212	264	38	1 484	2.22	68.2	6.9	28.6
Golden Valley	15.9	10.4	8.7	49.6	1 924	1 680	-12.7	8.2	135	109	119	803	2.19	55.8	3.0	39.7
Grand Forks	10.9	6.7	5.2	48.6	66 109	66 864	1.1	6.3	6 321	2 968	811	28 521	2.25	55.8	7.5	32.1
Grant	16.7	14.9	13.0	50.1	2 841	2 394	-15.7	-0.7	161	176	30	1 136	2.05	60.7	3.3	34.7
Griggs	16.8	16.6	13.5	48.4	2 754	2 420	-12.1	-5.9	124	248	-5	1 035	2.16	67.3	3.4	31.3
Hettinger	14.1	10.9	12.4	51.9	2 715	2 477	-8.8	6.1	192	212	168	1 091	2.25	72.1	6.7	25.1
Kidder	18.2	11.0	10.5	47.9	2 753	2 435	-11.6	-0.9	168	102	-66	1 084	2.24	73.0	2.7	23.9
LaMoure	16.9	11.2	13.8	48.5	4 701	4 139	-12.0	-0.7	265	273	16	1 840	2.20	65.2	3.8	31.7
Logan	15.1	12.8	14.0	48.5	2 308	1 990	-13.8	-2.5	125	160	-13	878	2.12	63.2	4.2	33.7
McHenry	14.7	10.0	9.2	48.2	5 987	5 395	-9.9	10.5	430	367	503	2 608	2.20	62.3	5.9	31.2
McIntosh	16.2	12.2	18.9	51.2	3 390	2 809	-17.1	-5.4	159	323	6	1 289	2.06	64.6	4.9	32.4
McKenzie	11.5	4.7	3.1	46.7	5 737	6 360	10.9	98.4	1 089	370	5 393	3 214	2.93	68.5	8.4	23.1
McLean	17.1	13.4	9.1	48.7	9 311	8 962	-3.7	8.6	734	654	703	4 234	2.18	67.0	5.4	29.4
Mercer	17.6	9.7	8.0	48.2	8 644	8 424	-2.5	2.3	652	516	154	3 673	2.31	68.3	6.2	27.7
Morton	13.5	8.8	6.8	49.6	25 303	27 471	8.6	12.2	2 753	1 647	2 152	12 308	2.30	64.8	8.0	26.3
Mountrail	12.8	6.9	4.2	45.7	6 631	7 673	15.7	33.5	968	503	2 040	3 206	2.83	66.1	11.8	29.7
Nelson	18.9	14.2	14.3	48.8	3 715	3 126	-15.9	-5.3	194	357	-8	1 522	1.95	58.4	6.6	38.5
Oliver	18.0	12.1	7.1	48.9	2 065	1 846	-10.6	1.3	136	75	-32	792	2.30	72.1	3.2	25.1
Pembina	17.5	11.6	11.2	48.1	8 585	7 410	-13.7	-4.6	502	528	-330	3 285	2.14	62.9	6.1	32.7
Pierce	14.3	10.9	12.3	49.5	4 675	4 357	-6.8	-2.1	296	404	22	2 018	2.08	60.2	6.0	32.8
Ramsey	14.7	10.0	9.0	49.8	12 066	11 451	-5.1	0.8	1 020	844	-51	5 016	2.20	56.5	7.9	37.6
Ransom	15.0	10.0	10.6	48.9	5 890	5 457	-7.4	-1.0	400	474	29	2 352	2.25	62.4	5.7	32.0
Renville	15.7	10.1	9.5	47.8	2 610	2 470	-5.4	3.2	196	161	46	1 020	2.46	64.9	4.2	30.6
Richland	15.0	8.2	8.1	48.6	17 998	16 321	-9.3	0.2	1 103	832	-248	6 621	2.28	63.0	6.2	29.6
Rolette	11.5	6.8	4.2	50.5	13 674	13 937	1.9	5.2	1 872	915	-252	4 774	3.00	72.0	24.9	24.9
Sargent	16.1	12.6	8.9	46.9	4 366	3 829	-12.3	1.6	246	210	38	1 728	2.22	63.3	5.6	30.2
Sheridan	18.6	13.5	15.4	48.9	1 710	1 321	-22.7	0.1	72	65	-7	653	2.05	67.8	4.6	30.6
Sioux	8.7	4.4	3.4	50.2	4 044	4 153	2.7	7.6	621	320	3	1 098	3.93	76.2	32.1	19.9
Slope	19.9	10.4	10.1	47.4	767	727	-5.2	5.0	52	19	8	322	2.09	64.3	6.2	33.2
Stark	11.5	6.1	6.5	47.5	22 636	24 199	6.9	28.9	2 880	1 440	5 440	11 379	2.44	63.2	7.1	28.0
Steele	15.9	13.0	12.1	48.4	2 258	1 975	-12.5	-0.7	133	106	-55	948	2.09	59.6	2.7	36.2
Stutsman	15.2	9.5	8.5	48.9	21 908	21 100	-3.7	0.1	1 473	1 490	96	9 061	2.15	58.3	7.2	36.3
Towner	17.3	12.0	11.8	49.2	2 876	2 246	-21.9	0.8	152	177	45	1 003	2.25	65.9	7.5	33.1
Traill	14.5	9.6	9.5	49.4	8 477	8 121	-4.2	-1.1	590	586	-83	3 278	2.35	60.3	6.1	35.3
Walsh	15.2	10.6	10.4	49.5	12 389	11 119	-10.3	-1.9	869	869	-169	4 929	2.15	63.9	6.9	32.3

1. No spouse present.

Table B. States and Counties — **Population, Vital Statistics, Health, and Crime**

STATE County	Persons in group quarters, 2016	Daytime population, 2011–2015 Number	Daytime population, 2011–2015 Employ-ment/ resi-dence ratio	Births, 2016 Total	Births, 2016 Rate[1]	Deaths, 2016 Number	Deaths, 2016 Rate[1]	Persons under 65 with no health insurance, 2015 Number	Persons under 65 with no health insurance, 2015 Percent	Medicare, 2015 Total Beneficiaries	Medicare, 2015 Enrolled in Original Medicare	Medicare, 2015 Enrolled in Medicare Advantage	Serious crimes known to police,[2] 2014 Total Number	Serious crimes known to police,[2] 2014 Total Rate[3]
	32	33	34	35	36	37	38	39	40	41	42	43	44	45
NORTH CAROLINA—Cont'd														
Swain............................	247	15 031	1.16	214	14.9	209	14.6	2 089	18.0	3 447	2 938	509	250	1 773
Transylvania	1 079	31 428	0.89	285	8.5	383	11.4	3 151	13.7	9 604	7 039	2 565	555	1 685
Tyrrell	595	4 222	1.05	40	9.7	37	8.9	525	19.2	786	680	106	60	1 483
Union	2 216	181 919	0.68	2 409	10.6	1 351	6.0	22 140	11.3	23 508	16 372	7 136	4 680	2 167
Vance	627	44 178	0.96	544	12.3	515	11.6	5 020	13.7	10 501	7 081	3 420	2 748	6 138
Wake	20 843	1 000 553	1.05	12 884	12.3	5 416	5.2	87 652	9.7	123 735	81 722	42 013	14 893	1 498
Warren	975	18 348	0.69	190	9.5	255	12.8	2 471	16.8	4 224	2 980	1 244	512	2 754
Washington	147	12 506	0.96	116	9.5	155	12.7	1 322	13.8	3 181	2 731	450	303	2 397
Watauga	5 818	55 645	1.15	367	6.8	355	6.6	5 258	13.2	7 376	5 158	2 218	865	1 637
Wayne	3 034	122 675	0.97	1 633	13.2	1 275	10.3	14 136	13.8	22 938	18 276	4 662	4 608	3 764
Wilkes	1 051	66 116	0.89	696	10.1	803	11.7	8 595	15.9	16 108	9 146	6 962	1 718	2 486
Wilson	1 593	85 430	1.11	949	11.6	876	10.7	10 020	15.0	16 256	13 523	2 733	2 966	3 723
Yadkin	303	33 451	0.71	351	9.4	419	11.2	4 422	14.6	8 314	3 398	4 916	952	2 630
Yancey	164	15 601	0.70	182	10.3	199	11.3	1 801	13.5	5 017	3 506	1 511	154	878
NORTH DAKOTA	26 100	758 777	1.10	11 824	15.6	6 172	8.1	54 797	8.7	115 295	93 623	21 672	17 565	2 375
Adams...........................	51	2 236	0.92	21	9.1	23	10.0	187	10.7	624	537	87	12	506
Barnes	514	10 769	0.94	108	9.9	132	12.1	707	8.4	2 342	1 886	456	199	1 767
Benson..........................	16	6 839	1.02	156	23.1	77	11.4	952	16.3	898	842	56	36	518
Billings	9	1 018	1.09	19	20.3	5	5.4	88	11.2	D	74	D	8	883
Bottineau	241	6 535	0.97	76	11.6	76	11.6	584	11.5	1 524	1 485	39	71	1 038
Bowman........................	62	3 264	1.03	46	14.2	30	9.3	278	10.4	706	619	87	17	524
Burke	2	2 065	0.87	41	18.7	21	9.6	211	11.0	D	441	D	14	581
Burleigh........................	3 487	90 867	1.05	1 422	15.0	744	7.9	4 929	6.4	14 838	11 133	3 705	2 134	2 356
Cass..............................	5 465	177 669	1.16	2 646	15.1	1 051	6.0	11 180	7.6	20 552	15 795	4 757	4 341	2 603
Cavalier	74	3 735	0.92	47	12.3	41	10.7	295	10.5	981	869	112	28	720
Dickey	205	5 107	0.97	70	13.8	67	13.2	388	10.0	1 101	940	161	27	513
Divide	115	2 564	1.20	31	12.8	19	7.9	164	8.6	D	424	D	3	126
Dunn	130	4 917	1.35	80	18.3	23	5.3	508	12.6	489	400	89	71	1 632
Eddy	83	2 134	0.80	29	12.3	44	18.7	195	10.9	554	491	63	26	1 075
Emmons........................	53	3 383	0.95	31	9.3	53	15.8	298	12.1	935	654	281	36	1 033
Foster	55	3 456	1.05	35	10.6	49	14.8	221	8.4	758	604	154	NA	NA
Golden Valley	52	1 806	0.98	25	13.8	7	3.9	138	9.5	D	350	D	10	535
Grand Forks...................	4 021	72 474	1.09	1 097	15.4	480	6.8	4 907	8.4	9 691	7 955	1 736	1 960	2 800
Grant	18	2 309	0.96	26	10.9	28	11.8	299	17.2	608	444	164	8	336
Griggs	45	2 328	1.00	17	7.5	39	17.1	194	11.8	626	521	105	8	351
Hettinger	171	2 535	0.93	31	11.8	21	8.0	204	10.5	685	538	147	41	1 508
Kidder	0	2 179	0.81	25	10.4	18	7.5	217	11.4	520	318	202	23	945
LaMoure	65	3 960	0.93	49	11.9	42	10.2	340	11.0	969	728	241	10	239
Logan	64	1 933	0.99	20	10.3	22	11.3	206	14.7	498	352	146	10	515
McHenry........................	50	4 715	0.61	73	12.2	58	9.7	513	10.7	1 307	1 070	237	40	657
McIntosh	93	2 851	1.07	28	10.5	45	16.9	226	11.9	901	639	262	7	255
McKenzie.......................	154	12 710	1.68	294	23.3	68	5.4	1 330	11.1	838	827	11	244	2 372
McLean..........................	150	9 490	1.01	130	13.4	98	10.1	785	10.3	2 282	1 844	438	156	1 610
Mercer	125	9 264	1.15	111	12.8	78	9.0	595	8.1	1 618	1 288	330	48	554
Morton...........................	679	24 144	0.70	494	16.0	252	8.2	2 096	8.2	5 188	3 734	1 454	753	2 555
Mountrail	556	11 763	1.56	182	17.8	89	8.7	1 281	13.8	1 188	1 166	22	168	1 700
Nelson..........................	80	2 829	0.85	32	10.8	48	16.2	194	9.3	982	956	26	49	1 581
Oliver	2	1 910	1.11	23	12.3	7	3.7	121	8.1	266	201	65	7	370
Pembina	152	7 699	1.14	86	12.2	83	11.7	527	9.6	1 642	1 382	260	62	867
Pierce...........................	239	4 390	1.00	45	10.5	58	13.6	362	11.3	942	634	308	65	1 448
Ramsey..........................	461	11 913	1.06	170	14.7	132	11.4	912	10.0	2 512	2 479	33	404	3 476
Ransom	181	5 409	0.98	70	13.0	76	14.1	373	8.7	1 161	1 008	153	47	846
Renville	54	2 382	0.86	31	12.2	19	7.5	155	7.4	D	453	D	51	1 923
Richland........................	1 014	16 315	1.00	192	11.7	131	8.0	958	7.5	2 599	1 945	654	296	1 804
Rolette	122	14 262	0.95	284	19.4	181	12.3	2 399	18.6	1 696	1 647	49	35	237
Sargent	39	4 927	1.52	48	12.3	37	9.5	240	7.9	960	841	119	25	637
Sheridan	3	1 227	0.82	8	6.1	8	6.1	132	14.2	355	277	78	21	1 606
Sioux	59	4 900	1.41	100	22.4	76	17.0	589	15.1	321	292	29	1	22
Slope............................	0	671	0.99	6	7.9	3	3.9	56	9.0	D	67	D	2	259
Stark.............................	577	31 011	1.15	593	19.0	243	7.8	2 162	7.7	4 142	3 353	789	796	2 709
Steele............................	1	1 861	0.88	25	12.7	11	5.6	146	9.8	379	331	48	2	102
Stutsman.......................	1 645	21 721	1.06	237	11.2	224	10.6	1 262	7.9	4 361	2 994	1 367	546	2 576
Towner..........................	33	2 244	0.95	24	10.6	26	11.5	219	12.7	540	523	17	3	128
Traill	347	7 745	0.92	95	11.8	104	13.0	449	7.2	1 590	1 324	266	48	578
Walsh............................	327	11 180	1.03	150	13.8	138	12.7	1 052	12.3	2 355	2 003	352	213	1 911

1. Per 1,000 estimated resident population.   2. Data for serious crimes have not been adjusted for underreporting; this may affect comparability between geographic areas and over time.
3. Per 100,000 population estimated by the FBI.

Items 32—45

Table B. States and Counties — **Crime, Education, Money Income, and Poverty**

STATE County	Serious crimes known to police, 2014 (cont.)[1] Rate[2]		Education School enrollment and attainment, 2011–2015				Local government expenditures,[5] 2013–2014		Money income, 2011–2015		Households			Income and poverty, 2015 Percent below poverty level		
			Enrollment[3]		Attainment[4] (percent)						Percent					
	Violent	Property	Total	Percent private	High school graduate or less	Bachelor's degree or more	Total current spending (mil dol)	Current spending per student (dollars)	Per capita income[6] (dollars)	Median income (dollars)	with income of less than $50,000	with income of $200,000 or more	Median household income (dollars)	All persons	Children under 18 years	Children 5 to 17 years in families
	46	47	48	49	50	51	52	53	54	55	56	57	58	59	60	61
NORTH CAROLINA—Cont'd																
Swain	206	1 567	3 260	7.6	50.7	15.9	21.4	9 768	20 409	33 931	63.5	1.9	36 103	16.2	26.0	25.8
Transylvania	143	1 543	6 632	22.9	40.0	29.7	37.3	9 966	24 080	45 114	56.1	1.8	45 792	15.4	29.6	28.1
Tyrrell	222	1 261	780	2.4	67.4	8.0	8.6	15 768	16 268	32 361	68.9	0.6	33 759	25.0	36.2	36.8
Union	168	1 999	64 425	17.6	36.2	33.4	321.9	7 595	29 662	65 903	37.0	7.5	71 690	9.7	12.7	10.9
Vance	646	5 493	11 094	6.9	60.8	11.4	69.0	9 197	18 606	33 316	66.4	1.4	32 698	24.6	37.3	35.3
Wake	126	1 373	283 361	17.5	24.9	49.0	1 251.9	7 770	34 202	67 309	36.9	7.5	70 629	11.1	14.7	13.1
Warren	226	2 528	3 842	10.6	57.0	15.4	26.7	11 320	19 354	34 254	64.7	1.5	34 149	27.3	37.1	36.6
Washington	261	2 136	2 982	8.9	58.5	10.4	20.1	11 291	20 067	34 538	66.1	1.1	35 146	23.4	40.9	40.0
Watauga	114	1 524	21 742	6.0	31.4	38.4	44.8	9 878	22 314	37 656	59.9	2.9	41 762	25.3	18.9	17.5
Wayne	372	3 392	31 918	14.0	47.0	18.4	155.0	7 989	21 204	40 390	58.2	1.5	41 161	18.4	28.1	28.0
Wilkes	207	2 279	14 746	8.4	57.1	12.8	85.4	8 531	19 163	33 232	67.3	1.5	40 647	18.7	27.4	24.9
Wilson	409	3 314	19 699	13.4	53.1	18.0	100.8	7 679	21 486	39 847	60.9	1.3	41 276	19.9	30.3	29.4
Yadkin	282	2 348	7 852	6.3	56.8	11.9	46.5	8 531	21 372	37 796	61.6	1.7	41 208	16.3	24.9	22.4
Yancey	28	849	3 527	18.5	50.8	19.3	21.8	9 417	20 798	37 484	64.0	0.9	36 418	19.3	29.2	26.4
NORTH DAKOTA	265	2 110	180 414	11.0	35.7	27.7	1 280.5	12 338	32 035	57 181	44.2	4.6	61 674	10.7	12.1	10.5
Adams	84	421	402	5.5	39.1	24.8	3.8	12 121	34 005	52 118	47.1	6.5	48 106	10.1	12.4	10.9
Barnes	231	1 536	2 577	5.4	39.7	25.4	19.2	13 807	33 016	53 141	47.4	3.7	51 053	12.4	13.5	11.3
Benson	14	503	1 902	0.9	47.4	14.6	16.4	14 782	20 697	41 296	58.5	3.4	39 969	27.9	39.0	35.7
Billings	0	883	127	0.0	44.4	25.2	2.5	27 886	42 729	70 469	37.3	10.3	76 913	7.1	5.9	5.4
Bottineau	102	936	1 313	5.9	41.5	20.9	13.3	15 758	33 541	56 349	44.7	4.1	56 645	10.6	13.7	12.0
Bowman	62	462	563	6.7	40.3	22.1	8.0	12 779	34 414	66 845	39.5	4.9	62 892	7.6	7.7	6.6
Burke	124	456	496	7.7	43.5	19.6	5.3	15 735	34 161	60 096	45.5	5.9	68 477	8.4	11.1	10.7
Burleigh	246	2 110	20 871	24.3	31.0	34.0	135.0	11 000	34 813	65 254	38.9	5.1	66 057	9.0	8.5	7.0
Cass	296	2 308	48 336	10.1	25.7	36.8	253.7	11 457	31 795	53 289	47.2	4.8	55 946	10.7	10.0	8.8
Cavalier	77	643	718	10.9	38.1	17.7	6.6	14 957	38 721	66 806	37.5	5.0	57 200	9.4	13.0	11.1
Dickey	95	418	1 226	15.1	42.1	26.6	8.5	10 338	27 825	53 750	45.7	3.6	56 325	10.3	14.3	11.9
Divide	0	126	269	0.0	45.0	20.6	5.1	14 156	41 625	56 042	46.8	8.1	62 922	8.6	11.2	10.1
Dunn	276	1 356	866	11.1	43.3	19.6	8.6	16 492	41 849	69 732	36.5	12.3	73 135	9.9	12.2	10.5
Eddy	41	1 034	508	3.5	40.2	22.0	5.4	15 178	31 806	48 583	51.6	4.1	47 804	11.3	15.0	12.3
Emmons	29	1 005	731	3.7	53.1	15.3	7.9	13 802	29 367	44 051	56.3	3.8	46 952	13.9	16.2	13.2
Foster	NA	NA	645	4.3	43.7	18.8	5.7	10 880	29 710	55 769	44.5	2.3	53 408	8.4	12.0	10.3
Golden Valley	107	428	424	5.4	32.3	22.7	5.2	16 040	27 650	40 179	51.9	2.7	56 948	10.2	12.3	10.8
Grand Forks	216	2 584	22 753	6.7	31.9	33.0	104.5	11 914	29 088	48 676	51.0	4.3	52 022	14.3	13.8	11.9
Grant	84	252	366	4.6	49.3	17.1	3.5	15 260	32 412	44 559	53.4	6.1	40 879	15.6	18.4	16.1
Griggs	88	264	403	5.5	49.3	18.3	5.9	15 789	29 639	48 355	51.2	4.3	47 222	10.0	9.5	7.9
Hettinger	0	1 508	492	14.8	48.3	14.8	7.0	16 198	28 132	52 169	47.3	3.3	53 403	10.6	10.2	8.3
Kidder	123	822	406	7.1	44.2	19.5	5.2	13 261	32 743	54 559	44.8	5.5	46 800	13.9	18.8	15.9
LaMoure	48	191	776	10.3	44.8	21.1	11.3	14 419	34 471	54 821	44.0	5.5	58 638	10.9	13.3	10.9
Logan	0	515	350	3.4	57.4	12.7	5.3	14 644	32 180	51 458	48.4	3.3	50 047	11.8	13.3	11.7
McHenry	49	608	1 055	8.6	47.3	18.8	13.1	13 490	34 169	57 386	44.3	4.6	56 351	11.1	13.0	11.0
McIntosh	146	109	455	2.0	51.7	18.7	5.6	13 897	28 735	42 277	56.9	2.8	48 494	12.5	16.4	15.0
McKenzie	447	1 925	2 363	18.2	36.7	22.8	20.2	13 566	37 045	72 794	31.3	10.5	82 906	8.4	10.2	8.5
McLean	83	1 528	1 936	6.3	42.6	19.0	20.6	12 621	31 777	55 686	44.5	3.1	62 480	10.0	12.0	10.2
Mercer	81	473	1 721	5.6	39.6	20.5	15.8	11 873	31 759	72 704	36.5	3.2	75 698	7.2	7.0	6.0
Morton	248	2 308	6 054	15.2	38.6	25.9	49.5	10 947	32 614	62 418	38.6	3.5	64 260	7.8	10.7	9.6
Mountrail	263	1 437	2 285	5.5	37.7	22.0	21.9	13 649	38 061	68 188	38.6	9.7	65 606	11.2	14.6	13.0
Nelson	129	1 452	461	12.6	40.0	19.2	6.7	14 549	32 259	51 085	48.5	4.1	48 196	11.6	16.5	14.2
Oliver	106	264	343	12.8	43.3	17.5	3.1	13 662	32 235	60 278	39.1	2.0	65 798	10.2	17.5	15.0
Pembina	126	741	1 383	6.1	49.0	19.0	15.4	15 018	31 244	53 504	47.2	3.3	58 683	8.8	11.2	9.6
Pierce	89	1 359	701	11.1	47.3	15.2	7.5	13 044	25 029	42 563	55.7	1.0	43 419	16.1	17.3	12.8
Ramsey	189	3 286	2 609	7.0	40.0	23.0	26.5	14 608	29 006	50 841	49.3	2.9	51 607	12.0	16.8	14.7
Ransom	108	738	1 216	4.6	46.5	18.1	10.6	11 002	30 779	56 500	44.3	3.4	60 122	9.1	12.3	10.3
Renville	75	1 848	547	4.6	37.0	15.9	8.4	13 687	31 281	65 125	36.3	3.6	65 651	7.6	8.1	7.0
Richland	140	1 664	4 295	7.5	37.1	21.8	31.8	13 904	28 413	55 390	45.2	2.4	56 942	10.2	11.5	9.4
Rolette	27	210	3 239	0.7	39.1	20.9	40.2	13 514	16 706	33 277	63.6	1.9	37 634	25.5	31.7	28.7
Sargent	51	586	785	2.2	41.1	19.8	8.8	13 520	32 280	57 125	41.7	2.7	58 626	7.8	10.4	9.4
Sheridan	153	1 453	204	9.8	50.7	15.2	2.2	21 243	32 095	48 102	53.1	4.1	38 234	17.6	18.7	15.5
Sioux	22	0	1 439	9.2	47.7	17.3	8.7	20 393	15 557	38 068	62.6	2.2	32 895	40.4	45.1	41.0
Slope	0	259	93	10.8	44.3	25.7	0.6	21 269	34 597	55 000	44.7	4.7	56 833	9.0	9.0	7.3
Stark	191	2 518	6 629	15.6	40.5	24.3	43.6	11 039	35 114	72 099	34.1	5.0	76 844	7.5	8.0	7.0
Steele	51	51	357	3.1	37.7	19.7	4.0	20 754	34 774	55 833	41.8	4.0	61 352	7.8	12.1	10.5
Stutsman	231	2 345	4 905	23.3	46.4	23.6	35.5	13 701	29 490	52 359	47.1	3.0	54 925	11.4	14.2	12.0
Towner	0	128	444	2.5	41.3	17.7	3.2	10 518	33 277	56 625	42.7	4.5	51 561	10.4	15.2	14.7
Traill	72	506	2 090	5.5	33.3	26.4	17.9	13 352	30 213	54 960	46.1	3.2	54 814	9.5	9.7	8.4
Walsh	144	1 767	2 161	5.6	49.8	17.2	23.8	14 738	30 154	49 411	50.7	2.8	51 749	10.8	13.3	11.7

1. Data for serious crimes have not been adjusted for underreporting; this may affect comparability between geographic areas and over time.   2. Per 100,000 population estimated by the FBI.
3. All persons 3 years old and over enrolled in nursery school through college.   4. Persons 25 years old and over.   5. Elementary and secondary education expenditures.
6. Based on population estimated by the American Community Survey, 2011–2015.

Table B. States and Counties — **Personal Income**

	Personal income, 2015										Earnings, 2015		
STATE County	Total (mil dol)	Percent change, 2014–2015	Per capita[1] Dollars	Per capita[1] Rank	Wages and salaries (mil dol)	Supplements to wages and salaries; employer contributions (mil dol) Pension and insurance	Supplements to wages and salaries; employer contributions (mil dol) Government social insurance	Proprietors' income (mil dol)	Dividends, interest, and rent (mil dol)	Personal transfer receipts (mil dol)	Total (mil dol)	Contributions for government social insurance (mil dol) From employee and self-employed	Contributions for government social insurance (mil dol) From employer
	62	63	64	65	66	67	68	69	70	71	72	73	74
NORTH CAROLINA— Cont'd													
Swain	461	5.9	31 971	2 758	241	40	20	31	81	150	332	22	20
Transylvania	1 179	4.5	35 487	2 260	314	53	25	102	316	355	494	39	25
Tyrrell	124	0.7	30 514	2 704	37	8	3	18	17	37	66	4	3
Union	9 727	6.4	43 669	1 043	2 708	415	214	591	1 295	1 284	3 928	247	214
Vance	1 417	3.4	31 792	2 711	547	94	44	81	208	499	767	54	44
Wake	53 029	5.5	51 776	400	30 287	4 079	2 266	3 347	9 203	5 492	39 979	2 374	2 266
Warren	569	1.6	28 220	2 889	118	26	9	24	89	203	177	15	9
Washington	406	2.0	32 755	2 414	105	21	8	11	62	158	145	12	8
Watauga	1 751	4.7	33 103	2 583	856	158	65	152	401	345	1 231	76	65
Wayne	4 444	1.7	35 801	1 909	1 884	387	156	324	726	1 132	2 750	160	156
Wilkes	2 223	4.1	32 449	2 586	811	153	62	181	364	717	1 207	87	62
Wilson	3 074	3.8	37 617	1 777	1 671	274	129	229	439	830	2 302	145	129
Yadkin	1 278	2.6	33 995	2 452	352	60	29	87	175	356	529	39	29
Yancey	554	3.2	31 481	2 745	124	24	10	43	105	196	201	17	10
NORTH DAKOTA	42 350	-1.2	55 956	X	23 452	3 123	1 939	4 378	9 208	5 326	32 892	1 932	1 939
Adams	109	-0.8	46 205	808	41	6	3	19	22	25	68	4	3
Barnes	534	-3.6	48 131	410	201	32	18	50	150	104	301	19	18
Benson	212	-4.2	31 402	2 446	85	20	7	9	45	65	121	7	7
Billings	87	-8.4	92 463	17	24	4	2	13	31	5	42	2	2
Bottineau	364	-5.4	54 176	172	118	20	10	48	104	64	195	12	10
Bowman	207	-7.0	62 919	84	81	11	6	39	54	26	137	8	6
Burke	185	-15.2	80 133	10	45	8	4	29	47	17	85	5	4
Burleigh	5 316	5.4	57 171	258	2 996	400	246	526	1 118	641	4 167	248	246
Cass	9 185	4.3	53 552	277	5 756	736	467	866	2 101	960	7 825	457	467
Cavalier	224	-11.0	58 604	65	68	10	6	49	61	38	133	7	6
Dickey	283	-8.6	55 408	145	75	12	6	19	129	51	112	7	6
Divide	165	-4.7	67 517	90	62	8	5	33	54	20	107	6	5
Dunn	371	-7.5	79 799	26	207	22	16	69	94	29	313	17	16
Eddy	95	-14.4	40 369	617	29	5	3	8	22	27	43	3	3
Emmons	156	6.5	45 828	1 028	34	6	3	41	36	35	84	5	3
Foster	184	-1.5	54 886	420	75	10	6	52	40	28	143	8	6
Golden Valley	93	-7.9	50 452	871	29	5	2	23	27	12	59	4	2
Grand Forks	3 271	3.1	46 129	743	1 957	323	169	204	751	453	2 653	151	169
Grant	101	-4.7	42 273	777	23	4	2	18	23	24	48	3	2
Griggs	110	-10.1	47 657	257	36	6	3	9	36	26	54	4	3
Hettinger	127	-18.0	46 969	210	35	6	3	-1	32	24	43	4	3
Kidder	126	0.5	52 029	380	27	5	2	36	29	22	70	3	2
LaMoure	200	-15.2	48 454	142	58	10	5	22	66	37	95	7	5
Logan	91	-23.5	46 920	78	22	4	2	16	27	20	44	3	2
McHenry	301	-5.6	50 497	292	60	11	5	62	49	50	138	8	5
McIntosh	126	-6.5	45 535	395	38	7	3	19	33	35	67	5	3
McKenzie	917	-4.5	71 519	27	870	85	71	110	216	55	1 136	64	71
McLean	542	-3.4	55 591	204	191	33	16	41	126	92	281	17	16
Mercer	487	6.4	55 020	331	359	62	32	29	87	68	482	27	32
Morton	1 502	4.3	49 539	718	571	84	53	139	253	229	848	54	53
Mountrail	711	-8.1	68 781	56	496	55	39	83	163	67	672	39	39
Nelson	146	-5.4	49 045	313	36	6	3	16	42	41	61	4	3
Oliver	80	-1.5	43 553	606	71	11	6	3	18	14	90	5	6
Pembina	359	0.5	50 665	430	173	27	16	31	106	64	247	15	16
Pierce	182	-0.2	42 238	1 263	74	11	6	32	39	41	123	8	6
Ramsey	530	-1.1	45 547	885	234	38	20	43	133	109	336	21	20
Ransom	256	2.7	46 948	762	85	14	8	20	61	54	127	8	8
Renville	131	-10.7	51 125	195	38	6	3	9	33	23	55	4	3
Richland	746	3.9	45 487	1 019	328	51	29	70	186	122	477	29	29
Rolette	494	7.1	33 727	2 637	181	46	16	54	71	159	297	17	16
Sargent	208	-2.3	53 579	356	127	21	11	24	70	30	184	10	11
Sheridan	38	-6.4	28 651	3 074	8	2	1	-3	13	15	8	1	1
Sioux	112	1.1	25 546	3 070	67	17	6	11	15	42	100	5	6
Slope	46	-14.4	60 199	170	11	1	1	14	15	5	27	1	1
Stark	2 755	-7.9	85 677	15	1 433	148	111	477	394	195	2 168	129	111
Steele	110	-5.4	56 009	254	32	5	3	17	40	14	57	3	3
Stutsman	993	-1.4	47 076	458	480	74	42	98	228	184	694	43	42
Towner	92	-15.4	40 421	490	27	5	2	5	29	25	39	3	2
Traill	412	4.6	51 420	690	142	23	13	53	105	70	232	14	13
Walsh	509	-0.8	46 728	559	200	32	18	47	140	103	296	19	18

1. Based on the resident population estimated as of July 1 of the year shown.

Table B. States and Counties — Earnings, Social Security, and Housing

STATE County	Earnings, 2015 (cont.)									Social Security beneficiaries, December 2015			Housing units, 2016	
	Percent by selected industries											Supplemental Security Income recipients, December 2015		
	Farm	Mining	Construction	Manufacturing	Information: professional, scientific, technical services	Retail trade	Finance, insurance, real estate and leasing	Health care and social assistance	Government	Number	Rate[1]		Total	Percent change, 2010–2016
	75	76	77	78	79	80	81	82	83	84	85	86	87	88
NORTH CAROLINA—Cont'd														
Swain	0.2	0.0	5.0	D	1.5	6.1	1.5	D	42.7	4 185	290	341	8 859	1.6
Transylvania	3.5	0.1	10.6	6.8	7.2	9.1	5.8	14.1	16.3	10 250	309	620	19 477	1.6
Tyrrell	21.1	0.0	4.4	6.3	D	6.0	D	D	33.8	905	219	130	2 063	-0.2
Union	2.4	D	14.0	19.7	6.1	7.3	3.4	4.7	13.3	32 320	145	2 368	79 377	8.9
Vance	1.3	D	4.0	11.4	5.3	10.6	4.8	14.3	18.1	11 370	256	2 332	19 952	-0.6
Wake	0.1	0.0	6.2	7.9	21.3	5.9	8.1	9.3	14.3	130 650	128	12 406	420 410	13.1
Warren	7.1	0.0	3.8	11.5	2.6	6.2	2.0	D	38.1	4 925	244	936	11 813	-0.1
Washington	0.8	0.0	D	14.9	D	7.3	3.8	11.6	27.3	3 635	294	679	6 424	-1.0
Watauga	1.1	0.1	6.2	2.0	5.5	8.5	6.3	16.4	29.2	9 035	170	597	33 521	4.3
Wayne	5.8	D	4.2	12.2	3.8	7.2	4.1	12.3	31.4	25 715	207	4 541	53 393	0.8
Wilkes	2.5	D	5.0	17.7	D	7.3	5.1	6.7	19.0	19 305	282	2 022	33 111	0.1
Wilson	2.6	0.1	6.9	23.8	6.2	7.6	5.9	9.8	12.3	20 070	246	3 032	35 882	1.0
Yadkin	6.2	0.0	9.9	24.3	4.8	6.0	2.7	5.7	14.9	9 465	252	823	17 258	-0.5
Yancey	4.6	D	13.9	9.3	4.0	9.1	2.6	D	21.1	5 780	329	608	11 127	0.8
NORTH DAKOTA	1.2	9.4	10.6	5.7	6.4	6.6	7.1	10.8	16.0	125 786	166	8 198	368 624	16.1
Adams	9.1	D	7.8	4.2	2.2	11.6	3.7	28.3	10.2	680	287	13	1 417	2.9
Barnes	1.0	D	11.7	12.2	4.7	6.8	4.5	12.9	20.1	2 710	246	134	5 817	2.0
Benson	0.6	0.1	6.8	D	D	1.3	D	2.0	63.7	1 170	173	185	3 006	1.9
Billings	5.8	D	3.8	4.0	D	4.2	0.0	0.6	21.7	145	158	0	551	13.8
Bottineau	3.4	17.4	9.7	3.7	3.8	8.0	5.0	D	18.9	1 665	248	54	4 459	2.7
Bowman	10.8	10.7	8.7	1.6	3.1	6.4	D	10.2	10.3	710	216	25	1 745	3.7
Burke	14.5	D	5.8	0.3	D	5.5	2.8	0.7	24.5	480	208	10	1 428	6.6
Burleigh	0.2	1.0	8.7	3.7	9.1	7.4	7.3	18.9	19.7	15 950	171	830	41 962	17.4
Cass	-0.2	D	9.4	8.3	10.1	8.0	11.6	13.9	12.4	22 590	132	1 902	80 248	18.1
Cavalier	21.2	D	10.4	0.9	D	6.0	D	6.8	10.8	1 090	285	21	2 343	1.5
Dickey	5.6	0.0	6.0	9.1	D	8.4	D	16.1	13.7	1 155	226	66	2 652	0.6
Divide	10.8	D	D	D	D	3.5	1.8	D	12.1	510	209	15	1 497	13.1
Dunn	8.0	25.6	D	D	D	1.9	D	1.4	6.0	670	146	22	2 446	14.7
Eddy	-4.8	3.5	D	D	D	5.6	D	21.4	19.0	635	268	36	1 355	2.4
Emmons	24.2	0.4	8.7	D	D	6.5	D	8.9	14.8	1 005	296	34	2 122	1.8
Foster	7.2	D	7.6	D	D	7.7	4.5	9.6	10.0	775	233	31	1 820	1.1
Golden Valley	-8.2	32.5	D	D	D	4.7	4.5	10.3	14.8	350	190	10	1 037	7.2
Grand Forks	0.5	0.6	9.1	4.5	5.5	9.2	5.2	16.9	28.8	10 025	142	741	32 639	11.2
Grant	20.1	0.4	6.0	7.4	D	3.6	4.5	14.9	16.1	685	286	33	1 711	1.4
Griggs	-4.0	0.5	7.5	15.4	D	7.4	D	10.4	16.2	695	301	22	1 463	0.1
Hettinger	-17.3	0.4	D	6.3	D	5.1	8.5	9.4	24.8	660	245	15	1 428	1.0
Kidder	33.0	D	3.7	4.1	D	4.9	D	2.5	11.7	600	249	27	1 695	1.3
LaMoure	-1.9	0.0	8.4	3.6	2.8	16.4	9.1	4.6	20.4	1 025	248	61	2 253	0.7
Logan	13.9	0.6	12.0	D	D	4.9	D	D	18.0	550	285	22	1 157	1.1
McHenry	22.2	1.2	D	D	2.3	2.9	4.7	2.8	14.5	1 320	221	51	3 101	5.2
McIntosh	10.7	0.3	D	D	D	6.5	5.0	19.9	14.3	925	336	34	1 859	0.1
McKenzie	1.3	19.7	25.4	D	D	2.2	4.5	D	10.9	1 070	84	47	6 592	113.3
McLean	4.1	D	8.3	2.4	D	3.0	D	D	16.6	2 465	253	93	6 120	9.5
Mercer	1.5	D	18.9	0.3	2.5	3.1	1.6	D	6.1	1 825	207	50	4 732	6.3
Morton	2.2	1.6	10.5	10.6	9.9	7.3	6.0	8.9	12.0	5 625	185	292	14 660	21.4
Mountrail	-0.9	27.9	9.5	1.5	D	4.4	D	2.7	7.3	1 380	134	69	4 969	20.6
Nelson	6.7	D	9.8	3.9	D	3.8	D	13.9	19.6	990	333	33	1 945	0.9
Oliver	1.3	D	11.2	D	D	0.4	D	D	5.6	430	233	0	947	4.6
Pembina	3.8	0.2	12.6	16.7	D	5.8	D	4.8	23.5	1 805	255	73	3 875	0.4
Pierce	2.3	0.2	D	6.2	2.9	6.2	D	D	12.1	1 040	242	44	2 225	1.2
Ramsey	-1.8	D	7.8	4.4	5.1	11.0	8.6	D	25.4	2 615	225	209	5 840	4.0
Ransom	6.9	D	8.8	11.9	D	4.4	5.7	12.9	20.1	1 215	223	44	2 677	0.8
Renville	-6.0	14.0	8.7	4.1	4.0	8.2	D	8.0	22.2	565	220	14	1 422	2.6
Richland	3.3	D	9.7	23.8	4.0	6.5	4.8	6.4	21.2	3 165	193	134	7 697	2.6
Rolette	4.9	D	7.7	3.2	0.6	7.9	D	57.9	22.2	2 220	151	836	5 513	2.6
Sargent	9.0	D	4.6	59.6	D	2.1	D	1.3	8.1	950	246	29	2 109	5.2
Sheridan	-105.9	1.8	23.8	D	D	D	D	D	61.0	420	323	21	899	0.6
Sioux	6.7	0.0	1.4	D	0.3	D	-0.1	D	82.4	515	117	205	1 334	1.8
Slope	27.0	D	D	0.6	0.6	3.9	1.2	0.7	5.4	165	216	0	438	0.5
Stark	-0.5	31.1	10.6	5.7	4.5	6.2	4.5	4.7	6.8	4 415	137	220	14 534	35.4
Steele	18.3	0.5	15.4	12.4	D	5.3	D	D	11.2	465	237	0	1 198	2.3
Stutsman	0.8	D	8.6	13.4	4.9	7.2	6.6	D	17.8	4 705	223	364	10 159	3.0
Towner	-8.9	0.4	8.2	5.3	D	3.9	D	D	19.4	655	289	15	1 448	-0.1
Traill	3.8	D	5.6	15.3	1.9	D	6.1	D	18.2	1 660	207	54	3 824	1.2
Walsh	4.1	D	6.9	10.8	4.4	5.6	5.9	D	21.3	2 660	243	132	5 587	1.6

1. Per 1,000 resident population estimated as of July 1 of the year shown.

Table B. States and Counties — Housing, Labor Force, and Employment

STATE County	Housing units, 2011–2015 Occupied units — Owner-occupied Total	Percent	Median value[1]	Median owner cost as a percent of income — With a mortgage	Without a mortgage[2]	Renter-occupied Median rent[3]	Median rent as a percent of income[2]	Sub-standard units[4] (percent)	Civilian labor force, 2016 Total	Percent change, 2015–2016	Unemployment Total	Rate[5]	Civilian employment,[6] 2011–2015 Total	Percent Management, business, science and arts	Construction, production, and maintenance occupations
	89	90	91	92	93	94	95	96	97	98	99	100	101	102	103
NORTH CAROLINA—Cont'd															
Swain	5 379	72.3	126 700	22.6	10.0	587	26.2	3.5	7 224	6.6	439	6.1	5 543	29.0	20.7
Transylvania	13 667	76.7	192 000	21.1	10.0	666	33.0	1.6	14 009	3.4	682	4.9	13 794	31.0	23.8
Tyrrell	1 451	73.9	98 800	31.2	15.1	675	29.4	1.1	1 519	-1.8	128	8.4	1 350	13.5	40.5
Union	70 711	79.9	197 400	21.4	11.1	868	30.4	2.9	116 393	3.6	5 053	4.3	99 712	38.5	21.4
Vance	16 589	62.8	97 900	24.1	13.0	644	33.5	3.7	18 079	0.2	1 300	7.2	17 461	23.0	30.1
Wake	364 669	64.2	234 000	20.1	10.0	948	28.5	2.8	558 950	3.6	23 681	4.2	499 197	49.3	12.7
Warren	7 817	70.1	96 400	26.9	15.6	633	28.3	1.9	7 240	0.4	527	7.3	6 958	25.7	25.1
Washington	5 216	68.7	82 700	23.0	14.2	635	37.5	1.5	4 921	-0.9	365	7.4	4 410	21.7	40.7
Watauga	19 996	57.9	231 700	23.6	10.8	825	50.0	1.5	27 991	2.2	1 246	4.5	23 928	35.4	14.5
Wayne	47 530	59.9	110 400	21.7	12.1	716	30.4	3.3	53 697	0.0	3 128	5.8	50 821	29.7	31.0
Wilkes	27 422	74.3	114 800	23.5	13.0	587	33.2	2.8	30 285	2.2	1 452	4.8	26 631	25.8	32.9
Wilson	32 003	60.0	116 300	23.5	14.8	715	31.8	3.7	36 717	-0.1	2 974	8.1	34 701	29.9	28.8
Yadkin	15 369	76.0	124 400	23.9	11.6	591	28.8	3.6	17 727	1.4	777	4.4	15 747	26.0	35.0
Yancey	7 416	75.5	140 500	23.5	11.1	600	33.0	3.4	7 535	1.6	389	5.2	6 992	29.3	30.8
NORTH DAKOTA	299 638	64.1	153 800	18.6	10.0	709	24.9	2.0	416 230	0.5	13 161	3.2	387 716	35.0	25.6
Adams	1 067	73.7	126 100	15.5	11.4	481	18.6	1.6	1 140	2.7	31	2.7	1 279	44.3	28.1
Barnes	5 056	68.7	97 600	18.4	10.0	582	22.5	0.5	5 626	-0.4	186	3.3	5 889	35.7	27.2
Benson	2 280	64.2	63 600	16.6	10.0	423	19.9	9.4	2 447	-1.6	101	4.1	2 461	38.1	26.7
Billings	407	74.0	145 300	20.6	10.0	863	14.3	1.2	443	-5.7	14	3.2	564	35.1	32.3
Bottineau	3 035	74.4	116 800	17.7	10.0	608	22.4	1.1	3 248	0.0	155	4.8	3 369	35.3	28.3
Bowman	1 377	74.0	135 000	16.4	10.0	582	16.1	0.7	1 839	-1.5	41	2.2	1 721	31.8	32.0
Burke	980	67.2	110 100	12.7	10.0	650	22.4	3.4	1 131	-4.0	55	4.9	1 084	32.7	33.7
Burleigh	37 061	69.9	199 200	19.3	10.0	755	24.4	2.9	50 923	3.9	1 336	2.6	49 375	38.5	21.9
Cass	68 776	52.1	172 100	19.8	10.1	712	25.9	1.4	100 569	5.6	2 283	2.3	94 675	37.9	21.3
Cavalier	1 746	85.8	86 700	14.5	10.0	485	25.5	0.1	2 110	2.3	58	2.7	1 968	43.5	27.6
Dickey	2 132	71.9	92 000	17.6	10.0	548	22.2	1.3	2 546	-0.4	50	2.0	2 755	35.4	27.0
Divide	1 081	79.4	100 400	15.0	10.0	546	20.9	0.7	1 710	-5.9	46	2.7	1 252	41.4	25.2
Dunn	1 557	81.0	146 400	13.5	10.0	771	21.4	2.0	3 426	-14.8	107	3.1	2 078	31.3	34.2
Eddy	1 060	74.1	68 500	15.4	10.0	441	25.8	0.1	1 271	-0.3	57	4.5	1 208	38.7	26.6
Emmons	1 599	80.6	79 900	17.6	11.3	430	23.8	1.2	1 580	2.1	71	4.5	1 583	39.2	24.3
Foster	1 484	73.9	96 300	16.0	10.0	512	21.9	0.8	1 691	3.7	52	3.1	1 786	31.6	30.9
Golden Valley	803	67.5	107 000	15.8	10.0	554	26.2	2.7	971	-0.6	27	2.8	964	36.4	23.3
Grand Forks	28 521	49.9	160 600	19.0	10.0	763	30.2	1.7	39 673	5.7	942	2.4	37 754	35.2	20.6
Grant	1 136	81.4	75 100	19.2	11.2	442	25.9	2.0	1 289	-2.5	41	3.2	1 205	47.5	23.5
Griggs	1 035	73.9	83 600	16.0	10.0	406	21.2	0.0	1 146	-1.0	34	3.0	1 203	32.5	26.1
Hettinger	1 091	83.0	95 700	14.9	10.0	565	19.0	2.6	1 551	-0.3	48	3.1	1 211	37.2	27.7
Kidder	1 084	80.9	87 600	19.3	10.0	465	21.3	1.3	1 380	2.5	54	3.9	1 337	41.3	25.8
LaMoure	1 840	78.5	85 200	18.1	10.0	578	22.2	0.5	2 308	1.5	57	2.5	2 073	37.0	29.3
Logan	878	83.5	71 000	16.2	10.0	630	26.3	1.6	958	0.8	34	3.5	952	38.2	27.2
McHenry	2 608	81.9	107 700	18.1	10.0	550	21.4	1.6	3 353	2.2	170	5.1	2 840	32.0	34.3
McIntosh	1 289	82.2	62 800	17.3	11.1	558	22.0	0.7	1 253	1.0	40	3.2	1 347	36.2	24.5
McKenzie	3 214	61.2	198 400	13.4	10.0	829	17.2	5.2	8 092	-11.8	311	3.8	4 766	32.5	34.4
McLean	4 234	76.2	130 500	16.9	10.0	588	21.0	1.5	5 044	2.0	182	3.6	4 541	33.8	29.0
Mercer	3 673	83.0	136 600	17.0	10.0	705	18.6	1.7	4 632	7.4	212	4.6	4 391	28.5	34.9
Morton	12 308	75.6	165 500	20.1	10.0	762	24.6	1.2	16 873	3.7	559	3.3	16 411	34.7	24.8
Mountrail	3 206	69.7	132 300	16.0	10.0	673	17.9	4.0	7 203	-11.4	220	3.1	4 607	33.4	27.1
Nelson	1 522	77.4	73 200	17.1	10.0	467	16.4	0.7	1 537	1.4	54	3.5	1 554	34.2	29.3
Oliver	792	81.1	120 300	16.3	10.0	534	19.6	2.3	903	2.3	49	5.4	857	38.5	30.1
Pembina	3 285	78.1	76 900	16.1	10.4	515	22.1	1.0	3 697	2.4	188	5.1	3 694	30.1	31.4
Pierce	2 018	73.2	97 900	18.5	11.4	584	29.3	1.7	1 898	3.1	77	4.1	2 194	32.2	28.7
Ramsey	5 016	63.4	102 400	17.5	10.0	525	24.0	3.1	6 277	10.2	180	2.9	5 910	34.9	21.6
Ransom	2 352	67.9	103 600	18.3	10.0	580	22.3	0.7	2 830	2.3	66	2.3	2 847	33.2	35.7
Renville	1 020	78.0	118 000	17.9	10.0	668	19.5	0.8	1 300	-2.8	53	4.1	1 301	36.0	28.4
Richland	6 621	71.3	102 000	17.9	10.0	520	22.5	1.3	8 922	3.8	252	2.8	8 800	31.7	32.8
Rolette	4 774	67.7	69 000	16.3	10.5	351	27.3	6.0	5 018	2.7	553	11.0	4 907	37.5	20.8
Sargent	1 728	75.5	77 900	16.5	10.0	577	18.4	0.5	2 350	4.1	46	2.0	2 078	31.0	42.4
Sheridan	653	81.5	69 600	17.1	10.0	356	42.9	1.1	726	-0.1	42	5.8	629	39.4	30.7
Sioux	1 098	41.3	66 200	14.3	10.5	470	16.3	12.4	1 336	3.2	59	4.4	1 291	40.8	13.2
Slope	322	85.7	101 100	13.7	10.0	663	14.7	0.6	443	-2.9	11	2.5	335	46.3	31.3
Stark	11 379	68.7	206 200	17.3	10.0	854	24.0	3.3	18 488	-9.0	735	4.0	16 062	27.7	33.0
Steele	948	77.4	74 900	14.7	10.0	463	17.2	1.5	1 066	0.1	23	2.2	1 035	33.0	34.8
Stutsman	9 061	66.7	111 200	17.8	10.0	620	26.0	0.5	11 150	3.9	281	2.5	11 144	31.6	26.4
Towner	1 003	77.9	70 400	14.0	10.0	464	23.8	3.3	1 333	7.2	30	2.3	1 059	45.0	17.8
Traill	3 278	73.2	105 600	18.1	10.2	560	24.9	1.6	4 595	3.1	131	2.9	4 085	33.3	29.6
Walsh	4 929	74.3	75 400	17.5	10.0	514	25.1	1.1	5 678	1.6	220	3.9	5 457	30.9	34.5

1. Specified owner-occupied units.   2. A value of 10.0 represents 10 percent or less; a value of 50.0 represents 50 percent or more.   3. Specified renter-occupied units.
4. Overcrowded or lacking complete plumbing facilities.   5. Percent of civilian labor force.   6. Civilian employed persons 16 years old and over.

Table B. States and Counties — Nonfarm Employment and Agriculture

STATE County	Number of establishments	Employment Total	Health care and social assistance	Manufacturing	Retail trade	Finance and insurance	Professional, scientific, and technical services	Annual payroll Total (mil dol)	Average per employee (dollars)	Farms Number	Fewer than 50 acres	500 acres or more	Farm operators whose principal occupation is farming (percent)
	104	105	106	107	108	109	110	111	112	113	114	115	116
NORTH CAROLINA—Cont'd													
Swain	360	3 512	835	D	524	87	35	110	31 273	94	62.8	1.1	26.6
Transylvania	798	7 194	1 384	553	1 463	211	230	221	30 773	221	63.8	2.3	46.6
Tyrrell	72	414	24	25	145	16	D	12	30 075	78	21.8	28.2	57.7
Union	4 358	52 968	5 591	11 209	7 294	1 064	1 489	2 044	38 597	1 059	55.6	6.8	53.0
Vance	835	12 709	2 393	1 446	2 249	238	308	422	33 240	242	36.4	10.7	36.8
Wake	27 405	431 040	56 975	12 595	56 872	22 278	48 696	22 263	51 650	783	57.0	4.5	49.0
Warren	255	2 407	611	377	369	53	45	65	26 875	256	34.0	11.7	42.6
Washington	234	3 002	617	847	463	59	58	114	37 906	156	25.6	30.1	59.0
Watauga	1 580	17 196	2 691	635	3 569	366	670	539	31 316	609	49.4	2.0	44.7
Wayne	2 174	33 461	7 316	5 679	5 998	1 115	753	1 151	34 404	563	40.1	18.1	60.9
Wilkes	1 178	18 766	2 888	4 850	2 443	388	547	773	41 205	972	44.9	3.9	50.6
Wilson	1 725	31 970	5 754	7 638	3 657	2 915	675	1 240	38 772	297	42.4	17.8	61.3
Yadkin	589	9 059	951	2 376	795	147	174	278	30 685	952	55.6	2.7	44.9
Yancey	309	3 217	415	875	588	76	80	106	33 099	450	57.3	0.7	31.1
NORTH DAKOTA	24 848	365 893	59 272	25 361	52 005	18 128	16 113	17 185	46 967	30 961	11.0	48.8	56.6
Adams	98	767	336	D	172	34	D	28	36 026	392	12.8	48.7	60.2
Barnes	361	4 012	1 084	587	506	149	78	131	32 686	855	11.6	40.6	52.4
Benson	95	1 166	D	69	64	65	D	37	31 738	563	6.9	54.2	64.5
Billings	61	384	260	NA	15	D	4	22	58 042	197	4.6	68.5	68.0
Bottineau	279	1 925	NA	123	357	121	75	80	41 785	863	8.5	41.7	48.8
Bowman	162	1 243	248	34	221	89	42	51	41 333	348	8.6	55.5	54.3
Burke	87	430	12	NA	83	36	56	21	48 412	488	6.4	47.3	54.3
Burleigh	3 040	47 707	10 085	1 200	7 604	2 285	2 533	2 234	46 824	1 014	23.1	34.7	42.3
Cass	5 436	102 901	17 925	8 985	13 482	8 180	5 893	4 656	45 245	968	21.0	49.8	66.3
Cavalier	161	1 256	235	24	227	102	18	49	38 869	667	7.5	57.1	63.4
Dickey	215	1 850	413	221	338	57	34	55	29 803	543	11.0	45.7	53.8
Divide	119	857	D	6	72	31	11	39	45 939	452	5.5	54.4	54.6
Dunn	190	3 084	D	D	198	35	136	176	57 165	628	13.1	56.5	66.1
Eddy	81	479	209	D	53	22	8	17	36 376	331	8.8	50.2	46.2
Emmons	128	719	178	D	106	50	18	23	31 391	609	6.6	58.1	55.2
Foster	146	1 412	294	D	249	60	9	57	40 110	310	10.3	49.7	61.0
Golden Valley	75	447	119	D	97	27	20	17	37 418	251	7.2	58.6	62.2
Grand Forks	1 918	34 034	7 135	2 304	6 444	912	1 600	1 306	38 382	970	12.3	35.8	62.7
Grant	78	424	190	D	32	25	D	13	31 038	508	8.3	59.4	65.2
Griggs	93	653	D	150	52	26	23	23	34 590	456	6.6	45.8	52.9
Hettinger	99	522	98	D	66	47	17	18	34 628	494	5.9	50.4	54.9
Kidder	65	518	63	5	71	38	22	20	37 797	559	6.4	54.2	49.7
LaMoure	153	1 010	151	82	129	117	NA	37	36 899	642	8.6	49.2	59.0
Logan	68	445	119	D	55	34	D	13	29 097	379	7.4	56.2	64.8
McHenry	125	765	120	D	206	45	17	30	39 633	911	9.2	48.8	64.3
McIntosh	119	862	317	72	131	53	26	26	29 838	471	7.4	51.4	59.7
McKenzie	536	7 444	314	D	611	100	245	490	65 843	574	10.5	59.4	61.1
McLean	258	2 574	425	75	352	114	15	146	56 749	868	7.3	51.6	51.6
Mercer	243	4 404	484	57	472	131	51	307	69 639	422	12.3	46.2	54.3
Morton	833	9 862	1 704	883	1 389	410	1 411	446	45 177	887	20.3	47.9	55.2
Mountrail	394	4 915	249	132	626	68	174	288	58 499	670	4.6	57.9	66.4
Nelson	119	746	258	D	93	64	10	24	32 135	603	6.8	35.8	36.5
Oliver	40	668	19	23	D	D	D	57	84 756	290	13.4	48.3	53.4
Pembina	277	2 484	351	707	356	117	33	102	41 195	584	12.3	45.0	62.3
Pierce	162	1 533	D	D	266	83	64	55	36 036	521	7.5	53.7	58.3
Ramsey	431	4 603	662	148	1 005	296	58	155	33 757	573	11.0	48.5	51.5
Ransom	193	1 541	395	268	233	75	49	53	34 644	548	11.7	36.3	48.7
Renville	111	657	92	D	107	29	16	24	36 626	304	8.2	68.1	73.4
Richland	536	6 232	617	2 007	849	172	133	239	38 331	854	15.6	47.9	64.3
Rolette	200	2 483	566	181	479	100	32	76	30 470	649	9.1	38.8	48.8
Sargent	127	2 383	76	D	176	49	17	116	48 802	537	6.5	45.4	55.9
Sheridan	43	154	25	2	22	16	D	4	27 390	370	7.8	53.5	54.6
Sioux	25	955	D	D	54	D	D	28	29 184	176	10.8	67.0	66.5
Slope	18	88	D	NA	D	NA	NA	6	69 250	221	9.5	62.4	62.0
Stark	1 225	17 543	2 080	1 083	2 600	465	546	913	52 061	837	20.2	39.1	48.6
Steele	58	473	D	115	60	49	10	21	43 611	355	8.7	52.4	63.1
Stutsman	693	9 349	2 665	862	1 442	459	223	346	37 054	1 028	10.1	49.8	55.2
Towner	81	510	D	63	34	54	25	15	30 300	529	7.2	62.4	61.1
Traill	291	2 847	614	420	332	154	38	114	39 912	468	17.3	48.3	63.7
Walsh	408	3 533	681	635	520	179	88	123	34 817	962	13.7	38.9	47.3

Table B. States and Counties — **Agriculture**

STATE County	Land in farms					Value of land and buildings (dollars)		Value of machinery and equipment, average per farm (dollars)	Value of products sold				Percent of farms with sales of:		Government payments	
	Acreage (1,000)	Percent change, 2007–2012	Acres: Average size of farm	Total irrigated (1,000)	Total cropland (1,000)	Average per farm	Average per acre		Total (mil dol)	Average per farm (dollars)	Percent from: Crops	Live-stock and poultry products	$10,000 or more	$100,000 or more	Total ($1,000)	Percent of farms
	117	118	119	120	121	122	123	124	125	126	127	128	129	130	131	132
NORTH CAROLINA—Cont'd																
Swain	D	D	D	0.0	D	349 085	D	37 309	0.7	7 202	48.3	51.7	16.0	1.1	17	10.6
Transylvania	18	11.7	81	0.4	6.6	716 964	8 838	43 715	20.4	92 131	81.5	18.5	34.8	11.3	200	12.7
Tyrrell	65	19.9	828	0.0	57.8	2 107 192	2 545	343 936	59.6	763 474	D	D	62.8	42.3	772	83.3
Union	202	13.2	190	0.4	148.3	1 075 361	5 647	112 638	535.8	505 977	24.0	76.0	43.6	25.9	1 807	17.4
Vance	55	-0.4	227	1.6	19.5	784 640	3 460	79 628	17.3	71 463	97.7	2.3	26.4	11.2	446	45.9
Wake	84	-0.9	108	3.2	44.4	1 029 967	9 575	68 049	65.2	83 324	94.1	5.9	33.0	9.6	848	24.8
Warren	66	-9.6	257	0.8	26.0	657 488	2 562	60 867	25.6	100 156	53.7	46.3	37.9	14.5	678	57.4
Washington	91	-5.7	586	4.4	75.9	1 767 526	3 017	301 814	68.4	438 237	95.5	4.5	52.6	35.9	1 639	76.3
Watauga	56	21.8	92	0.0	14.5	684 361	7 474	51 750	15.3	25 108	38.4	61.6	34.5	5.1	222	22.5
Wayne	191	9.1	340	4.8	146.8	1 400 607	4 124	199 504	577.2	1 025 265	27.4	72.6	61.5	44.8	2 943	56.5
Wilkes	111	1.0	114	0.1	36.2	553 577	4 842	80 330	284.9	293 140	6.6	93.4	42.1	19.1	329	6.6
Wilson	111	6.4	375	1.4	86.4	1 431 529	3 817	266 391	179.6	604 822	84.3	15.7	46.5	30.6	1 876	62.3
Yadkin	100	-4.5	106	0.5	53.5	555 887	5 267	68 082	124.7	130 956	26.8	73.2	33.8	12.3	921	25.7
Yancey	31	-7.3	69	0.1	6.2	446 533	6 482	28 402	5.7	12 758	71.8	28.2	23.8	2.7	532	23.3
NORTH DAKOTA	39 263	-1.0	1 268	218.4	27 147.2	1 808 801	1 426	300 285	10 950.7	353 693	88.3	11.7	59.0	40.6	381 710	80.1
Adams	601	-4.1	1 534	D	380.0	1 236 143	806	192 020	107.5	274 329	77.3	22.7	54.1	36.7	4 734	81.9
Barnes	937	3.3	1 096	1.7	836.5	2 449 174	2 235	342 849	376.4	440 175	97.5	2.5	54.9	39.5	11 719	83.6
Benson	802	5.6	1 425	1.2	644.4	1 841 764	1 293	354 654	240.6	427 405	92.7	7.3	62.0	46.0	7 551	83.5
Billings	722	-0.3	3 666	0.0	131.3	2 888 964	788	226 416	36.7	186 127	48.1	51.9	78.7	41.1	1 365	68.5
Bottineau	899	-12.6	1 042	D	773.0	1 408 030	1 351	275 319	254.0	294 359	95.1	4.9	53.3	34.9	9 818	83.4
Bowman	730	1.3	2 099	1.5	372.6	1 577 514	752	251 733	111.4	320 164	54.1	45.9	61.5	41.4	4 005	80.2
Burke	595	4.3	1 219	D	434.6	1 023 576	839	247 330	105.1	215 455	91.7	8.3	50.4	32.4	5 413	86.9
Burleigh	951	8.1	938	4.6	494.7	1 320 447	1 408	162 938	179.6	177 132	72.9	27.1	50.2	23.6	5 300	53.9
Cass	1 107	6.6	1 144	9.3	1 044.5	3 277 384	2 865	455 639	567.1	585 855	96.8	3.2	68.0	54.3	14 691	78.3
Cavalier	940	7.7	1 410	0.0	871.5	2 681 525	1 902	456 447	334.5	501 547	98.2	1.8	65.1	54.4	15 805	92.2
Dickey	633	-9.2	1 166	16.3	481.1	2 629 105	2 254	359 029	266.8	491 398	88.2	11.8	57.8	43.1	10 047	79.4
Divide	565	-20.2	1 250	2.4	419.2	807 018	646	241 810	93.8	207 496	90.9	9.1	55.1	38.3	4 848	90.5
Dunn	1 031	-1.2	1 642	0.4	374.3	1 498 726	913	250 261	124.8	198 707	60.6	39.4	72.3	39.3	3 189	70.9
Eddy	396	5.1	1 196	0.2	288.7	1 600 341	1 338	283 166	105.1	317 538	90.2	9.8	52.0	37.2	4 696	87.9
Emmons	744	-14.7	1 222	3.9	443.9	1 439 232	1 178	269 821	171.3	281 255	80.9	19.1	62.7	47.0	5 117	87.8
Foster	374	-6.5	1 206	2.6	314.3	2 254 016	1 868	422 081	169.4	546 484	80.4	19.6	65.5	51.3	4 700	78.4
Golden Valley	562	-1.4	2 241	D	242.6	1 887 992	843	258 785	59.6	237 327	73.3	26.7	63.3	38.2	4 251	79.7
Grand Forks	816	-1.1	842	18.9	749.2	1 768 300	2 101	322 178	428.8	442 023	94.8	5.2	51.3	39.3	11 254	90.9
Grant	1 050	-0.8	2 067	2.4	504.0	1 904 955	922	235 537	157.1	309 232	70.3	29.7	68.1	45.9	5 753	84.8
Griggs	445	9.7	977	2.8	342.4	1 781 884	1 824	254 471	127.8	280 325	91.5	8.5	53.7	35.5	8 891	88.4
Hettinger	716	1.1	1 449	0.0	558.5	1 624 585	1 121	263 455	159.0	321 927	91.4	8.6	49.4	34.4	8 615	88.7
Kidder	780	3.6	1 396	15.0	429.8	1 290 878	925	198 445	148.3	265 326	72.2	27.8	59.9	40.4	4 079	84.6
LaMoure	726	5.5	1 131	7.4	611.3	2 445 422	2 163	342 617	292.4	455 500	88.9	11.1	63.6	50.9	7 967	85.7
Logan	572	-1.0	1 508	1.5	333.3	1 541 950	1 022	285 359	172.1	454 087	50.0	50.0	63.1	48.3	3 296	90.0
McHenry	1 061	-2.0	1 165	1.2	624.8	1 047 299	899	161 514	198.2	217 581	72.3	27.7	56.4	34.7	8 289	77.9
McIntosh	590	7.3	1 252	D	397.2	1 472 964	1 176	214 769	139.8	296 754	75.3	24.7	66.7	42.7	3 350	79.6
McKenzie	1 064	-1.0	1 854	19.9	425.6	1 366 373	737	246 225	114.4	199 387	69.0	31.0	62.9	38.5	4 116	70.0
McLean	1 113	-4.3	1 282	7.4	838.7	1 681 880	1 312	307 744	293.4	338 025	92.3	7.7	62.2	41.6	11 766	82.8
Mercer	503	-1.3	1 192	1.4	231.0	1 135 981	953	188 306	76.7	181 765	73.3	26.7	65.6	32.5	2 572	70.9
Morton	1 220	4.7	1 375	7.6	549.1	1 405 868	1 022	208 989	225.2	253 934	67.6	32.4	62.8	34.6	5 558	62.0
Mountrail	964	-7.0	1 438	0.2	578.8	1 308 849	910	278 960	154.9	231 166	86.8	13.2	60.3	37.0	7 195	77.0
Nelson	560	1.9	929	2.1	474.9	1 092 551	1 175	230 488	145.8	241 725	93.3	6.7	37.3	24.5	9 207	95.5
Oliver	395	4.4	1 360	5.9	165.1	1 388 955	1 021	192 590	85.5	294 810	60.2	39.8	74.8	39.3	2 057	75.2
Pembina	692	6.6	1 185	5.7	632.8	3 054 467	2 577	574 476	406.0	695 164	98.7	1.3	60.3	44.9	8 554	77.7
Pierce	598	2.9	1 148	1.0	479.8	1 180 380	1 028	257 340	142.1	272 649	90.5	9.5	55.9	41.8	6 473	90.6
Ramsey	698	-2.3	1 219	D	622.7	1 696 558	1 392	394 349	236.1	412 005	96.7	3.3	51.0	41.2	10 448	85.3
Ransom	502	-4.9	915	14.8	339.3	1 673 436	1 828	213 192	179.3	327 126	85.4	14.6	50.2	32.5	9 311	81.6
Renville	500	-9.8	1 645	0.0	445.8	2 659 974	1 617	536 164	156.4	514 605	97.8	2.2	80.6	66.1	6 902	84.2
Richland	869	-4.1	1 017	3.7	788.5	3 021 842	2 970	437 697	535.7	627 234	95.1	4.9	67.7	54.3	15 676	82.2
Rolette	534	-5.9	823	D	365.5	925 470	1 124	187 112	107.9	166 301	90.8	9.2	50.7	24.8	5 631	68.1
Sargent	513	1.5	955	13.7	432.5	2 265 119	2 372	338 054	243.4	453 311	90.3	9.7	55.5	45.8	9 185	87.2
Sheridan	514	2.7	1 388	D	347.3	1 297 773	935	230 697	107.8	291 295	91.1	8.9	53.8	38.9	4 293	82.7
Sioux	573	-21.5	3 256	D	155.9	2 912 585	894	265 188	62.7	356 421	47.1	52.9	71.6	52.3	1 476	58.5
Slope	674	-12.3	3 051	D	245.0	2 603 290	853	329 502	67.6	305 688	72.0	28.0	64.3	41.6	3 166	72.4
Stark	830	-0.9	991	0.8	498.8	1 345 419	1 358	207 119	152.6	182 298	77.8	22.2	52.9	27.4	4 741	66.3
Steele	426	5.9	1 200	6.0	397.0	2 218 885	1 850	483 662	210.6	593 158	98.3	1.7	63.7	57.2	6 646	94.6
Stutsman	1 303	9.2	1 267	8.2	1 030.6	2 212 500	1 746	385 059	464.6	451 914	90.0	10.0	60.1	41.3	13 278	78.3
Towner	645	6.3	1 220	0.4	573.3	1 565 902	1 283	320 216	196.8	372 049	91.2	8.8	60.5	53.1	7 528	87.1
Traill	548	0.8	1 170	2.0	526.2	3 395 635	2 901	477 162	308.8	659 887	99.3	0.7	68.2	54.9	8 804	80.6
Walsh	802	0.9	834	3.4	714.5	1 982 913	2 377	308 740	424.0	440 783	98.3	1.7	49.7	37.8	14 445	87.1

Table B. States and Counties — Water Use, Wholesale Trade, Retail Trade, and Real Estate

STATE County	Water use, 2010 — Total water withdrawn (mil gal/day)	Gallons withdrawn per person per day	Wholesale trade,[1] 2012 — Number of establishments	Number of employees	Sales (mil dol)	Annual payroll (mil dol)	Retail trade,[2] 2012 — Number of establishments	Number of employees	Sales (mil dol)	Annual payroll (mil dol)	Real estate and rental and leasing,[2] 2012 — Number of establishments	Number of employees	Receipts (mil dol)	Annual payroll (mil dol)
	133	134	135	136	137	138	139	140	141	142	143	144	145	146
NORTH CAROLINA—Cont'd														
Swain	15.0	1 073	4	D	D	D	96	472	107.1	9.1	7	23	2.0	0.4
Transylvania	811.1	24 513	15	D	D	D	125	1 352	311.3	30.2	48	91	13.4	2.7
Tyrrell	0.6	134	1	D	D	D	20	135	36.0	2.3	2	D	D	D
Union	42.2	210	266	2 658	1 449.1	126.9	492	6 803	1 943.6	156.4	144	304	60.2	11.2
Vance	9.8	216	31	D	D	D	179	2 186	527.9	49.0	51	211	27.5	5.1
Wake	114.5	127	1 082	18 108	18 602.6	1 401.0	3 161	51 026	14 359.3	1 264.2	1 320	7 360	1 683.3	391.9
Warren	2.6	123	9	21	10.2	0.6	44	314	72.4	6.0	9	D	D	D
Washington	5.8	438	12	185	174.1	4.1	48	465	127.7	8.7	4	D	D	D
Watauga	11.0	215	37	299	140.2	14.7	318	3 471	762.9	70.2	100	382	55.2	10.0
Wayne	34.3	280	95	1 822	1 244.8	74.4	464	5 709	1 557.5	125.8	63	257	29.3	7.1
Wilkes	14.3	206	47	D	D	D	223	2 500	1 365.2	53.5	44	185	46.8	7.0
Wilson	26.0	320	99	D	D	D	319	3 606	992.7	83.6	76	247	43.1	6.3
Yadkin	15.3	399	29	222	87.7	7.8	108	760	242.9	16.0	14	D	D	D
Yancey	12.8	716	7	24	3.7	0.4	61	522	144.9	12.3	17	D	D	D
NORTH DAKOTA	1 147.1	1 705	1 430	18 880	28 150.8	1 078.2	3 185	47 186	15 519.8	1 204.4	912	5 157	1 445.1	247.5
Adams	0.5	222	10	49	120.6	1.7	16	169	43.1	4.1	2	D	D	D
Barnes	2.2	194	22	192	329.6	9.2	48	479	121.7	10.3	11	86	4.5	1.8
Benson	2.1	321	14	86	228.9	4.1	9	55	12.3	1.4	2	D	D	D
Billings	2.1	2 669	1	D	D	D	10	D	D	D	1	D	D	D
Bottineau	3.2	496	16	120	99.0	5.6	34	337	95.5	6.8	8	16	1.1	0.1
Bowman	2.1	673	13	123	96.6	7.6	19	251	93.2	5.5	3	2	0.2	0.0
Burke	1.1	549	6	60	454.5	3.6	10	96	38.5	2.5	3	2	0.7	0.1
Burleigh	16.2	199	132	2 094	1 483.2	113.2	373	6 905	1 995.1	177.7	132	404	107.3	13.9
Cass	17.2	115	333	6 020	5 497.7	335.9	645	12 500	3 790.4	302.8	277	1 716	302.9	64.8
Cavalier	0.9	215	15	D	D	D	29	213	125.7	5.2	1	D	D	D
Dickey	7.6	1 431	16	152	450.1	7.0	41	324	96.3	7.2	1	D	D	D
Divide	2.2	1 067	2	D	D	D	9	86	21.1	1.8	1	D	D	D
Dunn	3.0	834	8	50	86.8	2.7	13	161	69.1	3.5	1	D	D	D
Eddy	2.0	818	4	D	D	D	10	72	16.7	1.7	2	D	D	D
Emmons	5.7	1 606	14	95	236.9	3.5	20	106	30.7	2.3	NA	NA	NA	NA
Foster	1.8	523	19	119	210.8	6.6	28	247	133.0	7.2	2	D	D	D
Golden Valley	0.6	339	5	68	87.3	3.2	15	134	72.7	2.8	NA	NA	NA	NA
Grand Forks	17.5	262	92	1 235	1 214.9	65.6	314	5 860	1 562.2	130.9	79	504	86.1	14.7
Grant	9.6	3 989	8	50	98.4	2.4	10	31	7.2	0.7	1	D	D	D
Griggs	3.1	1 269	6	104	66.5	5.2	12	60	18.1	1.4	1	D	D	D
Hettinger	0.3	113	4	D	D	D	14	87	128.6	2.7	2	D	D	D
Kidder	13.9	5 696	6	17	27.9	0.7	8	66	48.4	1.7	2	D	D	D
LaMoure	5.3	1 285	23	213	391.6	9.9	16	142	133.1	3.8	2	D	D	D
Logan	2.8	1 392	6	D	D	D	11	46	30.5	1.7	1	D	D	D
McHenry	22.0	4 085	5	D	D	D	17	122	26.5	2.5	5	D	D	D
McIntosh	0.9	313	11	103	277.1	3.5	19	140	52.1	3.6	3	9	0.8	0.1
McKenzie	37.7	5 925	14	172	263.6	25.7	24	301	166.1	10.6	15	69	27.6	5.0
McLean	21.6	2 407	20	216	528.9	9.4	38	293	132.5	7.2	2	D	D	D
Mercer	372.6	44 230	6	28	21.5	1.5	39	420	125.2	9.6	5	5	0.3	0.1
Morton	51.2	1 865	34	D	D	D	99	1 230	586.1	40.3	43	118	16.8	3.3
Mountrail	3.4	446	12	140	406.4	9.1	41	475	274.0	15.4	6	16	1.1	0.3
Nelson	1.0	326	13	107	449.2	6.2	19	103	31.5	1.6	4	4	0.1	0.0
Oliver	433.1	234 588	1	D	D	D	2	D	D	D	NA	NA	NA	NA
Pembina	2.1	286	35	352	847.9	13.4	45	403	82.9	7.8	3	1	0.3	0.0
Pierce	1.3	287	11	112	201.5	5.3	22	263	92.6	6.2	2	D	D	D
Ramsey	0.3	26	29	207	622.1	11.0	80	962	311.7	27.1	6	192	7.4	4.6
Ransom	10.6	1 933	13	187	292.1	10.4	30	252	66.2	4.8	4	4	0.7	0.1
Renville	1.4	579	12	89	250.5	4.3	13	142	81.1	3.7	2	D	D	D
Richland	6.2	379	34	D	D	D	75	899	277.3	19.6	18	50	5.6	1.1
Rolette	2.1	149	7	48	103.6	2.9	45	496	132.9	9.7	2	D	D	D
Sargent	4.5	1 183	12	74	145.1	2.9	17	124	20.9	1.8	4	D	D	D
Sheridan	0.4	310	3	D	D	D	6	20	5.5	0.2	2	D	D	D
Sioux	0.7	166	NA	NA	NA	NA	8	D	D	D	NA	NA	NA	NA
Slope	6.1	8 391	NA	NA	NA	NA	1	D	D	D	NA	NA	NA	NA
Stark	3.2	132	53	745	1 186.8	44.7	160	2 050	883.4	62.8	43	211	72.4	12.0
Steele	0.8	400	6	D	D	D	10	61	34.4	1.7	1	D	D	D
Stutsman	9.1	430	39	470	875.5	24.3	101	1 328	379.1	32.3	28	79	20.9	2.0
Towner	0.5	205	8	64	193.8	3.4	13	51	30.4	1.3	2	D	D	D
Traill	1.1	132	30	334	1 733.4	16.3	42	313	97.2	7.1	7	9	0.7	0.2
Walsh	1.0	92	35	374	599.7	18.9	58	535	123.1	10.4	11	13	1.0	0.3

1. Merchant wholesalers, except manufacturers' sales branches and offices.   2. Employer establishments.

Table B. States and Counties — Professional Services, Manufacturing, and Accommodation and Food Services

STATE County	Professional, scientific, and technical services, 2012				Manufacturing, 2012				Accommodation and food services, 2012			
	Number of establishments	Number of employees	Receipts (mil dol)	Annual payroll (mil dol)	Number of establishments	Number of employees	Receipts (mil dol)	Annual payroll (mil dol)	Number of establishments	Number of employees	Sales (mil dol)	Annual payroll (mil dol)
	147	148	149	150	151	152	153	154	155	156	157	158
NORTH CAROLINA—Cont'd												
Swain	11	D	D	D	11	414	D	17.1	82	765	50.0	12.4
Transylvania	67	D	D	D	24	440	61.1	18.3	83	1 106	68.5	21.3
Tyrrell	3	D	D	D	3	105	9.6	2.3	6	D	D	D
Union	395	1 221	156.5	54.2	231	9 760	3 645.4	444.3	264	4 159	192.9	50.8
Vance	46	196	16.4	6.9	41	1 581	756.2	66.1	67	1 239	57.0	15.0
Wake	4 332	40 850	7 315.9	3 072.9	576	12 902	13 105.2	696.6	2 102	42 326	2 165.2	606.3
Warren	14	52	3.8	0.9	9	494	128.9	14.7	23	207	8.9	2.3
Washington	12	66	7.5	1.8	12	780	394.6	47.0	27	D	D	D
Watauga	149	723	47.9	20.0	47	667	108.0	23.6	174	3 416	142.1	43.2
Wayne	147	816	76.0	27.4	83	5 833	1 691.3	243.8	186	3 284	161.7	42.0
Wilkes	83	418	36.5	15.0	73	4 288	1 156.1	138.7	105	1 568	65.7	17.9
Wilson	112	769	95.4	36.3	91	7 809	13 159.9	393.6	138	2 749	139.3	34.2
Yadkin	41	230	20.6	8.1	41	2 064	748.3	79.1	58	875	34.4	9.6
Yancey	17	75	5.0	1.5	12	686	145.0	28.9	21	282	11.6	3.4
NORTH DAKOTA	1 722	13 715	1 846.9	735.7	745	23 541	14 427.4	1 042.8	1 935	35 698	2 045.1	521.3
Adams	4	D	D	D	NA	NA	NA	NA	11	D	D	D
Barnes	15	79	9.6	3.6	10	500	D	23.1	31	356	14.1	3.4
Benson	6	14	1.9	0.9	4	102	D	D	16	D	D	D
Billings	3	5	1.0	0.3	3	13	D	D	14	131	19.0	5.4
Bottineau	20	67	6.4	2.9	10	92	D	4.6	28	237	11.0	2.7
Bowman	4	D	D	D	7	35	D	1.0	17	118	5.1	1.2
Burke	4	D	D	D	NA	NA	NA	NA	12	48	4.4	0.5
Burleigh	308	1 969	314.8	118.4	68	900	D	39.3	173	4 980	242.1	70.7
Cass	481	D	D	D	186	8 566	3 451.1	395.7	388	9 671	446.8	130.9
Cavalier	6	16	1.3	0.6	5	14	3.1	0.6	18	D	D	D
Dickey	9	37	2.6	0.9	13	225	60.0	9.4	19	145	4.6	1.1
Divide	6	15	1.6	0.4	3	6	D	D	7	D	D	D
Dunn	4	16	2.2	0.9	5	D	D	D	9	165	24.6	3.5
Eddy	4	10	1.1	0.2	NA	NA	NA	NA	11	30	1.4	0.3
Emmons	9	12	0.9	0.3	3	6	D	D	10	88	2.8	0.8
Foster	7	10	3.4	0.5	3	D	D	D	10	125	5.2	1.5
Golden Valley	5	18	1.8	0.5	NA	NA	NA	NA	4	D	D	D
Grand Forks	130	1 473	167.2	79.1	55	2 166	590.7	78.4	196	4 191	177.6	52.5
Grant	3	7	0.6	0.1	3	27	D	D	6	D	D	D
Griggs	9	43	4.7	1.6	5	155	21.4	5.1	11	D	D	D
Hettinger	5	15	0.9	0.4	3	5	D	D	5	35	1.3	0.2
Kidder	4	D	D	D	3	6	D	D	8	43	2.0	0.6
LaMoure	2	D	D	D	7	52	D	1.9	16	D	D	D
Logan	2	D	D	D	NA	NA	NA	NA	9	57	1.3	0.3
McHenry	6	14	2.1	0.6	4	D	D	D	7	24	1.3	0.3
McIntosh	6	24	1.6	0.6	4	109	D	3.3	10	D	D	D
McKenzie	32	134	46.7	13.9	5	17	1.6	0.4	28	460	31.8	6.5
McLean	7	20	1.6	0.5	5	67	D	3.2	28	181	9.8	2.1
Mercer	11	69	7.2	2.2	7	35	5.7	0.9	30	348	12.4	3.5
Morton	61	D	D	D	36	913	D	56.0	52	D	D	D
Mountrail	18	44	8.9	2.3	3	D	D	1.4	30	167	18.8	3.1
Nelson	5	12	0.8	0.3	3	57	D	0.7	15	106	3.4	0.8
Oliver	3	D	D	D	5	D	D	D	3	9	0.3	0.1
Pembina	14	27	2.8	0.6	15	520	477.1	22.5	20	D	D	D
Pierce	13	58	4.4	1.1	NA	NA	NA	NA	12	171	5.6	1.5
Ramsey	19	61	7.9	2.4	9	219	D	9.8	47	681	29.6	7.9
Ransom	15	52	4.7	1.3	8	405	D	12.3	19	129	4.8	1.2
Renville	7	14	1.1	0.3	NA	NA	NA	NA	10	30	1.4	0.2
Richland	32	D	D	D	35	1 871	1 276.7	87.2	47	821	89.6	16.1
Rolette	6	8	0.9	0.3	8	231	D	7.4	25	582	43.1	12.5
Sargent	9	34	3.5	1.5	6	D	D	D	14	D	D	D
Sheridan	4	D	D	D	3	43	D	D	2	D	D	D
Sioux	2	D	D	D	NA	NA	NA	NA	6	D	D	D
Slope	NA	NA	NA	NA	NA	NA	NA	NA	1	D	D	D
Stark	71	430	75.9	23.3	28	898	431.8	44.6	80	1 431	111.6	25.8
Steele	3	3	0.3	0.1	8	158	D	4.9	5	20	1.0	0.1
Stutsman	34	174	16.4	6.4	24	902	500.6	37.7	60	926	40.2	11.9
Towner	8	21	1.9	0.5	4	49	D	1.0	9	32	1.3	0.3
Traill	10	31	3.1	1.4	15	311	D	12.3	26	203	7.7	2.0
Walsh	24	88	8.5	3.0	10	522	111.2	17.8	36	259	12.0	2.7

1. Establishment subject to federal tax.

Health Care and Social Assistance, Other Services, Nonemployer Businesses, and Residential Construction

STATE County	Health care and social assistance, 2012				Other services, 2012				Nonemployer businesses, 2015		Value of residential construction authorized by building permits, 2016	
	Number of establishments	Number of employees	Receipts (mil dol)	Annual payroll (mil dol)	Number of establishments	Number of employees	Receipts (mil dol)	Annual payroll (mil dol)	Number	Receipts (mil dol)	New Construction ($1,000)	Number of housing units
	159	160	161	162	163	164	165	166	167	168	169	170
NORTH CAROLINA—Cont'd												
Swain	31	736	89.3	26.7	18	D	D	D	1 346	45.4	14 398	91
Transylvania	70	1 589	148.7	57.5	46	248	21.0	6.0	3 113	128.8	39 649	104
Tyrrell	8	D	D	D	7	44	4.2	1.4	298	10.5	65	1
Union	292	5 038	533.9	201.5	281	1 255	109.2	32.8	17 148	776.7	356 214	1 572
Vance	101	2 512	205.0	83.0	48	225	22.7	6.1	2 500	94.1	5 668	35
Wake	2 688	47 097	5 110.4	2 066.2	1 699	12 705	1 463.3	420.1	84 397	3 906.3	2 025 574	11 050
Warren	23	446	20.0	9.7	12	D	D	D	1 004	34.2	12 052	40
Washington	34	665	34.7	15.0	11	D	D	D	638	18.8	1 340	8
Watauga	140	3 419	624.9	144.3	82	349	28.4	7.6	4 774	205.3	56 267	198
Wayne	254	6 896	606.6	265.8	142	939	69.3	20.3	6 147	229.8	45 235	269
Wilkes	147	2 783	233.7	91.5	72	338	23.2	8.4	4 460	184.2	22 560	144
Wilson	200	5 103	408.7	169.3	114	619	54.4	15.0	4 650	170.9	26 272	117
Yadkin	52	982	60.4	24.8	35	D	D	D	2 414	91.8	2 721	5
Yancey	32	D	D	D	24	86	7.5	2.2	1 606	53.9	10 417	51
NORTH DAKOTA	1 856	56 639	5 418.4	2 414.4	1 716	9 232	1 064.0	253.7	53 263	2 746.0	714 175	3 981
Adams	13	D	D	D	9	D	D	D	208	8.3	1 036	5
Barnes	37	1 156	53.4	26.8	28	147	10.5	2.9	881	45.6	7 940	54
Benson	6	50	1.5	0.8	3	10	1.8	0.2	298	11.3	0	0
Billings	NA	NA	NA	NA	4	14	1.7	0.4	102	7.1	800	3
Bottineau	6	256	14.3	6.8	9	D	D	D	654	27.2	3 170	11
Bowman	11	226	16.7	8.3	14	D	D	D	272	11.6	0	0
Burke	5	D	D	D	2	D	D	D	214	11.5	1 042	6
Burleigh	271	10 591	1 080.5	488.2	254	1 691	208.8	53.8	7 132	399.6	104 858	553
Cass	439	15 347	1 909.7	815.0	380	2 549	278.0	71.4	11 937	719.3	326 936	1 903
Cavalier	10	242	15.7	5.7	11	D	D	D	390	14.1	2 110	6
Dickey	23	409	31.5	13.0	20	67	5.9	1.6	441	14.9	1 030	2
Divide	6	D	D	D	5	D	D	D	214	9.3	1 544	13
Dunn	4	D	D	D	11	D	D	D	334	22.7	3 213	10
Eddy	9	223	11.3	6.5	7	D	D	D	197	7.5	430	2
Emmons	11	213	10.1	5.7	7	12	0.7	0.1	270	8.3	2 350	10
Foster	11	302	22.9	10.1	7	17	1.2	0.3	287	13.7	1 345	5
Golden Valley	5	114	7.0	3.3	7	28	1.2	0.4	191	7.1	175	1
Grand Forks	160	6 865	668.9	301.2	148	827	103.2	21.7	4 000	196.3	57 171	339
Grant	7	224	12.1	5.3	5	D	D	D	220	7.8	898	7
Griggs	5	D	D	D	7	D	D	D	211	8.9	110	1
Hettinger	10	110	5.1	2.6	8	D	D	D	213	8.2	0	0
Kidder	6	47	1.7	0.8	3	D	D	D	241	10.9	0	0
LaMoure	13	D	D	D	13	49	4.4	0.9	342	13.8	1 050	2
Logan	7	148	4.6	2.5	7	D	D	D	182	7.6	0	0
McHenry	6	D	D	D	7	D	D	D	425	17.6	2 488	13
McIntosh	10	308	17.0	8.9	7	19	1.0	0.2	239	10.6	450	3
McKenzie	9	184	15.1	6.1	27	112	10.6	2.6	769	48.5	20 527	126
McLean	19	443	23.8	12.0	19	D	D	D	701	30.4	10 330	48
Mercer	18	445	26.7	12.7	16	44	4.0	0.9	635	17.8	3 286	15
Morton	64	1 627	99.3	48.3	58	D	D	D	2 320	125.4	57 171	299
Mountrail	13	196	12.5	6.2	19	83	10.1	2.5	711	39.6	2 085	17
Nelson	10	256	11.5	5.6	12	D	D	D	292	10.3	1 047	6
Oliver	4	D	D	D	2	D	D	D	129	5.6	1 190	4
Pembina	16	336	19.1	7.2	18	D	D	D	558	22.9	105	1
Pierce	9	D	D	D	14	D	D	D	356	14.4	2 314	8
Ramsey	41	888	56.7	26.1	28	131	10.9	2.2	891	37.2	361	4
Ransom	25	420	26.5	11.9	22	75	6.5	1.3	365	16.2	995	5
Renville	7	D	D	D	3	D	D	D	180	8.0	200	1
Richland	45	578	35.6	18.7	38	143	11.2	3.0	1 148	55.7	6 757	33
Rolette	25	549	54.7	24.7	9	D	D	D	662	17.2	300	1
Sargent	7	65	3.0	1.8	8	31	5.1	0.8	294	13.1	4 145	21
Sheridan	2	D	D	D	5	D	D	D	109	4.1	580	10
Sioux	1	D	D	D	2	D	D	D	94	3.9	0	0
Slope	NA	NA	NA	NA	1	D	D	D	59	4.1	0	0
Stark	91	1 927	131.4	60.4	79	585	78.6	16.0	2 542	139.0	19 638	86
Steele	1	D	D	D	4	7	1.2	0.2	153	9.2	145	2
Stutsman	62	2 423	154.8	88.7	54	299	23.6	6.9	1 347	59.0	13 056	48
Towner	3	D	D	D	6	30	2.5	0.4	246	8.5	0	0
Traill	20	595	34.4	17.5	23	80	15.9	2.2	578	25.3	3 530	13
Walsh	39	726	45.8	21.7	38	101	7.0	1.9	786	33.4	654	4

Government Employment and Payroll, and Local Government Finances

		Government employment and payroll, 2012								Local government finances, 2012				
			March payroll (percent of total)							General revenue				
													Taxes	
													Per capita[1] (dollars)	
STATE County	Full-time equivalent employees	March payroll (dollars)	Adminis-tration, judicial, and legal	Police and Corrections	Fire Protection	Highways and transpor-tation	Health and Welfare	Natural resources and utilities	Education and libraries	Total (mil dol)	Inter-govern-mental (mil dol)	Total (mil dol)	Total	Property
	171	172	173	174	175	176	177	178	179	180	181	182	183	184
NORTH CAROLINA—Cont'd														
Swain	570	1 634 935	2.8	6.9	0.0	0.2	15.2	3.5	58.7	39.0	24.0	8.3	586	366
Transylvania	1 211	3 349 488	5.1	9.9	0.5	1.7	16.3	4.8	52.7	82.0	34.9	38.2	1 162	930
Tyrrell	212	788 126	5.4	5.1	0.0	0.3	6.1	4.4	76.8	19.0	12.0	4.7	1 091	930
Union	6 960	22 437 486	4.7	8.5	1.4	0.7	5.2	5.8	72.3	593.9	274.3	239.3	1 148	942
Vance	2 151	6 716 262	3.1	6.3	2.9	1.8	9.0	3.0	71.8	166.4	101.2	37.4	828	618
Wake	31 235	120 436 016	3.6	9.3	3.7	3.7	7.3	6.6	61.6	3 180.9	1 227.2	1 366.9	1 436	1 077
Warren	682	2 143 055	2.8	7.9	0.0	0.0	10.7	3.8	61.2	57.4	29.8	20.1	976	845
Washington	551	1 546 357	6.0	8.2	0.0	0.4	15.3	5.7	59.9	40.0	25.2	10.3	805	588
Watauga	1 481	4 632 704	6.0	11.0	2.1	4.5	13.2	7.1	47.6	137.3	56.5	63.0	1 214	855
Wayne	5 237	14 176 474	3.0	6.2	2.1	1.3	9.2	6.0	66.2	346.7	199.6	101.5	817	585
Wilkes	3 431	10 259 077	2.0	4.8	0.3	0.9	32.4	1.6	56.6	184.5	95.3	58.2	840	635
Wilson	3 417	11 244 041	5.5	9.5	3.3	2.4	11.6	11.2	53.8	288.2	140.0	90.5	1 105	863
Yadkin	1 268	3 737 818	3.9	5.9	0.1	0.5	11.5	3.0	70.9	88.3	50.5	29.0	763	624
Yancey	773	2 283 963	4.6	6.2	0.2	1.0	23.0	3.1	60.9	45.5	25.0	17.2	973	798
NORTH DAKOTA	X	X	X	X	X	X	X	X	X	X	X	X	X	X
Adams	92	255 672	10.2	8.6	0.0	6.4	7.5	3.3	62.1	8.2	3.6	3.0	1 313	1 054
Barnes	418	1 392 699	15.6	9.1	0.5	3.9	5.1	9.8	55.6	66.9	40.2	17.6	1 597	1 448
Benson	305	941 315	6.1	1.3	0.6	5.7	5.8	1.7	78.6	27.9	19.5	4.6	683	672
Billings	71	278 902	16.6	9.9	1.1	28.8	4.2	4.9	31.5	14.4	10.4	1.7	1 884	1 457
Bottineau	258	801 858	8.7	5.1	0.1	7.5	5.5	8.6	64.2	29.2	15.4	8.8	1 337	1 194
Bowman	154	498 076	10.9	6.0	0.1	7.5	7.8	4.7	63.1	25.9	15.6	5.2	1 630	1 395
Burke	132	476 712	12.0	4.9	0.0	8.5	2.8	2.4	67.3	11.4	4.8	4.8	2 215	1 096
Burleigh	2 640	9 881 026	4.2	8.2	4.2	3.6	6.6	9.1	61.0	347.2	171.6	100.7	1 174	925
Cass	4 659	18 693 995	4.8	9.4	2.9	4.9	9.6	7.5	60.1	694.2	293.1	246.4	1 578	1 145
Cavalier	150	482 792	10.3	7.1	0.0	7.2	5.9	7.5	58.4	17.1	7.4	6.7	1 688	1 662
Dickey	177	602 013	11.3	6.4	0.0	5.8	12.2	3.2	59.7	28.7	12.8	9.2	1 751	1 617
Divide	112	399 142	14.1	7.5	0.0	19.6	4.6	5.6	47.0	17.6	9.2	3.7	1 673	1 505
Dunn	163	514 670	8.7	4.7	0.8	11.8	6.5	2.4	65.0	27.2	19.0	3.9	992	865
Eddy	101	291 076	9.8	5.2	0.0	6.4	5.8	4.1	67.8	12.9	6.6	3.2	1 370	1 257
Emmons	160	461 725	8.9	3.7	0.1	7.4	1.9	9.4	68.6	16.2	7.3	6.2	1 777	1 711
Foster	109	345 480	14.5	2.4	0.1	5.2	6.9	1.6	67.7	14.4	6.3	5.0	1 462	1 302
Golden Valley	168	598 525	4.4	2.4	0.0	4.3	3.1	1.4	83.6	12.6	6.8	3.5	1 923	1 846
Grand Forks	2 414	9 092 121	5.6	9.8	3.4	6.3	6.5	11.9	54.2	280.6	106.1	94.4	1 399	1 054
Grant	103	251 784	10.0	5.5	0.0	9.2	10.7	3.2	60.2	8.5	3.8	3.4	1 448	1 414
Griggs	112	363 293	9.3	4.3	0.0	8.1	9.0	2.0	65.6	13.5	5.4	5.3	2 241	2 176
Hettinger	147	439 881	7.5	2.1	0.1	8.1	4.0	22.4	54.8	15.0	6.5	5.4	2 133	1 985
Kidder	100	305 849	4.8	4.8	0.0	1.6	8.6	4.8	75.3	16.0	7.8	3.7	1 533	1 484
LaMoure	228	740 715	7.4	3.3	0.0	6.3	2.2	19.6	60.3	63.8	47.3	9.5	2 316	2 252
Logan	83	243 512	4.2	4.7	0.0	5.7	6.1	5.0	73.3	10.5	5.6	3.9	2 040	2 023
McHenry	239	766 397	8.6	2.6	0.1	4.2	4.4	4.0	74.9	20.6	10.3	7.3	1 263	1 225
McIntosh	139	432 649	7.6	5.1	0.1	10.8	4.4	16.0	55.9	10.7	5.5	3.7	1 328	1 289
McKenzie	313	1 128 904	9.9	9.8	0.0	9.8	6.5	4.0	57.4	54.1	24.6	7.4	930	751
McLean	438	1 374 148	6.7	7.0	0.0	5.7	12.1	3.3	64.5	43.6	23.1	11.4	1 229	1 093
Mercer	347	1 135 199	9.4	9.5	0.0	9.4	2.8	4.7	62.2	34.8	17.4	9.3	1 093	917
Morton	946	3 200 962	5.4	9.1	1.2	7.7	8.1	5.9	61.5	106.1	48.2	35.2	1 253	1 139
Mountrail	385	1 261 569	8.3	7.4	0.0	8.6	6.2	3.5	65.1	85.8	57.9	12.5	1 434	1 307
Nelson	146	457 045	9.7	3.0	0.0	8.5	4.7	8.9	63.6	17.3	8.0	6.7	2 183	2 144
Oliver	76	233 042	14.9	6.8	0.0	9.6	2.9	7.5	56.4	9.0	3.8	3.7	2 018	1 749
Pembina	393	1 633 628	6.4	4.3	0.0	3.1	4.1	45.4	36.2	40.0	15.7	16.1	2 221	2 125
Pierce	154	464 990	7.2	8.4	0.0	4.1	5.0	3.6	69.5	21.3	8.8	5.5	1 245	1 151
Ramsey	543	1 755 199	7.3	12.7	1.3	4.3	10.4	5.8	57.4	84.1	57.8	15.4	1 331	1 034
Ransom	223	692 010	8.7	4.1	0.8	4.5	6.6	5.2	68.5	23.4	12.3	7.8	1 436	1 220
Renville	140	452 741	8.2	6.0	0.0	8.7	3.5	2.3	70.0	19.2	9.5	5.9	2 288	2 255
Richland	582	2 019 868	4.8	9.7	0.0	6.5	9.5	7.4	61.0	75.6	33.2	29.0	1 787	1 613
Rolette	726	2 856 302	1.9	2.3	0.2	1.2	3.8	2.8	87.6	53.9	44.3	5.9	409	382
Sargent	167	536 100	9.7	3.9	0.0	3.3	5.4	6.8	70.4	21.4	9.5	8.1	2 073	2 002
Sheridan	59	160 666	12.8	0.0	0.0	8.5	0.2	3.7	73.9	5.6	2.2	2.9	2 255	2 229
Sioux	129	394 909	4.4	0.8	1.7	4.0	0.3	1.7	86.3	11.5	9.3	1.5	349	348
Slope	36	114 876	15.1	4.2	0.0	6.9	0.2	2.1	68.6	5.2	3.3	1.0	1 297	1 208
Stark	970	3 430 314	4.3	17.8	1.0	4.4	10.3	9.5	51.8	103.5	43.2	33.0	1 232	836
Steele	76	279 013	12.8	4.5	0.1	2.6	1.4	2.1	76.4	12.4	4.6	4.9	2 441	2 369
Stutsman	738	2 551 998	5.2	10.8	0.9	5.8	9.7	7.6	58.2	88.6	38.8	29.6	1 413	1 195
Towner	120	341 158	12.4	5.1	0.0	10.5	3.7	3.7	63.4	10.1	3.9	3.9	1 695	1 626
Traill	299	1 042 936	6.6	4.5	0.0	5.7	5.6	2.7	74.1	35.7	16.3	11.8	1 468	1 367
Walsh	425	1 396 845	7.5	5.6	0.0	5.1	6.2	9.3	63.8	46.8	22.8	16.0	1 451	1 295

1. Based on the resident population estimated as of July 1 of the year shown.

Table B. States and Counties — Local Government Finances, Government Employment, and Income Taxes

	Local government finances, 2012 (cont.)									Government employment, 2015			Individual income tax returns, 2014		
	Direct general expenditure							Debt outstanding							
					Percent of total for:										
STATE County	Total (mil dol)	Per capita[1] (dollars)	Educa-tion	Health and hospitals	Police protec-tion	Public welfare	High-ways	Total (mil dol)	Per capita[1] (dollars)	Federal civilian	Federal military	State and local	Number of returns	Mean adjusted gross income	Mean income tax
	185	186	187	188	189	190	191	192	193	194	195	196	197	198	199
NORTH CAROLINA—Cont'd															
Swain	40.3	2 852	47.4	5.4	7.2	14.3	0.2	10.7	758	158	34	2 439	7 770	38 862	3 295
Transylvania	80.6	2 453	45.7	4.8	9.9	7.4	1.1	13.0	395	131	77	1 351	13 990	50 238	5 328
Tyrrell	18.9	4 355	54.4	1.2	9.5	7.3	0.7	10.3	2 385	20	D	439	1 660	34 275	2 963
Union	614.4	2 946	53.1	2.0	6.1	4.7	1.0	748.0	3 587	261	529	8 934	92 200	75 452	9 989
Vance	164.7	3 650	56.0	9.8	6.5	7.1	0.6	48.5	1 074	90	105	2 706	18 640	37 730	3 457
Wake	3 282.9	3 448	42.3	4.0	6.5	3.3	2.2	9 085.4	9 542	5 220	2 989	78 474	466 560	77 325	10 874
Warren	54.2	2 635	50.1	5.1	10.5	10.6	0.3	7.2	348	33	46	1 303	7 610	36 937	2 883
Washington	43.9	3 443	43.6	0.4	7.2	13.8	1.5	7.6	594	27	29	793	5 220	36 883	3 043
Watauga	128.3	2 473	32.3	4.5	9.1	5.1	3.7	134.7	2 596	106	118	6 346	18 820	51 111	5 961
Wayne	344.7	2 774	55.1	4.8	6.3	6.3	1.4	151.3	1 217	1 225	4 290	8 001	51 660	45 681	4 468
Wilkes	183.3	2 645	60.4	4.2	5.5	7.8	0.6	49.6	715	178	162	4 209	27 120	43 413	4 127
Wilson	278.4	3 401	41.7	5.4	8.2	8.1	1.5	192.4	2 351	130	192	4 985	35 720	44 434	4 402
Yadkin	87.9	2 308	57.4	4.6	6.9	10.0	0.9	50.3	1 322	68	89	1 419	16 050	45 225	4 185
Yancey	44.5	2 522	51.4	2.5	6.4	10.3	0.6	14.3	810	45	42	835	7 190	40 707	3 421
NORTH DAKOTA	X	X	X	X	X	X	X	X	X	9 214	11 440	66 448	370 550	73 305	11 130
Adams	8.2	3 529	45.9	0.0	4.8	3.9	18.8	0.1	33	16	14	133	1 140	52 905	5 873
Barnes	64.0	5 811	34.3	4.3	8.8	3.5	21.8	18.2	1 650	79	66	1 065	5 420	59 565	7 142
Benson	27.4	4 053	65.7	0.2	1.4	3.3	17.2	0.6	85	145	42	1 434	2 590	43 967	4 822
Billings	17.0	18 828	14.4	6.5	9.0	0.0	56.2	0.1	133	33	D	125	490	87 637	13 316
Bottineau	32.3	4 914	41.2	2.2	4.2	0.0	32.5	11.5	1 748	67	41	611	3 320	70 620	10 264
Bowman	21.3	6 655	38.7	2.4	2.9	1.6	30.5	1.3	409	22	20	246	1 680	76 255	11 606
Burke	10.7	4 949	47.9	0.4	2.6	2.0	26.1	0.1	67	90	14	174	1 280	81 300	12 039
Burleigh	313.0	3 649	41.6	1.2	5.7	1.7	12.7	181.5	2 116	1 099	568	10 648	46 370	78 960	12 016
Cass	703.9	4 508	39.9	0.1	5.6	3.0	13.2	1 204.5	7 713	2 313	1 066	11 723	83 860	71 498	10 755
Cavalier	16.8	4 263	40.9	2.0	4.3	4.3	23.7	11.4	2 878	36	24	211	1 990	65 824	8 882
Dickey	36.5	6 935	38.3	1.4	3.0	1.6	13.3	34.3	6 520	26	31	306	2 520	57 949	7 515
Divide	23.6	10 577	21.6	1.5	4.6	0.7	33.8	0.9	389	33	15	155	1 270	96 745	16 731
Dunn	24.7	6 221	37.5	0.0	3.7	1.5	33.1	0.3	74	16	28	298	2 260	113 461	22 676
Eddy	13.4	5 660	43.4	0.1	4.4	2.5	14.8	1.6	686	21	14	162	1 150	52 049	5 869
Emmons	14.9	4 274	52.4	1.3	1.9	2.0	14.2	3.8	1 081	22	21	230	1 610	46 817	5 534
Foster	13.8	4 065	45.3	1.9	3.7	2.8	14.1	10.6	3 116	26	21	222	1 720	70 229	10 280
Golden Valley	12.7	7 062	41.7	1.5	3.3	2.2	17.1	4.6	2 568	10	11	177	890	66 792	8 618
Grand Forks	251.5	3 728	47.0	1.0	5.1	1.4	4.7	705.5	10 456	1 031	1 915	9 296	33 630	61 150	8 214
Grant	8.1	3 453	49.5	18.0	2.5	2.6	12.7	1.2	524	22	15	141	1 140	42 115	4 898
Griggs	13.1	5 527	43.9	3.5	2.8	2.9	21.9	3.7	1 562	20	14	169	1 210	58 927	7 020
Hettinger	16.2	6 357	49.8	0.0	2.6	2.3	14.4	1.9	738	18	16	188	1 270	61 451	7 926
Kidder	15.9	6 560	32.7	24.9	1.7	1.4	20.1	2.4	973	20	15	157	1 160	50 340	5 601
LaMoure	23.0	5 581	54.0	0.0	2.5	2.6	15.6	7.0	1 691	40	25	305	1 980	63 359	8 149
Logan	8.8	4 566	63.4	1.0	2.8	0.2	13.9	1.7	867	19	12	142	930	43 719	4 642
McHenry	20.8	3 592	61.0	0.0	2.3	2.7	13.3	1.0	180	47	37	319	2 850	58 115	7 325
McIntosh	10.1	3 663	56.1	1.5	2.9	2.7	15.9	1.7	619	18	17	194	1 360	48 765	5 207
McKenzie	61.8	7 738	29.9	3.0	3.5	1.3	31.4	15.2	1 897	66	80	1 840	5 160	154 013	34 776
McLean	38.0	4 086	53.6	1.4	4.7	3.8	12.0	18.4	1 973	118	60	725	4 700	65 364	8 102
Mercer	37.5	4 418	49.3	0.5	5.7	1.3	17.4	59.3	6 990	35	55	559	4 380	71 195	8 887
Morton	106.7	3 797	49.8	2.5	5.2	2.3	6.9	103.5	3 685	96	186	1 675	15 320	66 491	8 887
Mountrail	86.5	9 907	36.3	0.5	1.9	1.2	37.1	26.9	3 081	45	61	715	4 810	120 396	25 764
Nelson	16.3	5 277	44.9	2.6	2.2	1.3	18.7	14.3	4 644	22	18	228	1 560	55 557	6 745
Oliver	7.8	4 256	42.5	0.0	3.8	0.0	8.3	20.2	10 993	D	12	106	890	64 139	7 854
Pembina	37.7	5 190	45.2	0.5	3.9	2.4	8.5	14.9	2 043	235	83	551	3 590	65 282	9 132
Pierce	24.3	5 462	53.5	2.7	4.5	1.9	9.5	4.3	974	22	26	257	2 090	55 777	6 319
Ramsey	75.8	6 569	35.0	0.9	2.9	2.1	20.4	33.0	2 865	158	70	1 375	5 810	57 999	7 241
Ransom	25.2	4 634	45.6	1.6	2.9	1.7	12.3	21.6	3 965	37	33	488	2 850	55 161	5 992
Renville	20.6	8 041	40.3	0.1	2.1	0.0	28.2	3.6	1 387	22	16	205	1 300	67 638	8 553
Richland	75.3	4 645	43.4	4.4	4.5	1.9	13.1	88.9	5 482	62	100	1 903	7 810	61 636	7 617
Rolette	53.3	3 703	79.0	1.4	2.2	2.2	5.1	6.0	419	928	91	2 022	5 520	41 889	3 743
Sargent	19.0	4 886	48.6	1.5	1.7	2.4	13.8	11.5	2 940	40	24	251	2 070	58 362	7 114
Sheridan	5.5	4 306	39.7	1.2	1.7	1.0	20.2	0.2	179	12	D	106	660	50 894	5 674
Sioux	11.0	2 521	85.3	0.0	0.5	4.1	5.3	3.0	686	213	27	1 275	1 320	33 271	2 445
Slope	3.6	4 734	14.2	2.9	4.4	0.0	33.2	0.4	538	D	D	42	330	105 285	12 703
Stark	96.5	3 605	41.6	0.9	4.4	3.4	11.2	19.1	712	182	197	2 210	16 820	92 395	15 878
Steele	11.3	5 664	42.7	0.0	2.8	4.2	26.4	5.7	2 876	13	12	110	960	70 348	9 070
Stutsman	83.3	3 978	42.4	3.2	5.0	2.2	13.9	57.9	2 766	177	122	1 863	10 300	58 943	7 463
Towner	8.9	3 844	45.7	5.0	3.3	2.3	18.6	2.2	931	19	14	126	1 140	54 828	6 361
Traill	35.4	4 390	54.9	0.9	3.8	2.9	12.5	42.5	5 269	38	48	844	3 740	65 251	8 010
Walsh	51.9	4 703	54.4	1.3	4.4	2.5	9.7	23.8	2 156	61	67	1 107	5 480	54 923	6 534

1. Based on the resident population estimated as of July 1 of the year shown.

Table B. States and Counties — Land Area and Population

STATE/ County code	CBSA code[1]	County type[2]	STATE County	Land area,[3] (sq mi) 2016	Total persons 2016	Rank	Per square mile	White	Black	American Indian, Alaska Native	Asian and Pacific Islander	Percent Hispanic or Latino[4]	Under 5 years	5 to 17 years	18 to 24 years	25 to 34 years	35 to 44 years	45 to 54 years
				1	2	3	4	5	6	7	8	9	10	11	12	13	14	15
			NORTH DAKOTA—Cont'd															
38 101	33500	5	Ward	2 013.2	70 210	765	34.9	85.6	5.4	3.1	2.4	6.1	8.1	15.4	14.5	18.3	11.5	10.1
38 103	...	9	Wells	1 270.7	4 098	2 895	3.2	97.7	0.9	1.1	0.4	1.0	5.2	14.5	5.9	9.3	7.8	13.5
38 105	48780	7	Williams	2 077.7	34 337	1 315	16.5	84.2	4.7	5.6	1.6	6.8	9.4	18.3	9.5	18.6	12.4	11.6
39 000	...	0	OHIO	40 862.4	11 614 373	X	284.2	81.3	13.7	0.7	2.7	3.7	6.0	16.5	9.3	13.0	11.9	13.3
39 001	...	6	Adams	583.9	27 907	1 492	47.8	97.7	1.0	1.2	0.4	1.0	5.8	18.3	7.3	11.0	12.2	13.8
39 003	30620	3	Allen	402.5	103 742	580	257.7	83.6	14.3	0.7	1.2	3.0	6.1	17.2	9.9	12.2	11.5	12.5
39 005	11740	4	Ashland	423.0	53 652	937	126.8	96.9	1.4	0.6	1.1	1.3	6.0	16.8	10.8	11.0	10.8	12.6
39 007	11780	4	Ashtabula	701.9	98 231	604	140.0	91.6	4.8	0.8	0.7	4.1	5.5	16.7	7.8	11.5	11.3	14.1
39 009	11900	4	Athens	503.6	66 186	805	131.4	91.4	3.6	1.1	4.3	1.9	4.1	10.8	29.6	12.6	9.8	10.4
39 011	47540	4	Auglaize	401.4	45 894	1 053	114.3	97.0	1.1	0.5	0.9	1.5	5.9	18.2	7.9	11.2	11.4	13.2
39 013	48540	3	Belmont	532.1	68 673	777	129.1	94.3	4.9	0.6	0.7	0.9	5.1	13.9	7.7	12.7	11.7	13.3
39 015	17140	1	Brown	490.0	43 759	1 098	89.3	97.7	1.3	0.8	0.4	0.9	5.6	17.3	7.6	11.0	12.3	14.1
39 017	17140	1	Butler	467.0	377 537	182	808.4	83.9	9.4	0.6	3.7	4.6	6.2	17.6	12.4	11.7	12.0	13.3
39 019	15940	2	Carroll	394.6	27 669	1 506	70.1	97.3	1.1	0.9	0.5	1.3	4.8	16.2	7.5	10.2	11.2	13.8
39 021	46500	6	Champaign	428.4	38 747	1 208	90.4	95.2	3.4	1.0	0.9	1.6	5.3	17.5	8.6	11.1	11.4	14.6
39 023	44220	3	Clark	397.5	134 786	469	339.1	86.8	10.6	0.9	1.2	3.3	6.0	16.8	8.6	11.7	10.9	13.3
39 025	17140	1	Clermont	452.1	203 022	324	449.1	95.2	2.1	0.6	1.6	1.8	5.9	17.7	7.7	12.5	12.4	14.2
39 027	48940	6	Clinton	408.7	41 902	1 130	102.5	95.3	3.4	0.8	0.9	1.6	6.2	17.5	9.4	11.6	11.7	13.3
39 029	41400	4	Columbiana	531.9	103 685	581	194.9	95.5	3.1	0.6	0.6	1.6	5.1	15.6	7.3	11.3	12.1	13.7
39 031	18740	6	Coshocton	563.9	36 602	1 261	64.9	97.1	1.9	0.6	0.5	1.0	6.4	17.3	7.4	11.5	11.2	13.2
39 033	15340	4	Crawford	401.8	42 083	1 128	104.7	96.8	1.7	0.5	0.7	1.5	5.8	16.1	7.8	10.8	11.8	13.3
39 035	17460	1	Cuyahoga	457.2	1 249 352	32	2 732.6	61.1	30.9	0.6	3.7	5.7	5.8	15.4	9.1	13.6	11.4	13.2
39 037	24820	6	Darke	598.1	51 778	962	86.6	97.3	1.2	0.6	0.6	1.5	6.2	17.8	7.8	10.4	11.4	13.4
39 039	19580	4	Defiance	411.5	38 158	1 219	92.7	88.0	2.3	0.7	0.6	9.7	5.7	17.3	9.1	11.5	11.8	12.5
39 041	18140	1	Delaware	443.2	196 463	337	443.3	87.7	4.2	0.5	7.0	2.6	6.3	20.7	7.6	10.0	15.2	15.5
39 043	41780	4	Erie	251.6	75 107	734	298.5	86.0	10.5	0.8	1.0	4.4	5.2	15.3	8.1	11.1	10.5	13.3
39 045	18140	1	Fairfield	504.4	152 597	429	302.5	88.7	8.6	0.8	1.9	2.1	5.8	18.2	8.4	12.0	12.8	14.6
39 047	47920	6	Fayette	406.4	28 676	1 468	70.6	94.7	3.5	0.7	1.1	2.0	6.2	17.2	7.7	12.1	12.1	13.5
39 049	18140	1	Franklin	532.4	1 264 518	31	2 375.1	66.8	24.2	0.9	5.9	5.3	7.3	16.3	9.8	18.2	13.3	12.4
39 051	45780	2	Fulton	405.4	42 514	1 122	104.9	90.4	1.0	0.6	0.6	8.5	6.1	17.9	8.1	10.9	11.7	13.5
39 053	38580	6	Gallia	466.5	30 015	1 432	64.3	95.2	3.4	1.0	0.8	1.3	6.4	16.7	8.5	11.8	11.5	12.9
39 055	17460	1	Geauga	400.2	94 060	622	235.0	96.6	1.6	0.4	1.0	1.4	5.3	18.2	8.4	8.2	10.4	14.7
39 057	19380	2	Greene	413.7	164 765	391	398.3	86.6	8.4	0.9	4.1	2.8	5.6	15.1	12.0	13.5	11.0	12.7
39 059	15740	6	Guernsey	522.3	39 063	1 205	74.8	96.6	2.7	0.9	0.7	1.2	5.9	16.4	8.1	11.7	11.1	13.7
39 061	17140	1	Hamilton	405.9	809 099	74	1 993.3	67.9	27.6	0.7	3.2	3.1	6.7	16.6	9.3	15.1	11.6	12.7
39 063	22300	4	Hancock	531.4	75 872	729	142.8	91.1	2.5	0.5	2.2	5.3	6.2	16.4	9.3	13.2	11.5	13.0
39 065	...	6	Hardin	470.4	31 474	1 396	66.9	96.4	1.6	0.7	1.0	1.6	6.2	17.0	15.2	10.4	11.1	12.1
39 067	...	6	Harrison	402.3	15 307	2 075	38.0	96.4	3.1	0.6	0.4	1.0	5.3	15.8	6.8	10.2	11.0	13.8
39 069	...	6	Henry	416.0	27 629	1 508	66.4	90.9	1.0	0.6	0.7	7.6	5.7	17.5	7.7	11.4	11.6	13.0
39 071	...	6	Highland	553.1	43 029	1 111	77.8	96.9	2.4	0.8	0.6	1.0	6.2	17.8	7.6	11.3	12.0	13.6
39 073	18140	1	Hocking	421.3	28 340	1 475	67.3	97.7	1.2	0.9	0.5	0.9	5.6	16.7	7.5	11.0	11.9	14.3
39 075	...	7	Holmes	422.5	43 936	1 095	104.0	98.3	0.6	0.3	0.3	1.0	8.7	23.6	9.7	12.6	10.9	10.8
39 077	35940	4	Huron	491.5	58 439	886	118.9	91.9	2.0	0.7	0.6	6.3	6.3	17.9	8.5	11.4	11.8	13.7
39 079	27160	7	Jackson	420.3	32 505	1 369	77.3	97.5	1.2	1.1	0.5	1.0	6.5	17.3	7.8	12.1	12.5	13.3
39 081	48260	3	Jefferson	408.2	66 704	792	163.4	92.4	6.8	0.6	0.8	1.4	5.1	14.5	9.4	10.8	10.8	13.3
39 083	34540	4	Knox	525.5	60 814	857	115.7	96.6	1.6	0.6	1.0	1.5	5.8	17.0	11.6	10.9	10.8	12.6
39 085	17460	1	Lake	229.3	228 614	285	997.0	90.4	4.7	0.4	1.8	4.2	4.9	15.4	7.9	11.6	11.5	14.2
39 087	26580	2	Lawrence	453.4	60 872	855	134.3	96.3	3.1	0.7	0.6	0.9	5.8	16.2	7.6	11.8	12.4	14.0
39 089	18140	1	Licking	682.4	172 198	377	252.3	92.9	5.0	0.8	1.6	1.8	6.2	17.3	8.9	11.7	12.0	14.2
39 091	13340	6	Logan	458.4	45 165	1 071	98.5	95.6	3.2	0.8	1.1	1.5	5.9	17.7	7.9	11.1	11.9	13.6
39 093	17460	1	Lorain	491.1	306 365	225	623.8	80.9	9.4	0.8	1.6	9.8	5.7	16.7	8.7	11.1	12.2	14.0
39 095	45780	2	Lucas	340.9	432 488	163	1 268.7	71.7	21.2	0.8	2.2	6.9	6.4	16.7	9.3	14.0	11.6	12.8
39 097	18140	1	Madison	465.9	43 419	1 105	93.2	90.3	6.9	0.7	1.7	1.9	5.2	15.8	8.1	13.1	14.4	15.1
39 099	49660	2	Mahoning	411.5	230 008	284	559.0	78.1	16.3	0.7	1.3	5.6	5.2	15.1	8.6	11.4	11.2	13.0
39 101	32020	4	Marion	403.8	65 096	813	161.2	90.1	7.6	0.7	0.9	2.6	5.7	15.1	8.3	13.1	12.6	14.2
39 103	17460	1	Medina	421.4	177 221	367	420.6	95.3	1.9	0.5	1.6	2.0	5.5	17.5	7.7	10.6	12.5	15.3
39 105	...	6	Meigs	430.1	23 125	1 673	53.8	97.8	1.4	0.9	0.4	0.7	4.9	16.6	6.8	11.1	12.3	14.1
39 107	16380	7	Mercer	462.4	40 909	1 156	88.5	96.6	0.9	0.5	1.1	1.9	6.9	18.5	8.2	11.5	10.6	12.3
39 109	19380	2	Miami	406.6	104 679	570	257.4	94.4	3.5	0.6	1.8	1.6	5.9	17.1	7.3	11.9	11.9	13.7
39 111	...	8	Monroe	455.7	14 210	2 150	31.2	98.5	1.1	0.9	0.3	0.5	5.1	15.7	6.8	9.8	10.9	13.6
39 113	19380	2	Montgomery	461.6	531 239	128	1 150.9	73.6	22.6	0.9	2.9	2.8	6.1	16.1	9.3	13.3	11.4	12.9
39 115	...	6	Morgan	416.4	14 804	2 116	35.6	95.4	5.1	1.7	0.7	0.9	4.9	16.5	7.4	10.6	11.2	13.5
39 117	18140	1	Morrow	406.1	35 036	1 302	86.3	97.4	1.2	0.9	0.6	1.4	5.5	18.4	7.2	10.8	12.5	14.2
39 119	49780	4	Muskingum	664.6	86 068	666	129.5	94.3	5.8	0.9	0.8	1.1	6.1	16.8	9.1	11.9	11.6	13.3
39 121	...	7	Noble	398.0	14 294	2 146	35.9	96.0	3.1	0.7	0.4	0.7	4.9	13.7	6.0	9.7	8.3	12.7

1. CBSA = Core Based Statistical Area. See Appendix A for explanation. See Appendix B for list of metropolitan areas with component counties.
Service of USDA Rural-Urban Continuum Codes. See Appendix A for definition. 3. Dry land or land partially or temporarily covered by water.
2. County type code from the Economic Research
4. May be of any race.

Table B. States and Counties — Population and Households

STATE County	55 to 64 years (16)	65 to 74 years (17)	75 years and over (18)	Percent female (19)	Total persons 2000 (20)	Total persons 2010 (21)	Percent change 2000–2010 (22)	Percent change 2010–2016 (23)	Births (24)	Deaths (25)	Net migration (26)	Number (27)	Persons per household (28)	Family households (29)	Female family householder[1] (30)	One person (31)
NORTH DAKOTA—Cont'd																
Ward	10.3	6.2	5.6	46.8	58 795	61 675	4.9	13.8	7 444	3 037	4 078	26 131	2.49	61.2	7.4	29.9
Wells	16.1	12.6	15.1	49.8	5 102	4 207	-17.5	-2.6	246	422	59	2 008	2.04	62.4	4.8	35.2
Williams	11.2	4.8	4.2	46.2	19 761	22 398	13.3	53.3	3 530	1 429	9 642	12 082	2.40	63.2	7.5	26.0
OHIO	13.8	9.3	6.9	51.0	11 353 140	11 536 727	1.6	0.7	865 493	706 188	-70 390	4 585 084	2.46	64.1	12.8	30.0
Adams	14.4	10.1	7.2	50.3	27 330	28 554	4.5	-2.3	2 081	2 044	-646	10 858	2.56	68.5	12.7	27.5
Allen	13.7	9.4	7.4	49.5	108 473	106 326	-2.0	-2.4	7 975	6 743	-3 736	39 986	2.53	65.5	14.4	28.7
Ashland	13.9	10.1	7.9	50.9	52 523	53 139	1.2	1.0	3 844	3 449	67	20 427	2.50	68.4	9.6	26.1
Ashtabula	14.9	10.5	7.6	49.6	102 728	101 488	-1.2	-3.2	6 812	7 171	-2 769	38 890	2.48	64.8	12.4	29.2
Athens	11.0	7.2	4.6	50.1	62 223	64 772	4.1	2.2	3 463	3 016	971	22 486	2.47	55.4	9.4	32.7
Auglaize	14.3	9.7	8.2	50.3	46 611	45 949	-1.4	-0.1	3 344	3 011	-518	18 193	2.49	68.5	7.9	26.3
Belmont	15.8	11.0	8.7	48.9	70 226	70 402	0.3	-2.5	4 360	5 533	-370	27 935	2.35	64.6	9.8	30.9
Brown	14.4	10.2	7.4	50.3	42 285	44 843	6.0	-2.4	3 089	2 958	-1 203	16 672	2.62	72.3	12.9	23.3
Butler	12.9	8.3	5.7	51.0	332 807	368 135	10.6	2.6	28 183	19 535	802	134 720	2.68	69.3	12.0	24.4
Carroll	16.0	12.1	8.3	49.8	28 836	28 836	0.0	-4.0	1 715	1 885	-948	10 972	2.54	71.2	8.1	23.2
Champaign	14.2	10.2	7.1	50.0	38 890	40 097	3.1	-3.4	2 461	2 394	-1 407	15 237	2.53	71.1	11.3	23.0
Clark	14.1	10.6	8.1	51.5	144 742	138 333	-4.4	-2.6	9 962	10 424	-2 946	54 809	2.44	65.6	14.6	28.8
Clermont	14.5	9.3	5.8	50.7	177 977	197 363	10.9	2.9	14 624	10 147	1 164	74 812	2.65	71.2	10.4	24.0
Clinton	14.2	9.5	6.7	50.5	40 543	42 037	3.7	-0.3	3 192	2 714	-588	16 073	2.53	69.0	11.9	25.9
Columbiana	15.8	10.9	8.2	49.5	112 075	107 841	-3.8	-3.9	6 738	7 439	-3 310	42 087	2.43	68.0	12.2	27.0
Coshocton	14.5	10.4	8.0	50.5	36 655	36 898	0.7	-0.8	2 825	2 492	-546	14 335	2.53	69.5	10.2	26.3
Crawford	14.4	11.0	9.0	51.1	46 966	43 785	-6.8	-3.9	3 001	3 195	-1 453	17 798	2.37	65.9	10.2	29.2
Cuyahoga	14.4	9.3	7.8	52.3	1 393 978	1 280 109	-8.2	-2.4	93 526	85 069	-37 303	534 719	2.31	57.2	15.9	37.2
Darke	13.9	10.5	8.6	50.7	53 309	52 959	-0.7	-2.2	3 934	3 585	-1 501	20 865	2.48	67.8	9.3	28.4
Defiance	14.4	10.1	7.7	50.4	39 500	39 027	-1.2	-2.2	2 755	2 421	-1 208	15 279	2.49	69.1	11.1	25.6
Delaware	12.1	7.8	4.7	50.5	109 989	174 189	58.4	12.8	13 566	6 319	14 550	65 648	2.78	76.6	7.7	19.8
Erie	15.5	12.0	8.8	51.3	79 551	77 079	-3.1	-2.6	4 929	5 707	-1 188	31 767	2.35	63.5	12.7	31.2
Fairfield	13.1	9.1	6.1	50.2	122 759	146 177	19.1	4.4	10 238	7 477	3 499	55 032	2.66	72.6	11.2	22.7
Fayette	13.8	10.1	7.3	50.8	28 433	29 028	2.1	-1.2	2 155	2 133	-373	11 589	2.44	66.2	12.3	28.8
Franklin	11.4	6.8	4.5	51.2	1 068 978	1 163 529	8.8	8.7	115 794	56 290	43 097	480 946	2.47	58.1	14.1	32.6
Fulton	14.7	9.8	7.4	50.5	42 084	42 698	1.5	-0.4	3 117	2 551	-881	16 229	2.59	73.6	8.5	23.1
Gallia	14.5	10.2	7.5	50.7	31 069	30 946	-0.4	-3.0	2 371	2 248	-1 001	11 590	2.56	70.8	12.0	25.8
Geauga	15.7	11.1	8.0	50.5	90 895	93 410	2.8	0.7	5 727	4 892	-143	34 774	2.67	75.1	8.7	20.5
Greene	13.8	9.5	7.0	50.8	147 886	161 577	9.3	2.0	11 106	8 501	585	64 182	2.41	65.8	10.4	28.4
Guernsey	14.8	10.8	7.5	50.3	40 792	40 091	-1.7	-2.6	2 856	2 788	-967	15 558	2.51	66.2	12.2	28.0
Hamilton	13.4	8.2	6.5	51.8	845 303	802 368	-5.1	0.8	68 487	48 318	-11 581	331 638	2.37	58.5	15.3	34.6
Hancock	13.7	9.3	7.3	51.0	71 295	74 789	4.9	1.4	5 780	4 319	-396	31 083	2.37	64.8	10.0	28.7
Hardin	12.5	9.0	6.5	50.3	31 945	32 060	0.4	-1.8	2 375	1 974	-996	11 540	2.55	66.6	10.0	28.1
Harrison	16.8	11.8	8.7	50.5	15 856	15 862	0.0	-3.5	1 015	1 263	-273	6 271	2.45	70.5	9.9	25.0
Henry	14.6	9.6	8.9	50.6	29 210	28 215	-3.4	-2.1	2 000	1 678	-1 033	10 958	2.52	70.3	9.9	24.9
Highland	13.7	10.3	7.4	50.9	40 875	43 600	6.7	-1.3	3 310	2 960	-870	16 696	2.55	67.3	11.2	26.8
Hocking	15.0	10.9	7.3	50.6	28 241	29 375	4.0	-3.5	1 941	1 887	-913	11 387	2.48	68.9	11.2	26.8
Holmes	10.7	7.3	5.7	49.9	38 943	42 366	8.8	3.7	4 894	1 882	-1 421	12 685	3.36	80.2	6.0	16.8
Huron	13.9	9.8	6.8	50.6	59 487	59 626	0.2	-2.0	4 546	3 593	-2 134	22 527	2.58	69.9	12.0	24.3
Jackson	13.9	10.1	6.6	51.0	32 641	33 224	1.8	-2.2	2 620	2 481	-814	12 981	2.50	66.2	12.6	29.3
Jefferson	15.9	11.3	8.9	51.4	73 894	69 709	-5.7	-4.3	4 114	5 977	-947	27 958	2.35	65.1	11.7	29.9
Knox	14.1	10.0	7.2	51.0	54 500	60 930	11.8	-0.2	4 447	3 771	-736	22 759	2.53	67.1	9.3	26.4
Lake	15.6	10.8	8.2	51.1	227 511	230 050	1.1	-0.6	14 080	14 839	-451	94 815	2.39	65.1	10.5	29.6
Lawrence	14.2	10.4	7.5	51.2	62 319	62 448	0.2	-2.5	4 374	4 245	-1 543	23 548	2.60	67.8	13.2	27.7
Licking	13.9	9.5	6.3	50.9	145 491	166 492	14.4	3.4	12 503	9 483	2 779	64 230	2.57	70.4	11.3	24.7
Logan	14.8	10.2	6.9	50.5	46 005	45 854	-0.3	-1.5	3 370	3 008	-1 031	18 640	2.42	68.3	12.2	25.5
Lorain	14.3	10.0	7.2	50.7	284 664	301 356	5.9	1.7	21 229	18 153	1 872	117 298	2.50	68.0	14.0	27.1
Lucas	13.8	8.9	6.4	51.5	455 054	441 815	-2.9	-2.1	35 368	27 353	-16 857	177 619	2.40	60.0	15.8	33.1
Madison	13.5	8.6	6.1	46.1	40 213	43 430	8.0	0.0	2 647	2 442	-196	14 906	2.57	70.6	10.8	25.1
Mahoning	15.5	10.8	9.1	51.2	257 555	238 807	-7.3	-3.7	14 888	18 954	-4 102	97 790	2.32	62.3	15.1	33.0
Marion	14.2	9.7	6.9	46.7	66 217	66 501	0.4	-2.1	4 693	4 362	-1 645	24 478	2.43	68.5	13.7	27.1
Medina	14.3	10.1	6.6	50.5	151 095	172 333	14.1	2.8	11 247	8 751	2 170	66 002	2.63	72.6	8.9	23.2
Meigs	15.4	11.0	7.8	50.9	23 072	23 767	3.0	-2.7	1 473	1 664	-423	9 322	2.49	68.9	10.3	26.3
Mercer	14.6	9.4	8.0	49.7	40 924	40 814	-0.3	0.2	3 412	2 525	-829	15 919	2.54	69.7	7.1	25.9
Miami	14.2	10.4	7.5	50.8	98 868	102 506	3.7	2.1	7 361	6 299	1 192	41 135	2.49	67.6	10.2	26.4
Monroe	15.2	13.2	9.8	49.9	15 180	14 642	-3.5	-3.0	941	1 144	-258	6 056	2.37	69.4	10.3	26.4
Montgomery	13.6	9.7	7.7	51.8	559 062	535 136	-4.3	-0.7	41 467	36 077	-8 336	222 687	2.32	60.1	15.1	34.3
Morgan	15.4	11.4	9.2	49.8	14 897	15 048	1.0	-1.6	915	999	-128	6 120	2.41	71.5	9.9	25.2
Morrow	15.1	9.7	6.8	49.9	31 628	34 827	10.1	0.6	2 393	1 952	-242	12 700	2.73	74.0	9.8	22.0
Muskingum	13.9	9.8	7.5	51.5	84 585	86 086	1.8	0.0	6 494	5 924	-499	34 261	2.45	66.8	13.3	27.6
Noble	20.1	15.4	9.2	41.5	14 058	14 645	4.2	-2.4	894	789	-446	4 886	2.45	68.8	7.0	28.1

1. No spouse present.

Table B. States and Counties — Population, Vital Statistics, Health, and Crime

STATE County	Persons in group quarters, 2016	Daytime population, 2011–2015 Number	Employment/ residence ratio	Births, 2016 Total	Rate[1]	Deaths, 2016 Number	Rate[1]	Persons under 65 with no health insurance, 2015 Number	Percent	Medicare, 2015 Total Beneficiaries	Enrolled in Original Medicare	Enrolled in Medicare Advantage	Serious crimes known to police,[2] 2014 Total Number	Rate[3]
	32	33	34	35	36	37	38	39	40	41	42	43	44	45
NORTH DAKOTA—Cont'd														
Ward	3 313	69 980	1.06	1 323	18.8	491	7.0	4 884	8.1	8 940	7 561	1 379	1 678	2 404
Wells	100	4 376	1.08	41	10.0	54	13.2	288	9.6	1 192	1 155	37	47	1 113
Williams	546	38 806	1.58	781	22.7	222	6.5	2 801	8.7	3 285	3 229	56	1 787	5 618
OHIO	313 225	11 589 548	1.00	138 012	11.9	115 938	10.0	735 492	7.7	2 090 290	1 153 908	936 382	357 558	3 084
Adams	338	25 321	0.71	310	11.1	333	11.9	2 145	9.3	6 487	4 307	2 180	455	1 623
Allen	5 977	111 378	1.13	1 252	12.1	1 085	10.5	6 108	7.4	20 220	14 645	5 575	3 862	3 672
Ashland	2 331	49 409	0.84	606	11.3	579	10.8	4 045	9.7	9 972	5 828	4 144	841	1 589
Ashtabula	3 452	92 632	0.82	1 035	10.5	1 118	11.4	6 975	8.9	21 363	15 338	6 025	NA	NA
Athens	10 338	65 902	1.04	554	8.4	491	7.4	4 132	8.5	10 018	6 402	3 616	1 247	1 958
Auglaize	526	43 831	0.91	532	11.6	500	10.9	2 360	6.3	10 550	7 664	2 886	384	1 111
Belmont	3 817	64 199	0.82	688	10.0	853	12.4	3 684	7.0	14 251	7 045	7 206	681	1 145
Brown	575	35 463	0.52	458	10.5	484	11.1	3 330	9.3	7 994	4 596	3 398	559	1 275
Butler	11 711	350 764	0.87	4 434	11.7	3 405	9.0	23 673	7.5	59 013	31 342	27 671	10 943	3 059
Carroll	405	23 745	0.63	265	9.6	289	10.4	1 993	9.0	4 341	2 241	2 100	246	984
Champaign	702	33 716	0.68	372	9.6	399	10.3	2 231	7.0	7 096	3 782	3 314	751	1 908
Clark	2 785	127 449	0.84	1 566	11.6	1 676	12.4	8 631	7.9	29 014	13 443	15 571	6 145	4 539
Clermont	1 718	164 382	0.63	2 285	11.3	1 717	8.5	12 017	7.0	26 914	13 594	13 320	5 703	2 835
Clinton	1 113	42 227	1.02	519	12.4	449	10.7	2 558	7.5	8 582	4 986	3 596	832	2 203
Columbiana	3 951	93 441	0.72	1 014	9.8	1 166	11.2	7 098	8.6	23 575	13 022	10 553	617	750
Coshocton	428	34 617	0.86	458	12.5	379	10.4	2 792	9.4	7 130	4 996	2 134	561	1 525
Crawford	579	39 380	0.81	491	11.7	471	11.2	2 601	7.7	10 118	7 170	2 948	1 645	4 309
Cuyahoga	30 191	1 397 624	1.24	14 941	12.0	13 563	10.9	80 109	7.8	232 711	120 948	111 763	38 478	3 569
Darke	607	47 960	0.81	655	12.7	600	11.6	3 269	7.8	10 036	7 006	3 030	678	1 349
Defiance	723	37 406	0.93	423	11.1	409	10.7	2 373	7.6	8 540	6 459	2 081	643	1 673
Delaware	2 285	167 846	0.81	2 230	11.4	1 154	5.9	6 923	4.1	18 792	9 683	9 109	2 547	1 620
Erie	1 679	76 197	1.00	775	10.3	912	12.1	3 927	6.6	18 628	13 801	4 827	1 945	2 838
Fairfield	3 338	122 923	0.62	1 593	10.4	1 346	8.8	8 088	6.4	24 541	12 108	12 433	3 701	2 845
Fayette	593	28 845	1.01	315	11.0	310	10.8	1 928	8.2	5 276	2 917	2 359	1 181	4 103
Franklin	27 636	1 328 307	1.19	18 942	15.0	9 784	7.7	99 694	9.2	163 506	76 619	86 887	49 469	4 146
Fulton	391	40 033	0.88	511	12.0	424	10.0	2 528	7.2	8 783	5 640	3 143	469	1 229
Gallia	799	31 332	1.07	377	12.6	349	11.6	2 174	9.0	7 073	5 157	1 916	1 064	3 497
Geauga	864	83 642	0.78	911	9.7	809	8.6	6 989	9.1	15 731	9 300	6 431	703	747
Greene	8 064	168 703	1.06	1 784	10.8	1 449	8.8	7 874	6.0	20 566	11 104	9 462	3 898	2 439
Guernsey	510	39 601	1.00	456	11.7	447	11.4	2 542	8.0	8 873	5 935	2 938	693	1 771
Hamilton	21 046	925 363	1.32	10 989	13.6	7 955	9.8	50 791	7.5	142 549	76 689	65 860	34 335	4 462
Hancock	1 641	84 548	1.25	959	12.6	684	9.0	3 865	6.2	13 236	9 417	3 819	1 786	2 439
Hardin	1 940	28 702	0.77	370	11.8	323	10.3	2 403	9.7	5 684	4 185	1 499	690	2 185
Harrison	232	14 199	0.78	172	11.2	204	13.3	985	8.1	3 675	2 230	1 445	107	723
Henry	346	25 598	0.82	293	10.6	249	9.0	1 550	6.9	5 518	4 046	1 472	448	1 670
Highland	484	38 331	0.71	513	11.9	485	11.3	3 056	8.7	7 770	5 085	2 685	835	1 941
Hocking	310	25 008	0.67	294	10.7	302	10.7	1 819	7.8	5 550	3 801	1 749	444	1 557
Holmes	765	45 834	1.13	759	17.3	333	7.6	8 397	22.2	3 719	1 996	1 723	326	747
Huron	578	55 893	0.88	728	12.5	564	9.7	4 187	8.6	13 135	9 985	3 150	NA	NA
Jackson	325	31 399	0.89	399	12.3	365	11.2	2 535	9.4	6 279	4 548	1 731	852	2 604
Jefferson	2 290	64 032	0.85	665	10.0	964	14.5	3 781	7.3	16 834	10 602	6 232	NA	NA
Knox	3 448	56 844	0.85	697	11.5	628	10.3	4 199	8.8	11 187	6 983	4 204	1 265	2 080
Lake	2 802	209 521	0.83	2 182	9.5	2 473	10.8	13 063	7.0	46 476	26 220	20 256	NA	NA
Lawrence	669	51 311	0.56	689	11.3	718	11.8	3 977	8.0	13 914	10 683	3 231	1 525	2 503
Licking	3 436	150 628	0.77	2 092	12.1	1 595	9.3	10 241	7.3	28 785	15 784	13 001	4 408	3 136
Logan	450	44 664	0.96	515	11.4	508	11.2	2 729	7.3	9 338	6 424	2 914	1 113	2 572
Lorain	9 008	273 017	0.78	3 429	11.2	2 930	9.6	16 125	6.5	55 683	33 461	22 222	NA	NA
Lucas	10 362	455 009	1.10	5 579	12.9	4 515	10.4	28 344	7.9	76 347	40 042	36 305	11 822	2 860
Madison	4 510	41 928	0.92	426	9.8	392	9.0	2 457	7.5	7 832	3 484	4 348	796	1 853
Mahoning	7 962	235 579	1.01	2 377	10.3	2 991	13.0	13 736	7.6	52 101	23 833	28 268	8 153	3 583
Marion	6 274	66 330	1.02	693	10.6	710	10.9	3 681	7.5	13 970	8 831	5 139	2 868	4 355
Medina	1 199	148 985	0.70	1 868	10.5	1 441	8.1	8 874	6.0	30 172	16 575	13 597	1 736	988
Meigs	212	18 928	0.47	203	8.8	267	11.5	1 761	9.4	4 530	3 380	1 150	334	1 490
Mercer	439	38 624	0.89	553	13.5	387	9.5	2 183	6.5	7 441	5 236	2 205	609	1 491
Miami	1 056	96 633	0.86	1 216	11.6	1 010	9.6	6 248	7.3	21 362	12 679	8 683	2 908	2 933
Monroe	165	14 060	0.91	146	10.3	214	15.1	997	9.0	3 316	1 682	1 634	66	540
Montgomery	15 240	555 005	1.09	6 488	12.2	5 845	11.0	35 818	8.3	109 600	52 198	57 402	20 599	3 909
Morgan	188	12 699	0.60	151	10.2	148	10.0	1 036	8.9	2 818	1 805	1 013	250	1 679
Morrow	366	26 109	0.44	373	10.6	319	9.1	2 117	7.3	4 909	3 033	1 876	355	1 144
Muskingum	1 762	85 417	0.98	1 038	12.1	962	11.2	5 273	7.5	19 842	13 425	6 417	2 776	3 326
Noble	2 678	13 695	0.82	137	9.6	131	9.2	744	8.0	1 837	1 197	640	NA	NA

1. Per 1,000 estimated resident population.   2. Data for serious crimes have not been adjusted for underreporting; this may affect comparability between geographic areas and over time.
3. Per 100,000 population estimated by the FBI.

Table B. States and Counties — Crime, Education, Money Income, and Poverty

STATE County	Serious crimes known to police, 2014 (cont.)[1] Rate[2]		Education School enrollment and attainment, 2011–2015				Local government expenditures,[5] 2013–2014		Money income, 2011–2015		Households			Income and poverty, 2015 Percent below poverty level		
			Enrollment[3]		Attainment[4] (percent)							Percent				
	Violent	Property	Total	Percent private	High school graduate or less	Bachelor's degree or more	Total current spending (mil dol)	Current spending per student (dollars)	Per capita income[6] (dollars)	Median income (dollars)	with income of less than $50,000	with income of $200,000 or more	Median household income (dollars)	All persons	Children under 18 years	Children 5 to 17 years in families
	46	47	48	49	50	51	52	53	54	55	56	57	58	59	60	61
NORTH DAKOTA—Cont'd																
Ward	271	2 133	16 167	8.1	36.3	25.8	118.1	11 692	31 215	61 393	40.7	3.5	61 170	8.4	9.6	8.4
Wells	47	1 066	690	7.2	50.1	19.8	7.5	13 600	30 514	48 098	51.7	2.9	51 857	10.4	11.7	10.0
Williams	516	5 103	6 267	10.4	37.8	21.0	56.9	12 240	43 946	88 013	27.2	10.4	89 860	7.8	9.3	8.3
OHIO	285	2 799	2 972 026	18.1	45.0	26.1	19 266.6	11 175	26 953	49 429	50.5	3.4	51 086	14.8	21.2	19.3
Adams	96	1 527	6 281	7.9	65.6	10.5	46.5	9 692	18 556	35 560	64.4	0.7	36 609	21.3	29.3	27.0
Allen	386	3 286	28 220	18.7	50.4	17.4	156.2	10 384	22 922	44 103	55.1	2.1	49 297	15.5	23.4	21.4
Ashland	68	1 521	14 022	30.5	55.0	20.4	88.6	10 393	22 928	48 003	52.3	1.3	48 338	14.1	20.1	17.3
Ashtabula	NA	NA	22 338	13.6	59.4	13.3	147.3	10 530	20 378	40 544	59.1	0.7	44 258	18.6	28.6	26.3
Athens	99	1 859	27 613	4.2	42.5	29.1	95.2	12 991	17 868	33 872	64.5	1.4	38 400	31.5	29.1	25.9
Auglaize	52	1 059	10 969	10.1	51.4	17.5	77.7	9 962	25 727	54 274	46.5	1.8	58 840	8.7	11.5	10.0
Belmont	118	1 027	13 852	12.0	54.0	15.1	81.9	9 439	23 684	43 833	56.5	2.0	45 675	14.6	21.1	19.4
Brown	57	1 218	9 730	6.2	64.3	12.1	72.6	10 121	22 133	45 568	54.2	1.8	47 202	14.9	23.6	21.6
Butler	223	2 835	105 496	14.7	44.3	28.4	578.0	10 113	27 490	57 540	43.7	4.1	58 954	14.4	18.3	17.1
Carroll	80	904	6 178	12.9	60.5	11.4	31.3	9 527	23 706	47 075	52.4	2.2	52 166	13.0	20.0	17.2
Champaign	109	1 799	9 410	16.6	57.3	15.5	77.7	10 566	23 513	50 974	48.9	1.4	58 837	10.8	16.2	14.3
Clark	369	4 171	33 496	18.0	49.6	18.1	218.7	10 468	23 445	43 625	56.1	1.5	47 651	15.1	25.1	23.2
Clermont	106	2 729	49 639	19.5	44.5	27.1	260.6	9 640	29 288	60 805	41.1	4.3	62 214	9.5	13.5	11.5
Clinton	90	2 113	10 447	16.4	52.6	15.8	70.7	8 854	23 039	46 787	53.1	1.7	47 055	13.6	21.1	20.7
Columbiana	51	699	22 456	11.5	59.4	13.9	162.4	10 629	23 348	44 497	55.1	1.8	42 301	14.7	22.3	19.5
Coshocton	92	1 433	7 976	17.0	65.3	12.1	53.0	10 825	20 713	41 701	58.3	0.8	41 643	15.1	23.4	21.1
Crawford	144	4 165	9 271	12.8	57.3	12.6	65.1	9 788	22 499	40 795	59.3	0.9	41 471	16.5	24.4	20.8
Cuyahoga	561	3 008	318 982	25.8	40.3	30.5	2 365.5	13 483	28 215	44 190	54.7	3.9	45 506	18.2	26.2	24.9
Darke	117	1 231	12 499	9.5	61.7	12.3	80.1	9 449	22 832	44 632	55.5	1.4	51 131	9.6	15.2	13.5
Defiance	104	1 569	9 778	22.2	54.2	16.7	58.8	9 256	24 143	50 663	49.3	1.6	53 936	10.2	16.2	14.6
Delaware	82	1 538	54 865	20.1	24.0	51.8	287.8	10 027	41 824	91 955	25.5	12.1	97 679	4.4	4.7	3.8
Erie	133	2 705	17 613	14.1	49.2	21.2	160.2	13 393	27 249	48 011	52.0	2.4	48 129	12.7	22.3	20.6
Fairfield	153	2 692	39 502	14.7	42.8	26.0	240.0	9 759	28 130	60 567	41.8	3.6	61 450	9.1	12.4	10.4
Fayette	205	3 898	6 788	6.1	61.3	14.1	41.3	8 636	21 632	40 503	59.6	1.6	45 068	16.3	26.2	22.9
Franklin	422	3 724	334 850	16.9	35.2	37.6	2 370.7	11 706	29 244	52 341	47.7	4.4	53 939	17.1	24.5	23.3
Fulton	84	1 145	10 819	13.9	50.6	17.2	101.4	13 355	26 470	55 120	44.7	2.0	58 782	8.5	12.4	11.2
Gallia	151	3 346	7 161	10.6	60.7	15.1	57.9	13 647	21 195	37 319	61.9	1.6	38 738	21.7	32.4	31.2
Geauga	30	717	22 854	27.9	36.3	37.0	139.3	12 523	37 021	72 430	32.7	8.5	76 315	6.7	8.8	7.5
Greene	114	2 325	48 847	21.3	33.4	37.1	231.2	10 798	31 075	60 113	42.0	5.2	61 250	12.7	16.2	13.9
Guernsey	135	1 636	9 028	12.0	57.9	13.5	58.0	12 303	21 564	40 930	58.7	1.0	41 630	18.6	28.7	25.1
Hamilton	457	4 005	213 600	24.0	37.5	35.0	1 286.7	11 794	30 360	49 013	50.7	5.1	51 070	16.6	23.1	22.9
Hancock	117	2 321	19 374	26.2	44.6	25.8	121.8	10 099	27 129	50 895	48.9	3.3	55 265	10.6	14.6	14.2
Hardin	95	2 090	9 222	32.8	60.0	13.5	43.8	10 203	20 332	42 703	58.3	1.1	44 101	16.5	21.2	18.3
Harrison	203	521	3 039	8.0	61.7	8.6	15.3	9 444	22 197	43 173	59.2	1.1	44 221	15.5	24.3	21.8
Henry	63	1 607	6 920	12.6	53.7	16.1	62.3	14 213	25 205	53 835	46.1	2.4	56 986	9.4	13.9	12.4
Highland	67	1 873	10 261	7.9	58.7	12.1	67.0	9 003	20 240	39 858	60.4	1.0	41 494	17.9	27.6	25.2
Hocking	102	1 456	6 972	10.3	55.8	15.1	39.2	9 922	21 360	42 170	56.7	1.1	43 598	15.7	23.8	21.9
Holmes	18	728	9 321	43.7	77.4	7.8	41.4	9 951	18 906	51 996	48.0	2.7	53 540	10.8	15.7	14.2
Huron	NA	NA	14 246	15.7	60.2	13.1	102.4	9 385	23 158	48 745	51.2	1.5	48 838	13.1	20.7	18.8
Jackson	113	2 491	7 737	11.1	59.1	17.2	49.7	9 506	20 697	39 460	61.4	1.1	42 828	20.4	29.2	29.0
Jefferson	NA	NA	15 777	25.7	52.4	15.1	90.9	10 100	23 188	41 942	58.4	1.7	43 306	17.8	28.5	25.5
Knox	112	1 968	15 895	33.0	52.3	21.8	85.8	11 081	23 520	48 533	51.4	2.1	50 914	14.8	19.9	18.7
Lake	NA	NA	53 723	17.9	42.2	26.3	361.5	11 202	30 094	58 029	43.7	3.2	60 782	8.3	12.6	11.3
Lawrence	141	2 362	14 047	9.5	57.1	14.7	122.4	12 694	21 955	42 874	56.1	1.0	39 698	21.0	30.1	29.4
Licking	125	3 010	44 158	18.2	47.3	22.8	266.9	10 029	27 389	56 549	44.6	3.0	59 119	12.6	17.4	15.1
Logan	102	2 470	10 142	13.8	61.0	15.7	79.2	11 972	25 428	49 783	50.3	1.9	49 690	10.9	17.3	15.6
Lorain	NA	NA	78 939	19.7	44.3	22.8	467.0	10 582	26 804	52 457	47.3	3.1	52 779	13.5	20.9	17.7
Lucas	782	2 078	116 659	18.2	42.9	24.2	784.1	10 335	24 816	41 777	56.7	2.7	43 136	19.5	28.9	26.0
Madison	70	1 784	10 434	16.4	54.3	17.1	56.2	12 177	25 159	57 406	41.5	3.6	63 736	9.3	14.0	12.8
Mahoning	281	3 302	55 948	15.4	48.7	22.2	376.8	11 499	24 056	41 375	58.0	2.1	42 443	16.8	26.8	24.6
Marion	200	4 154	14 428	8.4	56.4	12.4	115.8	10 283	20 811	42 966	56.6	1.1	43 529	18.2	27.7	26.2
Medina	47	941	44 567	15.8	30.8	32.8	263.6	9 763	31 760	66 952	35.6	4.8	70 576	7.0	8.8	7.0
Meigs	129	1 361	5 021	10.8	59.4	12.9	35.4	10 594	19 999	37 813	62.0	0.8	38 479	22.8	31.3	27.3
Mercer	95	1 395	9 752	5.6	57.5	15.7	95.4	11 812	24 978	53 099	46.8	1.9	56 124	7.8	10.6	9.6
Miami	102	2 831	25 294	11.5	48.3	20.6	171.6	11 181	26 320	51 569	48.4	2.1	51 685	10.7	14.0	12.1
Monroe	57	483	2 805	17.0	65.2	9.9	23.9	10 118	22 522	41 528	59.8	1.5	41 754	18.3	24.4	23.3
Montgomery	362	3 546	141 736	22.4	39.7	25.7	891.7	11 610	25 734	43 829	55.5	2.6	46 696	17.7	27.0	24.9
Morgan	262	1 417	2 978	8.1	60.8	11.1	20.9	10 357	20 180	37 067	61.0	1.7	39 969	19.0	29.1	25.5
Morrow	58	1 086	8 655	11.9	59.0	13.9	50.2	9 325	23 420	51 993	48.3	1.1	52 312	11.3	19.4	17.4
Muskingum	182	3 144	20 895	13.1	56.3	15.1	177.0	11 997	21 274	41 130	58.5	1.2	43 324	16.5	26.7	23.8
Noble	NA	NA	2 106	7.2	69.1	9.3	18.6	11 047	21 788	41 708	58.7	1.2	47 714	15.0	17.8	16.5

1. Data for serious crimes have not been adjusted for underreporting; this may affect comparability between geographic areas and over time.   2. Per 100,000 population estimated by the FBI.
3. All persons 3 years old and over enrolled in nursery school through college.   4. Persons 25 years old and over.   5. Elementary and secondary education expenditures.
6. Based on population estimated by the American Community Survey, 2011–2015.

Table B. States and Counties — Personal Income

STATE County	Personal income, 2015										Earnings, 2015		
	Total (mil dol)	Percent change, 2014–2015	Per capita[1] Dollars	Per capita[1] Rank	Wages and salaries (mil dol)	Supplements to wages and salaries; employer contributions (mil dol) Pension and insurance	Government social insurance	Proprietors' income (mil dol)	Dividends, interest, and rent (mil dol)	Personal transfer receipts (mil dol)	Total (mil dol)	Contributions for government social insurance (mil dol) From employee and self-employed	From employer
	62	63	64	65	66	67	68	69	70	71	72	73	74
NORTH DAKOTA—Cont'd													
Ward	3 981	-1.9	55 852	197	2 116	320	191	383	795	439	3 010	169	191
Wells	201	-6.9	48 167	318	66	10	6	16	71	47	99	7	6
Williams	3 587	-12.9	101 645	4	2 857	247	210	282	576	184	3 596	206	210
OHIO	505 950	3.5	43 597	X	265 273	46 534	18 638	37 311	78 001	101 930	367 756	20 738	18 638
Adams	827	3.4	29 507	2 885	234	58	15	76	97	306	383	24	15
Allen	3 913	2.9	37 469	1 752	2 255	435	163	254	543	983	3 107	179	163
Ashland	1 842	3.1	34 615	2 114	755	146	55	122	253	428	1 078	65	55
Ashtabula	3 444	3.0	34 918	2 213	1 201	252	89	197	419	1 087	1 739	110	89
Athens	2 083	3.6	31 613	2 588	925	292	46	123	322	528	1 386	57	46
Auglaize	1 961	1.9	42 736	1 014	930	173	67	126	331	353	1 296	75	67
Belmont	2 586	1.3	37 393	1 457	1 039	189	70	122	360	681	1 419	89	70
Brown	1 422	2.5	32 436	2 376	308	78	21	83	162	422	491	33	21
Butler	15 631	4.3	41 534	1 076	7 522	1 276	528	1 077	2 070	2 931	10 403	591	528
Carroll	999	1.9	35 927	1 849	278	54	21	89	126	254	443	28	21
Champaign	1 453	2.5	37 256	1 619	460	94	32	86	177	333	672	41	32
Clark	5 055	3.4	37 183	1 672	1 992	382	143	221	723	1 417	2 738	171	143
Clermont	9 345	5.7	46 267	849	2 750	455	197	1 101	1 096	1 575	4 502	263	197
Clinton	1 633	3.1	38 947	1 820	741	144	53	259	216	368	1 197	67	53
Columbiana	3 701	2.8	35 314	2 131	1 205	250	88	254	462	1 051	1 797	113	88
Coshocton	1 284	6.9	35 107	2 045	548	102	40	102	155	358	792	48	40
Crawford	1 467	1.6	34 675	2 080	533	113	39	68	203	435	754	49	39
Cuyahoga	60 919	2.6	48 506	455	41 986	6 663	2 939	4 234	11 742	12 358	55 821	3 138	2 939
Darke	1 998	2.0	38 360	1 379	748	145	55	208	288	441	1 156	65	55
Defiance	1 386	-1.5	36 128	1 633	713	126	53	90	172	344	983	60	53
Delaware	12 475	5.8	64 634	95	4 840	695	331	753	1 772	1 025	6 619	375	331
Erie	3 723	2.7	49 283	848	1 469	288	106	795	526	745	2 658	146	106
Fairfield	6 230	4.5	41 145	1 136	1 668	323	117	306	797	1 153	2 413	146	117
Fayette	992	2.6	34 591	1 905	417	79	30	49	136	288	574	35	30
Franklin	58 767	5.0	46 949	664	42 189	7 368	2 791	5 026	8 839	9 281	57 374	2 948	2 791
Fulton	1 719	3.7	40 414	1 333	766	147	56	157	226	340	1 126	65	56
Gallia	1 059	1.9	35 129	2 088	428	103	30	79	155	362	640	38	30
Geauga	5 771	3.2	61 323	196	1 525	265	113	689	1 103	680	2 592	148	113
Greene	7 377	3.8	44 862	776	4 189	963	316	342	1 334	1 289	5 809	308	316
Guernsey	1 457	3.6	37 121	2 036	676	132	48	116	177	427	973	58	48
Hamilton	42 061	1.9	52 081	322	31 294	4 655	2 194	3 148	8 961	6 999	41 291	2 322	2 194
Hancock	3 695	8.3	48 896	791	2 231	364	157	624	466	564	3 377	190	157
Hardin	1 014	-1.2	32 009	2 373	334	75	24	83	124	254	516	29	24
Harrison	556	2.6	36 008	2 041	172	39	12	30	63	158	252	16	12
Henry	1 081	1.5	38 865	1 462	464	94	34	88	144	245	680	38	34
Highland	1 357	2.9	31 541	2 721	360	89	25	123	159	421	598	37	25
Hocking	959	3.8	33 675	2 370	235	59	15	59	109	289	368	23	15
Holmes	1 635	6.4	37 232	2 318	753	130	57	555	191	211	1 496	75	57
Huron	2 131	3.0	36 453	1 828	954	172	81	122	288	518	1 329	81	81
Jackson	1 083	2.3	33 227	2 334	389	80	28	66	138	347	562	35	28
Jefferson	2 391	3.5	35 496	2 031	879	182	66	91	299	765	1 218	79	66
Knox	2 402	3.7	39 345	1 486	913	172	68	177	393	563	1 330	79	68
Lake	10 498	3.3	45 793	761	4 475	822	321	483	1 448	1 997	6 102	357	321
Lawrence	2 099	2.3	34 353	2 298	481	110	34	91	225	702	717	49	34
Licking	7 093	4.9	41 581	1 202	2 329	431	165	462	930	1 360	3 388	198	165
Logan	1 749	3.1	38 540	1 340	903	155	65	122	217	393	1 245	74	65
Lorain	12 624	3.8	41 371	1 192	4 436	856	319	588	1 692	2 697	6 199	369	319
Lucas	18 247	4.0	42 075	1 099	10 367	1 875	737	1 462	2 538	4 286	14 440	801	737
Madison	1 620	3.0	36 730	1 684	724	155	48	116	211	309	1 043	56	48
Mahoning	9 321	2.7	40 192	1 178	4 027	767	292	713	1 453	2 507	5 799	346	292
Marion	2 152	3.5	32 935	2 200	1 018	224	73	83	273	630	1 397	83	73
Medina	8 660	4.6	49 097	524	2 652	469	190	561	1 111	1 263	3 872	230	190
Meigs	698	2.5	30 029	2 834	124	33	8	35	76	243	200	15	8
Mercer	1 850	0.7	45 167	829	798	156	56	268	278	301	1 278	68	56
Miami	4 355	1.7	41 781	1 139	1 739	321	127	203	639	872	2 389	143	127
Monroe	441	-0.8	30 590	2 657	110	27	8	27	66	148	172	12	8
Montgomery	22 474	3.6	42 223	1 083	12 528	2 173	910	1 469	3 897	5 081	17 080	977	910
Morgan	445	1.5	30 128	2 734	105	25	7	28	55	143	164	11	7
Morrow	1 199	3.2	34 181	2 303	244	55	16	71	127	290	387	25	16
Muskingum	3 267	4.7	37 855	1 891	1 380	267	97	226	423	871	1 971	117	97
Noble	420	3.6	29 300	2 988	130	35	8	36	50	102	209	11	8

1. Based on the resident population estimated as of July 1 of the year shown.

Table B. States and Counties — Earnings, Social Security, and Housing

STATE County	Earnings, 2015 (cont.)									Social Security beneficiaries, December 2015		Housing units, 2016		
	Percent by selected industries													
	Farm	Mining	Construction	Manu-facturing	Infor-mation: professional, scientific, technical services	Retail trade	Finance, insur-ance, real estate and leasing	Health care and social assistance	Govern-ment	Number	Rate[1]	Supple-mental Security Income recipients, December 2015	Total	Percent change, 2010–2016
	75	76	77	78	79	80	81	82	83	84	85	86	87	88
NORTH DAKOTA—Cont'd														
Ward	0.4	8.1	9.6	1.1	4.4	7.6	8.1	11.4	25.8	9 265	130	584	32 808	22.7
Wells	0.3	D	9.2	2.3	2.3	7.8	6.4	D	13.6	1 175	282	48	2 504	0.9
Williams	0.7	36.7	14.5	1.3	4.0	3.5	5.9	2.8	4.3	3 550	100	179	19 357	85.0
OHIO	0.3	0.5	5.4	14.8	9.0	5.9	7.2	13.0	15.3	2 290 813	197	312 351	5 164 361	0.7
Adams	1.6	D	8.3	17.7	3.3	9.0	2.8	9.5	22.2	6 655	238	1 798	12 716	-2.0
Allen	-0.1	D	4.9	25.7	3.7	6.5	3.4	18.5	13.4	22 500	216	3 105	44 812	-0.4
Ashland	0.2	0.2	7.2	20.7	8.5	6.3	3.0	D	14.4	11 480	215	782	22 112	-0.1
Ashtabula	-0.3	0.4	8.6	26.9	D	6.3	2.8	14.6	15.9	23 230	236	3 091	45 790	-0.7
Athens	0.0	D	3.5	D	4.9	6.5	3.3	12.3	51.3	9 600	146	2 563	26 348	-0.2
Auglaize	1.4	D	5.5	45.8	3.0	5.1	4.0	8.1	10.8	9 270	202	526	19 733	0.8
Belmont	0.3	17.0	6.8	4.0	D	10.0	5.7	12.5	16.0	16 790	243	2 053	31 993	-1.4
Brown	-0.9	D	D	9.6	2.9	6.7	3.3	D	24.5	10 260	234	1 177	19 764	2.4
Butler	0.1	0.1	6.8	19.6	4.2	7.2	9.1	10.4	13.0	66 400	177	7 362	150 645	1.6
Carroll	2.2	3.6	17.3	18.6	2.7	6.2	4.6	6.1	12.4	6 590	237	443	13 471	-1.6
Champaign	3.2	D	4.8	39.6	D	4.8	2.9	D	16.4	8 240	211	653	16 664	-0.5
Clark	0.1	0.4	4.0	16.5	3.2	6.9	8.4	14.6	16.2	30 990	228	4 111	61 031	-0.6
Clermont	0.1	D	7.5	10.1	9.3	7.7	8.4	7.4	11.4	38 470	191	3 349	82 195	1.9
Clinton	0.4	D	3.6	19.0	3.9	4.8	6.1	D	12.8	8 890	212	1 074	18 026	-0.6
Columbiana	1.4	1.1	6.4	20.0	2.9	9.3	3.4	13.7	17.9	25 285	242	3 118	46 408	-1.4
Coshocton	2.2	2.0	19.8	23.8	2.4	5.4	2.5	9.5	11.8	8 615	235	912	16 278	-1.6
Crawford	0.7	D	4.5	24.1	4.2	6.4	7.6	D	15.4	10 960	259	1 147	19 948	-1.1
Cuyahoga	0.0	0.7	3.6	10.5	12.8	4.2	9.5	15.7	14.0	251 985	201	51 041	617 519	-0.7
Darke	8.1	D	8.4	24.3	D	5.9	4.5	10.7	11.4	12 025	231	842	22 782	0.2
Defiance	-0.5	0.0	4.2	34.5	3.6	9.2	5.6	D	12.7	9 025	235	798	16 673	-0.3
Delaware	0.1	D	3.2	8.1	12.6	6.4	13.7	6.9	8.5	25 845	134	1 259	71 399	7.6
Erie	0.6	D	2.8	15.5	2.3	5.5	3.0	11.5	13.5	18 645	247	1 637	37 679	-0.4
Fairfield	0.3	0.4	7.5	11.3	4.6	9.2	4.0	16.5	19.0	28 100	186	2 505	60 264	2.7
Fayette	0.9	0.0	5.4	17.1	D	12.1	5.9	D	18.2	6 575	230	944	12 680	-0.1
Franklin	0.0	D	4.1	6.0	12.3	5.1	9.9	11.5	19.3	170 960	137	33 155	549 421	4.2
Fulton	0.8	D	9.9	37.0	D	5.7	2.6	D	13.0	8 955	211	571	17 381	-0.1
Gallia	0.2	D	5.5	6.3	D	8.0	4.3	D	16.4	7 190	239	1 676	13 657	-2.0
Geauga	0.3	D	15.2	20.8	5.5	6.6	4.0	9.4	10.0	18 535	197	749	36 892	0.9
Greene	0.0	D	3.1	4.4	16.8	5.2	2.8	7.0	47.0	29 150	178	2 566	69 572	2.0
Guernsey	0.4	D	12.0	21.7	4.7	6.6	2.7	13.3	14.9	9 645	246	1 513	19 117	-0.4
Hamilton	0.0	0.1	4.8	11.7	13.5	4.3	9.3	14.5	10.2	144 185	179	24 695	377 769	0.1
Hancock	-0.2	D	2.9	24.8	3.5	4.7	2.7	9.4	6.4	15 000	198	1 070	33 773	1.8
Hardin	8.7	0.0	3.3	25.1	2.1	5.7	3.8	D	15.7	6 350	201	666	13 074	-0.2
Harrison	1.7	20.8	12.3	7.9	D	3.4	3.2	8.0	16.2	3 815	247	561	8 005	-2.0
Henry	1.4	D	10.2	33.0	2.4	5.2	3.6	9.4	18.0	6 090	219	350	11 999	0.3
Highland	2.0	0.4	10.4	17.9	D	9.3	5.2	10.6	22.3	10 025	233	1 473	19 090	-1.5
Hocking	0.1	D	9.1	14.5	2.4	7.7	5.0	8.9	30.2	6 800	239	1 034	13 261	-1.1
Holmes	4.4	0.9	16.1	35.0	D	9.9	2.8	D	6.4	4 795	109	405	13 503	-1.2
Huron	2.7	D	11.6	27.2	2.4	5.6	3.7	10.5	11.6	12 515	214	1 252	25 108	-0.3
Jackson	0.2	0.9	7.3	29.7	D	8.6	3.5	12.0	17.1	7 620	234	1 540	14 590	0.0
Jefferson	0.1	D	D	7.3	D	8.1	2.6	D	15.5	17 815	265	2 592	32 323	-1.5
Knox	1.0	0.7	7.6	29.6	3.6	6.4	2.9	11.9	12.6	12 745	209	1 170	25 573	1.8
Lake	0.6	D	6.2	28.3	5.3	7.1	3.5	9.8	13.0	50 205	219	2 849	102 470	1.3
Lawrence	0.1	D	10.9	D	3.2	8.4	3.0	16.9	24.9	15 120	248	3 586	27 210	-1.4
Licking	1.9	0.5	9.1	13.6	6.2	9.4	8.0	11.4	16.0	33 580	197	3 206	70 228	1.4
Logan	1.1	0.2	5.6	35.0	D	4.7	2.6	8.3	10.6	9 865	218	874	23 183	0.0
Lorain	0.7	0.0	5.7	23.4	4.4	7.1	4.3	11.3	17.8	63 385	208	7 061	129 892	2.2
Lucas	0.1	0.1	5.4	15.8	7.3	6.3	7.3	16.8	15.7	85 095	196	17 766	202 411	-0.1
Madison	1.2	0.0	5.8	27.6	D	6.7	2.0	D	21.8	7 505	170	725	15 960	0.2
Mahoning	0.2	1.1	7.2	10.2	5.9	7.7	5.5	17.7	16.9	56 725	245	8 840	111 131	-0.6
Marion	1.0	0.6	3.8	28.7	2.9	6.7	1.3	17.0	18.3	14 410	221	2 251	27 756	-0.3
Medina	0.2	0.1	12.0	16.3	5.7	8.1	4.3	8.4	12.2	33 575	190	1 460	71 687	3.6
Meigs	0.6	4.0	9.7	3.9	D	11.0	3.9	D	31.0	5 600	241	1 168	10 957	-2.1
Mercer	5.8	D	8.6	32.1	D	6.0	5.4	D	12.7	8 310	203	421	17 831	1.1
Miami	0.3	D	6.1	29.7	4.0	7.6	3.3	9.2	13.3	22 670	218	1 747	44 181	-0.2
Monroe	2.0	D	12.3	D	D	6.0	6.3	D	23.9	3 970	276	456	7 413	-2.0
Montgomery	0.1	0.0	4.8	12.5	11.2	5.1	6.7	19.0	15.6	111 215	209	16 163	254 233	-0.2
Morgan	0.6	D	10.2	19.9	2.8	6.1	2.8	8.9	22.6	3 505	237	529	7 828	-0.8
Morrow	1.1	0.2	20.8	16.3	D	5.9	2.3	D	24.2	7 120	203	579	14 085	-0.5
Muskingum	0.6	3.1	5.4	10.7	4.6	8.8	4.0	D	16.2	20 575	238	3 462	37 644	-1.1
Noble	1.2	11.1	8.8	4.8	4.6	4.3	5.0	5.4	31.1	2 700	188	285	6 052	0.0

1. Per 1,000 resident population estimated as of July 1 of the year shown.

Table B. States and Counties — Housing, Labor Force, and Employment

STATE County	Housing units, 2011–2015								Civilian labor force, 2016				Civilian employment,[6] 2011–2015		
	Occupied units										Unemployment			Percent	
			Owner-occupied			Renter-occupied										
				Median owner cost as a percent of income											Construction, production, and maintenance occupations
	Total	Percent	Median value[1]	With a mortgage	Without a mortgage[2]	Median rent[3]	Median rent as a percent of income[2]	Substandard units[4] (percent)	Total	Percent change, 2015–2016	Total	Rate[5]	Total	Management, business, science and arts	
	89	90	91	92	93	94	95	96	97	98	99	100	101	102	103
NORTH DAKOTA—Cont'd															
Ward	26 131	61.3	189 500	19.4	10.0	919	25.7	2.0	33 943	-1.2	1 427	4.2	35 580	30.5	27.4
Wells	2 008	78.5	73 700	17.4	10.0	443	19.9	1.1	2 181	0.1	88	4.0	2 055	33.3	30.3
Williams	12 082	64.0	201 400	14.7	10.0	898	20.3	3.4	23 133	-19.8	1 022	4.4	16 193	29.9	36.8
OHIO	4 585 084	66.3	129 900	21.2	12.3	730	29.5	1.7	5 713 093	0.4	282 301	4.9	5 366 673	35.1	23.5
Adams	10 858	69.0	87 900	22.0	12.1	562	34.4	3.2	10 794	1.1	807	7.5	10 135	27.9	35.5
Allen	39 986	67.2	105 400	20.1	12.1	639	31.4	1.9	47 957	0.3	2 377	5.0	47 604	26.9	30.0
Ashland	20 427	71.9	120 800	21.6	12.4	676	23.8	2.9	26 024	0.2	1 293	5.0	24 172	30.4	30.9
Ashtabula	38 890	71.2	106 000	22.0	12.9	628	32.1	2.2	44 101	-0.5	2 653	6.0	40 422	25.3	33.9
Athens	22 486	56.3	117 700	21.4	12.3	705	40.6	2.3	28 096	0.7	1 736	6.2	26 794	36.7	16.5
Auglaize	18 193	74.2	133 300	19.3	11.3	642	23.7	1.5	24 547	0.4	898	3.7	22 719	29.4	35.5
Belmont	27 935	74.2	91 700	19.3	11.1	552	26.5	0.8	30 772	-1.2	2 281	7.4	29 728	26.4	29.9
Brown	16 672	75.7	113 800	22.7	13.2	649	26.8	1.9	19 518	0.2	1 109	5.7	18 693	25.7	32.2
Butler	134 720	69.4	157 200	21.1	11.8	817	29.6	1.6	188 853	0.8	8 349	4.4	176 782	36.7	21.4
Carroll	10 972	78.3	112 200	21.2	11.2	599	26.8	2.6	13 385	0.3	907	6.8	12 657	24.7	36.9
Champaign	15 237	75.0	123 200	21.1	12.6	700	27.6	1.7	19 833	-0.1	883	4.5	18 230	26.5	36.1
Clark	54 809	66.2	103 600	20.4	11.9	675	30.8	1.8	63 318	-1.1	3 289	5.2	59 111	29.2	28.2
Clermont	74 812	73.6	155 500	20.8	11.8	764	28.2	1.3	103 378	0.7	4 513	4.4	97 207	35.5	22.9
Clinton	16 073	64.4	120 000	21.9	11.7	707	26.9	1.9	17 001	1.9	984	5.8	18 460	28.0	29.3
Columbiana	42 087	71.1	101 100	19.8	11.5	615	25.8	1.9	48 266	-2.2	3 186	6.6	46 577	25.4	33.3
Coshocton	14 335	74.4	96 500	21.2	11.4	565	26.2	2.5	14 971	-5.5	1 043	7.0	15 576	21.8	41.1
Crawford	17 798	68.6	86 700	21.3	12.0	631	26.4	0.9	18 992	-0.4	1 138	6.0	18 142	26.3	35.1
Cuyahoga	534 719	59.3	121 800	22.3	13.8	730	31.1	1.6	610 483	0.3	33 257	5.4	576 603	39.0	17.9
Darke	20 865	72.1	109 900	21.1	11.9	610	27.7	1.3	26 306	0.4	1 072	4.1	23 751	24.9	40.2
Defiance	15 279	74.9	108 900	20.2	12.1	664	27.1	1.6	18 432	-1.2	893	4.8	18 092	26.4	33.9
Delaware	65 648	81.5	256 800	21.6	11.6	953	27.0	0.9	103 569	1.3	3 665	3.5	94 424	51.9	12.1
Erie	31 767	68.6	131 400	21.3	13.1	707	26.4	0.9	37 127	-0.6	2 027	5.5	35 636	29.5	26.1
Fairfield	55 032	70.5	163 100	20.7	11.0	799	29.7	2.0	75 754	1.3	3 204	4.2	69 708	36.2	21.2
Fayette	11 589	60.1	107 400	23.6	12.4	688	29.5	1.8	14 427	3.0	631	4.4	12 385	24.6	31.7
Franklin	480 946	53.8	150 600	21.6	12.7	845	28.8	2.4	663 620	1.3	26 773	4.0	616 368	41.6	16.0
Fulton	16 229	78.5	129 500	20.2	11.8	641	27.3	1.9	22 643	1.0	1 036	4.6	20 872	28.5	34.5
Gallia	11 590	76.6	94 900	21.9	12.9	601	26.1	3.0	12 173	-0.2	812	6.7	11 344	28.4	30.4
Geauga	34 774	85.1	218 800	21.6	11.3	800	26.7	2.6	48 714	0.0	2 152	4.4	46 540	40.3	22.1
Greene	64 182	67.3	159 400	20.6	11.9	848	28.7	1.2	80 630	0.4	3 471	4.3	76 109	44.4	16.4
Guernsey	15 558	73.0	95 600	19.9	11.7	595	32.1	1.8	18 852	-1.8	1 321	7.0	16 310	26.4	33.2
Hamilton	331 638	58.3	142 000	21.3	12.6	709	30.8	1.8	404 217	0.7	17 566	4.3	383 555	40.1	16.9
Hancock	31 083	70.6	127 100	19.8	11.1	679	26.7	0.7	41 243	1.2	1 497	3.6	37 580	32.5	30.9
Hardin	11 540	70.9	94 000	20.3	12.4	630	29.4	3.3	14 305	-1.3	713	5.0	13 828	26.5	33.3
Harrison	6 271	79.6	85 400	19.9	11.8	606	26.1	2.7	7 011	-2.4	527	7.5	6 740	23.1	39.6
Henry	10 958	80.5	111 000	19.8	12.4	686	25.8	1.2	13 639	0.7	717	5.3	13 436	29.0	37.4
Highland	16 696	70.6	103 500	23.4	11.8	643	31.7	2.1	16 783	-0.9	1 051	6.3	16 962	26.5	38.6
Hocking	11 387	74.3	110 600	21.8	12.4	587	27.5	2.3	13 137	1.1	713	5.4	12 199	29.8	29.7
Holmes	12 685	76.2	161 100	20.5	10.0	561	22.6	5.9	20 969	1.7	736	3.5	19 207	20.8	46.3
Huron	22 527	70.7	116 100	21.0	11.5	630	26.5	1.9	27 864	1.0	1 801	6.5	26 987	23.5	40.0
Jackson	12 981	67.7	91 200	22.3	13.2	637	30.3	2.1	12 729	-2.4	989	7.8	13 191	32.2	32.0
Jefferson	27 958	70.8	86 200	18.6	12.5	594	28.4	1.8	28 797	-2.0	2 384	8.3	27 871	28.5	26.8
Knox	22 759	70.8	132 500	22.3	12.9	699	28.6	2.5	31 290	0.3	1 416	4.5	28 165	30.3	29.8
Lake	94 815	73.9	147 900	21.4	12.1	814	28.9	1.2	123 935	0.3	5 972	4.8	117 389	35.6	22.6
Lawrence	23 548	74.2	98 900	20.3	12.1	652	31.2	2.5	24 652	-0.9	1 589	6.4	24 489	29.7	28.1
Licking	64 230	72.1	152 200	21.1	12.4	760	29.8	1.7	87 863	1.2	3 781	4.3	81 446	35.0	23.2
Logan	18 640	73.6	119 400	19.7	12.6	694	27.7	2.4	23 092	0.0	961	4.2	20 773	27.5	39.9
Lorain	117 298	71.3	137 400	21.2	12.6	741	30.7	1.5	150 470	0.4	8 897	5.9	138 469	32.4	24.8
Lucas	177 619	60.9	104 200	21.4	13.2	666	31.0	1.3	210 587	0.9	10 741	5.1	193 466	32.6	24.0
Madison	14 906	70.3	149 200	20.1	12.2	734	25.5	2.6	20 754	1.4	798	3.8	18 617	31.7	29.1
Mahoning	97 790	68.2	97 400	20.9	12.2	627	31.2	1.2	105 735	-1.1	6 671	6.3	103 169	31.1	24.4
Marion	24 478	67.9	96 400	20.1	11.6	693	31.1	1.7	27 631	-0.4	1 387	5.0	25 608	27.7	34.2
Medina	66 002	79.4	179 500	21.2	11.4	824	28.3	1.6	94 725	0.2	4 117	4.3	88 911	38.1	21.0
Meigs	9 322	78.5	84 900	21.7	12.2	541	31.5	2.6	8 982	-1.2	748	8.3	8 770	26.8	32.7
Mercer	15 919	76.6	130 200	19.6	11.2	653	24.7	1.3	23 430	1.9	755	3.2	20 476	24.7	41.0
Miami	41 135	70.3	136 800	20.6	11.0	730	27.2	1.3	52 576	0.4	2 260	4.3	49 186	30.4	31.3
Monroe	6 056	77.4	92 200	19.4	10.0	533	28.2	1.7	5 244	-5.3	584	11.1	5 571	22.6	39.4
Montgomery	222 687	60.9	109 900	21.9	13.5	728	30.9	1.7	249 484	0.2	12 099	4.8	236 657	35.6	20.7
Morgan	6 120	77.0	88 300	21.5	12.0	549	31.6	3.2	6 750	0.8	549	8.1	5 678	29.8	38.0
Morrow	12 700	81.1	132 800	21.3	13.2	677	31.5	2.6	16 861	1.2	830	4.9	16 096	28.0	35.4
Muskingum	34 261	66.8	108 600	20.9	12.7	641	29.8	2.0	39 383	1.6	2 357	6.0	37 501	26.4	28.7
Noble	4 886	83.4	87 100	22.1	11.1	595	28.9	2.4	4 915	-1.1	421	8.6	4 641	22.9	36.2

1. Specified owner-occupied units.   2. A value of 10.0 represents 10 percent or less; a value of 50.0 represents 50 percent or more.   3. Specified renter-occupied units.
4. Overcrowded or lacking complete plumbing facilities.   5. Percent of civilian labor force.   6. Civilian employed persons 16 years old and over.

Table B. States and Counties — Nonfarm Employment and Agriculture

	Private nonfarm establishments, employment and payroll, 2015								Agriculture, 2012			
		Employment					Annual payroll		Farms			
										Percent with:		
STATE County	Number of establishments	Total	Health care and social assistance	Manufacturing	Retail trade	Finance and insurance	Professional, scientific, and technical services	Total (mil dol)	Average per employee (dollars)	Number	Fewer than 50 acres	500 acres or more	Farm operators whose principal occupation is farming (percent)
	104	105	106	107	108	109	110	111	112	113	114	115	116
NORTH DAKOTA—Cont'd													
Ward	2 150	29 739	4 647	545	6 330	1 044	1 043	1 337	44 963	961	15.3	47.9	60.1
Wells	195	1 395	508	55	231	90	14	45	32 553	543	8.1	50.8	56.9
Williams	1 564	26 379	1 302	395	2 303	419	891	1 789	67 804	758	8.8	52.1	52.4
OHIO	251 668	4 719 985	824 772	663 884	565 140	241 764	250 042	213 161	45 161	75 462	41.1	8.3	43.9
Adams	382	4 173	1 068	702	878	101	84	145	34 735	1 351	38.0	4.2	37.2
Allen	2 404	46 122	11 656	7 767	6 063	1 142	916	1 843	39 964	904	38.8	11.8	42.9
Ashland	1 013	16 036	2 556	3 656	2 096	322	1 023	579	36 085	1 034	36.4	5.4	46.8
Ashtabula	1 909	24 585	5 121	6 358	3 635	563	748	855	34 775	1 099	41.6	6.7	46.8
Athens	1 040	12 298	2 978	244	2 691	389	587	360	29 310	722	31.2	3.3	37.8
Auglaize	990	19 938	2 535	8 967	2 114	319	453	813	40 764	1 040	34.6	9.8	42.5
Belmont	1 446	19 595	4 158	921	4 177	792	586	684	34 917	700	27.1	4.9	42.1
Brown	536	5 769	1 201	872	896	187	119	182	31 543	1 379	40.4	5.7	39.7
Butler	7 115	128 552	16 713	18 279	17 612	7 761	3 604	5 608	43 625	865	51.0	6.6	43.9
Carroll	471	5 485	753	1 527	783	81	108	176	32 103	733	33.2	5.5	40.9
Champaign	565	9 239	938	3 868	943	192	244	388	42 046	873	46.0	11.6	46.2
Clark	2 281	41 116	8 063	6 242	5 454	2 830	1 314	1 471	35 772	785	53.2	11.3	49.6
Clermont	3 586	50 075	5 940	5 174	9 988	2 401	2 663	2 026	40 463	822	60.1	5.0	38.6
Clinton	730	14 035	1 825	3 063	1 566	338	251	557	39 714	759	42.2	15.5	53.1
Columbiana	2 039	27 137	5 596	6 292	4 045	572	449	881	32 453	1 045	44.7	4.5	42.0
Coshocton	627	9 310	2 028	2 475	1 373	198	140	340	36 563	1 122	32.6	5.4	40.6
Crawford	820	12 738	2 644	4 130	1 351	652	447	434	34 061	634	33.1	18.6	50.9
Cuyahoga	33 161	667 784	139 333	68 081	62 232	44 242	43 360	33 928	50 807	114	87.7	0.0	40.4
Darke	1 147	16 624	2 256	5 740	2 100	552	305	618	37 178	1 693	41.8	10.8	41.2
Defiance	813	13 809	2 100	3 444	2 346	606	210	539	39 016	1 030	37.5	12.1	38.5
Delaware	4 257	75 808	7 072	5 738	12 068	13 745	3 552	3 878	51 152	755	56.4	9.9	43.8
Erie	1 854	30 596	4 886	6 718	4 683	624	623	1 153	37 673	345	42.9	12.2	48.1
Fairfield	2 644	35 103	6 786	4 018	6 892	802	1 008	1 170	33 342	1 184	51.2	8.2	43.2
Fayette	584	9 527	1 125	1 478	2 433	163	67	305	31 988	504	35.5	24.2	56.5
Franklin	27 758	614 311	109 542	31 905	67 008	53 264	41 775	30 865	50 243	388	62.9	8.2	40.5
Fulton	951	15 413	1 943	7 072	1 730	364	241	621	40 277	825	42.4	13.3	42.8
Gallia	557	9 175	2 676	433	1 506	346	78	365	39 789	957	34.6	2.7	39.0
Geauga	2 750	29 107	4 369	7 766	3 719	680	1 126	1 239	42 583	959	55.2	2.2	49.8
Greene	3 071	51 017	6 555	3 418	9 271	1 259	10 588	2 059	40 360	800	61.6	9.0	39.4
Guernsey	855	14 621	2 972	2 883	1 862	247	276	515	35 255	1 228	36.6	1.6	34.6
Hamilton	20 925	471 497	86 149	39 830	45 032	33 038	39 629	26 396	55 983	295	67.1	3.1	42.4
Hancock	1 715	43 062	5 529	12 082	4 180	680	1 270	1 949	45 268	831	32.7	15.4	45.5
Hardin	448	6 964	655	2 003	855	211	112	227	32 588	793	31.3	14.1	52.2
Harrison	267	3 359	563	375	336	47	32	141	42 063	444	26.6	6.8	46.2
Henry	572	8 560	1 334	2 997	961	226	184	345	40 313	848	33.1	15.7	47.9
Highland	661	8 573	1 652	1 779	1 610	583	110	290	33 841	1 412	38.3	7.9	45.1
Hocking	482	4 986	1 005	768	803	145	88	149	29 834	367	38.4	3.0	40.9
Holmes	1 221	17 712	1 421	6 834	2 082	394	279	606	34 233	1 969	36.7	2.4	50.0
Huron	1 132	16 689	2 743	4 895	2 157	428	406	669	40 079	865	38.7	12.7	47.1
Jackson	599	8 638	1 351	3 138	1 407	263	153	273	31 593	526	32.3	4.9	41.8
Jefferson	1 261	19 017	4 542	1 173	3 155	326	281	673	35 386	493	26.0	4.1	39.4
Knox	1 060	19 381	3 030	4 522	2 115	438	343	778	40 158	1 374	45.8	5.5	44.6
Lake	6 059	87 838	10 819	20 073	13 127	1 752	3 201	3 948	44 948	214	70.6	1.4	55.6
Lawrence	794	10 486	2 874	826	1 870	277	299	342	32 608	592	26.2	1.9	41.9
Licking	2 942	48 933	8 078	8 193	6 943	3 341	2 014	1 909	39 017	1 484	51.1	5.7	39.8
Logan	843	15 618	1 935	4 369	1 689	306	711	673	43 103	868	40.4	12.3	39.2
Lorain	5 588	85 649	14 958	16 320	13 664	2 149	3 216	3 439	40 148	768	52.7	6.0	46.4
Lucas	9 570	204 127	38 790	22 691	23 436	6 099	9 798	8 598	42 119	330	52.7	2.4	58.2
Madison	668	12 821	1 267	3 661	1 749	135	521	526	40 998	699	40.1	21.9	53.2
Mahoning	5 485	86 074	20 809	9 327	12 276	2 232	3 758	3 101	36 022	578	44.5	4.2	48.3
Marion	1 119	21 288	4 599	6 123	2 890	362	274	783	36 782	578	34.1	16.6	41.9
Medina	3 993	53 040	7 981	8 718	8 971	2 446	2 070	2 178	41 063	920	63.0	4.0	50.2
Meigs	304	2 373	427	75	603	123	56	66	27 671	588	27.0	3.2	53.2
Mercer	974	15 371	2 128	4 367	2 039	557	321	576	37 461	1 208	35.3	12.0	45.0
Miami	2 104	36 454	4 580	11 245	4 827	664	897	1 409	38 661	1 068	54.6	10.0	41.8
Monroe	249	2 381	190	71	378	170	44	108	45 415	823	26.5	2.8	41.9
Montgomery	11 401	231 331	51 728	27 961	26 161	9 573	13 332	10 681	46 171	770	63.8	6.6	42.7
Morgan	159	2 061	465	658	299	90	43	66	32 129	510	22.2	5.5	39.4
Morrow	375	3 722	983	881	458	66	151	126	33 815	824	43.9	8.7	43.0
Muskingum	1 736	28 380	6 430	2 886	4 638	743	470	1 094	38 545	1 259	35.3	4.8	38.4
Noble	217	2 011	338	279	314	92	87	59	29 327	595	27.2	4.2	33.3

Table B. States and Counties — **Agriculture**

STATE County	Agriculture, 2012 (cont.)															
	Land in farms					Value of land and buildings (dollars)		Value of products sold					Percent of farms with sales of:		Government payments	
			Acres								Percent from:					
	Acreage (1,000)	Percent change, 2007–2012	Average size of farm	Total irrigated (1,000)	Total cropland (1,000)	Average per farm	Average per acre	Value of machinery and equipment, average per farm (dollars)	Total (mil dol)	Average per farm (dollars)	Crops	Live-stock and poultry products	$10,000 or more	$100,000 or more	Total ($1,000)	Percent of farms
	117	118	119	120	121	122	123	124	125	126	127	128	129	130	131	132
NORTH DAKOTA—Cont'd																
Ward	1 073	0.7	1 117	0.2	829.4	1 716 400	1 537	298 381	274.5	285 596	93.3	6.7	62.7	39.2	9 875	71.4
Wells	738	-2.5	1 359	0.8	622.3	2 198 269	1 617	364 245	272.0	500 842	95.1	4.9	58.2	44.6	7 746	85.6
Williams	1 063	-7.1	1 403	15.6	739.1	1 044 598	745	289 881	178.7	235 756	93.8	6.2	59.4	36.7	6 315	72.2
OHIO	13 961	0.0	185	46.6	10 748.6	894 933	4 837	116 896	10 064.1	133 366	65.6	34.4	47.4	20.3	228 858	45.9
Adams	172	-6.3	128	0.2	84.4	365 260	2 862	59 237	38.9	28 798	68.6	31.4	33.6	6.6	2 316	55.4
Allen	183	-2.2	203	D	163.0	1 070 715	5 284	144 872	144.1	159 393	76.2	23.8	61.7	30.3	3 593	74.4
Ashland	153	1.6	148	0.2	110.9	677 328	4 578	93 800	103.6	100 214	53.0	47.0	52.5	17.5	2 061	45.4
Ashtabula	166	2.6	151	0.2	109.0	494 527	3 275	114 303	82.3	74 846	74.4	25.6	38.8	13.2	1 609	28.7
Athens	90	10.1	125	0.1	28.0	348 506	2 781	47 575	9.5	13 224	57.2	42.8	21.3	2.1	320	16.8
Auglaize	210	-1.5	202	0.0	191.5	1 220 936	6 044	176 234	190.6	183 235	60.6	39.4	66.1	34.0	5 338	77.1
Belmont	113	-12.3	162	0.0	35.0	540 911	3 344	59 970	20.1	28 764	21.9	78.1	37.4	4.1	613	9.7
Brown	206	-14.1	150	0.1	139.3	539 260	3 602	89 819	82.6	59 891	88.5	11.5	41.8	12.2	3 795	57.9
Butler	146	14.8	169	0.3	116.4	986 918	5 845	107 817	65.0	75 191	80.4	19.6	36.6	12.4	2 379	32.4
Carroll	106	-9.1	145	0.4	58.4	539 031	3 718	86 621	39.2	53 478	51.6	48.4	40.5	10.2	989	28.0
Champaign	190	-7.2	218	3.7	164.9	1 166 636	5 359	147 490	130.4	149 386	86.6	13.4	49.7	24.6	3 854	56.2
Clark	174	-1.7	222	1.6	149.8	1 141 031	5 138	147 288	145.1	184 896	80.4	19.6	45.1	23.8	2 754	47.6
Clermont	121	15.7	147	0.2	88.5	752 370	5 106	83 123	58.0	70 583	93.3	6.7	25.5	8.4	1 264	29.7
Clinton	208	-4.7	274	0.1	187.7	1 360 628	4 962	172 278	163.8	215 867	90.5	9.5	60.1	34.8	3 825	63.8
Columbiana	128	-2.4	122	0.3	81.7	594 740	4 861	98 871	99.3	95 020	38.4	61.6	45.0	15.4	1 509	24.8
Coshocton	170	-0.8	151	0.6	88.7	518 983	3 430	87 948	81.7	72 781	39.9	60.1	39.2	13.4	1 530	30.7
Crawford	240	9.3	379	0.1	221.9	1 772 235	4 681	250 994	193.1	304 645	74.0	26.0	67.2	43.7	4 734	75.6
Cuyahoga	3	-10.4	23	0.1	0.6	391 509	17 113	56 079	10.2	89 605	98.5	1.5	25.4	8.8	12	3.5
Darke	340	-3.0	201	1.1	311.6	1 425 144	7 097	175 760	559.5	330 475	32.2	67.8	65.2	32.9	6 902	69.5
Defiance	225	-3.4	219	0.0	198.1	980 354	4 483	116 630	113.5	110 232	75.9	24.1	48.4	21.8	6 297	85.8
Delaware	141	2.0	187	0.8	123.4	1 108 061	5 937	144 164	121.9	161 464	88.5	11.5	45.0	20.5	2 396	45.2
Erie	83	-0.9	242	0.4	71.9	1 137 035	4 708	184 907	88.2	255 583	92.2	7.8	56.8	31.6	1 343	55.1
Fairfield	207	16.3	175	0.3	162.9	833 232	4 773	114 217	105.8	89 394	79.4	20.6	36.5	15.8	3 782	48.0
Fayette	197	-10.0	390	0.0	180.6	2 134 145	5 473	226 067	143.5	284 808	87.9	12.1	59.9	39.3	4 144	73.0
Franklin	62	4.1	160	0.3	53.5	983 101	6 151	118 101	48.2	124 299	96.2	3.8	44.8	17.5	853	37.9
Fulton	195	6.2	237	0.5	179.6	1 315 518	5 556	166 076	175.7	213 023	69.4	30.6	60.7	35.4	4 204	67.3
Gallia	116	-0.9	121	0.2	34.6	393 862	3 254	51 183	15.1	15 827	51.6	48.4	22.6	2.9	734	23.6
Geauga	67	18.1	70	0.3	32.7	494 216	7 094	47 110	43.6	45 477	41.0	59.0	40.0	9.1	345	5.6
Greene	146	-10.3	182	0.6	124.7	1 095 626	6 012	120 653	95.9	119 883	90.7	9.3	39.6	17.1	2 173	46.6
Guernsey	144	4.5	117	0.0	51.7	336 147	2 871	49 570	21.5	17 502	36.6	63.4	24.9	2.9	291	10.2
Hamilton	22	1.5	73	0.2	10.0	533 654	7 282	73 278	23.6	80 153	61.3	38.7	32.5	10.5	257	13.2
Hancock	230	-7.1	277	0.0	212.8	1 310 924	4 731	164 752	160.2	192 834	91.7	8.3	71.2	41.2	4 142	77.1
Hardin	248	-3.5	313	0.4	222.6	1 527 226	4 887	171 834	272.5	343 571	53.8	46.2	61.9	34.6	4 779	72.1
Harrison	95	2.2	215	0.0	38.1	645 957	3 007	68 225	18.2	41 081	42.6	57.4	32.9	7.9	245	14.4
Henry	236	1.6	278	0.6	221.4	1 570 350	5 645	170 375	155.5	183 383	91.6	8.4	72.3	36.0	4 449	85.6
Highland	265	-2.0	187	0.2	197.7	677 928	3 619	97 353	128.6	91 069	82.6	17.4	43.9	16.3	6 128	62.6
Hocking	38	-9.3	104	0.0	14.0	372 025	3 585	44 937	5.3	14 450	80.2	19.8	22.9	2.7	212	19.3
Holmes	221	17.7	112	0.3	124.1	653 282	5 822	64 655	204.9	104 045	20.9	79.1	59.6	24.3	1 796	12.9
Huron	238	8.6	275	3.2	208.7	1 235 467	4 485	165 143	190.7	220 421	81.0	19.0	55.8	32.1	3 680	57.9
Jackson	72	-0.3	136	0.1	27.2	321 939	2 362	58 485	10.7	20 293	44.2	55.8	29.3	5.9	525	32.3
Jefferson	68	-1.6	139	0.0	25.9	381 974	2 755	68 801	7.8	15 880	48.4	51.6	30.2	3.4	218	19.9
Knox	186	-6.2	135	0.1	128.7	647 124	4 779	91 124	121.4	88 386	66.0	34.0	42.4	15.0	2 491	35.7
Lake	17	6.6	80	1.9	8.6	604 140	7 550	111 075	81.8	382 351	99.4	0.6	48.1	17.8	23	8.9
Lawrence	65	-1.8	109	0.1	17.0	266 258	2 441	50 843	4.8	8 189	57.3	42.7	15.7	1.5	366	18.2
Licking	224	-0.8	151	0.2	161.4	738 829	4 894	103 000	194.8	131 270	52.2	47.8	36.8	12.1	2 331	25.5
Logan	213	5.8	245	0.3	177.7	1 221 374	4 979	135 014	147.9	170 409	82.6	17.4	49.5	23.4	4 046	58.8
Lorain	123	-1.1	160	1.4	102.7	750 453	4 698	125 251	179.1	233 203	89.7	10.3	51.8	20.6	1 519	41.5
Lucas	63	0.2	191	1.5	59.7	1 103 406	5 778	138 709	66.2	200 521	95.2	4.8	58.2	31.8	964	55.2
Madison	263	6.2	377	0.1	244.2	1 917 923	5 092	202 773	193.8	277 230	79.4	20.6	58.4	39.9	5 148	66.0
Mahoning	75	17.0	130	0.9	54.5	644 289	4 968	119 341	65.4	113 234	45.9	54.1	48.1	19.9	847	32.9
Marion	189	-8.5	327	D	174.8	1 562 507	4 773	199 900	151.4	261 990	74.2	25.8	55.0	32.0	4 497	73.5
Medina	95	-0.5	103	0.6	72.4	656 848	6 363	94 628	60.5	65 797	70.1	29.9	37.1	11.6	1 274	20.8
Meigs	76	-2.5	129	0.3	24.6	312 980	2 428	53 207	14.5	24 622	66.8	33.2	29.1	4.3	748	17.9
Mercer	273	-6.8	226	0.1	248.7	1 775 939	7 854	213 011	596.4	493 681	25.7	74.3	76.3	49.7	7 650	79.1
Miami	184	-6.5	173	2.3	164.8	983 794	5 703	103 808	110.0	102 998	91.9	8.1	51.2	21.7	3 147	59.2
Monroe	111	11.9	135	0.0	29.7	311 759	2 308	58 011	13.7	16 612	32.4	67.6	23.2	2.6	264	6.3
Montgomery	124	11.8	161	1.2	104.7	944 147	5 858	111 271	76.8	99 695	84.6	15.4	38.8	13.0	1 656	44.4
Morgan	95	-6.9	187	0.0	30.0	448 463	2 403	64 149	12.2	23 975	41.5	58.5	34.1	5.1	370	22.7
Morrow	168	1.6	204	0.2	139.2	952 987	4 682	131 218	131.7	159 848	70.9	29.1	50.7	20.0	2 689	43.8
Muskingum	173	4.1	138	0.1	79.2	449 031	3 263	70 551	58.1	46 149	51.8	48.2	34.4	7.8	1 298	24.1
Noble	86	-3.6	145	0.1	28.8	368 677	2 547	55 652	9.8	16 403	37.1	62.9	31.9	2.2	78	4.9

Table B. States and Counties — Water Use, Wholesale Trade, Retail Trade, and Real Estate

STATE County	Water use, 2010 Total water withdrawn (mil gal/day)	Gallons withdrawn per person per day	Wholesale trade,[1] 2012 Number of establishments	Number of employees	Sales (mil dol)	Annual payroll (mil dol)	Retail trade,[2] 2012 Number of establishments	Number of employees	Sales (mil dol)	Annual payroll (mil dol)	Real estate and rental and leasing,[2] 2012 Number of establishments	Number of employees	Receipts (mil dol)	Annual payroll (mil dol)
	133	134	135	136	137	138	139	140	141	142	143	144	145	146
NORTH DAKOTA—Cont'd														
Ward	7.7	125	102	1 621	2 898.0	100.1	297	5 634	1 902.3	162.9	79	735	195.1	37.9
Wells	1.0	226	19	D	D	D	36	209	80.4	4.5	3	D	D	D
Williams	21.1	942	91	1 527	1 868.5	119.2	114	1 833	797.5	62.2	77	819	573.6	82.4
OHIO	9 442.8	819	11 744	182 791	155 426.0	9 627.2	36 531	549 152	153 554.0	13 099.3	9 932	60 966	16 132.7	2 441.8
Adams	588.8	20 622	9	114	77.9	3.9	77	853	224.9	18.0	8	27	3.0	0.8
Allen	34.6	325	124	2 287	1 388.8	91.6	417	6 072	1 641.5	134.3	85	376	55.2	11.0
Ashland	5.6	105	39	D	D	D	156	2 036	486.1	46.1	31	156	12.8	3.4
Ashtabula	189.6	1 868	48	385	220.1	14.2	327	3 635	1 081.1	80.6	70	199	26.7	5.3
Athens	9.5	147	28	D	D	D	192	2 783	695.1	58.7	61	213	24.8	4.5
Auglaize	10.8	234	35	D	D	D	165	2 096	491.8	43.1	31	193	14.4	5.9
Belmont	179.5	2 550	38	D	D	D	299	3 837	1 042.5	82.2	54	320	44.1	8.0
Brown	4.8	107	23	138	72.3	4.5	102	979	256.4	21.6	14	51	6.0	1.0
Butler	131.6	357	435	9 727	8 239.8	545.4	1 011	17 718	7 072.0	482.8	264	1 283	289.6	45.7
Carroll	3.1	107	17	D	D	D	65	671	204.9	16.8	12	57	6.7	1.5
Champaign	9.4	233	25	D	D	D	95	980	271.3	21.4	22	56	10.3	1.5
Clark	25.8	187	88	2 274	2 697.8	111.4	403	5 708	1 541.5	128.0	95	468	56.8	12.5
Clermont	384.0	1 946	148	1 560	1 051.1	83.5	520	9 185	2 659.3	227.7	140	608	105.3	19.7
Clinton	4.1	98	29	383	425.2	17.4	127	1 531	443.1	37.0	27	186	37.4	5.4
Columbiana	10.3	96	88	1 108	584.6	49.7	338	3 922	1 126.4	88.9	55	215	25.7	5.9
Coshocton	147.3	3 993	16	D	D	D	107	1 219	307.3	25.5	18	D	D	D
Crawford	5.5	125	35	D	D	D	135	1 330	348.9	30.4	27	64	7.3	1.3
Cuyahoga	466.0	364	1 930	31 718	21 584.9	1 742.5	4 302	59 458	15 072.5	1 412.8	1 534	13 977	4 931.1	691.5
Darke	8.5	161	56	628	528.3	25.4	170	1 956	480.6	43.3	36	131	14.3	3.9
Defiance	11.2	286	33	445	422.8	19.7	150	2 344	593.9	54.0	25	95	13.5	2.2
Delaware	28.3	162	151	D	D	D	587	11 363	3 178.6	273.5	162	697	146.6	28.0
Erie	34.2	443	65	743	1 145.5	35.5	309	4 531	1 072.4	96.7	74	282	41.0	9.2
Fairfield	14.6	100	75	D	D	D	412	6 930	1 678.8	151.1	130	491	63.7	10.5
Fayette	4.2	146	25	D	D	D	183	2 411	675.2	44.9	15	58	20.8	1.5
Franklin	177.8	153	1 274	25 263	20 890.3	1 441.5	3 613	65 130	21 384.9	1 810.6	1 394	9 626	2 688.7	420.3
Fulton	4.5	104	42	429	382.8	15.7	157	1 651	433.7	37.4	19	70	6.1	1.6
Gallia	1 109.4	35 863	17	209	68.3	6.3	120	1 320	336.3	28.7	22	65	9.0	1.6
Geauga	9.8	105	135	1 382	592.0	74.1	283	3 696	1 007.8	87.6	65	299	30.3	10.1
Greene	15.6	97	79	979	1 101.9	46.9	505	9 080	2 121.3	192.5	128	472	96.7	13.6
Guernsey	6.5	163	23	D	D	D	144	1 667	547.0	37.8	34	99	25.3	2.6
Hamilton	382.5	477	1 112	18 946	15 311.6	1 065.9	2 821	44 091	11 558.5	1 077.1	979	6 913	1 634.4	313.1
Hancock	19.2	257	72	964	953.4	47.8	263	4 090	1 103.7	90.6	60	432	55.4	14.2
Hardin	4.6	143	16	115	216.4	4.8	90	930	200.0	18.0	13	49	8.0	0.8
Harrison	1.3	83	8	D	D	D	33	281	70.9	5.1	5	D	D	D
Henry	11.7	413	26	221	305.7	9.6	79	943	290.7	19.0	19	75	24.6	2.2
Highland	3.4	78	14	131	95.8	4.4	139	1 532	393.0	34.1	26	65	10.1	1.7
Hocking	3.0	101	5	D	D	D	67	799	213.2	17.5	28	110	10.2	2.5
Holmes	6.4	151	60	631	332.2	22.7	157	1 976	456.7	45.1	15	40	10.3	1.2
Huron	7.1	120	46	607	601.6	27.7	174	1 993	538.4	43.5	47	151	23.3	4.0
Jackson	2.3	70	20	123	60.4	4.3	117	1 410	339.5	29.9	24	79	10.4	2.1
Jefferson	1 734.0	24 875	45	D	D	D	216	3 082	723.2	65.7	43	196	23.1	6.0
Knox	9.0	147	43	D	D	D	177	2 051	585.2	47.6	38	137	16.7	3.2
Lake	818.4	3 558	296	2 993	1 406.6	149.5	789	12 537	3 505.0	293.4	189	711	150.6	23.6
Lawrence	9.4	150	20	180	100.3	6.3	154	1 870	553.8	42.4	22	59	8.1	1.5
Licking	19.9	119	96	1 574	1 634.8	76.6	444	6 954	2 454.9	167.9	110	357	69.0	10.3
Logan	6.1	134	28	1 381	748.8	63.3	148	1 685	442.3	38.2	32	153	28.4	4.0
Lorain	464.5	1 541	246	2 943	1 826.6	130.4	814	12 995	3 707.3	310.4	192	1 116	116.2	26.5
Lucas	685.3	1 551	440	6 310	5 058.6	327.0	1 459	23 721	5 977.9	561.0	411	2 688	2 530.9	161.2
Madison	7.0	162	23	D	D	D	103	1 719	1 116.1	44.8	30	87	13.6	1.9
Mahoning	7.4	31	279	3 666	1 814.7	178.6	893	12 319	3 104.3	262.6	177	2 348	184.5	59.3
Marion	12.4	186	36	541	620.1	25.7	181	2 822	745.3	69.5	44	191	28.9	6.0
Medina	9.7	56	233	3 012	1 536.8	162.5	486	8 741	2 651.4	199.7	131	487	85.4	13.7
Meigs	9.0	379	7	68	13.2	1.7	63	510	155.5	10.1	8	16	1.8	0.2
Mercer	8.9	218	49	1 039	790.3	39.4	168	1 930	496.5	46.4	28	69	10.2	1.7
Miami	16.5	161	84	820	740.7	35.7	307	4 558	1 239.3	108.0	73	300	44.1	8.8
Monroe	2.9	197	6	D	D	D	47	360	74.4	6.5	1	D	D	D
Montgomery	141.2	264	521	7 997	15 523.2	450.6	1 675	26 113	6 490.7	605.1	534	3 167	524.5	110.7
Morgan	1.7	114	6	D	D	D	26	268	54.5	4.8	3	D	D	D
Morrow	3.4	99	14	D	D	D	51	475	164.1	9.7	6	11	2.2	0.2
Muskingum	16.5	192	54	868	707.1	33.6	338	4 448	1 117.8	94.1	56	265	41.2	8.3
Noble	1.3	89	5	28	16.7	1.1	34	327	105.0	6.7	3	2	0.7	0.1

1. Merchant wholesalers, except manufacturers' sales branches and offices. 2. Employer establishments.

Table B. States and Counties — Professional Services, Manufacturing, and Accommodation and Food Services

STATE County	Professional, scientific, and technical services, 2012				Manufacturing, 2012				Accommodation and food services, 2012			
	Number of establishments	Number of employees	Receipts (mil dol)	Annual payroll (mil dol)	Number of establishments	Number of employees	Receipts (mil dol)	Annual payroll (mil dol)	Number of establishments	Number of employees	Sales (mil dol)	Annual payroll (mil dol)
	147	148	149	150	151	152	153	154	155	156	157	158
NORTH DAKOTA—Cont'd												
Ward	144	763	116.9	49.4	54	561	D	21.8	173	3 932	211.6	59.1
Wells	9	25	2.0	0.8	7	51	30.0	1.9	17	114	4.8	1.0
Williams	99	558	123.8	37.5	33	250	125.1	12.4	94	2 152	259.1	44.0
OHIO	23 961	233 876	35 970.8	14 219.9	14 482	627 124	313 630.0	33 135.4	23 432	437 293	20 652.8	5 742.7
Adams	26	D	D	D	24	542	103.7	29.8	35	508	21.4	5.8
Allen	164	952	75.8	33.0	124	7 318	15 270.4	448.1	234	4 521	211.3	54.3
Ashland	69	962	127.1	42.8	83	3 655	1 069.9	156.6	91	1 500	61.9	17.2
Ashtabula	118	D	D	D	147	6 167	2 449.5	313.9	229	2 706	121.5	30.8
Athens	71	580	86.0	23.6	38	176	D	6.4	143	2 860	107.2	29.1
Auglaize	70	434	56.8	17.2	83	7 339	2 961.6	363.5	90	1 341	50.5	14.2
Belmont	81	551	55.9	20.1	45	893	D	37.5	127	2 374	112.2	31.4
Brown	28	131	9.2	3.5	32	526	95.1	21.4	67	825	33.0	9.3
Butler	590	3 574	441.6	174.1	402	17 369	10 342.8	997.0	640	12 799	611.8	166.0
Carroll	25	118	9.6	3.5	40	1 366	368.6	55.1	41	485	17.9	5.3
Champaign	47	271	14.6	14.2	41	3 393	1 387.0	170.0	48	701	29.9	7.6
Clark	166	1 172	141.2	58.3	158	6 116	2 832.4	275.0	235	4 288	197.0	53.2
Clermont	385	2 826	469.6	154.5	169	5 182	1 248.5	262.3	280	6 030	285.3	81.9
Clinton	49	D	D	D	41	2 604	1 029.1	128.4	74	1 371	75.2	17.6
Columbiana	106	435	36.3	13.8	171	5 294	1 443.2	213.0	174	2 587	102.9	28.0
Coshocton	29	132	10.8	3.1	52	2 358	1 195.1	113.0	51	717	32.8	9.2
Crawford	45	357	74.1	13.2	80	3 374	1 045.9	149.9	84	987	41.6	10.9
Cuyahoga	4 016	41 345	6 848.8	2 750.9	1 890	69 606	24 399.4	4 048.8	2 959	53 954	2 738.6	758.7
Darke	69	280	30.3	8.8	72	4 475	1 855.5	216.8	88	1 015	43.0	11.0
Defiance	45	221	20.5	7.4	43	3 278	1 018.0	203.5	81	1 228	50.1	13.2
Delaware	534	3 692	667.1	222.2	135	5 463	3 012.0	303.4	421	9 496	460.2	134.1
Erie	117	D	D	D	103	5 465	2 021.6	291.7	263	5 848	305.9	77.6
Fairfield	196	910	76.3	28.9	107	4 219	1 277.9	207.0	244	4 767	203.0	59.6
Fayette	21	72	8.3	2.1	25	1 670	1 343.7	75.9	59	1 053	46.9	12.5
Franklin	3 472	40 628	7 092.6	2 737.0	814	28 991	12 574.1	1 461.7	2 797	57 229	2 980.8	843.3
Fulton	47	D	D	D	93	6 102	3 394.5	290.9	73	936	35.3	10.3
Gallia	29	87	8.7	2.4	22	452	D	22.4	53	886	43.4	11.5
Geauga	349	1 109	207.7	58.4	195	7 259	2 787.3	353.1	171	2 404	98.7	28.5
Greene	437	8 729	1 756.2	651.4	102	3 221	877.9	170.4	311	6 674	319.9	86.5
Guernsey	43	235	30.7	11.1	55	2 634	1 562.7	120.8	89	1 465	71.0	18.0
Hamilton	2 536	40 955	6 599.1	2 839.3	990	45 901	23 167.3	2 800.1	1 853	39 506	2 004.4	569.6
Hancock	136	758	97.8	38.6	94	9 903	4 821.3	491.4	181	4 063	169.8	48.3
Hardin	25	85	7.0	2.4	30	1 722	475.3	73.3	51	868	37.2	12.1
Harrison	13	27	2.4	0.7	12	368	92.3	13.6	27	198	7.9	2.3
Henry	24	91	9.8	3.3	45	3 100	2 313.6	158.0	49	D	D	D
Highland	40	132	11.0	2.9	27	1 698	585.9	68.6	63	878	36.4	9.6
Hocking	26	D	D	D	24	847	287.1	39.3	57	885	45.8	12.6
Holmes	30	267	35.1	11.2	253	6 028	1 483.4	200.9	67	1 374	61.0	17.9
Huron	80	410	33.1	14.4	87	5 436	2 336.8	232.4	107	1 474	60.9	15.5
Jackson	36	153	11.6	3.3	32	3 492	D	117.6	53	884	35.8	9.8
Jefferson	87	D	D	D	35	1 333	D	76.0	142	1 808	76.2	20.0
Knox	54	335	33.4	12.1	69	4 976	2 166.3	300.4	91	1 438	60.7	16.5
Lake	555	3 056	413.5	170.9	617	19 183	6 045.2	970.0	529	9 279	406.8	111.6
Lawrence	42	271	18.0	7.8	34	915	D	30.6	66	1 124	58.9	14.3
Licking	229	1 795	144.3	114.4	151	7 809	2 958.9	358.2	280	4 975	212.7	61.7
Logan	54	766	62.7	27.2	48	4 584	6 790.1	305.7	98	1 214	56.5	15.0
Lorain	448	3 297	276.1	111.4	379	16 010	7 328.0	892.4	514	8 536	397.0	104.6
Lucas	864	8 875	1 182.6	474.5	460	18 286	27 736.6	1 154.6	1 025	19 099	823.0	237.3
Madison	42	D	D	D	44	2 895	1 157.9	135.8	46	844	36.0	10.6
Mahoning	447	3 570	307.8	142.2	326	8 756	1 978.7	398.9	490	9 022	397.2	105.6
Marion	71	303	29.8	9.6	71	5 966	3 681.7	276.5	106	1 893	86.9	22.1
Medina	407	2 028	230.8	83.7	277	8 543	2 970.4	405.6	288	4 897	223.0	61.9
Meigs	11	D	D	D	7	D	D	1.6	28	372	16.4	4.6
Mercer	44	295	31.7	10.6	82	3 807	1 136.9	172.5	85	1 192	44.8	11.9
Miami	159	1 000	112.6	41.6	216	10 888	3 923.9	542.3	188	3 816	159.8	45.7
Monroe	11	D	D	D	9	D	D	D	18	163	5.9	1.6
Montgomery	1 121	12 095	1 713.7	727.6	730	26 188	8 239.2	1 466.6	1 112	22 321	1 028.7	296.6
Morgan	8	D	D	D	9	582	D	27.8	16	159	5.1	1.5
Morrow	33	D	D	D	26	844	D	45.6	29	350	17.6	4.6
Muskingum	106	452	55.6	17.1	72	2 699	867.7	126.2	167	3 102	139.5	39.7
Noble	12	D	D	D	13	299	101.9	D	17	D	D	D

1. Establishment subject to federal tax.

STATE County	Health care and social assistance, 2012				Other services, 2012				Nonemployer businesses, 2015		Value of residential construction authorized by building permits, 2016	
	Number of establishments	Number of employees	Receipts (mil dol)	Annual payroll (mil dol)	Number of establishments	Number of employees	Receipts (mil dol)	Annual payroll (mil dol)	Number	Receipts (mil dol)	New Construction ($1,000)	Number of housing units
	159	160	161	162	163	164	165	166	167	168	169	170
NORTH DAKOTA—Cont'd												
Ward	152	D	D	D	134	751	69.7	19.7	4 303	212.2	17 936	79
Wells	17	461	21.8	10.8	16	D	D	D	378	17.1	12	1
Williams	65	1 485	131.6	57.6	78	467	82.0	17.0	2 562	147.1	27 664	200
OHIO	28 237	798 770	80 915.7	33 141.0	18 851	127 366	13 221.5	3 491.3	763 418	33 534.4	4 589 266	22 816
Adams	48	1 057	67.1	28.3	25	64	26.1	2.2	1 928	74.2	425	3
Allen	307	11 307	1 256.5	501.7	197	1 264	92.0	25.5	5 366	211.5	16 004	76
Ashland	112	2 220	188.6	71.4	91	563	44.3	14.7	3 413	150.1	9 370	58
Ashtabula	217	5 453	420.3	171.9	158	646	47.5	10.9	6 141	248.2	15 026	92
Athens	144	3 058	287.7	101.6	80	417	27.6	7.5	3 238	113.7	5 415	22
Auglaize	97	2 259	169.4	60.0	89	529	38.2	11.9	2 732	107.3	25 448	113
Belmont	208	4 715	311.7	127.6	124	654	41.0	12.0	3 232	133.3	1 801	10
Brown	58	1 461	112.6	42.2	42	180	13.1	3.8	2 734	106.3	11 153	70
Butler	730	15 022	1 491.8	566.6	520	4 178	373.1	108.0	21 945	955.4	203 759	1 140
Carroll	39	753	41.6	17.4	46	224	16.8	4.0	1 917	83.9	1 000	1
Champaign	49	1 362	89.1	35.5	48	165	14.0	3.1	2 208	92.4	9 322	53
Clark	313	10 029	912.0	334.8	212	1 363	134.3	40.5	6 681	244.8	13 160	55
Clermont	291	5 950	527.0	211.9	289	1 688	147.8	43.8	13 258	573.1	81 065	488
Clinton	90	1 751	176.2	64.2	60	260	21.5	6.2	2 711	108.7	9 640	48
Columbiana	291	5 444	415.4	161.9	184	857	69.0	18.4	5 919	242.8	11 417	90
Coshocton	84	1 783	143.5	56.0	60	267	22.0	5.0	2 312	92.7	464	3
Crawford	98	2 313	176.8	70.1	73	310	27.1	6.3	2 170	83.4	1 218	7
Cuyahoga	3 593	137 744	14 792.8	6 409.1	2 495	18 586	2 072.3	568.0	91 324	4 111.1	207 582	829
Darke	77	2 284	186.6	74.3	106	405	24.9	7.0	3 520	146.4	6 524	28
Defiance	85	2 403	194.0	80.8	70	386	31.2	7.1	2 164	87.7	7 474	42
Delaware	395	6 795	541.6	243.4	270	2 266	458.8	94.2	16 658	931.7	330 970	1 522
Erie	208	5 406	489.8	224.1	138	710	47.5	14.3	4 733	186.0	26 254	132
Fairfield	303	6 114	564.4	241.0	171	1 031	101.5	30.4	10 466	453.1	108 485	454
Fayette	53	1 432	114.4	45.8	40	193	10.7	3.2	1 509	59.3	5 588	33
Franklin	3 325	104 976	11 693.1	4 509.2	1 912	17 718	2 309.3	597.1	93 514	4 263.2	917 019	5 770
Fulton	93	2 330	197.1	76.4	71	254	25.9	6.0	2 952	128.0	9 252	49
Gallia	70	2 473	227.0	97.3	37	241	17.9	5.4	1 766	75.1	500	6
Geauga	237	3 833	360.2	157.2	176	1 179	108.6	36.7	10 873	624.3	45 927	148
Greene	341	5 861	608.5	219.4	212	1 244	99.7	27.9	9 864	395.1	188 186	718
Guernsey	123	2 653	221.2	74.6	60	276	31.0	6.1	2 249	100.9	6 868	34
Hamilton	2 371	80 058	10 054.4	4 272.5	1 488	11 624	1 292.3	344.2	57 438	2 662.5	255 373	1 340
Hancock	183	5 107	523.6	192.3	137	892	99.6	22.9	4 349	192.4	35 329	203
Hardin	48	645	48.9	18.9	32	117	8.9	2.3	1 509	59.2	8 483	52
Harrison	27	513	39.9	15.0	19	61	5.7	1.2	869	44.3	273	1
Henry	52	1 371	81.3	36.0	42	304	19.7	5.2	1 640	68.5	3 692	20
Highland	97	1 650	128.4	50.9	42	154	13.1	2.9	2 946	126.5	583	6
Hocking	47	1 075	74.7	29.9	35	199	22.2	4.2	1 898	72.1	743	8
Holmes	60	1 397	153.1	41.2	53	184	21.5	5.0	5 263	332.8	1 207	6
Huron	102	2 711	269.6	111.4	105	544	41.3	11.6	3 112	132.6	9 623	53
Jackson	74	1 372	120.4	42.5	40	157	16.7	3.6	1 682	64.9	16 607	69
Jefferson	155	4 577	438.1	164.5	101	590	41.0	11.9	3 074	104.3	2 277	9
Knox	130	2 971	231.6	93.2	77	499	42.7	11.7	4 822	208.5	26 885	148
Lake	608	11 077	944.7	408.2	470	2 718	214.6	66.8	15 490	693.6	85 263	384
Lawrence	123	D	D	D	55	281	28.2	6.3	2 773	100.4	655	12
Licking	262	7 491	625.0	254.5	203	1 190	103.1	27.8	11 823	505.1	72 585	291
Logan	94	2 122	180.1	69.5	67	505	79.3	13.1	2 821	118.4	11 380	91
Lorain	616	13 559	1 290.7	534.4	454	2 641	260.3	62.6	17 147	687.3	189 235	990
Lucas	1 275	38 102	4 107.7	1 677.1	731	5 136	444.5	130.0	24 644	1 073.9	126 064	505
Madison	73	D	D	D	46	159	11.9	3.3	2 709	111.0	9 446	45
Mahoning	767	19 562	1 823.7	717.0	382	2 612	216.7	58.4	15 421	646.7	32 244	146
Marion	157	4 315	369.2	151.5	95	648	40.1	11.0	2 997	108.5	6 253	39
Medina	369	7 484	580.7	238.2	300	1 639	128.9	41.0	13 229	632.4	160 598	702
Meigs	41	473	30.4	11.9	17	53	6.7	1.4	1 143	38.1	2 654	14
Mercer	76	2 104	132.6	57.7	86	436	43.3	10.9	2 718	126.5	15 484	67
Miami	197	4 449	374.8	135.0	178	900	81.3	20.7	6 715	263.2	47 601	153
Monroe	18	D	D	D	23	D	D	D	1 063	34.0	0	0
Montgomery	1 466	48 822	5 573.6	2 243.7	852	6 243	682.6	157.5	31 435	1 304.4	84 276	411
Morgan	16	340	20.2	7.7	13	D	D	D	808	26.2	8 078	36
Morrow	47	D	D	D	24	80	7.3	2.0	2 608	121.0	7 684	38
Muskingum	194	6 011	603.1	266.2	159	1 093	86.6	23.9	5 060	202.9	5 417	32
Noble	20	D	D	D	20	D	D	D	737	29.8	4 876	25

Table B. States and Counties — Government Employment and Payroll, and Local Government Finances

STATE County			March payroll (percent of total)												
	Government employment and payroll, 2012									Local government finances, 2012					
										General revenue					
												Taxes			
													Per capita[1] (dollars)		
	Full-time equivalent employees	March payroll (dollars)	Adminis- tration, judicial, and legal	Police and Corrections	Fire Protection	Highways and transpor- tation	Health and Welfare	Natural resources and utilities	Education and libraries	Total (mil dol)	Inter- govern- mental (mil dol)	Total (mil dol)	Total	Property
	171	172	173	174	175	176	177	178	179	180	181	182	183	184
NORTH DAKOTA— Cont'd														
Ward	2 136	7 851 589	4.3	7.5	2.8	4.2	5.4	5.7	68.4	241.7	117.3	80.2	1 238	819
Wells	201	657 258	11.8	3.8	0.0	9.3	11.4	5.1	54.7	18.7	8.8	6.5	1 519	1 436
Williams	864	3 064 820	7.6	11.5	0.1	4.9	6.8	4.6	59.1	140.3	49.9	59.7	2 236	1 126
OHIO	X	X	X	X	X	X	X	X	X	X	X	X	X	X
Adams	1 309	4 554 288	8.6	6.3	1.2	4.8	20.7	12.5	44.5	95.0	57.8	28.2	996	856
Allen	4 029	14 917 726	8.3	9.1	4.8	3.4	9.8	5.8	55.9	394.8	197.5	125.6	1 195	774
Ashland	1 952	6 407 247	7.9	9.8	3.4	8.4	11.1	4.1	54.7	148.8	65.0	62.1	1 172	812
Ashtabula	3 445	13 283 345	8.6	8.3	6.3	6.3	10.0	5.8	52.9	379.5	210.8	114.5	1 141	880
Athens	2 322	8 135 468	7.7	8.6	2.5	4.0	14.9	8.3	53.4	218.6	106.3	74.7	1 161	793
Auglaize	1 848	6 837 964	8.1	11.1	3.6	6.2	9.8	11.2	48.9	165.8	68.7	63.4	1 383	791
Belmont	2 607	9 128 313	8.1	10.6	2.1	10.5	11.9	10.3	46.0	191.0	101.3	63.6	913	616
Brown	1 467	5 037 757	10.7	6.4	1.0	3.0	3.9	4.5	68.2	139.2	79.2	35.6	803	573
Butler	12 086	48 616 602	7.6	9.8	5.5	2.6	6.4	6.6	59.8	1 333.8	510.2	553.1	1 493	1 108
Carroll	814	2 533 284	12.9	4.6	0.1	10.7	12.6	3.6	53.6	67.3	39.5	18.9	663	541
Champaign	1 507	5 457 874	8.0	11.9	3.0	4.5	7.3	4.2	60.0	133.3	67.8	46.2	1 167	749
Clark	5 386	19 627 638	7.6	10.0	4.2	2.3	8.2	4.4	57.6	501.3	270.1	168.3	1 227	774
Clermont	5 289	20 437 759	7.0	10.5	7.4	2.9	8.3	2.8	59.9	577.6	246.3	251.2	1 262	1 074
Clinton	1 809	5 888 599	9.0	8.5	2.2	3.7	8.2	6.6	60.3	157.7	71.7	54.0	1 288	849
Columbiana	3 495	11 243 471	8.0	8.4	2.1	5.7	10.5	5.6	58.7	309.6	171.8	94.5	887	570
Coshocton	1 280	4 337 624	6.8	5.0	9.6	5.4	10.8	3.0	57.6	122.4	67.8	38.8	1 056	791
Crawford	1 254	4 325 266	5.9	4.7	3.6	1.8	1.1	5.5	77.2	151.9	72.7	51.8	1 209	747
Cuyahoga	62 490	287 120 691	6.2	10.3	5.0	6.7	17.9	8.2	44.0	8 188.0	2 777.4	3 498.3	2 765	1 595
Darke	1 735	6 310 491	7.2	9.5	3.5	3.8	9.0	4.8	60.8	161.4	77.3	60.1	1 145	652
Defiance	1 658	5 904 403	6.0	5.9	1.8	3.6	22.5	5.1	51.1	159.4	60.4	46.4	1 200	722
Delaware	5 621	21 810 855	6.5	8.3	8.6	3.5	6.9	3.8	60.6	594.5	125.1	379.4	2 096	1 582
Erie	3 210	12 237 910	9.9	7.7	6.1	3.6	6.5	6.6	58.0	347.1	131.6	140.7	1 841	1 302
Fairfield	4 930	17 614 468	7.6	7.4	6.0	3.4	7.0	5.5	62.0	533.2	218.0	227.0	1 539	972
Fayette	1 569	5 994 441	8.4	7.6	3.1	4.0	30.8	6.0	35.4	151.4	51.3	42.0	1 454	900
Franklin	43 936	204 420 126	7.5	12.0	8.0	4.8	6.8	5.9	53.0	6 852.6	2 645.8	3 248.5	2 717	1 632
Fulton	1 714	6 275 872	9.2	6.4	2.8	7.9	4.5	5.4	60.4	175.3	77.4	66.6	1 566	1 017
Gallia	1 230	4 310 190	10.5	5.0	0.3	10.5	8.6	3.8	60.0	121.8	67.0	35.1	1 144	879
Geauga	2 853	10 934 381	6.8	10.3	1.9	6.2	6.6	5.0	60.8	321.0	103.8	177.1	1 890	1 605
Greene	5 165	20 150 214	7.8	10.0	5.1	2.9	8.5	4.8	58.8	586.4	206.6	277.8	1 698	1 294
Guernsey	1 477	4 435 295	10.2	6.1	1.9	6.0	6.7	6.6	52.4	132.8	73.2	38.5	968	624
Hamilton	30 330	130 350 382	7.8	13.0	8.0	5.1	7.5	8.7	47.8	4 236.2	1 499.4	1 927.5	2 403	1 479
Hancock	2 432	8 819 684	8.0	8.9	4.5	4.6	9.6	8.0	55.4	271.6	110.7	109.9	1 453	890
Hardin	1 423	4 258 899	9.1	8.7	1.2	4.7	11.9	3.6	57.1	110.9	55.5	32.7	1 034	564
Harrison	710	1 856 484	14.6	4.5	0.0	15.6	8.0	4.7	51.0	49.7	28.0	13.6	864	670
Henry	1 481	5 408 211	10.0	3.9	0.9	3.5	8.5	11.1	57.7	117.5	56.0	44.6	1 592	1 074
Highland	2 293	6 286 414	5.2	4.7	1.8	3.3	31.1	2.7	50.4	172.7	76.0	41.2	959	563
Hocking	914	2 885 727	10.2	5.6	1.4	5.5	5.2	3.2	67.0	114.8	42.6	28.6	978	747
Holmes	1 321	4 844 879	5.9	5.2	1.1	8.0	34.0	1.8	43.4	120.7	39.0	36.0	838	671
Huron	2 467	10 437 634	6.6	7.8	2.4	4.1	4.3	21.4	48.4	200.0	86.9	77.4	1 306	715
Jackson	1 363	4 190 837	9.9	7.6	2.0	7.6	8.5	6.5	56.1	108.3	64.9	23.7	718	505
Jefferson	2 754	8 388 400	8.2	12.7	2.8	7.2	11.7	7.8	48.7	279.5	143.1	76.7	1 121	730
Knox	2 080	6 852 809	7.4	6.9	4.1	5.9	8.2	4.9	60.0	183.1	81.3	75.5	1 244	918
Lake	9 604	40 201 055	7.4	10.0	6.0	4.6	9.6	6.7	54.4	980.1	328.7	481.4	2 097	1 489
Lawrence	2 540	8 380 560	7.9	7.5	1.5	3.4	6.7	4.8	67.2	216.7	128.7	37.7	607	431
Licking	5 717	20 737 584	8.7	10.0	5.7	3.6	5.5	4.6	60.9	579.7	236.0	255.6	1 525	1 041
Logan	1 959	6 311 962	5.8	5.7	2.0	5.4	16.7	4.0	58.9	181.6	83.8	65.2	1 434	1 028
Lorain	11 564	45 174 817	6.2	9.7	3.8	2.9	8.7	7.0	60.5	1 201.2	540.9	467.7	1 551	1 088
Lucas	14 739	62 111 336	9.0	11.4	4.7	4.8	10.1	5.0	50.5	2 086.3	910.4	780.9	1 783	1 087
Madison	1 659	6 453 004	10.2	8.0	6.0	3.9	8.2	4.3	57.6	145.7	58.9	62.4	1 448	1 020
Mahoning	8 773	31 345 985	6.1	10.6	3.5	4.0	7.9	7.9	58.9	868.3	433.7	320.4	1 363	887
Marion	2 295	8 158 244	7.0	10.0	5.7	2.9	9.1	2.6	60.7	238.0	129.7	65.6	990	651
Medina	5 924	23 018 921	7.1	9.8	2.3	4.3	7.5	6.6	61.1	592.1	209.5	282.6	1 627	1 274
Meigs	1 067	3 103 267	7.9	7.6	0.0	6.4	10.2	11.3	53.7	74.8	52.2	14.0	593	473
Mercer	1 924	6 814 130	6.9	4.9	1.1	2.5	23.6	3.3	56.9	205.3	75.3	58.0	1 418	907
Miami	3 473	13 601 040	7.3	8.3	2.8	3.5	7.7	7.6	59.9	385.2	159.1	157.7	1 531	850
Monroe	802	1 932 268	10.9	3.9	0.2	9.0	13.4	7.6	53.8	74.7	47.7	17.9	1 229	1 062
Montgomery	22 502	93 151 363	7.9	9.7	4.7	6.0	8.0	8.2	54.1	2 605.5	1 042.9	1 055.0	1 974	1 302
Morgan	442	1 318 311	13.5	4.8	0.0	6.2	1.1	3.1	69.8	48.1	33.5	10.1	676	539
Morrow	1 452	4 922 890	11.2	5.3	0.3	5.8	24.4	1.2	49.4	129.7	48.6	32.8	939	663
Muskingum	3 889	12 275 435	6.0	8.2	2.0	4.2	10.5	5.2	60.2	370.0	202.8	113.8	1 324	918
Noble	445	1 384 468	17.5	1.9	0.0	7.5	11.4	15.2	45.8	48.2	22.3	17.2	1 183	1 099

1. Based on the resident population estimated as of July 1 of the year shown.

Table B. States and Counties — Local Government Finances, Government Employment, and Income Taxes

STATE County	Local government finances, 2012 (cont.) Direct general expenditure — Total (mil dol)	Per capita[1] (dollars)	Educa-tion	Health and hospitals	Police protec-tion	Public welfare	High-ways	Debt outstanding Total (mil dol)	Per capita[1] (dollars)	Government employment, 2015 Federal civilian	Federal military	State and local	Individual income tax returns, 2014 Number of returns	Mean adjusted gross income	Mean income tax
	185	186	187	188	189	190	191	192	193	194	195	196	197	198	199
NORTH DAKOTA—Cont'd															
Ward	230.0	3 550	57.5	0.3	5.1	2.2	10.8	95.7	1 477	1 209	5 714	4 439	35 840	70 726	10 222
Wells	18.0	4 209	46.4	1.9	3.5	4.3	18.7	9.3	2 176	27	25	266	2 170	61 570	7 649
Williams	130.1	4 872	37.2	3.2	4.7	0.9	16.5	127.0	4 757	80	218	2 329	19 070	119 484	24 185
OHIO	X	X	X	X	X	X	X	X	X	76 607	35 702	682 926	5 559 640	56 373	6 978
Adams	85.9	3 030	56.6	4.4	3.7	6.7	8.9	48.9	1 726	64	71	1 449	10 870	40 014	3 262
Allen	385.4	3 665	49.5	5.4	6.9	4.3	6.7	180.7	1 719	322	258	5 794	47 950	49 038	5 391
Ashland	147.7	2 789	50.7	9.1	6.1	3.4	7.9	51.1	966	99	131	2 315	24 530	45 958	4 464
Ashtabula	389.2	3 877	53.0	7.0	3.8	6.1	7.1	243.8	2 429	189	262	4 331	44 610	43 429	3 791
Athens	231.8	3 605	47.4	7.2	2.6	14.9	4.9	68.3	1 062	225	156	10 845	22 100	46 800	5 020
Auglaize	176.4	3 848	52.8	1.4	5.8	4.8	6.3	154.1	3 362	92	116	2 263	23 480	52 869	5 716
Belmont	186.0	2 669	48.0	6.2	2.5	6.5	6.8	55.5	797	162	168	3 667	31 210	55 820	7 167
Brown	134.7	3 035	63.4	3.5	6.0	3.2	5.5	58.8	1 325	85	111	1 944	19 040	42 427	3 667
Butler	1 326.8	3 580	50.2	3.7	7.9	4.7	5.8	1 987.8	5 364	550	951	19 956	172 970	58 447	6 838
Carroll	59.8	2 092	47.0	8.7	3.5	6.9	10.6	17.3	605	48	70	959	12 910	52 335	5 919
Champaign	144.3	3 648	59.7	3.7	3.5	3.9	6.6	60.2	1 522	63	98	1 827	18 480	47 055	4 458
Clark	474.6	3 459	49.3	5.8	5.9	6.2	3.3	206.0	1 502	563	345	6 435	63 770	45 120	4 379
Clermont	582.2	2 924	49.6	6.2	6.8	6.0	5.4	332.6	1 671	342	514	7 288	96 950	59 902	7 196
Clinton	150.9	3 602	49.6	3.5	5.9	5.2	7.7	60.1	1 434	129	105	2 314	19 140	50 571	6 176
Columbiana	314.7	2 954	56.2	3.2	5.1	8.9	6.3	123.5	1 160	612	259	4 439	47 750	44 622	4 384
Coshocton	116.3	3 163	50.7	9.0	6.0	6.2	9.6	60.1	1 634	72	93	1 484	16 120	42 255	3 871
Crawford	163.0	3 804	50.5	4.3	4.1	5.0	8.0	99.7	2 328	80	107	1 780	20 570	40 318	3 371
Cuyahoga	8 005.7	6 328	36.6	14.5	5.9	3.6	2.9	11 286.9	8 922	16 106	3 574	77 812	627 120	59 631	8 252
Darke	165.9	3 160	56.8	4.8	5.9	4.6	7.2	76.5	1 457	102	132	2 146	25 240	45 939	4 558
Defiance	164.9	4 263	38.1	17.8	4.2	3.1	5.7	96.2	2 486	85	97	1 940	18 960	47 692	4 717
Delaware	580.7	3 207	51.8	3.6	4.6	2.2	6.9	734.5	4 057	222	495	7 264	89 940	101 616	16 483
Erie	360.9	4 724	52.1	2.5	5.2	3.9	4.2	232.7	3 046	287	191	5 041	39 770	49 308	5 588
Fairfield	537.8	3 647	55.2	5.3	4.9	3.9	3.7	791.1	5 364	232	402	6 557	69 870	57 337	6 361
Fayette	143.4	4 966	32.8	26.1	3.8	3.7	4.5	83.9	2 906	51	72	1 688	13 380	41 750	4 098
Franklin	6 511.1	5 446	38.1	3.0	6.3	6.0	4.2	8 029.0	6 716	12 811	3 655	117 393	612 920	58 651	7 603
Fulton	197.2	4 637	67.2	2.5	4.2	2.4	4.5	104.1	2 450	94	108	2 514	21 140	50 029	4 999
Gallia	123.5	4 023	57.7	2.3	5.6	5.4	6.2	74.2	2 416	73	75	1 642	12 050	45 699	4 525
Geauga	314.3	3 355	48.5	9.3	6.8	2.6	8.8	302.2	3 225	102	239	3 995	47 460	86 331	13 931
Greene	655.1	4 004	53.0	4.0	6.4	4.0	4.8	524.5	3 206	14 018	3 127	10 995	75 670	64 535	8 183
Guernsey	125.8	3 159	48.1	3.5	4.9	8.6	7.9	38.7	973	114	100	2 200	18 260	47 871	5 618
Hamilton	4 409.2	5 497	37.9	6.8	6.8	4.4	3.4	5 717.7	7 129	8 528	2 125	48 040	401 250	66 658	9 829
Hancock	295.5	3 905	53.3	7.9	3.8	2.7	4.3	240.6	3 180	152	190	3 144	37 220	57 165	7 117
Hardin	110.3	3 489	43.3	1.9	7.5	10.6	8.3	59.1	1 869	71	76	1 394	13 230	43 441	3 954
Harrison	46.0	2 927	48.6	1.1	3.7	9.2	14.1	4.8	305	49	39	723	6 690	52 090	5 861
Henry	116.8	4 166	57.4	9.8	4.3	0.3	7.0	51.0	1 819	71	71	1 988	14 130	49 637	5 037
Highland	157.5	3 663	45.3	24.8	5.4	4.0	5.4	55.6	1 293	95	109	2 201	18 250	40 251	3 315
Hocking	118.1	4 036	34.2	34.9	4.9	5.2	5.5	21.9	748	47	72	1 727	12 240	42 740	3 792
Holmes	122.6	2 851	35.9	29.5	3.5	5.1	8.0	35.7	830	63	111	1 532	17 100	48 757	5 137
Huron	227.6	3 839	59.2	1.8	3.8	5.5	5.6	177.4	2 992	142	149	2 348	28 820	44 743	4 214
Jackson	103.5	3 142	55.6	4.5	4.9	6.5	7.1	74.9	2 274	70	83	1 467	13 490	41 996	3 580
Jefferson	274.2	4 010	48.3	6.7	5.3	3.8	7.4	154.1	2 253	165	167	3 129	30 740	46 833	4 944
Knox	190.4	3 137	48.2	3.8	2.8	3.7	12.6	94.4	1 554	105	148	2 624	27 080	50 492	5 251
Lake	960.6	4 184	51.1	7.4	6.8	2.5	5.5	411.1	1 790	461	606	11 060	122 420	56 365	6 723
Lawrence	214.4	3 452	60.9	5.7	3.5	4.9	4.0	51.1	822	130	155	3 003	25 410	45 134	4 365
Licking	578.6	3 453	56.4	0.8	6.3	6.5	4.5	386.9	2 309	363	437	7 620	80 880	54 512	6 046
Logan	185.1	4 071	51.9	5.6	4.3	4.6	6.6	117.8	2 592	116	118	2 032	22 400	48 403	5 068
Lorain	1 206.9	4 003	55.2	4.3	5.8	3.9	4.7	1 730.7	5 741	1 105	783	14 230	147 360	54 761	6 310
Lucas	1 896.4	4 330	37.6	9.4	7.1	4.9	3.8	2 289.2	5 226	1 849	1 184	28 741	203 380	51 715	6 143
Madison	152.8	3 549	60.2	4.9	4.6	3.8	5.7	137.1	3 184	75	100	3 066	18 990	54 824	6 225
Mahoning	851.8	3 622	47.9	5.8	7.8	3.8	4.3	531.9	2 262	1 177	588	13 572	112 550	49 232	5 788
Marion	232.6	3 512	58.7	1.2	4.1	2.2	4.0	316.2	4 773	110	178	3 874	28 010	43 758	4 147
Medina	715.8	4 121	54.5	3.6	4.6	2.1	11.9	431.2	2 483	324	479	6 765	90 420	66 137	8 496
Meigs	70.8	3 002	53.3	2.8	2.8	10.1	10.2	25.4	1 075	58	59	1 067	9 120	41 814	3 499
Mercer	196.0	4 794	46.2	26.1	3.3	3.1	7.9	89.2	2 183	100	104	2 693	20 950	54 909	6 559
Miami	405.1	3 930	56.7	3.4	6.0	3.1	5.3	280.3	2 720	184	266	4 606	51 000	54 055	5 982
Monroe	83.7	5 754	66.8	2.8	2.6	8.8	8.9	2.9	200	47	37	748	6 400	69 711	10 103
Montgomery	2 652.7	4 965	44.5	3.0	6.4	8.6	5.3	2 338.6	4 377	4 241	3 765	26 960	255 760	51 140	5 890
Morgan	43.8	2 938	48.1	4.6	5.2	8.6	11.1	11.3	760	40	37	630	5 990	39 818	3 173
Morrow	139.5	3 994	47.5	22.8	1.4	3.0	5.3	60.5	1 733	45	89	1 601	15 410	46 571	4 239
Muskingum	340.0	3 956	54.4	3.3	4.9	6.1	6.4	122.4	1 424	216	217	5 117	39 390	48 410	5 326
Noble	36.8	2 523	50.8	2.9	4.1	7.6	14.3	3.0	208	21	30	940	5 350	63 831	9 387

1. Based on the resident population estimated as of July 1 of the year shown.

Table B. States and Counties — **Land Area and Population**

					Population, 2016			Population and population characteristics, 2016									
								Race alone or in combination, not Hispanic or Latino (percent)					Age (percent)					
STATE/ County code	CBSA code[1]	County type[2]	STATE County	Land area,[3] (sq mi) 2016	Total persons 2016	Rank	Per square mile	White	Black	American Indian, Alaska Native	Asian and Pacific Islander	Percent Hispanic or Latino[4]	Under 5 years	5 to 17 years	18 to 24 years	25 to 34 years	35 to 44 years	45 to 54 years
				1	2	3	4	5	6	7	8	9	10	11	12	13	14	15
			OHIO—Cont'd															
39 123	38840	4	Ottawa	254.9	40 636	1 161	159.4	93.6	1.5	0.5	0.6	4.9	4.4	14.4	6.7	9.5	10.1	13.6
39 125	...	6	Paulding	416.4	18 865	1 880	45.3	93.6	1.5	0.7	0.6	4.8	5.8	17.8	7.9	11.1	11.3	13.5
39 127	18140	1	Perry	408.0	35 927	1 274	88.1	98.1	0.9	1.1	0.4	0.8	6.2	17.7	7.8	11.9	12.1	14.2
39 129	18140	1	Pickaway	501.2	57 565	893	114.9	94.1	4.5	0.7	0.8	1.4	5.5	16.3	9.1	13.2	13.6	14.4
39 131	...	7	Pike	440.3	28 160	1 483	64.0	96.8	1.8	1.4	0.7	1.0	6.1	18.0	7.5	11.6	12.3	13.8
39 133	10420	2	Portage	487.4	161 921	397	332.2	91.6	5.4	0.7	2.6	1.7	4.7	14.3	16.5	11.3	10.6	13.3
39 135	...	6	Preble	424.2	41 247	1 146	97.2	97.5	1.1	0.8	1.0	0.8	5.3	17.5	7.3	11.2	11.8	13.8
39 137	...	6	Putnam	482.5	34 056	1 325	70.6	93.1	0.7	0.3	0.4	6.1	6.8	18.8	8.2	11.0	11.2	13.2
39 139	31900	3	Richland	495.3	121 107	515	244.5	87.7	10.7	0.7	1.1	1.8	5.7	15.9	8.4	12.3	11.8	12.9
39 141	17060	4	Ross	689.2	77 000	718	111.7	92.0	7.2	1.1	0.9	1.2	5.6	15.8	7.9	12.5	13.2	14.8
39 143	23380	4	Sandusky	408.5	59 330	873	145.2	86.5	4.2	0.6	0.7	9.8	5.5	17.3	7.8	11.3	11.8	13.5
39 145	39020	4	Scioto	610.2	76 088	725	124.7	95.2	3.4	1.3	0.6	1.3	5.7	16.1	8.8	12.9	12.3	13.1
39 147	45660	4	Seneca	551.0	55 353	914	100.5	91.6	3.5	0.6	0.9	5.0	5.3	16.9	10.5	11.4	11.6	12.6
39 149	43380	4	Shelby	407.7	48 623	1 008	119.3	94.9	3.5	0.6	1.4	1.5	6.5	19.0	8.3	11.1	11.7	13.9
39 151	15940	2	Stark	575.3	373 612	184	649.4	89.1	9.4	0.8	1.3	2.0	5.6	16.1	8.7	11.8	11.3	13.4
39 153	10420	2	Summit	412.8	540 300	124	1 308.9	79.7	16.1	0.8	3.9	2.0	5.7	15.6	8.7	13.1	11.6	13.8
39 155	49660	2	Trumbull	618.3	201 825	326	326.4	89.1	9.6	0.7	0.9	1.7	5.2	15.5	7.9	11.2	11.1	13.3
39 157	35420	4	Tuscarawas	567.4	92 420	633	162.9	95.9	1.4	0.6	0.7	2.6	6.1	16.6	7.7	11.7	11.6	13.0
39 159	18140	1	Union	431.7	55 457	912	128.5	91.7	3.2	0.6	4.3	1.6	6.0	18.8	8.2	13.0	14.9	15.3
39 161	46780	6	Van Wert	409.2	28 362	1 474	69.3	95.4	1.8	0.5	0.6	3.1	6.0	17.3	8.0	11.2	11.6	13.0
39 163	...	8	Vinton	412.4	12 921	2 231	31.3	97.8	1.0	1.2	0.5	0.9	5.0	17.4	7.9	10.9	12.7	14.0
39 165	17140	1	Warren	401.3	227 063	287	565.8	88.3	4.1	0.5	5.9	2.7	5.8	19.4	7.9	11.1	13.6	15.5
39 167	31930	4	Washington	632.0	60 610	862	95.9	96.7	1.9	1.0	1.0	1.1	5.0	14.8	8.7	11.2	11.3	13.2
39 169	49300	4	Wayne	554.9	116 470	526	209.9	95.2	2.4	0.6	1.4	1.9	6.7	17.7	10.0	11.7	11.0	12.4
39 171	...	6	Williams	421.0	37 017	1 251	87.9	93.7	1.6	0.6	0.8	4.4	5.8	17.0	7.8	11.4	11.7	13.0
39 173	45780	2	Wood	617.2	130 219	485	211.0	89.9	3.3	0.6	2.2	5.5	5.4	15.1	17.5	12.1	11.1	11.7
39 175	...	7	Wyandot	406.9	22 118	1 724	54.4	96.1	0.7	0.5	0.8	2.7	5.9	17.0	7.7	11.1	12.1	13.2
40 000	...	0	OKLAHOMA	68 596.4	3 923 561	X	57.2	71.2	8.9	12.4	3.0	10.3	6.8	17.7	9.8	13.9	12.2	12.1
40 001	...	6	Adair	573.5	22 098	1 725	38.5	50.3	1.1	51.6	0.9	6.4	7.4	19.4	8.8	11.9	12.1	13.0
40 003	...	9	Alfalfa	866.5	5 827	2 767	6.7	85.9	5.3	5.3	0.6	5.4	5.7	14.5	6.3	10.9	15.2	16.0
40 005	...	9	Atoka	975.5	13 810	2 180	14.2	77.8	5.0	19.9	1.0	3.6	6.4	16.6	8.1	12.9	12.0	12.4
40 007	...	9	Beaver	1 814.7	5 382	2 809	3.0	75.5	1.2	2.4	0.6	22.2	6.0	20.1	7.6	10.4	11.3	12.4
40 009	21120	7	Beckham	901.8	22 519	1 709	25.0	78.2	4.6	4.1	1.1	14.2	7.4	17.6	8.9	15.9	12.7	11.9
40 011	...	6	Blaine	928.4	9 643	2 457	10.4	77.2	4.7	11.3	0.8	10.3	7.9	19.1	7.2	10.8	10.2	11.7
40 013	20460	6	Bryan	904.5	45 573	1 061	50.4	78.4	2.6	19.4	1.0	5.7	6.7	16.9	9.6	14.1	11.5	11.9
40 015	...	6	Caddo	1 278.3	29 557	1 442	23.1	61.9	4.1	26.5	0.8	12.2	7.1	18.5	8.4	13.5	11.6	12.6
40 017	36420	1	Canadian	896.6	136 532	465	152.3	80.8	3.9	7.2	4.0	8.4	7.0	19.3	7.6	14.8	14.2	12.8
40 019	11620	5	Carter	822.2	48 556	1 010	59.1	75.7	8.5	13.5	1.5	7.0	6.9	18.5	8.2	12.5	12.3	12.4
40 021	45140	6	Cherokee	749.4	48 700	1 007	65.0	56.8	2.2	42.3	1.0	6.9	5.9	16.6	15.4	12.1	11.0	11.2
40 023	...	7	Choctaw	770.4	14 885	2 108	19.3	67.4	12.5	21.9	0.9	4.0	6.6	17.3	7.3	11.5	10.8	11.9
40 025	...	9	Cimarron	1 834.8	2 162	3 034	1.2	74.9	1.5	2.8	0.7	22.8	6.8	17.5	6.3	10.0	9.2	12.5
40 027	36420	1	Cleveland	538.8	278 655	245	517.2	77.3	6.3	7.8	5.7	8.4	5.7	14.6	15.1	12.7	11.6	11.6
40 029	...	9	Coal	516.7	5 651	2 787	10.9	77.5	1.8	23.8	0.7	4.4	5.7	17.7	7.8	11.0	11.3	11.6
40 031	30020	3	Comanche	1 069.3	122 136	513	114.2	61.4	19.5	7.9	5.0	12.7	7.2	16.8	12.8	16.6	12.2	11.4
40 033	30020	3	Cotton	632.7	5 941	2 758	9.4	80.4	3.2	12.8	1.0	7.7	5.9	17.0	8.1	11.2	10.9	13.6
40 035	...	6	Craig	761.4	14 625	2 124	19.2	72.0	4.3	27.8	1.3	3.5	6.0	16.3	8.0	11.5	11.5	13.7
40 037	46140	2	Creek	950.2	71 312	759	75.0	82.8	3.4	15.6	1.0	4.0	6.2	17.8	8.0	11.7	12.0	13.2
40 039	48220	7	Custer	988.8	29 293	1 451	29.6	73.9	3.7	8.4	1.7	17.5	7.7	17.3	16.7	13.7	10.4	9.9
40 041	...	6	Delaware	738.2	41 598	1 137	56.4	71.5	0.8	30.3	1.4	3.8	5.0	15.5	7.3	9.9	10.3	12.7
40 043	...	9	Dewey	999.5	4 819	2 846	4.8	85.6	1.4	7.9	1.3	7.2	6.8	19.1	7.4	11.1	10.9	11.9
40 045	...	9	Ellis	1 231.5	4 080	2 897	3.3	89.2	1.4	3.7	0.4	7.4	6.0	17.5	7.9	9.3	12.0	11.3
40 047	21420	5	Garfield	1 058.5	62 603	843	59.1	78.1	4.3	4.2	4.6	12.5	7.5	18.3	8.7	14.2	11.6	11.5
40 049	...	6	Garvin	802.1	27 838	1 496	34.7	80.7	3.2	11.9	0.9	8.3	7.1	18.3	7.6	12.5	12.1	11.9
40 051	36420	1	Grady	1 100.5	54 655	923	49.7	85.7	3.2	9.1	0.9	5.7	5.9	18.3	8.2	12.4	12.6	13.4
40 053	...	9	Grant	1 000.9	4 465	2 865	4.5	90.9	2.4	3.9	0.6	4.9	5.6	18.8	6.4	11.2	9.9	12.4
40 055	...	7	Greer	639.3	5 998	2 750	9.4	77.5	9.0	4.5	0.6	11.4	5.8	14.4	8.2	15.9	13.3	13.2
40 057	...	9	Harmon	537.2	2 704	2 989	5.0	60.7	9.6	3.4	1.5	28.6	6.8	17.7	7.4	11.9	10.7	12.2
40 059	...	9	Harper	1 039.0	3 717	2 921	3.6	75.8	0.8	2.0	0.5	22.7	6.8	19.4	7.2	10.9	10.9	11.8
40 061	...	6	Haskell	576.5	12 747	2 246	22.1	78.1	1.3	22.5	1.2	4.1	6.7	17.3	7.6	11.1	11.2	12.3
40 063	...	7	Hughes	804.6	13 566	2 193	16.9	69.9	6.6	24.4	0.8	5.2	5.4	15.9	8.6	13.7	12.1	12.6
40 065	11060	7	Jackson	802.7	25 497	1 585	31.8	66.2	8.1	3.3	2.3	23.3	8.0	17.7	10.2	15.3	11.6	11.1
40 067	...	8	Jefferson	758.8	6 230	2 734	8.2	82.5	2.0	8.6	1.0	10.1	7.2	16.8	7.5	10.9	10.9	12.2
40 069	...	9	Johnston	642.9	11 087	2 348	17.2	77.2	3.1	21.3	1.1	5.2	6.6	17.6	9.1	11.8	11.0	12.4
40 071	38620	5	Kay	919.7	44 943	1 075	48.9	79.9	3.0	13.4	1.2	7.6	6.9	18.2	8.8	11.8	11.1	11.5
40 073	...	6	Kingfisher	898.2	15 638	2 064	17.4	79.3	1.8	5.5	0.6	15.6	7.1	20.3	7.9	11.5	12.0	12.5

1. CBSA = Core Based Statistical Area. See Appendix A for explanation. See Appendix B for list of metropolitan areas with component counties. Service of USDA Rural-Urban Continuum Codes. See Appendix A for definition. 3. Dry land or land partially or temporarily covered by water. 2. County type code from the Economic Research 4. May be of any race.

Table B. States and Counties — **Population and Households**

STATE County	55 to 64 years (16)	65 to 74 years (17)	75 years and over (18)	Percent female (19)	Total persons 2000 (20)	2010 (21)	Percent change 2000–2010 (22)	2010–2016 (23)	Births (24)	Deaths (25)	Net migration (26)	Number (27)	Persons per household (28)	Family households (29)	Female family householder[1] (30)	One person (31)
OHIO—Cont'd																
Ottawa	17.5	14.2	9.5	50.5	40 985	41 434	1.1	-1.9	2 179	3 001	-21	17 334	2.33	69.4	9.8	26.3
Paulding	14.8	10.5	7.3	50.2	20 293	19 616	-3.3	-3.8	1 377	1 184	-931	7 699	2.48	68.9	7.9	27.3
Perry	14.5	9.8	5.7	49.9	34 078	36 039	5.8	-0.3	2 685	2 222	-502	13 780	2.59	73.0	12.1	22.6
Pickaway	12.9	8.7	6.3	47.2	52 727	55 678	5.6	3.4	3 787	3 210	1 327	19 460	2.68	72.8	11.2	22.7
Pike	14.0	9.5	7.2	50.1	27 695	28 702	3.6	-1.9	2 194	2 081	-596	10 940	2.55	66.3	13.4	28.5
Portage	13.9	9.3	6.2	50.9	152 061	161 421	6.2	0.3	9 249	8 520	40	61 055	2.54	65.5	11.4	25.8
Preble	14.7	10.8	7.5	50.4	42 337	42 270	-0.2	-2.4	2 729	2 818	-861	16 124	2.56	70.8	10.4	24.6
Putnam	14.4	8.9	7.5	50.0	34 726	34 497	-0.7	-1.3	2 885	1 914	-1 422	13 049	2.60	73.0	5.7	23.3
Richland	14.1	10.4	8.4	49.1	128 852	124 475	-3.4	-2.7	8 612	8 475	-3 411	48 103	2.40	63.3	12.1	31.7
Ross	14.4	9.4	6.5	47.5	73 345	78 062	6.4	-1.4	5 323	5 047	-1 209	28 269	2.52	69.4	13.7	25.7
Sandusky	14.9	10.0	7.8	50.6	61 792	60 946	-1.4	-2.7	4 109	3 889	-1 755	23 626	2.49	67.1	12.1	27.8
Scioto	13.8	9.8	7.6	50.6	79 195	79 499	0.4	-4.3	5 467	5 867	-2 902	29 700	2.50	62.9	11.5	30.8
Seneca	14.4	9.7	7.6	50.1	58 683	56 742	-3.3	-2.4	3 612	3 638	-1 336	21 538	2.45	67.0	11.3	27.8
Shelby	13.9	9.0	6.6	49.8	47 910	49 420	3.2	-1.6	3 859	2 662	-2 008	18 537	2.62	72.2	10.5	23.2
Stark	14.6	10.4	8.1	51.5	378 098	375 592	-0.7	-0.5	26 002	25 251	-1 995	150 385	2.43	65.7	12.3	29.0
Summit	14.5	9.7	7.3	51.5	542 899	541 782	-0.2	-0.3	38 424	35 041	-3 879	220 902	2.41	62.6	13.3	31.5
Trumbull	15.3	11.5	8.9	51.2	225 116	210 318	-6.6	-4.0	13 035	15 567	-5 552	86 828	2.33	63.8	13.2	31.8
Tuscarawas	14.5	10.3	8.4	50.6	90 914	92 582	1.8	-0.2	6 963	6 218	-827	36 713	2.49	68.8	10.8	26.1
Union	12.0	7.1	4.6	52.2	40 909	52 267	27.8	6.1	3 844	2 107	1 375	18 431	2.73	75.0	8.6	21.1
Van Wert	14.3	10.2	8.5	50.9	29 659	28 744	-3.1	-1.3	2 048	1 921	-566	11 355	2.49	69.1	9.5	26.3
Vinton	15.6	10.1	6.4	49.9	12 806	13 430	4.9	-3.8	877	905	-451	4 992	2.63	69.4	11.1	25.9
Warren	12.9	8.3	5.6	49.8	158 383	212 868	34.4	6.7	15 106	9 935	8 699	78 359	2.73	75.2	7.7	20.3
Washington	15.5	11.5	8.8	50.8	63 251	61 778	-2.3	-1.9	3 755	4 468	-319	25 064	2.38	65.4	9.9	29.7
Wayne	13.5	9.6	7.4	50.4	111 564	114 514	2.6	1.7	9 549	6 708	-819	42 910	2.60	70.9	9.1	25.3
Williams	14.8	10.0	8.4	50.5	39 188	37 650	-3.9	-1.7	2 655	2 404	-874	15 150	2.39	64.8	9.7	29.4
Wood	12.4	8.6	6.3	50.6	121 065	125 488	3.7	3.8	8 531	6 452	2 379	50 091	2.44	61.9	8.7	28.8
Wyandot	14.3	10.2	8.6	50.5	22 908	22 615	-1.3	-2.2	1 616	1 486	-617	9 327	2.38	66.9	9.8	25.7
OKLAHOMA	12.4	8.7	6.3	50.5	3 450 654	3 751 615	8.7	4.6	331 103	238 568	78 417	1 455 321	2.57	66.4	12.4	28.1
Adair	12.2	9.2	6.0	50.1	21 038	22 683	7.8	-2.6	1 910	1 491	-963	7 968	2.78	74.2	16.1	22.2
Alfalfa	13.6	9.4	8.3	40.1	6 105	5 642	-7.6	3.3	360	409	266	2 072	2.28	65.6	6.9	28.1
Atoka	13.3	10.9	7.3	47.9	13 879	14 183	2.2	-2.6	1 038	890	-462	5 258	2.37	71.3	14.4	25.0
Beaver	14.0	10.1	8.0	49.9	5 857	5 636	-3.8	-4.5	374	282	-336	2 017	2.70	74.6	7.2	23.6
Beckham	12.0	7.6	5.9	46.2	19 799	22 119	11.7	1.8	2 278	1 521	-398	7 535	2.87	68.6	13.4	24.1
Blaine	14.3	10.1	8.6	50.8	11 976	11 943	-0.3	-19.3	987	748	-2 673	3 580	2.25	64.7	12.0	31.0
Bryan	11.9	10.2	7.3	51.1	36 534	42 416	16.1	7.4	3 659	2 962	2 404	16 632	2.58	63.9	12.0	30.3
Caddo	12.3	9.2	6.8	47.6	30 150	29 600	-1.8	-0.1	2 625	2 216	-392	10 202	2.77	68.2	14.0	27.4
Canadian	11.7	7.7	4.8	50.3	87 697	115 541	31.8	18.2	10 591	5 579	15 520	43 063	2.88	73.9	10.6	22.0
Carter	13.1	9.2	7.1	51.4	45 621	47 726	4.6	1.7	4 133	3 903	575	17 867	2.67	65.7	11.8	30.4
Cherokee	11.9	9.5	6.4	50.8	42 521	46 985	10.5	3.7	3 739	3 064	1 022	16 324	2.81	65.4	12.9	29.2
Choctaw	14.7	11.7	8.3	51.6	15 342	15 205	-0.9	-2.1	1 194	1 299	-185	5 924	2.52	62.9	16.7	33.6
Cimarron	13.8	12.5	11.5	48.7	3 148	2 475	-21.4	-12.6	157	162	-324	1 017	2.28	65.3	9.2	31.9
Cleveland	11.3	7.7	5.0	50.1	208 016	255 761	23.0	9.0	19 193	11 763	14 861	99 276	2.59	66.2	11.1	25.9
Coal	14.4	11.3	9.1	50.9	6 031	5 925	-1.8	-4.6	387	504	-184	2 288	2.51	70.2	14.0	26.9
Comanche	11.1	6.8	5.1	48.2	114 996	124 098	7.9	-1.6	12 295	6 231	-8 043	43 240	2.69	65.4	14.7	29.0
Cotton	14.5	10.8	7.9	50.1	6 614	6 193	-6.4	-4.1	430	500	-180	2 429	2.48	71.8	11.2	24.6
Craig	13.4	11.2	8.6	48.9	14 950	15 025	0.5	-2.7	1 079	1 309	-100	5 418	2.52	67.6	11.6	29.4
Creek	13.7	10.2	7.3	50.5	67 367	69 967	3.9	1.9	5 465	5 253	1 077	26 204	2.67	71.1	11.3	25.1
Custer	10.8	7.2	6.4	50.0	26 142	27 469	5.1	6.6	2 914	1 804	697	10 364	2.63	68.8	10.4	22.8
Delaware	15.2	14.7	9.3	50.6	37 077	41 489	11.9	0.3	2 423	3 200	950	16 561	2.47	68.1	10.7	27.7
Dewey	13.3	10.6	8.8	50.9	4 743	4 810	1.4	0.2	359	439	88	1 851	2.57	69.2	5.5	27.2
Ellis	15.4	11.2	9.4	51.0	4 075	4 151	1.9	-1.7	287	334	-32	1 710	2.38	65.9	8.1	32.2
Garfield	12.4	8.4	7.3	49.9	57 813	60 580	4.8	3.3	6 061	4 255	306	23 937	2.52	70.6	11.5	26.0
Garvin	13.4	9.5	7.6	50.3	27 210	27 576	1.3	1.0	2 391	2 339	284	10 531	2.57	66.0	10.0	30.2
Grady	13.9	9.1	6.2	50.1	45 516	52 430	15.2	4.2	3 811	3 325	1 807	19 589	2.70	73.1	10.2	23.1
Grant	14.5	10.3	10.9	50.0	5 144	4 527	-12.0	-1.4	316	383	11	1 968	2.26	67.5	8.5	29.6
Greer	11.6	8.4	9.3	42.8	6 061	6 239	2.9	-3.9	444	482	-202	2 186	2.30	61.7	9.3	35.0
Harmon	13.1	10.3	9.9	51.5	3 283	2 922	-11.0	-7.5	209	216	-215	1 174	2.35	69.9	13.6	26.8
Harper	15.1	9.0	9.0	49.9	3 562	3 685	3.5	0.9	313	294	14	1 444	2.57	67.9	6.0	30.0
Haskell	13.5	11.9	8.4	50.0	11 792	12 769	8.3	-0.2	976	919	-26	4 903	2.60	68.9	11.3	26.4
Hughes	12.5	10.5	8.7	46.3	14 154	14 003	-1.1	-3.1	900	1 163	-190	4 454	2.70	67.0	11.7	30.3
Jackson	11.8	7.9	6.4	49.9	28 439	26 446	-7.0	-3.6	2 681	1 545	-2 093	10 220	2.48	65.5	11.6	29.7
Jefferson	14.6	11.5	8.5	49.5	6 818	6 472	-5.1	-3.7	458	593	-104	2 471	2.50	66.2	9.8	30.9
Johnston	13.1	10.7	7.7	50.4	10 513	10 957	4.2	1.2	832	881	178	4 164	2.58	65.3	13.4	32.2
Kay	12.9	10.2	8.5	50.4	48 080	46 562	-3.2	-3.5	3 886	3 546	-1 859	18 115	2.46	63.8	12.0	31.6
Kingfisher	13.1	8.2	7.4	50.0	13 926	15 029	7.9	4.1	1 315	920	215	5 741	2.64	72.9	10.1	24.6

1. No spouse present.

STATE County	Persons in group quarters, 2016	Daytime population, 2011–2015 Number	Daytime population, 2011–2015 Employ-ment/ resi-dence ratio	Births, 2016 Total	Births, 2016 Rate[1]	Deaths, 2016 Number	Deaths, 2016 Rate[1]	Persons under 65 with no health insurance, 2015 Number	Persons under 65 with no health insurance, 2015 Percent	Medicare, 2015 Total Beneficiaries	Medicare, 2015 Enrolled in Original Medicare	Medicare, 2015 Enrolled in Medicare Advantage	Serious crimes known to police,[2] 2014 Total Number	Serious crimes known to police,[2] 2014 Total Rate[3]
	32	33	34	35	36	37	38	39	40	41	42	43	44	45
OHIO—Cont'd														
Ottawa	495	37 019	0.78	358	8.8	520	12.8	1 967	6.3	10 457	6 756	3 701	564	1 637
Paulding	85	15 776	0.60	219	11.6	193	10.2	1 247	8.0	3 649	2 615	1 034	184	978
Perry	307	29 137	0.52	428	11.9	382	10.6	2 549	8.4	7 456	4 969	2 487	594	1 707
Pickaway	4 894	48 690	0.68	614	10.7	567	9.8	2 878	6.5	9 360	4 475	4 885	1 493	2 642
Pike	496	28 951	1.06	355	12.6	369	13.1	2 183	9.4	5 022	3 635	1 387	360	1 271
Portage	7 891	144 068	0.77	1 506	9.3	1 404	8.7	9 019	6.9	25 973	12 795	13 178	2 794	1 831
Preble	386	35 138	0.65	428	10.4	434	10.5	2 785	8.3	8 044	4 534	3 510	420	1 299
Putnam	303	28 705	0.68	465	13.7	327	9.6	1 682	5.9	6 115	4 615	1 500	250	767
Richland	7 386	124 114	1.04	1 319	10.9	1 348	11.1	7 466	8.0	27 057	19 561	7 496	5 689	4 880
Ross	5 710	77 344	1.00	893	11.6	818	10.6	4 533	7.6	16 334	10 244	6 090	3 239	4 154
Sandusky	902	59 523	0.98	616	10.4	608	10.2	3 229	6.6	10 700	7 420	3 280	1 339	2 453
Scioto	3 291	75 898	0.92	816	10.7	912	12.0	4 906	8.1	16 456	12 527	3 929	2 815	3 613
Seneca	2 547	50 535	0.78	567	10.2	568	10.3	3 248	7.4	12 288	9 350	2 938	637	1 491
Shelby	589	53 394	1.19	619	12.7	427	8.8	2 591	6.3	7 929	5 341	2 588	1 164	2 414
Stark	9 007	367 882	0.96	4 175	11.2	4 035	10.8	22 386	7.4	82 772	36 422	46 350	11 219	3 272
Summit	10 357	560 398	1.07	6 135	11.4	5 789	10.7	33 505	7.5	98 188	43 250	54 938	16 807	3 362
Trumbull	3 974	197 728	0.90	2 035	10.1	2 487	12.3	13 492	8.4	46 446	22 361	24 085	5 045	2 681
Tuscarawas	1 251	87 556	0.88	1 123	12.2	1 010	10.9	6 796	9.0	19 232	10 452	8 780	714	775
Union	2 959	60 382	1.28	633	11.4	346	6.2	2 570	5.7	5 689	2 943	2 746	508	948
Van Wert	396	26 893	0.87	341	12.0	305	10.8	1 524	6.6	5 079	3 589	1 490	507	1 782
Vinton	68	10 788	0.50	128	9.9	155	12.0	1 006	9.3	2 280	1 603	677	229	1 727
Warren	5 825	204 061	0.85	2 358	10.4	1 806	8.0	9 184	4.8	29 151	15 383	13 768	2 652	1 290
Washington	1 562	61 217	0.99	562	9.3	724	11.9	3 673	7.7	14 411	11 113	3 298	687	1 131
Wayne	3 839	112 652	0.95	1 523	13.1	1 127	9.7	9 714	10.4	21 923	11 509	10 414	1 930	1 775
Williams	990	37 781	1.02	413	11.2	393	10.6	2 151	7.2	7 781	5 171	2 610	NA	NA
Wood	6 855	131 469	1.04	1 388	10.7	1 074	8.2	6 055	5.8	20 683	11 329	9 354	1 944	1 635
Wyandot	251	20 281	0.80	250	11.3	248	11.2	1 390	7.7	4 712	3 329	1 383	159	736
OKLAHOMA	109 868	3 842 100	1.00	53 175	13.6	39 588	10.1	522 022	16.1	659 820	535 844	123 976	131 726	3 397
Adair	92	20 311	0.77	329	14.9	274	12.4	4 186	22.6	4 026	3 824	202	458	2 074
Alfalfa	1 054	5 960	1.10	59	10.1	48	8.2	551	14.3	1 112	1 064	48	51	863
Atoka	750	13 067	0.81	166	12.0	119	8.6	2 138	20.3	2 594	2 415	179	250	1 805
Beaver	43	5 146	0.85	67	12.4	51	9.5	799	18.0	883	863	20	82	1 477
Beckham	1 925	25 918	1.28	348	15.5	270	12.0	2 876	15.2	3 103	2 910	193	593	2 463
Blaine	107	10 197	1.12	160	16.6	109	11.3	1 351	16.9	2 045	1 927	118	153	1 580
Bryan	1 134	42 916	0.94	600	13.2	525	11.5	6 287	17.4	8 804	8 117	687	1 448	3 240
Caddo	1 933	27 195	0.79	404	13.7	382	12.9	4 637	20.4	5 804	5 455	349	596	2 013
Canadian	2 486	99 314	0.56	1 805	13.2	974	7.1	12 946	11.2	16 176	11 658	4 518	4 259	3 306
Carter	913	51 853	1.17	685	14.1	667	13.7	6 801	16.8	10 371	9 431	940	2 661	5 457
Cherokee	2 009	45 783	0.88	567	11.6	499	10.2	7 763	19.8	7 598	6 818	780	1 382	2 862
Choctaw	172	14 893	0.96	185	12.4	210	14.1	2 364	19.9	3 595	3 326	269	385	2 564
Cimarron	7	2 227	0.90	23	10.6	15	6.9	413	24.6	553	541	12	30	1 300
Cleveland	10 545	224 974	0.67	3 098	11.1	2 008	7.2	29 380	12.7	29 338	23 576	5 762	9 452	3 465
Coal	61	5 243	0.74	55	9.7	79	14.0	910	20.5	1 213	1 127	86	73	1 245
Comanche	10 328	128 465	1.05	1 838	15.0	1 072	8.8	13 764	13.7	17 422	16 305	1 117	5 745	4 598
Cotton	48	5 378	0.72	70	11.8	83	14.0	809	16.6	1 209	1 143	66	33	536
Craig	1 050	15 171	1.08	186	12.7	232	15.9	2 026	18.1	4 795	4 263	532	201	1 378
Creek	1 062	61 632	0.69	879	12.3	917	12.9	9 021	15.5	13 373	9 013	4 360	1 474	2 087
Custer	1 519	29 407	1.03	462	15.8	283	9.7	4 497	18.3	4 444	4 131	313	612	2 047
Delaware	356	37 671	0.76	398	9.6	547	13.1	6 832	21.8	8 948	7 689	1 259	466	1 126
Dewey	93	4 708	0.92	57	11.8	79	16.4	608	15.2	1 072	1 030	42	69	1 421
Ellis	46	3 907	0.88	57	14.0	54	13.2	460	13.6	854	767	87	96	2 298
Garfield	1 797	63 122	1.03	988	15.8	661	10.6	8 690	16.5	11 365	10 537	828	2 459	3 921
Garvin	317	28 740	1.12	390	14.0	335	12.0	3 801	16.7	6 257	5 684	573	683	2 501
Grady	1 079	45 591	0.66	594	10.9	504	9.2	6 583	14.5	8 419	7 182	1 237	968	1 791
Grant	73	4 375	0.93	51	11.4	53	11.9	485	13.6	971	930	41	46	1 015
Greer	1 142	5 445	0.71	76	12.7	60	10.0	636	16.3	1 212	1 179	33	44	713
Harmon	100	2 729	0.88	29	10.7	38	14.1	478	22.1	587	564	23	111	3 881
Harper	41	3 612	0.91	42	11.3	69	18.6	602	19.7	752	727	25	25	650
Haskell	78	12 281	0.87	173	13.6	144	11.3	2 200	21.6	2 970	2 674	296	85	647
Hughes	1 561	13 105	0.85	147	10.8	178	13.1	1 923	19.9	2 745	2 457	288	219	1 588
Jackson	686	26 706	1.06	396	15.5	206	8.1	3 411	16.0	3 991	3 826	165	752	2 890
Jefferson	144	5 633	0.72	69	11.1	83	13.3	979	19.9	1 534	1 409	125	73	1 135
Johnston	292	10 268	0.81	138	12.4	169	15.2	1 656	19.1	2 306	2 162	144	110	1 000
Kay	1 273	46 615	1.05	591	13.1	559	12.4	6 197	17.1	10 109	9 046	1 063	1 830	4 024
Kingfisher	155	15 056	0.97	231	14.8	129	8.2	2 221	16.9	2 687	2 455	232	215	1 401

1. Per 1,000 estimated resident population.   2. Data for serious crimes have not been adjusted for underreporting; this may affect comparability between geographic areas and over time.
3. Per 100,000 population estimated by the FBI.

Table B. States and Counties — Crime, Education, Money Income, and Poverty

STATE County	Serious crimes known to police, 2014 (cont.)[1] Rate[2] Violent	Property	Education — School enrollment and attainment, 2011–2015 Enrollment[3] Total	Percent private	Attainment[4] (percent) High school graduate or less	Bachelor's degree or more	Local government expenditures,[5] 2013–2014 Total current spending (mil dol)	Current spending per student (dollars)	Money income, 2011–2015 Per capita income[6] (dollars)	Median income (dollars)	Households Percent with income of less than $50,000	with income of $200,000 or more	Income and poverty, 2015 Median household income (dollars)	Percent below poverty level All persons	Children under 18 years	Children 5 to 17 years in families
	46	47	48	49	50	51	52	53	54	55	56	57	58	59	60	61
OHIO—Cont'd																
Ottawa	107	1 529	8 591	8.8	46.0	21.7	70.7	11 238	29 343	53 914	46.3	3.1	58 793	9.7	15.3	13.5
Paulding	27	952	4 456	12.3	60.5	12.7	35.8	11 744	23 836	45 550	55.1	2.4	49 796	10.9	17.3	15.0
Perry	124	1 583	8 804	9.4	60.5	11.0	63.4	10 873	20 302	42 017	57.9	1.1	44 738	18.8	25.9	23.2
Pickaway	124	2 518	13 519	11.5	56.4	17.1	94.7	10 241	24 921	57 439	43.2	2.3	58 472	12.4	17.6	15.4
Pike	67	1 204	6 495	4.7	64.1	11.8	52.3	10 982	20 790	40 283	59.2	1.2	39 851	21.4	33.3	30.5
Portage	111	1 720	47 567	10.2	46.4	26.0	249.9	11 087	26 042	52 552	47.4	2.6	53 609	13.6	16.1	13.3
Preble	68	1 231	10 138	9.2	57.9	11.8	65.0	10 166	23 414	47 818	52.1	1.4	51 042	12.7	18.9	16.0
Putnam	64	702	8 865	13.2	50.1	19.4	62.5	10 637	26 269	60 524	39.4	2.1	60 036	7.2	8.7	7.8
Richland	218	4 662	28 303	20.1	54.5	15.7	199.9	12 135	22 367	41 877	58.0	1.6	45 273	15.1	23.4	21.4
Ross	210	3 944	17 952	9.5	58.2	14.7	125.4	11 250	21 365	43 345	55.9	2.0	45 615	17.8	25.9	23.9
Sandusky	86	2 367	14 528	14.3	53.1	14.5	91.4	10 836	23 782	47 209	52.9	1.5	49 994	12.2	18.3	15.9
Scioto	184	3 429	19 127	8.3	58.0	14.4	130.5	10 744	19 769	35 903	62.4	1.4	37 277	23.0	32.1	28.9
Seneca	147	1 344	15 047	27.1	55.5	14.2	68.8	11 746	23 020	45 444	53.4	1.5	48 617	13.6	19.8	17.4
Shelby	114	2 300	12 616	11.9	54.0	16.3	81.2	9 580	26 741	54 550	46.5	2.3	59 149	8.9	13.6	11.7
Stark	318	2 954	94 275	17.4	48.3	21.9	577.0	10 005	25 547	47 137	52.8	2.5	48 976	13.4	20.2	18.3
Summit	335	3 027	137 747	15.5	41.4	30.3	842.7	11 325	28 986	50 765	49.2	4.0	51 434	14.4	21.5	19.5
Trumbull	219	2 461	44 585	11.1	56.8	17.3	315.4	10 932	23 509	43 073	56.8	1.5	42 831	17.6	26.9	22.4
Tuscarawas	38	737	21 208	11.8	61.1	14.4	166.9	10 404	23 314	45 310	54.5	1.8	47 588	13.0	18.0	15.2
Union	50	897	14 122	13.3	44.6	26.2	93.1	9 493	28 549	67 382	37.5	4.9	76 116	7.6	8.8	7.2
Van Wert	112	1 670	6 864	15.3	57.1	15.7	54.6	11 191	24 422	48 060	51.4	1.7	51 264	11.2	15.3	14.3
Vinton	60	1 667	3 100	8.1	64.0	9.1	24.0	10 429	18 330	40 680	61.9	0.3	41 675	18.9	32.9	29.8
Warren	58	1 232	60 523	18.0	33.8	39.6	362.8	9 977	34 271	74 379	30.3	8.6	81 383	5.2	6.6	5.6
Washington	79	1 052	13 583	21.8	51.9	17.5	83.4	10 432	24 013	43 509	56.0	2.0	44 697	15.0	21.5	18.8
Wayne	107	1 668	28 561	23.8	55.9	21.2	170.9	10 954	23 695	50 383	49.5	2.0	52 717	11.3	16.9	15.3
Williams	NA	NA	8 843	15.1	56.4	13.9	56.4	10 115	22 234	42 492	57.6	1.3	49 031	12.0	17.5	15.8
Wood	66	1 569	41 828	10.6	37.3	31.1	234.9	12 758	27 477	53 577	46.7	3.2	57 390	11.7	10.9	9.8
Wyandot	79	657	5 193	10.1	58.1	14.1	32.6	9 496	24 246	47 555	51.7	1.7	51 109	8.8	11.7	10.6
OKLAHOMA	406	2 991	998 861	10.8	44.8	24.1	5 254.2	7 681	25 032	46 879	52.7	3.1	48 595	16.0	22.0	20.4
Adair	389	1 684	5 662	2.6	63.6	13.8	40.2	8 849	16 247	33 404	68.5	0.7	31 572	28.4	42.7	40.8
Alfalfa	118	745	1 084	8.5	52.4	20.2	11.3	11 919	28 233	50 156	49.7	3.7	52 551	14.6	16.3	14.9
Atoka	116	1 689	3 107	6.4	59.0	14.0	21.2	9 188	18 810	36 661	66.2	2.1	34 850	23.0	30.6	27.9
Beaver	90	1 387	1 344	3.6	55.0	20.1	12.2	11 100	26 258	52 090	47.3	3.3	59 544	11.1	14.1	12.0
Beckham	158	2 305	4 920	6.0	57.1	17.6	32.4	7 508	25 156	48 601	51.7	5.3	51 394	13.9	18.2	17.0
Blaine	165	1 415	2 093	3.7	54.0	16.3	22.5	9 579	19 576	41 972	58.1	2.0	43 540	16.3	25.3	24.7
Bryan	206	3 034	10 740	7.4	54.3	21.5	64.6	8 572	20 688	38 847	61.6	1.7	40 875	18.1	25.9	25.0
Caddo	250	1 763	7 017	2.6	56.7	15.8	45.1	8 183	20 003	40 674	58.9	1.7	43 548	21.3	27.7	25.8
Canadian	418	2 888	34 417	10.1	37.6	25.5	177.0	7 036	28 246	64 505	36.2	3.8	63 291	9.8	11.2	10.7
Carter	929	4 528	12 359	9.7	53.8	18.8	73.1	7 795	22 870	44 531	55.3	2.3	45 287	16.3	23.2	22.3
Cherokee	249	2 614	13 953	5.1	45.5	24.4	67.8	8 618	19 509	38 694	60.4	1.4	40 600	21.5	28.6	26.3
Choctaw	306	2 258	3 339	2.1	59.9	13.2	22.7	8 385	18 269	30 617	67.6	1.2	30 572	29.9	40.2	35.4
Cimarron	130	1 170	489	7.0	52.0	13.9	5.3	12 164	26 981	46 680	53.7	4.2	44 023	17.0	29.6	26.9
Cleveland	318	3 146	83 616	9.8	35.3	31.0	316.1	7 160	27 745	56 452	43.5	3.7	59 417	11.5	12.8	12.2
Coal	85	1 160	1 350	4.0	60.0	14.8	12.9	11 033	22 977	38 243	60.1	2.4	38 954	19.4	28.5	24.6
Comanche	739	3 860	33 376	6.6	43.9	20.8	168.1	7 672	23 264	46 241	53.6	2.3	46 821	15.1	20.7	20.3
Cotton	16	520	1 398	7.9	56.0	15.4	8.7	7 742	21 640	46 361	52.7	0.6	42 901	16.8	23.5	21.0
Craig	137	1 241	3 308	7.7	55.7	13.9	24.4	8 475	19 623	38 876	62.4	0.8	41 119	18.2	27.4	25.4
Creek	212	1 875	16 208	8.2	54.6	15.0	99.5	7 676	23 010	45 016	53.8	2.3	47 395	15.7	21.9	20.6
Custer	164	1 883	9 018	3.1	48.8	26.9	40.9	7 618	23 044	46 125	54.3	1.8	47 745	17.9	20.4	20.0
Delaware	143	984	8 626	8.1	52.4	16.8	54.6	8 113	21 736	37 942	61.9	2.1	38 840	20.5	32.8	29.6
Dewey	21	1 400	1 117	4.5	52.4	21.8	12.4	12 143	25 942	50 904	48.7	4.5	53 004	13.1	17.8	15.9
Ellis	215	2 082	923	5.0	49.1	22.0	12.2	13 925	28 417	50 855	49.2	4.0	57 524	11.9	17.0	14.1
Garfield	319	3 602	14 517	10.2	49.1	20.6	86.2	7 607	24 928	48 238	51.5	2.5	49 070	14.5	20.2	19.6
Garvin	205	2 296	5 670	4.1	58.9	15.2	43.2	7 910	21 644	40 524	59.5	2.4	46 139	14.2	20.3	18.2
Grady	200	1 591	13 447	6.4	50.9	17.6	66.2	7 064	24 965	52 279	48.0	3.1	53 208	13.1	17.7	15.3
Grant	66	949	971	6.8	44.8	23.5	9.5	11 942	28 552	50 250	49.6	2.5	50 729	11.4	15.4	13.5
Greer	97	616	1 207	1.8	52.7	13.1	8.2	8 097	19 552	40 125	62.3	2.9	36 495	23.7	26.6	24.3
Harmon	280	3 601	697	3.9	47.3	22.8	4.8	8 829	20 891	31 250	67.0	0.3	33 144	23.6	31.8	31.6
Harper	52	598	870	5.1	55.3	20.7	7.6	9 764	24 364	48 359	52.9	1.7	52 635	9.8	13.4	13.3
Haskell	30	616	2 905	3.3	59.9	11.5	19.2	8 070	18 858	35 252	64.1	1.0	36 888	18.1	27.7	26.1
Hughes	131	1 457	2 933	3.3	58.6	12.2	20.1	8 493	17 723	35 563	63.5	2.1	37 676	20.1	28.9	26.3
Jackson	288	2 602	6 409	6.4	44.9	19.7	38.1	7 623	21 923	41 560	58.6	1.5	44 723	17.2	24.8	24.0
Jefferson	109	1 026	1 392	4.9	60.3	11.7	11.0	9 023	19 409	33 449	66.8	0.9	36 227	19.9	30.0	29.3
Johnston	100	900	2 728	4.9	53.6	16.1	16.6	8 531	20 425	38 776	62.2	2.2	38 980	21.4	29.1	27.2
Kay	517	3 507	11 146	8.2	47.6	18.4	69.1	8 189	23 044	42 134	57.8	2.2	43 373	18.7	27.0	24.5
Kingfisher	91	1 310	3 968	9.7	48.9	19.7	29.1	8 222	27 733	60 034	41.7	2.9	59 462	10.6	13.4	12.4

1. Data for serious crimes have not been adjusted for underreporting; this may affect comparability between geographic areas and over time.   2. Per 100,000 population estimated by the FBI.
3. All persons 3 years old and over enrolled in nursery school through college.   4. Persons 25 years old and over.   5. Elementary and secondary education expenditures.
6. Based on population estimated by the American Community Survey, 2011–2015.

Table B. States and Counties — Personal Income

STATE County	Personal income, 2015										Earnings, 2015		
	Total (mil dol)	Percent change, 2014–2015	Per capita[1] Dollars	Per capita[1] Rank	Wages and salaries (mil dol)	Supplements to wages and salaries; employer contributions (mil dol) Pension and insurance	Government social insurance	Proprietors' income (mil dol)	Dividends, interest, and rent (mil dol)	Personal transfer receipts (mil dol)	Total (mil dol)	Contributions for government social insurance (mil dol) From employee and self-employed	From employer
	62	63	64	65	66	67	68	69	70	71	72	73	74
OHIO—Cont'd													
Ottawa	1 839	2.6	44 978	742	596	124	44	90	301	434	853	54	44
Paulding	683	-2.0	36 010	1 699	186	42	13	49	99	165	290	16	13
Perry	1 204	4.4	33 469	2 574	207	52	14	74	116	344	347	24	14
Pickaway	2 096	3.8	36 775	1 972	620	155	39	172	247	460	985	52	39
Pike	936	3.2	33 176	2 429	474	75	34	110	104	327	693	42	34
Portage	6 488	3.5	39 982	1 323	2 568	568	168	383	906	1 273	3 688	197	168
Preble	1 500	1.4	36 288	1 974	408	85	29	104	190	366	626	39	29
Putnam	1 481	1.0	43 512	883	468	93	34	126	209	250	721	43	34
Richland	4 331	2.7	35 588	2 086	2 024	419	148	235	629	1 168	2 825	166	148
Ross	2 628	4.4	34 061	2 413	1 278	280	91	131	319	737	1 780	100	91
Sandusky	2 254	2.9	37 765	1 698	1 096	238	83	116	278	536	1 532	89	83
Scioto	2 522	2.2	32 826	2 505	948	221	68	125	301	930	1 361	81	68
Seneca	2 091	6.6	37 592	2 025	744	158	56	201	261	520	1 159	69	56
Shelby	2 051	2.5	41 942	1 352	1 392	240	101	243	253	365	1 976	110	101
Stark	15 409	3.1	41 072	1 129	6 907	1 244	508	974	2 275	3 521	9 633	574	508
Summit	24 969	3.5	46 071	699	13 697	2 274	963	1 714	3 891	4 778	18 647	1 069	963
Trumbull	7 504	2.6	36 831	1 997	3 059	574	228	551	1 072	2 151	4 412	276	228
Tuscarawas	3 707	4.0	39 893	1 761	1 499	298	109	430	481	811	2 336	135	109
Union	2 505	5.1	46 143	888	1 887	293	129	131	290	324	2 440	134	129
Van Wert	1 044	-0.7	36 556	1 644	422	88	30	64	137	248	603	36	30
Vinton	398	2.4	30 478	2 796	86	25	5	17	45	136	133	8	5
Warren	11 572	4.5	51 553	408	4 464	710	315	599	1 486	1 424	6 087	348	315
Washington	2 356	2.5	38 548	1 578	1 199	225	88	165	346	590	1 677	100	88
Wayne	4 467	3.1	38 489	1 900	2 110	398	149	573	650	879	3 231	180	149
Williams	1 417	3.5	38 167	1 737	707	144	53	114	187	324	1 017	59	53
Wood	5 537	4.0	42 679	1 063	3 005	577	218	317	789	923	4 116	223	218
Wyandot	867	3.1	38 988	1 581	386	77	27	89	112	181	579	31	27
OKLAHOMA	178 250	1.8	45 619	X	76 876	13 040	5 803	32 364	30 499	31 253	128 083	6 554	5 803
Adair	598	3.9	27 161	3 044	162	39	13	73	75	210	287	16	13
Alfalfa	282	1.1	48 046	436	81	18	6	55	72	39	159	7	6
Atoka	419	1.2	30 372	2 645	110	24	9	66	54	134	209	12	9
Beaver	286	-1.8	52 751	226	72	14	5	99	48	36	190	6	5
Beckham	949	-9.4	39 940	739	537	76	40	192	162	157	844	44	40
Blaine	418	2.1	42 540	1 058	127	23	10	75	82	85	235	12	10
Bryan	1 393	3.5	31 039	2 646	610	109	46	101	216	402	866	53	46
Caddo	908	1.3	30 931	2 639	295	65	23	89	158	253	472	28	23
Canadian	5 812	4.0	43 573	975	1 414	234	108	500	826	797	2 256	126	108
Carter	2 124	1.2	43 630	788	1 069	183	81	240	398	450	1 573	88	81
Cherokee	1 411	2.8	29 127	2 783	557	111	41	97	231	418	807	47	41
Choctaw	469	1.6	31 298	2 590	152	33	12	53	56	174	250	15	12
Cimarron	145	8.0	65 254	209	25	5	2	71	18	22	103	2	2
Cleveland	11 724	3.3	42 716	1 064	3 464	646	262	1 056	2 101	1 792	5 428	297	262
Coal	205	2.7	36 331	1 790	41	9	3	32	31	56	85	5	3
Comanche	4 761	2.9	38 195	1 572	2 425	568	213	255	870	1 000	3 461	172	213
Cotton	236	-1.2	39 298	1 097	60	14	4	26	36	53	105	6	4
Craig	517	0.6	34 900	1 680	208	44	16	68	73	160	335	19	16
Creek	2 701	1.7	38 096	1 286	818	140	64	209	423	652	1 230	78	64
Custer	1 160	-2.6	39 014	1 037	567	100	42	140	235	196	848	45	42
Delaware	1 323	5.2	31 899	2 602	305	57	24	165	241	397	551	34	24
Dewey	218	-7.6	43 630	234	67	13	5	41	44	38	125	6	5
Ellis	267	-4.6	63 065	70	54	11	4	101	55	29	170	5	4
Garfield	2 860	0.3	44 985	675	1 414	238	108	256	568	516	2 016	112	108
Garvin	1 120	-2.0	40 337	1 049	457	84	35	134	175	267	709	41	35
Grady	2 114	2.3	38 678	1 393	515	90	40	211	317	408	856	49	40
Grant	228	-2.7	50 348	293	96	16	7	40	55	40	158	8	7
Greer	149	-8.3	24 508	3 024	42	11	3	8	28	57	65	5	3
Harmon	105	-3.0	37 510	1 625	26	6	2	31	15	26	65	3	2
Harper	190	-0.9	50 607	596	40	9	3	67	32	25	119	4	3
Haskell	443	4.0	34 501	1 845	113	22	9	89	57	141	233	12	9
Hughes	451	2.3	32 856	2 067	112	23	9	63	73	137	206	12	9
Jackson	968	-1.2	37 858	1 433	446	110	38	59	190	212	653	34	38
Jefferson	227	-2.8	36 208	1 912	44	9	3	47	31	61	103	5	3
Johnston	352	1.1	32 082	2 419	111	25	9	29	49	118	173	11	9
Kay	1 744	0.7	38 443	1 295	794	131	60	159	332	428	1 144	69	60
Kingfisher	726	1.3	46 574	677	279	48	20	137	139	114	484	25	20

1. Based on the resident population estimated as of July 1 of the year shown.

Table B. States and Counties — Earnings, Social Security, and Housing

STATE County	Earnings, 2015 (cont.) Percent by selected industries									Social Security beneficiaries, December 2015		Housing units, 2016	
	Farm	Mining	Construction	Manu-facturing	Infor-mation: professional, scientific, technical services	Retail trade	Finance, insur-ance, real estate and leasing	Health care and social assistance	Govern-ment	Number	Rate[1]	Supple-mental Security Income recipients, December 2015	Total	Percent change, 2010–2016
	75	76	77	78	79	80	81	82	83	84	85	86	87	88
OHIO—Cont'd														
Ottawa	-0.4	D	6.7	18.7	D	6.0	4.0	9.3	17.1	11 150	273	570	28 092	0.7
Paulding	12.9	0.3	5.5	26.4	2.6	5.3	2.8	D	21.5	4 410	232	360	8 689	-0.7
Perry	-0.5	4.2	13.8	12.3	2.7	6.4	3.4	D	25.4	7 950	221	1 317	15 110	-0.6
Pickaway	3.4	D	8.4	22.1	D	5.5	2.7	8.3	28.4	11 015	193	1 175	21 116	-0.7
Pike	0.4	D	9.2	6.4	D	4.6	2.3	9.6	12.7	6 630	235	1 583	12 575	0.8
Portage	0.1	0.9	6.3	21.4	5.2	5.9	2.4	7.7	25.1	29 690	183	2 421	68 447	1.4
Preble	3.5	D	7.2	33.2	D	7.2	2.6	D	16.2	9 215	223	738	17 833	-0.3
Putnam	-0.2	D	9.7	36.0	3.8	6.2	4.3	5.9	13.0	6 670	196	328	13 800	0.5
Richland	0.7	D	6.4	21.9	4.4	8.0	3.7	14.2	18.2	28 770	237	3 448	54 013	-1.1
Ross	0.7	0.1	4.3	20.4	2.3	7.3	2.3	18.2	27.3	16 270	211	2 926	31 668	-1.5
Sandusky	-0.2	D	6.0	40.7	2.2	6.6	4.0	D	13.1	13 380	225	1 072	26 202	-0.7
Scioto	0.1	D	4.5	7.7	4.0	7.4	4.3	28.7	24.2	16 980	221	5 544	34 124	-0.1
Seneca	0.4	0.8	7.1	30.2	D	6.9	3.4	8.9	13.7	12 420	223	1 192	23 946	-0.7
Shelby	1.0	0.0	8.2	49.9	D	3.5	2.5	5.6	8.2	9 625	197	830	20 335	0.8
Stark	0.5	1.0	6.7	20.3	5.9	7.0	6.2	16.0	12.7	85 635	228	9 888	165 957	0.4
Summit	0.0	1.0	4.9	11.9	9.0	7.8	6.0	14.8	11.8	107 850	199	14 593	245 193	0.0
Trumbull	-0.1	0.2	6.1	25.3	2.9	7.9	4.1	12.9	14.4	52 915	260	6 088	95 211	-1.0
Tuscarawas	1.0	5.5	8.8	22.9	3.8	7.7	3.7	10.8	13.2	20 665	223	1 962	39 854	-0.9
Union	0.5	D	4.4	33.5	D	3.6	2.0	3.3	10.5	7 980	147	443	20 629	6.2
Van Wert	0.5	D	5.7	28.2	D	6.7	9.7	12.4	14.1	6 620	232	445	12 642	0.2
Vinton	0.4	D	5.8	23.0	D	3.3	4.7	D	29.9	2 730	210	613	6 134	-2.5
Warren	0.1	0.0	6.5	16.0	9.3	8.0	7.7	9.3	11.2	35 140	157	1 861	85 617	6.0
Washington	0.3	3.2	8.2	19.4	4.2	6.0	5.5	19.8	11.1	15 245	250	1 917	27 955	-1.5
Wayne	2.5	3.4	7.2	31.8	3.3	6.2	4.2	6.9	12.7	22 565	194	1 943	46 179	0.7
Williams	1.3	D	4.2	42.8	D	7.8	2.5	9.6	12.1	8 460	228	606	16 526	-0.9
Wood	0.3	0.1	8.6	25.8	4.8	5.1	3.7	6.8	17.5	22 145	171	1 386	53 442	0.1
Wyandot	7.1	1.8	11.6	34.7	D	4.9	3.8	D	15.0	4 945	222	346	9 882	0.1
OKLAHOMA	1.6	10.8	6.1	8.2	6.7	5.7	5.1	9.5	17.5	758 912	194	96 921	1 721 045	3.4
Adair	14.3	D	6.3	20.6	1.8	5.3	2.4	9.1	25.0	4 990	226	931	9 256	1.2
Alfalfa	22.6	D	6.3	2.0	D	4.9	D	3.2	18.8	1 195	205	92	2 743	-0.7
Atoka	3.3	4.4	4.2	3.1	D	11.1	6.1	D	27.9	3 380	245	534	6 348	0.6
Beaver	41.6	9.7	11.5	1.3	D	1.4	D	0.6	13.1	1 085	200	47	2 660	-0.4
Beckham	0.9	31.0	10.3	2.7	D	7.7	5.8	D	7.1	3 995	169	554	10 035	4.0
Blaine	15.5	5.6	10.3	15.0	3.5	3.3	5.7	4.3	16.5	2 250	230	245	5 175	-0.3
Bryan	1.7	0.9	6.1	6.2	4.2	6.0	2.9	12.6	36.5	9 720	216	1 680	20 039	2.3
Caddo	6.4	5.9	10.3	1.2	6.9	6.0	D	D	30.2	6 415	218	1 002	13 184	0.3
Canadian	1.4	8.4	9.6	14.1	4.2	6.7	6.2	6.1	16.3	20 260	152	1 116	48 033	4.9
Carter	0.4	14.8	7.5	17.2	4.4	6.4	5.2	11.5	11.8	11 320	233	1 580	21 571	2.0
Cherokee	3.2	0.3	4.4	1.2	2.5	7.2	3.8	7.5	54.1	9 970	206	1 556	21 813	1.7
Choctaw	7.2	D	4.1	2.4	4.4	5.8	3.0	11.0	28.9	4 040	269	874	7 554	0.4
Cimarron	62.3	D	D	D	D	2.6	2.1	D	11.2	645	293	36	1 571	-1.0
Cleveland	0.1	2.4	8.6	5.2	9.2	8.7	5.3	8.8	28.7	42 715	156	3 432	113 535	8.3
Coal	11.2	14.9	7.8	4.4	D	5.3	D	11.0	22.1	1 325	235	236	2 800	-0.3
Comanche	0.2	0.3	3.6	8.4	6.6	5.4	3.6	5.2	52.9	19 880	160	3 196	51 733	2.0
Cotton	13.9	1.8	11.9	D	D	3.6	2.6	2.6	41.8	1 415	237	130	3 004	-0.4
Craig	10.6	D	3.5	4.7	D	7.4	4.0	8.7	27.6	4 060	274	706	6 724	-0.3
Creek	0.8	7.4	13.2	22.6	D	5.6	3.7	9.5	15.2	16 555	233	1 746	30 278	1.7
Custer	3.4	13.0	6.0	7.2	5.1	6.4	5.7	D	17.9	4 825	163	540	12 508	2.5
Delaware	15.2	D	7.5	9.1	D	7.0	3.4	D	22.5	11 100	268	1 244	24 998	0.7
Dewey	5.7	17.2	9.1	4.4	D	4.9	D	3.4	17.0	1 180	239	70	2 440	-0.2
Ellis	37.7	18.8	2.6	0.4	D	2.3	D	3.0	12.8	935	221	51	2 271	-0.6
Garfield	1.0	14.8	8.2	7.6	6.8	6.3	5.1	10.5	16.7	12 415	196	1 303	26 885	0.2
Garvin	1.9	15.3	11.1	13.5	2.8	7.5	3.1	6.6	12.9	6 775	244	890	12 847	0.2
Grady	6.7	8.9	11.1	9.5	4.8	7.5	5.6	6.9	17.2	10 575	194	1 193	22 688	2.1
Grant	10.1	33.2	12.3	0.6	D	3.2	D	2.8	10.9	1 080	240	72	2 480	-0.2
Greer	3.3	D	2.2	D	D	5.6	D	15.9	46.2	1 425	235	198	2 727	-0.4
Harmon	30.8	1.0	D	D	D	2.9	D	2.8	22.3	690	249	155	1 544	0.0
Harper	45.1	6.1	D	D	D	3.7	D	2.2	17.4	755	200	40	1 888	-1.0
Haskell	21.3	7.0	5.7	2.9	D	6.6	D	21.4	13.8	3 540	277	526	6 072	0.7
Hughes	20.0	10.7	3.2	6.5	D	5.6	D	D	23.5	3 605	263	457	6 238	0.9
Jackson	1.6	D	2.3	7.4	D	6.4	4.0	4.7	52.9	4 575	179	674	12 169	0.8
Jefferson	26.7	2.6	D	D	D	5.7	6.4	D	19.5	1 650	264	248	3 390	0.4
Johnston	4.2	9.4	3.7	15.8	D	3.6	D	16.0	28.8	2 760	252	444	5 150	0.5
Kay	1.2	4.3	7.8	12.2	D	7.0	4.0	9.3	17.9	11 240	248	1 130	21 607	-0.5
Kingfisher	3.2	27.8	9.6	7.0	9.3	5.6	4.0	4.5	8.7	2 980	191	205	6 499	1.4

1. Per 1,000 resident population estimated as of July 1 of the year shown.

Table B. States and Counties — Housing, Labor Force, and Employment

STATE County	Housing units, 2011–2015 Occupied units Total	Percent	Owner-occupied Median value[1]	Median owner cost as a percent of income With a mortgage	Without a mortgage[2]	Renter-occupied Median rent[3]	Median rent as a percent of income[2]	Sub-standard units[4] (percent)	Civilian labor force, 2016 Total	Percent change, 2015–2016	Unemployment Total	Rate[5]	Civilian employment,[6] 2011–2015 Percent Total	Management, business, science and arts	Construction, production, and maintenance occupations
	89	90	91	92	93	94	95	96	97	98	99	100	101	102	103
OHIO—Cont'd															
Ottawa	17 334	79.5	138 800	20.8	12.0	696	27.8	1.1	20 931	-0.4	1 339	6.4	19 539	30.0	29.6
Paulding	7 699	78.1	91 900	18.8	12.8	587	25.0	2.4	8 860	-0.5	404	4.6	8 638	23.5	41.4
Perry	13 780	73.2	91 800	21.5	12.6	588	29.3	2.1	15 988	1.2	998	6.2	14 630	26.1	34.1
Pickaway	19 460	73.8	147 700	21.4	12.1	747	27.8	1.6	26 073	1.4	1 235	4.7	24 777	32.8	27.4
Pike	10 940	68.2	95 000	20.8	12.3	665	35.0	3.5	10 732	2.5	796	7.4	9 887	31.1	31.5
Portage	61 055	68.7	150 900	21.4	11.9	802	32.3	1.1	86 787	0.0	4 313	5.0	81 544	31.9	25.0
Preble	16 124	76.7	112 700	22.3	13.2	702	29.6	1.8	21 014	0.2	982	4.7	19 308	24.8	34.6
Putnam	13 049	82.5	138 900	18.9	10.1	684	24.5	1.0	18 808	0.8	683	3.6	17 579	31.6	34.9
Richland	48 103	68.6	102 500	21.5	11.7	624	28.8	1.4	53 352	-0.3	2 918	5.5	50 632	26.7	29.5
Ross	28 269	71.7	110 300	20.8	12.1	670	30.0	2.5	33 672	-0.1	1 838	5.5	30 096	27.0	30.4
Sandusky	23 626	74.2	110 100	21.0	12.1	634	28.5	0.9	30 908	-1.4	1 443	4.7	28 181	24.2	39.7
Scioto	29 700	68.5	90 200	19.7	13.3	550	32.6	2.1	29 928	1.2	2 279	7.6	27 592	32.7	24.1
Seneca	21 538	71.3	96 900	19.4	12.0	645	26.4	1.0	27 164	0.1	1 309	4.8	25 327	25.4	38.0
Shelby	18 537	70.9	130 000	19.7	11.1	684	23.8	1.3	23 987	-0.3	984	4.1	23 649	27.8	37.6
Stark	150 385	68.9	122 900	20.3	11.6	680	28.4	1.4	185 571	-0.5	10 033	5.4	174 941	31.7	25.4
Summit	220 902	66.3	133 500	20.8	12.3	744	30.0	1.1	271 529	0.0	13 668	5.0	258 416	37.5	19.8
Trumbull	86 828	70.9	97 000	20.7	11.6	627	29.5	1.4	90 355	-1.1	6 036	6.7	88 133	26.6	30.9
Tuscarawas	36 713	70.3	111 100	20.7	11.8	674	28.0	1.2	44 979	-1.0	2 554	5.7	42 879	25.9	33.7
Union	18 431	77.5	171 200	22.3	13.9	805	27.0	1.5	27 340	1.3	1 028	3.8	25 357	37.0	26.1
Van Wert	11 355	75.7	95 800	19.7	10.6	635	26.4	1.3	14 273	-0.3	570	4.0	13 163	24.8	39.7
Vinton	4 992	77.1	81 000	21.9	13.0	600	32.0	3.2	5 434	-0.4	379	7.0	5 060	23.8	37.6
Warren	78 359	77.2	190 900	20.7	11.7	923	25.9	0.8	113 310	0.8	4 624	4.1	105 433	46.2	16.6
Washington	25 064	75.2	110 700	19.8	10.6	600	29.5	1.4	27 779	-0.9	1 914	6.9	26 082	30.4	27.3
Wayne	42 910	73.1	135 700	21.3	10.8	657	27.2	3.1	60 680	1.2	2 387	3.9	54 503	29.9	32.2
Williams	15 150	74.6	95 800	21.1	12.4	633	29.0	1.5	19 121	0.6	846	4.4	17 119	24.1	41.2
Wood	50 091	66.8	146 300	20.9	12.4	727	29.1	1.1	70 261	1.0	2 889	4.1	65 406	35.3	23.8
Wyandot	9 327	72.2	106 200	19.3	10.9	618	25.8	1.2	12 668	2.6	465	3.7	11 017	25.0	40.8
OKLAHOMA	1 455 321	66.1	117 900	20.5	10.6	727	28.3	3.2	1 828 423	-0.3	89 054	4.9	1 719 541	33.3	24.9
Adair	7 968	70.3	76 600	21.3	10.7	526	25.1	5.7	8 112	-0.8	483	6.0	8 336	24.9	38.0
Alfalfa	2 072	76.0	64 600	15.9	10.0	639	21.6	1.6	2 956	-6.7	100	3.4	2 176	32.2	35.4
Atoka	5 258	73.1	85 400	20.9	11.8	583	29.6	2.2	4 995	2.6	337	6.7	4 695	28.5	31.0
Beaver	2 017	79.0	89 300	19.1	10.0	682	19.4	1.2	2 869	-5.3	92	3.2	2 555	33.0	34.8
Beckham	7 535	63.9	122 400	20.1	10.0	702	22.2	1.8	10 877	-11.1	817	7.5	9 611	24.3	33.2
Blaine	3 580	75.1	77 900	18.0	10.0	549	28.3	1.6	4 341	-3.4	167	3.8	3 270	34.6	22.2
Bryan	16 632	64.6	90 100	19.6	11.4	666	30.4	4.0	19 372	5.4	844	4.4	18 472	30.1	26.8
Caddo	10 202	70.1	78 400	18.5	10.6	545	22.8	3.2	11 765	-0.8	638	5.4	11 208	28.1	33.5
Canadian	43 063	76.9	144 600	21.1	10.0	886	25.1	2.5	68 568	0.2	2 776	4.0	63 025	36.0	22.2
Carter	17 867	69.9	97 000	19.7	11.0	676	26.1	3.4	22 592	0.0	1 186	5.2	20 820	27.7	29.5
Cherokee	16 324	66.8	108 100	20.2	10.6	580	30.7	4.3	19 222	-0.4	1 073	5.6	19 314	32.4	22.4
Choctaw	5 924	70.9	80 900	21.3	11.9	530	33.2	3.2	5 763	-2.7	447	7.8	5 308	27.8	29.7
Cimarron	1 017	72.9	59 500	18.8	10.0	393	14.4	4.2	1 421	3.1	36	2.5	1 131	38.5	31.7
Cleveland	99 276	66.4	146 100	20.2	10.7	831	29.3	2.7	138 580	0.1	5 343	3.9	133 949	39.5	18.1
Coal	2 288	72.5	80 100	19.0	10.4	589	28.0	4.9	2 315	-0.3	173	7.5	2 296	31.5	32.1
Comanche	43 240	55.2	115 800	20.6	10.1	784	27.2	2.3	49 507	-0.5	2 329	4.7	49 641	32.3	23.4
Cotton	2 429	75.7	79 900	18.3	11.6	565	28.1	4.2	2 869	0.1	140	4.9	2 607	31.8	27.9
Craig	5 418	75.5	90 600	20.8	10.0	621	28.4	2.3	6 278	0.1	307	4.9	5 781	27.3	29.3
Creek	26 204	75.0	105 000	21.2	10.6	689	26.8	4.2	31 496	0.3	1 850	5.9	29 749	28.1	32.1
Custer	10 364	59.7	119 000	18.1	10.0	625	24.6	3.9	15 084	-3.8	705	4.7	14 072	27.4	30.4
Delaware	16 561	75.6	109 000	24.7	11.9	621	28.9	3.9	17 851	2.0	889	5.0	15 991	27.7	29.5
Dewey	1 851	72.9	84 200	17.2	10.2	618	17.2	2.9	2 679	7.1	111	4.1	2 061	31.7	37.7
Ellis	1 710	77.1	81 800	16.1	10.0	645	19.3	1.2	2 275	-5.0	88	3.9	1 824	35.9	33.3
Garfield	23 937	66.6	96 900	19.8	10.1	726	22.8	3.3	29 953	-0.6	1 298	4.3	28 056	26.5	32.5
Garvin	10 531	69.4	88 000	19.7	11.2	598	24.0	3.2	12 621	-1.8	684	5.4	10 668	28.3	33.0
Grady	19 589	75.9	111 200	19.7	10.0	663	25.3	2.7	26 355	0.3	1 310	5.0	24 086	29.2	30.3
Grant	1 968	75.5	73 200	17.8	10.0	606	20.8	1.3	3 001	-9.0	99	3.3	2 098	36.8	32.4
Greer	2 186	66.0	61 600	18.8	12.1	664	24.1	3.7	2 218	2.1	166	7.5	2 344	31.8	25.0
Harmon	1 174	69.3	51 300	20.1	11.9	480	25.8	1.4	1 307	0.2	51	3.9	1 139	34.9	26.2
Harper	1 444	80.3	74 100	15.0	10.0	569	23.6	1.3	1 909	-4.1	74	3.9	1 779	32.9	32.4
Haskell	4 903	73.2	80 100	22.1	10.3	563	29.6	3.4	4 499	0.3	380	8.4	4 585	27.0	36.0
Hughes	4 454	75.3	67 600	20.3	12.2	553	27.0	2.4	5 476	-4.6	410	7.5	4 546	28.1	32.9
Jackson	10 220	58.7	90 300	19.4	11.7	708	26.7	3.2	10 939	0.4	492	4.5	10 388	25.8	30.9
Jefferson	2 471	71.6	56 600	19.4	11.9	468	26.1	2.3	2 731	1.8	197	7.2	2 497	24.3	36.4
Johnston	4 164	72.7	78 200	19.0	11.5	579	28.2	2.3	4 455	12.0	261	5.9	4 078	33.3	34.0
Kay	18 115	68.9	78 800	19.8	11.4	620	25.4	3.0	18 960	-1.4	1 217	6.4	19 588	28.5	29.1
Kingfisher	5 741	76.4	122 100	18.3	10.0	708	23.3	1.9	8 380	1.1	284	3.4	7 289	31.3	33.0

1. Specified owner-occupied units. 2. A value of 10.0 represents 10 percent or less; a value of 50.0 represents 50 percent or more. 3. Specified renter-occupied units.
4. Overcrowded or lacking complete plumbing facilities. 5. Percent of civilian labor force. 6. Civilian employed persons 16 years old and over.

Table B. States and Counties — Nonfarm Employment and Agriculture

STATE County	Private nonfarm establishments, employment and payroll, 2015									Agriculture, 2012			
		Employment						Annual payroll		Farms			
												Percent with:	
	Number of establishments	Total	Health care and social assistance	Manufacturing	Retail trade	Finance and insurance	Professional, scientific, and technical services	Total (mil dol)	Average per employee (dollars)	Number	Fewer than 50 acres	500 acres or more	Farm operators whose principal occupation is farming (percent)
	104	105	106	107	108	109	110	111	112	113	114	115	116

OHIO—Cont'd

Ottawa	1 026	10 053	1 837	2 036	1 350	258	177	432	43 012	620	45.2	8.4	40.5
Paulding	299	3 551	556	1 219	408	101	61	122	34 259	676	34.8	18.2	39.8
Perry	440	4 176	862	724	680	143	139	135	32 346	699	39.1	4.9	29.3
Pickaway	790	11 272	2 194	2 437	1 507	303	184	433	38 445	803	39.6	18.3	52.3
Pike	404	8 615	1 525	1 559	1 023	223	1 907	419	48 622	490	27.6	5.3	38.0
Portage	3 011	45 887	6 129	9 980	8 012	694	1 341	1 759	38 324	847	56.6	3.0	42.9
Preble	640	8 832	1 047	3 345	1 265	214	217	314	35 564	1 088	45.9	11.9	41.8
Putnam	742	10 094	1 126	3 755	1 044	307	217	348	34 484	1 272	27.6	12.2	40.8
Richland	2 618	44 133	7 685	8 574	6 418	1 048	963	1 487	33 692	1 010	37.2	5.0	52.0
Ross	1 228	23 194	6 178	4 368	3 795	469	410	1 057	45 573	980	35.1	9.0	48.1
Sandusky	1 321	23 195	3 467	9 031	2 491	488	404	848	36 576	737	36.9	14.8	47.2
Scioto	1 298	18 394	6 949	1 536	3 134	489	657	611	33 241	689	39.2	4.9	40.3
Seneca	1 128	17 109	2 680	4 208	2 315	409	385	572	33 420	1 113	28.4	14.7	41.3
Shelby	972	24 112	2 009	12 325	1 987	309	387	1 137	47 136	986	32.4	11.1	41.3
Stark	8 210	142 085	28 306	25 494	20 077	5 656	4 279	5 450	38 357	1 168	56.1	3.3	46.5
Summit	13 475	248 240	45 861	29 997	30 799	10 439	14 530	11 319	45 596	304	72.4	1.6	41.4
Trumbull	4 074	66 127	10 589	17 474	9 734	1 554	1 461	2 504	37 872	888	41.6	4.2	46.7
Tuscarawas	2 165	32 236	5 397	7 782	4 507	633	903	1 155	35 834	1 014	39.2	4.7	41.3
Union	1 005	25 670	1 740	6 263	2 150	357	3 321	1 472	57 340	995	48.2	11.1	44.5
Van Wert	544	9 772	1 403	3 387	1 124	752	321	353	36 097	655	29.2	23.1	55.7
Vinton	135	1 865	329	509	164	88	19	63	33 955	226	25.7	3.5	36.3
Warren	4 120	76 870	10 169	10 614	9 827	3 692	5 027	3 959	51 504	942	67.3	4.7	42.3
Washington	1 402	22 603	4 751	3 403	2 901	747	789	938	41 490	1 122	31.0	2.7	48.7
Wayne	2 481	40 201	5 806	12 540	4 742	1 121	1 705	1 635	40 672	1 928	41.7	5.2	52.0
Williams	807	15 539	1 927	7 158	1 295	267	228	566	36 400	984	35.6	9.8	37.5
Wood	2 744	51 941	5 325	12 613	6 130	860	2 150	2 264	43 595	1 091	42.4	13.7	44.6
Wyandot	515	7 993	783	3 202	800	266	77	311	38 857	593	32.2	21.2	42.2
OKLAHOMA	93 093	1 370 988	214 372	140 997	183 726	58 894	70 888	59 125	43 126	80 245	25.0	19.0	42.1
Adair	228	3 063	556	1 046	547	132	78	92	30 134	1 129	26.5	10.5	43.8
Alfalfa	144	1 236	135	38	200	80	28	54	43 936	645	6.8	41.4	55.5
Atoka	284	2 334	343	197	489	131	45	74	31 905	1 103	17.9	16.1	37.0
Beaver	158	1 422	83	D	119	56	30	59	41 840	965	6.1	40.3	32.7
Beckham	847	10 795	1 172	397	1 778	272	318	460	42 608	1 016	15.0	28.0	33.0
Blaine	285	2 334	354	401	388	145	61	86	36 889	798	8.5	35.5	54.1
Bryan	750	10 514	2 147	1 146	1 614	540	347	317	30 161	1 484	23.9	13.9	40.9
Caddo	460	4 522	642	81	867	202	395	157	34 825	1 461	12.3	26.7	46.5
Canadian	2 589	27 577	2 791	3 206	3 980	857	1 645	1 042	37 779	1 307	32.8	19.3	47.1
Carter	1 610	21 188	3 401	3 459	3 153	688	658	860	40 579	1 321	22.6	15.7	34.1
Cherokee	746	9 132	2 791	135	1 732	336	133	276	30 273	1 233	29.4	8.5	38.8
Choctaw	285	3 100	1 194	87	492	118	85	89	28 811	965	18.4	18.7	50.3
Cimarron	76	335	D	D	78	36	6	9	26 349	554	3.4	52.0	49.6
Cleveland	5 703	70 988	12 911	3 766	12 215	2 477	3 720	2 539	35 768	1 081	53.6	4.8	45.1
Coal	89	843	191	87	181	53	13	25	29 725	571	16.5	23.1	43.1
Comanche	2 201	33 267	6 339	3 516	5 801	1 515	1 380	1 121	33 689	1 107	22.6	23.7	43.8
Cotton	79	1 158	73	D	99	45	19	38	32 782	500	11.4	37.0	51.4
Craig	342	4 197	1 379	346	704	207	83	142	33 845	1 263	21.9	13.9	43.9
Creek	1 352	17 344	2 056	4 751	2 185	468	462	693	39 952	1 777	39.0	6.9	31.6
Custer	923	10 397	1 509	1 320	1 863	379	279	412	39 638	877	15.7	36.7	41.7
Delaware	718	7 184	1 113	631	1 444	326	138	217	30 225	1 345	27.7	8.0	46.4
Dewey	161	973	89	63	209	68	23	40	40 846	743	7.1	41.6	40.5
Ellis	127	1 209	160	D	265	56	31	40	33 445	760	5.3	39.7	42.2
Garfield	1 708	22 318	3 724	2 318	3 741	781	605	833	37 332	1 098	16.8	31.5	46.8
Garvin	721	8 294	1 147	1 180	1 362	258	166	334	40 299	1 498	25.3	15.3	36.5
Grady	1 112	11 794	1 798	1 860	1 680	410	419	383	32 499	1 666	26.8	17.6	45.3
Grant	120	1 085	148	6	168	58	16	53	48 868	801	8.1	36.6	50.1
Greer	86	703	217	D	162	40	15	19	27 606	498	5.4	38.6	40.2
Harmon	53	533	119	D	77	D	7	24	44 184	366	4.6	43.7	44.3
Harper	99	613	132	D	118	33	34	19	31 801	532	4.7	49.1	46.1
Haskell	221	2 457	769	79	486	65	46	71	28 831	864	19.8	14.5	46.9
Hughes	219	2 186	697	101	364	81	23	60	27 439	921	15.4	20.7	47.8
Jackson	531	8 319	1 239	1 101	1 301	346	120	291	34 951	694	16.7	34.6	44.2
Jefferson	104	757	94	26	120	202	36	32	41 639	417	8.4	42.0	48.2
Johnston	178	2 081	552	477	261	33	36	76	36 724	645	18.0	16.3	42.6
Kay	1 105	15 768	2 357	3 431	2 201	407	469	634	40 201	993	22.7	25.0	43.5
Kingfisher	475	5 412	525	455	624	198	200	247	45 622	1 021	13.0	33.7	49.8

STATE County	Land in farms					Value of land and buildings (dollars)		Value of machinery and equipment, average per farm (dollars)	Value of products sold				Percent of farms with sales of:		Government payments	
	Acreage (1,000)	Percent change, 2007–2012	Acres			Average per farm	Average per acre		Total (mil dol)	Average per farm (dollars)	Percent from:		$10,000 or more	$100,000 or more	Total ($1,000)	Percent of farms
			Average size of farm	Total irrigated (1,000)	Total cropland (1,000)						Crops	Live-stock and poultry products				
	117	118	119	120	121	122	123	124	125	126	127	128	129	130	131	132
OHIO—Cont'd																
Ottawa	113	-2.1	182	1.5	103.6	863 753	4 753	119 450	79.1	127 503	98.5	1.5	59.5	26.8	2 390	74.0
Paulding	221	-13.6	327	0.0	205.3	1 583 920	4 848	188 343	187.2	276 864	55.0	45.0	57.8	27.5	5 581	86.1
Perry	107	9.5	153	0.0	67.8	556 103	3 625	82 957	37.1	53 074	82.3	17.7	31.3	7.2	866	21.3
Pickaway	294	1.7	366	0.8	265.8	1 752 654	4 792	200 377	172.3	214 609	78.8	21.2	51.4	28.0	6 106	64.8
Pike	97	20.8	199	0.7	53.2	631 647	3 176	71 429	26.9	54 855	85.3	14.7	35.5	8.4	992	35.7
Portage	83	0.7	98	0.4	58.7	511 001	5 195	78 929	43.7	51 571	73.7	26.3	32.9	7.8	618	18.5
Preble	224	-2.8	206	0.2	195.1	1 083 226	5 256	148 121	154.8	142 302	65.9	34.1	50.6	24.9	4 689	55.9
Putnam	306	0.6	240	0.6	287.2	1 208 173	5 029	175 040	243.2	191 203	74.8	25.2	78.0	41.4	5 606	84.4
Richland	161	9.6	159	0.1	120.3	789 172	4 962	110 557	128.7	127 408	51.7	48.3	55.0	29.5	1 806	32.5
Ross	222	-0.9	226	D	153.7	816 043	3 607	92 039	79.8	81 432	87.5	12.5	35.5	14.3	6 567	57.1
Sandusky	181	0.1	246	0.8	166.3	1 159 189	4 709	160 579	135.3	183 525	93.5	6.5	65.9	37.9	3 636	76.5
Scioto	94	-7.5	137	0.1	42.0	385 210	2 813	67 393	22.2	32 229	63.5	36.5	25.5	6.1	995	25.5
Seneca	291	7.8	261	0.2	258.1	1 272 024	4 873	163 428	174.6	156 848	85.0	15.0	69.7	33.2	4 919	80.8
Shelby	206	-5.4	209	0.0	183.2	1 245 277	5 952	149 865	207.9	210 807	59.5	40.5	68.6	37.9	3 948	77.1
Stark	136	-1.7	116	0.5	105.4	640 866	5 514	101 840	130.7	111 895	50.6	49.4	46.0	16.5	1 693	26.5
Summit	17	9.1	54	0.3	9.6	459 954	8 451	59 490	11.3	37 118	86.7	13.3	32.2	7.6	112	8.2
Trumbull	114	-9.0	128	0.1	77.5	514 001	4 007	112 287	66.5	74 841	72.0	28.0	44.7	14.8	1 117	30.4
Tuscarawas	138	-3.2	136	0.0	78.4	521 749	3 831	95 939	92.3	91 066	25.6	74.4	38.4	12.5	1 562	25.1
Union	242	10.6	243	0.2	216.6	1 248 834	5 136	151 144	169.0	169 875	84.5	15.5	48.0	22.9	4 372	58.6
Van Wert	227	-7.8	347	0.8	214.8	2 177 867	6 276	212 111	209.7	320 087	73.0	27.0	78.0	48.7	5 103	85.0
Vinton	33	-9.3	148	0.0	11.8	358 668	2 427	42 867	4.7	20 805	82.4	17.6	27.9	2.7	195	35.8
Warren	107	13.0	113	0.7	80.2	809 270	7 150	85 670	66.7	70 815	91.1	8.9	30.7	10.1	1 061	24.3
Washington	139	12.0	124	1.8	49.5	331 367	2 676	58 988	30.5	27 165	59.2	40.8	30.7	5.4	1 152	22.1
Wayne	272	9.4	141	0.8	209.6	878 912	6 238	113 697	381.0	197 614	27.2	72.8	64.0	28.8	4 320	29.2
Williams	208	-2.1	211	1.3	181.6	809 134	3 828	101 897	126.0	128 026	66.2	33.8	44.0	20.6	5 771	79.3
Wood	268	-2.8	246	1.0	252.2	1 429 592	5 821	162 243	227.7	208 712	85.0	15.0	63.2	34.8	5 520	80.8
Wyandot	221	0.6	372	0.0	202.0	1 872 809	5 029	211 556	196.7	331 749	66.8	33.2	63.1	38.1	4 364	86.0
OKLAHOMA	34 356	-2.1	428	479.8	11 279.0	573 858	1 340	74 209	7 129.6	88 848	26.3	73.7	40.8	10.0	256 845	37.1
Adair	252	1.1	223	0.2	44.5	441 987	1 979	56 876	164.2	145 455	1.5	98.5	41.5	10.7	1 278	20.4
Alfalfa	545	0.4	845	1.3	326.6	1 201 132	1 421	186 451	168.5	261 298	36.7	63.3	72.1	34.3	5 814	82.8
Atoka	353	-13.5	320	0.1	59.9	447 024	1 396	52 142	24.5	22 249	17.1	82.9	35.4	2.8	1 311	23.5
Beaver	1 116	-1.2	1 156	24.6	351.9	772 084	668	100 918	187.0	193 772	17.6	82.4	37.8	15.8	7 765	74.1
Beckham	568	9.3	559	6.2	159.8	617 433	1 105	74 880	44.3	43 574	43.5	56.5	35.2	9.1	5 558	66.4
Blaine	522	-10.9	654	3.1	247.1	778 357	1 190	124 377	138.2	173 231	30.2	69.8	65.3	21.2	4 901	77.8
Bryan	441	-10.1	297	8.1	111.8	526 677	1 771	56 929	60.9	41 060	31.9	68.1	40.2	6.3	1 971	26.3
Caddo	708	-5.6	484	30.3	276.1	647 626	1 337	93 927	128.9	88 215	46.9	53.1	54.2	15.2	9 454	61.7
Canadian	501	-1.6	383	10.0	253.8	737 861	1 926	107 595	145.8	111 524	35.7	64.3	44.0	16.1	4 250	42.1
Carter	457	13.3	346	1.1	79.5	545 662	1 579	53 157	33.0	24 953	17.0	83.0	30.2	4.6	1 055	14.8
Cherokee	236	-4.2	191	1.1	46.0	453 732	2 370	56 633	138.7	112 483	75.8	24.2	33.4	3.6	1 083	15.0
Choctaw	330	1.3	342	1.1	63.2	503 597	1 471	63 712	47.5	49 178	13.2	86.8	44.7	8.1	1 810	29.3
Cimarron	1 157	10.8	2 089	39.4	426.9	1 055 505	505	132 971	376.7	679 890	17.4	82.6	46.8	29.8	9 997	86.6
Cleveland	134	-16.3	124	1.4	36.1	386 582	3 125	42 396	14.9	13 764	44.7	55.3	19.7	2.2	585	12.1
Coal	274	1.6	479	0.4	45.1	603 704	1 260	65 790	22.4	39 282	18.5	81.5	43.8	8.4	856	20.0
Comanche	463	-6.9	418	0.7	137.1	577 613	1 381	62 284	47.4	42 794	35.9	64.1	40.3	9.5	2 995	43.9
Cotton	400	9.0	800	0.1	185.5	900 322	1 126	122 376	64.4	128 862	46.0	54.0	61.0	24.2	5 699	79.0
Craig	462	1.1	366	D	110.9	582 744	1 592	61 639	97.3	77 075	11.9	88.1	51.1	8.4	1 725	33.9
Creek	347	-8.1	195	0.4	71.1	349 067	1 788	43 752	23.5	13 238	19.0	81.0	23.5	2.1	384	8.3
Custer	623	9.5	710	8.2	254.9	951 593	1 340	134 592	103.2	117 636	48.3	51.7	58.6	20.4	6 729	69.3
Delaware	283	-8.3	211	0.1	62.4	488 390	2 319	62 352	254.4	189 144	1.8	98.2	48.9	13.8	1 183	27.9
Dewey	625	6.1	841	2.4	165.1	852 131	1 013	90 935	42.0	56 580	49.7	50.3	51.4	13.3	5 420	76.6
Ellis	758	5.6	998	8.7	168.7	796 726	798	83 476	119.8	157 616	11.0	89.0	45.5	15.3	4 705	74.5
Garfield	666	0.4	607	8.4	433.0	870 574	1 434	146 813	151.8	138 239	61.8	38.2	64.4	24.7	9 317	69.1
Garvin	463	-7.5	309	1.1	111.0	488 585	1 580	72 700	44.9	29 975	38.2	61.8	39.6	6.3	2 210	32.0
Grady	583	-4.1	350	14.3	182.7	563 619	1 610	77 691	138.9	83 344	21.0	79.0	40.3	9.8	3 014	33.0
Grant	582	-8.0	727	1.3	409.2	992 482	1 365	152 116	96.9	120 953	73.4	26.6	58.9	24.2	8 734	87.3
Greer	402	7.0	806	3.7	142.9	690 175	856	99 878	32.7	65 681	61.5	38.5	54.0	17.1	4 991	84.5
Harmon	341	5.7	931	25.2	167.1	886 842	953	143 131	53.6	146 579	51.7	48.3	48.1	20.8	4 837	86.6
Harper	618	0.1	1 161	5.9	201.9	884 026	761	78 647	148.7	279 560	9.4	90.6	47.4	20.1	5 563	82.0
Haskell	256	-11.8	296	0.5	46.7	448 627	1 514	60 922	98.8	114 407	2.5	97.5	45.7	10.6	810	23.4
Hughes	436	-1.1	474	1.8	64.0	590 418	1 247	68 746	90.2	97 958	6.1	93.9	41.4	7.5	2 392	36.4
Jackson	479	0.9	690	14.1	295.6	690 865	1 001	154 581	53.2	76 591	78.7	21.3	45.5	20.3	7 021	77.2
Jefferson	475	3.3	1 140	0.1	79.3	1 153 223	1 011	87 902	82.4	197 511	7.5	92.5	63.3	24.0	1 921	59.7
Johnston	284	-15.1	440	0.5	40.9	591 054	1 344	55 721	21.6	33 541	17.6	82.4	42.5	4.8	766	33.6
Kay	484	-1.6	488	1.8	307.1	659 226	1 352	109 617	86.7	87 312	66.5	33.5	54.7	17.3	8 096	67.4
Kingfisher	568	0.2	556	9.1	327.5	757 269	1 362	135 742	161.8	158 497	39.2	60.8	65.2	27.9	4 945	69.9

Table B. States and Counties — **Water Use, Wholesale Trade, Retail Trade, and Real Estate**

STATE County	Water use, 2010 Total water withdrawn (mil gal/day) [133]	Gallons withdrawn per person per day [134]	Wholesale trade,[1] 2012 Number of establishments [135]	Number of employees [136]	Sales (mil dol) [137]	Annual payroll (mil dol) [138]	Retail trade,[2] 2012 Number of establishments [139]	Number of employees [140]	Sales (mil dol) [141]	Annual payroll (mil dol) [142]	Real estate and rental and leasing,[2] 2012 Number of establishments [143]	Number of employees [144]	Receipts (mil dol) [145]	Annual payroll (mil dol) [146]
OHIO—Cont'd														
Ottawa	37.1	896	27	156	127.5	6.4	144	1 433	427.7	38.2	44	120	15.1	3.4
Paulding	2.6	132	15	201	120.1	7.7	48	385	113.0	7.6	6	D	D	D
Perry	2.7	75	15	D	D	D	70	626	173.4	13.1	10	16	2.7	0.4
Pickaway	23.4	420	38	D	D	D	124	1 402	437.9	32.6	25	85	12.7	2.1
Pike	7.6	263	14	133	46.9	4.5	79	890	219.1	18.4	10	71	11.1	2.1
Portage	50.5	313	138	2 930	2 204.2	174.6	438	7 363	1 944.3	159.4	105	621	108.5	25.6
Preble	5.0	118	26	221	159.9	8.8	106	1 319	415.5	29.3	13	70	13.3	2.3
Putnam	6.1	178	35	354	297.1	13.6	110	1 054	274.8	21.6	10	28	2.5	0.8
Richland	17.0	137	104	1 993	939.2	78.9	438	6 528	1 501.2	139.9	102	417	49.2	9.1
Ross	40.9	524	44	D	D	D	236	3 582	938.9	77.8	51	198	34.7	6.2
Sandusky	14.7	241	47	662	764.0	28.1	199	2 366	629.2	54.7	34	172	17.8	3.5
Scioto	11.8	149	25	D	D	D	253	3 085	784.0	70.0	45	246	30.4	5.6
Seneca	6.5	115	49	646	504.3	27.0	159	2 064	586.5	49.8	29	71	10.6	1.6
Shelby	8.0	161	43	979	543.0	35.6	142	1 754	490.0	39.2	37	132	15.4	3.6
Stark	45.2	120	329	4 584	2 551.8	212.6	1 261	19 983	5 330.3	453.5	284	1 295	215.7	41.5
Summit	24.3	45	821	13 158	7 841.2	752.5	1 755	29 142	8 439.7	745.7	476	2 570	473.6	92.7
Trumbull	176.8	840	170	2 528	2 288.6	124.1	685	9 608	2 495.3	201.1	135	1 323	200.4	47.1
Tuscarawas	38.8	419	81	758	321.3	28.6	361	4 334	1 180.3	95.1	61	267	38.0	7.4
Union	14.3	272	55	689	2 150.6	38.2	121	1 911	631.1	50.4	42	158	24.2	4.2
Van Wert	6.5	226	28	D	D	D	87	1 202	282.7	24.6	13	56	16.5	3.1
Vinton	0.8	61	1	D	D	D	30	209	43.7	3.4	1	D	D	D
Warren	23.4	110	167	3 371	3 109.6	221.0	532	9 726	2 924.2	246.2	151	664	124.7	20.3
Washington	777.3	12 582	68	D	D	D	227	2 724	756.3	62.9	39	D	D	D
Wayne	16.6	145	124	D	D	D	366	4 524	1 060.0	100.6	62	217	46.9	7.0
Williams	4.9	130	46	680	413.0	25.1	125	1 266	326.6	25.4	23	80	13.3	2.5
Wood	11.7	94	167	2 958	2 057.6	137.0	385	6 264	1 813.4	134.2	117	527	127.2	20.7
Wyandot	7.4	328	27	342	270.2	13.8	66	786	228.8	16.2	8	D	D	D
OKLAHOMA	3 168.2	845	3 909	50 660	71 892.9	2 718.6	13 051	168 839	50 256.2	4 055.1	4 000	21 261	4 269.6	898.0
Adair	10.3	452	8	63	27.9	1.7	58	549	123.4	9.4	7	12	1.4	0.4
Alfalfa	8.2	1 456	9	D	D	D	24	163	57.1	3.4	1	D	D	D
Atoka	24.4	1 721	9	35	34.0	1.2	45	438	129.8	9.8	7	D	D	D
Beaver	42.0	7 452	6	D	D	D	19	106	37.5	1.8	5	5	1.6	0.1
Beckham	11.2	508	36	547	305.4	29.2	141	1 657	715.4	41.0	40	421	138.4	27.2
Blaine	10.3	863	13	D	D	D	47	272	89.7	4.5	4	D	D	D
Bryan	13.9	327	28	D	D	D	124	1 441	432.8	31.5	26	70	12.2	2.4
Caddo	65.9	2 227	17	237	191.5	9.4	89	767	283.9	19.1	9	39	12.1	1.4
Canadian	15.3	132	102	877	512.8	42.6	255	3 567	1 306.8	88.1	123	721	212.0	41.9
Carter	438.1	9 212	64	866	872.1	32.3	247	2 700	889.7	65.6	70	345	83.0	16.6
Cherokee	9.6	203	16	738	111.3	16.4	143	1 710	390.6	33.7	35	146	25.8	3.5
Choctaw	9.4	617	6	31	27.6	1.1	43	481	118.8	9.5	3	8	0.5	0.1
Cimarron	55.4	22 347	6	17	30.3	1.0	11	81	38.5	1.7	NA	NA	NA	NA
Cleveland	39.1	153	140	1 360	737.9	70.9	710	10 983	3 168.9	262.2	335	1 479	231.0	52.6
Coal	3.3	552	2	D	D	D	20	153	41.9	3.1	1	D	D	D
Comanche	25.4	204	62	D	D	D	409	5 286	1 407.8	117.9	125	D	D	D
Cotton	6.8	1 095	2	D	D	D	15	124	36.9	1.6	1	D	D	D
Craig	2.0	134	16	135	73.4	5.8	62	720	204.9	15.7	5	9	1.3	0.2
Creek	216.7	3 096	64	1 061	579.7	49.4	181	1 877	570.5	43.7	34	103	14.2	2.9
Custer	9.0	327	36	338	442.9	21.7	149	1 655	530.9	37.2	45	383	96.6	34.7
Delaware	7.2	174	19	100	26.0	3.4	141	1 428	369.2	30.7	36	279	45.2	11.6
Dewey	30.0	6 239	8	25	17.5	1.0	33	246	74.9	3.8	2	D	D	D
Ellis	23.3	5 602	5	69	39.6	3.9	25	269	53.0	3.0	1	D	D	D
Garfield	9.8	162	73	D	D	D	267	3 387	926.8	84.3	80	328	57.5	12.4
Garvin	44.6	1 617	25	177	105.5	7.2	110	1 117	433.7	30.3	12	36	15.6	2.2
Grady	37.1	707	42	525	324.9	25.9	152	1 602	491.7	34.7	33	164	38.8	8.1
Grant	15.3	3 369	10	40	69.6	1.5	19	D	D	D	1	D	D	D
Greer	4.5	723	4	26	7.8	0.7	13	145	30.2	2.7	2	D	D	D
Harmon	31.0	10 620	1	D	D	D	13	D	D	D	1	D	D	D
Harper	9.0	2 432	3	D	D	D	17	127	26.5	2.4	3	D	D	D
Haskell	5.0	388	4	60	18.9	1.5	33	473	142.9	10.2	4	6	0.7	0.1
Hughes	9.3	664	5	D	D	D	47	427	111.5	7.8	8	34	3.2	1.2
Jackson	74.2	2 805	24	D	D	D	99	1 241	358.3	27.0	20	146	20.1	3.1
Jefferson	12.3	1 904	3	D	D	D	25	149	46.0	2.4	1	D	D	D
Johnston	4.6	418	9	68	36.1	2.3	34	229	61.1	4.7	3	5	0.4	0.1
Kay	46.5	998	43	D	D	D	183	2 126	631.8	48.2	40	132	22.6	4.0
Kingfisher	10.3	683	22	331	450.2	16.1	53	556	198.9	14.1	4	4	2.3	0.5

1. Merchant wholesalers, except manufacturers' sales branches and offices.   2. Employer establishments.

Table B. States and Counties — Professional Services, Manufacturing, and Accommodation and Food Services

STATE County	Professional, scientific, and technical services, 2012				Manufacturing, 2012				Accommodation and food services, 2012			
	Number of establishments	Number of employees	Receipts (mil dol)	Annual payroll (mil dol)	Number of establishments	Number of employees	Receipts (mil dol)	Annual payroll (mil dol)	Number of establishments	Number of employees	Sales (mil dol)	Annual payroll (mil dol)
	147	148	149	150	151	152	153	154	155	156	157	158
OHIO—Cont'd												
Ottawa	54	D	D	D	53	2 150	811.8	117.7	165	1 703	115.1	30.4
Paulding	12	52	3.2	1.2	38	1 132	282.8	44.9	25	296	11.0	2.7
Perry	21	D	D	D	22	738	D	28.4	47	355	16.6	4.1
Pickaway	56	429	28.7	9.9	35	2 221	900.0	125.1	70	1 254	51.4	14.0
Pike	21	D	D	D	22	1 388	D	88.8	36	597	28.7	7.2
Portage	224	D	D	D	244	9 585	3 010.8	468.2	304	4 925	250.5	61.7
Preble	38	188	11.4	4.9	55	2 761	1 141.7	148.9	56	882	37.4	10.6
Putnam	35	171	18.0	6.0	53	3 209	2 677.9	145.8	60	D	D	D
Richland	187	925	113.1	36.0	168	8 064	3 122.7	385.9	239	4 556	190.1	54.1
Ross	74	645	37.1	15.7	33	4 270	3 928.5	276.6	123	2 486	115.2	30.7
Sandusky	85	431	39.1	12.2	108	8 458	3 878.0	388.4	117	1 844	76.4	19.8
Scioto	80	792	74.0	37.4	43	1 439	1 190.6	64.3	142	2 485	112.8	29.9
Seneca	69	377	29.3	11.9	79	3 498	1 262.6	152.8	106	1 481	53.4	14.5
Shelby	52	364	48.0	18.6	122	10 052	7 166.1	536.9	80	1 300	58.2	14.4
Stark	675	D	D	D	506	22 667	12 182.9	1 061.2	769	13 844	630.1	174.7
Summit	1 500	14 776	2 443.4	856.7	837	27 965	9 557.1	1 402.7	1 195	21 494	974.7	268.9
Trumbull	306	1 436	175.5	49.5	218	15 764	9 668.4	1 095.3	396	11 386	516.3	156.0
Tuscarawas	140	D	D	D	211	7 401	2 276.1	346.3	194	2 700	112.1	30.6
Union	93	2 362	706.6	211.2	53	6 143	10 102.7	424.9	80	1 335	63.9	17.5
Van Wert	36	141	14.7	6.3	39	3 323	1 505.7	130.2	45	798	31.2	7.8
Vinton	7	D	D	D	15	453	98.2	27.5	13	D	D	D
Warren	473	3 934	567.7	234.9	198	9 523	3 803.4	493.3	350	7 767	386.6	107.1
Washington	96	D	D	D	88	3 628	D	222.3	112	D	D	D
Wayne	153	1 668	117.3	88.3	254	10 257	3 203.8	471.4	171	2 937	125.6	36.6
Williams	40	301	23.3	11.2	113	6 337	2 466.3	274.4	71	927	35.0	9.7
Wood	216	1 658	195.1	93.1	179	11 030	4 256.0	623.3	322	6 468	263.9	73.2
Wyandot	23	76	7.9	2.0	41	3 055	958.8	130.8	49	568	22.6	5.5
OKLAHOMA	9 470	71 997	10 991.3	4 115.2	3 610	133 064	74 295.4	6 416.0	7 403	143 561	7 121.2	1 908.3
Adair	17	D	D	D	16	1 075	485.0	38.3	20	198	7.2	2.2
Alfalfa	9	D	D	D	NA	NA	NA	NA	8	44	3.1	0.7
Atoka	10	D	D	D	17	178	47.0	6.6	25	D	D	D
Beaver	18	D	D	D	3	29	D	D	9	D	D	D
Beckham	80	273	47.2	14.3	17	D	D	D	72	999	51.9	10.7
Blaine	21	183	17.1	7.0	7	391	D	16.8	16	129	6.0	1.5
Bryan	63	382	39.7	15.0	35	1 076	243.2	35.3	76	1 573	73.5	21.1
Caddo	34	D	D	D	10	46	D	1.6	36	339	14.1	3.6
Canadian	232	846	172.5	59.6	79	2 979	1 035.6	114.1	171	3 310	160.6	41.7
Carter	134	722	61.5	33.7	43	2 984	4 853.5	178.2	116	2 397	106.7	29.4
Cherokee	45	129	10.4	2.8	21	107	15.1	3.5	88	1 226	53.1	13.5
Choctaw	18	D	D	D	11	133	D	2.7	24	542	18.1	8.1
Cimarron	4	D	D	D	NA	NA	NA	NA	10	82	4.1	1.0
Cleveland	676	3 166	396.5	131.5	132	3 659	1 495.7	158.7	506	11 290	512.4	140.7
Coal	2	D	D	D	5	73	D	2.9	6	D	D	D
Comanche	162	1 129	114.8	49.8	45	3 487	D	183.7	227	4 863	220.5	66.2
Cotton	6	14	1.0	0.4	4	8	D	D	7	64	2.7	0.6
Craig	24	D	D	D	14	440	89.9	16.8	25	345	14.4	3.7
Creek	104	299	35.1	10.4	124	4 057	1 649.9	212.4	90	D	D	D
Custer	74	D	D	D	32	1 184	429.8	57.3	68	1 284	61.3	14.4
Delaware	54	D	D	D	27	693	87.1	22.0	63	1 816	165.8	40.2
Dewey	4	D	D	D	4	28	D	1.4	6	64	1.9	0.6
Ellis	9	29	6.1	0.8	NA	NA	NA	NA	8	D	D	D
Garfield	118	D	D	D	61	2 451	1 668.7	96.5	125	2 198	112.7	26.8
Garvin	61	D	D	D	31	1 067	2 819.8	53.9	49	660	33.1	7.9
Grady	105	300	35.7	11.5	64	1 505	564.1	57.0	62	1 240	53.2	13.6
Grant	6	D	D	D	3	12	2.1	0.3	5	D	D	D
Greer	9	D	D	D	NA	NA	NA	NA	6	55	1.8	0.5
Harmon	4	D	D	D	NA	NA	NA	NA	2	D	D	D
Harper	7	D	D	D	NA	NA	NA	NA	6	D	D	D
Haskell	23	D	D	D	7	70	D	D	13	D	D	D
Hughes	9	D	D	D	6	29	D	1.0	19	202	7.2	2.1
Jackson	41	D	D	D	13	821	225.6	D	56	1 103	42.0	11.4
Jefferson	5	D	D	D	7	28	D	0.9	8	78	3.0	0.8
Johnston	12	D	D	D	9	285	D	9.4	9	D	D	D
Kay	90	509	52.8	21.7	65	2 983	D	171.0	90	1 350	65.2	15.9
Kingfisher	27	277	41.3	18.4	18	470	130.2	22.5	34	370	16.7	4.4

1. Establishment subject to federal tax.

STATE County	Health care and social assistance, 2012				Other services, 2012				Nonemployer businesses, 2015		Value of residential construction authorized by building permits, 2016	
	Number of establishments	Number of employees	Receipts (mil dol)	Annual payroll (mil dol)	Number of establishments	Number of employees	Receipts (mil dol)	Annual payroll (mil dol)	Number	Receipts (mil dol)	New Construction ($1,000)	Number of housing units
	159	160	161	162	163	164	165	166	167	168	169	170
OHIO—Cont'd												
Ottawa	76	1 771	123.0	49.8	79	311	28.6	8.4	2 938	120.8	41 866	135
Paulding	32	604	36.0	15.8	17	61	6.0	1.2	1 037	36.3	4 461	21
Perry	61	709	40.0	18.5	28	158	11.4	2.4	2 057	69.5	7 034	38
Pickaway	86	2 266	189.6	73.5	51	179	18.2	4.3	3 336	135.9	14 386	84
Pike	60	1 610	118.0	44.4	21	69	6.6	1.4	1 525	60.8	14 708	58
Portage	267	5 974	418.5	181.0	227	1 518	120.6	40.8	10 202	445.0	62 356	273
Preble	61	975	60.4	21.6	59	235	20.8	5.4	2 442	99.4	6 286	34
Putnam	54	990	49.0	20.9	55	274	30.3	6.4	1 991	82.5	14 107	57
Richland	316	7 570	674.5	274.6	209	1 186	108.4	25.3	6 844	281.9	16 502	69
Ross	158	6 268	754.2	373.1	85	490	35.3	9.7	3 843	147.6	1 585	19
Sandusky	160	3 660	283.4	113.3	99	635	42.3	14.1	3 153	111.8	6 773	37
Scioto	214	6 155	591.9	206.7	89	336	30.4	6.8	3 830	124.1	3 763	163
Seneca	145	2 536	180.6	69.9	104	505	32.0	8.2	2 903	109.6	8 413	76
Shelby	98	1 929	169.1	64.1	69	342	36.3	9.7	2 730	114.5	13 293	53
Stark	996	28 010	2 455.5	1 090.0	694	4 770	460.7	131.2	23 344	964.4	108 088	553
Summit	1 519	45 181	4 649.6	1 869.0	1 084	7 398	853.5	202.2	37 373	1 665.0	164 313	636
Trumbull	578	10 720	991.1	378.8	313	1 771	128.1	36.8	12 603	533.9	29 871	241
Tuscarawas	200	5 156	397.5	157.3	190	1 096	125.2	27.8	5 953	267.6	12 857	67
Union	78	1 732	166.1	63.3	68	354	29.6	8.9	3 566	164.2	107 019	387
Van Wert	60	1 505	113.3	41.8	45	234	20.2	3.6	1 649	72.0	3 756	20
Vinton	22	D	D	D	8	D	D	D	678	23.3	0	0
Warren	433	9 527	853.7	325.5	244	1 944	175.3	56.3	16 024	786.5	322 851	1 287
Washington	139	5 586	453.2	195.2	110	D	D	D	3 753	155.3	1 317	15
Wayne	235	5 274	415.5	178.6	169	891	97.0	20.4	9 040	415.9	37 842	173
Williams	65	2 006	169.7	71.6	66	372	30.3	7.1	2 227	89.6	7 952	38
Wood	243	4 906	384.2	164.5	210	1 433	126.7	38.6	7 604	328.0	67 133	273
Wyandot	37	772	55.6	21.1	56	240	21.5	5.6	1 333	52.9	3 555	19
OKLAHOMA	10 654	213 226	22 795.4	8 289.9	5 411	32 388	4 037.3	939.7	276 218	12 862.1	2 155 011	12 092
Adair	17	562	33.0	16.5	11	28	1.9	0.4	1 456	49.9	2 890	15
Alfalfa	11	111	6.6	2.9	6	D	D	D	411	14.7	40	1
Atoka	22	466	26.2	9.8	15	D	D	D	950	48.1	4 800	32
Beaver	6	75	7.1	2.3	11	D	D	D	466	19.7	0	0
Beckham	87	1 235	111.5	39.4	39	247	33.4	7.6	1 848	98.2	1 226	5
Blaine	27	365	21.3	10.0	14	28	3.5	0.4	716	30.0	170	2
Bryan	124	2 092	204.5	66.4	34	159	12.8	3.6	2 885	135.0	7 777	73
Caddo	34	618	29.7	13.1	19	88	12.4	3.3	1 536	65.9	900	4
Canadian	233	2 849	228.1	88.7	159	1 006	184.0	32.9	10 084	450.3	54 859	257
Carter	217	3 790	323.6	121.1	93	974	148.1	46.4	3 352	148.1	12 163	70
Cherokee	114	2 633	244.7	106.7	41	279	20.4	5.8	2 857	121.0	8 305	81
Choctaw	40	975	59.7	27.0	13	D	D	D	912	42.7	0	0
Cimarron	4	D	D	D	4	D	D	D	205	10.4	0	0
Cleveland	755	12 359	1 158.1	435.8	308	1 761	301.9	44.6	20 619	947.9	248 908	1 950
Coal	11	242	10.4	5.5	4	D	D	D	451	42.6	0	0
Comanche	275	6 918	704.6	271.8	136	830	69.0	20.9	4 735	208.7	18 427	99
Cotton	7	42	5.1	1.4	5	16	1.6	0.3	328	11.2	80	1
Craig	74	1 329	83.1	43.5	16	43	4.4	1.2	934	41.8	0	0
Creek	113	2 166	147.1	56.4	82	306	35.9	8.1	4 812	198.8	15 723	85
Custer	92	1 668	158.5	59.7	51	302	30.3	8.3	2 190	105.8	6 007	31
Delaware	84	1 440	133.1	47.2	54	241	21.8	5.3	2 751	121.9	7 436	100
Dewey	9	D	D	D	9	42	8.4	1.1	489	21.1	NA	NA
Ellis	10	192	15.5	6.9	5	D	D	D	345	13.2	0	0
Garfield	208	4 158	427.0	151.8	118	586	58.8	14.5	4 267	183.3	13 841	70
Garvin	64	1 277	78.3	30.7	26	129	23.9	4.8	2 107	100.9	593	4
Grady	87	D	D	D	65	328	37.1	8.2	3 707	176.4	17 171	88
Grant	7	119	5.1	2.5	4	D	D	D	366	15.7	200	1
Greer	17	D	D	D	7	15	1.5	0.2	291	11.3	0	0
Harmon	6	122	8.5	3.8	2	D	D	D	161	6.5	NA	NA
Harper	9	127	7.5	3.5	6	D	D	D	327	13.4	0	0
Haskell	29	819	53.7	22.3	11	31	2.4	0.4	1 012	46.0	550	2
Hughes	40	D	D	D	10	D	D	D	733	29.8	290	2
Jackson	48	1 389	111.1	47.6	34	151	10.6	2.7	1 406	57.8	5 380	34
Jefferson	7	D	D	D	3	D	D	D	435	16.6	NA	NA
Johnston	30	586	31.8	15.3	10	32	3.3	0.8	618	27.8	567	7
Kay	143	2 252	176.8	65.7	75	335	31.6	8.3	2 578	101.3	957	9
Kingfisher	39	479	33.3	13.6	29	D	D	D	1 566	83.2	3 746	12

	Government employment and payroll, 2012									Local government finances, 2012				
			March payroll (percent of total)							General revenue				
												Taxes		
													Per capita[1] (dollars)	
STATE County	Full-time equivalent employees	March payroll (dollars)	Administration, judicial, and legal	Police and Corrections	Fire Protection	Highways and transportation	Health and Welfare	Natural resources and utilities	Education and libraries	Total (mil dol)	Inter-governmental (mil dol)	Total (mil dol)	Total	Property
	171	172	173	174	175	176	177	178	179	180	181	182	183	184
OHIO—Cont'd														
Ottawa	1 807	6 970 433	8.9	9.2	2.9	11.6	10.2	7.2	48.1	169.9	58.3	72.2	1 746	1 408
Paulding	840	2 899 437	7.0	5.4	0.3	5.0	30.9	2.1	47.9	78.4	30.7	20.4	1 057	705
Perry	1 584	4 562 693	8.5	5.7	0.8	9.1	10.2	4.3	60.2	119.5	77.0	27.9	775	640
Pickaway	2 330	14 643 979	43.7	3.1	0.9	1.5	14.8	1.6	34.2	261.8	90.0	68.3	1 211	848
Pike	1 231	4 378 557	9.2	6.9	1.1	6.4	9.9	6.4	59.2	142.7	70.7	26.2	920	694
Portage	6 776	25 510 983	5.9	7.0	4.0	6.3	23.8	3.4	48.7	675.5	218.5	230.1	1 425	1 010
Preble	1 714	6 190 256	11.3	8.4	1.2	8.8	6.9	4.8	52.3	137.6	66.2	50.4	1 204	713
Putnam	1 034	3 725 218	9.3	7.5	0.0	5.3	1.5	3.8	72.3	126.1	61.7	46.9	1 371	814
Richland	5 091	18 513 991	8.5	9.4	5.0	4.1	11.2	8.3	52.0	473.0	237.7	163.9	1 336	864
Ross	2 848	9 604 595	8.8	6.4	2.9	4.7	10.0	4.2	62.4	240.8	134.0	79.9	1 032	625
Sandusky	2 171	7 625 048	7.2	8.4	1.7	3.5	12.3	6.5	58.8	231.5	116.4	82.4	1 362	773
Scioto	2 809	9 457 558	7.1	6.9	2.7	3.9	7.6	6.7	64.1	259.9	167.7	61.3	781	581
Seneca	1 825	6 110 506	9.4	11.2	4.5	4.6	9.9	4.4	55.0	195.7	93.8	60.1	1 073	657
Shelby	1 460	5 397 171	6.3	6.1	4.3	3.0	5.5	5.6	68.3	184.8	82.0	67.4	1 370	761
Stark	11 531	42 201 589	4.3	6.8	4.8	4.1	1.9	6.1	71.3	1 313.7	628.2	474.7	1 266	949
Summit	20 065	81 863 137	7.5	10.7	5.8	4.7	7.7	7.2	54.5	2 401.2	877.7	1 094.2	2 023	1 303
Trumbull	7 911	27 957 859	8.3	9.9	5.3	3.3	10.3	6.6	55.2	724.1	366.6	245.2	1 182	844
Tuscarawas	3 307	11 310 698	8.3	7.0	2.8	5.4	6.0	9.0	58.9	309.5	126.6	106.5	1 152	825
Union	2 131	8 121 953	6.0	5.6	3.5	2.1	30.6	3.2	47.7	262.5	68.5	90.7	1 720	1 149
Van Wert	1 050	4 217 502	8.6	7.4	2.1	8.6	3.4	13.7	52.1	118.7	67.2	36.2	1 260	753
Vinton	591	1 697 854	7.1	2.3	0.0	6.1	13.7	1.9	66.2	47.0	34.8	7.8	590	511
Warren	5 863	22 314 741	4.2	7.3	6.2	2.1	0.6	3.3	75.2	748.9	233.0	383.6	1 766	1 359
Washington	2 326	7 490 510	7.9	9.4	3.2	6.0	8.9	3.7	59.9	189.5	93.8	66.4	1 080	769
Wayne	4 495	16 994 820	7.3	7.8	2.6	5.0	22.5	5.7	48.6	484.9	177.5	144.9	1 261	926
Williams	1 758	5 321 575	7.9	5.7	0.7	4.6	15.8	10.1	54.0	135.0	55.5	50.2	1 339	733
Wood	4 470	17 275 956	8.6	10.8	3.6	3.3	9.2	6.1	56.1	532.6	184.0	232.7	1 815	1 163
Wyandot	1 084	3 936 981	8.9	7.2	0.8	3.5	33.2	5.1	40.6	97.2	30.4	25.4	1 124	531
OKLAHOMA	X	X	X	X	X	X	X	X	X	X	X	X	X	X
Adair	986	2 539 434	3.7	4.1	0.2	2.8	2.6	7.8	77.6	58.2	42.9	7.8	352	205
Alfalfa	248	605 307	12.0	6.9	0.5	12.8	1.7	4.7	59.3	13.7	4.5	6.9	1 225	981
Atoka	901	3 031 357	2.1	2.9	0.0	0.7	13.5	14.8	65.5	69.1	37.2	9.2	658	295
Beaver	349	1 030 481	7.5	3.5	0.0	11.8	12.7	7.2	56.4	23.3	11.7	9.1	1 626	1 124
Beckham	996	2 808 433	5.1	8.4	3.6	5.8	2.7	8.0	63.2	78.3	28.3	36.4	1 577	607
Blaine	619	1 556 580	6.7	6.5	0.9	6.6	23.9	4.9	49.9	45.9	14.5	14.0	1 429	639
Bryan	1 434	4 012 582	7.3	9.9	3.7	4.8	3.9	6.2	62.9	108.1	53.8	36.2	833	407
Caddo	1 563	4 548 760	3.7	5.7	1.7	6.2	8.5	8.8	64.8	96.6	61.1	21.0	708	392
Canadian	3 819	11 398 884	4.8	10.1	3.4	2.2	6.5	2.2	69.3	291.7	123.9	127.1	1 037	614
Carter	1 811	5 386 589	5.3	10.5	3.1	4.9	1.1	6.3	67.9	152.0	61.4	59.3	1 233	591
Cherokee	2 005	6 302 718	3.9	5.1	1.3	3.4	35.5	5.3	44.2	165.4	56.2	22.0	457	230
Choctaw	795	2 289 614	6.3	3.7	1.7	3.9	19.7	5.9	57.8	37.7	23.4	8.9	588	233
Cimarron	196	450 099	9.5	5.4	0.0	14.3	1.7	5.6	54.3	9.9	3.7	3.1	1 291	950
Cleveland	9 950	35 955 536	3.3	6.4	4.0	1.7	32.0	2.8	48.9	893.3	214.7	278.1	1 047	619
Coal	319	840 600	8.4	5.3	4.4	7.5	6.5	3.4	64.6	24.3	13.0	8.5	1 425	897
Comanche	6 240	22 060 234	3.6	5.7	3.0	2.1	37.2	3.2	44.6	505.2	159.3	103.2	817	354
Cotton	263	656 798	7.9	5.3	1.5	6.9	1.4	7.9	66.9	18.1	12.3	3.0	492	352
Craig	859	2 734 367	4.9	5.6	1.6	5.0	35.0	3.8	42.2	46.2	23.2	13.9	943	509
Creek	2 475	7 871 373	5.1	6.6	4.0	2.5	1.9	5.1	74.1	169.5	81.2	61.8	874	489
Custer	1 316	3 555 785	5.3	7.5	2.4	3.8	17.0	5.5	56.6	88.8	32.3	37.3	1 306	656
Delaware	1 264	3 298 724	6.6	7.0	0.4	4.1	1.2	4.6	74.6	80.2	42.1	28.6	690	467
Dewey	334	940 532	8.5	5.7	0.5	11.7	14.3	4.1	54.3	35.1	7.3	21.9	4 581	2 207
Ellis	243	705 922	9.0	9.1	0.0	18.9	2.9	2.2	56.6	31.4	7.5	8.4	2 051	1 616
Garfield	2 242	6 971 075	5.4	9.4	5.9	4.5	1.4	5.0	66.7	176.9	68.5	75.4	1 232	577
Garvin	1 260	3 212 232	6.5	6.6	2.1	5.0	14.9	6.4	57.8	92.3	43.7	25.1	920	451
Grady	1 921	5 776 643	3.4	5.2	3.6	3.2	26.9	2.4	54.3	157.9	56.1	41.4	779	442
Grant	233	634 768	12.0	7.0	0.1	21.2	0.0	6.1	53.1	15.2	6.4	5.9	1 313	1 043
Greer	288	950 821	5.8	5.3	2.0	1.0	29.5	6.4	48.4	16.6	9.5	2.9	481	285
Harmon	242	611 023	7.5	4.4	0.0	5.4	40.8	2.6	38.3	7.4	4.3	1.9	648	388
Harper	266	708 452	8.7	5.5	0.0	9.6	26.4	4.5	45.3	14.8	7.0	5.9	1 592	1 096
Haskell	614	1 704 293	4.5	5.0	0.0	5.1	27.6	1.6	53.4	31.8	20.1	7.0	543	274
Hughes	768	2 037 752	4.4	2.9	0.8	3.3	28.1	3.9	55.8	38.4	20.3	12.6	908	604
Jackson	1 759	6 015 452	3.3	4.6	2.2	1.8	47.3	5.6	33.9	146.2	38.1	20.7	788	304
Jefferson	350	958 729	7.0	3.6	0.7	3.6	15.4	11.0	58.0	49.9	41.2	3.0	470	281
Johnston	410	1 050 719	7.1	6.5	0.6	3.4	2.9	5.1	73.6	22.7	13.6	6.2	561	357
Kay	2 026	5 686 908	6.0	8.0	6.7	4.3	2.5	9.9	60.6	149.2	58.1	50.8	1 108	557
Kingfisher	634	1 825 978	7.8	7.8	3.3	9.1	1.5	4.9	65.1	48.4	22.2	18.8	1 254	825

1. Based on the resident population estimated as of July 1 of the year shown.

Table B. States and Counties — Local Government Finances, Government Employment, and Income Taxes

STATE County	Local government finances, 2012 (cont.)									Government employment, 2015			Individual income tax returns, 2014		
	Direct general expenditure							Debt outstanding							
				Percent of total for:											
	Total (mil dol)	Per capita[1] (dollars)	Education	Health and hospitals	Police protection	Public welfare	Highways	Total (mil dol)	Per capita[1] (dollars)	Federal civilian	Federal military	State and local	Number of returns	Mean adjusted gross income	Mean income tax
	185	186	187	188	189	190	191	192	193	194	195	196	197	198	199
OHIO—Cont'd															
Ottawa	183.7	4 444	50.5	4.7	6.9	9.8	7.3	162.5	3 930	183	142	2 100	21 570	53 704	5 906
Paulding	83.9	4 350	53.2	21.6	2.3	1.9	7.4	20.8	1 079	48	49	1 046	8 960	45 546	4 428
Perry	127.1	3 530	59.9	5.5	4.7	7.4	7.0	19.6	543	62	92	1 483	15 190	42 870	3 768
Pickaway	245.9	4 360	42.1	29.7	3.7	2.8	4.2	155.1	2 750	92	135	3 813	24 370	50 669	4 986
Pike	136.0	4 775	54.3	20.5	2.3	3.4	5.2	25.3	889	72	71	1 385	11 100	41 908	3 714
Portage	676.4	4 190	37.6	28.6	4.0	3.4	4.1	295.0	1 827	335	407	14 724	75 960	54 873	6 566
Preble	135.2	3 229	56.4	4.3	5.3	6.0	7.0	22.8	546	70	105	1 768	19 410	45 377	4 092
Putnam	148.9	4 353	62.5	3.1	4.2	4.4	6.0	72.4	2 117	72	87	1 556	17 430	57 523	6 832
Richland	480.9	3 920	52.3	8.7	5.0	4.8	5.5	209.0	1 703	626	295	7 108	56 820	44 570	4 473
Ross	234.3	3 026	58.4	0.5	5.1	7.8	4.6	264.6	3 418	1 627	183	5 098	32 500	45 292	4 369
Sandusky	231.1	3 819	59.9	4.6	7.5	4.6	4.8	105.5	1 744	108	151	3 268	30 110	45 384	4 338
Scioto	262.2	3 341	61.1	5.0	1.9	4.1	4.6	211.5	2 694	168	190	5 171	29 020	44 750	4 380
Seneca	196.2	3 502	52.9	6.1	6.7	3.7	7.6	729.9	13 029	122	136	2 480	26 540	43 646	3 992
Shelby	185.3	3 769	51.8	0.7	3.4	11.7	9.7	191.1	3 887	71	124	2 480	23 980	52 274	5 803
Stark	1 278.7	3 411	55.1	4.6	5.7	5.0	5.4	444.1	1 185	935	971	17 862	184 130	51 403	5 867
Summit	2 276.4	4 209	43.9	4.8	5.6	4.3	3.4	4 224.1	7 811	1 787	1 386	28 974	268 810	58 526	7 622
Trumbull	736.8	3 552	53.3	5.9	6.4	5.6	3.7	248.1	1 196	514	541	9 221	100 310	44 277	4 471
Tuscarawas	292.0	3 160	50.0	4.4	5.1	6.3	5.1	119.9	1 297	258	235	4 944	45 050	49 077	5 298
Union	256.7	4 870	31.4	31.2	3.9	1.4	6.7	364.0	6 906	69	132	3 432	24 680	68 900	8 766
Van Wert	130.4	4 536	67.9	0.9	3.8	2.9	7.3	64.6	2 247	49	72	1 389	14 150	46 654	4 566
Vinton	47.0	3 548	53.9	4.2	3.0	10.0	10.2	7.8	588	15	33	675	5 130	39 014	3 135
Warren	743.8	3 424	50.7	0.4	7.2	6.1	4.8	599.3	2 759	302	588	9 651	105 790	77 705	10 970
Washington	192.0	3 124	48.4	9.0	6.4	6.0	9.1	94.7	1 541	214	153	2 826	29 090	56 354	7 188
Wayne	466.4	4 061	44.9	24.0	3.9	6.3	4.1	103.7	903	257	289	6 548	54 010	51 332	5 493
Williams	124.0	3 304	51.6	1.0	5.4	10.9	7.1	67.6	1 801	83	93	2 067	18 310	45 204	4 390
Wood	538.0	4 197	50.7	2.8	4.6	11.9	5.6	402.7	3 142	199	332	11 489	60 820	59 513	7 125
Wyandot	101.5	4 489	33.1	34.8	4.5	8.4	7.7	18.8	830	55	56	1 449	11 120	47 220	4 740
OKLAHOMA	X	X	X	X	X	X	X	X	X	47 014	33 551	292 218	1 639 760	59 518	7 625
Adair	58.1	2 606	75.3	1.7	3.3	0.0	6.3	8.0	359	43	83	1 436	7 850	34 515	2 383
Alfalfa	13.7	2 424	57.6	1.3	4.0	0.0	1.2	6.6	1 158	37	18	549	2 150	107 170	21 015
Atoka	56.5	4 036	38.0	13.0	4.0	0.0	9.5	27.1	1 931	38	49	1 142	5 190	42 394	3 628
Beaver	21.3	3 811	59.5	6.4	2.9	0.1	14.8	3.5	632	31	20	489	2 370	64 921	8 423
Beckham	65.5	2 839	44.5	3.2	6.9	0.0	8.4	42.2	1 830	51	83	1 090	9 480	72 576	10 276
Blaine	43.3	4 420	45.4	22.1	2.7	0.0	10.7	12.1	1 232	54	37	830	4 090	58 139	7 165
Bryan	107.3	2 473	57.5	3.2	6.5	0.0	4.5	150.1	3 458	96	166	6 061	17 020	44 687	4 343
Caddo	102.4	3 449	54.1	1.6	3.8	0.0	12.2	21.8	736	507	104	2 275	10 820	45 299	4 318
Canadian	275.3	2 246	65.8	0.4	5.8	0.0	4.1	217.3	1 773	565	544	5 761	57 890	67 085	7 809
Carter	138.7	2 885	55.4	3.2	6.9	0.0	8.9	72.9	1 517	101	181	3 323	21 230	56 447	7 194
Cherokee	168.8	3 505	38.7	45.6	2.0	0.0	2.6	38.5	800	252	176	8 152	17 680	42 575	3 758
Choctaw	38.5	2 537	57.0	7.0	5.1	0.5	14.4	11.0	728	44	56	1 533	5 630	38 247	3 066
Cimarron	9.8	4 126	56.2	20.2	2.6	0.0	5.2	1.3	527	14	D	250	1 130	40 179	4 361
Cleveland	909.8	3 425	38.7	32.5	4.4	0.0	4.9	703.2	2 647	706	1 054	23 755	119 270	62 763	8 070
Coal	24.2	4 050	54.5	2.2	3.3	0.0	16.0	1.2	199	15	21	389	2 050	49 033	4 867
Comanche	515.7	4 080	36.9	40.3	4.3	0.0	3.0	244.6	1 935	4 058	11 409	9 862	49 300	45 512	4 211
Cotton	18.1	2 940	59.1	0.3	2.7	0.0	14.7	9.2	1 490	23	23	950	2 420	45 164	4 223
Craig	47.8	3 238	66.7	1.2	4.4	0.0	10.2	13.5	915	54	52	1 664	5 540	43 234	3 519
Creek	169.8	2 404	59.1	3.0	5.7	0.0	7.1	161.0	2 279	261	265	3 180	29 220	54 412	5 919
Custer	81.3	2 850	57.0	0.1	7.9	0.0	10.2	57.0	1 999	187	107	2 737	12 070	60 929	7 649
Delaware	80.1	1 934	71.5	1.7	5.9	0.0	2.4	56.3	1 357	71	156	2 586	15 450	44 283	4 295
Dewey	31.7	6 636	49.7	0.2	2.9	9.2	14.3	8.2	1 718	28	19	412	2 160	62 157	7 584
Ellis	30.2	7 367	36.1	47.3	0.6	0.0	4.4	13.0	3 179	23	16	378	1 850	74 041	10 843
Garfield	196.4	3 209	47.9	2.4	5.3	0.1	7.4	189.6	3 098	481	1 395	3 379	28 170	62 303	8 579
Garvin	89.3	3 271	48.3	13.4	4.7	0.0	8.8	23.0	841	78	104	1 718	11 180	50 747	5 543
Grady	154.9	2 916	45.5	28.8	4.1	0.0	7.2	30.5	575	89	203	2 548	21 720	59 081	6 804
Grant	14.3	3 176	61.0	1.3	3.6	0.0	8.2	4.8	1 069	25	17	343	1 960	75 108	12 518
Greer	17.2	2 824	46.1	10.9	6.9	0.0	14.6	3.8	617	26	19	597	1 980	43 276	3 739
Harmon	8.0	2 738	65.6	4.3	8.1	0.0	0.4	0.3	109	22	10	294	1 010	44 267	5 114
Harper	17.7	4 809	42.7	7.9	3.9	0.0	26.2	2.4	653	26	14	417	1 630	54 591	5 380
Haskell	31.5	2 434	63.9	0.9	4.0	0.2	11.6	2.2	171	59	48	578	4 600	38 290	3 180
Hughes	38.5	2 780	61.1	4.7	3.7	0.0	13.2	24.3	1 755	35	46	988	4 780	42 319	4 159
Jackson	175.1	6 672	28.3	40.8	3.6	0.0	5.4	32.6	1 243	1 366	1 321	2 364	10 800	48 375	4 706
Jefferson	21.5	3 367	52.8	2.1	2.8	0.0	12.1	30.4	4 768	28	23	382	2 230	43 965	4 352
Johnston	21.5	1 952	72.5	4.2	4.8	0.0	3.1	3.8	343	48	41	1 005	4 190	42 885	4 045
Kay	166.0	3 621	41.7	1.9	7.4	0.0	9.5	127.9	2 790	102	167	4 244	19 350	52 258	5 852
Kingfisher	52.9	3 526	63.6	1.6	4.5	0.0	9.8	16.6	1 106	45	59	843	6 940	76 031	10 767

1. Based on the resident population estimated as of July 1 of the year shown.

Table B. States and Counties — **Land Area and Population**

STATE/ County code	CBSA code[1]	County type[2]	STATE County	Land area,[3] (sq mi) 2016	Total persons 2016	Rank	Per square mile	White	Black	American Indian, Alaska Native	Asian and Pacific Islander	Percent Hispanic or Latino[4]	Under 5 years	5 to 17 years	18 to 24 years	25 to 34 years	35 to 44 years	45 to 54 years
				Population, 2016				Race alone or in combination, not Hispanic or Latino (percent)					Age (percent)					
				1	2	3	4	5	6	7	8	9	10	11	12	13	14	15
			OKLAHOMA—Cont'd															
40 075	...	6	Kiowa	1 015.1	9 077	2 501	8.9	77.5	4.8	8.3	0.9	11.9	6.6	16.8	7.9	11.1	10.8	12.2
40 077	...	7	Latimer	722.1	10 414	2 395	14.4	73.0	2.0	28.6	1.1	3.5	5.5	16.4	10.3	11.4	10.4	12.6
40 079	22900	2	Le Flore	1 589.3	49 873	986	31.4	77.2	2.8	17.7	1.1	6.9	6.6	17.6	8.4	12.2	12.0	12.8
40 081	36420	1	Lincoln	952.3	35 129	1 299	36.9	87.5	2.6	11.0	0.8	3.2	6.2	18.3	7.5	11.3	11.0	13.6
40 083	36420	1	Logan	743.8	46 588	1 038	62.6	81.4	9.6	6.1	1.1	5.9	5.7	17.5	10.5	11.5	12.3	12.9
40 085	...	9	Love	514.0	9 997	2 434	19.4	75.6	3.0	9.8	1.0	15.3	6.3	18.7	7.9	12.9	11.0	11.9
40 087	36420	1	McClain	570.7	38 682	1 210	67.8	84.6	1.3	10.6	0.9	7.8	5.9	19.5	7.8	12.1	13.2	13.2
40 089	...	7	McCurtain	1 850.6	32 822	1 361	17.7	68.9	9.6	20.7	1.8	5.9	7.1	18.5	8.4	11.7	11.4	12.6
40 091	...	6	McIntosh	618.5	19 815	1 839	32.0	75.0	4.5	24.6	1.0	2.7	5.1	14.8	6.9	9.8	9.8	12.7
40 093	...	9	Major	955.0	7 772	2 613	8.1	87.2	1.5	3.4	0.7	9.5	7.4	18.6	6.5	11.0	11.3	11.2
40 095	...	6	Marshall	371.3	16 191	2 029	43.6	70.6	2.3	14.4	0.6	17.5	5.7	17.7	7.7	10.1	11.0	12.4
40 097	...	6	Mayes	655.4	40 920	1 155	62.4	74.1	1.1	29.9	0.7	3.4	6.1	17.8	8.2	11.7	11.6	12.7
40 099	...	7	Murray	416.5	13 918	2 171	33.4	78.9	2.3	18.2	0.8	6.2	5.7	17.6	7.4	11.6	11.6	12.6
40 101	34780	4	Muskogee	810.4	69 477	771	85.7	63.7	12.8	24.9	1.0	6.0	6.8	17.7	9.0	12.9	12.0	12.2
40 103	...	6	Noble	731.9	11 384	2 336	15.6	85.5	2.6	11.5	1.0	3.7	5.7	18.0	7.5	11.4	10.9	13.7
40 105	...	6	Nowata	565.8	10 419	2 393	18.4	75.8	3.5	26.5	0.7	2.9	5.5	16.9	8.1	11.6	11.1	13.2
40 107	...	6	Okfuskee	618.6	12 167	2 281	19.7	67.6	8.9	25.3	0.8	3.9	6.0	17.4	8.3	12.4	12.2	13.3
40 109	36420	1	Oklahoma	708.8	782 970	80	1 104.6	60.5	17.2	5.8	4.5	17.0	7.8	18.0	9.1	15.9	12.7	11.7
40 111	46140	2	Okmulgee	697.3	39 213	1 195	56.2	70.1	10.5	23.4	1.0	3.9	6.4	17.6	9.7	11.8	11.2	12.1
40 113	46140	2	Osage	2 246.6	47 806	1 021	21.3	70.2	12.4	20.7	0.7	3.4	5.1	17.3	7.5	11.4	11.2	13.2
40 115	33060	6	Ottawa	470.8	31 691	1 387	67.3	73.0	1.6	25.6	1.9	5.6	7.2	17.8	9.8	11.4	11.2	11.9
40 117	46140	2	Pawnee	568.2	16 485	2 009	29.0	82.5	1.6	17.9	0.8	3.1	6.2	17.7	7.7	10.7	11.6	13.5
40 119	44660	4	Payne	684.7	81 131	693	118.5	82.0	5.0	8.2	5.5	4.7	5.4	13.9	27.3	13.8	9.7	8.8
40 121	32540	5	Pittsburg	1 305.5	44 173	1 088	33.8	76.7	4.5	20.7	0.9	4.9	6.1	16.3	7.8	13.2	11.8	12.7
40 123	10220	7	Pontotoc	720.4	38 330	1 216	53.2	72.9	3.8	24.4	1.4	5.3	6.7	17.1	11.2	14.1	11.3	11.6
40 125	43060	4	Pottawatomie	787.7	72 290	749	91.8	78.7	4.4	17.3	1.3	4.9	6.3	17.8	9.6	12.9	12.2	12.7
40 127	...	9	Pushmataha	1 395.8	11 057	2 350	7.9	77.3	1.6	22.3	0.7	3.6	5.9	15.7	7.0	10.7	10.3	13.2
40 129	...	9	Roger Mills	1 141.1	3 640	2 931	3.2	86.2	1.6	6.6	0.9	7.1	6.3	19.8	6.8	10.1	11.4	12.1
40 131	46140	2	Rogers	675.7	91 766	638	135.8	80.1	1.8	20.1	1.8	4.4	6.0	18.0	8.8	12.1	11.8	13.8
40 133	...	7	Seminole	632.8	25 207	1 601	39.8	71.2	6.4	24.1	0.8	4.8	6.6	18.7	8.9	11.4	11.3	12.4
40 135	22900	2	Sequoyah	673.3	41 294	1 145	61.3	72.0	2.7	29.8	1.1	4.0	6.3	17.3	8.4	11.7	11.9	13.7
40 137	20340	4	Stephens	870.2	44 090	1 090	50.7	84.7	2.8	8.7	1.0	7.4	6.1	17.5	7.6	11.9	11.7	12.2
40 139	25100	7	Texas	2 041.3	21 098	1 770	10.3	46.0	5.1	1.5	3.4	45.4	8.4	19.5	10.9	14.9	12.9	11.7
40 141	...	6	Tillman	871.1	7 465	2 635	8.6	62.1	8.6	4.9	0.9	26.5	6.9	17.7	7.8	11.4	11.1	13.0
40 143	46140	2	Tulsa	570.3	642 940	102	1 127.4	67.5	12.1	9.9	3.9	12.3	7.3	18.2	9.0	14.8	12.8	12.3
40 145	46140	2	Wagoner	561.6	77 679	714	138.3	78.7	4.6	16.0	2.2	5.9	6.3	18.6	7.4	12.8	13.0	13.2
40 147	12780	4	Washington	415.5	52 087	961	125.4	79.0	3.7	15.1	2.7	5.8	6.2	17.3	8.0	12.6	11.4	11.9
40 149	...	7	Washita	1 003.2	11 447	2 328	11.4	86.2	1.9	4.6	0.5	9.6	7.2	18.4	7.4	12.5	11.4	11.8
40 151	...	7	Woods	1 286.5	9 201	2 491	7.2	85.6	4.1	4.1	1.5	7.3	6.4	14.2	17.0	14.4	10.1	10.3
40 153	49260	7	Woodward	1 242.4	20 814	1 782	16.8	81.9	2.4	4.3	1.0	12.4	7.2	18.0	8.4	14.3	13.3	12.1
41 000	...	0	**OREGON**	95 986.6	4 093 465	X	42.6	79.3	2.6	2.4	6.3	12.8	5.8	15.5	8.9	14.0	13.0	12.6
41 001	...	7	Baker	3 068.0	16 059	2 036	5.2	93.1	1.2	2.5	1.5	4.2	5.4	14.3	6.8	10.6	9.6	11.5
41 003	18700	3	Benton	675.2	89 385	648	132.4	84.2	1.7	1.6	8.8	7.3	4.1	12.4	22.8	13.2	9.8	10.1
41 005	38900	1	Clackamas	1 870.7	408 062	172	218.1	85.3	1.6	1.6	6.2	8.4	5.5	16.3	7.8	12.1	12.8	13.8
41 007	11820	4	Clatsop	828.3	38 632	1 211	46.6	88.0	1.1	2.2	2.9	8.5	5.4	14.0	8.0	12.4	11.4	12.0
41 009	38900	1	Columbia	658.0	50 785	976	77.2	91.9	1.1	3.0	2.5	4.9	5.2	16.3	7.3	11.2	12.1	14.2
41 011	18300	5	Coos	1 596.0	63 761	832	40.0	88.8	1.0	5.2	2.5	6.5	5.0	13.7	7.0	11.0	10.1	11.7
41 013	39260	6	Crook	2 978.9	22 570	1 708	7.6	89.9	0.7	2.5	1.0	7.6	5.1	14.3	6.5	10.1	10.6	11.8
41 015	15060	7	Curry	1 628.4	22 713	1 694	13.9	89.6	0.8	4.4	1.7	6.8	3.9	10.8	5.1	8.7	8.4	11.7
41 017	13460	3	Deschutes	3 017.6	181 307	359	60.1	89.7	0.9	1.7	2.2	7.8	5.3	15.4	6.9	12.7	12.8	12.9
41 019	40700	4	Douglas	5 035.7	108 457	554	21.5	90.9	0.8	3.7	2.1	5.6	5.3	14.1	6.9	10.9	10.2	12.0
41 021	...	9	Gilliam	1 204.7	1 854	3 064	1.5	91.4	1.0	2.2	1.6	5.8	5.2	14.4	5.6	8.0	10.8	11.3
41 023	...	9	Grant	4 527.8	7 158	2 659	1.6	93.9	0.9	2.8	1.2	3.7	4.9	13.6	5.4	9.6	9.7	11.0
41 025	...	7	Harney	10 134.4	7 292	2 646	0.7	90.3	1.2	5.1	1.4	5.2	5.9	15.1	7.0	10.5	10.7	11.7
41 027	26220	6	Hood River	522.1	23 232	1 668	44.5	65.9	0.8	1.5	2.6	31.3	6.7	17.9	8.1	12.2	13.0	13.4
41 029	32780	3	Jackson	2 783.2	216 520	305	77.8	84.1	1.3	2.4	2.7	12.5	5.6	15.0	7.9	12.5	11.2	12.0
41 031	...	6	Jefferson	1 782.2	23 080	1 676	13.0	62.1	1.3	17.5	1.6	20.0	6.6	17.1	8.0	12.3	11.0	12.5
41 033	24420	3	Josephine	1 638.7	85 904	667	52.4	89.8	0.9	2.9	2.0	7.3	5.1	14.5	6.7	10.3	10.2	11.9
41 035	28900	5	Klamath	5 942.7	66 443	799	11.2	81.6	1.4	6.0	2.0	12.5	6.1	15.5	8.3	12.5	10.6	11.9
41 037	...	7	Lake	8 138.6	7 837	2 608	1.0	88.5	1.2	4.1	1.8	7.8	5.3	13.2	6.4	9.9	11.4	12.8
41 039	21660	2	Lane	4 555.7	369 519	188	81.1	86.1	1.9	2.8	4.8	8.5	5.1	13.7	12.8	12.9	11.6	11.6
41 041	35440	5	Lincoln	980.4	47 806	1 021	48.8	85.6	1.0	5.3	2.3	9.0	4.7	12.5	5.9	9.9	10.0	11.8
41 043	10540	3	Linn	2 287.1	122 849	510	53.7	88.1	1.0	2.7	2.2	8.8	6.0	16.8	7.8	13.3	11.7	12.4
41 045	36620	6	Malheur	9 887.6	30 439	1 422	3.1	63.1	1.6	1.6	2.2	33.1	7.0	18.4	9.6	13.2	12.2	11.6
41 047	41420	2	Marion	1 180.5	336 316	203	284.9	68.5	1.7	2.1	4.3	26.2	6.7	18.2	9.4	13.7	12.5	12.0

1. CBSA = Core Based Statistical Area. See Appendix A for explanation. See Appendix B for list of metropolitan areas with component counties.   2. County type code from the Economic Research Service of USDA Rural-Urban Continuum Codes. See Appendix A for definition.   3. Dry land or land partially or temporarily covered by water.   4. May be of any race.

STATE County	55 to 64 years	65 to 74 years	75 years and over	Percent female	2000	2010	2000–2010	2010–2016	Births	Deaths	Net migration	Number	Persons per house-hold	Family house-holds	Female family house-holder[1]	One per-son
	16	17	18	19	20	21	22	23	24	25	26	27	28	29	30	31
OKLAHOMA—Cont'd																
Kiowa	15.2	11.0	8.4	50.4	10 227	9 446	-7.6	-3.9	730	821	-265	3 939	2.31	64.6	10.7	30.3
Latimer	13.2	10.9	9.3	49.4	10 692	11 154	4.3	-6.6	742	716	-764	4 135	2.50	70.9	13.0	24.9
Le Flore	13.1	10.3	7.1	49.9	48 109	50 384	4.7	-1.0	3 771	3 740	-500	18 164	2.67	69.4	11.5	25.8
Lincoln	14.2	10.6	7.3	50.4	32 080	34 273	6.8	2.5	2 547	2 242	511	13 231	2.58	71.1	10.5	25.3
Logan	13.7	9.4	6.5	50.4	33 924	41 853	23.4	11.3	3 040	2 217	3 638	15 091	2.83	73.4	9.5	23.6
Love	12.8	10.8	7.7	50.5	8 831	9 421	6.7	6.1	764	718	539	3 202	2.98	74.2	11.2	23.2
McClain	13.1	9.3	6.0	50.4	27 740	34 506	24.4	12.1	2 620	2 028	3 513	13 244	2.74	75.5	8.5	22.0
McCurtain	12.9	10.1	7.2	51.0	34 402	33 154	-3.6	-1.0	2 907	2 502	-679	12 908	2.53	70.5	15.5	26.2
McIntosh	15.7	14.2	11.0	50.5	19 456	20 252	4.1	-2.2	1 277	2 021	276	8 373	2.38	68.9	10.9	28.0
Major	14.9	9.8	9.4	50.8	7 545	7 527	-0.2	3.3	677	504	84	3 051	2.49	71.5	8.3	28.9
Marshall	14.0	12.4	9.1	50.2	13 184	15 836	20.1	2.2	1 143	1 147	319	5 965	2.64	66.9	8.7	28.9
Mayes	14.1	10.5	7.2	50.2	38 369	41 264	7.5	-0.8	3 133	3 061	-308	15 740	2.56	71.3	11.9	25.2
Murray	14.3	11.1	8.2	50.0	12 623	13 488	6.9	3.2	978	1 177	588	5 343	2.50	65.7	9.9	28.3
Muskogee	12.9	9.6	6.9	51.2	69 451	70 988	2.2	-2.1	5 894	5 671	-1 777	26 349	2.53	67.0	14.6	28.5
Noble	14.0	10.3	8.5	50.3	11 411	11 561	1.3	-1.5	834	814	-200	4 670	2.41	74.2	9.7	22.9
Nowata	14.1	10.6	8.8	50.6	10 569	10 536	-0.3	-1.1	706	839	33	4 046	2.56	70.2	11.3	26.5
Okfuskee	13.0	9.9	7.4	46.3	11 814	12 191	3.2	-0.2	1 057	1 042	-32	4 048	2.72	69.8	13.8	26.0
Oklahoma	11.9	7.5	5.4	51.1	660 448	718 627	8.8	9.0	76 899	43 102	30 778	291 390	2.53	62.3	13.8	31.2
Okmulgee	13.3	10.1	7.7	50.7	39 685	40 069	1.0	-2.1	3 206	3 214	-817	15 022	2.53	64.7	14.6	30.7
Osage	14.6	11.6	8.1	49.7	44 437	47 480	6.8	0.7	2 787	2 990	320	18 271	2.55	68.8	10.1	27.4
Ottawa	12.5	10.3	7.9	51.0	33 194	31 848	-4.1	-0.5	2 765	2 729	-241	12 061	2.58	68.0	13.3	27.6
Pawnee	14.1	10.8	7.7	50.1	16 612	16 579	-0.2	-0.6	1 235	1 282	-56	6 278	2.60	72.4	11.6	23.1
Payne	9.4	6.6	5.1	48.9	68 190	77 350	13.4	4.9	5 677	3 459	1 525	30 164	2.36	54.9	8.5	31.4
Pittsburg	13.5	10.8	7.9	49.1	43 953	45 837	4.3	-3.6	3 351	3 751	-1 191	18 087	2.36	66.4	12.4	28.6
Pontotoc	11.8	8.8	7.3	51.3	35 143	37 492	6.7	2.2	3 392	2 737	203	14 591	2.52	64.1	13.3	29.1
Pottawatomie	12.5	9.4	6.6	52.1	65 521	69 442	6.0	4.1	5 864	4 959	1 910	25 996	2.61	69.4	13.0	26.6
Pushmataha	14.5	12.8	9.9	50.6	11 667	11 572	-0.8	-4.5	807	1 018	-280	4 749	2.34	62.7	11.0	33.3
Roger Mills	14.5	10.1	9.0	50.2	3 436	3 647	6.1	-0.2	301	207	-125	1 340	2.80	63.6	8.7	30.1
Rogers	13.3	9.6	6.6	50.2	70 641	86 911	23.0	5.6	6 277	5 022	3 373	33 358	2.64	75.7	9.7	20.7
Seminole	13.1	9.9	7.7	51.0	24 894	25 482	2.4	-1.1	2 093	2 118	-185	9 202	2.70	68.7	13.3	26.9
Sequoyah	13.1	10.5	7.2	50.6	38 972	42 439	8.9	-2.7	2 830	3 097	-874	15 552	2.64	71.6	14.1	24.9
Stephens	14.3	10.3	8.4	51.5	43 182	45 048	4.3	-2.1	3 486	3 479	-941	17 868	2.48	67.3	10.0	29.0
Texas	10.7	6.2	4.8	46.3	20 107	20 640	2.7	2.2	2 264	863	-934	7 173	2.93	71.1	9.3	24.7
Tillman	13.8	10.3	8.0	49.8	9 287	7 992	-13.9	-6.6	648	554	-593	3 057	2.40	69.9	15.6	27.2
Tulsa	12.1	7.9	5.7	51.3	563 299	603 438	7.1	6.5	58 720	35 530	16 391	246 080	2.50	63.6	13.8	30.2
Wagoner	13.1	9.9	5.7	50.4	57 491	73 087	27.1	6.3	5 602	3 929	2 851	27 452	2.74	75.5	11.1	20.6
Washington	13.7	9.7	9.2	51.3	48 996	50 974	4.0	2.2	3 992	3 787	994	21 001	2.43	67.5	11.2	28.4
Washita	14.3	9.2	7.8	50.2	11 508	11 629	1.1	-1.6	980	893	-255	4 640	2.46	71.1	10.4	25.5
Woods	11.1	8.2	8.4	46.7	9 089	8 878	-2.3	3.6	693	628	236	3 426	2.37	59.4	7.2	31.9
Woodward	12.1	8.1	6.6	47.3	18 486	20 081	8.6	3.7	1 944	1 236	38	7 367	2.70	68.4	11.0	26.8
OREGON	13.4	10.2	6.7	50.5	3 421 399	3 831 072	12.0	6.8	284 655	210 571	184 204	1 533 430	2.51	63.4	10.5	27.9
Baker	16.0	14.8	11.1	49.5	16 741	16 138	-3.6	-0.5	1 065	1 279	198	7 160	2.16	62.2	8.0	32.9
Benton	12.3	9.2	6.0	49.9	78 153	85 581	9.5	4.4	4 601	3 485	2 656	33 840	2.40	55.7	7.1	28.8
Clackamas	14.5	10.5	6.7	50.8	338 391	375 998	11.1	8.5	25 124	19 913	25 987	149 522	2.59	68.8	9.7	24.4
Clatsop	16.2	13.2	7.4	50.6	35 630	37 029	3.9	4.3	2 607	2 406	1 403	15 726	2.32	61.1	10.3	32.4
Columbia	15.6	11.5	6.6	50.1	43 560	49 353	13.3	2.9	3 022	2 645	1 075	18 785	2.60	68.1	9.4	25.8
Coos	16.6	14.5	10.5	50.8	62 779	63 043	0.4	1.1	3 880	5 441	2 175	25 888	2.38	60.5	9.4	32.6
Crook	16.8	15.4	9.4	50.4	19 182	20 978	9.4	7.6	1 237	1 433	1 755	9 079	2.29	65.0	7.6	27.5
Curry	18.7	19.3	13.3	50.9	21 137	22 364	5.8	1.6	1 074	2 248	1 443	10 454	2.11	57.7	7.4	33.6
Deschutes	14.7	12.3	7.0	50.7	115 367	157 733	36.7	14.9	10 916	8 439	20 568	66 337	2.49	66.9	9.1	25.2
Douglas	15.9	14.1	10.6	50.8	100 399	107 667	7.2	0.7	6 792	8 647	2 594	43 798	2.41	66.5	11.7	26.0
Gilliam	17.7	14.5	12.5	49.0	1 915	1 873	-2.2	-1.0	110	129	-9	833	2.24	62.5	8.2	33.5
Grant	17.3	15.9	12.7	49.9	7 935	7 445	-6.2	-3.9	387	473	-200	3 149	2.26	62.0	7.8	32.3
Harney	16.4	13.1	9.5	49.8	7 609	7 422	-2.5	-1.8	530	502	-154	3 038	2.32	70.0	9.9	24.6
Hood River	13.5	8.7	6.4	50.1	20 411	22 346	9.5	4.0	1 836	1 093	102	8 189	2.66	64.2	6.3	26.6
Jackson	14.5	12.5	8.8	51.2	181 269	203 206	12.1	6.6	14 480	13 992	12 380	83 487	2.45	63.9	11.4	28.9
Jefferson	13.8	11.9	6.8	48.2	19 009	21 719	14.3	6.3	1 804	1 320	821	7 692	2.76	70.0	13.7	23.9
Josephine	15.8	14.8	10.8	51.2	75 726	82 713	9.2	3.9	5 221	7 247	5 091	34 527	2.38	64.0	10.4	29.2
Klamath	14.7	12.3	8.0	50.1	63 775	66 380	4.1	0.1	4 983	4 651	-228	27 188	2.39	65.4	11.4	26.4
Lake	17.0	14.2	9.7	46.5	7 422	7 886	6.3	-0.6	467	523	-3	3 526	2.08	55.4	6.6	37.3
Lane	13.8	11.1	7.4	50.8	322 959	351 724	8.9	5.1	22 445	20 818	15 588	146 235	2.39	59.3	10.6	29.3
Lincoln	18.5	17.1	9.5	51.6	44 479	46 032	3.5	3.9	2 705	3 578	2 693	20 566	2.22	60.7	8.7	31.4
Linn	13.9	10.7	7.4	50.5	103 069	116 672	13.2	5.3	9 006	7 447	4 360	45 100	2.61	68.1	11.8	24.7
Malheur	11.9	8.8	7.3	45.6	31 615	31 312	-1.0	-2.8	2 640	1 778	-1 732	10 286	2.62	66.5	11.7	29.2
Marion	12.3	8.9	6.2	50.2	284 834	315 335	10.7	6.7	27 530	16 636	9 872	113 996	2.75	69.2	13.7	25.2

1. No spouse present.

Table B. States and Counties — Population, Vital Statistics, Health, and Crime

STATE County	Persons in group quarters, 2016	Daytime population, 2011–2015 Number	Employ-ment/resi-dence ratio	Births, 2016 Total	Rate[1]	Deaths, 2016 Number	Rate[1]	Persons under 65 with no health insurance, 2015 Number	Percent	Medicare, 2015 Total Beneficiaries	Enrolled in Original Medicare	Enrolled in Medicare Advantage	Serious crimes known to police[2] 2014 Total Number	Rate[3]
	32	33	34	35	36	37	38	39	40	41	42	43	44	45
OKLAHOMA—Cont'd														
Kiowa	171	8 524	0.80	120	13.2	116	12.8	1 203	16.7	2 184	2 014	170	190	2 037
Latimer	574	10 470	0.92	120	11.5	104	10.0	1 411	17.7	1 698	1 538	160	169	1 580
Le Flore	1 614	45 997	0.78	640	12.8	681	13.7	8 184	20.7	11 139	9 617	1 522	1 209	2 435
Lincoln	386	28 823	0.60	428	12.2	343	9.8	4 846	16.9	6 246	5 113	1 133	635	1 846
Logan	2 184	33 557	0.45	507	10.9	389	8.3	5 150	13.8	5 222	4 134	1 088	773	1 715
Love	88	11 069	1.35	119	11.9	120	12.0	1 400	17.5	1 949	1 830	119	128	1 302
McClain	194	30 448	0.63	428	11.1	334	8.6	4 948	15.3	6 928	5 934	994	683	1 845
McCurtain	454	32 848	0.98	465	14.2	439	13.4	5 494	20.4	7 049	6 391	658	982	2 970
McIntosh	345	18 617	0.76	190	9.6	321	16.2	2 979	20.1	5 538	5 008	530	446	2 169
Major	77	7 401	0.91	112	14.4	74	9.5	894	14.2	1 518	1 458	60	98	1 267
Marshall	329	15 055	0.84	180	11.1	149	9.2	2 849	22.6	3 594	3 314	280	253	1 577
Mayes	566	39 317	0.90	489	12.0	544	13.3	5 905	17.7	8 238	6 923	1 315	762	1 871
Murray	313	12 958	0.87	159	11.4	201	14.4	1 865	16.9	2 772	2 589	183	274	1 989
Muskogee	3 518	73 625	1.13	896	12.9	905	13.0	9 978	18.2	15 851	14 048	1 803	2 412	3 437
Noble	273	11 403	0.98	123	10.8	127	11.2	1 317	14.0	2 134	2 021	113	171	1 496
Nowata	157	8 773	0.57	110	10.6	136	13.1	1 655	19.7	2 288	2 106	182	137	1 295
Okfuskee	1 228	11 231	0.74	152	12.5	157	12.9	1 805	19.7	2 434	2 161	273	296	2 382
Oklahoma	14 742	861 832	1.31	12 351	15.8	7 006	8.9	108 899	16.4	122 690	92 042	30 648	34 472	4 507
Okmulgee	1 375	36 530	0.80	502	12.8	525	13.4	4 950	15.9	8 082	6 875	1 207	964	2 452
Osage	1 504	39 053	0.53	434	9.1	559	11.7	5 415	14.5	3 882	3 245	637	1 074	2 229
Ottawa	968	32 092	1.00	453	14.3	499	15.7	4 996	19.7	7 369	6 642	727	741	2 289
Pawnee	194	13 993	0.63	202	12.3	190	11.5	2 243	16.9	3 524	3 070	454	190	1 151
Payne	7 778	81 359	1.05	895	11.0	582	7.2	10 018	15.6	11 361	10 708	653	2 361	2 967
Pittsburg	2 424	45 785	1.05	528	12.0	574	13.0	6 475	18.9	9 603	8 739	864	1 437	3 231
Pontotoc	1 700	39 968	1.11	515	13.4	510	13.3	5 666	18.5	7 462	6 837	625	1 463	3 837
Pottawatomie	3 050	68 197	0.90	918	12.7	823	11.4	9 374	16.3	13 915	11 133	2 782	2 941	4 107
Pushmataha	110	10 459	0.80	132	11.9	164	14.8	1 785	20.7	2 808	2 531	277	160	1 434
Roger Mills	11	3 886	1.06	42	11.5	24	6.6	470	15.3	695	674	21	75	1 987
Rogers	1 216	76 851	0.70	1 040	11.3	828	9.0	9 442	12.4	13 307	9 170	4 137	1 297	1 447
Seminole	581	24 694	0.91	325	12.9	341	13.5	3 885	18.9	5 140	4 482	658	633	2 488
Sequoyah	464	36 727	0.69	533	12.9	537	13.0	6 073	18.1	8 934	7 444	1 490	1 138	2 778
Stephens	540	44 565	0.99	563	12.8	546	12.4	5 748	15.9	8 788	7 724	1 064	1 728	3 847
Texas	572	20 777	0.93	390	18.5	142	6.7	4 446	24.0	2 251	2 073	178	362	1 614
Tillman	267	7 110	0.80	104	13.9	73	9.8	1 178	20.1	1 602	1 516	86	194	2 535
Tulsa	9 869	685 612	1.21	9 429	14.7	6 003	9.3	86 346	15.8	111 175	74 855	36 320	28 040	4 469
Wagoner	319	53 434	0.35	923	11.9	673	8.7	9 441	14.6	6 429	4 403	2 026	1 689	2 212
Washington	798	52 797	1.05	645	12.4	654	12.6	6 933	16.6	11 686	10 568	1 118	1 109	2 143
Washita	206	9 888	0.65	177	15.5	153	13.4	1 503	15.6	2 321	2 181	140	189	1 614
Woods	1 001	9 887	1.20	121	13.2	101	11.0	893	13.0	1 559	1 460	99	108	1 188
Woodward	1 237	21 874	1.10	302	14.5	256	12.3	2 679	15.4	3 218	3 048	170	583	2 704
OREGON	88 778	3 985 279	1.03	46 198	11.3	35 371	8.6	278 293	8.4	733 837	385 029	348 808	123 529	3 111
Baker	373	15 775	0.96	165	10.3	213	13.3	1 029	8.9	4 503	4 198	305	423	2 633
Benton	5 097	87 884	1.04	757	8.5	581	6.5	4 995	7.1	12 034	6 066	5 968	2 620	3 004
Clackamas	2 961	357 082	0.82	4 221	10.3	3 462	8.5	20 763	6.2	70 394	24 643	45 751	NA	NA
Clatsop	870	38 672	1.08	410	10.6	398	10.3	2 756	9.3	9 160	6 709	2 451	924	2 981
Columbia	455	40 465	0.55	484	9.5	477	9.4	2 867	7.1	9 802	4 482	5 320	661	1 388
Coos	1 145	62 805	1.00	627	9.8	903	14.2	4 261	9.2	18 230	16 007	2 223	2 164	3 613
Crook	239	20 016	0.88	240	10.6	236	10.5	1 406	8.7	5 897	4 442	1 455	536	2 567
Curry	304	22 221	0.98	151	6.6	355	15.6	1 493	9.9	7 889	6 901	988	291	1 367
Deschutes	1 083	166 682	1.00	1 853	10.2	1 455	8.0	12 206	8.6	37 153	25 532	11 621	4 379	2 595
Douglas	1 715	106 369	0.98	1 103	10.2	1 371	12.6	6 551	8.1	29 809	19 389	10 420	3 123	3 009
Gilliam	21	2 017	1.18	14	7.6	29	15.6	98	7.1	535	495	40	30	1 519
Grant	95	7 142	0.95	61	8.5	74	10.3	448	8.8	2 037	1 650	387	87	1 196
Harney	141	7 297	1.02	91	12.5	72	9.9	539	10.0	1 806	1 652	154	156	2 193
Hood River	789	23 886	1.10	308	13.3	172	7.4	2 246	11.4	3 681	2 683	998	410	1 796
Jackson	4 781	209 175	1.01	2 314	10.7	2 258	10.4	14 683	8.9	50 319	33 485	16 834	9 061	4 300
Jefferson	899	21 391	0.92	280	12.1	250	10.8	2 224	12.7	4 814	3 461	1 353	620	2 938
Josephine	1 537	81 968	0.95	885	10.3	1 147	13.4	5 518	8.9	24 070	14 899	9 171	2 896	3 457
Klamath	1 030	65 225	0.97	791	11.9	787	11.8	5 303	10.3	14 756	11 321	3 435	1 936	2 967
Lake	466	7 896	1.02	80	10.2	92	11.7	613	11.1	1 998	1 829	169	NA	NA
Lane	8 142	358 568	1.01	3 752	10.2	3 422	9.3	25 609	8.8	74 183	34 566	39 617	NA	NA
Lincoln	761	46 525	1.01	432	9.0	576	12.0	3 958	11.5	13 216	10 233	2 983	1 737	3 725
Linn	1 212	114 597	0.91	1 436	11.7	1 290	10.5	8 152	8.3	27 369	12 819	14 550	4 028	3 364
Malheur	3 346	34 056	1.34	388	12.7	249	8.2	2 626	11.9	5 779	5 072	707	821	3 017
Marion	10 598	329 482	1.05	4 451	13.2	2 848	8.5	26 364	9.7	54 294	21 126	33 168	11 416	3 492

1. Per 1,000 estimated resident population.   2. Data for serious crimes have not been adjusted for underreporting; this may affect comparability between geographic areas and over time.
3. Per 100,000 population estimated by the FBI.

Table B. States and Counties — Crime, Education, Money Income, and Poverty

STATE County	Serious crimes known to police, 2014 (cont.)[1] Rate[2] Violent	Property	Education — School enrollment and attainment, 2011–2015 Enrollment[3] (percent) Total	Per-cent private	Attainment[4] (percent) High school graduate or less	Bach-elor's degree or more	Local government expenditures,[5] 2013–2014 Total current spending (mil dol)	Current spending per student (dollars)	Money income, 2011–2015 Per capita income[6] (dollars)	Households Median income (dollars)	Percent with income of less than $50,000	with income of $200,000 or more	Income and poverty, 2015 Median house-hold income (dollars)	Percent below poverty level All per-sons	Children under 18 years	Children 5 to 17 years in families
	46	47	48	49	50	51	52	53	54	55	56	57	58	59	60	61
OKLAHOMA—Cont'd																
Kiowa	289	1 747	2 103	4.1	50.1	18.8	14.4	8 619	23 260	39 909	62.2	1.5	37 721	21.1	29.3	26.9
Latimer	290	1 290	2 595	5.3	50.9	14.0	13.1	8 623	22 343	39 205	60.3	2.3	38 313	19.4	26.9	24.8
Le Flore	213	2 222	11 777	4.6	58.3	13.8	78.9	7 915	18 881	36 490	63.5	1.2	38 261	19.3	27.4	25.4
Lincoln	189	1 657	8 277	9.5	54.9	13.4	41.3	7 349	23 072	45 149	55.2	1.8	46 976	14.7	20.5	18.5
Logan	144	1 570	11 538	12.4	44.1	26.1	35.5	7 466	27 402	55 299	45.3	5.4	57 892	13.1	16.4	15.0
Love	81	1 221	2 216	9.4	58.4	14.2	14.0	7 802	20 589	44 549	53.7	1.8	45 223	12.4	21.2	19.7
McClain	92	1 754	9 486	8.1	47.3	22.4	50.4	6 648	26 562	56 088	44.2	3.1	56 700	10.7	14.2	12.7
McCurtain	200	2 770	7 986	6.0	60.6	13.4	56.2	8 122	17 898	32 324	67.6	1.3	31 723	25.3	32.3	30.7
McIntosh	170	1 998	3 932	5.6	55.3	13.8	25.4	8 094	20 599	36 011	64.6	1.5	35 775	21.3	31.9	28.6
Major	26	1 241	1 705	8.2	53.9	16.7	9.3	8 246	27 877	51 571	47.8	3.4	55 020	10.8	13.6	12.5
Marshall	137	1 440	3 693	6.5	55.4	13.4	23.7	7 861	20 339	40 475	60.1	1.4	41 312	17.1	25.5	23.4
Mayes	346	1 525	9 859	6.7	51.3	16.3	58.2	7 984	20 884	42 071	57.0	1.2	46 373	18.5	25.9	24.2
Murray	167	1 822	2 979	1.9	56.9	20.2	18.1	6 735	23 146	47 077	53.6	2.3	45 560	14.4	19.4	17.3
Muskogee	735	2 702	17 308	8.3	50.7	18.4	105.5	7 633	20 516	39 984	59.7	1.3	40 340	21.1	27.6	26.3
Noble	175	1 321	2 838	3.2	46.7	22.7	18.4	8 513	25 368	48 285	51.8	2.7	51 977	11.8	17.3	14.8
Nowata	265	1 031	2 459	7.1	57.0	13.8	15.3	8 019	20 524	39 875	62.0	0.9	43 341	16.4	25.3	22.6
Okfuskee	249	2 132	2 709	7.9	57.3	12.1	17.2	8 794	16 818	36 216	64.4	1.0	37 289	23.9	31.4	30.3
Oklahoma	595	3 912	199 704	13.9	39.1	30.6	957.6	7 232	27 401	47 437	52.0	4.2	49 750	16.2	23.5	22.2
Okmulgee	252	2 200	9 872	5.0	50.1	15.2	70.5	7 600	20 313	38 843	61.1	1.1	39 825	22.5	32.2	29.5
Osage	235	1 995	11 469	10.7	54.4	16.1	33.1	8 480	22 935	45 443	53.7	1.4	46 093	16.3	23.9	21.5
Ottawa	182	2 107	7 872	6.2	52.7	13.7	47.5	7 813	18 136	36 347	64.7	0.7	36 166	23.0	33.0	30.9
Pawnee	273	878	3 725	8.0	55.1	16.5	20.2	7 617	22 603	45 765	54.1	1.6	45 184	16.0	23.6	20.8
Payne	264	2 704	31 812	3.8	36.1	36.9	83.6	7 717	21 469	37 667	61.9	3.0	41 747	22.7	18.0	17.5
Pittsburg	148	3 083	9 597	9.0	51.2	16.2	66.7	8 423	23 311	42 576	56.5	2.1	43 257	17.0	23.3	22.0
Pontotoc	422	3 414	10 168	4.9	45.6	27.1	58.3	8 139	21 827	43 261	56.2	1.3	44 798	15.4	20.6	19.5
Pottawatomie	459	3 647	17 749	12.8	48.5	18.1	98.3	7 305	21 974	44 688	55.0	2.2	43 587	17.0	22.6	21.7
Pushmataha	242	1 192	2 175	4.5	58.2	13.2	20.8	9 224	20 802	32 445	67.6	2.4	34 910	21.1	30.6	29.7
Roger Mills	132	1 854	883	6.1	49.1	20.4	11.0	14 199	26 257	50 739	49.0	3.8	57 063	10.8	15.5	14.0
Rogers	221	1 226	23 287	13.5	42.0	23.4	104.4	7 443	28 057	58 139	42.4	3.2	63 263	10.0	13.8	12.1
Seminole	279	2 209	6 471	4.0	52.8	13.7	43.1	8 281	19 141	36 068	63.6	2.0	39 102	20.7	30.5	28.0
Sequoyah	315	2 463	9 838	5.6	57.7	13.5	66.3	7 804	18 451	35 736	64.0	1.0	36 718	24.4	32.7	29.9
Stephens	158	3 689	10 481	6.3	53.3	17.3	62.0	7 543	24 291	43 781	55.2	2.7	47 949	15.6	21.9	20.1
Texas	214	1 400	5 547	4.1	58.7	19.1	37.2	8 148	21 809	50 242	49.8	1.2	51 092	11.4	15.8	15.1
Tillman	248	2 287	1 728	1.3	59.3	16.7	15.1	9 600	19 057	37 759	63.1	1.9	38 247	23.1	30.2	27.7
Tulsa	591	3 878	162 905	18.3	37.0	30.4	915.4	7 712	28 350	49 759	50.2	4.2	51 366	15.9	22.6	20.5
Wagoner	270	1 942	19 612	12.6	45.7	21.8	45.7	6 888	25 535	55 715	44.2	2.6	57 948	10.2	14.7	13.3
Washington	186	1 957	12 188	13.0	43.4	26.9	64.0	7 149	28 145	50 023	50.0	4.3	52 056	13.5	19.7	17.6
Washita	307	1 306	2 677	5.4	53.1	20.0	18.8	8 485	25 493	49 632	50.3	2.7	49 606	15.8	21.4	19.7
Woods	99	1 089	2 342	9.4	45.5	27.2	14.6	10 398	26 700	55 315	45.5	2.9	52 920	13.8	15.6	15.3
Woodward	278	2 425	4 975	4.6	53.0	18.1	31.2	7 871	26 124	55 300	46.1	2.4	60 290	11.8	16.1	15.6
OREGON	232	2 879	964 738	15.1	34.5	30.8	5 634.0	9 760	27 684	51 243	48.8	3.8	54 074	15.2	19.8	18.1
Baker	454	2 178	3 277	14.8	42.4	20.6	22.3	8 867	24 360	41 098	60.9	1.9	40 855	15.3	27.0	26.1
Benton	127	2 877	32 337	6.8	20.0	52.8	84.8	9 763	27 888	49 802	50.2	3.8	54 773	18.3	15.0	12.7
Clackamas	NA	NA	94 218	16.3	30.4	33.1	532.4	9 134	34 047	65 965	37.4	6.6	69 523	9.4	12.3	10.4
Clatsop	187	2 794	7 924	11.7	35.1	23.6	51.3	10 300	26 294	46 408	53.5	2.0	47 340	13.9	21.5	19.7
Columbia	90	1 297	11 120	12.6	44.1	18.2	68.5	8 767	25 885	53 179	46.3	1.8	52 060	13.4	16.6	14.4
Coos	144	3 470	11 289	8.4	43.5	18.3	87.6	9 176	22 667	38 605	63.2	1.5	38 934	18.7	29.8	26.8
Crook	196	2 370	4 046	9.9	50.7	15.5	27.8	8 293	21 496	37 106	61.5	0.9	45 046	15.9	25.6	22.1
Curry	99	1 268	3 179	12.0	37.6	23.5	23.4	10 116	24 682	40 884	60.1	0.9	38 126	17.2	27.0	26.3
Deschutes	181	2 414	39 247	12.0	29.4	32.6	245.9	9 802	29 158	51 223	49.0	3.9	56 911	13.4	18.2	15.6
Douglas	206	2 803	21 204	11.4	43.4	15.7	145.9	10 204	22 591	41 312	58.6	1.6	41 696	19.5	30.7	26.3
Gilliam	0	1 519	361	6.1	48.1	16.1	6.5	22 604	25 227	44 293	55.9	1.7	50 694	12.9	17.9	18.5
Grant	41	1 155	1 299	9.7	43.5	19.1	14.0	15 720	22 538	38 046	62.2	0.9	43 105	16.4	26.4	23.4
Harney	70	2 123	1 599	18.1	46.3	17.0	16.3	15 520	21 040	37 580	63.2	1.2	40 468	16.3	25.5	24.8
Hood River	158	1 638	5 124	8.7	44.4	31.7	44.1	10 725	27 719	55 827	42.1	4.1	53 726	11.5	17.9	16.1
Jackson	319	3 981	45 769	12.9	38.6	25.6	282.0	9 745	24 605	44 028	55.4	2.2	44 855	19.3	25.2	23.0
Jefferson	190	2 749	5 280	3.8	45.5	16.0	43.3	11 849	21 341	46 366	53.9	1.0	42 325	21.9	31.7	30.1
Josephine	222	3 235	16 347	11.3	43.0	16.7	102.5	9 557	22 470	37 665	62.4	2.3	40 569	21.9	34.4	32.6
Klamath	218	2 749	15 446	11.0	41.8	19.7	94.4	9 973	22 177	40 336	60.1	1.4	42 384	19.9	29.4	26.3
Lake	NA	NA	1 448	5.2	49.0	17.7	14.5	11 906	20 142	32 369	67.6	0.2	39 878	18.6	26.1	23.1
Lane	NA	NA	95 618	10.0	33.9	28.4	445.8	9 901	24 960	44 103	55.0	2.3	47 254	19.0	23.1	20.9
Lincoln	347	3 377	7 886	12.4	39.3	23.7	50.2	9 690	25 124	42 101	58.6	1.9	41 118	17.0	27.9	26.5
Linn	109	3 255	28 556	10.0	41.5	17.3	185.7	8 265	21 706	45 644	53.9	1.2	47 757	15.8	22.4	20.1
Malheur	294	2 723	8 057	12.0	49.7	13.8	58.6	11 312	16 867	35 418	61.9	1.6	37 604	24.9	33.9	31.1
Marion	237	3 255	84 662	16.0	42.8	22.0	622.5	8 848	22 490	48 432	51.3	1.9	51 623	16.8	24.1	21.6

1. Data for serious crimes have not been adjusted for underreporting; this may affect comparability between geographic areas and over time.   2. Per 100,000 population estimated by the FBI.
3. All persons 3 years old and over enrolled in nursery school through college.   4. Persons 25 years old and over.   5. Elementary and secondary education expenditures.
6. Based on population estimated by the American Community Survey, 2011–2015.

STATE County	Total (mil dol)	Percent change, 2014–2015	Per capita[1]		Wages and salaries (mil dol)	Supplements to wages and salaries; employer contributions (mil dol)		Proprietors' income (mil dol)	Dividends, interest, and rent (mil dol)	Personal transfer receipts (mil dol)	Total (mil dol)	Contributions for government social insurance (mil dol)	
			Dollars	Rank		Pension and insurance	Government social insurance					From employee and self-employed	From employer
	62	63	64	65	66	67	68	69	70	71	72	73	74
OKLAHOMA—Cont'd													
Kiowa	292	-6.2	31 899	2 176	81	19	6	32	49	92	138	9	6
Latimer	349	0.2	33 297	2 101	145	32	11	22	52	115	210	13	11
Le Flore	1 579	3.3	31 837	2 540	512	97	41	199	192	494	848	49	41
Lincoln	1 226	3.6	34 985	2 117	256	48	19	142	172	290	464	28	19
Logan	1 796	2.9	39 036	672	272	46	21	131	271	326	472	30	21
Love	357	2.9	36 197	1 883	196	47	15	30	51	90	288	16	15
McClain	1 618	1.9	42 507	1 070	346	58	26	139	225	287	569	33	26
McCurtain	1 021	3.8	30 880	2 680	404	77	33	115	127	339	630	38	33
McIntosh	649	1.4	32 448	2 280	132	26	10	51	98	250	219	17	10
Major	331	-9.1	42 611	462	115	21	8	52	63	58	197	10	8
Marshall	553	2.6	34 055	2 023	157	30	13	40	85	162	240	16	13
Mayes	1 473	3.8	36 035	2 072	567	98	44	112	201	389	820	50	44
Murray	579	5.6	41 565	1 210	228	53	17	59	85	132	358	20	17
Muskogee	2 369	3.2	33 990	2 216	1 303	263	104	185	393	727	1 855	109	104
Noble	459	3.1	33 694	1 456	208	40	15	40	93	97	304	17	15
Nowata	370	3.6	35 141	2 089	62	13	5	41	51	99	121	8	5
Okfuskee	349	0.1	28 624	2 866	82	19	6	39	54	119	147	9	6
Oklahoma	38 303	6.6	49 304	330	24 880	4 026	1 836	6 231	7 169	5 802	36 973	1 925	1 836
Okmulgee	1 253	1.8	31 985	2 524	378	75	29	78	174	404	560	37	29
Osage	1 599	0.7	33 397	1 636	279	55	21	182	230	364	538	32	21
Ottawa	1 098	4.5	34 331	2 291	409	82	31	111	168	339	633	38	31
Pawnee	557	2.4	33 897	2 171	147	30	12	39	81	160	226	15	12
Payne	2 972	0.9	36 757	1 449	1 474	317	109	268	572	507	2 168	115	109
Pittsburg	1 586	3.2	35 556	1 922	726	148	57	106	305	419	1 036	62	57
Pontotoc	1 535	3.1	40 180	1 261	748	153	57	130	257	359	1 088	61	57
Pottawatomie	2 587	2.5	35 999	1 916	865	154	66	333	399	635	1 419	81	66
Pushmataha	336	7.8	30 016	2 686	95	21	7	33	47	128	156	11	7
Roger Mills	196	-6.6	51 686	412	36	8	3	45	67	24	92	4	3
Rogers	3 739	2.3	41 178	903	1 344	218	103	226	563	693	1 891	114	103
Seminole	855	1.2	33 474	2 335	284	58	22	130	126	257	494	28	22
Sequoyah	1 268	1.3	30 807	2 638	276	61	22	83	201	421	442	32	22
Stephens	2 084	-2.6	46 750	411	730	113	54	453	375	406	1 351	70	54
Texas	988	1.0	45 962	639	389	70	28	323	116	108	811	29	28
Tillman	265	-5.3	35 271	1 484	75	17	6	45	42	70	142	7	6
Tulsa	44 001	-1.9	68 833	186	18 674	2 698	1 399	15 619	7 544	4 719	38 390	1 690	1 399
Wagoner	2 780	2.9	36 313	1 977	404	69	31	155	341	539	659	46	31
Washington	3 025	3.3	58 148	537	1 152	194	81	884	485	447	2 310	109	81
Washita	396	-5.1	33 932	1 987	82	18	6	47	73	88	153	9	6
Woods	442	2.7	47 537	910	183	37	13	64	157	61	297	15	13
Woodward	1 015	-9.5	47 068	216	474	76	35	216	176	137	801	39	35
OREGON	176 401	6.5	43 830	X	91 124	13 186	7 930	14 136	34 064	35 702	126 376	7 954	7 930
Baker	563	4.9	35 153	2 157	196	39	18	35	137	183	287	20	18
Benton	3 650	6.1	41 676	1 227	1 839	348	155	242	895	550	2 584	157	155
Clackamas	19 901	6.3	49 565	449	7 953	1 017	703	1 174	3 979	2 840	10 848	704	703
Clatsop	1 524	5.7	40 278	1 494	687	112	64	143	298	396	1 007	66	64
Columbia	1 927	6.2	38 845	1 652	427	75	40	81	268	488	622	47	40
Coos	2 429	5.7	38 475	1 693	876	164	83	203	442	830	1 327	92	83
Crook	782	8.8	36 153	2 100	273	45	24	69	154	253	411	29	24
Curry	870	6.3	38 707	1 817	240	43	23	69	203	305	375	30	23
Deschutes	7 788	9.3	44 435	987	3 196	466	298	1 091	1 737	1 637	5 051	331	298
Douglas	3 874	5.5	35 977	2 021	1 485	262	141	211	738	1 323	2 099	152	141
Gilliam	81	7.6	43 694	1 091	36	6	3	11	16	20	56	3	3
Grant	278	5.4	38 647	1 705	96	24	9	27	61	79	155	10	9
Harney	275	8.2	38 253	1 817	90	22	8	42	51	77	162	9	8
Hood River	1 061	7.6	45 856	1 041	479	71	45	110	256	172	705	40	45
Jackson	8 651	6.5	40 698	1 505	3 488	551	323	845	1 891	2 262	5 207	350	323
Jefferson	729	6.2	32 178	2 620	254	53	23	30	116	251	360	25	23
Josephine	3 052	6.2	36 013	2 179	929	150	89	279	593	1 089	1 447	111	89
Klamath	2 325	6.8	35 216	2 218	897	163	85	148	414	769	1 293	87	85
Lake	289	4.5	36 944	1 711	97	24	8	33	65	83	163	9	8
Lane	14 469	6.6	39 871	1 542	6 493	1 056	590	1 208	2 909	3 512	9 347	613	590
Lincoln	1 833	5.5	38 968	1 740	677	116	63	188	401	533	1 044	74	63
Linn	4 503	6.7	37 355	2 075	1 837	291	173	310	705	1 361	2 611	176	173
Malheur	919	7.1	30 255	2 942	458	92	42	116	162	317	708	40	42
Marion	12 302	7.3	37 199	1 839	6 376	1 137	566	945	2 070	3 244	9 025	553	566

1. Based on the resident population estimated as of July 1 of the year shown.

STATE County	Farm	Mining	Construction	Manu-facturing	Information: professional, scientific, technical services	Retail trade	Finance, insurance, real estate and leasing	Health care and social assistance	Govern-ment	Social Security beneficiaries, December 2015 Number	Rate[1]	Supplemental Security Income recipients, December 2015	Housing units, 2016 Total	Percent change, 2010–2016
	75	76	77	78	79	80	81	82	83	84	85	86	87	88
OKLAHOMA—Cont'd														
Kiowa	10.4	10.6	D	D	D	4.9	5.3	9.1	26.4	2 435	266	342	5 166	-1.0
Latimer	3.5	D	D	D	D	3.3	1.7	4.4	25.4	2 845	271	416	4 980	0.0
Le Flore	14.7	7.4	6.0	6.4	D	5.9	2.7	D	30.5	11 895	239	1 917	21 825	1.8
Lincoln	0.6	D	12.9	7.2	2.8	8.0	9.8	6.0	18.6	7 935	227	758	15 236	0.2
Logan	2.0	6.9	14.2	4.9	D	9.3	5.9	10.6	15.3	8 170	178	650	17 329	0.8
Love	2.0	1.6	2.9	1.9	D	4.1	1.2	D	54.8	2 385	243	231	4 532	-0.1
McClain	2.5	6.9	18.5	2.7	5.4	9.5	5.0	6.9	16.9	7 435	196	588	15 233	8.8
McCurtain	8.3	D	7.2	22.3	D	7.1	2.5	D	19.6	8 275	250	1 559	15 580	0.3
McIntosh	2.5	3.3	7.8	1.1	D	14.4	4.8	D	25.9	6 495	326	779	13 494	1.1
Major	14.4	23.4	10.8	5.3	D	3.9	D	5.1	9.1	1 740	225	87	3 665	-0.2
Marshall	3.2	2.3	3.8	29.4	D	7.9	4.7	9.1	17.1	4 155	256	451	10 042	0.4
Mayes	2.2	3.6	16.8	23.1	4.5	8.2	2.7	D	19.3	9 835	241	1 187	19 296	0.3
Murray	2.5	3.6	7.9	7.9	D	6.6	2.6	D	43.7	3 370	242	348	6 791	0.7
Muskogee	0.6	0.2	6.0	13.9	2.9	6.5	4.3	D	33.0	16 760	241	3 022	30 926	0.1
Noble	5.1	1.1	3.3	D	D	3.4	3.2	D	19.7	2 700	234	248	5 315	-0.5
Nowata	15.6	4.7	7.0	10.1	D	3.8	4.6	8.2	23.5	2 750	261	250	4 834	0.1
Okfuskee	8.8	5.6	8.9	4.7	D	5.0	3.7	8.3	39.0	2 865	236	600	5 293	0.2
Oklahoma	0.0	10.5	5.1	5.3	8.4	5.6	6.9	12.7	18.7	127 135	164	19 460	337 554	5.5
Okmulgee	1.4	2.7	4.3	18.5	3.1	8.3	3.7	D	34.8	10 055	257	1 552	17 792	-0.6
Osage	13.1	11.2	11.1	6.5	2.9	3.6	2.9	D	26.8	10 315	216	791	21 568	2.0
Ottawa	6.8	1.2	4.1	12.0	1.9	6.7	3.1	10.7	39.0	8 835	277	1 490	14 050	-0.1
Pawnee	1.5	D	7.7	2.9	D	7.4	D	7.9	27.8	4 285	260	413	7 721	-0.3
Payne	0.1	4.0	5.7	5.2	5.1	8.0	4.6	6.0	42.5	12 165	151	1 352	35 932	5.7
Pittsburg	0.8	10.0	8.0	7.4	D	6.3	3.3	D	36.0	11 005	247	1 501	22 992	1.6
Pontotoc	1.1	3.8	4.7	7.5	6.3	5.3	4.7	10.9	39.3	8 445	221	1 271	16 796	1.2
Pottawatomie	0.6	5.0	5.1	11.6	D	6.7	4.2	10.6	21.4	15 950	222	2 029	29 729	2.0
Pushmataha	3.1	D	7.1	4.6	D	6.9	4.3	19.8	30.2	3 450	309	576	6 114	0.1
Roger Mills	13.2	D	D	D	D	2.3	D	0.4	25.0	730	194	66	1 900	-0.3
Rogers	0.9	0.8	15.1	22.4	D	6.2	3.1	6.7	20.8	18 120	200	1 260	37 325	6.2
Seminole	5.2	18.3	4.7	12.8	2.1	9.1	2.9	D	21.8	6 000	235	1 029	11 656	0.1
Sequoyah	1.3	D	6.9	1.7	D	9.6	4.8	D	35.6	10 670	259	1 958	18 963	1.6
Stephens	1.1	D	4.7	12.9	D	6.2	4.3	8.5	8.4	10 890	244	1 079	20 717	0.3
Texas	33.1	2.8	4.8	17.4	6.0	3.7	2.3	2.3	10.6	2 740	128	159	8 168	-0.5
Tillman	25.6	0.7	D	D	D	2.7	D	2.8	25.1	1 830	243	309	4 040	-0.9
Tulsa	0.0	14.8	4.9	8.4	7.4	4.5	4.6	8.8	5.6	111 725	175	15 121	281 932	5.0
Wagoner	0.8	0.6	16.4	23.7	D	6.5	3.1	D	15.9	14 650	191	1 203	31 538	6.2
Washington	0.6	27.1	2.4	7.7	4.0	4.1	3.4	7.4	5.5	12 635	242	1 119	23 707	1.1
Washita	6.7	12.3	11.3	3.0	D	4.9	5.8	4.7	25.7	2 405	205	240	5 451	-0.5
Woods	9.3	30.3	3.6	2.7	D	5.7	5.6	D	19.1	1 660	178	92	4 435	-1.0
Woodward	8.7	24.7	7.9	5.7	2.9	5.1	4.7	5.7	11.0	3 850	179	285	8 971	1.5
OREGON	1.4	0.1	6.0	12.3	10.4	6.6	6.2	12.6	16.3	818 228	203	86 153	1 732 786	3.4
Baker	8.0	D	4.1	9.7	4.4	8.3	3.7	D	24.6	4 980	312	453	8 828	0.0
Benton	1.3	0.1	3.4	11.2	11.4	4.7	3.8	16.0	31.0	14 940	169	994	37 786	4.2
Clackamas	1.7	0.1	8.4	13.5	12.0	7.5	6.0	13.3	10.2	78 665	196	5 217	163 756	4.3
Clatsop	0.3	D	5.5	14.0	3.4	9.8	3.8	14.5	19.2	9 915	262	818	22 083	2.5
Columbia	1.2	1.0	7.6	17.4	D	7.8	4.8	8.8	20.5	11 995	242	1 000	20 815	0.5
Coos	2.2	0.1	5.3	8.2	4.1	8.6	3.9	12.6	28.2	20 340	323	2 422	30 496	-0.3
Crook	4.3	D	7.8	7.7	8.8	4.8	3.1	8.7	20.4	6 755	312	460	10 462	2.5
Curry	2.8	D	7.5	9.7	5.9	9.2	4.0	D	21.9	8 885	397	661	12 658	0.4
Deschutes	0.0	0.1	11.8	6.1	11.2	8.8	7.7	17.7	12.4	41 100	235	2 346	85 933	7.2
Douglas	1.3	0.5	5.5	11.9	3.5	7.2	4.4	14.4	23.3	33 920	315	3 376	49 203	0.6
Gilliam	21.0	0.0	5.5	D	D	2.8	D	2.9	21.0	530	284	42	1 155	-0.2
Grant	8.8	D	5.2	4.6	5.1	5.1	D	D	43.5	2 250	313	171	4 297	-1.1
Harney	21.0	0.0	3.9	0.2	2.1	6.4	1.8	D	41.0	2 085	290	230	3 799	-0.9
Hood River	8.5	0.0	4.0	13.9	12.8	7.4	3.7	13.5	11.8	4 145	180	271	9 661	4.2
Jackson	0.8	0.1	6.0	9.0	6.6	10.5	5.8	19.3	14.6	54 825	257	4 715	93 371	2.7
Jefferson	1.8	D	3.2	16.0	D	5.4	2.3	9.6	39.9	5 380	238	592	9 801	-0.1
Josephine	0.4	D	6.0	11.0	4.8	11.9	6.1	19.8	13.9	26 860	317	2 793	38 274	0.7
Klamath	3.9	0.1	4.7	7.8	D	8.0	4.4	15.7	25.1	17 295	262	2 026	32 822	0.1
Lake	18.1	D	3.7	6.3	2.9	4.5	1.8	D	43.3	2 275	292	243	4 385	-1.1
Lane	0.6	0.2	5.9	9.8	8.9	8.1	6.7	16.4	18.8	82 335	227	9 236	159 693	2.3
Lincoln	1.1	D	6.9	7.8	D	9.6	3.6	12.2	23.8	15 420	329	1 282	30 945	1.1
Linn	2.1	0.0	7.6	21.0	3.5	8.6	3.5	11.7	15.3	28 890	240	3 425	49 397	1.2
Malheur	12.0	D	2.1	5.2	D	9.4	2.9	11.6	29.3	6 365	210	974	11 640	-0.4
Marion	2.7	0.2	7.1	6.2	4.9	7.0	5.4	15.7	30.2	62 895	191	7 328	124 162	2.7

1. Per 1,000 resident population estimated as of July 1 of the year shown.

Table B. States and Counties — **Housing, Labor Force, and Employment**

STATE County	Housing units, 2011–2015								Civilian labor force, 2016				Civilian employment,[6] 2011–2015		
	Occupied units										Unemployment			Percent	
			Owner-occupied			Renter-occupied									
				Median owner cost as a percent of income											Construction, production, and maintenance occupations
				With a mortgage	Without a mortgage[2]		Median rent as a percent of income[2]	Sub-stand-ard units[4] (percent)		Percent change, 2015–2016				Manage-ment, business, science and arts	
	Total	Percent	Median value[1]			Median rent[3]			Total		Total	Rate[5]	Total		
	89	90	91	92	93	94	95	96	97	98	99	100	101	102	103

OKLAHOMA—Cont'd

Kiowa	3 939	69.5	60 300	17.5	10.0	508	23.7	3.5	4 125	-1.1	224	5.4	4 037	30.2	31.2
Latimer	4 135	68.5	80 500	19.3	10.0	506	25.9	3.8	3 708	-4.1	327	8.8	4 068	32.1	32.5
Le Flore	18 164	73.3	81 600	21.2	11.6	570	28.6	3.5	19 780	0.6	1 379	7.0	18 311	25.8	33.5
Lincoln	13 231	77.2	99 800	20.7	10.0	620	27.9	3.4	15 999	0.6	848	5.3	14 625	27.7	32.3
Logan	15 091	79.1	142 900	20.0	10.0	695	24.2	4.4	21 532	0.1	879	4.1	20 281	35.5	23.0
Love	3 202	76.4	89 000	19.0	10.9	653	22.1	2.8	6 507	8.6	208	3.2	4 127	25.0	33.5
McClain	13 244	80.2	152 600	21.8	10.2	688	26.0	2.3	18 853	0.3	784	4.2	16 746	33.8	24.6
McCurtain	12 908	69.0	73 700	21.7	11.4	556	28.3	4.9	14 843	0.5	1 074	7.2	12 348	23.2	38.1
McIntosh	8 373	78.3	90 100	22.1	10.7	566	28.7	5.2	7 086	-0.1	640	9.0	6 944	28.6	31.1
Major	3 051	74.5	89 300	16.5	10.0	570	19.8	2.9	3 996	-7.2	166	4.2	3 518	29.4	34.5
Marshall	5 965	76.5	85 700	19.9	10.4	622	24.8	4.7	6 589	-3.0	338	5.1	6 038	22.0	36.3
Mayes	15 740	73.3	104 000	21.3	10.4	629	27.0	4.6	19 329	-0.6	997	5.2	16 849	28.3	31.9
Murray	5 343	67.0	88 500	19.7	10.0	622	21.8	4.8	6 347	-6.4	288	4.5	6 115	28.2	24.9
Muskogee	26 349	67.0	91 500	20.3	10.7	643	31.1	2.7	29 480	-0.5	1 635	5.5	27 158	28.2	28.5
Noble	4 670	75.2	87 500	18.3	10.4	582	31.2	2.6	5 724	1.3	209	3.7	5 141	35.6	28.9
Nowata	4 046	77.8	76 300	18.3	12.2	618	27.5	2.9	4 685	-2.5	291	6.2	4 248	26.2	33.2
Okfuskee	4 048	74.1	76 400	20.0	10.0	501	27.4	4.4	4 564	0.3	282	6.2	3 942	29.2	34.3
Oklahoma	291 390	58.7	133 400	21.3	11.0	780	29.8	3.2	376 333	0.2	16 269	4.3	353 043	35.7	21.1
Okmulgee	15 022	69.3	78 800	20.1	11.4	608	27.0	2.4	16 239	-0.1	1 177	7.2	14 956	28.5	29.6
Osage	18 271	77.7	100 000	20.8	10.9	628	26.5	3.2	21 219	-0.2	1 226	5.8	19 274	30.0	31.1
Ottawa	12 061	69.9	82 600	22.3	11.2	627	29.5	4.9	14 394	0.0	740	5.1	12 922	26.5	28.8
Pawnee	6 278	76.2	85 100	20.3	10.9	644	23.3	4.0	7 511	0.3	503	6.7	6 890	28.6	34.9
Payne	30 164	50.2	135 600	22.1	10.6	735	38.6	2.9	38 578	0.3	1 462	3.8	36 780	37.3	20.2
Pittsburg	18 087	72.4	94 500	19.6	10.2	670	26.9	3.7	17 479	0.1	1 101	6.3	18 459	28.6	29.2
Pontotoc	14 591	64.1	107 800	21.1	10.0	638	28.4	3.1	18 322	0.2	760	4.1	17 465	32.6	23.6
Pottawatomie	25 996	68.8	102 700	19.8	10.0	650	27.1	3.4	32 818	0.1	1 538	4.7	29 366	31.0	26.2
Pushmataha	4 749	74.3	72 600	19.4	11.7	516	29.6	4.8	4 821	-2.0	364	7.6	4 074	30.9	31.6
Roger Mills	1 340	72.7	86 100	16.6	10.0	515	21.0	1.8	1 817	-1.3	95	5.2	1 698	28.9	31.1
Rogers	33 358	78.9	144 600	20.8	10.0	779	26.0	3.1	44 666	-0.1	2 264	5.1	42 093	34.1	26.2
Seminole	9 202	72.5	69 200	20.4	10.3	551	25.8	3.6	9 401	-2.3	666	7.1	9 379	27.2	31.4
Sequoyah	15 552	71.5	89 600	21.6	11.6	604	31.1	5.0	16 895	0.5	1 068	6.3	15 545	28.0	29.7
Stephens	17 868	70.3	98 400	19.5	10.9	649	26.3	2.4	19 023	-6.3	1 839	9.7	19 029	28.8	30.4
Texas	7 173	62.1	92 700	19.0	10.0	683	23.3	7.3	9 404	-3.2	328	3.5	11 144	24.5	41.9
Tillman	3 057	73.1	56 600	21.2	11.7	606	26.1	3.3	3 278	-2.5	149	4.5	3 098	29.4	33.4
Tulsa	246 080	59.7	138 500	20.6	11.2	774	28.5	3.0	318 212	-0.1	14 992	4.7	302 471	36.4	21.2
Wagoner	27 452	79.7	141 700	20.6	11.0	784	26.7	2.6	36 304	0.0	1 759	4.8	34 531	32.4	26.7
Washington	21 001	72.3	111 300	19.0	10.0	683	27.1	2.2	23 902	-2.4	1 178	4.9	23 028	36.4	22.0
Washita	4 640	72.0	77 600	17.1	10.0	644	18.2	3.0	5 278	-6.0	378	7.2	5 057	31.2	31.2
Woods	3 426	69.2	88 200	16.4	10.0	624	21.3	1.0	5 255	-2.3	171	3.3	4 365	28.2	26.2
Woodward	7 367	71.2	115 400	15.3	10.0	680	23.7	2.1	9 536	-7.6	604	6.3	9 345	28.2	36.6
OREGON	1 533 430	61.3	237 300	24.7	12.4	907	32.1	3.5	2 055 120	3.9	100 296	4.9	1 789 807	37.0	20.9
Baker	7 160	66.1	146 600	21.5	12.0	608	28.4	3.6	6 972	4.5	449	6.4	6 376	36.7	26.6
Benton	33 840	57.5	269 700	22.3	10.6	862	37.2	2.5	46 888	3.2	1 837	3.9	39 915	49.4	13.9
Clackamas	149 522	68.2	301 000	24.8	12.8	1 037	30.2	2.9	213 012	3.8	9 461	4.4	185 660	37.9	20.1
Clatsop	15 726	60.7	246 500	24.9	13.0	846	31.2	3.1	19 043	3.8	908	4.8	16 843	28.8	23.6
Columbia	18 785	73.4	206 100	23.6	12.1	791	31.2	1.7	23 494	3.6	1 460	6.2	20 362	28.1	31.0
Coos	25 888	65.0	170 500	25.2	13.2	709	32.8	2.6	26 521	2.2	1 719	6.5	23 458	27.0	26.6
Crook	9 079	68.7	166 900	27.4	11.4	771	33.1	4.3	9 354	3.7	654	7.0	8 014	22.3	26.5
Curry	10 454	65.4	218 200	29.2	12.5	824	33.6	3.1	9 080	4.2	624	6.9	7 930	32.0	21.5
Deschutes	66 337	64.7	253 400	25.9	12.2	939	32.3	2.2	89 943	6.1	4 408	4.9	74 599	37.3	19.3
Douglas	43 798	67.4	169 700	25.6	12.2	751	32.1	3.0	45 891	3.4	2 932	6.4	39 563	28.1	28.1
Gilliam	833	60.7	117 900	23.8	10.7	742	25.9	2.3	842	4.1	50	5.9	783	28.1	37.8
Grant	3 149	72.3	143 000	23.3	12.2	615	27.5	3.1	3 131	1.3	243	7.8	2 878	34.8	25.4
Harney	3 038	69.0	122 500	21.5	11.5	563	23.7	2.9	3 442	4.2	217	6.3	2 901	36.1	25.6
Hood River	8 189	64.9	321 300	26.5	10.5	888	30.5	4.1	13 975	3.3	587	4.2	11 251	35.6	29.9
Jackson	83 487	62.0	218 100	26.5	13.7	886	35.7	3.3	101 776	3.8	5 891	5.8	87 699	32.1	21.2
Jefferson	7 692	66.8	149 100	24.3	11.4	751	25.8	3.6	9 859	2.3	659	6.7	8 167	26.3	30.9
Josephine	34 527	66.4	215 900	27.4	12.7	837	36.9	3.3	34 465	3.6	2 260	6.6	28 510	29.7	24.6
Klamath	27 188	64.8	151 500	23.4	10.9	723	32.1	3.3	29 426	2.7	2 019	6.9	25 753	30.2	26.6
Lake	3 526	60.0	129 100	25.9	11.2	604	29.9	2.8	3 482	1.4	224	6.4	3 037	29.8	31.5
Lane	146 235	58.7	215 300	25.2	12.5	866	35.0	2.5	179 242	3.9	9 230	5.1	158 490	34.5	20.2
Lincoln	20 566	63.8	219 100	27.0	13.2	830	30.3	3.2	20 986	2.3	1 192	5.7	19 454	28.0	19.9
Linn	45 100	64.3	170 300	24.2	12.5	810	32.3	3.1	57 129	3.5	3 290	5.8	48 892	28.3	29.8
Malheur	10 286	59.7	127 000	23.2	11.4	604	35.0	5.6	12 539	4.9	706	5.6	10 595	28.6	30.9
Marion	113 996	59.8	186 700	25.0	12.4	798	31.4	5.4	158 561	3.9	8 103	5.1	137 706	30.2	26.2

1. Specified owner-occupied units.   2. A value of 10.0 represents 10 percent or less; a value of 50.0 represents 50 percent or more.   3. Specified renter-occupied units.
4. Overcrowded or lacking complete plumbing facilities.   5. Percent of civilian labor force.   6. Civilian employed persons 16 years old and over.

Table B. States and Counties — Nonfarm Employment and Agriculture

STATE County	Private nonfarm establishments, employment and payroll, 2015									Agriculture, 2012			
		Employment						Annual payroll		Farms			
											Percent with:		
	Number of establishments	Total	Health care and social assistance	Manufacturing	Retail trade	Finance and insurance	Professional, scientific, and technical services	Total (mil dol)	Average per employee (dollars)	Number	Fewer than 50 acres	500 acres or more	Farm operators whose principal occupation is farming (percent)
	104	105	106	107	108	109	110	111	112	113	114	115	116

OKLAHOMA—Cont'd													
Kiowa	180	1 650	480	D	296	105	31	47	28 483	667	9.0	44.8	53.2
Latimer	167	1 644	331	D	295	61	56	66	40 027	691	27.2	13.9	36.3
Le Flore	795	8 360	2 753	399	1 596	401	271	270	32 285	1 843	32.2	8.4	48.0
Lincoln	559	5 235	495	690	838	424	140	188	35 908	2 121	26.0	10.6	43.9
Logan	828	6 294	1 049	346	1 080	250	186	194	30 848	1 203	27.2	14.8	37.1
Love	151	5 053	124	147	146	49	47	154	30 492	621	22.9	15.5	45.7
McClain	841	8 067	1 267	472	1 494	266	295	259	32 164	1 239	39.9	12.2	38.7
McCurtain	595	8 699	1 595	2 456	1 248	236	85	279	32 031	1 577	28.0	8.1	39.9
McIntosh	360	3 091	839	61	929	146	118	98	31 570	1 018	25.8	9.4	36.7
Major	264	2 226	230	57	269	77	57	107	48 112	901	13.7	32.6	45.3
Marshall	281	3 777	563	1 362	588	169	110	123	32 441	525	26.5	15.6	40.8
Mayes	781	10 404	1 124	2 806	1 803	293	410	414	39 785	1 551	36.6	7.7	42.5
Murray	281	3 476	507	339	647	139	70	118	33 834	470	22.1	17.0	37.4
Muskogee	1 422	22 957	5 600	3 484	3 521	593	556	873	38 028	1 735	34.2	8.4	46.0
Noble	221	4 357	357	D	308	155	40	186	42 646	828	15.5	27.5	39.4
Nowata	159	1 302	295	241	134	69	27	39	29 839	889	22.5	14.3	44.2
Okfuskee	168	2 628	1 608	120	238	71	23	85	32 301	881	18.5	15.7	39.5
Oklahoma	23 592	374 351	57 301	21 273	46 079	19 968	25 336	17 815	47 589	1 180	56.6	5.7	44.4
Okmulgee	675	6 768	1 577	1 317	1 292	318	186	205	30 320	1 329	32.3	10.8	44.6
Osage	578	5 663	707	391	814	168	132	179	31 634	1 325	28.5	25.6	47.8
Ottawa	597	9 099	1 464	1 516	966	348	309	279	30 674	1 020	36.4	7.9	38.6
Pawnee	251	2 607	485	229	456	97	D	117	44 774	813	21.4	18.2	31.5
Payne	1 855	22 744	3 399	1 544	4 290	899	1 090	738	32 443	1 466	34.9	10.5	34.1
Pittsburg	948	11 424	2 581	1 031	2 090	404	389	393	34 384	1 567	21.7	15.8	39.8
Pontotoc	962	12 654	3 359	1 192	1 727	494	907	446	35 270	1 313	26.9	10.1	38.2
Pottawatomie	1 302	17 943	2 713	2 849	2 823	688	681	574	32 001	1 643	32.0	9.6	39.6
Pushmataha	199	1 987	756	171	324	128	110	50	25 102	732	15.4	15.8	47.0
Roger Mills	90	530	D	D	97	D	13	17	33 009	678	9.9	42.6	49.6
Rogers	1 738	28 986	3 127	7 543	2 961	807	836	1 352	46 659	1 733	47.8	8.1	33.8
Seminole	450	5 341	973	747	832	211	185	186	34 861	1 054	20.7	10.5	36.2
Sequoyah	575	7 278	2 421	276	1 219	344	114	181	24 821	1 204	37.7	6.9	42.6
Stephens	1 112	12 881	1 955	2 192	1 991	635	557	487	37 830	1 286	23.6	17.1	33.0
Texas	483	8 470	468	D	931	254	107	386	45 616	1 024	8.4	42.6	38.7
Tillman	136	1 252	221	D	154	76	20	38	30 205	556	8.1	44.4	52.2
Tulsa	18 725	332 919	50 940	40 841	40 140	14 859	20 307	16 026	48 139	1 036	57.6	3.8	40.0
Wagoner	922	8 857	770	2 209	1 463	264	246	317	35 787	1 090	44.7	7.5	35.0
Washington	1 194	19 927	2 972	957	2 446	742	1 378	997	50 048	811	37.5	9.5	41.2
Washita	244	1 497	247	123	301	100	44	46	30 697	973	12.3	36.2	50.5
Woods	285	3 335	363	53	516	153	82	144	43 164	751	13.6	41.9	52.2
Woodward	800	8 196	1 077	497	1 307	290	150	347	42 369	882	15.3	33.9	39.1
OREGON	112 393	1 498 727	234 608	159 648	202 996	59 584	90 894	71 007	47 378	35 439	61.5	10.6	49.9
Baker	522	4 055	623	526	813	117	176	132	32 668	645	31.0	28.7	60.5
Benton	2 111	25 919	5 819	1 896	3 797	607	2 128	1 091	42 075	886	71.4	5.6	46.3
Clackamas	11 499	137 872	20 340	17 204	19 356	5 692	8 553	6 595	47 833	3 745	81.4	1.1	41.1
Clatsop	1 440	14 137	1 916	1 854	2 607	265	320	501	35 443	199	55.3	2.5	45.7
Columbia	897	8 045	1 428	1 414	1 456	291	274	266	33 089	751	69.9	2.4	45.7
Coos	1 561	17 782	3 843	1 505	2 935	470	407	625	35 140	654	41.4	9.5	56.9
Crook	500	3 926	531	727	604	97	113	137	34 938	551	49.9	16.7	51.0
Curry	686	5 064	1 065	669	959	165	107	160	31 626	197	37.6	21.3	60.4
Deschutes	6 530	60 309	10 657	4 426	10 331	1 911	2 990	2 398	39 764	1 283	78.9	4.0	44.0
Douglas	2 492	28 630	5 442	3 785	4 563	1 138	807	1 089	38 032	1 927	50.9	8.1	48.3
Gilliam	71	765	73	NA	107	16	D	32	42 339	170	4.1	77.6	63.5
Grant	232	1 435	377	D	231	86	67	50	34 889	398	28.1	36.9	54.3
Harney	185	1 350	382	13	280	43	64	44	32 430	497	21.5	42.3	57.1
Hood River	1 036	9 963	1 515	1 508	1 433	165	394	324	32 471	554	74.9	0.5	56.7
Jackson	6 091	70 228	13 346	6 414	12 287	2 065	2 252	2 583	36 780	1 722	72.1	2.4	56.2
Jefferson	366	3 950	562	1 163	535	63	54	131	33 147	474	42.2	18.4	53.2
Josephine	1 907	21 420	4 544	2 831	4 409	620	849	719	33 581	617	76.3	0.6	55.8
Klamath	1 512	17 275	3 223	2 074	3 261	984	653	632	36 569	955	38.7	19.4	63.7
Lake	190	1 230	312	231	161	29	41	44	36 059	373	21.4	40.2	70.2
Lane	9 696	123 022	23 373	13 710	19 813	4 732	5 041	4 826	39 231	2 660	73.9	2.9	44.5
Lincoln	1 521	13 889	1 808	883	2 863	241	290	449	32 294	362	63.3	3.9	48.3
Linn	2 511	35 251	5 284	7 300	5 029	1 023	916	1 354	38 420	2 083	64.8	6.7	48.7
Malheur	706	8 370	1 605	1 048	1 958	191	214	246	29 445	1 113	33.9	20.8	64.1
Marion	7 837	100 793	18 444	10 306	16 573	2 897	3 716	3 761	37 312	2 567	72.5	5.6	47.1

Table B. States and Counties — **Agriculture**

STATE County	Land in farms					Value of land and buildings (dollars)			Value of products sold				Percent of farms with sales of:		Government payments	
	Acreage (1,000)	Percent change, 2007-2012	Acres					Value of machinery and equipment, average per farm (dollars)			Percent from:					
			Average size of farm	Total irrigated (1,000)	Total cropland (1,000)	Average per farm	Average per acre		Total (mil dol)	Average per farm (dollars)	Crops	Live-stock and poultry products	$10,000 or more	$100,000 or more	Total ($1,000)	Percent of farms
	117	118	119	120	121	122	123	124	125	126	127	128	129	130	131	132
OKLAHOMA—Cont'd																
Kiowa	593	5.1	890	2.7	302.3	854 510	961	144 499	107.8	161 627	59.1	40.9	61.3	28.0	8 081	79.2
Latimer	221	3.3	319	0.1	38.2	425 538	1 333	56 986	24.6	35 570	8.5	91.5	34.6	4.6	1 268	15.8
Le Flore	395	-15.3	214	6.1	103.7	425 397	1 985	57 896	287.3	155 883	6.6	93.4	38.0	12.0	2 522	25.6
Lincoln	454	-6.9	214	0.8	106.5	369 323	1 724	54 060	38.7	18 260	26.8	73.2	31.7	3.2	1 147	16.3
Logan	367	-9.0	305	1.1	133.7	575 341	1 884	63 051	44.0	36 563	47.2	52.8	37.2	5.5	2 181	38.3
Love	219	-16.2	353	1.1	48.8	611 282	1 730	56 594	23.9	38 472	19.5	80.5	40.7	7.4	1 234	29.0
McClain	283	-16.1	228	1.7	78.9	466 267	2 043	61 161	48.5	39 117	26.2	73.8	32.6	7.7	1 349	24.8
McCurtain	317	-6.8	201	1.5	70.3	349 785	1 742	57 386	163.1	103 452	7.2	92.8	36.6	7.8	1 573	24.0
McIntosh	236	-4.4	232	0.2	58.1	357 114	1 541	52 882	22.3	21 872	13.1	86.9	37.7	3.6	672	23.3
Major	537	3.8	596	10.1	217.0	668 974	1 122	95 212	105.4	116 986	39.2	60.8	59.4	20.3	3 795	65.7
Marshall	192	21.6	365	0.7	41.8	610 888	1 672	64 185	18.4	34 983	20.8	79.2	37.0	5.3	830	24.0
Mayes	285	-9.0	184	0.4	85.2	388 246	2 112	56 484	76.0	48 985	8.0	92.0	37.0	6.8	1 628	24.2
Murray	208	5.6	443	0.0	24.3	613 813	1 386	65 602	28.0	59 557	8.2	91.8	36.6	4.9	709	33.0
Muskogee	350	-6.5	202	7.3	120.2	356 096	1 765	55 445	50.6	29 140	42.3	57.7	33.9	4.0	2 161	29.6
Noble	443	-5.2	535	1.9	193.3	762 217	1 425	79 824	61.3	73 995	48.4	51.6	51.1	16.2	4 809	64.4
Nowata	292	-17.6	329	0.1	64.8	544 327	1 657	53 998	40.0	45 009	12.3	87.7	46.1	5.5	1 267	31.7
Okfuskee	320	7.0	363	0.7	60.1	463 053	1 276	57 190	34.7	39 373	13.3	86.7	39.7	5.3	922	26.4
Oklahoma	144	-9.8	122	2.3	47.9	378 664	3 099	43 969	20.4	17 300	71.0	29.0	19.7	3.6	502	14.4
Okmulgee	300	2.0	226	0.7	78.0	406 784	1 801	51 241	27.1	20 421	27.7	72.3	30.5	3.8	908	21.6
Osage	1 217	-5.7	918	1.3	131.4	968 906	1 055	58 483	121.5	91 682	6.2	93.8	42.9	11.2	4 433	23.2
Ottawa	193	-18.8	189	0.2	87.9	436 945	2 306	76 215	117.6	115 291	43.1	56.9	39.0	7.8	1 622	25.5
Pawnee	286	-3.9	352	0.0	52.2	468 352	1 331	55 888	26.7	32 864	14.6	85.4	37.8	7.4	1 400	30.3
Payne	350	-2.0	239	0.4	105.1	451 118	1 891	52 108	34.1	23 231	26.5	73.5	33.4	4.1	1 737	23.5
Pittsburg	524	-4.3	334	1.8	95.6	454 824	1 361	54 429	41.6	26 535	15.7	84.3	35.4	4.8	1 898	16.1
Pontotoc	325	-14.4	247	0.9	69.0	434 772	1 759	49 674	36.0	27 438	17.6	82.3	34.4	2.4	1 242	16.4
Pottawatomie	335	-15.1	204	0.9	86.9	358 388	1 756	52 875	35.4	21 523	24.0	76.0	26.0	2.7	1 346	14.2
Pushmataha	297	2.4	406	D	37.9	462 504	1 138	44 060	14.6	19 939	9.7	90.3	36.9	4.4	2 454	23.9
Roger Mills	719	0.0	1 061	5.3	117.5	1 093 820	1 031	96 844	46.0	67 827	28.1	71.9	47.8	14.0	4 532	58.1
Rogers	302	-18.7	174	1.0	71.8	429 069	2 464	44 947	66.4	38 290	11.7	88.3	31.2	4.5	1 186	15.5
Seminole	243	-3.0	231	0.2	48.0	325 588	1 411	46 705	38.1	36 162	10.4	89.6	29.9	2.2	875	20.8
Sequoyah	215	-7.3	179	3.3	63.8	357 679	2 002	52 061	55.5	46 084	23.0	77.0	31.2	3.9	1 620	9.1
Stephens	481	2.3	374	0.1	75.9	474 056	1 268	58 719	42.2	32 782	12.5	87.5	35.1	5.6	2 539	29.9
Texas	1 287	6.7	1 257	153.0	678.8	1 005 370	800	180 940	1 013.9	990 157	15.0	85.0	42.1	19.9	12 943	78.5
Tillman	541	16.7	974	10.6	290.0	977 950	1 004	163 739	102.4	184 257	53.7	46.3	62.4	25.7	6 753	79.0
Tulsa	106	-19.0	103	4.7	42.7	372 738	3 635	35 707	21.0	20 313	70.3	29.7	23.9	2.9	692	10.0
Wagoner	199	-24.3	182	4.0	78.6	443 074	2 428	53 862	33.8	31 050	57.8	42.2	31.1	4.7	1 257	26.2
Washington	231	1.9	285	D	55.6	476 007	1 672	50 665	37.4	46 086	19.2	80.8	35.4	7.5	590	22.3
Washita	633	7.2	651	7.0	343.6	780 371	1 199	136 291	114.7	117 867	54.3	45.7	64.5	23.2	10 153	80.5
Woods	808	-3.0	1 077	2.8	231.1	1 167 659	1 085	114 887	82.5	109 875	43.0	57.0	55.7	23.7	4 609	71.0
Woodward	715	-8.7	810	4.6	149.9	898 007	1 108	85 655	116.5	132 078	13.4	86.6	46.1	13.4	4 264	56.5
OREGON	16 302	-0.6	460	1 629.7	4 690.4	865 613	1 882	90 222	4 883.7	137 805	66.5	33.5	35.6	13.1	85 840	15.1
Baker	711	-0.1	1 102	100.9	107.5	1 117 372	1 014	118 667	93.3	144 583	49.4	50.6	52.2	21.6	1 883	25.7
Benton	124	8.2	140	11.3	68.2	830 059	5 932	68 867	103.3	116 597	78.2	21.8	28.6	10.4	486	6.4
Clackamas	163	-11.0	43	22.2	84.0	585 754	13 486	53 573	325.2	86 833	76.7	23.3	27.5	7.1	607	3.8
Clatsop	16	-22.7	82	0.7	5.3	456 739	5 548	53 940	11.5	58 010	12.3	87.7	22.1	6.0	50	6.0
Columbia	57	-1.9	75	1.9	18.0	414 475	5 493	41 466	39.4	52 413	D	D	17.6	1.6	232	4.1
Coos	157	8.1	241	11.2	20.9	776 687	3 225	60 953	50.4	77 018	21.5	78.6	43.6	12.2	678	10.7
Crook	823	8.0	1 493	61.9	57.0	1 357 530	909	76 437	42.3	76 766	32.1	67.9	38.3	9.4	554	9.3
Curry	63	-14.8	322	3.2	5.2	1 095 939	3 408	71 112	21.4	108 411	44.9	55.1	53.8	19.3	524	17.3
Deschutes	131	1.3	102	34.0	28.9	716 430	7 015	52 158	20.6	16 033	54.1	45.9	22.1	2.4	241	3.4
Douglas	382	-3.7	198	14.6	49.2	611 961	3 084	44 231	64.8	33 629	36.3	63.7	27.3	4.7	730	5.3
Gilliam	723	-1.4	4 255	6.5	331.7	2 117 900	498	293 047	44.1	259 141	84.6	15.4	50.6	40.0	7 931	90.0
Grant	656	-13.8	1 649	31.6	96.4	1 326 967	805	79 166	25.4	63 719	22.3	77.7	50.8	14.8	900	14.8
Harney	1 505	3.0	3 029	165.7	223.0	1 660 966	548	163 302	88.9	178 966	41.7	58.3	55.7	30.0	1 414	24.9
Hood River	26	-4.2	47	14.1	16.3	885 421	19 000	90 121	77.1	139 200	D	D	49.8	26.9	777	13.4
Jackson	214	-12.3	124	36.5	32.8	582 023	4 682	40 415	64.1	37 240	57.6	42.4	25.7	3.4	252	3.8
Jefferson	817	15.2	1 724	41.1	62.9	1 104 840	641	154 973	65.0	137 198	72.7	27.3	40.7	19.4	1 182	32.7
Josephine	28	-25.1	46	9.0	8.4	460 319	10 052	35 806	18.8	30 481	D	D	25.0	4.7	129	2.9
Klamath	650	-3.7	681	159.9	205.2	1 004 853	1 475	136 301	181.5	190 037	56.5	43.5	48.7	21.8	1 951	21.4
Lake	657	-5.2	1 762	148.9	131.1	1 791 244	1 017	171 150	85.6	229 614	52.6	47.4	61.7	33.8	716	20.6
Lane	220	-10.6	83	19.3	100.0	563 427	6 824	49 734	142.5	53 574	74.6	25.4	23.5	5.6	575	5.1
Lincoln	30	-3.1	83	0.4	5.1	400 392	4 795	35 680	5.5	15 293	30.6	69.4	22.7	1.7	93	3.6
Linn	331	-12.0	159	28.7	227.5	769 891	4 840	89 696	241.2	115 812	77.1	22.9	31.3	11.7	882	6.8
Malheur	1 077	-8.0	967	183.0	204.8	1 136 094	1 174	174 964	359.3	322 829	50.7	49.3	68.3	32.6	2 574	40.2
Marion	286	-7.0	111	84.9	213.8	885 406	7 942	130 593	592.9	230 953	81.5	18.5	41.0	17.7	1 583	9.8

Table B. States and Counties — **Water Use, Wholesale Trade, Retail Trade, and Real Estate**

STATE County	Water use, 2010		Wholesale trade,[1] 2012				Retail trade,[2] 2012				Real estate and rental and leasing,[2] 2012			
	Total water withdrawn (mil gal/day)	Gallons withdrawn per person per day	Number of establish-ments	Number of employees	Sales (mil dol)	Annual payroll (mil dol)	Number of establish-ments	Number of employees	Sales (mil dol)	Annual payroll (mil dol)	Number of establish-ments	Number of employees	Receipts (mil dol)	Annual payroll (mil dol)
	133	134	135	136	137	138	139	140	141	142	143	144	145	146
OKLAHOMA—Cont'd														
Kiowa	13.8	1 456	8	D	D	D	40	286	58.3	5.5	4	11	1.1	0.2
Latimer	2.9	261	5	54	73.5	3.9	24	259	52.5	5.1	4	D	D	D
Le Flore	23.7	470	21	D	D	D	145	1 490	406.8	30.3	22	44	5.9	0.9
Lincoln	21.3	620	27	183	117.3	8.1	87	814	239.1	17.3	19	69	9.9	2.1
Logan	11.2	267	15	63	26.3	2.4	87	1 001	343.9	22.2	40	155	30.2	4.5
Love	5.5	585	5	12	9.4	0.5	26	176	77.4	3.8	6	D	D	D
McClain	8.1	234	18	103	38.7	3.8	118	1 389	463.6	37.5	27	66	39.7	4.5
McCurtain	9.9	298	27	97	86.7	3.7	100	1 156	275.2	24.4	19	78	8.0	1.8
McIntosh	5.0	246	6	28	14.6	1.6	68	847	289.7	18.7	12	D	D	D
Major	17.3	2 300	16	100	55.5	3.9	32	264	93.7	5.3	6	D	D	D
Marshall	7.2	452	5	64	19.0	4.0	52	542	159.8	12.2	9	31	2.5	0.6
Mayes	111.1	2 692	34	344	382.6	18.1	137	1 663	466.8	35.2	20	41	5.4	0.7
Murray	21.3	1 577	7	D	D	D	48	578	196.9	14.2	11	D	D	D
Muskogee	48.0	677	57	1 022	509.1	45.7	258	3 194	927.9	75.8	56	211	29.6	5.7
Noble	35.6	3 079	8	81	30.9	2.3	32	326	127.6	7.5	7	17	2.1	0.2
Nowata	51.1	4 845	9	79	33.6	2.1	18	129	36.8	2.7	7	22	1.3	0.5
Okfuskee	5.8	479	4	15	2.3	0.2	28	210	88.7	4.8	2	D	D	D
Oklahoma	131.1	182	1 128	18 305	43 903.7	1 065.3	2 909	42 001	13 117.1	1 116.5	1 136	6 497	1 502.8	293.8
Okmulgee	18.9	471	21	D	D	D	123	1 315	341.0	26.3	16	36	4.7	0.9
Osage	19.1	402	15	D	D	D	88	869	216.3	16.8	17	95	21.2	4.7
Ottawa	4.9	152	21	180	44.6	6.4	100	993	232.9	20.8	19	46	6.8	1.2
Pawnee	13.3	800	5	D	D	D	39	423	115.7	8.8	6	37	8.9	1.9
Payne	11.9	153	50	D	D	D	297	4 027	1 021.0	84.7	85	298	53.0	8.3
Pittsburg	17.3	377	39	D	D	D	176	2 047	603.8	46.3	44	181	34.5	6.8
Pontotoc	152.5	4 066	41	407	438.3	18.7	167	1 809	437.4	37.8	42	293	65.5	12.6
Pottawatomie	22.9	330	38	305	180.3	12.6	238	2 904	755.0	63.6	47	162	23.5	4.5
Pushmataha	1.3	110	2	D	D	D	36	328	70.6	5.0	7	22	6.2	0.7
Roger Mills	7.8	2 137	2	D	D	D	16	92	31.6	1.7	1	D	D	D
Rogers	90.3	1 039	73	957	1 885.4	53.1	205	2 530	777.3	62.6	77	222	48.4	7.5
Seminole	342.0	13 423	23	386	161.7	14.2	75	862	233.5	17.6	14	31	6.7	1.4
Sequoyah	10.4	244	14	D	D	D	118	1 179	387.7	24.9	14	37	3.8	0.6
Stephens	137.0	3 040	48	D	D	D	194	1 961	550.4	43.9	26	106	23.9	3.8
Texas	301.9	14 629	33	D	D	D	76	890	226.5	18.4	15	42	4.3	0.8
Tillman	11.4	1 431	11	100	83.8	3.7	21	177	27.8	2.7	NA	NA	NA	NA
Tulsa	15.4	26	996	14 271	13 182.2	854.3	2 315	36 091	10 454.5	894.5	919	6 119	981.5	242.8
Wagoner	14.1	192	36	244	117.8	11.4	115	1 360	389.7	29.0	28	41	4.3	1.0
Washington	11.6	228	29	173	194.6	7.4	181	2 270	652.2	53.8	42	195	29.5	5.9
Washita	9.1	780	7	131	49.9	5.6	46	283	86.0	5.5	8	69	9.5	2.3
Woods	11.3	1 277	21	186	218.8	9.0	46	465	168.6	10.2	6	10	2.0	0.2
Woodward	24.4	1 217	42	D	D	D	114	1 224	435.2	30.3	33	148	31.4	7.2
OREGON	6 734.5	1 758	4 393	59 523	48 325.3	3 233.0	13 879	187 402	49 481.1	4 831.5	5 644	26 016	4 649.6	902.8
Baker	496.0	30 744	15	84	30.5	3.0	86	797	198.9	17.6	10	39	4.1	1.7
Benton	38.8	454	44	346	452.5	22.6	262	3 455	731.0	82.5	105	453	53.3	10.2
Clackamas	299.2	796	563	8 015	5 388.6	456.3	1 188	18 541	5 125.3	486.9	564	2 440	451.9	96.8
Clatsop	65.5	1 769	22	210	110.4	9.1	284	2 756	704.1	67.4	75	239	30.4	6.0
Columbia	39.5	801	16	D	D	D	120	1 349	318.1	31.5	37	108	12.8	2.6
Coos	27.5	435	42	399	287.8	15.3	262	2 930	745.8	73.8	58	215	26.4	5.1
Crook	225.6	10 755	13	D	D	D	70	583	184.2	14.6	24	33	6.5	0.8
Curry	21.2	948	12	35	14.6	0.7	97	988	244.6	23.8	45	81	10.1	1.5
Deschutes	157.5	998	215	1 262	794.9	57.1	755	9 365	2 476.6	244.0	388	1 252	186.1	40.0
Douglas	72.3	671	54	D	D	D	378	4 419	1 103.4	102.1	120	329	43.4	7.6
Gilliam	18.9	10 086	5	D	D	D	11	52	10.5	1.1	NA	NA	NA	NA
Grant	130.8	17 574	7	D	D	D	38	241	67.4	5.6	10	20	1.2	0.4
Harney	422.9	56 975	3	D	D	D	27	279	107.3	7.2	8	22	2.1	0.4
Hood River	83.1	3 718	24	360	110.5	14.7	157	1 287	315.4	33.5	31	71	10.0	2.0
Jackson	392.4	1 931	206	1 771	828.4	76.8	865	11 223	3 202.7	297.5	306	1 043	164.1	26.3
Jefferson	172.1	7 925	20	194	156.4	9.5	47	506	133.1	11.3	24	65	6.0	1.6
Josephine	30.2	365	49	D	D	D	312	4 150	987.9	105.1	106	354	44.8	8.5
Klamath	661.6	9 967	49	533	210.9	21.0	237	2 902	757.5	69.9	72	199	23.5	5.2
Lake	465.5	58 958	8	D	D	D	30	200	74.9	4.8	5	D	D	D
Lane	224.2	637	384	4 860	2 852.0	229.0	1 270	18 265	4 291.5	449.9	505	2 115	314.3	58.4
Lincoln	28.9	627	27	D	D	D	307	2 758	580.8	62.2	74	320	40.2	7.0
Linn	122.6	1 051	110	1 396	1 066.7	61.3	343	4 753	1 181.6	112.6	112	360	48.5	10.2
Malheur	616.4	19 684	36	584	340.7	17.6	120	1 834	534.5	45.8	29	55	9.0	1.4
Marion	281.5	893	264	3 694	3 190.0	177.6	1 103	15 497	3 862.2	377.0	417	1 991	269.7	58.6

1. Merchant wholesalers, except manufacturers' sales branches and offices.   2. Employer establishments.

Table B. States and Counties — Professional Services, Manufacturing, and Accommodation and Food Services

STATE County	Professional, scientific, and technical services, 2012				Manufacturing, 2012				Accommodation and food services, 2012			
	Number of establishments	Number of employees	Receipts (mil dol)	Annual payroll (mil dol)	Number of establishments	Number of employees	Receipts (mil dol)	Annual payroll (mil dol)	Number of establishments	Number of employees	Sales (mil dol)	Annual payroll (mil dol)
	147	148	149	150	151	152	153	154	155	156	157	158
OKLAHOMA—Cont'd												
Kiowa	16	D	D	D	5	D	D	D	15	D	D	D
Latimer	17	D	D	D	NA	NA	NA	NA	8	D	D	D
Le Flore	86	307	22.1	6.9	30	492	D	17.9	47	D	D	D
Lincoln	40	129	16.7	4.0	29	790	231.5	31.3	44	564	22.6	6.2
Logan	60	160	18.5	5.2	23	363	97.6	14.7	60	837	37.3	9.8
Love	14	D	D	D	5	111	D	4.6	29	579	53.8	10.4
McClain	72	269	40.4	10.4	22	385	103.5	13.9	62	1 110	46.3	12.8
McCurtain	34	D	D	D	29	2 477	1 342.0	91.7	53	691	37.0	7.5
McIntosh	37	D	D	D	14	62	9.5	2.2	34	465	20.8	5.4
Major	17	D	D	D	8	44	D	1.5	11	D	D	D
Marshall	23	D	D	D	20	1 097	245.2	43.8	28	289	17.4	4.1
Mayes	60	D	D	D	58	2 608	1 224.7	130.6	72	940	40.2	10.4
Murray	27	D	D	D	16	451	D	21.5	30	339	17.6	4.8
Muskogee	93	D	D	D	55	3 660	1 489.7	181.3	133	2 384	104.4	27.7
Noble	14	D	D	D	9	1 451	D	80.4	22	D	D	D
Nowata	8	D	D	D	11	254	D	11.3	9	D	D	D
Okfuskee	6	D	D	D	7	132	D	4.5	7	D	D	D
Oklahoma	2 947	22 906	3 372.4	1 360.6	701	21 353	7 681.0	948.9	1 780	39 515	1 909.4	525.0
Okmulgee	44	192	15.1	4.9	34	1 438	533.8	66.3	49	737	32.1	8.0
Osage	45	D	D	D	28	270	D	11.7	43	554	24.7	7.6
Ottawa	50	333	32.3	11.5	43	1 495	D	57.2	58	2 101	228.3	40.2
Pawnee	26	124	36.3	5.4	17	250	D	10.5	22	D	D	D
Payne	150	1 195	131.6	50.4	64	1 538	473.0	62.3	181	3 661	155.0	41.9
Pittsburg	98	422	46.8	18.0	31	999	332.7	50.2	96	1 560	74.2	18.2
Pontotoc	80	342	35.6	12.4	32	1 114	270.3	41.1	69	1 374	62.1	16.7
Pottawatomie	106	681	95.3	29.4	57	2 911	1 112.5	134.5	120	2 528	107.9	29.7
Pushmataha	14	D	D	D	7	85	D	2.7	15	124	4.4	1.2
Roger Mills	6	D	D	D	NA	NA	NA	NA	4	D	D	D
Rogers	135	782	110.8	44.2	150	6 775	3 040.1	365.1	109	3 258	308.2	77.7
Seminole	27	D	D	D	24	738	129.7	29.1	35	553	23.6	6.0
Sequoyah	41	126	10.5	3.2	22	104	D	4.4	59	D	D	D
Stephens	82	427	49.8	15.7	62	2 512	1 935.5	132.0	77	1 098	50.1	12.8
Texas	31	D	D	D	11	D	D	D	50	670	29.2	7.2
Tillman	8	D	D	D	5	D	D	D	10	86	3.5	0.9
Tulsa	2 382	19 526	3 446.4	1 198.9	903	37 197	18 770.2	1 997.1	1 519	30 477	1 425.3	414.5
Wagoner	72	199	18.0	6.1	61	2 163	746.5	111.5	69	D	D	D
Washington	89	D	D	D	36	965	253.2	53.4	111	1 831	91.0	23.2
Washita	20	D	D	D	10	39	D	1.4	14	D	D	D
Woods	23	D	D	D	5	40	D	1.9	33	332	19.2	3.8
Woodward	53	D	D	D	24	498	448.4	32.2	55	862	50.9	11.6
OREGON	11 663	84 493	11 386.1	5 841.1	5 289	D	D	D	10 610	150 482	8 466.8	2 438.5
Baker	40	172	18.4	5.4	29	494	105.1	18.0	56	557	27.5	8.2
Benton	284	1 996	332.6	125.1	93	1 613	412.7	71.4	209	3 087	142.8	41.6
Clackamas	1 231	7 805	1 215.9	525.9	553	15 789	5 371.5	901.1	777	11 638	637.5	188.3
Clatsop	87	326	22.1	7.2	47	1 671	905.8	103.1	248	3 138	210.1	59.7
Columbia	78	275	23.3	8.6	52	1 350	458.3	64.6	85	964	42.9	12.3
Coos	115	439	44.3	16.2	70	1 352	315.7	48.4	165	2 129	126.2	34.9
Crook	34	109	12.2	3.7	30	728	150.8	25.4	44	479	23.7	8.0
Curry	36	105	16.6	2.8	20	578	176.0	27.4	107	880	46.5	12.2
Deschutes	708	2 631	332.0	120.7	279	3 672	801.8	165.8	498	7 635	435.6	133.5
Douglas	157	777	64.4	26.5	126	3 640	1 017.3	158.4	262	3 391	217.2	57.2
Gilliam	3	D	D	D	NA	NA	NA	NA	9	68	1.5	0.6
Grant	18	D	D	D	4	D	D	D	24	135	6.0	1.8
Harney	11	45	2.8	1.2	4	D	D	D	32	186	11.5	2.9
Hood River	125	423	84.4	18.2	63	1 055	304.3	44.5	96	1 306	62.1	19.3
Jackson	506	D	D	D	308	5 370	1 624.6	217.4	586	7 381	382.2	112.5
Jefferson	21	55	3.8	1.3	19	838	168.3	32.4	45	404	21.3	5.9
Josephine	140	563	40.6	13.5	106	2 190	434.8	89.6	199	2 483	124.5	35.8
Klamath	125	625	107.1	24.7	56	1 662	449.9	63.8	171	1 978	110.7	30.1
Lake	12	D	D	D	11	190	34.5	7.2	31	144	6.6	1.6
Lane	948	5 301	583.9	226.2	529	12 345	4 039.3	581.3	937	13 627	711.8	203.7
Lincoln	95	289	27.6	9.8	50	965	579.4	61.0	274	3 593	216.4	63.4
Linn	164	802	84.8	27.8	181	6 318	2 253.6	355.2	216	2 796	130.4	35.5
Malheur	46	185	17.2	7.1	35	1 078	D	34.2	84	1 008	50.8	13.6
Marion	664	3 815	448.4	170.5	352	9 155	2 540.3	347.6	667	D	D	D

1. Establishment subject to federal tax.

STATE County	Health care and social assistance, 2012				Other services, 2012				Nonemployer businesses, 2015		Value of residential construction authorized by building permits, 2016	
	Number of establishments	Number of employees	Receipts (mil dol)	Annual payroll (mil dol)	Number of establishments	Number of employees	Receipts (mil dol)	Annual payroll (mil dol)	Number	Receipts (mil dol)	New Construction ($1,000)	Number of housing units
	159	160	161	162	163	164	165	166	167	168	169	170
OKLAHOMA—Cont'd												
Kiowa	24	577	30.6	13.8	8	28	3.5	0.8	606	27.1	85	1
Latimer	25	357	23.0	9.2	8	D	D	D	762	30.1	0	0
Le Flore	95	2 706	202.8	86.1	44	D	D	D	3 042	129.8	8 681	78
Lincoln	57	D	D	D	21	D	D	D	2 478	111.0	944	7
Logan	61	D	D	D	52	176	19.8	3.9	3 673	170.9	3 890	28
Love	10	133	5.5	2.6	6	62	3.1	1.3	630	28.8	0	0
McClain	68	D	D	D	48	D	D	D	3 308	151.8	60 473	302
McCurtain	60	1 634	79.5	37.0	37	146	11.1	3.8	2 241	97.1	700	4
McIntosh	49	916	71.0	25.3	23	102	13.1	3.1	1 412	58.2	475	3
Major	14	231	13.3	6.4	11	D	D	D	701	28.2	1 333	6
Marshall	26	590	70.0	23.2	14	50	4.2	1.1	1 054	46.8	3 594	31
Mayes	86	955	101.6	35.3	46	132	10.6	2.6	2 595	104.9	1 789	13
Murray	31	595	42.3	16.4	11	32	2.8	0.6	882	34.7	5 307	46
Muskogee	230	5 700	616.6	250.4	84	587	57.9	14.6	3 859	171.4	2 345	11
Noble	18	395	24.3	9.8	13	66	5.4	1.2	824	30.3	450	2
Nowata	16	D	D	D	10	30	2.2	0.6	670	24.7	257	4
Okfuskee	43	1 619	104.4	30.0	10	9	3.0	0.7	730	30.0	0	0
Oklahoma	2 873	56 884	7 921.4	2 618.1	1 414	9 503	1 063.4	285.5	61 687	3 142.2	869 521	4 108
Okmulgee	124	2 032	117.5	50.5	39	174	12.7	2.9	2 306	86.1	1 443	3
Osage	42	732	37.4	15.8	24	76	9.5	1.9	2 923	119.6	20 535	128
Ottawa	72	1 402	110.0	47.6	33	138	12.5	2.8	1 771	70.7	506	8
Pawnee	29	459	27.8	11.4	9	29	2.8	0.8	1 025	41.6	1 220	8
Payne	160	3 570	305.4	118.4	109	763	167.3	20.9	5 203	224.7	50 248	358
Pittsburg	116	2 560	218.9	87.2	54	340	24.5	7.3	2 659	111.9	2 823	28
Pontotoc	130	3 418	350.1	128.5	46	194	18.0	4.5	2 800	114.3	14 431	73
Pottawatomie	167	2 451	257.4	100.5	72	350	27.9	8.2	4 314	200.4	17 800	121
Pushmataha	24	732	43.3	16.6	7	28	2.5	0.7	800	36.0	0	0
Roger Mills	5	D	D	D	3	D	D	D	359	18.2	0	0
Rogers	193	2 953	268.3	108.2	83	392	43.2	11.7	6 563	288.4	75 546	508
Seminole	43	1 079	81.4	28.1	21	D	D	D	1 362	55.0	281	5
Sequoyah	79	2 345	105.4	46.6	29	D	D	D	2 733	116.9	7 878	71
Stephens	101	2 121	177.1	63.3	69	361	68.5	11.3	3 069	145.0	6 564	42
Texas	39	500	44.8	18.0	28	110	12.3	2.2	1 149	54.2	432	2
Tillman	18	298	18.3	7.2	7	D	D	D	442	15.7	0	0
Tulsa	2 063	48 166	5 808.5	2 135.3	1 184	8 068	1 123.9	251.1	49 147	2 414.4	492 309	2 656
Wagoner	76	816	52.8	21.9	58	172	25.9	4.9	5 338	241.2	59 993	364
Washington	172	3 091	284.1	113.0	78	473	38.5	11.9	3 135	135.7	7 832	29
Washita	14	297	13.9	7.4	10	27	3.3	0.6	800	31.3	0	0
Woods	20	D	D	D	18	D	D	D	783	31.1	150	1
Woodward	81	1 029	96.4	34.9	41	262	34.3	8.7	1 477	74.9	2 173	8
OREGON	12 475	217 584	24 956.8	9 689.3	6 894	37 941	4 435.0	1 149.1	278 839	13 308.1	21 920 553	148
Baker	53	664	54.6	22.9	37	D	D	D	1 136	39.9	10 525	37
Benton	271	5 258	588.1	258.8	147	891	153.8	30.3	5 783	238.1	45 824	195
Clackamas	1 136	17 962	2 424.2	896.7	677	D	D	D	30 579	1 680.3	525 560	2 450
Clatsop	137	2 163	213.9	89.8	91	D	D	D	2 935	132.9	35 569	162
Columbia	114	1 239	62.2	25.8	64	D	D	D	2 678	108.6	22 461	100
Coos	193	3 539	350.3	143.7	86	D	D	D	3 647	153.5	9 141	39
Crook	35	D	D	D	41	D	D	D	1 447	62.6	32 366	110
Curry	89	885	79.9	31.4	28	D	D	D	1 860	78.8	11 562	54
Deschutes	608	9 398	1 114.0	442.5	329	1 526	156.8	41.9	16 935	880.3	483 576	2 274
Douglas	312	4 830	544.3	244.2	135	657	134.1	17.3	5 739	244.6	52 272	215
Gilliam	9	D	D	D	5	D	D	D	110	3.1	NA	NA
Grant	22	D	D	D	14	D	D	D	475	16.8	NA	NA
Harney	22	309	29.8	10.8	14	D	D	D	517	16.9	2 124	10
Hood River	96	1 759	130.8	59.4	55	244	20.7	6.1	1 878	99.9	29 024	105
Jackson	674	12 116	1 443.8	510.7	315	1 836	157.3	51.0	16 786	753.1	192 114	912
Jefferson	40	622	51.2	24.1	22	D	D	D	1 003	42.1	13 781	56
Josephine	269	4 376	418.5	151.1	103	D	D	D	5 738	251.2	56 075	213
Klamath	203	3 067	323.5	122.2	102	D	D	D	3 350	150.4	23 324	105
Lake	21	292	28.6	12.1	10	D	D	D	481	17.2	1 398	6
Lane	1 135	20 576	2 247.4	828.6	611	3 480	443.9	97.7	23 337	1 040.8	221 914	1 174
Lincoln	119	1 657	169.4	73.8	111	D	D	D	3 442	175.5	30 905	167
Linn	216	4 660	422.3	174.0	142	D	D	D	5 859	241.4	98 763	405
Malheur	112	1 563	133.1	53.6	57	D	D	D	1 361	56.8	5 782	25
Marion	971	17 456	1 787.0	758.3	484	2 394	215.7	66.8	16 362	790.2	240 128	1 199

STATE County	Full-time equivalent employees (171)	March payroll (dollars) (172)	Administration, judicial, and legal (173)	Police and Corrections (174)	Fire Protection (175)	Highways and transportation (176)	Health and Welfare (177)	Natural resources and utilities (178)	Education and libraries (179)	Total (mil dol) (180)	Intergovernmental (mil dol) (181)	Taxes Total (mil dol) (182)	Per capita Total (183)	Per capita Property (184)
OKLAHOMA—Cont'd														
Kiowa	554	1 581 546	4.8	5.3	0.8	4.5	36.0	6.1	41.7	28.0	15.7	7.6	812	529
Latimer	754	2 593 866	3.2	2.1	0.0	3.7	15.7	2.1	72.9	31.9	13.6	7.0	636	318
Le Flore	1 864	5 014 735	3.3	6.0	0.4	3.5	3.6	5.5	75.8	125.0	71.3	28.8	578	300
Lincoln	1 059	2 802 834	6.5	7.7	1.4	5.3	0.3	7.8	70.0	71.7	38.3	21.4	627	358
Logan	875	2 347 456	7.2	7.5	3.8	5.0	0.6	6.6	67.9	60.0	30.1	18.4	421	259
Love	481	1 481 165	6.9	3.8	0.0	3.5	40.8	1.2	43.6	19.3	11.3	5.6	581	387
McClain	1 466	3 975 638	5.5	7.7	3.1	4.0	13.2	3.3	60.7	113.4	39.8	57.3	1 609	1 149
McCurtain	1 454	3 983 530	2.5	5.7	1.1	5.2	4.9	5.0	74.7	93.6	55.4	21.0	632	354
McIntosh	617	1 761 398	8.2	6.9	0.0	2.0	1.7	6.5	74.4	51.2	28.1	16.0	778	358
Major	407	1 118 428	9.8	3.5	0.5	9.3	27.6	2.4	45.6	26.8	10.8	7.7	1 002	610
Marshall	530	1 477 680	5.8	6.2	1.0	4.3	3.0	4.0	74.8	36.0	20.4	10.5	660	446
Mayes	1 472	4 043 970	8.9	5.6	0.7	3.0	3.2	7.1	70.0	95.9	51.9	32.6	792	421
Murray	655	1 707 493	6.8	7.5	3.1	2.3	19.7	11.8	48.5	44.1	24.1	10.4	762	306
Muskogee	3 141	8 727 804	4.0	8.5	4.5	4.3	6.8	5.1	65.6	275.3	85.7	75.6	1 071	547
Noble	622	1 661 200	5.9	6.7	2.5	6.0	18.5	6.1	53.2	44.6	16.7	14.0	1 213	863
Nowata	422	1 000 994	6.4	5.5	1.0	6.4	3.0	5.6	71.4	24.0	14.4	5.9	556	321
Okfuskee	460	1 098 562	3.9	6.1	0.0	6.2	0.9	3.6	76.5	34.2	24.4	6.6	531	326
Oklahoma	24 286	88 713 472	5.8	14.1	10.2	3.4	2.9	6.5	56.5	2 544.3	761.2	1 182.3	1 594	722
Okmulgee	1 552	4 277 777	5.1	5.1	2.9	3.2	3.2	5.9	73.4	89.1	52.5	23.2	586	272
Osage	1 130	2 941 818	9.3	7.0	1.1	14.2	11.3	6.8	48.8	74.5	39.5	19.7	410	229
Ottawa	1 421	4 097 793	5.8	5.3	2.3	2.7	1.7	8.0	73.0	80.7	44.3	21.1	654	269
Pawnee	597	1 604 091	5.8	5.4	1.0	3.9	18.9	7.0	56.7	35.2	20.6	8.5	514	277
Payne	3 634	11 234 115	4.8	7.5	4.2	1.9	31.7	8.2	40.1	192.3	66.9	89.1	1 137	592
Pittsburg	2 380	5 927 369	5.7	11.0	5.4	4.2	4.8	9.9	55.6	254.4	76.4	76.1	1 689	1 039
Pontotoc	1 436	4 130 846	4.3	6.5	3.1	5.4	2.1	5.4	70.4	103.9	50.5	34.4	905	337
Pottawatomie	2 336	6 720 266	6.0	7.2	4.0	2.8	0.1	7.4	71.9	167.8	93.6	52.1	737	301
Pushmataha	607	1 521 960	2.8	3.2	1.8	5.1	17.4	5.2	63.2	38.1	21.2	5.6	504	248
Roger Mills	256	746 029	12.5	6.7	0.0	25.4	12.9	5.1	34.8	20.6	10.5	6.4	1 687	1 138
Rogers	2 835	7 580 674	6.2	6.2	5.0	5.0	1.0	15.1	60.3	197.1	79.1	87.2	986	621
Seminole	1 164	2 881 448	5.7	5.9	2.6	4.0	1.0	5.8	73.2	80.4	47.5	19.7	772	340
Sequoyah	1 722	4 751 418	4.1	6.5	0.8	2.8	13.0	2.9	69.8	115.2	65.1	22.1	534	266
Stephens	1 530	4 875 145	5.7	8.9	3.8	3.6	0.3	5.9	70.1	109.2	51.3	39.9	891	426
Texas	1 138	3 387 767	5.5	7.8	2.0	6.4	23.7	3.4	50.3	93.1	28.0	34.4	1 601	1 035
Tillman	545	1 405 251	6.0	9.3	2.4	4.7	24.1	6.9	45.0	21.8	14.4	3.8	490	335
Tulsa	23 532	78 482 436	5.7	10.6	6.5	3.9	2.1	5.2	62.5	2 206.7	679.3	1 020.7	1 663	890
Wagoner	1 330	3 590 004	7.0	7.2	2.6	4.0	2.4	9.2	64.5	85.8	39.9	34.9	465	232
Washington	1 747	5 123 970	4.5	9.2	5.9	3.5	2.6	6.6	65.7	123.9	52.2	47.3	915	518
Washita	621	1 807 048	6.4	5.9	0.7	7.4	8.9	3.3	66.3	43.9	25.8	12.0	1 030	518
Woods	575	1 537 398	8.0	4.6	2.6	8.1	31.6	4.9	39.0	38.5	13.1	16.6	1 883	804
Woodward	891	2 568 486	5.9	8.6	3.5	5.0	7.2	4.7	61.8	69.5	25.7	32.5	1 583	708
OREGON	X	X	X	X	X	X	X	X	X	X	X	X	X	X
Baker	487	1 718 138	10.0	12.3	6.0	4.4	2.9	7.2	54.6	56.2	31.8	15.5	977	900
Benton	1 834	7 923 562	9.3	13.4	6.2	3.8	7.4	9.4	45.7	259.6	93.0	115.4	1 335	1 185
Clackamas	10 411	44 609 746	8.2	11.7	6.1	3.3	4.7	6.1	57.9	1 431.7	520.8	623.0	1 623	1 458
Clatsop	1 540	5 672 121	8.9	12.5	2.7	5.7	8.3	8.9	49.7	172.7	53.4	71.3	1 912	1 596
Columbia	1 444	6 022 192	7.2	9.3	8.1	2.1	0.4	16.3	52.3	192.4	87.9	59.7	1 211	1 123
Coos	3 079	13 113 856	2.7	5.5	1.8	2.4	45.7	3.7	37.5	386.2	116.4	74.2	1 187	1 048
Crook	584	2 274 092	9.3	15.0	2.6	3.8	3.7	7.2	51.7	72.1	28.3	22.8	1 099	940
Curry	803	3 143 734	7.1	10.1	0.4	5.5	38.6	5.6	31.1	90.5	25.4	26.9	1 211	1 076
Deschutes	4 773	21 188 503	8.1	12.1	5.4	2.6	5.0	7.0	55.3	649.0	217.1	283.8	1 749	1 579
Douglas	3 555	13 196 754	6.3	8.9	6.6	3.1	10.3	6.1	57.1	374.6	196.1	94.6	883	829
Gilliam	145	510 580	18.3	7.1	1.3	10.8	8.3	8.3	45.2	24.4	3.8	15.2	7 770	6 077
Grant	485	1 961 339	5.0	4.3	0.1	3.5	41.5	3.5	38.1	55.0	23.8	7.9	1 083	1 049
Harney	427	1 530 704	6.7	5.9	0.4	3.5	37.4	2.0	42.0	51.3	21.5	7.2	998	925
Hood River	639	2 757 629	6.9	8.8	4.6	6.5	3.0	12.1	54.2	95.2	38.6	26.4	1 171	1 023
Jackson	4 931	20 369 335	9.1	14.6	6.5	6.1	5.2	6.8	50.0	668.0	291.3	260.8	1 263	1 068
Jefferson	1 028	3 923 905	4.1	6.5	1.3	1.7	29.3	8.4	46.4	112.4	50.4	24.0	1 101	997
Josephine	2 192	8 995 230	6.6	12.9	2.5	3.4	1.3	3.1	68.4	243.6	119.9	70.8	854	781
Klamath	1 819	7 192 100	5.9	8.2	6.2	6.2	7.0	7.1	56.2	234.1	125.3	59.4	901	796
Lake	460	1 602 079	5.2	5.5	1.6	6.9	38.3	7.3	33.1	51.6	18.7	10.7	1 372	1 263
Lane	11 647	50 155 119	7.2	10.9	5.2	6.9	4.1	11.4	48.1	1 390.4	585.1	463.2	1 306	1 120
Lincoln	1 465	6 826 571	10.2	14.7	2.9	4.9	8.2	27.9	29.0	200.9	55.6	104.1	2 255	1 881
Linn	3 984	16 207 525	6.1	11.2	5.6	4.0	5.1	4.9	61.9	447.9	223.4	146.4	1 237	1 133
Malheur	1 459	4 992 780	4.9	8.6	1.3	2.7	8.2	7.2	66.0	146.8	85.7	25.2	821	712
Marion	12 046	53 396 211	5.2	8.9	3.6	3.2	3.6	3.7	69.6	1 311.4	678.7	400.1	1 250	1 131

1. Based on the resident population estimated as of July 1 of the year shown.

Table B. States and Counties — Local Government Finances, Government Employment, and Income Taxes

STATE County	Local government finances, 2012 (cont.)									Government employment, 2015			Individual income tax returns, 2014		
	Direct general expenditure							Debt outstanding							
			Percent of total for:												
	Total (mil dol)	Per capita[1] (dollars)	Education	Health and hospitals	Police protection	Public welfare	Highways	Total (mil dol)	Per capita[1] (dollars)	Federal civilian	Federal military	State and local	Number of returns	Mean adjusted gross income	Mean income tax
	185	186	187	188	189	190	191	192	193	194	195	196	197	198	199
OKLAHOMA—Cont'd															
Kiowa	28.9	3 103	50.8	1.7	5.1	0.0	11.2	18.6	1 994	46	34	695	3 650	40 977	3 632
Latimer	33.5	3 038	45.3	21.6	2.5	0.0	11.1	4.0	365	29	38	1 117	4 250	46 081	4 115
Le Flore	128.2	2 571	63.3	5.2	3.9	0.1	7.2	41.9	840	160	182	4 769	17 950	42 280	3 556
Lincoln	69.8	2 043	62.1	1.0	6.3	0.0	9.1	22.4	656	79	131	1 709	13 590	47 610	4 594
Logan	60.7	1 390	56.3	2.5	8.0	0.0	8.8	34.1	782	61	166	1 309	18 080	63 636	7 824
Love	22.3	2 329	73.8	2.7	1.9	0.0	7.2	4.8	506	19	37	2 959	4 150	44 883	4 178
McClain	115.0	3 229	69.2	1.7	5.3	0.0	6.8	54.5	1 531	69	144	1 677	16 450	64 007	7 687
McCurtain	89.7	2 703	65.8	3.0	3.2	0.0	7.5	40.6	1 222	131	124	2 354	12 600	37 564	3 042
McIntosh	48.8	2 370	65.3	1.5	5.7	0.0	9.6	27.7	1 344	35	75	1 144	7 520	42 028	3 784
Major	27.0	3 519	43.6	21.9	3.4	0.2	15.4	8.4	1 096	27	29	376	3 410	64 383	7 426
Marshall	35.6	2 234	67.7	3.5	3.9	0.0	4.1	8.2	513	23	60	802	6 270	44 060	4 237
Mayes	94.4	2 293	68.5	1.3	6.4	0.0	6.3	46.9	1 140	65	153	2 473	16 020	49 569	5 097
Murray	43.2	3 162	41.5	28.0	3.6	0.0	4.3	20.9	1 532	67	52	2 950	5 790	51 798	5 851
Muskogee	284.3	4 027	38.4	31.9	3.5	0.0	3.0	95.6	1 354	2 920	252	6 422	27 150	46 244	4 580
Noble	44.7	3 877	46.3	20.3	3.8	0.0	12.0	32.4	2 812	33	43	1 238	4 850	60 096	7 267
Nowata	24.4	2 295	64.3	0.0	4.0	0.0	11.1	7.8	734	30	39	615	4 240	45 665	4 136
Okfuskee	34.0	2 753	77.0	0.0	2.3	0.0	10.3	17.9	1 449	24	42	1 121	4 020	40 042	3 162
Oklahoma	2 264.8	3 053	44.4	0.4	10.3	0.2	5.6	2 878.7	3 881	26 004	8 458	59 244	341 380	63 753	9 395
Okmulgee	89.9	2 270	65.7	0.5	4.7	0.0	7.2	96.2	2 428	124	143	3 503	15 170	43 149	3 777
Osage	73.9	1 543	50.5	8.5	2.4	0.8	12.7	17.6	367	175	184	2 587	17 600	57 651	6 409
Ottawa	87.3	2 709	53.9	2.6	5.3	0.0	11.8	33.9	1 051	102	118	5 600	12 860	38 419	3 183
Pawnee	33.0	2 003	61.8	3.2	3.7	0.0	10.4	20.5	1 247	221	62	971	6 320	49 788	4 960
Payne	185.3	2 363	48.5	0.4	11.8	0.1	8.4	115.8	1 477	233	291	14 721	29 670	57 767	7 006
Pittsburg	209.1	4 642	32.4	36.3	4.6	0.0	4.1	129.8	2 882	1 709	162	3 918	17 970	47 533	4 805
Pontotoc	100.3	2 643	61.6	0.6	5.6	0.0	7.3	22.3	586	162	138	6 835	16 290	51 577	5 585
Pottawatomie	171.7	2 427	59.2	0.4	6.1	0.0	8.2	62.2	879	142	262	6 231	28 670	47 954	4 870
Pushmataha	38.0	3 395	55.0	22.5	3.5	0.2	8.3	9.5	847	28	42	888	4 280	38 891	3 011
Roger Mills	21.1	5 590	33.6	1.3	3.6	0.0	42.2	0.7	196	39	14	366	1 590	90 151	13 250
Rogers	198.7	2 249	54.8	0.9	4.1	0.0	9.8	136.5	1 544	450	340	6 313	39 320	64 397	7 809
Seminole	79.1	3 109	54.5	1.3	3.6	0.0	6.2	27.2	1 070	142	95	1 946	9 350	45 114	4 628
Sequoyah	115.1	2 781	61.2	12.8	4.0	0.7	4.6	67.9	1 639	131	171	3 161	15 540	41 161	3 632
Stephens	108.9	2 432	55.9	0.5	5.5	0.0	9.4	48.1	1 074	78	167	2 049	18 340	65 524	8 901
Texas	98.3	4 570	36.3	26.0	2.2	0.1	7.6	39.3	1 829	72	79	1 697	9 830	47 933	4 486
Tillman	23.0	2 944	65.1	1.9	5.6	0.0	12.8	6.9	884	33	28	703	2 960	39 399	3 219
Tulsa	2 175.2	3 544	44.8	4.4	6.3	0.8	7.9	3 349.0	5 456	3 349	2 434	31 490	287 480	71 600	10 495
Wagoner	88.4	1 178	62.5	2.4	6.7	0.0	8.5	84.6	1 128	70	303	1 853	31 730	57 842	6 169
Washington	127.7	2 473	49.2	0.7	6.0	0.0	8.3	98.7	1 911	89	194	2 384	23 370	62 971	8 082
Washita	39.5	3 402	50.0	0.3	4.5	0.0	20.5	17.5	1 502	42	43	730	4 810	56 217	6 398
Woods	34.4	3 894	39.3	5.7	3.4	0.0	14.9	7.3	829	29	31	1 137	3 950	88 187	15 768
Woodward	71.3	3 469	43.9	1.0	6.2	0.0	7.9	53.7	2 613	83	77	1 657	9 230	70 432	9 935
OREGON	X	X	X	X	X	X	X	X	X	27 820	11 722	242 640	1 825 020	59 775	7 199
Baker	54.2	3 408	42.8	7.5	5.5	1.6	8.5	12.0	754	210	40	877	6 820	43 306	4 022
Benton	259.2	2 999	46.3	7.4	9.6	0.0	4.2	233.8	2 705	502	250	10 731	37 890	64 358	7 693
Clackamas	1 519.2	3 958	45.7	4.4	7.2	1.0	4.3	2 524.7	6 577	1 026	1 117	14 153	189 480	74 173	10 279
Clatsop	169.8	4 551	35.4	2.0	7.8	5.6	4.9	220.8	5 921	187	505	2 435	17 610	48 983	4 788
Columbia	192.3	3 902	51.6	1.9	4.3	0.2	3.0	214.6	4 353	71	127	1 782	21 810	56 582	5 634
Coos	396.6	6 341	32.9	41.8	2.9	0.1	2.5	240.2	3 841	322	369	4 880	26 900	44 244	4 265
Crook	64.9	3 132	41.4	3.3	7.3	0.2	6.7	59.1	2 852	288	55	859	9 200	46 693	4 367
Curry	101.4	4 557	23.1	33.1	4.3	2.7	5.0	92.8	4 173	85	101	1 085	10 330	44 685	4 603
Deschutes	663.5	4 089	49.1	3.5	7.4	0.4	5.0	1 093.2	6 736	884	451	7 789	81 790	61 347	7 575
Douglas	388.7	3 627	47.5	11.2	5.7	0.2	5.6	258.0	2 407	1 460	314	5 744	44 920	45 720	4 426
Gilliam	26.0	13 296	30.4	4.8	3.1	0.9	11.5	62.9	32 197	D	D	218	820	53 182	5 404
Grant	58.7	8 019	29.3	28.9	3.0	0.6	14.1	17.9	2 444	287	18	688	3 040	40 793	3 882
Harney	51.9	7 203	32.1	38.3	1.6	0.5	8.2	34.0	4 719	241	18	740	2 970	39 286	3 330
Hood River	99.3	4 399	46.3	2.2	2.8	0.6	8.1	98.9	4 381	109	58	1 108	11 600	55 160	6 029
Jackson	678.0	3 285	42.6	5.3	8.6	0.0	6.1	887.0	4 297	1 834	542	8 837	96 950	51 323	5 622
Jefferson	108.0	4 966	39.6	27.4	3.8	0.4	3.9	71.9	3 306	125	56	2 282	9 050	39 882	3 365
Josephine	253.3	3 055	59.6	2.9	7.1	0.1	5.0	145.0	1 748	273	215	2 768	35 560	43 823	4 370
Klamath	233.2	3 538	47.7	4.6	6.8	0.2	7.6	72.7	1 103	867	250	3 861	27 160	44 203	4 224
Lake	52.0	6 689	27.7	39.5	2.5	0.3	10.2	44.6	5 745	252	19	779	3 080	43 175	3 984
Lane	1 390.2	3 921	44.2	5.1	6.9	2.2	4.3	1 580.1	4 457	1 617	1 013	23 484	161 290	54 292	6 247
Lincoln	229.9	4 981	36.4	6.6	7.4	0.1	6.6	316.8	6 864	322	210	3 293	21 590	46 611	4 645
Linn	449.1	3 794	51.6	3.6	6.2	0.4	4.4	449.9	3 801	313	309	6 048	51 380	47 517	4 324
Malheur	157.2	5 132	62.3	4.3	3.4	0.2	3.8	62.8	2 050	223	70	2 856	10 590	39 542	3 333
Marion	1 325.2	4 141	57.0	3.6	5.0	0.2	4.6	1 931.4	6 036	1 280	836	33 135	140 350	50 928	5 096

1. Based on the resident population estimated as of July 1 of the year shown.

Table B. States and Counties — **Land Area and Population**

					Population, 2016			Population and population characteristics, 2016									
								Race alone or in combination, not Hispanic or Latino (percent)					Age (percent)					
STATE/ County code	CBSA code[1]	County type[2]	STATE County	Land area,[3] (sq mi) 2016	Total persons 2016	Rank	Per square mile	White	Black	American Indian, Alaska Native	Asian and Pacific Islander	Percent Hispanic or Latino[4]	Under 5 years	5 to 17 years	18 to 24 years	25 to 34 years	35 to 44 years	45 to 54 years
				1	2	3	4	5	6	7	8	9	10	11	12	13	14	15
			OREGON—Cont'd															
41 049	25840	6	Morrow	2 030.5	11 274	2 340	5.6	61.0	1.1	2.2	1.3	36.3	7.3	20.8	8.9	11.1	11.4	11.4
41 051	38900	1	Multnomah	431.1	799 766	76	1 855.2	74.1	6.8	1.9	10.0	11.4	5.8	13.6	8.2	18.8	16.1	13.1
41 053	41420	2	Polk	740.9	81 823	685	110.4	81.3	1.5	3.1	3.6	13.7	5.9	17.2	12.6	11.7	11.3	11.4
41 055	...	9	Sherman	823.6	1 710	3 072	2.1	90.5	1.1	2.5	0.9	6.8	5.1	13.7	6.1	10.1	10.9	11.4
41 057	...	6	Tillamook	1 102.4	26 143	1 556	23.7	86.5	0.9	2.4	2.2	10.5	5.2	14.0	6.6	11.0	10.0	11.8
41 059	25840	4	Umatilla	3 215.4	76 456	722	23.8	68.2	1.3	4.4	1.7	26.4	6.9	18.8	9.2	13.7	12.3	12.2
41 061	29260	7	Union	2 036.9	26 087	1 559	12.8	91.1	1.3	2.2	3.2	4.7	6.1	16.1	11.7	11.8	10.4	10.4
41 063	...	9	Wallowa	3 145.9	6 946	2 677	2.2	95.4	1.0	1.7	1.4	2.8	4.6	14.1	4.5	9.8	9.7	10.9
41 065	45520	6	Wasco	2 381.1	26 115	1 558	11.0	77.1	0.9	4.2	2.5	17.4	6.4	16.0	7.7	12.5	10.9	11.1
41 067	38900	1	Washington	724.3	582 779	112	804.6	70.2	2.8	1.3	13.2	16.5	6.4	17.2	8.2	15.4	14.9	13.5
41 069	...	9	Wheeler	1 716.0	1 344	3 091	0.8	92.0	1.6	3.6	1.4	5.2	3.6	11.0	5.2	7.4	8.3	10.3
41 071	38900	1	Yamhill	715.9	105 035	567	146.7	80.0	1.4	2.4	3.1	15.7	5.6	16.9	10.7	12.2	12.5	12.4
42 000	...	0	PENNSYLVANIA	44 742.4	12 784 227	X	285.7	78.5	11.8	0.5	3.9	7.0	5.6	15.4	9.3	13.1	11.6	13.6
42 001	23900	3	Adams	518.7	102 180	591	197.0	90.4	2.2	0.5	1.1	7.0	5.0	15.3	9.5	10.7	10.7	14.5
42 003	38300	1	Allegheny	730.1	1 225 365	35	1 678.4	80.7	14.5	0.5	4.3	2.0	5.3	13.6	9.0	15.3	11.4	12.8
42 005	38300	1	Armstrong	653.2	66 486	798	101.8	97.9	1.3	0.4	0.5	0.8	4.9	14.4	7.0	10.7	11.2	14.3
42 007	38300	1	Beaver	434.7	167 429	385	385.2	91.5	7.6	0.5	0.9	1.5	5.3	14.4	7.7	11.6	11.0	13.8
42 009	...	6	Bedford	1 012.3	48 325	1 014	47.7	97.7	1.0	0.5	0.5	1.2	4.8	15.2	7.1	10.1	11.2	14.4
42 011	39740	2	Berks	856.4	414 812	168	484.4	74.1	5.1	0.4	1.8	20.0	5.9	16.8	9.7	12.2	11.5	14.0
42 013	11020	3	Blair	525.8	124 650	504	237.1	96.1	2.6	0.4	1.0	1.2	5.3	15.3	7.8	12.1	11.4	13.1
42 015	42380	6	Bradford	1 147.4	60 770	860	53.0	97.2	0.9	0.7	0.9	1.5	5.9	16.1	7.3	10.7	10.4	14.0
42 017	37980	1	Bucks	604.4	626 399	106	1 036.4	85.9	4.6	0.5	5.4	5.2	4.9	16.0	8.0	11.0	11.6	15.3
42 019	38300	1	Butler	788.6	186 847	348	236.9	95.9	1.6	0.4	1.7	1.4	5.1	15.2	8.7	11.2	11.6	14.8
42 021	27780	3	Cambria	688.4	134 732	470	195.7	94.3	4.4	0.4	0.8	1.6	4.9	14.4	9.2	10.4	10.9	13.1
42 023	...	7	Cameron	396.2	4 677	2 853	11.8	97.7	1.1	0.7	0.7	1.0	5.2	12.2	7.0	9.0	9.0	14.2
42 025	10900	2	Carbon	381.5	63 594	834	166.7	93.0	2.0	0.5	0.9	4.4	4.6	14.8	6.7	10.9	11.4	15.1
42 027	44300	3	Centre	1 109.9	161 464	401	145.5	87.1	4.1	0.4	7.1	2.9	4.1	11.1	24.1	14.6	10.4	11.4
42 029	37980	1	Chester	750.5	516 312	132	688.0	81.4	6.7	0.5	5.8	7.3	5.7	17.5	9.1	11.4	12.2	14.8
42 031	...	6	Clarion	600.8	38 513	1 212	64.1	97.0	1.7	0.5	1.0	0.9	4.9	13.8	12.7	11.9	10.3	13.0
42 033	20180	4	Clearfield	1 144.7	80 596	697	70.4	93.8	2.7	0.3	0.9	3.0	4.6	13.8	7.9	11.9	12.3	15.0
42 035	30820	4	Clinton	888.0	39 233	1 193	44.2	96.1	2.0	0.4	0.9	1.4	5.5	14.9	15.1	11.1	10.4	12.0
42 037	14100	3	Columbia	483.1	66 420	803	137.5	94.2	2.3	0.5	1.4	2.7	4.7	13.1	16.2	10.7	10.3	12.8
42 039	32740	4	Crawford	1 012.3	86 257	665	85.2	96.1	2.5	0.5	0.8	1.2	5.6	15.7	9.2	10.9	10.8	13.6
42 041	25420	2	Cumberland	545.5	248 506	271	455.6	88.2	4.7	0.5	4.9	3.7	5.5	14.9	9.8	13.1	12.1	13.5
42 043	25420	2	Dauphin	525.1	273 707	249	521.2	68.9	19.3	0.7	5.0	8.9	6.4	16.1	8.4	13.7	11.9	13.4
42 045	37980	1	Delaware	183.9	563 402	116	3 063.6	69.2	22.2	0.6	6.4	3.7	6.0	16.2	10.1	12.9	11.8	13.5
42 047	41260	7	Elk	827.4	30 480	1 419	36.8	98.2	0.8	0.4	0.6	0.8	4.9	14.4	7.4	9.4	10.5	15.4
42 049	21500	2	Erie	799.2	276 207	246	345.6	86.8	8.6	0.5	2.1	4.1	5.7	16.0	10.1	13.3	11.1	12.9
42 051	38300	1	Fayette	790.3	132 733	477	168.0	93.4	5.7	0.5	0.8	1.1	5.1	14.3	7.5	11.7	11.5	14.0
42 053	...	9	Forest	427.3	7 321	2 642	17.1	73.7	19.8	0.5	0.4	6.2	0.9	4.2	10.8	18.2	12.5	14.7
42 055	16540	3	Franklin	772.2	153 851	424	199.2	89.9	4.4	0.5	1.4	5.5	5.8	16.6	7.7	12.1	11.8	13.7
42 057	...	8	Fulton	437.6	14 640	2 123	33.5	97.2	1.7	0.6	0.4	1.2	5.3	15.3	7.7	10.4	11.6	14.9
42 059	...	6	Greene	575.9	37 197	1 245	64.6	94.6	3.7	0.7	0.6	1.4	5.2	14.1	9.3	12.4	12.4	14.0
42 061	26500	6	Huntingdon	874.7	45 634	1 058	52.2	91.9	6.0	0.4	0.8	2.0	5.0	13.9	9.4	12.3	12.0	13.9
42 063	26860	4	Indiana	827.0	86 364	663	104.4	94.9	2.9	0.4	1.4	1.3	4.8	13.4	16.8	10.7	9.8	12.1
42 065	...	7	Jefferson	652.4	44 073	1 091	67.6	98.1	0.8	0.6	0.5	1.0	5.7	15.4	7.6	11.4	10.9	13.3
42 067	...	6	Juniata	391.4	24 863	1 614	63.5	95.3	1.0	0.4	0.6	3.5	5.4	16.9	7.2	11.1	11.1	13.9
42 069	42540	2	Lackawanna	458.8	211 321	311	460.6	87.5	3.4	0.4	3.1	7.1	5.3	14.9	9.0	12.5	11.1	13.4
42 071	29540	2	Lancaster	943.9	538 500	125	570.5	83.8	4.5	0.4	2.6	10.2	6.6	17.2	9.1	13.0	11.3	12.7
42 073	35260	4	Lawrence	358.2	87 294	662	243.7	94.1	5.2	0.4	0.8	1.4	5.3	14.8	8.4	10.6	10.8	13.3
42 075	30140	3	Lebanon	361.8	138 863	461	383.8	83.8	2.5	0.4	1.7	12.7	6.1	16.9	8.4	11.6	11.6	13.1
42 077	10900	2	Lehigh	345.2	363 147	191	1 052.0	67.3	6.7	0.4	4.0	23.3	5.9	16.8	9.1	13.0	12.3	13.4
42 079	42540	2	Luzerne	890.3	316 383	216	355.4	84.3	4.4	0.4	1.5	10.7	5.0	14.5	8.8	12.4	11.4	14.1
42 081	48700	3	Lycoming	1 228.6	115 248	534	93.8	92.7	5.8	0.6	1.0	1.9	5.7	14.9	9.1	13.3	10.8	13.1
42 083	14620	7	McKean	979.2	41 883	1 132	42.8	94.2	3.1	0.6	0.8	2.2	4.8	14.8	9.5	11.7	11.9	13.6
42 085	49660	2	Mercer	672.6	112 913	542	167.9	91.9	6.8	0.5	1.1	1.4	4.9	14.9	9.9	10.4	10.5	13.6
42 087	30380	4	Mifflin	411.0	46 342	1 041	112.8	97.0	1.3	0.4	0.9	1.5	6.0	16.2	7.3	11.0	10.8	13.8
42 089	20700	3	Monroe	608.3	166 098	386	273.1	68.7	14.2	0.8	2.9	15.4	4.5	15.7	11.0	10.8	10.6	15.7
42 091	37980	1	Montgomery	483.0	821 725	72	1 701.3	78.0	10.2	0.4	8.3	5.0	5.5	16.2	8.1	12.4	12.3	14.3
42 093	14100	3	Montour	130.2	18 343	1 899	140.9	92.6	2.2	0.4	3.3	2.6	5.5	14.6	6.8	13.3	10.9	12.9
42 095	10900	2	Northampton	369.6	302 294	229	817.9	78.9	6.1	0.4	3.3	12.9	5.0	15.3	10.0	11.7	11.6	14.1
42 097	44980	4	Northumberland	458.0	92 541	631	202.1	93.7	2.9	0.4	0.7	3.4	5.2	14.7	7.3	12.2	11.5	13.8
42 099	25420	2	Perry	551.4	45 820	1 054	83.1	96.5	1.3	0.5	0.7	1.9	5.8	15.9	7.5	11.7	11.8	15.0
42 101	37980	1	Philadelphia	134.2	1 567 872	23	11 683.1	36.4	42.6	0.8	8.0	14.3	6.8	15.2	10.5	18.9	12.2	11.9
42 103	35620	1	Pike	545.0	55 562	910	101.9	82.3	6.2	0.8	1.7	10.7	3.6	15.1	8.0	8.9	10.5	16.0

1. CBSA = Core Based Statistical Area. See Appendix A for explanation. See Appendix B for list of metropolitan areas with component counties.   2. County type code from the Economic Research Service of USDA Rural-Urban Continuum Codes. See Appendix A for definition.   3. Dry land or land partially or temporarily covered by water.   4. May be of any race.

Table B. States and Counties — Population and Households

STATE County	55 to 64 years	65 to 74 years	75 years and over	Percent female	Total persons 2000	Total persons 2010	Percent change 2000–2010	Percent change 2010–2016	Births	Deaths	Net migration	Number	Persons per household	Family households	Female family householder[1]	One person
	16	17	18	19	20	21	22	23	24	25	26	27	28	29	30	31
OREGON—Cont'd																
Morrow	14.1	9.1	5.8	48.5	10 995	11 177	1.7	0.9	1 005	515	-379	3 772	2.96	73.0	9.6	23.4
Multnomah	11.9	7.9	4.7	50.4	660 486	735 169	11.3	8.8	59 356	35 062	40 277	310 669	2.41	54.4	10.6	32.9
Polk	12.3	10.4	7.3	51.3	62 380	75 404	20.9	8.5	5 426	4 142	4 915	28 458	2.65	68.0	9.4	23.4
Sherman	17.4	13.2	12.2	49.5	1 934	1 766	-8.7	-3.2	106	96	-66	804	2.22	58.6	7.2	33.3
Tillamook	17.1	15.3	9.0	49.5	24 262	25 258	4.1	3.5	1 588	1 775	1 168	10 094	2.45	63.4	8.5	29.5
Umatilla	12.2	8.6	6.2	47.8	70 548	75 885	7.6	0.8	6 718	3 921	-2 055	26 794	2.70	68.3	13.5	26.2
Union	14.0	11.0	8.4	50.6	24 530	25 744	4.9	1.3	1 867	1 655	183	10 130	2.46	63.5	8.2	27.6
Wallowa	18.7	16.2	11.4	51.2	7 226	7 008	-3.0	-0.9	361	499	118	3 082	2.18	62.5	10.8	34.8
Wasco	14.6	11.9	8.9	50.2	23 791	25 211	6.0	3.6	1 879	1 849	819	9 704	2.50	67.0	10.4	27.6
Washington	11.7	7.6	5.0	50.6	445 342	529 872	19.0	10.0	44 807	19 539	27 019	206 426	2.66	67.7	10.3	24.7
Wheeler	18.7	19.3	16.1	49.7	1 547	1 439	-7.0	-6.6	62	116	-42	671	1.97	60.7	4.6	35.3
Yamhill	13.0	9.6	7.0	50.2	84 992	99 190	16.7	5.9	7 018	5 279	3 812	34 425	2.78	71.2	11.6	22.6
PENNSYLVANIA	14.1	9.7	7.7	51.0	12 281 054	12 702 857	3.4	0.6	887 430	804 358	11 424	4 958 859	2.49	64.6	12.0	29.5
Adams	14.8	11.2	8.3	50.7	91 292	101 417	11.1	0.8	6 268	6 010	271	38 193	2.55	71.7	9.5	23.6
Allegheny	14.7	9.7	8.3	51.7	1 281 666	1 223 338	-4.6	0.2	82 636	85 530	8 028	529 534	2.26	57.7	11.7	35.3
Armstrong	16.2	11.8	9.5	50.3	72 392	68 938	-4.8	-3.6	4 104	5 343	-1 153	28 524	2.36	67.1	10.1	28.7
Beaver	15.9	11.0	9.5	51.5	181 412	170 539	-6.0	-1.8	10 892	12 993	-626	70 079	2.38	65.6	11.6	30.0
Bedford	15.9	11.4	9.9	50.0	49 984	49 768	-0.4	-2.9	2 931	3 342	-1 003	20 000	2.43	69.6	9.0	25.8
Berks	13.5	9.2	7.3	50.8	373 638	411 572	10.2	0.8	30 533	23 373	-3 275	153 312	2.61	69.1	12.3	24.8
Blair	14.8	11.0	9.2	51.1	129 144	127 076	-1.6	-1.9	8 435	9 973	-1 039	51 034	2.41	64.2	11.1	30.7
Bradford	15.3	11.6	8.7	50.4	62 761	62 622	-0.2	-3.0	4 461	4 226	-1 905	24 358	2.52	68.4	9.5	26.1
Bucks	15.6	9.9	7.7	50.9	597 635	625 255	4.6	0.2	36 753	35 161	-592	233 066	2.65	71.5	9.6	24.1
Butler	15.3	10.1	8.0	50.5	174 083	183 862	5.6	1.6	11 207	11 794	3 227	74 476	2.42	68.2	8.5	26.2
Cambria	15.8	11.6	9.8	50.9	152 598	143 674	-5.8	-6.2	8 273	11 319	-5 721	57 465	2.28	63.6	11.6	32.0
Cameron	18.1	14.7	10.5	50.4	5 974	5 085	-14.9	-8.0	310	402	-306	2 170	2.20	60.8	9.5	33.6
Carbon	16.1	11.8	8.5	50.4	58 802	65 250	11.0	-2.5	3 665	4 940	-264	25 751	2.48	67.1	10.8	25.9
Centre	11.2	7.3	5.7	47.4	135 758	154 027	13.5	4.8	8 165	5 940	5 400	57 183	2.47	56.9	6.5	28.6
Chester	14.0	8.9	6.5	50.8	433 501	499 146	15.1	3.4	34 524	23 659	6 578	186 057	2.66	70.2	8.6	23.6
Clarion	14.6	10.3	8.4	51.1	41 765	39 991	-4.2	-3.7	2 408	2 675	-1 218	15 830	2.39	62.6	8.4	28.0
Clearfield	14.7	10.8	9.0	47.7	83 382	81 597	-2.1	-1.2	4 647	5 839	184	31 817	2.38	66.6	9.3	29.4
Clinton	13.2	9.7	8.2	51.1	37 914	39 241	3.5	0.0	2 637	2 490	-96	14 796	2.52	67.0	10.9	26.4
Columbia	14.0	10.3	7.8	51.8	64 151	67 296	4.9	-1.3	3 868	4 264	-464	26 178	2.40	64.0	9.8	27.4
Crawford	15.0	11.4	7.8	51.0	90 366	88 761	-1.8	-2.8	6 020	6 084	-2 219	34 575	2.42	67.5	10.6	27.1
Cumberland	13.4	9.9	7.8	50.5	213 674	235 408	10.2	5.6	16 172	13 893	10 691	95 950	2.38	64.9	8.7	29.2
Dauphin	14.2	9.3	6.7	51.4	251 798	268 100	6.5	2.1	21 726	15 265	-199	109 623	2.41	63.2	13.9	30.6
Delaware	13.9	8.5	7.2	51.9	550 864	558 726	1.4	0.8	42 121	33 928	-2 479	203 817	2.65	67.0	14.6	28.5
Elk	16.5	11.4	10.0	49.8	35 112	31 946	-9.0	-4.6	1 830	2 431	-821	13 244	2.34	64.6	8.8	32.3
Erie	14.2	9.4	7.2	50.6	280 843	280 564	-0.1	-1.6	19 902	17 561	-6 229	109 934	2.43	63.6	13.2	30.0
Fayette	15.6	11.4	8.9	50.5	148 644	136 602	-8.1	-2.8	8 639	11 282	-1 023	53 997	2.41	63.9	12.4	31.5
Forest	16.2	13.8	8.7	32.3	4 946	7 716	56.0	-5.1	195	539	-55	1 974	1.86	59.1	7.8	36.0
Franklin	13.4	10.4	8.4	50.8	129 313	149 618	15.7	2.8	11 289	9 084	1 956	58 570	2.56	69.3	9.5	26.2
Fulton	14.6	11.8	8.4	49.4	14 261	14 844	4.1	-1.4	946	865	-220	5 960	2.46	69.8	7.7	25.4
Greene	14.7	10.6	7.3	48.1	40 672	38 686	-4.9	-3.8	2 379	2 705	-1 091	14 394	2.33	66.8	11.9	27.5
Huntingdon	14.0	11.2	8.3	46.8	45 586	46 031	1.0	-0.9	2 765	2 869	-242	17 225	2.36	68.3	8.8	27.8
Indiana	14.2	10.1	8.0	49.9	89 605	88 893	-0.8	-2.8	5 389	5 586	-2 254	34 061	2.41	62.6	8.1	28.9
Jefferson	15.5	10.9	9.2	50.3	45 932	45 196	-1.6	-2.5	3 129	3 533	-662	18 479	2.38	66.5	9.4	29.2
Juniata	14.0	11.1	9.3	50.0	22 821	24 636	8.0	0.9	1 685	1 573	-14	9 393	2.61	68.3	7.4	26.2
Lackawanna	14.2	10.6	8.9	51.6	213 295	214 440	0.5	-1.5	13 708	16 661	61	85 034	2.41	61.6	11.9	32.6
Lancaster	13.0	9.2	7.9	51.0	470 658	519 448	10.4	3.7	44 405	29 685	3 922	195 330	2.64	70.2	9.6	24.0
Lawrence	15.9	11.1	9.7	51.6	94 643	91 140	-3.7	-4.2	5 684	6 912	-2 498	36 435	2.38	66.5	12.5	29.5
Lebanon	13.5	10.3	8.6	50.9	120 327	133 577	11.0	4.0	10 218	8 832	3 836	52 267	2.54	68.8	11.3	26.4
Lehigh	13.1	9.0	7.4	51.2	312 090	349 626	12.0	3.9	26 003	20 873	8 668	133 960	2.60	67.1	13.4	26.9
Luzerne	14.2	10.6	8.9	50.6	319 250	320 918	0.5	-1.4	19 750	24 878	1 293	128 692	2.39	63.5	13.4	31.8
Lycoming	14.7	10.2	8.2	50.9	120 044	116 108	-3.3	-0.7	8 073	7 938	-905	45 906	2.42	64.3	10.7	29.2
McKean	14.9	10.2	8.6	48.3	45 936	43 450	-5.4	-3.6	2 602	3 287	-795	17 400	2.29	63.4	12.5	30.8
Mercer	15.1	11.0	9.7	50.6	120 293	116 674	-3.0	-3.2	7 168	8 664	-2 149	45 546	2.37	66.2	12.3	29.6
Mifflin	13.9	11.3	9.7	50.9	46 486	46 682	0.4	-0.7	3 493	3 254	-515	18 714	2.46	67.0	11.3	27.0
Monroe	15.6	9.9	6.1	50.5	138 687	169 842	22.5	-2.2	8 892	8 539	-3 912	57 297	2.89	72.9	12.1	21.0
Montgomery	14.0	9.3	7.9	51.4	750 097	799 884	6.6	2.7	55 741	46 084	12 054	308 626	2.57	68.3	9.5	26.4
Montour	15.4	10.3	10.3	51.8	18 236	18 267	0.2	0.4	1 325	1 341	60	7 380	2.41	63.1	9.8	31.5
Northampton	14.3	10.0	8.1	50.8	267 066	297 735	11.5	1.5	18 078	17 903	4 324	112 927	2.56	69.4	11.5	24.9
Northumberland	15.0	11.1	9.2	49.8	94 556	94 514	0.0	-2.1	6 032	7 201	-672	39 375	2.27	63.1	10.5	31.9
Perry	15.3	10.6	6.4	49.4	43 602	45 965	5.4	-0.3	3 463	2 665	-908	18 085	2.49	70.6	9.6	23.7
Philadelphia	11.6	7.3	5.5	52.7	1 517 550	1 526 006	0.6	2.7	141 911	90 607	-6 623	581 050	2.59	53.3	20.5	39.0
Pike	16.2	13.2	8.6	49.8	46 302	57 344	23.8	-3.1	2 326	2 712	-1 579	21 079	2.66	72.1	9.3	23.6

1. No spouse present.

Table B. States and Counties — Population, Vital Statistics, Health, and Crime

STATE County	Persons in group quarters, 2016	Daytime population, 2011–2015 Number	Employ-ment/resi-dence ratio	Births, 2016 Total	Rate[1]	Deaths, 2016 Number	Rate[1]	Persons under 65 with no health insurance, 2015 Number	Percent	Medicare, 2015 Total Beneficiaries	Enrolled in Original Medicare	Enrolled in Medicare Advantage	Serious crimes known to police,[2] 2014 Total Number	Rate[3]
	32	33	34	35	36	37	38	39	40	41	42	43	44	45
OREGON—Cont'd														
Morrow	23	11 796	1.13	172	15.3	98	8.7	1 078	11.4	1 779	1 484	295	244	2 137
Multnomah	19 766	867 458	1.26	9 547	11.9	5 998	7.5	55 817	8.2	111 768	41 248	70 520	43 289	5 573
Polk	1 799	65 481	0.63	881	10.8	704	8.6	5 140	8.1	16 960	6 675	10 285	2 280	2 945
Sherman	0	1 911	1.16	20	11.7	14	8.2	103	8.2	473	371	102	18	1 042
Tillamook	468	25 406	1.00	270	10.3	288	11.0	1 928	10.2	6 940	5 093	1 847	530	2 083
Umatilla	4 080	75 539	0.96	1 016	13.3	648	8.5	7 053	11.5	12 474	10 448	2 026	2 050	2 678
Union	733	25 770	1.00	289	11.1	290	11.1	1 578	7.8	5 716	5 045	671	559	2 172
Wallowa	108	6 837	0.99	55	7.9	60	8.6	408	8.2	2 102	1 973	129	60	884
Wasco	741	25 436	0.99	312	11.9	276	10.6	2 416	12.0	5 895	4 414	1 481	724	2 824
Washington	7 003	557 049	1.00	7 181	12.3	3 405	5.8	38 483	7.7	67 968	26 007	41 961	10 645	1 889
Wheeler	24	1 315	0.94	9	6.7	17	12.6	80	9.1	389	311	78	10	729
Yamhill	5 973	94 085	0.84	1 152	11.0	856	8.1	7 501	9.3	17 645	8 300	9 345	2 075	2 044
PENNSYLVANIA	427 424	12 720 839	0.99	140 897	11.0	133 053	10.4	786 343	7.6	2 450 138	1 381 208	1 068 930	287 180	2 246
Adams	4 069	87 088	0.70	997	9.8	992	9.7	6 309	7.9	19 405	13 172	6 233	1 224	1 205
Allegheny	36 519	1 319 619	1.15	13 193	10.8	13 995	11.4	58 815	6.0	236 393	77 008	159 385	29 394	2 384
Armstrong	650	58 197	0.67	592	8.9	898	13.5	3 781	7.2	17 502	5 688	11 814	688	1 013
Beaver	3 244	149 875	0.75	1 764	10.5	2 129	12.7	7 272	5.5	38 255	12 234	26 021	4 073	2 460
Bedford	551	44 686	0.80	441	9.1	531	11.0	3 229	8.5	11 610	5 728	5 882	633	1 331
Berks	11 795	395 419	0.90	4 879	11.8	3 821	9.2	29 080	8.6	75 804	47 843	27 961	8 699	2 102
Blair	3 754	131 739	1.09	1 287	10.3	1 673	13.4	6 281	6.4	30 417	14 595	15 822	2 368	1 878
Bradford	577	63 784	1.06	715	11.8	716	11.8	3 963	8.1	14 067	10 179	3 888	1 129	1 814
Bucks	8 178	573 024	0.83	5 999	9.6	6 027	9.6	29 954	5.8	112 787	72 972	39 815	10 254	1 635
Butler	5 501	186 266	1.01	1 777	9.5	1 967	10.5	7 359	4.9	37 227	12 966	24 261	2 616	1 408
Cambria	6 281	136 364	0.95	1 259	9.3	1 794	13.3	6 794	6.6	34 839	12 496	22 343	2 707	1 937
Cameron	92	4 920	1.02	55	11.8	70	15.0	263	7.4	1 376	950	426	58	1 198
Carbon	700	53 468	0.60	572	9.0	785	12.3	3 616	7.1	14 684	11 655	3 029	1 273	1 969
Centre	19 306	165 051	1.10	1 335	8.3	1 039	6.4	9 576	7.9	21 242	10 614	10 628	1 970	1 265
Chester	13 417	502 557	0.97	5 536	10.7	4 092	7.9	27 417	6.4	75 507	55 591	19 916	6 857	1 344
Clarion	1 376	37 438	0.88	372	9.7	436	11.3	2 487	8.1	8 208	5 257	2 951	590	1 515
Clearfield	5 576	80 424	0.97	737	9.1	952	11.8	4 411	7.3	18 548	11 165	7 383	1 593	1 965
Clinton	2 437	37 776	0.90	407	10.4	395	10.1	2 290	7.6	7 493	4 226	3 267	730	1 819
Columbia	4 280	64 958	0.93	602	9.1	711	10.7	3 410	6.7	14 381	8 348	6 033	1 188	1 782
Crawford	3 825	84 340	0.92	989	11.5	957	11.1	6 520	9.8	19 856	13 078	6 778	1 256	1 443
Cumberland	12 631	250 745	1.08	2 661	10.7	2 282	9.2	13 126	6.8	49 074	28 714	20 360	3 813	1 572
Dauphin	6 787	321 381	1.39	3 509	12.8	2 537	9.3	16 831	7.4	48 607	23 622	24 985	7 509	2 765
Delaware	22 516	513 110	0.82	6 755	12.0	5 534	9.8	31 131	6.8	94 294	64 775	29 519	13 741	2 442
Elk	355	31 000	0.97	281	9.2	376	12.3	1 455	6.0	7 441	5 804	1 637	553	1 762
Erie	12 787	284 645	1.04	3 107	11.2	2 808	10.2	15 455	6.9	54 419	28 345	26 074	6 587	2 351
Fayette	4 245	122 186	0.76	1 371	10.3	1 872	14.1	7 878	7.5	31 750	13 116	18 634	2 951	2 192
Forest	2 558	8 526	1.78	26	3.6	87	11.9	275	8.3	1 670	1 048	622	109	1 432
Franklin	2 544	143 225	0.87	1 755	11.4	1 602	10.4	11 645	9.4	31 071	23 354	7 717	3 321	2 176
Fulton	122	13 699	0.85	152	10.4	139	9.5	904	7.8	3 422	2 653	769	200	1 368
Greene	2 958	39 971	1.14	378	10.2	441	11.9	1 843	6.5	7 863	3 807	4 056	772	2 051
Huntingdon	4 814	42 729	0.83	451	9.9	519	11.4	2 247	7.0	9 944	6 050	3 894	586	1 366
Indiana	5 537	87 695	0.99	852	9.9	898	10.4	5 784	8.7	17 995	6 497	11 498	1 441	1 648
Jefferson	775	42 794	0.90	488	11.1	530	12.0	3 108	8.8	10 459	6 373	4 086	412	918
Juniata	292	21 401	0.69	265	10.7	262	10.5	1 949	9.9	4 804	2 577	2 227	265	1 096
Lackawanna	7 900	216 216	1.03	2 164	10.2	2 607	12.3	12 874	7.8	46 775	33 155	13 620	4 326	2 044
Lancaster	12 803	516 582	0.95	7 185	13.3	5 035	9.4	48 546	11.1	98 269	59 292	38 977	9 261	1 741
Lawrence	2 089	82 874	0.84	912	10.4	1 102	12.6	4 855	7.1	22 432	8 741	13 691	1 903	2 157
Lebanon	3 666	126 532	0.85	1 623	11.7	1 478	10.6	9 522	8.7	28 398	16 618	11 780	2 350	1 729
Lehigh	9 024	370 357	1.08	4 182	11.5	3 373	9.3	25 413	8.6	67 704	44 633	23 071	9 145	2 567
Luzerne	11 832	321 092	1.01	3 138	9.9	4 046	12.8	19 419	7.8	69 123	50 999	18 124	8 077	2 532
Lycoming	5 311	119 398	1.05	1 298	11.3	1 336	11.6	6 492	7.2	24 934	16 242	8 692	2 479	2 121
McKean	3 379	41 891	0.94	403	9.6	519	12.4	2 310	7.2	9 305	7 135	2 170	762	1 777
Mercer	6 591	117 423	1.04	1 166	10.5	1 476	13.1	6 738	7.9	27 159	13 908	13 251	2 360	2 055
Mifflin	560	44 267	0.88	543	11.7	525	11.3	3 940	10.7	10 460	5 768	4 692	764	1 640
Monroe	4 452	155 923	0.84	1 421	8.6	1 521	9.2	11 641	8.5	29 333	23 320	6 013	4 401	2 644
Montgomery	21 566	877 155	1.16	8 792	10.7	7 797	9.5	35 795	5.3	145 546	100 767	44 779	15 053	1 847
Montour	841	25 671	1.87	218	11.9	220	12.0	730	5.0	3 980	1 941	2 039	219	1 178
Northampton	11 042	275 248	0.83	2 818	9.3	2 946	9.7	16 415	6.9	60 221	42 865	17 356	5 713	1 903
Northumberland	3 687	84 511	0.76	956	10.3	1 111	12.0	5 236	7.3	21 817	13 714	8 103	1 667	1 774
Perry	659	33 249	0.45	564	12.3	430	9.4	3 535	9.3	9 080	4 626	4 454	677	1 490
Philadelphia	56 675	1 660 037	1.17	22 169	14.1	15 245	9.7	144 593	11.0	233 709	121 577	112 132	68 761	4 410
Pike	478	46 375	0.57	389	7.0	497	8.9	3 753	8.6	9 216	7 982	1 234	907	1 608

1. Per 1,000 estimated resident population. 2. Data for serious crimes have not been adjusted for underreporting; this may affect comparability between geographic areas and over time.
3. Per 100,000 population estimated by the FBI.

Table B. States and Counties — Crime, Education, Money Income, and Poverty

STATE County	Serious crimes known to police, 2014 (cont.)[1] Rate[2] Violent	Property	Education — Enrollment[3] Total	Percent private	Attainment[4] (percent) High school graduate or less	Bachelor's degree or more	Local government expenditures,[5] 2013–2014 Total current spending (mil dol)	Current spending per student (dollars)	Money income, 2011–2015 Per capita income[6] (dollars)	Households Median income (dollars)	Percent with income of less than $50,000	with income of $200,000 or more	Income and poverty, 2015 Median household income (dollars)	Percent below poverty level All persons	Children under 18 years	Children 5 to 17 years in families
	46	47	48	49	50	51	52	53	54	55	56	57	58	59	60	61
OREGON—Cont'd																
Morrow	184	1 953	2 849	5.2	59.4	10.5	25.2	10 616	20 497	50 918	48.0	0.6	53 774	15.0	22.9	20.6
Multnomah	467	5 106	186 536	21.0	28.0	41.3	997.5	10 627	31 544	54 102	46.6	5.3	58 764	15.7	18.5	18.0
Polk	220	2 725	21 876	10.2	35.5	29.4	61.8	9 198	23 967	52 821	46.5	2.0	55 342	13.7	18.1	15.2
Sherman	58	984	316	13.0	44.8	17.3	3.7	15 237	26 178	38 362	58.1	3.1	51 448	16.3	20.7	18.5
Tillamook	114	1 969	4 606	14.4	45.1	21.0	39.7	12 493	22 426	42 581	58.5	1.8	44 972	15.5	25.2	22.9
Umatilla	209	2 469	19 238	7.0	45.7	16.3	152.8	11 115	21 214	48 101	51.7	1.8	49 016	19.2	26.3	24.0
Union	128	2 044	6 717	15.1	41.1	23.2	36.5	9 648	23 764	43 822	56.4	2.8	46 378	16.5	21.2	19.5
Wallowa	0	884	1 218	11.6	39.7	24.3	14.4	16 403	24 386	40 581	60.5	1.1	44 045	16.1	26.2	23.0
Wasco	129	2 695	5 641	12.8	43.7	18.7	39.1	10 821	22 828	43 422	57.0	1.7	45 110	16.0	24.1	22.8
Washington	154	1 736	143 789	18.1	28.3	40.7	830.7	9 622	32 369	66 754	37.2	6.2	70 417	10.5	12.3	12.2
Wheeler	219	511	226	9.7	46.9	15.4	4.7	14 403	23 535	33 487	66.3	1.6	34 157	21.4	43.6	41.4
Yamhill	123	1 921	26 433	25.0	42.4	23.2	157.6	9 382	25 047	53 423	47.5	3.2	52 806	13.3	18.1	15.2
PENNSYLVANIA	314	1 932	3 074 221	23.9	47.2	28.6	24 037.0	13 860	29 291	53 599	46.7	4.6	55 683	13.1	19.1	17.9
Adams	103	1 102	24 291	26.4	54.6	21.7	279.1	9 925	27 870	60 356	40.6	3.0	60 558	8.5	13.5	12.3
Allegheny	401	1 983	289 969	25.5	36.3	37.8	2 276.8	15 200	32 848	53 040	47.2	5.0	54 412	12.2	16.5	16.1
Armstrong	105	909	13 007	13.3	60.5	15.0	110.8	14 846	24 391	44 942	54.4	1.7	44 893	12.6	19.2	18.0
Beaver	285	2 175	35 365	16.8	47.4	22.8	413.8	12 312	27 233	50 581	49.5	2.3	50 131	13.1	20.3	20.1
Bedford	90	1 241	9 570	13.2	64.8	13.5	85.3	11 724	23 195	45 930	53.7	1.3	45 988	13.9	19.0	17.4
Berks	328	1 774	105 252	17.5	53.3	23.2	896.1	13 113	27 146	55 936	44.5	3.5	56 167	12.6	19.9	19.4
Blair	235	1 643	26 793	13.5	57.6	19.6	219.2	12 355	23 865	43 981	55.2	2.3	44 880	15.3	22.5	21.1
Bradford	182	1 633	12 808	13.2	59.6	17.6	125.0	13 119	25 577	48 987	50.8	2.6	49 367	13.0	19.8	18.9
Bucks	92	1 543	150 561	24.2	37.2	37.4	1 354.6	15 620	38 795	77 568	31.4	9.8	80 512	6.3	7.8	7.0
Butler	93	1 315	45 112	16.5	41.9	32.3	309.5	11 404	32 301	60 934	40.5	5.4	67 892	9.5	11.3	10.4
Cambria	173	1 764	31 287	23.0	56.7	19.1	220.4	12 020	23 410	42 107	57.5	1.7	43 786	14.9	21.5	19.5
Cameron	103	1 095	814	9.8	59.2	15.7	9.5	15 157	25 240	39 897	60.4	1.6	42 452	13.3	22.4	21.8
Carbon	213	1 755	13 261	13.1	57.5	15.5	111.0	12 806	25 398	49 973	50.0	1.4	52 121	11.5	18.8	17.4
Centre	82	1 184	58 874	8.6	38.4	41.4	186.4	14 094	26 492	52 186	48.0	4.3	55 084	16.1	12.2	11.1
Chester	134	1 210	136 261	24.0	30.5	49.1	1 336.0	14 986	42 556	85 976	28.7	13.8	90 555	6.0	7.4	6.5
Clarion	139	1 376	10 142	7.8	58.3	20.1	88.5	16 985	22 136	42 536	57.0	1.5	39 988	17.4	21.3	20.4
Clearfield	260	1 705	15 400	12.7	63.8	13.2	155.5	13 658	21 362	42 257	57.7	1.0	44 336	16.6	26.2	22.7
Clinton	164	1 655	10 450	12.2	58.5	16.9	59.9	13 005	21 937	45 078	54.0	1.0	45 897	16.0	22.3	21.2
Columbia	180	1 602	18 224	8.6	57.2	21.1	81.3	12 728	23 580	45 374	53.8	2.0	44 763	15.0	18.5	17.6
Crawford	99	1 344	19 556	24.7	57.4	19.8	142.1	12 671	22 726	44 579	55.3	1.7	45 989	15.3	23.5	20.9
Cumberland	98	1 475	58 716	22.3	43.5	32.7	354.8	13 685	32 398	61 820	39.4	4.7	63 926	7.3	10.4	9.4
Dauphin	370	2 395	62 636	18.1	46.0	28.4	537.1	12 551	29 461	53 754	46.0	3.9	54 198	13.6	23.4	20.2
Delaware	416	2 027	152 381	33.3	39.6	36.0	1 110.9	15 242	34 064	65 123	39.3	7.9	67 184	10.4	14.4	13.1
Elk	70	1 692	6 179	24.4	59.2	16.8	43.4	11 908	24 647	46 671	53.1	1.3	47 826	9.3	14.2	12.9
Erie	228	2 124	71 083	23.9	49.2	26.1	497.5	12 584	24 856	45 971	53.5	2.5	47 118	17.1	26.3	23.5
Fayette	184	2 009	26 094	12.7	63.1	14.2	212.4	12 482	22 014	39 636	59.3	1.3	40 293	20.1	31.2	29.0
Forest	460	972	782	40.5	73.1	8.5	16.5	14 942	13 645	35 533	68.0	0.7	37 388	24.3	46.4	41.1
Franklin	149	2 027	32 887	16.8	57.9	19.0	250.3	10 953	26 025	53 916	46.3	1.9	56 975	9.4	14.9	14.5
Fulton	260	1 108	3 063	10.0	66.0	13.1	27.1	12 493	23 435	48 311	51.3	1.3	49 378	11.6	19.4	17.9
Greene	244	1 807	7 873	23.9	60.4	17.7	75.6	14 577	23 232	46 661	52.3	1.6	50 714	15.1	21.5	19.7
Huntingdon	201	1 166	9 447	23.5	62.9	14.3	63.1	10 942	21 714	44 396	55.9	0.8	44 875	14.3	20.7	19.9
Indiana	300	1 348	24 607	9.7	55.4	22.6	164.6	16 738	23 450	45 195	54.8	2.2	45 448	18.2	22.3	21.0
Jefferson	107	811	8 967	14.9	62.6	14.6	67.0	13 962	22 282	42 903	57.0	1.0	45 499	14.6	21.9	20.3
Juniata	87	1 009	4 818	24.4	69.3	13.1	28.2	9 508	22 170	47 398	52.6	1.4	50 008	12.8	19.0	17.3
Lackawanna	196	1 848	50 410	31.8	47.8	25.9	346.9	12 369	25 608	46 271	53.7	2.6	48 000	15.3	22.4	21.3
Lancaster	165	1 577	126 455	25.4	53.6	25.2	945.0	14 011	27 158	57 721	43.0	3.3	59 231	10.6	15.5	14.9
Lawrence	211	1 946	18 848	15.3	55.8	19.7	152.7	12 427	24 450	44 571	55.0	2.2	43 944	17.5	26.6	24.4
Lebanon	149	1 580	30 137	24.0	58.3	19.6	215.2	11 310	26 526	55 499	44.1	2.4	52 829	11.6	17.4	16.3
Lehigh	228	2 339	86 662	21.7	45.7	28.5	692.8	13 690	28 688	56 117	44.6	4.3	56 352	12.1	19.1	18.2
Luzerne	264	2 268	70 827	21.9	50.6	21.4	554.5	12 531	25 224	45 897	53.3	2.3	49 589	15.1	23.9	22.2
Lycoming	218	1 903	26 049	15.8	53.1	20.4	221.7	13 785	24 194	47 313	52.5	2.0	49 941	14.8	23.1	18.8
McKean	303	1 474	9 708	13.2	58.5	16.7	97.8	15 597	23 554	43 965	56.8	1.6	46 039	16.9	25.6	24.2
Mercer	218	1 837	26 254	23.8	55.3	21.5	249.8	15 593	23 683	44 156	55.4	1.9	46 319	14.2	24.0	24.0
Mifflin	137	1 502	9 025	22.8	68.0	11.6	91.7	17 398	20 769	41 288	59.8	1.3	42 296	15.4	26.4	24.0
Monroe	218	2 426	44 327	14.2	47.0	23.0	422.8	15 395	25 022	57 365	43.1	3.0	57 152	12.7	17.6	15.7
Montgomery	148	1 699	203 808	30.4	31.1	46.9	1 801.2	16 599	42 275	80 675	30.6	11.6	83 258	6.6	7.5	7.0
Montour	301	877	3 787	17.5	50.4	28.8	28.2	12 035	30 272	54 648	47.2	4.7	57 056	9.0	15.2	14.1
Northampton	168	1 735	74 238	28.2	45.5	27.2	631.9	14 277	30 176	60 972	40.8	4.6	62 129	8.8	13.4	11.8
Northumberland	237	1 536	17 212	18.3	64.7	14.6	184.4	15 357	23 291	42 406	57.1	1.4	44 221	13.1	20.2	18.6
Perry	207	1 283	9 456	17.6	57.5	16.0	72.4	11 702	27 019	57 177	42.8	2.2	54 818	9.6	14.3	13.1
Philadelphia	1 022	3 388	411 245	34.2	51.8	25.4	2 558.9	12 900	22 919	38 253	60.4	2.8	41 210	25.4	38.4	38.4
Pike	144	1 465	12 785	11.6	44.9	23.7	118.9	14 553	28 533	60 180	40.9	3.3	60 436	10.9	17.1	15.3

1. Data for serious crimes have not been adjusted for underreporting; this may affect comparability between geographic areas and over time.   2. Per 100,000 population estimated by the FBI.
3. All persons 3 years old and over enrolled in nursery school through college.   4. Persons 25 years old and over.   5. Elementary and secondary education expenditures.
6. Based on population estimated by the American Community Survey, 2011–2015.

Table B. States and Counties — **Personal Income**

STATE County	Personal income, 2015										Earnings, 2015		
	Total (mil dol)	Percent change, 2014–2015	Per capita[1] Dollars	Per capita[1] Rank	Wages and salaries (mil dol)	Supplements to wages and salaries; employer contributions (mil dol) Pension and insurance	Supplements to wages and salaries; employer contributions (mil dol) Government social insurance	Proprietors' income (mil dol)	Dividends, interest, and rent (mil dol)	Personal transfer receipts (mil dol)	Total (mil dol)	Contributions for government social insurance (mil dol) From employee and self-employed	Contributions for government social insurance (mil dol) From employer
	62	63	64	65	66	67	68	69	70	71	72	73	74
OREGON—Cont'd													
Morrow	496	5.9	44 281	947	313	49	29	111	57	94	501	22	29
Multnomah	38 906	6.1	49 230	519	27 594	3 865	2 405	3 378	7 466	6 032	37 242	2 237	2 405
Polk	2 921	6.9	36 797	2 064	706	137	65	160	529	685	1 068	76	65
Sherman	97	-0.4	57 526	156	42	9	4	20	15	22	75	4	4
Tillamook	982	4.5	38 276	1 678	347	62	32	104	212	293	545	36	32
Umatilla	2 788	6.0	36 434	2 059	1 192	213	117	198	427	709	1 720	105	117
Union	935	4.6	36 268	2 047	399	75	39	56	170	274	568	38	39
Wallowa	288	4.9	41 949	990	87	18	8	33	71	82	146	9	8
Wasco	1 056	5.8	40 989	1 322	450	74	40	127	173	270	690	40	40
Washington	29 813	6.8	51 909	544	19 150	2 108	1 478	2 021	5 651	3 749	24 757	1 522	1 478
Wheeler	49	8.6	36 294	2 427	10	2	1	5	12	16	18	1	1
Yamhill	3 996	6.9	38 920	1 688	1 457	247	135	314	722	899	2 152	135	135
PENNSYLVANIA	636 857	3.8	49 786	X	308 208	56 609	24 035	59 538	107 385	122 229	448 390	25 963	24 035
Adams	4 606	4.4	45 023	873	1 377	287	115	315	740	863	2 095	127	115
Allegheny	66 556	3.9	54 090	235	42 843	6 833	3 255	5 270	11 479	11 714	58 201	3 357	3 255
Armstrong	2 780	2.7	41 456	1 100	730	172	60	272	379	717	1 234	82	60
Beaver	7 321	4.3	43 355	1 050	2 369	527	198	379	904	1 845	3 473	227	198
Bedford	1 799	3.9	37 022	1 889	581	129	50	205	241	491	965	62	50
Berks	18 609	4.1	44 813	864	8 442	1 710	683	1 321	2 984	3 769	12 157	703	683
Blair	5 139	4.2	40 919	1 415	2 472	542	215	418	782	1 370	3 646	222	215
Bradford	2 410	1.4	39 329	1 401	1 137	232	91	161	413	577	1 622	100	91
Bucks	40 343	4.1	64 306	106	13 797	2 341	1 103	2 952	6 737	5 399	20 193	1 175	1 103
Butler	9 675	4.7	51 790	438	4 477	854	355	610	1 498	1 596	6 296	369	355
Cambria	5 253	2.8	38 512	1 521	2 116	488	179	251	795	1 640	3 035	200	179
Cameron	212	3.0	44 865	1 046	79	20	7	22	38	62	129	8	7
Carbon	2 803	3.8	43 829	1 338	633	157	53	498	367	639	1 341	79	53
Centre	6 639	2.8	41 344	1 180	3 622	1 426	273	560	1 201	1 000	5 883	289	273
Chester	38 078	3.4	73 803	50	18 361	2 689	1 292	3 287	7 348	3 739	25 629	1 424	1 292
Clarion	1 439	2.6	36 426	1 738	506	144	42	138	236	402	831	50	42
Clearfield	3 206	3.9	39 578	1 425	1 180	273	99	182	415	824	1 735	111	99
Clinton	1 443	2.2	36 586	1 787	568	150	47	100	197	364	865	52	47
Columbia	2 487	3.6	37 307	1 744	1 033	265	86	144	376	603	1 528	93	86
Crawford	3 197	2.5	36 967	1 925	1 229	283	104	322	440	874	1 937	119	104
Cumberland	12 503	4.7	50 757	472	6 861	1 288	560	971	2 233	2 000	9 680	549	560
Dauphin	12 790	4.5	46 851	638	10 032	2 197	771	793	1 953	2 513	13 794	760	771
Delaware	32 568	4.0	57 756	207	13 361	2 224	1 008	2 075	5 974	5 227	18 668	1 087	1 008
Elk	1 347	1.4	43 625	928	622	144	53	63	208	326	882	54	53
Erie	11 240	3.8	40 425	1 429	5 455	1 192	444	696	1 829	2 768	7 787	460	444
Fayette	5 159	4.4	38 609	1 592	1 578	374	134	345	699	1 567	2 431	166	134
Forest	186	2.1	25 039	3 096	100	37	8	16	44	66	160	9	8
Franklin	6 417	3.2	41 768	1 181	2 476	524	210	481	1 045	1 334	3 691	220	210
Fulton	539	2.9	36 837	1 811	224	53	19	44	80	143	340	21	19
Greene	1 717	1.6	45 760	841	888	177	69	202	219	379	1 335	78	69
Huntingdon	1 653	3.8	36 195	1 990	486	135	40	120	229	435	781	50	40
Indiana	3 132	3.7	36 013	1 616	1 482	392	117	243	489	805	2 234	132	117
Jefferson	1 699	2.3	38 242	1 765	622	139	53	175	257	468	988	62	53
Juniata	944	5.0	38 152	1 667	230	51	20	135	131	209	436	26	20
Lackawanna	9 041	3.8	42 662	1 038	4 105	850	342	556	1 515	2 244	5 853	357	342
Lancaster	24 146	5.3	44 995	979	10 740	1 968	872	3 454	3 981	4 326	17 033	952	872
Lawrence	3 514	3.8	39 893	1 419	1 212	257	102	222	486	997	1 793	119	102
Lebanon	5 906	4.2	43 090	1 056	2 021	470	169	516	910	1 250	3 177	187	169
Lehigh	17 146	3.9	47 537	659	10 063	1 714	779	1 517	2 635	3 226	14 073	808	779
Luzerne	12 976	3.9	40 746	1 215	6 202	1 306	524	640	2 053	3 267	8 672	528	524
Lycoming	4 778	2.7	41 171	1 214	2 410	535	195	250	774	1 099	3 389	203	195
McKean	1 709	1.5	40 291	1 279	677	168	55	147	315	437	1 048	64	55
Mercer	4 320	3.2	37 820	1 779	2 003	421	166	283	644	1 239	2 874	181	166
Mifflin	1 634	3.9	35 139	2 173	612	137	51	179	211	475	979	62	51
Monroe	6 330	3.9	38 043	1 723	2 390	566	197	395	906	1 377	3 547	211	197
Montgomery	58 418	3.3	71 306	38	34 476	4 923	2 538	908	15 850	6 844	42 845	2 628	2 538
Montour	944	3.8	50 859	220	1 013	172	67	51	129	185	1 303	74	67
Northampton	14 372	4.2	47 776	652	5 332	1 038	439	950	2 278	2 769	7 759	468	439
Northumberland	3 514	3.2	37 689	1 749	1 098	261	94	185	550	959	1 637	109	94
Perry	1 822	3.6	39 884	1 435	270	76	23	150	243	386	519	35	23
Philadelphia	77 904	3.3	49 701	887	43 875	7 615	3 355	19 961	9 606	18 456	74 805	3 932	3 355
Pike	2 279	4.5	40 738	1 309	392	102	33	142	369	543	670	47	33

1. Based on the resident population estimated as of July 1 of the year shown.

Table B. States and Counties — Earnings, Social Security, and Housing

| STATE County | Earnings, 2015 (cont.) Percent by selected industries | | | | | | | | | Social Security beneficiaries, December 2015 | | Housing units, 2016 | | |
	Farm	Mining	Construction	Manu-facturing	Infor-mation: professional, scientific, technical services	Retail trade	Finance, insur-ance, real estate and leasing	Health care and social assistance	Govern-ment	Number	Rate[1]	Supple-mental Security Income recipients, December 2015	Total	Percent change, 2010–2016
	75	76	77	78	79	80	81	82	83	84	85	86	87	88
OREGON—Cont'd														
Morrow	27.8	D	11.6	21.3	D	1.2	1.0	1.7	11.1	2 085	187	247	4 482	0.9
Multnomah	0.1	D	5.1	7.0	15.7	5.2	7.7	11.5	17.0	117 235	149	20 907	340 290	4.8
Polk	4.2	D	7.4	10.9	3.7	4.9	3.9	12.1	29.1	17 215	217	1 371	31 470	3.9
Sherman	23.2	0.2	D	D	0.3	3.0	D	0.7	32.8	510	304	40	914	-0.5
Tillamook	7.1	0.1	8.0	14.9	3.5	6.8	3.5	11.3	21.9	7 955	311	538	18 625	1.4
Umatilla	5.5	0.1	5.4	9.6	3.0	6.6	3.6	11.5	26.1	14 025	184	1 686	29 883	0.6
Union	1.3	0.0	5.7	15.0	3.7	8.4	4.0	16.8	23.9	6 130	238	598	11 580	0.8
Wallowa	14.7	0.1	7.8	3.7	4.4	6.4	4.9	8.4	27.1	2 350	344	154	4 097	-0.3
Wasco	14.1	D	4.5	4.8	8.6	8.7	2.7	19.8	19.8	6 240	242	668	11 429	-0.5
Washington	0.5	0.1	4.8	24.7	10.2	5.4	6.2	8.2	6.6	80 655	141	7 251	225 473	6.1
Wheeler	20.6	0.4	D	D	D	7.9	D	D	30.8	500	371	33	889	-0.6
Yamhill	6.4	0.2	5.7	21.5	4.9	6.1	5.1	12.4	13.9	20 280	198	1 585	38 232	3.0
PENNSYLVANIA	0.4	1.0	5.7	10.0	14.7	5.5	7.8	13.8	13.4	2 744 424	215	368 212	5 612 002	0.8
Adams	3.3	D	7.9	19.8	4.8	6.3	3.5	D	15.6	23 900	234	1 112	41 610	1.9
Allegheny	0.0	0.8	5.6	5.2	15.4	4.7	10.6	14.6	10.0	265 610	216	35 062	592 261	0.5
Armstrong	-0.1	20.7	5.8	11.2	4.5	6.1	3.4	13.0	15.9	17 950	268	1 824	32 302	-0.7
Beaver	0.0	0.6	7.2	14.0	6.5	7.0	3.8	16.1	15.9	43 965	260	4 754	78 241	0.0
Bedford	2.2	D	12.4	12.4	2.6	9.2	3.7	D	15.1	13 540	279	1 327	24 001	0.2
Berks	1.2	0.1	6.9	19.1	7.2	6.0	5.3	13.8	13.5	85 440	206	10 548	164 954	0.1
Blair	0.5	D	5.7	13.0	5.8	8.2	4.1	19.5	16.0	30 470	243	4 711	55 974	-0.5
Bradford	0.7	9.0	7.6	15.8	3.5	5.8	4.4	21.3	13.1	15 725	256	1 832	30 159	0.6
Bucks	0.1	0.1	9.8	11.1	12.3	7.2	5.9	14.6	10.4	130 000	207	7 002	247 865	0.8
Butler	0.0	1.6	7.4	15.9	8.4	6.6	4.5	11.3	13.9	41 660	223	3 307	81 554	4.3
Cambria	0.2	0.6	4.7	8.7	7.7	7.5	5.8	22.7	18.1	38 305	281	5 068	65 004	-1.0
Cameron	-0.1	D	2.2	48.8	D	2.8	D	4.4	19.4	1 585	334	132	4 374	-1.8
Carbon	0.1	0.1	4.7	8.9	D	5.4	2.6	13.0	13.7	16 805	263	1 348	34 368	0.2
Centre	0.1	2.4	4.4	4.7	7.8	4.5	3.9	9.7	49.5	23 680	148	1 522	65 762	3.9
Chester	0.7	0.0	4.8	8.1	19.8	7.1	15.0	8.4	8.2	87 095	169	4 217	197 706	2.7
Clarion	0.3	5.2	8.0	10.7	3.2	7.7	4.0	15.0	26.5	9 825	253	1 302	20 245	1.4
Clearfield	0.0	2.5	4.7	8.2	3.4	8.1	3.8	20.6	19.4	20 970	259	2 456	38 645	0.1
Clinton	3.3	3.6	7.0	23.9	2.4	6.5	2.5	D	24.4	9 060	230	1 050	18 974	-0.6
Columbia	0.1	D	5.8	20.6	4.9	7.5	4.0	11.0	21.9	15 535	233	1 478	29 687	0.6
Crawford	1.1	1.4	6.1	25.8	3.7	6.5	3.2	15.7	15.4	22 120	255	2 974	44 239	-1.0
Cumberland	0.4	0.1	4.3	5.9	12.0	6.0	10.2	12.0	16.5	50 650	205	2 692	104 178	4.2
Dauphin	0.3	0.0	3.7	7.9	7.6	3.6	8.7	15.4	24.9	55 140	202	7 565	122 650	1.9
Delaware	0.0	D	6.9	9.5	11.1	5.0	11.8	13.6	11.4	105 060	187	12 440	221 765	-0.5
Elk	-0.1	0.6	4.5	49.1	3.1	4.9	2.8	10.7	10.0	8 565	277	647	17 528	-0.3
Erie	0.2	0.2	4.6	21.8	4.6	6.7	7.7	17.4	16.0	62 080	223	11 172	120 087	0.8
Fayette	0.0	4.4	7.7	9.7	4.3	8.5	3.0	15.4	20.0	37 355	279	8 295	62 783	0.0
Forest	0.0	7.6	D	D	D	1.5	D	9.9	57.0	1 810	244	155	8 629	-1.5
Franklin	2.6	0.1	5.7	17.9	4.6	7.6	3.3	14.7	16.7	35 510	232	2 499	64 409	1.9
Fulton	2.1	D	10.4	39.9	1.3	3.7	1.8	10.9	13.8	3 900	267	373	7 116	-0.1
Greene	-0.3	D	8.5	1.6	5.4	4.5	3.3	D	15.1	8 920	238	1 733	16 439	-0.1
Huntingdon	2.9	1.1	6.7	8.9	2.5	5.7	4.1	D	30.1	11 190	245	1 168	22 382	0.1
Indiana	0.2	12.4	6.1	5.8	3.9	6.2	3.6	11.4	24.3	20 100	231	2 792	38 458	0.6
Jefferson	0.5	10.2	6.1	23.1	3.9	5.0	2.3	15.3	13.2	11 750	265	1 448	22 369	-0.3
Juniata	6.5	D	8.7	31.0	D	5.6	3.6	5.8	11.6	5 660	229	483	11 016	0.3
Lackawanna	0.0	0.1	5.8	10.0	7.9	7.1	8.3	18.1	14.3	53 320	251	6 711	98 706	1.9
Lancaster	2.3	0.1	11.0	15.9	6.8	7.6	6.5	13.3	9.1	108 810	203	9 766	207 811	2.4
Lawrence	0.4	0.7	10.4	13.6	5.1	7.4	6.3	15.2	14.6	23 870	271	3 520	40 622	-0.9
Lebanon	3.6	D	6.3	17.2	5.2	7.7	3.2	12.3	19.9	31 785	231	2 441	56 640	1.9
Lehigh	0.1	D	4.5	12.7	7.4	4.9	6.2	20.0	9.3	74 265	206	9 896	144 230	1.1
Luzerne	0.0	0.4	4.7	11.2	5.8	7.2	5.8	15.8	16.3	78 855	248	10 022	147 871	-0.6
Lycoming	0.1	6.3	7.1	15.8	5.0	6.4	4.5	15.2	18.6	27 590	238	3 299	52 694	0.4
McKean	0.0	14.3	5.7	20.5	2.6	5.3	1.9	12.9	16.5	11 095	262	1 638	20 972	-1.2
Mercer	0.0	1.2	5.0	21.6	3.2	7.8	5.5	18.1	13.1	30 895	271	3 941	51 533	-0.4
Mifflin	2.5	0.0	6.5	26.3	2.2	7.3	3.2	16.5	12.5	12 105	260	1 440	21 522	-0.1
Monroe	0.0	0.2	5.2	14.6	3.1	8.3	2.9	12.1	26.1	34 705	208	3 045	80 756	0.5
Montgomery	0.0	0.0	6.0	10.4	22.3	5.7	9.9	12.9	7.5	153 660	188	8 399	329 376	1.1
Montour	0.5	D	1.7	2.4	D	1.7	8.2	D	8.2	4 515	246	455	8 064	1.3
Northampton	-0.1	0.1	6.4	15.8	8.1	6.4	6.8	9.9	14.4	68 350	227	6 553	121 638	1.1
Northumberland	2.0	0.8	5.6	17.6	3.6	6.4	2.9	13.0	18.4	24 305	261	2 830	44 799	-0.7
Perry	5.9	D	14.3	5.4	3.9	7.8	4.8	7.2	24.9	10 240	224	747	20 505	0.4
Philadelphia	0.0	0.0	1.8	2.4	32.5	2.5	7.6	13.5	13.9	257 475	165	109 532	674 464	0.6
Pike	0.1	D	D	D	6.7	9.3	3.8	8.5	29.2	14 495	259	683	38 539	0.5

1. Per 1,000 resident population estimated as of July 1 of the year shown.

Table B. States and Counties — Housing, Labor Force, and Employment

STATE County	Housing units, 2011–2015								Civilian labor force, 2016				Civilian employment,[6] 2011–2015		
	Occupied units										Unemployment		Percent		
			Owner-occupied			Renter-occupied									
				Median owner cost as a percent of income											Con-struction, produc-tion, and mainte-nance occu-pations
	Total	Percent	Median value[1]	With a mort-gage	Without a mort-gage[2]	Median rent[3]	Median rent as a per-cent of income[2]	Sub-stand-ard units[4] (percent)	Total	Percent change, 2015–2016	Total	Rate[5]	Total	Manage-ment, business, science and arts	
	89	90	91	92	93	94	95	96	97	98	99	100	101	102	103

OREGON—Cont'd															
Morrow	3 772	69.9	121 800	19.3	12.2	663	23.9	9.0	5 733	3.5	288	5.0	4 827	27.1	40.1
Multnomah	310 669	53.8	278 300	24.9	13.6	964	32.4	4.0	446 379	3.9	19 128	4.3	394 637	43.1	16.5
Polk	28 458	64.3	209 200	23.6	11.7	795	32.6	3.0	38 120	4.2	1 957	5.1	32 687	36.0	21.7
Sherman	804	61.6	140 500	19.3	13.0	701	31.6	1.9	900	1.4	41	4.6	746	35.0	31.4
Tillamook	10 094	72.4	222 900	25.8	12.5	837	36.8	2.0	11 668	2.5	585	5.0	9 747	25.5	35.4
Umatilla	26 794	62.7	144 000	22.6	10.6	676	25.1	5.0	36 291	3.0	1 966	5.4	32 450	26.9	32.0
Union	10 130	63.8	163 200	20.8	11.2	705	33.3	3.2	12 073	3.2	717	5.9	11 024	28.9	25.3
Wallowa	3 082	67.4	204 500	23.1	13.1	656	31.9	2.6	3 334	2.8	225	6.7	2 898	34.5	23.8
Wasco	9 704	64.5	174 800	24.2	12.2	754	36.7	2.6	13 789	5.9	673	4.9	10 907	28.0	27.1
Washington	206 426	60.4	285 100	23.6	11.3	1 055	30.0	3.6	314 169	4.2	13 087	4.2	276 371	43.9	16.7
Wheeler	671	70.3	113 800	30.5	14.5	544	23.2	2.2	690	-0.3	30	4.3	563	36.9	29.8
Yamhill	34 425	67.4	220 800	24.7	12.2	900	32.9	3.3	52 921	4.1	2 476	4.7	44 114	31.5	27.4
PENNSYLVANIA	4 958 859	69.2	166 000	22.2	13.4	840	30.3	1.7	6 471 996	0.7	351 962	5.4	6 001 889	36.7	21.7
Adams	38 193	77.3	193 100	23.2	13.6	838	30.4	1.9	55 490	0.8	2 223	4.0	50 517	29.1	31.2
Allegheny	529 534	64.8	129 600	19.6	12.8	780	28.6	1.1	649 725	0.3	34 008	5.2	612 259	43.7	14.7
Armstrong	28 524	75.1	96 000	19.9	12.5	607	24.8	1.4	33 354	0.9	2 521	7.6	29 897	27.4	32.2
Beaver	70 079	73.0	120 100	20.2	12.8	645	28.2	1.3	86 003	0.3	5 377	6.3	80 816	32.4	24.0
Bedford	20 000	79.7	122 700	21.7	11.8	630	29.1	2.6	24 137	0.0	1 425	5.9	22 499	25.8	35.0
Berks	153 312	71.9	168 200	23.2	14.8	851	32.0	2.0	214 132	0.7	10 738	5.0	197 703	31.3	28.1
Blair	51 034	71.8	110 600	19.7	12.4	638	29.4	1.3	61 079	0.1	3 249	5.3	57 253	30.6	24.7
Bradford	24 358	74.6	135 900	20.5	12.2	673	28.4	2.3	30 314	-3.4	2 006	6.6	26 689	28.3	34.6
Bucks	233 066	76.4	308 800	24.1	14.7	1 137	30.7	1.3	342 598	1.4	15 926	4.6	321 488	42.1	18.0
Butler	74 476	76.8	178 100	20.1	12.0	752	28.9	1.1	98 546	0.4	5 057	5.1	91 888	36.6	22.2
Cambria	57 465	73.9	87 100	19.7	13.3	566	28.0	1.1	61 630	-1.2	4 236	6.9	58 018	32.1	24.6
Cameron	2 170	70.3	70 600	19.8	11.2	576	27.7	1.0	2 238	-1.2	167	7.5	2 254	23.6	42.5
Carbon	25 751	78.3	144 700	24.6	14.3	773	30.8	1.8	31 793	1.0	1 903	6.0	28 973	27.2	31.2
Centre	57 183	60.5	197 200	21.6	11.3	900	34.4	3.0	79 084	1.6	3 329	4.2	75 314	44.6	16.5
Chester	186 057	75.1	325 800	22.9	13.6	1 197	29.8	1.5	281 139	1.4	10 992	3.9	260 731	48.8	15.0
Clarion	15 830	69.3	107 100	19.1	11.3	608	31.4	2.1	18 154	-0.7	1 155	6.4	17 055	29.8	28.4
Clearfield	31 817	77.2	87 300	21.0	13.6	582	28.6	1.5	36 447	0.0	2 686	7.4	34 110	26.8	32.0
Clinton	14 796	71.3	117 400	20.8	13.7	661	28.3	1.3	18 701	-0.4	1 333	7.1	17 861	24.8	31.5
Columbia	26 178	70.4	140 600	21.1	14.0	707	31.7	1.1	33 883	0.4	1 898	5.6	30 123	31.3	27.9
Crawford	34 575	73.5	104 800	20.7	12.8	619	28.6	2.9	41 007	-0.3	2 460	6.0	37 783	30.4	30.7
Cumberland	95 950	70.7	188 400	21.2	12.0	886	28.3	1.4	129 793	1.0	5 336	4.1	121 280	38.6	19.4
Dauphin	109 623	63.5	159 200	21.5	12.5	847	28.7	1.7	142 626	1.1	6 854	4.8	132 283	37.9	18.6
Delaware	203 817	69.9	232 700	23.8	14.8	983	32.5	1.4	295 542	1.3	14 516	4.9	269 220	41.9	15.8
Elk	13 244	78.1	90 700	18.0	11.6	546	26.0	0.7	16 366	0.1	915	5.6	14 947	23.6	42.6
Erie	109 934	65.7	118 200	20.1	12.4	689	30.3	1.8	134 326	-0.4	8 807	6.6	128 541	33.7	23.2
Fayette	53 997	71.7	88 900	20.2	12.6	593	28.7	2.4	58 805	0.7	4 808	8.2	53 707	26.5	30.6
Forest	1 974	82.7	84 400	22.1	12.3	541	27.5	1.9	1 892	-0.4	152	8.0	1 256	26.2	20.9
Franklin	58 570	71.7	173 400	22.8	11.6	809	27.4	1.8	77 872	-0.1	4 021	5.2	71 278	30.7	29.0
Fulton	5 960	79.1	153 200	23.1	11.0	644	27.0	1.7	7 334	-1.5	467	6.4	6 598	23.9	37.5
Greene	14 394	73.1	97 400	18.7	11.2	630	26.7	1.3	17 502	-3.8	1 363	7.8	14 728	30.0	30.3
Huntingdon	17 225	76.2	119 000	21.5	12.3	554	27.2	1.3	19 740	0.3	1 393	7.1	18 580	28.7	31.0
Indiana	34 061	70.8	107 000	20.2	12.1	694	32.6	3.1	40 491	-3.1	2 973	7.3	38 903	29.4	27.8
Jefferson	18 479	74.7	90 300	20.4	11.4	577	26.3	2.8	20 733	-1.1	1 439	6.9	19 756	25.1	36.3
Juniata	9 393	75.4	141 700	22.1	11.3	587	25.8	2.7	12 184	1.5	659	5.4	11 152	25.9	39.1
Lackawanna	85 034	66.6	144 800	22.3	14.9	709	28.8	1.3	106 830	0.3	6 107	5.7	97 589	34.9	22.4
Lancaster	195 330	68.9	189 200	23.1	12.7	908	31.0	2.3	280 499	1.6	11 662	4.2	259 601	32.8	27.4
Lawrence	36 435	73.9	97 300	20.6	12.8	630	30.9	1.8	41 701	-1.1	2 839	6.8	39 340	29.9	27.2
Lebanon	52 267	70.5	163 800	22.2	12.8	768	27.3	2.1	70 711	0.8	3 182	4.5	65 090	29.0	28.8
Lehigh	133 960	66.6	191 700	23.7	14.4	929	32.3	2.2	188 118	1.2	10 190	5.4	170 448	34.3	23.4
Luzerne	128 692	67.6	122 700	21.4	14.4	702	29.0	1.5	159 459	0.3	10 181	6.4	147 243	30.5	24.6
Lycoming	45 906	70.1	138 500	21.4	13.7	723	29.8	1.6	59 014	-3.2	3 959	6.7	54 324	29.8	26.8
McKean	17 400	73.7	76 200	19.3	11.2	598	29.5	1.0	18 653	-1.8	1 243	6.7	18 277	30.7	31.1
Mercer	45 546	73.7	107 900	20.1	12.4	621	29.0	2.1	52 953	-0.2	3 189	6.0	50 055	30.4	25.8
Mifflin	18 714	70.4	97 800	22.8	14.0	619	26.7	3.8	20 886	-0.2	1 204	5.8	19 860	24.1	37.0
Monroe	57 297	78.4	174 500	28.0	17.3	1 014	34.3	2.0	81 990	1.4	5 185	6.3	76 767	32.2	22.4
Montgomery	308 626	72.6	292 300	22.9	13.7	1 158	29.6	1.2	447 689	1.5	18 686	4.2	418 411	49.0	14.3
Montour	7 380	72.4	163 400	20.7	12.7	725	26.2	0.7	9 193	0.4	398	4.3	8 391	39.4	22.0
Northampton	112 927	71.8	206 100	24.1	15.2	957	31.9	1.6	158 347	1.0	8 269	5.2	144 854	35.0	23.0
Northumberland	39 375	71.2	104 300	20.7	13.7	613	27.0	1.7	43 886	1.0	2 785	6.3	41 033	27.8	29.5
Perry	18 085	78.8	159 900	23.0	11.9	734	25.1	1.9	24 357	1.0	1 133	4.7	22 893	28.7	31.4
Philadelphia	581 050	52.6	145 300	24.5	14.8	922	34.5	3.0	707 571	1.7	48 148	6.8	640 661	36.0	16.3
Pike	21 079	84.1	183 200	24.8	14.4	1 118	37.1	1.5	25 105	0.4	1 616	6.4	24 320	31.9	23.2

1. Specified owner-occupied units.   2. A value of 10.0 represents 10 percent or less; a value of 50.0 represents 50 percent or more.   3. Specified renter-occupied units.   4. Overcrowded or lacking complete plumbing facilities.   5. Percent of civilian labor force.   6. Civilian employed persons 16 years old and over.

Table B. States and Counties — Nonfarm Employment and Agriculture

STATE County	Number of establishments	Total	Health care and social assistance	Manufacturing	Retail trade	Finance and insurance	Professional, scientific, and technical services	Annual payroll Total (mil dol)	Average per employee (dollars)	Farms Number	Percent with: Fewer than 50 acres	500 acres or more	Farm operators whose principal occupation is farming (percent)
	104	105	106	107	108	109	110	111	112	113	114	115	116
OREGON—Cont'd													
Morrow	188	3 701	270	1 370	117	94	D	163	43 944	401	27.7	51.9	63.1
Multnomah	26 618	418 505	62 804	34 298	41 973	20 218	34 615	21 891	52 308	598	84.8	1.7	44.5
Polk	1 407	13 844	2 662	1 797	1 586	244	396	457	32 978	1 143	66.0	5.2	52.2
Sherman	50	471	12	D	104	D	D	18	37 423	186	5.4	76.3	73.7
Tillamook	713	6 969	971	1 421	1 028	164	106	241	34 637	280	45.4	3.2	68.2
Umatilla	1 564	21 584	3 103	2 908	2 854	466	706	773	35 818	1 603	49.0	25.0	49.0
Union	734	7 163	1 483	1 351	1 388	222	224	252	35 143	829	46.4	18.2	46.9
Wallowa	374	1 874	409	84	320	62	91	66	35 054	522	37.0	27.4	47.9
Wasco	692	7 087	1 865	270	1 534	216	314	251	35 463	670	39.4	24.2	52.1
Washington	15 075	259 419	29 572	28 394	32 004	12 399	21 788	16 818	64 829	1 643	74.4	3.0	44.7
Wheeler	31	153	D	D	34	D	NA	3	21 882	153	10.5	51.0	58.8
Yamhill	2 412	29 107	4 777	6 141	3 684	666	652	1 082	37 160	2 028	73.7	3.8	47.0
PENNSYLVANIA	299 695	5 306 896	985 243	551 797	664 898	266 704	323 826	257 627	48 546	59 309	39.3	4.1	51.7
Adams	1 942	28 508	4 838	5 683	3 358	510	561	990	34 714	1 188	48.2	6.3	50.9
Allegheny	33 818	701 226	129 092	35 303	72 798	48 855	57 230	36 314	51 786	428	50.7	0.9	41.6
Armstrong	1 323	14 386	3 469	1 503	2 084	643	402	500	34 782	783	25.0	6.1	42.0
Beaver	3 380	49 345	10 207	7 098	7 229	890	2 220	1 901	38 526	646	45.2	1.9	47.5
Bedford	1 050	13 211	1 840	1 932	2 157	327	214	433	32 774	1 210	25.0	6.5	50.6
Berks	8 404	154 975	25 371	31 436	20 908	5 723	6 744	7 072	45 633	2 039	47.8	3.5	61.4
Blair	3 191	54 469	D	7 138	8 719	1 500	1 962	1 971	36 179	525	35.8	5.9	58.5
Bradford	1 378	19 925	5 112	3 212	3 104	787	603	809	40 601	1 629	25.8	7.6	45.8
Bucks	19 037	249 874	42 794	25 113	38 216	8 168	16 482	11 179	44 740	827	71.1	2.7	51.3
Butler	4 860	81 472	13 736	12 706	11 207	2 240	6 409	3 671	45 053	1 061	39.9	4.1	45.6
Cambria	3 194	46 531	11 291	4 670	6 909	2 008	2 303	1 599	34 357	551	33.4	5.6	37.4
Cameron	112	1 581	197	941	130	21	14	56	35 355	36	25.0	11.1	50.0
Carbon	1 126	13 664	3 257	1 742	2 096	302	344	412	30 182	195	46.2	2.6	37.4
Centre	3 313	44 884	8 343	3 970	8 074	1 261	3 024	1 701	37 900	1 192	40.1	4.8	57.4
Chester	14 189	246 768	34 843	16 808	28 453	24 493	26 425	17 415	70 574	1 730	57.1	2.5	60.7
Clarion	916	11 230	2 917	1 603	1 812	284	253	355	31 635	652	22.1	6.3	39.3
Clearfield	1 993	26 045	5 629	2 768	4 807	597	591	903	34 663	533	34.3	4.3	45.0
Clinton	761	10 785	1 264	2 919	1 880	178	213	399	36 961	469	37.1	3.8	51.0
Columbia	1 447	22 530	3 898	5 328	3 431	681	782	797	35 376	944	37.3	4.6	39.8
Crawford	1 983	27 766	5 338	7 444	3 686	575	766	954	34 371	1 351	31.1	6.0	51.5
Cumberland	5 930	120 450	17 213	8 495	16 987	9 004	8 832	5 321	44 175	1 415	47.0	3.5	53.1
Dauphin	6 769	144 748	33 291	8 493	15 609	10 247	7 514	7 061	48 778	811	40.9	2.7	44.9
Delaware	12 789	211 953	39 580	12 817	26 324	12 964	10 768	11 959	56 423	76	64.5	0.0	48.7
Elk	874	14 584	1 786	7 195	1 440	246	294	555	38 077	271	45.4	1.5	33.6
Erie	6 163	114 164	24 363	20 764	15 674	5 160	3 681	4 394	38 486	1 422	41.2	4.1	48.7
Fayette	2 671	37 436	7 947	3 025	6 470	560	946	1 218	32 544	941	34.0	3.4	47.8
Forest	109	1 091	370	242	95	17	D	35	32 278	56	25.0	3.6	41.1
Franklin	3 048	49 464	8 173	8 312	7 588	1 144	1 716	1 819	36 779	1 596	35.9	6.3	60.8
Fulton	264	5 590	668	D	332	76	22	266	47 518	656	22.6	5.2	38.6
Greene	767	13 641	1 598	345	2 435	326	279	641	46 982	876	27.2	3.3	40.4
Huntingdon	821	9 270	1 909	1 151	1 470	398	265	291	31 445	833	25.1	7.1	45.9
Indiana	1 877	26 726	4 946	2 388	5 081	1 309	1 116	1 020	38 163	1 166	38.0	3.9	50.2
Jefferson	1 138	14 424	3 080	3 548	1 702	269	428	510	35 340	577	25.0	5.7	51.5
Juniata	465	5 961	808	2 665	586	232	78	198	33 145	737	42.3	3.0	47.6
Lackawanna	5 333	94 184	21 582	8 617	12 983	5 232	3 104	3 412	36 232	303	25.1	1.3	43.6
Lancaster	12 594	226 286	35 183	34 391	31 253	7 501	11 527	9 467	41 837	5 657	44.1	1.3	72.2
Lawrence	1 956	26 998	6 834	3 780	3 651	1 175	698	958	35 498	659	33.4	3.6	50.4
Lebanon	2 684	44 109	8 261	9 263	6 910	974	1 110	1 654	37 508	1 219	48.2	2.3	58.9
Lehigh	8 446	171 963	40 602	18 100	22 168	6 291	6 418	8 964	52 126	486	58.8	5.8	56.2
Luzerne	7 182	131 537	23 993	17 008	17 810	5 150	6 172	5 087	38 671	556	38.8	3.6	42.3
Lycoming	2 817	46 211	8 912	7 801	7 609	1 518	1 552	1 759	38 071	1 207	40.1	3.7	44.0
McKean	1 032	13 224	2 750	3 277	1 790	251	219	478	36 141	290	37.2	3.1	36.9
Mercer	2 754	45 277	10 373	8 452	7 274	1 371	827	1 548	34 182	1 185	32.3	4.1	45.1
Mifflin	968	14 092	3 390	3 962	2 189	374	179	521	36 991	808	35.4	2.1	49.0
Monroe	3 368	44 970	7 144	5 290	9 522	975	1 549	1 651	36 723	283	53.0	2.5	55.1
Montgomery	26 076	489 771	81 519	41 333	59 484	34 846	43 771	30 085	61 427	596	75.2	1.0	55.0
Montour	489	14 308	7 400	605	691	1 351	441	961	67 143	459	43.1	1.5	45.3
Northampton	6 265	99 553	13 885	11 824	13 837	3 944	4 163	4 352	43 714	498	62.9	6.0	50.6
Northumberland	1 660	24 270	5 510	4 314	3 409	646	603	864	35 604	847	43.0	6.5	54.7
Perry	779	6 335	1 039	670	1 194	235	195	166	26 254	889	32.6	4.8	50.6
Philadelphia	27 287	606 822	143 629	21 345	52 370	30 142	47 431	33 869	55 814	22	81.8	0.0	45.5
Pike	889	8 033	965	266	1 907	163	186	222	27 582	50	46.0	14.0	34.0

Table B. States and Counties — **Agriculture**

STATE County	Agriculture, 2012 (cont.)															
	Land in farms					Value of land and buildings (dollars)			Value of products sold				Percent of farms with sales of:		Government payments	
			Acres								Percent from:					
	Acreage (1,000)	Percent change, 2007–2012	Average size of farm	Total irrigated (1,000)	Total cropland (1,000)	Average per farm	Average per acre	Value of machinery and equipment, average per farm (dollars)	Total (mil dol)	Average per farm (dollars)	Crops	Live-stock and poultry products	$10,000 or more	$100,000 or more	Total ($1,000)	Percent of farms
	117	118	119	120	121	122	123	124	125	126	127	128	129	130	131	132
OREGON—Cont'd																
Morrow	1 165	5.5	2 906	65.6	486.4	2 762 863	951	302 516	568.1	1 416 736	34.3	65.7	50.4	34.9	11 900	61.1
Multnomah	30	5.2	50	4.6	17.4	598 075	11 928	72 756	68.9	115 278	D	D	30.1	9.5	242	6.0
Polk	145	-13.1	127	20.4	101.0	777 650	6 141	85 558	149.8	131 099	77.6	22.4	33.3	12.8	912	16.1
Sherman	514	-0.1	2 762	2.2	365.1	1 645 672	596	308 538	54.5	292 914	D	D	61.8	44.6	8 820	93.5
Tillamook	37	-3.3	131	7.1	14.5	817 064	6 259	115 754	117.1	418 361	2.6	97.4	53.6	38.6	1 553	34.3
Umatilla	1 308	-9.6	816	147.8	769.7	1 332 795	1 633	163 995	423.3	264 089	87.9	12.1	42.1	22.2	18 381	40.8
Union	412	-15.6	497	49.0	119.2	768 875	1 548	101 823	68.4	82 473	75.0	25.0	39.0	12.2	2 713	30.0
Wallowa	453	-14.3	867	38.0	88.5	1 094 554	1 263	101 395	46.6	89 310	47.5	52.5	45.8	20.5	2 746	38.5
Wasco	1 427	50.3	2 130	50.6	210.0	1 605 100	753	118 193	89.8	134 005	88.7	11.3	41.3	18.4	6 871	39.3
Washington	136	6.1	83	20.3	82.0	774 189	9 371	81 491	238.0	144 840	94.7	5.3	38.5	12.8	1 544	15.0
Wheeler	649	-14.3	4 242	10.4	24.8	2 749 542	648	97 634	14.2	92 536	22.9	77.1	45.1	19.6	748	26.1
Yamhill	177	-1.9	87	22.1	108.5	801 316	9 162	76 411	280.9	138 487	78.9	21.1	32.8	10.8	2 466	16.2
PENNSYLVANIA	7 704	-1.3	130	39.0	4 546.1	704 712	5 425	89 730	7 400.8	124 783	37.6	62.4	48.1	19.9	86 359	27.0
Adams	171	-1.9	144	2.2	125.6	898 623	6 232	113 572	201.7	169 817	56.5	43.5	48.6	19.2	1 818	28.5
Allegheny	35	-8.4	81	0.2	14.1	428 841	5 269	53 269	10.4	24 292	84.2	15.8	31.3	5.1	41	7.9
Armstrong	129	5.6	165	0.2	66.6	474 018	2 875	83 686	35.9	45 800	56.3	43.7	42.1	9.2	924	24.8
Beaver	56	-16.8	86	0.2	28.5	415 333	4 809	67 373	20.9	32 373	52.0	48.0	32.8	6.0	500	16.1
Bedford	210	-0.6	173	0.1	104.3	640 069	3 692	95 976	122.8	101 504	29.7	70.3	48.1	21.7	1 863	29.4
Berks	234	5.2	115	1.6	182.3	1 015 554	8 859	120 253	528.7	259 299	42.6	57.4	58.5	30.2	3 646	28.3
Blair	90	3.1	172	0.3	63.3	783 611	4 565	106 916	107.7	205 145	16.2	83.8	54.1	29.0	1 416	32.6
Bradford	308	15.5	189	0.2	163.3	700 259	3 704	89 510	128.8	79 063	22.6	77.4	43.1	15.3	6 994	43.0
Bucks	64	-15.6	77	0.8	48.0	950 716	12 280	89 245	62.4	75 475	75.1	24.9	41.0	13.7	579	13.7
Butler	136	4.9	128	0.6	77.1	609 486	4 747	89 819	52.9	49 863	69.6	30.4	41.3	10.0	1 502	26.6
Cambria	77	-12.6	140	0.1	45.4	457 327	3 277	82 508	32.6	59 240	55.5	44.5	42.3	8.5	775	31.9
Cameron	6	22.1	173	0.0	1.6	337 472	1 955	55 528	0.7	19 222	45.4	54.6	44.4	0.0	55	38.9
Carbon	21	5.6	109	0.2	13.4	710 523	6 547	99 005	9.3	47 892	91.4	8.6	46.7	8.2	191	42.1
Centre	162	9.1	136	1.1	84.9	736 207	5 416	86 739	91.6	76 830	34.3	65.7	47.2	20.0	1 985	30.3
Chester	164	-1.4	95	1.2	107.1	1 242 743	13 070	110 712	660.7	381 933	81.0	19.0	52.6	27.7	1 631	15.8
Clarion	116	-12.2	178	0.1	60.5	524 998	2 951	75 406	36.1	55 423	55.7	44.3	41.7	10.3	960	33.3
Clearfield	69	10.4	130	0.1	34.8	344 137	2 649	68 355	13.7	25 687	53.2	46.8	36.4	6.9	392	21.6
Clinton	53	-6.9	112	0.8	29.1	608 542	5 414	85 166	60.6	129 122	20.2	79.8	57.1	31.8	951	29.2
Columbia	123	0.1	130	0.6	85.1	610 161	4 693	89 506	74.4	78 762	65.5	34.5	40.7	13.8	2 088	48.9
Crawford	228	-1.9	169	0.3	130.3	475 734	2 822	91 693	116.1	85 918	44.3	55.7	46.3	15.4	2 095	26.6
Cumberland	155	-1.6	109	1.6	119.7	853 018	7 793	95 594	195.4	138 061	30.4	69.6	55.3	26.6	1 997	28.5
Dauphin	129	44.5	160	0.7	60.0	724 409	4 541	94 716	122.6	151 158	23.4	76.6	49.3	20.1	724	27.1
Delaware	5	8.3	62	0.1	1.2	857 868	13 799	57 684	9.8	128 697	99.0	1.0	32.9	6.6	D	2.6
Elk	23	-29.4	87	0.0	9.7	296 376	3 420	49 461	4.2	15 605	47.6	52.4	30.6	2.2	66	8.5
Erie	169	-2.6	119	0.9	96.2	407 705	3 438	75 158	91.7	64 469	76.5	23.5	41.5	12.8	1 693	20.5
Fayette	113	-19.8	120	0.0	55.2	398 345	3 321	66 763	27.0	28 717	52.6	47.4	31.6	5.3	588	17.7
Forest	8	-22.8	148	0.0	2.5	356 125	2 408	69 071	1.8	32 500	38.8	61.2	35.7	5.4	25	17.9
Franklin	265	9.0	166	2.8	201.8	1 101 504	6 646	133 634	413.8	259 277	21.6	78.4	66.3	40.4	4 302	34.1
Fulton	112	8.4	171	0.1	61.1	622 541	3 639	84 477	53.0	80 755	24.7	75.3	41.9	12.0	1 033	53.5
Greene	112	-25.2	128	D	36.3	385 629	3 007	66 540	14.6	16 637	39.3	60.7	28.3	2.2	189	7.2
Huntingdon	158	6.8	190	0.8	77.2	728 200	3 832	89 801	93.5	112 249	19.5	80.5	42.3	14.4	2 274	35.4
Indiana	154	-18.1	132	D	85.4	369 054	2 799	70 768	67.3	57 725	58.4	41.6	38.3	9.9	1 078	22.7
Jefferson	91	4.9	158	0.1	53.2	410 645	2 596	71 778	27.7	48 057	44.9	55.1	44.5	10.2	436	16.1
Juniata	91	-6.8	124	0.3	53.8	622 389	5 039	92 383	101.4	137 639	14.1	85.9	51.4	24.6	1 913	44.6
Lackawanna	33	-17.6	108	0.1	16.1	529 017	4 894	68 812	13.2	43 687	71.2	28.8	32.0	7.3	127	17.5
Lancaster	439	3.3	78	6.1	332.0	973 388	12 529	101 987	1 475.0	260 731	17.7	82.3	74.2	48.4	5 843	18.4
Lawrence	80	-12.9	122	0.1	46.8	501 196	4 105	84 781	38.5	58 451	53.5	46.5	48.7	10.3	652	25.9
Lebanon	121	7.0	100	1.5	97.4	1 052 028	10 562	122 164	348.9	286 245	13.1	86.9	64.1	37.6	2 250	26.6
Lehigh	76	-9.8	157	0.8	63.2	1 308 144	8 329	109 327	90.8	186 899	69.6	30.4	51.4	14.4	701	25.3
Luzerne	61	-8.5	110	0.3	34.4	491 933	4 489	67 198	21.0	37 757	82.2	17.8	31.7	9.2	970	41.4
Lycoming	158	-1.2	131	0.6	79.7	559 934	4 265	73 065	72.2	59 819	53.8	46.2	41.6	13.2	2 246	39.1
McKean	36	-12.5	125	0.0	13.2	258 072	2 062	49 907	5.0	17 076	49.3	50.7	31.4	4.5	192	24.5
Mercer	163	-5.1	138	0.1	97.7	470 815	3 420	88 056	82.7	69 747	56.5	43.5	47.8	14.8	1 376	29.9
Mifflin	91	-3.8	112	0.1	53.2	550 040	4 908	76 090	94.0	116 365	17.7	82.3	55.6	24.8	1 361	26.6
Monroe	26	-9.2	94	0.1	13.0	735 583	7 861	71 198	11.0	38 777	66.8	33.2	35.7	8.5	174	15.5
Montgomery	31	-26.6	52	0.8	18.7	725 669	14 051	52 896	25.6	42 943	71.9	28.1	39.8	8.1	293	10.6
Montour	43	-13.5	95	0.1	29.6	519 508	5 483	62 275	47.4	103 322	60.1	39.9	44.2	17.6	678	36.4
Northampton	66	-3.7	132	0.3	55.6	1 084 882	8 218	115 108	43.5	87 341	82.9	17.1	44.6	16.9	845	23.3
Northumberland	130	-12.3	153	1.4	92.8	748 819	4 898	101 762	154.3	182 218	37.0	63.0	54.0	24.7	2 014	43.1
Perry	135	-6.4	152	0.3	81.3	767 425	5 051	104 962	140.4	157 931	19.7	80.3	52.2	25.5	1 816	36.2
Philadelphia	0	8.8	13	0.0	0.1	587 318	45 337	29 864	0.8	34 909	94.7	5.2	50.0	9.1	0	0.0
Pike	28	2.5	565	0.0	3.4	1 037 120	1 835	55 680	3.0	59 300	91.3	8.7	40.0	10.0	D	6.0

Table B. States and Counties — Water Use, Wholesale Trade, Retail Trade, and Real Estate

STATE County	Water use, 2010 — Total water withdrawn (mil gal/day)	Gallons withdrawn per person per day	Wholesale trade,[1] 2012 — Number of establishments	Number of employees	Sales (mil dol)	Annual payroll (mil dol)	Retail trade,[2] 2012 — Number of establishments	Number of employees	Sales (mil dol)	Annual payroll (mil dol)	Real estate and rental and leasing,[2] 2012 — Number of establishments	Number of employees	Receipts (mil dol)	Annual payroll (mil dol)
	133	134	135	136	137	138	139	140	141	142	143	144	145	146
OREGON—Cont'd														
Morrow	412.1	36 879	11	60	51.2	3.8	13	79	19.6	2.1	10	11	1.4	0.2
Multnomah	58.3	79	1 233	21 805	21 267.8	1 275.5	2 888	37 805	9 982.9	1 016.1	1 373	8 734	1 569.3	369.5
Polk	42.6	565	29	264	100.9	10.4	125	1 546	360.7	36.9	59	167	19.4	3.0
Sherman	11.3	6 380	4	D	D	D	7	D	D	D	NA	NA	NA	NA
Tillamook	47.5	1 882	9	105	42.3	3.2	114	1 032	248.9	24.4	27	91	8.0	1.7
Umatilla	383.3	5 051	65	953	738.7	45.4	224	2 922	802.8	70.8	60	148	21.1	4.0
Union	206.1	8 006	22	209	140.3	8.4	103	1 313	318.5	31.6	17	70	9.6	1.8
Wallowa	138.6	19 773	2	D	D	D	51	284	63.6	7.0	18	D	D	D
Wasco	125.6	4 982	25	628	213.6	14.6	123	1 506	389.4	37.1	42	102	10.9	2.6
Washington	103.5	195	734	9 915	8 667.6	618.5	1 573	28 336	8 389.7	790.3	809	4 492	1 207.1	158.0
Wheeler	35.9	24 892	1	D	D	D	6	D	D	D	2	D	D	D
Yamhill	75.7	763	70	D	D	D	283	3 325	886.6	84.9	102	263	36.4	6.1
PENNSYLVANIA	8 134.9	640	12 568	195 004	191 170.1	11 203.8	43 952	643 903	178 794.9	15 330.6	9 438	58 585	13 364.0	2 617.5
Adams	20.2	199	61	D	D	D	333	3 231	801.2	74.4	47	210	35.8	7.0
Allegheny	641.5	524	1 497	21 265	27 237.9	1 195.1	4 423	72 737	20 553.7	1 730.3	1 291	9 005	2 208.0	414.5
Armstrong	180.4	2 617	35	525	217.2	24.2	215	2 105	551.2	42.1	27	270	33.8	10.0
Beaver	432.3	2 535	112	1 508	1 179.5	74.3	517	7 307	1 590.2	149.3	92	398	83.2	14.2
Bedford	17.8	358	39	382	350.6	21.8	183	2 088	576.2	43.0	11	86	21.2	4.9
Berks	57.1	139	354	6 912	4 277.4	362.2	1 256	20 219	5 719.4	494.3	246	1 249	213.0	41.4
Blair	22.8	179	119	1 832	2 258.4	80.7	561	8 383	2 286.7	189.4	87	349	72.9	11.3
Bradford	11.9	191	49	D	D	D	252	3 127	903.7	72.7	30	223	52.6	9.9
Bucks	182.4	292	1 152	14 950	12 999.7	854.9	2 408	38 063	10 185.1	975.9	589	3 494	855.9	147.2
Butler	15.7	85	253	4 444	3 353.8	249.0	680	11 085	2 902.2	245.0	148	714	160.4	23.9
Cambria	27.1	189	115	1 365	664.9	51.0	561	6 927	1 733.8	148.6	86	408	48.3	12.2
Cameron	0.8	157	2	D	D	D	17	174	30.9	3.3	1	D	D	D
Carbon	25.1	385	19	D	D	D	194	2 142	562.6	49.3	36	121	21.1	3.4
Centre	45.4	295	90	873	538.9	42.5	481	7 570	1 748.7	155.7	133	1 036	255.5	34.7
Chester	191.4	384	711	12 642	19 155.1	1 204.8	1 517	27 549	12 474.9	984.2	457	2 360	781.2	143.1
Clarion	5.1	126	30	385	167.3	14.2	185	1 879	460.4	40.7	21	104	11.0	3.4
Clearfield	304.3	3 727	68	771	703.6	30.4	350	4 731	1 331.3	105.4	43	344	35.9	8.7
Clinton	16.9	430	18	D	D	D	121	1 773	582.6	39.5	37	165	26.6	4.3
Columbia	10.4	155	46	419	118.4	15.8	236	3 413	904.8	70.4	43	205	33.9	6.4
Crawford	14.0	157	57	372	136.3	12.8	317	3 577	973.5	85.5	51	176	24.5	4.3
Cumberland	33.0	140	189	2 607	2 666.3	124.9	858	16 016	4 812.9	376.3	222	1 366	316.8	66.3
Dauphin	100.4	374	295	6 839	6 655.5	390.2	981	15 280	3 943.9	348.2	218	1 608	505.1	90.5
Delaware	782.2	1 399	522	6 961	5 482.3	536.3	1 700	24 271	6 468.8	602.2	409	2 945	776.4	169.8
Elk	21.6	676	26	D	D	D	124	1 496	314.5	28.8	11	46	6.3	1.2
Erie	49.4	176	264	3 127	1 242.5	145.7	958	15 221	3 752.8	326.4	182	1 042	158.5	32.3
Fayette	45.1	330	107	1 002	496.6	37.7	487	6 040	1 638.8	129.7	69	299	50.9	9.9
Forest	2.0	264	1	D	D	D	18	101	24.8	2.0	1	D	D	D
Franklin	19.1	127	108	D	D	D	486	7 106	1 809.5	157.6	87	328	54.9	10.4
Fulton	2.9	193	12	142	139.8	4.6	42	374	102.9	7.3	3	12	1.2	0.5
Greene	35.7	922	26	350	302.8	17.5	138	2 444	883.7	63.3	12	47	6.7	1.1
Huntingdon	14.0	306	29	344	94.9	11.6	141	1 424	354.3	28.8	10	28	9.8	1.0
Indiana	59.8	673	67	D	D	D	309	5 016	1 318.8	112.7	45	163	26.2	3.8
Jefferson	4.7	105	39	441	245.5	17.9	176	1 857	556.2	37.7	24	128	32.2	4.6
Juniata	3.8	154	18	133	54.5	5.0	69	601	204.4	13.1	6	12	1.3	0.2
Lackawanna	52.1	243	251	3 800	4 374.5	168.9	916	13 197	3 186.3	278.2	138	690	128.5	21.1
Lancaster	78.2	151	582	10 776	8 764.0	496.7	1 917	29 783	6 899.6	669.6	342	2 009	396.6	79.1
Lawrence	100.3	1 101	86	D	D	D	292	3 391	838.7	75.6	44	279	29.7	7.0
Lebanon	14.6	109	99	2 679	3 913.7	112.7	431	6 597	1 695.7	158.6	70	309	40.5	7.8
Lehigh	50.9	146	408	9 182	8 062.4	577.2	1 239	20 261	5 550.4	467.5	315	1 587	324.0	58.2
Luzerne	85.3	266	300	5 656	3 435.9	242.3	1 247	18 177	8 097.0	413.8	210	923	214.7	34.0
Lycoming	16.0	138	108	2 110	1 271.2	82.6	503	7 404	1 878.1	154.7	89	618	120.0	24.4
McKean	12.9	298	31	D	D	D	158	1 551	401.8	34.7	16	62	6.4	1.4
Mercer	30.6	263	89	1 099	644.7	42.4	516	7 109	1 527.3	147.2	72	275	101.6	7.8
Mifflin	9.3	199	35	D	D	D	162	2 063	539.4	46.9	23	71	11.0	1.7
Monroe	33.1	195	97	D	D	D	634	8 710	2 140.4	187.8	123	507	86.8	15.2
Montgomery	114.8	143	1 237	19 422	17 692.1	1 444.8	3 261	56 471	16 036.3	1 489.8	931	7 713	1 767.3	412.8
Montour	18.8	1 030	13	149	190.2	6.1	54	662	167.2	13.6	6	18	2.9	0.6
Northampton	267.2	897	250	3 917	9 979.8	192.8	873	13 238	3 627.4	316.9	178	726	260.6	27.4
Northumberland	22.9	242	56	945	1 152.0	46.6	280	3 188	909.7	76.7	38	182	37.4	7.7
Perry	3.9	85	16	144	81.4	6.1	134	1 166	317.8	25.6	10	23	3.4	0.7
Philadelphia	374.8	246	1 047	16 940	13 181.9	973.0	4 506	50 185	12 241.3	1 165.5	1 079	8 856	1 951.0	443.5
Pike	4.6	79	15	98	31.8	5.4	134	1 862	471.4	40.0	40	442	41.9	10.9

1. Merchant wholesalers, except manufacturers' sales branches and offices. 2. Employer establishments.

Table B. States and Counties — Professional Services, Manufacturing, and Accommodation and Food Services

STATE County	Professional, scientific, and technical services, 2012				Manufacturing, 2012				Accommodation and food services, 2012			
	Number of establishments	Number of employees	Receipts (mil dol)	Annual payroll (mil dol)	Number of establishments	Number of employees	Receipts (mil dol)	Annual payroll (mil dol)	Number of establishments	Number of employees	Sales (mil dol)	Annual payroll (mil dol)
	147	148	149	150	151	152	153	154	155	156	157	158
OREGON—Cont'd												
Morrow	3	6	1.2	0.2	11	1 120	753.5	46.9	19	125	6.8	2.0
Multnomah	3 682	31 457	5 611.6	2 186.1	1 095	32 206	10 278.1	1 633.4	2 799	42 709	2 506.2	736.3
Polk	117	407	36.2	12.6	60	1 801	424.7	68.1	142	D	D	D
Sherman	1	D	D	D	NA	NA	NA	NA	7	60	4.6	1.2
Tillamook	41	D	D	D	30	1 224	708.3	55.8	120	950	51.2	14.5
Umatilla	102	844	74.3	36.3	70	2 522	858.1	90.3	163	2 903	194.5	47.1
Union	47	225	19.2	7.9	28	1 097	275.9	43.1	65	806	33.8	9.4
Wallowa	24	82	7.5	2.6	15	85	D	2.9	47	139	9.7	2.3
Wasco	48	267	25.0	10.0	30	273	93.6	10.8	85	1 288	66.7	20.8
Washington	1 750	21 129	1 788.4	2 119.1	708	D	D	D	1 141	17 404	970.6	277.9
Wheeler	NA	NA	NA	NA	NA	NA	NA	NA	5	18	0.9	0.2
Yamhill	200	638	67.4	24.7	225	5 407	1 893.6	280.4	195	2 486	129.3	40.0
PENNSYLVANIA	29 297	316 658	54 833.8	22 621.5	13 988	543 641	231 396.2	28 057.8	27 646	439 159	23 504.2	6 377.4
Adams	126	D	D	D	113	5 745	2 148.7	240.8	222	3 521	185.7	53.0
Allegheny	3 864	59 880	11 007.2	4 362.7	1 086	36 428	16 279.5	2 073.3	3 170	57 039	2 940.6	827.4
Armstrong	77	361	37.8	11.5	65	1 468	324.1	62.6	95	1 153	42.7	11.0
Beaver	254	3 560	262.0	143.0	175	7 556	4 615.0	397.5	309	4 456	191.8	51.1
Bedford	45	194	18.5	4.7	64	2 065	863.0	83.5	107	1 607	78.6	24.7
Berks	703	D	D	D	498	29 439	10 905.1	1 547.9	754	12 294	548.8	155.6
Blair	221	1 789	208.3	74.8	135	6 943	2 115.6	298.8	280	4 634	199.4	56.5
Bradford	88	549	64.0	21.4	61	3 921	1 975.5	185.0	125	1 576	76.2	20.4
Bucks	2 331	18 164	3 140.0	1 196.9	1 045	27 061	9 681.4	1 428.8	1 385	21 398	1 136.1	302.9
Butler	426	7 354	2 293.3	622.6	266	12 782	4 630.0	687.1	363	6 841	326.6	89.7
Cambria	228	3 359	380.3	168.2	127	5 232	1 798.8	241.6	300	4 070	179.0	47.8
Cameron	6	D	D	D	23	858	D	38.2	13	D	D	D
Carbon	60	241	19.8	9.7	55	1 678	415.0	68.8	116	1 939	112.0	29.9
Centre	365	3 204	432.1	191.2	145	3 960	1 053.5	181.9	311	6 352	289.0	79.7
Chester	2 239	20 472	4 199.5	1 774.2	533	16 067	6 633.5	961.4	932	15 867	846.1	251.0
Clarion	38	238	22.1	9.9	33	1 293	471.2	52.1	95	1 400	57.4	14.2
Clearfield	106	610	56.1	19.7	108	2 613	962.4	99.9	179	2 407	99.5	27.1
Clinton	48	235	24.0	7.9	47	2 836	1 676.8	130.3	83	1 266	58.0	15.3
Columbia	92	677	54.0	22.0	73	5 484	1 613.4	224.9	159	2 484	109.3	29.6
Crawford	115	800	84.1	32.2	277	7 093	1 759.2	318.1	185	2 349	102.8	27.4
Cumberland	649	7 932	1 161.1	522.0	186	7 550	3 776.4	353.2	506	9 403	465.0	129.1
Dauphin	712	7 608	1 178.0	481.8	186	7 679	3 228.9	404.2	679	12 533	718.3	199.6
Delaware	1 525	12 084	2 383.7	903.0	367	12 929	7 364.9	974.8	1 105	16 283	878.1	236.0
Elk	40	1 020	26.4	17.0	135	6 587	1 732.6	295.0	72	763	28.3	7.1
Erie	412	3 028	375.8	135.3	476	21 490	9 437.7	1 179.0	630	10 877	485.4	128.2
Fayette	137	961	143.0	40.5	111	3 088	1 324.2	157.8	285	4 101	211.8	62.0
Forest	2	D	D	D	5	D	D	D	21	125	7.5	1.8
Franklin	223	2 067	234.8	100.3	196	8 182	3 180.0	403.9	270	D	D	D
Fulton	12	31	1.8	0.5	15	D	D	D	18	255	10.5	3.1
Greene	39	230	23.1	7.4	24	370	101.5	15.8	59	1 087	53.3	14.4
Huntingdon	54	256	17.5	7.6	43	1 884	667.4	75.8	84	964	50.3	13.6
Indiana	125	D	D	D	89	2 570	509.6	101.4	178	2 955	117.6	30.0
Jefferson	69	380	42.1	13.9	101	3 475	887.6	151.7	94	942	41.6	10.2
Juniata	22	60	4.3	1.1	59	1 977	337.1	64.7	31	371	15.4	4.4
Lackawanna	488	2 922	363.3	132.4	237	8 611	D	370.4	590	8 685	411.7	107.9
Lancaster	957	12 486	1 249.1	1 037.2	856	33 212	13 655.7	1 638.7	998	17 833	878.4	246.9
Lawrence	138	D	D	D	140	3 465	1 819.4	192.3	163	2 163	89.0	23.9
Lebanon	197	1 083	151.2	48.6	205	8 099	2 743.8	336.5	232	3 320	146.1	40.5
Lehigh	754	D	D	D	378	15 977	9 889.5	867.6	735	12 283	633.0	175.9
Luzerne	575	5 266	528.3	207.3	314	16 701	6 628.0	728.6	740	10 730	515.6	134.1
Lycoming	200	2 151	184.5	74.5	160	8 162	3 186.7	371.5	296	4 696	237.9	62.6
McKean	60	202	16.3	6.2	51	3 290	1 615.8	170.4	102	954	44.6	11.3
Mercer	164	801	77.1	26.6	186	7 405	3 309.4	351.2	254	4 138	188.3	47.6
Mifflin	38	164	11.7	3.6	86	3 696	1 163.0	184.0	84	1 107	45.2	12.3
Monroe	306	D	D	D	111	4 449	D	358.1	387	8 392	724.8	155.1
Montgomery	3 696	45 260	7 823.6	3 663.3	987	39 566	14 574.7	2 433.5	1 901	29 320	1 723.2	489.4
Montour	37	449	134.9	25.4	18	424	140.7	13.9	39	708	38.7	9.9
Northampton	590	4 342	588.8	252.6	328	11 374	4 081.2	571.4	678	11 011	941.1	198.3
Northumberland	104	534	45.0	17.4	78	3 710	1 194.3	150.7	172	1 549	66.2	17.8
Perry	50	218	18.1	6.6	36	665	102.6	22.0	71	449	21.1	5.2
Philadelphia	2 845	47 158	10 464.6	4 249.2	765	22 558	19 718.6	1 198.5	3 669	53 533	3 551.7	982.4
Pike	77	243	30.6	8.6	20	150	27.1	6.2	103	1 826	127.2	36.3

1. Establishment subject to federal tax.

Table B. States and Counties — Health Care and Social Assistance, Other Services, Nonemployer Businesses, and Residential Construction

STATE County	Health care and social assistance, 2012				Other services, 2012				Nonemployer businesses, 2015		Value of residential construction authorized by building permits, 2016	
	Number of establishments	Number of employees	Receipts (mil dol)	Annual payroll (mil dol)	Number of establishments	Number of employees	Receipts (mil dol)	Annual payroll (mil dol)	Number	Receipts (mil dol)	New Construction ($1,000)	Number of housing units
	159	160	161	162	163	164	165	166	167	168	169	170
OREGON—Cont'd												
Morrow	15	139	9.8	3.6	12	31	2.8	0.8	486	23.6	4 349	18
Multnomah	2 950	62 033	7 703.7	2 988.1	1 867	12 391	1 810.6	423.2	68 862	3 404.8	748 869	5 092
Polk	191	2 531	168.6	75.0	87	332	25.7	7.5	4 175	168.1	56 816	279
Sherman	4	23	0.3	0.1	2	D	D	D	118	5.6	NA	NA
Tillamook	52	810	87.3	36.0	44	D	D	D	1 900	85.3	32 552	141
Umatilla	207	2 923	312.6	115.8	104	500	58.4	17.3	3 374	152.8	17 497	87
Union	103	1 388	127.5	55.3	54	D	D	D	1 557	58.5	12 316	49
Wallowa	35	412	33.9	13.4	19	D	D	D	775	38.7	4 652	20
Wasco	74	1 769	148.2	78.4	48	173	13.4	4.1	1 382	51.7	NA	NA
Washington	1 722	25 903	3 238.1	1 205.9	843	5 106	530.2	179.2	36 696	1 777.3	798 492	3 327
Wheeler	5	D	D	D	1	D	D	D	154	7.6	NA	NA
Yamhill	260	4 241	433.6	151.6	133	D	D	D	5 922	259.4	102 755	412
PENNSYLVANIA	36 552	955 479	96 329.2	39 326.6	25 231	154 319	17 736.7	4 366.6	811 890	39 393.2	4 515 560	23 303
Adams	182	4 634	448.2	167.1	150	909	75.1	19.8	6 528	274.8	79 900	347
Allegheny	4 423	123 336	12 756.2	5 392.7	2 872	19 874	2 346.4	604.4	80 279	3 734.4	437 576	2 325
Armstrong	188	3 504	246.4	106.5	113	499	38.4	10.5	3 571	150.9	15 633	61
Beaver	470	9 380	779.6	351.2	316	1 324	113.6	30.6	8 736	351.9	56 955	391
Bedford	120	1 769	148.9	54.8	95	373	27.1	6.8	3 257	150.1	12 120	65
Berks	827	25 605	2 588.9	1 067.0	767	4 046	363.5	101.5	24 122	1 151.4	84 612	436
Blair	438	11 356	1 149.5	472.4	283	1 573	118.4	36.7	6 105	298.3	30 900	183
Bradford	148	4 744	561.0	228.0	120	558	43.9	11.3	3 574	151.5	25 498	102
Bucks	2 014	40 065	3 735.6	1 582.5	1 424	8 400	746.1	234.1	51 912	2 997.1	221 123	1 091
Butler	608	12 564	1 198.6	493.0	388	2 309	203.4	54.3	11 898	570.8	204 938	841
Cambria	540	11 708	1 047.3	444.7	312	1 690	133.9	34.2	6 206	243.2	40 318	164
Cameron	11	D	D	D	11	62	3.5	0.6	219	7.2	0	0
Carbon	160	3 302	219.0	97.4	91	310	28.7	6.8	3 290	142.9	10 913	54
Centre	363	7 882	767.4	316.6	249	1 471	131.7	37.0	9 780	464.7	90 561	393
Chester	1 440	34 065	3 442.7	1 431.8	1 042	8 068	1 969.8	300.6	41 543	2 533.0	234 846	1 158
Clarion	137	3 052	197.3	84.0	72	494	53.1	11.3	2 423	109.9	6 574	31
Clearfield	260	6 187	576.4	238.7	165	1 169	90.7	26.1	4 207	170.6	13 359	74
Clinton	71	1 241	98.3	39.3	66	315	30.9	5.5	1 835	77.1	17 714	36
Columbia	164	D	D	D	114	493	48.6	9.8	3 199	137.9	20 563	95
Crawford	238	5 129	424.6	183.6	174	816	70.2	16.4	5 316	233.7	11 601	69
Cumberland	662	15 684	1 650.9	675.6	535	4 185	521.6	130.0	15 426	786.3	165 789	913
Dauphin	820	26 291	2 182.0	899.1	685	4 728	580.5	175.7	15 923	724.5	106 556	609
Delaware	1 608	39 002	3 952.6	1 724.6	1 116	6 740	863.0	212.3	41 247	2 079.8	115 827	452
Elk	108	2 117	146.6	66.5	78	340	21.9	5.4	1 533	64.5	7 526	44
Erie	850	24 899	2 216.5	923.1	563	3 591	322.7	80.2	13 841	594.6	41 380	338
Fayette	408	7 929	619.8	259.5	240	1 181	118.1	28.1	6 254	276.7	41 502	165
Forest	10	456	35.9	14.2	6	13	1.2	0.2	281	11.8	266	2
Franklin	305	8 178	820.5	349.3	287	1 558	131.5	32.7	8 947	374.7	58 876	327
Fulton	25	D	D	D	27	97	9.7	2.1	931	41.9	3 742	16
Greene	105	1 588	141.3	52.5	72	369	46.9	10.3	1 462	63.3	5 879	36
Huntingdon	95	1 859	147.4	61.7	79	301	27.3	5.5	2 468	106.1	11 343	52
Indiana	252	4 406	360.6	149.4	151	954	109.1	25.6	4 876	210.1	11 969	71
Jefferson	150	2 991	236.6	100.0	103	426	32.6	7.9	2 921	141.6	8 242	54
Juniata	34	561	37.3	14.2	32	108	9.9	2.5	1 844	96.2	6 497	39
Lackawanna	730	19 120	1 805.5	768.9	401	2 181	180.8	53.0	11 887	585.8	144 530	617
Lancaster	1 110	34 977	3 387.5	1 411.1	1 031	6 339	588.6	161.3	41 260	2 188.1	281 242	1 287
Lawrence	291	6 467	501.7	214.0	174	853	71.5	19.5	5 074	209.0	16 799	98
Lebanon	279	8 165	772.4	341.9	233	1 086	110.1	27.5	8 125	388.0	71 057	432
Lehigh	1 170	40 184	4 351.2	1 715.9	719	4 730	428.3	127.0	22 130	1 007.0	108 010	623
Luzerne	967	23 680	2 273.1	934.5	559	2 803	292.8	71.8	16 739	812.0	64 315	375
Lycoming	287	8 233	825.8	345.7	240	1 546	152.8	35.4	6 254	281.5	20 313	93
McKean	151	2 764	209.7	88.5	95	472	37.9	9.1	2 126	84.2	4 141	24
Mercer	410	10 413	866.4	358.8	251	1 144	97.7	22.7	6 301	283.2	17 769	79
Mifflin	127	3 113	251.0	104.4	67	249	21.1	5.2	2 691	114.1	10 840	62
Monroe	393	7 031	643.1	276.0	309	1 571	115.7	37.0	10 328	473.6	58 815	246
Montgomery	3 023	71 373	7 980.2	3 199.4	1 908	11 847	1 609.1	359.9	69 365	4 281.1	380 261	2 406
Montour	100	D	D	D	35	234	62.0	8.7	1 040	48.6	11 355	55
Northampton	776	13 343	1 137.2	468.0	547	2 875	233.2	71.8	17 843	874.7	73 013	329
Northumberland	206	5 305	340.8	149.5	146	772	46.7	13.8	4 496	211.5	11 902	55
Perry	80	1 007	49.6	23.6	65	245	22.9	4.8	2 864	126.4	26 024	105
Philadelphia	3 920	152 972	17 972.6	6 847.5	2 493	17 972	2 408.7	632.4	88 920	3 306.9	534 322	3 175
Pike	86	961	64.2	26.0	97	950	70.1	19.4	3 860	191.0	19 882	75

Table B. States and Counties — Government Employment and Payroll, and Local Government Finances

	Government employment and payroll, 2012									Local government finances, 2012				
			March payroll (percent of total)							General revenue				
												Taxes		
													Per capita[1] (dollars)	
STATE County	Full-time equivalent employees	March payroll (dollars)	Adminis- tration, judicial, and legal	Police and Corrections	Fire Protection	Highways and transpor- tation	Health and Welfare	Natural resources and utilities	Education and libraries	Total (mil dol)	Inter- govern- mental (mil dol)	Total (mil dol)	Total	Property
	171	172	173	174	175	176	177	178	179	180	181	182	183	184
OREGON—Cont'd														
Morrow	611	2 174 057	7.8	9.3	1.6	5.2	17.4	6.6	45.7	79.1	31.3	21.7	1 928	1 801
Multnomah	29 478	148 927 675	7.5	11.9	4.2	13.6	6.4	9.0	42.8	4 680.8	1 700.4	1 856.1	2 445	1 660
Polk	1 230	4 842 625	12.3	13.6	2.4	1.9	8.6	6.6	52.1	138.5	77.6	42.1	1 152	500
Sherman	121	446 146	20.7	9.6	8.8	9.9	11.4	7.5	29.5	23.4	4.3	6.6	3 808	3 775
Tillamook	1 081	4 310 792	8.6	7.5	1.5	5.0	4.7	26.1	44.4	116.8	36.6	46.1	1 822	1 701
Umatilla	2 519	9 346 604	6.6	11.0	3.9	3.0	1.9	7.4	65.3	307.6	163.2	86.2	1 122	1 020
Union	750	2 655 712	8.7	12.0	2.8	4.4	0.9	8.8	60.1	87.0	50.9	20.7	802	722
Wallowa	382	1 406 470	6.1	5.5	0.3	3.8	43.8	3.1	36.5	46.2	14.1	8.6	1 262	1 113
Wasco	982	3 676 060	6.9	6.4	4.7	3.8	3.2	15.2	58.1	115.4	52.3	37.4	1 468	1 319
Washington	14 620	63 993 061	6.8	11.2	6.7	2.5	2.0	7.5	60.1	1 882.7	665.8	834.1	1 523	1 366
Wheeler	106	329 289	21.3	2.9	0.0	9.3	0.0	7.4	57.6	8.1	5.1	1.6	1 126	1 092
Yamhill	2 820	11 200 226	7.7	9.1	4.6	1.7	6.0	8.9	59.7	320.3	146.1	104.5	1 043	942
PENNSYLVANIA	X	X	X	X	X	X	X	X	X	X	X	X	X	X
Adams	2 548	9 790 732	7.8	9.5	0.9	2.6	2.1	3.4	73.2	374.0	165.8	167.3	1 648	1 256
Allegheny	43 945	195 375 705	6.5	12.8	2.4	11.5	5.4	5.9	53.8	6 769.1	2 823.5	2 739.2	2 228	1 525
Armstrong	2 222	7 529 691	6.9	7.0	0.0	4.1	6.8	5.5	68.9	227.1	114.7	81.0	1 185	1 004
Beaver	5 422	21 094 763	6.4	10.1	0.3	4.8	6.7	6.8	64.1	785.3	350.5	233.6	1 372	1 124
Bedford	1 369	4 444 835	5.3	5.6	0.8	4.2	1.7	5.0	77.4	128.7	70.2	45.3	918	675
Berks	14 566	69 528 665	6.1	16.3	5.1	2.6	4.7	5.3	58.7	2 039.3	792.5	835.6	2 021	1 642
Blair	4 030	13 533 958	4.8	8.4	2.3	5.0	8.5	7.0	62.6	402.4	214.5	126.2	993	707
Bradford	2 246	8 350 493	7.8	4.9	0.5	5.3	11.4	1.9	67.4	247.1	119.2	78.6	1 252	972
Bucks	18 333	88 124 851	6.0	11.7	0.6	4.0	4.0	3.9	68.9	2 731.2	688.4	1 517.1	2 419	2 074
Butler	4 890	20 031 417	6.5	6.1	0.5	3.3	5.6	4.7	72.2	629.8	252.7	262.6	1 420	1 090
Cambria	4 484	15 273 184	8.2	8.3	1.4	5.9	5.7	6.0	63.9	555.1	293.7	143.3	1 012	781
Cameron	214	664 238	8.3	4.9	0.0	5.0	7.5	2.5	70.2	17.3	9.0	6.0	1 223	1 052
Carbon	2 113	7 282 054	7.7	9.6	0.0	3.5	11.6	5.7	60.5	211.1	71.9	108.6	1 671	1 438
Centre	3 965	14 048 206	7.5	8.6	0.0	7.9	9.9	5.8	58.3	455.2	154.4	216.4	1 394	1 018
Chester	13 231	61 935 244	7.1	9.3	0.2	2.2	4.5	2.8	71.3	2 107.9	567.4	1 254.5	2 476	2 063
Clarion	1 226	4 224 897	6.3	6.9	0.0	3.1	1.8	3.0	78.3	155.3	103.3	39.4	993	773
Clearfield	2 608	9 251 789	4.9	5.4	0.0	3.3	1.6	4.7	78.9	261.5	141.7	88.1	1 086	853
Clinton	1 129	4 364 621	9.8	5.9	2.2	2.6	11.0	7.0	59.8	138.0	54.0	44.3	1 121	835
Columbia	1 917	7 059 353	6.5	11.0	0.0	3.3	2.0	3.1	73.5	197.2	86.4	83.5	1 248	914
Crawford	2 501	8 880 019	8.6	8.3	1.6	5.0	10.3	5.8	59.4	270.2	125.4	98.7	1 127	906
Cumberland	7 023	27 433 306	6.6	8.7	0.0	2.7	6.7	4.9	68.9	914.8	308.3	434.2	1 820	1 330
Dauphin	10 041	42 265 280	7.7	13.4	1.0	4.7	1.7	5.4	64.3	1 441.8	522.5	527.9	1 958	1 407
Delaware	18 047	76 207 314	10.5	9.6	1.0	2.0	6.2	4.1	65.6	2 712.5	932.9	1 199.8	2 138	1 938
Elk	1 009	3 366 414	8.9	6.3	0.0	12.9	2.6	6.2	61.7	108.1	52.0	37.3	1 181	901
Erie	8 523	32 472 819	5.3	9.7	2.6	5.6	3.9	6.0	65.7	1 197.6	616.5	364.0	1 297	1 046
Fayette	3 546	14 568 652	6.8	9.1	0.4	5.2	7.7	9.3	61.2	411.7	262.1	104.7	772	570
Forest	197	632 875	20.3	3.4	0.0	3.6	5.7	3.9	62.0	19.5	9.4	7.5	980	863
Franklin	3 820	13 644 359	7.7	8.8	1.7	2.3	9.1	6.1	63.5	415.1	130.8	191.4	1 265	978
Fulton	454	1 468 178	11.3	2.6	0.0	2.5	0.0	2.1	81.0	47.4	25.7	16.4	1 112	912
Greene	1 301	4 613 569	10.4	5.2	0.0	6.2	4.1	7.8	65.3	144.0	67.6	57.8	1 518	1 258
Huntingdon	1 125	3 453 282	9.3	7.1	0.0	3.2	3.8	5.2	70.1	118.4	66.3	38.4	837	613
Indiana	2 289	9 093 274	6.9	6.4	0.1	4.5	4.9	5.1	70.9	313.8	170.3	97.7	1 107	879
Jefferson	1 211	4 334 856	6.6	7.0	0.0	4.9	1.4	6.4	72.3	125.7	68.4	38.4	858	661
Juniata	563	1 993 044	11.0	5.3	1.3	2.6	0.1	1.9	75.5	49.2	23.8	21.6	867	690
Lackawanna	6 361	25 493 690	6.8	11.8	3.2	4.1	6.5	6.5	59.1	757.3	291.3	324.8	1 515	1 101
Lancaster	12 622	54 624 168	5.9	11.7	0.8	2.8	3.4	3.5	70.9	1 833.2	668.6	843.7	1 601	1 327
Lawrence	2 433	9 509 559	8.0	8.4	1.5	4.9	1.0	3.8	71.8	318.9	174.0	106.5	1 185	905
Lebanon	4 116	14 939 586	6.1	9.0	1.7	2.8	9.0	5.5	65.4	485.8	160.6	191.5	1 416	1 136
Lehigh	11 303	49 829 858	7.3	10.7	1.9	4.5	9.3	4.5	60.4	1 670.5	674.3	669.0	1 883	1 523
Luzerne	9 404	36 055 331	7.5	12.5	3.5	3.7	4.7	5.2	62.1	1 080.5	466.5	439.6	1 369	1 039
Lycoming	3 615	14 906 594	7.7	7.9	1.8	4.3	2.7	6.0	68.7	451.3	198.0	155.7	1 329	953
McKean	1 616	5 647 554	6.9	7.4	1.5	4.5	8.7	8.2	62.2	167.7	97.2	44.6	1 033	829
Mercer	3 570	12 446 506	8.5	9.8	1.2	3.2	1.2	4.2	70.1	402.4	216.5	133.0	1 150	861
Mifflin	1 135	4 324 228	8.8	6.8	1.1	5.0	2.7	9.1	64.8	153.4	81.3	46.8	1 002	733
Monroe	5 957	25 067 544	5.7	4.3	0.0	5.4	1.6	1.5	80.9	719.0	225.3	441.5	2 616	2 404
Montgomery	23 690	112 151 487	6.4	12.2	0.4	2.4	5.0	4.0	68.6	3 430.1	888.0	2 054.1	2 541	2 087
Montour	515	1 746 307	6.4	6.4	0.0	4.4	0.9	6.3	73.4	92.9	26.6	26.3	1 431	915
Northampton	10 782	47 706 434	7.1	11.9	1.8	2.5	7.7	4.9	61.8	1 411.9	496.8	671.7	2 244	1 804
Northumberland	3 162	10 304 053	9.0	7.6	0.0	3.1	16.2	4.4	59.0	273.2	137.2	88.2	934	631
Perry	1 241	4 130 390	6.3	5.0	0.0	3.3	5.0	1.5	77.8	139.6	62.3	60.0	1 312	977
Philadelphia	60 937	311 591 353	8.6	18.6	4.6	16.9	6.0	8.1	36.4	11 133.9	5 530.3	4 080.0	2 636	743
Pike	1 166	4 430 795	9.4	13.5	0.0	2.5	4.3	1.7	67.0	128.4	48.7	71.2	1 252	1 185

1. Based on the resident population estimated as of July 1 of the year shown.

Table B. States and Counties — Local Government Finances, Government Employment, and Income Taxes

STATE County	Total (mil dol)	Per capita[1] (dollars)	Education	Health and hospitals	Police protection	Public welfare	Highways	Total (mil dol)	Per capita[1] (dollars)	Federal civilian	Federal military	State and local	Number of returns	Mean adjusted gross income	Mean income tax
	185	186	187	188	189	190	191	192	193	194	195	196	197	198	199
OREGON—Cont'd															
Morrow	78.1	6 947	32.8	11.0	4.6	0.3	5.8	136.8	12 168	57	35	779	4 770	46 154	3 940
Multnomah	4 425.0	5 828	31.5	4.6	5.2	4.0	6.5	7 864.7	10 358	12 293	2 377	59 390	385 290	64 185	8 601
Polk	140.8	1 844	43.0	8.4	8.3	1.0	5.6	271.5	3 556	72	200	5 110	33 540	54 792	5 456
Sherman	18.9	10 932	20.7	4.0	4.0	1.4	11.8	3.5	2 023	128	D	180	830	54 310	5 854
Tillamook	118.4	4 684	38.3	7.8	3.6	0.3	5.5	166.8	6 595	103	103	1 686	11 750	45 772	4 337
Umatilla	311.2	4 051	58.5	1.4	4.4	0.0	4.1	422.0	5 493	525	187	6 236	31 430	47 810	4 552
Union	90.0	3 495	44.0	3.4	5.7	0.4	5.1	30.5	1 185	228	65	1 977	11 210	47 881	4 543
Wallowa	44.0	6 453	31.6	33.8	3.6	0.8	8.6	38.3	5 620	93	17	515	3 310	43 708	3 876
Wasco	106.5	4 180	48.5	2.2	4.8	0.4	4.4	159.3	6 251	283	65	1 694	11 200	46 187	4 414
Washington	1 940.6	3 543	44.5	2.9	7.1	0.0	5.6	2 532.1	4 623	765	1 468	20 708	265 690	73 754	9 503
Wheeler	9.5	6 659	47.9	0.8	2.6	1.5	12.0	2.0	1 419	D	D	103	570	32 488	2 530
Yamhill	320.3	3 195	49.5	5.9	5.8	0.1	3.1	445.1	4 439	481	250	3 830	43 410	56 291	5 882
PENNSYLVANIA	X	X	X	X	X	X	X	X	X	96 059	35 786	642 693	6 168 840	63 073	8 549
Adams	458.0	4 513	68.9	3.6	1.4	3.2	2.7	405.6	3 997	714	258	3 299	50 750	56 743	6 719
Allegheny	6 640.6	5 402	42.9	7.9	4.6	4.6	3.0	13 494.2	10 977	12 928	3 584	52 005	630 440	67 595	9 938
Armstrong	246.9	3 609	57.6	1.5	1.2	7.5	5.0	239.3	3 498	187	174	2 559	32 440	47 512	4 714
Beaver	789.6	4 638	46.6	3.5	3.0	14.1	3.9	1 928.6	11 328	299	437	7 282	86 300	52 413	5 755
Bedford	155.3	3 148	66.4	0.0	0.4	2.0	4.8	224.7	4 556	99	126	2 118	22 920	44 333	4 085
Berks	2 024.3	4 896	54.5	3.4	4.1	7.2	2.8	3 478.7	8 413	915	1 064	21 503	201 400	56 873	6 724
Blair	409.0	3 217	49.0	3.1	3.0	8.6	3.9	474.2	3 730	999	321	7 569	59 330	49 488	5 676
Bradford	244.7	3 898	54.4	2.0	1.6	7.3	6.2	751.2	11 963	210	160	2 831	29 020	54 789	6 488
Bucks	2 875.9	4 586	57.6	0.8	5.5	7.0	4.5	3 960.3	6 316	1 109	1 648	21 314	328 200	84 824	13 342
Butler	656.7	3 550	51.5	4.2	2.4	9.5	4.4	1 305.0	7 055	2 821	482	8 422	93 330	69 347	9 428
Cambria	571.5	4 037	49.2	3.2	5.7	14.0	3.6	641.5	4 531	1 036	365	6 888	64 240	46 259	4 842
Cameron	19.1	3 864	59.4	3.8	1.2	2.5	5.9	30.2	6 117	12	12	370	2 450	41 652	3 883
Carbon	219.0	3 370	60.5	0.1	2.6	4.4	3.4	265.0	4 076	109	166	2 551	30 840	47 118	4 663
Centre	453.5	2 923	51.0	2.2	3.5	7.9	6.1	486.7	3 136	459	450	47 937	59 660	63 804	8 068
Chester	2 204.4	4 352	57.7	5.2	3.8	3.4	3.3	2 995.8	5 914	2 399	1 322	23 179	250 820	106 387	18 788
Clarion	168.8	4 258	67.2	3.0	1.9	2.5	3.4	87.7	2 213	99	98	3 323	17 270	45 841	4 325
Clearfield	261.5	3 221	66.6	0.0	3.5	3.1	4.8	310.5	3 824	240	200	4 452	36 760	44 895	4 430
Clinton	137.3	3 474	41.4	0.3	1.3	4.6	4.0	99.3	2 514	141	99	2 969	17 010	45 977	4 351
Columbia	207.5	3 102	63.6	0.0	3.1	3.7	4.7	212.5	3 176	144	164	5 134	29 620	48 910	5 130
Crawford	281.4	3 212	48.8	2.8	1.9	9.1	5.8	238.2	2 719	263	218	3 789	38 740	46 619	4 819
Cumberland	1 033.3	4 330	58.9	3.0	2.8	6.7	2.5	1 275.7	5 346	4 502	1 416	12 705	123 000	67 313	9 148
Dauphin	1 554.4	5 764	46.5	4.7	3.9	9.1	2.6	2 450.3	9 087	2 662	762	38 923	140 820	55 896	6 860
Delaware	2 744.1	4 891	50.1	2.1	4.9	11.1	2.0	4 601.2	8 200	2 093	1 473	23 611	275 390	78 729	12 297
Elk	92.2	2 921	46.8	0.2	2.8	1.8	8.2	287.8	9 123	106	80	1 249	16 640	48 598	5 269
Erie	1 203.4	4 288	44.0	5.6	2.7	14.2	3.5	1 705.3	6 076	1 517	738	15 584	130 660	50 095	5 750
Fayette	427.6	3 152	56.8	10.4	1.2	3.1	3.6	909.8	6 706	352	340	6 095	61 800	45 738	4 656
Forest	20.2	2 638	52.6	4.6	0.8	4.0	10.1	11.6	1 515	65	13	948	2 250	41 433	3 932
Franklin	452.7	2 992	54.1	4.1	1.9	5.5	4.8	619.1	4 092	2 205	401	5 892	75 390	52 079	5 305
Fulton	47.5	3 214	61.6	0.0	3.7	4.3	4.1	65.3	4 419	27	38	712	7 060	45 642	4 140
Greene	138.0	3 624	59.6	4.6	1.0	1.6	6.1	149.4	3 923	118	91	2 422	16 150	67 276	9 735
Huntingdon	134.9	2 937	57.1	1.3	1.8	2.3	5.0	147.7	3 216	111	107	2 933	19 090	45 776	4 320
Indiana	303.7	3 442	61.2	0.1	1.0	6.1	4.2	387.8	4 396	192	220	7 461	36 500	50 386	5 496
Jefferson	139.0	3 104	60.2	0.0	1.5	3.9	5.0	213.5	4 770	107	115	1 844	21 380	45 565	4 690
Juniata	46.0	1 848	65.2	0.1	0.9	2.6	5.4	13.7	550	64	64	678	11 110	45 447	4 112
Lackawanna	820.1	3 824	47.2	0.3	3.9	6.6	3.0	968.6	4 516	932	544	9 939	102 910	50 714	5 914
Lancaster	2 018.4	3 831	55.1	5.4	4.3	5.1	3.3	3 447.0	6 543	1 216	1 379	19 280	261 550	58 202	6 956
Lawrence	334.2	3 719	50.8	2.1	3.0	11.6	4.1	469.7	5 226	207	227	3 373	41 940	48 563	5 131
Lebanon	507.4	3 752	47.7	2.2	2.9	15.0	5.1	705.4	5 215	3 023	352	4 943	67 730	52 410	5 543
Lehigh	1 756.6	4 945	46.2	3.6	3.3	11.2	2.9	3 948.1	11 114	815	936	15 984	179 430	59 158	7 507
Luzerne	1 193.5	3 718	50.4	0.4	3.0	3.8	4.8	1 386.1	4 318	3 220	827	14 772	156 410	48 483	5 417
Lycoming	560.5	4 783	43.8	0.0	2.2	3.1	4.4	997.6	8 514	356	293	8 957	54 980	50 198	5 465
McKean	182.4	4 229	57.8	3.7	2.0	4.1	3.6	130.5	3 026	423	103	1 990	19 070	48 058	5 193
Mercer	435.3	3 764	63.5	2.3	3.0	2.6	3.9	444.6	3 844	250	302	4 919	53 650	47 800	5 045
Mifflin	166.3	3 555	61.5	4.0	1.7	0.4	3.1	218.1	4 664	85	121	1 712	20 920	42 600	3 817
Monroe	739.9	4 384	67.9	0.1	3.0	3.9	2.5	1 201.0	7 115	3 243	455	8 254	76 980	52 041	5 668
Montgomery	3 494.4	4 322	56.9	1.9	5.0	6.2	3.6	4 364.3	5 398	2 562	2 265	32 315	415 720	100 589	17 301
Montour	79.5	4 333	44.5	0.0	1.9	1.3	3.9	895.8	48 800	37	48	1 487	9 100	64 457	8 913
Northampton	1 501.3	5 017	49.8	3.1	4.0	11.6	2.7	2 550.6	8 523	1 081	766	13 488	149 540	62 752	7 934
Northumberland	266.3	2 820	54.3	3.8	5.1	7.1	3.9	255.4	2 704	162	235	4 094	43 740	43 841	4 196
Perry	128.6	2 813	61.7	2.5	0.8	7.4	4.3	107.1	2 343	79	118	1 837	22 560	48 759	4 532
Philadelphia	9 802.9	6 334	34.2	13.8	6.2	5.8	1.1	18 737.5	12 107	29 832	5 198	72 844	671 090	47 363	5 604
Pike	135.9	2 388	49.0	0.4	1.9	5.8	3.9	42.8	752	223	146	2 312	26 650	54 831	5 979

1. Based on the resident population estimated as of July 1 of the year shown.

Table B. States and Counties — Land Area and Population

					Population, 2016			Population and population characteristics, 2016										
								Race alone or in combination, not Hispanic or Latino (percent)					Age (percent)					
STATE/ County code	CBSA code[1]	County type[2]	STATE County	Land area,[3] (sq mi) 2016	Total persons 2016	Rank	Per square mile	White	Black	American Indian, Alaska Native	Asian and Pacific Islander	Percent Hispanic or Latino[4]	Under 5 years	5 to 17 years	18 to 24 years	25 to 34 years	35 to 44 years	45 to 54 years
				1	2	3	4	5	6	7	8	9	10	11	12	13	14	15
			PENNSYLVANIA—Cont'd															
42 105	...	9	Potter	1 081.3	16 885	1 985	15.6	97.5	0.8	0.7	0.6	1.3	5.4	15.5	7.2	9.9	10.0	13.4
42 107	39060	4	Schuylkill	778.6	143 573	449	184.4	92.5	3.3	0.4	0.8	4.0	4.8	14.7	7.2	11.8	12.1	14.6
42 109	42780	7	Snyder	328.8	40 468	1 165	123.1	95.7	1.5	0.4	0.9	2.3	5.7	15.8	11.7	11.4	10.9	13.5
42 111	43740	4	Somerset	1 074.4	75 061	735	69.9	95.1	3.1	0.4	0.7	1.5	4.6	13.6	7.3	11.4	11.9	14.1
42 113	...	8	Sullivan	449.9	6 137	2 742	13.6	93.9	3.8	0.8	0.6	1.8	3.0	8.6	8.8	9.8	9.6	13.5
42 115	...	6	Susquehanna	823.5	40 862	1 157	49.6	97.1	0.9	0.5	0.7	1.8	4.5	14.6	7.3	10.1	10.1	14.6
42 117	...	6	Tioga	1 133.8	41 467	1 141	36.6	97.2	1.2	0.6	0.8	1.3	5.3	14.6	9.6	11.3	10.4	13.0
42 119	30260	2	Union	316.0	45 565	1 062	144.2	84.9	7.7	0.6	2.2	5.9	4.4	13.2	13.4	13.8	13.2	13.1
42 121	36340	4	Venango	674.3	52 582	953	78.0	97.0	1.8	0.5	0.7	1.1	5.1	15.0	7.0	10.3	10.8	13.5
42 123	47620	6	Warren	884.1	40 025	1 173	45.3	97.6	0.9	0.6	0.8	1.1	5.0	14.6	7.2	10.4	10.7	14.4
42 125	38300	1	Washington	857.0	207 981	317	242.7	94.0	4.2	0.5	1.4	1.7	5.1	14.6	8.5	11.1	11.4	14.0
42 127	...	6	Wayne	725.6	50 710	977	69.9	91.5	3.7	0.5	0.9	4.3	4.1	12.9	7.2	11.2	11.2	14.8
42 129	38300	1	Westmoreland	1 027.6	355 458	195	345.9	95.3	3.4	0.4	1.2	1.1	4.5	14.0	7.8	10.4	10.8	14.4
42 131	42540	2	Wyoming	397.3	27 521	1 512	69.3	96.5	1.3	0.6	0.7	1.9	4.9	15.1	8.8	10.9	11.1	13.8
42 133	49620	2	York	904.2	443 744	159	490.8	85.6	6.7	0.5	1.9	7.2	5.7	16.6	8.2	12.3	12.0	14.5
44 000	...	0	RHODE ISLAND	1 033.9	1 056 426	X	1 021.8	75.1	7.0	1.1	4.2	14.9	5.2	14.5	10.8	13.5	11.6	13.9
44 001	39300	1	Bristol	24.2	49 067	999	2 027.6	93.7	1.6	0.7	2.7	2.9	3.9	15.2	11.0	9.8	10.7	14.7
44 003	39300	1	Kent	168.5	164 614	392	976.9	90.9	2.4	0.8	3.1	4.6	4.9	14.1	7.2	12.9	11.9	15.2
44 005	39300	1	Newport	102.4	82 784	680	808.4	87.9	5.1	1.0	2.9	5.8	4.4	13.3	9.8	12.3	11.2	14.0
44 007	39300	1	Providence	409.5	633 673	105	1 547.4	64.4	9.9	1.1	5.1	22.1	5.8	15.0	11.1	15.0	12.1	13.4
44 009	39300	1	Washington	329.3	126 288	497	383.5	92.7	2.0	1.4	2.6	3.1	3.7	13.4	14.8	9.1	9.5	14.2
45 000	...	0	SOUTH CAROLINA	30 062.6	4 961 119	X	165.0	65.3	27.9	0.8	2.1	5.5	5.9	16.2	9.4	13.2	12.1	13.1
45 001	24940	6	Abbeville	490.5	24 872	1 612	50.7	70.1	28.7	0.7	0.6	1.4	5.3	15.9	9.4	10.5	10.6	13.2
45 003	12260	2	Aiken	1 071.1	167 458	384	156.3	68.1	25.7	1.0	1.4	5.7	5.7	16.2	8.1	12.6	11.4	13.1
45 005	...	6	Allendale	408.1	9 045	2 507	22.2	22.8	73.2	0.6	0.7	3.4	4.7	14.4	8.9	13.7	11.4	14.1
45 007	24860	2	Anderson	715.5	196 569	336	274.7	79.1	17.0	0.6	1.3	3.6	6.0	17.0	8.3	12.0	11.9	13.7
45 009	...	7	Bamberg	393.4	14 434	2 133	36.7	36.6	60.6	0.7	0.7	2.3	5.0	15.2	12.5	9.9	10.0	13.0
45 011	...	6	Barnwell	548.4	21 483	1 754	39.2	52.5	44.7	1.0	0.9	2.3	6.5	18.0	8.6	11.1	11.5	13.2
45 013	25940	3	Beaufort	576.3	183 149	354	317.8	69.1	19.0	0.6	1.9	11.1	5.5	13.8	9.3	11.5	10.2	10.7
45 015	16700	2	Berkeley	1 098.5	210 898	312	191.9	66.3	25.3	1.2	3.6	6.3	6.6	17.6	9.6	14.8	13.1	13.1
45 017	17900	2	Calhoun	381.2	14 796	2 117	38.8	54.4	41.7	0.8	0.5	3.7	4.9	14.9	7.4	10.5	10.4	14.1
45 019	16700	2	Charleston	917.4	396 484	175	432.2	65.7	28.0	0.7	2.2	5.0	6.0	13.9	9.1	17.4	12.6	12.6
45 021	23500	4	Cherokee	392.7	56 646	990	144.2	74.2	21.5	0.7	0.8	4.3	6.0	17.6	9.4	12.4	12.2	13.7
45 023	16740	1	Chester	580.7	32 181	1 377	55.4	60.4	37.7	1.0	0.7	1.9	5.9	16.8	7.8	11.7	11.1	14.3
45 025	...	6	Chesterfield	799.1	46 013	1 047	57.6	61.7	33.7	1.0	0.8	4.3	5.7	17.0	8.4	11.4	11.9	14.6
45 027	...	6	Clarendon	606.9	33 951	1 328	55.9	48.3	48.0	0.5	0.9	3.1	4.9	15.3	9.3	11.5	10.2	12.7
45 029	...	6	Colleton	1 056.5	37 923	1 226	35.9	57.9	38.4	1.2	0.7	3.2	5.9	16.6	7.8	11.2	10.8	13.4
45 031	22500	3	Darlington	561.2	67 234	788	119.8	56.1	41.8	0.7	0.7	1.9	5.9	16.8	8.9	11.3	11.7	13.4
45 033	...	6	Dillon	404.8	30 858	1 412	76.2	47.7	47.7	3.1	0.7	2.7	6.7	18.8	8.3	12.2	11.9	12.6
45 035	16700	2	Dorchester	573.3	153 773	426	268.2	66.9	26.6	1.2	2.9	5.2	6.4	18.7	8.2	14.1	13.4	14.2
45 037	12260	2	Edgefield	500.4	26 358	1 547	52.7	57.7	36.2	0.7	0.8	5.9	4.3	14.5	8.5	12.9	13.0	14.7
45 039	17900	2	Fairfield	686.3	22 653	1 701	33.0	39.4	58.6	0.8	0.8	2.1	4.8	14.8	7.9	10.6	10.9	14.1
45 041	22500	3	Florence	800.0	138 742	462	173.4	53.2	43.0	0.7	1.7	2.6	6.3	17.7	8.9	12.6	12.4	13.0
45 043	23860	4	Georgetown	813.6	61 399	851	75.5	64.6	32.0	0.5	0.8	3.0	4.7	14.5	6.9	9.4	10.0	12.5
45 045	24860	2	Greenville	785.2	498 766	140	635.2	70.4	19.0	0.6	2.8	9.0	6.4	16.9	8.9	13.8	12.9	13.6
45 047	24940	4	Greenwood	454.7	70 133	766	154.2	60.8	32.4	0.5	1.4	6.1	6.3	16.8	9.3	12.7	11.5	13.0
45 049	...	6	Hampton	559.9	19 922	1 832	35.6	41.9	53.8	0.7	0.8	4.0	5.3	16.4	8.3	13.0	12.8	13.3
45 051	34820	2	Horry	1 133.9	322 342	212	284.3	79.1	14.0	1.0	1.8	6.0	5.0	13.7	7.5	12.1	11.4	12.8
45 053	25940	3	Jasper	655.3	28 465	1 471	43.4	43.5	43.0	0.6	1.0	13.0	5.9	14.9	8.9	13.6	11.7	12.9
45 055	17900	2	Kershaw	726.6	64 097	826	88.2	70.5	25.4	0.7	1.0	4.3	5.9	17.6	7.5	11.7	11.9	13.8
45 057	16740	1	Lancaster	549.2	89 594	646	163.1	71.6	22.4	0.6	1.5	5.2	6.1	15.8	6.7	12.2	13.2	13.1
45 059	24860	2	Laurens	713.8	66 777	791	93.6	69.4	26.1	0.6	0.7	4.6	5.6	16.4	9.3	12.0	11.2	13.7
45 061	...	6	Lee	410.2	17 635	1 936	43.0	33.8	63.4	0.6	0.7	2.6	5.1	15.5	9.3	13.6	11.1	12.8
45 063	17900	2	Lexington	699.1	286 196	240	409.4	76.9	15.8	0.9	2.4	5.8	6.0	17.4	7.8	13.4	13.0	14.1
45 065	...	8	McCormick	359.1	9 643	2 457	26.9	51.2	47.2	0.5	0.8	1.4	3.1	9.5	5.4	10.4	9.8	13.0
45 067	...	6	Marion	489.3	31 726	1 386	64.8	39.9	56.8	0.9	1.0	2.6	6.1	17.4	8.3	11.3	11.6	12.5
45 069	13500	6	Marlboro	479.7	26 945	1 529	56.2	40.6	51.6	5.4	0.8	3.4	5.5	14.8	8.4	14.4	13.3	13.8
45 071	35140	6	Newberry	630.0	38 079	1 223	60.4	61.1	31.3	0.6	0.9	7.4	6.0	16.0	9.6	11.2	11.0	13.1
45 073	42860	4	Oconee	626.3	76 355	723	121.9	86.1	8.5	0.7	1.1	5.1	5.1	15.0	7.2	11.3	10.7	12.9
45 075	36700	4	Orangeburg	1 106.1	87 903	659	79.5	34.4	62.5	1.1	1.3	2.1	5.9	16.6	10.3	12.1	10.2	12.7
45 077	24860	2	Pickens	496.3	122 863	509	247.6	87.6	7.5	0.7	2.3	3.6	5.1	14.3	17.5	11.8	10.7	12.4
45 079	17900	2	Richland	757.2	409 549	170	540.9	44.7	48.1	0.8	3.6	5.1	5.9	15.7	16.0	14.9	12.2	12.0
45 081	17900	2	Saluda	452.8	20 197	1 821	44.6	59.1	25.6	0.7	0.5	15.2	6.2	16.0	7.5	11.8	11.5	13.8
45 083	43900	2	Spartanburg	808.0	301 463	230	373.1	70.1	21.6	0.6	2.7	6.6	6.1	17.2	9.3	13.1	12.1	13.7

1. CBSA = Core Based Statistical Area. See Appendix A for explanation. See Appendix B for list of metropolitan areas with component counties. 2. County type code from the Economic Research Service of USDA Rural-Urban Continuum Codes. See Appendix A for definition. 3. Dry land or land partially or temporarily covered by water. 4. May be of any race.

STATE County	55 to 64 years	65 to 74 years	75 years and over	Percent female	2000	2010	2000–2010	2010–2016	Births	Deaths	Net migration	Number	Persons per house-hold	Family house-holds	Female family house-holder[1]	One per-son
	16	17	18	19	20	21	22	23	24	25	26	27	28	29	30	31
PENNSYLVANIA—Cont'd																
Potter	15.8	12.8	10.0	50.0	18 080	17 458	-3.4	-3.3	1 164	1 281	-396	6 669	2.57	65.3	8.3	30.1
Schuylkill	14.8	11.0	9.0	48.9	150 336	148 289	-1.4	-3.2	8 563	11 970	-1 030	58 554	2.38	65.0	11.3	30.0
Snyder	13.6	9.7	7.6	50.6	37 546	39 709	5.8	1.9	2 801	2 207	194	14 442	2.62	72.7	9.4	22.6
Somerset	15.7	11.6	9.8	47.9	80 023	77 746	-2.8	-3.5	4 325	5 873	-1 020	29 619	2.42	69.4	8.6	26.8
Sullivan	18.9	15.6	12.2	47.7	6 556	6 428	-2.0	-4.5	298	685	81	2 669	2.22	62.2	5.4	33.0
Susquehanna	17.3	12.6	8.8	49.7	42 238	43 352	2.6	-5.7	2 305	2 764	-2 078	17 487	2.41	67.8	8.6	26.5
Tioga	15.1	11.7	9.1	50.4	41 373	41 983	1.5	-1.2	2 768	2 760	-474	16 611	2.47	67.4	8.6	26.8
Union	12.2	8.7	7.9	44.7	41 624	44 949	8.0	1.4	2 510	2 365	475	14 916	2.38	67.8	8.2	25.5
Venango	17.1	11.9	9.2	50.7	57 565	54 983	-4.5	-4.4	3 487	4 110	-1 680	22 129	2.38	68.1	11.3	28.1
Warren	16.6	12.1	9.5	49.8	43 863	41 815	-4.7	-4.3	2 492	3 122	-1 027	17 113	2.35	64.4	8.4	30.9
Washington	15.6	11.1	8.6	51.0	202 897	207 848	2.4	0.1	12 461	15 622	3 572	83 739	2.42	66.1	10.1	28.6
Wayne	16.7	13.4	8.6	46.8	47 722	52 825	10.7	-4.0	2 538	3 678	-1 100	19 306	2.47	68.7	9.3	26.6
Westmoreland	16.4	12.0	9.7	51.2	369 993	365 164	-1.3	-2.7	19 640	27 612	-1 179	151 173	2.33	66.6	10.4	28.9
Wyoming	15.5	12.2	7.7	49.8	28 080	28 269	0.7	-2.6	1 780	1 870	-637	10 894	2.52	67.5	10.8	26.3
York	14.2	9.6	7.0	50.6	381 751	434 998	13.9	2.0	30 522	23 932	2 896	167 416	2.57	69.6	11.2	24.7
RHODE ISLAND	13.9	9.2	7.3	51.4	1 048 319	1 052 940	0.4	0.3	68 094	60 437	-3 159	410 602	2.46	62.7	13.9	30.2
Bristol	15.4	10.3	9.1	51.7	50 648	49 875	-1.5	-1.6	2 174	3 118	130	19 290	2.38	66.1	9.1	28.2
Kent	15.5	10.3	8.1	51.8	167 090	166 158	-0.6	-0.9	9 874	10 776	-515	68 616	2.38	62.8	10.5	30.7
Newport	15.0	11.6	8.6	50.5	85 433	83 141	-2.7	-0.4	4 376	4 396	-123	34 848	2.27	60.2	9.8	32.3
Providence	12.8	8.0	6.7	51.4	621 602	626 672	0.8	1.1	45 976	35 272	-2 927	238 284	2.53	62.1	16.7	30.8
Washington	15.8	11.4	7.9	51.7	123 546	127 094	2.9	-0.6	5 694	6 875	276	49 564	2.42	65.9	9.8	26.3
SOUTH CAROLINA	13.3	10.3	6.4	51.5	4 012 012	4 625 410	15.3	7.3	358 823	277 145	243 861	1 815 094	2.56	66.8	15.0	28.0
Abbeville	14.6	12.3	8.2	51.5	26 167	25 416	-2.9	-2.1	1 575	1 702	-404	9 573	2.52	68.2	15.9	29.2
Aiken	14.3	11.1	7.4	51.6	142 552	160 106	12.3	4.6	11 825	10 369	5 574	63 706	2.53	67.7	14.2	28.2
Allendale	14.1	12.2	6.3	47.0	11 211	10 419	-7.1	-13.2	613	694	-1 299	3 346	2.58	60.7	24.1	36.6
Anderson	13.4	10.5	7.2	51.9	165 740	187 123	12.9	5.0	14 020	12 542	7 707	74 023	2.55	69.2	13.4	26.9
Bamberg	14.6	11.6	8.1	51.8	16 658	15 987	-4.0	-9.7	948	1 099	-1 371	5 921	2.41	61.0	18.6	36.5
Barnwell	14.2	10.5	6.5	52.3	23 478	22 621	-3.7	-5.0	1 788	1 636	-1 307	8 344	2.61	67.7	20.6	28.6
Beaufort	13.4	15.8	9.8	50.8	120 937	162 233	34.1	12.9	12 847	8 920	16 207	65 975	2.51	68.1	10.2	26.5
Berkeley	12.2	8.6	4.4	50.3	142 651	177 867	24.7	18.6	16 306	7 992	23 676	69 030	2.75	71.2	14.5	23.7
Calhoun	16.2	13.7	7.8	51.8	15 185	15 176	-0.1	-2.5	890	1 068	-253	6 028	2.45	67.5	15.6	29.0
Charleston	13.1	9.5	5.8	51.6	309 969	350 196	13.0	13.2	30 224	18 960	33 450	148 018	2.44	58.9	13.4	31.9
Cherokee	12.9	9.6	6.2	51.2	52 537	55 471	5.6	2.1	4 267	3 699	749	20 523	2.68	66.4	14.7	30.1
Chester	14.6	10.8	6.9	51.6	34 068	33 140	-2.7	-2.9	2 468	2 422	-941	12 385	2.61	65.2	19.3	31.6
Chesterfield	14.0	10.4	6.4	51.4	42 768	46 737	9.3	-1.5	3 216	3 157	-734	18 022	2.52	70.1	17.7	26.7
Clarendon	15.0	13.1	8.0	50.7	32 502	34 966	7.6	-2.9	2 167	2 340	-766	13 161	2.47	66.9	18.4	29.7
Colleton	14.5	12.2	7.7	52.0	38 264	38 892	1.6	-2.5	2 841	3 137	-803	14 774	2.53	66.7	19.5	29.2
Darlington	14.3	10.9	6.9	52.7	67 394	68 692	1.9	-2.1	4 976	5 062	-1 277	26 417	2.52	68.4	19.5	27.7
Dillon	13.5	9.6	6.4	52.5	30 722	32 062	4.4	-3.8	2 676	2 299	-1 602	11 514	2.69	69.8	24.0	27.9
Dorchester	12.4	8.3	4.4	51.3	96 413	136 581	41.7	12.6	11 476	5 967	11 074	51 856	2.77	71.6	15.4	23.9
Edgefield	14.9	10.8	6.4	46.2	24 595	26 978	9.7	-2.3	1 242	1 333	-573	9 096	2.60	71.0	14.8	26.9
Fairfield	17.2	12.4	7.3	52.2	23 454	23 956	2.1	-5.4	1 374	1 784	-861	8 990	2.52	68.1	18.1	30.0
Florence	13.1	9.8	6.3	53.3	125 761	136 879	8.8	1.4	11 023	9 204	88	51 847	2.61	68.7	18.7	27.6
Georgetown	16.1	16.3	9.6	52.4	55 797	60 158	7.8	2.1	3 621	4 482	1 843	23 566	2.55	69.6	14.5	27.0
Greenville	12.6	9.0	6.0	51.5	379 616	451 221	18.9	10.5	38 822	24 578	32 161	179 862	2.58	67.1	12.9	28.2
Greenwood	12.8	9.9	7.8	53.3	66 271	69 661	5.1	0.7	5 503	4 421	-590	26 709	2.52	65.7	17.4	29.1
Hampton	13.6	10.5	6.8	48.6	21 386	21 090	-1.4	-5.5	1 393	1 345	-1 246	7 530	2.53	65.8	19.7	31.7
Horry	15.3	14.8	7.5	51.7	196 629	269 291	37.0	19.7	19 261	18 558	50 457	118 738	2.43	64.4	11.7	28.9
Jasper	13.6	12.2	6.2	49.2	20 678	24 777	19.8	14.9	2 109	1 461	2 953	9 095	2.85	68.6	18.7	25.2
Kershaw	14.4	10.6	6.6	51.6	52 647	61 570	16.9	4.1	4 512	4 050	2 065	24 194	2.58	70.1	16.0	25.7
Lancaster	12.6	12.9	7.3	51.3	61 351	76 652	24.9	16.9	5 937	5 026	11 478	29 395	2.70	69.1	16.4	27.4
Laurens	14.2	10.5	7.2	51.7	69 567	66 539	-4.4	0.4	4 768	5 000	414	25 160	2.54	71.9	18.2	24.3
Lee	14.6	11.0	7.0	49.0	20 119	19 222	-4.5	-8.3	1 105	1 452	-1 281	6 385	2.63	65.8	22.6	31.2
Lexington	13.4	9.3	5.7	51.3	216 014	262 396	21.5	9.1	20 315	14 109	17 069	106 637	2.54	68.0	13.0	26.3
McCormick	16.5	20.7	11.7	45.9	9 958	10 233	2.8	-5.8	376	791	-191	4 003	2.15	69.5	15.7	27.1
Marion	14.6	11.4	6.9	53.9	35 466	33 062	-6.8	-4.0	2 498	2 682	-1 113	11 958	2.67	67.0	23.2	28.6
Marlboro	13.5	10.3	6.1	47.4	28 818	28 933	0.4	-6.9	1 913	2 024	-1 878	9 950	2.50	67.4	18.2	29.2
Newberry	14.2	11.4	7.5	51.1	36 108	37 508	3.9	1.5	2 786	2 618	389	14 287	2.55	68.7	17.2	27.5
Oconee	15.4	13.8	8.5	50.8	66 215	74 275	12.2	2.8	4 916	5 328	2 557	30 556	2.43	69.2	12.3	26.3
Orangeburg	14.0	11.0	7.2	53.2	91 582	92 495	1.0	-5.0	6 710	6 618	-4 593	33 410	2.63	63.5	19.2	33.6
Pickens	12.3	9.4	6.5	50.1	110 757	119 226	7.6	3.1	7 652	6 972	2 780	44 646	2.53	65.0	10.0	26.3
Richland	11.3	7.5	4.6	51.5	320 677	384 507	19.9	6.5	30 259	17 967	12 706	145 069	2.53	60.9	17.5	31.7
Saluda	13.9	11.3	8.0	49.6	19 181	19 872	3.6	1.6	1 554	1 243	17	7 059	2.78	70.6	14.8	25.6
Spartanburg	12.7	9.5	6.2	51.5	253 791	284 305	12.0	6.0	22 363	17 866	12 372	109 892	2.58	69.6	15.9	26.1

1. No spouse present.

Table B. States and Counties — **Population, Vital Statistics, Health, and Crime**

STATE County	Persons in group quarters, 2016	Daytime population, 2011–2015 Number	Daytime population, 2011–2015 Employment/residence ratio	Births, 2016 Total	Births, 2016 Rate[1]	Deaths, 2016 Number	Deaths, 2016 Rate[1]	Persons under 65 with no health insurance, 2015 Number	Persons under 65 with no health insurance, 2015 Percent	Medicare, 2015 Total Beneficiaries	Medicare, 2015 Enrolled in Original Medicare	Medicare, 2015 Enrolled in Medicare Advantage	Serious crimes known to police,[2] 2014 Total Number	Serious crimes known to police,[2] 2014 Total Rate[3]
	32	33	34	35	36	37	38	39	40	41	42	43	44	45
PENNSYLVANIA—Cont'd														
Potter	217	17 153	0.97	179	10.6	215	12.7	1 027	7.8	4 262	3 000	1 262	207	1 222
Schuylkill	6 602	136 017	0.83	1 326	9.2	1 849	12.9	8 756	7.9	33 407	23 279	10 128	2 541	1 756
Snyder	2 591	39 187	0.95	455	11.2	356	8.8	3 275	10.5	7 650	4 190	3 460	579	1 513
Somerset	4 958	71 684	0.85	693	9.2	960	12.8	4 843	8.7	18 032	7 108	10 924	870	1 142
Sullivan	439	5 939	0.83	43	7.0	102	16.6	407	8.9	1 712	1 200	512	76	1 199
Susquehanna	282	36 447	0.68	359	8.8	433	10.6	3 068	9.3	9 057	7 048	2 009	506	1 276
Tioga	1 578	41 579	0.96	447	10.8	461	11.1	2 738	8.6	9 707	7 176	2 531	528	1 240
Union	9 370	47 328	1.14	386	8.5	408	9.0	2 624	8.9	7 736	4 680	3 056	409	912
Venango	1 301	52 383	0.93	533	10.1	680	12.9	3 042	7.3	13 161	8 188	4 973	872	1 626
Warren	760	39 891	0.94	394	9.8	519	13.0	2 243	7.1	9 281	7 062	2 219	616	1 515
Washington	5 516	201 498	0.93	2 001	9.6	2 541	12.2	9 400	5.7	47 156	16 294	30 862	3 898	1 896
Wayne	3 881	48 183	0.83	399	7.9	560	11.0	2 991	8.1	16 723	13 763	2 960	724	1 414
Westmoreland	6 973	335 568	0.85	3 040	8.6	4 523	12.7	16 343	5.9	84 112	26 664	57 448	5 864	1 640
Wyoming	607	27 967	0.99	270	9.8	318	11.6	1 506	6.9	6 594	4 494	2 100	411	1 471
York	8 745	405 114	0.84	4 872	11.0	3 997	9.0	25 815	7.1	81 673	51 279	30 394	8 253	1 877
RHODE ISLAND	42 752	1 031 168	0.96	10 770	10.2	9 849	9.3	56 939	6.7	189 994	114 997	74 997	25 248	2 393
Bristol	2 709	40 217	0.63	334	6.8	536	10.9	1 683	4.4	9 440	5 289	4 151	684	1 389
Kent	1 565	154 494	0.87	1 566	9.5	1 716	10.4	6 521	4.8	33 885	19 444	14 441	3 257	1 969
Newport	3 973	84 818	1.05	672	8.1	729	8.8	3 220	5.0	17 224	12 496	4 728	1 987	2 406
Providence	27 473	633 057	1.01	7 312	11.5	5 674	9.0	41 503	8.0	105 069	61 569	43 500	17 326	2 744
Washington	7 032	118 582	0.88	886	7.0	1 194	9.5	4 012	4.1	24 376	16 199	8 177	1 912	1 511
SOUTH CAROLINA	136 582	4 742 106	0.98	57 926	11.7	47 514	9.6	517 674	13.0	928 369	691 524	236 845	191 269	3 958
Abbeville	963	21 611	0.63	245	9.9	261	10.5	2 528	13.1	4 705	3 257	1 448	605	2 622
Aiken	2 268	160 097	0.94	1 927	11.5	1 766	10.5	16 143	12.1	33 992	25 977	8 015	6 600	3 980
Allendale	1 185	10 080	1.09	82	9.1	103	11.4	821	12.7	1 857	1 091	766	178	2 257
Anderson	2 907	179 472	0.85	2 273	11.6	2 130	10.8	20 262	12.8	39 590	26 546	13 044	10 786	5 608
Bamberg	995	14 813	0.88	132	9.1	179	12.4	1 513	13.6	2 968	2 018	950	521	3 390
Barnwell	285	21 126	0.88	251	11.7	277	12.9	2 252	12.6	4 400	3 100	1 300	996	4 508
Beaufort	5 234	175 206	1.05	2 058	11.2	1 557	8.5	20 613	15.9	43 663	35 782	7 881	5 313	3 040
Berkeley	3 611	165 169	0.67	2 695	12.8	1 454	6.9	22 299	12.9	22 804	17 429	5 375	5 600	2 822
Calhoun	155	11 754	0.48	134	9.1	186	12.6	1 562	13.4	2 297	1 661	636	402	2 738
Charleston	10 617	432 545	1.33	5 051	12.7	3 412	8.6	40 689	12.6	71 066	56 558	14 508	12 662	3 342
Cherokee	1 181	53 936	0.91	680	12.0	591	10.4	6 218	13.3	10 457	6 971	3 486	2 026	3 603
Chester	218	28 982	0.70	378	11.7	402	12.5	3 132	11.8	7 165	5 229	1 936	1 245	3 820
Chesterfield	874	45 309	0.95	512	11.1	549	11.9	5 639	14.8	8 503	6 933	1 570	1 649	3 562
Clarendon	1 598	31 169	0.73	334	9.8	375	11.0	3 548	14.1	7 598	5 610	1 988	1 401	4 077
Colleton	388	35 401	0.82	456	12.0	569	15.0	4 841	16.0	8 316	5 942	2 374	1 859	4 934
Darlington	1 378	64 022	0.85	807	12.0	824	12.3	7 198	13.1	13 339	10 805	2 534	2 867	4 212
Dillon	482	30 505	0.91	404	13.1	375	12.2	4 286	16.5	5 896	4 452	1 444	1 967	6 313
Dorchester	1 879	117 251	0.58	1 916	12.5	1 086	7.1	14 476	10.9	21 065	16 093	4 972	5 426	3 715
Edgefield	2 806	23 487	0.70	202	7.7	260	9.9	2 433	12.5	3 366	2 348	1 018	458	1 733
Fairfield	397	21 789	0.84	194	8.6	282	12.4	2 374	13.0	4 681	3 268	1 413	906	3 934
Florence	3 314	148 040	1.17	1 705	12.3	1 516	10.9	13 281	11.6	29 072	24 580	4 492	6 414	4 647
Georgetown	553	60 360	0.99	558	9.1	813	13.2	6 300	13.8	18 215	14 421	3 794	2 385	3 931
Greenville	11 155	506 511	1.15	6 441	12.9	4 224	8.5	55 783	13.6	84 146	55 992	28 154	19 328	4 010
Greenwood	2 431	70 954	1.04	844	12.0	777	11.1	8 469	15.3	15 964	11 777	4 187	3 311	4 728
Hampton	1 533	19 492	0.87	209	10.5	237	11.9	1 889	12.4	4 669	3 338	1 331	567	3 364
Horry	3 725	292 246	1.01	3 133	9.7	3 302	10.2	41 618	17.4	75 011	61 271	13 740	16 896	5 709
Jasper	1 488	23 295	0.72	366	12.9	261	9.2	4 149	19.2	3 775	2 564	1 211	1 076	3 957
Kershaw	402	56 173	0.75	739	11.5	740	11.5	6 740	12.8	13 422	10 590	2 832	1 614	2 562
Lancaster	1 962	72 420	0.73	1 043	11.6	886	9.9	8 582	12.8	12 491	10 099	2 392	2 991	3 660
Laurens	2 402	61 750	0.83	746	11.2	831	12.4	7 802	14.7	13 310	9 069	4 241	2 811	4 230
Lee	1 651	16 135	0.61	161	9.1	284	16.1	1 661	12.6	3 311	2 491	820	764	4 193
Lexington	2 336	257 860	0.88	3 220	11.3	2 384	8.3	26 590	11.1	45 846	35 720	10 126	8 259	3 000
McCormick	1 119	9 201	0.75	67	6.9	144	14.9	680	12.3	3 410	2 261	1 149	157	1 583
Marion	204	28 266	0.66	386	12.2	443	14.0	3 356	13.0	7 623	6 089	1 534	2 096	6 551
Marlboro	2 909	26 396	0.83	310	11.5	305	11.3	2 868	14.4	6 160	4 674	1 486	1 323	4 741
Newberry	1 191	37 105	0.96	451	11.8	441	11.6	4 311	14.4	8 578	6 324	2 254	1 088	2 888
Oconee	792	73 657	0.95	782	10.2	904	11.8	7 946	13.6	19 271	14 217	5 054	2 396	3 171
Orangeburg	2 932	90 218	0.99	954	10.9	1 118	12.7	9 411	13.4	19 354	12 934	6 420	4 299	4 801
Pickens	6 829	110 798	0.81	1 284	10.5	1 141	9.3	13 794	14.3	25 004	16 388	8 616	4 655	3 862
Richland	31 335	435 222	1.20	4 888	11.9	3 108	7.6	35 001	10.6	56 286	44 147	12 139	19 952	4 932
Saluda	265	17 865	0.73	254	12.6	192	9.5	3 032	18.8	2 998	2 110	888	361	1 785
Spartanburg	8 228	297 692	1.05	3 604	12.0	2 986	9.9	31 694	13.0	62 395	38 817	23 578	9 989	3 399

1. Per 1,000 estimated resident population.   2. Data for serious crimes have not been adjusted for underreporting; this may affect comparability between geographic areas and over time.
3. Per 100,000 population estimated by the FBI.

Table B. States and Counties — Crime, Education, Money Income, and Poverty

STATE County	Serious crimes known to police, 2014 (cont.)[1] Rate[2] Violent	Property	Education — School enrollment and attainment, 2011–2015 — Enrollment[3] Total	Percent private	Attainment[4] (percent) High school graduate or less	Bachelor's degree or more	Local government expenditures,[5] 2013–2014 Total current spending (mil dol)	Current spending per student (dollars)	Money income, 2011–2015 Per capita income[6] (dollars)	Median income (dollars)	Households Percent with income of less than $50,000	with income of $200,000 or more	Income and poverty, 2015 Median household income (dollars)	Percent below poverty level All persons	Children under 18 years	Children 5 to 17 years in families
	46	47	48	49	50	51	52	53	54	55	56	57	58	59	60	61
PENNSYLVANIA—Cont'd																
Potter	183	1 039	3 565	10.8	60.4	15.7	32.8	13 456	22 318	40 654	58.9	1.9	41 754	14.3	23.6	22.0
Schuylkill	158	1 598	29 280	14.4	60.3	15.4	242.4	13 055	23 682	45 535	53.5	1.7	45 733	13.0	19.0	17.6
Snyder	167	1 346	9 760	34.5	63.6	16.5	54.9	11 224	23 836	49 917	50.1	2.7	49 803	11.7	18.0	17.0
Somerset	105	1 037	13 928	14.4	62.8	15.3	120.6	12 666	22 980	44 587	55.5	1.8	43 608	14.4	21.8	19.7
Sullivan	79	1 121	962	12.9	59.5	16.1	11.7	19 429	25 054	44 189	55.8	1.6	43 844	13.5	20.7	19.8
Susquehanna	96	1 180	8 278	16.5	57.6	17.1	96.2	15 019	25 958	50 477	49.5	2.3	50 141	12.6	19.6	18.3
Tioga	101	1 139	9 101	13.5	56.2	19.6	71.3	13 125	23 980	46 494	53.3	1.8	48 186	13.1	18.9	17.6
Union	74	839	11 433	49.2	57.3	20.5	51.4	12 932	22 863	49 803	50.3	4.1	57 862	12.4	13.6	12.5
Venango	125	1 501	10 725	13.2	60.6	15.8	81.0	13 127	23 380	43 644	56.3	1.2	44 916	13.5	23.2	22.1
Warren	152	1 362	7 933	14.5	56.7	18.1	61.0	12 525	24 830	44 020	56.3	1.3	45 362	12.2	22.7	21.2
Washington	167	1 729	46 431	17.9	48.0	27.4	378.2	13 538	30 605	56 450	44.4	4.6	57 622	10.1	13.8	12.4
Wayne	102	1 313	9 640	15.0	55.0	19.7	77.0	15 830	24 539	49 919	50.1	2.3	49 927	13.3	20.7	19.2
Westmoreland	165	1 475	76 053	18.4	46.2	26.4	589.2	12 210	29 472	52 247	47.4	3.5	53 422	11.3	15.5	13.4
Wyoming	79	1 393	6 010	21.0	57.0	18.2	54.6	14 902	26 087	51 004	49.1	2.5	51 797	11.1	17.7	16.6
York	206	1 671	103 359	19.7	52.7	22.8	818.4	12 189	28 403	58 269	42.5	3.0	58 527	10.4	15.2	15.3
RHODE ISLAND	219	2 174	269 928	26.2	41.2	31.9	2 138.1	15 071	31 118	56 852	44.6	5.2	57 265	14.1	20.6	19.3
Bristol	65	1 324	13 450	39.1	31.6	45.1	96.1	14 209	39 196	72 458	35.9	9.6	75 324	9.3	9.7	8.4
Kent	115	1 854	36 570	21.5	37.9	30.9	347.4	15 773	34 824	64 383	39.0	4.9	65 332	8.7	12.5	11.3
Newport	180	2 226	19 574	33.1	30.3	45.1	151.6	15 875	40 320	69 526	36.9	7.8	66 096	11.1	13.8	11.9
Providence	290	2 455	164 533	28.1	46.7	26.8	1 282.9	14 615	27 162	49 943	50.2	4.0	50 364	17.2	25.7	24.7
Washington	73	1 438	35 621	13.6	29.8	44.1	260.1	16 511	36 851	72 807	34.4	7.5	71 951	9.9	11.3	10.0
SOUTH CAROLINA	498	3 460	1 202 214	14.5	44.2	25.8	7 211.5	9 671	24 604	45 483	53.9	2.9	47 308	16.8	24.4	23.5
Abbeville	316	2 306	5 797	17.8	59.4	12.3	28.7	9 170	18 112	34 799	66.2	0.9	35 932	19.1	26.2	24.9
Aiken	370	3 610	38 840	13.6	45.6	25.3	203.3	8 226	25 321	45 759	53.5	2.5	48 012	18.1	27.1	25.4
Allendale	469	1 788	2 139	7.9	64.7	12.6	19.0	14 435	12 199	25 327	78.8	0.1	27 089	41.0	50.6	49.1
Anderson	546	5 062	46 034	14.1	48.7	19.5	286.3	9 092	22 400	42 143	57.2	1.8	44 745	17.2	25.1	23.4
Bamberg	416	2 974	4 480	12.1	48.7	18.2	26.0	12 022	18 215	31 314	71.4	0.9	29 642	32.7	43.9	42.7
Barnwell	738	3 770	5 817	10.3	58.3	11.9	42.2	10 093	19 026	34 336	64.5	0.3	33 280	27.3	38.2	37.6
Beaufort	469	2 570	35 462	17.4	31.3	38.8	223.7	10 792	32 401	57 048	43.6	6.2	60 071	12.9	21.3	20.1
Berkeley	307	2 515	49 485	15.9	43.3	22.3	275.5	8 672	24 826	52 506	47.0	2.6	55 876	13.0	18.7	18.3
Calhoun	368	2 370	3 396	24.4	53.2	16.8	18.8	10 668	24 900	43 531	57.2	2.9	41 277	21.3	29.4	27.4
Charleston	418	2 923	93 066	17.3	31.9	40.4	507.1	11 107	32 162	53 437	46.8	6.1	56 244	14.9	22.9	22.7
Cherokee	363	3 240	13 473	12.3	59.2	15.3	83.4	9 133	19 279	35 389	64.3	1.2	37 098	20.3	29.7	29.2
Chester	706	3 114	7 522	10.7	57.9	13.8	52.9	9 721	18 819	31 914	66.4	1.0	35 006	25.7	38.0	36.9
Chesterfield	402	3 160	10 722	8.2	63.3	11.8	69.2	9 332	17 840	32 083	67.9	0.7	36 520	23.5	33.7	31.5
Clarendon	512	3 565	7 522	15.2	57.1	14.3	48.1	9 580	18 535	33 162	68.0	1.6	34 654	25.4	38.1	36.5
Colleton	865	4 068	8 719	7.7	55.7	14.0	55.9	9 145	19 015	32 804	66.7	1.4	33 745	23.1	36.7	35.5
Darlington	436	3 776	16 547	14.3	55.8	16.9	97.8	9 437	19 810	35 409	63.7	1.4	36 719	21.5	33.4	32.0
Dillon	867	5 447	7 734	7.6	66.0	9.0	48.8	8 158	14 736	28 938	72.0	0.4	31 094	31.2	42.8	40.4
Dorchester	412	3 302	39 331	15.4	39.2	25.0	230.8	8 681	25 223	54 901	45.2	2.4	55 595	13.6	18.8	17.5
Edgefield	117	1 616	6 064	12.5	54.9	18.3	35.9	10 495	21 723	46 637	53.2	1.2	46 430	18.9	27.1	24.3
Fairfield	677	3 256	4 718	11.8	59.8	14.3	42.0	14 185	20 401	36 004	64.7	1.7	36 622	23.0	33.4	31.0
Florence	490	4 158	36 845	13.3	49.5	21.7	219.4	9 375	22 877	42 080	56.8	2.5	41 197	20.3	28.7	27.5
Georgetown	458	3 473	12 587	10.5	45.1	25.8	101.1	10 413	25 216	42 835	54.8	3.7	44 395	19.3	32.0	30.8
Greenville	584	3 427	119 737	23.0	39.6	32.1	622.9	8 363	27 200	50 540	49.4	3.9	52 017	13.8	17.7	17.5
Greenwood	578	4 149	18 501	9.8	49.0	23.0	103.1	8 741	21 287	37 060	61.3	2.3	42 240	19.1	26.2	24.5
Hampton	611	2 753	4 510	6.5	64.0	10.6	37.0	11 047	20 046	31 410	66.2	1.6	30 772	23.6	35.1	34.0
Horry	536	5 173	61 196	9.9	44.2	22.8	418.1	10 213	24 094	43 299	57.0	2.0	47 083	16.7	29.6	28.4
Jasper	276	3 681	5 995	18.9	58.0	15.0	35.8	12 569	17 565	37 141	68.6	0.6	37 231	23.2	40.1	40.3
Kershaw	317	2 244	14 991	9.7	49.6	20.3	93.4	8 901	22 434	46 022	55.4	1.8	48 233	15.5	23.3	22.5
Lancaster	497	3 163	17 765	9.8	49.7	21.9	104.5	8 736	22 647	44 016	56.0	2.1	47 279	14.4	21.0	20.0
Laurens	582	3 648	15 416	11.9	56.2	14.6	85.0	9 294	20 072	38 515	62.4	1.2	39 731	18.9	30.7	28.0
Lee	653	3 540	4 276	14.0	64.1	10.7	22.3	9 956	15 662	30 954	70.6	0.6	31 525	28.3	38.6	37.6
Lexington	340	2 660	68 646	12.3	39.3	29.2	390.3	10 097	27 248	53 857	46.0	3.1	55 413	13.2	19.1	18.0
McCormick	121	1 462	1 548	13.8	51.4	18.0	10.6	12 419	22 201	38 712	60.5	2.5	41 589	19.2	35.2	34.5
Marion	700	5 851	7 931	14.6	57.8	15.6	49.1	9 496	17 553	29 874	69.9	0.7	30 528	24.4	41.1	40.0
Marlboro	914	3 827	6 034	5.4	67.1	8.5	40.2	9 441	15 682	30 767	70.1	1.1	32 485	28.2	37.9	37.1
Newberry	289	2 598	8 876	16.7	56.5	16.6	61.6	10 140	21 267	40 127	57.4	1.4	41 120	19.1	28.5	27.7
Oconee	449	2 723	16 623	10.0	48.6	22.8	111.4	10 559	24 666	41 237	57.4	3.0	44 819	18.0	25.1	23.6
Orangeburg	530	4 270	23 870	13.1	52.5	19.3	158.3	11 414	17 889	34 218	65.9	0.9	37 651	24.0	36.8	36.0
Pickens	316	3 546	38 114	19.6	48.3	22.4	131.4	7 858	21 222	41 459	58.8	1.6	44 091	18.1	19.4	18.4
Richland	805	4 128	124 416	15.7	32.4	36.4	913.0	10 945	26 026	49 131	50.6	3.5	51 065	15.8	22.3	21.5
Saluda	242	1 543	4 058	9.8	61.9	14.0	20.9	9 583	20 430	38 827	61.1	1.8	41 409	18.3	29.6	29.4
Spartanburg	380	3 019	75 028	14.9	46.6	22.7	463.9	9 782	22 618	43 907	55.3	2.1	45 768	15.0	21.5	20.8

1. Data for serious crimes have not been adjusted for underreporting; this may affect comparability between geographic areas and over time.   2. Per 100,000 population estimated by the FBI.
3. All persons 3 years old and over enrolled in nursery school through college.   4. Persons 25 years old and over.   5. Elementary and secondary education expenditures.
6. Based on population estimated by the American Community Survey, 2011–2015.

Table B. States and Counties — Personal Income

STATE County	Personal income, 2015										Earnings, 2015		
	Total (mil dol)	Percent change, 2014–2015	Per capita[1] Dollars	Rank	Wages and salaries (mil dol)	Supplements to wages and salaries; employer contributions (mil dol) Pension and insurance	Government social insurance	Proprietors' income (mil dol)	Dividends, interest, and rent (mil dol)	Personal transfer receipts (mil dol)	Total (mil dol)	Contributions for government social insurance (mil dol) From employee and self-employed	From employer
	62	63	64	65	66	67	68	69	70	71	72	73	74
PENNSYLVANIA—Cont'd													
Potter	602	2.0	35 208	1 798	216	56	18	65	94	181	356	22	18
Schuylkill	5 717	3.8	39 539	1 478	2 043	470	174	299	861	1 541	2 985	191	174
Snyder	1 558	5.0	38 519	1 768	546	128	47	172	222	414	893	52	47
Somerset	2 769	2.0	36 671	1 838	946	236	79	220	465	758	1 481	96	79
Sullivan	253	3.7	39 995	1 489	67	18	6	19	63	74	109	8	6
Susquehanna	1 680	3.0	40 317	1 532	388	97	31	197	320	379	713	46	31
Tioga	1 502	1.8	35 877	2 053	553	142	45	106	259	398	847	53	45
Union	1 636	3.6	36 391	1 989	763	169	64	193	265	311	1 189	67	64
Venango	2 029	2.1	38 205	1 755	741	195	61	108	309	658	1 105	72	61
Warren	1 686	-1.6	41 745	1 471	602	146	49	243	271	417	1 039	62	49
Washington	11 201	7.9	53 783	466	5 134	871	383	1 391	1 675	2 084	7 779	456	383
Wayne	1 917	3.6	37 447	1 943	587	144	48	166	377	522	945	62	48
Westmoreland	16 739	3.7	46 764	723	5 973	1 182	493	992	2 641	3 701	8 641	550	493
Wyoming	1 150	3.0	41 369	1 559	488	97	40	121	181	251	746	44	40
York	19 774	4.0	44 651	842	8 301	1 630	682	975	2 966	3 734	11 588	693	682
RHODE ISLAND	52 834	4.3	50 050	X	25 577	4 130	2 104	3 646	9 477	10 670	35 458	2 340	2 104
Bristol	3 390	3.9	69 066	75	646	114	54	202	924	421	1 016	75	54
Kent	8 862	4.1	53 776	316	3 707	571	314	467	1 387	1 650	5 058	347	314
Newport	5 083	3.4	61 666	164	2 272	438	202	405	1 335	790	3 317	207	202
Providence	28 126	4.6	44 399	778	16 356	2 484	1 318	1 873	4 302	6 673	22 032	1 451	1 318
Washington	7 373	4.0	58 274	231	2 597	523	216	699	1 528	1 135	4 035	261	216
SOUTH CAROLINA	187 532	5.4	38 312	X	90 324	15 152	6 993	12 530	31 309	42 679	124 999	8 058	6 993
Abbeville	760	4.4	30 468	2 775	223	47	19	46	96	252	335	26	19
Aiken	6 200	4.3	37 389	1 560	3 031	429	233	267	991	1 499	3 960	268	233
Allendale	266	1.3	28 199	2 894	116	26	9	9	39	99	160	11	9
Anderson	6 872	4.6	35 297	2 077	2 619	461	204	335	947	1 798	3 620	254	204
Bamberg	444	-1.1	29 845	2 761	147	32	11	16	61	164	206	15	11
Barnwell	602	1.3	27 704	2 969	190	39	15	23	91	216	268	20	15
Beaufort	8 644	4.8	48 134	588	3 123	563	259	607	2 882	1 686	4 552	292	259
Berkeley	7 033	6.3	34 684	1 965	2 485	382	186	323	986	1 418	3 377	224	186
Calhoun	501	3.2	33 874	1 834	199	39	15	18	77	145	271	19	15
Charleston	19 789	5.3	50 838	486	12 611	2 132	978	2 425	4 485	2 962	18 145	1 064	978
Cherokee	1 652	4.5	29 394	2 901	736	124	60	72	207	519	993	70	60
Chester	982	4.8	30 441	2 797	375	68	29	42	120	329	513	37	29
Chesterfield	1 379	4.9	29 962	2 847	573	101	45	64	154	419	782	54	45
Clarendon	935	3.4	27 692	2 973	248	52	19	43	137	374	362	30	19
Colleton	1 250	4.8	33 120	2 440	379	70	30	62	177	420	541	41	30
Darlington	2 275	3.1	33 680	2 307	993	169	75	44	302	693	1 281	91	75
Dillon	795	4.1	25 461	3 071	299	54	25	7	93	311	384	31	25
Dorchester	5 484	6.4	35 966	2 245	1 287	225	100	225	742	1 165	1 837	129	100
Edgefield	827	4.5	31 173	2 786	236	48	18	47	115	217	349	25	18
Fairfield	765	4.3	33 633	2 533	691	113	53	25	103	239	883	55	53
Florence	5 184	3.9	37 322	1 709	2 855	485	216	258	723	1 374	3 814	247	216
Georgetown	2 445	4.6	39 888	1 209	965	160	75	136	598	716	1 336	97	75
Greenville	21 215	6.2	43 132	1 089	13 148	1 881	1 000	1 738	3 130	3 769	17 766	1 110	1 000
Greenwood	2 355	4.4	33 723	2 293	1 198	236	91	99	373	688	1 623	107	91
Hampton	549	2.2	27 398	2 967	201	40	15	10	80	194	266	21	15
Horry	10 151	6.4	32 830	2 438	4 363	677	352	734	1 885	3 091	6 125	436	352
Jasper	722	8.2	25 951	3 075	340	55	26	52	90	231	473	33	26
Kershaw	2 364	5.6	37 163	1 817	787	137	61	141	317	599	1 127	76	61
Lancaster	3 266	8.3	38 043	1 948	1 072	177	80	356	420	807	1 685	118	80
Laurens	2 092	4.0	31 406	2 701	929	163	72	72	262	717	1 237	88	72
Lee	473	2.6	26 425	3 020	132	27	10	12	59	194	182	15	10
Lexington	11 770	6.7	41 764	1 189	5 067	839	386	945	1 590	2 138	7 236	460	386
McCormick	326	4.1	33 608	2 571	62	16	5	13	71	126	95	10	5
Marion	910	3.5	28 674	2 778	235	46	19	26	108	348	326	28	19
Marlboro	692	1.8	25 161	3 068	317	59	25	3	89	275	403	31	25
Newberry	1 318	5.0	34 660	2 163	521	97	41	49	184	366	708	49	41
Oconee	2 859	4.4	37 761	1 807	1 199	227	91	124	529	769	1 641	116	91
Orangeburg	2 728	3.3	30 578	2 763	1 182	218	94	77	358	926	1 572	111	94
Pickens	4 127	4.7	33 911	2 385	1 444	279	109	218	628	1 012	2 050	143	109
Richland	16 699	5.5	41 025	1 351	10 906	1 996	842	1 160	2 721	3 175	14 904	870	842
Saluda	644	5.1	32 113	2 703	153	32	12	35	81	180	232	17	12
Spartanburg	11 501	5.6	38 686	1 671	6 238	980	475	820	2 166	2 563	8 512	552	475

1. Based on the resident population estimated as of July 1 of the year shown.

Table B. States and Counties — Earnings, Social Security, and Housing

STATE County	Earnings, 2015 (cont.) Percent by selected industries									Social Security beneficiaries, December 2015			Housing units, 2016	
	Farm	Mining	Construction	Manufacturing	Information: professional, scientific, technical services	Retail trade	Finance, insurance, real estate and leasing	Health care and social assistance	Government	Number	Rate[1]	Supplemental Security Income recipients, December 2015	Total	Percent change, 2010–2016
	75	76	77	78	79	80	81	82	83	84	85	86	87	88
PENNSYLVANIA—Cont'd														
Potter	2.2	0.8	7.0	10.6	13.7	4.9	3.1	D	18.6	4 940	290	475	12 789	-1.1
Schuylkill	1.2	1.4	4.6	23.2	4.0	6.2	3.4	13.4	18.7	38 170	264	3 862	68 854	-0.7
Snyder	4.8	D	6.5	22.9	3.3	10.8	3.2	D	17.8	8 875	219	649	16 178	0.9
Somerset	0.7	4.2	6.7	11.2	4.0	7.1	4.5	12.9	22.0	20 285	268	2 242	37 886	-0.6
Sullivan	0.5	D	16.3	D	D	5.2	D	D	23.8	1 925	306	142	6 289	-0.2
Susquehanna	0.2	13.7	17.7	4.2	4.7	6.4	4.4	D	18.2	10 880	262	913	23 035	0.3
Tioga	1.0	4.9	6.3	14.3	5.7	7.3	4.2	D	21.9	10 955	263	1 097	21 472	0.5
Union	4.1	D	5.9	7.1	2.7	6.0	3.4	D	22.3	8 500	187	549	17 084	0.5
Venango	-0.3	1.4	4.7	24.1	2.6	7.2	3.6	14.8	21.7	15 460	291	2 124	27 195	-1.0
Warren	0.1	13.3	4.5	16.7	3.2	6.3	5.8	12.0	14.2	11 120	276	949	23 273	-1.2
Washington	0.0	11.3	11.3	9.4	7.8	4.8	7.6	10.3	9.3	52 595	253	5 061	94 548	1.7
Wayne	0.6	0.4	12.5	2.9	4.3	9.3	5.4	15.0	26.3	14 465	283	1 120	31 930	0.9
Westmoreland	0.0	1.2	8.7	15.1	7.1	8.2	4.8	12.8	13.6	94 915	265	8 607	168 225	0.0
Wyoming	1.3	9.4	7.0	26.6	4.0	6.0	2.6	D	11.0	7 075	255	648	13 311	0.4
York	0.1	0.3	9.1	19.5	5.5	6.3	3.9	13.7	14.2	93 000	210	8 368	181 457	1.6
RHODE ISLAND	0.1	D	5.5	8.7	9.8	6.3	9.9	14.3	17.1	217 881	206	33 114	462 589	-0.2
Bristol	0.1	-0.1	D	D	8.6	5.1	6.4	11.4	18.2	11 050	224	674	20 784	-0.3
Kent	0.0	D	6.0	11.0	10.1	8.9	9.1	13.8	13.4	38 695	235	3 515	73 599	-0.1
Newport	0.1	D	D	D	11.4	7.3	5.4	6.9	35.1	18 510	223	1 400	41 990	0.5
Providence	0.0	0.0	5.1	6.9	10.0	4.8	11.9	16.3	14.4	121 395	192	25 949	263 048	-0.7
Washington	0.2	0.1	6.4	17.0	6.7	10.4	4.5	11.2	21.4	28 230	223	1 576	63 168	1.5
SOUTH CAROLINA	0.1	0.1	5.8	14.2	8.9	6.9	7.4	9.5	20.6	1 066 150	218	118 080	2 236 153	4.6
Abbeville	1.7	0.0	8.0	31.9	3.5	3.7	2.0	3.4	23.4	6 555	263	621	12 003	-0.6
Aiken	-0.2	D	8.7	14.2	11.2	5.9	5.2	7.6	12.1	38 555	232	3 953	75 009	3.8
Allendale	3.2	0.0	1.2	36.2	D	2.6	1.6	D	33.2	2 350	249	612	4 441	-1.0
Anderson	0.3	0.2	5.5	25.4	3.9	8.2	3.3	8.2	20.7	47 110	242	4 323	86 750	2.3
Bamberg	1.3	0.0	2.6	21.8	D	7.3	D	8.5	23.9	3 710	254	699	7 588	-1.7
Barnwell	-0.8	D	5.9	27.6	D	8.9	2.4	D	27.1	5 020	231	1 120	10 373	-1.1
Beaufort	0.2	0.0	7.1	1.0	9.7	7.8	7.4	9.4	32.1	46 065	256	2 032	96 893	4.2
Berkeley	0.0	D	8.4	14.8	22.9	6.4	3.8	3.4	17.9	34 765	171	3 129	81 029	10.4
Calhoun	-1.7	0.1	9.6	40.8	D	2.7	D	D	14.5	3 845	260	434	7 291	-0.6
Charleston	0.1	0.0	6.0	8.3	10.7	6.5	9.9	10.9	24.4	69 790	179	7 363	184 086	8.3
Cherokee	0.7	D	D	36.6	1.9	6.8	3.4	D	13.2	13 855	245	1 630	24 077	0.3
Chester	2.4	0.0	6.9	35.0	D	4.9	D	D	17.4	8 410	260	1 179	14 559	-1.0
Chesterfield	1.6	D	4.9	37.8	D	5.3	1.9	8.3	13.7	10 790	234	1 545	21 255	-1.1
Clarendon	-0.1	-0.1	4.6	5.3	6.6	12.0	3.4	7.6	38.0	9 310	275	1 598	17 407	-0.3
Colleton	-0.5	D	7.3	8.1	D	8.3	4.9	15.4	19.6	10 485	278	1 696	19 671	-1.2
Darlington	-1.4	-0.1	3.7	29.5	2.2	5.2	2.5	10.4	13.1	16 785	249	2 893	30 291	0.0
Dillon	-6.2	0.0	1.4	21.8	D	11.0	3.7	D	20.0	7 215	231	1 593	13 525	-1.6
Dorchester	-0.1	D	9.8	19.1	5.0	8.0	4.0	7.4	18.9	26 835	176	2 878	59 257	7.3
Edgefield	3.2	D	6.6	17.5	D	5.0	3.1	D	31.1	5 635	213	806	10 704	1.4
Fairfield	1.0	D	1.9	41.4	D	2.0	0.6	D	8.8	5 760	252	847	11 684	0.0
Florence	-0.3	D	3.5	12.2	7.1	7.8	12.8	13.9	21.1	31 080	224	5 954	59 342	1.2
Georgetown	0.2	0.1	6.9	13.9	6.6	7.4	6.7	11.2	23.4	19 810	323	1 867	34 488	2.4
Greenville	0.0	0.0	6.5	13.0	12.2	6.1	9.3	9.8	11.8	95 820	195	9 746	207 276	6.0
Greenwood	0.1	D	4.5	25.5	3.2	6.9	3.2	12.0	25.3	16 730	239	1 771	31 260	0.7
Hampton	-5.1	0.0	4.9	9.3	D	8.4	D	D	33.8	4 835	241	989	8 986	-1.7
Horry	0.0	0.1	6.9	2.8	7.0	12.3	10.3	12.0	16.4	87 010	281	5 733	199 551	7.3
Jasper	0.5	0.0	13.4	3.1	D	19.1	3.6	13.9	15.9	5 750	206	667	11 362	10.3
Kershaw	3.5	2.2	7.7	20.1	4.2	8.3	6.1	6.2	17.2	14 970	236	1 527	28 416	3.4
Lancaster	1.3	0.1	3.3	13.8	29.5	5.9	3.4	10.6	12.1	21 480	250	1 737	36 077	10.4
Laurens	0.5	D	3.4	39.0	4.4	5.1	1.8	D	16.6	17 450	262	2 134	30 658	-0.2
Lee	0.5	0.0	3.0	16.7	D	6.5	D	15.3	31.8	4 455	249	733	7 641	-1.7
Lexington	0.0	0.1	7.0	14.6	6.1	8.0	5.1	6.4	19.1	53 200	189	4 523	121 288	6.4
McCormick	1.1	0.0	D	10.4	D	4.5	D	D	48.4	3 620	373	310	5 499	0.8
Marion	-0.9	D	3.5	13.9	D	11.7	6.1	D	22.7	8 450	266	1 671	14 736	-1.5
Marlboro	-3.4	D	1.5	38.1	7.3	7.5	2.7	D	27.3	7 065	257	1 462	11 902	-1.4
Newberry	1.5	0.0	6.3	39.3	D	6.0	1.6	D	18.6	9 525	251	1 014	18 009	0.5
Oconee	0.4	D	5.5	27.4	4.7	6.1	2.9	7.3	14.9	21 865	289	1 509	39 417	1.7
Orangeburg	-0.4	0.0	3.4	22.5	3.0	8.6	3.6	8.0	27.8	21 950	247	4 090	42 061	-1.0
Pickens	0.0	D	5.8	17.2	4.1	8.2	3.9	8.0	33.9	26 880	221	2 282	52 870	3.2
Richland	0.0	D	3.6	5.5	11.2	5.3	11.6	11.6	30.5	65 070	160	8 528	171 098	5.8
Saluda	11.5	D	3.9	34.9	D	4.2	1.0	D	21.7	4 695	233	462	9 268	-0.2
Spartanburg	0.1	0.1	6.2	24.4	5.2	6.5	5.2	6.9	16.1	66 245	223	7 277	126 534	3.2

1. Per 1,000 resident population estimated as of July 1 of the year shown.

STATE County	Housing units, 2011–2015 Occupied units								Civilian labor force, 2016				Civilian employment,[6] 2011–2015		
	Owner-occupied			Median owner cost as a percent of income		Renter-occupied					Unemployment			Percent	
	Total	Percent	Median value[1]	With a mortgage	Without a mortgage[2]	Median rent[3]	Median rent as a percent of income[2]	Substandard units[4] (percent)	Total	Percent change, 2015–2016	Total	Rate[5]	Total	Management, business, science and arts	Construction, production, and maintenance occupations
	89	90	91	92	93	94	95	96	97	98	99	100	101	102	103
PENNSYLVANIA—Cont'd															
Potter	6 669	77.1	101 200	22.1	13.8	609	30.5	1.5	7 425	0.6	588	7.9	6 956	28.3	37.0
Schuylkill	58 554	74.9	93 000	21.3	14.4	635	26.6	1.2	67 900	-0.5	4 236	6.2	63 264	27.8	32.5
Snyder	14 442	74.6	144 700	21.2	12.1	694	26.8	2.7	20 540	2.3	970	4.7	19 403	26.5	32.3
Somerset	29 619	78.6	98 800	21.3	13.2	580	26.9	1.2	34 257	-0.7	2 494	7.3	33 159	28.2	31.1
Sullivan	2 669	83.3	145 800	22.7	14.5	578	24.7	1.3	2 887	-4.9	209	7.2	2 632	25.9	38.2
Susquehanna	17 487	76.7	150 700	21.8	13.5	714	28.8	1.6	20 965	-2.1	1 205	5.7	19 048	27.7	34.0
Tioga	16 611	74.3	124 700	22.1	13.3	688	27.9	1.5	19 973	-1.8	1 446	7.2	18 289	28.8	33.1
Union	14 916	71.5	160 200	21.8	12.9	697	28.2	1.8	19 752	2.2	946	4.8	17 585	32.4	26.4
Venango	22 129	76.3	81 200	19.3	11.3	578	28.5	1.1	23 815	-2.7	1 745	7.3	23 527	28.1	29.5
Warren	17 113	76.6	89 700	19.2	11.8	576	27.1	1.6	19 767	-1.0	1 096	5.5	18 545	30.1	32.0
Washington	83 739	75.8	152 400	19.2	11.0	675	26.2	1.2	107 354	0.6	6 643	6.2	99 731	34.8	23.5
Wayne	19 306	80.2	179 000	26.6	13.4	826	34.2	1.1	22 462	0.8	1 315	5.9	21 211	27.9	29.5
Westmoreland	151 173	76.6	138 500	19.8	12.0	654	27.0	0.8	183 949	0.5	10 847	5.9	173 533	34.9	24.3
Wyoming	10 894	77.9	159 500	22.2	13.8	736	28.9	1.9	14 197	0.5	887	6.2	13 003	25.8	33.6
York	167 416	74.2	168 400	23.2	14.1	851	30.3	1.4	235 131	0.9	10 967	4.7	217 393	32.4	27.4
RHODE ISLAND	410 602	60.1	238 000	24.9	15.3	925	30.6	2.0	552 220	-0.3	29 408	5.3	518 170	36.9	18.5
Bristol	19 290	70.9	330 100	24.5	16.2	993	32.2	1.1	26 105	-0.3	1 194	4.6	24 777	47.7	13.2
Kent	68 616	70.3	208 500	24.4	15.2	975	30.0	1.2	90 550	-0.2	4 374	4.8	86 274	36.9	18.6
Newport	34 848	61.9	349 200	24.8	14.6	1 111	29.5	1.2	43 897	-0.3	2 061	4.7	40 977	43.1	14.4
Providence	238 284	53.4	211 200	25.3	15.9	887	30.8	2.6	322 544	-0.2	18 458	5.7	301 318	33.6	20.2
Washington	49 564	73.1	311 600	24.4	14.4	1 050	30.5	1.0	69 124	-0.6	3 321	4.8	64 824	44.1	14.9
SOUTH CAROLINA	1 815 094	68.6	139 900	22.0	11.1	790	31.1	2.2	2 297 814	1.2	111 070	4.8	2 075 274	33.1	23.8
Abbeville	9 573	79.1	88 300	22.9	12.9	562	39.1	1.7	10 396	0.4	552	5.3	9 294	25.4	36.4
Aiken	63 706	73.9	128 800	20.2	10.6	696	31.6	2.3	74 613	0.9	3 597	4.8	69 420	34.7	25.7
Allendale	3 346	63.9	56 300	29.2	14.8	578	29.5	1.9	2 693	-2.1	228	8.5	2 866	17.2	34.2
Anderson	74 023	71.9	128 100	21.2	10.0	675	30.7	2.2	89 362	1.0	3 968	4.4	81 226	30.3	27.9
Bamberg	5 921	75.7	63 900	20.6	13.8	607	36.4	3.7	5 328	-2.5	481	9.0	5 527	29.1	31.0
Barnwell	8 344	72.9	74 100	22.5	13.0	604	32.6	2.9	8 348	-0.4	582	7.0	8 026	26.7	33.4
Beaufort	65 975	70.0	274 700	27.6	11.7	1 048	30.7	2.9	72 683	1.4	3 335	4.6	70 487	33.6	17.3
Berkeley	69 030	69.9	153 500	22.6	11.0	981	30.2	1.7	95 753	2.4	4 223	4.4	84 494	32.9	26.3
Calhoun	6 028	77.5	100 100	22.0	12.8	681	28.1	2.9	6 939	0.6	415	6.0	6 455	28.3	34.2
Charleston	148 018	60.6	243 200	24.4	12.8	992	32.8	1.9	203 308	2.5	7 968	3.9	183 111	39.4	17.0
Cherokee	20 523	67.9	86 500	19.8	11.5	633	29.3	2.8	23 618	0.6	1 349	5.7	20 966	25.7	33.6
Chester	12 385	72.3	86 700	21.5	10.0	591	33.4	2.5	13 712	1.9	941	6.9	12 296	22.3	35.3
Chesterfield	18 022	69.9	77 600	22.6	10.8	577	35.6	3.5	21 935	2.3	1 053	4.8	17 730	24.4	37.3
Clarendon	13 161	73.2	88 500	24.2	12.2	568	30.9	3.0	12 967	-0.8	823	6.3	11 443	27.7	30.4
Colleton	14 774	73.4	86 000	25.1	13.4	705	31.6	2.2	16 974	1.5	915	5.4	14 841	24.6	29.7
Darlington	26 417	67.7	86 800	19.9	11.2	623	33.0	2.2	30 079	0.0	1 819	6.0	25 949	28.8	28.5
Dillon	11 514	65.7	63 500	22.0	13.6	530	30.9	4.0	12 867	1.5	843	6.6	10 805	18.7	38.2
Dorchester	51 856	69.4	168 000	23.2	11.7	947	31.1	1.7	74 457	2.4	3 264	4.4	66 723	34.5	22.7
Edgefield	9 096	75.9	114 900	20.0	11.0	583	30.4	2.4	10 780	1.0	589	5.5	10 099	27.5	35.6
Fairfield	8 990	72.7	97 700	21.9	13.6	666	41.7	1.1	10 100	0.7	706	7.0	8 693	24.1	33.3
Florence	51 847	66.2	122 200	20.8	10.9	676	29.4	2.6	65 550	0.0	3 361	5.1	58 296	34.1	21.6
Georgetown	23 566	76.8	159 600	27.3	13.0	821	28.6	1.8	25 415	0.7	1 652	6.5	22 756	31.6	22.6
Greenville	179 862	66.0	156 200	20.2	10.0	771	28.7	1.9	245 768	1.1	10 093	4.1	219 810	37.0	21.5
Greenwood	26 709	65.3	104 900	20.7	10.5	657	32.6	2.1	31 482	0.6	1 581	5.0	28 506	31.9	29.6
Hampton	7 530	75.1	76 400	22.5	13.7	628	26.4	3.0	8 296	-0.7	473	5.7	7 787	23.2	31.3
Horry	118 738	69.0	159 700	25.1	11.6	843	33.7	2.4	139 212	1.3	7 770	5.6	129 161	28.2	17.7
Jasper	9 095	70.7	99 300	29.1	12.6	784	30.4	1.4	11 991	1.4	506	4.2	11 707	19.7	31.1
Kershaw	24 194	78.8	117 600	22.4	10.9	680	26.5	1.2	29 228	0.9	1 483	5.1	26 360	31.0	29.1
Lancaster	29 395	76.8	150 200	22.0	11.3	687	33.4	1.8	37 589	2.3	1 945	5.2	33 151	29.9	25.7
Laurens	25 160	71.6	83 900	19.9	10.0	654	29.7	2.4	30 403	0.3	1 530	5.0	27 397	24.8	35.0
Lee	6 385	73.9	69 800	23.1	12.1	596	34.2	3.1	6 497	0.5	446	6.9	6 146	21.6	31.0
Lexington	106 637	73.6	140 500	20.2	10.0	837	29.0	2.1	146 929	1.0	5 836	4.0	132 105	36.6	22.0
McCormick	4 003	76.8	109 400	25.6	11.9	507	29.3	0.6	3 427	-0.4	188	5.5	2 970	25.5	31.3
Marion	11 958	69.6	75 000	22.9	13.8	496	36.1	1.5	12 791	-0.6	1 075	8.4	11 875	28.4	31.5
Marlboro	9 950	65.6	60 200	20.3	11.8	567	31.9	3.7	9 350	-3.1	771	8.2	9 600	23.0	38.4
Newberry	14 287	73.2	100 800	20.3	11.6	668	28.9	3.1	19 121	1.1	832	4.4	15 784	25.4	35.3
Oconee	30 556	74.1	147 000	22.1	10.1	670	33.1	2.1	34 598	0.3	1 721	5.0	28 796	31.0	29.0
Orangeburg	33 410	69.1	87 600	23.9	13.0	661	32.3	2.9	36 035	-2.5	3 098	8.6	33 811	28.2	30.4
Pickens	44 646	69.2	123 000	20.4	11.1	704	34.1	2.0	56 655	1.0	2 738	4.8	50 816	33.6	25.9
Richland	145 069	59.3	149 700	21.7	10.3	875	32.2	2.1	200 628	0.9	9 413	4.7	184 364	38.7	15.2
Saluda	7 059	71.8	92 700	21.9	10.9	652	26.5	1.3	8 901	0.7	392	4.4	8 107	21.9	42.0
Spartanburg	109 892	68.6	123 800	20.1	10.0	707	30.2	2.5	142 477	1.8	6 524	4.6	128 253	30.8	29.4

1. Specified owner-occupied units.   2. A value of 10.0 represents 10 percent or less; a value of 50.0 represents 50 percent or more.   3. Specified renter-occupied units.
4. Overcrowded or lacking complete plumbing facilities.   5. Percent of civilian labor force.   6. Civilian employed persons 16 years old and over.

Table B. States and Counties — Nonfarm Employment and Agriculture

STATE County	Private nonfarm establishments, employment and payroll, 2015									Agriculture, 2012			
		Employment						Annual payroll		Farms			
												Percent with:	
	Number of establishments	Total	Health care and social assistance	Manufacturing	Retail trade	Finance and insurance	Professional, scientific, and technical services	Total (mil dol)	Average per employee (dollars)	Number	Fewer than 50 acres	500 acres or more	Farm operators whose principal occupation is farming (percent)
	104	105	106	107	108	109	110	111	112	113	114	115	116
PENNSYLVANIA—Cont'd													
Potter	358	4 304	942	511	532	66	209	154	35 755	442	23.8	9.3	55.9
Schuylkill	2 795	40 970	7 298	9 930	5 678	982	995	1 510	36 866	791	41.5	5.4	49.7
Snyder	875	14 678	1 689	3 959	2 890	291	194	413	28 170	933	46.7	2.9	47.9
Somerset	1 707	18 560	3 534	2 866	2 702	747	612	651	35 097	1 140	22.5	7.2	48.3
Sullivan	163	1 171	433	75	226	27	24	31	26 516	179	24.6	8.9	50.3
Susquehanna	889	7 216	1 152	537	1 257	176	325	225	31 124	1 005	29.7	5.5	51.0
Tioga	876	10 910	1 929	2 114	1 887	410	249	400	36 621	1 125	21.0	7.0	49.5
Union	914	15 983	4 081	1 437	1 605	440	394	577	36 103	613	37.8	2.3	61.5
Venango	1 189	16 087	3 354	3 862	2 640	328	379	537	33 351	464	33.0	5.4	48.1
Warren	916	14 135	2 986	2 937	2 269	1 021	268	517	36 608	602	34.7	4.5	39.0
Washington	5 131	84 328	13 284	8 863	8 464	1 460	3 678	4 483	53 156	1 915	36.1	1.8	44.6
Wayne	1 310	12 233	2 544	619	2 569	453	291	408	33 339	711	24.9	4.1	50.4
Westmoreland	8 675	126 336	20 272	18 975	19 407	2 812	6 455	5 106	40 419	1 274	37.3	3.1	46.2
Wyoming	670	10 866	515	2 289	1 347	205	466	551	50 741	508	30.9	3.1	46.1
York	8 675	164 072	23 886	30 511	22 218	3 696	5 907	6 859	41 803	2 171	56.6	4.4	48.9
RHODE ISLAND	28 387	425 748	86 655	39 160	49 837	25 582	22 850	19 705	46 283	1 243	71.1	0.9	49.8
Bristol	1 237	13 764	2 758	1 676	1 381	221	428	461	33 464	42	73.8	0.0	57.1
Kent	4 682	69 893	12 665	5 787	11 524	5 094	4 095	2 997	42 885	126	65.9	1.6	41.3
Newport	2 748	30 220	5 036	1 988	4 141	1 200	3 095	1 313	43 440	214	72.4	0.9	55.6
Providence	15 696	264 537	58 266	22 452	26 133	17 722	12 475	12 697	47 997	425	73.2	0.2	45.6
Washington	3 772	42 441	7 716	7 255	6 652	979	1 565	1 975	46 536	436	69.7	1.4	52.8
SOUTH CAROLINA	103 973	1 662 251	224 365	224 665	236 944	67 755	82 841	66 120	39 778	25 266	44.1	8.1	41.0
Abbeville	332	4 743	523	2 164	477	132	48	151	31 887	574	32.2	5.9	34.1
Aiken	2 716	49 157	5 891	7 802	7 195	1 131	1 940	2 130	43 329	1 102	46.5	4.6	33.9
Allendale	124	1 665	275	853	123	29	31	70	41 986	141	22.0	27.0	54.6
Anderson	3 658	55 324	8 527	11 044	9 129	1 083	2 128	2 080	37 594	1 498	50.9	2.9	35.6
Bamberg	264	2 983	453	1 001	448	92	56	93	31 074	315	19.4	15.6	40.3
Barnwell	350	4 436	660	1 445	773	126	112	140	31 449	397	36.5	11.8	44.6
Beaufort	5 025	52 777	7 891	550	9 706	1 879	2 360	1 784	33 811	137	56.9	16.1	39.4
Berkeley	2 852	43 588	2 344	5 086	6 950	923	3 249	2 033	46 643	373	57.4	9.7	45.8
Calhoun	236	3 595	394	1 467	246	40	42	150	41 830	412	31.1	14.3	45.4
Charleston	12 858	194 144	30 741	14 691	27 879	6 217	14 957	8 265	42 572	359	64.1	3.6	42.9
Cherokee	943	17 651	1 281	5 672	2 763	305	185	550	31 134	490	43.1	3.9	31.4
Chester	520	6 674	641	2 284	960	151	135	269	40 274	477	33.5	8.6	39.8
Chesterfield	686	12 756	1 672	5 577	1 229	203	79	487	38 196	717	36.8	7.9	34.0
Clarendon	463	5 630	1 557	704	1 257	237	73	153	27 101	422	29.6	17.1	55.2
Colleton	731	7 479	1 343	796	1 528	257	214	237	31 750	530	40.4	13.0	42.1
Darlington	1 096	17 146	2 439	3 090	2 365	396	253	758	44 229	385	36.9	20.0	46.2
Dillon	480	7 461	1 201	2 192	1 154	173	415	190	25 445	228	21.1	24.6	46.5
Dorchester	2 206	25 134	2 950	4 262	4 209	689	906	870	34 614	411	48.7	7.5	46.7
Edgefield	319	4 954	533	1 230	432	57	61	177	35 651	389	40.1	9.0	36.2
Fairfield	308	8 139	536	1 221	621	61	D	559	68 732	194	32.5	10.3	40.2
Florence	3 101	56 982	13 741	7 069	9 133	3 768	2 394	2 120	37 196	632	33.4	11.1	44.3
Georgetown	1 797	19 329	3 541	2 264	3 235	479	736	701	36 242	209	39.7	13.9	44.0
Greenville	12 592	220 394	26 246	27 593	26 603	9 062	16 067	9 831	44 606	1 101	62.7	1.4	33.9
Greenwood	1 341	22 604	4 508	5 311	3 695	507	804	812	35 942	476	44.1	4.6	49.6
Hampton	322	3 272	517	638	582	125	101	235	71 901	323	28.5	18.6	46.1
Horry	8 520	102 242	10 747	2 529	22 308	3 550	3 265	3 089	30 210	938	44.1	9.8	50.5
Jasper	604	7 338	1 155	230	1 871	100	207	276	37 559	115	40.9	23.5	65.2
Kershaw	1 108	15 494	2 257	3 251	2 355	523	390	568	36 680	483	44.7	6.8	39.3
Lancaster	1 294	17 505	2 461	1 927	2 962	1 188	712	765	43 700	577	47.1	4.0	47.1
Laurens	953	17 032	1 944	6 743	1 778	385	398	643	37 747	826	40.0	5.3	35.4
Lee	182	1 712	216	189	366	77	48	49	28 625	386	26.2	16.8	45.3
Lexington	6 249	95 496	13 071	9 009	16 127	3 061	3 503	3 635	38 069	1 011	56.2	3.8	42.0
McCormick	77	918	217	265	98	17	17	26	27 997	93	24.7	21.5	35.5
Marion	496	5 381	648	910	1 102	296	73	149	27 699	275	40.7	17.1	41.8
Marlboro	329	5 070	1 118	2 069	770	114	60	163	32 072	224	26.8	20.1	44.6
Newberry	702	11 428	1 326	4 614	1 396	188	152	394	34 487	594	36.2	7.7	38.9
Oconee	1 489	20 074	2 274	5 318	2 996	484	526	808	40 253	884	60.7	1.7	39.3
Orangeburg	1 603	25 588	4 187	6 570	3 912	676	455	893	34 896	1 056	34.2	12.7	42.2
Pickens	1 959	29 654	3 389	5 294	4 971	575	786	845	28 506	727	69.6	1.1	44.0
Richland	8 775	158 565	27 190	9 505	18 944	18 004	10 991	6 730	42 443	398	52.0	4.5	38.9
Saluda	245	3 695	434	2 013	320	46	123	111	29 957	587	30.7	9.2	44.6
Spartanburg	6 142	124 510	14 917	28 569	14 379	2 055	4 005	5 370	43 131	1 338	57.6	1.4	43.7

Table B. States and Counties — **Agriculture**

STATE County	Land in farms		Acres			Value of land and buildings (dollars)		Value of machinery and equipment, average per farm (dollars)	Value of products sold		Percent from:		Percent of farms with sales of:		Government payments	
	Acreage (1,000)	Percent change, 2007–2012	Average size of farm	Total irrigated (1,000)	Total cropland (1,000)	Average per farm	Average per acre		Total (mil dol)	Average per farm (dollars)	Crops	Live-stock and poultry products	$10,000 or more	$100,000 or more	Total ($1,000)	Percent of farms
	117	118	119	120	121	122	123	124	125	126	127	128	129	130	131	132
PENNSYLVANIA—Cont'd																
Potter	97	9.3	219	0.0	42.0	601 247	2 749	87 593	35.5	80 204	31.7	68.3	36.2	12.9	1 364	52.0
Schuylkill	106	-10.8	134	1.7	72.1	860 377	6 436	105 598	165.9	209 675	46.3	53.7	47.0	21.0	1 486	42.7
Snyder	91	-9.0	98	0.8	59.7	568 781	5 820	67 891	165.5	177 377	16.4	83.6	56.2	24.9	1 273	25.3
Somerset	215	3.8	188	0.1	119.4	495 161	2 631	91 144	104.2	91 411	26.0	74.0	52.8	21.1	1 602	30.9
Sullivan	37	34.7	209	0.0	15.4	645 698	3 084	97 117	9.5	53 168	26.7	73.3	33.5	8.9	461	43.6
Susquehanna	166	5.2	166	0.1	73.7	675 315	4 079	80 360	43.3	43 106	20.7	79.3	35.2	11.3	1 585	35.2
Tioga	205	11.4	182	0.2	109.0	626 933	3 438	78 940	80.3	71 340	26.5	73.5	43.6	13.3	2 590	42.0
Union	93	46.2	152	0.1	52.7	820 065	5 391	101 024	136.0	221 811	19.1	80.9	73.2	45.0	713	27.2
Venango	62	-5.0	133	0.0	29.0	410 136	3 093	81 901	15.8	33 998	64.5	35.5	39.2	6.7	489	22.8
Warren	82	-17.2	137	0.1	27.6	321 166	2 346	63 495	20.7	34 464	32.9	67.1	28.9	6.6	464	15.9
Washington	206	-2.5	107	0.8	86.4	489 897	4 558	68 244	35.4	18 492	53.1	46.9	28.1	2.7	841	10.9
Wayne	113	21.6	159	0.1	43.2	592 875	3 730	76 821	32.4	45 502	21.0	79.0	43.5	11.4	696	20.0
Westmoreland	143	-14.6	112	0.4	81.9	534 291	4 758	92 900	48.6	38 155	55.6	44.4	37.1	7.1	1 118	25.3
Wyoming	69	-11.8	135	0.1	32.4	542 844	4 011	79 911	14.6	28 772	57.3	42.7	32.7	7.7	633	31.7
York	262	-10.4	121	0.8	195.0	910 957	7 547	87 005	234.1	107 814	62.9	37.1	45.3	16.5	2 746	22.2
RHODE ISLAND	70	2.6	56	4.0	22.6	786 093	14 041	56 065	59.7	47 990	82.1	17.9	35.7	8.7	2 345	15.3
Bristol	D	D	D	0.1	1.1	977 024	D	52 190	2.7	63 548	80.4	19.5	47.6	16.7	D	2.4
Kent	D	D	D	0.2	1.9	790 095	D	39 087	4.4	34 548	80.4	19.6	38.1	7.9	D	7.9
Newport	12	13.9	54	0.5	6.5	1 201 720	22 248	63 850	14.6	68 365	83.1	16.9	47.2	12.6	390	22.4
Providence	D	D	D	0.6	4.9	600 586	D	41 569	14.1	33 127	77.8	22.2	31.3	5.2	949	17.9
Washington	27	10.8	63	2.6	8.2	743 369	11 870	71 654	23.9	54 865	84.6	15.4	32.6	9.6	936	12.6
SOUTH CAROLINA	4 971	1.7	197	159.2	1 967.3	586 518	2 981	72 400	3 040.1	120 323	42.6	57.4	27.0	8.6	46 616	26.9
Abbeville	92	0.9	160	D	23.7	444 972	2 775	52 261	9.6	16 786	31.0	69.0	26.1	1.2	631	19.9
Aiken	154	-3.1	140	1.3	55.8	532 257	3 800	54 850	96.3	87 426	16.3	83.7	26.9	7.1	892	16.1
Allendale	124	-0.7	882	6.5	39.1	1 949 496	2 211	94 773	25.6	181 532	89.3	10.7	27.0	12.8	946	68.8
Anderson	159	-8.1	106	0.6	46.5	463 880	4 367	51 636	62.8	41 918	D	D	23.5	4.3	779	12.3
Bamberg	93	-25.9	294	7.4	36.6	650 460	2 215	93 587	37.2	118 187	69.9	30.1	36.5	15.6	1 408	67.9
Barnwell	88	-5.2	221	4.4	37.5	539 234	2 437	79 058	48.4	121 867	D	D	29.5	13.9	1 091	48.9
Beaufort	42	-14.6	308	3.2	6.4	1 041 226	3 382	99 153	D		D	D	32.1	6.6	51	10.9
Berkeley	75	42.4	201	0.4	19.5	718 094	3 568	54 810	6.9	18 413	87.5	12.5	27.1	4.3	388	18.8
Calhoun	118	7.1	287	14.9	64.5	802 779	2 794	154 303	79.7	193 354	69.6	30.4	40.0	19.4	1 632	45.9
Charleston	35	-15.0	99	1.6	8.8	615 329	6 234	49 072	D	D	D	D	28.1	5.8	76	4.7
Cherokee	65	3.0	132	D	16.6	399 810	3 033	43 643	24.0	49 078	40.7	59.3	20.8	2.0	625	15.9
Chester	96	-14.6	200	0.5	19.0	564 608	2 820	65 338	42.6	89 329	D	D	29.8	6.1	376	10.3
Chesterfield	131	-6.8	183	1.2	42.4	500 552	2 739	59 743	121.2	169 050	D	D	23.2	7.8	1 047	37.1
Clarendon	174	12.3	412	8.5	98.1	758 033	1 840	152 725	139.6	330 829	53.2	46.8	42.2	20.1	1 972	68.7
Colleton	188	7.4	354	2.8	45.9	955 200	2 697	90 266	33.6	63 330	95.4	4.6	28.7	6.6	707	36.2
Darlington	177	2.4	459	7.3	113.7	1 132 418	2 465	182 395	129.2	335 509	58.4	41.6	45.7	26.5	2 806	47.3
Dillon	107	1.7	468	1.3	75.2	1 218 289	2 602	169 167	132.2	579 724	38.6	61.4	43.4	28.1	2 245	69.3
Dorchester	75	14.6	181	2.1	34.5	623 706	3 440	74 095	50.0	121 572	47.1	52.9	28.5	10.7	853	29.2
Edgefield	81	6.4	210	6.0	20.9	619 203	2 955	80 298	44.7	114 854	73.3	26.7	23.7	5.1	540	24.2
Fairfield	45	-14.2	229	D	7.3	640 268	2 791	51 732	30.9	159 237	5.0	95.0	26.8	6.7	137	9.8
Florence	156	-1.7	247	1.8	94.3	546 794	2 215	91 321	54.0	85 517	98.4	1.6	35.1	11.6	2 303	49.8
Georgetown	66	15.1	318	0.5	12.4	747 407	2 354	71 541	12.8	61 287	98.3	1.7	23.0	8.6	313	56.5
Greenville	73	0.3	66	1.6	20.6	430 060	6 498	38 996	16.6	15 044	81.7	18.4	15.8	1.7	180	5.3
Greenwood	86	21.0	180	0.2	12.7	432 540	2 407	46 794	6.7	14 023	33.3	66.7	23.3	1.7	311	11.1
Hampton	139	9.7	431	6.3	51.7	1 032 814	2 398	85 718	34.6	107 266	98.8	1.2	31.6	13.3	1 584	64.4
Horry	178	8.5	189	5.6	108.0	571 035	3 016	93 665	101.3	107 988	78.6	21.4	31.4	14.0	2 149	45.7
Jasper	69	31.6	597	D	8.7	1 620 974	2 717	69 043	6.4	55 626	93.5	6.5	26.1	5.2	60	17.4
Kershaw	83	-3.1	172	1.1	16.7	524 702	3 058	60 770	147.2	304 687	3.3	96.7	23.6	10.8	499	16.6
Lancaster	65	-0.2	113	0.3	14.0	443 986	3 936	45 899	78.0	135 208	4.5	95.5	24.4	7.5	86	8.8
Laurens	123	-5.7	148	0.7	35.0	503 297	3 389	47 098	40.9	49 530	D	D	28.8	4.8	1 085	15.0
Lee	142	1.0	369	7.4	93.2	835 806	2 265	151 886	118.6	307 225	51.3	48.7	31.6	18.9	2 289	66.8
Lexington	108	19.2	107	10.7	49.0	424 407	3 984	64 111	164.6	162 818	25.9	74.1	27.2	10.1	660	13.2
McCormick	30	20.5	323	0.2	3.6	570 806	1 767	42 785	5.2	55 946	22.6	77.4	21.5	5.4	155	32.3
Marion	80	15.4	292	1.1	44.5	679 087	2 328	107 269	40.6	147 815	69.8	30.2	29.5	14.2	931	66.5
Marlboro	113	-7.5	506	2.7	71.1	1 096 866	2 169	123 723	61.8	276 063	73.5	26.5	33.0	23.2	2 154	62.5
Newberry	104	3.7	176	0.8	31.7	476 949	2 711	66 958	139.5	234 891	D	D	31.1	7.2	1 004	22.2
Oconee	68	-4.0	77	0.3	15.4	407 562	5 308	49 633	121.4	137 313	5.0	95.0	21.4	7.9	382	6.3
Orangeburg	283	-1.5	268	25.4	152.9	677 763	2 528	124 560	231.5	219 264	53.8	46.2	33.3	16.3	3 506	43.9
Pickens	45	-12.3	62	0.8	13.0	344 880	5 575	41 396	8.4	11 611	66.3	33.7	12.5	1.0	167	4.0
Richland	61	3.5	153	2.0	31.1	536 626	3 511	68 653	30.0	75 472	76.9	23.1	24.6	5.8	507	10.1
Saluda	108	-1.7	184	4.4	29.6	524 673	2 853	81 700	126.3	215 130	21.8	78.2	37.0	11.6	750	25.6
Spartanburg	102	-7.3	76	1.9	37.7	377 862	4 964	38 547	34.6	25 829	56.6	43.4	18.1	2.2	833	8.1

Table B. States and Counties — Water Use, Wholesale Trade, Retail Trade, and Real Estate

STATE County	Water use, 2010		Wholesale trade,[1] 2012				Retail trade,[2] 2012				Real estate and rental and leasing,[2] 2012			
	Total water withdrawn (mil gal/day)	Gallons withdrawn per person per day	Number of establishments	Number of employees	Sales (mil dol)	Annual payroll (mil dol)	Number of establishments	Number of employees	Sales (mil dol)	Annual payroll (mil dol)	Number of establishments	Number of employees	Receipts (mil dol)	Annual payroll (mil dol)
	133	134	135	136	137	138	139	140	141	142	143	144	145	146
PENNSYLVANIA—Cont'd														
Potter	6.3	358	6	D	D	D	68	546	152.7	13.6	5	16	1.0	0.2
Schuylkill	36.7	247	99	1 562	916.6	55.0	504	5 677	1 381.9	119.1	60	240	40.7	6.6
Snyder	276.6	6 967	26	D	D	D	198	2 867	630.2	54.9	13	47	11.1	1.7
Somerset	29.7	382	65	894	443.1	34.6	253	2 643	781.1	60.2	46	151	43.6	5.8
Sullivan	0.6	95	2	D	D	D	30	279	64.7	4.5	4	D	D	D
Susquehanna	4.4	102	34	267	569.9	8.6	146	1 269	533.6	28.0	15	88	24.5	4.7
Tioga	8.0	190	28	394	237.7	17.5	155	2 002	563.9	44.5	23	56	8.9	1.6
Union	6.4	142	30	D	D	D	130	1 561	479.2	37.0	28	158	19.0	3.4
Venango	8.2	149	43	D	D	D	204	2 565	636.9	53.9	26	79	12.6	1.9
Warren	14.0	334	27	211	142.0	8.8	130	2 394	674.6	55.4	18	71	7.3	1.4
Washington	357.6	1 721	227	3 257	2 869.3	186.9	691	8 657	2 342.1	194.5	145	772	221.8	38.3
Wayne	5.8	110	24	D	D	D	223	2 560	711.1	60.4	27	62	11.5	2.0
Westmoreland	40.0	110	330	5 958	7 333.3	308.5	1 258	18 183	4 671.7	416.7	262	1 106	240.4	38.0
Wyoming	13.1	464	18	389	106.5	14.5	114	1 334	393.5	28.0	9	27	10.4	2.0
York	2 641.2	6 072	359	6 685	4 340.8	301.4	1 297	21 024	5 192.4	463.9	258	1 470	263.7	51.8
RHODE ISLAND	375.5	357	1 158	15 697	22 310.4	1 000.2	3 795	47 688	12 063.9	1 206.6	1 058	5 615	1 119.8	218.5
Bristol	1.6	32	48	385	204.9	21.5	145	1 355	288.1	32.2	43	127	24.2	3.8
Kent	4.0	24	213	2 683	1 670.6	156.9	676	11 126	2 984.2	285.3	177	1 298	261.8	49.5
Newport	11.7	142	69	390	331.1	22.0	430	4 211	1 116.5	116.3	112	769	100.9	23.1
Providence	330.8	528	701	11 014	19 000.6	720.6	1 996	24 365	5 999.4	594.4	598	3 063	659.5	130.0
Washington	27.4	216	127	1 225	1 103.3	79.3	548	6 631	1 675.7	178.4	128	358	73.5	12.2
SOUTH CAROLINA	6 782.2	1 466	4 337	54 949	45 520.9	2 806.2	17 586	220 438	58 093.8	4 954.6	4 692	23 189	4 334.4	825.9
Abbeville	4.4	172	6	52	22.1	2.1	62	439	91.4	7.6	2	D	D	D
Aiken	207.9	1 298	69	505	399.4	20.0	508	6 601	1 749.5	139.6	106	331	53.6	9.8
Allendale	12.8	1 229	8	46	55.2	1.8	26	136	33.9	2.7	4	D	D	D
Anderson	266.7	1 425	167	2 514	2 641.3	105.6	697	8 472	2 189.6	188.1	125	422	91.7	13.1
Bamberg	5.4	337	6	D	D	D	56	462	95.3	9.6	2	D	D	D
Barnwell	5.6	247	4	D	D	D	74	782	167.1	14.9	10	18	2.2	0.4
Beaufort	24.4	150	113	470	295.6	21.4	734	9 080	2 090.5	203.1	379	1 718	267.1	62.8
Berkeley	571.4	3 213	151	2 343	3 248.3	125.6	396	6 173	1 730.6	141.6	130	699	132.4	26.1
Calhoun	91.5	6 031	9	D	D	D	35	224	65.9	3.6	3	D	D	D
Charleston	53.5	153	468	5 049	2 875.4	264.4	1 935	26 034	6 707.7	628.9	695	3 295	599.2	118.4
Cherokee	11.5	208	22	432	131.6	14.6	235	2 648	800.6	49.4	39	153	24.2	2.6
Chester	5.3	160	12	175	302.1	10.0	100	828	234.1	17.1	14	D	D	D
Chesterfield	9.7	207	27	305	96.4	10.0	135	1 271	317.7	22.8	16	37	4.1	0.8
Clarendon	6.4	183	16	113	74.2	3.8	124	1 247	336.3	24.9	16	34	3.9	1.0
Colleton	12.3	316	28	195	107.2	7.3	157	1 635	408.3	32.5	44	144	22.5	3.7
Darlington	216.8	3 156	73	592	859.7	25.3	235	2 246	536.6	45.2	37	102	46.5	2.7
Dillon	5.6	174	20	443	391.7	15.4	121	1 159	394.2	22.2	21	62	4.9	1.1
Dorchester	33.6	246	73	562	215.3	27.5	297	3 697	973.2	78.7	104	332	65.0	11.3
Edgefield	11.4	422	8	125	62.7	6.1	54	405	152.1	9.5	8	22	1.7	0.5
Fairfield	772.0	32 227	10	D	D	D	54	539	224.9	12.1	11	D	D	D
Florence	42.8	313	158	2 493	1 585.7	105.5	701	8 277	2 149.6	178.9	130	555	104.3	19.7
Georgetown	833.2	13 850	40	280	135.3	10.2	303	2 776	703.3	62.9	86	417	54.8	13.3
Greenville	41.7	93	711	9 278	10 153.0	521.9	1 757	24 790	6 380.5	593.2	534	2 681	838.1	113.6
Greenwood	13.0	186	49	421	837.9	19.1	275	3 224	758.9	67.6	44	D	D	D
Hampton	8.3	394	10	182	118.2	10.0	92	678	164.8	13.2	7	23	2.1	0.8
Horry	141.7	526	238	1 605	734.3	65.4	1 666	20 687	5 240.2	455.3	590	4 496	506.6	131.1
Jasper	29.2	1 178	27	258	146.8	12.6	104	1 425	574.8	40.5	18	69	13.6	3.2
Kershaw	11.2	182	16	70	43.5	4.8	178	2 122	586.3	44.0	32	83	14.0	3.2
Lancaster	20.5	268	47	1 106	719.7	38.8	238	2 673	732.9	60.3	43	D	D	D
Laurens	7.3	109	32	227	115.2	10.6	180	1 680	412.1	32.8	20	50	6.3	1.0
Lee	3.9	203	11	80	138.2	3.8	42	381	86.0	7.3	2	D	D	D
Lexington	257.7	982	302	5 744	3 889.3	292.0	1 046	15 123	3 974.5	338.3	243	1 277	227.9	43.8
McCormick	1.5	149	1	D	D	D	22	122	31.9	2.1	2	D	D	D
Marion	4.5	135	21	338	208.4	16.5	128	1 042	239.0	21.0	10	30	3.5	0.9
Marlboro	32.7	1 130	13	114	43.5	4.2	98	704	185.5	14.9	13	29	4.3	0.6
Newberry	9.3	247	26	238	160.5	10.0	133	1 389	428.1	29.2	17	65	14.9	2.2
Oconee	2 537.7	34 167	39	388	201.2	13.4	254	2 920	741.0	63.9	64	153	26.0	5.5
Orangeburg	32.4	351	66	529	387.8	21.6	370	4 070	1 016.6	80.2	53	241	25.7	7.9
Pickens	48.8	409	66	403	301.3	21.5	324	4 215	1 163.1	97.9	68	345	44.5	9.4
Richland	78.0	203	417	5 489	4 191.3	303.2	1 254	18 443	4 780.7	433.4	408	2 792	736.4	133.1
Saluda	6.1	308	8	45	14.4	1.4	49	414	115.1	8.5	4	D	D	D
Spartanburg	42.1	148	414	5 813	5 340.5	297.1	1 069	13 459	3 966.7	316.7	227	999	180.6	37.3

1. Merchant wholesalers, except manufacturers' sales branches and offices.   2. Employer establishments.

Table B. States and Counties — Professional Services, Manufacturing, and Accommodation and Food Services

STATE County	Professional, scientific, and technical services, 2012				Manufacturing, 2012				Accommodation and food services, 2012			
	Number of establish-ments	Number of employees	Receipts (mil dol)	Annual payroll (mil dol)	Number of establish-ments	Number of employees	Receipts (mil dol)	Annual payroll (mil dol)	Number of establish-ments	Number of employees	Sales (mil dol)	Annual payroll (mil dol)
	147	148	149	150	151	152	153	154	155	156	157	158
PENNSYLVANIA—Cont'd												
Potter	23	113	12.9	4.9	23	513	69.5	19.0	40	254	12.3	2.9
Schuylkill	157	1 040	113.9	49.6	177	8 882	3 400.0	397.6	271	2 671	124.4	31.5
Snyder	44	204	17.3	7.0	62	3 627	678.7	139.7	85	1 743	79.9	20.6
Somerset	96	D	D	D	107	2 854	836.1	130.8	165	3 112	137.2	39.2
Sullivan	10	16	1.7	0.7	5	D	D	D	26	D	D	D
Susquehanna	46	213	26.1	8.5	61	659	124.0	23.8	83	752	44.1	10.8
Tioga	53	306	29.4	11.8	42	2 316	591.7	90.9	104	1 451	65.5	16.9
Union	68	345	25.1	10.0	38	1 343	353.3	55.9	92	2 165	89.3	24.1
Venango	69	365	46.7	14.4	80	4 048	1 388.1	219.2	112	1 325	55.0	15.2
Warren	52	277	25.3	12.6	61	2 652	3 515.5	136.9	78	904	42.3	10.8
Washington	408	3 276	608.1	189.3	247	9 931	3 561.9	514.0	396	6 603	318.0	81.4
Wayne	84	305	30.9	11.0	53	523	104.1	20.1	158	1 490	144.6	39.6
Westmoreland	705	5 812	1 053.4	328.6	556	18 854	7 681.5	920.2	756	12 356	516.6	143.6
Wyoming	48	292	33.6	12.7	30	2 541	D	156.9	60	763	33.7	7.9
York	705	5 671	635.2	279.4	568	31 890	11 489.4	1 602.6	791	13 391	593.3	165.9
RHODE ISLAND	2 997	21 165	3 338.2	1 310.1	1 509	39 608	11 262.2	2 076.5	2 973	44 063	2 481.3	705.9
Bristol	109	381	52.9	19.8	92	1 633	325.1	70.6	124	1 496	72.8	19.9
Kent	503	2 948	418.3	160.4	218	7 609	2 643.0	439.1	467	8 013	412.0	118.5
Newport	326	3 168	545.6	229.0	74	1 860	284.1	148.0	358	5 945	411.2	121.4
Providence	1 719	13 021	2 040.1	803.1	962	21 885	6 126.4	1 026.7	1 563	23 354	1 242.9	351.4
Washington	340	1 647	281.3	97.9	163	6 621	1 883.6	392.1	461	5 255	342.4	94.7
SOUTH CAROLINA	9 721	79 824	12 721.7	4 817.3	3 854	207 396	99 160.8	10 082.1	9 828	185 282	9 763.8	2 650.5
Abbeville	17	43	3.4	0.9	34	1 686	598.8	71.9	26	332	12.5	3.8
Aiken	243	4 751	1 548.2	471.3	82	6 845	4 639.3	390.4	253	D	D	D
Allendale	6	D	D	D	6	719	447.0	35.3	6	D	D	D
Anderson	278	1 822	209.0	74.8	196	10 223	5 435.0	439.9	383	6 019	272.2	75.5
Bamberg	17	66	7.5	1.9	21	823	177.0	32.6	21	235	9.7	2.5
Barnwell	24	D	D	D	20	1 918	564.1	83.1	32	419	16.9	4.3
Beaufort	554	2 876	339.1	144.8	71	524	82.2	20.2	501	10 502	656.6	193.0
Berkeley	246	2 735	477.7	164.5	88	5 106	6 261.6	332.3	241	4 605	195.9	52.6
Calhoun	13	D	D	D	22	1 278	D	80.6	10	D	D	D
Charleston	1 561	15 343	2 760.7	1 096.9	288	13 984	5 668.1	818.4	1 192	26 575	1 640.0	455.0
Cherokee	48	179	16.2	6.0	58	5 455	3 050.6	220.7	86	1 758	73.4	20.5
Chester	32	157	19.9	6.8	40	2 245	1 140.7	105.3	41	536	25.5	6.6
Chesterfield	27	81	7.0	2.0	49	4 375	1 345.2	188.7	63	848	37.8	9.7
Clarendon	18	77	9.5	4.7	18	403	235.2	13.6	58	624	28.3	7.1
Colleton	45	229	34.3	9.3	26	620	137.8	20.1	70	1 205	65.6	18.5
Darlington	60	255	26.5	8.0	50	3 092	1 693.0	171.0	88	1 188	53.2	13.7
Dillon	24	302	8.4	4.0	16	2 214	470.1	54.2	56	872	34.8	9.4
Dorchester	194	796	102.4	34.6	89	4 439	2 026.4	228.4	183	2 879	132.4	36.2
Edgefield	17	42	4.4	1.1	20	1 213	389.5	41.5	22	D	D	D
Fairfield	15	D	D	D	18	754	232.3	30.9	24	234	9.1	2.5
Florence	208	2 429	267.8	104.8	98	5 860	2 633.5	308.5	296	5 423	272.5	71.9
Georgetown	168	837	129.0	34.9	45	2 010	1 032.6	115.9	171	2 819	152.0	44.5
Greenville	1 529	14 537	2 095.5	888.9	555	26 782	9 628.1	1 280.1	1 073	19 791	999.9	271.7
Greenwood	119	1 166	140.8	58.2	62	5 498	2 478.9	251.8	135	2 387	102.5	26.1
Hampton	16	D	D	D	15	621	156.6	26.5	31	347	16.6	3.6
Horry	670	3 059	342.9	121.5	145	2 693	759.8	121.4	1 218	25 903	1 716.7	451.1
Jasper	25	123	13.6	5.4	19	190	46.2	7.3	54	687	32.3	8.9
Kershaw	77	D	D	D	58	3 122	1 419.7	149.0	91	1 308	55.5	14.8
Lancaster	88	559	73.8	28.6	47	1 916	1 292.5	87.0	95	1 491	65.9	16.5
Laurens	46	186	13.3	6.6	78	5 398	1 728.2	230.9	84	1 275	56.6	14.7
Lee	11	D	D	D	11	214	D	11.1	18	234	10.1	2.7
Lexington	579	3 175	367.3	140.1	206	8 527	3 620.3	402.0	513	10 122	455.2	127.3
McCormick	6	D	D	D	5	298	D	12.5	7	D	D	D
Marion	22	69	4.9	1.8	19	714	214.1	26.9	44	708	32.0	8.2
Marlboro	14	55	4.6	1.4	20	1 912	881.9	76.8	27	317	14.7	4.0
Newberry	42	153	12.3	4.4	44	4 831	1 651.5	185.2	61	826	36.6	9.0
Oconee	117	469	42.1	16.8	76	5 151	2 135.2	242.5	119	1 672	81.5	19.2
Orangeburg	80	334	42.9	16.1	70	6 332	2 470.4	275.8	175	3 222	152.1	37.5
Pickens	157	846	92.1	34.2	113	4 713	1 500.8	200.3	235	4 212	186.9	48.9
Richland	1 213	13 037	2 328.9	859.4	204	9 355	5 375.0	536.0	844	17 706	862.2	238.3
Saluda	14	D	D	D	8	1 953	D	52.0	18	D	D	D
Spartanburg	452	4 804	692.5	263.5	397	23 972	15 038.1	1 288.2	550	10 059	477.9	128.0

1. Establishment subject to federal tax.

Table B. States and Counties — Health Care and Social Assistance, Other Services, Nonemployer Businesses, and Residential Construction

STATE County	Health care and social assistance, 2012				Other services, 2012				Nonemployer businesses, 2015		Value of residential construction authorized by building permits, 2016	
	Number of establishments	Number of employees	Receipts (mil dol)	Annual payroll (mil dol)	Number of establishments	Number of employees	Receipts (mil dol)	Annual payroll (mil dol)	Number	Receipts (mil dol)	New Construction ($1,000)	Number of housing units
	159	160	161	162	163	164	165	166	167	168	169	170
PENNSYLVANIA—Cont'd												
Potter	33	907	88.3	36.1	27	115	8.9	1.9	1 329	52.3	2 098	12
Schuylkill	336	7 975	597.1	259.1	250	1 103	83.9	24.3	6 685	317.8	18 029	96
Snyder	83	1 134	104.6	39.4	69	286	27.4	6.1	2 875	141.7	15 880	79
Somerset	193	3 627	292.2	119.0	143	654	52.9	12.9	4 492	182.5	14 520	63
Sullivan	16	D	D	D	13	61	2.3	0.6	466	20.9	2 438	11
Susquehanna	65	1 136	77.9	34.3	70	291	24.5	5.5	3 119	160.3	14 651	59
Tioga	104	1 901	153.8	62.4	69	255	27.8	6.0	2 536	103.7	7 292	37
Union	144	3 740	315.4	142.1	66	306	23.5	5.9	2 757	138.9	21 707	99
Venango	170	3 475	226.6	114.7	107	419	35.6	8.4	2 759	112.4	6 363	32
Warren	107	3 221	254.0	114.2	85	529	31.4	7.4	2 118	82.5	6 533	34
Washington	690	13 512	1 301.5	518.0	421	2 455	227.6	63.9	12 428	636.2	84 697	292
Wayne	125	2 510	188.0	80.0	103	706	55.4	15.5	3 863	183.0	17 215	87
Westmoreland	1 155	20 603	1 809.4	737.8	805	4 447	477.2	105.5	21 539	962.4	86 016	328
Wyoming	67	687	42.1	18.8	52	237	24.5	6.5	1 792	77.0	6 147	26
York	924	24 161	2 604.4	1 031.9	783	5 242	651.3	139.7	25 875	1 231.5	156 288	878
RHODE ISLAND	3 236	84 067	8 223.0	3 556.0	2 276	13 046	1 444.6	390.9	76 747	3 488.7	236 512	1 226
Bristol	126	2 848	133.7	70.6	121	449	34.9	10.8	4 329	206.8	11 372	47
Kent	570	11 802	1 113.1	455.6	369	2 083	219.7	60.9	11 589	543.6	24 010	178
Newport	250	4 845	375.1	154.4	208	1 133	120.4	35.0	7 698	378.7	34 320	128
Providence	1 898	57 002	5 943.2	2 600.1	1 310	8 075	940.3	249.7	41 595	1 801.1	72 364	480
Washington	392	7 570	658.1	275.4	268	1 306	129.3	34.6	11 536	558.6	94 445	393
SOUTH CAROLINA	9 848	212 444	22 941.3	8 687.3	6 666	44 374	4 464.9	1 302.3	329 431	13 960.9	6 723 604	32 165
Abbeville	27	486	37.9	15.6	23	67	6.7	1.4	1 332	47.7	5 798	39
Aiken	310	6 330	519.8	199.6	169	950	79.6	20.4	10 327	376.5	179 229	887
Allendale	12	283	22.5	8.5	8	D	D	D	484	11.4	2 665	2
Anderson	365	8 273	928.6	343.8	235	3 448	371.8	169.8	12 016	487.2	155 582	813
Bamberg	41	693	36.4	20.5	23	D	D	D	786	19.9	705	7
Barnwell	34	723	48.5	20.6	26	131	16.9	4.0	1 390	33.8	2 955	26
Beaufort	426	5 819	661.3	222.0	309	2 700	244.6	82.6	15 277	804.8	550 489	1 551
Berkeley	210	2 318	154.7	65.5	187	1 068	86.9	26.2	12 414	492.9	416 862	1 964
Calhoun	22	D	D	D	16	D	D	D	882	38.0	4 704	36
Charleston	1 250	30 476	4 338.2	1 412.0	768	5 340	579.2	155.9	36 656	1 921.2	789 150	3 970
Cherokee	75	1 180	84.5	36.1	70	319	32.0	7.8	2 518	79.9	13 267	109
Chester	49	707	75.3	27.2	36	141	12.3	3.4	1 647	58.4	8 993	49
Chesterfield	90	1 624	125.4	47.2	40	119	8.7	2.3	2 264	74.4	8 553	51
Clarendon	41	1 456	95.5	41.2	33	194	13.2	4.1	2 097	76.5	6 213	44
Colleton	71	1 443	158.5	60.6	35	145	9.6	2.4	2 892	110.8	16 193	51
Darlington	96	2 444	218.8	83.4	79	345	29.9	7.6	3 709	122.6	17 896	107
Dillon	47	1 170	87.2	37.1	37	83	7.3	1.6	1 613	51.3	2 404	23
Dorchester	209	3 170	271.0	100.7	165	832	67.7	23.0	9 329	348.7	232 340	1 040
Edgefield	20	526	34.3	14.1	24	65	5.9	1.5	1 418	49.4	23 043	106
Fairfield	27	D	D	D	12	D	D	D	1 415	44.5	9 885	47
Florence	354	13 444	1 565.1	585.4	196	1 348	135.8	32.3	8 638	334.4	55 486	388
Georgetown	215	3 742	467.2	164.1	115	619	44.0	12.7	5 305	234.1	82 834	366
Greenville	1 120	21 857	2 261.7	996.1	706	5 185	651.9	157.1	36 919	1 682.3	812 575	3 799
Greenwood	144	4 752	585.2	207.9	78	548	33.4	10.1	3 822	143.4	14 174	133
Hampton	28	520	39.8	17.1	23	105	7.8	1.8	1 232	37.6	4 094	34
Horry	657	10 903	1 274.1	443.5	504	2 720	279.6	65.9	23 599	1 091.9	757 617	4 097
Jasper	44	975	89.8	27.6	42	162	14.1	3.5	1 602	74.8	56 633	233
Kershaw	96	D	D	D	82	373	29.3	8.4	4 055	156.6	48 177	358
Lancaster	136	2 266	229.0	88.2	97	495	50.3	27.5	5 282	203.4	323 534	1 231
Laurens	90	2 033	179.0	68.5	60	278	24.4	7.3	3 235	116.3	17 066	115
Lee	25	323	18.9	8.3	14	D	D	D	876	24.0	1 093	8
Lexington	527	12 620	1 058.8	436.7	491	2 905	277.8	88.1	19 393	837.0	453 818	2 000
McCormick	9	214	12.1	5.0	7	D	D	D	531	18.0	11 562	50
Marion	60	711	51.2	24.2	36	112	9.6	2.2	1 740	50.9	1 767	13
Marlboro	43	971	73.1	27.9	22	45	4.0	1.1	995	28.3	1 997	15
Newberry	58	1 175	107.3	42.0	55	232	20.0	5.9	1 873	61.5	17 339	92
Oconee	139	2 882	274.5	107.9	94	542	40.5	12.6	4 691	176.1	92 471	387
Orangeburg	220	3 904	381.9	158.5	98	474	37.5	10.6	5 024	159.6	6 830	48
Pickens	195	3 459	296.7	121.6	137	692	117.3	17.6	7 494	309.2	167 897	1 026
Richland	944	26 658	3 202.5	1 277.0	609	4 986	475.4	141.8	27 333	1 151.2	265 932	2 151
Saluda	21	D	D	D	14	D	D	D	973	37.3	7 515	35
Spartanburg	583	D	D	D	413	2 940	326.3	80.2	19 027	847.1	324 663	1 901

Table B. States and Counties — Government Employment and Payroll, and Local Government Finances

STATE County	Government employment and payroll, 2012		March payroll (percent of total)							Local government finances, 2012				
										General revenue		Taxes		
													Per capita[1] (dollars)	
	Full-time equivalent employees	March payroll (dollars)	Adminis-tration, judicial, and legal	Police and Corrections	Fire Protection	Highways and transpor-tation	Health and Welfare	Natural resources and utilities	Education and libraries	Total (mil dol)	Inter-govern-mental	Total (mil dol)	Total	Property
	171	172	173	174	175	176	177	178	179	180	181	182	183	184
PENNSYLVANIA— Cont'd														
Potter	590	2 437 639	12.0	6.7	1.0	7.4	0.9	10.0	61.5	73.9	41.6	21.8	1 241	1 052
Schuylkill	4 186	15 090 961	8.1	8.5	0.1	3.8	7.3	7.1	64.1	485.2	233.0	166.2	1 130	842
Snyder	1 018	3 558 017	6.3	8.1	0.0	2.9	3.5	3.8	74.2	107.4	42.7	49.5	1 247	859
Somerset	2 210	7 165 165	8.8	4.3	0.0	5.7	1.8	4.2	70.6	225.8	112.7	81.2	1 055	857
Sullivan	201	742 784	15.2	1.7	1.1	5.2	3.8	5.3	67.2	22.1	7.8	11.8	1 822	1 657
Susquehanna	1 464	5 097 993	5.6	5.6	0.6	4.5	1.7	2.4	79.2	139.9	73.6	54.2	1 268	1 138
Tioga	1 450	4 927 182	7.0	6.0	0.6	3.5	10.4	7.0	64.2	150.3	76.5	54.9	1 290	1 005
Union	883	3 323 742	9.7	6.0	0.0	3.9	4.3	8.9	66.1	157.6	75.7	51.5	1 145	812
Venango	2 052	6 987 537	7.7	7.9	3.0	3.8	5.2	5.7	65.4	196.8	112.6	57.2	1 053	811
Warren	1 409	4 668 630	8.7	7.2	1.1	5.4	17.0	2.6	57.5	113.1	58.7	41.3	1 004	762
Washington	5 853	22 585 416	6.8	9.1	1.4	4.1	7.0	4.9	65.0	790.8	371.8	291.3	1 396	1 069
Wayne	2 592	9 809 084	4.6	4.1	0.0	2.0	28.2	1.9	57.7	212.3	71.7	119.1	2 293	2 175
Westmoreland	10 354	41 162 785	6.1	8.6	0.9	4.3	6.4	9.3	63.6	1 302.8	557.8	500.8	1 378	1 099
Wyoming	947	3 123 745	15.3	5.7	0.0	2.7	0.3	2.0	71.4	97.3	46.7	41.6	1 479	1 225
York	12 293	50 416 660	6.7	12.2	1.5	2.7	6.3	3.6	64.5	1 771.5	572.5	787.5	1 799	1 467
RHODE ISLAND	X	X	X	X	X	X	X	X	X	X	X	X	X	X
Bristol	1 397	7 178 253	3.0	7.9	2.0	3.0	1.9	4.4	77.5	205.0	41.5	148.0	3 011	2 942
Kent	4 694	24 743 968	2.8	9.9	10.7	2.0	1.3	3.7	68.1	624.4	144.3	407.2	2 470	2 403
Newport	2 527	11 716 139	5.0	10.6	9.2	2.6	0.2	5.5	65.4	364.6	76.1	229.2	2 793	2 650
Providence	17 322	86 400 418	3.8	11.7	9.5	2.0	0.4	5.9	66.0	2 313.9	791.5	1 215.6	1 935	1 896
Washington	4 199	20 282 486	4.3	9.4	3.8	3.0	1.3	3.8	73.7	552.3	102.2	401.4	3 187	3 138
SOUTH CAROLINA	X	X	X	X	X	X	X	X	X	X	X	X	X	X
Abbeville	815	2 384 457	7.4	9.5	1.1	1.8	7.5	8.4	63.9	60.8	30.4	21.1	840	689
Aiken	4 376	15 335 939	9.0	9.9	1.0	4.3	3.0	6.2	65.7	401.1	181.9	160.3	984	738
Allendale	625	1 746 281	7.6	6.7	0.0	2.9	29.6	2.5	49.5	29.1	16.4	9.0	902	790
Anderson	5 484	17 493 225	6.4	10.0	1.2	2.0	1.3	5.3	72.7	476.2	210.0	176.3	931	827
Bamberg	819	2 552 389	7.1	5.8	0.6	1.4	37.3	0.9	45.9	39.6	22.1	13.7	867	775
Barnwell	1 118	3 299 448	5.3	8.6	0.4	1.1	16.7	7.6	59.3	70.5	38.2	23.1	1 038	893
Beaufort	5 616	22 420 841	6.5	9.3	6.0	1.7	27.9	4.2	42.3	768.1	132.7	391.8	2 332	1 843
Berkeley	4 857	15 229 373	6.7	8.6	2.0	1.9	2.3	2.1	74.3	476.5	201.9	143.2	755	670
Calhoun	495	1 790 689	3.0	5.0	0.5	1.8	4.1	1.1	81.6	33.4	14.6	15.0	1 004	980
Charleston	13 396	47 281 757	9.0	15.4	8.8	3.6	4.8	11.4	43.8	1 612.3	402.2	924.2	2 531	1 581
Cherokee	1 933	5 953 218	3.7	7.2	1.7	1.1	6.9	7.7	68.8	146.3	65.3	61.5	1 104	806
Chester	1 174	3 574 024	8.6	9.3	2.2	0.6	4.9	8.2	64.8	79.0	35.9	29.6	909	770
Chesterfield	1 558	4 244 462	5.6	8.8	0.8	1.2	1.7	2.9	77.8	100.3	53.6	36.7	796	594
Clarendon	1 529	4 986 545	5.1	7.6	1.8	1.2	37.8	2.0	42.4	136.5	40.9	33.6	977	747
Colleton	1 758	4 967 648	10.1	9.9	7.4	1.9	2.9	2.2	63.4	116.4	49.6	49.9	1 307	1 182
Darlington	2 194	6 310 138	4.5	9.9	1.9	2.4	4.0	4.0	70.6	151.5	78.7	44.0	646	554
Dillon	1 167	2 987 274	6.2	10.5	1.5	1.1	5.2	3.0	70.1	74.9	42.2	21.2	675	561
Dorchester	4 560	14 338 815	6.9	8.6	2.2	1.2	2.7	4.6	73.0	360.3	155.5	139.0	976	789
Edgefield	1 053	2 997 459	5.4	8.0	0.1	1.3	20.4	4.5	59.7	56.1	29.4	18.1	688	606
Fairfield	1 055	3 207 938	8.3	8.3	1.2	2.5	4.8	5.3	67.8	73.7	26.6	41.9	1 793	1 684
Florence	4 772	15 317 333	6.1	8.9	1.8	2.8	7.2	5.8	66.2	387.1	172.1	134.7	976	696
Georgetown	2 430	7 765 625	7.3	7.7	6.1	2.1	3.9	7.3	63.7	209.0	63.2	106.1	1 762	1 609
Greenville	21 594	81 147 575	3.3	5.4	3.5	1.1	44.4	4.7	36.9	2 639.7	456.3	485.5	1 038	884
Greenwood	2 547	7 901 666	5.9	7.9	1.9	1.7	4.3	10.3	62.2	563.0	100.6	69.9	1 002	786
Hampton	938	2 724 640	7.1	11.8	1.3	1.6	5.2	2.5	69.3	58.5	31.0	21.3	1 028	897
Horry	9 820	34 724 743	8.4	11.7	5.0	3.5	2.7	7.6	58.9	1 161.7	254.9	609.6	2 160	1 278
Jasper	809	2 603 546	11.5	13.8	11.9	2.4	1.3	2.1	56.6	69.7	25.2	37.2	1 441	1 298
Kershaw	2 730	9 680 043	3.3	4.0	1.9	0.5	41.5	2.8	45.5	255.3	130.9	56.4	904	774
Lancaster	2 327	7 452 417	5.3	8.0	1.9	1.0	4.2	8.2	68.9	189.5	79.8	80.0	1 012	782
Laurens	2 310	7 353 314	3.4	6.7	2.3	0.9	31.0	8.0	45.9	214.0	83.0	50.0	755	651
Lee	612	1 602 678	12.0	8.7	1.3	2.9	9.6	3.4	62.1	41.4	23.3	12.5	672	517
Lexington	14 886	59 502 218	2.4	4.2	1.3	0.5	41.6	2.7	46.6	1 461.3	374.4	370.5	1 370	1 163
McCormick	304	811 090	7.2	12.7	0.0	1.9	8.7	11.9	53.4	21.6	7.9	10.9	1 095	1 058
Marion	1 230	3 302 618	5.6	10.1	1.2	1.8	3.5	3.5	72.9	78.2	42.6	22.7	700	520
Marlboro	985	2 122 399	9.2	11.9	1.6	1.6	3.1	6.4	62.6	68.7	37.5	16.6	591	514
Newberry	1 757	5 725 610	5.0	8.2	1.1	1.3	25.7	9.1	48.9	109.3	44.6	46.1	1 227	1 069
Oconee	2 527	8 134 083	7.1	8.0	2.1	2.9	2.0	10.1	66.8	184.8	66.5	95.0	1 272	1 175
Orangeburg	4 563	16 266 007	3.4	5.4	0.2	1.1	46.5	2.7	38.9	425.4	101.6	103.8	1 135	920
Pickens	3 247	10 077 389	5.7	8.6	2.0	3.3	4.7	5.9	66.7	262.7	109.4	112.3	939	722
Richland	13 444	45 241 826	6.4	9.8	3.8	1.6	2.7	7.7	65.0	1 390.8	394.8	589.3	1 496	1 309
Saluda	474	1 331 037	7.6	11.4	2.9	2.3	1.5	2.7	69.2	35.8	16.8	14.0	705	629
Spartanburg	14 164	55 750 441	3.2	4.9	1.6	0.6	47.1	3.9	37.9	1 488.8	350.6	322.9	1 118	988

1. Based on the resident population estimated as of July 1 of the year shown.

Table B. States and Counties — Local Government Finances, Government Employment, and Income Taxes

STATE County	Local government finances, 2012 (cont.) Direct general expenditure Total (mil dol)	Per capita[1] (dollars)	Percent of total for: Education	Health and hospitals	Police protection	Public welfare	Highways	Debt outstanding Total (mil dol)	Per capita[1] (dollars)	Government employment, 2015 Federal civilian	Federal military	State and local	Individual income tax returns, 2014 Number of returns	Mean adjusted gross income	Mean income tax
	185	186	187	188	189	190	191	192	193	194	195	196	197	198	199
PENNSYLVANIA—Cont'd															
Potter	70.3	3 999	50.7	1.3	1.0	9.1	10.6	81.5	4 636	45	44	1 037	7 670	46 075	5 031
Schuylkill	520.8	3 541	55.0	1.5	2.5	6.8	4.7	555.0	3 774	606	364	7 192	67 940	47 330	5 388
Snyder	122.1	3 077	62.0	2.4	4.4	0.0	4.2	222.5	5 610	86	101	2 129	18 200	45 886	4 282
Somerset	213.0	2 768	61.0	0.1	2.5	5.7	5.5	286.3	3 720	186	185	4 185	34 760	46 705	4 643
Sullivan	25.1	3 889	63.1	2.1	0.7	2.7	8.5	9.0	1 396	17	15	363	2 950	52 973	6 124
Susquehanna	148.2	3 471	72.6	0.9	1.4	2.1	5.8	59.8	1 401	100	109	1 814	19 880	58 394	7 654
Tioga	137.5	3 229	52.4	0.0	1.2	10.9	7.3	119.5	2 807	143	105	2 812	18 800	48 972	5 079
Union	203.9	4 535	63.4	1.3	1.3	2.6	2.9	249.6	5 553	1 576	99	1 370	17 140	58 083	6 987
Venango	206.3	3 800	58.4	2.1	1.5	7.2	5.3	271.4	5 001	104	136	3 304	25 080	44 862	4 442
Warren	109.9	2 672	58.9	0.5	2.9	0.7	5.6	93.3	2 267	168	104	1 817	19 530	48 004	5 204
Washington	804.7	3 855	54.3	1.5	2.6	11.8	4.2	903.0	4 326	448	558	9 780	103 600	70 583	10 258
Wayne	210.9	4 059	64.5	2.4	0.7	4.4	3.0	262.7	5 056	504	124	2 505	24 650	49 279	5 291
Westmoreland	1 328.7	3 656	53.4	2.5	2.9	10.3	4.0	1 848.5	5 087	829	944	14 219	183 080	58 185	7 192
Wyoming	92.1	3 276	63.0	0.1	3.2	5.3	6.8	54.9	1 953	61	71	1 105	13 640	56 009	6 885
York	1 790.5	4 089	47.4	3.5	3.3	9.2	2.6	2 454.1	5 605	4 136	1 306	16 010	219 430	56 561	6 387
RHODE ISLAND	X	X	X	X	X	X	X	X	X	10 494	6 991	54 023	521 890	62 294	8 211
Bristol	201.6	4 102	66.6	0.2	4.1	0.1	4.2	147.6	3 004	93	220	2 006	24 030	106 368	17 958
Kent	593.7	3 601	58.4	0.1	6.4	0.5	2.8	449.3	2 725	719	761	7 259	87 440	63 947	8 380
Newport	357.9	4 363	48.4	2.1	8.0	0.4	3.0	203.9	2 486	4 624	2 550	3 363	42 940	85 040	13 054
Providence	2 229.9	3 549	53.2	0.2	8.2	0.1	2.8	1 836.7	2 923	4 458	2 877	29 577	303 100	52 460	6 220
Washington	532.3	4 226	67.5	0.5	5.4	0.4	3.5	302.1	2 398	600	583	11 818	64 390	74 715	10 486
SOUTH CAROLINA	X	X	X	X	X	X	X	X	X	32 872	53 382	319 402	2 123 820	52 428	5 960
Abbeville	59.7	2 377	50.1	3.0	7.7	0.0	1.3	24.7	985	39	96	1 376	9 580	40 333	3 181
Aiken	373.4	2 294	57.5	1.3	7.7	0.1	2.4	155.5	955	671	651	7 066	71 560	53 255	5 672
Allendale	27.5	2 758	69.3	1.7	5.0	0.0	1.5	14.8	1 477	17	32	1 087	3 230	32 958	2 855
Anderson	483.1	2 551	63.5	0.3	6.2	0.2	2.1	1 327.5	7 010	316	767	11 874	81 950	48 954	5 004
Bamberg	61.7	3 917	76.9	0.2	5.2	0.0	0.8	38.4	2 439	34	54	977	5 450	36 331	3 104
Barnwell	71.5	3 218	57.8	0.4	6.7	0.2	2.1	37.0	1 667	48	85	1 439	8 720	37 271	2 935
Beaufort	752.2	4 476	32.2	19.6	6.0	1.1	2.3	1 451.5	8 637	2 211	10 439	7 766	80 770	73 468	10 489
Berkeley	500.4	2 637	57.1	1.2	5.3	0.4	2.8	2 158.7	11 375	888	813	8 163	87 860	51 187	5 392
Calhoun	36.1	2 418	56.3	3.7	6.6	1.8	1.0	42.7	2 864	25	58	789	6 240	45 779	4 039
Charleston	1 363.0	3 733	36.6	1.0	11.9	0.2	4.7	2 857.4	7 825	9 382	11 583	37 372	182 410	67 499	9 707
Cherokee	132.3	2 378	65.3	1.5	6.6	5.1	2.3	1 423.8	25 579	101	220	2 234	22 680	39 652	3 266
Chester	89.7	2 756	62.9	3.1	5.0	0.0	0.4	59.0	1 811	59	127	1 555	13 820	37 786	3 032
Chesterfield	104.7	2 271	63.2	0.0	8.7	0.0	2.6	194.8	4 224	88	180	2 007	17 670	38 087	3 144
Clarendon	138.9	4 044	34.7	40.8	4.1	0.0	1.0	88.7	2 583	54	129	2 309	13 220	36 187	3 085
Colleton	127.8	3 350	47.8	0.7	8.0	0.8	3.0	141.2	3 701	95	157	1 926	16 340	36 388	3 076
Darlington	148.0	2 173	64.2	0.4	7.0	0.0	2.0	103.9	1 525	149	263	3 045	27 790	42 297	4 086
Dillon	76.7	2 441	64.6	0.3	6.0	3.0	2.1	10.2	324	80	122	1 438	12 240	32 856	2 325
Dorchester	349.2	2 451	64.0	1.4	6.0	0.0	7.4	507.4	3 561	205	601	6 197	67 460	50 874	4 839
Edgefield	58.3	2 211	67.5	2.4	6.3	0.5	2.0	25.9	981	417	94	1 252	10 500	46 394	4 453
Fairfield	86.5	3 704	53.6	6.2	5.9	0.0	1.7	21.4	917	39	89	1 390	9 890	40 467	3 818
Florence	382.5	2 773	59.5	5.9	6.5	0.2	1.7	270.2	1 958	544	567	12 647	59 150	46 168	4 817
Georgetown	194.2	3 227	56.8	1.4	5.1	0.6	2.7	502.9	8 355	121	276	4 758	28 890	55 262	6 903
Greenville	2 628.6	5 621	23.1	51.4	2.7	0.2	1.1	3 479.0	7 440	2 020	1 969	29 790	218 620	61 056	7 693
Greenwood	506.5	7 261	23.9	58.7	2.1	0.0	0.7	466.2	6 684	135	268	6 896	29 560	44 521	4 265
Hampton	68.8	3 318	69.0	2.5	7.3	0.9	1.8	31.5	1 522	343	74	1 138	7 840	38 999	3 699
Horry	1 100.1	3 897	39.1	12.4	5.6	0.1	5.5	1 603.2	5 679	610	1 219	15 414	144 120	44 299	4 836
Jasper	67.2	2 600	51.4	0.2	8.9	0.4	1.9	79.1	3 062	54	105	1 269	10 800	39 164	3 377
Kershaw	253.6	4 068	36.7	41.9	2.8	0.2	1.0	291.1	4 669	93	251	3 252	27 320	46 766	4 407
Lancaster	185.7	2 347	54.7	4.0	5.6	0.0	2.8	219.5	2 775	99	333	3 621	35 300	54 097	5 779
Laurens	231.7	3 499	34.1	32.5	3.9	0.1	2.1	194.1	2 931	100	258	3 740	26 960	39 827	3 231
Lee	37.3	1 999	57.1	4.7	6.6	0.1	2.1	54.1	2 902	26	64	1 092	6 950	32 460	2 317
Lexington	1 529.8	5 658	44.1	37.4	3.3	0.0	0.9	1 531.8	5 665	620	1 112	19 809	124 410	55 151	6 136
McCormick	18.6	1 873	57.9	5.8	5.0	0.0	2.0	32.0	3 218	81	34	799	3 840	47 461	4 471
Marion	79.9	2 460	61.3	1.8	8.6	0.0	2.4	5.2	159	69	129	1 395	13 380	30 312	2 095
Marlboro	80.0	2 841	65.4	1.7	6.2	2.2	0.0	67.2	2 386	366	97	1 415	10 590	31 193	2 085
Newberry	116.7	3 107	49.9	1.3	5.2	0.5	1.6	134.2	3 573	103	146	2 298	16 470	42 598	3 744
Oconee	188.2	2 522	59.7	0.5	7.2	0.2	3.1	171.5	2 298	154	298	3 926	31 690	54 857	6 189
Orangeburg	436.4	4 771	34.3	43.8	4.1	0.1	3.6	296.9	3 246	212	347	6 747	37 190	37 093	3 289
Pickens	329.4	2 752	64.3	1.5	5.1	0.1	3.3	469.0	3 919	183	472	9 567	48 130	50 257	5 273
Richland	1 388.2	3 525	44.0	0.2	4.6	0.1	1.1	5 237.8	13 300	9 428	10 789	46 600	176 280	54 144	6 402
Saluda	34.3	1 725	55.3	2.1	7.5	0.1	2.3	31.1	1 565	35	79	948	8 550	39 859	3 384
Spartanburg	1 501.9	5 202	32.3	48.4	2.8	0.4	1.0	1 018.7	3 528	505	1 154	19 895	127 830	51 647	5 710

1. Based on the resident population estimated as of July 1 of the year shown.

Table B. States and Counties — Land Area and Population

STATE/ County code	CBSA code[1]	County type[2]	STATE County	Land area[3] (sq mi) 2016	Total persons 2016	Rank	Per square mile	White	Black	American Indian, Alaska Native	Asian and Pacific Islander[4]	Percent Hispanic or Latino[4]	Under 5 years	5 to 17 years	18 to 24 years	25 to 34 years	35 to 44 years	45 to 54 years
				1	2	3	4	5	6	7	8	9	10	11	12	13	14	15
			SOUTH CAROLINA—Cont'd															
45 085	44940	3	Sumter	665.1	107 396	557	161.5	46.9	48.2	0.9	2.1	3.8	6.9	17.5	10.2	13.9	11.1	12.4
45 087	43900	2	Union	514.2	27 673	1 503	53.8	66.5	32.6	0.6	0.6	1.4	5.6	15.9	7.7	10.8	11.5	14.0
45 089		6	Williamsburg	934.2	31 955	1 379	34.2	32.1	65.1	0.6	0.7	2.3	5.3	16.2	8.2	11.6	11.5	12.9
45 091	16740	1	York	680.7	258 526	262	379.8	72.8	20.2	1.3	2.4	5.3	6.2	18.3	8.5	12.4	13.7	14.6
46 000	...	0	**SOUTH DAKOTA**	75 810.5	865 454	X	11.4	84.4	2.5	9.6	1.9	3.7	7.1	17.6	9.8	13.0	11.4	11.8
46 003	...	9	Aurora	708.4	2 736	2 988	3.9	90.9	1.3	2.9	0.9	5.2	6.5	19.7	6.5	10.3	10.3	11.9
46 005	26700	7	Beadle	1 258.7	18 101	1 911	14.4	80.3	1.6	1.6	8.5	9.4	8.9	18.2	7.4	11.9	10.3	11.9
46 007	...	9	Bennett	1 184.7	3 460	2 942	2.9	37.7	1.0	60.2	1.1	4.9	9.9	23.6	10.8	12.1	9.1	11.0
46 009	...	9	Bon Homme	563.7	6 984	2 673	12.4	88.2	1.5	8.5	0.4	2.6	5.1	13.8	9.1	13.3	12.0	12.7
46 011	15100	5	Brookings	792.2	34 135	1 322	43.1	92.1	1.8	1.6	3.2	2.5	6.4	13.9	26.4	13.1	10.2	9.0
46 013	10100	5	Brown	1 713.0	39 128	1 203	22.8	89.4	2.1	4.2	3.4	2.7	6.5	17.3	9.7	13.5	11.2	12.1
46 015	...	9	Brule	817.2	5 238	2 815	6.4	87.7	0.7	11.5	0.7	2.6	6.9	19.2	7.8	9.9	10.5	12.9
46 017	...	9	Buffalo	471.4	2 043	3 045	4.3	17.1	1.2	79.7	0.2	3.7	11.0	27.7	9.7	14.2	10.7	9.1
46 019	...	6	Butte	2 250.0	10 205	2 415	4.5	93.5	0.8	3.6	0.7	3.6	6.1	18.1	7.2	10.9	10.5	12.1
46 021	...	9	Campbell	733.7	1 378	3 086	1.9	96.4	0.6	1.4	0.4	2.0	4.0	13.0	7.0	6.9	8.2	15.2
46 023	...	9	Charles Mix	1 097.5	9 396	2 475	8.6	65.8	0.9	32.2	0.7	3.4	9.1	20.6	8.8	10.2	9.7	11.0
46 025	...	9	Clark	957.6	3 656	2 928	3.8	94.7	2.2	0.6	0.7	2.7	5.0	15.3	8.3	10.6	9.2	11.2
46 027	46820	6	Clay	412.2	14 086	2 158	34.2	90.2	2.5	4.1	2.9	2.6	6.7	17.8	8.4	12.9	11.6	12.7
46 029	47980	5	Codington	688.1	28 063	1 488	40.8	93.8	1.0	2.8	1.3	2.3	6.7	17.8	8.4	12.9	11.6	12.7
46 031	...	9	Corson	2 469.7	4 132	2 891	1.7	33.3	0.9	63.4	1.2	4.6	9.8	25.6	9.0	12.1	9.9	10.6
46 033	39660	3	Custer	1 557.0	8 596	2 542	5.5	92.2	0.9	4.9	0.8	3.2	3.8	12.1	5.2	7.7	9.4	13.2
46 035	33580	7	Davison	435.5	19 903	1 835	45.7	92.8	1.2	3.6	1.0	2.9	6.4	16.9	9.9	12.8	11.2	11.4
46 037	...	9	Day	1 027.9	5 571	2 796	5.4	87.4	0.8	10.4	0.8	2.4	5.9	16.5	6.7	9.1	9.7	11.1
46 039	...	9	Deuel	622.7	4 231	2 880	6.8	95.7	1.1	0.9	0.4	2.9	5.5	17.6	6.8	9.9	10.7	13.1
46 041	...	9	Dewey	2 302.5	5 742	2 775	2.5	24.6	0.9	73.5	0.7	4.6	12.3	24.4	9.7	12.4	10.5	11.2
46 043	...	9	Douglas	431.8	2 932	2 978	6.8	95.4	0.8	2.8	0.5	1.5	6.7	16.2	7.1	9.2	7.8	11.8
46 045	10100	9	Edmunds	1 126.0	3 952	2 904	3.5	96.6	0.8	1.2	0.7	1.8	7.1	16.1	7.1	9.3	10.1	13.1
46 047	...	6	Fall River	1 739.8	6 849	2 688	3.9	87.7	1.8	8.3	1.2	4.1	4.6	13.3	6.2	7.8	9.8	12.5
46 049	...	9	Faulk	981.7	2 354	3 019	2.4	98.2	0.8	0.7	0.3	0.9	8.0	15.6	7.2	9.7	9.4	11.4
46 051	...	7	Grant	681.5	7 148	2 660	10.5	94.2	1.0	1.6	0.7	3.9	6.2	16.5	7.8	9.0	11.1	12.5
46 053	...	9	Gregory	1 015.0	4 171	2 886	4.1	90.4	0.9	9.1	0.8	1.6	6.2	17.2	7.0	8.0	10.3	10.9
46 055	...	8	Haakon	1 810.5	1 892	3 058	1.0	95.1	1.6	3.5	1.3	1.7	5.5	17.0	7.1	8.5	10.0	9.7
46 057	...	9	Hamlin	507.2	6 028	2 749	11.9	94.8	0.6	0.8	0.4	4.1	9.2	21.8	7.8	9.7	10.5	11.0
46 059	...	9	Hand	1 436.6	3 319	2 951	2.3	97.7	0.4	0.9	0.8	1.1	5.5	15.4	7.5	9.3	8.6	12.4
46 061	33580	8	Hanson	434.5	3 374	2 945	7.8	97.3	0.7	0.9	0.8	1.1	8.4	23.5	7.7	8.8	12.6	12.0
46 063	...	9	Harding	2 671.6	1 278	3 097	0.5	94.8	1.2	3.4	0.4	2.0	6.3	17.6	7.1	13.0	10.0	12.9
46 065	38180	7	Hughes	741.5	17 600	1 939	23.7	85.0	1.2	12.1	1.1	3.1	7.0	16.7	7.7	13.7	11.6	12.7
46 067	...	8	Hutchinson	812.9	7 368	2 638	9.1	95.6	1.4	1.4	0.4	2.1	8.1	16.4	7.6	9.2	9.9	11.4
46 069	...	9	Hyde	860.5	1 352	3 090	1.6	90.1	1.0	9.4	0.4	1.3	5.2	15.0	7.5	9.8	10.5	10.8
46 071	...	8	Jackson	1 863.9	3 326	2 950	1.8	45.1	1.5	53.1	0.6	4.1	10.6	22.9	10.7	11.5	9.3	10.4
46 073	...	9	Jerauld	526.2	2 004	3 048	3.8	94.4	0.4	1.1	0.6	4.4	7.2	16.8	4.4	9.9	10.8	10.1
46 075	...	9	Jones	969.7	927	3 109	1.0	92.0	1.4	5.9	1.1	2.7	4.6	15.5	5.6	10.1	9.6	12.5
46 077	...	9	Kingsbury	832.2	5 001	2 834	6.0	96.2	0.8	1.6	0.7	2.0	5.9	15.9	7.5	9.4	10.2	12.1
46 079	...	6	Lake	563.3	12 909	2 233	22.9	94.3	1.2	1.6	1.7	2.4	5.5	14.3	10.6	9.4	9.4	11.4
46 081	43940	6	Lawrence	800.0	25 281	1 596	31.6	92.9	1.2	3.3	1.4	3.0	4.7	13.5	12.1	12.2	10.2	11.3
46 083	43620	3	Lincoln	577.3	54 469	924	94.4	94.9	2.0	1.0	1.7	1.9	7.6	20.1	7.0	14.9	14.9	12.1
46 085	...	9	Lyman	1 642.2	3 894	2 911	2.4	58.6	1.1	40.9	0.7	2.0	9.0	20.1	8.9	12.1	10.3	10.4
46 087	43620	3	McCook	574.2	5 625	2 790	9.8	95.3	0.7	1.3	0.4	3.2	7.5	19.1	7.3	9.3	11.4	11.3
46 089	...	9	McPherson	1 136.6	2 438	3 009	2.1	97.9	0.7	0.6	0.3	1.3	7.1	16.0	6.0	8.2	9.1	10.9
46 091	...	9	Marshall	838.1	4 801	2 847	5.7	84.9	1.0	7.4	0.4	7.5	7.2	15.5	7.9	11.5	10.1	12.6
46 093	39660	3	Meade	3 470.9	27 693	1 502	8.0	90.0	2.4	4.0	1.9	4.3	6.1	17.4	10.9	14.5	11.7	11.4
46 095	...	9	Mellette	1 307.3	2 102	3 039	1.6	43.1	1.3	56.5	0.8	3.5	8.3	22.6	9.3	11.0	9.1	11.6
46 097	...	8	Miner	570.2	2 281	3 024	4.0	95.7	1.8	0.9	0.6	2.4	5.6	17.9	7.2	8.5	9.3	12.4
46 099	43620	3	Minnehaha	807.2	187 318	346	232.1	85.3	6.2	3.2	2.8	4.8	7.8	17.5	9.2	15.5	12.6	12.3
46 101	...	8	Moody	519.4	6 505	2 714	12.5	79.5	2.3	15.1	2.1	3.9	7.4	18.5	8.3	10.5	10.4	12.8
46 102	...	0	Oglala Lakota	2 093.8	14 415	2 135	6.9	5.6	0.6	91.3	0.4	3.6	11.0	26.7	11.4	15.2	10.3	10.2
46 103	39660	3	Pennington	2 776.6	109 372	552	39.4	83.6	2.1	11.0	2.0	4.9	6.7	16.7	8.4	13.6	11.4	11.7
46 105	...	8	Perkins	2 870.5	2 983	2 972	1.0	95.8	1.0	2.1	0.5	1.5	5.6	15.4	7.4	8.7	9.9	12.0
46 107	...	9	Potter	861.1	2 299	3 023	2.7	95.2	0.9	2.6	0.6	2.2	4.9	15.8	6.3	7.4	8.9	11.7
46 109	...	9	Roberts	1 101.0	10 255	2 406	9.3	60.4	1.2	38.2	0.7	2.8	8.8	19.3	9.1	9.6	9.4	11.7
46 111	...	9	Sanborn	569.3	2 396	3 016	4.2	96.0	0.5	1.3	0.4	3.0	8.2	15.6	7.1	11.9	10.9	11.1
46 115	...	9	Spink	1 503.5	6 420	2 722	4.3	96.1	0.9	2.0	0.3	1.8	5.8	17.4	8.2	10.6	9.8	12.0
46 117	38180	9	Stanley	1 444.4	2 993	2 971	2.1	90.2	1.5	8.2	0.7	2.1	6.7	17.8	6.7	11.0	11.7	13.8
46 119	38180	9	Sully	1 006.8	1 421	3 083	1.4	94.2	1.0	3.3	0.3	3.0	6.5	15.6	6.8	10.8	9.5	12.6
46 121	...	9	Todd	1 388.5	10 155	2 423	7.3	10.5	0.7	86.2	0.4	4.3	12.7	28.1	10.2	13.9	10.0	9.1

1. CBSA = Core Based Statistical Area. See Appendix A for explanation. See Appendix B for list of metropolitan areas with component counties. 2. County type code from the Economic Research Service of USDA Rural-Urban Continuum Codes. See Appendix A for definition. 3. Dry land or land partially or temporarily covered by water. 4. May be of any race.

Table B. States and Counties — **Population and Households**

STATE County	Age (percent) 55 to 64 years	65 to 74 years	75 years and over	Percent female	Total persons 2000	2010	Percent change 2000–2010	2010–2016	Components of change 2010–2016 Births	Deaths	Net migration	Households, 2011–2015 Number	Persons per household	Family households	Female family householder[1]	One person
	16	17	18	19	20	21	22	23	24	25	26	27	28	29	30	31
SOUTH CAROLINA—Cont'd																
Sumter	12.6	8.9	6.5	51.7	104 646	107 463	2.7	-0.1	9 384	6 425	-3 103	40 571	2.60	68.4	19.4	27.3
Union	15.2	11.3	8.0	52.5	29 881	28 963	-3.1	-4.5	1 935	2 321	-903	11 666	2.37	67.0	17.1	30.5
Williamsburg	14.9	12.1	7.5	51.9	37 217	34 419	-7.5	-7.2	2 157	2 544	-2 099	11 885	2.64	66.4	21.1	30.6
York	12.6	8.6	5.1	51.7	164 614	226 074	37.3	14.4	18 212	11 878	25 243	90 322	2.61	71.3	13.7	24.1
SOUTH DAKOTA	13.4	9.0	7.1	49.6	754 844	814 195	7.9	6.3	75 478	45 707	21 072	330 858	2.45	64.4	9.7	29.5
Aurora	14.4	10.5	9.9	47.7	3 058	2 710	-11.4	1.0	219	167	-6	1 157	2.24	65.2	5.5	29.8
Beadle	14.1	8.7	8.6	49.5	17 023	17 398	2.2	4.0	2 014	1 223	-67	7 565	2.31	62.6	9.0	32.6
Bennett	11.0	6.3	6.2	51.5	3 574	3 431	-4.0	0.8	440	191	-212	1 050	3.24	72.6	17.0	24.9
Bon Homme	13.6	9.9	10.4	41.2	7 260	7 067	-2.7	-1.2	404	461	-31	2 480	2.23	64.6	4.4	31.1
Brookings	9.9	6.2	4.9	48.8	28 220	31 965	13.3	6.8	2 568	1 219	822	12 325	2.38	58.2	6.1	30.4
Brown	13.4	8.2	8.0	50.6	35 460	36 531	3.0	7.1	3 048	2 330	1 920	15 996	2.29	62.3	9.1	32.9
Brule	14.7	9.1	8.9	50.5	5 364	5 255	-2.0	-0.3	472	343	-144	2 067	2.47	71.8	10.0	23.2
Buffalo	9.7	5.3	2.6	50.0	2 032	1 912	-5.9	6.9	315	118	-59	546	3.73	79.7	28.9	18.5
Butte	15.5	11.3	8.4	50.0	9 094	10 110	11.2	0.9	786	653	-47	4 079	2.49	62.5	6.5	30.3
Campbell	20.3	11.4	14.1	48.5	1 782	1 466	-17.7	-6.0	71	79	-72	683	2.27	61.5	1.6	35.4
Charles Mix	12.9	8.9	8.9	50.3	9 350	9 129	-2.4	2.9	997	600	-127	3 171	2.78	65.5	12.4	30.1
Clark	15.3	10.5	10.0	49.4	4 143	3 691	-10.9	-0.9	334	289	-81	1 488	2.21	59.2	3.9	36.2
Clay	9.2	6.6	5.2	50.4	13 537	13 868	2.4	1.6	924	611	-101	5 335	2.21	48.6	5.8	28.8
Codington	13.7	8.6	7.7	49.9	25 897	27 227	5.1	3.1	2 371	1 495	-5	11 934	2.28	61.2	9.8	30.3
Corson	12.0	6.8	4.3	49.7	4 181	4 048	-3.2	2.1	534	288	-175	1 229	3.37	76.6	22.8	19.7
Custer	21.5	17.8	9.2	50.4	7 275	8 216	12.9	4.6	455	511	442	3 759	2.12	68.1	7.6	26.4
Davison	13.5	8.8	9.2	50.1	18 741	19 504	4.1	2.0	1 620	1 288	75	8 580	2.20	61.5	8.5	31.8
Day	15.7	13.6	11.6	48.9	6 267	5 710	-8.9	-2.4	395	461	-58	2 533	2.15	62.8	9.6	34.9
Deuel	14.8	11.4	10.3	48.1	4 498	4 364	-3.0	-3.0	288	247	-165	1 900	2.25	65.5	5.2	32.3
Dewey	10.0	5.2	4.4	50.9	5 972	5 303	-11.2	8.3	894	442	-7	1 640	3.36	67.2	20.6	27.0
Douglas	15.6	12.3	13.2	51.0	3 458	3 002	-13.2	-2.3	225	262	-39	1 296	2.22	67.5	3.1	27.7
Edmunds	15.7	10.8	10.7	49.5	4 367	4 071	-6.8	-2.9	285	275	-108	1 586	2.30	68.8	6.6	26.9
Fall River	18.1	16.6	11.2	49.8	7 453	7 094	-4.8	-3.5	365	704	71	3 087	2.14	59.2	8.8	37.9
Faulk	15.5	10.2	13.0	49.6	2 640	2 364	-10.5	-0.4	187	166	-36	951	2.16	58.6	3.2	35.4
Grant	15.8	11.4	9.8	48.2	7 847	7 356	-6.3	-2.8	511	508	-212	3 209	2.20	69.3	5.3	26.6
Gregory	15.9	11.9	12.5	48.1	4 792	4 271	-10.9	-2.3	311	387	-22	1 970	2.12	60.1	10.0	37.4
Haakon	18.8	11.2	12.2	49.5	2 196	1 937	-11.8	-2.3	126	146	-15	855	2.39	70.4	5.1	26.5
Hamlin	12.2	9.4	8.4	49.2	5 540	5 903	6.6	2.1	736	414	-209	2 178	2.64	74.4	4.2	19.5
Hand	16.0	10.9	14.4	49.9	3 741	3 431	-8.3	-3.3	225	265	-81	1 510	2.19	61.8	6.4	35.2
Hanson	13.2	10.2	3.7	49.6	3 139	3 331	6.1	1.3	292	127	-120	1 056	2.96	75.4	4.2	23.1
Harding	16.5	8.9	7.6	46.2	1 353	1 255	-7.2	1.8	101	50	-32	507	2.48	67.5	6.3	29.8
Hughes	14.3	9.2	7.1	50.7	16 481	17 022	3.3	3.4	1 486	875	-30	7 117	2.30	59.3	5.2	37.0
Hutchinson	14.8	9.6	13.0	50.6	8 075	7 343	-9.1	0.3	605	696	100	2 942	2.23	66.5	7.9	31.5
Hyde	16.3	10.8	14.1	49.4	1 671	1 420	-15.0	-4.8	86	97	-54	545	2.52	65.5	7.3	33.0
Jackson	11.2	7.0	6.5	49.6	2 930	3 031	3.4	9.7	444	202	50	1 032	3.05	68.8	12.3	26.0
Jerauld	15.5	12.5	12.8	50.0	2 295	2 071	-9.8	-3.2	153	158	-68	863	2.31	69.4	6.6	26.3
Jones	19.5	11.4	11.0	51.2	1 193	1 006	-15.7	-7.9	62	56	-103	426	1.83	50.2	4.2	47.9
Kingsbury	16.3	11.4	11.2	49.2	5 815	5 148	-11.5	-2.9	385	434	-116	2 283	2.18	63.5	4.0	30.7
Lake	17.4	14.3	7.6	48.0	11 276	11 200	-0.7	15.3	817	682	1 495	4 764	2.38	65.2	6.4	30.5
Lawrence	16.4	11.6	8.0	50.0	21 802	24 094	10.5	4.9	1 475	1 374	1 070	10 528	2.22	61.5	7.4	30.6
Lincoln	11.0	7.1	4.6	50.3	24 131	44 823	85.7	21.5	4 880	1 281	5 834	18 037	2.74	74.1	9.0	20.5
Lyman	14.5	8.1	6.7	47.5	3 895	3 755	-3.6	3.7	434	198	-99	1 394	2.74	67.9	12.4	27.0
McCook	14.2	9.8	10.1	49.6	5 832	5 618	-3.7	0.1	478	488	-20	2 253	2.37	68.5	7.5	26.5
McPherson	14.8	11.8	16.1	51.4	2 904	2 459	-15.3	-0.9	157	214	37	1 009	1.89	60.9	8.1	38.4
Marshall	15.1	11.7	8.5	46.2	4 576	4 656	1.7	3.1	396	324	89	1 765	2.52	63.5	7.7	30.0
Meade	13.3	9.0	5.7	47.9	24 253	25 459	5.0	8.8	1 969	1 119	1 363	10 593	2.42	71.4	7.7	23.1
Mellette	12.0	9.0	7.0	47.4	2 083	2 048	-1.7	2.6	210	134	-31	675	3.04	72.3	23.4	24.9
Miner	17.3	10.7	11.1	48.7	2 884	2 389	-17.2	-4.5	145	192	-60	1 006	2.24	63.2	5.4	32.7
Minnehaha	12.2	7.5	5.3	49.7	148 281	169 476	14.3	10.5	17 978	8 185	7 935	70 140	2.48	63.2	11.2	29.6
Moody	14.8	9.4	7.9	49.0	6 595	6 486	-1.7	0.3	566	315	-207	2 681	2.30	68.8	9.9	27.7
Oglala Lakota	8.3	4.4	2.5	50.8	12 466	13 586	9.0	6.1	2 112	878	-396	2 933	4.73	80.5	40.8	17.9
Pennington	14.4	9.9	7.0	49.6	88 565	100 937	14.0	8.4	9 598	5 142	3 869	41 670	2.46	63.7	10.9	30.3
Perkins	17.1	11.7	12.1	50.3	3 363	2 982	-11.3	0.0	209	261	47	1 306	2.21	63.9	7.0	34.2
Potter	15.1	15.7	14.4	51.2	2 693	2 329	-13.5	-1.3	144	218	41	1 056	2.11	60.9	6.3	37.4
Roberts	13.2	10.2	8.7	49.9	10 016	10 149	1.3	1.0	1 127	694	-327	3 652	2.74	66.5	13.3	29.4
Sanborn	16.6	9.5	9.0	47.7	2 675	2 355	-12.0	1.7	208	168	18	1 072	2.09	64.6	4.4	29.1
Spink	15.8	9.8	10.6	49.8	7 454	6 415	-13.9	0.1	467	463	-4	2 631	2.41	63.7	8.9	30.9
Stanley	13.3	11.6	7.3	48.8	2 772	2 966	7.0	0.9	236	109	-83	1 268	2.34	68.1	10.6	24.8
Sully	17.6	10.6	9.9	47.1	1 556	1 373	-11.8	3.5	97	54	6	622	2.34	64.3	3.7	32.6
Todd	8.2	4.9	2.9	51.4	9 050	9 612	6.2	5.6	1 717	642	-552	2 737	3.62	72.1	37.2	24.2

1. No spouse present.

Table B. States and Counties — Population, Vital Statistics, Health, and Crime

STATE County	Persons in group quarters, 2016	Daytime population, 2011–2015 Number	Employ- ment/ resi- dence ratio	Births, 2016 Total	Rate[1]	Deaths, 2016 Number	Rate[1]	Persons under 65 with no health insurance, 2015 Number	Percent	Medicare, 2015 Total Beneficiaries	Enrolled in Original Medicare	Enrolled in Medicare Advantage	Serious crimes known to police,[2] 2014 Total Number	Rate[3]
	32	33	34	35	36	37	38	39	40	41	42	43	44	45
SOUTH CAROLINA—Cont'd														
Sumter	2 666	108 369	1.01	1 446	13.5	1 055	9.8	11 693	13.2	20 552	16 637	3 915	4 780	4 395
Union	499	26 271	0.83	313	11.3	377	13.6	2 594	11.7	6 782	4 387	2 395	1 019	3 647
Williamsburg	1 284	31 262	0.82	347	10.9	395	12.4	3 236	12.9	6 937	4 858	2 079	1 164	3 537
York	3 956	220 824	0.83	2 944	11.4	2 012	7.8	22 367	10.4	46 059	34 699	11 360	6 425	2 637
SOUTH DAKOTA	34 010	846 023	1.01	12 114	14.0	7 296	8.4	82 558	11.8	152 107	120 130	31 977	18 688	2 190
Aurora	95	2 639	0.93	37	13.5	20	7.3	312	14.7	519	407	112	10	367
Beadle	621	18 211	1.00	327	18.1	198	10.9	2 210	14.7	4 114	3 223	891	403	2 206
Bennett	37	3 261	0.84	66	19.1	30	8.7	642	22.3	456	436	20	56	1 619
Bon Homme	1 544	6 418	0.78	66	9.5	67	9.6	546	12.8	1 512	1 264	248	2	28
Brookings	3 599	33 929	1.05	434	12.7	195	5.7	2 907	10.8	3 829	2 981	848	468	1 408
Brown	1 366	39 133	1.05	481	12.3	354	9.0	3 230	10.2	7 034	6 121	913	675	1 835
Brule	132	5 420	1.04	70	13.4	47	9.0	747	17.5	1 021	840	181	NA	NA
Buffalo	3	2 039	1.00	48	23.5	33	16.2	382	20.7	D	147	D	NA	NA
Butte	111	8 807	0.70	121	11.9	107	10.5	1 148	13.9	2 068	1 530	538	169	1 626
Campbell	0	1 458	0.88	12	8.7	7	5.1	117	11.3	560	466	94	5	384
Charles Mix	589	9 558	1.08	173	18.4	116	12.3	1 439	19.5	1 708	1 493	215	65	810
Clark	489	3 482	0.92	62	17.0	37	10.1	400	13.8	794	529	265	9	251
Clay	2 247	13 655	0.95	135	9.6	90	6.4	1 214	11.9	1 709	1 386	323	319	2 283
Codington	381	28 812	1.07	371	13.2	223	7.9	2 392	10.2	5 100	3 109	1 991	600	2 140
Corson	1	4 053	0.92	82	19.8	49	11.9	708	19.7	665	625	40	13	305
Custer	252	7 611	0.79	70	8.1	81	9.4	771	12.8	2 222	1 817	405	102	1 196
Davison	769	21 092	1.13	254	12.8	184	9.2	1 630	10.3	3 827	3 167	660	667	3 349
Day	139	5 416	0.92	63	11.3	76	13.6	680	16.6	1 403	995	408	NA	NA
Deuel	50	4 110	0.90	47	11.1	38	9.0	393	11.5	917	600	317	24	556
Dewey	19	5 872	1.16	145	25.3	92	16.0	1 098	22.1	686	663	23	11	194
Douglas	178	2 908	0.96	39	13.3	34	11.6	286	12.9	766	610	156	5	165
Edmunds	420	3 472	0.73	51	12.9	36	9.1	345	11.0	841	740	101	2	50
Fall River	211	7 113	1.07	61	8.9	100	14.6	594	12.3	2 244	1 920	324	NA	NA
Faulk	497	2 360	1.00	37	15.7	21	8.9	161	9.1	572	543	29	10	418
Grant	104	7 597	1.10	87	12.2	79	11.1	623	11.1	1 728	1 034	694	NA	NA
Gregory	44	4 083	0.93	55	13.2	49	11.7	520	16.7	1 151	914	237	NA	NA
Haakon	36	2 111	1.03	19	10.0	14	7.4	178	12.5	459	395	64	NA	NA
Hamlin	245	5 321	0.77	119	19.7	60	10.0	573	11.5	1 045	684	361	65	1 087
Hand	61	3 281	0.95	33	9.9	29	8.7	259	10.3	679	605	74	12	355
Hanson	520	2 568	0.51	39	11.6	10	3.0	330	11.3	1 253	1 046	207	15	438
Harding	29	1 374	1.07	19	14.9	4	3.1	133	12.7	186	155	31	1	79
Hughes	771	18 061	1.06	231	13.1	166	9.4	1 557	10.9	2 846	2 513	333	535	3 033
Hutchinson	832	6 719	0.86	115	15.6	107	14.5	629	11.4	1 833	1 369	464	25	352
Hyde	38	1 478	1.09	12	8.9	10	7.4	129	12.1	319	300	19	NA	NA
Jackson	42	3 170	0.94	69	20.7	29	8.7	618	22.2	404	352	52	NA	NA
Jerauld	176	2 269	1.24	23	11.5	19	9.5	172	11.5	515	442	73	2	97
Jones	0	738	0.91	8	8.6	7	7.6	122	17.3	216	184	32	NA	NA
Kingsbury	203	4 654	0.82	61	12.2	64	12.8	352	9.1	1 376	1 095	281	NA	NA
Lake	875	11 784	0.95	129	10.0	116	9.0	899	9.5	3 271	2 668	603	NA	NA
Lawrence	1 072	24 432	0.98	235	9.3	217	8.6	2 276	11.8	4 953	3 759	1 194	664	2 643
Lincoln	284	38 891	0.60	758	13.9	220	4.0	2 750	5.8	2 473	1 729	744	1 134	2 217
Lyman	36	3 776	0.96	74	19.0	25	6.4	568	17.8	595	515	80	NA	NA
McCook	312	4 611	0.66	81	14.4	77	13.7	454	10.2	999	777	222	47	829
McPherson	347	2 221	0.96	29	11.9	23	9.4	229	13.1	483	438	45	1	41
Marshall	373	4 463	0.90	74	15.4	41	8.5	656	17.1	955	832	123	52	1 084
Meade	798	21 075	0.61	303	10.9	190	6.9	2 526	11.3	4 105	3 210	895	297	1 073
Mellette	49	1 928	0.79	36	17.1	17	8.1	295	17.9	315	299	16	21	1 003
Miner	80	2 202	0.91	24	10.5	23	10.1	168	9.8	507	459	48	14	603
Minnehaha	6 275	195 965	1.17	2 974	15.9	1 396	7.5	16 547	10.5	32 744	24 510	8 234	5 216	2 861
Moody	164	5 746	0.79	96	14.8	46	7.1	773	14.6	978	772	206	55	861
Oglala Lakota	91	14 903	1.24	313	21.7	174	12.1	2 317	18.2	1 010	989	21	NA	NA
Pennington	2 568	111 919	1.11	1 493	13.7	892	8.2	11 707	13.1	21 470	17 199	4 271	3 702	3 460
Perkins	65	2 990	1.01	33	11.1	24	8.0	337	14.6	771	637	134	13	425
Potter	63	2 289	0.98	23	10.0	33	14.4	197	12.0	709	683	26	10	415
Roberts	281	10 014	0.93	175	17.1	96	9.4	1 480	18.0	1 825	1 428	397	55	535
Sanborn	174	1 965	0.70	37	15.4	15	6.3	230	12.0	507	426	81	NA	NA
Spink	405	6 414	0.95	67	10.4	74	11.5	608	12.0	1 495	1 291	204	35	525
Stanley	0	2 610	0.78	40	13.4	9	3.0	290	11.9	552	481	71	7	235
Sully	0	1 499	1.04	14	9.9	6	4.2	159	13.8	223	205	18	2	137
Todd	28	10 145	1.07	271	26.7	118	11.6	1 531	17.5	D	695	D	NA	NA

1. Per 1,000 estimated resident population.   2. Data for serious crimes have not been adjusted for underreporting; this may affect comparability between geographic areas and over time.
3. Per 100,000 population estimated by the FBI.

Table B. States and Counties — Crime, Education, Money Income, and Poverty

STATE County	Serious crimes known to police, 2014 (cont.)[1] Rate[2] Violent	Property	Education School enrollment and attainment, 2011–2015 Enrollment[3] Total	Percent private	Attainment[4] (percent) High school graduate or less	Bachelor's degree or more	Local government expenditures,[5] 2013–2014 Total current spending (mil dol)	Current spending per student (dollars)	Money income, 2011–2015 Per capita income[6] (dollars)	Median income (dollars)	Households Percent with income of less than $50,000	with income of $200,000 or more	Income and poverty, 2015 Median household income (dollars)	Percent below poverty level All persons	Children under 18 years	Children 5 to 17 years in families
	46	47	48	49	50	51	52	53	54	55	56	57	58	59	60	61
SOUTH CAROLINA—Cont'd																
Sumter	647	3 748	29 547	18.0	47.5	19.2	147.0	8 752	20 806	41 332	58.8	1.4	41 058	19.6	29.8	30.0
Union	523	3 124	6 396	10.6	59.8	12.2	35.7	8 522	19 087	34 033	66.4	0.7	35 467	23.2	33.8	32.7
Williamsburg	523	3 015	8 330	13.1	61.7	11.3	48.4	10 854	16 344	28 297	71.8	1.1	28 943	33.6	43.3	42.5
York	398	2 238	64 110	10.4	39.4	29.5	392.0	9 479	27 868	54 117	46.4	4.1	57 302	12.5	17.1	17.0
SOUTH DAKOTA	327	1 864	216 895	13.0	40.4	27.0	1 160.4	8 873	26 747	50 957	49.0	3.2	53 263	13.5	17.7	16.0
Aurora	37	330	654	10.7	49.1	17.9	6.8	11 911	25 965	48 750	51.4	2.4	50 392	9.6	12.0	10.6
Beadle	301	1 905	3 971	14.4	49.5	19.7	24.0	9 061	24 662	46 267	53.3	1.8	47 592	15.5	21.4	20.7
Bennett	318	1 301	1 139	6.7	49.2	17.5	5.8	11 550	16 549	42 171	59.5	1.5	40 529	35.1	47.0	42.5
Bon Homme	14	14	1 371	4.9	49.6	18.5	11.0	9 968	22 165	45 254	54.5	2.3	48 900	14.6	17.1	14.8
Brookings	99	1 309	13 574	5.5	31.5	40.8	37.0	8 267	25 727	50 082	49.9	2.9	55 749	14.5	11.2	10.2
Brown	242	1 593	9 658	19.0	40.7	28.3	41.4	7 738	28 841	53 100	45.9	3.7	52 065	10.2	12.6	11.1
Brule	NA	NA	1 072	15.4	45.2	24.3	12.2	10 219	22 591	49 531	50.2	2.1	50 604	12.7	17.6	15.8
Buffalo	NA	NA	642	19.2	61.5	9.5	NA	NA	11 372	31 163	67.8	0.0	22 894	36.8	43.5	45.3
Butte	173	1 453	2 397	14.3	46.9	17.7	13.8	7 899	23 267	41 920	54.4	3.2	43 572	13.9	20.1	18.0
Campbell	0	384	327	1.5	52.1	21.8	1.4	11 533	30 998	45 110	55.3	4.5	49 569	9.5	8.6	7.9
Charles Mix	125	685	2 501	16.0	49.3	18.3	18.9	11 020	20 814	43 109	56.6	2.8	41 005	23.3	34.6	31.7
Clark	84	167	687	2.8	47.6	21.3	5.8	9 146	25 250	49 600	50.5	2.8	60 544	12.6	21.1	20.4
Clay	279	2 004	6 679	3.5	32.1	45.0	10.8	8 890	21 121	36 608	63.2	1.4	43 902	19.0	17.7	16.1
Codington	225	1 915	6 825	11.7	48.5	20.3	35.1	7 796	26 767	48 912	51.7	2.7	53 073	10.8	12.4	11.0
Corson	0	305	1 218	1.6	52.2	16.1	12.6	14 226	13 848	31 676	69.5	1.4	31 621	47.4	59.8	54.3
Custer	47	1 149	1 384	12.5	37.9	26.0	8.5	8 760	29 934	52 218	47.6	4.0	54 309	10.7	17.7	15.8
Davison	346	3 002	4 903	22.9	35.9	27.2	27.4	8 567	25 844	49 991	50.0	2.0	47 591	13.4	15.1	13.3
Day	NA	NA	1 135	4.3	50.0	17.1	6.8	9 435	25 844	39 216	62.8	2.5	45 131	14.2	18.1	15.3
Deuel	46	510	887	4.1	50.8	20.3	4.2	7 759	30 511	53 152	47.4	4.2	54 087	10.0	12.4	10.6
Dewey	0	194	1 625	0.9	51.5	14.0	5.0	13 470	16 216	37 206	61.9	2.2	38 337	24.7	32.9	33.3
Douglas	99	66	595	22.4	55.2	19.3	3.3	10 470	29 235	52 500	47.5	5.4	51 915	10.4	12.2	10.6
Edmunds	0	50	907	8.5	45.0	24.0	6.5	9 919	27 487	56 000	44.3	3.3	56 304	10.7	14.9	12.8
Fall River	NA	NA	1 188	11.1	38.5	23.2	10.8	9 753	24 653	45 997	55.2	1.2	44 065	14.6	22.6	18.4
Faulk	0	418	521	22.5	43.5	23.2	2.9	8 991	26 958	43 679	54.3	3.5	47 802	12.9	14.4	12.8
Grant	NA	NA	1 362	10.6	52.7	17.1	10.5	9 094	26 741	51 272	49.1	2.2	51 251	9.2	11.0	10.3
Gregory	NA	NA	854	6.9	51.9	17.2	7.8	10 824	24 035	37 540	61.4	1.6	36 150	18.1	24.9	21.6
Haakon	NA	NA	462	7.8	47.6	20.1	2.6	8 852	23 599	41 518	56.5	2.2	50 221	10.8	14.8	13.7
Hamlin	0	1 087	1 448	5.2	51.9	20.1	12.2	9 385	26 153	58 602	40.2	3.5	57 278	9.0	11.4	10.7
Hand	0	355	652	11.8	44.8	22.5	4.3	9 479	29 723	47 163	52.3	3.5	52 718	8.5	10.9	9.6
Hanson	58	380	1 040	16.4	40.4	26.0	3.3	7 583	23 656	60 741	38.4	2.3	59 508	8.7	15.3	13.8
Harding	0	79	338	1.8	37.3	29.9	2.8	15 306	25 087	52 396	47.7	3.4	57 053	10.2	13.3	13.8
Hughes	431	2 602	3 671	11.5	36.6	32.9	19.6	7 451	29 642	59 177	42.8	2.2	60 582	10.8	13.3	12.5
Hutchinson	14	338	1 611	6.1	45.5	26.7	13.4	9 589	27 880	45 075	54.6	3.2	49 558	12.3	18.2	16.5
Hyde	NA	NA	260	1.5	55.6	16.1	3.0	11 090	26 239	51 776	47.5	0.9	49 820	11.1	14.9	13.0
Jackson	NA	NA	903	4.1	43.9	19.8	4.3	11 275	19 216	45 074	59.5	4.3	36 308	32.5	45.2	42.5
Jerauld	0	97	471	11.7	52.0	16.0	3.2	10 218	34 277	53 125	47.2	4.6	49 054	13.7	19.9	18.2
Jones	NA	NA	120	4.2	46.4	16.6	1.9	10 206	26 103	35 972	62.2	0.2	47 362	13.5	22.6	20.3
Kingsbury	NA	NA	942	7.6	46.2	21.8	10.0	9 875	29 747	53 828	46.7	3.2	54 543	9.5	12.2	11.7
Lake	NA	NA	3 454	4.1	38.9	32.4	16.6	8 134	29 610	54 535	47.1	3.9	55 300	10.1	11.7	10.5
Lawrence	179	2 464	6 158	10.8	39.0	29.5	26.0	8 662	27 083	45 548	53.6	2.4	51 553	12.9	16.0	13.4
Lincoln	268	1 949	13 968	17.3	26.3	40.4	52.5	7 908	35 559	76 094	30.1	6.5	77 540	4.3	4.8	-4.0
Lyman	NA	NA	930	8.6	48.0	19.2	5.4	12 833	20 912	43 030	55.8	2.2	39 527	22.7	35.2	31.7
McCook	0	829	1 317	12.7	42.6	23.9	11.8	10 133	30 086	56 954	42.1	2.9	56 382	9.5	13.7	12.7
McPherson	41	0	358	8.4	50.8	15.4	4.6	12 486	22 263	36 375	62.5	1.5	43 859	15.7	22.5	19.9
Marshall	229	854	1 016	13.7	43.3	22.3	6.0	8 733	25 161	51 788	46.5	2.4	50 216	12.3	21.3	20.3
Meade	90	982	6 664	9.5	39.9	23.0	22.2	7 761	27 123	52 473	47.8	2.9	55 515	9.9	13.2	11.4
Mellette	191	812	655	6.3	54.2	15.3	5.1	11 813	14 123	30 938	67.7	1.2	34 241	35.6	44.2	42.9
Miner	43	560	501	10.8	47.8	23.0	3.6	9 861	30 204	44 938	54.3	3.3	47 970	10.8	14.3	12.2
Minnehaha	372	2 489	45 032	18.6	38.3	29.4	251.0	8 106	27 387	53 525	46.7	3.0	55 605	12.2	14.5	13.4
Moody	204	657	1 569	5.7	43.0	25.6	7.7	8 720	26 918	52 446	47.4	3.4	54 729	10.7	14.6	13.6
Oglala Lakota	NA	NA	4 901	9.9	50.3	11.4	22.9	15 272	9 150	26 369	74.9	1.0	30 391	44.2	47.0	43.2
Pennington	497	2 962	26 717	13.9	35.6	28.2	151.4	8 861	27 298	50 890	49.1	3.5	52 217	12.2	18.4	16.6
Perkins	33	393	573	22.7	48.1	19.2	5.0	12 866	27 174	39 773	58.5	4.7	44 132	13.1	15.0	13.1
Potter	0	415	442	6.3	50.5	20.5	4.1	11 184	29 158	46 081	53.7	4.1	54 655	10.0	13.0	11.2
Roberts	126	409	2 538	4.0	50.9	16.7	16.3	10 839	23 010	48 614	51.4	2.8	42 744	20.0	29.0	27.3
Sanborn	NA	NA	374	10.4	47.4	17.5	4.0	9 221	29 952	50 541	49.3	3.8	49 638	11.9	18.1	17.2
Spink	15	510	1 451	8.3	45.6	22.3	12.8	9 794	28 165	48 217	52.0	4.4	46 504	12.1	15.2	11.9
Stanley	134	101	646	2.5	44.9	26.9	4.5	10 830	30 597	56 829	44.6	6.4	62 015	8.3	11.0	9.4
Sully	0	137	349	9.2	43.9	23.8	3.1	11 367	37 078	60 417	39.5	6.6	58 230	6.9	8.6	7.1
Todd	NA	NA	3 567	9.2	45.2	14.4	23.5	11 362	11 616	31 128	73.2	1.2	29 193	44.0	52.3	48.5

1. Data for serious crimes have not been adjusted for underreporting; this may affect comparability between geographic areas and over time.   2. Per 100,000 population estimated by the FBI.
3. All persons 3 years old and over enrolled in nursery school through college.   4. Persons 25 years old and over.   5. Elementary and secondary education expenditures.
6. Based on population estimated by the American Community Survey, 2011–2015.

STATE County	Total (mil dol)	Percent change, 2014–2015	Per capita[1] Dollars	Per capita[1] Rank	Wages and salaries (mil dol)	Supplements to wages and salaries; employer contributions (mil dol) Pension and insurance	Supplements to wages and salaries; employer contributions (mil dol) Government social insurance	Proprietors' income (mil dol)	Dividends, interest, and rent (mil dol)	Personal transfer receipts (mil dol)	Earnings, 2015 Total (mil dol)	Contributions for government social insurance (mil dol) From employee and self-employed	Contributions for government social insurance (mil dol) From employer
	62	63	64	65	66	67	68	69	70	71	72	73	74
SOUTH CAROLINA—Cont'd													
Sumter	3 959	2.9	36 834	1 770	1 845	396	158	177	653	1 050	2 576	153	158
Union	836	3.7	30 115	2 868	277	53	22	34	102	308	385	30	22
Williamsburg	899	3.1	27 637	2 994	386	86	30	23	113	358	525	39	30
York	9 992	6.8	39 778	1 468	3 941	618	303	519	1 175	1 780	5 381	348	303
SOUTH DAKOTA	41 104	4.8	47 912	X	17 761	3 235	1 308	7 179	8 612	6 088	29 483	1 696	1 308
Aurora	128	-1.6	46 921	416	27	6	2	41	24	18	76	3	2
Beadle	920	9.9	50 086	487	340	64	25	202	210	130	631	34	25
Bennett	101	-2.6	29 463	2 263	28	9	2	15	17	30	54	3	2
Bon Homme	247	0.2	35 431	1 593	62	16	5	54	50	49	137	8	5
Brookings	1 485	6.1	43 815	1 018	766	188	56	230	312	160	1 241	66	56
Brown	1 939	6.6	50 001	545	876	160	66	354	429	259	1 457	87	66
Brule	234	-3.2	44 245	478	66	14	5	70	48	37	155	7	5
Buffalo	53	6.9	25 341	2 980	20	6	2	8	8	18	36	2	2
Butte	348	-0.9	33 875	2 061	101	20	7	59	65	72	188	12	7
Campbell	58	-9.9	41 709	485	18	3	1	8	15	11	31	2	1
Charles Mix	386	2.2	41 119	874	111	27	8	122	72	77	269	12	8
Clark	163	-13.5	44 662	294	37	7	3	24	61	24	71	4	3
Clay	503	4.4	36 022	917	214	65	15	70	106	85	365	19	15
Codington	1 196	3.7	42 820	844	621	113	46	121	260	187	901	56	46
Corson	114	-10.9	27 107	2 396	32	9	2	26	19	32	70	3	2
Custer	358	1.9	42 405	965	86	20	7	28	95	73	141	10	7
Davison	996	7.6	50 132	496	487	85	37	186	225	146	795	48	37
Day	232	-1.4	41 809	726	64	14	5	36	60	51	118	7	5
Deuel	221	0.9	50 958	275	61	13	5	61	42	33	139	7	5
Dewey	200	-10.0	35 125	1 230	82	23	6	26	35	50	138	7	6
Douglas	165	7.9	55 554	281	42	8	3	61	28	24	115	5	3
Edmunds	192	-5.3	48 026	327	49	10	3	41	51	28	103	6	3
Fall River	301	0.4	43 766	900	106	26	11	43	67	82	186	12	11
Faulk	102	-18.8	43 730	239	24	5	2	24	28	19	54	3	2
Grant	453	15.2	63 456	763	166	28	12	182	78	57	388	22	12
Gregory	173	-3.6	41 240	1 184	47	10	3	38	38	38	99	5	3
Haakon	98	-9.9	52 801	109	30	6	2	33	20	13	72	3	2
Hamlin	224	5.8	37 084	1 926	65	13	5	31	44	36	114	7	5
Hand	176	-5.9	52 543	155	49	9	3	52	39	25	113	5	3
Hanson	218	0.5	64 310	108	24	5	2	46	70	37	77	4	2
Harding	70	-13.8	54 916	162	23	4	2	25	14	6	54	2	2
Hughes	862	1.7	49 087	484	461	108	33	84	184	113	687	39	33
Hutchinson	365	4.4	49 951	338	93	18	7	121	69	58	238	11	7
Hyde	64	-12.8	46 040	569	21	5	1	14	18	10	41	2	1
Jackson	85	-9.0	25 478	2 837	24	7	2	11	16	24	44	2	2
Jerauld	106	12.8	53 084	319	50	9	3	31	22	19	94	5	3
Jones	55	-10.3	59 561	163	14	3	1	17	13	6	36	1	1
Kingsbury	242	-7.0	48 486	296	63	13	5	41	53	40	122	7	5
Lake	736	12.9	58 299	398	192	42	14	202	164	115	449	26	14
Lawrence	1 092	4.1	43 984	954	414	75	31	96	288	183	615	40	31
Lincoln	3 342	10.3	63 242	208	952	137	68	548	630	221	1 705	99	68
Lyman	169	12.9	43 701	1 615	45	11	3	52	32	29	111	4	3
McCook	259	6.1	46 234	384	51	10	4	65	46	40	129	6	4
McPherson	99	-5.8	40 910	798	19	4	1	25	28	20	50	3	1
Marshall	217	0.0	45 420	555	62	12	5	57	47	32	136	6	5
Meade	1 043	2.1	38 645	601	302	75	24	114	192	172	515	32	24
Mellette	57	-11.4	27 659	2 610	10	4	1	9	9	17	23	1	1
Miner	106	1.1	47 356	754	24	5	2	25	23	18	56	3	2
Minnehaha	9 401	7.3	50 760	565	5 827	877	421	1 609	1 689	1 217	8 733	522	421
Moody	313	11.1	48 666	721	80	18	6	66	63	42	170	8	6
Oglala Lakota	336	-1.3	23 406	3 092	152	45	12	17	34	141	226	13	12
Pennington	5 053	3.7	46 480	1 015	2 462	442	188	526	1 265	895	3 618	220	188
Perkins	119	-12.9	39 255	385	39	9	3	26	25	24	77	4	3
Potter	192	-24.0	82 608	21	31	6	2	96	44	21	135	7	2
Roberts	344	5.7	33 377	2 426	121	30	9	38	74	81	198	12	9
Sanborn	120	27.7	51 165	1 047	20	5	1	41	19	15	68	2	1
Spink	334	1.7	51 167	256	89	22	6	81	77	76	198	10	6
Stanley	191	9.4	64 515	177	50	8	4	47	40	18	109	5	4
Sully	86	-30.3	60 007	18	22	4	2	23	23	9	51	2	2
Todd	244	1.2	24 500	3 081	104	30	8	18	28	90	160	8	8

1. Based on the resident population estimated as of July 1 of the year shown.

Table B. States and Counties — Earnings, Social Security, and Housing

STATE County	Earnings, 2015 (cont.)									Social Security beneficiaries, December 2015		Housing units, 2016		
	Percent by selected industries													
	Farm	Mining	Construction	Manufacturing	Information: professional, scientific, technical services	Retail trade	Finance, insurance, real estate and leasing	Health care and social assistance	Government	Number	Rate[1]	Supplemental Security Income recipients, December 2015	Total	Percent change, 2010–2016
	75	76	77	78	79	80	81	82	83	84	85	86	87	88
SOUTH CAROLINA—Cont'd														
Sumter	0.3	0.0	7.0	15.5	3.7	5.9	2.9	11.2	36.3	23 195	216	4 373	47 289	2.8
Union	2.3	D	2.7	25.2	D	7.2	3.2	D	25.9	8 350	301	1 057	13 967	-1.3
Williamsburg	-2.1	0.1	6.4	31.5	D	4.6	D	24.1	D	8 680	266	1 909	15 153	-1.3
York	0.5	0.0	5.5	15.6	8.0	7.5	8.5	10.8	13.4	45 125	180	3 804	104 112	10.5
SOUTH DAKOTA	6.3	0.2	6.7	11.3	6.1	7.6	10.0	13.7	16.1	168 626	197	14 834	383 838	5.6
Aurora	40.0	0.0	D	D	D	2.9	D	10.4	11.9	605	222	22	1 328	0.3
Beadle	13.0	D	5.4	21.7	2.7	5.8	5.8	D	13.1	3 575	196	410	8 390	1.0
Bennett	18.8	0.0	8.7	D	D	8.1	D	D	35.7	510	149	159	1 255	-0.6
Bon Homme	21.0	D	8.1	6.2	2.9	5.3	4.8	D	22.3	1 590	228	81	2 966	1.2
Brookings	6.0	D	5.5	26.0	3.5	4.9	4.9	3.4	25.1	4 340	128	267	14 228	8.3
Brown	2.1	D	6.8	17.3	4.8	8.1	8.1	15.0	12.7	7 390	191	557	17 803	6.6
Brule	34.7	D	6.0	1.2	3.0	5.4	4.8	7.9	13.5	980	186	118	2 515	3.4
Buffalo	22.3	0.0	D	0.0	D	D	D	D	66.3	265	126	100	606	-0.5
Butte	8.4	D	7.6	5.9	5.7	11.8	3.9	6.7	16.1	2 245	219	198	4 718	2.1
Campbell	20.6	0.0	D	D	D	5.7	D	2.4	10.3	400	285	14	977	-0.3
Charles Mix	32.7	0.0	5.1	3.5	2.0	5.9	3.4	D	23.5	1 880	201	260	3 861	0.3
Clark	27.0	0.0	11.5	10.4	D	4.9	D	4.8	15.2	775	211	87	1 812	6.0
Clay	11.5	0.0	2.7	3.7	2.2	5.3	3.7	7.3	48.2	1 995	143	175	5 894	4.5
Codington	2.0	D	7.6	21.4	4.3	9.8	8.3	12.5	14.2	5 570	200	367	12 937	4.4
Corson	34.5	0.0	1.5	1.8	1.4	1.6	D	D	43.0	580	138	242	1 535	-0.3
Custer	2.6	1.1	8.2	1.5	D	5.7	4.2	D	30.0	2 385	282	102	5 036	8.8
Davison	1.9	D	7.4	22.2	6.0	9.3	5.1	12.6	9.9	4 265	216	364	9 302	5.1
Day	20.3	0.0	7.7	10.2	D	6.7	D	7.9	16.8	1 565	281	98	3 721	2.5
Deuel	27.4	0.0	13.4	14.0	D	3.2	2.5	4.6	8.4	1 120	259	33	2 208	0.2
Dewey	10.4	D	2.0	1.2	D	7.0	2.0	D	61.1	845	148	355	2 005	0.1
Douglas	37.2	D	5.4	7.9	D	4.3	D	7.4	7.4	740	249	39	1 439	0.0
Edmunds	16.3	0.0	7.5	5.9	D	10.4	10.4	D	15.5	885	221	43	2 026	3.1
Fall River	12.8	0.5	5.1	1.4	D	4.2	2.3	D	35.4	2 305	337	181	4 166	-0.6
Faulk	31.3	0.0	7.6	D	D	2.2	9.4	D	11.1	520	223	55	1 153	1.5
Grant	3.3	0.4	11.3	12.3	1.3	40.4	D	4.1	4.7	1 820	256	87	3 572	1.3
Gregory	25.7	D	7.2	1.8	1.8	8.2	8.0	13.0	13.0	1 195	285	119	2 504	0.0
Haakon	32.7	0.0	4.7	7.5	5.8	5.2	5.8	D	8.6	425	229	0	1 009	-0.4
Hamlin	12.7	0.0	14.1	D	2.3	5.7	D	3.9	18.7	1 120	185	58	2 867	3.9
Hand	33.2	0.0	4.9	3.6	D	4.0	D	D	9.4	855	257	44	1 813	-0.1
Hanson	35.3	D	15.0	14.7	2.0	2.0	2.9	D	10.6	1 420	419	37	1 178	0.1
Harding	23.3	D	27.1	4.4	D	5.0	D	D	10.7	220	173	0	740	1.2
Hughes	2.3	0.0	4.3	2.4	6.9	6.7	8.0	11.4	41.2	3 325	190	248	7 930	4.0
Hutchinson	33.7	D	3.7	6.4	D	4.4	3.6	D	8.5	1 890	258	94	3 358	0.2
Hyde	30.5	0.0	3.8	3.8	D	5.2	D	D	20.3	335	240	15	701	-1.0
Jackson	19.6	0.0	4.2	D	D	5.7	D	D	43.3	530	160	141	1 187	-0.5
Jerauld	26.5	0.0	D	D	D	2.4	D	D	5.9	640	318	31	1 069	-0.1
Jones	40.2	0.0	D	0.1	D	10.4	3.0	1.6	16.8	245	266	0	609	3.4
Kingsbury	16.5	0.0	7.6	13.5	D	5.6	D	7.4	12.1	1 295	260	72	2 755	1.3
Lake	5.6	D	5.5	35.5	6.0	6.0	3.5	6.2	13.6	3 680	292	156	5 697	2.5
Lawrence	0.0	D	8.9	4.7	6.5	10.5	5.1	12.1	17.4	5 680	228	344	13 712	7.5
Lincoln	1.7	D	12.1	19.1	D	6.7	16.1	12.5	5.1	6 510	123	209	19 870	11.2
Lyman	41.7	0.0	D	D	D	5.9	D	0.2	29.9	730	188	83	1 729	1.5
McCook	33.2	D	6.0	D	4.7	4.4	4.6	8.0	10.4	1 200	215	73	2 535	1.8
McPherson	37.2	0.0	4.7	4.0	D	3.3	11.7	7.1	14.0	685	285	44	1 424	0.4
Marshall	36.2	D	6.5	17.1	2.7	3.8	D	D	12.2	1 035	216	72	2 591	2.2
Meade	3.0	D	12.1	3.7	3.8	7.2	4.4	4.7	38.9	5 345	198	286	11 742	6.6
Mellette	25.4	0.0	D	5.0	D	5.4	D	1.8	44.2	380	185	117	833	-0.6
Miner	27.3	0.0	D	9.6	D	4.1	D	7.1	14.1	570	254	32	1 337	2.2
Minnehaha	0.6	D	5.6	7.5	9.5	7.6	17.6	19.7	9.4	33 165	179	2 971	79 115	10.6
Moody	29.9	0.0	D	D	1.4	1.9	2.6	5.4	20.5	1 330	207	46	2 847	0.8
Oglala Lakota	5.6	0.0	0.6	D	D	D	D	D	77.0	1 495	104	1 119	3 582	-0.3
Pennington	0.0	0.1	8.4	4.1	6.9	8.3	7.6	19.9	20.8	23 700	218	1 988	47 631	6.0
Perkins	22.0	0.0	4.6	D	D	6.4	D	7.0	15.4	760	253	52	1 727	-0.7
Potter	6.3	0.0	4.7	2.2	D	61.2	D	3.0	5.8	670	290	21	1 498	-0.1
Roberts	9.3	D	4.5	9.6	2.6	5.5	D	D	39.9	2 260	220	227	4 958	1.1
Sanborn	51.4	0.0	D	D	D	2.0	D	D	10.3	510	216	21	1 186	1.2
Spink	22.1	0.4	4.4	7.3	3.4	4.7	8.3	D	24.8	1 550	239	160	3 182	1.4
Stanley	33.6	D	26.4	0.7	3.5	6.4	3.3	0.8	9.9	630	213	20	1 480	6.7
Sully	39.8	0.0	D	D	D	6.2	12.5	D	11.1	325	229	6	880	4.1
Todd	9.2	0.0	0.6	D	D	4.1	D	2.6	72.6	1 070	107	607	3 132	-0.3

1. Per 1,000 resident population estimated as of July 1 of the year shown.

Table B. States and Counties — Housing, Labor Force, and Employment

STATE County	Housing units, 2011–2015								Civilian labor force, 2016				Civilian employment,[6] 2011–2015		
	Occupied units										Unemployment			Percent	
		Owner-occupied				Renter-occupied									
				Median owner cost as a percent of income											Con-struction, produc-tion, and mainte-nance occu-pations[2]
	Total	Percent	Median value[1]	With a mort-gage	Without a mort-gage[2]	Median rent[3]	Median rent as a per-cent of income[2]	Sub-stand-ard units[4] (percent)	Total	Percent change, 2015–2016	Total	Rate[5]	Total	Manage-ment, business, science and arts	
	89	90	91	92	93	94	95	96	97	98	99	100	101	102	103
SOUTH CAROLINA—Cont'd															
Sumter	40 571	65.3	107 100	21.1	11.1	747	29.7	3.1	44 317	-0.2	2 543	5.7	41 972	28.6	29.1
Union	11 666	72.2	72 600	21.0	12.2	604	28.9	1.8	11 672	1.0	700	6.0	11 086	24.3	38.9
Williamsburg	11 885	73.5	68 300	26.3	15.0	569	33.4	2.1	12 658	-1.3	947	7.5	11 416	22.4	31.7
York	90 322	71.1	160 100	20.4	10.0	834	31.3	1.8	129 912	2.5	5 801	4.5	112 791	36.2	21.6
SOUTH DAKOTA	330 858	68.1	140 500	20.7	10.8	655	26.0	2.8	453 073	0.5	12 776	2.8	430 853	34.8	23.9
Aurora	1 157	78.4	69 400	17.6	10.8	618	20.8	1.8	1 519	-3.7	32	2.1	1 352	36.3	29.7
Beadle	7 565	65.2	96 500	18.4	10.4	549	23.6	5.8	9 517	0.1	235	2.5	9 189	27.0	33.6
Bennett	1 050	59.8	56 300	16.3	12.1	513	20.3	16.0	1 143	0.8	42	3.7	1 168	42.2	20.8
Bon Homme	2 480	78.3	69 900	19.0	10.3	467	24.9	4.2	2 955	-2.2	77	2.6	2 806	39.5	24.3
Brookings	12 325	59.5	156 000	21.5	10.6	658	30.0	1.1	19 004	2.0	492	2.6	19 007	34.9	26.2
Brown	15 996	68.6	143 100	19.6	11.4	610	25.3	1.4	21 102	0.2	532	2.5	20 762	33.0	26.5
Brule	2 067	73.0	102 900	20.7	11.8	582	17.9	3.1	2 490	-2.2	61	2.4	2 583	38.9	19.9
Buffalo	546	44.0	57 900	21.9	13.0	533	21.7	17.0	725	1.0	57	7.9	653	35.2	19.6
Butte	4 079	74.7	118 600	21.5	14.3	617	29.4	1.1	5 086	-0.5	165	3.2	5 015	29.2	33.3
Campbell	683	80.5	59 800	18.0	10.5	550	22.9	1.0	860	0.9	24	2.8	755	43.3	19.6
Charles Mix	3 171	70.1	82 700	19.2	10.4	508	22.5	4.9	3 907	-2.3	119	3.0	3 894	33.5	24.8
Clark	1 488	76.1	76 100	18.8	10.5	518	17.6	2.8	1 942	-1.5	72	3.7	1 826	38.9	28.2
Clay	5 335	51.5	135 000	20.8	10.2	679	39.2	1.6	7 045	0.2	198	2.8	7 510	39.6	18.0
Codington	11 934	67.7	145 500	20.9	10.6	618	24.9	2.4	15 257	-0.8	444	2.9	15 575	25.4	31.1
Corson	1 229	51.6	53 800	15.0	12.9	408	21.9	13.4	1 474	-1.4	62	4.2	1 240	43.0	23.4
Custer	3 759	81.3	208 900	22.6	13.7	796	24.2	1.8	3 952	-0.4	152	3.8	3 823	38.0	23.3
Davison	8 580	62.9	133 600	20.1	10.0	643	25.3	1.3	11 319	-0.4	256	2.3	10 359	35.3	24.6
Day	2 533	72.8	81 100	21.7	12.1	483	29.2	1.5	2 853	-0.6	116	4.1	2 652	35.7	26.8
Deuel	1 900	82.9	112 000	18.4	10.5	426	16.5	1.0	2 291	-1.2	105	4.6	2 317	35.2	32.4
Dewey	1 640	58.5	60 100	17.9	11.1	495	19.7	11.8	2 236	-2.7	191	8.5	1 900	42.4	20.2
Douglas	1 296	78.5	73 000	16.3	10.0	492	19.1	1.9	1 685	0.3	41	2.4	1 538	34.5	25.0
Edmunds	1 586	81.8	111 200	18.6	10.3	488	22.3	0.4	2 210	-0.8	48	2.2	2 070	39.1	24.3
Fall River	3 087	71.0	102 800	23.7	11.6	589	27.2	3.8	3 050	2.2	127	4.2	3 005	35.2	24.4
Faulk	951	77.0	78 600	21.6	10.0	535	18.8	0.9	1 105	-1.6	28	2.5	1 162	48.6	19.3
Grant	3 209	78.6	107 900	21.0	10.0	529	23.9	1.1	4 411	-6.6	136	3.1	3 953	27.9	32.4
Gregory	1 970	68.8	61 200	22.1	10.5	480	28.3	2.4	2 090	1.3	60	2.9	2 007	37.1	23.4
Haakon	855	78.5	76 800	24.7	10.0	614	18.7	1.2	1 101	0.0	25	2.3	1 018	47.0	20.7
Hamlin	2 178	79.9	112 100	20.8	10.0	608	23.5	4.1	3 180	1.1	102	3.2	2 874	32.1	33.5
Hand	1 510	70.4	96 100	20.5	10.0	474	21.8	1.0	1 881	0.0	38	2.0	1 768	36.9	26.3
Hanson	1 056	83.3	110 100	21.2	11.2	531	25.2	2.1	1 790	-0.8	57	3.2	1 673	37.8	28.9
Harding	507	72.8	87 200	20.0	10.4	483	15.8	0.6	765	-2.3	21	2.7	684	41.1	33.9
Hughes	7 117	66.0	167 800	18.8	10.0	578	22.7	2.9	10 158	2.3	226	2.2	9 620	45.0	17.4
Hutchinson	2 942	75.2	72 000	18.4	10.6	556	28.8	2.0	3 676	-0.3	88	2.4	3 745	38.1	24.9
Hyde	545	81.8	76 400	18.0	12.5	556	16.2	4.4	715	0.8	18	2.5	762	37.8	28.2
Jackson	1 032	61.5	57 800	17.8	10.7	460	17.8	13.3	1 315	-1.3	51	3.9	1 202	45.8	21.8
Jerauld	863	75.7	81 600	18.4	11.9	555	16.1	1.3	1 068	-5.4	24	2.2	1 033	33.3	35.9
Jones	426	68.5	58 300	23.3	12.0	391	22.1	1.4	573	-2.2	13	2.3	482	38.0	23.0
Kingsbury	2 283	77.0	88 800	16.3	10.4	453	19.8	1.7	2 735	-1.0	69	2.5	2 631	35.1	32.7
Lake	4 764	73.5	139 800	18.5	11.0	510	23.4	0.5	6 447	-1.3	206	3.2	6 468	30.8	26.8
Lawrence	10 528	66.9	180 100	24.2	11.4	629	26.5	2.5	13 051	2.2	405	3.1	13 004	30.6	23.0
Lincoln	18 037	78.4	193 600	20.5	10.2	835	22.5	1.0	30 863	1.4	627	2.0	27 623	44.7	18.4
Lyman	1 394	72.4	70 300	16.3	12.5	513	18.3	7.1	1 774	-1.4	79	4.5	1 719	42.2	19.1
McCook	2 253	77.9	109 500	18.9	10.0	588	20.5	1.2	3 155	0.7	74	2.3	2 974	35.8	27.6
McPherson	1 009	74.4	57 800	20.4	10.2	394	16.7	0.0	1 094	-2.1	36	3.3	1 017	39.8	24.5
Marshall	1 765	72.2	97 400	20.0	11.4	480	18.4	1.2	2 475	-1.4	90	3.6	2 394	34.8	31.3
Meade	10 593	72.0	162 700	22.7	13.2	772	28.8	3.4	13 419	0.6	402	3.0	12 907	33.4	25.8
Mellette	675	64.6	49 100	16.1	10.0	486	30.6	9.2	773	-3.5	30	3.9	740	48.1	22.8
Miner	1 006	76.9	67 000	17.7	12.6	476	18.9	1.4	1 204	-1.0	30	2.5	1 174	38.3	28.4
Minnehaha	70 140	63.6	155 400	20.6	10.0	713	26.6	2.5	107 721	1.4	2 607	2.4	98 459	33.2	22.2
Moody	2 681	71.5	122 900	20.4	12.5	540	19.9	2.9	3 946	-0.2	136	3.4	3 379	41.3	27.7
Oglala Lakota	2 933	52.7	20 400	13.2	12.6	435	19.3	34.1	3 646	1.4	364	10.0	3 226	37.2	17.1
Pennington	41 670	67.0	159 800	22.8	11.6	776	29.1	2.7	54 724	0.7	1 588	2.9	53 612	32.0	20.7
Perkins	1 306	71.7	65 100	20.0	10.5	487	25.2	1.2	1 589	0.5	44	2.8	1 490	40.2	28.3
Potter	1 056	81.1	75 400	16.7	12.8	536	19.1	0.5	1 173	-1.1	30	2.6	1 142	33.5	28.5
Roberts	3 652	70.5	90 900	21.0	10.6	519	23.1	3.3	4 858	-0.5	190	3.9	4 416	37.0	26.0
Sanborn	1 072	74.3	75 800	19.4	10.0	506	20.0	0.7	1 217	-1.1	34	2.8	1 289	31.9	35.5
Spink	2 631	73.5	74 200	18.3	10.0	540	21.5	1.7	3 323	-0.2	98	2.9	3 266	34.8	26.6
Stanley	1 268	80.9	124 100	22.0	11.6	671	25.5	4.2	1 867	1.4	42	2.2	1 674	38.4	28.9
Sully	622	69.3	94 600	17.2	10.0	540	13.2	2.1	871	-0.2	19	2.2	788	40.9	31.5
Todd	2 737	44.9	43 700	27.0	10.0	442	20.7	17.1	3 039	-0.6	184	6.1	2 901	35.5	17.6

1. Specified owner-occupied units.   2. A value of 10.0 represents 10 percent or less; a value of 50.0 represents 50 percent or more.   3. Specified renter-occupied units.
4. Overcrowded or lacking complete plumbing facilities.   5. Percent of civilian labor force.   6. Civilian employed persons 16 years old and over.

Table B. States and Counties — Nonfarm Employment and Agriculture

	Private nonfarm establishments, employment and payroll, 2015									Agriculture, 2012			
STATE County	Number of establish-ments	Employment						Annual payroll		Farms			
		Total	Health care and social assistance	Manufac-turing	Retail trade	Finance and insurance	Professional, scientific, and technical services	Total (mil dol)	Average per employee (dollars)	Number	Percent with:		Farm operators whose principal occu-pation is farming (percent)
											Fewer than 50 acres	500 acres or more	
	104	105	106	107	108	109	110	111	112	113	114	115	116
SOUTH CAROLINA—Cont'd													
Sumter	1 755	32 393	5 279	5 985	4 648	780	617	1 107	34 161	515	44.3	14.2	45.8
Union	418	6 357	878	1 515	876	188	85	198	31 160	264	33.0	7.2	33.7
Williamsburg	505	7 436	823	2 313	882	159	91	264	35 528	679	28.9	15.8	38.3
York	4 703	71 753	9 239	9 840	10 963	4 409	2 780	2 974	41 446	1 004	48.3	4.7	35.8
SOUTH DAKOTA	26 511	353 540	65 468	45 363	53 311	25 870	12 019	13 813	39 071	31 989	19.6	43.6	58.9
Aurora	82	603	191	D	59	44	67	20	32 784	442	12.2	47.5	60.6
Beadle	564	7 122	1 465	1 666	1 102	413	120	236	33 125	754	19.4	43.4	55.6
Bennett	66	665	152	D	119	D	D	18	26 808	219	7.3	68.5	68.0
Bon Homme	171	1 112	316	120	133	90	22	33	29 602	671	20.3	38.3	54.7
Brookings	891	13 865	1 477	4 961	1 826	572	598	505	36 458	1 023	31.7	23.9	46.2
Brown	1 289	18 885	3 226	2 969	3 058	1 000	510	716	37 890	1 056	23.6	38.9	57.4
Brule	218	1 887	407	29	269	80	54	58	30 659	407	21.4	47.2	61.9
Buffalo	12	180	28	D	D	NA	D	4	24 083	78	7.7	66.7	75.6
Butte	321	2 423	308	207	449	81	133	79	32 454	659	21.1	35.2	57.7
Campbell	58	275	26	D	31	D	10	9	31 338	242	7.9	56.6	63.2
Charles Mix	281	2 408	530	97	435	138	49	66	27 515	759	14.1	45.1	67.2
Clark	117	636	104	92	88	31	20	22	35 233	597	11.6	48.1	58.1
Clay	305	3 414	796	228	761	75	122	84	24 559	461	27.1	37.3	64.4
Codington	1 107	13 827	1 765	3 399	2 806	765	278	492	35 581	713	30.9	29.6	44.6
Corson	33	200	14	NA	59	15	NA	7	33 965	323	6.5	73.7	79.3
Custer	263	1 314	230	22	278	39	44	49	37 025	446	33.0	32.5	54.3
Davison	729	11 529	2 152	1 933	2 112	332	679	396	34 374	427	26.5	31.1	48.2
Day	190	1 511	300	212	291	83	34	47	31 184	693	14.0	35.9	46.0
Deuel	141	1 522	186	D	108	42	112	73	47 861	664	26.5	28.6	53.6
Dewey	78	601	133	D	76	D	12	22	36 017	342	14.6	65.2	55.6
Douglas	105	934	236	106	138	37	9	29	31 207	434	15.0	42.9	72.4
Edmunds	122	893	178	73	124	49	25	32	36 362	422	9.7	60.7	62.6
Fall River	207	2 515	D	14	276	38	43	136	53 927	327	18.7	51.1	64.5
Faulk	70	447	D	D	69	23	6	15	32 584	280	6.4	70.7	75.4
Grant	284	3 262	427	617	479	127	67	118	36 243	618	22.0	39.6	64.6
Gregory	187	1 133	317	D	266	75	34	30	26 304	505	10.1	52.3	65.3
Haakon	82	648	D	D	94	48	10	22	33 338	287	2.8	72.8	73.2
Hamlin	188	1 170	158	220	139	54	44	42	36 079	489	28.6	30.3	52.8
Hand	129	1 125	260	63	170	58	44	34	30 468	415	6.5	64.6	68.7
Hanson	73	354	11	88	38	29	6	13	36 932	370	16.8	44.1	60.0
Harding	41	416	82	NA	30	D	D	23	54 358	250	5.6	80.4	79.2
Hughes	672	6 801	1 439	82	1 381	472	333	227	33 320	338	33.1	34.3	50.0
Hutchinson	234	2 201	665	324	345	108	27	71	32 446	802	16.5	40.5	60.3
Hyde	44	480	D	NA	71	D	D	17	34 535	207	11.6	63.8	81.2
Jackson	54	289	D	D	110	D	D	7	22 990	299	7.7	70.6	70.6
Jerauld	74	1 258	133	D	49	26	13	47	37 325	233	18.5	46.4	49.8
Jones	51	284	D	NA	91	14	D	8	28 894	163	4.3	72.4	73.0
Kingsbury	176	1 395	217	393	175	117	13	51	36 751	518	14.9	45.8	64.1
Lake	361	3 653	610	806	472	153	155	128	34 965	502	29.1	30.3	51.6
Lawrence	1 028	9 655	1 437	503	1 459	274	267	293	30 324	312	28.8	17.9	42.0
Lincoln	1 388	15 125	2 943	2 188	1 821	1 306	505	623	41 162	899	34.8	27.5	50.3
Lyman	73	593	D	NA	254	33	D	14	24 051	430	6.3	62.3	53.7
McCook	190	1 013	266	4	171	39	35	32	31 504	568	25.0	37.5	53.5
McPherson	81	380	46	69	71	50	D	10	26 995	398	12.6	54.0	60.6
Marshall	149	1 360	181	519	210	47	28	47	34 308	518	14.5	41.5	53.7
Meade	703	5 312	1 431	359	729	156	177	247	46 509	891	21.2	50.4	56.9
Mellette	19	155	D	NA	51	D	D	3	21 110	229	3.1	76.4	83.8
Miner	81	518	112	36	58	24	19	16	31 822	486	17.5	36.8	55.6
Minnehaha	5 625	119 015	23 096	12 179	15 826	12 685	4 380	5 230	43 945	1 157	39.7	23.2	52.0
Moody	167	1 692	214	334	183	22	22	54	32 203	513	29.2	25.7	63.0
Oglala Lakota	67	1 776	270	D	209	34	D	56	31 572	174	4.6	69.5	77.0
Pennington	3 771	48 235	9 204	2 780	8 979	2 727	1 865	1 805	37 428	599	24.5	38.4	52.1
Perkins	130	794	126	D	144	48	14	24	30 394	437	8.9	72.3	69.6
Potter	98	765	113	D	82	D	11	30	39 582	247	11.3	56.3	68.0
Roberts	233	2 148	468	301	401	106	23	61	28 533	876	19.2	35.0	54.3
Sanborn	59	415	D	D	52	25	25	13	30 663	402	10.2	41.5	47.0
Spink	188	1 401	320	93	186	75	32	48	34 398	675	11.4	56.7	67.0
Stanley	112	1 054	20	D	117	38	D	36	33 734	183	7.1	71.0	66.1
Sully	68	317	5	D	89	19	D	13	41 555	191	6.3	66.0	72.8
Todd	58	1 206	259	D	276	D	D	38	31 325	231	10.4	63.2	70.6

Table B. States and Counties — Agriculture

STATE County	Agriculture, 2012 (cont.)														
	Land in farms				Value of land and buildings (dollars)			Value of products sold				Percent of farms with sales of:		Government payments	
			Acres							Percent from:					
	Acreage (1,000)	Percent change, 2007– 2012	Average size of farm	Total irrigated (1,000)	Total cropland (1,000)	Average per farm	Average per acre	Value of machinery and equipment, average per farm (dollars)	Total (mil dol)	Average per farm (dollars)	Crops	Live- stock and poultry products	$10,000 or more	$100,000 or more	Total ($1,000)	Percent of farms
	117	118	119	120	121	122	123	124	125	126	127	128	129	130	131	132
SOUTH CAROLINA—Cont'd																
Sumter	176	14.7	342	8.9	69.5	792 967	2 320	105 033	130.5	253 379	36.9	63.1	27.2	10.9	1 870	57.3
Union	47	4.0	179	0.1	9.0	394 534	2 201	43 322	15.3	58 121	12.3	87.7	29.5	1.9	303	14.4
Williamsburg	224	7.2	331	0.8	91.8	689 383	2 086	83 346	61.8	91 032	83.2	16.8	29.9	12.8	2 763	60.1
York	124	-0.2	123	0.7	38.1	621 009	5 031	48 627	96.8	96 452	D	D	23.4	4.1	572	14.6
SOUTH DAKOTA	43 257	-0.9	1 352	378.7	19 147.3	2 281 027	1 687	241 373	10 170.2	317 929	59.7	40.3	65.0	40.7	283 797	71.3
Aurora	442	21.2	1 000	D	267.7	2 361 032	2 361	226 367	127.3	287 910	53.6	46.4	71.7	45.5	3 875	81.4
Beadle	794	3.1	1 053	11.2	576.9	3 014 625	2 864	295 423	300.2	398 088	63.3	36.7	66.3	46.9	7 071	74.9
Bennett	606	-19.5	2 769	6.6	178.6	1 564 995	565	198 361	62.2	283 799	35.8	64.2	76.7	51.1	2 139	73.5
Bon Homme	352	13.9	524	6.6	277.2	1 529 963	2 920	189 478	107.9	160 744	38.3	61.7	66.0	30.3	4 954	86.3
Brookings	449	-2.9	439	16.9	327.4	1 870 065	4 261	195 803	312.5	305 506	51.9	48.1	52.9	29.9	7 038	68.3
Brown	1 079	-0.6	1 022	6.4	854.5	2 980 409	2 917	318 692	520.6	493 029	88.9	11.1	56.9	40.7	17 500	66.3
Brule	514	-0.9	1 263	3.7	263.9	2 876 440	2 278	244 592	150.9	370 715	51.0	49.0	70.0	42.8	2 702	68.8
Buffalo	296	-5.1	3 797	6.3	87.0	4 488 474	1 182	380 705	45.7	585 256	50.3	49.7	70.5	50.0	912	78.2
Butte	1 135	-0.5	1 722	45.4	116.8	1 066 480	619	99 675	75.4	114 340	23.0	77.0	67.2	26.1	3 255	46.7
Campbell	360	-10.1	1 489	2.3	211.0	1 898 711	1 275	321 665	98.9	408 607	62.8	37.2	71.1	51.7	2 928	85.5
Charles Mix	692	4.8	912	15.3	448.9	2 146 680	2 353	264 441	227.9	300 271	45.2	54.8	70.2	44.9	5 433	87.7
Clark	609	19.7	1 020	7.3	401.3	2 584 074	2 534	297 191	249.4	417 714	64.0	36.0	66.2	51.1	5 326	83.9
Clay	259	-3.0	561	20.8	237.6	2 481 560	4 422	279 267	96.8	210 037	82.3	17.7	64.2	46.6	4 323	79.4
Codington	369	0.6	518	4.3	255.9	1 389 913	2 684	168 854	172.4	241 811	62.8	37.2	56.2	33.4	3 757	62.6
Corson	1 242	-3.2	3 846	D	346.4	2 514 418	654	240 712	117.1	362 492	50.9	49.1	86.4	60.4	3 165	66.3
Custer	623	3.7	1 397	3.1	46.9	1 600 944	1 146	76 119	26.0	58 325	11.0	89.0	47.8	15.7	1 285	19.7
Davison	275	-1.5	645	1.7	210.2	2 187 288	3 393	215 440	78.8	184 515	63.7	36.3	55.7	31.4	2 594	65.6
Day	570	0.5	823	0.3	395.0	1 571 924	1 911	211 440	189.7	273 775	83.5	16.5	51.7	32.5	6 718	78.6
Deuel	342	7.8	515	1.1	207.6	1 519 508	2 951	183 530	177.8	267 700	52.5	47.5	54.2	32.2	4 206	78.2
Dewey	1 182	-18.5	3 455	0.0	214.4	1 979 599	573	171 526	69.3	202 535	42.2	57.8	76.9	44.7	4 224	64.9
Douglas	270	19.8	622	2.1	192.3	1 774 048	2 854	210 823	117.5	270 668	35.4	64.6	81.1	50.5	2 807	79.3
Edmunds	697	6.1	1 652	1.0	492.8	3 620 645	2 192	451 389	271.4	643 123	68.7	31.3	74.2	58.3	5 097	81.5
Fall River	1 089	14.6	3 330	7.5	63.8	1 714 394	515	112 138	116.9	357 364	5.5	94.5	59.3	30.3	1 885	40.4
Faulk	616	0.2	2 199	0.5	382.8	4 275 536	1 945	559 368	216.3	772 596	72.3	27.7	83.9	66.4	5 575	87.9
Grant	429	17.9	694	3.4	290.7	2 075 218	2 992	261 960	240.8	389 675	56.4	43.6	66.0	48.1	4 517	70.6
Gregory	635	-3.0	1 257	0.5	239.1	1 534 659	1 221	156 531	94.1	186 410	42.4	57.6	73.5	37.4	2 245	79.4
Haakon	1 133	-1.5	3 949	0.1	324.6	2 375 324	601	186 188	77.1	268 700	43.0	57.0	75.6	50.2	4 539	73.5
Hamlin	311	0.4	636	7.9	241.7	2 272 331	3 572	285 902	188.2	384 920	66.3	33.7	59.1	39.9	4 136	74.8
Hand	905	0.7	2 181	4.5	565.6	4 161 320	1 908	431 607	284.4	685 390	69.6	30.4	77.1	58.1	5 362	85.3
Hanson	274	25.1	741	1.1	212.2	2 773 749	3 745	316 603	110.7	299 054	60.7	39.3	67.6	46.8	2 701	75.1
Harding	1 467	-8.1	5 869	0.7	179.7	2 465 216	420	212 876	70.4	281 628	24.3	75.7	80.0	55.6	2 729	61.6
Hughes	431	4.8	1 275	9.8	269.5	2 502 944	1 963	213 530	107.3	317 577	81.2	18.8	54.7	32.8	3 532	62.1
Hutchinson	513	0.7	640	4.0	409.7	2 103 788	3 287	263 249	186.2	232 226	38.3	61.7	69.1	38.4	7 192	85.2
Hyde	515	7.0	2 486	0.3	216.3	3 454 498	1 390	317 135	94.3	455 705	66.9	33.1	80.7	57.5	2 441	75.4
Jackson	1 158	-2.2	3 873	0.6	176.6	3 077 278	795	179 492	51.9	173 619	34.6	65.4	71.2	41.8	2 083	58.2
Jerauld	333	1.3	1 428	1.4	181.6	2 811 747	1 968	300 974	99.3	426 206	62.4	37.6	67.8	40.8	2 191	73.4
Jones	612	17.9	3 757	0.7	210.1	2 730 785	727	235 785	65.3	400 319	61.5	38.5	74.8	58.3	2 535	81.0
Kingsbury	521	9.1	1 006	2.1	382.3	3 338 884	3 319	324 201	278.3	537 182	63.0	37.0	75.3	55.8	5 135	74.9
Lake	262	-16.9	521	1.8	207.3	2 128 008	4 081	237 606	168.8	336 323	66.6	33.4	56.6	41.8	3 352	75.5
Lawrence	159	18.9	509	2.7	29.7	722 071	1 419	76 962	19.1	61 064	12.7	87.3	41.0	11.9	315	22.1
Lincoln	366	9.8	407	2.9	329.9	2 211 686	5 440	198 632	172.3	191 619	60.0	40.0	61.4	33.1	6 946	71.4
Lyman	1 029	5.3	2 392	8.7	456.4	2 398 733	1 003	253 705	136.8	318 044	69.5	30.5	65.6	47.0	6 670	81.6
McCook	363	-0.1	639	D	299.5	2 713 745	4 248	278 900	157.0	276 347	61.6	38.4	65.0	40.1	3 979	72.9
McPherson	573	10.5	1 439	1.3	286.8	2 201 472	1 530	274 035	159.4	400 425	53.1	46.9	71.4	42.0	3 081	76.9
Marshall	532	-0.4	1 027	D	316.0	2 296 672	2 235	328 147	306.8	592 357	47.6	52.4	58.7	39.6	8 084	82.2
Meade	2 033	-8.0	2 281	4.0	349.8	1 537 875	674	117 736	116.4	130 688	21.8	78.2	60.3	28.5	4 935	42.4
Mellette	699	-4.2	3 051	D	117.4	2 181 253	715	174 258	46.2	201 799	30.1	69.9	82.5	52.8	1 048	65.1
Miner	357	19.1	735	D	231.5	2 361 718	3 212	260 222	123.7	254 517	60.6	39.4	57.4	40.1	4 341	82.5
Minnehaha	408	-3.2	353	1.7	322.4	1 814 344	5 146	191 197	270.2	233 576	60.8	39.2	56.3	34.4	5 753	67.2
Moody	254	-13.3	496	3.2	208.8	2 525 815	5 094	216 696	215.0	419 047	61.1	38.9	59.8	40.7	4 100	76.2
Oglala Lakota	1 101	-17.4	6 329	0.5	97.8	2 910 178	460	155 874	32.3	185 563	27.0	73.0	77.0	36.8	1 772	45.4
Pennington	1 074	-9.4	1 793	5.8	222.8	1 253 793	699	110 694	65.7	109 760	45.0	55.0	55.9	23.7	2 942	30.7
Perkins	1 631	-10.8	3 732	0.2	393.2	2 007 828	538	177 826	125.0	286 087	34.6	65.4	77.6	51.5	4 913	77.1
Potter	538	4.1	2 178	D	357.3	4 354 235	1 999	489 332	157.0	635 684	89.5	10.5	70.9	54.7	3 783	78.1
Roberts	623	5.1	711	2.3	429.3	1 800 643	2 531	225 765	251.2	286 725	79.7	20.3	57.1	36.6	9 142	79.2
Sanborn	360	13.2	896	D	221.8	2 130 490	2 377	270 057	118.8	295 401	58.4	41.6	60.9	39.8	3 561	78.1
Spink	945	4.1	1 400	19.2	714.7	4 166 481	2 976	425 689	447.6	663 096	74.7	25.3	72.3	56.4	12 003	87.4
Stanley	791	-14.1	4 323	0.2	219.4	3 968 497	918	248 842	64.0	349 896	63.7	36.3	77.6	50.3	2 309	62.3
Sully	628	3.2	3 289	24.6	501.0	5 131 304	1 560	595 026	225.6	1 181 042	82.7	17.3	77.5	61.3	3 981	77.0
Todd	860	-1.1	3 723	7.2	125.2	1 902 965	511	163 303	59.7	258 268	26.7	73.3	72.3	42.4	398	37.2

Table B. States and Counties — Water Use, Wholesale Trade, Retail Trade, and Real Estate

STATE County	Water use, 2010		Wholesale trade,[1] 2012				Retail trade,[2] 2012				Real estate and rental and leasing,[2] 2012			
	Total water withdrawn (mil gal/day)	Gallons withdrawn per person per day	Number of establishments	Number of employees	Sales (mil dol)	Annual payroll (mil dol)	Number of establishments	Number of employees	Sales (mil dol)	Annual payroll (mil dol)	Number of establishments	Number of employees	Receipts (mil dol)	Annual payroll (mil dol)
	133	134	135	136	137	138	139	140	141	142	143	144	145	146
SOUTH CAROLINA—Cont'd														
Sumter	23.5	219	69	635	342.0	28.8	398	4 416	1 096.8	85.4	78	258	28.9	6.4
Union	4.7	161	14	102	43.4	4.4	99	905	195.7	16.9	14	134	8.2	3.1
Williamsburg	5.4	155	19	249	145.1	8.6	115	927	225.2	18.0	17	45	4.5	1.0
York	217.1	960	233	4 335	3 237.0	292.2	656	9 498	2 845.2	218.4	202	717	125.3	25.3
SOUTH DAKOTA	625.8	769	1 317	15 827	20 411.1	756.9	3 843	49 867	13 791.8	1 127.3	962	3 526	582.8	105.7
Aurora	0.8	284	6	48	65.4	1.5	8	59	10.8	1.1	2	D	D	D
Beadle	5.7	329	28	351	615.6	17.8	79	1 084	257.8	23.7	31	155	14.0	2.5
Bennett	26.2	7 648	NA	NA	NA	NA	15	126	32.3	2.4	NA	NA	NA	NA
Bon Homme	6.9	976	11	101	76.2	2.9	32	206	47.1	3.7	4	7	0.4	0.1
Brookings	17.0	532	29	252	451.6	12.5	121	1 679	375.9	34.7	45	169	21.1	4.4
Brown	8.8	241	80	1 048	1 914.6	48.7	201	2 956	809.5	75.0	57	251	31.3	7.0
Brule	3.9	742	12	104	102.0	4.3	41	299	99.1	6.4	4	4	0.2	0.1
Buffalo	15.4	8 044	NA	NA	NA	NA	2	D	D	D	NA	NA	NA	NA
Butte	17.2	1 698	6	D	D	D	49	429	157.4	11.4	8	16	1.2	0.4
Campbell	15.8	10 764	5	D	D	D	6	25	10.9	0.4	1	D	D	D
Charles Mix	19.9	2 178	14	182	180.8	5.8	52	445	99.8	7.5	3	D	D	D
Clark	8.2	2 208	8	D	D	D	14	91	34.8	2.0	1	D	D	D
Clay	5.5	397	8	44	30.2	1.8	45	665	122.8	11.3	11	20	3.2	0.4
Codington	12.8	469	58	773	580.6	36.0	184	2 667	649.1	56.0	50	126	20.3	3.1
Corson	1.8	447	4	D	D	D	6	43	15.1	1.1	NA	NA	NA	NA
Custer	12.5	1 525	1	D	D	D	31	261	68.1	4.8	9	16	6.3	0.3
Davison	1.6	80	35	D	D	D	130	2 030	530.4	47.3	26	D	D	D
Day	8.5	1 490	9	139	212.7	4.8	29	264	62.2	4.6	2	D	D	D
Deuel	2.9	671	6	30	37.6	1.1	23	116	46.1	3.0	1	D	D	D
Dewey	1.1	208	5	73	50.1	2.0	14	97	22.0	1.2	4	22	0.9	0.2
Douglas	4.3	1 419	6	D	D	D	18	119	36.4	1.9	2	D	D	D
Edmunds	3.0	747	13	202	472.5	8.8	16	126	44.4	2.7	4	6	0.2	0.0
Fall River	7.1	1 001	3	D	D	D	31	239	68.5	4.1	7	11	1.1	0.2
Faulk	0.9	389	10	48	113.5	2.4	13	95	29.6	2.2	1	D	D	D
Grant	20.4	2 766	13	129	193.2	6.2	46	501	127.5	10.9	9	18	2.2	0.3
Gregory	3.1	716	6	27	39.7	1.0	29	221	67.0	4.5	2	D	D	D
Haakon	6.3	3 242	8	102	232.1	2.7	16	99	29.0	2.0	1	D	D	D
Hamlin	1.6	276	11	142	149.8	7.7	18	117	38.5	2.6	2	D	D	D
Hand	1.1	329	11	158	89.1	5.0	21	186	36.2	2.8	1	D	D	D
Hanson	1.6	477	7	D	D	D	4	32	6.2	0.5	1	D	D	D
Harding	0.8	622	NA	NA	NA	NA	7	33	11.4	0.6	NA	NA	NA	NA
Hughes	46.8	2 752	23	D	D	D	105	1 393	347.2	30.6	30	D	D	D
Hutchinson	1.9	261	28	336	480.0	12.5	41	321	81.1	6.2	2	D	D	D
Hyde	0.8	528	5	58	173.1	2.9	8	97	21.3	1.3	1	D	D	D
Jackson	2.1	683	2	D	D	D	14	118	33.6	1.8	NA	NA	NA	NA
Jerauld	1.2	594	5	D	D	D	9	65	21.3	1.5	2	D	D	D
Jones	2.7	2 674	2	D	D	D	12	87	32.8	2.0	NA	NA	NA	NA
Kingsbury	6.1	1 189	8	112	240.5	5.2	23	141	34.1	2.5	2	D	D	D
Lake	8.0	716	17	198	371.4	11.5	46	491	162.3	12.2	12	28	2.3	0.4
Lawrence	23.1	959	19	52	38.8	2.1	142	1 380	434.0	35.2	63	184	22.2	4.6
Lincoln	5.4	120	55	390	667.6	19.5	126	1 571	490.6	45.9	54	268	39.2	8.8
Lyman	5.5	1 475	4	D	D	D	16	301	54.5	5.0	1	D	D	D
McCook	1.6	287	10	73	100.0	3.4	24	161	52.1	2.9	6	D	D	D
McPherson	1.4	582	2	D	D	D	10	61	14.2	1.1	1	D	D	D
Marshall	8.8	1 881	10	60	69.1	2.5	24	194	74.3	4.6	1	D	D	D
Meade	10.3	403	21	D	D	D	78	615	211.0	16.2	23	75	11.6	1.9
Mellette	4.5	2 202	NA	NA	NA	NA	7	56	11.6	0.8	1	D	D	D
Miner	0.5	213	4	D	D	D	13	65	17.8	1.3	2	D	D	D
Minnehaha	34.2	202	359	5 704	3 841.7	291.7	798	14 467	4 264.7	332.8	229	1 189	254.0	44.9
Moody	4.4	680	4	31	18.8	1.6	20	188	50.5	3.0	5	5	0.5	0.1
Oglala Lakota	0.9	67	1	D	D	D	10	189	51.4	3.2	NA	NA	NA	NA
Pennington	51.8	513	158	1 858	1 248.7	83.0	574	8 278	2 250.8	198.6	160	554	97.2	15.8
Perkins	1.6	550	5	D	D	D	19	108	24.8	2.2	3	D	D	D
Potter	5.0	2 130	7	94	577.3	5.3	17	123	21.8	1.6	2	D	D	D
Roberts	8.8	862	14	101	421.8	4.8	41	359	112.5	6.6	2	D	D	D
Sanborn	0.7	301	4	19	25.5	0.8	5	D	D	D	NA	NA	NA	NA
Spink	18.3	2 846	18	202	491.8	11.6	23	184	46.1	3.6	3	4	0.6	0.1
Stanley	4.5	1 514	3	D	D	D	15	133	53.2	3.8	4	D	D	D
Sully	27.2	19 825	5	D	D	D	11	88	42.6	2.4	3	D	D	D
Todd	39.4	4 097	1	D	D	D	15	196	43.0	3.0	3	D	D	D

1. Merchant wholesalers, except manufacturers' sales branches and offices.   2. Employer establishments.

Table B. States and Counties — **Professional Services, Manufacturing, and Accommodation and Food Services**

STATE County	Professional, scientific, and technical services, 2012				Manufacturing, 2012				Accommodation and food services, 2012			
	Number of establishments	Number of employees	Receipts (mil dol)	Annual payroll (mil dol)	Number of establishments	Number of employees	Receipts (mil dol)	Annual payroll (mil dol)	Number of establishments	Number of employees	Sales (mil dol)	Annual payroll (mil dol)
	147	148	149	150	151	152	153	154	155	156	157	158
SOUTH CAROLINA—Cont'd												
Sumter	126	714	75.8	23.2	71	5 524	1 817.5	214.6	158	2 951	127.0	34.9
Union	22	100	5.7	1.8	28	1 483	524.5	63.7	36	485	21.0	6.0
Williamsburg	26	95	10.5	2.8	35	2 110	1 778.0	97.2	27	D	D	D
York	455	2 240	297.2	102.9	213	8 310	3 111.1	439.6	392	7 094	336.9	89.6
SOUTH DAKOTA	1 822	11 144	1 315.4	482.3	1 025	41 931	16 882.6	1 764.7	2 363	37 974	1 873.7	514.2
Aurora	8	D	D	D	5	44	D	1.5	14	35	1.6	0.4
Beadle	28	114	11.0	4.0	31	1 646	495.1	55.7	48	525	21.7	5.4
Bennett	4	5	0.3	0.1	NA	NA	NA	NA	5	46	1.6	0.4
Bon Homme	6	20	1.8	0.5	13	320	D	11.6	14	65	2.4	0.5
Brookings	71	348	43.3	16.2	40	4 565	2 282.1	206.1	84	1 540	55.9	16.0
Brown	80	430	54.7	18.4	40	2 827	D	114.8	108	1 951	81.1	23.8
Brule	22	41	3.3	1.2	3	12	4.6	0.5	24	209	11.4	2.7
Buffalo	1	D	D	D	NA	NA	NA	NA	1	D	D	D
Butte	21	84	6.5	2.5	16	123	60.9	5.2	30	257	11.4	3.3
Campbell	4	7	0.3	0.1	3	48	D	D	7	D	D	D
Charles Mix	10	52	4.5	1.4	8	86	D	3.1	21	438	19.8	7.2
Clark	6	18	2.4	0.4	8	121	D	3.6	9	20	1.3	0.4
Clay	14	50	2.8	1.1	10	275	D	11.5	43	837	28.4	7.5
Codington	72	294	46.2	10.6	78	3 388	1 029.9	140.7	92	1 884	82.6	22.6
Corson	NA	NA	NA	NA	NA	NA	NA	NA	3	D	D	D
Custer	19	D	D	D	12	43	D	1.2	54	366	31.1	7.9
Davison	48	D	D	D	39	1 676	D	75.4	67	1 365	55.9	15.2
Day	5	24	2.2	0.7	13	219	61.5	9.4	17	168	5.2	1.4
Deuel	5	D	D	D	4	D	D	D	13	88	4.3	1.0
Dewey	4	11	0.4	0.1	NA	NA	NA	NA	6	18	1.7	0.2
Douglas	5	10	0.8	0.2	9	105	14.4	3.1	5	D	D	D
Edmunds	6	21	2.6	0.7	5	63	D	2.5	9	72	2.3	0.7
Fall River	13	49	3.1	1.1	8	24	5.5	0.8	37	336	13.5	3.5
Faulk	3	D	D	D	3	13	D	D	13	49	2.5	0.3
Grant	14	46	4.7	1.6	14	580	844.6	25.9	25	286	10.5	2.3
Gregory	8	26	2.3	0.6	6	59	D	D	19	95	3.8	0.8
Haakon	5	14	1.7	0.5	4	62	D	D	7	36	1.6	0.3
Hamlin	3	D	D	D	8	233	D	8.9	11	33	1.4	0.2
Hand	9	30	3.5	1.1	6	40	D	1.6	13	95	3.0	0.6
Hanson	2	D	D	D	3	54	D	D	4	15	0.7	0.1
Harding	NA	NA	NA	NA	NA	NA	NA	NA	3	23	1.0	0.2
Hughes	53	279	35.9	12.3	6	44	D	2.1	51	984	40.9	11.7
Hutchinson	11	30	2.8	1.0	11	214	76.8	8.2	18	D	D	D
Hyde	2	D	D	D	NA	NA	NA	NA	1	D	D	D
Jackson	1	D	D	D	NA	NA	NA	NA	10	39	4.5	1.0
Jerauld	6	8	1.9	0.2	NA	NA	NA	NA	6	42	2.6	0.7
Jones	2	D	D	D	NA	NA	NA	NA	14	78	4.3	1.2
Kingsbury	7	20	2.2	0.5	12	401	75.1	14.3	13	101	3.5	0.9
Lake	29	126	18.1	4.6	21	872	374.0	32.1	36	463	14.3	4.0
Lawrence	69	263	24.8	8.5	41	445	130.9	17.1	137	2 704	197.1	46.4
Lincoln	82	D	D	D	69	2 313	D	97.6	53	D	D	D
Lyman	1	D	D	D	NA	NA	NA	NA	14	173	9.7	2.5
McCook	10	D	D	D	4	8	D	0.2	18	D	D	D
McPherson	4	D	D	D	7	47	4.7	1.6	5	20	0.7	0.2
Marshall	11	21	2.1	0.6	8	355	174.7	16.3	13	115	3.7	1.0
Meade	50	D	D	D	35	225	D	8.3	74	671	43.6	10.9
Mellette	1	D	D	D	NA	NA	NA	NA	4	10	0.4	0.1
Miner	3	16	1.1	0.4	4	32	D	1.3	8	D	D	D
Minnehaha	480	4 148	476.7	201.5	176	10 763	3 612.6	479.0	444	10 517	493.8	147.2
Moody	9	16	1.1	0.4	11	326	88.5	14.1	15	D	D	D
Oglala Lakota	2	D	D	D	NA	NA	NA	NA	10	305	20.3	5.9
Pennington	303	1 928	223.8	76.8	117	2 115	524.3	85.9	352	6 418	351.8	98.3
Perkins	5	11	0.8	0.2	4	D	D	D	8	D	D	D
Potter	3	D	D	D	4	44	D	1.6	12	65	4.8	1.0
Roberts	15	31	3.7	1.0	11	272	D	7.3	18	171	4.6	1.0
Sanborn	7	20	1.9	0.4	NA	NA	NA	NA	6	25	1.2	0.2
Spink	8	36	4.8	1.4	7	72	D	3.3	13	126	4.8	1.2
Stanley	4	D	D	D	3	D	D	D	13	D	D	D
Sully	2	D	D	D	NA	NA	NA	NA	8	D	D	D
Todd	2	D	D	D	3	37	7.0	1.4	3	19	0.6	0.2

1. Establishment subject to federal tax.

Table B. States and Counties — Health Care and Social Assistance, Other Services, Nonemployer Businesses, and Residential Construction

STATE County	Health care and social assistance, 2012				Other services, 2012				Nonemployer businesses, 2015		Value of residential construction authorized by building permits, 2016	
	Number of establishments	Number of employees	Receipts (mil dol)	Annual payroll (mil dol)	Number of establishments	Number of employees	Receipts (mil dol)	Annual payroll (mil dol)	Number	Receipts (mil dol)	New Construction ($1,000)	Number of housing units
	159	160	161	162	163	164	165	166	167	168	169	170
SOUTH CAROLINA—Cont'd												
Sumter	188	5 504	471.1	184.1	130	996	77.4	27.8	6 120	215.8	38 734	273
Union	30	D	D	D	30	132	8.0	2.3	1 115	32.1	3 948	20
Williamsburg	55	797	55.3	22.5	35	D	D	D	1 748	48.3	3 245	13
York	445	8 980	897.0	307.6	283	2 070	188.3	61.7	16 343	640.1	705 677	2 457
SOUTH DAKOTA	2 298	63 494	6 211.7	2 558.4	1 805	8 371	939.5	214.1	64 006	3 046.1	883 698	5 686
Aurora	10	D	D	D	6	D	D	D	236	8.8	2 378	14
Beadle	50	1 409	87.8	40.4	51	175	16.5	4.2	1 054	48.4	3 264	23
Bennett	5	156	9.1	5.1	2	D	D	D	162	5.3	0	0
Bon Homme	21	367	22.0	9.1	14	D	D	D	466	18.9	1 970	10
Brookings	75	1 396	99.0	43.4	66	354	64.9	9.1	2 050	95.8	32 042	253
Brown	112	2 867	240.5	116.1	79	D	D	D	2 881	141.8	7 661	98
Brule	24	457	24.7	10.8	17	69	8.8	1.9	474	20.7	450	8
Buffalo	3	D	D	D	1	D	D	D	31	0.4	0	0
Butte	31	282	18.8	8.1	22	D	D	D	898	36.8	5 240	44
Campbell	4	25	0.8	0.5	1	D	D	D	136	5.7	0	0
Charles Mix	22	524	31.9	14.5	26	D	D	D	683	25.8	5 328	22
Clark	10	140	6.1	2.4	11	D	D	D	271	11.3	3 725	11
Clay	30	721	50.5	17.8	24	113	12.1	2.5	887	39.1	8 688	46
Codington	89	1 691	191.5	65.1	79	327	31.2	7.8	2 136	86.5	8 711	68
Corson	6	19	1.0	0.6	NA	NA	NA	NA	144	5.8	0	0
Custer	20	D	D	D	16	78	6.6	2.1	902	41.6	12 450	104
Davison	79	D	D	D	52	D	D	D	1 449	66.4	20 568	194
Day	19	291	18.1	6.3	14	D	D	D	488	17.6	5 084	32
Deuel	5	161	10.6	4.2	5	D	D	D	376	15.7	394	2
Dewey	9	149	18.7	7.2	6	D	D	D	235	10.5	0	0
Douglas	7	265	13.6	6.7	11	28	4.3	0.7	255	11.7	1 325	9
Edmunds	11	197	8.8	3.8	6	D	D	D	374	21.7	2 757	11
Fall River	22	D	D	D	16	67	4.5	1.1	602	22.8	210	2
Faulk	4	D	D	D	5	D	D	D	203	9.9	3 693	13
Grant	24	415	30.1	11.4	18	72	7.3	1.5	645	25.5	1 261	11
Gregory	15	317	18.1	7.4	12	D	D	D	475	18.2	2 190	11
Haakon	7	D	D	D	4	17	1.6	0.5	230	11.5	0	0
Hamlin	12	198	6.5	2.9	7	16	2.3	0.4	444	19.3	3 020	24
Hand	8	229	13.5	6.8	11	19	1.5	0.2	329	15.9	1 174	4
Hanson	2	D	D	D	1	D	D	D	308	11.4	1 429	10
Harding	4	D	D	D	1	D	D	D	169	5.7	350	3
Hughes	58	1 269	110.1	45.7	76	347	50.8	11.6	1 451	62.6	8 477	34
Hutchinson	17	651	40.2	18.8	14	D	D	D	578	20.9	1 062	4
Hyde	3	D	D	D	2	D	D	D	113	5.8	0	0
Jackson	1	D	D	D	5	10	0.8	0.1	186	6.0	0	0
Jerauld	4	131	9.6	3.8	7	16	1.4	0.3	154	6.7	260	1
Jones	2	D	D	D	2	D	D	D	116	4.5	370	9
Kingsbury	14	240	13.2	5.3	13	33	3.0	0.6	494	21.8	4 275	23
Lake	33	694	40.7	18.5	20	D	D	D	1 098	54.9	13 661	58
Lawrence	87	1 401	126.3	54.9	58	233	21.0	5.3	2 407	111.4	52 703	194
Lincoln	132	3 237	232.2	96.7	80	D	D	D	4 607	259.1	48 027	277
Lyman	2	D	D	D	3	D	D	D	253	10.6	275	2
McCook	17	251	13.5	5.2	13	D	D	D	494	22.7	4 120	18
McPherson	7	53	3.2	1.1	6	D	D	D	188	9.1	200	1
Marshall	13	175	10.7	4.0	7	27	3.7	0.8	352	16.4	4 230	17
Meade	45	D	D	D	50	151	20.8	4.1	2 160	90.8	27 720	149
Mellette	2	D	D	D	1	D	D	D	99	3.8	254	2
Miner	9	156	7.2	3.3	4	12	1.3	0.4	196	8.3	1 560	10
Minnehaha	462	20 372	2 348.8	970.6	375	2 326	256.5	67.7	13 120	714.0	402 005	2 772
Moody	15	203	13.9	6.0	6	D	D	D	438	19.0	3 753	12
Oglala Lakota	13	285	30.3	10.4	3	11	0.8	0.2	323	6.4	NA	NA
Pennington	343	D	D	D	268	1 572	193.3	39.2	7 947	375.2	98 512	718
Perkins	16	142	7.8	3.4	16	38	3.3	0.9	275	11.0	0	0
Potter	13	70	6.4	2.8	8	D	D	D	246	13.8	300	2
Roberts	23	532	32.7	14.8	16	42	3.2	0.8	613	21.8	5 994	27
Sanborn	4	D	D	D	4	D	D	D	184	7.4	300	1
Spink	17	359	18.3	8.3	12	D	D	D	514	25.1	2 995	15
Stanley	3	D	D	D	11	D	D	D	301	14.5	3 394	12
Sully	3	D	D	D	2	D	D	D	180	7.9	1 290	7
Todd	7	283	37.6	16.2	3	7	0.4	0.1	202	3.5	75	2

Table B. States and Counties — **Government Employment and Payroll, and Local Government Finances**

STATE County	Government employment and payroll, 2012									Local government finances, 2012				
			March payroll (percent of total)							General revenue				
													Taxes	
														Per capita[1] (dollars)
	Full-time equivalent employees	March payroll (dollars)	Administration, judicial, and legal	Police and Corrections	Fire Protection	Highways and transportation	Health and Welfare	Natural resources and utilities	Education and libraries	Total (mil dol)	Inter-governmental (mil dol)	Total (mil dol)	Total	Property
	171	172	173	174	175	176	177	178	179	180	181	182	183	184
SOUTH CAROLINA— Cont'd														
Sumter	6 341	17 021 292	4.2	6.1	1.7	1.8	1.6	3.3	80.4	271.8	124.5	114.5	1 060	719
Union	1 425	4 994 326	5.2	7.0	0.2	1.0	39.3	5.0	41.2	156.7	60.9	39.0	1 380	1 287
Williamsburg	1 213	3 312 602	4.2	7.9	1.6	5.2	5.0	3.6	71.8	89.9	50.4	26.4	785	649
York	6 735	24 865 548	7.3	9.2	2.7	1.3	1.7	7.5	67.9	705.5	262.8	328.3	1 399	1 188
SOUTH DAKOTA	X	X	X	X	X	X	X	X	X	X	X	X	X	X
Aurora	140	322 496	9.8	3.3	0.0	8.6	1.1	1.5	66.8	11.3	4.4	5.5	2 022	1 782
Beadle	584	1 871 207	6.9	12.0	1.9	6.5	2.6	6.6	60.1	58.6	17.5	28.6	1 609	1 176
Bennett	147	346 133	7.8	7.3	0.0	5.0	1.7	2.9	72.7	11.6	7.6	3.2	943	754
Bon Homme	246	662 539	7.1	6.3	0.0	9.5	0.7	8.4	67.8	20.1	7.9	9.7	1 383	1 174
Brookings	1 332	4 813 095	7.8	6.0	0.3	3.2	25.9	9.5	35.5	157.9	19.7	49.9	1 530	1 086
Brown	1 246	3 689 884	7.8	11.6	5.1	6.3	2.4	10.7	55.2	123.6	32.4	67.9	1 819	1 288
Brule	271	673 549	6.8	6.7	0.0	5.9	4.3	5.0	71.0	23.2	8.9	9.4	1 779	1 325
Buffalo	8	22 528	50.6	21.1	0.0	22.9	5.5	0.0	0.0	0.8	0.4	0.4	192	185
Butte	371	1 001 042	7.3	7.8	0.0	4.9	3.0	11.2	62.8	30.3	11.5	12.6	1 233	945
Campbell	48	126 932	22.4	4.9	0.0	20.2	1.5	5.8	43.7	4.7	1.5	2.4	1 718	1 442
Charles Mix	442	1 244 510	5.7	6.5	0.0	4.7	3.0	7.5	71.5	43.1	25.6	13.6	1 477	1 206
Clark	179	456 728	7.7	2.5	0.0	10.5	1.0	1.7	74.5	13.4	3.7	8.2	2 276	2 032
Clay	330	1 043 813	10.4	13.3	0.4	5.7	5.0	14.2	48.1	31.3	7.5	16.6	1 174	904
Codington	1 090	3 894 294	3.6	7.6	3.8	3.8	1.7	14.6	62.8	104.2	32.6	43.8	1 587	1 028
Corson	271	904 657	3.0	2.6	0.0	2.6	0.1	2.2	88.7	21.6	17.7	2.5	623	555
Custer	232	684 633	12.9	6.8	0.0	6.7	2.7	5.5	65.3	24.6	3.9	16.5	1 973	1 606
Davison	843	2 644 986	5.7	9.5	3.2	6.0	2.9	7.3	64.6	80.5	25.5	35.2	1 779	1 145
Day	198	482 927	10.0	8.0	0.0	11.7	0.7	5.9	61.4	17.2	6.4	8.5	1 510	1 240
Deuel	127	393 062	16.5	8.2	0.0	17.0	0.4	1.9	51.5	10.7	2.3	7.0	1 607	1 351
Dewey	249	617 513	9.8	3.1	0.0	5.4	0.5	3.0	76.8	18.8	15.2	2.6	474	405
Douglas	103	390 547	16.4	4.6	0.0	12.5	2.5	2.3	56.5	11.6	4.6	5.2	1 737	1 444
Edmunds	292	715 008	7.1	3.1	0.0	7.8	38.4	2.4	38.6	22.4	5.8	9.6	2 374	2 086
Fall River	314	938 839	8.8	7.6	0.0	7.0	1.0	10.3	60.3	26.8	9.4	11.3	1 614	1 321
Faulk	160	527 286	5.6	4.5	0.5	2.3	56.7	2.0	27.9	16.8	4.1	5.1	2 160	1 927
Grant	245	716 131	9.0	6.4	0.0	8.2	1.2	3.8	68.1	23.2	5.9	13.7	1 887	1 505
Gregory	203	581 904	10.2	4.7	0.0	9.2	1.1	2.4	71.6	14.3	5.6	7.1	1 664	1 354
Haakon	81	213 827	13.1	5.5	0.0	16.5	0.4	2.6	58.3	6.5	2.3	3.6	1 879	1 523
Hamlin	251	731 928	6.3	2.3	0.0	5.0	20.2	5.1	60.7	25.7	8.6	10.9	1 835	1 641
Hand	128	359 355	11.0	4.7	0.0	11.4	0.2	8.6	63.0	11.0	2.9	6.5	1 921	1 624
Hanson	122	328 179	9.5	3.1	0.0	9.0	0.2	1.6	71.2	10.7	3.6	5.8	1 710	1 577
Harding	80	208 002	15.2	4.0	0.0	10.1	0.3	2.9	63.3	10.2	6.4	3.1	2 343	2 124
Hughes	626	1 983 352	7.7	12.8	0.3	6.2	2.7	9.5	57.1	62.6	25.1	25.5	1 463	989
Hutchinson	312	1 009 609	5.2	3.1	0.0	6.2	0.4	1.3	82.1	25.8	8.2	14.2	1 970	1 677
Hyde	72	227 594	10.2	2.5	0.0	8.4	0.0	1.6	77.3	7.5	1.8	4.3	2 988	2 608
Jackson	115	288 915	10.3	3.2	0.0	5.1	1.0	2.8	74.9	7.4	4.2	2.7	835	680
Jerauld	90	237 116	13.3	5.9	0.0	10.4	1.6	8.1	58.2	8.7	2.5	4.4	2 169	1 851
Jones	52	131 432	19.8	7.6	0.0	10.4	0.0	7.8	54.5	4.5	1.4	2.5	2 475	1 992
Kingsbury	244	603 141	5.3	3.1	0.0	8.6	0.5	3.3	72.9	19.8	5.2	12.1	2 312	2 048
Lake	462	1 563 214	5.5	6.2	2.0	5.6	2.5	13.5	62.4	39.3	10.2	19.2	1 628	1 310
Lawrence	692	2 469 903	12.9	15.3	0.3	6.8	1.3	10.2	51.2	81.2	20.9	45.9	1 883	1 338
Lincoln	1 033	2 768 370	9.1	4.4	0.0	3.8	0.9	2.0	77.7	90.9	26.1	51.6	1 069	947
Lyman	133	337 375	11.7	3.3	0.0	7.7	3.0	3.7	67.3	10.3	4.3	4.8	1 278	913
McCook	186	538 315	9.8	4.8	0.0	8.7	1.8	2.2	71.0	17.3	5.5	9.8	1 740	1 508
McPherson	123	336 878	14.7	3.6	0.0	5.4	0.4	2.0	72.6	9.5	2.9	5.6	2 295	1 958
Marshall	176	472 048	9.8	7.5	0.0	9.0	0.7	2.0	69.8	18.3	6.1	9.2	1 978	1 696
Meade	671	2 100 253	11.4	12.6	0.3	4.8	2.3	5.9	59.2	71.1	19.6	32.1	1 233	1 036
Mellette	114	303 196	8.5	5.7	0.0	4.1	0.4	0.8	78.5	7.4	5.3	1.6	750	650
Miner	106	326 794	11.4	7.0	0.0	13.4	1.2	6.7	59.0	10.3	2.7	6.3	2 717	2 393
Minnehaha	5 678	21 221 355	6.2	10.8	4.4	3.8	2.4	6.0	65.2	616.7	171.2	329.3	1 882	1 201
Moody	202	536 978	10.4	8.8	0.0	7.4	2.5	6.9	57.6	17.4	5.8	9.2	1 422	1 220
Oglala Lakota	423	1 199 764	0.8	0.3	0.0	0.8	0.1	0.1	98.0	32.0	30.4	0.8	60	34
Pennington	4 148	12 984 488	4.9	10.8	1.8	2.6	2.5	4.4	67.5	388.6	116.3	197.4	1 891	1 300
Perkins	118	328 373	10.9	5.6	0.1	9.6	2.5	6.3	62.1	12.4	5.3	5.7	1 878	1 506
Potter	120	307 306	11.7	3.9	0.0	9.7	0.1	2.7	67.9	9.5	3.0	5.6	2 367	2 004
Roberts	404	1 039 666	5.9	3.7	0.0	5.7	2.4	2.0	77.9	33.8	13.8	12.6	1 220	986
Sanborn	116	293 325	10.3	3.6	0.0	17.9	1.1	1.1	64.9	9.9	3.4	5.4	2 323	2 120
Spink	406	1 160 424	5.6	3.5	0.0	5.0	32.9	2.4	50.2	35.9	9.8	13.7	2 078	1 808
Stanley	129	372 565	10.6	5.4	0.0	9.7	1.2	9.7	61.3	12.9	5.5	6.2	2 082	1 623
Sully	83	220 042	14.4	4.9	0.0	19.2	0.0	3.4	56.8	8.2	1.3	6.2	4 370	3 985
Todd	452	1 136 660	0.9	0.9	0.0	1.9	0.0	0.5	95.5	33.5	29.5	2.7	275	165

1. Based on the resident population estimated as of July 1 of the year shown.

Table B. States and Counties — Local Government Finances, Government Employment, and Income Taxes

STATE County	Local government finances, 2012 (cont.) Direct general expenditure Total (mil dol)	Per capita¹ (dollars)	Percent of total for: Education	Health and hospitals	Police protection	Public welfare	High-ways	Debt outstanding Total (mil dol)	Per capita¹ (dollars)	Government employment, 2015 Federal civilian	Federal military	State and local	Individual income tax returns, 2014 Number of returns	Mean adjusted gross income	Mean income tax
	185	186	187	188	189	190	191	192	193	194	195	196	197	198	199
SOUTH CAROLINA—Cont'd															
Sumter	256.2	2 371	55.2	1.2	7.1	0.3	2.5	245.3	2 270	1 218	5 566	5 493	46 770	39 689	3 318
Union	153.8	5 444	47.1	30.4	4.0	0.0	1.3	64.7	2 291	56	108	1 891	11 070	35 790	2 614
Williamsburg	98.8	2 939	50.1	2.9	6.6	0.2	2.4	85.8	2 551	366	124	1 876	13 220	31 445	2 133
York	690.0	2 941	56.4	0.2	5.6	0.3	5.3	1 179.4	5 026	413	983	11 864	109 760	60 588	7 124
SOUTH DAKOTA	X	X	X	X	X	X	X	X	X	11 136	7 896	65 278	410 850	60 855	8 099
Aurora	10.8	3 945	58.5	0.4	3.0	0.2	16.5	1.6	575	20	15	193	1 340	48 215	4 597
Beadle	52.6	2 962	43.9	0.4	4.7	0.5	16.7	29.0	1 634	288	104	1 031	8 780	54 017	6 254
Bennett	9.4	2 748	64.2	0.1	4.4	0.1	6.8	1.2	356	28	20	342	1 150	35 212	3 023
Bon Homme	17.7	2 516	62.3	1.6	3.0	0.2	15.6	31.0	4 403	28	32	581	2 760	50 231	5 579
Brookings	154.9	4 746	25.5	21.6	2.6	0.2	6.1	90.0	2 758	150	182	5 928	13 820	61 910	7 875
Brown	117.1	3 136	36.3	1.3	5.8	0.9	19.9	125.1	3 352	468	219	2 673	18 970	63 243	8 898
Brule	20.0	3 782	59.2	3.2	3.6	0.4	11.2	7.8	1 479	35	30	363	2 570	48 136	5 488
Buffalo	0.8	373	0.0	0.1	9.4	0.1	48.9	0.0	0	146	12	302	710	28 911	1 592
Butte	26.8	2 623	51.6	0.6	5.1	0.1	7.2	14.4	1 409	49	59	600	4 790	46 610	4 684
Campbell	4.2	2 981	36.0	0.6	4.6	0.0	22.5	0.4	298	D	D	73	750	53 137	5 544
Charles Mix	36.8	3 989	58.4	1.9	2.5	0.1	9.6	8.3	898	183	51	1 101	3 760	45 566	4 887
Clark	12.5	3 493	42.0	1.9	2.9	0.4	29.1	4.5	1 242	25	19	239	1 800	56 002	7 143
Clay	28.7	2 034	37.0	1.5	8.1	0.3	17.6	30.7	2 172	31	72	3 476	5 270	52 233	5 897
Codington	112.1	4 060	54.8	0.3	6.8	0.1	7.1	80.3	2 910	193	161	1 994	13 870	57 397	7 203
Corson	23.4	5 738	86.2	0.1	2.0	0.0	5.0	0.0	0	65	25	562	1 320	37 799	3 050
Custer	27.8	3 331	34.7	5.4	4.4	0.4	11.1	31.7	3 801	173	48	516	4 100	57 266	6 130
Davison	79.9	4 042	50.0	4.3	4.8	0.5	9.4	39.7	2 006	125	112	1 252	9 870	54 651	6 587
Day	17.9	3 188	37.1	0.7	3.2	0.3	29.6	10.3	1 840	56	32	376	2 730	47 486	5 283
Deuel	11.0	2 511	38.7	3.1	3.5	0.4	20.6	3.8	861	23	25	243	2 140	54 058	6 837
Dewey	20.6	3 719	81.8	0.2	1.5	0.0	11.1	1.0	189	373	33	1 189	2 490	39 938	4 202
Douglas	13.1	4 408	29.4	0.6	2.1	0.1	14.6	4.2	1 429	24	16	171	1 400	56 531	6 489
Edmunds	19.8	4 926	31.7	14.2	1.7	12.6	18.5	5.7	1 415	20	21	326	1 900	64 737	9 525
Fall River	27.6	3 962	45.4	2.5	5.3	0.5	9.0	13.8	1 973	472	39	583	3 390	47 358	4 638
Faulk	15.6	6 550	19.0	49.2	1.5	0.1	14.5	9.5	4 005	18	11	126	1 000	58 335	6 799
Grant	24.5	3 375	44.5	0.6	3.4	0.2	18.1	33.2	4 576	31	41	349	3 710	52 723	6 036
Gregory	13.6	3 189	55.3	0.9	3.5	0.2	17.9	4.1	966	30	24	249	1 990	45 986	4 801
Haakon	5.9	3 054	42.6	5.8	5.5	0.1	21.5	1.1	586	18	11	99	980	54 073	5 960
Hamlin	22.8	3 851	49.4	1.4	2.0	13.5	15.0	12.1	2 042	16	34	453	2 590	56 990	6 681
Hand	10.6	3 130	41.2	0.5	4.5	0.1	26.1	19.0	5 596	20	19	205	1 660	56 621	6 708
Hanson	11.6	3 434	65.3	0.5	1.6	0.3	16.2	6.0	1 773	D	17	188	2 120	56 481	6 436
Harding	10.1	7 661	50.7	0.5	2.4	0.4	25.4	8.7	6 600	20	D	101	620	79 581	8 824
Hughes	62.3	3 568	31.3	0.8	5.8	0.2	8.1	67.4	3 862	273	99	3 693	8 950	60 315	7 385
Hutchinson	27.0	3 751	58.0	0.4	2.3	0.4	18.5	16.9	2 349	39	38	419	3 350	52 677	5 673
Hyde	6.9	4 834	48.1	0.3	2.2	0.2	22.1	3.4	2 354	D	D	169	660	55 392	5 447
Jackson	6.7	2 101	64.9	0.5	3.6	0.1	11.3	0.1	43	109	19	222	1 100	40 429	3 605
Jerauld	8.5	4 170	41.2	4.0	3.2	0.4	21.3	7.5	3 682	D	11	125	860	55 756	5 837
Jones	4.6	4 509	46.3	0.5	2.9	0.0	21.7	0.2	192	D	D	125	500	37 932	4 782
Kingsbury	18.6	3 559	52.1	0.8	2.8	0.4	20.1	7.7	1 482	36	28	271	2 690	60 021	7 696
Lake	36.5	3 105	51.8	0.5	4.3	0.3	14.7	90.9	7 721	57	69	1 142	6 630	62 384	8 276
Lawrence	77.3	3 170	35.3	0.4	7.0	0.2	6.3	116.0	4 753	153	139	1 878	12 430	61 031	8 425
Lincoln	90.3	1 871	58.4	0.4	3.1	0.3	11.9	267.9	5 547	50	341	1 491	25 020	94 806	16 844
Lyman	9.2	2 439	55.2	0.9	3.3	0.2	15.6	1.7	440	80	22	630	1 730	48 309	4 771
McCook	15.8	2 821	51.5	2.0	4.3	1.1	18.5	9.6	1 716	26	31	259	2 660	58 615	7 208
McPherson	9.4	3 852	48.9	0.7	3.2	0.2	24.6	1.4	581	11	12	148	970	57 653	6 553
Marshall	17.1	3 652	35.5	1.2	4.5	1.6	22.5	18.4	3 939	25	26	335	2 100	51 523	6 337
Meade	75.4	2 895	52.2	1.6	5.1	0.0	8.9	43.4	1 666	1 459	156	1 400	13 030	52 442	5 428
Mellette	6.7	3 182	72.5	0.9	4.5	0.0	7.6	0.1	43	12	12	238	730	39 197	3 411
Miner	10.4	4 490	36.7	2.2	3.5	0.3	27.2	3.8	1 655	18	13	149	1 080	54 005	5 996
Minnehaha	640.2	3 657	45.9	1.7	5.7	0.6	9.2	652.2	3 726	2 544	1 070	8 505	96 150	62 880	8 408
Moody	17.2	2 661	47.1	1.8	6.6	1.5	18.2	8.8	1 373	110	37	646	3 020	50 885	6 528
Oglala Lakota	33.5	2 386	97.4	0.1	0.3	0.0	1.0	0.0	1	630	84	2 456	3 930	29 784	1 780
Pennington	412.8	3 956	45.6	1.3	6.0	0.5	8.9	401.2	3 844	1 447	3 625	6 194	54 700	58 973	7 714
Perkins	12.2	4 029	44.2	1.4	4.2	1.5	18.1	0.6	203	30	17	231	1 380	51 862	5 344
Potter	9.5	4 047	43.5	2.0	3.4	0.0	20.1	1.6	667	15	13	164	1 260	64 329	9 422
Roberts	30.3	2 938	57.6	0.5	2.8	0.1	10.2	9.6	930	188	59	1 335	4 400	44 621	4 617
Sanborn	8.5	3 645	45.3	1.1	3.6	0.1	31.4	2.8	1 215	13	13	151	1 120	51 263	4 911
Spink	34.6	5 228	34.4	27.8	3.5	0.4	14.0	21.8	3 298	36	36	956	2 990	58 957	7 490
Stanley	13.1	4 413	38.6	0.8	6.2	0.1	30.5	9.4	3 157	D	17	186	1 560	65 719	8 487
Sully	7.0	4 938	44.2	0.2	5.0	0.4	25.5	3.3	2 332	11	D	114	760	68 161	10 891
Todd	28.4	2 854	92.0	0.1	0.7	0.0	2.9	1.4	137	251	58	2 016	2 900	30 141	1 982

1. Based on the resident population estimated as of July 1 of the year shown.

Table B. States and Counties — **Land Area and Population**

STATE/ County code	CBSA code[1]	County type[2]	STATE County	Land area,[3] (sq mi) 2016	Total persons 2016	Rank	Per square mile	White	Black	American Indian, Alaska Native	Asian and Pacific Islander	Percent Hispanic or Latino[4]	Under 5 years	5 to 17 years	18 to 24 years	25 to 34 years	35 to 44 years	45 to 54 years
				1	2	3	4	5	6	7	8	9	10	11	12	13	14	15
			SOUTH DAKOTA—Cont'd															
46 123	...	7	Tripp	1 612.5	5 492	2 804	3.4	83.7	0.7	15.0	0.9	1.9	6.4	16.5	8.0	10.2	9.5	12.3
46 125	43620	3	Turner	617.1	8 317	2 565	13.5	96.6	0.7	1.0	0.5	2.1	5.9	17.6	6.9	10.1	11.4	12.1
46 127	43580	3	Union	460.7	14 934	2 100	32.4	93.8	1.4	1.4	1.8	3.1	5.7	18.5	7.4	11.1	12.6	13.6
46 129	...	7	Walworth	708.6	5 610	2 793	7.9	81.3	1.1	16.5	2.4	2.0	6.9	16.5	6.7	10.4	9.6	11.6
46 135	49460	7	Yankton	521.2	22 616	1 707	43.4	90.4	2.5	3.7	1.1	4.0	5.8	15.3	9.0	12.4	11.5	13.5
46 137	...	8	Ziebach	1 961.2	2 801	2 987	1.4	27.3	1.4	69.9	0.5	4.8	6.4	26.3	11.1	11.2	13.9	12.9
47 000	...	0	**TENNESSEE**	41 234.8	6 651 194	X	161.3	75.8	17.7	0.8	2.3	5.2	6.1	16.5	9.3	13.4	12.5	13.4
47 001	28940	2	Anderson	337.2	75 936	727	225.2	91.4	5.1	0.9	1.9	2.7	5.4	15.4	7.6	11.6	11.7	13.8
47 003	43180	4	Bedford	473.6	47 484	1 028	100.3	79.3	8.7	0.8	1.4	11.8	6.6	19.1	8.4	12.5	12.7	13.6
47 005	...	7	Benton	394.3	16 014	2 038	40.6	94.1	3.0	1.2	0.9	2.3	5.1	14.6	7.0	9.8	11.0	14.2
47 007	...	8	Bledsoe	406.4	14 675	2 119	36.1	90.4	7.3	1.0	0.5	2.2	4.2	12.1	7.5	13.4	14.9	15.5
47 009	28940	2	Blount	558.8	128 670	489	230.3	92.7	3.6	0.9	1.2	3.2	5.1	15.5	8.0	11.3	11.8	14.6
47 011	17420	3	Bradley	328.8	104 490	575	317.8	87.9	5.5	0.9	1.4	6.1	5.8	16.3	9.6	12.7	12.6	13.9
47 013	28940	2	Campbell	480.2	39 714	1 184	82.7	97.6	0.7	1.0	0.5	1.2	5.3	15.6	7.3	11.2	12.3	14.3
47 015	34980	1	Cannon	265.6	14 027	2 160	52.8	95.5	2.2	1.1	0.5	2.3	5.5	15.3	7.5	12.0	12.0	14.8
47 017	...	6	Carroll	597.7	28 092	1 486	47.0	86.5	11.4	0.9	0.5	2.5	5.6	15.6	10.3	10.5	10.7	13.7
47 019	27740	3	Carter	341.2	56 502	905	165.6	96.0	2.0	0.8	0.7	1.8	4.6	14.5	7.2	12.2	11.7	14.5
47 021	34980	1	Cheatham	302.4	39 880	1 179	131.9	94.5	2.3	1.0	0.9	2.8	5.7	17.0	7.6	12.2	12.8	15.9
47 023	27180	3	Chester	285.7	17 453	1 948	61.1	87.8	9.9	1.0	0.7	2.4	5.6	16.3	13.9	11.0	11.8	12.3
47 025	...	6	Claiborne	434.6	31 757	1 385	73.1	96.5	1.5	1.0	0.9	1.3	4.9	14.4	9.2	12.2	11.9	13.8
47 027	...	9	Clay	236.5	7 752	2 614	32.8	95.7	2.1	0.8	0.3	2.5	5.2	14.8	6.8	9.6	10.6	14.4
47 029	35460	6	Cocke	434.5	35 219	1 298	81.1	94.8	2.7	1.1	0.6	2.2	5.4	15.0	7.3	10.6	11.5	14.4
47 031	46100	4	Coffee	429.0	54 682	922	127.5	90.7	4.7	0.9	1.5	4.1	6.4	17.7	7.9	12.2	11.9	13.6
47 033	27180	3	Crockett	265.5	14 411	2 136	54.3	75.7	14.5	0.7	0.4	10.4	6.2	17.7	7.9	11.9	11.5	13.6
47 035	18900	4	Cumberland	681.0	58 655	882	86.1	95.6	0.9	1.0	0.8	2.8	4.9	13.1	6.3	9.7	9.3	12.1
47 037	34980	1	Davidson	503.8	684 410	96	1 358.5	58.3	28.6	0.8	4.5	10.1	6.9	14.4	10.2	19.7	13.6	12.2
47 039	...	9	Decatur	333.8	11 769	2 307	35.3	92.9	3.5	0.8	0.7	3.3	5.6	15.7	6.7	10.2	11.0	12.7
47 041	...	6	DeKalb	304.4	19 361	1 855	63.6	90.1	2.0	0.8	0.9	7.3	6.2	15.8	7.4	12.1	12.0	14.3
47 043	34980	1	Dickson	489.9	52 170	957	106.5	91.5	5.2	0.9	0.9	3.3	6.2	17.1	7.8	12.6	12.5	14.5
47 045	20540	5	Dyer	512.3	37 708	1 232	73.6	81.6	14.9	0.7	0.9	3.4	6.2	17.9	8.2	12.1	11.9	13.8
47 047	32820	1	Fayette	704.8	39 590	1 187	56.2	69.0	27.9	0.6	0.9	2.5	5.2	15.0	7.0	10.7	11.5	14.2
47 049	...	9	Fentress	498.6	18 033	1 918	36.2	97.6	0.6	0.9	0.5	1.4	5.5	15.9	7.3	9.9	11.0	14.2
47 051	46100	4	Franklin	554.5	41 700	1 135	75.2	90.4	5.8	1.1	1.2	3.1	5.0	15.5	11.3	10.2	11.5	12.8
47 053	...	4	Gibson	602.7	49 401	991	82.0	78.6	19.1	0.6	0.4	2.7	6.4	17.9	7.7	11.7	12.2	13.0
47 055	...	6	Giles	610.9	29 307	1 450	48.0	86.4	11.3	1.0	0.8	2.4	5.5	15.6	8.5	11.1	13.0	14.0
47 057	28940	2	Grainger	280.6	23 072	1 677	82.2	95.6	1.1	0.8	0.3	3.3	5.0	15.8	7.4	10.4	12.1	15.4
47 059	24620	4	Greene	622.2	68 615	778	110.3	94.3	2.6	0.7	0.7	2.8	4.8	14.9	8.1	10.6	11.9	14.2
47 061	...	8	Grundy	360.4	13 389	2 205	37.2	97.2	0.9	1.4	0.5	1.1	5.6	16.1	7.6	10.9	11.8	13.1
47 063	34100	3	Hamblen	161.2	63 785	830	395.7	83.3	4.8	0.7	1.3	11.5	6.0	17.2	8.0	11.6	12.5	13.7
47 065	16860	2	Hamilton	542.4	357 738	193	659.5	72.8	20.2	0.8	2.5	5.4	5.8	15.2	8.9	14.2	12.4	13.2
47 067	...	8	Hancock	222.3	6 577	2 706	29.6	98.5	1.0	1.1	0.4	0.5	5.2	15.5	7.3	11.4	11.7	13.2
47 069	...	6	Hardeman	667.7	25 435	1 588	38.1	55.8	42.1	0.6	0.9	1.7	5.2	14.5	8.7	14.7	12.7	13.8
47 071	...	6	Hardin	577.3	25 679	1 579	44.5	93.4	4.1	1.0	0.8	2.1	5.4	15.2	7.4	10.5	11.1	13.8
47 073	28700	2	Hawkins	487.0	56 563	901	116.1	96.4	1.8	0.8	0.7	1.4	5.0	15.6	7.3	10.9	11.7	14.7
47 075	15140	6	Haywood	533.1	17 853	1 926	33.5	45.1	50.6	0.5	0.4	4.4	6.0	16.9	8.4	10.9	11.7	13.6
47 077	...	6	Henderson	520.0	27 822	1 497	53.5	89.6	9.1	0.6	0.5	2.1	5.8	17.3	7.6	12.0	12.5	13.9
47 079	37540	7	Henry	561.8	32 310	1 374	57.5	89.1	8.6	0.9	0.7	2.4	5.1	15.5	7.0	10.5	11.0	13.4
47 081	34980	1	Hickman	612.5	24 295	1 633	39.7	92.5	4.7	1.2	0.6	2.4	6.0	16.0	8.0	12.6	12.5	14.5
47 083	...	8	Houston	200.3	8 134	2 587	40.6	93.9	4.0	1.2	0.8	2.1	5.0	16.7	7.7	11.0	11.3	13.4
47 085	...	6	Humphreys	530.8	18 347	1 898	34.6	93.9	3.3	1.1	0.7	2.4	5.5	16.4	7.4	11.0	11.8	13.7
47 087	18260	8	Jackson	308.6	11 566	2 314	37.5	96.8	0.9	1.3	0.3	2.0	4.6	13.8	7.1	10.0	11.4	14.4
47 089	34100	3	Jefferson	274.9	53 535	939	194.7	93.6	2.6	0.8	0.8	3.4	5.1	15.1	8.9	10.9	11.6	14.3
47 091	...	6	Johnson	298.4	17 754	1 930	59.5	95.0	2.6	0.8	0.4	2.0	4.3	13.0	7.2	11.9	12.9	14.9
47 093	28940	2	Knox	508.2	456 132	150	897.5	84.6	9.8	0.8	2.8	4.0	5.8	15.4	12.1	13.4	12.4	13.1
47 095	...	9	Lake	165.8	7 560	2 628	45.6	69.2	29.1	0.9	0.4	2.2	4.1	10.7	10.8	18.1	14.9	14.1
47 097	...	6	Lauderdale	472.0	26 773	1 538	56.7	61.4	35.5	1.0	1.0	2.6	5.4	17.3	9.1	14.2	13.1	13.8
47 099	29980	6	Lawrence	617.1	43 081	1 109	69.8	95.2	2.3	1.1	0.7	2.1	6.9	18.3	7.7	11.9	11.3	13.5
47 101	...	6	Lewis	282.1	11 904	2 302	42.2	94.7	2.6	0.9	0.8	2.3	5.8	16.3	7.5	10.5	11.7	12.8
47 103	...	6	Lincoln	570.3	33 645	1 338	59.0	88.6	7.6	1.5	0.7	3.3	5.3	16.9	7.3	11.3	11.3	14.0
47 105	28940	2	Loudon	229.3	51 454	968	224.4	89.3	1.7	0.7	1.0	8.3	5.1	14.5	6.7	10.0	10.2	12.8
47 107	11940	4	McMinn	430.1	52 850	950	122.9	91.3	4.6	1.2	0.9	3.9	5.4	16.0	8.4	11.0	11.5	14.0
47 109	...	6	McNairy	562.8	25 935	1 566	46.1	91.5	6.7	0.9	0.4	2.0	5.2	16.9	7.6	10.5	12.1	13.5
47 111	34980	1	Macon	307.1	23 450	1 662	76.4	92.8	1.2	0.8	1.1	5.1	7.1	17.5	8.5	12.6	11.9	14.0
47 113	27180	3	Madison	557.1	97 663	607	175.3	57.6	38.2	0.5	1.5	3.7	6.4	16.5	10.7	12.3	11.5	13.0
47 115	16860	2	Marion	498.2	28 446	1 472	57.1	93.4	4.6	1.1	0.8	1.7	5.7	15.5	7.4	11.5	11.9	14.0

1. CBSA = Core Based Statistical Area. See Appendix A for explanation. See Appendix B for list of metropolitan areas with component counties. 2. County type code from the Economic Research Service of USDA Rural-Urban Continuum Codes. See Appendix A for definition. 3. Dry land or land partially or temporarily covered by water. 4. May be of any race.

Table B. States and Counties — Population and Households

STATE County	Age (percent) (cont.)				Population change and components of change, 2000–2016							Households, 2011–2015				
	55 to 64 years	65 to 74 years	75 years and over	Percent female	Total persons 2000	Total persons 2010	Percent change 2000–2010	Percent change 2010–2016	Components of change 2010–2016 Births	Deaths	Net migration	Number	Persons per household	Family households	Female family householder[1]	One person
	16	17	18	19	20	21	22	23	24	25	26	27	28	29	30	31
SOUTH DAKOTA—Cont'd																
Tripp	15.2	10.8	11.1	50.2	6 430	5 644	-12.2	-2.7	415	422	-131	2 579	2.08	57.9	6.3	36.9
Turner	15.2	10.7	10.1	49.8	8 849	8 347	-5.7	-0.4	554	632	34	3 520	2.31	67.7	5.3	26.9
Union	14.5	10.0	6.7	49.3	12 584	14 399	14.4	3.7	1 011	719	263	5 939	2.48	65.6	5.4	30.5
Walworth	13.7	12.2	12.3	50.6	5 974	5 438	-9.0	3.2	466	504	215	2 389	2.21	58.7	8.8	37.6
Yankton	14.4	9.6	8.6	48.1	21 652	22 438	3.6	0.8	1 640	1 363	-67	8 899	2.33	64.1	10.0	30.2
Ziebach	10.8	4.5	3.0	50.3	2 519	2 801	11.2	0.0	238	94	-145	810	3.50	80.7	28.8	16.3
TENNESSEE	13.0	9.4	6.3	51.2	5 689 283	6 346 298	11.5	4.8	502 451	392 451	191 384	2 504 556	2.53	66.5	13.4	28.1
Anderson	14.7	11.2	8.5	51.4	71 330	75 094	5.3	1.1	5 010	5 699	1 580	30 612	2.43	64.1	12.8	31.2
Bedford	12.1	9.4	5.7	50.8	37 586	45 056	19.9	5.4	3 856	2 800	1 323	16 721	2.72	72.9	12.0	21.6
Benton	15.0	14.1	9.2	50.7	16 537	16 491	-0.3	-2.9	994	1 505	34	6 786	2.37	63.6	10.1	32.4
Bledsoe	14.3	11.2	7.0	41.6	12 367	12 872	4.1	14.0	767	820	1 723	4 534	2.75	72.7	10.9	23.4
Blount	14.3	11.6	7.8	51.5	105 823	123 100	16.3	4.5	7 993	8 083	5 361	49 033	2.51	69.4	10.2	26.1
Bradley	12.6	9.8	6.7	51.5	87 965	98 932	12.5	5.6	7 361	6 092	4 131	38 466	2.58	68.8	11.5	26.8
Campbell	14.0	11.9	8.1	51.1	39 854	40 723	2.2	-2.5	2 629	3 377	-194	15 995	2.48	68.3	13.6	29.1
Cannon	14.2	10.7	7.9	50.6	12 826	13 816	7.7	1.5	914	1 060	344	5 388	2.53	69.2	11.2	26.7
Carroll	13.3	11.9	8.5	51.4	29 475	28 480	-3.4	-1.4	1 961	2 587	212	11 168	2.45	66.3	11.3	30.4
Carter	14.5	12.1	8.7	51.0	56 742	57 375	1.1	-1.5	3 313	4 164	-44	23 894	2.31	67.1	11.5	29.2
Cheatham	14.3	9.5	5.0	50.4	35 912	39 103	8.9	2.0	2 752	2 329	374	14 499	2.70	72.8	11.3	21.3
Chester	11.9	9.9	7.3	52.0	15 540	17 143	10.3	1.8	1 187	1 083	155	6 074	2.66	70.6	13.1	26.2
Claiborne	14.3	11.9	7.4	51.1	29 862	32 212	7.9	-1.4	1 937	2 639	246	12 705	2.40	68.1	12.5	28.7
Clay	14.1	14.0	10.3	50.5	7 976	7 860	-1.5	-1.4	491	710	58	3 242	2.37	71.1	10.2	26.2
Cocke	15.4	12.6	7.7	51.9	33 565	35 642	6.2	-1.2	2 416	3 006	195	14 710	2.38	66.9	14.7	29.6
Coffee	13.1	9.9	7.3	51.2	48 014	52 800	10.0	3.6	4 154	4 056	1 783	21 170	2.49	68.7	13.2	27.5
Crockett	13.1	10.3	7.8	52.0	14 532	14 576	0.3	-1.1	1 091	1 073	-162	5 453	2.64	67.0	12.9	28.4
Cumberland	14.9	17.4	12.3	51.1	46 802	56 062	19.8	4.6	3 502	4 837	3 759	24 177	2.35	69.1	9.2	27.0
Davidson	11.6	6.8	4.6	51.8	569 891	626 580	9.9	9.2	62 323	32 044	27 934	264 211	2.41	55.5	14.2	35.3
Decatur	14.9	13.1	10.0	50.6	11 731	11 750	0.2	0.2	741	1 069	339	4 978	2.30	68.2	12.2	28.3
DeKalb	14.0	11.2	7.0	50.7	17 423	18 720	7.4	3.4	1 437	1 499	711	6 920	2.70	70.2	13.4	25.4
Dickson	13.5	9.4	6.3	51.0	43 156	49 658	15.1	5.1	3 838	3 172	1 771	18 556	2.69	71.5	12.3	25.2
Dyer	12.8	10.1	7.0	51.9	37 279	38 330	2.8	-1.6	2 974	2 678	-932	14 931	2.51	70.3	14.2	24.6
Fayette	16.4	12.4	7.7	50.7	28 806	38 439	33.4	3.0	2 662	2 329	686	14 846	2.58	73.9	11.0	22.7
Fentress	15.0	13.6	7.6	51.1	16 625	17 960	8.0	0.4	1 180	1 488	329	7 304	2.43	68.8	12.7	27.1
Franklin	14.2	11.5	8.2	51.2	39 270	41 064	4.6	1.5	2 434	3 016	1 249	16 302	2.40	69.4	11.4	25.5
Gibson	13.0	10.0	8.0	52.0	48 152	49 691	3.2	-0.6	3 849	4 132	-5	19 449	2.49	68.1	15.6	28.4
Giles	14.9	11.5	8.1	51.5	29 447	29 489	0.1	-0.6	1 912	2 165	46	11 297	2.49	69.2	13.6	25.4
Grainger	14.7	12.4	6.9	49.6	20 659	22 656	9.7	1.8	1 408	1 689	705	8 952	2.52	71.0	9.1	25.0
Greene	14.6	12.5	8.4	50.8	62 909	68 825	9.4	-0.3	3 934	5 295	1 115	28 061	2.38	66.7	11.7	29.6
Grundy	13.5	12.8	8.5	50.6	14 332	13 726	-4.2	-2.5	972	1 228	-120	5 221	2.55	68.3	15.4	27.8
Hamblen	12.7	10.7	7.5	51.1	58 128	62 533	7.6	2.0	4 851	4 555	991	24 470	2.54	69.4	13.4	26.3
Hamilton	13.6	9.7	7.1	51.8	307 896	336 484	9.3	6.3	26 041	21 021	16 367	136 319	2.48	65.0	13.7	29.4
Hancock	15.8	12.4	7.4	50.5	6 786	6 815	0.4	-3.5	417	634	-30	2 754	2.35	65.9	12.6	30.9
Hardeman	13.2	10.4	6.8	45.2	28 105	27 247	-3.1	-6.7	1 697	1 738	-1 733	8 737	2.59	69.6	19.4	27.0
Hardin	14.6	12.9	9.1	51.6	25 578	26 012	1.7	-1.3	1 728	2 212	190	9 871	2.58	67.7	11.0	28.6
Hawkins	14.7	12.3	7.9	50.8	53 563	56 829	6.1	-0.5	3 408	4 243	555	23 167	2.42	68.8	12.9	27.8
Haywood	15.3	10.1	7.1	53.3	19 797	18 807	-5.0	-5.1	1 368	1 183	-1 163	7 008	2.57	62.2	15.6	34.3
Henderson	13.4	10.8	6.8	51.5	25 522	27 782	8.9	0.1	2 024	1 957	-17	10 809	2.57	69.2	12.0	27.5
Henry	14.9	13.4	9.2	51.7	31 115	32 354	4.0	-0.1	2 075	2 797	682	13 471	2.36	67.4	12.2	28.0
Hickman	13.9	9.9	6.6	48.0	22 295	24 689	10.7	-1.6	1 705	1 660	-448	8 769	2.60	69.8	10.8	27.7
Houston	14.4	12.1	8.3	51.1	8 088	8 425	4.2	-3.5	517	628	-153	3 247	2.49	69.3	10.2	26.7
Humphreys	14.7	11.5	7.9	50.4	17 929	18 535	3.4	-1.0	1 267	1 487	48	7 124	2.53	68.2	9.9	28.2
Jackson	17.2	13.2	8.2	50.1	10 984	11 632	5.9	-0.6	607	937	271	4 531	2.49	69.5	12.8	28.1
Jefferson	14.2	12.1	7.7	50.8	44 294	51 660	16.6	3.6	3 312	3 593	2 012	19 679	2.58	71.5	11.7	25.1
Johnson	14.3	13.2	8.4	46.2	17 499	18 244	4.3	-2.7	954	1 295	-177	7 009	2.29	67.3	8.5	29.5
Knox	12.6	9.0	6.2	51.4	382 032	432 266	13.1	5.5	32 607	25 983	16 846	180 729	2.39	61.1	10.4	31.9
Lake	12.3	8.7	6.5	35.9	7 954	7 832	-1.5	-3.5	417	584	-99	2 092	2.38	68.4	18.8	28.6
Lauderdale	12.5	8.9	5.6	47.6	27 101	27 822	2.7	-3.8	1 856	1 736	-1 165	9 800	2.50	69.2	20.5	27.4
Lawrence	12.8	10.2	7.5	51.0	39 926	41 851	4.8	2.9	3 537	3 174	908	16 104	2.59	70.7	12.3	26.2
Lewis	15.4	12.2	7.8	51.3	11 367	12 171	7.1	-2.2	812	867	-210	4 712	2.49	69.1	9.7	27.2
Lincoln	15.0	10.8	8.2	51.1	31 340	33 350	6.4	0.9	2 117	2 460	685	13 644	2.43	66.8	11.6	28.9
Loudon	15.1	15.6	10.1	51.0	39 086	48 548	24.2	6.0	3 300	3 739	3 192	20 009	2.49	74.3	9.2	22.6
McMinn	14.3	11.3	8.0	51.3	49 015	52 278	6.7	1.1	3 516	4 070	1 151	19 978	2.58	67.3	9.6	29.6
McNairy	13.8	12.2	8.3	50.8	24 653	26 077	5.8	-0.5	1 723	2 131	234	9 872	2.61	67.5	11.2	29.3
Macon	12.7	9.7	6.0	51.4	20 386	22 227	9.0	5.5	2 038	1 692	867	8 856	2.53	68.7	11.4	25.7
Madison	13.6	9.4	6.6	52.7	91 837	98 299	7.0	-0.6	7 817	5 883	-2 588	36 766	2.56	67.1	17.0	28.1
Marion	14.8	11.8	7.4	51.2	27 776	28 222	1.6	0.8	1 930	2 203	502	11 525	2.43	72.9	14.6	23.4

1. No spouse present.

Table B. States and Counties — Population, Vital Statistics, Health, and Crime

STATE County	Persons in group quarters, 2016	Daytime population, 2011–2015 Number	Employ-ment/resi-dence ratio	Births, 2016 Total	Rate[1]	Deaths, 2016 Number	Rate[1]	Persons under 65 with no health insurance, 2015 Number	Percent	Medicare, 2015 Total Beneficiaries	Enrolled in Original Medicare	Enrolled in Medicare Advantage	Serious crimes known to police,[2] 2014 Total Number	Rate[3]
	32	33	34	35	36	37	38	39	40	41	42	43	44	45
SOUTH DAKOTA—Cont'd														
Tripp	131	5 405	0.97	69	12.6	66	12.0	661	16.0	1 233	1 097	136	37	677
Turner	152	6 666	0.61	86	10.3	97	11.7	690	10.7	1 875	1 323	552	79	944
Union	89	15 882	1.14	152	10.2	107	7.2	864	6.8	2 806	2 143	663	123	948
Walworth	152	5 388	0.96	87	15.5	74	13.2	603	14.9	1 200	1 146	54	94	1 694
Yankton	2 295	24 016	1.12	267	11.8	213	9.4	1 740	10.2	4 504	3 606	898	570	2 502
Ziebach	0	2 571	0.72	32	11.4	25	8.9	456	18.2	D	113	D	5	176
TENNESSEE	152 979	6 543 697	1.02	81 443	12.2	65 454	9.8	656 235	12.0	1 217 102	761 146	455 956	240 295	3 669
Anderson	1 184	91 304	1.51	802	10.6	892	11.7	6 149	10.2	16 685	9 963	6 722	NA	NA
Bedford	545	43 456	0.87	628	13.2	444	9.4	6 702	16.8	8 367	5 591	2 776	1 030	2 229
Benton	162	15 278	0.83	156	9.7	246	15.4	1 790	14.5	4 616	3 592	1 024	319	1 959
Bledsoe	2 522	11 969	0.63	132	9.0	150	10.2	1 379	14.7	2 277	1 636	641	124	964
Blount	2 033	116 642	0.85	1 284	10.0	1 294	10.1	11 100	10.9	26 777	15 350	11 427	2 420	1 922
Bradley	2 685	101 261	0.98	1 181	11.3	1 029	9.8	10 934	12.9	20 574	12 316	8 258	4 316	4 198
Campbell	519	36 536	0.73	426	10.7	575	14.5	3 953	12.6	10 417	5 183	5 234	1 443	3 587
Cannon	164	10 552	0.42	154	11.0	156	11.1	1 439	12.8	2 955	1 984	971	133	963
Carroll	1 271	25 770	0.75	308	11.0	429	15.3	2 418	11.3	7 699	6 010	1 689	629	2 199
Carter	915	46 631	0.55	521	9.2	711	12.6	6 117	13.9	11 460	5 476	5 984	1 650	2 871
Cheatham	283	30 196	0.49	456	11.4	409	10.3	3 834	11.3	6 340	3 354	2 986	971	2 446
Chester	1 293	15 045	0.68	189	10.8	151	8.7	1 605	12.1	2 748	2 117	631	305	1 752
Claiborne	1 258	29 251	0.79	304	9.6	427	13.4	3 026	12.3	8 095	4 173	3 922	776	2 465
Clay	96	7 143	0.77	76	9.8	116	15.0	817	14.0	1 486	1 210	276	100	1 286
Cocke	294	31 380	0.71	385	10.9	489	13.9	3 252	11.7	9 579	4 886	4 693	1 495	4 207
Coffee	557	56 807	1.16	702	12.8	655	12.0	5 513	12.4	12 769	9 309	3 460	1 880	3 505
Crockett	194	13 186	0.75	167	11.6	180	12.5	1 839	15.4	3 200	2 653	547	320	2 187
Cumberland	636	57 648	1.01	560	9.5	819	14.0	5 643	13.8	18 323	14 052	4 271	2 264	3 908
Davidson	26 549	759 780	1.30	10 438	15.3	5 461	8.0	81 013	14.0	90 870	48 732	42 138	32 658	4 887
Decatur	213	10 480	0.73	127	10.8	170	14.4	1 254	14.1	2 758	2 084	674	278	2 381
DeKalb	298	17 939	0.85	237	12.2	218	11.3	2 395	15.5	4 182	2 242	1 940	447	2 313
Dickson	617	45 659	0.78	646	12.4	508	9.7	5 094	11.8	9 414	5 712	3 702	1 558	3 083
Dyer	516	38 317	1.02	466	12.4	439	11.6	3 207	10.3	8 576	6 903	1 673	2 006	5 239
Fayette	424	30 125	0.48	429	11.0	427	10.8	3 046	9.8	5 896	4 157	1 739	681	1 752
Fentress	132	16 708	0.79	185	10.3	255	14.1	1 897	13.5	4 980	3 972	1 008	460	2 562
Franklin	2 086	38 927	0.87	389	9.3	464	11.1	3 603	11.4	8 682	6 135	2 547	806	1 953
Gibson	991	44 501	0.75	618	12.5	664	13.4	4 375	10.9	11 414	9 159	2 255	1 567	3 164
Giles	702	27 454	0.87	319	10.9	350	11.9	2 882	12.6	6 557	5 116	1 441	713	2 488
Grainger	151	18 161	0.47	226	9.8	289	12.5	2 388	13.0	5 820	2 738	3 082	439	1 929
Greene	1 753	67 761	0.97	649	9.5	872	12.7	6 626	12.4	17 781	9 754	8 027	1 723	2 522
Grundy	180	11 764	0.61	150	11.2	188	14.0	1 553	14.9	3 670	2 347	1 323	301	2 233
Hamblen	918	68 144	1.21	766	12.0	711	11.1	7 414	14.4	13 933	7 874	6 059	2 240	3 533
Hamilton	9 599	390 237	1.26	4 227	11.8	3 529	9.9	32 463	11.3	68 791	43 088	25 703	17 270	4 899
Hancock	149	5 819	0.61	64	9.7	99	15.1	570	11.0	1 385	750	635	146	2 192
Hardeman	3 799	25 115	0.86	263	10.3	284	11.2	2 094	11.8	5 587	4 219	1 368	759	2 901
Hardin	371	25 232	0.93	271	10.6	344	13.4	2 819	14.1	6 206	4 959	1 247	905	3 468
Hawkins	456	48 252	0.60	551	9.7	725	12.8	4 926	11.0	14 055	5 735	8 320	1 413	2 482
Haywood	174	16 312	0.73	194	10.9	220	12.3	1 761	11.9	3 351	2 410	941	839	4 625
Henderson	218	26 273	0.84	317	11.4	329	11.8	2 515	10.9	6 198	4 554	1 644	757	2 686
Henry	491	31 964	0.98	314	9.7	469	14.5	3 227	13.1	8 830	7 035	1 795	1 095	3 394
Hickman	1 188	19 642	0.48	279	11.5	256	10.5	2 482	13.0	5 036	3 052	1 984	508	2 096
Houston	177	7 218	0.63	85	10.4	92	11.3	820	12.7	1 963	1 482	481	103	1 245
Humphreys	205	17 858	0.94	196	10.7	242	13.2	1 622	11.3	4 265	3 206	1 059	330	1 812
Jackson	177	9 842	0.55	94	8.1	168	14.5	1 201	13.5	2 205	1 671	534	202	1 754
Jefferson	1 640	45 738	0.70	542	10.1	652	12.2	5 024	12.1	14 459	7 888	6 571	1 340	2 556
Johnson	1 792	16 710	0.78	155	8.7	202	11.4	1 583	12.9	5 014	2 725	2 289	621	3 460
Knox	12 125	472 267	1.13	5 285	11.6	4 321	9.5	40 387	10.8	79 766	43 678	36 088	19 896	4 434
Lake	2 501	7 854	1.09	63	8.3	95	12.6	469	11.5	1 378	1 214	164	130	1 682
Lauderdale	2 505	26 461	0.89	286	10.7	277	10.3	2 437	11.9	5 261	3 918	1 343	1 004	3 602
Lawrence	407	38 222	0.75	574	13.3	502	11.7	4 437	12.8	11 011	8 566	2 445	1 264	3 002
Lewis	217	10 437	0.68	136	11.4	137	11.5	1 372	14.6	2 345	1 642	703	334	2 796
Lincoln	283	29 583	0.71	313	9.3	386	11.5	3 110	11.4	7 487	5 184	2 303	923	2 733
Loudon	480	46 297	0.80	511	9.9	588	11.4	5 135	13.5	15 073	8 698	6 375	1 145	2 244
McMinn	965	51 755	0.96	556	10.5	637	12.1	5 032	12.0	12 123	8 043	4 080	2 099	3 997
McNairy	313	24 007	0.76	254	9.8	338	13.0	2 667	12.9	7 938	6 330	1 608	585	2 230
Macon	269	19 461	0.65	356	15.2	276	11.8	2 851	14.8	4 162	2 790	1 372	340	1 487
Madison	4 431	113 450	1.36	1 219	12.5	990	10.1	8 540	10.8	18 908	14 519	4 389	4 492	4 533
Marion	250	25 032	0.72	322	11.3	354	12.4	2 636	11.5	5 871	3 657	2 214	578	2 029

1. Per 1,000 estimated resident population.   2. Data for serious crimes have not been adjusted for underreporting; this may affect comparability between geographic areas and over time.
3. Per 100,000 population estimated by the FBI.

Table B. States and Counties — Crime, Education, Money Income, and Poverty

STATE County	Serious crimes known to police, 2014 (cont.)[1] Rate[2]		Education School enrollment and attainment, 2011–2015				Local government expenditures,[5] 2013–2014		Money income, 2011–2015		Households		Income and poverty, 2015 Percent below poverty level			
			Enrollment[3]		Attainment[4] (percent)							Percent				
	Violent	Property	Total	Percent private	High school graduate or less	Bachelor's degree or more	Total current spending (mil dol)	Current spending per student (dollars)	Per capita income[6] (dollars)	Median income (dollars)	with income of less than $50,000	with income of $200,000 or more	Median household income (dollars)	All persons	Children under 18 years	Children 5 to 17 years in families
	46	47	48	49	50	51	52	53	54	55	56	57	58	59	60	61
SOUTH DAKOTA—Cont'd																
Tripp	128	549	1 096	4.7	48.0	22.1	8.3	8 857	24 560	37 153	62.0	2.6	48 289	17.7	25.9	23.6
Turner	48	896	1 781	9.7	44.3	21.0	13.2	8 854	26 958	53 378	47.3	2.1	54 134	10.0	9.6	8.4
Union	154	794	3 679	13.3	38.3	31.5	25.3	8 639	36 730	64 471	37.8	9.6	74 439	6.3	7.0	5.8
Walworth	144	1 550	1 143	13.5	48.3	21.7	7.5	8 847	25 553	43 221	58.3	1.3	44 480	14.8	20.3	18.2
Yankton	299	2 204	5 084	17.8	43.5	26.7	24.7	8 027	27 044	48 176	51.2	3.7	48 991	13.6	14.5	12.8
Ziebach	0	176	938	1.2	54.0	13.9	10.3	14 295	12 877	35 119	67.8	0.2	33 239	47.1	54.0	38.6
TENNESSEE	608	3 061	1 590 303	17.2	47.5	24.9	8 566.2	8 622	25 227	45 219	54.2	3.2	47 243	16.7	24.1	22.4
Anderson	NA	NA	16 176	14.3	44.8	24.0	122.2	10 045	25 590	42 880	56.3	2.3	44 488	19.7	30.0	25.2
Bedford	346	1 882	10 940	11.8	62.1	13.7	60.5	7 234	20 390	41 984	59.2	1.4	44 734	17.0	24.7	21.7
Benton	190	1 769	3 094	6.0	66.8	10.8	20.3	8 849	19 285	33 240	66.9	0.7	36 201	20.5	32.2	29.6
Bledsoe	140	824	2 407	17.9	67.6	10.7	16.2	8 202	18 061	37 013	63.8	2.4	39 730	26.1	34.5	31.8
Blount	272	1 649	27 425	16.5	47.3	22.8	160.2	8 793	25 916	48 286	51.7	2.6	49 532	13.1	19.3	16.3
Bradley	544	3 654	25 753	23.6	49.6	19.9	129.8	8 164	23 336	42 114	56.6	2.0	43 772	18.1	23.8	21.3
Campbell	370	3 217	8 245	13.8	69.6	10.2	42.3	7 149	18 117	32 028	69.2	0.7	33 092	26.2	39.4	36.9
Cannon	181	782	2 808	10.3	61.2	13.9	17.4	8 302	21 897	41 533	58.0	0.9	43 864	16.4	23.4	21.7
Carroll	252	1 948	6 520	18.4	63.0	14.2	38.7	8 215	19 086	35 508	65.3	1.2	38 412	21.1	31.1	29.9
Carter	231	2 639	11 984	13.0	58.4	16.1	70.7	8 738	19 166	33 213	67.1	0.8	35 053	23.6	33.1	32.4
Cheatham	315	2 131	9 685	14.1	52.6	19.3	48.6	7 339	23 922	51 857	47.8	1.6	56 447	10.6	16.3	14.8
Chester	276	1 477	4 818	25.8	55.9	15.7	20.6	7 360	19 440	40 167	56.7	1.6	43 452	19.0	26.5	24.2
Claiborne	394	2 071	7 198	27.7	64.0	14.2	38.9	8 412	18 817	34 899	66.3	1.1	35 193	21.6	33.1	30.8
Clay	244	1 042	1 419	6.6	69.1	14.7	9.1	8 448	16 881	28 804	72.5	0.2	32 750	23.7	34.8	32.9
Cocke	523	3 683	6 243	5.3	67.4	10.1	46.3	8 309	18 691	31 187	69.3	0.9	31 355	26.4	40.1	38.2
Coffee	464	3 041	12 181	7.9	54.9	18.3	86.4	9 143	21 680	41 590	59.0	1.9	44 452	15.9	24.2	21.6
Crockett	492	1 695	3 437	9.5	64.1	13.0	23.5	7 647	19 178	35 464	66.6	1.1	38 474	19.1	25.8	23.0
Cumberland	343	3 564	10 147	10.4	55.1	18.2	58.1	7 737	21 770	38 576	64.1	1.1	39 472	16.7	27.5	26.3
Davidson	1 120	3 767	162 130	30.3	36.8	37.3	894.5	10 280	29 589	48 368	51.4	4.4	51 999	17.1	26.5	26.5
Decatur	231	2 150	2 357	5.9	63.3	12.7	12.2	7 371	23 715	37 263	63.1	2.9	38 771	19.4	28.7	27.7
DeKalb	269	2 044	4 107	5.5	65.2	13.8	23.2	7 748	25 573	38 319	60.6	3.8	43 804	20.2	30.9	29.8
Dickson	455	2 628	11 490	12.4	60.2	14.5	66.1	7 882	22 369	44 680	56.1	2.6	47 621	16.4	23.3	22.8
Dyer	737	4 503	9 072	5.9	56.0	19.2	57.2	8 588	23 044	42 468	56.9	2.1	43 391	22.5	31.3	29.2
Fayette	275	1 477	8 331	31.3	48.4	22.9	28.8	7 818	29 431	54 890	45.6	5.4	56 710	13.8	21.5	20.7
Fentress	201	2 361	3 696	4.0	69.5	10.9	19.3	6 493	16 539	30 259	74.0	1.2	31 824	25.7	36.3	33.1
Franklin	346	1 606	9 755	23.2	54.2	19.5	47.7	8 225	22 889	42 773	57.1	2.5	47 286	15.0	21.7	19.6
Gibson	545	2 619	12 115	8.3	54.6	16.0	73.5	7 918	20 704	38 457	62.5	1.2	40 789	15.7	23.4	22.3
Giles	283	2 205	6 349	16.6	60.4	14.8	32.4	8 034	20 765	41 093	59.9	1.1	42 207	16.1	24.3	22.5
Grainger	180	1 749	4 507	9.5	67.0	11.1	27.8	7 625	18 974	35 391	65.7	1.4	38 103	18.7	27.9	26.0
Greene	328	2 194	14 053	12.3	61.6	15.0	83.1	8 215	20 398	35 196	66.2	1.4	36 309	18.0	25.2	22.4
Grundy	341	1 892	2 627	11.6	70.7	10.8	19.6	8 688	16 356	27 373	72.9	1.7	33 595	26.1	36.6	35.1
Hamblen	472	3 064	13 665	10.4	61.3	15.5	81.1	7 946	20 246	37 617	62.3	1.5	39 566	19.0	26.3	23.8
Hamilton	640	4 259	84 690	21.0	39.9	28.7	398.5	9 152	27 518	48 248	51.5	3.8	48 943	15.2	21.7	21.1
Hancock	195	1 996	1 414	15.3	66.1	10.6	9.9	10 224	15 169	26 898	75.5	0.6	27 987	30.1	44.3	42.0
Hardeman	688	2 213	5 244	10.8	67.6	10.1	35.0	8 651	15 671	31 801	67.6	0.8	37 729	24.2	31.1	29.4
Hardin	410	3 058	5 229	15.7	64.8	12.7	32.4	8 792	20 740	35 290	66.3	2.1	36 765	22.7	31.9	29.1
Hawkins	297	2 185	11 867	7.4	63.2	12.6	69.3	8 723	20 338	36 927	62.2	0.9	38 708	21.2	30.6	28.5
Haywood	1 064	3 561	4 813	7.1	63.0	12.8	28.6	8 558	19 027	34 182	68.3	1.7	35 216	22.5	33.1	31.1
Henderson	443	2 242	6 734	12.1	60.0	12.8	40.2	8 142	19 269	38 745	60.4	1.0	41 328	17.5	25.0	23.5
Henry	319	3 075	7 006	8.8	61.8	15.5	40.7	8 305	22 207	38 234	63.0	1.8	38 323	19.1	30.8	27.8
Hickman	371	1 725	5 220	10.5	67.0	10.6	29.3	8 103	17 957	36 334	63.3	1.0	39 682	20.4	29.3	27.9
Houston	242	1 003	1 933	5.8	66.8	10.5	11.6	8 361	18 234	39 401	62.5	1.1	39 999	19.5	29.9	28.2
Humphreys	209	1 603	3 977	9.0	59.2	13.4	25.4	8 329	22 329	41 949	56.5	1.7	43 657	15.9	25.2	23.8
Jackson	208	1 546	2 131	6.8	73.2	8.1	13.0	8 193	17 788	31 534	71.6	0.5	34 651	23.6	34.2	32.6
Jefferson	277	2 279	11 358	16.6	57.1	15.6	61.4	8 208	22 383	42 417	56.3	1.5	42 669	16.8	25.6	23.5
Johnson	579	2 880	3 220	15.7	66.1	9.2	21.4	9 492	16 916	30 763	69.4	1.0	33 402	27.2	34.9	33.3
Knox	481	3 952	112 467	16.5	36.3	34.5	510.3	8 591	28 337	48 701	51.0	4.2	52 136	15.6	19.8	18.5
Lake	181	1 501	1 470	14.8	72.9	8.9	8.4	8 856	12 810	30 086	68.0	1.0	29 908	43.1	47.9	47.9
Lauderdale	814	2 787	6 406	5.6	69.0	9.1	38.1	8 254	15 769	30 281	68.7	0.7	34 715	26.2	35.1	30.8
Lawrence	511	2 492	9 551	17.0	63.0	12.4	55.1	7 981	19 214	37 814	62.2	1.1	40 076	18.9	28.7	27.0
Lewis	385	2 411	2 274	13.9	60.9	12.1	14.3	7 448	18 236	36 621	66.3	0.1	38 198	17.9	29.7	28.2
Lincoln	391	2 342	7 174	12.3	59.5	16.7	43.3	7 827	21 655	40 389	59.9	0.8	43 694	16.0	25.3	22.1
Loudon	231	2 013	9 140	17.1	48.2	25.5	58.7	8 015	27 466	51 107	49.1	3.3	52 787	13.5	22.0	19.3
McMinn	489	3 508	11 546	16.0	60.1	15.0	64.1	8 005	20 215	38 535	61.7	0.9	39 207	23.0	31.6	28.9
McNairy	385	1 845	5 644	11.7	64.8	11.4	34.9	7 953	17 751	32 557	68.0	0.6	37 337	18.9	27.6	26.6
Macon	223	1 264	4 987	10.9	70.0	9.5	28.8	7 604	17 882	33 509	66.9	0.5	37 865	18.5	30.0	28.9
Madison	883	3 650	26 210	29.6	45.2	25.4	115.3	8 774	23 467	42 544	56.0	2.8	46 694	18.1	28.8	26.3
Marion	253	1 776	6 132	10.5	59.3	13.3	37.2	8 020	21 784	41 348	58.6	1.1	41 090	19.0	28.5	26.1

1. Data for serious crimes have not been adjusted for underreporting; this may affect comparability between geographic areas and over time.   2. Per 100,000 population estimated by the FBI.
3. All persons 3 years old and over enrolled in nursery school through college.   4. Persons 25 years old and over.   5. Elementary and secondary education expenditures.
6. Based on population estimated by the American Community Survey, 2011–2015.

Table B. States and Counties — **Personal Income**

STATE County	Personal income, 2015 Total (mil dol)	Percent change, 2014–2015	Per capita¹ Dollars	Per capita¹ Rank	Wages and salaries (mil dol)	Supplements to wages and salaries; employer contributions (mil dol) Pension and insurance	Government social insurance	Proprietors' income (mil dol)	Dividends, interest, and rent (mil dol)	Personal transfer receipts (mil dol)	Earnings, 2015 Total (mil dol)	Contributions for government social insurance (mil dol) From employee and self-employed	From employer
	62	63	64	65	66	67	68	69	70	71	72	73	74
SOUTH DAKOTA—Cont'd													
Tripp	250	-2.6	46 057	640	75	15	5	69	46	50	164	8	5
Turner	540	28.5	65 784	225	73	16	5	261	64	60	355	17	5
Union	1 323	7.3	88 707	32	488	66	32	226	384	96	813	46	32
Walworth	228	-3.0	41 952	839	77	16	6	20	63	49	119	8	6
Yankton	1 021	5.4	44 953	1 337	515	96	38	167	199	160	816	47	38
Ziebach	59	-23.2	20 944	2 992	12	3	1	17	9	16	34	1	1
TENNESSEE	277 832	5.5	42 127	X	137 424	20 530	9 482	37 442	39 047	57 156	204 878	12 247	9 482
Anderson	2 927	5.0	38 637	1 132	2 169	291	153	284	416	736	2 897	178	153
Bedford	1 633	5.7	34 618	2 284	733	133	52	182	219	385	1 100	66	52
Benton	539	3.5	33 443	2 344	139	31	10	34	69	194	215	17	10
Bledsoe	300	3.3	20 719	3 106	61	20	4	32	38	120	118	8	4
Blount	4 823	4.6	37 900	1 588	2 213	342	157	363	700	1 123	3 075	197	157
Bradley	3 874	5.1	37 216	1 220	1 755	294	128	423	559	913	2 601	160	128
Campbell	1 232	4.1	30 981	2 655	332	68	25	80	155	482	504	40	25
Cannon	462	5.4	33 416	2 078	78	17	5	33	60	134	134	11	5
Carroll	973	2.8	34 865	2 248	272	54	21	68	109	357	415	31	21
Carter	1 774	3.8	31 407	2 642	385	78	28	138	250	608	629	50	28
Cheatham	1 517	5.9	38 177	1 581	344	72	25	165	159	300	605	39	25
Chester	519	4.7	29 701	2 790	129	28	10	49	57	158	216	15	10
Claiborne	988	3.9	31 161	2 735	324	65	24	70	113	362	484	36	24
Clay	244	1.9	31 431	2 033	55	13	4	27	32	85	100	7	4
Cocke	1 027	4.0	29 206	2 900	281	57	20	66	112	394	423	34	20
Coffee	1 991	4.9	36 679	1 557	1 071	175	76	203	269	535	1 525	94	76
Crockett	525	2.1	35 968	1 691	152	31	11	85	54	156	278	18	11
Cumberland	1 978	3.6	33 973	2 273	615	105	44	223	352	724	987	76	44
Davidson	37 618	9.0	55 411	223	27 050	3 262	1 805	9 459	5 523	4 836	41 576	2 323	1 805
Decatur	398	3.0	34 149	2 134	131	26	9	29	48	160	196	14	9
DeKalb	647	6.5	33 746	2 337	213	41	16	85	83	179	355	23	16
Dickson	1 851	7.1	35 952	2 132	631	107	46	204	211	447	987	63	46
Dyer	1 446	3.1	38 153	1 610	615	119	45	193	188	412	971	59	45
Fayette	1 866	3.8	47 649	337	352	59	24	209	227	346	645	44	24
Fentress	528	2.6	29 490	2 603	150	30	11	65	61	219	256	19	11
Franklin	1 482	3.6	35 757	2 008	453	85	33	131	211	408	702	47	33
Gibson	1 778	3.1	36 002	2 000	515	101	38	181	206	574	835	56	38
Giles	1 048	5.8	36 189	1 924	405	70	29	73	147	303	577	39	29
Grainger	677	4.2	29 623	2 826	136	28	10	47	76	222	221	19	10
Greene	2 580	5.1	37 622	1 764	1 001	173	73	149	289	1 025	1 395	96	73
Grundy	389	4.7	28 975	2 925	67	18	5	45	45	155	136	11	5
Hamblen	2 200	5.0	34 696	2 401	1 186	203	84	256	275	605	1 729	108	84
Hamilton	16 451	4.5	46 460	752	9 715	1 471	680	2 209	2 601	3 070	14 075	823	680
Hancock	156	2.6	23 733	3 098	27	9	2	6	20	70	44	4	2
Hardeman	704	2.5	27 400	2 982	259	58	19	47	86	258	383	26	19
Hardin	889	2.6	34 499	1 882	313	59	22	63	131	326	457	33	22
Hawkins	1 773	3.2	31 391	2 740	497	96	36	83	209	595	712	57	36
Haywood	514	-2.0	28 546	2 759	197	43	14	11	76	184	264	19	14
Henderson	911	2.3	32 503	2 598	311	54	23	81	114	261	468	31	23
Henry	1 218	3.1	37 891	1 715	428	88	32	192	186	368	741	46	32
Hickman	712	5.7	29 238	2 984	141	33	10	68	74	225	253	19	10
Houston	258	1.6	31 624	2 484	51	13	4	17	31	95	84	6	4
Humphreys	654	5.1	36 082	2 068	290	56	21	57	85	201	423	27	21
Jackson	325	3.4	28 256	2 048	56	14	4	22	37	131	95	9	4
Jefferson	1 703	4.7	31 994	2 625	536	94	39	119	225	518	789	57	39
Johnson	545	6.1	30 543	2 843	171	37	12	34	72	191	253	19	12
Knox	20 242	5.0	44 849	846	11 288	1 646	786	2 419	3 335	3 465	16 139	950	786
Lake	184	-0.1	24 256	3 090	55	17	4	13	25	85	89	6	4
Lauderdale	717	1.9	26 617	3 049	221	50	16	41	90	253	328	23	16
Lawrence	1 359	5.4	31 919	2 722	364	74	27	164	158	425	629	44	27
Lewis	348	4.4	29 359	2 910	81	19	6	40	40	121	147	11	6
Lincoln	1 258	3.3	37 279	1 808	360	73	25	129	171	330	587	38	25
Loudon	2 197	4.9	42 971	1 163	612	95	43	191	411	538	941	66	43
McMinn	1 738	3.5	33 020	2 353	757	123	56	115	208	526	1 051	71	56
McNairy	759	2.8	29 105	2 934	193	48	14	64	89	296	319	25	14
Macon	715	6.4	30 845	2 769	165	36	12	85	81	217	299	20	12
Madison	3 737	4.5	38 288	1 514	2 395	432	168	387	539	901	3 381	197	168
Marion	980	3.5	34 388	2 237	272	50	19	69	114	282	411	30	19

1. Based on the resident population estimated as of July 1 of the year shown.

STATE County	Farm	Mining	Construction	Manu-facturing	Information: professional, scientific, technical services	Retail trade	Finance, insurance, real estate and leasing	Health care and social assistance	Govern-ment	Number	Rate[1]	Supplemental Security Income recipients, December 2015	Total	Percent change, 2010-2016
	75	76	77	78	79	80	81	82	83	84	85	86	87	88
SOUTH DAKOTA—Cont'd														
Tripp	31.3	D	3.8	2.3	4.1	7.6	D	D	12.3	1 360	251	146	3 079	0.2
Turner	19.0	D	3.8	43.7	3.6	1.5	D	D	5.0	1 840	224	85	3 983	1.1
Union	6.0	0.0	3.5	16.0	6.1	3.7	9.2	15.2	5.0	3 005	203	91	6 953	10.7
Walworth	0.6	D	7.9	2.4	D	9.0	7.9	D	17.2	1 500	272	113	3 019	0.5
Yankton	7.1	D	4.5	27.9	D	6.3	5.7	14.0	14.3	4 810	212	377	9 957	3.2
Ziebach	50.7	0.0	D	D	D	D	D	D	27.3	185	66	79	986	-0.1
TENNESSEE	0.2	0.2	6.1	11.9	9.0	6.9	7.3	16.1	13.8	1 392 164	211	181 992	2 919 671	3.8
Anderson	-0.1	D	5.5	29.1	19.8	3.9	4.0	9.9	12.9	19 315	255	2 089	34 866	0.5
Bedford	2.5	D	7.1	36.3	D	5.9	3.1	D	11.2	9 865	210	1 131	18 796	2.4
Benton	-0.4	D	7.1	17.4	D	10.5	6.4	D	26.3	5 220	324	598	8 967	-0.1
Bledsoe	10.1	D	8.7	1.9	D	4.4	3.7	6.4	46.8	3 225	221	428	5 684	-0.6
Blount	-0.1	D	10.1	18.8	4.6	8.3	6.0	8.7	15.3	31 535	248	2 646	56 926	2.9
Bradley	1.3	D	7.7	24.4	3.2	7.3	3.9	D	10.9	24 015	231	2 653	43 365	4.8
Campbell	-0.2	0.4	10.5	15.2	3.0	9.1	5.0	D	21.6	11 600	292	2 437	20 590	3.1
Cannon	-0.6	D	12.2	10.6	2.8	5.3	D	D	23.7	3 440	248	366	6 076	0.5
Carroll	-0.3	D	5.8	10.4	D	6.2	6.4	D	20.6	8 130	289	1 090	13 161	0.0
Carter	0.0	D	9.8	10.1	4.2	10.0	4.9	D	22.3	15 935	282	1 967	27 856	0.5
Cheatham	0.1	D	15.5	22.8	D	6.1	2.7	5.7	15.2	8 070	203	674	15 960	1.9
Chester	0.0	0.1	D	13.0	D	9.8	3.2	D	23.8	4 210	242	447	7 038	0.8
Claiborne	0.2	3.5	5.6	19.2	2.1	6.5	4.8	D	20.6	9 460	299	1 903	15 141	1.9
Clay	10.7	D	4.7	9.5	D	4.4	1.7	13.5	23.4	2 305	297	290	4 259	-0.5
Cocke	1.3	D	6.1	21.9	1.6	10.0	3.2	D	24.5	10 860	309	2 034	17 333	-0.7
Coffee	0.4	0.0	4.8	18.9	19.6	6.7	3.5	11.6	14.8	13 405	247	1 486	23 725	1.2
Crockett	-2.4	0.0	6.8	26.5	3.3	20.3	2.6	D	15.9	3 620	249	461	6 369	-0.8
Cumberland	0.5	1.1	8.5	13.1	5.8	10.9	4.1	14.3	13.8	21 560	370	1 560	29 041	3.2
Davidson	0.0	0.2	5.5	3.2	14.7	5.9	8.5	22.8	8.7	98 360	145	15 757	306 393	7.9
Decatur	-1.1	D	6.1	14.5	D	6.4	D	D	18.5	3 890	334	475	6 829	0.0
DeKalb	3.0	0.0	5.4	26.7	15.2	4.7	2.0	D	16.0	4 935	257	701	9 484	0.5
Dickson	-0.4	D	13.0	20.7	D	8.5	4.3	14.6	14.8	11 020	214	1 205	21 397	2.8
Dyer	0.5	0.0	9.4	25.7	D	8.1	4.8	13.0	15.4	9 570	253	1 550	16 837	0.8
Fayette	-1.4	D	13.1	30.9	D	5.8	3.9	6.8	11.9	9 680	247	1 244	16 646	6.2
Fentress	3.6	D	8.4	6.3	2.8	10.0	4.9	D	16.3	5 875	328	1 097	8 930	-0.4
Franklin	1.7	0.9	5.7	18.9	D	7.6	3.3	D	16.3	10 870	262	999	19 128	2.3
Gibson	2.6	0.0	11.3	17.3	2.9	10.7	5.5	D	19.3	12 860	260	1 645	22 487	2.2
Giles	-0.8	D	6.1	35.8	D	6.7	3.2	D	13.3	7 820	269	795	13 918	0.5
Grainger	0.7	D	11.5	23.6	D	5.6	D	4.1	23.4	6 445	282	1 055	10 880	-0.1
Greene	1.0	D	4.3	25.7	2.6	6.3	3.5	D	15.8	20 630	301	2 624	32 202	0.5
Grundy	1.1	D	9.5	8.1	D	10.7	D	D	28.3	4 225	314	786	6 374	-0.5
Hamblen	0.3	D	4.7	33.0	3.0	8.4	3.2	12.8	12.6	16 235	256	2 120	27 053	0.4
Hamilton	0.0	D	6.1	12.7	7.5	5.8	12.5	12.6	16.0	73 240	207	8 613	157 744	4.4
Hancock	-0.6	D	2.9	D	D	8.3	D	14.9	49.4	1 530	233	467	3 588	-0.9
Hardeman	0.0	0.1	4.6	29.2	D	4.6	2.9	D	26.1	6 570	255	1 358	10 909	0.6
Hardin	-0.7	D	4.9	32.5	3.4	10.0	3.6	D	19.2	8 115	316	1 102	13 983	0.3
Hawkins	0.1	D	5.6	34.8	D	5.3	1.8	D	18.6	17 090	303	1 962	26 878	0.0
Haywood	-5.0	0.1	3.4	30.0	D	6.2	4.9	6.8	26.2	4 510	250	980	8 414	1.1
Henderson	0.1	0.0	6.5	17.0	1.4	9.8	10.0	7.3	17.1	6 670	238	943	12 801	0.1
Henry	3.9	D	7.2	20.2	2.7	9.0	5.2	8.1	21.0	9 745	303	953	17 007	-0.3
Hickman	-1.0	0.0	D	11.0	D	7.0	D	D	25.8	5 660	233	714	10 320	0.1
Houston	1.0	0.0	11.0	12.5	D	4.9	3.1	17.7	31.3	2 050	252	296	4 167	-0.5
Humphreys	-0.2	D	8.4	33.9	4.9	6.3	2.1	D	19.3	5 005	276	505	8 873	0.1
Jackson	-0.8	0.0	11.7	11.8	D	4.3	D	D	28.8	3 410	296	431	5 814	-0.5
Jefferson	0.6	D	D	15.9	3.1	7.1	2.8	D	16.1	14 235	267	1 450	23 761	1.0
Johnson	0.6	D	7.7	22.3	3.4	4.1	3.3	8.6	22.2	5 515	309	890	8 904	-0.6
Knox	0.0	0.1	5.9	5.3	10.9	8.0	6.8	18.3	14.6	87 105	193	10 365	201 889	3.6
Lake	3.0	0.0	D	D	D	5.1	1.7	11.0	51.4	1 410	186	359	2 609	0.4
Lauderdale	0.1	0.0	3.8	20.2	D	6.9	6.6	8.4	29.3	6 025	223	1 285	11 265	0.1
Lawrence	1.9	D	8.3	18.1	4.1	10.4	3.4	10.9	18.7	11 285	265	1 377	18 140	-0.2
Lewis	-0.3	0.1	7.7	9.1	3.0	13.7	2.6	D	22.3	3 100	261	315	5 453	-0.3
Lincoln	2.3	D	6.5	28.3	3.9	8.4	3.3	5.0	20.7	8 630	256	824	15 340	0.7
Loudon	2.5	D	11.5	16.4	4.8	7.3	5.1	8.7	13.8	15 620	306	1 018	22 627	4.2
McMinn	0.4	D	4.9	39.9	D	7.0	4.1	D	12.5	13 725	261	1 702	23 250	-0.4
McNairy	-1.0	0.0	7.5	19.0	D	7.6	2.7	D	23.0	7 785	299	1 233	11 979	0.4
Macon	8.9	0.1	6.2	12.1	5.5	11.1	5.5	D	20.0	5 530	239	717	10 106	2.6
Madison	0.0	D	6.7	16.7	4.1	7.2	3.9	15.0	23.1	21 170	217	3 366	42 935	2.5
Marion	0.3	D	6.7	26.1	D	9.0	2.8	8.2	17.6	7 620	268	1 032	13 131	1.4

1. Per 1,000 resident population estimated as of July 1 of the year shown.

Table B. States and Counties — Housing, Labor Force, and Employment

STATE County	Housing units, 2011–2015								Civilian labor force, 2016				Civilian employment,[6] 2011–2015		
	Occupied units										Unemployment			Percent	
			Owner-occupied			Renter-occupied									
				Median owner cost as a percent of income				Sub-stand-ard units[4]						Manage-ment, business, science and arts	Con-struction, produc-tion, and mainte-nance occu-pations
	Total	Percent	Median value[1]	With a mort-gage	Without a mort-gage[2]	Median rent[3]	Median rent as a per-cent of income[2]	(percent)	Total	Percent change, 2015–2016	Total	Rate[5]	Total		
	89	90	91	92	93	94	95	96	97	98	99	100	101	102	103
SOUTH DAKOTA—Cont'd															
Tripp	2 579	65.8	71 200	19.2	13.4	557	28.4	1.6	3 037	-1.7	64	2.1	2 863	44.8	25.2
Turner	3 520	77.6	99 700	21.2	10.9	619	23.5	1.2	4 670	0.7	124	2.7	4 248	36.5	27.6
Union	5 939	74.6	159 700	17.9	10.4	772	23.8	0.7	8 053	0.0	237	2.9	7 576	41.8	20.2
Walworth	2 389	65.6	76 600	18.7	11.6	540	19.7	2.9	2 224	-2.2	107	4.8	2 595	32.8	25.1
Yankton	8 899	67.4	128 700	19.4	10.0	581	25.7	1.0	11 695	0.5	284	2.4	11 348	32.7	25.2
Ziebach	810	53.2	65 700	18.1	10.2	468	29.4	12.5	980	-0.6	41	4.2	948	48.7	20.9
TENNESSEE	2 504 556	66.8	142 100	22.1	10.7	764	30.3	2.4	3 135 102	2.1	150 842	4.8	2 888 742	33.8	24.3
Anderson	30 612	68.3	131 200	21.5	10.3	685	29.3	1.3	33 901	1.8	1 681	5.0	31 814	34.1	22.8
Bedford	16 721	68.2	115 700	22.6	10.6	675	29.0	4.3	19 812	2.0	1 003	5.1	19 939	24.0	38.8
Benton	6 786	76.3	86 400	22.2	12.0	559	34.6	3.5	6 747	-0.4	492	7.3	5 844	23.1	35.4
Bledsoe	4 534	76.8	115 400	25.4	11.9	541	31.5	4.7	4 319	1.5	305	7.1	4 739	24.4	36.0
Blount	49 033	73.8	166 500	22.1	10.0	746	30.1	1.3	60 719	1.9	2 703	4.5	56 262	32.4	24.8
Bradley	38 466	65.3	146 200	21.8	10.4	717	31.1	2.9	50 515	2.1	2 280	4.5	43 685	29.1	28.6
Campbell	15 995	69.9	89 400	23.0	12.4	556	29.7	1.8	14 882	1.6	1 040	7.0	13 897	23.8	33.3
Cannon	5 388	75.4	124 200	24.1	10.8	605	25.7	2.8	6 046	3.1	287	4.7	5 724	26.6	35.7
Carroll	11 168	74.2	83 500	21.5	11.4	566	30.9	2.0	11 953	-2.0	814	6.8	10 700	27.1	32.6
Carter	23 894	70.7	108 500	22.1	11.9	565	32.5	2.6	23 760	0.9	1 366	5.7	23 210	27.6	28.0
Cheatham	14 499	79.4	159 100	23.2	10.0	953	37.9	2.0	20 524	3.2	823	4.0	18 572	29.5	29.7
Chester	6 074	74.1	108 300	20.5	11.0	655	31.2	2.3	8 442	2.5	431	5.1	7 235	31.1	27.8
Claiborne	12 705	72.0	101 500	23.0	10.0	519	28.7	1.5	12 799	1.4	810	6.3	11 935	27.5	35.4
Clay	3 242	76.4	94 000	25.4	12.8	505	31.2	2.8	3 051	1.6	204	6.7	2 765	26.7	34.1
Cocke	14 710	68.8	99 500	23.8	10.9	556	30.6	2.4	14 447	0.2	937	6.5	14 071	21.4	33.7
Coffee	21 170	67.5	113 100	22.3	10.8	670	28.0	2.9	24 472	0.6	1 179	4.8	21 841	30.1	31.2
Crockett	5 453	68.8	92 000	23.2	13.3	637	30.8	3.4	6 966	2.0	372	5.3	5 766	28.4	35.3
Cumberland	24 177	78.6	139 500	22.5	10.0	630	30.6	1.4	23 667	3.1	1 427	6.0	20 279	27.2	29.6
Davidson	264 211	54.1	169 600	23.1	11.1	874	29.9	3.0	377 213	3.5	13 710	3.6	341 548	39.8	17.7
Decatur	4 978	77.1	90 500	20.2	10.4	533	32.2	0.8	4 672	-1.0	326	7.0	4 569	28.4	32.2
DeKalb	6 920	71.2	121 800	21.2	10.0	575	24.6	2.6	7 602	3.1	430	5.7	7 409	27.8	38.7
Dickson	18 556	72.1	140 300	22.5	10.4	722	29.7	2.7	24 885	3.2	1 101	4.4	21 847	28.3	29.6
Dyer	14 931	64.3	98 800	19.9	11.8	618	25.9	2.8	16 507	-1.0	1 036	6.3	16 095	31.0	33.4
Fayette	14 846	79.9	181 700	21.9	10.0	613	28.3	1.5	18 087	1.1	936	5.2	17 031	32.4	28.1
Fentress	7 304	77.3	95 300	22.8	12.6	506	27.9	2.9	7 101	1.3	449	6.3	5 998	23.3	34.5
Franklin	16 302	73.9	110 700	22.6	10.8	599	26.1	2.1	19 819	1.0	985	5.0	17 027	29.9	32.7
Gibson	19 449	72.2	89 200	23.5	11.6	605	28.6	2.3	21 317	1.3	1 274	6.0	20 201	27.1	29.3
Giles	11 297	72.7	108 100	22.5	11.3	603	29.6	2.0	15 236	4.6	620	4.1	11 881	26.7	36.0
Grainger	8 952	81.0	96 400	23.1	11.2	545	28.4	2.3	9 279	1.4	512	5.5	8 940	24.0	39.8
Greene	28 061	71.5	109 700	22.4	10.3	558	27.8	2.1	31 089	1.5	1 724	5.5	28 160	27.8	33.7
Grundy	5 221	77.6	80 400	23.6	13.0	525	27.7	3.9	4 791	-1.7	319	6.7	4 529	22.9	37.3
Hamblen	24 470	65.9	124 200	21.8	11.0	654	32.5	2.4	26 879	1.5	1 397	5.2	25 095	25.0	36.6
Hamilton	136 319	64.5	158 600	20.9	10.2	757	30.0	1.8	171 576	2.4	8 086	4.7	162 818	37.3	20.1
Hancock	2 754	76.4	80 400	22.3	11.7	358	29.1	3.0	2 059	-0.3	164	8.0	2 240	26.6	39.3
Hardeman	8 737	71.6	83 000	25.0	12.8	616	36.3	1.9	9 166	-1.4	581	6.3	8 256	26.0	33.9
Hardin	9 871	77.7	96 900	25.0	11.2	577	28.0	3.6	10 268	0.0	627	6.1	9 438	23.6	31.9
Hawkins	23 167	74.6	108 600	21.2	11.2	598	29.1	1.7	23 655	0.4	1 306	5.5	21 893	25.8	34.8
Haywood	7 008	62.1	99 100	24.6	13.3	598	31.5	1.9	7 724	1.2	510	6.6	7 194	25.0	38.1
Henderson	10 809	71.5	92 700	19.7	10.6	597	27.8	3.1	12 086	-1.6	840	7.0	11 115	26.1	37.4
Henry	13 471	74.1	94 300	22.1	10.1	601	28.8	1.9	13 990	0.7	832	5.9	12 592	27.0	32.3
Hickman	8 769	77.5	93 800	23.3	10.9	637	34.4	3.0	10 636	3.0	494	4.6	9 388	24.1	33.3
Houston	3 247	72.4	94 200	23.4	11.7	599	27.2	3.1	3 209	0.2	246	7.7	2 997	20.7	42.0
Humphreys	7 124	78.8	106 400	21.4	10.9	640	29.2	1.6	8 626	1.8	527	6.1	7 067	29.5	36.8
Jackson	4 531	78.3	101 400	26.3	13.4	479	31.4	1.6	4 490	0.5	323	7.2	3 842	24.3	40.9
Jefferson	19 679	73.4	128 800	21.9	10.3	642	27.9	2.2	23 655	1.5	1 272	5.4	23 000	26.0	32.1
Johnson	7 009	77.5	110 500	24.9	11.3	472	35.6	5.2	7 598	3.9	372	4.9	6 048	26.5	32.1
Knox	180 729	64.0	160 700	21.2	10.2	793	29.7	1.7	233 354	2.1	9 505	4.1	215 253	39.7	17.1
Lake	2 092	60.3	71 600	19.5	12.9	478	26.4	3.7	1 935	-1.9	153	7.9	1 840	25.7	27.0
Lauderdale	9 800	60.3	81 100	23.9	13.0	608	29.7	3.6	9 475	-1.3	743	7.8	9 099	23.3	35.7
Lawrence	16 104	74.9	98 600	21.7	10.7	563	29.2	4.1	17 825	0.5	1 039	5.8	16 607	24.0	38.0
Lewis	4 712	79.2	89 600	22.7	11.6	498	28.1	1.8	4 903	2.0	297	6.1	4 858	26.5	32.8
Lincoln	13 644	72.9	109 100	23.2	11.2	605	28.6	2.2	15 936	5.3	669	4.2	14 232	26.4	36.9
Loudon	20 009	76.8	178 000	21.3	10.0	712	27.9	2.2	22 346	1.8	1 063	4.8	19 909	30.8	30.5
McMinn	19 978	73.8	113 200	21.5	10.9	588	31.9	1.8	22 897	1.0	1 255	5.5	20 767	26.1	36.4
McNairy	9 872	75.7	85 000	23.2	12.5	578	30.2	2.2	8 822	0.6	627	7.1	8 901	26.5	37.6
Macon	8 856	70.3	100 700	23.1	12.1	539	26.3	2.9	10 287	3.2	457	4.4	9 657	22.0	41.9
Madison	36 766	64.6	117 300	22.7	11.1	767	34.8	1.3	47 607	2.4	2 366	5.0	43 039	32.9	22.5
Marion	11 525	72.6	119 100	22.6	10.6	632	29.6	3.5	12 033	2.6	766	6.4	11 895	27.0	34.5

1. Specified owner-occupied units.　　2.　A value of 10.0 represents 10 percent or less; a value of 50.0 represents 50 percent or more.　　3.　Specified renter-occupied units.
4. Overcrowded or lacking complete plumbing facilities.　　5.　Percent of civilian labor force.　　6.　Civilian employed persons 16 years old and over.

Table B. States and Counties — **Nonfarm Employment and Agriculture**

STATE County	Private nonfarm establishments, employment and payroll, 2015									Agriculture, 2012			
		Employment						Annual payroll		Farms			
												Percent with:	
	Number of establishments	Total	Health care and social assistance	Manufacturing	Retail trade	Finance and insurance	Professional, scientific, and technical services	Total (mil dol)	Average per employee (dollars)	Number	Fewer than 50 acres	500 acres or more	Farm operators whose principal occupation is farming (percent)
	104	105	106	107	108	109	110	111	112	113	114	115	116
SOUTH DAKOTA—Cont'd													
Tripp	203	1 607	461	43	378	69	61	49	30 431	629	12.6	58.8	65.5
Turner	260	1 522	393	186	244	70	47	51	33 721	794	26.4	30.6	57.4
Union	499	9 253	1 129	1 830	502	996	210	451	48 720	527	24.5	37.6	63.6
Walworth	219	2 007	373	D	330	77	72	62	30 718	256	18.0	48.8	60.5
Yankton	739	11 135	1 873	3 059	1 746	683	218	410	36 799	692	23.0	34.0	57.2
Ziebach	47	298	68	D	81	D	D	9	28 862	240	8.8	75.0	72.5
TENNESSEE	133 344	2 507 205	400 693	315 835	317 075	117 783	113 402	110 481	44 066	68 050	39.4	5.5	41.8
Anderson	1 524	37 332	3 900	9 433	3 324	876	8 435	2 260	60 541	441	52.4	1.4	34.0
Bedford	759	13 972	1 051	4 658	1 475	471	213	536	38 357	1 411	36.2	7.6	47.1
Benton	303	3 351	686	817	699	147	43	95	28 407	463	24.8	6.7	43.4
Bledsoe	93	433	63	51	101	54	7	13	29 947	579	28.5	5.4	40.6
Blount	2 270	41 286	6 141	5 907	5 712	2 153	3 949	1 909	46 247	980	52.0	2.7	45.6
Bradley	1 918	38 000	4 974	7 972	4 987	1 816	737	1 417	37 285	807	50.7	4.2	40.8
Campbell	596	7 439	1 871	1 733	1 574	270	107	222	29 897	370	41.9	1.4	41.9
Cannon	178	1 696	539	263	213	45	38	52	30 571	717	36.7	3.6	43.1
Carroll	416	6 144	1 502	808	799	272	91	194	31 503	732	31.3	7.9	44.4
Carter	694	8 984	1 824	1 039	1 786	324	156	258	28 748	493	51.7	1.6	37.7
Cheatham	592	6 022	665	1 795	859	151	145	239	39 700	415	38.8	2.9	46.5
Chester	237	3 084	426	480	444	102	55	84	27 200	391	32.5	4.3	26.6
Claiborne	420	7 366	1 180	1 981	791	265	142	248	33 612	945	36.3	3.6	40.2
Clay	107	1 060	296	280	139	34	14	29	27 331	424	23.6	7.8	47.2
Cocke	471	5 919	925	1 574	1 386	193	87	190	32 115	625	39.8	1.0	44.6
Coffee	1 242	19 933	2 944	4 248	3 008	766	2 541	829	41 588	895	47.4	7.9	36.0
Crockett	219	1 953	443	256	282	78	46	67	34 086	369	35.8	17.6	45.3
Cumberland	1 038	14 423	2 758	2 469	2 594	447	290	463	32 112	764	39.4	7.5	36.8
Davidson	19 088	426 687	81 277	19 072	40 697	26 714	26 015	22 720	53 248	360	49.2	2.2	40.8
Decatur	216	2 807	988	474	335	103	50	100	35 597	405	22.2	7.2	40.7
DeKalb	284	3 915	423	1 953	482	83	87	139	35 536	637	37.2	4.9	38.8
Dickson	921	13 419	2 161	3 162	2 413	464	199	456	33 970	1 143	36.7	3.8	33.8
Dyer	774	13 048	2 116	3 887	1 987	488	187	461	35 311	449	34.5	22.5	50.6
Fayette	577	6 685	569	1 753	821	209	100	284	42 423	745	33.0	12.8	41.3
Fentress	238	4 642	1 581	311	605	172	42	120	25 875	536	38.4	6.5	45.5
Franklin	686	11 229	1 584	3 231	1 435	260	175	443	39 485	861	48.0	5.3	40.0
Gibson	930	10 933	1 983	2 129	2 088	408	208	357	32 632	830	40.0	13.3	40.8
Giles	537	8 231	905	3 468	1 266	274	114	310	37 708	1 692	28.9	4.4	40.7
Grainger	229	2 331	186	943	365	39	58	72	30 964	885	40.7	0.8	43.3
Greene	1 092	21 861	4 221	6 321	2 764	587	270	730	33 406	2 529	49.8	1.4	46.9
Grundy	160	1 357	353	287	270	78	22	34	24 961	278	42.1	2.5	34.5
Hamblen	1 287	27 698	3 835	9 134	4 231	448	290	988	35 659	569	49.4	1.9	48.7
Hamilton	8 817	183 015	27 675	25 815	20 397	11 867	8 129	7 696	42 052	561	53.8	3.2	39.2
Hancock	50	386	166	NA	99	15	3	12	31 718	457	28.9	4.4	40.0
Hardeman	332	5 387	1 177	1 718	591	160	47	181	33 617	579	24.2	11.2	31.6
Hardin	493	6 355	1 155	1 717	1 292	214	67	247	38 861	589	29.2	11.9	37.4
Hawkins	598	9 104	1 385	3 460	1 342	239	106	313	34 377	1 437	42.7	1.3	45.4
Haywood	304	5 284	542	1 901	611	172	56	198	37 426	413	31.2	19.9	44.8
Henderson	498	6 257	1 020	1 598	1 042	398	90	198	31 700	844	24.6	6.5	32.0
Henry	694	8 480	1 390	1 371	1 703	342	281	282	33 230	826	30.4	10.8	41.3
Hickman	250	2 327	632	556	304	59	34	80	34 435	639	27.4	8.1	39.7
Houston	105	1 051	330	211	150	41	31	30	28 716	338	29.9	6.8	47.9
Humphreys	333	4 348	577	1 331	622	99	259	191	43 904	598	30.3	12.0	36.8
Jackson	100	1 065	129	D	118	26	37	43	40 453	499	32.5	5.6	38.7
Jefferson	675	10 608	1 105	1 703	1 727	259	166	376	35 431	981	45.9	1.4	43.7
Johnson	242	2 965	544	565	388	115	47	118	39 774	476	45.0	1.9	37.0
Knox	11 184	212 841	34 948	10 436	29 951	10 717	9 854	8 913	41 879	912	55.8	1.0	45.5
Lake	75	569	168	NA	123	15	D	16	27 736	60	16.7	41.7	58.3
Lauderdale	307	4 802	637	1 025	713	181	37	159	33 162	457	34.4	15.5	37.4
Lawrence	706	8 143	1 307	1 616	1 624	260	213	250	30 698	1 559	36.4	5.6	42.3
Lewis	212	1 947	505	340	421	74	47	53	27 470	222	40.5	5.9	44.6
Lincoln	574	7 900	861	2 832	1 369	210	131	275	34 802	1 595	33.1	6.1	37.6
Loudon	908	12 252	1 424	2 565	1 974	351	399	469	38 282	685	49.5	2.3	41.3
McMinn	878	16 013	2 227	6 166	2 180	528	277	587	36 682	1 043	44.8	3.9	44.1
McNairy	402	4 444	818	924	589	138	68	128	28 847	658	26.0	5.9	38.4
Macon	315	3 516	637	1 007	722	234	61	111	31 669	879	33.8	3.2	43.2
Madison	2 515	51 155	11 910	8 822	7 084	1 444	1 240	1 921	37 558	592	31.3	10.0	46.8
Marion	425	5 611	686	1 559	1 136	147	99	191	34 075	280	33.2	8.6	41.4

Table B. States and Counties — **Agriculture**

STATE County	Agriculture, 2012 (cont.)															
	Land in farms				Value of land and buildings (dollars)			Value of products sold					Percent of farms with sales of:		Government payments	
			Acres				Value of machinery and equipment, average per farm (dollars)				Percent from:					
	Acreage (1,000)	Percent change, 2007–2012	Average size of farm	Total irrigated (1,000)	Total cropland (1,000)	Average per farm	Average per acre		Total (mil dol)	Average per farm (dollars)	Crops	Live-stock and poultry products	$10,000 or more	$100,000 or more	Total ($1,000)	Percent of farms
	117	118	119	120	121	122	123	124	125	126	127	128	129	130	131	132
SOUTH DAKOTA—Cont'd																
Tripp	1 019	0.5	1 620	2.7	477.8	1 810 404	1 118	224 453	229.0	364 110	37.8	62.2	74.6	49.9	5 336	83.1
Turner	384	3.5	484	18.3	329.3	2 089 242	4 316	248 820	182.2	229 447	55.4	44.6	67.3	36.3	5 690	72.5
Union	288	3.4	547	41.4	259.3	2 743 670	5 012	281 402	158.4	300 653	67.2	32.8	70.2	45.2	4 998	80.8
Walworth	445	0.1	1 737	1.9	245.7	2 572 492	1 481	343 938	117.8	460 305	75.6	24.4	62.1	47.3	3 077	78.1
Yankton	328	1.7	474	15.5	265.0	1 962 231	4 142	221 565	117.4	169 691	48.4	51.6	62.4	33.1	4 604	81.5
Ziebach	1 108	4.7	4 618	0.0	175.6	2 194 488	475	163 100	49.8	207 504	38.7	61.3	75.0	42.9	2 580	56.7
TENNESSEE	10 868	-0.9	160	146.4	5 329.7	569 416	3 565	69 244	3 611.0	53 065	57.8	42.2	30.2	6.1	67 665	23.8
Anderson	36	-10.7	81	0.1	10.2	475 961	5 856	61 673	3.6	8 102	21.2	78.8	13.2	1.6	36	7.3
Bedford	232	0.5	165	0.5	88.6	629 255	3 821	62 006	107.3	76 062	9.8	90.2	37.7	8.9	811	18.9
Benton	88	21.2	190	0.0	38.5	425 503	2 241	67 212	10.8	23 348	67.9	32.1	29.4	3.9	606	39.1
Bledsoe	102	11.1	177	0.8	42.6	619 174	3 506	74 772	42.7	73 789	24.9	75.1	42.3	11.2	96	10.5
Blount	101	2.4	103	0.6	42.8	700 027	6 811	59 394	17.0	17 341	36.6	63.4	28.7	3.4	234	11.1
Bradley	87	-9.4	107	0.1	28.6	583 543	5 439	57 476	115.7	143 376	5.5	94.5	30.1	11.3	217	8.7
Campbell	33	-2.0	91	0.1	11.5	338 165	3 736	58 478	3.3	9 041	22.3	77.7	18.9	1.1	50	9.2
Cannon	96	-17.5	134	0.1	38.5	415 745	3 097	55 290	21.1	29 431	49.3	50.7	27.3	5.7	381	14.1
Carroll	178	-1.0	243	2.0	121.4	595 486	2 450	92 384	62.2	84 956	95.1	4.9	25.4	6.7	2 510	50.3
Carter	40	2.3	82	0.0	12.4	427 787	5 238	49 771	8.6	17 377	18.9	81.1	24.1	2.8	95	13.4
Cheatham	52	-17.0	126	0.2	20.8	539 161	4 270	71 566	11.4	27 436	73.7	26.3	30.1	6.3	155	18.3
Chester	61	-15.1	156	0.5	28.1	300 294	1 928	52 100	10.0	25 683	80.8	19.2	25.1	4.6	404	48.8
Claiborne	121	-2.6	129	0.0	34.4	394 144	3 066	52 611	18.7	19 773	12.1	87.9	25.0	1.7	380	31.2
Clay	80	2.5	188	0.0	27.3	522 627	2 779	67 042	36.3	85 526	12.0	88.0	44.3	9.0	373	24.3
Cocke	61	-4.8	98	0.8	20.4	358 320	3 668	49 451	27.9	44 584	36.7	63.3	22.4	2.7	189	16.6
Coffee	145	3.5	162	2.6	79.0	572 818	3 540	80 251	60.8	67 884	64.7	35.3	32.5	10.1	1 075	22.3
Crockett	131	-12.5	354	4.2	112.1	1 003 241	2 836	150 220	62.1	168 247	95.5	4.5	48.2	22.0	2 946	69.1
Cumberland	129	5.3	169	0.1	49.5	643 314	3 807	70 047	34.1	44 685	37.9	62.1	29.7	5.0	264	10.2
Davidson	35	-15.8	97	0.4	11.3	601 725	6 221	58 703	D	D	D	D	16.1	1.1	55	4.2
Decatur	77	1.2	191	0.0	25.0	410 128	2 150	60 484	8.1	20 037	55.6	44.4	30.1	2.5	301	34.3
DeKalb	90	-6.0	141	1.0	33.5	451 124	3 209	64 680	62.7	98 447	91.4	8.6	31.4	5.2	154	17.9
Dickson	149	6.7	130	0.2	46.1	432 552	3 329	52 872	14.0	12 209	40.0	60.0	23.6	1.7	153	11.6
Dyer	212	-11.3	471	16.5	188.3	1 182 490	2 508	188 944	108.4	241 408	94.9	5.1	51.4	26.9	2 426	63.3
Fayette	229	0.7	307	5.3	147.4	965 636	3 141	113 322	75.3	101 050	90.2	9.8	26.8	9.1	2 515	44.0
Fentress	91	7.7	169	0.0	26.3	543 444	3 207	70 149	41.0	76 515	8.9	91.1	41.4	9.5	400	17.4
Franklin	125	-13.1	146	1.9	74.8	567 243	3 897	82 614	81.4	94 565	43.9	56.1	37.0	10.9	683	23.9
Gibson	286	-0.2	345	5.0	250.2	1 065 437	3 090	153 169	145.2	174 923	94.6	5.4	39.2	16.6	4 101	62.3
Giles	270	3.3	160	2.4	88.4	468 997	2 938	62 255	45.8	27 075	36.8	63.2	32.8	3.3	955	19.3
Grainger	85	-7.2	96	0.4	25.8	366 236	3 803	49 200	18.9	21 367	57.7	42.3	27.2	2.4	233	22.4
Greene	226	-1.4	89	0.4	90.8	362 074	4 052	56 139	85.6	33 859	15.3	84.7	26.9	3.6	1 135	23.6
Grundy	33	-22.5	119	0.5	14.2	340 791	2 864	50 061	17.7	63 507	48.4	51.6	33.5	6.8	61	9.7
Hamblen	59	-15.2	103	D	27.3	484 123	4 682	60 812	29.0	51 051	38.3	61.7	28.8	3.7	313	13.5
Hamilton	52	-4.2	93	0.1	19.7	527 171	5 654	57 647	12.4	22 182	16.9	83.1	19.6	2.9	114	5.7
Hancock	64	6.2	141	D	15.6	323 665	2 297	44 394	5.5	11 993	10.3	89.7	28.7	1.5	162	28.2
Hardeman	154	4.0	266	1.1	78.2	678 563	2 554	73 984	30.3	52 252	87.2	12.8	22.3	6.0	1 411	50.4
Hardin	126	15.0	214	1.9	59.9	542 166	2 531	66 596	22.1	37 554	81.7	18.3	31.2	6.3	849	39.0
Hawkins	133	-11.7	93	0.2	42.3	326 872	3 522	45 740	18.1	12 602	36.4	63.6	20.9	1.1	451	26.8
Haywood	219	2.4	531	14.2	197.0	1 916 540	3 608	210 751	125.6	304 107	98.6	1.4	40.7	23.0	3 018	70.0
Henderson	162	-1.9	192	0.1	79.8	424 276	2 207	64 594	35.3	41 831	73.9	26.1	31.4	5.9	1 264	50.4
Henry	205	5.8	248	4.4	131.6	688 305	2 779	98 464	91.6	110 849	62.1	37.9	36.3	14.8	2 181	48.8
Hickman	121	7.7	189	0.4	39.3	452 828	2 394	56 521	12.9	20 233	50.4	49.6	32.1	2.7	291	20.3
Houston	50	6.6	149	D	11.8	337 740	2 269	57 231	9.0	26 521	4.9	95.1	26.3	7.4	94	12.4
Humphreys	123	4.3	207	0.3	40.8	587 381	2 844	66 271	15.3	25 517	56.4	43.6	28.9	4.2	343	12.2
Jackson	74	-2.5	148	0.0	19.5	427 545	2 894	46 649	5.0	9 928	47.5	52.5	17.2	1.0	452	23.8
Jefferson	96	-5.9	97	0.5	37.7	526 143	5 400	55 272	30.7	31 318	15.3	84.7	26.7	3.3	441	16.3
Johnson	47	8.8	100	0.0	16.1	474 284	4 764	55 954	9.1	19 046	24.0	76.0	29.6	3.6	226	21.2
Knox	65	-21.2	72	0.2	24.5	549 549	7 670	49 402	14.6	16 035	59.3	40.7	17.5	1.0	241	10.0
Lake	80	-5.2	1 329	15.4	78.1	4 373 900	3 291	611 450	51.8	863 000	99.8	0.2	83.3	51.7	868	90.0
Lauderdale	201	4.5	439	13.2	172.5	1 373 934	3 127	155 593	97.3	212 827	97.2	2.8	32.6	17.5	2 290	65.4
Lawrence	236	-1.1	151	0.8	105.5	400 664	2 649	55 580	65.3	41 875	51.0	49.0	34.3	5.6	1 223	23.8
Lewis	31	-13.6	138	0.1	9.6	360 077	2 602	44 788	3.1	13 860	15.8	84.2	27.0	4.5	46	14.4
Lincoln	266	1.9	167	4.0	108.2	562 043	3 371	70 241	110.5	69 283	33.5	66.5	37.2	6.7	1 066	17.5
Loudon	69	-9.9	101	0.1	33.1	549 140	5 422	77 477	77.5	113 093	77.3	22.7	24.7	4.2	177	17.7
McMinn	122	-0.1	117	0.2	48.2	480 752	4 098	61 846	37.9	36 379	12.1	87.9	24.7	4.0	473	13.0
McNairy	130	5.9	198	D	61.5	426 061	2 157	58 903	23.0	35 026	87.3	12.7	23.9	4.0	929	47.7
Macon	122	-4.6	139	0.2	47.6	474 719	3 424	56 597	44.7	50 857	59.8	40.2	33.0	7.4	869	34.6
Madison	166	-6.3	280	7.9	117.9	706 385	2 520	101 103	66.0	111 552	94.4	5.6	30.9	11.0	2 288	61.8
Marion	51	0.3	181	0.1	22.0	533 475	2 942	88 682	13.1	46 918	46.3	53.7	33.6	8.2	183	11.8

Table B. States and Counties — Water Use, Wholesale Trade, Retail Trade, and Real Estate

STATE County	Water use, 2010		Wholesale trade,[1] 2012				Retail trade,[2] 2012				Real estate and rental and leasing,[2] 2012			
	Total water withdrawn (mil gal/day)	Gallons withdrawn per person per day	Number of establishments	Number of employees	Sales (mil dol)	Annual payroll (mil dol)	Number of establishments	Number of employees	Sales (mil dol)	Annual payroll (mil dol)	Number of establishments	Number of employees	Receipts (mil dol)	Annual payroll (mil dol)
	133	134	135	136	137	138	139	140	141	142	143	144	145	146
SOUTH DAKOTA—Cont'd														
Tripp	11.5	2 032	14	132	130.1	5.2	47	384	104.3	8.4	4	2	0.4	0.0
Turner	4.4	524	16	107	250.4	4.9	33	269	46.6	4.1	4	D	D	D
Union	6.8	472	35	641	1 135.3	39.1	46	422	153.2	7.8	21	40	9.1	1.9
Walworth	13.5	2 473	9	73	351.0	3.3	41	366	88.8	6.6	6	D	D	D
Yankton	19.3	859	32	240	213.8	10.3	121	1 554	368.6	34.5	21	51	7.6	1.4
Ziebach	0.5	168	4	D	D	D	8	62	15.8	0.9	2	D	D	D
TENNESSEE	7 696.6	1 213	5 828	92 537	111 718.4	4 863.3	22 615	306 078	91 641.6	7 420.3	5 470	30 593	6 178.4	1 220.0
Anderson	307.7	4 096	41	449	591.5	19.5	242	3 510	916.1	76.6	57	184	38.5	6.9
Bedford	16.0	354	24	D	D	D	150	1 502	407.6	34.3	31	154	27.4	5.1
Benton	2.5	149	11	D	D	D	59	631	150.9	13.5	4	9	1.5	0.2
Bledsoe	3.1	238	3	D	D	D	19	127	53.2	3.8	4	6	0.9	0.2
Blount	16.0	130	86	D	D	D	360	5 651	1 441.2	144.2	84	334	70.7	10.9
Bradley	19.0	192	60	D	D	D	363	4 676	1 335.0	111.7	62	D	D	D
Campbell	4.7	115	13	58	46.9	2.5	132	1 492	401.5	33.0	24	62	8.1	1.5
Cannon	2.0	143	5	D	D	D	34	213	61.2	4.7	2	D	D	D
Carroll	5.6	198	14	D	D	D	98	846	204.4	16.6	13	57	7.1	0.9
Carter	20.2	351	12	D	D	D	131	1 692	431.2	35.0	23	61	9.5	1.6
Cheatham	4.4	112	10	D	D	D	76	797	225.8	18.0	17	37	7.4	0.9
Chester	1.9	110	8	38	35.3	1.1	57	440	132.9	10.0	8	15	2.8	0.3
Claiborne	4.3	132	10	D	D	D	86	768	170.1	16.5	19	48	5.3	1.2
Clay	13.7	1 744	2	D	D	D	26	159	37.7	2.8	6	25	1.5	0.2
Cocke	6.9	193	5	D	D	D	112	1 271	341.0	28.7	17	113	5.9	1.5
Coffee	9.3	176	38	456	269.6	20.1	255	2 834	827.6	67.1	39	144	20.9	4.2
Crockett	4.3	298	15	272	352.2	16.4	39	266	78.5	5.1	5	12	3.8	0.2
Cumberland	8.3	147	38	D	D	D	229	2 632	750.3	61.1	39	139	19.1	3.6
Davidson	163.4	261	923	17 595	17 607.0	1 115.0	2 575	37 506	10 138.3	989.0	897	6 348	1 410.7	284.0
Decatur	2.2	189	4	D	D	D	45	335	76.5	7.1	4	7	0.5	0.1
DeKalb	3.1	164	9	D	D	D	51	493	107.3	10.0	10	15	1.7	0.5
Dickson	6.2	125	28	525	513.7	22.7	179	2 198	714.7	49.8	32	74	10.8	1.8
Dyer	13.5	352	40	D	D	D	169	2 053	580.8	50.8	25	72	12.8	3.2
Fayette	6.9	179	24	D	D	D	86	924	216.1	19.8	14	24	4.4	0.6
Fentress	2.3	130	5	10	5.4	0.3	50	599	145.6	12.4	6	92	10.0	2.8
Franklin	41.1	1 000	12	D	D	D	144	1 379	410.4	32.4	16	D	D	D
Gibson	8.6	173	32	367	310.4	15.7	192	1 992	505.8	42.5	26	71	18.0	2.2
Giles	5.4	181	25	273	189.1	12.4	124	1 342	317.1	27.8	9	37	2.6	0.9
Grainger	4.4	195	1	D	D	D	51	351	89.9	7.3	10	7	1.4	0.2
Greene	12.6	184	31	365	181.8	12.3	205	2 642	686.2	56.2	34	129	18.4	2.6
Grundy	2.6	187	3	4	0.6	0.1	47	306	72.1	5.9	1	D	D	D
Hamblen	10.0	161	50	D	D	D	265	3 888	978.7	93.5	53	165	33.2	4.6
Hamilton	1 968.0	5 849	437	5 317	2 904.0	266.3	1 410	19 752	5 236.5	485.2	375	2 092	418.4	97.5
Hancock	0.7	103	2	D	D	D	16	107	24.7	1.8	3	D	D	D
Hardeman	4.2	155	11	76	69.5	3.0	77	629	147.9	12.6	6	22	1.5	0.5
Hardin	29.4	1 128	15	98	228.0	4.2	113	1 269	396.7	30.6	20	55	8.3	2.0
Hawkins	355.5	6 255	19	167	89.1	6.2	113	1 233	303.1	25.1	24	91	11.3	2.6
Haywood	7.6	407	10	107	68.1	3.5	59	630	207.6	12.7	9	30	3.2	0.9
Henderson	4.0	145	15	224	56.5	5.8	103	1 094	296.9	23.5	8	D	D	D
Henry	5.7	177	25	581	159.4	18.4	139	1 604	489.5	40.5	26	84	15.2	2.2
Hickman	3.3	134	13	58	45.3	2.1	48	293	71.4	5.9	5	16	0.8	0.2
Houston	1.4	171	1	D	D	D	21	154	35.3	3.2	2	D	D	D
Humphreys	737.3	39 775	13	86	111.3	5.4	65	585	185.7	12.0	8	19	1.3	0.3
Jackson	1.1	97	4	D	D	D	22	102	30.9	1.8	1	D	D	D
Jefferson	8.2	160	18	D	D	D	126	1 786	640.4	38.4	26	132	28.8	4.3
Johnson	2.8	152	4	D	D	D	55	453	108.8	8.3	14	34	3.5	0.4
Knox	71.8	166	655	9 371	5 382.5	494.3	1 764	29 577	7 926.7	733.1	559	3 312	618.3	123.8
Lake	5.3	679	6	D	D	D	21	154	29.8	2.6	3	8	1.0	0.2
Lauderdale	6.7	239	19	818	1 545.9	35.0	78	688	161.7	14.5	17	56	18.0	2.1
Lawrence	6.6	157	33	258	157.6	9.2	172	1 512	384.2	34.2	18	61	8.2	1.4
Lewis	2.1	169	5	D	D	D	41	394	179.5	10.1	3	6	0.7	0.1
Lincoln	9.5	286	22	248	385.1	11.7	128	1 240	316.8	30.7	19	122	8.5	2.8
Loudon	18.2	374	41	D	D	D	150	1 857	484.0	41.7	32	131	14.8	3.5
McMinn	68.9	1 318	29	D	D	D	172	1 940	542.4	42.9	33	132	18.2	3.3
McNairy	4.2	160	15	130	44.2	6.3	83	615	154.8	14.0	8	30	3.9	0.7
Macon	3.5	155	10	78	18.7	2.0	70	666	177.4	14.7	16	50	3.4	0.5
Madison	16.6	168	141	1 485	808.6	65.7	469	7 050	1 902.6	162.4	104	546	86.8	16.9
Marion	4.0	142	19	159	69.1	6.2	99	1 112	336.2	25.4	5	21	2.6	0.5

1. Merchant wholesalers, except manufacturers' sales branches and offices.   2. Employer establishments.

Table B. States and Counties — Professional Services, Manufacturing, and Accommodation and Food Services

STATE County	Professional, scientific, and technical services, 2012				Manufacturing, 2012				Accommodation and food services, 2012			
	Number of establish- ments	Number of employees	Receipts (mil dol)	Annual payroll (mil dol)	Number of establish- ments	Number of employees	Receipts (mil dol)	Annual payroll (mil dol)	Number of establish- ments	Number of employees	Sales (mil dol)	Annual payroll (mil dol)
	147	148	149	150	151	152	153	154	155	156	157	158
SOUTH DAKOTA—Cont'd												
Tripp	15	51	6.4	1.7	6	68	D	D	23	166	8.0	2.0
Turner	15	43	9.0	1.6	11	172	D	7.6	20	86	3.5	0.7
Union	49	188	30.9	9.8	23	1 502	D	63.3	40	416	18.5	4.6
Walworth	18	90	9.6	2.8	4	103	D	D	28	428	27.1	6.7
Yankton	45	228	28.4	9.1	29	2 808	849.2	114.8	65	1 013	44.8	12.3
Ziebach	2	D	D	D	NA	NA	NA	NA	4	D	D	D
TENNESSEE	10 863	104 552	14 199.5	6 129.5	5 823	293 646	139 960.5	14 180.5	12 004	241 348	12 499.0	3 546.5
Anderson	201	9 551	871.7	742.0	94	9 177	2 224.0	598.3	132	2 690	127.1	35.0
Bedford	48	218	18.8	6.0	52	3 882	1 121.4	138.4	54	833	40.2	10.9
Benton	14	56	4.2	1.3	19	596	96.3	19.1	30	D	D	D
Bledsoe	6	8	0.6	0.2	7	D	9.9	D	4	D	D	D
Blount	175	D	D	D	107	5 417	3 761.4	306.1	210	4 526	229.8	68.3
Bradley	142	853	76.2	32.0	113	7 961	D	339.8	178	3 538	168.3	44.5
Campbell	26	D	D	D	34	980	235.9	38.6	55	D	D	D
Cannon	12	27	1.9	0.6	14	290	26.1	8.8	10	D	D	D
Carroll	29	114	9.2	3.6	26	727	612.5	35.5	32	398	19.5	4.3
Carter	44	141	12.2	3.7	35	1 007	188.4	40.2	65	1 203	48.5	15.4
Cheatham	37	140	21.8	4.9	39	1 905	820.2	83.4	40	545	26.0	6.7
Chester	13	D	D	D	20	388	76.1	16.7	25	D	D	D
Claiborne	29	D	D	D	32	1 860	327.9	56.7	29	463	23.6	5.7
Clay	4	9	0.7	0.1	9	274	D	7.0	10	D	D	D
Cocke	27	102	7.5	2.4	30	1 486	659.6	69.1	65	915	48.2	13.1
Coffee	83	3 159	361.0	174.2	79	4 443	D	211.8	108	1 893	89.8	23.6
Crockett	10	D	D	D	14	238	127.9	13.7	10	D	D	D
Cumberland	68	248	30.5	7.7	58	2 099	678.0	79.4	97	1 570	101.2	24.9
Davidson	1 930	24 182	4 021.7	1 641.1	552	18 154	7 319.4	851.8	1 714	40 106	2 573.8	759.3
Decatur	16	D	D	D	22	443	117.0	19.0	20	159	7.9	1.7
DeKalb	24	105	7.8	2.9	20	2 359	672.0	80.2	22	284	13.1	3.8
Dickson	53	199	20.5	7.7	47	3 214	775.7	132.0	92	1 396	67.1	19.0
Dyer	45	191	18.5	5.9	40	3 705	1 455.6	146.6	58	949	42.4	10.8
Fayette	32	338	15.5	8.1	46	1 831	814.3	85.5	42	557	22.5	5.4
Fentress	14	43	3.7	0.8	20	298	39.1	10.6	19	D	D	D
Franklin	37	D	D	D	45	D	3 643.1	D	55	D	D	D
Gibson	47	219	14.3	4.8	58	2 620	737.8	116.9	65	985	45.0	11.0
Giles	36	151	12.8	5.2	43	2 376	1 040.2	107.9	46	639	24.8	6.4
Grainger	10	D	D	D	25	867	138.8	25.7	14	D	D	D
Greene	81	279	31.2	9.3	96	5 209	1 771.1	226.8	117	1 658	77.8	21.5
Grundy	7	D	D	D	16	359	D	8.6	13	157	7.2	1.9
Hamblen	70	281	24.8	10.1	101	8 609	3 235.8	357.6	110	1 995	99.2	26.1
Hamilton	787	7 803	1 053.0	390.3	411	25 092	12 127.5	1 323.1	830	17 426	903.3	256.9
Hancock	1	D	D	D	NA	NA	NA	NA	3	38	1.8	0.5
Hardeman	13	44	3.0	0.6	22	1 566	D	57.3	25	229	13.1	3.1
Hardin	31	94	7.5	2.1	34	1 674	743.9	91.7	54	653	31.7	8.2
Hawkins	34	90	11.5	3.1	41	3 475	1 328.3	151.3	67	911	38.1	10.8
Haywood	15	80	4.6	2.0	17	1 798	597.8	73.5	32	288	14.5	3.5
Henderson	32	D	D	D	35	1 202	362.4	48.2	37	656	26.2	6.2
Henry	40	264	18.3	8.4	39	1 358	277.8	51.4	65	798	33.1	9.2
Hickman	9	34	2.4	0.9	24	544	124.4	18.5	22	D	D	D
Houston	5	21	2.3	0.5	7	207	23.2	6.8	16	D	D	D
Humphreys	14	66	4.7	2.0	23	1 353	2 099.1	95.2	40	385	18.1	5.0
Jackson	5	D	D	D	NA	NA	NA	NA	5	D	D	D
Jefferson	40	157	23.9	4.1	43	1 596	988.3	60.5	68	1 070	53.1	14.5
Johnson	14	44	7.4	1.3	18	758	165.4	32.6	22	254	9.3	2.7
Knox	1 153	D	D	D	360	11 934	4 816.9	645.3	934	21 794	1 039.3	315.2
Lake	2	D	D	D	NA	NA	NA	NA	11	135	5.2	1.4
Lauderdale	13	33	3.4	0.8	12	953	209.1	36.4	19	D	D	D
Lawrence	42	177	19.9	5.5	50	1 683	397.6	64.6	49	851	44.6	10.8
Lewis	15	36	2.6	0.8	20	259	46.0	8.1	17	D	D	D
Lincoln	38	154	14.3	4.9	31	2 363	D	79.7	48	545	26.7	6.6
Loudon	53	D	D	D	50	2 804	1 424.2	136.8	77	1 366	64.6	19.3
McMinn	52	350	17.4	5.5	62	4 642	2 196.6	248.2	92	1 539	69.6	18.3
McNairy	19	68	6.2	1.6	49	1 328	352.1	47.6	31	435	15.4	4.4
Macon	25	53	6.3	1.7	35	771	214.2	27.3	24	221	12.0	2.6
Madison	171	1 810	129.4	70.3	101	8 726	4 374.7	406.6	221	4 750	222.5	62.9
Marion	20	77	6.1	2.7	27	1 374	D	59.6	51	D	D	D

1. Establishment subject to federal tax.

STATE County	Health care and social assistance, 2012				Other services, 2012				Nonemployer businesses, 2015		Value of residential construction authorized by building permits, 2016	
	Number of establishments	Number of employees	Receipts (mil dol)	Annual payroll (mil dol)	Number of establishments	Number of employees	Receipts (mil dol)	Annual payroll (mil dol)	Number	Receipts (mil dol)	New Construction ($1,000)	Number of housing units
	159	160	161	162	163	164	165	166	167	168	169	170
SOUTH DAKOTA—Cont'd												
Tripp	19	434	31.6	13.2	16	75	6.4	1.3	531	24.8	0	0
Turner	25	412	21.1	10.4	10	D	D	D	756	36.5	4 443	17
Union	57	1 070	143.3	54.5	30	D	D	D	1 357	88.5	36 467	156
Walworth	12	397	26.0	12.1	20	106	6.6	1.9	461	19.6	1 631	12
Yankton	72	2 028	193.2	83.9	58	243	21.8	5.0	1 543	61.8	19 985	107
Ziebach	8	D	D	D	1	D	D	D	76	3.0	NA	NA
TENNESSEE	14 897	380 453	42 383.7	16 227.9	8 117	55 990	6 525.8	1 711.4	495 703	22 845.7	6 580 600	36 157
Anderson	189	4 140	424.7	164.7	111	491	44.8	13.1	4 592	193.4	27 570	128
Bedford	96	986	86.8	32.6	38	257	19.5	6.2	2 961	125.4	39 269	191
Benton	38	672	51.6	18.0	19	D	D	D	999	34.4	443	10
Bledsoe	9	D	D	D	2	D	D	D	773	27.7	0	0
Blount	247	6 554	561.5	249.4	161	896	85.3	28.8	8 743	381.8	125 255	744
Bradley	230	4 659	622.9	188.2	94	851	70.9	21.4	6 798	352.2	56 864	368
Campbell	69	2 191	172.8	68.3	32	D	D	D	2 365	95.4	22 779	211
Cannon	17	377	24.8	11.3	10	D	D	D	1 039	42.6	1 640	13
Carroll	67	1 721	111.5	49.8	23	D	D	D	1 565	62.8	1 145	6
Carter	81	1 782	147.9	59.7	40	D	D	D	3 334	121.7	14 798	160
Cheatham	46	567	44.5	17.2	26	D	D	D	3 444	163.2	34 112	173
Chester	28	455	26.9	12.4	10	D	D	D	1 031	44.1	2 700	20
Claiborne	52	1 227	84.4	37.9	32	D	D	D	1 866	77.0	9 307	99
Clay	9	373	13.0	6.0	3	D	D	D	674	21.8	2 301	15
Cocke	40	1 017	102.7	37.5	26	D	D	D	2 157	66.7	358	6
Coffee	197	3 056	305.8	107.0	70	278	21.4	5.9	3 400	138.2	23 431	206
Crockett	29	515	31.6	13.3	10	D	D	D	909	35.0	5 246	35
Cumberland	138	3 018	386.0	91.9	66	580	33.4	12.8	4 604	197.3	57 257	247
Davidson	1 819	62 989	8 547.7	3 158.0	1 225	11 665	1 369.2	407.5	68 869	3 651.9	1 639 181	9 566
Decatur	27	1 019	67.4	39.5	10	D	D	D	798	28.7	0	0
DeKalb	29	533	40.9	15.7	16	D	D	D	1 350	50.6	8 221	62
Dickson	122	2 129	260.3	85.4	45	D	D	D	3 789	170.0	51 977	260
Dyer	108	2 005	200.6	71.7	45	207	20.8	5.2	2 370	86.9	8 452	76
Fayette	54	611	44.1	20.0	29	113	9.7	2.7	3 276	164.9	85 194	360
Fentress	29	D	D	D	15	D	D	D	1 468	78.3	0	0
Franklin	84	1 577	149.7	53.3	50	273	30.7	6.5	2 538	96.5	19 965	139
Gibson	111	2 106	139.7	56.2	53	D	D	D	2 875	111.3	17 901	95
Giles	57	889	77.5	28.3	28	D	D	D	1 776	81.7	9 876	82
Grainger	15	232	11.9	5.6	14	D	D	D	1 471	60.0	7 264	41
Greene	136	4 034	298.1	127.4	60	356	27.9	8.0	3 968	144.9	23 467	127
Grundy	18	379	24.4	11.7	8	D	D	D	1 164	42.6	1 212	4
Hamblen	164	4 246	358.7	147.7	73	349	28.6	8.9	3 567	162.4	16 144	93
Hamilton	1 038	26 382	3 179.1	1 255.6	580	D	D	D	25 662	1 307.8	306 509	2 049
Hancock	12	182	16.6	5.7	2	D	D	D	431	11.4	63	1
Hardeman	40	1 149	76.9	36.5	16	D	D	D	1 457	47.7	3 442	24
Hardin	59	1 155	100.4	40.4	23	D	D	D	1 762	73.6	421	7
Hawkins	54	1 433	102.5	41.7	44	D	D	D	3 016	102.3	11 040	94
Haywood	27	470	37.7	15.4	21	D	D	D	1 121	38.0	2 903	19
Henderson	56	886	60.1	22.9	34	D	D	D	1 695	64.6	1 003	4
Henry	83	1 466	142.0	53.3	52	D	D	D	2 226	100.7	1 506	17
Hickman	23	D	D	D	15	D	D	D	1 695	65.0	9 358	55
Houston	15	408	28.5	12.6	5	D	D	D	486	18.9	0	0
Humphreys	30	595	47.3	15.1	22	D	D	D	1 150	43.1	871	8
Jackson	9	D	D	D	4	D	D	D	784	28.3	0	0
Jefferson	66	1 434	132.5	42.1	41	177	13.8	4.1	3 102	127.8	34 535	143
Johnson	23	575	42.8	17.1	9	D	D	D	1 061	39.3	200	1
Knox	1 244	36 221	4 262.2	1 514.8	730	5 946	547.5	191.1	34 884	1 867.8	398 471	2 122
Lake	11	D	D	D	4	D	D	D	330	9.2	43	1
Lauderdale	30	611	62.9	17.6	13	D	D	D	1 309	47.2	1 820	14
Lawrence	76	1 311	107.0	38.8	40	119	10.7	3.2	2 797	123.7	1 839	11
Lewis	26	492	23.9	10.7	10	D	D	D	885	37.4	542	6
Lincoln	54	843	59.4	25.7	37	D	D	D	2 270	95.5	885	9
Loudon	97	1 796	142.9	55.0	46	216	27.6	6.0	3 456	165.0	71 994	307
McMinn	108	1 805	177.0	62.4	48	219	18.9	5.0	2 986	127.9	1 442	18
McNairy	47	799	63.9	24.5	20	D	D	D	1 702	69.4	557	5
Macon	37	657	50.7	19.2	22	D	D	D	1 651	65.3	19 531	93
Madison	313	11 842	1 172.9	484.4	131	D	D	D	6 368	283.3	40 069	223
Marion	44	D	D	D	31	D	D	D	1 759	70.5	23 034	117

STATE County	Full-time equivalent employees	March payroll (dollars)	Administration, judicial, and legal	Police and Corrections	Fire Protection	Highways and transportation	Health and Welfare	Natural resources and utilities	Education and libraries	Total (mil dol)	Inter-governmental (mil dol)	Total (mil dol)	Per capita[1] (dollars) Total	Property
	171	172	173	174	175	176	177	178	179	180	181	182	183	184
SOUTH DAKOTA— Cont'd														
Tripp	313	855 393	8.1	15.4	0.0	7.0	3.8	9.9	55.0	19.6	5.9	10.3	1 882	1 410
Turner	279	817 829	8.0	3.7	0.0	8.8	0.3	5.1	73.1	26.4	8.0	14.2	1 711	1 477
Union	512	1 673 489	7.8	8.7	0.3	5.6	0.6	5.0	68.1	61.5	22.0	30.6	2 059	1 752
Walworth	221	589 011	7.5	16.1	0.1	6.5	1.9	2.6	64.6	20.6	9.1	7.9	1 440	1 024
Yankton	681	2 403 085	7.3	8.7	0.5	6.7	3.4	8.0	64.3	65.0	16.6	35.8	1 586	1 147
Ziebach	95	280 194	7.1	2.1	0.0	3.4	0.6	0.4	86.0	6.0	4.4	1.4	474	432
TENNESSEE	X	X	X	X	X	X	X	X	X	X	X	X	X	X
Anderson	3 051	10 709 572	8.9	7.5	4.2	3.4	1.7	10.8	62.8	221.7	89.4	94.0	1 246	741
Bedford	2 341	6 860 633	3.8	5.9	2.6	2.3	32.4	8.2	44.3	114.2	59.7	38.4	842	542
Benton	474	1 606 363	5.8	8.8	0.2	3.6	4.0	12.7	63.7	37.9	21.5	12.7	775	443
Bledsoe	594	1 386 704	5.7	6.0	0.0	3.7	3.2	3.2	63.4	34.4	25.2	6.2	483	381
Blount	6 070	20 455 931	4.4	6.6	1.8	2.2	37.0	5.4	41.5	528.9	111.3	129.7	1 044	749
Bradley	3 454	10 166 787	4.0	11.4	6.6	3.1	10.6	1.9	61.3	246.4	112.5	81.3	804	494
Campbell	1 510	4 358 532	4.9	7.7	2.4	5.5	4.9	19.0	54.0	98.1	55.2	27.6	684	390
Cannon	555	1 372 374	3.7	6.2	1.4	2.5	4.5	3.9	73.3	29.2	18.5	7.5	546	395
Carroll	1 139	3 140 304	5.3	9.1	1.3	4.5	0.7	12.9	62.8	71.5	41.1	18.0	635	428
Carter	1 973	5 071 600	5.5	8.9	2.0	4.0	1.2	9.8	68.0	111.1	63.2	34.7	606	404
Cheatham	1 170	3 416 461	8.9	8.5	1.2	3.8	4.2	5.4	66.2	87.0	44.5	32.3	824	545
Chester	583	1 479 520	6.9	10.4	1.3	4.6	3.5	4.5	63.6	35.4	21.8	9.2	537	327
Claiborne	1 693	4 650 708	4.4	4.7	0.0	1.8	36.9	4.7	46.4	101.7	41.7	19.7	620	402
Clay	346	836 185	8.5	6.7	0.0	5.7	8.6	7.4	60.8	19.6	11.9	5.0	642	405
Cocke	1 225	3 330 780	5.4	6.8	3.2	4.8	1.6	3.4	73.7	82.1	45.4	25.0	704	410
Coffee	2 224	6 075 717	5.2	8.5	3.3	2.4	3.8	13.4	59.9	153.4	61.5	58.5	1 099	624
Crockett	563	1 474 498	6.0	8.0	0.1	3.9	5.1	5.6	69.5	39.4	25.3	9.5	647	455
Cumberland	1 971	4 871 298	10.5	9.2	1.5	7.6	3.6	6.6	59.6	116.9	58.5	44.1	773	397
Davidson	22 627	87 554 648	6.2	13.1	7.2	2.6	9.0	12.5	47.7	2 674.3	751.4	1 227.6	1 894	1 220
Decatur	576	1 686 615	5.4	7.1	0.0	3.3	24.4	5.4	52.2	40.6	17.7	8.4	718	421
DeKalb	735	1 938 173	2.6	5.5	0.0	2.8	3.4	27.2	58.1	43.2	24.6	12.8	677	446
Dickson	1 972	5 546 728	7.3	6.8	2.6	2.4	3.9	17.9	57.6	141.4	60.1	55.8	1 108	644
Dyer	1 460	4 541 888	6.2	11.6	5.0	4.0	2.4	8.4	60.7	128.0	69.8	34.0	890	593
Fayette	1 075	2 824 788	9.0	14.5	2.4	0.3	4.2	5.6	62.7	63.0	30.1	24.0	622	428
Fentress	636	1 503 203	9.4	7.6	0.0	4.8	9.5	5.6	62.4	35.7	20.4	10.5	583	350
Franklin	1 139	3 326 510	2.9	9.5	1.7	3.7	1.6	11.4	69.2	91.2	43.8	33.8	829	597
Gibson	1 945	5 303 575	3.3	10.5	3.0	4.3	1.1	8.6	68.2	134.8	75.7	35.9	723	550
Giles	1 369	3 634 496	12.1	7.4	0.5	8.8	4.0	4.5	61.5	61.4	31.0	24.0	827	523
Grainger	662	1 667 581	3.5	8.8	0.0	0.6	5.1	2.8	78.1	45.9	30.1	11.3	496	384
Greene	2 317	6 964 692	4.1	9.6	2.3	3.1	6.4	13.2	60.6	142.8	69.9	48.8	709	420
Grundy	608	1 426 124	5.2	4.3	0.0	3.5	2.0	5.6	77.2	32.3	23.7	6.9	507	359
Hamblen	1 973	6 233 306	5.6	9.2	4.7	2.5	1.7	12.8	60.0	162.1	67.7	63.4	1 011	537
Hamilton	14 734	56 385 621	6.4	7.3	3.0	3.5	37.2	11.3	30.7	1 780.1	395.6	494.7	1 432	1 127
Hancock	347	800 025	10.1	7.0	0.2	6.6	20.3	2.7	53.2	20.3	13.2	2.7	407	312
Hardeman	1 079	2 839 972	5.5	9.2	1.0	3.5	5.9	11.2	62.9	64.6	37.7	18.1	684	425
Hardin	1 366	3 651 007	4.5	6.1	0.3	2.3	39.7	2.3	43.0	104.2	34.3	23.2	893	480
Hawkins	2 067	6 744 656	3.8	5.3	0.4	2.2	8.6	5.8	73.1	111.4	61.3	40.6	717	506
Haywood	942	2 633 709	7.9	9.5	3.1	3.5	5.1	9.8	55.4	60.5	32.7	17.9	982	679
Henderson	1 113	2 867 377	7.3	13.1	1.5	3.4	1.2	16.3	56.3	63.0	35.8	20.0	714	394
Henry	1 119	3 290 953	5.3	9.3	2.1	1.8	1.8	14.7	63.3	150.2	42.7	24.7	765	442
Hickman	1 002	2 269 272	16.1	6.3	0.5	2.3	4.1	5.8	61.1	54.5	34.7	13.4	554	369
Houston	381	990 105	9.2	11.3	0.4	5.4	8.2	5.2	59.0	21.6	14.5	4.9	585	382
Humphreys	1 002	3 913 409	14.1	4.3	0.1	2.3	9.0	4.1	63.2	46.8	26.1	15.5	851	526
Jackson	425	1 046 407	9.7	7.7	0.0	7.2	3.9	4.7	66.8	24.4	16.5	5.7	497	349
Jefferson	1 433	4 289 878	5.4	8.6	1.0	4.2	5.2	9.0	66.5	126.4	54.0	43.3	829	545
Johnson	620	1 243 277	8.2	8.9	0.0	5.0	2.1	6.1	68.5	37.2	23.2	8.9	494	360
Knox	13 135	45 220 953	5.5	12.5	2.9	3.2	3.7	15.3	55.2	1 270.2	389.9	630.9	1 430	810
Lake	321	873 740	15.6	15.9	0.2	6.0	4.5	10.1	47.6	18.1	11.6	3.5	457	287
Lauderdale	1 033	2 753 225	7.4	11.7	2.0	4.8	4.6	4.1	64.7	70.8	41.8	18.4	664	441
Lawrence	1 270	4 176 846	6.6	9.0	1.9	3.7	3.6	13.3	60.8	96.9	50.8	33.0	783	468
Lewis	515	1 074 509	10.9	12.0	0.6	6.6	1.4	6.6	61.8	31.6	21.1	6.6	554	298
Lincoln	1 457	3 836 126	5.1	6.7	1.8	3.0	1.0	26.5	54.5	110.1	39.6	20.1	599	348
Loudon	1 628	5 601 296	4.4	6.8	2.4	2.3	1.4	30.5	50.4	114.9	46.7	47.0	944	641
McMinn	2 013	6 789 227	4.8	5.9	1.4	2.2	24.9	7.7	47.8	109.5	59.5	34.1	651	417
McNairy	1 044	2 736 738	6.7	5.8	0.7	3.7	0.6	11.6	68.0	61.0	40.2	14.3	547	361
Macon	840	2 132 533	7.7	8.1	1.0	0.1	5.9	5.3	70.4	49.3	29.8	13.4	597	355
Madison	7 853	28 936 219	2.2	6.4	2.6	1.2	64.3	4.4	18.6	921.0	113.3	137.5	1 393	781
Marion	942	2 790 775	7.6	7.6	0.6	2.9	2.4	9.1	69.0	67.8	35.6	24.6	870	523

1. Based on the resident population estimated as of July 1 of the year shown.

Table B. States and Counties — Local Government Finances, Government Employment, and Income Taxes

STATE County	Local government finances, 2012 (cont.) — Direct general expenditure							Debt outstanding		Government employment, 2015			Individual income tax returns, 2014		
	Total (mil dol)	Per capita¹ (dollars)	Percent of total for: Education	Health and hospitals	Police protection	Public welfare	Highways	Total (mil dol)	Per capita¹ (dollars)	Federal civilian	Federal military	State and local	Number of returns	Mean adjusted gross income	Mean income tax
	185	186	187	188	189	190	191	192	193	194	195	196	197	198	199
SOUTH DAKOTA—Cont'd															
Tripp	20.4	3 717	42.1	1.5	4.2	0.3	17.5	16.4	2 990	31	31	365	2 660	51 419	5 980
Turner	25.7	3 093	49.0	0.7	4.4	0.2	18.6	21.3	2 563	26	47	394	3 950	53 606	6 071
Union	61.7	4 151	39.7	0.2	4.0	0.0	10.5	55.2	3 718	52	87	726	7 450	120 238	24 176
Walworth	18.8	3 440	49.6	0.6	5.7	0.1	11.1	8.2	1 510	32	31	394	2 740	52 875	6 292
Yankton	61.7	2 730	45.1	1.7	5.7	0.5	12.7	62.1	2 746	198	119	1 700	10 820	57 156	7 215
Ziebach	6.0	2 081	73.9	0.5	2.6	0.0	10.9	0.0	0	D	16	167	500	38 442	2 884
TENNESSEE	X	X	X	X	X	X	X	X	X	49 614	21 650	371 541	2 928 220	55 000	7 032
Anderson	264.4	3 506	58.7	2.4	7.0	0.0	3.3	316.3	4 194	872	232	4 114	33 700	50 550	5 542
Bedford	117.2	2 572	51.0	2.6	5.8	0.2	4.7	126.0	2 764	65	144	2 344	20 400	42 696	4 453
Benton	36.9	2 254	60.4	2.4	7.0	0.3	8.6	25.4	1 550	58	49	998	6 580	40 600	3 677
Bledsoe	29.7	2 318	58.9	3.4	3.8	0.3	6.6	28.6	2 232	20	37	1 012	4 400	36 834	2 873
Blount	501.3	4 037	31.7	37.6	3.9	0.0	2.2	1 376.5	11 085	250	408	7 487	57 560	52 247	5 797
Bradley	234.0	2 314	53.1	8.4	7.2	0.1	4.8	222.5	2 200	208	313	4 743	45 170	47 818	5 204
Campbell	109.0	2 696	46.6	2.9	5.5	0.1	5.8	125.9	3 115	77	121	1 962	14 540	38 969	3 450
Cannon	28.5	2 064	58.3	3.3	7.4	0.4	8.5	13.9	1 008	29	42	580	5 900	42 143	3 569
Carroll	72.3	2 547	58.4	0.4	6.1	0.2	7.2	63.9	2 250	77	83	1 540	11 420	40 439	3 451
Carter	118.2	2 060	67.1	0.7	5.7	0.0	4.3	105.8	1 845	81	171	2 551	22 710	38 959	3 424
Cheatham	93.0	2 367	69.6	2.1	5.4	0.3	4.2	61.6	1 568	73	121	1 573	18 450	51 070	5 126
Chester	35.0	2 039	59.3	1.0	5.7	0.4	11.6	19.6	1 140	32	50	1 012	6 630	40 588	3 338
Claiborne	96.3	3 036	42.5	32.9	3.7	0.0	3.6	69.4	2 188	63	94	1 941	11 920	38 157	3 287
Clay	20.9	2 663	48.6	6.1	6.2	0.2	10.9	14.3	1 818	43	24	432	2 930	33 382	2 430
Cocke	89.1	2 504	59.3	1.2	4.9	0.0	6.9	71.6	2 014	62	107	1 932	14 420	34 084	2 655
Coffee	162.9	3 060	57.5	2.0	5.5	0.1	4.0	222.3	4 176	484	216	3 191	23 800	45 684	4 628
Crockett	40.8	2 791	61.9	3.1	4.8	0.9	7.7	29.0	1 982	37	44	834	6 050	40 710	4 153
Cumberland	113.1	1 983	49.3	6.2	5.6	0.0	4.0	134.0	2 349	108	177	2 409	25 550	45 291	4 556
Davidson	2 727.2	4 207	31.0	8.4	7.3	1.2	1.6	6 313.0	9 738	8 109	2 478	38 288	335 820	62 878	9 644
Decatur	37.9	3 249	38.3	26.2	3.3	0.3	5.7	26.0	2 228	28	35	773	4 500	39 061	3 132
DeKalb	40.9	2 165	55.5	3.0	7.5	0.1	5.8	23.6	1 246	39	58	980	7 770	38 595	3 844
Dickson	126.9	2 520	53.8	2.4	7.4	0.0	4.2	145.3	2 885	87	158	2 496	22 550	46 396	4 571
Dyer	131.4	3 436	50.7	0.2	7.3	0.6	6.4	99.2	2 594	97	115	2 605	16 020	44 515	4 473
Fayette	62.3	1 611	54.0	3.2	7.9	0.0	9.2	51.2	1 325	56	119	1 308	18 270	63 600	8 899
Fentress	35.1	1 954	57.6	4.3	4.7	0.6	7.7	14.5	810	37	55	790	6 510	36 052	3 239
Franklin	85.2	2 091	56.5	0.5	7.5	0.1	5.2	83.2	2 040	125	121	1 968	17 840	47 251	4 848
Gibson	141.6	2 854	58.9	2.2	5.8	0.4	6.0	112.6	2 270	145	149	2 763	21 000	44 369	4 340
Giles	61.6	2 118	59.8	4.3	3.0	0.1	8.6	25.0	859	68	87	1 396	12 480	43 453	4 078
Grainger	44.5	1 960	64.7	3.7	4.6	0.0	7.6	29.5	1 301	51	70	900	8 830	39 800	3 280
Greene	138.3	2 009	61.2	3.2	5.4	0.0	7.0	106.4	1 546	223	207	3 436	28 740	40 616	3 651
Grundy	31.5	2 310	69.9	0.6	3.4	0.2	7.5	12.0	880	20	41	762	5 410	35 064	2 763
Hamblen	158.5	2 526	53.0	0.6	6.2	0.2	4.7	224.6	3 579	164	193	3 649	26 780	43 390	4 249
Hamilton	1 693.1	4 900	23.2	34.8	4.9	0.9	2.5	1 512.3	4 377	5 329	1 117	21 868	162 350	59 959	8 201
Hancock	20.0	2 979	49.9	15.8	3.9	0.2	7.0	17.1	2 543	10	20	455	2 290	32 576	2 202
Hardeman	62.6	2 361	60.6	2.7	6.6	0.1	7.3	28.4	1 071	54	67	1 798	9 800	36 365	2 893
Hardin	104.9	4 042	36.7	35.8	2.7	2.7	4.6	72.4	2 789	111	78	1 609	10 380	41 333	4 070
Hawkins	108.4	1 915	66.6	0.9	4.8	0.3	4.8	126.4	2 234	133	172	2 249	23 010	41 685	3 715
Haywood	64.2	3 520	54.9	2.6	5.5	0.0	5.8	26.7	1 465	93	55	1 098	8 050	35 311	2 953
Henderson	60.8	2 170	65.5	0.2	6.4	0.1	5.4	92.9	3 314	55	86	1 382	11 640	41 955	3 731
Henry	154.5	4 776	27.8	50.9	2.8	0.0	4.3	81.7	2 525	109	128	2 510	13 740	42 902	4 695
Hickman	52.0	2 151	60.6	3.4	4.7	0.0	9.9	46.4	1 921	54	70	1 200	9 200	40 167	3 561
Houston	20.6	2 448	57.1	4.4	4.1	0.4	9.8	13.7	1 623	19	25	559	3 320	39 800	3 244
Humphreys	43.2	2 363	55.4	1.0	7.3	0.0	8.5	7.4	405	220	55	1 025	7 830	45 765	4 582
Jackson	23.3	2 034	61.8	2.9	4.3	0.2	9.2	4.9	428	26	35	537	4 350	35 774	2 722
Jefferson	135.7	2 600	53.6	3.3	4.7	9.4	4.4	112.4	2 153	114	161	2 289	21 840	42 686	3 983
Johnson	35.0	1 933	61.4	0.7	5.0	0.2	7.3	18.8	1 038	36	49	1 009	6 180	43 751	5 307
Knox	1 174.3	2 661	40.8	2.1	7.9	0.2	2.6	2 290.6	5 191	3 504	1 436	30 858	202 660	65 045	9 612
Lake	17.1	2 221	49.1	3.9	6.9	0.5	10.4	23.7	3 088	16	16	858	2 120	35 520	3 046
Lauderdale	69.4	2 504	56.8	2.7	7.3	0.6	7.8	45.4	1 639	53	75	1 807	9 690	36 336	2 960
Lawrence	93.3	2 217	57.9	3.0	6.7	0.0	7.8	110.6	2 628	116	130	1 980	16 360	41 080	3 500
Lewis	31.4	2 639	46.3	0.6	5.1	0.1	5.8	17.0	1 431	26	36	667	4 760	38 769	3 640
Lincoln	111.8	3 338	38.2	35.1	4.0	0.0	4.7	92.5	2 760	50	103	2 168	14 640	45 725	4 415
Loudon	111.4	2 238	57.9	0.6	7.1	0.2	4.5	662.5	13 305	134	156	1 898	23 360	60 913	7 454
McMinn	110.6	2 110	58.7	0.9	5.3	0.0	5.6	28.0	534	99	159	2 132	21 910	42 828	3 927
McNairy	55.7	2 129	62.1	0.2	4.9	0.0	6.8	28.4	1 086	82	79	1 376	10 200	39 319	3 190
Macon	53.2	2 366	60.7	4.0	6.0	0.1	7.6	27.7	1 232	38	71	1 177	9 250	36 857	3 032
Madison	890.5	9 027	13.8	63.1	3.2	0.0	1.8	1 017.8	10 317	430	290	11 591	43 490	49 659	5 963
Marion	61.4	2 169	58.5	0.8	8.3	0.0	5.6	57.5	2 034	64	87	1 297	11 930	45 591	4 535

1. Based on the resident population estimated as of July 1 of the year shown.

Table B. States and Counties — **Land Area and Population**

STATE/ County code	CBSA code[1]	County type[2]	STATE County	Land area,[3] (sq mi) 2016	Total persons 2016	Rank	Per square mile	White	Black	American Indian, Alaska Native	Asian and Pacific Islander	Percent Hispanic or Latino[4]	Under 5 years	5 to 17 years	18 to 24 years	25 to 34 years	35 to 44 years	45 to 54 years
				1	2	3	4	5	6	7	8	9	10	11	12	13	14	15
			TENNESSEE—Cont'd															
47 117	30280	6	Marshall	375.5	31 915	1 380	85.0	87.3	7.6	0.8	1.0	5.0	6.0	17.5	7.8	12.2	12.8	14.3
47 119	34980	1	Maury	613.1	89 981	645	146.8	81.5	12.7	0.8	1.2	5.7	6.5	16.9	7.6	13.8	12.7	12.9
47 121	...	8	Meigs	195.1	12 005	2 295	61.5	95.5	1.8	1.3	0.6	2.0	5.4	15.7	6.9	10.5	12.2	14.7
47 123	...	6	Monroe	635.6	45 970	1 050	72.3	92.7	2.5	1.4	0.7	4.2	5.7	16.1	7.5	10.9	11.4	13.7
47 125	17300	2	Montgomery	539.2	195 734	338	363.0	67.5	21.3	1.3	4.2	10.0	8.5	18.4	11.3	19.2	13.1	11.2
47 127	46100	9	Moore	129.2	6 323	2 731	48.9	94.8	3.1	0.9	0.9	1.9	4.2	15.4	7.4	10.2	12.2	13.7
47 129	28940	2	Morgan	522.2	21 554	1 749	41.3	94.6	3.9	1.2	0.5	1.2	4.9	15.0	8.2	13.0	13.3	15.2
47 131	46460	7	Obion	544.9	30 578	1 416	56.1	84.7	11.5	0.6	0.6	4.2	5.6	16.2	7.6	11.3	12.0	13.1
47 133	18260	7	Overton	433.5	22 051	1 726	50.9	97.3	1.1	1.0	0.5	1.4	5.3	16.4	7.7	10.6	12.2	13.5
47 135	...	8	Perry	414.8	7 964	2 602	19.2	94.5	3.1	1.4	0.7	2.5	6.3	15.6	7.6	11.1	10.9	12.4
47 137	...	9	Pickett	163.0	5 142	2 824	31.5	97.4	0.4	0.8	0.3	2.0	4.5	14.1	6.0	8.8	10.6	13.6
47 139	17420	3	Polk	434.6	16 772	1 994	38.6	96.6	1.0	1.3	0.5	2.1	4.7	15.3	7.4	10.6	12.3	15.3
47 141	18260	4	Putnam	401.1	75 931	728	189.3	90.0	2.8	0.8	1.7	6.2	5.9	15.2	14.6	12.8	11.1	12.1
47 143	19420	6	Rhea	315.4	32 442	1 372	102.9	92.1	2.8	1.0	0.7	4.8	5.9	17.1	8.7	11.5	11.6	13.7
47 145	28940	2	Roane	360.7	52 874	949	146.6	94.5	3.3	1.1	0.9	1.7	4.5	14.6	7.1	10.0	11.1	14.4
47 147	34980	1	Robertson	476.3	69 165	773	145.2	85.3	8.1	0.7	0.8	6.5	6.4	18.1	7.7	12.6	13.0	14.3
47 149	34980	1	Rutherford	619.4	308 251	222	497.7	74.2	15.9	0.8	4.0	7.6	6.7	18.2	12.7	14.6	14.1	13.2
47 151	...	6	Scott	532.3	21 947	1 730	41.2	98.5	0.4	0.9	0.4	0.8	6.6	17.9	7.7	12.1	12.9	13.9
47 153	16860	2	Sequatchie	265.9	14 897	2 106	56.0	95.1	1.1	1.1	0.6	3.4	5.1	16.4	7.2	10.7	12.1	13.8
47 155	42940	4	Sevier	592.5	96 673	613	163.2	91.8	1.4	0.9	1.6	5.6	5.5	15.4	7.9	11.7	11.9	14.2
47 157	32820	1	Shelby	763.6	934 603	55	1 223.9	37.3	54.4	0.6	3.1	6.1	7.2	18.0	9.7	14.5	12.5	13.0
47 159	34980	1	Smith	314.3	19 447	1 851	61.9	94.5	2.9	1.1	0.5	2.4	6.1	17.2	8.0	11.8	11.9	14.8
47 161	...	8	Stewart	459.3	13 182	2 218	28.7	93.7	2.4	1.6	1.4	2.7	5.1	15.7	7.4	10.4	11.7	15.1
47 163	28700	2	Sullivan	413.4	156 667	414	379.0	94.9	2.9	0.8	1.0	1.8	5.0	14.6	7.6	11.2	11.7	14.4
47 165	34980	1	Sumner	529.4	180 063	361	340.1	86.6	7.9	0.7	1.8	4.6	6.1	17.9	7.8	12.1	13.3	14.4
47 167	32820	1	Tipton	458.4	61 303	852	133.7	77.7	19.2	1.0	1.3	2.6	6.1	18.9	8.7	12.6	12.4	14.3
47 169	34980	1	Trousdale	114.3	8 271	2 569	72.4	87.5	9.9	1.0	0.5	3.0	6.1	16.9	8.1	12.8	12.0	14.5
47 171	27740	3	Unicoi	186.2	17 719	1 933	95.2	94.4	0.8	0.8	0.4	4.6	4.3	14.3	7.0	10.5	11.3	14.1
47 173	28940	2	Union	223.6	19 140	1 867	85.6	97.6	0.6	1.1	0.4	1.6	5.5	16.8	7.2	11.8	12.1	14.4
47 175	...	9	Van Buren	273.4	5 689	2 783	20.8	97.3	1.4	0.8	0.4	1.4	5.2	14.1	7.2	9.6	11.6	13.6
47 177	32660	6	Warren	432.7	40 516	1 163	93.6	87.2	3.8	0.8	0.9	8.7	6.0	17.8	7.5	11.8	12.9	13.3
47 179	27740	3	Washington	326.5	127 440	493	390.3	90.6	5.2	0.8	1.9	3.3	5.1	14.2	12.3	12.4	11.9	13.2
47 181	...	8	Wayne	734.1	16 713	1 999	22.8	90.9	6.8	0.8	0.5	2.0	4.2	13.3	8.1	14.1	13.2	14.7
47 183	32280	7	Weakley	580.4	33 507	1 341	57.7	88.4	8.6	0.7	1.5	2.2	5.2	14.4	16.3	10.9	10.4	12.5
47 185	...	7	White	376.7	26 653	1 540	70.8	94.8	2.5	0.9	0.6	2.6	5.8	16.1	6.9	12.1	11.5	13.8
47 187	34980	1	Williamson	582.6	219 107	302	376.1	86.6	4.9	0.5	4.9	4.6	6.0	21.6	7.7	9.2	14.3	15.8
47 189	34980	1	Wilson	571.1	132 781	476	232.5	87.3	7.5	0.8	2.1	4.0	6.0	18.0	7.5	11.7	13.7	14.7
48 000	...	0	**TEXAS**	261 249.7	27 862 596	X	106.7	43.9	12.5	0.7	5.4	39.1	7.2	18.9	9.9	14.7	13.4	12.6
48 001	37300	7	Anderson	1 062.6	57 734	889	54.3	60.6	21.5	0.8	1.0	17.5	5.2	14.3	7.8	16.1	16.0	14.6
48 003	11380	6	Andrews	1 500.7	17 760	1 928	11.8	41.3	1.8	1.0	0.7	56.0	9.2	21.8	9.4	15.3	12.2	11.6
48 005	31260	5	Angelina	797.8	87 791	660	110.0	62.1	15.4	0.6	1.2	21.7	6.9	19.0	8.9	12.7	12.0	12.7
48 007	18580	2	Aransas	252.1	25 721	1 575	102.0	69.0	1.9	1.4	2.1	26.8	5.2	13.3	7.2	9.9	9.6	11.8
48 009	48660	3	Archer	903.1	8 703	2 531	9.6	89.4	1.4	1.4	0.8	8.5	5.1	16.6	7.6	10.7	10.9	14.6
48 011	11100	2	Armstrong	909.1	1 876	3 059	2.1	88.6	1.3	1.4	0.4	9.2	6.4	17.0	6.4	9.2	11.6	10.9
48 013	41700	1	Atascosa	1 219.5	48 797	1 005	40.0	34.5	0.9	0.7	0.6	64.0	7.3	20.3	9.1	12.7	12.3	12.1
48 015	26420	1	Austin	646.5	29 758	1 436	46.0	63.8	9.2	0.7	0.8	26.5	6.4	17.9	8.1	10.8	11.3	12.7
48 017	...	7	Bailey	827.0	7 181	2 652	8.7	34.0	1.4	0.6	0.6	64.1	8.4	23.8	8.5	11.8	11.5	10.6
48 019	41700	1	Bandera	791.0	21 776	1 740	27.5	79.6	1.2	1.4	1.0	18.2	4.1	12.6	6.5	8.5	9.1	13.9
48 021	12420	1	Bastrop	888.2	82 733	681	93.1	54.9	7.6	1.0	1.2	36.8	6.7	19.0	8.2	12.0	12.3	13.6
48 023	...	8	Baylor	867.5	3 697	2 923	4.3	84.0	3.5	0.9	0.5	12.7	5.7	15.8	6.8	10.4	9.7	12.2
48 025	13300	6	Bee	880.2	32 750	1 363	37.2	32.2	8.3	0.5	0.7	58.9	6.1	15.6	11.4	17.4	14.5	13.0
48 027	28660	2	Bell	1 051.0	340 411	200	323.9	49.5	23.7	1.1	5.2	24.3	8.7	19.2	11.4	17.0	12.7	10.9
48 029	41700	1	Bexar	1 239.9	1 928 680	16	1 555.5	29.5	7.9	0.6	3.6	59.9	7.3	18.7	10.5	15.8	13.3	12.2
48 031	...	8	Blanco	709.3	11 392	2 332	16.1	78.2	1.4	1.1	1.1	19.2	4.2	14.4	6.8	8.7	10.5	13.4
48 033	...	8	Borden	897.4	633	3 132	0.7	78.0	0.9	1.4	0.8	20.2	5.8	16.9	7.4	8.7	12.5	15.3
48 035	...	6	Bosque	983.0	18 097	1 913	18.4	79.6	2.3	1.0	0.6	17.6	5.3	16.2	6.9	9.4	10.2	12.2
48 037	45500	3	Bowie	885.0	93 860	626	106.1	65.8	25.6	1.4	1.7	7.6	6.5	17.3	8.7	13.7	12.8	12.7
48 039	26420	1	Brazoria	1 357.8	354 195	196	260.9	49.9	13.9	0.8	7.1	30.0	7.1	19.5	8.3	14.0	14.5	13.5
48 041	17780	3	Brazos	585.5	220 417	300	376.5	57.8	11.1	0.6	6.9	25.1	6.2	14.3	27.0	16.2	10.6	9.1
48 043	...	7	Brewster	6 183.8	9 200	2 492	1.5	52.5	1.5	1.4	1.4	44.7	5.6	13.9	7.1	14.3	11.6	11.5
48 045	...	9	Briscoe	900.0	1 474	3 080	1.6	70.1	3.9	1.2	0.3	26.3	4.3	16.2	6.6	9.2	11.7	13.7
48 047	...	7	Brooks	943.4	7 214	2 650	7.6	7.5	0.7	0.2	1.4	90.4	8.4	19.6	9.3	12.6	10.4	10.4
48 049	15220	5	Brown	944.4	38 271	1 217	40.5	73.6	4.1	1.1	0.9	21.8	5.6	17.2	9.0	11.9	11.2	12.3
48 051	17780	3	Burleson	659.0	17 760	1 928	26.9	66.1	13.2	0.9	0.5	20.8	6.3	16.4	7.5	10.6	10.3	13.6
48 053	...	6	Burnet	994.3	46 243	1 044	46.5	74.9	2.1	1.1	1.0	22.1	5.5	16.0	7.7	10.6	10.7	12.2

1. CBSA = Core Based Statistical Area. See Appendix A for explanation. See Appendix B for list of metropolitan areas with component counties. 2. County type code from the Economic Research Service of USDA Rural-Urban Continuum Codes. See Appendix A for definition. 3. Dry land or land partially or temporarily covered by water. 4. May be of any race.

Table B. States and Counties — **Population and Households**

STATE County	55 to 64 years (16)	65 to 74 years (17)	75 years and over (18)	Percent female (19)	2000 (20)	2010 (21)	2000–2010 (22)	2010–2016 (23)	Births (24)	Deaths (25)	Net migration (26)	Number (27)	Persons per house-hold (28)	Family house-holds (29)	Female family house-holder[1] (30)	One person (31)
TENNESSEE—Cont'd																
Marshall	13.7	9.9	5.6	50.9	26 767	30 606	14.3	4.3	2 299	1 928	945	11 968	2.57	71.0	13.4	24.7
Maury	14.1	9.5	6.0	51.8	69 498	80 930	16.4	11.2	6 964	5 110	7 069	32 465	2.55	69.1	14.2	26.1
Meigs	14.4	13.3	6.9	50.1	11 086	11 768	6.2	2.0	730	925	409	4 620	2.51	70.5	12.6	24.7
Monroe	14.2	12.9	7.5	50.4	38 961	44 505	14.2	3.3	3 138	3 174	1 483	17 193	2.60	73.6	9.1	23.9
Montgomery	9.3	5.5	3.5	50.0	134 768	172 362	27.9	13.6	20 874	7 096	9 189	66 234	2.76	72.3	13.9	21.9
Moore	15.7	12.2	8.9	50.0	5 740	6 345	10.5	-0.3	320	401	59	2 454	2.55	71.6	9.7	24.0
Morgan	13.6	10.3	6.4	45.6	19 757	21 986	11.3	-2.0	1 262	1 405	-249	7 370	2.52	72.9	11.5	23.0
Obion	14.2	11.8	8.2	51.6	32 450	31 807	-2.0	-3.9	2 149	2 401	-951	12 665	2.42	70.4	14.8	24.7
Overton	14.1	12.1	8.0	50.7	20 118	22 084	9.8	-0.1	1 477	1 781	275	8 893	2.45	71.9	9.9	25.6
Perry	14.5	13.3	8.4	49.5	7 631	7 928	3.9	0.5	625	675	82	3 226	2.40	65.4	11.3	29.8
Pickett	15.5	16.0	10.9	50.2	4 945	5 077	2.7	1.3	268	410	169	2 223	2.25	79.6	13.2	18.3
Polk	14.2	12.4	7.8	50.2	16 050	16 826	4.8	-0.3	950	1 356	351	6 745	2.44	70.2	11.2	26.3
Putnam	11.8	9.8	6.7	50.3	62 315	72 347	16.1	5.0	5 559	4 750	2 767	29 721	2.38	63.9	12.5	27.6
Rhea	13.3	11.4	6.9	50.7	28 400	31 802	12.0	2.0	2 399	2 318	612	12 545	2.51	66.7	13.1	27.4
Roane	16.2	12.9	9.2	51.1	51 910	54 193	4.4	-2.4	2 938	4 336	178	21 887	2.40	65.1	9.8	29.5
Robertson	13.7	8.8	5.4	50.8	54 433	66 349	21.9	4.2	5 537	3 920	1 165	24 641	2.70	74.1	12.6	22.0
Rutherford	10.5	6.4	3.7	50.8	182 023	262 592	44.3	17.4	23 935	10 490	31 253	100 661	2.76	69.7	12.0	22.5
Scott	12.8	9.9	6.3	50.6	21 127	22 232	5.2	-1.3	1 700	1 689	-281	8 309	2.61	67.6	12.8	28.3
Sequatchie	14.4	12.7	7.5	50.5	11 370	14 121	24.2	5.5	947	974	770	5 615	2.56	72.5	10.9	24.0
Sevier	14.4	11.9	7.0	50.9	71 170	89 725	26.1	7.7	6 508	5 937	6 093	36 717	2.52	70.4	12.2	24.2
Shelby	12.5	7.6	4.9	52.4	897 472	927 684	3.4	0.7	85 792	48 939	-28 936	347 224	2.65	63.5	20.6	31.1
Smith	14.1	10.3	5.9	50.3	17 712	19 149	8.1	1.6	1 397	1 333	208	7 478	2.53	70.2	8.6	26.7
Stewart	15.1	12.0	7.6	49.8	12 370	13 313	7.6	-1.0	814	981	62	5 131	2.57	70.0	9.8	27.4
Sullivan	14.5	12.0	9.1	51.5	153 048	156 806	2.5	-0.1	9 756	12 450	2 745	66 421	2.32	66.2	11.2	29.5
Sumner	13.0	9.5	6.0	51.1	130 449	160 617	23.1	12.1	12 567	8 707	14 970	62 425	2.70	73.8	12.1	22.0
Tipton	13.0	8.6	5.4	50.7	51 271	61 006	19.0	0.5	4 618	3 440	-974	21 575	2.82	75.8	16.7	20.1
Trousdale	13.9	9.6	5.9	50.5	7 259	7 864	8.3	5.2	584	541	354	2 926	2.65	69.5	13.7	23.0
Unicoi	15.7	12.9	9.8	50.8	17 667	18 315	3.7	-3.3	969	1 627	62	7 428	2.36	64.9	8.5	32.4
Union	15.0	11.0	6.3	50.6	17 808	19 109	7.3	0.2	1 276	1 312	68	7 302	2.59	71.9	12.2	23.4
Van Buren	16.9	14.3	7.5	49.5	5 508	5 558	0.9	2.4	372	369	120	2 106	2.61	72.5	14.3	24.5
Warren	13.4	10.2	7.2	50.6	38 276	39 824	4.0	1.7	2 977	2 938	661	15 661	2.51	66.6	12.5	29.5
Washington	13.2	10.4	7.2	51.1	107 198	123 065	14.8	3.6	8 349	8 305	4 172	52 638	2.29	63.1	11.4	30.4
Wayne	13.6	10.9	7.9	45.0	16 842	17 027	1.1	-1.8	878	1 222	46	5 967	2.48	71.8	11.4	25.8
Weakley	12.5	10.2	7.7	51.3	34 895	35 015	0.3	-4.3	2 200	2 288	-1 399	13 678	2.32	64.7	10.4	28.2
White	13.7	11.6	8.4	50.9	23 102	25 836	11.8	3.2	1 865	2 243	1 136	9 731	2.65	69.5	10.0	27.9
Williamson	12.9	7.8	4.7	51.1	126 638	183 252	44.7	19.6	13 052	6 450	28 729	69 478	2.86	79.6	7.1	17.5
Wilson	13.3	9.7	5.5	51.0	88 809	114 057	28.4	16.4	8 773	6 044	15 548	44 528	2.72	73.9	12.0	22.4
TEXAS	11.2	7.2	4.8	50.4	20 851 820	25 146 100	20.6	10.8	2 437 794	1 117 880	1 375 776	9 149 196	2.84	69.6	14.3	25.0
Anderson	11.8	8.5	5.7	38.9	55 109	58 458	6.1	-1.2	3 664	3 963	-341	16 737	2.68	71.2	12.3	25.9
Andrews	10.2	5.8	4.5	49.0	13 004	14 786	13.7	20.1	1 953	740	1 740	5 476	3.05	77.8	10.0	18.6
Angelina	12.2	8.8	6.9	51.1	80 130	86 771	8.3	1.2	7 529	5 392	-1 159	30 583	2.77	74.2	16.5	22.9
Aransas	15.5	16.0	11.5	50.4	22 497	23 158	2.9	11.1	1 619	2 117	2 801	9 682	2.46	66.6	7.2	27.6
Archer	15.6	10.4	8.4	50.2	8 854	9 055	2.3	-3.9	458	466	-351	3 350	2.60	74.2	4.8	22.2
Armstrong	17.0	12.1	9.4	49.8	2 148	1 901	-11.5	-1.3	125	172	14	714	2.63	74.8	5.9	20.4
Atascosa	11.7	8.6	5.8	50.4	38 628	44 911	16.3	8.7	4 158	2 483	2 210	15 363	3.04	76.3	15.3	20.8
Austin	14.6	11.1	7.2	50.7	23 590	28 411	20.4	4.7	2 153	1 675	907	11 038	2.59	71.6	10.0	25.8
Bailey	11.2	7.3	6.9	49.5	6 594	7 165	8.7	0.2	748	361	-402	2 392	2.92	75.4	11.5	22.7
Bandera	19.3	16.5	9.6	50.6	17 645	20 485	16.1	6.3	1 012	1 257	1 465	8 292	2.45	66.8	7.1	29.4
Bastrop	13.9	9.3	5.0	49.2	57 733	74 159	28.5	11.6	5 919	3 902	6 347	25 454	2.94	72.1	11.0	22.8
Baylor	13.9	12.7	12.8	51.0	4 093	3 726	-9.0	-0.8	237	366	109	1 723	2.06	56.7	6.5	41.6
Bee	10.4	6.7	4.9	39.6	32 359	31 861	-1.5	2.8	2 407	1 545	109	8 762	2.85	70.5	18.5	24.7
Bell	9.4	6.3	4.2	50.2	237 974	310 244	30.4	9.7	39 499	12 573	2 714	109 844	2.89	72.0	15.1	23.8
Bexar	10.5	6.9	4.8	50.7	1 392 931	1 714 774	23.1	12.5	168 446	76 878	119 552	618 831	2.90	67.8	16.6	26.5
Blanco	18.0	15.3	8.8	50.0	8 418	10 499	24.7	8.5	569	700	1 005	4 164	2.55	73.1	8.7	24.3
Borden	12.8	12.2	8.4	49.0	729	641	-12.1	-1.2	41	33	-14	262	2.69	75.6	8.4	22.1
Bosque	15.1	13.9	10.8	50.8	17 204	18 212	5.9	-0.6	1 151	1 506	183	6 999	2.52	70.7	9.4	26.0
Bowie	12.4	9.2	6.8	49.8	89 306	92 565	3.6	1.4	7 620	6 238	-21	33 423	2.63	69.8	17.9	26.3
Brazoria	11.7	7.1	4.4	49.4	241 767	313 127	29.5	13.1	29 538	13 403	24 329	112 510	2.85	73.4	11.9	22.5
Brazos	8.2	5.0	3.6	49.3	152 415	194 861	27.8	13.1	17 046	5 941	14 130	73 858	2.58	54.8	11.1	28.0
Brewster	14.8	12.9	8.3	49.7	8 866	9 232	4.1	-0.3	688	454	-285	4 025	2.27	53.1	6.9	39.1
Briscoe	13.6	13.4	11.3	50.7	1 790	1 637	-8.5	-10.0	80	108	-139	675	2.47	72.4	11.7	24.6
Brooks	11.3	10.0	8.1	49.4	7 976	7 223	-9.4	-0.1	764	516	-248	2 080	3.31	71.9	21.7	24.6
Brown	13.1	11.3	8.4	50.8	37 674	38 106	1.1	0.4	2 633	3 028	545	13 295	2.71	69.3	9.9	27.0
Burleson	15.5	11.2	8.5	50.3	16 470	17 187	4.4	3.3	1 237	1 225	555	6 401	2.67	72.2	12.8	25.6
Burnet	15.2	12.9	9.1	51.0	34 147	42 707	25.1	8.3	2 950	2 872	3 209	16 940	2.58	71.8	10.7	24.6

1. No spouse present.

Table B. States and Counties — **Population, Vital Statistics, Health, and Crime**

STATE County	Persons in group quarters, 2016	Daytime population, 2011–2015 Number	Daytime population, 2011–2015 Employment/residence ratio	Births, 2016 Total	Births, 2016 Rate[1]	Deaths, 2016 Number	Deaths, 2016 Rate[1]	Persons under 65 with no health insurance, 2015 Number	Persons under 65 with no health insurance, 2015 Percent	Medicare, 2015 Total Beneficiaries	Medicare, 2015 Enrolled in Original Medicare	Medicare, 2015 Enrolled in Medicare Advantage	Serious crimes known to police,[2] 2014 Total Number	Serious crimes known to police,[2] 2014 Total Rate[3]
	32	33	34	35	36	37	38	39	40	41	42	43	44	45
TENNESSEE—Cont'd														
Marshall	359	28 077	0.77	384	12.0	332	10.4	3 113	11.8	5 901	3 870	2 031	652	2 081
Maury	1 009	78 928	0.87	1 157	12.9	912	10.1	8 447	11.5	18 226	12 385	5 841	2 319	2 740
Meigs	128	9 864	0.51	121	10.1	153	12.7	1 250	13.4	3 035	1 927	1 108	358	3 073
Monroe	520	43 425	0.88	505	11.0	547	11.9	5 183	14.3	11 142	6 301	4 841	1 324	2 907
Montgomery	3 476	164 653	0.74	3 452	17.6	1 243	6.4	15 248	8.8	21 008	15 857	5 151	6 243	3 330
Moore	104	5 191	0.61	49	7.7	48	7.6	558	11.2	772	611	161	89	1 411
Morgan	2 232	18 281	0.48	217	10.1	238	11.0	1 711	10.8	3 594	1 811	1 783	369	1 681
Obion	461	30 745	0.97	332	10.9	379	12.4	3 100	12.7	8 254	7 011	1 243	1 173	3 779
Overton	286	19 194	0.65	227	10.3	307	13.9	2 184	12.5	4 934	3 952	982	379	1 713
Perry	123	7 496	0.86	103	12.9	104	13.1	837	13.6	2 022	1 359	663	93	1 181
Pickett	74	4 577	0.74	54	10.5	56	10.9	476	12.5	1 179	947	232	48	939
Polk	244	13 895	0.56	157	9.4	220	13.1	1 620	12.2	4 595	3 219	1 376	375	2 246
Putnam	2 582	79 772	1.20	891	11.7	789	10.4	8 009	13.3	18 371	14 125	4 246	2 576	3 483
Rhea	799	34 952	1.21	379	11.7	395	12.2	3 359	13.0	7 683	5 454	2 229	815	2 488
Roane	646	48 683	0.78	437	8.3	714	13.5	4 577	11.2	13 736	7 722	6 014	1 420	2 845
Robertson	703	57 819	0.69	871	12.6	638	9.2	6 637	11.3	11 656	6 495	5 161	1 775	2 618
Rutherford	4 823	267 440	0.89	4 117	13.4	1 881	6.1	27 913	10.5	34 336	20 303	14 033	8 094	2 827
Scott	264	20 686	0.82	277	12.6	265	12.1	2 262	12.4	4 618	2 813	1 805	430	1 953
Sequatchie	188	12 125	0.56	150	10.1	174	11.7	1 357	11.6	2 858	1 931	927	437	2 941
Sevier	980	93 528	1.00	1 066	11.0	988	10.2	12 947	16.7	21 114	11 408	9 706	3 075	3 247
Shelby	18 227	1 014 106	1.18	13 448	14.4	8 326	8.9	110 137	13.6	133 302	92 826	40 476	57 798	6 118
Smith	159	16 871	0.72	223	11.5	201	10.3	1 638	10.1	3 597	2 446	1 151	328	1 716
Stewart	92	11 863	0.70	127	9.6	160	12.1	1 268	11.9	3 021	2 362	659	244	1 821
Sullivan	2 633	165 828	1.14	1 533	9.8	1 957	12.5	13 743	11.2	40 871	16 631	24 240	5 448	3 471
Sumner	1 252	144 998	0.70	2 135	11.9	1 567	8.7	16 182	10.9	28 504	15 272	13 232	2 842	1 659
Tipton	962	47 530	0.47	718	11.7	615	10.0	5 428	10.3	9 731	7 334	2 397	2 001	3 234
Trousdale	130	6 511	0.59	101	12.2	80	9.7	914	13.6	1 442	867	575	224	2 858
Unicoi	405	17 527	0.91	148	8.4	264	14.9	1 835	13.3	4 983	2 613	2 370	297	1 643
Union	152	15 284	0.43	193	10.1	218	11.4	2 409	15.3	3 457	1 480	1 977	551	2 877
Van Buren	94	4 826	0.64	66	11.6	45	7.9	539	12.3	1 036	787	249	128	2 283
Warren	580	39 663	0.98	469	11.6	467	11.5	4 952	15.0	9 821	7 068	2 753	1 124	2 803
Washington	4 199	132 871	1.13	1 321	10.4	1 324	10.4	11 612	11.5	28 911	14 976	13 935	3 622	2 864
Wayne	2 163	15 848	0.81	129	7.7	195	11.7	1 445	12.5	3 271	2 418	853	163	960
Weakley	1 786	31 789	0.81	346	10.3	363	10.8	2 719	10.3	6 380	5 393	987	612	1 779
White	382	24 230	0.79	291	10.9	356	13.4	2 825	13.4	6 763	4 882	1 881	803	3 039
Williamson	1 154	219 934	1.21	2 237	10.2	1 173	5.4	11 184	6.0	25 618	15 563	10 055	2 471	1 215
Wilson	1 285	107 874	0.75	1 509	11.4	1 060	8.0	10 120	9.3	19 792	11 934	7 858	2 693	2 169
TEXAS	608 204	26 534 489	1.00	404 533	14.5	192 814	6.9	4 536 765	19.2	3 501 633	2 215 695	1 285 938	923 348	3 425
Anderson	14 268	58 189	1.01	580	10.0	655	11.3	6 917	19.1	10 136	7 346	2 790	1 376	2 363
Andrews	78	16 728	0.99	348	19.6	119	6.7	3 177	19.5	1 872	1 463	409	515	2 950
Angelina	2 938	89 095	1.04	1 176	13.4	920	10.5	15 867	21.9	17 522	12 646	4 876	3 293	3 733
Aransas	445	22 216	0.77	279	10.8	354	13.8	3 946	21.7	6 299	3 877	2 422	1 128	4 540
Archer	55	6 658	0.50	78	9.0	75	8.6	1 241	17.6	1 223	1 029	194	NA	NA
Armstrong	54	1 491	0.52	17	9.1	27	14.4	273	18.1	403	326	77	16	810
Atascosa	352	43 569	0.82	710	14.6	428	8.8	7 750	18.7	6 854	3 881	2 973	856	1 784
Austin	212	25 910	0.78	363	12.2	272	9.1	4 292	17.8	5 814	4 420	1 394	541	1 855
Bailey	106	6 632	0.84	125	17.4	41	5.7	1 772	29.2	1 060	895	165	122	1 705
Bandera	300	16 942	0.56	160	7.3	209	9.6	2 696	17.2	5 144	3 808	1 336	311	1 498
Bastrop	2 348	63 341	0.57	1 082	13.1	685	8.3	13 903	20.7	12 603	9 068	3 535	1 830	2 384
Baylor	105	3 616	0.99	40	10.8	49	13.3	532	19.6	1 027	848	179	90	2 490
Bee	7 470	32 331	0.97	406	12.4	230	7.0	3 976	18.5	4 197	2 625	1 572	610	1 834
Bell	8 525	338 814	1.09	6 308	18.5	2 230	6.6	38 243	13.0	40 794	27 158	13 636	11 381	3 431
Bexar	43 247	1 869 746	1.05	28 283	14.7	13 458	7.0	274 865	16.8	251 475	130 099	121 376	97 028	5 229
Blanco	105	10 056	0.85	99	8.7	117	10.3	1 799	21.5	2 779	2 161	618	121	1 115
Borden	0	662	0.85	6	9.5	6	9.5	76	14.8	50	38	12	11	1 719
Bosque	329	15 298	0.62	181	10.0	221	12.2	3 068	22.7	4 516	2 921	1 595	210	1 278
Bowie	6 313	99 589	1.18	1 229	13.1	1 039	11.1	11 700	16.0	18 171	14 002	4 169	4 232	4 484
Brazoria	10 510	285 607	0.70	4 932	13.9	2 337	6.6	46 459	15.6	42 446	27 096	15 350	6 482	1 925
Brazos	15 208	209 214	1.04	2 954	13.4	1 084	4.9	31 952	17.4	19 524	15 303	4 221	6 144	2 974
Brewster	44	9 274	1.01	100	10.9	68	7.4	1 371	19.0	1 899	1 385	514	172	1 838
Briscoe	0	1 494	0.76	10	6.8	9	6.1	376	33.3	382	308	74	9	589
Brooks	59	7 578	1.15	113	15.7	81	11.2	1 097	18.7	1 510	938	572	138	1 891
Brown	1 831	38 288	1.03	421	11.0	477	12.5	5 057	17.2	8 736	6 979	1 757	1 200	3 163
Burleson	177	14 870	0.66	216	12.2	206	11.6	2 964	21.2	3 727	2 672	1 055	202	1 169
Burnet	1 196	41 326	0.85	499	10.8	497	10.7	7 640	22.1	12 229	9 013	3 216	900	2 080

1. Per 1,000 estimated resident population.   2. Data for serious crimes have not been adjusted for underreporting; this may affect comparability between geographic areas and over time.
3. Per 100,000 population estimated by the FBI.

Table B. States and Counties — Crime, Education, Money Income, and Poverty

STATE County	Serious crimes known to police, 2014 (cont.)[1] Rate[2] Violent	Property	School enrollment and attainment, 2011–2015 Enrollment[3] Total	Per-cent private	High school grad-uate or less	Bach-elor's degree or more	Local government expenditures,[5] 2013–2014 Total current spending (mil dol)	Current spend-ing per student (dollars)	Per capita income[6] (dollars)	Median income (dollars)	Households Percent with income of less than $50,000	with income of $200,000 or more	Median house-hold income (dollars)	All per-sons	Children under 18 years	Children 5 to 17 years in families
	46	47	48	49	50	51	52	53	54	55	56	57	58	59	60	61

TENNESSEE—Cont'd

STATE County	46	47	48	49	50	51	52	53	54	55	56	57	58	59	60	61
Marshall	575	1 507	7 002	13.3	60.0	13.4	43.0	8 021	21 962	42 661	57.3	1.9	46 788	13.8	20.5	19.0
Maury	419	2 320	18 809	17.6	49.1	19.2	96.8	8 056	24 155	47 692	51.9	2.3	50 868	13.2	19.4	18.6
Meigs	386	2 687	2 216	6.4	66.2	8.2	15.2	8 384	19 212	34 424	65.7	0.7	41 061	20.2	30.2	26.7
Monroe	369	2 538	8 501	9.3	63.1	12.1	58.2	8 127	19 351	35 291	63.2	1.0	37 867	18.6	28.9	26.0
Montgomery	596	2 734	54 378	11.7	38.9	24.6	258.7	8 274	22 916	50 344	49.5	1.9	49 603	13.4	18.4	18.2
Moore	111	1 300	1 372	15.6	53.0	17.6	8.7	8 992	28 841	49 427	51.0	3.4	52 911	11.8	18.8	16.7
Morgan	159	1 521	4 171	10.9	71.3	6.4	26.4	8 112	17 646	39 049	60.9	1.6	46 067	21.2	29.4	26.8
Obion	383	3 395	7 295	9.1	59.1	16.8	43.8	8 427	21 829	40 281	60.8	1.8	39 946	19.5	27.3	25.8
Overton	253	1 459	4 850	7.0	64.8	13.4	25.7	7 584	19 244	35 287	64.5	0.9	36 316	17.5	26.2	23.7
Perry	216	965	1 550	16.9	65.9	11.0	10.4	8 971	18 340	31 425	69.5	0.7	34 445	22.3	33.6	32.6
Pickett	78	861	845	1.1	61.0	11.4	6.2	7 963	20 526	36 773	63.9	0.2	34 714	18.9	29.3	25.8
Polk	198	2 048	3 204	10.7	64.9	9.8	21.0	7 990	21 404	38 925	62.6	1.9	38 923	18.4	28.3	26.3
Putnam	370	3 112	20 053	7.2	54.0	23.3	89.7	8 055	21 835	35 343	62.4	2.2	40 629	19.7	23.8	20.8
Rhea	284	2 204	7 345	10.3	62.4	12.9	41.6	7 830	19 927	36 146	63.2	2.2	39 863	23.3	32.8	29.1
Roane	339	2 506	10 296	12.2	51.7	18.4	61.6	8 685	23 287	40 854	58.6	1.5	43 939	17.6	25.2	23.2
Robertson	478	2 140	16 596	18.3	52.2	17.8	89.6	7 847	24 340	53 151	45.9	2.2	53 413	12.3	18.4	17.5
Rutherford	390	2 437	82 791	12.0	39.3	30.1	403.1	8 286	25 663	56 219	43.5	2.9	60 022	11.1	13.5	12.8
Scott	218	1 735	5 259	4.6	70.3	9.0	34.2	7 774	18 709	30 246	72.8	1.1	33 254	25.5	34.2	33.4
Sequatchie	370	2 570	3 210	12.8	58.2	13.0	16.7	7 143	21 818	45 408	54.7	1.2	43 207	18.7	28.6	27.9
Sevier	302	2 945	18 777	11.6	55.0	16.4	130.1	8 931	22 483	42 258	57.0	2.1	41 987	14.6	23.5	21.3
Shelby	1 306	4 812	258 976	20.5	40.3	30.2	1 381.5	9 221	26 285	46 224	52.9	4.3	46 998	20.2	31.4	28.9
Smith	272	1 444	4 422	8.6	66.3	10.2	25.5	7 932	22 854	43 914	55.0	1.8	44 556	18.1	25.2	23.4
Stewart	403	1 418	3 303	5.4	55.4	14.2	17.2	7 979	21 475	42 023	58.0	0.9	44 266	15.5	25.2	22.7
Sullivan	430	3 041	32 797	13.8	49.4	21.9	196.0	8 912	24 544	40 346	58.4	2.3	42 277	16.4	24.6	21.5
Sumner	246	1 413	42 461	14.5	43.6	24.6	226.1	7 874	28 883	57 382	43.0	4.2	59 816	10.1	13.9	12.5
Tipton	711	2 523	16 128	8.2	53.4	15.0	90.0	7 763	23 572	53 669	46.3	1.9	54 077	14.4	21.0	19.7
Trousdale	485	2 373	1 882	9.9	64.1	14.3	9.5	7 513	20 937	41 029	58.0	2.6	47 531	16.2	24.7	22.7
Unicoi	277	1 366	3 574	6.5	62.4	12.4	21.0	8 174	20 187	33 210	66.8	1.2	36 641	19.2	27.5	24.2
Union	313	2 564	3 943	12.5	69.9	9.1	40.2	6 875	18 654	37 351	64.5	1.3	36 878	23.9	33.9	31.1
Van Buren	232	2 051	1 125	19.3	70.4	12.6	7.1	9 188	20 351	40 439	62.2	0.8	39 348	18.9	30.9	29.3
Warren	434	2 369	9 014	9.0	64.4	13.5	52.6	7 983	20 534	35 376	63.9	1.8	39 357	21.2	30.1	27.2
Washington	316	2 549	33 526	11.1	42.5	30.6	141.7	8 418	26 176	42 817	57.5	3.0	45 261	17.2	22.1	19.3
Wayne	277	683	3 131	6.9	67.1	8.8	21.0	8 521	16 333	30 701	68.2	0.8	34 895	25.4	32.5	28.9
Weakley	204	1 576	10 594	6.7	56.0	20.4	34.6	7 624	19 694	37 037	63.2	1.4	38 025	18.2	24.6	22.9
White	242	2 797	5 605	10.2	64.1	12.1	31.1	7 603	17 451	34 901	67.8	0.4	38 649	18.2	28.4	26.9
Williamson	118	1 097	58 604	23.1	21.0	55.7	333.1	8 732	44 671	96 565	23.5	16.3	104 367	5.0	5.3	4.5
Wilson	323	1 846	30 127	17.4	42.6	28.3	155.8	7 592	28 994	61 070	40.5	4.2	65 372	8.4	11.7	10.8
TEXAS	406	3 019	7 438 819	11.0	43.2	27.6	44 179.3	8 572	26 999	53 207	47.0	5.3	55 668	15.9	22.9	21.9
Anderson	299	2 064	12 583	5.3	57.1	11.3	76.3	9 315	17 876	41 327	58.0	2.2	43 062	21.0	26.9	24.5
Andrews	538	2 412	4 241	5.2	59.1	11.7	35.7	9 471	29 423	70 423	37.7	6.3	72 184	10.4	13.4	12.8
Angelina	340	3 393	22 640	5.0	52.4	15.2	125.3	8 421	21 688	44 223	56.2	2.1	45 428	17.9	27.6	25.2
Aransas	427	4 114	4 153	9.2	46.6	19.5	31.1	9 661	28 472	41 690	56.5	3.6	41 560	18.2	32.9	30.4
Archer	NA	NA	2 080	6.2	47.8	20.6	17.3	9 379	29 380	60 275	42.4	3.4	60 414	9.5	12.8	10.7
Armstrong	152	658	392	3.6	33.6	23.0	3.9	10 466	28 669	59 737	38.4	1.3	55 198	10.4	14.3	13.2
Atascosa	119	1 665	12 484	6.1	60.2	14.0	84.4	9 236	22 493	52 192	47.4	1.7	49 047	20.4	29.9	30.8
Austin	274	1 581	6 948	12.3	45.9	20.1	51.1	8 938	27 658	53 687	46.3	3.8	57 960	12.7	18.9	17.5
Bailey	168	1 537	1 971	5.4	64.2	7.8	13.8	9 366	17 007	37 397	68.1	0.4	38 299	15.8	26.0	25.2
Bandera	96	1 402	3 922	15.0	43.4	22.6	24.3	9 177	26 663	49 863	50.2	2.5	53 662	13.3	23.8	21.7
Bastrop	317	2 068	19 420	8.9	49.8	17.9	137.1	8 691	24 812	54 821	45.1	2.6	56 866	12.7	21.7	20.3
Baylor	249	2 241	835	4.6	43.3	25.8	6.1	10 760	32 907	36 373	65.7	5.3	38 231	17.4	28.4	25.7
Bee	183	1 650	6 780	8.0	60.5	9.7	45.7	8 732	17 209	42 302	58.6	3.5	42 540	23.4	29.0	27.3
Bell	391	3 040	96 367	11.3	38.3	23.1	555.9	8 222	23 535	50 550	49.3	2.6	48 894	15.9	23.0	22.9
Bexar	454	4 775	526 332	13.7	41.9	26.7	2 998.4	8 702	24 735	51 150	48.9	3.9	52 230	15.6	22.2	21.0
Blanco	92	1 023	2 400	12.9	41.8	28.4	19.0	11 289	29 148	55 504	46.3	4.3	53 449	10.9	18.2	15.9
Borden	313	1 406	126	0.0	35.2	31.9	4.5	17 677	44 591	73 750	32.4	8.8	63 358	10.2	14.5	13.9
Bosque	116	1 162	3 824	6.0	52.9	17.0	24.4	10 434	24 658	44 674	55.0	3.1	47 135	15.0	24.6	22.8
Bowie	553	3 931	22 319	7.1	48.7	18.2	157.0	8 728	22 685	42 670	57.0	2.8	42 515	18.6	26.2	25.3
Brazoria	178	1 746	91 415	11.1	39.7	28.6	508.5	7 858	30 634	69 749	36.0	6.4	71 230	10.6	13.5	12.6
Brazos	285	2 689	88 142	5.2	35.0	38.9	241.0	8 350	22 648	39 808	57.8	3.7	44 767	24.0	19.7	18.0
Brewster	171	1 667	2 297	8.5	33.3	39.1	15.6	12 846	27 265	38 395	62.0	3.0	41 785	14.8	21.9	22.3
Briscoe	0	589	406	5.9	49.8	21.8	4.6	12 044	22 323	38 603	55.7	2.7	42 261	16.6	30.4	28.0
Brooks	260	1 631	1 480	2.4	67.0	11.7	16.7	10 844	13 179	22 741	74.8	0.7	30 124	31.7	46.5	48.6
Brown	301	2 863	9 148	13.0	52.4	17.9	60.1	9 089	21 916	41 962	58.8	2.5	41 981	18.2	25.7	24.3
Burleson	145	1 024	3 832	13.2	58.2	14.9	25.9	9 297	24 894	51 821	48.4	3.0	50 113	15.5	24.7	22.6
Burnet	250	1 830	9 411	10.4	46.9	22.7	65.8	9 098	26 578	49 732	50.2	3.4	53 086	13.2	22.3	20.3

1. Data for serious crimes have not been adjusted for underreporting; this may affect comparability between geographic areas and over time. 2. Per 100,000 population estimated by the FBI.
3. All persons 3 years old and over enrolled in nursery school through college. 4. Persons 25 years old and over. 5. Elementary and secondary education expenditures.
6. Based on population estimated by the American Community Survey, 2011–2015.

Table B. States and Counties — Personal Income

STATE County	Total (mil dol)	Percent change, 2014–2015	Per capita¹ Dollars	Per capita¹ Rank	Wages and salaries (mil dol)	Pension and insurance	Government social insurance	Proprietors' income (mil dol)	Dividends, interest, and rent (mil dol)	Personal transfer receipts (mil dol)	Total (mil dol)	From employee and self-employed	From employer
	62	63	64	65	66	67	68	69	70	71	72	73	74
TENNESSEE—Cont'd													
Marshall	1 057	5.2	33 513	2 392	335	65	24	86	131	263	510	33	24
Maury	3 330	7.3	37 947	1 659	1 383	237	99	305	376	767	2 025	126	99
Meigs	359	2.4	30 386	2 243	75	18	5	22	49	125	121	10	5
Monroe	1 395	6.1	30 470	2 784	534	101	40	102	172	458	776	55	40
Montgomery	7 623	4.2	39 400	1 225	1 953	372	140	504	1 231	1 436	2 970	174	140
Moore	241	3.1	38 179	1 690	86	24	6	22	30	61	139	8	6
Morgan	588	4.7	27 329	2 968	109	30	8	43	61	201	191	16	8
Obion	1 094	0.4	35 699	1 826	366	65	26	99	192	333	557	38	26
Overton	663	4.4	29 962	2 897	165	38	12	78	76	216	293	21	12
Perry	228	4.7	28 759	2 844	63	15	5	22	35	97	105	8	5
Pickett	177	7.3	34 472	2 666	38	8	3	28	22	63	76	6	3
Polk	519	1.5	30 937	2 640	79	20	6	40	56	163	144	12	6
Putnam	2 700	3.6	36 215	2 107	1 331	272	94	364	476	673	2 061	123	94
Rhea	1 059	4.0	32 573	2 612	513	107	40	54	119	335	715	46	40
Roane	1 975	4.1	37 441	1 880	1 102	146	72	102	267	608	1 422	95	72
Robertson	2 582	6.5	37 661	1 911	890	177	64	251	274	547	1 382	83	64
Rutherford	11 244	8.2	37 654	1 746	5 710	915	402	1 303	1 208	1 698	8 331	474	402
Scott	598	2.3	27 231	3 014	184	44	14	45	62	241	287	21	14
Sequatchie	498	4.0	33 653	2 404	98	23	7	34	67	161	162	13	7
Sevier	3 329	5.0	34 693	2 397	1 408	208	108	481	467	829	2 205	141	108
Shelby	42 356	3.3	45 153	703	27 177	3 703	1 824	4 509	6 524	7 595	37 213	2 146	1 824
Smith	679	5.2	35 182	2 076	214	43	15	68	100	166	340	22	15
Stewart	505	3.7	38 085	1 541	138	33	11	30	77	143	212	14	11
Sullivan	6 083	3.3	38 799	1 610	3 303	542	227	510	901	1 642	4 583	294	227
Sumner	7 581	6.7	43 079	1 349	2 223	348	157	908	901	1 347	3 637	224	157
Tipton	2 148	3.3	34 721	2 171	426	85	30	122	241	500	663	46	30
Trousdale	281	6.6	34 954	250	52	13	4	32	29	80	100	7	4
Unicoi	622	3.5	34 826	2 247	240	45	20	35	79	234	340	25	20
Union	547	5.1	28 611	3 027	83	20	6	49	58	179	158	14	6
Van Buren	152	6.3	26 693	3 002	29	8	2	15	19	65	54	5	2
Warren	1 299	4.3	32 135	2 624	534	95	38	105	175	401	773	51	38
Washington	4 930	4.1	39 034	1 623	2 507	467	176	450	722	1 151	3 600	218	176
Wayne	471	3.1	28 134	3 008	144	35	10	32	56	170	221	16	10
Weakley	1 106	1.0	32 575	2 354	440	106	31	110	159	343	687	41	31
White	821	3.7	30 967	2 787	243	46	18	89	105	275	396	28	18
Williamson	18 504	10.0	87 419	53	7 629	815	495	5 502	2 360	1 046	14 441	770	495
Wilson	5 602	8.2	43 458	1 034	1 851	255	126	508	655	951	2 741	172	126
TEXAS	1 289 604	4.5	47 015	X	661 654	92 939	44 568	186 307	210 222	190 023	985 468	49 963	44 568
Anderson	1 824	3.2	31 686	2 464	867	150	60	102	255	485	1 179	66	60
Andrews	947	-5.8	52 319	213	471	67	30	179	81	102	747	36	30
Angelina	3 471	5.0	39 328	1 579	1 500	249	103	460	516	865	2 312	124	103
Aransas	1 124	3.4	44 321	813	258	40	18	84	268	286	400	27	18
Archer	432	-2.9	49 597	289	82	15	5	78	65	72	181	9	5
Armstrong	86	4.4	44 078	814	17	3	1	10	16	20	31	2	1
Atascosa	1 862	3.5	38 437	1 575	602	94	40	181	340	389	917	51	40
Austin	1 515	6.6	51 260	542	491	70	34	214	274	246	809	42	34
Bailey	309	3.5	42 925	681	100	19	7	97	36	56	222	7	7
Bandera	890	4.2	41 827	1 080	118	21	8	82	200	202	229	15	8
Bastrop	2 635	7.6	32 723	2 667	650	119	45	246	383	571	1 060	62	45
Baylor	152	0.4	42 081	1 012	46	8	3	26	24	46	83	5	3
Bee	934	-3.1	28 423	2 808	374	76	23	68	174	248	541	28	23
Bell	13 925	5.4	41 574	1 174	7 732	1 744	657	866	2 395	2 690	10 999	508	657
Bexar	81 038	5.8	42 702	1 082	43 439	6 916	3 100	11 116	13 933	13 949	64 571	3 276	3 100
Blanco	531	4.2	48 239	158	131	22	9	61	152	95	222	12	9
Borden	37	15.2	57 151	442	9	2	1	8	14	4	19	1	1
Bosque	728	7.0	40 711	1 428	147	30	9	86	137	192	272	15	9
Bowie	3 462	4.7	37 066	1 806	1 714	333	125	261	617	881	2 432	134	125
Brazoria	15 538	4.7	44 867	898	5 964	918	398	1 180	1 655	2 157	8 461	447	398
Brazos	7 519	5.4	34 964	2 327	4 014	814	252	804	1 405	1 060	5 883	267	252
Brewster	387	4.4	42 337	1 112	153	32	10	32	106	75	227	12	10
Briscoe	63	8.2	42 123	958	13	3	1	13	13	14	30	1	1
Brooks	266	6.2	36 756	1 668	109	24	8	25	28	103	166	9	8
Brown	1 285	5.3	33 917	2 325	585	109	41	106	185	426	841	49	41
Burleson	731	4.9	41 880	1 160	190	30	13	84	119	168	317	18	13
Burnet	2 010	6.0	44 219	786	561	90	38	216	562	430	905	54	38

1. Based on the resident population estimated as of July 1 of the year shown.

Table B. States and Counties — Earnings, Social Security, and Housing

| STATE County | Earnings, 2015 (cont.) Percent by selected industries | | | | | | | | | Social Security beneficiaries, December 2015 | | Housing units, 2016 | | |
	Farm	Mining	Construction	Manu-facturing	Infor-mation: professional, scientific, technical services	Retail trade	Finance, insur-ance, real estate and leasing	Health care and social assistance	Govern-ment	Number	Rate[1]	Supple-mental Security Income recipients, December 2015	Total	Percent change, 2010–2016
	75	76	77	78	79	80	81	82	83	84	85	86	87	88
TENNESSEE—Cont'd														
Marshall	1.0	D	7.0	31.6	3.1	8.9	2.8	4.6	19.3	7 095	225	699	13 417	2.3
Maury	0.1	D	7.1	17.1	5.0	6.6	9.3	10.6	19.8	19 305	220	1 920	36 666	4.0
Meigs	-0.2	D	7.4	33.6	D	3.4	D	7.4	23.9	3 425	288	531	5 727	1.7
Monroe	0.0	D	4.6	37.3	3.2	8.2	2.9	8.9	13.8	13 030	285	1 716	20 877	0.5
Montgomery	0.3	D	7.8	9.5	5.9	10.4	5.3	13.4	24.3	26 160	135	3 345	79 455	13.3
Moore	4.5	D	4.7	D	D	1.4	0.6	D	27.8	1 475	234	71	3 003	3.2
Morgan	1.7	D	8.6	6.9	D	5.4	2.5	11.5	38.8	5 815	271	887	8 877	-0.4
Obion	3.0	D	6.2	15.8	D	13.3	6.6	9.4	17.0	8 710	284	1 090	14 610	-0.3
Overton	-0.1	1.1	9.9	16.7	3.1	8.8	5.5	15.3	20.5	6 280	283	703	10 250	-0.5
Perry	-1.2	D	5.6	24.2	D	7.8	D	D	23.3	2 320	293	264	4 578	-0.5
Pickett	3.7	0.1	11.9	D	1.2	12.5	3.9	D	18.1	1 710	333	160	3 452	-0.2
Polk	8.0	D	6.6	7.8	3.1	7.7	2.7	D	31.1	4 555	272	511	8 621	7.8
Putnam	-0.2	0.2	6.4	13.8	5.4	8.8	5.5	11.0	25.6	17 440	233	2 184	33 695	5.7
Rhea	0.3	D	3.7	28.2	3.0	4.1	2.0	D	40.8	8 220	254	1 227	14 434	0.5
Roane	-0.2	D	3.8	4.2	47.1	4.2	1.4	D	15.6	15 540	295	1 602	25 489	-0.9
Robertson	1.6	D	10.7	30.5	D	6.6	3.5	6.4	15.2	13 575	198	1 280	26 842	2.8
Rutherford	0.0	D	6.4	25.7	5.7	6.7	6.3	10.1	14.8	41 230	138	3 897	115 467	12.1
Scott	-0.3	1.5	9.4	21.9	2.0	7.4	2.6	D	26.0	5 800	264	1 472	9 861	-0.5
Sequatchie	1.1	3.4	6.6	10.8	4.1	7.5	7.0	8.5	28.2	4 130	279	492	6 388	0.3
Sevier	0.0	D	6.0	3.7	3.6	12.4	7.0	6.0	14.3	24 010	251	1 949	56 576	1.3
Shelby	0.0	0.0	4.3	10.5	6.5	6.4	8.1	13.6	13.8	153 890	164	33 964	406 022	1.9
Smith	0.6	D	D	22.7	2.2	7.9	3.6	7.5	17.2	4 430	230	519	8 638	1.3
Stewart	0.2	0.1	15.4	13.4	D	4.7	1.9	4.0	47.3	3 640	275	432	6 766	-0.1
Sullivan	-0.1	D	8.1	25.8	D	6.9	3.6	18.3	10.2	45 390	290	4 751	74 541	1.1
Sumner	0.2	D	12.1	12.7	8.4	7.9	5.7	13.5	12.6	34 245	195	2 567	69 844	5.9
Tipton	-1.9	D	15.1	14.1	D	7.3	3.4	D	24.5	11 795	191	1 455	23 571	1.7
Trousdale	2.6	0.0	D	11.4	4.8	8.1	D	D	26.5	1 925	240	245	3 503	4.1
Unicoi	0.4	D	7.4	37.1	D	4.1	1.3	8.0	15.1	5 240	294	636	8 835	0.0
Union	-1.3	D	D	15.2	D	7.9	D	D	26.7	4 945	259	760	9 152	2.1
Van Buren	1.3	D	D	21.2	D	3.2	D	D	36.9	1 735	305	187	2 648	-0.6
Warren	0.5	0.0	6.3	30.9	D	6.7	3.5	12.6	14.3	10 225	253	1 618	17 852	0.2
Washington	0.2	D	3.9	8.5	6.6	8.2	6.3	22.4	22.4	30 300	240	3 389	59 881	4.5
Wayne	1.3	D	3.5	9.5	D	5.3	4.2	17.3	33.0	4 360	260	428	7 236	-0.7
Weakley	4.9	1.6	3.1	10.5	D	6.0	14.0	D	28.2	7 940	235	865	15 514	0.1
White	-0.2	D	6.4	22.2	D	7.1	3.2	11.1	15.0	7 550	285	973	11 712	1.7
Williamson	0.0	D	5.5	1.4	14.8	5.9	11.2	29.7	4.9	29 080	137	1 034	78 585	14.7
Wilson	-0.3	0.2	9.3	11.3	5.9	12.5	5.4	8.8	11.2	25 115	195	1 599	51 488	12.9
TEXAS	0.6	8.5	7.6	9.1	11.3	5.8	8.1	8.9	13.8	3 928 648	143	666 218	10 753 629	7.8
Anderson	0.7	5.9	4.5	4.9	6.7	5.9	4.7	10.7	25.5	10 300	179	1 484	20 176	0.3
Andrews	0.4	35.1	11.1	2.4	D	3.4	5.3	D	11.9	2 240	124	268	6 213	6.9
Angelina	0.7	5.3	4.6	10.9	5.2	6.6	4.1	18.3	16.0	18 135	206	3 168	36 387	2.2
Aransas	-0.5	D	11.7	1.2	9.6	13.0	6.7	D	14.7	7 585	300	626	16 017	4.3
Archer	8.3	22.6	5.3	4.8	D	6.8	1.8	2.6	15.3	1 880	216	118	4 145	0.9
Armstrong	17.8	0.9	12.8	1.8	4.2	D	D	7.2	21.6	450	234	24	900	-0.4
Atascosa	1.3	19.2	10.0	3.6	3.7	7.8	7.4	6.8	15.0	8 660	179	1 442	17 988	2.0
Austin	6.7	2.9	13.0	14.1	D	10.9	4.9	4.1	9.8	5 980	202	557	13 061	1.1
Bailey	43.8	0.2	2.0	3.9	3.1	2.7	2.3	3.9	10.8	1 135	157	149	2 779	-0.2
Bandera	4.7	5.5	16.9	1.0	7.4	6.3	2.9	D	17.1	5 900	278	364	11 652	0.8
Bastrop	0.6	3.8	15.2	7.1	4.5	10.7	3.6	6.9	22.8	14 255	178	1 894	29 960	2.2
Baylor	13.4	D	9.4	3.3	D	4.8	D	D	14.6	1 075	293	122	2 650	-0.6
Bee	1.9	14.8	2.8	2.4	6.5	7.7	4.2	D	33.0	4 690	144	1 038	10 676	0.3
Bell	0.1	D	5.5	4.1	4.2	5.4	3.2	12.9	50.1	48 065	144	7 904	137 649	9.7
Bexar	0.0	6.9	5.2	3.7	9.6	6.1	11.9	10.9	21.1	286 170	151	56 006	687 624	3.7
Blanco	3.7	D	18.7	5.9	D	6.3	6.4	D	14.4	2 740	248	140	5 743	3.7
Borden	36.5	D	D	2.2	D	9.7	D	D	26.8	130	203	0	385	0.0
Bosque	16.3	D	10.7	12.1	3.9	4.0	3.3	D	23.1	4 890	273	418	9 653	0.3
Bowie	1.0	0.9	4.5	3.9	3.9	9.1	7.3	18.7	28.7	19 590	210	4 103	39 521	2.7
Brazoria	0.3	2.7	18.3	22.5	5.5	6.1	4.0	7.8	13.3	47 185	137	5 576	132 653	12.1
Brazos	0.5	4.5	6.2	4.8	8.8	6.7	5.2	10.0	35.2	21 250	98	3 582	86 775	11.7
Brewster	2.4	0.7	8.5	1.0	9.3	5.4	3.8	D	37.3	2 070	227	207	5 455	1.3
Briscoe	41.8	0.4	D	D	D	3.4	5.4	D	17.8	400	266	36	953	0.0
Brooks	9.6	11.3	2.5	0.1	1.0	4.8	D	6.0	43.5	1 725	239	536	3 231	-0.2
Brown	-0.1	2.5	6.9	23.4	D	8.1	4.2	D	18.6	9 335	246	1 265	18 635	1.9
Burleson	3.7	12.8	11.2	6.2	D	7.2	3.7	D	13.0	4 155	237	496	8 948	1.3
Burnet	0.2	1.8	14.3	10.5	7.8	9.3	5.3	10.7	15.4	11 690	259	728	22 031	5.7

1. Per 1,000 resident population estimated as of July 1 of the year shown.

Table B. States and Counties — Housing, Labor Force, and Employment

STATE County	Housing units, 2011–2015								Civilian labor force, 2016				Civilian employment,[6] 2011–2015		
	Occupied units							Sub-stand-ard units[4] (percent)		Percent change, 2015–2016	Unemployment			Percent	
			Owner-occupied			Renter-occupied								Manage-ment, business, science and arts	Con-struction, produc-tion, and mainte-nance occu-pations
				Median owner cost as a percent of income											
	Total	Percent	Median value[1]	With a mort-gage	Without a mort-gage[2]	Median rent[3]	Median rent as a per-cent of income[2]		Total		Total	Rate[5]	Total		
	89	90	91	92	93	94	95	96	97	98	99	100	101	102	103
TENNESSEE—Cont'd															
Marshall	11 968	72.8	112 300	20.4	11.4	653	29.1	3.2	15 188	2.8	705	4.6	13 637	24.7	36.0
Maury	32 465	68.6	140 800	21.9	10.8	723	29.8	2.2	43 751	3.2	1 802	4.1	38 831	31.3	23.8
Meigs	4 620	79.4	99 500	23.8	11.1	590	32.9	4.7	4 936	1.5	339	6.9	3 907	19.3	46.2
Monroe	17 193	75.5	113 600	22.4	11.0	596	31.9	2.8	19 350	1.5	1 041	5.4	16 178	26.2	34.5
Montgomery	66 234	59.1	145 900	21.7	10.0	876	28.4	2.6	79 415	0.9	4 129	5.2	73 139	32.2	24.2
Moore	2 454	85.1	152 500	21.3	10.4	634	18.7	2.1	3 384	2.3	131	3.9	3 045	24.1	37.9
Morgan	7 370	80.9	92 900	20.7	12.1	640	28.7	3.4	7 858	1.7	515	6.6	6 893	23.3	31.8
Obion	12 665	68.2	87 800	19.2	11.9	575	29.2	1.1	12 600	0.9	902	7.2	12 572	27.6	31.4
Overton	8 893	77.7	101 300	22.2	10.4	551	24.9	3.6	9 225	1.4	506	5.5	8 479	28.5	35.1
Perry	3 226	78.3	79 900	24.9	10.1	529	31.9	4.2	3 194	2.3	207	6.5	2 819	22.1	40.8
Pickett	2 223	82.8	106 700	18.0	11.1	458	26.5	2.3	2 327	-3.1	157	6.7	2 166	32.0	26.3
Polk	6 745	78.1	109 100	21.7	11.0	642	28.8	2.7	7 476	2.0	432	5.8	6 397	26.3	33.5
Putnam	29 721	62.3	144 600	23.3	10.8	616	33.9	2.8	33 210	2.2	1 648	5.0	30 346	33.1	23.3
Rhea	12 545	68.3	106 400	21.3	10.0	583	32.9	3.2	13 409	2.3	986	7.4	12 496	25.9	37.5
Roane	21 887	72.6	120 000	20.7	11.2	682	31.9	2.5	23 015	1.8	1 296	5.6	20 586	31.1	26.8
Robertson	24 641	75.7	155 800	22.6	11.4	813	27.8	2.2	35 045	3.5	1 473	4.2	31 579	31.3	30.9
Rutherford	100 661	66.3	160 700	21.4	10.0	890	29.1	2.6	161 297	3.6	6 067	3.8	141 737	34.6	23.6
Scott	8 309	73.0	84 500	22.8	13.7	537	34.3	0.8	8 021	-0.8	606	7.6	7 780	22.9	38.6
Sequatchie	5 615	74.1	135 700	21.4	10.0	608	29.3	5.2	5 934	2.3	350	5.9	5 676	26.0	32.0
Sevier	36 717	66.5	159 000	22.8	10.0	722	29.5	3.0	51 111	2.4	2 574	5.0	44 811	24.6	20.2
Shelby	347 224	57.3	130 800	23.3	12.3	859	33.7	3.0	435 626	1.2	23 764	5.5	425 295	35.1	22.1
Smith	7 478	76.2	114 000	22.8	10.0	538	28.0	2.8	8 759	3.1	405	4.6	8 121	24.8	37.4
Stewart	5 131	79.5	123 100	22.5	12.7	610	27.2	0.6	5 175	0.6	360	7.0	4 818	31.7	27.6
Sullivan	66 421	73.6	124 900	20.6	10.0	602	28.7	1.7	69 786	0.8	3 697	5.3	66 313	32.4	23.0
Sumner	62 425	72.1	178 000	22.4	10.0	885	28.4	1.9	91 795	3.5	3 611	3.9	82 224	35.1	22.5
Tipton	21 575	72.1	139 600	21.1	10.2	741	28.3	1.8	27 752	0.8	1 607	5.8	27 209	29.2	30.7
Trousdale	2 926	74.8	129 400	21.9	12.3	594	34.1	0.4	3 804	3.2	188	4.9	3 376	23.1	31.1
Unicoi	7 428	74.3	106 200	23.3	11.2	602	35.6	2.8	7 096	0.8	510	7.2	6 462	23.2	36.1
Union	7 302	78.3	106 800	22.9	10.0	585	28.3	4.1	7 338	1.5	429	5.8	6 792	23.7	36.4
Van Buren	2 106	85.9	90 700	21.0	10.0	506	28.8	1.2	2 051	-0.2	129	6.3	2 218	29.4	28.0
Warren	15 661	69.0	97 700	20.5	10.6	581	27.4	2.3	17 791	-0.2	863	4.9	16 304	24.9	38.2
Washington	52 638	66.2	145 800	21.3	10.0	692	29.9	1.7	58 468	1.0	2 864	4.9	57 193	38.5	18.4
Wayne	5 967	81.7	82 300	23.1	11.9	473	26.6	1.0	6 100	-1.5	409	6.7	5 703	24.0	31.7
Weakley	13 678	67.8	94 100	19.5	11.4	561	30.2	1.0	15 769	1.0	957	6.1	14 342	31.7	29.1
White	9 731	78.7	97 900	24.6	11.3	605	35.7	2.0	11 738	2.7	598	5.1	9 769	23.2	35.7
Williamson	69 478	81.0	348 600	20.4	10.0	1 181	28.0	1.2	111 585	3.6	3 873	3.5	97 869	54.8	9.4
Wilson	44 528	77.8	200 300	22.0	10.0	871	31.2	1.6	66 996	3.6	2 619	3.9	59 107	35.3	19.8
TEXAS	9 149 196	62.2	136 000	21.7	11.7	882	29.3	5.4	13 284 651	1.8	612 837	4.6	12 094 262	35.1	22.8
Anderson	16 737	70.4	83 000	22.0	12.9	721	29.2	4.6	23 751	4.3	1 018	4.3	19 859	23.4	28.9
Andrews	5 476	74.7	111 600	16.1	10.0	929	23.4	8.1	8 639	-6.8	417	4.8	7 923	22.2	42.1
Angelina	30 583	66.0	87 100	20.1	11.2	773	30.5	5.0	36 713	-1.5	2 198	6.0	36 182	26.8	30.0
Aransas	9 682	72.7	144 000	23.8	14.6	822	32.9	3.0	10 016	-0.1	574	5.7	9 464	28.6	28.8
Archer	3 350	83.3	107 500	19.6	10.4	659	24.3	1.9	4 074	-0.9	181	4.4	4 239	33.7	30.6
Armstrong	714	76.1	106 600	17.2	10.0	708	17.7	2.4	973	0.1	27	2.8	954	39.2	28.6
Atascosa	15 363	74.3	94 100	18.7	10.8	742	24.4	7.9	21 133	3.2	1 127	5.3	19 975	23.3	34.0
Austin	11 038	73.9	157 000	23.1	11.4	825	26.8	4.4	14 128	0.9	753	5.3	13 483	30.8	31.2
Bailey	2 392	69.4	58 300	26.8	10.4	683	24.2	13.7	2 707	-3.0	119	4.4	3 191	23.2	33.8
Bandera	8 292	83.5	146 100	21.1	12.1	834	28.6	2.6	9 402	2.8	388	4.1	9 010	35.8	24.5
Bastrop	25 454	78.1	129 500	21.9	12.0	917	27.9	5.6	38 735	3.5	1 443	3.7	32 343	31.5	28.2
Baylor	1 723	80.1	81 400	23.1	15.5	480	20.1	0.9	1 604	-1.0	58	3.6	1 486	37.6	28.5
Bee	8 762	61.8	72 900	20.5	12.3	802	27.4	6.8	10 272	-0.7	791	7.7	10 451	21.3	30.0
Bell	109 844	55.2	127 500	21.2	11.0	861	28.5	3.2	140 722	3.6	6 232	4.4	127 550	32.1	21.8
Bexar	618 831	58.5	129 400	21.8	11.3	876	29.5	4.9	902 623	3.0	33 598	3.7	824 123	34.6	19.4
Blanco	4 164	75.4	175 000	23.3	12.4	744	26.1	4.8	5 894	2.5	180	3.1	4 670	36.3	23.7
Borden	262	67.6	83 500	11.4	10.0	933	24.2	0.8	391	-4.9	14	3.6	282	52.8	21.3
Bosque	6 999	77.4	88 800	18.9	11.8	629	25.9	4.1	8 162	1.6	355	4.3	7 165	28.5	31.7
Bowie	33 423	66.0	101 800	21.2	11.3	721	32.5	3.2	39 529	1.3	1 869	4.7	35 959	29.7	25.9
Brazoria	112 510	71.8	152 900	20.1	10.0	904	26.2	4.8	168 419	1.1	8 702	5.2	154 290	41.0	23.8
Brazos	73 858	44.8	160 000	21.5	11.0	861	38.5	3.9	110 420	2.0	3 777	3.4	98 294	40.1	18.0
Brewster	4 025	57.8	112 700	20.2	10.0	617	24.0	4.5	3 968	1.8	150	3.8	4 385	43.4	18.4
Briscoe	675	74.1	60 000	17.4	10.0	618	25.0	3.0	549	-7.4	24	4.4	757	33.7	33.0
Brooks	2 080	68.8	52 100	28.9	14.8	538	37.7	6.9	2 420	-6.7	287	11.9	2 416	19.6	22.7
Brown	13 295	70.7	90 400	21.2	12.6	661	30.2	1.8	16 077	1.5	700	4.4	15 006	32.3	25.4
Burleson	6 401	80.2	93 100	20.1	10.0	712	24.9	6.3	7 876	1.8	369	4.7	7 352	27.4	33.5
Burnet	16 940	72.9	158 900	24.6	12.8	847	27.8	2.6	21 848	3.5	757	3.5	18 673	29.3	27.3

1. Specified owner-occupied units. 2. A value of 10.0 represents 10 percent or less; a value of 50.0 represents 50 percent or more. 3. Specified renter-occupied units. 4. Overcrowded or lacking complete plumbing facilities. 5. Percent of civilian labor force. 6. Civilian employed persons 16 years old and over.

Table B. States and Counties — **Nonfarm Employment and Agriculture**

STATE County	Number of establishments	Total	Health care and social assistance	Manufacturing	Retail trade	Finance and insurance	Professional, scientific, and technical services	Total (mil dol)	Average per employee (dollars)	Number	Fewer than 50 acres	500 acres or more	Farm operators whose principal occupation is farming (percent)
	104	105	106	107	108	109	110	111	112	113	114	115	116

Column group headers: Private nonfarm establishments, employment and payroll, 2015 — Employment (cols 105–110), Annual payroll (cols 111–112); Agriculture, 2012 — Farms (cols 113–115, with "Percent with:" over 114–115), col 116.

STATE County	104	105	106	107	108	109	110	111	112	113	114	115	116
TENNESSEE—Cont'd													
Marshall	477	8 195	716	3 559	1 079	202	107	305	37 231	1 025	34.4	5.4	50.4
Maury	1 732	25 489	5 247	3 822	4 437	1 724	636	1 016	39 879	1 513	39.4	6.3	40.0
Meigs	108	1 495	113	849	223	33	D	51	34 041	317	28.7	5.4	39.1
Monroe	708	11 490	1 332	4 861	1 741	313	186	383	33 295	872	42.0	4.0	48.2
Montgomery	2 776	42 060	7 695	5 461	8 504	1 275	1 620	1 390	33 056	783	38.6	7.8	34.4
Moore	65	1 014	124	D	105	12	12	52	51 076	358	32.1	7.8	45.3
Morgan	158	1 246	311	210	265	45	9	41	32 787	413	32.9	4.4	48.9
Obion	634	8 876	1 054	2 599	1 696	420	112	292	32 908	568	32.6	16.5	57.0
Overton	301	3 478	774	764	498	136	99	122	35 041	922	39.6	4.1	32.9
Perry	112	1 718	425	788	195	53	8	48	27 957	246	19.5	6.1	40.2
Pickett	83	705	137	67	96	46	8	23	32 177	316	34.2	3.5	30.4
Polk	215	1 401	321	119	314	68	9	40	28 360	255	45.5	6.7	58.0
Putnam	1 732	28 230	5 566	4 283	4 945	964	560	982	34 781	898	46.1	3.1	33.9
Rhea	492	8 247	1 046	3 625	1 130	217	103	274	33 219	411	40.1	5.6	44.8
Roane	731	8 107	1 977	1 033	1 660	228	551	239	29 423	519	45.9	1.2	34.9
Robertson	1 105	18 624	2 074	6 697	2 293	384	243	698	37 502	1 180	46.6	6.6	45.3
Rutherford	4 891	102 716	11 837	16 524	13 806	4 252	2 793	4 341	42 258	1 327	46.5	4.6	41.8
Scott	312	3 419	659	1 009	631	132	28	106	30 940	302	30.8	3.0	43.4
Sequatchie	175	1 977	498	163	429	170	52	55	27 885	188	39.4	8.5	38.8
Sevier	2 657	36 759	2 457	1 516	8 061	897	719	1 001	27 221	603	40.1	1.3	41.3
Shelby	19 311	430 779	67 976	28 117	46 337	15 813	18 008	21 122	49 032	411	53.3	7.8	42.1
Smith	261	3 851	458	1 154	609	112	71	143	37 138	850	24.4	4.4	45.1
Stewart	150	1 288	215	310	297	58	19	38	29 418	350	28.0	7.1	38.6
Sullivan	3 352	64 048	12 041	15 231	8 591	1 891	1 637	2 790	43 561	1 074	58.0	1.8	34.8
Sumner	3 059	43 607	6 484	8 218	6 033	1 545	1 653	1 781	40 844	1 355	48.6	4.1	40.7
Tipton	710	8 815	1 314	1 866	1 617	308	149	293	33 258	520	44.6	10.6	42.9
Trousdale	117	1 087	211	193	204	67	44	29	26 761	290	32.8	4.5	37.6
Unicoi	251	3 836	522	1 671	508	80	13	153	39 783	93	60.2	0.0	31.2
Union	183	1 614	133	516	360	35	32	47	29 064	408	38.0	1.5	42.4
Van Buren	35	444	D	D	28	D	D	14	31 396	245	42.0	5.7	55.1
Warren	718	10 257	1 575	3 625	1 591	319	116	362	35 305	1 122	41.5	6.3	50.4
Washington	2 797	50 837	14 168	4 432	8 669	2 629	1 544	1 979	38 923	1 312	55.6	2.1	49.0
Wayne	210	2 746	738	580	323	183	35	88	31 965	664	19.4	7.7	35.2
Weakley	564	7 681	1 545	1 411	1 248	313	103	223	28 991	861	33.7	12.8	45.5
White	388	5 160	839	1 916	803	133	41	181	35 101	927	38.9	5.0	38.9
Williamson	6 584	112 133	15 155	2 402	13 570	10 912	9 537	6 807	60 709	1 160	46.5	3.5	43.6
Wilson	2 516	36 481	3 999	4 046	5 878	1 087	1 077	1 459	40 001	1 473	37.4	3.7	41.8
TEXAS	569 091	10 239 710	1 449 547	811 053	1 279 651	508 715	684 780	521 096	50 890	248 809	37.7	15.8	42.1
Anderson	931	11 781	2 225	344	1 987	296	204	448	38 043	2 001	38.3	6.5	39.4
Andrews	409	5 991	572	387	557	118	258	318	53 154	169	37.3	39.1	30.8
Angelina	1 850	30 916	8 179	4 778	4 939	848	827	1 049	33 936	975	47.5	3.3	39.8
Aransas	511	4 166	488	45	1 037	163	151	124	29 793	100	49.0	8.0	34.0
Archer	208	1 277	89	134	116	20	46	48	37 550	531	17.1	36.2	47.1
Armstrong	39	308	67	NA	59	5	D	9	28 016	281	5.7	55.5	45.9
Atascosa	780	12 215	1 207	213	1 952	267	305	524	42 919	1 987	29.8	15.0	37.4
Austin	609	7 665	654	1 096	1 019	290	240	299	39 044	2 098	38.5	7.2	36.1
Bailey	151	1 379	226	305	221	63	36	40	29 323	494	9.5	39.3	46.6
Bandera	371	3 133	391	32	330	84	102	88	28 089	1 002	36.3	17.9	45.7
Bastrop	1 223	13 333	1 720	1 183	3 133	430	401	440	33 038	2 083	40.2	6.7	49.0
Baylor	115	849	387	D	105	43	25	21	24 744	277	7.6	38.3	58.1
Bee	492	5 632	1 036	225	1 151	179	234	194	34 516	974	31.6	16.9	45.2
Bell	4 952	89 907	25 771	6 156	14 659	3 170	3 255	3 533	39 293	2 533	50.8	6.3	34.2
Bexar	35 170	709 657	113 367	32 424	90 902	61 049	43 051	31 183	43 941	2 457	56.8	4.8	41.4
Blanco	274	2 023	168	223	212	77	97	79	39 009	792	29.8	24.6	41.7
Borden	8	17	NA	NA	D	NA	D	1	36 471	114	7.0	58.8	50.9
Bosque	275	2 439	505	511	366	115	52	80	32 614	1 265	26.1	17.9	41.6
Bowie	2 182	32 359	7 356	2 086	6 391	1 330	1 767	1 090	33 679	1 619	44.4	6.9	40.4
Brazoria	5 355	86 188	8 586	14 421	14 845	2 131	3 429	4 388	50 914	3 091	61.8	8.6	36.4
Brazos	4 139	64 393	9 314	5 328	10 925	1 524	3 406	2 225	34 546	1 412	46.0	7.5	34.7
Brewster	286	2 539	519	49	377	171	36	68	26 659	202	17.3	52.5	51.0
Briscoe	39	126	D	D	22	23	D	4	32 159	282	5.0	44.7	46.5
Brooks	131	1 546	295	NA	297	84	14	42	26 898	374	19.5	21.7	43.3
Brown	892	13 068	3 412	2 484	1 960	425	199	420	32 170	1 918	33.7	13.5	36.5
Burleson	331	3 116	300	440	611	107	171	125	40 005	1 429	30.9	10.6	49.1
Burnet	1 178	10 789	1 766	815	2 166	340	427	389	36 081	1 481	36.5	12.5	35.6

Table B. States and Counties — **Agriculture**

	Agriculture, 2012 (cont.)														
	Land in farms					Value of land and buildings (dollars)			Value of products sold				Percent of farms with sales of:		Government payments	
STATE County			Acres					Value of machinery and equipment, average per farm (dollars)			Percent from:					
	Acreage (1,000)	Percent change, 2007–2012	Average size of farm	Total irrigated (1,000)	Total cropland (1,000)	Average per farm	Average per acre		Total (mil dol)	Average per farm (dollars)	Crops	Live-stock and poultry products	$10,000 or more	$100,000 or more	Total ($1,000)	Percent of farms
	117	118	119	120	121	122	123	124	125	126	127	128	129	130	131	132
TENNESSEE—Cont'd																
Marshall	162	6.9	158	0.0	62.5	477 125	3 017	54 191	38.7	37 764	12.0	88.0	32.5	6.8	534	20.7
Maury	242	7.1	160	0.5	90.1	584 794	3 649	59 194	43.3	28 632	36.7	63.3	29.1	4.0	886	16.1
Meigs	53	7.7	167	0.1	20.0	587 246	3 520	57 767	6.9	21 647	19.3	80.7	30.9	3.8	153	19.6
Monroe	111	19.5	127	0.1	48.1	571 742	4 507	62 169	33.1	37 969	22.4	77.6	26.3	6.4	282	13.9
Montgomery	147	-2.7	188	0.7	77.1	811 156	4 310	79 954	47.3	60 350	77.0	23.0	35.0	8.9	1 031	31.5
Moore	59	13.3	164	0.0	14.8	578 542	3 528	69 791	22.6	63 045	D	D	38.0	9.8	128	13.4
Morgan	55	4.0	134	0.0	19.5	460 262	3 427	57 613	15.1	36 567	7.8	92.2	24.9	3.9	70	6.3
Obion	253	0.4	445	6.1	211.8	1 418 014	3 186	191 794	141.0	248 166	72.5	27.5	48.9	23.1	3 270	65.7
Overton	123	7.2	133	0.1	36.1	433 815	3 250	49 648	16.4	17 787	19.3	80.7	31.0	2.9	345	17.8
Perry	48	-6.3	194	0.0	13.8	384 012	1 981	41 463	2.4	9 951	33.9	66.1	26.0	1.6	155	31.3
Pickett	42	10.2	132	0.0	14.5	384 127	2 905	53 035	12.0	37 842	9.2	90.8	36.7	3.8	144	23.4
Polk	36	9.8	139	0.1	16.3	623 392	4 470	73 286	38.0	149 188	9.0	91.0	35.7	16.1	180	11.8
Putnam	96	-7.7	107	D	31.4	461 269	4 329	51 198	11.5	12 845	23.2	76.8	24.9	2.3	236	13.6
Rhea	58	2.7	140	0.8	24.4	490 925	3 499	56 000	16.8	40 886	55.2	44.8	28.5	4.4	194	16.3
Roane	47	-10.7	90	0.0	14.0	460 058	5 085	48 503	4.9	9 357	21.0	79.0	21.0	0.8	70	9.2
Robertson	209	-8.0	177	2.3	140.7	862 760	4 869	106 988	134.9	114 306	83.8	16.2	37.9	13.5	1 789	31.5
Rutherford	176	7.2	133	0.7	70.4	647 736	4 878	58 704	28.4	21 424	54.3	45.7	26.5	3.1	691	11.8
Scott	39	25.9	130	D	14.9	366 026	2 824	54 722	4.3	14 189	10.1	89.9	11.3	0.7	56	9.3
Sequatchie	31	7.0	163	D	10.0	528 037	3 236	72 968	7.0	37 404	15.1	84.9	31.9	8.0	66	17.0
Sevier	56	-1.6	92	0.0	17.1	545 836	5 926	48 391	5.3	8 713	22.1	77.9	24.0	0.7	61	13.8
Shelby	82	-11.3	199	4.3	60.4	913 324	4 586	77 803	31.8	77 387	94.2	5.8	26.3	8.0	733	22.9
Smith	130	2.0	153	0.2	36.8	405 628	2 658	52 353	18.9	22 205	40.3	59.7	32.2	3.3	507	19.5
Stewart	61	9.5	173	0.2	20.7	455 657	2 629	73 034	8.2	23 537	68.6	31.4	27.4	3.4	176	22.6
Sullivan	85	3.4	79	0.1	31.7	436 682	5 526	46 955	17.8	16 535	9.8	90.2	20.5	2.2	254	16.3
Sumner	167	-8.9	123	0.2	68.7	600 046	4 864	57 937	47.2	34 830	51.7	48.3	27.4	5.4	1 321	22.0
Tipton	155	-8.7	299	5.7	127.3	887 075	2 967	121 448	67.6	130 064	96.8	3.2	33.1	13.3	2 213	44.0
Trousdale	41	-6.2	142	0.1	13.9	548 321	3 854	65 507	8.2	28 259	36.4	63.6	41.4	4.5	90	24.1
Unicoi	5	14.4	58	D	1.9	321 409	5 511	32 602	D	D	D	D	9.7	2.2	7	7.5
Union	45	-1.5	111	0.0	12.8	320 044	2 887	57 931	3.3	8 039	14.1	85.9	20.8	0.7	183	17.6
Van Buren	37	6.1	151	D	11.0	561 576	3 721	60 033	5.6	22 727	17.5	82.5	29.4	3.3	221	20.0
Warren	163	1.7	146	5.4	83.7	519 646	3 569	73 327	88.2	78 595	79.6	20.4	48.1	13.3	531	13.9
Washington	112	-5.8	85	0.9	49.4	546 271	6 417	67 845	38.6	29 405	33.5	66.5	28.3	5.3	381	22.4
Wayne	133	15.7	201	0.2	36.7	404 798	2 014	52 301	22.3	33 581	15.1	84.9	39.8	4.7	533	20.3
Weakley	254	-0.6	295	3.2	203.8	878 358	2 976	140 220	129.6	150 479	66.0	34.0	42.5	19.0	2 897	51.8
White	122	-7.6	131	0.1	39.6	494 409	3 766	60 759	25.4	27 435	14.9	85.1	41.3	2.7	344	16.5
Williamson	139	-14.3	120	0.5	52.4	882 452	7 376	54 664	23.6	20 338	46.1	53.9	24.7	3.8	254	12.2
Wilson	188	-2.4	128	0.2	57.2	566 389	4 432	47 804	18.4	12 470	16.5	83.5	27.6	1.5	423	11.3
TEXAS	130 153	-0.2	523	4 489.2	29 147.5	876 614	1 676	72 180	25 375.6	101 988	29.0	71.0	29.7	7.0	643 993	21.1
Anderson	375	8.4	187	0.9	70.3	458 514	2 446	50 885	44.6	22 278	30.6	69.4	24.5	2.6	835	5.3
Andrews	752	-7.0	4 450	5.0	71.5	1 459 077	328	91 710	12.6	74 426	46.3	53.7	24.3	12.4	1 436	34.9
Angelina	117	1.5	120	0.2	21.7	378 739	3 157	45 106	46.4	47 639	9.2	90.8	24.3	3.3	168	2.6
Aransas	40	-21.8	398	0.0	2.6	679 110	1 704	43 180	1.1	10 750	18.4	81.6	14.0	2.0	93	24.0
Archer	541	6.7	1 020	0.2	115.6	1 002 917	984	87 567	76.8	144 674	16.6	83.4	53.5	21.8	2 480	40.7
Armstrong	434	-15.9	1 545	4.6	143.0	1 623 819	1 051	116 189	19.2	68 349	42.1	57.9	38.8	16.7	2 637	76.2
Atascosa	665	3.4	335	26.7	108.1	655 914	1 959	57 840	85.0	42 778	32.7	67.3	25.2	4.1	1 512	16.8
Austin	370	10.8	176	4.3	71.2	720 469	4 086	48 374	43.5	20 754	40.1	59.9	32.1	3.1	1 256	12.1
Bailey	472	-1.0	955	48.5	307.7	768 374	805	162 789	292.4	592 000	10.9	89.1	38.3	21.9	8 049	80.4
Bandera	402	22.2	402	0.6	34.1	1 082 003	2 694	42 303	11.2	11 166	11.3	88.7	16.3	0.8	455	7.1
Bastrop	388	-3.6	186	2.9	60.3	695 536	3 738	49 157	35.3	16 955	33.7	66.3	26.0	2.7	1 678	12.0
Baylor	544	-0.6	1 963	1.9	146.8	2 039 458	1 039	143 347	44.7	161 509	33.2	66.8	57.0	24.2	2 780	77.6
Bee	539	-1.7	553	5.1	70.4	1 032 344	1 866	56 745	26.0	26 739	38.2	61.8	25.6	4.4	1 051	17.9
Bell	421	-2.5	166	3.1	170.5	509 341	3 062	64 187	84.9	33 510	69.0	31.0	22.5	3.8	2 125	16.3
Bexar	343	-19.5	140	8.3	89.1	597 423	4 281	44 547	72.4	29 462	75.6	24.4	17.1	2.7	706	10.0
Blanco	364	-8.0	460	0.5	22.1	2 172 696	4 728	46 035	19.1	24 172	47.3	52.7	27.4	1.8	481	9.3
Borden	464	6.7	4 073	5.0	63.1	2 381 579	585	242 132	9.4	82 781	56.6	43.4	36.8	16.7	1 527	74.6
Bosque	570	3.4	450	0.7	70.3	1 089 916	2 420	55 434	78.3	61 894	64.1	35.9	31.9	5.2	466	11.2
Bowie	273	-6.4	169	5.9	77.8	382 695	2 269	51 216	66.0	40 780	21.2	78.8	29.4	5.4	1 209	13.1
Brazoria	631	19.3	204	20.4	175.9	619 773	3 036	59 444	118.2	38 252	60.5	39.5	21.8	3.5	4 831	9.4
Brazos	299	8.5	212	7.3	41.9	798 834	3 771	53 654	95.0	67 278	13.1	86.9	26.3	4.2	1 409	8.6
Brewster	1 913	9.5	9 469	0.5	47.1	4 436 252	469	85 431	9.9	49 025	10.5	89.5	31.2	12.4	1 041	15.8
Briscoe	524	-4.1	1 859	22.8	139.6	1 550 957	834	128 057	20.4	72 465	62.6	37.4	36.5	20.2	3 481	84.4
Brooks	573	4.4	1 532	1.1	26.0	1 628 016	1 063	53 329	50.8	135 743	1.1	98.9	26.7	2.9	320	25.4
Brown	595	6.3	310	3.5	84.6	635 187	2 046	45 413	40.7	21 209	18.5	81.5	22.1	2.1	1 191	18.0
Burleson	335	-7.1	235	19.6	81.2	674 186	2 873	67 470	90.1	63 022	38.1	61.9	32.7	5.6	1 432	10.9
Burnet	485	0.6	328	1.7	44.7	1 089 307	3 324	42 226	14.7	9 935	25.3	74.7	19.4	1.6	588	6.6

Table B. States and Counties — **Water Use, Wholesale Trade, Retail Trade, and Real Estate**

STATE County	Water use, 2010		Wholesale trade,[1] 2012				Retail trade,[2] 2012				Real estate and rental and leasing,[2] 2012			
	Total water withdrawn (mil gal/day)	Gallons withdrawn per person per day	Number of establishments	Number of employees	Sales (mil dol)	Annual payroll (mil dol)	Number of establishments	Number of employees	Sales (mil dol)	Annual payroll (mil dol)	Number of establishments	Number of employees	Receipts (mil dol)	Annual payroll (mil dol)
	133	134	135	136	137	138	139	140	141	142	143	144	145	146
TENNESSEE—Cont'd														
Marshall	4.8	155	14	D	D	D	102	1 033	289.1	23.3	16	35	4.7	0.8
Maury	13.4	165	61	977	474.0	46.8	327	4 023	1 132.0	94.1	68	238	46.4	7.6
Meigs	1.5	130	1	D	D	D	29	198	51.9	3.9	4	6	0.3	0.1
Monroe	10.2	228	23	133	36.7	4.6	141	1 630	412.1	36.4	27	44	6.6	1.0
Montgomery	25.4	148	77	1 020	587.5	46.0	533	8 205	2 146.2	199.1	145	623	103.9	19.2
Moore	1.7	270	2	D	D	D	15	80	16.3	1.3	1	D	D	D
Morgan	2.4	108	3	D	D	D	33	253	54.2	4.2	1	D	D	D
Obion	8.9	281	33	423	301.5	14.5	142	1 826	457.7	40.1	22	60	7.3	1.3
Overton	3.0	134	8	D	D	D	63	498	164.1	10.9	8	D	D	D
Perry	1.9	239	1	D	D	D	29	188	40.2	3.6	3	3	0.4	0.1
Pickett	0.9	177	1	D	D	D	26	121	30.0	2.7	1	D	D	D
Polk	4.7	276	5	D	D	D	46	370	84.3	7.1	4	D	D	D
Putnam	15.5	215	65	1 150	427.2	52.2	349	4 782	1 282.9	104.4	63	172	34.2	4.5
Rhea	24.9	781	7	D	D	D	107	1 150	281.1	22.7	21	97	8.4	1.7
Roane	272.2	5 023	20	D	D	D	151	1 746	472.3	39.4	20	65	11.1	1.9
Robertson	9.7	146	39	739	724.1	23.5	172	2 313	675.2	58.2	35	95	12.2	2.1
Rutherford	38.8	148	219	6 361	14 847.0	287.0	829	12 376	3 515.3	281.7	188	990	314.0	44.2
Scott	2.7	122	4	15	9.8	0.6	67	633	153.3	13.8	10	13	2.5	0.4
Sequatchie	1.4	96	9	55	83.4	1.4	37	391	104.0	9.1	7	21	4.1	0.5
Sevier	13.4	149	38	D	D	D	645	7 349	1 561.1	150.9	146	1 185	143.2	32.0
Shelby	646.3	697	1 180	24 270	35 454.3	1 374.8	3 056	46 778	22 058.5	1 261.1	923	6 988	1 437.0	306.3
Smith	2.8	144	7	D	D	D	60	579	158.9	14.4	9	21	2.6	0.5
Stewart	1 291.4	96 924	3	8	1.4	0.2	37	289	86.6	6.3	4	18	1.3	0.2
Sullivan	512.0	3 265	174	1 733	1 006.2	67.9	547	8 149	2 095.9	187.4	110	443	77.7	13.2
Sumner	622.2	3 873	117	1 572	2 117.7	72.8	449	5 756	1 503.6	136.8	131	785	152.0	41.4
Tipton	9.1	148	18	D	D	D	145	1 667	393.6	33.3	25	80	10.5	2.2
Trousdale	1.2	155	3	D	D	D	30	234	56.2	4.4	1	D	D	D
Unicoi	6.2	336	8	D	D	D	37	505	129.5	11.1	6	19	2.4	0.7
Union	1.8	94	7	D	D	D	40	346	87.6	6.8	4	D	D	D
Van Buren	1.4	243	1	D	D	D	10	60	9.4	0.8	2	D	D	D
Warren	10.6	266	26	D	D	D	157	1 618	376.4	34.6	22	51	11.8	1.5
Washington	23.3	190	118	1 259	791.3	52.2	520	8 260	2 011.5	174.7	114	588	91.7	18.0
Wayne	2.3	135	5	D	D	D	45	335	65.0	5.8	5	D	D	D
Weakley	5.4	153	27	295	243.0	13.6	123	1 178	297.4	24.5	20	57	9.3	1.1
White	4.4	168	15	D	D	D	82	811	209.4	18.6	14	32	2.4	0.6
Williamson	4.1	23	237	2 762	10 285.7	186.4	766	12 866	3 968.6	354.4	249	1 397	500.8	77.0
Wilson	17.0	149	88	1 646	1 362.9	88.5	403	5 471	1 432.6	123.7	106	542	94.8	18.5
TEXAS	24 796.7	986	27 752	408 692	691 242.6	24 826.1	78 281	1 150 148	356 116.4	28 835.5	26 639	169 941	38 757.4	7 751.8
Anderson	28.7	491	33	D	D	D	164	1 913	572.1	47.1	34	124	34.7	5.8
Andrews	64.0	4 329	15	D	D	D	30	344	169.8	12.5	15	114	26.7	8.5
Angelina	15.2	175	62	808	360.6	35.2	324	4 580	1 274.7	109.4	79	329	54.4	10.8
Aransas	0.7	29	8	63	10.5	1.1	73	920	288.9	25.0	36	79	13.3	1.9
Archer	7.0	768	13	D	D	D	14	102	25.5	1.8	3	D	D	D
Armstrong	4.7	2 462	3	D	D	D	4	D	D	D	1	D	D	D
Atascosa	41.2	917	38	D	D	D	115	1 709	564.7	38.8	35	226	66.5	11.6
Austin	7.0	246	23	679	728.8	34.1	83	939	272.4	22.4	20	47	9.5	1.5
Bailey	65.2	9 096	19	D	D	D	21	229	49.0	4.3	NA	NA	NA	NA
Bandera	3.4	165	5	28	8.1	1.1	49	299	81.2	5.7	8	18	2.8	0.6
Bastrop	223.3	3 011	34	D	D	D	175	2 462	867.8	59.6	44	132	24.8	3.7
Baylor	6.0	1 602	6	35	30.9	1.4	16	99	24.0	1.7	1	D	D	D
Bee	8.5	266	12	D	D	D	78	1 050	330.6	26.1	27	98	17.8	3.7
Bell	73.6	237	126	2 616	3 630.5	135.2	922	13 098	3 626.1	293.2	299	1 486	217.9	50.4
Bexar	1 342.1	783	1 464	D	D	D	4 845	80 840	26 480.6	1 994.5	1 718	13 472	3 054.2	601.3
Blanco	2.2	212	8	D	D	D	32	209	68.7	4.7	4	9	1.1	0.2
Borden	6.7	10 374	NA	NA	NA	NA	1	D	D	D	NA	NA	NA	NA
Bosque	9.7	533	10	77	22.0	2.9	53	417	90.7	8.1	10	23	2.1	0.5
Bowie	16.0	173	90	D	D	D	413	6 170	1 611.3	146.2	102	455	93.3	17.3
Brazoria	856.3	2 734	228	1 865	1 636.4	102.3	797	13 282	3 686.3	314.0	248	1 566	392.8	77.3
Brazos	67.9	349	140	1 704	1 191.8	86.6	629	9 807	2 672.0	207.8	231	1 299	260.8	43.5
Brewster	3.7	403	11	D	D	D	49	405	87.7	8.0	21	148	5.4	1.2
Briscoe	26.8	16 359	4	D	D	D	6	23	6.3	0.4	1	D	D	D
Brooks	3.3	457	2	D	D	D	18	297	85.8	6.7	4	10	2.1	0.3
Brown	16.0	420	35	D	D	D	181	1 872	509.0	41.5	36	132	20.0	3.9
Burleson	29.3	1 705	18	D	D	D	58	653	293.2	17.9	6	14	3.1	0.6
Burnet	16.9	396	41	336	163.1	14.8	182	2 015	617.7	52.1	46	148	25.8	5.2

1. Merchant wholesalers, except manufacturers' sales branches and offices.   2. Employer establishments.

STATE County	Professional, scientific, and technical services, 2012				Manufacturing, 2012				Accommodation and food services, 2012			
	Number of establishments	Number of employees	Receipts (mil dol)	Annual payroll (mil dol)	Number of establishments	Number of employees	Receipts (mil dol)	Annual payroll (mil dol)	Number of establishments	Number of employees	Sales (mil dol)	Annual payroll (mil dol)
	147	148	149	150	151	152	153	154	155	156	157	158
TENNESSEE—Cont'd												
Marshall	30	88	7.7	2.2	45	2 656	1 085.2	128.0	45	512	25.5	6.4
Maury	104	620	57.8	23.4	76	3 582	1 902.1	201.5	158	2 859	123.1	35.4
Meigs	3	D	D	D	11	753	233.0	28.2	15	D	D	D
Monroe	42	197	16.2	6.1	60	4 333	1 509.3	171.6	82	918	41.7	10.6
Montgomery	177	1 677	235.5	78.7	68	5 519	2 256.0	258.2	338	6 157	296.8	81.1
Moore	4	D	D	D	5	D	D	D	8	D	D	D
Morgan	6	D	D	D	20	330	63.3	12.8	8	D	D	D
Obion	32	119	14.1	4.3	39	2 439	1 195.0	82.2	57	822	33.4	8.4
Overton	22	D	D	D	28	D	D	D	25	D	D	D
Perry	4	D	D	D	11	515	D	17.2	8	D	D	D
Pickett	3	5	0.4	0.1	8	86	14.8	2.2	12	D	D	D
Polk	8	14	2.2	0.5	9	108	D	5.4	18	296	9.3	2.5
Putnam	141	584	70.8	25.4	99	4 301	1 214.4	162.2	159	3 666	158.8	45.1
Rhea	29	79	6.0	2.0	29	3 544	848.6	121.0	48	792	30.7	8.0
Roane	56	D	D	D	23	1 096	270.1	40.5	68	1 359	52.0	15.1
Robertson	64	208	21.2	7.3	78	5 788	1 793.0	218.1	91	1 536	65.6	18.4
Rutherford	340	2 304	265.6	117.2	200	14 761	11 539.0	818.0	469	11 020	502.7	146.5
Scott	13	41	3.8	2.1	31	738	113.7	22.2	24	387	14.4	3.9
Sequatchie	13	42	4.0	1.7	8	111	D	5.1	15	D	D	D
Sevier	151	779	69.9	25.3	69	939	263.2	41.2	508	11 751	832.7	221.2
Shelby	1 762	17 349	2 496.2	1 055.5	580	24 360	22 412.7	1 417.0	1 659	36 739	1 889.7	529.1
Smith	16	D	D	D	17	959	D	41.9	21	D	D	D
Stewart	4	D	D	D	9	194	37.1	6.2	19	D	D	D
Sullivan	266	1 875	232.4	89.4	143	15 287	6 361.4	1 030.5	317	6 340	286.4	82.4
Sumner	210	1 837	213.7	92.7	173	6 127	2 158.4	271.7	231	4 416	195.6	58.1
Tipton	33	131	11.1	3.3	26	1 591	446.3	56.2	63	882	39.5	10.1
Trousdale	8	35	2.5	0.8	6	195	D	6.8	9	108	4.3	1.1
Unicoi	7	16	2.0	0.6	19	1 698	440.7	90.4	32	344	15.9	4.1
Union	11	D	D	D	14	544	125.9	19.2	9	161	7.4	2.0
Van Buren	1	D	D	D	6	D	D	D	1	D	D	D
Warren	40	117	10.4	3.4	57	3 276	1 311.7	141.4	51	770	32.3	8.2
Washington	222	2 751	218.3	102.0	116	4 536	1 503.7	179.2	283	6 344	278.5	80.8
Wayne	10	19	1.4	0.4	21	530	79.9	16.4	17	170	7.1	2.0
Weakley	23	91	8.3	2.4	25	1 033	D	34.7	58	816	35.5	8.8
White	18	32	3.4	0.7	40	1 910	561.1	82.2	28	D	D	D
Williamson	792	7 610	1 465.0	580.1	119	2 237	558.3	92.9	437	9 418	485.2	138.0
Wilson	185	D	D	D	108	2 851	1 281.6	143.6	212	4 345	190.0	56.8
TEXAS	62 322	639 561	122 086.2	47 256.4	19 782	767 024	702 603.1	42 529.8	48 721	976 390	54 480.8	14 743.8
Anderson	81	238	32.0	10.6	24	245	D	10.8	68	D	D	D
Andrews	24	D	D	D	7	387	135.9	15.3	26	372	21.4	5.1
Angelina	147	768	91.7	33.6	65	4 602	1 451.6	177.8	144	3 162	141.5	40.1
Aransas	37	153	20.8	4.9	7	26	D	0.8	74	1 032	50.5	13.4
Archer	9	D	D	D	11	D	D	D	8	D	D	D
Armstrong	1	D	D	D	NA	NA	NA	NA	1	D	D	D
Atascosa	44	240	34.2	10.8	21	216	D	8.3	62	951	52.3	13.6
Austin	49	235	23.8	10.9	33	2 085	D	117.2	49	521	28.7	7.5
Bailey	12	38	4.2	1.5	7	148	D	5.2	14	212	7.9	2.3
Bandera	35	104	10.5	3.4	11	35	D	1.0	49	559	26.6	8.6
Bastrop	101	416	46.1	14.6	59	990	284.4	42.0	109	2 273	138.0	39.8
Baylor	7	24	1.4	0.8	4	44	D	1.1	9	71	5.5	0.7
Bee	38	D	D	D	9	92	D	4.3	56	725	40.5	10.5
Bell	365	3 505	407.6	164.2	136	5 724	1 962.5	237.3	584	11 467	552.0	149.9
Bexar	3 963	40 811	6 684.3	2 557.1	873	30 474	14 766.1	1 478.3	3 612	88 432	5 006.7	1 365.3
Blanco	26	D	D	D	13	109	26.4	4.6	27	277	11.5	3.6
Borden	1	D	D	D	NA	NA	NA	NA	NA	NA	NA	NA
Bosque	22	48	5.7	2.3	16	431	115.2	19.2	22	172	10.1	2.3
Bowie	156	846	86.5	29.2	56	1 840	462.7	78.9	184	4 141	193.8	55.7
Brazoria	456	2 433	316.1	126.5	212	12 119	32 864.6	1 016.8	474	9 303	462.5	127.2
Brazos	401	2 690	523.0	134.3	100	4 480	1 063.6	178.3	436	9 491	446.5	121.5
Brewster	17	49	5.6	1.6	11	27	5.9	0.9	40	617	31.5	8.5
Briscoe	1	D	D	D	NA	NA	NA	NA	3	10	0.3	0.1
Brooks	9	25	2.3	0.5	NA	NA	NA	NA	21	289	15.6	4.3
Brown	54	D	D	D	31	2 292	1 222.0	107.5	81	1 270	59.9	16.4
Burleson	23	149	12.4	4.2	15	353	D	16.9	40	266	14.1	3.3
Burnet	84	473	33.5	14.6	52	687	259.9	33.2	110	1 545	89.0	25.6

1. Establishment subject to federal tax.

STATE County	Health care and social assistance, 2012				Other services, 2012				Nonemployer businesses, 2015		Value of residential construction authorized by building permits, 2016	
	Number of establish-ments	Number of employees	Receipts (mil dol)	Annual payroll (mil dol)	Number of establish-ments	Number of employees	Receipts (mil dol)	Annual payroll (mil dol)	Number	Receipts (mil dol)	New Construction ($1,000)	Number of housing units
	159	160	161	162	163	164	165	166	167	168	169	170
TENNESSEE—Cont'd												
Marshall	56	724	57.3	19.8	25	111	11.9	2.8	2 020	88.5	28 538	155
Maury	213	5 384	539.7	208.3	107	661	60.5	18.1	6 193	268.9	244 499	1 226
Meigs	10	D	D	D	7	D	D	D	651	28.7	11 278	53
Monroe	72	1 480	118.5	42.1	40	D	D	D	2 736	120.2	5 387	80
Montgomery	331	7 170	662.2	251.9	184	975	76.1	21.2	9 927	434.7	192 025	1 531
Moore	6	187	12.5	7.5	5	9	0.6	0.1	420	20.0	5 873	32
Morgan	15	370	33.2	13.1	7	D	D	D	1 121	39.6	0	0
Obion	86	D	D	D	39	D	D	D	1 849	71.9	3 177	15
Overton	35	D	D	D	18	D	D	D	1 765	69.1	650	3
Perry	14	396	26.1	10.8	8	D	D	D	609	27.0	976	5
Pickett	5	D	D	D	4	D	D	D	477	23.9	NA	NA
Polk	18	395	30.9	12.7	8	22	2.0	0.4	1 046	37.7	29 540	164
Putnam	228	5 719	511.9	214.5	115	D	D	D	5 937	273.3	95 880	720
Rhea	68	968	68.2	28.4	26	89	7.6	2.1	1 595	59.9	11 540	85
Roane	91	1 892	128.8	53.5	46	192	20.3	5.0	3 064	116.0	375	6
Robertson	122	1 908	176.3	70.4	69	209	21.7	5.5	5 048	239.9	64 838	370
Rutherford	524	13 614	1 376.6	586.1	301	2 632	282.7	78.4	20 563	967.9	545 253	2 826
Scott	41	1 002	65.2	23.7	16	D	D	D	1 336	62.6	355	4
Sequatchie	22	D	D	D	8	21	1.8	0.4	1 056	36.7	345	4
Sevier	150	2 281	198.9	67.3	144	846	78.6	22.3	7 864	383.1	71 412	471
Shelby	2 338	68 016	8 166.7	3 140.9	1 202	10 502	1 938.8	366.1	78 921	2 943.8	388 430	2 338
Smith	26	D	D	D	12	D	D	D	1 363	53.7	10 988	62
Stewart	15	195	18.2	8.1	11	D	D	D	810	27.3	1 680	15
Sullivan	444	12 341	1 521.5	567.3	220	D	D	D	9 746	411.3	71 135	753
Sumner	334	5 369	599.5	219.1	197	944	98.6	24.6	14 653	738.5	288 337	1 341
Tipton	84	1 314	141.3	45.5	41	160	20.1	4.9	3 823	128.4	27 454	155
Trousdale	23	233	19.3	6.1	6	D	D	D	566	23.9	7 751	57
Unicoi	26	747	44.7	18.3	19	D	D	D	799	28.9	851	18
Union	20	177	11.6	4.8	15	47	4.9	1.3	1 239	45.3	10 510	78
Van Buren	2	D	D	D	2	D	D	D	377	15.1	0	0
Warren	98	1 428	114.7	43.6	48	D	D	D	2 972	122.8	10 145	70
Washington	351	14 010	1 641.3	737.0	175	910	69.9	22.6	8 037	372.7	64 364	355
Wayne	31	402	34.3	12.7	12	39	4.7	1.0	874	36.2	0	0
Weakley	81	1 582	134.6	50.9	37	168	15.2	4.2	1 670	71.7	6 053	37
White	38	856	68.3	24.3	27	D	D	D	1 879	77.4	10 353	103
Williamson	634	11 192	1 456.1	591.2	323	2 109	200.2	60.5	25 285	1 704.8	796 065	2 759
Wilson	268	3 941	392.5	151.2	149	1 091	95.2	31.3	10 834	531.9	329 137	1 381
TEXAS	61 342	1 345 664	145 035.1	54 570.6	34 116	259 128	30 172.2	8 454.5	2 205 149	108 490.6	29 242 398	165 853
Anderson	141	2 214	216.2	78.4	60	308	22.3	7.8	2 938	126.9	2 100	13
Andrews	26	475	64.0	22.8	23	D	D	D	1 333	82.1	2 372	8
Angelina	285	7 839	588.4	240.8	119	818	152.6	32.8	5 332	258.0	9 779	64
Aransas	44	518	46.2	14.8	47	150	14.1	3.4	2 650	124.7	27 831	189
Archer	12	D	D	D	10	D	D	D	901	46.9	1 085	5
Armstrong	4	93	3.1	1.6	2	D	D	D	174	7.7	1 129	7
Atascosa	80	1 309	115.4	43.0	48	217	23.8	5.2	3 381	142.9	5 404	34
Austin	44	D	D	D	31	114	11.6	2.8	2 729	134.4	4 817	28
Bailey	15	251	16.9	6.6	12	37	3.9	0.8	383	22.4	160	2
Bandera	24	339	21.4	8.4	32	105	11.4	2.8	2 299	107.1	210	1
Bastrop	108	1 983	155.1	62.7	78	330	31.1	8.6	6 110	286.9	18 104	168
Baylor	13	511	19.3	8.6	15	D	D	D	282	11.9	0	0
Bee	50	D	D	D	38	187	18.3	4.7	1 507	52.2	803	7
Bell	524	22 484	2 849.6	1 245.3	409	2 898	202.5	72.7	16 877	698.9	309 543	2 107
Bexar	4 314	110 407	12 143.6	4 363.8	2 461	17 571	1 645.4	478.9	131 716	6 106.2	1 066 142	7 600
Blanco	18	159	7.8	3.6	15	44	7.4	1.4	1 358	63.9	3 388	18
Borden	NA	NA	NA	NA	NA	NA	NA	NA	55	2.2	NA	NA
Bosque	20	606	42.2	16.4	21	69	5.4	1.4	1 500	64.7	40	1
Bowie	289	7 151	798.4	295.4	154	979	87.0	26.4	5 194	232.8	13 414	73
Brazoria	627	8 038	646.5	273.7	369	2 558	237.6	75.3	23 910	1 037.9	667 506	2 930
Brazos	399	8 166	1 040.0	376.0	266	1 939	374.6	53.6	13 193	608.9	367 763	2 769
Brewster	24	548	30.0	12.1	20	D	D	D	998	34.0	1 632	13
Briscoe	3	4	0.2	0.1	1	D	D	D	128	4.2	NA	NA
Brooks	20	339	10.7	5.3	11	31	3.3	0.7	612	12.7	50	1
Brown	136	3 126	206.2	77.2	69	381	24.3	6.9	2 508	103.9	15 559	88
Burleson	16	D	D	D	26	115	11.4	3.7	1 453	63.9	1 919	12
Burnet	106	1 302	145.3	51.5	71	303	24.0	6.9	5 113	294.2	98 660	452

Table B. States and Counties — Government Employment and Payroll, and Local Government Finances

	Government employment and payroll, 2012									Local government finances, 2012				
STATE County			March payroll (percent of total)							General revenue		Taxes		
													Per capita[1] (dollars)	
	Full-time equivalent employees	March payroll (dollars)	Administration, judicial, and legal	Police and Corrections	Fire Protection	Highways and transportation	Health and Welfare	Natural resources and utilities	Education and libraries	Total (mil dol)	Intergovernmental (mil dol)	Total (mil dol)	Total	Property
	171	172	173	174	175	176	177	178	179	180	181	182	183	184
TENNESSEE—Cont'd														
Marshall	1 203	3 538 766	7.5	9.0	3.9	2.6	5.0	17.4	52.4	86.1	36.7	29.2	947	612
Maury	4 616	17 056 047	3.2	6.1	2.9	2.0	47.4	6.3	30.7	499.9	86.1	89.0	1 086	702
Meigs	438	942 766	9.9	10.0	0.1	7.3	3.2	2.3	67.2	24.7	17.0	5.2	441	333
Monroe	1 373	3 993 045	7.7	8.8	1.3	3.3	4.4	9.7	64.2	96.5	51.5	31.4	696	447
Montgomery	6 061	19 419 026	4.6	11.0	3.6	3.7	5.7	6.1	63.4	519.4	202.5	207.0	1 122	681
Moore	237	724 102	2.2	14.7	0.1	9.4	3.2	8.5	61.9	15.5	8.0	5.6	884	707
Morgan	796	1 965 391	7.2	7.4	0.0	4.6	5.8	5.4	68.9	42.3	28.2	10.4	475	387
Obion	1 057	3 471 219	8.5	14.0	3.5	4.1	0.4	7.6	60.8	80.5	42.6	24.7	789	436
Overton	829	2 041 789	5.5	9.1	0.7	4.4	6.6	7.0	65.6	46.5	30.0	11.5	520	304
Perry	339	836 675	10.6	3.6	0.0	5.3	3.5	5.7	67.5	22.6	13.7	5.6	716	537
Pickett	180	540 892	11.1	15.0	0.6	9.3	3.5	4.7	55.8	13.0	8.2	3.4	670	349
Polk	595	1 517 421	15.7	1.5	0.0	7.2	2.1	5.6	67.4	36.3	22.3	11.2	674	514
Putnam	4 261	15 613 316	2.1	4.8	1.2	1.6	55.8	4.6	27.7	418.9	71.7	81.6	1 114	597
Rhea	1 269	3 661 964	5.1	6.0	0.8	2.6	18.6	8.5	54.3	86.8	39.8	20.0	621	367
Roane	1 700	6 055 393	5.5	6.7	3.8	2.6	1.3	17.4	61.6	147.3	59.5	50.7	948	593
Robertson	2 143	5 842 234	11.7	12.9	2.0	4.7	1.8	7.6	58.5	164.1	73.4	70.3	1 050	658
Rutherford	8 751	29 120 491	7.0	11.2	3.9	1.2	3.2	8.8	62.0	738.4	270.4	325.5	1 186	718
Scott	1 044	2 569 027	6.5	7.4	0.9	5.4	5.6	10.3	62.6	56.6	33.7	12.4	560	370
Sequatchie	429	1 170 657	6.1	8.5	0.0	0.5	5.6	7.1	71.3	32.3	19.5	9.3	645	457
Sevier	3 747	12 103 289	4.1	9.3	3.0	4.0	3.5	8.2	62.6	359.9	83.9	186.0	2 010	703
Shelby	39 378	138 123 866	7.0	15.4	7.3	4.6	11.4	14.4	38.1	4 311.3	1 448.6	1 719.3	1 828	1 235
Smith	725	1 800 266	8.4	11.3	0.6	6.1	2.0	7.1	61.0	45.3	25.5	13.2	693	395
Stewart	498	1 358 521	8.2	10.6	0.2	5.1	5.7	3.5	65.2	36.1	23.5	9.2	693	470
Sullivan	5 719	18 566 959	5.4	9.7	3.3	4.6	4.4	5.7	64.8	404.7	154.7	177.3	1 131	800
Sumner	5 626	16 827 689	5.9	10.4	4.6	1.7	3.7	8.6	63.7	406.0	171.8	163.0	981	658
Tipton	2 180	6 476 685	4.4	8.2	2.1	2.7	0.9	8.0	72.1	146.0	87.1	41.2	668	453
Trousdale	275	758 540	10.0	16.9	0.0	0.0	4.0	1.1	68.0	18.5	11.4	4.6	596	490
Unicoi	819	2 543 400	3.6	3.8	1.5	4.4	24.1	4.2	48.7	63.6	21.5	9.0	495	392
Union	593	1 652 593	8.9	6.9	0.0	4.2	0.9	6.7	72.2	47.6	34.6	8.9	466	312
Van Buren	275	698 479	8.3	7.1	1.3	19.0	5.9	2.5	55.9	13.1	8.7	3.1	554	397
Warren	1 148	3 625 874	6.8	9.9	2.3	1.1	6.3	13.7	58.4	97.8	53.6	31.0	779	452
Washington	4 114	12 590 200	5.8	10.1	3.4	7.7	2.2	15.3	53.6	294.8	106.3	133.5	1 068	712
Wayne	611	1 515 515	5.5	10.2	0.2	4.9	1.5	4.4	71.7	45.0	23.8	10.1	595	364
Weakley	1 333	3 550 802	5.6	11.2	2.3	5.4	9.1	13.8	50.6	73.0	37.4	20.2	579	318
White	908	2 433 483	6.9	8.8	0.8	3.2	3.5	9.7	65.1	53.2	31.7	14.3	548	338
Williamson	8 184	27 964 745	5.4	6.5	3.3	2.0	20.1	5.4	55.8	754.7	175.6	348.2	1 805	1 175
Wilson	3 881	11 949 351	7.0	10.1	4.4	3.3	1.0	8.4	64.6	281.9	110.9	131.1	1 102	707
TEXAS	X	X	X	X	X	X	X	X	X	X	X	X	X	X
Anderson	1 888	5 360 452	8.0	11.5	3.0	3.1	0.6	3.8	69.2	124.5	47.1	61.2	1 052	867
Andrews	1 090	4 021 801	5.8	6.7	0.0	2.3	33.8	5.1	46.1	121.7	9.4	81.6	5 063	4 756
Angelina	4 483	13 382 100	4.8	8.0	2.7	2.0	11.2	3.8	66.5	300.9	135.8	97.6	1 114	832
Aransas	888	2 584 176	9.4	13.5	0.0	5.1	2.4	5.8	61.2	78.8	13.5	50.4	2 117	1 856
Archer	436	1 231 876	8.0	6.2	0.0	2.7	1.6	4.3	76.7	26.8	10.9	12.0	1 378	1 224
Armstrong	112	284 475	10.7	2.6	0.0	2.6	2.2	3.2	77.2	9.5	3.3	3.2	1 666	1 480
Atascosa	2 208	6 519 286	5.0	7.2	0.0	2.0	13.3	3.4	67.8	191.3	123.7	49.0	1 056	822
Austin	1 209	3 635 525	7.8	10.5	0.0	3.4	2.6	5.7	69.1	87.7	23.7	51.5	1 801	1 613
Bailey	547	1 435 208	5.2	6.9	0.0	2.6	29.6	1.9	53.0	36.8	12.6	9.8	1 375	1 158
Bandera	640	2 084 125	8.5	10.8	0.2	3.9	4.1	2.5	68.5	46.4	8.5	32.2	1 567	1 462
Bastrop	2 838	9 520 485	5.2	12.2	0.0	2.3	0.8	3.0	76.0	243.4	86.4	112.0	1 498	1 314
Baylor	318	889 487	6.6	4.2	0.0	2.8	45.1	5.7	34.2	22.6	4.9	3.9	1 085	880
Bee	1 435	4 453 164	5.0	5.5	1.3	2.9	4.8	5.0	74.6	114.4	63.6	30.2	930	752
Bell	16 055	50 764 685	4.5	8.6	3.4	1.9	2.7	4.5	73.5	1 144.1	497.9	378.1	1 171	912
Bexar	76 821	296 304 428	4.1	8.7	3.4	4.0	10.0	11.6	57.2	7 217.6	2 547.6	2 991.4	1 675	1 345
Blanco	357	1 339 398	8.8	7.8	0.0	1.9	0.2	3.3	77.7	39.5	6.7	29.4	2 761	2 644
Borden	74	200 651	18.7	3.1	0.0	8.2	0.0	0.5	68.4	14.0	2.2	11.3	18 268	18 188
Bosque	689	2 029 654	8.4	7.1	0.0	2.6	0.4	2.1	77.7	47.1	20.0	22.7	1 253	1 100
Bowie	4 233	13 543 434	5.4	7.5	2.7	2.3	0.7	7.1	73.2	292.7	128.5	118.6	1 273	993
Brazoria	12 753	42 706 512	5.9	10.5	0.7	2.7	5.3	4.6	69.2	1 184.7	316.7	617.5	1 901	1 646
Brazos	7 250	22 942 099	8.3	13.0	5.1	4.6	3.7	12.3	47.5	549.9	134.9	310.5	1 547	1 241
Brewster	439	1 264 854	9.4	14.2	0.0	3.7	0.7	6.1	63.5	31.3	14.9	12.8	1 373	1 071
Briscoe	68	181 356	19.1	3.9	0.0	5.1	1.2	13.9	56.0	4.9	1.8	2.3	1 491	1 329
Brooks	470	1 100 857	8.0	8.1	0.4	3.7	1.2	7.4	70.9	40.5	15.5	18.6	2 598	2 321
Brown	1 839	5 391 982	6.8	9.8	2.3	3.3	10.4	7.5	59.2	125.8	54.0	52.8	1 397	1 099
Burleson	707	1 886 727	9.3	7.8	0.0	4.3	0.7	3.5	74.3	46.7	14.9	26.1	1 507	1 240
Burnet	1 778	6 073 530	9.9	14.7	4.3	2.7	0.2	7.3	59.5	155.5	24.4	99.6	2 293	2 003

1. Based on the resident population estimated as of July 1 of the year shown.

Table B. States and Counties — Local Government Finances, Government Employment, and Income Taxes

STATE County	Local government finances, 2012 (cont.) Direct general expenditure Total (mil dol)	Per capita[1] (dollars)	Percent of total for: Education	Health and hospitals	Police protection	Public welfare	Highways	Debt outstanding Total (mil dol)	Per capita[1] (dollars)	Government employment, 2015 Federal civilian	Federal military	State and local	Individual income tax returns, 2014 Number of returns	Mean adjusted gross income	Mean income tax
	185	186	187	188	189	190	191	192	193	194	195	196	197	198	199
TENNESSEE—Cont'd															
Marshall	82.9	2 684	52.1	3.0	8.4	0.2	5.3	93.9	3 039	64	96	1 662	13 940	43 298	4 080
Maury	491.1	5 990	19.6	56.1	3.7	0.0	3.1	294.5	3 592	173	268	6 255	40 490	49 116	5 070
Meigs	23.1	1 979	63.8	2.5	5.7	0.5	8.0	7.5	637	29	36	486	4 890	45 708	4 500
Monroe	104.4	2 314	64.5	4.7	5.5	0.1	5.1	101.6	2 250	89	139	1 972	18 470	42 321	3 818
Montgomery	461.9	2 504	57.1	3.0	7.0	0.0	4.1	4 359.0	23 630	1 846	622	9 267	80 520	44 951	4 110
Moore	15.3	2 419	59.1	2.9	4.2	0.1	11.9	10.0	1 582	D	19	860	2 760	53 293	5 738
Morgan	41.9	1 911	64.0	5.8	4.0	0.4	6.2	30.5	1 389	36	59	1 405	7 410	39 965	3 113
Obion	81.3	2 595	55.8	0.3	6.3	3.1	8.4	30.1	960	111	93	1 596	13 640	41 976	3 845
Overton	44.3	1 997	60.0	3.6	4.9	0.1	6.9	44.2	1 992	43	67	1 250	8 770	38 635	3 188
Perry	21.2	2 699	47.8	5.5	4.8	0.0	8.5	8.1	1 031	16	24	437	3 080	40 260	3 834
Pickett	13.0	2 545	48.4	5.3	3.9	0.0	10.4	3.4	663	10	16	284	2 070	48 001	6 691
Polk	34.7	2 079	61.1	2.7	6.5	0.1	8.0	19.5	1 171	71	51	743	6 950	39 659	3 421
Putnam	420.4	5 740	22.0	57.2	3.4	0.0	2.3	286.9	3 919	231	226	8 321	31 010	48 635	5 953
Rhea	100.3	3 111	50.3	17.1	4.9	0.0	5.3	141.2	4 378	1 182	97	1 666	13 130	43 671	4 103
Roane	135.7	2 538	58.0	2.9	4.6	0.2	4.6	117.8	2 203	431	160	3 314	22 430	51 732	5 485
Robertson	151.2	2 259	56.5	3.0	9.4	0.0	4.9	198.9	2 971	87	209	3 522	32 610	47 238	4 562
Rutherford	715.7	2 608	53.2	2.1	8.2	1.5	4.4	983.5	3 583	2 799	922	15 386	134 040	51 882	5 566
Scott	55.5	2 502	62.9	3.9	4.5	2.5	6.6	69.2	3 121	87	67	1 430	7 630	37 663	2 666
Sequatchie	28.3	1 960	60.8	3.3	6.5	0.0	5.5	20.7	1 434	12	45	909	5 910	43 372	4 143
Sevier	377.1	4 076	36.1	2.9	5.4	0.1	6.1	1 420.7	15 357	334	292	4 652	45 150	39 596	3 941
Shelby	4 592.5	4 882	44.5	8.2	8.9	1.1	2.0	5 549.0	5 898	13 361	3 809	51 088	439 940	57 086	7 942
Smith	46.3	2 421	56.5	3.9	7.0	0.1	6.8	37.3	1 955	122	59	1 009	8 170	43 998	3 845
Stewart	34.1	2 565	59.2	4.6	6.3	0.0	7.3	35.9	2 697	469	41	582	5 430	42 488	3 783
Sullivan	439.1	2 801	49.3	2.5	6.5	0.0	4.1	464.0	2 959	470	475	7 455	69 430	49 892	5 749
Sumner	387.5	2 333	56.0	2.5	7.6	0.1	4.7	365.1	2 198	473	538	7 386	80 120	60 798	7 738
Tipton	139.6	2 263	63.6	0.7	6.7	0.1	6.6	67.3	1 091	93	187	2 693	26 250	47 395	4 442
Trousdale	20.8	2 672	57.7	2.4	6.2	0.2	9.5	0.0	0	32	24	453	3 630	39 871	3 541
Unicoi	70.8	3 884	31.1	44.7	3.2	0.3	5.1	50.1	2 748	69	54	854	7 300	41 890	3 705
Union	45.7	2 387	70.7	3.8	4.1	0.2	4.9	34.2	1 787	19	58	798	7 120	39 112	3 287
Van Buren	17.4	3 085	70.1	3.3	3.6	0.0	8.9	9.0	1 604	12	17	364	2 280	34 968	2 669
Warren	107.0	2 687	60.0	3.5	4.8	0.0	5.4	47.1	1 181	91	123	1 877	16 570	39 157	3 563
Washington	308.7	2 467	44.9	1.3	7.5	0.5	5.7	609.5	4 872	2 682	412	9 747	55 110	52 099	6 278
Wayne	44.4	2 612	47.4	0.4	4.4	17.6	6.9	31.8	1 874	30	45	1 014	5 640	41 010	3 722
Weakley	68.4	1 967	54.8	0.5	6.6	11.4	8.3	23.7	682	120	103	3 636	12 890	43 049	4 088
White	50.7	1 943	60.1	2.7	5.8	0.3	5.6	21.8	835	50	80	1 258	10 590	37 994	3 054
Williamson	720.3	3 734	44.7	20.8	4.0	0.0	4.3	886.6	4 596	803	649	10 413	94 660	129 833	24 199
Wilson	304.2	2 557	61.0	0.4	7.4	0.0	4.9	398.5	3 350	199	393	4 921	59 550	62 655	7 648
TEXAS	X	X	X	X	X	X	X	X	X	195 091	172 422	1 647 199	11 991 140	67 079	10 026
Anderson	133.7	2 297	64.2	0.2	4.5	0.4	4.2	165.8	2 850	133	88	5 325	19 050	48 873	5 276
Andrews	109.9	6 817	50.8	29.4	3.5	0.0	1.1	185.6	11 518	13	37	1 346	7 600	80 193	11 939
Angelina	307.3	3 509	57.1	10.2	4.5	0.3	4.2	395.7	4 517	321	174	6 711	36 570	49 147	5 491
Aransas	80.8	3 391	53.6	1.1	9.5	1.2	4.4	116.6	4 897	19	51	1 062	11 440	61 092	9 097
Archer	26.8	3 072	60.0	1.1	6.2	0.4	7.7	257.0	29 423	22	66	492	3 900	72 089	10 544
Armstrong	8.5	4 369	44.7	28.9	3.6	0.2	4.8	4.2	2 172	D	D	141	830	61 113	7 777
Atascosa	210.7	4 536	43.4	9.8	2.8	0.8	23.3	433.1	9 325	52	98	2 479	20 230	59 204	8 485
Austin	84.2	2 944	55.5	4.8	7.5	0.0	7.6	104.0	3 635	71	60	1 406	14 110	73 205	11 872
Bailey	34.7	4 873	39.4	36.7	4.8	0.0	3.9	50.9	7 137	20	14	456	2 980	41 629	4 030
Bandera	43.7	2 128	59.1	2.9	6.1	0.5	5.8	35.4	1 721	14	43	708	9 320	62 733	8 727
Bastrop	242.4	3 242	50.0	11.5	5.2	0.6	5.9	413.3	5 529	376	159	3 582	34 050	50 659	5 445
Baylor	20.8	5 731	29.9	49.2	3.4	0.6	3.5	3.0	829	20	D	231	1 480	47 951	5 341
Bee	111.6	3 432	71.0	1.4	3.1	1.8	2.5	62.7	1 928	33	51	3 302	11 080	50 073	5 579
Bell	1 144.2	3 542	60.4	2.5	4.9	0.5	2.7	1 912.6	5 919	10 208	39 663	19 785	143 680	47 030	4 767
Bexar	7 362.8	4 123	44.0	14.4	5.4	2.0	2.3	18 461.5	10 338	34 243	33 308	108 883	840 050	56 862	7 613
Blanco	38.6	3 621	55.5	0.1	3.6	0.0	9.2	37.3	3 505	58	22	519	5 110	69 667	9 832
Borden	23.8	38 584	84.8	0.0	0.6	0.1	3.3	22.5	36 494	D	D	87	250	79 900	13 424
Bosque	45.2	2 493	68.1	0.1	4.3	0.7	4.0	30.9	1 705	63	36	1 201	7 590	52 698	6 056
Bowie	279.8	3 004	63.0	0.3	4.7	0.4	5.3	243.0	2 609	4 206	203	6 284	40 080	49 719	5 866
Brazoria	1 133.2	3 489	48.6	5.5	5.0	0.2	6.1	3 469.8	10 684	456	751	17 771	145 950	72 404	9 773
Brazos	577.4	2 877	45.4	2.3	6.2	0.4	5.6	1 281.3	6 385	730	485	36 254	78 710	61 340	8 464
Brewster	31.8	3 412	50.6	3.2	7.7	0.4	6.8	9.3	995	270	19	1 061	4 320	56 707	8 024
Briscoe	3.7	2 339	51.9	0.1	4.3	0.0	11.3	7.8	4 998	12	D	113	640	47 706	5 909
Brooks	42.3	5 904	45.4	2.3	10.2	0.3	5.0	40.3	5 626	332	15	532	3 020	36 848	3 028
Brown	120.7	3 191	51.3	7.8	5.5	0.5	4.3	150.8	3 986	126	74	2 767	15 810	46 620	4 687
Burleson	42.2	2 441	59.8	0.6	4.9	0.0	11.0	23.6	1 367	48	35	783	8 030	55 562	7 054
Burnet	148.6	3 420	46.0	1.6	5.8	0.4	3.8	219.9	5 061	75	90	2 447	20 880	70 184	10 438

1. Based on the resident population estimated as of July 1 of the year shown.

Table B. States and Counties — Land Area and Population

STATE/ County code	CBSA code[1]	County type[2]	STATE County	Land area,[3] (sq mi) 2016	Total persons 2016	Rank	Per square mile	White	Black	American Indian, Alaska Native	Asian and Pacific Islander	Percent Hispanic or Latino[4]	Under 5 years	5 to 17 years	18 to 24 years	25 to 34 years	35 to 44 years	45 to 54 years
				1	2	3	4	5	6	7	8	9	10	11	12	13	14	15
			TEXAS—Cont'd															
48 055	12420	1	Caldwell	545.2	41 161	1 149	75.5	41.8	6.5	0.7	1.1	50.9	6.3	17.4	11.6	13.3	12.4	12.7
48 057	38920	6	Calhoun	506.8	21 965	1 729	43.3	43.6	2.8	0.7	5.3	48.4	6.7	18.3	8.9	12.4	11.5	12.6
48 059	10180	3	Callahan	899.4	13 820	2 178	15.4	87.7	2.0	1.3	1.0	9.5	5.8	17.1	6.7	10.9	11.3	13.0
48 061	15180	2	Cameron	891.1	422 135	164	473.7	9.5	0.4	0.2	0.7	89.4	8.5	22.6	10.6	12.1	12.3	11.1
48 063	...	6	Camp	195.8	12 867	2 237	65.7	57.4	17.5	0.8	1.1	25.1	7.6	18.8	8.9	11.0	10.9	12.0
48 065	11100	2	Carson	920.2	6 057	2 746	6.6	87.4	1.4	2.0	0.7	10.1	6.3	19.0	7.7	11.6	11.7	12.5
48 067	...	6	Cass	937.0	30 375	1 424	32.4	77.8	17.4	1.0	0.8	4.5	6.1	16.5	7.5	10.1	10.8	12.8
48 069	...	6	Castro	894.4	7 669	2 617	8.6	32.9	2.1	0.6	0.6	64.1	7.9	21.4	10.0	10.8	11.7	10.7
48 071	26420	1	Chambers	597.1	39 899	1 177	66.8	67.9	8.6	0.9	1.6	22.2	6.9	20.8	8.7	13.2	14.0	13.4
48 073	27380	6	Cherokee	1 053.0	51 668	964	49.1	62.2	14.9	0.8	0.7	22.8	7.2	18.5	9.4	11.7	11.9	12.5
48 075	...	7	Childress	696.4	7 052	2 668	10.1	59.6	10.7	0.9	1.1	29.0	5.1	15.6	12.7	18.2	12.5	10.1
48 077	48660	3	Clay	1 088.7	10 193	2 416	9.4	91.9	1.1	2.1	0.7	5.9	4.7	16.1	6.9	9.5	11.2	13.7
48 079	...	9	Cochran	775.1	2 882	2 981	3.7	37.7	4.2	0.8	0.4	57.7	7.8	20.4	8.4	13.9	10.1	12.7
48 081	...	8	Coke	911.5	3 264	2 955	3.6	76.3	1.3	1.7	0.4	21.8	4.6	16.4	6.2	9.5	9.4	12.7
48 083	...	6	Coleman	1 261.9	8 420	2 558	6.7	78.2	3.2	1.1	1.1	17.7	5.2	16.5	6.5	9.1	10.2	12.6
48 085	19100	1	Collin	841.3	939 585	53	1 116.8	60.6	10.3	0.9	15.4	15.1	6.4	20.3	8.1	12.6	15.9	15.3
48 087	...	9	Collingsworth	918.4	3 016	2 968	3.3	59.3	5.6	2.2	0.5	34.0	7.3	19.9	8.6	11.9	9.9	11.8
48 089	...	6	Colorado	960.3	21 019	1 774	21.9	57.6	12.9	0.5	1.1	28.9	6.3	16.7	8.0	10.1	10.3	11.8
48 091	41700	1	Comal	559.5	134 788	468	240.9	69.6	2.3	0.9	1.5	26.9	5.9	16.9	7.7	11.0	11.7	13.9
48 093	...	7	Comanche	937.8	13 484	2 197	14.4	70.9	0.8	1.0	0.6	27.7	5.7	16.6	7.7	9.5	10.0	12.8
48 095	...	8	Concho	983.8	4 279	2 877	4.3	41.2	2.2	0.6	0.8	55.9	2.8	10.5	7.4	17.8	20.0	14.4
48 097	23620	6	Cooke	874.8	39 266	1 192	44.9	77.3	3.8	1.5	1.2	17.7	6.9	17.1	8.6	11.8	10.7	12.6
48 099	28660	2	Coryell	1 052.2	74 686	740	71.0	62.2	18.1	1.4	4.2	18.0	7.2	16.6	12.5	19.4	14.6	11.4
48 101	...	9	Cottle	900.6	1 402	3 084	1.6	65.0	10.8	0.5	0.4	24.5	5.3	18.0	6.6	9.9	10.2	11.1
48 103	...	6	Crane	785.1	4 830	2 845	6.2	33.0	3.0	1.0	0.5	63.2	7.8	21.9	8.7	13.5	12.1	12.3
48 105	...	7	Crockett	2 807.3	3 675	2 926	1.3	32.6	0.6	0.9	0.7	65.8	7.4	18.1	8.2	11.9	11.6	12.1
48 107	31180	2	Crosby	900.2	5 992	2 751	6.7	40.9	3.7	0.6	0.3	55.3	7.1	20.2	8.4	10.9	11.2	11.1
48 109	...	9	Culberson	3 812.2	2 198	3 031	0.6	23.2	1.8	1.6	2.2	72.8	6.6	17.7	8.3	12.2	9.8	13.1
48 111	...	7	Dallam	1 503.1	7 056	2 667	4.7	52.1	2.2	1.3	1.3	44.5	9.7	22.2	9.4	14.4	12.3	13.2
48 113	19100	1	Dallas	873.1	2 574 984	9	2 949.2	30.9	23.2	0.7	6.7	39.9	7.6	19.1	9.7	16.2	13.8	12.8
48 115	29500	7	Dawson	900.3	13 111	2 222	14.6	36.5	5.7	0.5	0.9	57.2	7.0	19.0	10.2	15.4	12.4	10.4
48 117	25820	6	Deaf Smith	1 496.8	18 830	1 882	12.6	26.1	1.3	0.6	0.7	72.0	8.8	22.7	9.9	12.7	12.0	10.9
48 119	...	8	Delta	256.8	5 215	2 817	20.3	84.2	7.3	2.8	1.4	6.9	6.1	16.3	7.2	10.6	10.5	12.7
48 121	19100	1	Denton	878.5	806 180	75	917.7	62.2	10.4	1.0	9.5	19.2	6.5	19.0	9.4	14.9	15.4	14.6
48 123	...	6	DeWitt	909.0	20 865	1 780	23.0	56.3	9.0	0.5	0.4	34.6	6.7	16.1	7.0	12.0	12.1	13.0
48 125	...	8	Dickens	901.7	2 184	3 033	2.4	62.6	4.9	1.4	1.2	30.6	3.9	15.2	8.5	12.6	14.1	10.2
48 127	...	6	Dimmit	1 328.9	10 794	2 372	8.1	11.5	1.3	0.2	0.6	86.6	8.8	21.0	9.6	12.5	11.1	11.0
48 129	...	8	Donley	926.9	3 405	2 943	3.7	82.6	6.0	1.2	0.8	10.7	4.8	15.8	12.5	9.8	9.8	10.9
48 131	...	7	Duval	1 793.5	11 428	2 330	6.4	9.2	1.0	0.3	0.4	89.4	7.5	18.3	10.4	12.4	11.3	11.5
48 133	...	6	Eastland	926.5	18 274	1 902	19.7	80.6	2.5	1.1	0.9	16.1	5.5	15.7	10.8	10.4	10.3	11.6
48 135	36220	3	Ector	897.7	157 462	412	175.4	34.4	4.7	0.8	1.3	59.7	9.3	20.9	10.4	16.5	12.3	10.8
48 137	...	9	Edwards	2 117.9	1 911	3 057	0.9	43.4	0.8	0.9	0.4	55.0	6.8	14.6	6.5	9.7	9.9	11.1
48 139	19100	1	Ellis	935.7	168 499	380	180.1	63.1	10.3	0.9	1.1	25.9	6.8	20.1	9.1	12.7	12.9	13.7
48 141	21340	2	El Paso	1 013.2	837 918	69	827.0	13.1	3.5	0.5	1.7	82.2	7.8	19.9	11.5	14.7	12.4	11.5
48 143	44500	4	Erath	1 083.1	41 659	1 136	38.5	76.3	2.1	1.1	1.0	20.8	5.9	14.8	21.8	12.7	9.8	10.7
48 145	47380	2	Falls	765.5	17 273	1 959	22.6	52.1	24.3	0.8	0.8	23.1	6.2	15.1	9.2	14.5	11.8	13.2
48 147	14300	6	Fannin	890.8	34 031	1 326	38.2	80.8	7.3	1.9	0.9	10.9	4.9	15.9	8.3	12.2	12.0	13.7
48 149	...	6	Fayette	950.0	25 149	1 604	26.5	72.2	6.7	0.6	0.6	20.8	5.1	15.7	7.5	9.0	10.2	12.0
48 151	...	8	Fisher	898.9	3 854	2 915	4.3	67.3	3.9	0.8	0.7	28.4	5.7	15.0	8.9	9.8	9.8	12.7
48 153	...	6	Floyd	992.1	5 917	2 763	6.0	37.4	3.5	0.4	0.5	58.7	5.8	21.2	9.0	11.4	10.3	11.2
48 155	...	9	Foard	704.4	1 183	3 100	1.7	75.7	5.9	0.4	1.2	17.8	4.1	15.1	6.4	9.8	8.5	15.8
48 157	26420	1	Fort Bend	861.9	741 237	86	860.0	35.5	20.9	0.6	20.7	24.2	7.1	20.6	8.3	12.4	15.2	14.0
48 159	...	7	Franklin	284.4	10 607	2 383	37.3	80.3	4.4	1.2	1.2	14.5	5.6	18.8	6.6	11.1	10.4	12.5
48 161	...	7	Freestone	877.7	19 624	1 846	22.4	68.3	16.3	0.9	0.6	15.0	5.9	17.3	6.7	11.3	13.5	13.0
48 163	...	6	Frio	1 133.5	18 956	1 876	16.7	15.5	3.4	0.4	2.4	78.8	6.9	17.5	13.2	18.7	12.1	10.7
48 165	...	7	Gaines	1 502.4	20 478	1 801	13.6	56.3	2.0	0.7	0.6	41.2	10.1	25.6	9.7	13.6	11.8	10.8
48 167	26420	1	Galveston	378.9	329 431	207	869.4	59.2	13.5	0.8	4.0	24.1	6.5	18.0	8.7	13.3	13.0	13.5
48 169	...	6	Garza	893.4	6 442	2 720	7.2	42.0	6.9	0.7	0.4	50.8	4.7	12.9	14.3	20.3	11.5	13.3
48 171	23240	7	Gillespie	1 058.2	26 521	1 545	25.1	76.1	0.6	0.7	0.7	22.6	4.9	14.6	6.7	8.5	9.1	11.1
48 173	13700	8	Glasscock	900.2	1 314	3 093	1.5	60.9	1.8	0.4	0.2	37.1	6.3	19.1	10.8	10.6	13.5	13.1
48 175	47020	3	Goliad	852.0	7 517	2 630	8.8	59.2	4.6	0.8	0.5	35.8	5.1	16.5	7.7	9.5	10.9	12.9
48 177	...	6	Gonzales	1 066.7	20 876	1 779	19.6	42.4	6.6	0.6	0.7	50.6	7.5	19.8	8.4	12.1	11.1	12.1
48 179	37420	6	Gray	926.0	22 725	1 691	24.5	64.8	5.5	1.4	0.8	28.9	7.3	18.2	7.7	13.7	13.1	12.8
48 181	43300	3	Grayson	932.8	128 235	491	137.5	78.3	6.8	2.4	1.9	13.0	6.4	17.4	8.6	12.2	11.4	12.9
48 183	30980	3	Gregg	273.4	123 745	507	452.6	59.3	21.1	0.9	1.8	18.6	7.7	18.3	9.6	13.7	11.7	11.9
48 185	...	6	Grimes	787.5	27 671	1 504	35.1	60.0	16.1	0.9	0.6	23.6	6.1	16.2	8.3	12.4	12.1	13.6

1. CBSA = Core Based Statistical Area. See Appendix A for explanation. See Appendix B for list of metropolitan areas with component counties.   2. County type code from the Economic Research Service of USDA Rural-Urban Continuum Codes. See Appendix A for definition.   3. Dry land or land partially or temporarily covered by water.   4. May be of any race.

Table B. States and Counties — **Population and Households**

STATE County	Age (percent) 55 to 64 years	Age (percent) 65 to 74 years	Age (percent) 75 years and over	Percent female	Total persons 2000	Total persons 2010	Percent change 2000–2010	Percent change 2010–2016	Components of change 2010–2016 Births	Deaths	Net migration	Households, 2011–2015 Number	Persons per household	Percent Family households	Percent Female family householder[1]	Percent One person
	16	17	18	19	20	21	22	23	24	25	26	27	28	29	30	31
TEXAS—Cont'd																
Caldwell	12.3	8.4	5.5	49.5	32 194	38 057	18.2	8.2	3 075	1 871	1 878	12 451	2.85	70.9	14.9	22.8
Calhoun	13.0	9.6	7.0	48.9	20 647	21 381	3.6	2.7	1 821	1 281	29	7 994	2.68	69.9	11.4	25.2
Callahan	15.1	11.3	8.7	50.7	12 905	13 544	5.0	2.0	857	1 065	504	5 273	2.55	62.0	9.1	35.8
Cameron	9.7	7.4	5.8	51.5	335 227	406 219	21.2	3.9	46 081	15 698	-14 858	121 097	3.42	79.3	21.1	18.3
Camp	13.0	10.2	7.6	51.4	11 549	12 401	7.4	3.8	1 195	874	193	4 431	2.81	73.8	16.1	24.3
Carson	14.5	9.2	7.5	50.0	6 516	6 182	-5.1	-2.0	380	394	-70	2 293	2.62	73.8	10.9	22.8
Cass	14.1	12.6	9.5	51.6	30 438	30 464	0.1	-0.3	2 244	2 519	45	11 691	2.56	68.0	13.5	28.5
Castro	13.1	7.2	7.2	49.1	8 285	8 062	-2.7	-4.9	786	345	-836	2 501	3.14	76.4	11.4	19.2
Chambers	11.8	7.3	3.8	49.5	26 031	35 099	34.8	13.7	2 982	1 629	3 403	13 018	2.84	75.9	7.0	21.1
Cherokee	12.4	9.8	6.8	48.9	46 659	50 834	8.9	1.6	4 749	3 170	-648	17 729	2.74	73.0	15.5	23.1
Childress	10.7	8.0	7.1	41.1	7 688	7 041	-8.4	0.2	473	414	-27	2 391	2.44	65.8	11.0	29.8
Clay	17.1	12.1	8.8	50.0	11 006	10 752	-2.3	-5.2	538	725	-340	4 146	2.51	69.9	7.3	26.5
Cochran	12.1	7.1	7.4	50.0	3 730	3 127	-16.2	-7.8	290	152	-390	1 030	2.79	70.4	13.3	27.8
Coke	14.9	13.5	12.8	50.8	3 864	3 319	-14.1	-1.7	182	308	95	1 601	1.95	64.1	7.3	30.6
Coleman	15.8	13.8	10.2	49.9	9 235	8 895	-3.7	-5.3	543	795	-215	3 405	2.49	72.0	11.2	25.3
Collin	10.9	6.7	3.8	50.9	491 675	782 459	59.1	20.1	66 672	22 894	110 713	305 827	2.81	74.1	10.1	21.2
Collingsworth	12.6	9.8	8.2	51.5	3 206	3 057	-4.6	-1.3	249	235	-52	1 109	2.70	72.4	10.9	24.3
Colorado	15.4	11.7	9.7	49.9	20 390	20 874	2.4	0.7	1 592	1 656	164	7 657	2.67	72.2	9.4	25.4
Comal	14.8	11.3	6.9	50.7	78 021	108 471	39.0	24.3	8 748	6 389	23 153	43 951	2.70	74.3	9.5	21.4
Comanche	13.7	13.6	10.3	50.6	14 026	13 961	-0.5	-3.4	968	1 065	-380	5 119	2.62	69.3	10.6	28.0
Concho	11.7	9.0	6.5	29.5	3 966	4 087	3.1	4.7	163	189	217	813	3.30	74.3	9.6	23.4
Cooke	14.2	10.5	7.6	50.2	36 363	38 437	5.7	2.2	3 356	2 514	34	14 598	2.61	71.4	11.6	24.0
Coryell	8.6	5.9	3.9	50.5	74 978	75 388	0.5	-0.9	6 425	2 664	-4 651	21 829	2.86	75.2	13.3	21.2
Cottle	15.1	13.3	10.6	51.4	1 904	1 505	-21.0	-6.8	97	148	-49	635	2.38	68.0	9.0	29.0
Crane	11.6	6.8	5.2	50.1	3 996	4 375	9.5	10.4	467	226	205	1 542	3.01	72.7	8.4	23.2
Crockett	14.4	9.7	6.7	49.3	4 099	3 719	-9.3	-1.2	347	205	-170	1 433	2.53	73.7	6.1	20.0
Crosby	12.4	10.4	8.2	50.8	7 072	6 056	-14.4	-1.1	502	434	-124	2 189	2.71	72.7	14.5	24.9
Culberson	13.6	10.0	8.7	50.6	2 975	2 398	-19.4	-8.3	180	88	-294	788	2.86	68.5	14.3	29.8
Dallam	10.0	5.5	3.3	48.7	6 222	6 700	7.7	5.3	865	247	-273	2 256	3.09	69.7	13.5	28.1
Dallas	10.8	6.1	4.0	50.8	2 218 899	2 366 672	6.7	8.8	245 482	94 768	61 704	881 279	2.79	65.4	16.2	28.4
Dawson	10.5	8.1	7.1	45.5	14 985	13 833	-7.7	-5.2	1 148	859	-1 049	4 232	2.74	69.4	13.1	27.8
Deaf Smith	10.7	6.9	5.5	50.2	18 561	19 372	4.4	-2.8	2 115	908	-1 733	6 194	3.05	73.0	12.8	24.6
Delta	14.4	12.8	9.3	50.8	5 327	5 231	-1.8	-0.3	389	473	46	1 928	2.67	74.8	13.3	22.4
Denton	10.7	6.2	3.2	50.8	432 976	662 387	53.0	21.7	59 887	19 640	101 158	257 275	2.80	71.0	11.3	22.1
DeWitt	13.5	10.3	9.2	47.6	20 013	20 097	0.4	3.8	1 626	1 562	669	7 061	2.66	71.3	13.6	26.0
Dickens	14.4	11.2	9.4	42.9	2 762	2 441	-11.6	-10.5	121	156	-219	878	2.36	63.8	9.1	34.3
Dimmit	10.8	8.8	6.4	51.0	10 248	9 996	-2.5	8.0	1 113	565	256	3 568	2.96	62.5	16.4	36.1
Donley	13.1	12.6	10.7	50.7	3 828	3 728	-2.6	-8.7	200	314	-195	1 311	2.53	64.5	13.0	33.0
Duval	10.6	9.7	8.2	48.7	13 120	11 782	-10.2	-3.0	1 099	823	-660	3 937	2.80	70.2	16.6	25.0
Eastland	14.1	12.1	9.4	50.6	18 297	18 583	1.6	-1.7	1 261	1 572	17	6 810	2.55	59.4	11.0	36.7
Ector	9.9	5.6	4.2	49.4	121 123	137 136	13.2	14.8	17 706	7 362	9 866	50 868	2.91	71.2	16.1	23.0
Edwards	15.3	15.8	10.3	47.3	2 162	2 002	-7.4	-4.5	155	116	-145	747	2.54	65.3	6.7	33.2
Ellis	12.2	7.8	4.6	50.7	111 360	149 597	34.3	12.6	12 731	6 957	12 904	52 653	2.95	78.4	11.8	17.8
El Paso	10.2	6.6	5.3	50.8	679 622	800 647	17.8	4.7	85 139	31 224	-16 861	259 612	3.14	75.1	19.4	21.6
Erath	10.4	7.9	5.9	50.6	33 001	37 900	14.8	9.9	3 055	1 955	2 528	14 572	2.62	61.0	8.8	28.2
Falls	13.0	9.4	7.6	52.4	18 576	17 863	-3.8	-3.3	1 289	1 124	-711	5 418	2.86	62.2	12.4	34.5
Fannin	13.8	11.2	7.9	47.0	31 242	33 910	8.5	0.4	2 085	2 541	555	11 974	2.56	71.0	12.5	24.9
Fayette	15.9	13.2	11.3	50.9	21 804	24 554	12.6	2.4	1 532	1 884	894	9 558	2.55	68.7	6.7	28.3
Fisher	15.1	11.7	11.3	50.1	4 344	3 974	-8.5	-3.0	251	316	-41	1 667	2.29	61.8	9.7	33.3
Floyd	12.6	9.4	9.2	50.2	7 771	6 446	-17.1	-8.2	496	414	-619	2 413	2.54	73.4	14.3	24.8
Foard	14.5	12.7	12.9	52.3	1 622	1 336	-17.6	-11.5	68	123	-97	507	2.30	51.5	8.5	46.7
Fort Bend	12.0	6.9	3.6	50.8	354 452	584 703	65.0	26.8	54 353	17 019	116 489	206 188	3.17	82.7	12.6	14.9
Franklin	14.3	12.4	8.4	50.3	9 458	10 603	12.1	0.0	662	708	78	4 259	2.46	71.5	14.0	24.4
Freestone	13.3	11.2	8.0	48.0	17 867	19 817	10.9	-1.0	1 367	1 347	-213	7 406	2.44	71.9	15.5	25.9
Frio	9.1	7.0	4.9	41.3	16 252	17 217	5.9	10.1	1 586	806	981	4 794	3.14	77.6	20.4	19.2
Gaines	9.4	4.9	4.1	49.6	14 467	17 526	21.1	16.8	2 443	732	1 183	5 615	3.35	77.8	8.1	19.0
Galveston	13.4	8.3	5.2	50.7	250 158	291 303	16.4	13.1	25 163	15 382	27 504	113 866	2.66	68.2	13.1	25.9
Garza	11.4	5.9	5.7	35.1	4 872	6 461	32.6	-0.3	404	321	-112	1 532	2.70	76.1	18.3	21.0
Gillespie	15.5	15.6	14.1	51.8	20 814	24 837	19.3	6.8	1 563	2 088	2 097	10 577	2.36	67.9	7.6	29.3
Glasscock	12.9	8.8	5.0	44.7	1 406	1 226	-12.8	7.2	88	40	51	431	2.74	78.2	0.9	21.8
Goliad	16.1	12.3	8.9	50.5	6 928	7 210	4.1	4.3	429	468	346	2 881	2.54	73.4	12.0	23.5
Gonzales	12.8	8.7	7.4	49.4	18 628	19 807	6.3	5.4	1 849	1 216	442	6 477	3.07	71.5	16.0	26.3
Gray	11.9	8.3	7.0	46.9	22 744	22 535	-0.9	0.8	2 094	1 614	-277	8 250	2.59	67.0	9.3	29.0
Grayson	13.7	10.1	7.1	51.1	110 595	120 864	9.3	6.1	9 535	8 538	6 176	47 215	2.55	68.4	13.1	26.6
Gregg	12.2	8.2	6.6	51.1	111 379	121 764	9.3	1.6	11 956	7 833	-2 268	45 618	2.61	67.0	16.5	28.7
Grimes	14.2	10.8	6.4	45.5	23 552	26 568	12.8	4.2	1 990	1 719	763	9 005	2.63	68.7	14.2	28.1

1. No spouse present.

Table B. States and Counties — Population, Vital Statistics, Health, and Crime

STATE County	Persons in group quarters, 2016	Daytime population, 2011–2015		Births, 2016		Deaths, 2016		Persons under 65 with no health insurance, 2015		Medicare, 2015			Serious crimes known to police,[2] 2014 Total	
		Number	Employ-ment/resi-dence ratio	Total	Rate[1]	Number	Rate[1]	Number	Percent	Total Beneficiaries	Enrolled in Original Medicare	Enrolled in Medicare Advantage	Number	Rate[3]
	32	33	34	35	36	37	38	39	40	41	42	43	44	45
TEXAS—Cont'd														
Caldwell	3 349	32 550	0.59	535	13.0	314	7.6	7 618	22.7	6 191	4 472	1 719	787	1 977
Calhoun	251	24 676	1.32	302	13.7	219	10.0	3 625	20.0	3 695	3 146	549	565	2 842
Callahan	77	11 151	0.52	155	11.2	177	12.8	2 040	18.9	2 766	2 111	655	202	1 482
Cameron	3 381	414 291	0.97	7 147	16.9	2 712	6.4	103 400	28.6	55 300	31 163	24 137	15 087	3 569
Camp	67	11 216	0.74	197	15.3	119	9.2	2 389	22.9	2 865	2 074	791	397	3 175
Carson	25	5 415	0.77	61	10.1	53	8.8	779	15.7	1 012	792	220	67	1 114
Cass	365	27 570	0.77	369	12.1	430	14.2	3 871	16.4	7 496	5 421	2 075	912	3 027
Castro	64	7 501	0.86	115	15.0	46	6.0	1 965	30.3	1 048	901	147	188	2 330
Chambers	221	36 039	0.92	503	12.6	259	6.5	5 343	15.5	2 944	2 017	927	1 087	2 900
Cherokee	2 904	47 817	0.83	782	15.1	527	10.2	8 775	21.7	8 106	5 635	2 471	1 487	2 913
Childress	1 424	7 301	1.10	73	10.4	58	8.2	637	13.8	1 215	920	295	NA	NA
Clay	61	7 890	0.42	80	7.8	125	12.3	1 373	16.7	1 675	1 394	281	152	1 450
Cochran	78	2 833	0.86	45	15.6	8	2.8	709	28.7	546	435	111	131	4 355
Coke	36	2 743	0.66	31	9.5	48	14.7	421	17.6	796	620	176	30	936
Coleman	40	7 839	0.78	77	9.1	112	13.3	1 382	21.8	2 312	1 928	384	NA	NA
Collin	4 800	813 256	0.89	11 045	11.8	4 344	4.6	89 681	11.0	84 720	59 992	24 728	16 724	1 903
Collingsworth	50	2 769	0.78	26	8.6	32	10.6	821	33.1	615	536	79	16	510
Colorado	350	20 291	0.95	266	12.7	253	12.0	3 221	19.7	4 253	3 622	631	291	1 394
Comal	1 243	117 759	0.96	1 597	11.8	1 085	8.0	16 838	16.0	26 481	18 614	7 867	3 122	2 564
Comanche	165	12 242	0.74	147	10.9	185	13.7	2 705	26.5	3 153	2 485	668	315	2 310
Concho	1 629	4 273	1.20	28	6.5	26	6.1	347	18.8	597	463	134	3	74
Cooke	649	37 835	0.95	561	14.3	414	10.5	6 232	19.6	6 656	5 162	1 494	NA	NA
Coryell	11 512	66 306	0.67	1 042	14.0	477	6.4	7 652	13.3	8 042	5 703	2 339	1 461	1 900
Cottle	0	1 474	0.94	16	11.4	18	12.8	301	27.6	406	316	90	14	966
Crane	90	4 745	1.01	77	15.9	23	4.8	877	19.8	550	429	121	48	977
Crockett	49	3 925	1.12	53	14.4	18	4.9	673	21.6	604	505	99	51	1 321
Crosby	60	5 293	0.71	92	15.4	68	11.3	1 158	24.0	1 142	792	350	35	720
Culberson	12	2 255	0.96	28	12.7	13	5.9	517	28.6	450	364	86	15	663
Dallam	40	7 572	1.17	144	20.4	27	3.8	1 867	29.0	1 395	1 169	226	187	2 603
Dallas	33 538	2 805 509	1.27	40 063	15.6	16 407	6.4	510 960	22.6	295 649	180 205	115 444	93 245	3 691
Dawson	1 357	13 517	0.99	182	13.9	130	9.9	2 264	23.2	2 197	1 754	443	486	3 496
Deaf Smith	343	19 468	1.03	322	17.1	165	8.8	4 046	24.6	2 546	2 072	474	559	2 904
Delta	62	4 280	0.48	65	12.5	59	11.3	707	17.5	1 258	1 026	232	66	1 251
Denton	11 423	598 809	0.65	10 153	12.6	3 692	4.6	90 301	12.9	58 819	39 461	19 358	14 355	1 912
DeWitt	1 845	21 428	1.11	285	13.7	235	11.3	2 607	17.1	3 588	3 048	540	590	2 841
Dickens	315	2 403	1.17	18	8.2	19	8.7	327	22.9	530	417	113	17	750
Dimmit	100	15 370	2.14	179	16.6	100	9.3	1 714	18.5	1 707	1 115	592	438	3 908
Donley	207	3 349	0.83	26	7.6	49	14.4	521	21.5	821	669	152	58	1 652
Duval	524	11 261	0.93	182	15.9	148	13.0	1 766	20.0	2 216	1 424	792	NA	NA
Eastland	886	18 234	0.99	201	11.0	250	13.7	2 828	20.7	4 364	3 362	1 002	445	2 543
Ector	2 636	149 961	1.01	3 145	20.0	1 247	7.9	30 616	21.5	18 182	14 241	3 941	7 375	4 797
Edwards	5	1 824	0.91	26	13.6	14	7.3	436	31.2	706	541	165	32	1 709
Ellis	1 675	134 418	0.69	2 182	12.9	1 236	7.3	25 446	17.9	24 264	17 255	7 009	3 200	2 028
El Paso	16 225	829 169	0.99	13 320	15.9	5 432	6.5	164 421	22.8	111 309	45 790	65 519	20 101	2 393
Erath	3 965	39 176	0.95	500	12.0	335	8.0	7 684	24.0	5 773	4 369	1 404	780	1 930
Falls	1 977	15 357	0.66	213	12.3	162	9.4	2 598	21.2	2 765	1 815	950	187	1 215
Fannin	3 061	30 065	0.72	327	9.6	439	12.9	4 838	19.5	6 891	5 527	1 364	441	1 411
Fayette	421	23 911	0.92	261	10.4	302	12.0	3 947	20.8	6 222	5 074	1 148	421	1 679
Fisher	22	3 355	0.71	51	13.2	51	13.2	495	16.9	835	659	176	152	3 937
Floyd	35	5 974	0.92	71	12.0	60	10.1	1 121	23.6	1 189	860	329	125	2 793
Foard	29	1 140	0.87	4	3.4	9	7.6	202	22.0	379	322	57	0	0
Fort Bend	5 397	518 857	0.55	9 870	13.3	3 317	4.5	81 599	12.8	51 655	31 119	20 536	12 516	1 858
Franklin	73	10 825	1.05	102	9.6	130	12.3	1 565	18.5	1 793	1 358	435	163	1 516
Freestone	1 634	18 390	0.84	211	10.8	200	10.2	3 004	20.6	3 592	2 771	821	268	1 357
Frio	3 377	20 579	1.37	261	13.8	145	7.6	2 692	20.3	2 357	1 579	778	475	2 580
Gaines	82	18 435	0.94	442	21.6	129	6.3	5 982	33.0	1 798	1 495	303	227	1 169
Galveston	5 039	275 732	0.77	4 259	12.9	2 796	8.5	41 972	15.2	47 909	33 049	14 860	9 911	3 170
Garza	2 151	6 689	1.14	64	9.9	43	6.7	823	23.1	796	552	244	64	1 011
Gillespie	365	25 498	1.01	262	9.9	343	12.9	4 214	23.0	7 296	5 953	1 343	363	1 414
Glasscock	0	1 527	1.70	14	10.7	5	3.8	191	16.8	147	125	22	11	869
Goliad	90	6 219	0.59	75	10.0	71	9.4	799	13.5	1 358	1 072	286	115	1 517
Gonzales	311	20 864	1.08	331	15.9	191	9.1	4 195	24.7	3 704	2 954	750	652	3 168
Gray	2 020	22 877	0.99	336	14.8	259	11.4	3 897	21.9	4 191	3 433	758	1 024	4 384
Grayson	2 251	117 540	0.90	1 582	12.3	1 402	10.9	20 594	20.1	26 011	20 343	5 668	2 961	2 417
Gregg	4 136	144 201	1.38	1 908	15.4	1 288	10.4	21 206	20.5	25 837	19 274	6 563	5 349	4 307
Grimes	2 919	24 647	0.76	337	12.2	251	9.1	4 308	21.2	4 849	3 448	1 401	600	2 212

1. Per 1,000 estimated resident population.   2. Data for serious crimes have not been adjusted for underreporting; this may affect comparability between geographic areas and over time.
3. Per 100,000 population estimated by the FBI.

Table B. States and Counties — Crime, Education, Money Income, and Poverty

STATE County	Violent [46]	Property [47]	Total [48]	Percent private [49]	High school graduate or less [50]	Bachelor's degree or more [51]	Total current spending (mil dol) [52]	Current spending per student (dollars) [53]	Per capita income (dollars) [54]	Median income (dollars) [55]	with income of less than $50,000 [56]	with income of $200,000 or more [57]	Median household income (dollars) [58]	All persons [59]	Children under 18 years [60]	Children 5 to 17 years in families [61]
TEXAS—Cont'd																
Caldwell	201	1 776	9 642	5.7	57.0	15.4	55.3	8 215	20 667	47 233	54.1	2.3	46 093	17.8	25.2	23.4
Calhoun	372	2 469	5 194	5.5	51.9	16.2	35.5	8 283	24 372	51 078	49.1	2.2	50 873	16.8	26.2	24.4
Callahan	110	1 372	2 935	11.4	51.2	14.3	22.4	9 134	22 387	40 981	58.8	2.4	44 450	13.0	21.0	19.4
Cameron	259	3 310	128 154	4.2	59.3	16.4	931.6	9 168	15 105	33 266	65.1	1.7	34 044	32.0	45.9	44.7
Camp	432	2 743	3 010	3.5	58.2	14.3	28.1	11 442	19 738	37 851	62.4	1.8	40 768	18.8	30.6	29.4
Carson	266	848	1 540	9.2	38.6	24.4	13.7	10 640	28 400	66 023	35.1	2.3	61 083	8.5	11.2	9.6
Cass	378	2 649	6 427	3.5	58.4	13.6	51.1	9 078	20 991	37 352	62.1	1.5	39 274	20.0	29.4	28.7
Castro	124	2 206	2 055	2.3	63.1	13.2	18.8	11 025	21 068	39 459	62.5	1.3	43 372	18.8	28.8	27.2
Chambers	277	2 623	9 909	6.7	48.8	18.7	72.5	9 887	30 572	70 544	38.2	5.7	77 282	9.6	12.0	11.2
Cherokee	380	2 533	12 943	10.8	55.1	16.3	89.4	8 155	19 420	39 595	61.6	1.6	41 355	19.0	27.6	26.6
Childress	NA	NA	1 432	11.0	53.2	16.7	10.2	8 996	19 861	36 633	57.5	1.6	37 732	22.3	27.5	25.5
Clay	124	1 326	2 316	11.1	50.7	15.9	17.7	10 341	26 339	48 297	51.5	3.6	51 234	12.3	18.9	17.5
Cochran	166	4 189	776	5.0	63.9	12.2	12.3	15 028	18 968	39 113	63.6	1.9	39 398	22.5	34.7	32.9
Coke	31	905	707	3.5	45.3	20.6	5.9	11 383	29 355	42 467	55.4	2.3	42 498	13.5	21.3	19.8
Coleman	NA	NA	1 563	6.4	58.9	11.8	13.4	10 506	20 085	35 156	67.9	1.2	35 922	20.0	33.6	31.0
Collin	159	1 744	249 604	13.0	22.1	49.8	1 477.8	7 998	38 883	84 735	28.2	11.0	86 823	6.6	8.2	7.4
Collingsworth	32	478	708	6.5	53.9	15.2	5.9	9 631	20 269	39 743	61.3	0.8	38 775	19.0	32.1	29.1
Colorado	187	1 207	4 362	14.1	56.3	18.2	32.0	9 049	25 578	46 618	54.4	3.4	47 783	14.5	23.6	21.6
Comal	301	2 264	27 795	13.6	35.1	33.4	199.9	7 190	32 838	65 833	37.7	6.5	68 362	8.3	12.7	11.6
Comanche	264	2 046	2 836	8.5	58.4	16.7	21.3	9 362	19 743	37 470	65.2	1.2	41 155	16.8	27.2	25.0
Concho	0	74	754	6.0	66.9	11.6	5.1	10 925	15 820	48 368	52.9	3.6	39 945	26.4	25.5	23.7
Cooke	NA	NA	9 095	11.5	45.0	21.0	56.2	8 895	26 742	52 406	47.7	3.1	54 534	13.2	20.5	19.4
Coryell	181	1 719	22 313	9.2	42.1	14.8	95.9	8 344	19 760	49 340	51.0	1.8	45 989	16.0	24.0	23.7
Cottle	483	483	358	16.5	55.6	15.2	2.8	13 352	18 926	34 955	69.3	0.9	35 602	21.4	36.1	29.9
Crane	142	834	1 288	4.3	58.2	12.8	14.4	12 545	23 808	58 333	41.4	3.1	65 883	9.6	12.8	11.8
Crockett	181	1 140	635	2.2	56.0	13.4	10.2	12 556	26 675	53 678	44.5	0.9	53 903	12.9	18.6	17.4
Crosby	103	617	1 501	7.5	61.0	11.7	15.7	13 167	18 692	37 434	64.4	1.5	34 562	22.8	34.8	31.6
Culberson	0	663	475	1.3	70.8	9.9	5.2	11 220	17 340	35 000	67.8	2.9	35 192	23.9	37.2	37.2
Dallam	612	1 990	2 033	10.6	58.7	11.1	16.8	8 663	19 997	41 345	59.3	2.2	47 559	12.0	17.7	17.0
Dallas	443	3 248	673 135	12.9	45.2	29.1	4 093.6	8 412	27 605	50 270	49.7	5.5	51 824	17.9	26.5	26.6
Dawson	403	3 093	3 142	2.5	64.9	11.0	29.7	11 058	19 889	41 095	58.4	3.5	42 589	21.9	29.5	28.6
Deaf Smith	301	2 602	5 778	6.6	58.7	14.8	36.3	8 281	18 846	43 373	57.1	1.8	45 713	19.4	28.1	25.7
Delta	38	1 213	1 120	6.3	48.1	18.8	7.4	9 313	20 704	42 432	55.2	1.5	42 846	18.5	28.4	26.7
Denton	167	1 745	223 446	12.1	27.4	41.3	1 114.7	8 131	34 914	75 050	32.1	8.5	75 898	8.0	9.0	8.3
DeWitt	611	2 229	4 172	6.8	58.9	14.5	34.4	11 569	28 418	49 736	50.2	7.3	47 365	19.2	27.2	25.7
Dickens	88	661	433	1.2	52.0	15.5	5.5	13 696	20 659	39 700	58.8	1.5	39 169	22.2	29.2	28.7
Dimmit	143	3 766	3 034	5.2	61.6	11.9	23.0	9 350	21 174	36 825	58.8	3.7	40 040	24.4	34.5	33.2
Donley	541	1 111	936	8.7	50.0	15.2	6.8	11 986	20 204	36 681	62.2	1.3	36 862	20.2	32.8	32.0
Duval	NA	NA	2 443	4.9	64.9	8.1	25.4	9 872	20 752	33 939	63.8	3.2	36 986	25.4	37.4	34.9
Eastland	200	2 343	4 161	9.1	53.2	14.4	27.6	9 424	22 135	34 888	67.6	2.5	41 944	18.1	27.9	26.8
Ector	911	3 886	41 691	9.6	54.5	14.6	236.0	7 368	26 135	57 150	44.0	4.0	62 519	12.6	17.4	16.8
Edwards	107	1 603	292	0.0	49.7	25.1	7.1	12 490	27 893	41 813	52.6	1.2	37 567	22.2	39.6	37.4
Ellis	114	1 914	44 547	11.0	45.1	21.2	263.4	8 083	26 357	62 465	39.5	4.3	66 811	10.9	15.6	13.6
El Paso	364	2 029	262 714	7.4	48.8	21.3	1 569.7	8 824	18 880	41 637	58.4	2.1	43 101	20.3	29.4	28.8
Erath	151	1 779	13 388	6.4	42.7	26.6	48.9	8 453	21 903	41 416	59.6	2.1	45 663	17.7	21.1	20.0
Falls	195	1 020	4 048	7.1	61.5	11.8	25.0	11 019	16 739	36 079	62.2	0.7	37 912	23.9	32.7	32.4
Fannin	147	1 264	7 495	8.8	52.7	16.0	51.8	9 321	20 545	44 071	54.9	1.4	43 733	16.4	23.0	23.3
Fayette	263	1 416	5 079	11.9	57.2	16.0	36.9	9 886	28 458	47 808	51.3	4.4	53 173	12.0	17.9	16.3
Fisher	285	3 652	714	3.6	50.3	16.3	6.1	11 285	26 855	41 406	58.4	1.2	43 082	15.2	22.6	19.4
Floyd	469	2 324	1 588	6.9	55.3	16.6	14.4	11 483	22 195	41 026	59.5	1.8	36 859	21.8	36.4	34.4
Foard	0	0	201	2.0	48.3	22.7	3.0	13 399	22 871	36 477	60.6	0.0	36 466	17.8	28.2	25.0
Fort Bend	267	1 591	203 007	13.7	28.6	43.7	1 381.4	7 921	35 962	89 152	26.3	13.4	95 117	7.0	9.7	8.8
Franklin	233	1 284	2 392	13.3	48.4	18.1	14.8	8 969	26 653	41 537	56.1	5.5	43 569	16.4	27.0	24.1
Freestone	167	1 190	4 360	3.3	52.1	12.3	39.5	10 749	24 087	44 301	54.1	2.6	48 057	15.8	21.9	20.2
Frio	299	2 281	4 367	9.4	68.2	8.0	33.4	10 005	17 017	36 404	61.5	2.9	38 809	29.3	35.8	34.3
Gaines	46	1 123	4 694	21.4	67.3	11.8	45.0	13 078	22 744	57 635	42.3	3.0	53 297	13.3	20.1	18.9
Galveston	274	2 895	84 391	10.8	37.0	29.3	647.8	8 080	31 585	62 313	40.8	6.8	66 173	14.0	19.1	18.9
Garza	79	932	1 270	7.1	68.2	9.4	10.0	10 499	18 125	48 508	52.4	4.6	54 606	26.8	27.3	24.8
Gillespie	51	1 364	4 963	22.7	39.9	33.5	35.5	9 962	30 859	54 859	45.9	4.9	54 180	10.4	18.0	17.0
Glasscock	0	869	364	0.0	46.6	24.6	6.1	20 545	35 054	67 303	37.8	12.5	74 854	7.8	10.5	9.2
Goliad	211	1 306	1 601	2.2	51.0	13.9	14.0	10 255	29 513	51 226	48.2	4.9	52 612	14.1	21.2	18.5
Gonzales	661	2 507	5 086	9.9	61.6	13.8	40.4	9 783	21 185	42 983	56.3	2.9	43 519	16.4	25.6	23.3
Gray	492	3 891	5 320	9.9	52.5	13.6	37.5	8 971	21 555	43 288	55.4	1.2	49 415	13.0	17.8	17.0
Grayson	272	2 145	30 443	11.3	44.8	20.3	190.8	8 828	25 033	47 952	51.5	2.7	48 164	15.2	22.6	20.5
Gregg	443	3 864	31 636	11.0	44.1	20.5	217.7	9 089	24 364	47 639	52.5	2.8	48 561	17.0	23.4	22.9
Grimes	498	1 714	6 388	6.9	57.5	11.5	41.6	9 358	20 891	46 195	53.2	2.7	44 226	17.8	25.3	24.8

1. Data for serious crimes have not been adjusted for underreporting; this may affect comparability between geographic areas and over time.   2. Per 100,000 population estimated by the FBI.
3. All persons 3 years old and over enrolled in nursery school through college.   4. Persons 25 years old and over.   5. Elementary and secondary education expenditures.
6. Based on population estimated by the American Community Survey, 2011–2015.

Table B. States and Counties — **Personal Income**

STATE County	Personal income, 2015										Earnings, 2015		
			Per capita[1]			Supplements to wages and salaries; employer contributions (mil dol)						Contributions for government social insurance (mil dol)	
	Total (mil dol)	Percent change, 2014–2015	Dollars	Rank	Wages and salaries (mil dol)	Pension and insurance	Government social insurance	Proprietors' income (mil dol)	Dividends, interest, and rent (mil dol)	Personal transfer receipts (mil dol)	Total (mil dol)	From employee and self-employed	From employer
	62	63	64	65	66	67	68	69	70	71	72	73	74
TEXAS—Cont'd													
Caldwell	1 253	6.5	30 925	2 798	324	56	23	115	184	324	519	31	23
Calhoun	846	1.1	38 618	1 319	767	126	52	71	114	200	1 016	54	52
Callahan	514	2.9	37 919	1 758	92	17	6	47	81	133	162	11	6
Cameron	11 325	5.2	26 826	3 057	4 642	951	332	1 143	1 380	3 587	7 068	380	332
Camp	495	8.0	39 031	1 786	153	27	10	78	83	129	268	14	10
Carson	270	5.8	45 244	684	352	36	24	44	36	45	456	24	24
Cass	1 035	3.4	34 149	2 136	279	55	20	100	146	367	452	28	20
Castro	487	21.3	63 583	268	117	17	7	242	38	64	383	7	7
Chambers	1 929	4.4	49 647	523	763	122	51	114	207	250	1 050	56	51
Cherokee	1 663	4.0	32 274	2 384	551	112	36	163	230	505	863	47	36
Childress	195	6.0	27 471	3 041	92	22	5	15	32	60	134	7	5
Clay	436	0.2	42 079	393	59	12	4	46	70	98	120	7	4
Cochran	122	0.1	41 223	628	35	7	2	31	15	29	76	2	2
Coke	113	1.8	34 766	2 178	26	6	2	11	22	38	44	3	2
Coleman	315	1.7	37 783	1 823	71	15	5	41	65	111	132	8	5
Collin	54 420	7.3	59 532	144	24 079	2 776	1 606	6 074	7 216	4 026	34 535	1 765	1 606
Collingsworth	111	1.1	36 558	1 536	39	7	3	12	20	34	61	3	3
Colorado	989	4.7	47 370	644	304	48	21	119	185	226	492	27	21
Comal	6 931	7.2	53 710	404	2 141	294	149	801	1 230	1 097	3 386	186	149
Comanche	494	-1.0	36 797	1 253	129	24	9	69	85	147	231	13	9
Concho	90	-2.5	22 008	3 082	37	6	3	4	19	32	50	3	3
Cooke	2 093	3.8	53 355	182	767	123	53	554	321	347	1 497	72	53
Coryell	2 441	4.3	32 334	2 338	612	132	39	86	476	530	869	45	39
Cottle	71	-0.9	50 074	190	13	3	1	5	29	18	22	1	1
Crane	200	-11.3	39 581	650	88	14	6	34	17	31	143	7	6
Crockett	165	0.7	44 453	1 004	82	15	5	18	39	28	120	6	5
Crosby	196	2.4	32 805	2 238	59	10	4	11	30	73	84	5	4
Culberson	92	1.8	41 138	1 713	51	9	4	4	13	25	67	4	4
Dallam	494	18.5	69 427	130	172	23	13	238	40	51	446	14	13
Dallas	135 803	4.9	53 186	282	108 826	12 700	7 335	25 335	26 461	15 977	154 196	7 800	7 335
Dawson	467	1.8	34 562	2 189	171	34	11	67	86	122	283	13	11
Deaf Smith	918	16.8	48 426	1 102	314	49	20	352	88	153	736	22	20
Delta	193	5.4	37 050	1 793	33	9	2	16	21	60	60	4	2
Denton	39 118	7.6	50 112	522	11 113	1 530	764	3 068	4 544	3 670	16 476	850	764
DeWitt	1 125	2.9	54 074	499	364	64	23	136	373	222	586	31	23
Dickens	69	7.4	31 260	2 789	21	5	1	5	13	24	33	2	1
Dimmit	529	-1.3	48 203	476	326	51	24	57	71	107	458	23	24
Donley	147	5.7	41 903	1 306	33	8	2	34	23	37	76	3	2
Duval	440	-4.1	38 675	1 208	153	30	10	26	49	154	220	13	10
Eastland	915	-3.4	50 345	69	359	60	26	35	293	222	479	28	26
Ector	7 303	-5.0	45 806	520	4 270	541	284	1 009	801	979	6 104	311	284
Edwards	76	5.3	39 920	1 272	16	3	1	9	9	22	30	2	1
Ellis	6 504	7.0	39 747	1 551	2 057	321	147	510	693	1 103	3 034	168	147
El Paso	27 252	4.9	32 614	2 463	13 109	2 760	1 003	2 041	4 362	6 357	18 913	966	1 003
Erath	1 363	3.5	33 144	2 423	564	107	37	193	220	310	901	43	37
Falls	549	0.4	31 999	2 194	129	32	8	45	76	185	215	12	8
Fannin	1 194	5.7	35 449	2 118	287	64	20	75	162	351	446	28	20
Fayette	1 285	3.2	51 176	515	385	64	25	118	363	265	593	34	25
Fisher	190	8.2	49 777	856	38	8	2	31	27	43	79	4	2
Floyd	268	7.6	45 346	1 110	62	12	4	89	32	65	167	5	4
Foard	49	-5.4	40 220	1 066	11	2	1	6	10	18	20	1	1
Fort Bend	40 162	5.9	56 086	215	9 353	1 206	611	3 535	4 806	3 197	14 704	757	611
Franklin	396	5.4	37 137	1 366	123	19	9	61	63	106	212	11	9
Freestone	669	3.2	33 956	1 732	285	50	20	55	126	176	410	24	20
Frio	688	-1.8	36 612	1 916	377	54	25	73	82	148	529	27	25
Gaines	809	10.1	40 365	1 717	325	53	21	231	84	106	631	26	21
Galveston	15 464	4.7	47 991	526	5 086	979	328	914	2 332	2 481	7 307	376	328
Garza	234	-3.7	36 549	60	75	13	5	63	46	44	156	7	5
Gillespie	1 413	5.3	54 441	323	390	62	27	150	515	280	629	38	27
Glasscock	103	1.0	78 529	81	28	5	2	11	53	6	46	2	2
Goliad	345	1.3	45 825	1 143	54	11	3	26	80	73	95	6	3
Gonzales	1 007	9.6	48 960	996	293	51	19	254	216	187	617	24	19
Gray	1 091	-0.8	47 024	500	437	74	28	208	206	188	747	35	28
Grayson	4 916	5.5	39 181	1 595	1 946	301	138	351	734	1 237	2 736	160	138
Gregg	5 791	-0.9	46 664	387	3 722	505	268	766	939	1 179	5 261	281	268
Grimes	1 018	5.2	36 985	1 937	390	67	26	84	163	224	567	32	26

1. Based on the resident population estimated as of July 1 of the year shown.

Table B. States and Counties — Earnings, Social Security, and Housing

| STATE County | Earnings, 2015 (cont.) | | | | | | | | | Social Security beneficiaries, December 2015 | | Housing units, 2016 | | |
| | Percent by selected industries | | | | | | | | | | | | | |
	Farm	Mining	Construction	Manufacturing	Information: professional, scientific, technical services	Retail trade	Finance, insurance, real estate and leasing	Health care and social assistance	Government	Number	Rate[1]	Supplemental Security Income recipients, December 2015	Total	Percent change 2010–2016
	75	76	77	78	79	80	81	82	83	84	85	86	87	88
TEXAS—Cont'd														
Caldwell	1.3	8.7	11.6	5.0	3.4	8.7	4.0	12.2	18.3	7 120	176	1 070	14 329	4.2
Calhoun	0.4	1.5	21.3	42.6	4.3	4.3	5.6	2.8	8.1	4 345	198	570	11 880	4.1
Callahan	3.0	5.4	19.5	5.2	4.3	10.7	3.1	5.2	20.5	3 340	246	313	6 604	0.8
Cameron	0.5	0.2	4.5	5.3	3.6	9.5	4.3	19.2	26.8	62 795	150	23 072	148 656	4.7
Camp	12.5	D	11.5	4.7	D	6.4	5.6	8.3	11.3	2 945	232	504	5 701	0.8
Carson	6.6	D	3.3	D	D	1.7	D	D	4.8	1 180	198	55	2 779	-0.2
Cass	5.2	2.6	9.3	20.6	D	6.0	3.5	D	18.5	8 160	269	1 200	14 463	0.6
Castro	68.8	1.0	0.7	0.8	2.0	1.7	2.0	0.6	7.7	1 220	159	151	3 182	0.5
Chambers	0.9	6.3	12.5	29.3	D	3.3	6.9	D	12.1	6 120	158	494	15 106	13.6
Cherokee	9.5	1.6	7.3	12.6	D	5.6	4.7	D	25.3	10 740	209	1 467	21 021	0.8
Childress	2.3	D	D	D	5.8	7.3	5.5	5.7	45.4	1 310	186	171	2 857	-0.9
Clay	15.2	11.4	7.1	5.2	D	6.9	3.2	D	21.7	2 555	247	166	5 161	0.2
Cochran	43.1	9.0	D	D	0.6	3.3	1.7	2.0	23.0	600	204	111	1 356	-0.3
Coke	3.0	11.1	8.6	D	D	7.9	D	2.1	31.2	905	280	74	2 667	0.1
Coleman	2.5	5.9	12.6	3.3	D	5.3	8.4	D	21.3	2 460	295	267	5 523	-0.4
Collin	0.0	2.1	6.1	8.2	19.1	7.7	12.7	9.9	8.8	97 680	107	8 197	351 306	16.7
Collingsworth	10.4	D	D	D	7.2	4.9	3.8	D	17.7	640	212	75	1 605	-0.7
Colorado	2.6	4.4	13.3	17.8	D	6.7	4.8	D	11.7	5 025	241	474	10 575	0.5
Comal	-0.1	2.1	15.4	6.0	7.2	10.4	5.5	10.5	10.8	27 890	216	1 449	54 803	16.3
Comanche	17.6	2.0	5.8	3.4	4.7	9.5	4.1	9.0	16.2	3 665	274	350	7 272	0.7
Concho	1.4	D	D	D	0.4	2.5	D	9.9	27.6	700	168	68	1 648	0.7
Cooke	0.8	24.7	4.3	23.5	3.1	4.6	4.1	D	10.7	7 825	200	611	16 765	1.0
Coryell	0.6	1.3	8.7	2.2	D	6.5	5.2	6.2	41.8	10 185	135	1 197	26 411	4.9
Cottle	19.5	0.5	8.5	0.9	D	10.4	D	3.9	29.3	440	307	52	956	-1.2
Crane	1.1	D	D	D	D	2.6	D	3.4	16.1	700	139	99	1 663	1.9
Crockett	4.1	42.4	D	D	D	4.9	5.3	D	16.7	705	188	53	1 873	0.4
Crosby	12.9	D	D	D	D	13.6	D	7.3	25.9	1 310	219	175	2 915	0.5
Culberson	3.9	D	D	D	D	13.2	D	D	31.4	525	235	119	1 153	1.4
Dallam	37.2	D	7.0	10.5	2.7	2.7	3.8	1.0	3.6	970	136	104	2 915	3.1
Dallas	0.0	5.2	6.1	7.6	17.1	4.9	12.3	9.1	8.9	309 025	121	65 901	1 002 962	6.4
Dawson	11.1	9.6	5.3	1.6	2.5	16.5	3.8	D	27.6	2 445	187	426	5 197	-0.4
Deaf Smith	43.7	D	2.9	12.8	1.7	4.8	2.4	1.7	10.1	2 835	151	424	7 069	-0.1
Delta	13.8	0.4	8.4	D	D	2.0	D	D	24.0	1 390	267	191	2 471	0.5
Denton	0.2	1.7	8.7	7.8	11.0	7.7	8.6	9.9	14.2	81 890	105	6 297	297 896	16.3
DeWitt	0.4	16.9	9.1	10.9	4.6	6.8	6.9	4.1	20.4	4 545	219	530	9 191	0.2
Dickens	10.3	D	D	D	D	5.9	D	1.3	24.1	580	264	42	1 281	0.0
Dimmit	3.8	23.9	14.1	1.1	D	4.0	2.4	D	20.3	1 990	181	578	4 371	0.5
Donley	37.2	D	D	D	D	4.6	6.1	3.3	24.6	880	258	77	2 131	-0.4
Duval	0.5	18.7	D	D	D	3.5	D	6.4	28.9	2 510	220	661	5 552	0.5
Eastland	1.0	13.4	11.8	6.6	3.0	5.5	9.9	D	22.5	4 635	256	606	10 257	0.0
Ector	0.0	20.2	13.8	9.3	3.8	7.0	5.3	5.1	10.8	19 630	123	3 453	57 602	8.6
Edwards	18.6	D	D	D	D	7.8	D	D	27.9	535	280	84	1 612	0.4
Ellis	0.3	0.7	10.5	24.5	D	7.1	3.8	6.7	13.6	25 545	156	2 932	59 390	9.3
El Paso	0.1	0.0	4.1	5.9	5.3	7.9	4.7	10.0	37.0	124 155	149	29 860	293 638	8.6
Erath	10.8	1.4	9.4	10.7	D	6.8	4.2	9.1	21.0	6 350	153	557	17 776	4.6
Falls	8.2	D	5.7	3.7	3.5	6.7	D	8.9	38.0	3 520	205	735	7 731	0.1
Fannin	1.1	D	7.3	8.9	2.9	9.6	5.2	D	35.8	7 820	232	853	14 291	0.7
Fayette	1.4	7.8	9.0	8.2	5.8	8.9	7.7	8.9	16.5	6 445	257	448	13 895	0.2
Fisher	21.6	1.7	D	D	D	4.1	6.0	3.6	20.6	975	253	96	2 207	-0.2
Floyd	51.4	D	1.4	2.0	D	2.9	D	2.9	15.9	1 260	214	175	2 997	-0.2
Foard	23.7	1.1	D	D	D	4.6	D	D	22.6	360	296	35	789	0.0
Fort Bend	0.1	5.6	14.2	10.5	10.3	8.6	5.8	8.8	10.6	74 075	104	10 385	242 441	23.2
Franklin	17.0	D	5.8	D	D	2.9	D	15.9	11.0	2 430	230	173	5 798	0.5
Freestone	2.7	23.9	10.2	2.2	4.0	6.2	4.2	D	17.8	4 015	204	421	9 317	0.6
Frio	6.6	22.2	6.4	3.5	D	4.0	5.5	D	15.4	2 735	144	720	5 914	1.2
Gaines	9.1	20.7	19.2	1.6	1.6	6.6	2.4	D	12.4	2 085	103	307	6 378	1.2
Galveston	0.0	1.5	8.4	12.4	6.3	6.9	7.2	6.7	27.6	52 540	163	6 772	144 508	9.1
Garza	1.6	38.8	5.6	2.9	D	3.5	1.8	D	13.0	840	132	107	2 217	-0.9
Gillespie	0.4	2.6	15.8	8.1	7.0	9.9	5.9	17.4	11.0	7 920	304	293	12 999	1.7
Glasscock	4.2	D	D	D	2.0	D	D	0.5	15.0	205	154	0	583	0.5
Goliad	-4.7	12.3	16.6	3.5	D	4.1	D	5.1	24.8	1 665	221	178	3 727	0.5
Gonzales	28.6	5.7	2.9	9.7	2.3	4.6	3.6	D	13.9	4 010	195	526	8 859	0.7
Gray	9.2	18.7	4.9	23.2	D	5.8	2.7	6.3	11.3	4 275	184	349	10 078	-0.8
Grayson	0.4	1.7	8.7	15.8	4.5	8.3	7.0	18.5	13.4	27 255	217	3 031	54 973	2.3
Gregg	0.0	14.3	10.7	11.1	6.7	8.0	5.0	12.9	8.1	24 260	196	4 611	51 829	4.6
Grimes	0.3	1.8	8.4	27.6	D	5.3	4.6	D	19.1	5 435	198	738	11 043	1.2

1. Per 1,000 resident population estimated as of July 1 of the year shown.

Table B. States and Counties — Housing, Labor Force, and Employment

STATE County	Housing units, 2011–2015								Civilian labor force, 2016				Civilian employment,[6] 2011–2015		
	Occupied units							Sub-stand-ard units[4] (percent)		Percent change, 2015–2016	Unemployment			Percent	
	Owner-occupied					Renter-occupied									
				Median owner cost as a percent of income											Con-struction, produc-tion, and mainte-nance occu-pations
	Total	Percent	Median value[1]	With a mort-gage	Without a mort-gage[2]	Median rent[3]	Median rent as a per-cent of income[2]		Total		Total	Rate[5]	Total	Manage-ment, business, science and arts	
	89	90	91	92	93	94	95	96	97	98	99	100	101	102	103

STATE County	89	90	91	92	93	94	95	96	97	98	99	100	101	102	103
TEXAS—Cont'd															
Caldwell	12 451	65.9	115 300	22.3	11.8	765	28.9	5.7	18 010	3.7	774	4.3	16 693	24.1	30.1
Calhoun	7 994	70.8	102 800	19.0	10.2	759	28.1	7.2	10 815	-4.2	602	5.6	9 416	27.6	37.2
Callahan	5 273	81.8	74 000	19.4	12.2	612	24.0	3.5	5 709	-0.1	246	4.3	5 092	25.9	32.6
Cameron	121 097	66.8	79 300	23.8	12.8	643	32.1	12.4	166 061	2.1	11 963	7.2	148 011	27.9	21.8
Camp	4 431	68.1	78 100	21.2	12.5	712	24.1	6.7	5 039	-0.7	343	6.8	5 039	22.0	36.5
Carson	2 293	89.2	93 700	18.6	10.0	718	25.5	2.5	3 065	0.2	103	3.4	2 902	34.9	30.7
Cass	11 691	76.8	81 000	20.4	12.3	540	28.4	4.4	12 249	1.0	896	7.3	11 964	21.3	35.1
Castro	2 501	70.0	70 600	19.7	12.3	671	27.7	7.2	3 502	-2.8	108	3.1	3 316	23.7	40.3
Chambers	13 018	80.9	151 200	18.9	12.5	871	22.8	2.6	17 991	1.4	1 093	6.1	15 166	34.4	36.0
Cherokee	17 729	71.7	84 500	22.5	12.9	661	29.5	5.2	21 117	1.4	1 093	5.2	19 729	26.9	30.8
Childress	2 391	64.0	73 300	19.6	16.1	702	23.4	0.9	2 958	3.4	91	3.1	2 600	34.2	25.8
Clay	4 146	83.5	83 600	20.0	11.9	629	23.5	1.4	4 846	-1.0	216	4.5	4 605	28.8	28.3
Cochran	1 030	78.9	32 300	19.1	10.0	445	19.5	9.9	1 185	-9.7	66	5.6	1 180	24.2	48.7
Coke	1 601	70.3	79 000	19.8	11.1	533	25.9	1.1	1 424	2.2	59	4.1	1 508	46.3	24.7
Coleman	3 405	68.3	60 000	26.4	11.8	529	27.9	1.3	3 061	0.7	182	5.9	3 235	26.2	28.9
Collin	305 827	66.5	223 400	21.0	11.2	1 119	26.5	2.4	506 100	3.9	17 818	3.5	444 189	52.1	11.0
Collingsworth	1 109	77.8	64 200	20.1	12.6	486	22.1	1.8	1 212	-4.3	43	3.5	1 345	25.4	40.5
Colorado	7 657	81.1	109 800	20.0	11.9	703	24.4	2.7	9 758	-1.2	464	4.8	9 169	29.0	33.6
Comal	43 951	75.9	214 400	21.6	10.2	982	28.8	3.6	63 539	3.0	2 310	3.6	54 190	37.8	19.9
Comanche	5 119	76.3	72 100	22.8	12.4	525	28.2	5.9	5 327	-0.3	230	4.3	5 338	26.9	36.7
Concho	813	78.5	86 000	21.2	12.0	597	25.3	0.2	1 305	-4.7	47	3.6	961	34.1	27.9
Cooke	14 598	69.5	122 700	19.6	11.9	707	28.3	4.1	18 825	-4.5	762	4.0	18 012	27.6	30.8
Coryell	21 829	57.2	102 700	19.9	10.9	921	27.5	2.7	25 286	3.5	1 145	4.5	22 684	30.4	20.4
Cottle	635	71.3	42 900	23.3	12.8	275	22.6	1.4	539	-0.9	29	5.4	615	31.4	23.1
Crane	1 542	75.6	75 900	14.7	10.0	650	23.4	5.9	1 772	-3.3	150	8.5	1 980	19.0	44.2
Crockett	1 433	73.7	79 000	17.7	10.0	588	21.6	2.2	1 726	-8.9	132	7.6	1 851	21.6	40.2
Crosby	2 189	67.7	53 900	19.3	12.1	581	23.6	7.0	2 633	-0.2	117	4.4	2 478	28.9	31.6
Culberson	788	71.6	60 700	21.3	13.7	575	32.3	4.3	1 071	3.3	41	3.8	1 020	20.1	23.5
Dallam	2 256	60.9	72 800	21.3	10.0	697	23.9	2.5	3 998	0.1	90	2.3	3 381	20.3	40.0
Dallas	881 279	51.2	132 700	23.6	12.6	907	29.3	7.0	1 305 202	3.7	51 868	4.0	1 191 958	33.3	24.0
Dawson	4 232	72.0	62 100	17.1	12.1	582	21.8	2.5	4 651	-2.2	239	5.1	4 844	24.9	32.5
Deaf Smith	6 194	66.0	86 700	21.5	10.3	699	26.7	6.0	8 614	-1.8	271	3.1	8 501	26.8	39.0
Delta	1 928	77.6	73 600	20.6	13.2	593	29.9	2.7	2 566	-0.8	102	4.0	1 830	32.6	30.5
Denton	257 275	64.4	197 600	21.2	11.5	991	28.2	2.6	443 801	3.9	15 190	3.4	387 884	43.9	14.9
DeWitt	7 061	76.1	98 200	17.3	10.0	640	27.2	4.3	9 376	-6.4	525	5.6	7 927	29.1	30.7
Dickens	878	74.8	49 600	17.9	13.2	481	15.0	3.0	690	-1.4	35	5.1	744	41.5	25.9
Dimmit	3 568	69.1	58 200	18.9	11.7	649	22.5	10.5	6 203	-13.1	444	7.2	4 210	19.3	25.3
Donley	1 311	76.2	59 900	19.4	14.0	494	27.3	3.5	1 554	-2.1	67	4.3	1 411	32.9	25.7
Duval	3 937	70.0	52 800	19.8	12.2	686	23.7	14.2	4 845	-7.2	540	11.1	4 336	18.1	35.6
Eastland	6 810	72.3	60 100	24.7	12.7	539	19.8	4.2	7 371	-8.0	405	5.5	6 803	30.7	27.8
Ector	50 868	66.3	103 200	18.4	10.0	903	24.8	7.1	75 790	-4.7	4 859	6.4	70 130	23.5	35.2
Edwards	747	90.2	70 900	15.8	12.8	481	18.1	4.7	857	-0.6	42	4.9	912	22.7	29.5
Ellis	52 653	72.0	145 400	21.4	11.8	907	30.3	3.8	83 699	3.7	3 142	3.8	74 703	31.7	26.8
El Paso	259 612	61.5	113 900	22.9	11.1	750	29.8	6.7	349 468	2.6	17 252	4.9	327 744	29.6	22.5
Erath	14 572	59.8	121 700	22.9	10.7	703	33.7	4.1	20 168	0.3	831	4.1	19 275	29.9	29.0
Falls	5 418	73.3	64 900	20.1	12.6	570	24.5	4.6	6 579	2.3	295	4.5	6 068	26.2	30.3
Fannin	11 974	74.5	94 600	21.3	13.2	688	30.6	3.9	15 770	2.9	596	3.8	13 259	31.5	29.3
Fayette	9 558	77.8	138 100	18.8	12.4	701	24.8	1.5	12 439	-2.3	462	3.7	11 669	22.7	34.2
Fisher	1 667	71.0	64 900	18.8	10.5	494	21.9	3.7	1 753	-2.3	78	4.4	1 767	28.9	28.9
Floyd	2 413	67.5	65 300	17.5	11.4	642	27.3	5.8	2 736	0.0	142	5.2	2 600	29.4	36.4
Foard	507	78.5	55 900	28.3	12.3	300	19.0	0.6	537	-2.2	21	3.9	446	31.8	19.3
Fort Bend	206 188	78.7	200 200	21.5	11.2	1 211	26.4	3.5	359 594	1.4	18 075	5.0	314 534	49.3	14.7
Franklin	4 259	72.7	103 200	22.2	10.5	700	27.4	2.8	4 499	-0.9	225	5.0	4 309	25.5	32.2
Freestone	7 406	75.7	81 400	20.2	12.4	653	22.6	3.0	6 865	-7.1	471	6.9	7 868	26.1	30.5
Frio	4 794	70.4	68 400	23.3	12.9	675	23.1	12.8	8 711	-10.9	434	5.0	6 618	18.5	34.0
Gaines	5 615	76.9	92 600	16.9	10.0	753	19.2	6.6	9 094	-3.0	339	3.7	7 868	24.3	44.3
Galveston	113 866	66.9	155 000	20.9	11.6	912	30.2	3.2	158 813	0.9	8 456	5.3	143 681	39.7	20.5
Garza	1 532	67.0	80 600	17.4	10.0	727	23.2	3.1	2 122	-0.1	83	3.9	2 018	24.0	31.8
Gillespie	10 577	76.5	238 300	25.0	12.3	866	31.2	4.4	12 923	2.5	368	2.8	11 230	35.4	23.3
Glasscock	431	66.6	190 200	14.8	10.0	1 095	21.9	3.0	755	-7.8	29	3.8	499	44.1	31.7
Goliad	2 881	84.7	116 300	14.6	11.2	679	24.2	4.5	3 345	-2.7	194	5.8	2 962	29.5	33.0
Gonzales	6 477	70.1	89 200	21.3	11.7	600	24.9	10.9	9 531	-1.4	410	4.3	8 422	22.5	36.3
Gray	8 250	73.5	74 800	18.1	10.7	674	28.4	3.1	8 475	-8.3	593	7.0	9 444	24.1	35.8
Grayson	47 215	66.9	107 000	21.0	12.7	780	27.7	3.5	60 832	1.7	2 340	3.8	54 835	31.4	25.5
Gregg	45 618	60.4	124 600	20.5	10.9	771	29.9	3.8	58 377	-1.2	3 556	6.1	55 402	27.7	29.5
Grimes	9 005	77.6	105 400	20.4	11.5	666	29.1	6.6	11 000	-4.2	736	6.7	9 951	24.7	36.5

1. Specified owner-occupied units.   2. A value of 10.0 represents 10 percent or less; a value of 50.0 represents 50 percent or more.   3. Specified renter-occupied units.
4. Overcrowded or lacking complete plumbing facilities.   5. Percent of civilian labor force.   6. Civilian employed persons 16 years old and over.

Table B. States and Counties — **Nonfarm Employment and Agriculture**

STATE County	Private nonfarm establishments, employment and payroll, 2015									Agriculture, 2012			
		Employment						Annual payroll		Farms			
												Percent with:	
	Number of establish- ments	Total	Health care and social assistance	Manufac- turing	Retail trade	Finance and insurance	Professional, scientific, and technical services	Total (mil dol)	Average per employee (dollars)	Number	Fewer than 50 acres	500 acres or more	Farm operators whose principal occu- pation is farming (percent)
	104	105	106	107	108	109	110	111	112	113	114	115	116

TEXAS—Cont'd

Caldwell	585	6 300	1 146	894	1 177	188	110	199	31 638	1 623	42.7	8.3	40.1
Calhoun	452	9 060	630	3 503	1 061	186	588	564	62 218	264	29.2	31.4	46.6
Callahan	210	1 432	137	146	325	59	76	51	35 899	992	27.6	21.3	43.3
Cameron	6 381	104 560	33 316	4 425	18 562	3 214	3 473	2 818	26 951	1 305	66.3	11.5	45.4
Camp	213	2 577	390	221	434	113	28	109	42 134	487	40.0	6.2	41.3
Carson	116	627	D	31	130	33	18	26	41 721	386	15.5	46.6	51.0
Cass	491	5 810	850	1 768	912	223	113	211	36 282	1 024	29.6	5.2	43.1
Castro	162	988	D	42	179	50	92	33	33 686	532	9.0	51.5	54.3
Chambers	584	11 356	607	2 506	1 085	118	243	692	60 949	734	56.0	17.7	39.6
Cherokee	763	10 089	2 204	2 273	1 410	351	216	349	34 613	1 574	34.2	6.5	46.9
Childress	157	1 249	110	D	451	63	43	34	26 974	383	5.2	34.5	41.3
Clay	137	749	103	D	218	44	20	21	28 354	861	16.4	27.1	43.4
Cochran	47	275	100	D	73	11	6	8	30 189	288	4.9	47.6	51.7
Coke	56	229	NA	D	84	28	D	6	27 148	443	9.3	40.6	44.9
Coleman	211	1 410	266	95	279	79	43	37	26 223	906	10.9	36.5	46.7
Collin	21 587	371 709	46 555	18 598	49 769	44 558	35 949	22 488	60 499	2 264	64.9	4.4	33.0
Collingsworth	61	493	117	D	80	D	15	18	35 696	383	6.3	41.3	45.2
Colorado	548	6 165	803	1 794	952	180	138	216	35 009	1 575	28.3	13.0	48.5
Comal	3 338	42 924	5 855	2 934	6 502	944	1 522	1 697	39 529	1 104	44.8	9.3	36.9
Comanche	259	2 253	450	112	476	156	83	73	32 212	1 435	26.8	18.6	50.6
Concho	51	697	167	D	76	D	D	23	33 311	401	5.7	51.4	56.9
Cooke	911	13 994	982	3 287	1 872	385	262	608	43 478	1 946	40.0	10.9	42.2
Coryell	690	9 763	1 189	492	1 869	425	845	255	26 078	1 308	31.3	16.8	42.3
Cottle	27	124	D	D	55	18	D	3	22 645	264	6.4	44.7	32.2
Crane	85	1 050	167	D	116	14	13	56	53 690	27	29.6	66.7	51.9
Crockett	129	1 350	28	D	213	35	11	61	45 241	216	4.2	68.1	63.4
Crosby	99	679	171	D	131	28	10	24	35 434	431	8.6	43.4	51.0
Culberson	53	553	78	D	165	D	D	15	27 635	77	9.1	75.3	68.8
Dallam	210	1 727	44	63	264	67	70	65	37 621	371	5.9	62.3	59.0
Dallas	64 505	1 412 852	166 355	95 503	125 839	97 737	134 862	85 149	60 267	839	68.2	5.0	39.7
Dawson	291	2 709	255	118	696	134	66	98	36 284	596	7.2	42.8	55.0
Deaf Smith	395	5 323	507	1 551	869	190	188	211	39 552	621	11.3	55.2	64.6
Delta	55	806	628	NA	50	D	12	11	13 558	529	33.1	10.2	41.2
Denton	13 606	202 674	26 081	13 129	31 802	12 746	9 657	8 724	43 043	3 203	73.2	3.8	34.9
DeWitt	458	5 666	875	547	683	252	141	237	41 882	1 711	24.1	14.0	45.7
Dickens	39	248	15	NA	54	D	D	9	36 319	437	4.8	34.3	35.5
Dimmit	255	6 457	406	29	523	28	46	306	47 415	367	23.2	35.7	36.8
Donley	79	517	114	D	112	21	23	10	19 818	380	8.9	29.7	44.5
Duval	166	2 402	371	D	197	57	36	92	38 361	1 436	11.0	25.0	45.5
Eastland	450	5 682	860	556	817	148	932	241	42 360	1 174	17.3	18.6	33.6
Ector	3 717	65 095	6 827	4 619	8 418	1 442	1 481	3 230	49 626	264	70.5	14.4	28.8
Edwards	38	169	4	D	78	D	D	5	26 840	419	6.4	50.6	51.1
Ellis	2 719	39 241	3 889	9 775	5 645	901	824	1 515	38 605	2 264	48.4	8.2	40.8
El Paso	14 178	229 310	44 588	12 959	39 185	6 507	10 539	7 283	31 762	657	81.6	7.6	39.7
Erath	931	12 231	1 632	2 719	2 054	311	350	437	35 709	2 161	30.2	13.7	44.6
Falls	221	1 722	399	124	415	63	37	50	28 899	1 263	26.5	13.2	53.4
Fannin	466	4 787	1 214	616	926	160	101	170	35 589	2 515	41.4	8.5	43.2
Fayette	753	7 136	1 125	1 121	1 363	266	203	243	34 079	2 822	30.8	6.7	41.5
Fisher	73	534	109	D	68	45	17	23	43 036	588	8.5	38.4	38.6
Floyd	158	1 035	232	46	104	56	14	33	31 835	589	7.3	39.4	39.9
Foard	28	163	77	D	30	D	D	4	24 988	194	8.8	42.3	46.4
Fort Bend	12 144	154 307	24 137	14 979	26 913	3 915	9 892	7 023	45 510	1 286	46.6	9.7	47.1
Franklin	155	5 732	3 576	D	298	94	29	108	18 803	520	28.1	12.1	47.5
Freestone	347	4 033	585	159	504	132	129	155	38 530	1 517	30.3	11.8	45.6
Frio	345	6 506	699	93	764	196	74	287	44 188	651	20.0	35.3	50.8
Gaines	418	3 969	309	222	495	91	69	187	47 035	644	10.6	50.2	55.9
Galveston	5 587	82 813	14 927	5 941	13 085	3 875	4 487	3 328	40 189	612	63.2	8.7	45.4
Garza	130	1 329	161	23	198	28	16	46	34 892	277	8.7	46.9	43.7
Gillespie	969	8 821	1 589	711	1 632	289	321	291	32 940	1 847	30.5	19.9	41.5
Glasscock	35	241	NA	D	D	D	D	13	52 191	186	4.3	70.4	59.7
Goliad	125	719	100	D	109	22	25	28	39 051	1 175	27.9	17.2	44.4
Gonzales	437	5 274	731	1 374	858	193	113	195	36 889	1 674	23.1	18.9	46.1
Gray	606	6 883	831	996	1 163	181	226	274	39 740	417	15.3	47.7	35.7
Grayson	2 511	39 777	8 664	7 000	6 222	1 831	919	1 373	34 508	2 562	50.8	5.6	44.1
Gregg	4 127	68 629	11 004	9 733	9 696	2 168	2 288	2 826	41 179	527	59.0	4.2	42.9
Grimes	408	6 245	393	2 690	650	139	133	248	39 710	1 683	37.3	10.5	39.7

Table B. States and Counties — **Agriculture**

STATE County	Land in farms				Value of land and buildings (dollars)		Value of machinery and equipment, average per farm (dollars)	Value of products sold				Percent of farms with sales of:		Government payments	
			Acres							Percent from:					
	Acreage (1,000)	Percent change, 2007–2012	Average size of farm	Total irrigated (1,000)	Total cropland (1,000)	Average per farm	Average per acre		Total (mil dol)	Average per farm (dollars)	Crops	Live-stock and poultry products	$10,000 or more	$100,000 or more	Total ($1,000)	Percent of farms
	117	118	119	120	121	122	123	124	125	126	127	128	129	130	131	132
TEXAS—Cont'd																
Caldwell	310	1.9	191	0.6	55.9	632 375	3 306	45 283	62.9	38 779	17.8	82.2	22.2	2.7	1 076	10.2
Calhoun	184	-20.1	697	5.8	60.5	1 223 477	1 755	114 295	42.1	159 489	67.2	32.8	49.2	20.5	1 664	46.2
Callahan	563	5.7	568	0.7	87.2	857 079	1 510	49 690	29.9	30 142	19.5	80.5	28.7	4.9	1 943	26.1
Cameron	310	-11.4	237	112.3	209.2	697 056	2 937	84 762	160.4	122 916	91.9	8.1	32.1	13.3	4 851	45.4
Camp	78	14.1	161	0.7	20.4	418 072	2 602	73 626	137.7	282 686	2.2	97.8	37.8	9.0	118	5.5
Carson	485	-9.8	1 256	49.4	269.8	1 156 262	920	200 505	83.0	214 990	61.0	39.0	44.8	23.8	5 875	75.1
Cass	168	-5.1	164	0.2	38.9	337 149	2 060	50 023	67.6	66 010	7.8	92.2	27.3	5.1	128	4.1
Castro	548	-3.4	1 030	154.9	411.0	1 131 530	1 098	323 836	1 312.1	2 466 429	11.9	88.1	62.0	45.5	10 759	80.5
Chambers	254	-5.1	346	15.2	92.8	690 097	1 996	80 785	25.6	34 868	58.8	41.2	27.1	7.9	3 018	17.2
Cherokee	301	2.4	191	1.4	67.8	472 935	2 470	58 168	134.0	85 123	66.9	33.1	34.1	5.7	736	3.9
Childress	444	11.1	1 159	9.2	142.1	891 243	769	90 394	19.9	51 883	65.5	34.5	38.6	11.2	3 104	80.4
Clay	633	-4.4	735	1.7	99.2	1 158 323	1 577	71 052	79.8	92 695	15.6	84.4	48.0	13.0	2 098	34.5
Cochran	449	-8.2	1 558	67.8	268.5	1 048 688	673	204 642	100.8	349 955	D	D	35.8	25.3	7 287	87.2
Coke	484	-1.4	1 093	1.0	49.0	1 141 964	1 045	62 172	7.0	15 826	29.4	70.6	26.0	3.4	967	34.5
Coleman	726	3.8	801	1.0	135.5	1 210 947	1 512	68 786	28.4	31 320	40.1	59.9	41.3	7.5	2 499	49.2
Collin	313	7.6	138	6.2	136.6	732 661	5 303	45 315	77.8	34 369	65.3	34.7	19.2	3.4	1 307	7.2
Collingsworth	495	-3.5	1 292	27.3	164.1	1 075 068	832	152 681	43.1	112 556	69.4	30.6	47.3	18.8	4 307	79.6
Colorado	485	-8.0	308	20.1	136.2	1 019 175	3 309	68 878	68.0	43 162	65.4	34.6	35.9	7.6	4 361	17.0
Comal	205	6.5	186	0.4	14.1	974 562	5 248	42 853	D	D	D	D	14.5	0.5	131	5.2
Comanche	517	-10.7	360	18.1	133.8	865 152	2 401	69 521	158.1	110 199	16.9	83.1	42.4	8.4	1 563	21.0
Concho	502	-9.0	1 251	2.1	106.6	1 979 873	1 583	117 608	22.8	56 933	62.3	37.7	54.6	13.2	3 244	67.8
Cooke	504	10.6	259	0.4	132.4	845 941	3 267	60 599	63.3	32 538	29.2	70.8	36.9	7.1	1 361	19.2
Coryell	463	-5.2	354	0.4	85.8	861 112	2 432	52 811	68.6	52 408	23.6	76.4	30.2	5.0	959	16.1
Cottle	565	5.6	2 139	2.9	98.4	1 323 023	619	96 019	15.9	60 246	33.5	66.5	33.3	9.1	2 297	81.4
Crane	239	-36.3	8 858	D	D	5 228 185	590	51 926	1.4	52 222	1.6	98.4	55.6	14.8	56	14.8
Crockett	1 546	-3.5	7 158	0.1	8.0	4 508 931	630	78 523	13.9	64 324	0.3	99.7	46.3	16.7	2 214	33.3
Crosby	558	1.0	1 296	111.7	299.6	1 107 218	855	231 005	71.6	166 100	93.9	6.1	53.1	36.2	7 549	88.6
Culberson	1 618	17.8	21 013	6.0	64.5	7 180 273	342	134 844	13.7	178 364	48.1	51.9	57.1	28.6	680	27.3
Dallam	852	-9.1	2 296	175.6	388.4	2 164 833	943	330 364	651.7	1 756 642	25.5	74.5	55.3	40.7	7 262	76.8
Dallas	84	-4.8	100	1.4	35.9	460 257	4 611	52 857	44.5	53 026	85.9	14.1	17.8	4.4	280	6.9
Dawson	558	-1.8	936	61.2	481.2	738 569	789	188 577	73.1	122 700	97.0	3.0	38.9	23.0	11 185	91.9
Deaf Smith	924	-2.4	1 487	119.9	606.7	1 470 176	989	259 588	1 379.1	2 220 734	5.8	94.2	50.4	37.5	13 023	78.9
Delta	131	-1.2	248	D	65.0	452 815	1 826	60 987	29.3	55 475	53.6	46.4	40.8	5.3	801	33.8
Denton	384	9.5	120	3.3	131.9	731 687	6 111	52 478	137.0	42 771	25.8	74.2	18.1	3.2	1 210	7.6
DeWitt	536	-2.3	314	0.6	49.7	819 210	2 613	61 814	61.4	35 856	12.4	87.6	40.9	4.7	1 068	10.0
Dickens	573	-0.3	1 310	13.4	128.3	958 899	732	87 062	18.5	42 394	43.7	56.3	31.1	8.5	3 468	78.9
Dimmit	677	-4.4	1 845	4.8	44.3	2 875 932	1 559	62 379	35.2	95 956	24.3	75.7	25.9	6.5	730	14.4
Donley	585	-0.7	1 540	14.9	68.0	1 659 213	1 078	89 887	95.1	250 337	14.1	85.9	36.3	12.9	2 000	63.4
Duval	960	-6.0	668	D	60.0	872 009	1 305	38 103	14.8	10 309	6.5	93.5	20.5	1.3	2 814	37.0
Eastland	504	-3.2	429	8.9	91.5	852 450	1 987	56 647	27.9	23 744	30.5	69.5	36.4	4.5	1 428	24.0
Ector	429	1.2	1 624	0.8	3.6	786 019	484	48 008	2.2	8 296	28.9	71.1	16.3	1.5	211	5.3
Edwards	970	-2.7	2 315	1.1	13.0	2 907 783	1 256	48 630	8.2	19 485	7.4	92.6	28.9	5.5	2 070	25.8
Ellis	474	7.0	209	0.4	224.4	665 859	3 181	73 345	91.4	40 367	73.7	26.3	24.1	4.5	2 825	24.3
El Paso	209	24.2	319	24.9	53.3	617 767	1 938	93 251	45.5	69 308	87.0	13.0	25.7	9.4	768	9.3
Erath	608	-2.5	281	12.3	124.4	903 801	3 215	72 397	256.4	118 670	7.2	92.8	32.2	7.2	1 814	8.5
Falls	383	-14.1	303	5.1	174.3	589 978	1 947	82 715	135.3	107 123	40.7	59.3	41.3	12.2	4 706	29.1
Fannin	514	8.4	204	1.2	200.0	523 141	2 561	54 400	71.1	28 287	56.0	44.0	28.2	4.9	2 381	20.3
Fayette	492	-13.0	174	1.1	95.4	738 387	4 235	49 415	66.4	23 515	20.8	79.2	32.0	2.3	1 428	15.1
Fisher	495	-9.2	842	2.6	210.1	527 309	1 083	109 594	31.1	52 872	64.8	35.2	36.6	11.9	4 632	78.7
Floyd	582	-7.3	988	96.7	392.9	1 131 611	1 145	188 253	282.7	480 039	D	D	37.0	21.2	9 002	89.8
Foard	368	-3.8	1 898	1.9	98.2	1 401 794	739	100 098	13.8	71 273	44.8	55.2	47.4	22.7	1 505	69.6
Fort Bend	339	-11.4	264	10.3	135.9	1 080 498	4 095	75 835	103.8	80 705	88.5	11.5	36.2	10.7	4 101	29.2
Franklin	113	-15.4	217	0.8	27.9	623 454	2 869	67 423	86.0	165 339	4.4	95.6	48.1	14.6	171	7.3
Freestone	421	5.4	278	0.4	47.1	583 104	2 100	56 028	44.1	29 059	13.1	86.9	30.5	4.1	433	6.7
Frio	713	10.5	1 096	60.5	152.9	2 238 931	2 043	113 647	183.7	282 138	59.4	40.6	35.9	16.0	2 765	26.3
Gaines	775	-18.2	1 203	227.0	570.6	1 167 174	970	255 823	180.5	280 233	97.2	2.8	53.4	38.4	17 390	83.5
Galveston	90	-13.4	146	0.4	17.6	527 309	3 604	49 598	D	D	D	D	24.3	1.0	756	8.3
Garza	456	-11.1	1 645	8.1	82.1	1 141 856	694	92 982	12.4	44 711	70.4	29.6	35.7	13.4	2 696	74.4
Gillespie	652	-0.1	353	1.9	66.4	1 504 356	4 260	41 480	46.1	24 981	24.5	75.5	28.0	3.1	1 901	20.8
Glasscock	434	-9.6	2 332	25.3	134.7	2 086 946	895	302 559	25.9	139 129	89.3	10.7	51.1	30.6	5 362	69.4
Goliad	495	5.4	421	0.7	33.0	871 038	2 068	55 077	19.4	16 549	19.6	80.4	29.7	3.8	751	9.4
Gonzales	610	-6.8	364	7.8	69.0	1 176 904	3 231	69 381	517.8	309 295	4.5	95.5	44.0	11.6	1 202	12.7
Gray	515	1.1	1 235	21.6	161.2	1 096 012	888	129 902	207.7	498 026	11.7	88.3	42.9	16.1	3 299	61.4
Grayson	431	7.7	168	3.5	176.4	632 363	3 757	58 110	91.9	35 889	72.7	27.3	24.6	4.3	1 948	14.2
Gregg	48	6.3	91	0.4	8.2	353 905	3 881	45 812	3.6	6 844	37.3	62.7	15.7	0.8	41	0.8
Grimes	417	-4.6	248	1.6	56.7	957 864	3 865	59 447	48.1	28 551	23.0	77.0	31.0	3.7	755	5.8

STATE County	Water use, 2010 Total water withdrawn (mil gal/day)	Gallons withdrawn per person per day	Wholesale trade,[1] 2012 Number of establishments	Number of employees	Sales (mil dol)	Annual payroll (mil dol)	Retail trade,[2] 2012 Number of establishments	Number of employees	Sales (mil dol)	Annual payroll (mil dol)	Real estate and rental and leasing,[2] 2012 Number of establishments	Number of employees	Receipts (mil dol)	Annual payroll (mil dol)
	133	134	135	136	137	138	139	140	141	142	143	144	145	146
TEXAS—Cont'd														
Caldwell	21.6	567	18	D	D	D	81	1 035	345.2	26.7	21	55	7.4	1.3
Calhoun	49.6	2 319	16	D	D	D	63	927	435.3	31.4	20	146	35.2	5.9
Callahan	2.7	200	7	32	11.7	1.0	38	330	157.0	10.5	8	D	D	D
Cameron	281.5	693	317	D	D	D	1 119	16 624	4 124.8	353.2	312	1 338	185.5	32.2
Camp	4.3	344	9	82	34.0	2.9	50	371	111.2	8.4	7	D	D	D
Carson	80.6	13 044	7	D	D	D	20	150	57.4	2.7	1	D	D	D
Cass	33.2	1 091	18	D	D	D	88	883	218.4	18.4	18	33	5.0	0.7
Castro	324.4	40 237	12	142	117.2	6.2	33	185	55.0	3.6	8	16	2.9	0.3
Chambers	265.5	7 565	32	407	138.9	18.5	85	588	283.2	13.7	22	68	37.5	3.4
Cherokee	68.1	1 339	31	D	D	D	132	1 438	383.2	31.8	29	60	8.8	1.6
Childress	9.3	1 318	3	D	D	D	29	370	90.4	7.3	4	D	D	D
Clay	5.4	500	3	D	D	D	28	226	88.8	6.4	5	D	D	D
Cochran	65.9	21 059	3	D	D	D	12	68	50.2	1.7	NA	NA	NA	NA
Coke	34.8	10 491	2	D	D	D	14	66	32.4	1.6	NA	NA	NA	NA
Coleman	52.6	5 915	7	48	23.3	2.1	32	259	68.2	5.0	10	15	1.6	0.4
Collin	327.8	419	817	13 530	18 366.8	1 074.2	2 433	44 931	14 623.9	1 209.9	928	6 910	1 363.0	316.6
Collingsworth	44.5	14 540	5	D	D	D	14	74	15.8	1.6	NA	NA	NA	NA
Colorado	143.7	6 886	32	262	151.7	9.7	101	905	256.5	21.3	18	194	49.0	7.9
Comal	44.4	410	123	D	D	D	380	5 498	1 894.5	147.7	165	800	131.4	29.0
Comanche	28.4	2 033	22	D	D	D	49	430	138.1	10.2	9	27	1.9	0.7
Concho	7.8	1 899	1	D	D	D	12	73	17.1	1.1	1	D	D	D
Cooke	12.4	323	46	D	D	D	145	1 787	543.4	43.4	30	102	21.5	3.1
Coryell	3.7	49	11	D	D	D	120	1 704	493.6	36.2	37	112	14.3	3.0
Cottle	2.0	1 336	NA	NA	NA	NA	5	44	11.6	1.0	NA	NA	NA	NA
Crane	23.5	5 365	4	23	16.9	1.3	12	109	30.2	2.0	2	D	D	D
Crockett	11.7	3 154	4	36	36.3	2.3	19	181	72.9	4.7	3	D	D	D
Crosby	74.7	12 327	8	D	D	D	19	133	35.8	2.8	2	D	D	D
Culberson	39.2	16 351	1	D	D	D	17	247	136.7	4.1	2	D	D	D
Dallam	329.6	49 172	20	354	394.1	14.3	23	203	89.8	5.8	5	D	D	D
Dallas	307.4	130	3 657	67 700	80 605.0	4 255.0	7 518	112 656	35 957.9	3 151.9	3 490	32 478	7 691.3	1 679.2
Dawson	79.0	5 712	21	104	78.5	4.8	43	659	316.8	19.0	7	D	D	D
Deaf Smith	173.9	8 978	34	D	D	D	66	747	275.8	17.7	14	53	4.5	1.0
Delta	2.6	501	3	17	16.3	0.6	14	33	11.7	0.6	2	D	D	D
Denton	166.3	251	513	8 395	16 900.0	539.7	1 625	26 041	8 274.0	645.1	582	3 180	655.5	129.7
DeWitt	6.6	326	14	213	124.9	11.4	61	667	220.2	16.2	13	195	52.1	10.3
Dickens	8.8	3 588	NA	NA	NA	NA	9	57	11.9	1.0	2	D	D	D
Dimmit	11.2	1 116	6	191	174.6	13.1	28	446	142.6	11.2	9	35	3.5	0.9
Donley	26.8	7 289	1	D	D	D	20	113	27.9	1.9	6	9	1.7	0.4
Duval	9.3	789	9	74	24.8	2.5	29	240	78.6	4.7	3	29	6.0	1.0
Eastland	9.8	527	12	D	D	D	81	807	314.0	19.2	19	34	4.6	0.9
Ector	60.2	439	298	4 659	3 608.8	330.5	451	7 286	2 711.7	218.7	176	1 482	604.9	101.9
Edwards	0.9	455	NA	NA	NA	NA	7	83	21.7	2.2	2	D	D	D
Ellis	23.4	156	113	D	D	D	360	5 007	1 459.4	115.4	122	381	66.0	10.7
El Paso	277.5	347	952	D	D	D	2 322	34 934	9 180.6	753.5	699	3 143	617.3	108.0
Erath	16.1	425	35	D	D	D	172	1 831	535.2	41.5	40	111	15.8	2.8
Falls	10.9	611	9	D	D	D	52	419	97.5	8.4	5	19	3.9	0.9
Fannin	55.1	1 624	11	D	D	D	80	924	281.9	24.3	12	121	8.9	3.1
Fayette	24.7	1 005	34	D	D	D	125	1 134	368.6	28.5	32	109	20.4	3.3
Fisher	7.8	1 968	2	D	D	D	13	70	15.6	1.4	1	D	D	D
Floyd	93.3	14 469	12	D	D	D	22	131	31.5	2.5	1	D	D	D
Foard	2.9	2 141	1	D	D	D	7	31	7.4	0.5	NA	NA	NA	NA
Fort Bend	995.3	1 700	579	5 593	6 110.2	302.2	1 423	23 132	7 147.2	561.9	457	1 521	428.0	61.4
Franklin	5.4	505	4	16	5.1	0.7	27	269	105.9	6.1	9	16	2.1	0.3
Freestone	816.1	41 182	13	168	127.5	9.6	63	498	221.3	11.3	12	102	22.6	5.2
Frio	56.4	3 276	13	D	D	D	54	619	250.4	12.7	11	30	6.4	1.2
Gaines	333.6	19 037	27	374	362.2	25.9	45	498	108.9	10.3	12	22	3.8	0.7
Galveston	57.3	197	197	1 701	1 933.8	83.5	876	11 165	3 523.0	294.5	283	1 422	252.3	50.3
Garza	14.3	2 219	4	D	D	D	21	203	58.5	3.4	5	13	4.1	0.6
Gillespie	7.4	297	33	D	D	D	167	1 490	327.8	33.7	39	182	24.1	6.5
Glasscock	56.7	46 215	2	D	D	D	1	D	D	D	NA	NA	NA	NA
Goliad	391.7	54 325	3	13	3.3	0.3	15	128	41.0	2.0	2	D	D	D
Gonzales	19.5	985	20	277	228.2	13.1	72	770	238.6	15.7	9	15	3.4	0.5
Gray	24.6	1 093	31	447	1 065.5	31.3	100	1 082	314.8	25.0	30	118	23.7	4.8
Grayson	22.3	185	100	905	906.6	36.6	417	5 685	1 620.2	137.9	109	327	48.9	8.6
Gregg	90.4	743	252	3 592	2 395.6	194.3	664	9 190	2 639.8	233.0	199	1 220	411.8	62.5
Grimes	308.2	11 585	19	195	189.0	9.5	67	713	213.1	16.7	14	44	5.1	1.2

1. Merchant wholesalers, except manufacturers' sales branches and offices. 2. Employer establishments.

Table B. States and Counties — Professional Services, Manufacturing, and Accommodation and Food Services

STATE County	Professional, scientific, and technical services, 2012				Manufacturing, 2012				Accommodation and food services, 2012			
	Number of establishments	Number of employees	Receipts (mil dol)	Annual payroll (mil dol)	Number of establishments	Number of employees	Receipts (mil dol)	Annual payroll (mil dol)	Number of establishments	Number of employees	Sales (mil dol)	Annual payroll (mil dol)
	147	148	149	150	151	152	153	154	155	156	157	158
TEXAS—Cont'd												
Caldwell	32	108	6.7	2.2	19	699	153.4	24.3	59	740	41.1	10.5
Calhoun	27	D	D	D	19	3 274	11 074.5	304.2	61	619	32.9	8.2
Callahan	11	49	6.8	2.1	10	126	D	4.9	19	D	D	D
Cameron	488	2 359	258.4	81.1	204	4 414	1 709.6	D	660	12 582	635.1	171.7
Camp	9	25	4.5	1.4	8	202	D	8.3	8	D	D	D
Carson	6	D	D	D	3	D	D	D	10	D	D	D
Cass	28	135	10.1	3.9	23	1 257	D	66.0	43	495	18.8	4.9
Castro	12	107	10.4	4.1	7	42	D	1.9	12	77	3.1	0.8
Chambers	32	190	29.1	10.1	30	2 135	D	184.1	54	876	48.7	12.2
Cherokee	56	277	48.0	12.9	66	2 711	458.5	93.6	58	828	39.4	10.4
Childress	11	43	5.0	1.2	NA	NA	NA	NA	26	344	16.6	4.0
Clay	6	D	D	D	NA	NA	NA	NA	7	D	D	D
Cochran	4	5	0.5	0.1	NA	NA	NA	NA	2	D	D	D
Coke	3	D	D	D	NA	NA	NA	NA	6	D	D	D
Coleman	20	35	4.3	1.0	10	168	D	7.2	20	D	D	D
Collin	3 138	D	D	D	419	18 588	8 652.9	1 309.7	1 620	34 192	1 892.3	540.8
Collingsworth	5	D	D	D	NA	NA	NA	NA	4	35	1.2	0.3
Colorado	37	88	11.5	3.5	37	1 597	556.6	78.7	44	578	33.4	7.4
Comal	304	1 340	188.4	58.3	110	3 244	960.3	134.7	318	5 723	304.9	80.1
Comanche	24	85	10.6	3.7	7	131	D	5.3	19	D	D	D
Concho	2	D	D	D	4	27	D	D	5	D	D	D
Cooke	65	223	25.4	8.9	57	2 953	999.7	133.0	71	1 325	61.6	16.6
Coryell	69	780	88.1	36.5	21	293	D	12.4	80	1 316	60.7	15.5
Cottle	NA	NA	NA	NA	NA	NA	NA	NA	4	D	D	D
Crane	5	24	2.3	1.0	NA	NA	NA	NA	6	D	D	D
Crockett	5	14	0.8	0.3	NA	NA	NA	NA	19	269	14.2	2.8
Crosby	3	D	D	D	3	28	D	1.0	5	D	D	D
Culberson	1	D	D	D	NA	NA	NA	NA	15	174	9.5	2.4
Dallam	14	D	D	D	7	57	D	2.4	20	249	13.8	3.2
Dallas	8 837	125 146	23 867.3	10 053.0	2 347	94 078	37 035.6	4 801.6	5 059	107 611	6 753.1	1 887.8
Dawson	18	D	D	D	15	121	22.0	5.7	27	335	17.8	4.1
Deaf Smith	28	224	25.1	9.5	25	1 469	1 084.2	59.8	27	D	D	D
Delta	4	D	D	D	NA	NA	NA	NA	4	D	D	D
Denton	1 626	8 428	1 246.8	446.6	366	12 933	6 886.9	651.8	1 117	22 142	1 138.8	307.1
DeWitt	37	121	14.8	4.8	18	594	D	16.1	51	440	27.3	6.2
Dickens	4	D	D	D	NA	NA	NA	NA	5	36	1.7	0.4
Dimmit	8	D	D	D	4	84	11.2	2.7	30	399	32.8	5.5
Donley	10	D	D	D	NA	NA	NA	NA	9	103	4.1	1.2
Duval	7	56	6.4	1.4	NA	NA	NA	NA	17	75	5.7	1.0
Eastland	28	365	51.8	21.6	20	511	D	20.9	46	530	24.9	6.6
Ector	227	1 832	205.4	80.1	251	4 756	1 706.3	265.7	261	6 150	389.0	94.0
Edwards	2	D	D	D	NA	NA	NA	NA	5	D	D	D
Ellis	179	D	D	D	160	8 301	4 129.7	407.5	207	3 753	177.7	49.5
El Paso	1 201	D	D	D	504	D	13 643.2	D	1 476	28 733	1 384.4	375.2
Erath	68	324	32.8	11.9	40	2 463	D	114.6	98	1 682	71.4	18.8
Falls	8	24	6.4	0.9	8	90	D	5.1	15	D	D	D
Fannin	30	130	10.3	3.3	27	606	135.7	20.3	38	925	44.5	11.8
Fayette	64	201	21.8	7.0	39	951	314.0	38.6	74	D	D	D
Fisher	4	D	D	D	NA	NA	NA	NA	6	D	D	D
Floyd	7	17	1.1	0.4	7	38	11.4	1.8	10	46	2.0	0.4
Foard	1	D	D	D	NA	NA	NA	NA	3	11	0.6	0.1
Fort Bend	1 505	10 000	1 749.9	911.6	342	13 045	4 791.5	722.0	889	16 733	885.3	244.6
Franklin	13	29	2.5	0.8	NA	NA	NA	NA	14	D	D	D
Freestone	28	68	8.2	2.7	12	222	D	7.9	30	549	25.0	6.5
Frio	13	68	4.0	1.7	3	50	D	2.2	40	449	34.2	6.5
Gaines	15	72	7.0	2.8	17	158	31.9	7.8	27	D	D	D
Galveston	541	6 889	778.8	347.9	154	6 236	41 294.9	613.6	646	14 121	763.3	212.4
Garza	6	9	0.8	0.2	NA	NA	NA	NA	9	D	D	D
Gillespie	71	D	D	D	56	544	114.7	20.7	104	1 472	72.7	22.9
Glasscock	2	D	D	D	NA	NA	NA	NA	1	D	D	D
Goliad	14	25	3.3	1.5	4	69	D	D	16	109	5.7	1.6
Gonzales	39	106	10.9	3.6	23	1 456	554.5	52.5	38	473	24.6	5.5
Gray	46	413	65.2	27.6	21	927	453.0	52.5	40	816	35.0	8.9
Grayson	227	844	99.0	32.7	112	6 886	2 574.9	288.3	224	4 305	200.2	57.1
Gregg	382	2 759	357.5	143.4	176	9 075	3 582.7	486.9	322	6 608	307.4	86.3
Grimes	26	142	16.1	5.5	37	2 617	1 501.4	138.9	34	323	20.3	4.7

1. Establishment subject to federal tax.

STATE County	Health care and social assistance, 2012				Other services, 2012				Nonemployer businesses, 2015		Value of residential construction authorized by building permits, 2016	
	Number of establishments	Number of employees	Receipts (mil dol)	Annual payroll (mil dol)	Number of establishments	Number of employees	Receipts (mil dol)	Annual payroll (mil dol)	Number	Receipts (mil dol)	New Construction ($1,000)	Number of housing units
	159	160	161	162	163	164	165	166	167	168	169	170
TEXAS—Cont'd												
Caldwell	65	1 279	93.7	46.7	33	106	11.9	3.0	2 744	125.2	53 054	332
Calhoun	34	582	44.8	17.9	34	244	28.4	8.8	1 408	61.0	13 515	60
Callahan	11	118	6.0	2.5	8	40	2.8	0.9	1 221	49.5	46	7
Cameron	1 003	31 018	1 911.3	844.7	402	2 159	163.6	44.6	31 024	1 152.8	188 323	1 569
Camp	22	459	41.0	13.1	9	D	D	D	803	30.3	485	6
Carson	4	D	D	D	8	D	D	D	414	11.5	1 538	7
Cass	46	1 096	63.5	29.2	37	186	16.9	4.8	1 852	79.1	958	5
Castro	5	165	14.0	5.2	14	49	7.4	1.4	453	24.6	91	2
Chambers	31	D	D	D	28	104	9.1	2.5	2 636	115.4	58 675	295
Cherokee	83	2 521	179.2	87.3	42	171	15.1	3.9	3 087	124.0	657	6
Childress	20	360	33.3	12.4	11	27	2.9	0.6	371	15.6	0	0
Clay	11	D	D	D	7	D	D	D	783	35.7	5 870	45
Cochran	9	96	6.9	2.8	3	D	D	D	170	5.7	130	3
Coke	1	D	D	D	4	D	D	D	276	12.8	0	0
Coleman	14	344	22.6	8.2	14	D	D	D	797	40.1	0	0
Collin	2 690	35 757	4 766.3	1 665.7	1 036	7 810	1 154.4	276.8	85 086	4 770.8	3 105 206	13 154
Collingsworth	5	D	D	D	5	16	0.8	0.1	216	6.0	320	1
Colorado	43	1 165	92.4	37.7	35	128	10.9	2.8	1 854	89.7	2 551	22
Comal	305	5 472	497.2	202.0	218	1 821	94.9	50.8	13 203	699.9	545 482	3 089
Comanche	19	466	32.6	13.3	19	46	3.3	0.9	987	41.5	60	1
Concho	6	141	10.5	4.7	2	D	D	D	233	7.3	186	1
Cooke	84	1 135	100.8	41.5	55	411	37.5	13.7	3 365	182.1	7 032	51
Coryell	57	1 136	70.1	30.9	75	360	29.2	7.8	2 807	115.0	23 025	176
Cottle	4	46	1.3	0.7	1	D	D	D	134	3.6	0	0
Crane	9	167	13.4	6.2	3	D	D	D	291	12.5	19 165	13
Crockett	6	35	2.6	1.3	5	25	2.1	0.5	332	10.9	NA	NA
Crosby	10	157	9.6	4.0	6	D	D	D	348	10.7	603	9
Culberson	4	D	D	D	2	D	D	D	191	8.3	166	3
Dallam	10	D	D	D	21	D	D	D	501	30.7	3 589	23
Dallas	6 754	155 579	19 683.2	7 652.7	3 427	32 368	4 510.7	1 244.5	224 664	12 502.9	2 741 849	18 059
Dawson	14	378	42.6	10.5	23	79	6.2	1.7	666	27.7	0	0
Deaf Smith	21	505	39.5	16.0	37	174	17.5	3.8	1 316	63.1	897	11
Delta	6	299	6.7	3.1	5	16	1.3	0.2	314	11.5	0	0
Denton	1 462	21 835	2 473.8	893.3	743	4 951	497.3	145.7	66 761	3 360.3	1 949 641	7 428
DeWitt	39	D	D	D	34	191	31.9	6.0	1 534	74.4	535	3
Dickens	5	D	D	D	3	D	D	D	158	4.2	NA	NA
Dimmit	24	419	45.1	13.0	19	D	D	D	720	25.9	1 821	7
Donley	9	99	4.8	2.3	8	20	2.5	0.6	306	9.7	0	0
Duval	19	351	14.5	9.0	6	D	D	D	832	26.8	NA	NA
Eastland	53	885	45.2	21.2	37	132	11.4	3.1	1 420	59.3	0	0
Ector	293	7 384	823.7	297.6	250	2 276	340.1	83.5	11 141	612.8	85 659	448
Edwards	3	13	0.6	0.1	3	D	D	D	206	11.7	NA	NA
Ellis	259	3 610	326.6	125.6	170	786	71.1	18.6	13 490	664.8	264 143	1 451
El Paso	1 523	D	D	D	907	5 672	464.4	129.3	56 344	2 428.1	656 311	3 054
Erath	75	1 839	152.9	56.8	73	381	40.5	9.2	3 159	157.3	14 569	221
Falls	27	470	42.9	13.7	18	44	2.8	0.9	921	40.0	600	3
Fannin	49	1 211	128.3	49.1	34	122	12.5	2.5	2 331	107.9	5 648	33
Fayette	64	D	D	D	51	278	22.1	6.8	2 554	122.0	1 397	8
Fisher	8	129	9.4	4.2	7	18	2.1	0.4	230	8.7	NA	NA
Floyd	15	265	18.3	7.7	14	37	3.9	0.9	371	12.1	0	0
Foard	5	D	D	D	3	D	D	D	113	3.8	NA	NA
Fort Bend	1 490	18 644	1 809.7	648.0	566	3 481	366.9	101.0	64 349	3 294.0	1 323 641	10 279
Franklin	21	3 787	85.5	42.1	18	109	7.1	1.7	802	37.9	0	0
Freestone	29	631	45.3	15.7	26	88	10.2	1.9	1 218	49.5	1 349	6
Frio	31	786	42.6	16.4	16	D	D	D	978	39.9	551	7
Gaines	15	300	29.9	10.0	31	D	D	D	1 714	132.8	0	0
Galveston	556	12 280	1 211.2	495.9	419	2 455	368.2	73.9	23 759	1 095.9	523 338	2 241
Garza	11	177	9.3	4.4	4	11	2.0	0.2	362	19.5	0	0
Gillespie	84	1 611	138.5	66.4	53	269	26.4	6.4	3 593	171.1	9 723	49
Glasscock	NA	NA	NA	NA	1	D	D	D	128	8.3	NA	NA
Goliad	10	107	4.5	1.8	7	10	0.4	0.1	596	24.5	150	3
Gonzales	31	734	49.2	22.2	30	89	8.6	2.2	1 314	58.1	1 395	9
Gray	58	879	87.3	31.7	45	170	19.9	5.0	1 347	62.3	0	0
Grayson	381	9 105	809.1	337.4	139	834	81.0	27.5	9 582	456.3	88 659	730
Gregg	435	10 345	1 323.8	420.7	246	1 979	256.7	80.9	9 389	484.7	26 657	157
Grimes	23	D	D	D	18	D	D	D	2 065	92.8	3 979	39

Table B. States and Counties — Government Employment and Payroll, and Local Government Finances

	Government employment and payroll, 2012									Local government finances, 2012				
			March payroll (percent of total)							General revenue				
													Taxes	
													Per capita[1] (dollars)	
STATE County	Full-time equivalent employees	March payroll (dollars)	Adminis-tration, judicial, and legal	Police and Corrections	Fire Protection	Highways and transpor-tation	Health and Welfare	Natural resources and utilities	Education and libraries	Total (mil dol)	Inter-govern-mental (mil dol)	Total (mil dol)	Total	Property
	171	172	173	174	175	176	177	178	179	180	181	182	183	184
TEXAS—Cont'd														
Caldwell	1 295	4 627 444	7.7	8.7	1.9	2.0	2.0	4.0	73.2	94.8	42.5	38.1	983	834
Calhoun	989	2 883 600	7.4	10.3	2.1	7.4	2.5	3.0	65.2	113.6	11.0	59.8	2 767	2 477
Callahan	610	1 550 184	5.1	6.1	0.1	2.1	0.9	3.3	80.5	36.2	16.2	14.8	1 095	992
Cameron	21 552	67 816 703	3.9	8.4	2.8	2.4	1.6	5.2	74.0	1 662.8	982.8	420.5	1 012	795
Camp	508	1 428 009	4.7	3.7	0.0	2.7	0.0	6.7	81.7	31.5	14.9	13.1	1 056	885
Carson	384	1 061 435	13.7	2.8	0.0	2.8	2.7	4.8	64.8	23.9	6.1	15.1	2 453	2 374
Cass	1 554	4 198 540	6.2	6.2	1.2	1.7	13.0	3.1	67.7	95.7	40.0	32.1	1 064	938
Castro	547	1 382 117	5.7	6.3	0.0	3.1	22.6	2.8	59.3	40.7	18.5	9.6	1 182	1 099
Chambers	1 626	5 773 846	8.8	6.1	0.0	3.1	10.0	6.3	64.8	164.5	34.4	100.6	2 780	2 551
Cherokee	1 869	5 488 563	6.6	9.7	2.3	2.5	5.7	2.1	69.7	129.7	67.3	48.0	938	770
Childress	583	1 738 210	4.7	11.1	1.6	1.8	46.8	4.4	29.0	62.7	9.4	6.1	867	753
Clay	559	1 694 976	3.7	2.8	0.0	4.0	14.3	8.9	63.3	47.0	12.1	16.9	1 605	1 445
Cochran	322	904 022	9.5	5.0	0.0	3.0	15.4	3.4	63.0	25.0	7.6	15.4	5 071	4 948
Coke	281	838 152	5.9	2.3	0.0	2.1	28.4	5.7	54.6	19.7	5.9	9.5	2 954	2 830
Coleman	629	1 691 631	4.4	5.0	0.9	13.7	19.1	6.3	48.7	34.6	18.7	11.3	1 301	1 096
Collin	28 433	113 769 771	4.6	8.7	4.4	3.5	1.7	4.9	69.6	3 611.2	681.0	1 995.2	2 390	2 038
Collingsworth	212	542 831	8.4	5.4	0.0	4.5	10.4	2.8	67.4	13.8	5.2	4.4	1 449	1 266
Colorado	861	2 596 959	7.5	9.0	0.0	6.1	1.1	3.8	71.4	68.4	17.2	35.5	1 716	1 501
Comal	4 722	16 455 274	5.9	10.7	5.6	2.4	1.7	4.9	65.1	413.5	81.4	279.4	2 443	2 055
Comanche	808	2 419 843	5.0	9.4	3.7	2.4	31.9	1.8	45.5	44.9	19.7	15.0	1 088	940
Concho	164	494 362	12.1	5.4	0.0	4.2	27.0	5.6	44.3	14.7	3.5	6.1	1 522	1 335
Cooke	2 150	7 756 968	4.6	7.0	2.3	2.2	22.1	3.1	58.0	192.9	53.2	71.4	1 846	1 489
Coryell	2 637	8 819 482	4.6	7.6	1.9	0.9	12.3	2.8	67.6	181.4	80.4	52.0	674	538
Cottle	98	244 407	17.9	5.3	0.0	6.5	0.0	11.3	51.6	5.8	2.0	2.8	1 867	1 769
Crane	326	1 145 731	9.6	10.7	0.0	1.4	1.7	18.9	57.2	40.3	6.9	31.6	6 922	6 690
Crockett	357	1 200 438	6.5	5.5	0.5	4.8	18.8	4.6	54.0	42.3	5.4	32.0	8 555	8 552
Crosby	396	1 113 076	6.6	6.1	0.0	1.6	0.7	8.5	76.2	24.3	14.0	7.8	1 271	1 153
Culberson	191	571 285	13.3	8.3	0.0	6.0	1.7	9.4	60.5	20.8	4.5	8.8	3 852	3 344
Dallam	459	1 265 633	7.6	10.7	0.5	2.5	1.7	3.2	73.1	27.7	8.8	15.1	2 154	1 701
Dallas	105 099	440 691 940	4.7	11.6	5.3	7.3	14.2	4.5	50.8	12 510.2	3 260.1	5 736.3	2 338	1 792
Dawson	1 027	2 968 415	3.1	5.5	0.8	1.9	24.1	9.3	55.0	56.2	16.2	34.3	2 514	2 311
Deaf Smith	1 045	3 343 534	6.0	8.2	0.3	2.5	18.1	3.3	61.2	124.1	26.6	28.5	1 470	1 181
Delta	249	617 205	10.2	5.7	0.1	0.9	0.0	6.2	76.6	18.1	9.8	6.9	1 304	1 174
Denton	21 018	80 654 351	6.5	9.2	4.5	1.3	2.5	6.0	68.8	2 022.8	459.3	1 266.0	1 790	1 527
DeWitt	1 484	4 135 234	4.5	4.4	0.5	2.2	24.6	3.4	59.6	97.2	42.1	29.7	1 450	1 280
Dickens	132	357 360	9.4	5.8	0.0	5.1	0.0	3.9	70.5	10.8	3.0	6.0	2 586	2 419
Dimmit	818	1 945 225	7.2	5.4	0.0	1.0	23.0	4.5	58.2	46.5	21.1	19.9	1 904	1 452
Donley	386	1 127 365	14.0	2.9	0.0	2.0	12.1	7.2	61.3	18.4	8.5	4.9	1 371	1 208
Duval	1 069	2 869 544	5.5	8.4	0.0	5.8	26.4	3.4	49.4	84.6	22.4	23.2	1 983	1 875
Eastland	1 310	3 783 362	4.4	5.2	0.7	1.4	13.7	3.5	70.8	84.5	34.9	24.4	1 322	1 079
Ector	6 915	26 339 816	4.0	7.3	3.2	1.3	27.3	2.1	53.3	690.5	140.4	269.5	1 867	1 389
Edwards	196	461 967	5.6	6.6	0.5	3.6	2.2	2.7	77.7	11.0	3.0	7.2	3 657	3 565
Ellis	6 187	19 866 741	5.2	9.5	4.1	1.8	0.8	3.8	73.5	481.2	162.1	262.5	1 705	1 483
El Paso	38 262	139 590 880	4.5	10.3	3.7	3.1	8.1	3.0	65.5	3 339.7	1 610.5	1 090.4	1 318	1 018
Erath	1 440	4 169 914	6.4	10.7	3.0	2.6	13.7	4.5	57.7	97.3	38.9	48.4	1 230	1 006
Falls	755	2 249 164	5.5	10.4	1.3	2.6	0.2	6.9	72.4	45.7	26.5	12.5	711	588
Fannin	1 308	3 305 390	7.2	6.5	4.5	3.2	0.4	4.6	72.9	79.2	36.7	29.9	885	758
Fayette	1 047	3 070 054	8.5	11.9	0.0	5.3	5.8	7.8	59.5	68.3	15.9	38.4	1 557	1 347
Fisher	274	819 484	9.8	4.3	0.0	4.0	33.9	2.2	42.7	20.3	6.6	7.5	1 949	1 549
Floyd	494	1 401 943	6.0	6.3	0.0	3.0	29.3	3.2	52.2	29.3	12.8	7.3	1 148	1 016
Foard	109	252 340	7.9	2.2	0.0	27.8	2.3	4.6	52.5	6.5	3.6	2.6	1 980	1 699
Fort Bend	16 162	56 081 173	6.1	10.9	2.4	2.1	1.2	2.8	73.5	1 700.0	419.7	1 031.0	1 644	1 484
Franklin	376	1 062 026	10.1	8.0	0.0	4.2	0.1	6.2	71.2	29.0	7.2	17.8	1 676	1 502
Freestone	870	2 743 049	6.9	7.9	0.0	2.8	1.7	3.3	77.1	162.3	33.5	110.1	5 642	5 300
Frio	734	2 179 421	2.5	6.3	0.0	4.5	0.2	6.1	79.7	65.4	34.3	19.5	1 102	928
Gaines	1 152	3 808 818	1.9	4.1	0.0	3.9	20.6	2.9	66.0	125.0	15.5	87.9	4 775	4 628
Galveston	16 441	61 971 543	4.8	11.2	1.9	2.4	3.8	5.1	69.9	1 645.8	615.8	806.4	2 684	2 330
Garza	293	892 400	9.4	14.2	0.0	2.3	1.8	3.0	68.2	25.0	4.6	15.2	2 373	2 062
Gillespie	1 151	3 952 390	6.0	8.2	0.8	2.5	3.0	27.3	49.9	76.0	11.8	50.4	2 005	1 655
Glasscock	71	223 571	6.0	3.1	0.0	7.3	0.0	3.2	74.8	20.5	1.8	16.3	12 932	12 861
Goliad	327	1 001 812	9.8	6.6	0.0	4.9	0.3	2.6	69.7	27.2	7.6	18.0	2 453	2 250
Gonzales	1 193	3 267 421	6.8	6.0	0.5	2.5	24.1	5.5	54.2	101.3	40.1	26.2	1 309	1 024
Gray	994	2 974 220	9.1	9.3	4.4	4.3	1.5	4.0	66.4	72.0	21.7	36.7	1 599	1 291
Grayson	5 248	18 290 717	5.6	9.2	3.5	2.7	4.2	4.8	69.0	414.8	144.6	188.3	1 544	1 271
Gregg	5 913	19 287 172	4.5	10.7	5.5	1.7	6.6	4.4	64.2	499.5	162.8	256.1	2 088	1 490
Grimes	917	2 789 960	7.3	9.4	0.7	2.4	1.2	2.1	74.4	77.3	25.0	42.7	1 594	1 464

1. Based on the resident population estimated as of July 1 of the year shown.

Table B. States and Counties — Local Government Finances, Government Employment, and Income Taxes

STATE County	Total (mil dol) 185	Per capita[1] (dollars) 186	Education 187	Health and hospitals 188	Police protection 189	Public welfare 190	Highways 191	Total (mil dol) 192	Per capita[1] (dollars) 193	Federal civilian 194	Federal military 195	State and local 196	Number of returns 197	Mean adjusted gross income 198	Mean income tax 199
TEXAS—Cont'd															
Caldwell	103.3	2 667	49.6	3.3	5.2	0.3	3.5	64.6	1 669	61	76	1 626	16 860	45 160	4 609
Calhoun	106.7	4 938	37.9	23.7	4.3	0.2	4.4	73.3	3 392	37	102	1 354	9 630	53 739	6 447
Callahan	33.7	2 494	68.1	0.5	5.7	0.0	2.9	34.4	2 546	44	27	602	5 800	49 137	4 959
Cameron	1 613.4	3 883	61.9	0.8	4.4	0.5	3.7	1 801.3	4 335	3 282	950	27 544	161 210	37 056	3 255
Camp	30.6	2 461	71.8	0.2	3.9	0.1	5.5	43.1	3 459	27	26	578	5 310	44 651	4 428
Carson	23.0	3 741	59.9	1.1	2.8	0.0	5.0	34.1	5 539	16	12	428	2 600	60 763	7 011
Cass	91.1	3 021	59.3	15.9	3.7	0.3	2.8	50.0	1 659	63	61	1 604	12 520	46 219	4 462
Castro	33.2	4 069	51.2	27.7	4.5	0.0	3.7	20.0	2 445	19	15	616	2 990	45 900	6 515
Chambers	168.5	4 656	51.2	9.0	4.2	0.4	4.6	360.8	9 968	55	79	1 986	18 080	75 107	9 722
Cherokee	167.4	3 268	66.5	4.9	3.9	0.1	4.5	85.5	1 669	71	99	4 147	20 170	45 493	4 685
Childress	54.2	7 712	18.8	64.6	2.7	0.0	2.7	6.3	898	19	11	1 091	2 540	43 654	4 161
Clay	46.1	4 377	39.2	17.7	2.7	0.1	5.6	119.9	11 385	24	21	513	4 550	54 733	5 904
Cochran	27.0	8 873	69.4	12.8	3.0	0.0	3.8	0.1	27	13	D	324	1 240	37 510	3 902
Coke	16.5	5 122	42.6	0.1	3.0	32.6	4.0	24.2	7 483	10	D	336	1 440	53 654	5 780
Coleman	34.1	3 930	44.6	22.9	4.1	0.1	3.7	15.9	1 837	41	17	553	3 620	46 984	6 505
Collin	4 140.4	4 961	43.1	0.7	3.6	0.1	8.6	16 872.8	20 216	1 697	1 939	44 160	404 120	95 226	15 866
Collingsworth	16.5	5 436	37.3	43.5	4.4	0.0	1.5	12.6	4 138	16	D	216	1 220	39 056	4 018
Colorado	71.5	3 453	50.2	14.9	5.5	0.1	5.4	63.0	3 042	47	42	1 039	9 660	65 313	9 287
Comal	446.0	3 899	56.1	0.9	6.3	0.6	5.0	943.7	8 251	171	261	5 649	60 900	79 364	12 076
Comanche	42.2	3 069	50.8	15.3	4.6	0.2	5.8	30.9	2 246	46	27	804	5 580	41 466	4 228
Concho	12.3	3 067	36.9	29.2	4.3	0.0	4.1	3.9	977	25	D	231	1 010	48 162	5 525
Cooke	191.9	4 961	48.0	22.9	5.0	0.1	3.7	159.4	4 119	59	79	2 802	17 890	72 899	11 516
Coryell	215.6	2 792	43.6	12.0	4.0	0.3	22.6	217.4	2 815	171	506	6 078	27 200	41 729	3 370
Cottle	5.4	3 651	50.1	1.6	2.9	0.1	3.3	1.4	940	10	D	138	650	32 906	3 482
Crane	40.9	8 956	77.6	0.0	3.1	0.0	1.6	6.3	1 384	D	10	376	2 120	65 180	7 481
Crockett	42.8	11 437	63.2	0.7	1.7	0.8	5.5	6.0	1 614	D	D	407	1 710	75 250	11 910
Crosby	24.1	3 941	70.8	0.1	3.8	1.1	3.7	0.5	83	16	12	464	2 390	42 906	3 878
Culberson	18.7	8 167	29.9	32.6	5.7	0.0	3.2	2.8	1 224	85	D	207	1 030	38 368	3 519
Dallam	28.3	4 044	60.6	0.3	5.2	0.0	6.8	30.2	4 320	19	14	272	3 390	45 923	5 847
Dallas	11 949.9	4 870	37.6	17.2	5.8	0.7	2.6	27 138.7	11 060	25 230	5 752	147 724	1 154 650	70 579	11 937
Dawson	56.4	4 132	73.5	0.6	3.9	0.1	3.1	165.8	12 154	60	24	1 355	5 120	55 373	7 268
Deaf Smith	135.2	6 983	26.5	25.1	2.4	0.1	2.8	2 436.8	125 866	48	38	1 302	8 080	36 735	3 703
Delta	15.4	2 898	62.3	0.0	6.5	0.3	5.4	19.5	3 660	16	11	301	1 970	44 395	4 084
Denton	2 006.9	2 837	52.0	1.7	5.6	0.1	6.2	6 231.1	8 810	1 618	1 615	32 891	345 710	79 343	11 804
DeWitt	94.1	4 596	46.6	28.3	3.1	0.2	3.8	56.7	2 773	31	39	2 262	8 590	117 037	28 597
Dickens	13.9	5 980	66.7	0.3	4.5	0.0	7.7	7.5	3 235	11	D	167	780	40 674	3 754
Dimmit	42.2	4 036	66.0	0.3	4.0	0.0	3.8	95.0	9 081	274	22	1 087	4 470	54 046	8 061
Donley	19.7	5 489	76.6	0.0	1.8	2.7	1.6	21.5	5 966	11	D	424	1 480	39 024	3 789
Duval	69.0	5 890	36.6	35.9	4.0	0.7	3.7	59.2	5 053	129	22	998	4 770	45 949	4 253
Eastland	81.8	4 441	62.6	14.7	2.7	0.2	2.9	42.9	2 328	50	476	1 406	7 300	51 751	5 206
Ector	691.3	4 790	36.3	40.0	3.5	0.0	2.4	385.4	2 670	179	321	9 721	70 810	67 171	9 441
Edwards	10.4	5 270	76.7	0.0	6.7	0.0	2.3	2.5	1 271	20	D	124	800	65 665	8 801
Ellis	446.9	2 903	57.1	0.3	6.0	0.3	3.9	1 320.0	8 573	223	330	7 092	71 900	58 947	6 791
El Paso	3 257.4	3 937	52.3	15.6	4.9	0.4	0.9	4 034.1	4 876	12 583	28 514	54 658	357 290	41 655	4 034
Erath	86.0	2 188	55.2	1.6	7.4	0.4	5.3	109.6	2 786	74	85	3 974	15 520	48 899	6 008
Falls	44.4	2 519	65.6	1.1	5.3	0.8	6.2	13.4	762	406	31	1 158	6 430	41 490	4 527
Fannin	76.7	2 268	61.1	2.7	7.1	0.7	5.8	54.2	1 601	695	62	1 897	13 120	46 848	4 651
Fayette	68.1	2 756	56.7	3.7	5.9	0.8	7.7	47.6	1 928	67	50	1 507	11 580	101 176	15 608
Fisher	21.3	5 529	41.6	30.6	4.6	0.1	5.1	3.0	779	17	D	308	1 590	53 025	5 499
Floyd	29.6	4 646	49.4	29.9	3.4	0.0	1.0	5.9	923	29	12	508	2 510	41 649	4 189
Foard	4.6	3 531	56.3	4.7	6.8	0.2	7.6	0.1	79	10	D	96	520	41 492	3 950
Fort Bend	1 722.6	2 746	46.9	0.7	4.7	0.3	7.2	5 183.8	8 264	728	1 480	23 096	305 380	94 806	15 672
Franklin	25.1	2 364	51.5	0.1	5.6	0.4	9.6	29.4	2 760	17	22	431	4 180	47 560	5 363
Freestone	159.6	8 177	39.9	10.8	11.9	0.0	12.6	91.4	4 681	36	37	1 355	7 870	53 251	6 052
Frio	58.9	3 327	54.3	3.8	5.2	0.0	3.8	93.0	5 256	115	31	1 347	6 490	51 452	7 222
Gaines	132.6	7 199	63.4	14.7	1.8	0.0	4.5	120.9	6 566	26	41	1 440	7 500	54 268	6 428
Galveston	1 667.3	5 549	43.5	4.3	5.0	0.5	5.1	3 060.4	10 185	892	1 036	26 063	146 440	72 546	10 687
Garza	22.3	3 480	59.5	0.1	9.6	0.7	5.7	14.9	2 330	13	D	378	1 870	64 312	10 073
Gillespie	76.0	3 023	58.0	2.8	9.2	0.3	5.1	26.7	1 061	50	52	1 151	13 080	73 919	11 610
Glasscock	21.4	16 992	83.0	6.7	0.3	0.0	0.7	8.1	6 411	D	D	136	640	181 375	48 978
Goliad	22.9	3 113	65.5	4.1	7.2	0.8	7.3	16.0	2 182	15	15	445	3 210	71 606	11 686
Gonzales	101.6	5 069	39.0	28.7	5.0	0.0	3.6	43.0	2 146	62	41	1 477	8 880	70 095	12 855
Gray	70.1	3 049	52.0	0.4	5.0	0.2	5.4	80.6	3 506	42	43	1 576	9 440	56 647	7 038
Grayson	423.3	3 471	54.8	3.3	5.1	0.0	6.0	717.6	5 885	331	252	6 240	55 050	52 057	5 938
Gregg	514.7	4 196	54.4	5.9	5.3	0.0	4.4	916.0	7 468	349	244	7 132	56 490	59 364	7 923
Grimes	84.3	3 146	51.8	0.3	3.8	0.0	6.3	95.1	3 549	48	50	1 811	11 390	52 543	6 592

1. Based on the resident population estimated as of July 1 of the year shown.

Table B. States and Counties — Land Area and Population

STATE/ County code	CBSA code[1]	County type[2]	STATE County	Population, 2016				Population and population characteristics, 2016										
								Race alone or in combination, not Hispanic or Latino (percent)					Age (percent)					
				Land area,[3] (sq mi) 2016	Total persons 2016	Rank	Per square mile	White	Black	American Indian, Alaska Native	Asian and Pacific Islander	Percent Hispanic or Latino[4]	Under 5 years	5 to 17 years	18 to 24 years	25 to 34 years	35 to 44 years	45 to 54 years
				1	2	3	4	5	6	7	8	9	10	11	12	13	14	15
			TEXAS—Cont'd															
48 187	41700	1	Guadalupe	711.3	155 265	419	218.3	52.9	8.1	0.8	2.7	37.6	6.4	19.2	9.0	12.7	13.8	13.8
48 189	38380	4	Hale	1 004.7	34 263	1 317	34.1	35.0	5.4	0.6	0.7	59.0	7.3	20.4	11.4	13.7	11.6	11.7
48 191	...	9	Hall	883.5	3 138	2 960	3.6	57.0	7.8	0.9	0.3	34.9	5.4	18.1	8.4	9.7	9.7	11.7
48 193	...	6	Hamilton	835.9	8 304	2 567	9.9	85.4	1.1	0.9	0.9	12.6	5.4	15.6	7.3	9.7	10.0	11.5
48 195	...	7	Hansford	919.8	5 538	2 799	6.0	52.2	1.0	0.5	0.5	46.5	7.2	22.2	9.5	10.9	11.6	12.5
48 197	...	9	Hardeman	695.1	3 906	2 909	5.6	70.2	5.9	1.1	0.9	23.6	5.3	18.3	7.1	10.5	12.2	13.0
48 199	13140	2	Hardin	890.6	56 322	907	63.2	88.0	5.9	0.9	0.9	5.5	6.5	18.2	7.7	12.4	12.3	13.1
48 201	26420	1	Harris	1 704.9	4 589 928	3	2 692.2	31.5	19.2	0.5	7.7	42.4	7.8	19.2	9.5	16.2	14.2	12.6
48 203	32220	4	Harrison	899.9	66 534	796	73.9	65.0	21.5	0.9	1.0	13.0	6.6	18.9	8.7	12.1	11.8	12.6
48 205	...	7	Hartley	1 462.0	5 747	2 773	3.9	66.6	6.5	0.9	0.9	26.1	5.4	16.7	6.5	13.5	16.6	14.8
48 207	...	6	Haskell	903.1	5 681	2 785	6.3	65.7	4.5	1.1	1.3	28.9	4.5	14.9	9.4	13.3	11.4	11.0
48 209	12420	1	Hays	678.0	204 470	321	301.6	56.3	4.2	0.8	2.2	38.1	6.3	16.9	17.1	14.4	12.9	11.4
48 211	...	7	Hemphill	906.3	4 129	2 892	4.6	65.2	0.6	1.2	1.1	33.0	7.8	24.4	7.2	12.2	12.7	11.3
48 213	11980	4	Henderson	873.8	79 901	701	91.4	80.2	7.0	1.3	0.9	12.2	5.6	16.0	7.8	10.8	10.6	12.8
48 215	32580	2	Hidalgo	1 570.9	849 843	67	541.0	6.7	0.5	0.1	1.0	91.8	9.6	23.7	11.0	13.2	12.8	10.7
48 217	...	6	Hill	958.9	35 077	1 300	36.6	72.5	7.0	0.9	0.7	20.3	6.0	17.5	8.3	11.1	10.4	12.5
48 219	30220	6	Hockley	908.4	23 275	1 666	25.6	48.2	4.1	0.8	0.7	47.1	6.8	19.4	12.3	13.1	11.2	11.2
48 221	19100	1	Hood	420.7	56 857	899	135.1	85.6	1.1	1.2	1.0	12.4	5.7	15.3	6.7	10.6	9.9	12.1
48 223	44860	6	Hopkins	767.2	36 400	1 266	47.4	75.1	7.9	1.0	1.0	16.5	6.5	18.5	8.1	12.0	11.2	12.8
48 225	...	7	Houston	1 231.0	22 754	1 688	18.5	63.3	25.5	0.8	0.8	10.7	5.1	14.2	7.1	11.9	12.4	13.9
48 227	13700	4	Howard	900.8	36 708	1 259	40.8	50.3	6.7	1.2	1.3	41.7	6.4	15.5	10.3	15.9	12.4	15.4
48 229	21340	2	Hudspeth	4 570.5	4 053	2 898	0.9	19.6	2.1	0.7	0.9	77.6	6.6	17.1	9.6	17.4	11.7	10.0
48 231	19100	1	Hunt	840.3	92 073	637	109.6	74.0	8.6	1.5	1.9	15.7	6.3	17.5	10.0	12.2	11.7	13.4
48 233	14420	6	Hutchinson	887.4	21 511	1 752	24.2	72.4	3.2	2.4	0.9	22.9	6.9	19.0	8.7	12.5	12.2	11.6
48 235	41660	3	Irion	1 051.5	1 557	3 077	1.5	71.2	1.5	1.5	0.7	26.6	6.1	18.0	6.9	10.2	10.9	12.2
48 237	...	6	Jack	910.7	8 744	2 528	9.6	78.5	4.4	0.8	0.9	16.3	5.7	16.0	9.5	13.9	11.9	14.0
48 239	...	6	Jackson	829.4	14 869	2 111	17.9	59.7	6.6	0.7	1.2	32.8	6.8	18.7	8.0	12.3	11.7	11.4
48 241	...	6	Jasper	938.7	35 648	1 286	38.0	75.6	17.0	1.0	1.0	6.9	6.2	18.0	7.8	11.4	11.0	12.8
48 243	...	9	Jeff Davis	2 264.6	2 200	3 029	1.0	63.4	0.9	1.6	1.4	34.5	1.5	7.6	5.4	8.4	9.5	13.4
48 245	13140	2	Jefferson	876.3	254 679	265	290.6	42.4	34.1	0.7	4.2	19.9	7.0	16.9	9.8	14.8	12.6	12.6
48 247	...	6	Jim Hogg	1 136.2	5 146	2 822	4.5	6.2	0.6	0.5	0.6	92.4	8.9	21.2	8.4	11.9	11.6	10.9
48 249	10860	4	Jim Wells	865.2	41 149	1 150	47.6	18.4	0.7	0.4	0.5	80.4	8.0	20.4	9.4	13.0	11.6	11.5
48 251	19100	1	Johnson	724.8	163 274	395	225.3	74.6	3.6	1.1	1.6	20.6	6.7	19.4	8.7	12.8	12.7	13.5
48 253	10180	3	Jones	928.6	20 009	1 827	21.5	59.3	12.5	0.7	0.8	27.6	4.5	13.2	10.2	17.0	15.0	14.0
48 255	...	6	Karnes	747.6	15 254	2 078	20.4	37.6	8.7	0.4	0.5	53.3	5.8	15.1	10.2	17.9	13.4	11.8
48 257	19100	1	Kaufman	780.7	118 350	524	151.6	67.2	11.4	1.1	1.5	20.5	7.2	20.3	8.1	13.1	13.9	13.3
48 259	41700	1	Kendall	662.5	42 540	1 119	64.2	74.2	1.2	1.0	1.4	23.3	5.1	18.2	7.8	9.4	11.9	13.8
48 261	28780	9	Kenedy	1 458.5	404	3 139	0.3	22.3	2.2	1.7	0.7	73.3	4.2	24.8	7.9	10.9	9.7	13.1
48 263	...	9	Kent	902.5	769	3 123	0.9	80.2	1.4	1.6	0.4	17.8	5.3	14.7	5.6	8.1	9.6	12.4
48 265	28500	4	Kerr	1 103.3	51 504	967	46.7	70.4	1.8	1.1	1.2	26.6	5.2	14.2	8.3	10.0	9.0	11.4
48 267	...	7	Kimble	1 251.0	4 423	2 869	3.5	74.6	0.6	0.8	0.8	23.7	4.9	13.9	6.8	8.9	9.8	11.9
48 269	...	9	King	910.9	289	3 140	0.3	82.7	1.0	1.7	0.0	16.6	4.5	23.9	4.5	11.4	10.7	14.5
48 271	...	7	Kinney	1 360.1	3 590	2 936	2.6	39.3	1.8	1.2	0.4	58.3	4.3	14.2	9.4	12.0	11.9	11.3
48 273	28780	4	Kleberg	881.3	31 690	1 388	36.0	21.7	3.9	0.5	2.4	72.5	7.1	17.2	20.7	14.0	9.9	9.2
48 275	...	9	Knox	850.6	3 806	2 919	4.5	60.6	5.7	1.2	0.6	33.3	7.3	19.7	7.7	10.6	10.0	11.3
48 277	37580	5	Lamar	907.2	49 791	988	54.9	77.0	14.2	2.6	1.2	7.7	6.9	17.0	8.3	12.2	10.9	13.0
48 279	...	6	Lamb	1 016.2	13 275	2 217	13.1	40.6	4.4	0.8	0.4	54.7	7.1	20.7	8.5	11.8	10.9	11.8
48 281	28660	2	Lampasas	712.8	20 760	1 786	29.1	74.8	4.4	1.8	2.3	19.2	5.9	17.2	7.6	10.9	11.8	13.9
48 283	...	6	La Salle	1 486.7	7 613	2 624	5.1	12.6	0.7	0.5	0.5	86.0	6.2	14.4	17.7	17.5	11.2	10.8
48 285	...	6	Lavaca	969.7	19 809	1 840	20.4	74.8	6.5	0.5	0.6	18.5	5.9	17.6	7.2	10.3	10.4	12.0
48 287	...	6	Lee	629.0	17 055	1 976	27.1	64.7	11.5	0.8	0.8	23.6	6.1	16.1	8.7	11.2	11.5	13.0
48 289	...	8	Leon	1 073.2	17 299	1 956	16.1	77.3	7.6	1.1	1.0	14.2	6.1	16.6	6.8	9.9	10.5	11.4
48 291	26420	1	Liberty	1 158.4	81 704	688	70.5	66.3	10.5	0.9	0.8	22.7	7.0	18.5	9.2	14.0	12.7	13.3
48 293	...	6	Limestone	905.3	23 468	1 660	25.9	59.9	17.9	0.8	0.9	21.9	6.6	16.4	8.6	12.9	11.7	12.1
48 295	...	9	Lipscomb	932.2	3 487	2 940	3.7	63.6	1.5	2.0	1.1	33.8	6.1	20.8	8.2	14.0	11.0	11.2
48 297	...	8	Live Oak	1 039.7	12 056	2 290	11.6	55.1	4.7	1.1	0.8	39.1	5.7	14.4	7.8	14.0	12.0	12.2
48 299	...	7	Llano	934.1	20 362	1 812	21.8	87.3	1.3	1.2	0.8	10.5	4.2	11.5	5.2	8.0	7.7	11.3
48 301	...	9	Loving	668.8	113	3 141	0.2	77.0	2.7	1.8	0.0	18.6	8.0	31.9	1.8	20.4	5.3	8.0
48 303	31180	2	Lubbock	895.6	303 137	228	338.5	55.2	7.5	0.7	2.8	35.0	6.8	17.3	17.0	14.7	11.3	10.4
48 305	31180	2	Lynn	891.9	5 711	2 779	6.4	50.0	2.6	0.8	0.3	47.2	6.9	19.9	7.6	12.2	11.1	12.9
48 307	...	7	McCulloch	1 065.6	8 172	2 581	7.7	65.8	2.2	0.9	0.7	31.4	5.7	16.9	7.9	10.5	10.1	12.1
48 309	47380	2	McLennan	1 037.1	247 934	272	239.1	58.0	15.0	0.7	2.2	25.8	7.1	17.7	14.9	12.8	11.1	11.2
48 311	...	9	McMullen	1 139.8	804	3 116	0.7	56.8	2.4	1.2	0.6	39.7	5.6	16.5	7.0	11.4	10.2	13.6
48 313	...	6	Madison	466.1	13 987	2 165	30.0	56.5	20.2	0.8	1.0	22.8	5.6	16.1	11.6	17.3	12.8	11.5
48 315	...	8	Marion	380.9	10 147	2 424	26.6	72.6	22.5	1.9	1.3	3.9	4.7	13.8	6.4	9.7	9.5	13.5
48 317	33260	3	Martin	915.0	5 723	2 777	6.3	51.2	2.1	0.7	0.6	46.1	9.3	21.9	8.8	14.0	11.4	12.0

1. CBSA = Core Based Statistical Area. See Appendix A for explanation. See Appendix B for list of metropolitan areas with component counties.   2. County type code from the Economic Research Service of USDA Rural-Urban Continuum Codes. See Appendix A for definition.   3. Dry land or land partially or temporarily covered by water.   4. May be of any race.

Table B. States and Counties — **Population and Households**

STATE County	Age (percent) (cont.) 55 to 64 years	65 to 74 years	75 years and over	Percent female	Total persons 2000	2010	Percent change 2000–2010	2010–2016	Components of change, 2010–2016 Births	Deaths	Net migration	Households, 2011–2015 Number	Persons per household	Percent Family households	Female family householder[1]	One person
	16	17	18	19	20	21	22	23	24	25	26	27	28	29	30	31
TEXAS—Cont'd																
Guadalupe	11.5	8.2	5.4	50.6	89 023	131 537	47.8	18.0	10 931	5 908	18 150	48 940	2.89	75.6	12.5	21.0
Hale	10.8	7.2	5.8	48.2	36 602	36 229	-1.0	-5.4	3 234	1 916	-3 383	11 513	2.86	73.8	16.8	22.7
Hall	13.9	12.0	11.0	51.0	3 782	3 353	-11.3	-6.4	195	293	-110	1 155	2.71	71.0	13.8	26.9
Hamilton	14.5	13.4	12.7	50.2	8 229	8 517	3.5	-2.5	553	852	65	3 166	2.52	69.6	8.3	29.2
Hansford	11.3	7.8	7.0	49.3	5 369	5 613	4.5	-1.3	511	310	-284	1 972	2.78	76.9	8.4	21.0
Hardeman	14.0	10.8	8.9	49.8	4 724	4 139	-12.4	-5.6	268	268	-221	1 634	2.42	60.6	10.5	34.9
Hardin	13.5	9.7	6.5	50.6	48 073	54 635	13.7	3.1	4 311	3 390	797	20 799	2.64	72.5	11.1	24.3
Harris	10.7	6.1	3.7	50.3	3 400 578	4 093 242	20.4	12.1	432 780	150 560	219 106	1 499 528	2.88	68.4	15.6	26.1
Harrison	13.3	9.5	6.4	51.2	62 110	65 629	5.7	1.4	5 311	3 881	-396	23 546	2.76	73.2	13.4	24.0
Hartley	10.8	7.7	7.9	41.2	5 537	6 062	9.5	-5.2	370	224	-501	1 769	2.61	73.9	3.3	23.5
Haskell	14.0	11.2	10.3	47.2	6 093	5 899	-3.2	-3.7	305	504	-23	2 285	2.20	65.7	11.2	30.4
Hays	10.4	6.9	3.7	50.3	97 589	157 089	61.0	30.2	13 968	5 535	38 023	61 360	2.78	64.3	10.1	23.1
Hemphill	10.5	7.8	6.1	50.9	3 351	3 807	13.6	8.5	424	200	91	1 466	2.77	78.6	7.9	19.6
Henderson	14.7	12.6	9.1	51.2	73 277	78 534	7.2	1.7	5 610	6 336	2 129	29 780	2.61	70.0	10.2	25.4
Hidalgo	8.2	6.2	4.8	51.1	569 463	774 770	36.1	9.7	101 020	24 660	-2 201	224 021	3.62	81.8	20.6	15.6
Hill	13.7	11.8	8.7	50.3	32 321	35 085	8.6	0.0	2 567	2 513	-73	12 902	2.63	69.1	11.8	26.4
Hockley	11.8	8.1	6.0	50.3	22 716	22 927	0.9	1.5	2 054	1 293	-393	8 089	2.80	74.3	13.6	22.5
Hood	15.2	14.0	10.4	51.1	41 100	51 168	24.5	11.1	3 675	3 992	5 880	20 932	2.51	68.5	8.3	26.8
Hopkins	12.9	10.4	7.5	51.0	31 960	35 161	10.0	3.5	2 905	2 383	635	13 273	2.65	74.4	13.3	21.6
Houston	14.3	11.6	9.5	46.8	23 185	23 732	2.4	-4.1	1 424	1 856	-533	8 046	2.45	63.5	13.9	33.9
Howard	11.7	6.8	5.6	42.9	33 627	35 012	4.1	4.8	2 889	2 400	1 188	11 206	2.73	67.2	14.9	28.0
Hudspeth	11.7	9.5	6.3	49.5	3 344	3 476	3.9	16.6	280	89	392	968	3.06	75.2	14.9	22.9
Hunt	13.3	9.3	6.4	50.6	76 596	86 161	12.5	6.9	6 845	5 491	4 472	30 832	2.77	68.2	11.2	27.0
Hutchinson	13.5	8.9	6.8	49.6	23 857	22 249	-6.7	-3.3	1 869	1 494	-1 077	8 297	2.62	66.2	12.1	31.0
Irion	15.7	10.5	9.3	49.3	1 771	1 599	-9.7	-2.6	89	79	-48	658	2.50	74.3	7.4	23.4
Jack	12.8	9.1	7.1	43.7	8 763	9 044	3.2	-3.3	614	539	-351	3 031	2.55	73.2	7.9	24.0
Jackson	13.6	9.4	8.0	50.4	14 391	14 075	-2.2	5.6	1 224	883	473	5 109	2.79	70.0	8.8	26.5
Jasper	13.8	11.1	7.8	50.6	35 604	35 710	0.3	-0.2	2 756	2 589	-194	12 310	2.83	67.3	11.8	30.2
Jeff Davis	22.0	20.1	12.1	49.4	2 207	2 342	6.1	-6.1	85	112	-105	1 023	2.12	62.5	5.5	33.8
Jefferson	12.6	7.7	6.0	48.7	252 051	252 277	0.1	1.0	22 192	15 248	-4 252	93 495	2.53	63.6	17.2	32.0
Jim Hogg	10.6	10.0	6.5	50.0	5 281	5 300	0.4	-2.9	562	331	-377	1 688	3.09	75.4	17.4	22.3
Jim Wells	11.3	8.5	6.3	50.8	39 326	40 838	3.8	0.8	4 137	2 536	-1 264	13 829	2.97	75.0	18.9	22.7
Johnson	12.4	8.6	5.3	50.1	126 811	150 944	19.0	8.2	12 489	7 886	7 542	53 685	2.84	76.5	11.1	19.5
Jones	11.6	8.1	6.4	36.9	20 785	20 198	-2.8	-0.9	1 068	1 180	-48	5 489	2.26	67.9	11.7	27.6
Karnes	11.4	7.5	6.8	41.0	15 446	14 824	-4.0	2.9	1 057	919	289	4 309	2.83	68.0	13.6	30.8
Kaufman	11.8	7.6	4.6	50.7	71 313	103 364	44.9	14.5	9 272	5 417	10 811	35 418	3.05	77.5	13.0	18.4
Kendall	14.1	11.6	8.1	51.3	23 743	33 419	40.8	27.3	2 172	2 115	8 749	13 552	2.72	74.6	10.6	22.7
Kenedy	14.1	7.7	7.7	50.0	414	413	-0.2	-2.2	24	9	-31	145	3.88	75.9	14.5	24.1
Kent	15.5	13.4	15.5	51.1	859	808	-5.9	-4.8	51	80	-3	372	2.07	57.8	3.5	40.9
Kerr	14.6	14.6	12.7	51.8	43 653	49 625	13.7	3.8	3 213	4 443	2 858	20 316	2.38	64.6	13.0	31.3
Kimble	15.6	15.7	12.6	50.6	4 468	4 605	3.1	-4.0	257	318	-107	1 990	2.22	65.8	9.3	29.0
King	13.1	8.7	8.7	51.2	356	286	-19.7	1.0	12	7	-6	113	2.36	68.1	4.4	21.2
Kinney	12.5	11.7	12.8	44.5	3 379	3 598	6.5	-0.2	203	225	26	1 079	3.00	67.7	7.7	26.2
Kleberg	8.8	7.5	5.6	49.1	31 549	32 061	1.6	-1.2	2 955	1 534	-1 815	10 906	2.76	64.0	16.4	25.1
Knox	13.3	9.9	10.2	50.6	4 253	3 719	-12.6	2.3	329	335	104	1 437	2.55	66.4	14.1	31.5
Lamar	12.7	11.0	7.9	51.8	48 499	49 789	2.7	0.0	4 185	3 839	-399	19 026	2.56	69.8	14.3	26.4
Lamb	12.2	8.3	8.6	50.5	14 709	13 977	-5.0	-5.0	1 233	954	-984	4 865	2.78	70.9	13.5	25.7
Lampasas	13.8	11.1	7.8	50.7	17 762	19 678	10.8	5.5	1 466	1 205	761	7 505	2.66	73.3	8.6	22.5
La Salle	8.3	8.2	5.7	40.7	5 866	6 886	17.4	10.6	618	310	394	1 971	3.19	67.5	14.2	29.9
Lavaca	14.1	12.1	10.4	50.9	19 210	19 263	0.3	2.8	1 394	1 519	674	7 701	2.48	72.3	8.8	25.4
Lee	15.3	10.4	7.7	49.7	15 657	16 610	6.1	2.7	1 265	1 000	199	5 996	2.69	71.1	8.5	24.8
Leon	14.9	13.9	10.0	50.1	15 335	16 801	9.6	3.0	1 302	1 368	542	6 142	2.72	71.2	11.7	24.1
Liberty	12.3	8.3	4.8	50.6	70 154	75 641	7.8	8.0	6 689	4 628	3 901	25 319	2.82	73.0	11.6	22.7
Limestone	13.5	10.7	7.6	48.5	22 051	23 386	6.1	0.4	1 936	1 612	-171	8 084	2.77	68.9	14.1	28.0
Lipscomb	13.1	8.3	7.3	47.9	3 057	3 302	8.0	5.6	290	162	59	1 198	2.87	72.5	7.8	25.1
Live Oak	13.5	11.6	8.8	45.8	12 309	11 528	-6.3	4.6	789	740	495	3 699	2.78	67.8	8.2	27.2
Llano	17.6	19.5	15.1	51.7	17 044	19 301	13.2	5.5	994	1 853	1 787	8 654	2.21	64.6	6.3	31.7
Loving	15.9	8.8	0.0	45.1	67	82	22.4	37.8	9	6	28	45	2.60	40.0	4.4	42.2
Lubbock	10.3	6.8	5.3	50.7	242 628	278 897	14.9	8.7	25 548	14 497	12 700	107 540	2.59	62.2	13.6	28.5
Lynn	13.0	8.6	7.8	48.8	6 550	5 915	-9.7	-3.4	456	299	-355	2 188	2.62	73.5	19.1	23.9
McCulloch	14.3	12.7	9.8	49.9	8 205	8 283	1.0	-1.3	581	708	17	3 145	2.59	68.3	10.1	26.7
McLennan	11.3	7.8	6.1	51.2	213 517	234 906	10.0	5.5	21 869	12 843	4 003	86 769	2.68	66.7	14.7	26.5
McMullen	12.8	9.7	13.2	48.8	851	707	-16.9	13.7	57	52	98	278	2.80	77.7	10.4	18.7
Madison	10.2	8.5	6.4	42.8	12 940	13 667	5.6	2.3	972	780	118	4 121	2.32	68.6	13.4	27.6
Marion	17.5	14.8	10.0	51.7	10 941	10 536	-3.7	-3.7	610	1 002	-23	4 463	2.26	62.5	9.3	33.3
Martin	10.7	7.3	4.6	49.9	4 746	4 799	1.1	19.3	595	250	575	1 630	3.18	71.8	13.4	24.0

1. No spouse present.

Table B. States and Counties — Population, Vital Statistics, Health, and Crime

STATE County	Persons in group quarters, 2016	Daytime population, 2011–2015 — Number	Daytime population, 2011–2015 — Employment/residence ratio	Births, 2016 — Total	Births, 2016 — Rate[1]	Deaths, 2016 — Number	Deaths, 2016 — Rate[1]	Persons under 65 with no health insurance, 2015 — Number	Persons under 65 with no health insurance, 2015 — Percent	Medicare, 2015 — Total Beneficiaries	Medicare, 2015 — Enrolled in Original Medicare	Medicare, 2015 — Enrolled in Medicare Advantage	Serious crimes known to police,[2] 2014 — Total Number	Serious crimes known to police,[2] 2014 — Total Rate[3]
	32	33	34	35	36	37	38	39	40	41	42	43	44	45
TEXAS—Cont'd														
Guadalupe	1 943	117 654	0.61	1 847	11.9	1 058	6.8	19 226	14.8	20 380	14 568	5 812	3 246	2 207
Hale	2 730	35 545	1.00	461	13.5	309	9.0	6 221	23.0	5 442	4 139	1 303	1 065	2 968
Hall	43	3 316	1.10	27	8.6	39	12.4	713	29.8	740	604	136	39	1 206
Hamilton	217	7 981	0.91	87	10.5	131	15.8	1 463	24.4	1 926	1 260	666	96	1 374
Hansford	73	5 369	0.93	87	15.7	39	7.0	1 330	27.9	877	778	99	34	772
Hardeman	21	3 659	0.80	44	11.3	37	9.5	704	23.0	889	733	156	75	2 251
Hardin	402	44 017	0.52	687	12.2	540	9.6	6 942	14.8	9 985	6 112	3 873	854	1 526
Harris	49 246	4 658 708	1.15	73 072	15.9	26 660	5.8	856 230	21.1	455 423	240 987	214 436	200 021	4 519
Harrison	1 241	61 791	0.83	844	12.7	685	10.3	10 094	18.3	10 130	7 545	2 585	1 585	2 342
Hartley	1 059	6 215	1.04	59	10.3	33	5.7	797	20.6	137	115	22	101	1 641
Haskell	524	5 685	0.92	56	9.9	54	9.5	823	20.6	1 304	1 030	274	63	1 064
Hays	7 890	157 050	0.76	2 553	12.5	1 011	4.9	26 625	16.0	20 446	14 127	6 319	3 889	2 136
Hemphill	45	4 957	1.47	74	17.9	28	6.8	802	21.8	504	441	63	81	1 890
Henderson	1 298	70 236	0.71	882	11.0	1 086	13.6	12 945	21.0	13 779	9 820	3 959	2 215	2 802
Hidalgo	7 577	806 894	0.96	16 144	19.0	4 395	5.2	236 321	32.0	90 323	41 092	49 231	30 676	3 689
Hill	776	31 110	0.73	401	11.4	416	11.9	6 008	22.1	7 764	5 690	2 074	727	2 077
Hockley	902	23 068	0.98	316	13.6	212	9.1	3 903	20.1	3 423	2 492	931	711	2 977
Hood	745	49 281	0.82	636	11.2	681	12.0	8 145	19.6	14 382	10 435	3 947	1 078	2 035
Hopkins	438	33 810	0.88	470	12.9	389	10.7	6 250	21.1	6 763	5 725	1 038	375	1 044
Houston	2 695	22 620	0.96	214	9.4	283	12.4	3 122	20.2	5 151	3 932	1 219	455	1 988
Howard	6 081	36 654	1.04	513	14.0	367	10.0	4 864	18.1	5 249	4 222	1 027	1 880	5 122
Hudspeth	86	3 531	1.18	46	11.3	9	2.2	822	30.9	566	331	235	23	696
Hunt	2 524	84 530	0.90	1 121	12.2	950	10.3	12 928	17.5	15 439	12 527	2 912	2 785	3 273
Hutchinson	232	22 506	1.07	294	13.7	234	10.9	3 571	19.5	3 773	3 116	657	707	3 527
Irion	0	2 263	1.78	10	6.4	5	3.2	170	13.6	279	232	47	46	2 831
Jack	1 077	9 016	1.02	101	11.6	71	8.1	1 431	22.4	1 424	1 156	268	222	2 465
Jackson	217	14 093	0.94	204	13.7	129	8.7	2 273	18.6	2 463	1 937	526	216	1 456
Jasper	945	34 598	0.90	427	12.0	432	12.1	4 817	17.1	6 965	4 905	2 060	1 078	3 006
Jeff Davis	88	2 299	1.06	11	5.0	22	10.0	414	29.6	585	466	119	12	535
Jefferson	16 083	278 403	1.25	3 684	14.5	2 578	10.1	44 842	21.9	42 075	26 014	16 061	10 924	4 298
Jim Hogg	16	5 185	0.97	89	17.3	45	8.7	821	19.0	872	617	255	22	417
Jim Wells	341	44 033	1.16	680	16.5	404	9.8	7 099	20.2	7 699	4 373	3 326	1 713	4 151
Johnson	2 709	131 082	0.64	2 085	12.8	1 336	8.2	25 807	18.9	27 867	15 425	12 442	3 126	1 995
Jones	5 290	19 325	0.87	174	8.7	176	8.8	2 319	19.3	2 680	2 112	568	593	2 979
Karnes	2 976	17 844	1.58	187	12.3	138	9.0	1 628	15.9	2 748	2 124	624	376	2 466
Kaufman	1 333	89 790	0.60	1 577	13.3	951	8.0	18 071	18.1	20 009	13 829	6 180	2 111	1 909
Kendall	509	35 065	0.86	391	9.2	389	9.1	5 262	16.3	10 122	7 446	2 676	524	1 338
Kenedy	0	892	2.77	2	5.0	0	0.0	78	22.7	61	46	15	12	2 899
Kent	45	878	1.15	8	10.4	10	13.0	105	19.2	178	139	39	11	1 355
Kerr	1 985	50 458	1.02	551	10.7	750	14.6	7 559	21.1	15 119	12 540	2 579	1 119	2 220
Kimble	43	4 273	0.90	40	9.0	45	10.2	758	24.0	1 076	869	207	52	1 159
King	0	271	1.02	0	0.0	0	0.0	51	22.1	D	D	D	1	348
Kinney	335	3 615	1.03	36	10.0	35	9.7	494	21.2	840	629	211	NA	NA
Kleberg	1 797	31 580	0.97	459	14.5	236	7.4	5 299	20.4	4 481	2 499	1 982	1 385	4 283
Knox	104	3 850	1.04	57	15.0	47	12.3	704	23.3	726	584	142	28	736
Lamar	719	50 264	1.03	688	13.8	665	13.4	8 137	20.4	11 175	9 780	1 395	1 673	3 368
Lamb	185	13 222	0.91	189	14.2	133	10.0	2 936	26.6	2 508	1 856	652	352	2 735
Lampasas	223	17 110	0.63	232	11.2	183	8.8	3 337	20.0	4 595	3 274	1 321	463	2 504
La Salle	1 645	10 154	2.32	110	14.4	45	5.9	922	18.6	1 038	667	371	49	649
Lavaca	420	17 667	0.79	242	12.2	250	12.6	2 731	17.8	5 434	4 493	941	272	1 373
Lee	491	16 077	0.92	220	12.9	156	9.1	2 759	20.4	2 906	2 163	743	310	1 850
Leon	107	17 162	1.05	212	12.3	225	13.0	2 912	22.4	4 973	3 707	1 266	194	1 236
Liberty	5 103	68 400	0.66	1 118	13.7	771	9.4	13 585	21.0	13 723	8 172	5 551	2 631	3 384
Limestone	1 592	23 646	1.02	320	13.6	269	11.5	3 747	21.1	4 342	3 044	1 298	827	3 525
Lipscomb	40	3 285	0.88	45	12.9	19	5.4	676	22.3	551	479	72	41	1 150
Live Oak	1 126	13 557	1.41	143	11.9	121	10.0	1 582	18.1	1 597	1 137	460	276	2 293
Llano	164	18 338	0.87	175	8.6	310	15.2	2 547	19.7	5 659	4 196	1 463	346	1 764
Loving	0	377	5.19	0	0.0	0	0.0	14	13.2	D	D	D	11	11 000
Lubbock	12 162	292 005	1.01	4 252	14.0	2 533	8.4	42 716	16.9	40 594	26 329	14 265	14 146	4 828
Lynn	43	4 981	0.67	64	11.2	36	6.3	1 190	25.2	1 018	758	260	58	1 014
McCulloch	102	8 529	1.07	90	11.0	114	14.0	1 389	21.5	1 945	1 660	285	114	1 354
McLennan	9 189	247 625	1.06	3 588	14.5	2 141	8.6	36 636	17.9	38 694	25 868	12 826	8 722	3 615
McMullen	0	1 851	4.60	11	13.7	9	11.2	102	15.7	163	112	51	45	5 740
Madison	2 518	14 610	1.19	158	11.3	112	8.0	2 067	21.6	2 136	1 563	573	343	2 469
Marion	164	8 643	0.58	94	9.3	141	13.9	1 362	17.9	2 182	1 618	564	337	3 291
Martin	43	5 359	1.05	113	19.7	43	7.5	1 046	21.3	723	602	121	118	2 151

1. Per 1,000 estimated resident population.   2. Data for serious crimes have not been adjusted for underreporting; this may affect comparability between geographic areas and over time.
3. Per 100,000 population estimated by the FBI.

STATE County	Serious crimes known to police, 2014 (cont.)[1] Rate[2] Violent	Serious crimes known to police, 2014 (cont.)[1] Rate[2] Property	Education School enrollment and attainment, 2011-2015 Enrollment[3] Total	Education School enrollment and attainment, 2011-2015 Enrollment[3] Percent private	Education School enrollment and attainment, 2011-2015 Attainment[4] (percent) High school graduate or less	Education School enrollment and attainment, 2011-2015 Attainment[4] (percent) Bachelor's degree or more	Education Local government expenditures,[5] 2013-2014 Total current spending (mil dol)	Education Local government expenditures,[5] 2013-2014 Current spending per student (dollars)	Money income, 2011-2015 Per capita income[6] (dollars)	Money income, 2011-2015 Households Median income (dollars)	Money income, 2011-2015 Households Percent with income of less than $50,000	Money income, 2011-2015 Households Percent with income of $200,000 or more	Income and poverty, 2015 Median household income (dollars)	Income and poverty, 2015 Percent below poverty level All persons	Income and poverty, 2015 Percent below poverty level Children under 18 years	Income and poverty, 2015 Percent below poverty level Children 5 to 17 years in families
	46	47	48	49	50	51	52	53	54	55	56	57	58	59	60	61
TEXAS—Cont'd																
Guadalupe	186	2 021	40 842	12.4	42.3	26.1	186.2	7 586	26 928	62 420	39.1	3.3	64 252	10.3	14.5	12.9
Hale	198	2 771	9 823	11.1	59.9	14.7	63.6	8 621	17 910	43 375	58.9	1.7	41 999	20.3	29.4	28.3
Hall	186	1 020	819	3.1	54.5	12.7	5.6	10 933	17 378	30 950	73.5	1.4	32 158	25.5	39.8	35.3
Hamilton	129	1 245	1 540	6.0	52.5	21.3	13.9	9 282	24 518	42 432	55.5	2.7	46 181	15.4	25.8	24.0
Hansford	318	454	1 473	5.4	54.3	19.4	16.5	11 632	22 867	44 219	54.0	3.0	55 215	11.7	16.9	14.8
Hardeman	30	2 221	977	1.4	53.8	17.7	9.5	12 751	20 374	37 174	61.3	1.3	38 154	18.0	29.7	28.1
Hardin	164	1 361	13 466	12.0	51.9	15.4	87.1	8 313	26 844	52 614	46.7	3.3	56 201	11.8	16.3	14.9
Harris	718	3 801	1 239 179	11.4	43.7	29.5	6 715.1	8 406	29 047	54 457	46.0	6.9	56 670	16.6	25.3	24.4
Harrison	371	1 971	16 117	11.0	50.2	19.1	109.9	8 378	24 114	45 974	53.4	2.9	46 593	18.5	26.9	25.1
Hartley	341	1 300	1 229	20.8	54.5	21.3	4.3	12 976	21 740	63 004	40.0	2.9	66 231	9.9	10.1	9.3
Haskell	101	963	1 033	7.1	60.8	14.7	10.7	11 979	22 140	39 850	58.5	2.2	36 085	22.3	30.6	28.4
Hays	253	1 883	62 359	6.7	32.5	36.1	258.4	8 001	27 398	58 583	43.9	4.9	61 121	13.6	14.1	12.1
Hemphill	373	1 517	1 214	4.9	43.4	24.4	9.8	10 057	30 082	62 813	36.8	4.8	71 177	8.6	13.1	12.1
Henderson	314	2 489	17 195	6.4	52.3	16.5	89.9	8 669	22 613	41 607	58.1	2.3	44 944	16.2	26.8	24.6
Hidalgo	329	3 360	267 739	5.7	61.1	16.7	2 083.4	9 216	14 689	34 782	63.9	1.9	35 441	31.1	42.9	42.3
Hill	157	1 920	8 359	4.8	53.7	14.8	64.1	9 875	21 281	41 382	57.9	1.8	44 965	17.8	29.2	25.2
Hockley	423	2 554	6 989	5.3	48.4	15.7	53.7	10 895	22 609	50 665	49.1	2.6	48 768	15.9	22.6	20.5
Hood	170	1 866	10 350	12.1	40.0	25.5	65.4	8 545	30 478	56 100	45.0	5.0	61 371	9.8	18.0	16.6
Hopkins	150	894	8 419	8.4	55.0	16.2	59.9	9 022	22 453	44 396	55.2	3.1	43 284	15.9	24.4	23.0
Houston	188	1 800	4 280	8.3	54.8	14.5	30.5	9 894	17 570	32 698	66.3	1.3	37 536	27.0	35.7	31.0
Howard	687	4 436	8 635	7.6	53.2	12.8	50.8	8 842	22 049	49 575	50.3	2.9	47 148	19.1	23.1	20.7
Hudspeth	91	605	798	2.5	73.2	8.2	9.0	13 299	15 990	26 384	74.0	1.4	33 048	25.0	38.4	36.3
Hunt	402	2 871	23 429	7.2	51.2	17.5	127.1	8 703	21 888	45 197	53.9	1.9	46 632	16.5	23.1	21.6
Hutchinson	659	2 869	5 484	6.5	47.1	15.1	39.2	9 137	24 875	49 353	50.5	2.3	53 085	14.2	19.8	18.5
Irion	62	2 769	399	5.8	46.1	14.7	4.2	12 888	30 963	58 500	39.5	5.0	64 777	7.9	11.2	10.6
Jack	178	2 287	1 788	7.3	60.9	11.1	17.3	11 001	23 573	50 324	49.5	3.1	51 711	17.1	21.0	18.5
Jackson	175	1 281	3 540	9.3	53.0	17.4	32.2	9 131	25 687	54 926	45.9	4.1	53 667	13.6	19.0	17.5
Jasper	323	2 682	8 046	9.3	59.9	9.6	58.8	9 092	20 121	40 820	56.7	1.0	46 541	15.7	24.8	24.1
Jeff Davis	312	223	398	1.8	40.3	36.6	4.4	16 326	26 693	50 165	49.6	1.1	47 654	13.3	35.9	34.8
Jefferson	652	3 646	60 809	7.9	50.3	18.4	371.5	8 859	24 154	43 540	55.7	3.2	47 620	16.9	23.6	22.9
Jim Hogg	114	304	1 373	0.4	58.8	12.8	11.8	10 717	17 122	35 521	65.8	2.4	36 048	23.2	33.9	33.5
Jim Wells	582	3 570	10 747	5.7	63.0	11.0	75.3	8 767	21 798	42 986	53.6	2.6	43 028	22.1	30.9	30.1
Johnson	155	1 840	40 458	12.0	48.4	17.3	265.8	8 244	25 310	58 135	42.6	2.8	58 685	11.4	17.2	16.2
Jones	317	2 663	3 560	5.6	65.1	9.7	28.4	10 538	15 006	43 897	56.9	2.7	41 871	21.4	25.1	24.8
Karnes	223	2 243	3 023	8.1	62.5	13.0	25.1	10 210	25 868	45 502	54.1	7.1	47 129	20.0	25.7	24.3
Kaufman	223	1 686	29 789	9.7	47.8	19.0	200.6	7 815	24 944	60 391	41.9	2.9	60 438	13.1	15.8	15.3
Kendall	130	1 208	9 649	13.0	30.3	40.8	69.6	8 245	36 126	73 240	35.3	9.0	79 108	8.0	11.7	10.0
Kenedy	483	2 415	162	11.1	65.7	15.1	2.2	27 341	14 251	36 438	66.9	0.0	40 082	16.5	26.5	22.0
Kent	246	1 108	98	1.0	47.4	24.8	3.2	23 543	27 962	47 024	51.1	3.0	45 338	11.3	18.1	15.5
Kerr	232	1 988	10 531	16.8	40.2	28.1	56.3	8 293	26 265	43 810	55.3	3.2	47 389	14.3	26.7	25.4
Kimble	111	1 047	628	0.3	52.3	17.1	6.1	9 123	26 749	40 125	58.1	2.6	37 448	20.0	37.0	35.5
King	0	348	39	0.0	59.5	21.8	3.2	28 434	30 269	63 250	42.5	7.1	69 588	11.0	16.2	17.0
Kinney	NA	NA	672	4.8	61.5	12.5	6.5	10 170	17 299	38 281	57.4	0.0	40 840	20.6	26.5	23.7
Kleberg	696	3 587	11 637	6.8	47.5	25.4	51.5	9 998	18 722	38 247	59.9	1.8	40 066	24.3	33.0	33.4
Knox	79	657	865	2.7	55.8	15.2	8.9	11 292	20 124	40 493	60.8	0.6	43 238	19.2	31.7	29.6
Lamar	364	3 003	12 355	7.0	49.6	16.2	76.8	8 850	22 344	40 748	58.4	2.6	39 433	18.8	28.9	27.9
Lamb	241	2 494	3 558	2.8	56.6	16.3	30.7	10 104	20 863	39 851	62.5	3.5	41 807	21.8	31.6	29.4
Lampasas	141	2 363	4 863	8.1	38.1	21.0	31.7	8 558	23 772	49 630	50.6	1.7	50 985	13.9	22.7	21.1
La Salle	80	570	1 735	2.4	71.2	14.9	14.9	10 858	22 127	37 292	69.9	5.3	42 500	27.9	33.3	34.2
Lavaca	162	1 212	4 300	19.3	59.8	15.9	37.6	9 674	27 288	48 677	51.3	3.8	49 752	12.2	17.4	16.0
Lee	269	1 582	4 027	9.5	56.0	17.2	28.1	9 192	25 006	53 902	46.7	3.1	54 747	12.4	18.2	16.9
Leon	45	1 192	3 317	3.6	52.4	17.2	31.6	10 248	27 535	49 802	50.2	4.8	47 740	13.8	21.4	20.8
Liberty	439	2 946	18 223	8.2	61.8	9.6	126.0	8 487	21 194	48 729	51.2	2.8	53 552	15.8	22.4	20.9
Limestone	367	3 158	5 170	7.1	55.3	13.8	39.2	9 377	20 430	37 554	61.8	1.6	40 655	19.1	28.9	28.3
Lipscomb	140	1 010	803	5.1	54.6	18.6	10.6	12 473	30 237	63 125	38.3	4.3	60 955	9.7	11.2	9.9
Live Oak	357	1 936	2 477	5.9	55.5	12.7	19.2	10 874	21 231	50 400	49.3	2.1	53 184	15.8	21.7	19.5
Llano	158	1 606	2 980	9.9	39.4	27.6	19.0	10 435	36 279	48 259	51.9	6.5	46 366	14.8	27.3	26.6
Loving	1 000	10 000	6	0.0	71.7	1.9	NA	NA	25 877	0	53.3	0.0	59 499	14.3	28.6	22.6
Lubbock	764	4 065	98 068	10.2	41.2	27.5	426.8	8 575	24 510	46 075	53.9	3.7	47 139	20.1	24.3	23.0
Lynn	87	926	1 401	8.7	54.5	16.5	15.9	11 631	23 341	39 526	58.8	3.8	38 922	20.5	31.1	28.6
McCulloch	48	1 307	1 483	2.7	53.6	15.6	16.1	10 344	22 194	40 561	57.8	1.6	39 900	18.6	29.2	26.9
McLennan	400	3 216	74 214	22.1	44.5	22.2	422.8	8 966	22 221	42 687	56.3	2.7	46 264	19.9	26.9	24.7
McMullen	128	5 612	143	12.6	52.8	15.4	4.6	18 645	27 608	46 250	54.0	7.2	60 709	10.0	15.8	13.2
Madison	274	2 196	2 263	2.7	60.3	10.6	22.8	8 493	15 894	39 390	62.1	1.0	40 857	19.2	26.1	24.3
Marion	645	2 646	2 065	11.2	54.1	14.3	11.7	9 635	22 755	34 175	64.7	3.5	35 152	23.4	36.4	34.0
Martin	219	1 933	1 405	5.3	56.0	17.5	14.6	13 065	26 130	55 682	47.7	6.7	60 815	11.4	16.2	15.1

1. Data for serious crimes have not been adjusted for underreporting; this may affect comparability between geographic areas and over time.   2. Per 100,000 population estimated by the FBI.
3. All persons 3 years old and over enrolled in nursery school through college.   4. Persons 25 years old and over.   5. Elementary and secondary education expenditures.
6. Based on population estimated by the American Community Survey, 2011-2015.

Table B. States and Counties — **Personal Income**

STATE County	Personal income, 2015 Total (mil dol)	Percent change, 2014–2015	Per capita[1] Dollars	Per capita[1] Rank	Wages and salaries (mil dol)	Supplements to wages and salaries; employer contributions (mil dol) Pension and insurance	Government social insurance	Proprietors' income (mil dol)	Dividends, interest, and rent (mil dol)	Personal transfer receipts (mil dol)	Earnings, 2015 Total (mil dol)	Contributions for government social insurance (mil dol) From employee and self-employed	From employer
	62	63	64	65	66	67	68	69	70	71	72	73	74
TEXAS—Cont'd													
Guadalupe	6 217	6.5	41 103	1 403	1 487	245	102	444	973	1 116	2 278	127	102
Hale	1 078	1.1	31 367	2 564	445	78	31	151	152	290	704	35	31
Hall	110	-1.3	34 959	1 775	32	6	2	11	16	38	52	3	2
Hamilton	446	4.7	54 640	375	87	17	6	33	191	96	143	9	6
Hansford	486	16.6	86 619	40	129	22	8	231	46	38	389	8	8
Hardeman	145	2.0	37 689	1 565	43	9	3	11	29	47	65	4	3
Hardin	2 352	4.5	42 096	818	566	87	41	97	261	513	792	51	41
Harris	249 989	3.9	55 088	175	167 541	19 979	10 680	47 528	42 257	27 387	245 728	12 278	10 680
Harrison	2 706	0.3	40 540	812	1 295	219	88	255	403	594	1 858	102	88
Hartley	443	21.6	71 581	249	114	19	7	255	52	23	395	6	7
Haskell	202	-2.2	35 145	1 729	62	11	4	21	33	64	97	6	4
Hays	7 398	10.3	37 990	1 944	2 442	414	165	767	1 136	1 085	3 788	193	165
Hemphill	376	-7.0	88 255	44	137	22	9	141	110	21	308	12	9
Henderson	2 920	3.1	36 711	1 915	597	113	41	320	417	886	1 071	70	41
Hidalgo	20 703	5.2	24 579	3 086	8 594	1 702	594	2 798	2 144	6 144	13 688	702	594
Hill	1 308	5.7	37 533	1 760	347	63	24	126	190	362	560	34	24
Hockley	963	-1.5	41 096	935	520	81	34	144	115	211	779	40	34
Hood	2 610	6.0	47 088	758	744	102	51	273	501	561	1 171	72	51
Hopkins	1 341	3.7	37 009	1 675	494	82	34	151	210	337	760	41	34
Houston	841	4.1	36 913	1 979	348	56	21	49	137	253	473	28	21
Howard	1 288	1.6	34 624	1 721	616	127	43	116	226	279	902	47	43
Hudspeth	97	6.1	28 621	2 961	67	17	5	9	14	24	98	5	5
Hunt	3 101	5.4	34 511	2 225	1 413	269	94	214	359	813	1 991	109	94
Hutchinson	897	2.9	41 275	1 124	524	96	36	61	108	181	717	38	36
Irion	108	1.4	69 555	116	45	7	3	21	28	12	76	4	3
Jack	376	-7.9	42 319	497	183	27	12	55	82	68	277	15	12
Jackson	613	0.9	41 364	1 123	250	42	17	58	86	139	367	20	17
Jasper	1 333	3.8	37 547	1 490	415	73	29	71	173	395	587	37	29
Jeff Davis	81	2.3	37 546	2 028	26	5	2	11	23	19	44	2	2
Jefferson	10 809	6.2	42 505	1 244	7 136	1 228	491	1 146	1 609	2 423	10 001	526	491
Jim Hogg	145	-0.5	27 961	2 226	74	19	5	5	21	54	103	6	5
Jim Wells	1 753	1.7	42 359	872	892	123	59	141	228	473	1 216	68	59
Johnson	6 165	6.2	38 533	1 452	1 991	312	138	433	741	1 266	2 874	166	138
Jones	595	3.4	29 819	2 862	186	44	11	60	85	171	302	16	11
Karnes	730	9.4	48 742	1 115	320	51	21	77	205	139	468	24	21
Kaufman	4 370	6.8	38 106	1 546	1 214	202	83	266	470	798	1 765	100	83
Kendall	3 055	6.5	75 638	82	680	94	46	419	804	329	1 238	63	46
Kenedy	28	22.6	67 830	188	39	5	2	14	4	2	61	2	2
Kent	36	-2.1	46 857	692	11	3	1	4	7	10	19	1	1
Kerr	2 332	4.2	45 770	757	746	122	52	289	726	540	1 209	71	52
Kimble	183	2.8	41 792	1 060	51	10	3	18	43	50	82	5	3
King	22	-6.5	78 216	92	10	1	1	9	3	1	21	1	1
Kinney	110	3.5	31 117	2 675	38	11	3	6	24	33	58	3	3
Kleberg	1 169	3.6	36 689	2 090	504	120	36	104	174	292	764	38	36
Knox	142	-2.5	36 733	1 291	53	10	3	15	19	46	82	4	3
Lamar	1 858	5.8	37 578	1 518	854	139	61	147	253	552	1 202	70	61
Lamb	527	6.0	39 396	1 734	157	27	10	141	50	130	336	12	10
Lampasas	977	4.2	47 478	549	161	30	11	86	190	238	289	18	11
La Salle	380	-3.3	49 861	631	219	29	14	40	126	55	303	16	14
Lavaca	990	4.0	49 897	796	237	41	16	147	260	225	441	25	16
Lee	775	2.4	45 849	822	341	53	23	72	135	151	489	27	23
Leon	710	3.9	41 575	1 162	276	41	19	96	133	193	432	25	19
Liberty	2 794	4.9	35 081	1 960	716	123	49	184	273	688	1 072	63	49
Limestone	776	1.8	33 287	2 185	322	73	20	42	107	271	458	26	20
Lipscomb	183	-3.1	51 316	574	63	11	4	34	48	21	113	5	4
Live Oak	550	1.7	44 968	715	244	46	16	60	137	93	366	19	16
Llano	899	3.3	45 404	1 246	180	29	12	128	275	236	348	23	12
Loving	4	35.0	32 321	2 204	2	0	0	0	1	0	3	0	0
Lubbock	11 546	4.3	38 557	1 503	5 802	981	387	1 178	1 829	2 212	8 348	426	387
Lynn	204	18.3	35 607	2 580	58	12	4	22	27	52	96	5	4
McCulloch	315	1.4	37 733	892	123	22	8	28	55	95	181	11	8
McLennan	9 154	5.6	37 260	1 864	4 871	786	341	797	1 391	1 984	6 795	369	341
McMullen	88	16.0	107 627	54	41	6	3	20	42	6	70	3	3
Madison	468	4.5	33 263	2 559	183	31	12	45	97	124	271	15	12
Marion	338	-0.4	33 292	2 003	65	13	5	19	50	132	103	8	5
Martin	289	1.3	51 211	429	95	17	6	44	63	41	161	7	6

1. Based on the resident population estimated as of July 1 of the year shown.

Table B. States and Counties — Earnings, Social Security, and Housing

STATE County	Earnings, 2015 (cont.) Percent by selected industries									Social Security beneficiaries, December 2015		Supplemental Security Income recipients, December 2015	Housing units, 2016	
	Farm	Mining	Construction	Manufacturing	Information: professional, scientific, technical services	Retail trade	Finance, insurance, real estate and leasing	Health care and social assistance	Government	Number	Rate[1]		Total	Percent change, 2010–2016
	75	76	77	78	79	80	81	82	83	84	85	86	87	88
TEXAS—Cont'd														
Guadalupe	0.5	2.1	10.2	22.8	4.2	7.6	4.3	6.3	16.6	24 465	162	1 966	56 505	13.0
Hale	11.2	0.9	4.6	6.0	D	11.7	3.7	D	18.4	5 705	167	932	13 472	-0.4
Hall	12.8	0.8	D	D	D	3.9	5.0	5.5	23.4	815	262	84	1 932	-0.6
Hamilton	4.0	D	11.8	6.7	4.9	9.3	3.3	8.0	25.7	2 320	285	174	4 566	0.0
Hansford	58.3	15.7	2.3	0.7	D	1.4	D	0.5	8.0	930	166	46	2 346	0.3
Hardeman	10.5	1.8	D	D	D	5.0	3.9	3.8	32.2	985	256	124	2 398	-0.8
Hardin	-0.2	5.5	14.6	8.3	5.4	10.3	2.7	14.0	14.5	11 495	206	1 254	24 007	6.2
Harris	0.0	12.1	8.2	10.0	13.4	4.2	7.7	6.9	8.6	503 905	111	106 644	1 751 802	9.6
Harrison	0.5	15.9	6.2	26.5	D	4.5	6.1	D	9.5	13 315	200	1 937	28 195	1.8
Hartley	66.3	0.4	D	D	D	1.8	D	D	11.1	610	106	10	2 001	2.8
Haskell	4.4	10.0	6.4	1.9	D	13.9	D	7.4	23.3	1 400	242	171	3 441	-0.1
Hays	0.1	1.2	13.3	8.8	8.0	9.9	4.9	8.7	20.6	24 720	127	2 168	75 482	27.1
Hemphill	10.4	34.3	10.2	1.1	1.7	1.7	6.6	0.4	8.8	545	128	26	1 688	3.6
Henderson	1.0	9.5	10.4	9.9	5.7	9.6	4.0	10.8	17.0	21 050	265	2 570	40 214	1.6
Hidalgo	0.9	1.9	4.9	2.8	3.8	10.6	4.8	17.8	25.3	103 115	123	42 644	268 765	8.2
Hill	0.8	3.1	23.7	8.6	4.6	9.9	3.1	D	19.2	8 580	246	964	16 166	0.3
Hockley	1.4	44.0	4.6	2.3	D	3.8	3.2	D	12.9	4 025	172	518	9 303	0.1
Hood	0.1	24.5	9.4	5.1	D	8.4	8.0	10.1	9.6	15 045	272	785	25 859	3.7
Hopkins	8.8	D	7.7	12.0	D	9.5	5.0	5.5	16.1	7 860	217	954	15 255	1.5
Houston	1.6	4.6	8.0	11.1	7.9	5.4	11.0	5.4	19.1	5 440	240	887	11 570	0.3
Howard	-0.3	11.0	7.5	13.7	3.2	6.1	3.2	D	26.8	5 650	152	846	13 225	0.8
Hudspeth	6.0	D	D	D	D	0.7	D	1.3	62.7	710	207	183	1 535	0.5
Hunt	0.6	D	6.3	36.7	4.0	6.0	2.5	6.7	20.2	18 135	202	2 444	37 159	1.2
Hutchinson	0.6	28.6	14.4	16.4	D	4.6	3.1	D	11.7	4 230	194	378	10 621	-0.1
Irion	2.8	60.3	D	D	D	1.5	D	D	8.1	345	223	22	857	0.1
Jack	-0.4	40.4	11.3	4.6	D	1.8	2.5	D	11.5	1 710	194	120	4 115	0.5
Jackson	1.9	10.7	17.2	D	5.7	4.0	2.5	2.8	15.9	3 025	204	319	6 619	0.4
Jasper	0.4	2.9	11.9	19.7	D	7.5	3.8	D	18.0	8 545	241	1 331	16 936	0.8
Jeff Davis	4.4	D	D	D	D	3.7	D	9.6	32.9	645	296	37	1 620	0.4
Jefferson	0.0	0.7	11.4	24.3	8.1	5.9	4.2	10.5	11.8	46 065	181	9 145	108 552	4.0
Jim Hogg	1.2	82.0	3.0	3.3	D	6.0	D	D	51.5	1 015	195	280	2 453	0.5
Jim Wells	1.1	38.1	3.2	3.4	3.0	5.2	5.9	10.7	9.9	8 270	199	1 829	16 266	0.7
Johnson	0.3	6.2	10.9	16.5	4.2	9.1	3.4	8.2	14.6	28 255	177	2 931	60 394	6.5
Jones	3.6	15.2	6.2	3.4	2.2	4.5	4.5	3.7	38.8	3 470	174	383	7 405	-0.2
Karnes	-0.8	19.7	3.5	5.4	D	15.7	4.9	D	20.8	2 775	182	440	5 918	4.7
Kaufman	0.2	0.2	13.8	14.1	D	8.4	3.9	7.3	20.7	18 810	164	2 071	40 074	4.5
Kendall	0.7	5.3	16.7	5.2	12.7	13.8	7.4	8.0	9.3	8 730	216	317	15 512	10.3
Kenedy	26.7	D	1.9	0.0	D	D	0.0	D	7.4	60	146	9	232	0.0
Kent	12.6	1.2	D	2.2	D	4.9	D	10.4	43.1	190	247	13	552	0.0
Kerr	1.2	2.0	11.0	6.7	6.8	9.8	6.1	15.9	16.9	15 350	301	1 004	24 184	1.5
Kimble	6.3	D	11.9	5.2	D	8.2	11.6	2.9	22.3	1 290	294	135	3 374	0.1
King	13.6	3.8	8.6	0.0	D	4.6	3.7	0.9	18.0	30	105	0	186	0.0
Kinney	7.8	D	D	D	0.1	2.5	D	1.2	60.0	920	259	117	1 945	0.3
Kleberg	2.5	6.3	4.9	3.5	D	6.2	3.5	D	42.6	5 095	161	1 117	13 317	4.1
Knox	14.7	23.4	D	D	D	5.9	D	2.2	25.6	860	223	123	2 044	0.0
Lamar	0.1	D	9.6	27.2	2.5	7.8	3.9	14.8	13.6	12 025	242	1 991	22 655	0.8
Lamb	41.0	0.0	3.5	1.7	D	5.0	D	3.2	14.9	2 760	207	444	6 096	-0.5
Lampasas	-1.1	D	12.0	9.8	4.0	25.1	5.3	D	18.3	4 905	239	464	9 266	6.3
La Salle	1.5	50.5	6.8	0.4	1.1	1.6	3.6	D	17.5	1 230	161	337	2 925	6.5
Lavaca	2.7	8.8	15.5	16.4	3.9	5.4	5.1	D	14.5	5 105	258	427	10 390	0.5
Lee	0.7	10.2	33.8	6.0	4.5	3.9	4.8	D	14.2	3 525	209	311	7 628	1.7
Leon	8.7	15.4	20.3	15.3	2.6	3.5	4.8	1.0	10.6	5 085	297	432	9 582	0.8
Liberty	0.1	7.0	10.4	9.0	D	9.5	3.8	6.2	22.2	14 220	178	2 628	30 110	4.7
Limestone	0.7	10.4	4.7	6.3	D	6.7	3.0	8.1	34.4	5 165	221	792	10 570	0.3
Lipscomb	7.0	8.0	D	D	D	2.8	D	0.9	16.8	585	165	29	1 514	0.1
Live Oak	-0.2	24.2	10.0	12.2	7.0	3.4	5.2	1.8	16.5	2 025	166	200	6 142	1.3
Llano	0.8	0.7	10.9	3.6	5.6	4.8	8.1	D	13.4	6 520	329	350	14 985	4.9
Loving	3.2	D	D	D	D	0.0	D	0.0	27.0	10	87	0	50	0.0
Lubbock	0.3	1.0	6.5	3.3	7.5	9.1	7.6	15.8	23.6	44 680	149	6 575	124 841	8.5
Lynn	19.7	1.7	3.8	3.3	D	2.2	5.6	1.7	27.9	1 130	198	159	2 676	0.0
McCulloch	0.3	21.0	7.3	7.5	1.9	8.5	3.3	4.3	18.6	2 085	251	308	4 276	-0.6
McLennan	0.3	0.4	8.2	18.7	5.5	6.1	8.0	10.5	15.4	43 265	176	7 447	100 059	5.2
McMullen	6.6	32.9	D	D	D	D	D	D	12.9	175	212	11	488	0.6
Madison	3.1	D	18.2	2.9	4.4	11.8	3.1	5.5	23.8	2 530	182	307	5 199	2.0
Marion	1.3	D	3.5	18.3	D	7.6	3.2	15.0	19.3	2 980	294	407	6 270	0.9
Martin	6.7	11.2	D	D	D	5.3	D	3.0	19.0	790	138	105	1 871	1.0

1. Per 1,000 resident population estimated as of July 1 of the year shown.

Table B. States and Counties — Housing, Labor Force, and Employment

STATE County	Housing units, 2011–2015								Civilian labor force, 2016				Civilian employment,[6] 2011–2015		
			Occupied units								Unemployment			Percent	
			Owner-occupied			Renter-occupied									
				Median owner cost as a percent of income											Construction, production, and maintenance occupations
	Total	Percent	Median value[1]	With a mortgage	Without a mortgage[2]	Median rent[3]	Median rent as a percent of income[2]	Substandard units[4] (percent)	Total	Percent change, 2015–2016	Total	Rate[5]	Total	Management, business, science and arts	
	89	90	91	92	93	94	95	96	97	98	99	100	101	102	103

TEXAS—Cont'd

Guadalupe	48 940	76.8	163 300	21.3	11.6	898	24.8	4.0	74 988	3.1	2 692	3.6	66 822	34.4	24.5
Hale	11 513	61.0	73 400	19.4	10.0	616	24.9	6.6	12 554	-2.3	715	5.7	14 265	24.5	34.0
Hall	1 155	68.0	36 500	22.8	12.8	497	25.8	2.2	1 146	-4.5	81	7.1	1 214	20.6	33.6
Hamilton	3 166	72.7	96 600	19.8	13.0	638	30.7	3.9	3 591	3.4	177	4.9	3 279	28.4	29.0
Hansford	1 972	75.4	81 300	18.0	12.2	638	25.6	4.2	2 961	-4.5	93	3.1	2 629	28.9	39.6
Hardeman	1 634	72.8	45 600	17.6	12.3	516	27.2	0.4	1 607	-0.5	63	3.9	1 671	30.6	34.1
Hardin	20 799	79.6	101 000	18.8	10.0	814	25.5	3.1	24 875	-0.1	1 527	6.1	23 933	32.2	31.1
Harris	1 499 528	54.9	137 800	21.8	11.3	906	29.7	6.3	2 255 093	1.2	119 025	5.3	2 081 889	34.7	24.4
Harrison	23 546	74.3	112 700	20.3	11.7	699	24.6	3.5	29 862	-4.0	1 807	6.1	28 650	32.1	30.5
Hartley	1 769	65.3	147 300	19.0	10.1	730	26.5	4.9	3 004	0.3	65	2.2	2 290	38.6	25.1
Haskell	2 285	76.6	48 200	19.8	10.7	421	29.1	5.3	2 519	-2.1	111	4.4	2 227	30.8	28.7
Hays	61 360	63.9	180 900	23.4	12.3	973	24.3	4.3	101 898	3.8	3 400	3.3	87 233	36.9	17.9
Hemphill	1 466	72.6	123 400	19.3	10.0	713	22.9	4.5	2 117	-7.7	80	3.8	1 812	28.9	29.2
Henderson	29 780	74.3	91 500	22.7	13.6	749	30.4	3.6	35 199	2.7	1 659	4.7	30 441	26.8	29.4
Hidalgo	224 021	68.1	79 200	24.1	13.1	661	32.4	14.7	335 276	1.6	26 303	7.8	298 030	25.9	24.3
Hill	12 902	72.2	85 000	21.1	13.1	651	29.5	5.3	15 804	1.5	704	4.5	14 271	26.0	31.0
Hockley	8 089	68.0	81 600	17.9	10.0	654	24.7	4.4	11 140	-4.6	519	4.7	10 729	26.1	32.6
Hood	20 932	76.8	153 000	22.5	11.0	847	31.6	3.3	24 984	2.1	1 183	4.7	22 208	34.6	25.9
Hopkins	13 273	71.1	92 800	20.9	11.0	676	29.5	4.8	17 241	1.7	698	4.0	15 235	28.7	29.8
Houston	8 046	68.7	76 500	23.5	13.5	635	37.4	2.6	10 381	4.8	472	4.5	7 694	24.5	28.9
Howard	11 206	67.3	73 800	17.9	10.0	779	25.1	4.0	13 169	-1.1	740	5.6	13 924	28.4	29.9
Hudspeth	968	82.5	42 600	22.3	16.0	605	18.8	11.8	1 298	1.6	87	6.7	1 141	24.0	30.0
Hunt	30 832	69.8	94 400	22.0	12.8	755	33.0	4.4	40 082	3.4	1 713	4.3	35 598	30.6	28.2
Hutchinson	8 297	76.8	73 500	16.9	10.0	694	24.5	3.6	9 652	-1.2	543	5.6	9 347	23.5	35.8
Irion	658	77.1	104 700	16.5	11.2	842	19.0	2.9	781	-2.0	25	3.2	805	36.8	31.1
Jack	3 031	77.6	76 700	15.7	10.3	717	23.3	3.8	3 918	-3.6	191	4.9	3 348	24.2	41.2
Jackson	5 109	74.8	87 600	17.6	10.2	805	19.9	4.5	7 246	-1.3	346	4.8	6 251	26.4	39.7
Jasper	12 310	76.7	86 500	19.7	11.1	677	32.1	3.3	13 406	-3.1	1 048	7.8	12 347	24.2	33.1
Jeff Davis	1 023	75.5	93 300	19.7	10.0	830	17.9	5.5	1 060	-1.5	31	2.9	1 074	33.1	28.6
Jefferson	93 495	63.0	97 900	21.6	11.7	761	30.8	3.5	106 985	-0.6	7 532	7.0	103 203	28.0	28.4
Jim Hogg	1 688	78.1	68 500	20.9	12.0	490	30.7	4.4	1 934	-4.4	185	9.6	1 786	24.7	40.3
Jim Wells	13 829	68.3	70 100	18.3	11.4	711	28.8	8.2	17 313	-9.6	1 844	10.7	16 674	28.2	30.4
Johnson	53 685	73.5	119 200	20.4	12.1	883	26.9	3.9	75 584	2.1	3 285	4.3	68 950	31.0	30.5
Jones	5 489	76.2	69 000	18.3	13.3	659	22.3	1.8	5 627	-0.4	330	5.9	5 003	28.3	26.8
Karnes	4 309	75.3	87 200	19.1	10.0	650	27.8	8.7	6 259	-2.3	305	4.9	5 251	27.3	31.6
Kaufman	35 418	77.4	134 700	23.5	12.9	902	30.5	4.0	56 920	3.7	2 155	3.8	49 359	33.0	24.4
Kendall	13 552	72.6	281 200	22.4	11.6	1 002	30.0	2.6	19 565	2.4	631	3.2	16 597	46.7	14.3
Kenedy	145	32.4	0	0.0	10.0	558	29.4	9.0	212	-24.8	11	5.2	185	24.9	20.5
Kent	372	69.6	72 300	13.4	10.0	511	18.9	4.0	465	-6.3	14	3.0	398	39.7	27.1
Kerr	20 316	69.6	158 200	23.4	12.2	780	28.1	5.1	21 236	0.6	764	3.6	20 523	31.6	19.6
Kimble	1 990	74.2	85 400	22.3	12.8	645	31.0	1.0	1 933	-3.1	76	3.9	2 129	29.5	27.0
King	113	30.1	73 000	0.0	16.7	743	14.6	8.8	177	-11.1	7	4.0	166	34.3	41.6
Kinney	1 079	79.2	72 200	25.0	10.0	578	26.5	2.4	1 166	-1.3	70	6.0	1 213	30.0	21.8
Kleberg	10 906	52.9	80 800	19.4	11.3	745	29.9	5.8	14 052	-2.1	967	6.9	13 466	30.6	27.2
Knox	1 437	72.7	42 900	14.7	10.8	464	25.1	4.9	1 596	-4.8	70	4.4	1 534	26.5	37.2
Lamar	19 026	65.3	85 900	18.9	11.8	661	29.5	3.3	23 186	4.9	1 077	4.6	20 953	27.6	28.3
Lamb	4 865	69.8	62 000	19.2	12.1	622	23.9	5.5	5 215	-5.0	342	6.6	5 709	29.5	35.7
Lampasas	7 505	72.7	133 300	21.2	12.8	772	28.0	2.9	9 307	3.1	382	4.1	8 245	30.8	27.9
La Salle	1 971	70.4	70 100	21.2	12.8	433	28.6	12.9	3 891	-8.6	204	5.2	2 307	25.1	42.0
Lavaca	7 701	78.0	119 300	18.5	10.2	632	20.3	7.5	8 699	-0.9	374	4.3	8 929	32.4	33.7
Lee	5 996	74.5	115 800	21.2	11.5	760	27.6	3.9	9 228	-0.5	350	3.8	7 706	24.7	28.1
Leon	6 142	82.1	102 800	19.0	11.9	621	23.4	4.3	6 463	-6.5	425	6.6	6 673	30.3	34.1
Liberty	25 319	75.4	87 900	20.3	12.0	762	27.0	5.2	31 191	1.1	2 358	7.6	27 767	23.9	37.8
Limestone	8 084	74.5	83 500	22.3	12.6	674	31.5	3.6	8 223	-3.9	471	5.7	9 384	29.5	30.9
Lipscomb	1 198	71.4	93 000	14.6	10.0	662	16.9	2.4	1 654	-3.8	76	4.6	1 662	32.1	42.5
Live Oak	3 699	80.9	86 900	18.0	11.5	699	23.5	4.4	5 176	-11.8	313	6.0	4 140	27.1	34.1
Llano	8 654	78.0	160 600	19.7	12.5	741	30.9	2.3	8 218	1.2	341	4.1	7 348	32.2	19.9
Loving	45	48.9	92 500	0.0	10.0	871	45.0	0.0	92	19.5	4	4.3	62	22.6	22.6
Lubbock	107 540	56.9	112 600	21.0	11.5	811	32.2	3.5	152 876	2.5	5 183	3.4	141 493	34.0	20.2
Lynn	2 188	72.3	69 900	22.6	10.4	580	30.5	2.7	2 757	0.1	111	4.0	2 409	29.4	28.5
McCulloch	3 145	78.5	67 500	20.3	14.2	658	29.6	5.7	3 703	-5.3	172	4.6	3 727	26.9	28.6
McLennan	86 769	58.6	114 700	22.3	12.8	765	32.0	3.4	115 341	2.8	4 586	4.0	107 737	32.4	24.3
McMullen	278	78.4	69 300	30.3	10.6	523	10.0	9.0	871	-9.8	19	2.2	324	25.9	21.0
Madison	4 121	67.0	103 100	27.9	10.8	751	26.6	8.4	4 719	-7.5	243	5.1	4 194	25.6	30.8
Marion	4 463	75.9	85 500	22.0	11.4	594	32.3	1.9	4 317	-1.9	306	7.1	3 940	26.7	31.8
Martin	1 630	75.5	99 400	18.4	10.0	768	22.6	6.7	2 457	-4.6	109	4.4	2 342	25.6	36.5

1. Specified owner-occupied units.   2. A value of 10.0 represents 10 percent or less; a value of 50.0 represents 50 percent or more.   3. Specified renter-occupied units.
4. Overcrowded or lacking complete plumbing facilities.   5. Percent of civilian labor force.   6. Civilian employed persons 16 years old and over.

Table B. States and Counties — Nonfarm Employment and Agriculture

| | Private nonfarm establishments, employment and payroll, 2015 | | | | | | | | | Agriculture, 2012 | | | |
| | Employment | | | | | | Annual payroll | | Farms | | | |
STATE County	Number of establishments	Total	Health care and social assistance	Manufacturing	Retail trade	Finance and insurance	Professional, scientific, and technical services	Total (mil dol)	Average per employee (dollars)	Number	Fewer than 50 acres	500 acres or more	Farm operators whose principal occupation is farming (percent)
	104	105	106	107	108	109	110	111	112	113	114	115	116
TEXAS—Cont'd													
Guadalupe	1 979	31 472	3 086	7 003	4 515	584	791	1 243	39 502	2 241	48.3	6.1	35.7
Hale	686	8 835	1 100	608	1 478	253	157	306	34 686	899	11.7	39.6	48.8
Hall	70	562	72	38	86	47	D	16	29 219	390	3.8	44.1	39.5
Hamilton	209	1 606	256	201	377	38	44	52	32 473	1 001	17.1	21.8	42.2
Hansford	153	1 202	270	17	167	92	42	47	39 479	263	5.7	62.7	70.0
Hardeman	85	717	137	D	118	70	D	27	37 158	357	8.4	42.0	37.5
Hardin	816	9 216	939	793	2 245	214	364	339	36 805	660	64.8	4.1	33.2
Harris	99 121	2 059 669	255 880	170 711	208 017	79 415	178 784	134 040	65 078	2 207	70.1	4.5	35.0
Harrison	1 295	20 691	1 721	5 198	2 106	940	1 040	840	40 614	1 298	43.4	7.1	41.1
Hartley	119	1 268	325	NA	234	29	17	47	36 739	255	6.7	65.5	64.7
Haskell	138	1 135	167	D	393	47	45	35	30 590	503	8.7	40.4	50.1
Hays	3 846	50 066	6 705	3 913	11 948	899	2 035	1 663	33 216	1 439	52.1	6.5	34.3
Hemphill	160	1 661	208	25	153	36	27	82	49 116	232	12.1	58.6	55.6
Henderson	1 293	12 855	2 168	1 517	2 618	427	848	410	31 866	1 961	45.2	6.2	42.4
Hidalgo	11 866	187 842	57 630	6 659	38 679	6 527	5 818	5 185	27 602	2 161	57.9	14.7	51.4
Hill	637	6 913	1 107	1 048	1 545	186	152	230	33 281	1 884	34.6	11.0	43.6
Hockley	512	7 912	1 459	239	922	251	90	364	45 976	781	14.7	34.1	45.6
Hood	1 256	14 577	2 225	465	2 850	438	409	568	38 943	1 286	57.1	6.8	42.8
Hopkins	733	10 482	1 224	1 813	1 639	485	173	370	35 288	2 113	31.5	8.8	42.0
Houston	345	3 599	643	565	632	152	110	119	33 093	1 505	23.3	13.2	49.9
Howard	715	9 413	1 596	851	1 467	276	218	367	38 976	475	21.3	34.3	48.8
Hudspeth	30	299	D	D	64	D	NA	14	45 462	167	13.2	53.9	60.5
Hunt	1 392	23 247	3 216	8 186	3 586	368	556	1 217	52 365	4 206	58.7	3.6	31.9
Hutchinson	480	6 602	543	1 679	1 049	158	228	351	53 094	247	27.1	38.9	44.1
Irion	62	588	D	NA	29	D	16	29	49 272	155	22.6	52.3	43.9
Jack	229	2 217	74	47	146	34	59	96	43 263	864	17.1	23.8	42.0
Jackson	312	4 955	285	D	538	149	161	219	44 251	811	23.7	25.2	45.3
Jasper	614	8 666	2 174	1 665	1 475	283	230	308	35 528	894	59.5	2.0	36.9
Jeff Davis	57	368	88	NA	48	25	24	10	27 693	84	16.7	69.0	57.1
Jefferson	5 652	103 964	17 027	15 132	14 261	2 461	5 109	5 368	51 631	764	48.0	18.3	45.5
Jim Hogg	89	738	210	64	195	44	4	23	30 779	263	15.2	45.2	39.2
Jim Wells	926	16 253	5 003	595	1 712	379	297	609	37 497	1 047	32.7	16.0	33.5
Johnson	2 721	37 170	3 577	6 032	5 659	781	975	1 448	38 952	3 023	61.4	4.3	35.6
Jones	284	2 364	464	204	233	104	43	94	39 708	1 014	25.0	20.9	37.6
Karnes	352	5 405	405	338	633	100	125	298	55 075	1 288	17.5	13.1	45.6
Kaufman	1 772	23 503	3 357	3 662	4 152	638	579	855	36 372	3 041	59.3	4.2	38.5
Kendall	1 220	11 833	1 560	957	2 618	368	912	481	40 641	1 387	42.4	13.6	39.3
Kenedy	17	182	D	NA	17	NA	NA	11	61 027	28	0.0	89.3	67.9
Kent	16	87	3 786	NA	2 905	D	NA	7	79 678	194	8.8	44.3	31.4
Kerr	1 418	15 539	NA	593	NA	491	803	578	37 189	1 034	28.9	20.6	38.9
Kimble	132	903	142	64	294	42	12	26	28 661	602	15.4	48.2	46.7
King	NA	NA	NA	NA	NA	NA	NA	NA	NA	59	0.0	59.3	23.7
Kinney	34	493	D	NA	54	NA	NA	13	27 351	196	12.8	57.1	43.4
Kleberg	570	7 097	1 597	109	1 587	332	153	215	30 336	401	50.9	10.2	37.7
Knox	87	655	96	NA	127	48	D	25	37 496	228	8.8	47.4	56.1
Lamar	1 187	17 053	3 459	4 552	2 550	514	360	631	37 020	1 843	32.0	11.7	34.6
Lamb	240	2 103	396	94	380	156	51	80	38 273	933	10.1	37.3	52.3
Lampasas	396	3 902	744	550	668	109	89	112	28 641	1 017	37.0	17.2	46.3
La Salle	150	3 331	117	NA	294	D	D	178	53 369	446	11.9	44.6	42.2
Lavaca	493	5 335	968	1 240	820	290	122	202	37 858	2 617	29.8	7.7	40.7
Lee	412	5 710	275	419	611	239	152	256	44 903	1 807	33.8	7.2	35.0
Leon	350	4 687	99	834	580	119	54	253	54 030	1 962	30.3	11.6	52.2
Liberty	1 049	12 787	1 799	1 290	2 658	340	369	497	38 866	1 470	50.7	7.6	46.0
Limestone	399	5 320	1 165	948	1 018	241	66	177	33 292	1 526	24.1	14.2	50.4
Lipscomb	94	925	D	D	169	64	21	41	44 298	277	6.5	56.0	46.2
Live Oak	295	3 477	148	D	426	89	98	199	57 342	892	13.5	28.5	42.3
Llano	442	3 739	544	82	535	175	132	111	29 730	740	25.8	31.6	42.7
Loving	3	4	NA	NA	NA	D	NA	1	128 000	10	0.0	100.0	80.0
Lubbock	7 049	112 299	22 836	5 312	18 437	6 072	4 343	3 999	35 613	1 116	36.0	26.8	45.6
Lynn	85	663	144	77	68	57	D	28	41 910	455	8.6	49.5	60.4
McCulloch	210	2 495	158	448	462	95	135	89	35 652	619	13.1	36.0	46.2
McLennan	5 056	101 496	17 100	14 027	12 086	4 955	2 511	3 691	36 369	3 278	55.3	5.8	38.8
McMullen	50	624	D	D	79	D	2	37	59 197	238	7.1	64.3	50.4
Madison	243	2 998	268	39	758	92	71	100	33 415	970	28.8	10.4	45.8
Marion	153	1 586	361	341	189	39	21	50	31 245	247	34.8	6.1	34.8
Martin	105	1 274	196	D	166	33	D	65	51 296	414	13.5	42.3	57.0

Table B. States and Counties — **Agriculture**

STATE County	Land in farms — Acreage (1,000) [117]	Percent change, 2007–2012 [118]	Acres — Average size of farm [119]	Total irrigated (1,000) [120]	Total cropland (1,000) [121]	Value of land and buildings — Average per farm [122]	Average per acre [123]	Value of machinery and equipment, average per farm (dollars) [124]	Value of products sold — Total (mil dol) [125]	Average per farm (dollars) [126]	Percent from: Crops [127]	Livestock and poultry products [128]	Percent of farms with sales of: $10,000 or more [129]	$100,000 or more [130]	Government payments — Total ($1,000) [131]	Percent of farms [132]
TEXAS—Cont'd																
Guadalupe	383	-0.5	171	1.9	112.1	614 506	3 595	50 088	61.6	27 484	49.2	50.8	25.0	4.0	2 230	12.2
Hale	641	8.8	713	202.2	479.7	844 726	1 185	232 068	409.9	455 984	31.5	68.5	47.2	30.4	15 250	85.4
Hall	509	-4.6	1 305	27.8	186.3	1 006 900	771	121 005	24.8	63 464	74.3	25.7	36.2	13.3	4 834	83.8
Hamilton	446	-5.3	445	0.6	75.6	1 105 527	2 482	58 377	55.8	55 772	19.2	80.8	40.4	6.8	1 233	23.7
Hansford	567	-3.2	2 155	98.1	294.4	1 994 289	925	403 190	783.2	2 977 973	14.1	85.9	74.1	50.2	4 906	81.7
Hardeman	355	-4.2	993	4.5	130.9	869 655	875	82 580	25.4	71 042	36.1	63.9	45.7	8.7	2 043	80.1
Hardin	69	-24.9	104	1.7	22.7	320 964	3 092	62 642	D	D	D	D	18.0	2.0	414	2.1
Harris	236	-8.7	107	5.9	59.9	572 259	5 342	45 283	65.2	29 538	72.8	27.2	20.8	3.4	1 072	6.2
Harrison	200	-0.6	154	0.5	40.9	437 530	2 845	50 800	19.0	14 631	26.2	73.8	23.5	1.9	274	3.3
Hartley	903	-0.9	3 541	155.5	270.3	3 557 855	1 005	348 706	1 180.9	4 630 969	16.4	83.6	68.2	60.0	4 317	72.5
Haskell	567	14.6	1 128	27.5	298.5	834 078	740	144 797	38.7	76 881	74.0	26.0	42.1	16.5	5 201	84.9
Hays	245	4.0	170	1.0	30.3	1 055 578	6 200	33 647	15.0	10 403	48.9	51.1	12.7	1.5	469	4.5
Hemphill	576	4.9	2 482	3.2	39.8	1 837 310	740	115 043	110.6	476 517	2.7	97.3	46.1	19.8	1 293	50.4
Henderson	346	8.5	176	1.4	81.9	525 054	2 979	50 080	49.5	25 253	35.0	65.0	26.8	3.0	193	1.8
Hidalgo	795	10.0	368	183.6	465.6	1 117 900	3 038	115 296	452.8	209 517	91.7	8.3	33.2	14.2	9 106	20.0
Hill	504	-4.0	268	0.9	231.9	602 704	2 252	72 047	119.9	63 662	67.1	32.9	33.4	8.1	3 921	28.7
Hockley	484	-0.1	619	106.9	400.1	643 108	1 038	182 472	78.7	100 790	89.1	10.9	37.5	20.0	10 093	81.6
Hood	224	9.0	174	2.8	43.3	712 228	4 085	52 253	18.7	14 574	45.7	54.3	20.5	2.2	162	5.8
Hopkins	423	8.2	200	1.3	127.7	442 861	2 214	64 010	205.9	97 466	6.3	93.7	40.3	9.8	1 817	9.2
Houston	468	6.2	311	6.0	83.6	697 706	2 244	55 639	49.6	32 944	28.1	71.9	34.7	4.9	1 461	14.6
Howard	498	-4.7	1 049	4.2	161.9	796 236	759	88 682	13.9	29 187	33.5	66.5	18.7	4.8	4 460	62.1
Hudspeth	2 251	-0.3	13 480	18.1	48.3	7 586 677	563	134 042	34.5	206 455	71.7	28.3	65.3	22.2	1 323	35.9
Hunt	455	17.0	108	5.4	180.3	330 262	3 056	41 054	69.3	16 485	64.6	35.4	18.7	1.9	1 324	8.4
Hutchinson	521	-6.5	2 109	35.1	97.8	1 606 478	762	154 777	55.9	226 219	57.5	42.5	39.3	21.9	1 984	30.4
Irion	496	-20.6	3 201	0.7	10.7	3 005 394	939	70 394	7.5	48 148	10.3	89.7	47.1	9.7	904	25.8
Jack	528	-8.4	611	0.4	35.8	1 195 220	1 956	55 066	22.5	26 042	10.1	89.9	35.3	5.9	751	11.9
Jackson	442	-10.3	545	13.1	151.8	1 151 591	2 114	118 181	101.8	125 568	72.7	27.3	48.3	16.5	6 538	36.6
Jasper	88	-8.1	99	0.4	16.3	310 437	3 149	49 808	10.1	11 263	55.8	44.2	18.2	0.7	26	1.3
Jeff Davis	1 255	-9.8	14 941	0.1	3.6	7 177 381	480	76 583	D	D	D	D	38.1	23.8	792	26.2
Jefferson	354	6.2	463	22.4	112.7	767 829	1 657	88 914	38.0	49 778	56.8	43.2	31.8	10.1	3 631	22.3
Jim Hogg	645	0.7	2 452	D	9.6	3 272 540	1 335	58 118	11.1	42 323	D	D	36.1	6.1	1 349	33.1
Jim Wells	504	8.9	481	4.8	192.0	878 878	1 827	85 848	82.9	79 137	42.5	57.5	25.5	4.8	2 904	22.5
Johnson	429	29.5	142	2.4	119.9	578 482	4 077	50 827	78.9	26 083	25.3	74.7	20.4	2.8	834	6.3
Jones	563	-1.8	555	3.6	301.9	617 260	1 112	88 348	43.3	42 685	68.6	31.4	29.2	8.4	5 627	53.7
Karnes	465	11.3	361	0.9	82.7	937 215	2 598	66 483	27.6	21 428	38.8	61.2	32.2	3.4	1 683	18.9
Kaufman	449	6.5	148	1.4	130.5	502 007	3 399	42 963	59.0	19 395	34.4	65.6	19.8	2.3	637	2.8
Kendall	370	8.0	267	0.9	27.5	1 277 133	4 788	32 921	12.5	9 034	16.9	83.1	19.3	1.2	835	6.3
Kenedy	916	0.8	32 728	0.7	3.1	21 522 643	658	288 179	23.7	845 964	D	D	75.0	28.6	44	10.7
Kent	563	-0.8	2 903	1.1	39.3	2 479 716	854	68 263	D	D	D	D	31.4	10.8	1 687	74.2
Kerr	582	-5.1	563	1.9	44.2	1 483 207	2 634	38 048	10.8	10 448	12.2	87.8	18.3	1.6	597	7.6
Kimble	694	12.0	1 153	8.5	15.5	2 044 718	1 773	53 435	D	D	D	D	23.8	2.8	2 269	26.4
King	418	-23.0	7 078	D	23.4	4 304 051	608	122 169	6.6	111 661	D	D	37.3	15.3	748	78.0
Kinney	577	-4.1	2 943	1.2	16.6	3 539 699	1 203	48 612	4.7	24 031	24.7	75.3	32.1	5.1	903	20.9
Kleberg	484	-2.9	1 207	0.1	71.2	2 274 983	1 884	79 327	61.8	154 157	D	D	25.4	4.7	1 570	27.9
Knox	451	-8.7	1 976	21.6	189.7	1 528 439	773	192 219	59.0	258 829	32.4	67.6	64.5	27.2	3 240	82.0
Lamar	497	-4.7	269	7.0	175.8	582 745	2 163	67 187	84.9	46 058	47.7	52.3	36.2	6.5	5 129	25.7
Lamb	616	-2.9	661	179.5	469.1	764 255	1 157	226 869	575.3	616 598	20.3	79.7	46.5	30.3	14 489	85.7
Lampasas	445	6.9	437	0.2	50.3	1 097 964	2 511	49 163	16.1	15 867	18.1	81.9	25.6	3.0	530	11.1
La Salle	635	-2.2	1 423	7.0	44.0	2 777 861	1 952	69 648	18.7	41 890	63.9	36.1	28.0	6.5	1 007	15.9
Lavaca	547	-3.5	209	4.3	80.8	612 201	2 931	46 957	61.9	23 655	20.3	79.7	36.4	3.3	1 440	10.4
Lee	318	-2.3	176	0.9	44.1	563 382	3 199	42 538	38.6	21 340	33.4	66.6	31.0	1.8	935	11.9
Leon	594	4.4	303	0.8	74.0	759 197	2 506	63 997	148.7	75 810	6.7	93.3	32.8	4.6	1 172	6.9
Liberty	287	-3.7	195	5.2	101.1	488 804	2 505	70 376	34.9	23 768	42.1	57.9	22.9	3.3	1 494	6.1
Limestone	487	-3.8	319	0.3	80.9	603 233	1 891	55 660	48.3	31 641	25.6	74.4	38.2	5.0	2 192	15.3
Lipscomb	591	3.5	2 135	23.3	118.4	1 725 505	808	137 588	52.7	190 188	16.9	83.1	44.8	23.5	2 756	75.1
Live Oak	541	7.9	606	0.7	55.7	1 161 267	1 916	63 307	17.9	20 082	15.8	84.2	34.9	4.5	1 774	26.2
Llano	528	-2.0	714	0.8	21.3	1 930 442	2 705	51 043	13.8	18 600	10.4	89.6	32.2	3.2	890	12.3
Loving	380	-11.1	37 952	0.0	0.6	7 543 900	199	74 000	0.9	91 200	0.0	100.0	90.0	30.0	136	60.0
Lubbock	503	-2.6	450	155.5	423.8	834 394	1 853	174 972	174.8	156 631	54.8	45.2	39.0	22.0	10 896	61.6
Lynn	472	-4.4	1 038	71.6	406.7	933 648	900	261 402	67.6	148 560	97.3	2.7	55.6	32.3	9 808	90.1
McCulloch	614	0.3	992	0.9	90.1	1 838 354	1 852	79 971	22.6	36 454	38.2	61.8	36.7	9.5	3 014	39.9
McLennan	554	4.5	169	3.5	244.0	437 533	2 591	54 417	183.1	55 852	40.9	59.1	21.2	4.5	3 662	17.3
McMullen	517	2.2	2 174	D	19.3	3 055 197	1 405	85 521	8.3	35 025	5.2	94.8	31.5	7.6	239	8.0
Madison	291	6.7	300	2.3	35.3	840 584	2 799	79 825	82.9	85 423	D	D	33.5	4.4	1 087	10.6
Marion	40	-5.1	162	0.2	8.3	361 308	2 224	40 939	3.4	13 563	16.5	83.5	16.6	0.8	62	4.9
Martin	454	-0.9	1 096	17.1	279.6	1 130 809	1 032	160 903	20.3	48 949	88.8	11.2	26.1	13.8	5 158	80.9

Table B. States and Counties — Water Use, Wholesale Trade, Retail Trade, and Real Estate

STATE County	Water use, 2010		Wholesale trade,[1] 2012				Retail trade,[2] 2012				Real estate and rental and leasing,[2] 2012			
	Total water withdrawn (mil gal/day)	Gallons withdrawn per person per day	Number of establish-ments	Number of employees	Sales (mil dol)	Annual payroll (mil dol)	Number of establish-ments	Number of employees	Sales (mil dol)	Annual payroll (mil dol)	Number of establish-ments	Number of employees	Receipts (mil dol)	Annual payroll (mil dol)
	133	134	135	136	137	138	139	140	141	142	143	144	145	146
TEXAS—Cont'd														
Guadalupe	61.1	465	92	D	D	D	270	3 756	1 166.8	90.5	89	373	70.1	14.2
Hale	208.4	5 744	45	D	D	D	114	1 464	346.9	29.0	31	103	15.9	2.4
Hall	30.9	9 219	2	D	D	D	15	94	48.3	1.7	1	D	D	D
Hamilton	2.5	298	6	85	32.9	3.7	52	366	87.1	7.8	1	D	D	D
Hansford	119.6	21 302	18	98	148.0	3.7	24	213	74.2	5.3	4	4	0.9	0.1
Hardeman	6.1	1 476	7	D	D	D	15	135	33.4	2.3	NA	NA	NA	NA
Hardin	6.5	119	19	D	D	D	155	2 033	712.6	51.4	26	54	7.3	1.4
Harris	443.8	108	6 363	100 988	340 775.7	6 909.3	12 644	189 299	61 669.4	4 940.5	4 930	37 842	9 174.7	1 850.8
Harrison	32.5	495	58	D	D	D	192	2 069	647.6	49.5	62	288	45.3	10.9
Hartley	311.1	51 321	10	78	85.2	4.2	13	D	D	D	5	13	4.2	1.0
Haskell	33.3	5 640	1	D	D	D	27	298	89.8	7.0	NA	NA	NA	NA
Hays	19.7	125	117	D	D	D	619	10 400	2 471.3	208.4	177	680	161.8	21.6
Hemphill	8.6	2 267	13	D	D	D	23	148	64.8	3.9	9	96	24.4	5.6
Henderson	37.6	478	34	D	D	D	230	2 599	671.8	58.0	56	201	26.4	5.8
Hidalgo	470.2	607	841	D	D	D	2 219	33 566	9 296.8	733.9	497	2 209	445.0	61.9
Hill	7.5	212	21	D	D	D	151	1 427	409.7	28.1	28	86	12.0	2.1
Hockley	126.9	5 533	23	D	D	D	61	850	221.0	18.8	12	63	13.4	4.7
Hood	25.6	501	55	396	222.5	19.5	195	2 394	747.6	60.6	70	376	50.0	11.9
Hopkins	37.7	1 073	31	904	1 176.6	42.2	147	1 659	496.7	37.5	28	116	15.8	2.7
Houston	10.1	426	11	D	D	D	60	640	160.7	13.6	9	45	4.8	1.2
Howard	29.6	846	27	D	D	D	108	D	D	D	41	156	30.1	4.5
Hudspeth	120.0	34 508	NA	NA	NA	NA	10	41	11.3	0.6	NA	NA	NA	NA
Hunt	17.2	200	51	D	D	D	247	3 428	966.3	90.9	66	182	28.5	4.8
Hutchinson	94.4	4 260	19	D	D	D	79	867	205.2	17.7	11	93	17.0	2.2
Irion	3.7	2 289	2	D	D	D	4	17	1.6	0.2	NA	NA	NA	NA
Jack	6.1	679	7	D	D	D	26	187	38.7	3.9	7	12	2.4	0.3
Jackson	90.4	6 419	15	124	230.1	7.4	38	511	165.6	10.8	10	D	D	D
Jasper	44.7	1 251	29	D	D	D	127	1 457	425.7	32.5	23	78	14.0	2.3
Jeff Davis	2.7	1 170	1	D	D	D	6	51	7.9	0.8	4	9	2.4	0.4
Jefferson	242.7	962	273	2 964	2 451.0	156.3	992	13 877	3 968.3	348.1	264	1 759	372.3	73.9
Jim Hogg	0.8	158	4	D	D	D	20	209	72.8	4.6	3	D	D	D
Jim Wells	7.0	171	39	D	D	D	142	1 708	641.6	43.8	46	527	128.1	30.9
Johnson	25.3	168	124	1 160	604.6	52.8	381	4 843	1 513.4	119.0	108	610	125.6	28.9
Jones	15.6	770	23	108	538.5	4.4	34	216	158.4	5.9	6	D	D	D
Karnes	5.1	344	13	69	45.3	2.7	39	479	192.0	11.9	11	8	2.1	0.5
Kaufman	59.6	577	62	D	D	D	291	3 480	1 021.0	84.9	50	150	27.6	4.8
Kendall	4.9	148	51	D	D	D	152	2 107	941.0	66.1	47	116	24.3	4.2
Kenedy	1.3	3 005	NA	NA	NA	NA	NA	NA	NA	NA	1	D	D	D
Kent	16.8	20 792	NA	NA	NA	NA	3	D	D	D	NA	NA	NA	NA
Kerr	10.1	203	44	D	D	D	215	3 006	791.7	72.0	84	229	31.7	8.2
Kimble	17.0	3 679	NA	NA	NA	NA	34	239	97.5	6.0	3	7	1.6	0.4
King	4.1	14 231	NA	NA	NA	NA	NA	NA	NA	NA	NA	NA	NA	NA
Kinney	2.2	620	2	D	D	D	8	58	9.8	0.8	2	D	D	D
Kleberg	3.2	100	5	D	D	D	110	1 490	524.3	33.8	27	D	D	D
Knox	26.9	7 220	11	D	D	D	15	139	31.6	2.1	3	4	0.2	0.1
Lamar	29.2	587	43	D	D	D	212	2 426	678.6	57.3	48	161	22.4	4.9
Lamb	184.9	13 231	19	172	123.6	8.4	40	374	93.0	7.8	1	D	D	D
Lampasas	3.5	176	6	D	D	D	51	604	208.9	15.1	14	42	9.5	2.0
La Salle	6.8	985	6	72	33.9	3.3	22	238	134.4	4.9	5	D	D	D
Lavaca	10.3	535	15	D	D	D	90	772	178.8	15.3	12	39	8.5	1.2
Lee	8.6	515	19	D	D	D	62	618	151.6	12.8	14	111	39.9	5.5
Leon	6.0	354	13	D	D	D	66	558	156.8	10.9	13	51	9.3	2.4
Liberty	56.6	748	45	500	239.1	25.8	197	2 468	796.6	60.9	32	192	33.0	8.3
Limestone	30.6	1 307	10	D	D	D	93	966	263.8	20.6	14	47	6.1	1.1
Lipscomb	30.2	9 140	4	D	D	D	20	120	98.1	3.6	1	D	D	D
Live Oak	5.3	455	15	D	D	D	39	347	263.0	9.5	10	40	20.1	1.8
Llano	74.5	3 859	15	236	79.0	10.1	68	480	135.3	11.0	22	39	9.1	1.4
Loving	2.1	26 098	NA	NA	NA	NA	NA	NA	NA	NA	NA	NA	NA	NA
Lubbock	131.7	472	377	5 273	4 815.9	259.1	1 046	16 460	4 796.6	405.0	394	1 559	270.4	49.7
Lynn	54.5	9 214	4	D	D	D	8	76	18.5	1.7	3	D	D	D
McCulloch	12.3	1 485	9	180	57.7	10.5	39	481	139.0	10.6	5	8	0.9	0.2
McLennan	73.7	314	239	2 976	1 634.7	123.0	846	11 099	3 223.8	250.4	223	1 512	286.8	63.8
McMullen	1.8	2 546	NA	NA	NA	NA	4	D	D	D	2	D	D	D
Madison	4.3	312	6	D	D	D	37	655	244.8	17.9	13	47	14.6	1.2
Marion	9.9	937	2	D	D	D	28	192	61.3	4.6	7	8	1.4	0.2
Martin	38.5	8 029	7	D	D	D	12	144	88.7	4.6	1	D	D	D

1. Merchant wholesalers, except manufacturers' sales branches and offices. 2. Employer establishments.

Table B. States and Counties — Professional Services, Manufacturing, and Accommodation and Food Services

STATE County	Professional, scientific, and technical services, 2012				Manufacturing, 2012				Accommodation and food services, 2012			
	Number of establishments	Number of employees	Receipts (mil dol)	Annual payroll (mil dol)	Number of establishments	Number of employees	Receipts (mil dol)	Annual payroll (mil dol)	Number of establishments	Number of employees	Sales (mil dol)	Annual payroll (mil dol)
	147	148	149	150	151	152	153	154	155	156	157	158
TEXAS—Cont'd												
Guadalupe	132	568	54.5	19.5	111	5 290	2 542.7	231.0	176	3 082	153.7	39.8
Hale	47	D	D	D	23	2 631	2 414.6	90.2	53	985	44.5	12.2
Hall	3	D	D	D	3	35	D	D	12	D	D	D
Hamilton	13	37	4.2	1.0	15	234	38.2	6.6	17	179	8.7	2.4
Hansford	9	39	4.8	1.8	3	16	2.1	0.6	12	D	D	D
Hardeman	3	D	D	D	NA	NA	NA	NA	8	D	D	D
Hardin	49	258	29.6	15.8	24	658	D	33.6	75	1 188	50.7	13.9
Harris	12 925	192 436	44 873.8	17 280.7	4 082	164 479	200 035.4	10 303.2	7 946	166 626	10 106.1	2 710.0
Harrison	115	825	141.8	53.9	77	4 454	2 856.9	183.1	106	1 784	78.2	23.1
Hartley	7	D	D	D	NA	NA	NA	NA	4	14	0.9	0.1
Haskell	7	D	D	D	NA	NA	NA	NA	17	120	5.6	1.2
Hays	381	1 870	198.0	77.7	136	3 908	1 179.0	203.9	361	7 110	348.3	99.3
Hemphill	10	35	15.3	1.4	4	21	D	1.0	12	91	8.0	1.8
Henderson	93	3 061	264.5	68.9	62	1 665	265.1	63.7	135	1 755	77.9	20.5
Hidalgo	886	5 381	566.0	169.6	268	5 713	1 675.4	216.0	1 014	19 468	985.9	247.1
Hill	38	139	15.7	5.2	40	850	265.3	34.0	69	954	43.9	12.5
Hockley	28	D	D	D	15	199	D	8.5	39	547	25.8	7.1
Hood	124	369	47.5	15.2	32	400	D	15.4	101	1 452	66.1	19.0
Hopkins	49	250	66.4	11.5	44	1 840	910.7	69.6	52	791	39.2	12.0
Houston	27	95	8.6	2.1	20	511	160.0	24.5	32	380	16.9	4.2
Howard	45	D	D	D	23	640	D	41.8	76	D	D	D
Hudspeth	1	D	D	D	NA	NA	NA	NA	5	24	1.1	0.3
Hunt	84	424	61.9	14.4	70	7 508	3 089.7	556.3	116	2 052	98.6	26.0
Hutchinson	33	208	25.2	10.5	22	1 712	D	156.7	46	709	31.3	8.8
Irion	4	4	0.7	0.1	NA	NA	NA	NA	1	D	D	D
Jack	10	D	D	D	5	50	D	2.1	17	D	D	D
Jackson	22	134	10.0	3.9	11	D	D	D	20	258	11.9	3.3
Jasper	43	151	18.2	4.1	19	1 335	771.2	90.0	56	777	31.7	8.5
Jeff Davis	5	D	D	D	NA	NA	NA	NA	13	159	8.9	2.4
Jefferson	510	5 909	985.5	383.2	202	13 123	80 760.5	1 106.7	478	10 150	485.5	132.2
Jim Hogg	1	D	D	D	6	69	D	4.1	10	82	3.5	0.8
Jim Wells	62	273	66.6	12.9	20	620	454.7	35.9	84	1 345	74.2	17.4
Johnson	199	1 032	131.0	45.3	161	4 977	1 498.0	245.1	230	3 690	170.9	47.6
Jones	14	44	4.4	1.7	11	182	D	5.5	16	D	D	D
Karnes	17	113	15.3	3.9	8	284	D	14.6	32	427	29.0	5.4
Kaufman	116	556	66.8	21.0	95	3 210	1 100.1	165.3	161	2 618	127.0	34.3
Kendall	136	793	131.1	46.6	36	1 003	D	41.1	96	1 486	64.7	20.7
Kenedy	NA	NA	NA	NA	NA	NA	NA	NA	1	D	D	D
Kent	NA	NA	NA	NA	NA	NA	NA	NA	1	D	D	D
Kerr	134	684	70.6	27.3	44	586	D	23.4	131	1 991	122.8	35.7
Kimble	10	D	D	D	6	68	D	2.8	15	D	D	D
King	NA	NA	NA	NA	NA	NA	NA	NA	NA	NA	NA	NA
Kinney	NA	NA	NA	NA	NA	NA	NA	NA	4	20	0.8	0.2
Kleberg	32	D	D	D	16	98	D	5.1	76	D	D	D
Knox	2	D	D	D	NA	NA	NA	NA	5	D	D	D
Lamar	53	D	D	D	56	3 525	2 152.6	177.8	105	1 568	73.1	20.4
Lamb	17	48	4.6	1.1	6	D	D	17.8	16	D	D	D
Lampasas	40	98	8.5	3.1	23	539	D	18.4	33	458	19.8	5.3
La Salle	1	D	D	D	NA	NA	NA	NA	18	D	D	D
Lavaca	40	136	17.1	5.8	35	1 554	377.5	54.6	31	371	19.5	4.9
Lee	26	117	15.9	4.6	19	418	108.6	20.8	38	316	15.9	4.0
Leon	20	D	D	D	20	751	D	48.8	42	346	18.0	3.9
Liberty	88	333	38.0	11.4	35	1 262	D	78.8	95	1 403	67.5	17.4
Limestone	25	71	7.3	2.4	11	818	193.2	33.5	40	430	22.1	5.2
Lipscomb	4	D	D	D	NA	NA	NA	NA	5	D	D	D
Live Oak	21	D	D	D	6	D	D	D	33	312	27.6	5.4
Llano	38	104	10.6	3.9	17	62	D	2.3	51	1 047	64.2	21.1
Loving	NA	NA	NA	NA	NA	NA	NA	NA	NA	NA	NA	NA
Lubbock	631	3 860	482.3	175.9	240	4 984	1 572.9	216.1	627	D	D	D
Lynn	6	D	D	D	3	63	D	1.9	6	D	D	D
McCulloch	20	D	D	D	12	435	D	16.8	23	265	11.5	2.9
McLennan	369	2 583	331.4	139.6	232	14 194	D	677.1	487	D	D	D
McMullen	3	D	D	D	NA	NA	NA	NA	3	6	0.5	0.1
Madison	19	73	8.4	2.3	8	33	6.8	1.5	36	386	23.0	4.9
Marion	10	D	D	D	9	182	D	7.4	21	211	11.2	2.8
Martin	4	12	1.3	0.7	NA	NA	NA	NA	6	D	D	D

1. Establishment subject to federal tax.

STATE County	Health care and social assistance, 2012				Other services, 2012				Nonemployer businesses, 2015		Value of residential construction authorized by building permits, 2016	
	Number of establishments	Number of employees	Receipts (mil dol)	Annual payroll (mil dol)	Number of establishments	Number of employees	Receipts (mil dol)	Annual payroll (mil dol)	Number	Receipts (mil dol)	New Construction ($1,000)	Number of housing units
	159	160	161	162	163	164	165	166	167	168	169	170
TEXAS—Cont'd												
Guadalupe	189	3 077	275.1	107.5	141	923	76.9	22.3	9 997	441.6	203 474	903
Hale	84	1 058	104.5	36.0	49	345	24.7	7.5	2 135	98.8	6 396	19
Hall	7	87	4.3	2.1	6	46	4.0	1.3	211	7.2	0	0
Hamilton	24	531	35.7	16.5	22	38	5.4	1.5	767	35.0	425	6
Hansford	7	D	D	D	12	42	4.9	1.3	510	23.3	220	2
Hardeman	13	210	18.3	7.7	10	51	3.1	0.9	286	10.3	0	0
Hardin	65	D	D	D	52	D	D	D	3 724	147.9	47 880	240
Harris	10 433	232 131	29 549.4	10 842.4	5 820	58 629	7 505.2	2 234.1	394 410	20 183.4	3 683 504	22 661
Harrison	123	1 881	203.6	66.2	77	923	89.0	32.8	4 646	203.3	9 023	68
Hartley	7	D	D	D	12	D	D	D	350	28.6	NA	NA
Haskell	11	D	D	D	15	55	5.7	1.0	444	17.2	75	2
Hays	309	5 778	603.3	220.8	203	1 170	114.0	35.3	16 320	765.5	383 593	2 441
Hemphill	10	169	12.7	5.7	8	D	D	D	430	21.8	0	0
Henderson	126	2 180	215.6	84.3	69	295	24.9	7.0	6 147	317.3	12 884	94
Hidalgo	2 048	54 356	3 479.0	1 471.2	571	3 701	350.3	84.2	69 823	2 680.3	637 566	4 568
Hill	50	1 168	79.0	33.0	38	178	11.6	3.2	2 344	108.7	1 102	8
Hockley	46	1 089	74.8	28.8	27	D	D	D	1 364	57.8	1 688	8
Hood	131	2 352	242.5	89.9	82	534	38.1	11.7	5 359	273.7	25 950	144
Hopkins	76	1 416	120.2	47.4	48	221	17.4	4.8	2 826	139.8	1 700	10
Houston	37	768	53.9	21.6	27	144	13.4	3.9	1 298	49.8	0	0
Howard	67	1 699	163.7	51.4	40	D	D	D	1 640	70.9	3 018	23
Hudspeth	2	D	D	D	3	4	0.1	0.0	242	7.3	NA	NA
Hunt	175	3 165	308.8	118.2	93	409	32.2	10.3	6 550	314.8	23 626	166
Hutchinson	44	486	49.7	16.7	34	223	25.8	6.9	1 057	40.0	4 013	49
Irion	1	D	D	D	3	D	D	D	176	10.4	0	0
Jack	13	D	D	D	12	87	16.2	2.7	774	41.9	1 193	2
Jackson	16	303	24.9	9.9	26	63	6.5	1.4	997	46.2	1 256	11
Jasper	80	2 341	107.3	47.8	35	137	11.5	2.9	2 486	100.8	948	7
Jeff Davis	4	D	D	D	5	D	D	D	270	9.5	NA	NA
Jefferson	810	17 453	1 760.8	625.3	362	2 712	286.6	81.2	15 329	709.0	100 711	602
Jim Hogg	11	645	13.9	8.0	4	9	0.7	0.2	422	11.1	NA	NA
Jim Wells	114	4 355	211.2	96.0	69	381	63.0	15.8	3 060	118.6	2 086	17
Johnson	240	D	D	D	183	1 110	118.5	42.2	12 435	599.8	126 318	754
Jones	20	632	32.3	15.2	16	54	3.8	1.1	1 186	48.9	0	0
Karnes	27	437	30.7	12.6	15	57	3.4	0.8	995	43.9	8 825	49
Kaufman	160	3 412	235.5	100.1	112	557	63.1	22.3	10 007	481.9	89 396	450
Kendall	129	1 548	125.3	44.9	69	365	30.6	8.4	5 229	333.9	90 375	533
Kenedy	NA	NA	NA	NA	4	D	D	D	26	0.5	NA	NA
Kent	2	D	D	D	NA	NA	NA	NA	57	2.2	NA	NA
Kerr	176	3 826	370.5	164.1	101	537	61.7	15.2	5 237	267.6	11 252	60
Kimble	8	141	8.6	4.1	6	19	1.4	0.4	597	19.7	0	0
King	NA	NA	NA	NA	NA	NA	NA	NA	31	1.2	NA	NA
Kinney	2	D	D	D	3	D	D	D	184	4.9	0	0
Kleberg	67	1 599	115.8	45.5	46	D	D	D	1 569	50.3	1 471	9
Knox	8	166	10.7	4.5	10	D	D	D	273	12.2	0	0
Lamar	177	3 747	326.1	121.7	86	425	39.7	10.4	3 871	172.5	4 913	46
Lamb	27	429	23.8	10.9	17	D	D	D	744	29.0	0	0
Lampasas	25	747	45.7	19.3	22	153	16.7	4.2	1 483	69.1	6 076	45
La Salle	9	D	D	D	4	14	1.5	0.4	589	21.1	508	3
Lavaca	38	981	65.3	24.5	47	140	13.3	2.6	1 728	78.7	3 341	27
Lee	29	325	20.8	8.3	25	85	9.3	2.2	1 395	58.6	1 939	13
Leon	19	291	11.6	5.5	25	114	6.9	2.0	1 527	66.4	0	0
Liberty	102	D	D	D	71	491	55.1	16.8	5 088	215.3	65 783	456
Limestone	49	1 120	84.0	31.2	21	D	D	D	1 313	56.9	405	3
Lipscomb	3	10	0.5	0.2	7	12	1.8	0.2	287	11.7	0	0
Live Oak	12	250	8.7	3.6	14	D	D	D	1 012	44.4	1 408	7
Llano	31	605	46.5	19.3	22	63	6.9	1.7	2 088	107.3	40 514	238
Loving	NA	NA	NA	NA	NA	NA	NA	NA	20	0.6	NA	NA
Lubbock	848	22 202	2 519.2	866.0	460	D	D	D	21 069	1 083.5	450 025	2 638
Lynn	6	131	9.2	3.1	6	D	D	D	347	11.2	207	1
McCulloch	16	267	19.9	8.2	19	78	6.3	1.8	705	24.9	4 354	73
McLennan	547	16 602	1 484.1	627.5	361	2 364	233.2	64.5	14 944	687.5	224 774	1 762
McMullen	1	D	D	D	NA	NA	NA	NA	132	5.7	NA	NA
Madison	19	306	24.8	11.3	15	D	D	D	995	43.8	463	11
Marion	13	354	15.7	9.7	13	D	D	D	701	29.2	600	8
Martin	7	135	11.6	4.7	8	21	3.2	0.6	442	23.1	634	4

Table B. States and Counties — Government Employment and Payroll, and Local Government Finances

STATE County	Government employment and payroll, 2012									Local government finances, 2012				
			March payroll (percent of total)							General revenue				
												Taxes		
													Per capita[1] (dollars)	
	Full-time equivalent employees	March payroll (dollars)	Adminis-tration, judicial, and legal	Police and Corrections	Fire Protection	Highways and transpor-tation	Health and Welfare	Natural resources and utilities	Education and libraries	Total (mil dol)	Inter-govern-mental (mil dol)	Total (mil dol)	Total	Property
	171	172	173	174	175	176	177	178	179	180	181	182	183	184
TEXAS—Cont'd														
Guadalupe	4 848	17 546 517	6.1	10.0	2.4	1.9	15.8	3.7	58.3	422.8	109.1	182.6	1 306	1 097
Hale	1 782	7 262 318	4.1	6.3	2.1	1.0	6.9	2.2	76.9	114.8	52.3	44.9	1 233	1 018
Hall	222	559 195	7.2	8.3	0.0	3.6	2.3	5.4	72.7	14.8	8.2	4.0	1 202	1 007
Hamilton	539	1 700 689	4.8	3.1	0.0	3.4	41.0	2.4	45.4	45.9	10.7	12.7	1 528	1 340
Hansford	494	1 557 868	4.9	2.9	0.1	2.2	32.4	1.8	53.8	31.7	6.9	19.4	3 509	3 267
Hardeman	417	1 303 943	5.8	4.2	0.7	1.9	46.4	3.2	37.5	42.6	8.4	16.1	1 160	1 008
Hardin	2 150	6 172 176	6.7	7.8	0.0	2.1	0.7	3.2	78.4	141.1	61.5	64.0	1 160	1 008
Harris	166 045	659 443 824	4.4	11.0	3.4	5.0	8.8	2.9	62.2	19 260.3	5 471.7	9 235.2	2 171	1 765
Harrison	2 833	8 500 249	3.8	8.6	2.9	1.9	0.3	3.6	77.3	193.7	50.6	119.6	1 773	1 592
Hartley	92	266 990	18.2	0.7	0.0	0.0	0.4	1.3	72.8	11.2	1.1	8.7	1 410	1 297
Haskell	331	767 433	9.1	5.5	0.1	3.6	22.4	5.8	53.3	22.1	9.1	7.4	1 260	1 097
Hays	7 053	24 108 223	5.6	10.9	2.6	1.5	6.6	5.7	64.1	545.5	162.4	287.7	1 703	1 398
Hemphill	358	1 141 524	8.4	5.9	0.0	4.6	27.8	4.3	48.3	47.6	3.4	36.2	8 863	8 415
Henderson	2 818	8 513 766	7.2	8.3	1.6	1.5	0.2	3.2	76.9	203.3	68.1	103.6	1 309	1 130
Hidalgo	39 042	129 583 687	3.7	6.7	1.7	1.6	2.9	3.9	78.6	3 159.2	1 926.2	864.1	1 071	868
Hill	1 782	5 391 972	5.2	8.8	1.2	2.0	0.1	2.7	79.5	122.0	52.4	48.3	1 376	1 175
Hockley	1 746	5 964 084	3.8	4.6	0.6	1.5	0.5	1.6	86.7	146.0	48.8	70.9	3 073	2 862
Hood	1 577	5 364 527	10.6	11.6	0.3	2.2	0.8	4.5	68.5	134.0	27.6	93.9	1 804	1 536
Hopkins	1 924	6 315 574	4.5	5.5	2.0	2.2	35.9	2.7	46.4	157.4	43.9	43.8	1 235	1 002
Houston	827	2 210 644	8.8	8.8	0.6	3.0	1.9	5.5	70.3	60.8	24.7	26.3	1 135	940
Howard	2 006	6 202 628	4.2	6.9	2.7	2.0	15.7	7.1	59.9	146.9	52.2	61.9	1 747	1 467
Hudspeth	286	780 976	7.7	13.3	0.0	2.9	1.1	7.6	67.2	19.0	10.0	7.0	1 250	1 039
Hunt	4 073	13 501 049	5.0	7.3	2.3	1.6	26.3	8.0	48.4	331.7	94.9	108.8	1 935	1 693
Hutchinson	1 204	3 868 672	7.3	8.9	2.7	2.5	1.7	5.0	70.3	90.0	30.2	42.4	1 935	1 693
Irion	111	320 492	16.7	8.2	0.0	4.3	0.8	7.7	60.9	14.0	1.4	12.0	7 598	7 380
Jack	453	1 551 359	5.7	9.9	0.3	1.9	21.3	3.8	56.6	35.4	3.7	28.0	3 118	2 834
Jackson	834	2 725 347	5.8	6.2	1.3	2.4	17.9	11.4	54.8	75.0	21.3	27.7	1 942	1 729
Jasper	1 516	4 363 997	5.7	7.7	0.0	3.0	2.1	6.7	72.0	103.2	47.1	43.9	1 222	1 064
Jeff Davis	113	390 447	7.2	8.1	0.0	0.0	1.2	1.2	81.3	9.9	6.7	3.0	1 289	1 181
Jefferson	10 830	41 244 326	6.6	14.9	6.1	3.8	6.0	8.0	53.1	1 149.2	304.3	568.5	2 258	1 850
Jim Hogg	316	819 818	7.4	11.3	0.9	0.2	7.1	5.0	62.8	22.9	9.1	11.0	2 095	1 786
Jim Wells	1 854	5 562 478	7.3	10.0	2.6	4.3	1.8	3.2	68.8	136.7	63.1	61.1	1 463	914
Johnson	6 428	20 663 672	6.4	10.8	3.7	2.3	0.9	4.4	69.6	540.8	136.3	306.3	1 996	1 658
Jones	1 148	3 124 966	5.6	5.9	0.0	1.6	32.6	5.2	48.8	55.2	25.7	15.1	754	677
Karnes	676	1 956 116	5.9	7.8	0.1	2.4	17.7	3.7	62.1	49.9	22.4	22.9	1 501	1 339
Kaufman	4 535	15 218 689	4.8	9.9	1.3	2.3	10.1	6.4	64.2	385.5	158.1	186.8	1 750	1 528
Kendall	1 662	5 537 436	9.0	8.0	1.1	3.0	1.6	5.5	70.6	133.9	20.6	100.2	2 786	2 470
Kenedy	35	84 678	6.2	3.9	0.0	0.0	0.5	0.4	86.0	11.6	0.2	10.5	24 369	24 346
Kent	75	243 441	11.6	3.7	0.1	21.1	0.0	2.6	60.8	8.5	1.3	6.8	8 151	8 082
Kerr	1 700	5 612 578	8.7	13.7	6.0	3.2	1.3	4.7	60.4	120.6	27.6	78.6	1 580	1 286
Kimble	171	555 031	11.3	14.1	0.0	6.0	2.2	4.9	60.8	13.0	3.2	6.7	1 472	1 379
King	59	195 445	17.5	2.0	0.0	2.6	0.0	0.5	77.5	9.5	1.7	7.1	25 620	25 616
Kinney	195	518 153	13.2	15.7	0.0	1.2	4.8	4.1	59.5	14.4	8.6	3.8	1 046	948
Kleberg	1 554	3 973 033	8.5	14.3	3.3	6.7	4.0	5.3	56.2	170.5	58.0	63.5	1 984	1 710
Knox	325	851 631	7.1	3.5	0.0	2.7	26.8	6.9	52.1	19.7	7.7	5.6	1 486	1 218
Lamar	2 237	7 154 454	5.0	8.6	0.2	1.3	0.9	4.5	77.8	165.7	68.1	68.9	1 384	1 087
Lamb	779	2 277 980	7.5	10.4	1.2	3.2	3.0	4.3	70.1	61.1	24.1	21.0	1 499	1 349
Lampasas	821	2 377 321	5.2	9.7	1.6	2.7	0.6	3.2	72.8	53.7	20.4	26.9	1 339	1 135
La Salle	315	950 554	9.0	9.5	0.0	3.2	0.2	4.1	71.9	22.1	6.6	13.4	1 887	1 739
Lavaca	808	2 421 042	9.6	8.5	3.3	4.6	17.2	10.0	41.0	73.1	14.0	28.2	1 446	1 296
Lee	700	2 033 290	5.6	8.6	0.0	3.2	0.0	4.3	74.9	49.3	14.2	29.5	1 776	1 564
Leon	757	2 170 423	7.7	7.0	0.0	3.1	1.2	2.4	78.4	47.5	14.0	28.8	1 714	1 601
Liberty	2 976	8 829 594	6.7	8.2	1.1	2.8	0.4	3.1	76.8	210.0	86.8	98.0	1 280	1 101
Limestone	1 302	3 748 599	6.3	12.5	1.9	3.5	15.2	4.0	56.2	116.3	27.5	51.1	2 165	1 970
Lipscomb	247	785 351	10.0	5.2	0.0	6.1	4.3	3.8	69.9	21.9	4.9	15.8	4 530	4 351
Live Oak	529	1 441 098	7.4	10.9	0.0	3.7	1.5	5.4	67.2	34.0	9.9	21.0	1 801	1 538
Llano	637	1 790 590	16.6	12.9	0.0	4.0	0.3	8.5	56.3	64.8	6.8	51.0	2 670	2 571
Loving	12	46 971	59.5	22.6	0.0	14.3	0.0	3.6	0.0	4.4	0.6	3.4	48 366	47 718
Lubbock	12 902	47 474 349	4.7	10.5	4.4	1.1	28.6	5.7	43.9	1 264.7	335.5	406.2	1 421	1 107
Lynn	453	1 252 881	5.2	5.1	0.0	1.3	20.1	4.2	62.8	30.1	12.7	8.8	1 516	1 374
McCulloch	585	1 662 784	6.4	5.5	1.5	2.1	23.0	8.4	50.7	33.3	13.2	11.4	1 371	1 168
McLennan	10 401	35 092 132	5.7	11.4	3.1	2.0	4.5	8.6	63.6	1 172.8	436.4	367.8	1 541	1 222
McMullen	82	296 876	20.7	8.4	0.0	8.2	1.7	1.9	58.1	10.8	0.8	9.1	12 590	12 296
Madison	473	1 465 387	9.1	5.4	0.0	2.2	0.6	3.0	77.1	37.7	16.3	14.6	1 066	920
Marion	304	892 993	8.9	7.6	0.0	4.1	0.5	2.4	76.0	19.4	6.6	11.1	1 074	952
Martin	332	1 249 120	9.9	4.5	0.0	9.6	23.0	3.5	48.5	39.6	3.4	28.7	5 722	5 575

1. Based on the resident population estimated as of July 1 of the year shown.

STATE County	Local government finances, 2012 (cont.)									Government employment, 2015			Individual income tax returns, 2014		
	Direct general expenditure							Debt outstanding							
				Percent of total for:											
	Total (mil dol)	Per capita¹ (dollars)	Education	Health and hospitals	Police protection	Public welfare	Highways	Total (mil dol)	Per capita¹ (dollars)	Federal civilian	Federal military	State and local	Number of returns	Mean adjusted gross income	Mean income tax
	185	186	187	188	189	190	191	192	193	194	195	196	197	198	199
TEXAS—Cont'd															
Guadalupe	411.4	2 942	44.3	19.5	5.0	0.8	3.8	852.5	6 096	211	304	6 039	68 020	59 659	6 973
Hale	116.3	3 196	62.2	9.1	7.7	0.6	2.8	79.2	2 177	74	64	2 337	13 470	39 503	3 643
Hall	13.5	4 104	66.2	1.9	3.1	0.1	5.0	0.2	72	18	D	260	1 250	37 072	3 467
Hamilton	41.2	4 960	31.5	48.5	2.0	0.3	2.3	24.5	2 949	32	16	717	3 580	51 477	7 721
Hansford	29.9	5 415	58.4	21.3	2.2	0.0	2.5	26.3	4 772	16	11	624	2 470	62 179	8 467
Hardeman	52.1	12 765	19.2	41.9	2.9	17.5	2.7	3.2	781	20	D	407	1 650	41 005	3 687
Hardin	129.3	2 342	65.3	0.6	6.8	0.5	3.7	120.4	2 181	72	113	2 253	23 950	63 199	7 550
Harris	18 773.0	4 413	44.4	10.5	5.7	0.1	4.8	54 673.5	12 853	24 720	10 124	245 919	1 999 680	76 003	12 888
Harrison	211.9	3 142	59.8	0.1	4.4	0.4	3.4	272.1	4 034	121	133	3 137	29 050	53 151	6 000
Hartley	10.5	1 709	39.9	0.0	7.7	0.2	15.4	0.2	32	D	10	819	1 860	72 973	11 289
Haskell	22.2	3 760	53.2	17.8	3.7	0.0	7.7	2.3	395	26	11	422	2 260	44 137	4 532
Hays	604.2	3 575	42.7	5.8	5.4	0.3	6.3	1 700.9	10 065	214	420	12 633	82 700	64 277	8 506
Hemphill	40.3	9 878	51.7	16.2	2.1	0.1	5.1	11.9	2 915	D	D	492	1 910	116 430	24 003
Henderson	213.8	2 703	68.0	1.9	5.3	0.0	3.7	147.7	1 868	84	160	3 396	32 470	47 347	5 208
Hidalgo	3 161.8	3 920	67.1	2.0	3.8	0.5	2.9	3 738.4	4 635	4 062	1 739	52 619	303 160	37 673	3 349
Hill	125.8	3 583	69.5	0.2	4.8	0.9	4.9	161.8	4 607	95	69	2 142	14 660	46 008	4 988
Hockley	161.5	7 000	72.9	0.5	2.3	0.2	2.4	78.0	3 383	39	46	2 008	9 450	55 777	6 869
Hood	131.2	2 521	60.0	0.3	6.6	0.1	3.8	144.0	2 767	90	111	1 892	24 760	68 466	9 193
Hopkins	166.2	4 685	40.6	33.8	3.5	0.0	3.4	140.0	3 947	71	73	2 320	15 210	46 283	4 766
Houston	60.7	2 619	51.0	8.0	6.2	0.1	5.3	62.1	2 682	71	41	1 638	8 310	44 593	4 699
Howard	188.2	5 315	65.7	10.8	3.1	0.2	2.0	576.8	16 289	920	63	2 669	13 950	62 068	8 341
Hudspeth	19.7	5 893	49.6	0.3	7.1	0.2	7.3	2.3	676	337	D	272	1 400	35 507	3 239
Hunt	326.3	3 747	36.3	30.6	4.6	0.2	2.6	436.0	5 007	255	249	7 069	36 840	48 860	5 087
Hutchinson	107.0	4 880	47.7	23.7	4.7	0.1	2.3	102.9	4 693	67	44	1 485	9 480	63 034	7 947
Irion	11.6	7 395	70.4	0.2	3.8	0.0	4.9	6.1	3 865	D	D	121	730	124 288	29 086
Jack	45.5	5 070	74.2	0.0	3.7	0.0	2.4	80.2	8 928	19	16	597	3 330	65 772	9 056
Jackson	78.6	5 513	49.1	25.8	3.2	0.1	3.9	106.4	7 462	29	30	1 075	6 700	55 158	6 249
Jasper	96.3	2 680	59.7	2.7	8.6	0.0	5.7	89.0	2 478	77	70	2 002	14 100	53 701	6 268
Jeff Davis	9.6	4 176	59.9	0.4	3.0	0.1	0.2	0.3	132	23	D	218	1 000	55 267	6 873
Jefferson	1 153.5	4 581	41.4	4.2	7.0	0.6	5.6	5 050.2	20 055	1 846	702	15 360	109 000	59 998	7 985
Jim Hogg	22.0	4 186	44.7	0.9	5.9	2.1	11.8	5.1	979	248	11	375	2 130	42 086	4 116
Jim Wells	136.5	3 268	62.9	0.3	5.4	0.2	3.5	108.5	2 599	85	104	2 206	17 810	57 580	8 258
Johnson	466.6	3 041	55.2	0.5	6.0	0.3	3.6	1 105.1	7 202	237	321	7 159	70 010	56 568	6 558
Jones	52.9	2 651	52.3	25.3	1.5	0.0	3.3	40.8	2 041	53	33	2 113	6 610	46 047	4 960
Karnes	43.7	2 867	55.3	6.6	2.9	0.5	5.2	10.2	671	62	25	1 656	5 890	129 392	33 190
Kaufman	387.6	3 631	51.9	6.6	4.1	0.3	7.0	686.1	6 427	177	231	6 345	49 830	55 377	5 860
Kendall	128.4	3 571	58.1	1.2	6.7	0.2	4.5	314.6	8 750	55	81	1 682	19 300	118 028	22 594
Kenedy	11.2	25 935	97.1	0.0	0.4	0.0	0.5	2.3	5 397	D	D	86	150	42 400	3 493
Kent	8.2	9 762	93.8	0.1	0.5	0.0	0.6	0.0	11	D	D	186	340	54 068	6 835
Kerr	109.6	2 202	53.6	0.5	9.0	0.7	3.7	92.9	1 865	477	101	2 652	24 130	62 551	8 737
Kimble	12.1	2 660	49.4	6.6	3.6	0.0	5.0	15.9	3 487	15	D	358	2 000	48 684	6 088
King	6.3	22 880	69.2	0.0	1.3	0.0	7.6	6.0	21 884	D	D	61	120	52 008	5 133
Kinney	13.4	3 722	44.0	4.4	9.1	0.6	3.6	2.9	792	149	D	302	1 290	47 503	4 867
Kleberg	174.6	5 453	30.3	33.2	3.9	0.0	12.4	115.3	3 599	879	429	3 984	13 270	49 957	5 947
Knox	18.2	4 797	47.6	28.6	3.0	0.3	3.7	1.1	293	28	D	410	1 510	42 441	4 579
Lamar	164.5	3 303	65.4	1.9	5.1	1.8	4.5	148.6	2 982	145	100	2 928	20 880	46 248	5 053
Lamb	58.4	4 171	54.5	18.7	5.0	0.0	4.5	16.0	1 139	38	27	965	5 450	35 834	3 842
Lampasas	51.3	2 552	61.5	0.3	7.0	0.3	5.8	67.4	3 353	41	41	1 007	9 020	50 872	5 367
La Salle	18.2	2 554	68.9	0.1	1.4	0.3	5.5	31.9	4 493	110	12	693	2 570	146 991	44 227
Lavaca	68.8	3 532	36.2	22.8	5.2	0.2	7.3	31.6	1 625	57	40	925	9 410	76 303	12 817
Lee	48.0	2 889	56.5	0.5	6.1	0.7	6.6	75.0	4 518	24	33	1 254	7 790	57 911	7 207
Leon	49.2	2 929	78.9	0.0	2.9	0.1	4.5	50.5	3 005	43	35	838	7 540	57 668	7 343
Liberty	200.4	2 617	61.0	0.6	5.8	0.5	5.2	218.2	2 850	109	152	4 298	31 060	53 263	5 814
Limestone	124.3	5 268	41.5	12.6	11.7	0.3	4.7	91.4	3 877	49	44	3 048	9 240	44 467	4 455
Lipscomb	21.7	6 247	73.2	0.5	3.5	0.1	5.7	7.8	2 241	21	D	380	1 540	78 682	13 236
Live Oak	41.2	3 535	63.8	0.2	3.3	0.0	5.5	61.8	5 297	257	23	608	4 910	80 546	14 773
Llano	64.4	3 376	59.1	0.1	6.5	0.0	4.8	33.0	1 727	30	40	778	8 430	67 479	10 486
Loving	1.8	25 817	0.0	0.0	11.2	0.0	10.5	0.0	0	0	0	15	30	88 500	0
Lubbock	1 336.0	4 675	34.3	32.4	4.8	0.0	2.2	2 306.4	8 071	1 300	624	27 574	126 580	55 511	7 331
Lynn	28.7	4 967	57.9	19.6	4.2	0.0	3.2	5.0	865	19	12	546	2 460	45 423	4 622
McCulloch	37.3	4 484	41.7	24.2	3.9	0.0	4.2	38.1	4 581	26	17	638	3 700	46 980	5 122
McLennan	1 142.6	4 787	41.4	2.5	5.0	0.6	1.6	11 590.0	48 553	2 647	573	14 321	104 520	50 610	5 896
McMullen	9.6	13 263	74.2	0.8	4.8	0.2	7.4	23.3	32 058	D	D	152	480	303 717	97 535
Madison	33.7	2 466	63.1	0.8	7.5	2.9	5.7	33.0	2 410	17	23	1 205	5 260	52 583	7 179
Marion	19.4	1 875	65.3	1.5	8.2	0.0	7.5	15.3	1 483	36	20	378	4 080	43 597	4 152
Martin	116.9	23 298	19.8	76.2	0.5	0.0	0.4	67.3	13 408	14	11	463	2 270	86 513	14 606

1. Based on the resident population estimated as of July 1 of the year shown.

Table B. States and Counties — **Land Area and Population**

STATE/ County code	CBSA code[1]	County type[2]	STATE County	Land area[3] (sq mi) 2016	Total persons 2016	Rank	Per square mile	White	Black	American Indian, Alaska Native	Asian and Pacific Islander	Percent Hispanic or Latino[4]	Under 5 years	5 to 17 years	18 to 24 years	25 to 34 years	35 to 44 years	45 to 54 years
				1	2	3	4	5	6	7	8	9	10	11	12	13	14	15
			TEXAS—Cont'd															
48 319	...	9	Mason	928.8	4 111	2 893	4.4	73.6	0.8	0.7	0.4	25.2	4.7	15.3	7.3	7.9	9.5	11.5
48 321	13060	4	Matagorda	1 092.9	37 187	1 246	34.0	45.0	10.9	0.7	2.3	42.1	7.2	18.3	9.0	12.6	10.7	12.4
48 323	20580	5	Maverick	1 279.5	57 685	891	45.1	2.9	0.3	1.1	0.5	95.3	9.5	22.4	11.6	12.8	11.7	11.0
48 325	41700	1	Medina	1 325.4	49 283	994	37.2	45.1	2.6	0.8	1.0	51.4	5.9	17.6	9.9	12.2	11.3	13.5
48 327	...	9	Menard	902.0	2 123	3 036	2.4	61.9	1.7	0.4	0.4	36.0	5.1	13.7	6.3	8.1	8.3	11.6
48 329	33260	3	Midland	900.3	162 565	396	180.6	47.2	6.5	0.8	2.2	44.4	8.9	19.5	9.3	17.8	12.5	11.0
48 331	...	6	Milam	1 016.9	24 871	1 613	24.5	63.5	9.5	0.8	1.0	26.3	6.5	18.2	8.2	10.6	10.5	12.2
48 333	...	9	Mills	748.3	4 907	2 840	6.6	80.1	1.2	0.7	0.4	18.6	4.7	17.3	7.2	7.4	9.6	12.2
48 335	...	7	Mitchell	911.1	8 720	2 530	9.6	48.8	10.5	1.1	0.7	39.8	5.6	14.3	12.0	17.4	13.5	12.2
48 337	...	6	Montague	930.9	19 414	1 853	20.9	87.0	1.0	1.6	0.6	11.1	5.8	17.2	7.2	10.9	10.6	12.6
48 339	26420	1	Montgomery	1 041.9	556 203	119	533.8	68.7	5.2	0.8	3.5	23.4	6.9	19.7	8.3	12.7	13.6	13.8
48 341	20300	7	Moore	899.7	22 120	1 723	24.6	33.6	3.4	0.9	8.5	54.4	9.7	22.0	10.1	13.8	12.2	11.3
48 343	...	6	Morris	252.0	12 593	2 255	50.0	66.8	23.7	1.3	1.0	9.3	6.2	16.4	7.8	11.1	10.9	11.4
48 345	...	9	Motley	989.6	1 160	3 102	1.2	80.8	2.4	1.1	0.2	16.0	3.4	15.1	7.3	10.3	7.9	10.8
48 347	34860	5	Nacogdoches	946.5	65 806	807	69.5	60.9	18.5	0.8	1.9	19.3	6.8	16.8	19.2	12.0	10.0	10.4
48 349	18620	4	Navarro	1 009.6	48 523	1 011	48.1	58.3	13.7	0.8	2.1	26.5	7.3	19.0	8.7	11.5	11.3	12.6
48 351	13140	2	Newton	933.7	14 003	2 164	15.0	74.8	20.8	1.4	1.1	3.5	5.1	15.8	9.0	11.9	11.2	13.8
48 353	45020	6	Nolan	912.0	14 993	2 096	16.4	57.6	5.3	0.9	0.8	36.8	7.2	18.7	8.8	12.1	11.0	12.0
48 355	18580	2	Nueces	838.3	361 350	192	431.1	30.7	3.9	0.5	2.5	63.4	6.9	18.1	10.1	14.7	12.4	12.0
48 357	...	7	Ochiltree	917.7	10 306	2 403	11.2	45.1	1.1	1.1	0.8	53.1	9.0	23.0	9.0	13.5	12.4	11.3
48 359	11100	2	Oldham	1 500.5	2 076	3 041	1.4	79.2	3.8	1.2	1.5	15.6	4.3	21.9	6.9	9.8	14.4	13.9
48 361	13140	2	Orange	333.8	84 964	670	254.5	82.6	9.0	1.1	1.5	7.2	7.0	17.9	8.3	12.9	12.0	13.0
48 363	33420	6	Palo Pinto	952.2	28 053	1 489	29.5	76.4	2.8	1.1	1.1	19.9	6.4	17.2	8.4	11.5	10.7	12.7
48 365	...	6	Panola	811.4	23 492	1 659	29.0	74.5	16.2	1.0	0.9	8.8	6.2	17.7	8.4	11.7	11.8	12.0
48 367	19100	1	Parker	903.5	129 441	487	143.3	85.5	1.7	1.4	1.0	11.8	6.1	18.4	7.9	11.5	12.3	14.3
48 369	...	7	Parmer	880.8	9 776	2 448	11.1	35.3	1.4	0.4	0.6	62.7	7.8	20.9	9.7	12.8	11.5	12.6
48 371	...	7	Pecos	4 763.8	15 970	2 040	3.4	26.5	4.0	0.7	0.9	68.5	7.0	17.9	9.0	15.5	13.9	13.0
48 373	...	6	Polk	1 057.0	47 916	1 020	45.3	72.3	10.9	2.3	1.0	14.7	5.4	15.1	7.6	11.9	11.6	12.9
48 375	11100	2	Potter	908.4	120 832	516	133.0	46.2	10.5	1.0	5.9	37.9	8.1	19.3	9.2	15.2	12.8	12.0
48 377	...	7	Presidio	3 855.3	6 958	2 675	1.8	12.7	1.0	0.7	2.4	83.8	8.2	18.6	9.0	10.2	10.9	10.9
48 379	...	8	Rains	229.5	11 314	2 338	49.3	86.9	3.0	1.5	1.3	8.8	4.8	14.6	6.8	10.1	10.3	12.9
48 381	11100	2	Randall	911.9	132 501	479	145.3	73.9	3.6	1.0	2.1	21.0	6.7	17.5	10.2	15.0	12.6	11.7
48 383	...	6	Reagan	1 175.3	3 608	2 934	3.1	28.9	3.1	0.7	0.7	67.7	8.3	21.3	9.6	13.2	12.7	12.4
48 385	...	9	Real	699.2	3 389	2 944	4.8	70.3	1.6	1.6	0.8	27.5	4.4	12.8	6.8	9.1	8.3	12.2
48 387	...	6	Red River	1 043.9	12 207	2 278	11.7	74.4	17.2	1.8	0.6	7.5	5.2	14.7	6.9	10.1	10.6	13.3
48 389	37780	7	Reeves	2 635.4	14 921	2 102	5.7	18.7	4.8	0.4	1.5	75.1	6.5	16.0	12.4	16.7	15.2	12.2
48 391	...	6	Refugio	770.5	7 321	2 642	9.5	42.8	6.5	0.9	0.9	50.0	6.7	17.3	8.0	11.6	10.1	12.4
48 393	...	9	Roberts	924.1	916	3 110	1.0	87.4	0.9	1.7	0.9	11.2	5.1	18.8	6.0	12.6	11.4	13.0
48 395	17780	3	Robertson	855.7	16 751	1 997	19.6	58.9	20.0	0.8	0.9	20.5	6.9	17.5	8.2	11.5	11.0	12.6
48 397	19100	1	Rockwall	127.1	93 978	625	739.4	73.5	6.6	0.9	3.5	17.1	6.2	20.9	8.1	11.0	14.7	14.6
48 399	...	6	Runnels	1 050.9	10 448	2 392	9.9	63.1	2.1	0.9	0.9	33.6	5.5	17.3	8.2	11.3	10.5	12.6
48 401	30980	3	Rusk	924.0	52 732	951	57.1	65.5	17.6	0.9	0.7	16.7	5.9	17.3	8.7	13.1	12.8	13.0
48 403	...	8	Sabine	491.4	10 303	2 404	21.0	87.4	7.9	1.2	0.6	4.5	4.5	14.4	6.4	8.6	8.4	11.9
48 405	...	9	San Augustine	530.7	8 320	2 564	15.7	70.1	23.1	0.8	0.5	6.8	5.4	14.4	6.9	9.7	8.8	13.2
48 407	...	8	San Jacinto	569.2	27 707	1 501	48.7	76.1	10.4	1.4	0.9	13.0	5.5	16.4	7.6	10.2	10.6	12.8
48 409	18580	2	San Patricio	693.4	67 655	785	97.6	39.8	1.9	0.7	1.4	57.1	7.4	19.6	9.1	13.3	12.3	12.2
48 411	...	7	San Saba	1 135.3	5 944	2 756	5.2	66.0	3.8	1.0	0.7	29.6	5.8	14.3	9.6	14.7	8.7	10.5
48 413	...	8	Schleicher	1 310.6	3 056	2 965	2.3	46.2	1.9	0.5	0.3	52.0	6.1	21.9	7.2	12.7	11.4	11.9
48 415	43660	7	Scurry	905.4	17 333	1 953	19.1	54.3	5.2	0.6	0.8	40.1	7.1	18.6	9.9	13.7	12.7	12.0
48 417	...	8	Shackelford	914.3	3 315	2 952	3.6	86.5	1.5	0.7	0.6	11.9	5.8	18.3	7.5	10.3	10.9	12.8
48 419	...	7	Shelby	795.6	25 579	1 580	32.2	62.5	17.8	0.6	1.9	18.3	7.0	19.5	8.6	12.0	11.3	12.5
48 421	...	9	Sherman	923.0	3 068	2 963	3.3	53.4	1.6	0.7	0.4	44.6	7.0	20.8	8.7	10.8	11.5	14.6
48 423	46340	3	Smith	921.5	225 290	293	244.5	61.4	18.1	0.8	2.0	19.2	7.0	17.8	9.9	13.7	11.6	11.9
48 425	19100	1	Somervell	186.5	8 775	2 525	47.1	78.3	1.5	1.5	1.1	19.2	5.1	17.6	8.5	10.5	11.9	13.6
48 427	40100	4	Starr	1 223.2	64 122	824	52.4	3.4	0.1	0.0	0.2	96.3	10.3	22.9	11.4	13.0	11.7	10.8
48 429	...	7	Stephens	896.7	9 906	2 439	11.0	71.4	3.3	0.9	0.9	24.3	5.4	15.8	10.4	13.5	11.5	11.8
48 431	...	8	Sterling	923.4	1 367	3 088	1.5	58.5	2.5	1.2	0.7	38.6	6.8	20.9	7.0	12.6	12.1	11.3
48 433	...	9	Stonewall	916.3	1 426	3 082	1.6	77.6	3.8	0.8	1.5	17.7	6.5	16.4	5.5	9.5	10.0	12.1
48 435	...	7	Sutton	1 453.9	3 869	2 913	2.7	37.7	0.7	0.2	0.4	61.2	5.9	18.9	7.9	12.0	11.0	13.6
48 437	...	6	Swisher	890.2	7 466	2 634	8.4	47.7	7.8	1.0	0.5	44.1	6.6	18.6	9.5	13.5	10.7	11.4
48 439	19100	1	Tarrant	863.7	2 016 872	15	2 335.2	49.5	16.9	0.9	6.3	28.4	7.2	19.5	9.3	14.8	13.6	13.4
48 441	10180	3	Taylor	915.6	136 535	464	149.1	66.1	8.2	0.9	2.9	24.0	7.4	17.3	14.5	14.5	10.7	10.4
48 443	...	9	Terrell	2 358.0	812	3 115	0.3	45.4	2.6	1.5	0.6	51.6	5.4	14.3	6.7	9.5	12.1	12.0
48 445	...	6	Terry	888.8	12 799	2 241	14.4	40.2	4.6	0.5	0.5	54.9	7.8	19.8	9.3	14.7	11.1	11.9
48 447	...	9	Throckmorton	912.6	1 533	3 078	1.7	84.6	1.3	1.0	0.8	13.2	4.9	16.4	7.1	9.7	9.7	12.9
48 449	34420	7	Titus	406.1	32 592	1 368	80.3	46.9	9.8	0.7	1.2	42.4	7.7	21.4	9.9	12.1	12.0	12.4

1. CBSA = Core Based Statistical Area. See Appendix A for explanation. See Appendix B for list of metropolitan areas with component counties.   2. County type code from the Economic Research Service of USDA Rural-Urban Continuum Codes. See Appendix A for definition.   3. Dry land or land partially or temporarily covered by water.   4. May be of any race.

STATE County	55 to 64 years	65 to 74 years	75 years and over	Percent female	Total persons 2000	Total persons 2010	Percent change 2000–2010	Percent change 2010–2016	Births	Deaths	Net migration	Number	Persons per house-hold	Family house-holds	Female family house-holder[1]	One person
	16	17	18	19	20	21	22	23	24	25	26	27	28	29	30	31
TEXAS—Cont'd																
Mason	15.0	15.8	12.8	49.6	3 738	4 012	7.3	2.5	227	266	148	1 714	2.37	63.3	7.1	33.3
Matagorda	13.6	9.3	6.8	50.0	37 957	36 702	-3.3	1.3	3 341	2 273	-505	13 382	2.70	69.0	13.5	28.6
Maverick	9.3	6.8	4.9	50.4	47 297	54 258	14.7	6.3	6 867	2 292	-1 184	16 030	3.48	80.9	19.9	17.8
Medina	13.4	9.7	6.4	48.2	39 304	46 006	17.1	7.1	3 432	2 440	2 230	14 975	2.98	76.8	12.7	19.4
Menard	16.6	16.7	13.5	50.0	2 360	2 242	-5.0	-5.3	116	201	-25	951	2.25	66.0	13.0	32.2
Midland	11.1	5.5	4.5	49.7	116 009	136 872	18.0	18.8	16 586	6 521	15 491	52 870	2.83	69.4	12.0	24.9
Milam	13.9	11.2	8.8	50.7	24 238	24 753	2.1	0.5	1 965	1 774	-61	9 346	2.56	64.6	12.1	32.3
Mills	14.7	14.8	12.0	50.7	5 151	4 936	-4.2	-0.6	278	394	79	1 848	2.55	71.2	8.3	28.4
Mitchell	10.8	8.0	6.2	40.1	9 698	9 403	-3.0	-7.3	604	596	-689	2 753	2.45	69.7	8.6	25.9
Montague	14.1	12.5	9.1	50.9	19 117	19 720	3.2	-1.6	1 436	1 672	-15	8 024	2.39	66.2	9.1	29.9
Montgomery	12.4	8.0	4.7	50.5	293 768	455 750	55.1	22.0	42 104	20 484	76 465	173 238	2.88	74.0	10.7	21.7
Moore	10.3	5.9	4.6	48.0	20 121	21 904	8.9	1.0	2 619	861	-1 531	6 893	3.21	79.4	10.7	16.0
Morris	14.7	11.3	10.1	52.1	13 048	12 934	-0.9	-2.6	967	1 024	-276	4 954	2.53	73.8	15.3	25.0
Motley	15.3	17.7	12.2	47.2	1 426	1 205	-15.5	-3.7	52	102	5	445	2.41	60.7	6.7	35.7
Nacogdoches	11.1	8.2	5.6	52.0	59 203	64 524	9.0	2.0	5 587	3 528	-852	23 888	2.52	62.8	12.7	30.6
Navarro	12.9	9.8	6.9	50.7	45 124	47 840	6.0	1.4	4 365	3 168	-583	17 477	2.70	71.5	15.0	24.0
Newton	14.5	11.4	7.2	47.9	15 072	14 445	-4.2	-3.1	881	978	-335	4 825	2.88	63.0	10.0	32.4
Nolan	12.5	9.9	7.7	50.3	15 802	15 217	-3.7	-1.5	1 292	1 110	-434	5 599	2.62	64.3	14.4	29.8
Nueces	12.1	8.0	5.6	50.7	313 645	340 223	8.5	6.2	30 706	17 395	8 230	126 900	2.72	68.6	17.0	24.6
Ochiltree	11.0	6.3	4.5	49.5	9 006	10 223	13.5	0.8	1 145	518	-545	3 696	2.86	74.9	12.0	21.0
Oldham	14.3	8.6	5.9	47.8	2 185	2 052	-6.1	1.2	133	89	-14	640	2.52	72.5	7.2	26.1
Orange	13.2	9.0	6.7	50.5	84 966	81 837	-3.7	3.8	7 043	5 739	1 797	32 054	2.57	70.0	12.6	25.8
Palo Pinto	14.3	11.3	7.4	50.9	27 026	28 122	4.1	-0.2	2 264	1 987	-282	10 562	2.62	66.7	11.9	28.2
Panola	14.3	10.5	7.5	50.5	22 756	23 796	4.6	-1.3	1 845	1 694	-457	8 923	2.63	69.3	13.2	26.4
Parker	13.9	9.7	5.8	50.2	88 495	116 948	32.2	10.7	8 552	6 262	9 861	42 781	2.78	76.1	9.2	20.8
Parmer	11.5	6.8	6.2	48.1	10 016	10 269	2.5	-4.8	940	452	-978	3 224	3.08	77.2	13.3	17.0
Pecos	11.1	7.2	5.5	43.2	16 809	15 507	-7.7	3.0	1 392	688	-212	4 339	3.17	66.4	7.6	29.6
Polk	16.2	13.0	6.4	46.5	41 133	45 414	10.4	5.5	3 146	3 912	3 285	17 480	2.40	70.9	15.1	25.5
Potter	11.2	6.9	5.3	48.4	113 546	121 078	6.6	-0.2	12 770	7 444	-5 709	43 227	2.68	64.3	16.7	30.6
Presidio	10.8	11.1	10.5	49.8	7 304	7 817	7.0	-11.0	763	270	-1 365	2 634	2.77	67.3	13.7	30.0
Rains	16.7	14.8	9.0	50.1	9 139	10 914	19.4	3.7	609	818	616	4 201	2.61	71.2	10.6	26.2
Randall	12.3	8.2	5.8	50.8	104 312	120 720	15.7	9.8	10 434	6 214	7 498	48 770	2.55	68.3	11.2	25.1
Reagan	11.6	6.3	4.6	47.4	3 326	3 367	1.2	7.2	351	139	19	1 217	2.93	72.6	6.6	23.4
Real	17.4	16.5	12.6	50.0	3 047	3 309	8.6	2.4	207	303	191	1 224	2.65	71.6	11.8	26.4
Red River	15.2	13.6	10.5	51.3	14 314	12 864	-10.1	-5.1	820	1 103	-350	5 196	2.38	62.8	14.2	33.6
Reeves	9.0	6.5	5.5	39.3	13 137	13 783	4.9	8.3	1 152	635	622	3 716	3.06	65.5	11.5	31.0
Refugio	13.0	11.7	9.1	50.9	7 828	7 383	-5.7	-0.8	557	558	-49	2 753	2.59	69.6	15.0	26.8
Roberts	14.2	12.0	7.0	49.5	887	929	4.7	-1.4	56	52	-16	350	2.66	78.3	10.9	21.7
Robertson	13.7	10.8	7.8	50.7	16 000	16 620	3.9	0.8	1 332	1 139	-30	6 065	2.69	69.6	15.8	26.3
Rockwall	11.9	7.6	5.0	50.7	43 080	78 326	81.8	20.0	6 160	3 228	12 493	28 457	2.98	81.5	10.5	15.3
Runnels	13.3	11.4	9.9	49.3	11 495	10 501	-8.6	-0.5	683	861	123	3 703	2.76	72.1	12.9	25.6
Rusk	13.3	9.3	6.6	47.5	47 372	53 304	12.5	-1.1	3 983	3 406	-1 097	17 753	2.75	71.3	13.9	25.6
Sabine	16.3	17.3	12.3	50.4	10 469	10 835	3.5	-4.9	567	1 019	-95	3 795	2.73	64.7	10.8	33.1
San Augustine	16.0	14.2	11.4	51.0	8 946	8 864	-0.9	-6.1	599	842	-239	2 882	2.93	63.9	12.7	32.2
San Jacinto	16.2	12.6	8.2	50.2	22 246	26 377	18.6	5.0	1 750	1 761	1 389	9 476	2.84	73.1	9.7	22.4
San Patricio	11.5	8.7	5.9	49.9	67 138	64 807	-3.5	4.4	6 068	3 873	609	22 781	2.87	75.4	14.9	21.0
San Saba	13.3	13.3	9.8	46.0	6 186	6 131	-0.9	-3.1	423	398	-215	2 126	2.45	64.3	9.5	29.8
Schleicher	11.9	10.2	6.7	49.3	2 935	3 461	17.9	-11.7	226	144	-509	1 074	3.00	76.4	17.1	20.1
Scurry	11.7	7.5	6.7	46.1	16 361	16 921	3.4	2.4	1 587	1 085	-73	5 832	2.65	70.9	8.5	25.3
Shackelford	15.8	10.6	8.1	51.2	3 302	3 378	2.3	-1.9	199	183	-65	1 377	2.42	69.4	9.5	27.5
Shelby	12.7	9.4	7.0	50.2	25 224	25 448	0.9	0.5	2 266	1 800	-281	9 396	2.72	66.4	14.2	31.8
Sherman	11.7	8.1	6.7	48.4	3 186	3 034	-4.8	1.1	243	177	-24	986	3.07	77.3	8.2	19.7
Smith	12.1	9.0	7.0	51.7	174 706	209 721	20.0	7.4	19 123	12 502	8 634	78 778	2.70	68.2	13.3	26.6
Somervell	13.8	11.5	7.5	51.4	6 809	8 491	24.7	3.3	529	520	247	3 386	2.45	75.9	12.4	21.0
Starr	8.4	6.5	5.1	51.4	53 597	60 968	13.8	5.2	8 491	2 423	-2 992	16 145	3.84	83.1	24.4	15.6
Stephens	13.0	10.3	8.2	45.3	9 674	9 630	-0.5	2.9	663	685	288	3 447	2.55	67.9	9.7	29.0
Sterling	12.8	8.8	7.6	48.8	1 393	1 143	-17.9	19.6	95	76	202	451	2.90	76.9	10.2	18.6
Stonewall	13.9	12.0	14.0	52.7	1 693	1 490	-12.0	-4.3	87	139	-20	580	2.35	67.4	5.7	31.2
Sutton	13.1	10.8	6.9	49.1	4 077	4 128	1.3	-6.3	320	201	-389	1 480	2.66	77.4	9.8	18.3
Swisher	11.4	9.4	8.7	46.9	8 378	7 854	-6.3	-4.9	665	483	-558	2 594	2.73	72.7	9.9	23.6
Tarrant	11.2	6.6	4.2	51.1	1 446 219	1 810 614	25.2	11.4	174 686	73 738	103 586	673 737	2.81	69.2	14.3	25.5
Taylor	10.9	7.7	6.6	51.0	126 555	131 510	3.9	3.8	12 883	7 988	66	49 476	2.59	65.6	12.7	27.3
Terrell	13.8	14.5	11.7	49.8	1 081	984	-9.0	-17.5	73	73	-178	466	1.98	55.4	11.8	36.1
Terry	10.9	7.8	6.6	46.8	12 761	12 651	-0.9	1.2	1 229	769	-297	4 046	2.86	70.0	17.3	26.5
Throckmorton	14.3	11.9	13.0	52.4	1 850	1 641	-11.3	-6.6	89	120	-72	701	2.17	64.8	10.4	34.0
Titus	10.7	7.9	5.9	50.7	28 118	32 334	15.0	0.8	3 162	1 659	-1 193	10 461	3.08	77.0	12.5	19.7

1. No spouse present.

Table B. States and Counties — **Population, Vital Statistics, Health, and Crime**

STATE County	Persons in group quarters, 2016	Daytime population, 2011–2015		Births, 2016		Deaths, 2016		Persons under 65 with no health insurance, 2015		Medicare, 2015			Serious crimes known to police,[2] 2014 Total	
		Number	Employ-ment/resi-dence ratio	Total	Rate[1]	Number	Rate[1]	Number	Percent	Total Beneficiaries	Enrolled in Original Medicare	Enrolled in Medicare Advantage	Number	Rate[3]
	32	33	34	35	36	37	38	39	40	41	42	43	44	45
TEXAS—Cont'd														
Mason	3	3 949	0.94	37	9.0	42	10.2	829	28.8	1 117	899	218	77	1 839
Matagorda	380	35 615	0.94	556	15.0	390	10.5	6 463	21.1	6 478	4 760	1 718	1 220	3 313
Maverick	1 002	53 587	0.85	1 159	20.1	393	6.8	14 293	28.8	9 045	5 933	3 112	1 355	2 389
Medina	2 355	39 820	0.61	607	12.3	432	8.8	7 049	18.2	7 369	4 560	2 809	652	1 390
Menard	38	2 070	0.86	19	8.9	20	9.4	464	30.7	619	508	111	15	700
Midland	1 667	164 517	1.17	3 031	18.6	1 087	6.7	24 337	16.9	16 035	12 706	3 329	4 583	2 929
Milam	433	22 443	0.79	338	13.6	275	11.1	3 684	19.0	5 345	3 245	2 100	546	2 255
Mills	145	4 697	0.90	46	9.4	61	12.4	877	24.6	1 233	818	415	31	629
Mitchell	1 898	8 840	0.89	89	10.2	86	9.9	1 118	19.2	1 392	1 105	287	198	2 091
Montague	248	18 020	0.82	226	11.6	263	13.5	3 216	21.4	4 874	4 111	763	481	2 590
Montgomery	3 551	454 259	0.79	7 371	13.3	3 816	6.9	73 190	15.6	67 652	40 887	26 765	9 493	1 849
Moore	153	23 183	1.09	425	19.2	139	6.3	5 347	27.0	2 200	1 863	337	470	2 301
Morris	145	12 543	0.96	146	11.6	157	12.5	1 871	19.2	3 287	2 198	1 089	358	2 774
Motley	0	1 018	0.88	6	5.2	13	11.2	214	26.0	335	259	76	13	1 082
Nacogdoches	4 955	64 402	0.96	867	13.2	602	9.1	10 501	20.1	10 325	7 946	2 379	1 884	2 855
Navarro	728	46 949	0.94	720	14.8	560	11.5	8 930	22.4	9 689	7 612	2 077	1 759	3 751
Newton	726	12 048	0.55	137	9.8	171	12.2	1 836	17.1	2 507	1 759	748	81	572
Nolan	367	15 757	1.11	219	14.6	177	11.8	2 228	18.2	3 030	2 384	646	382	2 530
Nueces	6 727	362 270	1.06	5 123	14.2	2 944	8.1	57 222	18.6	52 954	25 584	27 370	17 671	4 940
Ochiltree	27	11 692	1.21	195	18.9	72	7.0	2 541	26.5	1 150	1 025	125	86	778
Oldham	278	2 273	1.26	22	10.6	9	4.3	247	16.0	408	328	80	20	939
Orange	697	76 034	0.79	1 196	14.1	934	11.0	10 957	15.4	15 976	10 111	5 865	2 289	2 731
Palo Pinto	280	26 390	0.86	360	12.8	349	12.4	4 952	22.0	5 282	4 395	887	759	2 707
Panola	389	23 635	0.97	291	12.4	258	11.0	3 389	17.5	4 305	3 368	937	864	3 590
Parker	1 220	100 939	0.63	1 493	11.5	1 077	8.3	16 838	15.9	18 269	13 495	4 774	2 103	1 731
Parmer	79	11 018	1.22	151	15.4	50	5.1	2 373	28.2	1 302	1 184	118	92	924
Pecos	2 074	16 527	1.11	224	14.0	96	6.0	2 647	21.8	2 059	1 598	461	391	2 467
Polk	4 394	44 887	0.92	517	10.8	669	14.0	7 672	22.7	16 807	12 001	4 806	1 236	2 675
Potter	6 929	146 395	1.45	1 966	16.3	1 190	9.8	24 202	24.0	30 997	24 058	6 939	6 026	4 914
Presidio	0	7 146	0.94	123	17.7	45	6.5	1 628	30.5	1 651	1 362	289	27	381
Rains	66	9 143	0.57	96	8.5	127	11.2	1 791	21.1	2 610	2 042	568	128	1 145
Randall	2 583	101 213	0.60	1 723	13.0	1 045	7.9	14 551	13.2	4 860	3 864	996	5 429	4 216
Reagan	28	4 290	1.40	55	15.2	16	4.4	843	24.9	388	328	60	0	0
Real	72	3 259	0.90	34	10.0	43	12.7	609	26.5	1 090	883	207	23	680
Red River	177	10 697	0.59	117	9.6	180	14.7	2 014	21.1	3 227	2 698	529	304	2 438
Reeves	3 136	16 134	1.41	211	14.1	98	6.6	2 122	21.5	1 963	1 653	310	285	2 020
Refugio	117	6 862	0.87	100	13.7	76	10.4	1 054	18.5	1 678	1 286	392	117	1 593
Roberts	0	762	0.58	6	6.6	4	4.4	80	10.7	136	99	37	14	1 716
Robertson	194	15 241	0.80	233	13.9	158	9.4	2 746	20.4	3 074	2 313	761	383	2 310
Rockwall	823	75 128	0.74	1 039	11.1	549	5.8	10 718	13.5	11 132	8 092	3 040	1 155	1 320
Runnels	188	9 950	0.88	110	10.5	126	12.1	1 725	20.9	2 512	2 199	313	189	1 829
Rusk	4 820	48 803	0.78	595	11.3	558	10.6	8 767	21.8	7 623	5 661	1 962	1 369	2 647
Sabine	121	9 908	0.80	90	8.7	144	14.0	1 398	19.1	3 834	3 002	832	162	1 705
San Augustine	171	8 465	0.89	81	9.7	124	14.9	1 163	18.7	2 094	1 616	478	198	2 246
San Jacinto	129	20 925	0.38	294	10.6	288	10.4	4 889	22.4	4 089	2 512	1 577	613	2 258
San Patricio	645	58 968	0.75	1 040	15.4	594	8.8	10 729	18.8	12 525	6 154	6 371	2 186	3 261
San Saba	663	5 806	0.96	71	11.9	54	9.1	1 073	27.0	1 292	964	328	55	913
Schleicher	3	3 092	0.91	33	10.8	17	5.6	661	24.6	496	405	91	16	506
Scurry	1 688	17 839	1.08	247	14.3	182	10.5	2 622	19.3	2 656	2 108	548	644	3 676
Shackelford	11	3 352	1.00	30	9.0	27	8.1	495	18.3	628	520	108	31	911
Shelby	167	24 514	0.88	361	14.1	307	12.0	5 164	24.4	4 880	3 755	1 125	584	2 345
Sherman	29	2 741	0.78	39	12.7	25	8.1	769	29.3	452	399	53	35	1 117
Smith	5 046	223 806	1.07	3 146	14.0	2 095	9.3	34 968	19.0	41 188	31 180	10 008	7 096	3 269
Somervell	287	9 299	1.19	79	9.0	95	10.8	1 232	17.4	1 456	1 042	414	72	822
Starr	843	59 591	0.85	1 331	20.8	402	6.3	16 889	30.6	8 770	6 417	2 353	1 140	1 821
Stephens	1 135	9 221	0.94	111	11.2	90	9.1	1 714	24.4	1 777	1 418	359	139	1 506
Sterling	36	1 522	1.31	18	13.2	11	8.0	233	20.8	236	193	43	6	480
Stonewall	29	1 379	0.94	19	13.3	16	11.2	214	20.6	362	321	41	5	350
Sutton	13	4 123	1.09	48	12.4	24	6.2	728	22.4	655	616	39	23	572
Swisher	645	7 126	0.78	100	13.4	70	9.4	1 330	24.0	1 531	1 317	214	150	1 926
Tarrant	24 398	1 907 139	0.99	28 682	14.2	12 903	6.4	310 164	17.7	220 903	117 720	103 183	71 745	3 679
Taylor	4 973	137 461	1.05	2 116	15.5	1 402	10.3	18 193	16.0	23 460	18 340	5 120	6 089	4 488
Terrell	0	946	1.06	10	12.3	12	14.8	150	24.0	231	180	51	14	1 582
Terry	1 177	12 542	0.97	199	15.5	135	10.5	2 489	25.5	1 982	1 342	640	324	2 520
Throckmorton	13	1 551	1.01	10	6.5	20	13.0	261	22.0	361	310	51	5	312
Titus	614	35 358	1.21	515	15.8	269	8.3	6 772	24.3	4 915	3 752	1 163	952	2 897

1. Per 1,000 estimated resident population.   2. Data for serious crimes have not been adjusted for underreporting; this may affect comparability between geographic areas and over time.
3. Per 100,000 population estimated by the FBI.

Table B. States and Counties — Crime, Education, Money Income, and Poverty

STATE County	Serious crimes known to police, 2014 (cont.)[1] Rate[2] Violent	Property	School enrollment and attainment, 2011–2015 Enrollment[3] Total	Percent private	Attainment[4] (percent) High school graduate or less	Bachelor's degree or more	Local government expenditures,[5] 2013–2014 Total current spending (mil dol)	Current spending per student (dollars)	Money income, 2011–2015 Per capita income[6] (dollars)	Median income (dollars)	Households Percent with income of less than $50,000	with income of $200,000 or more	Income and poverty, 2015 Median household income (dollars)	Percent below poverty level All persons	Children under 18 years	Children 5 to 17 years in families
	46	47	48	49	50	51	52	53	54	55	56	57	58	59	60	61
TEXAS—Cont'd																
Mason	96	1 743	579	15.0	49.7	22.4	7.4	10 472	25 585	37 654	61.1	3.7	45 340	13.8	23.3	20.1
Matagorda	326	2 987	8 363	7.8	58.1	15.3	70.9	10 101	21 693	40 797	57.9	1.4	45 073	20.5	30.9	30.1
Maverick	178	2 211	17 548	5.5	63.3	10.7	125.8	8 319	15 249	33 747	64.4	1.2	34 687	23.9	32.2	30.6
Medina	143	1 247	12 402	10.9	50.2	18.9	80.5	8 505	23 830	57 338	43.6	4.0	52 831	14.8	21.4	18.4
Menard	514	187	560	0.0	53.1	17.4	4.6	14 454	22 016	34 464	66.8	3.2	34 308	20.8	38.2	38.2
Midland	326	2 603	39 475	14.6	40.6	25.6	232.7	8 941	35 537	68 806	36.3	9.1	79 829	8.9	13.1	11.8
Milam	235	2 020	5 783	9.0	56.1	16.7	41.6	8 915	22 130	38 929	58.4	2.2	46 433	16.9	27.5	26.0
Mills	20	608	1 271	5.7	43.9	22.1	12.7	14 585	22 804	43 920	57.3	2.9	40 958	16.6	26.1	23.5
Mitchell	243	1 848	2 240	5.6	59.5	11.0	16.7	11 494	18 764	49 870	50.2	1.6	41 977	19.7	24.9	23.3
Montague	162	2 429	4 206	7.6	51.7	15.8	31.6	9 354	25 846	46 172	55.3	2.2	49 653	15.2	22.1	19.8
Montgomery	179	1 670	134 855	13.2	38.0	32.2	748.1	7 678	34 215	68 838	36.8	9.8	72 428	10.1	13.9	13.0
Moore	245	2 057	6 228	3.2	62.0	12.0	45.3	8 822	19 495	49 802	50.1	1.5	49 345	14.4	20.3	20.5
Morris	333	2 441	2 762	6.2	51.5	14.5	20.2	9 486	20 900	39 453	61.1	1.2	37 236	19.5	31.6	31.0
Motley	0	1 082	245	2.4	47.9	17.2	2.7	16 579	20 322	31 683	69.2	0.9	40 575	17.0	28.6	24.2
Nacogdoches	288	2 567	22 231	5.3	46.1	25.1	94.9	8 430	21 113	39 538	59.6	2.5	39 556	24.5	30.9	30.2
Navarro	354	3 397	11 898	5.0	53.1	15.7	83.4	8 393	20 697	41 505	57.9	1.9	41 047	19.6	27.9	26.9
Newton	64	508	2 946	6.0	62.4	6.4	21.5	10 657	20 428	38 144	62.1	1.5	40 345	21.2	28.1	25.8
Nolan	391	2 140	3 761	4.6	56.1	12.1	35.0	10 564	20 444	37 102	62.8	1.6	40 052	20.0	30.6	27.5
Nueces	646	4 294	92 426	7.5	47.4	20.2	541.5	8 597	25 176	50 337	49.6	3.2	50 188	19.9	30.6	28.2
Ochiltree	127	652	2 996	7.0	54.5	15.2	20.1	8 260	25 995	51 517	46.7	3.7	67 136	8.8	13.3	12.4
Oldham	141	798	673	3.1	36.0	27.8	13.2	15 108	23 452	50 893	49.2	5.3	53 797	13.4	29.2	22.4
Orange	307	2 425	20 220	7.9	51.3	14.6	128.4	8 445	25 489	49 763	50.2	2.2	51 156	16.1	22.6	21.4
Palo Pinto	175	2 532	5 839	6.9	55.4	15.8	42.4	9 011	23 013	39 516	59.4	2.8	42 932	18.6	27.8	26.7
Panola	349	3 241	5 401	5.3	49.6	12.8	42.0	10 371	25 693	50 119	49.8	3.8	50 057	15.1	20.9	20.2
Parker	125	1 606	30 249	14.5	37.9	26.5	164.2	8 309	31 923	67 288	37.6	6.5	67 545	9.4	13.7	12.0
Parmer	80	844	2 741	10.4	62.7	15.3	24.3	10 207	20 381	45 326	53.3	2.1	46 827	14.5	21.1	20.2
Pecos	366	2 101	3 496	5.2	65.9	10.0	32.4	10 328	19 772	50 305	49.7	1.0	45 839	18.1	23.6	23.3
Polk	331	2 343	8 911	8.4	58.0	12.3	64.4	9 359	21 010	39 662	58.4	2.5	42 746	17.2	28.8	27.1
Potter	622	4 292	33 112	7.6	51.8	14.9	310.2	8 235	20 283	38 159	61.3	2.0	40 353	22.4	31.8	30.1
Presidio	113	268	1 792	1.0	59.9	25.9	21.0	11 936	16 507	32 132	68.6	0.0	33 218	22.4	32.3	32.7
Rains	98	1 047	2 182	6.8	56.5	10.6	14.4	8 906	23 443	48 448	51.3	1.4	46 698	14.4	26.8	24.6
Randall	534	3 682	35 325	7.7	30.4	30.4	92.3	9 577	30 480	60 972	40.1	3.6	62 080	8.5	12.0	11.3
Reagan	0	0	919	5.7	68.3	10.5	10.8	11 731	25 238	52 181	43.0	3.2	65 948	8.8	11.9	11.9
Real	0	680	576	3.3	47.4	22.0	6.4	13 967	19 549	36 523	63.2	0.3	34 031	19.4	34.6	37.2
Red River	297	2 142	2 576	11.0	59.7	13.1	23.2	10 600	19 482	31 563	67.8	1.4	36 347	20.2	31.0	29.9
Reeves	390	1 631	2 820	3.9	66.0	10.8	28.8	11 567	17 893	43 540	54.9	2.5	44 470	19.3	24.2	22.3
Refugio	245	1 348	1 556	4.8	56.0	9.7	18.4	13 067	24 902	44 240	54.0	4.0	45 562	15.4	22.9	21.1
Roberts	245	1 471	251	2.8	33.6	31.8	3.2	15 028	31 314	63 889	35.1	4.3	71 859	6.7	8.7	7.3
Robertson	537	1 773	4 022	7.8	57.6	16.5	38.2	11 855	21 781	46 501	53.5	1.5	53 635	16.6	28.8	28.0
Rockwall	90	1 229	24 622	12.9	30.7	36.9	157.9	8 039	36 163	87 524	26.4	9.9	92 150	6.0	8.2	7.3
Runnels	135	1 693	2 371	3.2	59.3	17.5	21.2	10 186	21 803	41 526	58.8	2.5	39 404	18.5	25.4	22.6
Rusk	298	2 349	11 564	7.5	53.3	13.7	72.1	8 739	22 272	46 173	53.6	2.6	49 347	16.6	22.3	21.3
Sabine	358	1 347	1 987	2.3	59.5	12.0	14.7	9 275	19 511	31 307	68.6	1.8	36 813	19.7	33.7	32.0
San Augustine	250	1 997	1 661	6.6	63.0	10.8	8.6	10 806	19 213	28 275	72.2	1.6	33 156	24.3	37.3	36.6
San Jacinto	243	2 015	5 651	4.8	63.5	11.4	32.0	9 328	22 363	43 029	55.5	3.1	42 371	18.1	30.1	27.6
San Patricio	340	2 921	16 627	6.2	53.6	15.1	130.5	8 880	24 211	52 261	47.2	2.8	52 952	15.5	23.3	22.1
San Saba	149	763	1 338	6.4	52.8	14.5	10.1	10 478	19 743	39 040	63.7	1.5	42 559	18.9	29.2	28.0
Schleicher	0	506	916	4.7	47.5	19.5	6.5	10 932	25 199	55 543	45.6	4.6	53 886	13.4	21.9	17.9
Scurry	485	3 191	4 681	6.2	49.4	15.3	32.2	9 895	24 584	56 842	44.0	2.8	57 385	12.7	18.1	17.6
Shackelford	147	764	811	9.2	48.0	22.6	7.0	11 623	23 826	48 750	51.1	2.3	51 685	13.1	19.4	17.4
Shelby	333	2 012	6 135	6.3	58.6	14.8	54.4	9 607	20 753	37 756	61.9	2.5	41 519	19.8	29.0	27.2
Sherman	96	1 022	745	6.2	54.5	20.6	8.1	8 095	22 436	51 987	46.9	2.5	54 010	12.8	18.7	17.0
Smith	342	2 927	58 914	10.9	41.2	24.9	289.8	8 419	24 964	46 929	52.7	3.7	49 364	16.0	23.2	21.4
Somervell	69	754	2 152	4.2	44.4	22.7	21.3	11 443	26 946	51 912	48.1	5.4	58 040	12.1	17.7	16.5
Starr	271	1 549	19 746	2.1	75.9	9.1	173.3	9 815	12 483	26 172	72.2	0.8	28 292	30.9	42.5	43.1
Stephens	173	1 333	2 058	7.7	53.7	19.1	12.6	8 326	22 241	43 951	55.8	2.2	45 410	18.2	27.7	25.6
Sterling	240	240	270	0.0	53.5	22.3	3.7	11 895	21 386	53 456	45.9	2.4	62 759	11.6	17.5	15.4
Stonewall	0	350	350	1.4	57.1	15.6	2.8	11 772	22 416	42 155	56.2	3.3	45 928	14.5	21.2	19.1
Sutton	224	348	973	0.7	53.6	20.2	11.8	12 494	25 650	51 667	48.8	3.7	60 310	12.5	18.4	18.4
Swisher	295	1 631	1 780	7.5	56.8	15.9	16.2	10 360	18 437	37 040	61.1	1.2	40 584	21.6	34.0	31.8
Tarrant	400	3 279	544 887	13.4	38.6	30.3	2 920.9	8 174	29 058	58 711	42.6	5.6	60 735	13.1	18.4	17.9
Taylor	442	4 046	38 871	25.8	42.8	24.6	198.8	8 499	23 896	45 396	53.8	2.7	47 388	14.8	21.7	21.1
Terrell	113	1 469	144	9.0	55.2	17.3	2.7	19 086	27 062	31 111	67.4	1.7	43 815	16.7	21.8	18.3
Terry	257	2 264	3 345	7.3	60.3	12.6	25.1	10 606	21 705	37 475	60.1	3.1	43 357	22.5	32.2	30.4
Throckmorton	0	312	281	8.9	45.5	21.9	3.9	13 353	28 305	41 042	56.1	3.0	43 225	13.6	26.9	23.9
Titus	344	2 553	8 959	4.2	56.8	15.0	58.9	8 295	19 472	44 178	56.4	1.5	41 538	20.1	28.8	25.8

1. Data for serious crimes have not been adjusted for underreporting; this may affect comparability between geographic areas and over time.   2. Per 100,000 population estimated by the FBI.
3. All persons 3 years old and over enrolled in nursery school through college.   4. Persons 25 years old and over.   5. Elementary and secondary education expenditures.
6. Based on population estimated by the American Community Survey, 2011–2015.

Table B. States and Counties — **Personal Income**

STATE County	Personal income, 2015										Earnings, 2015		
	Total (mil dol)	Percent change, 2014–2015	Per capita¹		Wages and salaries (mil dol)	Supplements to wages and salaries; employer contributions (mil dol)		Proprietors' income (mil dol)	Dividends, interest, and rent (mil dol)	Personal transfer receipts (mil dol)	Total (mil dol)	Contributions for government social insurance (mil dol)	
			Dollars	Rank		Pension and insurance	Government social insurance					From employee and self-employed	From employer
	62	63	64	65	66	67	68	69	70	71	72	73	74
TEXAS—Cont'd													
Mason	173	3.2	42 897	1 228	39	8	2	40	47	40	90	5	2
Matagorda	1 452	3.8	39 493	1 550	624	111	40	125	196	347	901	48	40
Maverick	1 557	5.9	26 982	3 047	587	138	41	162	137	512	928	50	41
Medina	1 777	5.3	36 697	1 860	358	71	23	133	296	408	584	34	23
Menard	75	4.0	34 867	2 190	14	3	1	12	17	26	30	2	1
Midland	17 169	-9.0	106 588	11	6 077	761	395	7 801	2 455	891	15 035	627	395
Milam	902	4.7	36 817	1 558	293	46	19	78	128	277	435	26	19
Mills	185	9.0	37 726	1 862	52	10	3	20	42	58	85	5	3
Mitchell	284	-1.0	31 319	2 441	101	25	6	19	44	78	150	8	6
Montague	907	-1.2	47 071	413	231	39	15	112	172	219	398	23	15
Montgomery	32 517	-0.6	60 490	203	9 298	1 194	616	4 708	4 678	3 246	15 817	794	616
Moore	859	9.3	38 581	1 511	477	91	32	172	81	129	772	32	32
Morris	516	-2.5	41 251	1 479	196	36	14	95	62	165	341	19	14
Motley	41	-0.5	36 071	1 735	12	2	1	6	8	12	22	1	1
Nacogdoches	2 250	5.6	34 258	2 399	840	160	56	348	359	573	1 404	68	56
Navarro	1 730	5.3	35 792	1 895	640	115	45	132	261	499	931	54	45
Newton	428	4.0	30 625	2 846	51	14	3	15	45	131	83	7	3
Nolan	562	2.0	37 222	1 687	263	47	18	40	96	162	368	21	18
Nueces	15 417	3.5	42 859	905	8 115	1 354	577	2 168	2 512	3 082	12 215	626	577
Ochiltree	782	-2.1	72 785	123	289	40	18	379	93	57	726	26	18
Oldham	113	6.9	54 690	350	55	8	4	43	13	14	110	4	4
Orange	3 512	5.9	41 679	1 190	1 200	202	82	181	363	861	1 665	100	82
Palo Pinto	1 065	3.3	38 171	1 679	377	62	24	90	198	272	554	32	24
Panola	964	-1.5	40 543	744	450	68	31	111	149	233	659	36	31
Parker	6 335	7.7	50 257	473	1 538	224	106	612	1 038	889	2 481	135	106
Parmer	566	17.4	58 088	535	221	34	16	262	43	67	533	13	16
Pecos	535	0.7	33 042	2 332	289	53	18	42	68	119	402	20	18
Polk	1 707	3.3	36 341	1 763	427	79	29	119	367	696	653	50	29
Potter	5 078	2.2	41 690	1 098	3 586	599	258	1 163	730	1 051	5 606	275	258
Presidio	238	1.2	34 618	2 351	91	21	6	25	55	63	143	7	6
Rains	360	6.1	32 293	2 476	61	12	4	28	52	115	105	8	4
Randall	5 891	4.9	45 223	956	1 336	185	85	676	922	791	2 281	122	85
Reagan	209	-7.2	55 073	143	121	19	8	28	24	21	175	9	8
Real	107	5.7	32 344	2 929	23	5	2	17	28	45	45	3	2
Red River	456	3.9	36 628	1 901	88	19	6	25	67	170	139	10	6
Reeves	452	8.2	30 692	2 965	187	37	12	71	68	107	307	15	12
Refugio	333	-3.1	45 644	651	107	19	7	32	64	83	165	9	7
Roberts	46	5.1	49 713	632	9	2	1	4	14	6	15	1	1
Robertson	669	5.2	40 181	736	185	35	12	67	120	173	299	16	12
Rockwall	4 841	7.7	53 285	361	1 118	159	78	456	632	502	1 811	96	78
Runnels	392	4.3	37 155	1 754	110	22	7	38	63	117	177	11	7
Rusk	1 936	-0.1	36 484	1 836	635	106	42	162	291	459	946	54	42
Sabine	372	5.1	35 859	2 059	84	17	6	30	66	154	137	10	6
San Augustine	298	9.0	35 172	2 368	61	14	4	38	44	129	117	7	4
San Jacinto	880	2.4	32 115	2 511	81	18	5	45	123	268	149	14	5
San Patricio	2 788	4.0	41 386	1 330	992	175	71	177	392	635	1 415	79	71
San Saba	207	13.9	35 057	1 980	57	12	4	28	43	61	101	6	4
Schleicher	134	-8.9	41 659	701	49	9	3	21	21	25	81	4	3
Scurry	889	-2.1	50 489	295	435	67	27	213	120	139	743	36	27
Shackelford	446	-12.0	132 989	8	79	13	5	285	55	31	382	14	5
Shelby	1 034	4.1	40 721	1 164	335	57	23	217	136	268	632	28	23
Sherman	252	28.1	81 876	87	42	7	3	162	15	16	213	3	3
Smith	11 197	1.1	50 224	821	4 551	683	317	3 105	1 701	1 943	8 656	419	317
Somervell	383	6.9	43 880	1 062	249	49	16	42	62	74	355	18	16
Starr	1 566	5.8	24 540	3 095	479	134	33	146	128	583	792	43	33
Stephens	471	-5.7	49 928	263	126	26	9	172	67	100	333	15	9
Sterling	80	-2.3	59 442	252	30	6	2	10	30	10	48	2	2
Stonewall	78	5.1	55 528	290	26	5	2	10	19	19	43	2	2
Sutton	214	-9.8	54 573	77	155	19	9	31	40	34	214	11	9
Swisher	356	13.5	47 284	1 026	72	16	4	153	39	72	245	6	4
Tarrant	96 601	4.7	48 727	582	47 416	6 707	3 342	13 088	15 906	12 128	70 553	3 595	3 342
Taylor	5 967	1.4	43 861	924	2 716	473	200	912	1 088	1 197	4 302	216	200
Terrell	59	16.8	70 192	212	29	5	2	2	16	9	38	2	2
Terry	455	4.5	35 729	2 143	166	28	11	68	54	122	273	13	11
Throckmorton	81	-8.1	51 480	298	20	4	1	18	14	19	43	2	1
Titus	1 069	4.7	32 760	2 560	598	112	42	113	145	264	866	44	42

1. Based on the resident population estimated as of July 1 of the year shown.

Table B. States and Counties — Earnings, Social Security, and Housing

STATE County	Earnings, 2015 (cont.) Percent by selected industries									Social Security beneficiaries, December 2015			Housing units, 2016	
	Farm	Mining	Construction	Manufacturing	Information: professional, scientific, technical services	Retail trade	Finance, insurance, real estate and leasing	Health care and social assistance	Government	Number	Rate[1]	Supplemental Security Income recipients, December 2015	Total	Percent change, 2010–2016
	75	76	77	78	79	80	81	82	83	84	85	86	87	88
TEXAS—Cont'd														
Mason	14.2	D	5.3	2.7	D	3.0	7.4	3.9	15.3	1 180	294	82	2 753	0.7
Matagorda	4.0	3.0	11.8	2.3	7.1	4.8	3.5	D	14.8	7 190	195	1 114	19 285	2.6
Maverick	1.3	1.0	5.3	3.6	2.3	10.3	2.8	D	39.3	10 195	177	3 587	18 249	4.5
Medina	3.1	8.6	12.6	1.1	5.2	8.3	5.9	D	27.6	9 050	187	1 110	18 216	1.3
Menard	19.3	D	D	D	D	8.1	8.8	D	28.2	635	294	58	1 707	0.3
Midland	0.0	60.2	3.6	2.3	3.8	2.8	6.0	2.9	4.3	18 450	114	2 069	60 491	11.3
Milam	5.2	2.2	16.0	14.1	3.2	4.6	4.1	13.9	14.5	5 985	244	810	11 399	0.8
Mills	9.3	D	7.9	4.5	D	9.4	4.9	12.6	21.3	1 380	283	114	2 856	0.4
Mitchell	1.9	21.7	2.5	2.5	D	5.6	D	1.8	43.7	1 550	175	214	4 053	-0.3
Montague	1.2	32.8	6.8	5.2	6.3	5.8	4.0	D	16.4	5 105	265	460	10 182	0.5
Montgomery	0.1	18.3	12.0	6.7	10.1	5.9	6.2	7.0	10.0	77 665	145	7 345	209 415	17.9
Moore	19.0	3.8	D	D	D	4.4	1.8	D	12.8	2 525	115	272	8 006	1.6
Morris	6.1	D	2.1	39.9	18.5	4.1	D	2.5	9.3	3 770	302	538	6 028	0.1
Motley	18.2	1.0	D	D	D	7.9	D	3.4	23.5	350	306	30	778	0.0
Nacogdoches	8.5	1.4	8.9	11.0	3.8	8.0	5.0	12.9	23.2	11 580	176	2 058	28 079	2.5
Navarro	-0.3	2.1	12.9	16.7	D	7.0	5.0	10.8	18.6	10 550	219	1 687	20 553	1.6
Newton	-2.4	D	4.5	8.1	D	8.4	D	12.1	34.9	2 815	201	582	7 186	0.6
Nolan	0.6	6.9	8.5	14.9	2.9	8.4	4.4	D	24.1	3 250	216	542	7 095	-0.8
Nueces	0.3	7.7	11.6	10.2	6.9	5.9	5.3	12.9	17.1	59 155	164	12 597	148 941	5.6
Ochiltree	17.6	43.5	7.5	3.5	1.7	3.0	2.0	1.0	5.9	1 325	124	97	4 062	0.0
Oldham	39.1	D	22.8	D	D	0.9	D	D	14.7	425	206	30	849	1.0
Orange	-0.3	0.6	13.6	33.5	3.6	5.9	4.0	4.4	13.9	18 475	219	2 477	36 755	4.1
Palo Pinto	1.0	14.0	7.6	22.2	3.3	6.9	3.1	D	17.9	6 225	223	746	15 344	0.8
Panola	4.0	15.8	23.9	6.9	3.8	5.1	3.6	4.8	11.7	5 155	217	653	11 021	0.9
Parker	1.2	10.6	13.5	8.6	5.7	8.6	4.1	7.5	12.3	22 735	180	1 339	48 725	4.5
Parmer	54.0	D	D	D	1.0	1.2	D	D	7.7	1 460	149	138	3 795	-0.1
Pecos	1.4	17.1	6.7	2.1	D	5.8	3.6	3.0	28.4	2 330	145	374	5 612	0.5
Polk	-0.5	1.7	8.6	11.3	4.6	8.8	4.5	10.0	23.7	18 665	397	1 769	24 855	9.6
Potter	0.1	7.1	4.9	8.8	7.2	7.0	7.3	17.0	17.7	18 660	154	3 124	49 796	5.3
Presidio	14.3	0.3	D	D	D	4.8	2.4	D	49.6	1 745	254	638	3 838	0.4
Rains	-1.6	D	12.4	4.8	D	12.5	D	D	22.2	3 010	270	265	5 309	0.8
Randall	7.4	2.4	11.1	4.1	6.4	12.0	5.6	7.8	10.4	20 445	157	1 292	54 320	5.3
Reagan	-1.0	35.5	3.9	1.0	D	3.2	D	D	12.9	445	119	53	1 398	1.9
Real	6.6	D	8.7	6.7	D	8.2	D	13.9	19.2	1 175	356	131	2 602	0.2
Red River	3.2	3.0	10.8	11.3	7.6	5.3	3.5	11.2	23.6	3 635	294	509	6 878	0.7
Reeves	3.0	9.8	8.1	0.5	2.1	7.2	4.1	1.3	32.1	2 240	151	431	4 624	-0.3
Refugio	0.7	27.7	12.7	0.4	5.7	5.4	5.2	2.8	23.7	1 805	245	234	3 735	0.2
Roberts	17.3	13.6	3.9	2.1	D	D	0.7	0.0	33.0	170	185	0	439	0.0
Robertson	10.6	7.8	7.3	2.8	3.3	4.8	3.6	4.3	18.4	3 735	224	634	8 661	2.1
Rockwall	0.0	0.8	11.4	7.0	10.3	9.8	5.9	16.8	12.2	12 785	141	747	32 693	17.0
Runnels	0.2	5.1	8.8	19.1	D	6.4	D	7.1	23.9	2 665	253	318	5 270	-0.5
Rusk	3.8	16.9	8.8	8.8	D	4.6	4.1	7.2	13.8	10 215	193	1 199	21 410	1.1
Sabine	4.5	10.3	6.3	18.0	D	5.1	D	11.4	19.6	3 675	354	340	8 051	0.8
San Augustine	24.5	D	7.1	3.2	D	4.6	D	11.5	17.6	2 585	308	438	5 366	0.5
San Jacinto	-3.7	2.5	14.0	5.4	7.3	4.4	4.0	D	30.8	6 195	227	737	13 315	1.0
San Patricio	0.5	8.0	18.2	10.3	5.9	6.4	3.0	4.7	24.2	13 435	199	2 411	27 944	5.4
San Saba	6.9	10.9	5.6	1.8	D	4.7	D	3.6	25.5	1 480	249	148	3 171	-0.2
Schleicher	9.9	25.5	D	D	D	2.2	D	4.0	15.7	575	180	62	1 495	0.4
Scurry	1.4	45.9	5.8	2.4	1.9	4.2	2.8	D	13.6	2 955	168	336	7 202	3.4
Shackelford	1.4	82.3	1.0	1.5	D	0.7	2.0	D	3.2	710	214	65	1 757	0.2
Shelby	24.6	8.6	5.6	14.9	D	5.9	3.5	4.4	11.7	5 455	215	1 025	11 973	0.8
Sherman	76.6	D	D	D	D	1.5	0.9	D	6.6	360	118	23	1 302	4.0
Smith	0.3	23.2	4.3	6.8	6.4	10.4	5.6	16.5	9.6	43 405	195	5 554	89 329	2.3
Somervell	2.1	D	7.7	1.4	5.0	1.7	1.1	D	13.5	1 685	193	110	3 754	2.1
Starr	3.1	2.5	3.1	0.5	2.4	8.9	1.9	D	45.8	9 700	152	4 965	19 698	0.9
Stephens	0.6	53.1	6.6	7.2	D	3.4	5.4	3.1	10.9	2 110	213	241	4 927	-0.2
Sterling	1.0	34.8	6.1	1.3	1.0	2.9	D	D	16.7	250	184	27	617	0.3
Stonewall	20.3	12.4	12.4	2.3	D	4.3	D	D	27.8	375	266	24	928	0.0
Sutton	4.3	26.7	5.9	5.3	D	2.6	2.1	D	11.6	725	186	68	2 033	0.1
Swisher	63.9	D	1.4	1.7	D	1.8	D	D	15.4	1 590	212	164	3 201	-0.6
Tarrant	0.0	7.3	7.9	11.7	7.5	6.2	8.2	9.6	11.6	252 210	127	36 448	756 517	5.8
Taylor	0.6	10.9	7.0	3.9	6.1	6.9	6.3	14.3	21.1	24 440	179	3 847	57 393	2.9
Terrell	4.5	0.3	2.9	0.0	1.3	2.6	D	D	35.9	220	257	27	700	0.0
Terry	12.7	15.7	4.5	3.7	D	16.2	D	D	21.2	2 210	173	363	4 859	0.6
Throckmorton	16.3	36.1	D	D	D	1.7	D	2.4	18.1	390	250	22	1 079	0.0
Titus	3.4	2.9	4.2	33.0	2.1	6.9	3.5	6.8	18.0	5 445	167	784	12 245	1.6

1. Per 1,000 resident population estimated as of July 1 of the year shown.

Table B. States and Counties — Housing, Labor Force, and Employment

STATE County	Housing units, 2011–2015								Civilian labor force, 2016		Unemployment		Civilian employment,[6] 2011–2015		
	Occupied units												Percent		
		Owner-occupied				Renter-occupied									
				Median owner cost as a percent of income											
	Total	Percent	Median value[1]	With a mortgage	Without a mortgage[2]	Median rent[3]	Median rent as a percent of income[2]	Substandard units[4] (percent)	Total	Percent change, 2015–2016	Total	Rate[5]	Total	Management, business, science and arts	Construction, production, and maintenance occupations
	89	90	91	92	93	94	95	96	97	98	99	100	101	102	103
TEXAS—Cont'd															
Mason	1 714	78.6	154 800	28.8	12.9	746	33.3	2.6	1 777	-1.2	66	3.7	2 018	23.4	35.0
Matagorda	13 382	67.8	93 700	20.2	12.6	658	25.0	4.4	16 833	-1.7	1 246	7.4	15 874	22.5	33.4
Maverick	16 030	70.0	88 700	24.9	13.5	589	26.3	13.9	24 087	2.2	2 721	11.3	20 309	22.0	28.9
Medina	14 975	81.1	125 100	19.7	11.0	708	24.6	4.8	20 893	2.6	924	4.4	19 610	31.9	25.1
Menard	951	71.2	56 200	18.9	13.0	534	29.1	5.3	822	-3.7	38	4.6	797	28.6	29.7
Midland	52 870	67.0	166 700	19.4	10.0	1 089	27.4	5.0	84 612	-4.0	3 740	4.4	76 743	32.3	28.2
Milam	9 346	65.8	80 600	19.3	11.9	652	29.3	3.9	10 275	1.8	537	5.2	9 212	30.0	30.3
Mills	1 848	81.5	120 100	24.8	11.6	520	24.3	2.9	1 916	-3.4	81	4.2	1 887	31.4	26.2
Mitchell	2 753	70.3	48 500	17.6	10.0	603	19.6	1.3	2 600	-5.0	188	7.2	2 955	30.5	32.0
Montague	8 024	73.5	96 000	20.2	12.9	727	31.9	3.1	8 963	-7.3	451	5.0	8 193	29.4	34.2
Montgomery	173 238	71.8	176 900	21.1	11.2	1 030	27.8	4.6	260 658	1.3	12 843	4.9	230 258	38.2	21.8
Moore	6 893	67.5	93 000	19.2	10.0	675	21.2	10.8	11 176	0.9	335	3.0	10 714	20.3	46.0
Morris	4 954	72.1	69 300	21.1	11.7	648	26.8	5.3	4 898	-7.6	539	11.0	4 588	27.7	31.7
Motley	445	71.9	53 100	22.0	14.7	541	27.7	3.6	508	3.7	19	3.7	459	38.8	30.3
Nacogdoches	23 888	55.7	110 400	20.5	10.5	730	30.7	3.8	28 621	2.1	1 348	4.7	27 638	33.7	26.4
Navarro	17 477	66.5	81 300	22.6	12.6	704	28.7	5.5	22 692	-0.5	958	4.2	20 159	25.2	32.4
Newton	4 825	76.6	74 900	22.6	10.5	703	23.6	0.8	5 334	-0.3	430	8.1	4 911	21.8	35.6
Nolan	5 599	67.3	57 200	18.3	11.7	579	25.3	4.9	6 847	-0.6	333	4.9	6 403	24.9	33.0
Nueces	126 900	57.3	113 200	21.5	12.0	887	29.5	5.4	165 431	0.1	9 418	5.7	162 895	28.7	25.5
Ochiltree	3 696	72.9	84 200	19.1	10.5	702	18.8	7.0	4 680	-11.0	251	5.4	5 081	21.3	38.6
Oldham	640	76.1	87 100	21.4	10.0	675	37.5	3.6	908	-0.3	27	3.0	773	39.2	21.9
Orange	32 054	76.5	97 800	20.9	10.0	748	27.7	3.5	36 931	-0.4	2 498	6.8	35 616	28.3	31.7
Palo Pinto	10 562	68.1	82 800	20.2	12.8	702	31.7	5.3	13 233	0.8	735	5.6	11 291	25.2	36.3
Panola	8 923	77.6	91 800	18.7	10.0	678	24.1	3.4	10 090	-12.5	746	7.4	10 154	22.0	38.1
Parker	42 781	77.7	161 800	19.7	11.4	900	28.4	3.2	60 534	1.9	2 479	4.1	56 235	37.6	23.2
Parmer	3 224	68.2	86 400	22.6	10.0	625	21.6	6.5	4 916	-0.7	124	2.5	4 665	23.9	43.6
Pecos	4 339	70.2	68 800	16.7	10.0	742	23.9	5.7	6 456	-5.7	383	5.9	6 447	18.9	37.2
Polk	17 480	78.7	81 500	22.7	11.7	644	28.6	4.9	17 289	1.8	1 095	6.3	16 267	25.2	29.3
Potter	43 227	57.8	88 200	22.1	11.5	716	30.6	6.1	56 795	1.3	1 897	3.3	53 420	25.2	29.2
Presidio	2 634	68.5	59 400	20.6	11.5	428	20.2	7.1	3 070	-1.2	329	10.7	2 610	33.9	22.7
Rains	4 201	81.0	98 400	23.4	13.2	662	28.3	4.4	5 510	2.2	222	4.0	4 468	28.6	32.6
Randall	48 770	68.8	149 000	19.4	11.0	832	28.1	2.4	69 711	1.2	2 074	3.0	65 270	36.8	18.3
Reagan	1 217	68.7	82 900	19.4	11.6	629	15.9	3.2	1 675	-12.9	111	6.6	1 778	20.1	47.1
Real	1 224	79.0	109 800	22.5	13.3	761	29.5	2.9	1 027	-3.1	59	5.7	996	33.7	20.1
Red River	5 196	71.9	69 200	21.9	13.6	536	29.9	2.2	5 030	2.8	295	5.9	4 697	22.5	38.6
Reeves	3 716	74.4	44 600	14.1	10.5	708	21.9	4.8	5 892	4.1	328	5.6	4 768	25.5	27.2
Refugio	2 753	73.9	74 500	17.6	10.9	645	30.6	5.2	3 108	-5.7	212	6.8	3 096	23.0	31.8
Roberts	350	84.6	109 300	15.6	11.6	844	20.8	1.4	428	-5.7	20	4.7	423	40.2	21.0
Robertson	6 065	71.1	92 600	18.9	10.9	605	33.5	2.6	7 332	1.5	369	5.0	6 776	28.6	31.5
Rockwall	28 457	80.4	193 300	21.2	13.6	1 231	28.0	2.7	46 423	3.7	1 629	3.5	41 300	45.3	16.8
Runnels	3 703	76.0	70 000	17.6	13.0	528	21.2	1.2	4 652	-0.1	190	4.1	4 292	28.4	30.9
Rusk	17 753	74.8	101 400	19.0	10.8	701	26.5	3.0	22 463	-1.4	1 310	5.8	21 219	24.2	35.8
Sabine	3 795	89.3	84 500	20.7	14.1	533	37.4	5.0	3 461	-0.9	333	9.6	2 882	23.7	34.5
San Augustine	2 882	80.5	79 000	24.3	13.8	575	28.7	3.5	2 822	1.1	258	9.1	2 237	20.5	40.6
San Jacinto	9 476	84.4	87 800	24.9	12.4	666	31.2	4.4	11 413	1.4	723	6.3	9 976	24.0	36.4
San Patricio	22 781	67.2	95 000	20.1	12.3	835	25.6	8.2	30 202	0.2	2 286	7.6	28 627	27.8	31.2
San Saba	2 126	74.0	72 700	22.6	12.4	612	33.2	2.5	2 440	9.0	84	3.4	2 329	26.5	38.9
Schleicher	1 074	75.0	79 200	16.3	10.0	503	25.5	10.5	1 377	-8.0	78	5.7	1 499	30.8	36.8
Scurry	5 832	75.8	89 000	18.7	10.0	716	23.4	4.7	7 463	-8.3	442	5.9	7 371	24.4	36.5
Shackelford	1 377	77.0	79 000	20.5	13.4	575	28.8	1.5	1 889	-9.0	73	3.9	1 502	31.5	24.8
Shelby	9 396	72.4	75 100	21.7	10.1	568	31.8	2.2	11 048	-2.6	664	6.0	10 162	27.0	38.9
Sherman	986	78.8	79 700	21.1	10.0	621	26.9	3.2	1 350	-4.7	39	2.9	1 497	29.9	39.7
Smith	78 778	65.5	130 600	22.1	12.0	840	30.6	4.2	105 569	2.1	4 742	4.5	95 841	34.3	24.5
Somervell	3 386	68.5	139 800	21.0	12.8	853	24.3	5.6	4 172	1.8	198	4.7	3 878	35.6	30.3
Starr	16 145	75.2	65 100	26.2	12.7	510	34.7	13.3	26 266	1.8	3 579	13.6	21 006	21.6	29.8
Stephens	3 447	76.7	83 900	21.7	12.2	561	26.3	3.5	3 979	-2.8	209	5.3	3 805	28.4	32.4
Sterling	451	75.6	86 300	17.4	10.0	820	30.0	2.4	664	-10.8	28	4.2	583	30.7	30.2
Stonewall	580	80.9	49 700	18.3	12.2	439	31.3	4.8	626	-5.2	29	4.6	553	34.9	29.8
Sutton	1 480	64.5	88 200	23.5	14.0	610	19.7	4.8	1 579	-7.9	127	8.0	1 771	25.8	45.1
Swisher	2 594	73.3	67 200	18.4	12.8	608	26.0	5.4	2 703	-0.8	116	4.3	2 784	27.4	33.8
Tarrant	673 737	60.9	141 000	21.8	12.1	913	29.4	4.7	1 008 020	2.0	39 774	3.9	924 741	36.3	22.0
Taylor	49 476	60.0	101 500	20.1	11.5	778	29.6	3.1	63 169	0.0	2 365	3.7	60 708	30.3	22.0
Terrell	466	66.3	64 200	16.8	14.1	743	15.6	0.0	418	-3.5	17	4.1	415	20.0	25.5
Terry	4 046	72.1	64 200	17.5	11.2	703	31.1	4.3	5 381	-0.1	262	4.9	4 767	32.1	31.2
Throckmorton	701	71.9	64 400	13.8	12.2	461	21.6	3.4	764	-1.8	28	3.7	686	30.5	29.3
Titus	10 461	67.8	97 500	21.1	11.0	638	25.8	8.5	12 879	1.4	803	6.2	13 867	22.6	40.6

1. Specified owner-occupied units.   2. A value of 10.0 represents 10 percent or less; a value of 50.0 represents 50 percent or more.   3. Specified renter-occupied units.
4. Overcrowded or lacking complete plumbing facilities.   5. Percent of civilian labor force.   6. Civilian employed persons 16 years old and over.

STATE County	Private nonfarm establishments, employment and payroll, 2015									Agriculture, 2012			
	Number of establishments	Employment						Annual payroll		Farms			
											Percent with:		
		Total	Health care and social assistance	Manufac-turing	Retail trade	Finance and insurance	Professional, scientific, and technical services	Total (mil dol)	Average per employee (dollars)	Number	Fewer than 50 acres	500 acres or more	Farm operators whose principal occu-pation is farming (percent)
	104	105	106	107	108	109	110	111	112	113	114	115	116

TEXAS—Cont'd

Mason	138	782	137	42	133	53	38	21	27 281	640	11.1	43.4	48.9
Matagorda	713	8 291	1 338	695	1 408	207	295	474	57 182	856	28.5	27.9	47.7
Maverick	794	12 340	3 897	537	2 855	381	226	302	24 505	294	53.4	20.4	34.4
Medina	725	7 309	938	315	1 431	292	473	234	32 083	1 976	31.9	15.9	50.2
Menard	46	194	D	D	54	23	9	4	21 825	325	14.5	45.2	48.6
Midland	5 194	90 213	6 970	3 183	9 096	2 051	4 591	5 395	59 799	540	47.6	19.8	24.3
Milam	407	4 302	1 212	210	632	213	132	198	46 039	1 909	32.6	12.2	44.9
Mills	109	833	148	83	188	61	17	25	29 556	870	20.3	26.0	43.1
Mitchell	130	1 383	D	D	294	51	34	51	36 803	482	12.2	25.9	32.2
Montague	428	4 081	392	254	653	178	143	181	44 300	1 454	26.2	15.3	39.8
Montgomery	10 759	149 976	17 855	11 936	23 756	5 237	9 563	8 477	56 523	1 601	63.1	3.7	30.7
Moore	442	7 932	641	3 504	907	151	98	334	42 132	261	10.0	58.2	64.8
Morris	231	3 829	174	2 032	428	124	74	147	38 433	412	34.7	8.7	50.0
Motley	30	156	D	D	D	D	D	4	24 288	224	3.6	53.1	39.3
Nacogdoches	1 304	17 520	3 224	3 572	2 819	562	483	566	32 280	1 196	28.6	7.6	43.0
Navarro	960	13 330	2 527	2 528	2 302	392	284	425	31 892	2 573	41.0	9.2	47.6
Newton	131	1 099	406	82	166	25	67	28	25 885	450	57.8	2.2	31.3
Nolan	354	4 438	562	893	824	142	90	163	36 623	478	15.1	32.4	39.7
Nueces	7 919	143 429	28 875	7 685	18 745	4 103	6 640	6 024	42 000	754	43.4	21.1	36.3
Ochiltree	364	4 103	313	51	427	130	178	215	52 284	348	8.3	54.3	51.1
Oldham	47	541	D	D	40	D	3	18	33 484	159	7.5	64.8	46.5
Orange	1 354	20 300	1 399	5 506	3 230	563	479	980	48 277	671	79.7	3.9	43.7
Palo Pinto	611	6 170	758	1 274	1 093	152	220	225	36 414	1 329	42.2	15.6	32.7
Panola	475	7 301	658	947	891	185	301	322	44 134	1 079	34.6	10.1	43.4
Parker	2 531	29 403	3 302	2 781	5 473	676	1 030	1 130	38 417	4 370	66.1	3.5	35.3
Parmer	193	3 331	180	D	172	78	62	126	37 838	570	8.6	47.9	59.3
Pecos	348	4 297	579	D	797	150	64	171	39 902	291	13.1	67.7	45.0
Polk	735	8 479	1 407	1 220	1 791	358	228	281	33 163	738	40.2	8.5	48.6
Potter	3 577	62 261	13 797	6 494	9 041	4 109	2 338	2 489	39 982	258	35.3	31.4	38.0
Presidio	121	862	43	D	255	58	D	19	22 202	162	8.6	63.6	45.1
Rains	162	1 324	122	56	398	43	208	35	26 495	682	47.5	7.9	44.7
Randall	2 503	31 748	3 498	4 664	5 927	1 078	847	1 251	39 400	892	30.5	27.4	36.4
Reagan	134	1 814	85	D	133	D	21	90	49 579	135	5.2	71.9	51.1
Real	79	488	32	29	73	D	6	12	24 514	241	19.9	40.7	44.4
Red River	165	1 395	277	356	278	88	23	41	29 365	1 139	22.3	17.1	45.7
Reeves	251	3 844	419	8	463	21	44	173	44 998	240	11.7	51.7	43.3
Refugio	154	1 924	225	11	274	42	30	83	43 360	259	31.3	35.9	43.2
Roberts	19	103	NA	NA	D	D	D	6	57 757	107	2.8	73.8	58.9
Robertson	274	2 759	288	136	410	97	34	106	38 583	1 520	28.7	12.0	49.5
Rockwall	2 035	23 810	4 157	1 405	4 793	666	1 141	859	36 073	440	71.8	6.4	35.7
Runnels	229	2 021	277	419	397	120	33	68	33 696	925	12.4	29.6	45.8
Rusk	828	11 998	1 474	1 368	1 415	465	1 005	502	41 822	1 390	30.9	7.8	35.1
Sabine	161	1 513	328	D	314	59	27	51	33 462	201	36.3	4.5	46.8
San Augustine	123	1 088	360	53	197	48	8	38	34 938	305	23.3	9.8	52.5
San Jacinto	203	1 074	128	145	213	37	39	33	31 186	791	48.5	2.8	44.6
San Patricio	1 060	16 120	1 590	3 219	2 587	422	1 381	744	46 179	701	47.9	21.8	41.8
San Saba	168	967	244	40	209	25	39	24	24 661	744	19.9	33.7	48.8
Schleicher	55	536	D	D	59	23	15	23	42 129	310	10.6	60.6	44.8
Scurry	438	5 790	564	84	824	127	78	269	46 430	677	16.4	32.9	39.0
Shackelford	123	1 250	40	157	97	49	5	60	48 030	233	7.7	47.6	43.3
Shelby	504	6 288	638	1 986	1 021	490	135	221	35 222	1 048	26.4	8.3	53.3
Sherman	64	329	D	D	95	25	D	14	42 398	313	5.8	59.1	48.6
Smith	5 776	91 548	22 769	6 663	13 025	4 745	4 888	3 821	41 735	2 961	54.8	3.0	45.3
Somervell	196	3 394	474	118	210	45	101	185	54 478	350	38.6	14.0	37.7
Starr	550	9 402	5 191	37	1 822	327	147	187	19 911	1 165	16.8	26.3	39.5
Stephens	249	2 290	257	363	378	104	50	88	38 646	452	7.3	40.9	30.3
Sterling	54	646	D	NA	42	14	13	37	56 938	73	4.1	80.8	56.2
Stonewall	50	436	D	NA	41	D	16	17	39 076	356	5.3	45.5	34.0
Sutton	130	1 047	72	D	137	27	29	43	41 309	218	6.9	71.1	54.1
Swisher	139	936	195	114	151	43	26	29	31 206	565	19.6	46.5	54.2
Tarrant	40 484	752 869	97 766	81 074	101 104	45 396	39 067	36 162	48 033	1 278	74.0	3.6	28.7
Taylor	3 405	56 202	12 451	2 553	8 206	2 505	1 804	1 985	35 324	1 149	29.8	19.1	38.7
Terrell	13	46	D	NA	18	D	D	2	34 435	86	0.0	86.0	57.0
Terry	235	2 590	482	49	458	97	56	95	36 807	630	11.4	37.5	55.7
Throckmorton	51	251	79	D	16	14	D	7	28 781	275	5.5	49.1	49.1
Titus	635	14 533	2 442	6 219	1 813	474	135	472	32 453	801	35.8	5.7	37.5

Table B. States and Counties — **Agriculture**

STATE County	Land in farms — Acreage (1,000)	Percent change, 2007–2012	Acres — Average size of farm	Acres — Total irrigated (1,000)	Acres — Total cropland (1,000)	Value of land and buildings (dollars) — Average per farm	Value of land and buildings (dollars) — Average per acre	Value of machinery and equipment, average per farm (dollars)	Value of products sold — Total (mil dol)	Value of products sold — Average per farm (dollars)	Percent from: Crops	Percent from: Live-stock and poultry products	Percent of farms with sales of: $10,000 or more	Percent of farms with sales of: $100,000 or more	Government payments — Total ($1,000)	Government payments — Percent of farms
	117	118	119	120	121	122	123	124	125	126	127	128	129	130	131	132
TEXAS—Cont'd																
Mason	551	2.8	861	3.0	28.9	2 039 833	2 368	59 491	51.4	80 389	9.7	90.3	43.8	8.4	1 749	32.5
Matagorda	568	-1.7	664	32.7	177.0	1 315 683	1 983	126 209	129.7	151 522	59.4	40.6	48.7	16.2	5 271	34.6
Maverick	541	14.2	1 840	13.0	13.8	2 169 796	1 179	59 840	32.6	110 912	8.0	92.0	24.1	8.5	410	7.5
Medina	834	11.4	422	51.4	141.4	1 095 775	2 598	66 329	115.5	58 461	56.2	43.8	28.5	7.2	3 298	19.4
Menard	537	9.2	1 651	1.5	20.7	2 408 895	1 459	54 991	9.6	29 646	13.0	87.0	42.8	7.1	1 249	30.8
Midland	404	-11.4	749	10.7	62.4	1 072 641	1 432	83 080	17.2	31 876	65.7	34.3	17.6	5.0	1 866	23.5
Milam	528	-2.0	277	2.5	143.0	990 114	3 581	65 371	144.7	75 814	26.6	73.4	33.1	7.2	3 451	22.0
Mills	471	-0.6	542	3.3	57.5	1 204 675	2 223	58 645	43.0	49 462	12.6	87.4	40.9	4.8	1 277	22.2
Mitchell	573	-0.3	1 189	4.2	146.7	938 568	789	84 627	21.2	43 956	61.0	39.0	24.1	8.7	7 078	77.8
Montague	489	-3.7	336	0.6	74.0	840 349	2 500	59 290	44.9	30 902	18.7	81.3	32.9	5.7	1 034	14.4
Montgomery	155	-8.6	97	1.2	31.6	573 034	5 905	48 231	23.8	14 888	48.2	51.8	18.4	2.4	227	3.4
Moore	524	-5.4	2 006	122.4	263.6	1 884 521	939	303 854	605.0	2 318 107	19.4	80.6	57.1	39.8	6 010	68.6
Morris	92	7.2	223	0.0	18.1	468 248	2 100	55 663	46.9	113 922	4.9	95.1	41.3	10.4	99	9.2
Motley	595	3.6	2 658	4.2	65.8	1 960 781	738	69 571	12.8	57 143	24.5	75.5	42.0	15.2	1 767	74.6
Nacogdoches	265	-0.1	221	0.3	43.7	558 234	2 521	73 452	322.4	269 544	1.8	98.2	37.0	11.8	595	7.3
Navarro	558	-4.9	217	0.9	146.1	445 243	2 053	57 970	66.4	25 798	47.3	52.7	27.4	3.5	2 633	13.6
Newton	59	-0.8	131	0.0	8.9	261 813	2 004	54 300	2.9	6 551	35.4	64.7	17.1	0.7	D	0.7
Nolan	465	-13.9	973	3.3	118.2	1 093 607	1 124	81 916	23.8	49 847	52.0	48.0	26.2	7.5	3 074	57.3
Nueces	524	2.9	695	0.4	362.6	1 076 476	1 549	160 967	84.9	112 557	92.2	7.8	33.2	12.9	5 340	34.7
Ochiltree	545	-6.0	1 565	48.2	304.6	1 566 761	1 001	223 842	424.6	1 220 129	14.6	85.4	59.2	33.0	6 098	77.3
Oldham	830	-5.7	5 223	3.4	94.8	3 082 126	590	134 522	113.0	710 415	2.4	97.6	45.9	27.0	2 473	81.8
Orange	53	-17.2	79	0.4	6.7	261 493	3 323	47 335	4.3	6 461	44.2	55.8	11.3	0.9	112	1.5
Palo Pinto	593	7.6	446	0.7	55.4	1 074 703	2 407	51 951	53.8	40 472	18.4	81.6	24.8	4.0	489	6.5
Panola	227	4.4	211	0.7	38.6	442 762	2 101	66 066	93.3	86 466	6.0	94.0	34.5	5.8	156	4.7
Parker	494	12.0	113	2.2	93.9	567 100	5 012	49 848	74.3	17 000	20.8	79.2	17.3	2.5	294	2.4
Parmer	554	-1.3	971	163.0	444.7	1 010 667	1 040	277 575	1 329.5	2 332 523	9.9	90.1	59.3	42.1	11 381	83.3
Pecos	2 948	1.4	10 130	13.9	63.7	5 133 601	507	136 553	47.5	163 127	58.1	41.9	47.1	17.5	2 077	33.3
Polk	139	5.7	189	0.4	23.2	515 232	2 732	57 919	7.8	10 618	30.7	69.3	25.2	1.5	106	2.4
Potter	569	-0.8	2 204	3.1	54.2	1 208 547	548	66 465	21.0	81 287	7.7	92.3	29.5	12.0	1 092	22.1
Presidio	1 656	6.1	10 219	0.6	24.5	4 712 426	461	101 093	D	D	D	D	34.6	13.6	555	21.6
Rains	117	19.7	171	0.2	34.3	432 129	2 522	43 035	15.3	22 361	31.2	68.8	26.5	4.7	329	6.5
Randall	571	-0.7	640	15.9	250.8	642 873	1 004	77 600	540.3	605 734	2.9	97.1	29.8	10.0	5 003	42.9
Reagan	699	2.2	5 174	12.1	46.7	2 516 941	486	233 267	11.1	82 259	64.3	35.7	50.4	22.2	1 681	63.0
Real	321	-13.9	1 330	0.5	5.5	1 966 274	1 478	38 465	1.6	6 842	12.2	87.8	14.5	0.4	270	15.8
Red River	449	-0.2	394	2.8	94.7	654 453	1 662	73 917	53.5	46 997	26.5	73.5	42.0	7.5	1 949	18.9
Reeves	1 236	18.8	5 149	10.6	98.2	1 384 817	269	85 475	54.2	225 858	20.0	80.0	33.8	15.4	2 698	58.3
Refugio	475	-3.2	1 833	1.2	86.5	1 673 463	913	151 490	43.0	166 201	76.1	23.9	46.3	18.1	1 669	33.6
Roberts	562	15.9	5 257	6.3	49.3	3 455 290	657	143 140	16.4	153 271	31.5	68.5	57.0	31.8	1 122	57.9
Robertson	468	2.7	308	19.7	107.9	736 551	2 394	70 166	136.4	89 766	24.3	75.7	37.0	6.3	2 945	13.7
Rockwall	45	21.3	103	0.1	14.1	602 114	5 836	38 743	4.1	9 348	48.8	51.2	14.3	1.1	63	2.7
Runnels	666	1.5	720	4.5	247.9	931 382	1 294	89 466	47.4	51 272	62.3	37.7	42.8	10.9	6 002	68.8
Rusk	274	-8.8	197	0.4	47.5	431 437	2 186	58 886	75.3	54 175	25.6	74.4	24.7	3.3	295	2.4
Sabine	29	-8.5	144	0.2	4.6	392 557	2 718	84 005	14.7	73 274	3.8	96.2	31.3	3.0	22	9.0
San Augustine	73	0.3	239	0.0	8.9	552 167	2 310	122 351	63.2	207 262	2.0	98.0	42.6	11.1	25	6.2
San Jacinto	112	17.2	141	0.5	24.3	400 991	2 835	54 541	8.5	10 783	27.9	72.1	19.3	1.4	110	1.6
San Patricio	374	1.2	534	5.6	247.7	852 438	1 597	189 071	86.2	122 989	79.2	20.8	32.5	14.6	3 794	36.9
San Saba	671	-6.5	902	3.6	53.2	2 198 733	2 438	66 862	30.0	40 351	31.1	68.9	43.1	8.9	1 166	18.8
Schleicher	834	4.1	2 689	1.4	32.5	2 490 152	926	79 410	13.6	43 903	20.6	79.4	46.1	10.6	2 325	46.8
Scurry	494	-4.8	730	3.7	206.4	620 700	850	98 991	29.0	42 876	44.9	55.1	23.3	7.4	4 295	69.3
Shackelford	505	-8.5	2 168	D	55.0	2 371 000	1 093	83 609	22.3	95 854	11.6	88.4	54.5	15.9	1 604	53.2
Shelby	197	-0.3	188	1.8	36.4	550 712	2 927	92 111	473.3	451 610	2.1	97.9	46.6	21.6	334	3.9
Sherman	583	-0.2	1 863	126.6	339.1	2 006 652	1 077	378 847	590.4	1 886 121	21.9	78.1	46.3	37.7	6 153	83.1
Smith	302	0.0	102	2.5	77.1	386 589	3 786	43 300	76.8	25 934	77.5	22.5	18.6	2.6	189	1.8
Somervell	91	10.6	261	0.1	12.3	1 016 549	3 894	47 343	4.3	12 294	27.5	72.5	22.0	2.3	42	5.4
Starr	669	2.4	574	8.6	131.3	1 015 723	1 770	66 303	108.5	93 173	25.0	75.0	23.5	4.4	4 099	40.3
Stephens	517	20.4	1 143	D	54.4	1 599 708	1 399	58 681	9.2	20 392	11.6	88.4	37.6	3.1	777	30.3
Sterling	585	1.2	8 015	0.6	12.7	4 225 370	527	140 699	D	D	D	D	71.2	27.4	712	39.7
Stonewall	473	-2.6	1 328	0.7	79.5	955 171	719	52 202	47.4	133 275	5.3	94.7	35.4	6.2	2 288	80.9
Sutton	911	1.8	4 179	1.3	11.0	3 946 307	944	77 894	10.9	49 872	4.6	95.5	45.9	15.1	1 066	26.6
Swisher	546	-3.1	966	65.3	351.1	888 986	921	164 150	586.8	1 038 602	7.6	92.4	45.7	21.2	10 082	86.9
Tarrant	146	-5.6	114	0.9	38.0	722 473	6 339	54 282	34.6	27 076	72.8	27.2	18.0	4.1	109	2.8
Taylor	579	-0.1	504	1.1	158.9	570 210	1 132	55 372	37.6	32 746	27.7	72.3	23.8	4.1	3 600	37.7
Terrell	1 101	-15.5	12 800	0.3	2.0	4 976 860	389	57 116	3.1	35 686	D	D	39.5	9.3	507	22.1
Terry	442	-11.0	702	98.2	377.0	799 537	1 139	189 140	125.8	199 687	70.2	29.8	46.2	27.9	13 162	88.6
Throckmorton	508	-11.5	1 847	D	107.6	2 215 240	1 199	84 844	24.8	90 316	35.1	64.9	54.2	11.6	1 749	60.0
Titus	147	-11.9	183	D	31.1	471 061	2 575	53 954	81.2	101 401	4.5	95.5	35.3	6.1	112	7.6

Table B. States and Counties — Water Use, Wholesale Trade, Retail Trade, and Real Estate

STATE County	Water use, 2010		Wholesale trade,[1] 2012				Retail trade,[2] 2012				Real estate and rental and leasing,[2] 2012			
	Total water withdrawn (mil gal/day)	Gallons withdrawn per person per day	Number of establishments	Number of employees	Sales (mil dol)	Annual payroll (mil dol)	Number of establishments	Number of employees	Sales (mil dol)	Annual payroll (mil dol)	Number of establishments	Number of employees	Receipts (mil dol)	Annual payroll (mil dol)
	133	134	135	136	137	138	139	140	141	142	143	144	145	146
TEXAS—Cont'd														
Mason	5.2	1 306	8	D	D	D	25	140	36.4	2.6	4	5	2.0	0.2
Matagorda	210.5	5 736	31	123	104.9	4.5	128	1 241	324.6	25.7	33	170	32.1	7.5
Maverick	56.2	1 035	44	D	D	D	166	2 511	585.6	49.4	26	71	12.5	1.9
Medina	52.7	1 145	24	D	D	D	100	1 112	436.7	30.3	25	42	5.3	0.9
Menard	2.8	1 240	4	D	D	D	9	49	11.9	0.8	NA	NA	NA	NA
Midland	35.3	258	265	4 659	3 749.7	289.5	503	7 463	2 930.6	216.9	266	D	D	D
Milam	45.7	1 844	16	138	110.5	5.3	64	681	186.9	14.6	16	38	5.0	0.9
Mills	5.2	1 062	1	D	D	D	23	203	65.2	5.3	2	D	D	D
Mitchell	18.0	1 911	4	10	4.3	0.6	30	284	71.3	6.2	2	D	D	D
Montague	10.9	554	22	68	35.2	3.0	69	686	192.6	15.3	9	12	3.1	0.4
Montgomery	89.2	196	501	4 711	9 996.3	290.2	1 313	21 292	6 297.8	535.2	482	2 134	489.6	108.6
Moore	156.4	7 139	29	D	D	D	75	898	276.4	19.4	13	31	5.0	0.8
Morris	29.4	2 270	12	631	212.7	35.0	39	316	63.6	6.1	7	33	4.8	0.8
Motley	6.4	5 322	3	D	D	D	4	24	3.3	0.4	NA	NA	NA	NA
Nacogdoches	16.1	250	45	D	D	D	241	2 944	880.8	70.7	54	168	29.3	4.5
Navarro	51.2	1 073	29	D	D	D	163	2 039	539.2	46.1	48	136	19.4	3.3
Newton	6.2	429	4	D	D	D	32	177	73.3	3.5	NA	NA	NA	NA
Nolan	11.3	743	19	D	D	D	53	691	210.1	14.5	10	47	5.3	0.7
Nueces	235.0	691	361	4 987	5 153.6	264.8	1 128	17 030	5 138.3	418.1	414	2 868	667.2	132.2
Ochiltree	58.5	5 721	30	D	D	D	37	448	127.2	11.0	16	90	44.2	5.5
Oldham	5.8	2 836	2	D	D	D	7	D	D	D	NA	NA	NA	NA
Orange	411.3	5 026	36	D	D	D	269	3 310	909.6	71.8	59	272	58.3	8.7
Palo Pinto	50.4	1 794	23	267	121.4	11.8	118	1 089	281.8	23.1	28	91	16.9	3.2
Panola	17.4	733	23	D	D	D	81	939	228.7	20.7	26	155	24.8	6.1
Parker	22.6	193	97	1 053	779.1	41.6	316	4 515	1 772.7	128.0	88	302	55.0	9.5
Parmer	239.6	23 332	26	201	426.9	6.7	25	167	43.9	3.3	4	4	0.6	0.1
Pecos	145.1	9 356	16	166	135.6	8.0	58	645	185.9	14.4	9	64	11.8	2.2
Polk	558.9	12 308	19	99	45.9	4.3	128	1 738	474.6	40.9	30	87	17.6	3.0
Potter	5.6	46	169	D	D	D	555	D	D	D	167	827	162.2	29.0
Presidio	5.3	682	2	D	D	D	27	212	51.3	3.6	2	D	D	D
Rains	2.2	202	5	D	D	D	27	408	149.0	11.2	5	10	1.5	0.2
Randall	26.8	222	79	D	D	D	352	5 343	1 805.1	142.0	142	D	D	D
Reagan	25.6	7 594	5	D	D	D	9	60	29.2	1.6	1	D	D	D
Real	1.0	311	3	4	1.0	0.1	12	45	14.6	1.0	4	6	0.9	0.1
Red River	7.1	550	5	D	D	D	40	249	54.8	4.2	5	5	0.7	0.1
Reeves	56.9	4 129	7	D	D	D	29	425	162.0	9.0	8	29	8.1	1.1
Refugio	12.0	1 624	5	D	D	D	22	252	101.1	5.0	7	29	3.9	0.7
Roberts	21.1	22 680	NA	NA	NA	NA	2	D	D	D	NA	NA	NA	NA
Robertson	433.8	26 099	2	D	D	D	49	370	148.6	8.1	7	39	7.7	2.1
Rockwall	0.6	7	66	D	D	D	251	4 179	1 444.8	108.4	76	289	56.0	9.1
Runnels	7.8	743	5	D	D	D	47	473	139.8	10.3	2	D	D	D
Rusk	1 594.9	29 906	27	255	152.4	11.8	126	1 410	442.1	34.2	22	68	12.7	2.7
Sabine	2.2	202	1	D	D	D	31	310	65.6	5.4	4	2	0.1	0.0
San Augustine	3.1	350	4	12	2.9	0.4	24	215	58.2	4.8	6	10	0.6	0.2
San Jacinto	2.9	109	7	D	D	D	29	229	59.6	4.5	13	D	D	D
San Patricio	11.4	176	38	D	D	D	150	2 298	712.2	52.4	54	162	26.4	4.2
San Saba	7.0	1 137	9	61	14.1	1.1	35	198	45.3	3.7	3	3	0.2	0.1
Schleicher	2.7	766	3	D	D	D	10	56	12.3	1.2	NA	NA	NA	NA
Scurry	38.9	2 297	25	D	D	D	63	739	242.3	18.1	14	88	16.6	4.4
Shackelford	1.8	524	8	53	24.1	2.8	14	100	16.1	2.0	5	8	0.7	0.2
Shelby	13.5	530	10	D	D	D	93	1 087	302.1	24.3	22	91	9.8	2.5
Sherman	213.9	70 501	6	D	D	D	10	92	28.5	2.7	1	D	D	D
Smith	30.8	147	215	D	D	D	829	11 883	3 388.9	293.6	281	1 477	301.0	61.6
Somervell	2 043.9	240 736	6	46	25.8	1.9	30	218	47.8	4.3	10	17	2.4	0.3
Starr	26.2	429	24	D	D	D	135	1 735	435.4	33.6	14	45	5.6	0.9
Stephens	36.8	3 826	6	D	D	D	36	380	84.0	8.4	6	D	D	D
Sterling	2.0	1 724	2	D	D	D	3	D	D	D	1	D	D	D
Stonewall	2.5	1 698	2	D	D	D	6	35	8.9	0.6	1	D	D	D
Sutton	3.2	766	8	D	D	D	20	139	49.5	3.0	3	D	D	D
Swisher	104.4	13 296	13	55	23.4	1.8	20	152	51.5	2.9	3	6	0.4	0.1
Tarrant	286.1	158	1 944	34 600	30 173.3	1 974.7	5 705	91 200	28 908.8	2 381.7	1 826	12 190	2 647.1	528.7
Taylor	3.6	27	146	1 803	2 007.0	90.0	563	7 825	2 223.5	185.7	166	885	150.3	27.1
Terrell	1.5	1 514	NA	NA	NA	NA	4	19	5.0	0.4	NA	NA	NA	NA
Terry	132.5	10 473	18	D	D	D	43	453	131.5	10.1	8	D	D	D
Throckmorton	1.4	853	6	17	5.9	0.5	5	19	7.1	0.4	NA	NA	NA	NA
Titus	1 950.7	60 330	31	D	D	D	133	1 732	477.8	41.7	25	65	10.4	1.6

1. Merchant wholesalers, except manufacturers' sales branches and offices.   2. Employer establishments.

Table B. States and Counties — Professional Services, Manufacturing, and Accommodation and Food Services

STATE County	Professional, scientific, and technical services, 2012				Manufacturing, 2012				Accommodation and food services, 2012			
	Number of establish-ments	Number of employees	Receipts (mil dol)	Annual payroll (mil dol)	Number of establish-ments	Number of employees	Receipts (mil dol)	Annual payroll (mil dol)	Number of establish-ments	Number of employees	Sales (mil dol)	Annual payroll (mil dol)
	147	148	149	150	151	152	153	154	155	156	157	158
TEXAS—Cont'd												
Mason	14	D	D	D	6	29	5.3	1.2	14	D	D	D
Matagorda	43	162	11.8	4.2	28	513	1 657.5	41.4	84	1 045	51.5	14.0
Maverick	40	D	D	D	14	339	49.0	9.0	72	2 103	211.4	34.6
Medina	62	380	32.8	11.7	21	247	D	9.2	73	872	41.7	11.1
Menard	2	D	D	D	NA	NA	NA	NA	3	24	1.1	0.3
Midland	495	4 727	1 004.8	266.6	142	D	D	D	298	D	D	D
Milam	41	117	9.1	3.3	14	278	D	14.9	44	381	16.7	4.1
Mills	7	D	D	D	8	59	D	1.6	10	100	4.0	1.1
Mitchell	10	35	4.6	1.2	NA	NA	NA	NA	15	D	D	D
Montague	39	112	18.6	4.6	15	270	D	8.2	30	418	16.2	4.5
Montgomery	1 341	8 823	1 351.7	629.7	407	10 599	D	571.8	782	16 697	944.9	253.2
Moore	21	D	D	D	14	D	D	165.0	47	685	32.6	8.7
Morris	15	D	D	D	15	1 945	1 327.1	136.4	20	275	12.1	3.1
Motley	1	D	D	D	NA	NA	NA	NA	3	10	0.3	0.1
Nacogdoches	94	D	D	D	59	3 883	1 258.7	113.2	115	2 516	99.7	27.7
Navarro	59	298	24.0	8.0	55	2 834	1 046.9	115.2	63	1 017	50.7	13.0
Newton	9	58	4.1	1.5	6	81	D	1.3	3	27	0.4	0.2
Nolan	28	D	D	D	11	665	203.7	38.3	39	506	26.2	6.2
Nueces	812	5 789	849.1	309.6	193	7 063	41 840.9	514.2	849	17 049	892.8	242.4
Ochiltree	23	167	30.6	11.5	9	40	7.3	1.3	19	270	16.3	3.6
Oldham	NA	NA	NA	NA	NA	NA	NA	NA	9	54	2.0	0.5
Orange	92	501	57.9	23.0	74	5 287	6 340.3	426.6	140	2 002	101.2	25.5
Palo Pinto	39	211	33.7	8.6	33	1 325	460.4	55.2	73	1 023	47.1	13.2
Panola	39	206	25.3	8.0	16	905	281.9	29.6	30	419	17.8	4.8
Parker	208	892	115.3	37.7	127	2 360	582.9	109.6	190	3 237	152.0	42.0
Parmer	9	23	1.8	0.4	6	D	D	D	6	D	D	D
Pecos	16	60	2.4	1.8	4	14	D	D	43	627	36.6	7.8
Polk	73	340	30.5	10.1	25	1 227	362.5	58.1	57	940	44.5	11.9
Potter	322	1 967	414.6	115.3	125	11 535	D	716.9	366	D	D	D
Presidio	5	14	0.5	0.2	3	13	D	D	23	185	9.5	2.5
Rains	13	D	D	D	7	85	D	3.0	20	154	7.1	1.8
Randall	199	2 294	123.3	66.7	72	1 297	D	65.8	184	3 387	164.3	43.0
Reagan	7	26	1.8	0.6	NA	NA	NA	NA	7	D	D	D
Real	5	D	D	D	5	23	D	0.9	13	74	4.9	1.1
Red River	8	25	3.2	1.1	14	242	D	8.6	15	D	D	D
Reeves	16	D	D	D	3	6	2.0	D	32	434	33.9	6.4
Refugio	4	20	2.1	0.8	4	5	0.3	0.1	21	D	D	D
Roberts	1	D	D	D	NA	NA	NA	NA	1	D	D	D
Robertson	17	38	4.4	1.0	8	70	D	3.0	26	327	15.8	4.9
Rockwall	226	D	D	D	55	1 081	285.0	56.3	169	3 686	194.1	56.5
Runnels	13	D	D	D	14	505	297.9	18.8	17	D	D	D
Rusk	75	793	150.0	53.9	34	1 297	333.1	51.7	67	D	D	D
Sabine	16	D	D	D	4	309	D	D	15	77	3.9	0.7
San Augustine	7	D	D	D	5	85	D	2.3	7	D	D	D
San Jacinto	22	D	D	D	14	137	D	7.4	11	111	4.4	1.4
San Patricio	78	436	58.0	23.8	38	3 861	D	260.3	125	2 052	103.0	24.1
San Saba	16	39	4.2	1.2	7	30	D	1.4	18	D	D	D
Schleicher	4	D	D	D	NA	NA	NA	NA	1	D	D	D
Scurry	23	D	D	D	16	119	43.0	5.1	49	591	29.4	7.1
Shackelford	5	D	D	D	6	148	D	6.6	9	D	D	D
Shelby	32	133	19.7	4.5	23	2 465	577.3	72.1	34	D	D	D
Sherman	1	D	D	D	NA	NA	NA	NA	2	D	D	D
Smith	596	4 265	689.9	244.8	189	6 739	5 066.1	318.0	405	9 236	427.1	124.3
Somervell	14	59	9.7	3.8	6	33	D	1.1	28	455	23.0	7.4
Starr	30	D	D	D	6	29	2.3	0.6	51	648	35.5	8.2
Stephens	20	92	8.2	2.6	15	348	D	13.7	18	D	D	D
Sterling	2	D	D	D	NA	NA	NA	NA	3	D	D	D
Stonewall	3	D	D	D	NA	NA	NA	NA	5	22	0.8	payroll
Sutton	10	21	1.6	0.4	4	D	D	D	15	203	12.0	2.7
Swisher	7	25	1.5	0.7	8	75	D	3.1	13	D	D	D
Tarrant	4 314	39 363	6 258.9	2 258.2	1 568	70 421	45 771.0	3 894.9	3 474	77 362	4 483.6	1 188.2
Taylor	274	1 775	183.3	72.7	95	2 098	913.9	87.8	301	6 435	303.2	85.3
Terrell	2	D	D	D	NA	NA	NA	NA	5	11	0.4	0.0
Terry	15	61	4.7	1.2	5	22	D	0.8	23	280	15.4	3.4
Throckmorton	2	D	D	D	NA	NA	NA	NA	4	D	D	D
Titus	29	D	D	D	40	5 865	1 341.0	162.5	62	1 229	54.8	15.2

1. Establishment subject to federal tax.

Table B. States and Counties — **Health Care and Social Assistance, Other Services, Nonemployer Businesses, and Residential Construction**

STATE County	Health care and social assistance, 2012				Other services, 2012				Nonemployer businesses, 2015		Value of residential construction authorized by building permits, 2016	
	Number of establish-ments	Number of employees	Receipts (mil dol)	Annual payroll (mil dol)	Number of establish-ments	Number of employees	Receipts (mil dol)	Annual payroll (mil dol)	Number	Receipts (mil dol)	New Construction ($1,000)	Number of housing units
	159	160	161	162	163	164	165	166	167	168	169	170
TEXAS—Cont'd												
Mason	11	98	5.1	2.7	8	19	2.5	0.4	604	24.2	262	3
Matagorda	79	1 418	151.0	48.1	60	282	31.9	9.3	2 706	118.3	24 098	82
Maverick	96	4 039	213.0	84.4	37	145	9.5	2.5	4 394	157.5	9 682	76
Medina	69	935	55.0	25.4	40	200	18.0	4.4	3 300	146.0	5 762	29
Menard	2	D	D	D	2	D	D	D	291	10.8	NA	NA
Midland	398	7 196	817.7	299.7	264	2 138	337.4	73.6	16 137	1 114.6	129 864	672
Milam	38	791	51.8	22.9	32	117	10.7	2.6	1 614	67.2	1 442	12
Mills	13	156	7.9	3.7	7	D	D	D	452	16.0	NA	NA
Mitchell	8	D	D	D	5	17	1.2	0.3	468	16.1	0	0
Montague	40	643	46.1	19.4	37	122	11.1	2.7	1 918	91.5	152	1
Montgomery	1 015	15 877	2 147.8	724.1	579	4 253	353.2	111.7	45 630	2 624.9	1 050 358	5 537
Moore	43	680	49.6	21.7	27	109	11.9	2.6	1 109	57.5	1 943	10
Morris	23	257	11.9	5.8	17	78	9.9	2.0	834	30.2	1 594	4
Motley	1	D	D	D	2	D	D	D	116	3.4	NA	NA
Nacogdoches	202	3 339	353.7	119.6	85	427	37.1	9.6	4 003	173.6	3 663	28
Navarro	130	2 338	163.0	65.3	63	214	21.0	5.1	3 257	135.0	21 050	178
Newton	9	D	D	D	5	D	D	D	611	21.3	NA	NA
Nolan	32	D	D	D	15	D	D	D	1 037	36.7	160	1
Nueces	1 045	28 174	2 640.5	984.5	522	4 501	525.5	143.9	23 811	1 070.6	231 224	1 237
Ochiltree	20	D	D	D	24	101	11.6	2.8	804	43.0	5 965	50
Oldham	2	D	D	D	2	D	D	D	204	8.1	512	2
Orange	141	1 419	119.6	43.3	85	D	D	D	4 861	180.1	46 629	252
Palo Pinto	49	670	89.0	31.5	37	145	16.9	3.9	2 167	107.2	1 838	9
Panola	43	653	56.1	19.7	27	126	12.7	3.2	1 670	76.5	1 200	6
Parker	207	D	D	D	150	914	79.0	23.9	12 490	698.5	99 356	465
Parmer	9	140	14.3	4.9	19	D	D	D	512	27.5	25	1
Pecos	17	470	51.9	17.6	23	114	10.6	3.1	939	37.2	1 751	112
Polk	72	1 413	121.7	45.6	43	268	19.6	5.5	3 748	172.1	96 408	471
Potter	460	D	D	D	237	1 916	253.5	60.9	8 268	444.3	158 078	639
Presidio	4	41	2.6	1.3	4	14	0.5	0.2	836	28.7	2 165	11
Rains	12	144	7.8	3.1	12	D	D	D	846	38.4	204	1
Randall	235	D	D	D	162	D	D	D	10 470	484.9	18 778	85
Reagan	5	D	D	D	8	D	D	D	398	14.9	204	1
Real	10	199	8.5	4.3	2	D	D	D	454	21.4	0	0
Red River	16	395	29.8	12.2	7	D	D	D	896	42.9	523	8
Reeves	10	D	D	D	11	D	D	D	701	38.5	540	3
Refugio	8	257	23.0	7.3	7	23	1.9	0.6	505	25.3	767	7
Roberts	NA	NA	NA	NA	NA	NA	NA	NA	97	3.4	NA	NA
Robertson	18	D	D	D	24	139	19.2	5.5	1 235	54.6	17 771	79
Rockwall	234	3 578	472.7	146.0	96	741	53.4	16.9	9 063	534.9	353 719	1 116
Runnels	19	387	24.8	12.0	14	D	D	D	886	33.1	385	2
Rusk	73	1 596	104.0	41.2	41	275	23.2	7.6	3 170	136.0	581	2
Sabine	14	320	12.7	6.3	14	45	3.7	0.9	715	28.0	418	3
San Augustine	17	393	20.8	8.4	5	D	D	D	518	18.8	0	0
San Jacinto	11	138	7.4	3.1	12	40	4.6	1.0	1 905	79.1	53 433	265
San Patricio	97	1 722	113.9	50.0	64	342	42.4	11.4	4 623	178.4	70 916	484
San Saba	17	194	15.3	4.6	6	D	D	D	576	22.7	743	7
Schleicher	3	D	D	D	1	D	D	D	322	12.4	120	1
Scurry	22	538	60.3	19.5	29	251	38.3	9.4	1 153	46.9	1 546	8
Shackelford	4	D	D	D	7	8	1.0	0.2	477	24.8	NA	NA
Shelby	40	820	49.2	19.4	30	D	D	D	1 656	77.7	0	0
Sherman	2	D	D	D	4	7	0.5	0.1	231	11.1	1 066	12
Smith	640	21 211	2 527.9	969.6	347	2 613	252.8	87.5	18 125	911.4	149 444	581
Somervell	15	D	D	D	12	D	D	D	730	34.7	3 012	31
Starr	100	5 009	170.5	85.9	21	D	D	D	6 653	175.0	80	4
Stephens	19	314	19.5	9.6	17	56	4.5	1.1	891	49.3	97	2
Sterling	2	D	D	D	2	D	D	D	170	6.7	NA	NA
Stonewall	6	D	D	D	3	6	0.5	0.1	142	6.0	NA	NA
Sutton	4	61	7.4	2.9	9	13	2.1	0.5	414	14.2	2 342	12
Swisher	10	206	15.7	5.9	15	D	D	D	485	15.2	0	0
Tarrant	4 575	91 404	11 276.2	4 009.1	2 390	19 504	2 118.4	563.0	162 998	7 691.1	2 113 588	12 506
Taylor	389	11 883	1 026.5	403.9	224	1 763	145.6	40.3	9 861	468.8	55 547	304
Terrell	1	D	D	D	2	D	D	D	91	2.2	NA	NA
Terry	21	446	31.9	12.1	22	63	5.1	1.6	615	24.3	0	0
Throckmorton	3	D	D	D	4	8	0.6	0.1	223	8.4	NA	NA
Titus	88	D	D	D	41	204	19.9	4.8	1 754	77.9	2 442	19

Table B. States and Counties — Government Employment and Payroll, and Local Government Finances

	Government employment and payroll, 2012									Local government finances, 2012				
			March payroll (percent of total)							General revenue				
												Taxes		
													Per capita[1] (dollars)	
STATE County	Full-time equivalent employees	March payroll (dollars)	Administration, judicial, and legal	Police and Corrections	Fire Protection	Highways and transportation	Health and Welfare	Natural resources and utilities	Education and libraries	Total (mil dol)	Inter-governmental (mil dol)	Total (mil dol)	Total	Property
	171	172	173	174	175	176	177	178	179	180	181	182	183	184
TEXAS—Cont'd														
Mason	187	574 614	8.5	5.1	0.0	5.6	6.2	8.5	64.4	12.7	4.9	6.2	1 550	1 351
Matagorda	1 950	6 092 071	4.5	8.9	0.0	2.4	17.9	4.6	60.5	272.8	55.1	91.7	2 509	2 321
Maverick	3 274	9 420 323	4.8	5.7	1.7	2.4	2.2	3.5	79.0	215.5	121.7	45.7	826	606
Medina	2 042	6 076 041	4.7	6.4	0.0	2.1	11.3	4.7	68.9	144.1	64.8	47.3	1 012	893
Menard	160	407 534	7.5	8.8	0.0	1.5	18.9	3.1	58.6	9.7	3.2	4.0	1 788	1 631
Midland	6 743	26 604 150	5.0	7.8	4.1	1.5	30.2	1.5	47.9	761.2	127.7	334.2	2 279	1 657
Milam	1 010	3 486 020	6.1	8.9	0.2	4.0	1.5	3.6	74.9	75.2	30.4	35.9	1 485	1 337
Mills	267	764 983	7.7	3.6	0.0	3.0	2.7	4.7	78.1	16.6	9.4	5.5	1 135	994
Mitchell	583	1 683 044	7.8	5.5	0.2	3.5	33.1	3.1	46.1	46.4	10.5	19.0	2 033	1 894
Montague	1 080	3 133 643	3.8	5.6	1.7	2.8	25.9	4.1	52.2	89.9	35.1	30.6	1 565	1 349
Montgomery	15 517	53 618 969	5.3	8.9	4.3	1.6	4.2	3.6	70.3	1 469.3	416.6	880.8	1 816	1 602
Moore	1 387	4 297 575	5.7	7.6	1.6	2.0	18.7	4.0	59.3	101.2	21.6	47.4	2 125	1 879
Morris	525	1 489 068	7.2	8.0	0.0	2.6	0.2	4.5	77.3	33.3	11.9	17.9	1 399	1 218
Motley	53	139 031	14.8	3.4	0.0	11.8	4.1	2.8	61.5	4.2	1.7	2.0	1 659	1 542
Nacogdoches	3 209	11 081 415	3.8	5.6	2.6	0.8	27.6	2.8	56.3	249.0	82.9	70.1	1 062	894
Navarro	2 582	8 615 927	4.3	7.4	1.8	2.3	3.2	3.1	74.7	198.0	85.4	69.3	1 444	1 208
Newton	492	1 402 695	9.9	5.3	0.0	3.1	1.3	4.5	74.9	46.4	14.2	18.8	1 321	1 309
Nolan	1 074	3 200 019	5.7	6.5	2.3	1.6	30.0	3.7	48.4	92.2	25.3	33.8	2 265	1 854
Nueces	15 002	50 012 628	4.7	10.3	4.3	5.0	3.5	5.4	62.9	1 333.3	434.9	623.4	1 793	1 377
Ochiltree	750	1 938 537	5.3	7.0	1.8	3.2	23.4	3.9	53.5	38.3	10.0	24.3	2 264	1 986
Oldham	268	808 206	6.5	4.6	0.0	1.8	0.0	1.4	85.2	17.9	9.3	4.2	2 028	1 796
Orange	3 533	11 142 459	7.8	12.4	2.2	3.6	1.2	10.2	61.9	284.3	105.6	118.8	1 432	1 208
Palo Pinto	1 439	4 512 709	5.6	7.4	0.8	3.8	30.1	2.6	48.2	125.0	32.7	53.6	1 926	1 663
Panola	1 035	3 674 945	5.9	7.4	0.6	4.5	0.6	2.7	77.7	119.5	26.6	78.0	3 248	3 005
Parker	3 910	13 841 811	8.1	6.9	2.5	2.7	2.3	3.6	72.3	342.4	84.3	203.7	1 701	1 506
Parmer	674	1 770 342	9.3	9.6	0.0	4.1	7.1	4.4	65.0	56.5	17.4	22.7	2 231	2 142
Pecos	928	3 033 599	8.3	7.8	0.0	4.3	11.7	7.2	58.4	127.5	16.7	76.1	4 873	4 588
Polk	1 509	6 360 260	11.3	19.6	0.0	3.8	2.1	6.1	56.0	118.9	38.8	47.9	1 049	878
Potter	8 893	30 669 359	4.8	10.2	6.1	3.0	6.5	3.7	64.1	740.4	307.7	290.5	2 375	1 650
Presidio	514	1 310 951	9.3	7.0	0.0	3.7	6.0	5.4	67.8	35.4	22.2	7.8	1 041	903
Rains	490	1 074 762	8.2	7.5	0.0	2.1	0.3	4.6	75.7	30.7	11.0	16.4	1 498	1 297
Randall	1 728	5 466 299	10.7	21.4	1.0	1.7	0.6	1.5	61.9	119.8	28.9	76.8	614	566
Reagan	366	1 075 023	9.6	7.2	0.4	4.0	23.8	3.8	50.1	44.4	3.9	33.4	9 618	8 897
Real	97	286 334	19.1	8.8	0.0	5.7	12.5	1.5	51.9	7.4	1.1	5.5	1 637	1 475
Red River	579	1 522 449	5.6	7.7	1.5	3.4	0.0	3.7	77.9	37.1	22.5	10.9	857	736
Reeves	1 448	3 858 596	5.2	36.7	1.3	1.5	16.8	4.5	33.4	149.1	13.2	27.3	1 981	1 689
Refugio	551	1 642 349	7.4	7.5	0.7	4.5	25.8	3.6	49.3	40.3	10.7	21.9	3 017	2 809
Roberts	81	227 300	16.9	8.7	0.0	5.2	2.4	7.8	59.0	9.8	1.4	7.9	9 265	8 938
Robertson	905	2 580 494	9.2	10.0	0.0	3.8	0.5	5.5	69.4	85.5	23.3	56.6	3 421	3 199
Rockwall	3 263	11 181 638	8.8	10.5	1.2	0.8	0.1	2.9	74.8	283.0	72.7	179.3	2 159	1 870
Runnels	671	2 087 986	8.8	8.8	0.6	3.6	22.7	8.6	45.9	42.1	20.2	12.8	1 230	1 099
Rusk	1 692	6 115 196	8.9	12.8	1.3	2.9	0.5	7.7	64.0	130.2	38.5	76.0	1 407	1 267
Sabine	470	1 232 799	8.2	5.9	0.0	2.1	12.7	6.2	63.1	31.3	14.1	9.8	938	790
San Augustine	376	978 889	9.7	7.9	0.0	4.2	0.9	5.0	71.7	33.0	20.0	10.7	1 214	1 066
San Jacinto	778	2 008 317	6.5	5.3	0.1	3.0	0.8	1.6	81.9	49.7	19.2	26.2	965	899
San Patricio	3 506	9 765 866	4.9	8.3	1.0	2.9	7.6	7.3	67.8	239.0	100.4	101.3	1 544	1 330
San Saba	434	1 149 764	5.8	3.1	0.0	36.7	1.6	5.8	45.2	25.2	16.5	6.7	1 112	1 001
Schleicher	239	526 633	7.5	4.0	0.0	5.0	19.5	5.6	57.3	13.1	4.2	6.5	2 000	1 918
Scurry	995	3 410 030	6.1	6.6	1.3	2.1	20.3	2.2	60.2	121.2	28.5	57.3	3 345	2 945
Shackelford	207	556 026	10.6	6.6	0.0	5.6	3.6	4.5	68.0	12.7	3.6	7.4	2 193	1 913
Shelby	1 249	3 791 323	5.4	6.0	0.5	2.4	0.0	3.4	81.5	78.9	40.8	30.6	1 176	971
Sherman	266	825 372	8.9	3.5	0.0	4.4	16.5	9.6	54.1	17.5	2.5	11.5	3 752	3 455
Smith	8 764	29 028 100	7.6	10.8	2.8	1.5	6.8	3.6	65.8	648.3	207.0	325.4	1 515	1 170
Somervell	476	1 533 907	6.3	9.3	0.2	6.9	1.2	3.4	65.6	85.7	11.9	48.2	5 603	5 421
Starr	4 112	12 165 296	5.7	7.0	1.5	2.0	8.1	2.5	71.6	268.0	173.1	50.8	825	734
Stephens	543	1 467 714	8.2	6.9	1.9	2.5	26.7	3.6	48.8	27.8	5.2	19.3	2 044	1 781
Sterling	86	271 999	21.3	6.6	0.0	4.1	0.0	5.7	60.3	15.5	4.1	9.5	8 008	7 790
Stonewall	209	553 406	6.8	2.8	0.0	10.2	50.6	1.9	26.7	13.8	2.1	5.3	3 967	3 683
Sutton	312	1 080 664	8.3	4.9	0.0	4.6	23.3	3.3	51.3	24.7	7.3	14.2	3 596	3 274
Swisher	403	1 118 598	6.5	7.0	0.0	2.6	0.9	4.3	77.3	36.9	14.7	7.6	964	823
Tarrant	76 274	291 509 259	6.4	12.5	4.8	1.5	9.8	4.8	58.6	7 673.3	2 064.9	3 815.1	2 029	1 629
Taylor	5 091	16 346 681	6.1	13.5	5.9	1.9	5.4	4.7	60.8	427.2	176.5	186.9	1 401	997
Terrell	108	366 799	22.2	0.0	0.0	7.7	5.5	4.7	44.6	12.5	1.9	9.9	10 751	10 482
Terry	926	2 466 610	5.9	8.0	1.0	2.6	26.1	3.6	51.2	56.3	12.9	26.6	2 108	1 903
Throckmorton	113	346 336	4.5	0.0	0.0	1.3	25.5	5.9	62.6	9.8	3.2	3.9	2 462	2 280
Titus	2 456	7 751 640	2.6	4.2	1.3	1.2	29.0	2.5	58.4	124.8	50.8	52.8	1 617	1 410

1. Based on the resident population estimated as of July 1 of the year shown.

Table B. States and Counties — Local Government Finances, Government Employment, and Income Taxes

STATE County	Local government finances, 2012 (cont.) Direct general expenditure Total (mil dol)	Per capita[1] (dollars)	Percent of total for: Education	Health and hospitals	Police protection	Public welfare	Highways	Debt outstanding Total (mil dol)	Per capita[1] (dollars)	Government employment, 2015 Federal civilian	Federal military	State and local	Individual income tax returns, 2014 Number of returns	Mean adjusted gross income	Mean income tax
	185	186	187	188	189	190	191	192	193	194	195	196	197	198	199
TEXAS—Cont'd															
Mason	11.2	2 787	63.4	2.7	6.9	0.1	5.9	3.4	853	14	D	272	1 820	51 318	6 833
Matagorda	250.1	6 844	32.2	45.6	2.8	0.0	2.5	242.4	6 631	82	74	2 342	16 240	54 182	6 188
Maverick	219.2	3 958	56.6	2.8	3.8	0.0	8.5	215.3	3 888	886	116	5 185	25 000	35 831	2 320
Medina	151.4	3 238	58.2	13.0	3.7	0.4	3.0	135.1	2 888	59	94	2 955	19 470	55 603	6 503
Menard	9.9	4 437	46.2	0.0	6.1	23.8	3.2	1.6	696	D	D	190	920	40 977	4 515
Midland	747.6	5 098	34.2	40.2	3.6	0.0	1.3	587.4	4 005	539	325	8 561	74 720	119 325	24 081
Milam	70.4	2 914	62.9	2.6	4.1	0.6	7.3	71.3	2 950	49	49	1 210	10 260	46 989	5 073
Mills	17.5	3 633	61.9	2.4	3.5	0.4	4.0	5.4	1 116	14	10	348	2 090	50 473	6 642
Mitchell	47.8	5 118	43.4	36.9	2.7	0.1	3.9	37.5	4 017	22	14	1 175	3 050	52 131	5 549
Montague	91.2	4 662	32.2	41.0	3.2	0.2	3.8	35.2	1 798	47	39	1 245	8 310	59 400	7 636
Montgomery	1 474.0	3 039	50.5	6.5	5.6	0.1	4.0	4 045.0	8 339	853	1 090	25 535	232 340	102 057	17 869
Moore	95.6	4 283	47.6	26.8	5.1	0.1	0.9	47.9	2 146	66	45	1 602	9 510	45 614	4 379
Morris	30.0	2 343	68.2	0.1	4.2	0.6	3.3	10.3	804	29	25	631	5 390	43 362	4 438
Motley	4.0	3 301	70.6	4.0	1.7	0.1	5.8	0.1	49	10	D	95	480	39 944	3 829
Nacogdoches	257.8	3 903	37.6	34.4	3.9	0.9	1.9	196.8	2 981	149	131	5 367	25 250	48 865	5 684
Navarro	194.1	4 045	64.8	2.1	5.7	0.3	4.2	235.6	4 910	93	97	3 237	20 230	45 643	4 945
Newton	45.7	3 222	44.4	0.0	8.1	1.7	3.7	33.4	2 356	21	27	611	4 880	47 891	4 509
Nolan	90.3	6 050	47.2	28.5	3.6	0.0	3.1	76.3	5 116	39	30	1 552	6 470	49 616	5 507
Nueces	1 384.5	3 982	48.2	4.5	6.3	0.1	3.8	2 805.4	8 069	6 007	2 970	21 752	157 370	57 421	7 842
Ochiltree	30.1	2 806	68.7	0.5	3.5	0.0	4.9	31.4	2 924	18	22	803	4 710	88 986	15 466
Oldham	17.7	8 594	83.4	0.0	4.2	0.0	2.0	4.6	2 220	D	D	284	910	51 315	5 286
Orange	269.5	3 248	46.6	0.7	7.3	0.2	3.2	736.8	8 880	100	170	4 094	36 920	56 922	6 427
Palo Pinto	119.5	4 289	40.7	32.3	3.8	0.0	3.5	91.1	3 271	55	56	1 712	11 820	54 027	6 996
Panola	120.9	5 033	70.2	0.4	3.5	0.2	6.0	54.6	2 272	70	48	1 369	9 980	67 527	10 137
Parker	370.5	3 095	53.1	7.2	4.5	0.0	11.8	720.3	6 017	176	255	5 126	56 030	78 324	11 919
Parmer	51.6	5 067	48.1	20.9	4.1	4.3	4.2	28.1	2 758	67	20	811	4 210	41 081	3 406
Pecos	125.4	8 031	44.7	24.0	3.2	0.0	4.0	74.8	4 792	54	29	1 878	6 250	54 746	6 612
Polk	109.6	2 400	62.3	0.6	6.0	0.2	7.5	278.0	6 089	77	87	2 916	22 130	52 408	5 780
Potter	749.2	6 124	53.7	5.1	5.8	0.0	2.4	762.3	6 231	1 964	368	13 002	51 760	51 906	7 198
Presidio	41.0	5 442	67.0	0.7	1.8	0.0	1.4	21.5	2 854	304	14	633	3 600	43 312	5 519
Rains	31.1	2 840	44.9	2.6	3.6	0.5	6.4	25.3	2 316	20	23	471	4 250	48 755	5 188
Randall	116.9	935	49.6	1.1	7.6	0.1	3.1	128.5	1 027	186	260	4 249	59 680	65 378	8 611
Reagan	38.8	11 153	53.5	17.4	3.8	0.3	7.7	32.0	9 222	13	D	399	1 690	75 921	11 593
Real	6.9	2 039	48.7	0.5	9.4	2.4	11.7	0.3	75	D	D	203	1 500	43 486	4 607
Red River	37.7	2 968	74.1	0.1	2.9	1.4	1.5	18.4	1 453	37	25	698	5 210	41 893	4 278
Reeves	138.8	10 063	21.0	12.8	3.3	0.0	1.6	136.0	9 859	68	24	1 573	5 090	62 298	10 052
Refugio	40.6	5 594	55.7	13.7	4.6	0.0	5.7	20.5	2 822	32	15	688	3 450	62 465	8 778
Roberts	9.1	10 678	90.1	0.4	2.2	0.0	2.1	0.7	768	D	D	104	410	88 573	15 754
Robertson	89.0	5 381	81.1	0.1	3.4	0.3	3.2	84.0	5 080	42	34	1 018	7 470	47 264	5 364
Rockwall	297.5	3 584	49.5	0.4	5.7	0.2	5.2	881.6	10 619	96	184	3 490	39 560	87 339	13 227
Runnels	43.0	4 112	51.2	23.8	1.8	0.0	4.7	11.5	1 101	40	21	798	4 650	45 420	4 504
Rusk	130.1	2 408	66.3	0.4	4.6	0.1	6.1	181.9	3 368	69	98	2 400	20 860	53 374	5 741
Sabine	29.1	2 787	50.7	22.5	5.3	0.0	6.3	11.3	1 081	45	21	500	4 240	51 396	5 703
San Augustine	28.0	3 179	73.4	1.6	6.1	0.0	0.7	34.8	3 949	20	17	399	3 300	41 028	3 632
San Jacinto	46.2	1 704	66.1	0.2	5.1	0.5	6.7	34.4	1 269	24	56	898	10 120	51 221	5 764
San Patricio	237.2	3 616	57.1	6.5	5.8	0.3	3.2	231.1	3 524	89	1 579	3 911	31 200	54 714	6 600
San Saba	18.5	3 087	57.6	1.7	4.5	1.1	6.8	15.9	2 642	21	11	482	2 410	45 006	5 024
Schleicher	13.7	4 190	45.0	27.0	0.7	0.0	3.4	34.9	10 699	15	D	266	1 270	64 328	8 669
Scurry	113.5	6 628	57.4	17.4	3.7	0.1	3.7	74.5	4 348	34	32	1 743	7 190	68 253	9 445
Shackelford	11.4	3 400	61.4	4.1	6.5	0.0	5.6	0.9	262	13	D	224	1 510	85 772	14 774
Shelby	75.6	2 905	71.6	0.6	5.1	0.0	6.1	42.1	1 619	72	51	1 310	10 350	46 425	4 896
Sherman	18.7	6 099	54.0	15.6	4.5	0.0	6.0	3.1	1 017	D	D	272	1 110	53 514	5 996
Smith	645.1	3 003	55.0	5.1	5.6	0.2	3.4	1 145.0	5 330	631	468	13 278	97 400	60 868	8 396
Somervell	86.1	10 008	49.0	29.8	3.5	0.5	3.8	65.4	7 610	13	17	874	3 720	64 218	7 876
Starr	254.5	4 130	66.2	11.4	3.9	0.0	3.6	277.9	4 510	748	128	5 243	24 290	31 960	1 751
Stephens	27.4	2 898	46.7	2.5	5.2	0.1	3.9	19.2	2 029	16	18	665	3 720	52 004	6 622
Sterling	17.5	14 668	64.5	1.9	2.1	15.3	2.0	10.2	8 554	D	D	164	570	113 530	24 233
Stonewall	23.1	15 635	13.2	76.1	1.3	0.0	2.7	0.1	57	14	D	233	620	55 060	6 769
Sutton	22.3	5 656	62.2	17.0	3.3	0.1	3.4	1.6	405	D	D	437	1 860	74 400	10 963
Swisher	30.7	3 895	48.7	32.1	4.0	0.0	0.8	3.2	409	25	14	722	2 860	41 955	4 414
Tarrant	7 651.9	4 070	42.5	12.1	6.9	0.1	3.7	19 647.2	10 450	14 446	5 448	96 074	896 590	67 932	9 889
Taylor	402.0	3 012	53.5	4.7	7.8	0.6	3.1	263.9	1 977	1 091	4 302	8 547	60 630	55 495	7 142
Terrell	12.1	13 215	63.5	3.9	7.6	0.0	8.3	21.1	22 972	57	D	123	360	57 425	6 422
Terry	59.1	4 683	48.8	27.3	3.7	0.4	3.1	17.6	1 397	22	24	1 072	4 850	41 929	4 098
Throckmorton	9.9	6 177	38.7	32.3	0.8	0.0	11.7	0.2	137	D	D	174	680	71 699	12 940
Titus	127.0	3 889	67.0	0.4	4.2	0.1	6.4	228.1	6 985	93	65	2 805	13 550	49 139	5 380

1. Based on the resident population estimated as of July 1 of the year shown.

Table B. States and Counties — **Land Area and Population**

STATE/ County code	CBSA code[1]	County type[2]	STATE County	Land area,[3] (sq mi) 2016	Total persons 2016	Rank	Per square mile	White	Black	American Indian, Alaska Native	Asian and Pacific Islander	Percent Hispanic or Latino[4]	Under 5 years	5 to 17 years	18 to 24 years	25 to 34 years	35 to 44 years	45 to 54 years
				1	2	3	4	5	6	7	8	9	10	11	12	13	14	15
			TEXAS—Cont'd															
48 451	41660	3	Tom Green	1 522.0	118 386	523	77.8	55.3	4.4	0.8	1.8	39.3	6.9	16.7	12.1	15.7	11.0	10.8
48 453	12420	1	Travis	991.8	1 199 323	36	1 209.2	51.1	8.7	0.7	7.7	33.8	6.6	15.9	9.4	20.1	15.7	12.8
48 455	26660	7	Trinity	693.6	14 442	2 132	20.8	80.1	9.9	1.2	0.6	9.6	5.0	15.0	6.9	9.5	10.1	12.2
48 457	...	6	Tyler	924.5	21 320	1 760	23.1	80.6	11.5	1.1	0.8	7.4	5.0	14.4	8.8	13.5	11.1	12.0
48 459	30980	3	Upshur	582.9	40 969	1 154	70.3	82.4	9.0	1.4	0.7	8.3	6.0	17.8	8.0	11.6	11.4	13.1
48 461	...	8	Upton	1 241.3	3 673	2 927	3.0	43.5	2.4	1.4	0.7	53.0	8.5	20.6	8.0	14.0	12.2	10.5
48 463	46620	6	Uvalde	1 551.9	27 285	1 521	17.6	27.4	0.8	0.5	0.8	71.0	7.5	20.1	10.7	12.6	11.2	10.8
48 465	19620	5	Val Verde	3 144.8	48 881	1 002	15.5	16.1	1.5	0.4	0.9	81.7	8.7	20.0	11.3	14.1	11.8	10.8
48 467	...	6	Van Zandt	842.6	54 355	926	64.5	85.5	3.3	1.4	0.6	10.6	5.7	17.4	7.5	10.4	11.1	13.4
48 469	47020	3	Victoria	882.1	92 467	632	104.8	46.1	6.4	0.5	1.6	46.3	7.1	18.7	9.4	14.2	11.8	11.5
48 471	26660	4	Walker	784.2	71 484	757	91.2	57.6	23.4	0.7	1.5	18.0	4.5	10.9	19.6	14.8	13.1	13.9
48 473	26420	1	Waller	513.3	50 115	983	97.6	44.1	25.6	0.7	1.2	29.6	6.6	17.5	21.5	10.5	10.0	11.1
48 475	...	6	Ward	835.6	11 600	2 313	13.9	41.8	4.8	1.1	0.8	52.9	8.0	20.4	8.7	13.9	12.1	11.4
48 477	14780	6	Washington	604.0	35 056	1 301	58.0	65.0	17.5	0.6	2.4	15.6	6.0	15.5	10.9	10.5	10.3	12.0
48 479	29700	2	Webb	3 361.5	271 193	250	80.7	3.7	0.3	0.1	0.6	95.5	10.0	23.8	11.4	13.3	12.9	11.2
48 481	20900	4	Wharton	1 086.2	41 735	1 134	38.4	45.6	13.3	0.4	0.6	40.7	6.7	19.2	9.1	12.2	11.0	12.3
48 483	...	9	Wheeler	914.5	5 546	2 797	6.1	69.2	3.5	1.1	1.1	26.7	7.5	18.6	8.0	11.6	11.2	10.9
48 485	48660	3	Wichita	627.8	131 838	482	210.0	67.7	11.3	1.4	3.0	18.9	6.6	15.9	13.5	15.0	11.2	11.3
48 487	46900	6	Wilbarger	970.9	12 892	2 235	13.3	60.2	8.4	1.5	3.2	28.5	6.2	16.8	9.4	13.5	10.9	11.9
48 489	39700	6	Willacy	590.6	21 810	1 735	36.9	9.2	2.0	0.2	0.7	88.1	6.6	17.6	13.4	15.5	13.1	10.6
48 491	12420	1	Williamson	1 118.3	528 718	130	472.8	62.5	7.1	0.8	7.7	24.1	6.7	19.6	7.9	13.9	16.1	13.6
48 493	41700	1	Wilson	803.7	48 480	1 013	60.3	58.6	1.8	0.8	0.7	39.0	6.0	18.3	8.4	11.2	12.2	14.4
48 495	...	6	Winkler	841.1	7 893	2 605	9.4	36.1	2.4	0.7	0.7	60.8	8.8	21.4	10.3	13.3	11.9	12.5
48 497	19100	1	Wise	904.4	64 455	821	71.3	78.5	1.7	1.3	0.8	18.9	6.4	18.5	7.9	12.5	11.9	14.2
48 499	...	6	Wood	645.2	44 227	1 087	68.5	84.0	5.7	1.1	0.8	9.7	4.9	14.6	8.1	9.5	9.4	11.6
48 501	...	7	Yoakum	799.7	8 488	2 553	10.6	32.6	1.3	0.6	0.7	65.4	9.2	23.5	9.3	12.9	11.3	11.0
48 503	...	7	Young	914.5	18 152	1 908	19.8	79.2	1.8	0.9	0.7	18.4	6.4	17.9	7.4	11.5	10.9	11.9
48 505	49820	6	Zapata	998.4	14 349	2 142	14.4	4.9	0.3	0.2	0.2	94.6	9.6	24.0	10.7	12.7	11.9	10.4
48 507	...	7	Zavala	1 297.4	12 023	2 292	9.3	5.7	0.4	0.2	0.2	93.6	8.4	21.7	12.1	12.8	11.3	10.4
49 000	...	0	UTAH	82 195.6	3 051 217	X	37.1	80.7	1.6	1.5	4.7	13.8	8.3	21.9	11.3	14.7	13.3	10.3
49 001	...	7	Beaver	2 582.9	6 463	2 716	2.5	85.8	0.7	1.3	2.2	11.5	8.8	22.8	9.1	11.2	12.3	9.5
49 003	36260	2	Box Elder	5 745.6	53 139	945	9.2	88.7	0.6	1.2	1.8	9.2	8.2	23.9	8.7	12.3	12.8	10.2
49 005	30860	3	Cache	1 164.7	122 753	511	105.4	85.5	0.9	0.9	3.8	10.5	8.9	21.8	19.1	14.0	11.4	8.1
49 007	39220	7	Carbon	1 479.2	20 399	1 811	13.8	84.4	1.1	1.7	1.4	13.1	6.9	19.7	9.2	12.5	12.0	10.3
49 009	...	9	Daggett	696.9	1 095	3 103	1.6	93.7	0.9	1.9	1.3	3.9	4.7	17.1	6.5	11.1	11.6	9.7
49 011	36260	2	Davis	299.0	342 281	199	1 144.8	86.2	1.8	0.8	4.1	9.4	8.8	23.9	9.3	14.3	14.3	10.5
49 013	...	7	Duchesne	3 235.3	20 337	1 813	6.3	87.4	0.7	4.7	1.4	8.1	10.2	24.5	7.8	13.7	13.1	9.4
49 015	...	7	Emery	4 462.3	10 216	2 414	2.3	91.8	0.6	1.2	0.9	6.5	6.9	22.8	7.9	10.8	12.1	10.0
49 017	...	9	Garfield	5 175.1	4 986	2 835	1.0	89.6	0.7	2.6	2.3	6.1	6.0	18.3	7.3	11.1	10.8	11.1
49 019	...	7	Grand	3 672.9	9 579	2 462	2.6	83.9	1.0	4.5	2.1	10.2	6.3	15.9	6.7	12.9	13.3	12.1
49 021	16260	4	Iron	3 296.3	49 937	985	15.1	87.6	0.9	2.5	2.1	8.6	8.3	20.8	14.9	13.5	11.5	9.1
49 023	39340	2	Juab	3 391.7	11 010	2 353	3.2	93.5	0.7	1.3	0.9	4.8	8.8	26.0	9.1	11.5	12.9	10.2
49 025	...	6	Kane	3 989.9	7 334	2 641	1.8	92.7	0.7	2.2	1.0	4.5	5.6	17.0	7.3	11.4	10.3	10.7
49 027	...	7	Millard	6 605.0	12 694	2 248	1.9	84.4	0.5	1.6	1.7	13.0	7.8	23.1	8.4	10.4	11.3	9.7
49 029	36260	2	Morgan	609.2	11 437	2 329	18.8	96.1	0.5	0.6	1.2	2.4	8.2	27.6	8.7	9.5	13.2	10.9
49 031	...	9	Piute	758.4	1 466	3 081	1.9	90.7	1.0	1.2	1.0	7.7	4.8	19.6	6.3	7.8	9.7	9.6
49 033	...	8	Rich	1 028.8	2 319	3 021	2.3	93.1	0.6	0.9	0.5	5.8	7.6	22.0	7.3	9.8	11.6	10.0
49 035	41620	1	Salt Lake	742.1	1 121 354	39	1 511.1	73.8	2.2	1.1	7.1	18.1	7.8	20.1	9.5	16.5	14.5	11.3
49 037	...	7	San Juan	7 820.0	16 895	1 984	2.2	45.2	0.7	49.5	1.1	5.5	7.9	24.4	10.8	11.7	11.1	11.1
49 039	...	6	Sanpete	1 589.9	29 409	1 446	18.5	86.9	1.2	1.4	2.3	9.7	6.4	20.1	15.4	12.7	12.2	9.8
49 041	...	7	Sevier	1 910.4	21 267	1 764	11.1	93.1	0.7	1.5	0.9	4.9	7.2	22.6	8.4	11.1	12.9	10.2
49 043	44920	4	Summit	1 870.6	40 307	1 169	21.5	86.0	0.9	0.6	2.5	11.3	5.7	19.8	8.2	11.3	13.3	15.7
49 045	41620	1	Tooele	6 942.0	64 833	815	9.3	85.1	1.2	1.3	2.0	12.0	8.3	25.1	8.6	13.2	15.2	11.3
49 047	46860	7	Uintah	4 482.4	36 373	1 268	8.1	83.6	0.7	7.8	1.5	8.4	9.5	24.4	8.2	15.2	13.3	9.8
49 049	39340	2	Utah	2 003.6	592 299	110	295.6	84.9	1.0	0.9	4.2	11.5	9.8	24.4	16.9	14.1	12.5	8.3
49 051	25720	6	Wasatch	1 177.0	30 528	1 418	25.9	84.6	0.7	0.8	1.6	13.5	7.9	24.4	8.0	12.1	14.5	11.4
49 053	41100	3	Washington	2 426.9	160 245	403	66.0	86.6	0.9	1.6	2.7	10.1	6.9	20.2	8.6	11.7	11.3	9.4
49 055	...	9	Wayne	2 461.1	2 702	2 990	1.1	92.9	0.7	0.9	1.4	5.4	6.3	18.9	7.6	10.1	10.5	11.3
49 057	36260	2	Weber	576.3	247 560	274	429.6	78.4	1.9	1.1	2.8	18.0	7.9	20.9	9.5	15.2	13.5	11.0
50 000	...	0	VERMONT	9 217.6	624 594	X	67.8	94.8	1.8	1.1	2.3	1.9	4.9	14.1	10.8	11.6	11.1	13.8
50 001	...	6	Addison	766.3	36 959	1 252	48.2	94.5	1.7	0.9	2.7	2.2	4.4	13.0	14.0	9.9	10.5	14.1
50 003	13540	6	Bennington	675.0	36 191	1 271	53.6	95.7	1.6	0.8	1.4	1.9	4.8	14.3	9.6	9.4	9.6	13.9
50 005	...	7	Caledonia	649.0	30 333	1 427	46.7	96.4	1.0	1.3	1.2	1.6	4.8	14.9	9.6	10.4	11.4	13.2

1. CBSA = Core Based Statistical Area. See Appendix A for explanation. See Appendix B for list of metropolitan areas with component counties.   2. County type code from the Economic Research Service of USDA Rural-Urban Continuum Codes. See Appendix A for definition.   3. Dry land or land partially or temporarily covered by water.   4. May be of any race.

STATE County	55 to 64 years	65 to 74 years	75 years and over	Percent female	2000	2010	2000– 2010	2010– 2016	Births	Deaths	Net migration	Number	Persons per house-hold	Family house-holds	Female family house-holder[1]	One per-son
	16	17	18	19	20	21	22	23	24	25	26	27	28	29	30	31
TEXAS—Cont'd																
Tom Green	11.7	8.3	6.7	50.3	104 010	110 224	6.0	7.4	9 971	6 292	4 514	42 825	2.54	64.0	13.0	30.1
Travis	10.4	5.7	3.3	49.6	812 280	1 024 478	26.1	17.1	99 899	31 692	104 738	428 220	2.57	57.1	10.9	30.8
Trinity	15.9	15.0	10.4	51.6	13 779	14 675	6.5	-1.6	892	1 330	200	5 325	2.69	63.2	10.6	34.0
Tyler	14.0	12.1	9.1	46.0	20 871	21 762	4.3	-2.0	1 365	1 662	-83	7 968	2.39	70.4	10.8	26.1
Upshur	14.4	10.4	7.2	50.3	35 291	39 316	11.4	4.2	2 992	2 722	1 439	13 844	2.85	73.0	9.7	23.0
Upton	12.8	6.7	6.6	48.4	3 404	3 349	-1.6	9.7	324	197	210	1 217	2.75	71.8	8.1	26.4
Uvalde	10.4	9.5	7.2	50.7	25 926	26 405	1.8	3.3	2 543	1 553	-101	8 435	3.13	69.5	14.8	26.1
Val Verde	9.0	7.9	6.5	49.0	44 856	48 879	9.0	0.0	5 478	2 177	-3 363	14 790	3.20	75.5	13.5	22.1
Van Zandt	14.2	11.6	8.7	51.0	48 140	52 560	9.2	3.4	3 586	3 968	2 208	18 613	2.79	69.4	10.1	26.3
Victoria	12.3	8.7	6.4	50.9	84 088	86 793	3.2	6.5	8 160	4 858	2 424	32 510	2.73	70.9	14.6	24.6
Walker	11.1	7.3	4.8	41.7	61 758	67 861	9.9	5.3	3 952	3 098	2 770	20 685	2.37	59.3	12.9	30.8
Waller	10.9	7.4	4.5	50.3	32 663	43 223	32.3	15.9	3 780	1 779	4 753	13 937	2.94	73.1	13.4	19.7
Ward	11.3	8.2	6.1	49.9	10 909	10 658	-2.3	8.8	1 096	698	541	3 883	2.86	68.4	14.0	28.7
Washington	14.0	11.0	9.8	50.9	30 373	33 700	11.0	4.0	2 561	2 364	1 054	11 952	2.68	70.4	14.1	24.4
Webb	8.4	5.3	3.7	51.1	193 117	250 304	29.6	8.3	34 078	7 932	-5 109	69 668	3.73	81.3	22.7	15.7
Wharton	13.0	9.1	7.4	51.0	41 188	41 280	0.2	1.1	3 450	2 583	-438	14 741	2.77	68.6	14.0	28.7
Wheeler	13.9	10.3	8.0	50.0	5 284	5 410	2.4	2.5	485	414	58	2 293	2.42	69.7	9.1	25.5
Wichita	12.1	7.9	6.6	48.3	131 664	131 669	0.0	0.1	11 110	8 201	-2 834	47 941	2.45	64.2	13.3	30.5
Wilbarger	13.8	9.6	7.8	50.3	14 676	13 535	-7.8	-4.8	1 052	945	-731	5 212	2.41	63.2	14.1	33.3
Willacy	9.8	7.5	5.9	44.9	20 082	22 137	10.2	-1.5	1 929	1 017	-1 268	5 553	3.51	82.2	24.1	16.3
Williamson	10.4	7.3	4.4	50.8	249 967	422 537	69.0	25.1	39 047	14 043	78 981	161 793	2.90	72.5	10.0	22.5
Wilson	13.8	9.6	6.1	49.9	32 408	42 913	32.4	13.0	3 154	2 291	4 536	15 477	2.90	77.6	10.9	18.6
Winkler	10.4	6.9	4.4	48.7	7 173	7 110	-0.9	11.0	795	383	359	2 628	2.84	72.7	13.0	25.2
Wise	13.7	9.2	5.6	49.9	48 793	59 110	21.1	9.0	4 877	3 239	3 573	21 068	2.86	75.9	11.2	20.1
Wood	15.1	15.7	11.1	50.2	36 752	41 961	14.2	5.4	2 576	3 795	3 404	16 064	2.57	71.6	10.2	24.4
Yoakum	10.7	6.9	5.2	49.7	7 322	7 879	7.6	7.7	942	362	23	2 727	3.01	76.7	9.9	21.8
Young	14.3	10.5	9.2	50.6	17 943	18 550	3.4	-2.1	1 427	1 595	-266	7 115	2.54	74.1	11.2	23.3
Zapata	8.8	7.1	4.8	50.2	12 182	14 018	15.1	2.4	1 827	533	-954	4 517	3.16	80.8	20.4	17.6
Zavala	10.0	7.8	5.4	49.8	11 600	11 677	0.7	3.0	1 242	554	-372	3 627	3.26	72.8	24.4	24.3
UTAH	9.5	6.3	4.3	49.7	2 233 169	2 763 888	23.8	10.4	321 460	99 031	65 017	906 292	3.15	75.0	9.6	19.5
Beaver	11.8	9.1	5.4	48.3	6 005	6 629	10.4	-2.5	697	409	-461	2 249	2.84	74.2	11.3	24.0
Box Elder	11.1	7.1	5.6	49.5	42 745	49 975	16.9	6.3	5 485	2 383	25	16 404	3.08	80.6	6.7	17.9
Cache	7.7	5.2	3.9	49.9	91 391	112 656	23.3	9.0	14 985	3 171	-1 835	35 685	3.19	74.4	7.5	17.9
Carbon	13.2	9.9	6.4	50.3	20 422	21 403	4.8	-4.7	1 883	1 516	-1 412	7 798	2.61	67.4	10.2	27.6
Daggett	16.3	15.1	8.0	41.5	921	1 061	15.2	3.2	73	58	12	263	2.43	70.7	4.2	27.0
Davis	9.4	5.6	3.9	49.6	238 994	306 486	28.2	11.7	36 328	9 532	9 020	97 910	3.29	81.3	9.5	15.4
Duchesne	9.9	6.7	4.7	49.6	14 371	18 609	29.5	9.3	2 707	963	-76	6 606	2.94	78.2	8.3	17.9
Emery	13.3	9.7	6.5	49.3	10 860	10 976	1.1	-6.9	966	582	-1 146	3 531	3.02	77.6	7.1	19.7
Garfield	14.4	12.9	8.2	47.4	4 735	5 172	9.2	-3.6	372	299	-281	1 751	2.75	69.3	7.8	25.8
Grand	15.8	10.5	6.5	49.8	8 485	9 225	8.7	3.8	793	531	96	3 789	2.44	59.6	7.9	35.5
Iron	9.8	7.5	4.6	49.9	33 779	46 163	36.7	8.2	5 331	1 784	172	15 095	3.07	71.7	8.8	22.0
Juab	9.3	7.4	4.9	48.4	8 238	10 246	24.4	7.5	1 143	484	46	3 106	3.29	81.5	9.3	17.3
Kane	14.9	14.4	8.4	49.3	6 046	7 125	17.8	2.9	495	477	181	2 789	2.55	60.6	6.0	32.4
Millard	12.5	9.7	7.1	49.1	12 405	12 503	0.8	1.5	1 202	638	-401	4 160	2.98	76.6	8.7	20.4
Morgan	10.5	6.9	4.5	48.5	7 129	9 469	32.8	20.8	1 010	343	1 304	3 024	3.40	85.8	2.8	11.6
Piute	15.4	15.8	10.8	49.0	1 435	1 557	8.5	-5.8	89	171	-30	557	3.28	72.5	7.2	25.7
Rich	13.1	12.6	5.9	49.0	1 961	2 264	15.5	2.4	217	186	6	640	3.57	81.4	8.8	16.1
Salt Lake	10.2	6.1	4.0	49.8	898 387	1 029 581	14.6	8.9	111 994	37 269	18 613	351 892	3.03	70.4	10.7	23.1
San Juan	11.5	7.1	4.3	50.2	14 413	14 749	2.3	14.6	1 519	790	1 405	3 923	3.75	74.5	15.4	23.5
Sanpete	9.9	8.1	5.3	47.7	22 763	27 822	22.2	5.7	2 470	1 118	218	7 943	3.13	77.5	6.6	16.9
Sevier	11.5	9.2	7.0	49.2	18 842	20 801	10.4	2.2	1 948	1 327	-204	7 050	2.90	74.5	7.7	23.5
Summit	14.7	7.9	3.3	48.9	29 736	36 327	22.2	11.0	2 703	869	2 202	13 927	2.75	74.6	7.5	18.0
Tooele	9.3	5.6	3.4	49.4	40 735	58 218	42.9	11.4	6 177	2 028	2 455	18 631	3.25	79.7	9.7	17.3
Uintah	9.8	5.7	4.1	49.2	25 224	32 584	29.2	11.6	4 350	1 318	715	10 981	3.22	74.6	9.0	21.0
Utah	6.6	4.4	3.0	49.5	368 536	516 640	40.2	14.6	75 132	13 103	13 365	148 464	3.62	82.3	8.0	12.0
Wasatch	11.3	6.9	3.3	48.9	15 215	23 525	54.6	29.8	2 606	751	5 056	8 095	3.27	76.5	7.6	19.4
Washington	11.0	11.6	9.2	50.5	90 354	138 115	52.9	16.0	13 981	6 987	14 471	48 920	2.99	76.0	9.4	19.7
Wayne	14.8	13.8	6.8	48.9	2 509	2 778	10.7	-2.7	205	154	-139	972	2.74	72.6	2.2	25.3
Weber	10.6	6.7	4.7	49.8	196 533	231 229	17.7	7.1	24 599	9 790	1 640	80 137	2.94	73.3	11.3	22.0
VERMONT	15.5	10.8	7.2	50.6	608 827	625 741	2.8	-0.2	37 939	34 505	-4 076	257 167	2.34	62.0	9.0	28.8
Addison	15.6	11.5	7.0	50.0	35 974	36 824	2.4	0.4	1 961	1 919	70	14 336	2.38	66.5	9.5	26.7
Bennington	16.2	12.2	9.9	51.3	36 994	37 125	0.4	-2.5	2 114	2 656	-344	15 636	2.25	64.3	11.0	29.3
Caledonia	16.3	12.1	7.4	50.1	29 702	31 232	5.2	-2.9	1 807	1 908	-792	12 287	2.43	61.8	9.5	30.9

1. No spouse present.

Table B. States and Counties — Population, Vital Statistics, Health, and Crime

STATE County	Persons in group quarters, 2016	Daytime population, 2011–2015 Number	Daytime population, 2011–2015 Employment/residence ratio	Births, 2016 Total	Births, 2016 Rate[1]	Deaths, 2016 Number	Deaths, 2016 Rate[1]	Persons under 65 with no health insurance, 2015 Number	Persons under 65 with no health insurance, 2015 Percent	Medicare, 2015 Total Beneficiaries	Medicare, 2015 Enrolled in Original Medicare	Medicare, 2015 Enrolled in Medicare Advantage	Serious crimes known to police,[2] 2014 Total Number	Serious crimes known to police,[2] 2014 Total Rate[3]
	32	33	34	35	36	37	38	39	40	41	42	43	44	45
TEXAS—Cont'd														
Tom Green	5 479	114 779	0.99	1 695	14.3	1 021	8.6	17 141	17.8	19 894	15 395	4 499	4 603	3 938
Travis	23 191	1 229 858	1.18	16 586	13.8	5 683	4.7	170 253	16.2	108 040	76 158	31 882	45 530	3 959
Trinity	135	12 789	0.66	148	10.2	209	14.5	2 327	21.7	3 919	2 842	1 077	275	1 904
Tyler	2 387	19 615	0.74	214	10.0	241	11.3	2 554	17.0	4 638	3 457	1 181	267	1 239
Upshur	471	32 456	0.53	472	11.5	434	10.6	6 187	18.6	7 333	5 200	2 133	1 154	2 948
Upton	63	3 986	1.44	58	15.8	18	4.9	615	19.7	515	402	113	14	411
Uvalde	513	27 006	1.01	413	15.1	249	9.1	5 185	23.2	4 852	3 404	1 448	999	3 667
Val Verde	1 934	48 233	0.96	883	18.1	363	7.4	8 997	22.3	7 599	5 509	2 090	1 089	2 228
Van Zandt	628	44 630	0.62	595	10.9	635	11.7	9 215	21.6	11 158	8 252	2 906	957	1 863
Victoria	1 825	92 562	1.06	1 341	14.5	836	9.0	13 916	18.0	16 491	12 340	4 151	3 206	3 504
Walker	17 117	70 698	1.06	679	9.5	563	7.9	8 267	18.1	8 666	5 613	3 053	1 555	2 238
Waller	4 291	43 380	0.87	664	13.2	308	6.1	9 120	23.5	4 722	3 068	1 654	1 004	2 183
Ward	128	11 164	0.99	189	16.3	103	8.9	2 086	21.0	1 774	1 364	410	332	2 889
Washington	2 120	36 167	1.13	416	11.9	378	10.8	4 961	18.9	7 782	6 188	1 594	751	2 177
Webb	3 553	263 472	1.00	5 387	19.9	1 342	4.9	66 469	27.6	27 734	20 613	7 121	11 100	4 153
Wharton	466	39 284	0.89	572	13.7	408	9.8	7 612	22.1	7 412	5 862	1 550	1 011	2 437
Wheeler	41	6 639	1.38	87	15.7	64	11.5	1 056	22.7	1 062	918	144	88	1 496
Wichita	12 400	136 328	1.07	1 726	13.1	1 328	10.1	17 073	16.8	23 954	20 189	3 765	5 317	4 079
Wilbarger	638	13 591	1.07	166	12.9	138	10.7	2 199	20.8	2 528	1 929	599	343	2 611
Willacy	3 307	21 186	0.85	285	13.1	171	7.8	3 638	23.2	3 192	1 914	1 278	984	4 471
Williamson	5 820	411 170	0.73	6 619	12.5	2 611	4.9	50 652	11.3	60 957	41 627	19 330	9 248	1 901
Wilson	524	35 656	0.51	548	11.3	398	8.2	6 427	16.0	6 600	4 173	2 427	722	1 557
Winkler	97	7 157	0.87	141	17.9	48	6.1	1 481	21.1	1 007	812	195	91	1 167
Wise	986	55 614	0.79	810	12.6	580	9.0	9 763	18.5	9 224	6 588	2 636	768	1 242
Wood	1 910	39 690	0.81	416	9.4	628	14.2	6 075	19.9	13 015	9 611	3 404	941	2 204
Yoakum	56	8 652	1.13	162	19.1	49	5.8	1 719	22.9	1 096	926	170	117	1 404
Young	273	18 278	0.99	225	12.4	234	12.9	3 289	22.7	4 057	3 692	365	373	2 024
Zapata	30	13 834	0.91	283	19.7	99	6.9	3 660	29.2	1 747	1 431	316	117	803
Zavala	413	11 455	0.86	193	16.1	96	8.0	2 037	20.1	1 922	1 165	757	NA	NA
UTAH	45 776	2 903 246	1.00	51 444	16.9	16 447	5.4	306 968	11.6	326 601	203 499	123 102	91 057	3 094
Beaver	38	6 686	1.08	100	15.5	49	7.6	787	14.6	1 031	958	73	119	2 141
Box Elder	339	48 287	0.87	885	16.7	341	6.4	4 131	9.1	7 104	4 453	2 651	1 096	2 281
Cache	3 487	116 464	0.98	2 395	19.5	506	4.1	10 037	9.5	11 082	5 800	5 282	1 507	1 275
Carbon	539	21 275	1.04	267	13.1	193	9.5	1 834	10.9	3 793	3 452	341	658	3 411
Daggett	72	768	0.96	10	9.1	7	6.4	92	11.2	D	156	D	9	784
Davis	3 040	289 289	0.77	5 861	17.1	1 642	4.8	25 462	8.4	31 589	19 564	12 025	5 822	1 781
Duchesne	233	20 826	1.13	449	22.1	129	6.3	3 135	17.1	2 620	1 962	658	626	3 006
Emery	43	10 393	0.92	130	12.7	81	7.9	953	10.9	1 793	1 724	69	121	1 128
Garfield	171	5 076	1.00	53	10.6	30	6.0	577	15.2	1 040	1 012	28	NA	NA
Grand	143	9 625	1.05	125	13.0	71	7.4	1 278	16.2	1 696	1 655	41	262	2 787
Iron	862	45 840	0.93	869	17.4	294	5.9	6 733	16.2	7 059	5 280	1 779	1 202	2 554
Juab	86	9 414	0.77	185	16.8	74	6.7	1 163	12.7	1 386	1 319	67	253	2 432
Kane	260	7 687	1.15	78	10.6	71	9.7	531	10.1	1 670	1 599	71	79	1 081
Millard	122	12 603	1.00	204	16.1	98	7.7	1 819	17.5	2 022	1 964	58	277	2 175
Morgan	0	7 956	0.45	172	15.0	38	3.3	808	8.2	1 272	843	429	14	135
Piute	37	1 693	0.73	16	10.9	11	7.5	174	16.0	D	369	D	7	465
Rich	1	2 341	1.07	37	16.0	15	6.5	238	12.5	362	286	76	39	1 693
Salt Lake	14 042	1 156 829	1.15	17 746	15.8	6 387	5.7	119 879	12.2	116 593	62 756	53 837	52 799	4 823
San Juan	372	15 396	1.05	240	14.2	112	6.6	2 669	19.9	1 685	1 651	34	216	1 434
Sanpete	2 755	26 754	0.85	394	13.4	172	5.8	3 054	13.6	3 943	3 543	400	313	1 244
Sevier	252	21 312	1.05	317	14.9	184	8.7	2 328	13.4	3 629	3 224	405	581	2 776
Summit	70	42 391	1.19	417	10.3	149	3.7	3 913	10.9	4 307	2 971	1 336	747	1 909
Tooele	354	51 833	0.65	982	15.1	317	4.9	5 230	9.2	5 970	4 336	1 634	1 766	2 870
Uintah	192	36 285	1.04	727	20.0	226	6.2	5 392	15.7	3 402	2 383	1 019	736	2 016
Utah	13 456	532 329	0.92	12 162	20.5	2 269	3.8	55 048	10.5	44 331	25 437	18 894	9 431	1 678
Wasatch	218	22 241	0.64	475	15.6	126	4.1	4 094	15.7	3 840	2 288	1 552	250	917
Washington	1 903	147 597	0.99	2 232	13.9	1 206	7.5	20 573	16.9	30 025	21 739	8 286	2 749	1 860
Wayne	9	2 660	0.95	35	13.0	24	8.9	346	16.2	545	521	24	10	364
Weber	2 680	231 396	0.93	3 881	15.7	1 625	6.6	24 690	11.6	32 225	20 254	11 971	7 110	2 951
VERMONT	25 240	625 444	1.00	6 035	9.7	5 547	8.9	23 229	4.7	126 963	116 221	10 742	10 173	1 624
Addison	2 849	34 026	0.85	309	8.4	318	8.6	1 375	4.9	6 698	5 947	751	445	1 210
Bennington	1 476	38 527	1.11	344	9.5	429	11.9	1 441	5.3	8 700	8 001	699	590	1 615
Caledonia	1 289	29 137	0.87	288	9.5	294	9.7	1 213	5.1	6 436	5 928	508	427	1 371

1. Per 1,000 estimated resident population.   2. Data for serious crimes have not been adjusted for underreporting; this may affect comparability between geographic areas and over time.
3. Per 100,000 population estimated by the FBI.

Table B. States and Counties — Crime, Education, Money Income, and Poverty

STATE County	Rate[2] Violent	Rate[2] Property	Enrollment[3] Total	Enrollment[3] Percent private	Attainment[4] High school graduate or less	Attainment[4] Bachelor's degree or more	Local government expenditures,[5] 2013–2014 Total current spending (mil dol)	Current spending per student (dollars)	Per capita income[6] (dollars)	Median income (dollars)	Percent with income of less than $50,000	with income of $200,000 or more	Median household income (dollars)	All persons	Children under 18 years	Children 5 to 17 years in families
	46	47	48	49	50	51	52	53	54	55	56	57	58	59	60	61
TEXAS—Cont'd																
Tom Green	298	3 640	28 995	8.5	47.1	22.1	166.4	8 598	25 274	46 711	52.6	3.3	47 756	15.6	21.7	20.5
Travis	355	3 604	308 897	13.8	29.3	46.0	1 489.0	9 265	35 168	61 451	41.3	8.4	65 244	13.2	17.8	17.3
Trinity	201	1 703	2 785	4.9	58.5	11.1	45.6	9 065	19 766	34 295	67.8	0.9	37 213	19.5	32.8	30.1
Tyler	227	1 012	3 707	8.6	57.6	11.2	34.5	9 673	20 242	41 360	57.7	0.8	40 820	19.9	25.1	23.9
Upshur	330	2 619	9 469	7.6	49.8	14.5	66.2	9 289	22 692	46 673	52.5	2.7	45 494	15.5	23.6	22.3
Upton	29	382	862	3.9	63.4	10.1	12.0	14 829	22 751	46 131	52.4	3.3	57 085	13.5	18.2	17.5
Uvalde	316	3 351	7 751	2.9	52.7	15.3	60.1	10 023	18 135	38 568	58.0	1.9	37 700	20.7	33.4	31.2
Val Verde	133	2 095	12 705	6.5	60.5	17.0	88.5	8 147	18 632	42 174	57.3	1.9	42 465	22.1	31.8	30.5
Van Zandt	189	1 674	11 913	10.7	53.8	15.5	83.6	8 487	23 257	44 002	55.3	2.5	47 252	15.9	22.3	20.3
Victoria	445	3 059	23 206	11.6	48.8	18.2	139.7	8 972	25 987	51 758	48.1	3.3	55 406	13.6	20.7	18.4
Walker	380	1 858	20 426	5.6	53.9	18.9	67.1	8 965	16 135	37 666	59.4	1.8	41 429	22.7	24.9	23.1
Waller	359	1 824	16 172	11.7	53.3	18.8	89.1	9 226	22 849	51 348	49.4	3.6	50 746	16.0	21.9	20.4
Ward	374	2 515	2 734	3.2	59.6	11.4	20.6	8 778	24 234	51 345	48.0	3.5	57 570	12.8	17.8	17.2
Washington	273	1 905	7 950	8.3	48.5	21.6	46.3	8 819	25 057	51 269	48.9	2.6	51 879	14.5	20.0	19.9
Webb	403	3 750	88 489	5.0	59.1	17.1	596.1	8 605	15 096	38 862	60.1	2.0	39 237	30.5	41.9	38.6
Wharton	460	1 976	10 071	6.9	57.1	14.1	78.2	9 434	21 581	45 176	54.3	1.9	45 198	17.2	24.9	22.5
Wheeler	68	1 428	1 231	8.2	50.0	16.9	15.6	13 106	26 184	52 221	46.7	2.7	51 114	12.9	19.0	17.0
Wichita	372	3 707	33 282	8.3	46.3	21.6	179.5	8 388	22 861	45 543	54.3	2.2	45 430	18.9	26.3	24.1
Wilbarger	175	2 436	3 302	9.0	51.0	16.5	21.9	9 151	20 752	41 630	56.1	0.9	43 073	16.5	25.0	24.6
Willacy	809	3 662	5 468	3.9	72.7	8.3	50.5	11 208	11 413	26 495	72.6	1.0	30 287	35.4	43.0	41.8
Williamson	156	1 745	134 716	13.5	28.1	39.3	886.1	8 032	31 876	73 750	31.7	5.8	78 531	6.6	8.7	7.8
Wilson	149	1 409	11 780	9.8	49.7	19.5	73.7	8 572	28 887	68 100	36.9	4.2	68 805	9.4	13.2	11.9
Winkler	205	962	1 862	2.1	59.9	11.1	22.6	12 282	22 656	55 756	45.1	2.1	55 331	13.3	18.5	16.9
Wise	150	1 091	14 656	7.1	52.7	16.5	85.7	9 626	27 208	56 897	43.2	3.5	58 367	12.1	17.4	15.8
Wood	192	2 012	8 453	12.9	50.2	17.0	55.7	8 996	24 561	45 686	54.5	2.5	45 753	16.6	27.7	25.9
Yoakum	168	1 236	2 231	4.7	58.8	14.7	23.5	10 725	23 125	56 153	46.8	3.6	59 752	11.1	14.8	14.4
Young	201	1 823	3 978	7.9	54.9	17.6	32.3	9 212	25 524	44 693	52.9	1.7	49 079	15.0	22.0	20.7
Zapata	96	707	4 103	2.6	72.7	8.4	32.8	9 066	16 619	32 162	68.9	1.5	35 754	30.9	45.2	41.4
Zavala	NA	NA	3 388	1.7	66.8	9.0	28.2	11 093	13 813	26 672	72.3	1.1	27 711	32.0	42.2	42.1
UTAH	216	2 878	942 989	13.7	32.0	31.1	4 040.1	6 459	24 686	60 727	40.3	4.2	62 961	11.2	12.8	11.5
Beaver	54	2 087	1 881	4.0	45.0	20.0	12.5	7 844	21 405	50 282	49.8	1.4	50 492	11.2	14.8	13.4
Box Elder	112	2 169	15 481	7.4	40.4	21.5	71.5	6 969	21 748	55 038	44.2	1.5	58 380	8.4	11.7	10.5
Cache	57	1 218	45 760	6.3	29.4	36.1	156.9	6 379	20 223	50 497	49.5	2.6	51 951	16.0	16.0	15.0
Carbon	124	3 286	5 754	5.3	38.9	15.1	31.8	7 850	21 287	46 900	52.1	0.9	47 894	16.3	20.6	18.9
Daggett	87	697	162	7.4	41.3	15.9	3.3	14 487	22 149	56 750	41.8	0.0	57 368	8.0	12.2	10.7
Davis	101	1 680	107 620	9.3	26.0	34.8	485.0	6 197	26 411	71 112	31.4	4.5	72 268	6.9	8.3	7.5
Duchesne	423	2 584	5 548	6.8	48.3	15.0	33.6	6 600	23 576	61 133	40.4	2.1	63 149	11.0	12.0	11.0
Emery	177	951	2 682	6.7	42.7	12.6	24.5	10 288	19 717	49 787	50.4	0.8	54 086	10.4	14.4	12.8
Garfield	NA	NA	1 213	4.5	43.2	19.7	9.4	9 451	19 971	42 614	57.3	1.9	45 509	11.2	18.0	16.4
Grand	149	2 638	1 972	11.8	34.0	24.7	13.9	8 685	22 635	41 312	63.2	1.7	44 858	13.0	21.5	20.9
Iron	270	2 284	15 766	7.0	33.0	28.6	60.7	6 138	18 995	43 855	55.6	2.1	45 118	18.3	22.4	21.0
Juab	77	2 355	3 401	5.9	43.9	15.8	18.1	7 022	18 447	54 761	42.6	1.5	55 201	10.5	14.2	13.2
Kane	260	821	1 539	10.3	33.5	24.8	12.4	9 963	24 729	50 194	49.8	2.8	47 530	11.3	17.0	15.8
Millard	259	1 916	3 494	3.4	41.1	20.0	25.0	8 382	20 602	51 593	48.4	0.6	52 206	13.1	19.2	18.2
Morgan	19	116	3 508	12.5	26.0	34.6	14.2	5 273	27 312	74 314	28.5	8.4	81 358	4.8	5.3	4.6
Piute	0	465	469	7.7	56.3	17.5	4.1	12 590	17 493	35 980	62.8	0.2	39 507	17.3	31.1	25.1
Rich	87	1 607	655	11.1	40.6	19.1	6.5	13 345	19 168	50 781	48.4	1.1	58 645	9.1	11.1	9.7
Salt Lake	350	4 472	322 134	13.0	33.2	32.1	1 356.7	6 459	27 314	62 117	39.2	5.1	65 549	10.8	12.8	11.3
San Juan	106	1 328	4 729	6.1	47.9	18.9	33.5	10 680	15 654	41 484	57.9	0.7	39 305	28.5	31.9	26.3
Sanpete	64	1 181	9 677	9.8	38.1	20.5	41.0	7 135	16 965	50 323	49.7	1.9	46 929	17.2	19.1	17.8
Sevier	81	2 695	6 216	5.3	43.3	16.4	32.6	6 810	19 261	46 291	53.7	1.0	48 711	14.0	18.8	16.5
Summit	138	1 771	10 130	13.6	22.1	50.8	74.5	9 391	47 733	91 773	23.1	16.8	93 235	6.2	8.1	7.1
Tooele	228	2 642	20 136	10.4	39.7	22.4	92.6	6 172	22 643	63 552	35.2	1.9	67 938	7.2	9.3	8.5
Uintah	129	1 888	10 489	12.8	47.9	15.9	52.5	6 684	24 720	66 815	35.8	4.0	67 561	9.9	11.4	10.2
Utah	74	1 604	219 614	23.8	23.5	37.3	780.2	5 833	21 335	62 180	39.1	3.8	65 425	12.5	11.6	10.2
Wasatch	92	825	8 048	11.0	29.1	33.5	49.6	7 970	26 397	66 486	35.2	4.4	75 112	6.9	9.2	8.5
Washington	135	1 725	44 953	11.4	32.0	27.1	223.8	7 288	22 459	50 774	49.2	3.0	54 398	13.2	18.5	17.8
Wayne	36	327	759	6.1	32.6	26.8	5.4	10 102	20 121	40 645	59.8	1.2	41 596	15.0	25.6	22.8
Weber	254	2 698	69 199	8.1	39.5	23.0	314.7	6 423	23 545	56 581	43.6	2.6	58 786	12.4	15.6	13.9
VERMONT	99	1 524	151 852	21.0	38.3	36.0	1 507.7	17 236	29 894	55 176	45.4	3.7	56 883	10.4	13.7	12.2
Addison	95	1 115	9 748	35.7	39.9	35.5	87.3	18 547	29 561	59 688	41.9	3.6	58 408	8.9	10.9	9.2
Bennington	134	1 481	8 464	29.6	39.9	33.5	83.0	15 751	29 296	49 573	50.5	3.4	50 506	11.8	17.8	15.7
Caledonia	106	1 265	6 983	22.1	46.0	27.0	59.4	14 175	23 919	45 323	55.5	1.8	46 403	11.5	17.8	15.2

1. Data for serious crimes have not been adjusted for underreporting; this may affect comparability between geographic areas and over time.   2. Per 100,000 population estimated by the FBI.
3. All persons 3 years old and over enrolled in nursery school through college.   4. Persons 25 years old and over.   5. Elementary and secondary education expenditures.
6. Based on population estimated by the American Community Survey, 2011–2015.

Table B. States and Counties — **Personal Income**

STATE County	Personal income, 2015										Earnings, 2015		
	Total (mil dol)	Percent change, 2014–2015	Per capita[1] Dollars	Per capita[1] Rank	Wages and salaries (mil dol)	Supplements to wages and salaries; employer contributions (mil dol) Pension and insurance	Supplements to wages and salaries; employer contributions (mil dol) Government social insurance	Proprietors' income (mil dol)	Dividends, interest, and rent (mil dol)	Personal transfer receipts (mil dol)	Total (mil dol)	Contributions for government social insurance (mil dol) From employee and self-employed	Contributions for government social insurance (mil dol) From employer
	62	63	64	65	66	67	68	69	70	71	72	73	74
TEXAS—Cont'd													
Tom Green	5 166	1.7	43 737	941	2 160	380	154	604	1 152	980	3 299	171	154
Travis	68 666	6.3	58 362	230	43 733	5 692	2 864	10 514	15 281	5 908	62 803	3 069	2 864
Trinity	487	4.5	33 789	2 478	84	16	6	40	67	177	145	12	6
Tyler	664	3.1	31 120	2 692	149	35	9	31	91	214	224	15	9
Upshur	1 445	1.5	35 588	1 872	291	57	20	125	165	381	493	31	20
Upton	208	-2.3	56 860	124	116	20	7	35	35	26	178	8	7
Uvalde	1 063	3.7	39 013	2 103	351	72	24	161	220	280	608	31	24
Val Verde	1 670	3.9	34 100	2 276	749	178	61	133	260	393	1 121	59	61
Van Zandt	1 879	6.3	35 086	2 214	386	68	26	156	234	533	637	42	26
Victoria	4 351	1.3	47 101	504	1 985	300	135	528	796	813	2 947	156	135
Walker	1 843	3.5	26 061	3 044	952	244	54	93	348	457	1 343	63	54
Waller	1 867	6.1	38 380	2 105	773	130	50	248	230	319	1 201	58	50
Ward	526	-2.8	44 886	474	291	43	19	55	57	89	408	22	19
Washington	1 776	2.9	51 080	419	620	109	41	289	385	375	1 059	55	41
Webb	8 032	5.0	29 778	2 890	3 639	704	256	1 184	1 033	1 877	5 783	287	256
Wharton	1 720	3.1	41 460	1 079	618	101	41	199	250	389	959	48	41
Wheeler	287	-1.5	50 711	291	106	18	7	50	83	57	181	8	7
Wichita	5 525	-0.1	41 947	1 108	2 372	458	176	898	1 033	1 192	3 904	194	176
Wilbarger	493	2.4	37 869	1 311	229	54	14	33	76	140	330	17	14
Willacy	615	3.7	28 078	3 048	136	28	9	132	49	224	305	13	9
Williamson	22 119	8.9	43 498	1 328	8 330	1 043	545	2 085	2 891	2 599	12 002	644	545
Wilson	2 021	5.7	42 537	1 282	293	57	19	152	304	356	521	30	19
Winkler	314	-4.2	39 174	1 125	155	25	10	38	42	59	228	12	10
Wise	2 697	5.0	42 837	944	1 017	163	67	316	378	451	1 564	82	67
Wood	1 550	3.7	35 745	2 160	370	70	26	159	250	544	624	43	26
Yoakum	367	-5.6	42 964	711	238	38	15	79	38	58	371	17	15
Young	913	-1.8	49 954	314	296	56	20	244	166	198	617	30	20
Zapata	397	-9.8	27 625	2 432	213	37	14	24	53	115	288	16	14
Zavala	329	5.0	26 855	3 080	104	21	8	28	52	122	162	9	8
UTAH	117 764	6.2	39 378	X	64 680	10 763	5 011	9 676	21 957	16 014	90 130	5 254	5 011
Beaver	222	-1.8	34 983	1 665	114	21	9	16	34	47	161	9	9
Box Elder	1 728	5.0	33 161	2 416	799	134	64	94	271	297	1 091	66	64
Cache	3 881	5.2	32 128	2 662	1 941	417	151	360	712	593	2 868	161	151
Carbon	704	1.4	34 392	2 142	379	70	31	30	108	180	510	32	31
Daggett	41	8.2	37 017	357	16	4	1	2	10	7	24	1	1
Davis	13 442	6.8	40 000	1 354	5 548	1 088	451	798	2 197	1 553	7 884	452	451
Duchesne	740	-7.2	35 488	1 239	423	79	31	74	113	115	607	35	31
Emery	319	0.8	30 738	2 631	151	34	12	9	44	77	206	13	12
Garfield	171	6.7	34 084	2 308	75	15	7	8	37	37	105	6	7
Grand	381	3.2	39 990	1 084	180	31	16	33	107	72	260	16	16
Iron	1 308	6.0	27 037	2 995	573	126	45	55	255	344	799	49	45
Juab	331	6.7	31 206	2 736	131	25	11	24	37	66	191	11	11
Kane	258	5.0	36 244	1 946	111	21	9	19	56	57	160	10	9
Millard	424	5.1	33 522	2 352	195	41	15	52	64	87	303	16	15
Morgan	497	8.5	44 916	834	86	15	6	35	79	50	142	9	6
Piute	42	6.6	27 399	3 051	8	2	1	6	8	15	16	1	1
Rich	90	0.7	38 888	1 297	24	5	2	20	21	13	51	2	2
Salt Lake	49 488	6.1	44 692	895	34 565	5 406	2 631	4 820	9 291	6 042	47 422	2 735	2 631
San Juan	369	3.5	23 399	3 094	167	40	13	15	63	99	235	14	13
Sanpete	771	10.5	26 808	3 050	243	63	19	105	122	182	430	23	19
Sevier	633	5.5	30 175	2 744	302	60	24	27	106	155	414	26	24
Summit	3 889	6.3	98 128	9	1 152	140	92	303	1 463	177	1 687	97	92
Tooele	2 070	7.8	32 890	2 539	674	125	53	58	264	296	911	55	53
Uintah	1 197	-6.4	31 549	1 994	683	113	51	93	191	163	939	55	51
Utah	19 720	7.9	34 283	2 405	9 526	1 483	737	1 792	3 255	2 506	13 539	787	737
Wasatch	1 186	7.1	40 670	1 373	318	52	25	37	278	123	431	28	25
Washington	4 881	7.2	31 368	2 764	2 047	351	165	365	1 128	1 172	2 928	195	165
Wayne	84	2.3	31 337	2 689	33	7	3	5	19	19	48	3	3
Weber	8 898	6.0	36 522	1 947	4 216	794	338	419	1 625	1 472	5 768	345	338
VERMONT	30 418	2.9	48 584	X	14 127	2 450	1 194	2 330	6 062	6 349	20 101	1 305	1 194
Addison	1 641	-0.6	44 311	760	664	109	56	132	355	302	961	62	56
Bennington	1 732	2.3	47 700	609	727	123	64	130	440	406	1 044	71	64
Caledonia	1 164	1.5	37 802	1 529	436	84	38	94	206	302	652	45	38

1. Based on the resident population estimated as of July 1 of the year shown.

Table B. States and Counties — Earnings, Social Security, and Housing

STATE County	Farm	Mining	Construction	Manufacturing	Information: professional, scientific, technical services	Retail trade	Finance, insurance, real estate and leasing	Health care and social assistance	Government	Social Security beneficiaries, December 2015 Number	Rate[1]	Supplemental Security Income recipients, December 2015	Housing units, 2016 Total	Percent change, 2010–2016
	75	76	77	78	79	80	81	82	83	84	85	86	87	88
TEXAS—Cont'd														
Tom Green	1.0	6.9	6.4	10.1	5.4	7.4	6.3	14.0	21.9	21 655	184	2 955	48 463	4.1
Travis	0.0	5.1	6.0	8.1	21.3	5.1	9.4	8.0	15.2	120 135	102	17 908	499 062	13.1
Trinity	0.0	D	6.0	9.6	D	4.7	3.6	D	20.6	4 485	311	610	8 784	0.8
Tyler	2.9	1.7	3.5	4.7	D	8.1	4.0	7.5	39.8	5 295	249	668	10 648	0.7
Upshur	4.3	5.0	17.9	4.9	10.6	5.1	4.1	6.6	18.3	8 990	222	1 128	16 825	1.3
Upton	3.0	40.4	D	D	1.7	D	D	D	16.4	615	170	75	1 551	0.3
Uvalde	2.4	2.6	15.0	3.5	3.6	10.4	3.5	D	27.7	5 435	200	1 122	11 039	2.1
Val Verde	0.8	0.2	3.1	7.6	2.3	9.4	3.3	8.6	45.1	8 495	174	2 253	18 947	1.6
Van Zandt	4.8	1.6	16.1	8.0	4.7	9.9	3.1	5.7	18.5	12 895	241	1 225	23 032	1.0
Victoria	0.0	14.3	8.0	8.9	4.6	7.9	5.5	13.8	13.1	17 475	189	2 579	36 964	4.4
Walker	0.7	0.6	3.5	5.3	3.8	6.3	3.4	8.0	57.4	9 620	136	1 362	25 407	5.6
Waller	2.5	4.0	10.1	24.8	4.0	3.7	1.5	2.8	19.5	6 340	130	910	16 434	3.8
Ward	-0.1	D	6.9	2.4	D	3.7	4.2	1.3	11.2	1 995	171	273	4 788	2.0
Washington	0.8	3.8	7.1	28.4	4.6	7.8	8.3	6.2	15.8	7 945	227	959	15 926	2.7
Webb	0.2	6.1	3.9	1.0	3.9	7.9	4.5	10.1	26.3	32 310	120	12 562	81 486	10.9
Wharton	11.6	8.6	6.2	9.3	3.2	8.6	4.9	7.8	15.3	8 180	197	1 167	17 489	2.1
Wheeler	12.2	26.1	10.7	0.8	D	4.7	4.0	2.4	17.6	1 140	201	71	2 715	-0.5
Wichita	-0.1	15.5	4.0	9.3	4.0	7.4	5.2	13.0	24.7	24 760	188	4 017	56 102	1.0
Wilbarger	0.7	1.3	2.1	19.4	3.5	7.1	3.9	3.7	37.6	2 795	214	406	6 262	-0.9
Willacy	33.7	D	2.4	0.8	D	6.2	2.2	6.6	21.4	3 750	171	1 332	7 333	4.1
Williamson	0.1	0.5	9.8	14.0	10.5	8.7	6.7	8.1	11.0	65 895	130	4 422	186 964	14.9
Wilson	2.3	8.1	14.8	4.2	5.3	9.9	3.5	6.9	24.0	8 180	172	705	17 180	2.5
Winkler	0.1	37.6	D	D	D	3.9	2.3	D	15.5	1 225	153	233	3 002	-0.8
Wise	0.7	23.4	7.9	10.3	D	6.4	2.8	D	16.1	11 185	178	767	24 142	1.6
Wood	4.4	4.8	10.2	11.7	6.7	8.0	5.9	D	15.7	13 820	317	1 044	21 035	0.8
Yoakum	6.4	37.9	10.0	2.1	D	2.8	3.6	D	12.0	1 255	147	143	3 027	1.6
Young	0.2	31.6	6.3	14.6	3.6	4.7	8.7	5.3	11.6	4 390	241	499	8 694	0.8
Zapata	-1.1	40.0	8.6	1.9	D	3.9	D	2.6	24.2	2 030	141	618	6 258	0.9
Zavala	5.1	4.2	3.8	9.6	D	4.3	3.8	7.8	25.4	2 175	178	787	4 321	0.9
UTAH	0.5	1.0	7.6	10.1	12.3	7.8	9.0	8.4	17.2	375 685	126	31 365	1 054 164	7.6
Beaver	14.3	D	4.8	5.9	0.9	5.9	D	2.0	24.2	1 125	177	66	2 952	1.5
Box Elder	3.6	0.1	8.4	37.3	D	5.1	2.7	6.3	13.1	8 315	160	550	18 419	6.3
Cache	1.4	0.0	4.9	22.7	9.3	6.8	6.7	9.7	21.3	13 100	109	868	40 108	8.3
Carbon	0.1	D	8.9	4.7	2.7	7.1	3.1	D	20.7	4 490	220	490	9 648	1.0
Daggett	7.8	D	8.3	D	D	D	D	D	-0.7	240	216	0	1 155	1.1
Davis	0.1	0.2	9.3	11.2	D	6.9	5.2	7.4	29.3	37 790	113	2 413	106 525	9.2
Duchesne	3.4	29.7	8.4	1.9	D	5.2	4.3	D	18.3	3 130	151	299	9 971	5.0
Emery	2.6	12.9	11.1	0.7	D	5.3	D	D	21.2	2 190	212	129	4 493	0.1
Garfield	5.1	D	2.4	1.8	D	3.8	1.4	D	30.1	1 145	229	38	3 842	3.1
Grand	0.3	D	7.9	0.6	D	11.3	5.7	8.7	22.0	1 940	204	136	5 186	7.7
Iron	2.9	0.8	5.5	10.3	3.2	8.9	6.7	9.7	29.6	7 705	160	666	20 484	4.2
Juab	3.7	2.7	12.4	23.7	D	3.6	D	D	18.3	1 665	158	124	3 642	4.0
Kane	1.4	D	4.8	4.1	2.9	6.7	2.9	2.8	25.6	1 850	260	67	5 861	0.8
Millard	17.9	2.8	2.1	4.7	D	4.7	1.9	D	18.0	2 405	190	125	4 961	0.4
Morgan	2.3	0.9	18.9	10.5	D	5.7	D	D	16.3	1 425	128	36	3 484	15.9
Piute	13.7	0.0	D	0.4	D	D	D	D	40.5	455	303	20	930	3.4
Rich	37.4	D	D	D	D	3.8	D	D	22.3	390	170	9	2 971	4.8
Salt Lake	0.0	0.5	6.8	8.8	13.5	7.5	12.1	7.7	15.3	134 470	122	13 639	386 400	6.2
San Juan	0.2	13.1	6.1	1.6	D	2.6	1.5	16.1	38.3	2 130	136	599	5 846	1.9
Sanpete	18.4	0.4	5.7	9.1	4.1	5.1	2.4	6.9	30.1	4 770	166	347	10 538	1.5
Sevier	2.6	9.5	3.6	5.2	4.0	10.2	3.4	D	21.4	4 280	204	308	8 604	1.8
Summit	0.3	0.5	7.3	4.2	13.0	8.6	12.0	4.9	9.9	4 730	120	105	27 570	3.8
Tooele	2.5	0.7	5.3	13.2	D	5.6	2.4	6.8	29.6	7 350	117	681	21 131	8.6
Uintah	0.9	25.6	10.7	0.8	4.1	6.6	4.3	5.0	18.8	4 275	113	359	13 514	12.9
Utah	0.5	0.0	9.7	9.9	18.4	10.1	4.9	9.0	11.8	53 135	92	4 151	166 794	12.4
Wasatch	0.1	D	19.9	4.2	11.1	7.4	2.8	10.0	20.8	3 415	117	106	12 550	18.7
Washington	0.1	0.3	9.8	5.5	7.2	9.7	6.7	17.0	15.3	33 725	217	1 338	65 472	13.4
Wayne	7.8	D	13.1	1.4	D	4.6	0.4	7.6	31.6	615	228	18	1 639	3.0
Weber	0.2	0.1	7.0	16.7	5.6	7.3	7.3	12.7	21.8	33 430	137	3 675	89 474	3.8
VERMONT	0.6	0.2	7.6	11.0	9.8	7.4	5.4	14.7	19.1	142 755	228	15 664	329 525	2.2
Addison	3.4	0.3	6.3	14.9	7.3	10.0	3.6	13.2	12.0	7 785	211	592	17 128	2.2
Bennington	0.3	0.0	7.0	14.5	D	9.7	3.9	18.6	13.6	9 915	272	1 232	20 921	0.0
Caledonia	0.8	D	10.7	12.0	6.2	8.5	3.2	16.0	19.1	7 505	244	989	16 129	1.2

1. Per 1,000 resident population estimated as of July 1 of the year shown.

Table B. States and Counties — Housing, Labor Force, and Employment

STATE County	Housing units, 2011–2015								Civilian labor force, 2016				Civilian employment,[6] 2011–2015		
	Occupied units										Unemployment			Percent	
			Owner-occupied			Renter-occupied									
				Median owner cost as a percent of income											Con-struction, produc-tion, and mainte-nance occu-pations
	Total	Percent	Median value[1]	With a mort-gage	Without a mort-gage[2]	Median rent[3]	Median rent as a per-cent of income[2]	Sub-stand-ard units[4] (percent)	Total	Percent change, 2015–2016	Total	Rate[5]	Total	Manage-ment, business, science and arts	
	89	90	91	92	93	94	95	96	97	98	99	100	101	102	103
TEXAS—Cont'd															
Tom Green	42 825	61.8	108 600	20.4	11.1	774	28.8	3.7	54 206	-0.3	2 442	4.5	51 528	31.1	25.8
Travis	428 220	51.7	237 100	22.8	12.2	1 054	30.1	4.8	678 367	3.8	21 282	3.1	599 597	46.2	14.6
Trinity	5 325	80.9	81 000	22.3	15.3	702	29.1	3.8	5 460	-0.1	344	6.3	4 922	23.7	24.7
Tyler	7 968	84.4	81 600	19.7	11.5	638	26.9	5.6	7 191	-2.1	546	7.6	7 230	23.7	30.9
Upshur	13 844	78.9	93 700	18.9	11.4	735	26.4	4.8	17 708	-1.2	1 149	6.5	16 849	27.1	31.7
Upton	1 217	75.1	57 600	17.2	10.0	650	20.7	5.3	1 583	-11.0	85	5.4	1 326	25.8	39.8
Uvalde	8 435	73.6	77 000	21.9	13.1	628	28.1	6.6	11 778	1.2	628	5.3	10 801	27.8	29.3
Val Verde	14 790	64.8	92 400	21.1	12.0	677	26.8	7.4	19 968	2.3	1 267	6.3	18 261	24.6	27.2
Van Zandt	18 613	78.0	103 400	21.5	13.1	711	30.5	3.1	24 738	2.5	1 063	4.3	21 856	29.6	27.9
Victoria	32 510	65.8	119 300	20.5	10.9	793	29.4	4.3	43 919	-2.8	2 361	5.4	41 513	27.9	27.8
Walker	20 685	55.3	116 100	21.4	11.7	786	37.4	2.3	23 663	3.3	1 249	5.3	22 612	31.5	16.2
Waller	13 937	69.0	144 200	22.1	11.7	798	34.1	7.3	21 841	1.1	1 236	5.7	20 127	28.0	25.3
Ward	3 883	72.9	72 200	14.8	10.8	651	19.8	4.2	5 340	-9.4	310	5.8	4 661	20.3	38.5
Washington	11 952	73.8	152 800	22.9	11.9	776	27.5	3.0	14 990	-2.1	769	5.1	14 380	30.0	30.1
Webb	69 668	63.1	109 500	25.2	14.0	758	34.2	16.2	113 533	1.9	5 556	4.9	98 996	26.2	23.0
Wharton	14 741	67.7	102 300	20.3	12.3	678	25.3	3.8	21 009	-0.7	1 055	5.0	18 584	27.2	33.2
Wheeler	2 293	69.9	84 000	21.6	10.0	618	23.4	5.5	2 484	-11.7	125	5.0	2 688	27.7	35.0
Wichita	47 941	61.4	89 700	21.1	12.2	738	28.1	3.2	55 044	-0.2	2 415	4.4	55 053	33.0	22.7
Wilbarger	5 212	65.4	69 200	19.2	13.3	549	23.7	4.1	5 035	-1.1	240	4.8	5 977	27.8	26.8
Willacy	5 553	77.4	49 700	22.3	13.4	498	34.9	11.4	6 500	-3.4	805	12.4	5 365	21.9	29.9
Williamson	161 793	68.5	196 500	22.0	11.0	1 072	27.9	2.8	273 363	3.9	9 125	3.3	233 418	45.4	15.1
Wilson	15 477	83.5	159 700	21.9	11.1	817	23.9	4.5	23 583	3.0	919	3.9	20 521	32.8	27.0
Winkler	2 628	79.3	45 200	14.2	10.0	619	13.9	4.6	3 027	-2.1	238	7.9	3 271	20.6	44.1
Wise	21 068	78.0	126 900	21.9	12.0	885	29.0	4.0	29 155	2.0	1 386	4.8	27 154	28.5	30.8
Wood	16 064	80.0	111 100	24.1	11.9	738	31.7	3.3	17 127	2.5	905	5.3	15 868	29.5	28.2
Yoakum	2 727	72.7	74 600	15.3	10.0	683	19.1	9.1	3 739	-7.3	177	4.7	3 546	25.8	45.9
Young	7 115	77.5	82 000	17.4	10.7	622	26.3	2.3	8 324	-1.4	369	4.4	8 288	30.4	30.5
Zapata	4 517	75.2	55 200	24.2	10.1	416	32.0	15.2	5 100	-17.4	561	11.0	5 184	16.7	37.9
Zavala	3 627	67.8	41 900	21.4	10.9	470	37.0	11.3	3 893	2.6	549	14.1	4 276	28.7	31.9
UTAH	906 292	69.5	215 900	22.8	10.0	887	29.0	3.8	1 511 467	3.1	51 762	3.4	1 337 646	36.8	21.4
Beaver	2 249	75.1	150 000	20.8	10.0	626	25.6	4.0	3 088	-1.2	153	5.0	2 881	28.7	29.2
Box Elder	16 404	77.5	167 500	21.9	10.0	672	24.6	2.5	24 694	2.6	857	3.5	21 534	30.4	34.1
Cache	35 685	65.3	191 900	22.6	10.0	686	29.0	3.1	61 443	2.0	1 881	3.1	54 566	37.4	23.8
Carbon	7 798	71.1	123 900	19.3	10.0	619	25.1	2.6	8 384	-4.1	498	5.9	9 197	26.1	29.3
Daggett	263	87.8	174 700	18.6	10.0	1 069	24.8	2.3	474	1.3	23	4.9	222	21.6	33.3
Davis	97 910	77.3	225 800	22.0	10.0	913	28.3	2.8	164 656	2.6	5 182	3.1	147 875	40.9	18.7
Duchesne	6 606	75.5	172 600	21.1	10.0	849	25.6	4.1	8 158	-7.7	730	8.9	7 875	29.7	38.0
Emery	3 531	82.6	132 700	19.3	10.0	593	26.7	3.3	4 284	-3.0	272	6.3	4 188	26.4	37.1
Garfield	1 751	80.5	156 600	21.5	11.1	633	19.7	2.7	2 780	0.6	233	8.4	2 000	27.6	22.0
Grand	3 789	68.2	224 800	23.2	10.2	758	35.0	2.8	5 773	2.5	337	5.8	4 741	26.1	18.7
Iron	15 095	63.6	165 900	23.6	10.0	661	29.8	3.2	21 491	5.3	930	4.3	19 636	33.5	24.6
Juab	3 106	82.2	165 200	21.9	10.0	761	26.1	4.4	5 178	4.5	187	3.6	4 422	26.5	32.1
Kane	2 789	79.6	175 300	21.8	10.0	858	26.3	3.2	3 685	1.3	140	3.8	3 201	27.7	21.7
Millard	4 160	78.3	138 400	19.5	10.0	657	24.7	4.0	6 275	2.1	209	3.3	5 499	25.8	37.4
Morgan	3 024	83.2	266 400	22.3	10.0	917	29.3	1.8	5 077	2.7	151	3.0	4 234	38.6	25.8
Piute	557	84.0	140 800	22.3	10.3	613	20.8	3.2	463	-0.9	28	6.0	653	35.4	20.4
Rich	640	79.1	173 500	21.3	10.0	614	33.6	3.4	1 111	5.8	35	3.2	731	32.7	32.4
Salt Lake	351 892	66.2	234 700	22.9	10.0	936	29.4	4.1	605 535	3.1	19 142	3.2	536 170	37.4	20.2
San Juan	3 923	79.1	139 400	21.8	10.0	607	21.3	10.9	5 696	-0.7	454	8.0	5 026	32.7	25.8
Sanpete	7 943	74.1	164 400	23.0	10.0	675	22.9	4.6	11 837	3.3	467	3.9	10 060	33.5	28.5
Sevier	7 050	77.2	149 400	22.3	10.0	696	25.2	2.8	9 641	1.0	421	4.4	8 449	26.2	31.2
Summit	13 927	74.6	497 300	22.5	10.0	1 220	25.3	2.4	24 030	3.8	745	3.1	20 741	44.3	15.1
Tooele	18 631	77.0	177 700	22.4	10.0	811	26.1	2.6	30 519	3.0	1 162	3.8	26 337	33.3	26.5
Uintah	10 981	76.2	189 400	21.1	10.0	972	22.2	4.5	14 370	-6.4	1 337	9.3	15 359	28.1	34.9
Utah	148 464	66.9	228 400	23.0	10.0	900	30.1	4.6	279 346	4.7	8 511	3.0	241 085	40.3	17.9
Wasatch	8 095	73.0	316 800	24.4	10.0	1 083	29.4	3.1	13 940	4.8	463	3.3	12 451	34.6	20.2
Washington	48 920	68.8	212 600	26.3	10.0	951	30.5	4.4	67 474	5.6	2 493	3.7	57 785	31.2	20.0
Wayne	972	82.8	198 600	23.3	10.0	544	19.4	4.0	1 439	1.4	111	7.7	1 254	31.1	25.1
Weber	80 137	71.2	168 000	22.6	10.0	793	28.5	3.3	120 626	2.6	4 610	3.8	109 474	31.6	27.2
VERMONT	257 167	71.0	217 500	24.6	16.5	895	30.9	2.1	344 889	-0.2	11 252	3.3	326 732	40.4	20.8
Addison	14 336	74.2	237 300	25.4	17.1	879	28.7	1.6	20 977	0.6	645	3.1	19 530	40.8	24.2
Bennington	15 636	71.9	211 300	27.2	17.6	868	30.7	2.2	18 474	-0.7	704	3.8	18 014	34.1	23.3
Caledonia	12 287	73.6	162 400	24.6	17.6	739	32.5	3.2	15 008	-0.5	620	4.1	14 773	35.2	25.2

1. Specified owner-occupied units.   2. A value of 10.0 represents 10 percent or less; a value of 50.0 represents 50 percent or more.   3. Specified renter-occupied units.
4. Overcrowded or lacking complete plumbing facilities.   5. Percent of civilian labor force.   6. Civilian employed persons 16 years old and over.

Table B. States and Counties — Nonfarm Employment and Agriculture

STATE County	Private nonfarm establishments, employment and payroll, 2015									Agriculture, 2012			
	Number of establishments	Employment						Annual payroll		Farms			Farm operators whose principal occupation is farming (percent)
		Total	Health care and social assistance	Manufacturing	Retail trade	Finance and insurance	Professional, scientific, and technical services	Total (mil dol)	Average per employee (dollars)	Number	Fewer than 50 acres	500 acres or more	
	104	105	106	107	108	109	110	111	112	113	114	115	116

TEXAS—Cont'd

Tom Green	2 798	40 825	8 059	3 162	6 658	1 595	1 384	1 489	36 481	1 203	44.1	20.3	40.1
Travis	33 397	562 990	64 144	26 017	61 926	27 310	66 901	32 073	56 969	1 132	51.7	8.0	42.7
Trinity	169	1 643	283	188	280	75	39	51	31 127	604	32.0	6.6	39.6
Tyler	267	2 574	547	214	787	79	62	71	27 459	727	46.9	4.4	41.8
Upshur	490	4 448	394	365	809	235	448	155	34 929	1 754	46.9	3.5	33.2
Upton	88	1 514	D	NA	80	22	D	83	54 847	101	8.9	68.3	47.5
Uvalde	640	7 112	1 487	380	1 555	252	248	204	28 713	640	17.7	33.9	49.8
Val Verde	767	10 765	3 079	401	2 175	482	186	269	25 008	421	40.9	35.2	42.5
Van Zandt	889	7 898	959	721	1 480	236	318	265	33 520	2 915	49.6	5.0	43.6
Victoria	2 422	35 554	6 542	2 167	6 185	933	1 158	1 534	43 136	1 533	41.6	12.1	41.6
Walker	962	12 214	2 072	949	2 703	407	444	359	29 427	1 560	55.5	6.7	43.3
Waller	715	11 651	1 129	3 727	987	107	262	502	43 117	1 927	59.2	5.6	41.7
Ward	307	4 125	255	71	342	95	85	211	51 125	93	30.1	33.3	26.9
Washington	883	12 936	1 795	3 312	2 049	784	359	448	34 594	2 697	42.7	4.2	35.8
Webb	5 259	75 850	15 232	605	13 739	2 656	1 982	2 186	28 820	696	15.1	48.6	48.6
Wharton	972	11 508	1 766	1 508	2 210	438	262	387	33 587	1 553	31.6	21.6	51.6
Wheeler	195	1 634	286	6	248	48	56	54	33 268	551	8.3	39.2	37.0
Wichita	3 113	45 176	11 115	4 680	7 410	1 658	1 619	1 593	35 268	639	40.2	15.5	38.3
Wilbarger	295	3 577	396	D	684	124	73	118	33 059	424	18.6	33.0	43.6
Willacy	192	2 458	428	D	454	94	31	64	26 046	321	47.0	26.2	50.2
Williamson	9 842	141 251	19 857	8 816	23 721	7 681	16 381	6 728	47 634	2 542	48.3	9.3	43.2
Wilson	684	6 631	1 237	326	1 395	192	244	218	32 891	2 444	38.1	7.2	38.4
Winkler	178	1 816	77	NA	243	60	15	110	60 593	43	30.2	60.5	32.6
Wise	1 307	20 352	2 670	2 077	2 272	379	356	898	44 127	3 095	54.2	6.4	37.6
Wood	806	8 514	1 187	914	1 408	350	914	272	31 930	1 465	44.6	4.9	47.4
Yoakum	190	2 652	D	128	271	86	15	149	56 348	339	5.0	58.1	50.1
Young	601	6 187	1 176	1 106	873	241	144	230	37 250	795	21.0	25.5	39.4
Zapata	150	1 796	232	D	269	84	9	68	37 919	449	9.4	49.9	49.4
Zavala	107	1 713	614	D	208	47	24	41	23 920	287	7.3	54.7	46.7
UTAH	75 463	1 203 954	133 442	118 196	150 671	62 207	93 945	51 453	42 737	18 027	57.9	12.3	38.5
Beaver	168	1 735	291	109	436	37	13	52	29 862	277	43.3	20.9	66.1
Box Elder	1 076	16 550	1 460	7 190	1 657	272	227	795	48 014	1 235	45.6	21.6	41.0
Cache	3 236	41 502	5 652	11 457	6 078	1 395	3 176	1 361	32 782	1 217	51.5	10.4	39.9
Carbon	504	6 322	967	496	1 087	228	121	248	39 163	319	63.3	13.8	46.7
Daggett	19	87	NA	NA	27	NA	D	3	37 379	51	37.3	21.6	31.4
Davis	6 900	82 478	10 118	10 692	14 440	2 279	8 825	3 155	38 256	493	79.9	2.4	32.9
Duchesne	706	6 989	1 026	220	859	106	253	316	45 278	1 058	39.0	13.7	35.4
Emery	187	2 228	165	11	479	48	60	115	51 409	587	48.9	12.4	42.9
Garfield	153	1 318	D	26	115	18	24	42	32 008	279	42.3	12.2	43.0
Grand	460	4 063	348	80	733	69	143	120	29 501	81	60.5	13.6	51.9
Iron	1 288	11 665	1 854	1 491	2 225	431	391	353	30 238	509	39.3	24.6	45.0
Juab	198	2 637	484	818	265	38	268	75	28 313	353	33.1	22.1	28.3
Kane	253	2 366	235	D	347	95	26	74	31 464	183	33.3	24.6	39.9
Millard	251	2 949	235	505	605	71	88	131	44 489	728	29.3	30.2	49.9
Morgan	252	1 614	157	158	164	55	101	67	41 639	301	59.8	10.6	37.5
Piute	19	63	D	NA	23	D	NA	1	23 794	123	23.6	15.4	54.5
Rich	88	408	D	D	28	D	22	15	37 245	158	29.1	54.4	61.4
Salt Lake	30 949	571 478	61 561	48 520	63 512	41 519	48 525	27 491	48 105	630	89.8	3.0	29.2
San Juan	233	2 663	657	191	335	62	26	81	30 474	746	53.8	22.8	54.7
Sanpete	413	4 868	910	699	934	133	572	139	28 471	901	52.5	13.1	38.5
Sevier	521	6 535	820	237	1 445	143	127	216	32 988	674	60.8	6.4	38.9
Summit	2 316	26 498	1 234	576	4 238	1 078	1 112	919	34 681	618	62.0	11.2	33.0
Tooele	823	10 569	1 241	1 728	1 831	170	525	382	36 172	476	60.1	14.5	31.3
Uintah	1 131	11 306	752	334	1 866	207	554	496	43 886	1 231	55.5	8.0	32.8
Utah	12 240	189 798	23 047	17 109	25 864	5 175	13 108	7 596	40 024	2 462	78.9	3.8	30.5
Wasatch	862	6 340	615	231	1 127	129	548	214	33 680	450	76.9	5.1	32.4
Washington	4 557	45 178	8 190	2 517	8 405	1 423	1 896	1 469	32 515	579	63.0	13.1	43.5
Wayne	85	565	103	4	113	NA	6	17	30 830	187	29.4	10.2	48.1
Weber	5 136	76 598	11 016	12 724	11 408	4 031	3 869	2 905	37 920	1 121	79.8	3.1	36.4
VERMONT	21 121	266 363	48 095	29 786	40 006	9 103	18 840	10 615	39 852	7 338	39.2	7.3	51.5
Addison	1 170	14 191	2 034	1 733	2 142	334	632	560	39 482	814	37.0	14.7	60.6
Bennington	1 395	15 456	3 341	2 371	3 013	333	369	551	35 671	305	48.9	3.9	46.6
Caledonia	901	8 739	1 790	1 499	1 615	294	230	325	37 160	560	38.8	5.7	47.1

Table B. States and Counties — **Agriculture**

	Agriculture, 2012 (cont.)														
	Land in farms				Value of land and buildings (dollars)			Value of products sold					Percent of farms with sales of:		Government payments	
			Acres							Percent from:						
STATE County	Acreage (1,000)	Percent change, 2007– 2012	Average size of farm	Total irrigated (1,000)	Total cropland (1,000)	Average per farm	Average per acre	Value of machinery and equipment, average per farm (dollars)	Total (mil dol)	Average per farm (dollars)	Crops	Live-stock and poultry products	$10,000 or more	$100,000 or more	Total ($1,000)	Percent of farms
	117	118	119	120	121	122	123	124	125	126	127	128	129	130	131	132
TEXAS—Cont'd																
Tom Green	957	3.6	795	31.1	168.2	906 863	1 140	87 951	131.4	109 257	24.8	75.2	26.9	9.4	5 161	25.4
Travis	253	-3.7	223	1.8	61.2	856 591	3 837	55 964	41.7	36 809	82.0	18.0	24.6	6.6	1 130	16.8
Trinity	111	2.1	184	0.2	17.9	427 030	2 318	57 775	7.1	11 672	24.1	75.9	31.1	1.3	161	7.3
Tyler	91	7.6	125	0.6	16.4	364 713	2 924	58 297	19.1	26 333	74.7	25.3	21.7	1.1	43	2.9
Upshur	202	2.1	115	0.4	43.1	330 283	2 863	43 263	60.6	34 526	7.6	92.4	21.8	3.2	298	2.7
Upton	686	8.2	6 794	8.9	46.1	3 991 644	587	142 505	12.7	125 584	63.6	36.4	54.5	34.7	1 495	41.6
Uvalde	977	-1.3	1 527	49.5	139.8	3 052 314	1 999	102 739	112.5	175 742	55.0	45.0	33.6	14.1	2 447	28.1
Val Verde	1 497	0.2	3 556	0.4	8.1	2 028 570	570	39 625	10.7	25 297	3.8	96.2	20.9	6.9	1 146	10.0
Van Zandt	371	-10.9	127	2.4	100.6	405 667	3 191	47 770	94.3	32 360	50.1	49.9	25.7	3.2	887	2.9
Victoria	438	-11.3	286	3.3	80.2	654 921	2 293	54 768	47.6	31 020	58.4	41.6	27.5	4.3	2 451	18.2
Walker	281	25.2	180	0.5	38.6	598 604	3 329	52 780	34.5	22 124	53.8	46.2	16.9	2.1	533	2.8
Waller	315	16.2	163	10.1	79.9	1 020 860	6 245	64 387	91.7	47 575	76.8	23.2	25.1	4.5	2 172	14.7
Ward	392	-9.5	4 211	0.2	5.9	1 560 022	370	53 290	1.8	19 054	6.5	93.5	19.4	3.2	214	18.3
Washington	369	9.0	137	1.4	89.4	758 889	5 549	51 747	45.7	16 955	24.9	75.1	25.9	1.9	914	8.4
Webb	2 098	13.1	3 015	2.6	25.2	3 265 045	1 083	57 487	30.3	43 476	2.8	97.2	31.2	7.0	1 169	14.1
Wharton	661	7.3	425	71.6	391.6	1 080 889	2 541	159 701	373.6	240 591	72.5	27.5	49.5	22.0	13 724	52.9
Wheeler	519	-11.0	942	11.2	99.6	773 481	821	83 860	111.2	201 826	8.2	91.8	40.8	10.2	2 651	61.0
Wichita	367	10.9	574	3.0	117.1	684 844	1 193	80 674	37.9	59 362	51.6	48.4	35.1	9.5	2 069	33.5
Wilbarger	587	-4.3	1 385	15.7	196.6	1 384 455	1 000	143 679	47.2	111 425	66.5	33.5	50.2	18.9	3 593	71.9
Willacy	336	-0.6	1 047	21.1	192.1	1 913 025	1 827	165 358	82.6	257 215	94.9	5.1	40.8	23.1	3 370	60.7
Williamson	559	3.1	220	1.3	211.6	853 775	3 885	61 058	129.6	51 002	57.8	42.2	25.5	6.7	3 659	26.2
Wilson	440	-5.9	180	12.4	103.3	537 404	2 987	50 097	102.1	41 775	27.3	72.7	27.5	3.0	1 988	20.7
Winkler	533	0.1	12 406	D	D	4 500 116	363	95 000	3.4	79 907	D	D	41.9	18.6	D	7.0
Wise	487	10.0	157	2.8	114.3	600 404	3 815	52 997	49.9	16 112	32.9	67.1	23.1	2.6	1 079	7.5
Wood	227	-2.8	155	1.6	52.5	442 703	2 853	57 063	105.9	72 270	6.2	93.8	27.2	5.3	267	3.3
Yoakum	488	10.1	1 441	90.4	265.9	1 166 307	809	247 257	80.0	236 012	91.6	8.4	47.2	32.4	7 563	81.7
Young	524	-0.7	659	0.2	97.8	911 345	1 384	68 309	23.7	29 801	33.8	66.2	33.8	5.2	1 385	30.1
Zapata	563	22.6	1 254	1.8	13.0	1 465 744	1 169	50 205	11.8	26 238	38.7	61.3	32.7	4.2	932	17.4
Zavala	693	-7.9	2 414	29.4	96.0	3 705 300	1 535	109 195	72.7	253 359	39.9	60.1	32.8	18.5	1 427	31.4
UTAH	10 974	-1.1	609	1 104.3	1 645.9	888 886	1 460	84 528	1 816.1	100 746	31.6	68.4	37.2	11.0	23 898	15.4
Beaver	190	20.0	686	37.6	37.1	1 370 004	1 997	140 502	288.5	1 041 520	7.5	92.5	57.8	33.6	419	31.4
Box Elder	1 171	-11.3	948	102.9	328.6	1 140 029	1 203	129 594	169.5	137 284	45.0	55.0	47.4	21.0	7 453	40.5
Cache	269	6.7	221	76.3	137.2	778 555	3 529	96 619	142.9	117 407	26.3	73.7	43.9	14.9	2 456	33.7
Carbon	241	11.6	754	11.1	20.9	918 621	1 218	59 596	9.0	28 248	27.0	73.0	31.3	5.3	239	5.6
Daggett	D	D	D	7.3	6.9	824 255	D	91 882	2.3	45 529	33.5	66.5	45.1	13.7	44	7.8
Davis	55	11.6	112	13.8	13.0	723 596	6 484	66 773	36.8	74 564	85.9	14.1	29.8	8.3	178	7.3
Duchesne	1 089	1.1	1 029	100.9	78.2	856 720	833	92 628	57.1	53 992	33.2	66.8	47.0	11.2	455	8.4
Emery	156	-23.7	266	51.7	41.6	452 336	1 700	65 775	14.1	23 978	36.2	63.8	37.8	6.0	306	16.7
Garfield	92	11.8	328	19.6	17.6	746 086	2 274	57 297	12.0	43 165	30.0	70.0	47.7	8.2	113	7.9
Grand	D	D	D	4.2	6.3	1 571 889	D	100 469	3.9	47 815	58.5	41.5	45.7	14.8	28	11.1
Iron	532	8.2	1 046	61.6	77.6	1 973 149	1 886	141 428	136.7	268 658	39.1	60.9	47.9	21.2	714	12.8
Juab	243	-6.7	688	20.5	47.9	825 640	1 200	86 938	28.4	80 331	40.7	59.3	45.6	11.6	997	35.4
Kane	125	10.6	685	4.0	4.5	966 694	1 410	50 333	4.7	25 590	16.8	83.2	43.2	2.7	214	10.4
Millard	577	1.9	793	115.2	151.6	1 114 356	1 405	200 816	180.6	248 110	41.4	58.6	64.3	27.6	2 312	38.3
Morgan	229	-24.1	760	9.0	15.8	1 196 671	1 575	63 116	20.4	67 648	16.7	83.3	36.5	12.6	71	10.0
Piute	38	-10.7	308	13.9	15.0	901 667	2 931	124 073	16.9	137 797	10.9	89.1	52.8	15.4	101	11.4
Rich	409	12.6	2 591	66.0	77.2	2 606 139	1 006	155 513	32.8	207 753	13.6	86.4	65.2	40.5	597	18.4
Salt Lake	78	-27.3	124	6.8	13.5	586 952	4 731	55 016	21.5	34 160	65.3	34.7	21.3	5.9	80	2.4
San Juan	1 609	4.0	2 157	4.3	113.0	805 649	374	43 488	13.4	17 906	32.6	67.4	16.6	5.2	1 543	23.9
Sanpete	284	-8.7	316	68.9	74.9	679 514	2 153	95 179	147.4	163 604	14.8	85.2	41.6	15.0	1 682	15.5
Sevier	122	-34.1	181	40.2	44.6	548 010	3 019	79 190	63.0	93 399	31.6	68.4	37.1	10.5	452	12.9
Summit	270	-34.9	437	20.8	25.2	996 972	2 281	51 511	24.2	39 079	13.0	87.0	34.0	7.0	154	2.4
Tooele	347	37.2	729	23.0	40.2	870 779	1 194	80 141	40.4	84 845	28.2	71.8	33.8	8.6	170	6.9
Uintah	D	D	D	69.0	62.5	930 444	D	75 442	46.6	37 877	45.7	54.3	33.5	6.3	653	6.6
Utah	343	-0.7	139	75.2	109.5	742 896	5 331	68 401	222.6	90 427	44.1	55.9	29.4	6.2	1 123	7.6
Wasatch	149	126.3	332	12.4	17.4	1 266 053	3 818	53 662	12.2	27 069	26.0	74.0	21.3	3.6	200	3.1
Washington	148	-15.0	256	14.8	20.2	934 487	3 656	50 485	12.6	21 843	51.1	48.9	29.2	5.5	210	7.8
Wayne	42	-6.3	227	15.7	15.3	914 588	4 037	78 561	15.7	84 144	19.3	80.7	62.6	14.4	500	35.3
Weber	117	10.5	105	37.7	32.9	609 955	5 823	60 135	39.9	35 568	41.9	58.1	23.5	4.4	436	8.0
VERMONT	1 252	1.5	171	3.6	488.3	546 627	3 205	86 935	776.1	105 765	22.9	77.1	40.6	15.1	13 930	21.3
Addison	208	11.1	256	0.3	126.8	779 307	3 044	130 227	185.5	227 928	15.3	84.7	47.1	21.4	3 796	32.7
Bennington	41	13.1	136	0.3	11.2	566 646	4 176	81 639	15.1	49 420	52.4	47.6	34.1	7.5	261	10.5
Caledonia	82	-0.1	146	0.1	29.1	464 918	3 182	76 234	37.2	66 509	18.1	81.9	40.4	13.6	628	15.7

Table B. States and Counties — Water Use, Wholesale Trade, Retail Trade, and Real Estate

STATE County	Water use, 2010		Wholesale trade,[1] 2012				Retail trade,[2] 2012				Real estate and rental and leasing,[2] 2012			
	Total water withdrawn (mil gal/day)	Gallons withdrawn per person per day	Number of establishments	Number of employees	Sales (mil dol)	Annual payroll (mil dol)	Number of establishments	Number of employees	Sales (mil dol)	Annual payroll (mil dol)	Number of establishments	Number of employees	Receipts (mil dol)	Annual payroll (mil dol)
	133	134	135	136	137	138	139	140	141	142	143	144	145	146
TEXAS—Cont'd														
Tom Green	55.9	507	113	D	D	D	418	5 963	1 821.7	149.8	134	595	92.7	16.5
Travis	293.3	286	1 166	21 735	56 614.8	1 470.9	3 469	54 094	15 583.7	1 443.3	1 771	10 798	2 455.1	539.0
Trinity	2.2	152	3	D	D	D	38	291	62.0	4.9	2	D	D	D
Tyler	5.1	236	7	47	39.7	3.6	53	531	115.8	10.0	4	21	1.0	0.2
Upshur	23.6	600	11	103	54.1	3.7	76	763	203.4	16.6	10	15	2.6	0.4
Upton	21.9	6 513	6	D	D	D	8	73	22.3	1.4	1	D	D	D
Uvalde	55.7	2 109	29	D	D	D	105	1 249	424.2	27.6	32	97	15.5	2.9
Val Verde	13.1	268	24	D	D	D	148	2 019	583.5	44.1	35	122	17.5	2.8
Van Zandt	11.3	216	29	263	72.3	11.3	147	1 406	430.7	31.2	29	83	6.2	1.4
Victoria	65.0	748	112	1 703	1 247.7	91.4	382	5 501	1 657.7	141.3	127	D	D	D
Walker	12.3	181	25	D	D	D	165	2 397	759.7	51.0	57	D	D	D
Waller	26.9	623	51	1 043	684.4	47.2	90	934	303.5	21.3	23	104	10.7	2.4
Ward	18.9	1 776	8	116	36.6	4.6	30	359	105.4	7.5	10	151	55.2	16.0
Washington	6.7	198	35	508	516.6	24.2	140	1 945	569.2	46.4	48	160	47.0	8.9
Webb	43.5	174	357	2 839	2 410.1	97.0	784	12 356	3 217.6	257.8	199	692	132.4	22.0
Wharton	223.6	5 416	49	890	572.2	37.2	163	1 999	563.8	49.1	39	168	29.4	7.5
Wheeler	17.9	3 303	9	D	D	D	33	239	71.6	5.1	6	8	1.1	0.2
Wichita	71.1	540	147	1 191	660.1	55.3	502	7 397	1 991.0	166.2	162	807	167.8	29.9
Wilbarger	34.8	2 567	12	D	D	D	48	664	254.6	14.3	10	22	2.7	0.6
Willacy	41.7	1 883	7	D	D	D	32	420	118.4	9.4	9	17	3.5	0.4
Williamson	64.1	152	306	D	D	D	1 277	21 844	8 585.0	593.3	408	1 550	348.9	65.5
Wilson	21.5	501	19	D	D	D	73	1 151	452.4	25.3	15	28	4.9	0.7
Winkler	14.5	2 032	7	D	D	D	20	195	53.6	4.4	7	D	D	D
Wise	68.4	1 157	57	609	658.0	31.9	154	2 174	757.1	62.1	46	291	61.3	13.8
Wood	53.0	1 262	31	257	169.8	7.6	129	1 345	393.7	33.4	30	133	31.0	4.9
Yoakum	211.9	26 888	11	135	43.6	8.9	28	211	61.6	5.2	6	D	D	D
Young	58.0	3 126	28	D	D	D	68	827	215.5	18.4	20	51	43.4	2.1
Zapata	7.4	527	1	D	D	D	32	263	75.7	5.3	4	26	5.7	0.7
Zavala	39.5	3 381	2	D	D	D	17	181	45.6	3.8	NA	NA	NA	NA
UTAH	4 463.8	1 615	3 015	43 523	30 927.9	2 364.4	9 095	133 535	38 024.5	3 334.9	4 446	16 197	3 226.1	604.8
Beaver	101.3	15 274	1	D	D	D	38	383	115.5	6.6	1	D	D	D
Box Elder	405.3	8 109	32	D	D	D	134	1 605	482.7	33.4	41	43	6.4	0.9
Cache	289.5	2 570	109	D	D	D	402	5 469	1 154.2	108.7	181	483	69.1	16.5
Carbon	41.3	1 929	30	D	D	D	86	1 084	311.3	26.0	15	57	17.9	1.9
Daggett	19.0	17 951	NA	NA	NA	NA	3	D	D	D	2	D	D	D
Davis	84.1	274	241	2 363	1 300.8	94.8	827	12 937	3 448.8	309.8	396	1 002	220.0	35.1
Duchesne	328.3	17 641	18	198	90.3	8.2	66	758	264.9	18.2	34	116	76.8	6.9
Emery	130.6	11 894	5	D	D	D	36	478	105.1	10.2	NA	NA	NA	NA
Garfield	64.5	12 477	4	D	D	D	23	116	29.9	2.2	2	D	D	D
Grand	17.1	1 857	13	D	D	D	79	678	170.1	16.0	31	131	14.0	2.7
Iron	210.1	4 551	33	261	246.0	9.7	172	1 892	567.8	43.3	72	165	28.7	4.8
Juab	56.1	5 478	9	62	36.3	2.2	33	313	114.5	5.0	2	D	D	D
Kane	17.6	2 466	4	7	1.3	0.2	41	337	77.1	6.4	16	26	3.6	0.7
Millard	291.1	23 281	13	D	D	D	61	549	122.1	9.1	3	4	0.3	0.1
Morgan	36.0	3 802	4	D	D	D	26	213	52.1	4.6	9	15	1.9	0.3
Piute	46.6	29 929	1	D	D	D	7	D	D	D	NA	NA	NA	NA
Rich	143.9	63 556	1	D	D	D	10	49	9.6	0.7	10	23	5.1	1.1
Salt Lake	410.8	399	1 653	27 748	19 734.9	1 640.3	3 395	55 808	17 178.4	1 536.0	1 931	8 980	1 927.6	378.3
San Juan	29.1	1 975	4	D	D	D	36	291	68.7	4.7	2	D	D	D
Sanpete	181.7	6 532	9	45	35.0	1.2	80	861	169.5	15.8	15	42	4.6	0.7
Sevier	143.9	6 916	13	90	211.9	3.4	88	1 255	331.8	29.2	14	85	17.7	2.9
Summit	70.9	1 952	43	551	378.7	32.0	295	4 105	1 013.6	101.5	245	900	124.1	27.6
Tooele	186.0	3 194	13	63	31.9	2.9	104	1 688	496.8	37.1	30	76	10.3	1.6
Uintah	274.6	8 426	45	D	D	D	135	1 575	503.2	43.4	79	453	104.1	21.8
Utah	366.1	709	368	5 770	3 112.6	298.4	1 520	22 096	6 039.4	529.6	684	D	D	D
Wasatch	56.3	2 391	17	35	11.0	1.0	88	1 021	267.4	20.7	44	105	27.3	3.4
Washington	122.2	885	149	1 284	1 514.7	47.4	574	7 375	1 900.8	168.4	306	702	95.2	18.7
Wayne	69.8	25 133	NA	NA	NA	NA	15	104	32.1	1.9	1	D	D	D
Weber	270.2	1 169	183	2 924	2 655.6	129.1	721	10 462	2 991.6	245.8	280	905	130.9	24.9
VERMONT	430.5	688	696	9 464	6 450.1	464.4	3 509	38 910	9 933.8	967.1	741	3 092	509.9	103.6
Addison	7.5	203	31	D	D	D	184	1 886	536.9	51.6	37	94	11.0	2.4
Bennington	5.3	142	27	D	D	D	271	3 051	806.2	79.8	53	222	29.9	6.7
Caledonia	4.0	128	29	D	D	D	173	1 687	451.4	43.1	30	D	D	D

1. Merchant wholesalers, except manufacturers' sales branches and offices.   2. Employer establishments.

Table B. States and Counties — Professional Services, Manufacturing, and Accommodation and Food Services

STATE County	Professional, scientific, and technical services, 2012				Manufacturing, 2012				Accommodation and food services, 2012			
	Number of establishments	Number of employees	Receipts (mil dol)	Annual payroll (mil dol)	Number of establishments	Number of employees	Receipts (mil dol)	Annual payroll (mil dol)	Number of establishments	Number of employees	Sales (mil dol)	Annual payroll (mil dol)
	147	148	149	150	151	152	153	154	155	156	157	158
TEXAS—Cont'd												
Tom Green	209	1 358	159.0	58.5	101	3 434	D	135.1	230	D	D	D
Travis	5 624	59 846	12 138.9	4 870.9	788	23 903	12 281.9	1 501.1	2 731	59 496	3 726.8	1 033.0
Trinity	11	42	3.3	1.0	9	158	79.9	8.8	15	223	14.7	3.2
Tyler	23	50	6.0	1.6	13	71	D	2.7	21	218	9.6	2.4
Upshur	51	446	47.0	16.6	23	285	113.3	13.4	37	D	D	D
Upton	3	D	D	D	NA	NA	NA	NA	11	D	D	D
Uvalde	41	D	D	D	17	409	149.5	12.1	80	1 063	58.1	13.3
Val Verde	45	D	D	D	22	321	D	11.0	94	1 647	77.8	19.8
Van Zandt	63	258	33.9	11.9	35	690	142.8	37.9	77	975	44.8	13.7
Victoria	159	874	115.1	41.1	73	2 021	D	D	188	3 593	187.0	49.2
Walker	90	473	42.9	14.2	41	761	352.7	37.3	103	1 875	92.1	24.8
Waller	62	490	72.7	40.2	70	2 744	919.4	160.1	46	647	33.2	7.8
Ward	18	62	7.4	2.6	4	38	D	2.1	28	326	22.3	5.0
Washington	59	339	48.1	13.8	45	2 967	883.6	128.4	86	1 084	54.9	14.8
Webb	317	1 803	186.1	58.6	69	635	339.6	22.0	389	8 216	423.7	106.2
Wharton	59	267	31.5	9.6	40	1 513	400.8	55.0	68	948	47.5	12.8
Wheeler	17	102	13.7	5.1	NA	NA	NA	NA	23	284	19.7	3.9
Wichita	235	D	D	D	129	4 885	1 400.8	230.7	271	D	D	D
Wilbarger	17	D	D	D	11	D	D	D	38	484	20.8	5.1
Willacy	10	D	D	D	3	12	D	D	23	253	13.1	2.9
Williamson	1 118	7 490	1 158.6	451.6	299	7 485	1 886.3	386.1	793	15 477	817.0	224.2
Wilson	37	166	22.8	11.9	24	327	121.9	15.2	62	763	36.8	9.6
Winkler	12	18	4.1	0.7	NA	NA	NA	NA	10	D	D	D
Wise	85	289	40.3	11.2	75	1 892	550.2	94.0	105	1 568	75.9	19.4
Wood	73	643	28.0	12.5	38	822	575.7	35.6	76	864	40.6	11.3
Yoakum	7	14	1.7	0.4	7	98	D	4.8	24	168	8.1	1.8
Young	34	102	13.7	5.2	22	881	252.2	42.5	42	474	21.9	6.0
Zapata	4	D	D	D	NA	NA	NA	NA	19	D	D	D
Zavala	7	27	1.0	0.2	3	D	D	D	17	200	8.8	2.1
UTAH	9 009	76 345	10 555.1	3 909.0	3 163	108 264	50 046.4	5 762.6	5 108	95 933	4 789.3	1 362.9
Beaver	5	11	1.0	0.2	6	79	D	2.9	29	244	12.0	3.1
Box Elder	53	213	23.6	7.1	72	6 206	D	469.2	69	1 174	47.5	14.8
Cache	368	2 487	245.2	87.2	207	10 515	4 516.6	434.4	162	2 969	125.1	33.8
Carbon	29	108	14.5	4.2	21	426	121.5	19.0	37	640	25.6	7.3
Daggett	1	D	D	D	NA	NA	NA	NA	7	64	5.1	1.5
Davis	868	6 369	974.4	320.4	265	9 506	5 982.0	459.4	420	8 178	350.5	96.9
Duchesne	50	168	27.0	6.9	22	209	D	9.9	33	396	21.7	4.8
Emery	14	149	7.8	3.5	4	17	D	0.9	20	192	8.2	2.0
Garfield	9	D	D	D	5	21	2.1	0.6	51	556	62.9	15.6
Grand	30	148	12.7	4.2	6	71	D	3.8	90	1 513	86.7	24.9
Iron	107	425	59.4	15.5	65	1 273	656.4	54.4	101	1 475	64.3	17.2
Juab	18	313	34.2	17.0	12	364	136.4	13.2	21	203	7.9	2.3
Kane	17	20	2.4	0.5	5	73	D	D	52	564	47.9	12.7
Millard	10	88	6.3	3.2	12	485	D	24.0	29	308	12.4	3.2
Morgan	23	86	7.8	2.6	12	143	D	9.2	8	111	4.5	1.7
Piute	NA	NA	NA	NA	NA	NA	NA	NA	5	22	0.8	0.3
Rich	6	10	1.3	0.5	NA	NA	NA	NA	14	79	9.5	2.7
Salt Lake	4 145	D	D	D	1 360	46 402	22 060.4	2 669.6	2 080	41 574	2 170.9	634.1
San Juan	13	23	1.6	0.7	7	230	D	10.8	52	744	65.0	14.3
Sanpete	22	92	7.2	2.3	25	657	174.7	22.5	36	390	10.5	3.1
Sevier	32	109	11.0	4.7	20	202	45.1	8.3	52	725	26.9	7.4
Summit	339	900	218.6	55.3	39	465	D	24.3	169	5 803	323.2	103.6
Tooele	68	D	D	D	34	1 705	884.3	92.3	69	1 028	46.4	12.4
Uintah	102	542	73.3	25.3	33	309	52.1	12.8	68	1 079	57.5	13.1
Utah	1 636	16 643	1 707.6	639.2	513	15 599	5 945.7	794.0	688	13 046	569.4	159.2
Wasatch	109	337	45.5	13.7	33	204	41.5	7.6	56	1 066	63.1	16.8
Washington	433	D	D	D	133	1 838	415.3	76.1	307	5 140	282.3	74.4
Wayne	3	D	D	D	4	D	1.7	D	25	157	12.8	2.4
Weber	499	4 180	401.7	195.7	247	11 260	4 799.0	540.7	358	6 493	268.6	77.3
VERMONT	2 113	15 948	1 782.0	739.9	1 013	31 487	9 315.5	1 594.3	1 920	31 365	1 564.3	494.0
Addison	123	D	D	D	57	1 472	D	82.1	86	873	55.2	18.8
Bennington	125	409	43.7	16.2	69	2 472	764.5	108.4	143	1 821	95.0	33.9
Caledonia	70	D	D	D	57	1 361	256.5	61.5	72	661	37.7	10.2

1. Establishment subject to federal tax.

Table B. States and Counties — **Health Care and Social Assistance, Other Services, Nonemployer Businesses, and Residential Construction**

STATE County	Health care and social assistance, 2012				Other services, 2012				Nonemployer businesses, 2015		Value of residential construction authorized by building permits, 2016	
	Number of establishments	Number of employees	Receipts (mil dol)	Annual payroll (mil dol)	Number of establishments	Number of employees	Receipts (mil dol)	Annual payroll (mil dol)	Number	Receipts (mil dol)	New Construction ($1,000)	Number of housing units
	159	160	161	162	163	164	165	166	167	168	169	170
TEXAS—Cont'd												
Tom Green	269	D	D	D	210	D	D	D	8 590	350.8	38 989	172
Travis	2 969	57 586	6 996.8	2 731.1	2 084	18 611	2 448.4	703.7	116 321	6 322.6	2 211 377	13 503
Trinity	22	320	24.4	9.7	17	64	4.1	0.8	968	36.2	89	1
Tyler	23	523	33.6	15.3	13	D	D	D	1 109	45.0	780	9
Upshur	35	634	40.6	17.7	24	95	8.2	2.5	2 821	124.2	325	5
Upton	5	D	D	D	NA	NA	NA	NA	280	15.8	0	0
Uvalde	73	1 731	130.7	45.8	33	D	D	D	2 743	127.3	1 818	23
Val Verde	92	2 819	89.9	45.2	47	255	15.1	4.4	3 063	108.1	14 573	93
Van Zandt	68	1 201	72.1	33.4	56	272	27.4	7.2	4 321	184.2	4 655	28
Victoria	304	6 591	679.7	274.5	151	1 165	162.8	46.8	6 213	287.6	12 785	62
Walker	97	2 179	180.2	75.2	54	297	23.6	6.1	4 082	150.8	32 146	156
Waller	38	D	D	D	43	195	25.2	5.7	3 673	193.3	18 045	305
Ward	12	229	15.9	8.7	13	168	21.6	6.8	699	36.2	372	3
Washington	98	1 906	98.3	43.0	53	212	17.4	5.1	3 134	151.5	6 846	84
Webb	536	14 678	926.2	373.6	203	1 129	101.1	27.1	24 479	1 146.6	212 895	1 158
Wharton	67	2 374	131.4	51.3	71	274	18.5	5.0	3 229	126.4	16 849	82
Wheeler	13	271	17.8	7.4	12	D	D	D	548	24.2	85	1
Wichita	391	10 832	1 051.7	391.7	225	1 212	118.8	31.1	7 732	360.3	31 975	176
Wilbarger	34	513	34.2	15.1	26	D	D	D	725	22.8	100	1
Willacy	33	547	27.1	12.8	12	39	2.4	0.5	1 307	39.5	4 826	37
Williamson	982	16 410	1 861.9	721.8	608	4 107	378.7	122.0	41 059	1 840.6	1 221 952	5 417
Wilson	55	1 158	69.5	29.3	46	140	11.8	2.7	3 454	171.1	10 618	52
Winkler	6	86	8.0	3.0	7	65	13.7	2.5	545	28.1	0	0
Wise	113	D	D	D	66	D	D	D	5 251	295.8	13 841	76
Wood	86	1 421	99.9	43.5	47	186	16.5	4.3	3 482	161.9	1 936	12
Yoakum	10	D	D	D	9	37	6.5	1.9	462	23.9	0	0
Young	58	1 032	77.3	31.7	37	147	13.3	3.6	2 075	126.1	1 702	10
Zapata	18	264	9.1	4.1	5	D	D	D	1 432	48.1	NA	NA
Zavala	12	D	D	D	2	D	D	D	844	21.7	817	4
UTAH	7 285	126 175	14 521.9	5 020.8	4 259	26 026	2 544.5	723.2	216 280	9 984.3	4 808 309	22 662
Beaver	21	D	D	D	10	26	3.6	0.8	433	15.3	3 116	19
Box Elder	116	D	D	D	66	D	D	D	3 203	126.5	41 023	186
Cache	348	5 106	494.3	161.6	172	810	60.7	17.8	8 411	324.8	152 831	837
Carbon	71	862	100.7	28.9	44	D	D	D	1 051	33.0	6 248	18
Daggett	NA	NA	NA	NA	NA	NA	NA	NA	96	4.6	1 262	5
Davis	667	9 466	888.6	340.7	395	2 471	182.9	54.0	22 514	1 006.9	388 398	1 770
Duchesne	50	D	D	D	34	D	D	D	1 464	64.1	10 541	74
Emery	17	D	D	D	15	D	D	D	584	15.5	1 936	10
Garfield	6	D	D	D	3	D	D	D	463	13.4	364	5
Grand	25	287	37.5	12.4	22	D	D	D	1 048	43.3	20 521	106
Iron	138	1 641	130.9	43.9	74	343	24.8	6.5	3 501	126.3	88 737	382
Juab	22	415	44.2	14.5	7	19	1.6	0.5	724	31.6	19 780	78
Kane	12	268	18.3	8.2	16	D	D	D	696	28.9	9 697	49
Millard	21	D	D	D	17	D	D	D	766	29.4	6 637	37
Morgan	21	D	D	D	8	D	D	D	998	41.9	31 372	85
Piute	1	D	D	D	1	D	D	D	110	5.8	3 485	19
Rich	2	D	D	D	6	D	D	D	237	8.2	10 108	42
Salt Lake	2 933	60 445	7 609.2	2 669.6	1 872	12 731	1 328.0	396.5	82 040	4 127.0	1 493 137	8 161
San Juan	34	701	76.0	28.2	11	D	D	D	794	23.3	5 400	32
Sanpete	47	856	58.7	23.0	25	D	D	D	1 783	69.8	5 797	48
Sevier	58	804	71.3	24.1	29	D	D	D	1 446	55.6	14 711	59
Summit	134	D	D	D	106	769	115.4	27.0	5 976	392.8	127 777	344
Tooele	92	1 267	125.5	45.5	58	239	20.9	5.5	2 890	98.8	123 112	570
Uintah	63	D	D	D	73	436	60.3	13.7	1 870	74.5	6 418	25
Utah	1 197	20 831	2 184.1	761.6	627	3 379	271.1	73.4	43 715	1 900.1	1 280 620	5 239
Wasatch	58	D	D	D	38	D	D	D	2 835	146.3	290 284	685
Washington	500	7 443	830.8	271.4	188	1 043	87.9	24.3	13 038	612.0	405 470	2 196
Wayne	4	D	D	D	2	D	D	D	346	12.9	2 270	12
Weber	627	10 695	1 335.5	418.8	340	1 964	166.7	47.1	13 248	551.7	257 259	1 569
VERMONT	2 096	44 198	4 458.0	1 789.2	1 588	7 211	755.4	199.3	60 312	2 610.4	315 195	1 771
Addison	120	2 091	159.6	72.5	88	330	55.0	10.1	3 848	146.9	27 151	122
Bennington	158	2 704	274.8	116.3	97	395	30.7	7.8	3 749	168.0	9 245	33
Caledonia	94	1 732	146.3	63.4	76	234	21.2	5.7	2 960	121.2	8 925	42

Table B. States and Counties — Government Employment and Payroll, and Local Government Finances

		Government employment and payroll, 2012								Local government finances, 2012				
			March payroll (percent of total)							General revenue				
												Taxes		
													Per capita[1] (dollars)	
STATE County	Full-time equivalent employees	March payroll (dollars)	Adminis- tration, judicial, and legal	Police and Corrections	Fire Protection	Highways and transpor- tation	Health and Welfare	Natural resources and utilities	Education and libraries	Total (mil dol)	Inter- govern- mental (mil dol)	Total (mil dol)	Total	Property
	171	172	173	174	175	176	177	178	179	180	181	182	183	184
TEXAS—Cont'd														
Tom Green	4 430	11 842 865	8.7	16.5	6.7	1.4	3.6	6.1	55.2	321.7	125.9	138.0	1 218	917
Travis	45 034	190 376 191	8.0	14.8	5.4	4.1	5.1	18.3	42.4	4 794.7	942.7	2 689.4	2 455	2 026
Trinity	657	1 816 086	6.2	7.0	0.0	3.0	19.3	2.2	60.4	42.8	22.8	13.7	954	889
Tyler	945	2 527 612	9.2	3.5	0.0	3.0	16.0	2.8	65.4	63.8	23.6	34.9	1 625	1 538
Upshur	1 527	4 228 679	4.9	8.6	0.6	1.7	0.1	2.3	81.6	91.7	43.7	38.4	961	866
Upton	396	1 316 616	8.8	8.6	0.0	3.5	31.5	4.4	42.2	64.5	4.8	53.2	16 191	16 022
Uvalde	2 058	6 807 776	3.6	5.1	0.2	1.9	25.8	2.2	60.5	171.9	70.8	36.8	1 374	1 094
Val Verde	2 194	5 580 787	14.3	6.2	5.3	3.0	2.4	6.1	61.0	177.1	111.3	44.7	918	690
Van Zandt	1 960	5 471 112	4.9	6.7	0.3	1.8	0.4	2.9	82.3	133.5	67.2	50.0	953	821
Victoria	5 364	18 189 328	3.7	10.4	3.1	1.8	31.4	3.0	46.0	455.8	105.2	155.9	1 746	1 294
Walker	1 980	6 982 834	14.0	12.7	0.8	2.6	1.0	18.0	43.7	157.3	53.4	61.8	904	699
Waller	1 643	5 642 929	7.6	7.4	0.3	2.5	0.1	3.3	77.2	129.4	49.0	69.2	1 560	1 448
Ward	559	1 720 115	12.0	13.3	0.1	4.4	3.1	7.7	57.1	58.5	9.0	35.1	3 231	2 922
Washington	2 307	7 486 978	4.8	5.4	0.9	1.6	2.0	4.0	80.0	171.2	48.3	57.0	1 671	1 323
Webb	14 741	48 977 584	5.1	9.2	5.1	3.0	3.0	3.7	70.4	1 245.0	614.2	391.8	1 512	1 216
Wharton	3 171	11 435 949	2.9	4.7	1.0	2.5	19.8	1.5	66.6	188.9	70.3	71.4	1 729	1 485
Wheeler	514	1 406 670	6.6	3.2	0.0	2.3	33.3	2.8	49.5	54.5	8.1	36.6	6 498	6 236
Wichita	5 729	18 326 731	6.5	14.8	7.0	2.9	9.1	5.0	51.8	380.0	131.8	178.0	1 353	1 020
Wilbarger	1 195	3 537 696	3.1	4.1	2.6	1.8	21.1	2.8	64.1	75.4	29.4	23.4	1 765	1 490
Willacy	988	3 020 755	5.5	5.6	0.0	2.6	0.6	4.5	80.4	77.1	48.6	20.8	941	793
Williamson	16 819	59 733 376	3.1	6.7	3.0	0.5	4.4	2.8	78.5	1 670.1	418.9	1 031.8	2 262	1 950
Wilson	1 799	5 521 367	3.9	4.2	0.0	1.3	11.3	8.0	71.0	127.9	49.4	47.4	1 067	977
Winkler	465	1 871 237	6.8	7.5	0.0	1.6	15.1	4.2	63.8	57.9	10.9	36.9	5 029	4 658
Wise	2 052	6 283 194	8.7	7.9	0.7	4.7	0.0	3.9	72.0	189.8	35.2	132.2	2 187	1 913
Wood	1 347	3 686 462	6.7	10.8	0.5	4.1	1.5	3.8	72.4	92.1	31.3	50.5	1 202	1 071
Yoakum	719	2 354 261	7.1	8.7	0.1	3.1	26.1	3.9	50.3	97.6	9.0	68.0	8 426	8 230
Young	1 189	3 441 113	4.9	6.9	1.2	1.6	33.2	3.4	47.6	89.6	22.2	26.3	1 434	1 181
Zapata	901	2 905 195	13.0	4.2	3.8	4.8	1.0	3.6	68.4	76.6	24.7	47.2	3 300	3 261
Zavala	676	1 796 547	3.7	8.4	0.0	2.9	3.4	5.7	71.6	42.2	30.7	7.7	641	557
UTAH	X	X	X	X	X	X	X	X	X	X	X	X	X	X
Beaver	339	1 182 302	5.5	2.7	0.0	0.6	31.1	8.3	50.7	51.1	10.9	13.4	2 054	1 709
Box Elder	1 701	4 888 324	8.2	9.3	0.8	3.1	2.0	5.8	69.8	163.1	71.5	66.7	1 329	1 068
Cache	3 328	10 972 734	7.5	7.4	2.7	3.6	8.3	6.1	61.3	309.3	134.5	108.6	940	578
Carbon	959	3 089 135	8.6	9.2	0.6	4.8	13.4	11.0	49.4	77.6	27.1	32.7	1 540	1 152
Daggett	101	367 263	17.3	30.4	0.1	4.2	2.7	2.2	42.0	12.0	5.2	2.8	2 550	2 139
Davis	10 391	37 610 946	5.6	7.5	2.5	1.4	4.5	5.5	63.0	900.2	374.8	329.2	1 042	745
Duchesne	667	2 048 894	10.0	11.8	0.7	5.0	1.5	5.8	62.3	84.8	40.2	33.0	1 715	1 314
Emery	466	1 718 363	11.2	10.6	0.0	4.9	2.1	8.1	62.3	62.8	21.5	29.4	2 685	2 355
Garfield	208	742 442	11.2	13.2	0.0	8.1	3.9	3.0	59.1	29.9	14.5	10.4	2 048	1 146
Grand	491	1 568 944	14.6	13.1	0.9	6.9	12.1	8.6	39.6	48.0	15.0	23.4	2 503	1 486
Iron	1 282	4 462 404	8.5	11.6	1.0	3.6	3.5	5.1	64.5	132.5	51.2	58.7	1 257	954
Juab	437	1 313 251	9.2	9.3	0.0	4.6	1.1	6.7	66.9	40.9	23.8	12.2	1 178	963
Kane	440	1 479 423	9.0	11.3	0.3	3.4	34.0	2.0	37.7	48.6	12.0	21.3	2 951	1 982
Millard	516	1 988 139	9.7	11.9	0.0	5.8	2.6	6.2	62.0	68.1	23.0	25.6	2 037	1 792
Morgan	299	975 455	9.6	3.4	0.9	2.2	0.0	4.1	79.3	26.9	11.8	11.1	1 126	946
Piute	89	242 632	8.4	6.3	0.0	5.8	1.4	1.1	68.5	7.9	5.5	1.6	1 026	813
Rich	110	395 515	10.7	7.4	1.1	3.8	1.8	4.6	67.9	13.2	5.2	6.2	2 714	2 297
Salt Lake	34 230	125 577 298	7.2	10.3	5.3	9.8	5.0	8.9	51.0	3 731.7	1 299.6	1 519.3	1 428	1 028
San Juan	708	2 586 369	5.3	6.4	0.5	6.1	20.5	1.9	57.4	84.2	52.5	14.9	994	908
Sanpete	1 157	3 481 157	6.7	6.0	0.2	1.8	18.6	4.4	59.7	95.1	43.9	20.5	734	527
Sevier	746	2 317 397	8.0	11.6	0.2	2.5	2.9	7.4	65.4	75.7	42.9	22.0	1 059	746
Summit	1 737	6 591 640	8.6	7.7	9.0	7.8	2.4	12.1	48.0	236.3	39.4	155.2	4 084	3 100
Tooele	2 049	6 240 915	9.0	10.6	1.0	2.9	5.1	6.2	64.3	202.7	99.2	53.2	888	639
Uintah	1 239	3 713 017	11.2	10.8	0.4	5.2	9.6	10.8	46.9	155.8	52.9	70.7	2 048	1 456
Utah	14 037	52 266 547	6.3	8.0	2.5	1.4	4.9	8.4	66.6	1 574.6	646.3	574.1	1 062	718
Wasatch	952	3 521 146	10.0	7.9	0.0	2.6	6.3	11.3	55.4	122.6	39.4	52.8	2 091	1 673
Washington	4 130	14 492 173	7.3	10.1	1.7	2.6	6.5	13.4	56.5	453.7	154.1	197.8	1 366	972
Wayne	114	391 098	6.2	5.1	0.5	6.5	3.8	4.8	70.9	13.2	9.5	2.6	961	721
Weber	7 494	26 228 893	6.1	11.2	4.3	1.7	7.0	6.9	60.7	668.4	249.5	273.1	1 154	796
VERMONT	X	X	X	X	X	X	X	X	X	X	X	X	X	X
Addison	1 255	4 519 763	4.3	2.9	0.0	5.3	0.9	2.2	84.0	127.5	92.7	23.2	632	604
Bennington	948	3 568 427	6.0	7.7	0.1	5.9	0.6	5.2	74.2	128.5	92.0	25.4	692	657
Caledonia	1 032	3 333 702	5.5	3.4	1.1	8.2	0.9	4.6	76.0	108.5	81.8	18.1	580	578

1. Based on the resident population estimated as of July 1 of the year shown.

Items 171—184

Table B. States and Counties — Local Government Finances, Government Employment, and Income Taxes

STATE County	Local government finances, 2012 (cont.) Direct general expenditure Total (mil dol)	Per capita¹ (dollars)	Percent of total for: Education	Health and hospitals	Police protection	Public welfare	Highways	Debt outstanding Total (mil dol)	Per capita¹ (dollars)	Government employment, 2015 Federal civilian	Federal military	State and local	Individual income tax returns, 2014 Number of returns	Mean adjusted gross income	Mean income tax
	185	186	187	188	189	190	191	192	193	194	195	196	197	198	199
TEXAS—Cont'd															
Tom Green	347.3	3 066	51.9	3.4	5.7	0.2	2.7	583.9	5 155	1 173	3 100	7 622	53 030	62 003	9 117
Travis	4 740.6	4 327	38.8	6.7	7.4	0.8	6.5	15 845.5	14 463	10 716	2 554	115 019	617 750	80 833	13 865
Trinity	41.5	2 899	53.9	9.1	1.8	0.5	4.9	18.1	1 265	24	29	595	5 740	41 212	3 825
Tyler	60.2	2 805	57.5	0.1	4.6	0.3	5.4	43.0	2 002	45	39	1 682	7 450	47 841	4 716
Upshur	91.6	2 291	72.4	0.0	4.3	0.1	3.6	89.1	2 229	58	82	1 705	16 110	48 985	4 910
Upton	68.5	20 851	78.3	16.8	0.3	0.1	0.7	15.4	4 703	D	D	495	1 520	82 938	14 709
Uvalde	177.9	6 652	45.7	29.2	4.7	0.7	3.6	95.4	3 566	220	54	2 568	11 940	46 429	5 694
Val Verde	202.3	4 154	44.6	1.1	4.3	0.6	18.1	196.2	4 027	2 136	1 398	2 823	21 010	43 393	3 761
Van Zandt	133.6	2 548	65.3	0.2	3.7	0.1	5.1	143.4	2 735	89	108	2 276	21 670	49 021	4 966
Victoria	447.8	5 016	35.0	30.9	5.7	0.0	7.0	427.6	4 790	194	192	6 380	42 430	66 153	9 942
Walker	336.2	4 914	20.8	2.8	2.4	0.0	2.2	2 119.8	30 987	132	145	12 848	23 780	51 508	6 491
Waller	122.5	2 761	63.3	0.0	5.3	0.2	5.2	201.4	4 540	59	96	4 297	18 820	61 210	8 677
Ward	50.2	4 618	39.7	22.1	5.2	0.5	5.1	27.1	2 491	12	24	796	5 130	70 768	10 886
Washington	177.9	5 218	67.6	1.5	3.7	0.2	9.5	209.7	6 151	73	67	2 946	16 230	65 343	9 394
Webb	1 204.4	4 647	58.3	1.3	6.0	0.4	1.5	1 569.6	6 056	3 233	542	18 957	108 850	40 922	4 024
Wharton	212.0	5 136	49.9	27.3	4.1	0.3	4.0	112.7	2 730	85	84	2 767	19 390	52 395	6 186
Wheeler	47.3	8 406	62.3	25.4	2.4	0.0	1.9	10.4	1 840	21	11	610	2 560	75 813	13 367
Wichita	367.1	2 790	48.2	3.9	7.6	0.8	4.0	311.8	2 370	1 898	4 532	9 426	54 180	55 182	7 017
Wilbarger	85.1	6 421	56.2	22.2	2.7	0.1	3.2	25.5	1 920	36	25	2 500	5 800	44 190	4 322
Willacy	71.7	3 250	69.9	2.0	3.8	0.0	3.5	245.2	11 115	29	38	1 208	7 440	32 749	2 325
Williamson	1 761.9	3 862	55.5	3.1	4.1	0.1	8.7	4 547.8	9 968	652	1 025	21 555	226 130	71 290	9 167
Wilson	123.3	2 779	58.0	17.0	2.5	0.0	3.5	291.4	6 568	82	96	2 307	20 310	66 607	8 608
Winkler	63.1	8 609	59.5	14.6	3.7	0.3	1.7	83.7	11 417	10	16	612	3 330	66 525	8 486
Wise	185.9	3 076	52.9	1.7	4.7	0.4	8.7	328.2	5 430	116	127	3 927	26 750	62 781	8 276
Wood	83.7	1 992	65.3	0.6	6.3	0.2	7.2	54.2	1 291	92	85	1 776	18 070	50 924	5 588
Yoakum	112.1	13 883	63.5	19.3	2.1	0.0	3.3	58.6	7 256	15	17	826	3 670	65 303	8 297
Young	85.3	4 653	35.5	36.5	4.0	0.1	3.6	63.6	3 466	39	37	1 384	7 920	62 662	8 686
Zapata	71.8	5 023	53.0	1.7	6.5	2.5	10.2	53.7	3 754	143	29	935	5 180	39 733	3 400
Zavala	39.0	3 260	64.7	0.8	4.7	0.6	3.1	27.4	2 292	D	24	915	4 690	40 340	4 452
UTAH	X	X	X	X	X	X	X	X	X	35 048	16 166	193 682	1 221 050	60 760	7 037
Beaver	56.0	8 618	45.5	16.6	4.4	0.1	4.4	64.4	9 900	42	27	693	2 610	44 803	3 349
Box Elder	160.8	3 204	53.7	1.5	5.9	0.0	5.0	153.6	3 061	191	219	2 535	21 030	50 631	4 068
Cache	279.8	2 422	51.7	4.7	6.0	0.3	5.2	189.4	1 640	338	499	10 247	45 850	51 997	4 803
Carbon	97.8	4 605	33.6	5.7	8.9	1.4	15.4	82.2	3 869	145	84	1 824	8 000	51 347	5 022
Daggett	10.8	9 932	41.8	0.6	12.0	0.0	4.4	7.7	7 049	58	D	155	430	45 672	4 158
Davis	883.2	2 797	54.5	3.5	5.9	0.7	2.9	783.9	2 482	12 608	4 814	13 746	136 370	65 710	7 131
Duchesne	87.6	4 553	62.9	1.4	3.7	0.6	5.4	67.8	3 525	68	86	2 034	7 940	70 135	8 966
Emery	55.4	5 071	43.3	1.6	9.6	0.2	10.6	197.2	18 039	55	43	817	3 890	50 378	4 230
Garfield	23.9	4 686	43.6	2.6	4.9	0.2	12.7	15.3	3 013	150	20	361	2 100	40 786	3 117
Grand	44.6	4 784	31.4	1.2	9.8	0.7	9.0	75.2	8 066	234	39	717	4 790	50 243	5 582
Iron	125.1	2 675	48.9	0.6	7.6	0.2	7.1	124.1	2 655	284	200	3 774	17 680	42 490	3 383
Juab	41.3	3 997	42.5	0.6	7.1	0.0	6.0	46.1	4 459	24	44	727	3 900	50 008	4 277
Kane	51.0	7 056	25.3	22.9	3.7	0.0	6.3	44.9	6 214	85	29	631	2 950	46 464	4 300
Millard	53.8	4 280	54.0	3.6	7.9	0.0	7.1	9.5	752	84	53	917	4 880	43 526	3 777
Morgan	30.5	3 110	65.1	1.3	3.6	0.0	3.2	31.7	3 228	11	46	458	4 300	86 888	11 134
Piute	8.4	5 526	63.5	0.9	6.3	0.0	8.4	7.6	5 012	D	D	135	520	41 496	2 767
Rich	11.4	5 038	56.3	0.8	5.5	2.9	8.5	10.7	4 710	11	10	198	880	48 831	3 680
Salt Lake	3 568.5	3 354	42.8	1.1	5.6	2.0	5.4	7 237.3	6 803	11 147	4 846	89 468	487 650	62 440	7 773
San Juan	80.3	5 367	48.8	16.3	2.8	0.1	14.7	21.4	1 432	162	65	1 451	4 210	43 891	3 360
Sanpete	90.3	3 237	50.5	20.9	4.6	0.0	3.0	121.5	4 352	76	110	2 505	8 970	43 019	3 174
Sevier	69.0	3 318	48.6	2.0	9.0	0.0	7.7	54.0	2 596	188	87	1 443	7 850	48 070	4 296
Summit	247.7	6 518	32.0	2.0	5.3	0.0	14.4	271.7	7 150	55	166	2 701	21 080	124 575	24 110
Tooele	205.1	3 426	44.3	2.1	5.5	2.9	3.0	186.1	3 109	1 256	297	2 570	24 040	54 651	4 577
Uintah	172.6	4 998	36.6	3.9	4.3	4.9	15.3	199.3	5 772	355	158	2 712	14 010	66 793	7 590
Utah	1 425.3	2 637	52.2	4.1	6.0	0.1	5.2	2 402.3	4 445	921	2 386	28 082	208 530	60 933	6 896
Wasatch	116.2	4 598	37.8	2.6	4.5	0.1	8.0	196.8	7 787	50	121	1 396	11 550	67 197	8 228
Washington	401.3	2 771	50.1	0.8	7.7	0.0	6.0	585.2	4 041	558	647	7 552	60 380	52 798	5 488
Wayne	11.3	4 138	49.8	0.3	9.5	0.0	14.9	0.8	300	82	11	177	1 080	38 985	2 937
Weber	687.2	2 904	45.7	2.1	6.6	3.6	2.8	686.2	2 900	5 805	1 049	13 656	103 740	52 397	5 047
VERMONT	X	X	X	X	X	X	X	X	X	6 794	4 370	47 114	322 850	57 587	6 825
Addison	134.4	3 658	71.2	0.1	2.3	0.1	11.8	60.1	1 636	106	240	1 729	18 060	56 642	6 038
Bennington	140.1	3 818	69.0	0.2	4.4	0.3	12.1	38.6	1 051	170	245	2 068	18 550	55 945	6 505
Caledonia	107.7	3 461	66.7	0.1	3.0	0.0	14.0	33.2	1 066	97	207	1 972	14 590	45 631	4 428

1. Based on the resident population estimated as of July 1 of the year shown.

Table B. States and Counties — **Land Area and Population**

STATE/ County code	CBSA code[1]	County type[2]	STATE County	Land area,[3] (sq mi) 2016	Total persons 2016	Rank	Per square mile	White	Black	American Indian, Alaska Native	Asian and Pacific Islander	Percent Hispanic or Latino[4]	Under 5 years	5 to 17 years	18 to 24 years	25 to 34 years	35 to 44 years	45 to 54 years
				1	2	3	4	5	6	7	8	9	10	11	12	13	14	15
			VERMONT—Cont'd															
50 007	15540	3	Chittenden	536.6	161 531	400	301.0	90.9	3.1	0.8	5.0	2.3	4.9	13.4	16.2	14.0	11.4	13.0
50 009	13620	9	Essex	663.6	6 176	2 737	9.3	97.0	1.0	1.4	0.8	1.4	4.9	13.4	6.1	8.5	10.3	15.0
50 011	15540	3	Franklin	633.8	48 915	1 001	77.2	96.2	1.1	2.4	1.0	1.5	6.3	16.6	7.9	12.2	12.7	14.9
50 013	15540	3	Grand Isle	81.8	6 919	2 680	84.6	95.7	1.4	3.3	0.9	1.7	4.8	14.0	6.7	10.8	10.7	15.0
50 015	...	8	Lamoille	458.9	25 333	1 592	55.2	96.3	1.3	1.3	1.1	1.7	5.2	15.6	9.4	12.2	12.9	14.0
50 017	17200	9	Orange	687.0	28 919	1 458	42.1	97.1	1.0	1.2	0.9	1.3	4.8	14.1	8.4	10.7	11.1	14.2
50 019	...	7	Orleans	693.6	26 863	1 534	38.7	97.0	1.1	1.5	0.8	1.4	5.1	14.4	7.5	11.0	11.2	13.5
50 021	40860	4	Rutland	929.8	59 310	874	63.8	96.8	1.0	0.8	1.2	1.5	4.7	13.4	9.3	10.6	10.1	14.3
50 023	12740	4	Washington	687.0	58 504	884	85.2	96.0	1.5	1.0	1.4	1.9	4.8	14.5	9.5	11.1	11.8	14.5
50 025	...	7	Windham	785.5	43 145	1 108	54.9	95.2	1.8	1.1	1.6	2.2	4.6	13.7	8.3	10.8	10.4	13.7
50 027	17200	7	Windsor	969.6	55 496	911	57.2	96.4	1.1	1.1	1.4	1.6	4.4	14.0	6.9	10.9	10.7	13.9
51 000	...	0	**VIRGINIA**	39 481.8	8 411 808	X	213.1	64.7	20.4	0.8	7.8	9.1	6.1	16.2	9.7	13.9	12.9	13.8
51 001	...	8	Accomack	449.3	32 947	1 357	73.3	62.0	28.7	0.9	1.1	8.9	5.6	15.0	6.8	10.9	10.2	12.7
51 003	16820	3	Albemarle	720.8	106 878	561	148.3	79.3	10.7	0.6	6.1	5.7	5.3	15.1	12.0	12.7	11.3	12.6
51 005	...	6	Alleghany	445.5	15 595	2 067	35.0	93.3	5.7	0.7	0.5	1.5	4.3	14.6	7.3	9.3	10.1	14.0
51 007	40060	1	Amelia	355.3	12 913	2 232	36.3	74.3	22.6	0.9	0.7	3.2	5.3	15.7	6.8	11.2	10.5	14.9
51 009	31340	2	Amherst	473.9	31 633	1 392	66.8	77.3	20.0	1.4	1.0	2.4	5.1	14.7	8.4	11.2	10.8	14.5
51 011	31340	2	Appomattox	333.5	15 475	2 071	46.4	78.4	20.8	0.6	0.7	1.4	6.0	15.9	7.3	11.9	11.1	13.4
51 013	47900	1	Arlington	26.0	230 050	283	8 848.1	64.9	9.6	0.7	12.3	15.4	6.1	11.7	8.0	25.1	16.7	12.8
51 015	44420	3	Augusta	967.0	74 997	736	77.6	92.3	4.8	0.6	0.9	2.7	4.7	14.8	7.7	11.2	11.5	14.9
51 017	...	8	Bath	529.2	4 476	2 863	8.5	92.2	5.1	0.7	0.7	2.5	4.7	11.1	7.0	9.4	9.5	15.6
51 019	31340	2	Bedford	759.9	77 960	710	102.6	89.5	7.7	0.7	1.6	2.1	4.7	15.5	7.6	9.7	10.7	15.0
51 021	...	8	Bland	357.7	6 513	2 713	18.2	94.9	4.0	0.5	0.6	0.8	4.0	12.2	6.7	12.0	13.7	15.0
51 023	40220	2	Botetourt	541.2	33 231	1 350	61.4	94.2	3.7	0.7	1.0	1.6	4.1	15.3	7.2	9.1	10.7	15.7
51 025	...	6	Brunswick	566.2	16 243	2 027	28.7	42.3	55.4	0.6	0.6	2.2	4.3	12.8	8.7	13.3	11.6	13.5
51 027	...	9	Buchanan	502.8	22 178	1 719	44.1	95.5	3.4	0.4	0.6	0.7	4.2	13.6	6.9	11.6	12.0	15.0
51 029	16820	3	Buckingham	579.7	17 048	1 977	29.4	62.6	35.3	0.7	0.6	2.6	4.8	13.8	7.7	13.5	13.0	15.0
51 031	31340	2	Campbell	503.9	54 952	918	109.1	82.0	15.6	0.8	1.4	2.2	4.7	15.2	8.2	12.9	11.5	14.1
51 033	40060	1	Caroline	527.5	30 178	1 429	57.2	66.3	29.5	1.5	1.6	4.6	6.7	16.7	7.0	13.7	12.6	13.6
51 035	...	7	Carroll	474.7	29 531	1 443	62.2	95.8	1.1	0.4	0.3	3.0	4.6	14.4	6.5	9.9	11.3	14.7
51 036	40060	1	Charles City	182.8	7 071	2 665	38.7	43.9	48.0	8.0	1.3	2.1	4.3	11.2	7.1	9.9	9.7	16.2
51 037	...	8	Charlotte	475.3	12 129	2 286	25.5	69.0	29.0	0.8	0.5	2.1	6.0	15.6	7.9	10.3	10.1	13.8
51 041	40060	1	Chesterfield	423.4	339 009	202	800.7	64.5	24.2	0.8	4.6	8.4	5.9	18.1	9.0	11.8	13.4	14.5
51 043	47900	1	Clarke	175.9	14 374	2 140	81.7	88.3	5.8	1.0	1.9	5.3	4.6	16.3	7.3	9.1	10.2	16.1
51 045	40220	2	Craig	329.5	5 158	2 821	15.7	97.9	0.6	0.5	0.3	1.4	4.2	14.7	7.0	9.7	11.1	14.7
51 047	47900	1	Culpeper	379.2	50 083	984	132.1	73.5	16.1	0.8	2.1	10.1	6.5	18.5	7.7	12.0	12.7	14.5
51 049	...	8	Cumberland	297.5	9 652	2 456	32.4	64.7	33.1	1.0	0.9	2.7	5.1	15.0	8.0	11.3	10.3	14.9
51 051	13720	9	Dickenson	330.5	14 968	2 098	45.3	98.3	0.7	0.5	0.3	0.8	5.2	14.7	7.2	11.4	13.0	13.5
51 053	40060	1	Dinwiddie	503.7	28 144	1 484	55.9	63.0	33.1	0.7	1.2	3.5	4.8	15.2	9.1	12.3	11.2	15.6
51 057	...	6	Essex	257.1	11 123	2 346	43.3	56.9	39.3	1.2	1.6	3.4	5.5	14.2	7.3	11.2	10.2	14.1
51 059	47900	1	Fairfax	390.9	1 138 652	37	2 912.9	54.3	10.5	0.6	21.8	16.1	6.5	17.3	8.4	13.4	14.5	14.8
51 061	47900	1	Fauquier	647.7	69 069	774	106.6	82.7	8.8	0.8	2.3	7.8	5.8	17.7	8.0	10.7	11.5	15.9
51 063	13980	3	Floyd	380.9	15 731	2 057	41.3	94.3	2.5	0.6	1.0	2.8	4.7	15.5	6.5	9.7	11.6	14.6
51 065	16820	3	Fluvanna	286.0	26 271	1 551	91.9	80.6	16.1	0.8	1.3	3.4	5.0	15.6	7.2	11.1	13.1	14.3
51 067	40220	2	Franklin	690.4	56 069	908	81.2	88.5	8.8	0.5	0.7	2.8	4.6	14.8	8.2	9.9	10.2	14.3
51 069	49020	3	Frederick	413.5	84 421	674	204.2	85.9	5.2	0.6	2.2	8.0	5.8	17.2	7.8	12.0	12.4	14.8
51 071	13980	3	Giles	355.8	16 857	1 987	47.4	95.8	2.1	0.5	1.0	1.7	5.3	15.5	7.3	10.9	11.8	14.9
51 073	47260	1	Gloucester	217.8	37 214	1 244	170.9	87.1	9.1	1.2	1.7	3.5	5.2	15.2	7.5	11.7	11.3	14.7
51 075	40060	1	Goochland	281.4	22 668	1 699	80.6	78.8	17.3	0.7	1.9	2.8	4.3	14.4	6.8	9.3	11.1	15.8
51 077	...	9	Grayson	442.2	15 107	2 090	34.2	94.0	3.0	0.6	0.4	3.2	4.9	13.2	6.6	9.5	10.5	14.3
51 079	16820	3	Greene	156.1	19 371	1 854	124.1	85.6	8.0	0.7	2.2	5.7	6.1	18.0	6.8	11.9	12.4	14.7
51 081	...	6	Greensville	295.2	11 706	2 310	39.7	37.8	59.5	0.5	1.0	2.2	4.7	11.9	8.3	15.7	14.9	16.1
51 083	...	6	Halifax	817.7	34 992	1 304	42.8	60.8	36.9	0.6	0.9	2.0	5.2	15.3	7.8	10.1	10.2	13.0
51 085	40060	1	Hanover	468.6	104 392	576	222.8	85.9	9.9	0.8	2.3	2.9	5.0	17.3	8.9	10.1	11.7	15.5
51 087	40060	1	Henrico	233.7	326 501	211	1 397.1	55.9	31.0	0.8	9.3	5.3	6.2	17.0	8.0	14.1	13.4	13.9
51 089	32300	4	Henry	382.3	51 445	969	134.6	71.6	23.2	0.6	0.9	5.4	4.8	15.1	6.9	10.4	10.4	14.5
51 091	...	8	Highland	415.2	2 216	3 028	5.3	97.1	0.9	0.2	0.5	1.6	3.5	10.2	4.9	7.2	8.6	12.1
51 093	47260	1	Isle of Wight	315.6	36 596	1 262	116.0	72.7	23.8	0.9	1.8	2.9	5.3	15.8	7.4	10.8	11.1	15.1
51 095	47260	1	James City	142.5	74 404	742	522.1	78.2	14.3	0.8	3.9	5.4	4.9	15.3	7.0	10.3	10.8	13.3
51 097	...	8	King and Queen	315.2	7 159	2 656	22.7	67.7	28.6	2.2	1.0	2.9	4.8	13.8	6.8	11.0	9.9	14.5
51 099	...	6	King George	179.6	25 984	1 564	144.7	76.7	18.0	1.3	2.7	4.9	6.2	19.2	8.5	12.5	13.5	15.0
51 101	40060	1	King William	273.9	16 334	2 019	59.6	78.3	17.8	2.1	1.4	2.5	5.5	17.6	7.3	13.0	12.3	14.7
51 103	...	9	Lancaster	133.3	10 972	2 357	82.3	69.5	28.4	0.5	1.0	1.9	3.9	11.1	5.4	8.3	7.1	10.6
51 105	...	8	Lee	435.5	24 179	1 636	55.5	93.5	4.1	0.8	0.6	1.9	4.7	14.0	6.7	12.8	13.1	13.7
51 107	47900	1	Loudoun	515.8	385 945	179	748.2	60.2	8.4	0.6	20.7	13.7	7.3	21.5	7.3	12.2	17.2	15.9

1. CBSA = Core Based Statistical Area. See Appendix A for explanation. See Appendix B for list of metropolitan areas with component counties. 2. County type code from the Economic Research Service of USDA Rural-Urban Continuum Codes. See Appendix A for definition. 3. Dry land or land partially or temporarily covered by water. 4. May be of any race.

STATE County	55 to 64 years	65 to 74 years	75 years and over	Percent female	Total persons 2000	Total persons 2010	Percent change 2000–2010	Percent change 2010–2016	Births	Deaths	Net migration	Number	Persons per house-hold	Family house-holds	Female family house-holder[1]	One per-son
	16	17	18	19	20	21	22	23	24	25	26	27	28	29	30	31
VERMONT—Cont'd																
Chittenden	13.3	8.0	5.8	51.0	146 571	156 540	6.8	3.2	9 905	6 484	1 488	63 498	2.36	58.2	8.1	27.6
Essex	17.8	14.6	9.3	49.5	6 459	6 306	-2.4	-2.1	337	352	-126	2 701	2.29	64.6	10.9	30.0
Franklin	14.8	9.1	5.6	50.2	45 417	47 752	5.1	2.4	3 720	2 436	-89	18 685	2.57	69.4	9.9	23.7
Grand Isle	19.2	13.2	5.7	49.9	6 901	6 970	1.0	-0.7	380	356	-55	2 965	2.34	69.8	7.8	25.1
Lamoille	14.5	9.6	6.6	50.0	23 233	24 475	5.3	3.5	1 640	1 218	467	10 176	2.39	59.9	7.8	31.5
Orange	17.5	12.1	7.1	50.0	28 226	28 937	2.5	-0.1	1 703	1 582	-74	12 148	2.32	66.1	9.5	26.1
Orleans	15.7	12.9	8.7	49.7	26 277	27 234	3.6	-1.4	1 704	1 892	-139	11 200	2.35	64.2	9.7	28.5
Rutland	16.7	12.5	8.4	50.7	63 400	61 646	-2.8	-3.8	3 432	4 121	-1 567	25 459	2.29	61.1	9.1	31.5
Washington	15.5	11.0	7.3	50.5	58 039	59 526	2.6	-1.7	3 647	3 293	-1 312	24 512	2.32	61.8	9.5	30.0
Windham	17.5	12.9	8.0	50.9	44 216	44 513	0.7	-3.1	2 530	2 680	-1 074	19 057	2.21	59.6	8.2	31.1
Windsor	17.3	13.1	8.9	51.1	57 418	56 661	-1.3	-2.1	3 059	3 608	-529	24 507	2.25	61.8	8.5	30.2
VIRGINIA	12.8	8.7	5.9	50.8	7 078 515	8 001 041	13.0	5.1	641 455	392 605	157 996	3 062 783	2.62	67.1	12.3	26.6
Accomack	16.5	13.2	9.1	51.3	38 305	33 164	-13.4	-0.7	2 496	2 794	56	13 961	2.29	65.5	13.3	29.7
Albemarle	13.4	9.9	7.8	52.2	79 236	98 998	24.9	8.0	6 880	4 904	5 582	38 853	2.45	64.0	9.1	29.2
Alleghany	15.1	14.5	10.6	51.1	17 215	16 261	-5.5	-4.1	884	1 483	-144	6 781	2.33	64.6	8.5	30.6
Amelia	16.3	11.7	7.6	51.0	11 400	12 695	11.4	1.7	846	808	188	4 704	2.68	78.8	14.5	18.0
Amherst	15.2	11.8	8.3	51.8	31 894	32 354	1.4	-2.2	2 019	2 165	-559	12 502	2.48	67.3	13.4	28.5
Appomattox	14.8	11.6	8.2	51.5	13 705	14 977	9.3	3.3	1 119	1 007	383	5 931	2.55	76.4	16.0	21.0
Arlington	10.0	6.0	3.7	50.1	189 453	207 676	9.6	10.8	19 642	6 011	8 646	98 441	2.04	46.5	5.8	39.8
Augusta	15.0	11.9	8.2	49.2	65 615	73 732	12.4	1.7	4 256	4 366	1 223	28 150	2.50	73.6	9.6	22.9
Bath	16.3	14.7	11.5	49.4	5 048	4 727	-6.4	-5.3	253	381	-101	2 146	2.10	54.9	3.6	35.4
Bedford	16.4	12.6	7.9	50.6	60 371	74 871	24.0	4.1	4 514	4 697	3 223	30 591	2.48	70.6	8.5	25.1
Bland	14.4	13.5	8.5	44.8	6 871	6 824	-0.7	-4.6	294	534	-63	2 614	2.19	67.6	9.4	29.5
Botetourt	16.5	13.0	8.4	50.5	30 496	33 148	8.7	0.3	1 555	1 976	459	12 913	2.55	74.9	8.4	20.7
Brunswick	15.2	11.6	8.9	47.5	18 419	17 425	-5.4	-6.8	914	1 245	-834	5 916	2.51	67.2	18.7	29.5
Buchanan	16.1	12.4	8.3	49.1	26 978	24 095	-10.7	-8.0	1 270	1 812	-1 383	9 442	2.37	69.7	13.8	26.0
Buckingham	14.3	10.9	7.0	45.1	15 623	17 140	9.7	-0.5	1 017	975	-115	5 603	2.68	69.0	13.8	27.4
Campbell	14.6	10.9	8.0	51.5	51 078	54 849	7.4	0.2	3 384	3 255	-13	21 791	2.50	70.5	12.3	25.6
Caroline	13.6	10.0	6.0	51.0	22 121	28 558	29.1	5.7	2 503	1 598	669	10 970	2.48	74.6	16.8	19.2
Carroll	15.9	13.6	9.1	50.5	29 245	30 067	2.8	-1.8	1 648	2 310	159	12 548	2.37	68.1	10.1	27.9
Charles City	18.4	14.6	8.6	51.5	6 926	7 256	4.8	-2.5	372	500	-79	2 883	2.47	64.4	14.7	30.3
Charlotte	15.3	12.1	9.0	50.1	12 472	12 591	1.0	-3.7	871	962	-362	4 723	2.57	65.7	14.4	29.4
Chesterfield	13.4	9.0	4.9	51.8	259 903	316 262	21.7	7.2	23 575	13 480	12 422	116 797	2.78	71.8	12.2	23.7
Clarke	16.5	12.0	7.8	50.4	12 652	14 029	10.9	2.5	805	935	480	5 526	2.55	66.5	13.2	27.3
Craig	16.7	13.1	8.9	49.9	5 091	5 173	1.6	-0.3	243	325	54	2 214	2.35	60.9	7.7	34.5
Culpeper	13.2	9.1	5.6	49.9	34 262	46 691	36.3	7.3	3 951	2 408	1 790	16 515	2.83	75.3	11.6	20.1
Cumberland	14.9	12.7	7.9	51.8	9 017	10 039	11.3	-3.9	643	579	-436	4 012	2.45	67.9	15.6	27.4
Dickenson	15.2	12.0	7.8	49.2	16 395	15 892	-3.1	-5.8	1 011	1 281	-611	6 205	2.43	70.6	10.1	26.8
Dinwiddie	14.8	10.2	6.9	51.4	24 533	28 005	14.2	0.5	1 720	1 581	-20	9 939	2.74	71.2	16.4	24.3
Essex	16.1	12.7	8.7	52.8	9 989	11 146	11.6	-0.2	781	775	-46	4 332	2.53	62.7	10.8	30.6
Fairfax	12.7	7.7	4.7	50.5	969 749	1 081 685	11.5	5.3	94 044	31 091	-4 918	392 355	2.85	71.4	9.2	22.4
Fauquier	14.4	9.7	6.3	50.5	55 139	65 275	18.4	5.8	4 704	3 312	2 269	23 595	2.84	73.5	7.6	21.3
Floyd	15.8	13.2	8.5	49.6	13 874	15 292	10.2	2.9	913	942	472	6 271	2.46	68.2	7.3	26.8
Fluvanna	14.3	11.7	7.7	54.0	20 047	25 704	28.2	2.2	1 649	1 242	142	9 891	2.50	73.3	8.8	22.0
Franklin	16.0	13.9	8.2	50.6	47 286	56 138	18.7	-0.1	3 136	3 606	482	23 189	2.36	71.5	10.1	25.1
Frederick	13.3	9.8	6.7	50.2	59 209	78 308	32.3	7.8	5 819	3 856	3 955	29 455	2.72	73.8	9.7	20.5
Giles	13.8	12.8	7.9	50.9	16 657	17 286	3.8	-2.5	1 122	1 331	-182	7 230	2.32	67.1	12.9	26.7
Gloucester	16.1	11.1	7.3	50.6	34 780	36 858	6.0	1.0	2 283	2 273	289	14 280	2.57	71.5	9.9	24.0
Goochland	17.5	13.5	7.3	50.7	16 863	21 699	28.7	4.5	1 106	1 085	829	8 148	2.50	77.5	7.3	20.4
Grayson	16.5	13.7	10.7	50.8	17 917	15 552	-13.2	-2.9	900	1 333	-9	6 795	2.24	64.6	10.4	31.4
Greene	13.5	10.6	6.1	50.8	15 244	18 410	20.8	5.2	1 379	921	487	7 111	2.64	71.0	8.9	20.9
Greensville	12.8	9.8	5.7	38.1	11 560	12 245	5.9	-4.4	724	743	-570	3 486	2.17	71.6	17.2	24.6
Halifax	15.2	13.3	9.8	52.1	37 355	36 241	-3.0	-3.4	2 235	2 963	-509	14 300	2.43	65.2	14.0	32.0
Hanover	14.8	10.0	6.7	51.0	86 320	99 850	15.7	4.5	5 699	5 182	3 886	37 463	2.65	75.3	9.9	20.3
Henrico	12.9	8.4	6.2	52.7	262 300	306 974	17.0	6.4	25 272	16 049	10 265	124 589	2.54	63.8	14.8	29.7
Henry	15.3	12.6	10.0	51.8	57 930	54 185	-6.5	-5.1	3 083	4 395	-1 439	22 415	2.32	66.5	14.1	30.3
Highland	22.3	18.6	12.6	49.7	2 536	2 319	-8.6	-4.4	97	169	-32	1 071	2.10	65.0	8.2	30.2
Isle of Wight	16.2	11.2	7.1	51.1	29 728	35 274	18.7	3.7	2 171	2 175	1 259	13 769	2.57	73.9	10.3	21.8
James City	14.1	13.7	10.6	51.8	48 102	67 393	40.1	10.4	4 231	3 967	6 532	28 000	2.49	71.0	10.5	24.7
King and Queen	17.1	13.2	8.9	49.5	6 630	6 945	4.8	3.1	409	453	230	2 894	2.46	67.6	13.6	27.3
King George	12.5	7.9	4.8	49.5	16 803	23 584	40.4	10.2	1 895	960	1 391	8 379	2.96	75.8	9.9	18.9
King William	14.2	9.8	5.6	51.1	13 146	15 927	21.2	2.6	1 162	859	122	6 036	2.66	75.4	11.2	20.4
Lancaster	17.0	18.6	18.0	52.9	11 567	11 394	-1.5	-3.7	520	1 256	261	5 164	2.13	58.2	10.1	37.1
Lee	15.0	12.0	8.0	48.0	23 589	25 583	8.5	-5.5	1 479	1 847	-1 092	9 445	2.52	67.6	9.8	29.8
Loudoun	9.9	5.3	3.4	50.5	169 599	312 336	84.2	23.6	31 526	7 241	48 399	113 432	3.08	77.5	8.4	17.2

1. No spouse present.

Table B. States and Counties — Population, Vital Statistics, Health, and Crime

STATE County	Persons in group quarters, 2016	Daytime population, 2011–2015 Number	Daytime population, 2011–2015 Employment/residence ratio	Births, 2016 Total	Births, 2016 Rate[1]	Deaths, 2016 Number	Deaths, 2016 Rate[1]	Persons under 65 with no health insurance, 2015 Number	Persons under 65 with no health insurance, 2015 Percent	Medicare, 2015 Total Beneficiaries	Medicare, 2015 Enrolled in Original Medicare	Medicare, 2015 Enrolled in Medicare Advantage	Serious crimes known to police,[2] 2014 Total Number	Serious crimes known to police,[2] 2014 Total Rate[3]
	32	33	34	35	36	37	38	39	40	41	42	43	44	45
VERMONT—Cont'd														
Chittenden	9 687	173 895	1.16	1 595	9.9	1 097	6.8	5 606	4.3	19 983	18 063	1 920	3 404	2 126
Essex	16	5 001	0.53	53	8.6	63	10.2	301	6.5	1 855	1 723	132	15	242
Franklin	598	42 648	0.77	620	12.7	398	8.1	1 791	4.3	8 227	7 465	762	797	1 647
Grand Isle	0	4 806	0.41	67	9.7	52	7.5	296	5.3	1 644	1 439	205	100	1 430
Lamoille	696	24 382	0.95	256	10.1	195	7.7	1 107	5.4	9 835	8 953	882	158	627
Orange	737	23 655	0.65	268	9.3	268	9.3	1 095	4.8	5 781	5 448	333	253	876
Orleans	777	26 849	0.97	273	10.2	301	11.2	1 204	5.8	6 531	6 055	476	406	1 496
Rutland	2 324	59 985	0.98	544	9.2	642	10.8	2 222	4.9	15 641	14 543	1 098	1 036	1 724
Washington	2 404	62 030	1.09	566	9.7	512	8.8	1 798	3.9	12 755	11 744	1 011	870	1 469
Windham	1 500	46 639	1.13	385	8.9	425	9.9	1 708	5.1	9 745	8 964	781	894	2 047
Windsor	887	53 864	0.92	467	8.4	553	10.0	2 072	4.8	13 132	11 948	1 184	717	1 282
VIRGINIA	241 626	8 156 254	0.98	102 366	12.2	66 558	7.9	722 551	10.4	1 282 336	1 001 158	281 178	177 060	2 127
Accomack	429	31 983	0.92	378	11.5	469	14.2	4 712	18.5	8 351	7 053	1 298	550	1 659
Albemarle	6 547	111 347	1.17	1 054	9.9	876	8.2	8 024	9.8	9 690	8 330	1 360	1 960	1 884
Alleghany	281	16 145	1.01	121	7.8	265	17.0	1 214	10.4	2 089	1 535	554	207	1 281
Amelia	128	9 974	0.50	129	10.0	140	10.8	1 402	13.4	2 634	1 949	685	130	1 019
Amherst	1 286	27 203	0.66	315	10.0	376	11.9	3 040	12.3	6 800	5 622	1 178	430	1 334
Appomattox	56	12 278	0.55	193	12.5	168	10.9	1 544	12.5	2 957	2 485	472	132	862
Arlington	2 921	271 927	1.34	3 127	13.6	1 054	4.6	13 809	6.7	18 660	15 126	3 534	4 311	1 882
Augusta	2 797	68 424	0.83	698	9.3	758	10.1	6 589	11.5	9 979	8 222	1 757	917	1 238
Bath	53	4 436	0.93	49	10.9	49	10.9	354	10.7	1 379	1 207	172	40	871
Bedford	547	60 746	0.55	626	8.0	833	10.2	6 337	10.2	19 381	15 249	4 132	1 064	1 400
Bland	686	6 125	0.78	49	7.5	87	13.4	448	9.9	1 631	1 263	368	51	759
Botetourt	278	27 153	0.62	246	7.4	344	10.4	2 023	7.7	6 967	5 246	1 721	294	892
Brunswick	1 847	14 697	0.65	141	8.7	228	14.0	1 471	12.9	3 615	2 709	906	119	705
Buchanan	1 153	24 057	1.08	169	7.6	308	13.9	2 256	13.1	6 089	3 556	2 533	403	1 715
Buckingham	2 204	14 908	0.65	147	8.6	152	8.9	1 709	14.2	2 548	1 928	620	220	1 283
Campbell	437	49 246	0.78	438	8.0	528	9.6	5 461	12.3	10 314	8 429	1 885	910	1 644
Caroline	513	21 613	0.46	389	12.9	277	9.2	3 020	12.1	4 749	3 732	1 017	433	1 468
Carroll	337	25 973	0.70	279	9.4	390	13.2	3 216	13.9	5 900	4 923	977	409	1 370
Charles City	0	5 566	0.53	63	8.9	95	13.4	962	17.5	2 101	1 567	534	31	437
Charlotte	175	10 213	0.59	147	12.1	161	13.3	1 466	15.4	3 901	3 195	706	66	539
Chesterfield	4 326	284 831	0.73	3 780	11.2	2 361	7.0	25 443	8.9	43 096	32 003	11 093	6 803	2 058
Clarke	180	11 674	0.61	135	9.4	144	10.0	1 285	11.1	2 553	2 234	319	174	1 206
Craig	9	3 708	0.27	37	7.2	71	13.8	402	9.8	1 029	768	261	22	422
Culpeper	1 426	43 185	0.76	643	12.8	410	8.2	5 172	12.6	8 124	6 683	1 441	739	1 509
Cumberland	37	6 895	0.33	85	8.8	105	10.9	1 021	13.2	1 364	985	379	68	694
Dickenson	564	14 404	0.78	140	9.4	189	12.6	1 523	12.9	4 335	2 609	1 726	175	1 137
Dinwiddie	719	22 897	0.58	181	6.4	262	9.3	2 558	11.3	3 704	2 858	846	432	1 549
Essex	190	10 403	0.85	125	11.2	113	10.2	1 194	13.6	2 575	2 033	542	205	1 822
Fairfax	10 071	1 140 363	1.02	14 298	12.6	5 610	4.9	87 578	8.8	99 132	83 100	16 032	16 399	1 435
Fauquier	389	57 913	0.72	749	10.8	602	8.7	5 475	9.4	9 890	8 829	1 061	631	941
Floyd	85	12 511	0.58	126	8.0	159	10.1	1 520	12.3	3 267	2 506	761	153	982
Fluvanna	1 177	18 617	0.38	263	10.0	204	7.8	2 094	10.4	5 149	4 272	877	241	925
Franklin	1 362	48 467	0.68	487	8.7	633	11.3	5 439	12.6	10 250	7 068	3 182	735	1 303
Frederick	1 114	71 851	0.76	916	10.9	654	7.7	7 685	11.1	8 565	7 514	1 051	1 695	2 065
Giles	136	15 125	0.76	183	10.9	203	12.0	1 512	11.4	4 373	3 098	1 275	277	1 645
Gloucester	346	29 879	0.60	368	9.9	436	11.7	3 001	9.9	7 163	5 787	1 376	599	1 626
Goochland	934	23 897	1.21	193	8.5	169	7.5	894	5.3	3 261	2 527	734	187	866
Grayson	249	13 695	0.70	139	9.2	193	12.8	1 476	12.8	3 449	2 975	474	174	1 153
Greene	137	13 941	0.43	217	11.2	141	7.3	2 240	14.0	3 065	2 529	536	245	1 296
Greensville	3 318	12 574	1.25	161	13.8	124	10.5	706	10.5	D	D	D	98	830
Halifax	753	34 938	0.96	364	10.4	498	14.2	3 342	12.5	9 355	8 027	1 328	784	2 225
Hanover	2 024	93 678	0.85	970	9.3	800	7.7	6 252	7.4	20 752	16 074	4 678	1 389	1 365
Henrico	2 609	325 803	1.04	4 034	12.4	2 682	8.2	28 430	10.3	30 735	23 019	7 716	8 387	2 608
Henry	561	48 237	0.79	445	8.7	714	13.9	5 637	14.1	10 871	7 628	3 243	1 298	2 483
Highland	0	2 202	0.96	14	6.3	23	10.4	305	19.9	656	582	74	6	273
Isle of Wight	310	28 758	0.60	385	10.5	369	10.1	2 693	9.0	6 757	5 106	1 651	492	1 375
James City	1 083	67 267	0.89	736	9.9	657	8.8	4 815	8.7	4 945	4 213	732	1 139	1 596
King and Queen	0	5 302	0.44	71	9.9	82	11.5	783	14.0	1 486	1 181	305	71	990
King George	301	25 255	1.03	287	11.0	150	5.8	1 547	7.0	3 083	2 688	395	344	1 362
King William	72	12 628	0.56	173	10.6	136	8.3	1 373	9.9	2 849	2 384	465	96	595
Lancaster	183	11 768	1.14	90	8.2	204	18.6	824	11.8	4 481	3 731	750	73	658
Lee	1 629	22 855	0.69	221	9.1	323	13.4	2 408	13.2	5 818	3 652	2 166	523	2 083
Loudoun	1 362	322 624	0.85	5 105	13.2	1 392	3.6	23 045	6.7	26 418	21 375	5 043	3 697	1 030

1. Per 1,000 estimated resident population. 2. Data for serious crimes have not been adjusted for underreporting; this may affect comparability between geographic areas and over time.
3. Per 100,000 population estimated by the FBI.

Items 32—45

STATE County	Serious crimes known to police, 2014 (cont.)[1] Rate[2]		Education School enrollment and attainment, 2011–2015 Enrollment[3]		Attainment[4] (percent)		Local government expenditures,[5] 2013–2014		Money income, 2011–2015		Households Percent		Income and poverty, 2015	Percent below poverty level	
	Violent	Property	Total	Percent private	High school graduate or less	Bachelor's degree or more	Total current spending (mil dol)	Current spending per student (dollars)	Per capita income[6] (dollars)	Median income (dollars)	with income of less than $50,000	with income of $200,000 or more	Median household income (dollars)	All persons	Children under 18 years	Children 5 to 17 years in families
	46	47	48	49	50	51	52	53	54	55	56	57	58	59	60	61
VERMONT—Cont'd																
Chittenden	90	2 036	46 624	20.8	26.8	48.7	383.9	17 782	33 977	65 350	38.5	5.7	67 112	10.4	10.2	9.2
Essex	0	242	1 149	12.3	58.8	16.0	13.7	20 344	21 338	36 599	62.2	1.0	41 764	14.3	22.8	20.6
Franklin	130	1 517	10 878	8.8	48.1	23.6	122.8	14 747	28 394	58 199	42.2	2.8	59 280	8.1	13.0	11.6
Grand Isle	72	1 359	1 480	17.2	35.8	35.1	12.1	12 514	35 214	62 608	38.7	5.6	68 342	8.3	13.2	12.0
Lamoille	44	583	5 843	10.3	36.5	36.2	61.6	16 381	27 390	50 939	48.9	3.9	54 076	10.2	13.7	11.9
Orange	24	851	6 254	16.8	43.4	30.8	65.9	16 278	27 755	53 869	45.6	2.2	54 552	9.8	14.8	13.3
Orleans	85	1 411	5 556	13.6	52.4	22.1	73.7	18 702	23 213	42 831	55.6	1.8	42 884	13.3	20.0	18.0
Rutland	160	1 564	13 727	15.2	43.5	29.1	150.5	19 619	27 219	49 372	50.6	2.3	51 164	11.4	17.0	15.1
Washington	76	1 393	13 749	27.8	35.3	39.9	145.1	16 816	30 598	58 788	42.1	3.3	56 333	9.3	11.1	10.0
Windham	167	1 880	9 583	27.3	39.1	35.8	107.5	17 838	28 473	51 045	49.0	2.7	49 298	13.2	18.1	15.4
Windsor	93	1 189	11 814	19.7	39.3	35.1	141.4	18 394	32 474	52 965	47.0	4.5	53 984	9.1	12.6	11.4
VIRGINIA	196	1 930	2 161 031	17.1	36.5	36.3	13 970.7	10 968	34 152	65 015	38.8	8.1	66 263	11.2	15.0	14.0
Accomack	244	1 415	6 176	13.1	59.5	18.8	51.1	9 731	23 231	39 412	60.3	1.9	38 690	20.4	31.0	33.4
Albemarle	100	1 784	30 575	17.2	26.9	51.7	[7]221.8	[7]12 489	37 474	68 449	36.8	10.1	71 293	9.5	9.6	8.5
Alleghany	130	1 151	3 148	16.5	53.4	15.7	26.3	10 648	24 118	45 007	54.6	1.1	45 210	18.2	24.0	21.7
Amelia	71	949	2 765	15.5	54.3	14.5	17.1	9 555	24 868	56 850	44.1	1.7	53 078	11.1	17.0	16.2
Amherst	133	1 201	7 233	24.2	52.9	18.3	43.4	10 115	23 469	47 558	52.0	1.2	48 646	15.0	20.6	19.1
Appomattox	104	757	3 568	17.5	52.1	17.7	19.9	8 505	23 941	48 823	51.6	1.2	49 461	14.2	20.9	20.3
Arlington	138	1 744	46 631	29.8	14.8	72.9	423.0	17 999	63 579	105 763	20.6	19.8	104 354	7.1	8.8	8.9
Augusta	150	1 088	14 723	19.1	54.2	22.0	98.5	9 234	27 000	54 558	45.9	3.0	56 867	9.3	12.9	11.6
Bath	0	871	844	13.6	51.0	21.8	9.9	15 608	32 166	43 646	58.6	1.4	44 401	10.3	14.6	13.4
Bedford	97	1 302	18 062	21.0	42.9	26.7	114.1	11 080	28 524	56 316	44.1	3.2	54 153	9.1	12.8	11.3
Bland	119	640	1 213	9.5	54.2	14.1	8.8	10 221	20 169	45 294	56.1	0.0	44 727	13.6	17.8	15.7
Botetourt	100	792	7 666	17.2	43.9	26.2	50.3	10 359	31 160	60 454	39.5	3.5	62 591	7.4	9.3	7.9
Brunswick	136	569	3 866	15.3	59.8	13.1	20.8	10 845	18 245	36 919	61.3	1.6	39 748	22.1	29.2	27.1
Buchanan	179	1 536	4 601	13.4	64.5	9.9	34.9	10 893	17 883	29 679	68.3	0.7	32 443	28.8	33.6	32.6
Buckingham	140	1 143	3 577	19.0	66.3	10.4	22.1	10 241	18 204	40 331	57.3	0.4	43 774	20.2	27.5	26.9
Campbell	173	1 471	12 690	26.7	51.3	19.3	73.4	8 801	24 192	47 699	51.9	1.9	46 938	11.7	16.3	15.1
Caroline	136	1 333	6 024	14.8	54.5	19.2	39.5	9 003	26 761	59 227	41.3	2.7	54 696	12.0	17.2	16.7
Carroll	111	1 259	5 892	9.3	54.7	14.5	40.0	9 972	21 145	35 000	65.0	0.7	42 790	15.0	24.3	21.6
Charles City	84	352	1 250	11.5	63.7	13.0	9.8	13 332	29 018	49 563	50.4	2.6	51 645	11.6	19.5	17.6
Charlotte	204	335	2 576	4.6	59.6	14.0	22.4	11 185	18 719	35 079	68.6	1.2	37 819	19.2	28.4	27.4
Chesterfield	129	1 929	91 150	14.6	33.1	36.9	524.1	8 855	33 220	72 609	32.1	6.6	75 107	6.9	9.5	8.7
Clarke	28	1 178	3 159	21.4	40.3	31.0	21.0	10 446	37 558	71 295	34.1	10.1	71 789	8.4	10.4	9.1
Craig	38	383	1 179	11.8	58.8	14.7	7.1	10 164	22 456	44 330	55.9	0.0	47 832	11.9	21.7	20.0
Culpeper	147	1 362	11 646	15.6	50.3	21.9	74.7	9 242	28 104	66 697	36.4	4.1	63 728	10.2	14.9	13.5
Cumberland	143	551	2 199	12.9	59.0	14.5	14.6	10 175	22 860	39 301	58.9	0.6	40 958	19.6	30.8	27.0
Dickenson	162	974	2 944	9.1	60.5	11.0	24.0	10 257	20 275	33 624	65.3	0.8	32 620	25.0	33.0	29.1
Dinwiddie	265	1 283	6 242	10.9	57.9	15.3	41.3	9 343	23 395	51 397	48.1	1.5	52 694	12.4	17.5	16.1
Essex	213	1 609	2 203	10.6	56.2	15.2	16.0	10 271	23 448	42 760	55.8	1.5	47 427	15.5	26.7	27.1
Fairfax	91	1 344	308 243	19.6	21.0	59.9	[8]2 515.2	[8]13 710	51 025	112 552	17.8	20.9	112 844	6.2	7.5	6.9
Fauquier	54	887	17 257	20.1	37.3	33.5	128.4	11 524	41 255	91 609	25.2	10.9	89 610	6.8	8.3	7.1
Floyd	64	918	2 996	29.1	52.5	18.2	19.1	9 133	23 885	48 005	51.9	2.4	48 448	11.9	18.2	17.1
Fluvanna	77	848	6 199	17.1	39.8	31.5	34.5	9 340	28 669	63 938	39.4	2.7	65 899	7.8	10.4	9.3
Franklin	129	1 174	12 111	24.0	48.0	20.5	72.5	9 794	25 219	46 870	52.5	2.4	49 117	13.1	19.1	17.3
Frederick	122	1 943	20 080	18.2	43.1	29.1	[9]186.1	[9]10 708	30 769	69 098	35.7	4.4	69 991	7.7	10.7	9.5
Giles	178	1 466	3 285	14.1	56.0	15.8	23.0	9 388	25 241	46 390	54.6	2.9	46 727	10.6	17.6	16.2
Gloucester	114	1 512	8 425	15.4	43.6	22.1	54.4	9 652	29 867	61 121	39.8	3.2	63 742	9.3	14.7	13.6
Goochland	130	736	4 528	33.9	36.9	37.4	26.9	10 971	46 366	79 330	29.4	14.3	86 257	7.4	9.8	8.6
Grayson	119	1 033	2 684	4.0	62.5	10.0	22.0	12 149	19 742	29 942	70.4	1.1	37 684	20.1	29.4	28.1
Greene	116	1 180	4 439	16.7	50.2	23.7	28.9	9 248	28 209	61 550	37.3	2.0	60 406	9.3	13.9	13.2
Greensville	161	669	2 217	9.2	66.1	8.6	[10]24.3	[10]9 373	14 450	38 012	62.7	1.4	40 252	27.9	28.7	28.6
Halifax	199	2 027	7 645	9.2	56.7	15.5	53.5	9 596	19 782	35 240	63.3	1.0	40 432	16.9	25.6	23.5
Hanover	128	1 237	27 257	17.2	35.4	35.7	164.1	8 984	34 701	78 645	29.9	6.8	81 900	6.2	7.1	6.1
Henrico	156	2 451	81 855	16.8	32.2	40.7	449.6	8 890	33 634	61 934	39.8	6.6	65 524	9.3	13.0	12.3
Henry	230	2 253	10 539	9.8	55.7	11.4	67.3	9 104	20 159	35 293	66.6	0.9	36 695	19.6	30.5	26.9
Highland	0	273	321	29.6	54.9	21.6	3.6	17 182	26 809	43 914	57.2	2.8	42 363	13.8	24.2	22.7
Isle of Wight	157	1 219	8 591	19.6	41.4	26.9	51.9	9 426	31 460	65 741	38.4	3.6	67 480	9.9	13.1	11.4
James City	123	1 472	17 046	13.8	27.3	47.0	[11]122.2	[11]10 832	39 802	75 710	30.8	8.1	77 668	7.1	10.2	9.1
King and Queen	28	962	1 390	16.5	56.3	18.1	10.4	12 657	25 498	48 292	52.8	1.8	47 513	14.0	20.5	18.0
King George	115	1 247	6 566	18.4	37.7	32.3	37.0	8 547	34 529	81 688	26.6	8.1	81 128	7.1	9.6	8.9
King William	43	552	3 877	13.2	51.8	18.4	30.7	10 089	28 300	62 031	36.1	2.2	64 651	7.9	12.2	11.3
Lancaster	126	532	1 782	12.3	42.9	27.9	14.7	11 704	31 062	50 374	49.7	3.8	47 098	13.1	26.2	25.1
Lee	151	1 932	4 949	11.5	59.1	12.0	33.8	9 941	17 899	31 086	68.4	1.2	32 135	25.9	36.3	32.9
Loudoun	80	949	107 167	17.5	20.2	58.2	883.4	12 485	47 495	123 453	14.9	21.7	125 900	3.7	4.0	3.4

1. Data for serious crimes have not been adjusted for underreporting; this may affect comparability between geographic areas and over time.   2. Per 100,000 population estimated by the FBI.
3. All persons 3 years old and over enrolled in nursery school through college.   4. Persons 25 years old and over.   5. Elementary and secondary education expenditures.
6. Based on population estimated by the American Community Survey, 2011–2015.   7. Charlottesville city is included with Albemarle county.   8. Fairfax city is included with Fairfax county.   9. Winchester city is included with Frederick county.   10. Emporia city is included with Greensville county.   11. Williamsburg city is included with James City county.

STATE County	Personal income, 2015										Earnings, 2015		
	Total (mil dol)	Percent change, 2014–2015	Per capita[1]		Wages and salaries (mil dol)	Supplements to wages and salaries; employer contributions (mil dol)		Proprietors' income (mil dol)	Dividends, interest, and rent (mil dol)	Personal transfer receipts (mil dol)	Total (mil dol)	Contributions for government social insurance (mil dol)	
			Dollars	Rank		Pension and insurance	Government social insurance					From employee and self-employed	From employer
	62	63	64	65	66	67	68	69	70	71	72	73	74

VERMONT—Cont'd													
Chittenden	8 837	3.8	54 756	300	5 388	872	447	660	1 793	1 342	7 367	457	447
Essex	213	4.0	34 497	2 043	40	10	4	17	33	62	71	6	4
Franklin	1 987	0.9	40 728	1 002	789	163	68	115	284	397	1 135	72	68
Grand Isle	368	0.8	53 604	389	42	9	4	34	83	60	89	7	4
Lamoille	1 216	3.9	48 196	648	471	78	42	134	288	221	725	47	42
Orange	1 238	2.7	42 836	1 081	308	62	26	109	218	266	506	35	26
Orleans	1 100	1.9	40 603	1 149	403	79	37	98	189	330	618	42	37
Rutland	2 849	2.9	47 694	617	1 169	216	101	139	458	933	1 626	112	101
Washington	3 080	4.0	52 541	434	1 645	284	134	243	556	668	2 306	148	134
Windham	2 062	3.9	47 526	749	1 007	169	84	198	438	476	1 458	96	84
Windsor	2 931	3.5	52 588	437	1 038	192	90	225	721	585	1 545	105	90
VIRGINIA	436 350	4.6	52 148	X	225 441	37 068	16 518	26 241	87 062	59 304	305 268	18 130	16 518
Accomack	1 275	3.8	38 683	1 605	513	109	38	81	266	340	742	49	38
Albemarle	[3]9 183	[3]5.8	[3]60 294	[3]149	[3]5 187	[3]1 017	[3]366	[3]741	[3]2 977	[3]952	[3]7 311	[3]416	[3]366
Alleghany	[4]789	[4]5.1	[4]36 989	[4]1 971	[4]363	[4]66	[4]27	[4]28	[4]129	[4]240	[4]484	[4]35	[4]27
Amelia	523	3.9	40 511	1 130	98	18	7	59	73	116	182	12	7
Amherst	1 084	3.3	33 981	2 303	341	74	25	37	175	290	477	35	25
Appomattox	538	5.0	34 915	2 184	106	23	7	24	76	149	160	14	7
Arlington	19 745	4.9	86 161	24	16 432	2 512	1 206	1 214	4 100	909	21 364	1 190	1 206
Augusta	[5]4 809	[5]4.8	[5]40 000	[5]1 380	[5]1 998	[5]375	[5]146	[5]349	[5]902	[5]1 040	[5]2 868	[5]189	[5]146
Bath	225	4.5	50 326	568	96	16	7	11	75	47	130	9	7
Bedford	[6]3 227	[6]3.8	[6]41 514	[6]1 027	[6]775	[6]135	[6]58	[6]155	[6]591	[6]673	[6]1 123	[6]85	[6]58
Bland	215	3.3	32 752	2 500	87	23	6	7	38	61	124	9	6
Botetourt	1 561	5.2	46 811	674	453	79	34	59	265	286	625	45	34
Brunswick	523	4.7	31 332	2 597	152	32	11	14	78	177	210	16	11
Buchanan	730	-1.1	32 032	1 865	336	66	25	26	103	292	452	35	25
Buckingham	468	5.0	27 449	2 915	134	32	9	26	70	138	201	15	9
Campbell	[7]4 797	[7]2.4	[7]35 559	[7]2 037	[7]3 228	[7]514	[7]238	[7]188	[7]904	[7]1 314	[7]4 168	[7]263	[7]238
Caroline	1 140	5.1	38 035	1 512	239	55	18	23	171	228	334	24	18
Carroll	[8]1 196	[8]4.3	[8]32 642	[8]2 530	[8]412	[8]85	[8]32	[8]66	[8]182	[8]409	[8]594	[8]44	[8]32
Charles City	296	6.2	42 002	1 188	71	13	5	20	53	66	109	8	5
Charlotte	391	5.3	32 048	2 600	105	25	8	22	69	124	159	13	8
Chesterfield	16 285	5.5	48 513	498	6 511	1 046	476	662	2 605	2 270	8 694	538	476
Clarke	810	3.1	56 372	227	183	29	13	44	204	101	270	18	13
Craig	181	4.7	34 690	2 152	27	6	2	7	31	46	42	4	2
Culpeper	2 062	4.5	41 724	1 199	686	127	51	136	354	345	999	64	51
Cumberland	336	3.5	34 599	2 392	46	11	3	25	50	90	85	7	3
Dickenson	430	1.3	28 443	2 903	155	33	11	14	56	187	213	18	11
Dinwiddie	[9]2 970	[9]3.9	[9]38 010	[9]1 635	[9]1 279	[9]239	[9]97	[9]84	[9]529	[9]846	[9]1 699	[9]111	[9]97
Essex	430	3.4	38 644	1 500	138	25	10	14	81	112	187	14	10
Fairfax	[10]88 419	[10]4.0	[10]74 923	[10]41	[10]56 307	[10]6 858	[10]3 851	[10]6 126	[10]19 911	[10]5 790	[10]73 142	[10]4 268	[10]3 851
Fauquier	4 249	4.2	61 780	112	1 115	180	81	254	1 010	440	1 630	102	81
Floyd	543	5.1	34 703	2 222	102	21	8	32	93	137	162	13	8
Fluvanna	1 040	5.1	39 659	1 586	192	40	14	30	211	194	277	21	14
Franklin	2 063	3.6	36 668	2 005	528	99	40	115	400	511	783	60	40
Frederick	[11]4 957	[11]4.5	[11]44 871	[11]881	[11]2 556	[11]429	[11]188	[11]353	[11]859	[11]763	[11]3 526	[11]214	[11]188
Giles	623	4.0	37 295	1 956	199	42	15	24	95	169	280	21	15
Gloucester	1 661	3.4	44 728	784	332	69	24	53	316	317	478	35	24
Goochland	1 875	4.9	84 253	20	1 400	148	86	61	542	197	1 695	103	86
Grayson	474	4.1	29 627	2 766	88	24	7	23	84	160	140	13	7
Greene	760	6.5	39 681	1 621	137	26	10	48	119	137	221	16	10
Greensville	[12]523	[12]2.0	[12]30 101	[12]2 653	[12]288	[12]62	[12]21	[12]6	[12]76	[12]169	[12]377	[12]25	[12]21
Halifax	1 193	3.4	33 960	2 282	468	98	35	47	199	382	648	46	35
Hanover	5 571	6.2	53 971	324	2 280	338	169	398	898	715	3 184	198	169
Henrico	19 006	5.6	58 452	391	10 818	1 467	774	2 967	3 330	2 227	16 026	948	774
Henry	[13]2 291	[13]3.9	[13]34 968	[13]2 207	[13]884	[13]169	[13]68	[13]101	[13]428	[13]776	[13]1 222	[13]92	[13]68
Highland	99	0.1	44 498	725	17	5	1	10	37	23	34	2	1
Isle of Wight	1 839	4.3	50 643	417	521	83	36	59	293	306	699	47	36
James City	[14]5 160	[14]4.2	[14]58 504	[14]165	[14]1 723	[14]309	[14]127	[14]246	[14]1 383	[14]774	[14]2 404	[14]154	[14]127
King and Queen	258	5.2	35 980	1 676	41	9	3	11	40	65	63	6	3
King George	1 279	3.1	50 109	512	874	213	72	104	236	151	1 263	69	72
King William	694	5.3	42 633	1 219	177	30	13	25	101	125	245	17	13
Lancaster	557	3.9	50 763	424	173	30	13	26	215	141	241	19	13
Lee	673	2.8	27 219	2 971	165	44	13	19	101	271	240	21	13
Loudoun	26 255	7.1	69 895	72	10 442	1 394	718	1 325	3 460	1 305	13 879	808	718

1. Based on the resident population estimated as of July 1 of the year shown.   3. Charlottesville city is included with Albemarle county.   4. Covington city is included with Alleghany county.   5. Staunton and Waynesboro cities are included with Augusta county.   6. Bedford city is included with Bedford county.   7. Lynchburg city is included with Campbell county.   8. Galax city is included with Carroll county.   9. Petersburg and Colonial Heights cities are included with Dinwiddie county.   10. Fairfax city and Falls Church city are included with Fairfax county.   11. Winchester city is included with Frederick county.   12. Emporia city is included with Greensville county.   13. Martinsville city is included with Henry county.   14. Williamsburg city is included with James City county.

STATE County	Farm	Mining	Construction	Manufacturing	Information: professional, scientific, technical services	Retail trade	Finance, insurance, real estate and leasing	Health care and social assistance	Government	Social Security beneficiaries, December 2015 — Number	Rate¹	Supplemental Security Income recipients, December 2015	Housing units, 2016 — Total	Percent change, 2010–2016
	75	76	77	78	79	80	81	82	83	84	85	86	87	88
VERMONT—Cont'd														
Chittenden	0.1	0.0	6.2	11.4	14.9	6.7	6.2	15.2	18.6	28 605	177	3 121	68 520	4.3
Essex	3.8	D	14.3	8.6	D	3.0	D	D	36.7	2 130	346	219	5 094	1.5
Franklin	2.6	0.2	5.9	17.9	D	6.9	2.0	12.7	30.1	8 865	181	1 250	22 174	2.7
Grand Isle	4.9	D	19.1	2.3	D	8.0	D	D	18.5	1 890	275	139	5 181	2.6
Lamoille	0.1	D	11.6	5.0	8.2	7.7	3.5	14.4	14.5	5 170	205	495	13 374	3.1
Orange	2.2	0.1	14.2	6.9	D	6.7	D		22.1	6 775	235	686	15 155	2.1
Orleans	2.7	D	10.6	11.8	D	9.3	3.5	16.0	20.8	7 460	275	1 001	17 151	6.1
Rutland	0.2	1.8	8.5	13.9	4.6	8.4	3.3	17.5	16.9	16 665	279	1 990	33 935	0.5
Washington	0.2	0.2	6.5	6.6	8.0	7.0	11.8	12.3	23.1	13 625	232	1 431	30 287	1.2
Windham	0.3	D	9.1	9.7	D	7.5	3.9	14.4	11.9	11 295	261	1 240	30 148	1.4
Windsor	0.2	0.2	9.2	7.4	11.0	6.6	3.9	11.8	24.1	15 070	271	1 279	34 328	0.6
VIRGINIA	0.1	0.1	5.5	5.9	20.0	5.2	6.8	9.0	23.7	1 443 127	172	156 517	3 491 054	3.7
Accomack	2.9	0.0	4.9	18.5	13.4	5.2	3.2	D	27.7	9 305	282	1 183	21 049	0.2
Albemarle	(3)0.0	(3)0.1	(3)4.5	(3)3.5	(3)14.3	(3)4.5	(3)7.1	(3)10.0	(3)35.4	18 335	174	948	44 684	6.1
Alleghany	(4)-0.6	(4)D	(4)6.3	(4)D	(4)D	(4)5.8	(4)2.0	(4)D	(4)17.4	4 595	293	315	8 039	-0.5
Amelia	12.1	D	12.7	11.0	D	7.7	1.6		15.6	3 225	251	313	5 471	2.1
Amherst	-0.1	0.0	7.6	20.6	3.3	7.6	2.3	D	30.1	8 220	260	839	14 123	1.0
Appomattox	-0.6	D	10.2	3.4	D	14.5	2.4	D	27.2	4 115	267	535	7 152	3.3
Arlington	0.0	D	1.6	0.6	34.1	1.7	4.6	3.4	30.8	19 270	85	2 251	112 963	7.2
Augusta	(5)1.5	(5)D	(5)D	(5)17.6	(5)6.7	(5)6.8	(5)3.8	(5)D	(5)17.4	18 125	243	632	32 285	3.5
Bath	0.5	0.0	5.1	2.0	9.3	2.1	1.8	D	15.8	1 355	301	95	3 296	0.9
Bedford	(6)-0.3	(6)0.0	(6)9.3	(6)12.9	(6)8.7	(6)7.0	(6)5.7	(6)10.7	(6)14.5	19 885	256	1 186	36 352	4.3
Bland	0.1	D	2.5	36.6	D	D	D	D	26.7	1 880	286	131	3 265	0.0
Botetourt	-0.1	D	8.5	20.3	4.5	D	3.2	6.2	13.2	8 450	253	727	14 803	1.7
Brunswick	2.5	D	6.2	8.0	D	4.6	3.0	D	24.7	4 400	267	680	8 130	-0.4
Buchanan	-0.1	31.5	6.2	5.0	D	5.1	2.7	7.1	19.2	8 425	370	1 650	11 370	-1.8
Buckingham	3.3	D	9.2	3.0	3.0	5.3	1.6	10.9	37.8	3 735	220	457	7 314	1.0
Campbell	(7)0.0	(7)D	(7)D	(7)20.3	(7)10.0	(7)6.4	(7)6.5	(7)16.8	(7)10.4	13 525	245	1 102	25 559	3.2
Caroline	-1.7	D	8.3	5.6	D	4.6	1.4	D	35.0	5 965	199	506	12 095	3.1
Carroll	(8)1.0	(8)0.0	(8)D	(8)18.7	(8)4.4	(8)9.3	(8)2.7	(8)16.6	(8)21.8	8 670	292	561	16 632	0.3
Charles City	0.4	D	13.9	15.8	D	2.6	D	D	17.3	1 985	281	121	3 319	2.8
Charlotte	-0.2	D	4.9	14.4	D	4.7	2.2	D	30.1	3 645	299	574	6 288	0.2
Chesterfield	0.0	D	7.9	9.2	10.7	8.3	6.9	10.4	16.4	57 140	170	4 348	129 011	5.3
Clarke	1.2	D	9.6	13.3	17.2	2.8	5.5	D	14.6	3 060	214	157	6 333	1.6
Craig	-2.7	0.0	7.5	D	D	6.2	6.1	D	30.3	1 440	277	108	2 880	2.7
Culpeper	-0.1	0.5	9.7	9.2	12.0	9.0	3.8	12.9	20.8	9 200	186	859	18 484	4.7
Cumberland	13.1	0.0	12.0	8.7	D	7.0	D	D	28.2	2 440	252	221	4 676	1.1
Dickenson	-0.9	38.6	6.8	1.2	D	5.6	D	6.5	21.0	5 465	361	947	7 476	-1.3
Dinwiddie	(9)0.0	(9)D	(9)6.1	(9)9.1	(9)2.8	(9)9.6	(9)4.4	(9)D	(9)23.2	6 130	219	491	11 630	1.8
Essex	-2.0	0.0	5.3	9.9	D	14.4	7.3	19.0	16.0	3 055	275	364	5 802	0.8
Fairfax	(10)0.0	(10)0.0	(10)4.8	(10)0.6	(10)38.5	(10)4.0	(10)7.8	(10)6.2	(10)16.6	122 415	108	10 932	414 268	1.5
Fauquier	-1.0	0.3	12.7	3.2	16.4	7.7	7.7	10.7	20.7	11 630	169	569	26 610	3.8
Floyd	2.3	D	10.6	11.9	D	5.9	5.9	11.2	21.1	4 100	262	303	7 961	2.1
Fluvanna	-0.8	D	9.5	2.4	5.0	3.7	2.5	D	29.5	5 725	219	247	10 823	4.2
Franklin	1.5	D	12.0	18.1	4.3	8.3	4.0		16.3	14 955	266	1 215	29 559	0.9
Frederick	(11)0.1	(11)D	(11)D	(11)14.0	(11)D	(11)8.6	(11)7.0	(11)17.2	(11)17.4	15 530	187	909	33 381	6.5
Giles	-0.2	0.0	D	29.7	5.3	8.0	2.1	D	15.8	4 900	292	594	8 324	0.1
Gloucester	0.0	D	9.2	2.0	D	12.5	4.4	15.3	27.6	8 540	230	644	16 345	3.1
Goochland	-0.2	D	5.3	2.1	3.3	1.3	D	1.7	4.9	5 280	237	240	9 133	6.1
Grayson	3.0	0.0	5.3	14.0	D	3.1	7.9	D	36.0	4 965	327	367	9 158	0.0
Greene	0.4	D	12.1	1.7	12.6	9.6	2.0	D	22.4	3 730	194	245	8 131	8.3
Greensville	(12)0.3	(12)D	(12)3.1	(12)24.5	(12)1.0	(12)5.7	(12)D	(12)14.9	(12)28.0	2 535	214	68	4 133	1.1
Halifax	0.9	D	6.1	17.8	3.0	6.1	2.3	17.0	17.6	10 580	301	1 577	18 102	0.5
Hanover	-0.2	0.2	13.0	7.0	6.5	9.1	3.8	11.8	9.4	20 015	194	926	40 907	6.7
Henrico	0.0	0.0	4.2	3.3	12.7	5.5	15.4	13.7	8.3	54 820	169	4 950	136 815	3.0
Henry	(13)0.2	(13)D	(13)D	(13)20.6	(13)D	(13)10.4	(13)3.6	(13)13.7	(13)17.5	17 135	331	2 362	26 036	-1.0
Highland	24.3	0.0	8.0	3.5	D	3.9	D	D	25.1	760	344	24	1 867	1.8
Isle of Wight	0.4	0.0	4.8	26.7	D	3.6	3.4	D	12.8	8 155	224	514	15 452	5.6
James City	(14)-0.1	(14)D	(14)5.0	(14)6.5	(14)D	(14)8.4	(14)D	(14)11.2	(14)23.9	18 700	256	798	32 810	9.2
King and Queen	-0.9	D	13.4	11.1	D	D	D	D	23.5	1 835	255	153	3 452	1.1
King George	-0.2	D	2.1	5.6	19.0	1.9	1.4	1.5	62.0	3 670	144	255	9 953	5.0
King William	-1.1	1.5	8.8	28.6	4.5	14.3	4.1	D	17.6	3 450	213	212	6 824	4.7
Lancaster	-1.2	D	8.1	2.3	8.5	9.7	12.1	22.4	12.4	4 335	395	293	7 607	2.8
Lee	-0.8	5.0	6.5	1.6	D	8.7	3.0	12.0	41.8	7 305	296	1 633	11 669	-0.6
Loudoun	-0.2	D	9.4	5.6	30.9	5.0	5.4	5.9	13.7	30 760	82	1 964	129 914	18.7

1. Per 1,000 resident population estimated as of July 1 of the year shown. 3. Charlottesville city is included with Albemarle county. 4. Covington city is included with Alleghany county. 5. Staunton and Waynesboro cities are included with Augusta county. 6. Bedford city is included with Bedford county. 7. Lynchburg city is included with Campbell county. 8. Galax city is included with Carroll county. 9. Petersburg and Colonial Heights cities are included with Dinwiddie county. 10. Fairfax city and Falls Church city are included with Fairfax county. 11. Winchester city is included with Frederick county. 12. Emporia city is included with Greensville county. 13. Martinsville city is included with Henry county. 14. Williamsburg city is included with James City county.

Table B. States and Counties — Housing, Labor Force, and Employment

STATE County	Housing units, 2011–2015 — Occupied units								Civilian labor force, 2016				Civilian employment,[6] 2011–2015		
			Owner-occupied			Renter-occupied					Unemployment			Percent	
				Median owner cost as a percent of income											
	Total	Percent	Median value[1]	With a mortgage	Without a mortgage[2]	Median rent[3]	Median rent as a percent of income[2]	Sub-stand-ard units[4] (percent)	Total	Percent change, 2015–2016	Total	Rate[5]	Total	Manage-ment, business, science and arts	Con-struction, produc-tion, and mainte-nance occu-pations
	89	90	91	92	93	94	95	96	97	98	99	100	101	102	103
VERMONT—Cont'd															
Chittenden	63 498	64.9	271 300	23.7	14.3	1 102	32.2	1.6	95 198	0.3	2 353	2.5	89 268	47.2	14.3
Essex	2 701	79.8	122 800	24.6	17.7	689	30.6	2.2	2 717	-2.8	159	5.9	2 683	29.8	32.1
Franklin	18 685	74.2	203 000	23.4	14.5	870	30.0	2.5	27 347	-0.1	867	3.2	25 416	36.2	27.2
Grand Isle	2 965	79.4	261 300	24.3	18.6	1 039	33.4	1.6	3 955	0.2	157	4.0	3 697	38.4	21.2
Lamoille	10 176	72.3	220 700	28.1	17.9	866	31.9	2.0	13 853	0.2	599	4.3	13 147	37.0	21.6
Orange	12 148	79.8	189 400	25.8	16.5	836	30.9	2.4	15 895	-0.2	495	3.1	15 314	39.0	23.8
Orleans	11 200	78.5	154 500	25.6	17.1	700	31.0	2.1	13 553	-0.8	709	5.2	12 168	32.6	28.9
Rutland	25 459	70.1	178 500	24.7	16.9	785	30.2	3.1	31 152	-0.6	1 211	3.9	30 125	34.7	23.7
Washington	24 512	73.6	211 200	23.3	17.0	862	29.4	1.8	34 013	-0.3	1 090	3.2	31 774	43.4	17.5
Windham	19 057	69.2	209 200	26.8	17.6	849	30.7	2.6	23 330	-0.7	778	3.3	22 336	39.9	22.4
Windsor	24 507	70.0	216 300	25.4	17.8	868	30.0	2.0	29 417	-0.4	865	2.9	28 487	39.5	22.4
VIRGINIA	3 062 783	66.2	245 000	22.7	10.5	1 116	29.9	2.3	4 240 416	0.7	170 151	4.0	3 990 770	42.7	17.9
Accomack	13 961	71.0	153 300	22.6	12.5	733	27.3	3.3	15 799	-0.4	761	4.8	14 296	33.1	29.6
Albemarle	38 853	65.1	313 800	21.3	10.0	1 117	29.3	1.1	54 092	0.4	1 892	3.5	48 206	54.1	12.6
Alleghany	6 781	78.7	112 000	19.0	10.6	591	28.3	1.9	6 922	-1.7	351	5.1	6 539	29.0	35.1
Amelia	4 704	81.3	170 800	23.2	10.0	693	46.5	1.2	6 226	0.7	261	4.2	5 686	26.2	26.5
Amherst	12 502	76.3	150 100	21.2	10.3	679	25.8	1.9	15 140	-0.8	658	4.3	14 663	28.5	25.8
Appomattox	5 931	80.8	148 200	20.9	10.0	695	34.2	1.6	6 974	-0.8	322	4.6	6 532	30.9	28.9
Arlington	98 441	44.4	607 700	20.9	10.0	1 827	26.5	2.5	146 487	1.6	3 785	2.6	141 305	68.0	6.2
Augusta	28 150	79.4	197 400	22.4	10.0	832	28.6	1.2	36 855	0.7	1 334	3.6	34 285	31.1	29.3
Bath	2 146	69.7	153 700	17.1	13.7	535	14.5	2.9	2 502	-1.2	92	3.7	2 310	28.5	23.1
Bedford	30 591	81.2	196 500	21.3	10.0	754	29.0	0.5	37 890	-0.8	1 537	4.1	35 756	34.6	25.9
Bland	2 614	79.9	100 300	18.9	10.1	580	24.3	2.1	2 747	-1.1	144	5.2	2 504	25.6	28.5
Botetourt	12 913	87.6	208 500	22.5	10.0	831	26.6	1.3	17 398	0.2	629	3.6	16 257	38.3	22.0
Brunswick	5 916	73.0	105 200	23.8	14.4	674	34.9	2.0	6 246	-1.2	376	6.0	6 601	26.1	29.2
Buchanan	9 442	78.9	71 500	24.1	10.7	637	36.7	2.1	6 826	-6.1	736	10.8	7 120	22.8	36.0
Buckingham	5 603	77.6	131 800	23.3	11.8	685	34.6	2.0	6 285	0.0	336	5.3	6 406	24.2	28.6
Campbell	21 791	76.0	151 500	20.7	10.0	725	28.7	1.3	26 026	-0.6	1 141	4.4	26 131	32.3	28.5
Caroline	10 970	80.7	186 800	23.2	10.3	1 050	29.1	1.3	14 841	0.9	649	4.4	13 539	30.4	27.3
Carroll	12 548	79.0	107 900	24.0	10.5	534	30.7	1.0	12 928	-0.8	664	5.1	13 033	26.8	35.0
Charles City	2 883	81.3	159 600	23.8	10.9	871	28.9	1.5	3 726	0.4	169	4.5	3 323	22.1	33.5
Charlotte	4 723	69.5	94 300	23.7	12.8	566	30.6	3.5	5 253	0.2	264	5.0	5 266	25.1	30.2
Chesterfield	116 797	76.3	216 800	21.9	10.0	1 123	29.3	1.4	180 031	1.3	6 890	3.8	164 842	42.4	17.5
Clarke	5 526	75.9	329 500	23.9	10.0	1 032	30.7	0.8	7 457	0.5	261	3.5	6 908	43.6	19.9
Craig	2 214	81.0	153 000	24.3	10.0	547	24.1	0.0	2 370	-0.3	111	4.7	2 101	24.9	38.0
Culpeper	16 515	72.8	251 600	24.5	10.4	1 050	31.9	2.8	23 235	0.7	889	3.8	22 103	35.9	23.7
Cumberland	4 012	72.1	137 800	24.4	13.4	867	29.6	3.4	4 605	1.2	211	4.6	4 567	28.7	30.7
Dickenson	6 205	77.4	74 100	19.9	10.0	528	36.9	2.8	4 535	-7.6	451	9.9	5 017	27.1	28.5
Dinwiddie	9 939	76.6	155 300	23.9	11.8	933	27.9	1.8	13 379	0.6	646	4.8	12 653	27.2	31.0
Essex	4 332	73.6	164 400	25.5	12.3	834	32.8	1.4	5 516	0.2	266	4.8	5 211	22.5	27.1
Fairfax	392 355	67.7	501 200	21.7	10.0	1 747	28.0	3.3	621 364	1.4	19 747	3.2	603 966	56.1	9.9
Fauquier	23 595	79.1	357 200	23.3	10.3	1 169	27.2	1.0	35 922	0.7	1 235	3.4	34 515	42.6	19.7
Floyd	6 271	77.7	155 300	20.7	10.0	527	18.6	2.6	8 226	-0.7	326	4.0	7 494	29.7	34.1
Fluvanna	9 891	82.1	215 600	24.8	12.4	1 282	26.2	2.0	13 223	0.6	440	3.3	12 076	43.2	17.5
Franklin	23 189	77.4	168 400	22.7	10.0	659	28.5	2.3	26 435	0.1	1 126	4.3	25 149	31.5	30.0
Frederick	29 455	78.1	225 300	22.0	11.0	1 073	27.6	2.7	44 971	0.9	1 556	3.5	40 973	38.9	23.1
Giles	7 230	76.1	104 700	19.9	10.0	593	24.2	1.5	7 956	0.3	422	5.3	7 510	24.8	37.7
Gloucester	14 280	79.0	224 100	22.9	10.0	873	27.0	1.2	19 019	-0.3	695	3.7	17 612	28.6	26.8
Goochland	8 148	87.0	318 400	21.6	10.0	1 027	24.6	0.8	10 694	0.9	401	3.7	10 325	46.6	16.1
Grayson	6 795	74.5	91 500	23.3	11.4	552	28.9	1.0	7 034	0.0	369	5.2	6 262	23.1	35.9
Greene	7 111	77.5	241 800	23.7	10.0	928	26.9	1.9	9 866	0.3	317	3.2	8 932	37.4	18.3
Greensville	3 486	71.6	99 800	23.4	14.4	716	32.2	2.2	4 186	0.5	215	5.1	3 365	22.8	26.2
Halifax	14 300	72.3	104 700	22.0	11.8	549	31.7	1.9	14 904	-1.8	862	5.8	14 234	26.6	29.9
Hanover	37 463	81.0	255 400	21.3	10.0	1 044	27.8	1.2	56 875	1.3	1 979	3.5	52 677	43.1	17.0
Henrico	124 589	62.9	216 300	22.1	10.0	1 035	28.9	1.7	179 138	1.4	6 880	3.8	164 877	43.4	14.0
Henry	22 415	74.6	95 400	22.1	12.0	584	27.8	2.5	22 095	-1.0	1 229	5.6	21 466	25.0	31.8
Highland	1 071	82.4	169 100	19.8	10.0	473	26.5	2.3	1 300	-2.8	41	3.2	1 006	28.7	30.0
Isle of Wight	13 769	78.1	243 000	23.6	11.4	959	29.8	1.1	18 750	-0.2	810	4.3	17 246	36.2	26.6
James City	28 000	74.9	319 100	23.0	10.0	1 159	32.1	1.0	34 206	-0.1	1 323	3.9	31 685	45.1	13.4
King and Queen	2 894	75.9	155 800	22.2	10.0	863	23.1	3.0	3 613	-0.4	151	4.2	3 335	26.7	35.3
King George	8 379	73.0	282 500	21.8	10.0	1 098	25.0	1.5	12 268	1.9	512	4.2	12 096	41.5	19.3
King William	6 036	81.7	198 500	24.3	10.0	1 026	35.2	1.9	8 761	0.8	326	3.7	7 972	32.4	31.9
Lancaster	5 164	75.0	229 100	27.8	10.3	870	27.7	1.1	5 100	-0.4	286	5.6	4 690	30.3	15.8
Lee	9 445	73.1	78 400	22.2	10.0	497	32.7	4.3	8 479	-1.0	577	6.8	7 942	31.5	25.2
Loudoun	113 432	77.1	452 300	22.8	10.0	1 668	27.7	2.1	202 652	1.4	6 407	3.2	186 474	56.4	9.9

1. Specified owner-occupied units.   2. A value of 10.0 represents 10 percent or less; a value of 50.0 represents 50 percent or more.   3. Specified renter-occupied units.
4. Overcrowded or lacking complete plumbing facilities.   5. Percent of civilian labor force.   6. Civilian employed persons 16 years old and over.

Table B. States and Counties — Nonfarm Employment and Agriculture

STATE County	Number of establish-ments	Private nonfarm establishments, employment and payroll, 2015						Annual payroll		Agriculture, 2012			
		Employment								Farms		
		Total	Health care and social assistance	Manufac-turing	Retail trade	Finance and insurance	Professional, scientific, and technical services	Total (mil dol)	Average per employee (dollars)	Number	Fewer than 50 acres	500 acres or more	Farm operators whose principal occu-pation is farming (percent)
	104	105	106	107	108	109	110	111	112	113	114	115	116
VERMONT—Cont'd													
Chittenden	5 607	88 809	16 407	8 780	13 005	2 984	6 768	3 974	44 748	587	50.4	3.9	50.6
Essex	116	484	67	136	91	10	17	16	33 107	93	26.9	18.3	47.3
Franklin	1 011	12 599	2 777	2 745	2 357	300	255	484	38 401	736	28.3	12.1	54.5
Grand Isle	185	660	44	44	166	20	44	23	35 238	121	44.6	7.4	59.5
Lamoille	950	11 502	1 756	549	1 489	221	320	351	30 558	349	42.4	6.9	36.1
Orange	753	6 312	1 582	701	986	158	330	246	39 003	748	38.2	4.0	49.9
Orleans	777	8 244	1 652	1 295	1 324	203	173	276	33 507	638	31.7	9.7	60.3
Rutland	2 135	23 780	4 534	3 205	4 214	576	602	890	37 416	640	38.4	7.0	47.8
Washington	2 242	27 085	4 584	2 457	4 344	2 482	1 054	1 162	42 904	532	40.0	3.2	50.4
Windham	1 696	21 452	3 534	2 022	2 431	574	500	815	37 983	447	46.1	4.7	52.3
Windsor	2 006	19 901	3 916	2 249	2 825	488	1 053	799	40 173	768	42.1	4.7	48.7
VIRGINIA	197 384	3 198 718	435 558	236 645	423 864	157 892	437 548	165 789	51 830	46 030	38.6	7.7	45.1
Accomack	738	8 344	1 128	2 865	1 420	162	296	241	28 902	226	46.0	15.5	63.7
Albemarle	2 660	38 540	7 478	2 895	5 990	3 002	3 480	1 880	48 775	946	38.1	8.0	41.4
Alleghany	242	2 261	812	245	285	59	25	74	32 640	207	25.6	6.8	32.4
Amelia	272	1 847	377	192	232	34	57	56	30 550	407	30.5	9.3	44.5
Amherst	572	6 346	781	1 218	1 155	137	272	206	32 446	426	27.9	10.1	39.0
Appomattox	288	2 301	451	141	641	84	83	59	25 828	410	21.0	10.5	43.4
Arlington	6 307	132 147	9 324	190	8 931	3 362	41 467	10 294	77 902	6	100.0	0.0	50.0
Augusta	1 409	19 147	4 408	3 767	1 940	263	427	782	40 825	1 706	42.3	6.2	48.8
Bath	125	2 216	261	43	71	25	115	75	34 013	116	17.2	15.5	45.7
Bedford	1 684	15 509	2 055	2 986	2 643	457	776	563	36 327	1 369	34.2	5.0	42.7
Bland	76	1 390	156	592	62	D	D	61	44 167	362	23.2	9.1	44.8
Botetourt	723	10 691	919	2 385	812	178	235	435	40 666	584	33.0	6.5	46.7
Brunswick	251	2 344	204	191	357	48	38	76	32 625	312	19.6	10.3	44.6
Buchanan	414	5 240	616	225	799	188	205	235	44 867	103	46.6	2.9	33.0
Buckingham	265	1 928	351	130	279	28	78	69	35 985	391	24.0	13.0	52.9
Campbell	1 176	16 925	1 126	4 745	2 232	389	805	735	43 420	761	28.1	8.9	37.2
Caroline	375	3 680	311	271	564	D	196	128	34 752	221	38.5	12.2	45.2
Carroll	416	4 383	696	1 002	744	92	105	119	27 214	980	34.3	6.5	39.2
Charles City	141	1 474	D	255	96	D	20	59	40 257	79	43.0	16.5	58.2
Charlotte	224	1 729	355	346	254	47	33	54	31 040	518	26.8	11.4	42.9
Chesterfield	7 146	110 731	12 836	9 307	17 853	5 214	7 735	4 656	42 052	197	56.3	2.5	44.7
Clarke	356	2 901	430	529	245	115	149	130	44 825	477	47.2	4.4	46.5
Craig	57	321	57	D	107	22	13	9	28 601	207	27.5	9.7	51.7
Culpeper	988	12 492	1 788	1 552	2 310	222	739	502	40 206	731	45.7	8.1	40.9
Cumberland	137	883	76	D	215	16	D	27	30 287	262	30.2	11.1	52.7
Dickenson	200	1 996	356	36	438	67	226	68	34 127	147	48.3	4.8	51.7
Dinwiddie	346	4 287	302	648	511	127	62	182	42 502	383	32.6	9.1	45.4
Essex	302	3 470	598	537	866	122	86	104	30 075	98	36.7	26.5	43.9
Fairfax	30 403	578 448	56 888	5 840	52 048	29 766	188 301	44 447	76 838	148	77.7	2.0	34.5
Fauquier	1 821	17 393	2 640	973	2 861	691	1 742	765	43 958	1 258	48.2	7.8	43.6
Floyd	318	2 138	445	366	321	84	58	59	27 456	863	29.9	6.7	48.2
Fluvanna	387	2 503	241	148	360	48	74	85	34 095	303	36.0	6.6	43.2
Franklin	1 166	12 437	1 494	2 460	1 944	258	280	347	27 910	1 023	30.7	6.6	45.2
Frederick	1 474	24 607	1 764	4 575	3 634	1 852	1 811	976	39 662	681	45.1	5.9	36.9
Giles	286	3 794	492	931	722	80	416	149	39 345	378	27.0	5.3	40.2
Gloucester	861	7 126	1 301	224	1 950	256	291	203	28 449	136	62.5	8.8	39.0
Goochland	644	16 499	509	189	528	6 179	313	1 365	82 714	315	52.1	6.0	41.0
Grayson	150	1 822	185	958	149	100	18	52	28 266	764	34.6	7.6	44.2
Greene	329	2 553	208	56	813	44	136	75	29 412	216	34.7	4.6	50.0
Greensville	101	1 977	D	D	218	D	D	56	28 536	151	29.1	19.2	38.4
Halifax	696	9 777	1 651	2 050	1 417	193	153	336	34 384	935	17.9	9.7	44.0
Hanover	3 117	45 384	5 667	4 029	6 480	650	1 342	1 713	37 745	600	53.2	5.7	51.8
Henrico	9 137	168 398	23 884	5 378	22 404	23 863	14 066	8 466	50 271	117	58.1	3.4	41.9
Henry	808	11 236	780	3 107	1 555	283	301	344	30 651	290	35.2	2.8	26.2
Highland	92	369	51	D	45	D	8	9	24 434	261	14.2	22.6	51.0
Isle of Wight	648	8 760	697	3 607	896	215	293	370	42 242	213	47.4	20.7	51.2
James City	1 669	27 276	4 654	2 457	3 776	588	1 505	997	36 569	83	61.4	1.2	28.9
King and Queen	97	529	14	54	32	D	23	18	34 212	127	40.2	13.4	66.1
King George	506	6 232	299	103	844	167	2 810	337	54 122	160	40.6	8.1	38.1
King William	317	2 957	276	404	418	90	98	153	51 746	135	37.0	18.5	50.4
Lancaster	461	3 826	1 045	103	765	302	249	137	35 690	61	39.3	8.2	45.9
Lee	273	2 705	535	100	903	176	59	71	26 065	1 012	38.7	3.6	37.2
Loudoun	9 867	141 629	11 041	5 636	18 989	3 074	21 699	8 568	60 495	1 396	69.0	3.4	37.0

STATE County	Land in farms					Value of land and buildings (dollars)		Value of machinery and equipment, average per farm (dollars)	Value of products sold				Percent of farms with sales of:		Government payments	
	Acreage (1,000)	Percent change, 2007–2012	Acres			Average per farm	Average per acre		Total (mil dol)	Average per farm (dollars)	Percent from:		$10,000 or more	$100,000 or more	Total ($1,000)	Percent of farms
			Average size of farm	Total irrigated (1,000)	Total cropland (1,000)						Crops	Live-stock and poultry products				
	117	118	119	120	121	122	123	124	125	126	127	128	129	130	131	132
VERMONT—Cont'd																
Chittenden	74	-11.8	125	0.5	25.9	538 598	4 297	75 608	42.2	71 951	47.0	53.0	40.9	12.3	609	21.8
Essex	25	-4.6	274	0.0	8.0	510 731	1 863	95 505	11.7	125 280	33.9	66.1	47.3	19.4	124	31.2
Franklin	186	3.5	253	0.6	80.2	708 868	2 801	145 685	184.4	250 497	17.1	82.9	55.8	31.4	2 937	34.2
Grand Isle	19	11.0	157	0.1	13.8	598 289	3 806	103 231	19.1	157 579	29.6	70.4	53.7	26.4	458	27.3
Lamoille	52	4.7	149	0.1	12.6	544 129	3 645	73 444	21.3	61 129	44.6	55.4	37.8	12.3	362	18.3
Orange	105	3.5	141	0.2	33.2	435 761	3 097	65 348	53.5	71 578	25.2	74.8	35.7	13.9	730	15.8
Orleans	130	0.1	204	0.2	52.5	497 260	2 432	90 815	99.3	155 655	14.4	85.6	48.6	20.5	1 342	24.3
Rutland	108	-16.9	170	0.2	36.5	460 703	2 718	73 945	30.8	48 114	33.2	66.8	36.9	10.2	1 131	25.9
Washington	67	10.4	127	0.2	21.1	508 002	4 013	70 991	27.1	50 972	25.9	74.1	35.3	8.8	535	14.5
Windham	51	0.0	114	0.5	14.0	454 076	3 998	64 159	26.4	59 116	43.0	57.0	36.9	8.5	499	17.4
Windsor	101	5.6	132	0.2	23.6	500 858	3 795	58 762	22.4	29 188	34.8	65.2	27.2	7.2	517	9.6
VIRGINIA	8 302	2.4	180	68.7	2 990.6	776 719	4 306	72 555	3 753.3	81 540	36.2	63.8	37.9	9.6	82 318	23.2
Accomack	77	-17.5	342	5.4	64.3	1 254 991	3 665	153 013	172.2	761 934	34.7	65.3	68.1	39.4	2 020	44.2
Albemarle	169	6.7	179	1.5	46.6	1 563 048	8 756	61 092	31.0	32 780	62.8	37.2	32.2	4.2	377	9.2
Alleghany	37	28.0	179	0.0	8.1	554 908	3 108	53 285	2.9	14 227	D	D	28.0	1.0	11	10.1
Amelia	88	-3.5	217	0.4	28.2	664 813	3 065	77 044	99.8	245 288	13.0	87.0	37.6	13.5	1 496	42.8
Amherst	99	11.9	232	D	19.4	846 944	3 646	60 845	9.3	21 758	35.2	64.8	35.4	2.6	175	10.6
Appomattox	96	26.9	235	0.1	28.7	668 800	2 847	63 924	12.6	30 788	35.1	64.9	42.0	7.8	367	30.0
Arlington	0	0.0	6	D	D	322 667	53 778	10 000	0.0	3 000	D	D	0.0	0.0	0	0.0
Augusta	260	-9.1	152	3.3	89.6	953 997	6 256	79 364	232.1	136 059	11.9	88.1	49.1	15.1	1 677	18.2
Bath	41	7.6	356	0.0	10.0	1 484 267	4 166	63 353	6.1	52 216	22.1	77.9	44.8	12.9	31	13.8
Bedford	207	-2.7	151	0.1	59.1	668 345	4 430	58 744	28.3	20 660	24.6	75.4	33.9	2.8	897	11.8
Bland	77	-4.1	214	D	14.1	690 022	3 225	64 199	9.3	25 785	13.1	86.9	44.2	5.2	179	18.8
Botetourt	89	1.6	153	0.1	26.2	668 360	4 370	69 147	18.7	32 027	32.4	67.6	34.1	6.0	397	15.8
Brunswick	90	3.6	288	1.3	25.2	601 074	2 088	73 490	25.7	82 349	67.1	32.9	32.7	7.7	1 243	52.9
Buchanan	10	2.4	93	D	0.8	245 175	2 642	29 864	0.5	4 651	46.3	53.7	8.7	0.0	166	23.3
Buckingham	84	8.6	215	0.0	24.5	660 348	3 077	66 338	39.9	101 997	16.2	83.8	40.9	10.2	215	19.9
Campbell	151	7.4	198	0.3	44.1	591 091	2 985	60 756	24.2	31 846	26.8	73.2	36.7	5.4	895	28.8
Caroline	56	1.5	255	2.0	37.8	1 052 570	4 128	114 928	20.4	92 172	96.6	3.4	29.9	13.1	1 149	24.9
Carroll	140	13.6	143	1.1	41.5	488 210	3 406	53 584	43.4	44 305	25.7	74.3	44.6	7.2	359	13.5
Charles City	31	13.4	395	1.4	21.4	1 482 443	3 756	221 367	23.7	299 747	D	D	40.5	24.1	744	30.4
Charlotte	149	19.0	288	0.8	41.0	654 878	2 271	58 116	21.7	41 849	51.2	48.8	40.5	7.1	1 200	34.4
Chesterfield	20	-7.3	101	0.1	6.9	539 970	5 329	73 452	6.4	32 487	59.4	40.6	18.8	6.6	259	13.7
Clarke	67	-1.4	140	0.2	27.6	1 105 929	7 880	59 356	25.9	54 333	33.1	66.9	33.5	7.3	235	10.5
Craig	47	12.0	225	0.0	9.9	714 005	3 170	76 580	4.9	23 604	26.6	73.4	43.5	2.4	106	18.4
Culpeper	126	13.5	173	0.6	58.0	1 115 272	6 450	80 141	42.8	58 534	59.9	40.1	36.3	7.3	1 059	14.5
Cumberland	57	0.6	218	0.0	15.6	782 668	3 588	66 351	44.9	171 260	8.6	91.4	37.8	11.8	377	27.9
Dickenson	15	4.9	102	0.0	2.6	303 755	2 967	43 837	0.8	5 313	21.4	78.7	16.3	0.0	72	8.8
Dinwiddie	89	13.2	233	1.2	39.0	699 723	3 003	73 689	24.8	64 747	82.3	17.7	36.3	6.3	2 425	49.3
Essex	57	6.3	579	D	38.7	1 761 745	3 045	258 112	22.8	232 418	98.5	1.5	44.9	29.6	873	48.0
Fairfax	8	11.7	53	0.1	1.4	804 507	15 156	42 581	3.4	23 243	94.0	6.0	19.6	2.7	26	6.8
Fauquier	228	2.6	181	0.4	82.2	1 439 924	7 935	73 037	53.9	42 884	40.0	60.0	32.6	6.4	865	9.9
Floyd	145	12.2	168	0.2	41.5	607 145	3 622	59 109	34.7	40 210	41.4	58.6	40.7	4.6	320	8.1
Fluvanna	47	-3.7	155	0.1	13.6	791 934	5 097	55 584	4.7	15 584	62.8	37.2	29.7	2.3	123	14.9
Franklin	165	-1.2	161	0.9	58.2	570 110	3 544	76 026	65.4	63 971	22.5	77.5	34.3	8.5	1 084	17.9
Frederick	101	2.5	148	0.2	39.7	872 966	5 903	57 128	34.3	50 389	72.5	27.5	34.4	5.4	398	5.6
Giles	66	0.1	173	0.0	12.2	458 352	2 642	53 362	8.1	21 402	20.0	80.0	35.4	5.0	55	3.2
Gloucester	20	-11.6	149	0.0	13.7	750 375	5 027	96 426	11.3	82 890	94.8	5.2	31.6	12.5	421	18.4
Goochland	50	-15.4	159	0.0	19.5	868 708	5 457	61 886	16.6	52 578	50.2	49.8	23.5	4.4	291	9.5
Grayson	132	-3.5	173	0.0	27.9	724 361	4 195	55 518	31.6	41 408	18.9	81.1	42.8	6.9	419	23.8
Greene	27	-12.0	126	0.0	7.6	868 801	6 880	62 347	9.9	45 759	15.9	84.1	34.7	4.2	40	22.7
Greensville	58	19.5	386	0.2	31.9	782 781	2 029	109 563	21.3	140 775	96.8	3.2	29.8	15.9	1 359	63.6
Halifax	212	9.2	226	2.2	61.5	520 118	2 298	77 607	36.5	39 065	63.4	36.6	35.2	7.8	3 737	53.7
Hanover	94	2.7	157	3.3	55.2	874 698	5 566	82 075	55.3	92 120	85.0	15.0	34.2	8.7	1 370	10.8
Henrico	13	-35.9	110	D	9.5	724 744	6 578	59 342	9.4	80 094	98.4	1.6	24.8	11.1	130	13.7
Henry	43	-15.4	148	0.1	9.3	400 117	2 700	50 052	D	D	D	D	27.2	2.8	177	13.1
Highland	93	21.3	357	0.0	11.6	1 205 379	3 380	69 057	30.1	115 199	4.5	95.5	61.7	18.4	252	13.4
Isle of Wight	76	3.0	355	0.7	50.0	1 262 986	3 556	165 127	45.6	214 202	72.4	27.6	49.8	22.5	1 689	51.2
James City	6	-4.9	67	0.0	3.0	585 530	8 766	72 687	D	D	D	D	36.1	1.2	94	12.0
King and Queen	42	-21.0	331	D	29.0	1 020 906	3 089	132 559	17.3	136 567	D	D	35.4	16.5	1 051	32.3
King George	24	-33.8	152	0.4	10.1	764 544	5 033	57 250	3.8	23 788	83.7	16.3	29.4	5.6	174	33.8
King William	54	16.3	397	1.1	28.6	1 481 511	3 734	107 889	16.6	123 296	84.4	15.6	32.6	17.8	735	18.5
Lancaster	11	-24.1	175	D	7.4	802 885	4 579	112 082	4.9	79 738	96.4	3.6	50.8	13.1	278	42.6
Lee	117	-0.5	116	0.1	30.4	255 115	2 202	47 907	18.2	18 026	23.8	76.2	30.8	3.3	1 007	44.5
Loudoun	135	-5.4	97	0.6	56.2	1 156 476	11 977	56 777	37.1	26 577	70.3	29.7	23.4	3.2	497	8.0

Table B. States and Counties — Water Use, Wholesale Trade, Retail Trade, and Real Estate

STATE County	Water use, 2010		Wholesale trade,[1] 2012				Retail trade,[2] 2012				Real estate and rental and leasing,[2] 2012			
	Total water withdrawn (mil gal/day)	Gallons withdrawn per person per day	Number of establishments	Number of employees	Sales (mil dol)	Annual payroll (mil dol)	Number of establishments	Number of employees	Sales (mil dol)	Annual payroll (mil dol)	Number of establishments	Number of employees	Receipts (mil dol)	Annual payroll (mil dol)
	133	134	135	136	137	138	139	140	141	142	143	144	145	146
VERMONT—Cont'd														
Chittenden	18.0	115	246	4 085	3 133.9	239.1	839	12 464	2 959.4	308.4	232	1 297	275.2	49.5
Essex	0.7	103	3	2	0.4	0.0	20	93	19.0	1.3	2	D	D	D
Franklin	7.4	156	46	794	1 257.8	32.1	195	2 139	628.6	50.7	26	74	7.4	1.8
Grand Isle	4.0	574	5	6	3.4	0.2	30	165	50.0	3.6	7	6	1.5	0.2
Lamoille	2.6	107	23	D	D	D	163	1 508	360.4	36.5	32	103	13.7	3.3
Orange	2.8	97	24	182	78.4	7.8	102	1 001	245.4	23.6	19	34	4.9	1.1
Orleans	3.8	138	23	D	D	D	147	1 285	350.3	31.3	21	94	14.2	2.7
Rutland	9.7	157	73	D	D	D	411	4 139	1 082.8	97.7	67	276	30.8	7.8
Washington	6.2	104	70	D	D	D	380	4 258	1 112.6	105.1	65	277	45.6	7.9
Windham	349.8	7 858	43	D	D	D	283	2 540	604.4	63.9	69	258	32.0	8.6
Windsor	8.9	157	53	670	276.6	32.1	311	2 694	726.3	70.5	81	265	30.9	8.7
VIRGINIA	7 648.0	956	6 232	88 353	86 613.6	4 983.1	27 415	410 918	110 002.4	10 007.9	8 862	54 246	11 758.9	2 378.3
Accomack	15.2	458	28	159	78.9	5.1	169	1 402	348.2	28.8	38	103	13.0	2.5
Albemarle	19.2	194	66	1 102	574.5	67.1	325	5 511	1 497.5	147.8	151	766	129.5	25.7
Alleghany	43.1	2 649	5	30	7.7	1.0	38	280	75.1	6.3	4	16	2.1	0.3
Amelia	7.9	623	6	D	D	D	30	227	71.1	4.9	6	7	0.5	0.1
Amherst	17.0	525	11	D	D	D	94	1 137	273.4	22.7	17	38	3.7	0.7
Appomattox	1.5	100	7	75	9.9	2.4	56	631	143.8	12.9	12	19	5.1	0.4
Arlington	0.3	1	85	1 090	935.3	88.8	613	9 610	2 608.8	265.6	404	5 188	1 493.4	219.8
Augusta	40.2	545	52	737	249.6	33.1	208	1 941	621.3	46.5	61	185	18.9	4.1
Bath	109.1	23 063	2	D	D	D	21	94	17.2	1.4	8	37	3.6	1.9
Bedford	21.6	314	53	503	342.0	20.4	216	2 512	652.3	57.9	79	143	24.1	4.4
Bland	2.9	422	7	D	D	D	12	64	33.8	1.2	2	D	D	D
Botetourt	8.7	261	37	D	D	D	85	873	321.4	18.5	19	D	D	D
Brunswick	28.4	1 629	6	45	27.1	1.6	45	326	103.6	6.3	5	D	D	D
Buchanan	0.9	36	21	231	265.3	13.2	79	834	173.0	14.5	12	29	4.8	0.9
Buckingham	2.3	136	8	D	D	D	38	293	83.0	6.0	3	D	D	D
Campbell	7.4	135	38	D	D	D	188	1 904	601.0	43.3	52	126	18.2	3.2
Caroline	9.0	314	8	D	D	D	49	655	404.2	15.5	12	24	4.3	0.5
Carroll	2.4	81	15	121	40.2	2.8	89	748	285.7	14.6	14	43	5.2	0.9
Charles City	0.9	127	8	D	D	D	10	57	14.7	2.0	6	20	3.8	0.6
Charlotte	1.5	118	9	68	29.6	2.2	32	230	56.5	4.3	5	12	0.7	0.2
Chesterfield	897.5	2 838	290	3 411	1 729.4	182.3	933	17 142	4 657.3	410.9	281	1 511	331.7	65.3
Clarke	1.9	133	9	D	D	D	35	229	81.5	4.6	17	D	D	D
Craig	3.1	588	3	D	D	D	11	110	18.6	1.7	2	D	D	D
Culpeper	5.1	109	24	448	296.8	16.5	157	2 120	550.1	52.5	43	239	31.2	9.2
Cumberland	5.9	587	1	D	D	D	34	204	40.4	3.9	3	D	D	D
Dickenson	4.8	300	7	20	5.3	0.4	44	451	102.3	9.4	4	5	0.4	0.1
Dinwiddie	2.1	76	8	D	D	D	56	541	144.9	9.8	7	52	7.5	1.8
Essex	2.0	182	7	D	D	D	60	826	236.6	20.3	10	73	7.1	2.6
Fairfax	14.9	14	750	11 158	25 177.2	930.7	2 735	50 244	14 589.5	1 418.8	1 447	10 962	2 918.3	687.9
Fauquier	6.6	101	38	445	159.7	20.1	223	2 632	920.8	75.7	77	203	34.6	8.1
Floyd	1.8	116	11	D	D	D	42	321	70.7	5.9	5	5	1.9	0.2
Fluvanna	118.8	4 625	11	117	76.0	5.4	39	308	75.3	6.3	15	20	3.6	0.7
Franklin	5.6	99	39	424	291.4	26.7	190	1 857	459.0	42.0	46	103	17.8	3.2
Frederick	16.2	206	84	D	D	D	197	3 512	1 346.1	91.3	54	143	30.4	6.0
Giles	149.0	8 619	8	D	D	D	62	694	184.0	14.8	11	22	3.1	0.7
Gloucester	3.5	95	23	87	22.7	2.9	141	1 905	496.2	45.7	43	110	11.6	2.6
Goochland	2.0	93	32	D	D	D	62	491	215.5	13.9	13	102	13.4	5.3
Grayson	1.9	123	6	D	D	D	24	161	40.5	2.8	5	3	0.8	0.1
Greene	1.7	95	9	60	14.6	2.8	52	764	183.9	16.9	9	D	D	D
Greensville	1.8	146	5	24	1.8	0.7	25	209	130.8	3.7	4	18	2.0	0.4
Halifax	18.5	510	20	244	99.2	8.8	133	1 436	358.1	30.3	21	69	12.1	1.6
Hanover	8.5	85	216	4 016	3 161.4	205.6	358	5 917	1 752.1	151.6	106	466	176.3	22.0
Henrico	31.0	101	405	7 312	7 293.9	446.7	1 277	22 637	5 519.9	538.8	447	3 659	718.5	164.4
Henry	11.4	211	44	D	D	D	167	1 715	581.5	41.4	25	110	16.1	2.9
Highland	9.3	4 020	2	D	D	D	17	44	8.6	0.6	1	D	D	D
Isle of Wight	23.9	678	16	75	51.2	3.4	104	950	246.9	16.8	29	80	11.3	2.5
James City	14.3	213	47	335	131.6	14.4	281	3 679	630.2	66.6	82	502	102.7	19.9
King and Queen	2.0	285	4	D	D	D	11	31	12.4	0.6	4	4	0.4	0.1
King George	3.9	165	8	D	D	D	54	721	232.4	15.4	16	46	8.7	1.3
King William	22.9	1 438	7	35	12.0	1.3	49	437	133.3	10.1	11	26	2.3	0.7
Lancaster	1.3	115	15	114	83.9	3.3	79	805	161.5	18.1	17	38	5.4	0.8
Lee	3.7	144	12	68	33.4	2.1	68	828	208.1	16.6	10	26	2.5	0.5
Loudoun	22.5	72	243	3 225	2 319.4	236.1	952	17 774	5 140.4	481.0	341	1 877	528.1	82.5

1. Merchant wholesalers, except manufacturers' sales branches and offices.　　2. Employer establishments.

Table B. States and Counties — Professional Services, Manufacturing, and Accommodation and Food Services

STATE County	Professional, scientific, and technical services, 2012				Manufacturing, 2012				Accommodation and food services, 2012			
	Number of establishments	Number of employees	Receipts (mil dol)	Annual payroll (mil dol)	Number of establishments	Number of employees	Receipts (mil dol)	Annual payroll (mil dol)	Number of establishments	Number of employees	Sales (mil dol)	Annual payroll (mil dol)
	147	148	149	150	151	152	153	154	155	156	157	158
VERMONT—Cont'd												
Chittenden	752	6 327	941.2	403.6	189	9 861	3 388.0	556.6	433	8 124	459.9	133.8
Essex	5	25	2.8	1.4	7	129	11.4	4.2	13	58	2.4	0.7
Franklin	62	236	26.7	11.9	55	2 770	D	132.8	88	771	44.6	13.6
Grand Isle	21	48	4.4	1.6	7	40	D	1.1	25	111	9.4	2.9
Lamoille	88	394	71.3	20.3	49	406	D	18.4	112	4 203	183.7	73.0
Orange	73	352	60.4	18.7	49	673	133.0	28.6	59	589	40.0	12.5
Orleans	48	169	16.5	6.5	41	1 108	D	36.8	68	1 446	54.1	20.4
Rutland	178	D	D	D	105	3 126	613.1	164.0	247	2 795	130.1	37.8
Washington	251	D	D	D	126	3 959	819.8	225.4	163	2 923	123.9	41.2
Windham	124	476	49.9	20.9	92	2 049	421.4	87.5	212	3 498	151.5	44.2
Windsor	193	5 011	265.8	108.4	110	2 062	442.6	86.8	199	3 492	176.8	50.9
VIRGINIA	29 368	429 690	92 775.9	36 364.7	5 101	228 197	96 389.9	11 586.1	16 832	320 514	17 795.9	4 908.6
Accomack	64	410	79.3	19.9	18	3 001	667.9	78.1	101	993	53.6	13.9
Albemarle	353	3 204	501.5	204.2	68	2 855	786.4	172.2	182	3 780	230.6	67.5
Alleghany	11	24	2.4	0.6	8	468	D	19.7	26	299	14.0	3.7
Amelia	14	46	3.1	1.0	19	247	98.4	7.6	11	93	5.0	1.1
Amherst	43	253	32.2	13.5	39	1 314	572.0	67.7	44	D	D	D
Appomattox	14	D	D	D	13	71	D	2.4	14	D	D	D
Arlington	1 829	42 070	11 167.3	4 296.3	34	220	54.1	7.4	647	17 342	1 362.4	363.6
Augusta	93	413	39.9	15.0	73	4 382	1 884.2	221.4	79	1 229	56.5	15.9
Bath	9	D	D	D	4	47	D	D	18	1 021	63.5	26.8
Bedford	166	630	76.4	23.0	71	3 393	D	181.0	106	1 231	50.8	14.2
Bland	2	D	D	D	8	488	D	25.5	6	46	2.3	0.6
Botetourt	63	D	D	D	30	D	812.0	114.2	49	D	D	D
Brunswick	13	36	3.3	1.0	17	217	69.1	10.5	11	D	D	D
Buchanan	35	277	20.9	7.4	10	238	91.7	13.8	22	317	15.3	4.2
Buckingham	15	100	12.9	5.2	11	116	D	3.5	7	D	D	D
Campbell	85	741	84.8	52.2	70	2 632	1 555.4	128.0	82	1 511	64.3	16.9
Caroline	30	206	19.9	8.7	17	279	76.1	10.8	30	332	18.5	4.9
Carroll	26	89	6.6	2.8	20	1 109	D	31.0	38	613	34.4	7.6
Charles City	3	D	D	D	18	292	D	10.6	4	D	D	D
Charlotte	9	40	2.3	0.8	15	419	74.8	13.3	10	91	4.5	1.3
Chesterfield	813	6 640	891.7	359.6	168	8 594	3 845.3	536.1	528	10 919	514.5	142.1
Clarke	44	113	16.4	6.6	14	706	89.8	27.0	21	D	D	D
Craig	7	D	D	D	NA	NA	NA	NA	4	D	D	D
Culpeper	92	674	96.9	31.4	39	1 382	563.6	63.6	77	1 193	59.3	14.7
Cumberland	5	D	D	D	3	D	D	D	4	44	1.4	0.4
Dickenson	11	163	8.9	3.7	6	43	D	1.9	13	D	D	D
Dinwiddie	24	64	4.1	1.7	10	652	D	D	18	270	15.4	3.6
Essex	23	93	6.4	2.7	14	609	90.7	16.7	30	459	19.6	5.8
Fairfax	8 232	197 134	48 404.9	18 643.4	357	6 199	1 408.8	349.1	2 158	39 514	2 795.4	731.2
Fauquier	267	1 590	287.5	115.2	58	872	137.8	39.7	110	2 008	108.1	29.8
Floyd	22	48	4.1	1.5	30	331	D	12.6	18	230	7.6	2.5
Fluvanna	29	71	7.6	2.0	10	89	D	3.0	22	D	D	D
Franklin	83	299	25.8	9.0	53	2 440	D	D	68	958	44.7	12.3
Frederick	114	D	D	D	84	4 514	2 537.6	220.9	129	2 381	117.5	30.6
Giles	15	264	19.2	10.1	13	994	D	60.1	35	429	18.3	4.9
Gloucester	74	283	24.2	9.8	15	181	22.1	6.5	65	934	40.4	12.1
Goochland	65	275	36.7	12.1	19	154	27.1	7.0	42	372	25.6	7.7
Grayson	11	20	2.1	0.6	17	819	D	27.4	14	110	4.4	1.4
Greene	30	336	23.7	20.0	11	48	D	1.9	27	299	14.9	4.0
Greensville	1	D	D	D	6	818	261.5	27.8	15	191	11.4	2.2
Halifax	35	157	17.6	4.9	37	1 685	573.4	73.0	62	914	36.0	10.1
Hanover	270	1 418	191.6	66.3	147	3 629	917.2	155.3	200	3 482	164.7	44.1
Henrico	1 142	11 253	1 505.7	630.6	175	5 104	1 808.2	262.6	720	16 249	832.8	238.8
Henry	33	270	13.4	6.6	69	2 885	834.7	115.5	55	1 003	41.3	10.9
Highland	5	7	0.9	0.3	NA	NA	NA	NA	5	D	D	D
Isle of Wight	60	296	30.2	11.8	15	D	D	83.1	50	766	34.1	9.8
James City	222	D	D	D	31	1 661	1 621.3	96.9	117	3 412	264.1	84.6
King and Queen	8	20	2.4	0.9	5	32	D	D	2	D	D	D
King George	108	2 415	459.4	194.9	8	82	D	3.3	37	369	21.8	5.4
King William	29	137	9.4	3.3	11	465	209.2	22.8	20	232	10.6	2.6
Lancaster	54	319	33.4	17.1	15	152	D	7.5	32	510	18.9	8.1
Lee	19	49	4.0	1.2	8	85	D	2.2	17	D	D	D
Loudoun	2 266	19 300	3 985.2	1 741.2	158	4 462	1 636.9	345.1	611	13 152	877.0	245.2

1. Establishment subject to federal tax.

STATE County	Health care and social assistance, 2012				Other services, 2012				Nonemployer businesses, 2015		Value of residential construction authorized by building permits, 2016	
	Number of establishments	Number of employees	Receipts (mil dol)	Annual payroll (mil dol)	Number of establishments	Number of employees	Receipts (mil dol)	Annual payroll (mil dol)	Number	Receipts (mil dol)	New Construction ($1,000)	Number of housing units
	159	160	161	162	163	164	165	166	167	168	169	170
VERMONT—Cont'd												
Chittenden	565	14 159	1 652.4	588.8	414	2 291	223.5	65.9	14 274	720.5	96 874	667
Essex	9	64	3.5	1.9	9	45	3.6	0.5	542	22.4	3 235	14
Franklin	108	D	D	D	69	264	25.9	6.1	3 626	153.4	34 414	173
Grand Isle	12	D	D	D	10	17	3.2	0.4	709	28.5	5 166	21
Lamoille	84	1 532	133.6	57.6	65	289	45.0	7.3	2 777	123.4	26 085	154
Orange	82	1 466	153.7	54.2	42	135	13.6	3.8	2 960	116.1	5 272	22
Orleans	75	1 714	152.5	67.2	69	217	18.9	4.3	2 542	103.0	13 575	154
Rutland	207	4 898	440.4	179.6	154	715	58.7	16.8	4 952	187.7	7 133	38
Washington	232	4 359	408.5	162.1	220	1 030	128.7	37.2	6 158	247.5	31 134	127
Windham	183	3 103	278.5	124.6	129	489	44.7	11.4	5 166	209.6	22 413	83
Windsor	167	3 691	436.7	204.6	146	760	82.6	21.9	6 049	262.2	24 572	121
VIRGINIA	18 774	411 108	47 705.0	18 628.8	14 726	112 430	17 079.4	4 471.2	576 446	25 410.0	5 473 492	31 132
Accomack	57	1 101	62.7	28.0	60	332	22.1	7.0	2 347	92.2	4 024	54
Albemarle	314	6 428	950.1	372.5	151	1 445	308.7	75.0	9 240	432.6	187 279	708
Alleghany	34	867	85.7	33.7	22	117	10.6	2.6	680	21.5	1 448	12
Amelia	24	369	21.6	9.9	20	D	D	D	869	31.2	9 108	44
Amherst	41	D	D	D	55	152	12.2	3.2	1 504	49.0	8 701	47
Appomattox	25	D	D	D	19	74	6.9	1.9	899	31.7	13 005	74
Arlington	484	8 987	1 450.6	465.6	642	10 355	2 577.8	721.4	19 400	1 004.0	350 024	1 914
Augusta	110	3 916	512.2	177.0	100	472	43.7	14.1	4 577	195.2	36 303	209
Bath	4	D	D	D	6	D	D	D	327	10.4	2 038	10
Bedford	145	1 295	82.4	34.3	118	601	62.3	17.6	5 155	210.1	74 017	288
Bland	7	81	7.6	3.2	6	D	D	D	287	9.9	2 286	22
Botetourt	48	D	D	D	57	D	D	D	2 353	87.9	15 664	69
Brunswick	12	189	10.4	4.7	20	D	D	D	687	24.9	5 248	23
Buchanan	43	655	53.4	23.0	26	D	D	D	817	28.8	394	2
Buckingham	15	375	17.4	11.2	16	70	7.9	2.2	697	25.7	4 186	29
Campbell	93	D	D	D	87	332	25.0	7.0	2 917	96.0	15 306	100
Caroline	19	283	18.2	9.2	30	172	15.1	3.8	1 663	57.8	21 092	110
Carroll	41	569	39.1	17.3	25	D	D	D	1 648	58.7	0	0
Charles City	3	D	D	D	7	D	D	D	393	12.2	3 123	17
Charlotte	23	284	13.2	7.7	17	D	D	D	650	26.0	1 454	9
Chesterfield	757	11 169	1 338.3	518.8	479	3 341	368.3	87.3	22 032	945.7	332 707	1 713
Clarke	25	D	D	D	30	79	10.1	3.0	1 291	60.3	23 029	60
Craig	5	D	D	D	3	D	D	D	305	9.9	2 090	12
Culpeper	74	2 007	204.3	84.8	75	539	47.4	17.3	3 580	168.6	54 847	213
Cumberland	10	115	3.3	2.1	9	D	D	D	526	18.2	2 625	17
Dickenson	27	402	24.7	12.2	19	D	D	D	434	12.7	255	3
Dinwiddie	26	263	15.5	6.7	32	D	D	D	1 288	49.1	1 163	61
Essex	35	623	68.4	19.7	23	D	D	D	791	34.4	3 697	24
Fairfax	2 860	52 008	6 870.2	2 622.2	1 950	17 487	2 708.3	760.6	104 930	5 419.8	375 044	2 670
Fauquier	125	2 571	274.8	114.2	128	875	82.3	28.9	6 012	309.7	105 524	325
Floyd	23	320	45.0	8.4	24	D	D	D	1 302	40.3	7 767	51
Fluvanna	22	199	11.7	5.5	22	138	9.4	3.0	1 729	60.1	21 848	109
Franklin	74	D	D	D	91	287	25.6	6.5	3 669	134.2	36 819	117
Frederick	88	1 551	114.1	45.9	104	591	55.8	17.4	5 427	210.5	151 827	791
Giles	29	500	46.1	16.5	26	D	D	D	842	31.3	3 089	20
Gloucester	69	1 282	128.1	45.2	75	323	22.5	7.2	2 389	87.2	34 247	185
Goochland	28	D	D	D	38	D	D	D	2 135	121.6	33 694	129
Grayson	17	197	11.3	4.5	9	D	D	D	1 036	33.1	4 311	21
Greene	15	D	D	D	20	103	9.2	2.5	1 362	47.6	17 313	140
Greensville	3	D	D	D	3	D	D	D	373	10.6	2 201	14
Halifax	82	1 767	159.9	73.5	50	173	16.1	3.9	1 748	61.5	300	4
Hanover	258	4 764	706.4	221.0	258	1 649	150.5	44.8	7 751	355.6	117 847	584
Henrico	977	24 726	2 887.9	1 138.2	635	4 883	735.9	163.0	22 959	1 027.7	136 160	958
Henry	55	1 005	51.9	23.4	47	257	20.5	6.3	2 295	72.9	5 353	30
Highland	5	58	3.3	1.4	9	D	D	D	245	6.2	1 616	12
Isle of Wight	50	648	44.0	21.2	64	309	29.2	9.7	2 203	82.5	33 813	171
James City	159	3 572	305.5	138.8	108	D	D	D	5 318	233.4	110 175	455
King and Queen	3	D	D	D	5	D	D	D	400	15.4	4 541	25
King George	21	321	21.3	8.8	29	D	D	D	1 443	47.9	24 476	103
King William	23	327	17.5	8.8	29	111	8.9	2.3	1 057	46.2	15 709	129
Lancaster	35	1 088	87.0	41.1	42	177	13.5	4.4	1 039	47.3	14 295	42
Lee	32	786	53.3	24.8	17	D	D	D	1 093	33.4	2 453	22
Loudoun	759	9 585	1 188.5	459.1	566	4 756	597.3	217.1	31 649	1 574.8	628 704	3 296

Table B. States and Counties — Government Employment and Payroll, and Local Government Finances

	Government employment and payroll, 2012									Local government finances, 2012				
		March payroll (percent of total)								General revenue				
												Taxes		
													Per capita[1] (dollars)	
STATE County	Full-time equivalent employees	March payroll (dollars)	Administration, judicial, and legal	Police and Corrections	Fire Protection	Highways and transportation	Health and Welfare	Natural resources and utilities	Education and libraries	Total (mil dol)	Inter-governmental (mil dol)	Total (mil dol)	Total	Property
	171	172	173	174	175	176	177	178	179	180	181	182	183	184
VERMONT—Cont'd														
Chittenden	6 092	25 796 817	4.3	6.7	2.8	6.4	0.8	8.4	68.8	648.3	401.0	117.0	738	613
Essex	227	673 088	8.5	1.1	0.0	5.4	1.1	1.2	82.3	22.3	16.5	3.7	588	586
Franklin	1 780	6 015 525	5.6	3.3	0.4	4.9	1.2	3.1	80.8	156.8	118.8	21.4	443	432
Grand Isle	201	726 392	10.7	0.0	0.0	6.8	2.7	2.1	76.7	25.5	17.3	7.2	1 026	1 022
Lamoille	1 075	3 560 151	5.3	4.1	0.1	5.4	1.5	5.9	77.1	94.8	63.4	20.8	832	792
Orange	1 252	3 813 072	7.2	1.2	0.1	5.8	0.2	0.5	84.5	109.1	85.0	17.9	618	616
Orleans	1 359	3 619 393	5.7	2.4	0.1	7.1	0.3	1.7	82.4	103.1	75.1	19.7	725	721
Rutland	2 343	8 318 234	5.3	3.7	1.6	7.2	0.7	4.0	76.9	234.3	164.7	46.5	764	726
Washington	2 492	8 165 965	5.6	4.3	2.3	5.1	1.2	3.5	77.0	224.6	150.4	42.0	707	701
Windham	1 877	6 583 583	5.5	4.5	2.2	6.1	1.0	3.8	75.7	202.3	137.1	44.4	1 010	989
Windsor	2 421	8 862 072	5.4	5.6	2.7	6.6	1.1	3.8	74.2	247.7	169.7	49.6	883	878
VIRGINIA	X	X	X	X	X	X	X	X	X	X	X	X	X	X
Accomack	1 352	3 776 224	8.2	7.7	0.6	0.7	9.6	1.0	70.7	104.5	55.5	39.6	1 188	876
Albemarle	3 014	10 671 438	7.3	10.3	3.1	1.0	4.5	4.6	65.3	368.6	114.7	187.5	1 833	1 375
Alleghany	689	2 172 894	9.7	10.5	0.3	0.7	8.8	8.3	59.0	58.7	31.2	19.1	1 178	989
Amelia	422	1 273 101	3.9	5.8	0.0	0.0	1.9	1.5	85.8	26.8	15.3	8.2	645	518
Amherst	989	3 067 237	5.7	5.9	0.0	0.0	5.8	6.4	73.5	75.6	42.9	26.1	807	633
Appomattox	535	1 345 618	8.3	5.6	2.3	0.0	7.7	3.3	71.1	37.2	20.5	13.3	878	716
Arlington	9 317	49 809 798	6.9	10.3	4.2	20.3	7.8	5.4	41.2	2 574.1	624.2	861.8	3 899	3 016
Augusta	2 388	6 901 173	5.3	10.5	2.9	0.7	5.8	1.4	72.4	160.8	85.2	60.8	826	604
Bath	219	806 860	8.1	6.7	0.0	0.0	0.7	2.2	80.7	19.6	4.6	14.0	3 000	2 445
Bedford	2 625	7 051 188	4.0	20.1	0.0	0.0	9.1	1.8	63.5	181.5	95.3	61.4	882	750
Bland	206	534 449	5.2	7.3	0.0	0.0	2.6	3.3	70.3	17.5	11.4	4.6	690	588
Botetourt	1 128	3 464 230	7.8	10.1	0.0	0.0	5.0	2.6	72.5	84.1	39.8	37.2	1 122	904
Brunswick	651	1 620 721	7.3	12.5	0.0	0.2	9.0	1.7	67.5	39.3	24.2	10.4	610	490
Buchanan	834	2 368 397	7.1	6.9	0.7	1.0	4.4	1.1	76.6	101.0	43.8	50.0	2 095	742
Buckingham	544	1 683 523	4.7	32.1	0.0	0.0	2.0	2.6	57.1	44.0	28.4	13.4	782	682
Campbell	1 839	5 409 816	5.0	6.0	1.2	0.4	4.4	1.8	78.6	131.1	70.6	44.2	801	613
Caroline	918	2 716 780	8.5	9.8	2.1	0.0	5.6	2.6	68.0	76.7	35.1	35.8	1 236	1 010
Carroll	1 015	2 970 573	6.2	5.3	1.8	0.4	12.0	2.7	68.4	74.0	35.3	24.9	836	659
Charles City	243	709 888	11.5	6.6	0.0	0.0	0.0	4.7	70.0	21.2	9.1	8.1	1 137	1 012
Charlotte	499	1 413 313	6.4	8.9	0.0	0.1	7.7	2.4	72.2	35.7	24.5	8.0	646	537
Chesterfield	12 105	41 117 167	7.5	9.1	5.5	0.2	7.4	4.0	62.3	1 045.1	437.5	443.8	1 370	1 103
Clarke	531	1 954 739	5.8	7.2	0.0	1.3	3.8	2.9	72.3	48.5	15.8	21.7	1 516	1 292
Craig	169	483 380	9.9	7.8	0.0	0.0	5.9	2.1	74.4	13.0	8.1	3.8	730	626
Culpeper	1 841	5 945 989	8.3	10.6	0.9	1.1	9.5	4.7	63.2	142.8	61.0	63.9	1 333	1 025
Cumberland	297	961 120	9.9	8.2	0.0	0.0	1.6	1.1	72.0	23.9	13.9	8.8	889	758
Dickenson	610	1 668 965	6.7	7.4	0.0	0.0	4.2	7.9	70.6	68.6	37.7	20.1	1 282	855
Dinwiddie	890	2 870 612	6.8	7.8	0.3	0.0	11.1	3.2	67.5	79.3	43.7	31.3	1 119	925
Essex	422	1 333 678	8.5	8.1	3.2	2.6	2.1	8.3	64.6	32.1	12.9	16.4	1 462	1 109
Fairfax	43 275	208 710 868	5.3	8.1	5.1	0.4	7.2	5.9	62.9	5 025.9	1 140.8	3 142.7	2 810	2 292
Fauquier	2 840	9 833 163	6.6	9.0	2.5	0.7	3.2	5.4	69.2	232.3	78.6	133.9	2 012	1 727
Floyd	421	1 524 813	5.3	6.1	0.0	0.0	3.6	2.2	81.6	27.7	14.4	11.9	771	609
Fluvanna	723	2 499 361	7.1	4.3	0.0	0.0	3.5	1.7	78.2	61.3	29.9	28.7	1 105	989
Franklin	1 773	5 802 144	5.5	5.8	2.1	0.7	4.3	1.4	79.1	131.8	64.9	58.9	1 044	833
Frederick	3 183	9 479 873	6.7	10.3	3.6	0.6	2.4	2.0	72.9	235.3	97.7	114.5	1 425	1 069
Giles	586	1 588 082	11.1	11.9	0.0	1.6	2.9	6.0	64.6	54.9	29.9	17.0	1 002	801
Gloucester	1 208	3 733 992	8.5	8.9	0.0	0.0	3.3	3.6	71.8	99.1	42.2	45.2	1 224	938
Goochland	541	1 850 764	13.7	7.7	3.4	0.0	1.5	3.0	67.1	56.0	13.5	37.7	1 768	1 342
Grayson	541	1 324 989	8.4	7.8	0.0	0.3	3.4	2.6	76.5	36.9	21.4	11.7	771	658
Greene	657	1 764 870	6.8	4.8	0.0	2.2	0.6	0.4	80.2	51.3	25.0	19.5	1 040	871
Greensville	571	1 743 841	9.5	15.1	0.0	0.0	1.0	4.8	67.5	48.9	30.7	8.1	686	540
Halifax	1 547	3 858 184	6.4	5.9	1.6	1.0	5.8	2.5	75.9	111.3	60.8	33.7	940	669
Hanover	4 522	15 814 948	6.9	13.8	4.2	0.4	5.6	3.8	63.1	349.4	131.9	160.0	1 590	1 262
Henrico	11 822	42 600 655	5.0	12.2	6.3	3.6	7.0	2.9	59.3	1 060.7	406.5	484.0	1 537	1 115
Henry	1 709	4 761 002	6.5	7.7	0.9	0.0	9.6	0.7	71.0	124.5	75.9	32.9	620	403
Highland	101	285 647	13.1	13.3	0.0	0.0	5.6	0.9	63.7	8.1	4.2	3.1	1 401	1 221
Isle of Wight	1 226	4 460 998	6.8	4.8	1.2	1.8	1.9	2.5	75.6	106.3	46.2	51.6	1 459	1 145
James City	3 104	11 075 839	5.4	9.6	5.6	1.6	3.8	10.2	60.5	257.6	89.5	138.2	2 003	1 605
King and Queen	300	906 918	6.2	30.6	0.0	0.0	0.5	0.0	57.6	23.5	13.1	6.2	884	787
King George	1 018	3 118 233	7.1	5.5	4.7	0.0	3.5	3.8	73.7	80.3	31.9	31.4	1 282	770
King William	608	1 988 526	5.8	6.3	0.6	0.6	2.4	1.7	79.0	49.7	22.6	23.3	1 459	1 282
Lancaster	380	818 567	17.4	17.6	0.0	0.5	6.5	2.5	53.6	32.1	11.5	18.8	1 669	1 337
Lee	981	2 345 408	5.5	6.0	0.0	0.7	1.6	1.9	83.8	61.5	44.1	13.2	519	363
Loudoun	13 775	59 560 641	6.5	6.9	4.6	0.5	5.4	3.9	70.0	1 546.7	373.1	1 012.0	3 004	2 472

1. Based on the resident population estimated as of July 1 of the year shown.

Table B. States and Counties — Local Government Finances, Government Employment, and Income Taxes

STATE County	Local government finances, 2012 (cont.) Direct general expenditure — Total (mil dol)	Per capita¹ (dollars)	Percent of total for: Education	Health and hospitals	Police protection	Public welfare	Highways	Debt outstanding — Total (mil dol)	Per capita¹ (dollars)	Government employment, 2015 — Federal civilian	Federal military	State and local	Individual income tax returns, 2014 — Number of returns	Mean adjusted gross income	Mean income tax
	185	186	187	188	189	190	191	192	193	194	195	196	197	198	199
VERMONT—Cont'd															
Chittenden	643.2	4 058	61.0	0.2	5.1	0.1	5.6	564.9	3 564	2 331	1 171	15 162	83 840	71 205	9 633
Essex	23.3	3 739	69.1	0.2	1.7	0.1	14.9	1.6	258	85	43	309	2 860	36 116	2 924
Franklin	162.7	3 374	75.1	0.6	4.0	0.0	8.1	53.3	1 106	1 491	339	2 960	24 260	51 406	5 232
Grand Isle	24.7	3 541	70.6	0.0	3.4	0.1	10.5	14.7	2 098	18	48	289	3 810	65 428	8 231
Lamoille	96.7	3 874	66.5	0.9	8.2	0.2	8.6	76.2	3 054	62	172	1 580	13 360	61 088	7 833
Orange	114.2	3 950	75.9	0.6	1.8	0.1	10.2	35.3	1 220	80	198	1 908	14 710	48 970	4 860
Orleans	106.7	3 935	76.0	0.3	1.8	0.0	9.3	33.0	1 219	233	185	1 861	13 470	42 160	4 020
Rutland	244.1	4 010	70.6	0.1	3.7	0.0	7.9	67.5	1 108	292	404	4 033	31 220	48 837	5 184
Washington	229.0	3 852	62.5	0.9	3.6	0.1	11.1	117.9	1 983	247	430	6 988	30 870	58 387	6 955
Windham	233.0	5 297	58.8	0.2	2.3	0.2	13.5	108.8	2 474	139	294	2 786	22 640	48 577	5 236
Windsor	275.6	4 903	62.8	0.8	3.4	0.0	12.6	98.2	1 746	1 443	394	3 469	30 130	57 556	6 841
VIRGINIA	X	X	X	X	X	X	X	X	X	196 453	139 516	536 052	3 871 420	72 257	9 918
Accomack	93.0	2 789	51.9	1.1	4.4	4.8	1.7	62.8	1 884	640	272	2 229	16 130	43 744	4 141
Albemarle	356.2	3 484	49.8	9.7	4.8	4.1	0.2	444.7	4 349	(3)1 259	(3)937	(3)29 540	48 060	96 582	15 682
Alleghany	59.6	3 670	51.9	0.6	5.0	6.2	1.3	32.8	2 020	(4)67	(4)66	(4)1 522	6 890	47 350	4 400
Amelia	26.9	2 108	60.3	2.6	6.3	6.1	1.7	4.0	313	22	40	471	5 990	48 057	4 214
Amherst	71.6	2 212	62.9	0.8	7.1	6.1	0.1	27.2	840	48	96	2 555	14 090	45 979	4 043
Appomattox	35.6	2 351	57.9	1.0	6.3	6.5	0.0	34.6	2 285	46	48	758	6 820	45 908	4 098
Arlington	2 639.2	11 940	16.7	1.1	2.2	3.0	2.0	8 672.6	39 235	27 767	8 649	12 281	124 450	112 006	20 110
Augusta	170.0	2 308	65.1	0.6	3.9	8.2	0.9	103.4	1 404	(5)258	(5)369	(5)8 373	34 230	51 934	5 147
Bath	17.3	3 728	54.1	1.3	5.9	4.2	0.0	9.3	1 990	28	14	349	2 220	50 977	5 376
Bedford	182.3	2 619	49.8	0.5	3.6	8.7	0.1	152.7	2 194	(6)129	(6)243	(6)2 906	35 450	60 958	6 994
Bland	15.8	2 338	54.4	0.9	6.4	8.4	6.8	5.0	743	13	18	602	2 580	45 607	4 002
Botetourt	82.4	2 486	63.3	0.6	6.0	3.8	0.0	55.7	1 681	55	104	1 416	16 040	64 024	7 371
Brunswick	41.2	2 421	57.0	0.6	6.4	7.4	0.2	19.3	1 133	39	46	1 038	6 490	39 509	3 214
Buchanan	84.4	3 538	45.9	0.7	4.7	11.2	11.3	12.4	520	65	68	1 561	7 870	44 577	4 408
Buckingham	45.4	2 658	45.9	1.1	3.9	6.2	0.1	68.7	4 022	29	47	1 290	6 220	40 522	3 437
Campbell	128.3	2 326	59.4	5.8	4.7	7.0	2.3	58.2	1 055	(7)341	(7)430	(7)7 021	25 040	46 784	4 265
Caroline	67.8	2 338	54.8	0.4	8.4	6.1	3.4	132.8	4 584	444	132	1 234	13 620	51 002	4 758
Carroll	84.4	2 829	57.3	7.7	4.7	6.3	0.7	59.6	1 996	(8)95	(8)113	(8)2 395	12 110	38 820	3 069
Charles City	20.4	2 844	63.8	0.5	3.9	5.3	0.0	2.7	382	17	22	319	3 530	50 012	5 395
Charlotte	37.5	3 022	59.8	2.5	5.0	11.4	0.1	6.2	500	39	38	912	5 090	39 264	3 239
Chesterfield	985.4	3 043	54.6	5.0	6.6	4.1	1.2	716.3	2 212	3 008	1 087	17 532	161 200	68 455	8 514
Clarke	61.0	4 259	55.3	0.7	3.6	3.6	0.4	147.7	10 315	29	45	652	6 930	74 778	10 046
Craig	12.6	2 425	55.8	1.3	6.8	12.8	0.3	4.1	793	15	16	237	2 200	45 790	4 010
Culpeper	140.4	2 931	53.3	0.9	7.6	9.8	2.8	122.9	2 566	213	151	3 119	21 830	61 714	6 879
Cumberland	23.1	2 345	63.3	1.2	6.5	4.8	0.0	44.0	4 466	11	30	468	4 250	41 622	3 598
Dickenson	61.5	3 918	45.4	5.6	3.7	9.6	1.7	13.6	869	37	46	921	4 990	40 747	3 351
Dinwiddie	72.2	2 580	60.9	3.9	5.4	4.8	0.1	113.2	4 044	(9)232	(9)249	(9)6 040	12 850	49 799	4 750
Essex	34.5	3 071	55.7	0.0	5.0	9.0	1.4	48.6	4 329	15	34	524	5 330	49 939	5 630
Fairfax	4 854.2	4 340	51.6	4.1	4.6	6.0	2.1	5 037.1	4 503	(10)46 059	(10)9 892	(10)61 262	547 180	112 913	19 335
Fauquier	242.3	3 641	59.7	0.4	7.0	4.2	1.2	187.2	2 813	586	215	3 645	33 340	90 420	13 386
Floyd	26.9	1 751	66.1	2.5	5.5	3.9	0.0	15.6	1 013	51	49	611	6 650	46 333	4 392
Fluvanna	74.8	2 882	70.0	0.8	3.4	6.6	0.3	91.0	3 506	29	78	1 308	11 810	58 463	5 807
Franklin	130.9	2 320	61.7	0.5	4.3	7.9	1.1	36.2	641	97	182	2 290	23 700	49 959	5 065
Frederick	220.1	2 740	72.6	0.5	5.1	2.7	0.1	196.2	2 443	(11)1 951	(11)358	(11)5 994	39 090	60 469	6 706
Giles	49.2	2 909	47.4	0.4	7.2	7.5	2.9	61.0	3 603	34	52	875	7 410	46 862	4 316
Gloucester	94.6	2 564	65.7	1.1	5.1	5.2	0.1	62.6	1 698	78	116	2 084	17 990	55 565	5 483
Goochland	45.4	2 128	55.2	1.1	5.8	4.2	0.5	133.0	6 229	36	67	1 349	10 610	132 318	25 516
Grayson	35.4	2 329	60.0	0.4	6.1	6.7	0.3	38.8	2 555	29	47	1 022	6 140	37 658	2 704
Greene	53.8	2 869	65.7	0.8	5.7	5.5	1.9	57.6	3 067	34	60	840	8 760	56 417	5 739
Greensville	52.0	4 385	49.3	0.3	4.8	5.4	0.4	56.1	4 732	(12)34	(12)43	(12)1 772	3 730	36 996	2 786
Halifax	113.2	3 157	52.4	10.5	5.0	6.6	2.0	72.1	2 012	85	108	2 194	14 870	42 139	3 746
Hanover	342.5	3 403	52.1	0.4	6.9	6.6	1.7	364.1	3 617	156	319	4 778	50 620	73 301	9 157
Henrico	1 095.4	3 478	45.2	3.0	6.3	2.5	4.7	980.8	3 114	2 200	1 014	17 062	160 310	69 322	9 448
Henry	127.8	2 414	68.2	0.9	4.2	6.1	0.0	28.3	534	(13)135	(13)203	(13)3 906	22 120	38 118	3 079
Highland	7.7	3 440	49.1	2.3	7.9	4.4	7.0	0.7	311	D	D	164	1 070	42 763	3 864
Isle of Wight	103.6	2 926	49.8	4.9	5.6	3.1	1.0	149.3	4 218	85	113	1 413	17 480	64 865	7 238
James City	260.7	3 781	54.2	6.4	4.7	1.9	0.0	269.9	3 914	(14)229	(14)399	(14)8 239	36 100	86 823	12 227
King and Queen	25.3	3 591	43.8	0.8	5.0	7.9	0.0	5.0	707	D	23	272	3 170	47 196	4 242
King George	72.4	2 957	53.1	0.9	9.0	6.0	0.1	190.9	7 793	4 547	543	1 058	11 350	68 991	7 735
King William	48.1	3 007	64.8	0.3	6.0	3.6	0.6	39.7	2 483	25	51	749	8 000	55 391	5 326
Lancaster	31.1	2 771	52.2	1.4	6.6	6.9	0.5	18.4	1 636	31	34	538	5 760	60 815	6 845
Lee	59.5	2 335	64.3	1.3	5.4	10.3	0.9	7.4	290	443	72	1 138	7 700	37 465	2 936
Loudoun	1 488.4	4 418	60.1	2.4	5.3	2.4	1.9	1 679.5	4 985	3 790	1 181	19 314	169 340	111 440	17 513

1. Based on the resident population estimated as of July 1 of the year shown. 3. Charlottesville city is included with Albemarle county. 4. Covington city is included with Alleghany county. 5. Staunton and Waynesboro cities are included with Augusta county. 6. Bedford city is included with Bedford county. 7. Lynchburg city is included with Campbell county. 8. Galax city is included with Carroll county. 9. Petersburg and Colonial Heights cities are included with Dinwiddie county. 10. Fairfax city and Falls Church city are included with Fairfax county. 11. Winchester city is included with Frederick county. 12. Emporia city is included with Greensville county. 13. Martinsville city is included with Henry county. 14. Williamsburg city is included with James City county.

Table B. States and Counties — Land Area and Population

					Population, 2016			Population and population characteristics, 2016								
								Race alone or in combination, not Hispanic or Latino (percent)				Age (percent)					
STATE/ County code	CBSA code[1]	County type[2]	STATE County	Land area,[3] (sq mi) 2016	Total persons 2016	Rank	Per square mile	White	Black	American Indian, Alaska Native	Asian and Pacific Islander	Percent Hispanic or Latino[4]	Under 5 years	5 to 17 years	18 to 24 years	25 to 34 years	35 to 44 years	45 to 54 years
				1	2	3	4	5	6	7	8	9	10	11	12	13	14	15

			VIRGINIA—Cont'd															
51 109	...	8	Louisa	496.3	35 236	1 296	71.0	80.0	17.4	0.9	1.1	2.7	5.4	15.3	6.8	11.3	11.3	15.0
51 111	...	9	Lunenburg	431.7	12 273	2 274	28.4	61.3	34.2	0.9	0.7	4.6	5.1	13.6	7.1	11.8	12.1	13.5
51 113	...	8	Madison	320.7	13 078	2 226	40.8	87.5	10.6	0.9	1.1	2.4	4.6	15.7	7.2	10.2	10.9	13.7
51 115	47260	1	Mathews	85.9	8 782	2 524	102.2	87.0	9.8	1.2	1.4	2.7	3.7	12.4	6.4	8.3	8.8	13.5
51 117	...	7	Mecklenburg	625.5	30 892	1 410	49.4	61.7	35.0	0.8	1.3	2.9	4.7	14.2	7.2	9.8	10.3	13.1
51 119	...	8	Middlesex	130.3	10 778	2 374	82.7	79.5	18.0	1.0	0.9	2.4	4.2	11.6	6.2	9.1	8.1	12.6
51 121	13980	3	Montgomery	386.5	98 602	600	255.1	86.0	4.8	0.6	7.7	3.1	4.7	11.4	27.5	14.7	10.0	10.3
51 125	16820	3	Nelson	470.9	14 869	2 111	31.6	83.0	12.7	0.9	1.0	4.0	4.3	14.5	6.2	9.3	10.1	13.1
51 127	40060	1	New Kent	209.7	21 147	1 768	100.8	81.7	13.9	2.0	1.9	2.9	4.9	15.6	7.4	12.0	11.9	15.7
51 131	...	8	Northampton	211.7	12 139	2 284	57.3	55.6	35.3	0.8	1.2	8.8	5.8	14.4	6.5	10.1	9.2	11.2
51 133	...	9	Northumberland	191.3	12 222	2 277	63.9	70.7	25.7	0.8	0.7	3.6	4.0	11.2	5.8	7.7	7.3	11.5
51 135	...	6	Nottoway	314.4	15 595	2 067	49.6	55.9	40.0	0.8	0.8	3.9	5.5	14.0	8.1	13.9	11.7	14.1
51 137	...	6	Orange	340.8	35 533	1 291	104.3	80.7	14.4	0.9	1.8	4.6	5.7	15.9	7.1	11.5	11.3	14.2
51 139	...	6	Page	310.8	23 654	1 653	76.1	95.4	2.5	0.6	0.8	1.9	5.0	15.0	7.1	11.0	11.5	14.9
51 141	...	8	Patrick	483.0	17 923	1 924	37.1	90.7	6.2	0.6	0.5	3.0	4.0	13.8	6.4	8.4	10.9	14.9
51 143	19260	4	Pittsylvania	968.9	61 687	850	63.7	75.2	22.0	0.6	0.7	2.6	4.2	15.2	7.2	10.2	10.9	14.9
51 145	40060	1	Powhatan	260.2	28 443	1 473	109.3	86.3	11.1	0.7	1.1	2.1	4.3	14.5	7.9	10.1	12.8	17.6
51 147	...	6	Prince Edward	350.0	23 142	1 672	66.1	63.7	32.9	0.7	1.9	2.4	4.6	11.5	26.3	10.7	8.7	10.4
51 149	40060	1	Prince George	265.2	37 845	1 227	142.7	57.8	32.8	1.2	3.0	7.8	5.6	16.2	9.0	15.4	15.0	13.6
51 153	47900	1	Prince William	336.4	455 210	152	1 353.2	47.2	22.4	0.9	10.6	22.9	7.5	20.1	8.8	13.8	15.2	14.7
51 155	13980	3	Pulaski	319.9	34 203	1 320	106.9	92.4	5.9	0.6	0.9	1.8	4.8	13.3	7.4	10.9	11.6	15.0
51 157	47900	1	Rappahannock	266.4	7 388	2 637	27.7	90.4	5.4	0.9	1.5	3.8	4.2	13.5	6.2	9.2	9.1	14.2
51 159	...	9	Richmond	191.5	8 774	2 526	45.8	62.9	30.1	0.8	1.1	6.9	3.9	13.0	7.0	13.7	13.0	14.6
51 161	40220	2	Roanoke	250.6	94 031	623	375.2	87.7	6.6	0.5	3.9	2.9	4.7	15.7	7.9	10.9	11.7	14.2
51 163	...	6	Rockbridge	597.6	22 392	1 712	37.5	94.2	3.4	1.2	0.9	1.7	4.4	13.2	6.6	10.4	10.3	13.9
51 165	25500	3	Rockingham	849.1	79 744	702	93.9	90.3	2.6	0.5	1.1	6.7	5.6	16.6	9.0	11.4	11.5	13.5
51 167	...	7	Russell	473.8	27 370	1 517	57.8	97.4	1.1	0.5	0.4	1.3	4.9	14.6	7.0	10.9	12.1	14.0
51 169	28700	2	Scott	535.5	21 930	1 731	41.0	97.4	1.1	0.6	0.4	1.3	4.1	14.2	6.9	10.8	11.8	14.3
51 171	...	6	Shenandoah	508.3	43 175	1 107	84.9	89.7	3.0	0.7	1.1	7.0	5.6	15.7	7.3	11.1	10.9	14.1
51 173	...	7	Smyth	450.9	31 062	1 406	68.9	94.9	2.9	0.6	0.6	2.1	4.7	14.8	7.5	10.8	12.2	14.3
51 175	...	6	Southampton	599.1	18 057	1 917	30.1	62.4	36.1	0.8	0.8	1.6	4.6	14.7	7.0	10.4	10.8	16.9
51 177	47900	1	Spotsylvania	401.5	132 010	481	328.8	71.9	17.3	0.9	3.8	9.3	6.3	18.9	8.6	12.5	12.8	15.1
51 179	47900	1	Stafford	269.1	144 361	446	536.5	66.2	19.4	1.1	5.0	12.3	6.3	19.9	10.0	13.1	13.6	15.6
51 181	...	8	Surry	278.9	6 544	2 711	23.5	53.8	44.1	0.9	1.0	2.0	4.4	13.2	7.8	10.0	9.2	16.3
51 183	40060	1	Sussex	490.2	11 504	2 320	23.5	39.6	57.2	0.6	0.7	3.0	4.6	11.4	9.4	17.4	12.2	14.3
51 185	14140	5	Tazewell	518.8	42 150	1 126	81.2	95.0	3.8	0.5	0.9	1.0	5.0	14.4	7.5	11.1	12.4	13.3
51 187	47900	1	Warren	213.8	39 155	1 201	183.1	89.5	5.8	0.9	1.8	4.2	6.1	16.4	8.6	12.7	11.6	15.2
51 191	28700	2	Washington	561.0	54 214	928	96.6	96.4	1.8	0.5	0.8	1.4	4.7	14.2	7.6	10.5	11.9	14.1
51 193	...	6	Westmoreland	229.4	17 592	1 940	76.7	65.7	27.8	1.1	1.4	6.3	5.3	13.5	6.6	11.5	9.8	12.5
51 195	13720	7	Wise	403.2	39 228	1 194	97.3	92.6	6.2	0.5	0.7	1.2	5.2	14.8	9.3	13.6	12.6	13.3
51 197	...	6	Wythe	461.8	29 016	1 454	62.8	95.2	3.7	0.6	0.9	1.2	5.3	14.9	6.8	11.1	11.9	14.8
51 199	47260	1	York	104.7	67 976	781	649.2	74.3	14.5	0.9	7.5	6.1	5.8	18.6	9.0	11.8	12.5	14.1
	...		Independent cities															
51 510	47900	1	Alexandria city	15.0	155 810	417	10 387.3	53.9	23.2	0.7	8.2	16.8	7.3	11.0	5.9	22.3	18.4	13.8
51 520	28700	2	Bristol city	13.0	16 960	1 981	1 304.6	90.8	6.9	0.8	1.5	2.2	4.5	15.4	7.5	13.1	12.3	13.3
51 530	...	6	Buena Vista city	6.7	6 452	2 718	963.0	89.8	6.2	1.9	1.4	3.0	4.7	15.3	14.1	12.2	10.1	12.3
51 540	16820	3	Charlottesville city	10.2	46 912	1 035	4 599.2	68.2	19.8	0.6	8.9	5.3	5.8	10.3	20.3	21.0	12.0	10.5
51 550	47260	1	Chesapeake city	338.5	237 940	280	702.9	60.8	30.9	1.0	4.9	5.7	6.4	17.8	8.8	14.2	13.2	14.0
51 570	40060	1	Colonial Heights city	7.5	17 772	1 927	2 369.6	75.3	15.5	1.1	4.7	5.9	6.3	16.4	8.4	12.3	11.0	12.5
51 580	...	6	Covington city	5.5	5 518	2 801	1 003.3	83.3	14.7	1.0	1.3	2.0	4.2	15.0	7.8	12.0	11.5	14.8
51 590	19260	4	Danville city	42.9	41 898	1 131	976.6	44.5	50.7	0.6	1.5	4.1	6.4	15.8	8.6	12.4	10.0	12.1
51 595	...	6	Emporia city	6.9	5 305	2 811	768.8	30.0	63.3	0.5	1.5	5.9	4.6	19.3	8.0	12.6	11.0	13.4
51 600	47900	1	Fairfax city	6.2	24 164	1 637	3 897.4	59.7	6.1	0.8	19.1	17.1	8.5	14.0	8.5	13.7	12.5	14.1
51 610	47900	1	Falls Church city	2.1	14 014	2 163	6 673.3	74.7	6.2	0.9	11.6	10.3	8.4	19.1	7.1	11.5	14.2	15.0
51 620	...	6	Franklin city	8.2	8 306	2 566	1 012.9	39.4	58.2	0.9	1.4	2.3	6.5	17.2	7.6	12.7	10.0	12.4
51 630	47900	1	Fredericksburg city	10.4	28 297	1 478	2 720.9	63.2	24.7	0.9	4.3	10.7	7.0	14.0	20.2	15.3	11.8	11.0
51 640	...	7	Galax city	8.3	6 775	2 691	816.3	77.6	7.1	0.6	1.0	15.4	5.9	16.6	7.9	10.9	11.2	12.8
51 650	47260	1	Hampton city	51.5	135 410	467	2 629.3	41.7	51.6	1.5	3.7	5.5	6.1	15.3	11.8	15.7	11.0	12.2
51 660	25500	3	Harrisonburg city	17.3	53 078	946	3 068.1	69.5	8.3	0.5	5.2	18.9	5.0	11.2	32.8	15.5	10.2	8.9
51 670	40060	1	Hopewell city	10.3	22 735	1 690	2 207.3	50.4	41.9	1.1	2.1	7.7	8.0	18.0	8.5	14.2	11.5	12.3
51 678	...	6	Lexington city	2.5	7 045	2 670	2 818.0	83.7	9.9	0.8	4.2	3.8	2.1	7.3	45.5	8.9	6.4	6.6
51 680	31340	2	Lynchburg city	49.1	80 212	698	1 633.6	65.1	29.4	0.8	3.5	3.5	6.2	13.1	24.9	13.4	8.7	9.4
51 683	47900	1	Manassas city	9.9	41 483	1 139	4 190.2	44.2	14.8	0.8	6.9	35.9	8.4	18.2	9.5	15.1	14.6	13.6
51 685	47900	1	Manassas Park city	2.5	15 915	2 046	6 366.0	37.6	13.9	0.9	11.6	38.6	5.8	19.9	9.0	16.4	16.3	14.9

1. CBSA = Core Based Statistical Area. See Appendix A for explanation. See Appendix B for list of metropolitan areas with component counties. 2. County type code from the Economic Research Service of USDA Rural-Urban Continuum Codes. See Appendix A for definition. 3. Dry land or land partially or temporarily covered by water. 4. May be of any race.

Table B. States and Counties — Population and Households

STATE County	Population, 2016 (cont.) Age (percent) (cont.) 55 to 64 years	65 to 74 years	75 years and over	Percent female	Population change and components of change, 2000–2016 Total persons 2000	2010	Percent change 2000–2010	2010–2016	Components of change, 2010–2016 Births	Deaths	Net migration	Households, 2011–2015 Number	Persons per house-hold	Percent Family house-holds	Female family house-holder[1]	One per-son
	16	17	18	19	20	21	22	23	24	25	26	27	28	29	30	31
VIRGINIA—Cont'd																
Louisa	16.3	12.0	6.7	50.6	25 627	33 223	29.6	6.1	2 319	1 864	1 507	12 829	2.64	72.3	9.7	21.7
Lunenburg	15.7	12.4	8.6	47.0	13 146	12 916	-1.7	-5.0	752	934	-464	4 516	2.48	68.7	15.5	28.6
Madison	16.3	12.6	8.9	51.6	12 520	13 308	6.3	-1.7	711	822	-121	5 003	2.58	68.1	10.9	26.0
Mathews	16.8	17.4	12.8	51.7	9 207	8 976	-2.5	-2.2	368	698	166	3 806	2.30	70.5	6.0	26.2
Mecklenburg	15.9	14.3	10.5	51.6	32 380	32 721	1.1	-5.6	1 823	2 768	-874	12 482	2.41	62.4	15.2	34.2
Middlesex	17.9	17.7	12.5	51.0	9 932	10 959	10.3	-1.7	549	909	178	4 342	2.38	67.0	9.2	28.3
Montgomery	9.9	6.7	4.8	47.8	83 629	94 412	12.9	4.4	5 624	3 742	2 430	35 199	2.48	54.0	7.3	27.6
Nelson	17.1	15.9	9.4	51.3	14 445	15 020	4.0	-1.0	837	1 101	169	6 339	2.33	63.1	14.9	29.5
New Kent	16.0	11.3	5.0	48.9	13 462	18 432	36.9	14.7	1 162	873	2 349	7 299	2.61	77.5	10.8	18.3
Northampton	17.0	14.8	11.0	51.8	13 093	12 389	-5.4	-2.0	864	1 208	36	5 248	2.26	59.4	15.3	35.2
Northumberland	17.6	20.5	14.5	50.7	12 259	12 327	0.6	-0.9	589	1 062	391	5 861	2.10	68.6	11.5	27.9
Nottoway	13.6	10.6	8.6	45.8	15 725	15 852	0.8	-1.6	1 095	1 246	-149	5 589	2.54	67.4	17.3	28.9
Orange	14.0	11.7	8.6	51.1	25 881	33 434	29.2	6.3	2 408	2 158	1 874	12 810	2.66	72.7	10.9	23.3
Page	14.7	12.2	8.7	50.6	23 177	24 055	3.8	-1.7	1 453	1 772	-84	9 372	2.52	71.2	12.2	23.2
Patrick	16.2	14.6	10.9	50.8	19 407	18 495	-4.7	-3.1	880	1 564	131	7 790	2.31	65.1	10.7	30.3
Pittsylvania	16.1	12.7	8.5	50.8	61 745	63 491	2.8	-2.8	3 260	4 428	-608	26 204	2.36	69.0	13.5	27.3
Powhatan	15.6	11.5	5.8	47.7	22 377	28 062	25.4	1.4	1 493	1 253	68	9 730	2.63	80.2	10.4	17.2
Prince Edward	11.5	8.9	7.4	50.2	19 720	23 357	18.4	-0.9	1 311	1 372	-202	7 409	2.49	64.4	14.8	26.8
Prince George	12.1	8.2	5.1	45.8	33 047	35 714	8.1	6.0	2 453	1 445	1 139	11 102	3.03	79.3	11.1	18.6
Prince William	10.8	6.0	3.1	50.2	280 813	401 972	43.1	13.2	41 736	10 632	22 043	136 794	3.17	77.4	11.5	18.0
Pulaski	15.2	13.3	8.4	49.9	35 127	34 859	-0.8	-1.9	2 018	2 672	70	14 619	2.30	67.4	12.3	27.5
Rappahannock	17.5	16.4	9.7	50.6	6 983	7 506	7.5	-1.6	384	448	-68	3 273	2.26	69.5	4.9	25.8
Richmond	13.7	10.6	10.5	44.8	8 809	9 254	5.1	-5.2	417	632	-301	2 875	2.47	70.9	16.4	24.0
Roanoke	14.3	11.8	9.0	51.9	85 778	92 439	7.8	1.7	5 151	6 051	2 372	38 164	2.40	68.2	10.4	27.5
Rockbridge	16.3	13.8	11.3	50.5	20 808	22 310	7.2	0.4	1 151	1 476	352	9 319	2.39	66.7	8.4	26.6
Rockingham	13.8	10.2	8.4	50.8	67 725	76 310	12.7	4.5	5 330	4 407	2 298	29 625	2.57	72.1	9.7	22.8
Russell	16.4	11.9	8.2	51.0	30 308	28 896	-4.7	-5.3	1 628	2 233	-866	11 045	2.51	66.8	9.4	30.5
Scott	15.3	12.8	9.7	49.8	23 403	23 170	-1.0	-5.4	1 165	1 884	-537	9 379	2.34	69.0	9.9	28.3
Shenandoah	14.2	12.1	9.1	51.1	35 075	41 993	19.7	2.8	2 936	2 880	1 081	17 096	2.47	68.8	9.3	27.0
Smyth	14.6	12.0	9.1	50.9	33 081	32 208	-2.6	-3.6	1 852	2 685	-286	12 795	2.43	67.2	11.6	28.0
Southampton	16.6	11.0	8.0	47.9	17 482	18 570	6.2	-2.8	1 043	1 209	-383	6 682	2.53	73.6	17.7	22.4
Spotsylvania	12.6	8.4	4.9	50.9	90 395	122 660	35.7	7.6	9 932	5 064	4 321	42 823	2.97	78.3	12.5	17.5
Stafford	11.4	6.3	3.7	49.6	92 446	128 952	39.5	11.9	10 662	4 126	8 661	43 405	3.08	82.0	11.5	14.5
Surry	18.4	12.7	7.9	51.2	6 829	7 065	3.5	-7.4	359	431	-414	2 668	2.56	73.5	15.1	22.3
Sussex	13.6	10.0	7.0	40.9	12 504	12 070	-3.5	-4.7	646	823	-399	3 149	2.08	60.7	15.6	33.8
Tazewell	15.4	12.3	8.5	50.1	44 598	45 078	1.1	-6.5	2 784	3 928	-1 761	17 832	2.38	67.5	9.9	28.7
Warren	14.6	9.2	5.7	50.1	31 584	37 431	18.5	4.6	2 971	2 256	925	14 364	2.62	70.4	12.3	23.5
Washington	15.6	12.7	8.8	50.8	51 103	54 870	7.4	-1.2	3 181	3 803	33	22 673	2.35	66.9	10.8	29.1
Westmoreland	16.6	14.3	10.0	51.3	16 718	17 454	4.4	0.8	1 132	1 293	280	6 944	2.51	61.9	10.5	31.5
Wise	14.2	10.3	6.6	47.9	40 123	41 476	3.4	-5.4	2 737	3 078	-1 919	15 254	2.46	66.7	13.0	28.6
Wythe	14.7	12.0	8.5	51.1	27 599	29 232	5.9	-0.7	1 814	2 192	193	11 863	2.44	67.2	10.1	29.6
York	13.1	8.9	6.3	50.9	56 297	65 189	15.8	4.3	4 132	2 582	1 170	23 997	2.73	78.8	11.0	17.4
Independent cities																
Alexandria city	10.9	6.7	3.8	51.8	128 283	140 006	9.1	11.3	17 206	4 641	3 315	66 879	2.21	48.4	8.6	41.9
Bristol city	13.6	11.3	9.0	52.5	17 367	17 841	2.7	-4.9	1 019	1 589	-283	7 718	2.22	63.5	17.6	32.2
Buena Vista city	12.5	11.0	7.9	53.4	6 349	6 651	4.8	-3.0	409	447	-177	2 737	2.26	65.0	10.3	30.2
Charlottesville city	10.4	6.1	3.7	51.6	45 049	43 435	-3.6	8.0	3 441	1 674	1 678	17 752	2.39	44.4	10.6	36.8
Chesapeake city	13.0	7.8	4.8	51.2	199 184	222 306	11.6	7.0	18 008	10 421	7 908	81 518	2.75	75.2	15.5	20.8
Colonial Heights city	12.7	10.2	10.2	53.8	16 897	17 412	3.0	2.1	1 327	1 340	388	7 106	2.44	62.7	14.6	31.2
Covington city	14.6	11.9	8.2	51.2	6 303	5 954	-5.5	-7.3	295	427	-335	2 476	2.28	57.2	14.4	39.2
Danville city	14.3	10.9	9.4	53.7	48 411	43 059	-11.1	-2.7	3 368	4 241	-368	18 559	2.20	58.1	19.8	37.0
Emporia city	12.8	8.9	9.3	54.4	5 665	5 925	4.6	-10.5	334	545	-420	2 459	2.21	61.4	22.6	37.8
Fairfax city	12.2	9.0	7.6	50.7	21 498	22 542	4.9	7.2	2 354	1 209	348	8 467	2.70	68.4	9.3	19.9
Falls Church city	13.0	7.4	4.4	50.9	10 377	12 289	18.4	14.0	1 152	434	1 054	5 166	2.57	63.5	7.9	32.1
Franklin city	14.6	10.6	8.4	54.6	8 346	8 580	2.8	-3.2	656	743	-198	3 453	2.41	63.3	28.4	33.4
Fredericksburg city	9.9	6.1	4.6	54.2	19 279	24 023	24.6	17.8	2 595	1 163	2 684	10 080	2.46	56.2	19.4	35.7
Galax city	13.7	10.8	10.3	53.7	6 837	7 000	2.4	-3.2	581	649	-190	2 961	2.19	60.5	17.3	36.3
Hampton city	13.4	8.5	6.1	51.9	146 437	137 384	-6.2	-1.4	11 392	7 477	-5 764	52 940	2.51	62.1	18.5	31.2
Harrisonburg city	7.8	4.6	4.0	52.1	40 468	48 907	20.9	8.5	3 432	1 542	2 120	16 409	2.69	50.2	9.5	28.6
Hopewell city	11.9	8.9	6.7	53.5	22 354	22 602	1.1	0.6	2 186	1 725	-350	8 706	2.53	59.7	22.4	35.0
Lexington city	8.2	7.9	7.1	43.4	6 867	7 038	2.5	0.1	183	360	136	1 638	2.04	48.2	12.5	45.8
Lynchburg city	9.8	7.5	7.0	53.1	65 269	75 608	15.8	6.1	6 587	4 854	2 699	28 528	2.37	57.4	16.2	33.6
Manassas city	11.5	5.9	3.2	50.2	35 135	37 839	7.7	9.6	4 261	1 150	478	12 433	3.27	73.9	12.7	21.4
Manassas Park city	9.7	5.1	2.9	48.9	10 290	14 241	38.4	11.8	1 224	226	607	4 723	3.31	71.6	12.6	21.6

1. No spouse present.

Table B. States and Counties — Population, Vital Statistics, Health, and Crime

STATE County	Persons in group quarters, 2016	Daytime population, 2011–2015 Number	Daytime population, 2011–2015 Employment/residence ratio	Births, 2016 Total	Births, 2016 Rate[1]	Deaths, 2016 Number	Deaths, 2016 Rate[1]	Persons under 65 with no health insurance, 2015 Number	Persons under 65 with no health insurance, 2015 Percent	Medicare, 2015 Total Beneficiaries	Medicare, 2015 Enrolled in Original Medicare	Medicare, 2015 Enrolled in Medicare Advantage	Serious crimes known to police,[2] 2014 Total Number	Serious crimes known to police,[2] 2014 Total Rate[3]
	32	33	34	35	36	37	38	39	40	41	42	43	44	45
VIRGINIA—Cont'd														
Louisa	211	27 758	0.61	360	10.2	341	9.7	3 628	12.8	6 956	5 512	1 444	700	2 051
Lunenburg	973	10 777	0.60	116	9.5	167	13.6	1 342	15.2	2 229	1 776	453	91	731
Madison	193	10 821	0.60	106	8.1	113	8.6	1 437	13.9	2 371	1 953	418	114	865
Mathews	86	7 108	0.54	63	7.2	125	14.2	650	10.4	2 664	2 238	426	92	1 036
Mecklenburg	905	32 610	1.09	298	9.6	471	15.2	3 352	14.6	8 653	7 037	1 616	621	1 995
Middlesex	409	9 658	0.76	101	9.4	134	12.4	787	11.0	3 496	2 871	625	157	1 465
Montgomery	9 817	102 283	1.13	915	9.3	618	6.3	8 634	11.1	12 142	9 546	2 596	1 493	1 544
Nelson	102	12 875	0.69	129	8.7	149	10.0	1 492	13.4	4 749	3 925	824	189	1 281
New Kent	552	14 111	0.45	196	9.3	129	6.1	1 609	9.7	3 217	2 589	628	331	1 675
Northampton	258	12 511	1.07	126	10.4	214	17.6	1 402	15.6	3 272	2 585	687	179	1 484
Northumberland	0	10 481	0.63	89	7.3	176	14.4	1 103	13.9	3 968	3 371	597	133	1 093
Nottoway	2 295	16 827	1.20	178	11.4	208	13.3	1 474	13.6	3 474	2 663	811	297	1 884
Orange	601	28 475	0.58	406	11.4	312	8.8	3 303	11.8	8 817	7 443	1 374	439	1 254
Page	194	20 117	0.63	223	9.4	283	12.0	2 615	13.9	5 534	4 778	756	414	1 741
Patrick	261	16 474	0.74	136	7.6	234	13.1	1 882	14.0	5 074	3 614	1 460	280	1 526
Pittsylvania	1 067	51 205	0.57	470	7.6	735	11.9	5 934	12.2	10 565	8 470	2 095	502	808
Powhatan	1 390	22 402	0.55	240	8.4	239	8.4	2 072	9.4	5 305	4 088	1 217	314	1 109
Prince Edward	4 228	25 064	1.24	226	9.8	229	9.9	2 076	13.5	5 204	3 972	1 232	432	1 905
Prince George	4 411	42 938	1.36	373	9.9	251	6.6	2 618	9.2	3 611	3 077	534	410	1 088
Prince William	2 669	348 690	0.61	6 793	14.9	1 919	4.2	45 547	11.1	27 763	21 914	5 849	6 835	1 528
Pulaski	1 156	34 342	0.99	317	9.3	426	12.5	2 559	9.8	7 665	5 882	1 783	936	2 717
Rappahannock	35	6 332	0.68	55	7.4	73	9.9	836	15.1	2 326	2 108	218	39	522
Richmond	1 489	9 107	1.04	68	7.8	98	11.2	781	13.9	1 868	1 438	430	77	867
Roanoke	2 331	85 166	0.81	786	8.4	975	10.4	6 081	8.2	8 962	7 102	1 860	1 621	1 728
Rockbridge	196	19 676	0.71	147	6.6	231	10.3	2 088	12.5	3 024	2 395	629	395	1 769
Rockingham	1 660	74 715	0.92	845	10.6	749	9.4	8 176	13.0	12 287	9 952	2 335	774	991
Russell	429	25 977	0.77	250	9.1	369	13.5	2 797	12.5	7 299	4 772	2 527	439	1 560
Scott	805	19 681	0.65	170	7.8	289	13.2	1 832	11.0	6 406	3 149	3 257	353	1 567
Shenandoah	427	37 681	0.75	478	11.1	471	10.9	4 497	13.2	9 563	8 344	1 219	602	1 404
Smyth	845	31 099	0.95	263	8.5	467	15.0	2 720	11.1	8 150	6 237	1 913	573	1 817
Southampton	1 671	14 621	0.52	141	7.8	211	11.7	1 604	12.1	2 642	2 087	555	277	1 536
Spotsylvania	524	102 448	0.59	1 603	12.1	932	7.1	11 807	10.4	10 541	8 925	1 616	2 199	1 711
Stafford	3 612	111 759	0.63	1 736	12.0	726	5.0	9 460	7.6	15 915	13 827	2 088	2 362	1 703
Surry	0	6 205	0.80	45	6.9	63	9.6	597	11.1	1 368	993	375	71	1 060
Sussex	2 548	12 661	1.32	98	8.5	136	11.8	997	13.7	2 647	1 913	734	145	1 232
Tazewell	1 629	44 384	1.03	446	10.6	639	15.2	4 146	12.6	12 137	8 320	3 817	1 064	2 425
Warren	942	33 530	0.73	496	12.7	376	9.6	3 671	11.2	6 157	5 477	680	811	2 078
Washington	1 494	54 364	0.98	588	10.8	617	11.4	4 620	11.0	11 290	7 712	3 578	1 100	2 002
Westmoreland	70	14 390	0.56	163	9.3	212	12.1	1 935	14.5	4 315	3 606	709	262	1 483
Wise	2 963	44 408	1.29	426	10.9	472	12.0	3 612	11.8	10 614	6 692	3 922	976	2 418
Wythe	260	29 690	1.04	325	11.2	373	12.9	2 873	12.4	8 660	6 399	2 261	379	1 290
York	649	58 730	0.76	740	10.9	507	7.5	4 551	8.0	17 699	15 332	2 367	1 217	1 828
Independent cities														
Alexandria city	1 834	154 597	1.06	2 824	18.1	798	5.1	16 233	11.9	16 288	13 466	2 822	3 263	2 160
Bristol city	219	21 580	1.57	68	4.0	244	14.4	1 554	11.4	7 542	4 454	3 088	537	3 118
Buena Vista city	426	5 858	0.71	4	0.6	72	11.2	534	10.6	1 881	1 392	489	63	941
Charlottesville city	2 420	59 360	1.61	660	14.1	302	6.4	5 606	13.9	13 595	11 381	2 214	1 550	3 477
Chesapeake city	4 158	215 853	0.87	3 013	12.7	1 823	7.7	16 887	8.3	31 164	24 400	6 764	7 428	3 195
Colonial Heights city	171	19 723	1.29	258	14.5	196	11.0	1 476	10.4	4 865	3 997	868	905	5 111
Covington city	87	5 532	0.91	0	0.0	55	10.0	524	11.7	4 216	3 503	713	122	2 109
Danville city	1 586	51 431	1.55	560	13.4	666	15.9	3 826	11.8	15 039	12 396	2 643	1 965	4 577
Emporia city	246	6 670	1.48	0	0.0	74	13.9	534	11.9	2 580	1 746	834	306	5 553
Fairfax city	521	47 161	2.90	698	28.9	248	10.3	2 054	10.3	15 107	12 628	2 479	464	1 906
Falls Church city	42	16 834	1.48	280	20.0	79	5.6	591	4.8	2 027	1 668	359	239	1 733
Franklin city	129	9 243	1.24	65	7.8	92	11.1	864	12.5	2 951	2 331	620	NA	NA
Fredericksburg city	2 602	40 926	2.02	408	14.4	235	8.3	2 440	10.7	7 320	6 085	1 235	1 333	4 572
Galax city	377	7 968	1.39	59	8.7	90	13.3	894	16.4	4 015	3 576	439	312	4 438
Hampton city	4 777	137 965	1.01	1 699	12.5	1 267	9.4	11 611	10.3	23 285	17 199	6 086	4 790	3 507
Harrisonburg city	7 624	60 917	1.41	604	11.4	253	4.8	6 301	15.3	5 646	4 822	824	1 257	2 416
Hopewell city	237	20 932	0.85	368	16.2	285	12.5	2 372	12.7	4 997	3 886	1 111	764	3 464
Lexington city	2 707	10 207	2.53	0	0.0	42	6.0	361	10.2	3 622	3 097	525	60	833
Lynchburg city	10 812	101 093	1.68	1 213	15.1	710	8.9	6 845	11.7	17 569	14 638	2 931	2 372	3 016
Manassas city	46	43 006	1.11	747	18.0	167	4.0	6 022	15.9	14 559	11 346	3 213	866	2 031
Manassas Park city	6	10 877	0.40	19	1.2	42	2.6	2 747	19.0	D	D	D	177	1 065

1. Per 1,000 estimated resident population.   2. Data for serious crimes have not been adjusted for underreporting; this may affect comparability between geographic areas and over time.
3. Per 100,000 population estimated by the FBI.

STATE County	Serious crimes known to police, 2014 (cont.)[1] Rate[2]		Education School enrollment and attainment, 2011–2015				Local government expenditures,[5] 2013–2014		Money income, 2011–2015				Income and poverty, 2015			
			Enrollment[3]		Attainment[4] (percent)						Households			Percent below poverty level		
											Percent					
	Violent	Property	Total	Per- cent private	High school grad- uate or less	Bach- elor's degree or more	Total current spending (mil dol)	Current spend- ing per student (dollars)	Per capita income[6] (dollars)	Median income (dollars)	with income of less than $50,000	with income of $200,000 or more	Median house- hold income (dollars)	All per- sons	Children under 18 years	Children 5 to 17 years in families
	46	47	48	49	50	51	52	53	54	55	56	57	58	59	60	61
VIRGINIA—Cont'd																
Louisa	196	1 855	6 766	14.3	54.2	20.6	51.1	10 659	28 323	57 829	43.8	2.8	57 015	10.6	16.7	15.8
Lunenburg	169	563	2 680	15.9	60.4	12.2	15.3	9 743	18 428	39 506	60.0	1.2	38 941	21.1	29.0	26.2
Madison	76	789	2 765	19.7	53.4	23.2	18.6	9 882	25 349	47 736	52.0	3.1	53 655	10.4	18.2	16.2
Mathews	11	1 024	1 524	9.3	41.1	29.2	12.3	10 644	32 397	63 845	40.9	3.2	56 119	10.2	17.9	16.2
Mecklenburg	292	1 702	6 242	11.4	53.6	15.6	41.0	8 847	20 618	37 356	62.7	1.3	33 650	20.4	27.5	25.0
Middlesex	252	1 213	1 943	13.2	44.8	24.2	12.2	9 975	30 297	54 654	45.4	5.0	52 407	12.8	25.1	23.3
Montgomery	118	1 426	41 400	8.2	30.6	45.7	97.2	9 994	25 368	46 663	52.6	4.8	51 157	20.8	15.2	14.4
Nelson	61	1 220	2 708	14.1	49.7	28.2	24.7	12 539	27 528	47 118	51.2	1.9	49 621	13.9	23.2	21.5
New Kent	147	1 528	4 963	17.8	42.9	24.6	27.4	9 220	33 689	73 041	29.7	5.4	79 322	6.7	10.2	8.9
Northampton	75	1 409	2 021	21.2	54.5	20.6	19.9	11 819	22 490	35 055	62.5	2.6	37 515	20.5	33.7	32.3
Northumberland	115	978	1 988	11.0	43.0	25.4	15.4	10 808	31 280	51 885	47.6	2.8	52 075	13.7	29.0	27.1
Nottoway	355	1 529	3 339	11.8	59.4	15.2	22.0	9 437	18 917	36 284	60.9	0.2	39 544	23.7	28.7	28.5
Orange	120	1 134	7 742	15.4	46.8	25.1	48.4	9 349	29 748	65 166	38.9	4.1	59 482	10.4	15.2	13.8
Page	168	1 573	4 963	12.7	65.8	12.8	33.7	9 521	22 241	43 895	55.9	1.9	43 313	15.0	23.2	20.8
Patrick	109	1 417	3 515	6.7	57.2	12.6	24.5	8 821	19 311	33 982	67.2	0.5	37 360	17.0	25.5	22.2
Pittsylvania	79	729	13 966	11.7	54.6	14.1	81.3	8 745	21 667	41 824	60.0	0.9	42 390	17.1	25.6	23.4
Powhatan	74	1 035	6 346	17.1	39.5	27.9	42.5	9 979	32 110	77 896	30.5	6.8	77 761	6.4	8.5	7.4
Prince Edward	251	1 654	8 398	25.0	52.6	24.4	24.5	10 726	17 901	41 697	58.4	0.7	41 088	22.3	29.1	27.6
Prince George	111	976	9 377	12.6	45.7	21.3	58.3	9 134	24 785	61 857	38.6	2.5	63 320	9.9	12.3	10.9
Prince William	176	1 353	130 070	15.4	32.0	38.8	873.0	10 216	37 215	98 657	21.0	13.1	99 206	6.7	9.0	8.2
Pulaski	232	2 485	6 617	6.4	50.2	17.8	45.0	10 070	25 556	47 495	52.1	1.7	48 218	15.0	22.1	19.8
Rappahannock	67	455	1 332	14.7	39.2	35.1	11.8	12 991	36 567	57 210	42.7	6.7	62 729	9.8	15.6	14.0
Richmond	124	743	1 762	5.8	61.1	12.7	13.9	11 262	19 407	47 288	51.7	1.8	43 888	17.7	23.0	20.7
Roanoke	168	1 559	22 123	17.4	34.5	34.2	131.8	9 192	31 370	60 519	40.0	3.9	63 372	7.3	9.4	8.5
Rockbridge	130	1 639	3 811	21.1	50.5	25.5	28.7	10 089	26 767	48 901	50.9	3.2	47 561	12.8	18.6	16.9
Rockingham	101	889	18 474	20.4	54.2	23.8	[7]181.0	[7]10 479	26 472	53 744	45.8	2.7	52 953	11.0	14.0	12.8
Russell	160	1 400	5 421	13.2	60.1	12.4	37.0	8 847	20 053	35 045	62.5	0.7	38 386	21.2	28.2	25.4
Scott	98	1 469	4 118	6.5	59.7	11.7	33.2	8 698	21 295	37 240	63.3	1.5	37 567	19.2	24.5	21.7
Shenandoah	180	1 225	9 134	15.6	55.0	19.0	59.7	9 626	25 253	49 406	50.4	1.7	54 281	11.5	17.7	16.7
Smyth	152	1 665	6 320	8.3	57.1	15.0	44.6	9 324	21 927	37 983	62.8	1.6	38 933	18.1	27.6	24.7
Southampton	122	1 414	4 227	10.0	54.3	15.0	27.9	9 731	23 259	48 962	51.0	2.0	48 119	15.2	20.9	18.8
Spotsylvania	170	1 541	34 474	13.7	42.1	29.3	234.4	9 834	32 105	78 125	29.4	6.6	76 181	7.7	10.9	9.8
Stafford	178	1 525	41 389	12.4	30.4	36.8	266.6	9 709	37 198	97 144	20.7	12.9	95 666	5.4	7.1	6.4
Surry	209	851	1 393	15.8	47.5	21.2	14.9	15 941	24 660	53 673	43.9	1.2	51 331	13.0	20.0	19.0
Sussex	85	1 147	2 350	11.4	69.6	9.6	18.5	16 594	15 143	39 194	60.6	0.8	39 900	22.1	29.0	28.8
Tazewell	210	2 216	8 752	11.6	56.6	13.5	55.2	8 702	22 721	37 664	63.6	2.4	40 476	17.2	24.1	22.1
Warren	110	1 968	9 230	26.6	51.1	20.7	50.4	9 201	29 522	61 454	39.6	3.7	58 047	10.8	15.1	14.0
Washington	142	1 860	11 723	19.0	48.8	23.3	72.6	9 790	25 351	43 310	56.3	2.7	45 864	16.3	22.7	21.1
Westmoreland	147	1 336	3 510	6.4	55.2	18.3	24.3	10 611	25 992	47 911	51.8	1.6	47 581	14.1	28.9	28.4
Wise	206	2 212	8 867	7.1	58.4	14.0	57.8	9 337	20 321	37 407	61.7	1.5	36 076	22.7	30.9	28.3
Wythe	109	1 181	5 592	7.3	55.2	16.0	40.6	9 394	23 770	41 360	59.5	1.9	42 883	14.4	21.3	19.8
York	141	1 687	18 577	13.8	25.5	42.2	119.8	9 606	35 876	81 749	28.1	6.5	83 007	5.3	6.8	5.8
Independent cities																
Alexandria city	185	1 975	29 434	26.9	20.6	61.4	236.5	17 359	54 861	89 134	25.2	14.6	89 177	9.1	14.5	15.2
Bristol city	313	2 804	3 878	19.4	50.3	23.3	25.3	10 884	20 777	35 368	66.2	1.2	38 745	19.3	33.4	29.8
Buena Vista city	134	807	1 891	37.8	58.6	16.4	10.0	9 393	15 707	29 097	75.0	0.7	38 962	17.3	24.6	23.9
Charlottesville city	431	3 047	16 395	12.3	32.0	49.8	[8]	[8]	30 378	49 775	50.1	6.2	54 876	20.7	22.6	24.2
Chesapeake city	430	2 765	64 723	13.6	35.4	29.6	421.7	10 613	29 703	68 620	34.7	4.6	67 296	9.7	13.9	12.8
Colonial Heights city	215	4 897	4 149	5.2	47.3	21.7	34.3	12 205	27 572	50 304	49.7	2.8	45 283	10.6	16.7	17.3
Covington city	173	1 936	1 129	7.4	60.2	9.3	10.5	10 698	20 055	34 746	68.4	0.4	35 374	18.3	28.6	27.0
Danville city	447	4 129	10 391	16.6	49.4	17.9	66.2	10 487	20 933	32 315	68.4	1.8	32 369	23.5	39.4	39.4
Emporia city	526	5 026	1 392	5.2	57.9	18.1	[9]	[9]	20 417	28 601	69.7	1.5	33 904	22.5	38.3	35.4
Fairfax city	74	1 832	6 183	15.1	22.8	54.9	[10]	[10]	45 545	105 297	20.9	17.4	99 671	7.3	7.8	8.2
Falls Church city	130	1 602	3 895	22.1	9.8	78.8	39.3	16 219	65 600	120 522	18.2	26.1	122 092	3.4	3.3	2.7
Franklin city	NA	NA	2 397	12.4	44.7	26.2	15.9	12 595	21 621	32 399	64.3	3.0	36 004	19.4	35.2	35.9
Fredericksburg city	449	4 122	8 539	12.1	35.9	37.3	41.2	11 903	29 090	51 762	48.7	5.1	50 710	15.9	22.8	24.7
Galax city	327	4 111	1 450	4.8	61.3	11.6	13.3	9 942	21 515	30 604	69.9	1.2	32 829	24.2	36.5	36.4
Hampton city	256	3 251	38 449	22.5	37.5	23.2	215.1	10 166	25 029	49 190	50.7	1.9	50 191	15.2	23.5	23.4
Harrisonburg city	198	2 218	23 928	6.9	42.4	35.8	[7]	[7]	18 324	38 750	62.0	2.0	39 967	30.9	23.7	22.7
Hopewell city	381	3 083	5 211	9.1	57.4	12.3	42.3	9 768	20 700	39 064	59.0	1.3	37 193	20.6	33.7	33.3
Lexington city	69	764	4 782	20.0	38.1	43.8	5.0	9 541	14 792	34 017	64.8	4.3	44 392	22.9	18.4	11.5
Lynchburg city	472	2 545	29 433	55.4	36.8	33.1	93.2	10 857	21 650	39 589	60.6	2.4	39 939	23.1	28.4	30.7
Manassas city	326	1 705	11 298	14.9	44.5	28.8	91.7	12 658	29 424	72 890	29.6	5.8	72 562	9.6	15.4	15.3
Manassas Park city	150	915	4 310	11.8	43.8	28.3	33.7	10 471	28 164	73 528	25.3	5.5	75 429	7.7	12.7	11.1

1. Data for serious crimes have not been adjusted for underreporting; this may affect comparability between geographic areas and over time.   2. Per 100,000 population estimated by the FBI.
3. All persons 3 years old and over enrolled in nursery school through college.   4. Persons 25 years old and over.   5. Elementary and secondary education expenditures.
6. Based on population estimated by the American Community Survey, 2011–2015.   7. Harrisonburg city is included with Rockingham county.   8. Charlottesville city is included with Albemarle county.   9. Emporia city is included with Greensville county.   10. Fairfax city is included with Fairfax county.

Table B. States and Counties — **Personal Income**

STATE County	Personal income, 2015										Earnings, 2015		
			Per capita[1]			Supplements to wages and salaries; employer contributions (mil dol)						Contributions for government social insurance (mil dol)	
	Total (mil dol)	Percent change, 2014–2015	Dollars	Rank	Wages and salaries (mil dol)	Pension and insurance	Government social insurance	Proprietors' income (mil dol)	Dividends, interest, and rent (mil dol)	Personal transfer receipts (mil dol)	Total (mil dol)	From employee and self-employed	From employer
	62	63	64	65	66	67	68	69	70	71	72	73	74
VIRGINIA—Cont'd													
Louisa	1 469	6.6	42 445	561	497	92	36	55	223	278	680	45	36
Lunenburg	378	1.9	30 733	2 691	97	22	7	9	72	117	135	11	7
Madison	575	2.9	43 775	1 036	118	23	9	73	123	102	222	16	9
Mathews	450	3.9	50 774	349	49	10	4	26	129	97	89	8	4
Mecklenburg	1 061	4.3	34 137	2 256	422	80	32	29	213	350	563	42	32
Middlesex	482	4.7	45 488	911	120	27	9	32	131	123	188	14	9
Montgomery	[3]3 818	[3]4.6	[3]33 184	[3]2 518	[3]2 169	[3]523	[3]158	[3]178	[3]826	[3]643	[3]3 028	[3]174	[3]158
Nelson	666	5.4	45 055	912	140	29	10	52	149	157	231	17	10
New Kent	1 119	6.7	54 876	391	167	32	13	44	157	149	256	18	13
Northampton	460	4.6	37 804	1 781	177	33	13	21	115	141	245	17	13
Northumberland	523	1.3	42 790	907	101	19	8	16	190	150	144	14	8
Nottoway	558	5.0	35 630	2 087	222	62	18	13	98	172	315	21	18
Orange	1 492	5.2	42 166	1 297	367	71	27	60	310	309	526	38	27
Page	849	3.2	35 766	2 091	187	40	15	65	153	218	308	22	15
Patrick	556	3.4	30 794	2 801	162	36	12	31	95	185	241	20	12
Pittsylvania	[4]3 558	[4]3.6	[4]34 119	[4]2 329	[4]1 459	[4]275	[4]110	[4]139	[4]614	[4]1 141	[4]982	[4]141	[4]110
Powhatan	1 376	5.5	49 105	663	299	60	21	62	223	194	442	30	21
Prince Edward	670	5.0	29 186	2 993	332	73	25	37	120	192	468	30	25
Prince George	[5]2 240	[5]5.3	[5]37 178	[5]1 701	[5]1 837	[5]490	[5]163	[5]37	[5]483	[5]492	[5]2 527	[5]127	[5]163
Prince William	[6]25 621	[6]5.1	[6]50 315	[6]479	[6]8 285	[6]1 462	[6]633	[6]1 339	[6]3 815	[6]2 417	[6]11 719	[6]667	[6]633
Pulaski	1 262	4.9	36 770	1 976	573	110	45	50	199	348	779	53	45
Rappahannock	421	3.6	57 071	178	87	14	5	41	133	62	147	10	5
Richmond	286	4.4	32 128	2 606	115	27	8	9	60	75	160	11	8
Roanoke	[7]5 758	[7]4.9	[7]48 047	[7]633	[7]2 986	[7]511	[7]213	[7]393	[7]1 068	[7]1 006	[7]4 103	[7]258	[7]213
Rockbridge	[8]1 348	[8]3.3	[8]37 210	[8]1 962	[8]515	[8]102	[8]41	[8]91	[8]333	[8]316	[8]750	[8]51	[8]41
Rockingham	[9]4 681	[9]3.6	[9]35 700	[9]2 160	[9]2 619	[9]484	[9]190	[9]505	[9]879	[9]827	[9]3 798	[9]222	[9]190
Russell	894	3.4	32 047	2 627	309	57	24	25	127	303	416	34	24
Scott	681	2.8	30 767	2 794	172	37	13	15	109	248	237	22	13
Shenandoah	1 697	3.9	39 291	1 469	523	99	39	122	339	363	782	53	39
Smyth	1 073	4.2	34 090	2 536	472	103	36	77	161	332	688	47	36
Southampton	[10]931	[10]3.2	[10]34 987	[10]2 242	[10]305	[10]69	[10]22	[10]28	[10]184	[10]262	[10]424	[10]30	[10]22
Spotsylvania	[11]7 359	[11]4.8	[11]46 401	[11]704	[11]2 557	[11]415	[11]186	[11]367	[11]1 303	[11]1 054	[11]3 524	[11]216	[11]186
Stafford	7 110	5.0	50 067	459	2 263	444	168	223	1 165	799	3 099	181	168
Surry	266	1.6	39 631	1 378	211	45	15	4	43	62	275	16	15
Sussex	339	3.2	28 943	2 947	152	35	11	8	60	102	206	14	11
Tazewell	1 464	0.7	34 121	2 251	564	119	43	65	248	483	791	59	43
Warren	1 634	4.0	41 815	1 157	506	90	39	71	273	285	705	46	39
Washington	[12]2 926	[12]1.9	[12]40 787	[12]1 113	[12]1 216	[12]237	[12]90	[12]341	[12]650	[12]706	[12]1 884	[12]126	[12]90
Westmoreland	687	4.1	38 991	1 391	115	25	9	10	178	176	159	14	9
Wise	[13]1 302	[13]1.5	[13]29 829	[13]2 849	[13]618	[13]137	[13]46	[13]39	[13]200	[13]507	[13]841	[13]60	[13]46
Wythe	1 023	4.3	35 120	2 240	419	88	32	45	158	287	583	40	32
York	[14]4 403	[14]4.8	[14]55 111	[14]248	[14]1 042	[14]199	[14]81	[14]144	[14]933	[14]529	[14]1 466	[14]91	[14]81
Independent cities													
Alexandria city	12 693	4.2	82 683	35	7 602	1 187	577	942	2 875	748	10 308	580	577
Bristol city	(12)	(12)	(12)	(12)	(12)	(12)	(12)	(12)	(12)	(12)	(12)	(12)	(12)
Buena Vista city	(8)	(8)	(8)	(8)	(8)	(8)	(8)	(8)	(8)	(8)	(8)	(8)	(8)
Charlottesville city	(15)	(15)	(15)	(15)	(15)	(15)	(15)	(15)	(15)	(15)	(15)	(15)	(15)
Chesapeake city	11 011	4.8	46 769	627	4 475	742	334	314	1 900	1 625	5 865	355	334
Colonial Heights city	(16)	(16)	(16)	(16)	(16)	(16)	(16)	(16)	(16)	(16)	(16)	(16)	(16)
Covington city	(17)	(17)	(17)	(17)	(17)	(17)	(17)	(17)	(17)	(17)	(17)	(17)	(17)
Danville city	(4)	(4)	(4)	(4)	(4)	(4)	(4)	(4)	(4)	(4)	(4)	(4)	(4)
Emporia city	(18)	(18)	(18)	(18)	(18)	(18)	(18)	(18)	(18)	(18)	(18)	(18)	(18)
Fairfax city	(19)	(19)	(19)	(19)	(19)	(19)	(19)	(19)	(19)	(19)	(19)	(19)	(19)
Falls Church city	(19)	(19)	(19)	(19)	(19)	(19)	(19)	(19)	(19)	(19)	(19)	(19)	(19)
Franklin city	(10)	(10)	(10)	(10)	(10)	(10)	(10)	(10)	(10)	(10)	(10)	(10)	(10)
Fredericksburg city	(11)	(11)	(11)	(11)	(11)	(11)	(11)	(11)	(11)	(11)	(11)	(11)	(11)
Galax city	(20)	(20)	(20)	(20)	(20)	(20)	(20)	(20)	(20)	(20)	(20)	(20)	(20)
Hampton city	5 562	3.5	40 759	1 226	3 116	709	258	140	1 132	1 200	4 224	237	258
Harrisonburg city	(9)	(9)	(9)	(9)	(9)	(9)	(9)	(9)	(9)	(9)	(9)	(9)	(9)
Hopewell city	(5)	(5)	(5)	(5)	(5)	(5)	(5)	(5)	(5)	(5)	(5)	(5)	(5)
Lexington city	(8)	(8)	(8)	(8)	(8)	(8)	(8)	(8)	(8)	(8)	(8)	(8)	(8)
Lynchburg city	(21)	(21)	(21)	(21)	(21)	(21)	(21)	(21)	(21)	(21)	(21)	(21)	(21)
Manassas city	(6)	(6)	(6)	(6)	(6)	(6)	(6)	(6)	(6)	(6)	(6)	(6)	(6)
Manassas Park city	(6)	(6)	(6)	(6)	(6)	(6)	(6)	(6)	(6)	(6)	(6)	(6)	(6)

1. Based on the resident population estimated as of July 1 of the year shown.　3. Radford city is included with Montgomery county.　4. Danville city is included with Pittsylvania county.　5. Hopewell city is included with Prince George county.　6. Manassas and Manassas Park cities are included with Prince William county.　7. Salem city is included with Roanoke county.　8. Buena Vista and Lexington cities are included with Rockbridge county.　9. Harrisonburg city is included with Rockingham county.　10. Franklin city is included with Southhampton county.　11. Fredericksburg city is included with Spotsylvania county.　12. Bristol city is included with Washington county.　13. Norton city is included with Wise county.　14. Poquoson city is included with York county.　15. Charlottesville city is included with Albemarle county.　16. Petersburg and Colonial Heights cities are included with Dinwiddie county.　17. Covington city is included with Alleghany county.　18. Emporia city is included with Greensville county.　19. Fairfax city and Falls Church city are included with Fairfax county.　20. Galax city is included with Carroll county.　21. Lynchburg city is included with Campbell county.

Table B. States and Counties — Earnings, Social Security, and Housing

STATE County	Earnings, 2015 (cont.) — Percent by selected industries									Social Security beneficiaries, December 2015		Supplemental Security Income recipients, December 2015	Housing units, 2016	
	Farm	Mining	Construction	Manufacturing	Information: professional, scientific, technical services	Retail trade	Finance, insurance, real estate and leasing	Health care and social assistance	Government	Number	Rate[1]		Total	Percent change, 2010–2016
	75	76	77	78	79	80	81	82	83	84	85	86	87	88
VIRGINIA—Cont'd														
Louisa	-0.2	D	15.5	15.5	D	5.2	1.8	3.5	13.0	7 950	230	653	17 101	4.6
Lunenburg	1.4	0.0	8.5	12.0	D	5.0	D	D	31.6	3 215	261	374	5 932	-0.1
Madison	0.0	-0.4	9.6	7.5	D	37.1	1.1	D	15.1	3 015	230	180	6 053	2.0
Mathews	-0.6	0.0	10.9	4.6	D	6.2	8.6	D	24.2	2 885	325	143	5 740	1.3
Mecklenburg	-0.1	D	8.0	11.0	6.4	8.0	3.9	16.8	18.0	9 935	320	1 232	18 719	0.7
Middlesex	0.0	0.0	10.3	5.2	D	6.6	5.8	D	27.8	3 665	343	251	7 280	2.1
Montgomery	[3]0.1	[3]0.2	[3]D	[3]15.1	[3]9.1	[3]5.6	[3]3.6	[3]9.0	[3]40.1	13 725	141	1 120	39 659	2.8
Nelson	1.1	D	10.8	10.2	D	3.7	3.9	D	17.9	4 555	308	374	10 112	1.8
New Kent	-0.6	0.0	27.7	3.5	5.2	6.1	3.4	10.1	22.5	4 235	207	215	8 217	12.6
Northampton	3.8	0.0	3.8	12.9	D	5.5	3.1	22.1	22.5	3 705	305	605	7 378	1.1
Northumberland	-1.8	D	8.8	28.7	9.0	6.4	3.5	2.8	19.0	4 630	378	243	9 193	2.2
Nottoway	1.8	0.0	4.3	6.1	2.0	5.3	2.4	D	51.5	3 840	245	618	6 739	1.4
Orange	-0.3	0.0	8.3	12.2	5.7	8.2	6.3	4.6	23.1	8 720	247	627	14 910	2.1
Page	10.0	0.0	7.6	10.5	5.3	7.1	4.0	9.9	23.4	6 510	275	576	11 674	0.6
Patrick	-0.2	0.0	5.6	26.9	8.0	6.4	2.1	D	17.8	5 575	309	562	10 087	0.0
Pittsylvania	[4]1.4	[4]D	[4]D	[4]21.7	[4]3.6	[4]8.1	[4]3.6	[4]15.0	[4]18.3	17 365	280	1 562	31 321	0.1
Powhatan	-0.2	D	20.9	3.3	10.4	6.1	3.6	4.6	30.1	5 835	208	258	10 706	6.6
Prince Edward	0.5	D	4.5	1.5	2.8	8.9	3.6	D	30.3	4 880	210	912	9 327	2.0
Prince George	[5]-0.2	[5]-0.1	[5]D	[5]11.7	[5]3.3	[5]2.0	[5]1.0	[5]4.2	[5]63.1	6 055	158	344	12 366	2.6
Prince William	[6]0.0	[6]D	[6]D	[6]3.4	[6]D	[6]D	[6]3.9	[6]D	[6]28.7	42 870	95	3 985	147 509	7.6
Pulaski	0.5	D	4.0	42.2	D	6.6	1.8	D	15.7	9 770	285	888	17 260	0.2
Rappahannock	-1.0	0.0	13.3	3.0	38.3	3.8	2.6	2.2	13.4	1 965	266	72	3 980	2.1
Richmond	-0.4	0.0	6.5	5.3	D	4.9	D	D	38.7	1 990	227	245	3 921	1.8
Roanoke	[7]0.0	[7]D	[7]D	[7]20.5	[7]7.9	[7]6.0	[7]7.4	[7]D	[7]15.5	22 200	236	929	41 022	2.4
Rockbridge	[8]0.0	[8]D	[8]8.0	[8]13.6	[8]D	[8]6.7	[8]2.7	[8]7.1	[8]21.6	5 985	267	306	11 365	1.9
Rockingham	[9]4.1	[9]D	[9]6.2	[9]17.6	[9]6.6	[9]6.6	[9]4.7	[9]11.7	[9]17.7	17 275	219	859	34 975	3.9
Russell	0.1	5.3	7.8	4.5	12.5	6.5	3.4	D	19.9	8 750	315	1 458	13 363	-0.9
Scott	-2.3	0.0	3.5	18.9	D	7.8	2.8	14.0	27.5	7 275	328	1 292	11 836	-0.7
Shenandoah	2.9	D	7.1	21.6	5.5	7.8	3.8	8.7	15.3	10 790	251	706	21 163	1.4
Smyth	1.4	D	5.3	31.0	2.9	5.0	1.8	D	22.7	9 790	312	1 248	15 294	-0.9
Southampton	[10]-1.0	[10]0.0	[10]2.5	[10]8.1	[10]4.1	[10]8.7	[10]4.3	[10]18.2	[10]32.1	4 405	242	357	7 554	1.1
Spotsylvania	[11]0.0	[11]D	[11]6.0	[11]1.3	[11]11.8	[11]12.4	[11]5.6	[11]19.4	[11]17.5	19 935	153	1 327	46 883	3.5
Stafford	-0.1	D	6.9	1.3	12.2	5.5	D	5.9	35.2	15 960	113	1 061	47 953	9.0
Surry	-0.7	0.0	6.8	D	2.5	0.5	0.1	D	11.1	1 670	250	148	3 529	2.4
Sussex	0.5	D	4.3	2.3	D	6.4	1.5	D	38.8	2 630	224	482	4 720	0.6
Tazewell	0.4	6.6	4.8	9.3	3.9	11.6	4.0	D	20.8	13 190	307	1 855	20 601	-1.1
Warren	-0.3	0.0	9.3	11.1	4.8	7.1	D	11.1	17.6	7 630	195	649	16 268	1.9
Washington	[12]0.1	[12]D	[12]D	[12]19.4	[12]4.4	[12]8.2	[12]3.9	[12]10.3	[12]15.3	15 980	294	1 567	25 714	0.4
Westmoreland	-0.9	0.0	6.3	16.1	D	7.6	3.6	D	28.4	4 915	280	443	10 880	2.5
Wise	[13]0.2	[13]7.4	[13]D	[13]2.6	[13]6.5	[13]9.4	[13]2.5	[13]16.6	[13]29.3	11 915	300	2 333	17 740	-1.2
Wythe	1.0	1.0	5.0	22.9	4.0	10.2	3.8	11.2	21.7	8 315	285	839	14 222	1.0
York	[14]0.0	[14]D	[14]10.7	[14]2.3	[14]D	[14]8.6	[14]6.1	[14]D	[14]30.5	11 170	164	337	27 742	3.9
Independent cities														
Alexandria city	0.0	D	2.0	D	28.1	4.6	5.9	4.5	31.5	14 620	95	1 801	76 571	5.8
Bristol city	[12]	[12]	[12]	[12]	[12]	[12]	[12]	[12]	[12]	4 910	286	808	8 804	-0.3
Buena Vista city	[8]	[8]	[8]	[8]	[8]	[8]	[8]	[8]	[8]	1 620	246	259	2 908	-1.0
Charlottesville city	[15]	[15]	[15]	[15]	[15]	[15]	[15]	[15]	[15]	6 175	134	1 031	20 611	7.4
Chesapeake city	0.0	0.1	9.8	5.8	13.5	9.0	6.3	7.5	18.5	36 865	157	3 594	90 115	8.3
Colonial Heights city	[16]	[16]	[16]	[16]	[16]	[16]	[16]	[16]	[16]	4 400	249	499	7 793	-0.5
Covington city	[17]	[17]	[17]	[17]	[17]	[17]	[17]	[17]	[17]	1 945	348	463	3 024	-1.3
Danville city	[4]	[4]	[4]	[4]	[4]	[4]	[4]	[4]	[4]	12 705	302	2 927	22 266	-0.8
Emporia city	[18]	[18]	[18]	[18]	[18]	[18]	[18]	[18]	[18]	1 460	266	639	2 622	2.1
Fairfax city	[19]	[19]	[19]	[19]	[19]	[19]	[19]	[19]	[19]	3 390	143	17	8 866	2.2
Falls Church city	[19]	[19]	[19]	[19]	[19]	[19]	[19]	[19]	[19]	1 520	109	118	6 046	10.4
Franklin city	[10]	[10]	[10]	[10]	[10]	[10]	[10]	[10]	[10]	2 175	259	659	3 875	-0.6
Fredericksburg city	[11]	[11]	[11]	[11]	[11]	[11]	[11]	[11]	[11]	3 935	141	506	11 501	10.9
Galax city	[20]	[20]	[20]	[20]	[20]	[20]	[20]	[20]	[20]	2 210	322	590	3 203	-1.1
Hampton city	0.0	0.0	3.2	3.6	11.4	5.5	2.5	9.8	48.4	26 030	191	3 346	60 416	1.5
Harrisonburg city	[9]	[9]	[9]	[9]	[9]	[9]	[9]	[9]	[9]	5 615	107	999	18 225	4.5
Hopewell city	[5]	[5]	[5]	[5]	[5]	[5]	[5]	[5]	[5]	5 020	225	1 106	10 355	2.3
Lexington city	[8]	[8]	[8]	[8]	[8]	[8]	[8]	[8]	[8]	1 670	236	228	2 529	-0.6
Lynchburg city	[21]	[21]	[21]	[21]	[21]	[21]	[21]	[21]	[21]	15 790	199	2 764	32 585	1.8
Manassas city	[6]	[6]	[6]	[6]	[6]	[6]	[6]	[6]	[6]	4 355	105	476	13 612	3.7
Manassas Park city	[6]	[6]	[6]	[6]	[6]	[6]	[6]	[6]	[6]	1 195	75	10	4 910	0.3

1. Per 1,000 resident population estimated as of July 1 of the year shown. 3. Radford city is included with Montgomery county. 4. Danville city is included with Pittsylvania county. 5. Hopewell city is included with Prince George county. 6. Manassas and Manassas Park cities are included with Prince William county. 7. Salem city is included with Roanoke county. 8. Buena Vista and Lexington cities are included with Rockbridge county. 9. Harrisonburg city is included with Rockingham county. 10. Franklin city is included with Southhampton county. 11. Fredericksburg city is included with Spotsylvania county. 12. Bristol city included with Washington county. 13. Norton city is included with Wise county. 14. Poquoson city is included with York county. 15. Charlottesville city is included with Albemarle county. 16. Petersburg and Colonial Heights cities are included with Dinwiddie county. 17. Covington city is included with Alleghany county. 18. Emporia city is included with Greensville county. 19. Fairfax city and Falls Church city are included with Fairfax county. 20. Galax city is included with Carroll county. 21. Lynchburg city is included with Campbell county.

Table B. States and Counties — Housing, Labor Force, and Employment

	Housing units, 2011–2015								Civilian labor force, 2016		Unemployment		Civilian employment,[6] 2011–2015		
	Occupied units													Percent	
		Owner-occupied				Renter-occupied									
				Median owner cost as a percent of income											
STATE County	Total	Percent	Median value[1]	With a mortgage	Without a mortgage[2]	Median rent[3]	Median rent as a percent of income[2]	Substandard units[4] (percent)	Total	Percent change, 2015–2016	Total	Rate[5]	Total	Management, business, science and arts	Construction, production, and maintenance occupations
	89	90	91	92	93	94	95	96	97	98	99	100	101	102	103

VIRGINIA—Cont'd

	89	90	91	92	93	94	95	96	97	98	99	100	101	102	103
Louisa	12 829	79.5	193 700	22.7	11.0	936	28.3	1.8	18 457	-1.7	695	3.8	16 077	33.1	26.6
Lunenburg	4 516	73.6	106 600	24.4	11.3	685	30.4	3.0	5 252	-0.5	241	4.6	4 523	27.0	30.4
Madison	5 003	72.7	241 200	25.6	12.4	775	30.6	4.6	7 182	-0.5	221	3.1	5 965	30.7	26.6
Mathews	3 806	82.8	250 900	20.5	10.0	942	24.2	0.3	4 067	0.0	161	4.0	3 901	34.8	25.7
Mecklenburg	12 482	74.0	125 400	25.0	13.0	683	29.1	2.5	12 420	-0.6	698	5.6	12 460	30.2	23.3
Middlesex	4 342	83.2	245 800	25.9	10.0	781	27.3	1.6	4 985	0.2	188	3.8	4 404	31.1	23.4
Montgomery	35 199	54.2	205 100	20.5	10.0	861	37.1	1.3	49 782	0.2	2 006	4.0	45 648	46.6	13.2
Nelson	6 339	72.1	212 000	24.8	10.7	709	25.8	3.8	7 223	-0.5	257	3.6	6 694	33.1	23.6
New Kent	7 299	85.5	245 000	22.2	10.0	883	24.1	1.1	11 325	1.1	383	3.4	9 896	36.1	23.8
Northampton	5 248	68.9	160 900	22.8	15.0	694	31.4	2.2	5 905	-3.1	338	5.7	4 830	30.9	27.4
Northumberland	5 861	83.7	242 000	25.4	10.6	720	31.8	3.1	5 452	-0.1	295	5.4	5 021	35.3	19.1
Nottoway	5 589	65.3	132 900	23.7	11.0	783	40.8	2.0	7 050	-1.0	278	3.9	5 644	27.3	24.9
Orange	12 810	75.5	231 000	22.6	10.0	879	30.5	3.1	16 375	2.1	658	4.0	15 024	33.2	27.6
Page	9 372	70.4	176 000	22.2	10.7	711	28.4	2.4	11 534	-0.8	641	5.6	10 379	26.0	28.7
Patrick	7 790	76.7	111 100	23.3	11.2	532	31.8	2.9	8 034	5.3	386	4.8	6 971	25.9	39.7
Pittsylvania	26 204	76.8	111 900	21.7	11.1	645	27.2	1.8	29 629	-1.3	1 398	4.7	27 803	25.6	34.4
Powhatan	9 730	87.3	257 300	22.0	10.0	970	23.8	1.3	13 523	1.1	480	3.5	13 301	38.2	21.3
Prince Edward	7 409	64.8	151 500	24.4	10.1	749	26.4	2.4	10 140	0.9	541	5.3	8 771	30.9	22.3
Prince George	11 102	70.6	207 500	21.7	10.0	1 279	32.2	1.5	15 022	1.1	721	4.8	14 315	35.8	22.9
Prince William	136 794	71.5	333 100	22.6	10.0	1 547	30.9	3.4	234 139	1.3	8 402	3.6	223 939	43.2	16.3
Pulaski	14 619	71.2	135 700	20.4	10.0	596	26.2	1.6	16 498	1.3	959	5.8	15 480	29.7	31.1
Rappahannock	3 273	76.1	367 000	24.8	12.3	1 036	30.5	1.3	3 720	-0.3	130	3.5	3 570	35.1	19.6
Richmond	2 875	74.4	150 000	22.6	11.8	773	28.4	1.6	3 897	0.1	145	3.7	3 199	26.2	28.2
Roanoke	38 164	74.7	189 200	21.5	10.0	872	25.0	1.2	49 286	0.6	1 747	3.5	45 358	40.6	17.0
Rockbridge	9 319	74.3	188 500	25.5	10.0	684	29.6	1.9	10 336	0.3	456	4.4	9 789	33.3	27.4
Rockingham	29 625	75.8	197 300	23.1	10.0	809	27.2	2.9	40 447	1.0	1 399	3.5	38 108	32.0	28.9
Russell	11 045	78.0	96 000	24.6	10.0	536	35.4	0.9	11 162	-2.2	723	6.5	10 211	30.8	31.5
Scott	9 379	77.7	91 900	19.5	10.3	503	32.4	3.0	9 471	-0.2	457	4.8	8 509	23.8	32.6
Shenandoah	17 096	72.6	198 900	23.9	11.0	781	31.4	2.8	20 845	-0.8	777	3.7	19 990	28.6	31.8
Smyth	12 795	69.9	88 900	19.2	11.0	574	28.1	1.3	13 728	2.1	792	5.8	13 278	28.5	31.9
Southampton	6 682	69.7	159 700	22.6	11.0	729	32.5	1.8	9 038	-1.6	352	3.9	7 948	29.2	29.1
Spotsylvania	42 823	76.1	248 500	22.6	10.0	1 346	31.3	1.5	64 475	1.2	2 618	4.1	62 469	39.0	19.2
Stafford	43 405	76.8	305 300	21.7	10.0	1 445	32.0	1.7	67 494	1.4	2 636	3.9	64 619	45.9	14.8
Surry	2 668	80.0	169 000	21.8	13.2	823	26.2	2.4	3 649	-1.7	192	5.3	3 209	23.1	38.7
Sussex	3 149	65.4	140 400	22.7	10.9	728	32.8	0.8	4 037	-0.7	248	6.1	2 551	26.1	27.9
Tazewell	17 832	75.4	91 400	20.7	12.1	585	28.1	1.0	15 969	-3.8	1 205	7.5	16 752	28.6	29.5
Warren	14 364	76.7	213 500	22.5	11.1	915	29.5	1.1	19 746	0.8	790	4.0	18 689	32.7	26.9
Washington	22 673	76.2	130 200	20.8	10.1	614	28.0	1.1	26 933	-0.1	1 208	4.5	24 442	34.4	23.7
Westmoreland	6 944	74.6	191 600	26.2	11.6	910	29.0	0.8	8 926	0.2	410	4.6	7 423	29.4	24.7
Wise	15 254	69.7	87 500	18.4	10.7	600	32.6	2.2	13 063	-5.1	1 115	8.5	13 736	33.5	29.2
Wythe	11 863	69.7	123 900	21.4	10.0	611	28.0	1.0	13 588	-0.3	773	5.7	12 631	27.8	30.3
York	23 997	73.0	312 600	21.9	10.0	1 389	29.8	1.0	31 985	0.1	1 244	3.9	30 160	48.2	16.3
Independent cities															
Alexandria city	66 879	42.5	502 500	22.1	10.8	1 555	27.7	3.9	95 389	1.4	2 740	2.9	92 575	58.1	8.9
Bristol city	7 718	55.2	114 500	20.7	12.9	649	31.4	1.3	7 501	0.0	379	5.1	7 306	32.7	18.1
Buena Vista city	2 737	58.6	115 000	27.9	13.8	691	40.3	2.5	3 262	-0.9	167	5.1	2 824	16.2	34.0
Charlottesville city	17 752	43.6	285 300	21.8	11.2	998	31.2	1.4	24 830	0.9	831	3.3	23 605	49.5	9.5
Chesapeake city	81 518	70.4	253 800	25.1	12.1	1 176	31.7	2.1	116 459	0.3	4 973	4.3	105 953	39.1	20.4
Colonial Heights city	7 106	62.8	169 300	23.8	10.1	940	30.4	1.6	8 784	1.5	388	4.4	7 672	35.6	19.1
Covington city	2 476	74.1	68 600	19.7	12.9	590	29.0	4.2	2 379	-1.5	138	5.8	2 160	18.7	34.9
Danville city	18 559	54.0	88 600	21.5	11.8	601	28.8	2.7	19 036	-0.3	1 144	6.0	16 682	31.6	23.9
Emporia city	2 459	42.7	115 000	24.5	13.2	680	33.8	2.6	2 230	-0.5	144	6.5	2 074	30.5	28.3
Fairfax city	8 467	70.0	470 300	21.1	10.0	1 692	31.2	3.0	12 950	1.3	394	3.0	12 724	51.8	9.4
Falls Church city	5 166	58.7	718 900	21.4	10.0	1 517	27.4	2.4	7 948	1.4	216	2.7	7 347	74.0	3.9
Franklin city	3 453	47.7	178 700	27.2	18.7	781	39.6	1.1	3 547	-1.6	211	5.9	3 429	30.1	22.7
Fredericksburg city	10 080	34.5	317 900	20.0	10.0	1 058	30.5	0.7	13 530	1.3	639	4.7	13 384	42.1	11.9
Galax city	2 961	59.6	91 000	25.0	12.3	529	25.9	5.9	2 905	-1.3	145	5.0	2 842	21.6	34.0
Hampton city	52 940	57.6	188 000	24.5	12.8	1 009	35.0	5.8	64 276	0.1	3 614	5.6	60 826	32.5	22.4
Harrisonburg city	16 409	36.1	199 400	22.2	10.0	837	32.7	4.9	24 269	1.7	1 142	4.7	24 011	34.5	18.6
Hopewell city	8 706	51.3	123 800	22.0	13.0	835	30.2	3.4	9 681	0.7	629	6.5	9 041	23.0	32.7
Lexington city	1 638	57.4	242 700	32.7	14.1	744	28.1	0.0	2 255	0.2	142	6.3	2 082	46.6	4.5
Lynchburg city	28 528	50.7	149 200	21.7	11.5	778	34.4	1.7	35 374	-0.6	1 825	5.2	34 404	38.9	16.0
Manassas city	12 433	64.2	276 700	23.4	12.4	1 327	30.7	7.3	21 834	1.2	776	3.6	21 549	31.5	22.6
Manassas Park city	4 723	68.7	248 300	27.4	13.4	1 470	25.9	4.1	8 410	1.0	298	3.5	7 991	33.6	25.6

1. Specified owner-occupied units.   2. A value of 10.0 represents 10 percent or less; a value of 50.0 represents 50 percent or more.   3. Specified renter-occupied units.
4. Overcrowded or lacking complete plumbing facilities.   5. Percent of civilian labor force.   6. Civilian employed persons 16 years old and over.

	Private nonfarm establishments, employment and payroll, 2015								Agriculture, 2012			
	Employment						Annual payroll		Farms			
										Percent with:		
STATE County	Number of establishments	Total	Health care and social assistance	Manufacturing	Retail trade	Finance and insurance	Professional, scientific, and technical services	Total (mil dol)	Average per employee (dollars)	Number	Fewer than 50 acres	500 acres or more	Farm operators whose principal occupation is farming (percent)
	104	105	106	107	108	109	110	111	112	113	114	115	116
VIRGINIA—Cont'd												
Louisa	545	6 535	300	1 170	1 073	89	154	311	47 601	485	39.6	8.2	40.6
Lunenburg	180	1 875	266	512	422	68	56	53	28 070	371	20.2	9.7	46.9
Madison	280	2 816	333	297	931	23	59	89	31 620	522	36.2	10.3	49.6
Mathews	174	1 068	248	D	209	19	37	25	23 752	55	72.7	5.5	47.3
Mecklenburg	780	9 619	1 704	1 416	1 799	288	583	314	32 682	527	20.5	12.0	44.8
Middlesex	322	2 179	367	137	490	70	170	65	29 665	73	43.8	12.3	61.6
Montgomery	1 931	29 367	4 288	5 024	5 156	651	2 122	1 106	37 648	603	39.5	6.6	39.6
Nelson	373	3 128	230	445	283	41	163	87	27 768	455	29.0	5.9	36.0
New Kent	357	2 826	566	147	442	24	109	89	31 631	137	52.6	5.1	49.6
Northampton	327	2 931	812	355	471	51	81	97	33 243	147	40.8	24.5	57.1
Northumberland	323	1 623	98	331	306	70	96	57	35 400	98	39.8	27.6	64.3
Nottoway	316	3 835	1 398	423	621	115	107	104	27 139	356	31.2	6.5	56.2
Orange	639	6 720	422	1 161	1 253	133	457	269	40 065	547	35.5	7.5	47.5
Page	403	3 935	512	462	705	142	195	118	29 939	545	45.0	5.3	56.7
Patrick	284	4 118	671	1 362	498	82	63	109	26 539	566	35.5	3.7	40.6
Pittsylvania	822	8 364	1 309	1 880	887	134	157	267	31 929	1 354	25.2	10.1	56.6
Powhatan	682	4 816	277	141	807	128	261	179	37 172	250	42.0	5.2	48.4
Prince Edward	533	6 551	1 749	114	1 457	181	103	206	31 474	413	28.8	8.5	32.4
Prince George	472	9 610	380	1 051	812	91	838	320	33 280	167	32.9	9.6	59.3
Prince William	7 859	96 400	10 471	1 457	22 196	1 921	10 564	3 981	41 292	330	68.2	4.8	53.0
Pulaski	601	11 702	1 251	5 326	1 644	155	186	455	38 898	445	38.7	11.5	42.2
Rappahannock	199	1 028	42	59	158	13	83	36	34 659	397	46.6	7.3	51.9
Richmond	177	1 957	728	133	225	56	27	58	29 425	90	34.4	21.1	54.4
Roanoke	1 990	29 156	4 779	3 434	3 841	3 860	1 602	1 084	37 163	280	52.9	4.3	44.3
Rockbridge	428	4 661	313	1 064	1 278	75	162	133	28 523	833	28.3	8.5	42.4
Rockingham	1 415	26 501	4 571	6 873	1 852	375	506	1 092	41 188	1 902	43.2	2.8	54.6
Russell	447	5 822	1 185	569	919	228	788	205	35 182	995	34.8	7.1	41.5
Scott	283	3 616	681	840	722	93	114	118	32 700	1 292	33.7	3.0	41.4
Shenandoah	865	11 878	1 434	3 591	1 645	293	309	402	33 857	980	45.7	4.9	50.1
Smyth	505	9 494	2 331	3 378	1 191	178	171	320	33 688	792	40.8	9.2	41.2
Southampton	220	2 088	121	750	264	21	41	83	39 678	335	26.3	31.6	60.0
Spotsylvania	2 395	30 220	3 654	1 300	7 577	567	2 836	1 225	40 539	369	56.9	5.4	43.6
Stafford	2 161	30 742	3 265	960	4 742	4 386	4 165	1 286	41 817	215	62.3	1.4	41.9
Surry	72	1 302	D	116	41	D	22	123	94 473	127	43.3	21.3	50.4
Sussex	179	2 025	356	257	328	30	21	66	32 415	123	29.3	26.8	61.8
Tazewell	1 042	13 101	2 392	1 179	3 172	664	343	449	34 276	584	31.8	15.6	43.5
Warren	785	9 980	1 383	922	1 765	237	268	351	35 175	346	58.1	5.8	43.1
Washington	1 148	17 431	2 761	3 678	3 293	472	667	669	38 374	1 602	48.3	4.2	39.7
Westmoreland	316	2 504	210	597	468	83	170	70	28 135	152	18.4	21.7	50.7
Wise	751	8 716	1 670	208	2 018	226	406	284	32 569	165	49.7	6.1	32.7
Wythe	666	9 449	1 254	2 037	1 953	234	234	299	31 626	952	34.2	8.3	47.8
York	1 398	17 770	1 776	293	3 827	414	1 887	586	32 991	47	63.8	2.1	70.2
Independent cities												
Alexandria city	4 725	84 399	8 090	1 112	7 641	2 907	18 287	5 157	61 104	NA	NA	NA	NA
Bristol city	623	10 449	794	1 334	1 524	339	178	441	42 221	NA	NA	NA	NA
Buena Vista city	106	2 147	145	1 153	86	31	18	74	34 436	NA	NA	NA	NA
Charlottesville city	2 029	33 654	9 492	594	3 909	855	2 311	1 772	52 640	NA	NA	NA	NA
Chesapeake city	5 354	88 569	9 848	4 082	15 574	3 876	8 309	3 608	40 739	253	71.1	8.7	44.7
Colonial Heights city	668	9 681	1 633	199	3 357	281	414	243	25 107	NA	NA	NA	NA
Covington city	224	4 070	178	D	768	94	42	197	48 340	NA	NA	NA	NA
Danville city	1 282	23 322	5 210	4 362	4 373	846	376	789	33 812	NA	NA	NA	NA
Emporia city	233	3 806	1 122	891	590	88	57	115	30 204	NA	NA	NA	NA
Fairfax city	2 277	32 385	4 202	162	6 605	1 301	7 339	1 749	54 000	NA	NA	NA	NA
Falls Church city	863	9 665	1 926	76	1 039	197	1 522	475	49 198	NA	NA	NA	NA
Franklin city	276	3 558	1 180	34	1 065	181	140	103	29 035	NA	NA	NA	NA
Fredericksburg city	1 333	18 958	4 438	227	4 041	578	1 432	778	41 059	NA	NA	NA	NA
Galax city	296	4 949	1 458	671	1 196	116	133	153	30 993	NA	NA	NA	NA
Hampton city	2 373	40 789	7 461	1 964	7 126	935	4 017	1 613	39 552	NA	NA	NA	NA
Harrisonburg city	1 557	24 958	2 980	2 418	5 468	847	1 058	789	31 612	NA	NA	NA	NA
Hopewell city	421	6 102	1 117	1 594	653	119	260	309	50 578	NA	NA	NA	NA
Lexington city	279	3 739	647	19	395	98	147	147	39 442	NA	NA	NA	NA
Lynchburg city	2 188	56 062	9 678	7 009	7 510	2 907	3 513	2 200	39 245	NA	NA	NA	NA
Manassas city	1 486	19 179	3 404	3 539	2 506	426	1 412	1 039	54 168	NA	NA	NA	NA
Manassas Park city	337	3 115	99	284	225	25	149	144	46 261	NA	NA	NA	NA

Table B. States and Counties — **Agriculture**

STATE County	Land in farms					Value of land and buildings (dollars)		Value of machinery and equipment, average per farm (dollars)	Value of products sold				Percent of farms with sales of:		Government payments	
	Acreage (1,000)	Percent change, 2007–2012	Acres: Average size of farm	Total irrigated (1,000)	Total cropland (1,000)	Average per farm	Average per acre		Total (mil dol)	Average per farm (dollars)	Crops	Live-stock and poultry products	$10,000 or more	$100,000 or more	Total ($1,000)	Percent of farms
	117	118	119	120	121	122	123	124	125	126	127	128	129	130	131	132
VIRGINIA—Cont'd																
Louisa	80	2.2	165	0.3	30.1	946 557	5 723	61 971	14.5	29 928	46.9	53.1	36.3	6.0	784	24.5
Lunenburg	83	-0.6	223	0.4	27.7	530 593	2 380	77 668	18.5	49 846	73.2	26.8	33.7	7.3	1 085	33.4
Madison	107	4.1	205	0.1	40.1	1 294 623	6 316	74 799	29.0	55 517	39.8	60.2	51.1	9.2	389	18.2
Mathews	5	5.3	84	0.0	3.2	523 182	6 193	57 909	2.4	43 691	93.0	6.9	32.7	7.3	67	12.7
Mecklenburg	145	-7.5	276	2.8	50.8	710 928	2 575	100 488	42.9	81 395	82.5	17.5	35.9	11.6	1 229	35.5
Middlesex	19	8.3	263	0.5	13.7	1 013 082	3 855	139 068	11.3	154 233	92.5	7.5	38.4	19.2	384	39.7
Montgomery	107	20.0	178	0.3	31.6	867 716	4 878	68 212	23.7	39 315	28.2	71.8	34.7	6.6	219	12.1
Nelson	80	9.3	176	0.9	22.4	805 229	4 581	63 396	15.8	34 741	65.6	34.4	40.7	4.4	116	10.5
New Kent	20	-3.2	144	D	10.5	794 927	5 525	58 759	7.0	51 117	95.9	4.1	24.1	8.0	381	19.0
Northampton	56	-12.1	381	6.3	42.8	1 646 782	4 319	259 687	93.1	633 054	66.0	34.0	73.5	47.6	1 892	50.3
Northumberland	43	-2.5	442	0.0	33.5	1 324 908	3 001	220 061	21.4	217 929	98.3	1.7	60.2	33.7	1 104	60.2
Nottoway	62	-5.7	173	0.1	22.6	539 621	3 120	75 242	48.7	136 778	12.7	87.3	34.6	9.6	413	29.8
Orange	105	0.2	192	0.6	40.5	1 292 497	6 746	95 737	90.6	165 589	71.7	28.3	42.6	9.3	1 081	16.5
Page	71	10.5	131	1.0	28.2	767 554	5 881	84 549	141.1	258 894	4.4	95.6	51.6	25.3	472	17.2
Patrick	79	-1.1	140	0.1	22.9	466 200	3 336	52 781	16.5	29 125	45.3	54.7	36.2	3.0	555	19.6
Pittsylvania	287	4.7	212	3.7	100.4	515 637	2 430	80 956	86.9	64 211	42.5	57.5	38.3	10.0	3 886	36.0
Powhatan	32	7.7	128	0.1	10.6	735 120	5 729	48 592	10.0	40 036	39.1	60.9	25.2	4.0	128	16.0
Prince Edward	79	-4.1	191	0.1	19.7	612 015	3 203	58 479	16.5	39 993	11.6	88.4	29.5	4.8	641	51.6
Prince George	37	-18.2	220	0.0	19.0	922 305	4 202	102 784	10.8	64 449	91.8	8.2	34.7	11.4	903	47.9
Prince William	36	8.6	108	1.0	19.0	953 252	8 827	70 982	12.0	36 467	48.3	51.7	26.1	7.0	240	8.5
Pulaski	97	28.0	217	0.0	26.7	667 404	3 074	78 555	28.1	63 234	8.5	91.5	44.0	7.9	337	11.0
Rappahannock	63	-3.5	158	0.1	17.3	1 335 914	8 443	54 128	9.3	23 378	39.5	60.5	33.0	7.6	147	9.1
Richmond	32	-13.3	360	0.1	22.3	1 036 744	2 882	158 744	15.5	171 856	94.7	5.3	55.6	26.7	684	63.3
Roanoke	31	7.8	112	0.1	7.6	480 689	4 275	47 568	4.1	14 786	D	D	20.0	3.2	13	8.6
Rockbridge	168	21.7	202	0.1	42.1	868 321	4 296	57 385	31.8	38 148	21.9	78.1	41.3	5.3	649	14.3
Rockingham	222	-4.7	117	5.6	100.5	823 606	7 055	88 252	659.0	346 475	7.2	92.8	58.4	35.0	2 741	15.9
Russell	188	23.8	189	0.0	34.0	409 282	2 171	53 826	32.2	32 326	9.1	90.9	36.3	7.2	2 525	32.9
Scott	158	2.9	123	0.1	33.4	254 430	2 076	48 673	14.1	10 892	30.1	69.9	25.3	1.3	999	38.0
Shenandoah	134	-5.5	136	0.7	52.7	760 234	5 580	74 039	128.8	131 394	15.1	84.9	43.2	15.0	1 242	13.7
Smyth	167	30.9	210	0.0	34.3	586 822	2 789	64 580	58.0	73 184	6.6	93.4	43.4	13.8	760	38.1
Southampton	154	-4.8	459	3.2	94.3	1 224 988	2 668	183 934	79.2	236 310	84.6	15.4	53.7	31.9	6 268	75.8
Spotsylvania	42	-19.2	114	0.1	18.7	700 862	6 130	85 612	11.0	29 800	36.4	63.6	27.4	3.3	331	16.0
Stafford	15	-23.0	71	0.0	6.6	650 702	9 168	59 926	2.7	12 740	49.0	51.0	22.3	1.4	71	11.2
Surry	45	9.8	355	1.2	34.0	1 272 142	3 581	126 425	27.7	218 291	69.9	30.1	53.5	23.6	1 198	46.5
Sussex	64	-13.4	522	1.4	39.4	1 189 211	2 277	199 992	37.3	303 065	D	D	56.1	26.8	2 190	71.5
Tazewell	150	-2.3	257	0.0	29.1	569 505	2 215	63 351	27.0	46 267	7.2	92.8	42.3	10.8	572	21.2
Warren	48	0.8	139	0.0	15.8	990 098	7 138	60 844	5.7	16 572	37.4	62.6	24.6	2.6	40	3.2
Washington	192	-3.4	120	0.2	54.2	471 998	3 936	51 363	76.5	47 753	8.7	91.3	35.3	8.1	4 522	38.1
Westmoreland	59	-7.2	391	1.6	36.0	1 396 757	3 576	161 632	35.8	235 250	85.9	14.1	65.8	32.2	1 184	52.6
Wise	26	16.9	157	0.0	3.5	432 818	2 756	42 079	D	D	D	D	20.0	0.6	25	6.1
Wythe	174	9.4	183	0.1	49.5	619 529	3 386	69 486	51.4	54 034	13.0	87.0	47.7	10.7	840	20.7
York	3	116.4	60	0.0	D	298 723	4 991	77 489	2.4	50 830	86.9	13.1	29.8	10.6	5	6.4
Independent cities																
Alexandria city	NA	NA	NA	NA	NA	NA	NA	NA	NA	NA	NA	NA	NA	NA	NA	NA
Bristol city	NA	NA	NA	NA	NA	NA	NA	NA	NA	NA	NA	NA	NA	NA	NA	NA
Buena Vista city	NA	NA	NA	NA	NA	NA	NA	NA	NA	NA	NA	NA	NA	NA	NA	NA
Charlottesville city	NA	NA	NA	NA	NA	NA	NA	NA	NA	NA	NA	NA	NA	NA	NA	NA
Chesapeake city	45	-11.7	178	0.3	37.0	776 672	4 355	98 379	40.5	160 028	D	D	33.2	13.8	570	24.1
Colonial Heights city	NA	NA	NA	NA	NA	NA	NA	NA	NA	NA	NA	NA	NA	NA	NA	NA
Covington city	NA	NA	NA	NA	NA	NA	NA	NA	NA	NA	NA	NA	NA	NA	NA	NA
Danville city	NA	NA	NA	NA	NA	NA	NA	NA	NA	NA	NA	NA	NA	NA	NA	NA
Emporia city	NA	NA	NA	NA	NA	NA	NA	NA	NA	NA	NA	NA	NA	NA	NA	NA
Fairfax city	NA	NA	NA	NA	NA	NA	NA	NA	NA	NA	NA	NA	NA	NA	NA	NA
Falls Church city	NA	NA	NA	NA	NA	NA	NA	NA	NA	NA	NA	NA	NA	NA	NA	NA
Franklin city	NA	NA	NA	NA	NA	NA	NA	NA	NA	NA	NA	NA	NA	NA	NA	NA
Fredericksburg city	NA	NA	NA	NA	NA	NA	NA	NA	NA	NA	NA	NA	NA	NA	NA	NA
Galax city	NA	NA	NA	NA	NA	NA	NA	NA	NA	NA	NA	NA	NA	NA	NA	NA
Hampton city	NA	NA	NA	NA	NA	NA	NA	NA	NA	NA	NA	NA	NA	NA	NA	NA
Harrisonburg city	NA	NA	NA	NA	NA	NA	NA	NA	NA	NA	NA	NA	NA	NA	NA	NA
Hopewell city	NA	NA	NA	NA	NA	NA	NA	NA	NA	NA	NA	NA	NA	NA	NA	NA
Lexington city	NA	NA	NA	NA	NA	NA	NA	NA	NA	NA	NA	NA	NA	NA	NA	NA
Lynchburg city	NA	NA	NA	NA	NA	NA	NA	NA	NA	NA	NA	NA	NA	NA	NA	NA
Manassas city	NA	NA	NA	NA	NA	NA	NA	NA	NA	NA	NA	NA	NA	NA	NA	NA
Manassas Park city	NA	NA	NA	NA	NA	NA	NA	NA	NA	NA	NA	NA	NA	NA	NA	NA

Table B. States and Counties — Water Use, Wholesale Trade, Retail Trade, and Real Estate

STATE County	Water use, 2010		Wholesale trade,[1] 2012				Retail trade,[2] 2012				Real estate and rental and leasing,[2] 2012			
	Total water withdrawn (mil gal/day)	Gallons withdrawn per person per day	Number of establish-ments	Number of employees	Sales (mil dol)	Annual payroll (mil dol)	Number of establish-ments	Number of employees	Sales (mil dol)	Annual payroll (mil dol)	Number of establish-ments	Number of employees	Receipts (mil dol)	Annual payroll (mil dol)
	133	134	135	136	137	138	139	140	141	142	143	144	145	146
VIRGINIA—Cont'd														
Louisa	1 823.7	55 010	11	100	45.3	6.3	77	1 086	276.4	22.9	20	71	10.4	2.5
Lunenburg	5.2	406	6	112	111.2	7.3	36	250	51.3	5.0	1	D	D	D
Madison	2.5	185	13	74	16.5	2.6	40	635	186.4	15.0	4	6	1.0	0.1
Mathews	2.1	231	5	D	D	D	25	232	54.4	4.5	10	D	D	D
Mecklenburg	7.9	241	31	263	159.0	11.1	160	1 677	417.1	35.7	33	131	14.3	3.2
Middlesex	1.9	171	12	83	25.7	3.0	56	437	101.3	9.8	13	D	D	D
Montgomery	33.1	350	46	808	593.0	35.8	324	4 992	1 280.6	108.9	91	535	103.8	19.0
Nelson	5.9	395	4	D	D	D	50	299	115.1	6.3	12	D	D	D
New Kent	30.0	1 628	4	28	13.6	1.2	39	488	155.0	8.8	14	21	2.0	0.5
Northampton	4.2	335	18	160	167.1	5.2	72	543	117.9	10.4	13	43	6.8	0.8
Northumberland	4.2	340	12	69	31.4	2.6	48	352	85.3	7.6	18	39	5.2	1.6
Nottoway	2.4	149	12	98	85.2	3.4	62	607	126.6	12.9	6	14	2.0	0.4
Orange	5.6	166	7	D	D	D	107	970	311.6	24.5	23	41	6.1	1.1
Page	4.0	166	8	D	D	D	76	772	173.9	17.3	11	35	5.5	0.7
Patrick	3.4	183	6	52	21.7	1.9	54	550	204.6	11.0	6	6	0.4	0.1
Pittsylvania	7.6	119	29	771	381.0	21.7	133	868	242.8	16.8	24	86	12.8	1.9
Powhatan	4.3	153	21	156	51.0	6.3	66	550	264.2	17.5	22	67	12.0	1.9
Prince Edward	4.9	209	14	140	41.7	4.8	99	1 488	390.5	35.9	25	99	11.0	1.9
Prince George	17.4	487	24	D	D	D	73	977	260.7	22.7	19	41	9.1	0.9
Prince William	66.2	165	172	2 387	2 222.7	138.3	1 083	20 117	5 638.2	516.7	306	1 242	339.7	50.4
Pulaski	6.8	194	17	114	36.0	3.4	110	1 599	352.7	32.1	21	65	7.8	1.5
Rappahannock	0.8	110	5	22	2.4	0.6	26	150	29.3	3.6	4	D	D	D
Richmond	0.8	84	7	68	72.2	2.5	38	252	68.2	5.6	7	19	1.6	0.3
Roanoke	17.2	186	98	1 168	700.2	66.9	260	3 609	891.0	84.3	104	352	60.4	12.0
Rockbridge	5.0	226	9	53	16.5	1.5	74	1 175	360.1	25.8	13	38	3.6	0.8
Rockingham	38.0	498	56	946	626.3	48.3	206	1 871	429.8	40.3	44	568	110.4	23.9
Russell	11.5	399	14	53	30.0	2.0	81	934	233.2	20.3	13	43	3.5	1.1
Scott	2.2	94	10	D	D	D	78	709	210.5	13.5	5	11	1.5	0.3
Shenandoah	30.5	727	18	440	519.7	15.5	150	1 705	499.5	36.1	30	D	D	D
Smyth	19.8	614	16	D	D	D	114	1 202	272.0	24.0	15	43	7.1	1.4
Southampton	8.6	461	10	142	131.2	5.9	30	236	55.7	4.4	8	20	2.5	0.4
Spotsylvania	13.9	113	64	678	341.7	31.3	402	6 758	2 160.1	184.4	113	508	77.9	18.1
Stafford	13.7	106	47	D	D	D	253	4 489	1 247.9	111.3	89	298	58.1	10.2
Surry	1 908.5	270 397	1	D	D	D	12	53	14.9	1.0	3	D	D	D
Sussex	2.1	171	9	D	D	D	43	332	112.6	6.8	5	13	2.2	0.4
Tazewell	5.0	110	60	527	265.7	22.1	212	3 044	804.6	65.9	50	170	24.9	4.6
Warren	11.4	303	7	D	D	D	137	1 718	444.6	40.2	22	71	9.9	1.9
Washington	59.9	1 091	38	D	D	D	206	3 207	820.5	67.8	46	127	26.1	5.1
Westmoreland	4.8	273	16	48	31.2	1.7	45	415	109.8	8.7	12	22	2.1	0.4
Wise	5.3	127	37	345	299.7	16.4	168	2 092	500.9	45.1	23	69	7.3	1.5
Wythe	16.6	567	13	D	D	D	137	1 922	905.5	44.0	22	75	21.7	2.5
York	781.4	11 936	34	139	80.0	6.1	220	3 922	884.4	86.9	50	256	28.2	7.9
Independent cities														
Alexandria city	0.0	0	82	1 139	502.8	61.6	480	7 180	2 416.0	222.6	240	1 475	524.1	76.6
Bristol city	0.0	0	34	802	370.4	22.5	157	1 732	349.9	33.6	23	69	9.9	2.0
Buena Vista city	0.2	24	1	D	D	D	19	156	34.8	3.0	3	4	0.4	0.0
Charlottesville city	0.2	4	48	513	183.3	23.7	331	3 925	747.9	82.8	99	502	107.6	19.7
Chesapeake city	544.0	2 448	239	3 447	2 225.2	169.7	789	15 088	4 114.9	336.7	273	1 227	291.6	52.9
Colonial Heights city	0.0	1	10	53	19.7	2.0	180	3 498	763.3	65.3	27	151	31.6	4.5
Covington city	2.0	330	6	D	D	D	60	734	158.3	15.8	9	24	2.5	0.5
Danville city	7.2	168	50	545	285.2	24.5	306	4 165	965.0	87.2	64	339	48.7	9.1
Emporia city	0.0	7	3	D	D	D	52	620	136.5	13.5	11	36	4.6	0.8
Fairfax city	0.1	5	40	372	408.9	18.2	251	5 526	1 757.5	176.4	60	261	61.3	13.5
Falls Church city	0.0	2	18	D	D	D	92	1 010	310.2	35.9	35	192	71.7	9.3
Franklin city	1.1	122	7	52	28.3	1.8	63	979	228.3	21.6	11	D	D	D
Fredericksburg city	0.3	14	21	224	95.3	11.8	253	4 098	1 075.0	88.1	70	308	63.3	12.5
Galax city	1.9	275	5	69	117.5	3.0	64	1 105	259.6	24.3	13	52	9.9	1.6
Hampton city	0.3	2	71	886	344.7	39.3	436	6 791	1 512.5	148.3	114	750	117.3	23.7
Harrisonburg city	0.4	8	57	1 006	405.9	43.2	334	5 664	1 519.8	144.6	72	351	75.9	10.9
Hopewell city	130.5	5 775	11	84	26.9	3.5	73	586	164.8	13.1	22	97	20.3	3.7
Lexington city	0.0	0	NA	NA	NA	NA	44	458	92.7	9.4	17	32	4.4	1.0
Lynchburg city	0.2	2	69	877	509.0	39.0	385	7 371	1 995.2	178.2	109	447	79.9	14.5
Manassas city	0.1	2	41	D	D	D	194	2 778	895.3	86.1	52	229	64.0	11.4
Manassas Park city	0.0	1	23	281	170.8	17.1	31	240	124.7	7.5	9	33	7.3	1.3

1. Merchant wholesalers, except manufacturers' sales branches and offices.   2. Employer establishments.

Table B. States and Counties — Professional Services, Manufacturing, and Accommodation and Food Services

STATE County	Professional, scientific, and technical services, 2012				Manufacturing, 2012				Accommodation and food services, 2012			
	Number of establishments	Number of employees	Receipts (mil dol)	Annual payroll (mil dol)	Number of establishments	Number of employees	Receipts (mil dol)	Annual payroll (mil dol)	Number of establishments	Number of employees	Sales (mil dol)	Annual payroll (mil dol)
	147	148	149	150	151	152	153	154	155	156	157	158
VIRGINIA—Cont'd												
Louisa	57	188	16.2	5.4	32	1 162	426.8	58.2	30	348	18.2	4.8
Lunenburg	10	44	3.9	1.1	7	429	99.4	12.9	8	D	D	D
Madison	22	51	5.4	1.6	18	250	D	8.5	18	190	9.4	2.8
Mathews	19	D	D	D	3	D	D	D	13	178	6.4	1.7
Mecklenburg	49	264	26.3	9.2	34	1 338	298.0	49.4	67	1 179	46.6	12.7
Middlesex	28	150	8.7	4.7	12	133	D	4.9	26	190	9.5	3.1
Montgomery	267	2 714	265.2	142.7	50	3 054	936.8	159.8	197	4 223	186.5	53.5
Nelson	42	140	14.7	5.5	27	268	D	9.0	20	168	6.4	1.9
New Kent	28	94	7.7	3.4	14	157	D	4.6	29	D	29.0	6.9
Northampton	21	56	4.7	1.8	9	397	D	13.8	40	476	D	D
Northumberland	21	91	20.4	4.5	21	426	D	14.9	20	134	5.7	2.0
Nottoway	19	93	6.8	2.5	12	329	104.3	12.7	27	335	12.7	3.8
Orange	74	302	52.6	14.7	18	836	230.0	34.0	58	850	36.3	10.3
Page	25	164	15.4	5.3	13	552	161.5	15.6	56	652	39.9	11.1
Patrick	18	67	3.4	1.4	35	1 342	189.2	39.9	20	163	7.0	1.7
Pittsylvania	47	149	19.3	4.8	45	1 959	615.9	82.0	38	421	15.5	4.7
Powhatan	62	249	27.4	11.1	19	99	D	D	25	494	17.1	5.4
Prince Edward	34	111	8.6	3.0	14	107	D	2.9	49	1 148	49.9	13.9
Prince George	49	695	89.4	35.1	24	839	602.9	42.3	45	668	39.3	8.8
Prince William	1 067	10 927	1 557.4	753.1	94	1 634	353.1	75.2	633	11 867	673.7	177.6
Pulaski	38	170	17.2	7.8	39	3 797	2 861.3	183.6	74	1 148	53.4	14.1
Rappahannock	29	77	9.1	3.2	7	36	D	0.9	14	D	D	D
Richmond	13	42	4.8	2.4	7	122	D	4.8	13	122	6.2	1.6
Roanoke	217	1 101	124.5	49.8	63	3 134	815.7	164.8	132	2 663	128.3	32.4
Rockbridge	28	89	7.8	2.9	20	1 203	197.6	42.3	52	802	44.3	11.9
Rockingham	76	565	75.6	32.5	88	7 047	5 397.1	323.0	91	2 128	82.7	35.7
Russell	46	634	80.9	42.0	9	345	D	10.7	38	504	19.3	5.7
Scott	22	102	10.6	3.9	9	962	486.8	37.8	24	D	D	D
Shenandoah	63	262	33.2	14.4	35	3 271	796.2	109.7	81	1 365	56.0	17.1
Smyth	37	198	14.7	6.4	40	3 129	833.0	128.8	45	727	29.0	8.1
Southampton	11	D	D	D	12	411	106.4	15.0	13	84	3.8	1.0
Spotsylvania	227	2 219	424.7	190.8	59	1 517	D	67.7	203	3 880	190.4	53.4
Stafford	318	3 786	677.6	268.6	39	768	171.1	31.7	183	3 102	161.4	40.9
Surry	7	21	1.2	0.5	3	108	D	3.7	5	39	1.6	0.4
Sussex	7	D	D	D	9	120	D	6.2	13	239	11.7	3.1
Tazewell	60	443	39.8	16.3	53	1 294	297.8	60.0	71	1 245	59.6	16.1
Warren	77	277	28.3	12.8	25	810	811.8	41.1	79	1 203	61.2	18.0
Washington	94	642	49.0	26.5	66	3 763	1 095.6	153.6	96	D	D	D
Westmoreland	30	235	14.4	8.3	9	560	167.0	12.9	31	D	D	D
Wise	58	423	38.4	18.1	26	303	D	12.4	55	1 130	42.1	12.2
Wythe	43	204	20.8	8.9	40	1 705	1 292.9	71.6	83	1 509	78.3	19.4
York	177	D	D	D	27	D	D	8.9	155	3 804	269.9	56.2
Independent cities												
Alexandria city	1 238	18 505	3 799.3	1 692.1	72	1 332	273.0	57.9	387	8 051	647.5	180.7
Bristol city	44	239	24.2	13.0	23	1 057	302.3	48.6	82	1 811	86.8	23.8
Buena Vista city	6	20	1.3	0.5	14	894	351.4	39.1	12	D	D	D
Charlottesville city	322	2 555	406.5	164.9	46	455	98.7	21.6	*466	5 199	293.3	75.9
Chesapeake city	510	D	D	D	130	3 965	1 504.2	211.6	466	10 267	447.6	121.1
Colonial Heights city	50	491	21.5	8.3	8	129	D	5.4	82	2 180	99.9	27.8
Covington city	19	52	6.5	1.2	6	D	D	D	20	D	D	D
Danville city	74	522	71.0	31.7	46	4 635	1 703.0	223.7	139	2 850	120.4	33.6
Emporia city	18	79	4.7	1.9	9	850	203.7	35.3	26	586	25.1	7.2
Fairfax city	647	6 022	1 368.7	522.1	29	158	18.8	6.3	192	3 608	218.6	60.9
Falls Church city	157	1 798	352.4	136.3	17	74	16.1	3.4	119	1 098	73.5	19.1
Franklin city	20	200	12.5	6.2	6	27	8.5	1.3	28	484	20.3	5.1
Fredericksburg city	180	1 390	227.1	99.5	26	221	57.0	8.3	165	3 718	179.5	55.4
Galax city	26	138	12.8	4.4	12	719	157.9	18.6	39	540	22.7	7.1
Hampton city	279	3 711	648.1	289.6	68	2 189	508.3	114.9	250	5 380	249.0	72.2
Harrisonburg city	139	924	98.8	43.9	46	2 556	832.6	99.4	186	4 468	216.0	58.8
Hopewell city	35	184	16.8	7.5	16	1 338	1 930.8	110.8	52	728	33.5	8.2
Lexington city	29	121	10.5	3.7	5	14	D	D	52	540	34.2	9.3
Lynchburg city	200	3 395	969.0	265.2	83	8 339	2 749.6	504.3	215	5 071	216.4	61.0
Manassas city	213	3 462	612.2	285.9	32	4 012	1 365.7	366.4	109	1 587	91.4	24.7
Manassas Park city	23	153	18.2	10.3	12	237	29.6	8.1	14	89	5.6	1.8

1. Establishment subject to federal tax.

Health Care and Social Assistance, Other Services, Nonemployer Businesses, and Residential Construction

STATE County	Health care and social assistance, 2012				Other services, 2012				Nonemployer businesses, 2015		Value of residential construction authorized by building permits, 2016	
	Number of establishments	Number of employees	Receipts (mil dol)	Annual payroll (mil dol)	Number of establishments	Number of employees	Receipts (mil dol)	Annual payroll (mil dol)	Number	Receipts (mil dol)	New Construction ($1,000)	Number of housing units
	159	160	161	162	163	164	165	166	167	168	169	170
VIRGINIA—Cont'd												
Louisa	25	299	24.6	10.4	47	D	D	D	2 214	85.9	47 206	249
Lunenburg	16	326	11.3	5.5	12	D	D	D	561	22.2	4 830	24
Madison	21	286	13.8	6.7	21	D	D	D	1 144	39.6	12 616	44
Mathews	9	D	D	D	12	D	D	D	795	31.4	5 790	26
Mecklenburg	75	1 843	153.7	62.3	68	333	23.7	6.9	1 626	67.8	15 370	67
Middlesex	20	440	23.2	9.5	25	D	D	D	1 057	40.7	1 000	33
Montgomery	224	3 898	489.7	167.8	148	814	165.6	23.1	5 024	211.5	65 363	422
Nelson	20	D	D	D	21	181	13.1	4.9	1 289	53.0	13 414	51
New Kent	25	610	37.2	17.0	29	D	D	D	1 593	64.3	39 582	221
Northampton	40	942	97.8	34.3	20	D	D	D	1 013	37.1	6 158	31
Northumberland	11	84	3.1	1.6	26	D	D	D	1 128	44.2	14 737	68
Nottoway	28	959	48.7	25.9	25	D	D	D	647	18.3	4 033	28
Orange	45	389	23.9	10.0	56	373	36.9	10.8	2 326	89.9	29 846	132
Page	24	479	46.8	17.6	35	D	D	D	1 441	51.2	7 880	59
Patrick	23	673	40.5	17.4	13	D	D	D	1 037	31.7	5 828	27
Pittsylvania	52	1 120	51.6	23.3	72	281	23.5	6.5	3 143	103.1	10 648	52
Powhatan	27	D	D	D	57	344	24.2	7.6	2 087	97.6	40 256	210
Prince Edward	82	1 697	135.0	59.4	35	160	14.5	3.5	990	32.6	6 878	49
Prince George	25	159	18.1	8.3	32	143	12.2	4.4	1 517	53.2	12 273	81
Prince William	718	9 320	993.6	387.7	537	3 703	653.2	116.1	34 412	1 366.8	289 196	1 916
Pulaski	57	1 109	108.8	43.8	43	208	20.8	5.5	1 490	48.0	6 831	35
Rappahannock	10	D	D	D	9	D	D	D	976	46.8	4 121	18
Richmond	15	802	27.2	13.5	12	D	D	D	545	18.5	17 693	35
Roanoke	229	4 773	381.7	174.4	142	695	53.8	17.5	5 566	222.4	27 686	154
Rockbridge	39	356	24.2	9.8	28	D	D	D	1 549	58.6	12 207	60
Rockingham	100	4 573	496.7	202.5	104	474	42.1	13.5	5 469	241.0	117 601	493
Russell	65	1 199	97.1	41.9	27	D	D	D	1 109	33.3	3 453	21
Scott	37	679	39.4	18.5	15	D	D	D	883	27.1	2 315	20
Shenandoah	74	1 273	109.4	46.0	81	379	33.6	9.0	2 860	104.7	18 048	104
Smyth	65	1 756	143.8	66.6	35	179	18.5	4.7	1 450	51.5	3 835	19
Southampton	10	143	7.8	3.9	14	D	D	D	876	26.9	5 892	40
Spotsylvania	198	3 021	262.5	122.9	173	1 021	86.9	26.8	8 320	330.3	109 564	420
Stafford	173	3 363	287.0	118.9	199	1 195	107.4	35.2	8 520	331.7	246 900	1 370
Surry	4	11	0.9	0.4	2	D	D	D	334	11.0	4 033	27
Sussex	14	D	D	D	19	D	D	D	435	14.2	3 720	24
Tazewell	140	2 377	209.2	80.2	92	605	71.7	20.8	2 078	73.2	2 999	12
Warren	61	D	D	D	68	517	74.3	13.5	2 653	109.3	32 592	145
Washington	150	2 410	258.4	108.1	62	D	D	D	3 409	127.1	15 952	74
Westmoreland	18	238	13.2	6.7	27	88	4.8	1.4	1 250	40.9	10 375	72
Wise	93	1 598	125.1	46.5	53	D	D	D	1 555	43.8	1 470	11
Wythe	75	1 274	108.6	47.1	55	324	27.2	8.7	1 503	55.7	11 723	63
York	107	1 667	215.8	81.2	116	D	D	D	3 659	137.0	18 599	88
Independent cities												
Alexandria city	397	7 356	1 041.6	376.9	584	9 997	2 626.4	670.0	15 348	733.5	84 900	621
Bristol city	48	654	54.7	18.6	46	D	D	D	968	38.2	5 361	51
Buena Vista city	12	183	5.1	2.7	9	D	D	D	284	9.4	100	1
Charlottesville city	175	D	D	D	151	1 444	318.3	52.5	4 048	222.1	34 689	197
Chesapeake city	497	9 693	978.2	435.2	399	2 990	313.4	95.8	13 636	510.4	297 574	1 065
Colonial Heights city	108	1 746	139.9	56.8	50	357	25.0	8.8	948	41.0	553	4
Covington city	17	•178	8.8	2.9	22	D	D	D	231	9.4	0	0
Danville city	194	4 803	441.4	188.5	101	535	49.2	11.2	2 422	76.2	660	5
Emporia city	37	1 078	80.1	34.4	18	D	D	D	275	9.3	225	3
Fairfax city	265	3 637	339.1	135.3	146	1 531	424.5	77.8	3 362	254.3	22 467	274
Falls Church city	108	D	D	D	93	588	69.5	22.6	1 355	88.7	8 275	20
Franklin city	52	1 200	105.1	39.4	26	182	12.3	3.1	440	14.7	0	0
Fredericksburg city	189	5 216	789.2	335.8	104	860	69.9	22.8	1 954	105.4	23 019	190
Galax city	45	D	D	D	24	D	D	D	408	13.1	291	4
Hampton city	265	7 739	888.7	394.2	176	1 056	87.5	25.0	6 773	190.6	9 214	149
Harrisonburg city	163	2 860	211.7	96.1	127	690	67.3	18.2	2 588	118.4	24 849	151
Hopewell city	49	1 450	144.0	60.4	38	200	16.7	5.1	860	24.4	4 260	47
Lexington city	41	669	69.2	23.4	34	229	31.0	7.4	437	15.1	5 691	6
Lynchburg city	268	9 339	1 046.5	427.9	173	1 161	100.6	30.6	4 157	155.0	16 471	154
Manassas city	174	3 297	418.2	176.8	141	848	93.5	26.4	3 302	151.9	20 436	145
Manassas Park city	5	D	D	D	52	D	D	D	1 249	56.9	0	0

Table B. States and Counties — Government Employment and Payroll, and Local Government Finances

STATE County	Government employment and payroll, 2012									Local government finances, 2012				
			March payroll (percent of total)							General revenue				
												Taxes		
													Per capita[1] (dollars)	
	Full-time equivalent employees	March payroll (dollars)	Administration, judicial, and legal	Police and Corrections	Fire Protection	Highways and transportation	Health and Welfare	Natural resources and utilities	Education and libraries	Total (mil dol)	Inter-governmental (mil dol)	Total (mil dol)	Total	Property
	171	172	173	174	175	176	177	178	179	180	181	182	183	184
VIRGINIA—Cont'd														
Louisa	1 124	3 411 101	8.2	6.8	4.2	0.0	1.1	4.9	73.3	96.7	33.7	53.8	1 609	1 418
Lunenburg	403	1 190 954	9.0	11.5	0.0	0.0	2.3	2.4	72.9	33.1	20.6	9.9	790	676
Madison	403	1 326 277	10.7	6.4	0.0	0.0	5.8	0.3	69.8	34.3	15.7	16.2	1 227	1 036
Mathews	358	848 780	8.9	7.2	0.0	0.0	5.4	0.0	74.9	23.0	9.7	12.1	1 364	1 166
Mecklenburg	1 375	3 603 811	7.0	12.8	0.2	1.1	10.7	2.6	62.8	94.5	47.2	37.6	1 185	856
Middlesex	280	843 355	10.1	15.3	0.0	0.0	3.5	0.8	70.3	25.5	8.9	15.3	1 409	1 212
Montgomery	2 699	8 781 181	9.0	11.9	0.5	4.6	2.7	5.5	61.5	255.0	103.6	112.5	1 182	829
Nelson	457	1 391 646	8.9	4.1	0.0	0.0	1.6	0.5	80.1	45.2	17.7	23.6	1 590	1 346
New Kent	638	2 123 526	10.3	8.3	5.3	0.3	4.1	7.3	63.1	52.7	21.7	26.8	1 400	1 195
Northampton	850	3 278 000	5.0	9.0	0.0	20.1	6.5	3.2	55.2	101.7	23.0	21.3	1 740	1 417
Northumberland	358	1 244 110	8.2	7.7	0.0	0.0	4.8	0.9	77.1	28.9	10.2	17.4	1 407	1 269
Nottoway	548	1 646 561	8.1	8.7	0.0	2.8	5.9	4.4	67.2	39.4	23.9	10.3	650	454
Orange	1 173	3 380 570	7.0	14.3	3.2	1.7	2.2	2.9	67.7	89.1	37.1	42.7	1 247	997
Page	878	2 456 816	8.1	13.4	0.0	0.6	1.8	3.8	71.0	65.3	32.2	27.2	1 138	890
Patrick	695	1 689 450	5.6	12.0	0.0	0.0	4.5	0.8	75.3	43.9	24.0	14.5	784	617
Pittsylvania	1 563	4 924 209	5.8	7.5	0.1	0.5	1.4	1.2	80.6	127.9	84.1	37.6	599	478
Powhatan	855	2 784 066	7.2	7.7	0.5	0.0	3.4	1.3	77.9	69.7	28.5	38.3	1 361	1 230
Prince Edward	701	2 116 144	10.4	10.6	0.3	3.1	2.0	3.4	66.4	54.6	29.8	19.8	852	490
Prince George	1 519	5 308 620	5.9	28.6	0.9	0.0	2.5	1.5	58.6	118.9	72.6	36.1	976	765
Prince William	15 485	68 447 361	3.7	8.8	4.5	3.3	4.4	3.5	69.0	1 578.6	659.7	752.7	1 749	1 412
Pulaski	1 288	4 175 730	6.1	8.3	0.9	1.1	3.6	5.9	68.5	117.9	56.3	35.2	1 013	707
Rappahannock	256	760 848	9.7	11.1	0.0	0.0	6.5	0.8	68.9	20.6	4.6	14.7	1 978	1 804
Richmond	326	1 099 371	6.8	32.6	0.0	0.0	0.6	2.6	56.3	32.9	20.4	9.1	1 002	790
Roanoke	3 729	13 158 244	7.7	7.6	6.2	0.3	4.8	9.4	62.7	353.7	116.0	158.3	1 704	1 275
Rockbridge	661	1 852 653	7.0	8.7	0.0	0.3	5.5	2.1	74.0	71.1	30.7	29.1	1 299	943
Rockingham	2 706	8 346 966	7.1	8.4	3.0	0.8	4.8	4.5	70.2	227.8	108.4	83.5	1 079	895
Russell	1 094	4 018 658	3.7	6.4	0.2	1.1	0.2	2.5	83.0	73.8	48.1	20.2	710	482
Scott	721	2 170 415	5.9	6.0	0.0	0.8	3.3	2.2	79.1	62.5	41.3	16.4	722	496
Shenandoah	1 504	4 472 709	7.1	9.2	3.6	1.5	4.6	6.2	65.6	123.4	60.3	48.9	1 149	882
Smyth	1 259	3 570 921	6.6	8.1	0.4	1.0	11.3	5.6	65.4	92.2	58.8	22.8	718	494
Southampton	717	2 092 925	8.4	10.2	0.0	0.2	6.0	3.3	70.4	53.2	26.3	21.4	1 162	1 013
Spotsylvania	3 637	13 506 224	7.0	5.7	4.9	0.0	3.5	3.8	72.0	382.7	163.4	188.0	1 496	1 158
Stafford	4 475	17 648 377	6.1	5.1	2.8	0.2	2.7	4.7	77.1	448.6	192.3	213.9	1 592	1 307
Surry	386	1 034 084	6.2	6.4	0.0	0.0	0.8	3.6	77.4	29.5	7.5	21.1	3 078	2 927
Sussex	423	1 312 782	12.9	14.1	0.0	0.2	7.5	2.3	61.1	40.7	22.0	10.1	843	685
Tazewell	1 644	4 416 984	7.8	8.5	0.4	2.1	7.4	4.0	67.6	142.1	75.0	40.0	903	580
Warren	1 201	3 547 039	8.8	13.4	0.9	2.4	2.5	5.2	65.3	103.2	45.3	48.1	1 264	942
Washington	2 294	6 382 778	4.2	19.7	0.0	2.6	2.7	7.4	62.3	154.9	83.7	51.1	926	645
Westmoreland	590	1 733 294	11.3	10.8	0.0	0.5	7.2	2.7	66.0	47.8	21.1	21.6	1 230	999
Wise	1 524	4 814 554	7.6	7.5	0.1	1.5	2.6	6.1	72.2	146.0	82.3	52.0	1 271	712
Wythe	1 424	3 649 638	5.6	26.2	0.3	2.6	1.1	5.5	55.4	100.6	52.2	30.2	1 032	628
York	2 630	9 095 299	7.9	5.3	7.7	0.0	3.3	2.6	66.6	226.0	92.7	107.0	1 618	1 182
Independent cities														
Alexandria city	5 221	27 072 935	10.0	12.5	7.7	2.6	11.9	7.2	44.7	658.7	76.2	498.6	3 408	2 503
Bristol city	765	2 448 312	7.6	15.4	6.1	3.8	8.9	3.5	53.6	72.5	36.3	26.8	1 519	788
Buena Vista city	329	965 276	10.8	5.3	0.0	3.3	1.3	7.0	71.5	22.5	12.2	6.9	1 023	765
Charlottesville city	2 284	8 528 975	9.8	5.8	3.3	6.0	4.6	8.3	55.8	212.5	76.7	93.0	2 116	1 314
Chesapeake city	11 013	41 054 055	4.1	9.2	5.0	1.7	24.6	3.7	49.6	1 127.4	370.1	422.6	2 297	1 225
Colonial Heights city	802	3 016 516	7.0	9.3	9.1	2.9	0.6	5.1	64.2	74.5	26.0	40.1	1 850	1 301
Covington city	279	921 554	6.6	10.3	0.0	0.0	7.9	9.3	65.9	26.1	10.0	11.0	1 904	1 291
Danville city	2 451	7 816 325	9.2	11.3	5.7	3.0	4.1	10.7	51.6	173.3	85.4	50.7	1 180	635
Emporia city	121	358 410	26.1	32.7	0.8	10.3	9.0	14.9	0.0	22.4	7.1	10.4	1 814	786
Fairfax city	414	2 320 342	17.7	23.1	21.4	10.9	3.8	13.9	0.0	121.0	20.6	87.1	3 711	2 469
Falls Church city	720	3 347 248	12.1	9.0	0.2	2.9	0.5	11.6	62.0	84.9	11.0	58.9	4 454	3 374
Franklin city	602	1 874 981	4.7	34.1	3.4	2.6	4.5	7.4	40.0	43.1	23.9	11.8	1 389	766
Fredericksburg city	1 610	5 694 248	7.8	27.8	4.3	5.6	3.2	3.1	44.2	149.0	48.1	67.8	2 483	1 244
Galax city	414	1 172 160	3.5	10.4	0.0	4.3	9.1	11.5	57.5	25.9	13.1	8.9	1 283	595
Hampton city	6 125	20 173 326	6.9	11.1	6.0	1.0	6.7	5.9	61.4	526.3	220.7	218.7	1 599	1 068
Harrisonburg city	1 474	5 157 943	4.1	7.6	6.7	5.8	3.6	11.7	53.6	162.1	48.7	63.4	1 244	631
Hopewell city	1 107	3 758 446	8.1	8.6	4.7	2.5	4.1	11.7	58.7	102.8	47.0	32.3	1 448	1 059
Lexington city	273	881 406	8.8	24.4	4.0	7.7	2.1	13.4	30.0	22.6	6.6	7.8	1 109	687
Lynchburg city	3 057	9 313 489	8.7	9.6	8.0	2.9	7.1	8.5	52.5	265.1	109.0	117.5	1 524	905
Manassas city	1 551	7 149 920	5.0	8.7	4.1	2.5	2.9	8.2	67.1	180.9	61.7	83.5	2 055	1 564
Manassas Park city	547	2 174 966	6.3	8.6	5.6	0.7	1.8	6.3	67.3	58.7	24.8	25.4	1 608	1 293

1. Based on the resident population estimated as of July 1 of the year shown.

STATE County	Local government finances, 2012 (cont.)									Government employment, 2015			Individual income tax returns, 2014		
	Direct general expenditure							Debt outstanding							
			Percent of total for:												
	Total (mil dol)	Per capita[1] (dollars)	Education	Health and hospitals	Police protection	Public welfare	Highways	Total (mil dol)	Per capita[1] (dollars)	Federal civilian	Federal military	State and local	Number of returns	Mean adjusted gross income	Mean income tax
	185	186	187	188	189	190	191	192	193	194	195	196	197	198	199
VIRGINIA—Cont'd															
Louisa	99.6	2 980	58.3	1.2	5.3	6.6	0.3	25.5	763	55	108	1 528	15 470	56 163	5 902
Lunenburg	35.6	2 826	62.6	1.1	5.0	6.7	2.1	26.9	2 134	18	36	766	4 850	40 259	3 361
Madison	32.1	2 431	58.6	4.5	8.2	11.2	0.0	15.3	1 157	64	41	537	6 040	55 246	5 953
Mathews	20.3	2 283	58.0	0.8	7.8	7.9	0.7	9.8	1 108	15	64	363	4 240	59 824	6 934
Mecklenburg	89.8	2 829	48.3	6.5	7.0	4.6	2.7	33.6	1 059	113	95	1 796	13 360	42 904	4 113
Middlesex	23.8	2 198	52.5	2.0	5.6	6.1	0.0	22.7	2 100	18	32	1 009	5 150	54 681	5 980
Montgomery	258.1	2 711	48.5	0.4	8.4	3.5	4.9	475.3	4 993	[3]335	[3]389	[3]17 511	34 650	59 307	7 059
Nelson	40.8	2 750	59.8	0.5	7.1	4.4	0.7	45.5	3 068	58	46	679	7 300	55 848	6 148
New Kent	49.4	2 579	54.5	1.0	4.6	4.2	0.0	60.4	3 152	41	62	936	9 840	77 808	10 568
Northampton	81.1	6 632	27.6	1.0	3.1	3.3	15.7	159.5	13 045	31	65	911	5 910	45 738	4 903
Northumberland	27.3	2 213	57.8	1.2	7.1	6.9	1.7	42.0	3 401	28	38	446	5 930	58 994	6 680
Nottoway	38.9	2 460	57.3	0.4	7.7	6.1	2.3	16.5	1 044	345	55	2 528	6 120	42 297	3 566
Orange	87.3	2 548	55.7	0.6	6.4	3.0	2.0	124.0	3 620	54	109	2 195	16 370	56 994	5 953
Page	66.1	2 765	55.3	0.9	7.9	5.0	2.0	77.1	3 228	185	74	1 135	10 570	41 251	3 520
Patrick	36.7	1 989	67.6	1.0	5.6	2.7	0.2	44.5	2 411	44	56	820	7 230	40 148	3 377
Pittsylvania	127.3	2 026	65.4	0.5	5.2	7.6	0.3	112.9	1 797	[4]198	[4]321	[4]6 527	26 780	44 086	4 054
Powhatan	65.5	2 328	65.3	0.3	6.2	5.1	0.0	103.3	3 675	49	84	2 115	12 950	74 084	9 355
Prince Edward	54.4	2 342	50.0	0.5	7.0	7.1	5.6	67.7	2 914	74	59	2 305	7 830	42 367	3 797
Prince George	134.6	3 644	45.1	2.0	4.5	2.6	0.3	173.0	4 684	[5]5 150	[5]9 011	[5]3 117	15 320	56 999	5 534
Prince William	1 678.9	3 902	57.5	1.9	5.9	2.5	1.6	1 440.8	3 349	[6]7 209	[6]8 712	[6]23 612	209 820	74 249	8 984
Pulaski	110.5	3 181	43.4	0.7	5.8	9.2	2.0	71.9	2 069	35	104	2 384	14 550	46 199	4 262
Rappahannock	21.0	2 817	57.1	0.7	5.0	4.4	0.0	10.8	1 446	20	23	303	3 610	68 827	9 352
Richmond	32.3	3 565	42.0	0.6	4.9	5.4	0.1	11.6	1 280	28	25	1 058	3 360	44 572	3 790
Roanoke	397.1	4 275	42.0	6.5	5.5	3.6	0.2	497.3	5 353	[7]2 191	[7]364	[7]6 772	45 860	64 845	7 954
Rockbridge	69.2	3 088	45.1	10.9	3.4	9.5	0.0	67.1	2 995	[8]94	[8]146	[8]2 586	9 980	52 599	5 498
Rockingham	234.6	3 031	52.1	2.8	3.5	11.4	1.3	200.1	2 585	[9]349	[9]393	[9]10 814	36 250	54 069	5 601
Russell	71.0	2 495	57.5	0.7	4.1	8.4	6.4	22.5	790	63	86	1 387	10 000	43 816	3 975
Scott	60.2	2 640	60.3	0.7	6.9	7.1	1.4	30.5	1 339	56	67	1 168	8 170	40 167	3 176
Shenandoah	116.2	2 729	54.8	0.6	6.7	6.1	3.0	146.9	3 449	130	134	1 986	20 450	49 338	4 905
Smyth	94.6	2 984	50.5	0.9	6.6	10.5	2.3	141.0	4 444	76	96	2 913	12 710	39 938	3 085
Southampton	56.0	3 044	56.1	0.8	3.6	3.8	0.2	67.3	3 657	[10]72	[10]78	[10]2 536	7 570	48 100	4 287
Spotsylvania	378.7	3 013	60.7	0.4	4.3	4.3	2.1	483.9	3 850	[11]404	[11]491	[11]9 716	60 050	65 371	7 373
Stafford	443.1	3 298	62.9	0.3	5.0	3.4	1.5	601.1	4 474	4 444	602	6 238	62 560	76 271	9 050
Surry	27.8	4 061	61.1	1.2	4.9	7.5	0.0	16.2	2 369	D	21	520	3 180	49 181	4 555
Sussex	39.1	3 269	58.6	0.5	7.2	7.5	0.1	26.7	2 229	50	29	1 271	4 470	39 191	3 165
Tazewell	136.7	3 088	44.7	17.2	6.0	6.5	4.1	52.5	1 186	71	129	3 391	16 070	50 128	5 407
Warren	120.1	3 155	38.6	12.5	6.5	5.4	1.5	214.6	5 637	176	120	1 836	18 260	55 668	5 863
Washington	172.4	3 125	41.6	10.5	5.9	3.9	1.1	101.3	1 835	[12]224	[12]223	[12]4 699	22 510	53 296	6 262
Westmoreland	49.6	2 832	53.8	0.8	8.0	6.1	1.5	23.2	1 322	50	55	836	8 340	49 317	4 965
Wise	142.7	3 487	49.3	6.0	6.1	9.8	4.4	186.8	4 565	[13]217	[13]128	[13]4 234	13 850	42 577	3 918
Wythe	103.2	3 530	39.8	0.1	5.8	6.6	2.0	150.9	5 159	87	91	2 357	12 560	43 208	3 837
York	226.9	3 430	55.6	0.6	4.0	2.9	0.0	176.3	2 665	[14]1 025	[14]1 766	[14]3 616	31 660	74 359	9 205
Independent cities															
Alexandria city	692.1	4 731	34.7	6.0	9.7	6.4	3.7	714.3	4 882	14 793	1 402	8 220	83 210	99 708	16 906
Bristol city	80.9	4 578	41.9	3.1	10.9	5.1	11.6	60.4	3 418	[12]	[12]	[12]	7 120	44 853	3 924
Buena Vista city	21.2	3 164	51.2	2.1	6.2	6.2	4.2	43.1	6 424	[8]	[8]	[8]	2 830	35 481	2 572
Charlottesville city	227.5	5 176	31.3	8.0	7.2	11.1	6.4	151.8	3 454	[15]	[15]	[15]	20 320	87 852	14 555
Chesapeake city	1 112.4	4 870	42.2	24.6	3.6	2.6	4.4	886.9	3 883	1 110	1 603	14 452	110 410	60 066	6 448
Colonial Heights city	69.5	3 974	51.8	0.0	5.3	0.6	4.6	61.6	3 526	[16]	[16]	[16]	8 900	47 820	4 380
Covington city	33.2	5 752	46.0	0.3	7.1	5.4	4.1	55.3	9 583	[17]	[17]	[17]	2 780	38 717	3 227
Danville city	179.2	4 169	41.3	2.3	5.5	4.2	5.7	156.0	3 628	[4]	[4]	[4]	18 330	38 617	3 790
Emporia city	22.3	3 882	17.9	1.2	14.0	1.4	4.2	14.6	2 551	[18]	[18]	[18]	2 670	33 213	2 598
Fairfax city	112.7	4 804	34.1	0.9	9.6	1.5	4.8	321.3	13 695	[19]	[19]	[19]	12 300	89 025	12 972
Falls Church city	76.6	5 787	47.6	0.3	8.2	2.3	6.9	97.9	7 399	[19]	[19]	[19]	6 430	137 665	24 957
Franklin city	51.8	6 072	32.0	0.5	5.3	3.8	4.2	22.8	2 673	[10]	[10]	[10]	3 870	44 212	3 967
Fredericksburg city	158.1	5 789	24.4	0.5	4.5	4.2	4.1	451.1	16 521	[11]	[11]	[11]	12 580	60 848	8 127
Galax city	28.7	4 153	45.2	0.7	8.9	5.8	7.1	10.9	1 575	[20]	[20]	[20]	2 970	38 664	3 716
Hampton city	524.9	3 836	44.8	0.8	5.1	5.6	1.2	438.4	3 204	7 216	7 408	8 750	65 570	45 381	4 112
Harrisonburg city	165.9	3 255	39.0	0.7	4.7	1.8	11.4	529.2	10 380	[9]	[9]	[9]	17 430	43 580	4 145
Hopewell city	116.0	5 192	43.8	0.5	4.4	5.9	3.4	114.6	5 128	[5]	[5]	[5]	10 290	37 068	2 839
Lexington city	28.1	4 013	24.4	2.6	5.2	2.6	4.3	34.5	4 926	[8]	[8]	[8]	2 380	69 524	9 131
Lynchburg city	262.8	3 408	36.6	0.8	6.5	7.2	2.8	337.4	4 375	[21]	[21]	[21]	31 580	53 958	6 676
Manassas city	169.8	4 182	54.0	2.2	7.8	0.7	6.2	130.5	3 213	[6]	[6]	[6]	20 450	58 943	6 451
Manassas Park city	60.1	3 803	52.0	0.2	7.5	2.3	0.9	123.4	7 811	[6]	[6]	[6]	7 460	53 094	5 058

1. Based on the resident population estimated as of July 1 of the year shown.   3. Radford city is included with Montgomery county.   4. Danville city is included with Pittsylvania county.   5. Hopewell city is included with Prince George county.   6. Manassas and Manassas Park cities are included with Prince William county.   7. Salem city is included with Roanoke county.   8. Buena Vista and Lexington cities are included with Rockbridge county.   9. Harrisonburg city is included with Rockingham county.   10. Franklin city is included with Southhampton county.   11. Fredericksburg city is included with Spotsylvania county.   12. Bristol city included with Washington county.   13. Norton city is included with Wise county.   14. Poquoson city is included with York county.   15. Charlottesville city is included with Albemarle county.   16. Petersburg and Colonial Heights cities are included with Dinwiddie county.   17. Covington city is included with Alleghany county.   18. Emporia city is included with Greensville county.   19. Fairfax city and Falls Church city are included with Fairfax county.   20. Galax city is included with Carroll county.   21. Lynchburg city is included with Campbell county.

Table B. States and Counties — Land Area and Population

STATE/ County code	CBSA code[1]	County type[2]	STATE County	Population, 2016				Race alone or in combination, not Hispanic or Latino (percent)					Age (percent)					
				Land area,[3] (sq mi) 2016	Total persons 2016	Rank	Per square mile	White	Black	American Indian, Alaska Native	Asian and Pacific Islander	Percent Hispanic or Latino[4]	Under 5 years	5 to 17 years	18 to 24 years	25 to 34 years	35 to 44 years	45 to 54 years
				1	2	3	4	5	6	7	8	9	10	11	12	13	14	15
			VIRGINIA—Cont'd															
51 690	32300	4	Martinsville city	11.0	13 445	2 199	1 222.3	47.9	46.9	0.7	1.3	5.1	6.9	16.3	7.2	11.0	10.4	13.5
51 700	47260	1	Newport News city	69.1	181 825	357	2 631.3	46.9	42.3	1.3	4.7	8.8	7.2	16.0	12.4	17.1	11.6	11.8
51 710	47260	1	Norfolk city	53.3	245 115	275	4 598.8	46.3	43.1	1.3	5.1	7.8	6.7	13.4	17.9	19.3	11.2	10.4
51 720	13720	7	Norton city	7.5	3 864	2 914	515.2	88.1	7.5	0.7	1.9	3.8	4.9	15.8	8.9	14.3	12.8	12.5
51 730	40060	1	Petersburg city	22.9	31 882	1 382	1 392.2	16.5	78.1	1.0	1.8	4.9	7.9	13.7	9.8	15.4	9.7	13.6
51 735	47260	1	Poquoson city	15.4	12 017	2 294	780.3	93.4	1.9	0.7	3.4	2.4	4.4	17.1	8.1	9.9	11.9	15.3
51 740	47260	1	Portsmouth city	33.3	95 252	618	2 860.4	40.2	54.9	1.2	2.2	4.2	7.4	16.1	9.5	16.7	11.8	11.6
51 750	13980	3	Radford city	9.9	17 483	1 946	1 766.0	84.7	11.1	0.7	2.8	3.1	3.8	9.3	39.2	12.7	8.6	9.4
51 760	40060	1	Richmond city	59.8	223 170	296	3 731.9	42.1	49.6	0.8	3.1	6.5	6.0	12.0	13.1	21.6	11.5	11.7
51 770	40220	2	Roanoke city	42.5	99 660	597	2 344.9	61.5	30.9	0.8	3.5	6.2	7.0	15.2	8.0	15.3	12.4	13.1
51 775	40220	2	Salem city	14.4	25 549	1 583	1 774.2	86.5	8.2	0.6	2.6	3.8	5.3	14.3	12.9	11.8	10.9	12.9
51 790	44420	3	Staunton city	20.0	24 363	1 630	1 218.2	84.0	13.1	0.7	1.9	2.9	5.8	12.7	8.9	13.4	11.7	12.5
51 800	47260	1	Suffolk city	399.2	89 273	650	223.6	51.6	43.2	0.8	2.7	4.1	6.7	18.1	8.0	13.4	12.8	14.6
51 810	47260	1	Virginia Beach city	244.7	452 602	154	1 849.6	65.2	20.9	1.0	8.8	8.1	6.4	16.0	9.8	16.6	12.8	13.1
51 820	44420	3	Waynesboro city	15.0	21 887	1 733	1 459.1	78.6	13.9	0.9	1.6	8.1	6.8	16.3	7.3	14.5	11.8	12.2
51 830	47260	1	Williamsburg city	8.9	15 214	2 081	1 709.4	71.1	16.1	0.8	7.6	7.5	3.3	7.7	36.1	12.5	7.1	7.7
51 840	49020	3	Winchester city	9.2	27 516	1 513	2 990.9	69.5	12.8	0.7	3.1	16.8	6.5	15.8	10.8	14.2	12.2	12.9
53 000	...	0	WASHINGTON	66 453.4	7 288 000	X	109.7	73.1	5.0	2.5	11.3	12.4	6.2	16.1	9.1	14.8	12.9	13.0
53 001	36830	6	Adams	1 925.0	19 238	1 861	10.0	35.2	0.8	0.7	1.1	63.0	10.1	25.6	10.3	11.8	11.4	10.7
53 003	30300	3	Asotin	636.1	22 306	1 715	35.1	93.1	1.2	2.5	1.7	3.8	5.6	15.2	6.8	11.7	10.7	12.5
53 005	28420	2	Benton	1 699.8	193 686	341	113.9	73.3	2.1	1.5	4.2	21.4	7.2	19.6	8.7	13.6	12.1	12.1
53 007	48300	3	Chelan	2 921.2	76 338	724	26.1	69.7	0.9	1.7	1.8	27.7	6.5	17.4	8.2	12.3	11.3	11.8
53 009	38820	5	Clallam	1 738.7	74 570	741	42.9	86.3	1.5	6.6	3.1	6.1	4.8	12.6	6.4	10.6	9.6	10.9
53 011	38900	1	Clark	628.4	467 018	147	743.2	82.5	3.1	1.8	7.2	9.3	6.3	18.4	8.1	12.9	13.2	13.5
53 013	47460	3	Columbia	868.6	3 938	2 905	4.5	89.1	1.5	2.1	1.9	7.5	4.4	13.4	5.8	9.4	9.1	13.1
53 015	31020	3	Cowlitz	1 140.4	105 160	565	92.2	86.9	1.5	3.1	2.9	8.8	5.9	16.7	7.7	11.9	11.5	12.9
53 017	48300	3	Douglas	1 819.3	41 327	1 144	22.7	65.9	0.9	1.6	1.7	31.5	6.8	19.4	8.7	12.1	11.6	12.0
53 019	...	9	Ferry	2 203.2	7 614	2 623	3.5	77.7	1.4	18.8	2.1	4.5	5.1	12.3	8.2	9.0	9.9	12.3
53 021	28420	2	Franklin	1 241.6	90 160	643	72.6	42.1	2.6	1.0	2.9	53.0	9.3	23.8	9.6	15.5	13.6	10.6
53 023	...	8	Garfield	710.8	2 247	3 027	3.2	93.3	1.1	0.9	2.0	4.5	5.5	14.5	6.0	8.6	10.7	11.4
53 025	34180	5	Grant	2 679.5	93 546	628	34.9	56.1	1.4	1.7	1.5	41.0	8.1	21.7	9.9	13.1	11.6	11.2
53 027	10140	4	Grays Harbor	1 901.3	71 628	756	37.7	82.8	1.9	6.2	2.8	9.9	5.5	15.3	7.3	11.8	11.4	12.7
53 029	36020	4	Island	208.3	82 636	682	396.7	83.5	3.8	2.0	7.7	7.4	5.6	12.8	9.1	13.4	9.7	10.9
53 031	...	6	Jefferson	1 803.8	31 139	1 405	17.3	91.1	1.4	3.5	3.0	3.9	3.1	9.5	5.0	8.4	8.2	11.0
53 033	42660	1	King	2 115.6	2 149 970	13	1 016.2	65.0	7.8	1.7	20.9	9.5	6.0	14.6	8.4	17.6	14.7	13.8
53 035	14740	2	Kitsap	395.1	264 811	256	670.2	81.8	4.1	2.9	9.4	7.6	5.9	14.8	10.3	14.2	11.2	12.6
53 037	21260	4	Kittitas	2 297.3	44 866	1 077	19.5	86.6	1.6	2.1	3.7	8.8	4.6	12.8	21.9	12.4	9.7	10.7
53 039	...	6	Klickitat	1 871.6	21 301	1 761	11.4	83.9	0.7	3.5	1.7	12.5	5.0	14.6	6.7	9.5	11.5	12.7
53 041	16500	4	Lewis	2 402.8	77 066	717	32.1	86.5	1.3	2.9	2.2	10.1	5.7	15.9	7.6	11.6	11.2	11.6
53 043	...	8	Lincoln	2 310.5	10 350	2 401	4.5	93.7	0.9	3.1	1.4	3.3	4.9	16.5	6.4	8.4	10.0	11.6
53 045	43220	4	Mason	959.4	62 198	847	64.8	84.4	1.8	5.1	3.0	9.4	5.1	14.0	7.3	11.4	10.7	12.4
53 047	...	6	Okanogan	5 266.1	41 554	1 138	7.9	67.9	1.1	12.5	1.6	19.5	6.2	16.8	7.3	10.4	11.0	11.5
53 049	...	7	Pacific	932.8	21 249	1 765	22.8	85.1	1.3	4.4	3.1	9.4	4.3	12.2	6.0	9.2	9.3	11.7
53 051	44060	2	Pend Oreille	1 400.3	13 123	2 221	9.4	91.0	1.2	4.9	1.7	3.5	4.5	14.7	6.4	8.8	9.2	13.2
53 053	42660	1	Pierce	1 668.5	861 312	65	516.2	72.9	9.4	2.7	11.2	10.6	6.8	16.9	9.3	15.3	12.7	13.0
53 055	...	9	San Juan	173.9	16 339	2 018	94.0	91.0	1.0	1.8	2.3	6.1	2.9	10.6	5.3	7.4	9.3	12.2
53 057	34580	3	Skagit	1 730.1	123 681	508	71.5	77.1	1.3	2.8	3.3	18.0	6.1	15.9	8.1	12.3	11.3	12.0
53 059	38900	1	Skamania	1 658.3	11 510	2 318	6.9	90.4	1.1	3.0	2.0	6.2	4.4	15.2	6.8	9.7	11.7	14.6
53 061	42660	1	Snohomish	2 086.6	787 620	78	377.5	74.6	4.2	2.2	13.5	9.9	6.3	16.5	8.1	14.6	13.7	14.4
53 063	44060	2	Spokane	1 763.9	499 072	139	282.9	88.3	3.0	2.6	4.3	5.5	6.1	16.1	9.9	14.8	11.9	12.5
53 065	44060	2	Stevens	2 477.4	44 439	1 082	17.9	89.5	0.9	7.2	1.8	3.6	5.5	16.4	7.0	8.9	10.0	12.6
53 067	36500	2	Thurston	722.5	275 222	247	380.9	79.9	4.6	2.7	9.4	8.6	5.9	15.8	8.4	14.3	12.9	12.8
53 069	...	8	Wahkiakum	262.9	4 139	2 889	15.7	91.6	1.1	3.0	2.5	4.7	3.9	13.8	5.8	7.1	8.5	12.2
53 071	47460	3	Walla Walla	1 270.0	60 340	865	47.5	74.1	2.5	1.6	2.8	21.2	5.7	15.7	13.1	12.5	11.2	11.7
53 073	13380	3	Whatcom	2 107.9	216 800	304	102.9	82.5	1.8	3.8	6.3	9.2	5.5	14.2	14.4	13.2	11.5	11.9
53 075	39420	4	Whitman	2 159.2	48 851	1 003	22.6	82.3	3.3	1.5	10.7	6.2	4.5	10.8	35.3	14.6	8.4	7.8
53 077	49420	3	Yakima	4 294.5	249 636	269	58.1	45.4	1.2	4.6	1.8	48.8	8.3	21.6	9.8	13.0	11.8	11.3
54 000	...	0	WEST VIRGINIA	24 040.9	1 831 102	X	76.2	93.8	4.4	0.7	1.2	1.5	5.5	15.0	8.8	12.0	12.2	13.3
54 001	...	6	Barbour	341.1	16 831	1 991	49.3	96.9	1.9	1.3	0.5	1.0	5.2	15.0	12.1	10.7	11.3	13.0
54 003	25180	2	Berkeley	321.1	113 525	540	353.6	87.4	9.0	0.8	1.6	4.1	6.4	17.5	7.4	13.9	13.2	14.5
54 005	16620	3	Boone	501.5	22 816	1 686	45.5	98.4	1.1	0.4	0.2	0.6	5.2	16.6	7.1	10.2	13.5	13.5
54 007	...	8	Braxton	510.8	14 471	2 131	28.3	97.8	1.1	0.8	0.6	0.7	5.4	14.5	6.8	11.2	11.7	13.7
54 009	48260	3	Brooke	89.2	22 977	1 683	257.6	97.1	2.1	0.5	0.7	0.9	4.2	13.4	9.8	9.8	11.0	12.9
54 011	26580	2	Cabell	281.0	95 987	616	341.6	92.0	6.2	0.7	1.8	1.4	5.8	14.2	13.6	12.5	11.8	11.8

1. CBSA = Core Based Statistical Area. See Appendix A for explanation. See Appendix B for list of metropolitan areas with component counties. 2. County type code from the Economic Research Service of USDA Rural-Urban Continuum Codes. See Appendix A for definition. 3. Dry land or land partially or temporarily covered by water. 4. May be of any race.

Table B. States and Counties — **Population and Households**

STATE County	Age (percent) (cont.)				Population change and components of change, 2000–2016							Households, 2011–2015				
					Total persons		Percent change		Components of change, 2010–2016						Percent	
	55 to 64 years	65 to 74 years	75 years and over	Percent female	2000	2010	2000–2010	2010–2016	Births	Deaths	Net migration	Number	Persons per house-hold	Family house-holds	Female family house-holder[1]	One per-son
	16	17	18	19	20	21	22	23	24	25	26	27	28	29	30	31
VIRGINIA—Cont'd																
Martinsville city	13.7	10.9	10.1	54.1	15 416	13 811	-10.4	-2.7	1 165	1 373	-196	5 857	2.26	55.3	19.6	40.8
Newport News city	11.6	7.1	5.2	51.4	180 150	181 039	0.5	0.4	17 703	9 041	-7 731	69 073	2.50	61.9	18.1	31.8
Norfolk city	10.8	6.1	4.3	47.8	234 403	242 823	3.6	0.9	23 042	12 146	-8 364	87 045	2.53	57.7	18.1	32.5
Norton city	14.0	9.3	7.5	52.1	3 904	3 951	1.2	-2.2	270	224	-136	1 783	2.21	53.6	15.9	39.1
Petersburg city	13.8	9.2	6.9	53.8	33 740	32 436	-3.9	-1.7	3 405	2 624	-1 367	12 803	2.44	54.8	24.1	37.6
Poquoson city	14.2	11.1	8.1	50.5	11 566	12 157	5.1	-1.2	576	617	-92	4 642	2.59	73.8	8.4	22.1
Portsmouth city	12.5	8.2	6.2	52.0	100 565	95 527	-5.0	-0.3	9 526	6 487	-3 183	36 757	2.54	63.2	21.8	31.5
Radford city	9.0	4.6	3.5	52.3	15 859	16 408	3.5	6.6	830	570	790	5 477	2.57	43.8	10.4	34.3
Richmond city	12.4	7.0	4.8	52.5	197 790	204 142	3.2	9.3	18 102	11 966	12 817	87 224	2.33	46.5	18.1	41.7
Roanoke city	13.4	9.1	6.5	52.1	94 911	96 919	2.1	2.8	9 065	7 319	1 057	42 239	2.29	55.9	17.3	36.6
Salem city	14.1	9.9	7.9	52.4	24 747	24 848	0.4	2.8	1 638	1 817	794	10 045	2.29	63.0	12.8	31.8
Staunton city	13.7	11.7	9.7	54.5	23 853	23 746	-0.4	2.6	1 790	2 111	918	10 387	2.21	56.0	12.1	36.7
Suffolk city	12.8	8.3	5.4	51.6	63 677	84 570	32.8	5.6	7 036	4 583	2 141	30 990	2.75	73.6	17.3	22.3
Virginia Beach city	12.0	7.8	5.4	50.9	425 257	437 907	3.0	3.4	38 251	18 568	-5 120	166 242	2.63	68.8	14.1	24.3
Waynesboro city	12.6	10.0	8.5	52.0	19 520	21 024	7.7	4.1	1 883	1 514	424	9 031	2.32	62.8	15.6	30.9
Williamsburg city	9.3	9.0	7.3	54.1	11 998	13 681	14.0	11.2	641	672	1 397	4 538	2.37	47.9	8.8	41.3
Winchester city	12.3	8.6	6.7	50.7	23 585	26 201	11.1	5.0	2 386	1 714	629	10 608	2.47	56.9	13.2	33.6
WASHINGTON	13.0	9.0	5.8	50.0	5 894 121	6 724 545	14.1	8.4	549 553	323 987	333 395	2 668 912	2.56	64.5	10.2	27.5
Adams	9.6	6.1	4.4	49.1	16 428	18 728	14.0	2.7	2 512	733	-1 258	5 802	3.24	78.5	13.3	18.3
Asotin	15.9	12.2	9.5	51.2	20 551	21 623	5.2	3.2	1 530	1 481	650	9 341	2.34	64.6	11.0	30.1
Benton	12.7	8.5	5.6	49.9	142 475	175 171	22.9	10.6	16 292	8 066	10 001	67 430	2.72	69.3	11.1	25.9
Chelan	14.1	10.7	7.7	50.1	66 616	72 464	8.8	5.3	5 861	4 155	2 062	27 052	2.70	67.5	9.9	27.0
Clallam	16.8	16.5	11.8	50.6	64 525	71 404	10.7	4.4	4 221	5 906	4 573	31 321	2.27	59.1	8.5	32.8
Clark	12.9	9.3	5.5	50.6	345 238	425 360	23.2	9.8	34 335	19 900	26 131	162 441	2.71	69.6	11.3	23.8
Columbia	16.4	16.4	12.0	50.8	4 064	4 078	0.3	-3.4	215	303	-37	1 686	2.31	64.2	11.0	27.3
Cowlitz	14.4	11.3	7.5	50.5	92 948	102 408	10.2	2.7	7 423	6 643	1 827	39 763	2.54	65.6	11.4	27.8
Douglas	12.7	10.0	6.8	49.5	32 603	38 431	17.9	7.5	3 293	1 933	1 545	14 212	2.76	76.5	10.4	19.2
Ferry	18.1	16.1	8.9	48.3	7 260	7 554	4.0	0.8	459	523	139	3 103	2.39	63.9	11.5	31.5
Franklin	9.0	5.5	3.1	48.4	49 347	78 163	58.4	15.3	10 375	2 414	3 893	24 725	3.40	77.2	17.1	18.1
Garfield	17.6	14.4	11.3	50.6	2 397	2 266	-5.5	-0.8	131	160	18	953	2.30	63.9	4.2	32.3
Grant	11.1	8.0	5.2	49.5	74 698	89 120	19.3	5.0	9 579	4 140	-761	30 358	3.00	72.6	12.0	22.3
Grays Harbor	15.8	12.6	7.6	48.7	67 194	72 804	8.3	-1.6	4 910	5 058	-979	27 219	2.51	63.8	11.9	29.1
Island	14.8	14.6	9.2	50.1	71 558	78 506	9.7	5.3	5 617	4 116	2 420	33 125	2.33	67.5	8.3	27.0
Jefferson	20.1	22.1	12.6	50.8	25 953	29 872	15.1	4.2	1 191	2 170	2 113	13 422	2.18	60.3	6.6	32.6
King	12.2	7.6	5.1	50.0	1 737 034	1 931 281	11.2	11.3	157 110	78 629	141 448	819 651	2.45	59.5	8.8	30.6
Kitsap	14.1	10.7	6.3	48.9	231 969	251 137	8.3	5.4	18 934	13 050	7 185	97 739	2.54	67.0	9.6	26.2
Kittitas	12.6	9.5	6.0	49.6	33 362	40 906	22.6	9.7	2 500	1 784	3 191	16 953	2.34	55.7	7.4	30.8
Klickitat	17.3	14.3	8.3	49.4	19 161	20 317	6.0	4.8	1 302	1 162	881	7 863	2.62	67.2	7.3	26.1
Lewis	14.8	12.4	8.4	49.9	68 600	75 457	10.0	2.1	5 489	5 133	1 090	29 515	2.52	66.5	10.4	27.0
Lincoln	17.2	14.7	10.2	49.4	10 184	10 570	3.8	-2.1	613	721	-79	4 370	2.34	65.9	7.5	28.1
Mason	16.6	14.1	8.4	48.4	49 405	60 696	22.9	2.5	3 903	3 919	1 648	23 026	2.58	65.3	9.1	28.1
Okanogan	15.9	13.0	8.0	49.8	39 564	41 117	3.9	1.1	3 306	2 707	-97	16 619	2.42	67.0	9.1	27.3
Pacific	18.4	18.0	10.9	50.0	20 984	20 920	-0.3	1.6	1 229	1 921	986	9 100	2.24	60.7	8.1	33.0
Pend Oreille	18.6	16.2	8.4	49.2	11 732	13 001	10.8	0.9	699	909	378	5 396	2.38	68.3	10.9	26.6
Pierce	12.5	8.1	5.2	50.3	700 820	795 219	13.5	8.3	70 916	38 444	32 836	303 586	2.65	66.7	11.8	26.4
San Juan	20.5	20.6	11.2	51.5	14 077	15 769	12.0	3.6	555	825	844	7 708	2.04	60.6	8.2	30.8
Skagit	14.4	11.9	8.0	50.5	102 979	116 901	13.5	5.8	9 048	7 096	4 506	45 841	2.56	66.0	10.8	25.2
Skamania	18.8	12.0	6.7	49.1	9 872	11 070	12.1	4.0	601	505	404	4 495	2.49	66.2	8.3	28.6
Snohomish	13.5	7.9	4.9	49.8	606 024	713 308	17.7	10.4	58 442	31 039	45 666	274 766	2.68	68.2	10.3	24.4
Spokane	13.2	9.3	6.3	50.4	417 939	471 225	12.7	5.9	37 153	26 365	16 541	189 471	2.45	63.2	10.8	29.0
Stevens	17.5	14.1	8.0	50.2	40 066	43 527	8.6	2.1	2 819	2 730	902	17 679	2.44	69.4	8.8	25.4
Thurston	13.5	10.2	6.3	51.1	207 355	252 258	21.7	9.1	19 467	12 650	15 858	102 631	2.52	66.5	11.1	26.4
Wahkiakum	17.3	19.9	11.4	49.5	3 824	3 978	4.0	4.0	180	290	290	1 716	2.31	69.3	8.6	28.6
Walla Walla	12.8	9.5	7.8	49.0	55 180	58 781	6.5	2.7	4 226	3 498	722	21 696	2.50	63.1	10.1	32.1
Whatcom	12.7	10.2	6.4	50.4	166 814	201 140	20.6	7.8	14 362	9 502	10 642	79 767	2.53	61.8	9.8	27.4
Whitman	8.6	5.8	4.2	49.1	40 740	44 778	9.9	9.1	2 806	1 569	2 825	17 399	2.31	49.9	6.8	30.7
Yakima	10.8	7.8	5.6	50.0	222 581	243 237	9.3	2.6	25 949	11 838	-7 609	79 972	3.05	72.0	15.1	22.9
WEST VIRGINIA	14.5	11.1	7.7	50.5	1 808 344	1 853 011	2.5	-1.2	127 578	137 344	-10 139	740 890	2.43	64.8	11.4	30.0
Barbour	13.9	11.1	7.7	51.2	15 557	16 589	6.6	1.5	1 068	1 202	384	6 041	2.68	70.2	11.4	24.4
Berkeley	13.0	9.1	4.9	50.5	75 905	104 172	37.2	9.0	8 557	5 831	6 458	40 991	2.63	70.2	12.5	24.5
Boone	15.5	11.3	6.9	50.4	25 535	24 627	-3.6	-7.4	1 630	1 978	-1 431	9 547	2.50	70.1	12.3	26.3
Braxton	15.2	13.0	8.5	49.4	14 702	14 519	-1.2	-0.3	981	1 077	58	5 607	2.51	67.8	8.4	28.4
Brooke	16.1	12.5	10.2	50.9	25 447	24 071	-5.4	-4.5	1 188	2 068	-220	10 030	2.26	63.3	9.8	32.3
Cabell	12.6	10.1	7.7	51.0	96 784	96 316	-0.5	-0.3	7 258	7 261	-12	39 973	2.32	57.7	12.4	34.7

1. No spouse present.

Table B. States and Counties — **Population, Vital Statistics, Health, and Crime**

STATE County	Daytime population, 2011–2015 Persons in group quarters, 2016	Number	Employ-ment/resi-dence ratio	Births, 2016 Total	Rate[1]	Deaths, 2016 Number	Rate[1]	Persons under 65 with no health insurance, 2015 Number	Percent	Medicare, 2015 Total Beneficiaries	Enrolled in Original Medicare	Enrolled in Medicare Advantage	Serious crimes known to police,[2] 2014 Total Number	Rate[3]
	32	33	34	35	36	37	38	39	40	41	42	43	44	45
VIRGINIA—Cont'd														
Martinsville city	377	16 904	1.64	220	16.4	210	15.6	1 277	12.1	8 527	6 256	2 271	437	3 175
Newport News city	8 481	204 525	1.26	2 751	15.1	1 518	8.3	16 387	10.8	26 390	19 022	7 368	6 334	3 473
Norfolk city	32 949	305 408	1.49	3 596	14.7	2 096	8.6	24 535	13.0	29 835	21 163	8 672	10 981	4 444
Norton city	68	3 532	0.73	17	4.4	27	7.0	375	11.3	1 530	1 010	520	210	5 211
Petersburg city	887	34 469	1.18	694	21.8	454	14.2	3 286	12.2	8 258	6 136	2 122	1 036	3 183
Poquoson city	51	8 450	0.39	102	8.5	99	8.2	725	7.4	1 461	1 280	181	103	851
Portsmouth city	3 162	106 962	1.26	1 464	15.4	1 061	11.1	9 293	11.6	16 805	11 841	4 964	5 451	5 653
Radford city	3 004	17 033	1.00	147	8.4	69	3.9	1 205	9.2	3 117	2 388	729	477	2 744
Richmond city	13 685	282 848	1.68	2 987	13.4	2 054	9.2	26 530	14.5	56 756	37 123	19 633	9 690	4 471
Roanoke city	2 117	124 301	1.56	1 477	14.8	1 164	11.7	11 197	13.4	30 947	21 728	9 219	4 476	4 524
Salem city	1 929	36 265	1.90	348	13.6	305	11.9	1 940	10.1	8 072	6 385	1 687	530	2 085
Staunton city	1 097	24 966	1.07	313	12.8	312	12.8	2 114	11.4	9 081	7 493	1 588	623	2 543
Suffolk city	1 068	77 293	0.78	1 201	13.5	789	8.8	6 718	8.9	14 271	10 923	3 348	2 485	2 890
Virginia Beach city	9 495	415 671	0.86	6 068	13.4	3 238	7.2	35 902	9.3	61 508	49 925	11 583	10 532	2 335
Waynesboro city	192	20 957	0.98	339	15.5	224	10.2	2 201	12.5	7 003	5 752	1 251	688	3 227
Williamsburg city	4 416	22 871	2.40	91	6.0	104	6.8	1 075	13.0	6 445	5 577	868	205	1 323
Winchester city	933	39 756	2.01	395	14.4	264	9.6	3 589	16.1	10 635	9 307	1 328	1 171	4 261
WASHINGTON	142 590	6 938 842	0.99	89 982	12.3	55 979	7.7	459 596	7.6	1 142 661	763 395	379 266	281 842	3 991
Adams	162	19 228	1.02	374	19.4	116	6.0	2 444	14.4	1 541	1 326	215	771	4 010
Asotin	174	19 065	0.68	247	11.1	250	11.2	1 230	7.1	5 550	4 590	960	701	3 142
Benton	1 425	187 913	1.04	2 708	14.0	1 385	7.2	11 974	7.4	29 544	25 717	3 827	4 849	2 588
Chelan	931	79 256	1.15	938	12.3	663	8.7	5 941	9.7	11 269	8 935	2 334	1 689	2 264
Clallam	1 889	71 476	0.97	689	9.2	998	13.4	4 919	9.5	23 184	21 260	1 924	2 222	3 051
Clark	3 427	398 985	0.77	5 698	12.2	3 524	7.5	27 179	6.9	74 226	31 264	42 962	10 389	2 308
Columbia	75	4 010	1.01	35	8.9	38	9.6	211	7.4	1 101	1 067	34	127	3 151
Cowlitz	1 208	101 019	0.97	1 195	11.4	1 094	10.4	6 675	8.0	21 837	11 397	10 440	3 982	3 897
Douglas	190	33 381	0.65	536	13.0	321	7.8	3 772	11.2	11 244	8 667	2 577	814	2 041
Ferry	252	7 451	0.91	82	10.8	77	10.1	683	11.9	1 664	1 588	76	52	675
Franklin	2 840	81 740	0.87	1 628	18.1	457	5.1	9 813	12.6	8 298	7 230	1 068	1 862	2 091
Garfield	36	2 113	0.86	25	11.1	24	10.7	93	5.6	636	616	20	40	1 768
Grant	1 244	93 773	1.05	1 469	15.7	660	7.1	10 885	13.6	14 331	11 903	2 428	3 963	4 341
Grays Harbor	2 697	69 756	0.94	757	10.6	825	11.5	5 657	10.3	17 432	15 935	1 497	2 174	3 135
Island	1 895	70 409	0.75	918	11.1	695	8.4	3 750	6.2	19 951	13 841	6 110	1 124	1 439
Jefferson	631	29 626	0.96	179	5.7	362	11.6	1 473	7.4	10 482	9 818	664	843	2 787
King	38 777	2 212 056	1.16	25 905	12.0	13 580	6.3	118 624	6.5	273 656	168 112	105 544	100 616	4 834
Kitsap	9 514	244 936	0.91	3 240	12.2	2 295	8.7	12 163	5.8	46 096	36 165	9 931	7 909	3 093
Kittitas	2 362	40 544	0.91	391	8.7	286	6.4	3 068	8.9	6 820	6 225	595	1 186	2 814
Klickitat	198	20 249	0.92	203	9.5	199	9.3	1 572	9.6	5 100	4 719	381	290	1 375
Lewis	943	73 572	0.93	870	11.3	838	10.9	5 436	9.1	18 784	12 750	6 034	2 135	2 886
Lincoln	94	9 943	0.89	97	9.4	121	11.7	533	6.9	2 778	2 668	110	170	1 654
Mason	2 507	55 495	0.76	607	9.8	621	10.0	4 848	10.7	14 335	11 310	3 025	2 201	3 626
Okanogan	640	41 602	1.02	499	12.0	476	11.5	4 709	14.5	9 508	8 520	988	970	2 345
Pacific	287	20 300	0.95	204	9.6	326	15.3	1 545	10.5	6 844	6 524	320	428	2 089
Pend Oreille	98	12 421	0.87	113	8.6	143	10.9	750	7.6	3 366	2 942	424	388	2 999
Pierce	16 754	775 700	0.88	11 775	13.7	6 964	8.1	52 712	7.3	127 444	86 684	40 760	35 442	4 272
San Juan	187	16 013	1.01	89	5.4	125	7.7	1 182	10.6	4 763	3 617	1 146	164	1 027
Skagit	1 626	121 135	1.04	1 447	11.7	1 229	9.9	9 527	9.8	26 644	18 153	8 491	4 588	3 829
Skamania	25	9 311	0.57	91	7.9	96	8.3	647	7.0	1 663	1 473	190	121	1 064
Snohomish	9 881	670 042	0.79	9 732	12.4	5 545	7.0	46 978	7.0	99 405	50 987	48 418	27 604	3 663
Spokane	14 982	489 638	1.04	5 961	11.9	4 510	9.0	25 764	6.4	90 211	56 963	33 248	29 502	6 103
Stevens	266	39 853	0.76	476	10.7	460	10.4	2 917	8.5	9 808	8 516	1 292	900	2 064
Thurston	4 027	249 506	0.89	3 172	11.5	2 172	7.9	14 801	6.6	48 843	31 268	17 575	7 956	2 991
Wahkiakum	48	3 888	0.88	22	5.3	47	11.4	227	8.2	1 280	921	359	37	907
Walla Walla	4 629	63 381	1.14	672	11.1	612	10.1	4 120	9.0	11 404	9 977	1 427	2 267	3 781
Whatcom	5 836	203 888	0.97	2 371	10.9	1 580	7.3	15 806	9.1	38 100	23 847	14 253	7 219	3 462
Whitman	6 338	49 538	1.13	454	9.3	232	4.7	2 220	6.0	5 061	4 872	189	870	1 871
Yakima	3 495	246 630	0.99	4 113	16.5	2 033	8.1	32 748	15.5	38 458	31 028	7 430	8 831	3 549
WEST VIRGINIA	48 027	1 834 771	0.98	19 799	10.8	22 479	12.3	106 941	7.3	412 392	294 131	118 261	43 236	2 337
Barbour	1 037	14 059	0.57	169	10.0	198	11.8	1 068	8.3	3 535	2 683	852	NA	NA
Berkeley	896	92 125	0.66	1 371	12.1	1 001	8.8	6 979	7.3	18 386	14 526	3 860	2 041	1 864
Boone	131	25 042	1.14	224	9.8	305	13.4	1 414	7.4	5 127	3 702	1 425	407	1 789
Braxton	370	13 797	0.87	154	10.6	181	12.5	991	8.9	3 026	2 074	952	101	840
Brooke	851	21 610	0.80	199	8.7	323	14.1	1 039	6.0	4 832	3 034	1 798	191	845
Cabell	4 131	109 686	1.33	1 128	11.8	1 114	11.6	5 600	7.3	23 554	16 128	7 426	1 797	1 850

1. Per 1,000 estimated resident population. 2. Data for serious crimes have not been adjusted for underreporting; this may affect comparability between geographic areas and over time.
3. Per 100,000 population estimated by the FBI.

Table B. States and Counties — Crime, Education, Money Income, and Poverty

STATE County	Serious crimes known to police, 2014 (cont.)[1] Rate[2] Violent	Property	Education — School enrollment and attainment, 2011–2015 — Enrollment[3] (percent) Total	Per cent private	Attainment[4] (percent) High school graduate or less	Bachelor's degree or more	Local government expenditures,[5] 2013–2014 Total current spending (mil dol)	Current spending per student (dollars)	Money income, 2011–2015 Per capita income[6] (dollars)	Median income (dollars)	Households Percent with income of less than $50,000	with income of $200,000 or more	Income and poverty, 2015 Median household income (dollars)	Percent below poverty level All persons	Children under 18 years	Children 5 to 17 years in families
	46	47	48	49	50	51	52	53	54	55	56	57	58	59	60	61
VIRGINIA—Cont'd																
Martinsville city..................	356	2 819	3 169	10.5	51.6	17.8	24.4	10 801	21 899	29 587	66.7	2.8	32 541	23.7	37.1	35.7
Newport News city	429	3 044	51 135	14.1	39.2	24.0	299.9	10 071	25 369	50 077	49.9	2.5	48 127	16.8	25.7	24.3
Norfolk city.......................	520	3 924	68 903	11.7	39.9	26.1	342.6	10 509	24 657	44 480	55.3	2.7	45 094	21.5	29.6	28.9
Norton city........................	298	4 913	888	1.9	37.4	19.6	7.6	8 988	19 647	27 731	69.4	1.9	31 287	23.7	37.5	30.9
Petersburg city	593	2 590	6 355	12.6	56.1	15.9	47.3	10 600	19 149	31 798	69.0	0.5	31 645	28.4	43.0	44.0
Poquoson city	91	760	3 250	9.7	33.4	37.1	19.9	9 388	38 428	83 735	27.6	7.2	86 135	5.4	6.6	5.2
Portsmouth city	610	5 043	24 922	12.9	45.3	20.8	148.5	9 922	23 075	45 676	54.2	1.6	46 308	18.6	30.5	29.7
Radford city.......................	598	2 146	9 788	3.9	33.2	35.5	14.9	9 213	15 556	29 912	68.7	1.4	35 259	32.8	21.5	20.3
Richmond city.....................	583	3 887	55 505	19.1	39.8	36.0	299.4	12 328	28 023	40 758	58.8	4.4	40 161	24.4	36.3	39.3
Roanoke city......................	344	4 180	21 631	14.2	46.0	23.6	157.6	11 642	23 685	39 930	59.3	2.0	39 587	21.3	32.9	34.5
Salem city.........................	114	1 971	6 957	25.9	39.8	28.4	40.6	10 570	27 560	50 068	49.9	4.1	47 600	10.2	13.8	12.9
Staunton city......................	127	2 416	5 318	26.9	43.7	31.3	30.1	10 683	25 182	40 842	58.5	1.9	43 401	15.2	23.0	21.8
Suffolk city........................	272	2 618	24 389	20.3	40.7	26.4	135.1	9 334	29 620	65 499	38.6	4.5	61 171	13.1	18.0	16.3
Virginia Beach city	148	2 187	119 788	18.0	29.0	33.8	734.7	10 413	32 269	66 634	35.5	5.0	67 032	8.2	12.4	12.1
Waynesboro city..................	155	3 072	4 469	8.6	53.6	18.4	32.4	10 183	22 156	45 643	54.8	0.9	43 500	16.0	26.2	24.9
Williamsburg city.................	161	1 162	7 218	3.7	23.8	52.4	(7)	(7)	24 127	48 639	51.2	5.3	47 971	22.0	25.1	24.5
Winchester city...................	313	3 948	6 926	27.2	46.2	28.3	(8)	(8)	26 182	45 363	54.5	4.6	47 679	17.8	25.6	23.9
WASHINGTON.................	285	3 706	1 719 835	14.9	32.8	32.9	10 791.3	10 194	31 762	61 062	41.0	5.7	64 080	12.2	15.7	14.6
Adams..............................	291	3 719	5 323	4.4	59.3	13.6	46.9	10 178	17 564	46 564	53.5	1.2	48 127	16.5	21.5	20.4
Asotin..............................	238	2 904	5 078	8.4	41.1	18.2	34.1	10 252	25 132	44 394	55.8	1.4	46 573	15.7	24.4	22.0
Benton.............................	193	2 395	48 230	10.7	35.5	29.4	324.1	9 413	28 758	60 251	41.6	4.8	62 698	14.2	19.7	16.2
Chelan.............................	135	2 128	17 268	9.7	46.7	24.5	137.4	10 443	25 564	51 837	47.9	3.0	53 604	12.7	18.3	17.4
Clallam............................	255	2 796	14 032	10.4	35.6	24.7	102.6	9 842	27 000	47 253	53.2	2.2	46 708	15.6	24.2	21.5
Clark...............................	209	2 099	116 825	12.9	33.4	27.2	757.7	9 668	28 801	60 756	40.3	4.3	64 282	10.6	14.5	13.1
Columbia..........................	0	3 151	775	13.5	37.5	23.0	5.9	12 558	24 400	38 581	59.9	2.0	40 209	15.2	25.2	22.3
Cowlitz.............................	250	3 648	23 177	10.1	43.1	16.0	166.3	9 935	24 260	47 452	52.5	1.7	50 502	15.7	22.8	20.3
Douglas...........................	85	1 956	9 690	6.2	46.9	17.4	80.4	10 321	23 598	53 636	46.3	1.9	51 400	13.5	21.0	19.1
Ferry...............................	117	558	1 545	12.8	43.9	16.7	13.3	14 390	20 602	38 125	63.7	0.3	40 747	20.4	30.5	27.5
Franklin............................	234	1 858	25 397	7.9	53.7	15.9	185.6	9 830	20 412	56 980	43.9	2.6	58 246	15.6	21.3	19.8
Garfield............................	88	1 679	412	3.6	33.8	24.5	4.3	13 098	22 884	45 855	54.0	0.8	47 087	15.2	22.4	19.3
Grant...............................	289	4 052	24 860	6.4	51.3	16.4	191.6	10 097	20 251	48 714	51.2	2.0	50 573	16.1	20.6	20.0
Grays Harbor......................	274	2 861	15 177	6.4	44.2	14.7	116.1	11 225	22 387	43 538	56.5	1.4	44 345	16.0	24.9	23.5
Island..............................	102	1 336	15 675	15.1	28.8	31.7	77.6	9 626	31 836	58 815	42.1	3.5	60 567	8.4	12.7	12.0
Jefferson..........................	291	2 496	4 397	14.7	29.1	37.0	31.5	10 623	28 593	49 279	50.7	2.6	53 421	11.9	23.3	21.4
King................................	334	4 500	488 675	19.1	24.2	47.9	2 665.7	10 504	41 664	75 302	33.7	10.6	81 816	9.8	10.6	10.1
Kitsap..............................	267	2 827	58 689	13.2	28.7	30.3	360.4	10 047	32 063	62 941	38.6	4.4	65 814	9.9	11.8	10.6
Kittitas.............................	109	2 705	13 994	9.9	35.2	33.6	48.9	9 909	24 014	46 458	52.7	1.4	47 378	20.0	16.3	15.2
Klickitat............................	71	1 304	4 266	16.8	40.3	23.5	36.0	11 389	22 456	48 319	52.7	0.6	50 043	17.2	23.6	21.5
Lewis...............................	207	2 679	16 672	12.1	44.5	15.4	120.9	10 219	22 480	44 100	55.0	1.1	47 619	15.3	22.0	20.8
Lincoln.............................	68	1 585	2 211	7.5	42.0	20.6	29.1	14 404	24 951	46 069	54.5	1.6	49 774	14.0	18.6	16.6
Mason..............................	232	3 394	11 690	8.3	42.8	17.7	83.3	10 520	25 015	50 406	49.9	2.1	54 175	16.9	27.0	24.7
Okanogan..........................	174	2 171	8 586	13.6	46.9	18.5	90.5	9 166	22 460	40 730	60.1	1.7	41 844	20.5	28.2	25.5
Pacific.............................	156	1 933	3 607	5.4	44.2	16.8	35.4	11 118	21 923	37 684	62.8	1.0	41 088	18.8	25.8	25.0
Pend Oreille.......................	62	2 938	2 667	20.4	41.3	17.1	19.6	12 544	22 008	40 599	57.9	1.4	41 526	19.6	31.0	27.7
Pierce..............................	432	3 840	205 583	15.3	37.9	24.7	1 312.7	10 199	28 824	59 953	41.0	3.9	60 168	12.4	16.7	15.2
San Juan..........................	44	983	2 464	25.2	21.8	46.6	21.0	10 765	39 266	55 960	45.9	6.2	59 859	11.5	18.5	16.3
Skagit..............................	206	3 622	26 151	11.5	38.3	24.8	204.5	10 784	27 794	54 129	45.9	3.1	56 891	14.9	20.4	19.3
Skamania..........................	106	959	2 158	17.5	38.5	22.0	12.5	11 026	29 878	52 374	47.3	3.5	53 733	14.5	20.5	17.8
Snohomish.........................	183	3 480	183 152	14.7	32.7	29.9	1 287.3	9 904	32 542	70 722	34.3	5.3	76 053	9.3	11.5	10.6
Spokane...........................	345	5 758	124 158	18.1	32.8	28.6	752.5	10 235	26 093	50 079	49.9	2.8	48 676	15.5	19.6	18.3
Stevens............................	99	1 965	9 357	12.9	44.1	16.7	68.9	11 022	22 221	41 978	57.5	1.7	42 845	19.7	27.2	25.1
Thurston...........................	228	2 764	63 778	13.5	29.3	33.4	408.8	9 926	29 741	61 677	38.6	3.4	62 299	12.2	15.0	14.2
Wahkiakum........................	25	883	792	12.6	40.7	14.5	4.5	10 835	24 483	44 485	56.1	2.0	50 402	12.6	25.0	23.0
Walla Walla........................	217	3 565	15 884	28.2	33.9	27.2	94.1	10 536	23 520	47 946	51.7	2.2	50 120	16.5	20.9	20.7
Whatcom...........................	188	3 274	57 321	12.3	31.8	32.5	267.5	10 162	27 223	53 145	46.8	2.8	55 073	14.4	14.5	13.4
Whitman............................	179	1 693	23 572	4.7	21.8	48.9	54.4	11 892	21 188	36 631	60.9	3.1	43 817	20.8	14.4	13.4
Yakima.............................	244	3 305	66 547	7.9	55.9	15.7	537.7	10 201	19 793	44 749	55.8	1.9	46 891	19.1	27.4	26.1
WEST VIRGINIA.............	302	2 035	410 745	10.3	55.8	19.2	3 116.3	11 092	23 450	41 751	57.8	2.1	41 969	18.0	24.7	22.9
Barbour............................	NA	NA	4 043	21.2	66.0	11.9	24.7	10 078	18 039	37 066	66.5	0.4	37 330	20.1	28.2	24.8
Berkeley...........................	155	1 709	27 246	13.6	51.2	19.7	199.9	10 973	26 469	55 239	44.5	2.2	54 217	12.5	18.5	17.3
Boone..............................	229	1 560	4 898	4.3	71.0	8.8	57.4	12 645	21 387	39 958	58.9	1.1	37 971	23.4	30.6	28.5
Braxton............................	233	607	2 645	8.5	68.6	12.0	22.1	10 408	19 409	32 750	63.0	0.9	35 892	23.7	33.3	31.4
Brooke.............................	53	792	5 300	20.4	52.9	18.5	38.1	11 741	23 819	46 215	53.4	1.5	45 272	14.9	20.3	17.8
Cabell..............................	55	1 796	24 770	10.1	45.0	26.9	143.6	11 641	23 908	38 344	60.2	3.0	39 044	20.2	26.5	24.8

1. Data for serious crimes have not been adjusted for underreporting; this may affect comparability between geographic areas and over time.   2. Per 100,000 population estimated by the FBI.
3. All persons 3 years old and over enrolled in nursery school through college.   4. Persons 25 years old and over.   5. Elementary and secondary education expenditures.
6. Based on population estimated by the American Community Survey, 2011–2015.   7. Williamsburg city is included with James City county.   8. Winchester city is included with Frederick county.

STATE County	Total (mil dol)	Percent change, 2014–2015	Per capita[1] Dollars	Per capita Rank	Wages and salaries (mil dol)	Supplements to wages and salaries; employer contributions (mil dol) — Pension and insurance	Government social insurance	Proprietors' income (mil dol)	Dividends, interest, and rent (mil dol)	Personal transfer receipts (mil dol)	Earnings, 2015 — Total (mil dol)	Contributions for government social insurance (mil dol) — From employee and self-employed	From employer
	62	63	64	65	66	67	68	69	70	71	72	73	74
VIRGINIA—Cont'd	(3)	(3)	(3)	(3)	(3)	(3)	(3)	(3)	(3)	(3)	(3)	(3)	(3)
Martinsville city	7 378	4.1	40 453	1 390	5 828	1 186	444	338	1 472	1 408	7 796	431	444
Newport News city	9 530	4.5	38 676	1 400	10 691	2 472	913	302	2 411	1 853	14 377	727	913
Norfolk city	(4)	(4)	(4)	(4)	(4)	(4)	(4)	(4)	(4)	(4)	(4)	(4)	(4)
Norton city	(5)	(5)	(5)	(5)	(5)	(5)	(5)	(5)	(5)	(5)	(5)	(5)	(5)
Petersburg city	(6)	(6)	(6)	(6)	(6)	(6)	(6)	(6)	(6)	(6)	(6)	(6)	(6)
Poquoson city	3 781	5.4	39 301	1 344	2 851	754	243	105	743	928	3 953	213	243
Portsmouth city	(7)	(7)	(7)	(7)	(7)	(7)	(7)	(7)	(7)	(7)	(7)	(7)	(7)
Radford city													
Richmond city	10 717	3.1	48 652	536	9 507	1 666	666	847	2 814	1 819	12 686	745	666
Roanoke city	4 091	4.6	40 947	1 265	3 382	545	266	259	877	997	4 452	272	266
Salem city	(8)	(8)	(8)	(8)	(8)	(8)	(8)	(8)	(8)	(8)	(8)	(8)	(8)
Staunton city	(9)	(9)	(9)	(9)	(9)	(9)	(9)	(9)	(9)	(9)	(9)	(9)	(9)
Suffolk city	4 191	5.1	47 533	643	1 497	266	112	140	739	719	2 014	125	112
Virginia Beach city	23 649	4.4	52 235	326	8 966	1 665	701	1 266	5 396	3 147	12 598	721	701
Waynesboro city	(9)	(9)	(9)	(9)	(9)	(9)	(9)	(9)	(9)	(9)	(9)	(9)	(9)
Williamsburg city	(10)	(10)	(10)	(10)	(10)	(10)	(10)	(10)	(10)	(10)	(10)	(10)	(10)
Winchester city	(11)	(11)	(11)	(11)	(11)	(11)	(11)	(11)	(11)	(11)	(11)	(11)	(11)
WASHINGTON	372 125	4.6	51 971	X	191 805	27 293	16 490	30 359	77 925	56 395	265 947	15 309	16 490
Adams	808	10.3	41 962	1 537	285	49	28	171	167	158	533	22	28
Asotin	910	3.3	41 162	1 249	224	40	22	68	193	248	353	25	22
Benton	8 280	8.4	43 507	1 068	4 519	603	420	914	1 263	1 478	6 456	359	420
Chelan	3 389	5.2	44 797	876	1 702	271	167	341	747	713	2 481	136	167
Clallam	2 920	2.9	39 738	1 262	926	193	88	187	778	885	1 394	98	88
Clark	20 710	6.1	45 070	831	7 483	1 119	684	1 305	3 962	3 519	10 591	656	684
Columbia	192	10.5	48 769	893	54	12	5	39	36	50	110	5	5
Cowlitz	4 177	4.7	40 371	1 435	1 844	278	176	371	651	1 118	2 670	172	176
Douglas	1 472	8.5	36 310	2 228	424	72	40	111	275	323	647	36	40
Ferry	240	2.3	31 681	2 629	72	19	6	10	50	87	107	8	6
Franklin	3 015	6.9	33 955	2 553	1 333	223	136	455	375	596	2 146	103	136
Garfield	102	10.9	45 898	1 256	32	10	3	16	20	25	60	3	3
Grant	3 551	8.9	38 081	2 040	1 545	274	150	586	536	779	2 555	115	150
Grays Harbor	2 534	2.7	35 625	2 058	922	175	88	147	448	809	1 331	89	88
Island	3 873	4.6	48 060	552	1 012	256	102	272	1 082	787	1 642	96	102
Jefferson	1 439	4.3	47 222	811	330	68	31	118	471	380	547	41	31
King	153 554	4.1	72 530	64	98 579	11 342	7 823	13 594	36 735	13 715	131 339	7 509	7 823
Kitsap	12 474	4.7	47 953	554	4 937	1 146	463	622	3 064	2 118	7 168	404	463
Kittitas	1 694	5.5	39 157	1 488	579	117	55	134	377	338	885	51	55
Klickitat	910	2.9	43 290	630	335	60	32	81	199	240	509	30	32
Lewis	2 844	4.8	37 486	1 728	1 046	181	101	216	476	844	1 544	99	101
Lincoln	464	9.1	44 958	964	109	27	10	82	96	112	229	12	10
Mason	2 235	3.7	36 623	1 815	575	122	53	99	469	642	849	61	53
Okanogan	1 575	6.7	37 934	1 516	581	120	56	159	314	450	916	51	56
Pacific	866	4.5	41 560	1 268	242	51	24	68	179	284	384	27	24
Pend Oreille	460	3.5	35 151	2 193	145	32	13	22	90	155	212	15	13
Pierce	37 640	4.8	44 600	792	16 500	2 934	1 574	2 621	6 626	6 914	23 629	1 333	1 574
San Juan	1 077	2.2	66 255	136	207	33	20	107	579	162	367	25	20
Skagit	5 419	4.6	44 470	869	2 276	412	215	447	1 186	1 168	3 351	201	215
Skamania	439	4.0	38 725	1 602	84	17	8	19	93	96	128	9	8
Snohomish	36 633	5.0	47 421	679	16 747	2 521	1 468	2 504	5 447	5 045	23 240	1 358	1 468
Spokane	19 796	4.2	40 322	1 312	10 331	1 621	958	1 157	3 803	4 440	14 067	853	958
Stevens	1 519	3.0	34 694	2 265	408	83	38	99	278	478	627	45	38
Thurston	11 901	4.4	44 155	850	5 314	1 024	475	724	2 420	2 300	7 536	440	475
Wahkiakum	146	0.4	36 153	1 850	29	7	3	6	38	48	45	4	3
Walla Walla	2 529	5.9	41 912	1 232	1 143	207	105	305	503	535	1 760	92	105
Whatcom	9 024	4.4	42 511	1 085	3 968	674	370	868	1 914	1 699	5 880	344	370
Whitman	1 726	7.8	35 834	2 132	844	242	73	202	357	292	1 360	65	73
Yakima	9 587	3.6	38 527	1 506	4 122	658	408	1 114	1 628	2 365	6 301	317	408
WEST VIRGINIA	67 787	2.5	36 820	X	30 238	5 436	2 404	4 165	9 818	19 118	42 243	2 879	2 404
Barbour	499	0.9	29 889	2 760	127	25	10	26	59	162	188	15	10
Berkeley	4 135	4.7	36 950	1 801	1 385	284	116	177	518	790	1 962	128	116
Boone	733	1.5	31 352	2 523	302	52	23	22	73	266	400	30	23
Braxton	422	3.6	29 277	2 894	142	27	11	25	58	147	206	16	11
Brooke	870	3.1	37 261	1 741	339	60	27	48	126	247	474	34	27
Cabell	3 708	3.0	38 287	1 527	2 301	388	188	218	603	1 045	3 095	199	188

1. Based on the resident population estimated as of July 1 of the year shown. 3. Martinsville city is included with Henry county. 4. Norton city is included with Wise county. 5. Petersburg and Colonial Heights cities are included with Dinwiddie county. 6. Poquoson city is included with York county. 7. Radford city is included with Montgomery county. 8. Salem city is included with Roanoke county. 9. Staunton and Waynesboro cities are included with Augusta county. 10. Williamsburg city is included with James City county. 11. Winchester city is included with Frederick county.

Table B. States and Counties — Earnings, Social Security, and Housing

STATE County	Earnings, 2015 (cont.) — Percent by selected industries									Social Security beneficiaries, December 2015		Supplemental Security Income recipients, December 2015	Housing units, 2016	
	Farm	Mining	Construction	Manu-facturing	Information: professional, scientific, technical services	Retail trade	Finance, insurance, real estate and leasing	Health care and social assistance	Govern-ment	Number	Rate[1]		Total	Percent change, 2010–2016
	75	76	77	78	79	80	81	82	83	84	85	86	87	88
VIRGINIA—Cont'd														
Martinsville city	(3)	(3)	(3)	(3)	(3)	(3)	(3)	(3)	(3)	4 110	303	49	7 132	-0.9
Newport News city	0.0	D	2.4	31.0	7.5	4.2	3.2	9.9	24.7	29 115	160	4 810	78 025	2.2
Norfolk city	0.0	D	D	3.1	7.5	2.7	4.6	9.7	51.9	34 040	138	7 562	97 854	3.0
Norton city	(4)	(4)	(4)	(4)	(4)	(4)	(4)	(4)	(4)	1 430	364	375	1 932	-0.6
Petersburg city	(5)	(5)	(5)	(5)	(5)	(5)	(5)	(5)	(5)	8 025	250	3 058	16 481	0.9
Poquoson city	(6)	(6)	(6)	(6)	(6)	(6)	(6)	(6)	(6)	2 465	204	61	4 774	1.0
Portsmouth city	0.0	0.0	5.3	2.5	3.8	2.4	1.2	10.4	60.7	18 720	194	3 908	41 155	0.9
Radford city	(7)	(7)	(7)	(7)	(7)	(7)	(7)	(7)	(7)	2 315	133	376	6 549	1.9
Richmond city	0.0	D	3.3	D	16.5	2.3	9.0	12.2	27.0	34 660	158	9 581	100 672	2.4
Roanoke city	0.0	D	6.9	D	8.6	6.5	8.1	20.2	13.0	21 350	214	4 702	47 384	0.0
Salem city	(8)	(8)	(8)	(8)	(8)	(8)	(8)	(8)	(8)	6 220	245	560	10 886	0.4
Staunton city	(9)	(9)	(9)	(9)	(9)	(9)	(9)	(9)	(9)	6 720	276	787	11 866	1.1
Suffolk city	0.5	0.0	3.9	8.1	17.2	5.8	3.6	12.8	26.6	16 120	183	2 267	36 200	9.6
Virginia Beach city	-0.1	D	7.8	3.1	11.4	6.9	10.2	11.4	28.1	69 585	154	5 541	184 358	3.7
Waynesboro city	(9)	(9)	(9)	(9)	(9)	(9)	(9)	(9)	(9)	5 320	246	751	10 082	3.7
Williamsburg city	(10)	(10)	(10)	(10)	(10)	(10)	(10)	(10)	(10)	2 405	159	13	5 237	6.5
Winchester city	(11)	(11)	(11)	(11)	(11)	(11)	(11)	(11)	(11)	5 385	197	746	11 907	0.3
WASHINGTON	1.7	0.2	6.4	10.4	16.3	7.3	6.5	10.0	18.7	1 260 474	176	151 062	3 025 685	4.9
Adams	30.4	0.0	2.3	13.3	1.2	3.7	3.8	D	17.3	2 535	132	342	6 462	3.5
Asotin	1.2	D	12.9	7.1	4.9	12.8	5.0	D	18.7	6 325	286	718	9 855	-0.2
Benton	6.3	0.0	7.3	5.3	18.3	5.5	3.7	10.6	16.7	33 190	174	3 794	73 949	7.8
Chelan	8.6	D	6.6	5.9	4.3	7.7	3.9	17.0	19.9	16 590	220	1 470	36 731	3.6
Clallam	0.3	0.1	6.5	5.8	4.8	9.3	3.6	9.3	38.5	24 825	338	1 976	36 071	1.4
Clark	0.3	D	9.0	9.0	10.3	6.9	6.9	13.2	17.6	81 065	177	8 315	177 829	6.2
Columbia	26.5	D	9.5	2.2	1.2	3.0	1.7	6.3	30.0	1 285	326	143	2 121	-0.7
Cowlitz	0.5	0.6	13.8	21.1	3.5	6.4	3.6	13.9	14.8	26 715	258	3 790	43 625	0.4
Douglas	17.7	0.0	7.5	4.5	8.4	8.7	3.5	5.2	25.4	7 680	189	560	16 502	3.1
Ferry	2.0	D	D	D	2.3	3.4	1.6	D	53.5	2 290	302	265	4 408	0.1
Franklin	17.3	D	6.8	9.1	1.9	7.1	3.3	6.3	19.8	9 840	111	1 794	27 009	10.6
Garfield	17.8	0.2	D	0.6	D	4.3	1.9	2.6	53.3	655	294	44	1 216	-1.4
Grant	25.6	D	4.2	12.9	2.1	5.0	3.0	4.9	23.5	15 520	167	2 141	35 970	2.5
Grays Harbor	0.9	D	6.5	13.8	3.9	7.6	3.3	10.2	30.8	19 445	274	2 951	35 373	0.6
Island	0.4	D	6.9	3.2	D	5.4	3.6	5.2	53.7	21 210	263	1 038	41 050	2.0
Jefferson	0.7	D	10.4	8.7	7.7	7.5	4.9	6.9	30.8	11 555	380	616	18 131	2.0
King	0.0	0.3	5.4	8.8	25.9	8.0	7.7	7.9	12.0	284 770	135	38 350	910 098	6.9
Kitsap	0.0	0.1	5.3	2.0	8.1	5.6	3.6	10.2	52.7	49 975	192	5 048	110 381	2.8
Kittitas	4.8	D	9.7	3.2	4.8	7.6	5.0	6.2	35.6	8 100	188	563	23 012	5.1
Klickitat	10.9	D	4.9	22.6	D	2.6	2.8	3.3	21.7	5 955	284	607	10 084	3.1
Lewis	6.7	0.7	5.7	15.9	3.0	8.6	3.0	13.0	20.3	20 955	277	2 708	34 165	0.3
Lincoln	27.1	D	7.3	D	D	3.5	5.5	D	31.3	3 045	295	247	5 860	1.5
Mason	1.0	D	6.1	9.9	3.9	7.9	4.0	5.4	42.9	17 000	279	1 570	32 664	0.4
Okanogan	14.0	2.1	6.1	3.3	D	7.9	2.5	7.7	33.5	10 690	258	1 310	22 619	1.7
Pacific	3.6	0.5	5.8	10.1	2.8	5.4	5.4	D	33.2	7 730	370	667	15 756	1.4
Pend Oreille	0.5	D	7.3	10.1	3.3	3.2	2.6	D	48.1	3 995	306	501	8 052	1.5
Pierce	0.3	0.1	7.2	5.9	4.8	6.5	5.1	16.0	32.2	144 675	172	19 866	338 560	4.1
San Juan	0.5	D	16.8	2.9	D	9.6	6.6	5.6	14.6	5 080	313	125	13 882	4.3
Skagit	3.5	0.1	9.4	15.5	5.7	8.5	5.8	8.0	23.2	28 855	237	2 486	52 526	2.0
Skamania	0.4	D	7.2	14.2	6.6	4.1	1.7	D	32.2	2 435	215	196	5 698	1.2
Snohomish	0.2	0.1	8.8	31.1	7.9	6.6	5.9	8.3	14.5	115 640	150	12 288	303 552	5.9
Spokane	0.3	0.1	6.1	7.4	7.4	7.2	8.7	17.3	19.9	98 025	200	14 217	210 553	4.5
Stevens	1.9	0.8	8.1	13.8	3.7	6.5	3.0	13.4	27.9	12 375	283	1 324	21 160	0.0
Thurston	0.9	0.0	5.3	3.1	6.3	6.3	4.9	12.7	39.3	55 735	207	5 207	113 324	4.8
Wahkiakum	3.0	0.1	10.9	5.9	D	2.6	1.9	D	32.2	1 455	362	99	2 081	0.6
Walla Walla	14.2	D	3.9	14.2	D	4.8	4.4	14.8	22.8	12 390	206	1 401	24 172	3.1
Whatcom	3.1	D	9.7	13.4	7.3	8.6	5.6	12.4	18.8	41 775	197	4 423	94 171	3.9
Whitman	7.8	D	2.6	16.1	2.2	4.5	2.6	5.3	46.7	5 705	118	415	20 285	5.0
Yakima	17.5	0.1	4.2	8.0	2.9	6.5	3.3	13.2	18.2	43 390	175	7 487	86 728	1.5
WEST VIRGINIA	-0.1	6.5	6.9	8.1	7.6	7.0	4.5	15.7	21.1	468 120	254	76 375	886 640	0.5
Barbour	-0.1	D	10.1	D	D	5.2	2.9	D	19.7	4 240	250	793	7 869	0.3
Berkeley	0.2	D	5.6	4.6	9.7	6.6	3.7	13.5	34.1	21 520	193	2 305	47 353	5.8
Boone	0.0	37.0	1.4	0.7	D	5.2	D	D	22.0	6 805	293	1 385	10 997	-0.7
Braxton	0.0	D	11.3	9.1	3.3	15.3	2.6	11.9	20.8	3 835	265	684	7 363	-0.7
Brooke	0.0	D	D	25.8	1.8	7.5	3.0	D	10.0	6 465	277	532	10 874	-0.9
Cabell	0.0	0.4	5.8	10.7	6.4	7.9	4.8	26.4	16.4	22 585	234	4 553	46 474	0.7

1. Per 1,000 resident population estimated as of July 1 of the year shown. 3. Martinsville city is included with Henry county. 4. Norton city is included with Wise county. 5. Petersburg and Colonial Heights cities are included with Dinwiddie county. 6. Poquoson city is included with York county. 7. Radford city is included with Montgomery county. 8. Salem city is included with Roanoke county. 9. Staunton and Waynesboro cities are included with Augusta county. 10. Williamsburg city is included with James City county. 11. Winchester city is included with Frederick county.

Table B. States and Counties — Housing, Labor Force, and Employment

STATE County	Housing units, 2011–2015								Civilian labor force, 2016				Civilian employment,[6] 2011–2015		
	Occupied units							Sub-stand-ard units[4] (percent)		Percent change, 2015–2016	Unemployment			Percent	
	Owner-occupied					Renter-occupied									Management, business, science and arts	Con-struction, produc-tion, and mainte-nance occu-pations
	Total	Percent	Median value[1]	Median owner cost as a percent of income		Median rent[3]	Median rent as a per-cent of income[2]		Total		Total	Rate[5]	Total		
				With a mort-gage	Without a mort-gage[2]										
	89	90	91	92	93	94	95	96	97	98	99	100	101	102	103
VIRGINIA—Cont'd															
Martinsville city	5 857	52.9	89 100	20.7	14.9	589	31.5	1.4	5 165	-3.5	366	7.1	5 156	25.6	29.5
Newport News city	69 073	50.2	193 100	23.9	12.4	964	31.4	2.8	88 891	0.2	4 516	5.1	82 572	33.1	21.7
Norfolk city	87 045	43.5	193 400	27.1	13.9	970	33.7	2.7	110 644	0.2	5 794	5.2	101 764	32.4	22.7
Norton city	1 783	50.9	91 600	25.0	11.7	557	26.6	2.7	1 649	-4.7	112	6.8	1 811	33.7	17.4
Petersburg city	12 803	41.4	111 900	24.1	13.9	842	36.0	2.4	13 509	0.2	1 033	7.6	12 898	25.4	21.9
Poquoson city	4 642	82.1	307 800	22.9	14.2	1 154	24.7	0.4	6 178	-0.2	218	3.5	5 932	50.0	16.2
Portsmouth city	36 757	54.8	169 800	26.9	16.2	964	33.5	2.4	44 370	0.4	2 688	6.1	41 039	29.9	25.5
Radford city	5 477	43.7	148 600	21.8	11.7	705	42.9	0.0	8 316	0.4	447	5.4	6 797	33.5	14.4
Richmond city	87 224	42.3	193 700	24.6	14.5	896	33.3	2.6	113 825	1.1	5 226	4.6	104 547	40.1	14.9
Roanoke city	42 239	53.7	134 400	23.6	12.7	728	29.1	2.0	48 994	0.3	2 085	4.3	46 331	32.1	22.0
Salem city	10 045	66.2	173 100	22.0	11.6	836	30.6	2.4	12 824	0.6	505	3.9	12 506	38.3	17.3
Staunton city	10 387	56.8	165 400	22.1	12.3	795	32.8	2.5	11 933	1.2	462	3.9	11 297	36.3	19.1
Suffolk city	30 990	70.6	235 300	25.3	11.9	1 031	31.5	1.7	42 341	0.2	1 983	4.7	39 589	38.1	22.7
Virginia Beach city	166 242	63.5	259 900	25.1	11.7	1 236	31.7	1.5	228 787	0.1	9 012	3.9	214 968	39.6	17.1
Waynesboro city	9 031	57.7	156 200	24.2	12.7	794	31.2	2.5	10 105	1.1	414	4.1	9 655	27.3	24.9
Williamsburg city	4 538	46.0	320 600	24.2	10.0	1 093	34.7	2.7	6 630	-0.3	370	5.6	5 953	47.3	11.2
Winchester city	10 608	44.9	216 300	21.4	12.6	936	32.4	4.5	14 289	0.7	563	3.9	12 748	34.7	20.5
WASHINGTON	2 668 912	62.5	259 500	24.2	11.8	1 014	30.0	3.5	3 643 885	2.8	198 002	5.4	3 259 877	39.0	20.9
Adams	5 802	65.3	138 400	23.0	10.0	680	28.8	12.5	8 699	1.0	592	6.8	7 698	23.9	47.5
Asotin	9 341	67.0	171 900	22.4	10.9	694	28.0	2.9	9 993	3.3	511	5.1	9 439	30.3	23.8
Benton	67 430	67.5	184 200	19.4	10.0	834	28.8	3.9	94 454	3.0	6 185	6.5	82 427	37.7	23.9
Chelan	27 052	65.7	246 300	24.7	10.2	788	25.1	4.5	43 917	3.1	2 578	5.9	33 140	29.3	30.8
Clallam	31 321	69.8	217 100	25.7	11.2	822	32.1	2.5	27 450	2.4	2 172	7.9	27 697	29.0	23.7
Clark	162 441	64.3	234 800	24.1	11.2	990	30.1	3.2	220 608	3.0	13 797	6.3	201 261	34.9	23.1
Columbia	1 686	73.7	154 800	25.9	12.6	721	34.3	3.3	1 732	2.2	118	6.8	1 557	34.9	21.5
Cowlitz	39 763	65.6	175 300	23.6	11.9	765	33.7	3.3	44 859	1.7	3 358	7.5	40 418	27.3	30.7
Douglas	14 212	71.8	209 700	23.7	10.2	824	26.6	8.3	20 661	4.5	1 469	7.1	18 034	24.9	36.9
Ferry	3 103	71.2	166 000	26.8	10.2	550	29.5	5.8	2 497	0.9	270	10.8	2 452	34.6	32.4
Franklin	24 725	67.1	166 800	21.5	10.0	807	29.0	11.5	39 969	2.6	3 056	7.6	36 259	23.8	40.0
Garfield	953	68.2	140 900	19.4	12.1	658	31.3	2.8	922	-0.9	55	6.0	883	35.6	21.4
Grant	30 358	60.5	157 500	21.9	10.5	696	24.9	7.5	44 807	0.3	3 321	7.4	38 314	27.6	40.4
Grays Harbor	27 219	67.8	158 300	23.6	12.0	729	29.8	3.0	27 373	1.7	2 384	8.7	26 197	25.0	27.0
Island	33 125	67.8	290 900	25.5	11.8	1 076	29.9	1.5	32 821	3.4	1 977	6.0	31 525	35.1	23.1
Jefferson	13 422	75.0	284 500	27.7	12.5	845	32.2	2.4	11 509	2.8	836	7.3	11 518	33.5	21.1
King	819 651	57.4	384 300	24.0	12.5	1 204	28.8	3.4	1 208 334	2.5	47 600	3.9	1 079 601	49.1	14.2
Kitsap	97 739	67.2	258 700	24.3	11.7	1 042	30.8	2.1	117 931	2.3	6 816	5.8	107 745	37.9	20.6
Kittitas	16 953	57.6	242 900	25.2	10.7	798	37.0	3.6	21 648	3.9	1 304	6.0	19 811	32.2	23.6
Klickitat	7 863	68.6	200 600	25.1	10.3	809	31.2	3.9	9 663	2.2	683	7.1	7 766	35.6	27.2
Lewis	29 515	67.4	174 000	24.2	12.3	801	32.3	3.3	32 094	2.8	2 595	8.1	29 297	25.9	30.5
Lincoln	4 370	79.0	142 500	22.9	11.7	644	23.8	3.4	4 885	0.2	280	5.7	4 050	35.3	26.8
Mason	23 026	77.0	204 300	26.5	10.8	884	34.4	3.2	23 597	2.5	1 849	7.8	22 155	27.6	26.7
Okanogan	16 619	68.2	162 700	22.6	10.3	621	28.7	7.5	21 548	1.5	1 493	6.9	16 969	30.8	30.0
Pacific	9 100	72.2	156 200	23.7	13.6	703	29.8	2.0	8 334	2.9	692	8.3	7 141	26.7	32.1
Pend Oreille	5 396	75.4	179 200	23.6	10.4	781	32.0	4.2	4 723	2.7	429	9.1	4 217	33.1	28.3
Pierce	303 586	61.0	232 600	25.0	12.7	1 029	31.3	3.0	405 717	3.4	25 462	6.3	365 152	33.3	23.7
San Juan	7 708	71.4	465 500	29.1	11.5	962	29.8	6.1	7 902	2.4	381	4.8	7 633	37.7	21.2
Skagit	45 841	66.8	249 800	25.4	12.7	954	32.9	5.5	58 138	2.6	3 945	6.8	51 761	31.6	26.3
Skamania	4 495	70.4	243 000	24.2	11.7	716	29.0	2.1	5 081	2.7	366	7.2	4 742	34.8	29.2
Snohomish	274 766	66.0	293 000	25.3	12.4	1 153	30.0	3.1	412 178	2.6	17 961	4.4	367 655	37.2	22.1
Spokane	189 471	62.9	183 300	23.2	11.0	782	31.5	2.0	234 518	3.0	14 865	6.3	211 522	35.8	19.0
Stevens	17 679	75.0	172 600	25.4	11.0	672	31.3	4.3	17 931	2.8	1 536	8.6	16 259	29.0	29.3
Thurston	102 631	64.6	239 400	24.6	11.2	1 054	29.8	2.7	130 653	3.9	7 604	5.8	119 123	40.0	17.9
Wahkiakum	1 716	78.8	178 400	21.7	11.4	653	45.4	1.5	1 296	0.2	116	9.0	1 248	28.0	34.9
Walla Walla	21 696	64.3	192 400	23.8	12.0	739	31.0	3.1	28 890	3.0	1 629	5.6	26 112	35.2	21.4
Whatcom	79 767	63.1	274 700	25.0	12.2	925	34.1	2.4	107 690	3.3	6 478	6.0	98 265	34.0	21.9
Whitman	17 399	44.5	181 800	20.7	10.0	695	41.3	1.1	23 069	1.4	1 184	5.1	21 665	46.8	14.5
Yakima	79 972	62.5	158 200	23.7	11.6	774	31.1	8.4	125 794	3.3	10 055	8.0	101 169	24.8	37.1
WEST VIRGINIA	740 890	72.5	103 800	19.1	10.0	643	28.9	1.9	783 468	0.0	47 043	6.0	751 252	32.2	24.8
Barbour	6 041	72.9	92 600	19.6	10.0	540	29.6	1.5	6 896	-0.2	460	6.7	6 345	21.3	28.8
Berkeley	40 991	73.2	162 500	22.5	10.0	919	28.6	3.0	54 596	1.1	2 085	3.8	49 941	32.6	26.1
Boone	9 547	76.6	75 700	19.7	10.0	572	29.7	2.7	8 103	-1.1	721	8.9	7 592	26.5	32.6
Braxton	5 607	74.9	79 500	17.3	10.0	488	29.8	2.4	5 494	0.5	473	8.6	5 280	25.6	30.8
Brooke	10 030	73.3	86 500	16.5	10.0	573	26.8	1.8	10 030	-0.7	696	6.9	10 360	29.8	25.8
Cabell	39 973	61.1	112 800	19.3	10.0	653	31.3	1.2	41 344	0.0	1 952	4.7	40 103	37.8	15.7

1. Specified owner-occupied units.　2. A value of 10.0 represents 10 percent or less; a value of 50.0 represents 50 percent or more.　3. Specified renter-occupied units.　4. Overcrowded or lacking complete plumbing facilities.　5. Percent of civilian labor force.　6. Civilian employed persons 16 years old and over.

Table B. States and Counties — Nonfarm Employment and Agriculture

	Private nonfarm establishments, employment and payroll, 2015									Agriculture, 2012			
		Employment						Annual payroll		Farms			
												Percent with:	
STATE County	Number of establishments	Total	Health care and social assistance	Manufacturing	Retail trade	Finance and insurance	Professional, scientific, and technical services	Total (mil dol)	Average per employee (dollars)	Number	Fewer than 50 acres	500 acres or more	Farm operators whose principal occupation is farming (percent)
	104	105	106	107	108	109	110	111	112	113	114	115	116
VIRGINIA—Cont'd													
Martinsville city	540	9 309	2 228	1 334	1 402	224	269	282	30 343	NA	NA	NA	NA
Newport News city	3 769	88 526	13 919	28 947	10 375	1 723	5 117	4 473	50 530	NA	NA	NA	NA
Norfolk city	5 302	107 775	19 065	7 000	12 132	4 634	10 500	4 949	45 920	NA	NA	NA	NA
Norton city	242	5 337	1 267	690	815	75	164	220	41 182	NA	NA	NA	NA
Petersburg city	702	14 008	6 391	1 239	1 440	194	151	471	33 596	NA	NA	NA	NA
Poquoson city	193	1 236	161	D	318	43	68	33	26 757	NA	NA	NA	NA
Portsmouth city	1 645	27 047	7 163	1 666	3 072	534	1 469	1 052	38 909	NA	NA	NA	NA
Radford city	302	4 174	539	1 145	592	132	198	150	36 015	NA	NA	NA	NA
Richmond city	6 044	119 124	27 044	4 722	9 174	10 606	11 727	7 090	59 520	NA	NA	NA	NA
Roanoke city	3 149	67 925	13 864	4 132	9 752	3 254	2 978	2 917	42 949	NA	NA	NA	NA
Salem city	978	18 312	4 710	3 199	1 915	518	551	875	47 807	NA	NA	NA	NA
Staunton city	757	11 051	2 983	524	1 970	324	291	310	28 089	NA	NA	NA	NA
Suffolk city	1 549	21 200	4 585	1 968	3 573	763	1 105	823	38 828	308	57.8	10.7	56.2
Virginia Beach city	10 977	152 137	19 453	5 809	23 493	11 302	15 572	5 984	39 330	187	64.7	7.0	48.1
Waynesboro city	608	9 598	721	1 680	2 288	388	285	326	33 981	NA	NA	NA	NA
Williamsburg city	533	8 685	671	20	1 744	170	129	264	30 408	NA	NA	NA	NA
Winchester city	1 350	24 843	7 115	1 842	4 239	619	909	983	39 549	NA	NA	NA	NA
WASHINGTON	182 913	2 602 408	392 857	262 314	330 705	96 389	193 065	149 259	57 354	37 249	63.2	11.0	47.4
Adams	369	4 495	763	1 152	677	85	40	179	39 831	713	17.8	46.6	54.8
Asotin	436	4 660	1 033	362	1 093	155	274	164	35 290	185	35.1	40.0	60.5
Benton	4 243	60 744	7 972	3 883	10 152	1 580	7 306	3 011	49 564	1 509	76.0	7.8	44.8
Chelan	2 491	28 899	5 965	1 900	4 459	680	1 116	1 240	42 908	890	72.2	2.9	55.7
Clallam	2 049	17 104	3 939	1 118	3 575	469	666	598	34 947	536	79.7	0.6	45.9
Clark	10 257	124 531	21 046	13 437	17 296	5 427	8 603	6 031	48 433	1 929	86.3	0.5	35.4
Columbia	124	774	164	83	115	18	26	29	37 261	308	23.1	37.7	42.5
Cowlitz	2 099	30 598	5 471	6 382	4 879	811	708	1 398	45 674	492	72.4	2.8	46.7
Douglas	724	6 751	876	389	1 680	192	184	221	32 707	849	43.0	25.9	55.9
Ferry	139	1 076	148	171	142	22	23	61	56 545	255	27.8	16.1	52.2
Franklin	1 489	18 917	1 797	2 965	3 112	347	474	786	41 546	883	37.5	27.2	62.7
Garfield	46	312	110	NA	48	13	7	11	34 154	211	15.6	51.2	56.9
Grant	1 799	20 843	2 891	4 095	3 395	522	416	825	39 563	1 552	31.2	25.9	66.6
Grays Harbor	1 618	15 448	2 723	2 009	2 861	545	391	575	37 232	557	63.9	4.7	44.7
Island	1 706	12 224	2 636	731	2 193	380	713	434	35 492	377	80.6	0.8	46.7
Jefferson	1 029	6 578	1 351	758	1 061	147	315	238	36 131	221	64.7	0.9	49.3
King	66 891	1 133 727	146 533	84 658	106 380	41 504	104 444	83 213	73 398	1 837	90.5	0.4	44.3
Kitsap	5 676	57 374	12 273	1 970	11 203	1 937	3 999	2 188	38 141	706	94.9	0.1	44.6
Kittitas	1 193	11 086	1 610	543	1 669	197	247	370	33 355	1 006	66.4	6.7	48.9
Klickitat	532	3 748	598	613	371	65	276	149	39 796	760	44.5	22.8	51.7
Lewis	1 848	19 400	3 428	2 916	3 766	385	495	741	38 213	1 647	63.8	2.1	41.0
Lincoln	249	1 554	427	40	290	70	105	67	43 025	897	16.7	48.6	54.3
Mason	1 005	9 770	1 838	1 003	1 687	292	246	361	36 904	377	83.8	1.9	40.6
Okanogan	1 109	8 609	1 676	572	1 936	211	466	267	31 061	1 449	52.3	11.5	48.5
Pacific	580	3 838	650	559	552	161	112	128	33 342	330	61.8	6.1	45.8
Pend Oreille	219	1 626	361	263	237	49	66	66	40 704	288	45.5	4.2	37.8
Pierce	17 012	244 855	47 157	18 032	35 621	10 228	9 253	10 815	44 169	1 478	85.3	0.3	47.0
San Juan	1 003	4 441	378	192	677	132	234	168	37 744	274	73.0	1.5	52.9
Skagit	3 417	39 772	6 933	6 000	7 130	1 402	1 585	1 724	43 353	1 074	73.0	4.4	48.0
Skamania	189	1 488	145	333	141	21	54	47	31 358	144	75.0	0.0	45.8
Snohomish	17 851	247 650	29 358	62 521	35 938	8 546	11 865	12 868	51 960	1 438	82.3	1.2	35.5
Spokane	12 679	181 186	35 903	14 690	26 777	10 573	8 706	7 877	43 475	2 501	59.7	9.2	41.5
Stevens	852	7 013	1 625	1 091	1 251	188	216	255	36 379	1 148	44.3	11.1	46.7
Thurston	6 039	68 684	14 080	2 657	12 558	2 612	4 539	2 709	39 435	1 336	79.3	2.0	30.7
Wahkiakum	82	437	33	50	39	16	16	14	32 233	109	50.5	1.8	50.5
Walla Walla	1 359	19 348	4 040	3 493	2 200	666	461	731	37 806	943	53.0	24.0	48.4
Whatcom	6 401	73 743	9 648	9 979	11 754	2 345	3 325	3 052	41 387	1 702	74.7	2.5	45.4
Whitman	856	10 100	1 830	D	1 355	204	340	388	38 398	1 195	21.5	45.4	59.5
Yakima	4 680	66 044	12 845	8 574	10 402	1 520	1 747	2 542	38 496	3 143	73.9	5.5	51.9
WEST VIRGINIA	36 993	565 435	130 862	48 347	85 720	17 458	26 802	22 159	39 189	21 489	28.3	5.8	42.6
Barbour	228	3 183	768	121	325	71	101	83	26 172	513	22.4	6.0	41.1
Berkeley	1 574	22 961	5 816	2 446	4 241	589	1 029	904	39 359	676	57.5	3.7	34.5
Boone	283	4 869	801	117	675	118	83	234	48 093	19	21.1		73.7
Braxton	259	3 623	884	342	603	74	53	138	38 029	386	16.6	12.2	50.3
Brooke	391	7 399	2 173	1 652	857	118	86	275	37 110	96	29.2	8.3	45.8
Cabell	2 398	46 688	13 468	4 409	6 966	1 312	1 997	1 790	38 344	383	33.2	2.9	31.6

Table B. States and Counties — **Agriculture**

STATE County	Land in farms Acreage (1,000)	Percent change, 2007–2012	Acres Average size of farm	Total irrigated (1,000)	Total cropland (1,000)	Value of land and buildings (dollars) Average per farm	Average per acre	Value of machinery and equipment, average per farm (dollars)	Value of products sold Total (mil dol)	Average per farm (dollars)	Percent from: Crops	Live-stock and poultry products	Percent of farms with sales of: $10,000 or more	$100,000 or more	Government payments Total ($1,000)	Percent of farms
	117	118	119	120	121	122	123	124	125	126	127	128	129	130	131	132
VIRGINIA—Cont'd																
Martinsville city	NA	NA	NA	NA	NA	NA	NA	NA	NA	NA	NA	NA	NA	NA	NA	NA
Newport News city	NA	NA	NA	NA	NA	NA	NA	NA	NA	NA	NA	NA	NA	NA	NA	NA
Norfolk city	NA	NA	NA	NA	NA	NA	NA	NA	NA	NA	NA	NA	NA	NA	NA	NA
Norton city	NA	NA	NA	NA	NA	NA	NA	NA	NA	NA	NA	NA	NA	NA	NA	NA
Petersburg city	NA	NA	NA	NA	NA	NA	NA	NA	NA	NA	NA	NA	NA	NA	NA	NA
Poquoson city	NA	NA	NA	NA	NA	NA	NA	NA	NA	NA	NA	NA	NA	NA	NA	NA
Portsmouth city	NA	NA	NA	NA	NA	NA	NA	NA	NA	NA	NA	NA	NA	NA	NA	NA
Radford city	NA	NA	NA	NA	NA	NA	NA	NA	NA	NA	NA	NA	NA	NA	NA	NA
Richmond city	NA	NA	NA	NA	NA	NA	NA	NA	NA	NA	NA	NA	NA	NA	NA	NA
Roanoke city	NA	NA	NA	NA	NA	NA	NA	NA	NA	NA	NA	NA	NA	NA	NA	NA
Salem city	NA	NA	NA	NA	NA	NA	NA	NA	NA	NA	NA	NA	NA	NA	NA	NA
Staunton city	NA	NA	NA	NA	NA	NA	NA	NA	NA	NA	NA	NA	NA	NA	NA	NA
Suffolk city	69	-3.0	225	0.4	50.9	1 016 494	4 521	155 899	62.5	202 760	94.4	5.6	37.3	15.6	2 466	47.4
Virginia Beach city	26	-1.8	140	0.2	21.2	744 428	5 317	93 203	17.7	94 631	95.0	5.0	36.9	13.9	373	23.0
Waynesboro city	NA	NA	NA	NA	NA	NA	NA	NA	NA	NA	NA	NA	NA	NA	NA	NA
Williamsburg city	NA	NA	NA	NA	NA	NA	NA	NA	NA	NA	NA	NA	NA	NA	NA	NA
Winchester city	NA	NA	NA	NA	NA	NA	NA	NA	NA	NA	NA	NA	NA	NA	NA	NA
WASHINGTON	14 748	-1.5	396	1 633.6	7 526.7	910 249	2 299	98 588	9 120.7	244 859	71.2	28.8	34.2	16.4	159 269	19.4
Adams	1 037	-5.6	1 454	127.0	815.0	1 790 387	1 231	252 728	430.2	603 303	79.0	21.0	50.5	39.4	15 567	68.2
Asotin	263	-3.9	1 423	0.5	84.3	1 210 465	851	103 357	20.5	110 854	79.9	20.2	40.5	25.4	2 504	49.2
Benton	704	11.2	466	197.3	519.1	1 276 306	2 738	127 966	923.2	611 771	D	D	34.5	15.0	6 225	10.9
Chelan	76	-19.2	85	22.8	31.5	746 306	8 760	64 446	206.5	231 999	98.2	1.8	65.6	33.7	658	7.0
Clallam	24	3.6	44	4.2	8.1	549 722	12 464	36 032	10.6	19 866	38.8	61.1	16.6	3.9	47	2.2
Clark	75	-4.6	39	3.7	29.0	490 328	12 652	38 798	50.9	26 367	37.1	62.9	16.4	2.6	293	2.4
Columbia	297	-5.1	966	4.1	184.5	1 038 701	1 076	177 896	57.7	187 442	93.4	6.6	39.3	24.0	5 273	73.4
Cowlitz	39	27.1	79	7.6	18.6	689 236	8 693	67 535	28.8	58 482	D	D	19.5	6.9	44	1.6
Douglas	814	-7.8	959	18.3	545.4	976 847	1 019	130 582	199.0	234 442	98.4	1.6	55.2	35.7	12 940	48.5
Ferry	792	5.7	3 107	2.8	19.4	1 320 859	425	55 478	5.3	20 906	54.0	46.0	28.2	7.5	159	13.3
Franklin	625	2.6	708	207.2	452.2	2 071 813	2 927	302 318	740.0	838 068	68.0	32.0	60.6	46.2	8 142	38.7
Garfield	308	0.1	1 462	0.8	187.5	1 384 441	947	153 076	48.2	228 474	92.0	8.0	50.7	37.0	4 878	80.6
Grant	964	-11.4	621	428.2	720.0	2 128 600	3 428	291 085	1 762.3	1 135 499	75.6	24.4	63.0	47.1	11 429	38.5
Grays Harbor	119	0.1	214	8.6	22.8	450 820	2 102	66 575	31.4	56 289	53.3	46.7	22.6	6.8	186	5.4
Island	15	-13.8	40	1.6	7.4	575 838	14 236	41 111	11.5	30 416	28.6	71.4	24.1	3.4	56	4.2
Jefferson	16	22.3	70	1.2	4.2	643 059	9 136	36 900	7.7	34 647	22.7	77.3	33.0	7.2	94	9.0
King	47	-5.2	25	4.1	19.7	545 036	21 432	39 027	120.7	65 732	36.4	63.6	22.8	4.6	791	4.0
Kitsap	10	-34.2	14	0.5	2.5	377 215	26 446	27 010	5.3	7 513	70.0	30.0	14.3	1.4	30	2.5
Kittitas	183	-4.2	182	66.9	68.3	804 841	4 421	77 593	68.9	68 500	68.4	31.6	35.5	12.2	875	10.3
Klickitat	551	-8.3	725	21.7	192.3	1 033 424	1 425	83 599	72.4	95 246	80.3	19.7	31.6	11.4	4 275	37.8
Lewis	133	1.0	81	8.2	54.3	507 676	6 294	48 523	132.3	80 345	22.0	78.0	24.0	6.3	879	6.8
Lincoln	1 115	2.3	1 243	34.7	808.5	1 383 491	1 113	173 996	183.2	204 285	94.7	5.3	46.5	33.8	20 307	77.6
Mason	24	-5.7	63	0.8	4.8	522 432	8 295	40 891	40.8	108 247	6.2	93.8	24.7	8.8	57	2.1
Okanogan	1 205	0.0	832	51.7	129.2	1 103 226	1 326	73 568	287.1	198 150	87.0	13.0	42.1	21.0	2 383	9.5
Pacific	52	-15.5	158	2.5	13.0	546 279	3 456	60 573	36.8	111 461	20.2	79.8	43.3	16.1	305	9.4
Pend Oreille	44	-20.8	151	0.9	15.3	462 514	3 054	45 521	4.0	13 729	58.5	41.5	15.3	2.4	27	2.8
Pierce	49	3.8	33	2.8	11.5	476 152	14 222	35 548	90.9	61 524	26.3	73.7	17.9	3.0	96	1.3
San Juan	16	-27.0	57	0.3	5.5	756 471	13 228	28 427	4.2	15 493	60.8	39.2	33.9	2.9	41	3.6
Skagit	107	-1.8	99	19.2	66.8	752 365	7 585	118 998	272.3	253 515	73.8	26.2	29.1	12.2	1 442	11.1
Skamania	6	18.3	45	0.4	1.3	456 965	10 166	36 611	5.5	38 458	27.7	72.3	25.0	6.9	0	0.0
Snohomish	71	-7.8	49	5.3	29.1	791 114	16 054	40 122	139.5	97 000	45.3	54.7	21.8	6.5	620	4.9
Spokane	537	-14.2	215	10.3	369.6	611 087	2 844	72 631	149.8	59 880	88.7	11.3	25.6	9.3	7 355	24.7
Stevens	527	-0.7	459	6.7	88.8	722 020	1 572	49 637	36.3	31 660	47.9	52.1	32.3	7.3	926	12.6
Thurston	77	-4.9	57	5.3	23.1	498 439	8 689	40 468	122.4	91 634	39.9	60.1	19.5	5.2	267	2.4
Wahkiakum	10	-20.5	88	0.0	2.7	411 376	4 692	38 826	3.5	31 991	8.3	91.7	31.2	7.3	92	11.9
Walla Walla	645	-5.5	684	91.1	565.8	1 426 922	2 086	175 634	437.4	463 795	D	D	42.2	23.5	12 372	45.2
Whatcom	116	12.9	68	35.5	78.7	786 343	11 554	80 437	357.3	209 937	33.5	66.5	31.2	15.5	3 425	17.6
Whitman	1 275	0.3	1 067	4.3	1 020.0	1 490 631	1 397	214 180	370.8	310 294	95.0	5.0	50.5	40.4	28 405	77.9
Yakima	1 780	8.0	566	224.4	306.9	1 021 212	1 803	118 874	1 645.5	523 548	65.0	35.0	45.7	22.4	5 804	11.5
WEST VIRGINIA	3 607	-2.5	168	2.1	804.0	413 407	2 463	50 020	806.8	37 544	17.2	82.8	25.3	4.0	7 034	10.2
Barbour	85	-6.9	165	0.0	19.2	323 021	1 955	52 060	6.6	12 930	17.5	82.5	28.8	1.9	109	8.2
Berkeley	70	-6.7	104	0.1	33.3	596 855	5 757	53 351	30.5	45 185	78.5	21.5	25.7	4.7	374	14.5
Boone	2	-2.9	117	0.0	0.1	203 895	1 736	26 526	0.0	2 526	43.8	56.3	5.3	0.0	D	10.5
Braxton	89	11.9	230	0.0	14.7	376 614	1 635	40 829	4.9	12 586	20.0	80.0	27.7	1.3	147	9.3
Brooke	15	-4.5	153	D	4.3	298 448	1 948	68 323	1.4	14 406	20.4	79.5	30.2	3.1	D	3.1
Cabell	42	-10.9	111	0.0	6.3	332 266	2 998	42 608	2.0	5 198	50.3	49.7	9.4	0.5	60	16.2

Table B. States and Counties — Water Use, Wholesale Trade, Retail Trade, and Real Estate

STATE County	Water use, 2010		Wholesale trade,[1] 2012				Retail trade,[2] 2012				Real estate and rental and leasing,[2] 2012			
	Total water withdrawn (mil gal/day)	Gallons withdrawn per person per day	Number of establishments	Number of employees	Sales (mil dol)	Annual payroll (mil dol)	Number of establishments	Number of employees	Sales (mil dol)	Annual payroll (mil dol)	Number of establishments	Number of employees	Receipts (mil dol)	Annual payroll (mil dol)
	133	134	135	136	137	138	139	140	141	142	143	144	145	146
VIRGINIA—Cont'd														
Martinsville city	0.0	0	16	D	D	D	111	1 578	317.8	34.4	31	104	14.3	2.3
Newport News city	28.6	158	110	1 438	851.3	72.7	686	9 879	2 480.8	229.7	254	1 672	276.5	60.3
Norfolk city	1.0	4	209	3 287	3 195.3	161.6	867	12 440	2 683.2	281.6	291	2 496	430.8	127.7
Norton city	0.8	200	8	123	78.3	7.1	48	786	219.7	19.3	11	42	5.0	1.0
Petersburg city	0.1	3	21	570	560.1	16.2	145	1 426	334.5	33.0	32	223	27.2	5.8
Poquoson city	0.0	0	4	D	D	D	28	305	63.8	6.1	12	20	3.2	0.6
Portsmouth city	1.4	15	48	688	249.5	32.0	273	3 081	699.5	71.1	71	332	52.6	9.7
Radford city	2.1	128	8	51	84.6	2.3	39	537	105.8	11.8	21	83	12.5	2.5
Richmond city	65.6	321	269	3 767	3 288.5	201.3	808	8 666	1 955.2	206.1	258	1 539	304.3	67.1
Roanoke city	5.3	54	180	2 727	1 398.0	130.3	535	9 912	2 461.0	230.1	155	950	141.8	31.0
Salem city	4.6	187	77	1 567	1 228.3	89.3	145	1 995	507.8	48.3	35	176	50.4	7.2
Staunton city	0.2	10	22	200	76.0	7.1	134	1 862	432.7	42.6	43	D	D	D
Suffolk city	82.8	979	54	961	666.0	49.8	226	3 536	958.9	79.1	67	243	37.5	8.1
Virginia Beach city	1.7	4	391	6 893	8 187.6	477.1	1 500	22 723	5 671.5	521.6	649	6 165	902.5	210.7
Waynesboro city	6.0	286	16	253	113.3	12.7	123	2 123	474.3	45.2	30	D	D	D
Williamsburg city	1.0	70	7	49	31.9	3.2	119	1 931	348.7	37.9	24	D	D	D
Winchester city	0.1	4	39	677	286.8	26.1	283	4 126	888.5	94.4	59	260	56.4	8.0
WASHINGTON	4 955.8	737	7 733	103 307	83 313.4	5 789.8	21 588	307 089	118 924.0	8 722.5	9 913	45 209	9 695.5	1 895.1
Adams	217.3	11 602	26	D	D	D	51	548	157.8	13.1	10	21	3.4	0.4
Asotin	4.9	227	13	D	D	D	59	1 094	285.9	30.3	21	143	11.8	3.1
Benton	415.5	2 372	109	999	1 230.3	44.5	583	9 216	2 463.5	222.7	244	1 004	179.4	30.2
Chelan	68.6	947	89	2 118	1 018.7	76.5	379	4 154	1 004.5	106.7	118	399	51.9	11.3
Clallam	21.0	294	38	D	D	D	287	3 476	812.0	92.1	87	246	35.3	7.0
Clark	134.1	315	414	4 410	4 395.4	253.2	1 011	15 547	4 276.5	419.9	465	D	D	D
Columbia	8.4	2 048	18	D	D	D	18	111	30.5	2.6	7	12	0.8	0.2
Cowlitz	146.6	1 431	85	1 036	2 021.4	53.2	333	4 644	1 188.3	113.8	104	337	50.7	8.5
Douglas	35.2	915	38	D	D	D	98	1 547	430.0	40.2	27	76	11.1	2.2
Ferry	6.3	837	1	D	D	D	27	167	45.4	3.8	6	20	0.7	0.3
Franklin	479.3	6 132	113	1 513	1 741.6	67.8	189	2 719	918.9	84.7	56	240	41.0	7.1
Garfield	3.0	1 337	9	D	D	D	11	55	10.4	1.0	NA	NA	NA	NA
Grant	1 074.9	12 061	117	D	D	D	287	3 160	825.6	77.4	81	203	28.2	5.1
Grays Harbor	34.3	471	52	D	D	D	264	2 871	761.5	73.3	82	246	24.5	5.6
Island	9.0	115	36	145	57.5	6.3	212	2 181	456.3	52.5	82	238	36.8	6.6
Jefferson	5.6	187	20	D	D	D	144	1 012	209.9	26.0	49	116	14.5	2.6
King	259.7	134	3 235	49 268	42 092.5	3 183.4	6 524	97 959	61 598.2	3 159.8	4 186	23 233	5 825.0	1 180.7
Kitsap	32.1	128	147	953	407.9	43.7	731	10 343	2 674.2	276.3	338	979	198.5	32.7
Kittitas	132.0	3 227	41	442	398.7	23.6	159	1 646	516.0	39.0	54	140	25.6	4.1
Klickitat	40.6	1 997	16	D	D	D	47	330	64.5	7.0	21	23	3.6	0.4
Lewis	39.2	519	60	D	D	D	314	3 521	912.2	87.0	75	251	34.4	7.7
Lincoln	32.3	3 057	27	D	D	D	46	292	106.9	8.1	5	6	0.5	0.1
Mason	43.8	722	33	D	D	D	134	1 557	404.3	40.4	44	233	17.6	5.1
Okanogan	98.7	2 400	39	D	D	D	199	1 836	447.0	44.5	60	154	11.5	2.3
Pacific	9.2	441	6	D	D	D	89	555	107.9	14.2	22	52	4.5	1.0
Pend Oreille	4.0	308	4	D	D	D	32	249	58.3	5.0	7	14	0.8	0.2
Pierce	197.2	248	686	9 171	7 705.6	449.9	2 154	33 111	10 114.4	944.9	947	4 673	837.6	158.6
San Juan	1.8	113	14	61	12.7	2.0	111	608	150.6	19.6	52	92	12.9	2.0
Skagit	45.3	388	104	1 277	793.5	58.2	553	6 801	1 999.2	186.8	158	467	81.8	14.4
Skamania	23.1	2 083	5	24	10.7	1.0	21	134	25.2	2.7	3	D	D	D
Snohomish	201.9	283	731	7 287	5 652.7	407.7	2 184	32 776	9 130.8	903.2	863	3 131	710.2	122.0
Spokane	185.1	393	561	8 334	4 946.9	400.8	1 617	24 749	6 560.8	668.0	614	3 053	518.3	102.2
Stevens	29.9	688	21	D	D	D	128	1 214	283.2	27.5	23	76	12.1	2.0
Thurston	52.3	207	169	1 824	1 252.0	90.8	769	12 317	3 330.8	324.6	325	994	202.1	31.3
Wahkiakum	0.7	173	2	D	D	D	9	51	10.1	1.0	6	9	0.4	0.1
Walla Walla	160.2	2 725	70	D	D	D	183	2 322	555.5	56.5	55	175	22.2	5.0
Whatcom	85.5	425	289	D	D	D	818	11 310	3 103.6	272.4	317	1 131	230.9	34.3
Whitman	8.9	199	61	D	D	D	100	1 331	333.6	28.0	50	194	21.5	4.6
Yakima	608.4	2 501	234	4 373	3 335.1	198.3	713	9 575	2 560.2	246.1	249	974	132.0	26.7
WEST VIRGINIA	3 533.0	1 907	1 334	16 906	14 295.4	761.9	6 393	85 305	22 637.9	1 908.5	1 405	6 011	1 255.8	203.8
Barbour	2.1	128	4	8	1.3	0.2	37	378	89.6	7.0	6	13	0.8	0.3
Berkeley	28.8	276	40	840	709.5	39.3	247	3 879	939.2	82.4	67	264	32.9	6.6
Boone	3.0	123	10	D	D	D	63	790	227.4	17.7	5	D	D	D
Braxton	2.3	160	8	59	23.3	2.1	67	572	171.1	13.5	8	26	3.4	0.6
Brooke	12.5	518	13	D	D	D	63	931	236.8	20.4	2	D	D	D
Cabell	29.3	304	106	1 754	873.6	82.4	439	6 687	1 570.9	145.2	97	362	69.0	12.4

1. Merchant wholesalers, except manufacturers' sales branches and offices.　　2. Employer establishments.

Table B. States and Counties — Professional Services, Manufacturing, and Accommodation and Food Services

STATE County	Professional, scientific, and technical services, 2012				Manufacturing, 2012				Accommodation and food services, 2012			
	Number of establish-ments	Number of employees	Receipts (mil dol)	Annual payroll (mil dol)	Number of establish-ments	Number of employees	Receipts (mil dol)	Annual payroll (mil dol)	Number of establish-ments	Number of employees	Sales (mil dol)	Annual payroll (mil dol)
	147	148	149	150	151	152	153	154	155	156	157	158
VIRGINIA—Cont'd												
Martinsville city	48	241	21.6	8.9	24	1 041	192.7	33.0	46	718	28.8	7.8
Newport News city	364	4 971	762.0	292.6	91	26 503	5 578.9	1 558.5	386	6 621	323.8	87.6
Norfolk city	708	12 065	2 415.0	1 025.2	130	6 866	1 812.5	328.2	593	11 264	547.1	148.4
Norton city	21	173	12.9	5.7	8	585	109.8	22.2	24	D	D	D
Petersburg city	36	175	20.5	8.0	28	1 646	D	91.0	79	885	39.1	10.2
Poquoson city	22	85	7.2	3.1	3	D	1.0	D	21	278	10.0	2.9
Portsmouth city	147	D	D	D	56	2 196	447.1	97.6	172	2 624	107.1	29.3
Radford city	25	196	20.1	7.9	18	2 794	712.0	149.8	49	934	36.0	9.3
Richmond city	856	10 406	2 522.3	894.5	187	5 882	16 885.9	386.3	618	11 470	576.5	184.1
Roanoke city	328	2 920	390.6	170.1	100	3 869	1 629.7	174.8	320	6 509	308.1	94.4
Salem city	75	552	66.4	24.2	61	3 558	1 335.7	199.7	92	1 825	75.6	22.7
Staunton city	52	295	30.7	11.9	23	430	87.3	19.1	80	1 433	59.5	18.2
Suffolk city	123	D	D	D	46	1 996	1 521.0	103.6	147	2 477	122.9	30.6
Virginia Beach city	1 395	17 405	3 911.2	1 197.5	207	5 616	1 954.2	255.1	1 153	21 910	1 202.7	324.3
Waynesboro city	42	761	21.7	43.4	28	1 856	465.5	79.5	68	1 330	67.9	18.2
Williamsburg city	39	154	12.5	4.6	3	D	1.0	0.3	143	4 043	217.5	71.5
Winchester city	131	1 122	98.6	47.9	23	2 197	866.2	117.6	130	2 518	119.1	33.1
WASHINGTON	20 047	167 512	28 283.6	11 976.5	6 992	248 192	131 530.6	14 461.8	16 333	234 145	14 297.3	4 159.7
Adams	13	D	D	D	10	1 243	D	43.2	37	341	18.7	4.6
Asotin	32	1 182	19.7	11.9	25	277	50.5	10.1	40	581	25.2	8.5
Benton	436	8 899	1 654.5	668.2	144	3 990	1 828.0	217.8	375	5 996	311.6	88.4
Chelan	181	886	100.9	38.8	89	1 702	572.6	83.5	289	3 364	197.2	61.8
Clallam	170	850	77.1	33.7	82	1 215	372.2	57.4	224	2 050	113.3	33.5
Clark	1 141	7 197	1 005.6	364.9	409	11 562	D	630.8	721	10 524	550.7	163.9
Columbia	8	21	1.1	0.5	6	57	D	2.7	12	62	3.2	0.8
Cowlitz	140	830	86.5	34.9	116	5 722	3 264.5	385.6	215	2 796	124.2	39.2
Douglas	36	184	15.3	6.5	20	304	62.4	16.1	52	810	36.1	11.4
Ferry	7	D	D	D	6	141	D	5.2	17	D	D	D
Franklin	75	442	46.6	19.0	53	2 774	993.7	109.3	117	1 740	94.2	26.1
Garfield	4	D	D	D	NA	NA	NA	NA	6	12	0.3	0.1
Grant	101	406	40.6	14.5	73	4 074	1 458.5	182.3	189	1 935	117.2	29.7
Grays Harbor	91	427	43.9	18.6	84	2 580	874.2	121.2	232	1 902	104.2	29.5
Island	181	D	D	D	65	705	125.7	25.7	159	D	D	D
Jefferson	108	256	25.2	10.1	70	676	D	30.2	108	939	44.9	14.4
King	9 676	97 576	18 749.2	7 992.6	2 233	79 631	D	4 816.6	5 861	93 388	6 223.8	1 864.5
Kitsap	710	D	D	D	161	1 817	328.2	80.7	468	7 138	426.0	124.0
Kittitas	66	252	23.1	8.9	29	640	D	15.5	161	1 990	101.4	35.4
Klickitat	61	298	59.5	11.4	33	638	139.0	26.9	50	298	20.8	5.7
Lewis	118	D	D	D	123	3 270	1 238.1	139.7	188	1 842	93.6	26.6
Lincoln	11	D	D	D	8	36	D	1.5	24	D	D	D
Mason	73	D	D	D	47	942	268.5	40.2	95	D	D	D
Okanogan	76	227	23.8	6.6	35	354	123.7	12.4	124	1 031	54.8	16.6
Pacific	38	104	10.4	4.0	32	566	154.9	21.2	110	698	46.1	11.6
Pend Oreille	15	D	D	D	10	298	D	19.5	27	176	8.7	2.6
Pierce	1 427	9 464	1 043.4	546.3	566	16 027	4 461.0	796.5	1 553	22 535	1 363.0	368.8
San Juan	96	230	35.7	12.2	37	207	D	7.2	100	699	67.8	21.8
Skagit	300	D	D	D	174	5 269	11 529.4	295.7	330	4 195	291.5	79.1
Skamania	17	55	8.5	4.1	16	192	D	8.9	25	517	32.9	10.2
Snohomish	1 548	10 150	1 514.0	712.6	785	60 156	D	4 264.2	1 550	19 757	1 168.5	324.6
Spokane	1 259	D	D	D	512	13 940	3 943.1	660.3	1 057	17 949	1 062.6	299.7
Stevens	63	208	18.1	7.3	44	987	282.2	43.8	87	567	28.4	7.9
Thurston	593	D	D	D	168	2 883	910.5	123.8	533	7 785	419.2	120.5
Wahkiakum	7	D	D	D	6	D	D	D	7	D	D	D
Walla Walla	109	438	44.8	17.1	131	3 394	D	156.8	135	1 936	92.7	27.6
Whatcom	685	D	D	D	330	9 613	14 932.2	552.3	509	8 282	492.9	140.6
Whitman	56	D	D	D	27	2 136	D	128.4	130	1 463	62.1	17.1
Yakima	319	2 023	193.3	80.5	232	8 152	2 622.2	327.3	416	5 364	281.5	79.8
WEST VIRGINIA	2 974	24 816	3 104.8	1 143.4	1 245	48 686	24 553.1	2 603.9	3 629	66 302	4 036.3	975.9
Barbour	16	116	8.6	3.2	10	101	28.6	D	24	D	D	D
Berkeley	136	963	133.6	48.4	41	2 210	866.6	98.0	171	2 660	127.5	36.5
Boone	18	D	D	D	4	34	D	1.1	20	D	D	D
Braxton	12	50	4.5	1.5	12	258	148.2	12.2	27	D	D	D
Brooke	21	D	D	D	22	1 800	1 641.4	102.4	55	D	D	D
Cabell	202	2 070	204.9	77.5	90	4 818	2 345.2	298.5	269	4 968	237.4	64.9

1. Establishment subject to federal tax.

STATE County	Health care and social assistance, 2012				Other services, 2012				Nonemployer businesses, 2015		Value of residential construction authorized by building permits, 2016	
	Number of establishments	Number of employees	Receipts (mil dol)	Annual payroll (mil dol)	Number of establishments	Number of employees	Receipts (mil dol)	Annual payroll (mil dol)	Number	Receipts (mil dol)	New Construction ($1,000)	Number of housing units
	159	160	161	162	163	164	165	166	167	168	169	170
VIRGINIA—Cont'd												
Martinsville city	109	2 135	205.5	80.8	46	231	20.6	4.7	741	30.8	324	5
Newport News city	390	13 476	1 546.8	651.1	289	1 963	210.3	60.0	8 964	310.3	15 601	232
Norfolk city	533	18 651	2 391.6	900.9	374	3 245	443.7	110.7	12 014	473.5	78 709	1 045
Norton city	52	1 379	141.0	51.2	15	D	D	D	230	8.6	0	0
Petersburg city	126	4 740	437.7	175.4	74	554	43.2	14.7	1 241	47.9	3 768	77
Poquoson city	14	204	12.6	5.3	26	D	D	D	802	32.2	10 783	43
Portsmouth city	207	7 793	815.7	310.9	148	1 100	134.6	38.1	4 589	127.7	15 135	124
Radford city	39	507	40.4	17.4	29	D	D	D	628	28.7	1 482	15
Richmond city	597	25 804	3 769.4	1 303.8	516	3 904	445.6	125.1	15 278	672.0	72 308	510
Roanoke city	314	12 451	1 582.3	615.0	250	2 083	159.3	47.5	5 748	262.5	21 281	153
Salem city	114	5 223	737.8	266.3	101	563	33.6	12.8	1 424	62.7	8 865	37
Staunton city	86	2 194	154.1	74.3	85	436	38.3	11.3	1 550	65.0	4 125	71
Suffolk city	177	4 087	494.9	192.3	94	593	43.3	13.3	5 167	185.2	73 334	707
Virginia Beach city	997	18 362	1 959.4	814.7	829	4 778	618.6	119.9	29 786	1 449.5	219 498	1 583
Waynesboro city	48	875	66.9	24.1	52	364	39.4	11.5	1 059	43.5	298	22
Williamsburg city	44	D	D	D	29	276	33.3	12.4	830	38.7	7 615	49
Winchester city	261	6 460	885.3	355.8	85	506	36.7	10.9	2 054	122.5	6 584	30
WASHINGTON	19 833	374 227	43 966.9	17 833.2	12 425	69 976	13 185.2	2 203.3	444 135	21 910.1	9 116 339	44 077
Adams	27	716	64.2	30.7	28	D	D	D	739	43.5	4 670	31
Asotin	54	995	99.1	36.8	23	D	D	D	1 058	44.6	6 957	32
Benton	544	9 802	1 108.3	436.7	250	1 506	120.3	39.1	8 849	375.9	320 439	1 357
Chelan	221	5 233	642.6	288.8	162	571	67.6	15.7	4 626	212.5	80 408	393
Clallam	273	4 062	329.7	146.7	148	D	D	D	4 492	160.9	50 701	247
Clark	1 075	20 893	2 251.1	1 011.9	682	D	D	D	28 706	1 471.1	775 340	3 310
Columbia	11	164	11.9	5.8	8	D	D	D	231	8.3	423	2
Cowlitz	240	5 444	567.0	232.1	148	D	D	D	4 469	182.6	65 525	308
Douglas	64	1 042	59.3	25.6	43	149	12.1	3.3	1 624	60.9	44 147	181
Ferry	13	165	12.4	4.7	8	D	D	D	361	11.9	3 994	21
Franklin	118	1 737	201.5	83.8	95	462	41.3	11.1	3 305	168.7	130 252	530
Garfield	4	D	D	D	1	D	D	D	139	4.4	80	1
Grant	146	2 710	255.6	104.2	125	D	D	D	3 633	183.7	89 108	650
Grays Harbor	202	2 882	263.9	107.1	104	D	D	D	3 023	118.2	41 256	207
Island	172	2 326	228.3	94.4	96	401	28.1	9.1	5 790	234.6	97 855	373
Jefferson	108	1 370	127.3	54.3	88	D	D	D	3 158	108.7	39 944	238
King	7 309	135 353	17 719.2	7 109.5	4 537	29 268	9 324.7	1 074.5	166 065	9 336.7	3 375 978	17 699
Kitsap	685	11 861	1 272.8	484.3	382	1 789	149.7	48.6	14 249	624.0	275 354	1 059
Kittitas	96	1 613	114.9	48.7	76	D	D	D	2 613	119.2	84 452	323
Klickitat	40	599	63.7	26.3	33	103	7.3	2.2	1 439	61.7	20 548	123
Lewis	202	3 432	350.3	140.9	116	D	D	D	3 533	143.3	30 562	232
Lincoln	16	441	42.4	19.2	11	D	D	D	687	24.8	9 063	50
Mason	94	1 658	161.5	65.4	80	D	D	D	2 313	89.1	20 006	133
Okanogan	116	1 704	143.8	64.2	68	D	D	D	2 313	104.0	44 738	77
Pacific	44	618	55.6	23.5	39	32	4.9	0.8	1 353	52.2	12 457	59
Pend Oreille	19	D	D	D	15	32	4.9	0.8	714	22.4	13 113	
Pierce	1 915	43 245	5 369.3	2 118.8	1 328	8 133	760.7	241.0	42 238	1 986.6	907 635	3 865
San Juan	61	352	26.5	10.4	62	D	D	D	2 640	113.0	26 987	124
Skagit	330	7 152	700.3	296.6	252	1 128	106.0	31.3	7 712	369.9	99 532	505
Skamania	15	128	5.6	3.0	11	22	2.2	0.5	678	28.6	7 909	38
Snohomish	1 770	28 491	2 931.5	1 217.9	1 223	6 446	572.5	178.0	44 811	2 034.0	990 903	3 925
Spokane	1 497	33 772	3 968.0	1 576.7	813	4 742	415.5	126.4	29 100	1 335.7	618 523	3 596
Stevens	82	1 627	128.4	54.5	60	D	D	D	2 452	95.4	21 909	109
Thurston	790	13 079	1 584.8	619.1	483	2 769	331.1	98.1	14 707	630.2	371 772	2 081
Wahkiakum	7	D	D	D	2	D	D	D	316	10.5	3 200	15
Walla Walla	160	4 194	443.5	198.7	80	D	D	D	3 234	136.7	46 229	218
Whatcom	659	9 901	1 026.2	422.5	404	2 282	239.2	70.4	14 916	703.1	245 847	1 183
Whitman	97	D	D	D	60	D	D	D	2 100	69.2	35 839	194
Yakima	557	12 903	1 431.4	574.7	281	1 449	130.9	34.3	9 242	429.4	102 684	422
WEST VIRGINIA	4 939	129 075	12 259.4	4 824.5	2 661	16 583	1 773.3	443.6	88 136	3 380.3	397 382	2 544
Barbour	31	842	43.7	18.2	17	D	D	D	662	19.2	100	1
Berkeley	197	5 667	629.5	296.9	116	635	55.2	15.7	5 687	224.0	136 346	755
Boone	37	835	45.1	22.0	23	D	D	D	755	20.4	1 744	13
Braxton	19	842	48.3	17.5	17	D	D	D	550	19.0	0	0
Brooke	65	1 959	171.3	66.2	32	165	9.7	3.2	959	38.2	2 837	12
Cabell	372	12 905	1 426.9	570.0	170	1 053	161.2	32.3	4 724	190.0	13 438	93

— **Government Employment and Payroll, and Local Government Finances**

STATE County			March payroll (percent of total)							Local government finances, 2012				
	Full-time equivalent employees	March payroll (dollars)	Administration, judicial, and legal	Police and Corrections	Fire Protection	Highways and transportation	Health and Welfare	Natural resources and utilities	Education and libraries	Total (mil dol)	Inter-governmental (mil dol)	Total (mil dol)	Per capita[1] (dollars) Total	Property
	171	172	173	174	175	176	177	178	179	180	181	182	183	184
VIRGINIA—Cont'd														
Martinsville city.............	769	2 241 998	9.4	13.6	4.4	3.9	2.0	9.5	54.3	58.0	32.0	15.8	1 148	628
Newport News city........	8 482	34 753 223	6.1	10.1	4.5	2.1	4.5	9.1	62.7	786.5	332.1	322.2	1 783	1 269
Norfolk city....................	14 612	55 628 038	4.8	10.3	4.2	8.7	8.6	7.9	54.2	1 422.2	577.3	416.3	1 694	1 029
Norton city....................	226	662 054	8.5	13.0	0.5	4.4	8.7	6.7	55.1	22.2	11.9	7.7	1 884	632
Petersburg city.............	1 476	4 759 064	5.8	19.4	8.6	4.3	5.8	7.7	45.6	126.3	70.3	45.2	1 415	1 044
Poquoson city	447	1 474 638	7.0	6.8	6.8	3.3	0.8	2.3	70.5	38.2	15.0	19.1	1 576	1 340
Portsmouth city.............	4 358	16 114 476	6.2	15.8	6.6	0.8	6.9	6.3	55.4	449.4	234.6	161.2	1 671	1 219
Radford city..................	450	1 533 350	9.5	10.2	2.3	3.6	4.7	13.6	53.1	37.9	20.4	11.1	664	455
Richmond city	8 977	34 059 020	8.8	19.1	5.9	2.9	6.0	10.3	41.5	1 102.8	456.7	412.6	1 962	1 249
Roanoke city.................	3 900	14 209 461	8.0	12.7	8.2	3.3	6.2	4.1	55.6	398.1	176.5	172.9	1 774	1 086
Salem city	1 239	4 093 202	12.6	9.6	6.7	6.7	2.4	12.1	49.5	108.5	42.3	49.5	1 982	1 301
Staunton city................	1 131	3 120 624	7.9	23.4	4.4	2.5	1.7	5.3	51.1	82.8	39.3	32.3	1 349	839
Suffolk city...................	3 558	11 946 187	10.3	7.7	9.6	2.9	4.4	6.4	58.0	305.1	145.8	134.5	1 579	1 162
Virginia Beach city	19 058	68 439 433	3.5	9.0	3.4	0.3	6.4	12.4	57.0	1 816.6	615.1	810.1	1 812	1 218
Waynesboro city............	795	2 593 698	8.5	8.2	4.6	3.4	1.3	8.3	60.2	77.5	33.4	33.2	1 574	946
Williamsburg city............	407	1 404 121	11.0	37.6	9.6	3.3	4.2	10.1	21.2	46.8	11.2	29.9	1 971	766
Winchester city.............	1 491	5 190 139	6.6	22.4	6.4	2.6	4.2	6.7	49.4	137.9	46.7	61.6	2 292	1 298
WASHINGTON	X	X	X	X	X	X	X	X	X	X	X	X	X	X
Adams.........................	1 040	3 937 847	5.7	6.6	0.8	5.5	21.8	10.0	47.7	141.3	72.5	24.1	1 269	906
Asotin.........................	728	2 891 078	6.7	8.1	3.6	6.7	12.3	6.0	54.9	69.3	39.9	19.3	881	674
Benton.........................	7 559	41 657 634	4.9	6.8	3.2	4.4	13.0	32.6	34.0	876.0	367.1	242.6	1 330	745
Chelan........................	3 427	16 843 859	4.7	6.8	2.3	5.4	9.3	32.8	36.9	368.1	151.3	114.2	1 550	1 003
Clallam........................	3 439	16 962 339	5.9	7.8	3.5	5.3	38.0	11.5	26.0	416.5	135.2	89.7	1 249	834
Clark...........................	11 478	56 406 570	6.0	8.5	5.1	6.1	1.9	9.2	59.4	1 575.0	717.2	576.6	1 316	967
Columbia.....................	318	1 186 883	10.8	5.9	1.0	8.9	38.0	7.4	25.7	32.7	11.4	6.7	1 687	1 352
Cowlitz........................	3 301	15 112 407	7.8	11.6	3.0	7.2	3.7	14.2	51.3	420.9	170.2	127.1	1 246	848
Douglas.......................	1 297	6 128 626	5.0	6.0	1.5	6.7	0.5	26.3	52.5	145.0	88.5	39.7	1 008	759
Ferry...........................	420	1 474 156	7.4	5.9	0.4	5.7	31.9	8.5	39.8	44.5	24.8	5.0	651	505
Franklin.......................	2 593	11 637 558	6.0	7.6	3.3	4.6	0.0	14.4	62.8	318.4	176.1	82.9	965	615
Garfield.......................	229	842 190	7.7	6.5	0.9	9.8	47.5	1.7	24.6	29.1	16.3	3.5	1 591	960
Grant...........................	4 837	22 986 238	4.1	5.2	1.2	2.7	20.7	28.8	35.5	555.0	232.9	128.7	1 403	1 005
Grays Harbor	2 841	12 751 235	7.3	9.1	6.2	10.1	5.9	14.9	44.7	305.6	124.6	95.4	1 330	817
Island.........................	2 321	11 320 614	5.9	5.9	5.9	8.0	32.6	3.6	36.8	280.9	92.9	87.2	1 101	776
Jefferson.....................	1 311	6 130 951	7.9	5.4	5.8	9.2	41.3	2.8	26.6	158.5	38.9	46.4	1 556	1 102
King............................	65 821	388 288 446	8.0	10.3	5.9	13.1	13.5	13.9	33.3	12 411.3	3 474.5	5 105.6	2 543	1 381
Kitsap.........................	6 732	32 797 634	7.2	7.7	9.1	6.6	1.0	9.5	56.8	1 053.2	532.7	344.8	1 352	960
Kittitas........................	1 664	7 365 807	8.8	8.2	3.6	3.8	32.4	9.0	32.4	197.1	81.5	58.9	1 412	1 006
Klickitat.......................	1 119	4 905 212	5.9	6.8	0.4	4.5	31.9	13.1	35.6	136.0	44.1	27.2	1 316	1 015
Lewis..........................	2 603	11 808 449	7.8	9.5	3.2	6.0	10.1	11.8	47.1	268.0	123.6	81.1	1 072	750
Lincoln........................	806	3 420 386	7.1	4.6	0.1	8.4	38.7	1.4	38.6	95.2	44.6	15.2	1 458	1 199
Mason.........................	2 164	10 240 656	6.6	6.6	4.0	5.9	26.0	11.1	37.8	268.3	97.3	72.6	1 193	869
Okanogan.....................	1 848	8 014 386	6.5	8.2	0.5	3.7	30.9	10.5	38.5	228.9	90.9	42.6	1 031	722
Pacific.........................	1 032	5 269 056	8.5	7.3	3.7	6.5	27.8	11.0	33.1	126.6	42.8	31.2	1 518	1 146
Pend Oreille	786	3 517 534	6.4	5.1	0.4	3.4	34.6	21.7	26.3	81.4	36.0	10.4	799	627
Pierce.........................	23 934	131 701 698	8.7	9.5	9.2	8.4	2.7	12.1	47.1	3 300.2	1 329.7	1 234.7	1 521	1 076
San Juan.....................	551	2 448 595	14.0	7.8	3.9	9.0	9.8	11.9	39.1	76.6	25.1	34.7	2 196	1 573
Skagit.........................	5 963	27 675 332	5.4	5.4	2.0	4.5	41.5	4.7	33.8	852.8	275.6	199.6	1 688	1 157
Skamania.....................	390	1 668 143	14.8	12.9	0.3	6.4	8.7	12.8	38.8	36.0	20.0	8.7	781	588
Snohomish....................	19 389	108 720 406	6.9	9.4	6.5	8.0	5.4	13.4	47.9	2 865.2	1 091.9	1 077.6	1 470	1 030
Spokane.......................	13 368	67 439 060	9.4	11.5	7.6	7.3	3.7	7.0	51.9	1 818.7	806.0	639.3	1 344	862
Stevens.......................	1 254	5 040 095	8.1	7.4	1.3	6.3	7.8	4.7	61.9	143.8	97.8	31.2	717	541
Thurston......................	7 290	36 403 899	10.9	9.6	5.9	9.3	2.0	8.9	51.8	946.4	372.7	391.6	1 516	997
Wahkiakum	161	658 898	16.0	9.8	0.1	7.0	12.6	16.9	31.8	27.2	18.9	3.6	909	651
Walla Walla	1 801	7 900 373	8.1	11.4	5.9	6.2	5.5	3.9	55.3	236.4	107.1	76.1	1 281	877
Whatcom......................	5 120	25 193 563	10.0	10.9	7.5	8.7	1.8	7.1	50.4	696.1	261.3	292.4	1 424	871
Whitman.......................	1 636	7 215 336	5.6	5.7	3.5	8.0	37.2	2.3	36.4	210.9	64.2	44.8	961	644
Yakima........................	8 019	34 900 911	7.0	10.7	3.2	2.8	3.3	5.9	66.0	970.4	601.4	232.4	941	607
WEST VIRGINIA..........	X	X	X	X	X	X	X	X	X	X	X	X	X	X
Barbour........................	525	1 593 938	6.5	3.2	0.0	1.0	6.3	5.7	74.1	35.3	22.1	6.7	408	324
Berkeley	3 583	11 743 879	4.1	3.5	2.1	0.6	1.2	4.4	82.8	263.0	125.8	97.1	907	806
Boone..........................	1 129	3 935 149	4.3	3.0	1.1	0.8	17.5	1.2	69.9	102.4	38.1	37.4	1 528	1 483
Braxton........................	464	1 418 168	6.8	3.5	5.0	0.8	1.9	4.6	76.8	34.7	20.6	7.6	528	481
Brooke.........................	700	2 209 915	5.0	5.9	0.0	2.9	3.5	5.7	73.7	55.0	24.1	20.4	854	747
Cabell.........................	2 866	9 646 891	2.5	7.4	3.4	4.5	2.0	4.8	70.4	298.6	122.6	110.8	1 142	895

1. Based on the resident population estimated as of July 1 of the year shown.

Table B. States and Counties — Local Government Finances, Government Employment, and Income Taxes

STATE County	Direct general expenditure — Total (mil dol)	Per capita¹ (dollars)	Education	Health and hospitals	Police protection	Public welfare	Highways	Debt outstanding — Total (mil dol)	Per capita¹ (dollars)	Federal civilian	Federal military	State and local	Number of returns	Mean adjusted gross income	Mean income tax
	185	186	187	188	189	190	191	192	193	194	195	196	197	198	199
VIRGINIA—Cont'd															
Martinsville city	59.6	4 339	42.2	0.5	6.3	0.5	5.7	35.1	2 555	(3)	(3)	(3)	6 100	42 298	4 166
Newport News city	820.9	4 542	41.6	8.3	5.6	5.0	3.9	1 041.2	5 761	5 493	6 634	11 175	86 040	45 382	4 285
Norfolk city	1 457.9	5 932	43.5	5.0	4.7	5.2	3.6	2 294.3	9 335	20 070	42 361	20 623	104 840	46 843	5 185
Norton city	20.8	5 109	39.7	0.5	9.9	6.6	7.9	19.6	4 823	(4)	(4)	(4)	1 670	42 643	4 162
Petersburg city	134.0	4 190	38.8	1.0	8.8	11.1	4.6	60.3	1 887	(5)	(5)	(5)	16 200	32 359	2 397
Poquoson city	38.6	3 191	55.1	1.5	6.4	1.1	7.3	56.8	4 694	(6)	(6)	(6)	5 950	79 365	10 426
Portsmouth city	543.5	5 633	31.4	2.0	6.5	4.7	1.3	647.6	6 713	13 576	6 499	5 349	45 690	41 108	3 456
Radford city	44.5	2 667	45.2	0.5	8.1	5.6	5.3	28.4	1 701	(7)	(7)	(7)	5 210	46 583	4 907
Richmond city	1 081.3	5 141	30.1	4.3	8.5	1.5	3.8	1 910.6	9 085	5 438	1 209	37 541	100 430	62 121	9 250
Roanoke city	391.0	4 011	38.2	0.8	5.9	14.8	3.4	597.7	6 132	1 516	331	6 728	46 790	43 475	5 114
Salem city	120.6	4 828	38.5	0.7	5.3	1.5	4.9	167.0	6 689	(8)	(8)	(8)	11 720	54 727	6 076
Staunton city	94.0	3 928	32.9	8.4	5.8	5.6	5.2	98.6	4 122	(9)	(9)	(9)	11 620	47 758	4 718
Suffolk city	324.3	3 808	45.2	0.2	6.3	4.4	6.8	654.0	7 677	1 322	447	4 954	39 730	61 174	6 723
Virginia Beach city	2 062.0	4 613	40.8	2.6	4.3	3.3	4.2	2 582.9	5 778	6 245	18 358	22 661	222 370	64 070	8 139
Waynesboro city	75.1	3 556	42.8	0.6	5.0	4.9	6.7	92.3	4 374	(9)	(9)	(9)	10 350	44 639	4 242
Williamsburg city	53.2	3 510	14.0	0.9	7.4	3.7	3.5	32.4	2 134	(10)	(10)	(10)	5 490	59 213	7 506
Winchester city	131.6	4 897	37.2	0.9	5.5	5.5	4.3	337.1	12 539	(11)	(11)	(11)	13 340	57 694	7 851
WASHINGTON	X	X	X	X	X	X	X	X	X	73 286	76 001	481 139	3 342 610	73 083	10 459
Adams	135.7	7 140	46.3	18.1	2.6	0.0	5.7	62.9	3 309	34	52	1 559	8 270	44 937	4 248
Asotin	68.8	3 142	46.9	7.4	5.3	0.0	7.3	21.9	1 003	49	60	1 130	9 840	54 936	6 254
Benton	835.7	4 582	38.0	28.0	4.0	0.0	3.3	6 728.4	36 888	765	529	12 065	83 130	63 467	7 659
Chelan	345.4	4 688	41.8	14.6	4.2	0.0	5.4	1 594.5	21 638	604	204	6 114	36 560	60 014	8 014
Clallam	403.3	5 612	25.3	39.7	3.3	0.0	3.6	172.3	2 398	447	516	7 015	33 750	53 427	5 677
Clark	1 525.7	3 481	51.0	3.7	4.0	0.5	5.8	2 123.7	4 845	3 202	1 287	21 252	207 890	66 736	8 523
Columbia	29.1	7 286	21.7	37.4	4.2	0.0	7.5	17.2	4 300	70	11	441	1 700	50 454	4 954
Cowlitz	424.6	4 163	38.6	3.9	5.4	0.0	4.9	609.4	5 974	226	279	5 696	44 530	52 586	5 509
Douglas	142.5	3 622	59.9	8.3	5.1	0.0	6.7	350.0	8 893	253	110	1 932	18 110	50 095	5 021
Ferry	39.2	5 090	46.3	22.7	2.6	0.0	9.2	9.5	1 236	160	20	752	2 730	46 287	4 492
Franklin	294.3	3 429	60.6	1.4	3.9	0.0	4.7	315.8	3 679	463	234	5 730	35 720	49 349	4 910
Garfield	32.0	14 354	37.5	23.0	2.9	0.0	17.9	7.7	3 442	128	D	345	950	48 532	4 598
Grant	519.5	5 664	37.4	28.7	3.4	0.6	4.6	1 451.0	15 819	766	250	7 366	39 880	47 470	4 656
Grays Harbor	303.0	4 227	38.5	9.5	5.7	0.2	6.2	405.8	5 660	178	226	6 120	28 990	46 993	4 683
Island	257.0	3 246	28.7	33.0	3.3	0.2	7.4	171.2	2 163	1 340	6 032	3 235	38 880	63 891	7 442
Jefferson	155.4	5 205	19.1	39.9	3.6	0.3	5.2	145.8	4 885	170	92	2 162	15 380	64 294	8 147
King	11 212.0	5 585	28.9	12.4	5.0	1.2	5.5	22 389.4	11 153	20 229	7 390	154 124	1 055 960	101 319	17 577
Kitsap	1 054.5	4 135	42.3	4.6	3.5	0.0	3.5	748.5	2 935	18 676	11 130	12 862	120 700	67 761	8 533
Kittitas	186.9	4 485	26.5	30.6	4.7	0.0	6.5	110.8	2 658	142	124	3 956	18 060	52 400	6 035
Klickitat	118.4	5 721	34.2	32.3	3.9	0.0	8.0	215.9	10 431	89	57	1 573	9 500	56 164	6 687
Lewis	254.6	3 367	47.6	10.3	5.3	0.0	6.3	343.9	4 547	224	204	4 803	32 750	47 808	4 646
Lincoln	96.3	9 226	34.5	30.0	2.8	0.0	10.9	34.2	3 279	59	28	1 221	4 480	53 967	5 535
Mason	257.4	4 232	32.2	26.8	3.0	0.0	4.3	295.3	4 854	68	160	5 497	25 630	52 802	5 394
Okanogan	207.5	5 027	35.7	32.4	4.0	0.1	3.7	126.1	3 056	410	111	4 405	18 060	42 509	3 926
Pacific	123.7	6 010	30.5	32.4	3.3	0.0	4.1	113.3	5 509	63	164	1 756	9 380	47 655	4 981
Pend Oreille	75.9	5 850	25.2	33.2	3.2	0.1	6.9	158.1	12 178	99	35	1 369	5 210	52 759	5 749
Pierce	3 273.5	4 033	43.7	2.1	5.8	0.6	5.6	4 565.2	5 624	11 877	33 160	45 220	388 380	60 462	7 163
San Juan	74.8	4 726	30.2	8.5	3.4	0.3	9.8	34.2	2 159	55	44	761	8 600	84 108	13 593
Skagit	797.6	6 747	26.4	43.2	2.9	0.1	3.4	556.4	4 706	388	327	10 706	56 960	59 113	6 844
Skamania	41.2	3 682	35.3	7.8	6.4	0.2	7.2	16.3	1 455	112	31	492	4 710	60 776	7 104
Snohomish	2 730.6	3 725	42.2	8.8	4.8	0.6	4.4	3 753.7	5 121	2 014	6 446	36 130	361 970	68 698	8 648
Spokane	1 872.4	3 936	45.5	5.1	5.4	0.2	4.0	1 560.2	3 280	4 589	4 069	30 956	220 870	56 523	6 882
Stevens	148.2	3 405	61.9	5.5	3.5	0.0	7.0	45.9	1 055	334	118	2 562	17 900	48 172	4 566
Thurston	952.8	3 688	42.4	5.4	4.0	0.0	7.1	917.5	3 552	863	776	36 001	127 650	59 576	6 794
Wahkiakum	25.9	6 484	20.6	41.0	3.8	0.0	7.9	4.8	1 207	14	11	254	1 760	49 307	4 819
Walla Walla	228.3	3 844	45.7	5.8	5.9	0.0	7.1	249.9	4 207	1 262	154	4 268	25 190	55 903	6 511
Whatcom	644.4	3 139	42.5	4.3	6.1	0.0	5.7	595.5	2 901	1 389	630	14 117	97 860	59 200	7 276
Whitman	199.6	4 282	27.1	40.8	3.9	0.3	4.7	87.2	1 870	230	122	9 156	17 040	51 931	5 711
Yakima	1 052.2	4 260	60.9	3.2	4.2	0.8	4.9	606.3	2 455	1 245	802	16 036	107 840	47 135	5 284
WEST VIRGINIA	X	X	X	X	X	X	X	X	X	23 310	8 753	123 118	782 830	50 148	5 511
Barbour	38.2	2 315	63.0	3.6	3.6	0.0	1.0	23.1	1 402	31	75	699	6 440	42 171	3 855
Berkeley	274.3	2 561	76.5	0.5	4.5	0.0	0.7	319.3	2 981	3 490	569	4 810	51 770	49 535	4 771
Boone	117.1	4 784	50.3	15.4	4.9	0.2	0.5	11.7	479	64	110	1 541	8 490	46 477	4 281
Braxton	39.8	2 754	58.6	1.2	2.1	0.0	0.5	106.5	7 361	60	66	905	5 330	42 913	4 168
Brooke	57.1	2 394	62.3	1.0	9.7	0.1	2.8	99.9	4 186	28	106	926	10 770	47 868	4 990
Cabell	294.4	3 035	46.5	1.1	6.6	0.4	1.3	141.0	1 454	940	557	7 399	40 440	51 651	6 252

1. Based on the resident population estimated as of July 1 of the year shown.   3. Martinsville city is included with Henry county.   4. Norton city is included with Wise county.   5. Petersburg and Colonial Heights cities are included with Dinwiddie county.   6. Poquoson city is included with York county.   7. Radford city is included with Montgomery county.   8. Salem city is included with Roanoke county.   9. Staunton and Waynesboro cities are included with Augusta county.   10. Williamsburg city is included with James City county.   11. Winchester city is included with Frederick county.

Table B. States and Counties — Land Area and Population

STATE/ County code	CBSA code[1]	County type[2]	STATE County	Land area[3] (sq mi) 2016	Total persons 2016	Rank	Per square mile	White	Black	American Indian, Alaska Native	Asian and Pacific Islander	Percent Hispanic or Latino[4]	Under 5 years	5 to 17 years	18 to 24 years	25 to 34 years	35 to 44 years	45 to 54 years
				1	2	3	4	5	6	7	8	9	10	11	12	13	14	15
			WEST VIRGINIA—Cont'd															
54 013	...	8	Calhoun	279.2	7 336	2 640	26.3	98.1	0.6	0.8	0.3	1.2	4.9	14.1	6.2	10.0	11.4	14.2
54 015	16620	3	Clay	341.9	8 859	2 517	25.9	98.7	0.5	0.8	0.2	0.7	5.6	16.9	7.0	9.7	11.8	13.6
54 017	17220	9	Doddridge	319.7	8 413	2 559	26.3	96.3	2.6	0.9	0.5	1.0	4.1	13.9	9.9	11.9	12.6	14.8
54 019	13220	3	Fayette	661.6	44 323	1 084	67.0	94.0	5.2	0.8	0.3	1.1	5.9	14.8	7.4	11.1	12.5	13.0
54 021	...	7	Gilmer	338.5	8 249	2 573	24.4	82.4	11.3	1.2	1.1	5.5	3.8	10.5	15.1	15.1	14.1	13.2
54 023	...	7	Grant	477.4	11 732	2 309	24.6	97.6	1.3	0.5	0.3	1.3	5.2	14.4	6.9	10.0	10.9	14.3
54 025	49020	6	Greenbrier	1 019.7	35 279	1 293	34.6	94.8	3.9	0.9	0.7	1.4	5.1	14.4	7.1	11.0	11.1	13.3
54 027	49020	3	Hampshire	640.4	23 301	1 664	36.4	96.8	1.7	0.6	0.5	1.4	4.9	15.0	6.9	10.2	11.2	15.2
54 029	48260	3	Hancock	82.6	29 590	1 440	358.2	95.3	3.4	0.6	0.7	1.6	4.8	14.6	6.7	10.5	11.9	13.9
54 031	...	6	Hardy	582.3	13 889	2 175	23.9	91.2	3.7	0.7	0.9	4.8	5.2	14.9	6.5	10.9	12.1	14.4
54 033	17220	5	Harrison	416.0	68 400	780	164.4	95.9	2.5	0.8	0.9	1.6	5.8	15.9	7.3	12.1	12.4	13.6
54 035	...	6	Jackson	464.4	29 152	1 452	62.8	98.3	0.8	0.6	0.5	0.8	5.4	16.2	7.4	10.8	12.0	13.9
54 037	47900	1	Jefferson	209.7	56 368	906	268.8	86.2	7.6	0.9	2.3	5.5	5.6	17.2	8.4	11.5	12.9	15.6
54 039	16620	3	Kanawha	901.6	186 241	349	206.6	89.9	9.0	0.9	1.6	1.1	5.6	14.7	7.7	12.2	12.2	12.9
54 041	...	7	Lewis	386.9	16 309	2 024	42.2	97.5	1.1	0.7	0.6	1.2	5.9	14.8	7.1	11.3	12.4	14.0
54 043	26580	2	Lincoln	437.0	21 232	1 766	48.6	98.7	0.6	0.6	0.3	0.7	6.0	16.4	6.9	10.6	12.6	14.2
54 045	30880	6	Logan	453.8	33 700	1 336	74.3	96.9	2.2	0.4	0.5	0.9	5.6	14.9	7.1	11.1	13.5	13.0
54 047	...	7	McDowell	533.5	19 141	1 866	35.9	90.0	9.5	0.7	0.3	0.9	5.8	14.8	6.7	10.4	12.1	13.0
54 049	21900	4	Marion	308.7	56 538	902	183.1	94.5	4.3	0.7	0.9	1.2	5.7	14.4	11.5	11.6	11.9	12.5
54 051	48540	3	Marshall	305.4	31 793	1 383	104.1	97.7	1.3	0.6	0.5	1.0	5.3	14.5	7.4	11.0	11.7	13.4
54 053	38580	6	Mason	430.7	26 825	1 535	62.3	97.9	1.4	0.7	0.5	0.7	5.3	15.9	6.8	11.4	12.3	13.2
54 055	14140	4	Mercer	419.0	60 468	864	144.3	92.0	7.1	0.7	0.8	1.1	5.9	14.9	8.2	11.8	11.8	12.4
54 057	19060	3	Mineral	327.9	27 411	1 516	83.6	95.4	3.9	0.6	0.7	0.9	5.5	14.6	9.0	11.2	10.9	13.9
54 059	...	7	Mingo	423.1	24 647	1 621	58.3	96.9	2.5	0.5	0.5	0.8	6.5	16.1	6.6	11.7	13.1	13.6
54 061	34060	3	Monongalia	360.1	104 622	571	290.5	90.3	5.0	0.6	4.2	2.1	5.3	11.9	21.2	17.8	11.7	10.6
54 063	...	8	Monroe	472.8	13 370	2 207	28.3	97.7	1.3	1.1	0.5	0.9	5.0	15.5	6.4	9.9	11.0	14.0
54 065	...	8	Morgan	229.1	17 632	1 937	77.0	96.9	1.3	1.0	0.7	1.5	4.4	14.0	7.1	9.5	11.0	15.2
54 067	...	6	Nicholas	646.8	25 311	1 595	39.1	98.2	0.5	1.0	0.5	0.8	5.4	15.0	6.8	11.1	11.8	13.5
54 069	48540	3	Ohio	105.8	42 516	1 121	401.9	94.1	5.0	0.6	1.3	1.2	5.3	14.0	10.2	11.6	10.9	12.3
54 071	...	8	Pendleton	696.0	7 051	2 669	10.1	96.3	2.6	0.7	0.4	1.2	4.5	13.0	6.8	8.8	9.9	13.0
54 073	...	6	Pleasants	130.1	7 591	2 625	58.3	97.1	1.8	0.8	0.4	1.0	4.2	14.5	8.2	11.4	13.1	14.8
54 075	...	9	Pocahontas	940.3	8 501	2 551	9.0	96.7	1.6	1.1	0.5	1.6	4.6	12.8	6.2	10.8	10.8	14.0
54 077	34060	3	Preston	648.8	33 758	1 331	52.0	97.3	1.6	0.7	0.4	1.0	5.3	14.0	7.1	13.5	13.0	14.0
54 079	26580	2	Putnam	345.7	56 941	896	164.7	96.6	1.7	0.7	1.1	1.1	5.8	17.0	6.8	11.1	13.4	14.1
54 081	13220	3	Raleigh	605.4	76 601	721	126.5	89.0	9.1	0.9	1.4	1.6	5.7	15.5	7.5	12.4	13.2	12.0
54 083	21180	7	Randolph	1 039.7	29 006	1 455	27.9	96.9	2.0	0.7	0.6	0.9	5.4	13.7	8.4	12.0	11.5	13.5
54 085	...	8	Ritchie	452.0	9 875	2 442	21.8	98.6	0.7	0.7	0.3	0.7	5.0	15.0	7.1	10.0	11.3	14.8
54 087	...	6	Roane	483.6	14 208	2 151	29.4	97.9	0.8	0.8	0.6	1.1	5.3	16.2	6.3	9.7	12.0	13.5
54 089	...	6	Summers	360.6	12 872	2 236	35.7	93.1	5.3	1.1	0.6	1.7	3.8	13.1	6.1	10.9	12.8	14.0
54 091	17220	6	Taylor	172.8	16 859	1 986	97.6	97.1	1.6	0.6	0.6	1.0	5.0	14.9	6.7	12.3	12.7	14.7
54 093	...	8	Tucker	419.0	6 926	2 678	16.5	98.3	0.8	0.6	0.5	0.7	4.8	12.3	6.9	10.3	11.0	14.9
54 095	...	9	Tyler	256.3	8 972	2 511	35.0	98.6	0.5	0.5	0.4	0.8	5.4	14.6	6.6	10.0	11.1	14.6
54 097	...	7	Upshur	354.6	24 658	1 619	69.5	97.1	1.4	0.7	0.7	1.3	5.8	14.9	10.8	11.5	11.2	12.7
54 099	26580	2	Wayne	506.0	40 531	1 162	80.1	98.2	0.8	0.7	0.6	0.6	5.2	16.0	7.3	11.2	12.4	13.9
54 101	...	9	Webster	553.5	8 646	2 537	15.6	98.4	0.9	0.7	0.4	0.7	5.3	15.1	6.8	9.3	11.2	13.9
54 103	...	6	Wetzel	358.1	15 640	2 063	43.7	98.1	0.9	0.5	0.5	0.9	5.4	14.6	7.6	10.2	10.9	14.0
54 105	37620	3	Wirt	232.5	5 806	2 768	25.0	98.2	1.1	0.8	0.4	0.8	5.2	15.8	6.4	10.7	11.3	14.3
54 107	37620	3	Wood	366.3	85 643	668	233.8	96.8	2.0	0.7	0.9	1.1	5.7	15.6	7.4	11.7	12.0	13.8
54 109	...	6	Wyoming	499.5	21 763	1 743	43.6	98.3	1.1	0.7	0.3	0.6	5.3	15.8	6.9	10.7	13.0	12.9
55 000	...	0	WISCONSIN	54 159.9	5 778 708	X	106.7	83.2	7.1	1.4	3.3	6.7	5.8	16.5	9.7	12.6	11.9	13.5
55 001	...	8	Adams	645.6	20 069	1 824	31.1	91.7	3.2	1.5	0.9	3.9	3.6	11.2	5.7	9.6	9.6	13.1
55 003	...	7	Ashland	1 045.0	15 714	2 099	15.0	85.6	1.0	13.3	1.0	2.6	5.8	16.6	9.2	10.9	10.5	12.9
55 005	...	6	Barron	862.7	45 412	1 066	52.6	94.7	1.8	1.3	1.0	2.5	5.7	15.9	7.3	10.8	10.8	13.2
55 007	...	8	Bayfield	1 477.9	14 891	2 107	10.1	87.3	1.0	11.8	0.8	1.8	4.2	13.2	6.3	8.0	9.0	13.9
55 009	24580	2	Brown	529.7	260 401	261	491.6	83.3	3.4	3.2	3.7	8.5	6.5	17.5	9.3	13.6	12.4	13.7
55 011	...	8	Buffalo	671.6	13 099	2 224	19.5	96.7	0.7	0.7	0.5	2.2	5.3	15.7	7.2	10.2	10.4	14.2
55 013	...	8	Burnett	821.6	15 213	2 082	18.5	93.0	1.1	5.9	0.8	1.6	4.4	13.6	5.9	7.9	9.1	13.1
55 015	11540	3	Calumet	318.2	49 553	990	155.7	92.3	1.1	0.8	2.8	4.2	5.8	19.0	7.8	10.8	13.0	15.6
55 017	20740	3	Chippewa	1 008.4	63 649	833	63.1	94.7	2.0	0.9	1.7	1.7	5.7	16.7	7.2	12.5	12.3	14.0
55 019	...	6	Clark	1 209.7	34 557	1 310	28.6	94.0	0.7	0.8	0.8	4.5	8.1	21.2	7.8	10.0	10.6	12.4
55 021	31540	2	Columbia	765.5	56 927	897	74.4	93.7	2.0	0.9	1.1	3.4	5.5	16.4	7.4	11.7	12.4	14.6
55 023	...	7	Crawford	570.7	16 321	2 022	28.6	95.6	2.4	0.7	0.9	1.4	4.8	16.0	7.5	10.3	10.2	13.4
55 025	31540	2	Dane	1 196.4	531 273	127	444.1	82.1	6.3	0.7	6.9	6.3	5.9	15.0	13.9	15.4	12.8	12.3
55 027	13180	4	Dodge	875.7	88 068	656	100.6	91.1	3.5	0.8	0.9	4.7	4.8	15.4	7.9	12.4	12.5	14.9
55 029	...	6	Door	482.0	27 587	1 510	57.2	95.4	1.1	1.1	0.7	2.9	3.6	12.6	6.2	8.2	9.8	12.5

1. CBSA = Core Based Statistical Area. See Appendix A for explanation. See Appendix B for list of metropolitan areas with component counties. Service of USDA Rural-Urban Continuum Codes. See Appendix A for definition. 3. Dry land or land partially or temporarily covered by water. 2. County type code from the Economic Research Service of USDA Rural-Urban Continuum Codes. See Appendix A for definition. 4. May be of any race.

Table B. States and Counties — **Population and Households**

STATE County	55 to 64 years (16)	65 to 74 years (17)	75 years and over (18)	Percent female (19)	2000 (20)	2010 (21)	2000–2010 (22)	2010–2016 (23)	Births (24)	Deaths (25)	Net migration (26)	Number (27)	Persons per household (28)	Family households (29)	Female family householder[1] (30)	One person (31)
WEST VIRGINIA—Cont'd																
Calhoun	16.8	13.3	9.1	50.3	7 582	7 627	0.6	-3.8	481	559	-206	3 090	2.44	67.8	9.5	27.2
Clay	15.2	11.8	8.4	49.5	10 330	9 386	-9.1	-5.6	664	675	-544	3 460	2.62	70.0	8.6	21.6
Doddridge	15.3	11.0	6.6	44.4	7 403	8 198	10.7	2.6	414	512	253	2 674	2.85	65.8	8.3	30.3
Fayette	15.4	11.7	8.2	49.7	47 579	46 039	-3.2	-3.7	3 351	4 131	-920	17 669	2.47	68.3	13.7	27.4
Gilmer	11.9	8.7	7.6	40.6	7 160	8 697	21.5	-5.2	424	454	-416	2 744	2.40	62.9	6.7	29.0
Grant	14.7	13.9	9.8	50.1	11 299	11 937	5.6	-1.7	746	816	-159	4 175	2.80	66.3	6.2	26.9
Greenbrier	15.4	13.3	9.3	51.3	34 453	35 480	3.0	-0.6	2 225	2 984	567	15 339	2.28	64.4	11.6	30.8
Hampshire	15.6	13.4	7.5	49.1	20 203	23 971	18.7	-2.8	1 462	1 597	-496	10 194	2.25	45.0	8.4	52.3
Hancock	16.4	11.9	9.4	51.1	32 667	30 675	-6.1	-3.5	1 791	2 527	-320	12 894	2.32	64.3	12.3	31.8
Hardy	15.0	12.6	8.3	49.8	12 669	14 025	10.7	-1.0	913	933	-162	5 156	2.69	67.8	7.7	28.6
Harrison	14.4	10.6	7.9	51.0	68 652	69 108	0.7	-1.0	4 993	5 381	-128	27 502	2.48	64.6	11.4	31.2
Jackson	14.7	10.8	8.8	50.4	28 000	29 211	4.3	-0.2	2 020	2 155	138	11 118	2.62	69.0	10.3	26.8
Jefferson	13.7	9.7	5.4	50.4	42 190	53 488	26.8	5.4	3 810	2 805	1 859	20 331	2.65	70.6	11.4	22.9
Kanawha	15.3	11.1	8.1	51.8	200 073	193 058	-3.5	-3.5	13 479	15 275	-4 546	82 250	2.28	62.0	13.5	32.4
Lewis	14.5	11.9	8.1	50.2	16 919	16 372	-3.2	-0.4	1 243	1 361	77	6 526	2.48	67.2	11.7	26.8
Lincoln	14.7	11.3	7.2	50.2	22 108	21 720	-1.8	-2.2	1 675	1 746	-439	7 994	2.69	68.3	11.6	28.4
Logan	15.9	11.7	7.2	50.8	37 710	36 745	-2.6	-8.3	2 548	3 276	-2 351	14 043	2.50	70.2	12.1	25.3
McDowell	17.3	11.8	8.0	51.0	27 329	22 111	-19.1	-13.4	1 569	2 197	-2 344	8 180	2.39	66.0	15.4	29.3
Marion	13.7	10.7	8.1	50.7	56 598	56 418	-0.3	0.2	4 069	4 072	248	22 481	2.47	65.6	11.2	28.7
Marshall	16.0	12.4	8.3	50.5	35 519	33 107	-6.8	-4.0	2 030	2 558	-711	13 569	2.36	68.9	9.5	25.9
Mason	15.7	11.2	8.2	51.7	25 957	27 326	5.3	-1.8	1 756	2 097	-187	10 838	2.44	66.8	12.9	28.6
Mercer	14.5	12.1	8.5	52.2	62 980	62 267	-1.1	-2.9	4 608	5 641	-690	25 451	2.39	65.8	13.0	29.1
Mineral	14.3	12.5	8.1	50.3	27 078	28 205	4.2	-2.8	1 825	2 025	-532	11 265	2.40	57.1	10.3	40.6
Mingo	15.6	10.7	6.1	50.7	28 253	26 834	-5.0	-8.2	2 133	2 320	-1 950	10 844	2.38	69.8	13.6	26.9
Monongalia	10.8	6.9	4.5	48.5	81 866	96 189	17.5	8.8	6 932	4 107	5 655	37 035	2.56	52.3	8.3	35.9
Monroe	14.7	14.0	9.5	50.3	14 583	13 500	-7.4	-1.0	816	1 055	166	5 822	2.30	70.8	13.3	26.3
Morgan	16.5	13.3	9.1	50.2	14 943	17 541	17.4	0.5	921	1 333	523	7 348	2.36	54.5	6.2	40.1
Nicholas	15.4	12.7	8.2	50.6	26 562	26 233	-1.2	-3.5	1 749	2 102	-586	10 787	2.39	70.2	9.3	25.3
Ohio	15.5	10.9	9.3	51.7	47 427	44 442	-6.3	-4.3	2 893	3 630	-1 007	18 408	2.24	57.4	10.9	37.4
Pendleton	17.2	13.8	13.0	49.4	8 196	7 695	-6.1	-8.4	435	568	-502	3 095	2.35	64.9	6.8	29.7
Pleasants	14.1	11.7	8.1	46.1	7 514	7 605	1.2	-0.2	407	568	133	2 893	2.43	72.2	10.0	22.2
Pocahontas	17.0	14.1	9.6	48.5	9 131	8 722	-4.5	-2.5	520	670	-57	3 737	2.24	63.3	6.8	30.2
Preston	14.5	11.0	7.4	48.5	29 334	33 520	14.3	0.7	2 198	2 174	281	12 472	2.52	69.7	8.1	25.1
Putnam	14.2	10.6	7.1	51.0	51 589	55 508	7.6	2.6	3 796	3 454	1 033	21 707	2.60	73.2	10.5	22.9
Raleigh	14.4	11.5	7.9	49.8	79 220	78 862	-0.5	-2.9	5 747	6 309	-1 549	31 274	2.40	66.5	12.2	28.2
Randolph	14.6	12.3	8.5	48.3	28 262	29 405	4.0	-1.4	1 970	2 271	-61	11 563	2.35	66.9	10.0	28.5
Ritchie	15.8	12.4	8.7	49.9	10 343	10 449	1.0	-5.5	612	810	-339	3 942	2.56	63.9	9.6	32.9
Roane	16.1	12.3	8.5	50.5	15 446	14 926	-3.4	-4.8	964	1 168	-483	5 872	2.48	65.1	9.6	28.9
Summers	16.6	13.3	9.5	54.8	12 999	13 927	7.1	-7.6	664	1 134	-536	5 584	2.22	65.6	11.0	31.5
Taylor	14.7	11.2	7.8	49.2	16 089	16 890	5.0	-0.2	1 054	1 214	145	6 732	2.45	68.5	13.1	27.7
Tucker	15.6	14.6	9.6	49.3	7 321	7 141	-2.5	-3.0	417	585	-62	3 010	2.26	67.6	5.6	27.7
Tyler	16.4	12.2	9.0	50.2	9 592	9 211	-4.0	-2.6	558	744	-54	3 616	2.48	66.5	10.1	30.1
Upshur	13.8	11.4	7.9	50.4	23 404	24 254	3.6	1.7	1 723	1 665	369	9 093	2.57	69.1	10.2	26.8
Wayne	14.4	11.6	8.0	51.4	42 903	42 484	-1.0	-4.6	2 637	3 030	-1 550	16 691	2.47	65.4	12.8	31.5
Webster	16.1	13.8	8.5	50.4	9 719	9 154	-5.8	-5.5	605	763	-380	3 887	2.28	67.7	12.9	27.0
Wetzel	14.9	12.7	9.7	50.6	17 693	16 580	-6.3	-5.7	1 068	1 429	-586	6 525	2.46	65.6	10.6	30.5
Wirt	17.1	11.8	7.3	49.1	5 873	5 717	-2.7	1.6	374	367	85	2 430	2.40	66.1	10.7	26.4
Wood	14.5	11.1	8.1	51.6	87 986	86 956	-1.2	-1.5	6 147	6 540	-736	36 192	2.37	64.4	11.5	30.9
Wyoming	16.2	12.3	7.0	50.7	25 708	23 801	-7.4	-8.6	1 460	2 140	-1 319	9 199	2.48	70.7	10.8	26.1
WISCONSIN	14.0	9.2	6.9	50.3	5 363 675	5 687 289	6.0	1.6	419 490	307 115	-20 083	2 299 107	2.43	63.9	10.0	29.0
Adams	18.8	17.2	11.1	46.5	18 643	20 875	12.0	-3.9	826	1 561	-74	7 786	2.47	65.1	6.8	29.7
Ashland	15.5	10.9	7.8	49.5	16 866	16 157	-4.2	-2.7	1 115	1 158	-396	6 718	2.29	58.2	9.9	35.2
Barron	15.2	12.1	8.9	49.7	44 963	45 870	2.0	-1.0	3 196	3 086	-513	19 120	2.35	65.8	7.8	28.2
Bayfield	19.7	16.2	9.6	48.9	15 013	15 014	0.0	-0.8	761	995	140	6 919	2.16	62.9	6.5	30.9
Brown	13.0	8.1	5.9	50.3	226 778	248 007	9.4	5.0	21 197	11 425	2 648	100 640	2.46	64.7	10.2	28.4
Buffalo	16.1	11.7	9.2	48.9	13 804	13 587	-1.6	-3.6	882	810	-535	5 771	2.29	65.3	7.5	29.8
Burnett	18.7	16.1	11.2	49.2	15 674	15 457	-1.4	-1.6	824	1 083	85	7 312	2.08	63.4	7.9	30.4
Calumet	14.0	8.2	5.8	49.8	40 631	48 971	20.5	1.2	3 468	1 955	-925	18 583	2.66	74.8	7.8	20.2
Chippewa	14.5	10.0	7.2	48.1	55 195	62 505	13.2	1.8	4 503	3 465	148	24 873	2.44	67.2	7.7	26.7
Clark	13.5	8.7	7.6	49.5	33 557	34 691	3.4	-0.4	3 546	2 101	-1 534	12 797	2.65	69.5	7.7	25.8
Columbia	15.1	10.0	7.0	49.0	52 468	56 833	8.3	0.2	3 773	3 304	-411	22 615	2.44	68.1	9.0	26.8
Crawford	15.7	12.7	9.4	48.1	17 243	16 644	-3.5	-1.9	1 029	1 095	-239	6 623	2.38	63.2	7.1	32.4
Dane	11.8	7.8	5.1	50.3	426 526	488 075	14.4	8.9	38 526	19 309	23 305	211 114	2.35	57.9	8.7	30.6
Dodge	14.8	9.3	7.9	47.2	85 897	88 761	3.3	-0.8	5 230	5 508	-572	33 322	2.51	66.4	8.0	28.7
Door	18.4	17.1	11.5	50.6	27 961	27 785	-0.6	-0.7	1 290	2 027	479	12 968	2.11	65.4	5.4	28.4

1. No spouse present.

Table B. States and Counties — Population, Vital Statistics, Health, and Crime

STATE County	Persons in group quarters, 2016	Daytime population, 2011–2015 Number	Daytime population, 2011–2015 Employment/residence ratio	Births, 2016 Total	Births, 2016 Rate[1]	Deaths, 2016 Number	Deaths, 2016 Rate[1]	Persons under 65 with no health insurance, 2015 Number	Persons under 65 with no health insurance, 2015 Percent	Medicare, 2015 Total Beneficiaries	Medicare, 2015 Enrolled in Original Medicare	Medicare, 2015 Enrolled in Medicare Advantage	Serious crimes known to police,[2] 2014 Total Number	Serious crimes known to police,[2] 2014 Total Rate[3]
	32	33	34	35	36	37	38	39	40	41	42	43	44	45
WEST VIRGINIA—Cont'd														
Calhoun	22	6 912	0.73	71	9.7	80	10.9	518	8.9	1 749	1 387	362	NA	NA
Clay	74	8 064	0.62	93	10.5	107	12.1	663	9.3	2 648	1 786	862	NA	NA
Doddridge	990	7 053	0.59	67	8.0	73	8.7	397	6.6	1 084	771	313	NA	NA
Fayette	1 833	41 665	0.75	490	11.1	693	15.6	2 857	8.2	11 117	7 939	3 178	1 027	2 466
Gilmer	1 927	8 718	1.03	63	7.6	80	9.7	491	9.5	1 438	993	445	NA	NA
Grant	126	11 220	0.88	115	9.8	127	10.8	693	7.7	3 945	3 109	836	70	780
Greenbrier	616	37 017	1.10	328	9.3	502	14.2	2 101	7.7	8 816	6 734	2 082	405	1 187
Hampshire	402	19 463	0.53	229	9.8	250	10.7	1 710	9.4	5 017	3 993	1 024	194	846
Hancock	226	29 002	0.91	283	9.6	429	14.5	1 652	7.0	8 101	6 158	1 943	337	1 160
Hardy	58	13 859	0.99	138	9.9	166	12.0	1 065	9.7	2 995	2 331	664	145	1 067
Harrison	867	76 512	1.26	783	11.4	882	12.9	3 654	6.6	16 060	11 764	4 296	NA	NA
Jackson	180	26 712	0.76	317	10.9	361	12.4	1 657	7.1	7 055	5 246	1 809	208	824
Jefferson	1 219	47 508	0.70	580	10.3	481	8.5	3 257	6.9	8 959	7 135	1 824	787	1 557
Kanawha	3 177	211 375	1.25	2 093	11.2	2 507	13.5	10 276	6.8	45 106	29 808	15 298	8 347	4 539
Lewis	248	16 989	1.09	195	12.0	238	14.6	952	7.3	4 250	2 811	1 439	167	1 016
Lincoln	66	17 566	0.44	254	12.0	304	14.3	1 443	8.3	5 102	3 473	1 629	NA	NA
Logan	551	37 020	1.11	350	10.4	500	14.8	2 253	8.1	9 609	6 731	2 878	650	1 996
McDowell	139	21 329	1.12	209	10.9	342	17.9	1 502	9.4	6 111	4 254	1 857	238	1 419
Marion	1 344	52 258	0.82	628	11.1	691	12.2	3 143	6.9	13 121	9 250	3 871	560	1 119
Marshall	584	30 754	0.87	331	10.4	396	12.5	1 516	6.0	6 270	3 592	2 678	571	1 938
Mason	687	25 029	0.76	268	10.0	350	13.0	1 470	6.9	6 096	4 690	1 406	417	1 695
Mercer	1 110	61 197	0.97	684	11.3	913	15.1	3 663	7.6	16 643	12 027	4 616	928	1 535
Mineral	654	24 808	0.72	284	10.4	339	12.4	1 433	6.8	5 557	4 736	821	474	1 822
Mingo	85	25 116	0.89	321	13.0	371	15.1	1 872	8.9	6 639	4 601	2 038	293	1 232
Monongalia	6 332	113 692	1.25	1 228	11.7	693	6.6	5 258	6.1	11 927	7 843	4 084	2 025	2 079
Monroe	57	11 014	0.51	123	9.2	154	11.5	912	8.8	3 971	3 065	906	101	751
Morgan	123	14 167	0.53	144	8.2	223	12.6	1 189	8.7	3 927	3 261	666	218	1 333
Nicholas	162	25 491	0.95	252	10.0	347	13.7	1 518	7.5	6 654	4 311	2 343	563	2 363
Ohio	2 380	54 145	1.53	450	10.6	595	14.0	1 999	6.1	11 466	6 572	4 894	1 201	2 815
Pendleton	117	6 702	0.76	59	8.4	68	9.6	448	8.4	1 992	1 526	466	NA	NA
Pleasants	670	7 622	1.00	60	7.9	76	10.0	310	5.5	1 581	1 110	471	NA	NA
Pocahontas	318	8 542	0.96	77	9.1	115	13.5	544	8.6	2 143	1 633	510	58	764
Preston	2 187	28 862	0.63	354	10.5	359	10.6	1 890	7.4	6 829	5 050	1 779	260	841
Putnam	249	52 104	0.82	619	10.9	585	10.3	2 621	5.6	10 378	6 800	3 578	1 067	1 913
Raleigh	3 823	81 291	1.10	836	10.9	1 068	13.9	4 836	8.1	18 674	14 129	4 545	3 161	4 098
Randolph	2 298	29 969	1.05	320	11.0	372	12.8	1 740	8.2	7 307	5 624	1 683	325	1 107
Ritchie	106	10 431	1.08	106	10.7	147	14.9	691	8.7	2 508	1 881	627	104	1 170
Roane	98	13 097	0.68	142	10.0	183	12.9	1 098	9.6	3 525	2 533	992	191	1 311
Summers	1 095	11 814	0.63	92	7.1	153	11.9	745	8.0	2 998	2 248	750	181	1 346
Taylor	509	13 715	0.51	146	8.7	194	11.5	921	6.9	3 130	2 422	708	33	195
Tucker	131	6 709	0.91	68	9.8	112	16.2	378	7.2	1 710	1 153	557	NA	NA
Tyler	67	8 213	0.75	87	9.7	111	12.4	476	6.8	1 889	1 261	628	66	813
Upshur	1 224	24 564	1.00	278	11.3	274	11.1	1 530	8.1	5 206	3 373	1 833	310	1 254
Wayne	246	37 694	0.73	406	10.0	515	12.7	2 456	7.4	7 062	4 960	2 102	795	2 112
Webster	58	8 362	0.80	86	9.9	124	14.3	620	9.1	2 395	1 613	782	NA	NA
Wetzel	124	17 141	1.18	175	11.2	239	15.3	926	7.5	4 581	2 810	1 771	NA	NA
Wirt	0	4 439	0.37	60	10.3	48	8.3	345	7.2	1 500	1 121	379	144	2 428
Wood	996	89 749	1.09	990	11.6	1 061	12.4	4 661	6.7	21 505	16 585	4 920	1 820	2 110
Wyoming	56	21 777	0.83	222	10.2	359	16.5	1 500	8.3	5 586	3 781	1 805	512	2 482
WISCONSIN	146 260	5 696 052	0.98	66 079	11.4	49 823	8.6	314 933	6.6	1 037 367	617 888	419 479	136 952	2 379
Adams	1 159	17 476	0.60	128	6.4	251	12.5	1 111	8.4	3 490	2 682	808	449	2 202
Ashland	569	17 127	1.15	175	11.1	175	11.1	1 058	8.5	3 888	2 579	1 309	432	2 703
Barron	612	45 881	1.01	478	10.5	464	10.2	2 675	7.5	11 087	6 972	4 115	207	555
Bayfield	110	12 976	0.69	114	7.7	180	12.1	1 128	10.2	3 644	2 413	1 231	170	1 119
Brown	6 526	273 949	1.15	3 345	12.8	1 843	7.1	16 501	7.6	42 088	19 885	22 203	4 332	1 812
Buffalo	92	10 816	0.63	142	10.8	123	9.4	756	7.3	3 122	2 423	699	111	834
Burnett	134	14 200	0.82	132	8.7	167	11.0	962	8.8	4 316	2 792	1 524	502	3 278
Calumet	179	38 240	0.57	527	10.6	347	7.0	1 862	4.3	4 819	1 573	3 246	551	1 107
Chippewa	2 646	58 501	0.85	704	11.1	597	9.4	3 399	6.7	11 878	7 968	3 910	920	1 453
Clark	516	32 180	0.85	553	16.0	331	9.6	5 029	17.7	6 402	3 214	3 188	193	558
Columbia	1 419	48 803	0.73	607	10.7	528	9.3	2 462	5.3	12 399	8 636	3 763	688	1 418
Crawford	770	16 703	1.03	164	10.0	168	10.3	807	6.6	3 425	2 235	1 190	270	1 652
Dane	12 739	547 016	1.13	6 246	11.8	3 177	6.0	24 052	5.4	69 654	51 847	17 807	12 261	2 447
Dodge	6 302	81 827	0.84	805	9.1	905	10.3	3 446	5.0	12 062	8 019	4 043	1 186	1 343
Door	335	27 107	0.95	204	7.4	356	12.9	1 373	6.9	8 117	5 883	2 234	308	1 102

1. Per 1,000 estimated resident population.   2. Data for serious crimes have not been adjusted for underreporting; this may affect comparability between geographic areas and over time.
3. Per 100,000 population estimated by the FBI.

Table B. States and Counties — Crime, Education, Money Income, and Poverty

	Serious crimes known to police, 2014 (cont.)[1]		Education						Money income, 2011–2015				Income and poverty, 2015			
	Rate[2]		School enrollment and attainment, 2011–2015				Local government expenditures,[5] 2013–2014				Households			Percent below poverty level		
			Enrollment[3]		Attainment[4] (percent)							Percent					
STATE County	Violent	Property	Total	Percent private	High school graduate or less	Bachelor's degree or more	Total current spending (mil dol)	Current spending per student (dollars)	Per capita income[6] (dollars)	Median income (dollars)	with income of less than $50,000	with income of $200,000 or more	Median household income (dollars)	All persons	Children under 18 years	Children 5 to 17 years in families
	46	47	48	49	50	51	52	53	54	55	56	57	58	59	60	61
WEST VIRGINIA—Cont'd																
Calhoun	NA	NA	1 588	5.2	71.9	10.4	12.1	11 318	19 635	35 568	63.6	0.8	36 403	20.0	30.0	29.7
Clay	NA	NA	1 984	1.0	75.4	9.8	21.1	10 673	16 827	31 325	70.0	0.9	30 369	27.7	37.4	35.7
Doddridge	NA	NA	1 526	6.4	62.5	13.5	16.7	14 440	19 992	39 974	60.0	0.9	41 115	18.1	25.8	22.3
Fayette	279	2 188	8 936	12.7	64.2	12.4	76.0	11 155	19 232	36 293	65.5	1.0	36 235	19.9	28.9	27.8
Gilmer	NA	NA	2 152	16.8	58.3	16.6	11.0	12 152	17 115	37 536	62.0	0.3	36 392	25.8	26.3	26.5
Grant	189	591	2 338	6.9	68.4	12.3	18.1	9 975	20 052	39 088	63.4	0.7	38 370	15.9	24.4	22.6
Greenbrier	108	1 079	6 953	8.8	59.2	18.1	58.1	11 185	22 340	39 746	61.6	1.9	38 209	19.0	27.1	24.0
Hampshire	227	619	4 801	8.5	71.8	10.1	36.5	10 298	18 477	27 995	72.8	0.3	40 293	18.6	27.9	25.5
Hancock	120	1 040	6 372	11.5	55.9	17.8	46.6	11 136	23 845	39 959	60.0	1.9	42 009	13.7	21.5	19.5
Hardy	390	677	2 731	7.0	68.3	14.0	22.9	9 884	22 195	40 303	62.1	1.7	41 344	14.4	23.9	22.2
Harrison	NA	NA	14 635	9.4	52.0	20.4	121.7	11 149	24 415	43 987	55.6	2.4	46 979	16.0	21.9	20.7
Jackson	214	610	5 860	8.0	54.7	17.6	55.4	11 278	23 090	41 314	57.7	2.5	44 675	15.4	22.8	21.3
Jefferson	154	1 403	14 496	12.6	44.0	28.4	99.1	10 933	30 912	66 677	36.7	5.2	67 821	10.6	13.8	11.9
Kanawha	562	3 977	39 404	13.4	49.1	25.1	304.6	10 522	27 642	45 882	54.0	3.2	44 849	16.5	24.8	22.9
Lewis	73	943	3 019	9.3	63.0	14.1	28.8	10 980	21 067	37 849	62.8	1.5	39 601	20.6	27.5	25.8
Lincoln	NA	NA	4 263	3.5	65.0	9.5	42.5	11 514	19 114	35 800	64.1	0.7	35 249	28.3	36.6	34.1
Logan	547	1 449	6 835	5.2	65.2	8.1	69.8	11 136	20 477	36 763	60.1	1.0	35 615	22.4	29.9	29.8
McDowell	352	1 067	3 119	3.5	79.4	5.1	46.5	13 537	14 874	24 921	76.4	0.8	26 413	34.5	46.8	45.4
Marion	210	910	12 968	7.9	52.5	21.4	91.8	11 429	23 807	43 165	55.7	1.5	43 654	16.0	22.1	20.3
Marshall	210	1 728	6 860	12.2	55.9	16.8	62.9	13 359	23 543	45 182	54.8	1.8	48 109	12.6	20.6	19.3
Mason	126	1 569	5 646	7.9	63.4	10.4	47.7	11 068	19 694	36 448	63.5	0.4	35 717	22.3	30.2	26.8
Mercer	246	1 289	13 328	10.4	55.5	18.8	101.5	10 585	20 942	36 195	63.9	0.9	35 342	21.1	29.9	30.1
Mineral	234	1 587	5 758	5.3	62.2	12.9	48.5	11 582	19 111	31 790	66.2	0.4	43 159	15.4	21.5	20.2
Mingo	315	916	5 254	3.1	67.4	10.2	50.9	11 568	20 417	33 221	64.9	1.6	31 742	29.0	38.7	35.6
Monongalia	246	1 833	36 777	6.0	38.4	39.7	124.6	11 135	26 314	45 467	53.3	4.5	46 718	19.6	15.5	14.6
Monroe	97	654	2 577	7.3	67.5	13.3	19.7	10 820	20 678	36 918	65.0	1.2	34 974	18.5	24.7	22.5
Morgan	465	869	3 223	10.6	58.0	18.6	27.9	10 822	23 456	39 324	61.7	1.4	45 628	14.1	22.0	19.3
Nicholas	772	1 591	5 113	5.1	64.2	13.9	43.3	10 942	23 404	39 171	61.9	2.9	38 912	18.5	27.0	24.6
Ohio	588	2 227	10 139	23.1	43.4	29.8	63.9	11 776	27 053	40 569	57.5	3.0	46 315	14.0	19.5	18.5
Pendleton	NA	NA	1 312	10.8	65.9	15.3	13.2	13 209	21 979	36 953	65.4	2.0	40 257	16.4	25.7	24.2
Pleasants	NA	NA	1 480	2.8	61.7	13.0	15.7	12 734	23 291	44 288	55.0	1.6	48 308	15.4	19.8	17.6
Pocahontas	158	606	1 429	9.5	62.2	16.7	14.9	13 366	21 847	36 827	64.1	1.5	36 822	18.9	30.1	30.1
Preston	165	676	6 119	10.1	64.3	14.6	42.2	9 197	21 097	45 064	55.1	1.1	43 804	17.0	23.2	21.8
Putnam	448	1 465	12 632	11.3	46.6	25.4	106.8	10 775	29 412	56 774	44.8	4.1	58 933	10.4	13.0	11.6
Raleigh	450	3 648	16 381	12.3	56.9	18.3	133.2	10 595	22 405	41 032	58.8	1.7	38 564	19.9	27.9	25.1
Randolph	249	858	5 592	15.5	62.4	19.3	45.5	10 762	21 139	39 457	61.7	1.4	37 185	19.8	28.4	26.0
Ritchie	68	1 103	2 039	9.8	66.5	10.5	17.3	11 387	19 632	37 636	63.4	0.5	39 501	18.5	25.6	22.7
Roane	206	1 105	2 950	6.7	68.0	11.3	24.5	10 038	18 957	31 813	66.2	1.5	36 176	21.1	30.1	28.0
Summers	119	1 227	2 514	4.7	58.6	13.6	16.5	10 312	20 347	36 651	65.5	0.4	35 676	26.4	35.9	32.4
Taylor	24	171	3 379	14.1	58.5	16.6	25.2	10 409	22 799	43 970	56.8	1.8	43 652	16.2	22.8	21.0
Tucker	NA	NA	1 184	9.8	65.2	14.2	12.5	12 167	22 321	40 533	59.0	0.3	38 000	17.1	24.1	22.9
Tyler	185	628	1 794	4.4	62.8	11.3	17.1	12 719	21 018	38 854	60.1	1.4	42 696	16.3	23.3	21.2
Upshur	32	1 222	5 748	24.3	64.3	16.3	41.3	10 802	20 230	40 330	60.3	1.6	40 766	17.3	26.1	23.9
Wayne	136	1 977	9 538	4.6	62.2	12.3	78.2	10 501	19 867	36 318	63.1	1.3	35 537	22.5	31.1	27.8
Webster	NA	NA	1 536	4.4	72.0	9.3	16.0	11 035	17 864	29 086	71.2	0.7	30 673	29.6	41.0	39.1
Wetzel	NA	NA	2 983	3.3	64.8	10.4	35.6	12 924	21 619	39 096	61.7	1.0	41 833	20.0	29.1	28.5
Wirt	270	2 159	1 121	7.0	61.7	12.0	11.4	11 161	22 125	39 352	59.9	2.1	42 309	17.9	27.0	25.4
Wood	196	1 914	18 919	10.6	48.9	18.8	143.4	10 817	24 364	41 884	58.6	1.8	41 133	17.3	25.3	23.5
Wyoming	911	1 570	4 538	4.9	70.8	7.9	49.7	11 674	19 009	33 730	64.6	1.0	35 020	22.5	31.6	27.8
WISCONSIN	290	2 088	1 477 783	16.8	41.0	27.8	9 677.5	11 067	28 340	53 357	46.7	3.3	55 623	12.1	16.5	14.9
Adams	177	2 026	3 319	8.6	56.5	12.8	38.9	11 379	22 783	43 640	57.4	1.8	42 844	17.4	29.3	25.7
Ashland	282	2 422	3 809	18.0	42.7	23.2	31.3	11 273	22 196	39 381	61.7	1.3	40 163	17.2	25.1	24.9
Barron	32	523	9 309	9.8	50.3	16.6	92.1	11 784	23 852	45 714	54.9	1.5	51 056	10.5	17.0	15.5
Bayfield	178	941	2 868	11.4	36.3	29.3	23.5	15 835	26 485	46 665	52.9	1.7	50 080	11.1	20.7	19.1
Brown	258	1 554	67 692	15.2	40.7	27.9	464.9	10 566	27 876	53 527	46.5	3.6	56 003	11.1	14.4	13.0
Buffalo	68	766	2 950	12.3	51.2	18.0	23.1	11 032	26 170	50 196	49.8	1.7	53 892	10.2	13.5	12.6
Burnett	222	3 056	2 842	11.2	48.6	17.7	26.4	10 429	23 963	41 135	59.9	1.2	44 858	13.1	22.3	20.2
Calumet	119	988	13 013	15.3	40.9	28.4	40.4	10 476	29 479	67 427	34.3	3.2	71 298	6.2	7.6	6.6
Chippewa	134	1 319	14 074	10.3	46.7	19.2	95.5	10 755	25 651	52 109	47.7	1.9	53 209	10.8	15.3	13.7
Clark	23	535	7 584	24.6	61.9	11.5	54.6	11 071	21 699	45 048	55.3	2.0	50 187	13.9	21.0	18.8
Columbia	150	1 267	13 248	12.0	42.4	22.1	97.3	11 138	28 967	59 769	40.9	2.6	60 837	8.9	12.6	10.7
Crawford	116	1 536	3 550	14.7	52.8	15.1	27.4	12 496	23 020	44 459	55.3	1.5	44 895	14.5	20.6	18.4
Dane	229	2 218	149 599	12.0	24.0	47.9	861.0	11 339	34 562	62 865	39.9	5.3	65 416	11.2	10.4	9.5
Dodge	74	1 270	19 404	19.3	52.0	16.4	118.2	10 889	25 372	53 783	45.8	1.8	56 514	8.7	11.7	10.6
Door	43	1 059	4 950	10.3	39.3	29.7	44.0	12 435	30 920	51 928	47.3	3.1	55 047	8.5	14.5	12.8

1. Data for serious crimes have not been adjusted for underreporting; this may affect comparability between geographic areas and over time.   2. Per 100,000 population estimated by the FBI.
3. All persons 3 years old and over enrolled in nursery school through college.   4. Persons 25 years old and over.   5. Elementary and secondary education expenditures.
6. Based on population estimated by the American Community Survey, 2011–2015.

STATE County	Personal income, 2015										Earnings, 2015		
	Total (mil dol)	Percent change, 2014–2015	Per capita[1]		Wages and salaries (mil dol)	Supplements to wages and salaries; employer contributions (mil dol)		Proprietors' income (mil dol)	Dividends, interest, and rent (mil dol)	Personal transfer receipts (mil dol)	Contributions for government social insurance (mil dol)		
			Dollars	Rank		Pension and insurance	Government social insurance				Total (mil dol)	From employee and self-employed	From employer
	62	63	64	65	66	67	68	69	70	71	72	73	74
WEST VIRGINIA—Cont'd													
Calhoun	204	-3.7	27 324	2 883	68	11	5	5	24	85	89	8	5
Clay	259	1.9	29 045	2 952	48	10	4	18	26	92	79	8	4
Doddridge	221	2.9	26 971	3 109	69	14	5	12	36	53	99	7	5
Fayette	1 371	2.1	30 462	2 675	420	81	33	67	161	525	601	47	33
Gilmer	216	-1.5	25 376	3 009	98	25	8	10	43	71	141	9	8
Grant	381	2.7	32 372	2 474	144	30	12	27	60	129	212	16	12
Greenbrier	1 279	6.6	36 008	1 941	515	86	44	130	202	420	776	56	44
Hampshire	722	3.8	30 920	2 723	139	29	12	38	101	203	217	19	12
Hancock	1 142	3.9	38 290	1 803	389	76	32	43	145	333	540	39	32
Hardy	385	-1.1	27 814	2 876	193	37	18	9	60	114	257	18	18
Harrison	3 016	2.3	43 898	840	1 750	329	139	351	467	690	2 569	163	139
Jackson	1 000	2.6	34 203	2 182	314	56	25	60	114	288	455	34	25
Jefferson	2 532	3.9	44 834	748	701	126	58	100	379	454	984	64	58
Kanawha	8 283	1.7	43 980	759	5 062	843	389	752	1 345	2 218	7 046	451	389
Lewis	602	0.3	36 621	1 647	340	56	26	47	94	168	469	32	26
Lincoln	592	1.3	27 661	2 975	110	21	9	20	59	209	159	16	9
Logan	1 164	2.3	33 546	2 206	449	77	36	26	129	478	587	44	36
McDowell	538	-1.2	27 107	2 979	211	45	17	11	68	266	283	24	17
Marion	2 220	2.2	39 007	1 358	871	148	67	138	298	570	1 224	85	67
Marshall	1 171	0.7	36 617	1 175	564	101	40	46	181	312	752	51	40
Mason	803	3.5	29 716	2 870	254	53	19	27	93	284	353	27	19
Mercer	2 081	1.6	34 029	2 188	770	140	65	123	279	811	1 097	83	65
Mineral	984	2.9	35 838	1 840	320	65	27	34	120	294	446	33	27
Mingo	744	-2.0	29 416	2 731	279	51	24	20	92	325	374	30	24
Monongalia	4 318	4.5	41 429	1 134	2 894	521	214	287	702	744	3 916	231	214
Monroe	390	0.5	28 845	2 874	78	20	6	24	51	133	129	12	6
Morgan	576	2.9	32 875	2 415	98	19	8	28	88	180	152	14	8
Nicholas	824	1.2	32 184	2 361	295	52	25	40	118	299	412	32	25
Ohio	2 097	1.7	48 687	707	1 243	201	97	161	433	506	1 702	109	97
Pendleton	251	0.3	34 764	2 024	55	12	4	10	49	81	81	7	4
Pleasants	297	3.5	38 674	1 363	148	30	11	18	37	96	208	14	11
Pocahontas	293	2.8	34 094	2 162	100	19	9	18	53	120	147	11	9
Preston	1 123	2.8	33 100	2 311	310	68	26	54	139	303	458	34	26
Putnam	2 383	2.7	41 923	1 045	1 075	155	88	127	307	468	1 444	96	88
Raleigh	2 738	0.2	35 324	1 748	1 358	242	109	116	398	918	1 825	125	109
Randolph	968	3.7	33 244	2 435	403	78	34	78	139	334	592	41	34
Ritchie	319	0.4	31 985	2 545	147	27	12	23	51	105	209	15	12
Roane	453	2.8	31 411	2 632	114	22	9	22	54	164	166	15	9
Summers	370	2.5	27 914	2 999	89	17	8	13	52	168	127	12	8
Taylor	588	2.6	34 761	2 050	146	27	12	20	76	157	205	16	12
Tucker	227	4.1	32 635	2 461	101	19	8	12	35	81	140	10	8
Tyler	300	2.8	33 402	2 537	113	24	8	9	49	92	154	11	8
Upshur	781	2.0	31 565	2 557	309	55	26	61	115	221	451	32	26
Wayne	1 209	1.3	29 498	2 748	412	92	34	59	143	363	597	45	34
Webster	242	2.3	27 673	3 000	77	16	6	11	32	103	110	10	6
Wetzel	542	1.8	34 292	2 341	163	31	13	18	99	188	225	18	13
Wirt	172	5.1	29 315	2 989	20	5	2	9	23	53	35	4	2
Wood	3 396	3.8	39 276	1 584	1 580	296	127	306	498	933	2 309	157	127
Wyoming	651	-2.0	29 369	2 835	236	42	18	16	66	255	312	26	18
WISCONSIN	264 988	3.6	45 942	X	135 408	24 270	10 493	19 077	47 544	46 005	189 248	11 418	10 493
Adams	710	4.6	35 222	1 444	165	39	14	56	118	232	274	20	14
Ashland	570	2.4	36 003	2 066	315	74	26	48	97	169	463	28	26
Barron	2 017	3.6	44 261	765	875	182	70	158	424	443	1 284	78	70
Bayfield	627	2.7	41 869	1 185	127	38	11	40	150	160	216	16	11
Brown	12 052	3.5	46 584	621	7 788	1 284	590	862	2 202	1 721	10 525	623	590
Buffalo	555	3.9	42 066	685	153	35	12	48	99	118	247	15	12
Burnett	577	3.3	38 063	1 460	162	43	13	37	115	177	256	19	13
Calumet	2 234	3.0	44 892	733	544	102	44	130	354	277	820	50	44
Chippewa	2 701	3.0	42 518	1 069	1 027	203	83	310	410	525	1 623	98	83
Clark	1 259	-1.0	36 538	1 612	436	94	35	208	217	261	771	42	35
Columbia	2 687	4.6	47 346	806	913	189	75	328	444	432	1 506	93	75
Crawford	609	2.2	37 161	1 594	274	56	23	42	114	158	395	25	23
Dane	28 122	5.5	53 705	310	17 585	3 372	1 310	1 782	5 584	3 206	24 049	1 371	1 310
Dodge	3 633	2.7	41 055	1 204	1 583	294	128	362	555	646	2 367	144	128
Door	1 482	4.6	53 773	368	491	101	43	118	430	288	753	49	43

1. Based on the resident population estimated as of July 1 of the year shown.

Table B. States and Counties — Earnings, Social Security, and Housing

STATE County	Earnings, 2015 (cont.) Percent by selected industries									Social Security beneficiaries, December 2015			Housing units, 2016	
	Farm	Mining	Construction	Manu-facturing	Infor-mation: professional, scientific, technical services	Retail trade	Finance, insur-ance, real estate and leasing	Health care and social assistance	Govern-ment	Number	Rate[1]	Supple-mental Security Income recipients, December 2015	Total	Percent change, 2010–2016
	75	76	77	78	79	80	81	82	83	84	85	86	87	88
WEST VIRGINIA—Cont'd														
Calhoun	-1.7	D	37.7	0.9	2.8	3.5	D	D	16.7	2 270	306	582	3 949	-0.4
Clay	0.0	D	D	D	D	6.7	D	12.3	28.6	2 795	314	708	4 570	0.0
Doddridge	-1.5	26.4	D	D	D	5.4	3.0	3.8	26.6	1 800	212	214	3 904	-1.0
Fayette	-0.1	7.9	3.9	3.7	4.0	8.7	3.5	14.7	27.4	12 350	276	2 670	21 465	-0.7
Gilmer	2.0	D	8.7	6.1	D	3.5	D	D	45.3	1 605	193	330	3 499	1.4
Grant	-1.0	D	12.4	6.2	D	6.9	3.2	D	22.7	3 450	293	389	6 583	3.4
Greenbrier	0.8	11.0	4.3	5.0	3.8	8.6	2.9	18.6	16.5	10 355	292	1 440	19 141	0.9
Hampshire	-1.6	D	8.9	3.7	D	8.4	5.2	D	30.0	6 085	261	723	13 870	1.3
Hancock	0.0	0.6	3.4	36.4	4.8	4.4	5.2	7.6	13.0	8 595	288	955	14 401	-1.0
Hardy	-2.2	0.0	2.4	D	4.0	6.4	3.9	D	15.3	3 645	262	404	8 168	1.1
Harrison	-0.2	8.8	7.9	4.4	10.1	6.4	3.8	12.9	24.4	17 100	249	2 793	31 584	0.5
Jackson	-0.2	1.9	8.2	24.8	5.5	8.2	4.7	D	16.3	7 870	270	1 268	13 244	-0.5
Jefferson	0.6	D	5.9	4.7	9.9	5.6	3.8	6.1	30.7	10 325	184	820	22 977	4.3
Kanawha	0.0	3.3	6.6	4.2	12.5	5.6	7.7	18.8	18.7	49 790	265	7 346	92 536	-0.1
Lewis	-0.1	28.9	8.3	1.7	1.9	5.5	2.6	D	15.7	4 660	283	910	7 905	-0.7
Lincoln	-0.2	D	18.2	0.2	4.9	6.3	1.4	11.9	28.7	6 000	281	1 744	9 785	-1.0
Logan	0.0	20.4	2.2	4.3	5.7	9.9	2.5	D	19.3	10 365	300	2 272	16 689	-0.3
McDowell	0.0	26.8	4.2	0.3	D	6.2	2.0	D	36.9	6 730	342	2 759	11 136	-1.6
Marion	-0.2	D	6.9	4.2	8.8	7.9	4.7	9.0	18.8	14 265	251	2 035	26 319	-0.5
Marshall	-0.7	30.2	5.3	14.4	D	6.0	2.0	D	12.7	7 830	244	878	15 787	-0.8
Mason	1.9	0.7	D	12.0	3.2	4.9	2.5	15.2	21.4	7 345	272	1 323	12 921	-0.7
Mercer	0.2	1.1	5.0	5.1	4.6	11.3	3.9	18.2	24.5	17 725	290	3 787	29 755	-1.2
Mineral	-0.7	0.4	6.0	31.7	9.3	7.0	2.4	D	18.8	6 810	248	754	13 106	0.5
Mingo	0.0	36.4	2.8	3.5	4.1	3.6	2.1	D	17.6	7 895	313	2 741	12 615	-0.7
Monongalia	-0.1	1.7	6.0	10.2	8.9	5.3	3.0	19.5	25.2	13 980	134	1 672	44 681	3.3
Monroe	-2.2	0.1	8.3	23.4	D	2.2	D	6.7	36.0	3 995	296	443	7 559	-0.5
Morgan	-0.3	D	8.9	5.0	4.3	7.6	5.0	17.2	22.9	4 790	273	336	9 877	1.3
Nicholas	0.2	9.6	6.2	10.3	4.8	12.0	2.3	D	23.3	7 860	308	1 268	12 975	-0.7
Ohio	-0.1	D	D	4.0	10.8	7.5	5.6	23.6	12.3	11 595	270	1 372	21 103	-0.3
Pendleton	0.0	D	D	D	5.5	5.7	4.9	D	29.9	2 295	319	206	5 179	0.9
Pleasants	-0.1	D	9.6	21.3	3.2	3.1	D	5.8	14.7	1 960	258	238	3 370	-0.6
Pocahontas	1.0	D	5.5	7.3	D	5.8	3.4	D	27.7	2 490	291	291	8 836	-0.2
Preston	-1.0	0.7	16.7	7.0	D	6.7	2.9	D	38.4	7 970	236	1 111	15 023	-0.5
Putnam	0.2	0.4	15.9	13.0	6.6	6.0	5.3	8.8	9.8	13 100	231	1 079	23 981	2.3
Raleigh	-0.1	9.9	4.6	2.5	6.7	9.7	3.5	20.0	21.3	21 820	282	3 347	35 996	0.2
Randolph	0.2	3.7	9.1	9.4	3.5	9.2	3.3	D	18.8	7 710	264	1 254	14 171	-0.1
Ritchie	-1.2	32.9	6.7	20.3	D	5.1	3.5	D	11.5	2 980	298	518	5 824	-0.3
Roane	-1.8	16.4	8.1	5.9	4.0	9.6	6.1	D	18.2	4 560	316	1 015	7 389	0.5
Summers	-1.4	D	12.5	1.0	D	6.4	3.9	D	25.3	3 455	264	775	7 671	-0.1
Taylor	-0.9	D	7.1	D	D	7.6	D	D	26.5	3 850	228	682	7 499	-0.5
Tucker	0.4	D	D	10.5	D	4.6	3.4	9.1	20.5	1 960	283	199	5 357	0.2
Tyler	-0.4	4.4	2.7	40.4	D	3.7	D	8.8	19.1	2 620	293	296	4 987	-0.3
Upshur	-0.2	7.2	11.6	9.4	5.0	9.2	3.8	D	14.8	6 150	249	1 039	11 302	1.8
Wayne	-0.1	D	7.4	9.3	3.2	4.5	1.5	D	38.8	10 585	258	2 035	19 153	-0.4
Webster	-0.1	D	1.5	8.9	D	5.1	D	8.4	28.2	2 820	323	716	5 400	-0.5
Wetzel	-0.3	D	12.6	2.9	D	12.4	4.4	D	25.9	4 440	281	751	8 134	-0.5
Wirt	-0.5	5.2	10.3	D	D	7.8	D	11.1	36.7	1 655	283	340	3 278	1.5
Wood	-0.2	4.8	7.3	10.8	5.2	9.0	6.6	14.9	19.9	23 315	270	3 647	40 300	0.2
Wyoming	-0.1	38.8	3.6	1.1	5.8	5.7	5.7	1.5	D	19.8	7 055	318	1 648	10 756	-1.9
WISCONSIN	1.4	0.2	5.8	18.2	8.1	6.0	7.6	12.3	15.0	1 170 705	203	118 556	2 668 444	1.7
Adams	14.3	0.0	5.0	6.5	D	5.1	D	8.0	28.7	7 075	351	411	17 406	-0.2
Ashland	0.6	0.0	8.6	13.9	D	7.4	3.2	D	26.1	4 210	265	415	9 585	-0.7
Barron	5.8	1.7	5.3	23.3	2.5	7.8	3.0	15.0	17.9	12 220	269	913	23 814	0.8
Bayfield	0.8	0.1	11.8	4.1	D	6.3	2.7	D	37.4	4 785	320	250	13 203	1.6
Brown	1.1	0.1	5.6	16.4	7.6	4.9	9.9	13.6	12.0	46 460	180	4 742	108 692	4.1
Buffalo	8.9	D	7.3	4.5	D	3.4	3.8	D	20.6	3 420	259	202	6 723	0.9
Burnett	1.4	D	7.5	21.1	2.4	6.8	2.2	D	31.3	5 435	359	269	15 490	1.4
Calumet	7.5	1.1	6.4	31.0	D	6.1	6.1	6.9	11.2	8 160	164	237	20 479	4.0
Chippewa	3.7	1.4	9.6	27.7	3.4	9.1	1.9	9.6	14.6	13 985	220	1 164	28 022	3.1
Clark	14.4	D	9.1	23.0	1.6	6.6	D	D	15.0	6 965	202	502	15 027	-0.3
Columbia	1.7	D	5.8	27.0	3.6	5.7	2.8	10.2	15.2	12 655	223	758	26 392	1.0
Crawford	3.3	D	4.6	24.8	D	15.1	2.3	D	16.2	4 460	272	312	8 849	0.5
Dane	0.5	0.1	5.4	8.0	16.6	5.3	9.1	9.2	23.1	80 100	153	7 521	228 287	5.7
Dodge	2.2	D	13.4	30.5	2.7	5.0	2.3	9.7	14.5	17 935	203	823	37 469	1.3
Door	2.5	D	9.7	19.9	D	9.3	4.5	11.5	15.2	9 190	334	271	24 601	2.6

1. Per 1,000 resident population estimated as of July 1 of the year shown.

Table B. States and Counties — Housing, Labor Force, and Employment

	Housing units, 2011–2015								Civilian labor force, 2016				Civilian employment,[6] 2011–2015		
	Occupied units							Sub-stand-ard units[4] (percent)			Unemployment			Percent	
	Owner-occupied					Renter-occupied									
				Median owner cost as a percent of income										Manage-ment, business, science and arts	Con-struction, produc-tion, and mainte-nance occu-pations
STATE County	Total	Percent	Median value[1]	With a mort-gage	Without a mort-gage[2]	Median rent[3]	Median rent as a per-cent of income[2]		Total	Percent change, 2015–2016	Total	Rate[5]	Total		
	89	90	91	92	93	94	95	96	97	98	99	100	101	102	103
WEST VIRGINIA—Cont'd															
Calhoun	3 090	80.4	71 100	17.8	10.0	551	27.9	0.8	2 652	-4.1	334	12.6	2 511	23.5	38.3
Clay	3 460	82.3	78 000	22.1	10.0	477	32.8	2.9	3 248	-0.9	332	10.2	2 891	24.2	35.9
Doddridge	2 674	85.6	92 000	17.8	10.0	532	31.7	1.0	3 747	2.8	185	4.9	2 831	26.5	32.2
Fayette	17 669	76.8	77 100	19.1	10.3	585	27.9	2.7	15 998	-1.8	1 257	7.9	15 837	27.0	27.6
Gilmer	2 744	77.4	78 700	16.2	10.0	561	28.0	2.1	2 533	-6.5	208	8.2	2 791	31.3	24.5
Grant	4 175	78.7	124 900	21.1	10.2	569	23.8	0.4	5 982	3.6	349	5.8	4 974	20.9	41.1
Greenbrier	15 339	73.3	105 300	20.5	10.0	630	28.9	2.2	15 612	1.5	833	5.3	14 116	31.9	27.1
Hampshire	10 194	54.4	121 400	23.9	10.3	531	28.3	2.0	9 986	3.6	424	4.2	8 878	19.3	40.3
Hancock	12 894	73.5	86 400	18.1	10.2	629	28.6	1.0	12 817	-1.5	888	6.9	13 236	27.3	28.9
Hardy	5 156	76.2	118 800	22.4	10.0	600	25.0	2.0	5 695	4.0	321	5.6	6 129	20.4	41.1
Harrison	27 502	73.6	97 800	17.2	10.0	648	28.5	1.8	32 181	0.9	1 864	5.8	29 587	32.8	24.0
Jackson	11 118	78.0	111 600	18.0	10.0	567	25.3	2.4	11 951	0.2	766	6.4	11 050	32.0	26.6
Jefferson	20 331	74.0	207 300	22.0	10.0	887	29.6	1.7	28 743	3.4	943	3.3	26 418	39.9	19.1
Kanawha	82 250	69.5	103 100	18.5	10.0	698	26.4	1.6	85 541	-0.9	4 604	5.4	84 406	37.9	17.5
Lewis	6 526	70.3	95 500	18.0	10.0	546	27.8	3.4	6 802	-2.6	573	8.4	6 259	24.2	31.7
Lincoln	7 994	76.9	81 000	17.7	10.0	524	39.5	3.1	7 307	-0.8	615	8.4	7 245	23.9	30.1
Logan	14 043	75.9	82 100	19.2	10.1	562	29.1	1.6	11 139	-3.2	1 129	10.1	11 765	26.3	32.8
McDowell	8 180	76.7	35 500	17.5	10.0	521	40.7	3.7	5 095	-4.8	615	12.1	4 627	23.4	31.1
Marion	22 481	76.6	99 800	17.1	10.3	681	30.0	2.2	25 675	-1.4	1 650	6.4	25 422	33.1	25.0
Marshall	13 569	77.4	94 600	17.7	10.0	578	24.0	1.3	13 974	-0.7	1 104	7.9	13 530	28.1	29.7
Mason	10 838	79.5	79 600	19.1	10.0	504	31.7	2.0	9 990	0.1	706	7.1	9 116	25.3	35.2
Mercer	25 451	72.0	85 200	19.2	10.0	596	31.3	1.3	22 044	0.2	1 434	6.5	23 443	31.2	21.6
Mineral	11 265	57.3	118 800	20.2	10.0	531	30.5	1.2	11 857	1.9	699	5.9	10 716	24.8	31.9
Mingo	10 844	75.9	73 200	18.4	10.6	584	28.2	2.5	6 717	-7.4	840	12.5	7 951	27.7	36.1
Monongalia	37 035	57.2	167 600	17.9	10.0	747	33.7	2.7	51 187	1.3	2 186	4.3	48 349	43.0	16.1
Monroe	5 822	80.7	101 600	19.3	10.1	575	26.2	2.9	5 962	3.6	267	4.5	5 348	27.3	34.6
Morgan	7 348	70.7	165 000	23.7	11.4	710	26.6	2.2	7 656	2.3	328	4.3	7 144	30.9	31.0
Nicholas	10 787	79.2	83 100	19.5	10.0	548	27.5	2.8	9 507	-4.4	836	8.8	9 824	24.2	32.9
Ohio	18 408	68.4	107 500	18.0	10.0	566	31.0	1.4	20 642	-0.2	1 134	5.5	20 291	34.0	19.8
Pendleton	3 095	78.5	100 500	20.3	10.0	607	22.6	2.6	3 660	2.3	141	3.9	2 833	25.9	36.6
Pleasants	2 893	83.2	100 800	17.4	10.0	629	24.1	1.5	2 953	-1.2	238	8.1	2 915	31.2	33.3
Pocahontas	3 737	80.6	115 500	20.2	10.0	550	26.9	2.2	3 683	2.4	244	6.6	3 723	30.1	28.8
Preston	12 472	79.7	107 100	18.4	10.0	584	26.9	1.7	14 945	2.0	843	5.6	13 842	26.4	32.6
Putnam	21 707	82.9	148 600	18.1	10.0	731	25.4	0.8	25 593	0.1	1 234	4.8	25 964	37.5	18.9
Raleigh	31 274	72.8	101 700	18.5	10.4	641	26.8	1.2	29 873	-1.7	2 060	6.9	29 014	31.3	23.7
Randolph	11 563	72.9	101 200	20.6	10.0	560	28.9	2.5	12 130	1.8	719	5.9	11 833	29.1	23.3
Ritchie	3 942	79.4	73 100	19.0	10.0	578	26.5	0.9	4 597	2.2	297	6.5	3 730	25.1	35.7
Roane	5 872	76.4	88 900	19.8	10.0	456	30.5	2.4	5 233	0.1	528	10.1	4 892	26.5	30.6
Summers	5 584	78.3	89 200	17.6	10.0	561	30.8	3.4	4 591	1.5	280	6.1	4 857	29.4	31.1
Taylor	6 732	78.9	88 800	18.9	10.0	587	25.9	1.0	7 806	0.7	433	5.5	6 784	33.7	29.3
Tucker	3 010	79.1	104 000	19.7	10.0	525	23.9	1.5	3 505	2.3	185	5.3	3 052	29.6	30.2
Tyler	3 616	77.1	87 100	18.1	10.0	556	32.6	1.5	3 569	-2.5	310	8.7	3 296	25.2	31.0
Upshur	9 093	76.0	108 800	19.4	10.0	591	24.2	1.5	9 891	2.3	731	7.4	9 682	31.8	30.0
Wayne	16 691	76.9	82 800	19.2	10.0	589	32.1	1.9	15 604	0.1	1 011	6.5	14 542	30.1	25.7
Webster	3 887	73.8	64 800	20.9	11.3	489	39.0	1.1	3 476	0.0	287	8.3	2 945	18.0	37.4
Wetzel	6 525	79.2	83 500	15.7	10.0	515	34.5	1.7	7 182	0.2	659	9.2	5 548	23.4	36.5
Wirt	2 430	81.5	80 300	17.5	10.0	495	19.1	2.6	2 239	-0.9	194	8.7	2 265	28.1	35.8
Wood	36 192	71.3	107 000	19.2	10.0	622	31.0	1.6	36 845	-0.7	2 089	5.7	36 778	30.7	23.1
Wyoming	9 199	81.1	60 200	16.7	10.1	551	26.8	3.8	7 390	-4.7	749	10.1	6 451	27.6	33.0
WISCONSIN	2 299 107	67.3	165 800	22.6	13.5	776	28.9	2.1	3 120 236	0.8	129 201	4.1	2 883 390	34.5	25.4
Adams	7 786	84.6	131 600	25.6	14.8	695	29.4	1.6	8 303	-0.4	517	6.2	7 457	23.5	31.5
Ashland	6 718	69.3	109 000	22.6	13.9	614	27.4	3.2	7 956	0.3	446	5.6	7 475	30.0	26.8
Barron	19 120	73.0	134 100	23.8	13.9	646	26.0	2.1	24 472	0.0	1 146	4.7	22 257	26.6	35.7
Bayfield	6 919	82.3	161 300	24.0	14.5	613	26.6	3.4	7 527	-0.1	536	7.1	6 859	34.6	26.6
Brown	100 640	65.9	158 400	21.3	12.5	712	27.7	2.6	140 771	1.0	5 262	3.7	130 354	33.4	25.1
Buffalo	5 771	75.4	145 500	23.0	14.2	621	26.5	2.1	6 593	0.8	305	4.6	7 013	31.6	34.3
Burnett	7 312	80.4	148 800	26.5	14.6	624	28.9	2.3	7 152	-1.8	445	6.2	6 464	26.9	30.2
Calumet	18 583	81.1	165 200	20.1	12.0	707	25.6	1.4	27 977	1.8	920	3.3	26 679	33.8	28.6
Chippewa	24 873	72.5	148 500	21.7	12.3	724	27.9	1.8	33 481	0.9	1 461	4.4	31 085	29.5	32.0
Clark	12 797	77.1	113 100	22.5	13.3	586	23.8	5.0	17 563	0.7	705	4.0	15 579	28.6	39.3
Columbia	22 615	74.4	175 300	23.0	13.2	744	26.7	1.5	31 803	1.4	1 172	3.7	29 483	31.6	28.6
Crawford	6 623	74.2	123 500	22.7	14.1	569	29.7	2.6	7 967	0.7	399	5.0	7 491	24.6	36.3
Dane	211 114	58.1	230 800	22.7	12.5	923	29.8	2.2	316 545	1.8	9 287	2.9	287 151	48.8	13.9
Dodge	33 322	72.3	153 100	23.3	14.1	761	26.2	1.5	47 871	0.6	1 810	3.8	43 362	26.6	36.3
Door	12 968	78.7	194 100	24.6	13.7	692	27.1	1.2	15 494	0.0	794	5.1	13 169	31.7	24.9

1. Specified owner-occupied units.   2. A value of 10.0 represents 10 percent or less; a value of 50.0 represents 50 percent or more.   3. Specified renter-occupied units.
4. Overcrowded or lacking complete plumbing facilities.   5. Percent of civilian labor force.   6. Civilian employed persons 16 years old and over.

Table B. States and Counties — Nonfarm Employment and Agriculture

	Private nonfarm establishments, employment and payroll, 2015									Agriculture, 2012			
		Employment						Annual payroll		Farms			
												Percent with:	
STATE County	Number of establishments	Total	Health care and social assistance	Manufacturing	Retail trade	Finance and insurance	Professional, scientific, and technical services	Total (mil dol)	Average per employee (dollars)	Number	Fewer than 50 acres	500 acres or more	Farm operators whose principal occupation is farming (percent)
	104	105	106	107	108	109	110	111	112	113	114	115	116
WEST VIRGINIA—Cont'd													
Calhoun	99	807	273	25	106	51	21	41	50 898	227	16.7	8.8	35.7
Clay	83	796	322	29	130	D	D	24	30 175	114	20.2	3.5	34.2
Doddridge	69	1 440	144	D	93	D	D	170	117 859	352	19.6	5.4	49.4
Fayette	758	8 152	1 978	561	1 523	227	155	305	37 450	232	39.7	1.3	40.1
Gilmer	130	1 195	255	188	167	25	20	36	30 211	235	9.4	11.1	46.4
Grant	231	2 623	760	289	376	109	40	101	38 600	486	24.5	12.1	45.7
Greenbrier	907	10 950	2 789	851	1 995	239	237	352	32 114	819	29.9	10.4	40.2
Hampshire	325	2 660	799	189	515	174	87	75	28 246	798	40.6	8.8	43.4
Hancock	579	9 570	1 104	2 754	971	284	432	322	33 678	96	47.9	1.0	30.2
Hardy	249	4 776	465	2 636	599	190	52	139	29 029	494	33.8	13.4	52.8
Harrison	1 829	28 561	6 854	1 594	4 769	577	1 882	1 180	41 314	778	26.2	4.4	34.8
Jackson	505	6 919	1 184	1 573	1 185	226	260	274	39 541	732	24.2	3.6	41.7
Jefferson	837	13 375	1 152	852	1 931	344	365	427	31 909	501	51.7	5.6	50.7
Kanawha	4 977	84 023	18 271	3 220	11 396	4 669	5 383	3 626	43 155	210	34.8	1.0	41.0
Lewis	394	5 537	1 193	102	1 109	99	51	236	42 533	476	20.6	5.5	42.9
Lincoln	195	1 628	579	D	333	56	50	49	30 289	149	14.8	4.0	47.7
Logan	622	9 558	1 912	546	1 742	194	248	400	41 876	11	54.5	9.1	45.5
McDowell	258	2 687	948	D	596	119	71	87	32 235	11	72.7	9.1	54.5
Marion	1 201	16 937	2 684	879	2 376	449	1 031	665	39 265	557	34.1	0.9	53.5
Marshall	498	9 481	1 602	513	1 259	230	263	408	43 005	682	23.3	1.6	43.5
Mason	324	3 944	1 009	520	612	104	65	177	44 931	875	26.2	4.0	38.9
Mercer	1 241	17 688	4 876	1 228	3 153	420	567	566	31 985	400	30.8	3.5	40.8
Mineral	451	5 774	1 452	1 273	968	121	188	220	38 130	429	34.3	7.5	33.3
Mingo	388	3 081	609	83	392	162	369	97	31 626	20	70.0	10.0	55.0
Monongalia	2 338	46 042	14 406	3 858	6 257	785	2 705	2 043	44 375	458	26.4	2.6	34.3
Monroe	169	1 393	287	D	128	51	49	47	33 884	796	27.4	7.8	41.7
Morgan	232	1 981	552	161	396	86	75	60	30 220	196	42.9	2.0	46.9
Nicholas	569	6 725	1 681	751	1 571	118	172	210	31 231	393	31.3	5.1	52.2
Ohio	1 402	27 702	7 067	1 056	3 338	1 098	1 781	1 039	37 509	197	26.4	5.1	38.1
Pendleton	142	1 137	347	160	176	62	19	32	28 314	556	17.3	16.2	51.8
Pleasants	124	2 043	373	448	151	74	43	104	50 943	150	27.3	5.3	44.0
Pocahontas	209	3 101	429	282	330	48	D	72	23 266	389	18.5	14.7	44.7
Preston	522	5 150	1 108	542	891	162	110	177	34 390	1 084	26.2	3.6	46.1
Putnam	1 213	18 296	2 088	2 316	2 434	463	736	816	44 626	544	28.9	1.5	41.9
Raleigh	1 829	26 779	6 949	882	5 136	513	872	1 002	37 433	332	44.9	2.4	51.5
Randolph	679	9 409	2 716	1 208	1 458	255	222	273	29 023	405	27.7	10.9	44.2
Ritchie	207	2 555	209	980	233	71	66	109	42 832	428	17.5	7.7	42.1
Roane	243	2 387	675	179	484	94	40	87	36 469	575	15.5	7.1	45.2
Summers	161	1 400	421	35	239	43	53	41	29 221	345	21.4	3.8	43.5
Taylor	230	2 446	557	D	476	35	42	106	43 225	404	36.4	4.2	40.1
Tucker	152	2 059	268	231	225	42	23	59	28 762	162	20.4	9.9	52.5
Tyler	105	1 886	534	656	139	113	17	82	43 628	286	18.9	5.2	44.1
Upshur	521	6 228	1 497	749	775	97	241	221	35 477	456	27.9	4.8	42.3
Wayne	509	7 018	2 161	702	1 079	134	166	288	41 092	197	21.8	4.6	39.1
Webster	136	1 187	454	220	160	29	8	37	31 355	70	28.6	0.0	44.3
Wetzel	346	4 330	757	905	908	130	211	172	39 798	249	13.7	2.0	44.6
Wirt	51	293	D	D	65	14	7	7	25 273	217	19.4	6.0	37.3
Wood	2 044	31 964	7 078	2 244	6 107	965	1 047	1 135	35 522	816	30.3	1.3	34.1
Wyoming	282	3 048	825	63	597	79	78	128	41 876	27	33.3	3.7	33.3
WISCONSIN	139 500	2 503 532	394 420	450 924	309 366	137 219	107 911	112 406	44 899	69 754	32.2	8.8	49.8
Adams	334	3 275	443	406	518	51	63	99	30 195	313	19.8	16.6	55.3
Ashland	515	6 322	1 371	1 122	951	204	148	229	36 281	187	23.5	13.4	35.3
Barron	1 299	16 361	2 568	4 847	3 086	505	320	595	36 350	1 322	25.3	11.0	54.5
Bayfield	431	2 280	321	184	412	78	28	66	29 156	352	27.3	9.9	51.4
Brown	6 418	144 065	20 798	25 125	15 790	8 925	5 394	6 513	45 206	1 111	52.7	6.0	54.3
Buffalo	314	2 843	252	310	302	136	76	104	36 663	1 061	20.3	14.8	49.8
Burnett	407	3 271	703	773	529	88	69	108	32 989	406	27.1	10.6	42.9
Calumet	885	13 472	1 237	3 917	1 710	676	207	516	38 316	719	36.7	9.2	53.3
Chippewa	1 555	21 679	3 161	5 907	3 878	366	532	851	39 252	1 757	29.5	9.6	47.2
Clark	741	8 849	920	3 537	930	172	159	319	36 016	2 317	23.3	7.1	64.7
Columbia	1 417	19 650	2 567	4 688	3 056	393	468	708	36 039	1 564	39.5	9.6	52.9
Crawford	388	6 455	876	1 481	995	155	595	196	30 364	1 105	24.1	6.9	43.5
Dane	13 828	275 333	46 594	24 489	31 123	24 175	22 113	14 202	51 580	2 749	43.0	7.8	47.3
Dodge	1 736	30 462	4 139	9 607	3 414	664	550	1 500	49 230	2 012	36.9	9.7	47.5
Door	1 280	10 353	1 441	2 356	1 692	337	232	374	36 158	803	40.6	6.2	45.0

Table B. States and Counties — **Agriculture**

STATE County	Land in farms — Acreage (1,000)	Percent change, 2007–2012	Acres — Average size of farm	Total irrigated (1,000)	Total cropland (1,000)	Value of land and buildings (dollars) Average per farm	Average per acre	Value of machinery and equipment, average per farm (dollars)	Value of products sold — Total (mil dol)	Average per farm (dollars)	Percent from: Crops	Live-stock and poultry products	Percent of farms with sales of: $10,000 or more	$100,000 or more	Government payments Total ($1,000)	Percent of farms
	117	118	119	120	121	122	123	124	125	126	127	128	129	130	131	132
WEST VIRGINIA—Cont'd																
Calhoun	49	-11.7	218	0.0	7.4	331 432	1 521	38 423	2.1	9 326	17.9	82.1	17.2	2.6	40	6.6
Clay	20	0.6	176	D	2.2	329 789	1 873	34 000	0.5	4 570	30.3	69.7	10.5	0.0	37	6.1
Doddridge	65	-19.6	186	D	10.0	349 517	1 882	41 406	2.3	6 452	33.7	66.3	15.3	0.3	66	7.3
Fayette	23	-13.2	100	0.0	6.1	245 427	2 458	43 509	1.7	7 478	41.5	58.5	18.1	0.9	66	7.3
Gilmer	70	9.9	300	0.0	11.7	440 783	1 472	55 600	8.8	37 634	4.4	95.6	25.1	3.0	139	10.2
Grant	112	3.2	231	0.0	21.3	549 519	2 377	44 138	51.3	105 498	2.4	97.6	37.2	11.7	253	19.1
Greenbrier	190	7.4	232	0.0	35.7	658 885	2 837	71 835	76.8	93 722	2.8	97.2	37.6	8.5	461	15.4
Hampshire	142	10.0	178	0.1	34.8	641 143	3 601	51 271	39.2	49 102	19.3	80.7	26.2	5.5	227	16.9
Hancock	9	-7.9	93	D	3.1	271 469	2 932	59 625	0.6	6 750	53.1	46.9	13.5	1.0	2	5.2
Hardy	155	15.6	314	0.0	29.2	891 816	2 837	87 621	189.0	382 530	2.7	97.3	46.6	27.7	336	15.4
Harrison	117	4.8	150	0.0	25.7	318 695	2 119	45 731	9.5	12 264	25.2	74.8	20.3	2.1	71	3.3
Jackson	105	-19.1	143	0.0	25.8	315 790	2 207	42 680	7.4	10 067	28.8	71.2	20.8	1.2	256	8.9
Jefferson	67	-7.1	134	0.3	41.4	918 731	6 874	74 527	35.5	70 920	45.0	55.0	36.7	9.6	852	24.8
Kanawha	26	9.5	124	0.0	4.1	268 152	2 165	31 386	1.3	6 310	33.3	66.7	18.6	0.5	25	8.1
Lewis	82	-10.5	173	D	16.2	341 069	1 969	42 935	7.0	14 735	14.0	86.0	35.1	1.5	73	3.6
Lincoln	26	-20.8	172	0.0	3.3	348 013	2 021	38 450	0.9	6 087	37.6	62.4	12.8	1.3	63	24.8
Logan	1	-40.3	76	D	0.0	147 273	1 949	34 455	0.1	5 364	89.8	10.2	18.2	0.0	0	0.0
McDowell	1	-29.7	95	0.0	0.2	227 091	2 400	47 091	D	D	D	D	9.1	9.1	0	0.0
Marion	53	-8.0	96	0.0	12.7	206 381	2 155	42 246	2.4	4 370	39.1	60.9	11.8	0.0	49	3.6
Marshall	86	-10.3	126	0.0	22.8	277 150	2 199	46 801	3.3	4 890	40.9	59.1	11.9	0.0	121	7.6
Mason	139	5.0	159	0.3	39.7	335 312	2 114	52 757	34.1	38 965	74.1	25.9	24.1	4.6	465	17.5
Mercer	52	-4.0	129	0.0	9.7	287 660	2 222	45 280	3.9	9 790	33.2	66.8	19.8	1.8	34	2.8
Mineral	76	-2.3	178	0.1	16.7	533 772	3 006	49 399	22.2	51 849	6.9	93.1	22.6	5.6	257	11.7
Mingo	2	-49.2	102	0.0	0.1	143 850	1 417	23 300	0.1	5 300	D	D	10.0	0.0	0	0.0
Monongalia	58	-2.1	127	0.0	14.9	391 255	3 090	48 055	4.0	8 784	27.8	72.2	21.8	0.9	165	6.1
Monroe	145	8.9	182	0.0	29.2	414 754	2 283	52 758	31.4	39 447	9.5	90.5	36.8	7.5	426	15.8
Morgan	18	-18.1	94	0.1	7.8	419 311	4 470	39 770	3.0	15 408	77.2	22.8	19.4	3.1	86	6.6
Nicholas	58	13.2	148	0.0	13.6	377 216	2 552	42 771	4.6	11 649	16.8	83.2	22.9	2.0	37	8.7
Ohio	30	-2.4	153	D	11.9	353 061	2 312	80 888	3.5	17 660	20.5	79.5	28.4	5.6	64	24.4
Pendleton	170	0.1	306	D	24.4	711 710	2 326	68 344	118.8	213 608	2.4	97.6	58.6	21.0	207	17.1
Pleasants	21	-16.6	143	D	4.1	277 013	1 933	55 173	D	D	D	D	14.7	2.7	D	1.3
Pocahontas	118	-2.8	305	0.0	18.7	670 208	2 201	61 131	9.3	23 779	11.3	88.7	40.1	4.4	174	21.9
Preston	161	5.5	148	0.1	44.9	365 799	2 467	55 455	18.2	16 749	28.1	71.9	31.5	2.8	222	8.4
Putnam	60	-9.7	110	0.1	12.2	281 868	2 556	39 509	10.1	18 603	83.1	16.9	14.3	1.1	85	9.6
Raleigh	37	-15.1	111	0.0	8.1	276 123	2 487	47 337	3.0	9 036	24.6	75.4	17.2	0.9	47	6.0
Randolph	94	-9.9	232	D	19.8	422 042	1 815	54 812	9.4	23 173	21.8	78.2	35.1	3.2	147	9.9
Ritchie	89	-2.3	207	0.0	17.6	331 741	1 599	54 668	7.6	17 776	15.1	84.9	21.7	1.2	57	4.0
Roane	111	-5.7	193	D	21.6	330 957	1 716	42 193	5.6	9 781	26.2	73.8	23.1	0.7	209	9.6
Summers	58	-2.8	168	0.0	10.9	369 194	2 198	42 614	5.0	14 365	25.7	74.3	25.2	3.5	45	6.7
Taylor	49	-8.7	122	0.0	10.4	301 597	2 481	50 545	3.7	9 228	19.2	80.8	18.1	1.5	131	4.2
Tucker	34	-2.7	210	D	6.7	641 191	3 059	47 975	2.2	13 580	22.6	77.4	29.0	1.9	37	9.9
Tyler	48	1.4	169	0.0	11.5	309 413	1 836	41 035	2.2	7 829	35.1	64.9	26.2	0.3	34	7.0
Upshur	68	-3.4	150	0.0	15.0	348 270	2 320	46 175	6.8	14 925	18.8	81.3	24.6	2.6	48	3.9
Wayne	30	-24.2	153	0.0	3.7	288 345	1 880	36 102	1.0	5 183	40.7	59.2	12.2	1.0	24	4.1
Webster	8	-31.2	113	0.0	1.8	248 500	2 194	25 086	0.3	4 743	62.7	37.3	15.7	0.0	D	2.9
Wetzel	38	-26.5	153	D	7.6	279 361	1 826	34 867	1.2	4 727	43.9	56.1	6.8	0.4	45	4.4
Wirt	38	-7.8	175	D	7.7	287 650	1 642	42 065	2.2	10 286	28.8	71.2	20.3	1.4	55	8.8
Wood	88	-1.3	108	0.0	21.8	251 165	2 333	34 237	6.1	7 496	30.9	69.1	14.0	0.2	102	3.4
Wyoming	3	-26.5	110	D	0.5	227 889	2 072	42 407	0.1	2 556	15.9	84.1	3.7	0.0	0	0.0
WISCONSIN	14 569	-4.1	209	421.7	9 911.0	819 551	3 924	129 561	11 744.5	168 370	39.2	60.8	52.3	24.6	237 304	55.8
Adams	118	2.6	378	44.3	87.5	1 467 256	3 879	173 677	105.7	337 601	88.5	11.5	52.4	23.0	882	54.3
Ashland	46	-17.3	245	0.0	21.2	450 973	1 841	83 807	12.0	64 364	20.9	79.1	42.2	8.0	214	18.2
Barron	310	-4.5	234	11.7	202.9	655 775	2 799	148 573	343.1	259 503	29.1	70.9	58.5	29.0	4 643	59.5
Bayfield	72	-19.6	204	0.1	36.3	414 466	2 031	70 830	13.9	39 528	35.3	64.7	34.9	10.8	267	19.6
Brown	181	-3.2	163	0.5	151.3	884 833	5 425	149 589	307.5	276 792	17.4	82.6	52.8	27.2	3 585	48.7
Buffalo	305	-0.6	288	4.6	162.7	968 225	3 365	147 399	225.8	212 814	32.1	67.9	58.9	30.3	4 876	68.7
Burnett	84	-13.1	206	0.2	44.4	506 421	2 459	84 613	37.2	91 626	38.8	61.2	39.7	13.5	661	42.4
Calumet	142	-6.1	198	0.0	120.9	1 092 981	5 520	172 268	213.2	296 527	25.5	74.5	64.4	33.1	3 196	64.0
Chippewa	385	8.8	219	5.7	249.9	597 028	2 727	114 201	253.2	144 107	38.1	61.9	51.5	24.6	5 088	54.5
Clark	458	4.1	198	0.6	310.9	618 134	3 126	119 200	401.9	173 441	22.9	77.1	64.2	38.2	5 774	38.1
Columbia	308	-2.6	197	1.6	234.1	993 045	5 043	129 485	214.3	137 021	55.7	44.3	51.0	20.5	5 783	51.3
Crawford	217	-9.1	196	0.2	98.4	530 437	2 706	78 187	74.9	67 783	50.3	49.7	48.1	15.3	2 373	61.3
Dane	504	-5.8	183	4.6	396.3	1 111 346	6 057	145 729	471.6	171 553	39.1	60.9	50.5	23.2	12 023	62.2
Dodge	402	-2.6	200	0.8	332.6	1 069 970	5 355	169 021	373.5	185 612	45.8	54.2	57.6	30.2	7 872	58.2
Door	132	-1.9	164	0.9	94.3	668 813	4 070	99 567	82.6	102 905	46.1	53.9	45.0	16.4	1 826	50.7

Table B. States and Counties — Water Use, Wholesale Trade, Retail Trade, and Real Estate

STATE County	Water use, 2010 Total water withdrawn (mil gal/day)	Gallons withdrawn per person per day	Wholesale trade,[1] 2012 Number of establishments	Number of employees	Sales (mil dol)	Annual payroll (mil dol)	Retail trade,[2] 2012 Number of establishments	Number of employees	Sales (mil dol)	Annual payroll (mil dol)	Real estate and rental and leasing,[2] 2012 Number of establishments	Number of employees	Receipts (mil dol)	Annual payroll (mil dol)
	133	134	135	136	137	138	139	140	141	142	143	144	145	146
WEST VIRGINIA—Cont'd														
Calhoun	0.8	106	NA	NA	NA	NA	19	128	27.3	2.4	3	6	0.5	0.1
Clay	1.1	121	1	D	D	D	17	134	45.7	2.7	1	D	D	D
Doddridge	1.1	135	1	D	D	D	10	90	22.8	1.4	1	D	D	D
Fayette	7.8	169	25	D	D	D	134	1 683	413.8	37.0	21	56	8.6	1.2
Gilmer	2.9	331	4	D	D	D	22	157	38.3	3.2	2	D	D	D
Grant	1 120.9	93 903	2	D	D	D	38	377	115.2	7.7	5	10	0.9	0.2
Greenbrier	8.9	250	17	D	D	D	173	2 029	543.4	47.6	42	118	23.3	3.7
Hampshire	2.6	110	6	D	D	D	57	480	123.6	9.6	14	29	3.6	0.8
Hancock	78.7	2 565	13	154	105.9	4.9	93	1 000	235.3	19.2	22	D	D	D
Hardy	16.4	1 172	4	D	D	D	45	599	133.3	12.2	7	20	2.2	0.4
Harrison	55.4	802	74	867	381.8	37.0	327	4 727	1 314.7	104.5	62	508	161.0	24.8
Jackson	4.1	139	18	254	191.4	9.9	96	1 138	348.2	25.9	14	49	24.9	2.1
Jefferson	9.9	184	14	58	51.0	2.8	142	1 866	451.4	40.8	43	117	18.0	3.4
Kanawha	590.8	3 060	256	3 709	2 518.9	183.3	760	11 292	3 186.6	274.2	238	1 208	278.6	42.3
Lewis	2.5	151	14	116	109.9	5.8	75	1 063	301.2	23.6	9	39	5.2	0.8
Lincoln	1.9	88	3	D	D	D	38	312	80.3	6.5	2	D	D	D
Logan	9.4	256	34	411	138.2	18.1	118	1 726	551.2	42.6	20	86	9.3	2.4
McDowell	3.6	162	5	D	D	D	53	650	131.2	12.7	6	29	17.9	3.1
Marion	16.4	291	44	D	D	D	189	2 291	743.2	55.4	35	128	24.0	4.4
Marshall	433.9	13 105	16	D	D	D	85	1 224	344.7	27.3	7	D	D	D
Mason	643.1	23 536	5	D	D	D	54	575	143.9	11.9	14	51	6.1	1.2
Mercer	10.2	163	52	590	355.8	28.1	251	3 183	929.1	78.2	38	126	61.9	4.6
Mineral	4.3	153	12	D	D	D	71	999	237.3	20.4	15	37	4.7	0.8
Mingo	6.6	246	14	197	55.0	8.2	62	445	119.7	11.2	15	D	D	D
Monongalia	115.4	1 199	56	401	340.9	14.5	382	6 325	1 608.6	129.8	132	D	D	D
Monroe	3.1	230	6	16	3.6	0.4	31	145	26.6	2.7	3	4	0.6	0.1
Morgan	4.4	249	3	D	D	D	48	397	90.3	8.2	10	29	3.4	0.6
Nicholas	4.8	185	17	149	59.3	6.3	109	1 505	432.5	34.7	18	46	9.0	1.5
Ohio	10.5	236	72	D	D	D	201	3 486	896.0	79.7	56	D	D	D
Pendleton	9.7	1 257	3	D	D	D	24	204	37.2	3.5	2	D	D	D
Pleasants	67.7	8 899	NA	NA	NA	NA	16	168	45.7	3.7	2	D	D	D
Pocahontas	5.7	649	1	D	D	D	33	327	75.7	6.0	11	47	6.2	1.0
Preston	7.9	236	15	85	33.3	2.9	94	854	234.5	16.9	20	D	D	D
Putnam	47.7	859	74	D	D	D	174	2 359	748.5	55.8	57	316	112.1	18.1
Raleigh	12.3	156	96	D	D	D	346	5 057	1 452.4	124.3	74	287	50.0	9.8
Randolph	13.6	461	24	238	368.9	8.9	142	1 477	352.7	32.6	21	100	14.7	3.3
Ritchie	1.6	154	5	D	D	D	34	288	73.2	5.6	4	8	0.5	0.1
Roane	2.3	151	9	78	50.8	2.2	41	513	132.6	11.3	10	22	1.8	0.4
Summers	5.7	406	6	D	D	D	29	259	68.4	5.6	3	6	0.5	0.1
Taylor	2.3	134	7	D	D	D	33	448	110.9	10.3	2	D	D	D
Tucker	1.5	210	1	D	D	D	28	223	50.1	4.8	10	52	3.8	1.1
Tyler	13.5	1 468	NA	NA	NA	NA	21	139	44.1	2.7	1	D	D	D
Upshur	5.0	205	12	154	171.6	6.6	82	874	264.2	20.4	19	65	8.8	1.7
Wayne	13.0	305	15	252	140.5	11.4	107	1 048	254.9	20.8	19	D	D	D
Webster	3.5	387	3	D	D	D	21	153	42.9	3.2	3	D	D	D
Wetzel	4.0	242	12	93	27.6	2.4	77	879	208.7	18.7	13	34	4.4	1.0
Wirt	0.5	93	1	D	D	D	13	77	19.8	1.2	1	D	D	D
Wood	63.3	728	76	699	332.7	27.9	390	6 018	1 396.6	129.2	84	332	68.8	10.4
Wyoming	2.9	124	5	D	D	D	72	677	154.3	12.6	9	28	3.1	0.7
WISCONSIN	6 157.6	1 083	5 990	97 040	77 066.9	5 253.6	19 272	296 956	78 201.8	6 835.0	4 509	23 762	4 358.9	801.1
Adams	50.9	2 436	6	32	10.3	0.8	44	454	192.3	11.7	13	41	4.8	1.1
Ashland	35.1	2 169	11	90	33.7	3.2	87	897	214.2	20.0	9	38	2.7	0.5
Barron	11.6	253	41	319	166.0	11.3	220	3 033	713.3	67.7	33	80	12.8	2.0
Bayfield	10.7	713	8	D	D	D	69	391	84.5	6.6	9	18	2.1	0.3
Brown	312.8	1 261	329	6 081	4 360.8	321.1	864	14 521	3 686.2	322.1	203	1 407	203.8	43.4
Buffalo	344.1	25 322	9	117	62.3	5.9	46	281	77.8	5.6	10	24	2.5	0.3
Burnett	2.7	177	4	D	D	D	63	588	121.0	10.8	15	18	4.3	0.5
Calumet	5.9	119	44	498	222.9	22.9	109	1 796	418.6	37.0	13	50	3.1	0.8
Chippewa	19.3	310	62	671	408.4	24.9	213	3 500	1 064.9	82.6	34	95	13.8	2.5
Clark	6.1	174	41	331	256.0	16.9	99	820	260.6	18.1	7	15	1.7	0.3
Columbia	29.0	510	46	494	342.4	23.0	197	3 292	795.2	76.2	41	D	D	D
Crawford	3.4	204	11	D	D	D	78	1 034	216.6	22.0	8	21	2.1	0.3
Dane	72.2	148	597	11 599	8 106.6	613.2	1 687	29 330	8 516.2	743.4	620	4 076	952.3	158.3
Dodge	12.3	138	71	978	474.7	40.7	234	3 189	833.0	69.8	40	100	18.3	2.9
Door	5.1	183	25	144	62.9	6.0	259	1 682	414.1	40.8	46	188	20.7	4.4

1. Merchant wholesalers, except manufacturers' sales branches and offices.   2. Employer establishments.

Table B. States and Counties — **Professional Services, Manufacturing, and Accommodation and Food Services**

STATE County	Professional, scientific, and technical services, 2012				Manufacturing, 2012				Accommodation and food services, 2012			
	Number of establish-ments	Number of employees	Receipts (mil dol)	Annual payroll (mil dol)	Number of establish-ments	Number of employees	Receipts (mil dol)	Annual payroll (mil dol)	Number of establish-ments	Number of employees	Sales (mil dol)	Annual payroll (mil dol)
	147	148	149	150	151	152	153	154	155	156	157	158
WEST VIRGINIA—Cont'd												
Calhoun	5	21	1.8	0.6	6	33	D	0.7	4	22	1.1	0.4
Clay	2	D	D	D	4	43	D	2.4	5	D	D	D
Doddridge	1	D	D	D	NA	NA	NA	NA	3	D	D	D
Fayette	50	222	25.1	9.9	31	583	275.0	31.0	73	989	58.6	16.9
Gilmer	8	55	5.4	2.0	5	214	D	6.4	11	D	D	D
Grant	12	58	4.2	1.6	7	221	68.9	8.8	21	D	D	D
Greenbrier	75	295	24.0	7.7	35	774	D	30.8	88	2 455	190.7	67.3
Hampshire	24	D	D	D	12	153	66.0	7.7	35	310	18.7	5.2
Hancock	47	487	36.2	13.1	20	2 689	D	136.6	79	D	D	D
Hardy	15	48	4.4	1.3	11	2 575	D	71.4	28	309	13.9	3.9
Harrison	139	1 674	270.5	99.6	52	1 752	D	D	155	3 196	155.3	41.2
Jackson	43	236	29.9	11.9	15	1 188	D	78.3	52	852	39.1	10.4
Jefferson	84	360	48.6	18.6	17	816	206.7	35.2	127	D	D	D
Kanawha	565	5 965	884.4	340.3	121	2 985	2 196.6	185.5	458	9 306	552.9	145.9
Lewis	15	56	5.5	1.6	15	124	D	4.6	37	596	34.3	11.0
Lincoln	9	71	8.0	2.6	4	11	2.2	0.5	15	D	D	D
Logan	39	246	17.7	7.5	36	734	157.8	31.1	62	979	48.3	12.7
McDowell	13	D	D	D	4	26	D	0.8	22	D	D	D
Marion	119	1 060	130.7	59.5	50	1 154	469.5	50.6	113	2 043	93.7	23.7
Marshall	33	173	15.7	5.5	19	473	D	24.3	60	792	32.4	8.5
Mason	25	87	9.1	3.0	19	696	D	41.2	33	344	14.2	4.2
Mercer	92	639	71.4	20.2	57	1 246	241.5	50.6	106	2 177	100.9	27.6
Mineral	27	195	11.2	4.5	16	1 821	D	117.3	50	D	D	D
Mingo	47	D	D	D	13	173	D	4.2	31	322	11.2	3.4
Monongalia	205	2 723	394.9	120.9	53	3 668	2 034.3	256.4	281	5 885	253.5	70.4
Monroe	9	30	2.2	0.6	5	411	D	19.0	11	D	D	D
Morgan	13	79	13.2	6.3	6	140	D	D	27	D	D	D
Nicholas	45	246	14.7	7.7	25	709	212.9	30.6	59	844	36.9	10.3
Ohio	154	1 777	215.8	80.0	42	1 520	337.5	55.6	135	2 984	226.7	45.3
Pendleton	5	D	D	D	5	127	D	5.3	11	D	D	D
Pleasants	4	D	D	D	8	565	305.6	32.5	12	D	D	D
Pocahontas	6	D	D	D	6	261	38.1	7.9	24	1 360	51.4	16.8
Preston	29	111	10.4	3.8	25	465	147.1	17.4	36	280	13.6	3.4
Putnam	105	1 037	117.0	42.1	41	1 989	1 948.4	115.1	91	1 535	74.3	19.6
Raleigh	123	864	107.0	41.2	60	1 058	278.6	48.3	149	3 189	177.8	48.3
Randolph	49	226	17.8	6.8	24	1 069	189.4	37.2	54	776	38.4	10.6
Ritchie	14	51	3.8	1.6	13	741	D	31.8	17	D	D	D
Roane	16	46	4.2	1.4	16	226	45.2	8.1	13	D	D	D
Summers	11	70	6.8	2.5	7	19	3.1	0.7	19	247	9.6	2.5
Taylor	10	D	D	D	8	D	D	D	26	D	D	D
Tucker	7	D	D	D	15	224	D	9.9	32	D	D	D
Tyler	8	19	1.4	0.3	4	514	D	46.2	6	D	D	D
Upshur	37	228	15.8	6.4	18	665	285.3	32.5	48	644	30.0	8.5
Wayne	22	158	17.4	5.7	26	523	446.1	26.7	52	D	D	D
Webster	5	D	D	D	7	114	D	3.1	11	D	D	D
Wetzel	19	117	8.9	3.3	10	850	D	70.5	42	606	28.2	6.6
Wirt	4	D	D	D	4	D	D	2.2	8	D	D	D
Wood	161	986	105.9	42.2	59	D	2 261.9	205.7	210	4 070	181.8	53.1
Wyoming	19	55	4.5	1.4	9	51	D	2.5	21	D	D	D
WISCONSIN	11 301	99 162	15 135.0	5 738.3	8 995	436 777	177 728.9	21 879.3	14 137	221 567	10 303.3	2 764.3
Adams	15	57	4.6	1.6	12	377	D	18.3	60	1 117	55.1	17.9
Ashland	29	161	15.2	7.2	23	1 107	219.8	51.9	62	588	28.9	7.9
Barron	66	317	28.2	12.4	92	4 865	1 520.7	199.1	137	1 474	59.1	15.8
Bayfield	9	28	2.0	0.6	21	170	D	5.5	90	515	31.8	9.0
Brown	526	4 885	709.5	255.6	442	24 628	11 068.4	1 230.8	593	11 889	479.2	141.4
Buffalo	18	63	4.8	1.3	20	386	303.2	17.7	41	286	10.5	2.6
Burnett	22	62	7.1	2.3	25	790	286.6	34.5	65	456	20.9	5.8
Calumet	64	206	18.6	7.8	71	3 827	1 616.8	174.4	95	1 502	47.0	12.7
Chippewa	86	383	48.5	17.9	125	5 030	1 930.5	237.5	165	1 801	70.0	17.0
Clark	33	165	13.4	5.1	77	3 513	2 021.0	136.7	57	508	17.8	4.9
Columbia	80	465	41.3	15.9	94	4 732	2 530.5	220.7	167	3 440	158.0	45.2
Crawford	21	227	10.0	4.7	24	1 534	1 054.2	66.7	55	638	27.6	7.0
Dane	1 741	19 907	3 387.5	1 313.8	521	23 154	7 205.3	1 210.9	1 265	24 284	1 111.2	316.1
Dodge	78	467	52.4	19.0	148	10 011	3 727.6	462.8	155	1 801	69.5	18.2
Door	74	237	28.7	9.4	56	1 968	416.7	88.3	238	1 999	147.6	36.9

1. Establishment subject to federal tax.

STATE County	Health care and social assistance, 2012				Other services, 2012				Nonemployer businesses, 2015		Value of residential construction authorized by building permits, 2016	
	Number of establishments	Number of employees	Receipts (mil dol)	Annual payroll (mil dol)	Number of establishments	Number of employees	Receipts (mil dol)	Annual payroll (mil dol)	Number	Receipts (mil dol)	New Construction ($1,000)	Number of housing units
	159	160	161	162	163	164	165	166	167	168	169	170
WEST VIRGINIA—Cont'd												
Calhoun	9	294	17.0	10.0	5	D	D	D	465	9.9	NA	NA
Clay	12	283	10.6	5.2	5	D	D	D	366	11.5	302	8
Doddridge	11	176	4.2	2.4	2	D	D	D	237	7.4	0	0
Fayette	105	2 040	162.6	65.2	56	372	37.0	9.1	1 749	55.4	3 319	30
Gilmer	13	255	14.2	7.1	9	32	2.6	0.6	354	8.6	1 983	18
Grant	28	738	45.9	19.5	19	D	D	D	689	25.2	5 102	64
Greenbrier	145	3 028	238.4	101.2	55	291	26.7	7.9	2 245	82.7	18 288	115
Hampshire	34	752	52.1	21.9	26	107	9.1	2.3	1 422	57.2	7 908	61
Hancock	75	1 251	73.4	31.6	46	198	13.8	3.4	1 221	43.0	4 112	14
Hardy	30	451	28.4	12.1	19	54	5.6	0.9	875	26.9	8 577	90
Harrison	237	6 341	666.5	275.1	134	D	D	D	3 765	154.7	28 301	240
Jackson	62	1 111	71.6	30.1	27	D	D	D	1 467	59.6	3 917	34
Jefferson	77	1 217	103.1	41.8	72	541	76.6	15.1	3 572	137.1	42 962	159
Kanawha	746	18 799	2 083.3	768.4	388	D	D	D	9 094	391.6	18 422	164
Lewis	35	1 261	112.6	42.7	30	103	8.6	2.2	830	35.2	199	1
Lincoln	18	D	D	D	15	66	4.4	1.3	760	21.6	1 806	14
Logan	96	1 880	186.3	68.7	60	486	87.4	15.9	1 136	44.1	0	0
McDowell	34	867	58.5	21.8	19	D	D	D	491	13.1	623	6
Marion	163	2 878	259.9	99.2	107	761	59.1	20.2	2 605	88.4	9 278	81
Marshall	79	D	D	D	42	208	16.0	4.2	1 131	36.2	214	1
Mason	38	1 034	93.9	37.5	28	111	9.7	2.5	907	27.8	977	8
Mercer	244	4 629	432.9	161.6	94	831	81.3	25.1	3 001	122.7	1 026	8
Mineral	64	1 382	70.4	28.4	41	180	14.1	3.8	1 379	44.8	6 550	44
Mingo	48	686	71.0	23.7	21	211	19.8	6.8	914	29.3	0	0
Monongalia	233	13 029	1 513.8	539.2	143	1 104	170.3	29.1	5 447	260.9	2 721	17
Monroe	19	338	18.5	7.2	8	29	1.9	0.5	743	26.8	0	0
Morgan	20	558	44.9	16.3	22	66	4.4	1.1	1 168	44.2	6 914	53
Nicholas	58	1 626	100.1	47.2	35	168	19.3	5.1	1 187	44.7	0	0
Ohio	234	D	D	D	125	1 074	117.3	28.9	2 463	114.4	4 696	23
Pendleton	17	325	18.4	7.9	11	49	5.6	1.3	492	14.3	2 281	17
Pleasants	15	497	21.0	8.8	7	D	D	D	304	8.6	1 371	5
Pocahontas	20	415	24.2	9.9	17	104	7.1	1.8	534	22.1	240	4
Preston	62	1 149	68.3	30.3	34	212	20.4	5.2	1 611	65.2	331	4
Putnam	120	D	D	D	64	418	51.5	12.8	2 938	120.8	18 615	95
Raleigh	284	7 414	735.3	289.5	112	796	87.8	23.4	3 432	129.8	7 347	42
Randolph	107	2 872	183.3	82.9	44	217	19.9	5.5	1 476	48.5	402	3
Ritchie	18	208	11.7	5.3	11	D	D	D	656	23.8	1 214	9
Roane	22	665	48.6	20.5	8	D	D	D	857	28.0	0	0
Summers	20	426	33.6	12.7	14	D	D	D	479	13.8	2 128	19
Taylor	27	552	47.1	17.7	23	D	D	D	710	20.3	0	0
Tucker	10	284	12.8	6.4	11	101	9.8	2.5	401	14.0	100	1
Tyler	12	544	26.7	13.1	16	53	2.7	0.8	373	8.7	1 344	8
Upshur	77	1 626	100.5	53.6	30	124	11.7	2.5	1 254	50.3	5 353	37
Wayne	72	2 462	312.9	122.2	32	150	14.5	4.2	1 555	51.0	1 851	21
Webster	13	462	25.8	12.5	2	D	D	D	322	10.1	0	0
Wetzel	41	717	52.7	19.7	32	152	9.5	2.6	561	16.6	1 055	18
Wirt	5	73	4.1	1.5	2	D	D	D	278	8.6	1 064	7
Wood	282	7 096	635.4	247.0	150	859	83.5	20.6	4 134	168.7	19 748	125
Wyoming	27	778	36.1	17.6	13	D	D	D	749	21.3	277	2
WISCONSIN	14 659	386 141	40 680.6	16 257.6	10 210	62 054	6 406.7	1 732.2	341 935	15 999.3	3 732 635	19 274
Adams	30	454	31.0	12.0	25	121	10.9	3.4	1 101	47.1	12 813	61
Ashland	62	1 629	143.1	62.5	36	121	9.1	2.7	1 079	40.4	2 630	13
Barron	127	2 646	282.3	112.2	96	316	27.8	7.1	3 148	141.8	20 837	99
Bayfield	21	248	12.4	6.7	24	41	5.2	1.4	1 570	61.1	13 336	78
Brown	593	19 588	2 446.2	907.0	433	2 833	241.9	67.9	13 616	694.3	178 219	822
Buffalo	23	293	14.0	6.3	19	D	D	D	1 030	49.7	6 246	41
Burnett	30	587	34.7	16.6	22	63	6.4	1.4	1 154	42.7	17 621	79
Calumet	79	1 175	95.3	37.3	58	261	18.5	5.1	2 484	99.3	41 638	238
Chippewa	175	3 185	260.2	110.4	101	545	58.6	15.3	3 992	203.5	45 922	238
Clark	61	904	54.5	26.0	62	D	D	D	2 189	127.0	6 626	36
Columbia	132	2 563	206.1	91.7	91	398	37.1	9.9	3 679	164.7	61 996	325
Crawford	48	1 129	74.6	35.1	34	107	9.5	2.4	1 104	49.0	4 095	27
Dane	1 217	43 351	5 188.2	2 019.6	1 094	8 233	1 237.6	280.6	37 088	1 833.0	814 455	4 512
Dodge	205	4 611	437.1	170.0	133	452	39.3	10.9	4 474	199.1	26 866	113
Door	78	1 630	131.8	61.6	98	472	53.9	11.6	2 866	121.0	32 463	169

Table B. States and Counties — Government Employment and Payroll, and Local Government Finances

STATE County	Government employment and payroll, 2012									Local government finances, 2012				
			March payroll (percent of total)							General revenue				
												Taxes		
													Per capita[1] (dollars)	
	Full-time equivalent employees	March payroll (dollars)	Administration, judicial, and legal	Police and Corrections	Fire Protection	Highways and transportation	Health and Welfare	Natural resources and utilities	Education and libraries	Total (mil dol)	Inter-governmental (mil dol)	Total (mil dol)	Total	Property
	171	172	173	174	175	176	177	178	179	180	181	182	183	184

WEST VIRGINIA— Cont'd														
Calhoun	235	856 049	5.0	1.6	0.0	0.1	2.0	2.3	88.7	15.2	10.3	3.4	451	395
Clay	380	1 124 468	6.3	1.8	0.0	0.0	5.2	2.2	84.1	27.4	19.9	4.1	442	430
Doddridge	298	898 174	6.8	2.9	0.0	0.0	5.3	2.4	82.0	22.4	10.1	9.7	1 188	1 164
Fayette	1 528	4 553 455	4.1	5.0	0.3	1.5	1.0	5.1	80.2	107.2	57.1	37.1	808	664
Gilmer	243	631 014	10.3	2.7	0.0	0.5	1.7	3.3	80.9	15.5	7.0	5.8	665	612
Grant	680	2 034 759	3.4	1.7	0.0	3.5	45.2	3.2	40.6	59.3	13.0	10.1	852	816
Greenbrier	1 170	3 506 733	7.6	5.7	0.3	0.6	1.5	5.0	78.7	105.9	52.9	33.6	939	809
Hampshire	737	2 045 370	7.4	3.3	0.0	0.4	2.4	3.6	80.9	45.1	25.8	14.3	602	574
Hancock	1 042	3 202 337	5.3	8.5	2.6	2.7	1.3	6.7	66.6	87.7	34.1	29.9	986	818
Hardy	415	1 314 488	8.0	4.5	0.0	1.3	3.9	3.7	78.2	29.6	15.9	10.0	724	691
Harrison	2 683	9 099 926	6.8	6.1	3.8	3.1	1.3	6.8	71.1	209.4	84.1	90.4	1 308	979
Jackson	990	3 308 041	4.4	4.8	0.0	0.8	4.8	4.0	80.4	73.7	39.2	26.2	895	804
Jefferson	1 638	5 678 847	10.1	5.7	0.0	0.8	0.7	3.3	76.3	146.5	52.8	59.7	1 096	978
Kanawha	6 718	23 530 157	5.6	7.2	4.5	3.9	6.5	3.5	65.5	605.2	237.9	258.2	1 344	860
Lewis	544	1 762 505	8.2	4.5	0.7	0.9	5.8	2.3	77.1	39.7	21.5	16.2	990	848
Lincoln	667	2 364 650	4.5	2.3	0.0	1.6	1.0	3.2	85.7	53.6	38.2	11.4	526	507
Logan	1 162	3 939 889	5.9	3.5	0.7	0.2	1.5	5.1	81.4	91.3	48.4	36.2	1 001	949
McDowell	898	2 888 117	9.6	3.1	0.0	0.2	2.7	2.7	81.5	73.1	34.6	20.5	959	873
Marion	1 717	5 814 952	5.2	6.4	2.4	3.4	0.7	6.1	74.1	167.3	77.9	56.2	991	827
Marshall	1 141	3 323 871	5.8	8.5	0.5	1.2	2.2	5.2	75.5	112.7	45.9	46.4	1 420	1 271
Mason	808	2 759 625	5.8	3.8	1.1	0.5	1.8	4.4	81.7	67.3	31.9	24.3	894	820
Mercer	2 791	9 567 647	3.0	2.7	1.1	1.6	34.9	3.3	53.2	241.4	83.0	39.7	634	442
Mineral	785	2 765 305	6.5	4.1	0.0	1.4	1.0	5.1	80.1	68.4	36.1	19.1	682	591
Mingo	985	3 045 535	7.8	3.4	0.6	0.0	0.8	5.9	81.3	90.1	46.0	25.0	959	895
Monongalia	2 739	8 098 611	6.5	7.5	2.5	4.8	3.8	8.2	63.2	216.0	81.0	90.9	906	711
Monroe	414	1 100 622	5.2	1.8	0.0	0.0	1.4	2.7	86.0	27.7	19.5	5.8	431	417
Morgan	518	1 614 401	8.1	3.1	0.0	0.2	3.5	2.2	81.4	35.9	14.8	15.4	884	845
Nicholas	1 289	3 992 571	5.3	3.7	0.0	1.2	46.4	3.6	39.7	111.9	37.5	19.6	748	569
Ohio	2 026	6 205 898	4.8	7.0	5.8	5.4	1.5	21.6	51.3	195.9	55.2	71.7	1 626	865
Pendleton	226	700 064	8.4	1.3	0.0	0.8	2.2	3.9	80.7	15.5	10.2	4.1	537	478
Pleasants	324	1 102 661	10.6	2.5	0.0	0.4	3.5	3.5	79.3	32.6	11.4	12.9	1 701	1 664
Pocahontas	405	1 184 054	6.2	3.0	0.0	0.0	30.8	3.2	53.8	31.5	10.0	9.0	1 038	857
Preston	940	2 685 410	7.1	3.2	0.9	1.2	1.0	4.1	82.2	66.4	36.1	18.3	541	504
Putnam	1 860	6 184 199	4.2	3.8	0.1	0.5	2.8	5.9	81.7	150.7	66.0	58.4	1 035	970
Raleigh	2 440	7 917 866	5.4	5.4	1.7	1.5	2.8	5.6	75.8	223.2	112.9	76.2	964	750
Randolph	999	2 905 572	3.8	2.3	0.5	0.9	3.4	6.7	80.2	72.1	40.5	17.4	593	462
Ritchie	297	909 321	8.7	3.8	0.0	1.0	0.1	2.4	84.1	24.5	12.7	8.6	838	761
Roane	376	1 154 052	6.1	3.9	0.0	1.0	2.1	6.9	79.1	31.0	21.0	6.6	447	384
Summers	287	926 192	9.8	3.8	1.5	1.2	2.4	1.1	80.2	23.4	14.8	6.1	443	343
Taylor	364	895 244	5.7	4.2	1.5	2.1	4.6	11.1	66.9	51.2	18.8	11.0	648	459
Tucker	275	825 484	9.3	1.5	0.0	1.3	7.1	3.8	69.5	25.7	10.2	7.0	1 003	837
Tyler	484	1 507 476	5.2	4.0	0.0	1.0	29.5	1.8	58.1	30.4	11.4	7.0	778	752
Upshur	769	2 460 649	3.9	3.4	0.6	1.2	4.6	5.0	78.3	57.1	29.8	16.0	654	566
Wayne	1 363	3 245 672	6.1	5.2	0.0	0.5	1.6	4.5	81.4	101.8	63.8	27.0	648	573
Webster	358	989 930	7.5	2.5	2.2	1.0	1.1	6.1	78.1	23.4	16.4	3.8	420	365
Wetzel	861	2 789 337	4.5	3.5	0.0	0.7	30.1	6.0	54.4	69.9	21.7	17.0	1 038	859
Wirt	221	579 537	5.0	1.0	0.0	0.0	0.0	1.9	92.1	12.0	8.3	2.5	428	408
Wood	2 923	9 783 040	4.6	5.6	2.1	2.8	2.7	6.6	73.9	223.4	105.4	75.1	866	645
Wyoming	818	2 431 168	7.1	3.1	0.0	0.1	2.6	2.9	82.3	59.6	32.3	21.1	906	862
WISCONSIN	X	X	X	X	X	X	X	X	X	X	X	X	X	X
Adams	752	2 398 694	11.0	12.5	0.7	11.1	19.9	3.2	40.0	75.0	26.6	36.5	1 766	1 664
Ashland	751	2 545 721	7.6	8.1	4.1	10.6	10.7	7.0	49.8	79.8	47.9	22.4	1 398	1 298
Barron	1 838	6 618 589	8.0	8.4	1.3	6.3	10.3	4.0	60.6	190.4	84.2	79.1	1 729	1 625
Bayfield	707	2 315 340	13.5	8.9	0.8	14.7	14.5	4.4	42.0	70.7	26.8	33.0	2 186	2 071
Brown	9 417	41 301 919	3.9	9.3	3.3	3.0	7.6	3.8	67.8	1 182.5	506.0	459.7	1 817	1 685
Buffalo	479	1 597 741	7.7	7.1	0.2	11.0	7.2	3.7	62.0	50.4	28.0	18.4	1 378	1 318
Burnett	687	2 258 798	11.7	9.6	0.3	13.5	8.5	4.2	51.0	63.0	23.4	33.2	2 157	2 077
Calumet	1 110	4 057 590	8.1	8.8	0.2	5.3	10.0	4.7	61.8	111.1	46.0	47.5	956	941
Chippewa	1 941	7 086 033	6.6	8.6	2.6	10.3	6.3	4.1	60.8	196.6	102.1	74.2	1 179	1 086
Clark	1 398	4 771 022	6.3	8.0	0.1	9.4	23.0	4.1	48.3	140.3	73.6	38.4	1 115	1 055
Columbia	2 325	8 247 107	8.1	9.2	0.4	3.5	8.2	3.5	65.9	255.2	98.3	121.8	2 154	2 025
Crawford	593	1 975 908	11.0	8.6	0.2	10.4	5.2	3.1	60.2	77.0	46.6	24.3	1 469	1 348
Dane	19 136	83 118 268	5.7	10.6	3.0	6.3	5.9	6.9	59.9	2 389.4	787.6	1 194.7	2 373	2 225
Dodge	2 529	9 541 340	7.2	13.4	1.1	6.9	16.7	4.2	48.9	269.1	119.0	102.8	1 162	1 082
Door	1 091	4 311 224	10.3	10.3	2.4	7.1	11.5	5.3	51.6	140.6	38.4	81.9	2 946	2 757

1. Based on the resident population estimated as of July 1 of the year shown.

Table B. States and Counties — Local Government Finances, Government Employment, and Income Taxes

STATE County	Local government finances, 2012 (cont.) Direct general expenditure Total (mil dol)	Per capita[1] (dollars)	Education	Health and hospitals	Police protection	Public welfare	Highways	Debt outstanding Total (mil dol)	Per capita[1] (dollars)	Government employment, 2015 Federal civilian	Federal military	State and local	Individual income tax returns, 2014 Number of returns	Mean adjusted gross income	Mean income tax
				Percent of total for:											
	185	186	187	188	189	190	191	192	193	194	195	196	197	198	199
WEST VIRGINIA—Cont'd															
Calhoun	16.5	2 170	67.3	0.0	4.6	0.1	0.1	13.0	1 714	12	35	279	2 600	44 813	4 462
Clay	29.0	3 117	78.1	4.6	7.4	0.0	0.0	1.2	128	12	42	478	3 250	39 126	3 027
Doddridge	22.0	2 695	75.1	2.0	2.2	0.0	0.2	8.1	994	10	35	524	2 890	58 538	6 184
Fayette	113.9	2 482	68.7	0.5	5.7	0.0	1.6	47.9	1 045	249	210	2 909	17 400	40 501	3 572
Gilmer	17.4	1 988	61.7	1.3	6.6	0.0	0.4	4.5	516	334	30	649	2 590	46 451	4 702
Grant	59.2	5 007	30.0	52.8	2.8	0.0	0.1	13.9	1 177	47	55	890	5 100	40 692	3 342
Greenbrier	128.0	3 574	63.2	0.6	4.9	0.1	1.0	116.1	3 241	91	164	2 229	15 230	44 068	4 294
Hampshire	52.8	2 229	71.4	1.4	6.3	0.0	0.5	31.5	1 328	40	108	1 313	9 570	41 711	3 595
Hancock	95.4	3 148	57.0	1.9	5.9	0.4	3.5	88.0	2 903	60	139	1 312	14 700	46 058	4 623
Hardy	30.9	2 227	67.5	1.2	3.9	0.1	1.5	61.4	4 426	46	65	767	6 380	36 903	3 023
Harrison	213.8	3 092	57.6	0.7	4.7	0.0	3.1	154.5	2 234	3 920	321	3 839	31 780	55 412	6 747
Jackson	77.4	2 647	65.9	3.3	6.4	0.0	0.9	34.3	1 172	74	137	1 256	12 270	48 242	5 051
Jefferson	165.6	3 037	64.7	0.4	7.7	0.0	1.5	64.5	1 183	1 194	260	2 907	25 420	62 453	7 134
Kanawha	630.4	3 280	49.5	0.7	6.4	0.0	3.1	316.3	1 646	2 095	915	20 007	88 150	54 613	6 951
Lewis	44.9	2 740	61.9	2.9	2.7	0.3	0.8	5.9	361	56	76	1 374	7 880	47 662	4 949
Lincoln	56.1	2 593	81.6	0.7	1.6	0.1	0.0	11.6	535	38	101	841	7 550	42 284	3 529
Logan	90.2	2 493	72.3	0.9	1.5	0.0	1.1	10.2	281	91	161	2 056	12 290	45 183	4 243
McDowell	77.6	3 641	65.1	0.4	3.6	0.0	1.0	12.9	606	374	92	1 623	5 990	36 605	2 791
Marion	168.8	2 978	58.1	1.2	4.9	0.0	1.1	273.1	4 819	182	262	4 181	26 040	48 891	4 906
Marshall	98.2	3 004	56.7	2.0	5.2	0.2	2.1	187.9	5 751	48	149	1 803	14 750	52 109	5 818
Mason	71.4	2 625	63.5	7.2	3.0	0.1	1.4	29.8	1 097	107	124	1 358	10 150	44 022	3 998
Mercer	244.7	3 914	40.5	39.9	4.2	0.0	1.0	92.7	1 483	167	283	4 810	24 630	42 072	3 985
Mineral	67.8	2 426	67.5	0.9	6.0	0.1	1.0	39.5	1 413	94	126	1 486	12 320	45 531	4 240
Mingo	98.5	3 774	63.6	0.6	2.1	0.1	1.1	29.5	1 128	67	119	1 232	8 340	42 424	3 643
Monongalia	226.2	2 254	54.5	2.7	5.6	0.4	2.1	196.0	1 954	1 204	477	14 711	42 020	63 631	8 924
Monroe	25.2	1 875	79.9	0.7	5.6	0.1	0.8	11.1	828	211	63	467	5 460	40 666	3 290
Morgan	37.8	2 162	73.4	1.3	6.3	0.0	0.5	22.3	1 279	26	82	679	7 750	43 334	3 823
Nicholas	110.3	4 207	42.1	40.3	4.8	0.0	1.0	40.6	1 546	88	120	1 679	10 200	45 425	4 434
Ohio	204.2	4 634	34.0	0.9	7.3	0.2	3.3	309.3	7 017	393	192	3 654	20 980	61 136	8 870
Pendleton	16.3	2 160	74.5	2.0	1.0	0.0	0.2	4.2	549	65	71	318	3 260	38 624	3 164
Pleasants	31.1	4 098	51.5	1.1	2.8	1.2	0.9	168.6	22 201	11	33	656	3 180	54 658	6 243
Pocahontas	32.3	3 712	42.6	29.0	6.8	0.3	0.3	7.5	861	58	39	778	3 790	37 524	3 060
Preston	67.7	2 001	71.9	0.8	3.4	0.0	0.8	71.7	2 120	897	149	1 604	11 770	46 169	4 393
Putnam	187.6	3 324	75.3	0.9	5.2	0.0	0.4	178.8	3 168	209	268	2 082	25 680	60 962	7 180
Raleigh	227.9	2 884	60.0	0.6	7.4	0.1	1.6	109.6	1 387	1 761	363	3 884	31 220	50 110	5 485
Randolph	78.4	2 667	59.6	0.4	4.2	0.1	1.6	33.1	1 126	160	126	1 892	12 310	43 539	3 923
Ritchie	26.4	2 577	64.5	8.2	3.8	0.1	1.0	5.0	492	25	47	510	4 280	51 859	6 540
Roane	32.6	2 218	76.9	1.3	2.2	0.0	1.1	10.7	731	27	68	581	5 420	42 989	3 961
Summers	26.4	1 922	59.2	1.1	4.3	0.0	1.2	7.1	514	36	57	757	4 380	38 638	3 169
Taylor	50.1	2 947	47.3	30.5	3.2	0.0	2.7	25.2	1 485	46	77	1 069	7 290	48 715	4 898
Tucker	25.6	3 656	47.4	5.2	1.8	0.0	0.6	6.1	873	48	32	565	3 230	40 306	3 366
Tyler	31.5	3 490	53.3	28.3	3.8	0.0	0.6	14.5	1 606	15	42	560	3 880	57 376	7 677
Upshur	57.5	2 351	66.4	0.5	2.2	0.1	1.6	23.7	969	112	111	1 176	10 150	46 800	4 713
Wayne	99.1	2 380	75.7	1.2	4.2	0.1	0.6	56.7	1 362	1 441	192	1 786	15 380	43 823	3 878
Webster	23.6	2 613	67.1	0.1	6.5	0.0	0.6	2.3	257	14	41	566	3 060	38 446	3 261
Wetzel	76.4	4 650	43.1	35.0	3.3	0.0	1.3	24.0	1 459	36	74	1 144	7 000	50 823	5 548
Wirt	12.5	2 133	82.9	0.0	0.1	0.0	0.6	1.6	280	12	28	249	2 290	41 365	3 537
Wood	223.9	2 582	63.1	0.1	5.4	0.0	4.0	189.9	2 190	2 293	405	4 339	39 300	51 350	5 756
Wyoming	60.0	2 578	76.4	0.9	3.5	0.1	0.4	21.2	910	101	104	1 009	7 280	43 041	3 724
WISCONSIN	X	X	X	X	X	X	X	X	X	28 898	15 938	389 220	2 811 160	59 614	7 358
Adams	74.9	3 623	28.9	10.0	7.1	4.2	20.2	54.3	2 624	305	51	836	8 930	42 032	3 782
Ashland	80.3	5 021	41.4	3.1	6.4	7.4	11.1	35.5	2 221	161	41	1 917	7 410	41 385	3 612
Barron	194.8	4 259	48.2	0.6	5.4	8.5	14.2	109.9	2 402	137	120	3 868	22 710	49 072	5 318
Bayfield	74.2	4 916	33.4	7.0	4.7	0.1	19.4	43.1	2 852	118	56	1 386	7 690	52 800	5 985
Brown	1 202.2	4 751	49.8	5.5	6.3	4.1	6.6	1 130.3	4 467	1 173	705	17 355	127 710	61 894	8 192
Buffalo	53.1	3 982	48.0	1.8	3.5	5.5	22.8	23.0	1 723	159	35	658	6 700	45 430	4 108
Burnett	66.0	4 292	45.3	5.0	4.3	3.4	18.5	34.6	2 248	29	40	1 560	7 680	43 883	4 055
Calumet	110.0	2 217	42.6	3.7	6.9	6.6	12.0	109.5	2 206	96	134	1 329	23 970	64 806	7 312
Chippewa	206.5	3 282	53.4	4.8	4.8	2.5	14.8	127.7	2 030	181	164	3 374	30 320	51 956	5 371
Clark	143.7	4 173	42.9	4.9	4.0	14.6	11.4	69.7	2 024	110	91	1 964	14 830	48 492	5 198
Columbia	257.0	4 546	51.3	1.4	5.7	6.8	11.3	215.7	3 815	167	148	3 533	29 450	55 874	6 281
Crawford	74.8	4 519	39.3	3.0	5.3	4.1	18.5	47.8	2 889	62	42	1 033	7 840	42 802	4 573
Dane	2 429.4	4 825	46.4	1.9	6.1	8.3	5.9	2 890.1	5 740	5 095	1 467	74 498	262 120	72 618	10 061
Dodge	312.6	3 536	31.9	3.5	7.1	19.1	11.6	247.2	2 795	176	221	4 969	42 350	53 123	5 677
Door	143.6	5 161	33.0	8.5	5.0	3.5	16.6	112.6	4 047	70	145	1 782	15 390	56 969	6 437

1. Based on the resident population estimated as of July 1 of the year shown.

Table B. States and Counties — Land Area and Population

STATE/ County code	CBSA code[1]	County type[2]	STATE County	Land area,[3] (sq mi) 2016	Total persons 2016	Rank	Per square mile	Population and population characteristics, 2016 — Race alone or in combination, not Hispanic or Latino (percent) — White	Black	American Indian, Alaska Native	Asian and Pacific Islander	Percent Hispanic or Latino[4]	Age (percent) — Under 5 years	5 to 17 years	18 to 24 years	25 to 34 years	35 to 44 years	45 to 54 years
				1	2	3	4	5	6	7	8	9	10	11	12	13	14	15
			WISCONSIN—Cont'd															
55 031	20260	2	Douglas	1 304.1	43 509	1 101	33.4	94.4	1.9	3.3	1.5	1.6	5.0	14.9	8.8	12.8	11.8	13.7
55 033	32860	6	Dunn	850.2	44 704	1 078	52.6	94.2	1.1	0.8	3.2	1.9	5.2	14.5	18.8	11.2	10.7	11.6
55 035	20740	3	Eau Claire	637.9	102 965	583	161.4	92.0	1.7	0.9	4.7	2.3	5.8	14.7	16.7	13.7	10.9	11.4
55 037	27020	9	Florence	488.1	4 456	2 866	9.1	97.2	0.7	1.5	0.8	1.1	3.4	11.2	5.5	8.3	8.6	15.8
55 039	22540	3	Fond du Lac	719.6	102 144	592	141.9	91.2	2.2	0.8	1.9	5.1	5.5	16.3	8.6	11.7	11.8	14.0
55 041	...	9	Forest	1 014.2	9 064	2 502	8.9	82.2	1.8	15.6	0.9	2.3	5.8	14.3	8.8	9.5	9.6	12.8
55 043	38420	6	Grant	1 146.9	52 214	956	45.5	95.9	1.7	0.4	1.2	1.6	5.4	15.0	18.2	10.7	9.7	11.0
55 045	31540	2	Green	584.0	37 075	1 250	63.5	95.4	1.2	0.5	0.9	3.0	5.4	17.1	7.4	10.7	11.9	14.2
55 047	...	6	Green Lake	349.3	18 719	1 884	53.6	93.4	1.0	0.6	0.9	4.8	5.4	16.7	6.9	9.4	10.0	13.6
55 049	31540	2	Iowa	762.7	23 654	1 653	31.0	96.8	1.1	0.5	1.1	1.6	5.6	17.3	6.8	10.7	11.7	14.3
55 051	...	9	Iron	758.2	5 726	2 776	7.6	97.0	0.8	1.7	0.7	1.4	3.1	12.1	5.4	7.3	9.2	13.6
55 053	...	6	Jackson	987.7	20 562	1 796	20.8	87.8	2.6	7.0	1.0	3.3	6.2	16.0	7.6	12.0	11.3	14.1
55 055	48020	4	Jefferson	556.5	84 625	671	152.1	90.8	1.3	0.7	1.3	7.1	5.2	16.5	9.7	11.6	12.4	14.3
55 057	...	7	Juneau	767.0	26 274	1 550	34.3	92.7	2.6	1.8	0.8	3.2	5.3	14.7	6.8	11.2	11.9	14.8
55 059	16980	1	Kenosha	272.0	168 183	381	618.3	78.2	8.1	0.8	2.2	13.0	5.9	17.7	9.8	12.7	12.6	14.7
55 061	24580	2	Kewaunee	342.4	20 405	1 810	59.6	95.8	0.9	1.0	0.7	2.8	5.0	16.7	7.3	9.9	11.6	14.4
55 063	29100	3	La Crosse	451.8	118 122	525	261.4	91.7	2.2	0.8	5.2	1.8	5.2	14.8	16.3	12.7	10.9	11.8
55 065	...	8	Lafayette	633.6	16 753	1 996	26.4	95.1	0.8	0.5	0.6	3.7	6.6	18.5	7.6	10.9	10.4	13.2
55 067	...	6	Langlade	870.6	19 221	1 862	22.1	95.7	1.3	1.8	0.7	2.0	5.0	14.6	6.9	9.4	9.9	14.0
55 069	32980	6	Lincoln	878.8	27 902	1 494	31.8	96.6	1.3	0.9	0.9	1.5	4.6	14.2	7.1	9.5	11.2	15.4
55 071	31820	4	Manitowoc	589.4	79 536	703	134.9	92.1	1.2	0.9	3.1	3.8	5.3	15.5	7.7	10.4	11.0	14.5
55 073	48140	3	Marathon	1 545.0	135 603	466	87.8	90.2	1.3	0.8	6.3	2.8	5.9	17.1	8.0	11.9	11.9	14.0
55 075	31940	6	Marinette	1 399.4	40 491	1 164	28.9	96.7	0.8	1.2	0.9	1.5	4.6	14.6	6.6	9.8	10.2	13.7
55 077	...	8	Marquette	455.7	15 067	2 093	33.1	94.9	1.1	1.2	1.0	3.2	5.1	14.8	5.6	9.2	9.9	14.3
55 078	43020	8	Menominee	357.6	4 533	2 860	12.7	13.8	1.4	79.5	2.0	5.8	9.7	23.6	9.5	10.8	8.8	11.8
55 079	33340	1	Milwaukee	241.6	951 448	50	3 938.1	53.9	27.7	1.2	4.8	14.8	7.0	17.3	9.9	16.4	12.6	12.1
55 081	...	6	Monroe	900.9	45 623	1 060	50.6	92.3	1.8	1.6	1.3	4.2	6.9	18.4	7.2	11.6	11.8	13.1
55 083	24580	2	Oconto	997.2	37 430	1 238	37.5	96.1	0.6	1.9	0.7	1.7	4.9	15.6	6.6	9.6	11.3	15.4
55 085	...	7	Oneida	1 113.9	35 601	1 287	32.0	96.4	0.8	1.8	0.9	1.5	4.5	12.7	6.5	9.5	9.4	14.1
55 087	11540	3	Outagamie	637.6	184 526	352	289.4	89.5	1.9	2.1	3.9	4.2	6.3	17.5	8.8	13.2	12.7	14.3
55 089	33340	1	Ozaukee	233.1	88 314	655	378.9	92.9	1.9	0.6	3.1	2.8	5.1	16.6	9.1	9.6	11.0	14.6
55 091	...	8	Pepin	232.0	7 307	2 644	31.5	97.3	0.5	0.6	0.4	1.8	5.5	15.6	7.3	9.4	10.3	13.6
55 093	33460	1	Pierce	573.7	41 238	1 147	71.9	96.0	1.2	0.9	1.4	2.0	5.0	15.9	15.9	10.9	11.4	13.5
55 095	...	6	Polk	914.1	43 481	1 102	47.6	96.1	0.8	1.5	0.9	1.9	5.1	16.4	7.2	9.6	11.3	14.7
55 097	44620	4	Portage	800.8	70 447	763	88.0	92.7	1.3	0.7	3.5	3.1	4.9	14.4	16.8	11.8	10.6	12.5
55 099	...	9	Price	1 254.0	13 517	2 194	10.8	95.9	0.9	1.2	1.7	1.6	4.2	13.4	6.2	7.6	10.1	14.3
55 101	39540	3	Racine	332.5	195 140	340	586.9	74.2	12.5	0.8	1.7	12.9	6.2	17.4	8.4	11.9	11.9	14.3
55 103	...	6	Richland	586.2	17 476	1 947	29.8	96.0	1.2	0.7	0.9	2.2	5.1	16.9	7.4	9.6	10.5	12.6
55 105	27500	3	Rock	718.1	161 620	399	225.1	85.0	6.1	0.7	1.7	8.6	6.0	17.6	8.7	12.1	12.2	13.8
55 107	...	6	Rusk	913.6	14 127	2 155	15.5	96.0	1.4	1.2	0.9	1.8	4.8	15.9	7.0	8.2	10.0	13.7
55 109	33460	1	St. Croix	722.5	88 029	657	121.8	95.4	1.3	0.7	1.7	2.3	6.2	19.3	7.4	11.6	13.8	14.8
55 111	12660	4	Sauk	831.5	63 949	828	76.9	92.2	1.4	1.6	1.1	4.9	6.0	16.8	7.7	12.0	11.9	13.7
55 113	...	7	Sawyer	1 257.3	16 369	2 016	13.0	80.0	1.1	19.1	0.6	2.4	5.2	14.6	6.5	8.8	9.2	12.9
55 115	43020	6	Shawano	893.2	41 062	1 152	46.0	88.9	0.7	8.9	0.8	2.6	5.3	16.2	7.1	10.1	10.9	14.6
55 117	43100	3	Sheboygan	511.3	115 427	533	225.8	86.0	2.5	0.8	5.9	6.3	5.5	17.0	8.3	11.5	11.7	14.1
55 119	...	6	Taylor	975.0	20 439	1 806	21.0	96.8	0.7	0.7	0.7	1.9	5.6	18.2	6.8	9.6	11.4	13.7
55 121	...	6	Trempealeau	733.0	29 633	1 439	40.4	90.8	0.7	0.6	0.8	7.9	7.1	17.6	7.5	11.0	11.3	14.0
55 123	...	6	Vernon	791.6	30 814	1 414	38.9	97.2	0.9	0.6	0.8	1.6	7.0	18.9	7.1	9.4	10.3	12.6
55 125	...	9	Vilas	857.7	21 435	1 757	25.0	86.5	0.7	11.2	0.8	2.3	4.3	12.3	5.6	7.6	8.3	13.5
55 127	48580	4	Walworth	555.3	102 959	584	185.4	86.4	1.5	0.6	1.4	11.2	5.1	16.3	12.8	10.4	11.0	13.5
55 129	...	7	Washburn	797.1	15 648	2 061	19.6	95.9	0.7	2.5	0.8	1.7	4.5	14.5	6.0	8.4	9.6	13.5
55 131	33340	1	Washington	430.6	134 296	473	311.9	94.0	1.6	0.5	1.8	3.1	5.3	17.2	7.3	10.7	12.1	15.7
55 133	33340	1	Waukesha	549.7	398 424	174	724.8	90.1	1.9	0.5	4.1	4.7	5.1	16.7	7.9	10.4	12.0	14.8
55 135	...	6	Waupaca	747.7	51 533	966	68.9	95.5	0.7	1.0	0.7	3.0	5.1	15.6	7.3	10.2	11.3	14.4
55 137	...	6	Waushara	626.2	24 162	1 638	38.6	90.5	2.4	1.0	0.8	6.4	5.0	13.7	6.4	10.0	10.2	14.4
55 139	36780	3	Winnebago	434.5	169 886	379	391.0	90.6	2.7	1.0	3.3	4.0	5.5	15.2	12.0	13.2	11.8	13.5
55 141	49220	4	Wood	792.9	73 107	747	92.2	93.7	1.3	1.1	2.2	2.9	5.6	16.0	7.5	11.1	10.8	13.9
56 000	...	0	**WYOMING**	97 091.2	585 501	X	6.0	85.7	1.6	2.9	1.6	10.0	6.5	17.2	9.4	14.0	12.2	11.8
56 001	29660	4	Albany	4 274.3	38 256	1 218	9.0	84.9	2.1	1.3	4.2	9.4	5.1	11.4	28.4	16.5	9.8	8.2
56 003	...	9	Big Horn	3 136.5	12 005	2 295	3.8	89.0	0.8	1.7	0.7	9.0	6.3	19.3	7.4	10.8	10.5	11.7
56 005	23940	5	Campbell	4 802.3	48 803	1 004	10.2	89.1	0.9	1.9	1.2	8.6	7.9	20.3	8.4	16.3	13.6	12.1
56 007	...	7	Carbon	7 897.6	15 618	2 066	2.0	78.2	1.5	1.8	1.2	18.7	6.4	17.5	7.7	15.1	12.1	12.0
56 009	...	6	Converse	4 254.9	14 191	2 152	3.3	89.7	1.0	1.6	1.0	8.1	7.5	18.1	7.2	13.2	11.8	13.0
56 011	...	9	Crook	2 854.5	7 464	2 636	2.6	95.5	1.2	1.6	0.6	2.5	6.9	17.4	6.2	10.5	10.2	12.9
56 013	40180	7	Fremont	9 183.8	40 242	1 170	4.4	72.5	0.7	21.6	0.9	6.9	7.2	18.3	8.0	12.5	11.0	11.3

1. CBSA = Core Based Statistical Area. See Appendix A for explanation. See Appendix B for list of metropolitan areas with component counties. 2. County type code from the Economic Research Service of USDA Rural-Urban Continuum Codes. See Appendix A for definition. 3. Dry land or land partially or temporarily covered by water. 4. May be of any race.

Table B. States and Counties — **Population and Households**

STATE County	55 to 64 years (16)	65 to 74 years (17)	75 years and over (18)	Percent female (19)	2000 (20)	2010 (21)	2000–2010 (22)	2010–2016 (23)	Births (24)	Deaths (25)	Net migration (26)	Number (27)	Persons per house-hold (28)	Family house-holds (29)	Female family house-holder[1] (30)	One person (31)
WISCONSIN—Cont'd																
Douglas	15.4	10.4	7.1	49.8	43 287	44 159	2.0	-1.5	2 717	2 603	-708	18 581	2.28	61.2	11.0	32.2
Dunn	12.3	9.0	6.6	49.6	39 858	43 857	10.0	1.9	2 835	1 951	-140	16 441	2.48	63.3	7.6	26.6
Eau Claire	12.0	8.6	6.2	50.7	93 142	98 885	6.2	4.1	7 429	4 973	1 698	39 893	2.43	58.6	7.5	30.5
Florence	20.3	15.4	11.5	48.2	5 088	4 423	-13.1	0.7	169	318	147	1 904	2.32	67.5	5.7	26.9
Fond du Lac	14.6	9.9	7.7	50.9	97 296	101 630	4.5	0.5	6 851	5 769	-416	41 069	2.40	66.3	8.6	28.3
Forest	16.5	12.7	9.9	49.5	10 024	9 304	-7.2	-2.6	684	711	-184	3 810	2.33	66.3	8.8	28.9
Grant	13.0	8.8	8.0	48.0	49 597	51 208	3.2	2.0	3 407	3 041	644	19 447	2.44	62.0	6.5	27.5
Green	15.5	10.0	7.8	50.4	33 647	36 842	9.5	0.6	2 436	2 146	-131	14 819	2.47	68.1	8.3	26.4
Green Lake	16.2	12.3	9.5	49.9	19 105	19 051	-0.3	-1.7	1 245	1 398	-155	7 939	2.36	65.9	7.9	30.7
Iowa	15.7	10.6	7.3	49.9	22 780	23 687	4.0	-0.1	1 652	1 289	-498	9 689	2.43	66.9	6.6	25.9
Iron	19.2	16.5	13.6	49.5	6 861	5 916	-13.8	-3.2	230	527	93	2 910	1.99	61.7	7.0	33.2
Jackson	14.5	10.8	7.6	46.4	19 100	20 441	7.0	0.6	1 568	1 254	-178	7 960	2.42	66.0	9.7	28.2
Jefferson	14.3	9.4	6.5	50.0	74 021	83 681	13.1	1.1	5 536	3 960	-506	32 413	2.49	67.9	9.1	25.3
Juneau	15.7	11.4	8.1	46.9	24 316	26 664	9.7	-1.5	1 699	1 725	-284	9 984	2.48	63.7	8.8	29.9
Kenosha	13.4	7.6	5.6	50.5	149 577	166 426	11.3	1.1	12 267	8 488	-1 932	62 330	2.62	66.7	13.6	26.4
Kewaunee	15.3	10.9	8.9	49.2	20 187	20 574	1.9	-0.8	1 217	1 130	-235	8 138	2.49	66.5	5.5	28.6
La Crosse	12.7	8.7	7.0	51.2	107 120	114 638	7.0	3.0	7 908	6 031	1 594	46 345	2.41	60.5	8.8	28.3
Lafayette	15.5	9.0	8.4	49.7	16 137	16 836	4.3	-0.5	1 332	812	-628	6 646	2.51	68.5	7.9	26.8
Langlade	16.8	12.8	10.7	49.5	20 740	19 977	-3.7	-3.8	1 197	1 470	-528	8 713	2.21	62.2	7.8	31.3
Lincoln	17.3	11.4	9.3	49.6	29 641	28 743	-3.0	-2.9	1 655	2 036	-430	12 419	2.22	65.6	7.1	27.4
Manitowoc	16.1	10.7	8.7	50.1	82 887	81 442	-1.7	-2.3	5 107	5 257	-1 721	33 927	2.34	64.6	7.4	30.7
Marathon	14.3	9.4	7.5	49.7	125 834	134 063	6.5	1.1	10 060	7 115	-1 524	53 848	2.48	67.4	8.4	26.9
Marinette	17.4	13.0	10.0	49.8	43 384	41 749	-3.8	-3.0	2 339	3 104	-413	18 319	2.20	61.9	7.8	33.0
Marquette	18.1	13.5	9.6	49.4	15 832	15 404	-2.7	-2.2	953	1 110	-177	6 332	2.36	66.6	7.4	27.1
Menominee	12.5	8.3	5.0	50.2	4 562	4 232	-7.2	7.1	599	268	-39	1 259	3.48	73.5	25.2	22.1
Milwaukee	12.1	7.2	5.5	51.6	940 164	947 736	0.8	0.4	87 471	50 904	-31 406	381 715	2.44	57.0	16.7	35.0
Monroe	14.3	9.8	6.9	49.5	40 899	44 675	9.2	2.1	3 844	2 555	-362	17 794	2.49	66.3	9.7	27.8
Oconto	17.1	11.5	7.8	48.9	35 634	37 660	5.7	-0.6	2 230	2 149	-260	15 486	2.40	70.2	6.8	24.3
Oneida	18.2	14.3	10.8	50.0	36 776	35 998	-2.1	-1.1	1 870	2 803	574	15 044	2.33	64.2	5.5	30.9
Outagamie	13.3	8.1	5.8	50.1	160 971	176 695	9.8	4.4	14 324	8 145	1 647	70 505	2.51	67.6	9.2	26.1
Ozaukee	15.5	10.6	8.1	50.8	82 317	86 395	5.0	2.2	5 067	4 575	1 373	34 543	2.50	70.7	7.2	24.9
Pepin	16.9	11.5	9.8	49.6	7 213	7 469	3.5	-2.2	488	454	-202	2 954	2.45	68.5	5.7	27.0
Pierce	13.8	8.2	5.5	50.4	36 804	41 019	11.5	0.5	2 424	1 597	-620	15 177	2.51	67.6	7.2	23.2
Polk	16.2	11.4	8.1	49.4	41 319	44 205	7.0	-1.6	2 662	2 649	-721	17 994	2.39	68.7	8.5	26.0
Portage	13.4	8.9	6.6	49.7	67 182	70 019	4.2	0.6	4 338	3 263	-607	27 768	2.41	62.4	7.2	27.4
Price	18.9	14.2	11.1	49.1	15 822	14 159	-10.5	-4.5	690	1 106	-230	6 700	2.03	63.5	6.1	30.3
Racine	14.4	9.0	6.6	50.6	188 831	195 428	3.5	-0.1	14 992	10 682	-4 386	75 183	2.53	66.8	12.1	27.4
Richland	16.4	11.5	9.9	49.6	17 924	18 021	0.5	-3.0	1 114	1 092	-579	7 547	2.29	65.9	7.0	29.4
Rock	13.8	8.9	6.9	50.8	152 307	160 331	5.3	0.8	12 087	9 017	-1 720	63 845	2.47	65.9	13.0	27.6
Rusk	17.3	12.9	10.1	49.3	15 347	14 755	-3.9	-4.3	886	1 120	-346	6 239	2.27	66.1	9.6	28.6
St. Croix	13.7	8.0	5.2	50.1	63 155	84 345	33.6	4.4	6 633	3 488	472	32 459	2.63	73.8	8.9	20.7
Sauk	14.1	10.1	7.7	50.2	55 225	61 976	12.2	3.2	4 787	3 668	753	25 331	2.45	65.5	9.6	28.6
Sawyer	18.1	15.0	9.7	49.2	16 196	16 557	2.2	-1.1	1 031	1 260	98	7 359	2.19	66.3	11.1	27.4
Shawano	15.1	11.5	9.1	49.9	40 664	41 955	3.2	-2.1	2 656	2 811	-792	16 957	2.41	66.7	8.3	27.9
Sheboygan	14.7	9.6	7.5	49.7	112 646	115 510	2.5	-0.1	7 895	6 704	-1 359	46 701	2.40	66.2	8.7	28.5
Taylor	15.8	9.8	9.2	49.3	19 680	20 689	5.1	-1.2	1 419	1 141	-586	8 756	2.32	65.0	7.4	29.4
Trempealeau	14.1	9.7	7.7	49.3	27 010	28 816	6.7	2.8	2 498	1 700	52	11 796	2.45	66.9	9.0	27.2
Vernon	15.5	10.6	8.6	49.9	28 056	29 771	6.1	3.5	2 633	1 835	152	11 758	2.54	67.5	6.9	27.3
Vilas	18.4	17.4	12.6	49.3	21 033	21 430	1.9	0.0	1 116	1 789	760	10 646	1.99	63.1	8.4	31.0
Walworth	14.2	9.8	6.8	50.1	93 759	102 228	9.0	0.7	6 526	5 604	-303	39 648	2.53	65.6	9.1	26.5
Washburn	18.1	15.1	10.2	50.6	16 036	15 911	-0.8	-1.7	920	1 281	99	7 141	2.16	64.4	7.8	29.9
Washington	14.9	9.7	7.2	50.2	117 493	131 887	12.3	1.8	8 429	6 606	457	52 897	2.49	71.6	7.5	23.2
Waukesha	15.5	9.9	7.6	50.9	360 767	389 936	8.1	2.2	23 659	19 998	4 687	154 991	2.51	70.0	6.6	25.1
Waupaca	15.9	10.9	9.2	49.6	51 731	52 410	1.3	-1.7	3 244	4 451	382	21 532	2.35	65.2	8.1	28.9
Waushara	17.1	13.5	9.7	47.2	23 154	24 496	5.8	-1.4	1 445	1 644	-114	9 689	2.39	66.5	5.8	29.4
Winnebago	13.3	8.6	7.0	49.6	156 763	166 994	6.5	1.7	11 721	8 933	38	68 939	2.33	60.5	9.0	31.2
Wood	15.5	10.6	9.0	50.7	75 555	74 749	-1.1	-2.2	5 133	4 723	-1 989	31 717	2.30	63.5	8.5	30.7
WYOMING	13.9	9.1	5.9	48.9	493 782	563 767	14.2	3.9	47 402	28 731	2 864	226 865	2.49	64.9	8.4	28.0
Albany	10.1	6.6	3.9	47.5	32 014	36 299	13.4	5.4	2 654	1 163	445	15 662	2.26	48.5	5.3	30.7
Big Horn	13.8	11.8	8.3	49.7	11 461	11 668	1.8	2.9	886	832	278	4 491	2.59	66.1	5.4	29.6
Campbell	13.3	5.6	2.5	48.1	33 698	46 133	36.9	5.8	4 721	1 656	-457	17 510	2.71	69.6	8.1	23.4
Carbon	14.4	9.4	5.4	46.1	15 639	15 885	1.6	-1.7	1 257	801	-682	6 108	2.44	66.6	9.6	27.9
Converse	14.4	9.0	5.8	49.4	12 052	13 833	14.8	2.6	1 218	732	-106	5 677	2.47	71.1	8.2	26.8
Crook	17.1	11.5	7.3	49.3	5 887	7 083	20.3	5.4	606	390	181	2 958	2.43	72.8	6.9	24.2
Fremont	14.4	10.3	7.0	49.9	35 804	40 123	12.1	0.3	3 716	2 725	-879	15 330	2.61	66.0	10.7	27.1

1. No spouse present.

Table B. States and Counties — Population, Vital Statistics, Health, and Crime

STATE County	Persons in group quarters, 2016	Daytime population, 2011–2015 Number	Daytime population Employment/residence ratio	Births, 2016 Total	Births, 2016 Rate[1]	Deaths, 2016 Number	Deaths, 2016 Rate[1]	Persons under 65 with no health insurance, 2015 Number	Persons under 65 with no health insurance, 2015 Percent	Medicare, 2015 Total Beneficiaries	Medicare, 2015 Enrolled in Original Medicare	Medicare, 2015 Enrolled in Medicare Advantage	Serious crimes known to police,[2] 2014 Total Number	Serious crimes known to police,[2] 2014 Total Rate[3]
	32	33	34	35	36	37	38	39	40	41	42	43	44	45
WISCONSIN—Cont'd														
Douglas	1 379	40 546	0.85	411	9.4	399	9.2	2 331	6.7	9 775	5 826	3 949	2 116	4 829
Dunn	3 253	40 827	0.85	444	9.9	325	7.3	2 158	6.2	7 000	4 488	2 512	810	1 833
Eau Claire	4 921	108 186	1.13	1 211	11.8	811	7.9	4 823	5.8	20 505	14 752	5 753	2 169	2 124
Florence	53	3 728	0.60	29	6.5	55	12.3	286	8.7	948	700	248	107	2 351
Fond du Lac	3 532	97 796	0.92	1 050	10.3	880	8.6	4 651	5.7	20 919	10 785	10 134	1 801	1 768
Forest	361	8 901	0.93	110	12.1	114	12.6	749	10.9	2 473	1 630	843	123	1 354
Grant	4 881	47 544	0.85	563	10.8	496	9.5	2 936	7.5	11 175	7 031	4 144	623	1 266
Green	344	34 640	0.88	387	10.4	357	9.6	1 782	5.8	7 003	5 727	1 276	509	1 370
Green Lake	157	18 114	0.90	189	10.1	221	11.8	1 400	9.6	4 629	2 127	2 502	330	1 742
Iowa	188	22 830	0.92	246	10.4	211	8.9	1 143	5.8	4 085	2 590	1 495	250	1 051
Iron	82	5 336	0.77	32	5.6	92	16.1	313	7.7	1 715	1 002	713	98	1 665
Jackson	1 320	19 538	0.89	268	13.0	189	9.2	1 517	9.7	3 695	2 221	1 474	365	1 764
Jefferson	3 246	73 909	0.76	839	9.9	670	7.9	4 398	6.4	15 176	10 418	4 758	1 269	1 608
Juneau	1 689	25 161	0.88	270	10.3	271	10.3	1 676	8.4	5 893	4 584	1 309	389	1 467
Kenosha	4 361	148 877	0.76	1 910	11.4	1 342	8.0	10 203	7.1	24 637	18 085	6 552	3 750	2 231
Kewaunee	177	18 172	0.78	188	9.2	183	9.0	956	5.8	4 198	2 128	2 070	200	976
La Crosse	5 748	126 422	1.15	1 254	10.6	960	8.1	5 077	5.3	20 721	11 699	9 022	2 559	2 183
Lafayette	95	14 007	0.67	225	13.4	128	7.6	1 295	9.4	3 002	2 075	927	168	1 015
Langlade	257	18 842	0.92	179	9.3	232	12.1	1 164	8.0	4 877	2 834	2 043	554	2 842
Lincoln	656	25 894	0.83	252	9.0	313	11.2	1 351	6.2	7 353	4 309	3 044	NA	NA
Manitowoc	1 038	77 006	0.91	784	9.9	859	10.8	3 859	6.0	17 729	9 941	7 788	1 594	1 980
Marathon	1 591	137 263	1.03	1 582	11.7	1 141	8.4	7 037	6.2	23 766	13 075	10 691	1 906	1 424
Marinette	615	42 766	1.08	359	8.9	494	12.2	2 101	6.7	11 843	7 295	4 548	694	1 669
Marquette	134	12 769	0.64	148	9.8	179	11.9	858	7.5	4 659	3 090	1 569	203	1 342
Menominee	57	5 502	1.76	89	19.6	60	13.2	399	10.3	647	464	183	33	761
Milwaukee	23 538	990 166	1.08	13 675	14.4	8 176	8.6	69 693	8.6	143 339	78 329	65 010	48 786	5 092
Monroe	818	46 736	1.07	604	13.2	415	9.1	2 831	7.5	7 645	5 054	2 591	630	1 401
Oconto	272	28 730	0.53	359	9.6	359	9.6	2 058	6.8	7 367	3 522	3 845	NA	NA
Oneida	510	36 363	1.04	286	8.0	472	13.3	1 678	6.3	11 402	7 564	3 838	616	1 729
Outagamie	3 025	185 378	1.05	2 295	12.4	1 358	7.4	9 257	5.9	32 666	12 921	19 745	3 201	1 766
Ozaukee	2 019	83 203	0.91	826	9.4	799	9.0	2 818	4.0	16 837	10 070	6 767	797	913
Pepin	125	6 604	0.79	77	10.5	79	10.8	443	7.8	1 655	1 274	381	74	1 008
Pierce	2 457	30 016	0.51	372	9.0	272	6.6	1 814	5.4	7 102	4 043	3 059	604	1 475
Polk	433	39 076	0.78	414	9.5	441	10.1	2 629	7.5	8 694	4 982	3 712	573	1 323
Portage	3 505	70 762	1.01	674	9.6	507	7.2	2 945	5.2	11 309	6 458	4 851	1 068	1 515
Price	165	14 108	1.05	114	8.4	165	12.2	689	6.8	3 894	2 431	1 463	200	1 457
Racine	4 792	182 495	0.86	2 353	12.1	1 676	8.6	10 844	6.7	37 755	23 503	14 252	4 833	2 479
Richland	346	16 441	0.84	171	9.8	183	10.5	1 017	7.4	3 484	2 865	619	81	459
Rock	2 665	149 330	0.85	1 923	11.9	1 440	8.9	10 915	8.1	30 399	20 348	10 051	4 401	2 735
Rusk	157	14 250	0.98	139	9.8	170	12.0	936	8.6	3 400	2 032	1 368	195	1 362
St. Croix	811	74 552	0.74	1 043	11.8	591	6.7	3 301	4.3	11 336	6 280	5 056	1 176	1 406
Sauk	733	65 705	1.08	760	11.9	624	9.8	3 690	7.1	11 855	7 029	4 826	1 635	2 576
Sawyer	314	16 802	1.05	155	9.5	200	12.2	1 290	10.7	4 252	2 867	1 385	234	1 418
Shawano	732	36 533	0.75	396	9.6	402	9.8	2 836	8.7	8 592	3 774	4 818	570	1 371
Sheboygan	2 818	116 120	1.02	1 226	10.6	1 086	9.4	5 577	5.9	22 261	12 646	9 615	2 162	1 883
Taylor	219	20 002	0.94	233	11.4	196	9.6	1 254	7.6	3 549	1 975	1 574	198	961
Trempealeau	466	29 186	0.98	411	13.9	269	9.1	1 888	7.8	6 205	3 767	2 438	238	799
Vernon	358	27 393	0.78	429	13.9	318	10.3	2 350	9.6	6 216	3 037	3 179	289	1 038
Vilas	190	21 123	0.97	174	8.1	289	13.5	1 538	10.4	7 039	4 916	2 123	235	1 100
Walworth	2 683	97 147	0.88	1 047	10.2	910	8.8	6 909	8.2	17 230	13 500	3 730	1 694	1 642
Washburn	205	15 474	0.97	127	8.1	200	12.8	813	7.0	6 174	3 953	2 221	324	2 073
Washington	1 073	116 362	0.77	1 337	10.0	1 100	8.2	5 129	4.6	24 229	14 636	9 593	1 805	1 595
Waukesha	5 308	420 677	1.13	3 751	9.4	3 351	8.4	11 998	3.7	75 517	45 021	30 496	4 860	1 369
Waupaca	1 545	49 304	0.89	515	10.0	731	14.2	2 698	6.6	13 172	5 847	7 325	1 005	1 923
Waushara	1 222	21 252	0.70	232	9.6	252	10.4	1 516	8.8	5 428	2 695	2 733	317	1 305
Winnebago	7 714	179 482	1.12	1 833	10.8	1 449	8.5	7 061	5.2	28 976	12 763	16 213	3 126	1 837
Wood	799	77 902	1.11	785	10.7	749	10.2	3 434	5.8	19 574	9 789	9 785	1 308	1 773
WYOMING	14 290	586 600	1.02	7 590	13.0	4 838	8.3	65 487	13.4	92 579	88 392	4 187	12 619	2 160
Albany	2 289	37 085	0.98	437	11.4	183	4.8	3 791	11.9	4 087	3 803	284	962	2 568
Big Horn	183	11 732	0.97	149	12.4	121	10.1	1 784	18.8	2 399	2 353	46	74	692
Campbell	422	51 607	1.14	767	15.7	333	6.8	5 302	11.7	4 082	4 023	59	1 283	2 650
Carbon	809	15 506	0.97	200	12.8	138	8.8	2 005	16.0	2 439	2 311	128	279	1 835
Converse	103	14 096	1.00	210	14.8	112	7.9	1 348	11.1	2 146	2 110	36	300	2 089
Crook	34	6 373	0.77	98	13.1	66	8.8	741	12.2	1 322	1 254	68	90	1 256
Fremont	888	40 270	0.97	562	14.0	481	12.0	6 165	18.9	7 550	6 921	629	853	2 082

1. Per 1,000 estimated resident population. 2. Data for serious crimes have not been adjusted for underreporting; this may affect comparability between geographic areas and over time.
3. Per 100,000 population estimated by the FBI.

STATE County	Serious crimes known to police, 2014 (cont.)[1] Rate[2]		Education School enrollment and attainment, 2011-2015				Local government expenditures,[5] 2013-2014		Money income, 2011-2015		Households			Income and poverty, 2015 Percent below poverty level		
			Enrollment[3]		Attainment[4] (percent)							Percent				
	Violent	Property	Total	Percent private	High school graduate or less	Bachelor's degree or more	Total current spending (mil dol)	Current spending per student (dollars)	Per capita income[6] (dollars)	Median income (dollars)	with income of less than $50,000	with income of $200,000 or more	Median household income (dollars)	All persons	Children under 18 years	Children 5 to 17 years in families
	46	47	48	49	50	51	52	53	54	55	56	57	58	59	60	61
WISCONSIN—Cont'd																
Douglas	194	4 635	10 741	7.8	39.9	22.5	72.8	11 490	25 191	47 095	52.5	1.4	48 715	14.8	20.1	18.3
Dunn	156	1 677	14 619	5.5	41.8	25.6	63.3	10 356	24 098	49 788	50.2	2.1	53 082	13.5	16.2	15.3
Eau Claire	130	1 994	30 970	9.4	33.7	31.1	153.4	10 845	26 034	49 513	50.4	2.7	51 937	13.6	15.7	15.1
Florence	66	2 285	769	3.5	48.1	17.1	6.5	15 936	25 142	48 643	51.0	1.5	46 193	12.2	20.2	17.8
Fond du Lac	200	1 568	24 108	23.4	47.2	21.5	143.9	10 704	27 474	55 473	44.3	2.1	58 049	9.4	12.3	11.1
Forest	198	1 155	1 917	4.5	53.9	13.8	20.1	12 753	21 623	40 636	58.8	1.0	44 098	14.5	22.3	22.1
Grant	122	1 144	15 357	10.5	47.3	21.3	84.1	12 007	22 937	49 067	51.0	1.6	51 008	14.0	16.7	15.2
Green	89	1 281	8 618	8.2	46.8	21.9	65.5	11 464	28 187	56 219	44.4	2.3	59 155	7.5	10.7	9.4
Green Lake	53	1 689	3 869	16.6	54.3	16.9	35.1	11 126	25 466	46 780	53.6	1.6	49 493	12.2	19.9	18.5
Iowa	135	917	5 437	11.9	43.2	22.9	44.4	12 449	27 664	55 188	45.1	2.5	58 092	9.5	12.3	11.0
Iron	119	1 546	962	6.0	42.9	21.0	10.2	13 118	25 435	42 543	59.4	1.1	42 328	13.0	20.5	19.1
Jackson	82	1 682	4 170	8.7	55.2	13.8	34.5	10 680	23 299	47 851	52.0	1.9	50 653	12.4	19.6	18.2
Jefferson	117	1 491	21 972	17.9	45.3	22.6	149.5	10 982	26 935	56 877	43.1	2.4	61 622	9.2	12.4	10.6
Juneau	219	1 248	5 517	13.2	56.8	12.3	44.7	11 847	22 363	44 961	54.8	1.6	46 051	14.5	21.2	19.6
Kenosha	207	2 024	45 881	13.2	42.6	24.5	333.1	11 213	26 514	54 918	45.6	3.1	56 414	12.7	18.9	17.0
Kewaunee	44	932	4 543	16.5	52.3	15.8	35.6	10 113	26 655	56 863	44.8	2.0	60 572	8.2	10.3	9.1
La Crosse	124	2 060	35 896	13.6	33.3	30.9	196.9	12 191	27 550	50 539	49.4	3.1	51 428	14.4	12.4	11.2
Lafayette	72	942	3 913	11.8	51.8	17.5	34.5	12 008	25 258	51 445	48.5	2.3	56 428	10.5	16.9	16.4
Langlade	67	2 776	4 059	15.4	53.3	14.9	35.4	11 641	23 857	41 775	58.7	1.4	44 635	14.4	22.8	20.7
Lincoln	NA	NA	6 107	15.8	50.6	15.3	48.6	10 097	25 856	49 721	50.2	1.5	51 406	9.8	14.7	13.4
Manitowoc	156	1 823	17 698	18.8	49.6	19.7	116.6	10 800	26 096	48 398	51.4	1.7	51 951	10.7	15.1	12.9
Marathon	96	1 328	32 861	13.8	46.1	23.7	224.6	11 141	28 457	54 083	46.2	2.8	56 347	9.5	13.5	12.6
Marinette	41	1 628	8 938	13.0	51.6	14.4	67.4	10 809	24 450	43 425	56.2	1.4	48 545	12.7	18.6	16.4
Marquette	13	1 329	2 916	14.2	55.9	12.8	20.4	11 435	24 054	46 242	53.8	0.9	48 508	12.0	19.6	17.9
Menominee	0	761	1 287	3.8	54.0	16.1	15.8	18 803	14 482	35 343	66.4	0.3	33 410	35.2	50.9	54.4
Milwaukee	1 002	4 089	267 793	25.8	41.6	29.1	1 559.4	11 080	24 984	43 873	55.3	2.5	45 905	20.3	29.5	27.4
Monroe	131	1 270	10 775	12.4	50.1	17.1	77.2	11 013	23 709	50 694	49.2	1.4	52 975	12.8	19.6	18.2
Oconto	NA	NA	7 887	7.3	53.5	15.4	52.8	12 483	26 914	52 765	47.2	1.7	53 243	9.7	13.9	12.5
Oneida	205	1 524	6 669	13.6	41.8	25.0	57.5	13 512	26 432	46 516	52.6	2.0	50 297	9.5	16.2	15.2
Outagamie	144	1 622	47 347	16.5	40.7	27.7	353.6	10 105	28 679	58 765	41.8	2.8	60 649	9.0	12.0	10.9
Ozaukee	56	857	23 030	24.5	26.1	46.1	136.5	10 752	43 543	76 433	32.2	10.4	80 135	5.2	5.2	4.4
Pepin	109	899	1 529	18.0	52.2	17.4	15.5	13 080	24 951	49 516	50.4	2.1	50 094	10.1	16.9	15.2
Pierce	76	1 399	13 228	10.7	38.1	27.5	79.9	10 489	29 068	61 611	41.2	3.3	63 735	9.8	9.2	7.8
Polk	235	1 087	9 382	8.4	46.8	19.5	84.4	11 325	26 450	50 714	49.2	2.2	54 946	10.1	14.2	13.2
Portage	99	1 416	21 776	8.0	41.2	29.2	97.0	10 278	26 071	51 613	48.2	2.3	57 010	12.2	12.1	10.8
Price	87	1 369	2 392	11.0	51.7	16.6	22.9	11 444	25 055	43 137	58.0	1.3	44 932	13.0	18.2	16.1
Racine	200	2 279	49 295	19.9	42.5	23.7	349.9	11 755	27 895	55 584	43.9	3.3	57 367	12.4	18.4	17.7
Richland	17	442	3 909	18.1	51.8	16.6	19.8	11 248	23 765	44 810	55.5	1.4	46 998	14.2	21.8	19.9
Rock	232	2 503	40 106	13.8	47.9	20.4	305.6	10 934	25 219	50 324	49.7	2.1	54 107	13.9	20.1	18.1
Rusk	133	1 229	2 797	16.1	55.1	15.0	25.1	12 406	21 975	39 194	62.4	1.1	42 900	14.0	23.2	21.2
St. Croix	62	1 344	22 695	13.8	32.6	32.3	142.4	9 917	32 955	70 886	32.5	5.1	74 624	5.7	6.9	5.9
Sauk	95	2 482	14 207	12.6	46.6	22.2	112.3	10 982	26 335	51 055	48.9	2.0	52 025	11.7	16.8	14.7
Sawyer	188	1 230	3 226	8.6	43.5	22.6	26.0	11 408	25 284	41 665	59.1	2.4	44 556	15.5	27.8	27.0
Shawano	63	1 308	9 092	12.0	55.0	15.5	61.3	11 008	24 638	47 861	52.0	1.6	50 948	11.6	18.8	16.6
Sheboygan	162	1 721	28 116	17.4	45.7	23.4	207.8	10 727	27 034	53 713	45.8	2.0	58 190	9.0	11.8	9.7
Taylor	87	873	4 542	12.7	58.7	13.3	33.9	10 995	24 300	45 420	54.9	2.1	48 951	12.4	19.5	16.6
Trempealeau	57	742	6 537	8.9	50.3	19.2	66.2	11 361	25 502	51 077	49.0	1.9	53 695	9.4	13.5	13.0
Vernon	79	959	6 721	23.0	49.8	20.5	47.0	11 520	23 985	47 675	52.0	2.1	49 217	14.8	26.4	24.7
Vilas	47	1 054	3 894	6.3	38.9	26.0	43.4	16 368	26 304	41 061	60.6	2.1	42 993	13.4	22.8	21.1
Walworth	73	1 569	28 807	10.6	41.7	26.8	188.6	11 649	27 410	53 445	46.5	3.0	58 554	12.4	14.7	13.7
Washburn	218	1 856	2 864	10.4	47.4	20.7	32.8	12 383	25 575	42 368	56.7	1.8	45 043	13.5	22.7	21.6
Washington	79	1 516	32 150	22.0	36.7	28.9	208.0	10 341	33 744	69 237	33.9	4.6	70 778	5.3	6.4	5.5
Waukesha	67	1 302	100 398	22.8	28.6	41.2	674.2	10 760	38 684	76 545	31.4	7.8	78 689	4.7	5.1	4.5
Waupaca	140	1 783	11 223	13.0	53.4	16.9	94.7	10 730	27 257	51 994	48.1	1.9	54 849	10.7	14.4	12.3
Waushara	91	1 214	4 538	11.0	55.5	14.6	31.9	12 037	23 977	45 166	54.8	1.8	49 912	11.8	20.2	19.3
Winnebago	172	1 665	42 755	11.6	42.0	26.6	235.7	10 430	27 770	52 018	47.6	2.8	52 725	11.3	13.3	12.6
Wood	34	1 739	16 767	12.8	47.3	19.6	139.1	11 150	26 516	48 961	50.8	1.9	51 025	11.3	16.1	14.0
WYOMING	195	1 965	148 169	9.9	37.1	25.7	1 464.9	15 885	29 803	58 840	42.7	3.2	61 213	10.6	13.0	11.2
Albany	152	2 416	16 651	7.9	20.4	49.3	60.9	16 176	24 946	42 834	56.7	2.6	44 455	20.1	15.9	14.5
Big Horn	122	571	2 916	5.7	42.5	19.6	42.3	17 050	23 812	51 679	47.4	0.8	50 056	12.1	13.9	11.6
Campbell	174	2 477	12 084	8.2	43.1	19.3	131.8	14 935	33 925	80 060	28.9	4.2	83 042	7.5	8.9	7.3
Carbon	303	1 532	3 613	10.5	44.8	19.5	43.0	17 008	26 706	56 825	44.1	1.9	60 209	11.4	13.7	11.8
Converse	272	1 818	3 117	14.2	46.7	17.5	39.4	16 213	30 249	62 307	40.2	1.7	70 307	8.5	11.3	9.6
Crook	195	1 061	1 532	8.7	41.7	18.8	20.1	18 012	32 083	60 445	40.1	4.9	64 851	7.7	10.7	9.7
Fremont	142	1 941	10 281	8.9	39.9	21.3	127.0	18 860	25 293	52 773	48.0	2.5	52 408	12.9	18.2	15.9

1. Data for serious crimes have not been adjusted for underreporting; this may affect comparability between geographic areas and over time. 2. Per 100,000 population estimated by the FBI.
3. All persons 3 years old and over enrolled in nursery school through college. 4. Persons 25 years old and over. 5. Elementary and secondary education expenditures.
6. Based on population estimated by the American Community Survey, 2011-2015.

Table B. States and Counties — **Personal Income**

STATE County	Personal income, 2015											Earnings, 2015		
			Per capita[1]			Supplements to wages and salaries; employer contributions (mil dol)							Contributions for government social insurance (mil dol)		
	Total (mil dol)	Percent change, 2014–2015	Dollars	Rank	Wages and salaries (mil dol)	Pension and insurance	Government social insurance	Proprietors' income (mil dol)	Dividends, interest, and rent (mil dol)	Personal transfer receipts (mil dol)		Total (mil dol)	From employee and self-employed	From employer
	62	63	64	65	66	67	68	69	70	71		72	73	74

WISCONSIN—Cont'd														
Douglas	1 683	3.2	38 603	1 646	753	155	68	78	266	431		1 054	70	68
Dunn	1 616	-0.2	36 316	1 835	732	167	58	112	259	346		1 069	64	58
Eau Claire	4 467	2.9	43 747	870	2 622	478	201	294	881	774		3 595	216	201
Florence	209	5.4	46 793	1 161	30	8	2	32	39	49		73	5	2
Fond du Lac	4 463	3.3	43 764	908	2 134	383	173	315	714	815		3 004	182	173
Forest	313	2.6	34 520	2 006	117	35	9	22	59	100		183	12	9
Grant	2 007	1.9	38 413	1 427	733	190	57	231	338	408		1 211	70	57
Green	1 724	3.6	46 367	819	648	133	51	170	317	272		1 001	59	51
Green Lake	864	3.2	45 805	795	269	55	22	75	206	172		421	27	22
Iowa	1 045	2.8	43 877	916	444	79	36	107	185	170		666	39	36
Iron	248	2.5	42 744	528	57	14	5	19	60	75		95	7	5
Jackson	829	1.3	40 316	1 061	379	85	30	61	162	169		555	32	30
Jefferson	3 447	4.2	40 761	1 250	1 398	279	110	211	536	625		1 998	123	110
Juneau	980	3.9	37 356	1 730	380	89	30	63	144	242		563	34	30
Kenosha	6 969	5.1	41 373	1 217	2 746	510	217	350	948	1 275		3 823	238	217
Kewaunee	873	0.2	42 855	937	277	57	22	97	135	156		453	25	22
La Crosse	5 267	3.1	44 557	925	3 146	586	252	358	998	914		4 342	260	252
Lafayette	718	1.4	42 640	968	157	37	12	131	125	121		337	17	12
Langlade	767	2.4	39 900	1 273	273	58	22	84	130	210		437	28	22
Lincoln	1 117	2.9	39 916	1 397	465	93	37	64	168	273		660	43	37
Manitowoc	3 576	1.8	44 803	898	1 515	286	121	356	574	690		2 278	139	121
Marathon	5 967	2.5	43 921	852	3 324	581	256	466	956	970		4 628	277	256
Marinette	1 622	2.7	39 681	1 237	818	167	66	86	252	447		1 137	73	66
Marquette	543	2.4	35 995	1 870	134	31	11	31	90	151		207	15	11
Menominee	[3]124	[3]7.0	[3]27 013	[3]3 033	[3]76	[3]33	[3]5	[3]9	[3]16	[3]45		[3]123	[3]7	[3]5
Milwaukee	41 202	3.3	43 020	1 009	26 772	4 378	2 045	3 135	6 982	9 055		36 329	2 177	2 045
Monroe	1 716	3.9	37 678	1 772	861	198	72	141	309	351		1 271	74	72
Oconto	1 529	3.2	40 842	1 222	315	77	26	122	221	317		539	36	26
Oneida	1 652	4.0	46 451	673	706	127	55	130	348	405		1 019	68	55
Outagamie	8 325	4.1	45 429	789	5 156	841	405	528	1 328	1 174		6 931	413	405
Ozaukee	6 454	3.3	73 462	55	2 056	350	157	337	1 669	639		2 900	178	157
Pepin	324	2.3	44 487	1 021	89	19	7	27	56	76		142	9	7
Pierce	1 752	3.9	42 855	1 155	408	119	32	123	288	267		683	41	32
Polk	1 815	3.7	41 777	1 207	633	137	51	121	298	393		942	60	51
Portage	2 917	3.9	41 434	1 245	1 583	298	126	202	486	530		2 208	130	126
Price	588	2.0	43 128	1 252	231	50	18	58	103	159		357	23	18
Racine	8 483	3.6	43 486	1 020	3 684	691	282	325	1 497	1 646		4 982	313	282
Richland	662	0.9	37 838	1 454	237	59	18	64	104	161		378	22	18
Rock	6 462	4.2	40 026	1 362	2 976	543	236	320	1 145	1 328		4 074	259	236
Rusk	508	2.1	35 984	2 211	195	47	17	44	84	151		303	19	17
St. Croix	4 235	4.7	48 392	667	1 389	262	111	254	640	522		2 016	123	111
Sauk	2 785	4.8	43 763	1 095	1 472	266	119	326	460	487		2 183	132	119
Sawyer	668	2.5	40 778	1 304	239	57	19	58	150	193		373	25	19
Shawano	1 535	1.2	37 167	1 613	465	104	38	124	242	356		731	47	38
Sheboygan	5 304	1.9	45 896	573	2 858	478	221	336	1 053	855		3 892	237	221
Taylor	735	1.4	35 931	2 069	317	62	26	95	120	154		499	30	26
Trempealeau	1 249	3.2	42 272	1 071	614	118	48	73	198	251		853	51	48
Vernon	1 130	2.6	37 057	1 852	334	76	26	127	181	251		563	35	26
Vilas	1 052	3.9	49 212	902	263	61	22	191	277	266		537	37	22
Walworth	4 364	3.3	42 446	1 114	1 674	359	134	276	852	756		2 442	149	134
Washburn	680	2.4	43 727	1 135	215	51	17	63	141	196		346	24	17
Washington	6 832	3.6	51 110	454	2 558	433	199	421	1 129	917		3 611	225	199
Waukesha	25 373	4.1	63 995	117	13 569	1 970	1 040	1 841	4 993	2 834		18 421	1 111	1 040
Waupaca	2 193	2.1	42 216	1 057	789	169	63	142	357	509		1 163	75	63
Waushara	928	2.9	38 620	1 648	215	54	17	80	164	225		367	25	17
Winnebago	7 189	3.6	42 399	1 120	4 779	805	365	408	1 309	1 204		6 357	384	365
Wood	3 076	3.5	41 883	1 296	1 696	316	131	232	491	662		2 375	147	131
WYOMING	32 870	0.4	56 038	X	14 260	2 614	1 384	3 647	9 637	4 138		21 904	1 228	1 384
Albany	1 482	3.6	39 052	1 474	676	188	65	97	349	211		1 026	54	65
Big Horn	444	0.9	36 964	1 685	197	44	20	26	78	93		287	17	20
Campbell	2 690	1.0	54 653	450	1 743	264	161	502	378	232		2 670	145	161
Carbon	775	1.8	49 787	439	390	91	39	25	171	106		545	31	39
Converse	783	1.4	55 012	311	369	67	36	87	124	105		559	32	36
Crook	328	-0.7	44 121	557	106	22	10	41	77	49		179	10	10
Fremont	1 654	-0.7	41 019	1 065	720	153	69	96	362	352		1 037	63	69

1. Based on the resident population estimated as of July 1 of the year shown.   3. Menominee county included with Shawano county.

Table B. States and Counties — Earnings, Social Security, and Housing

STATE County	Earnings, 2015 (cont.) — Percent by selected industries									Social Security beneficiaries, December 2015		Supplemental Security Income recipients, December 2015	Housing units, 2016	
	Farm	Mining	Construction	Manufacturing	Information: professional, scientific, technical services	Retail trade	Finance, insurance, real estate and leasing	Health care and social assistance	Government	Number	Rate[1]		Total	Percent change, 2010–2016
	75	76	77	78	79	80	81	82	83	84	85	86	87	88
WISCONSIN—Cont'd														
Douglas	0.0	D	9.6	11.0	3.3	6.6	2.9	7.3	20.1	9 675	222	1 173	22 924	0.4
Dunn	4.0	D	6.2	18.8	4.0	5.2	3.6	10.4	25.1	9 280	208	743	18 230	1.5
Eau Claire	0.3	D	5.0	9.1	5.9	8.1	6.7	23.1	16.1	19 790	194	1 995	43 504	3.2
Florence	0.3	0.3	4.3	D	D	D	2.9	2.2	20.6	1 490	334	65	4 850	1.4
Fond du Lac	3.7	0.4	8.2	25.4	4.5	6.3	4.7	12.7	12.8	21 605	212	1 513	44 706	1.8
Forest	0.0	D	3.7	8.2	D	3.7	1.8	D	57.2	2 740	303	211	9 084	1.3
Grant	9.4	D	6.0	12.1	4.5	6.0	3.7	8.9	27.6	11 130	213	790	21 905	1.5
Green	3.6	D	5.0	25.7	D	12.0	3.7	12.9	12.8	7 955	214	419	15 887	0.2
Green Lake	3.6	1.5	10.8	15.5	D	6.4	5.4	16.2	15.5	5 070	269	295	10 629	0.1
Iowa	7.4	D	8.3	10.7	2.3	28.7	2.6	D	12.9	5 065	213	353	10 802	0.8
Iron	1.5	D	12.1	8.6	4.1	7.9	D	14.9	25.4	2 140	370	128	6 039	0.7
Jackson	6.2	2.9	15.3	9.7	1.2	4.1	2.8	D	25.8	4 715	229	379	9 783	0.6
Jefferson	1.8	D	7.0	31.9	3.7	6.2	3.4	8.8	13.1	16 930	200	964	35 467	0.9
Juneau	6.1	0.0	4.5	23.7	1.8	5.5	2.2	D	28.0	6 835	261	657	14 858	1.3
Kenosha	0.3	D	4.6	14.5	3.6	7.3	3.7	13.9	17.8	30 125	179	3 731	69 880	0.9
Kewaunee	18.6	D	7.2	24.2	D	4.0	3.3	D	15.9	4 650	228	221	9 353	0.5
La Crosse	0.2	D	5.4	11.2	4.8	6.1	8.1	21.4	15.5	22 355	189	2 202	49 783	2.9
Lafayette	27.3	D	7.6	12.5	D	3.0	4.5	3.0	18.2	3 610	215	197	7 241	0.2
Langlade	7.5	D	4.5	18.5	2.5	12.7	4.9	D	15.7	5 830	304	446	12 441	0.6
Lincoln	1.1	D	6.3	25.3	1.8	6.5	13.7	7.8	17.4	7 745	277	471	16 957	1.0
Manitowoc	4.5	0.2	5.3	31.9	3.1	5.1	3.5	10.6	11.9	19 960	250	1 363	37 236	0.1
Marathon	2.1	0.2	5.4	22.2	5.3	7.2	9.6	15.8	11.5	27 840	205	2 026	58 725	1.7
Marinette	2.6	D	5.3	38.8	2.4	5.5	2.9	D	12.2	12 435	304	849	30 392	0.0
Marquette	7.3	0.0	4.9	33.1	3.0	4.4	2.2	D	21.7	4 640	308	331	9 839	-0.6
Menominee	[3]0.0	[3]0.0	[3]0.1	[3]D	[3]D	[3]D	[3]D	[3]0.1	[3]89.7	960	213	226	2 270	0.8
Milwaukee	0.0	0.1	2.8	12.3	10.6	4.6	10.6	15.1	13.2	162 335	170	43 486	417 284	-0.2
Monroe	3.3	2.4	6.2	19.4	2.1	4.9	2.5	6.9	29.7	9 250	203	829	19 630	2.2
Oconto	8.5	D	8.5	21.0	D	6.4	2.6	10.6	21.1	9 530	254	593	23 792	1.1
Oneida	0.9	0.0	8.2	10.9	4.8	12.3	4.1	21.2	15.5	11 740	330	629	30 666	1.8
Outagamie	0.9	0.1	8.7	21.2	6.2	6.4	9.0	11.6	11.7	33 675	184	2 680	76 355	4.4
Ozaukee	0.6	D	4.3	24.8	10.6	5.6	10.2	13.3	9.2	18 575	211	508	37 042	2.1
Pepin	5.4	0.0	11.5	5.7	4.2	7.9	4.8	9.6	18.0	2 110	289	107	3 632	1.5
Pierce	4.7	D	6.9	13.3	3.1	4.1	3.9	D	35.6	7 210	176	401	16 399	1.7
Polk	2.9	0.9	6.0	22.9	D	5.9	3.3	17.1	17.6	10 960	252	650	24 352	0.4
Portage	4.2	D	3.4	11.8	5.1	7.0	19.1	9.9	16.7	13 650	194	875	30 605	1.8
Price	2.5	D	3.4	37.6	5.8	5.0	2.4	9.6	14.7	4 430	324	290	11 220	0.9
Racine	0.3	0.1	5.0	34.1	3.9	5.5	4.4	12.3	14.3	41 265	212	5 485	82 367	0.2
Richland	9.9	D	5.6	23.9	1.7	7.6	2.5	12.6	22.1	4 260	244	375	8 885	0.2
Rock	1.0	0.3	6.6	17.2	5.1	7.1	3.6	16.1	15.4	34 510	214	3 926	68 527	0.2
Rusk	4.8	D	4.5	29.7	D	5.6	2.4	5.8	22.0	4 185	296	366	9 075	2.2
St. Croix	1.3	D	8.3	21.3	6.6	7.5	5.0	12.2	14.3	14 160	162	629	35 224	3.7
Sauk	1.6	D	11.4	17.8	4.5	7.9	5.2	10.5	15.2	13 825	217	888	30 007	1.0
Sawyer	0.8	D	8.9	10.4	3.5	10.0	4.2	D	28.8	5 480	335	374	16 344	2.3
Shawano	7.7	0.0	6.4	16.5	D	6.9	3.5	10.9	20.8	10 175	247	680	20 695	-0.1
Sheboygan	1.3	D	4.7	39.8	2.8	5.5	6.3	11.8	9.9	24 955	216	1 784	50 599	-0.3
Taylor	7.0	D	7.5	23.3	D	5.7	3.5	9.0	11.9	4 335	212	238	10 626	0.4
Trempealeau	2.6	D	4.4	43.8	D	3.6	2.8	D	16.3	6 455	218	463	12 953	2.6
Vernon	8.8	D	7.9	7.8	4.2	7.2	3.1	15.2	18.2	7 340	240	637	13 863	1.0
Vilas	1.0	D	13.0	2.9	2.8	6.1	3.4	6.0	23.1	8 380	392	335	25 711	2.4
Walworth	1.2	D	6.1	23.7	4.5	6.5	4.1	7.5	21.8	20 560	200	1 251	51 901	0.7
Washburn	1.9	D	5.6	17.7	D	8.9	3.0	D	24.3	5 315	342	398	13 127	1.1
Washington	0.8	0.2	6.9	29.3	4.5	6.4	7.5	10.6	10.3	26 845	201	927	56 111	2.6
Waukesha	0.1	0.2	7.7	19.8	11.3	7.2	9.5	9.7	7.0	81 035	204	2 931	164 319	2.1
Waupaca	3.2	D	6.2	34.5	3.5	6.5	2.9	9.2	18.1	13 565	261	871	25 526	0.5
Waushara	11.8	D	6.4	14.0	3.1	6.1	2.6	D	23.4	6 995	291	399	14 927	0.6
Winnebago	0.3	D	7.1	29.1	7.2	4.8	5.6	9.6	12.5	33 535	198	2 502	75 104	2.4
Wood	1.6	D	5.9	16.9	6.4	5.8	3.5	20.8	14.1	18 440	252	1 511	34 752	1.9
WYOMING	1.2	14.3	9.0	4.1	5.5	5.7	5.1	6.9	24.3	103 689	177	6 697	270 600	3.3
Albany	2.6	0.9	5.4	2.0	7.8	5.9	5.3	7.9	49.3	4 600	121	305	18 869	5.2
Big Horn	4.3	14.4	8.4	6.5	D	3.2	2.6	D	33.8	2 605	217	160	5 355	-0.4
Campbell	-0.1	42.5	7.6	2.0	2.8	4.7	2.9	2.6	14.3	5 160	105	298	19 810	4.5
Carbon	1.8	D	13.4	D	3.9	5.8	2.1	D	25.7	2 665	171	142	8 585	0.1
Converse	1.0	26.5	10.8	2.4	3.8	3.4	5.2	D	21.4	2 430	170	151	6 555	2.4
Crook	3.9	14.2	13.7	7.9	D	4.3	2.7	D	25.5	1 530	206	35	3 558	-1.0
Fremont	1.0	9.1	6.7	1.4	4.9	6.7	5.0	D	36.6	8 605	213	868	17 652	-0.8

1. Per 1,000 resident population estimated as of July 1 of the year shown.   3. Menominee county included with Shawano county.

Table B. States and Counties — Housing, Labor Force, and Employment

STATE County	Housing units, 2011–2015 Occupied units								Civilian labor force, 2016		Unemployment		Civilian employment,[6] 2011–2015		
			Owner-occupied			Renter-occupied							Percent		
				Median owner cost as a percent of income				Sub-stand-ard units[4] (percent)		Percent change, 2015–2016				Manage-ment, business, science and arts	Con-struction, produc-tion, and mainte-nance occu-pations
	Total	Percent	Median value[1]	With a mort-gage	Without a mort-gage[2]	Median rent[3]	Median rent as a per-cent of income[2]		Total		Total	Rate[5]	Total		
	89	90	91	92	93	94	95	96	97	98	99	100	101	102	103
WISCONSIN—Cont'd															
Douglas	18 581	68.2	131 200	22.0	13.1	696	29.3	2.3	23 538	0.7	1 285	5.5	21 340	29.5	25.1
Dunn	16 441	67.6	153 700	22.8	13.4	721	28.7	2.1	24 383	2.5	1 023	4.2	22 494	31.4	28.8
Eau Claire	39 893	61.9	152 000	21.2	12.9	746	31.0	2.1	58 705	0.9	2 066	3.5	54 079	34.7	21.1
Florence	1 904	86.9	140 700	23.6	13.3	506	25.1	2.8	2 210	-0.3	136	6.2	1 942	27.2	32.7
Fond du Lac	41 069	71.5	146 100	21.9	13.1	688	26.4	1.9	57 183	0.2	2 067	3.6	52 846	29.3	32.8
Forest	3 810	76.8	126 500	23.8	13.8	461	24.9	2.3	3 996	-0.1	257	6.4	3 559	29.2	31.2
Grant	19 447	70.8	133 200	22.0	12.3	677	26.5	2.8	28 130	-0.2	1 141	4.1	26 157	30.0	31.3
Green	14 819	73.4	160 200	22.7	15.0	689	26.8	1.3	21 485	1.8	730	3.4	19 815	31.8	30.1
Green Lake	7 939	73.5	140 300	22.8	13.7	615	25.3	2.4	9 770	-2.3	491	5.0	9 016	25.8	37.4
Iowa	9 689	76.9	163 300	23.8	14.5	687	26.1	1.7	13 923	1.6	497	3.6	12 424	32.4	28.1
Iron	2 910	81.4	104 700	22.4	13.4	485	28.7	1.5	2 662	1.4	204	7.7	2 560	27.6	29.6
Jackson	7 960	74.1	127 000	23.1	13.8	621	26.0	2.8	10 354	0.0	466	4.5	9 294	26.4	32.8
Jefferson	32 413	71.4	173 000	23.2	13.8	775	26.5	1.4	45 748	0.1	1 846	4.0	44 424	30.5	29.4
Juneau	9 984	76.6	116 800	24.8	14.8	690	27.2	2.0	13 520	0.0	621	4.6	11 520	23.9	32.7
Kenosha	62 330	66.7	161 800	23.8	14.7	857	31.5	2.3	88 641	1.0	4 263	4.8	79 753	32.9	25.2
Kewaunee	8 138	81.2	148 100	22.5	13.6	602	24.3	1.7	11 054	1.4	419	3.8	10 404	29.3	36.2
La Crosse	46 345	64.9	156 700	21.5	12.9	748	28.9	1.4	67 673	1.5	2 525	3.7	62 292	35.2	21.7
Lafayette	6 646	76.5	124 000	23.6	13.3	635	24.0	2.1	9 897	1.5	325	3.3	8 705	30.5	34.1
Langlade	8 713	75.0	109 700	22.4	12.7	597	32.8	3.7	9 573	0.9	512	5.3	8 779	25.8	32.9
Lincoln	12 419	75.5	132 600	21.0	13.2	616	23.8	1.5	15 277	0.0	694	4.5	13 973	25.9	33.1
Manitowoc	33 927	75.2	126 700	21.3	13.5	614	25.8	1.4	41 835	-0.2	1 868	4.5	40 799	27.3	34.6
Marathon	53 848	73.2	144 500	21.2	12.7	697	28.3	2.0	73 935	0.6	2 715	3.7	69 834	33.6	28.1
Marinette	18 319	75.6	110 500	21.3	13.7	628	27.9	1.7	20 509	-1.2	1 156	5.6	18 969	24.9	37.7
Marquette	6 332	80.4	144 500	24.7	14.9	731	24.7	2.7	7 570	0.9	397	5.2	6 809	22.5	37.9
Menominee	1 259	69.5	83 500	17.9	11.4	469	25.8	9.2	1 587	-1.1	124	7.8	1 403	25.5	23.7
Milwaukee	381 715	49.9	151 700	24.2	15.0	806	32.3	3.0	479 090	0.3	24 615	5.1	445 174	35.3	21.2
Monroe	17 794	67.5	135 300	22.2	12.5	767	25.2	3.8	22 997	0.6	912	4.0	20 936	28.0	32.2
Oconto	15 486	83.6	150 900	22.7	13.5	606	26.7	1.8	20 548	0.9	937	4.6	19 075	27.8	36.8
Oneida	15 044	83.3	162 600	24.0	14.4	725	30.6	0.9	18 706	0.3	937	5.0	16 557	30.9	25.3
Outagamie	70 505	71.2	155 900	21.2	12.8	735	25.8	1.8	103 735	1.7	3 778	3.6	96 532	33.0	27.4
Ozaukee	34 543	76.7	245 700	21.4	12.9	845	25.5	0.8	48 705	0.9	1 690	3.5	45 522	46.5	17.0
Pepin	2 954	81.7	141 800	24.0	14.4	567	26.8	2.2	4 197	2.1	165	3.9	3 618	31.8	32.0
Pierce	15 177	72.4	191 000	22.9	13.3	750	29.6	1.8	24 695	2.2	1 031	4.2	22 567	31.8	29.5
Polk	17 994	77.0	155 100	25.5	14.5	710	27.7	1.6	24 911	1.2	1 178	4.7	21 085	29.1	33.8
Portage	27 768	68.6	151 700	21.0	11.8	675	29.7	1.7	39 586	-0.1	1 556	3.9	36 371	31.7	24.8
Price	6 700	77.1	116 700	23.3	14.0	573	26.9	2.0	6 961	1.5	307	4.4	6 662	28.4	36.9
Racine	75 183	69.9	164 600	22.7	14.0	783	30.3	1.6	99 649	0.2	5 094	5.1	91 796	32.5	27.7
Richland	7 547	72.9	124 200	23.4	13.4	589	27.9	3.9	9 274	-0.3	357	3.8	8 332	26.0	36.1
Rock	63 845	69.2	131 800	22.6	12.9	744	30.0	2.0	84 378	1.2	3 840	4.6	75 824	30.0	30.5
Rusk	6 239	77.6	105 200	24.9	13.4	646	27.2	2.7	6 993	-0.1	369	5.3	6 462	24.0	38.5
St. Croix	32 459	77.0	205 400	22.0	11.9	883	27.7	2.4	49 807	2.0	1 924	3.9	45 882	36.7	23.9
Sauk	25 331	69.2	166 700	22.8	14.0	731	28.7	2.6	35 120	-0.6	1 296	3.7	32 534	28.3	27.4
Sawyer	7 359	75.0	160 400	24.0	13.2	648	29.2	3.4	7 838	0.2	511	6.5	6 957	30.6	24.6
Shawano	16 957	76.2	131 500	22.6	14.6	615	24.1	1.6	21 375	0.3	916	4.3	20 281	27.5	32.4
Sheboygan	46 701	70.7	148 200	21.4	13.3	658	25.1	1.7	61 961	1.1	2 171	3.5	59 133	29.1	32.0
Taylor	8 756	77.1	127 200	23.5	13.7	556	29.0	2.6	10 951	2.3	471	4.3	10 090	27.7	42.8
Trempealeau	11 796	72.9	140 800	22.3	13.9	647	24.2	2.8	16 706	0.5	634	3.8	15 166	30.3	37.1
Vernon	11 758	79.1	140 900	23.0	13.7	621	27.6	6.3	15 785	1.8	591	3.7	13 450	30.4	31.2
Vilas	10 646	75.8	194 900	27.2	14.7	673	29.0	1.8	10 033	0.2	584	5.8	8 986	31.2	22.3
Walworth	39 648	68.1	189 600	24.6	14.5	812	30.2	2.2	57 780	1.3	2 381	4.1	52 048	30.2	27.8
Washburn	7 141	77.8	143 600	24.2	13.7	654	28.4	1.6	7 972	0.1	413	5.2	6 880	28.2	30.3
Washington	52 897	78.0	215 400	22.6	13.4	829	26.1	0.9	76 703	0.8	2 663	3.5	72 365	35.4	25.6
Waukesha	154 991	76.3	249 300	21.8	13.0	933	27.2	1.3	223 338	0.8	8 008	3.6	209 461	43.6	17.8
Waupaca	21 532	75.2	137 300	22.1	14.0	668	24.5	1.3	27 118	0.2	1 111	4.1	25 703	25.3	37.5
Waushara	9 689	81.1	137 300	23.5	14.1	660	29.4	2.1	11 464	-0.3	596	5.2	10 458	24.8	38.4
Winnebago	68 939	65.1	143 100	21.5	13.0	678	26.5	1.3	93 042	1.7	3 435	3.7	85 970	30.1	27.5
Wood	31 717	74.5	120 100	20.3	12.2	617	28.0	1.3	34 185	-0.8	1 697	5.0	36 445	30.4	30.3
WYOMING	226 865	69.1	194 800	20.7	10.0	789	25.6	2.4	302 335	-0.9	15 960	5.3	293 949	32.5	28.4
Albany	15 662	48.5	216 100	22.0	10.0	727	37.9	2.7	21 083	1.8	667	3.2	20 577	42.0	17.0
Big Horn	4 491	73.9	141 400	21.0	10.0	595	20.2	2.6	5 584	0.1	274	4.9	5 288	32.4	32.1
Campbell	17 510	72.3	212 200	19.0	10.0	936	26.2	3.0	24 650	-4.8	1 751	7.1	26 387	25.0	38.9
Carbon	6 108	69.0	146 200	19.2	10.0	794	20.4	2.8	8 454	-0.1	391	4.6	7 851	28.6	35.5
Converse	5 677	74.5	190 300	19.9	10.0	647	22.2	4.2	7 937	-4.9	489	6.2	7 303	26.6	35.0
Crook	2 958	78.3	205 800	19.1	10.0	743	16.7	3.9	3 766	1.2	171	4.5	3 754	28.3	37.9
Fremont	15 330	70.9	186 500	21.7	10.0	708	24.7	4.5	20 132	-0.9	1 438	7.1	18 736	33.5	25.8

1. Specified owner-occupied units.   2. A value of 10.0 represents 10 percent or less; a value of 50.0 represents 50 percent or more.   3. Specified renter-occupied units.
4. Overcrowded or lacking complete plumbing facilities.   5. Percent of civilian labor force.   6. Civilian employed persons 16 years old and over.

Table B. States and Counties — Nonfarm Employment and Agriculture

	Private nonfarm establishments, employment and payroll, 2015								Agriculture, 2012			
		Employment					Annual payroll		Farms			
											Percent with:	
STATE County	Number of establishments	Total	Health care and social assistance	Manufacturing	Retail trade	Finance and insurance	Professional, scientific, and technical services	Total (mil dol)	Average per employee (dollars)	Number	Fewer than 50 acres	500 acres or more	Farm operators whose principal occupation is farming (percent)
	104	105	106	107	108	109	110	111	112	113	114	115	116
WISCONSIN—Cont'd													
Douglas	1 032	13 650	1 997	1 589	2 253	320	390	518	37 963	364	29.4	5.8	42.0
Dunn	891	13 631	2 380	2 850	1 815	452	383	534	39 174	1 404	24.0	12.0	45.4
Eau Claire	2 719	51 174	11 170	5 276	7 035	2 612	2 209	1 965	38 389	1 313	31.7	4.0	42.3
Florence	110	610	D	122	81	36	8	16	26 525	90	31.1	0.0	38.9
Fond du Lac	2 361	42 920	6 379	8 776	5 966	1 662	1 462	1 687	39 305	1 399	31.9	10.7	59.0
Forest	240	1 731	330	293	256	68	72	63	36 217	127	21.3	9.4	54.3
Grant	1 218	13 678	2 123	2 173	2 547	700	521	463	33 834	2 436	25.6	10.7	53.8
Green	948	13 068	2 054	3 392	1 540	339	323	512	39 154	1 545	42.0	7.4	45.8
Green Lake	463	5 772	1 119	1 251	971	272	67	231	39 944	608	26.8	13.2	48.4
Iowa	572	8 865	1 071	1 139	3 984	191	160	355	40 070	1 588	25.8	9.9	47.2
Iron	205	1 339	311	160	237	32	26	36	27 251	61	34.4	8.2	32.8
Jackson	433	5 843	1 000	620	847	191	101	275	47 049	864	23.0	11.5	49.4
Jefferson	1 937	29 597	4 038	8 871	4 105	652	586	1 154	38 975	1 225	37.7	6.9	46.1
Juneau	554	6 503	1 043	2 285	1 004	168	60	239	36 722	827	29.7	8.1	39.4
Kenosha	3 116	51 852	8 688	6 958	9 866	827	1 275	2 104	40 583	359	51.5	11.1	46.8
Kewaunee	467	5 073	494	1 945	603	152	159	189	37 342	734	27.9	9.4	49.7
La Crosse	3 032	61 378	11 164	7 721	8 757	2 146	1 914	2 355	38 366	748	23.7	10.0	46.9
Lafayette	365	3 110	256	829	410	150	65	100	32 056	1 252	28.9	13.1	57.1
Langlade	546	6 344	981	1 487	1 289	284	132	222	35 015	396	24.2	14.6	56.3
Lincoln	671	8 791	884	2 554	1 375	936	107	336	38 207	449	28.1	6.2	48.8
Manitowoc	1 776	29 976	4 410	10 413	3 650	750	554	1 229	40 991	1 224	39.1	7.9	47.7
Marathon	3 273	64 477	9 922	17 087	9 960	3 708	1 953	2 664	41 315	2 266	23.2	7.5	55.0
Marinette	1 053	15 988	2 698	6 164	2 170	415	243	610	38 166	535	31.2	11.8	51.6
Marquette	289	3 740	329	1 252	326	45	80	122	32 549	478	28.0	9.2	52.1
Menominee	27	867	D	D	38	NA	144	18	20 595	5	60.0	0.0	0.0
Milwaukee	19 557	452 727	91 407	46 309	43 772	34 670	22 459	23 197	51 239	82	76.8	2.4	59.8
Monroe	961	15 434	2 438	3 718	1 821	419	489	614	39 754	1 926	25.7	6.1	44.3
Oconto	788	6 953	1 461	2 117	947	170	141	226	32 555	929	35.1	9.1	48.1
Oneida	1 350	13 906	2 586	1 355	4 044	322	342	503	36 149	150	43.3	9.3	28.0
Outagamie	5 013	98 890	12 753	17 562	12 726	5 596	3 886	4 267	43 153	1 170	38.7	10.7	56.0
Ozaukee	2 776	39 703	5 891	9 129	4 896	2 314	2 485	1 722	43 382	416	38.5	7.0	53.4
Pepin	223	1 797	305	152	241	98	42	68	37 721	459	22.9	10.0	47.3
Pierce	801	7 079	1 033	1 374	973	291	175	226	31 985	1 259	31.6	7.8	52.2
Polk	1 121	12 911	2 548	4 130	1 853	266	297	430	33 310	1 313	30.1	8.1	47.8
Portage	1 634	29 800	3 229	4 078	3 922	4 884	989	1 184	39 732	969	27.1	11.8	51.2
Price	414	4 634	836	1 937	564	145	92	174	37 496	472	26.1	7.8	47.2
Racine	4 004	69 285	11 236	16 579	9 298	2 144	1 955	3 149	45 445	575	51.0	8.2	45.6
Richland	369	4 846	916	1 554	879	160	55	163	33 595	1 260	27.9	6.7	44.4
Rock	3 275	56 646	9 055	9 453	8 900	1 343	1 939	2 373	41 895	1 509	44.1	10.3	50.0
Rusk	322	4 391	776	1 706	620	110	41	145	32 922	529	16.8	10.0	62.9
St. Croix	2 203	29 343	4 187	6 003	4 419	881	1 432	1 130	38 507	1 417	39.0	8.0	41.6
Sauk	1 783	30 785	3 736	6 304	4 067	965	1 075	1 142	37 080	1 665	29.1	8.2	51.2
Sawyer	655	4 985	817	627	984	186	147	167	33 546	172	26.7	11.0	47.1
Shawano	867	10 285	1 529	2 252	1 520	287	201	346	33 624	1 278	26.7	8.1	54.4
Sheboygan	2 651	54 832	6 543	17 664	6 113	2 060	1 255	2 351	42 868	986	42.4	10.1	52.7
Taylor	476	7 166	937	2 555	895	314	97	256	35 675	967	25.9	8.8	52.7
Trempealeau	625	12 706	947	7 110	1 033	307	224	493	38 800	1 436	26.5	9.5	48.7
Vernon	630	7 087	1 796	933	1 159	269	168	236	33 337	2 228	31.7	4.2	49.2
Vilas	929	5 645	584	308	1 068	184	116	169	30 005	47	59.6	6.4	40.4
Walworth	2 654	35 798	3 978	9 066	4 723	781	1 042	1 283	35 833	870	45.3	11.1	51.8
Washburn	513	4 533	1 040	1 162	723	118	168	134	29 601	405	27.4	7.4	39.8
Washington	3 164	50 881	6 124	14 166	7 205	2 015	1 858	2 159	42 424	712	43.3	8.6	51.4
Waukesha	12 473	232 600	27 777	42 834	24 821	13 236	13 745	11 964	51 437	557	54.0	7.7	51.2
Waupaca	1 203	16 398	2 885	5 849	2 367	486	278	592	36 096	1 145	30.0	7.9	49.8
Waushara	468	4 608	746	912	691	110	164	138	29 883	592	27.2	9.6	44.6
Winnebago	3 499	82 979	12 118	21 930	8 607	3 346	2 882	4 160	50 129	1 117	48.5	6.0	39.2
Wood	1 770	35 358	9 210	6 138	3 992	1 365	1 001	1 549	43 811	1 067	27.8	9.3	56.7
WYOMING	21 040	219 881	32 521	9 904	32 372	6 677	10 113	10 094	45 907	11 736	28.8	36.3	49.8
Albany	1 026	9 892	2 043	359	1 760	458	795	324	32 703	448	26.8	45.5	40.4
Big Horn	315	2 722	366	221	384	95	53	113	41 639	627	32.1	26.6	54.4
Campbell	1 525	22 709	1 616	625	2 853	376	776	1 373	60 477	744	30.4	44.9	36.4
Carbon	533	4 397	553	D	872	127	102	194	44 045	319	16.3	59.9	60.2
Converse	459	5 193	671	250	484	119	134	271	52 257	410	18.3	51.7	57.8
Crook	229	1 561	203	136	158	62	30	73	46 791	482	10.4	58.5	61.8
Fremont	1 333	11 234	1 846	321	2 081	302	500	428	38 080	1 363	37.0	20.4	55.0

Table B. States and Counties — **Agriculture**

STATE County	Land in farms Acreage (1,000)	Percent change, 2007–2012	Acres Average size of farm	Total irrigated (1,000)	Total cropland (1,000)	Value of land and buildings (dollars) Average per farm	Average per acre	Value of machinery and equipment, average per farm (dollars)	Value of products sold Total (mil dol)	Average per farm (dollars)	Percent from: Crops	Live-stock and poultry products	Percent of farms with sales of: $10,000 or more	$100,000 or more	Government payments Total ($1,000)	Percent of farms
	117	118	119	120	121	122	123	124	125	126	127	128	129	130	131	132
WISCONSIN—Cont'd																
Douglas	71	-2.9	194	0.1	29.1	336 918	1 738	55 228	7.8	21 434	52.1	48.0	25.0	5.5	74	4.9
Dunn	372	-2.7	265	36.3	252.5	879 304	3 316	141 909	263.2	187 452	48.9	51.1	52.4	23.5	4 915	59.5
Eau Claire	204	-0.8	155	3.1	128.8	465 939	3 003	79 664	113.3	86 287	49.6	50.4	43.0	15.2	3 239	52.9
Florence	13	-33.9	149	0.0	4.9	463 544	3 115	43 489	1.0	11 067	D	D	24.4	1.1	28	26.7
Fond du Lac	316	-6.0	226	2.1	262.1	1 128 100	5 001	182 828	412.3	294 743	26.9	73.1	62.2	37.8	7 648	74.2
Forest	30	-10.5	238	D	10.3	490 488	2 059	82 496	2.9	22 449	62.0	38.0	28.3	3.1	33	15.7
Grant	588	-3.8	241	1.3	361.3	1 004 051	4 163	147 729	404.8	166 171	31.9	68.1	58.2	31.1	11 713	70.4
Green	302	-1.5	196	3.4	238.6	855 977	4 375	130 524	200.3	129 669	36.3	63.7	47.4	25.6	6 293	61.5
Green Lake	155	8.3	254	4.6	119.9	1 155 334	4 544	166 630	102.5	168 615	59.6	40.4	58.7	26.5	1 945	55.6
Iowa	351	-3.9	221	4.6	198.2	881 751	3 991	116 704	195.3	123 008	29.9	70.1	47.4	22.0	7 074	74.4
Iron	10	1.0	167	0.2	4.9	386 016	2 307	91 934	5.6	91 967	D	D	24.6	8.2	63	13.1
Jackson	240	0.4	278	7.2	139.3	859 022	3 093	155 612	169.6	196 263	53.2	46.8	54.5	27.0	3 186	60.1
Jefferson	228	-6.7	186	9.5	181.8	964 365	5 184	134 604	256.1	209 024	42.4	57.6	53.2	22.7	4 367	68.7
Juneau	180	-0.6	218	7.4	108.8	670 272	3 079	129 543	124.8	150 871	62.5	37.5	45.2	17.0	2 210	56.5
Kenosha	77	-9.1	213	0.2	68.1	1 075 507	5 038	145 295	68.9	191 827	70.1	29.9	51.3	28.4	1 592	46.8
Kewaunee	177	0.7	241	0.2	144.7	1 047 736	4 351	177 185	276.6	376 865	21.3	78.7	59.3	34.3	4 137	72.6
La Crosse	159	-4.0	212	1.0	86.9	709 759	3 345	118 472	86.5	115 671	44.7	55.3	53.5	21.4	2 565	62.7
Lafayette	369	7.6	294	0.2	276.1	1 440 604	4 895	191 424	287.3	229 493	34.4	65.6	62.1	35.8	8 268	73.6
Langlade	114	-7.3	288	19.7	73.1	796 227	2 769	178 447	103.9	262 381	58.4	41.6	51.8	28.0	1 114	48.0
Lincoln	77	-11.4	171	0.2	38.2	422 924	2 471	75 920	29.9	66 588	33.6	66.3	41.0	10.9	415	26.9
Manitowoc	231	-7.1	189	1.1	186.9	995 194	5 279	142 426	343.8	280 845	21.8	78.2	52.9	29.5	5 698	64.4
Marathon	479	-2.4	211	6.2	320.1	616 429	2 916	136 874	391.1	172 605	24.8	75.2	61.9	32.7	6 615	48.5
Marinette	132	-8.5	247	2.8	84.7	749 350	3 035	124 665	101.4	189 608	28.7	71.3	44.5	22.2	1 557	41.7
Marquette	120	-11.6	251	8.5	84.2	862 079	3 429	127 736	69.7	145 774	54.9	45.1	43.1	15.7	1 410	45.6
Menominee	1	76.4	112	0.0	0.4	144 200	1 285	29 200	0.0	4 200	0.0	100.0	0.0	0.0	D	20.0
Milwaukee	5	-16.4	56	0.1	3.5	526 354	9 459	56 915	7.6	92 878	99.6	0.4	57.3	19.5	64	19.5
Monroe	338	-3.8	175	4.3	173.2	562 429	3 206	98 238	202.0	104 903	45.4	54.6	50.4	17.2	4 423	50.9
Oconto	189	-8.0	204	1.2	141.0	667 081	3 272	114 002	165.9	178 589	39.2	60.8	48.2	26.5	2 856	54.6
Oneida	35	-10.8	233	3.0	12.1	975 653	4 190	86 700	20.2	134 973	84.8	15.2	30.7	12.7	D	12.0
Outagamie	251	1.3	214	0.4	210.1	1 129 579	5 271	174 059	302.2	258 319	34.9	65.1	60.2	37.2	5 994	65.0
Ozaukee	65	-8.1	156	0.3	51.7	876 038	5 608	110 024	64.7	155 505	37.4	62.6	55.5	25.7	1 218	51.0
Pepin	104	-4.4	226	3.6	63.0	741 634	3 286	130 987	71.7	156 288	38.8	61.2	58.4	27.5	1 966	69.7
Pierce	246	-9.3	195	0.5	166.3	773 024	3 957	130 292	178.7	141 902	52.8	47.2	50.8	25.3	4 639	62.0
Polk	256	-11.4	195	1.5	159.9	555 723	2 851	93 011	167.0	127 214	40.5	59.5	42.3	18.3	3 252	51.0
Portage	279	-1.0	288	92.5	201.4	946 737	3 292	203 829	295.1	304 528	71.8	28.2	53.3	23.3	2 782	52.0
Price	92	-9.9	196	D	39.4	371 648	1 901	65 871	31.6	66 892	22.8	77.2	38.3	10.6	537	25.0
Racine	110	-8.7	191	1.9	92.6	1 042 289	5 450	127 732	94.8	164 887	77.6	22.4	50.3	21.7	1 972	50.6
Richland	228	-10.2	181	1.7	111.8	544 504	3 011	83 011	115.5	91 628	28.2	71.8	41.9	14.6	2 969	63.1
Rock	354	2.7	234	16.2	303.7	1 294 782	5 523	154 109	274.4	181 858	60.4	39.6	49.8	23.5	7 892	68.2
Rusk	134	-16.8	253	0.1	70.1	514 170	2 036	104 786	64.2	121 367	28.4	71.6	58.6	24.8	1 236	47.6
St. Croix	268	-13.2	189	8.3	196.1	793 838	4 202	115 975	214.3	151 251	50.1	49.9	49.4	20.5	4 492	59.6
Sauk	333	-7.3	200	19.7	209.8	775 477	3 881	132 189	207.1	124 356	34.4	65.6	49.4	22.3	5 597	57.4
Sawyer	44	-7.5	253	1.0	21.9	580 750	2 293	124 134	25.3	147 145	40.0	60.0	48.3	20.3	552	32.0
Shawano	261	-3.9	204	0.3	183.5	734 011	3 592	133 984	254.1	198 858	26.0	74.0	61.4	33.6	4 470	61.8
Sheboygan	190	-0.8	193	0.2	155.9	1 011 178	5 243	162 747	242.1	245 507	27.1	72.9	59.2	29.8	3 790	51.4
Taylor	217	-10.7	224	0.1	120.0	491 262	2 189	102 087	136.5	141 155	24.7	75.3	51.3	26.1	2 265	43.2
Trempealeau	323	-5.3	225	7.9	197.8	719 451	3 197	124 753	268.9	187 243	32.6	67.4	52.3	24.4	4 772	67.7
Vernon	346	-3.1	155	0.5	181.5	512 496	3 301	76 915	221.4	99 359	32.2	67.8	52.4	16.3	3 703	46.0
Vilas	7	-30.8	146	1.0	2.8	783 574	5 352	94 830	10.2	216 894	95.6	4.4	40.4	17.0	42	21.3
Walworth	188	-13.7	216	2.8	163.9	1 323 506	6 134	154 289	168.6	193 830	46.9	53.1	53.8	23.8	4 539	60.2
Washburn	87	-14.2	216	0.8	38.2	535 677	2 483	81 933	32.5	80 294	48.1	51.9	36.0	12.3	494	33.0
Washington	133	2.8	187	0.5	107.3	1 093 001	5 832	165 548	122.7	172 313	39.9	60.1	55.3	25.8	2 609	48.0
Waukesha	92	6.5	166	1.3	75.6	1 080 562	6 527	104 210	55.1	98 860	75.9	24.1	40.6	16.9	1 587	33.9
Waupaca	215	-8.1	188	7.0	141.5	722 332	3 841	120 088	160.0	139 767	31.6	68.4	50.8	22.7	4 066	53.5
Waushara	145	-2.5	245	39.9	108.7	848 429	3 459	129 704	134.1	226 603	77.6	22.4	50.7	19.4	1 156	40.7
Winnebago	156	-5.2	139	0.4	126.2	585 332	4 204	97 747	126.6	113 315	41.3	58.7	41.5	20.1	3 245	54.3
Wood	223	0.3	209	6.2	132.9	656 817	3 147	127 231	160.3	150 256	53.2	46.8	59.0	26.1	2 887	48.2
WYOMING	30 364	0.6	2 587	1 435.7	2 418.9	1 759 200	680	114 212	1 689.4	143 952	26.0	74.0	48.8	23.5	28 146	23.9
Albany	1 964	5.8	4 385	94.4	120.4	2 466 013	562	99 815	93.4	208 509	8.6	91.4	48.0	23.2	473	8.5
Big Horn	303	-30.9	483	108.7	99.2	736 719	1 527	116 603	88.8	141 684	59.7	40.3	48.5	23.0	900	32.7
Campbell	2 878	22.7	3 868	1.8	140.7	2 239 153	579	94 640	67.2	90 269	5.3	94.7	41.4	18.7	2 305	20.6
Carbon	2 374	9.3	7 442	165.5	126.4	4 187 091	563	144 317	78.6	246 326	14.3	85.7	56.4	37.0	362	6.0
Converse	2 447	3.4	5 969	31.9	60.9	2 256 332	378	125 300	48.6	118 507	12.7	87.3	57.1	27.3	1 303	15.9
Crook	1 587	1.1	3 292	7.8	151.3	2 920 595	887	130 118	67.1	139 137	8.6	91.4	57.3	26.8	1 205	43.2
Fremont	1 710	-5.0	1 255	157.1	168.0	1 091 768	870	103 492	102.5	75 189	49.8	50.2	45.3	21.4	2 052	17.2

Table B. States and Counties — Water Use, Wholesale Trade, Retail Trade, and Real Estate

STATE County	Water use, 2010 Total water withdrawn (mil gal/day)	Gallons withdrawn per person per day	Wholesale trade,[1] 2012 Number of establishments	Number of employees	Sales (mil dol)	Annual payroll (mil dol)	Retail trade,[2] 2012 Number of establishments	Number of employees	Sales (mil dol)	Annual payroll (mil dol)	Real estate and rental and leasing,[2] 2012 Number of establishments	Number of employees	Receipts (mil dol)	Annual payroll (mil dol)
	133	134	135	136	137	138	139	140	141	142	143	144	145	146
WISCONSIN—Cont'd														
Douglas	7.0	159	44	701	840.6	33.1	150	1 993	577.7	48.7	37	110	14.9	2.5
Dunn	19.2	437	36	D	D	D	113	1 755	440.6	35.2	29	D	D	D
Eau Claire	13.9	141	95	1 601	1 013.6	69.6	402	6 995	1 658.9	143.1	107	564	77.4	16.0
Florence	0.2	43	5	D	D	D	11	61	19.9	1.2	2	D	D	D
Fond du Lac	14.4	142	111	1 541	1 372.0	74.4	354	5 462	1 402.4	130.0	64	235	37.7	6.0
Forest	0.8	89	4	D	D	D	33	276	72.2	5.3	5	13	0.8	0.2
Grant	136.9	2 673	61	481	213.7	17.9	191	2 379	657.0	51.2	49	118	16.7	3.8
Green	7.5	203	41	699	269.3	29.2	150	2 325	1 003.2	71.1	25	D	D	D
Green Lake	11.8	620	14	87	77.4	4.4	71	952	253.1	21.9	13	45	3.9	0.8
Iowa	7.8	330	25	280	252.3	13.7	89	3 980	1 426.1	151.6	9	D	D	D
Iron	2.1	357	9	91	21.3	2.3	30	232	54.3	4.9	8	D	D	D
Jackson	18.0	882	15	174	97.9	5.6	66	784	327.5	16.8	7	15	1.6	0.2
Jefferson	17.3	207	66	1 356	793.8	55.6	273	3 891	911.0	77.6	60	219	33.6	6.6
Juneau	19.1	718	17	205	110.5	5.8	92	1 030	335.5	20.9	11	21	6.8	0.4
Kenosha	30.2	181	101	1 639	1 779.7	86.5	491	8 523	2 134.1	213.6	115	460	73.0	11.2
Kewaunee	550.9	26 778	12	151	75.3	5.0	65	561	146.3	11.7	7	7	0.8	0.2
La Crosse	34.9	304	121	2 592	6 131.4	115.3	421	8 393	1 891.1	173.4	121	791	99.3	20.6
Lafayette	3.4	201	20	260	187.3	9.4	50	433	119.5	8.0	6	D	D	D
Langlade	22.3	1 115	26	352	450.3	17.7	89	1 310	428.7	31.0	13	32	3.3	0.6
Lincoln	14.1	491	21	328	143.7	13.0	111	1 222	308.7	26.0	14	68	7.3	2.1
Manitowoc	787.1	9 664	68	837	497.0	38.1	254	3 473	848.6	76.0	43	D	D	D
Marathon	126.8	946	180	2 955	1 276.6	126.2	472	9 545	2 572.4	208.5	83	412	79.2	11.9
Marinette	15.5	370	22	D	D	D	181	2 109	532.5	43.8	17	D	D	D
Marquette	6.4	414	8	D	D	D	35	319	70.9	5.2	8	D	D	D
Menominee	0.5	121	NA	NA	NA	NA	5	29	6.6	0.4	NA	NA	NA	NA
Milwaukee	1 753.0	1 850	848	17 873	12 445.3	1 263.2	2 724	41 381	10 427.9	945.7	795	5 063	1 085.5	208.1
Monroe	44.0	984	36	538	510.0	28.7	150	1 865	575.3	40.8	31	106	10.0	2.9
Oconto	6.4	170	23	143	54.9	5.4	100	872	261.1	19.8	23	71	4.9	1.2
Oneida	17.2	479	29	359	171.1	17.6	221	3 450	959.5	84.1	59	178	26.6	4.5
Outagamie	67.2	380	273	4 591	7 397.7	236.8	729	12 738	3 277.8	277.5	138	859	160.7	27.8
Ozaukee	473.9	5 485	150	1 479	1 677.6	75.9	303	4 642	1 228.0	108.0	94	312	59.5	10.0
Pepin	3.2	432	12	154	145.0	6.5	41	246	80.2	6.1	3	3	1.8	0.2
Pierce	5.7	139	18	D	D	D	102	984	256.5	19.3	23	D	D	D
Polk	9.6	218	37	465	183.9	20.1	165	1 889	452.0	38.6	36	59	7.8	1.2
Portage	79.6	1 137	70	D	D	D	230	3 758	933.9	79.2	45	188	21.4	4.3
Price	15.4	1 085	19	122	63.5	6.6	73	536	126.4	11.4	11	25	2.8	0.6
Racine	28.6	146	170	2 243	1 702.5	118.6	591	8 542	2 182.0	181.6	100	327	58.9	9.7
Richland	3.8	213	13	74	50.3	2.3	66	878	200.3	17.1	12	37	6.8	1.1
Rock	28.3	176	149	3 035	3 225.1	155.1	502	8 396	2 215.2	208.2	101	400	148.1	18.7
Rusk	3.6	241	6	101	18.9	3.6	52	595	145.3	12.0	5	11	0.6	0.2
St. Croix	17.3	205	99	1 072	1 907.3	55.0	263	3 935	1 107.7	90.4	64	D	D	D
Sauk	16.4	264	54	1 341	929.1	66.9	322	3 971	990.8	84.9	59	255	45.0	9.5
Sawyer	4.3	258	14	159	61.0	5.7	103	946	238.1	22.3	27	63	8.7	1.3
Shawano	12.2	291	38	1 219	498.6	54.1	122	1 441	397.1	30.9	13	43	5.0	1.0
Sheboygan	328.5	2 844	86	1 002	593.9	47.9	395	6 124	1 400.0	133.5	73	298	58.2	10.4
Taylor	2.5	123	9	82	36.0	3.2	76	838	238.3	17.1	9	26	3.4	0.4
Trempealeau	7.6	262	32	253	163.6	9.8	105	1 163	322.8	26.2	7	D	D	D
Vernon	101.9	3 421	18	D	D	D	98	1 138	320.4	25.7	18	29	2.2	0.5
Vilas	6.5	305	11	123	68.3	4.8	151	989	269.1	23.0	22	70	7.4	1.6
Walworth	13.0	127	107	1 395	1 544.6	67.7	358	4 521	1 234.4	106.2	88	350	54.8	10.4
Washburn	4.4	277	10	62	17.2	2.4	78	828	196.0	16.4	18	39	4.2	0.9
Washington	13.3	101	167	2 850	2 053.3	159.7	369	7 039	1 813.6	152.1	75	223	35.6	6.4
Waukesha	40.1	103	816	12 343	6 986.1	744.7	1 299	24 751	6 616.8	600.8	390	3 505	456.2	119.2
Waupaca	11.1	211	35	429	286.6	14.2	191	2 247	541.6	50.7	33	150	15.6	3.3
Waushara	40.3	1 643	19	154	100.6	6.9	73	706	219.5	13.9	11	19	2.6	0.5
Winnebago	35.3	211	136	D	D	D	473	7 892	2 064.9	174.5	113	576	219.2	19.9
Wood	174.4	2 333	59	913	626.2	46.6	279	4 815	1 101.7	105.6	59	210	37.8	4.6
WYOMING	4 701.5	8 342	709	7 003	5 597.9	398.7	2 681	30 088	9 446.0	796.0	1 076	4 546	1 259.1	215.6
Albany	189.3	5 215	23	115	132.8	4.6	141	1 729	479.6	36.8	53	147	22.5	3.2
Big Horn	392.8	33 664	10	57	43.7	2.3	47	403	90.7	8.4	9	15	2.1	0.4
Campbell	121.4	2 632	76	1 403	758.3	81.2	184	2 533	896.0	74.8	76	304	86.9	11.5
Carbon	375.7	23 651	4	D	D	D	86	683	305.5	17.3	25	83	25.0	2.5
Converse	156.1	11 284	9	45	19.3	1.9	57	486	141.5	9.6	21	55	6.1	0.9
Crook	50.5	7 124	8	D	D	D	26	160	39.6	3.4	8	D	D	D
Fremont	510.0	12 711	42	D	D	D	165	2 096	581.8	53.8	71	459	130.6	27.0

1. Merchant wholesalers, except manufacturers' sales branches and offices. 2. Employer establishments.

Table B. States and Counties — **Professional Services, Manufacturing, and Accommodation and Food Services**

STATE County	Professional, scientific, and technical services, 2012				Manufacturing, 2012				Accommodation and food services, 2012			
	Number of establishments	Number of employees	Receipts (mil dol)	Annual payroll (mil dol)	Number of establishments	Number of employees	Receipts (mil dol)	Annual payroll (mil dol)	Number of establishments	Number of employees	Sales (mil dol)	Annual payroll (mil dol)
	147	148	149	150	151	152	153	154	155	156	157	158
WISCONSIN—Cont'd												
Douglas	72	343	37.1	15.0	46	1 222	D	78.5	157	1 906	72.1	19.7
Dunn	66	388	38.5	16.9	58	2 369	1 528.6	118.7	89	1 222	42.9	11.9
Eau Claire	179	1 706	203.6	84.9	84	4 938	1 690.9	207.0	275	5 130	206.6	58.5
Florence	7	11	0.5	0.2	9	112	D	3.8	26	154	6.4	1.4
Fond du Lac	154	1 337	154.4	76.3	144	9 140	3 989.9	407.6	240	3 872	140.8	39.8
Forest	10	91	11.2	3.5	19	223	D	7.6	36	D	D	D
Grant	64	518	59.4	26.7	67	2 315	965.2	101.1	122	1 205	47.1	11.7
Green	57	280	73.7	13.7	82	2 934	1 420.7	131.1	84	966	37.9	10.2
Green Lake	22	76	6.8	2.3	37	1 335	390.1	53.5	50	538	21.9	7.5
Iowa	39	128	12.4	4.8	37	846	1 335.1	32.8	51	525	23.3	6.8
Iron	8	28	2.5	0.8	16	191	D	6.3	54	D	D	D
Jackson	22	93	6.0	2.5	29	921	499.5	47.3	59	661	27.9	7.1
Jefferson	129	672	92.1	24.4	152	8 385	3 842.9	415.5	186	2 126	88.3	22.0
Juneau	17	51	4.3	1.7	50	2 136	719.2	92.2	76	604	26.8	6.7
Kenosha	223	1 212	123.1	50.9	168	5 704	2 370.3	260.6	362	5 510	237.8	66.8
Kewaunee	27	135	13.2	5.4	37	1 771	466.7	81.3	50	518	15.4	4.2
La Crosse	250	1 855	177.7	85.7	157	6 805	1 941.7	266.0	330	6 383	243.7	72.1
Lafayette	16	55	6.2	2.0	23	681	270.2	22.8	36	D	D	D
Langlade	22	110	6.5	4.6	47	1 494	330.2	57.0	59	583	26.1	7.0
Lincoln	32	111	7.3	3.4	50	2 329	772.4	103.1	90	681	27.6	7.0
Manitowoc	103	646	92.8	23.7	179	9 968	3 138.3	457.1	174	2 443	87.7	24.9
Marathon	225	1 943	284.9	113.9	238	14 472	4 306.0	654.1	305	4 458	180.7	51.8
Marinette	49	243	22.8	11.0	90	6 302	1 889.6	300.4	161	1 398	61.1	15.5
Marquette	17	54	6.2	1.5	21	1 325	D	53.5	40	282	13.4	3.0
Menominee	3	D	D	D	NA	NA	NA	NA	3	D	D	D
Milwaukee	1 955	23 788	3 849.6	1 598.9	991	48 963	19 176.2	2 974.2	1 900	36 303	1 831.0	496.0
Monroe	72	545	48.6	19.5	59	3 937	1 364.2	163.2	112	1 540	60.0	16.6
Oconto	47	159	14.4	5.2	56	1 897	522.3	72.7	98	669	29.1	7.2
Oneida	81	363	51.2	12.4	46	1 397	330.5	69.2	186	1 503	82.0	22.2
Outagamie	385	3 279	499.0	179.5	357	17 963	7 208.5	888.2	453	8 198	330.0	91.7
Ozaukee	336	2 169	353.2	112.6	206	8 663	2 762.9	473.0	207	3 307	134.8	38.9
Pepin	15	43	4.9	1.6	13	140	D	5.4	28	D	D	D
Pierce	66	177	22.6	7.2	47	1 250	516.5	57.4	99	994	38.2	10.3
Polk	84	352	46.2	12.6	105	3 117	995.3	133.7	118	1 108	42.2	11.0
Portage	100	892	84.9	35.0	75	3 912	1 383.0	165.0	204	2 827	112.4	31.4
Price	20	83	5.2	2.0	44	1 973	502.0	85.5	48	319	11.8	3.1
Racine	310	1 967	234.8	91.7	325	15 444	8 100.1	844.4	382	5 974	251.7	70.5
Richland	18	60	3.6	1.3	30	1 545	682.1	61.8	29	333	11.3	2.9
Rock	208	1 172	129.3	49.5	224	8 850	4 474.2	421.3	363	5 355	236.2	63.7
Rusk	12	59	3.3	1.2	27	1 579	423.5	48.3	29	210	8.9	2.2
St. Croix	221	1 273	228.3	68.9	161	5 838	1 307.7	269.4	184	2 922	122.9	33.9
Sauk	120	982	118.6	49.3	94	5 001	1 669.5	223.1	238	7 576	542.6	133.3
Sawyer	41	136	21.1	5.1	46	561	256.7	27.1	115	1 022	67.2	19.5
Shawano	36	D	D	D	66	D	633.2	84.7	115	D	D	D
Sheboygan	179	1 240	207.9	65.8	230	16 716	7 346.2	825.1	269	4 151	188.8	53.4
Taylor	18	116	10.2	3.8	45	2 483	817.6	85.0	43	495	13.0	5.1
Trempealeau	38	195	15.3	5.9	58	6 418	1 786.7	248.4	81	649	25.4	6.6
Vernon	42	170	11.0	4.6	33	981	275.8	40.7	53	626	19.5	5.8
Vilas	37	91	13.8	3.0	28	257	39.0	8.7	207	1 941	126.0	34.1
Walworth	192	1 000	135.9	43.3	207	7 974	2 705.8	384.6	298	6 109	288.1	81.2
Washburn	28	193	25.2	8.0	29	969	198.9	28.4	81	505	25.0	6.7
Washington	222	1 643	278.9	95.9	318	13 257	3 740.7	676.5	248	4 147	165.4	43.7
Waukesha	1 328	13 383	2 265.1	822.6	950	43 232	15 221.2	2 481.1	824	16 092	725.2	202.0
Waupaca	62	309	29.2	10.8	89	5 784	2 587.2	277.4	151	1 621	64.5	17.6
Waushara	17	153	8.9	3.4	27	873	369.5	33.4	68	582	24.8	6.1
Winnebago	247	2 575	514.5	134.8	300	23 892	11 476.5	1 321.6	367	5 963	234.6	65.3
Wood	89	589	69.7	25.6	117	5 757	2 482.4	285.9	179	1 972	78.6	21.2
WYOMING	2 141	9 134	1 297.4	467.0	553	10 094	10 783.8	630.6	1 799	27 580	1 644.8	468.7
Albany	116	832	115.7	41.0	31	341	D	16.1	113	2 074	79.6	23.3
Big Horn	23	67	6.9	2.2	16	185	D	8.5	27	D	D	D
Campbell	113	757	97.8	37.2	35	632	267.8	38.4	105	1 678	95.1	26.6
Carbon	36	126	14.5	4.5	9	390	D	D	83	718	47.7	13.2
Converse	32	108	13.0	5.0	16	129	D	7.1	45	D	D	D
Crook	14	30	4.0	1.1	7	139	D	5.4	27	156	8.5	1.9
Fremont	129	494	66.2	25.4	35	246	57.0	10.4	128	1 373	66.1	18.5

1. Establishment subject to federal tax.

STATE County	Health care and social assistance, 2012				Other services, 2012				Nonemployer businesses, 2015		Value of residential construction authorized by building permits, 2016	
	Number of establishments	Number of employees	Receipts (mil dol)	Annual payroll (mil dol)	Number of establishments	Number of employees	Receipts (mil dol)	Annual payroll (mil dol)	Number	Receipts (mil dol)	New Construction ($1,000)	Number of housing units
	159	160	161	162	163	164	165	166	167	168	169	170
WISCONSIN—Cont'd												
Douglas	114	2 066	129.1	51.7	77	590	36.4	12.2	2 139	93.7	17 580	113
Dunn	92	2 779	170.5	76.9	71	301	23.1	7.1	2 541	116.1	19 591	122
Eau Claire	364	11 109	1 261.7	552.5	201	1 283	103.5	29.9	5 917	308.9	94 839	525
Florence	3	D	D	D	7	11	1.6	0.3	305	11.2	2 044	17
Fond du Lac	281	5 764	758.8	248.8	191	1 245	114.4	31.3	4 931	234.3	47 244	365
Forest	17	294	10.6	5.9	14	25	2.8	0.8	709	35.3	3 081	30
Grant	113	2 435	145.0	65.9	114	399	45.3	9.6	3 298	147.8	17 990	93
Green	71	2 048	206.9	91.7	77	286	27.5	6.7	2 496	115.6	14 262	67
Green Lake	48	1 111	101.2	44.7	33	108	8.8	3.1	1 346	63.3	13 691	44
Iowa	53	1 116	83.5	36.3	36	117	12.1	2.8	1 933	81.9	9 920	49
Iron	13	321	12.6	7.3	8	D	D	D	504	21.5	5 013	24
Jackson	48	1 012	82.3	37.1	27	D	D	D	1 124	49.2	8 194	45
Jefferson	229	4 021	395.0	134.6	139	607	53.3	15.0	4 860	233.8	45 227	209
Juneau	52	1 138	105.4	43.9	48	184	24.0	5.5	1 445	67.5	19 315	89
Kenosha	415	8 620	831.7	339.9	241	1 485	101.2	31.0	8 366	369.9	67 429	528
Kewaunee	37	495	21.2	10.9	28	61	7.4	1.4	1 232	50.0	7 782	37
La Crosse	282	11 223	1 472.4	520.9	233	1 679	148.1	44.8	6 251	273.8	58 435	256
Lafayette	23	232	19.5	6.2	29	D	D	D	1 317	66.6	2 379	13
Langlade	45	984	114.5	40.4	47	164	13.1	4.1	1 270	53.3	7 392	50
Lincoln	60	D	D	D	59	242	18.3	5.1	1 748	75.5	13 864	102
Manitowoc	175	4 731	382.0	176.8	130	553	54.3	12.0	3 936	171.1	26 318	154
Marathon	367	10 123	1 133.0	459.7	221	1 313	138.5	37.7	7 863	385.9	59 611	245
Marinette	117	2 875	251.2	109.4	77	322	27.1	7.6	2 274	102.8	15 963	101
Marquette	24	273	10.0	4.9	28	D	D	D	1 016	41.3	5 041	29
Menominee	1	D	D	D	3	15	1.0	0.4	92	3.5	3 028	11
Milwaukee	2 847	86 674	9 866.4	3 872.0	1 476	11 203	1 438.2	368.4	47 560	2 011.1	249 316	1 721
Monroe	83	2 640	255.6	138.7	73	427	28.9	8.7	2 600	121.8	23 138	134
Oconto	71	1 578	111.1	46.5	44	125	12.0	2.9	2 259	107.8	31 876	149
Oneida	139	2 895	335.8	115.0	98	387	32.7	8.9	2 919	117.6	42 881	243
Outagamie	464	11 090	1 289.6	521.0	361	2 827	247.8	73.7	9 860	498.6	116 157	505
Ozaukee	289	5 256	623.2	242.1	183	1 178	81.0	27.0	6 823	374.1	101 128	443
Pepin	15	286	26.7	9.3	18	D	D	D	558	25.4	5 751	26
Pierce	63	909	53.8	23.5	60	203	20.9	4.6	2 658	112.9	29 534	140
Polk	99	2 477	227.0	88.9	79	246	18.9	5.3	3 267	129.0	28 416	152
Portage	154	3 797	385.8	155.9	119	759	72.6	19.6	3 762	173.2	36 728	198
Price	43	890	55.9	26.2	29	81	6.2	1.8	1 128	42.7	8 002	54
Racine	459	10 588	764.4	335.7	317	1 839	140.4	44.5	9 535	395.1	70 010	358
Richland	48	898	71.3	31.4	25	D	D	D	1 223	58.3	4 853	32
Rock	320	9 667	1 120.9	438.4	268	1 417	105.0	30.8	7 974	342.7	49 421	257
Rusk	34	780	62.4	27.9	20	D	D	D	1 017	42.7	11 706	55
St. Croix	189	4 427	353.4	151.4	148	696	56.8	15.7	6 318	287.4	93 510	429
Sauk	144	3 910	340.6	147.5	129	541	50.6	16.3	4 438	216.5	46 401	225
Sawyer	39	832	71.5	28.7	40	168	15.1	3.9	1 570	67.3	23 262	107
Shawano	79	D	D	D	61	233	20.2	5.4	2 420	114.0	13 801	63
Sheboygan	299	6 483	597.2	247.8	202	992	67.4	19.5	5 705	239.4	54 961	307
Taylor	49	1 017	81.1	35.5	39	92	6.9	1.9	1 408	74.4	6 058	38
Trempealeau	53	1 344	86.0	38.7	40	110	11.2	2.8	1 963	88.2	16 784	108
Vernon	66	1 768	131.7	55.8	38	97	8.0	1.6	2 420	105.4	17 768	132
Vilas	51	519	46.7	16.1	59	216	15.1	4.5	2 418	101.5	50 135	227
Walworth	219	4 385	342.3	133.0	192	877	80.9	20.6	6 945	334.6	71 349	299
Washburn	49	992	59.8	26.2	37	131	9.6	2.7	1 461	62.1	12 727	78
Washington	263	6 231	482.2	208.8	265	1 450	113.4	34.6	8 240	417.3	120 406	585
Waukesha	1 333	25 812	2 722.5	1 122.9	812	6 537	634.5	206.3	27 220	1 534.8	369 268	1 306
Waupaca	114	2 577	198.7	73.5	91	322	30.0	7.9	3 022	126.9	20 841	108
Waushara	42	806	46.1	20.3	32	D	D	D	1 538	74.5	10 689	54
Winnebago	439	13 580	1 272.0	555.0	257	2 279	221.0	68.1	8 307	383.1	101 057	411
Wood	178	9 523	1 234.5	493.6	133	798	64.2	17.6	3 912	171.2	23 705	161
WYOMING	1 898	31 340	3 291.5	1 361.9	1 373	6 655	884.6	214.9	48 140	2 340.9	570 418	1 727
Albany	127	2 241	178.2	80.9	87	433	33.9	9.7	2 603	89.8	25 083	151
Big Horn	21	373	23.9	12.2	19	48	4.0	0.9	914	29.7	1 363	8
Campbell	97	1 738	264.5	91.6	132	989	146.5	41.5	3 340	155.1	15 918	53
Carbon	49	642	51.4	22.1	37	130	15.8	3.5	1 062	41.4	15 061	35
Converse	29	568	67.3	25.4	37	119	12.6	2.8	1 019	53.8	770	3
Crook	15	D	D	D	9	D	D	D	733	31.8	1 621	6
Fremont	161	1 985	181.5	72.1	82	349	37.2	9.5	2 957	112.2	3 094	19

Table B. States and Counties — Government Employment and Payroll, and Local Government Finances

			Government employment and payroll, 2012							Local government finances, 2012				
				March payroll (percent of total)						General revenue				
												Taxes		
													Per capita[1] (dollars)	
STATE County	Full-time equivalent employees	March payroll (dollars)	Administration, judicial, and legal	Police and Corrections	Fire Protection	Highways and transportation	Health and Welfare	Natural resources and utilities	Education and libraries	Total (mil dol)	Intergovernmental (mil dol)	Total (mil dol)	Total	Property
	171	172	173	174	175	176	177	178	179	180	181	182	183	184
WISCONSIN—Cont'd														
Douglas	2 164	7 766 579	6.6	9.7	2.6	4.7	3.9	4.3	66.9	239.4	102.3	103.0	2 352	2 221
Dunn	1 509	5 639 405	7.9	8.3	2.6	8.0	16.0	4.0	50.9	163.0	74.1	60.7	1 377	1 302
Eau Claire	3 593	14 808 173	5.9	7.8	3.1	4.5	5.6	4.3	67.1	406.0	166.9	179.3	1 781	1 647
Florence	185	612 638	17.1	13.9	0.2	11.3	10.7	4.5	42.3	20.9	8.4	9.9	2 211	2 114
Fond du Lac	3 703	15 389 801	4.9	9.2	2.4	4.4	10.7	3.5	63.8	424.7	174.4	182.3	1 790	1 688
Forest	493	1 528 680	11.1	10.4	0.1	9.6	6.8	1.9	59.2	43.8	19.4	21.0	2 284	2 224
Grant	2 070	7 484 129	5.4	5.9	0.1	7.1	11.1	4.5	64.9	195.5	97.7	59.2	1 159	1 089
Green	1 522	5 434 245	4.8	8.5	0.3	10.0	14.6	4.1	57.2	147.1	64.1	57.3	1 551	1 465
Green Lake	764	2 599 596	7.3	12.4	0.1	5.7	12.4	4.5	56.6	82.2	28.8	43.6	2 290	2 188
Iowa	1 004	3 519 446	8.0	6.3	0.3	11.9	9.5	4.0	59.0	96.3	43.2	39.1	1 641	1 551
Iron	343	1 294 139	9.8	10.2	0.3	17.8	25.1	5.0	30.4	30.8	12.7	13.2	2 218	2 077
Jackson	903	2 811 059	8.8	7.7	0.2	16.9	6.6	2.7	55.8	82.1	42.1	26.7	1 304	1 221
Jefferson	2 850	11 172 911	7.2	10.2	3.2	5.1	9.1	5.9	58.7	312.5	124.7	137.1	1 622	1 528
Juneau	1 087	3 617 443	10.2	11.0	0.2	10.0	8.0	7.6	51.7	107.4	51.9	43.2	1 624	1 536
Kenosha	6 796	30 615 896	4.1	10.1	3.6	2.9	5.4	4.3	68.6	855.8	363.2	367.3	2 187	2 088
Kewaunee	848	3 565 289	8.2	10.2	0.1	10.8	12.1	3.4	53.7	87.1	41.2	29.7	1 440	1 419
La Crosse	4 828	18 746 528	5.8	8.4	2.7	4.3	18.1	4.4	55.5	639.3	314.3	218.1	1 873	1 730
Lafayette	850	2 868 337	5.6	5.1	0.3	8.3	23.6	4.4	52.0	87.8	38.3	24.8	1 472	1 414
Langlade	760	2 800 264	10.3	8.9	3.8	7.9	3.0	5.0	60.4	84.0	40.2	32.5	1 656	1 556
Lincoln	1 136	4 470 314	7.0	8.8	2.5	7.1	16.7	4.1	52.4	126.6	51.7	46.2	1 628	1 550
Manitowoc	2 832	11 154 230	5.9	8.4	4.1	9.0	10.6	8.0	52.8	283.3	138.4	103.3	1 281	1 252
Marathon	5 721	22 517 091	4.6	6.0	1.9	5.6	19.3	2.6	59.4	701.3	346.1	232.0	1 722	1 622
Marinette	1 554	5 323 156	6.8	9.6	2.0	8.0	9.0	6.7	56.8	164.4	77.1	65.5	1 576	1 476
Marquette	499	1 734 369	8.4	12.2	0.1	8.1	10.6	1.6	56.1	50.8	18.7	27.4	1 805	1 741
Menominee	308	1 058 752	4.7	7.1	0.5	4.3	17.3	0.5	64.4	30.1	23.2	5.7	1 306	1 299
Milwaukee	34 086	166 779 941	5.4	14.8	5.3	4.3	9.0	4.7	53.9	5 067.2	2 122.5	1 803.2	1 888	1 733
Monroe	1 770	5 806 833	5.3	7.6	0.2	6.8	15.8	3.7	59.6	171.3	88.6	56.7	1 258	1 152
Oconto	1 242	4 597 591	8.0	8.3	1.4	7.3	18.7	4.2	50.7	129.3	64.1	50.5	1 349	1 293
Oneida	1 507	5 601 172	7.6	9.0	2.1	9.2	4.7	4.2	61.9	177.2	45.0	110.8	3 102	2 972
Outagamie	6 670	30 535 826	4.5	7.0	2.4	3.0	7.4	3.1	70.7	783.6	353.3	271.9	1 521	1 483
Ozaukee	2 849	10 891 062	5.8	12.2	1.1	5.8	11.9	5.0	57.3	314.5	88.3	173.0	1 993	1 870
Pepin	383	1 190 672	6.0	7.9	0.0	9.8	16.0	3.3	54.8	32.7	15.7	13.8	1 862	1 799
Pierce	1 550	5 604 968	7.8	8.1	0.6	7.2	7.5	3.9	64.3	161.3	69.8	71.2	1 743	1 678
Polk	1 872	6 676 347	6.7	6.6	0.1	8.1	13.3	2.7	61.5	182.9	73.8	81.7	1 873	1 795
Portage	2 267	8 603 550	8.0	9.1	2.6	7.5	10.8	4.0	57.1	239.8	105.3	94.6	1 343	1 237
Price	681	1 985 878	8.8	8.8	0.2	14.3	8.2	2.4	55.9	60.2	26.4	26.8	1 934	1 859
Racine	6 208	25 453 020	4.3	13.6	5.6	3.5	5.9	4.0	61.9	757.1	345.7	302.7	1 554	1 513
Richland	693	2 209 583	6.2	8.6	0.0	9.2	22.4	9.3	43.6	68.8	31.9	17.8	999	928
Rock	6 252	25 471 665	5.9	9.6	3.9	4.4	7.9	4.5	62.6	723.4	387.9	249.8	1 557	1 471
Rusk	655	2 410 554	18.7	7.8	0.0	7.6	8.7	4.6	51.6	86.0	34.2	18.5	1 293	1 209
St. Croix	2 777	10 535 818	8.9	8.5	0.6	5.0	10.3	3.3	61.9	287.9	124.7	126.4	1 483	1 393
Sauk	2 740	9 073 443	5.8	14.7	0.2	6.1	14.5	4.3	52.3	342.6	171.4	136.3	2 178	1 826
Sawyer	647	2 033 247	11.4	10.0	0.3	11.0	9.7	2.2	53.1	68.2	23.3	37.0	2 229	2 110
Shawano	1 508	5 334 917	7.7	11.2	0.3	6.9	9.6	4.4	58.3	146.4	73.0	52.6	1 294	1 190
Sheboygan	4 469	19 622 392	8.8	8.8	2.1	5.2	8.0	3.0	63.5	489.1	213.6	207.1	1 801	1 746
Taylor	791	2 632 338	8.6	8.5	0.1	7.8	13.4	3.7	56.2	77.9	42.6	26.0	1 270	1 206
Trempealeau	1 609	5 095 842	6.3	7.1	0.0	5.3	19.8	4.5	56.5	151.2	71.4	42.1	1 437	1 369
Vernon	1 200	3 885 090	13.0	10.1	0.0	9.9	7.7	3.8	53.3	116.3	57.2	38.4	1 270	1 203
Vilas	838	2 943 859	11.7	11.7	1.3	12.5	6.2	4.2	50.1	90.0	23.9	58.7	2 751	2 602
Walworth	3 935	15 369 324	8.6	14.6	5.1	5.4	7.1	4.6	53.9	432.3	127.0	247.7	2 409	2 279
Washburn	809	2 970 221	6.5	8.7	0.0	6.2	26.7	4.1	45.5	75.6	23.6	43.2	2 729	2 639
Washington	3 924	16 777 590	5.5	11.3	2.0	3.5	11.1	4.9	60.4	533.8	224.7	238.1	1 795	1 685
Waukesha	12 148	56 004 430	5.2	10.5	3.1	3.9	3.5	4.4	68.1	1 501.6	376.8	897.3	2 287	2 229
Waupaca	2 041	7 209 482	6.6	9.8	1.0	6.0	8.5	3.2	64.1	213.4	94.7	87.0	1 668	1 589
Waushara	768	2 669 797	12.8	9.7	0.0	7.3	14.0	2.2	51.2	79.8	31.6	38.3	1 565	1 495
Winnebago	5 300	21 156 305	4.4	11.7	4.6	5.5	11.2	7.1	54.5	697.9	338.4	249.0	1 475	1 436
Wood	3 170	12 767 826	6.1	9.1	3.2	5.9	6.1	3.5	65.8	337.6	146.1	136.7	1 837	1 741
WYOMING	X	X	X	X	X	X	X	X	X	X	X	X	X	X
Albany	2 004	7 113 079	5.9	6.8	3.8	1.8	26.8	5.7	48.8	203.8	74.7	35.3	948	550
Big Horn	940	3 298 694	4.9	6.2	0.2	2.2	30.5	4.5	51.0	99.0	52.6	18.8	1 595	1 308
Campbell	3 518	15 943 966	6.3	7.1	1.0	2.6	31.3	5.6	43.0	513.4	102.2	227.8	4 757	4 113
Carbon	1 195	4 095 546	7.4	9.7	1.4	3.4	23.3	5.9	44.5	136.5	41.4	57.8	3 691	2 846
Converse	1 098	4 194 426	4.6	6.9	0.0	1.8	33.4	4.4	47.4	123.9	29.5	48.7	3 477	2 778
Crook	486	1 567 725	9.6	7.3	0.1	2.9	16.3	2.3	60.3	47.3	23.8	13.5	1 893	1 459
Fremont	2 549	9 152 411	3.7	7.9	0.4	2.1	3.0	9.4	71.6	264.6	168.1	62.0	1 509	1 270

1. Based on the resident population estimated as of July 1 of the year shown.

Table B. States and Counties — Local Government Finances, Government Employment, and Income Taxes

	Local government finances, 2012 (cont.)									Government employment, 2015			Individual income tax returns, 2014		
	Direct general expenditure							Debt outstanding							
STATE County			Percent of total for:												
	Total (mil dol)	Per capita[1] (dollars)	Education	Health and hospitals	Police protection	Public welfare	Highways	Total (mil dol)	Per capita[1] (dollars)	Federal civilian	Federal military	State and local	Number of returns	Mean adjusted gross income	Mean income tax
	185	186	187	188	189	190	191	192	193	194	195	196	197	198	199
WISCONSIN—Cont'd															
Douglas	245.2	5 600	52.1	1.4	5.6	3.7	10.6	236.8	5 408	170	113	3 108	20 610	49 539	4 961
Dunn	163.3	3 704	41.6	2.5	5.7	12.3	12.7	105.8	2 402	90	110	4 514	18 900	50 608	5 139
Eau Claire	470.2	4 671	54.2	3.8	7.3	3.4	9.5	361.0	3 586	346	261	8 312	47 830	64 222	9 648
Florence	21.2	4 727	37.2	8.9	7.2	0.6	19.4	5.9	1 314	13	12	259	2 210	46 510	4 458
Fond du Lac	449.6	4 415	51.8	7.3	5.2	3.9	9.0	580.9	5 704	198	266	5 405	50 060	56 385	6 378
Forest	45.1	4 904	47.2	2.3	5.4	5.0	13.7	7.9	854	97	23	1 689	4 180	47 156	4 922
Grant	214.5	4 199	52.3	3.3	4.2	7.2	12.4	147.8	2 894	147	126	5 578	22 580	45 506	4 429
Green	151.7	4 109	48.0	2.6	6.1	10.5	13.8	103.5	2 805	83	99	2 024	18 680	55 678	6 270
Green Lake	81.9	4 301	48.2	3.2	6.9	5.3	9.5	68.9	3 620	53	50	1 074	9 360	49 701	5 329
Iowa	95.1	3 993	48.5	1.0	5.7	8.7	15.3	45.1	1 896	77	63	1 337	11 730	54 415	5 833
Iron	31.8	5 354	32.4	7.4	7.7	0.5	21.4	22.9	3 853	15	15	362	2 970	43 855	4 091
Jackson	85.1	4 152	52.3	2.5	4.5	6.0	13.4	40.6	1 983	47	51	2 481	9 460	48 305	5 279
Jefferson	322.8	3 820	49.7	5.1	6.2	5.7	8.1	312.0	3 693	173	217	3 957	40 500	52 639	5 366
Juneau	108.2	4 063	46.9	4.1	5.3	3.2	12.3	117.9	4 426	258	92	1 983	12 130	42 079	3 910
Kenosha	850.4	5 064	53.7	3.4	6.5	6.9	5.1	759.4	4 522	255	467	9 456	79 570	55 027	6 156
Kewaunee	102.8	4 983	40.7	9.0	4.0	5.5	16.5	50.3	2 438	65	54	1 143	9 990	51 745	4 969
La Crosse	639.1	5 488	42.3	2.8	3.9	23.8	4.9	409.7	3 518	456	305	9 940	55 660	58 732	7 104
Lafayette	90.2	5 355	43.0	14.6	2.7	11.4	12.9	33.1	1 965	50	45	1 021	8 210	45 611	4 281
Langlade	87.8	4 467	47.1	4.3	4.7	3.7	13.7	55.1	2 802	42	51	1 069	9 540	43 949	4 069
Lincoln	128.6	4 529	40.0	5.5	5.8	12.3	13.4	69.0	2 431	57	73	1 662	11 390	48 387	4 626
Manitowoc	296.5	3 675	42.9	1.3	6.2	6.4	9.3	337.8	4 187	193	234	3 804	40 140	54 056	6 119
Marathon	710.6	5 274	41.9	10.2	3.9	18.8	7.9	440.9	3 273	433	361	7 598	67 140	57 287	7 008
Marinette	165.7	3 988	44.3	5.4	5.8	7.1	14.3	116.0	2 790	151	113	2 110	20 080	46 923	4 745
Marquette	54.9	3 612	43.4	5.5	7.6	3.4	17.9	23.8	1 566	52	40	705	7 470	43 747	4 244
Menominee	30.7	7 067	60.2	0.0	5.9	18.3	5.8	5.7	1 309	[3]D	[3]12	[3]2 101	1 750	32 307	2 133
Milwaukee	5 034.7	5 271	40.9	10.3	8.2	1.9	4.9	6 485.7	6 790	9 495	2 847	51 755	449 660	52 939	6 315
Monroe	165.6	3 672	50.0	1.1	5.0	10.2	11.3	105.8	2 346	2 495	283	2 553	21 230	47 038	4 385
Oconto	134.4	3 590	40.5	9.2	4.7	5.0	18.4	80.7	2 154	90	99	1 841	18 160	50 876	4 925
Oneida	201.2	5 634	52.6	2.8	6.1	3.2	10.2	98.0	2 743	188	94	2 049	19 340	52 672	5 906
Outagamie	855.9	4 786	56.0	2.4	5.0	4.7	8.6	649.4	3 632	567	511	10 780	91 960	61 346	7 400
Ozaukee	321.3	3 701	46.5	2.6	7.4	7.0	10.8	290.2	3 342	151	230	3 539	45 370	103 570	18 091
Pepin	34.1	4 609	48.2	4.5	4.1	3.3	20.4	10.3	1 392	32	19	460	3 490	56 047	6 782
Pierce	163.8	4 014	51.4	3.3	5.2	3.2	16.2	140.8	3 451	83	103	4 136	18 840	62 259	7 073
Polk	186.0	4 265	50.3	5.5	4.6	6.5	13.2	178.6	4 095	127	115	2 636	21 390	49 888	4 859
Portage	238.8	3 391	43.8	5.1	6.1	6.5	12.7	142.9	2 029	167	187	6 003	33 500	55 640	6 448
Price	60.0	4 326	45.1	2.0	5.7	8.2	16.4	25.8	1 862	76	36	870	7 010	44 350	4 140
Racine	764.1	3 923	45.5	3.8	9.7	5.3	7.3	710.7	3 648	346	510	8 680	95 040	57 036	6 642
Richland	68.5	3 844	34.6	2.0	4.7	20.1	12.9	25.0	1 405	57	46	1 375	7 810	42 048	3 765
Rock	729.2	4 546	49.6	7.4	6.2	7.1	5.3	614.8	3 833	291	425	8 628	77 980	51 470	5 516
Rusk	90.1	6 292	32.1	22.9	3.9	8.8	12.1	51.6	3 603	42	37	1 067	6 580	40 626	3 609
St. Croix	287.7	3 375	50.6	2.2	5.7	8.2	13.4	288.4	3 383	156	232	4 371	42 230	75 142	9 958
Sauk	331.0	5 288	35.3	5.0	4.8	22.8	8.1	211.8	3 384	152	169	5 471	33 100	49 473	5 214
Sawyer	72.4	4 365	38.2	6.1	5.3	7.8	21.4	22.8	1 377	74	43	1 878	8 220	46 237	4 770
Shawano	157.1	3 776	42.7	6.0	5.5	4.6	17.3	107.1	2 575	112	109	2 750	19 460	45 937	4 193
Sheboygan	492.9	4 286	55.2	3.6	5.7	6.1	8.2	375.9	3 269	200	320	5 513	58 030	56 722	6 405
Taylor	77.2	3 770	44.9	3.6	5.2	8.1	16.4	38.0	1 857	55	54	955	9 070	46 384	4 416
Trempealeau	154.8	5 283	44.9	1.8	4.6	18.1	10.5	112.0	3 824	121	78	2 261	15 100	47 991	4 557
Vernon	117.6	3 887	43.6	1.7	3.8	13.5	14.5	68.6	2 265	112	81	1 750	13 300	45 330	4 264
Vilas	84.7	3 971	43.9	2.5	7.8	5.4	13.1	52.1	2 443	63	57	2 064	11 140	48 578	5 352
Walworth	423.9	4 121	48.5	3.3	9.0	4.8	9.2	448.4	4 360	186	268	8 234	48 980	58 638	7 123
Washburn	75.7	4 781	45.6	1.7	4.0	5.9	18.7	56.9	3 597	87	41	1 264	7 980	46 172	4 365
Washington	537.2	4 049	42.6	2.9	6.1	19.2	7.1	398.2	3 001	267	355	5 213	68 430	67 589	8 234
Waukesha	1 525.8	3 890	54.5	2.7	7.1	2.3	6.8	1 282.0	3 268	767	1 049	16 896	203 710	86 360	13 148
Waupaca	217.6	4 174	48.6	2.1	6.1	7.4	12.8	224.2	4 301	129	135	3 333	25 350	51 246	5 162
Waushara	86.2	3 523	39.0	3.9	8.2	9.2	13.7	34.2	1 400	46	61	1 313	11 090	44 859	4 444
Winnebago	708.5	4 197	35.6	2.5	5.6	20.8	8.3	688.0	4 076	407	437	11 858	82 080	57 666	6 859
Wood	353.7	4 752	52.5	6.5	5.5	4.9	9.8	274.0	3 681	192	194	4 970	37 080	51 682	5 616
WYOMING	X	X	X	X	X	X	X	X	X	7 372	6 003	62 366	279 900	77 766	11 760
Albany	193.6	5 194	32.5	30.5	5.1	0.3	6.1	57.2	1 535	155	199	7 961	16 170	54 001	6 318
Big Horn	99.3	8 416	44.8	21.5	3.8	0.1	2.7	33.3	2 823	102	62	1 412	5 070	50 945	5 804
Campbell	532.9	11 131	37.0	22.6	3.1	1.5	5.4	188.2	3 931	87	258	4 988	23 470	79 699	11 986
Carbon	136.8	8 731	40.1	19.3	4.0	0.4	2.9	63.8	4 069	190	78	1 749	7 300	65 117	8 486
Converse	125.0	8 921	39.9	31.1	4.0	0.2	6.5	11.6	826	63	75	1 528	6 840	74 430	10 943
Crook	47.5	6 641	47.4	16.7	4.3	0.1	7.7	3.6	504	88	39	619	3 340	73 065	10 046
Fremont	258.8	6 295	73.2	1.1	4.0	0.4	3.3	31.2	759	467	208	5 290	18 200	56 717	6 773

1. Based on the resident population estimated as of July 1 of the year shown.   3. Menominee county included with Shawano county.

Table B. States and Counties — **Land Area and Population**

STATE/ County code	CBSA code[1]	County type[2]	STATE County	Land area,[3] (sq mi) 2016	Total persons 2016	Rank	Per square mile	White	Black	American Indian, Alaska Native	Asian and Pacific Islander	Percent Hispanic or Latino[4]	Under 5 years	5 to 17 years	18 to 24 years	25 to 34 years	35 to 44 years	45 to 54 years
				1	2	3	4	5	6	7	8	9	10	11	12	13	14	15
			WYOMING—Cont'd															
56 015	...	7	Goshen	2 225.4	13 390	2 204	6.0	87.4	1.2	1.2	0.9	10.4	5.4	15.0	9.2	11.5	10.9	11.6
56 017	...	7	Hot Springs	2 004.1	4 679	2 852	2.3	92.9	0.9	2.3	0.9	4.4	5.3	15.3	5.7	10.1	10.1	11.2
56 019	...	7	Johnson	4 154.2	8 486	2 554	2.0	92.6	1.2	1.8	1.2	4.6	5.3	16.7	6.0	10.3	11.3	11.9
56 021	16940	3	Laramie	2 685.9	98 136	605	36.5	80.7	3.4	1.4	2.1	14.6	6.4	17.0	9.5	14.7	12.0	12.3
56 023	...	7	Lincoln	4 076.2	19 110	1 868	4.7	93.8	0.7	1.2	0.9	4.5	6.9	20.2	6.8	10.4	12.6	12.0
56 025	16220	3	Natrona	5 340.5	81 039	695	15.2	88.5	1.8	1.6	1.5	8.5	7.0	17.3	8.3	15.4	12.8	11.8
56 027	...	9	Niobrara	2 626.0	2 480	3 008	0.9	93.4	1.5	2.7	1.1	3.4	5.2	13.1	7.7	12.8	13.4	11.4
56 029	...	7	Park	6 939.8	29 353	1 448	4.2	92.0	1.2	1.3	1.2	5.7	5.7	15.0	8.3	11.5	10.6	11.5
56 031	...	7	Platte	2 084.2	8 680	2 533	4.2	90.0	1.0	1.1	1.1	8.2	5.4	14.7	6.7	10.4	9.9	12.9
56 033	43260	7	Sheridan	2 523.4	30 200	1 428	12.0	93.0	1.1	1.9	1.3	4.0	5.5	15.8	8.3	11.6	11.5	12.0
56 035	...	9	Sublette	4 886.5	9 769	2 449	2.0	89.2	1.3	1.3	1.3	8.1	6.6	17.6	6.3	12.3	14.0	13.9
56 037	40540	5	Sweetwater	10 426.7	44 165	1 089	4.2	81.2	1.6	1.5	1.3	16.1	7.0	19.8	8.6	15.0	13.8	11.8
56 039	27220	7	Teton	3 995.9	23 191	1 669	5.8	82.7	0.9	0.8	1.9	15.1	5.2	13.6	5.8	18.7	16.2	13.4
56 041	21740	7	Uinta	2 081.8	20 773	1 784	10.0	88.9	1.0	1.4	1.2	9.0	7.9	21.5	7.5	12.4	12.9	11.2
56 043	...	7	Washakie	2 238.6	8 235	2 576	3.7	84.2	1.0	1.4	1.1	13.9	5.8	18.1	6.6	10.0	12.1	12.1
56 045	...	7	Weston	2 398.1	7 236	2 649	3.0	93.6	1.0	2.3	1.0	4.0	6.0	15.4	7.3	12.3	11.5	12.4

1. CBSA = Core Based Statistical Area. See Appendix A for explanation. See Appendix B for list of metropolitan areas with component counties.   2. County type code from the Economic Research Service of USDA Rural-Urban Continuum Codes. See Appendix A for definition.   3. Dry land or land partially or temporarily covered by water.   4. May be of any race.

Table B. States and Counties — **Population and Households**

STATE County	Population, 2016 (cont.) Age (percent) (cont.)				Population change and components of change, 2000–2016								Households, 2011–2015				
					Total persons		Percent change		Components of change, 2010–2016						Percent		
	55 to 64 years	65 to 74 years	75 years and over	Percent female	2000	2010	2000–2010	2010–2016	Births	Deaths	Net migration	Number	Persons per house-hold	Family house-holds	Female family house-holder[1]	One per-son
	16	17	18	19	20	21	22	23	24	25	26	27	28	29	30	31
WYOMING—Cont'd																
Goshen	15.0	11.9	9.4	47.8	12 538	13 247	5.7	1.1	880	857	111	5 384	2.35	63.9	7.3	31.9
Hot Springs	17.3	13.7	11.3	49.5	4 882	4 812	-1.4	-2.8	320	417	-31	2 182	2.15	59.9	4.8	36.3
Johnson	16.0	13.0	9.4	49.5	7 075	8 569	21.1	-1.0	578	504	-162	3 649	2.34	58.9	5.2	36.1
Laramie	13.1	8.9	6.2	49.3	81 607	91 881	12.6	6.8	7 896	4 852	3 191	37 294	2.51	66.9	6.0	22.0
Lincoln	15.4	10.1	5.6	49.0	14 573	18 106	24.2	5.5	1 527	763	235	6 797	2.68	72.4	6.0	22.0
Natrona	13.6	8.1	5.7	49.5	66 533	75 450	13.4	7.4	7 111	4 370	2 815	32 131	2.44	63.1	9.4	29.9
Niobrara	15.7	11.2	9.6	54.4	2 407	2 484	3.2	-0.2	144	151	0	1 045	2.15	56.8	2.9	37.1
Park	16.0	12.8	8.6	50.2	25 786	28 205	9.4	4.1	1 954	1 658	862	11 822	2.38	65.8	8.4	28.9
Platte	16.1	13.6	10.3	49.0	8 807	8 667	-1.6	0.1	536	595	96	3 758	2.30	63.7	11.0	32.4
Sheridan	15.5	11.9	7.8	49.7	26 560	29 116	9.6	3.7	2 067	1 917	845	12 578	2.28	62.9	6.4	32.0
Sublette	14.8	9.7	4.8	46.6	5 920	10 247	73.1	-4.7	799	306	-1 010	3 623	2.74	73.5	5.9	21.8
Sweetwater	13.4	6.8	3.6	48.2	37 613	43 806	16.5	0.8	3 915	1 700	-1 836	16 679	2.64	68.4	8.5	25.8
Teton	13.5	8.9	4.6	48.4	18 251	21 294	16.7	8.9	1 553	500	806	8 187	2.63	59.1	5.7	26.6
Uinta	14.0	8.4	4.2	49.4	19 742	21 118	7.0	-1.6	1 966	842	-1 486	7 502	2.76	71.2	11.5	24.3
Washakie	14.3	11.5	9.4	49.7	8 289	8 533	2.9	-3.5	611	553	-343	3 512	2.34	63.6	7.5	32.1
Weston	16.4	10.4	8.3	47.3	6 644	7 208	8.5	0.4	487	447	-9	2 986	2.27	63.2	5.4	32.8

1. No spouse present.

Table B. States and Counties — **Population, Vital Statistics, Health, and Crime**

STATE County	Persons in group quarters, 2016	Daytime population, 2011–2015 Number	Daytime population, 2011–2015 Employment/residence ratio	Births, 2016 Total	Births, 2016 Rate[1]	Deaths, 2016 Number	Deaths, 2016 Rate[1]	Persons under 65 with no health insurance, 2015 Number	Persons under 65 with no health insurance, 2015 Percent	Medicare, 2015 Total Beneficiaries	Medicare, 2015 Enrolled in Original Medicare	Medicare, 2015 Enrolled in Medicare Advantage	Serious crimes known to police,[2] 2014 Total Number	Serious crimes known to police,[2] 2014 Total Rate[3]
	32	33	34	35	36	37	38	39	40	41	42	43	44	45
WYOMING—Cont'd														
Goshen	1 219	12 918	0.90	147	11.0	138	10.3	1 482	15.6	2 852	2 813	39	212	1 560
Hot Springs	86	4 700	0.95	49	10.5	69	14.7	587	16.5	1 301	1 286	15	39	807
Johnson	71	7 676	0.78	84	9.9	76	9.0	1 003	14.9	1 845	1 814	31	165	1 920
Laramie	1 945	98 153	1.06	1 252	12.8	850	8.7	9 272	11.4	16 401	15 662	739	2 495	2 593
Lincoln	71	16 716	0.81	241	12.6	121	6.3	2 046	13.0	3 047	2 932	115	176	1 020
Natrona	1 767	80 929	1.02	1 216	15.0	729	9.0	9 652	13.8	12 294	11 678	616	2 102	2 565
Niobrara	250	2 558	1.04	25	10.1	21	8.5	266	15.1	D	536	D	NA	NA
Park	793	29 178	1.01	317	10.8	260	8.9	3 026	13.4	6 701	6 561	140	497	1 696
Platte	102	8 842	1.02	86	9.9	82	9.4	898	13.4	2 152	2 108	44	164	1 877
Sheridan	1 036	29 279	0.97	315	10.4	334	11.1	2 907	12.3	6 313	5 974	339	499	1 673
Sublette	550	11 062	1.18	118	12.1	58	5.9	1 099	12.9	D	1 207	D	86	865
Sweetwater	684	46 979	1.10	604	13.7	275	6.2	4 905	12.4	5 252	5 017	235	954	2 101
Teton	267	25 861	1.26	239	10.3	87	3.8	3 060	15.3	2 831	2 674	157	NA	NA
Uinta	254	20 001	0.91	309	14.9	134	6.5	2 242	12.3	2 681	2 361	320	432	2 292
Washakie	140	8 578	1.05	98	11.9	93	11.3	1 140	17.4	1 710	1 697	13	63	750
Weston	327	6 501	0.80	67	9.3	77	10.6	766	13.6	1 392	1 297	95	87	1 445

1. Per 1,000 estimated resident population.   2. Data for serious crimes have not been adjusted for underreporting; this may affect comparability between geographic areas and over time.
3. Per 100,000 population estimated by the FBI.

Table B. States and Counties — **Crime, Education, Money Income, and Poverty**

STATE County	Serious crimes known to police, 2014 (cont.)[1] Rate[2]		Education						Money income, 2011–2015					Income and poverty, 2015		
			School enrollment and attainment, 2011–2015				Local government expenditures,[5] 2013–2014			Households			Median house-hold income (dollars)	Percent below poverty level		
			Enrollment[3]		Attainment[4] (percent)							Percent					
	Violent	Property	Total	Per-cent private	High school grad-uate or less	Bach-elor's degree or more	Total current spending (mil dol)	Current spend-ing per student (dollars)	Per capita income[6] (dollars)	Median income (dollars)	with income of less than $50,000	with income of $200,000 or more		All per-sons	Children under 18 years	Children 5 to 17 years in families
	46	47	48	49	50	51	52	53	54	55	56	57	58	59	60	61
WYOMING—Cont'd																
Goshen	309	1 251	3 145	16.3	39.1	22.8	31.6	18 541	25 105	42 689	57.3	1.5	48 146	15.1	19.3	16.7
Hot Springs	41	766	1 067	9.0	39.9	20.6	11.6	18 756	27 259	45 278	55.2	2.4	46 021	11.9	16.3	13.7
Johnson	128	1 792	1 678	15.7	41.7	25.3	22.3	17 442	30 144	54 065	46.0	1.8	56 845	8.2	10.6	9.0
Laramie	160	2 433	24 548	10.0	33.2	27.8	226.0	15 489	30 047	60 706	41.3	2.9	59 147	10.6	13.6	12.1
Lincoln	87	933	4 605	6.9	38.1	21.5	50.3	15 463	29 915	66 647	35.0	4.4	62 364	8.8	10.6	8.6
Natrona	184	2 380	19 720	9.8	36.2	21.9	186.4	14 564	30 783	56 871	44.0	3.8	56 703	11.0	14.2	12.3
Niobrara	NA	NA	455	9.7	37.6	21.3	12.9	12 935	25 272	40 398	57.1	3.5	46 693	13.3	19.0	16.7
Park	201	1 494	6 585	9.1	35.3	28.4	62.0	15 615	29 411	56 363	42.7	2.1	55 527	9.6	13.8	12.1
Platte	137	1 740	1 618	12.9	38.6	21.7	23.7	18 957	25 899	38 500	56.8	1.2	51 863	11.7	17.4	15.0
Sheridan	151	1 522	6 719	14.8	32.7	29.4	67.9	15 509	29 892	55 455	45.4	2.6	57 122	9.5	13.2	11.4
Sublette	101	765	2 582	9.1	39.8	22.9	29.1	17 259	33 193	81 772	30.4	3.2	77 581	6.1	7.1	5.8
Sweetwater	295	1 806	11 717	9.6	44.9	19.6	119.8	14 366	30 568	69 022	35.5	2.5	71 867	8.5	10.2	8.7
Teton	NA	NA	4 428	16.2	22.0	53.9	45.7	17 606	44 231	75 325	29.4	11.7	83 290	6.6	7.6	6.7
Uinta	48	2 245	5 732	6.2	46.5	19.3	65.9	15 074	25 772	56 569	45.0	2.9	62 968	9.8	11.9	9.9
Washakie	83	667	1 855	11.3	41.9	21.1	26.0	17 595	27 394	47 652	52.2	2.4	56 088	11.2	15.7	13.4
Weston	183	1 262	1 521	13.1	44.2	18.1	19.4	18 676	30 245	57 738	43.1	3.1	60 986	9.8	13.1	11.8

1. Data for serious crimes have not been adjusted for underreporting; this may affect comparability between geographic areas and over time.   2. Per 100,000 population estimated by the FBI.
3. All persons 3 years old and over enrolled in nursery school through college.   4. Persons 25 years old and over.   5. Elementary and secondary education expenditures.
6. Based on population estimated by the American Community Survey, 2011–2015.

Table B. States and Counties — **Personal Income**

STATE County	Personal income, 2015										Earnings, 2015		
	Total (mil dol)	Percent change, 2014–2015	Per capita[1]		Wages and salaries (mil dol)	Supplements to wages and salaries; employer contributions (mil dol)		Proprietors' income (mil dol)	Dividends, interest, and rent (mil dol)	Personal transfer receipts (mil dol)	Total (mil dol)	Contributions for government social insurance (mil dol)	
			Dollars	Rank		Pension and insurance	Government social insurance					From employee and self-employed	From employer
	62	63	64	65	66	67	68	69	70	71	72	73	74
WYOMING—Cont'd													
Goshen	567	3.2	42 346	1 104	182	41	18	69	108	115	310	17	18
Hot Springs	244	4.9	51 418	655	81	18	8	45	45	54	151	9	8
Johnson	382	-2.0	44 439	563	129	28	13	59	97	66	230	13	13
Laramie	4 836	2.0	49 796	426	2 414	517	245	312	1 091	770	3 487	196	245
Lincoln	743	4.2	39 683	1 146	285	63	26	44	183	123	419	25	26
Natrona	5 645	-3.1	68 692	134	2 240	311	211	1 373	1 375	574	4 135	217	211
Niobrara	118	-6.5	46 341	421	39	11	4	18	28	22	72	4	4
Park	1 423	2.2	48 692	492	597	116	59	137	405	252	908	54	59
Platte	399	2.5	45 275	702	187	39	19	46	75	84	292	17	19
Sheridan	1 653	2.9	55 089	286	593	116	62	124	549	245	894	54	62
Sublette	484	-5.0	48 881	309	46	46	24	61	142	48	406	22	24
Sweetwater	2 172	0.2	48 681	201	1 472	234	133	220	277	258	2 059	117	133
Teton	4 506	0.6	194 861	1	905	109	98	154	3 434	116	1 267	75	98
Uinta	854	-0.3	41 005	914	393	77	38	37	140	140	545	32	38
Washakie	362	2.2	43 460	951	166	33	17	30	86	67	246	15	17
Weston	326	-0.1	44 997	154	102	27	10	43	61	56	181	10	10

1. Based on the resident population estimated as of July 1 of the year shown.

STATE County	Earnings, 2015 (cont.)									Social Security beneficiaries, December 2015			Housing units, 2016	
	Percent by selected industries											Supplemental Security Income recipients, December 2015		
	Farm	Mining	Construction	Manu-facturing	Information: professional, scientific, technical services	Retail trade	Finance, insurance, real estate and leasing	Health care and social assistance	Govern-ment	Number	Rate[1]		Total	Percent change, 2010–2016
	75	76	77	78	79	80	81	82	83	84	85	86	87	88
WYOMING—Cont'd														
Goshen	14.1	0.0	5.2	4.0	2.6	4.4	4.0	13.8	30.6	3 095	228	225	5 922	-0.8
Hot Springs	0.9	D	4.2	4.1	2.9	D	2.4	8.5	23.7	1 455	307	98	2 534	-1.9
Johnson	6.3	5.7	12.5	0.8	4.8	4.5	10.7	D	31.4	2 085	243	47	4 536	-0.4
Laramie	0.8	1.1	7.1	3.8	7.1	6.6	6.7	7.7	40.1	17 560	181	1 490	42 284	4.5
Lincoln	1.1	18.6	12.9	2.0	6.1	5.0	2.7	3.3	30.0	3 535	188	148	9 139	2.1
Natrona	0.2	12.0	9.3	3.5	4.7	5.6	6.2	10.9	11.0	13 880	169	1 161	36 240	7.2
Niobrara	8.7	4.8	5.7	D	D	D	3.3	D	41.7	595	238	30	1 341	0.2
Park	1.2	6.6	10.6	4.2	6.3	7.1	4.9	10.9	27.9	7 455	257	275	14 119	4.1
Platte	8.6	2.1	11.4	1.7	3.2	5.5	4.0	6.1	20.3	2 325	264	78	4 718	1.1
Sheridan	1.6	3.4	10.6	3.3	7.5	7.5	4.6	8.3	30.5	6 700	223	302	14 532	4.3
Sublette	2.2	35.5	12.8	0.7	4.1	3.1	4.3	D	20.3	1 480	150	40	5 894	2.1
Sweetwater	0.0	32.9	8.2	8.9	2.6	4.7	4.5	3.0	16.0	6 200	139	383	19 268	2.8
Teton	0.2	0.2	12.2	0.5	14.8	7.1	6.8	4.9	15.5	2 920	127	45	13 611	6.2
Uinta	0.6	10.1	14.0	3.6	7.6	6.1	4.9	D	25.3	3 275	157	271	8 796	1.0
Washakie	2.2	6.5	8.6	12.4	5.5	5.6	4.4	D	23.3	1 930	232	86	3 799	-0.9
Weston	4.9	7.8	10.7	9.5	2.5	4.4	3.7	D	28.8	1 605	222	59	3 483	-1.4

1. Per 1,000 resident population estimated as of July 1 of the year shown.

Table B. States and Counties — **Housing, Labor Force, and Employment**

STATE County	Housing units, 2011–2015								Civilian labor force, 2016				Civilian employment,[6] 2011–2015		
	Occupied units										Unemployment			Percent	
		Owner-occupied				Renter-occupied									
				Median owner cost as a percent of income											Con-struction, produc-tion, and mainte-nance occu-pations
	Total	Percent	Median value[1]	With a mort-gage	Without a mort-gage[2]	Median rent[3]	Median rent as a per-cent of income[2]	Sub-stand-ard units[4] (percent)	Total	Percent change, 2015–2016	Total	Rate[5]	Total	Manage-ment, business, science and arts	
	89	90	91	92	93	94	95	96	97	98	99	100	101	102	103
WYOMING—Cont'd															
Goshen........................	5 384	76.6	148 700	19.8	12.3	669	26.3	0.9	7 130	0.4	243	3.4	6 080	33.6	27.9
Hot Springs	2 182	74.3	151 600	24.8	10.0	669	21.7	2.0	2 460	2.2	117	4.8	2 292	36.3	23.8
Johnson........................	3 649	71.9	227 700	20.7	12.2	854	23.0	0.1	4 227	0.2	225	5.3	4 300	32.5	30.5
Laramie........................	37 294	68.7	190 000	21.3	10.0	827	26.5	1.2	48 880	0.2	2 011	4.1	46 206	37.2	23.0
Lincoln........................	6 797	80.9	201 700	20.9	10.0	796	22.8	3.3	8 771	3.9	404	4.6	8 724	30.6	33.1
Natrona........................	32 131	66.6	185 600	20.7	10.0	826	25.2	1.9	41 220	-4.1	2 928	7.1	41 415	29.8	28.1
Niobrara........................	1 045	68.4	157 900	21.8	14.0	588	24.7	0.1	1 362	2.3	44	3.2	1 114	38.8	23.3
Park........................	11 822	72.0	221 300	21.1	10.7	692	21.6	1.6	16 027	1.3	751	4.7	15 305	30.3	24.9
Platte........................	3 758	77.0	155 500	23.3	12.4	592	27.8	0.6	4 806	-2.5	231	4.8	4 133	32.5	29.8
Sheridan........................	12 578	68.3	228 000	21.1	10.8	731	26.0	2.1	16 200	1.3	753	4.6	14 336	38.7	23.5
Sublette........................	3 623	73.5	275 600	19.1	10.0	1 171	21.3	1.5	4 281	-6.6	273	6.4	5 541	37.9	36.7
Sweetwater........................	16 679	71.0	190 900	18.7	10.0	892	21.8	3.1	22 265	-2.4	1 332	6.0	23 010	25.4	38.7
Teton........................	8 187	60.5	689 000	23.0	10.0	1 113	27.1	4.7	15 369	4.2	524	3.4	14 298	39.1	15.6
Uinta........................	7 502	73.0	176 700	20.6	10.0	641	24.3	2.8	9 468	-2.4	546	5.8	10 064	30.1	32.5
Washakie........................	3 512	73.7	160 800	21.1	11.7	605	23.8	3.0	4 270	-0.3	200	4.7	3 892	29.3	33.1
Weston........................	2 986	78.0	178 200	20.8	10.0	740	19.6	4.9	3 993	0.4	197	4.9	3 343	32.1	41.3

1. Specified owner-occupied units.   2. A value of 10.0 represents 10 percent or less; a value of 50.0 represents 50 percent or more.   3. Specified renter-occupied units.
4. Overcrowded or lacking complete plumbing facilities.   5. Percent of civilian labor force.   6. Civilian employed persons 16 years old and over.

	Private nonfarm establishments, employment and payroll, 2015								Agriculture, 2012			
		Employment						Annual payroll	Farms			
											Percent with:	
STATE County	Number of establish-ments	Total	Health care and social assistance	Manufac-turing	Retail trade	Finance and insurance	Professional, scientific, and technical services	Total (mil dol)	Average per employee (dollars)	Number	Fewer than 50 acres	500 acres or more	Farm operators whose principal occu-pation is farming (percent)
	104	105	106	107	108	109	110	111	112	113	114	115	116
WYOMING—Cont'd													
Goshen	351	2 998	691	232	399	132	146	97	32 321	790	15.4	43.0	59.6
Hot Springs	180	1 576	413	48	171	36	50	57	35 984	178	32.6	31.5	42.7
Johnson	422	2 292	395	71	342	141	174	80	35 062	358	19.0	53.4	51.7
Laramie	3 139	35 530	7 511	1 273	6 226	1 620	2 317	1 413	39 761	1 116	33.5	31.2	37.3
Lincoln	655	4 268	726	272	668	111	104	189	44 180	608	41.0	20.1	46.4
Natrona	3 006	36 096	5 566	1 688	5 325	941	1 651	1 700	47 094	397	31.5	33.5	49.4
Niobrara	89	404	56	D	106	20	9	12	29 886	234	6.0	82.5	80.8
Park	1 201	9 818	1 929	560	1 677	301	414	407	41 430	860	37.4	18.8	47.4
Platte	270	2 304	323	170	403	108	46	102	44 316	505	18.2	46.9	59.4
Sheridan	1 168	10 477	2 138	379	1 787	333	713	381	36 405	702	36.3	31.8	45.9
Sublette	434	3 524	166	49	357	73	129	248	70 502	398	32.4	41.5	51.5
Sweetwater	1 326	17 108	1 386	1 824	2 484	327	491	976	57 035	255	27.8	36.9	30.6
Teton	2 066	17 246	1 293	137	2 076	436	945	723	41 942	154	50.6	12.3	41.6
Uinta	573	8 481	1 458	203	1 094	151	288	371	43 777	315	28.9	33.3	44.1
Washakie	354	2 872	766	313	363	96	134	104	36 063	209	39.2	35.4	52.6
Weston	221	1 694	364	D	301	58	34	65	38 582	264	7.2	50.4	51.1

STATE County	Land in farms					Value of land and buildings (dollars)		Value of machinery and equipment, average per farm (dollars)	Value of products sold				Percent of farms with sales of:		Government payments	
	Acreage (1,000)	Percent change, 2007–2012	Acres			Average per farm	Average per acre		Total (mil dol)	Average per farm (dollars)	Percent from:		$10,000 or more	$100,000 or more	Total ($1,000)	Percent of farms
			Average size of farm	Total irrigated (1,000)	Total cropland (1,000)						Crops	Live-stock and poultry products				
	117	118	119	120	121	122	123	124	125	126	127	128	129	130	131	132
WYOMING—Cont'd																
Goshen	1 370	0.1	1 735	109.2	241.5	1 346 967	777	141 356	246.6	312 103	26.8	73.2	58.1	33.3	4 662	55.6
Hot Springs	517	-5.4	2 906	12.6	28.1	2 030 427	699	84 197	16.4	92 388	12.7	87.3	49.4	17.4	361	10.7
Johnson	2 036	4.6	5 686	40.0	59.8	3 452 782	607	119 444	51.7	144 441	8.9	91.1	57.8	32.4	750	14.5
Laramie	1 676	-0.9	1 502	59.3	338.1	1 079 159	719	110 585	190.7	170 918	24.4	75.6	37.0	17.6	4 938	32.7
Lincoln	344	0.3	565	72.7	98.5	1 017 597	1 800	87 056	40.8	67 153	30.7	69.3	45.6	19.9	732	27.8
Natrona	1 691	-22.5	4 259	28.9	43.3	2 656 418	624	133 912	42.9	108 118	16.5	83.5	49.6	23.7	634	11.3
Niobrara	1 359	-6.2	5 807	14.6	75.4	3 112 043	536	122 726	45.3	193 684	18.0	82.0	78.6	49.6	1 331	39.7
Park	813	-7.8	946	110.3	109.9	1 324 298	1 401	105 421	100.3	116 611	63.4	36.6	42.8	18.3	1 271	27.1
Platte	1 224	-6.4	2 424	72.2	147.9	1 743 954	719	178 135	130.4	258 151	23.3	76.7	61.0	32.3	2 397	40.0
Sheridan	1 305	6.6	1 859	49.8	74.6	1 532 138	824	87 229	59.8	85 190	16.5	83.5	46.0	17.1	537	10.5
Sublette	778	29.7	1 954	143.1	122.6	2 626 852	1 345	104 369	54.2	136 116	14.5	85.5	43.5	24.6	373	5.5
Sweetwater	1 665	12.0	6 531	28.4	36.0	1 321 392	202	106 012	21.1	82 894	35.2	64.8	49.8	14.9	250	16.5
Teton	40	-24.1	261	14.7	10.5	829 494	3 181	69 526	9.0	58 675	24.2	75.8	34.4	7.1	16	1.9
Uinta	650	-12.5	2 064	70.1	68.7	1 518 038	735	99 092	29.9	94 816	10.2	89.8	53.7	21.6	88	3.8
Washakie	341	-27.3	1 633	38.4	39.9	1 450 273	888	172 411	51.9	248 153	51.2	48.8	57.9	29.7	451	20.6
Weston	1 290	-2.9	4 888	4.2	57.0	2 282 818	467	132 371	52.2	197 833	4.3	95.7	45.5	26.9	757	27.3

Items 117—132

Water Use, Wholesale Trade, Retail Trade, and Real Estate

STATE County	Water use, 2010		Wholesale trade,[1] 2012				Retail trade,[2] 2012				Real estate and rental and leasing,[2] 2012			
	Total water withdrawn (mil gal/day)	Gallons withdrawn per person per day	Number of establish-ments	Number of employees	Sales (mil dol)	Annual payroll (mil dol)	Number of establish-ments	Number of employees	Sales (mil dol)	Annual payroll (mil dol)	Number of establish-ments	Number of employees	Receipts (mil dol)	Annual payroll (mil dol)
	133	134	135	136	137	138	139	140	141	142	143	144	145	146
WYOMING—Cont'd														
Goshen	395.2	29 829	20	156	69.8	5.8	51	402	107.4	8.7	14	25	3.5	0.6
Hot Springs	78.3	16 268	4	30	13.1	2.3	26	195	48.2	3.0	6	D	D	D
Johnson	118.4	13 814	6	27	8.6	0.7	52	359	91.4	8.1	17	46	4.8	1.5
Laramie	236.4	2 577	121	1 105	722.2	67.0	370	5 513	1 896.2	161.3	142	461	99.5	16.5
Lincoln	204.3	11 282	8	55	17.8	1.7	79	659	180.6	13.3	13	17	2.2	0.4
Natrona	172.3	2 283	163	1 890	2 052.7	115.2	363	4 796	1 487.5	132.1	166	1 281	502.0	79.4
Niobrara	68.9	27 738	2	D	D	D	13	110	28.8	2.3	5	3	1.7	0.2
Park	305.0	10 813	40	270	227.9	12.3	185	1 523	417.5	37.1	57	117	15.1	2.3
Platte	350.2	40 404	5	28	22.0	0.8	35	371	87.5	8.0	11	44	15.2	2.2
Sheridan	198.2	6 808	34	187	84.7	6.8	151	1 559	475.9	42.5	60	204	28.6	5.9
Sublette	167.1	16 311	8	46	41.6	2.7	41	401	94.7	9.7	31	151	27.9	6.4
Sweetwater	169.0	3 859	61	D	D	D	199	2 461	921.4	69.9	85	377	115.4	21.0
Teton	31.2	1 466	32	D	D	D	241	1 929	512.6	55.6	146	527	128.8	26.0
Uinta	217.9	10 316	20	216	153.9	11.3	92	1 119	389.9	24.3	39	148	29.8	5.1
Washakie	165.5	19 393	8	42	15.8	1.3	46	334	95.4	10.0	17	D	D	D
Weston	27.9	3 869	5	40	27.6	1.7	31	267	76.5	6.1	4	6	1.1	0.2

1. Merchant wholesalers, except manufacturers' sales branches and offices.   2. Employer establishments.

STATE County	Professional, scientific, and technical services, 2012				Manufacturing, 2012				Accommodation and food services, 2012			
	Number of establish-ments	Number of employees	Receipts (mil dol)	Annual payroll (mil dol)	Number of establish-ments	Number of employees	Receipts (mil dol)	Annual payroll (mil dol)	Number of establish-ments	Number of employees	Sales (mil dol)	Annual payroll (mil dol)
	147	148	149	150	151	152	153	154	155	156	157	158
WYOMING—Cont'd												
Goshen	24	158	8.4	4.3	12	308	D	9.9	30	320	15.9	3.8
Hot Springs	15	49	4.2	1.7	4	32	8.0	2.1	26	D	D	D
Johnson	49	149	18.1	6.6	12	64	D	2.8	42	403	23.3	7.2
Laramie	458	1 860	279.8	99.7	67	1 190	2 549.8	76.8	207	3 980	224.8	59.8
Lincoln	62	106	12.6	4.0	18	371	D	22.2	60	406	18.0	4.4
Natrona	278	1 537	222.4	83.2	83	2 428	1 780.3	163.0	200	3 814	198.2	57.4
Niobrara	5	9	0.7	0.1	3	D	D	1.4	13	95	5.1	1.2
Park	99	338	36.9	14.6	44	410	90.4	18.5	124	1 891	170.9	49.7
Platte	16	51	6.2	1.3	14	64	10.8	2.3	36	346	21.3	4.1
Sheridan	127	675	92.3	31.2	28	383	102.3	19.3	92	1 213	68.7	19.2
Sublette	54	139	20.1	6.7	9	31	D	1.5	40	358	24.4	6.9
Sweetwater	121	493	90.2	31.7	35	1 772	1 575.5	148.7	113	1 771	128.9	28.1
Teton	268	744	139.3	46.8	34	254	34.1	8.0	186	4 598	344.0	114.7
Uinta	54	285	33.8	13.8	24	233	204.2	9.8	48	875	35.5	9.9
Washakie	37	104	11.9	4.1	14	387	187.5	18.5	32	284	11.6	3.2
Weston	11	23	2.4	0.7	3	D	D	D	22	190	9.4	2.4

1. Establishment subject to federal tax.

STATE County	Health care and social assistance, 2012				Other services, 2012				Nonemployer businesses, 2015		Value of residential construction authorized by building permits, 2016	
	Number of establish-ments	Number of employees	Receipts (mil dol)	Annual payroll (mil dol)	Number of establish-ments	Number of employees	Receipts (mil dol)	Annual payroll (mil dol)	Number	Receipts (mil dol)	New Construction ($1,000)	Number of housing units
	159	160	161	162	163	164	165	166	167	168	169	170
WYOMING—Cont'd												
Goshen	27	803	60.5	25.6	28	89	9.3	2.3	914	37.1	648	2
Hot Springs	19	395	34.2	15.5	14	58	3.9	1.1	374	12.4	0	0
Johnson	32	375	32.1	13.2	22	104	7.6	2.8	1 200	63.5	1 950	8
Laramie	323	6 700	647.9	305.2	189	943	93.6	27.1	7 665	480.1	81 396	476
Lincoln	56	643	58.5	24.1	38	77	9.9	2.2	1 916	81.2	39 475	144
Natrona	305	5 141	687.2	266.3	207	1 333	227.6	49.8	5 884	301.6	37 169	165
Niobrara	7	D	D	D	7	28	6.7	1.3	244	10.7	2 014	7
Park	116	1 399	146.3	55.5	70	248	24.9	6.5	3 077	129.0	32 368	140
Platte	22	325	27.7	10.9	13	50	3.7	0.9	716	26.5	7 369	44
Sheridan	128	2 705	302.2	125.1	74	334	31.1	8.6	2 720	115.4	34 898	148
Sublette	23	207	13.3	6.8	32	162	25.1	6.3	991	41.5	8 121	30
Sweetwater	104	1 285	150.2	51.2	88	464	58.7	16.1	2 139	95.1	19 804	72
Teton	117	1 120	158.9	60.5	113	450	109.0	17.0	4 983	325.2	232 043	163
Uinta	67	1 265	110.3	53.9	35	D	D	D	1 398	63.5	9 039	46
Washakie	29	787	51.6	23.0	28	94	9.7	1.8	681	21.1	400	4
Weston	24	352	25.3	10.5	12	38	3.1	0.8	610	23.1	815	3

Table B. States and Counties — Government Employment and Payroll, and Local Government Finances

STATE County	Government employment and payroll, 2012									Local government finances, 2012				
			March payroll (percent of total)							General revenue				
												Taxes		
													Per capita[1] (dollars)	
	Full-time equivalent employees	March payroll (dollars)	Adminis- tration, judicial, and legal	Police and Corrections	Fire Protection	Highways and transpor- tation	Health and Welfare	Natural resources and utilities	Education and libraries	Total (mil dol)	Inter- govern- mental (mil dol)	Total (mil dol)	Total	Property
	171	172	173	174	175	176	177	178	179	180	181	182	183	184
WYOMING—Cont'd														
Goshen	800	2 841 581	5.6	7.0	0.0	2.4	1.3	5.3	77.7	86.6	58.5	10.5	773	552
Hot Springs	363	1 248 475	7.7	7.2	0.0	3.0	30.6	3.5	46.8	44.5	12.8	14.8	3 062	2 366
Johnson	670	2 461 238	5.8	13.9	1.0	2.9	30.1	3.1	42.7	83.0	14.4	44.9	5 208	4 585
Laramie	6 173	27 578 286	2.8	4.6	1.9	1.8	39.8	1.5	46.1	796.0	292.8	103.3	1 094	589
Lincoln	1 211	4 847 475	5.1	5.7	0.0	2.9	30.1	3.4	50.4	146.8	60.4	43.1	2 402	2 075
Natrona	3 954	15 321 295	4.4	7.8	3.5	2.3	2.0	5.1	72.5	442.5	254.7	108.8	1 384	938
Niobrara	300	1 035 735	7.3	4.9	0.0	2.2	34.2	5.3	43.5	21.1	9.3	5.8	2 352	1 687
Park	2 084	8 399 901	4.2	4.7	0.4	2.6	27.2	5.2	52.8	238.1	92.8	47.9	1 668	1 494
Platte	543	2 168 168	5.1	7.9	0.2	2.2	1.5	6.3	74.9	46.5	26.6	13.3	1 519	995
Sheridan	2 207	8 719 701	3.2	4.7	1.0	2.3	30.0	3.0	54.6	234.1	106.6	40.1	1 354	946
Sublette	677	2 840 346	8.1	15.4	0.0	10.5	11.9	4.2	49.3	142.2	33.5	91.3	8 805	8 657
Sweetwater	2 985	12 809 450	6.0	8.4	2.4	2.6	20.2	5.8	52.6	382.6	116.8	165.8	3 662	2 797
Teton	1 475	6 340 874	5.4	7.3	1.5	7.9	37.5	5.7	32.3	225.0	41.2	80.1	3 695	2 344
Uinta	1 240	4 518 508	5.8	7.1	0.8	2.5	1.9	5.2	73.2	117.5	70.3	38.1	1 811	1 505
Washakie	459	1 506 233	5.8	5.8	0.7	2.9	2.6	6.0	75.1	45.2	28.7	12.2	1 442	998
Weston	521	1 865 375	4.5	8.0	0.4	2.9	23.8	5.3	54.7	44.2	22.9	9.7	1 375	1 062

1. Based on the resident population estimated as of July 1 of the year shown.

Table B. States and Counties — **Local Government Finances, Government Employment, and Income Taxes**

	Local government finances, 2012 (cont.)										Government employment, 2015			Individual income tax returns, 2014		
STATE County	Direct general expenditure							Debt outstanding								
			Percent of total for:													
	Total (mil dol)	Per capita[1] (dollars)	Educa-tion	Health and hospitals	Police protec-tion	Public welfare	High-ways	Total (mil dol)	Per capita[1] (dollars)	Federal civilian	Federal military	State and local	Number of returns	Mean adjusted gross income	Mean income tax
	185	186	187	188	189	190	191	192	193	194	195	196	197	198	199
WYOMING—Cont'd															
Goshen	86.2	6 325	66.3	1.5	3.7	0.9	7.3	10.3	756	77	64	1 388	5 790	47 722	4 943
Hot Springs	44.9	9 306	33.3	31.7	3.7	0.0	5.2	4.5	931	15	25	552	2 330	52 191	5 877
Johnson	95.5	11 080	33.0	26.7	3.3	0.5	6.3	14.7	1 711	122	45	864	4 290	62 446	8 155
Laramie	781.4	8 270	37.0	40.5	2.5	0.2	3.1	132.4	1 401	2 643	3 465	11 395	47 590	60 985	7 432
Lincoln	144.3	8 033	47.9	26.3	3.6	0.1	4.8	60.9	3 388	108	98	1 691	8 060	71 253	9 208
Natrona	436.0	5 546	59.1	0.4	4.8	0.7	4.1	147.1	1 871	638	426	5 210	40 340	85 124	14 977
Niobrara	27.9	11 371	45.7	24.9	4.4	0.1	4.6	111.4	45 347	12	12	445	1 160	58 328	6 909
Park	277.9	9 682	41.4	36.2	2.5	0.0	2.9	79.0	2 754	767	150	2 801	14 670	63 701	8 216
Platte	48.9	5 582	54.4	2.9	7.4	0.1	4.1	8.7	993	107	57	808	4 420	53 794	6 446
Sheridan	252.8	8 543	49.0	26.5	2.5	0.0	5.2	33.2	1 121	761	153	2 727	14 980	80 233	11 715
Sublette	154.1	14 868	43.1	8.2	4.0	1.8	11.0	9.5	919	122	49	979	4 270	91 521	16 120
Sweetwater	389.7	8 609	48.2	17.5	5.5	0.3	4.3	69.5	1 536	201	232	4 325	20 970	71 545	9 518
Teton	218.0	10 059	24.1	34.3	3.8	0.0	2.4	92.9	4 287	422	121	1 980	14 190	248 949	52 177
Uinta	121.7	5 787	64.9	0.8	5.8	0.9	4.8	14.0	665	68	108	2 146	9 300	64 849	7 780
Washakie	52.1	6 153	68.3	0.8	4.1	0.4	3.0	12.8	1 512	108	43	763	3 930	61 809	8 459
Weston	48.0	6 780	47.5	21.6	4.2	0.6	10.3	2.0	286	49	36	745	3 310	65 335	8 707

1. Based on the resident population estimated as of July 1 of the year shown.

Metropolitan Areas

(For explanation of symbols, see page viii)

Part C—Metropolitan Areas

Metropolitan Area Highlights and Rankings

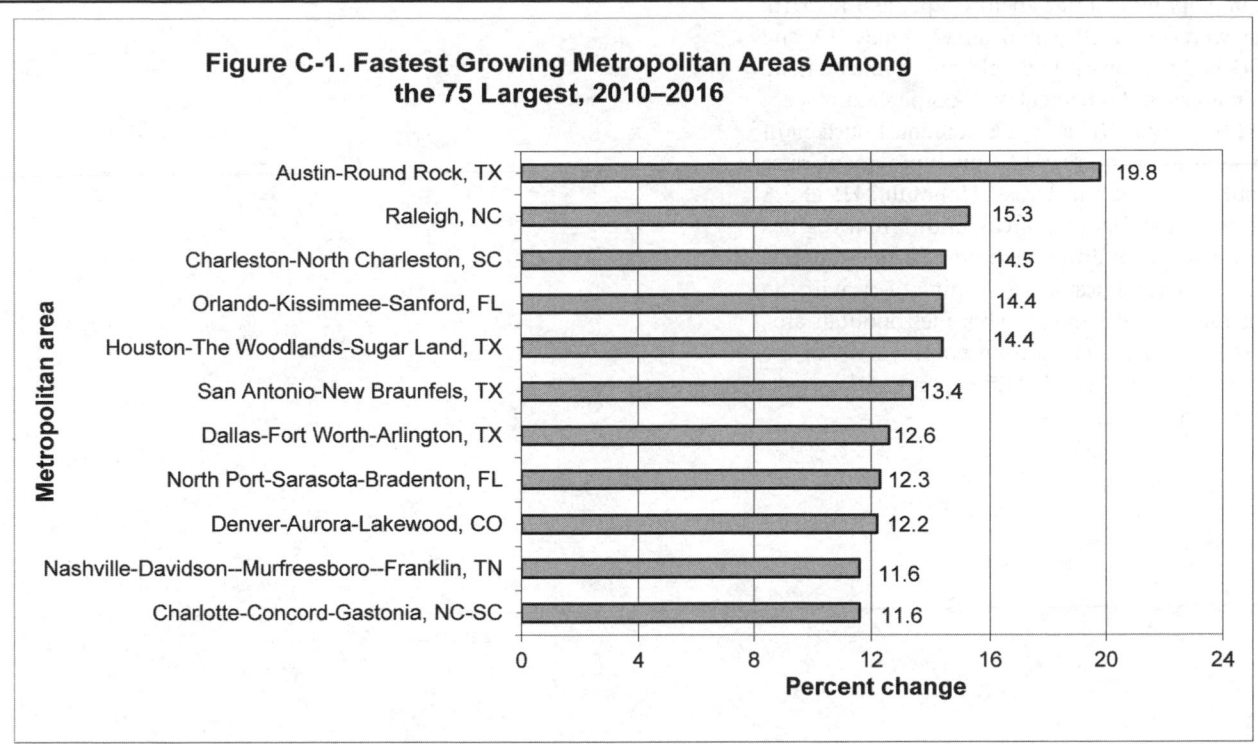

Figure C-1. Fastest Growing Metropolitan Areas Among the 75 Largest, 2010–2016

Metropolitan area (y-axis), Percent change (x-axis)

- Austin-Round Rock, TX: 19.8
- Raleigh, NC: 15.3
- Charleston-North Charleston, SC: 14.5
- Orlando-Kissimmee-Sanford, FL: 14.4
- Houston-The Woodlands-Sugar Land, TX: 14.4
- San Antonio-New Braunfels, TX: 13.4
- Dallas-Fort Worth-Arlington, TX: 12.6
- North Port-Sarasota-Bradenton, FL: 12.3
- Denver-Aurora-Lakewood, CO: 12.2
- Nashville-Davidson--Murfreesboro--Franklin, TN: 11.6
- Charlotte-Concord-Gastonia, NC-SC: 11.6

In 2016, 85.7 percent of Americans lived in metropolitan areas, but these metropolitan areas made up a mere 28 percent of the nation's land area. After nearly a decade of research and development, the Office of Management and Budget (OMB) first established new rules for defining metropolitan areas and issued a completely new list after the 2000 census. This scheme defines a variety of areas called "Core Based Statistical Areas" (CBSAs). Along with the new definition of metropolitan areas, OMB defined a new type of area—called a micropolitan area—that defines the many American communities with population clusters that are too small to meet the 50,000 minimum that defines a metropolitan area. Appendix C lists these micropolitan areas as of July 2015 but, because of size constraints, *County and City Extra* continues to include only metropolitan area data in Table C. In 2013, the Census Bureau released data for new metropolitan and micropolitan areas based on the 2010 census, and these were updated in 2015 This edition of *County and City Extra* uses these 2015 metropolitan area delineations. Most of the data producers are now releasing data for the new metropolitan areas. For a few data sources, the counties have been aggregated to the new areas.

With over 20 million people, the New York metropolitan area was the largest, followed by Los Angeles with a population of over 13 million. Chicago ranked third with 9.5 million people. Another 11 metropolitan areas had more than 4 million residents (Dallas, Houston, Washington, Philadelphia, Miami, Atlanta, Boston, San Francisco, Phoenix, Riverside, and Detroit), while 39 other metropolitan areas had between 1 million and 4 million people. Fifty-six percent of the U.S. population lived in these 53 metropolitan areas with one million or more residents.

One hundred-fifty-one metropolitan areas grew by 5 percent or more between 2010 and 2016. The Villages, FL had the highest growth rate, increasing by 32.7 percent to a 2016 population of 123,996 residents. Among the 75 largest metropolitan areas, Austin-Round Rock, TX had the largest increase at 19.8 percent followed by Raleigh, NC at 15.3 percent Six of the most populous metropolitan areas lost population since 2010—Pittsburgh, PA; Hartford-West Hartford-East Hartford, CT; New Haven-Milford, CT; Cleveland-Elyria, OH, Rochester, NY and Buffalo-Cheektowaga-Niagara Falls, NY.

Among metropolitan areas, New York and Los Angeles shared the top spots for density as well as for total population. With 2,745.1 persons per square mile, Los Angeles-Long Beach-Anaheim, CA was the most densely populated metropolitan area in the country. At the other extreme, eight of the largest metropolitan areas had fewer than 200 persons per square mile. These areas typically had large land areas and were located in the west and south.

In 2016, six metropolitan areas had unemployment rates at 10 percent or higher. In contrast, 131 metropolitan areas had unemployment rates at 10 percent or higher in 2010. Topping the list are El Centro, CA and Yuma, AZ, two metropolitan areas with large agricultural workforces and unemployment rates at 23.5 percent and 18.6 percent respectively. Eight of the 10 metropolitan areas with the highest unemployment were in California. Among the 75 most populous metropolitan areas, Bakersfield, CA was the only MSA with an unemployment rate above 10 percent. Over two hundred metropolitan areas had unemployment rates below 5 percent in 2016. Many of them were relatively small areas. Ames, IA and Sioux Falls, SD had the lowest unemployment rates among all metropolitan areas at 2.4 percent and 2.3 percent respectively followed by Fargo, ND at at 2.6 percent. Fourteen of the 75 largest metropolitan areas had unemployment rates below 4 percent, the lowest in Urban Honolulu, HI at 2.8 percent. These were metropolitan areas in different regions of the country, and with different employment patterns. Among them was Grand Rapids-Wyoming, MI with an unemployment rate of 3.4 percent. This metropolitan area had the highest level of manufacturing employment of the 75 largest metropolitan areas, with 21.8 percent of the workforce in manufacturing industries.

75 Largest Metropolitan Areas by 2016 Population
Selected Rankings

Population rank	Metropolitan area	Population [col 2]	Popu-lation rank	Land area rank	Metropolitan area	Land area (square miles) [col 1]
	Population, 2016				**Total land area, 2016**	
1	New York-Newark-Jersey City, NY-NJ-PA	20 153 634	13	1	Riverside-San Bernardino-Ontario, CA	27 264
2	Los Angeles-Long Beach-Anaheim, CA	13 310 447	12	2	Phoenix-Mesa-Scottsdale, AZ	14 565
3	Chicago-Naperville-Elgin, IL-IN-WI	9 512 999	60	3	Albuquerque, NM	9 281
4	Dallas-Fort Worth-Arlington, TX	7 233 323	4	4	Dallas-Fort Worth-Arlington, TX	9 280
5	Houston-The Woodlands-Sugar Land, TX	6 772 470	53	5	Tucson, AZ	9 187
6	Washington-Arlington-Alexandria, DC-VA-MD-WV	6 131 977	9	6	Atlanta-Sandy Springs-Roswell, GA	8 681
7	Philadelphia-Camden-Wilmington, PA-NJ-DE-MD	6 070 500	19	7	Denver-Aurora-Lakewood, CO	8 346
8	Miami-Fort Lauderdale-West Palm Beach, FL	6 066 387	1	8	New York-Newark-Jersey City, NY-NJ-PA	8 295
9	Atlanta-Sandy Springs-Roswell, GA	5 789 700	5	9	Houston-The Woodlands-Sugar Land, TX	8 261
10	Boston-Cambridge-Newton, MA-NH	4 794 447	62	10	Bakersfield, CA	8 132
11	San Francisco-Oakland-Hayward, CA	4 679 166	29	11	Las Vegas-Henderson-Paradise, NV	7 892
12	Phoenix-Mesa-Scottsdale, AZ	4 661 537	20	12	St. Louis, MO-IL	7 864
13	Riverside-San Bernardino-Ontario, CA	4 527 837	48	13	Salt Lake City, UT	7 684
14	Detroit-Warren-Dearborn, MI	4 297 617	16	14	Minneapolis-St. Paul-Bloomington, MN	7 637
15	Seattle-Tacoma-Bellevue, WA	3 798 902	24	15	San Antonio-New Braunfels, TX	7 313
16	Minneapolis-St. Paul-Bloomington, MN	3 551 036	30	16	Kansas City, MO-KS	7 256
17	San Diego-Carlsbad, CA	3 317 749	3	17	Chicago-Naperville-Elgin, IL-IN-WI	7 197
18	Tampa-St. Petersburg-Clearwater, FL	3 032 171	25	18	Portland-Vancouver-Hillsboro, OR-WA	6 687
19	Denver-Aurora-Lakewood, CO	2 853 077	36	19	Nashville-Davidson—Murfreesboro—Franklin, TN	6 302
20	St. Louis, MO-IL	2 807 002	55	20	Tulsa, OK	6 270
21	Baltimore-Columbia-Towson, MD	2 798 886	6	21	Washington-Arlington-Alexandria, DC-VA-MD-WV	6 247
22	Charlotte-Concord-Gastonia, NC-SC	2 474 314	56	22	Fresno, CA	5 959
23	Orlando-Kissimmee-Sanford, FL	2 441 257	15	23	Seattle-Tacoma-Bellevue, WA	5 871
24	San Antonio-New Braunfels, TX	2 429 609	68	24	El Paso, TX	5 584
25	Portland-Vancouver-Hillsboro, OR-WA	2 424 955	41	25	Oklahoma City, OK	5 512
26	Pittsburgh, PA	2 342 299	26	26	Pittsburgh, PA	5 281
27	Sacramento—Roseville—Arden-Arcade, CA	2 296 418	49	27	Birmingham-Hoover, AL	5 280
28	Cincinnati, OH-KY-IN	2 165 139	27	28	Sacramento—Roseville—Arden-Arcade, CA	5 095
29	Las Vegas-Henderson-Paradise, NV	2 155 664	8	29	Miami-Fort Lauderdale-West Palm Beach, FL	5 076
30	Kansas City, MO-KS	2 104 509	22	30	Charlotte-Concord-Gastonia, NC-SC	5 065
31	Austin-Round Rock, TX	2 056 405	42	31	Memphis, TN-MS-AR	4 986
32	Cleveland-Elyria, OH	2 055 612	2	32	Los Angeles-Long Beach-Anaheim, CA	4 849
33	Columbus, OH	2 041 520	33	33	Columbus, OH	4 797
34	Indianapolis-Carmel-Anderson, IN	2 004 230	7	34	Philadelphia-Camden-Wilmington, PA-NJ-DE-MD	4 603
35	San Jose-Sunnyvale-Santa Clara, CA	1 978 816	45	35	Richmond, VA	4 576
36	Nashville-Davidson—Murfreesboro—Franklin, TN	1 865 298	59	36	Omaha-Council Bluffs, NE-IA	4 350
37	Virginia Beach-Norfolk-Newport News, VA-NC	1 726 907	34	37	Indianapolis-Carmel-Anderson, IN	4 307
38	Providence-Warwick, RI-MA	1 614 750	31	38	Austin-Round Rock, TX	4 222
39	Milwaukee-Waukesha-West Allis, WI	1 572 482	17	39	San Diego-Carlsbad, CA	4 207
40	Jacksonville, FL	1 478 212	28	40	Cincinnati, OH-KY-IN	4 166
41	Oklahoma City, OK	1 373 211	70	41	Baton Rouge, LA	4 027
42	Memphis, TN-MS-AR	1 342 842	14	42	Detroit-Warren-Dearborn, MI	3 889
43	Raleigh, NC	1 302 946	71	43	Columbia, SC	3 703
44	Louisville/Jefferson County, KY-IN	1 283 430	44	44	Louisville/Jefferson County, KY-IN	3 578
45	Richmond, VA	1 281 708	64	45	Knoxville, TN	3 501
46	New Orleans-Metairie, LA	1 268 883	10	46	Boston-Cambridge-Newton, MA-NH	3 486
47	Hartford-West Hartford-East Hartford, CT	1 206 836	23	47	Orlando-Kissimmee-Sanford, FL	3 481
48	Salt Lake City, UT	1 186 187	51	48	Rochester, NY	3 266
49	Birmingham-Hoover, AL	1 147 417	46	49	New Orleans-Metairie, LA	3 202
50	Buffalo-Cheektowaga-Niagara Falls, NY	1 132 804	40	50	Jacksonville, FL	3 202
51	Rochester, NY	1 078 879	63	51	Albany-Schenectady-Troy, NY	2 812
52	Grand Rapids-Wyoming, MI	1 047 099	61	52	Greenville-Anderson-Mauldin, SC	2 711
53	Tucson, AZ	1 016 206	37	53	Virginia Beach-Norfolk-Newport News, VA-NC	2 683
54	Urban Honolulu, HI	992 605	35	54	San Jose-Sunnyvale-Santa Clara, CA	2 680
55	Tulsa, OK	987 201	52	55	Grand Rapids-Wyoming, MI	2 670
56	Fresno, CA	979 915	21	56	Baltimore-Columbia-Towson, MD	2 602
57	Bridgeport-Stamford-Norwalk, CT	944 177	74	57	Charleston-North Charleston, SC	2 590
58	Worcester, MA-CT	935 781	18	58	Tampa-St. Petersburg-Clearwater, FL	2 515
59	Omaha-Council Bluffs, NE-IA	924 129	11	59	San Francisco-Oakland-Hayward, CA	2 478
60	Albuquerque, NM	909 906	43	60	Raleigh, NC	2 118
61	Greenville-Anderson-Mauldin, SC	884 975	58	61	Worcester, MA-CT	2 024
62	Bakersfield, CA	884 788	32	62	Cleveland-Elyria, OH	1 999
63	Albany-Schenectady-Troy, NY	881 839	75	63	Greensboro-High Point, NC	1 994
64	Knoxville, TN	868 546	67	64	Oxnard-Thousand Oaks-Ventura, CA	1 843
65	New Haven-Milford, CT	856 875	38	65	Providence-Warwick, RI-MA	1 587
66	McAllen-Edinburg-Mission, TX	849 843	66	66	McAllen-Edinburg-Mission, TX	1 571
67	Oxnard-Thousand Oaks-Ventura, CA	849 738	50	67	Buffalo-Cheektowaga-Niagara Falls, NY	1 565
68	El Paso, TX	841 971	47	68	Hartford-West Hartford-East Hartford, CT	1 515
69	Allentown-Bethlehem-Easton, PA-NJ	835 652	39	69	Milwaukee-Waukesha-West Allis, WI	1 455
70	Baton Rouge, LA	835 175	69	70	Allentown-Bethlehem-Easton, PA-NJ	1 453
71	Columbia, SC	817 488	73	71	North Port-Sarasota-Bradenton, FL	1 299
72	Dayton, OH	800 683	72	72	Dayton, OH	1 282
73	North Port-Sarasota-Bradenton, FL	788 457	57	73	Bridgeport-Stamford-Norwalk, CT	625
74	Charleston-North Charleston, SC	761 155	65	74	New Haven-Milford, CT	604
75	Greensboro-High Point, NC	756 139	54	75	Urban Honolulu, HI	601

75 Largest Metropolitan Areas by 2016 Population
Selected Rankings

Population rank	Density rank	Metropolitan area (Population density, 2016)	Density (per square kilometer) [col 4]	Population rank	Percent change rank	Metropolitan area (Percent population change, 2010 – 2016)	Percent change [col 23]
2	1	Los Angeles-Long Beach-Anaheim, CA	2 745.1	31	1	Austin-Round Rock, TX	19.8
1	2	New York-Newark-Jersey City, NY-NJ-PA	2 429.7	43	2	Raleigh, NC	15.3
11	3	San Francisco-Oakland-Hayward, CA	1 888.4	74	3	Charleston-North Charleston, SC	14.5
54	4	Urban Honolulu, HI	1 652.7	5	4	Houston-The Woodlands-Sugar Land, TX	14.4
57	5	Bridgeport-Stamford-Norwalk, CT	1 510.7	23	4	Orlando-Kissimmee-Sanford, FL	14.4
65	6	New Haven-Milford, CT	1 417.5	24	6	San Antonio-New Braunfels, TX	13.4
10	7	Boston-Cambridge-Newton, MA-NH	1 375.4	4	7	Dallas-Fort Worth-Arlington, TX	12.6
3	8	Chicago-Naperville-Elgin, IL-IN-WI	1 321.9	73	8	North Port-Sarasota-Bradenton, FL	12.3
7	9	Philadelphia-Camden-Wilmington, PA-NJ-DE-MD	1 318.9	19	9	Denver-Aurora-Lakewood, CO	12.2
18	10	Tampa-St. Petersburg-Clearwater, FL	1 205.8	22	10	Charlotte-Concord-Gastonia, NC-SC	11.6
8	11	Miami-Fort Lauderdale-West Palm Beach, FL	1 195.2	36	10	Nashville-Davidson—Murfreesboro—Franklin, TN	11.6
14	12	Detroit-Warren-Dearborn, MI	1 105.0	12	12	Phoenix-Mesa-Scottsdale, AZ	11.2
39	13	Milwaukee-Waukesha-West Allis, WI	1 080.7	29	13	Las Vegas-Henderson-Paradise, NV	10.5
21	14	Baltimore-Columbia-Towson, MD	1 075.9	15	14	Seattle-Tacoma-Bellevue, WA	10.4
32	15	Cleveland-Elyria, OH	1 028.3	40	15	Jacksonville, FL	9.9
38	16	Providence-Warwick, RI-MA	1 017.5	66	16	McAllen-Edinburg-Mission, TX	9.7
6	17	Washington-Arlington-Alexandria, DC-VA-MD-WV	981.6	41	17	Oklahoma City, OK	9.6
5	18	Houston-The Woodlands-Sugar Land, TX	819.8	9	18	Atlanta-Sandy Springs-Roswell, GA	9.5
47	19	Hartford-West Hartford-East Hartford, CT	796.7	8	19	Miami-Fort Lauderdale-West Palm Beach, FL	9.0
17	20	San Diego-Carlsbad, CA	788.7	48	19	Salt Lake City, UT	9.0
4	21	Dallas-Fort Worth-Arlington, TX	779.4	18	21	Tampa-St. Petersburg-Clearwater, FL	8.9
35	22	San Jose-Sunnyvale-Santa Clara, CA	738.4	25	21	Portland-Vancouver-Hillsboro, OR-WA	8.9
50	23	Buffalo-Cheektowaga-Niagara Falls, NY	723.8	6	23	Washington-Arlington-Alexandria, DC-VA-MD-WV	8.8
23	24	Orlando-Kissimmee-Sanford, FL	701.2	11	24	San Francisco-Oakland-Hayward, CA	7.9
9	25	Atlanta-Sandy Springs-Roswell, GA	666.9	35	25	San Jose-Sunnyvale-Santa Clara, CA	7.7
15	26	Seattle-Tacoma-Bellevue, WA	647.1	61	26	Greenville-Anderson-Mauldin, SC	7.4
37	27	Virginia Beach-Norfolk-Newport News, VA-NC	643.7	33	27	Columbus, OH	7.3
72	28	Dayton, OH	624.6	13	28	Riverside-San Bernardino-Ontario, CA	7.2
43	29	Raleigh, NC	615.2	17	28	San Diego-Carlsbad, CA	7.2
73	30	North Port-Sarasota-Bradenton, FL	607.0	27	30	Sacramento—Roseville—Arden-Arcade, CA	6.9
69	31	Allentown-Bethlehem-Easton, PA-NJ	575.2	59	31	Omaha-Council Bluffs, NE-IA	6.8
66	32	McAllen-Edinburg-Mission, TX	541.0	46	32	New Orleans-Metairie, LA	6.6
28	33	Cincinnati, OH-KY-IN	519.8	71	33	Columbia, SC	6.5
22	34	Charlotte-Concord-Gastonia, NC-SC	488.6	34	34	Indianapolis-Carmel-Anderson, IN	6.2
31	35	Austin-Round Rock, TX	487.1	45	35	Richmond, VA	6.1
34	36	Indianapolis-Carmel-Anderson, IN	465.4	16	36	Minneapolis-St. Paul-Bloomington, MN	6.0
16	37	Minneapolis-St. Paul-Bloomington, MN	465.0	52	37	Grand Rapids-Wyoming, MI	5.9
58	38	Worcester, MA-CT	462.5	62	38	Bakersfield, CA	5.4
40	39	Jacksonville, FL	461.7	10	39	Boston-Cambridge-Newton, MA-NH	5.3
67	40	Oxnard-Thousand Oaks-Ventura, CA	461.1	55	39	Tulsa, OK	5.3
27	41	Sacramento—Roseville—Arden-Arcade, CA	450.7	56	39	Fresno, CA	5.3
26	42	Pittsburgh, PA	443.5	30	42	Kansas City, MO-KS	4.7
33	43	Columbus, OH	425.6	68	42	El Paso, TX	4.7
46	44	New Orleans-Metairie, LA	396.3	75	44	Greensboro-High Point, NC	4.5
52	45	Grand Rapids-Wyoming, MI	392.2	54	45	Urban Honolulu, HI	4.1
75	46	Greensboro-High Point, NC	379.3	70	45	Baton Rouge, LA	4.1
25	47	Portland-Vancouver-Hillsboro, OR-WA	362.7	44	47	Louisville/Jefferson County, KY-IN	3.9
44	48	Louisville/Jefferson County, KY-IN	358.7	2	48	Los Angeles-Long Beach-Anaheim, CA	3.8
20	49	St. Louis, MO-IL	357.0	53	49	Tucson, AZ	3.7
19	50	Denver-Aurora-Lakewood, CO	341.9	64	49	Knoxville, TN	3.7
24	51	San Antonio-New Braunfels, TX	332.2	21	51	Baltimore-Columbia-Towson, MD	3.3
51	52	Rochester, NY	330.3	67	52	Oxnard-Thousand Oaks-Ventura, CA	3.2
61	53	Greenville-Anderson-Mauldin, SC	326.5	1	53	New York-Newark-Jersey City, NY-NJ-PA	3.0
12	54	Phoenix-Mesa-Scottsdale, AZ	320.1	37	53	Virginia Beach-Norfolk-Newport News, VA-NC	3.0
63	55	Albany-Schenectady-Troy, NY	313.6	57	53	Bridgeport-Stamford-Norwalk, CT	3.0
36	56	Nashville-Davidson—Murfreesboro—Franklin, TN	296.0	60	56	Albuquerque, NM	2.6
74	57	Charleston-North Charleston, SC	293.9	28	57	Cincinnati, OH-KY-IN	2.4
30	58	Kansas City, MO-KS	290.0	58	58	Worcester, MA-CT	2.1
45	59	Richmond, VA	280.1	7	59	Philadelphia-Camden-Wilmington, PA-NJ-DE-MD	1.8
29	60	Las Vegas-Henderson-Paradise, NV	273.2	69	59	Allentown-Bethlehem-Easton, PA-NJ	1.8
42	61	Memphis, TN-MS-AR	269.3	49	61	Birmingham-Hoover, AL	1.7
41	62	Oklahoma City, OK	249.1	42	62	Memphis, TN-MS-AR	1.4
64	63	Knoxville, TN	248.1	63	63	Albany-Schenectady-Troy, NY	1.3
71	64	Columbia, SC	220.8	39	64	Milwaukee-Waukesha-West Allis, WI	1.1
49	65	Birmingham-Hoover, AL	217.3	38	65	Providence-Warwick, RI-MA	0.8
59	66	Omaha-Council Bluffs, NE-IA	212.4	20	66	St. Louis, MO-IL	0.7
70	67	Baton Rouge, LA	207.4	3	67	Chicago-Naperville-Elgin, IL-IN-WI	0.5
13	68	Riverside-San Bernardino-Ontario, CA	166.1	72	68	Dayton, OH	0.2
56	69	Fresno, CA	164.4	14	69	Detroit-Warren-Dearborn, MI	0.0
55	70	Tulsa, OK	157.5	51	70	Rochester, NY	-0.1
48	71	Salt Lake City, UT	154.4	50	71	Buffalo-Cheektowaga-Niagara Falls, NY	-0.2
68	72	El Paso, TX	150.8	47	72	Hartford-West Hartford-East Hartford, CT	-0.5
53	73	Tucson, AZ	110.6	26	73	Pittsburgh, PA	-0.6
62	74	Bakersfield, CA	108.8	65	73	New Haven-Milford, CT	-0.6
60	75	Albuquerque, NM	98.0	32	75	Cleveland-Elyria, OH	-1.0

75 Largest Metropolitan Areas by 2016 Population
Selected Rankings

Percent White, not Hispanic or Latino, alone or in combination, 2016				Percent Black, not Hispanic or Latino, alone or in combination, 2016			
Population rank	White rank	Metropolitan area	Percent White [col 5]	Population rank	Black rank	Metropolitan area	Percent Black [col 6]
64	1	Knoxville, TN	88.7	42	1	Memphis, TN-MS-AR	47.9
26	2	Pittsburgh, PA	87.3	70	2	Baton Rouge, LA	36.2
63	3	Albany-Schenectady-Troy, NY	82.3	46	3	New Orleans-Metairie, LA	35.4
28	4	Cincinnati, OH-KY-IN	81.7	9	4	Atlanta-Sandy Springs-Roswell, GA	34.7
52	5	Grand Rapids-Wyoming, MI	81.1	71	5	Columbia, SC	34.6
58	6	Worcester, MA-CT	80.0	37	6	Virginia Beach-Norfolk-Newport News, VA-NC	32.0
50	7	Buffalo-Cheektowaga-Niagara Falls, NY	79.3	45	7	Richmond, VA	31.0
73	8	North Port-Sarasota-Bradenton, FL	79.2	21	8	Baltimore-Columbia-Towson, MD	30.3
72	9	Dayton, OH	79.0	49	9	Birmingham-Hoover, AL	29.5
38	10	Providence-Warwick, RI-MA	78.7	75	10	Greensboro-High Point, NC	27.8
16	11	Minneapolis-St. Paul-Bloomington, MN	78.6	74	11	Charleston-North Charleston, SC	27.0
44	11	Louisville/Jefferson County, KY-IN	78.6	6	12	Washington-Arlington-Alexandria, DC-VA-MD-WV	26.5
59	11	Omaha-Council Bluffs, NE-IA	78.6	22	13	Charlotte-Concord-Gastonia, NC-SC	23.5
51	14	Rochester, NY	78.5	14	14	Detroit-Warren-Dearborn, MI	23.3
25	15	Portland-Vancouver-Hillsboro, OR-WA	77.4	40	15	Jacksonville, FL	22.3
33	16	Columbus, OH	76.1	7	16	Philadelphia-Camden-Wilmington, PA-NJ-DE-MD	21.6
20	17	St. Louis, MO-IL	75.7	8	17	Miami-Fort Lauderdale-West Palm Beach, FL	21.1
69	18	Allentown-Bethlehem-Easton, PA-NJ	75.6	32	18	Cleveland-Elyria, OH	21.0
30	19	Kansas City, MO-KS	75.1	43	19	Raleigh, NC	20.8
34	20	Indianapolis-Carmel-Anderson, IN	74.9	20	20	St. Louis, MO-IL	19.4
36	21	Nashville-Davidson—Murfreesboro—Franklin, TN	74.6	5	21	Houston-The Woodlands-Sugar Land, TX	17.5
61	21	Greenville-Anderson-Mauldin, SC	74.6	39	21	Milwaukee-Waukesha-West Allis, WI	17.5
48	23	Salt Lake City, UT	74.4	61	21	Greenville-Anderson-Mauldin, SC	17.5
10	24	Boston-Cambridge-Newton, MA-NH	73.2	3	24	Chicago-Naperville-Elgin, IL-IN-WI	17.2
32	25	Cleveland-Elyria, OH	71.9	72	24	Dayton, OH	17.2
55	26	Tulsa, OK	71.2	33	26	Columbus, OH	16.9
47	27	Hartford-West Hartford-East Hartford, CT	69.4	1	27	New York-Newark-Jersey City, NY-NJ-PA	16.7
41	28	Oklahoma City, OK	69.0	23	27	Orlando-Kissimmee-Sanford, FL	16.7
15	29	Seattle-Tacoma-Bellevue, WA	68.8	34	29	Indianapolis-Carmel-Anderson, IN	16.4
39	30	Milwaukee-Waukesha-West Allis, WI	68.7	36	30	Nashville-Davidson—Murfreesboro—Franklin, TN	16.3
14	31	Detroit-Warren-Dearborn, MI	68.6	4	31	Dallas-Fort Worth-Arlington, TX	16.2
19	32	Denver-Aurora-Lakewood, CO	66.7	44	32	Louisville/Jefferson County, KY-IN	15.7
74	33	Charleston-North Charleston, SC	66.1	30	33	Kansas City, MO-KS	13.7
18	34	Tampa-St. Petersburg-Clearwater, FL	65.8	28	34	Cincinnati, OH-KY-IN	13.6
40	34	Jacksonville, FL	65.8	65	34	New Haven-Milford, CT	13.6
65	36	New Haven-Milford, CT	65.2	50	36	Buffalo-Cheektowaga-Niagara Falls, NY	13.0
49	37	Birmingham-Hoover, AL	64.9	18	37	Tampa-St. Petersburg-Clearwater, FL	12.6
7	38	Philadelphia-Camden-Wilmington, PA-NJ-DE-MD	63.9	29	38	Las Vegas-Henderson-Paradise, NV	12.5
57	39	Bridgeport-Stamford-Norwalk, CT	63.8	51	39	Rochester, NY	12.2
43	40	Raleigh, NC	63.6	41	40	Oklahoma City, OK	12.0
22	41	Charlotte-Concord-Gastonia, NC-SC	63.4	47	41	Hartford-West Hartford-East Hartford, CT	11.7
75	42	Greensboro-High Point, NC	60.7	57	42	Bridgeport-Stamford-Norwalk, CT	11.6
45	43	Richmond, VA	59.6	55	43	Tulsa, OK	9.7
21	44	Baltimore-Columbia-Towson, MD	59.1	26	44	Pittsburgh, PA	9.5
71	45	Columbia, SC	58.4	16	45	Minneapolis-St. Paul-Bloomington, MN	9.4
37	46	Virginia Beach-Norfolk-Newport News, VA-NC	58.3	63	46	Albany-Schenectady-Troy, NY	9.1
12	47	Phoenix-Mesa-Scottsdale, AZ	58.1	59	47	Omaha-Council Bluffs, NE-IA	8.8
70	48	Baton Rouge, LA	57.9	10	48	Boston-Cambridge-Newton, MA-NH	8.5
27	49	Sacramento—Roseville—Arden-Arcade, CA	56.5	11	48	San Francisco-Oakland-Hayward, CA	8.5
3	50	Chicago-Naperville-Elgin, IL-IN-WI	54.5	27	48	Sacramento—Roseville—Arden-Arcade, CA	8.5
31	50	Austin-Round Rock, TX	54.5	13	51	Riverside-San Bernardino-Ontario, CA	8.0
53	52	Tucson, AZ	54.2	31	52	Austin-Round Rock, TX	7.8
46	53	New Orleans-Metairie, LA	53.1	52	53	Grand Rapids-Wyoming, MI	7.7
23	54	Orlando-Kissimmee-Sanford, FL	49.8	15	54	Seattle-Tacoma-Bellevue, WA	7.4
9	55	Atlanta-Sandy Springs-Roswell, GA	49.5	2	55	Los Angeles-Long Beach-Anaheim, CA	7.1
17	56	San Diego-Carlsbad, CA	48.9	24	55	San Antonio-New Braunfels, TX	7.1
4	57	Dallas-Fort Worth-Arlington, TX	48.8	73	55	North Port-Sarasota-Bradenton, FL	7.1
6	58	Washington-Arlington-Alexandria, DC-VA-MD-WV	48.4	64	58	Knoxville, TN	6.6
1	59	New York-Newark-Jersey City, NY-NJ-PA	48.0	19	59	Denver-Aurora-Lakewood, CO	6.4
67	60	Oxnard-Thousand Oaks-Ventura, CA	47.9	38	60	Providence-Warwick, RI-MA	6.3
29	61	Las Vegas-Henderson-Paradise, NV	46.5	12	61	Phoenix-Mesa-Scottsdale, AZ	6.1
42	62	Memphis, TN-MS-AR	45.1	62	62	Bakersfield, CA	5.9
11	63	San Francisco-Oakland-Hayward, CA	43.5	69	62	Allentown-Bethlehem-Easton, PA-NJ	5.9
60	64	Albuquerque, NM	41.3	17	64	San Diego-Carlsbad, CA	5.7
5	65	Houston-The Woodlands-Sugar Land, TX	38.2	56	65	Fresno, CA	5.3
62	66	Bakersfield, CA	36.5	58	66	Worcester, MA-CT	5.0
24	67	San Antonio-New Braunfels, TX	35.4	53	67	Tucson, AZ	4.1
35	68	San Jose-Sunnyvale-Santa Clara, CA	35.1	25	68	Portland-Vancouver-Hillsboro, OR-WA	3.9
13	69	Riverside-San Bernardino-Ontario, CA	34.9	54	69	Urban Honolulu, HI	3.6
8	70	Miami-Fort Lauderdale-West Palm Beach, FL	32.2	68	70	El Paso, TX	3.5
54	71	Urban Honolulu, HI	32.1	35	71	San Jose-Sunnyvale-Santa Clara, CA	2.9
2	72	Los Angeles-Long Beach-Anaheim, CA	31.9	60	71	Albuquerque, NM	2.9
56	73	Fresno, CA	31.6	67	73	Oxnard-Thousand Oaks-Ventura, CA	2.2
68	74	El Paso, TX	13.1	48	74	Salt Lake City, UT	2.1
66	75	McAllen-Edinburg-Mission, TX	6.7	66	75	McAllen-Edinburg-Mission, TX	0.5

75 Largest Metropolitan Areas by 2016 Population
Selected Rankings

Percent American Indian, Alaska Native, alone or in combination, 2016				Percent Asian and Pacific Islander, alone or in combination, 2016			
Population rank	American Indian Alaska native rank	Metropolitan area	Percent American Indian, Alaska Native [col 7]	Population rank	Asian and Pacific Islander rank	Metropolitan area	Percent Asian and Pacific Islander [col 8]
55	1	Tulsa, OK	12.9	54	1	Urban Honolulu, HI	78.2
41	2	Oklahoma City, OK	6.7	35	2	San Jose-Sunnyvale-Santa Clara, CA	37.7
60	3	Albuquerque, NM	6.1	11	3	San Francisco-Oakland-Hayward, CA	29.5
53	4	Tucson, AZ	3.1	2	4	Los Angeles-Long Beach-Anaheim, CA	17.6
12	5	Phoenix-Mesa-Scottsdale, AZ	2.5	15	5	Seattle-Tacoma-Bellevue, WA	17.2
15	6	Seattle-Tacoma-Bellevue, WA	2.0	27	6	Sacramento—Roseville—Arden-Arcade, CA	16.6
25	7	Portland-Vancouver-Hillsboro, OR-WA	1.7	17	7	San Diego-Carlsbad, CA	14.5
27	8	Sacramento—Roseville—Arden-Arcade, CA	1.5	29	8	Las Vegas-Henderson-Paradise, NV	13.0
54	8	Urban Honolulu, HI	1.5	1	9	New York-Newark-Jersey City, NY-NJ-PA	12.1
16	10	Minneapolis-St. Paul-Bloomington, MN	1.3	6	10	Washington-Arlington-Alexandria, DC-VA-MD-WV	11.9
62	10	Bakersfield, CA	1.3	56	11	Fresno, CA	11.2
30	12	Kansas City, MO-KS	1.2	25	12	Portland-Vancouver-Hillsboro, OR-WA	9.1
19	13	Denver-Aurora-Lakewood, CO	1.1	67	13	Oxnard-Thousand Oaks-Ventura, CA	9.0
29	13	Las Vegas-Henderson-Paradise, NV	1.1	10	14	Boston-Cambridge-Newton, MA-NH	8.8
37	13	Virginia Beach-Norfolk-Newport News, VA-NC	1.1	5	15	Houston-The Woodlands-Sugar Land, TX	8.4
48	13	Salt Lake City, UT	1.1	13	16	Riverside-San Bernardino-Ontario, CA	8.1
50	13	Buffalo-Cheektowaga-Niagara Falls, NY	1.1	16	17	Minneapolis-St. Paul-Bloomington, MN	7.6
56	13	Fresno, CA	1.1	4	18	Dallas-Fort Worth-Arlington, TX	7.4
13	19	Riverside-San Bernardino-Ontario, CA	1.0	3	19	Chicago-Naperville-Elgin, IL-IN-WI	7.3
17	19	San Diego-Carlsbad, CA	1.0	48	20	Salt Lake City, UT	6.8
59	19	Omaha-Council Bluffs, NE-IA	1.0	21	21	Baltimore-Columbia-Towson, MD	6.7
75	19	Greensboro-High Point, NC	1.0	31	21	Austin-Round Rock, TX	6.7
4	23	Dallas-Fort Worth-Arlington, TX	0.9	7	23	Philadelphia-Camden-Wilmington, PA-NJ-DE-MD	6.6
14	23	Detroit-Warren-Dearborn, MI	0.9	9	23	Atlanta-Sandy Springs-Roswell, GA	6.6
22	23	Charlotte-Concord-Gastonia, NC-SC	0.9	43	25	Raleigh, NC	6.4
38	23	Providence-Warwick, RI-MA	0.9	57	26	Bridgeport-Stamford-Norwalk, CT	6.3
39	23	Milwaukee-Waukesha-West Allis, WI	0.9	62	27	Bakersfield, CA	5.6
43	23	Raleigh, NC	0.9	47	28	Hartford-West Hartford-East Hartford, CT	5.5
45	23	Richmond, VA	0.9	37	29	Virginia Beach-Norfolk-Newport News, VA-NC	5.4
46	23	New Orleans-Metairie, LA	0.9	19	30	Denver-Aurora-Lakewood, CO	5.3
52	23	Grand Rapids-Wyoming, MI	0.9	23	30	Orlando-Kissimmee-Sanford, FL	5.3
64	23	Knoxville, TN	0.9	63	30	Albany-Schenectady-Troy, NY	5.3
74	23	Charleston-North Charleston, SC	0.9	40	33	Jacksonville, FL	5.1
6	34	Washington-Arlington-Alexandria, DC-VA-MD-WV	0.8	58	33	Worcester, MA-CT	5.1
11	34	San Francisco-Oakland-Hayward, CA	0.8	12	35	Phoenix-Mesa-Scottsdale, AZ	5.0
21	34	Baltimore-Columbia-Towson, MD	0.8	14	35	Detroit-Warren-Dearborn, MI	5.0
31	34	Austin-Round Rock, TX	0.8	33	37	Columbus, OH	4.8
33	34	Columbus, OH	0.8	65	37	New Haven-Milford, CT	4.8
36	34	Nashville-Davidson—Murfreesboro—Franklin, TN	0.8	45	39	Richmond, VA	4.7
40	34	Jacksonville, FL	0.8	39	40	Milwaukee-Waukesha-West Allis, WI	4.3
67	34	Oxnard-Thousand Oaks-Ventura, CA	0.8	18	41	Tampa-St. Petersburg-Clearwater, FL	4.2
71	34	Columbia, SC	0.8	22	41	Charlotte-Concord-Gastonia, NC-SC	4.2
72	34	Dayton, OH	0.8	41	41	Oklahoma City, OK	4.2
9	44	Atlanta-Sandy Springs-Roswell, GA	0.7	75	41	Greensboro-High Point, NC	4.2
18	44	Tampa-St. Petersburg-Clearwater, FL	0.7	53	45	Tucson, AZ	3.9
20	44	St. Louis, MO-IL	0.7	30	46	Kansas City, MO-KS	3.7
35	44	San Jose-Sunnyvale-Santa Clara, CA	0.7	38	46	Providence-Warwick, RI-MA	3.7
44	44	Louisville/Jefferson County, KY-IN	0.7	50	46	Buffalo-Cheektowaga-Niagara Falls, NY	3.7
49	44	Birmingham-Hoover, AL	0.7	34	49	Indianapolis-Carmel-Anderson, IN	3.6
70	44	Baton Rouge, LA	0.7	59	49	Omaha-Council Bluffs, NE-IA	3.6
2	51	Los Angeles-Long Beach-Anaheim, CA	0.6	51	51	Rochester, NY	3.5
5	51	Houston-The Woodlands-Sugar Land, TX	0.6	36	52	Nashville-Davidson—Murfreesboro—Franklin, TN	3.4
7	51	Philadelphia-Camden-Wilmington, PA-NJ-DE-MD	0.6	46	52	New Orleans-Metairie, LA	3.4
23	51	Orlando-Kissimmee-Sanford, FL	0.6	69	52	Allentown-Bethlehem-Easton, PA-NJ	3.4
24	51	San Antonio-New Braunfels, TX	0.6	20	55	St. Louis, MO-IL	3.2
28	51	Cincinnati, OH-KY-IN	0.6	24	55	San Antonio-New Braunfels, TX	3.2
32	51	Cleveland-Elyria, OH	0.6	52	55	Grand Rapids-Wyoming, MI	3.2
34	51	Indianapolis-Carmel-Anderson, IN	0.6	8	58	Miami-Fort Lauderdale-West Palm Beach, FL	3.1
42	51	Memphis, TN-MS-AR	0.6	28	58	Cincinnati, OH-KY-IN	3.1
47	51	Hartford-West Hartford-East Hartford, CT	0.6	55	58	Tulsa, OK	3.1
51	51	Rochester, NY	0.6	72	61	Dayton, OH	3.0
58	51	Worcester, MA-CT	0.6	32	62	Cleveland-Elyria, OH	2.9
61	51	Greenville-Anderson-Mauldin, SC	0.6	60	62	Albuquerque, NM	2.9
63	51	Albany-Schenectady-Troy, NY	0.6	26	64	Pittsburgh, PA	2.8
65	51	New Haven-Milford, CT	0.6	71	64	Columbia, SC	2.8
73	51	North Port-Sarasota-Bradenton, FL	0.6	74	66	Charleston-North Charleston, SC	2.7
1	67	New York-Newark-Jersey City, NY-NJ-PA	0.5	44	67	Louisville/Jefferson County, KY-IN	2.6
3	67	Chicago-Naperville-Elgin, IL-IN-WI	0.5	70	67	Baton Rouge, LA	2.6
10	67	Boston-Cambridge-Newton, MA-NH	0.5	42	69	Memphis, TN-MS-AR	2.5
26	67	Pittsburgh, PA	0.5	73	70	North Port-Sarasota-Bradenton, FL	2.3
68	67	El Paso, TX	0.5	61	71	Greenville-Anderson-Mauldin, SC	2.2
57	72	Bridgeport-Stamford-Norwalk, CT	0.4	64	72	Knoxville, TN	2.0
69	72	Allentown-Bethlehem-Easton, PA-NJ	0.4	49	73	Birmingham-Hoover, AL	1.8
8	74	Miami-Fort Lauderdale-West Palm Beach, FL	0.3	68	74	El Paso, TX	1.7
66	75	McAllen-Edinburg-Mission, TX	0.1	66	75	McAllen-Edinburg-Mission, TX	1.0

75 Largest Metropolitan Areas by 2016 Population
Selected Rankings

		Percent Hispanic or Latino,[1] 2016				Percent under 18 years old, 2016		
Popu-lation rank	Hispanic or Latino rank	Metropolitan area	Percent Hispanic or Latino [col 9]	Popu-lation rank	Under 18 years old rank	Metropolitan area	Percent Under 18 years old [cols 10 and 11]
66	1	McAllen-Edinburg-Mission, TX	91.8	66	1	McAllen-Edinburg-Mission, TX	9.6
68	2	El Paso, TX	82.2	62	2	Bakersfield, CA	8.1
24	3	San Antonio-New Braunfels, TX	55.2	56	2	Fresno, CA	8.1
56	4	Fresno, CA	52.8	48	4	Salt Lake City, UT	7.8
62	4	Bakersfield, CA	52.8	68	4	El Paso, TX	7.8
13	6	Riverside-San Bernardino-Ontario, CA	50.5	5	6	Houston-The Woodlands-Sugar Land, TX	7.5
60	7	Albuquerque, NM	48.7	4	7	Dallas-Fort Worth-Arlington, TX	7.1
2	8	Los Angeles-Long Beach-Anaheim, CA	45.1	13	8	Riverside-San Bernardino-Ontario, CA	6.9
8	9	Miami-Fort Lauderdale-West Palm Beach, FL	44.4	59	9	Omaha-Council Bluffs, NE-IA	7.3
67	10	Oxnard-Thousand Oaks-Ventura, CA	42.5	24	10	San Antonio-New Braunfels, TX	7.0
5	11	Houston-The Woodlands-Sugar Land, TX	36.8	42	11	Memphis, TN-MS-AR	6.9
53	11	Tucson, AZ	36.8	9	12	Atlanta-Sandy Springs-Roswell, GA	6.5
17	13	San Diego-Carlsbad, CA	33.5	34	13	Indianapolis-Carmel-Anderson, IN	6.8
31	14	Austin-Round Rock, TX	32.2	55	14	Tulsa, OK	6.9
29	15	Las Vegas-Henderson-Paradise, NV	30.9	41	15	Oklahoma City, OK	7.0
12	16	Phoenix-Mesa-Scottsdale, AZ	30.6	30	16	Kansas City, MO-KS	6.6
23	17	Orlando-Kissimmee-Sanford, FL	29.5	43	17	Raleigh, NC	6.3
4	18	Dallas-Fort Worth-Arlington, TX	28.5	12	18	Phoenix-Mesa-Scottsdale, AZ	6.6
35	19	San Jose-Sunnyvale-Santa Clara, CA	26.9	52	18	Grand Rapids-Wyoming, MI	6.6
1	20	New York-Newark-Jersey City, NY-NJ-PA	24.3	22	20	Charlotte-Concord-Gastonia, NC-SC	6.3
19	21	Denver-Aurora-Lakewood, CO	22.9	16	21	Minneapolis-St. Paul-Bloomington, MN	6.6
3	22	Chicago-Naperville-Elgin, IL-IN-WI	22.1	33	22	Columbus, OH	6.8
11	23	San Francisco-Oakland-Hayward, CA	21.9	28	23	Cincinnati, OH-KY-IN	6.3
27	24	Sacramento—Roseville—Arden-Arcade, CA	21.4	31	24	Austin-Round Rock, TX	6.6
57	25	Bridgeport-Stamford-Norwalk, CT	19.4	70	24	Baton Rouge, LA	6.6
18	26	Tampa-St. Petersburg-Clearwater, FL	18.6	29	26	Las Vegas-Henderson-Paradise, NV	6.4
48	27	Salt Lake City, UT	17.7	36	27	Nashville-Davidson—Murfreesboro—Franklin, TN ..	6.5
65	28	New Haven-Milford, CT	17.6	67	28	Oxnard-Thousand Oaks-Ventura, CA	6.1
69	29	Allentown-Bethlehem-Easton, PA-NJ	16.3	39	29	Milwaukee-Waukesha-West Allis, WI	6.3
6	30	Washington-Arlington-Alexandria, DC-VA-MD-WV ...	15.5	3	30	Chicago-Naperville-Elgin, IL-IN-WI	6.1
47	31	Hartford-West Hartford-East Hartford, CT	14.5	6	31	Washington-Arlington-Alexandria, DC-VA-MD-WV ..	6.6
41	32	Oklahoma City, OK	13.0	19	32	Denver-Aurora-Lakewood, CO	6.2
38	33	Providence-Warwick, RI-MA	12.4	27	33	Sacramento—Roseville—Arden-Arcade, CA	6.1
73	34	North Port-Sarasota-Bradenton, FL	12.3	49	34	Birmingham-Hoover, AL	6.3
25	35	Portland-Vancouver-Hillsboro, OR-WA	11.7	57	35	Bridgeport-Stamford-Norwalk, CT	5.6
58	36	Worcester, MA-CT	11.1	44	36	Louisville/Jefferson County, KY-IN	6.2
10	37	Boston-Cambridge-Newton, MA-NH	10.8	60	37	Albuquerque, NM	5.8
9	38	Atlanta-Sandy Springs-Roswell, GA	10.6	35	38	San Jose-Sunnyvale-Santa Clara, CA	6.2
39	38	Milwaukee-Waukesha-West Allis, WI	10.6	61	39	Greenville-Anderson-Mauldin, SC	6.1
43	40	Raleigh, NC	10.4	14	40	Detroit-Warren-Dearborn, MI	5.9
59	41	Omaha-Council Bluffs, NE-IA	10.3	20	41	St. Louis, MO-IL	6.0
22	42	Charlotte-Concord-Gastonia, NC-SC	10.0	40	42	Jacksonville, FL	6.2
15	43	Seattle-Tacoma-Bellevue, WA	9.9	46	42	New Orleans-Metairie, LA	6.2
54	44	Urban Honolulu, HI	9.7	75	44	Greensboro-High Point, NC	5.8
55	45	Tulsa, OK	9.5	37	45	Virginia Beach-Norfolk-Newport News, VA-NC	6.4
52	46	Grand Rapids-Wyoming, MI	9.3	71	46	Columbia, SC	5.9
7	47	Philadelphia-Camden-Wilmington, PA-NJ-DE-MD ...	9.2	2	47	Los Angeles-Long Beach-Anaheim, CA	6.1
30	48	Kansas City, MO-KS	8.9	23	48	Orlando-Kissimmee-Sanford, FL	6.0
46	49	New Orleans-Metairie, LA	8.8	74	49	Charleston-North Charleston, SC	6.3
40	50	Jacksonville, FL	8.5	21	50	Baltimore-Columbia-Towson, MD	6.0
75	51	Greensboro-High Point, NC	8.3	7	51	Philadelphia-Camden-Wilmington, PA-NJ-DE-MD ...	5.9
51	52	Rochester, NY	7.2	45	51	Richmond, VA	5.9
36	53	Nashville-Davidson—Murfreesboro—Franklin, TN ...	7.1	72	53	Dayton, OH	6.0
61	54	Greenville-Anderson-Mauldin, SC	6.7	17	54	San Diego-Carlsbad, CA	6.4
34	55	Indianapolis-Carmel-Anderson, IN	6.6	25	55	Portland-Vancouver-Hillsboro, OR-WA	5.9
37	55	Virginia Beach-Norfolk-Newport News, VA-NC	6.6	1	56	New York-Newark-Jersey City, NY-NJ-PA	6.1
45	57	Richmond, VA	5.9	15	57	Seattle-Tacoma-Bellevue, WA	6.3
16	58	Minneapolis-St. Paul-Bloomington, MN	5.7	32	58	Cleveland-Elyria, OH	5.7
21	59	Baltimore-Columbia-Towson, MD	5.6	53	59	Tucson, AZ	5.8
32	59	Cleveland-Elyria, OH	5.6	54	60	Urban Honolulu, HI	6.5
42	61	Memphis, TN-MS-AR	5.4	58	61	Worcester, MA-CT	5.4
71	61	Columbia, SC	5.4	69	62	Allentown-Bethlehem-Easton, PA-NJ	5.3
74	61	Charleston-North Charleston, SC	5.4	51	63	Rochester, NY	5.4
63	64	Albany-Schenectady-Troy, NY	5.1	64	64	Knoxville, TN	5.5
50	65	Buffalo-Cheektowaga-Niagara Falls, NY	4.9	65	65	New Haven-Milford, CT	5.2
44	66	Louisville/Jefferson County, KY-IN	4.5	8	66	Miami-Fort Lauderdale-West Palm Beach, FL	5.7
14	67	Detroit-Warren-Dearborn, MI	4.3	47	67	Hartford-West Hartford-East Hartford, CT	5.0
49	67	Birmingham-Hoover, AL	4.3	50	68	Buffalo-Cheektowaga-Niagara Falls, NY	5.5
33	69	Columbus, OH	4.0	18	69	Tampa-St. Petersburg-Clearwater, FL	5.5
70	70	Baton Rouge, LA	3.9	10	70	Boston-Cambridge-Newton, MA-NH	5.4
64	71	Knoxville, TN	3.6	11	71	San Francisco-Oakland-Hayward, CA	5.6
28	72	Cincinnati, OH-KY-IN	3.1	38	72	Providence-Warwick, RI-MA	5.2
20	73	St. Louis, MO-IL	3.0	63	73	Albany-Schenectady-Troy, NY	5.3
72	74	Dayton, OH	2.6	26	74	Pittsburgh, PA	5.1
26	75	Pittsburgh, PA	1.7	73	75	North Port-Sarasota-Bradenton, FL	4.3

75 Largest Metropolitan Areas by 2016 Population
Selected Rankings

Population rank	65 years old and over rank	Metropolitan area	Percent 65 years old and over [cols 17 + 18]	Population rank	Female households rank	Metropolitan area	Percent female households [col 30]
73	1	North Port-Sarasota-Bradenton, FL	16.5	66	1	McAllen-Edinburg-Mission, TX	22.1
18	2	Tampa-St. Petersburg-Clearwater, FL	10.8	42	2	Memphis, TN-MS-AR	19.7
26	3	Pittsburgh, PA	10.5	56	3	Fresno, CA	18.2
53	4	Tucson, AZ	10.9	62	4	Bakersfield, CA	17.0
8	5	Miami-Fort Lauderdale-West Palm Beach, FL	9.4	68	4	El Paso, TX	17.0
64	6	Knoxville, TN	10.5	46	6	New Orleans-Metairie, LA	16.4
32	7	Cleveland-Elyria, OH	9.8	8	7	Miami-Fort Lauderdale-West Palm Beach, FL	15.9
69	8	Allentown-Bethlehem-Easton, PA-NJ	9.7	13	8	Riverside-San Bernardino-Ontario, CA	15.4
50	9	Buffalo-Cheektowaga-Niagara Falls, NY	9.6	71	8	Columbia, SC	15.4
72	10	Dayton, OH	9.7	49	10	Birmingham-Hoover, AL	15.2
51	10	Rochester, NY	9.7	5	11	Houston-The Woodlands-Sugar Land, TX	15.0
54	12	Urban Honolulu, HI	9.0	24	12	San Antonio-New Braunfels, TX	14.9
38	13	Providence-Warwick, RI-MA	9.2	1	13	New York-Newark-Jersey City, NY-NJ-PA	14.8
47	13	Hartford-West Hartford-East Hartford, CT	9.2	23	13	Orlando-Kissimmee-Sanford, FL	14.8
63	15	Albany-Schenectady-Troy, NY	9.5	70	15	Baton Rouge, LA	14.7
65	16	New Haven-Milford, CT	9.1	7	16	Philadelphia-Camden-Wilmington, PA-NJ-DE-MD	14.5
61	17	Greenville-Anderson-Mauldin, SC	9.5	37	16	Virginia Beach-Norfolk-Newport News, VA-NC	14.5
20	18	St. Louis, MO-IL	8.9	40	16	Jacksonville, FL	14.5
60	19	Albuquerque, NM	9.4	2	19	Los Angeles-Long Beach-Anaheim, CA	14.3
75	20	Greensboro-High Point, NC	9.1	9	19	Atlanta-Sandy Springs-Roswell, GA	14.3
14	21	Detroit-Warren-Dearborn, MI	9.0	38	21	Providence-Warwick, RI-MA	14.2
49	22	Birmingham-Hoover, AL	9.1	21	22	Baltimore-Columbia-Towson, MD	14.1
7	23	Philadelphia-Camden-Wilmington, PA-NJ-DE-MD	8.6	29	22	Las Vegas-Henderson-Paradise, NV	14.1
12	24	Phoenix-Mesa-Scottsdale, AZ	8.9	14	24	Detroit-Warren-Dearborn, MI	14.0
40	25	Jacksonville, FL	9.3	32	24	Cleveland-Elyria, OH	14.0
44	26	Louisville/Jefferson County, KY-IN	9.0	65	26	New Haven-Milford, CT	13.9
10	27	Boston-Cambridge-Newton, MA-NH	8.6	4	27	Dallas-Fort Worth-Arlington, TX	13.6
58	28	Worcester, MA-CT	8.7	22	27	Charlotte-Concord-Gastonia, NC-SC	13.6
27	29	Sacramento—Roseville—Arden-Arcade, CA	8.6	50	27	Buffalo-Cheektowaga-Niagara Falls, NY	13.6
55	30	Tulsa, OK	8.7	45	30	Richmond, VA	13.5
57	31	Bridgeport-Stamford-Norwalk, CT	8.1	74	30	Charleston-North Charleston, SC	13.5
1	32	New York-Newark-Jersey City, NY-NJ-PA	8.3	3	32	Chicago-Naperville-Elgin, IL-IN-WI	13.4
21	33	Baltimore-Columbia-Towson, MD	8.6	75	32	Greensboro-High Point, NC	13.4
11	34	San Francisco-Oakland-Hayward, CA	8.4	20	34	St. Louis, MO-IL	13.3
39	35	Milwaukee-Waukesha-West Allis, WI	8.3	44	34	Louisville/Jefferson County, KY-IN	13.3
45	36	Richmond, VA	8.9	72	34	Dayton, OH	13.3
67	37	Oxnard-Thousand Oaks-Ventura, CA	8.5	58	37	Worcester, MA-CT	13.1
46	38	New Orleans-Metairie, LA	8.8	27	38	Sacramento—Roseville—Arden-Arcade, CA	13.0
23	39	Orlando-Kissimmee-Sanford, FL	8.4	51	38	Rochester, NY	13.0
28	39	Cincinnati, OH-KY-IN	8.4	18	40	Tampa-St. Petersburg-Clearwater, FL	12.9
74	41	Charleston-North Charleston, SC	9.0	28	40	Cincinnati, OH-KY-IN	12.9
25	42	Portland-Vancouver-Hillsboro, OR-WA	8.7	53	40	Tucson, AZ	12.9
29	43	Las Vegas-Henderson-Paradise, NV	8.8	47	43	Hartford-West Hartford-East Hartford, CT	12.8
71	44	Columbia, SC	8.7	55	43	Tulsa, OK	12.8
30	45	Kansas City, MO-KS	8.2	33	45	Columbus, OH	12.7
37	45	Virginia Beach-Norfolk-Newport News, VA-NC	8.2	67	45	Oxnard-Thousand Oaks-Ventura, CA	12.7
52	47	Grand Rapids-Wyoming, MI	7.9	34	47	Indianapolis-Carmel-Anderson, IN	12.6
3	47	Chicago-Naperville-Elgin, IL-IN-WI	7.9	61	47	Greenville-Anderson-Mauldin, SC	12.6
17	49	San Diego-Carlsbad, CA	7.7	41	49	Oklahoma City, OK	12.5
2	50	Los Angeles-Long Beach-Anaheim, CA	7.5	12	50	Phoenix-Mesa-Scottsdale, AZ	12.4
41	51	Oklahoma City, OK	7.8	39	51	Milwaukee-Waukesha-West Allis, WI	12.3
70	52	Baton Rouge, LA	8.1	60	51	Albuquerque, NM	12.3
16	53	Minneapolis-St. Paul-Bloomington, MN	7.7	57	53	Bridgeport-Stamford-Norwalk, CT	12.2
22	54	Charlotte-Concord-Gastonia, NC-SC	8.0	69	53	Allentown-Bethlehem-Easton, PA-NJ	12.2
34	55	Indianapolis-Carmel-Anderson, IN	7.7	36	55	Nashville-Davidson—Murfreesboro—Franklin, TN	12.1
42	56	Memphis, TN-MS-AR	7.9	6	56	Washington-Arlington-Alexandria, DC-VA-MD-WV	12.0
15	57	Seattle-Tacoma-Bellevue, WA	7.8	54	57	Urban Honolulu, HI	11.8
59	58	Omaha-Council Bluffs, NE-IA	7.6	10	58	Boston-Cambridge-Newton, MA-NH	11.6
35	59	San Jose-Sunnyvale-Santa Clara, CA	7.2	17	58	San Diego-Carlsbad, CA	11.6
24	60	San Antonio-New Braunfels, TX	7.6	30	58	Kansas City, MO-KS	11.6
36	61	Nashville-Davidson—Murfreesboro—Franklin, TN	7.8	43	58	Raleigh, NC	11.6
13	62	Riverside-San Bernardino-Ontario, CA	7.4	64	58	Knoxville, TN	11.6
33	63	Columbus, OH	7.6	59	63	Omaha-Council Bluffs, NE-IA	11.4
19	63	Denver-Aurora-Lakewood, CO	7.6	52	64	Grand Rapids-Wyoming, MI	11.3
6	65	Washington-Arlington-Alexandria, DC-VA-MD-WV	7.4	26	65	Pittsburgh, PA	11.0
68	66	El Paso, TX	6.7	11	66	San Francisco-Oakland-Hayward, CA	10.7
56	67	Fresno, CA	6.9	48	67	Salt Lake City, UT	10.6
9	68	Atlanta-Sandy Springs-Roswell, GA	7.3	73	68	North Port-Sarasota-Bradenton, FL	10.5
43	69	Raleigh, NC	7.0	35	69	San Jose-Sunnyvale-Santa Clara, CA	10.1
66	70	McAllen-Edinburg-Mission, TX	6.2	19	70	Denver-Aurora-Lakewood, CO	10.0
4	71	Dallas-Fort Worth-Arlington, TX	6.7	25	70	Portland-Vancouver-Hillsboro, OR-WA	10.0
5	72	Houston-The Woodlands-Sugar Land, TX	6.6	63	70	Albany-Schenectady-Troy, NY	10.0
62	73	Bakersfield, CA	6.3	16	73	Minneapolis-St. Paul-Bloomington, MN	9.7
31	74	Austin-Round Rock, TX	6.5	31	73	Austin-Round Rock, TX	9.7
48	75	Salt Lake City, UT	6.1	15	75	Seattle-Tacoma-Bellevue, WA	9.5

75 Largest Metropolitan Areas by 2016 Population
Selected Rankings

		Birth rate, 2016				Percent under 65 who have no health insurance, 2015	
Population rank	Birth rate rank	Metropolitan area	Births (per 1,000 population) [col 36]	Population rank	No health insurance rank	Metropolitan area	Percent with no health insurance [col 40]
66	1	McAllen-Edinburg-Mission, TX	19.0	66	1	McAllen-Edinburg-Mission, TX	32.0
56	2	Fresno, CA	16.1	68	2	El Paso, TX	22.8
62	3	Bakersfield, CA	16.0	5	3	Houston-The Woodlands-Sugar Land, TX	19.2
68	4	El Paso, TX	15.9	8	4	Miami-Fort Lauderdale-West Palm Beach, FL	18.8
48	5	Salt Lake City, UT	15.8	4	5	Dallas-Fort Worth-Arlington, TX	18.0
5	6	Houston-The Woodlands-Sugar Land, TX	15.1	73	6	North Port-Sarasota-Bradenton, FL	17.0
59	7	Omaha-Council Bluffs, NE-IA	14.6	24	7	San Antonio-New Braunfels, TX	16.6
24	8	San Antonio-New Braunfels, TX	14.1	9	8	Atlanta-Sandy Springs-Roswell, GA	15.3
4	9	Dallas-Fort Worth-Arlington, TX	14.0	55	8	Tulsa, OK	15.3
41	9	Oklahoma City, OK	14.0	31	10	Austin-Round Rock, TX	15.2
42	11	Memphis, TN-MS-AR	13.8	23	11	Orlando-Kissimmee-Sanford, FL	15.1
13	12	Riverside-San Bernardino-Ontario, CA	13.7	41	12	Oklahoma City, OK	15.0
55	13	Tulsa, OK	13.6	18	13	Tampa-St. Petersburg-Clearwater, FL	14.5
17	14	San Diego-Carlsbad, CA	13.5	29	13	Las Vegas-Henderson-Paradise, NV	14.5
33	14	Columbus, OH	13.5	46	15	New Orleans-Metairie, LA	13.9
70	16	Baton Rouge, LA	13.4	75	16	Greensboro-High Point, NC	13.7
31	17	Austin-Round Rock, TX	13.3	61	17	Greenville-Anderson-Mauldin, SC	13.6
34	17	Indianapolis-Carmel-Anderson, IN	13.3	42	18	Memphis, TN-MS-AR	12.9
54	17	Urban Honolulu, HI	13.3	12	19	Phoenix-Mesa-Scottsdale, AZ	12.5
6	20	Washington-Arlington-Alexandria, DC-VA-MD-WV	13.2	40	19	Jacksonville, FL	12.5
36	20	Nashville-Davidson—Murfreesboro—Franklin, TN	13.2	22	21	Charlotte-Concord-Gastonia, NC-SC	12.3
30	22	Kansas City, MO-KS	13.1	74	21	Charleston-North Charleston, SC	12.3
37	22	Virginia Beach-Norfolk-Newport News, VA-NC	13.1	53	23	Tucson, AZ	12.2
52	22	Grand Rapids-Wyoming, MI	13.1	48	24	Salt Lake City, UT	12.0
12	25	Phoenix-Mesa-Scottsdale, AZ	13.0	60	24	Albuquerque, NM	12.0
16	26	Minneapolis-St. Paul-Bloomington, MN	12.9	2	26	Los Angeles-Long Beach-Anaheim, CA	11.9
46	26	New Orleans-Metairie, LA	12.9	70	27	Baton Rouge, LA	11.6
9	28	Atlanta-Sandy Springs-Roswell, GA	12.7	36	28	Nashville-Davidson—Murfreesboro—Franklin, TN	11.4
29	28	Las Vegas-Henderson-Paradise, NV	12.7	71	29	Columbia, SC	11.3
74	28	Charleston-North Charleston, SC	12.7	64	30	Knoxville, TN	11.2
19	31	Denver-Aurora-Lakewood, CO	12.6	49	31	Birmingham-Hoover, AL	11.1
49	31	Birmingham-Hoover, AL	12.6	34	32	Indianapolis-Carmel-Anderson, IN	10.8
2	33	Los Angeles-Long Beach-Anaheim, CA	12.5	56	32	Fresno, CA	10.8
15	33	Seattle-Tacoma-Bellevue, WA	12.5	43	34	Raleigh, NC	10.5
22	33	Charlotte-Concord-Gastonia, NC-SC	12.5	45	34	Richmond, VA	10.5
28	33	Cincinnati, OH-KY-IN	12.5	13	36	Riverside-San Bernardino-Ontario, CA	10.3
39	33	Milwaukee-Waukesha-West Allis, WI	12.5	30	37	Kansas City, MO-KS	10.0
3	38	Chicago-Naperville-Elgin, IL-IN-WI	12.4	37	37	Virginia Beach-Norfolk-Newport News, VA-NC	10.0
35	38	San Jose-Sunnyvale-Santa Clara, CA	12.4	67	39	Oxnard-Thousand Oaks-Ventura, CA	9.9
1	40	New York-Newark-Jersey City, NY-NJ-PA	12.3	62	40	Bakersfield, CA	9.7
40	40	Jacksonville, FL	12.3	1	41	New York-Newark-Jersey City, NY-NJ-PA	9.6
44	40	Louisville/Jefferson County, KY-IN	12.3	17	42	San Diego-Carlsbad, CA	9.5
43	43	Raleigh, NC	12.2	3	43	Chicago-Naperville-Elgin, IL-IN-WI	9.3
67	43	Oxnard-Thousand Oaks-Ventura, CA	12.2	19	43	Denver-Aurora-Lakewood, CO	9.3
21	45	Baltimore-Columbia-Towson, MD	12.1	57	45	Bridgeport-Stamford-Norwalk, CT	9.2
27	45	Sacramento—Roseville—Arden-Arcade, CA	12.1	6	46	Washington-Arlington-Alexandria, DC-VA-MD-WV	8.5
61	45	Greenville-Anderson-Mauldin, SC	12.1	20	46	St. Louis, MO-IL	8.5
20	48	St. Louis, MO-IL	11.9	33	48	Columbus, OH	8.1
7	49	Philadelphia-Camden-Wilmington, PA-NJ-DE-MD	11.8	59	49	Omaha-Council Bluffs, NE-IA	8.0
23	49	Orlando-Kissimmee-Sanford, FL	11.8	69	50	Allentown-Bethlehem-Easton, PA-NJ	7.8
45	49	Richmond, VA	11.8	72	51	Dayton, OH	7.7
72	49	Dayton, OH	11.8	7	52	Philadelphia-Camden-Wilmington, PA-NJ-DE-MD	7.6
14	53	Detroit-Warren-Dearborn, MI	11.7	25	53	Portland-Vancouver-Hillsboro, OR-WA	7.5
25	53	Portland-Vancouver-Hillsboro, OR-WA	11.7	32	54	Cleveland-Elyria, OH	7.4
53	55	Tucson, AZ	11.6	44	54	Louisville/Jefferson County, KY-IN	7.4
71	56	Columbia, SC	11.5	14	56	Detroit-Warren-Dearborn, MI	7.3
11	57	San Francisco-Oakland-Hayward, CA	11.4	65	57	New Haven-Milford, CT	7.0
8	58	Miami-Fort Lauderdale-West Palm Beach, FL	11.3	27	58	Sacramento—Roseville—Arden-Arcade, CA	6.9
32	58	Cleveland-Elyria, OH	11.3	28	58	Cincinnati, OH-KY-IN	6.9
60	58	Albuquerque, NM	11.3	52	58	Grand Rapids-Wyoming, MI	6.9
75	58	Greensboro-High Point, NC	11.3	15	61	Seattle-Tacoma-Bellevue, WA	6.8
10	62	Boston-Cambridge-Newton, MA-NH	10.8	39	61	Milwaukee-Waukesha-West Allis, WI	6.8
50	62	Buffalo-Cheektowaga-Niagara Falls, NY	10.8	11	63	San Francisco-Oakland-Hayward, CA	6.2
64	62	Knoxville, TN	10.8	21	63	Baltimore-Columbia-Towson, MD	6.2
18	65	Tampa-St. Petersburg-Clearwater, FL	10.7	35	65	San Jose-Sunnyvale-Santa Clara, CA	6.1
51	65	Rochester, NY	10.7	26	66	Pittsburgh, PA	5.9
57	67	Bridgeport-Stamford-Norwalk, CT	10.6	51	67	Rochester, NY	5.8
63	68	Albany-Schenectady-Troy, NY	10.4	38	68	Providence-Warwick, RI-MA	5.6
58	69	Worcester, MA-CT	10.3	47	69	Hartford-West Hartford-East Hartford, CT	5.4
38	70	Providence-Warwick, RI-MA	10.2	50	69	Buffalo-Cheektowaga-Niagara Falls, NY	5.4
65	70	New Haven-Milford, CT	10.2	63	71	Albany-Schenectady-Troy, NY	5.3
69	70	Allentown-Bethlehem-Easton, PA-NJ	10.2	16	72	Minneapolis-St. Paul-Bloomington, MN	5.0
26	73	Pittsburgh, PA	10.1	54	73	Urban Honolulu, HI	4.4
47	74	Hartford-West Hartford-East Hartford, CT	9.8	10	74	Boston-Cambridge-Newton, MA-NH	3.5
73	75	North Port-Sarasota-Bradenton, FL	8.3	58	75	Worcester, MA-CT	3.3

75 Largest Metropolitan Areas by 2016 Population
Selected Rankings

Percent college graduates (bachelor's degree or more), 2015				Median household income, 2015			
Population rank	Percent college graduates rank	Metropolitan area	Percent college graduates [col 51]	Population rank	Median income rank	Metropolitan area	Median income (dollars) [col 55]
6	1	Washington-Arlington-Alexandria, DC-VA-MD-WV	49.3	57	1	Bridgeport-Stamford-Norwalk, CT	137 438
35	2	San Jose-Sunnyvale-Santa Clara, CA	48.7	35	2	San Jose-Sunnyvale-Santa Clara, CA	136 386
11	3	San Francisco-Oakland-Hayward, CA	47.2	11	3	San Francisco-Oakland-Hayward, CA	124 194
57	4	Bridgeport-Stamford-Norwalk, CT	46.3	6	4	Washington-Arlington-Alexandria, DC-VA-MD-WV	121 072
10	5	Boston-Cambridge-Newton, MA-NH	46.0	10	5	Boston-Cambridge-Newton, MA-NH	106 840
43	6	Raleigh, NC	44.4	67	6	Oxnard-Thousand Oaks-Ventura, CA	104 004
31	7	Austin-Round Rock, TX	42.6	1	7	New York-Newark-Jersey City, NY-NJ-PA	101 934
19	8	Denver-Aurora-Lakewood, CO	41.8	15	8	Seattle-Tacoma-Bellevue, WA	99 442
15	9	Seattle-Tacoma-Bellevue, WA	41.2	54	9	Urban Honolulu, HI	98 463
16	10	Minneapolis-St. Paul-Bloomington, MN	40.3	21	10	Baltimore-Columbia-Towson, MD	95 598
21	11	Baltimore-Columbia-Towson, MD	38.6	47	11	Hartford-West Hartford-East Hartford, CT	94 753
1	12	New York-Newark-Jersey City, NY-NJ-PA	38.4	19	12	Denver-Aurora-Lakewood, CO	93 705
47	13	Hartford-West Hartford-East Hartford, CT	38.3	31	13	Austin-Round Rock, TX	92 495
25	14	Portland-Vancouver-Hillsboro, OR-WA	37.9	16	14	Minneapolis-St. Paul-Bloomington, MN	92 395
17	15	San Diego-Carlsbad, CA	37.2	2	15	Los Angeles-Long Beach-Anaheim, CA	90 892
9	16	Atlanta-Sandy Springs-Roswell, GA	37.0	17	16	San Diego-Carlsbad, CA	90 125
3	17	Chicago-Naperville-Elgin, IL-IN-WI	36.0	7	17	Philadelphia-Camden-Wilmington, PA-NJ-DE-MD	89 851
7	17	Philadelphia-Camden-Wilmington, PA-NJ-DE-MD	36.0	5	18	Houston-The Woodlands-Sugar Land, TX	89 171
30	19	Kansas City, MO-KS	35.8	3	19	Chicago-Naperville-Elgin, IL-IN-WI	88 925
63	20	Albany-Schenectady-Troy, NY	35.3	43	20	Raleigh, NC	87 155
45	21	Richmond, VA	35.2	4	21	Dallas-Fort Worth-Arlington, TX	86 871
33	22	Columbus, OH	35.1	58	22	Worcester, MA-CT	85 490
59	23	Omaha-Council Bluffs, NE-IA	34.7	25	23	Portland-Vancouver-Hillsboro, OR-WA	84 633
74	23	Charleston-North Charleston, SC	34.7	65	24	New Haven-Milford, CT	83 327
65	25	New Haven-Milford, CT	34.3	48	25	Salt Lake City, UT	83 088
39	26	Milwaukee-Waukesha-West Allis, WI	33.9	27	26	Sacramento—Roseville—Arden-Arcade, CA	82 648
36	27	Nashville-Davidson—Murfreesboro—Franklin, TN	33.6	45	27	Richmond, VA	82 209
22	28	Charlotte-Concord-Gastonia, NC-SC	33.5	9	28	Atlanta-Sandy Springs-Roswell, GA	81 825
4	29	Dallas-Fort Worth-Arlington, TX	33.4	63	29	Albany-Schenectady-Troy, NY	81 725
58	30	Worcester, MA-CT	33.3	30	30	Kansas City, MO-KS	80 465
54	31	Urban Honolulu, HI	33.2	59	31	Omaha-Council Bluffs, NE-IA	79 771
26	32	Pittsburgh, PA	33.0	36	32	Nashville-Davidson—Murfreesboro—Franklin, TN	79 665
51	32	Rochester, NY	33.0	69	33	Allentown-Bethlehem-Easton, PA-NJ	78 853
34	34	Indianapolis-Carmel-Anderson, IN	32.9	33	34	Columbus, OH	78 054
2	35	Los Angeles-Long Beach-Anaheim, CA	32.7	74	35	Charleston-North Charleston, SC	77 932
48	35	Salt Lake City, UT	32.7	20	36	St. Louis, MO-IL	77 901
67	35	Oxnard-Thousand Oaks-Ventura, CA	32.7	22	37	Charlotte-Concord-Gastonia, NC-SC	77 789
20	38	St. Louis, MO-IL	32.5	38	38	Providence-Warwick, RI-MA	77 620
27	39	Sacramento—Roseville—Arden-Arcade, CA	32.2	39	39	Milwaukee-Waukesha-West Allis, WI	77 011
28	40	Cincinnati, OH-KY-IN	32.1	28	40	Cincinnati, OH-KY-IN	76 779
5	41	Houston-The Woodlands-Sugar Land, TX	31.5	8	41	Miami-Fort Lauderdale-West Palm Beach, FL	76 284
71	42	Columbia, SC	31.4	12	42	Phoenix-Mesa-Scottsdale, AZ	76 146
73	43	North Port-Sarasota-Bradenton, FL	31.3	37	43	Virginia Beach-Norfolk-Newport News, VA-NC	75 461
52	44	Grand Rapids-Wyoming, MI	31.1	34	44	Indianapolis-Carmel-Anderson, IN	75 178
53	44	Tucson, AZ	31.1	73	45	North Port-Sarasota-Bradenton, FL	75 124
8	46	Miami-Fort Lauderdale-West Palm Beach, FL	30.9	40	46	Jacksonville, FL	74 960
38	47	Providence-Warwick, RI-MA	30.6	70	47	Baton Rouge, LA	74 487
50	48	Buffalo-Cheektowaga-Niagara Falls, NY	30.3	26	48	Pittsburgh, PA	74 452
37	49	Virginia Beach-Norfolk-Newport News, VA-NC	30.2	14	49	Detroit-Warren-Dearborn, MI	74 403
60	49	Albuquerque, NM	30.2	52	50	Grand Rapids-Wyoming, MI	74 005
40	51	Jacksonville, FL	30.0	24	51	San Antonio-New Braunfels, TX	73 771
23	52	Orlando-Kissimmee-Sanford, FL	29.9	13	52	Riverside-San Bernardino-Ontario, CA	73 425
14	53	Detroit-Warren-Dearborn, MI	29.5	41	53	Oklahoma City, OK	72 437
12	54	Phoenix-Mesa-Scottsdale, AZ	29.4	51	54	Rochester, NY	72 186
32	54	Cleveland-Elyria, OH	29.4	44	55	Louisville/Jefferson County, KY-IN	71 307
41	56	Oklahoma City, OK	29.3	32	56	Cleveland-Elyria, OH	70 990
18	57	Tampa-St. Petersburg-Clearwater, FL	28.9	55	57	Tulsa, OK	70 968
44	58	Louisville/Jefferson County, KY-IN	28.7	23	58	Orlando-Kissimmee-Sanford, FL	70 292
46	59	New Orleans-Metairie, LA	28.6	49	59	Birmingham-Hoover, AL	70 090
49	59	Birmingham-Hoover, AL	28.6	29	60	Las Vegas-Henderson-Paradise, NV	69 724
72	61	Dayton, OH	28.5	62	61	Bakersfield, CA	69 017
69	62	Allentown-Bethlehem-Easton, PA-NJ	28.2	42	62	Memphis, TN-MS-AR	68 861
70	62	Baton Rouge, LA	28.2	50	63	Buffalo-Cheektowaga-Niagara Falls, NY	68 689
75	64	Greensboro-High Point, NC	28.0	46	64	New Orleans-Metairie, LA	68 409
64	65	Knoxville, TN	27.9	18	65	Tampa-St. Petersburg-Clearwater, FL	68 251
42	66	Memphis, TN-MS-AR	26.9	71	66	Columbia, SC	67 564
55	67	Tulsa, OK	26.7	64	67	Knoxville, TN	66 566
61	67	Greenville-Anderson-Mauldin, SC	26.7	60	68	Albuquerque, NM	65 938
24	69	San Antonio-New Braunfels, TX	26.6	72	69	Dayton, OH	65 586
29	70	Las Vegas-Henderson-Paradise, NV	23.1	56	70	Fresno, CA	64 716
68	71	El Paso, TX	22.8	75	71	Greensboro-High Point, NC	64 628
13	72	Riverside-San Bernardino-Ontario, CA	20.1	53	72	Tucson, AZ	64 613
56	73	Fresno, CA	19.2	61	73	Greenville-Anderson-Mauldin, SC	63 602
66	74	McAllen-Edinburg-Mission, TX	17.3	68	74	El Paso, TX	56 608
62	75	Bakersfield, CA	16.2	66	75	McAllen-Edinburg-Mission, TX	53 857

75 Largest Metropolitan Areas by 2016 Population
Selected Rankings

Percent of population below the poverty level, 2015				Percent of children under 18 years old below the poverty level, 2015			
Population rank	Poverty rate rank	Metropolitan area	Poverty rate [col 59]	Population rank	Poverty rate rank	Metropolitan area	Poverty rate [col 60]
66	1	McAllen-Edinburg-Mission, TX	31.5	66	1	McAllen-Edinburg-Mission, TX	43.8
56	2	Fresno, CA	25.3	56	2	Fresno, CA	36.9
62	3	Bakersfield, CA	21.9	62	3	Bakersfield, CA	31.9
68	4	El Paso, TX	20.1	68	4	El Paso, TX	29.3
53	5	Tucson, AZ	18.9	42	5	Memphis, TN-MS-AR	28.8
60	6	Albuquerque, NM	18.7	53	6	Tucson, AZ	28.3
42	7	Memphis, TN-MS-AR	18.4	46	7	New Orleans-Metairie, LA	27.7
46	8	New Orleans-Metairie, LA	18.0	60	8	Albuquerque, NM	25.7
13	9	Riverside-San Bernardino-Ontario, CA	17.5	50	9	Buffalo-Cheektowaga-Niagara Falls, NY	25.4
64	10	Knoxville, TN	16.8	13	10	Riverside-San Bernardino-Ontario, CA	25.0
8	11	Miami-Fort Lauderdale-West Palm Beach, FL	16.5	64	11	Knoxville, TN	24.4
12	12	Phoenix-Mesa-Scottsdale, AZ	16.2	72	11	Dayton, OH	24.4
70	12	Baton Rouge, LA	16.2	14	13	Detroit-Warren-Dearborn, MI	24.0
72	12	Dayton, OH	16.2	75	13	Greensboro-High Point, NC	24.0
14	15	Detroit-Warren-Dearborn, MI	16.1	8	15	Miami-Fort Lauderdale-West Palm Beach, FL	23.5
75	15	Greensboro-High Point, NC	16.1	55	15	Tulsa, OK	23.5
2	17	Los Angeles-Long Beach-Anaheim, CA	15.7	12	17	Phoenix-Mesa-Scottsdale, AZ	23.0
49	17	Birmingham-Hoover, AL	15.7	70	18	Baton Rouge, LA	22.5
50	17	Buffalo-Cheektowaga-Niagara Falls, NY	15.7	49	19	Birmingham-Hoover, AL	22.3
61	17	Greenville-Anderson-Mauldin, SC	15.7	29	20	Las Vegas-Henderson-Paradise, NV	22.0
55	21	Tulsa, OK	15.4	5	21	Houston-The Woodlands-Sugar Land, TX	21.9
29	22	Las Vegas-Henderson-Paradise, NV	15.1	23	22	Orlando-Kissimmee-Sanford, FL	21.8
71	22	Columbia, SC	15.1	2	23	Los Angeles-Long Beach-Anaheim, CA	21.7
23	24	Orlando-Kissimmee-Sanford, FL	15.0	32	23	Cleveland-Elyria, OH	21.7
27	24	Sacramento—Roseville—Arden-Arcade, CA	15.0	71	25	Columbia, SC	21.2
32	26	Cleveland-Elyria, OH	14.8	24	26	San Antonio-New Braunfels, TX	21.1
18	27	Tampa-St. Petersburg-Clearwater, FL	14.7	40	27	Jacksonville, FL	21.0
5	28	Houston-The Woodlands-Sugar Land, TX	14.6	61	28	Greenville-Anderson-Mauldin, SC	20.8
24	28	San Antonio-New Braunfels, TX	14.6	65	29	New Haven-Milford, CT	20.6
41	30	Oklahoma City, OK	14.5	34	30	Indianapolis-Carmel-Anderson, IN	20.5
40	31	Jacksonville, FL	14.3	18	31	Tampa-St. Petersburg-Clearwater, FL	20.4
33	32	Columbus, OH	14.2	39	32	Milwaukee-Waukesha-West Allis, WI	20.3
74	32	Charleston-North Charleston, SC	14.2	9	33	Atlanta-Sandy Springs-Roswell, GA	20.2
1	34	New York-Newark-Jersey City, NY-NJ-PA	14.1	51	33	Rochester, NY	20.2
22	34	Charlotte-Concord-Gastonia, NC-SC	14.1	41	35	Oklahoma City, OK	20.1
39	36	Milwaukee-Waukesha-West Allis, WI	14.0	74	35	Charleston-North Charleston, SC	20.1
9	37	Atlanta-Sandy Springs-Roswell, GA	13.9	-1	37	New York-Newark-Jersey City, NY-NJ-PA	20.0
34	37	Indianapolis-Carmel-Anderson, IN	13.9	73	37	North Port-Sarasota-Bradenton, FL	20.0
17	39	San Diego-Carlsbad, CA	13.8	33	39	Columbus, OH	19.6
51	39	Rochester, NY	13.8	44	40	Louisville/Jefferson County, KY-IN	19.5
65	41	New Haven-Milford, CT	13.7	22	41	Charlotte-Concord-Gastonia, NC-SC	19.4
4	42	Dallas-Fort Worth-Arlington, TX	13.4	27	41	Sacramento—Roseville—Arden-Arcade, CA	19.4
38	42	Providence-Warwick, RI-MA	13.4	3	43	Chicago-Naperville-Elgin, IL-IN-WI	19.3
44	42	Louisville/Jefferson County, KY-IN	13.4	4	44	Dallas-Fort Worth-Arlington, TX	19.2
3	45	Chicago-Naperville-Elgin, IL-IN-WI	13.3	37	45	Virginia Beach-Norfolk-Newport News, VA-NC	18.9
28	46	Cincinnati, OH-KY-IN	13.2	38	46	Providence-Warwick, RI-MA	18.8
7	47	Philadelphia-Camden-Wilmington, PA-NJ-DE-MD	13.1	7	47	Philadelphia-Camden-Wilmington, PA-NJ-DE-MD	18.7
52	48	Grand Rapids-Wyoming, MI	12.9	59	48	Omaha-Council Bluffs, NE-IA	18.3
36	49	Nashville-Davidson—Murfreesboro—Franklin, TN	12.7	28	49	Cincinnati, OH-KY-IN	17.9
26	50	Pittsburgh, PA	12.3	17	50	San Diego-Carlsbad, CA	17.7
37	50	Virginia Beach-Norfolk-Newport News, VA-NC	12.3	26	51	Pittsburgh, PA	17.6
59	50	Omaha-Council Bluffs, NE-IA	12.3	20	52	St. Louis, MO-IL	17.4
20	53	St. Louis, MO-IL	12.2	36	52	Nashville-Davidson—Murfreesboro—Franklin, TN	17.4
25	53	Portland-Vancouver-Hillsboro, OR-WA	12.2	52	54	Grand Rapids-Wyoming, MI	17.3
58	55	Worcester, MA-CT	11.9	30	55	Kansas City, MO-KS	17.2
30	56	Kansas City, MO-KS	11.8	45	56	Richmond, VA	16.5
45	56	Richmond, VA	11.8	43	57	Raleigh, NC	16.0
73	56	North Port-Sarasota-Bradenton, FL	11.8	58	58	Worcester, MA-CT	15.7
31	59	Austin-Round Rock, TX	11.7	69	58	Allentown-Bethlehem-Easton, PA-NJ	15.7
43	60	Raleigh, NC	11.6	31	60	Austin-Round Rock, TX	15.2
11	61	San Francisco-Oakland-Hayward, CA	10.6	25	61	Portland-Vancouver-Hillsboro, OR-WA	14.9
21	61	Baltimore-Columbia-Towson, MD	10.6	19	62	Denver-Aurora-Lakewood, CO	13.9
19	63	Denver-Aurora-Lakewood, CO	10.3	63	62	Albany-Schenectady-Troy, NY	13.9
10	64	Boston-Cambridge-Newton, MA-NH	10.2	21	64	Baltimore-Columbia-Towson, MD	13.8
15	64	Seattle-Tacoma-Bellevue, WA	10.2	67	65	Oxnard-Thousand Oaks-Ventura, CA	13.7
48	64	Salt Lake City, UT	10.2	47	66	Hartford-West Hartford-East Hartford, CT	13.0
63	64	Albany-Schenectady-Troy, NY	10.2	10	67	Boston-Cambridge-Newton, MA-NH	12.6
47	68	Hartford-West Hartford-East Hartford, CT	9.9	16	68	Minneapolis-St. Paul-Bloomington, MN	12.4
69	68	Allentown-Bethlehem-Easton, PA-NJ	9.9	15	69	Seattle-Tacoma-Bellevue, WA	12.3
67	70	Oxnard-Thousand Oaks-Ventura, CA	9.6	11	70	San Francisco-Oakland-Hayward, CA	12.2
16	71	Minneapolis-St. Paul-Bloomington, MN	9.3	48	71	Salt Lake City, UT	11.7
54	72	Urban Honolulu, HI	9.2	54	72	Urban Honolulu, HI	11.0
57	73	Bridgeport-Stamford-Norwalk, CT	8.9	57	73	Bridgeport-Stamford-Norwalk, CT	10.7
6	74	Washington-Arlington-Alexandria, DC-VA-MD-WV	8.3	6	74	Washington-Arlington-Alexandria, DC-VA-MD-WV	10.6
35	75	San Jose-Sunnyvale-Santa Clara, CA	8.1	35	75	San Jose-Sunnyvale-Santa Clara, CA	8.3

75 Largest Metropolitan Areas by 2016 Population
Selected Rankings

		Median value of owner-occupied housing units, 2015				Median gross rent of renter-occupied housing units, 2015	
Population rank	Median value rank	Metropolitan area	Median value (dollars) [col 91]	Population rank	Median gross rent	Metropolitan area	Median rent (dollars) [col 94]
35	1	San Jose-Sunnyvale-Santa Clara, CA	823 700	35	1	San Jose-Sunnyvale-Santa Clara, CA	1 894
11	2	San Francisco-Oakland-Hayward, CA	718 400	54	2	Urban Honolulu, HI	1 638
54	3	Urban Honolulu, HI	629 900	11	3	San Francisco-Oakland-Hayward, CA	1 623
2	4	Los Angeles-Long Beach-Anaheim, CA	540 600	67	4	Oxnard-Thousand Oaks-Ventura, CA	1 564
67	5	Oxnard-Thousand Oaks-Ventura, CA	528 700	6	5	Washington-Arlington-Alexandria, DC-VA-MD-WV	1 553
17	6	San Diego-Carlsbad, CA	485 900	57	6	Bridgeport-Stamford-Norwalk, CT	1 428
57	7	Bridgeport-Stamford-Norwalk, CT	420 900	17	7	San Diego-Carlsbad, CA	1 427
1	8	New York-Newark-Jersey City, NY-NJ-PA	414 000	2	8	Los Angeles-Long Beach-Anaheim, CA	1 348
6	9	Washington-Arlington-Alexandria, DC-VA-MD-WV	401 500	10	9	Boston-Cambridge-Newton, MA-NH	1 316
10	10	Boston-Cambridge-Newton, MA-NH	393 000	1	10	New York-Newark-Jersey City, NY-NJ-PA	1 308
15	11	Seattle-Tacoma-Bellevue, WA	361 500	15	11	Seattle-Tacoma-Bellevue, WA	1 263
27	12	Sacramento—Roseville—Arden-Arcade, CA	339 900	8	12	Miami-Fort Lauderdale-West Palm Beach, FL	1 208
19	13	Denver-Aurora-Lakewood, CO	314 400	19	13	Denver-Aurora-Lakewood, CO	1 184
25	14	Portland-Vancouver-Hillsboro, OR-WA	303 100	21	13	Baltimore-Columbia-Towson, MD	1 184
13	15	Riverside-San Bernardino-Ontario, CA	299 300	13	15	Riverside-San Bernardino-Ontario, CA	1 166
21	16	Baltimore-Columbia-Towson, MD	290 300	31	16	Austin-Round Rock, TX	1 131
38	17	Providence-Warwick, RI-MA	254 500	27	17	Sacramento—Roseville—Arden-Arcade, CA	1 109
48	18	Salt Lake City, UT	251 200	37	18	Virginia Beach-Norfolk-Newport News, VA-NC	1 106
58	19	Worcester, MA-CT	247 600	25	19	Portland-Vancouver-Hillsboro, OR-WA	1 071
47	20	Hartford-West Hartford-East Hartford, CT	247 000	23	20	Orlando-Kissimmee-Sanford, FL	1 070
65	21	New Haven-Milford, CT	244 400	65	20	New Haven-Milford, CT	1 070
8	22	Miami-Fort Lauderdale-West Palm Beach, FL	241 700	7	22	Philadelphia-Camden-Wilmington, PA-NJ-DE-MD	1 062
31	23	Austin-Round Rock, TX	241 100	73	23	North Port-Sarasota-Bradenton, FL	1 056
7	24	Philadelphia-Camden-Wilmington, PA-NJ-DE-MD	240 900	47	24	Hartford-West Hartford-East Hartford, CT	1 039
37	25	Virginia Beach-Norfolk-Newport News, VA-NC	236 900	74	25	Charleston-North Charleston, SC	1 034
16	26	Minneapolis-St. Paul-Bloomington, MN	231 800	45	26	Richmond, VA	1 019
43	27	Raleigh, NC	225 000	9	27	Atlanta-Sandy Springs-Roswell, GA	1 015
3	28	Chicago-Naperville-Elgin, IL-IN-WI	224 300	3	28	Chicago-Naperville-Elgin, IL-IN-WI	1 012
56	29	Fresno, CA	220 100	29	29	Las Vegas-Henderson-Paradise, NV	1 007
45	30	Richmond, VA	219 700	69	30	Allentown-Bethlehem-Easton, PA-NJ	995
12	31	Phoenix-Mesa-Scottsdale, AZ	219 100	40	31	Jacksonville, FL	994
29	32	Las Vegas-Henderson-Paradise, NV	217 300	4	32	Dallas-Fort Worth-Arlington, TX	992
74	33	Charleston-North Charleston, SC	210 400	12	33	Phoenix-Mesa-Scottsdale, AZ	986
73	34	North Port-Sarasota-Bradenton, FL	208 100	16	34	Minneapolis-St. Paul-Bloomington, MN	979
69	35	Allentown-Bethlehem-Easton, PA-NJ	203 500	5	35	Houston-The Woodlands-Sugar Land, TX	978
63	36	Albany-Schenectady-Troy, NY	201 000	18	36	Tampa-St. Petersburg-Clearwater, FL	976
39	37	Milwaukee-Waukesha-West Allis, WI	198 600	58	37	Worcester, MA-CT	972
62	38	Bakersfield, CA	197 100	43	38	Raleigh, NC	971
36	39	Nashville-Davidson—Murfreesboro—Franklin, TN	192 200	48	39	Salt Lake City, UT	964
46	40	New Orleans-Metairie, LA	188 300	24	40	San Antonio-New Braunfels, TX	926
9	41	Atlanta-Sandy Springs-Roswell, GA	186 300	63	41	Albany-Schenectady-Troy, NY	923
60	42	Albuquerque, NM	181 800	46	42	New Orleans-Metairie, LA	920
70	43	Baton Rouge, LA	176 400	36	43	Nashville-Davidson—Murfreesboro—Franklin, TN	917
23	44	Orlando-Kissimmee-Sanford, FL	176 100	22	44	Charlotte-Concord-Gastonia, NC-SC	915
22	45	Charlotte-Concord-Gastonia, NC-SC	173 900	38	45	Providence-Warwick, RI-MA	910
40	46	Jacksonville, FL	172 800	62	46	Bakersfield, CA	906
4	47	Dallas-Fort Worth-Arlington, TX	172 500	56	47	Fresno, CA	897
5	48	Houston-The Woodlands-Sugar Land, TX	168 300	14	48	Detroit-Warren-Dearborn, MI	871
33	49	Columbus, OH	166 600	33	49	Columbus, OH	869
53	50	Tucson, AZ	165 900	30	50	Kansas City, MO-KS	859
18	51	Tampa-St. Petersburg-Clearwater, FL	165 600	71	51	Columbia, SC	857
30	52	Kansas City, MO-KS	164 700	42	52	Memphis, TN-MS-AR	852
20	53	St. Louis, MO-IL	164 200	70	53	Baton Rouge, LA	850
28	54	Cincinnati, OH-KY-IN	159 200	39	54	Milwaukee-Waukesha-West Allis, WI	848
64	55	Knoxville, TN	158 300	20	55	St. Louis, MO-IL	839
49	56	Birmingham-Hoover, AL	156 900	59	56	Omaha-Council Bluffs, NE-IA	835
59	57	Omaha-Council Bluffs, NE-IA	155 200	51	57	Rochester, NY	833
44	58	Louisville/Jefferson County, KY-IN	154 000	60	58	Albuquerque, NM	826
24	59	San Antonio-New Braunfels, TX	151 400	34	59	Indianapolis-Carmel-Anderson, IN	825
52	60	Grand Rapids-Wyoming, MI	151 300	53	60	Tucson, AZ	824
14	61	Detroit-Warren-Dearborn, MI	151 000	41	61	Oklahoma City, OK	821
34	62	Indianapolis-Carmel-Anderson, IN	148 000	49	62	Birmingham-Hoover, AL	809
71	63	Columbia, SC	147 500	52	63	Grand Rapids-Wyoming, MI	794
61	64	Greenville-Anderson-Mauldin, SC	146 400	55	64	Tulsa, OK	791
41	65	Oklahoma City, OK	146 100	44	65	Louisville/Jefferson County, KY-IN	777
75	66	Greensboro-High Point, NC	144 900	28	66	Cincinnati, OH-KY-IN	775
26	67	Pittsburgh, PA	143 200	61	67	Greenville-Anderson-Mauldin, SC	768
32	68	Cleveland-Elyria, OH	143 100	75	67	Greensboro-High Point, NC	768
55	69	Tulsa, OK	141 800	68	69	El Paso, TX	757
42	70	Memphis, TN-MS-AR	139 800	26	70	Pittsburgh, PA	756
51	71	Rochester, NY	138 900	64	70	Knoxville, TN	756
50	72	Buffalo-Cheektowaga-Niagara Falls, NY	135 200	72	72	Dayton, OH	748
72	73	Dayton, OH	124 500	32	73	Cleveland-Elyria, OH	746
68	74	El Paso, TX	113 900	50	74	Buffalo-Cheektowaga-Niagara Falls, NY	733
66	75	McAllen-Edinburg-Mission, TX	81 700	66	75	McAllen-Edinburg-Mission, TX	690

75 Largest Metropolitan Areas by 2016 Population
Selected Rankings

	Unemployment rate, 2016					Mean income tax, 2014	
Population rank	Unemployment rate rank	Metropolitan area	Unemployment rate [col 100]	Population rank	Mean income tax rank	Metropolitan area	Mean income tax [col 199]
62	1	Bakersfield, CA..............	10.3	57	1	Bridgeport-Stamford-Norwalk, CT...............	$34 778
56	2	Fresno, CA..............	9.4	35	2	San Jose-Sunnyvale-Santa Clara, CA	$24 221
66	3	McAllen-Edinburg-Mission, TX...............	7.8	11	3	San Francisco-Oakland-Hayward, CA..........	$20 363
60	4	Albuquerque, NM..............	6.1	10	4	Boston-Cambridge-Newton, MA-NH..........	$16 340
13	5	Riverside-San Bernardino-Ontario, CA........	5.9	1	5	New York-Newark-Jersey City, NY-NJ-PA......	$15 248
3	6	Chicago-Naperville-Elgin, IL-IN-WI	5.8	15	6	Seattle-Tacoma-Bellevue, WA...............	$13 548
29	6	Las Vegas-Henderson-Paradise, NV	5.8	6	7	Washington-Arlington-Alexandria, DC-VA-MD-WV	$13 440
26	8	Pittsburgh, PA...............	5.7	5	8	Houston-The Woodlands-Sugar Land, TX	$13 183
49	9	Birmingham-Hoover, AL..............	5.6	31	9	Austin-Round Rock, TX	$11 872
46	10	New Orleans-Metairie, LA..............	5.5	73	10	North Port-Sarasota-Bradenton, FL...........	$11 488
65	10	New Haven-Milford, CT...............	5.5	4	11	Dallas-Fort Worth-Arlington, TX	$11 392
14	12	Detroit-Warren-Dearborn, MI..............	5.4	3	12	Chicago-Naperville-Elgin, IL-IN-WI	$11 287
32	13	Cleveland-Elyria, OH	5.3	19	13	Denver-Aurora-Lakewood, CO	$11 237
42	13	Memphis, TN-MS-AR	5.3	8	14	Miami-Fort Lauderdale-West Palm Beach, FL	$11 131
69	13	Allentown-Bethlehem-Easton, PA-NJ........	5.3	7	15	Philadelphia-Camden-Wilmington, PA-NJ-DE-MD	$10 939
5	16	Houston-The Woodlands-Sugar Land, TX	5.2	16	16	Minneapolis-St. Paul-Bloomington, MN	$10 849
27	16	Sacramento—Roseville—Arden-Arcade, CA........	5.2	2	17	Los Angeles-Long Beach-Anaheim, CA........	$10 837
67	16	Oxnard-Thousand Oaks-Ventura, CA.........	5.2	47	18	Hartford-West Hartford-East Hartford, CT	$10 548
70	16	Baton Rouge, LA..............	5.2	67	19	Oxnard-Thousand Oaks-Ventura, CA.........	$10 045
75	16	Greensboro-High Point, NC	5.2	63	20	Albany-Schenectady-Troy, NY...............	$10 043
7	21	Philadelphia-Camden-Wilmington, PA-NJ-DE-MD......	5.1	21	21	Baltimore-Columbia-Towson, MD	$9 965
9	21	Atlanta-Sandy Springs-Roswell, GA	5.1	17	22	San Diego-Carlsbad, CA	$9 808
38	21	Providence-Warwick, RI-MA	5.1	43	23	Raleigh, NC...............	$9 784
47	21	Hartford-West Hartford-East Hartford, CT	5.1	65	24	New Haven-Milford, CT..............	$9 416
8	25	Miami-Fort Lauderdale-West Palm Beach, FL.....	5.0	36	25	Nashville-Davidson—Murfreesboro—Franklin, TN......	$9 397
50	25	Buffalo-Cheektowaga-Niagara Falls, NY	5.0	9	26	Atlanta-Sandy Springs-Roswell, GA	$9 227
55	25	Tulsa, OK..............	5.0	59	27	Omaha-Council Bluffs, NE-IA	$9 218
2	28	Los Angeles-Long Beach-Anaheim, CA	4.9	55	28	Tulsa, OK..............	$9 124
53	28	Tucson, AZ..............	4.9	20	29	St. Louis, MO-IL	$9 096
68	28	El Paso, TX..............	4.9	30	30	Kansas City, MO-KS	$9 006
1	31	New York-Newark-Jersey City, NY-NJ-PA	4.8	39	31	Milwaukee-Waukesha-West Allis, WI	$8 997
57	31	Bridgeport-Stamford-Norwalk, CT	4.8	25	32	Portland-Vancouver-Hillsboro, OR-WA	$8 915
17	33	San Diego-Carlsbad, CA...............	4.7	26	33	Pittsburgh, PA...............	$8 784
22	33	Charlotte-Concord-Gastonia, NC-SC.........	4.7	22	34	Charlotte-Concord-Gastonia, NC-SC.........	$8 773
25	33	Portland-Vancouver-Hillsboro, OR-WA........	4.7	58	35	Worcester, MA-CT	$8 762
40	33	Jacksonville, FL	4.7	28	36	Cincinnati, OH-KY-IN	$8 702
51	33	Rochester, NY	4.7	46	37	New Orleans-Metairie, LA..............	$8 687
72	33	Dayton, OH	4.7	41	38	Oklahoma City, OK	$8 668
12	39	Phoenix-Mesa-Scottsdale, AZ..............	4.6	45	39	Richmond, VA	$8 583
18	39	Tampa-St. Petersburg-Clearwater, FL	4.6	40	40	Jacksonville, FL	$8 513
20	39	St. Louis, MO-IL	4.6	14	41	Detroit-Warren-Dearborn, MI..............	$8 508
37	39	Virginia Beach-Norfolk-Newport News, VA-NC	4.6	70	42	Baton Rouge, LA	$8 245
73	39	North Port-Sarasota-Bradenton, FL	4.6	49	43	Birmingham-Hoover, AL..............	$8 244
15	44	Seattle-Tacoma-Bellevue, WA	4.5	24	44	San Antonio-New Braunfels, TX.............	$8 127
23	44	Orlando-Kissimmee-Sanford, FL	4.5	32	45	Cleveland-Elyria, OH	$8 076
39	44	Milwaukee-Waukesha-West Allis, WI	4.5	12	46	Phoenix-Mesa-Scottsdale, AZ	$8 062
64	44	Knoxville, TN	4.5	34	47	Indianapolis-Carmel-Anderson, IN..........	$7 989
71	44	Columbia, SC	4.5	33	48	Columbus, OH	$7 984
21	49	Baltimore-Columbia-Towson, MD	4.4	38	49	Providence-Warwick, RI-MA	$7 949
28	50	Cincinnati, OH-KY-IN	4.3	18	50	Tampa-St. Petersburg-Clearwater, FL........	$7 912
30	50	Kansas City, MO-KS	4.3	27	51	Sacramento—Roseville—Arden-Arcade, CA......	$7 888
43	50	Raleigh, NC	4.3	29	52	Las Vegas-Henderson-Paradise, NV	$7 755
61	50	Greenville-Anderson-Mauldin, SC	4.3	64	53	Knoxville, TN	$7 656
41	54	Oklahoma City, OK	4.2	52	54	Grand Rapids-Wyoming, MI	$7 635
44	54	Louisville/Jefferson County, KY-IN..........	4.2	48	55	Salt Lake City, UT	$7 623
33	56	Columbus, OH	4.1	74	56	Charleston-North Charleston, SC	$7 612
45	56	Richmond, VA	4.1	69	57	Allentown-Bethlehem-Easton, PA-NJ	$7 511
58	56	Worcester, MA-CT	4.1	54	58	Urban Honolulu, HI	$7 170
63	56	Albany-Schenectady-Troy, NY	4.1	42	59	Memphis, TN-MS-AR	$7 082
74	56	Charleston-North Charleston, SC	4.1	51	60	Rochester, NY	$7 052
34	61	Indianapolis-Carmel-Anderson, IN	4.0	44	61	Louisville/Jefferson County, KY-IN..........	$7 006
4	62	Dallas-Fort Worth-Arlington, TX	3.8	50	62	Buffalo-Cheektowaga-Niagara Falls, NY	$6 830
6	62	Washington-Arlington-Alexandria, DC-VA-MD-WV	3.8	23	63	Orlando-Kissimmee-Sanford, FL	$6 823
11	62	San Francisco-Oakland-Hayward, CA........	3.8	37	64	Virginia Beach-Norfolk-Newport News, VA-NC	$6 547
35	62	San Jose-Sunnyvale-Santa Clara, CA	3.8	75	65	Greensboro-High Point, NC	$6 515
36	62	Nashville-Davidson—Murfreesboro—Franklin, TN	3.8	61	66	Greenville-Anderson-Mauldin, SC	$6 476
24	67	San Antonio-New Braunfels, TX	3.7	72	67	Dayton, OH	$6 356
16	68	Minneapolis-St. Paul-Bloomington, MN	3.6	53	68	Tucson, AZ	$6 327
52	69	Grand Rapids-Wyoming, MI	3.4	60	69	Albuquerque, NM	$6 083
59	69	Omaha-Council Bluffs, NE-IA	3.4	71	70	Columbia, SC	$5 966
10	71	Boston-Cambridge-Newton, MA-NH	3.3	56	71	Fresno, CA	$5 490
31	72	Austin-Round Rock, TX	3.2	62	72	Bakersfield, CA	$5 479
48	72	Salt Lake City, UT	3.2	13	73	Riverside-San Bernardino-Ontario, CA........	$4 923
19	74	Denver-Aurora-Lakewood, CO	3.1	68	74	El Paso, TX	$4 031
54	75	Urban Honolulu, HI	2.8	66	75	McAllen-Edinburg-Mission, TX...............	$3 349

75 Largest Metropolitan Areas by 2016 Population
Selected Rankings

	Employment in manufacturing as a percent of total nonfarm employment, 2015				Employment in professional, scientific, and technical services as a percent of total nonfarm employment, 2015		
Population rank	Manufacturing rank	Metropolitan area	Percent employed in manufacturing [col 107/col 105]	Population rank	Professional services rank	Metropolitan area	Percent employed in services [col 110/col 105]
52	1	Grand Rapids-Wyoming, MI	21.8	6	1	Washington-Arlington-Alexandria, DC-VA-MD-WV	20.3
75	2	Greensboro-High Point, NC	16.6	35	2	San Jose-Sunnyvale-Santa Clara, CA	12.9
61	3	Greenville-Anderson-Mauldin, SC	15.7	11	3	San Francisco-Oakland-Hayward, CA	11.5
39	4	Milwaukee-Waukesha-West Allis, WI	14.5	21	3	Baltimore-Columbia-Towson, MD	11.5
55	5	Tulsa, OK	14.2	31	5	Austin-Round Rock, TX	11.1
72	6	Dayton, OH	13.4	17	6	San Diego-Carlsbad, CA	11.0
14	7	Detroit-Warren-Dearborn, MI	13.2	43	7	Raleigh, NC	10.4
32	8	Cleveland-Elyria, OH	13.1	10	8	Boston-Cambridge-Newton, MA-NH	10.0
44	9	Louisville/Jefferson County, KY-IN	12.5	14	9	Detroit-Warren-Dearborn, MI	9.9
51	10	Rochester, NY	12.1	2	10	Los Angeles-Long Beach-Anaheim, CA	9.6
58	11	Worcester, MA-CT	11.9	1	11	New York-Newark-Jersey City, NY-NJ-PA	9.2
69	12	Allentown-Bethlehem-Easton, PA-NJ	11.3	18	12	Tampa-St. Petersburg-Clearwater, FL	8.7
28	13	Cincinnati, OH-KY-IN	10.9	19	12	Denver-Aurora-Lakewood, CO	8.7
47	13	Hartford-West Hartford-East Hartford, CT	10.9	57	12	Bridgeport-Stamford-Norwalk, CT	8.7
50	15	Buffalo-Cheektowaga-Niagara Falls, NY	10.8	67	15	Oxnard-Thousand Oaks-Ventura, CA	8.6
38	16	Providence-Warwick, RI-MA	10.4	9	16	Atlanta-Sandy Springs-Roswell, GA	8.5
16	17	Minneapolis-St. Paul-Bloomington, MN	10.3	63	16	Albany-Schenectady-Troy, NY	8.5
25	17	Portland-Vancouver-Hillsboro, OR-WA	10.3	30	18	Kansas City, MO-KS	8.4
15	19	Seattle-Tacoma-Bellevue, WA	10.2	37	18	Virginia Beach-Norfolk-Newport News, VA-NC	8.4
64	20	Knoxville, TN	10.1	48	18	Salt Lake City, UT	8.4
67	21	Oxnard-Thousand Oaks-Ventura, CA	9.7	3	21	Chicago-Naperville-Elgin, IL-IN-WI	8.2
22	22	Charlotte-Concord-Gastonia, NC-SC	9.6	5	22	Houston-The Woodlands-Sugar Land, TX	8.0
37	22	Virginia Beach-Norfolk-Newport News, VA-NC	9.6	7	23	Philadelphia-Camden-Wilmington, PA-NJ-DE-MD	7.9
3	24	Chicago-Naperville-Elgin, IL-IN-WI	9.3	72	24	Dayton, OH	7.8
56	24	Fresno, CA	9.3	15	25	Seattle-Tacoma-Bellevue, WA	7.7
71	24	Columbia, SC	9.3	27	25	Sacramento—Roseville—Arden-Arcade, CA	7.7
2	27	Los Angeles-Long Beach-Anaheim, CA	9.2	4	27	Dallas-Fort Worth-Arlington, TX	7.6
65	27	New Haven-Milford, CT	9.2	25	27	Portland-Vancouver-Hillsboro, OR-WA	7.6
74	29	Charleston-North Charleston, SC	9.1	8	29	Miami-Fort Lauderdale-West Palm Beach, FL	7.5
5	30	Houston-The Woodlands-Sugar Land, TX	8.8	70	30	Baton Rouge, LA	7.4
20	30	St. Louis, MO-IL	8.8	74	31	Charleston-North Charleston, SC	7.3
30	30	Kansas City, MO-KS	8.8	45	32	Richmond, VA	7.2
35	33	San Jose-Sunnyvale-Santa Clara, CA	8.7	64	32	Knoxville, TN	7.2
36	34	Nashville-Davidson—Murfreesboro—Franklin, TN	8.6	26	34	Pittsburgh, PA	7.1
48	34	Salt Lake City, UT	8.6	12	35	Phoenix-Mesa-Scottsdale, AZ	7.0
13	36	Riverside-San Bernardino-Ontario, CA	8.5	16	35	Minneapolis-St. Paul-Bloomington, MN	7.0
34	36	Indianapolis-Carmel-Anderson, IN	8.5	20	37	St. Louis, MO-IL	6.9
49	36	Birmingham-Hoover, AL	8.5	34	37	Indianapolis-Carmel-Anderson, IN	6.9
4	39	Dallas-Fort Worth-Arlington, TX	8.2	46	39	New Orleans-Metairie, LA	6.7
17	40	San Diego-Carlsbad, CA	8.1	50	40	Buffalo-Cheektowaga-Niagara Falls, NY	6.5
26	41	Pittsburgh, PA	8.0	23	41	Orlando-Kissimmee-Sanford, FL	6.4
57	41	Bridgeport-Stamford-Norwalk, CT	8.0	28	41	Cincinnati, OH-KY-IN	6.4
33	43	Columbus, OH	7.7	71	41	Columbia, SC	6.4
59	44	Omaha-Council Bluffs, NE-IA	7.5	22	44	Charlotte-Concord-Gastonia, NC-SC	6.3
42	45	Memphis, TN-MS-AR	7.4	33	44	Columbus, OH	6.3
70	46	Baton Rouge, LA	7.3	41	44	Oklahoma City, OK	6.3
53	47	Tucson, AZ	7.2	40	47	Jacksonville, FL	6.2
7	48	Philadelphia-Camden-Wilmington, PA-NJ-DE-MD	6.6	59	48	Omaha-Council Bluffs, NE-IA	6.1
73	48	North Port-Sarasota-Bradenton, FL	6.6	62	48	Bakersfield, CA	6.1
9	50	Atlanta-Sandy Springs-Roswell, GA	6.4	58	50	Worcester, MA-CT	6.0
63	50	Albany-Schenectady-Troy, NY	6.4	61	50	Greenville-Anderson-Mauldin, SC	6.0
12	52	Phoenix-Mesa-Scottsdale, AZ	6.3	47	52	Hartford-West Hartford-East Hartford, CT	5.9
41	52	Oklahoma City, OK	6.3	51	52	Rochester, NY	5.9
62	52	Bakersfield, CA	6.3	73	54	North Port-Sarasota-Bradenton, FL	5.8
10	55	Boston-Cambridge-Newton, MA-NH	6.2	24	55	San Antonio-New Braunfels, TX	5.7
45	56	Richmond, VA	5.7	32	55	Cleveland-Elyria, OH	5.7
11	57	San Francisco-Oakland-Hayward, CA	5.6	55	57	Tulsa, OK	5.6
68	57	El Paso, TX	5.6	29	58	Las Vegas-Henderson-Paradise, NV	5.3
24	59	San Antonio-New Braunfels, TX	5.4	36	58	Nashville-Davidson—Murfreesboro—Franklin, TN	5.3
31	60	Austin-Round Rock, TX	5.3	39	60	Milwaukee-Waukesha-West Allis, WI	5.2
46	60	New Orleans-Metairie, LA	5.3	53	60	Tucson, AZ	5.2
60	60	Albuquerque, NM	5.3	54	62	Urban Honolulu, HI	5.0
18	63	Tampa-St. Petersburg-Clearwater, FL	5.1	44	63	Louisville/Jefferson County, KY-IN	4.9
27	64	Sacramento—Roseville—Arden-Arcade, CA	4.9	49	63	Birmingham-Hoover, AL	4.9
40	65	Jacksonville, FL	4.8	68	65	El Paso, TX	4.6
43	65	Raleigh, NC	4.8	38	66	Providence-Warwick, RI-MA	4.5
19	67	Denver-Aurora-Lakewood, CO	4.6	65	66	New Haven-Milford, CT	4.5
21	68	Baltimore-Columbia-Towson, MD	4.5	56	68	Fresno, CA	4.1
1	69	New York-Newark-Jersey City, NY-NJ-PA	4.1	75	68	Greensboro-High Point, NC	4.1
23	70	Orlando-Kissimmee-Sanford, FL	3.7	52	70	Grand Rapids-Wyoming, MI	4.0
66	71	McAllen-Edinburg-Mission, TX	3.5	69	71	Allentown-Bethlehem-Easton, PA-NJ	3.8
8	72	Miami-Fort Lauderdale-West Palm Beach, FL	3.3	42	72	Memphis, TN-MS-AR	3.7
54	73	Urban Honolulu, HI	2.7	13	73	Riverside-San Bernardino-Ontario, CA	3.3
29	74	Las Vegas-Henderson-Paradise, NV	2.4	66	74	McAllen-Edinburg-Mission, TX	3.1
6	75	Washington-Arlington-Alexandria, DC-VA-MD-WV	1.9	60	75	Albuquerque, NM	0.0

75 Largest Metropolitan Areas by 2016 Population
Selected Rankings

Per capita local government taxes, 2012				Violent crime rate, 2014 (violent crimes known to police)			
Population rank	Local taxes rank	Metropolitan area	Local per capita taxes (dollars) [col 183]	Population rank	Crime rate rank	Metropolitan area	Crime rate (per 100,000 population) [col 46]
1	1	New York-Newark-Jersey City, NY-NJ-PA	4 280	42	1	Memphis, TN-MS-AR	1 104
57	2	Bridgeport-Stamford-Norwalk, CT	3 419	29	2	Las Vegas-Henderson-Paradise, NV	743
6	3	Washington-Arlington-Alexandria, DC-VA-MD-WV	3 255	60	3	Albuquerque, NM	732
3	4	Chicago-Naperville-Elgin, IL-IN-WI	2 701	34	4	Indianapolis-Carmel-Anderson, IN	715
11	5	San Francisco-Oakland-Hayward, CA	2 658	39	5	Milwaukee-Waukesha-West Allis, WI	659
63	6	Albany-Schenectady-Troy, NY	2 620	36	6	Nashville-Davidson—Murfreesboro—Franklin, TN	614
35	7	San Jose-Sunnyvale-Santa Clara, CA	2 585	49	7	Birmingham-Hoover, AL	590
47	8	Hartford-West Hartford-East Hartford, CT	2 512	21	8	Baltimore-Columbia-Towson, MD	584
51	9	Rochester, NY	2 381	71	9	Columbia, SC	581
32	10	Cleveland-Elyria, OH	2 378	5	10	Houston-The Woodlands-Sugar Land, TX	568
10	11	Boston-Cambridge-Newton, MA-NH	2 362	61	11	Greenville-Anderson-Mauldin, SC	538
65	12	New Haven-Milford, CT	2 358	14	12	Detroit-Warren-Dearborn, MI	534
7	13	Philadelphia-Camden-Wilmington, PA-NJ-DE-MD	2 356	23	13	Orlando-Kissimmee-Sanford, FL	531
50	14	Buffalo-Cheektowaga-Niagara Falls, NY	2 326	40	14	Jacksonville, FL	528
33	15	Columbus, OH	2 274	46	15	New Orleans-Metairie, LA	522
31	16	Austin-Round Rock, TX	2 267	8	16	Miami-Fort Lauderdale-West Palm Beach, FL	520
19	17	Denver-Aurora-Lakewood, CO	2 240	70	17	Baton Rouge, LA	514
21	18	Baltimore-Columbia-Towson, MD	2 145	62	18	Bakersfield, CA	510
4	19	Dallas-Fort Worth-Arlington, TX	2 139	11	19	San Francisco-Oakland-Hayward, CA	498
8	20	Miami-Fort Lauderdale-West Palm Beach, FL	2 106	30	20	Kansas City, MO-KS	486
69	20	Allentown-Bethlehem-Easton, PA-NJ	2 106	56	21	Fresno, CA	471
15	22	Seattle-Tacoma-Bellevue, WA	2 088	55	22	Tulsa, OK	467
5	23	Houston-The Woodlands-Sugar Land, TX	2 087	41	23	Oklahoma City, OK	466
30	24	Kansas City, MO-KS	2 040	7	24	Philadelphia-Camden-Wilmington, PA-NJ-DE-MD	460
59	25	Omaha-Council Bluffs, NE-IA	2 037	53	25	Tucson, AZ	443
38	26	Providence-Warwick, RI-MA	2 018	20	26	St. Louis, MO-IL	440
46	27	New Orleans-Metairie, LA	1 991	50	27	Buffalo-Cheektowaga-Niagara Falls, NY	431
39	28	Milwaukee-Waukesha-West Allis, WI	1 986	58	28	Worcester, MA-CT	419
2	29	Los Angeles-Long Beach-Anaheim, CA	1 870	27	29	Sacramento—Roseville—Arden-Arcade, CA	411
72	30	Dayton, OH	1 861	9	30	Atlanta-Sandy Springs-Roswell, GA	407
20	31	St. Louis, MO-IL	1 841	24	31	San Antonio-New Braunfels, TX	402
17	32	San Diego-Carlsbad, CA	1 791	44	31	Louisville/Jefferson County, KY-IN	402
28	33	Cincinnati, OH-KY-IN	1 786	73	31	North Port-Sarasota-Bradenton, FL	402
26	34	Pittsburgh, PA	1 785	32	34	Cleveland-Elyria, OH	395
25	35	Portland-Vancouver-Hillsboro, OR-WA	1 774	22	35	Charlotte-Concord-Gastonia, NC-SC	392
70	36	Baton Rouge, LA	1 760	64	36	Knoxville, TN	387
9	37	Atlanta-Sandy Springs-Roswell, GA	1 744	74	36	Charleston-North Charleston, SC	387
37	38	Virginia Beach-Norfolk-Newport News, VA-NC	1 733	3	38	Chicago-Naperville-Elgin, IL-IN-WI	382
74	39	Charleston-North Charleston, SC	1 730	1	39	New York-Newark-Jersey City, NY-NJ-PA	372
73	40	North Port-Sarasota-Bradenton, FL	1 684	18	39	Tampa-St. Petersburg-Clearwater, FL	372
24	41	San Antonio-New Braunfels, TX	1 669	2	41	Los Angeles-Long Beach-Anaheim, CA	369
67	42	Oxnard-Thousand Oaks-Ventura, CA	1 650	12	41	Phoenix-Mesa-Scottsdale, AZ	369
58	43	Worcester, MA-CT	1 628	59	43	Omaha-Council Bluffs, NE-IA	365
23	44	Orlando-Kissimmee-Sanford, FL	1 583	68	44	El Paso, TX	344
16	45	Minneapolis-St. Paul-Bloomington, MN	1 558	48	45	Salt Lake City, UT	344
42	46	Memphis, TN-MS-AR	1 555	10	46	Boston-Cambridge-Newton, MA-NH	333
45	47	Richmond, VA	1 521	65	46	New Haven-Milford, CT	333
27	48	Sacramento—Roseville—Arden-Arcade, CA	1 504	4	48	Dallas-Fort Worth-Arlington, TX	332
22	49	Charlotte-Concord-Gastonia, NC-SC	1 487	19	48	Denver-Aurora-Lakewood, CO	332
49	50	Birmingham-Hoover, AL	1 483	38	50	Providence-Warwick, RI-MA	329
12	51	Phoenix-Mesa-Scottsdale, AZ	1 447	66	50	McAllen-Edinburg-Mission, TX	329
36	52	Nashville-Davidson—Murfreesboro—Franklin, TN	1 445	13	52	Riverside-San Bernardino-Ontario, CA	327
40	52	Jacksonville, FL	1 445	15	53	Seattle-Tacoma-Bellevue, WA	325
53	54	Tucson, AZ	1 438	17	53	San Diego-Carlsbad, CA	325
34	55	Indianapolis-Carmel-Anderson, IN	1 402	75	55	Greensboro-High Point, NC	321
48	56	Salt Lake City, UT	1 399	6	56	Washington-Arlington-Alexandria, DC-VA-MD-WV	317
71	57	Columbia, SC	1 385	52	57	Grand Rapids-Wyoming, MI	315
18	58	Tampa-St. Petersburg-Clearwater, FL	1 381	37	58	Virginia Beach-Norfolk-Newport News, VA-NC	309
14	59	Detroit-Warren-Dearborn, MI	1 374	33	59	Columbus, OH	308
29	60	Las Vegas-Henderson-Paradise, NV	1 367	26	60	Pittsburgh, PA	291
62	61	Bakersfield, CA	1 365	31	60	Austin-Round Rock, TX	291
54	62	Urban Honolulu, HI	1 348	72	62	Dayton, OH	279
43	63	Raleigh, NC	1 332	63	63	Albany-Schenectady-Troy, NY	274
41	64	Oklahoma City, OK	1 331	25	64	Portland-Vancouver-Hillsboro, OR-WA	272
13	65	Riverside-San Bernardino-Ontario, CA	1 326	51	65	Rochester, NY	266
68	66	El Paso, TX	1 321	28	66	Cincinnati, OH-KY-IN	263
55	67	Tulsa, OK	1 319	16	67	Minneapolis-St. Paul-Bloomington, MN	261
44	68	Louisville/Jefferson County, KY-IN	1 265	47	68	Hartford-West Hartford-East Hartford, CT	253
75	69	Greensboro-High Point, NC	1 262	35	69	San Jose-Sunnyvale-Santa Clara, CA	250
60	70	Albuquerque, NM	1 208	57	70	Bridgeport-Stamford-Norwalk, CT	246
64	71	Knoxville, TN	1 191	45	71	Richmond, VA	231
52	72	Grand Rapids-Wyoming, MI	1 159	67	72	Oxnard-Thousand Oaks-Ventura, CA	223
56	73	Fresno, CA	1 131	69	73	Allentown-Bethlehem-Easton, PA-NJ	185
66	74	McAllen-Edinburg-Mission, TX	1 071	43	74	Raleigh, NC	136
61	75	Greenville-Anderson-Mauldin, SC	978	54	75	Urban Honolulu, HI	72

All Metropolitan Areas
Selected Rankings

	Nonemployer businesses, 2015				Value of residential construction authorized by building permits, 2016		
Population rank	Non-employer businesses rank	Metropolitan area	Non-employer businesses [col 167]	Population rank	New construction rank	Metropolitan area	New construction [col 169]
1	1	New York-Newark-Jersey City, NY-NJ-PA	1 861 540	4	1	Dallas-Fort Worth-Arlington, TX	10 909 645
2	2	Los Angeles-Long Beach-Anaheim, CA	1 323 907	5	2	Houston-The Woodlands-Sugar Land, TX	7 395 667
8	3	Miami-Fort Lauderdale-West Palm Beach, FL	885 524	2	3	Los Angeles-Long Beach-Anaheim, CA	7 355 806
3	4	Chicago-Naperville-Elgin, IL-IN-WI	779 014	1	4	New York-Newark-Jersey City, NY-NJ-PA	7 227 359
4	5	Dallas-Fort Worth-Arlington, TX	614 884	9	5	Atlanta-Sandy Springs-Roswell, GA	6 468 321
5	6	Houston-The Woodlands-Sugar Land, TX	566 184	12	6	Phoenix-Mesa-Scottsdale, AZ	6 432 518
9	7	Atlanta-Sandy Springs-Roswell, GA	564 061	15	7	Seattle-Tacoma-Bellevue, WA	5 274 516
6	8	Washington-Arlington-Alexandria, DC-VA-MD-WV	526 235	23	8	Orlando-Kissimmee-Sanford, FL	4 969 432
11	9	San Francisco-Oakland-Hayward, CA	437 632	19	9	Denver-Aurora-Lakewood, CO	4 343 273
7	10	Philadelphia-Camden-Wilmington, PA-NJ-DE-MD	410 065	6	10	Washington-Arlington-Alexandria, DC-VA-MD-WV	4 317 156
10	11	Boston-Cambridge-Newton, MA-NH	379 934	8	11	Miami-Fort Lauderdale-West Palm Beach, FL	4 207 477
14	12	Detroit-Warren-Dearborn, MI	334 728	22	12	Charlotte-Concord-Gastonia, NC-SC	4 065 100
12	13	Phoenix-Mesa-Scottsdale, AZ	316 042	11	13	San Francisco-Oakland-Hayward, CA	4 057 153
13	14	Riverside-San Bernardino-Ontario, CA	302 786	36	14	Nashville-Davidson—Murfreesboro—Franklin, TN	4 042 667
17	15	San Diego-Carlsbad, CA	268 900	18	15	Tampa-St. Petersburg-Clearwater, FL	3 959 582
16	16	Minneapolis-St. Paul-Bloomington, MN	264 395	3	16	Chicago-Naperville-Elgin, IL-IN-WI	3 898 390
15	17	Seattle-Tacoma-Bellevue, WA	253 114	31	17	Austin-Round Rock, TX	3 888 080
19	18	Denver-Aurora-Lakewood, CO	248 548	16	18	Minneapolis-St. Paul-Bloomington, MN	3 346 588
18	19	Tampa-St. Petersburg-Clearwater, FL	244 186	10	19	Boston-Cambridge-Newton, MA-NH	3 058 384
23	20	Orlando-Kissimmee-Sanford, FL	221 721	25	20	Portland-Vancouver-Hillsboro, OR-WA	2 981 386
21	21	Baltimore-Columbia-Towson, MD	207 633	40	21	Jacksonville, FL	2 494 462
22	22	Charlotte-Concord-Gastonia, NC-SC	187 409	13	22	Riverside-San Bernardino-Ontario, CA	2 447 666
20	23	St. Louis, MO-IL	183 648	43	23	Raleigh, NC	2 439 918
31	24	Austin-Round Rock, TX	182 554	17	24	San Diego-Carlsbad, CA	2 223 118
25	25	Portland-Vancouver-Hillsboro, OR-WA	174 121	27	25	Sacramento—Roseville—Arden-Arcade, CA	2 026 916
24	26	San Antonio-New Braunfels, TX	172 579	29	26	Las Vegas-Henderson-Paradise, NV	2 016 831
36	27	Nashville-Davidson—Murfreesboro—Franklin, TN	164 992	24	27	San Antonio-New Braunfels, TX	1 927 467
27	28	Sacramento—Roseville—Arden-Arcade, CA	161 569	7	28	Philadelphia-Camden-Wilmington, PA-NJ-DE-MD	1 925 175
29	29	Las Vegas-Henderson-Paradise, NV	154 711	30	29	Kansas City, MO-KS	1 884 251
33	30	Columbus, OH	148 635	34	30	Indianapolis-Carmel-Anderson, IN	1 852 768
32	31	Cleveland-Elyria, OH	148 063	73	31	North Port-Sarasota-Bradenton, FL	1 814 455
26	32	Pittsburgh, PA	144 705	14	32	Detroit-Warren-Dearborn, MI	1 792 551
35	33	San Jose-Sunnyvale-Santa Clara, CA	142 700	20	33	St. Louis, MO-IL	1 643 546
30	34	Kansas City, MO-KS	142 397	48	34	Salt Lake City, UT	1 616 249
28	35	Cincinnati, OH-KY-IN	140 795	33	35	Columbus, OH	1 575 371
34	36	Indianapolis-Carmel-Anderson, IN	137 653	74	36	Charleston-North Charleston, SC	1 438 352
46	37	New Orleans-Metairie, LA	116 471	21	37	Baltimore-Columbia-Towson, MD	1 427 438
38	38	Providence-Warwick, RI-MA	108 621	35	38	San Jose-Sunnyvale-Santa Clara, CA	1 295 220
42	39	Memphis, TN-MS-AR	108 553	41	39	Oklahoma City, OK	1 255 766
40	40	Jacksonville, FL	107 122	61	40	Greenville-Anderson-Mauldin, SC	1 153 120
41	41	Oklahoma City, OK	105 556	28	41	Cincinnati, OH-KY-IN	1 115 979
43	42	Raleigh, NC	100 662	37	42	Virginia Beach-Norfolk-Newport News, VA-NC	1 011 272
37	43	Virginia Beach-Norfolk-Newport News, VA-NC	99 469	26	43	Pittsburgh, PA	927 317
57	44	Bridgeport-Stamford-Norwalk, CT	91 902	52	44	Grand Rapids-Wyoming, MI	901 880
39	45	Milwaukee-Waukesha-West Allis, WI	89 843	45	45	Richmond, VA	847 323
44	46	Louisville/Jefferson County, KY-IN	85 248	39	46	Milwaukee-Waukesha-West Allis, WI	840 118
48	47	Salt Lake City, UT	84 930	44	47	Louisville/Jefferson County, KY-IN	815 393
45	48	Richmond, VA	84 106	71	48	Columbia, SC	790 031
47	49	Hartford-West Hartford-East Hartford, CT	80 958	56	49	Fresno, CA	729 163
49	50	Birmingham-Hoover, AL	80 676	49	50	Birmingham-Hoover, AL	725 467
55	51	Tulsa, OK	72 114	42	51	Memphis, TN-MS-AR	724 436
52	52	Grand Rapids-Wyoming, MI	71 476	70	52	Baton Rouge, LA	719 939
73	53	North Port-Sarasota-Bradenton, FL	71 186	53	53	Tucson, AZ	693 032
66	54	McAllen-Edinburg-Mission, TX	69 823	32	54	Cleveland-Elyria, OH	688 605
67	55	Oxnard-Thousand Oaks-Ventura, CA	67 736	55	55	Tulsa, OK	666 769
54	56	Urban Honolulu, HI	64 258	64	56	Knoxville, TN	664 218
53	57	Tucson, AZ	64 179	59	57	Omaha-Council Bluffs, NE-IA	663 605
51	58	Rochester, NY	63 347	68	58	El Paso, TX	656 311
64	59	Knoxville, TN	60 935	46	59	New Orleans-Metairie, LA	655 424
70	60	Baton Rouge, LA	60 652	54	60	Urban Honolulu, HI	641 470
61	61	Greenville-Anderson-Mauldin, SC	59 664	66	61	McAllen-Edinburg-Mission, TX	637 566
65	62	New Haven-Milford, CT	59 574	57	62	Bridgeport-Stamford-Norwalk, CT	621 925
59	63	Omaha-Council Bluffs, NE-IA	58 505	75	63	Greensboro-High Point, NC	545 301
74	64	Charleston-North Charleston, SC	58 399	63	64	Albany-Schenectady-Troy, NY	512 057
58	65	Worcester, MA-CT	58 294	62	65	Bakersfield, CA	488 500
50	66	Buffalo-Cheektowaga-Niagara Falls, NY	57 231	60	66	Albuquerque, NM	453 259
68	67	El Paso, TX	56 586	38	67	Providence-Warwick, RI-MA	450 988
75	68	Greensboro-High Point, NC	54 458	50	68	Buffalo-Cheektowaga-Niagara Falls, NY	391 181
71	69	Columbia, SC	54 051	51	69	Rochester, NY	370 848
63	70	Albany-Schenectady-Troy, NY	52 482	67	70	Oxnard-Thousand Oaks-Ventura, CA	340 979
60	71	Albuquerque, NM	51 935	58	71	Worcester, MA-CT	320 758
56	72	Fresno, CA	50 405	72	72	Dayton, OH	320 063
69	73	Allentown-Bethlehem-Easton, PA-NJ	50 343	47	73	Hartford-West Hartford-East Hartford, CT	296 855
72	74	Dayton, OH	48 014	69	74	Allentown-Bethlehem-Easton, PA-NJ	216 467
62	75	Bakersfield, CA	45 226	65	75	New Haven-Milford, CT	147 953

75 Metropolitan Areas with Highest Agricultural Sales
Selected rankings

	Value of agricultural products sold, 2012				Number of farms, 2012	
Value of sales rank	Metropolitan area	Value of sales (millions of dollars) [col 125]	Value of sales rank	Number of farms rank	Metropolitan area	Number of farms [col 113]
1	Fresno, CA	4 973.0	56	1	Dallas-Fort Worth-Arlington, TX	29 659
2	Visalia-Porterville, CA	4 017.1	9	2	Minneapolis-St. Paul-Bloomington, MN	13 251
3	Bakersfield, CA	3 999.0	51	3	Kansas City, MO-KS	12 757
4	Salinas, CA	2 979.7	26	4	St. Louis, MO-IL	11 270
5	Merced, CA	2 967.5	35	5	Portland-Vancouver-Hillsboro, OR-WA	10 838
6	Stockton-Lodi, CA	2 250.2	28	6	Columbus, OH	8 198
7	Modesto, CA	2 228.1	32	7	Madison, WI	7 446
8	Chicago-Naperville-Elgin, IL-IN-WI	2 187.2	8	8	Chicago-Naperville-Elgin, IL-IN-WI	6 841
9	Minneapolis-St. Paul-Bloomington, MN	2 169.8	24	9	Fayetteville-Springdale-Rogers, AR-MO	6 835
10	Phoenix-Mesa-Scottsdale, AZ	1 931.2	25	10	Philadelphia-Camden-Wilmington, PA-NJ-DE-MD	6 543
11	El Centro, CA	1 888.6	36	11	Indianapolis-Carmel-Anderson, IN	6 205
12	Greeley, CO	1 860.7	16	12	Omaha-Council Bluffs, NE-IA	6 055
13	Hanford-Corcoran, CA	1 829.2	58	13	San Diego-Carlsbad, CA	5 732
14	Kennewick-Richland, WA	1 663.2	1	14	Fresno, CA	5 683
15	Miami-Fort Lauderdale-West Palm Beach, FL	1 650.7	21	15	Lancaster, PA	5 657
16	Omaha-Council Bluffs, NE-IA	1 649.3	49	16	Wichita, KS	5 345
17	Yakima, WA	1 645.5	33	17	Boise City, ID	5 077
18	Riverside-San Bernardino-Ontario, CA	1 621.2	42	18	Sacramento—Roseville—Arden-Arcade, CA	5 076
19	Madera, CA	1 602.8	15	19	Miami-Fort Lauderdale-West Palm Beach, FL	4 978
20	Salisbury, MD-DE	1 575.7	2	20	Visalia-Porterville, CA	4 931
21	Lancaster, PA	1 475.0	48	21	Des Moines-West Des Moines, IA	4 898
22	Sioux City, IA-NE-SD	1 460.1	30	22	Grand Rapids-Wyoming, MI	4 680
23	Oxnard-Thousand Oaks-Ventura, CA	1 440.1	38	23	St. Cloud, MN	4 459
24	Fayetteville-Springdale-Rogers, AR-MO	1 356.1	44	24	Rochester, NY	4 268
25	Philadelphia-Camden-Wilmington, PA-NJ-DE-MD	1 264.9	31	25	Rochester, MN	4 233
26	St. Louis, MO-IL	1 235.6	18	26	Riverside-San Bernardino-Ontario, CA	4 198
27	Grand Island, NE	1 227.8	64	27	Jackson, MS	4 186
28	Columbus, OH	1 180.0	7	28	Modesto, CA	4 143
29	Santa Maria-Santa Barbara, CA	1 177.9	61	29	Memphis, TN-MS-AR	3 934
30	Grand Rapids-Wyoming, MI	1 120.3	57	30	Salem, OR	3 710
31	Rochester, MN	1 111.6	46	31	Cedar Rapids, IA	3 678
32	Madison, WI	1 081.6	22	32	Sioux City, IA-NE-SD	3 644
33	Boise City, ID	1 071.7	43	33	Peoria, IL	3 605
34	Grand Forks, ND-MN	1 023.3	6	34	Stockton-Lodi, CA	3 580
35	Portland-Vancouver-Hillsboro, OR-WA	1 008.7	39	35	Santa Rosa, CA	3 579
36	Indianapolis-Carmel-Anderson, IN	985.1	12	36	Greeley, CO	3 525
37	Yuma, AZ	985.0	41	37	Davenport-Moline-Rock Island, IA-IL	3 513
38	St. Cloud, MN	976.0	53	38	Sioux Falls, SD	3 418
39	Santa Rosa, CA	974.4	10	39	Phoenix-Mesa-Scottsdale, AZ	3 417
40	Fargo, ND-MN	965.2	17	40	Yakima, WA	3 143
41	Davenport-Moline-Rock Island, IA-IL	964.4	73	41	Orlando-Kissimmee-Sanford, FL	3 123
42	Sacramento—Roseville—Arden-Arcade, CA	961.8	66	42	Columbia, SC	3 085
43	Peoria, IL	960.8	55	43	Green Bay, WI	2 774
44	Rochester, NY	930.7	60	44	San Luis Obispo-Paso Robles-Arroyo Grande, CA	2 666
45	Waterloo-Cedar Falls, IA	921.7	45	45	Waterloo-Cedar Falls, IA	2 643
46	Cedar Rapids, IA	918.4	5	46	Merced, CA	2 486
47	Mankato-North Mankato, MN	892.1	52	47	Iowa City, IA	2 481
48	Des Moines-West Des Moines, IA	891.6	14	48	Kennewick-Richland, WA	2 392
49	Wichita, KS	864.4	20	49	Salisbury, MD-DE	2 384
50	Champaign-Urbana, IL	802.9	69	50	Bismarck, ND	2 367
51	Kansas City, MO-KS	785.7	27	51	Grand Island, NE	2 339
52	Iowa City, IA	785.1	34	52	Grand Forks, ND-MN	2 292
53	Sioux Falls, SD	781.7	50	53	Champaign-Urbana, IL	2 284
54	Amarillo, TX	776.4	59	54	Yuba City, CA	2 153
55	Green Bay, WI	750.0	23	55	Oxnard-Thousand Oaks-Ventura, CA	2 150
56	Dallas-Fort Worth-Arlington, TX	743.8	71	56	Chico, CA	2 056
57	Salem, OR	742.7	75	57	Reading, PA	2 039
58	San Diego-Carlsbad, CA	726.0	63	58	Bloomington, IL	2 000
59	Yuba City, CA	701.6	54	59	Amarillo, TX	1 976
60	San Luis Obispo-Paso Robles-Arroyo Grande, CA	665.0	3	60	Bakersfield, CA	1 938
61	Memphis, TN-MS-AR	661.4	62	61	Harrisonburg, VA	1 902
62	Harrisonburg, VA	659.0	47	62	Mankato-North Mankato, MN	1 834
63	Bloomington, IL	655.9	40	63	Fargo, ND-MN	1 772
64	Jackson, MS	633.0	74	64	Napa, CA	1 685
65	Lafayette-West Lafayette, IN	583.0	29	65	Santa Maria-Santa Barbara, CA	1 597
66	Columbia, SC	578.6	65	66	Lafayette-West Lafayette, IN	1 574
67	Goldsboro, NC	577.2	19	67	Madera, CA	1 507
68	Santa Cruz-Watsonville, CA	565.8	4	68	Salinas, CA	1 179
69	Bismarck, ND	553.1	13	69	Hanford-Corcoran, CA	1 056
70	Jonesboro, AR	549.0	72	70	Pine Bluff, AR	1 032
71	Chico, CA	541.3	70	71	Jonesboro, AR	980
72	Pine Bluff, AR	540.5	68	72	Santa Cruz-Watsonville, CA	667
73	Orlando-Kissimmee-Sanford, FL	539.8	67	73	Goldsboro, NC	563
74	Napa, CA	536.1	37	74	Yuma, AZ	562
75	Reading, PA	528.7	11	75	El Centro, CA	421

75 Metropolitan Areas with Highest Agricultural Sales
Selected rankings

Value of sales rank	Land in farms rank	Metropolitan area	Land in farms (1,000 acres) [col 117]	Value of sales rank	Value per Acre rank	Metropolitan area	Value per acre (1,000 acres) [col 123]
56	1	Dallas-Fort Worth-Arlington, TX	4 075	74	1	Napa, CA	21 801
69	2	Bismarck, ND	3 139	58	2	San Diego-Carlsbad, CA	17 964
51	3	Kansas City, MO-KS	3 124	23	3	Oxnard-Thousand Oaks-Ventura, CA	15 621
26	4	St. Louis, MO-IL	2 912	39	4	Santa Rosa, CA	14 620
54	5	Amarillo, TX	2 889	21	5	Lancaster, PA	12 529
49	6	Wichita, KS	2 856	68	6	Santa Cruz-Watsonville, CA	12 390
9	7	Minneapolis-St. Paul-Bloomington, MN	2 598	18	7	Riverside-San Bernardino-Ontario, CA	10 807
16	8	Omaha-Council Bluffs, NE-IA	2 373	25	8	Philadelphia-Camden-Wilmington, PA-NJ-DE-MD	10 682
3	9	Bakersfield, CA	2 330	35	9	Portland-Vancouver-Hillsboro, OR-WA	10 520
8	10	Chicago-Naperville-Elgin, IL-IN-WI	2 232	6	10	Stockton-Lodi, CA	10 090
12	11	Greeley, CO	1 956	15	11	Miami-Fort Lauderdale-West Palm Beach, FL	9 911
34	12	Grand Forks, ND-MN	1 911	7	12	Modesto, CA	9 636
17	13	Yakima, WA	1 780	75	13	Reading, PA	8 859
28	14	Columbus, OH	1 746	1	14	Fresno, CA	8 286
22	15	Sioux City, IA-NE-SD	1 733	50	15	Champaign-Urbana, IL	8 014
1	16	Fresno, CA	1 721	63	16	Bloomington, IL	7 961
40	17	Fargo, ND-MN	1 718	45	17	Waterloo-Cedar Falls, IA	7 913
36	18	Indianapolis-Carmel-Anderson, IN	1 689	5	18	Merced, CA	7 737
10	19	Phoenix-Mesa-Scottsdale, AZ	1 651	19	19	Madera, CA	7 614
61	20	Memphis, TN-MS-AR	1 573	71	20	Chico, CA	7 599
53	21	Sioux Falls, SD	1 521	2	21	Visalia-Porterville, CA	7 535
32	22	Madison, WI	1 466	29	22	Santa Maria-Santa Barbara, CA	7 365
33	23	Boise City, ID	1 376	57	23	Salem, OR	7 337
48	24	Des Moines-West Des Moines, IA	1 371	43	24	Peoria, IL	7 332
60	25	San Luis Obispo-Paso Robles-Arroyo Grande, CA	1 339	8	25	Chicago-Naperville-Elgin, IL-IN-WI	7 285
14	26	Kennewick-Richland, WA	1 329	37	26	Yuma, AZ	7 220
43	27	Peoria, IL	1 288	62	27	Harrisonburg, VA	7 055
4	28	Salinas, CA	1 268	11	28	El Centro, CA	7 002
2	29	Visalia-Porterville, CA	1 239	20	29	Salisbury, MD-DE	6 943
50	30	Champaign-Urbana, IL	1 184	46	30	Cedar Rapids, IA	6 910
27	31	Grand Island, NE	1 181	42	31	Sacramento—Roseville—Arden-Arcade, CA	6 892
31	32	Rochester, MN	1 158	41	32	Davenport-Moline-Rock Island, IA-IL	6 834
64	33	Jackson, MS	1 156	65	33	Lafayette-West Lafayette, IN	6 657
41	34	Davenport-Moline-Rock Island, IA-IL	1 101	52	34	Iowa City, IA	6 496
46	35	Cedar Rapids, IA	1 075	47	35	Mankato-North Mankato, MN	6 445
24	36	Fayetteville-Springdale-Rogers, AR-MO	1 073	59	36	Yuba City, CA	6 343
5	37	Merced, CA	979	16	37	Omaha-Council Bluffs, NE-IA	6 064
38	38	St. Cloud, MN	946	13	38	Hanford-Corcoran, CA	6 031
42	39	Sacramento—Roseville—Arden-Arcade, CA	927	48	39	Des Moines-West Des Moines, IA	5 875
44	39	Rochester, NY	927	22	40	Sioux City, IA-NE-SD	5 823
63	41	Bloomington, IL	888	36	41	Indianapolis-Carmel-Anderson, IN	5 724
45	42	Waterloo-Cedar Falls, IA	886	73	42	Orlando-Kissimmee-Sanford, FL	5 374
73	43	Orlando-Kissimmee-Sanford, FL	853	26	43	St. Louis, MO-IL	5 260
6	44	Stockton-Lodi, CA	787	9	44	Minneapolis-St. Paul-Bloomington, MN	5 180
7	45	Modesto, CA	768	31	45	Rochester, MN	5 117
30	46	Grand Rapids-Wyoming, MI	746	32	46	Madison, WI	5 002
70	47	Jonesboro, AR	723	28	47	Columbus, OH	4 928
29	48	Santa Maria-Santa Barbara, CA	701	4	48	Salinas, CA	4 893
65	49	Lafayette-West Lafayette, IN	679	53	49	Sioux Falls, SD	4 792
13	50	Hanford-Corcoran, CA	674	30	50	Grand Rapids-Wyoming, MI	4 790
19	51	Madera, CA	654	27	51	Grand Island, NE	4 451
25	52	Philadelphia-Camden-Wilmington, PA-NJ-DE-MD	653	3	52	Bakersfield, CA	4 435
47	53	Mankato-North Mankato, MN	651	55	53	Green Bay, WI	4 333
35	54	Portland-Vancouver-Hillsboro, OR-WA	644	56	54	Dallas-Fort Worth-Arlington, TX	4 260
52	55	Iowa City, IA	643	60	55	San Luis Obispo-Paso Robles-Arroyo Grande, CA	4 212
15	56	Miami-Fort Lauderdale-West Palm Beach, FL	610	67	56	Goldsboro, NC	4 124
39	57	Santa Rosa, CA	590	38	57	St. Cloud, MN	3 808
59	58	Yuba City, CA	563	24	58	Fayetteville-Springdale-Rogers, AR-MO	3 541
55	59	Green Bay, WI	547	10	59	Phoenix-Mesa-Scottsdale, AZ	3 326
66	60	Columbia, SC	522	66	60	Columbia, SC	3 177
20	61	Salisbury, MD-DE	520	70	61	Jonesboro, AR	3 134
72	62	Pine Bluff, AR	519	40	62	Fargo, ND-MN	3 097
11	63	El Centro, CA	516	51	63	Kansas City, MO-KS	3 062
21	64	Lancaster, PA	439	44	64	Rochester, NY	3 055
57	65	Salem, OR	431	72	65	Pine Bluff, AR	2 912
18	66	Riverside-San Bernardino-Ontario, CA	421	14	66	Kennewick-Richland, WA	2 827
71	67	Chico, CA	381	33	67	Boise City, ID	2 809
23	68	Oxnard-Thousand Oaks-Ventura, CA	281	61	68	Memphis, TN-MS-AR	2 682
74	69	Napa, CA	253	34	69	Grand Forks, ND-MN	2 559
75	70	Reading, PA	234	64	70	Jackson, MS	2 409
58	71	San Diego-Carlsbad, CA	222	12	71	Greeley, CO	1 979
62	71	Harrisonburg, VA	222	49	72	Wichita, KS	1 907
37	73	Yuma, AZ	215	17	73	Yakima, WA	1 803
67	74	Goldsboro, NC	191	69	74	Bismarck, ND	1 116
68	75	Santa Cruz-Watsonville, CA	100	54	75	Amarillo, TX	788

Table C. Metropolitan Areas — **Land Area and Population**

CBSA/ DIV code[1]	Area name	Population 2016				Population characteristics, 2016									
						Race alone or in combination, not Hispanic or Latino (percent)					Age (percent)				
		Land area,[2] 2016 (sq mi)	Total persons	Rank	Per square mile	White	Black	American Indian, Alaska Native	Asian and Pacific Islander	Percent Hispanic or Latino[3]	Under 5 years	5 to 17 years	18 to 24 years	25 to 34 years	35 to 44 years	45 to 54 years
		1	2	3	4	5	6	7	8	9	10	11	12	13	14	15

1. CBSA = Core Based Statistical Area. DIV = Metropolitan Division. See Appendix A for explanation. See Appendix B for list of metropolitan areas identified by type. 2. Dry land or land partially or temporarily covered by water. 3. May be of any race.

Table C. Metropolitan Areas — **Population and Households**

Area name	Population, 2016 (cont.)				Population change and components of change, 2000–2016							Households, 2015				
	Age (percent) (cont.)				Total persons		Percent change		Components of change, 2010–2016					Percent		
	55 to 64 years	65 to 74 years	75 years and over	Percent female	2000	2010	2000–2010	2010–2016	Births	Deaths	Net migration	Number	Persons per household	Family households	Female family householder[1]	One person
	16	17	18	19	20	21	22	23	24	25	26	27	28	29	30	31

1. No spouse present.

Table C. Metropolitan Areas — **Population, Vital Statistics, Health, and Crime**

Area name	Daytime population, 2015		Births, 2016		Deaths, 2016		Persons under 65 with no health insurance 2015		Medicare, 2015			Serious crimes known to police,[2] 2014	
												Total	
	Persons in group quarters, 2016	Number	Employment/ residence ratio	Total	Rate[1]	Number	Rate[1]	Number	Percent	Total Beneficiaries	Enrolled in Original Medicare	Enrolled in Medicare Advantage	Number	Rate[3]
	32	33	34	35	36	37	38	39	40	41	42	43	44	45

1. Per 1,000 estimated resident population. 2. Data for serious crimes have not been adjusted for underreporting; this may affect comparability between geographic areas and over time. 3. Per 100,000 population estimated by the FBI.

Table C. Metropolitan Areas — **Crime, Education, Money Income, and Poverty**

Area name	Serious crimes known to police, 2014 (cont.)[1]		Education						Income and Poverty, 2015							
	Rate[2]		School enrollment and attainment, 2015				Local government expenditures,[5] 2013–2014							Percent below poverty level		
			Enrollment[3]		Attainment[4] (percent)							Percent of households with income of less than $50,000	Percent of households with income of $200,000 or more			
	Violent	Property	Total	Percent private	High school graduate or less	Bachelor's degree or more	Total current expenditures (mil dol)	Current expenditures per student (dollars)	Per capita income[6] (dollars)	Mean household income (dollars)	Median household income			All persons	Children under 18 years	Age 65 years and older
	46	47	48	49	50	51	52	53	54	55	56	57	58	59	60	61

1. Data for serious crimes have not been adjusted for underreporting; this may affect comparability between geographic areas and over time. 2. Per 100,000 population estimated by the FBI. 3. All persons 3 years old and over enrolled in nursery school through college. 4. Persons 25 years old and over. 5. Elementary and secondary education expenditures. 6. Based on resident population estimated in the 2015 American Community Survey.

Table C. Metropolitan Areas — **Personal Income**

Area name	Personal income, 2015										Earnings, 2015		
			Per capita[1]			Supplements to wages and salaries; employer contributions (mil dol)						Contributions for government social insurance (mil dol)	
	Total (mil dol)	Percent change 2014–2015	Dollars	Rank	Wages and salaries (mil dol)	Pension and insurance	Government social insurance	Proprietors' income (mil dol)	Dividends, interest, and rent (mil dol)	Personal transfer receipts (mil dol)	Total (mil dol)	From employee and self-employed	From employer
	62	63	64	65	66	67	68	69	70	71	72	73	74

1. Based on the resident population estimated as of July 1 of the year shown.

Table C. Metropolitan Areas — **Earnings, Social Security, and Housing**

Area name	Earnings, 2015 (cont.)									Social Security beneficiaries, December 2015		Supplemental Security Income recipients, December 2015	Housing units, 2016	
	Percent by selected industries													
	Farm	Mining	Construction	Manufacturing	Information, professional, scientific, technical services	Retail trade	Finance, insurance, real estate, rental and leasing	Health care and social assistance	Government	Number	Rate[1]		Total	Percent change, 2010–2016
	75	76	77	78	79	80	81	82	83	84	85	86	87	88

1. Per 1,000 resident population estimated as of July 1, 2011 of the year shown.

Table C. Metropolitan Areas — **Housing, Labor Force, and Employment**

Area name	Housing units, 2015								Civilian labor force, 2016				Civilian employment[5], 2015		
	Occupied units										Unemployment			Percent	
			Owner-occupied			Renter-occupied									
				Median owner cost as a percent of income											
	Total	Percent	Median value[1]	With a mortgage	Without a mortgage[2]	Median rent[3]	Median rent as a percent of income	Percent with a computer	Total	Percent change, 2015–2016	Total	Rate[4]	Total employed	Management, professional, and related occupations	Construction, production, and related occupations
	89	90	91	92	93	94	95	96	97	98	99	100	101	102	103

1. Specified owner-occupied units.   2. A value of 10.0 represents 10 percent or less.   3. Specified renter-occupied units.   4. Percent of civilian labor force.
5. Civilian employed persons 16 years old and over.

Table C. Metropolitan Areas — **Nonfarm Employment and Agriculture**

Area name	Private nonfarm establishments, employment and payroll, 2015									Agriculture, 2012			
		Employment						Annual payroll		Farms			
											Percent with:		
	Number of establishments	Total	Health care and social assistance	Manufacturing	Retail trade	Finance and insurance	Professional, scientific, and technical services	Total (mil dol)	Average per employee (dollars)	Number	Fewer than 50 acres	500 acres or more	Farm operators whose principal occupation is farming (percent)
	104	105	106	107	108	109	110	111	112	113	114	115	116

Table C. Metropolitan Areas — Agriculture

Area name	Agriculture, 2012 (cont.)															
	Land in farms					Value of land and buildings (dollars)			Value of products sold				Percent of farms with sales of:		Government payments	
			Acres								Percent from:					
	Acreage (1,000)	Percent change, 2007–2012	Average size of farm	Total irrigated (1,000)	Total cropland (1,000)	Average per farm	Average per acre	Value of machinery and equipment, average per farm (dollars)	Total (mil dol)	Average per farm (dollars)	Crops	Live-stock and poultry products	$10,000 or more	$100,000 or more	Total ($1,000)	Percent of farms
	117	118	119	120	121	122	123	124	125	126	127	128	129	130	131	132

Table C. Metropolitan Areas — Water Use, Wholesale Trade, Retail Trade, and Real Estate

Area name	Water use, 2010		Wholesale trade,[1] 2012				Retail trade, 2012				Real estate and rental and leasing, 2012			
	Total water withdrawn (mil gal/day)	Gallons withdrawn per person per day	Number of establish-ments	Number of employees	Sales (mil dol)	Annual payroll (mil dol)	Number of establish-ments	Number of employees	Sales (mil dol)	Annual payroll (mil dol)	Number of establish-ments	Number of employees	Receipts (mil dol)	Annual payroll (mil dol)
	133	134	135	136	137	138	139	140	141	142	143	144	145	146

1. Merchant wholesalers, except manufacturers' sales branches and offices.

Table C. Metropolitan Areas — Professional Services, Manufacturing, and Accommodation and Food Services

Area name	Professional, scientific, and technical services, 2012				Manufacturing, 2012				Accommodation and food services, 2012			
	Number of establish-ments	Number of employees	Sales (mil dol)	Annual payroll (mil dol)	Number of establish-ments	Number of employees	Sales (mil dol)	Annual payroll (mil dol)	Number of establish-ments	Number of employees	Sales (mil dol)	Annual payroll (mil dol)
	147	148	149	150	151	152	153	154	155	156	157	158

Table C. Metropolitan Areas — Health Care and Social Assistance, Other Services, Nonemployer Business and Residential Construction

Area name	Health care and social assistance, 2012				Other services, 2012				Nonemployer business, 2015		Value of residential construction authorized by building permits, 2016	
	Number of establish-ments	Number of employees	Receipts (mil dol)	Annual payroll (mil dol)	Number of establish-ments	Number of employees	Receipts (mil dol)	Annual payroll (mil dol)	Number	Receipts (mil dol)	New construc-tion ($1,000)	Number of housing units
	159	160	161	162	163	164	165	166	167	168	169	170

Table C. Metropolitan Areas — Government Employment and Payroll and Local Government Finances

Area name	Government employment and payroll, 2012									Local government finances, 2012				
			March payroll (percent of total)							General revenue				
												Taxes		
													Per capita[1] (dollars)	
	Full-time equivalent employees	March Payroll (dollars)	Administration, judicial, and legal	Police and corrections	Fire protection	Highways and transportation	Health and welfare	Natural resources and utilities	Education and libraries	Total (mil dol)	Inter-governmental (mil dol)	Total (mil dol)	Total	Property
	171	172	173	174	175	176	177	178	179	180	181	182	183	184

1. Based on the resident population estimated as of July 1 of the year shown.

Table C. Metropolitan Areas — Local Government Finances, Government Employment, and Income Taxes

Area name	Local government finances, 2012 (cont.)							Debt outstanding		Government employment, 2015			Individual income tax returns, 2014		
	Direct general expenditure														
			Percent of total for:												
	Total (mil dol)	Per capita[1] (dollars)	Education	Health and hospitals	Police protection	Public welfare	Highways	Total (mil dol)	Per capita[1] (dollars)	Federal civilian	Federal military	State and local	Number of returns	Mean Adjusted Gross income	Mean income tax
	185	186	187	188	189	190	191	192	193	194	195	196	197	198	199

1. Based on the resident population estimated as of July 1 of the year shown.

Table C. Metropolitan Areas — **Land Area and Population**

CBSA/ DIV code[1]	Area name	Land area,[2] 2016 (sq mi)	Total persons	Rank	Per square mile	White	Black	American Indian, Alaska Native	Asian and Pacific Islander	Percent Hispanic or Latino[3]	Under 5 years	5 to 17 years	18 to 24 years	25 to 34 years	35 to 44 years	45 to 54 years
		1	2	3	4	5	6	7	8	9	10	11	12	13	14	15
10180	Abilene, TX	2 743.5	170 364	243	62.1	67.0	8.2	0.9	2.5	23.3	6.9	16.8	13.4	14.5	11.3	11.1
10420	Akron, OH	900.2	702 221	80	780.1	82.4	13.7	0.7	3.6	1.9	5.5	15.3	10.5	12.7	11.3	13.7
10500	Albany, GA	1 932.6	152 219	269	78.8	42.3	54.1	0.6	1.5	2.7	6.5	18.1	10.1	13.0	11.9	12.4
10540	Albany, OR	2 287.1	122 849	318	53.7	88.1	1.0	2.7	2.2	8.8	6.0	16.8	7.8	13.3	11.7	12.4
10580	Albany-Schenectady-Troy, NY	2 811.7	881 839	63	313.6	82.3	9.1	0.6	5.3	5.1	5.3	14.7	11.3	12.8	11.8	13.9
10740	Albuquerque, NM	9 281.0	909 906	60	98.0	41.3	2.9	6.1	2.9	48.7	5.8	17.0	8.9	14.3	12.4	12.7
10780	Alexandria, LA	1 961.0	154 789	262	78.9	64.9	30.3	1.5	1.7	3.4	6.7	17.9	8.7	13.7	12.3	12.6
10900	Allentown-Bethlehem-Easton, PA-NJ	1 452.8	835 652	69	575.2	75.6	5.9	0.4	3.4	16.3	5.3	16.0	9.2	12.1	11.8	14.2
11020	Altoona, PA	525.8	124 650	314	237.1	96.1	2.6	0.4	1.0	1.2	5.3	15.3	7.8	12.1	11.4	13.1
11100	Amarillo, TX	5 150.2	263 342	184	51.1	61.6	6.7	1.0	3.8	28.4	7.3	18.4	9.6	14.9	12.7	11.9
11180	Ames, IA	572.7	97 090	359	169.5	85.6	3.4	0.5	9.0	3.3	4.6	12.1	31.8	13.1	9.3	8.6
11260	Anchorage, AK	26 314.5	402 557	133	15.3	70.3	6.0	11.6	11.9	7.9	7.2	18.2	10.0	16.7	12.8	12.7
11460	Ann Arbor, MI	706.0	364 709	146	516.6	73.5	13.9	1.0	10.4	4.6	5.0	13.9	19.0	14.2	11.3	12.1
11500	Anniston-Oxford-Jacksonville, AL	605.9	114 611	335	189.2	74.2	21.6	1.0	1.4	3.6	5.6	16.2	9.1	13.2	12.0	13.1
11540	Appleton, WI	955.8	234 079	193	244.9	90.1	1.7	1.8	3.7	4.2	6.2	17.8	8.6	12.6	12.7	14.6
11700	Asheville, NC	2 032.6	452 319	116	222.5	87.0	5.3	1.0	1.6	6.8	5.0	13.9	7.5	12.2	12.3	13.2
12020	Athens-Clarke County, GA	1 024.9	205 290	216	200.3	67.4	21.0	0.5	4.4	8.4	5.5	14.7	19.4	14.2	11.8	11.2
12060	Atlanta-Sandy Springs-Roswell, GA	8 681.3	5 789 700	9	666.9	49.5	34.7	0.7	6.6	10.6	6.5	18.6	9.2	14.0	14.1	14.5
12100	Atlantic City-Hammonton, NJ	555.6	270 991	176	487.7	57.7	15.6	0.6	9.2	18.8	5.7	16.0	9.3	12.0	11.4	14.2
12220	Auburn-Opelika, AL	607.6	158 991	259	261.7	68.9	23.9	0.7	4.3	3.8	5.3	15.6	18.9	14.5	12.0	11.8
12260	Augusta-Richmond County, GA-SC	3 480.7	594 919	93	170.9	56.9	36.3	0.9	2.8	5.4	6.3	17.2	9.3	14.2	12.0	12.8
12420	Austin-Round Rock, TX	4 221.5	2 056 405	31	487.1	54.5	7.8	0.8	6.7	32.2	6.6	17.1	9.8	17.5	15.4	12.9
12540	Bakersfield, CA	8 131.9	884 788	62	108.8	36.5	5.9	1.3	5.6	52.8	8.1	21.1	10.5	15.4	12.5	11.6
12580	Baltimore-Columbia-Towson, MD	2 601.5	2 798 886	21	1 075.9	59.1	30.3	0.8	6.7	5.6	6.0	16.1	9.0	14.6	12.4	13.9
12620	Bangor, ME	3 397.2	151 806	270	44.7	95.5	1.3	2.0	1.5	1.3	4.7	13.7	10.7	13.4	11.1	13.9
12700	Barnstable Town, MA	394.2	214 276	207	543.6	92.1	3.6	1.2	2.0	2.9	3.6	11.8	7.2	8.8	8.6	13.2
12940	Baton Rouge, LA	4 026.9	835 175	70	207.4	57.9	36.2	0.7	2.6	3.9	6.6	17.1	11.4	14.6	12.5	12.5
12980	Battle Creek, MI	706.3	134 386	300	190.3	80.9	12.8	1.4	3.0	5.0	6.2	16.9	8.9	12.1	11.6	13.1
13020	Bay City, MI	442.3	104 747	345	236.8	92.0	2.6	1.2	0.9	5.2	5.0	15.6	7.8	12.2	11.3	13.5
13140	Beaumont-Port Arthur, TX	3 034.4	409 968	130	135.1	58.1	24.6	0.8	3.1	14.8	6.9	17.2	9.2	14.0	12.4	12.8
13220	Beckley, WV	1 266.9	120 924	322	95.4	90.8	7.7	0.9	1.0	1.4	5.7	15.2	7.5	11.9	12.9	12.4
13380	Bellingham, WA	2 107.9	216 800	203	102.9	82.5	1.8	3.8	6.3	9.2	5.5	14.2	14.4	13.2	11.5	11.9
13460	Bend-Redmond, OR	3 017.6	181 307	229	60.1	89.7	0.9	1.7	2.2	7.8	5.3	15.4	6.9	12.7	12.8	12.9
13740	Billings, MT	5 855.9	169 728	246	29.0	89.6	1.3	5.1	1.3	5.3	6.3	16.8	8.0	13.6	12.1	12.4
13780	Binghamton, NY	1 224.4	244 094	189	199.4	87.9	5.5	0.7	4.5	3.6	5.3	14.7	13.0	11.1	10.1	12.9
13820	Birmingham-Hoover, AL	5 280.0	1 147 417	49	217.3	64.9	29.5	0.7	1.8	4.3	6.3	16.9	8.5	13.6	12.9	13.3
13900	Bismarck, ND	5 375.5	131 635	302	24.5	88.7	2.2	7.3	1.1	2.5	7.3	16.4	9.1	14.9	12.4	12.0
13980	Blacksburg-Christiansburg-Radford, VA	1 453.0	182 876	228	125.9	88.7	5.2	0.6	4.8	2.7	4.7	12.3	21.2	13.0	10.5	11.9
14010	Bloomington, IL	1 580.9	188 644	226	119.3	83.1	8.2	0.5	5.7	4.6	5.8	15.9	16.9	12.8	12.0	12.0
14020	Bloomington, IN	779.8	166 336	251	213.3	87.4	4.0	0.8	7.0	3.1	4.6	12.0	24.4	14.5	10.3	10.4
14100	Bloomsburg-Berwick, PA	613.3	84 763	370	138.2	93.8	2.3	0.4	1.8	2.7	4.9	13.4	14.2	11.2	10.4	12.8
14260	Boise City, ID	11 765.3	691 423	81	58.8	82.7	1.4	1.3	3.4	13.5	6.5	19.3	8.7	13.9	13.3	12.6
14460	Boston-Cambridge-Newton, MA-NH	3 485.9	4 794 447	10	1 375.4	73.2	8.5	0.5	8.8	10.8	5.4	14.8	10.2	14.8	12.4	14.2
14460	Boston, MA Div 14454	1 113.2	1 994 976	X	1 792.1	67.5	13.9	0.6	8.5	11.3	5.4	14.4	10.8	16.2	12.3	13.7
14460	Cambridge-Newton-Framingham, MA Div 15764	1 310.1	2 368 792	X	1 808.1	74.3	5.2	0.4	10.1	11.9	5.5	15.2	9.8	14.2	12.6	14.3
14460	Rockingham County-Strafford County, NH 40484	1 062.6	430 679	X	405.3	93.9	1.3	0.6	3.0	2.6	4.7	15.0	10.2	11.8	11.5	15.6
14500	Boulder, CO	726.3	322 226	155	443.7	80.3	1.5	0.9	5.9	13.8	4.7	14.9	15.2	13.6	12.5	13.1
14540	Bowling Green, KY	1 614.9	171 122	241	106.0	85.7	8.1	0.7	3.2	4.4	6.2	16.2	14.2	13.0	12.2	12.3
14740	Bremerton-Silverdale, WA	395.1	264 811	182	670.2	81.8	4.1	2.9	9.4	7.6	5.9	14.8	10.3	14.2	11.2	12.6
14860	Bridgeport-Stamford-Norwalk, CT	625.0	944 177	57	1 510.7	63.8	11.6	0.4	6.3	19.4	5.6	17.5	9.2	11.5	12.6	15.3
15180	Brownsville-Harlingen, TX	891.1	422 135	126	473.7	9.5	0.4	0.2	0.7	89.4	8.5	22.6	10.6	12.1	12.3	11.1
15260	Brunswick, GA	1 286.5	116 784	329	90.8	69.5	24.3	0.8	1.7	5.6	5.7	16.6	8.1	11.7	11.5	13.3
15380	Buffalo-Cheektowaga-Niagara Falls, NY	1 565.1	1 132 804	50	723.8	79.3	13.0	1.1	3.7	4.9	5.4	15.1	9.4	13.7	11.0	13.6
15500	Burlington, NC	423.4	159 688	258	377.2	66.1	20.4	0.8	1.9	12.6	5.8	16.8	9.7	12.2	11.8	14.1
15540	Burlington-South Burlington, VT	1 252.2	217 365	202	173.6	92.2	2.6	1.3	4.0	2.1	5.2	14.1	14.0	13.5	11.6	13.5
15680	California-Lexington Park, MD	357.4	112 587	337	315.0	77.6	15.7	0.9	4.0	5.0	6.4	18.1	9.5	14.1	12.1	14.8
15940	Canton-Massillon, OH	969.9	401 281	134	413.7	89.6	8.8	0.8	1.2	1.9	5.6	16.1	8.6	11.7	11.3	13.4
15980	Cape Coral-Fort Myers, FL	784.1	722 336	78	921.2	69.5	8.8	0.5	2.1	20.5	4.8	13.4	6.9	10.9	10.3	12.1
16020	Cape Girardeau, MO-IL	1 432.0	97 443	358	68.0	87.6	9.5	0.9	1.7	2.2	5.8	15.8	12.9	12.1	11.2	12.2
16060	Carbondale-Marion, IL	1 004.2	126 430	310	125.9	84.7	10.3	0.8	3.0	3.3	5.7	14.4	14.2	13.7	11.5	11.7
16180	Carson City, NV	144.7	54 742	382	378.3	69.9	2.3	2.9	3.5	23.6	5.3	15.0	7.9	12.5	11.1	13.2
16220	Casper, WY	5 340.5	81 039	376	15.2	88.5	1.8	1.6	1.5	8.5	7.0	17.3	8.3	15.4	12.8	11.8

1. CBSA = Core Based Statistical Area. DIV = Metropolitan Division. See Appendix A for explanation. See Appendix B for list of metropolitan areas identified by type. 2. Dry land or land partially or temporarily covered by water. 3. May be of any race.

Table C. Metropolitan Areas — Population and Households

Area name	55 to 64 years	65 to 74 years	75 years and over	Percent female	2000	2010	2000–2010	2010–2016	Births	Deaths	Net migration	Number	Persons per household	Family households	Female family householder[1]	One person
	16	17	18	19	20	21	22	23	24	25	26	27	28	29	30	31
Abilene, TX	11.3	8.0	6.8	49.3	160 245	165 252	3.1	3.1	14 808	10 233	522	59 372	2.60	63.4	12.3	29.0
Akron, OH	14.4	9.6	7.0	51.3	694 960	703 203	1.2	-0.1	47 673	43 561	-3 839	282 456	2.44	62.9	12.6	30.2
Albany, GA	12.9	9.0	5.9	52.7	157 833	157 500	-0.2	-3.4	13 277	8 919	-9 768	57 597	2.63	65.5	22.2	29.7
Albany, OR	13.9	10.7	7.4	50.5	103 069	116 672	13.2	5.3	9 006	7 447	4 360	46 315	2.58	67.9	11.3	25.0
Albany-Schenectady-Troy, NY	13.8	9.5	6.9	51.0	825 875	870 692	5.4	1.3	57 223	48 211	3 810	342 766	2.48	59.5	10.0	33.4
Albuquerque, NM	13.3	9.4	6.2	50.8	729 649	887 080	21.6	2.6	66 702	43 741	-80	342 590	2.61	61.9	12.3	31.3
Alexandria, LA	12.7	9.0	6.5	50.6	145 035	153 922	6.1	0.6	13 061	10 009	-2 028	54 406	2.69	66.9	18.6	28.6
Allentown-Bethlehem-Easton, PA-NJ	14.0	9.7	7.7	51.0	740 395	821 266	10.9	1.8	53 935	49 553	10 342	314 985	2.57	68.7	12.2	25.1
Altoona, PA	14.8	11.0	9.2	51.1	129 144	127 076	-1.6	-1.9	8 435	9 973	-1 039	52 830	2.32	63.1	11.2	31.9
Amarillo, TX	11.9	7.6	5.6	49.7	228 707	251 933	10.2	4.5	23 842	14 313	1 719	95 626	2.65	65.2	13.5	30.0
Ames, IA	9.4	6.1	5.0	47.8	79 981	89 542	12.0	8.4	5 828	3 022	4 858	37 264	2.29	52.7	7.2	24.8
Anchorage, AK	12.3	6.8	3.3	48.7	319 605	380 821	19.2	5.7	37 941	13 419	-2 706	135 601	2.88	66.0	12.6	25.8
Ann Arbor, MI	11.5	7.8	5.1	50.5	322 895	345 066	6.9	5.7	23 359	13 512	9 891	138 099	2.46	57.1	9.4	30.1
Anniston-Oxford-Jacksonville, AL	13.9	10.1	6.8	51.9	112 249	118 586	5.6	-3.4	8 211	8 667	-3 373	44 323	2.54	66.4	18.9	29.8
Appleton, WI	13.5	8.1	5.8	50.0	201 602	225 666	11.9	3.7	17 792	10 100	722	90 489	2.54	69.4	11.8	25.3
Asheville, NC	14.4	12.4	9.0	51.9	369 171	424 853	15.1	6.5	27 684	29 606	28 029	184 983	2.36	61.1	9.0	32.9
Athens-Clarke County, GA	10.8	7.6	4.9	51.7	166 079	192 541	15.9	6.6	13 898	8 307	6 884	76 704	2.49	56.6	11.6	31.7
Atlanta-Sandy Springs-Roswell, GA	11.6	7.3	4.2	51.6	4 263 438	5 286 725	24.0	9.5	455 443	213 954	257 589	2 028 705	2.77	67.4	14.3	26.6
Atlantic City-Hammonton, NJ	14.5	9.8	7.1	51.6	252 552	274 540	8.7	-1.3	20 046	16 264	-7 210	101 813	2.64	66.9	15.8	27.5
Auburn-Opelika, AL	10.4	6.9	4.1	50.7	115 092	140 296	21.9	13.3	11 163	6 234	13 421	58 191	2.60	64.9	13.8	27.2
Augusta-Richmond County, GA-SC	13.2	9.2	5.8	51.3	508 032	564 873	11.2	5.3	46 349	32 477	15 493	210 854	2.72	68.2	16.6	26.6
Austin-Round Rock, TX	10.6	6.5	3.7	50.0	1 249 763	1 716 320	37.3	19.8	161 908	57 043	229 967	723 914	2.71	61.5	9.7	28.2
Bakersfield, CA	10.4	6.3	4.1	48.7	661 645	839 627	26.9	5.4	89 042	35 445	-7 445	263 273	3.23	75.5	17.0	19.6
Baltimore-Columbia-Towson, MD	13.3	8.6	6.1	51.8	2 552 994	2 710 583	6.2	3.3	211 423	148 256	28 008	1 037 443	2.63	65.1	14.1	28.2
Bangor, ME	14.9	10.2	7.5	50.5	144 919	153 920	6.2	-1.4	9 058	9 467	-1 668	59 099	2.47	63.3	9.0	27.7
Barnstable Town, MA	17.5	16.5	12.8	52.2	222 230	215 868	-2.9	-0.7	9 771	17 790	6 338	97 451	2.17	61.1	9.2	31.8
Baton Rouge, LA	12.2	8.1	5.1	51.0	705 973	802 500	13.7	4.1	69 142	41 433	5 190	300 535	2.68	64.4	14.7	29.1
Battle Creek, MI	14.0	9.6	7.5	51.1	137 985	136 148	-1.3	-1.3	10 355	9 055	-2 917	53 076	2.46	63.5	13.2	30.9
Bay City, MI	15.4	11.0	8.4	50.8	110 157	107 771	-2.2	-2.8	6 654	7 308	-2 288	42 799	2.44	61.4	10.2	31.4
Beaumont-Port Arthur, TX	12.9	8.4	6.3	49.3	400 162	403 194	0.8	1.7	34 427	25 355	-1 993	153 283	2.55	64.9	14.1	30.4
Beckley, WV	14.8	11.6	8.0	49.8	126 799	124 901	-1.5	-3.2	9 098	10 440	-2 469	49 070	2.41	63.8	11.0	31.0
Bellingham, WA	12.7	10.2	6.4	50.4	166 814	201 140	20.6	7.8	14 362	9 502	10 642	80 023	2.58	59.9	8.6	28.7
Bend-Redmond, OR	14.7	12.3	7.0	50.7	115 367	157 733	36.7	14.9	10 916	8 439	20 568	69 424	2.51	66.5	8.7	24.7
Billings, MT	14.0	9.7	7.1	50.7	139 946	158 934	13.6	6.8	13 041	9 381	7 059	68 021	2.44	61.5	8.3	30.4
Binghamton, NY	14.5	9.8	8.6	50.8	252 320	251 737	-0.2	-3.0	16 150	15 830	-7 656	97 883	2.40	60.0	11.5	31.5
Birmingham-Hoover, AL	13.3	9.1	6.3	51.9	1 052 238	1 128 056	7.2	1.7	90 968	71 781	875	441 762	2.54	66.1	15.2	29.5
Bismarck, ND	13.1	8.3	6.6	49.7	100 828	114 778	13.8	14.7	11 442	6 300	11 335	55 092	2.28	62.6	8.0	28.0
Blacksburg-Christiansburg-Radford, VA	11.7	8.9	6.0	49.1	165 146	178 257	7.9	2.6	10 507	9 257	3 580	69 396	2.39	58.7	11.4	27.6
Bloomington, IL	11.6	7.4	5.5	51.3	167 231	186 133	11.3	1.3	14 093	8 266	-3 192	72 767	2.49	63.8	6.4	27.4
Bloomington, IN	11.1	7.5	5.2	50.1	142 349	159 542	12.1	4.3	9 506	6 871	4 243	62 702	2.40	52.9	7.8	33.1
Bloomsburg-Berwick, PA	14.3	10.3	8.4	51.8	82 387	85 563	3.9	-0.9	5 193	5 605	-404	33 140	2.40	64.2	10.1	30.2
Boise City, ID	11.8	8.5	5.3	50.0	464 840	616 561	32.6	12.1	53 837	26 849	46 396	245 109	2.71	63.5	9.8	30.4
Boston-Cambridge-Newton, MA-NH	13.2	8.6	6.4	51.4	4 391 344	4 552 595	3.7	5.3	323 794	220 701	145 718	1 782 655	2.58	63.5	11.6	28.0
Boston, MA Div 14454	12.6	8.3	6.3	51.7	1 812 937	1 888 013	4.1	5.7	136 751	91 577	64 283	743 723	2.56	59.9	13.2	30.3
Cambridge-Newton-Framingham, MA Div 15764	13.2	8.6	6.6	51.3	2 188 815	2 246 228	2.6	5.5	162 992	109 338	73 161	872 640	2.62	65.5	10.8	26.9
Rockingham County-Strafford County, NH 40484	15.3	9.6	6.2	50.7	389 592	418 354	7.4	2.9	24 051	19 786	8 274	166 292	2.51	68.7	9.2	23.2
Boulder, CO	12.7	8.1	5.1	49.7	269 814	294 571	9.2	9.4	18 373	10 443	19 518	124 615	2.47	58.0	7.6	28.3
Bowling Green, KY	11.8	8.4	5.6	50.7	134 976	158 599	17.5	7.9	12 900	8 721	8 308	62 500	2.55	68.3	13.0	25.7
Bremerton-Silverdale, WA	14.1	10.7	6.3	48.9	231 969	251 137	8.3	5.4	18 934	13 050	7 185	98 490	2.57	68.0	9.1	25.3
Bridgeport-Stamford-Norwalk, CT	13.6	8.1	6.7	51.3	882 567	916 846	3.9	3.0	63 616	40 998	6 322	333 528	2.79	69.6	12.2	24.8
Brownsville-Harlingen, TX	9.7	7.4	5.8	51.5	335 227	406 219	21.2	3.9	46 081	15 698	-14 858	122 468	3.41	79.1	18.9	17.9
Brunswick, GA	14.3	11.5	7.2	52.1	93 044	112 368	20.8	3.9	8 260	6 944	2 957	46 647	2.50	69.7	16.4	25.9
Buffalo-Cheektowaga-Niagara Falls, NY	14.6	9.6	7.7	51.5	1 170 111	1 135 617	-2.9	-0.2	75 964	75 206	-800	467 992	2.36	59.4	13.6	33.7
Burlington, NC	12.9	9.4	7.3	52.5	130 800	151 144	15.6	5.7	11 063	9 759	7 016	63 093	2.43	62.5	15.9	32.1
Burlington-South Burlington, VT	13.8	8.4	5.8	50.8	198 889	211 262	6.2	2.9	14 005	9 276	1 344	85 553	2.41	58.8	7.7	27.0
California-Lexington Park, MD	12.3	7.5	5.1	50.1	86 211	105 148	22.0	7.1	8 985	4 691	3 010	39 029	2.78	71.3	14.2	22.9
Canton-Massillon, OH	14.7	10.5	8.1	51.4	406 934	404 428	-0.6	-0.8	27 717	27 136	-2 943	162 868	2.42	64.0	13.1	29.8
Cape Coral-Fort Myers, FL	14.1	15.6	11.8	51.1	440 888	618 754	40.3	16.7	40 165	40 337	100 863	263 694	2.62	65.2	10.1	28.7
Cape Girardeau, MO-IL	13.2	9.3	7.5	51.4	90 312	96 275	6.6	1.2	7 216	6 020	-11	35 273	2.64	63.7	8.7	29.0
Carbondale-Marion, IL	12.5	9.3	6.9	49.9	120 908	126 580	4.7	-0.1	9 209	7 585	-1 722	48 012	2.51	61.0	10.0	32.9
Carson City, NV	14.6	11.6	8.7	48.9	52 457	55 274	5.4	-1.0	3 572	4 115	-152	22 687	2.32	59.1	15.4	33.9
Casper, WY	13.6	8.1	5.7	49.5	66 533	75 450	13.4	7.4	7 111	4 370	2 815	32 564	2.47	58.4	9.6	33.9

1. No spouse present.

Table C. Metropolitan Areas — Population, Vital Statistics, Health, and Crime

Area name	Persons in group quarters, 2016	Daytime population, 2015		Births, 2016		Deaths, 2016		Persons under 65 with no health insurance 2015		Medicare, 2015			Serious crimes known to police,[2] 2014 Total	
		Number	Employ-ment/ residence ratio	Total	Rate[1]	Number	Rate[1]	Number	Percent	Total Benefici-aries	Enrolled in Original Medicare	Enrolled in Medicare Advantage	Number	Rate[3]
	32	33	34	35	36	37	38	39	40	41	42	43	44	45
Abilene, TX	10 340	168 757	1.00	2 445	14.4	1 755	10.3	22 552	16.5	28 906	22 563	6 343	6 884	4 069
Akron, OH	18 248	703 285	1.00	7 641	10.9	7 193	10.2	42 524	7.4	124 161	56 045	68 116	19 601	3 004
Albany, GA	5 377	156 670	0.99	1 937	12.7	1 515	10.0	20 239	16.0	26 571	18 277	8 294	7 193	4 726
Albany, OR	1 212	115 133	0.89	1 436	11.7	1 290	10.5	8 152	8.3	27 369	12 819	14 550	4 028	3 364
Albany-Schenectady-Troy, NY	32 651	891 606	1.02	9 158	10.4	8 058	9.1	38 228	5.3	157 720	86 731	70 989	22 003	2 497
Albuquerque, NM	14 872	903 318	0.99	10 272	11.3	7 602	8.4	90 725	12.0	146 530	67 668	78 862	44 988	4 981
Alexandria, LA	7 452	156 902	1.04	2 152	13.9	1 621	10.5	17 727	14.1	29 928	24 666	5 262	7 957	5 284
Allentown-Bethlehem-Easton, PA-NJ	22 737	793 705	0.90	8 556	10.2	8 032	9.6	52 623	7.8	162 655	117 156	45 499	17 658	2 132
Altoona, PA	3 754	131 390	1.11	1 287	10.3	1 673	13.4	6 281	6.4	30 417	14 595	15 822	2 368	1 878
Amarillo, TX	9 869	261 292	0.98	3 789	14.4	2 324	8.8	40 052	18.3	37 680	29 368	8 312	11 558	4 420
Ames, IA	11 836	99 174	1.06	886	9.1	502	5.2	3 751	5.0	11 896	10 436	1 460	1 647	1 903
Anchorage, AK	10 551	395 681	0.98	6 074	15.1	2 347	5.8	50 803	14.4	41 185	40 603	582	14 136	4 692
Ann Arbor, MI	22 313	396 568	1.21	3 709	10.2	2 323	6.4	16 409	5.5	49 455	33 816	15 639	7 632	2 139
Anniston-Oxford-Jacksonville, AL	2 776	114 583	0.98	1 237	10.8	1 441	12.6	10 764	11.4	27 423	22 648	4 775	4 615	3 965
Appleton, WI	3 204	229 443	0.97	2 822	12.1	1 705	7.3	11 119	5.6	37 485	14 494	22 991	3 752	1 624
Asheville, NC	11 151	448 613	1.01	4 510	10.0	5 077	11.2	46 650	13.5	106 356	76 796	29 560	10 990	2 507
Athens-Clarke County, GA	10 756	210 285	1.09	2 226	10.8	1 390	6.8	28 448	17.1	29 176	20 250	8 926	6 304	3 175
Atlanta-Sandy Springs-Roswell, GA	83 840	5 716 935	1.00	73 772	12.7	38 161	6.6	762 817	15.3	689 975	420 933	269 042	210 035	3 757
Atlantic City-Hammonton, NJ	6 219	278 448	1.03	3 019	11.1	2 779	10.3	24 496	10.9	49 844	45 101	4 743	9 170	3 315
Auburn-Opelika, AL	4 955	145 429	0.84	1 904	12.0	1 056	6.6	15 691	11.5	18 480	15 379	3 101	4 155	2 704
Augusta-Richmond County, GA-SC	17 301	592 403	1.01	7 494	12.6	5 570	9.4	63 742	13.1	99 160	67 808	31 352	14 158	2 446
Austin-Round Rock, TX	42 598	2 009 515	1.01	27 375	13.3	10 304	5.0	269 051	15.2	208 237	145 452	62 785	61 284	3 167
Bakersfield, CA	32 350	888 522	1.02	14 173	16.0	6 094	6.9	73 282	9.7	101 349	60 756	40 593	32 748	3 744
Baltimore-Columbia-Towson, MD	70 465	2 781 405	0.99	33 978	12.1	25 713	9.2	145 854	6.2	418 572	375 250	43 322	93 199	3 340
Bangor, ME	7 476	156 904	1.06	1 380	9.1	1 577	10.4	13 784	11.5	33 833	25 971	7 862	3 585	2 337
Barnstable Town, MA	4 148	213 222	0.99	1 506	7.0	2 908	13.6	5 212	3.5	67 818	59 246	8 572	5 243	2 434
Baton Rouge, LA	25 640	840 363	1.03	11 167	13.4	7 038	8.4	81 531	11.6	120 380	60 641	59 739	32 228	3 920
Battle Creek, MI	4 129	140 449	1.11	1 638	12.2	1 405	10.5	8 045	7.4	28 844	19 560	9 284	4 563	3 383
Bay City, MI	1 438	93 820	0.75	1 011	9.7	1 168	11.2	5 598	6.6	24 340	17 056	7 284	2 436	2 283
Beaumont-Port Arthur, TX	17 908	410 501	1.01	5 704	13.9	4 223	10.3	64 577	19.4	70 543	43 996	26 547	14 148	3 467
Beckley, WV	5 656	121 552	0.98	1 326	11.0	1 761	14.6	7 693	8.2	29 791	22 068	7 723	4 188	3 526
Bellingham, WA	5 836	209 237	0.97	2 371	10.9	1 580	7.3	15 806	9.1	38 100	23 847	14 253	7 219	3 462
Bend-Redmond, OR	1 083	177 412	1.03	1 853	10.2	1 455	8.0	12 206	8.6	37 153	25 532	11 621	4 379	2 595
Billings, MT	3 862	168 966	1.00	2 096	12.3	1 547	9.1	17 462	12.6	29 975	23 154	6 821	6 379	3 814
Binghamton, NY	11 286	243 503	0.98	2 600	10.7	2 606	10.7	12 009	6.2	52 783	32 370	20 413	6 892	2 787
Birmingham-Hoover, AL	24 924	1 146 009	1.00	14 413	12.6	12 010	10.5	106 218	11.1	210 435	117 711	92 724	41 803	4 137
Bismarck, ND	4 227	127 018	0.96	2 039	15.5	1 079	8.2	7 735	7.2	20 613	15 360	5 253	2 895	2 290
Blacksburg-Christiansburg-Radford, VA	14 198	182 255	1.03	1 688	9.2	1 475	8.1	15 430	10.8	30 564	23 420	7 144	3 336	1 844
Bloomington, IL	10 851	193 275	1.05	2 135	11.3	1 415	7.5	7 350	4.7	26 773	18 260	8 513	3 780	2 011
Bloomington, IN	15 273	169 325	1.05	1 513	9.1	1 132	6.8	16 031	12.3	22 922	18 295	4 627	4 188	2 932
Bloomsburg-Berwick, PA	5 121	89 716	1.12	820	9.7	931	11.0	4 140	6.3	18 361	10 289	8 072	1 407	1 651
Boise City, ID	14 402	675 906	1.00	8 753	12.7	4 596	6.6	67 623	11.8	102 629	51 292	51 337	13 451	2 029
Boston-Cambridge-Newton, MA-NH	168 405	4 938 015	1.07	51 964	10.8	37 646	7.9	137 373	3.5	736 810	578 298	158 512	94 798	2 048
Boston, MA Div 14454	80 414	2 176 883	1.19	21 964	11.0	15 701	7.9	53 414	3.3	293 732	230 575	63 157	45 762	2 430
Cambridge-Newton-Framingham, MA Div 15764	76 515	2 361 842	1.00	26 110	11.0	18 561	7.8	60 250	3.1	368 685	279 469	89 216	40 834	1 751
Rockingham County-Strafford County, NH 40484	11 476	NA	NA	3 890	9.0	3 384	7.9	23 709	6.7	74 393	68 254	6 139	8 202	1 985
Boulder, CO	11 247	345 245	1.15	2 911	9.0	1 860	5.8	19 657	7.3	46 352	26 420	19 932	6 581	2 617
Bowling Green, KY	7 207	170 255	1.05	2 146	12.5	1 434	8.4	11 224	8.1	28 565	21 599	6 966	4 118	2 497
Bremerton-Silverdale, WA	9 514	250 132	0.92	3 240	12.2	2 295	8.7	12 163	5.8	46 096	36 165	9 931	7 909	3 093
Bridgeport-Stamford-Norwalk, CT	19 530	952 509	1.01	10 050	10.6	6 800	7.2	73 657	9.2	135 618	101 362	34 256	17 221	1 857
Brownsville-Harlingen, TX	3 381	415 037	0.95	7 147	16.9	2 712	6.4	103 400	28.6	55 300	31 163	24 137	15 087	3 569
Brunswick, GA	1 431	117 685	1.00	1 307	11.2	1 192	10.2	16 374	17.4	22 274	15 995	6 279	5 151	4 573
Buffalo-Cheektowaga-Niagara Falls, NY	32 461	1 142 075	1.01	12 241	10.8	12 167	10.7	50 045	5.4	224 368	89 014	135 354	34 654	3 052
Burlington, NC	4 620	149 009	0.87	1 788	11.2	1 638	10.3	18 182	14.1	30 212	13 925	16 287	4 880	3 140
Burlington-South Burlington, VT	10 285	221 439	1.04	2 282	10.5	1 547	7.1	7 693	4.3	29 854	26 967	2 887	4 301	1 996
California-Lexington Park, MD	2 809	104 906	0.88	1 479	13.1	822	7.3	4 797	5.0	14 028	13 558	470	2 474	2 232
Canton-Massillon, OH	9 412	389 273	0.93	4 440	11.1	4 324	10.8	24 379	7.5	87 113	38 663	48 450	11 465	3 116
Cape Coral-Fort Myers, FL	8 473	689 312	0.95	6 666	9.2	7 324	10.1	100 793	19.9	163 550	109 102	54 448	15 855	2 342
Cape Girardeau, MO-IL	6 219	99 629	1.07	1 126	11.6	952	9.8	8 533	10.9	18 923	16 882	2 041	3 056	3 125
Carbondale-Marion, IL	5 983	129 816	1.05	1 510	11.9	1 240	9.8	6 495	6.4	23 007	18 296	4 711	2 917	2 381
Carson City, NV	2 810	NA	NA	579	10.6	658	12.0	5 645	13.7	13 973	12 203	1 770	1 035	1 906
Casper, WY	1 767	83 643	1.04	1 216	15.0	729	9.0	9 652	13.8	12 294	11 678	616	2 102	2 565

1. Per 1,000 estimated resident population.　　2. Data for serious crimes have not been adjusted for underreporting; this may affect comparability between geographic areas and over time.
3. Per 100,000 population estimated by the FBI.

Items 32—45

Table C. Metropolitan Areas — Crime, Education, Money Income, and Poverty

Area name	Serious crimes known to police, 2014 (cont.)[1] Rate[2] Violent	Property	Enrollment[3] Total	Percent private	Attainment[4] (percent) High school graduate or less	Bachelor's degree or more	Local government expenditures,[5] 2013–2014 Total current expenditures (mil dol)	Current expenditures per student (dollars)	Per capita income[6] (dollars)	Mean household income (dollars)	Median household income	Percent of households with income of less than $50,000	Percent of households with income of $200,000 or more	Percent below poverty level All persons	Children under 18 years	Age 65 years and older
	46	47	48	49	50	51	52	53	54	55	56	57	58	59	60	61
Abilene, TX	400	3 668	44 634	25.5	44.9	20.7	249.7	8 747	24 257	65 183	47 420	51.8	3.2	13.9	17.3	7.5
Akron, OH	282	2 721	178 124	15.5	41.9	30.1	1 092.6	11 269	29 020	70 288	51 580	48.3	3.8	14.2	21.0	6.4
Albany, GA	635	4 091	47 192	8.3	48.9	21.1	264.8	9 721	21 393	56 072	40 143	58.6	2.0	24.6	34.6	13.1
Albany, OR	109	3 255	28 325	10.6	40.2	17.2	185.7	8 265	23 050	58 294	47 527	52.5	1.7	15.9	20.8	8.4
Albany-Schenectady-Troy, NY	274	2 224	223 650	22.2	35.3	35.3	2 003.6	16 280	33 183	81 725	63 080	38.8	5.3	10.2	13.9	6.0
Albuquerque, NM	732	4 249	237 162	11.1	37.9	30.2	1 294.3	9 253	26 347	65 938	48 937	50.9	3.1	18.7	25.7	10.4
Alexandria, LA	823	4 462	37 457	15.5	56.1	17.7	252.3	9 248	22 199	58 070	42 778	56.5	3.1	22.0	33.9	15.0
Allentown-Bethlehem-Easton, PA-NJ	185	1 947	197 349	22.3	44.5	28.2	1 732.9	14 338	30 461	78 853	60 671	40.8	4.9	9.9	15.7	5.5
Altoona, PA	235	1 643	26 812	11.5	56.3	21.9	219.2	12 355	25 249	58 940	45 432	53.5	2.4	15.3	23.4	9.1
Amarillo, TX	563	3 857	74 424	9.4	40.3	24.5	433.3	8 694	26 859	70 285	51 734	47.4	3.5	14.4	20.2	8.5
Ames, IA	127	1 776	44 153	4.6	19.9	51.6	110.0	9 830	27 241	69 284	50 811	48.1	5.7	20.7	8.5	5.4
Anchorage, AK	865	3 827	104 332	14.7	32.5	31.7	1 031.6	15 563	36 733	101 231	78 238	31.0	7.8	8.7	13.3	4.2
Ann Arbor, MI	288	1 851	123 432	9.7	20.2	55.2	507.5	11 550	35 292	86 381	61 977	40.4	7.8	14.6	13.7	6.0
Anniston-Oxford-Jacksonville, AL	618	3 348	27 912	10.4	48.1	17.3	166.0	9 003	21 169	53 327	42 346	55.6	0.4	20.0	32.1	11.1
Appleton, WI	138	1 485	59 073	13.2	40.0	29.0	394.0	10 142	29 343	73 971	61 245	40.8	2.7	9.4	15.9	4.9
Asheville, NC	205	2 302	92 124	13.6	37.2	32.8	468.4	8 636	27 243	63 112	44 826	55.0	3.4	15.4	23.6	7.2
Athens-Clarke County, GA	300	2 875	73 307	6.7	39.6	38.0	280.5	10 527	23 945	60 127	38 643	60.0	3.8	27.1	31.6	9.9
Atlanta-Sandy Springs-Roswell, GA	407	3 350	1 572 170	16.3	35.8	37.0	8 844.5	9 022	30 203	81 825	60 219	41.7	6.3	13.9	20.2	8.0
Atlantic City-Hammonton, NJ	384	2 931	67 266	11.4	47.2	27.2	822.8	17 934	29 745	77 622	54 052	46.5	5.6	14.3	22.3	8.2
Auburn-Opelika, AL	241	2 463	53 689	8.3	32.0	34.3	196.8	8 933	24 097	62 399	46 589	52.6	3.1	21.9	21.3	11.7
Augusta-Richmond County, GA-SC	201	2 244	141 875	15.2	44.6	24.6	842.3	8 868	24 760	65 803	49 721	50.2	3.0	19.1	29.0	9.7
Austin-Round Rock, TX	291	2 876	550 590	12.6	30.5	42.6	2 825.9	8 673	34 959	92 495	67 195	37.1	8.1	11.7	15.2	7.5
Bakersfield, CA	510	3 234	253 211	8.1	55.8	16.2	1 735.4	9 658	21 775	69 017	51 342	48.5	3.5	21.9	31.9	9.9
Baltimore-Columbia-Towson, MD	584	2 757	727 157	21.1	35.2	38.6	5 523.4	13 930	36 652	95 598	72 520	34.0	8.5	10.6	13.8	7.9
Bangor, ME	77	2 260	39 033	15.7	43.7	24.5	264.8	11 992	23 921	57 899	44 173	54.5	1.9	18.0	20.8	8.7
Barnstable Town, MA	431	2 003	39 286	15.2	29.3	40.1	441.9	17 258	39 675	87 839	66 102	37.5	6.3	6.6	6.6	4.6
Baton Rouge, LA	514	3 406	225 018	18.6	44.9	28.2	1 365.6	11 042	28 215	74 487	54 774	46.1	4.4	16.2	22.5	9.2
Battle Creek, MI	548	2 835	31 670	14.3	48.0	20.0	246.4	12 173	22 818	56 042	43 084	55.5	1.7	15.8	21.0	9.9
Bay City, MI	284	1 999	24 212	11.7	44.8	18.0	162.7	11 191	23 284	54 876	46 560	52.9	1.6	14.6	20.1	8.0
Beaumont-Port Arthur, TX	494	2 973	96 431	8.9	50.7	17.5	608.5	8 739	26 217	66 644	49 787	50.2	3.0	15.7	20.2	10.2
Beckley, WV	390	3 136	24 426	10.4	60.0	14.8	209.1	10 792	20 310	48 467	37 101	64.5	0.9	18.0	25.7	7.1
Bellingham, WA	188	3 274	59 111	13.8	31.8	33.0	267.5	10 162	29 137	74 237	55 016	44.3	3.6	14.5	12.0	8.6
Bend-Redmond, OR	181	2 414	38 929	13.9	24.9	36.5	245.9	9 802	32 472	78 510	57 373	44.4	4.8	14.8	21.7	6.4
Billings, MT	327	3 487	37 870	11.8	38.2	29.9	238.7	9 717	30 051	73 166	57 249	42.5	3.9	9.6	13.5	6.4
Binghamton, NY	259	2 528	65 310	10.3	41.3	27.1	610.7	17 525	26 875	65 121	49 386	50.4	3.2	16.5	21.0	6.5
Birmingham-Hoover, AL	590	3 546	281 264	14.9	40.4	28.6	1 654.4	9 997	27 886	70 090	51 459	48.2	4.3	15.7	22.3	9.2
Bismarck, ND	236	2 053	27 064	28.2	32.8	33.9	196.4	11 252	36 851	87 334	65 173	39.4	5.7	10.5	11.4	7.5
Blacksburg-Christiansburg-Radford, VA	187	1 657	64 306	9.1	37.7	35.2	199.2	9 787	27 195	67 926	50 947	48.9	3.7	19.0	11.6	5.5
Bloomington, IL	272	1 739	61 327	14.2	32.2	44.0	313.8	10 851	33 497	85 814	63 842	38.5	6.3	11.5	7.3	5.8
Bloomington, IN	286	2 645	63 309	8.0	33.8	40.4	156.2	9 353	24 480	62 122	44 376	54.9	2.5	24.2	22.1	5.4
Bloomsburg-Berwick, PA	206	1 444	21 420	12.8	53.3	24.0	109.5	12 542	25 021	61 003	46 688	52.3	2.7	13.3	17.1	7.3
Boise City, ID	230	1 799	176 290	13.1	34.6	30.1	764.0	6 171	26 257	68 779	51 925	47.8	3.3	13.4	14.7	7.9
Boston-Cambridge-Newton, MA-NH	333	1 715	1 220 741	28.4	32.0	46.0	10 126.4	15 316	41 334	106 840	78 800	33.1	12.1	10.2	12.6	9.2
Boston, MA Div 14454	470	1 960	517 473	31.2	33.7	43.9	4 228.7	15 800	40 480	103 571	73 628	36.2	11.2	12.6	15.9	11.7
Cambridge-Newton-Framingham, MA Div 15764	254	1 497	598 156	28.4	30.6	48.8	5 050.5	15 221	42 480	111 158	82 394	31.2	13.5	8.9	10.8	8.0
Rockingham County-Strafford County, NH 40484	158	1 827	105 112	15.2	31.7	39.9	847.2	13 726	38 971	98 803	80 441	29.5	8.5	6.5	8.0	5.0
Boulder, CO	246	2 372	97 337	11.8	18.4	60.6	571.5	9 409	41 012	103 222	72 009	36.4	11.7	12.9	12.0	5.4
Bowling Green, KY	162	2 335	43 356	9.0	45.1	25.7	213.8	8 277	23 703	60 314	43 437	55.1	3.0	19.7	26.0	13.1
Bremerton-Silverdale, WA	267	2 827	58 772	11.8	28.3	30.5	360.4	10 047	31 879	81 047	66 090	36.3	4.7	9.6	9.3	5.4
Bridgeport-Stamford-Norwalk, CT	246	1 611	250 460	22.9	33.1	46.3	2 617.7	17 962	50 104	137 438	86 414	31.5	18.3	8.9	10.7	6.9
Brownsville-Harlingen, TX	259	3 310	120 849	4.8	59.7	15.2	931.6	9 168	15 597	50 664	34 074	65.6	1.9	32.4	47.5	18.8
Brunswick, GA	420	4 153	27 164	7.5	45.3	24.1	169.6	9 410	26 775	65 613	44 347	56.1	3.5	19.7	30.5	6.9
Buffalo-Cheektowaga-Niagara Falls, NY	431	2 620	269 800	16.1	39.2	30.3	2 498.1	15 704	29 207	69 889	51 772	48.2	3.1	15.7	25.4	8.2
Burlington, NC	372	2 768	39 797	21.3	43.9	22.9	189.9	7 933	23 004	55 884	39 541	59.5	1.5	20.1	29.7	13.3
Burlington-South Burlington, VT	98	1 897	58 990	24.5	31.4	43.4	518.8	16 799	33 831	84 490	66 807	36.5	5.3	10.4	12.3	5.8
California-Lexington Park, MD	237	1 995	32 687	16.2	36.3	33.3	222.3	12 463	37 859	102 544	85 163	25.7	9.4	8.0	13.1	5.3
Canton-Massillon, OH	302	2 814	95 906	16.8	48.2	21.2	608.3	9 979	27 437	65 874	49 313	50.6	3.0	13.2	20.2	7.2
Cape Coral-Fort Myers, FL	340	2 002	140 380	12.6	44.2	26.2	772.0	8 830	28 494	70 064	50 651	49.1	3.9	16.4	26.5	8.5
Cape Girardeau, MO-IL	400	2 725	27 087	14.4	44.8	24.9	114.2	8 897	26 687	69 223	47 824	52.5	3.8	19.6	28.2	7.2
Carbondale-Marion, IL	238	2 144	36 538	6.1	37.4	27.4	201.1	11 344	24 072	60 541	42 284	57.6	3.2	18.9	24.7	5.2
Carson City, NV	295	1 611	11 732	8.7	40.6	21.7	185.0	7 807	28 491	67 227	42 251	56.0	3.9	18.7	28.3	16.1
Casper, WY	184	2 380	21 508	9.5	40.1	22.2	186.4	14 564	31 017	73 985	52 886	46.8	3.1	11.6	18.7	5.0

1. Data for serious crimes have not been adjusted for underreporting; this may affect comparability between geographic areas and over time.   2. Per 100,000 population estimated by the FBI.
3. All persons 3 years old and over enrolled in nursery school through college.   4. Persons 25 years old and over.   5. Elementary and secondary education expenditures.   6. Based on resident population estimated in the 2015 American Community Survey.

Table C. Metropolitan Areas — **Personal Income**

Area name	Total (mil dol)	Percent change 2014– 2015	Dollars	Rank	Wages and salaries (mil dol)	Pension and insurance	Government social insurance	Proprietors' income (mil dol)	Dividends, interest, and rent (mil dol)	Personal transfer receipts (mil dol)	Total (mil dol)	From employee and self-employed	From employer
	62	63	64	65	66	67	68	69	70	71	72	73	74
Abilene, TX	7 077	1.7	41 732	186	2 994	535	217	1 019	1 254	1 501	4 765	242	217
Akron, OH.............................	31 457	3.5	44 668	117	16 265	2 842	1 130	2 097	4 796	6 050	22 335	1 266	1 130
Albany, GA............................	5 270	1.3	34 326	352	2 485	461	176	298	883	1 417	3 421	205	176
Albany, OR............................	4 503	6.7	37 355	285	1 837	291	173	310	705	1 361	2 611	176	173
Albany-Schenectady-Troy, NY	46 648	4.3	52 899	36	24 235	6 081	1 984	2 751	8 288	7 986	35 051	1 810	1 984
Albuquerque, NM	34 988	4.7	38 563	257	17 852	2 954	1 518	1 577	6 243	7 727	23 901	1 537	1 518
Alexandria, LA......................	6 305	4.4	40 812	203	2 626	507	173	666	992	1 765	3 973	218	173
Allentown-Bethlehem-Easton, PA-NJ	39 761	4.1	47 770	79	17 783	3 226	1 411	3 331	6 108	7 553	25 750	1 519	1 411
Altoona, PA	5 139	4.2	40 919	200	2 472	542	215	418	782	1 370	3 646	222	215
Amarillo, TX	11 438	3.7	43 648	142	5 346	831	372	1 936	1 718	1 922	8 484	426	372
Ames, IA	3 764	5.6	39 204	243	2 182	515	158	378	833	500	3 233	186	158
Anchorage, AK......................	23 443	3.1	58 638	17	11 438	2 566	874	1 911	3 847	3 415	16 789	878	874
Ann Arbor, MI.......................	18 447	5.0	51 400	46	10 893	2 138	786	983	3 799	2 378	14 801	844	786
Anniston-Oxford-Jacksonville, AL	3 864	2.7	33 418	365	1 729	353	131	229	695	1 130	2 442	161	131
Appleton, WI	10 559	3.9	45 314	104	5 700	943	450	658	1 682	1 451	7 751	463	450
Asheville, NC	17 351	5.2	38 831	251	7 656	1 242	605	1 412	3 728	4 223	10 915	732	605
Athens-Clarke County, GA ...	7 029	4.7	34 596	347	3 788	771	247	516	1 370	1 345	5 322	291	247
Atlanta-Sandy Springs-Roswell, GA	257 510	5.4	45 092	108	150 970	19 894	10 216	21 036	42 259	35 016	202 116	11 833	10 216
Atlantic City-Hammonton, NJ	11 982	3.7	43 695	140	6 046	1 101	496	947	2 024	2 739	8 590	520	496
Auburn-Opelika, AL..............	5 278	5.1	33 622	361	2 169	408	159	249	957	956	2 985	187	159
Augusta-Richmond County, GA-SC.................................	21 924	5.0	37 151	289	11 022	2 064	826	1 145	3 634	5 030	15 057	891	826
Austin-Round Rock, TX	102 072	7.2	51 014	48	55 479	7 325	3 641	13 728	19 874	10 488	80 171	3 997	3 641
Bakersfield, CA	32 953	2.8	37 355	285	15 561	3 540	1 096	3 698	4 849	6 598	23 895	1 231	1 096
Baltimore-Columbia-Towson, MD...................	154 626	3.5	55 275	23	84 125	14 098	6 321	9 512	28 606	24 120	114 056	6 609	6 321
Bangor, ME...........................	5 654	3.4	37 032	297	2 962	560	219	279	832	1 491	4 020	259	219
Barnstable Town, MA	13 874	4.9	64 730	10	4 496	850	327	1 366	4 003	2 634	7 039	406	327
Baton Rouge, LA	36 104	3.9	43 474	146	20 595	3 407	1 296	2 463	5 580	6 441	27 761	1 472	1 296
Battle Creek, MI	4 964	4.6	36 958	298	2 947	487	224	184	780	1 374	3 842	244	224
Bay City, MI	4 003	3.2	37 884	273	1 602	271	122	174	631	1 182	2 168	150	122
Beaumont-Port Arthur, TX	17 101	5.9	41 872	182	8 953	1 531	618	1 439	2 279	3 929	12 541	684	618
Beckley, WV.........................	4 109	0.8	33 538	363	1 778	323	142	183	559	1 443	2 426	172	142
Bellingham, WA	9 024	4.4	42 511	163	3 968	674	370	868	1 914	1 699	5 880	344	370
Bend-Redmond, OR	7 788	9.3	44 435	124	3 196	466	298	1 091	1 737	1 637	5 051	331	298
Billings, MT	7 750	3.7	46 052	94	3 953	564	354	917	1 447	1 239	5 788	371	354
Binghamton, NY	9 771	3.5	39 714	232	4 359	1 207	364	558	1 514	2 422	6 487	361	364
Birmingham-Hoover, AL........	51 059	3.2	44 568	120	26 302	3 751	1 887	4 453	9 195	9 644	36 393	2 338	1 887
Bismarck, ND	7 010	5.0	54 124	30	3 705	512	310	678	1 404	926	5 205	312	310
Blacksburg-Christiansburg-Radford, VA	6 247	4.7	34 370	351	3 043	697	226	284	1 213	1 297	4 249	261	226
Bloomington, IL	8 409	1.8	44 397	127	5 285	876	335	519	1 304	1 119	7 015	377	335
Bloomington, IN	5 829	4.8	35 203	340	3 003	670	218	256	1 198	1 093	4 146	244	218
Bloomsburg-Berwick, PA	3 431	3.7	40 258	217	2 046	437	152	195	505	788	2 830	167	152
Boise City, ID	27 047	5.3	39 956	228	13 060	1 968	1 114	3 341	5 223	4 507	19 484	1 225	1 114
Boston-Cambridge-Newton, MA-NH	326 046	5.6	68 292	7	194 209	27 408	12 577	27 426	65 685	40 188	261 620	14 030	12 577
Boston, MA Div 14454........	137 843	5.9	69 458	X	92 246	13 189	5 841	13 475	27 370	18 477	124 752	6 568	5 841
Cambridge-Newton-Framingham, MA Div 15764	162 946	5.5	69 010	X	91 143	12 482	6 006	11 801	33 918	18 631	121 432	6 551	6 006
Rockingham County-Strafford County, NH 40484	25 257	4.7	58 928	X	10 820	1 737	729	2 151	4 397	3 080	15 437	912	729
Boulder, CO	19 233	4.0	60 220	15	11 431	1 299	787	1 403	5 241	1 778	14 920	819	787
Bowling Green, KY	5 805	5.3	34 461	349	2 891	537	224	454	774	1 419	4 106	250	224
Bremerton-Silverdale, WA	12 474	4.7	47 953	75	4 937	1 146	463	622	3 064	2 118	7 168	404	463
Bridgeport-Stamford-Norwalk, CT	100 856	2.1	106 382	1	38 548	4 754	2 323	15 075	27 096	7 521	60 699	3 117	2 323
Brownsville-Harlingen, TX.....	11 325	5.2	26 826	381	4 642	951	332	1 143	1 380	3 587	7 068	380	332
Brunswick, GA	4 141	5.4	35 696	327	1 758	325	123	217	967	983	2 424	152	123
Buffalo-Cheektowaga-Niagara Falls, NY	51 958	4.1	45 769	97	25 553	5 904	2 136	3 184	8 069	11 275	36 777	1 991	2 136
Burlington, NC......................	5 673	4.6	35 839	323	2 406	368	191	326	889	1 310	3 291	222	191
Burlington-South Burlington, VT	11 192	3.2	51 565	44	6 219	1 044	519	809	2 160	1 799	8 591	535	519
California-Lexington Park, MD	5 792	4.6	51 990	42	3 154	659	253	208	1 065	757	4 274	237	253
Canton-Massillon, OH..........	16 408	3.1	40 717	206	7 185	1 299	529	1 063	2 401	3 774	10 076	603	529
Cape Coral-Fort Myers, FL...	31 296	5.3	44 583	119	11 112	1 721	780	2 437	11 014	6 686	16 050	1 114	780
Cape Girardeau, MO-IL	3 713	2.9	38 070	270	1 821	337	132	347	602	849	2 636	158	132
Carbondale-Marion, IL	4 703	2.9	37 084	294	2 365	598	158	272	809	1 055	3 393	176	158
Carson City, NV	2 369	9.0	43 443	148	1 369	420	81	260	493	538	2 130	97	81
Casper, WY	5 645	-3.1	68 692	6	2 240	311	211	1 373	1 375	574	4 135	217	211

1. Based on the resident population estimated as of July 1 of the year shown.

Table C. Metropolitan Areas — Earnings, Social Security, and Housing

Area name	Earnings, 2015 (cont.) Percent by selected industries									Social Security beneficiaries, December 2015			Housing units, 2016	
	Farm	Mining	Construction	Manufacturing	Information, professional, scientific, technical services	Retail trade	Finance, insurance, real estate, rental and leasing	Health care and social assistance	Government	Number	Rate[1]	Supplemental Security Income recipients, December 2015	Total	Percent change, 2010–2016
	75	76	77	78	79	80	81	82	83	84	85	86	87	88
Abilene, TX	0.9	11.0	7.4	3.9	5.8	6.9	6.1	13.3	22.2	31 250	184	4 543	71 402	2.4
Akron, OH	0.0	1.0	5.1	13.5	8.4	7.5	5.4	13.7	14.0	137 540	196	17 014	313 640	0.3
Albany, GA	2.8	D	D	D	6.6	6.3	D	17.0	23.4	31 130	203	7 087	66 538	0.6
Albany, OR	2.1	0.0	7.6	21.0	3.5	8.6	3.5	11.7	15.3	28 890	240	3 425	49 397	1.2
Albany-Schenectady-Troy, NY	0.1	0.8	5.6	7.5	12.3	6.1	7.3	11.1	28.8	180 110	204	19 964	401 308	2.0
Albuquerque, NM	0.1	D	6.1	5.5	D	6.8	D	12.6	25.8	169 870	188	24 019	383 092	2.3
Alexandria, LA	0.5	1.5	7.2	8.4	D	10.0	D	D	22.6	32 705	211	7 755	66 642	3.2
Allentown-Bethlehem-Easton, PA-NJ	0.1	D	D	13.3	8.9	5.8	5.8	15.9	12.0	181 555	218	19 285	345 687	1.0
Altoona, PA	0.5	D	5.7	13.0	5.8	8.2	4.1	19.5	16.0	30 470	243	4 711	55 974	-0.5
Amarillo, TX	3.0	5.4	6.7	10.8	D	D	6.4	D	15.0	41 160	157	4 525	108 644	5.1
Ames, IA	0.9	D	6.3	14.0	7.6	4.7	4.0	7.4	38.9	12 375	128	623	39 126	6.4
Anchorage, AK	0.0	5.2	8.1	1.1	11.0	6.0	5.0	12.9	27.3	47 810	120	7 511	157 031	1.7
Ann Arbor, MI	0.1	0.0	2.7	7.9	16.9	4.3	5.1	11.2	35.1	56 060	155	5 585	149 948	1.6
Anniston-Oxford-Jacksonville, AL	1.0	D	3.2	14.5	4.5	8.4	3.6	10.7	32.8	30 045	261	4 758	53 344	0.1
Appleton, WI	1.6	0.2	8.4	22.2	D	6.3	8.7	11.1	11.7	41 835	180	2 917	96 834	4.3
Asheville, NC	0.5	0.1	6.2	12.6	D	8.4	5.3	D	14.6	115 195	258	10 131	220 276	3.1
Athens-Clarke County, GA	2.9	0.2	3.5	9.5	D	6.2	7.2	14.7	30.9	32 950	162	4 774	84 837	3.8
Atlanta-Sandy Springs-Roswell, GA	0.1	D	D	6.6	19.7	6.1	9.2	8.8	11.4	810 330	142	113 504	2 265 967	4.3
Atlantic City-Hammonton, NJ	0.7	D	6.8	D	6.6	8.1	4.3	15.5	25.1	57 475	211	6 917	127 994	1.1
Auburn-Opelika, AL	0.1	0.2	5.1	12.8	5.4	6.9	4.1	6.4	35.0	24 080	154	3 394	67 159	7.6
Augusta-Richmond County, GA-SC	0.4	0.1	6.1	10.2	D	6.0	4.8	11.4	28.5	116 690	198	16 810	253 619	4.9
Austin-Round Rock, TX	0.1	4.2	7.0	9.0	18.7	5.9	8.7	8.0	15.0	232 125	116	27 462	805 797	14.1
Bakersfield, CA	7.5	9.2	6.0	4.9	5.2	6.0	3.6	8.3	24.0	116 820	133	33 746	295 213	3.8
Baltimore-Columbia-Towson, MD	0.1	0.0	6.0	4.4	15.5	4.8	8.0	12.7	23.3	471 465	169	69 408	1 161 504	2.6
Bangor, ME	0.2	D	5.9	4.7	5.3	9.4	4.4	22.3	21.4	36 880	242	5 468	74 690	1.1
Barnstable Town, MA	0.0	D	13.2	D	8.9	9.5	5.7	16.1	18.7	69 870	326	3 271	162 500	1.4
Baton Rouge, LA	0.2	0.6	15.0	11.9	10.3	6.0	D	10.6	16.9	136 595	165	25 375	348 670	5.7
Battle Creek, MI	0.5	D	4.0	22.3	D	4.9	2.5	13.8	20.7	32 580	242	4 943	60 541	-0.8
Bay City, MI	0.6	0.2	3.8	13.6	13.8	7.5	4.4	18.3	17.3	28 550	270	3 250	48 017	-0.4
Beaumont-Port Arthur, TX	0.0	D	11.9	24.4	D	6.2	D	9.9	12.4	78 850	193	13 458	176 500	4.1
Beckley, WV	-0.1	9.4	4.4	2.8	6.0	9.5	3.5	18.7	22.8	34 170	279	6 017	57 461	-0.2
Bellingham, WA	3.1	D	9.7	13.4	7.3	8.6	5.6	12.4	18.8	41 775	197	4 423	94 171	3.9
Bend-Redmond, OR	0.0	0.1	11.8	6.1	11.2	8.8	7.7	17.7	12.4	41 100	235	2 346	85 933	7.2
Billings, MT	1.0	D	D	D	D	D	D	D	11.5	32 710	195	2 647	76 055	7.3
Binghamton, NY	0.1	0.2	5.3	15.8	D	6.7	4.4	14.8	26.3	59 100	240	7 908	111 773	-0.9
Birmingham-Hoover, AL	0.2	0.6	6.8	7.5	D	5.8	12.0	14.7	14.6	245 855	215	36 294	512 758	2.5
Bismarck, ND	0.7	D	8.9	D	D	D	D	16.6	19.4	22 520	174	1 327	58 903	17.7
Blacksburg-Christiansburg-Radford, VA	0.3	0.2	3.9	20.9	D	5.9	3.2	9.0	33.3	34 810	192	3 281	79 753	1.8
Bloomington, IL	0.4	D	4.0	5.0	D	5.4	34.9	D	15.3	29 035	154	1 988	79 274	2.7
Bloomington, IN	0.1	0.3	5.0	15.0	D	5.7	4.6	D	32.9	26 325	159	2 212	70 766	2.3
Bloomsburg-Berwick, PA	0.3	D	3.9	12.2	D	4.8	5.9	D	15.6	20 050	236	1 933	37 751	0.8
Boise City, ID	1.6	1.5	7.9	12.7	D	9.2	D	D	14.4	117 235	173	12 252	265 352	7.8
Boston-Cambridge-Newton, MA-NH	0.0	D	D	D	21.6	4.2	12.4	12.5	11.1	795 310	167	107 309	1 928 579	2.4
Boston, MA Div 14454	0.0	D	5.0	D	18.8	3.8	19.6	14.5	12.0	318 640	161	54 672	810 438	3.1
Cambridge-Newton-Framingham, MA Div 15764	0.1	D	4.9	12.4	25.6	4.1	5.5	10.7	9.9	391 040	166	48 313	935 053	1.8
Rockingham County-Strafford County, NH 40484	0.1	D	D	D	13.2	8.2	9.3	9.9	12.2	85 630	200	4 324	183 088	2.6
Boulder, CO	0.1	0.4	2.9	12.1	31.6	4.5	5.7	9.8	15.0	42 510	133	2 426	133 773	5.3
Bowling Green, KY	1.3	D	D	D	D	6.4	D	13.4	16.7	32 140	191	5 421	73 003	6.0
Bremerton-Silverdale, WA	0.0	0.1	5.3	2.0	8.1	5.6	3.6	10.2	52.7	49 975	192	5 048	110 381	2.8
Bridgeport-Stamford-Norwalk, CT	0.0	-0.1	4.1	12.1	13.5	5.5	23.5	8.0	7.1	148 805	158	12 213	367 985	1.9
Brownsville-Harlingen, TX	0.5	0.2	4.5	5.3	3.6	9.5	4.3	19.2	26.8	62 795	150	23 072	148 656	4.7
Brunswick, GA	0.1	D	4.3	D	5.7	7.6	4.4	7.6	31.7	25 540	220	2 896	59 580	2.7
Buffalo-Cheektowaga-Niagara Falls, NY	0.2	D	4.6	11.9	8.6	6.7	7.3	12.4	22.0	256 185	226	33 301	521 530	0.5
Burlington, NC	0.1	0.1	6.2	16.3	4.3	8.1	5.5	20.1	11.5	33 560	213	3 430	69 159	3.9
Burlington-South Burlington, VT	0.5	D	6.3	12.1	D	6.7	5.6	D	20.1	39 360	181	4 510	95 875	3.8
California-Lexington Park, MD	-0.1	D	3.9	0.7	24.3	3.8	2.0	6.3	46.7	15 520	139	1 599	44 184	7.0
Canton-Massillon, OH	0.5	1.1	7.1	20.2	5.8	7.0	6.1	15.6	12.7	92 225	229	10 331	179 428	0.3
Cape Coral-Fort Myers, FL	0.3	0.1	7.7	2.6	10.6	10.0	6.8	11.4	18.1	179 170	256	12 789	385 070	3.8
Cape Girardeau, MO-IL	0.2	0.3	D	12.4	D	8.1	D	D	15.5	21 150	217	2 537	43 033	1.3
Carbondale-Marion, IL	0.2	3.3	5.0	6.6	D	6.7	4.7	17.1	36.2	24 875	196	3 225	59 610	1.1
Carson City, NV	0.1	D	5.3	8.6	6.7	6.4	2.8	14.0	38.3	12 875	237	1 003	23 436	-0.4
Casper, WY	0.2	12.0	9.3	3.5	4.7	5.6	6.2	10.9	11.0	13 880	169	1 161	36 240	7.2

1. Per 1,000 resident population estimated as of July 1, 2011 of the year shown.

Table C. Metropolitan Areas — Housing, Labor Force, and Employment

Area name	Housing units, 2015 Occupied units Owner-occupied Total	Percent	Median value[1]	Median owner cost as a percent of income With a mortgage	Without a mortgage[2]	Renter-occupied Median rent[3]	Median rent as a percent of income	Percent with a computer	Civilian labor force, 2016 Total	Percent change, 2015–2016	Unemployment Total	Rate[4]	Civilian employment[5], 2015 Total employed	Percent Management, professional, and related occupations	Construction, production, and related occupations
	89	90	91	92	93	94	95	96	97	98	99	100	101	102	103
Abilene, TX	59 372	60.7	107 400	20.0	11.4	796	27.3	84.4	74 505	0.0	2 941	3.9	73 064	30.6	24.2
Akron, OH	282 456	65.5	146 300	19.6	12.0	757	29.4	86.1	358 316	0.0	17 981	5.0	344 296	37.4	20.1
Albany, GA	57 597	54.7	110 200	19.8	12.6	711	30.6	78.8	66 454	1.3	4 178	6.3	60 786	35.3	25.2
Albany, OR	46 315	59.3	176 300	23.4	12.0	806	29.1	86.9	57 129	3.5	3 290	5.8	49 437	30.9	31.1
Albany-Schenectady-Troy, NY	342 766	63.9	201 000	21.2	12.1	923	29.3	88.8	448 044	-0.1	18 397	4.1	444 595	42.1	15.3
Albuquerque, NM	342 590	66.5	181 800	22.8	10.0	826	31.9	84.5	422 321	1.5	25 775	6.1	405 223	38.2	17.0
Alexandria, LA	54 406	57.4	134 800	19.3	10.0	731	31.8	79.7	65 948	-1.3	4 126	6.3	62 106	30.8	23.2
Allentown-Bethlehem-Easton, PA-NJ	314 985	69.0	203 500	23.6	14.2	995	30.9	87.5	435 144	0.9	22 965	5.3	408 363	34.7	23.9
Altoona, PA	52 830	70.6	114 800	19.2	11.8	655	29.6	80.6	61 079	0.1	3 249	5.3	56 198	34.0	21.6
Amarillo, TX	95 626	63.8	127 800	20.4	10.9	795	29.6	86.5	131 452	1.2	4 128	3.1	126 843	32.4	24.7
Ames, IA	37 264	53.3	177 400	18.1	11.7	832	32.2	95.0	57 150	-0.6	1 348	2.4	50 910	48.7	14.4
Anchorage, AK	135 601	64.7	283 000	22.0	10.2	1 210	29.5	94.2	202 177	-0.2	11 935	5.9	193 525	38.8	19.8
Ann Arbor, MI	138 099	58.7	234 200	19.9	12.1	978	29.3	93.1	191 860	1.9	6 586	3.4	181 977	52.9	12.9
Anniston-Oxford-Jacksonville, AL	44 323	69.4	111 400	18.2	11.2	711	33.3	83.0	45 794	-0.6	3 067	6.7	47 309	28.0	30.7
Appleton, WI	90 489	73.7	159 600	19.4	12.4	775	27.6	90.5	131 712	1.7	4 698	3.6	127 104	34.2	27.5
Asheville, NC	184 983	66.6	195 800	22.1	10.6	777	32.3	83.8	225 491	3.4	9 180	4.1	200 070	38.4	23.2
Athens-Clarke County, GA ...	76 704	53.5	158 600	21.3	12.2	799	36.1	83.6	97 042	3.2	5 064	5.2	92 507	40.4	19.3
Atlanta-Sandy Springs-Roswell, GA	2 028 705	61.6	186 300	20.9	10.0	1 015	29.4	91.9	2 938 616	3.2	150 138	5.1	2 764 512	40.0	19.8
Atlantic City-Hammonton, NJ	101 813	67.9	223 400	28.7	21.9	1 070	37.1	87.0	124 251	-2.7	9 198	7.4	128 434	30.2	16.8
Auburn-Opelika, AL	58 191	58.1	169 000	19.3	11.4	840	35.5	90.5	72 893	1.8	3 827	5.3	73 205	38.0	22.8
Augusta-Richmond County, GA-SC	210 854	66.6	135 100	20.1	10.3	796	32.0	82.1	263 236	1.7	14 767	5.6	242 071	34.0	23.4
Austin-Round Rock, TX	723 914	57.5	241 100	21.9	11.9	1 131	29.2	92.1	1 110 373	3.8	36 024	3.2	1 050 323	44.5	16.4
Bakersfield, CA	263 273	56.6	197 100	22.5	10.4	906	31.6	80.4	389 091	-0.4	40 169	10.3	344 626	25.4	35.6
Baltimore-Columbia-Towson, MD	1 037 443	65.6	290 300	22.2	11.4	1 184	29.8	89.1	1 484 142	0.6	65 443	4.4	1 383 041	45.3	15.1
Bangor, ME	59 099	68.6	143 100	21.2	13.3	738	32.3	86.9	76 955	0.3	3 362	4.4	68 454	37.3	19.5
Barnstable Town, MA	97 451	77.4	375 300	27.2	13.8	1 187	31.7	91.3	110 749	-0.4	5 225	4.7	104 949	36.3	19.8
Baton Rouge, LA	300 535	69.5	176 400	19.1	10.0	850	31.5	86.5	418 406	-0.8	21 873	5.2	388 290	37.5	21.8
Battle Creek, MI	53 076	69.3	101 400	19.4	14.1	682	32.8	81.8	52 090	-0.2	2 731	5.2	47 249	26.6	32.7
Bay City, MI	42 799	76.9	94 100	19.8	14.6	626	26.7	83.6	52 326	-0.5	11 987	6.9	47 249	27.6	23.4
Beaumont-Port Arthur, TX ...	153 283	67.4	106 000	20.2	10.5	797	27.3	77.3	174 125	-0.5	11 987	6.9	170 461	28.7	31.0
Beckley, WV	49 070	72.9	99 600	18.3	10.2	599	29.3	77.2	45 871	-1.7	3 317	7.2	43 662	32.2	23.2
Bellingham, WA	80 023	63.7	293 700	24.2	11.5	930	34.6	91.8	107 690	3.3	6 478	6.0	102 163	34.2	23.7
Bend-Redmond, OR	69 424	64.2	312 600	23.3	10.9	982	31.1	95.1	89 943	6.1	4 408	4.9	82 207	39.4	19.4
Billings, MT	68 021	67.5	211 500	22.1	10.8	858	28.0	90.1	87 934	1.2	3 179	3.6	85 638	34.9	22.9
Binghamton, NY	97 883	67.4	113 600	20.5	12.9	702	31.9	85.6	109 050	-1.3	5 828	5.3	112 244	36.8	20.2
Birmingham-Hoover, AL	441 762	68.9	156 900	19.9	11.0	809	30.4	83.9	535 725	0.6	29 982	5.6	515 386	37.1	21.5
Bismarck, ND	55 092	67.8	226 300	18.9	10.0	796	24.8	87.1	70 079	3.8	2 003	2.9	72 079	37.8	24.0
Blacksburg-Christiansburg-Radford, VA	69 396	61.8	172 300	20.0	10.0	846	31.6	87.7	90 778	0.4	4 160	4.6	83 789	42.2	20.6
Bloomington, IL	72 767	65.8	163 000	18.6	11.1	817	28.5	91.8	97 525	-1.4	5 022	5.1	99 549	42.4	13.0
Bloomington, IN	62 702	56.9	154 200	19.6	10.5	833	36.5	88.4	77 510	1.0	3 670	4.7	81 252	38.7	17.0
Bloomsburg-Berwick, PA	33 140	71.3	159 400	21.7	13.2	729	27.9	80.6	43 076	0.4	2 296	5.3	37 317	36.7	23.7
Boise City, ID	245 109	68.4	193 100	20.8	10.0	849	29.9	90.1	335 119	3.2	12 376	3.7	311 753	37.4	19.9
Boston-Cambridge-Newton, MA-NH	1 782 655	61.2	393 000	23.5	14.5	1 316	30.4	90.2	2 589 247	0.6	85 598	3.3	2 553 286	47.8	14.2
Boston, MA Div 14454	743 723	56.5	395 600	23.9	14.6	1 357	31.6	89.6	1 062 481	0.6	36 866	3.5	1 050 671	45.5	13.6
Cambridge-Newton-Framingham, MA Div 15764	872 640	62.8	423 900	23.3	14.1	1 324	29.5	90.2	1 273 796	0.5	41 544	3.3	1 261 990	50.7	13.6
Rockingham County-Strafford County, NH 40484	166 292	73.7	275 000	23.2	15.4	1 050	29.0	92.9	252 970	1.5	7 188	2.8	240 625	42.7	19.7
Boulder, CO	124 615	60.0	416 500	20.4	10.0	1 287	34.8	94.6	180 909	2.1	4 892	2.7	172 041	52.6	10.3
Bowling Green, KY	62 500	61.5	127 100	20.3	10.0	710	27.9	82.8	79 010	2.9	3 260	4.1	74 982	32.6	27.4
Bremerton-Silverdale, WA	98 490	68.2	269 200	22.7	10.9	1 057	29.5	94.2	117 931	2.3	6 816	5.8	109 920	37.2	22.5
Bridgeport-Stamford-Norwalk, CT	333 528	67.4	420 900	25.0	17.9	1 428	33.2	91.1	482 418	0.4	23 180	4.8	472 541	45.9	14.7
Brownsville-Harlingen, TX.....	122 468	66.0	82 800	22.8	12.4	643	32.6	70.8	166 061	2.1	11 993	7.2	154 177	27.0	22.1
Brunswick, GA	46 647	62.9	134 200	20.5	10.8	866	30.2	82.4	52 326	3.8	2 903	5.5	51 415	32.5	21.8
Buffalo-Cheektowaga-Niagara Falls, NY	467 992	65.2	135 200	19.2	12.3	733	30.4	83.7	547 390	-0.7	27 622	5.0	550 823	37.0	18.6
Burlington, NC	63 093	62.6	141 100	20.3	11.5	743	34.7	83.8	78 973	2.2	3 737	4.7	72 763	29.7	26.5
Burlington-South Burlington, VT	85 553	65.7	266 800	22.9	14.9	1 118	31.4	90.3	126 500	0.2	3 377	2.7	121 252	45.1	17.1
California-Lexington Park, MD	39 029	70.8	293 700	22.2	10.0	1 361	26.3	87.9	54 683	0.0	2 243	4.1	55 428	49.1	15.3
Canton-Massillon, OH	162 868	69.0	126 400	19.0	11.2	687	27.6	84.9	198 956	-0.4	10 940	5.5	197 031	31.9	27.1
Cape Coral-Fort Myers, FL...	263 694	69.3	184 200	25.0	12.6	1 003	31.7	90.4	328 512	3.0	15 077	4.6	277 323	29.0	21.0
Cape Girardeau, MO-IL	35 273	66.1	146 500	18.0	10.9	641	26.7	81.0	49 008	0.0	2 278	4.6	45 759	36.0	22.4
Carbondale-Marion, IL	48 012	64.8	98 800	19.5	10.8	654	32.1	82.0	60 763	0.3	3 541	5.8	55 521	37.2	20.6
Carson City, NV	22 687	54.3	218 100	24.6	11.8	837	27.3	87.6	24 766	-0.5	1 508	6.1	24 602	25.8	27.1
Casper, WY	32 564	62.0	206 400	21.3	10.3	812	25.5	87.5	41 220	-4.1	2 928	7.1	40 357	28.0	28.0

1. Specified owner-occupied units. 2. A value of 10.0 represents 10 percent or less. 3. Specified renter-occupied units. 4. Percent of civilian labor force.
5. Civilian employed persons 16 years old and over.

Table C. Metropolitan Areas — Nonfarm Employment and Agriculture

Area name	Private nonfarm establishments, employment and payroll, 2015									Agriculture, 2012			
	Number of establishments	Employment						Annual payroll		Farms			Farm operators whose principal occupation is farming (percent)
		Total	Health care and social assistance	Manufacturing	Retail trade	Finance and insurance	Professional, scientific, and technical services	Total (mil dol)	Average per employee (dollars)	Number	Percent with:		
											Fewer than 50 acres	500 acres or more	
	104	105	106	107	108	109	110	111	112	113	114	115	116
Abilene, TX	3 899	59 998	13 052	2 903	8 764	2 668	1 923	2 131	35 510	3 155	27.5	20.3	39.8
Akron, OH	16 486	294 127	51 990	39 977	38 811	11 133	15 871	13 077	44 462	1 151	60.7	2.6	42.5
Albany, GA	3 123	45 814	9 602	3 887	8 120	1 260	2 987	1 652	36 052	1 198	26.8	25.6	51.3
Albany, OR	2 511	35 251	5 284	7 300	5 029	1 023	916	1 354	38 420	2 083	64.8	6.7	48.7
Albany-Schenectady-Troy, NY	21 298	344 504	65 553	22 059	48 485	19 862	29 190	15 919	46 210	2 273	36.8	5.7	55.3
Albuquerque, NM	18 592	293 984	55 656	15 476	42 372	12 235	D	12 172	41 402	4 231	70.2	11.9	45.3
Alexandria, LA	3 325	49 098	14 114	4 136	8 278	1 457	1 957	1 799	36 633	1 091	50.4	9.6	45.6
Allentown-Bethlehem-Easton, PA-NJ	18 293	313 182	62 966	35 238	44 098	11 109	11 932	14 969	47 796	1 963	61.2	4.5	50.2
Altoona, PA	3 191	54 469	D	7 138	8 719	1 500	1 962	1 971	36 179	525	35.8	5.9	58.5
Amarillo, TX	6 282	95 485	17 702	11 204	15 197	5 231	3 210	3 793	39 724	1 976	22.8	38.7	41.6
Ames, IA	2 045	32 074	5 273	5 106	5 163	708	1 387	1 274	39 730	966	42.8	20.9	49.1
Anchorage, AK	10 887	166 243	29 713	2 095	20 106	5 256	15 171	10 168	61 162	291	56.7	5.8	56.4
Ann Arbor, MI	8 096	148 265	37 043	14 120	17 126	3 541	14 640	7 805	52 642	1 236	55.3	6.9	48.8
Anniston-Oxford-Jacksonville, AL	2 300	35 910	6 088	6 145	6 355	926	960	1 166	32 472	592	45.4	3.5	46.1
Appleton, WI	5 898	112 362	13 990	21 479	14 436	6 272	4 093	4 784	42 573	1 889	38.0	10.1	54.9
Asheville, NC	12 163	159 295	34 060	19 709	26 452	3 848	5 760	5 976	37 514	2 844	60.2	1.6	46.2
Athens-Clarke County, GA	4 592	59 932	11 319	6 512	9 924	1 595	2 481	2 199	36 688	1 616	44.1	3.8	45.4
Atlanta-Sandy Springs-Roswell, GA	137 077	2 241 972	256 203	143 591	268 261	116 561	191 475	121 373	54 137	7 760	52.7	3.4	47.1
Atlantic City-Hammonton, NJ	6 329	103 524	18 734	1 472	16 163	2 539	4 479	3 964	38 292	402	69.4	2.2	61.4
Auburn-Opelika, AL	2 658	41 553	5 983	6 927	6 957	1 037	1 412	1 323	31 850	315	32.7	7.6	37.1
Augusta-Richmond County, GA-SC	10 395	186 878	35 993	21 304	26 824	4 510	12 460	7 746	41 450	2 510	43.7	8.4	37.1
Austin-Round Rock, TX	48 893	773 940	93 572	40 823	101 905	36 508	85 828	41 104	53 110	8 819	46.4	7.9	42.5
Bakersfield, CA	12 642	194 840	29 994	12 248	31 869	5 869	11 808	8 445	43 345	1 938	40.6	26.6	63.2
Baltimore-Columbia-Towson, MD	66 489	1 139 580	199 937	51 634	140 615	53 049	131 177	61 487	53 956	3 518	57.8	6.3	45.2
Bangor, ME	4 109	57 350	14 412	3 635	11 036	1 870	1 745	2 160	37 658	677	36.9	7.7	51.7
Barnstable Town, MA	8 488	74 140	16 078	2 045	15 376	2 165	4 721	3 293	44 414	333	91.9	0.0	58.0
Baton Rouge, LA	18 098	337 264	47 614	24 635	45 474	14 627	25 028	16 344	48 461	2 686	48.6	11.1	41.9
Battle Creek, MI	2 614	53 395	9 209	14 145	6 107	990	2 115	2 463	46 130	1 023	35.1	10.8	45.7
Bay City, MI	2 193	30 703	7 328	3 933	5 582	995	1 350	1 178	38 370	766	36.9	14.6	54.4
Beaumont-Port Arthur, TX	7 953	134 579	19 771	21 513	19 902	3 263	6 019	6 715	49 900	2 545	62.5	8.0	39.3
Beckley, WV	2 587	34 931	8 927	1 443	6 659	740	1 027	1 308	37 437	564	42.7	2.0	46.8
Bellingham, WA	6 401	73 743	9 648	9 979	11 754	2 345	3 325	3 052	41 387	1 702	74.7	2.5	45.4
Bend-Redmond, OR	6 530	60 309	10 657	4 426	10 331	1 911	2 990	2 398	39 764	1 283	78.9	3.0	44.0
Billings, MT	5 994	72 287	13 529	3 270	11 493	4 386	3 573	3 044	42 106	2 213	37.5	28.2	51.1
Binghamton, NY	5 045	79 217	16 228	8 501	12 813	2 141	4 077	3 018	38 098	1 099	28.7	5.8	51.4
Birmingham-Hoover, AL	25 544	445 349	67 903	37 729	58 441	34 072	21 702	21 596	48 492	3 790	43.5	4.7	44.9
Bismarck, ND	3 938	59 192	11 816	2 107	9 078	2 708	3 952	2 764	46 693	2 367	19.9	43.7	50.3
Blacksburg-Christiansburg-Radford, VA	3 438	51 175	7 015	12 792	8 435	1 102	2 980	1 919	37 501	2 289	33.6	7.4	43.5
Bloomington, IL	4 006	82 343	9 122	4 771	10 721	21 467	2 850	4 181	50 774	2 000	33.3	27.9	55.6
Bloomington, IN	3 305	52 204	10 758	8 175	7 261	1 773	2 061	2 010	38 500	1 011	43.5	5.5	39.1
Bloomsburg-Berwick, PA	1 936	36 838	11 298	5 933	4 122	2 032	1 223	1 758	47 714	1 403	39.2	3.6	41.6
Boise City, ID	17 296	242 687	39 870	23 147	33 835	10 457	16 012	10 391	42 817	5 077	68.9	8.0	48.3
Boston-Cambridge-Newton, MA-NH	127 170	2 421 578	444 491	150 651	266 068	156 366	242 031	164 242	67 824	3 363	72.9	1.0	51.7
Boston, MA Div 14454	NA	NA	NA	NA	NA	NA	NA	NA	NA	1 090	75.3	1.7	51.9
Cambridge-Newton-Framingham, MA Div 15764	NA	NA	NA	NA	NA	NA	NA	NA	NA	1 261	76.8	0.5	54.0
Rockingham County-Strafford County, NH 40484	NA	NA	NA	NA	NA	NA	NA	NA	NA	1 012	65.6	0.9	48.7
Boulder, CO	12 073	150 110	19 934	13 645	17 570	3 544	29 655	9 668	64 407	855	72.0	4.3	44.9
Bowling Green, KY	3 539	57 912	9 880	9 768	8 423	1 815	1 989	2 171	37 494	4 063	37.3	5.2	37.4
Bremerton-Silverdale, WA	5 676	57 374	12 273	1 970	11 203	1 937	3 999	2 188	38 141	706	94.9	0.1	44.6
Bridgeport-Stamford-Norwalk, CT	27 190	421 295	65 971	33 818	49 732	47 425	36 802	35 200	83 551	439	82.2	1.6	57.9
Brownsville-Harlingen, TX	6 381	104 560	33 316	4 425	18 562	3 214	3 473	2 818	26 951	1 305	66.3	11.5	45.4
Brunswick, GA	2 855	32 901	4 561	2 342	5 866	821	998	1 142	34 700	324	56.2	3.7	47.8
Buffalo-Cheektowaga-Niagara Falls, NY	27 251	476 709	85 903	51 486	65 143	30 530	30 966	20 425	42 846	1 804	46.1	5.9	55.5
Burlington, NC	3 153	56 328	11 846	9 382	8 815	1 469	1 309	2 167	38 467	732	42.5	4.6	41.7
Burlington-South Burlington, VT	6 803	102 068	19 228	11 569	15 528	3 304	7 067	4 481	43 903	1 444	38.6	8.4	53.3
California-Lexington Park, MD	1 909	28 799	4 441	292	4 597	473	8 146	1 431	49 700	632	48.3	3.3	53.6
Canton-Massillon, OH	8 681	147 570	29 059	27 021	20 860	5 737	4 387	5 626	38 125	1 901	47.2	4.1	44.3
Cape Coral-Fort Myers, FL	17 459	201 523	34 908	4 754	38 959	5 713	11 139	7 656	37 991	844	79.5	4.5	48.1
Cape Girardeau, MO-IL	2 764	40 052	10 773	4 039	6 656	1 301	1 241	1 465	36 580	2 071	24.4	11.8	46.4
Carbondale-Marion, IL	2 953	40 758	10 529	3 667	7 636	1 916	1 349	1 413	34 663	1 485	39.5	8.6	40.9
Carson City, NV	1 960	21 200	3 716	2 710	3 504	1 032	1 244	923	43 555	21	81.0	4.8	47.6
Casper, WY	3 006	36 096	5 566	1 688	5 325	941	1 651	1 700	47 094	397	31.5	33.5	49.4

Table C. Metropolitan Areas — **Agriculture**

	Agriculture, 2012 (cont.)														
	Land in farms					Value of land and buildings (dollars)		Value of machinery and equipment, average per farm (dollars)	Value of products sold				Percent of farms with sales of:		Government payments	
			Acres								Percent from:					
Area name	Acreage (1,000)	Percent change, 2007–2012	Average size of farm	Total irrigated (1,000)	Total cropland (1,000)	Average per farm	Average per acre		Total (mil dol)	Average per farm (dollars)	Crops	Live-stock and poultry products	$10,000 or more	$100,000 or more	Total ($1,000)	Percent of farms
	117	118	119	120	121	122	123	124	125	126	127	128	129	130	131	132
Abilene, TX	1 705	1.2	540	5.4	548.0	675 529	1 250	64 184	110.8	35 122	41.5	58.5	27.1	5.7	11 170	39.2
Akron, OH	100	2.0	87	0.6	68.4	497 519	5 734	73 795	55.0	47 754	76.4	23.6	32.8	7.7	730	15.8
Albany, GA	667	-1.6	557	133.4	343.6	1 500 641	2 694	179 389	412.2	344 040	D	D	40.2	26.3	14 085	67.6
Albany, OR	331	-12.0	159	28.7	227.5	769 891	4 840	89 696	241.2	115 812	77.1	22.9	31.3	11.7	882	6.8
Albany-Schenectady-Troy, NY	349	3.8	154	2.1	195.0	515 614	3 356	92 574	222.7	97 955	43.5	56.5	44.1	12.2	2 936	21.7
Albuquerque, NM	3 835	22.5	906	62.8	101.5	520 688	574	45 045	143.0	33 799	34.8	65.2	16.8	3.0	4 887	10.8
Alexandria, LA	259	13.1	237	21.5	149.1	585 570	2 467	92 173	140.1	128 375	87.5	12.5	39.2	14.7	4 367	22.2
Allentown-Bethlehem-Easton, PA-NJ	235	-5.0	120	3.0	178.6	1 046 204	8 721	96 891	234.9	119 650	69.2	30.8	41.4	13.2	2 510	23.3
Altoona, PA	90	3.1	172	0.3	63.3	783 611	4 565	106 916	107.7	205 145	16.2	83.8	54.1	29.0	1 416	32.6
Amarillo, TX	2 889	-6.3	1 462	76.3	812.6	1 152 791	788	110 223	776.4	392 933	10.2	89.8	35.3	15.3	17 080	54.4
Ames, IA	306	-13.1	317	0.4	279.4	2 482 983	7 838	205 934	292.8	303 082	79.6	20.4	60.0	37.3	6 566	73.5
Anchorage, AK	36	-5.2	125	1.3	17.1	879 979	7 039	92 491	30.0	103 158	47.3	52.7	46.0	14.8	354	17.5
Ann Arbor, MI	170	2.0	138	3.6	133.5	701 358	5 095	92 338	87.8	71 004	77.0	23.0	42.5	14.6	3 466	31.7
Anniston-Oxford-Jacksonville, AL	81	6.6	137	0.9	21.4	418 128	3 046	61 630	92.4	156 052	11.8	88.2	30.1	7.3	406	17.4
Appleton, WI	393	-1.5	208	0.5	330.9	1 115 648	5 361	173 377	515.4	272 862	31.0	69.0	61.8	35.6	9 190	64.6
Asheville, NC	212	-8.8	75	4.9	54.9	530 540	7 101	45 581	136.0	47 831	76.2	23.8	23.8	5.0	4 540	21.5
Athens-Clarke County, GA	206	-7.3	128	3.1	51.5	642 869	5 039	60 082	508.8	314 880	D	D	40.8	20.5	1 712	22.3
Atlanta-Sandy Springs-Roswell, GA	856	-11.2	110	D	215.3	543 881	4 933	53 993	D	D	D	89.5	28.3	9.1	4 842	13.1
Atlantic City-Hammonton, NJ	29	-2.9	73	11.3	18.9	903 438	12 320	135 682	125.4	312 040	98.2	1.8	51.7	25.4	247	8.2
Auburn-Opelika, AL	59	-6.6	187	0.9	12.2	707 330	3 775	71 403	D	D	D	D	32.4	4.8	692	19.0
Augusta-Richmond County, GA-SC	486	-7.1	194	35.2	183.2	584 162	3 018	74 457	284.3	113 255	D	D	27.8	8.0	5 008	22.2
Austin-Round Rock, TX	1 754	0.4	199	7.7	419.3	808 944	4 067	50 217	284.5	32 265	49.0	51.0	22.8	4.2	8 012	15.2
Bakersfield, CA	2 330	-1.3	1 202	730.0	899.4	5 332 548	4 435	332 960	3 999.0	2 063 462	80.8	19.2	62.0	43.8	5 306	15.5
Baltimore-Columbia-Towson, MD	491	-2.0	140	18.6	347.9	1 191 135	8 534	104 999	452.4	128 582	71.1	28.9	36.1	15.2	9 885	34.4
Bangor, ME	113	-1.4	167	2.3	35.6	336 186	2 015	63 316	50.2	74 084	32.3	67.7	33.4	9.0	1 044	13.3
Barnstable Town, MA	5	-10.6	14	1.2	1.5	500 691	35 657	50 009	19.1	57 438	50.8	49.2	40.5	11.4	358	7.5
Baton Rouge, LA	778	11.7	290	9.9	343.2	876 897	3 026	117 136	323.6	120 465	81.1	18.9	34.9	8.5	4 656	17.8
Battle Creek, MI	225	-1.4	220	10.7	175.6	807 980	3 676	117 543	133.0	130 044	64.6	35.4	43.4	17.5	3 618	47.7
Bay City, MI	194	4.0	253	6.3	174.5	1 015 918	4 017	198 977	165.3	215 789	95.1	4.9	58.6	31.9	2 628	68.0
Beaumont-Port Arthur, TX	534	-2.4	210	24.5	151.1	428 972	2 044	65 018	D	61.3	D	20.2	3.9	D	7.7	
Beckley, WV	60	-14.3	106	0.1	14.3	263 496	2 476	45 762	4.7	8 395	30.8	69.2	17.6	0.9	113	6.6
Bellingham, WA	116	12.9	68	35.5	78.7	786 343	11 554	80 437	357.3	209 937	33.5	66.5	31.2	15.5	3 425	17.6
Bend-Redmond, OR	131	1.3	102	34.0	28.9	716 430	7 015	52 158	20.6	16 033	54.1	45.9	22.1	2.4	241	3.4
Billings, MT	3 168	2.8	1 431	153.0	623.2	1 177 360	822	103 667	315.1	142 371	29.9	70.1	43.6	18.2	7 886	34.5
Binghamton, NY	188	-3.0	171	0.8	88.8	383 313	2 246	75 197	67.5	61 384	27.2	72.8	38.1	10.1	1 882	27.6
Birmingham-Hoover, AL	513	-2.6	135	2.7	128.0	458 537	3 386	57 174	D	D	D	85.7	31.0	7.8	2 312	11.9
Bismarck, ND	3 139	-0.4	1 326	D	1 364.8	1 479 235	1 116	191 431	553.1	233 661	65.8	34.2	59.5	31.8	14 391	59.9
Blacksburg-Christiansburg-Radford, VA	414	15.3	181	0.6	112.1	662 932	3 664	64 339	94.6	41 344	26.5	73.5	38.9	5.9	931	8.9
Bloomington, IL	888	1.5	444	1.7	836.5	3 533 991	7 961	280 254	655.9	327 951	88.7	11.3	65.4	44.9	16 405	79.7
Bloomington, IN	148	4.9	147	0.2	90.1	573 007	3 907	66 578	36.5	36 101	77.0	23.0	28.7	6.9	2 291	40.3
Bloomsburg-Berwick, PA	166	-3.8	118	0.8	114.7	580 503	4 899	80 597	121.8	86 797	63.4	36.6	41.8	15.0	2 766	44.8
Boise City, ID	1 376	9.6	271	450.6	446.8	761 085	2 809	98 357	1 071.7	211 086	40.0	60.0	38.2	14.9	5 503	19.9
Boston-Cambridge-Newton, MA-NH	191	4.6	57	D	D	712 383	12 555	55 708	253.6	75 420	84.7	15.3	34.7	10.3	D	8.9
Boston, MA Div 14454	74	19.8	67	D	D	891 116	13 214	60 695	120.7	110 755	90.5	9.5	43.8	17.3	D	10.9
Cambridge-Newton-Framingham, MA Div 15764	51	-18.0	40	2.3	19.9	798 193	19 881	52 883	101.7	80 665	85.3	14.7	33.8	9.3	689	7.1
Rockingham County-Strafford County, NH 40484	67	12.4	66	0.6	16.6	412 952	6 267	53 856	31.2	30 825	59.9	40.1	26.1	4.1	647	8.9
Boulder, CO	133	-3.4	155	30.1	39.2	888 591	5 715	49 384	33.9	39 629	D	D	22.8	5.8	474	12.0
Bowling Green, KY	630	-10.3	155	0.9	296.1	450 659	2 907	60 060	230.6	56 745	43.0	57.0	32.9	7.2	12 288	43.1
Bremerton-Silverdale, WA	10	-34.2	14	0.5	2.5	377 215	26 446	27 010	5.3	7 513	70.0	30.0	14.3	1.4	30	2.5
Bridgeport-Stamford-Norwalk, CT	54	36.4	123	0.3	5.0	1 492 513	12 145	68 132	34.8	79 317	60.1	39.9	35.3	7.5	160	5.5
Brownsville-Harlingen, TX	310	-11.4	237	112.3	209.2	697 056	2 937	84 762	160.4	122 916	91.9	8.1	32.1	13.3	4 851	45.4
Brunswick, GA	44	9.4	136	1.1	8.7	388 679	2 857	67 997	11.6	35 846	55.8	44.2	34.9	5.6	164	18.2
Buffalo-Cheektowaga-Niagara Falls, NY	285	-2.2	158	4.8	212.4	415 481	2 625	122 739	255.8	141 808	53.9	46.1	43.5	15.7	3 547	25.3
Burlington, NC	84	-4.9	114	0.9	31.8	538 171	4 715	60 452	32.9	44 986	46.8	53.2	30.3	9.2	470	17.5
Burlington-South Burlington, VT	279	-0.6	193	1.2	119.8	630 386	3 264	113 641	245.7	170 130	23.2	76.8	49.6	23.2	4 004	28.6
California-Lexington Park, MD	67	-2.3	106	0.7	41.2	700 921	6 603	80 758	21.8	34 494	87.4	12.6	42.6	6.6	783	30.1
Canton-Massillon, OH	242	-5.1	127	0.9	163.8	601 600	4 726	95 972	169.9	89 370	50.8	49.2	43.9	14.1	2 682	27.0
Cape Coral-Fort Myers, FL	87	1.6	103	13.6	22.8	979 161	9 485	53 895	105.9	125 478	95.8	4.2	32.8	7.3	61	1.7
Cape Girardeau, MO-IL	516	-7.6	249	23.3	288.5	677 065	2 720	76 665	135.0	65 193	69.5	30.5	45.0	10.6	5 488	50.7
Carbondale-Marion, IL	318	-0.3	214	1.5	245.1	874 978	4 091	111 110	89.9	60 533	84.5	15.5	29.9	10.2	4 275	53.7
Carson City, NV	D	D	D	D	D	665 048	D	108 429	5.8	275 476	D	D	23.8	19.0	0	0.0
Casper, WY	1 691	-22.5	4 259	28.9	43.3	2 656 418	624	133 912	42.9	108 118	16.5	83.5	49.6	23.7	634	11.3

Table C. Metropolitan Areas — Water Use, Wholesale Trade, Retail Trade, and Real Estate

Area name	Water use, 2010		Wholesale trade,[1] 2012				Retail trade, 2012				Real estate and rental and leasing, 2012			
	Total water withdrawn (mil gal/day)	Gallons withdrawn per person per day	Number of establishments	Number of employees	Sales (mil dol)	Annual payroll (mil dol)	Number of establishments	Number of employees	Sales (mil dol)	Annual payroll (mil dol)	Number of establishments	Number of employees	Receipts (mil dol)	Annual payroll (mil dol)
	133	134	135	136	137	138	139	140	141	142	143	144	145	146
Abilene, TX	21.8	132	176	1 943	2 557.2	95.4	635	8 371	2 538.9	202.1	180	928	155.6	28.5
Akron, OH	74.8	106	959	16 088	10 045.5	927.1	2 193	36 505	10 384.1	905.1	581	3 191	582.1	118.3
Albany, GA	207.0	1 316	166	2 133	1 897.2	109.2	661	7 757	1 874.7	166.1	173	654	113.5	20.4
Albany, OR	122.6	1 051	110	1 396	1 066.7	61.3	343	4 753	1 181.6	112.6	112	360	48.5	10.2
Albany-Schenectady-Troy, NY	321.9	370	768	10 035	9 506.1	543.4	3 028	46 426	12 455.2	1 118.7	852	4 632	1 021.3	171.6
Albuquerque, NM	433.7	489	858	10 480	5 775.8	508.1	2 448	39 437	11 245.8	996.7	1 062	4 578	876.4	161.5
Alexandria, LA	553.2	3 594	125	1 550	829.5	59.6	611	7 996	2 294.7	193.6	139	605	92.0	18.4
Allentown-Bethlehem-Easton, PA-NJ	369.3	450	772	D	D	D	2 695	41 717	11 314.2	976.6	587	2 615	648.7	95.6
Altoona, PA	22.8	179	119	1 832	2 258.4	80.7	561	8 383	2 286.7	189.4	87	349	72.9	11.3
Amarillo, TX	123.5	490	260	D	D	D	938	13 922	4 425.5	331.7	311	1 431	287.9	48.9
Ames, IA	12.5	140	74	D	D	D	288	4 708	1 084.2	98.5	97	465	75.5	16.1
Anchorage, AK	80.0	210	376	5 526	3 282.6	311.4	1 104	18 668	6 005.9	551.5	458	2 584	669.6	118.4
Ann Arbor, MI	34.8	101	276	3 580	4 695.9	221.8	1 106	16 577	4 461.1	411.4	306	2 409	727.2	115.9
Anniston-Oxford-Jacksonville, AL	29.3	247	97	1 792	1 808.8	73.6	477	5 954	1 463.5	134.1	73	299	48.9	8.0
Appleton, WI	73.0	324	317	5 089	7 620.6	259.7	838	14 534	3 696.4	314.4	151	909	163.8	28.6
Asheville, NC	424.0	998	417	3 984	2 143.2	168.3	1 837	23 933	6 137.5	569.6	585	1 756	316.6	56.7
Athens-Clarke County, GA	27.9	145	148	2 155	2 079.7	100.6	698	9 141	2 257.6	195.6	262	1 199	223.1	41.9
Atlanta-Sandy Springs-Roswell, GA	727.7	138	6 996	107 280	102 221.8	6 641.1	16 888	246 883	69 477.9	6 136.7	6 808	39 825	11 502.2	2 232.5
Atlantic City-Hammonton, NJ	60.1	219	188	D	D	D	1 227	16 099	4 292.7	394.9	227	1 383	351.1	52.0
Auburn-Opelika, AL	18.2	130	75	613	504.3	28.3	477	6 450	1 632.1	141.6	113	544	81.0	16.0
Augusta-Richmond County, GA-SC	436.2	772	357	3 678	1 952.8	163.5	1 851	25 118	6 639.8	563.7	437	1 920	386.4	62.5
Austin-Round Rock, TX	622.0	362	1 641	32 902	77 904.9	2 642.0	5 621	89 835	27 852.9	2 331.3	2 421	13 215	2 998.0	631.2
Bakersfield, CA	2 159.9	2 572	582	7 990	6 987.9	447.4	1 867	27 918	8 640.6	700.7	634	3 492	733.6	141.3
Baltimore-Columbia-Towson, MD	1 090.7	402	2 653	43 211	33 873.6	2 572.3	8 871	136 209	36 505.4	3 449.0	2 795	19 455	6 677.9	965.9
Bangor, ME	58.4	379	162	1 794	955.4	82.3	735	10 931	3 203.1	249.6	172	692	123.3	22.9
Barnstable Town, MA	60.8	282	178	1 152	563.1	57.0	1 503	14 395	3 856.9	401.4	331	1 361	260.5	53.1
Baton Rouge, LA	1 239.1	1 544	845	10 959	7 974.1	590.2	2 873	41 392	11 292.1	987.8	756	4 551	944.6	171.3
Battle Creek, MI	28.1	206	94	D	D	D	488	5 858	1 702.3	133.4	87	373	53.9	10.5
Bay City, MI	608.3	5 644	87	D	D	D	419	5 526	1 303.0	124.5	65	212	29.3	4.7
Beaumont-Port Arthur, TX	666.7	1 654	332	D	D	D	1 448	19 217	5 663.9	474.7	349	2 085	437.8	84.0
Beckley, WV	20.1	161	121	1 426	797.4	63.4	480	6 740	1 866.3	161.3	95	343	58.6	10.9
Bellingham, WA	85.5	425	289	D	D	D	818	11 310	3 103.6	272.4	317	1 131	230.9	34.3
Bend-Redmond, OR	157.5	998	215	1 262	794.9	57.1	755	9 365	2 476.6	244.0	388	1 252	186.1	40.0
Billings, MT	877.3	5 520	322	4 747	3 237.2	233.6	785	10 572	3 334.4	283.3	295	944	166.8	30.7
Binghamton, NY	53.6	213	221	4 201	3 365.7	177.8	851	12 657	3 114.1	278.6	172	857	183.5	28.1
Birmingham-Hoover, AL	1 815.0	1 609	1 513	21 833	21 530.8	1 180.9	4 281	55 841	15 249.7	1 379.9	996	8 182	1 597.3	354.4
Bismarck, ND	501.2	4 367	167	2 362	2 105.2	126.5	482	8 216	2 621.2	219.6	175	522	124.1	17.1
Blacksburg-Christiansburg-Radford, VA	192.7	1 081	90	1 056	758.2	44.7	577	8 143	1 993.7	173.5	149	710	129.1	23.9
Bloomington, IL	781.5	4 199	196	2 867	9 734.4	185.1	632	10 111	2 662.2	218.4	152	748	151.6	23.1
Bloomington, IN	20.8	130	92	D	D	D	496	7 814	1 773.2	154.5	170	872	153.9	27.8
Bloomsburg-Berwick, PA	29.3	342	59	568	308.6	21.9	290	4 075	1 072.1	84.0	49	223	36.9	7.0
Boise City, ID	2 865.1	4 647	717	9 901	8 538.3	497.1	1 977	28 218	8 072.2	735.4	879	3 055	510.1	96.5
Boston-Cambridge-Newton, MA-NH	2 405.3	528	5 066	88 499	106 488.4	6 697.2	16 564	252 652	67 308.1	6 697.1	4 796	35 738	12 052.3	2 087.3
Boston, MA Div 14454	663.8	352	2 008	33 191	36 166.3	2 246.6	6 851	101 678	27 541.6	2 754.3	2 231	19 179	5 940.4	1 278.7
Cambridge-Newton-Framingham, MA Div 15764	851.4	379	2 486	47 467	61 732.6	3 937.2	7 741	118 530	31 382.5	3 150.4	2 169	14 713	5 717.1	730.1
Rockingham County-Strafford County, NH 40484	890.2	2 128	572	7 841	8 589.5	513.4	1 972	32 444	8 384.0	792.4	396	1 846	394.9	78.5
Boulder, CO	231.6	786	392	D	D	D	1 174	16 623	4 498.3	478.9	648	1 954	434.3	74.5
Bowling Green, KY	26.0	164	146	2 040	2 960.5	92.7	612	7 922	1 892.4	170.4	138	455	86.7	13.4
Bremerton-Silverdale, WA	32.1	128	147	953	407.9	43.7	731	10 343	2 674.2	276.3	338	979	198.5	32.7
Bridgeport-Stamford-Norwalk, CT	494.3	539	1 190	18 611	130 674.8	1 622.4	3 459	49 401	15 166.5	1 553.9	1 077	6 971	1 808.6	418.1
Brownsville-Harlingen, TX	281.5	693	317	D	D	D	1 119	16 624	4 124.8	353.2	312	1 338	185.5	32.2
Brunswick, GA	67.9	604	74	557	307.6	22.2	550	5 299	1 579.2	123.8	151	526	71.9	16.6
Buffalo-Cheektowaga-Niagara Falls, NY	850.2	749	1 177	20 641	20 849.6	1 106.2	4 078	62 656	14 627.6	1 352.0	929	6 446	944.0	207.0
Burlington, NC	23.9	158	143	1 642	627.2	70.0	624	8 756	2 108.4	178.0	119	607	142.0	24.4
Burlington-South Burlington, VT	29.4	139	297	4 885	4 395.2	271.4	1 064	14 768	3 638.0	362.7	265	1 377	284.2	51.6
California-Lexington Park, MD	7.9	75	39	397	189.5	17.6	294	4 835	1 227.0	109.5	83	312	94.7	11.4
Canton-Massillon, OH	48.2	119	346	D	D	D	1 326	20 654	5 535.1	470.3	296	1 352	222.3	43.0
Cape Coral-Fort Myers, FL	746.6	1 207	585	5 144	2 481.0	232.6	2 517	34 453	9 445.3	850.6	1 218	3 992	856.4	135.9
Cape Girardeau, MO-IL	52.7	548	147	1 565	935.9	65.4	468	6 306	1 709.0	140.0	117	357	56.4	9.7
Carbondale-Marion, IL	287.2	2 269	86	962	442.8	38.2	496	7 467	2 124.6	170.2	128	537	79.1	12.7
Carson City, NV	17.0	307	89	519	276.4	25.2	212	3 139	918.2	92.6	111	304	51.7	9.5
Casper, WY	172.3	2 283	163	1 890	2 052.7	115.2	363	4 796	1 487.5	132.1	166	1 281	502.0	79.4

1. Merchant wholesalers, except manufacturers' sales branches and offices.

Table C. Metropolitan Areas — Professional Services, Manufacturing, and Accommodation and Food Services

Area name	Professional, scientific, and technical services, 2012				Manufacturing, 2012				Accommodation and food services, 2012			
	Number of establishments	Number of employees	Sales (mil dol)	Annual payroll (mil dol)	Number of establishments	Number of employees	Sales (mil dol)	Annual payroll (mil dol)	Number of establishments	Number of employees	Sales (mil dol)	Annual payroll (mil dol)
	147	148	149	150	151	152	153	154	155	156	157	158
Abilene, TX	299	1 868	194.5	76.5	116	2 406	992.5	98.2	336	6 732	316.9	88.9
Akron, OH	1 724	D	D	D	1 081	37 550	12 567.9	1 871.0	1 499	26 419	1 225.2	330.6
Albany, GA	275	D	D	D	94	4 213	3 493.7	214.9	265	4 706	212.9	55.7
Albany, OR	164	802	84.8	27.8	181	6 318	2 253.6	355.2	216	2 796	130.4	35.5
Albany-Schenectady-Troy, NY	2 313	26 033	4 405.1	1 717.2	595	20 698	8 060.7	1 223.8	2 284	31 820	1 736.9	489.3
Albuquerque, NM	2 521	19 811	3 610.6	1 150.8	673	16 378	18 058.5	841.3	1 667	37 340	1 989.1	578.5
Alexandria, LA	291	2 261	243.0	96.9	83	4 158	3 339.5	228.1	242	4 406	219.3	59.1
Allentown-Bethlehem-Easton, PA-NJ	1 634	D	D	D	869	32 882	16 436.0	1 734.7	1 774	27 527	1 808.3	436.2
Altoona, PA	221	1 789	208.3	74.8	135	6 943	2 115.6	298.8	280	4 634	199.4	56.5
Amarillo, TX	528	4 274	538.8	182.4	202	12 867	D	784.6	570	11 176	558.8	151.3
Ames, IA	203	1 114	118.0	53.3	77	4 821	2 787.2	256.8	229	4 269	172.6	48.0
Anchorage, AK	1 306	14 431	2 646.4	1 004.2	227	2 272	533.7	104.8	988	16 739	1 241.7	373.4
Ann Arbor, MI	1 284	13 390	2 329.9	928.1	332	13 232	5 419.9	725.8	766	14 879	764.9	216.3
Anniston-Oxford-Jacksonville, AL	167	1 140	137.1	43.1	114	5 957	2 713.2	256.9	212	4 673	199.1	53.0
Appleton, WI	449	3 485	517.6	187.4	428	21 791	8 825.3	1 062.6	548	9 700	377.0	104.3
Asheville, NC	1 233	5 652	612.7	253.5	461	21 831	6 553.6	987.3	1 127	20 288	1 165.0	336.4
Athens-Clarke County, GA	490	D	D	D	138	5 949	2 145.1	259.3	423	7 878	354.2	96.4
Atlanta-Sandy Springs-Roswell, GA	20 920	192 024	36 037.1	13 725.0	3 762	131 702	60 486.1	6 477.2	10 694	208 494	11 868.4	3 260.4
Atlantic City-Hammonton, NJ	579	D	D	D	96	1 730	285.4	72.3	860	46 661	4 008.5	1 282.5
Auburn-Opelika, AL	202	1 474	138.0	55.1	111	5 903	2 386.1	248.4	323	5 947	271.6	70.4
Augusta-Richmond County, GA-SC	996	10 922	2 764.6	797.1	318	21 316	13 266.7	1 143.5	960	18 609	852.8	232.8
Austin-Round Rock, TX	7 256	69 730	13 548.4	5 417.0	1 301	36 984	15 784.9	2 157.4	4 053	85 096	5 071.2	1 406.8
Bakersfield, CA	1 204	11 757	1 641.3	637.3	391	12 257	6 890.7	558.2	1 278	19 829	1 092.2	284.0
Baltimore-Columbia-Towson, MD	9 506	117 982	27 098.7	9 886.3	1 631	53 494	22 199.6	3 275.5	5 570	101 810	6 089.2	1 659.1
Bangor, ME	328	1 831	179.4	84.5	134	3 749	977.7	164.0	315	5 639	313.9	86.7
Barnstable Town, MA	733	4 806	932.9	341.7	187	2 157	478.6	119.4	1 143	13 117	1 000.4	291.5
Baton Rouge, LA	2 138	19 451	3 087.2	1 126.7	600	24 133	84 643.9	1 778.4	1 507	31 681	1 626.7	447.9
Battle Creek, MI	191	1 058	93.0	55.5	148	11 179	5 445.1	599.3	280	6 023	471.2	104.3
Bay City, MI	152	1 360	111.0	57.1	123	3 650	1 149.4	190.6	233	4 039	172.0	47.6
Beaumont-Port Arthur, TX	660	6 726	1 077.1	423.5	306	19 149	87 422.5	1 568.3	696	13 367	637.8	171.8
Beckley, WV	173	1 086	132.0	51.1	91	1 641	553.6	79.4	222	4 178	236.4	65.2
Bellingham, WA	685	D	D	D	330	9 613	14 932.2	552.3	509	8 282	492.9	140.6
Bend-Redmond, OR	708	2 631	332.0	120.7	279	3 672	801.8	165.8	498	7 635	435.6	133.5
Billings, MT	633	6 931	634.7	205.6	194	3 225	6 885.5	187.0	459	8 438	477.5	128.8
Binghamton, NY	367	6 531	973.4	425.8	217	8 946	2 639.1	451.7	611	8 814	423.6	115.1
Birmingham-Hoover, AL	2 690	22 265	3 914.9	1 383.4	950	36 531	14 836.4	1 827.0	2 010	38 797	2 033.2	578.4
Bismarck, ND	374	3 124	490.9	182.4	110	1 833	2 998.6	96.0	234	6 184	336.0	92.0
Blacksburg-Christiansburg-Radford, VA	367	3 392	325.8	170.0	150	10 969	5 682.6	565.9	373	6 964	301.9	84.2
Bloomington, IL	386	2 942	289.8	127.8	106	4 393	1 771.6	220.2	417	8 625	412.8	114.3
Bloomington, IN	311	2 082	246.1	100.7	121	7 695	1 717.9	331.8	386	8 168	348.3	95.8
Bloomsburg-Berwick, PA	129	1 126	188.9	47.4	91	5 908	1 754.0	238.8	198	3 192	148.0	39.5
Boise City, ID	1 928	13 673	1 947.4	772.0	589	22 032	7 099.3	1 212.2	1 277	21 430	964.4	276.0
Boston-Cambridge-Newton, MA-NH	17 311	225 723	55 357.8	21 911.7	4 533	156 284	58 110.8	10 067.9	11 697	202 244	13 543.1	3 886.6
Boston, MA Div 14454	7 073	89 222	22 948.5	8 531.9	1 450	39 895	17 097.4	2 241.3	5 103	100 153	7 073.7	2 041.1
Cambridge-Newton-Framingham, MA Div 15764	8 954	126 579	31 082.5	12 822.1	2 521	97 905	35 508.6	6 773.6	5 459	84 611	5 476.4	1 556.1
Rockingham County-Strafford County, NH 40484	1 284	9 922	1 326.8	557.7	562	18 483	5 504.8	1 052.9	1 135	17 480	993.0	289.4
Boulder, CO	2 679	27 395	4 767.9	2 011.5	536	14 305	5 061.5	998.4	866	15 855	842.2	252.2
Bowling Green, KY	234	2 203	185.8	65.7	139	8 810	5 362.6	440.2	302	6 331	297.6	79.1
Bremerton-Silverdale, WA	710	D	D	D	161	1 817	328.2	80.7	468	7 138	426.0	124.0
Bridgeport-Stamford-Norwalk, CT	3 481	40 694	8 738.6	3 975.9	837	35 507	13 412.5	2 338.2	2 266	30 574	2 153.3	604.6
Brownsville-Harlingen, TX	488	2 359	258.4	81.1	204	4 414	1 709.6	D	660	12 582	635.1	171.7
Brunswick, GA	292	912	121.5	41.1	69	2 197	1 010.8	131.0	298	7 042	409.6	125.3
Buffalo-Cheektowaga-Niagara Falls, NY	2 463	30 722	3 833.2	1 742.2	1 281	50 593	18 970.4	2 713.2	2 800	50 984	2 927.8	734.8
Burlington, NC	218	1 375	133.0	55.8	200	9 268	3 138.4	399.3	293	5 761	254.4	71.8
Burlington-South Burlington, VT	835	6 611	972.3	417.1	251	12 671	4 891.5	690.5	546	9 006	513.9	150.4
California-Lexington Park, MD	309	8 327	1 654.0	640.7	28	225	D	9.6	184	3 670	166.6	48.1
Canton-Massillon, OH	700	D	D	D	546	24 034	12 551.4	1 116.3	810	14 329	648.0	180.0
Cape Coral-Fort Myers, FL	1 893	12 312	2 202.7	844.3	366	4 010	812.8	165.1	1 189	25 851	1 346.6	402.6
Cape Girardeau, MO-IL	172	D	D	D	113	3 999	D	193.2	192	4 338	177.5	50.6
Carbondale-Marion, IL	229	1 325	133.9	48.4	81	2 421	971.3	104.4	288	5 651	235.2	66.8
Carson City, NV	295	1 180	170.1	60.0	122	2 798	634.0	162.7	159	2 740	133.4	41.2
Casper, WY	278	1 537	222.4	83.2	83	2 428	1 780.3	163.0	200	3 814	198.2	57.4

Table C. Metropolitan Areas — Health Care and Social Assistance, Other Services, Nonemployer Business and Residential Construction

Area name	Health care and social assistance, 2012				Other services, 2012				Nonemployer business, 2015		Value of residential construction authorized by building permits, 2016	
	Number of establishments	Number of employees	Receipts (mil dol)	Annual payroll (mil dol)	Number of establishments	Number of employees	Receipts (mil dol)	Annual payroll (mil dol)	Number	Receipts (mil dol)	New construction ($1,000)	Number of housing units
	159	160	161	162	163	164	165	166	167	168	169	170
Abilene, TX	420	12 633	1 064.8	421.7	248	1 857	152.3	42.3	12 268	567.3	55 593	306
Akron, OH	1 786	51 155	5 068.1	2 050.0	1 311	8 916	974.1	243.0	47 575	2 110.0	226 669	909
Albany, GA	382	9 907	968.2	368.4	222	1 234	112.6	30.5	11 645	363.3	28 679	230
Albany, OR	216	4 660	422.3	174.0	142	D	D	D	5 859	241.4	98 763	405
Albany-Schenectady-Troy, NY	2 412	64 310	6 091.5	2 533.7	1 611	10 243	1 081.3	347.0	52 482	2 465.3	512 057	2 853
Albuquerque, NM	2 205	54 420	5 690.4	2 313.8	1 276	8 132	814.0	238.6	51 935	2 067.7	453 259	2 465
Alexandria, LA	523	14 367	1 529.4	560.2	209	1 068	107.6	28.5	8 971	407.3	73 119	390
Allentown-Bethlehem-Easton, PA-NJ	2 401	61 400	6 250.5	2 499.5	1 579	9 010	803.1	234.6	50 343	2 392.3	216 467	1 263
Altoona, PA	438	11 356	1 149.5	472.4	283	1 573	118.4	36.7	6 105	298.3	30 900	183
Amarillo, TX	705	17 438	1 952.4	701.1	411	2 866	350.5	85.9	19 530	956.6	180 035	740
Ames, IA	192	4 855	513.2	206.0	146	1 000	136.1	27.5	5 459	227.4	116 036	709
Anchorage, AK	1 432	29 237	4 067.7	1 509.4	703	4 435	578.7	152.7	27 304	1 378.4	276 192	1 046
Ann Arbor, MI	964	36 873	4 710.2	2 219.2	537	3 891	489.6	143.2	29 232	1 273.4	114 638	438
Anniston-Oxford-Jacksonville, AL	273	5 785	573.5	221.0	177	785	80.2	23.3	6 440	244.1	9 578	77
Appleton, WI	543	12 265	1 384.9	558.4	419	3 088	266.3	78.8	12 344	597.9	157 795	743
Asheville, NC	1 307	30 548	3 452.0	1 394.1	737	3 776	386.7	106.2	42 010	1 710.5	574 041	3 203
Athens-Clarke County, GA	602	10 408	1 274.7	512.7	271	1 723	235.1	52.1	15 372	624.8	125 555	584
Atlanta-Sandy Springs-Roswell, GA	13 077	230 926	28 008.1	10 487.2	8 560	59 105	7 668.8	1 894.6	564 061	23 084.3	6 468 321	36 357
Atlantic City-Hammonton, NJ	846	17 487	1 969.3	780.4	563	3 588	293.9	85.2	16 682	831.5	129 263	1 083
Auburn-Opelika, AL	235	5 923	541.5	218.4	172	787	72.8	18.6	9 855	416.4	241 301	891
Augusta-Richmond County, GA-SC	1 277	35 811	4 187.5	1 602.4	658	3 832	374.8	102.8	37 013	1 347.4	518 650	2 968
Austin-Round Rock, TX	4 433	83 036	9 710.8	3 783.2	3 006	24 324	2 984.0	872.5	182 554	9 340.7	3 888 080	21 861
Bakersfield, CA	1 550	27 833	3 675.0	1 265.4	835	5 099	567.8	153.6	45 226	2 186.4	488 500	2 256
Baltimore-Columbia-Towson, MD	7 428	200 484	23 846.6	9 213.0	4 781	37 448	4 255.3	1 233.4	207 633	9 257.4	1 427 438	8 070
Bangor, ME	547	14 740	1 570.2	624.9	273	1 395	142.7	36.9	9 201	361.0	49 775	271
Barnstable Town, MA	811	15 781	1 766.8	730.5	590	3 176	320.4	95.6	25 597	1 336.3	202 512	505
Baton Rouge, LA	1 918	48 310	4 807.8	1 827.7	1 261	11 145	1 308.9	452.0	60 652	2 431.4	719 939	3 426
Battle Creek, MI	323	9 313	966.4	421.9	208	1 173	448.4	41.7	6 424	242.1	8 825	44
Bay City, MI	329	7 152	682.5	261.2	190	928	70.8	21.3	5 472	199.7	14 474	71
Beaumont-Port Arthur, TX	1 025	20 354	1 951.3	701.4	504	3 670	393.6	111.7	24 525	1 058.3	195 220	1 094
Beckley, WV	389	9 454	898.0	354.7	168	1 168	124.8	32.5	5 181	185.2	10 666	72
Bellingham, WA	659	9 901	1 026.2	422.5	404	2 282	239.2	70.4	14 916	703.1	245 847	1 183
Bend-Redmond, OR	608	9 398	1 114.0	442.5	329	1 526	156.8	41.9	16 935	880.3	483 576	2 274
Billings, MT	592	12 939	1 549.9	590.1	389	2 186	239.0	59.9	12 648	658.5	137 655	1 206
Binghamton, NY	503	15 897	1 582.1	639.3	406	2 142	171.4	48.5	12 785	523.9	30 727	338
Birmingham-Hoover, AL	2 524	70 853	8 979.9	3 315.2	1 607	12 325	1 613.1	398.1	80 676	3 624.3	725 467	3 312
Bismarck, ND	340	12 237	1 180.9	537.1	316	1 975	246.8	63.0	9 675	534.4	163 219	856
Blacksburg-Christiansburg-Radford, VA	372	6 334	730.0	254.0	270	1 359	225.8	39.1	9 286	359.8	84 532	543
Bloomington, IL	399	9 128	1 008.2	385.5	286	2 409	221.6	77.3	10 402	426.3	44 640	342
Bloomington, IN	352	9 328	950.4	366.4	231	1 973	270.3	56.9	10 556	400.4	93 676	501
Bloomsburg-Berwick, PA	264	11 077	1 817.3	664.3	149	727	110.5	18.4	4 239	186.5	31 918	150
Boise City, ID	1 829	37 600	3 759.2	1 594.3	1 010	5 254	477.6	141.0	50 698	2 272.7	1 336 262	6 758
Boston-Cambridge-Newton, MA-NH	13 000	422 688	48 286.9	20 807.5	10 259	72 079	8 446.7	2 368.1	379 934	21 411.7	3 058 384	13 247
Boston, MA Div 14454	5 263	214 091	25 294.2	10 889.4	4 533	34 135	4 287.4	1 114.9	NA	NA	1 617 716	6 401
Cambridge-Newton-Framingham, MA Div 15764	6 569	186 471	20 460.6	8 918.9	4 846	33 113	3 711.6	1 116.2	NA	NA	1 175 953	5 401
Rockingham County-Strafford County, NH 40484	1 168	22 126	2 532.1	999.2	880	4 831	447.8	137.0	NA	NA	264 715	1 445
Boulder, CO	1 332	18 386	2 129.6	841.9	717	4 415	670.1	176.7	38 414	1 972.3	380 649	1 849
Bowling Green, KY	444	8 799	924.0	349.4	242	1 169	98.7	28.3	12 129	642.8	163 668	1 345
Bremerton-Silverdale, WA	685	11 861	1 272.8	484.3	382	1 789	149.7	48.6	14 249	624.0	275 354	1 059
Bridgeport-Stamford-Norwalk, CT	2 827	63 963	8 087.6	3 291.8	2 103	13 041	1 654.3	420.8	91 902	6 611.0	621 925	1 903
Brownsville-Harlingen, TX	1 003	31 018	1 911.3	844.7	402	2 159	163.6	44.6	31 024	1 152.8	188 323	1 569
Brunswick, GA	291	5 206	657.2	240.4	169	806	89.7	19.1	8 611	372.4	155 187	526
Buffalo-Cheektowaga-Niagara Falls, NY	3 187	85 040	8 321.9	3 500.3	2 093	12 616	1 168.9	314.5	57 231	2 543.0	391 181	1 964
Burlington, NC	379	8 367	801.9	369.4	190	1 097	100.7	29.2	9 727	371.5	175 101	1 353
Burlington-South Burlington, VT	685	16 844	1 869.8	685.4	493	2 572	252.7	72.4	18 609	902.5	136 454	861
California-Lexington Park, MD	179	4 110	379.9	172.2	142	865	80.7	30.1	6 732	259.4	143 497	698
Canton-Massillon, OH	1 035	28 763	2 497.1	1 107.4	740	4 994	477.5	135.2	25 261	1 048.3	109 088	554
Cape Coral-Fort Myers, FL	1 488	26 009	3 362.1	1 226.1	1 209	6 696	580.1	164.2	63 927	3 068.8	1 260 040	5 417
Cape Girardeau, MO-IL	345	11 469	1 176.6	468.0	181	864	84.3	21.1	6 339	267.8	33 128	172
Carbondale-Marion, IL	371	9 440	1 194.8	410.7	186	915	94.1	22.5	7 454	265.3	19 490	136
Carson City, NV	224	3 744	510.8	182.9	126	660	62.8	19.0	4 817	412.4	34 002	159
Casper, WY	305	5 141	687.2	266.3	207	1 333	227.6	49.8	5 884	301.6	37 169	165

1. Establishments subject to federal tax.

Table C. Metropolitan Areas — Government Employment and Payroll and Local Government Finances

Area name	Full-time equivalent employees	March Payroll (dollars)	Adminis-tration, judicial, and legal	Police and corrections	Fire protection	Highways and transporta-tion	Health and welfare	Natural resources and utilities	Education and libraries	Total (mil dol)	Inter-govern-mental (mil dol)	Total (mil dol)	Total	Property
			March payroll (percent of total)							General revenue		Taxes	Per capita¹ (dollars)	
	171	172	173	174	175	176	177	178	179	180	181	182	183	184
Abilene, TX	6 849	21 021 831	5.9	11.8	4.6	1.9	9.1	4.7	60.5	518.5	218.5	216.8	1 298	958
Akron, OH	26 841	107 374 120	7.1	9.8	5.3	5.1	11.5	6.3	53.1	3 076.7	1 096.1	1 324.2	1 886	1 236
Albany, GA	7 162	21 657 598	7.9	10.7	4.5	3.1	5.4	7.1	58.2	562.0	254.3	209.6	1 331	844
Albany, OR	3 984	16 207 525	6.1	11.2	5.6	4.0	5.1	4.9	61.9	447.9	223.4	146.4	1 237	1 133
Albany-Schenectady-Troy, NY	36 516	166 624 101	5.4	11.1	2.5	4.0	8.5	3.7	63.1	4 760.1	1 679.6	2 291.7	2 620	1 927
Albuquerque, NM	30 074	112 231 236	6.2	14.9	5.8	5.5	4.5	5.9	55.8	3 116.0	1 545.5	1 089.1	1 208	691
Alexandria, LA	6 219	18 920 106	10.2	14.7	7.3	3.5	1.6	5.7	54.5	537.9	262.7	207.5	1 343	529
Allentown-Bethlehem-Easton, PA-NJ	28 544	125 365 734	7.1	11.0	1.6	3.5	8.4	4.3	62.3	3 830.4	1 426.8	1 741.8	2 106	1 770
Altoona, PA	4 030	13 533 958	4.8	8.4	2.3	5.0	8.5	7.0	62.6	402.4	214.5	126.2	993	707
Amarillo, TX	11 385	38 289 774	6.0	11.5	5.0	2.8	5.4	3.4	64.4	911.4	355.4	389.8	1 513	1 141
Ames, IA	2 892	10 932 541	7.4	7.6	2.9	7.7	10.1	9.9	52.8	476.0	102.3	138.3	1 518	1 219
Anchorage, AK	12 850	64 974 760	5.2	7.0	5.6	4.8	2.6	8.4	65.2	1 699.8	812.1	683.6	1 741	1 513
Ann Arbor, MI	9 997	45 620 706	8.5	10.1	3.0	4.2	5.2	5.4	62.0	1 472.6	631.4	577.8	1 646	1 596
Anniston-Oxford-Jacksonville, AL	5 708	17 129 463	3.6	6.8	2.8	2.8	32.2	7.0	43.2	507.7	169.3	112.4	958	366
Appleton, WI	7 780	34 593 416	4.9	7.3	2.2	3.3	7.7	3.3	69.6	894.7	399.3	319.4	1 398	1 365
Asheville, NC	17 505	58 826 655	4.2	7.0	2.1	1.1	24.6	5.0	53.1	1 741.6	575.9	513.1	1 187	868
Athens-Clarke County, GA	7 394	23 449 444	6.9	10.8	3.3	3.2	5.2	6.6	61.6	987.4	199.2	256.9	1 308	933
Atlanta-Sandy Springs-Roswell, GA	203 403	731 570 783	7.2	9.5	4.1	4.5	5.7	5.0	62.5	20 074.6	5 922.8	9 520.7	1 744	1 190
Atlantic City-Hammonton, NJ	14 001	71 971 044	5.3	13.7	4.7	1.7	5.3	3.8	63.4	1 749.6	507.4	1 016.6	3 691	3 639
Auburn-Opelika, AL	6 506	23 295 526	2.9	5.8	2.5	1.6	40.7	4.1	41.4	640.1	158.1	164.2	1 115	594
Augusta-Richmond County, GA-SC	20 099	65 183 308	7.2	9.6	2.7	2.9	4.2	5.7	66.1	1 739.1	746.8	669.1	1 162	761
Austin-Round Rock, TX	73 039	288 365 719	6.7	12.6	4.5	3.0	4.9	13.3	53.3	7 348.5	1 653.0	4 159.1	2 267	1 895
Bakersfield, CA	32 191	158 787 344	5.1	10.1	4.5	2.2	16.0	4.2	56.8	6 098.2	2 797.6	1 169.0	1 365	1 151
Baltimore-Columbia-Towson, MD	99 896	465 911 722	4.8	11.2	4.8	2.5	4.4	5.4	65.0	11 911.4	4 396.6	5 905.6	2 145	1 222
Bangor, ME	5 352	18 128 721	5.6	7.8	5.2	7.6	1.3	6.1	64.9	466.9	185.2	205.7	1 338	1 324
Barnstable Town, MA	7 548	35 968 725	7.2	11.5	10.0	4.2	3.5	6.4	53.6	1 003.5	207.7	645.0	2 994	2 809
Baton Rouge, LA	30 360	102 896 811	8.5	10.0	4.5	3.6	6.5	7.1	57.0	3 050.2	1 092.8	1 434.7	1 760	767
Battle Creek, MI	4 008	16 572 500	10.0	11.0	3.1	3.3	5.9	4.4	61.4	671.0	371.6	175.1	1 296	1 142
Bay City, MI	4 027	15 471 429	6.7	5.7	2.4	4.8	13.5	5.1	61.1	536.8	284.0	123.7	1 157	1 137
Beaumont-Port Arthur, TX	17 005	59 961 656	6.9	13.5	4.6	3.6	4.5	7.9	57.9	1 621.0	485.7	770.1	1 905	1 584
Beckley, WV	3 968	12 471 321	4.9	5.2	1.2	1.5	2.1	5.4	77.4	330.4	170.0	113.2	907	718
Bellingham, WA	5 120	25 193 563	10.0	10.9	7.5	8.7	1.8	7.1	50.4	696.1	261.3	292.4	1 424	871
Bend-Redmond, OR	4 773	21 188 503	8.1	12.1	5.4	2.6	5.0	7.0	55.3	649.0	217.1	283.8	1 749	1 579
Billings, MT	5 275	20 966 552	5.5	8.5	4.5	5.0	8.4	5.9	55.7	507.5	191.1	179.3	1 101	1 025
Binghamton, NY	11 995	45 564 792	4.9	8.0	2.3	4.3	9.9	2.6	66.0	1 446.5	620.9	619.4	2 492	1 689
Birmingham-Hoover, AL	41 677	145 061 797	5.5	12.3	6.2	3.5	6.2	8.1	54.6	3 941.4	1 461.0	1 685.8	1 483	659
Bismarck, ND	3 791	13 709 939	4.6	8.1	3.4	4.7	6.7	8.1	61.8	473.7	232.8	141.1	1 176	966
Blacksburg-Christiansburg-Radford, VA	5 444	17 603 156	8.2	10.4	0.7	3.0	3.2	6.1	64.4	493.5	224.5	187.6	1 048	749
Bloomington, IL	7 152	27 482 356	6.5	10.1	4.3	4.2	7.4	5.2	60.3	732.2	198.8	386.9	2 050	1 720
Bloomington, IN	4 067	13 951 012	10.1	10.5	4.9	5.1	2.9	7.9	58.1	391.1	166.8	163.4	1 006	789
Bloomsburg-Berwick, PA	2 432	8 805 660	6.5	10.1	0.0	3.5	1.8	3.7	73.5	290.1	113.0	109.7	1 287	914
Boise City, ID	19 235	61 842 070	8.7	13.8	5.3	3.5	3.2	5.5	58.0	1 734.2	757.9	596.2	935	874
Boston-Cambridge-Newton, MA-NH	153 708	758 103 739	4.2	10.4	7.6	2.3	4.2	5.6	63.4	20 238.4	6 374.7	10 961.5	2 362	2 272
Boston, MA Div 14454	62 159	318 038 206	3.6	12.1	8.7	2.3	3.8	6.0	61.6	8 478.9	2 834.2	4 659.2	2 419	2 297
Cambridge-Newton-Framingham, MA Div 15764	76 602	380 709 237	4.6	9.0	6.9	2.4	4.4	5.7	64.4	10 119.6	3 073.3	5 273.3	2 300	2 225
Rockingham County-Strafford County, NH 40484	14 947	59 356 296	4.6	10.5	5.5	2.5	4.3	3.2	67.3	1 639.9	467.1	1 028.9	2 439	2 409
Boulder, CO	11 666	48 102 144	8.2	10.8	5.0	2.7	5.3	10.3	53.3	1 374.3	334.5	816.3	2 674	1 840
Bowling Green, KY	5 785	16 747 663	3.0	7.9	3.3	1.9	4.2	9.0	67.7	397.4	175.4	150.8	930	466
Bremerton-Silverdale, WA	6 732	32 797 634	7.2	7.7	9.1	6.6	1.0	9.5	56.8	1 053.2	532.7	344.8	1 352	960
Bridgeport-Stamford-Norwalk, CT	32 029	179 963 079	3.5	9.1	5.1	3.1	3.2	3.7	70.6	4 597.7	963.2	3 193.1	3 419	3 370
Brownsville-Harlingen, TX	21 552	67 816 703	3.9	8.4	2.8	2.4	1.6	5.2	74.0	1 662.8	982.8	420.5	1 012	795
Brunswick, GA	6 136	22 282 830	5.0	6.9	2.5	1.3	40.1	3.5	40.2	600.6	116.0	196.4	1 731	1 127
Buffalo-Cheektowaga-Niagara Falls, NY	44 201	202 514 083	3.8	12.1	3.3	3.0	5.4	4.9	65.5	6 495.4	2 759.6	2 637.8	2 326	1 539
Burlington, NC	1 005 835	17 822 770	4.1	10.8	2.8	1.7	7.8	5.8	64.0	420.3	210.4	147.7	960	694
Burlington-South Burlington, VT	8 073	32 538 734	4.7	5.9	2.3	6.1	0.9	7.3	71.2	830.6	537.1	145.5	681	585
California-Lexington Park, MD	3 187	14 069 480	5.9	10.5	0.0	2.3	1.5	4.3	73.2	356.5	125.4	191.8	1 760	923
Canton-Massillon, OH	12 345	44 734 873	4.8	6.7	4.6	4.4	2.5	5.9	70.3	1 381.0	667.7	493.7	1 224	920
Cape Coral-Fort Myers, FL	29 739	118 190 826	4.0	7.9	5.4	3.4	39.4	4.7	33.6	3 672.5	586.2	1 065.4	1 651	1 448
Cape Girardeau, MO-IL	3 276	8 670 805	6.6	8.7	4.7	6.8	1.2	9.4	60.9	259.7	107.2	113.5	1 169	651
Carbondale-Marion, IL	4 224	14 371 667	6.4	9.2	3.2	3.8	4.1	6.6	65.5	411.6	200.9	146.7	1 158	929
Carson City, NV	1 396	6 652 347	9.5	13.4	7.3	4.2	3.5	6.4	53.3	189.1	96.1	54.9	1 001	717
Casper, WY	3 954	15 321 295	4.4	7.8	3.5	2.3	2.0	5.1	72.5	442.5	254.7	108.8	1 384	938

1. Based on the resident population estimated as of July 1 of the year shown.

Table C. Metropolitan Areas — Local Government Finances, Government Employment, and Income Taxes

Area name	Total (mil dol)	Per capita[1] (dollars)	Education	Health and hospitals	Police protection	Public welfare	Highways	Total (mil dol)	Per capita[1] (dollars)	Federal civilian	Federal military	State and local	Number of returns	Mean Adjusted Gross income	Mean income tax
	185	186	187	188	189	190	191	192	193	194	195	196	197	198	199
Abilene, TX	488.6	2 927	54.4	6.6	7.0	0.5	3.1	339.1	2 031	1 188	4 362	11 262	73 040	54 135	6 771
Akron, OH	2 952.8	4 205	42.5	10.2	5.2	4.1	3.5	4 519.2	6 435	2 122	1 793	43 698	344 770	57 721	7 389
Albany, GA	576.8	3 665	46.3	10.0	6.0	0.1	3.2	314.8	2 000	2 767	743	9 984	65 010	43 271	4 251
Albany, OR	449.1	3 794	51.6	3.6	6.2	0.4	4.4	449.9	3 801	313	309	6 048	51 380	47 517	4 324
Albany-Schenectady-Troy, NY	4 877.2	5 576	47.3	3.9	3.9	11.4	4.6	4 658.9	5 327	6 428	3 291	93 481	434 410	71 824	10 043
Albuquerque, NM	2 976.7	3 301	50.0	1.6	8.3	1.5	5.0	4 360.6	4 836	14 324	5 640	66 893	403 520	53 075	6 083
Alexandria, LA	559.7	3 624	51.4	0.1	8.2	0.1	5.0	528.4	3 421	3 028	659	10 491	65 590	51 606	5 770
Allentown-Bethlehem-Easton, PA-NJ	4 050.8	4 897	50.0	3.0	3.6	9.9	3.0	7 000.9	8 464	2 224	2 082	37 594	413 080	60 583	7 511
Altoona, PA	409.0	3 217	49.0	3.1	3.0	8.6	3.9	474.2	3 730	999	321	7 569	59 330	49 488	5 676
Amarillo, TX	915.3	3 553	53.8	4.6	5.9	0.0	2.6	933.7	3 625	2 177	648	18 104	115 780	59 110	7 911
Ames, IA	440.2	4 830	30.3	42.8	3.2	0.5	3.7	391.5	4 295	958	344	19 019	36 480	64 591	7 794
Anchorage, AK	1 661.6	4 233	54.5	2.2	8.1	0.0	6.1	2 262.7	5 764	8 690	13 644	24 835	198 530	73 183	10 799
Ann Arbor, MI	1 495.8	4 262	46.0	12.6	6.5	0.9	4.9	2 033.3	5 794	4 073	606	69 709	163 820	75 953	11 320
Anniston-Oxford-Jacksonville, AL	517.7	4 414	32.7	36.2	5.9	0.0	3.9	358.0	3 052	3 745	569	8 416	48 040	44 419	4 104
Appleton, WI	965.9	4 228	54.4	2.6	5.2	4.9	9.0	758.9	3 322	663	645	12 109	115 930	62 061	7 382
Asheville, NC	1 591.2	3 680	36.5	20.8	7.4	7.0	1.7	929.8	2 150	3 306	1 107	22 007	207 530	51 577	5 833
Athens-Clarke County, GA	1 058.7	5 390	28.8	41.0	3.3	0.2	2.0	748.8	3 812	1 128	612	26 183	79 140	55 865	7 031
Atlanta-Sandy Springs-Roswell, GA	19 663.2	3 603	49.2	7.0	6.1	0.9	3.6	35 894.1	6 577	45 314	16 634	274 746	2 551 400	65 877	9 227
Atlantic City-Hammonton, NJ	1 718.6	6 240	52.7	0.6	6.1	2.1	1.7	1 314.6	4 773	2 631	975	20 217	135 430	51 604	5 721
Auburn-Opelika, AL	638.8	4 338	33.9	39.7	4.1	0.0	2.6	782.4	5 313	288	726	16 744	61 750	53 067	5 827
Augusta-Richmond County, GA-SC	1 747.7	3 035	52.5	4.4	5.9	0.3	3.6	1 584.4	2 751	9 022	13 075	39 491	251 250	51 002	5 376
Austin-Round Rock, TX	7 452.3	4 063	43.6	5.9	6.4	0.6	7.0	22 572.2	12 306	12 019	4 234	154 415	977 490	75 558	11 872
Bakersfield, CA	5 683.5	6 638	55.4	8.5	3.6	6.7	3.0	3 571.0	4 171	9 995	3 854	51 324	334 400	51 787	5 479
Baltimore-Columbia-Towson, MD	12 715.1	4 618	49.6	1.9	6.8	0.5	4.0	11 152.6	4 051	79 890	26 775	167 892	1 344 970	72 935	9 965
Bangor, ME	527.2	3 429	48.1	1.1	3.8	0.2	4.2	409.3	2 662	1 181	485	12 865	67 550	49 699	5 308
Barnstable Town, MA	1 041.6	4 835	45.9	1.1	5.3	0.2	3.5	892.5	4 143	1 685	1 182	13 356	124 250	68 293	9 131
Baton Rouge, LA	3 383.6	4 150	44.3	5.0	6.4	0.2	4.9	3 940.9	4 834	2 832	3 749	67 688	362 460	61 374	8 245
Battle Creek, MI	680.5	5 037	45.5	17.6	4.3	2.6	5.4	473.1	3 502	2 970	273	7 828	61 870	47 322	4 882
Bay City, MI	521.5	4 877	44.7	20.6	3.3	4.5	4.2	246.5	2 305	246	231	5 568	53 070	46 817	4 876
Beaumont-Port Arthur, TX	1 598.1	3 954	44.3	3.2	7.1	0.5	5.0	5 940.9	14 699	2 039	1 012	22 318	174 750	59 448	7 499
Beckley, WV	341.8	2 737	62.9	0.6	6.8	0.1	1.6	157.5	1 261	2 010	573	6 793	48 620	46 671	4 800
Bellingham, WA	644.4	3 139	42.5	4.3	6.1	0.0	5.7	595.5	2 901	1 389	630	14 117	97 860	59 200	7 276
Bend-Redmond, OR	663.5	4 089	49.1	3.5	7.4	0.4	5.0	1 093.2	6 736	884	451	7 789	81 790	61 347	7 575
Billings, MT	545.0	3 346	48.4	6.7	5.9	0.2	6.4	248.2	1 524	1 817	800	7 725	82 270	62 027	8 042
Binghamton, NY	1 497.1	6 024	49.5	3.4	2.7	11.2	4.5	1 460.3	5 875	672	387	20 924	112 740	50 885	5 560
Birmingham-Hoover, AL	3 959.1	3 483	45.9	4.8	7.2	0.1	4.3	8 903.8	7 833	9 042	5 350	69 611	495 930	62 140	8 244
Bismarck, ND	438.5	3 652	44.7	1.5	5.4	1.8	11.0	308.2	2 567	1 415	793	13 704	63 900	74 820	11 011
Blacksburg-Christiansburg-Radford, VA	489.3	2 734	47.9	0.6	7.5	5.4	3.8	652.1	3 644	455	594	21 381	68 470	52 947	5 745
Bloomington, IL	735.9	3 900	45.5	3.6	4.9	1.2	5.6	815.8	4 323	510	368	15 786	85 480	67 434	8 787
Bloomington, IN	330.0	2 032	47.5	1.0	4.6	0.4	4.3	424.9	2 617	337	506	22 606	66 590	53 750	6 451
Bloomsburg-Berwick, PA	287.0	3 367	58.3	0.0	2.7	3.0	4.5	1 108.2	13 001	181	212	6 621	38 720	52 564	6 019
Boise City, ID	1 619.0	2 538	42.6	1.3	9.7	0.9	6.7	1 042.0	1 633	6 118	2 343	38 714	288 570	57 773	7 057
Boston-Cambridge-Newton, MA-NH	19 978.0	4 305	50.4	5.7	5.4	0.8	2.6	12 543.9	2 703	35 594	14 504	268 310	2 378 260	95 644	16 340
Boston, MA Div 14454	8 442.8	4 384	47.1	3.7	6.6	0.7	2.2	5 428.2	2 818	19 133	5 968	127 802	NA	NA	NA
Cambridge-Newton-Framingham, MA Div 15764	9 961.0	4 344	52.0	8.3	4.3	0.2	2.7	6 297.2	2 746	15 146	6 877	115 769	NA	NA	NA
Rockingham County-Strafford County, NH 40484	1 574.2	3 731	58.3	0.3	6.2	4.9	4.0	818.5	1 940	1 315	1 659	24 739	NA	NA	NA
Boulder, CO	1 414.6	4 633	43.6	2.5	8.2	2.3	4.6	1 940.0	6 354	1 995	890	31 577	155 670	88 774	14 569
Bowling Green, KY	401.0	2 472	50.4	4.6	5.8	0.1	3.9	1 131.7	6 976	647	514	11 555	69 720	47 744	4 991
Bremerton-Silverdale, WA	1 054.5	4 135	42.3	4.6	3.5	0.0	3.5	748.5	2 935	18 676	11 130	12 862	120 700	67 761	8 533
Bridgeport-Stamford-Norwalk, CT	4 616.9	4 944	50.9	1.2	6.6	1.0	3.1	4 013.1	4 297	2 764	1 899	45 274	457 540	158 253	34 778
Brownsville-Harlingen, TX	1 613.4	3 883	61.9	0.8	4.4	0.5	3.7	1 801.3	4 335	3 282	950	27 544	161 210	37 056	3 255
Brunswick, GA	608.7	5 365	32.5	39.7	4.6	0.1	2.6	370.2	3 264	1 795	386	8 385	48 270	51 901	6 303
Buffalo-Cheektowaga-Niagara Falls, NY	6 848.3	6 038	44.7	9.1	3.7	9.2	3.7	6 125.0	5 400	9 171	2 053	78 476	551 180	56 254	6 830
Burlington, NC	427.7	2 779	50.9	3.4	8.3	5.8	1.6	182.0	1 183	224	369	6 866	68 920	48 536	4 909
Burlington-South Burlington, VT	830.6	3 887	64.1	0.3	4.8	0.1	6.2	632.9	2 962	3 840	1 558	18 411	111 910	66 716	8 631
California-Lexington Park, MD	331.8	3 045	62.8	2.2	6.2	0.9	2.7	197.3	1 810	9 518	2 521	4 681	50 850	72 300	8 533
Canton-Massillon, OH	1 338.5	3 318	54.8	4.8	5.6	5.1	5.6	461.4	1 144	983	1 041	18 821	197 040	51 464	5 871
Cape Coral-Fort Myers, FL	3 730.8	5 782	25.4	32.3	4.8	0.5	3.9	5 119.6	7 934	2 563	1 333	37 394	318 780	67 501	10 238
Cape Girardeau, MO-IL	263.0	2 710	55.0	0.5	5.3	0.1	9.3	203.7	2 098	420	338	6 811	42 450	52 236	5 952
Carbondale-Marion, IL	466.0	3 677	59.1	1.7	5.1	2.0	4.7	325.9	2 572	1 873	258	16 153	53 390	49 718	5 524
Carson City, NV	205.0	3 738	48.3	2.1	8.1	1.2	5.3	391.1	7 131	528	147	8 931	26 560	49 430	6 288
Casper, WY	436.0	5 546	59.1	0.4	4.8	0.7	4.1	147.1	1 871	638	426	5 210	40 340	85 124	14 977

1. Based on the resident population estimated as of July 1 of the year shown.

Table C. Metropolitan Areas — **Land Area and Population**

CBSA/ DIV code[1]	Area name	Land area,[2] 2016 (sq mi)	Population 2016 Total persons	Rank	Per square mile	White	Black	Amer- ican Indian, Alaska Native	Asian and Pacific Islander	Percent Hispanic or Latino[3]	Under 5 years	5 to 17 years	18 to 24 years	25 to 34 years	35 to 44 years	45 to 54 years
		1	2	3	4	5	6	7	8	9	10	11	12	13	14	15
16300	Cedar Rapids, IA	2 008.8	267 799	179	133.3	90.3	5.7	0.6	2.7	2.9	6.3	17.2	8.9	13.2	12.5	13.3
16540	Chambersburg-Waynesb- oro, PA	772.2	153 851	266	199.2	89.9	4.4	0.5	1.4	5.5	5.8	16.6	7.7	12.1	11.8	13.7
16580	Champaign-Urbana, IL	1 921.0	238 554	191	124.2	73.8	12.4	0.5	10.5	5.3	5.6	13.8	21.2	14.2	11.0	10.3
16620	Charleston, WV	1 745.1	217 916	200	124.9	91.1	7.8	0.8	1.4	1.1	5.6	15.0	7.6	11.9	12.3	13.0
16700	Charleston-North Charles- ton, SC	2 589.6	761 155	74	293.9	66.1	27.0	0.9	2.7	5.4	6.3	15.9	9.0	16.0	12.9	13.0
16740	Charlotte-Concord-Gasto- nia, NC-SC	5 064.6	2 474 314	22	488.6	63.4	23.5	0.9	4.2	10.0	6.3	17.9	8.6	13.9	14.0	14.4
16820	Charlottesville, VA	2 223.7	231 349	195	104.0	76.7	14.9	0.7	5.1	5.0	5.3	14.3	12.0	14.0	11.8	12.7
16860	Chattanooga, TN-GA..........	2 089.0	551 632	100	264.1	79.9	14.5	0.8	2.1	4.4	5.7	15.7	8.6	13.3	12.5	13.4
16940	Cheyenne, WY	2 685.9	98 136	356	36.5	80.7	3.4	1.4	2.1	14.6	6.4	17.0	9.5	14.7	12.0	12.3
16980	Chicago-Naperville-Elgin, IL-IN-WI	7 196.7	9 512 999	3	1 321.9	54.5	17.2	0.5	7.3	22.1	6.1	17.2	9.3	14.3	13.3	13.6
16980	Chicago-Naperville-Arling- ton Heights, IL Div 16974	3 451.0	7 304 532	X	2 116.6	51.4	19.2	0.4	8.1	22.4	6.2	16.8	9.1	15.1	13.5	13.5
16980	Elgin, IL Div 20994	1 151.5	636 243	X	552.5	62.0	6.3	0.4	4.3	28.4	6.4	19.2	10.8	12.2	13.1	13.9
16980	Gary, IN Div 23844	1 878.3	700 994	X	373.2	65.2	18.2	0.6	1.8	15.7	6.0	17.6	8.9	12.2	12.6	13.2
16980	Lake County-Kenosha County, IL-WI Div 29404	715.9	871 230	X	1 217.0	66.6	7.7	0.5	7.3	19.8	5.9	18.7	10.3	11.3	12.6	14.8
17020	Chico, CA	1 636.5	226 864	197	138.6	76.0	2.5	3.0	6.3	16.0	5.5	14.6	14.6	12.8	10.5	10.9
17140	Cincinnati, OH-KY-IN..........	4 165.6	2 165 139	28	519.8	81.7	13.6	0.6	3.1	3.1	6.3	17.5	9.3	13.3	12.3	13.6
17300	Clarksville, TN-KY..............	1 698.1	282 349	168	166.3	68.9	21.0	1.2	3.7	9.0	8.6	18.1	12.2	18.0	12.3	10.8
17420	Cleveland, TN	763.4	121 262	319	158.8	89.1	4.8	0.9	1.3	5.5	5.6	16.2	9.3	12.4	12.6	14.1
17460	Cleveland-Elyria, OH	1 999.1	2 055 612	32	1 028.3	71.9	21.0	0.6	2.9	5.6	5.7	15.9	8.7	12.5	11.6	13.7
17660	Coeur d'Alene, ID	1 237.6	154 311	264	124.7	92.9	0.7	2.3	2.0	4.4	6.1	17.2	7.8	12.7	11.7	12.6
17780	College Station-Bryan, TX ...	2 100.2	254 928	187	121.4	58.4	11.8	0.7	6.1	24.5	6.3	14.6	24.4	15.5	10.6	9.6
17820	Colorado Springs, CO	2 683.9	712 327	79	265.4	73.8	7.5	1.5	4.8	16.3	6.8	17.5	11.2	15.2	12.3	12.5
17860	Columbia, MO....................	685.6	176 594	237	257.6	82.1	10.9	1.0	5.7	3.3	5.9	14.3	19.9	15.4	11.4	10.8
17900	Columbia, SC....................	3 703.0	817 488	71	220.8	58.4	34.6	0.8	2.8	5.4	5.9	16.4	11.9	13.8	12.4	13.0
17980	Columbus, GA-AL..............	1 936.2	308 755	161	159.5	49.2	42.3	1.0	3.1	7.0	7.0	17.0	10.7	15.4	12.3	12.2
18020	Columbus, IN	406.9	81 402	375	200.1	84.4	2.9	0.6	7.1	6.5	6.7	17.2	8.3	14.4	12.6	12.9
18140	Columbus, OH....................	4 796.6	2 041 520	33	425.6	76.1	16.9	0.8	4.8	4.0	6.8	17.1	9.2	15.6	13.3	13.3
18580	Corpus Christi, TX	1 783.8	454 726	115	254.9	34.2	3.5	0.6	2.3	60.4	6.9	18.1	9.8	14.2	12.2	12.0
18700	Corvallis, OR......................	675.2	89 385	366	132.4	84.2	1.7	1.6	8.8	7.3	4.1	12.4	22.8	13.2	9.8	10.1
18880	Crestview-Fort Walton Beach-Destin, FL..........	1 968.0	267 059	180	135.7	79.9	9.8	1.4	4.4	8.0	6.5	15.1	8.4	15.3	11.6	12.7
19060	Cumberland, MD-WV..........	752.0	99 541	355	132.4	90.7	7.8	0.5	1.2	1.5	4.8	13.4	11.5	12.3	11.4	13.1
19100	Dallas-Fort Worth-Arlington, TX	9 280.1	7 233 323	4	779.4	48.8	16.2	0.9	7.4	28.5	7.1	19.4	9.2	14.7	14.1	13.6
19100	Dallas-Plano-Irving, TX Div 19124	5 276.7	4 793 649	X	908.5	45.7	17.2	0.8	8.4	29.7	7.1	19.4	9.2	14.9	14.4	13.7
19100	Fort Worth-Arlington, TX Div 23104	4 003.4	2 439 674	X	609.4	54.8	14.3	0.9	5.4	26.4	7.1	19.3	9.1	14.4	13.3	13.5
19140	Dalton, GA........................	635.0	143 904	286	226.6	66.7	3.4	0.6	1.5	29.0	6.6	19.7	9.1	13.1	12.9	13.8
19180	Danville, IL	898.4	78 111	378	86.9	80.5	14.8	0.6	1.2	5.0	6.3	17.5	8.1	12.0	11.6	12.6
19300	Daphne-Fairhope-Foley, AL	1 589.8	208 563	212	131.2	84.7	9.7	1.4	1.5	4.4	5.6	16.1	7.4	11.4	12.1	13.5
19340	Davenport-Moline-Rock Island, IA-IL	2 269.7	382 268	138	168.4	81.6	8.8	0.7	2.8	8.6	6.2	16.8	8.4	12.6	12.2	12.8
19380	Dayton, OH........................	1 281.9	800 683	72	624.6	79.0	17.2	0.8	3.0	2.6	6.0	16.0	9.6	13.1	11.4	13.0
19460	Decatur, AL........................	1 270.0	152 256	268	119.9	78.5	12.9	3.4	1.0	6.8	5.7	16.9	7.9	12.3	12.2	14.3
19500	Decatur, IL........................	580.7	106 550	342	183.5	79.1	19.1	0.6	1.7	2.2	6.0	16.3	9.0	11.7	11.5	12.3
19660	Deltona-Daytona Beach- Ormond Beach, FL	1 586.7	637 674	88	401.9	74.7	11.2	0.8	2.5	12.6	4.6	13.1	7.8	11.0	10.3	12.8
19740	Denver-Aurora-Lakewood, CO	8 345.9	2 853 077	19	341.9	66.7	6.4	1.1	5.3	22.9	6.2	17.0	8.3	16.3	14.4	13.4
19780	Des Moines-West Des Moines, IA....................	2 883.5	634 725	89	220.1	83.0	6.3	0.6	4.8	7.2	7.3	18.2	8.5	14.9	13.6	13.0
19820	Detroit-Warren-Dearborn, MI	3 889.1	4 297 617	14	1 105.0	68.6	23.3	0.9	5.0	4.3	5.9	16.6	8.6	12.9	12.1	14.3
19820	Detroit-Dearborn-Livonia, MI Div 19804	612.0	1 749 366	X	2 858.4	51.6	40.0	1.1	4.0	5.8	6.6	17.4	9.1	13.6	12.0	13.5
19820	Warren-Troy-Farmington Hills, MI Div 47664	3 277.1	2 548 251	X	777.6	80.4	11.9	0.9	5.7	3.3	5.4	16.1	8.2	12.5	12.2	14.9
20020	Dothan, AL........................	1 716.0	147 834	281	86.2	71.8	24.4	1.1	1.2	3.3	5.8	17.0	7.6	12.5	12.2	13.3
20100	Dover, DE..........................	586.3	174 827	238	298.2	65.0	26.8	1.4	3.3	6.9	6.3	16.8	10.3	13.5	11.5	12.9
20220	Dubuque, IA......................	608.3	97 003	361	159.5	92.7	3.9	0.5	2.1	2.3	6.3	16.7	10.2	12.8	10.8	12.8
20260	Duluth, MN-WI	8 413.0	279 227	171	33.2	93.2	2.3	3.8	1.5	1.6	5.1	14.6	11.5	11.9	11.2	12.6
20500	Durham-Chapel Hill, NC	1 757.7	559 535	97	318.3	56.4	27.8	0.9	5.7	11.3	5.9	15.1	11.5	14.9	13.0	12.9
20700	East Stroudsburg, PA.........	608.3	166 098	252	273.1	68.7	14.2	0.8	2.9	15.4	4.5	15.7	11.0	10.8	10.6	15.7
20740	Eau Claire, WI	1 646.3	166 614	250	101.2	93.0	1.9	0.9	3.6	2.1	5.7	15.5	13.1	13.3	11.4	12.4
20940	El Centro, CA.....................	4 176.6	180 883	230	43.3	11.6	2.6	1.0	1.6	83.8	8.5	20.2	10.5	14.4	11.9	11.6
21060	Elizabethtown-Fort Knox, KY	1 190.3	149 538	277	125.6	83.0	11.2	1.1	3.0	4.9	6.3	17.8	9.1	13.2	12.7	13.9
21140	Elkhart-Goshen, IN	463.2	203 781	218	439.9	77.4	7.0	0.7	1.5	15.5	7.6	20.3	8.9	12.7	12.2	12.6
21300	Elmira, NY........................	407.4	86 322	367	211.9	89.0	7.9	0.7	2.1	3.0	5.6	16.0	8.8	12.2	11.6	13.6
21340	El Paso, TX........................	5 583.7	841 971	68	150.8	13.1	3.5	0.5	1.7	82.2	7.8	19.9	11.5	14.7	12.4	11.5
21420	Enid, OK	1 058.5	62 603	381	59.1	78.1	4.3	4.2	4.6	12.5	7.5	18.3	8.7	14.2	11.6	11.5
21500	Erie, PA	799.2	276 207	172	345.6	86.8	8.6	0.5	2.1	4.1	5.7	16.0	10.1	13.3	11.1	12.9
21660	Eugene, OR........................	4 555.7	369 519	144	81.1	86.1	1.9	2.8	4.8	8.5	5.1	13.7	12.8	12.9	11.6	11.6

1. CBSA = Core Based Statistical Area. DIV = Metropolitan Division. See Appendix A for explanation. See Appendix B for list of metropolitan areas identified by type.   2. Dry land or land partially or temporarily covered by water.   3. May be of any race.

Table C. Metropolitan Areas — Population and Households

Area name	Population, 2016 (cont.) Age (percent) (cont.) 55 to 64 years	65 to 74 years	75 years and over	Percent female	Population change and components of change, 2000–2016 Total persons 2000	2010	Percent change 2000–2010	2010–2016	Components of change, 2010–2016 Births	Deaths	Net migration	Households, 2015 Number	Persons per house-hold	Percent Family house-holds	Female family house-holder[1]	One person
	16	17	18	19	20	21	22	23	24	25	26	27	28	29	30	31
Cedar Rapids, IA	13.0	8.7	6.8	50.4	237 230	257 941	8.7	3.8	20 408	13 122	2 829	107 586	2.41	63.1	9.2	29.6
Chambersburg-Waynesboro, PA	13.4	10.4	8.4	50.8	129 313	149 618	15.7	2.8	11 289	9 084	1 956	59 486	2.55	72.8	10.8	22.8
Champaign-Urbana, IL	11.2	7.2	5.5	50.1	210 275	231 889	10.3	2.9	16 978	10 179	-59	92 268	2.42	53.2	9.1	35.9
Charleston, WV	15.4	11.2	8.0	51.6	235 938	227 071	-3.8	-4.0	15 773	17 928	-6 521	94 533	2.28	62.9	14.9	31.3
Charleston-North Charleston, SC	12.7	9.0	5.2	51.2	549 033	664 644	21.1	14.5	58 006	32 919	68 200	273 722	2.66	63.7	13.5	29.1
Charlotte-Concord-Gastonia, NC-SC	11.9	8.0	5.0	51.5	1 717 372	2 216 974	29.1	11.6	185 968	108 326	175 616	905 696	2.64	66.5	13.6	27.1
Charlottesville, VA	13.2	9.8	6.9	51.6	189 644	218 707	15.3	5.8	15 203	10 817	7 943	87 949	2.47	62.0	10.6	26.9
Chattanooga, TN-GA	13.6	10.0	7.0	51.5	476 531	528 152	10.8	4.4	39 165	33 227	17 626	209 340	2.54	66.8	12.8	27.7
Cheyenne, WY	13.1	8.9	6.2	49.3	81 607	91 881	12.6	6.8	7 896	4 852	3 191	37 740	2.52	64.2	11.4	29.5
Chicago-Naperville-Elgin, IL-IN-WI	12.7	7.9	5.6	51.0	9 098 316	9 461 550	4.0	0.5	752 946	431 416	-260 662	3 470 993	2.71	65.4	13.4	28.5
Chicago-Naperville-Arlington Heights, IL Div 16974	12.5	7.8	5.6	51.2	7 135 324	7 263 183	1.8	0.6	588 011	331 243	-206 219	2 686 830	2.69	63.8	13.6	29.7
Elgin, IL Div 20994	11.9	7.5	5.0	50.3	493 088	620 418	25.8	2.6	50 555	23 388	-11 980	212 458	2.94	72.0	10.5	22.3
Gary, IN Div 23844	14.0	9.1	6.5	51.2	675 971	708 119	4.8	-1.0	52 255	41 247	-17 303	266 576	2.60	67.4	15.9	27.7
Lake County-Kenosha County, IL-WI Div 29404	13.4	7.7	5.3	50.1	793 933	869 830	9.6	0.2	62 125	35 538	-25 160	305 129	2.79	72.7	11.2	22.6
Chico, CA	13.1	10.4	7.6	50.5	203 171	220 000	8.3	3.1	15 302	14 220	5 611	85 289	2.58	59.6	9.1	26.8
Cincinnati, OH-KY-IN	13.3	8.4	5.9	51.0	1 994 830	2 114 751	6.0	2.4	169 405	116 499	-517	832 607	2.54	64.9	12.9	28.8
Clarksville, TN-KY	9.5	6.2	4.2	49.2	219 630	260 635	18.7	8.3	31 466	11 920	1 602	101 265	2.66	68.0	12.7	26.2
Cleveland, TN	12.8	10.2	6.8	51.3	104 015	115 758	11.3	4.8	8 311	7 448	4 482	46 389	2.56	67.6	11.2	28.3
Cleveland-Elyria, OH	14.6	9.8	7.7	51.7	2 148 143	2 077 258	-3.3	-1.0	145 809	131 704	-33 855	849 475	2.37	61.0	14.0	33.5
Coeur d'Alene, ID	13.7	11.1	7.1	50.7	108 685	138 464	27.4	11.4	10 965	7 885	12 327	58 675	2.53	67.5	8.1	25.8
College Station-Bryan, TX	9.1	5.8	4.2	49.5	184 885	228 668	23.7	11.5	19 615	8 305	14 655	90 526	2.59	56.8	11.1	27.8
Colorado Springs, CO	12.1	7.7	4.7	49.5	537 484	645 611	20.1	10.3	59 225	25 982	32 811	261 435	2.61	69.3	10.3	24.8
Columbia, MO	10.8	6.7	4.6	51.5	135 454	162 645	20.1	8.6	13 231	6 358	6 951	69 152	2.39	53.6	6.5	33.3
Columbia, SC	12.6	8.7	5.4	51.4	647 158	767 477	18.6	6.5	58 904	40 221	30 743	302 634	2.56	64.0	15.4	30.1
Columbus, GA-AL	12.0	7.9	5.4	50.4	281 768	295 531	4.9	4.5	28 899	16 966	752	112 983	2.66	63.2	16.3	32.3
Columbus, IN	12.4	8.9	6.5	49.9	71 435	76 786	7.5	6.0	6 543	4 495	2 668	31 131	2.58	65.0	10.3	27.4
Columbus, OH	12.1	7.6	5.0	50.8	1 675 013	1 902 003	13.6	7.3	169 398	93 389	64 774	772 304	2.55	63.9	12.7	28.4
Corpus Christi, TX	12.2	8.5	6.0	50.5	403 280	428 188	6.2	6.2	38 393	23 385	11 640	161 634	2.73	67.3	14.4	26.3
Corvallis, OR	12.3	9.2	6.0	49.9	78 153	85 581	9.5	4.4	4 601	3 485	2 656	35 062	2.34	55.7	7.2	30.8
Crestview-Fort Walton Beach-Destin, FL	13.6	9.9	6.8	49.3	211 099	235 865	11.7	13.2	21 398	13 781	22 826	102 729	2.48	63.8	10.7	30.0
Cumberland, MD-WV	13.5	11.2	8.6	48.6	102 008	103 292	1.3	-3.6	6 089	7 700	-1 934	39 120	2.34	61.1	11.9	32.4
Dallas-Fort Worth-Arlington, TX	11.2	6.7	4.1	50.8	5 204 126	6 426 241	23.5	12.6	611 857	254 032	444 944	2 479 995	2.83	69.5	13.6	24.9
Dallas-Plano-Irving, TX Div 19124	10.9	6.4	3.9	50.8	3 445 899	4 228 966	22.7	13.4	407 049	158 395	314 255	1 653 468	2.82	68.8	13.2	25.2
Fort Worth-Arlington, TX Div 23104	11.6	7.1	4.6	50.9	1 758 227	2 197 275	25.0	11.0	204 808	95 637	130 689	826 527	2.86	70.9	14.3	24.3
Dalton, GA	11.4	8.2	5.3	50.4	120 031	142 227	18.5	1.2	11 892	7 130	-3 030	48 631	2.93	72.8	11.0	21.3
Danville, IL	13.9	10.1	7.9	50.2	83 919	81 625	-2.7	-4.3	6 364	5 936	-3 803	30 927	2.47	65.0	14.0	30.3
Daphne-Fairhope-Foley, AL	14.1	11.9	7.8	51.5	140 415	182 265	29.8	14.4	13 682	12 324	23 779	72 269	2.78	63.5	9.4	32.2
Davenport-Moline-Rock Island, IA-IL	13.9	9.7	7.5	50.7	376 019	379 689	1.0	0.7	29 737	22 801	-3 855	155 753	2.41	63.7	10.7	30.7
Dayton, OH	13.7	9.7	7.5	51.5	805 816	799 219	-0.8	0.2	59 934	50 877	-6 559	330 430	2.34	61.7	13.3	31.6
Decatur, AL	13.7	10.1	6.8	50.9	145 867	153 825	5.5	-1.0	11 037	10 175	-2 269	60 697	2.48	69.4	13.9	26.5
Decatur, IL	14.4	10.4	8.4	52.0	114 706	110 768	-3.4	-3.8	8 446	7 475	-5 016	44 429	2.33	61.0	14.6	34.8
Deltona-Daytona Beach-Ormond Beach, FL	15.3	14.2	10.8	51.4	493 175	590 294	19.7	8.0	34 662	47 982	58 804	248 938	2.46	62.3	11.1	30.4
Denver-Aurora-Lakewood, CO	12.2	7.6	4.7	50.1	2 179 240	2 543 600	16.7	12.2	218 000	103 306	191 814	1 075 919	2.58	63.5	10.0	28.0
Des Moines-West Des Moines, IA	11.7	7.5	5.3	50.7	481 394	569 633	18.3	11.4	54 799	26 883	36 563	242 022	2.52	64.7	10.7	28.3
Detroit-Warren-Dearborn, MI	14.0	9.0	6.4	51.4	4 452 557	4 296 313	-3.5	0.0	314 182	251 625	-58 684	1 674 251	2.54	64.3	14.0	30.3
Detroit-Dearborn-Livonia, MI Div 19804	13.4	8.4	6.0	51.9	2 061 162	1 820 641	-11.7	-3.9	146 578	112 285	-104 909	667 521	2.60	61.3	19.1	33.5
Warren-Troy-Farmington Hills, MI Div 47664	14.5	9.5	6.7	51.0	2 391 395	2 475 672	3.5	2.9	167 604	139 340	46 225	1 006 730	2.50	66.4	10.7	28.2
Dothan, AL	13.5	10.6	7.3	51.8	130 861	145 643	11.3	1.5	11 048	10 056	1 287	55 973	2.62	66.9	14.8	28.8
Dover, DE	12.4	9.8	6.6	51.8	126 697	162 349	28.1	7.7	13 743	9 272	7 638	62 477	2.70	68.2	13.8	24.0
Dubuque, IA	13.5	9.0	7.9	50.6	89 143	93 653	5.1	3.6	7 542	5 554	1 389	37 784	2.46	66.7	9.8	27.9
Duluth, MN-WI	15.2	10.3	7.7	49.6	275 486	279 771	1.6	-0.2	17 760	17 834	56	116 212	2.30	59.3	8.9	33.3
Durham-Chapel Hill, NC	12.5	8.6	5.6	52.2	426 493	506 646	18.8	10.4	41 185	22 888	33 387	215 294	2.45	58.8	12.5	31.9
East Stroudsburg, PA	15.6	9.9	6.1	50.5	138 687	169 842	22.5	-2.2	8 892	8 539	-3 912	55 681	2.95	71.3	8.4	22.6
Eau Claire, WI	12.9	9.1	6.6	49.7	148 337	161 390	8.8	3.2	11 932	8 438	1 846	63 854	2.49	61.5	7.0	29.4
El Centro, CA	10.3	6.9	5.7	49.0	142 361	174 528	22.6	3.6	19 505	6 075	-7 347	45 158	3.77	76.7	19.6	20.9
Elizabethtown-Fort Knox, KY	13.0	8.2	5.7	50.1	133 896	148 351	10.8	0.8	12 533	7 894	-3 721	56 899	2.55	68.7	12.0	26.5
Elkhart-Goshen, IN	11.8	7.9	6.0	50.5	182 791	197 561	8.1	3.1	19 060	10 009	-2 626	68 498	2.92	69.8	10.2	24.2
Elmira, NY	14.4	9.9	7.9	50.4	91 070	88 842	-2.4	-2.8	6 200	5 817	-2 771	34 546	2.39	63.0	12.0	29.8
El Paso, TX	10.2	6.7	5.3	50.9	682 966	804 123	17.7	4.7	85 419	31 313	-16 469	261 529	3.14	74.2	17.0	22.7
Enid, OK	12.4	8.4	7.3	49.9	57 813	60 580	4.8	3.3	6 061	4 255	306	NA	NA	NA	NA	NA
Erie, PA	14.2	9.4	7.2	50.6	280 843	280 564	-0.1	-1.6	19 902	17 561	-6 229	110 138	2.41	63.8	14.6	30.0
Eugene, OR	13.8	11.1	7.4	50.8	322 959	351 724	8.9	5.1	22 445	20 818	15 588	146 602	2.42	59.9	10.5	30.1

1. No spouse present.

Table C. Metropolitan Areas — Population, Vital Statistics, Health, and Crime

Area name	Daytime population, 2015 — Persons in group quarters, 2016	Number	Employment/ residence ratio	Births, 2016 — Total	Rate[1]	Deaths, 2016 — Number	Rate[1]	Persons under 65 with no health insurance 2015 — Number	Percent	Medicare, 2015 — Total Beneficiaries	Enrolled in Original Medicare	Enrolled in Medicare Advantage	Serious crimes known to police,[2] 2014 — Total Number	Rate[3]
	32	33	34	35	36	37	38	39	40	41	42	43	44	45
Cedar Rapids, IA	6 552	270 190	1.03	3 326	12.4	2 200	8.2	10 428	4.7	45 098	32 861	12 237	6 786	2 595
Chambersburg-Waynesboro, PA...........	2 544	145 289	0.88	1 755	11.4	1 602	10.4	11 645	9.4	31 071	23 354	7 717	3 321	2 176
Champaign-Urbana, IL..........	16 708	244 243	1.04	2 751	11.5	1 713	7.2	12 517	6.4	31 857	16 935	14 922	6 554	2 821
Charleston, WV	3 382	239 004	1.22	2 410	11.1	2 919	13.4	12 353	7.0	52 881	35 296	17 585	8 831	4 274
Charleston-North Charleston, SC	16 107	747 931	1.01	9 662	12.7	5 952	7.8	77 464	12.3	114 935	90 080	24 855	23 688	3 274
Charlotte-Concord-Gastonia, NC-SC.................	36 649	2 444 034	1.02	30 815	12.5	18 767	7.6	257 555	12.3	356 578	238 493	118 085	75 601	3 212
Charlottesville, VA..............	12 587	237 227	1.06	2 470	10.7	1 824	7.9	21 165	11.7	38 796	32 365	6 431	4 405	1 954
Chattanooga, TN-GA	12 775	556 010	1.04	6 318	11.5	5 678	10.3	53 662	12.0	105 268	67 512	37 756	26 726	4 890
Cheyenne, WY	1 945	NA	NA	1 252	12.8	850	8.7	9 272	11.4	16 401	15 662	739	2 495	2 593
Chicago-Naperville-Elgin, IL-IN-WI	161 899	9 585 174	1.01	117 773	12.4	73 126	7.7	756 862	9.3	1 306 456	972 947	333 509	236 496	2 525
Chicago-Naperville-Arlington Heights, IL Div 16974	115 119	7 444 670	1.03	91 950	12.6	56 161	7.7	581 920	9.3	983 586	713 838	269 748	191 275	2 641
Elgin, IL Div 20994	12 873	600 051	0.89	7 958	12.5	4 081	6.4	52 466	9.6	85 433	63 681	21 752	9 755	1 584
Gary, IN Div 23844	11 002	671 549	0.90	8 182	11.7	6 953	9.9	63 682	10.8	121 098	100 130	20 968	19 681	3 075
Lake County-Kenosha County, IL-WI Div 29404	22 905	NA	NA	9 683	11.1	5 931	6.8	58 794	7.9	116 339	95 298	21 041	15 785	1 821
Chico, CA	5 396	225 668	1.00	2 520	11.1	2 444	10.8	14 769	8.1	46 872	45 740	1 132	7 309	3 265
Cincinnati, OH-KY-IN	48 958	2 168 893	1.01	27 134	12.5	19 766	9.1	125 732	6.9	345 707	192 111	153 596	64 200	3 174
Clarksville, TN-KY	8 948	277 842	0.98	5 205	18.4	2 032	7.2	20 309	8.3	35 198	26 781	8 417	8 209	2 982
Cleveland, TN	2 929	118 438	0.94	1 338	11.0	1 249	10.3	12 554	12.8	25 169	15 535	9 634	4 691	3 925
Cleveland-Elyria, OH	44 064	2 103 504	1.04	23 331	11.3	21 216	10.3	125 160	7.4	380 773	206 504	174 269	47 693	2 778
Coeur d'Alene, ID	1 489	145 294	0.93	1 834	11.9	1 354	8.8	14 296	11.6	31 622	21 428	10 194	4 328	2 951
College Station-Bryan, TX ...	15 579	251 485	1.01	3 403	13.3	1 448	5.7	37 662	17.8	26 325	20 288	6 037	6 729	2 799
Colorado Springs, CO........	18 468	691 055	0.98	9 813	13.8	4 601	6.5	48 109	8.1	93 191	62 245	30 946	22 584	3 276
Columbia, MO	9 019	181 927	1.08	2 119	12.0	1 064	6.0	14 185	9.6	22 689	18 936	3 753	5 735	3 316
Columbia, SC	34 890	814 047	1.01	9 429	11.5	6 892	8.4	75 299	11.3	125 530	97 496	28 034	31 494	3 933
Columbus, GA-AL	11 402	325 755	1.10	4 446	14.4	2 939	9.5	33 426	12.8	51 923	35 772	16 151	17 594	5 513
Columbus, IN	1 147	91 443	1.26	1 064	13.1	711	8.7	6 974	10.2	15 485	12 455	3 030	2 664	3 316
Columbus, OH	50 041	2 052 325	1.03	27 625	13.5	16 187	7.9	139 336	8.1	276 420	136 899	139 521	64 315	3 442
Corpus Christi, TX	7 817	455 703	1.03	6 442	14.2	3 892	8.6	71 897	18.8	71 778	35 615	36 163	20 985	4 668
Corvallis, OR	5 097	91 258	1.09	757	8.5	581	6.5	4 995	7.1	12 034	6 066	5 968	2 620	3 004
Crestview-Fort Walton Beach-Destin, FL	6 603	268 979	1.06	3 618	13.5	2 455	9.2	29 314	13.7	46 940	38 843	8 097	7 270	2 801
Cumberland, MD-WV	8 254	100 324	1.01	951	9.6	1 267	12.7	4 795	6.5	22 584	20 905	1 679	3 054	3 075
Dallas-Fort Worth-Arlington, TX	86 461	7 125 836	1.01	100 965	14.0	44 801	6.2	1 130 054	18.0	802 133	496 066	306 067	212 467	3 058
Dallas-Plano-Irving, TX Div 19124	56 116	4 776 972	1.03	67 180	14.0	28 129	5.9	758 105	18.1	510 032	331 361	178 671	133 575	2 906
Fort Worth-Arlington, TX Div 23104...................	30 345	2 348 864	0.96	33 785	13.8	16 672	6.8	371 949	17.7	292 101	164 705	127 396	78 892	3 354
Dalton, GA	1 265	147 871	1.06	1 874	13.0	1 205	8.4	26 668	21.6	22 845	18 583	4 262	4 111	2 932
Danville, IL	2 925	78 799	0.98	918	11.8	940	12.0	3 869	6.2	17 126	9 995	7 131	3 240	4 120
Daphne-Fairhope-Foley, AL..	2 341	191 362	0.86	2 274	10.9	2 113	10.1	18 751	11.5	44 243	28 689	15 554	4 227	2 189
Davenport-Moline-Rock Island, IA-IL	8 978	387 917	1.02	4 690	12.3	3 644	9.5	17 614	5.6	72 533	56 128	16 405	10 400	2 845
Dayton, OH	24 360	815 053	1.04	9 488	11.8	8 304	10.4	49 940	7.7	151 528	75 981	75 547	27 405	3 487
Decatur, AL........................	2 350	142 491	0.84	1 711	11.2	1 653	10.9	17 190	13.7	31 767	26 896	4 871	3 792	2 504
Decatur, IL	4 215	113 543	1.13	1 317	12.4	1 171	11.0	4 965	5.9	23 218	18 166	5 052	3 039	2 793
Deltona-Daytona Beach-Ormond Beach, FL	14 343	592 268	0.87	5 714	9.0	8 151	12.8	71 212	15.5	163 395	87 117	76 278	19 947	3 290
Denver-Aurora-Lakewood, CO...........................	34 201	2 805 103	0.99	35 834	12.6	18 291	6.4	228 576	9.3	343 062	159 802	183 260	81 271	2 956
Des Moines-West Des Moines, IA	12 360	635 302	1.04	9 081	14.3	4 604	7.3	28 825	5.4	86 897	69 729	17 168	17 232	2 833
Detroit-Warren-Dearborn, MI	48 806	4 319 340	1.01	50 265	11.7	41 532	9.7	265 501	7.3	763 454	460 929	302 525	117 769	2 745
Detroit-Dearborn-Livonia, MI Div 19804	22 889	1 816 074	1.08	23 209	13.3	18 231	10.4	125 477	8.4	312 807	174 361	138 446	75 016	4 268
Warren-Troy-Farmington Hills, MI Div 47664.......	25 917	2 503 266	0.97	27 056	10.6	23 301	9.1	140 024	6.6	450 647	286 568	164 079	42 753	1 688
Dothan, AL.........................	1 848	150 069	1.03	1 732	11.7	1 688	11.4	15 224	12.6	31 901	26 506	5 395	3 613	2 446
Dover, DE	4 719	164 700	0.89	2 147	12.3	1 651	9.4	9 821	6.9	31 093	28 287	2 806	5 424	3 160
Dubuque, IA	4 343	105 456	1.17	1 237	12.8	900	9.3	3 629	4.7	19 085	10 957	8 128	1 908	1 980
Duluth, MN-WI	12 391	282 504	1.02	2 777	9.9	2 849	10.2	11 530	5.2	59 610	29 444	30 166	9 449	3 371
Durham-Chapel Hill, NC	23 105	598 564	1.17	6 650	11.9	3 979	7.1	58 864	12.9	76 149	49 117	27 032	19 974	3 681
East Stroudsburg, PA	4 452	155 195	0.85	1 421	8.6	1 521	9.2	11 641	8.5	29 333	23 320	6 013	4 401	2 644
Eau Claire, WI....................	7 567	168 167	1.03	1 915	11.5	1 408	8.5	8 222	6.1	32 383	22 720	9 663	3 089	1 867
El Centro, CA.....................	8 870	179 165	0.98	3 201	17.7	1 019	5.6	15 794	10.6	25 245	22 980	2 265	6 119	3 577
Elizabethtown-Fort Knox, KY	3 782	144 892	0.95	1 821	12.2	1 315	8.8	7 828	6.3	26 219	21 417	4 802	2 173	1 429
Elkhart-Goshen, IN	3 797	232 175	1.32	3 128	15.3	1 622	8.0	27 967	16.2	31 610	22 074	9 536	5 051	2 507
Elmira, NY	4 616	86 527	0.99	955	11.1	950	11.0	3 462	5.1	18 768	12 109	6 659	2 151	2 430
El Paso, TX........................	16 311	838 989	1.00	13 366	15.9	5 441	6.5	165 243	22.8	111 875	46 121	65 754	20 124	2 386
Enid, OK	1 797	NA	NA	988	15.8	661	10.6	8 690	16.5	11 365	10 537	828		
Erie, PA	12 787	282 654	1.04	3 107	11.2	2 808	10.2	15 455	6.9	54 419	28 345	26 074	6 587	2 351
Eugene, OR	8 142	364 534	1.01	3 752	10.2	3 422	9.3	25 609	8.8	74 183	34 566	39 617	NA	NA

1. Per 1,000 estimated resident population.   2. Data for serious crimes have not been adjusted for underreporting; this may affect comparability between geographic areas and over time.
3. Per 100,000 population estimated by the FBI.

Table C. Metropolitan Areas — Crime, Education, Money Income, and Poverty

Area name	Serious crimes known to police, 2014 (cont.)[1] Rate[2] Violent	Property	Education School enrollment and attainment, 2015 Enrollment[3] Total	Percent private	Attainment[4] (percent) High school graduate or less	Bachelor's degree or more	Local government expenditures,[5] 2013–2014 Total current expenditures (mil dol)	Current expenditures per student (dollars)	Income and Poverty, 2015 Per capita income[6] (dollars)	Mean household income (dollars)	Median household income	Percent of households with income of less than $50,000	Percent of households with income of $200,000 or more	Percent below poverty level All persons	Children under 18 years	Age 65 years and older
	46	47	48	49	50	51	52	53	54	55	56	57	58	59	60	61
Cedar Rapids, IA	193	2 402	68 309	14.3	36.4	28.1	490.3	11 203	31 277	75 182	58 015	43.1	3.9	11.1	13.4	5.3
Chambersburg-Waynesboro, PA..........	149	2 027	33 875	17.1	56.8	20.2	250.3	10 953	27 507	70 642	57 960	43.9	2.7	8.9	13.5	7.8
Champaign-Urbana, IL.......	444	2 377	87 220	8.9	30.1	42.6	370.4	12 012	27 572	51 600	48.6	4.4	19.0	15.0	9.6	(see below)
Charleston, WV	528	3 745	42 489	14.4	53.7	22.8	383.2	10 803	25 137	57 505	42 526	57.1	2.3	18.6	29.6	8.6
Charleston-North Charleston, SC	387	2 888	181 764	15.2	35.6	34.7	1 013.4	9 744	30 769	77 932	56 430	43.5	5.5	14.2	20.1	9.7
Charlotte-Concord-Gastonia, NC-SC	392	2 819	609 188	15.2	36.7	33.5	3 155.8	8 185	30 005	77 789	54 836	45.4	5.9	14.1	19.4	8.4
Charlottesville, VA	165	1 789	61 519	17.1	32.8	40.9	332.0	11 576	34 093	88 050	63 918	39.2	7.5	13.1	11.3	5.4
Chattanooga, TN-GA	592	4 298	125 096	17.5	45.9	25.1	668.8	9 018	26 208	64 851	47 809	51.6	3.4	15.3	21.3	11.6
Cheyenne, WY	160	2 433	23 523	6.7	33.8	27.5	226.0	15 489	33 278	80 196	60 599	41.1	3.9	12.6	17.9	10.8
Chicago-Naperville-Elgin, IL-IN-WI........	382	2 143	2 499 757	19.7	36.7	36.0	21 342.8	13 593	33 437	88 925	63 153	40.1	7.8	13.3	19.3	9.0
Chicago-Naperville-Arlington Heights, IL Div 16974	430	2 211	1 896 666	21.3	36.0	37.2	16 166.3	14 142	33 669	88 805	62 505	40.5	7.9	13.7	19.5	9.7
Elgin, IL Div 20994	174	1 410	187 374	14.7	38.5	31.2	1 661.8	11 848	30 926	88 886	66 980	36.4	6.5	12.1	17.5	7.7
Gary, IN Div 23844	350	2 724	180 853	14.4	46.4	22.5	1 134.8	9 475	26 663	68 753	53 026	46.8	3.5	15.3	25.9	6.3
Lake County-Kenosha County, IL-WI Div 29404	160	1 661	234 864	14.4	33.2	40.2	2 379.9	14 254	38 758	107 632	75 548	33.2	11.5	9.7	14.0	6.1
Chico, CA	303	2 962	66 550	8.8	32.7	27.8	316.8	10 197	23 867	61 627	45 644	55.3	3.0	21.8	21.4	9.2
Cincinnati, OH-KY-IN	263	2 911	561 826	19.5	39.5	32.1	3 256.5	10 327	30 333	76 779	56 826	44.0	5.1	13.2	17.9	7.1
Clarksville, TN-KY	463	2 519	78 806	9.6	41.0	24.0	362.2	8 477	21 911	57 129	46 070	54.5	1.2	15.3	20.4	10.0
Cleveland, TN	495	3 430	29 265	24.7	50.3	18.5	150.8	8 139	24 612	63 662	42 380	56.2	3.3	19.6	27.1	9.0
Cleveland-Elyria, OH	395	2 383	496 583	23.8	40.1	29.4	3 596.8	12 404	29 859	70 990	51 049	48.8	4.4	14.8	21.7	8.4
Coeur d'Alene, ID	279	2 672	35 848	11.7	35.7	23.2	140.1	6 163	25 858	63 639	47 860	53.3	2.9	15.7	24.0	8.3
College Station-Bryan, TX	292	2 506	96 530	6.1	35.9	36.3	305.1	8 750	24 670	65 896	46 341	53.1	4.0	23.0	16.9	7.3
Colorado Springs, CO..........	382	2 893	194 994	11.5	27.3	36.5	999.7	8 348	29 809	78 073	60 458	40.9	4.8	10.6	14.7	5.9
Columbia, MO	342	2 974	64 400	13.1	27.1	48.5	228.1	9 806	26 609	66 751	50 520	49.3	2.9	18.5	10.4	9.0
Columbia, SC.......................	581	3 352	219 266	14.4	37.9	31.4	1 478.3	10 600	26 866	67 564	51 369	48.4	3.8	15.1	21.2	8.5
Columbus, GA-AL.................	434	5 079	83 717	10.6	41.7	23.3	479.0	9 545	23 184	58 076	41 592	58.5	2.6	21.1	31.4	11.5
Columbus, IN	110	3 206	19 282	18.2	41.7	29.6	115.0	9 146	28 193	70 857	54 447	44.9	3.2	13.9	20.4	10.0
Columbus, OH	308	3 134	536 167	15.7	37.5	35.1	3 562.3	11 088	30 559	78 054	58 192	43.1	5.2	14.2	19.6	7.6
Corpus Christi, TX	588	4 079	112 964	5.2	48.9	20.5	703.1	8 690	25 575	68 985	50 253	49.7	3.7	19.0	30.2	11.3
Corvallis, OR	127	2 877	32 759	3.2	20.5	55.1	84.8	9 763	31 618	75 743	52 852	47.7	5.2	20.1	16.5	6.8
Crestview-Fort Walton Beach-Destin, FL	391	2 410	57 115	10.0	34.8	28.5	337.0	8 800	29 802	73 686	53 488	46.7	4.6	11.8	19.8	5.6
Cumberland, MD-WV............	264	2 811	22 996	4.9	55.6	15.3	175.7	13 457	20 358	50 152	39 408	61.0	1.8	19.2	30.1	12.8
Dallas-Fort Worth-Arlington, TX	332	2 726	1 947 129	12.1	38.1	33.4	10 958.3	8 247	31 379	86 871	61 644	40.4	7.1	13.4	19.2	8.2
Dallas-Plano-Irving, TX Div 19124	320	2 586	1 291 819	11.8	37.2	35.5	7 435.0	8 252	32 096	88 680	62 142	40.2	7.5	13.6	19.5	9.0
Fort Worth-Arlington, TX Div 23104............	356	2 998	655 310	12.6	39.8	29.3	3 523.3	8 237	29 969	83 254	60 756	40.7	6.5	12.8	18.5	6.9
Dalton, GA	218	2 714	38 584	4.0	61.3	13.4	251.9	8 813	21 336	60 688	45 632	54.0	3.1	15.2	22.6	6.1
Danville, IL	598	3 523	16 804	5.0	53.4	13.0	148.2	11 198	23 665	59 412	45 098	54.5	2.1	18.1	27.8	6.7
Daphne-Fairhope-Foley, AL..	189	2 000	44 872	14.8	40.9	29.5	267.2	8 824	28 497	73 408	52 003	47.1	5.6	12.8	18.0	6.7
Davenport-Moline-Rock Island, IA-IL..................	366	2 479	95 750	15.5	41.3	26.0	683.0	10 831	28 492	68 844	55 496	44.6	2.8	11.9	16.0	8.4
Dayton, OH	279	3 208	203 224	23.9	38.8	28.5	1 294.5	11 399	27 551	65 586	49 504	50.4	3.4	16.2	24.4	8.3
Decatur, AL	156	2 349	33 791	12.1	49.4	19.9	232.8	9 495	24 700	60 268	46 157	54.7	2.3	17.3	25.2	9.0
Decatur, IL	364	2 429	24 830	20.9	45.1	23.4	215.8	13 117	28 185	66 687	48 040	51.7	4.1	18.3	27.0	6.4
Deltona-Daytona Beach-Ormond Beach, FL	402	2 887	131 336	16.8	42.7	23.1	607.9	8 215	25 220	59 514	43 284	56.6	2.2	15.3	22.8	7.5
Denver-Aurora-Lakewood, CO...........	332	2 624	697 574	14.2	29.6	41.8	4 142.8	9 041	36 733	93 705	70 283	34.9	7.8	10.3	13.9	6.8
Des Moines-West Des Moines, IA............	323	2 510	164 293	18.1	33.9	35.1	1 125.4	10 585	32 520	81 722	62 024	38.9	5.2	10.7	13.8	6.5
Detroit-Warren-Dearborn, MI	534	2 211	1 065 012	12.7	37.7	29.5	7 305.5	10 896	29 736	74 403	53 628	46.5	4.9	16.1	24.0	8.2
Detroit-Dearborn-Livonia, MI Div 19804............	995	3 273	451 319	12.0	44.9	22.6	3 134.0	10 969	23 789	60 145	41 557	56.6	3.1	24.8	37.5	12.1
Warren-Troy-Farmington Hills, MI Div 47664.......	214	1 474	613 693	13.2	33.0	34.1	4 171.5	10 842	33 850	83 857	62 593	39.8	6.1	10.1	13.8	5.8
Dothan, AL	291	2 155	34 101	18.3	48.8	19.0	193.0	8 657	23 731	59 338	42 492	58.4	3.1	17.9	27.1	8.2
Dover, DE	422	2 737	46 928	12.8	47.3	21.3	329.8	12 828	26 387	71 135	56 778	44.4	3.6	14.6	22.4	6.8
Dubuque, IA	177	1 803	25 889	36.7	40.6	30.9	154.8	10 616	28 508	70 651	58 487	41.9	2.7	12.9	16.9	9.3
Duluth, MN-WI	223	3 148	67 000	11.8	37.0	26.5	411.1	10 882	27 740	64 985	50 566	49.3	2.6	13.5	14.5	8.5
Durham-Chapel Hill, NC	426	3 255	155 149	19.2	31.8	45.1	723.3	9 862	32 362	80 006	54 160	46.2	7.2	15.9	22.8	8.9
East Stroudsburg, PA	218	2 426	42 600	9.5	47.1	24.9	422.8	15 395	24 664	69 094	57 318	43.9	2.7	12.5	16.2	10.0
Eau Claire, WI	132	1 736	42 444	8.2	37.0	26.5	248.9	10 810	26 964	66 647	52 094	46.9	2.7	12.5	14.9	10.2
El Centro, CA	341	3 236	52 374	5.5	54.7	14.3	376.5	10 183	15 757	55 930	40 852	57.7	1.9	25.1	31.6	18.0
Elizabethtown-Fort Knox, KY	97	1 332	39 543	11.4	44.8	20.1	213.0	8 559	24 204	59 973	48 955	51.2	1.4	15.7	24.7	8.0
Elkhart-Goshen, IN	357	2 149	49 262	13.5	55.0	18.3	340.2	9 409	22 971	64 099	49 556	50.6	2.7	15.1	22.7	7.1
Elmira, NY	186	2 243	17 312	21.5	44.4	24.2	179.0	15 173	26 372	65 125	53 119	46.0	2.4	13.9	20.0	8.8
El Paso, TX	363	2 024	260 039	9.2	47.7	22.8	1 578.6	8 841	19 258	56 608	43 633	56.4	1.5	20.1	29.3	16.3
Enid, OK.	NA	NA	NA	NA	NA	NA	86.2	7 607	NA	NA	NA	NA	NA	NA	NA	NA
Erie, PA.	228	2 124	69 903	25.3	47.4	26.4	497.5	12 584	26 152	64 276	47 386	51.5	3.0	17.5	27.2	7.0
Eugene, OR	NA	NA	90 032	10.0	33.3	29.1	445.8	9 901	25 892	62 572	47 318	52.2	2.7	19.4	24.6	6.2

1. Data for serious crimes have not been adjusted for underreporting; this may affect comparability between geographic areas and over time.   2. Per 100,000 population estimated by the FBI.
3. All persons 3 years old and over enrolled in nursery school through college.   4. Persons 25 years old and over.   5. Elementary and secondary education expenditures.   6. Based on resident population estimated in the 2015 American Community Survey.

Table C. Metropolitan Areas — Personal Income

Area name	Total (mil dol)	Percent change 2014–2015	Per capita[1] Dollars	Per capita Rank	Wages and salaries (mil dol)	Pension and insurance	Government social insurance	Proprietors' income (mil dol)	Dividends, interest, and rent (mil dol)	Personal transfer receipts (mil dol)	Total (mil dol)	From employee and self-employed	From employer
	62	63	64	65	66	67	68	69	70	71	72	73	74
Cedar Rapids, IA	12 628	3.6	47 468	82	7 252	1 081	541	765	2 233	2 015	9 639	602	541
Chambersburg-Waynesboro, PA	6 417	3.2	41 768	184	2 476	524	210	481	1 045	1 334	3 691	220	210
Champaign-Urbana, IL	10 244	2.3	42 863	158	5 092	1 252	315	1 261	1 843	1 396	7 919	378	315
Charleston, WV	9 274	1.7	42 039	178	5 412	905	416	792	1 444	2 576	7 525	488	416
Charleston-North Charleston, SC	32 307	5.7	43 393	150	16 383	2 738	1 264	2 973	6 213	5 544	23 358	1 417	1 264
Charlotte-Concord-Gastonia, NC-SC	109 028	6.5	44 935	113	64 737	8 633	4 825	9 812	15 937	17 037	88 007	5 363	4 825
Charlottesville, VA	12 117	5.7	52 795	37	5 789	1 145	410	896	3 544	1 578	8 241	486	410
Chattanooga, TN-GA	22 582	4.3	41 225	194	11 244	1 772	791	2 633	3 352	4 761	16 440	994	791
Cheyenne, WY	4 836	2.0	49 796	62	2 414	517	245	312	1 091	770	3 487	196	245
Chicago-Naperville-Elgin, IL-IN-WI	514 662	4.4	53 886	31	287 143	41 916	19 555	40 782	98 622	71 573	389 395	21 520	19 555
Chicago-Naperville-Arlington Heights, IL Div 16974	401 636	4.4	54 715	X	232 482	33 234	15 849	34 286	78 001	56 154	315 851	17 367	15 849
Elgin, IL Div 20994	27 725	4.5	43 647	X	12 339	2 270	866	1 352	4 144	3 695	16 828	903	866
Gary, IN Div 23844	29 181	4.7	41 507	X	12 649	1 985	944	1 674	4 057	6 185	17 253	1 085	944
Lake County-Kenosha County, IL-WI Div 29404	56 121	3.7	64 333	X	29 672	4 426	1 895	3 469	12 421	5 539	39 463	2 165	1 895
Chico, CA	9 010	7.0	39 971	227	3 349	786	241	810	1 733	2 441	5 185	315	241
Cincinnati, OH-KY-IN	101 960	3.3	47 254	84	55 933	8 748	3 987	7 264	17 415	17 149	75 932	4 372	3 987
Clarksville, TN-KY	10 834	3.8	38 554	258	5 248	1 261	466	739	1 872	2 175	7 715	385	466
Cleveland, TN	4 393	4.7	36 344	314	1 834	314	134	463	615	1 076	2 746	172	134
Cleveland-Elyria, OH	98 472	3.1	47 783	78	55 074	9 075	3 882	6 555	17 096	18 994	74 587	4 243	3 882
Coeur d'Alene, ID	5 804	5.5	38 605	256	2 184	371	198	447	1 248	1 216	3 201	218	198
College Station-Bryan, TX	8 919	5.3	35 797	325	4 388	879	277	954	1 644	1 401	6 498	301	277
Colorado Springs, CO	30 320	4.3	43 447	147	15 460	2 476	1 232	1 638	6 176	5 275	20 805	1 106	1 232
Columbia, MO	7 402	4.3	42 302	171	4 184	942	284	471	1 310	1 137	5 880	311	284
Columbia, SC	32 743	5.8	40 420	215	17 803	3 156	1 370	2 325	4 888	6 477	24 653	1 497	1 370
Columbus, GA-AL	11 447	3.7	36 484	310	6 515	1 328	505	395	2 620	2 715	8 743	480	505
Columbus, IN	3 699	3.8	45 575	99	2 718	408	201	214	597	624	3 541	212	201
Columbus, OH	94 148	4.9	46 570	87	54 942	9 585	3 666	7 171	13 437	14 835	75 364	3 980	3 666
Corpus Christi, TX	19 328	3.6	42 721	161	9 366	1 569	667	2 428	3 173	4 002	14 030	732	667
Corvallis, OR	3 650	6.1	41 676	188	1 839	348	155	242	895	550	2 584	157	155
Crestview-Fort Walton Beach-Destin, FL	12 149	4.4	46 340	91	5 783	1 145	465	636	3 487	2 217	8 028	458	465
Cumberland, MD-WV	3 683	2.8	36 836	302	1 560	325	131	165	595	1 159	2 180	146	131
Dallas-Fort Worth-Arlington, TX	362 948	5.7	51 099	47	202 776	25 516	13 826	50 688	59 000	42 257	292 806	14 958	13 826
Dallas-Plano-Irving, TX Div 19124	248 157	6.0	52 719	X	149 820	17 958	10 106	35 923	40 375	26 888	213 808	10 889	10 106
Fort Worth-Arlington, TX Div 23104	114 790	5.0	47 916	X	52 956	7 558	3 720	14 765	18 625	15 369	78 998	4 069	3 720
Dalton, GA	4 535	3.4	31 539	375	2 825	427	211	410	709	1 043	3 872	232	211
Danville, IL	2 825	-0.1	35 630	328	1 250	269	92	164	432	773	1 776	106	92
Daphne-Fairhope-Foley, AL	8 173	4.9	40 121	221	2 532	372	190	532	1 637	1 759	3 626	260	190
Davenport-Moline-Rock Island, IA-IL	17 039	2.0	44 418	126	9 032	1 503	651	1 008	3 191	3 273	12 194	734	651
Dayton, OH	34 205	3.4	42 707	162	18 457	3 456	1 352	2 014	5 870	7 241	25 278	1 427	1 352
Decatur, AL	5 416	2.5	35 472	333	2 281	384	170	317	837	1 345	3 152	214	170
Decatur, IL	4 762	1.9	44 383	128	2 710	455	199	363	780	1 041	3 727	216	199
Deltona-Daytona Beach-Ormond Beach, FL	23 808	5.7	38 197	267	7 553	1 232	542	1 082	5 442	6 566	10 409	783	542
Denver-Aurora-Lakewood, CO	157 532	4.1	55 975	22	88 839	9 949	6 237	19 460	29 394	17 825	124 486	6 912	6 237
Des Moines-West Des Moines, IA	30 781	4.5	49 415	65	18 715	2 582	1 361	2 293	5 198	4 112	24 952	1 534	1 361
Detroit-Warren-Dearborn, MI	201 741	4.9	46 894	86	110 751	14 766	8 301	15 152	33 028	40 125	148 970	9 274	8 301
Detroit-Dearborn-Livonia, MI Div 19804	NA	NA	NA	X	NA	NA	NA	NA	NA	NA	NA	NA	NA
Warren-Troy-Farmington Hills, MI Div 47664	NA	NA	NA	X	NA	NA	NA	NA	NA	NA	NA	NA	NA
Dothan, AL	5 464	2.7	36 879	300	2 294	380	169	405	919	1 430	3 248	217	169
Dover, DE	6 625	4.7	38 178	268	3 020	702	240	377	1 062	1 656	4 339	254	240
Dubuque, IA	4 273	2.8	43 997	136	2 548	385	191	272	865	768	3 396	218	191
Duluth, MN-WI	11 610	2.6	41 523	189	5 800	984	464	673	1 922	2 846	7 920	511	464
Durham-Chapel Hill, NC	26 250	4.6	47 513	81	18 553	2 837	1 336	1 909	5 218	3 871	24 634	1 454	1 336
East Stroudsburg, PA	6 330	3.9	38 043	271	2 390	566	197	395	906	1 377	3 547	211	197
Eau Claire, WI	7 168	2.9	43 276	153	3 649	682	284	604	1 291	1 299	5 218	314	284
El Centro, CA	6 052	5.3	33 584	362	2 488	752	179	784	761	1 628	4 203	202	179
Elizabethtown-Fort Knox, KY	5 596	1.8	37 656	281	2 658	624	225	326	966	1 323	3 833	215	225
Elkhart-Goshen, IN	8 115	5.3	39 882	229	5 850	934	461	800	1 211	1 479	8 045	471	461
Elmira, NY	3 496	2.8	40 149	220	1 701	426	140	156	478	908	2 424	135	140
El Paso, TX	27 349	4.9	32 598	369	13 176	2 777	1 008	2 050	4 377	6 381	19 012	971	1 008
Enid, OK	2 860	0.3	44 985	111	1 414	238	108	256	568	516	2 016	112	108
Erie, PA	11 240	3.8	40 425	214	5 455	1 192	444	696	1 829	2 768	7 787	460	444
Eugene, OR	14 469	6.6	39 871	230	6 493	1 056	590	1 208	2 909	3 512	9 347	613	590

1. Based on the resident population estimated as of July 1 of the year shown.

Table C. Metropolitan Areas — **Earnings, Social Security, and Housing**

Area name	Earnings, 2015 (cont.)									Social Security beneficiaries, December 2015		Housing units, 2016		
	Percent by selected industries													
	Farm	Mining	Construction	Manufacturing	Information, professional, scientific, technical services	Retail trade	Finance, insurance, real estate, rental and leasing	Health care and social assistance	Government	Number	Rate[1]	Supplemental Security Income recipients, December 2015	Total	Percent change, 2010-2016
	75	76	77	78	79	80	81	82	83	84	85	86	87	88
Cedar Rapids, IA	1.1	0.1	7.2	21.2	8.8	5.5	9.8	10.6	11.3	50 835	191	4 286	116 265	3.6
Chambersburg-Waynesboro, PA	2.6	0.1	5.7	17.9	4.6	7.6	3.3	14.7	16.7	35 510	232	2 499	64 409	1.9
Champaign-Urbana, IL	0.6	D	4.1	6.5	D	12.2	4.8	D	34.9	33 475	141	3 434	105 196	4.0
Charleston, WV	0.0	D	D	D	D	5.6	D	D	19.0	59 390	269	9 439	108 103	-0.1
Charleston-North Charleston, SC	0.0	0.1	6.6	10.1	12.0	6.6	8.5	9.5	23.1	131 390	176	13 370	324 372	8.7
Charlotte-Concord-Gastonia, NC-SC	0.4	0.1	6.7	9.0	D	5.7	D	D	11.8	404 580	167	42 977	1 005 693	7.4
Charlottesville, VA	0.1	0.2	5.2	3.6	D	4.6	6.5	9.7	34.5	42 255	185	3 302	101 675	5.5
Chattanooga, TN-GA	0.3	0.1	D	14.0	D	6.2	11.4	12.1	16.5	119 005	218	13 657	241 705	3.1
Cheyenne, WY	0.8	1.1	7.1	3.8	7.1	6.6	6.7	7.7	40.1	17 560	181	1 490	42 284	4.5
Chicago-Naperville-Elgin, IL-IN-WI	0.0	D	4.8	10.2	D	4.9	11.3	D	12.3	1 463 825	154	206 567	3 820 782	0.6
Chicago-Naperville-Arlington Heights, IL Div 16974	0.0	0.1	4.6	7.8	17.3	4.5	12.6	9.7	11.9	1 103 600	151	173 083	2 962 548	0.4
Elgin, IL Div 20994	-0.3	D	8.1	16.0	8.0	5.5	5.5	D	19.9	87 165	137	5 957	226 966	1.7
Gary, IN Div 23844	0.4	0.1	8.6	21.2	4.7	6.5	4.0	14.6	11.0	141 170	201	15 662	298 785	1.6
Lake County-Kenosha County, IL-WI Div 29404	0.1	0.0	3.8	22.6	9.3	7.1	6.3	7.0	13.1	131 890	151	11 865	332 483	0.9
Chico, CA	3.6	0.1	6.5	5.1	6.6	9.0	5.9	20.1	22.6	51 035	227	11 390	98 430	2.7
Cincinnati, OH-KY-IN	0.0	D	5.6	D	10.3	5.5	8.7	12.3	11.6	386 085	179	48 734	925 049	1.5
Clarksville, TN-KY	0.5	0.4	4.2	8.9	3.8	5.4	3.1	D	50.7	42 240	150	6 140	117 096	9.1
Cleveland, TN	1.7	0.1	7.7	23.5	3.2	7.3	3.9	D	12.0	28 570	237	3 164	51 986	5.3
Cleveland-Elyria, OH	0.1	D	4.8	13.7	10.9	5.0	8.1	14.3	14.0	417 685	203	63 160	958 460	0.3
Coeur d'Alene, ID	0.1	0.7	9.0	8.7	7.1	10.6	7.0	12.5	21.0	35 530	236	2 682	68 281	8.1
College Station-Bryan, TX	1.1	5.1	6.5	4.7	D	6.7	5.1	D	33.4	29 140	117	4 712	104 384	9.9
Colorado Springs, CO	0.0	D	6.3	D	15.8	6.2	6.2	9.6	32.5	105 505	151	9 237	285 558	7.6
Columbia, MO	0.1	0.0	4.5	4.5	7.8	7.0	6.9	11.2	36.3	25 230	145	2 692	75 719	8.9
Columbia, SC	0.3	0.2	4.8	10.8	D	6.1	D	9.3	25.5	147 540	182	16 321	349 045	5.3
Columbus, GA-AL	0.3	D	3.0	D	6.4	5.0	D	D	37.5	58 710	188	10 249	133 373	4.0
Columbus, IN	0.3	D	3.7	48.5	5.0	4.0	3.9	7.1	9.2	16 305	201	1 255	33 886	2.4
Columbus, OH	0.2	0.1	4.6	8.2	D	5.6	9.4	10.8	18.2	306 855	152	45 398	851 473	3.7
Corpus Christi, TX	0.3	D	12.3	9.9	6.9	6.1	5.1	D	17.8	80 175	177	15 634	192 902	5.5
Corvallis, OR	1.3	0.1	3.4	11.2	11.4	4.7	3.8	16.0	31.0	14 940	169	994	37 786	4.2
Crestview-Fort Walton Beach-Destin, FL	0.2	0.1	4.3	3.6	11.2	8.0	5.6	7.9	38.2	53 575	204	4 123	145 996	6.1
Cumberland, MD-WV	-0.1	0.3	4.4	13.9	D	7.4	4.0	D	24.6	24 215	242	3 071	46 220	-0.3
Dallas-Fort Worth-Arlington, TX	0.1	5.2	6.9	9.2	13.9	5.9	10.7	D	10.2	894 985	126	130 969	2 740 871	8.4
Dallas-Plano-Irving, TX Div 19124	0.0	4.2	6.5	8.3	16.5	5.7	11.8	9.3	9.6	563 870	120	88 589	1 821 480	9.9
Fort Worth-Arlington, TX Div 23104	0.1	7.9	8.2	11.6	7.2	6.4	7.8	9.3	11.8	331 115	138	42 380	919 391	5.5
Dalton, GA	1.1	D	2.0	35.3	D	7.4	4.0	D	10.1	26 675	186	3 710	55 330	-1.0
Danville, IL	0.7	D	3.2	21.9	2.3	6.7	5.0	9.7	22.5	18 715	237	2 789	35 888	-1.2
Daphne-Fairhope-Foley, AL	0.5	0.3	8.9	6.9	5.8	12.8	6.9	13.0	14.4	50 340	247	3 510	110 608	6.3
Davenport-Moline-Rock Island, IA-IL	0.2	D	7.2	15.4	D	6.2	5.5	11.8	16.2	79 300	207	7 540	169 011	1.1
Dayton, OH	0.1	0.1	4.5	12.3	11.8	5.4	5.5	15.3	22.6	163 035	204	20 476	367 986	0.2
Decatur, AL	1.5	D	7.9	30.4	D	6.6	4.1	D	14.9	36 995	243	4 789	66 860	0.7
Decatur, IL	0.6	0.0	7.3	30.8	4.7	5.0	4.2	12.5	10.7	24 915	232	3 276	50 241	-0.5
Deltona-Daytona Beach-Ormond Beach, FL	0.4	D	5.6	7.3	8.6	10.2	5.9	17.9	15.0	180 585	290	13 926	308 512	1.9
Denver-Aurora-Lakewood, CO	0.0	6.5	6.5	5.0	17.4	4.6	D	8.3	12.3	375 295	134	36 329	1 149 023	6.5
Des Moines-West Des Moines, IA	0.6	D	7.1	5.9	9.9	5.6	22.0	10.4	12.9	98 185	158	9 002	263 361	9.6
Detroit-Warren-Dearborn, MI	0.1	0.1	4.7	14.6	D	5.5	8.4	11.9	9.9	869 975	202	133 705	1 899 233	0.7
Detroit-Dearborn-Livonia, MI Div 19804	NA	NA	NA	NA	NA	NA	NA	NA	NA	356 595	203	84 892	814 282	-0.9
Warren-Troy-Farmington Hills, MI Div 47664	NA	NA	NA	NA	NA	NA	NA	NA	NA	513 380	202	48 813	1 084 951	1.9
Dothan, AL	2.6	D	5.7	7.3	D	9.7	4.8	D	18.8	37 495	253	5 937	68 517	2.4
Dover, DE	2.3	D	4.6	D	4.7	7.4	5.5	12.3	37.9	35 740	206	3 472	69 761	6.7
Dubuque, IA	1.8	D	6.2	20.0	8.2	6.1	10.4	14.0	8.4	20 540	212	1 583	40 880	5.0
Duluth, MN-WI	0.0	5.6	7.0	6.9	5.9	6.9	4.7	20.7	19.6	64 020	229	6 912	142 592	0.7
Durham-Chapel Hill, NC	0.4	0.0	2.6	15.6	16.1	3.6	6.6	15.4	19.9	89 660	163	9 808	239 780	7.7
East Stroudsburg, PA	0.0	0.2	5.2	14.6	3.1	8.3	2.9	12.1	26.1	34 705	208	3 045	80 756	0.5
Eau Claire, WI	1.4	D	6.4	14.8	5.2	8.4	5.2	18.9	15.6	33 775	204	3 159	71 526	3.2
El Centro, CA	12.7	0.9	3.6	1.7	2.3	7.9	2.6	6.0	38.8	30 815	171	10 421	57 384	2.3
Elizabethtown-Fort Knox, KY	0.3	D	4.1	14.5	D	6.0	D	D	42.8	29 445	198	4 399	64 762	5.8
Elkhart-Goshen, IN	1.0	D	3.5	49.1	2.6	4.2	2.9	7.8	6.0	35 415	174	3 058	78 179	0.5
Elmira, NY	0.0	1.8	4.7	16.5	3.8	7.2	5.5	15.6	25.0	21 295	244	3 144	38 320	-0.1
El Paso, TX	0.1	D	D	D	D	7.8	D	9.9	37.1	124 865	149	30 043	295 173	8.6
Enid, OK	1.0	14.8	8.2	7.6	6.8	6.3	5.1	10.5	16.7	12 415	196	1 303	26 885	0.2
Erie, PA	0.2	0.2	4.6	21.8	4.6	6.7	7.7	17.4	16.0	62 080	223	11 172	120 087	0.8
Eugene, OR	0.6	0.2	5.9	9.8	8.9	8.1	6.7	16.4	18.8	82 335	227	9 236	159 693	2.3

1. Per 1,000 resident population estimated as of July 1, 2011 of the year shown.

Table C. Metropolitan Areas — **Housing, Labor Force, and Employment**

Area name	Housing units, 2015								Civilian labor force, 2016				Civilian employment⁵, 2015		
	Occupied units										Unemployment			Percent	
	Owner-occupied					Renter-occupied									
				Median owner cost as a percent of income											
	Total	Percent	Median value¹	With a mortgage	Without a mortgage²	Median rent³	Median rent as a percent of income	Percent with a computer	Total	Percent change, 2015–2016	Total	Rate⁴	Total employed	Management, professional, and related occupations	Construction, production, and related occupations
	89	90	91	92	93	94	95	96	97	98	99	100	101	102	103
Cedar Rapids, IA	107 586	73.2	149 000	20.0	11.8	699	28.0	86.5	143 459	-1.0	5 393	3.8	140 190	37.2	25.4
Chambersburg-Waynesboro, PA...........	59 486	71.3	175 200	22.1	11.7	829	22.4	82.5	77 872	-0.1	4 021	5.2	72 851	29.2	28.5
Champaign-Urbana, IL........	92 268	57.6	152 600	20.0	10.3	854	30.0	90.8	120 140	0.4	6 151	5.1	116 838	44.9	18.6
Charleston, WV	94 533	68.9	104 100	18.4	10.0	692	27.0	82.0	96 892	-0.9	5 657	5.8	89 735	36.7	18.4
Charleston-North Charleston, SC	273 722	65.5	210 400	22.4	11.6	1 034	28.9	88.1	373 518	2.5	15 455	4.1	358 859	38.0	20.1
Charlotte-Concord-Gastonia, NC-SC	905 696	64.6	173 900	20.2	10.2	915	29.0	89.3	1 282 617	3.4	60 914	4.7	1 179 781	38.3	21.9
Charlottesville, VA	87 949	65.2	271 900	22.0	10.0	1 106	28.9	90.1	115 519	0.5	4 073	3.5	115 424	47.9	14.4
Chattanooga, TN-GA	209 340	67.1	150 300	20.3	10.5	744	28.5	83.0	260 045	2.5	12 854	4.9	251 262	34.2	22.9
Cheyenne, WY	37 740	65.4	204 500	20.6	10.9	926	28.2	89.9	48 880	0.2	2 011	4.1	45 849	37.3	25.1
Chicago-Naperville-Elgin, IL-IN-WI	3 470 993	63.2	224 300	23.1	14.1	1 012	30.4	87.6	4 926 476	0.8	286 615	5.8	4 672 798	38.6	20.3
Chicago-Naperville-Arlington Heights, IL Div 16974	2 686 830	61.3	234 700	23.6	14.5	1 033	30.6	87.0	3 801 497	0.8	224 718	5.9	3 607 889	39.5	19.2
Elgin, IL Div 20994	212 458	68.2	215 800	22.9	13.7	1 008	29.6	91.3	322 906	0.1	17 805	5.5	316 681	34.1	25.4
Gary, IN Div 23844	266 576	70.4	147 800	20.5	10.8	847	29.8	84.9	342 021	1.2	20 390	6.0	313 152	31.4	28.4
Lake County-Kenosha County, IL-WI Div 29404	305 129	70.9	232 300	22.2	14.4	1 015	29.9	92.4	460 052	0.8	23 702	5.2	435 076	39.7	20.0
Chico, CA	85 289	57.5	246 700	24.0	11.5	942	36.8	87.9	102 319	1.0	6 693	6.5	92 602	37.3	16.9
Cincinnati, OH-KY-IN	832 607	65.4	159 200	19.9	11.8	775	28.2	88.0	1 083 434	0.9	46 628	4.3	1 049 469	39.6	20.1
Clarksville, TN-KY	101 265	56.3	140 600	20.6	10.0	874	28.6	87.8	109 838	0.9	5 936	5.4	106 849	32.6	27.5
Cleveland, TN	46 389	62.7	149 000	19.8	10.0	707	30.0	78.9	57 991	2.1	2 712	4.7	52 963	31.9	30.7
Cleveland-Elyria, OH	849 475	64.5	143 100	20.6	12.9	746	29.2	84.8	1 028 327	0.3	54 395	5.3	980 254	37.5	20.3
Coeur d'Alene, ID	58 675	69.9	197 700	23.4	11.0	865	31.1	90.0	73 499	2.4	3 501	4.8	69 862	33.1	21.8
College Station-Bryan, TX	90 526	49.5	166 300	19.8	10.0	860	33.5	89.7	125 628	2.0	4 515	3.6	121 751	39.9	19.0
Colorado Springs, CO........	261 435	61.8	234 100	21.6	10.0	1 049	30.5	92.7	326 527	2.1	12 365	3.8	320 538	39.4	17.1
Columbia, MO	69 152	55.8	181 000	20.2	10.1	769	32.1	93.4	99 372	-0.2	3 227	3.2	90 460	48.3	13.1
Columbia, SC	302 634	66.6	147 500	20.4	10.0	857	30.7	86.0	402 725	0.9	18 245	4.5	381 265	37.7	19.4
Columbus, GA-AL	112 983	52.2	138 900	22.6	11.8	818	31.3	82.1	124 045	-0.2	7 975	6.4	123 789	32.6	23.8
Columbus, IN	31 131	71.2	136 800	19.3	10.8	844	22.0	87.1	44 457	1.9	1 502	3.4	40 420	38.5	27.3
Columbus, OH	772 304	60.5	166 600	20.5	12.1	869	28.2	89.0	1 050 959	1.3	43 025	4.1	1 011 096	41.5	18.1
Corpus Christi, TX	161 634	57.3	123 900	20.4	12.8	924	29.3	85.3	205 649	0.1	12 278	6.0	202 524	28.7	26.4
Corvallis, OR	35 062	58.2	275 800	21.6	11.0	885	34.1	93.1	46 888	3.2	1 837	3.9	41 755	52.6	13.2
Crestview-Fort Walton Beach-Destin, FL	102 729	62.9	203 500	22.3	10.6	1 041	31.5	87.7	122 288	2.4	4 984	4.1	112 924	36.2	17.0
Cumberland, MD-WV...........	39 120	65.7	119 400	19.2	12.2	659	31.3	72.6	44 284	0.7	2 662	6.0	39 185	27.2	24.4
Dallas-Fort Worth-Arlington, TX	2 479 995	59.3	172 500	21.4	11.8	992	28.8	90.3	3 684 676	3.2	141 820	3.8	3 513 490	38.1	21.3
Dallas-Plano-Irving, TX Div 19124	1 653 468	57.7	189 000	21.8	11.9	1 009	28.7	90.0	2 482 227	3.8	93 515	3.8	2 356 544	39.5	20.1
Fort Worth-Arlington, TX Div 23104	826 527	62.4	153 700	20.8	11.7	963	29.3	90.8	1 202 449	2.0	48 305	4.0	1 156 946	35.4	23.8
Dalton, GA	48 631	64.6	125 600	20.2	10.0	673	26.2	83.4	62 621	1.6	3 860	6.2	65 596	18.2	48.1
Danville, IL	30 927	67.0	73 800	17.6	10.0	649	25.2	78.9	34 974	-1.5	2 528	7.2	31 947	25.8	31.8
Daphne-Fairhope-Foley, AL..	72 269	73.7	177 800	21.2	10.0	914	26.6	88.6	89 931	2.5	4 870	5.4	87 864	32.7	18.0
Davenport-Moline-Rock Island, IA-IL	155 753	70.4	128 900	19.2	11.3	712	27.5	83.5	191 559	-0.9	10 553	5.5	184 536	31.8	27.6
Dayton, OH	330 430	63.0	124 500	20.0	12.3	748	28.7	87.0	382 690	0.3	17 830	4.7	369 610	37.4	21.4
Decatur, AL	60 697	73.1	125 700	19.3	10.0	597	27.1	82.5	69 060	-0.1	4 062	5.9	63 109	30.3	32.6
Decatur, IL	44 429	67.5	98 200	18.2	10.6	630	28.3	82.1	50 325	-0.6	3 328	6.6	47 989	34.3	23.9
Deltona-Daytona Beach-Ormond Beach, FL	248 938	70.4	151 000	25.3	12.8	958	35.5	88.4	290 610	3.1	15 020	5.2	248 236	32.0	20.0
Denver-Aurora-Lakewood, CO	1 075 919	62.9	314 400	21.1	10.0	1 184	29.4	92.6	1 541 195	2.1	48 155	3.1	1 498 349	42.9	17.3
Des Moines-West Des Moines, IA	242 022	68.4	164 700	19.0	11.9	825	27.7	90.7	343 853	1.0	11 633	3.4	329 295	39.8	19.8
Detroit-Warren-Dearborn, MI	1 674 251	68.0	151 000	20.0	13.0	871	31.1	87.1	2 066 593	2.1	110 986	5.4	1 959 298	37.6	21.4
Detroit-Dearborn-Livonia, MI Div 19804	667 521	61.3	92 400	20.8	14.2	809	33.5	83.4	773 086	1.8	49 298	6.4	712 421	31.4	24.9
Warren-Troy-Farmington Hills, MI Div 47664.......	1 006 730	72.5	178 400	19.7	12.1	931	29.2	89.5	1 293 507	2.3	61 688	4.8	1 246 877	41.2	19.5
Dothan, AL	55 973	66.4	120 500	20.4	10.7	671	27.9	78.8	62 385	0.1	3 717	6.0	60 847	31.6	26.2
Dover, DE	62 477	67.8	215 200	21.8	10.9	995	31.9	88.3	77 541	1.2	3 681	4.7	77 287	32.0	23.1
Dubuque, IA	37 784	71.9	161 700	18.6	11.6	693	24.9	86.4	55 049	-1.3	1 991	3.6	50 502	37.5	21.4
Duluth, MN-WI	116 212	72.1	147 300	20.5	11.5	686	28.2	84.4	142 305	0.2	8 115	5.7	138 618	34.3	22.3
Durham-Chapel Hill, NC	215 294	58.3	204 700	19.5	11.4	915	28.7	89.3	288 706	2.7	12 893	4.5	283 410	48.0	17.7
East Stroudsburg, PA	55 681	77.3	166 700	28.0	15.1	977	32.2	88.5	81 990	1.4	5 185	6.3	78 375	31.2	21.7
Eau Claire, WI	63 854	69.0	151 500	20.1	13.0	763	30.1	86.2	92 186	0.9	3 527	3.8	86 515	34.9	25.2
El Centro, CA	45 158	56.3	169 000	24.5	12.2	783	35.9	83.8	76 863	-1.6	18 079	23.5	59 958	24.6	24.2
Elizabethtown-Fort Knox, KY	56 899	65.4	141 500	21.4	10.0	748	27.0	87.9	65 272	2.1	2 954	4.5	64 449	26.0	31.3
Elkhart-Goshen, IN	68 498	69.0	134 900	18.9	10.0	729	27.9	81.0	107 999	3.0	3 768	3.5	92 706	25.5	39.9
Elmira, NY	34 546	71.1	98 600	18.9	11.2	750	30.3	85.0	36 376	-3.2	2 060	5.7	39 100	34.2	22.3
El Paso, TX	261 529	61.5	113 900	22.0	10.8	757	27.8	81.3	350 766	2.6	17 339	4.9	343 700	29.0	22.8
Enid, OK	NA	NA	NA	NA	NA	NA	NA	NA	29 953	-0.6	1 298	4.3	NA	NA	NA
Erie, PA	110 138	64.1	121 800	19.3	12.1	701	29.5	85.8	134 326	-0.4	8 807	6.6	127 249	34.0	23.0
Eugene, OR	146 602	58.3	235 800	24.1	11.6	881	34.0	89.9	179 242	3.9	9 230	5.1	165 490	35.6	20.9

1. Specified owner-occupied units. 2. A value of 10.0 represents 10 percent or less. 3. Specified renter-occupied units. 4. Percent of civilian labor force.
5. Civilian employed persons 16 years old and over.

Table C. Metropolitan Areas — Nonfarm Employment and Agriculture

Area name	Number of establish-ments	Employment Total	Health care and social assistance	Manufac-turing	Retail trade	Finance and insurance	Professional, scientific, and technical services	Annual payroll Total (mil dol)	Average per employee (dollars)	Farms Number	Percent with: Fewer than 50 acres	500 acres or more	Farm operators whose principal occu-pation is farming (percent)
	104	105	106	107	108	109	110	111	112	113	114	115	116
Cedar Rapids, IA	6 472	129 661	17 376	18 424	17 190	11 096	6 282	5 978	46 101	3 678	32.5	19.9	55.6
Chambersburg-Waynesboro, PA...........	3 048	49 464	8 173	8 312	7 588	1 144	1 716	1 819	36 779	1 596	35.9	6.3	60.8
Champaign-Urbana, IL........	4 900	75 399	14 034	8 007	11 326	3 230	2 979	3 013	39 955	2 284	28.5	32.7	56.8
Charleston, WV...................	5 343	89 688	19 394	3 366	12 201	4 823	5 473	3 884	43 308	343	29.2	1.7	40.5
Charleston-North Charles-ton, SC.........................	17 916	262 866	36 035	24 039	39 038	7 829	19 112	11 168	42 486	1 143	56.3	7.0	45.2
Charlotte-Concord-Gastonia, NC-SC.........................	57 660	988 186	126 660	95 255	119 774	80 992	61 844	51 678	52 296	7 328	50.8	4.6	44.6
Charlottesville, VA...............	6 043	82 306	18 000	4 268	11 634	4 018	6 242	3 968	48 211	2 311	33.3	8.0	43.4
Chattanooga, TN-GA	11 213	215 347	31 815	33 725	26 566	12 961	9 082	8 762	40 689	2 018	44.2	5.0	43.8
Cheyenne, WY	3 139	35 530	7 511	1 273	6 226	1 620	2 317	1 413	39 761	1 116	33.5	31.2	37.3
Chicago-Naperville-Elgin, IL-IN-WI	243 420	4 120 166	590 677	384 784	470 112	259 724	338 120	236 637	57 434	6 841	47.6	18.3	56.1
Chicago-Naperville-Arling-ton Heights, IL Div 16974	NA	NA	NA	NA	NA	NA	NA	NA	NA	2 789	48.8	16.7	58.6
Elgin, IL Div 20994	NA	NA	NA	NA	NA	NA	NA	NA	NA	1 470	40.2	22.6	63.2
Gary, IN Div 23844	NA	NA	NA	NA	NA	NA	NA	NA	NA	1 874	45.0	21.5	48.8
Lake County-Kenosha County, IL-WI Div 29404	NA	NA	NA	NA	NA	NA	NA	NA	NA	708	65.4	7.8	51.4
Chico, CA.........................	4 663	59 475	14 232	4 534	10 954	2 405	2 398	2 177	36 612	2 056	66.8	7.0	59.4
Cincinnati, OH-KY-IN	45 916	907 677	142 003	98 582	105 975	57 065	57 917	45 510	50 138	9 242	46.3	4.5	40.7
Clarksville, TN-KY...............	4 328	68 582	11 199	12 332	11 991	2 015	2 376	2 316	33 775	2 359	31.5	9.6	41.3
Cleveland, TN	2 133	39 401	5 295	8 091	5 301	1 884	746	1 457	36 968	1 062	49.4	4.8	44.9
Cleveland-Elyria, OH	51 551	923 418	177 460	120 958	101 713	51 269	52 973	44 732	48 442	2 975	59.3	3.6	49.1
Coeur d'Alene, ID	4 513	47 532	9 300	5 019	8 390	2 094	2 148	1 781	37 466	824	58.4	6.7	48.1
College Station-Bryan, TX	4 744	70 268	9 902	5 904	11 946	1 728	3 611	2 456	34 947	4 361	35.0	10.1	44.6
Colorado Springs, CO..........	17 221	232 291	36 192	11 442	32 223	10 563	20 478	10 163	43 752	1 329	45.4	17.6	48.5
Columbia, MO	4 649	75 408	17 295	4 115	13 056	6 843	3 956	2 813	37 299	1 171	39.5	8.6	38.3
Columbia, SC.....................	16 921	284 984	43 882	26 466	38 613	21 735	18 159	11 754	41 245	3 085	44.1	7.2	42.0
Columbus, GA-AL................	5 663	95 823	16 267	10 656	14 224	12 846	3 118	3 713	38 747	770	32.2	13.1	42.2
Columbus, IN	1 821	46 808	4 732	12 257	4 663	1 068	3 098	2 238	47 810	623	44.1	14.4	44.8
Columbus, OH	41 361	836 802	139 529	64 588	100 258	72 301	52 753	40 663	48 593	8 198	47.4	9.9	43.1
Corpus Christi, TX	9 490	163 715	30 953	10 949	22 369	4 688	8 172	6 893	42 101	1 555	45.8	20.6	38.6
Corvallis, OR......................	2 111	25 919	5 819	1 896	3 797	607	2 128	1 091	42 075	886	71.4	5.6	46.3
Crestview-Fort Walton Beach-Destin, FL	7 243	78 046	10 784	2 000	16 597	2 556	6 735	2 818	36 102	1 147	46.7	5.8	41.9
Cumberland, MD-WV...........	2 005	31 188	7 532	3 597	4 868	979	1 601	1 067	34 203	720	32.9	5.3	37.2
Dallas-Fort Worth-Arlington, TX	156 111	2 954 801	363 624	242 805	343 154	205 329	225 506	161 197	54 554	29 659	61.7	4.8	35.8
Dallas-Plano-Irving, TX Div 19124	NA	NA	NA	NA	NA	NA	NA	NA	NA	16 257	61.9	4.6	35.6
Fort Worth-Arlington, TX Div 23104....................	NA	NA	NA	NA	NA	NA	NA	NA	NA	13 402	61.5	4.9	36.1
Dalton, GA	2 545	56 250	4 941	22 294	5 573	780	1 769	2 204	39 175	698	46.7	3.2	44.6
Danville, IL	1 426	24 983	5 453	4 913	3 855	1 155	430	969	38 775	956	36.6	29.5	54.5
Daphne-Fairhope-Foley, AL..	5 127	58 868	7 507	4 248	13 794	1 590	1 927	1 887	32 059	989	52.6	8.1	45.8
Davenport-Moline-Rock Island, IA-IL.................	8 883	159 359	24 026	24 308	22 271	5 828	6 464	7 039	44 171	3 513	34.0	19.0	55.7
Dayton, OH	16 576	318 802	62 863	42 624	40 259	11 496	24 817	14 149	44 382	2 638	59.4	8.7	41.3
Decatur, AL........................	2 951	44 878	6 442	11 980	6 384	1 495	1 469	1 843	41 073	2 788	42.7	4.1	42.7
Decatur, IL.........................	2 461	45 585	8 070	6 635	5 915	1 525	1 167	1 948	42 738	674	35.9	29.5	59.1
Deltona-Daytona Beach-Ormond Beach, FL	14 380	158 021	30 214	9 181	29 413	5 165	7 361	5 498	34 794	1 481	78.8	3.4	55.0
Denver-Aurora-Lakewood, CO.................................	80 560	1 211 011	154 450	55 300	139 858	71 819	105 773	67 827	56 009	4 856	52.4	14.4	43.8
Des Moines-West Des Moines, IA	15 629	307 055	41 399	19 197	40 252	48 454	17 705	14 988	48 813	4 898	41.1	16.0	44.2
Detroit-Warren-Dearborn, MI	98 561	1 709 983	266 708	226 099	205 523	77 072	169 769	90 896	53 156	4 242	56.9	5.8	54.0
Detroit-Dearborn-Livonia, MI Div 19804	NA	NA	NA	NA	NA	NA	NA	NA	NA	287	77.7	1.4	59.9
Warren-Troy-Farmington Hills, MI Div 47664.......	NA	NA	NA	NA	NA	NA	NA	NA	NA	3 955	55.3	6.1	53.5
Dothan, AL........................	3 402	49 354	10 223	5 084	9 007	1 343	1 335	1 880	38 094	2 331	31.5	12.2	43.5
Dover, DE..........................	3 323	51 662	10 568	4 609	9 216	1 453	2 404	1 954	37 832	863	54.5	9.0	56.8
Dubuque, IA.......................	2 762	55 142	7 879	9 172	7 261	3 680	2 475	2 269	41 147	1 462	28.3	10.3	52.5
Duluth, MN-WI	7 071	109 624	28 531	7 149	16 217	4 082	4 076	4 453	40 621	1 550	25.4	6.1	41.0
Durham-Chapel Hill, NC	12 362	241 065	46 050	17 124	25 238	10 972	31 217	13 886	57 605	2 410	48.6	4.0	46.7
East Stroudsburg, PA	3 368	44 970	7 144	5 290	9 522	975	1 549	1 651	36 723	283	53.0	2.5	55.1
Eau Claire, WI	4 274	72 853	14 331	11 183	10 913	2 978	2 741	2 815	38 646	3 070	30.4	7.2	45.1
El Centro, CA.....................	2 494	33 153	5 025	3 612	8 719	838	796	1 064	32 103	421	29.7	40.6	69.4
Elizabethtown-Fort Knox, KY	2 932	40 291	8 136	6 924	6 584	1 567	1 626	1 452	36 035	2 831	44.0	5.5	44.5
Elkhart-Goshen, IN	4 866	123 927	10 868	63 752	9 233	2 094	1 959	5 353	43 192	1 724	62.8	3.9	38.3
Elmira, NY.........................	1 806	31 597	6 613	5 576	5 288	960	774	1 233	39 031	372	27.2	4.3	53.8
El Paso, TX........................	14 208	229 609	44 605	12 967	39 249	6 514	10 539	7 297	31 779	824	67.7	17.0	43.9
Enid, OK...........................	NA	NA	NA	NA	NA	NA	NA	NA	NA				
Erie, PA............................	6 163	114 164	24 363	20 764	15 674	5 160	3 681	4 394	38 486	1 422	41.2	4.1	48.7
Eugene, OR........................	9 696	123 022	23 373	13 710	19 813	4 732	5 041	4 826	39 231	2 660	73.9	2.9	44.5

Table C. Metropolitan Areas — **Agriculture**

Area name	Land in farms					Value of land and buildings (dollars)		Value of machinery and equipment, average per farm (dollars)	Value of products sold				Percent of farms with sales of:		Government payments	
	Acreage (1,000)	Percent change, 2007–2012	Acres			Average per farm	Average per acre		Total (mil dol)	Average per farm (dollars)	Percent from:		$10,000 or more	$100,000 or more	Total ($1,000)	Percent of farms
			Average size of farm	Total irrigated (1,000)	Total cropland (1,000)						Crops	Live-stock and poultry products				
	117	118	119	120	121	122	123	124	125	126	127	128	129	130	131	132
Cedar Rapids, IA	1 075	1.4	292	0.4	930.0	2 020 529	6 910	203 111	918.4	249 694	69.5	30.5	63.3	38.3	28 988	76.7
Chambersburg-Waynesboro, PA	265	9.0	166	2.8	201.8	1 101 504	6 646	133 634	413.8	259 277	21.6	78.4	66.3	40.4	4 302	34.1
Champaign-Urbana, IL	1 184	8.8	518	19.6	1 140.6	4 153 230	8 014	311 067	802.9	351 514	92.5	7.5	73.2	50.6	21 102	84.3
Charleston, WV	48	5.0	141	D	6.4	285 079	2 024	31 985	1.9	5 522	32.7	67.3	15.2	0.3	D	7.6
Charleston-North Charleston, SC	185	16.1	162	4.0	62.8	651 877	4 027	59 942	D	D	D	52.2	27.9	7.1	1 317	18.1
Charlotte-Concord-Gastonia, NC-SC	939	2.4	128	5.0	437.2	717 330	5 599	71 406	D	D	D	D	31.1	10.8	D	13.6
Charlottesville, VA	407	4.8	176	2.5	114.7	1 095 125	6 216	61 828	101.3	43 836	40.3	59.7	35.3	5.0	871	13.3
Chattanooga, TN-GA	267	2.2	132	D	94.7	532 958	4 035	67 110	213.6	105 852	10.7	89.3	31.1	9.0	1 684	11.3
Cheyenne, WY	1 676	-0.9	1 502	59.3	338.1	1 079 159	719	110 585	190.7	170 918	24.4	75.6	37.0	17.6	4 938	32.7
Chicago-Naperville-Elgin, IL-IN-WI	2 232	-2.6	326	D	2 069.2	2 377 211	7 285	210 709	2 187.2	319 717	75.5	24.5	57.9	36.1	44 738	55.3
Chicago-Naperville-Arlington Heights, IL Div 16974	831	-0.5	298	D	776.8	2 382 011	7 995	200 859	604.2	216 622	89.5	10.5	58.1	33.3	14 208	51.8
Elgin, IL Div 20994	566	0.6	385	5.1	537.8	3 142 503	8 157	253 384	671.1	456 510	74.7	25.3	66.4	48.0	16 157	63.7
Gary, IN Div 23844	728	-5.9	389	45.5	664.5	2 295 203	5 904	227 225	807.7	430 977	66.3	33.7	55.1	36.6	12 509	64.2
Lake County-Kenosha County, IL-WI Div 29404	107	-10.3	151	0.7	90.1	986 410	6 547	117 194	104.3	147 323	70.9	29.1	47.2	21.6	1 864	28.2
Chico, CA	381	1.9	185	199.7	227.3	1 408 199	7 599	135 591	541.3	263 266	97.3	2.7	59.7	26.2	9 386	13.7
Cincinnati, OH-KY-IN	1 216	-5.6	132	D	698.5	582 601	4 427	73 512	418.6	45 298	82.2	17.8	31.2	7.8	14 347	34.1
Clarksville, TN-KY	637	0.5	270	5.5	401.2	958 646	3 552	104 747	280.3	118 814	80.1	19.9	43.1	15.8	9 847	46.5
Cleveland, TN	122	-4.6	115	0.2	44.8	593 111	5 157	61 272	153.7	144 771	6.4	93.6	31.5	12.4	397	9.4
Cleveland-Elyria, OH	304	3.1	102	4.4	217.0	614 628	6 011	86 924	375.3	126 146	83.2	16.8	42.2	13.4	3 173	19.7
Coeur d'Alene, ID	124	-5.1	151	13.8	64.3	624 138	4 139	57 726	23.7	28 750	83.8	16.2	19.5	4.1	1 075	20.1
College Station-Bryan, TX	1 102	0.9	253	46.6	231.0	736 281	2 914	63 936	321.5	73 722	24.9	75.1	32.1	5.4	5 786	11.1
Colorado Springs, CO	720	4.4	542	8.3	57.0	696 877	1 287	43 971	45.2	33 977	46.2	53.8	23.9	4.8	1 334	10.2
Columbia, MO	241	-7.0	206	5.3	144.4	749 119	3 644	69 631	52.2	44 565	66.0	34.0	34.9	8.1	1 837	31.0
Columbia, SC	522	3.0	169	D	198.1	537 771	3 177	78 787	578.6	187 568	26.8	73.2	29.9	11.0	4 185	19.8
Columbus, GA-AL	206	-3.8	267	5.7	51.8	724 603	2 715	63 508	58.6	76 142	D	D	25.8	6.0	1 166	26.8
Columbus, IN	172	3.2	275	13.5	153.4	1 619 191	5 878	151 406	95.6	153 387	89.5	10.5	54.9	27.1	4 647	63.7
Columbus, OH	1 746	5.0	213	2.9	1 448.9	1 049 293	4 928	131 542	1 180.0	143 942	76.3	23.7	42.8	18.9	28 755	43.7
Corpus Christi, TX	938	0.9	603	6.0	612.9	949 925	1 575	166 062	172.2	110 713	85.3	14.8	31.6	12.9	9 227	35.0
Corvallis, OR	124	8.2	140	11.3	68.2	830 059	5 932	68 867	103.3	116 597	78.2	21.8	28.6	10.4	486	6.4
Crestview-Fort Walton Beach-Destin, FL	209	8.7	183	1.5	49.3	565 418	3 097	49 066	38.8	33 870	49.0	51.0	22.1	5.3	1 802	27.6
Cumberland, MD-WV	112	-1.9	156	0.1	28.5	493 965	3 163	50 556	25.4	35 232	13.4	86.6	25.8	3.8	510	19.7
Dallas-Fort Worth-Arlington, TX	4 075	10.8	137	29.3	1 275.6	585 215	4 260	50 241	743.8	25 077	46.4	53.6	19.6	2.8	10 166	7.2
Dallas-Plano-Irving, TX Div 19124	2 203	9.1	136	18.2	853.9	558 320	4 120	49 299	483.1	29 718	53.6	46.4	19.4	2.9	7 646	9.0
Fort Worth-Arlington, TX Div 23104	1 872	12.9	140	11.1	421.7	617 838	4 424	51 384	260.7	19 449	33.3	66.7	19.9	2.7	2 520	4.9
Dalton, GA	86	4.1	123	0.6	29.3	560 004	4 542	73 451	222.9	319 338	5.8	94.2	37.8	17.3	358	11.6
Danville, IL	434	-5.0	454	0.2	409.5	3 200 276	7 043	259 283	283.6	296 653	95.7	4.3	60.4	41.8	7 122	76.2
Daphne-Fairhope-Foley, AL	192	1.3	194	7.7	100.9	773 980	3 980	107 905	135.6	137 070	85.3	14.7	35.2	11.7	2 649	26.7
Davenport-Moline-Rock Island, IA-IL	1 101	-10.0	313	21.3	970.1	2 141 963	6 834	206 181	964.4	274 514	77.8	22.2	59.6	39.0	28 824	74.8
Dayton, OH	454	-3.5	172	4.2	394.2	1 006 136	5 845	111 095	282.7	107 154	89.5	10.5	44.1	17.8	6 976	51.1
Decatur, AL	396	3.2	142	5.0	167.3	471 748	3 318	68 907	301.3	108 081	23.3	76.7	32.3	11.8	6 226	31.2
Decatur, IL	337	15.8	499	0.0	321.7	3 911 432	7 833	294 921	211.3	313 540	95.7	4.3	66.0	42.7	5 762	80.1
Deltona-Daytona Beach-Ormond Beach, FL	150	5.6	101	12.9	28.8	564 216	5 584	45 579	128.4	86 726	90.0	10.0	35.0	9.6	D	7.6
Denver-Aurora-Lakewood, CO	2 490	-8.7	513	D	923.4	890 955	1 737	67 853	D	D	D	D	24.4	6.5	D	17.4
Des Moines-West Des Moines, IA	1 371	-3.9	280	D	1 079.5	1 644 653	5 875	143 481	891.6	182 028	70.5	29.5	49.3	22.9	32 090	65.6
Detroit-Warren-Dearborn, MI	557	2.2	131	7.3	437.7	626 459	4 770	106 037	399.2	94 113	83.9	16.1	41.1	14.6	6 302	21.4
Detroit-Dearborn-Livonia, MI Div 19804	16	-9.6	55	0.3	10.9	408 840	7 442	80 902	26.5	92 456	98.2	1.8	36.9	8.4	102	9.4
Warren-Troy-Farmington Hills, MI Div 47664	541	2.6	137	7.0	426.9	642 251	4 692	107 860	372.7	94 233	82.9	17.1	41.4	15.1	6 200	22.3
Dothan, AL	587	-0.7	252	20.0	263.4	586 922	2 332	93 694	342.7	147 028	44.1	55.9	34.8	15.3	13 121	60.3
Dover, DE	172	-0.9	200	31.8	147.4	1 596 656	7 999	121 074	277.7	321 816	D	D	53.3	29.8	2 550	37.2
Dubuque, IA	291	-6.2	199	0.0	224.3	1 214 544	6 093	172 274	387.8	265 260	31.0	69.0	67.5	39.7	11 080	81.2
Duluth, MN-WI	290	-9.1	187	0.2	131.9	345 245	1 843	52 513	35.8	23 111	54.9	45.1	34.8	3.6	D	7.3
Durham-Chapel Hill, NC	285	-1.5	118	5.1	104.5	611 832	5 181	58 915	245.0	101 639	28.0	72.0	35.7	9.9	2 245	21.0
East Stroudsburg, PA	26	-9.2	94	0.1	13.0	735 583	7 861	71 198	11.0	38 777	66.8	33.2	35.7	8.5	174	15.5
Eau Claire, WI	588	5.3	192	8.7	378.7	540 963	2 823	99 430	366.5	119 378	41.7	58.3	47.9	20.6	8 327	53.8
El Centro, CA	516	20.7	1 225	455.0	487.9	8 577 865	7 002	745 304	1 888.6	4 486 078	69.4	30.6	84.3	66.7	2 788	29.5
Elizabethtown-Fort Knox, KY	434	-7.4	153	0.9	245.1	523 605	3 412	77 721	136.4	48 180	66.5	33.5	36.8	7.3	4 749	44.3
Elkhart-Goshen, IN	173	5.8	100	25.5	140.2	808 782	8 067	83 012	296.8	172 178	28.0	72.0	51.8	27.4	2 785	20.1
Elmira, NY	58	-10.8	156	0.2	28.1	376 065	2 407	75 599	16.0	43 143	41.2	58.8	28.5	8.6	482	22.8
El Paso, TX	2 461	1.4	2 986	43.0	101.6	2 030 155	680	101 518	80.0	97 103	80.4	19.6	33.7	12.0	2 091	14.7
Enid, OK																
Erie, PA	169	-2.6	119	0.9	96.2	407 705	3 438	75 158	91.7	64 469	76.5	23.5	41.5	12.8	1 693	20.5
Eugene, OR	220	-10.6	83	19.3	100.0	563 427	6 824	49 734	142.5	53 574	74.6	25.4	23.5	5.6	575	5.1

Area name	Water use, 2010		Wholesale trade,[1] 2012				Retail trade, 2012				Real estate and rental and leasing, 2012			
	Total water withdrawn (mil gal/day)	Gallons withdrawn per person per day	Number of establishments	Number of employees	Sales (mil dol)	Annual payroll (mil dol)	Number of establishments	Number of employees	Sales (mil dol)	Annual payroll (mil dol)	Number of establishments	Number of employees	Receipts (mil dol)	Annual payroll (mil dol)
	133	134	135	136	137	138	139	140	141	142	143	144	145	146
Cedar Rapids, IA	153.4	595	364	5 483	4 229.0	284.7	882	16 193	4 949.8	393.1	239	1 022	210.4	36.0
Chambersburg-Waynesboro, PA	19.1	127	108	D	D	D	486	7 106	1 809.5	157.6	87	328	54.9	10.4
Champaign-Urbana, IL	42.0	181	235	3 501	3 586.0	161.9	724	11 239	2 735.2	241.0	213	3 033	562.6	119.0
Charleston, WV	595.0	2 620	267	3 771	2 568.6	186.0	840	12 216	3 459.6	294.5	244	1 220	279.9	42.5
Charleston-North Charleston, SC	658.6	991	692	7 954	6 339.0	417.6	2 628	35 904	9 411.5	849.2	929	4 326	796.6	155.8
Charlotte-Concord-Gastonia, NC-SC	4 214.7	1 901	3 185	46 227	33 695.9	2 696.6	7 467	107 892	29 996.8	2 541.1	2 704	13 096	2 885.5	646.3
Charlottesville, VA	148.2	678	146	1 853	868.8	100.8	835	11 100	2 702.8	266.0	289	1 356	248.1	48.0
Chattanooga, TN-GA	1 991.2	3 770	543	6 354	3 413.3	305.2	1 932	25 651	6 903.8	613.2	445	2 309	453.4	103.9
Cheyenne, WY	236.4	2 577	121	1 105	722.2	67.0	370	5 513	1 896.2	161.3	142	461	99.5	16.5
Chicago-Naperville-Elgin, IL-IN-WI	7 722.8	816	12 340	204 598	231 996.5	13 565.0	28 181	437 310	127 688.0	11 090.7	9 629	64 763	21 668.7	3 443.4
Chicago-Naperville-Arlington Heights, IL Div 16974	4 602.2	634	9 720	158 870	187 061.2	10 316.5	21 489	331 143	93 728.7	8 416.8	7 713	55 585	19 420.2	3 045.0
Elgin, IL Div 20994	76.2	123	801	9 957	9 982.0	598.8	1 767	27 240	6 733.8	599.9	508	2 492	684.0	97.9
Gary, IN Div 23844	2 357.1	3 329	612	6 761	6 918.2	335.4	2 125	32 702	10 190.7	748.4	548	2 840	496.9	96.3
Lake County-Kenosha County, IL-WI Div 29404	687.4	790	1 207	29 010	28 035.2	2 314.3	2 800	46 225	17 034.7	1 325.6	860	3 846	1 067.6	204.2
Chico, CA	715.3	3 252	148	D	D	D	725	9 231	2 576.9	240.4	234	1 160	147.6	28.3
Cincinnati, OH-KY-IN	1 580.1	747	2 292	43 770	51 641.2	2 634.6	6 428	104 296	30 586.2	2 564.2	1 911	11 621	2 614.7	482.8
Clarksville, TN-KY	46.0	176	147	1 921	1 653.1	79.5	828	11 849	3 261.3	284.6	211	958	146.6	29.3
Cleveland, TN	23.6	204	65	D	D	D	409	5 046	1 419.3	118.8	66	294	38.3	8.6
Cleveland-Elyria, OH	1 768.5	851	2 840	42 048	26 946.9	2 259.0	6 674	97 427	25 943.9	2 303.9	2 111	16 590	5 313.5	765.5
Coeur d'Alene, ID	56.5	408	132	D	D	D	574	7 996	2 501.7	207.0	201	623	122.6	19.1
College Station-Bryan, TX	531.0	2 322	160	1 805	1 275.7	91.1	736	10 830	3 113.8	233.7	244	1 352	271.6	46.2
Colorado Springs, CO	123.7	192	442	4 431	2 576.6	248.6	2 025	29 505	8 137.0	775.0	1 074	3 427	669.1	122.3
Columbia, MO	18.7	115	135	1 461	631.4	73.2	627	11 563	3 741.0	287.7	227	920	160.6	28.8
Columbia, SC	1 216.5	1 585	762	11 901	8 591.9	627.6	2 616	36 865	9 747.3	839.7	701	4 198	985.9	181.5
Columbus, GA-AL	95.8	325	182	2 405	1 716.5	95.0	1 034	13 671	3 475.8	300.0	289	1 615	285.7	59.6
Columbus, IN	18.2	237	77	998	774.4	52.7	306	4 701	1 113.1	99.4	72	303	57.0	9.4
Columbus, OH	294.4	155	1 746	30 642	33 473.9	1 742.1	5 592	97 309	31 432.9	2 571.3	1 937	11 638	3 033.5	480.4
Corpus Christi, TX	247.1	577	407	D	D	D	1 351	20 248	6 139.4	495.5	504	3 109	706.8	138.3
Corvallis, OR	38.8	454	44	346	452.5	22.6	262	3 455	731.0	82.5	105	453	53.3	10.2
Crestview-Fort Walton Beach-Destin, FL	40.1	170	184	1 624	883.8	79.2	1 194	14 773	3 704.0	346.5	528	2 300	404.8	86.3
Cumberland, MD-WV	46.5	450	57	596	234.7	25.5	359	4 853	1 160.1	102.0	67	236	34.0	6.4
Dallas-Fort Worth-Arlington, TX	3 374.1	525	7 562	130 067	150 841.7	8 112.6	19 506	305 066	97 494.7	8 162.1	7 462	57 356	12 829.3	2 748.1
Dallas-Plano-Irving, TX Div 19124	902.2	213	5 279	92 203	118 378.4	5 990.3	12 725	199 722	63 747.3	5 406.4	5 314	43 570	9 887.9	2 154.9
Fort Worth-Arlington, TX Div 23104	2 471.9	1 126	2 283	37 864	32 463.3	2 122.4	6 781	105 344	33 747.3	2 755.7	2 148	13 786	2 941.5	593.2
Dalton, GA	26.4	186	217	3 003	1 320.0	120.1	525	5 401	1 500.4	123.7	75	349	133.7	13.2
Danville, IL	14.0	171	77	1 788	3 136.5	84.3	255	3 401	850.3	74.3	45	158	28.7	4.5
Daphne-Fairhope-Foley, AL	64.4	353	175	1 868	1 118.2	84.1	950	12 072	3 145.8	280.0	292	1 760	250.3	53.8
Davenport-Moline-Rock Island, IA-IL	1 271.5	3 349	496	7 650	7 471.4	414.1	1 314	21 284	5 530.5	501.3	326	1 311	309.0	42.9
Dayton, OH	173.3	217	684	9 796	17 365.8	533.2	2 487	39 751	9 851.3	905.5	735	3 939	665.2	133.2
Decatur, AL	196.5	1 277	164	2 144	1 455.9	91.4	583	6 300	1 891.5	144.5	87	351	78.8	12.7
Decatur, IL	39.4	356	112	D	D	D	395	5 724	1 494.2	133.7	88	471	105.2	13.8
Deltona-Daytona Beach-Ormond Beach, FL	251.7	426	474	3 222	1 725.6	154.7	2 104	26 736	6 941.6	642.5	792	2 866	478.1	88.2
Denver-Aurora-Lakewood, CO	748.1	294	3 311	48 922	53 628.2	3 061.7	8 302	123 338	35 076.0	3 331.1	4 455	20 864	5 461.1	959.7
Des Moines-West Des Moines, IA	71.5	126	795	12 805	10 596.6	699.5	1 966	35 339	9 452.9	842.5	654	3 714	759.0	160.6
Detroit-Warren-Dearborn, MI	3 379.8	787	4 655	66 120	60 968.3	4 010.0	15 127	194 583	54 637.0	4 845.5	3 605	25 561	8 298.0	1 035.2
Detroit-Dearborn-Livonia, MI Div 19804	1 797.3	987	1 483	23 525	25 358.3	1 417.5	6 091	65 409	17 409.4	1 539.9	1 070	6 044	4 464.6	225.3
Warren-Troy-Farmington Hills, MI Div 47664	1 582.5	639	3 172	42 595	35 609.9	2 592.5	9 036	129 174	37 227.6	3 305.6	2 535	19 517	3 833.4	810.0
Dothan, AL	132.0	906	196	2 986	8 979.2	154.7	716	8 675	2 426.0	204.9	110	440	74.7	16.4
Dover, DE	43.3	267	94	D	D	D	561	8 856	2 690.8	214.1	127	459	92.2	17.0
Dubuque, IA	40.5	432	158	2 353	2 083.1	107.4	442	7 157	1 659.1	149.1	110	381	72.4	12.2
Duluth, MN-WI	376.0	1 344	267	3 351	2 368.2	158.6	1 168	15 179	3 937.6	340.4	260	1 098	180.2	30.4
Durham-Chapel Hill, NC	1 319.2	2 616	355	9 817	7 270.2	1 042.0	1 626	23 631	5 748.8	553.7	503	2 351	485.6	94.3
East Stroudsburg, PA	33.1	195	97	D	D	D	634	8 710	2 140.4	187.8	123	507	86.8	15.2
Eau Claire, WI	33.3	206	157	2 272	1 422.0	94.5	615	10 495	2 723.8	225.7	141	659	91.2	18.5
El Centro, CA	1 169.2	6 699	197	1 801	1 599.1	72.5	446	7 322	1 676.9	160.3	119	574	92.6	15.9
Elizabethtown-Fort Knox, KY	27.6	186	74	D	D	D	501	6 618	1 900.3	154.9	129	543	68.2	12.9
Elkhart-Goshen, IN	33.0	167	340	5 803	3 329.9	249.5	678	8 754	2 440.4	206.9	157	768	134.5	25.4
Elmira, NY	9.8	111	85	1 193	765.0	51.5	350	5 044	1 174.8	115.8	84	382	106.6	17.0
El Paso, TX	397.4	494	952	D	D	D	2 332	34 975	9 192.0	754.1	699	3 143	617.3	108.0
Enid, OK														
Erie, PA	49.4	176	264	3 127	1 242.5	145.7	958	15 221	3 752.8	326.4	182	1 042	158.5	32.3
Eugene, OR	224.2	637	384	4 860	2 852.0	229.0	1 270	18 265	4 291.5	449.9	505	2 115	314.3	58.4

1. Merchant wholesalers, except manufacturers' sales branches and offices.

Table C. Metropolitan Areas — Professional Services, Manufacturing, and Accommodation and Food Services

Area name	Professional, scientific, and technical services, 2012				Manufacturing, 2012				Accommodation and food services, 2012			
	Number of establishments	Number of employees	Sales (mil dol)	Annual payroll (mil dol)	Number of establishments	Number of employees	Sales (mil dol)	Annual payroll (mil dol)	Number of establishments	Number of employees	Sales (mil dol)	Annual payroll (mil dol)
	147	148	149	150	151	152	153	154	155	156	157	158
Cedar Rapids, IA	564	5 682	747.4	328.4	265	19 213	10 486.4	1 348.3	570	9 449	410.9	119.2
Chambersburg-Waynesboro, PA	223	2 067	234.8	100.3	196	8 182	3 180.0	403.9	270	D	D	D
Champaign-Urbana, IL	485	2 967	381.1	144.2	162	7 807	3 700.2	345.5	579	10 454	459.4	126.4
Charleston, WV	585	6 079	898.7	344.1	129	3 062	2 207.6	188.9	483	9 649	568.7	150.6
Charleston-North Charleston, SC	2 001	18 874	3 340.8	1 296.0	465	23 529	13 956.2	1 379.1	1 616	34 059	1 968.3	543.8
Charlotte-Concord-Gastonia, NC-SC	6 214	58 864	10 186.8	3 891.2	2 340	86 773	36 489.5	4 175.6	4 465	87 966	4 719.8	1 269.1
Charlottesville, VA	791	6 406	967.0	401.8	173	3 830	977.5	211.2	551	9 857	561.8	153.9
Chattanooga, TN-GA	942	D	D	D	557	32 303	14 940.6	1 610.2	1 056	21 292	1 089.7	306.5
Cheyenne, WY	458	1 860	279.8	99.7	67	1 190	2 549.8	76.8	207	3 980	224.8	59.8
Chicago-Naperville-Elgin, IL-IN-WI	33 178	323 636	64 623.4	26 279.3	10 473	383 870	194 249.9	21 208.1	19 708	355 344	22 899.9	6 279.1
Chicago-Naperville-Arlington Heights, IL Div 16974	26 911	277 996	58 343.8	23 040.6	8 005	274 717	127 047.1	14 762.8	15 390	281 814	18 925.7	5 214.3
Elgin, IL Div 20994	1 690	10 006	1 667.7	598.1	909	33 826	11 678.1	1 702.8	1 064	18 219	856.3	243.1
Gary, IN Div 23844	1 302	8 302	1 004.9	369.3	545	34 450	41 108.4	2 531.9	1 394	25 099	1 480.8	349.3
Lake County-Kenosha County, IL-WI Div 29404	3 275	27 332	3 606.9	2 271.3	1 014	40 878	14 416.3	2 210.6	1 860	30 212	1 637.1	472.3
Chico, CA	424	2 394	388.0	97.2	177	4 126	1 341.1	168.3	397	7 091	350.5	96.4
Cincinnati, OH-KY-IN	D	D	D	D	2 239	100 872	47 994.7	5 697.6	4 151	88 347	4 798.4	1 274.3
Clarksville, TN-KY	297	2 668	337.7	120.4	155	10 702	4 287.4	484.5	470	8 759	408.6	113.4
Cleveland, TN	150	867	78.4	32.6	122	8 069	5 718.3	345.2	196	3 834	177.5	47.1
Cleveland-Elyria, OH	5 775	50 835	7 976.9	3 175.2	3 358	120 600	43 530.2	6 669.9	4 461	79 070	3 864.1	1 065.2
Coeur d'Alene, ID	442	D	D	D	241	4 011	D	170.2	362	D	D	D
College Station-Bryan, TX	441	2 877	539.8	139.6	123	4 903	1 180.0	198.2	502	10 084	476.3	129.7
Colorado Springs, CO	2 505	20 151	3 041.6	1 280.6	479	10 471	3 382.5	562.2	1 371	28 383	1 554.0	427.2
Columbia, MO	414	3 570	424.0	156.7	99	3 994	2 042.1	173.3	419	9 006	373.2	104.7
Columbia, SC	1 911	16 971	2 745.8	1 045.8	516	24 989	13 694.4	1 250.5	1 500	29 589	1 391.3	385.3
Columbus, GA-AL	463	3 050	359.1	133.7	186	11 255	3 755.5	471.4	562	12 474	617.9	173.3
Columbus, IN	159	3 550	299.0	234.7	142	11 663	5 636.4	553.6	201	4 243	198.6	54.2
Columbus, OH	4 702	50 668	8 800.6	3 360.9	1 411	60 169	33 070.4	3 129.4	4 071	81 490	4 087.9	1 162.2
Corpus Christi, TX	927	6 378	928.0	338.3	238	10 950	44 697.1	775.4	1 048	20 133	1 046.4	279.9
Corvallis, OR	284	1 996	332.6	125.1	93	1 613	412.7	71.4	209	3 087	142.8	41.6
Crestview-Fort Walton Beach-Destin, FL	811	6 485	975.9	407.7	113	2 832	572.2	139.7	666	16 040	940.1	278.4
Cumberland, MD-WV	123	681	53.9	22.8	68	4 367	1 470.3	236.5	231	D	D	D
Dallas-Fort Worth-Arlington, TX	19 150	210 153	39 787.8	15 548.4	5 481	225 780	109 647.6	12 308.6	12 577	263 818	15 353.0	4 225.5
Dallas-Plano-Irving, TX Div 19124	14 206	168 149	33 185.1	13 176.9	3 512	145 699	61 179.9	7 948.5	8 449	176 054	10 381.6	2 902.0
Fort Worth-Arlington, TX Div 23104	4 944	42 004	6 602.7	2 371.5	1 969	80 081	48 467.8	4 360.1	4 128	87 764	4 971.4	1 323.5
Dalton, GA	188	D	D	D	330	17 966	7 111.9	668.8	213	3 781	196.4	50.1
Danville, IL	84	428	46.7	16.6	96	5 168	2 353.2	256.1	143	2 161	86.0	25.4
Daphne-Fairhope-Foley, AL	450	1 899	211.5	86.2	146	3 780	1 438.8	166.8	462	10 726	560.6	161.1
Davenport-Moline-Rock Island, IA-IL	776	5 712	1 007.7	280.0	402	24 533	16 677.3	1 289.9	872	15 809	832.3	208.7
Dayton, OH	1 717	21 824	3 582.6	1 420.6	1 048	40 297	13 041.0	2 179.3	1 611	32 811	1 508.4	428.8
Decatur, AL	230	1 483	167.8	69.3	202	12 048	10 543.3	718.5	243	4 370	197.9	54.9
Decatur, IL	157	1 216	142.7	54.0	109	8 240	13 379.3	435.3	225	4 331	189.8	55.6
Deltona-Daytona Beach-Ormond Beach, FL	1 510	7 316	886.3	301.5	380	8 224	2 024.2	367.4	1 156	22 876	1 134.5	341.5
Denver-Aurora-Lakewood, CO	12 927	108 529	22 675.3	8 365.9	2 237	52 525	24 861.3	2 880.5	5 846	115 312	7 069.5	2 014.3
Des Moines-West Des Moines, IA	1 686	15 965	2 633.1	966.8	427	19 669	11 785.8	953.5	1 354	24 834	1 211.0	348.2
Detroit-Warren-Dearborn, MI	11 419	163 997	24 342.5	12 026.3	5 353	199 394	110 685.0	11 620.7	8 168	153 118	8 567.2	2 275.4
Detroit-Dearborn-Livonia, MI Div 19804	2 848	46 825	7 135.0	3 444.6	1 483	71 526	56 638.5	4 413.5	3 184	61 446	4 238.8	1 050.2
Warren-Troy-Farmington Hills, MI Div 47664	8 571	117 172	17 207.5	8 581.7	3 870	127 869	54 046.5	7 207.2	4 984	91 672	4 328.4	1 225.2
Dothan, AL	261	1 359	162.4	59.6	132	4 834	1 646.4	182.8	280	5 084	231.9	61.9
Dover, DE	278	D	D	D	74	4 797	1 930.8	218.9	272	6 183	475.8	101.1
Dubuque, IA	166	2 956	450.9	147.7	144	8 498	6 036.4	434.6	242	4 456	169.5	49.8
Duluth, MN-WI	510	D	D	D	286	6 999	12 135.4	375.2	754	12 463	632.6	155.0
Durham-Chapel Hill, NC	1 838	35 056	6 112.3	2 966.1	350	15 118	10 445.6	957.9	1 179	22 267	1 248.1	344.0
East Stroudsburg, PA	306	D	D	D	111	4 449	D	358.1	387	8 392	724.8	155.1
Eau Claire, WI	265	2 089	252.1	102.8	209	9 968	3 621.4	444.4	440	6 931	276.6	75.5
El Centro, CA	179	787	79.1	30.4	50	2 218	1 466.0	95.4	258	3 516	182.6	47.9
Elizabethtown-Fort Knox, KY	270	1 809	184.5	69.0	88	5 679	2 366.8	262.1	229	5 034	220.3	61.7
Elkhart-Goshen, IN	313	2 004	220.2	81.0	795	53 705	14 833.3	2 288.0	348	6 500	280.7	75.8
Elmira, NY	111	774	83.5	36.1	85	5 495	1 247.0	278.8	202	3 534	154.5	43.3
El Paso, TX	1 202	D	D	D	505	13 129	D	543.2	1 481	28 757	1 385.5	375.5
Enid, OK												
Erie, PA	412	3 028	375.8	135.3	476	21 490	9 437.7	1 179.0	630	10 877	485.4	128.2
Eugene, OR	948	5 301	583.9	226.2	529	12 345	4 039.3	581.3	937	13 627	711.8	203.7

Area name	Health care and social assistance, 2012				Other services, 2012				Nonemployer business, 2015		Value of residential construction authorized by building permits, 2016	
	Number of establishments	Number of employees	Receipts (mil dol)	Annual payroll (mil dol)	Number of establishments	Number of employees	Receipts (mil dol)	Annual payroll (mil dol)	Number	Receipts (mil dol)	New construction ($1,000)	Number of housing units
	159	160	161	162	163	164	165	166	167	168	169	170
Cedar Rapids, IA	663	16 556	1 557.5	658.3	469	2 866	281.8	83.6	16 415	714.1	93 527	787
Chambersburg-Waynesboro, PA	305	8 178	820.5	349.3	287	1 558	131.5	32.7	8 947	374.7	58 876	327
Champaign-Urbana, IL	420	13 306	1 770.8	610.5	317	2 293	414.2	69.0	14 015	538.0	173 290	1 011
Charleston, WV	795	19 917	2 139.0	795.7	416	3 070	299.4	91.1	10 215	423.5	20 468	185
Charleston-North Charleston, SC	1 669	35 964	4 763.9	1 578.2	1 120	7 240	733.9	205.1	58 399	2 762.8	1 438 352	6 974
Charlotte-Concord-Gastonia, NC-SC	5 167	113 438	13 463.8	5 178.0	3 490	22 305	2 609.7	674.3	187 409	8 167.0	4 065 100	20 574
Charlottesville, VA	561	16 296	2 372.6	999.2	381	3 381	666.6	140.0	18 365	841.0	278 729	1 234
Chattanooga, TN-GA	1 275	31 220	3 602.0	1 420.4	716	5 022	569.2	149.4	37 716	1 790.7	379 787	2 487
Cheyenne, WY	323	6 700	647.9	305.2	189	943	93.6	27.1	7 665	480.1	81 396	476
Chicago-Naperville-Elgin, IL-IN-WI	25 714	569 844	63 927.3	24 944.8	17 586	132 350	17 826.4	4 831.8	779 014	35 080.6	3 898 390	19 941
Chicago-Naperville-Arlington Heights, IL Div 16974	20 277	459 774	51 473.0	20 190.9	13 870	107 796	15 518.3	4 150.1	NA	NA	2 873 397	15 072
Elgin, IL Div 20994	1 382	26 345	2 910.1	1 147.8	968	6 879	664.2	187.5	NA	NA	293 787	1 670
Gary, IN Div 23844	1 691	41 436	4 686.3	1 716.8	1 231	8 564	814.5	239.1	NA	NA	411 352	1 829
Lake County-Kenosha County, IL-WI Div 29404	2 364	42 289	4 858.0	1 889.3	1 517	9 111	829.4	255.1	NA	NA	319 854	1 370
Chico, CA	716	12 868	1 434.5	560.2	321	2 158	190.0	56.0	13 528	626.5	95 201	697
Cincinnati, OH-KY-IN	4 831	134 554	15 421.0	6 374.0	3 255	24 339	2 431.1	681.1	140 795	6 340.4	1 115 979	5 867
Clarksville, TN-KY	510	10 678	986.1	367.7	285	1 577	129.3	36.8	14 072	608.0	204 522	1 679
Cleveland, TN	248	5 054	653.8	200.8	102	873	73.0	21.8	7 844	389.9	86 404	532
Cleveland-Elyria, OH	5 423	173 697	17 969.1	7 747.1	3 895	26 763	2 784.6	775.0	148 063	6 748.7	688 605	3 053
Coeur d'Alene, ID	509	8 630	806.2	308.4	236	D	D	D	11 983	520.3	315 990	1 666
College Station-Bryan, TX	433	8 794	1 080.7	395.8	316	2 193	405.2	62.8	15 881	727.4	387 453	2 860
Colorado Springs, CO	1 955	31 286	3 300.0	1 327.9	1 128	8 548	1 816.7	326.1	50 936	2 028.6	1 688 749	5 166
Columbia, MO	602	16 725	2 033.5	699.4	327	1 985	187.4	53.2	11 463	561.3	261 329	1 304
Columbia, SC	1 637	42 874	4 546.9	1 828.4	1 224	8 398	794.5	241.2	54 051	2 264.5	790 031	4 627
Columbus, GA-AL	691	16 540	1 625.9	635.9	404	2 693	259.9	74.2	19 419	650.9	140 003	709
Columbus, IN	221	4 824	512.8	203.1	111	692	82.5	19.7	4 184	169.7	52 293	300
Columbus, OH	4 677	133 376	14 049.2	5 491.7	2 808	23 334	3 073.2	774.6	148 635	6 826.8	1 575 371	8 637
Corpus Christi, TX	1 186	30 414	2 800.7	1 049.3	633	4 993	581.9	158.7	31 084	1 373.6	329 971	1 910
Corvallis, OR	271	5 258	588.1	258.8	147	891	153.8	30.3	5 783	238.1	45 824	195
Crestview-Fort Walton Beach-Destin, FL	658	11 275	1 378.0	474.1	435	2 145	198.0	56.5	23 311	1 273.6	858 592	2 529
Cumberland, MD-WV	314	7 665	686.5	263.5	180	960	72.1	20.7	4 410	153.8	13 696	85
Dallas-Fort Worth-Arlington, TX	17 015	331 041	40 730.9	15 173.9	8 560	70 090	8 772.4	2 385.7	614 884	32 224.1	10 909 645	55 800
Dallas-Plano-Irving, TX Div 19124	11 734	226 936	28 266.9	10 701.7	5 677	47 622	6 382.3	1 735.2	NA	NA	8 527 580	41 824
Fort Worth-Arlington, TX Div 23104	5 281	104 105	12 464.0	4 472.2	2 883	22 468	2 390.1	650.5	NA	NA	2 382 065	13 976
Dalton, GA	225	4 744	525.2	198.0	141	958	85.2	28.7	7 888	375.2	28 749	173
Danville, IL	143	4 736	514.4	235.4	121	540	47.4	13.3	4 239	136.9	1 406	10
Daphne-Fairhope-Foley, AL	444	7 029	622.5	265.3	269	1 203	110.5	31.9	17 876	863.8	490 227	2 520
Davenport-Moline-Rock Island, IA-IL	1 010	22 953	2 081.4	893.8	684	4 209	364.7	106.2	20 884	869.4	126 691	647
Dayton, OH	2 004	59 132	6 556.8	2 598.1	1 242	8 387	863.6	206.1	48 014	1 962.8	320 063	1 282
Decatur, AL	376	6 469	541.2	207.7	180	1 060	103.0	29.5	9 484	370.2	33 426	194
Decatur, IL	291	8 193	886.2	332.1	176	1 170	239.1	37.3	5 713	183.7	12 547	56
Deltona-Daytona Beach-Ormond Beach, FL	1 542	28 190	3 112.5	1 157.7	1 150	5 517	584.5	186.5	48 879	2 051.3	739 140	2 696
Denver-Aurora-Lakewood, CO	7 163	130 863	15 988.2	6 540.4	5 189	35 432	4 395.4	1 161.3	248 548	12 303.7	4 343 273	21 947
Des Moines-West Des Moines, IA	1 414	39 163	4 078.1	1 844.6	1 143	8 007	992.9	271.6	43 795	2 108.2	1 331 602	6 697
Detroit-Warren-Dearborn, MI	12 474	254 643	28 793.7	11 432.0	6 992	44 589	4 734.0	1 273.7	334 728	14 798.5	1 792 551	7 659
Detroit-Dearborn-Livonia, MI Div 19804	4 091	101 848	12 420.4	4 712.3	2 645	16 865	1 763.8	497.5	NA	NA	358 370	1 729
Warren-Troy-Farmington Hills, MI Div 47664	8 383	152 795	16 373.3	6 719.7	4 347	27 724	2 970.2	776.2	NA	NA	1 434 181	5 930
Dothan, AL	375	10 243	1 127.1	486.2	221	D	D	D	9 860	433.1	72 076	360
Dover, DE	398	9 405	990.6	379.5	233	1 325	105.5	32.0	9 585	574.1	183 853	1 276
Dubuque, IA	271	7 806	702.0	318.7	201	1 157	109.4	28.1	6 335	278.9	79 185	368
Duluth, MN-WI	931	28 824	2 484.4	1 168.0	525	3 338	297.5	76.6	15 509	613.1	118 701	621
Durham-Chapel Hill, NC	1 373	42 120	5 452.9	1 974.5	755	6 461	1 033.8	248.0	43 648	1 700.7	794 613	4 382
East Stroudsburg, PA	393	7 031	643.1	276.0	309	1 571	115.7	37.0	10 328	473.6	58 815	246
Eau Claire, WI	539	14 294	1 521.9	662.8	302	1 828	162.1	45.1	9 909	512.4	140 761	763
El Centro, CA	268	4 536	511.1	182.9	142	608	53.4	16.5	9 817	338.8	44 156	215
Elizabethtown-Fort Knox, KY	398	8 120	728.7	319.5	182	1 053	95.6	24.0	7 918	317.9	60 372	467
Elkhart-Goshen, IN	362	10 105	1 160.8	413.6	336	2 069	261.0	61.1	12 754	562.7	74 728	354
Elmira, NY	211	6 421	621.6	294.0	128	670	57.3	15.6	3 875	141.9	17 326	41
El Paso, TX	1 525	41 470	4 304.3	1 488.3	910	5 676	464.5	129.4	56 586	2 435.5	656 311	3 054
Enid, OK									NA	NA	13 841	70
Erie, PA	850	24 899	2 216.5	923.1	563	3 591	322.7	80.2	13 841	594.6	41 380	338
Eugene, OR	1 135	20 576	2 247.4	828.6	611	3 480	443.9	97.7	23 337	1 040.8	221 914	1 174

1. Establishments subject to federal tax.

Table C. Metropolitan Areas — Government Employment and Payroll and Local Government Finances

Area name	Government employment and payroll, 2012									Local government finances, 2012				
			March payroll (percent of total)							General revenue				
												Taxes		
													Per capita[1] (dollars)	
	Full-time equivalent employees	March Payroll (dollars)	Administration, judicial, and legal	Police and corrections	Fire protection	Highways and transportation	Health and welfare	Natural resources and utilities	Education and libraries	Total (mil dol)	Inter-governmental (mil dol)	Total (mil dol)	Total	Property
	171	172	173	174	175	176	177	178	179	180	181	182	183	184
Cedar Rapids, IA..................	10 705	42 251 213	4.0	6.0	2.5	6.3	2.3	4.9	72.2	1 343.4	584.3	503.5	1 924	1 486
Chambersburg-Waynesboro, PA	3 820	13 644 359	7.7	8.8	1.7	2.3	9.1	6.1	63.5	415.1	130.8	191.4	1 265	978
Champaign-Urbana, IL...........	8 553	32 026 460	5.7	8.9	3.4	7.5	6.1	5.5	61.1	891.5	342.7	404.0	1 728	1 506
Charleston, WV....................	8 227	28 589 774	5.5	6.5	3.8	3.3	7.9	3.1	66.9	735.0	295.9	299.7	1 326	910
Charleston-North Charleston, SC ...	22 813	76 849 945	8.2	12.8	6.2	2.8	3.9	8.3	55.3	2 449.1	759.7	1 206.4	1 730	1 171
Charlotte-Concord-Gastonia, NC-SC...	106 366	436 927 670	3.6	7.0	2.3	1.5	39.9	4.1	40.2	12 067.6	3 110.9	3 416.0	1 487	1 141
Charlottesville, VA................	7 679	26 539 813	8.0	9.0	2.3	2.5	3.9	4.9	64.7	782.8	292.5	365.6	1 641	1 221
Chattanooga, TN-GA	19 778	70 912 137	6.7	7.6	2.9	3.3	31.0	10.3	37.0	2 452.8	620.7	669.9	1 245	910
Cheyenne, WY	6 173	27 578 286	2.8	4.6	1.9	1.8	39.8	1.5	46.1	796.0	292.8	103.3	1 094	589
Chicago-Naperville-Elgin, IL-IN-WI	358 119	1 755 095 339	5.6	15.8	4.2	6.1	4.0	6.3	56.6	49 995.8	16 211.6	25 716.1	2 701	2 261
Chicago-Naperville-Arlington Heights, IL Div 16974 ...	272 297	1 388 594 555	5.4	17.5	4.2	7.0	4.3	6.3	54.0	39 231.9	12 680.6	19 977.9	2 730	2 208
Elgin, IL Div 20994.............	25 482	114 832 272	5.3	10.3	5.2	2.2	1.5	6.6	67.5	3 172.7	934.1	1 826.9	2 913	2 670
Gary, IN Div 23844.............	25 614	86 646 440	8.5	10.0	3.9	4.2	3.6	7.3	60.8	3 048.3	1 320.8	1 243.6	1 759	1 670
Lake County-Kenosha County, IL-WI Div 29404.........	34 726	165 022 072	5.5	8.7	3.9	2.4	4.0	6.2	68.5	4 542.9	1 276.0	2 667.7	3 066	2 896
Chico, CA..........................	8 734	37 694 370	6.4	9.6	2.6	2.0	12.6	5.9	58.9	1 079.1	643.7	243.0	1 097	878
Cincinnati, OH-KY-IN	72 643	287 857 130	6.6	10.8	6.5	4.5	6.9	6.8	56.1	8 861.6	3 178.0	3 802.3	1 786	1 197
Clarksville, TN-KY	8 620	27 138 883	4.3	10.6	3.8	3.1	6.5	6.8	62.4	701.2	298.6	267.5	975	569
Cleveland, TN	4 049	11 684 208	5.5	10.1	5.8	3.7	9.5	2.4	62.1	282.7	134.8	92.6	786	497
Cleveland-Elyria, OH.............	92 435	406 449 865	6.4	10.2	4.7	5.9	15.2	7.7	48.3	11 282.4	3 960.2	4 907.0	2 378	1 483
Coeur d'Alene, ID...............	6 580	25 436 541	6.0	8.3	3.6	2.4	37.6	3.3	38.1	678.7	158.8	148.1	1 040	972
College Station-Bryan, TX	8 862	27 409 320	8.4	12.4	4.3	4.5	3.2	11.0	51.4	682.0	173.0	393.1	1 676	1 379
Colorado Springs, CO	25 178	98 225 856	5.3	9.9	3.8	2.2	15.3	15.2	45.7	2 631.8	836.0	850.3	1 272	745
Columbia, MO	6 008	20 052 275	7.9	5.3	3.3	2.8	2.7	11.3	63.5	497.3	161.0	228.2	1 354	805
Columbia, SC......................	33 084	120 753 751	4.2	6.5	2.3	1.0	25.0	4.6	54.7	3 250.3	958.1	1 087.0	1 385	1 204
Columbus, GA-AL	13 084	41 360 235	6.9	10.8	4.0	2.6	6.1	6.8	60.6	1 009.9	422.9	376.5	1 213	848
Columbus, IN	4 371	15 688 309	3.2	6.6	2.9	1.3	44.5	3.1	37.7	469.7	111.3	106.7	1 348	1 076
Columbus, OH.....................	70 274	306 173 279	9.4	10.4	7.0	4.4	8.1	5.2	53.9	9 594.0	3 610.3	4 421.2	2 274	1 428
Corpus Christi, TX................	19 396	62 362 670	4.9	10.1	3.6	4.7	4.1	5.7	63.6	1 651.1	548.8	775.1	1 773	1 396
Corvallis, OR	1 834	7 923 562	9.3	13.4	6.2	3.8	7.4	9.4	45.7	259.6	93.0	115.4	1 335	1 185
Crestview-Fort Walton Beach-Destin, FL	8 719	30 209 052	6.5	11.1	6.5	3.5	2.3	6.1	60.8	813.5	261.8	380.6	1 537	1 209
Cumberland, MD-WV	3 611	14 623 810	4.0	5.7	1.6	3.1	0.5	6.1	76.2	340.7	169.2	105.4	1 034	723
Dallas-Fort Worth-Arlington, TX	263 325	1 034 080 549	5.5	11.1	4.7	4.3	9.8	4.8	58.2	28 591.5	7 248.4	14 334.2	2 139	1 724
Dallas-Plano-Irving, TX Div 19124	172 608	694 884 179	5.0	10.6	4.8	5.5	10.3	4.8	57.3	19 625.6	4 888.2	9 734.9	2 199	1 766
Fort Worth-Arlington, TX Div 23104	90 717	339 196 370	6.6	12.1	4.4	1.7	8.6	4.7	60.2	8 965.9	2 360.2	4 599.3	2 022	1 644
Dalton, GA..........................	5 343	18 100 335	4.0	6.7	3.7	3.2	5.9	9.7	65.2	440.0	199.5	149.2	1 045	674
Danville, IL	3 642	12 242 579	7.0	7.8	2.7	3.5	3.6	4.2	67.9	289.5	151.8	91.4	1 132	940
Daphne-Fairhope-Foley, AL...	7 374	22 581 577	7.4	8.0	2.9	4.3	20.7	5.6	47.7	640.7	189.9	231.1	1 211	537
Davenport-Moline-Rock Island, IA-IL..................	14 533	58 873 005	5.4	9.2	3.4	4.7	5.9	5.6	64.3	1 610.6	616.3	675.0	1 764	1 489
Dayton, OH	31 140	126 902 617	7.8	9.6	4.5	5.3	8.1	7.6	55.4	3 577.2	1 408.5	1 490.6	1 861	1 242
Decatur, AL........................	6 083	20 609 391	3.2	7.4	2.8	2.6	21.3	8.4	53.1	589.6	255.2	134.1	870	438
Decatur, IL.........................	4 204	17 133 160	5.9	11.8	4.5	3.0	2.0	8.2	63.3	407.1	180.7	163.9	1 488	1 260
Deltona-Daytona Beach-Ormond Beach, FL	23 653	83 363 572	6.3	11.3	4.7	2.1	21.7	6.5	45.3	2 404.0	575.9	895.2	1 504	1 170
Denver-Aurora-Lakewood, CO	95 098	432 423 959	6.6	12.7	5.6	6.2	10.7	9.5	46.7	13 355.6	3 846.7	5 924.4	2 240	1 358
Des Moines-West Des Moines, IA	22 853	93 893 961	5.5	8.0	3.0	4.3	8.9	5.3	63.7	2 778.1	968.6	1 212.2	2 058	1 784
Detroit-Warren-Dearborn, MI .	115 282	533 695 857	7.4	12.9	5.0	4.6	2.5	4.5	60.8	18 679.3	8 819.4	5 896.0	1 374	1 225
Detroit-Dearborn-Livonia, MI Div 19804	52 078	243 918 311	7.3	16.2	6.7	6.5	2.2	6.4	52.0	9 260.6	4 384.4	2 686.6	1 499	1 195
Warren-Troy-Farmington Hills, MI Div 47664........	63 204	289 777 546	7.4	10.1	3.5	3.0	2.7	2.9	68.2	9 418.7	4 435.0	3 209.5	1 284	1 246
Dothan, AL.........................	7 365	24 527 281	3.9	6.4	3.0	2.7	40.1	5.5	36.7	730.7	179.2	156.0	1 057	387
Dover, DE	4 210	17 226 252	4.7	6.0	0.1	0.6	1.6	5.6	79.4	494.8	323.1	88.0	525	459
Dubuque, IA	3 261	12 486 456	6.7	9.6	3.9	7.2	5.0	6.0	60.6	400.9	169.8	165.8	1 743	1 320
Duluth, MN-WI.....................	11 586	52 151 960	6.8	9.8	2.9	6.5	13.3	7.0	48.7	1 488.3	728.3	373.6	1 337	1 215
Durham-Chapel Hill, NC	18 475	63 324 374	5.8	6.4	1.4	2.2	10.3	6.8	63.0	1 793.6	701.9	824.7	1 577	1 277
East Stroudsburg, PA	5 957	25 067 544	5.7	4.3	0.0	5.4	1.6	1.5	80.9	719.0	225.3	441.5	2 616	2 404
Eau Claire, WI	5 534	21 894 206	6.1	8.1	3.0	6.4	5.8	4.3	65.0	602.6	268.9	253.5	1 549	1 431
El Centro, CA......................	10 122	49 143 599	4.2	6.0	1.7	1.1	19.5	16.2	45.5	1 293.3	740.8	180.2	1 019	733
Elizabethtown-Fort Knox, KY .	6 654	21 761 001	1.7	4.2	1.5	1.3	37.6	3.5	49.3	547.6	189.2	112.2	746	448
Elkhart-Goshen, IN	6 985	24 411 992	5.4	8.4	4.1	2.5	1.6	3.6	73.6	630.5	315.1	218.4	1 094	907
Elmira, NY	3 853	14 858 297	5.0	9.7	2.9	4.0	13.2	3.8	59.7	476.3	219.3	175.3	1 971	1 236
El Paso, TX.........................	38 548	140 371 856	4.5	10.4	3.7	3.1	8.1	3.1	65.5	3 358.7	1 620.5	1 097.5	1 321	1 022
Enid, OK............................														
Erie, PA	8 523	32 472 819	5.3	9.7	2.6	5.6	3.9	6.0	65.7	1 197.6	616.5	364.0	1 297	1 046
Eugene, OR	11 647	50 155 119	7.2	10.9	5.2	6.9	4.1	11.4	48.1	1 390.4	585.1	463.2	1 306	1 120

1. Based on the resident population estimated as of July 1 of the year shown.

Table C. Metropolitan Areas — Local Government Finances, Government Employment, and Income Taxes

Area name	Local government finances, 2012 (cont.)									Government employment, 2015			Individual income tax returns, 2014		
	Direct general expenditure							Debt outstanding							
			Percent of total for:												
	Total (mil dol)	Per capita[1] (dollars)	Education	Health and hospitals	Police protection	Public welfare	Highways	Total (mil dol)	Per capita[1] (dollars)	Federal civilian	Federal military	State and local	Number of returns	Mean Adjusted Gross income	Mean income tax
	185	186	187	188	189	190	191	192	193	194	195	196	197	198	199
Cedar Rapids, IA	1 498.7	5 725	47.4	3.1	3.7	1.0	5.5	1 735.1	6 629	1 139	982	15 433	126 620	64 725	7 900
Chambersburg-Waynesboro, PA	452.7	2 992	54.1	4.1	1.9	5.5	4.8	619.1	4 092	2 205	401	5 892	75 390	52 079	5 305
Champaign-Urbana, IL	941.0	4 025	49.1	2.4	5.0	2.5	6.1	728.3	3 115	1 367	482	37 362	100 150	59 602	7 302
Charleston, WV	776.4	3 436	50.7	3.1	6.2	0.1	2.6	329.2	1 457	2 171	1 067	22 026	99 890	53 417	6 597
Charleston-North Charleston, SC	2 212.6	3 173	45.5	1.1	9.5	0.2	4.7	5 523.5	7 920	10 475	12 997	51 732	337 730	59 934	7 612
Charlotte-Concord-Gastonia, NC-SC	11 496.9	5 006	29.1	35.1	5.3	2.9	2.0	12 295.6	5 354	10 158	6 416	138 778	1 081 420	64 713	8 773
Charlottesville, VA	798.6	3 583	47.8	6.8	5.5	6.6	2.1	859.4	3 856	1 409	1 168	33 657	102 470	80 719	12 048
Chattanooga, TN-GA	2 273.9	4 228	31.4	31.0	4.8	0.8	2.7	1 828.1	3 399	5 605	1 663	30 440	238 120	55 132	6 903
Cheyenne, WY	781.4	8 270	37.0	40.5	2.5	0.2	3.1	132.4	1 401	2 643	3 465	11 395	47 590	60 985	7 432
Chicago-Naperville-Elgin, IL-IN-WI	48 512.9	5 095	44.9	3.1	7.1	1.3	4.3	81 674.3	8 577	54 109	31 815	512 060	4 608 660	73 945	11 287
Chicago-Naperville-Arlington Heights, IL Div 16974	38 566.5	5 270	42.7	3.4	7.4	1.3	4.3	70 331.4	9 610	44 687	15 206	389 747	NA	NA	NA
Elgin, IL Div 20994	3 112.0	4 962	53.7	0.6	6.3	0.5	5.5	4 822.0	7 688	1 829	1 265	42 650	NA	NA	NA
Gary, IN Div 23844	2 464.8	3 487	47.7	2.5	4.8	0.9	2.2	2 682.0	3 795	1 921	2 141	33 178	NA	NA	NA
Lake County-Kenosha County, IL-WI Div 29404	4 369.5	5 022	56.1	2.3	6.1	1.8	4.4	3 838.9	4 412	5 672	13 203	46 485	NA	NA	NA
Chico, CA	1 098.2	4 957	46.2	6.8	4.4	11.8	3.6	480.5	2 169	543	335	15 445	90 320	51 866	5 720
Cincinnati, OH-KY-IN	9 065.0	4 259	41.6	5.6	6.4	3.8	4.1	13 076.8	6 143	15 459	5 874	111 366	1 029 540	64 684	8 702
Clarksville, TN-KY	654.4	2 385	56.0	3.0	7.0	0.1	4.1	4 800.5	17 498	5 721	30 013	13 534	117 050	43 725	4 004
Cleveland, TN	268.7	2 281	54.1	7.7	7.1	0.1	5.2	242.0	2 054	279	364	5 486	52 120	46 730	4 966
Cleveland-Elyria, OH	11 203.3	5 429	41.3	12.0	5.9	3.4	4.1	14 162.1	6 863	18 098	5 681	113 862	1 034 780	60 344	8 076
Coeur d'Alene, ID	637.0	4 475	29.8	40.2	5.8	0.4	3.9	121.1	851	596	507	10 065	69 710	51 389	5 560
College Station-Bryan, TX	708.6	3 022	50.7	1.9	5.8	0.4	5.6	1 389.0	5 923	820	554	38 055	94 210	59 731	8 098
Colorado Springs, CO	2 586.9	3 871	37.1	21.4	6.1	2.0	8.1	4 453.6	6 663	12 680	38 522	37 876	315 700	58 689	6 820
Columbia, MO	580.4	3 444	44.8	3.1	4.3	0.2	6.2	2 592.5	15 382	2 515	596	28 535	77 110	57 855	7 272
Columbia, SC	3 328.6	4 242	44.0	20.7	4.0	0.1	1.1	7 155.9	9 119	10 240	12 378	72 788	352 690	53 050	5 966
Columbus, GA-AL	1 107.4	3 566	50.3	6.1	5.6	1.9	4.1	1 051.1	3 385	6 893	22 047	17 651	131 460	46 680	4 826
Columbus, IN	465.6	5 883	32.7	40.9	1.8	0.5	0.9	364.3	4 603	168	247	6 143	39 650	59 621	7 060
Columbus, OH	9 248.5	4 757	41.8	5.3	5.8	5.4	4.5	10 699.7	5 504	14 018	5 609	153 956	964 490	61 557	7 984
Corpus Christi, TX	1 702.5	3 895	49.7	4.7	6.4	0.2	3.7	3 153.1	7 214	6 115	4 600	26 725	200 010	57 209	7 720
Corvallis, OR	259.2	2 999	46.3	7.4	9.6	0.0	4.2	233.8	2 705	502	250	10 731	37 890	64 358	7 693
Crestview-Fort Walton Beach-Destin, FL	907.3	3 663	47.7	3.2	7.3	0.3	4.4	501.5	2 025	8 553	16 003	10 999	127 480	59 465	8 663
Cumberland, MD-WV	335.7	3 292	62.0	0.8	3.9	0.5	4.1	213.3	2 092	605	333	7 233	41 390	45 595	4 330
Dallas-Fort Worth-Arlington, TX	28 447.6	4 245	42.1	11.3	5.7	0.4	4.3	75 576.3	11 278	44 374	16 579	363 823	3 180 470	73 111	11 392
Dallas-Plano-Irving, TX Div 19124	19 555.5	4 418	41.1	11.5	5.2	0.5	4.4	53 566.2	12 101	29 296	10 300	248 771	NA	NA	NA
Fort Worth-Arlington, TX Div 23104	8 892.1	3 910	44.2	11.0	6.7	0.1	4.1	22 010.2	9 677	15 078	6 279	115 052	NA	NA	NA
Dalton, GA	487.6	3 416	54.9	8.7	3.9	0.4	4.8	143.3	1 004	232	399	6 737	56 980	44 437	4 443
Danville, IL	308.3	3 819	56.4	0.7	6.4	3.5	6.3	102.1	1 265	1 510	155	4 261	34 250	45 174	4 421
Daphne-Fairhope-Foley, AL	700.0	3 669	34.5	19.2	6.1	0.1	7.7	911.0	4 775	334	898	8 876	90 890	57 717	7 109
Davenport-Moline-Rock Island, IA-IL	1 675.1	4 378	48.5	5.0	5.5	1.5	4.6	1 215.2	3 176	5 707	1 508	20 271	185 230	58 851	7 165
Dayton, OH	3 712.9	4 635	47.4	3.3	6.4	7.2	5.2	3 143.4	3 924	18 443	7 158	42 560	382 430	54 179	6 356
Decatur, AL	670.1	4 345	54.9	16.9	4.4	0.3	3.3	924.8	5 996	393	670	7 834	66 190	49 609	5 079
Decatur, IL	452.8	4 112	52.8	2.0	7.8	0.1	8.1	462.5	4 200	318	219	5 457	49 350	55 564	6 655
Deltona-Daytona Beach-Ormond Beach, FL	2 484.9	4 174	30.8	22.3	7.3	0.4	3.9	3 027.1	5 085	1 331	1 187	21 548	288 090	48 941	6 008
Denver-Aurora-Lakewood, CO	12 432.0	4 700	33.7	6.3	6.2	4.2	4.8	24 877.2	9 405	28 418	10 005	171 507	1 352 010	75 606	11 237
Des Moines-West Des Moines, IA	3 004.6	5 101	48.5	8.3	4.2	1.2	5.5	3 647.7	6 193	6 206	2 445	37 201	292 040	69 832	9 217
Detroit-Warren-Dearborn, MI	19 021.2	4 432	43.4	5.7	6.5	3.0	3.8	31 478.0	7 334	27 749	7 985	161 902	2 084 370	61 525	8 508
Detroit-Dearborn-Livonia, MI Div 19804	9 500.3	5 300	36.3	3.3	7.0	5.2	2.9	21 084.6	11 764	14 043	3 275	73 079	NA	NA	NA
Warren-Troy-Farmington Hills, MI Div 47664	9 520.9	3 809	50.5	8.0	6.0	0.9	4.7	10 393.4	4 158	13 706	4 710	88 823	NA	NA	NA
Dothan, AL	704.8	4 774	29.3	42.3	4.1	0.1	4.1	485.5	3 289	399	685	10 294	61 920	47 771	5 449
Dover, DE	527.3	3 145	73.4	1.1	4.4	0.0	1.5	478.7	2 856	1 742	4 164	17 468	78 250	49 048	4 846
Dubuque, IA	405.9	4 268	37.6	4.5	4.7	2.0	7.0	372.4	3 916	259	368	4 482	47 230	58 936	7 178
Duluth, MN-WI	1 639.0	5 865	37.0	6.4	5.3	6.4	9.4	1 391.0	4 977	1 665	1 051	23 296	130 650	54 587	6 004
Durham-Chapel Hill, NC	1 919.0	3 670	40.5	5.6	8.2	5.6	2.1	1 899.7	3 633	6 520	1 461	58 201	247 710	68 028	9 283
East Stroudsburg, PA	739.9	4 384	67.9	0.1	3.0	3.9	2.5	1 201.0	7 115	3 243	455	8 254	76 980	52 041	5 668
Eau Claire, WI	676.7	4 137	54.0	4.1	6.5	3.1	11.1	488.8	2 988	527	425	11 686	78 150	59 464	7 989
El Centro, CA	1 172.3	6 625	40.7	23.6	4.1	7.5	2.9	1 408.8	7 962	2 228	374	15 783	77 590	38 477	3 234
Elizabethtown-Fort Knox, KY	515.1	3 425	39.9	37.7	2.7	0.0	2.2	447.0	2 972	5 996	5 447	8 751	65 070	47 895	4 529
Elkhart-Goshen, IN	609.8	3 055	58.2	1.0	3.9	0.2	3.5	758.8	3 801	260	617	8 464	93 840	52 688	6 184
Elmira, NY	467.0	5 252	42.9	3.0	3.0	18.1	8.9	490.6	5 518	214	132	5 912	39 660	51 976	5 720
El Paso, TX	3 277.0	3 945	52.3	15.5	5.0	0.4	1.0	4 036.3	4 859	12 920	28 521	54 930	358 690	41 631	4 031
Enid, OK										481	1 395	3 379	28 170	62 303	8 579
Erie, PA	1 203.4	4 288	44.0	5.6	2.7	14.2	3.5	1 705.3	6 076	1 517	738	15 584	130 660	50 095	5 750
Eugene, OR	1 390.2	3 921	44.2	5.1	6.9	2.2	4.3	1 580.1	4 457	1 617	1 013	23 484	161 290	54 292	6 247

1. Based on the resident population estimated as of July 1 of the year shown.

Table C. Metropolitan Areas — **Land Area and Population**

CBSA/ DIV code[1]	Area name	Land area,[2] 2016 (sq mi)	Population 2016			Population characteristics, 2016										
						Race alone or in combination, not Hispanic or Latino (percent)					Age (percent)					
			Total persons	Rank	Per square mile	White	Black	American Indian, Alaska Native	Asian and Pacific Islander	Percent Hispanic or Latino[3]	Under 5 years	5 to 17 years	18 to 24 years	25 to 34 years	35 to 44 years	45 to 54 years
		1	2	3	4	5	6	7	8	9	10	11	12	13	14	15
21780	Evansville, IN-KY	1 464.5	315 948	158	215.7	89.1	8.3	0.6	1.9	2.3	6.0	16.6	9.0	13.2	11.9	12.8
21820	Fairbanks, AK	7 343.3	100 605	352	13.7	75.8	6.3	10.7	5.7	7.9	7.8	16.6	13.9	18.8	12.1	10.8
22020	Fargo, ND-MN	2 810.2	238 124	192	84.7	88.4	5.2	2.0	3.3	3.1	7.3	15.5	15.2	16.4	12.4	10.8
22140	Farmington, NM	5 513.2	115 079	334	20.9	43.5	1.1	35.8	1.0	20.6	7.0	18.8	8.4	13.9	12.0	11.7
22180	Fayetteville, NC	1 042.6	380 389	139	364.8	46.3	38.7	3.5	4.1	11.6	7.9	17.9	11.7	17.2	12.1	11.4
22220	Fayetteville-Springdale-Rogers, AR-MO...	3 163.2	525 032	105	166.0	76.0	3.0	2.6	5.0	15.9	7.0	18.7	11.0	14.6	13.4	12.2
22380	Flagstaff, AZ	18 618.7	140 908	291	7.6	56.8	1.9	27.1	2.9	13.8	5.8	15.4	20.0	13.6	10.7	10.6
22420	Flint, MI	637.0	408 615	131	641.5	74.7	21.7	1.3	1.5	3.4	6.0	17.0	8.8	11.9	11.9	13.8
22500	Florence, SC	1 361.1	205 976	214	151.3	54.2	42.6	0.7	1.4	2.4	6.2	17.4	8.9	12.2	12.2	13.1
22520	Florence-Muscle Shoals, AL	1 260.3	146 534	283	116.3	84.0	13.0	1.0	1.0	2.5	5.3	15.2	10.1	12.0	11.2	13.3
22540	Fond du Lac, WI	719.6	102 144	350	141.9	91.2	2.2	0.8	1.9	5.1	5.5	16.3	8.6	11.7	11.8	14.0
22660	Fort Collins, CO	2 596.2	339 993	150	131.0	85.0	1.5	1.1	3.3	11.2	5.3	14.7	14.8	14.2	12.1	11.4
22900	Fort Smith, AR-OK	3 385.6	281 227	169	83.1	76.8	4.8	9.8	3.2	9.8	6.4	17.8	8.6	12.8	12.1	13.3
23060	Fort Wayne, IN	1 361.0	431 802	125	317.3	79.5	11.6	0.8	4.0	6.6	7.0	18.7	9.0	13.3	12.3	12.7
23420	Fresno, CA	5 958.8	979 915	56	164.4	31.6	5.3	1.1	11.2	52.8	8.1	20.6	10.3	15.2	12.2	11.4
23460	Gadsden, AL	535.3	102 564	348	191.6	79.5	16.2	1.1	1.0	3.8	5.6	16.2	8.3	12.0	12.4	13.6
23540	Gainesville, FL	1 224.7	280 708	170	229.2	65.7	20.3	0.7	6.7	9.2	5.5	12.8	20.4	15.3	10.5	10.3
23580	Gainesville, GA	392.8	196 637	221	500.6	62.5	8.0	0.6	2.3	28.0	6.6	19.4	9.0	12.9	12.8	13.7
23900	Gettysburg, PA	518.7	102 180	349	197.0	90.4	2.2	0.5	1.1	7.0	5.0	15.3	9.5	10.7	10.7	14.5
24020	Glens Falls, NY.................	1 698.4	126 367	311	74.4	94.4	2.6	0.7	1.0	2.5	4.7	14.2	7.8	12.0	11.2	14.9
24140	Goldsboro, NC	553.9	124 150	315	224.1	55.3	32.4	0.9	1.9	11.5	6.7	17.1	9.9	13.4	11.7	12.8
24220	Grand Forks, ND-MN	3 407.5	102 743	347	30.2	87.5	4.1	3.2	2.9	4.7	6.9	14.7	17.6	14.9	10.1	10.3
24260	Grand Island, NE	2 143.4	85 148	369	39.7	75.9	2.3	0.7	1.4	20.6	7.3	19.1	8.4	12.3	12.0	12.4
24300	Grand Junction, CO...........	3 328.9	150 083	275	45.1	83.2	1.2	1.4	1.6	14.4	5.9	16.1	9.8	13.1	11.6	11.6
24340	Grand Rapids-Wyoming, MI	2 669.7	1 047 099	52	392.2	81.1	7.7	0.9	3.2	9.3	6.6	17.7	10.4	14.2	12.0	12.8
24420	Grants Pass, OR	1 638.7	85 904	368	52.4	89.8	0.9	2.9	2.0	7.3	5.1	14.5	6.7	10.3	10.2	11.9
24500	Great Falls, MT	2 698.2	81 755	374	30.3	88.9	2.3	6.3	2.0	4.3	6.7	15.7	9.8	13.9	10.7	11.6
24540	Greeley, CO	3 987.2	294 932	163	74.0	67.7	1.5	1.1	2.2	29.1	7.2	19.3	9.6	14.8	13.3	12.4
24580	Green Bay, WI	1 869.4	318 236	157	170.2	85.6	2.9	2.9	3.1	7.4	6.3	17.2	8.9	12.9	12.2	13.9
24660	Greensboro-High Point, NC.	1 993.7	756 139	75	379.3	60.7	27.8	1.0	4.2	8.3	5.8	16.6	9.8	12.9	12.3	14.1
24780	Greenville, NC	652.4	177 220	236	271.6	56.5	35.7	0.7	2.7	6.2	5.9	16.0	18.0	13.8	11.7	11.5
24860	Greenville-Anderson-Mauldin, SC ...	2 710.8	884 975	61	326.5	74.6	17.5	0.6	2.2	6.7	6.1	16.5	10.0	13.0	12.3	13.5
25060	Gulfport-Biloxi-Pascagoula, MS ...	1 770.7	391 266	136	221.0	70.0	22.5	1.0	3.2	5.5	6.3	17.6	8.9	13.6	12.3	13.2
25180	Hagerstown-Martinsburg, MD-WV ...	778.9	263 817	183	338.7	84.4	11.1	0.7	2.1	4.4	6.1	16.9	7.8	13.3	12.7	14.6
25220	Hammond, LA	791.3	130 710	303	165.2	64.6	30.7	0.8	1.1	4.2	7.3	17.3	10.2	15.0	12.0	12.0
25260	Hanford-Corcoran, CA........	1 389.4	149 785	276	107.8	34.6	6.8	1.4	5.2	54.2	7.8	19.5	11.3	16.8	13.5	12.0
25420	Harrisburg-Carlisle, PA........	1 622.0	568 033	96	350.2	79.6	11.5	0.6	4.6	6.1	5.9	15.5	8.9	13.3	11.9	13.6
25500	Harrisonburg, VA	866.5	132 822	301	153.3	82.0	4.9	0.5	2.8	11.6	5.3	14.4	18.5	13.0	11.0	11.6
25540	Hartford-West Hartford-East Hartford, CT ...	1 514.8	1 206 836	47	796.7	69.4	11.7	0.6	5.5	14.5	5.0	15.5	10.4	12.6	11.7	14.4
25620	Hattiesburg, MS	1 610.4	149 138	279	92.6	66.8	29.6	0.6	1.5	2.7	6.4	17.5	12.0	15.0	12.6	12.0
25860	Hickory-Lenoir-Morganton, NC ...	1 639.5	364 187	147	222.1	82.7	7.7	0.7	3.3	7.2	5.3	16.0	8.2	11.2	12.0	14.9
25940	Hilton Head Island-Bluffton-Beaufort, NC...	1 231.6	211 614	209	171.8	65.6	22.2	0.6	1.8	11.3	5.6	14.0	9.2	11.8	10.4	11.0
25980	Hinesville, GA	916.8	81 007	377	88.4	47.2	39.9	1.2	3.6	12.2	9.5	18.7	13.4	18.9	11.5	10.1
26140	Homosassa Springs, FL	581.9	143 621	287	246.8	89.8	3.4	0.9	2.0	5.4	3.8	10.9	5.5	8.1	7.7	11.6
26300	Hot Springs, AR	677.8	97 477	357	143.8	84.6	9.5	1.5	1.3	5.4	5.5	15.1	7.4	11.4	11.1	12.6
26380	Houma-Thibodaux, LA.........	2 300.1	211 525	210	92.0	73.2	17.4	5.3	1.4	4.8	6.8	17.9	8.6	14.6	12.1	13.4
26420	Houston-The Woodlands-Sugar Land, TX	8 260.8	6 772 470	5	819.8	38.2	17.5	0.6	8.4	36.8	7.5	19.4	9.3	15.1	14.2	12.9
26580	Huntington-Ashland, WV-KY-OH ...	2 527.4	359 588	148	142.3	95.4	3.2	0.7	1.0	1.2	5.8	15.7	8.9	11.7	12.4	13.4
26620	Huntsville, AL	1 361.5	449 720	117	330.3	69.5	23.1	1.5	3.3	5.0	5.8	16.5	9.2	13.8	12.4	14.7
26820	Idaho Falls, ID	5 196.0	142 572	289	27.4	85.7	0.9	1.2	1.6	12.2	8.6	23.0	8.3	13.4	12.5	10.6
26900	Indianapolis-Carmel-Anderson, IN ...	4 306.5	2 004 230	34	465.4	74.9	16.4	0.6	3.6	6.6	6.8	18.2	8.8	14.3	13.2	13.4
26980	Iowa City, IA	1 182.9	168 828	248	142.7	82.6	6.7	0.6	6.6	5.6	6.2	14.6	19.4	15.2	11.6	10.6
27060	Ithaca, NY	474.6	104 871	344	221.0	79.7	5.0	0.8	12.4	5.0	4.1	10.8	27.1	13.0	10.1	10.4
27100	Jackson, MI......................	701.7	158 460	260	225.8	87.3	9.7	1.0	1.2	3.5	5.7	16.1	8.9	12.3	11.7	14.0
27140	Jackson, MS	4 648.1	579 229	94	124.6	47.2	49.6	0.4	1.5	2.3	6.4	18.1	9.6	14.1	12.9	12.7
27180	Jackson, TN	1 108.4	129 527	305	116.9	63.7	31.8	0.6	1.2	4.3	6.2	16.6	10.9	12.1	11.5	13.0
27260	Jacksonville, FL	3 202.0	1 478 212	40	461.7	65.8	22.3	0.8	5.1	8.5	6.2	16.3	8.5	14.6	12.5	13.6
27340	Jacksonville, NC	762.1	187 136	227	245.6	69.8	16.9	1.4	3.8	12.2	9.3	15.9	19.8	18.8	10.5	8.3
27500	Janesville-Beloit, WI	718.1	161 620	255	225.1	85.0	6.1	0.7	1.7	8.6	6.0	17.6	8.7	12.1	12.2	13.8
27620	Jefferson City, MO	2 247.7	151 391	272	67.4	88.1	8.7	1.0	1.3	2.7	5.9	16.5	9.4	13.3	12.6	13.7
27740	Johnson City, TN	853.8	201 661	219	236.2	92.5	3.9	0.8	1.4	3.0	4.9	14.3	10.4	12.1	11.8	13.6
27780	Johnstown, PA	688.4	134 732	299	195.7	94.3	4.4	0.4	0.8	1.6	4.9	14.4	9.2	10.4	10.9	13.1

1. CBSA = Core Based Statistical Area. DIV = Metropolitan Division. See Appendix A for explanation. See Appendix B for list of metropolitan areas identified by type.   2. Dry land or land partially or temporarily covered by water.   3. May be of any race.

Table C. Metropolitan Areas — **Population and Households**

Area name	Population, 2016 (cont.) Age (percent) (cont.)				Population change and components of change, 2000–2016							Households, 2015				
	55 to 64 years	65 to 74 years	75 years and over	Percent female	Total persons		Percent change		Components of change, 2010–2016				Persons per house-hold	Percent		
					2000	2010	2000–2010	2010–2016	Births	Deaths	Net migration	Number		Family house-holds	Female family house-holder[1]	One person
	16	17	18	19	20	21	22	23	24	25	26	27	28	29	30	31
Evansville, IN-KY	14.2	9.3	7.0	51.3	296 195	311 552	5.2	1.4	23 474	19 758	1 069	124 936	2.45	64.7	10.6	30.7
Fairbanks, AK	11.1	6.2	2.7	45.9	82 840	97 585	17.8	3.1	10 636	2 895	-4 733	35 475	2.69	64.7	7.1	28.1
Fargo, ND-MN	10.7	6.5	5.2	49.6	174 367	208 777	19.7	14.1	20 414	8 888	17 437	96 142	2.34	58.3	9.3	31.2
Farmington, NM	13.0	8.7	6.3	50.4	113 801	130 045	14.3	-11.5	11 561	5 911	-20 770	43 030	2.72	69.1	17.1	25.1
Fayetteville, NC	10.6	6.7	4.5	50.9	336 609	366 311	8.8	3.8	41 226	16 779	-10 770	137 158	2.66	65.2	17.6	30.8
Fayetteville-Springdale-Rogers, AR-MO	10.6	7.4	5.1	50.2	347 045	463 210	33.5	13.3	44 433	21 718	38 174	190 860	2.64	67.8	9.1	25.9
Flagstaff, AZ	11.9	7.6	4.3	50.7	116 320	134 437	15.6	4.8	10 636	4 778	556	45 911	2.74	61.4	11.0	25.5
Flint, MI	14.2	9.5	6.9	51.8	436 141	425 790	-2.4	-4.0	31 085	27 239	-20 784	163 488	2.48	63.0	15.9	31.1
Florence, SC	13.5	10.2	6.5	53.1	193 155	205 571	6.4	0.2	15 999	14 266	-1 189	79 914	2.53	64.6	18.5	31.0
Florence-Muscle Shoals, AL	13.9	10.9	8.2	52.0	142 950	147 137	2.9	-0.4	9 593	11 028	1 040	60 663	2.38	64.6	12.8	29.9
Fond du Lac, WI	14.6	9.9	7.7	50.9	97 296	101 630	4.5	0.5	6 851	5 769	-416	40 295	2.45	67.1	8.4	27.3
Fort Collins, CO	12.8	9.1	5.7	50.1	251 494	299 629	19.1	13.5	21 461	12 580	30 319	129 210	2.51	60.4	7.3	24.1
Fort Smith, AR-OK	12.9	9.5	6.6	50.7	255 399	280 547	9.8	0.2	22 052	18 376	-2 895	107 375	2.57	68.9	12.5	26.3
Fort Wayne, IN	12.8	8.4	5.9	51.0	390 156	416 254	6.7	3.7	37 239	22 175	958	165 857	2.55	66.5	12.9	28.3
Fresno, CA	10.4	6.9	5.0	50.1	799 407	930 491	16.4	5.3	99 284	40 558	-9 483	304 209	3.15	71.7	18.2	22.3
Gadsden, AL	13.9	10.9	7.3	51.6	103 459	104 427	0.9	-1.8	7 290	8 690	-340	39 332	2.59	70.0	13.4	27.1
Gainesville, FL	11.4	8.3	5.5	51.5	232 392	264 274	13.7	6.2	19 212	12 410	9 284	102 219	2.52	59.4	11.9	30.3
Gainesville, GA	11.3	8.6	5.8	50.3	139 277	179 684	29.0	9.4	15 990	8 412	9 028	63 989	3.00	77.2	12.5	18.8
Gettysburg, PA	14.8	11.2	8.3	50.7	91 292	101 417	11.1	0.8	6 268	6 010	271	38 459	2.55	70.1	8.6	25.4
Glens Falls, NY	15.5	11.6	8.1	49.6	124 345	128 942	3.7	-2.0	7 459	7 984	-1 889	48 814	2.52	62.8	10.4	29.2
Goldsboro, NC	13.1	8.9	6.4	51.0	113 329	122 638	8.2	1.2	10 594	7 097	-1 834	47 490	2.55	64.3	16.3	29.7
Grand Forks, ND-MN	11.8	7.5	6.1	48.9	97 478	98 464	1.0	4.3	8 831	5 108	517	42 166	2.28	57.9	6.1	31.0
Grand Island, NE	12.6	8.6	7.3	49.7	77 708	81 850	5.3	4.0	7 625	4 667	353	31 703	2.64	68.0	13.2	25.8
Grand Junction, CO	13.9	10.4	7.5	50.4	116 255	146 717	26.2	2.3	11 423	8 697	383	59 066	2.45	65.7	12.5	27.1
Grand Rapids-Wyoming, MI	12.5	7.9	5.8	50.5	930 670	988 940	6.3	5.9	84 889	45 935	19 433	383 194	2.65	68.0	11.3	24.9
Grants Pass, OR	15.8	14.8	10.8	51.2	75 726	82 713	9.2	3.9	5 221	7 247	5 091	35 918	2.33	61.8	9.8	28.8
Great Falls, MT	13.6	9.9	8.0	49.4	80 357	81 324	1.2	0.5	7 312	5 070	-1 784	34 375	2.31	62.2	10.6	31.6
Greeley, CO	11.6	7.3	4.4	49.6	180 926	252 831	39.7	16.7	24 362	9 904	26 711	97 822	2.85	72.8	9.5	20.8
Green Bay, WI	13.6	8.7	6.3	50.1	282 599	306 241	8.4	3.9	24 644	14 704	2 153	127 779	2.42	63.8	9.0	29.3
Greensboro-High Point, NC	13.1	9.1	6.4	52.1	643 430	723 854	12.5	4.5	53 896	40 733	19 257	291 088	2.52	64.0	13.4	30.2
Greenville, NC	11.2	7.2	4.8	52.9	133 798	168 152	25.7	5.4	13 332	7 499	3 282	68 374	2.48	58.5	17.2	30.0
Greenville-Anderson-Mauldin, SC	12.8	9.5	6.4	51.4	725 680	824 109	13.6	7.4	65 262	49 092	43 082	332 740	2.56	65.6	12.6	28.6
Gulfport-Biloxi-Pascagoula, MS	13.2	9.0	5.9	50.8	363 988	370 787	1.9	5.5	30 767	22 368	11 740	146 228	2.62	65.8	16.5	28.1
Hagerstown-Martinsburg, MD-WV	13.1	9.3	6.3	49.7	207 828	251 602	21.1	4.9	19 448	15 168	7 619	97 209	2.59	67.0	11.6	26.5
Hammond, LA	12.6	8.6	5.0	51.6	100 588	121 101	20.4	7.9	11 845	7 306	4 867	46 263	2.71	65.6	15.9	29.9
Hanford-Corcoran, CA	9.4	5.6	4.1	44.9	129 461	152 982	18.2	-2.1	14 984	5 042	-13 302	42 692	3.13	73.4	16.8	19.5
Harrisburg-Carlisle, PA	13.9	9.7	7.2	50.9	509 074	549 473	7.9	3.4	41 361	31 823	9 584	225 810	2.41	65.4	12.5	29.2
Harrisonburg, VA	11.4	8.0	6.6	51.3	108 193	125 217	15.7	6.1	8 762	5 949	4 418	47 600	2.56	62.2	9.3	26.3
Hartford-West Hartford-East Hartford, CT	14.1	9.2	7.2	51.2	1 148 618	1 212 397	5.6	-0.5	75 283	64 669	-14 212	464 613	2.50	65.4	12.8	27.9
Hattiesburg, MS	11.3	7.7	5.5	52.2	123 812	142 857	15.4	4.4	12 322	7 773	1 526	54 780	2.63	65.0	17.2	26.8
Hickory-Lenoir-Morganton, NC	14.2	10.9	7.3	50.6	341 851	365 814	7.0	-0.4	23 709	24 281	-1 168	140 097	2.53	64.6	10.9	31.4
Hilton Head Island-Bluffton-Beaufort, NC	13.5	15.3	9.3	50.6	141 615	187 010	32.1	13.2	14 956	10 381	19 160	78 824	2.56	70.8	10.9	23.7
Hinesville, GA	9.4	5.6	2.8	49.0	71 914	77 915	8.3	4.0	10 418	2 584	-5 137	27 874	2.75	68.7	20.2	26.1
Homosassa Springs, FL	16.4	19.7	16.2	51.7	118 085	141 236	19.6	1.7	6 439	15 211	10 611	60 541	2.29	63.4	9.3	31.5
Hot Springs, AR	14.6	12.8	9.6	51.8	88 068	95 995	9.0	1.5	6 886	8 458	3 298	40 134	2.37	63.6	11.3	31.1
Houma-Thibodaux, LA	12.7	8.2	5.7	50.7	194 477	208 176	7.0	1.6	18 102	11 759	-2 891	77 548	2.69	66.5	13.6	26.3
Houston-The Woodlands-Sugar Land, TX	11.2	6.6	3.9	50.3	4 693 161	5 920 499	26.2	14.4	599 542	226 559	476 857	2 292 992	2.87	70.6	15.0	24.5
Huntington-Ashland, WV-KY-OH	13.9	10.7	7.7	51.0	362 346	364 928	0.7	-1.5	25 882	26 199	-4 440	140 735	2.51	64.7	11.7	29.3
Huntsville, AL	13.3	8.4	6.0	50.9	342 376	417 593	22.0	7.7	32 183	22 117	21 229	172 549	2.51	65.7	11.1	29.2
Idaho Falls, ID	11.0	7.5	5.2	50.1	104 576	133 333	27.5	6.9	15 239	5 892	-229	45 611	3.03	75.2	10.2	21.2
Indianapolis-Carmel-Anderson, IN	12.3	7.7	5.3	51.1	1 658 462	1 888 082	13.8	6.2	166 419	97 275	47 319	755 100	2.58	62.7	12.6	31.2
Iowa City, IA	10.6	7.2	4.9	50.4	131 676	152 586	15.9	10.6	13 085	5 653	8 671	64 183	2.47	58.0	8.1	27.7
Ithaca, NY	11.4	7.9	5.2	50.8	96 501	101 594	5.3	3.2	5 511	4 117	1 891	38 112	2.40	51.4	8.5	34.3
Jackson, MI	14.4	9.8	7.0	48.9	158 422	160 248	1.2	-1.1	11 280	10 018	-2 907	59 292	2.53	66.1	11.3	29.2
Jackson, MS	12.5	8.1	5.5	52.2	525 346	567 645	8.1	2.0	47 379	31 562	-4 259	210 443	2.65	67.9	20.0	28.3
Jackson, TN	13.3	9.6	6.9	52.5	121 909	130 018	6.7	-0.4	10 095	8 039	-2 595	49 318	2.53	69.8	16.7	25.8
Jacksonville, FL	13.2	9.3	5.8	51.3	1 122 750	1 345 595	19.8	9.9	111 062	74 073	92 809	536 299	2.65	65.9	14.5	27.2
Jacksonville, NC	8.0	5.5	3.8	45.8	150 355	177 787	18.2	5.3	26 951	5 932	-12 254	64 771	2.70	71.3	15.0	22.3
Janesville-Beloit, WI	13.8	8.9	6.9	50.8	152 307	160 331	5.3	0.8	12 087	9 017	-1 720	65 054	2.43	65.9	13.3	26.6
Jefferson City, MO	13.2	8.9	6.4	48.8	140 052	149 805	7.0	1.1	11 179	7 890	-1 563	55 448	2.54	63.6	9.8	31.9
Johnson City, TN	13.8	11.1	7.9	51.0	181 607	198 755	9.4	1.5	12 631	14 096	4 190	83 074	2.33	64.6	11.6	29.6
Johnstown, PA	15.8	11.6	9.8	50.9	152 598	143 674	-5.8	-6.2	8 273	11 319	-5 721	57 044	2.26	60.9	9.9	33.2

1. No spouse present.

Table C. Metropolitan Areas — **Population, Vital Statistics, Health, and Crime**

Area name	Persons in group quarters, 2016	Daytime population, 2015		Births, 2016		Deaths, 2016		Persons under 65 with no health insurance 2015		Medicare, 2015			Serious crimes known to police,[2] 2014 Total	
		Number	Employment/residence ratio	Total	Rate[1]	Number	Rate[1]	Number	Percent	Total Beneficiaries	Enrolled in Original Medicare	Enrolled in Medicare Advantage	Number	Rate[3]
	32	33	34	35	36	37	38	39	40	41	42	43	44	45
Evansville, IN-KY	9 683	320 671	1.03	3 679	11.6	3 276	10.4	22 553	8.7	60 368	43 700	16 668	11 210	3 557
Fairbanks, AK	4 868	NA	NA	1 676	16.7	471	4.7	12 273	14.1	8 424	8 317	107	NA	NA
Fargo, ND-MN	8 617	239 785	1.05	3 510	14.7	1 507	6.3	13 373	6.7	29 228	20 069	9 159	5 491	2 410
Farmington, NM	1 748	118 227	0.99	1 703	14.8	1 026	8.9	16 349	16.2	17 835	17 043	792	3 155	2 518
Fayetteville, NC	9 892	389 202	1.08	6 354	16.7	2 896	7.6	37 969	11.6	53 130	39 726	13 404	18 498	4 862
Fayetteville-Springdale-Rogers, AR-MO	10 686	519 878	1.02	7 266	13.8	3 606	6.9	56 327	12.8	73 056	51 076	21 980	10 917	2 587
Flagstaff, AZ	11 485	139 798	1.01	1 683	11.9	869	6.2	16 458	14.6	20 593	17 140	3 453	4 877	3 529
Flint, MI	5 821	393 955	0.90	4 831	11.8	4 510	11.0	23 029	8.7	88 034	54 781	33 253	13 935	3 374
Florence, SC	4 692	212 386	1.07	2 512	12.2	2 340	11.4	20 479	12.1	42 411	35 385	7 026	9 281	4 504
Florence-Muscle Shoals, AL	2 534	143 176	0.94	1 522	10.4	1 760	12.0	12 907	11.0	34 113	28 857	5 256	4 561	3 100
Fond du Lac, WI	3 532	98 629	0.94	1 050	10.3	880	8.6	4 651	5.7	20 919	10 785	10 134	1 801	1 768
Fort Collins, CO	9 367	326 677	0.96	3 591	10.6	2 182	6.4	19 543	7.0	49 169	34 161	15 008	7 548	2 345
Fort Smith, AR-OK	5 001	280 629	1.00	3 662	13.0	3 077	10.9	34 444	14.9	56 404	40 660	15 744	9 990	3 581
Fort Wayne, IN	7 020	434 519	1.02	6 001	13.9	3 634	8.4	42 404	11.6	69 975	37 776	32 199	11 143	2 761
Fresno, CA	17 435	980 021	1.01	15 767	16.1	7 049	7.2	91 282	10.8	118 408	77 591	40 817	37 082	3 837
Gadsden, AL	2 085	98 839	0.90	1 148	11.2	1 497	14.6	9 969	12.0	24 831	18 589	6 242	4 647	4 475
Gainesville, FL	14 692	290 785	1.11	3 120	11.1	2 149	7.7	29 528	12.9	43 106	33 815	9 291	9 313	3 411
Gainesville, GA	2 879	198 857	1.06	2 622	13.3	1 533	7.8	34 845	21.3	29 871	20 230	9 641	4 071	2 139
Gettysburg, PA	4 069	86 910	0.69	997	9.8	992	9.7	6 309	7.9	19 405	13 172	6 233	1 224	1 205
Glens Falls, NY	3 758	125 266	0.97	1 123	8.9	1 321	10.5	6 013	6.0	29 328	17 409	11 919	1 939	1 509
Goldsboro, NC	3 034	122 395	0.97	1 633	13.2	1 275	10.3	14 136	13.8	22 938	18 276	4 662	4 608	3 764
Grand Forks, ND-MN	5 293	103 709	1.02	1 503	14.6	828	8.1	6 254	7.5	15 714	10 821	4 893	2 449	2 410
Grand Island, NE	1 487	85 777	1.02	1 272	14.9	750	8.8	8 913	12.6	15 171	14 134	1 037	2 763	3 532
Grand Junction, CO	4 437	147 019	0.98	1 787	11.9	1 455	9.7	12 847	10.8	28 355	17 255	11 100	4 393	2 955
Grand Rapids-Wyoming, MI	23 776	1 056 190	1.03	13 727	13.1	7 687	7.3	61 266	6.9	166 763	78 301	88 462	21 473	2 106
Grants Pass, OR	1 537	81 453	0.89	885	10.3	1 147	13.4	5 518	8.9	24 070	14 899	9 171	2 896	3 457
Great Falls, MT	2 463	NA	NA	1 124	13.7	813	9.9	8 918	13.5	16 570	12 376	4 194	2 942	3 554
Greeley, CO	4 944	270 521	0.89	4 106	13.9	1 725	5.8	20 906	8.4	33 383	22 250	11 133	6 203	2 261
Green Bay, WI	6 975	322 555	1.04	3 892	12.2	2 385	7.5	19 515	7.4	53 653	25 535	28 118	4 664	1 767
Greensboro-High Point, NC	19 476	770 823	1.05	8 558	11.3	7 031	9.3	85 556	13.7	136 687	63 326	73 361	25 199	3 380
Greenville, NC	6 820	176 239	1.00	2 121	12.0	1 318	7.4	18 618	12.5	26 358	21 591	4 767	6 114	3 532
Greenville-Anderson-Mauldin, SC	23 293	877 535	1.01	10 744	12.1	8 326	9.4	97 641	13.6	162 050	107 995	54 055	37 580	4 363
Gulfport-Biloxi-Pascagoula, MS	6 868	394 187	1.03	5 016	12.8	3 665	9.4	52 150	16.0	67 580	52 135	15 445	14 048	3 973
Hagerstown-Martinsburg, MD-WV	9 131	249 862	0.90	3 112	11.8	2 539	9.6	15 181	7.1	45 865	39 214	6 651	5 756	2 215
Hammond, LA	3 656	116 816	0.79	1 909	14.6	1 283	9.8	16 380	15.1	22 199	14 664	7 535	7 591	6 096
Hanford-Corcoran, CA	16 201	149 628	0.98	2 324	15.5	849	5.7	10 670	8.9	14 906	12 621	2 285	4 171	2 754
Harrisburg-Carlisle, PA	20 077	614 857	1.18	6 734	11.9	5 249	9.2	33 492	7.3	106 761	56 962	49 799	11 999	2 145
Harrisonburg, VA	9 284	138 310	1.12	1 449	10.9	1 002	7.5	14 477	13.9	17 933	14 774	3 159	2 031	1 560
Hartford-West Hartford-East Hartford, CT	47 027	1 243 831	1.05	11 863	9.8	10 674	8.8	53 116	5.4	206 042	139 935	66 107	25 563	2 495
Hattiesburg, MS	3 667	150 458	1.03	1 885	12.6	1 257	8.4	18 565	14.7	25 554	20 518	5 036	NA	NA
Hickory-Lenoir-Morganton, NC	7 217	354 661	0.95	3 817	10.5	4 042	11.1	42 025	14.3	76 614	50 261	26 353	10 636	2 938
Hilton Head Island-Bluffton-Beaufort, NC	6 722	208 882	1.02	2 424	11.5	1 818	8.6	24 762	16.3	47 438	38 346	9 092	6 389	3 163
Hinesville, GA	2 763	79 729	1.03	1 612	19.9	449	5.5	9 635	13.6	6 842	4 984	1 858	2 413	2 945
Homosassa Springs, FL	2 250	134 101	0.84	1 017	7.1	2 577	17.9	13 320	14.9	47 793	31 532	16 261	NA	NA
Hot Springs, AR	2 176	98 604	1.04	1 068	11.0	1 324	13.6	9 611	12.9	31 441	24 189	7 252	6 561	3 118
Houma-Thibodaux, LA	3 109	221 189	1.10	2 925	13.8	1 950	9.2	30 483	16.8	34 809	27 625	7 184		
Houston-The Woodlands-Sugar Land, TX	83 570	6 678 270	1.01	102 152	15.1	40 536	6.0	1 131 790	19.2	692 288	390 815	301 473	243 686	3 776
Huntington-Ashland, WV-KY-OH	7 958	357 556	0.97	4 052	11.3	4 280	11.9	20 436	7.0	81 310	57 942	23 368	6 922	2 049
Huntsville, AL	10 835	470 403	1.13	5 262	11.7	3 856	8.6	39 689	10.7	71 336	57 797	13 539	16 049	3 646
Idaho Falls, ID	1 370	142 762	1.05	2 399	16.8	967	6.8	14 444	11.9	20 332	15 630	4 702	2 667	1 920
Indianapolis-Carmel-Anderson, IN	38 924	1 999 181	1.01	26 568	13.3	16 107	8.0	184 460	10.8	291 697	207 783	83 914	70 311	4 117
Iowa City, IA	8 843	170 392	1.04	2 124	12.6	961	5.7	9 006	6.4	19 753	16 758	2 995	3 390	2 072
Ithaca, NY	13 242	117 761	1.26	854	8.1	631	6.0	5 055	6.4	14 068	10 640	3 428	2 611	2 504
Jackson, MI	8 834	158 615	0.99	1 808	11.4	1 624	10.2	7 775	6.2	32 356	23 792	8 564	4 054	2 559
Jackson, MS	21 614	587 134	1.03	7 363	12.7	5 354	9.2	60 437	12.5	91 866	69 212	22 654	16 194	3 424
Jackson, TN	5 918	140 924	1.19	1 575	12.2	1 321	10.2	11 984	11.5	24 856	19 289	5 567	5 117	3 902
Jacksonville, FL	28 228	1 454 968	1.01	18 248	12.3	13 137	8.9	151 491	12.5	240 418	166 165	74 253	52 727	3 719
Jacksonville, NC	14 297	187 635	1.01	4 194	22.4	1 050	5.6	15 306	9.8	20 171	17 204	2 967	NA	NA
Janesville-Beloit, WI	2 665	149 129	0.84	1 923	11.9	1 440	8.9	10 915	8.1	30 399	20 348	10 051	4 401	2 735
Jefferson City, MO	10 754	155 972	1.07	1 750	11.6	1 327	8.8	12 792	10.8	26 706	22 628	4 078	3 302	2 190
Johnson City, TN	5 519	197 546	0.97	1 990	9.9	2 299	11.4	19 624	12.3	45 354	23 065	22 289	5 569	2 757
Johnstown, PA	6 281	131 742	0.92	1 259	9.3	1 794	13.3	6 794	6.6	34 839	12 496	22 343	2 707	1 937

1. Per 1,000 estimated resident population.   2. Data for serious crimes have not been adjusted for underreporting; this may affect comparability between geographic areas and over time.
3. Per 100,000 population estimated by the FBI.

Table C. Metropolitan Areas — Crime, Education, Money Income, and Poverty

	Serious crimes known to police, 2014 (cont.)[1]		Education						Income and Poverty, 2015							
	Rate[2]		School enrollment and attainment, 2015				Local government expenditures,[5] 2013–2014								Percent below poverty level		
			Enrollment[3]		Attainment[4] (percent)												
Area name	Violent	Property	Total	Percent private	High school graduate or less	Bachelor's degree or more	Total current expenditures (mil dol)	Current expenditures per student (dollars)	Per capita income[6] (dollars)	Mean household income (dollars)	Median household income	Percent of households with income of less than $50,000	Percent of households with income of $200,000 or more	All persons	Children under 18 years	Age 65 years and older
	46	47	48	49	50	51	52	53	54	55	56	57	58	59	60	61
Evansville, IN-KY	293	3 264	74 626	18.9	46.0	23.3	435.2	9 795	26 949	66 140	48 662	51.1	3.3	15.2	22.6	7.5
Fairbanks, AK	NA	NA	28 491	17.7	24.2	34.5	276.0	17 678	33 553	88 857	72 975	31.5	6.1	7.4	8.9	3.5
Fargo, ND-MN	253	2 156	68 636	12.7	28.7	34.5	344.8	10 895	31 585	75 184	56 051	45.6	4.9	11.1	8.5	6.4
Farmington, NM	535	1 983	32 419	8.3	51.6	14.1	231.3	9 421	24 055	63 911	49 613	50.3	2.0	19.6	25.2	13.7
Fayetteville, NC	459	4 404	107 346	17.9	35.1	25.2	486.2	8 067	21 960	56 366	41 921	58.0	1.7	19.4	28.2	11.4
Fayetteville-Springdale-Rogers, AR-MO	323	2 263	144 161	11.6	43.8	30.8	803.8	9 229	27 083	71 402	50 788	48.9	5.2	14.3	19.4	9.5
Flagstaff, AZ	346	3 183	48 026	7.2	32.8	33.1	170.0	8 991	25 412	73 662	53 152	45.8	4.6	20.0	17.3	16.1
Flint, MI	654	2 720	100 555	11.6	42.0	20.8	748.7	10 893	23 593	57 809	44 025	56.3	2.0	20.6	30.6	7.3
Florence, SC	472	4 031	50 153	14.1	52.3	19.8	317.2	9 394	22 819	56 846	38 062	60.2	2.1	19.5	26.7	12.6
Florence-Muscle Shoals, AL.	338	2 762	32 912	8.1	51.3	20.8	197.9	9 297	25 170	59 042	41 547	57.7	2.5	18.0	26.6	6.2
Fond du Lac, WI	200	1 568	24 034	24.2	46.3	21.7	143.9	10 704	28 546	70 979	57 620	42.5	2.6	9.2	11.0	7.6
Fort Collins, CO	190	2 156	96 370	10.3	24.2	46.2	395.4	8 644	32 861	83 773	64 919	38.9	5.9	12.7	10.8	4.8
Fort Smith, AR-OK	432	3 148	67 202	7.1	51.8	17.1	433.5	8 686	21 748	55 126	41 040	59.0	2.1	20.5	27.5	12.2
Fort Wayne, IN	237	2 524	112 318	21.4	41.2	26.9	595.5	9 359	27 350	69 038	50 856	48.8	3.6	13.7	20.0	5.3
Fresno, CA	471	3 367	288 180	7.6	49.0	19.2	1 911.6	9 794	21 079	64 716	46 949	52.0	3.5	25.3	36.9	10.8
Gadsden, AL	490	3 985	22 330	9.2	47.6	17.3	135.2	8 415	21 407	52 933	43 346	56.9	1.0	18.1	32.9	8.5
Gainesville, FL	552	2 859	94 253	9.7	30.4	42.0	275.1	8 622	26 189	67 719	46 949	52.4	4.3	21.9	22.4	9.3
Gainesville, GA	173	1 965	52 144	8.4	48.4	22.7	295.5	8 539	26 080	76 098	55 009	45.7	5.2	17.3	26.7	11.2
Gettysburg, PA	103	1 102	22 981	24.9	52.2	21.0	279.1	19 925	27 698	72 473	61 023	40.7	3.2	7.9	13.1	3.7
Glens Falls, NY	115	1 394	26 291	12.0	45.2	24.6	326.6	18 015	28 603	71 721	55 186	45.4	2.8	11.5	14.9	6.7
Goldsboro, NC	372	3 392	31 485	16.4	44.1	21.9	155.0	7 989	22 018	54 321	40 361	57.6	1.9	18.0	29.1	8.0
Grand Forks, ND-MN	214	2 197	29 268	9.7	32.5	32.8	158.2	11 432	31 571	75 004	53 443	46.6	3.4	14.2	17.1	11.0
Grand Island, NE	210	3 322	21 401	8.8	47.6	19.8	184.0	11 762	24 622	63 358	51 371	48.4	2.3	12.7	19.4	10.2
Grand Junction, CO	346	2 609	36 636	10.6	35.1	30.3	181.6	8 069	27 270	67 247	51 465	47.8	3.6	14.4	17.6	6.8
Grand Rapids-Wyoming, MI.	315	1 791	276 391	19.9	37.2	31.1	1 827.8	10 631	28 029	74 005	55 459	45.2	3.8	12.9	17.3	6.7
Grants Pass, OR	222	3 235	16 203	8.4	45.9	14.0	102.5	9 557	21 972	51 033	41 493	58.8	2.6	22.6	38.3	13.1
Great Falls, MT	249	3 305	18 558	10.1	42.5	25.6	112.4	9 660	28 455	65 494	45 606	55.4	3.5	14.3	20.5	9.2
Greeley, CO	285	1 976	80 511	10.8	39.5	25.9	337.3	8 515	28 322	79 555	70 256	36.3	4.5	11.3	13.3	7.7
Green Bay, WI	240	1 527	79 557	15.5	41.9	26.1	553.3	10 692	28 015	68 514	54 847	45.4	3.3	11.0	14.9	7.5
Greensboro-High Point, NC..	321	3 060	190 196	12.0	40.8	28.0	992.3	8 854	26 026	64 628	45 749	53.9	3.4	16.1	24.0	8.6
Greenville, NC	416	3 116	63 397	9.9	35.5	31.6	194.1	8 217	24 810	61 513	41 453	58.2	3.4	26.8	32.9	11.2
Greenville-Anderson-Mauldin, SC	538	3 826	220 139	17.7	43.2	26.7	1 125.6	8 538	25 009	63 602	48 180	51.5	2.8	15.7	20.8	7.6
Gulfport-Biloxi-Pascagoula, MS	216	3 758	97 138	8.8	45.1	20.4	532.2	8 555	22 734	57 861	44 328	55.4	2.0	20.0	29.1	9.3
Hagerstown-Martinsburg, MD-WV	250	1 965	64 539	11.8	51.5	19.1	487.2	11 966	26 622	69 301	55 142	45.9	2.4	12.1	18.7	7.4
Hammond, LA	789	5 308	37 310	17.3	51.2	19.1	182.4	9 136	23 738	61 415	42 962	54.1	2.6	24.6	36.5	15.4
Hanford-Corcoran, CA	460	2 295	45 516	12.5	51.2	16.1	270.5	10 440	20 377	67 033	45 744	52.5	3.1	23.6	32.7	9.6
Harrisburg-Carlisle, PA	239	1 906	129 134	19.8	45.0	29.6	964.3	12 873	30 489	74 009	58 166	42.1	4.0	10.5	17.7	6.0
Harrisonburg, VA	140	1 421	41 606	11.0	48.0	29.0	181.0	10 479	23 481	63 449	47 420	51.6	3.0	20.3	20.2	9.4
Hartford-West Hartford-East Hartford, CT	253	2 242	311 991	16.4	36.5	38.3	3 106.7	16 630	37 426	94 753	72 275	36.1	9.1	9.9	13.0	7.2
Hattiesburg, MS	NA	NA	46 548	15.0	41.6	26.8	204.3	8 615	21 004	55 818	41 938	56.9	2.3	23.5	25.8	9.7
Hickory-Lenoir-Morganton, NC	194	2 744	79 752	14.3	48.7	18.5	453.4	8 295	22 281	55 285	40 380	59.6	1.8	15.8	19.4	9.0
Hilton Head Island-Bluffton-Beaufort, NC	443	2 720	43 113	23.1	33.7	37.3	259.5	11 007	31 391	78 273	55 923	46.0	4.7	14.3	26.3	5.8
Hinesville, GA	336	2 609	21 931	9.5	43.9	17.5	120.8	9 044	17 914	46 718	37 211	64.0	0.6	22.0	26.2	18.8
Homosassa Springs, FL	355	1 741	22 617	12.6	53.5	16.2	132.1	8 764	24 645	54 383	40 294	61.4	2.1	17.6	32.0	8.2
Hot Springs, AR	NA	NA	18 837	7.4	44.3	19.4	146.0	9 721	24 910	58 879	37 013	63.2	2.5	20.1	26.7	8.7
Houma-Thibodaux, LA	242	2 875	52 465	14.7	61.8	16.0	319.0	9 570	24 331	64 023	48 119	52.0	2.8	17.7	21.3	12.9
Houston-The Woodlands-Sugar Land, TX	568	3 209	1 849 065	12.3	41.1	31.5	10 339.6	8 251	31 668	89 171	61 465	40.9	8.6	14.6	21.9	9.5
Huntington-Ashland, WV-KY-OH	163	1 886	79 865	7.7	49.9	19.1	614.6	10 826	23 661	57 685	42 237	56.8	2.5	20.1	29.9	9.5
Huntsville, AL	476	3 170	115 040	15.2	34.2	38.1	603.4	9 254	31 093	78 342	57 792	44.0	5.1	13.8	19.6	7.7
Idaho Falls, ID	154	1 766	40 157	10.5	38.3	27.1	170.8	6 033	26 832	76 167	52 689	46.9	4.1	11.9	14.4	5.4
Indianapolis-Carmel-Anderson, IN	715	3 402	516 427	17.0	39.6	32.9	3 125.5	9 371	29 745	75 178	54 322	46.3	4.9	13.9	20.5	7.8
Iowa City, IA	260	1 812	57 536	11.8	29.2	43.6	211.8	10 131	29 990	76 186	55 332	44.7	5.5	19.4	16.2	4.8
Ithaca, NY	123	2 381	43 014	63.1	24.6	54.9	221.8	19 906	29 738	77 498	58 084	42.8	6.3	22.3	18.1	4.3
Jackson, MI	414	2 145	38 398	16.5	44.8	21.9	267.1	11 433	26 236	65 830	50 783	49.2	3.5	16.3	28.1	5.7
Jackson, MS	402	3 022	163 791	20.5	37.9	29.0	756.2	8 142	24 194	63 688	46 757	52.3	3.1	19.4	27.6	11.9
Jackson, TN	759	3 143	33 172	25.3	47.4	23.5	159.4	8 384	24 783	63 483	46 553	53.2	3.0	18.1	30.9	8.2
Jacksonville, FL	528	3 191	363 823	20.3	38.1	30.0	1 823.6	8 542	29 284	74 960	53 221	46.5	5.0	14.3	21.0	9.6
Jacksonville, NC	NA	NA	45 991	12.8	41.2	20.8	202.1	8 005	22 414	54 866	45 832	54.0	1.1	14.9	21.7	6.0
Janesville-Beloit, WI	232	2 503	38 502	14.2	47.0	21.8	305.6	10 934	26 694	65 408	53 777	45.3	3.0	14.5	22.3	5.3
Jefferson City, MO	236	1 954	36 463	27.1	44.8	27.1	176.3	7 892	25 639	67 077	55 069	44.8	2.5	13.5	21.9	7.2
Johnson City, TN	288	2 469	45 916	10.6	49.0	23.9	233.4	8 489	24 179	56 652	40 388	59.6	2.2	20.4	27.3	11.7
Johnstown, PA	173	1 764	31 139	24.2	54.2	21.1	220.4	12 020	23 827	56 001	44 179	55.3	1.4	14.9	22.3	8.4

1. Data for serious crimes have not been adjusted for underreporting; this may affect comparability between geographic areas and over time. 2. Per 100,000 population estimated by the FBI. 3. All persons 3 years old and over enrolled in nursery school through college. 4. Persons 25 years old and over. 5. Elementary and secondary education expenditures. 6. Based on resident population estimated in the 2015 American Community Survey.

Table C. Metropolitan Areas — **Personal Income**

Area name	Personal income, 2015										Earnings, 2015		
			Per capita[1]			Supplements to wages and salaries; employer contributions (mil dol)						Contributions for government social insurance (mil dol)	
	Total (mil dol)	Percent change 2014–2015	Dollars	Rank	Wages and salaries (mil dol)	Pension and insurance	Government social insurance	Proprietors' income (mil dol)	Dividends, interest, and rent (mil dol)	Personal transfer receipts (mil dol)	Total (mil dol)	From employee and self-employed	From employer
	62	63	64	65	66	67	68	69	70	71	72	73	74
Evansville, IN-KY	13 288	2.9	42 091	175	7 077	1 121	535	985	2 237	2 804	9 718	599	535
Fairbanks, AK	5 399	4.7	54 185	28	2 615	736	209	317	962	823	3 877	182	209
Fargo, ND-MN	11 689	4.2	49 987	58	6 566	874	537	1 082	2 471	1 441	9 059	537	537
Farmington, NM	4 485	2.0	37 777	278	2 448	411	194	176	610	1 009	3 227	202	194
Fayetteville, NC	13 727	3.6	36 460	311	8 836	2 190	814	517	3 009	3 429	12 357	615	814
Fayetteville-Springdale-Rogers, AR-MO	26 967	3.7	52 509	38	11 828	1 484	856	1 366	10 176	3 349	15 534	972	856
Flagstaff, AZ	5 705	4.7	41 018	199	2 702	546	200	338	1 208	1 097	3 786	222	200
Flint, MI	15 042	4.5	36 612	305	6 269	1 008	483	769	2 149	4 592	8 530	585	483
Florence, SC	7 459	3.7	36 130	319	3 848	654	291	301	1 025	2 067	5 094	338	291
Florence-Muscle Shoals, AL	5 206	2.1	35 427	335	2 160	369	161	327	938	1 384	3 017	211	161
Fond du Lac, WI	4 463	3.3	43 764	139	2 134	383	173	315	714	815	3 004	182	173
Fort Collins, CO	15 117	5.0	45 318	103	7 541	1 008	521	971	3 334	2 122	10 041	557	521
Fort Smith, AR-OK	9 546	2.2	34 065	356	4 427	684	352	919	1 398	2 603	6 383	414	352
Fort Wayne, IN	17 666	4.6	41 102	196	9 551	1 483	726	1 405	2 896	3 411	13 164	808	726
Fresno, CA	37 360	6.2	38 323	264	16 241	3 692	1 196	3 580	6 101	9 283	24 708	1 319	1 196
Gadsden, AL	3 513	3.1	34 086	355	1 347	217	102	230	514	1 084	1 897	137	102
Gainesville, FL	10 990	5.2	39 650	235	6 123	1 299	426	413	2 171	2 069	8 260	472	426
Gainesville, GA	7 083	5.9	36 597	306	3 877	589	253	515	1 092	1 371	5 235	316	253
Gettysburg, PA	4 606	4.4	45 023	109	1 377	287	115	315	740	863	2 095	127	115
Glens Falls, NY	5 343	3.2	42 101	174	2 314	582	199	302	842	1 244	3 398	188	199
Goldsboro, NC	4 444	1.7	35 801	324	1 884	387	156	324	726	1 132	2 750	160	156
Grand Forks, ND-MN	4 626	2.0	45 158	105	2 445	410	209	329	975	764	3 393	196	209
Grand Island, NE	3 460	2.1	40 671	208	1 731	285	127	420	619	616	2 563	149	127
Grand Junction, CO	5 772	1.6	38 863	250	2 708	355	205	399	1 140	1 215	3 667	222	205
Grand Rapids-Wyoming, MI	47 121	5.3	45 371	101	25 101	3 784	1 912	3 902	10 243	7 433	34 699	2 093	1 912
Grants Pass, OR	3 052	6.2	36 013	322	929	150	89	279	593	1 089	1 447	111	89
Great Falls, MT	3 460	3.4	42 053	177	1 621	290	151	263	759	706	2 324	147	151
Greeley, CO	12 202	8.1	42 787	159	5 114	633	374	1 789	1 672	1 734	7 910	418	374
Green Bay, WI	14 454	3.3	45 665	98	8 380	1 418	638	1 081	2 558	2 194	11 517	684	638
Greensboro-High Point, NC	29 532	4.1	39 263	240	16 772	2 507	1 302	2 083	4 999	6 175	22 664	1 426	1 302
Greenville, NC	6 514	3.6	37 042	296	3 429	676	257	429	1 109	1 396	4 791	282	257
Greenville-Anderson-Mauldin, SC	34 306	5.6	39 213	242	18 140	2 784	1 385	2 364	4 966	7 297	24 672	1 594	1 385
Gulfport-Biloxi-Pascagoula, MS	13 315	1.7	34 206	354	7 214	1 314	566	726	2 500	3 227	9 819	624	566
Hagerstown-Martinsburg, MD-WV	10 454	3.9	39 981	225	4 424	815	349	606	1 544	2 138	6 193	387	349
Hammond, LA	4 641	5.9	36 043	320	1 613	328	100	300	548	1 291	2 340	127	100
Hanford-Corcoran, CA	5 001	2.0	33 126	367	2 301	674	169	386	832	1 106	3 531	162	169
Harrisburg-Carlisle, PA	27 115	4.5	47 991	74	17 163	3 561	1 354	1 914	4 429	4 899	23 993	1 344	1 354
Harrisonburg, VA	4 681	3.6	35 700	326	2 619	484	190	505	879	827	3 798	222	190
Hartford-West Hartford-East Hartford, CT	71 227	3.4	58 801	16	41 145	6 537	2 903	6 721	11 606	10 811	57 307	3 020	2 903
Hattiesburg, MS	5 146	4.3	34 574	348	2 468	400	184	593	844	1 214	3 644	236	184
Hickory-Lenoir-Morganton, NC	12 835	5.0	35 406	337	6 000	1 013	484	870	1 958	3 299	8 367	551	484
Hilton Head Island-Bluffton-Beaufort, NC	9 366	5.0	45 158	105	3 463	618	285	659	2 972	1 916	5 025	325	285
Hinesville, GA	2 491	2.8	31 064	378	1 808	524	169	52	569	539	2 553	109	169
Homosassa Springs, FL	4 983	4.2	35 323	339	1 288	221	92	235	1 200	1 924	1 837	170	92
Hot Springs, AR	3 604	2.7	37 090	293	1 376	196	110	224	706	1 115	1 905	142	110
Houma-Thibodaux, LA	9 636	-2.0	45 390	100	5 317	798	340	672	1 698	1 701	7 127	398	340
Houston-The Woodlands-Sugar Land, TX	361 777	3.8	54 346	27	199 985	24 722	12 816	58 625	56 713	39 973	296 148	14 871	12 816
Huntington-Ashland, WV-KY-OH	13 070	2.4	36 146	318	5 960	1 055	479	660	1 706	3 774	8 154	548	479
Huntsville, AL	19 600	3.6	44 068	134	12 413	1 985	951	927	3 684	3 276	16 276	987	951
Idaho Falls, ID	5 293	4.9	37 873	274	2 657	376	229	772	989	924	4 034	250	229
Indianapolis-Carmel-Anderson, IN	96 004	4.6	48 272	72	51 612	7 539	3 796	12 946	14 093	15 029	75 893	4 410	3 796
Iowa City, IA	7 879	3.6	47 324	83	4 364	1 065	323	721	1 586	926	6 473	359	323
Ithaca, NY	4 312	5.2	41 095	197	2 621	522	226	319	838	664	3 688	187	226
Jackson, MI	5 808	4.1	36 413	313	2 662	478	204	294	861	1 514	3 639	236	204
Jackson, MS	24 251	2.1	41 900	181	12 124	1 867	892	2 797	4 051	4 875	17 680	1 131	892
Jackson, TN	4 781	4.3	36 870	301	2 675	491	189	520	651	1 216	3 875	231	189
Jacksonville, FL	64 095	5.5	44 219	130	33 764	5 073	2 432	2 979	13 156	11 884	44 248	2 713	2 432
Jacksonville, NC	8 189	-0.4	43 952	137	4 174	1 150	407	346	1 644	1 352	6 077	267	407
Janesville-Beloit, WI	6 462	4.2	40 026	222	2 976	543	236	320	1 145	1 328	4 074	259	236
Jefferson City, MO	5 970	2.5	39 497	236	3 158	749	217	496	947	1 162	4 620	253	217
Johnson City, TN	7 326	4.0	36 512	309	3 133	591	223	622	1 050	1 993	4 569	293	223
Johnstown, PA	5 253	2.8	38 512	261	2 116	488	179	251	795	1 640	3 035	200	179

1. Based on the resident population estimated as of July 1 of the year shown.

Table C. Metropolitan Areas — **Earnings, Social Security, and Housing**

Area name	Earnings, 2015 (cont.)									Social Security beneficiaries, December 2015		Housing units, 2016		
	Percent by selected industries													
	Farm	Mining	Construction	Manufacturing	Information, professional, scientific, technical services	Retail trade	Finance, insurance, real estate, rental and leasing	Health care and social assistance	Government	Number	Rate[1]	Supplemental Security Income recipients, December 2015	Total	Percent change, 2010–2016
	75	76	77	78	79	80	81	82	83	84	85	86	87	88
Evansville, IN-KY	0.5	0.7	8.3	20.5	6.1	6.2	4.5	D	9.7	68 000	215	7 315	141 039	1.7
Fairbanks, AK	0.1	2.4	10.9	1.1	4.1	5.5	2.8	9.4	46.4	10 360	104	1 055	41 557	-0.5
Fargo, ND-MN	0.0	D	9.1	8.6	9.3	7.9	10.6	D	13.7	32 530	139	2 954	106 226	15.6
Farmington, NM	0.4	21.0	8.5	2.4	D	8.2	3.3	11.9	21.2	21 405	180	3 982	49 665	0.7
Fayetteville, NC	0.4	D	3.4	4.6	D	4.5	2.0	D	62.6	61 860	163	11 414	165 644	7.8
Fayetteville-Springdale-Rogers, AR-MO	1.6	D	D	9.8	6.8	5.8	3.5	8.8	12.0	85 725	167	9 026	211 440	6.6
Flagstaff, AZ	0.2	0.2	4.7	10.4	3.7	6.9	3.9	15.0	32.5	19 330	139	2 624	65 271	3.1
Flint, MI	0.2	0.0	5.0	12.3	8.3	9.3	6.4	18.2	16.2	98 190	239	17 112	190 970	-0.6
Florence, SC	-0.6	D	3.6	16.6	5.9	7.1	10.2	13.0	19.1	47 865	232	8 847	89 633	0.7
Florence-Muscle Shoals, AL.	0.7	D	8.0	19.3	3.5	9.1	4.6	12.8	19.7	38 745	264	4 778	70 988	2.1
Fond du Lac, WI	3.7	0.4	8.2	25.4	4.5	6.3	4.7	12.7	12.8	21 605	212	1 513	44 706	1.8
Fort Collins, CO	0.4	0.4	8.1	13.6	13.2	6.8	5.6	8.7	22.1	53 095	159	2 537	143 268	7.9
Fort Smith, AR-OK	2.8	D	4.9	15.8	D	6.5	4.0	13.8	15.7	65 535	234	10 302	123 900	2.5
Fort Wayne, IN	0.0	D	6.7	19.4	D	6.2	8.0	17.8	9.7	81 255	189	8 736	182 522	2.5
Fresno, CA	6.2	0.2	5.2	6.6	6.0	6.7	5.5	13.9	22.8	132 645	136	43 429	327 780	3.9
Gadsden, AL	0.8	0.2	5.3	16.0	3.7	8.5	5.1	22.4	15.0	28 650	278	4 763	47 540	0.2
Gainesville, FL	1.0	D	3.3	3.8	7.7	5.5	5.3	D	38.7	46 390	168	7 005	122 775	2.3
Gainesville, GA	0.4	D	5.4	21.1	4.5	6.8	5.0	16.9	11.5	35 060	181	3 135	70 954	3.1
Gettysburg, PA	3.3	D	7.9	19.8	4.8	6.3	3.5	D	15.6	23 900	234	1 112	41 610	1.9
Glens Falls, NY	1.1	0.5	7.0	13.6	D	8.0	4.4	12.8	23.7	32 540	257	3 191	68 433	1.3
Goldsboro, NC	5.8	D	4.2	12.2	3.8	7.2	4.1	12.3	31.4	25 715	207	4 541	53 393	0.8
Grand Forks, ND-MN	2.3	0.5	8.9	6.8	5.0	8.6	5.0	D	27.0	16 815	164	1 330	47 376	7.8
Grand Island, NE	7.1	0.1	8.2	17.8	3.6	7.6	5.5	10.0	16.3	15 965	188	1 197	35 411	3.6
Grand Junction, CO	0.6	7.7	8.7	4.4	6.4	7.4	6.9	16.0	16.9	30 805	208	2 505	65 240	4.1
Grand Rapids-Wyoming, MI .	0.9	D	5.9	24.4	D	5.7	6.9	D	9.4	188 165	181	19 820	413 611	2.2
Grants Pass, OR	0.4	D	6.0	11.0	4.8	11.9	6.1	19.8	13.9	26 860	317	2 793	38 274	0.7
Great Falls, MT	0.8	0.1	7.4	3.6	6.3	9.0	7.1	17.0	26.9	18 060	220	1 862	38 062	2.1
Greeley, CO	5.6	11.0	14.8	11.5	4.0	5.9	5.0	6.9	11.1	39 210	138	3 410	105 474	9.5
Green Bay, WI	2.1	0.1	5.8	16.9	D	4.9	9.3	D	12.5	60 640	192	5 556	141 837	3.4
Greensboro-High Point, NC..	0.6	D	5.2	17.1	D	6.2	8.4	11.6	11.7	152 040	202	18 176	331 979	2.9
Greenville, NC	1.3	D	5.1	9.8	4.4	7.1	5.0	10.0	38.0	29 590	168	6 015	77 914	3.9
Greenville-Anderson-Mauldin, SC	0.1	0.0	6.1	16.5	9.9	6.5	7.6	D	15.2	187 260	214	18 485	377 554	4.2
Gulfport-Biloxi-Pascagoula, MS	0.0	D	6.3	17.1	6.5	6.0	3.5	7.4	29.2	79 360	204	10 901	177 700	6.3
Hagerstown-Martinsburg, MD-WV	0.5	0.1	5.5	9.3	6.7	8.9	9.3	13.8	21.1	52 905	203	5 841	108 878	3.1
Hammond, LA	0.3	1.1	4.9	5.6	4.8	12.6	5.0	12.2	27.2	22 955	178	5 260	53 763	7.4
Hanford-Corcoran, CA	10.4	0.0	2.7	9.0	2.2	4.4	2.2	9.3	45.8	17 510	116	4 591	45 765	4.3
Harrisburg-Carlisle, PA	0.4	D	4.2	7.0	9.3	4.7	9.2	13.8	21.5	116 030	205	11 004	247 333	2.7
Harrisonburg, VA	4.1	D	6.2	17.6	6.6	6.6	4.7	11.7	17.7	22 890	174	1 858	53 200	4.1
Hartford-West Hartford-East Hartford, CT	0.1	D	5.2	11.5	11.8	4.7	18.4	11.7	15.8	229 695	190	23 661	509 570	0.5
Hattiesburg, MS	0.4	1.4	5.8	6.8	D	11.1	D	17.0	23.3	27 700	186	4 810	62 779	1.4
Hickory-Lenoir-Morganton, NC	1.7	0.0	3.7	27.0	D	7.5	3.3	D	15.3	88 685	244	7 639	162 903	0.1
Hilton Head Island-Bluffton-Beaufort, NC	0.2	0.0	7.7	1.2	D	8.8	7.0	9.9	30.6	51 815	250	2 699	108 255	4.8
Hinesville, GA	0.2	D	D	D	D	2.4	1.5	1.9	76.1	9 140	114	1 460	34 150	4.2
Homosassa Springs, FL	0.1	0.2	9.2	1.4	7.2	11.8	4.1	22.7	13.9	57 725	409	3 326	77 900	-0.2
Hot Springs, AR	0.2	0.7	7.0	7.5	5.9	10.6	6.1	22.4	14.3	29 755	306	3 922	50 563	0.1
Houma-Thibodaux, LA	0.3	12.8	7.6	11.1	5.4	5.7	4.5	8.3	10.7	40 365	190	8 014	85 476	3.6
Houston-The Woodlands-Sugar Land, TX	0.1	11.5	9.1	10.4	D	4.7	7.3	D	9.5	788 030	119	141 311	2 555 530	11.4
Huntington-Ashland, WV-KY-OH	0.0	1.2	9.0	D	5.8	7.0	4.0	D	17.0	89 150	247	16 941	164 519	0.0
Huntsville, AL	0.3	0.0	4.1	12.1	23.5	5.4	3.3	7.2	29.1	81 275	183	9 096	194 847	7.4
Idaho Falls, ID	2.4	D	5.4	6.6	23.6	12.9	D	D	10.5	23 210	166	2 584	52 040	4.5
Indianapolis-Carmel-Anderson, IN	0.1	0.1	5.4	11.7	D	6.3	15.2	12.2	11.4	339 955	171	37 044	849 946	4.1
Iowa City, IA	2.0	D	5.2	6.8	6.3	5.3	4.9	7.2	42.9	22 800	137	1 980	71 447	9.1
Ithaca, NY	0.3	1.0	2.5	7.7	8.8	5.2	3.6	D	13.8	15 750	151	1 473	42 451	1.8
Jackson, MI	0.2	0.2	4.8	19.7	4.6	6.3	4.3	14.8	14.6	36 490	229	4 558	68 999	-0.7
Jackson, MS	0.7	D	5.8	7.4	8.8	7.4	7.7	12.8	21.4	109 455	189	20 548	240 597	3.4
Jackson, TN	-0.2	D	D	17.2	D	8.3	3.8	14.3	22.6	29 000	224	4 274	56 342	1.9
Jacksonville, FL	0.1	D	5.6	5.6	11.2	6.5	13.1	D	15.4	269 975	186	32 046	630 657	5.4
Jacksonville, NC	1.8	D	2.9	0.8	2.1	4.5	2.2	3.1	72.2	24 595	132	3 027	77 785	14.0
Janesville-Beloit, WI	1.0	0.3	6.6	17.2	5.1	7.1	3.6	16.1	15.4	34 510	214	3 926	68 527	0.2
Jefferson City, MO	1.4	D	6.2	9.1	D	5.9	5.1	8.9	33.1	31 345	208	2 497	64 301	1.2
Johnson City, TN	0.2	D	4.9	10.9	D	8.1	5.8	D	21.8	51 475	257	5 992	96 572	2.9
Johnstown, PA	0.2	0.6	4.7	8.7	7.7	7.5	5.8	22.7	18.1	38 305	281	5 068	65 004	-1.0

1. Per 1,000 resident population estimated as of July 1, 2011 of the year shown.

Table C. Metropolitan Areas — Housing, Labor Force, and Employment

Area name	Total	Percent	Median value[1]	With a mortgage	Without a mortgage[2]	Median rent[3]	Median rent as a percent of income	Percent with a computer	Total	Percent change, 2015–2016	Total	Rate[4]	Total employed	Management, professional, and related occupations	Construction, production, and related occupations
	89	90	91	92	93	94	95	96	97	98	99	100	101	102	103
Evansville, IN-KY	124 936	66.6	130 400	19.0	10.7	696	30.3	86.1	160 005	0.9	6 672	4.2	151 363	31.0	27.4
Fairbanks, AK	35 475	57.2	229 300	24.5	10.0	1 194	31.9	95.0	46 098	-0.5	2 607	5.7	48 100	31.9	24.6
Fargo, ND-MN	96 142	54.5	193 600	19.3	10.8	756	26.2	88.2	136 113	4.4	3 516	2.6	131 427	36.2	22.5
Farmington, NM	43 030	71.3	147 800	19.4	10.0	770	29.1	76.1	53 752	-2.5	4 799	8.9	51 078	27.0	28.3
Fayetteville, NC	137 158	52.2	127 800	22.5	12.8	888	31.5	87.7	147 834	1.2	9 397	6.4	140 806	33.0	20.3
Fayetteville-Springdale-Rogers, AR-MO	190 860	60.4	159 800	18.6	10.0	749	24.8	88.7	263 898	3.6	7 634	2.9	242 001	35.7	26.1
Flagstaff, AZ	45 911	61.1	228 600	20.8	10.0	1 093	32.5	87.2	74 287	1.4	4 397	5.9	65 735	37.3	16.8
Flint, MI	163 488	70.5	99 200	21.8	13.7	727	30.1	83.1	183 107	0.8	9 938	5.4	168 901	31.4	25.7
Florence, SC	79 914	65.4	115 300	19.8	11.7	699	29.5	80.0	95 629	0.0	5 180	5.4	85 295	33.3	24.0
Florence-Muscle Shoals, AL.	60 663	69.8	114 800	19.2	10.6	640	31.2	78.9	66 716	0.4	4 425	6.6	59 658	29.6	28.4
Fond du Lac, WI	40 295	74.2	146 700	20.4	12.6	667	26.8	84.2	57 183	0.2	2 067	3.6	53 310	31.4	30.6
Fort Collins, CO	129 210	64.5	298 100	21.0	10.0	1 112	32.8	94.2	187 235	3.4	5 306	2.8	174 576	44.6	16.0
Fort Smith, AR-OK	107 375	67.5	108 400	20.0	10.0	637	27.5	77.8	121 494	0.3	5 667	4.7	113 330	29.3	28.7
Fort Wayne, IN	165 857	69.5	123 700	17.8	10.0	715	27.5	87.6	212 155	1.3	8 867	4.2	206 340	33.9	27.7
Fresno, CA	304 209	52.1	220 100	23.6	10.0	897	34.1	85.0	446 228	1.1	42 094	9.4	397 209	28.8	28.9
Gadsden, AL	39 332	74.5	99 200	20.4	11.6	650	26.0	82.2	43 887	1.6	2 618	6.0	43 713	30.4	32.8
Gainesville, FL	102 219	55.5	164 400	19.7	11.0	858	33.2	87.0	138 968	2.3	5 980	4.3	127 725	46.9	12.3
Gainesville, GA	63 989	64.5	173 600	22.0	10.2	901	28.7	86.9	96 105	3.6	4 300	4.5	86 852	28.8	33.4
Gettysburg, PA	38 459	78.7	193 800	22.7	13.2	840	31.0	85.0	55 490	0.8	2 223	4.0	51 023	29.6	31.0
Glens Falls, NY	48 814	71.4	163 200	23.8	12.9	841	30.6	85.7	60 462	-1.0	2 999	5.0	62 435	32.2	23.6
Goldsboro, NC	47 490	61.5	119 600	19.7	12.0	718	28.9	85.4	53 697	0.0	3 128	5.8	51 874	30.2	28.1
Grand Forks, ND-MN	42 166	55.1	177 000	18.9	10.0	812	28.5	85.6	56 831	4.1	1 689	3.0	56 090	35.5	22.1
Grand Island, NE	31 703	64.7	134 200	20.3	11.4	682	24.3	82.6	43 492	-0.3	1 611	3.7	45 562	28.5	29.8
Grand Junction, CO	59 066	67.0	198 800	22.3	10.0	897	30.4	88.3	71 959	-0.1	3 882	5.4	69 184	35.6	21.7
Grand Rapids-Wyoming, MI .	383 194	72.1	151 300	19.3	11.4	794	28.9	89.3	567 416	2.7	19 487	3.4	520 509	33.4	27.3
Grants Pass, OR	35 918	65.6	232 700	24.2	12.2	838	34.8	86.0	34 465	3.6	2 260	6.6	31 876	26.6	29.8
Great Falls, MT	34 375	61.2	168 600	18.8	11.2	713	30.4	77.4	38 358	-0.2	1 524	4.0	37 292	36.8	20.8
Greeley, CO	97 822	70.3	242 700	20.5	10.0	983	28.9	88.8	149 365	0.8	5 135	3.4	139 270	33.7	27.1
Green Bay, WI	127 779	68.2	158 600	20.0	11.8	711	27.5	87.8	172 373	1.0	6 618	3.8	166 056	32.5	29.0
Greensboro-High Point, NC..	291 088	61.3	144 900	20.5	10.7	768	29.2	81.8	367 315	0.9	19 105	5.2	350 314	33.9	24.9
Greenville, NC	68 374	52.3	138 200	20.6	12.1	759	34.8	85.5	88 381	0.8	4 885	5.5	81 798	36.0	19.5
Greenville-Anderson-Mauldin, SC	332 740	66.9	146 400	19.4	10.0	768	27.9	82.5	422 188	1.0	18 329	4.3	396 669	34.4	24.4
Gulfport-Biloxi-Pascagoula, MS	146 228	61.8	134 200	21.8	10.6	819	29.0	81.5	165 190	0.7	9 814	5.9	157 634	29.7	26.5
Hagerstown-Martinsburg, MD-WV	97 209	68.7	186 900	21.8	11.4	900	26.6	83.4	131 535	0.5	5 835	4.4	119 497	32.4	25.1
Hammond, LA	46 263	64.3	136 700	19.1	10.0	794	34.8	82.6	54 225	-0.2	3 645	6.7	58 396	27.8	21.7
Hanford-Corcoran, CA	42 692	48.2	183 000	21.1	10.1	892	30.0	87.1	57 183	-1.2	5 699	10.0	52 823	26.9	29.2
Harrisburg-Carlisle, PA	225 810	67.3	172 600	20.8	12.2	884	28.1	86.5	296 776	1.0	13 323	4.5	281 708	38.0	19.3
Harrisonburg, VA	47 600	59.9	198 700	21.1	10.0	801	30.5	81.8	64 716	1.3	2 541	3.9	62 036	35.7	23.9
Hartford-West Hartford-East Hartford, CT	464 613	66.5	247 000	22.5	15.0	1 039	29.5	88.2	650 090	0.0	33 046	5.1	617 809	43.6	16.6
Hattiesburg, MS	54 780	59.6	136 800	19.2	11.2	736	34.8	85.3	67 446	1.6	3 570	5.3	63 584	34.3	21.6
Hickory-Lenoir-Morganton, NC..................................	140 097	70.3	122 000	21.2	11.3	615	27.5	79.0	170 825	2.0	8 227	4.8	155 633	30.0	33.8
Hilton Head Island-Bluffton-Beaufort, NC	78 824	70.1	253 500	26.4	11.3	1 055	30.2	90.0	84 674	1.4	3 841	4.5	84 769	34.1	19.2
Hinesville, GA	27 874	49.7	114 100	24.4	10.8	911	35.4	88.6	32 465	1.3	1 850	5.7	27 064	23.6	27.4
Homosassa Springs, FL	60 541	81.4	115 900	23.0	10.4	728	34.0	86.4	47 754	0.0	3 238	6.8	44 459	30.6	23.9
Hot Springs, AR	40 134	65.8	134 500	22.6	11.9	707	33.9	86.2	40 148	0.5	1 742	4.3	41 167	28.0	24.0
Houma-Thibodaux, LA	77 548	72.4	143 800	19.6	10.0	724	27.9	86.5	92 440	-7.4	6 174	6.7	92 297	26.8	32.8
Houston-The Woodlands-Sugar Land, TX	2 292 992	58.7	168 300	20.6	10.7	978	29.3	88.2	3 287 728	1.2	172 541	5.2	3 190 721	37.1	23.4
Huntington-Ashland, WV-KY-OH	140 735	70.8	115 700	18.8	10.2	653	32.1	81.9	146 194	-0.1	9 047	6.2	142 194	33.5	22.9
Huntsville, AL	172 549	68.9	171 800	18.0	10.0	758	29.2	87.9	213 870	1.7	11 167	5.2	202 518	45.1	17.7
Idaho Falls, ID	45 611	70.2	165 200	20.0	10.0	776	25.7	92.6	66 199	2.0	2 128	3.2	60 709	36.4	24.7
Indianapolis-Carmel-Anderson, IN	755 100	64.2	148 000	18.8	10.2	825	29.7	86.6	1 037 189	2.5	41 935	4.0	978 453	37.8	21.1
Iowa City, IA	64 183	59.9	186 600	18.8	11.0	868	33.5	90.7	97 052	0.7	2 579	2.7	94 463	41.2	19.4
Ithaca, NY	38 112	53.9	195 100	21.9	12.8	1 080	32.0	93.0	50 358	-0.4	2 079	4.1	50 549	55.0	12.3
Jackson, MI	59 292	70.5	127 800	19.6	11.8	696	29.8	87.3	74 432	2.0	3 495	4.7	64 672	28.6	27.8
Jackson, MS	210 443	67.1	145 300	20.8	10.7	834	32.2	81.7	270 767	1.6	13 284	4.9	255 733	36.2	22.1
Jackson, TN	49 318	66.6	129 200	20.5	11.3	811	31.9	82.0	63 085	2.3	3 169	5.0	59 719	34.4	24.7
Jacksonville, FL	536 299	63.2	172 800	22.1	10.8	994	30.5	88.9	734 244	2.1	34 713	4.7	667 491	37.2	18.3
Jacksonville, NC	64 771	51.9	147 400	25.5	10.0	937	32.0	93.6	63 729	0.0	3 498	5.5	64 037	27.2	21.0
Janesville-Beloit, WI..........	65 054	69.7	133 300	20.3	12.7	741	28.9	87.0	84 378	1.2	3 840	4.6	78 782	33.1	29.4
Jefferson City, MO	55 448	68.8	151 500	18.7	10.0	608	24.3	84.2	76 649	0.7	2 885	3.8	70 678	35.7	23.4
Johnson City, TN	83 074	69.7	137 800	22.2	10.0	662	29.8	81.5	89 324	0.9	4 740	5.3	85 582	35.5	21.2
Johnstown, PA	57 044	73.2	89 100	20.8	12.5	596	27.8	78.3	61 630	-1.2	4 236	6.9	58 413	31.6	26.1

1. Specified owner-occupied units.   2. A value of 10.0 represents 10 percent or less.   3. Specified renter-occupied units.   4. Percent of civilian labor force.
5. Civilian employed persons 16 years old and over.

Table C. Metropolitan Areas — **Nonfarm Employment and Agriculture**

	Private nonfarm establishments, employment and payroll, 2015								Agriculture, 2012			
	Employment						Annual payroll		Farms			
										Percent with:		
Area name	Number of establishments	Total	Health care and social assistance	Manufacturing	Retail trade	Finance and insurance	Professional, scientific, and technical services	Total (mil dol)	Average per employee (dollars)	Number	Fewer than 50 acres	500 acres or more	Farm operators whose principal occupation is farming (percent)
	104	105	106	107	108	109	110	111	112	113	114	115	116
Evansville, IN-KY	7 583	140 182	25 826	22 154	17 048	5 703	5 016	6 102	43 527	1 527	41.5	19.9	48.6
Fairbanks, AK	2 459	27 673	5 679	576	5 019	735	1 334	1 453	52 490	217	39.2	20.7	47.9
Fargo, ND-MN	6 725	120 979	22 090	9 950	16 384	8 607	6 372	5 250	43 397	1 772	20.8	42.4	60.1
Farmington, NM	2 721	39 736	6 819	1 751	6 389	973	1 400	1 802	45 344	2 628	61.7	20.8	54.2
Fayetteville, NC	6 046	97 042	20 492	7 318	17 520	2 018	5 097	3 284	33 844	591	43.3	11.7	48.6
Fayetteville-Springdale-Rogers, AR-MO	11 416	199 864	23 424	26 372	26 334	5 246	11 473	9 880	49 433	6 835	37.1	5.7	46.8
Flagstaff, AZ	3 527	50 051	8 007	5 480	8 063	830	1 708	1 933	38 627	2 239	92.0	3.8	72.5
Flint, MI	7 737	117 246	26 738	10 769	20 091	3 974	3 734	4 619	39 392	835	58.6	6.2	50.1
Florence, SC	4 197	74 128	16 180	10 159	11 498	4 164	2 647	2 878	38 823	1 017	34.7	14.5	45.0
Florence-Muscle Shoals, AL.	3 221	46 700	7 872	9 181	8 609	1 631	1 137	1 575	33 716	2 153	43.9	6.4	42.2
Fond du Lac, WI	2 361	42 920	6 379	8 776	5 966	1 662	1 462	1 687	39 305	1 399	31.9	10.7	59.0
Fort Collins, CO	10 291	120 470	18 944	11 520	18 928	3 769	10 001	5 575	46 274	1 625	60.7	8.5	46.5
Fort Smith, AR-OK	5 818	93 234	17 879	18 087	12 692	2 753	2 086	3 435	36 841	4 703	36.8	6.9	45.2
Fort Wayne, IN	10 377	191 745	35 793	33 386	23 670	8 911	6 135	7 847	40 923	3 071	52.7	9.9	42.5
Fresno, CA	16 350	249 702	42 438	23 328	37 805	8 998	10 210	10 056	40 273	5 683	59.7	11.2	59.6
Gadsden, AL	1 980	29 603	7 218	5 030	4 704	1 026	578	991	33 490	853	51.1	2.9	40.3
Gainesville, FL	6 285	92 134	24 949	3 809	14 029	4 148	5 564	3 553	38 562	2 243	68.8	5.0	42.9
Gainesville, GA	4 100	72 187	12 736	19 376	8 354	2 219	1 789	3 163	43 818	622	59.0	2.3	51.3
Gettysburg, PA	1 942	28 508	4 838	5 683	3 358	510	561	990	34 714	1 188	48.2	6.3	50.9
Glens Falls, NY	3 346	41 666	7 911	6 849	7 911	1 426	1 109	1 665	39 964	968	34.7	10.2	55.5
Goldsboro, NC	2 174	33 461	7 316	5 679	5 998	1 115	753	1 151	34 404	563	40.1	18.1	60.9
Grand Forks, ND-MN	2 703	43 601	9 433	4 245	7 922	1 158	1 842	1 641	37 633	2 292	11.9	36.6	58.9
Grand Island, NE	2 570	35 966	5 212	7 816	5 889	1 546	803	1 311	36 443	2 339	26.5	34.1	62.0
Grand Junction, CO	4 404	51 843	9 843	2 576	8 451	1 918	2 379	2 057	39 669	2 264	75.4	5.4	48.6
Grand Rapids-Wyoming, MI .	23 939	474 938	63 248	103 591	49 439	18 382	19 110	20 623	43 422	4 680	49.2	6.5	49.6
Grants Pass, OR	1 907	21 420	4 544	2 831	4 409	620	849	719	33 581	617	76.3	0.6	55.8
Great Falls, MT	2 433	30 802	6 753	1 345	5 118	1 460	1 105	1 068	34 658	1 105	36.0	29.3	47.8
Greeley, CO	5 830	85 157	8 443	13 025	9 914	3 289	2 736	4 019	47 195	3 525	35.5	19.6	49.8
Green Bay, WI	7 673	156 091	22 753	29 187	17 340	9 247	5 694	6 928	44 387	2 774	40.3	8.0	51.0
Greensboro-High Point, NC..	17 428	318 528	43 678	52 934	36 370	14 218	13 130	13 555	42 555	3 350	49.0	3.5	46.6
Greenville, NC	3 523	60 323	15 717	5 688	9 332	2 062	2 034	2 232	36 995	391	34.8	21.5	59.3
Greenville-Anderson-Mauldin, SC	19 162	322 404	40 106	50 674	42 481	11 105	19 379	13 399	41 559	4 152	55.1	2.7	36.6
Gulfport-Biloxi-Pascagoula, MS	7 132	127 159	20 439	19 996	18 476	3 750	5 833	5 128	40 331	988	59.6	2.0	39.9
Hagerstown-Martinsburg, MD-WV	4 993	83 253	16 031	8 622	14 158	7 332	2 803	3 190	38 323	1 536	51.2	4.6	43.0
Hammond, LA	2 317	35 571	8 589	2 161	6 994	2 310	1 010	1 265	35 569	1 070	52.1	3.0	44.1
Hanford-Corcoran, CA	1 585	23 393	4 519	4 236	4 192	546	681	908	38 830	1 056	51.2	18.6	66.0
Harrisburg-Carlisle, PA	13 478	271 533	51 543	17 658	33 790	19 486	16 541	12 548	46 211	3 115	43.4	3.7	50.2
Harrisonburg, VA	2 972	51 459	7 551	9 291	7 320	1 222	1 564	1 880	36 543	1 902	43.2	2.8	54.6
Hartford-West Hartford-East Hartford, CT	29 338	533 971	103 838	57 995	63 809	54 036	31 460	30 438	57 004	1 995	71.1	1.6	44.9
Hattiesburg, MS	3 294	50 122	11 789	4 126	9 658	1 601	1 630	1 826	36 425	1 093	43.8	4.0	39.5
Hickory-Lenoir-Morganton, NC	7 370	127 573	20 207	39 597	16 311	2 251	2 790	4 767	37 366	2 198	56.5	2.6	47.5
Hilton Head Island-Bluffton-Beaufort, NC	5 629	60 115	9 046	780	11 577	1 979	2 567	2 060	34 269	252	49.6	19.4	51.2
Hinesville, GA	872	12 898	2 035	2 041	2 015	377	768	485	37 611	113	39.8	7.1	41.6
Homosassa Springs, FL	2 715	27 791	9 121	282	5 742	666	844	938	33 764	559	73.9	3.4	49.7
Hot Springs, AR	2 697	32 412	7 369	2 371	6 009	972	1 470	1 032	31 825	361	49.3	2.5	55.4
Houma-Thibodaux, LA	4 766	81 983	11 650	9 078	11 308	1 920	3 402	3 901	47 587	596	44.5	12.1	43.6
Houston-The Woodlands-Sugar Land, TX	135 923	2 576 412	325 574	226 607	292 365	95 428	207 269	159 247	61 809	15 026	56.9	7.3	38.6
Huntington-Ashland, WV-KY-OH	6 967	111 891	28 216	10 932	17 330	3 080	4 188	4 516	40 363	2 683	28.7	2.6	39.7
Huntsville, AL	9 527	172 187	25 422	19 609	22 865	3 934	36 511	8 322	48 332	2 263	44.1	7.4	47.9
Idaho Falls, ID	3 920	50 584	8 497	3 775	8 320	1 333	6 717	2 056	40 647	1 883	49.7	19.3	44.7
Indianapolis-Carmel-Anderson, IN	45 981	856 951	137 987	73 038	97 521	44 347	59 200	40 088	46 780	6 205	54.5	14.8	46.0
Iowa City, IA	3 909	67 841	17 869	6 097	10 222	2 534	2 942	2 764	40 739	2 481	33.2	15.9	51.9
Ithaca, NY	2 369	49 525	5 709	2 600	4 922	1 105	2 239	1 830	36 957	558	43.9	6.8	50.5
Jackson, MI	2 892	48 974	9 622	8 901	7 341	1 259	2 760	2 193	44 769	1 073	48.7	7.7	45.4
Jackson, MS	13 128	216 677	46 158	18 504	30 789	11 368	10 424	8 882	40 990	4 186	30.1	12.6	43.3
Jackson, TN	2 971	56 192	12 779	9 558	7 810	1 624	1 341	2 072	36 869	1 352	32.8	10.4	40.5
Jacksonville, FL	36 198	534 828	76 730	25 492	74 613	48 835	33 395	24 245	45 332	1 768	74.4	3.8	46.2
Jacksonville, NC	2 763	35 491	5 360	888	8 758	1 002	1 856	977	27 532	347	48.4	7.2	54.2
Janesville-Beloit, WI	3 275	56 646	9 055	9 453	8 900	1 343	1 939	2 373	41 895	1 509	44.1	10.3	50.0
Jefferson City, MO	3 623	52 435	9 420	5 859	7 697	2 460	2 019	1 953	37 251	4 676	23.1	9.0	39.7
Johnson City, TN	3 742	63 657	16 514	7 142	10 963	3 033	1 713	2 390	37 539	1 898	54.8	1.9	45.2
Johnstown, PA	3 194	46 531	11 291	4 670	6 909	2 008	2 303	1 599	34 357	551	33.4	5.6	37.4

Table C. Metropolitan Areas — **Agriculture**

	Agriculture, 2012 (cont.)														
	Land in farms				Value of land and buildings (dollars)		Value of machinery and equipment, average per farm (dollars)	Value of products sold				Percent of farms with sales of:		Government payments	
Area name			Acres							Percent from:					
	Acreage (1,000)	Percent change, 2007–2012	Average size of farm	Total irrigated (1,000)	Total cropland (1,000)	Average per farm	Average per acre		Total (mil dol)	Average per farm (dollars)	Crops	Live-stock and poultry products	$10,000 or more	$100,000 or more	Total ($1,000)	Percent of farms
	117	118	119	120	121	122	123	124	125	126	127	128	129	130	131	132
Evansville, IN-KY	581	-0.1	380	D	524.8	1 668 276	4 386	228 634	294.2	192 650	90.1	9.9	51.7	27.9	10 066	67.8
Fairbanks, AK	100	-10.1	459	1.0	61.4	580 382	1 264	94 359	9.1	42 120	84.8	15.2	42.4	10.6	1 354	30.9
Fargo, ND-MN	1 718	4.0	970	19.2	1 599.8	3 003 294	3 097	390 421	965.2	544 686	94.1	5.9	65.4	48.4	22 932	77.1
Farmington, NM	2 580	58.2	982	85.9	115.6	341 496	348	41 084	71.3	27 135	88.9	11.1	13.3	1.2	1 023	14.0
Fayetteville, NC	141	-5.2	238	4.1	85.1	752 283	3 155	117 093	201.6	341 140	33.5	66.5	41.5	19.6	1 876	40.4
Fayetteville-Springdale-Rogers, AR-MO	1 073	3.0	157	2.0	278.5	555 647	3 541	64 923	1 356.1	198 410	1.4	98.6	44.7	13.9	6 743	15.3
Flagstaff, AZ	5 816	-4.7	2 597	1.9	8.3	543 406	209	23 731	25.8	11 528	9.1	90.9	9.6	1.4	987	23.0
Flint, MI	123	-4.6	148	1.5	102.6	570 910	3 867	107 984	91.3	109 389	88.7	11.3	38.4	12.9	2 131	32.2
Florence, SC	333	0.5	327	9.1	208.0	768 491	2 348	125 798	183.2	180 155	70.2	29.8	39.1	17.2	5 109	48.9
Florence-Muscle Shoals, AL.	364	2.2	169	4.0	165.6	491 966	2 907	64 124	139.4	64 748	55.0	45.0	31.2	7.4	4 969	33.6
Fond du Lac, WI	316	-6.0	226	2.1	262.1	1 128 100	5 001	182 828	412.3	294 743	26.9	73.1	62.2	37.8	7 648	74.2
Fort Collins, CO	450	-8.0	277	52.5	106.4	854 599	3 083	72 401	128.6	79 167	44.6	55.4	28.8	7.6	1 061	11.2
Fort Smith, AR-OK	854	-7.3	182	13.9	251.1	405 541	2 233	56 091	507.6	107 930	11.2	88.8	35.2	9.0	4 858	15.0
Fort Wayne, IN	611	4.3	199	2.7	550.8	1 191 722	5 987	120 572	498.0	162 173	73.6	26.4	52.0	24.7	12 089	58.8
Fresno, CA	1 721	5.2	303	968.7	1 153.4	2 509 484	8 286	161 509	4 973.0	875 073	74.4	25.6	71.9	41.9	10 149	9.0
Gadsden, AL	86	-8.6	101	0.1	19.5	359 368	3 559	51 635	83.7	98 161	6.5	93.5	27.8	8.2	450	11.8
Gainesville, FL	272	11.5	121	23.3	102.5	575 798	4 750	53 346	189.9	84 661	51.3	48.7	30.4	6.6	1 400	7.7
Gainesville, GA	52	-9.3	84	0.1	12.3	686 416	8 212	68 188	166.3	267 434	2.1	97.9	34.9	19.8	115	8.2
Gettysburg, PA	171	-1.9	144	2.2	125.6	898 623	6 232	113 572	201.7	169 817	56.5	43.5	48.6	19.2	1 818	28.5
Glens Falls, NY	199	-5.9	205	0.7	103.4	514 006	2 501	104 877	D	D	D	D	50.3	19.8	D	25.2
Goldsboro, NC	191	9.1	340	4.8	146.8	1 400 607	4 124	199 504	577.2	1 025 265	27.4	72.6	61.5	44.8	2 943	56.5
Grand Forks, ND-MN	1 911	-0.7	834	28.3	1 740.6	2 134 497	2 559	375 743	1 023.3	446 464	95.7	4.3	55.9	39.2	28 960	87.6
Grand Island, NE	1 181	0.6	505	726.0	901.2	2 248 299	4 451	272 145	1 227.8	524 935	63.4	36.6	71.4	50.1	18 245	71.1
Grand Junction, CO	387	3.9	171	75.3	71.4	575 360	3 367	51 431	84.6	37 360	48.1	51.9	25.7	6.1	821	7.1
Grand Rapids-Wyoming, MI .	746	-0.7	159	88.2	559.1	763 593	4 790	120 642	1 120.3	239 375	60.9	39.1	44.8	18.7	10 536	31.0
Grants Pass, OR	28	-25.1	46	9.0	8.4	460 319	10 052	35 806	18.8	30 481	D	D	25.0	4.7	129	2.9
Great Falls, MT	1 255	-9.1	1 136	33.4	427.7	1 197 706	1 055	96 719	111.1	100 568	48.2	51.8	40.9	16.2	5 952	51.5
Greeley, CO	1 956	-6.3	555	299.9	850.2	1 098 289	1 979	146 652	1 860.7	527 863	20.1	79.9	42.8	20.2	15 649	39.7
Green Bay, WI	547	-3.7	197	1.9	437.0	855 013	4 333	144 973	750.0	270 384	23.7	76.3	53.0	28.8	10 578	57.0
Greensboro-High Point, NC..	360	-0.3	107	6.0	135.9	527 298	4 910	60 005	327.4	97 730	24.8	75.2	30.5	10.7	2 649	17.5
Greenville, NC	172	0.2	439	3.6	131.7	1 397 719	3 181	233 246	215.9	552 194	51.5	48.5	60.1	38.9	3 877	57.3
Greenville-Anderson-Mauldin, SC	400	-6.4	96	3.7	115.1	441 917	4 592	45 588	128.7	30 999	D	D	20.6	3.1	2 211	9.5
Gulfport-Biloxi-Pascagoula, MS	87	-17.2	88	0.3	24.7	396 775	4 504	47 253	20.6	20 805	D	D	22.6	2.4	515	9.5
Hagerstown-Martinsburg, MD-WV	200	5.6	130	1.0	118.5	767 295	5 902	89 473	138.2	89 995	50.2	49.8	38.0	15.6	1 452	21.0
Hammond, LA	107	-13.8	100	0.7	36.3	410 570	4 117	54 967	45.7	42 694	40.2	59.8	29.1	7.2	790	17.3
Hanford-Corcoran, CA	674	-1.0	638	407.4	501.5	3 847 243	6 031	340 454	1 829.2	1 732 231	46.7	53.3	68.3	45.1	7 901	36.4
Harrisburg-Carlisle, PA	419	7.2	135	2.6	260.9	795 107	5 906	98 039	458.3	147 142	25.3	74.7	52.9	24.6	4 537	30.3
Harrisonburg, VA	222	-4.7	117	5.6	100.5	823 606	7 055	88 252	659.0	346 475	7.2	92.8	58.4	35.0	2 741	15.9
Hartford-West Hartford-East Hartford, CT	126	15.0	63	6.0	52.0	750 128	11 887	66 721	222.4	111 456	87.0	13.0	31.4	8.9	1 294	7.6
Hattiesburg, MS	150	-5.8	138	1.5	35.1	458 851	3 335	65 786	67.7	61 954	19.7	80.3	32.2	6.5	1 676	24.4
Hickory-Lenoir-Morganton, NC	192	2.0	87	3.5	75.0	487 357	5 573	57 925	318.1	144 744	16.2	83.8	34.3	14.5	839	9.2
Hilton Head Island-Bluffton-Beaufort, NC	111	9.1	440	D	15.2	1 305 794	2 970	85 413	D	D	D	14.2	29.4	6.0	111	13.9
Hinesville, GA	16	-26.8	146	D	3.4	339 894	2 330	48 301	11.8	104 841	7.2	92.8	32.7	7.1	143	31.0
Homosassa Springs, FL	41	1.3	73	0.7	7.3	480 195	6 621	29 451	14.1	25 190	54.9	45.1	17.7	3.4	146	3.6
Hot Springs, AR	36	-9.6	99	0.3	8.4	364 504	3 688	43 119	24.1	66 756	18.6	81.4	24.7	5.3	93	8.9
Houma-Thibodaux, LA	251	-11.8	421	1.0	73.9	919 569	2 183	127 193	95.1	159 572	61.9	38.1	39.8	8.7	146	4.5
Houston-The Woodlands-Sugar Land, TX	2 677	2.4	178	73.1	765.7	699 599	3 927	58 371	D	D	67.9	D	24.8	4.1	18 927	11.1
Huntington-Ashland, WV-KY-OH	323	-13.2	121	0.4	64.8	274 665	2 279	44 660	25.8	9 618	63.1	36.9	14.9	0.9	931	18.0
Huntsville, AL	456	4.5	202	18.2	271.4	787 164	3 906	96 602	206.9	91 443	72.1	27.9	33.9	9.6	6 761	34.3
Idaho Falls, ID	857	-4.7	455	367.6	538.5	1 055 110	2 318	147 762	500.6	265 869	65.4	34.6	48.1	23.4	8 915	45.0
Indianapolis-Carmel-Anderson, IN	1 689	7.5	272	13.4	1 525.2	1 558 263	5 724	150 794	985.1	158 753	D	D	44.8	22.9	28 897	50.0
Iowa City, IA	643	-0.6	259	0.4	549.7	1 683 794	6 496	164 372	785.1	316 447	43.6	56.4	59.0	36.6	21 083	71.5
Ithaca, NY	91	-16.5	163	0.3	54.4	448 507	2 757	113 717	67.4	120 772	33.7	66.3	43.7	16.1	900	25.8
Jackson, MI	183	0.4	171	3.9	136.0	652 247	3 822	85 794	78.2	72 866	69.2	30.8	36.4	12.0	4 210	32.1
Jackson, MS	1 156	-5.8	276	46.8	400.9	665 400	2 409	73 821	633.0	151 223	33.9	66.1	29.3	10.4	17 513	39.4
Jackson, TN	357	-10.2	264	12.6	258.1	669 964	2 534	100 337	138.2	102 192	93.9	6.1	33.9	12.1	5 638	60.1
Jacksonville, FL	186	16.2	105	13.8	38.5	565 515	5 383	56 509	117.4	66 417	77.0	23.0	20.4	3.5	D	3.5
Jacksonville, NC	58	4.4	166	1.5	38.4	634 349	3 819	115 625	187.7	540 928	15.6	84.4	46.4	30.5	1 001	38.3
Janesville-Beloit, WI	354	2.7	234	16.2	303.7	1 294 782	5 523	154 109	274.4	181 858	60.4	39.6	49.8	23.5	7 892	68.2
Jefferson City, MO	1 011	-3.2	216	8.8	410.6	590 339	2 731	71 559	375.4	80 288	19.9	80.1	49.5	9.2	6 757	35.2
Johnson City, TN	157	-3.3	83	D	63.6	504 477	6 084	61 423	D	D	31.1	D	26.3	4.5	483	19.3
Johnstown, PA	77	-12.6	140	0.1	45.4	457 327	3 277	82 508	32.6	59 240	55.5	44.5	42.3	8.5	775	31.9

Area name	Water use, 2010		Wholesale trade,[1] 2012				Retail trade, 2012				Real estate and rental and leasing, 2012			
	Total water withdrawn (mil gal/day)	Gallons withdrawn per person per day	Number of establishments	Number of employees	Sales (mil dol)	Annual payroll (mil dol)	Number of establishments	Number of employees	Sales (mil dol)	Annual payroll (mil dol)	Number of establishments	Number of employees	Receipts (mil dol)	Annual payroll (mil dol)
	133	134	135	136	137	138	139	140	141	142	143	144	145	146
Evansville, IN-KY	826.3	2 652	366	5 873	3 818.1	346.7	1 154	17 133	4 570.3	396.7	289	1 954	297.2	54.7
Fairbanks, AK	53.6	549	69	666	413.5	36.5	301	4 758	1 732.5	153.1	144	661	159.6	33.2
Fargo, ND-MN......................	23.8	114	401	6 920	6 673.0	383.0	805	15 182	4 455.4	360.4	318	1 876	322.0	68.5
Farmington, NM	343.7	2 643	156	1 412	663.0	73.8	450	6 210	1 801.6	157.4	107	750	205.0	36.8
Fayetteville, NC	71.9	196	173	2 711	1 078.4	106.5	1 128	16 393	4 631.9	382.0	345	1 903	368.3	63.2
Fayetteville-Springdale-Rogers, AR-MO.......................	414.0	894	484	5 216	4 145.6	273.4	1 522	22 576	6 183.1	524.0	498	3 276	367.4	100.3
Flagstaff, AZ........................	52.2	388	95	738	439.3	33.8	590	7 337	1 896.5	164.8	188	667	137.3	28.1
Flint, MI	13.4	31	272	3 969	3 673.6	218.5	1 459	19 368	5 307.9	444.9	318	1 843	255.8	57.1
Florence, SC	259.6	1 263	231	3 085	2 445.4	130.8	936	10 523	2 686.2	224.1	167	657	150.8	22.3
Florence-Muscle Shoals, AL.	1 361.8	9 255	154	2 097	1 235.0	71.4	647	7 749	2 202.1	181.0	127	522	70.0	14.0
Fond du Lac, WI	14.4	142	111	1 541	1 372.0	74.4	354	5 462	1 402.4	130.0	64	235	37.7	6.0
Fort Collins, CO	412.9	1 378	295	4 294	5 143.6	368.5	1 244	17 307	4 341.3	414.2	526	2 112	307.0	71.4
Fort Smith, AR-OK...............	72.5	258	291	3 410	2 259.1	145.2	990	12 490	3 264.4	271.3	246	1 167	176.1	37.3
Fort Wayne, IN.....................	60.2	145	556	9 321	14 090.5	435.5	1 465	22 309	5 772.6	520.2	428	2 005	385.3	70.5
Fresno, CA	2 813.2	3 024	819	12 981	9 266.3	663.0	2 421	32 954	9 117.8	836.0	769	4 299	715.1	139.6
Gadsden, AL........................	146.3	1 401	82	837	549.9	31.2	392	4 675	1 236.5	96.1	62	367	57.2	10.5
Gainesville, FL	62.9	238	205	1 896	1 356.0	92.7	958	13 245	3 261.2	286.8	325	1 727	232.5	52.3
Gainesville, GA	100.2	558	235	3 265	9 022.6	173.1	579	7 640	2 231.9	193.5	164	450	116.5	17.1
Gettysburg, PA.....................	20.2	199	61	D	D	D	333	3 231	801.2	74.4	47	210	35.8	7.0
Glens Falls, NY	86.8	673	89	D	D	D	633	8 195	2 047.9	191.9	91	286	49.8	10.0
Goldsboro, NC	34.3	280	95	1 822	1 244.8	74.4	464	5 709	1 557.5	125.8	63	257	29.3	7.1
Grand Forks, ND-MN...........	30.6	311	136	1 704	2 175.4	85.6	423	7 237	1 893.8	159.3	88	554	89.2	15.8
Grand Island, NE	555.2	6 783	144	1 833	1 868.6	92.9	397	5 589	1 497.8	123.6	89	315	58.5	10.2
Grand Junction, CO	754.7	5 144	219	2 076	876.5	96.2	604	7 966	2 173.3	202.6	263	889	170.7	33.7
Grand Rapids-Wyoming, MI .	1 010.0	1 021	1 336	26 242	20 615.3	1 444.6	3 218	44 758	12 253.0	1 107.9	882	4 947	859.4	175.3
Grants Pass, OR..................	30.2	365	49	D	D	D	312	4 150	987.9	105.1	106	354	44.8	8.5
Great Falls, MT	166.9	2 052	112	D	D	D	352	4 859	1 359.7	117.4	121	349	62.1	9.8
Greeley, CO	462.1	1 828	246	3 166	5 349.2	157.4	620	8 154	2 707.6	228.7	212	870	149.0	31.5
Green Bay, WI	870.1	2 841	364	6 375	4 491.1	331.5	1 029	15 954	4 093.6	353.6	233	1 485	209.4	44.7
Greensboro-High Point, NC..	222.8	308	1 157	16 682	15 345.7	893.5	2 570	34 286	8 953.9	831.4	791	4 726	773.8	181.8
Greenville, NC......................	28.8	171	144	1 597	1 028.7	69.5	633	8 597	2 354.8	193.0	176	681	115.5	22.7
Greenville-Anderson-Mauldin, SC.............................	364.5	442	976	12 422	13 210.8	659.6	2 958	39 157	10 145.3	912.0	747	3 498	980.5	137.0
Gulfport-Biloxi-Pascagoula, MS...................................	686.9	1 853	236	2 165	911.0	90.8	1 357	17 028	4 425.8	382.2	375	1 614	270.2	50.4
Hagerstown-Martinsburg, MD-WV	87.6	348	177	2 757	2 513.7	128.2	859	13 123	3 396.8	290.0	208	1 019	249.3	36.1
Hammond, LA	20.1	166	86	1 701	1 300.4	68.5	438	6 290	1 769.7	144.7	94	498	86.5	18.5
Hanford-Corcoran, CA	1 298.9	8 490	69	684	746.6	36.3	285	3 961	1 032.0	92.2	97	371	71.0	9.9
Harrisburg-Carlisle, PA	137.3	250	500	9 590	9 403.2	521.2	1 973	32 462	9 074.5	750.1	450	2 997	825.2	157.6
Harrisonburg, VA	38.5	307	113	1 952	1 032.2	91.5	540	7 535	1 949.6	185.0	116	919	186.3	34.8
Hartford-West Hartford-East Hartford, CT	350.3	289	1 192	21 837	17 564.8	1 261.3	4 166	63 342	17 268.0	1 593.2	1 082	6 148	1 269.1	270.7
Hattiesburg, MS	53.0	371	126	1 168	747.6	46.2	683	9 522	4 784.0	198.8	156	594	111.0	19.8
Hickory-Lenoir-Morganton, NC...................................	1 139.5	3 118	367	6 273	4 530.1	282.7	1 317	15 617	4 183.6	353.0	305	817	163.8	23.6
Hilton Head Island-Bluffton-Beaufort, NC....................	53.6	287	140	728	442.4	34.0	838	10 505	2 665.3	243.6	397	1 787	280.7	66.0
Hinesville, GA	18.8	241	12	217	151.6	12.1	183	1 990	580.2	42.0	51	187	24.9	5.6
Homosassa Springs, FL	1 201.2	8 505	80	D	D	D	455	5 122	1 421.0	121.8	172	415	54.4	10.4
Hot Springs, AR	17.6	183	79	D	D	D	513	5 877	1 564.0	133.8	133	439	65.0	13.0
Houma-Thibodaux, LA..........	49.5	238	257	2 970	1 943.9	160.2	793	11 090	2 895.0	256.2	233	2 023	530.3	113.4
Houston-The Woodlands-Sugar Land, TX	2 798.0	473	8 019	117 487	362 243.5	7 813.0	17 508	263 099	83 979.5	6 764.3	6 497	44 896	10 828.1	2 163.8
Huntington-Ashland, WV-KY-OH...........................	159.4	437	292	4 395	3 127.7	208.0	1 237	16 832	4 430.6	367.6	258	1 265	264.5	49.3
Huntsville, AL.......................	2 823.4	6 761	376	4 558	4 101.6	240.2	1 577	21 457	5 735.1	514.5	461	1 872	370.6	66.3
Idaho Falls, ID.....................	2 282.8	17 130	197	2 401	3 208.9	103.3	534	7 307	2 094.6	168.7	147	485	83.3	14.3
Indianapolis-Carmel-Anderson, IN...........................	611.0	324	2 120	36 502	30 286.1	2 075.0	5 917	94 488	28 311.3	2 293.9	2 162	15 619	3 839.4	666.8
Iowa City, IA.........................	42.5	279	127	1 695	1 284.8	74.3	612	9 834	2 117.8	218.0	146	560	132.6	21.1
Ithaca, NY	232.7	2 291	36	454	259.0	21.6	349	5 071	1 112.0	105.5	112	609	121.6	20.5
Jackson, MI	20.3	127	137	D	D	D	526	7 003	1 841.7	163.5	99	567	82.0	15.5
Jackson, MS	156.4	276	676	9 658	9 533.7	490.2	2 142	28 676	7 644.0	665.5	622	3 434	612.3	131.5
Jackson, TN	22.8	175	164	1 795	1 196.1	83.2	565	7 756	2 114.1	177.4	117	573	93.4	17.4
Jacksonville, FL....................	880.8	655	1 447	21 814	21 129.8	1 212.3	4 889	66 146	18 318.6	1 632.2	1 787	9 036	2 200.0	383.6
Jacksonville, NC...................	32.3	182	50	304	139.1	11.9	545	7 716	2 213.0	177.9	187	664	127.0	20.7
Janesville-Beloit, WI	28.3	176	149	3 035	3 225.1	155.1	502	8 396	2 215.2	208.2	101	400	148.1	18.7
Jefferson City, MO...............	104.5	697	115	2 595	1 154.4	77.3	531	7 253	1 924.3	158.9	100	344	54.1	9.2
Johnson City, TN	49.6	250	138	1 477	871.3	57.2	688	10 457	2 572.3	220.8	143	668	103.6	20.3
Johnstown, PA	27.1	189	115	1 365	664.9	51.0	561	6 927	1 733.8	148.6	86	408	48.3	12.2

1. Merchant wholesalers, except manufacturers' sales branches and offices.

Table C. Metropolitan Areas — Professional Services, Manufacturing, and Accommodation and Food Services

Area name	Professional, scientific, and technical services, 2012				Manufacturing, 2012				Accommodation and food services, 2012			
	Number of establishments	Number of employees	Sales (mil dol)	Annual payroll (mil dol)	Number of establishments	Number of employees	Sales (mil dol)	Annual payroll (mil dol)	Number of establishments	Number of employees	Sales (mil dol)	Annual payroll (mil dol)
	147	148	149	150	151	152	153	154	155	156	157	158
Evansville, IN-KY	640	5 050	D	228.1	398	20 872	15 137.5	1 118.6	656	14 254	694.8	185.7
Fairbanks, AK	237	1 683	293.4	86.5	67	641	1 941.2	36.2	213	3 092	255.3	66.4
Fargo, ND-MN	558	D	D	D	224	9 398	3 860.5	D	469	11 495	515.6	151.1
Farmington, NM	256	D	D	D	85	1 318	268.6	62.8	197	4 253	201.8	56.3
Fayetteville, NC	577	6 813	911.9	374.1	115	8 193	5 481.1	379.5	657	13 928	645.9	177.0
Fayetteville-Springdale-Rogers, AR-MO	1 226	9 359	1 413.8	541.7	409	25 466	7 229.0	917.4	950	17 956	786.9	224.0
Flagstaff, AZ	331	1 584	178.5	65.3	90	4 025	2 181.3	312.0	545	11 436	765.7	191.8
Flint, MI	639	3 544	370.3	143.2	273	10 675	9 418.1	684.4	704	13 207	563.9	157.4
Florence, SC	268	2 684	294.3	112.7	148	8 952	4 326.5	479.5	384	6 611	325.8	85.6
Florence-Muscle Shoals, AL.	246	1 071	110.4	40.5	181	7 761	3 325.2	322.7	268	5 455	231.8	66.1
Fond du Lac, WI	154	1 337	154.4	76.3	144	9 140	3 989.9	407.6	240	3 872	140.8	39.8
Fort Collins, CO	1 493	8 727	1 031.1	450.9	403	10 163	4 275.7	642.6	847	14 821	756.5	218.0
Fort Smith, AR-OK	534	2 168	304.8	80.0	298	18 435	6 525.7	709.7	458	8 769	433.6	117.5
Fort Wayne, IN	950	5 721	757.5	266.1	621	32 052	19 526.4	1 658.4	817	16 688	703.1	204.7
Fresno, CA	1 522	10 531	1 367.8	474.3	585	25 269	8 658.3	1 052.9	1 450	24 100	1 226.2	333.9
Gadsden, AL	130	1 250	82.2	35.5	96	4 715	1 355.8	194.1	172	3 231	153.0	40.0
Gainesville, FL	841	4 713	553.2	221.0	158	3 270	1 135.7	169.8	578	11 837	553.1	148.7
Gainesville, GA	402	D	D	D	225	17 020	7 629.2	647.1	283	4 742	298.3	67.4
Gettysburg, PA	126	D	D	D	113	5 745	2 148.7	240.8	222	3 521	185.7	53.0
Glens Falls, NY	229	1 111	141.8	49.2	163	6 709	2 135.1	358.7	540	4 750	344.1	95.6
Goldsboro, NC	147	816	76.0	27.4	83	5 833	1 691.3	243.8	186	3 284	161.7	42.0
Grand Forks, ND-MN	178	D	D	D	89	3 692	1 778.5	142.3	257	5 362	226.3	67.4
Grand Island, NE	143	767	90.3	30.2	114	7 947	7 126.4	313.9	198	2 852	128.6	36.5
Grand Junction, CO	561	2 529	289.0	119.8	159	2 388	520.6	95.1	300	6 052	282.6	88.8
Grand Rapids-Wyoming, MI.	2 215	17 189	2 524.8	982.1	1 735	94 665	30 246.9	4 672.9	1 735	34 865	1 559.5	448.7
Grants Pass, OR	140	563	40.6	13.5	106	2 190	434.8	89.6	199	2 483	124.5	35.8
Great Falls, MT	202	1 159	131.8	50.3	62	964	955.3	45.0	240	3 887	194.7	51.5
Greeley, CO	533	2 362	311.5	113.7	284	11 102	5 991.4	485.8	400	5 794	273.9	76.2
Green Bay, WI	600	5 179	737.1	266.2	535	28 296	12 057.4	1 384.8	741	13 076	523.8	152.8
Greensboro-High Point, NC..	1 717	D	D	D	1 019	53 589	35 757.7	2 468.5	1 494	28 185	1 408.2	385.3
Greenville, NC	311	1 893	247.9	84.4	87	4 905	2 160.8	248.8	362	8 055	357.6	96.7
Greenville-Anderson-Mauldin, SC	2 010	17 391	2 409.8	1 004.5	942	47 115	18 292.1	2 151.2	1 775	31 297	1 515.6	410.8
Gulfport-Biloxi-Pascagoula, MS	692	6 021	792.9	312.5	215	19 150	20 839.8	1 341.7	789	23 827	1 832.9	459.6
Hagerstown-Martinsburg, MD-WV	370	2 689	324.2	120.5	168	7 822	3 601.7	405.2	461	7 743	386.2	110.3
Hammond, LA	208	889	93.5	33.6	79	2 389	681.2	84.4	213	4 285	185.8	50.9
Hanford-Corcoran, CA	85	461	51.0	18.4	60	4 380	2 904.0	180.5	172	2 824	378.6	42.6
Harrisburg-Carlisle, PA	1 411	15 758	2 357.2	1 010.5	408	15 894	7 108.0	779.4	1 256	22 385	1 204.4	333.9
Harrisonburg, VA	215	1 489	174.5	76.4	134	9 603	6 229.7	422.4	277	6 596	298.7	94.5
Hartford-West Hartford-East Hartford, CT	2 801	30 314	5 830.7	2 201.0	1 638	69 502	21 474.5	4 621.6	2 685	42 030	2 453.9	706.2
Hattiesburg, MS	309	1 777	214.9	80.2	91	4 070	1 202.2	170.7	313	6 850	301.0	82.8
Hickory-Lenoir-Morganton, NC	548	2 538	742.2	102.2	727	37 686	10 405.1	1 403.5	624	10 992	481.6	134.1
Hilton Head Island-Bluffton-Beaufort, NC	579	2 999	352.7	150.2	90	713	128.5	27.5	555	11 189	688.9	202.0
Hinesville, GA	76	776	65.5	25.7	19	1 737	767.7	83.4	105	1 680	81.6	19.0
Homosassa Springs, FL	254	891	106.3	35.8	44	203	35.8	7.2	191	2 362	114.6	32.2
Hot Springs, AR	217	1 160	91.1	40.4	90	2 180	476.9	95.1	274	5 162	218.0	63.4
Houma-Thibodaux, LA	447	4 432	492.2	211.9	202	8 876	2 402.4	462.9	394	7 792	410.5	113.8
Houston-The Woodlands-Sugar Land, TX	16 999	221 829	49 233.9	19 369.0	5 365	214 702	290 261.2	13 767.5	10 981	226 927	13 340.3	3 592.4
Huntington-Ashland, WV-KY-OH	507	4 535	452.5	174.0	246	11 611	19 017.6	716.9	649	11 746	561.3	151.9
Huntsville, AL	1 442	33 281	7 765.6	2 691.5	344	20 108	8 833.7	1 121.3	828	16 350	810.1	224.6
Idaho Falls, ID	406	8 460	1 379.8	585.5	158	3 193	845.8	117.1	280	4 757	207.9	59.7
Indianapolis-Carmel-Anderson, IN	5 276	48 613	7 960.5	3 183.3	1 704	72 434	41 533.8	3 938.9	3 983	84 075	4 306.3	1 207.4
Iowa City, IA	328	2 127	314.1	96.7	125	6 061	3 799.2	276.4	419	8 252	436.6	114.4
Ithaca, NY	274	2 312	356.6	124.1	93	2 766	861.1	150.4	334	4 408	231.7	65.4
Jackson, MI	217	2 504	367.1	180.4	268	8 414	2 621.3	409.3	275	4 788	201.5	57.3
Jackson, MS	1 412	9 876	1 571.9	566.0	355	15 987	8 597.5	793.7	1 096	20 707	1 050.9	273.8
Jackson, TN	194	1 874	138.2	72.2	135	9 352	4 578.7	437.0	256	5 191	242.5	68.8
Jacksonville, FL	4 523	35 397	6 308.6	2 429.5	803	25 439	11 888.7	1 444.0	2 849	55 538	2 999.8	853.5
Jacksonville, NC	246	1 748	198.1	69.5	40	1 049	271.0	34.2	347	6 640	353.1	86.9
Janesville-Beloit, WI	208	1 172	129.3	49.5	224	8 850	4 474.2	421.3	363	5 355	236.2	63.7
Jefferson City, MO	290	1 937	279.3	93.1	147	5 562	3 774.8	238.7	279	4 545	185.2	54.0
Johnson City, TN	273	2 908	232.5	106.2	170	7 241	2 132.8	309.7	380	7 891	343.0	100.3
Johnstown, PA	228	3 359	380.3	168.2	127	5 232	1 798.8	241.6	300	4 070	179.0	47.8

Table C. Metropolitan Areas — Health Care and Social Assistance, Other Services, Nonemployer Business and Residential Construction

Area name	Health care and social assistance, 2012				Other services, 2012				Nonemployer business, 2015		Value of residential construction authorized by building permits, 2016	
	Number of establishments	Number of employees	Receipts (mil dol)	Annual payroll (mil dol)	Number of establishments	Number of employees	Receipts (mil dol)	Annual payroll (mil dol)	Number	Receipts (mil dol)	New construction ($1,000)	Number of housing units
	159	160	161	162	163	164	165	166	167	168	169	170
Evansville, IN-KY	852	24 213	2 658.0	999.2	548	3 988	441.5	121.4	17 072	694.9	152 221	947
Fairbanks, AK	290	5 748	746.9	305.5	185	842	88.8	25.6	5 587	230.5	2 931	11
Fargo, ND-MN	606	19 302	2 096.3	901.9	485	3 040	316.3	82.2	15 880	866.9	408 612	2 479
Farmington, NM	275	6 819	682.5	291.7	226	1 571	164.1	54.5	5 198	214.9	25 187	104
Fayetteville, NC	843	21 330	2 156.0	978.9	441	2 504	229.0	61.4	19 535	694.1	162 074	953
Fayetteville-Springdale-Rogers, AR-MO	1 084	22 894	2 307.6	908.9	596	3 738	472.9	101.8	35 197	1 561.9	880 826	4 421
Flagstaff, AZ	381	6 995	1 040.7	354.3	230	1 307	105.8	32.7	9 015	375.9	134 500	647
Flint, MI	1 294	25 418	2 787.5	1 148.7	562	3 406	376.2	91.1	27 934	979.0	69 253	374
Florence, SC	450	15 888	1 783.9	668.8	275	1 693	165.6	40.0	12 347	457.0	73 382	495
Florence-Muscle Shoals, AL	382	6 957	731.4	269.8	186	D	D	D	10 153	421.2	34 612	315
Fond du Lac, WI	281	5 764	758.8	248.8	191	1 245	114.4	31.3	4 931	234.3	47 244	365
Fort Collins, CO	1 021	18 142	1 988.2	783.2	658	3 536	374.1	96.2	30 473	1 392.6	680 813	3 532
Fort Smith, AR-OK	681	18 011	1 641.2	658.4	341	1 645	141.9	40.0	18 176	860.3	91 944	703
Fort Wayne, IN	1 069	31 129	3 035.1	1 282.7	791	5 195	491.7	147.2	26 989	1 090.5	292 120	1 536
Fresno, CA	2 204	42 281	5 325.6	1 997.0	1 000	7 367	747.6	200.1	50 405	2 577.2	729 163	2 904
Gadsden, AL	316	7 433	701.9	303.4	125	632	98.9	19.0	7 071	312.8	14 186	97
Gainesville, FL	757	22 437	2 752.6	1 043.5	392	2 664	465.2	93.2	19 003	733.8	150 144	1 110
Gainesville, GA	443	9 275	1 297.8	493.4	246	1 193	123.8	32.4	14 989	667.9	250 634	1 578
Gettysburg, PA	182	4 634	448.2	167.1	150	909	75.1	19.8	6 528	274.8	79 900	347
Glens Falls, NY	388	8 109	665.2	305.5	218	1 088	112.7	33.7	8 441	374.7	61 974	359
Goldsboro, NC	254	6 896	606.6	265.8	142	939	69.3	20.3	6 147	229.8	45 235	269
Grand Forks, ND-MN	250	9 377	823.3	372.6	204	1 128	126.4	27.2	6 206	287.5	75 168	443
Grand Island, NE	231	5 479	552.8	199.0	202	1 161	111.3	25.6	5 829	253.6	49 397	386
Grand Junction, CO	426	10 176	1 029.0	427.2	293	1 883	182.6	47.8	11 373	489.7	125 709	597
Grand Rapids-Wyoming, MI	2 285	64 137	6 540.1	2 608.2	1 690	11 582	1 100.9	313.1	71 476	3 485.7	901 880	4 717
Grants Pass, OR	269	4 376	418.5	151.1	103	D	D	D	5 738	251.2	56 075	213
Great Falls, MT	262	6 363	711.9	269.1	155	871	76.6	21.7	4 680	199.2	49 503	242
Greeley, CO	435	7 951	893.1	325.4	329	1 537	175.9	44.5	20 948	980.3	665 176	3 009
Green Bay, WI	701	21 661	2 578.4	964.5	505	3 019	261.3	72.2	17 107	852.0	217 877	1 008
Greensboro-High Point, NC	1 697	41 710	4 164.2	1 648.4	1 095	6 325	947.5	185.8	54 458	2 299.3	545 301	2 735
Greenville, NC	510	16 075	1 880.0	681.9	183	1 104	93.9	25.1	10 307	400.6	110 418	861
Greenville-Anderson-Mauldin, SC	1 770	35 622	3 666.0	1 530.0	1 138	9 603	1 165.4	351.8	59 664	2 594.9	1 153 120	5 753
Gulfport-Biloxi-Pascagoula, MS	789	18 643	2 454.1	1 001.3	462	2 663	247.4	73.3	26 655	1 040.7	276 958	1 776
Hagerstown-Martinsburg, MD-WV	637	15 877	1 685.9	725.3	377	2 229	191.8	54.1	14 130	590.7	185 659	955
Hammond, LA	301	8 143	655.2	261.4	149	966	98.1	25.5	9 340	324.9	94 783	698
Hanford-Corcoran, CA	231	4 770	587.8	203.5	94	382	37.4	9.9	4 378	196.1	126 276	605
Harrisburg-Carlisle, PA	1 562	42 982	3 882.5	1 598.3	1 285	9 158	1 124.9	310.5	34 213	1 637.2	298 369	1 627
Harrisonburg, VA	263	7 433	708.4	298.6	231	1 164	109.4	31.6	8 057	359.3	142 450	644
Hartford-West Hartford-East Hartford, CT	3 543	99 706	10 449.5	4 596.2	2 462	15 615	1 759.3	537.5	80 958	4 347.1	296 855	2 065
Hattiesburg, MS	368	11 108	1 237.7	562.0	168	943	83.1	22.5	10 465	484.5	14 391	174
Hickory-Lenoir-Morganton, NC	744	19 423	1 882.5	733.3	437	2 380	199.7	55.8	23 056	968.0	142 631	655
Hilton Head Island-Bluffton-Beaufort, NC	470	6 794	751.1	249.6	351	2 862	258.7	86.0	16 879	879.6	607 122	1 784
Hinesville, GA	81	2 055	251.1	101.6	68	435	32.7	9.5	3 442	101.3	86 668	417
Homosassa Springs, FL	390	7 932	819.7	307.1	212	744	53.2	15.5	8 892	346.1	88 490	516
Hot Springs, AR	319	7 374	717.5	275.4	161	766	53.3	16.2	7 961	329.6	14 287	45
Houma-Thibodaux, LA	478	11 115	1 181.6	466.8	285	2 135	304.2	92.7	15 024	688.5	116 879	682
Houston-The Woodlands-Sugar Land, TX	14 336	290 976	35 675.8	13 099.0	7 926	72 280	8 932.1	2 623.8	566 184	28 894.6	7 395 667	44 732
Huntington-Ashland, WV-KY-OH	1 054	28 659	3 170.0	1 241.0	457	3 096	360.0	96.4	17 197	651.9	41 539	250
Huntsville, AL	1 053	23 925	2 645.2	1 060.2	556	4 015	617.2	140.6	29 300	1 162.2	384 129	2 992
Idaho Falls, ID	577	8 114	865.6	297.5	194	892	91.4	22.7	10 566	481.0	135 709	881
Indianapolis-Carmel-Anderson, IN	4 724	131 895	15 661.0	6 100.5	3 192	26 908	4 270.6	900.2	137 653	5 891.9	1 852 768	7 773
Iowa City, IA	450	16 991	2 046.3	803.8	270	1 667	207.7	46.4	11 030	520.8	320 589	1 921
Ithaca, NY	271	5 283	483.0	199.8	152	966	122.9	23.9	7 389	276.1	79 641	575
Jackson, MI	351	9 060	936.8	409.4	210	1 361	129.7	37.1	8 894	342.6	29 927	136
Jackson, MS	1 446	44 764	4 786.6	1 894.4	853	5 442	604.1	185.0	48 768	2 124.1	389 115	1 673
Jackson, TN	370	12 812	1 231.3	510.1	151	812	66.4	20.5	8 308	362.4	48 015	278
Jacksonville, FL	3 685	74 724	9 238.6	3 315.2	2 369	13 420	2 219.2	438.7	107 122	4 416.8	2 494 462	11 768
Jacksonville, NC	257	5 765	491.7	197.5	210	1 172	89.9	26.6	9 253	331.3	109 646	803
Janesville-Beloit, WI	320	9 667	1 120.9	438.4	268	1 417	105.0	30.8	7 974	342.7	49 421	257
Jefferson City, MO	370	9 486	874.8	358.5	325	1 760	200.3	59.5	9 013	383.3	32 482	322
Johnson City, TN	458	16 539	1 833.8	815.0	234	1 347	100.5	32.1	12 170	523.4	80 013	533
Johnstown, PA	540	11 708	1 047.3	444.7	312	1 690	133.9	34.2	6 206	243.2	40 318	164

1. Establishments subject to federal tax.

Table C. Metropolitan Areas — Government Employment and Payroll and Local Government Finances

	Government employment and payroll, 2012									Local government finances, 2012				
			March payroll (percent of total)							General revenue				
												Taxes		
													Per capita[1] (dollars)	
Area name	Full-time equivalent employees	March Payroll (dollars)	Administration, judicial, and legal	Police and corrections	Fire protection	Highways and transportation	Health and welfare	Natural resources and utilities	Education and libraries	Total (mil dol)	Inter-governmental (mil dol)	Total (mil dol)	Total	Property
	171	172	173	174	175	176	177	178	179	180	181	182	183	184
Evansville, IN-KY	10 347	34 710 256	6.8	10.9	4.5	3.9	1.7	8.5	62.2	995.2	463.1	341.3	1 089	857
Fairbanks, AK	2 949	14 833 210	7.9	3.4	2.6	2.4	1.8	5.3	75.9	380.0	201.2	148.5	1 481	1 335
Fargo, ND-MN	6 888	27 847 634	5.1	9.5	2.7	4.4	9.5	7.5	60.2	969.4	445.6	298.8	1 381	1 058
Farmington, NM	5 857	21 149 302	4.2	11.0	2.6	2.0	1.9	8.4	68.4	491.8	290.9	126.9	987	702
Fayetteville, NC	20 611	71 938 105	1.4	6.0	1.8	0.8	38.1	3.6	42.6	1 147.7	620.9	372.5	995	717
Fayetteville-Springdale-Rogers, AR-MO	15 951	51 196 846	5.5	9.4	4.3	3.2	1.0	5.4	70.1	1 400.1	793.7	404.4	839	367
Flagstaff, AZ	4 575	17 536 070	11.8	13.5	9.2	3.5	4.5	6.4	48.1	469.7	159.1	223.4	1 643	979
Flint, MI	15 234	64 330 939	5.5	5.9	1.4	3.5	24.1	3.5	55.1	2 005.4	1 056.8	353.2	844	786
Florence, SC	6 966	21 627 471	5.6	9.2	1.9	2.7	6.2	5.3	67.5	538.5	250.7	178.7	867	649
Florence-Muscle Shoals, AL	5 882	19 596 410	3.1	6.8	3.3	3.2	20.6	13.8	47.1	488.1	192.2	137.3	934	418
Fond du Lac, WI	3 703	15 389 801	4.9	9.2	2.4	4.4	10.7	3.5	63.8	424.7	174.4	182.3	1 790	1 688
Fort Collins, CO	10 782	47 317 101	8.8	11.5	1.1	2.8	7.5	18.4	46.2	1 178.8	292.6	577.8	1 861	1 211
Fort Smith, AR-OK	9 950	33 824 806	6.1	6.9	2.1	3.1	5.0	11.1	65.4	795.9	453.2	202.5	722	305
Fort Wayne, IN	12 482	46 187 211	6.4	12.8	3.8	4.6	1.3	5.6	63.8	1 286.9	601.6	479.3	1 137	913
Fresno, CA	34 954	165 436 346	4.1	10.3	2.1	3.3	9.7	4.5	65.0	5 127.4	3 047.2	1 071.6	1 131	789
Gadsden, AL	3 980	11 900 349	4.3	10.5	6.2	3.7	6.9	8.4	56.6	284.1	137.1	99.7	955	293
Gainesville, FL	10 035	36 051 916	10.0	15.5	4.4	4.8	3.2	11.5	46.9	897.9	290.9	376.2	1 402	1 085
Gainesville, GA	6 523	22 620 107	6.4	9.1	7.3	1.6	4.4	4.9	65.4	563.5	217.3	266.2	1 436	890
Gettysburg, PA	2 548	9 790 732	7.8	9.5	0.9	2.6	2.1	3.4	73.2	374.0	165.8	167.3	1 648	1 256
Glens Falls, NY	6 698	24 733 643	6.0	8.2	0.4	6.9	8.7	2.7	65.0	745.4	272.2	360.1	2 803	2 155
Goldsboro, NC	5 237	14 176 474	3.0	6.2	2.1	1.3	9.2	6.0	66.2	346.7	199.6	101.5	817	585
Grand Forks, ND-MN	4 147	14 917 010	5.7	8.3	2.6	5.2	15.5	10.4	50.1	471.6	218.9	130.8	1 323	1 063
Grand Island, NE	4 036	14 835 732	5.6	6.7	2.9	4.0	6.4	15.9	57.5	355.7	117.9	148.0	1 773	1 410
Grand Junction, CO	5 197	18 735 519	8.2	13.3	5.0	4.1	7.0	9.6	48.8	498.4	180.8	228.0	1 542	966
Grand Rapids-Wyoming, MI	26 602	112 436 599	7.9	9.0	2.5	4.3	3.1	4.9	66.6	3 718.2	1 877.6	1 165.3	1 159	1 055
Grants Pass, OR	2 192	8 995 230	6.6	12.9	2.5	3.4	1.3	3.1	68.4	243.6	119.9	70.8	854	781
Great Falls, MT	2 704	9 771 107	6.8	13.0	3.8	5.6	3.7	6.9	59.0	238.3	103.2	77.2	944	913
Greeley, CO	8 663	35 763 495	8.2	17.4	4.0	5.2	6.6	11.0	45.5	919.9	308.8	411.9	1 562	1 194
Green Bay, WI	11 507	49 464 799	4.6	9.3	2.9	4.0	8.9	3.8	65.2	1 398.9	611.3	539.9	1 735	1 620
Greensboro-High Point, NC	26 780	99 652 358	4.7	9.7	3.6	2.0	7.2	5.5	64.4	2 394.5	1 098.1	928.6	1 262	995
Greenville, NC	6 107	20 619 861	3.8	8.9	3.2	2.0	4.2	10.9	60.2	555.7	265.7	167.7	972	677
Greenville-Anderson-Mauldin, SC	32 635	116 071 503	4.0	6.4	3.0	1.4	33.6	5.1	45.4	3 592.7	858.8	824.2	978	830
Gulfport-Biloxi-Pascagoula, MS	18 635	68 245 147	4.0	7.4	3.9	3.0	36.0	3.0	41.5	2 388.7	948.4	466.4	1 229	1 099
Hagerstown-Martinsburg, MD-WV	8 853	33 633 765	4.2	5.9	2.5	1.9	0.9	6.7	76.6	810.6	360.1	325.5	1 270	912
Hammond, LA	6 393	23 444 209	4.2	6.0	1.2	1.7	46.4	1.8	37.5	621.2	213.8	128.9	1 044	366
Hanford-Corcoran, CA	4 882	22 137 016	6.6	11.1	2.5	1.2	11.7	3.6	60.7	623.0	383.4	130.2	860	727
Harrisburg-Carlisle, PA	18 305	73 828 976	7.2	11.2	0.6	3.9	3.7	5.0	66.8	2 496.2	893.1	1 022.1	1 845	1 338
Harrisonburg, VA	4 180	13 504 909	5.9	8.1	4.4	2.7	4.3	7.2	63.8	389.9	157.1	146.9	1 145	791
Hartford-West Hartford-East Hartford, CT	41 889	212 590 921	3.4	7.9	3.6	2.6	3.3	4.5	73.1	5 466.8	1 915.2	3 050.0	2 512	2 484
Hattiesburg, MS	9 029	27 151 166	3.5	4.9	2.0	2.5	47.7	1.9	36.9	819.4	196.1	154.2	1 050	973
Hickory-Lenoir-Morganton, NC	15 251	50 474 252	3.6	5.9	2.0	1.2	24.3	3.5	56.8	1 280.9	597.8	326.4	898	671
Hilton Head Island-Bluffton-Beaufort, NC	6 425	25 024 387	7.0	9.7	6.6	1.7	25.2	3.9	43.8	837.8	157.8	429.0	2 213	1 771
Hinesville, GA	3 104	9 754 876	5.6	9.3	1.5	1.2	15.4	1.8	61.7	272.2	113.4	80.9	993	612
Homosassa Springs, FL	3 890	11 674 757	8.6	11.3	0.1	3.6	5.4	3.4	65.1	322.4	98.7	162.1	1 163	1 064
Hot Springs, AR	2 929	9 379 603	4.7	8.8	4.0	3.5	3.4	5.5	68.3	270.5	155.0	62.1	640	262
Houma-Thibodaux, LA	10 111	34 879 997	4.6	9.7	0.6	2.6	31.8	4.0	45.8	1 130.5	411.7	323.8	1 550	688
Houston-The Woodlands-Sugar Land, TX	234 372	897 703 915	4.7	10.8	3.1	4.2	7.4	3.2	64.5	25 851.7	7 434.4	12 890.3	2 087	1 738
Huntington-Ashland, WV-KY-OH	12 579	40 423 670	4.4	6.3	2.0	2.6	4.4	5.0	73.1	1 054.7	525.7	330.6	907	701
Huntsville, AL	20 024	74 872 202	3.7	6.3	3.0	2.8	37.7	7.5	35.8	2 192.6	900.1	428.1	994	510
Idaho Falls, ID	4 554	14 040 874	6.5	10.1	4.5	3.7	7.6	7.0	58.6	341.3	174.7	100.7	740	715
Indianapolis-Carmel-Anderson, IN	70 652	276 197 106	4.2	7.9	5.6	1.8	17.0	11.3	51.5	8 491.1	3 269.0	2 704.9	1 402	1 025
Iowa City, IA	3 919	16 365 120	7.2	7.7	1.2	4.7	10.4	5.1	60.1	620.3	195.2	302.5	1 912	1 555
Ithaca, NY	4 530	19 870 493	5.0	6.2	2.8	4.4	7.3	3.5	68.0	531.9	184.0	252.8	2 465	1 857
Jackson, MI	4 304	17 626 740	7.6	8.1	2.4	4.2	3.5	3.4	69.5	585.1	325.3	139.2	868	809
Jackson, MS	21 103	60 140 323	6.0	10.4	4.8	2.9	1.9	4.3	69.2	1 733.1	846.9	586.9	1 017	965
Jackson, TN	8 999	31 890 237	2.6	6.7	2.4	1.5	58.7	4.5	23.0	995.9	160.4	156.2	1 197	685
Jacksonville, FL	42 905	156 841 760	5.8	13.6	6.1	2.2	1.4	6.6	57.0	4 877.5	1 516.3	1 990.7	1 445	1 051
Jacksonville, NC	5 873	18 455 158	3.9	7.0	1.9	1.2	10.7	4.8	66.2	585.4	209.5	152.5	832	536
Janesville-Beloit, WI	6 252	25 471 665	5.9	9.6	3.9	4.4	7.9	4.5	62.6	723.4	387.9	249.8	1 557	1 471
Jefferson City, MO	4 566	13 402 962	7.4	8.2	3.3	4.3	4.8	6.3	65.4	359.6	122.3	173.3	1 154	721
Johnson City, TN	6 906	20 205 200	5.5	9.0	2.8	6.4	4.7	12.5	56.6	469.5	191.0	177.3	884	595
Johnstown, PA	4 484	15 273 184	8.2	8.3	1.4	5.9	5.7	6.0	63.9	555.1	293.7	143.3	1 012	781

1. Based on the resident population estimated as of July 1 of the year shown.

Table C. Metropolitan Areas — Local Government Finances, Government Employment, and Income Taxes

Area name	Local government finances, 2012 (cont.) Direct general expenditure — Total (mil dol)	Per capita¹ (dollars)	Percent of total for: Education	Health and hospitals	Police protection	Public welfare	Highways	Debt outstanding Total (mil dol)	Per capita¹ (dollars)	Government employment, 2015 Federal civilian	Federal military	State and local	Individual income tax returns, 2014 Number of returns	Mean Adjusted Gross income	Mean income tax
	185	186	187	188	189	190	191	192	193	194	195	196	197	198	199
Evansville, IN-KY	984.8	3 142	43.4	0.7	5.9	0.3	3.2	1 444.5	4 609	1 285	953	15 505	146 910	56 763	6 989
Fairbanks, AK	342.4	3 415	63.0	1.6	2.3	0.0	6.2	170.2	1 698	2 945	9 019	7 921	48 140	64 566	8 494
Fargo, ND-MN	990.1	4 577	37.7	0.6	5.3	4.1	12.4	1 641.6	7 589	2 435	1 278	16 041	111 780	67 371	9 482
Farmington, NM	551.0	4 287	55.6	3.3	6.3	1.2	4.3	2 140.3	16 652	1 491	308	9 836	51 650	52 699	5 948
Fayetteville, NC	1 203.8	3 214	51.4	3.6	7.6	6.4	1.2	604.8	1 615	14 786	48 640	25 090	161 820	43 246	3 906
Fayetteville-Springdale-Rogers, AR-MO	1 387.0	2 876	60.9	0.3	5.5	0.0	4.9	2 146.7	4 452	2 576	2 148	28 597	213 610	71 710	10 457
Flagstaff, AZ	457.2	3 361	35.9	3.4	6.5	1.6	7.6	377.9	2 779	2 706	301	16 135	58 640	52 565	6 064
Flint, MI	2 064.7	4 935	41.9	28.1	3.5	1.1	3.3	995.9	2 380	1 059	657	19 420	192 350	46 305	4 970
Florence, SC	530.6	2 575	60.9	4.4	6.7	0.2	1.8	374.1	1 815	693	830	15 692	86 940	44 930	4 584
Florence-Muscle Shoals, AL	484.2	3 294	44.6	19.9	4.8	0.1	5.0	444.4	3 023	965	647	8 869	61 830	51 119	5 689
Fond du Lac, WI	449.6	4 415	51.8	7.3	5.2	3.9	9.0	580.9	5 704	198	266	5 405	50 060	56 385	6 378
Fort Collins, CO	1 080.2	3 479	45.9	4.5	6.4	3.0	9.0	1 388.6	4 472	2 463	879	32 873	159 430	69 012	9 658
Fort Smith, AR-OK	802.3	2 860	58.0	2.8	5.0	0.2	6.3	1 030.6	3 674	1 326	1 188	16 684	110 950	47 824	5 076
Fort Wayne, IN	1 126.6	2 673	51.6	0.6	6.1	0.3	3.5	1 205.7	2 861	2 041	1 337	19 757	203 660	54 122	6 542
Fresno, CA	5 031.5	5 308	44.7	7.0	5.6	10.3	3.4	3 847.5	4 059	9 673	1 680	58 293	384 300	49 762	5 490
Gadsden, AL	278.9	2 672	46.7	1.9	11.2	0.2	4.8	218.9	2 097	290	449	5 080	41 710	44 077	4 205
Gainesville, FL	944.7	3 522	39.3	3.8	8.2	1.7	4.8	1 953.5	7 283	4 618	573	39 209	116 680	55 079	7 247
Gainesville, GA	566.0	3 053	55.8	6.1	4.5	0.8	2.5	1 522.9	8 213	467	535	10 076	82 640	55 230	6 595
Gettysburg, PA	458.0	4 513	68.9	3.6	1.4	3.2	2.7	405.6	3 997	714	258	3 299	50 750	56 743	6 719
Glens Falls, NY	755.6	5 881	49.4	4.6	2.6	10.7	7.9	575.7	4 481	319	196	9 487	62 350	51 670	5 817
Goldsboro, NC	344.7	2 774	55.1	4.8	6.3	6.3	1.4	151.3	1 217	1 225	4 290	8 001	51 660	45 681	4 468
Grand Forks, ND-MN	433.5	4 384	39.7	1.2	4.5	5.2	9.0	875.4	8 852	1 128	2 024	11 916	48 500	58 646	7 357
Grand Island, NE	357.6	4 284	52.8	8.0	4.1	0.3	5.6	317.1	3 799	721	298	6 052	40 390	53 858	6 383
Grand Junction, CO	517.8	3 502	35.4	1.7	13.1	5.6	9.4	476.5	3 223	1 470	396	8 337	67 630	56 379	6 712
Grand Rapids-Wyoming, MI	3 715.2	3 694	53.0	6.3	4.2	1.7	4.7	5 263.1	5 234	3 282	1 763	44 350	485 560	60 500	7 635
Grants Pass, OR	253.3	3 055	59.6	2.9	7.1	0.1	5.0	145.0	1 748	273	215	2 768	35 560	43 823	4 370
Great Falls, MT	242.5	2 968	53.0	1.0	9.7	1.4	5.2	90.0	1 101	1 639	3 466	4 070	40 090	49 525	5 350
Greeley, CO	839.9	3 185	42.6	1.2	7.3	4.0	6.6	868.6	3 294	596	736	16 010	122 060	63 749	8 183
Green Bay, WI	1 439.4	4 627	48.3	6.1	6.0	4.3	8.4	1 261.2	4 054	1 328	858	20 339	155 860	59 960	7 605
Greensboro-High Point, NC	2 532.1	3 440	46.9	4.0	7.4	4.8	2.6	2 453.8	3 334	4 301	1 817	39 312	334 310	54 010	6 515
Greenville, NC	557.6	3 232	46.8	1.8	9.9	5.2	2.1	400.7	2 322	685	448	25 720	70 570	51 426	5 913
Greenville-Anderson-Mauldin, SC	3 672.8	4 358	32.8	39.0	3.5	0.2	1.5	5 469.6	6 489	2 619	3 466	54 971	375 660	55 509	6 476
Gulfport-Biloxi-Pascagoula, MS	2 433.4	6 411	24.7	32.2	3.8	0.1	4.4	1 537.8	4 051	8 722	9 578	23 905	166 590	46 839	4 859
Hagerstown-Martinsburg, MD-WV	838.7	3 272	65.4	0.7	4.2	0.3	3.3	710.6	2 773	4 071	1 033	13 152	119 710	52 130	5 318
Hammond, LA	692.4	5 610	29.5	47.0	3.7	0.0	2.7	361.5	2 929	359	553	10 122	50 900	48 861	5 413
Hanford-Corcoran, CA	602.9	3 983	45.9	6.6	4.9	9.6	2.9	261.9	1 730	1 131	5 146	13 478	53 220	46 540	4 375
Harrisburg-Carlisle, PA	2 716.3	4 903	51.9	3.9	3.3	8.1	2.6	3 833.1	6 919	7 243	2 296	53 465	286 380	60 237	7 659
Harrisonburg, VA	400.5	3 120	46.7	1.9	4.0	7.4	5.5	729.3	5 681	349	393	10 814	53 680	50 663	5 128
Hartford-West Hartford-East Hartford, CT	5 447.0	4 485	58.0	0.9	5.6	0.7	4.2	3 350.1	2 759	6 177	2 449	93 778	596 270	74 530	10 548
Hattiesburg, MS	821.7	5 598	26.1	51.6	3.1	0.0	4.2	543.5	3 703	803	1 281	13 887	60 940	53 507	6 632
Hickory-Lenoir-Morganton, NC	1 270.8	3 495	44.3	23.2	5.0	6.0	1.2	476.3	1 310	660	854	22 429	155 770	47 010	4 867
Hilton Head Island-Bluffton-Beaufort, NC	819.4	4 226	33.8	18.0	6.2	1.1	2.3	1 530.6	7 895	2 265	10 544	9 035	91 570	69 422	9 650
Hinesville, GA	286.7	3 516	55.3	16.9	4.8	0.2	3.0	89.3	1 095	3 901	16 290	3 860	31 580	37 709	2 484
Homosassa Springs, FL	362.7	2 602	47.4	5.5	9.1	2.5	6.6	493.5	3 541	217	256	4 096	62 370	45 989	5 084
Hot Springs, AR	268.9	2 775	57.5	0.3	5.6	0.0	3.6	344.1	3 551	496	407	4 061	43 040	48 927	5 645
Houma-Thibodaux, LA	1 104.3	5 286	31.2	30.4	4.8	0.4	2.8	502.1	2 403	394	988	11 966	91 060	65 771	9 712
Houston-The Woodlands-Sugar Land, TX	25 345.7	4 103	45.4	8.8	5.5	0.2	5.0	71 316.9	11 545	27 943	14 868	350 371	2 911 860	79 342	13 183
Huntington-Ashland, WV-KY-OH	1 087.6	2 982	60.9	2.7	4.7	1.1	2.2	804.6	2 206	3 241	1 528	19 585	148 790	50 760	5 527
Huntsville, AL	2 106.9	4 891	33.3	37.0	3.8	0.1	2.7	2 214.6	5 141	19 448	2 729	29 366	200 850	64 292	8 143
Idaho Falls, ID	346.6	2 547	46.8	2.7	7.1	0.3	4.8	344.6	2 532	892	491	6 797	56 670	55 568	6 118
Indianapolis-Carmel-Anderson, IN	8 480.2	4 396	36.1	22.7	4.0	0.2	1.7	17 097.1	8 863	16 584	6 607	114 252	946 020	60 807	7 989
Iowa City, IA	652.2	4 122	35.8	7.3	3.9	0.8	6.6	863.6	5 458	2 052	638	35 443	74 050	66 170	8 489
Ithaca, NY	541.1	5 276	48.3	4.4	2.7	8.0	5.5	696.7	6 794	258	165	5 854	40 930	63 960	8 071
Jackson, MI	586.0	3 655	54.4	10.1	2.6	3.6	6.4	539.6	3 366	340	244	7 316	71 280	49 531	5 312
Jackson, MS	1 812.3	3 142	55.0	1.6	6.1	0.3	7.0	2 027.9	3 516	6 589	3 418	53 887	252 770	53 830	6 554
Jackson, TN	966.4	7 408	17.5	58.3	3.3	0.1	2.4	1 066.4	8 174	499	384	13 437	56 170	47 625	5 458
Jacksonville, FL	4 951.5	3 594	40.9	2.0	9.1	1.2	4.9	13 946.9	10 122	17 300	14 563	58 824	682 090	61 491	8 513
Jacksonville, NC	563.2	3 073	38.6	24.7	6.7	6.5	1.0	439.4	2 398	6 779	43 028	7 945	78 430	41 522	3 302
Janesville-Beloit, WI	729.2	4 546	49.6	7.4	6.2	7.1	5.3	614.8	3 833	291	425	8 628	77 980	51 470	5 516
Jefferson City, MO	363.3	2 419	52.7	3.5	8.9	0.0	8.7	294.3	1 960	829	501	24 750	68 150	50 747	5 271
Johnson City, TN	497.7	2 480	48.2	7.3	6.4	0.4	5.3	765.4	3 814	2 832	637	13 152	85 120	47 717	5 296
Johnstown, PA	571.5	4 037	49.2	3.2	5.7	14.0	3.6	641.5	4 531	1 036	365	6 888	64 240	46 259	4 842

1. Based on the resident population estimated as of July 1 of the year shown.

Table C. Metropolitan Areas — **Land Area and Population**

			Population 2016			Population characteristics, 2016										
						Race alone or in combination, not Hispanic or Latino (percent)					Age (percent)					
CBSA/ DIV code[1]	Area name	Land area,[2] 2016 (sq mi)	Total persons	Rank	Per square mile	White	Black	American Indian, Alaska Native	Asian and Pacific Islander	Percent Hispanic or Latino[3]	Under 5 years	5 to 17 years	18 to 24 years	25 to 34 years	35 to 44 years	45 to 54 years
		1	2	3	4	5	6	7	8	9	10	11	12	13	14	15
27860	Jonesboro, AR	1 465.6	129 858	304	88.6	80.4	14.6	0.8	1.3	4.5	6.9	17.7	10.3	14.9	12.5	12.2
27900	Joplin, MO	1 263.2	177 805	235	140.8	87.8	2.6	3.3	2.2	7.1	6.7	18.2	9.0	13.3	12.1	12.4
27980	Kahului-Wailuku-Lahaina, HI	1 173.5	165 474	253	141.0	44.1	1.4	1.8	67.6	11.1	6.1	16.0	7.3	12.8	13.0	13.8
28020	Kalamazoo-Portage, MI	1 170.0	336 877	152	287.9	81.4	11.3	1.3	2.9	6.3	6.1	16.1	14.0	12.9	11.4	11.9
28100	Kankakee, IL	676.6	110 008	339	162.6	73.4	16.0	0.5	1.4	10.4	5.9	17.7	10.2	12.1	12.1	13.0
28140	Kansas City, MO-KS...........	7 256.2	2 104 509	30	290.0	75.1	13.7	1.2	3.7	8.9	6.6	18.0	8.2	14.1	13.1	13.3
28420	Kennewick-Richland, WA	2 941.4	283 846	165	96.5	63.4	2.3	1.3	3.8	31.4	7.9	20.9	9.0	14.2	12.6	11.6
28660	Killeen-Temple, TX	2 816.1	435 857	123	154.8	52.9	21.8	1.2	4.9	22.9	8.3	18.7	11.4	17.1	13.0	11.1
28700	Kingsport-Bristol-Bristol, TN-VA.....................	2 010.0	306 334	162	152.4	95.4	2.6	0.7	0.9	1.6	4.9	14.7	7.5	11.1	11.7	14.3
28740	Kingston, NY	1 124.2	179 225	233	159.4	81.6	7.1	0.8	2.8	10.1	4.4	13.7	9.4	12.2	11.5	14.8
28940	Knoxville, TN.....................	3 500.7	868 546	64	248.1	88.7	6.6	0.9	2.0	3.6	5.5	15.4	9.9	12.3	12.0	13.6
29020	Kokomo, IN	293.0	82 568	373	281.8	88.0	8.8	0.9	1.7	3.3	6.1	16.6	8.1	11.7	11.5	13.2
29100	La Crosse-Onalaska, WI-MN	1 003.8	136 936	294	136.4	92.5	2.1	0.7	4.6	1.7	5.3	15.0	15.1	12.3	10.9	12.0
29180	Lafayette, LA.....................	3 408.9	491 528	108	144.2	69.0	25.7	0.7	2.1	4.0	7.0	17.9	8.9	15.2	12.3	12.7
29200	Lafayette-West Lafayette, IN	1 278.4	216 679	204	169.5	80.4	5.3	0.6	7.8	7.7	6.2	15.1	21.8	13.8	10.7	10.4
29340	Lake Charles, LA	2 349.2	207 483	213	88.3	70.2	25.6	1.1	1.7	3.3	6.9	17.9	8.9	14.7	12.0	12.4
29420	Lake Havasu City-Kingman, AZ	13 311.1	205 249	217	15.4	79.3	1.5	2.9	1.9	16.2	4.5	13.5	6.5	10.0	9.0	11.8
29460	Lakeland-Winter Haven, FL.	1 796.8	666 149	82	370.7	62.0	15.5	0.7	2.4	21.1	5.9	16.6	8.4	12.7	11.7	12.3
29540	Lancaster, PA	943.9	538 500	103	570.5	83.8	4.5	0.4	2.6	10.2	6.6	17.2	9.1	13.0	11.3	12.7
29620	Lansing-East Lansing, MI	1 697.7	475 099	110	279.8	79.2	10.5	1.2	5.5	6.6	5.6	15.2	15.4	13.4	11.2	12.2
29700	Laredo, TX........................	3 361.5	271 193	175	80.7	3.7	0.3	0.1	0.6	95.5	10.0	23.8	11.4	13.3	12.9	11.2
29740	Las Cruces, NM	3 808.2	214 207	208	56.2	28.7	1.7	1.2	1.5	68.0	6.7	18.4	14.8	12.5	10.7	10.7
29820	Las Vegas-Henderson-Paradise, NV	7 891.7	2 155 664	29	273.2	46.5	12.5	1.1	13.0	30.9	6.4	17.1	8.6	14.9	13.8	13.5
29940	Lawrence, KS	455.9	119 440	324	262.0	82.2	5.9	3.5	6.1	6.1	5.3	13.5	23.9	14.7	11.4	9.9
30020	Lawton, OK	1 701.9	128 077	307	75.3	62.3	18.7	8.1	4.8	12.4	7.2	16.8	12.6	16.4	12.2	11.5
30140	Lebanon, PA	361.8	138 863	292	383.8	83.8	2.5	0.4	1.7	12.7	6.1	16.9	8.4	11.6	11.6	13.1
30300	Lewiston, ID-WA	1 484.4	62 675	380	42.2	90.6	1.0	5.2	1.7	3.8	6.0	15.3	8.2	12.5	11.0	12.2
30340	Lewiston-Auburn, ME	467.9	107 319	341	229.4	93.1	4.8	1.1	1.4	1.8	6.0	15.8	8.7	12.3	11.9	14.4
30460	Lexington-Fayette, KY	1 468.6	506 751	106	345.1	79.9	12.3	0.7	3.4	5.9	6.3	15.9	12.4	14.3	13.0	12.8
30620	Lima, OH..........................	402.5	103 742	346	257.7	83.6	14.3	0.7	1.2	3.0	6.1	17.2	9.9	12.2	11.5	12.5
30700	Lincoln, NE	1 409.0	326 921	154	232.0	84.7	4.9	1.1	5.1	6.6	6.5	16.5	15.2	13.8	12.1	11.1
30780	Little Rock-North Little Rock-Conway, AR	4 084.4	734 622	76	179.9	69.2	24.2	1.1	2.2	5.2	6.5	17.2	9.5	14.3	12.8	12.6
30860	Logan, UT-ID	1 828.0	136 159	295	74.5	86.1	0.9	1.0	3.5	10.1	8.8	22.1	18.0	13.7	11.5	8.3
30980	Longview, TX	1 780.3	217 446	201	122.1	65.1	18.0	1.0	1.3	16.2	6.9	18.0	9.1	13.2	11.9	12.4
31020	Longview, WA.....................	1 140.4	105 160	343	92.2	86.9	1.5	3.1	2.9	8.8	5.9	16.7	7.7	11.9	11.5	12.9
31080	Los Angeles-Long Beach-Anaheim, CA	4 848.8	13 310 447	2	2 745.1	31.9	7.1	0.6	17.6	45.1	6.1	16.1	9.8	15.5	13.5	13.8
31080	Anaheim-Santa Ana-Irvine, CA Div 11244	790.6	3 172 532	X	4 012.8	43.5	2.1	0.6	22.3	34.3	6.0	16.5	9.5	14.3	13.0	14.4
31080	Los Angeles-Long Beach-Glendale, CA Div 31084..........	4 058.2	10 137 915	X	2 498.1	28.2	8.7	0.6	16.1	48.5	6.2	16.0	9.9	15.9	13.7	13.7
31140	Louisville/Jefferson County, KY-IN	3 578.4	1 283 430	44	358.7	78.6	15.7	0.7	2.6	4.5	6.2	16.6	8.3	13.7	12.8	13.7
31180	Lubbock, TX......................	2 687.7	314 840	159	117.1	54.9	7.4	0.7	2.7	35.6	6.8	17.4	16.6	14.6	11.3	10.5
31340	Lynchburg, VA	2 120.3	260 232	185	122.7	78.2	18.3	0.8	2.0	2.5	5.3	14.6	13.1	11.8	10.3	12.9
31420	Macon, GA........................	1 722.7	229 182	196	133.0	50.5	45.5	0.6	2.0	2.8	6.4	17.5	9.5	12.7	11.7	13.0
31460	Madera, CA.......................	2 137.1	154 697	263	72.4	36.0	3.6	1.8	2.7	57.4	7.5	20.0	9.8	13.8	12.4	11.8
31540	Madison, WI	3 308.7	648 929	86	196.1	84.4	5.5	0.7	5.8	5.7	5.8	15.3	12.7	14.7	12.7	12.7
31700	Manchester-Nashua, NH	876.4	407 761	132	465.3	87.1	2.8	0.7	4.6	6.5	5.3	15.7	8.9	13.2	12.2	15.5
31740	Manhattan, KS	1 450.8	97 004	360	66.9	82.8	6.5	1.3	5.2	7.2	6.4	13.6	26.4	17.0	10.0	8.0
31860	Mankato-North Mankato, MN	1 196.4	100 016	353	83.6	90.4	4.3	0.7	2.6	3.7	5.7	14.8	18.9	13.6	10.9	10.5
31900	Mansfield, OH	495.3	121 107	321	244.5	87.7	10.7	0.7	1.1	1.8	5.7	15.9	8.4	12.3	11.8	12.9
32580	McAllen-Edinburg-Mission, TX	1 570.9	849 843	66	541.0	6.7	0.5	0.1	1.0	91.8	9.6	23.7	11.0	13.2	12.8	10.7
32780	Medford, OR	2 783.2	216 527	205	77.8	84.1	1.3	2.4	2.7	12.5	5.6	15.0	7.9	12.5	11.2	12.0
32820	Memphis, TN-MS-AR..........	4 985.6	1 342 842	42	269.3	45.1	47.9	0.6	2.5	5.4	6.9	18.3	9.5	13.9	12.7	13.2
32900	Merced, CA.......................	1 935.2	268 672	178	138.8	30.0	3.6	0.9	8.5	58.9	7.9	21.9	11.2	14.4	12.2	11.5
33100	Miami-Fort Lauderdale-West Palm Beach, FL ..	5 075.5	6 066 387	8	1 195.2	32.2	21.1	0.3	3.1	44.4	5.7	14.8	8.2	13.6	13.1	14.4
33100	Fort Lauderdale-Pompano Beach-Deerfield Beach, FL Div 22744	1 207.0	1 909 632	X	1 582.1	38.9	29.1	0.5	4.6	28.7	5.8	15.5	8.1	13.6	13.2	14.6
33100	Miami-Miami Beach-Kendall, FL Div 33124	1 898.7	2 712 945	X	1 428.8	14.3	16.6	0.2	1.9	67.7	5.8	14.5	8.6	14.4	13.9	14.8
33100	West Palm Beach-Boca Raton-Delray Beach, FL Div 48424	1 969.9	1 443 810	X	732.9	57.0	19.1	0.4	3.4	21.5	5.2	14.2	7.6	11.9	11.4	13.3
33140	Michigan City-La Porte, IN ..	598.3	110 015	338	183.9	81.5	12.4	0.7	1.0	6.5	6.0	15.8	8.5	13.0	12.2	13.6
33220	Midland, MI	516.3	83 462	372	161.7	92.9	2.0	1.0	2.9	2.7	5.4	16.3	8.6	12.2	11.5	14.3
33260	Midland, TX......................	1 815.2	168 288	249	92.7	47.4	6.4	0.8	2.1	44.4	8.9	19.6	9.3	17.6	12.4	11.0
33340	Milwaukee-Waukesha-West Allis, WI	1 455.0	1 572 482	39	1 080.7	68.7	17.5	0.9	4.3	10.6	6.3	17.1	9.1	14.0	12.3	13.2
33460	Minneapolis-St. Paul-Bloomington, MN	7 637.1	3 551 036	16	465.0	78.6	9.4	1.3	7.6	5.7	6.6	17.3	8.7	14.6	13.0	13.8
33540	Missoula, MT	2 593.1	116 130	330	44.8	92.2	1.0	4.0	2.5	3.1	5.4	13.9	14.5	15.4	12.2	11.4

1. CBSA = Core Based Statistical Area. DIV = Metropolitan Division. See Appendix A for explanation. See Appendix B for list of metropolitan areas identified by type.　2. Dry land or land partially or temporarily covered by water.　3. May be of any race.

Table C. Metropolitan Areas — **Population and Households**

Area name	Population, 2016 (cont.) Age (percent) (cont.) 55 to 64 years	65 to 74 years	75 years and over	Percent female	Population change and components of change, 2000–2016 Total persons 2000	2010	Percent change 2000–2010	2010–2016	Components of change, 2010–2016 Births	Deaths	Net migration	Households, 2015 Number	Persons per house-hold	Percent Family house-holds	Female family house-holder[1]	One person
	16	17	18	19	20	21	22	23	24	25	26	27	28	29	30	31
Jonesboro, AR	11.3	8.2	5.9	51.4	107 762	121 026	12.3	7.3	10 979	7 615	5 348	48 943	2.54	64.2	14.6	29.2
Joplin, MO	12.6	9.0	6.7	51.0	157 322	175 516	11.6	1.3	15 160	10 985	-2 018	67 439	2.58	68.9	9.5	25.8
Kahului-Wailuku-Lahaina, HI	14.4	10.3	6.3	50.1	128 241	154 925	20.8	6.8	12 468	7 235	5 314	52 170	3.11	70.0	11.4	23.9
Kalamazoo-Portage, MI	12.7	8.7	6.2	50.8	314 866	326 592	3.7	3.1	25 318	17 358	2 371	129 792	2.51	62.0	11.5	29.5
Kankakee, IL	13.2	9.0	6.8	50.9	103 833	113 449	9.3	-3.0	8 355	6 770	-5 018	38 755	2.71	65.2	15.3	30.2
Kansas City, MO-KS	12.8	8.2	5.8	50.9	1 811 254	2 009 338	10.9	4.7	172 705	102 616	25 967	814 092	2.53	64.2	11.6	29.8
Kennewick-Richland, WA	11.5	7.6	4.8	49.4	191 822	253 334	32.1	12.0	26 667	10 480	13 894	94 423	2.91	73.4	12.5	20.6
Killeen-Temple, TX	9.5	6.4	4.3	50.3	330 714	405 310	22.6	7.5	47 390	16 442	-1 176	151 623	2.67	71.1	15.1	24.5
Kingsport-Bristol-Bristol, TN-VA	14.8	12.2	8.9	51.2	298 484	309 516	3.7	-1.0	18 529	23 969	2 513	126 840	2.36	66.1	11.5	30.5
Kingston, NY	15.3	11.0	7.7	50.4	177 749	182 512	2.7	-1.8	9 941	10 227	-2 758	69 594	2.42	60.4	8.7	32.2
Knoxville, TN	13.6	10.5	7.2	51.2	748 259	837 675	11.9	3.7	58 423	55 623	27 487	343 331	2.45	65.4	11.6	28.8
Kokomo, IN	13.9	10.7	8.1	51.5	84 964	82 752	-2.6	-0.2	6 203	5 777	-575	34 714	2.35	64.1	11.2	30.7
La Crosse-Onalaska, WI-MN	13.3	9.0	7.3	51.1	126 838	133 665	5.4	2.4	9 106	7 118	1 235	54 008	2.43	60.1	6.8	29.8
Lafayette, LA	12.7	7.8	5.4	51.2	425 020	466 747	9.8	5.3	42 807	25 419	7 254	180 902	2.67	66.7	15.1	26.8
Lafayette-West Lafayette, IN	10.4	6.8	4.9	49.0	178 541	201 798	13.0	7.4	16 240	8 607	7 505	81 069	2.45	54.8	9.4	31.6
Lake Charles, LA	13.0	8.4	5.8	51.2	193 568	199 629	3.1	3.9	17 386	12 379	3 119	79 853	2.52	65.1	16.2	29.0
Lake Havasu City-Kingman, AZ	16.2	16.7	11.9	49.6	155 032	200 185	29.1	2.5	11 655	16 725	9 221	83 801	2.41	65.9	12.1	26.0
Lakeland-Winter Haven, FL	12.4	11.5	8.5	51.0	483 924	602 095	24.4	10.6	46 080	39 039	55 293	227 122	2.81	69.2	14.4	24.9
Lancaster, PA	13.0	9.2	7.9	51.0	470 658	519 448	10.4	3.7	44 405	29 685	3 922	197 706	2.65	70.3	10.6	23.4
Lansing-East Lansing, MI	12.8	8.6	5.7	51.2	447 728	464 032	3.6	2.4	32 840	22 492	930	183 888	2.46	58.3	9.9	31.2
Laredo, TX	8.4	5.3	3.7	51.1	193 117	250 304	29.6	8.3	34 078	7 932	-5 109	72 259	3.69	77.5	21.1	18.6
Las Cruces, NM	11.1	8.8	6.4	50.8	174 682	209 235	19.8	2.4	19 011	9 352	-4 971	74 631	2.81	70.5	14.4	23.5
Las Vegas-Henderson-Paradise, NV	11.7	8.8	5.3	50.1	1 375 765	1 951 269	41.8	10.5	166 704	91 848	125 572	740 966	2.82	63.3	14.1	24.5
Lawrence, KS	10.0	6.7	4.5	50.1	99 962	110 826	10.9	7.8	7 675	4 004	4 926	42 817	2.55	56.1	7.8	30.7
Lawton, OK	11.3	7.0	5.2	48.3	121 610	130 291	7.1	-1.7	12 725	6 731	-8 223	43 678	2.77	65.3	14.4	28.0
Lebanon, PA	13.5	10.3	8.6	50.9	120 327	133 577	11.0	4.0	10 218	8 832	3 836	53 200	2.52	66.3	10.7	26.7
Lewiston, ID-WA	14.6	11.1	9.2	50.8	57 961	60 890	5.1	2.9	4 504	4 557	1 886	25 354	2.40	67.7	11.8	27.0
Lewiston-Auburn, ME	14.2	9.8	7.0	51.0	103 793	107 702	3.8	-0.4	8 025	6 471	-1 869	45 138	2.30	63.3	9.4	27.9
Lexington-Fayette, KY	12.1	7.9	5.3	51.0	408 326	472 102	15.6	7.3	39 374	23 211	18 594	199 299	2.43	63.9	13.7	26.9
Lima, OH	13.7	9.4	7.4	49.5	108 473	106 326	-2.0	-2.4	7 975	6 743	-3 736	40 234	2.50	66.1	13.7	28.2
Lincoln, NE	11.6	7.8	5.5	49.9	266 787	302 157	13.3	8.2	26 668	13 402	11 157	127 316	2.43	58.2	8.4	31.8
Little Rock-North Little Rock-Conway, AR	12.4	8.7	5.8	51.6	610 518	699 819	14.6	5.0	60 932	39 713	13 771	282 914	2.53	64.7	14.3	29.4
Logan, UT-ID	8.0	5.5	4.1	49.8	102 720	125 442	22.1	8.5	16 215	3 758	-1 852	40 927	3.20	74.2	7.0	17.7
Longview, TX	12.9	8.9	6.7	50.1	194 042	214 384	10.5	1.4	18 931	13 961	-1 926	76 401	2.72	68.8	15.1	25.3
Longview, WA	14.4	11.3	7.5	50.5	92 948	102 408	10.2	2.7	7 423	6 643	1 827	40 187	2.54	66.7	10.0	24.9
Los Angeles-Long Beach-Anaheim, CA	11.9	7.5	5.7	50.7	12 365 627	12 828 961	3.7	3.8	1 048 792	494 357	-57 111	4 315 637	3.04	68.1	14.3	24.5
Anaheim-Santa Ana-Irvine, CA Div 11244	12.3	7.9	6.0	50.7	2 846 289	3 010 261	5.8	5.4	238 043	117 213	43 160	1 022 542	3.06	71.6	11.9	21.3
Los Angeles-Long Beach-Glendale, CA Div 31084	11.7	7.3	5.6	50.7	9 519 338	9 818 700	3.1	3.3	810 749	377 144	-100 271	3 293 095	3.04	67.0	15.1	25.5
Louisville/Jefferson County, KY-IN	13.6	9.0	6.1	51.1	1 121 109	1 235 710	10.2	3.9	98 738	73 725	24 120	496 455	2.53	64.1	13.3	30.3
Lubbock, TX	10.4	6.9	5.4	50.6	256 250	290 868	13.5	8.2	26 506	15 230	12 221	112 853	2.67	61.5	14.6	28.8
Lynchburg, VA	13.7	10.5	7.7	51.8	228 616	252 659	10.5	3.0	17 623	15 978	5 733	100 497	2.46	67.9	13.0	26.3
Macon, GA	13.5	9.4	6.4	52.2	222 368	232 293	4.5	-1.3	18 957	14 874	-7 364	86 400	2.59	63.5	17.8	31.7
Madera, CA	11.1	8.2	5.4	51.7	123 109	150 843	22.5	2.6	14 523	6 594	-3 876	45 224	3.23	78.7	15.4	19.2
Madison, WI	12.5	8.2	5.5	50.2	535 421	605 437	13.1	7.2	46 387	26 048	22 265	264 340	2.36	58.4	8.8	29.5
Manchester-Nashua, NH	14.5	8.8	6.1	50.3	380 841	400 720	5.2	1.8	26 808	19 093	-457	156 678	2.54	66.1	11.1	25.4
Manhattan, KS	8.7	5.6	4.3	47.9	81 052	92 735	14.4	4.6	9 018	3 124	-1 806	34 806	2.57	55.6	5.3	28.4
Mankato-North Mankato, MN	11.6	7.7	6.3	49.5	85 712	96 740	12.9	3.4	7 055	4 242	423	38 444	2.40	57.9	9.7	27.9
Mansfield, OH	14.1	10.4	8.4	49.1	128 852	124 475	-3.4	-2.7	8 612	8 475	-3 411	46 989	2.44	61.2	11.8	32.1
McAllen-Edinburg-Mission, TX	8.2	6.2	4.8	51.1	569 463	774 770	36.1	9.7	101 020	24 660	-2 201	225 692	3.69	81.9	22.1	16.0
Medford, OR	14.5	12.5	8.8	51.2	181 269	203 206	12.1	6.6	14 480	13 992	12 380	83 876	2.49	63.1	11.3	28.4
Memphis, TN-MS-AR	12.6	7.9	5.1	52.1	1 213 230	1 324 824	9.2	1.4	117 652	70 812	-28 125	494 270	2.67	65.6	19.7	29.1
Merced, CA	9.9	6.4	4.5	49.6	210 554	255 798	21.5	5.0	26 416	10 143	-3 129	79 098	3.31	76.0	18.1	18.6
Miami-Fort Lauderdale-West Palm Beach, FL	12.6	9.4	8.4	51.5	5 007 564	5 566 298	11.2	9.0	419 349	298 402	374 706	2 077 362	2.85	65.3	15.9	28.5
Fort Lauderdale-Pompano Beach-Deerfield Beach, FL Div 22744	13.1	8.9	7.1	51.3	1 623 018	1 748 146	7.7	9.2	134 898	92 016	118 960	673 870	2.79	64.3	15.4	28.5
Miami-Miami Beach-Kendall, FL Div 33124	12.0	8.5	7.4	51.5	2 253 362	2 498 018	10.9	8.6	195 783	119 755	137 932	857 712	3.08	67.4	18.8	27.0
West Palm Beach-Boca Raton-Delray Beach, FL Div 48424	13.0	11.4	11.9	51.7	1 131 184	1 320 134	16.7	9.4	88 668	86 631	117 814	545 780	2.57	63.1	11.8	30.7
Michigan City-La Porte, IN	14.2	9.9	6.7	48.5	110 106	111 467	1.2	-1.3	8 207	7 209	-2 294	43 169	2.36	62.4	13.0	31.1
Midland, MI	14.3	9.5	7.9	50.7	82 874	83 629	0.9	-0.2	5 399	4 406	-1 133	32 977	2.50	68.9	9.4	26.5
Midland, TX	11.1	5.6	4.5	49.7	120 755	141 671	17.3	18.8	17 181	6 771	16 066	57 867	2.82	69.0	10.1	25.2
Milwaukee-Waukesha-West Allis, WI	13.4	8.3	6.3	51.3	1 500 741	1 555 954	3.7	1.1	124 626	82 083	-24 889	627 842	2.46	61.3	12.3	31.3
Minneapolis-St. Paul-Bloomington, MN	12.9	7.7	5.4	50.5	3 031 918	3 348 859	10.5	6.0	285 404	137 889	57 080	1 354 766	2.56	64.7	9.7	27.6
Missoula, MT	12.6	9.1	5.5	49.7	95 802	109 299	14.1	6.2	7 706	5 143	4 182	47 910	2.31	55.1	9.7	33.3

1. No spouse present.

Table C. Metropolitan Areas — **Population, Vital Statistics, Health, and Crime**

Area name	Persons in group quarters, 2016	Daytime population, 2015 Number	Employ-ment/residence ratio	Births, 2016 Total	Rate[1]	Deaths, 2016 Number	Rate[1]	Persons under 65 with no health insurance 2015 Number	Percent	Medicare, 2015 Total Benefici-aries	Enrolled in Original Medicare	Enrolled in Medicare Advantage	Serious crimes known to police,[2] 2014 Total Number	Rate[3]
	32	33	34	35	36	37	38	39	40	41	42	43	44	45
Jonesboro, AR	4 160	130 986	1.05	1 844	14.2	1 284	9.9	11 437	10.7	23 722	19 054	4 668	4 926	3 968
Joplin, MO..........................	3 364	180 205	1.04	2 374	13.4	1 705	9.6	21 307	14.5	33 086	24 759	8 327	8 073	4 606
Kahului-Wailuku-Lahaina, HI	2 830	NA	NA	1 933	11.7	1 329	8.0	7 500	5.4	23 798	10 776	13 022	6 309	3 889
Kalamazoo-Portage, MI	9 159	332 107	0.98	4 052	12.0	2 963	8.8	20 285	7.3	60 392	33 409	26 983	2 999	2 985
Kankakee, IL	5 160	107 923	0.94	1 278	11.6	1 140	10.4	6 396	7.1	20 056	15 855	4 201	2 999	3 053
Kansas City, MO-KS............	31 350	2 104 008	1.02	27 550	13.1	17 223	8.2	178 607	10.0	318 817	216 191	102 626	71 856	3 514
Kennewick-Richland, WA......	4 265	275 683	0.97	4 336	15.3	1 842	6.5	21 787	9.1	37 842	32 947	4 895	6 711	2 428
Killeen-Temple, TX	20 260	429 118	0.99	7 582	17.4	2 890	6.6	49 232	13.4	53 431	36 135	17 296	13 305	3 115
Kingsport-Bristol-Bristol, TN-VA..................................	5 607	306 363	1.00	2 910	9.5	3 832	12.5	26 675	11.1	80 164	37 681	42 483	8 851	2 868
Kingston, NY.......................	11 612	164 702	0.82	1 491	8.3	1 723	9.6	10 680	7.5	35 268	26 212	9 056	3 267	1 806
Knoxville, TN.......................	19 522	872 953	1.03	9 381	10.8	9 129	10.5	77 809	11.2	175 325	96 623	78 702	28 957	3 493
Kokomo, IN.........................	1 280	86 802	1.12	987	12.0	942	11.4	6 451	9.7	19 261	16 361	2 900	2 466	3 017
La Crosse-Onalaska, WI-MN	6 005	142 212	1.07	1 459	10.7	1 154	8.4	5 804	5.2	24 827	13 804	11 023	2 643	1 944
Lafayette, LA.......................	8 402	495 048	1.02	7 107	14.5	4 392	8.9	60 543	14.4	73 963	63 986	9 977	16 699	3 640
Lafayette-West Lafayette, IN	14 674	220 930	1.06	2 693	12.4	1 408	6.5	22 052	12.5	27 238	21 901	5 337	5 219	2 854
Lake Charles, LA	3 821	214 217	1.09	2 841	13.7	2 059	9.9	22 501	13.0	35 503	29 312	6 191	10 134	5 000
Lake Havasu City-Kingman, AZ	4 622	197 013	0.89	1 879	9.2	3 101	15.1	20 035	14.0	56 378	39 304	17 074	6 743	3 364
Lakeland-Winter Haven, FL..	13 208	627 349	0.91	7 678	11.5	6 786	10.2	78 735	15.4	128 042	63 733	64 309	19 500	3 080
Lancaster, PA	12 803	525 848	0.96	7 185	13.3	5 035	9.4	48 546	11.1	98 269	59 292	38 977	9 261	1 741
Lansing-East Lansing, MI	20 767	485 445	1.06	5 287	11.1	3 747	7.9	26 284	6.8	78 518	54 987	23 531	10 655	2 287
Laredo, TX	3 553	269 922	1.00	5 387	19.9	1 342	4.9	66 469	27.6	27 734	20 613	7 121	11 100	4 153
Las Cruces, NM	4 582	204 395	0.89	2 854	13.3	1 567	7.3	24 393	13.7	35 040	22 706	12 334	7 132	3 337
Las Vegas-Henderson-Para-dise, NV	23 321	2 118 398	1.00	27 352	12.7	16 501	7.7	261 500	14.5	283 581	161 821	121 760	72 994	3 532
Lawrence, KS	8 800	110 800	0.88	1 224	10.2	655	5.5	9 585	9.8	15 210	13 143	2 067	2 521	2 190
Lawton, OK	10 376	132 171	1.03	1 908	14.9	1 155	9.0	14 573	13.9	18 631	17 448	1 183	5 778	4 408
Lebanon, PA	3 666	128 307	0.87	1 623	11.7	1 478	10.6	9 522	8.7	28 398	16 618	11 780	2 350	1 729
Lewiston, ID-WA	1 229	62 546	1.01	724	11.6	720	11.5	4 799	9.8	15 291	11 985	3 306	1 996	3 185
Lewiston-Auburn, ME...........	2 833	100 864	0.88	1 215	11.3	1 052	9.8	8 068	9.3	23 261	16 229	7 032	2 474	2 297
Lexington-Fayette, KY	18 295	525 201	1.10	6 350	12.5	3 825	7.5	32 354	7.7	72 669	47 408	25 261	18 542	3 752
Lima, OH	5 977	109 292	1.10	1 252	12.1	1 085	10.5	6 108	7.4	20 220	14 645	5 575	3 862	3 672
Lincoln, NE	16 260	331 691	1.05	4 264	13.0	2 202	6.7	22 524	8.4	44 558	39 719	4 839	10 592	3 360
Little Rock-North Little Rock-Conway, AR.....................	15 724	739 939	1.03	9 532	13.0	6 581	9.0	57 539	9.3	120 613	97 720	22 893	36 769	5 041
Logan, UT-ID	3 589	130 096	0.94	2 578	18.9	587	4.3	11 553	9.9	13 045	7 530	5 515	1 649	1 257
Longview, TX	9 427	224 064	1.07	2 975	13.7	2 280	10.5	36 160	20.4	40 793	30 135	10 658	7 872	3 660
Longview, WA	1 208	101 376	0.95	1 195	11.4	1 094	10.4	6 675	8.0	21 837	11 397	10 440	3 982	3 897
Los Angeles-Long Beach-Anaheim, CA...................	219 602	13 580 367	1.04	166 913	12.5	87 009	6.5	1 364 099	11.9	1 678 195	707 993	970 202	321 229	2 419
Anaheim-Santa Ana-Irvine, CA Div 11244	42 892	3 263 629	1.06	38 433	12.1	20 520	6.5	271 391	10.0	425 459	195 503	229 956	61 011	1 933
Los Angeles-Long Beach-Glendale, CA Div 31084	176 710	10 316 738	1.03	128 480	12.7	66 489	6.6	1 092 708	12.5	1 252 736	512 490	740 246	260 218	2 571
Louisville/Jefferson County, KY-IN	26 405	1 295 910	1.03	15 821	12.3	12 081	9.4	79 189	7.4	222 865	155 829	67 036	46 200	3 749
Lubbock, TX........................	12 265	312 250	1.00	4 408	14.0	2 637	8.4	45 064	17.1	42 754	27 879	14 875	14 239	4 691
Lynchburg, VA	13 138	255 801	0.96	2 785	10.7	2 615	10.0	23 227	11.5	57 021	46 423	10 598	4 908	1 906
Macon, GA	7 705	238 889	1.08	2 931	12.8	2 573	11.2	28 391	15.1	42 372	26 883	15 489	NA	NA
Madera, CA	7 504	150 809	0.92	2 276	14.7	1 066	6.9	16 485	13.0	22 146	14 445	7 701	4 268	2 780
Madison, WI	14 690	669 371	1.08	7 486	11.5	4 273	6.6	29 439	5.4	93 141	68 800	24 341	13 708	2 245
Manchester-Nashua, NH	7 980	384 282	0.90	4 146	10.2	3 267	8.0	26 982	7.9	66 748	60 024	6 724	9 289	2 360
Manhattan, KS	9 379	96 190	0.95	1 414	14.6	537	5.5	6 615	8.2	10 328	9 600	728	1 707	1 718
Mankato-North Mankato, MN	7 023	104 013	1.09	1 102	11.0	697	7.0	3 465	4.3	16 149	7 509	8 640	2 344	2 364
Mansfield, OH	7 386	123 334	1.03	1 319	10.9	1 348	11.1	7 466	8.0	27 057	19 561	7 496	5 689	4 880
McAllen-Edinburg-Mission, TX	7 577	827 726	0.95	16 144	19.0	4 395	5.2	236 321	32.0	90 323	41 092	49 231	30 676	3 689
Medford, OR	4 781	215 324	1.03	2 314	10.7	2 258	10.4	14 683	8.9	50 319	33 485	16 834	9 061	4 300
Memphis, TN-MS-AR............	24 518	1 360 738	1.03	18 535	13.8	12 130	9.0	148 676	12.9	197 306	143 440	53 866	67 711	5 394
Merced, CA	5 747	253 972	0.85	4 188	15.6	1 730	6.4	23 618	10.1	31 409	27 892	3 517	8 611	3 233
Miami-Fort Lauderdale-West Palm Beach, FL	80 088	6 024 977	1.00	68 638	11.3	52 476	8.7	920 818	18.8	989 139	432 297	556 842	235 037	3 958
Fort Lauderdale-Pompano Beach-Deerfield Beach, FL Div 22744	16 914	1 816 477	0.91	22 170	11.6	15 864	8.3	261 839	16.5	279 598	117 988	161 610	64 848	3 457
Miami-Miami Beach-Ken-dall, FL Div 33124	41 977	2 767 212	1.06	31 772	11.7	21 405	7.9	473 278	21.2	418 594	137 534	281 060	122 865	4 606
West Palm Beach-Boca Raton-Delray Beach, FL Div 48424	21 197	1 441 288	1.03	14 696	10.2	15 207	10.5	185 701	17.2	290 947	176 775	114 172	47 324	3 391
Michigan City-La Porte, IN....	6 280	104 968	0.87	1 293	11.8	1 195	10.9	9 456	10.9	20 843	18 083	2 760	2 473	2 427
Midland, MI	1 272	87 706	1.11	883	10.6	734	8.8	4 044	5.9	15 648	10 296	5 352	1 148	1 366
Midland, TX	1 710	183 530	1.22	3 144	18.7	1 130	6.7	25 383	17.0	16 758	13 308	3 450	4 701	2 902
Milwaukee-Waukesha-West Allis, WI	31 938	1 619 152	1.06	19 589	12.5	13 426	8.5	89 638	6.8	259 922	148 056	111 866	56 248	3 716
Minneapolis-St. Paul-Bloomington, MN	64 633	3 545 678	1.01	45 944	12.9	23 322	6.6	152 975	5.0	483 310	190 020	293 290	95 940	2 751
Missoula, MT.......................	3 638	NA	NA	1 234	10.6	856	7.4	11 512	12.1	18 790	15 168	3 622	3 636	3 228

1. Per 1,000 estimated resident population.   2. Data for serious crimes have not been adjusted for underreporting; this may affect comparability between geographic areas and over time.
3. Per 100,000 population estimated by the FBI.

Table C. Metropolitan Areas — Crime, Education, Money Income, and Poverty

Area name	Serious crimes known to police, 2014 (cont.)[1] — Rate[2] Violent	Serious crimes known to police, 2014 (cont.)[1] — Rate[2] Property	Education — Enrollment[3] Total	Education — Enrollment[3] Percent private	Education — Attainment[4] (percent) High school graduate or less	Education — Attainment[4] (percent) Bachelor's degree or more	Local government expenditures,[5] 2013–2014 Total current expenditures (mil dol)	Local government expenditures,[5] 2013–2014 Current expenditures per student (dollars)	Income and Poverty, 2015 — Per capita income[6] (dollars)	Mean household income (dollars)	Median household income	Percent of households with income of less than $50,000	Percent of households with income of $200,000 or more	Percent below poverty level — All persons	Percent below poverty level — Children under 18 years	Percent below poverty level — Age 65 years and older
	46	47	48	49	50	51	52	53	54	55	56	57	58	59	60	61
Jonesboro, AR	412	3 557	36 494	4.9	48.1	21.7	198.7	8 888	21 762	54 177	37 378	60.5	1.7	18.2	26.9	8.1
Joplin, MO	329	4 276	44 130	14.8	45.4	22.7	239.7	7 938	23 207	60 416	45 089	55.4	2.4	14.2	19.3	8.0
Kahului-Wailuku-Lahaina, HI	314	3 575	36 121	23.3	39.9	25.3	NA	NA	29 590	86 521	70 468	32.8	5.3	9.7	12.5	9.1
Kalamazoo-Portage, MI	457	2 529	100 256	10.5	31.1	34.7	557.5	11 124	28 247	70 844	51 167	48.9	3.9	16.0	19.5	8.8
Kankakee, IL	329	2 724	29 802	19.7	47.2	20.8	211.6	11 118	25 129	66 017	53 850	45.8	3.3	15.1	21.5	8.8
Kansas City, MO-KS	486	3 028	525 251	15.6	35.1	35.8	3 125.7	9 108	32 147	80 465	60 502	41.6	5.1	11.8	17.2	7.0
Kennewick-Richland, WA	206	2 222	75 672	10.9	40.1	26.4	509.7	9 561	26 530	74 989	61 361	40.9	4.4	15.5	22.1	4.6
Killeen-Temple, TX	343	2 773	123 678	11.6	37.9	23.2	683.5	8 254	23 852	64 580	48 612	51.3	2.7	16.3	23.4	9.4
Kingsport-Bristol-Bristol, TN-VA	323	2 545	62 771	12.1	50.6	20.5	396.5	9 114	23 612	55 152	41 206	58.4	2.2	17.6	27.7	9.1
Kingston, NY	183	1 622	40 417	15.6	42.0	31.3	516.5	21 740	30 010	75 145	59 758	43.6	3.5	13.9	18.3	8.5
Knoxville, TN	387	3 105	198 095	16.5	44.5	27.9	1 049.6	8 544	27 299	66 566	48 382	51.3	3.7	16.8	24.4	8.5
Kokomo, IN	225	2 792	18 244	11.9	49.7	18.8	129.9	9 199	25 316	58 805	46 793	53.2	1.9	18.9	29.4	8.4
La Crosse-Onalaska, WI-MN	116	1 827	39 083	13.0	33.8	30.0	243.3	11 730	29 467	73 049	50 705	48.9	4.3	14.1	10.9	9.5
Lafayette, LA	439	3 201	121 531	16.5	52.7	21.2	712.2	9 775	26 910	70 185	48 370	50.8	4.8	19.0	25.6	17.9
Lafayette-West Lafayette, IN	232	2 622	76 032	12.1	38.3	32.5	252.2	9 385	25 038	64 297	50 088	49.9	3.1	18.5	17.6	4.2
Lake Charles, LA	544	4 456	53 495	11.5	48.5	21.6	372.1	10 742	26 712	66 182	46 229	52.5	3.5	17.4	27.6	8.9
Lake Havasu City-Kingman, AZ	202	3 162	36 061	19.9	53.3	11.9	172.2	7 050	22 926	54 325	40 908	58.6	1.5	16.2	24.4	6.3
Lakeland-Winter Haven, FL	349	2 732	148 537	14.7	52.3	19.1	843.3	8 610	21 494	57 817	44 061	55.7	1.8	17.2	26.5	7.8
Lancaster, PA	165	1 577	124 673	25.5	52.0	25.8	945.0	14 011	28 252	74 570	59 262	41.7	3.7	10.9	16.5	5.3
Lansing-East Lansing, MI	412	1 875	142 908	8.5	31.7	34.2	762.0	11 052	27 679	68 970	51 839	47.9	3.5	17.5	21.1	7.6
Laredo, TX	403	3 750	86 569	6.1	61.0	17.4	596.1	8 605	16 673	57 849	39 774	58.5	3.3	31.8	44.7	27.1
Las Cruces, NM	286	3 051	68 552	4.7	43.8	26.4	399.4	9 801	20 301	55 899	39 902	61.1	2.1	27.1	44.0	8.9
Las Vegas-Henderson-Paradise, NV	743	2 790	518 864	11.7	43.2	23.1	2 587.9	8 074	26 506	69 724	51 552	48.3	3.7	15.1	22.0	8.7
Lawrence, KS	203	1 986	43 163	12.7	27.5	47.0	143.5	9 548	29 796	76 075	52 964	47.7	4.9	21.3	11.5	9.5
Lawton, OK	705	3 703	35 220	7.9	44.5	19.9	176.8	7 676	22 700	62 333	47 617	52.2	2.3	14.1	15.8	9.0
Lebanon, PA	149	1 580	29 506	24.6	58.7	18.6	215.2	11 310	26 087	65 755	52 571	46.5	3.3	12.7	20.5	6.1
Lewiston, ID-WA	185	3 000	12 624	13.0	39.5	22.9	81.5	8 987	27 592	64 955	52 735	46.9	1.6	13.5	23.6	5.2
Lewiston-Auburn, ME	141	2 156	25 030	27.5	47.8	21.1	201.3	11 828	25 645	61 431	50 338	49.6	2.1	15.4	22.0	11.0
Lexington-Fayette, KY	263	3 488	135 044	14.8	36.0	35.5	695.3	9 857	29 968	74 283	53 117	47.3	4.5	18.7	26.3	8.3
Lima, OH	386	3 286	28 106	19.9	47.6	19.4	156.2	10 384	24 930	61 939	50 332	49.6	2.1	14.6	22.8	4.9
Lincoln, NE	303	3 057	98 832	14.9	28.3	36.7	488.6	10 710	28 672	71 196	54 002	45.2	3.6	13.7	14.0	6.5
Little Rock-North Little Rock-Conway, AR	688	4 354	186 892	15.0	39.0	30.0	1 110.7	9 676	27 288	68 055	49 066	50.8	4.1	17.0	23.7	8.9
Logan, UT-ID	54	1 203	49 376	5.3	31.1	33.4	174.3	6 261	20 912	66 322	51 555	48.7	3.3	16.6	19.6	4.7
Longview, TX	387	3 273	50 698	10.0	46.3	19.1	356.1	9 052	23 442	63 308	47 532	51.4	2.4	16.6	23.4	10.0
Longview, WA	250	3 648	23 727	12.8	42.9	17.2	166.3	9 935	25 178	65 206	49 949	50.1	1.9	15.1	20.5	11.7
Los Angeles-Long Beach-Anaheim, CA	369	2 050	3 575 803	14.7	40.7	32.7	20 254.4	9 864	30 888	90 892	62 544	40.8	8.8	15.7	21.7	12.1
Anaheim-Santa Ana-Irvine, CA Div 11244	198	1 735	859 952	14.4	33.1	38.8	4 450.8	8 890	35 651	106 144	78 428	32.5	12.3	12.7	16.7	9.4
Los Angeles-Long Beach-Glendale, CA Div 31084	422	2 149	2 715 851	14.8	43.1	30.8	15 803.6	10 178	29 403	86 156	59 134	43.4	7.7	16.6	23.3	13.1
Louisville/Jefferson County, KY-IN	402	3 346	310 015	19.5	40.9	28.7	1 864.2	10 125	28 736	71 307	52 898	47.2	3.9	13.4	19.5	8.0
Lubbock, TX	741	3 950	101 387	10.8	43.8	25.8	458.4	8 760	23 982	64 135	47 291	51.7	3.4	20.7	25.3	10.0
Lynchburg, VA	233	1 673	72 037	39.9	44.1	24.6	344.1	10 162	25 671	64 045	48 090	52.0	2.6	14.8	19.2	9.2
Macon, GA	NA	NA	62 241	23.4	48.6	23.6	348.3	9 531	25 885	62 249	40 067	58.9	2.9	23.7	36.6	14.2
Madera, CA	578	2 201	42 506	6.5	53.6	15.4	283.4	9 184	20 890	65 695	47 150	52.3	3.2	23.4	34.4	9.0
Madison, WI	211	2 035	174 568	11.3	27.0	43.5	1 068.2	11 370	35 237	84 372	64 174	37.9	5.8	10.8	10.4	4.6
Manchester-Nashua, NH	272	2 088	98 923	28.3	34.8	36.9	738.6	13 100	36 949	93 830	74 323	33.0	8.2	8.0	8.8	7.3
Manhattan, KS	235	1 482	36 038	8.5	26.3	40.0	116.2	10 061	23 836	64 010	50 354	49.4	2.7	20.8	10.1	6.5
Mankato-North Mankato, MN	180	2 184	32 776	19.0	29.3	33.7	140.1	10 861	26 846	66 888	52 497	47.7	3.0	16.8	12.2	7.1
Mansfield, OH	218	4 662	27 386	19.5	54.3	14.4	199.9	12 135	23 725	57 945	45 155	54.2	1.4	14.2	22.4	5.6
McAllen-Edinburg-Mission, TX	329	3 360	272 218	5.4	60.6	17.3	2 083.4	9 216	15 502	53 857	35 730	62.5	2.8	31.5	43.8	22.5
Medford, OR	319	3 981	43 954	15.8	39.8	25.6	282.0	9 745	24 590	59 897	43 948	54.4	2.6	20.3	27.3	10.9
Memphis, TN-MS-AR	1 104	4 291	350 930	18.2	43.4	26.9	1 924.3	8 672	26 336	68 861	48 524	51.1	4.0	18.4	28.8	10.2
Merced, CA	558	2 675	84 938	3.3	56.5	14.4	564.1	10 065	18 659	59 213	41 997	57.5	3.2	26.7	38.5	10.9
Miami-Fort Lauderdale-West Palm Beach, FL	520	3 438	1 453 587	20.4	42.3	30.9	7 247.9	8 996	28 511	76 284	50 441	49.5	5.7	16.5	23.5	15.2
Fort Lauderdale-Pompano Beach-Deerfield Beach, FL Div 22744	409	3 048	478 432	20.9	39.1	32.2	2 266.7	8 580	28 775	75 859	53 926	46.1	5.4	13.9	20.2	11.4
Miami-Miami Beach-Kendall, FL Div 33124	633	3 973	656 629	20.2	48.3	27.4	3 243.7	9 106	24 660	69 760	43 786	55.2	5.0	20.0	27.3	23.2
West Palm Beach-Boca Raton-Delray Beach, FL Div 48424	452	2 939	318 526	19.9	35.5	35.7	1 737.4	9 380	35 447	87 061	56 664	44.7	7.3	13.5	20.9	8.3
Michigan City-La Porte, IN	143	2 283	25 170	14.7	50.9	17.6	179.0	9 931	25 344	64 369	45 838	53.7	3.1	16.4	28.2	5.6
Midland, MI	125	1 241	19 904	18.2	37.7	34.0	133.3	11 114	30 370	80 370	59 292	39.4	6.1	11.5	16.3	6.2
Midland, TX	322	2 580	41 110	14.3	40.7	26.2	247.3	9 110	37 852	106 491	80 761	31.4	10.3	6.6	7.9	12.2
Milwaukee-Waukesha-West Allis, WI	659	3 057	409 113	23.7	35.5	33.9	2 578.1	10 915	31 506	77 011	56 247	44.4	4.8	14.0	20.3	7.0
Minneapolis-St. Paul-Bloomington, MN	261	2 489	905 867	16.9	28.7	40.3	6 400.9	11 423	36 284	92 395	71 008	34.7	7.3	9.3	12.4	6.0
Missoula, MT	274	2 954	33 207	10.9	28.2	42.9	143.1	10 635	26 594	60 771	42 815	54.4	3.4	16.0	15.4	6.3

1. Data for serious crimes have not been adjusted for underreporting; this may affect comparability between geographic areas and over time.   2. Per 100,000 population estimated by the FBI.
3. All persons 3 years old and over enrolled in nursery school through college.   4. Persons 25 years old and over.   5. Elementary and secondary education expenditures.   6. Based on resident population estimated in the 2015 American Community Survey.

Table C. Metropolitan Areas — **Personal Income**

Area name	Personal income, 2015 Total (mil dol) [62]	Percent change 2014–2015 [63]	Per capita[1] Dollars [64]	Per capita[1] Rank [65]	Wages and salaries (mil dol) [66]	Supplements to wages and salaries; employer contributions (mil dol) Pension and insurance [67]	Supplements Government social insurance [68]	Proprietors' income (mil dol) [69]	Dividends, interest, and rent (mil dol) [70]	Personal transfer receipts (mil dol) [71]	Earnings, 2015 Total (mil dol) [72]	Contributions for government social insurance (mil dol) From employee and self-employed [73]	From employer [74]
Jonesboro, AR	4 328	2.9	33 709	360	2 134	321	170	493	522	1 162	3 119	200	170
Joplin, MO	6 386	4.2	36 037	321	3 200	575	234	563	941	1 477	4 573	275	234
Kahului-Wailuku-Lahaina, HI	6 989	6.1	42 430	165	3 356	580	253	734	1 464	1 146	4 923	299	253
Kalamazoo-Portage, MI	14 004	4.8	41 760	185	6 884	1 149	517	785	2 649	2 806	9 335	574	517
Kankakee, IL	4 108	3.1	37 049	295	1 894	370	137	153	554	985	2 554	147	137
Kansas City, MO-KS	100 316	3.8	48 056	73	56 975	8 445	4 287	9 017	16 146	15 220	78 723	4 622	4 287
Kennewick-Richland, WA	11 295	8.0	40 468	212	5 852	825	556	1 369	1 638	2 074	8 602	462	556
Killeen-Temple, TX	17 343	5.2	40 237	218	8 505	1 907	707	1 038	3 061	3 458	12 157	571	707
Kingsport-Bristol-Bristol, TN-VA	11 462	2.9	37 322	287	5 188	912	367	949	1 869	3 201	7 416	498	367
Kingston, NY	8 002	3.8	44 422	125	2 601	758	220	543	1 447	1 835	4 122	228	220
Knoxville, TN	35 206	4.8	40 870	202	18 044	2 666	1 260	3 579	5 478	7 555	25 548	1 574	1 260
Kokomo, IN	3 084	3.2	37 356	284	1 961	302	152	117	453	861	2 532	165	152
La Crosse-Onalaska, WI-MN	6 141	3.1	44 831	114	3 318	622	266	438	1 153	1 079	4 643	280	266
Lafayette, LA	21 250	-1.5	43 325	151	10 672	1 559	684	2 668	3 596	3 853	15 583	851	684
Lafayette-West Lafayette, IN	7 528	2.6	35 120	342	4 308	817	318	511	1 283	1 289	5 954	345	318
Lake Charles, LA	8 788	6.7	42 743	160	5 179	889	334	759	1 304	1 740	7 161	388	334
Lake Havasu City-Kingman, AZ	6 041	5.2	29 505	380	1 830	301	137	378	1 019	2 139	2 646	218	137
Lakeland-Winter Haven, FL	21 923	4.7	33 723	359	9 146	1 488	640	1 164	4 143	5 978	12 438	854	640
Lancaster, PA	24 146	5.3	44 995	110	10 740	1 968	872	3 454	3 981	4 326	17 033	952	872
Lansing-East Lansing, MI	17 882	4.3	37 863	275	9 894	1 794	736	920	2 964	3 727	13 345	811	736
Laredo, TX	8 032	5.0	29 778	379	3 639	704	256	1 184	1 033	1 877	5 783	287	256
Las Cruces, NM	6 907	6.0	32 233	370	2 860	580	244	611	1 106	1 979	4 295	272	244
Las Vegas-Henderson-Paradise, NV	85 970	4.9	40 652	209	44 575	7 733	3 389	4 205	18 515	14 571	59 901	3 426	3 389
Lawrence, KS	4 567	6.3	38 686	253	1 975	416	153	304	849	658	2 848	163	153
Lawton, OK	4 997	2.7	38 246	265	2 485	582	217	281	906	1 053	3 566	178	217
Lebanon, PA	5 906	4.2	43 090	155	2 021	470	169	516	910	1 250	3 177	187	169
Lewiston, ID-WA	2 486	4.1	39 999	224	1 108	185	97	205	498	607	1 595	107	97
Lewiston-Auburn, ME	3 979	3.6	37 106	292	2 109	340	163	179	524	1 068	2 791	187	163
Lexington-Fayette, KY	21 555	5.4	43 065	156	12 690	2 255	963	1 468	3 835	3 751	17 376	1 004	963
Lima, OH	3 913	2.9	37 469	283	2 255	435	163	254	543	983	3 107	179	163
Lincoln, NE	14 281	3.7	44 133	132	8 058	1 363	603	947	2 736	2 052	10 970	656	603
Little Rock-North Little Rock-Conway, AR	30 042	2.8	41 062	198	16 575	2 476	1 299	2 091	4 780	6 409	22 442	1 415	1 299
Logan, UT-ID	4 300	5.1	32 121	372	2 047	439	160	423	773	670	3 070	172	160
Longview, TX	9 173	-0.4	42 118	173	4 648	667	330	1 054	1 395	2 020	6 699	365	330
Longview, WA	4 177	4.7	40 371	216	1 844	278	176	371	651	1 118	2 670	172	176
Los Angeles-Long Beach-Anaheim, CA	727 377	5.8	54 526	25	371 843	61 456	25 724	82 517	147 594	115 018	541 541	30 415	25 724
Anaheim-Santa Ana-Irvine, CA Div 11244	183 052	4.9	57 749	X	99 523	15 052	6 980	16 361	39 836	21 399	137 915	7 888	6 980
Los Angeles-Long Beach-Glendale, CA Div 31084	544 325	6.1	53 521	X	272 320	46 404	18 744	66 157	107 759	93 618	403 625	22 527	18 744
Louisville/Jefferson County, KY-IN	56 960	5.4	44 556	121	31 351	4 733	2 398	3 724	9 353	10 970	42 206	2 595	2 398
Lubbock, TX	11 946	4.5	38 392	263	5 919	1 004	394	1 210	1 886	2 337	8 528	436	394
Lynchburg, VA	9 646	3.1	37 107	291	4 449	747	328	404	1 746	2 426	5 927	397	328
Macon, GA	8 622	3.5	37 470	282	4 394	717	308	657	1 433	2 161	6 076	374	308
Madera, CA	5 450	3.0	35 165	341	1 976	495	143	1 014	824	1 215	3 628	170	143
Madison, WI	33 578	5.3	52 352	40	19 589	3 772	1 472	2 388	6 529	4 079	27 222	1 562	1 472
Manchester-Nashua, NH	23 254	5.1	57 180	20	12 284	1 868	831	1 852	4 083	3 026	16 836	982	831
Manhattan, KS	3 987	3.3	40 455	213	1 633	352	125	239	819	489	2 349	131	125
Mankato-North Mankato, MN	4 329	5.3	43 665	141	2 263	378	173	556	795	719	3 371	196	173
Mansfield, OH	4 331	2.7	35 588	330	2 024	419	148	235	629	1 168	2 825	166	148
McAllen-Edinburg-Mission, TX	20 703	5.2	24 579	382	8 594	1 702	594	2 798	2 144	6 144	13 688	702	594
Medford, OR	8 651	6.5	40 698	207	3 488	551	323	845	1 891	2 262	5 207	350	323
Memphis, TN-MS-AR	56 856	3.3	42 300	172	31 548	4 347	2 156	5 516	8 076	10 771	43 567	2 588	2 156
Merced, CA	9 714	5.6	36 185	317	3 180	848	223	1 478	1 393	2 477	5 729	258	223
Miami-Fort Lauderdale-West Palm Beach, FL	299 528	5.3	49 819	61	136 580	18 875	9 328	20 086	88 509	49 840	184 869	11 694	9 328
Fort Lauderdale-Pompano Beach-Deerfield Beach, FL Div 22744	85 167	6.1	44 909	X	42 101	5 804	2 909	5 158	18 994	13 896	55 971	3 485	2 909
Miami-Miami Beach-Kendall, FL Div 33124	116 553	5.0	43 278	X	61 605	8 782	4 219	10 112	26 235	23 160	84 718	5 351	4 219
West Palm Beach-Boca Raton-Delray Beach, FL Div 48424	97 807	5.0	68 743	X	32 874	4 289	2 200	4 816	43 280	12 784	44 179	2 858	2 200
Michigan City-La Porte, IN	4 194	3.8	37 827	277	1 711	288	133	276	633	969	2 407	154	133
Midland, MI	3 760	1.4	44 954	112	2 179	333	153	-216	783	730	2 449	208	153
Midland, TX	17 458	-8.9	104 714	2	6 172	779	401	7 845	2 518	932	15 196	634	401
Milwaukee-Waukesha-West Allis, WI	79 861	3.6	50 681	52	44 955	7 131	3 441	5 733	14 773	13 444	61 260	3 690	3 441
Minneapolis-St. Paul-Bloomington, MN	194 372	4.4	55 148	24	115 033	15 117	8 383	13 508	35 727	25 781	152 042	9 134	8 383
Missoula, MT	4 659	5.4	40 803	205	2 388	378	219	405	1 170	805	3 390	218	219

1. Based on the resident population estimated as of July 1 of the year shown.

Table C. Metropolitan Areas — **Earnings, Social Security, and Housing**

Area name	Earnings, 2015 (cont.)									Social Security beneficiaries, December 2015		Housing units, 2016		
	Percent by selected industries													
	Farm	Mining	Construction	Manufacturing	Information, professional, scientific, technical services	Retail trade	Finance, insurance, real estate, rental and leasing	Health care and social assistance	Government	Number	Rate[1]	Supplemental Security Income recipients, December 2015	Total	Percent change, 2010–2016
	75	76	77	78	79	80	81	82	83	84	85	86	87	88
Jonesboro, AR	2.8	D	6.3	13.7	4.1	7.7	5.0	20.7	15.8	26 700	208	5 557	55 326	7.6
Joplin, MO	2.1	D	4.7	20.2	3.5	7.8	4.3	15.4	11.2	37 570	212	4 587	76 432	1.9
Kahului-Wailuku-Lahaina, HI	1.6	D	8.5	1.5	4.3	8.2	5.7	7.2	17.3	28 685	175	2 056	72 251	2.5
Kalamazoo-Portage, MI	1.3	D	6.0	20.8	6.0	5.9	7.9	14.5	14.7	67 335	201	8 581	147 799	0.7
Kankakee, IL	0.4	D	4.3	19.0	D	6.8	5.4	18.0	16.6	22 380	202	2 658	45 181	-0.1
Kansas City, MO-KS	0.0	0.1	5.8	9.0	D	5.7	11.1	10.8	14.0	359 405	172	34 205	898 631	3.1
Kennewick-Richland, WA	9.0	D	7.2	6.2	14.2	5.9	3.6	9.5	17.5	43 030	154	5 588	100 958	8.5
Killeen-Temple, TX	0.1	D	5.9	4.1	D	5.9	3.4	D	48.8	63 155	147	9 565	173 326	8.8
Kingsport-Bristol-Bristol, TN-VA	-0.1	0.9	D	24.8	D	7.1	3.5	D	12.8	90 645	296	10 380	147 773	0.5
Kingston, NY	0.5	0.2	6.3	6.1	5.7	8.5	3.9	12.5	32.1	40 950	228	4 111	83 920	0.3
Knoxville, TN	0.1	D	D	10.4	12.6	7.3	D	14.9	15.0	197 920	230	22 859	391 296	2.7
Kokomo, IN	-0.3	D	3.0	47.7	2.5	6.0	3.7	12.2	9.9	21 310	258	2 199	39 106	1.1
La Crosse-Onalaska, WI-MN	0.9	D	5.7	11.2	5.0	6.0	7.7	20.6	15.8	26 810	196	2 423	58 457	2.6
Lafayette, LA	0.5	18.6	6.5	8.8	8.8	6.8	6.7	11.7	10.1	84 800	173	15 470	206 473	5.4
Lafayette-West Lafayette, IN	0.6	D	4.9	D	D	5.4	5.2	12.5	26.1	31 660	148	2 610	88 522	4.8
Lake Charles, LA	0.3	1.2	19.3	17.9	D	D	3.6	10.8	11.8	39 870	194	6 411	91 801	7.2
Lake Havasu City-Kingman, AZ	0.4	0.3	6.5	6.2	4.7	11.5	5.5	20.8	17.8	64 295	315	4 681	113 809	2.6
Lakeland-Winter Haven, FL	0.9	0.6	6.0	9.4	5.6	8.0	7.5	14.1	13.6	152 885	235	21 247	286 515	1.9
Lancaster, PA	2.3	0.1	11.0	15.9	6.8	7.6	6.5	13.3	9.1	108 810	203	9 766	207 811	2.4
Lansing-East Lansing, MI	0.5	0.2	4.6	11.8	D	5.2	8.7	12.5	27.0	88 405	187	10 282	201 068	1.0
Laredo, TX	0.2	6.1	3.9	1.0	3.9	7.9	4.5	10.1	26.3	32 310	120	12 562	81 486	10.9
Las Cruces, NM	2.9	0.0	6.0	3.5	8.0	6.3	4.4	15.5	32.0	38 890	182	8 093	85 226	4.6
Las Vegas-Henderson-Paradise, NV	0.0	0.0	6.1	2.5	8.4	7.2	6.8	9.3	15.7	332 650	158	41 203	881 165	4.9
Lawrence, KS	0.5	0.4	4.7	8.5	10.2	6.5	6.0	7.3	35.0	16 125	137	1 360	49 286	5.5
Lawton, OK	0.6	0.4	3.9	D	D	5.3	3.6	5.2	52.6	21 295	164	3 326	54 737	1.8
Lebanon, PA	3.6	D	6.3	17.2	5.2	7.7	3.2	12.3	19.9	31 785	231	2 441	56 640	1.9
Lewiston, ID-WA	0.2	D	7.3	18.3	4.7	9.5	7.4	D	18.1	16 465	265	1 682	27 348	0.1
Lewiston-Auburn, ME	0.6	D	7.2	11.4	6.9	7.7	5.8	21.4	11.8	25 510	238	4 113	49 053	-0.1
Lexington-Fayette, KY	0.4	0.2	6.3	14.7	9.4	5.8	5.0	10.8	21.4	82 980	166	11 437	218 343	4.4
Lima, OH	-0.1	D	4.9	25.7	3.7	6.5	3.4	18.5	13.4	22 500	216	3 105	44 812	-0.4
Lincoln, NE	1.0	D	5.8	8.7	9.0	5.9	9.5	D	21.9	48 575	150	4 965	135 840	6.3
Little Rock-North Little Rock-Conway, AR	0.2	0.8	5.5	6.2	10.5	7.5	D	12.8	23.2	146 075	200	24 846	322 361	5.0
Logan, UT-ID	2.5	D	5.1	21.7	9.0	6.9	6.6	D	21.3	15 365	115	1 044	44 822	7.9
Longview, TX	0.8	14.0	11.0	10.3	D	7.3	4.8	11.6	9.6	43 465	200	6 938	90 064	3.1
Longview, WA	0.5	0.6	13.8	21.1	3.5	6.4	3.6	13.9	14.8	26 715	258	3 790	43 625	0.4
Los Angeles-Long Beach-Anaheim, CA	0.0	0.3	4.3	8.5	19.7	5.7	11.0	9.3	13.9	1 733 435	131	493 416	4 610 681	2.6
Anaheim-Santa Ana-Irvine, CA Div 11244	0.0	0.1	7.0	11.1	16.2	5.8	14.3	8.8	10.9	433 330	137	74 589	1 090 054	3.9
Los Angeles-Long Beach-Glendale, CA Div 31084	0.0	0.4	3.4	7.6	20.9	5.7	9.8	9.4	14.9	1 300 105	129	418 827	3 520 627	2.2
Louisville/Jefferson County, KY-IN	0.2	0.1	D	D	8.8	5.5	D	12.1	12.7	253 240	198	35 264	554 189	2.5
Lubbock, TX	0.6	D	D	D	D	9.0	D	15.6	23.7	47 120	152	6 909	130 432	8.1
Lynchburg, VA	-0.1	D	D	18.5	D	6.8	5.9	14.7	13.2	61 535	237	6 426	115 771	2.9
Macon, GA	0.8	0.7	D	D	8.3	D	D	19.7	13.8	49 680	216	9 716	102 330	0.7
Madera, CA	21.5	D	4.0	7.6	2.3	4.8	2.2	13.9	21.4	24 685	160	4 806	50 204	2.2
Madison, WI	0.8	0.1	5.5	9.8	D	6.1	8.4	D	22.0	105 775	165	9 051	281 368	4.7
Manchester-Nashua, NH	0.0	D	D	14.2	15.3	8.0	10.6	11.3	10.3	77 720	191	7 233	168 693	1.6
Manhattan, KS	0.8	D	6.6	7.8	6.0	6.6	7.3	10.4	34.9	11 720	114	752	39 774	8.0
Mankato-North Mankato, MN	5.2	D	5.4	18.1	D	7.0	5.0	D	16.1	16 615	168	1 329	41 350	5.8
Mansfield, OH	0.7	D	6.4	21.9	4.4	8.0	3.7	14.2	18.2	28 770	237	3 448	54 013	-1.1
McAllen-Edinburg-Mission, TX	0.9	1.9	4.9	2.8	3.8	10.6	4.8	17.8	25.3	103 115	123	42 644	268 765	8.2
Medford, OR	0.8	0.1	6.0	9.0	6.6	10.5	5.8	19.3	14.6	54 825	257	4 715	93 371	2.7
Memphis, TN-MS-AR	0.1	0.0	5.1	10.6	6.0	D	7.5	13.1	14.1	233 505	174	46 875	569 329	2.6
Merced, CA	21.2	D	3.3	11.1	2.2	5.7	2.4	8.7	26.3	36 425	136	11 291	84 406	0.8
Miami-Fort Lauderdale-West Palm Beach, FL	0.3	0.0	5.3	3.3	14.6	7.7	10.0	11.6	13.4	1 030 970	172	231 832	2 527 979	2.6
Fort Lauderdale-Pompano Beach-Deerfield Beach, FL Div 22744	0.0	0.0	6.1	3.6	14.2	8.5	9.5	10.2	14.2	308 190	163	44 876	822 931	1.5
Miami-Miami Beach-Kendall, FL Div 33124	0.3	0.0	4.7	3.0	14.9	7.3	9.7	11.5	13.9	414 805	154	162 767	1 021 527	3.2
West Palm Beach-Boca Raton-Delray Beach, FL Div 48424	0.7	-0.2	5.5	3.6	14.7	7.4	11.5	13.3	11.4	307 975	217	24 189	683 521	2.8
Michigan City-La Porte, IN	1.1	D	8.6	20.8	3.3	6.7	4.2	13.9	15.1	24 230	219	2 214	48 837	0.8
Midland, MI	0.2	D	7.0	8.8	5.2	5.1	8.6	14.3	9.1	18 975	227	1 605	36 538	1.6
Midland, TX	0.1	59.6	D	D	D	2.8	D	2.9	4.4	19 240	115	2 174	62 362	11.0
Milwaukee-Waukesha-West Allis, WI	0.1	D	4.6	16.2	10.5	5.5	10.1	13.1	11.0	288 790	183	47 852	674 756	0.7
Minneapolis-St. Paul-Bloomington, MN	0.2	0.1	5.4	11.7	D	5.1	12.3	10.5	12.0	540 260	154	61 274	1 432 632	3.3
Missoula, MT	-0.1	0.1	6.7	3.0	9.6	8.6	7.0	18.3	19.4	20 575	181	2 129	52 321	4.4

1. Per 1,000 resident population estimated as of July 1, 2011 of the year shown.

Table C. Metropolitan Areas — Housing, Labor Force, and Employment

Area name	Housing units, 2015								Civilian labor force, 2016				Civilian employment[5], 2015		
	Occupied units										Unemployment			Percent	
	Owner-occupied					Renter-occupied									
				Median owner cost as a percent of income			Median rent as a percent of income								
	Total	Percent	Median value[1]	With a mortgage	Without a mortgage[2]	Median rent[3]		Percent with a computer	Total	Percent change, 2015–2016	Total	Rate[4]	Total employed	Management, professional, and related occupations	Construction, production, and related occupations
	89	90	91	92	93	94	95	96	97	98	99	100	101	102	103
Jonesboro, AR	48 943	58.8	122 100	18.8	10.7	678	30.4	87.2	62 354	2.1	2 138	3.4	57 367	31.0	29.4
Joplin, MO	67 439	65.2	123 300	19.3	11.6	739	25.5	83.5	87 076	0.0	3 644	4.2	85 148	31.0	25.6
Kahului-Wailuku-Lahaina, HI	52 170	58.5	569 300	28.2	10.0	1 416	30.3	89.0	85 457	1.9	2 719	3.2	83 258	31.3	18.4
Kalamazoo-Portage, MI	129 792	67.1	143 400	19.6	12.1	716	28.4	88.1	167 722	2.1	7 106	4.2	163 560	38.6	19.6
Kankakee, IL	38 755	67.9	136 300	22.0	12.9	846	28.8	84.4	54 834	0.0	3 534	6.4	48 556	31.8	29.0
Kansas City, MO-KS	814 092	65.3	164 700	19.9	11.6	859	27.0	88.5	1 128 132	1.0	48 496	4.3	1 051 623	39.1	20.1
Kennewick-Richland, WA	94 423	67.4	191 700	19.3	10.0	825	27.7	86.4	134 423	2.9	9 241	6.9	123 880	34.5	29.3
Killeen-Temple, TX	151 623	52.9	130 000	21.7	11.4	858	29.6	86.4	175 315	3.6	7 759	4.4	163 295	31.8	22.7
Kingsport-Bristol-Bristol, TN-VA	126 840	70.8	122 800	19.5	10.0	621	27.8	81.4	137 346	0.5	7 047	5.1	127 958	31.8	25.2
Kingston, NY	69 594	68.5	216 900	24.8	15.3	996	36.1	85.7	88 256	-0.4	3 889	4.4	86 146	37.6	19.7
Knoxville, TN	343 331	67.8	158 300	20.3	10.0	756	29.1	83.4	412 692	1.9	18 744	4.5	396 624	35.9	22.2
Kokomo, IN	34 714	68.4	100 800	17.1	10.0	640	32.2	80.7	38 176	3.1	1 780	4.7	35 488	30.3	32.4
La Crosse-Onalaska, WI-MN	54 008	66.8	159 000	20.9	13.4	746	29.7	86.9	78 154	1.4	2 943	3.8	73 374	34.8	20.7
Lafayette, LA	180 902	68.4	147 100	18.4	10.0	733	28.5	82.9	216 149	-5.2	15 363	7.1	224 114	32.7	23.0
Lafayette-West Lafayette, IN	81 069	56.2	138 300	18.8	10.0	782	30.0	91.7	109 969	1.9	4 423	4.0	108 749	35.4	27.6
Lake Charles, LA	79 853	68.7	139 700	18.9	10.0	764	29.7	83.1	106 685	3.5	5 077	4.8	93 008	30.8	29.0
Lake Havasu City-Kingman, AZ	83 801	67.2	139 400	22.9	10.0	742	27.9	84.9	80 432	1.1	5 294	6.6	71 494	22.3	26.0
Lakeland-Winter Haven, FL	227 122	67.1	123 100	23.0	11.9	890	31.9	83.4	284 936	1.9	16 069	5.6	258 761	29.0	22.3
Lancaster, PA	197 706	67.4	197 400	22.3	12.1	941	29.3	83.2	280 499	1.6	11 662	4.2	266 353	32.7	28.3
Lansing-East Lansing, MI	183 888	64.2	138 500	20.1	12.0	790	29.5	88.3	246 427	2.1	9 848	4.0	227 433	38.0	19.8
Laredo, TX	72 259	61.9	117 600	24.4	14.5	776	33.0	70.8	113 533	1.9	5 556	4.9	106 380	28.7	21.4
Las Cruces, NM	74 631	62.9	146 700	21.6	10.0	741	29.8	84.1	95 001	1.6	6 845	7.2	88 709	30.6	18.6
Las Vegas-Henderson-Paradise, NV	740 966	51.6	217 300	22.8	10.0	1 007	30.9	90.2	1 048 043	0.8	60 832	5.8	975 157	26.4	17.6
Lawrence, KS	42 817	53.8	179 700	19.0	10.0	827	32.9	91.9	65 556	0.4	2 351	3.6	63 871	44.1	15.1
Lawton, OK	43 678	53.5	118 200	19.3	10.2	766	26.4	84.8	52 376	-0.4	2 469	4.7	54 848	35.1	23.9
Lebanon, PA	53 200	67.8	162 700	21.4	13.5	786	27.0	80.4	70 711	0.8	3 182	4.5	67 361	27.8	27.2
Lewiston, ID-WA	25 354	70.8	178 500	20.0	10.0	727	26.5	86.7	30 877	1.8	1 211	3.9	28 504	33.4	21.9
Lewiston-Auburn, ME	45 138	63.0	147 500	22.8	14.5	721	29.1	87.2	55 377	1.1	1 993	3.6	54 658	33.6	24.2
Lexington-Fayette, KY	199 299	56.2	167 800	19.5	10.0	803	28.6	90.1	261 470	1.6	9 580	3.7	250 933	38.3	18.9
Lima, OH	40 234	65.9	113 500	19.7	11.0	642	30.1	83.0	47 957	0.3	2 377	5.0	49 872	30.1	30.9
Lincoln, NE	127 316	59.2	163 600	19.8	10.0	767	29.2	91.2	177 878	0.9	5 144	2.9	175 745	39.4	20.1
Little Rock-North Little Rock-Conway, AR	282 914	63.1	149 900	19.4	10.0	807	29.8	85.4	350 471	0.9	12 431	3.5	334 707	37.9	20.7
Logan, UT-ID	40 927	65.5	200 600	20.8	10.0	705	27.7	94.1	68 012	2.0	2 085	3.1	63 344	36.7	25.2
Longview, TX	76 401	66.4	123 900	19.0	11.9	779	28.6	84.9	98 548	-1.2	6 015	6.1	92 425	27.5	29.4
Longview, WA	40 187	66.2	187 900	21.7	11.7	820	29.4	87.1	44 859	1.7	3 358	7.5	43 976	27.2	32.8
Los Angeles-Long Beach-Anaheim, CA	4 315 637	47.9	540 600	27.2	10.9	1 348	34.3	89.3	6 645 625	0.9	328 840	4.9	6 390 533	37.6	19.9
Anaheim-Santa Ana-Irvine, CA Div 11244	1 022 542	56.6	625 300	26.0	10.1	1 624	33.7	92.6	1 602 371	0.9	64 345	4.0	1 559 173	40.9	17.7
Los Angeles-Long Beach-Glendale, CA Div 31084	3 293 095	45.1	497 200	27.7	11.2	1 279	34.5	88.3	5 043 254	0.9	264 495	5.2	4 831 360	36.5	20.6
Louisville/Jefferson County, KY-IN	496 455	66.4	154 000	19.6	10.8	777	28.5	84.7	641 524	2.3	27 166	4.2	619 385	36.2	24.2
Lubbock, TX	112 853	54.6	120 700	19.8	11.1	834	31.3	87.4	158 266	2.4	5 411	3.4	147 968	33.3	21.5
Lynchburg, VA	100 497	68.3	162 900	19.7	10.0	759	32.7	79.0	121 404	-0.7	5 483	4.5	120 389	35.3	22.4
Macon, GA	86 400	62.0	112 500	21.6	12.0	751	33.7	79.8	104 141	1.5	6 056	5.8	91 634	37.2	21.7
Madera, CA	45 224	61.8	232 800	23.0	13.3	947	33.7	82.8	61 468	2.4	5 632	9.2	58 279	22.9	39.2
Madison, WI	264 340	60.6	228 500	21.3	12.3	933	28.4	91.5	383 756	1.7	11 686	3.0	362 860	46.5	16.2
Manchester-Nashua, NH	156 678	66.5	256 200	22.9	14.9	1 107	28.3	92.7	231 348	1.0	6 884	3.0	221 277	40.3	19.1
Manhattan, KS	34 806	50.4	189 300	20.8	12.6	930	29.5	91.1	49 201	-0.8	1 659	3.4	44 871	38.2	16.9
Mankato-North Mankato, MN	38 444	66.6	172 400	21.0	11.0	782	31.2	88.4	59 808	1.0	1 845	3.1	57 219	36.5	21.7
Mansfield, OH	46 989	67.9	102 600	19.8	11.2	640	27.0	82.9	53 352	-0.3	2 918	5.5	51 798	24.3	31.6
McAllen-Edinburg-Mission, TX	225 692	69.5	81 700	23.5	12.4	690	30.6	78.7	335 276	1.6	26 303	7.8	309 408	26.4	23.9
Medford, OR	83 876	61.0	243 500	24.4	13.4	882	36.2	89.4	101 776	3.8	5 891	5.8	90 729	32.5	21.4
Memphis, TN-MS-AR	494 270	59.7	139 800	21.5	11.1	852	31.0	81.5	623 926	1.2	33 072	5.3	614 879	33.4	24.4
Merced, CA	79 098	51.2	210 100	24.9	10.7	874	34.9	88.4	115 037	0.6	12 056	10.5	98 425	23.0	36.8
Miami-Fort Lauderdale-West Palm Beach, FL	2 077 362	58.5	241 700	26.6	14.9	1 208	37.7	87.0	3 056 146	2.1	152 963	5.0	2 858 008	34.0	18.2
Fort Lauderdale-Pompano Beach-Deerfield Beach, FL Div 22744	673 870	61.5	222 900	26.4	15.7	1 256	36.7	89.7	1 004 123	1.7	46 241	4.6	942 614	35.3	17.7
Miami-Miami Beach-Kendall, FL Div 33124	857 712	50.6	251 900	28.3	15.2	1 162	39.2	83.5	1 341 510	1.8	72 494	5.4	1 261 863	31.7	19.7
West Palm Beach-Boca Raton-Delray Beach, FL Div 48424	545 780	67.3	246 200	24.6	14.3	1 241	35.6	89.0	710 513	3.0	34 228	4.8	653 531	36.6	16.1
Michigan City-La Porte, IN	43 169	69.9	126 000	20.0	11.4	694	29.8	84.6	48 521	-0.1	2 875	5.9	46 640	24.4	33.5
Midland, MI	32 977	75.5	138 500	19.3	10.3	739	27.9	85.8	41 182	-0.6	1 870	4.5	38 497	40.4	22.6
Midland, TX	57 867	70.9	195 800	18.8	10.0	1 196	27.6	92.1	87 069	-4.0	3 849	4.4	84 441	32.2	28.6
Milwaukee-Waukesha-West Allis, WI	627 842	58.9	198 600	21.8	13.6	848	29.5	86.0	827 836	0.5	36 976	4.5	794 353	39.0	20.3
Minneapolis-St. Paul-Bloomington, MN	1 354 766	68.9	231 800	20.3	10.7	979	29.0	91.8	1 938 645	1.2	69 215	3.6	1 911 709	43.3	18.2
Missoula, MT	47 910	58.7	246 400	24.1	11.4	770	30.0	91.7	61 742	1.6	2 310	3.7	60 583	41.4	14.8

1. Specified owner-occupied units.   2. A value of 10.0 represents 10 percent or less.   3. Specified renter-occupied units.   4. Percent of civilian labor force.
5. Civilian employed persons 16 years old and over.

Table C. Metropolitan Areas — Nonfarm Employment and Agriculture

Area name	Private nonfarm establishments, employment and payroll, 2015									Agriculture, 2012			
		Employment						Annual payroll		Farms			
												Percent with:	
	Number of establishments	Total	Health care and social assistance	Manufacturing	Retail trade	Finance and insurance	Professional, scientific, and technical services	Total (mil dol)	Average per employee (dollars)	Number	Fewer than 50 acres	500 acres or more	Farm operators whose principal occupation is farming (percent)
	104	105	106	107	108	109	110	111	112	113	114	115	116
Jonesboro, AR	2 808	44 177	10 656	6 207	7 640	1 116	962	1 574	35 634	980	31.9	39.2	57.8
Joplin, MO	3 978	69 998	12 797	12 250	9 944	1 702	1 935	2 557	36 524	2 877	35.9	6.1	39.6
Kahului-Wailuku-Lahaina, HI	4 546	61 999	6 189	1 157	9 782	900	1 512	2 390	38 549	1 128	89.0	3.5	54.0
Kalamazoo-Portage, MI	6 822	121 603	21 351	19 558	16 102	5 774	5 724	5 512	45 328	1 847	52.1	6.2	51.4
Kankakee, IL	2 339	36 979	7 466	5 807	5 949	1 387	790	1 367	36 967	818	33.7	24.4	56.8
Kansas City, MO-KS	52 739	923 782	137 606	81 733	109 781	60 139	77 663	46 167	49 976	12 757	35.5	10.8	42.8
Kennewick-Richland, WA	5 732	79 661	9 769	6 848	13 264	1 927	7 780	3 797	47 660	2 392	61.8	14.9	51.4
Killeen-Temple, TX	6 038	103 572	27 704	7 198	17 196	3 704	4 189	3 899	37 646	4 858	42.7	11.4	38.9
Kingsport-Bristol-Bristol, TN-VA	6 004	104 648	17 662	24 543	15 472	3 034	2 702	4 331	41 389	5 405	45.3	2.7	40.6
Kingston, NY	4 746	45 604	9 359	3 394	9 197	1 895	1 678	1 603	35 156	486	48.4	5.1	67.3
Knoxville, TN	17 783	324 448	50 891	32 776	45 185	14 714	23 394	14 173	43 683	5 613	46.9	1.8	42.6
Kokomo, IN	1 751	32 084	5 291	9 943	4 978	737	675	1 410	43 951	476	40.8	15.5	57.4
La Crosse-Onalaska, WI-MN	3 458	65 354	12 210	8 205	9 352	2 239	2 016	2 476	37 886	1 668	18.8	10.7	47.8
Lafayette, LA	13 273	195 811	33 114	15 316	27 440	5 317	11 266	8 695	44 406	3 276	53.8	10.9	47.0
Lafayette-West Lafayette, IN	4 042	69 714	10 819	17 235	10 130	1 673	2 649	2 830	40 594	1 574	42.7	22.9	48.7
Lake Charles, LA	4 597	75 839	14 005	8 595	11 271	1 996	4 991	3 373	44 474	1 244	44.3	12.4	35.4
Lake Havasu City-Kingman, AZ	3 677	41 520	8 699	2 830	9 538	919	905	1 342	32 324	335	59.1	23.9	51.3
Lakeland-Winter Haven, FL	11 218	174 572	27 755	14 558	26 277	10 929	5 973	6 858	39 285	2 415	64.4	7.2	45.3
Lancaster, PA	12 594	226 286	35 183	34 391	31 253	7 501	11 527	9 467	41 837	5 657	44.1	1.3	72.2
Lansing-East Lansing, MI	9 453	160 786	28 433	17 767	21 814	12 770	7 337	6 862	42 676	3 235	46.2	9.9	49.0
Laredo, TX	5 259	75 850	15 232	605	13 739	2 656	1 982	2 186	28 820	696	15.1	48.6	48.6
Las Cruces, NM	3 570	50 155	13 655	2 129	8 274	1 671	3 656	1 508	30 057	2 184	85.6	4.5	37.7
Las Vegas-Henderson-Paradise, NV	43 396	824 659	79 754	19 400	108 862	25 934	43 541	33 078	40 112	252	78.6	2.0	46.8
Lawrence, KS	2 698	40 240	6 103	3 558	6 179	1 324	1 656	1 197	29 741	945	38.5	9.7	35.8
Lawton, OK	2 280	34 425	6 412	3 519	5 900	1 560	1 399	1 159	33 659	1 607	19.1	27.8	46.2
Lebanon, PA	2 684	44 109	8 261	9 263	6 910	974	1 110	1 654	37 508	1 219	48.2	2.3	58.9
Lewiston, ID-WA	1 568	21 824	4 170	4 278	3 565	1 323	744	820	37 589	615	39.5	33.0	54.6
Lewiston-Auburn, ME	2 706	45 347	9 828	5 996	6 036	3 262	1 802	1 764	38 897	463	51.6	5.0	56.4
Lexington-Fayette, KY	12 282	219 269	36 951	27 686	27 984	6 046	15 385	9 298	42 405	4 727	44.1	7.6	46.4
Lima, OH	2 404	46 122	11 656	7 767	6 063	1 142	916	1 843	39 964	904	38.8	11.8	42.9
Lincoln, NE	8 759	139 267	24 813	13 619	19 211	11 187	8 581	5 546	39 822	2 828	46.0	17.8	38.7
Little Rock-North Little Rock-Conway, AR	17 801	275 443	53 238	21 931	38 818	15 213	13 744	11 520	41 825	3 534	40.0	9.0	42.9
Logan, UT-ID	3 531	43 653	6 008	11 780	6 625	1 457	3 237	1 425	32 652	2 051	46.9	14.0	41.4
Longview, TX	5 445	85 075	12 872	11 466	11 920	2 868	3 741	3 483	40 943	3 671	42.6	5.3	35.3
Longview, WA	2 099	30 598	5 471	6 382	4 879	811	708	1 398	45 674	492	72.4	2.8	46.7
Los Angeles-Long Beach-Anaheim, CA	357 910	5 456 991	683 766	500 241	578 582	242 979	524 561	293 613	53 805	1 606	88.2	3.3	60.2
Anaheim-Santa Ana-Irvine, CA Div 11244	NA	NA	NA	NA	NA	NA	NA	NA	NA	312	85.3	4.8	58.7
Los Angeles-Long Beach-Glendale, CA Div 31084	NA	NA	NA	NA	NA	NA	NA	NA	NA	1 294	88.9	2.9	60.6
Louisville/Jefferson County, KY-IN	29 101	560 894	86 095	69 883	63 122	34 327	27 340	25 189	44 908	7 555	48.0	4.9	43.3
Lubbock, TX	7 233	113 641	23 151	5 411	18 636	6 157	4 362	4 051	35 648	2 002	23.9	35.5	50.1
Lynchburg, VA	5 908	97 143	14 091	16 099	14 181	3 974	5 449	3 764	38 745	2 966	29.9	7.5	40.9
Macon, GA	5 112	82 500	17 297	5 574	11 631	8 938	2 738	3 194	38 712	734	38.4	6.7	44.0
Madera, CA	1 929	26 580	5 789	3 829	3 790	442	460	1 054	39 660	1 507	44.8	14.3	57.9
Madison, WI	16 765	316 916	52 286	33 708	39 703	25 098	23 064	15 777	49 782	7 446	38.4	8.5	48.1
Manchester-Nashua, NH	10 938	179 115	29 400	26 169	28 664	8 883	10 665	9 593	53 558	688	64.0	1.5	50.0
Manhattan, KS	2 189	29 258	4 783	2 327	5 991	1 052	1 344	954	32 603	1 383	23.1	23.4	43.5
Mankato-North Mankato, MN	2 587	48 648	11 265	7 963	7 228	1 195	1 545	1 795	36 904	1 834	25.5	21.8	57.4
Mansfield, OH	2 618	44 133	7 685	8 574	6 418	1 048	963	1 487	33 692	1 010	37.2	5.0	52.0
McAllen-Edinburg-Mission, TX	11 866	187 842	57 630	6 659	38 679	6 527	5 818	5 185	27 602	2 161	57.9	14.7	51.4
Medford, OR	6 091	70 228	13 346	6 414	12 287	2 065	2 252	2 583	36 780	1 722	72.1	2.4	56.2
Memphis, TN-MS-AR	25 206	527 509	79 956	39 025	61 751	18 133	19 642	24 325	46 114	3 934	32.7	15.3	44.0
Merced, CA	2 969	42 036	6 977	8 621	8 456	980	780	1 606	38 217	2 486	56.7	12.8	64.5
Miami-Fort Lauderdale-West Palm Beach, FL	188 379	2 122 149	306 915	69 181	332 199	99 215	159 903	99 310	46 797	4 978	92.1	1.9	55.8
Fort Lauderdale-Pompano Beach-Deerfield Beach, FL Div 22744	NA	NA	NA	NA	NA	NA	NA	NA	NA	615	93.7	1.3	50.1
Miami-Miami Beach-Kendall, FL Div 33124	NA	NA	NA	NA	NA	NA	NA	NA	NA	2 954	92.8	1.2	56.5
West Palm Beach-Boca Raton-Delray Beach, FL Div 48424	NA	NA	NA	NA	NA	NA	NA	NA	NA	1 409	90.0	3.5	56.7
Michigan City-La Porte, IN	2 303	34 473	6 041	7 413	5 951	729	768	1 307	37 911	731	43.8	17.1	51.4
Midland, MI	2 167	34 633	6 111	6 003	4 043	1 091	928	2 112	60 993	555	47.9	7.0	46.7
Midland, TX	5 299	91 487	7 166	3 195	9 262	2 084	4 600	5 460	59 681	954	32.8	29.6	38.5
Milwaukee-Waukesha-West Allis, WI	37 970	775 911	131 199	112 438	80 694	52 235	40 547	39 042	50 318	1 767	47.1	7.6	52.2
Minneapolis-St. Paul-Bloomington, MN	94 806	1 778 005	279 890	183 788	187 226	122 175	124 029	98 597	55 454	13 251	40.4	9.2	49.4
Missoula, MT	4 296	49 149	9 621	1 806	8 286	1 958	2 929	1 725	35 092	637	58.4	10.0	38.3

Table C. Metropolitan Areas — Agriculture

Area name	Land in farms — Acreage (1,000) [117]	Percent change, 2007–2012 [118]	Average size of farm [119]	Total irrigated (1,000) [120]	Total cropland (1,000) [121]	Value of land and buildings (dollars) Average per farm [122]	Average per acre [123]	Value of machinery and equipment, average per farm (dollars) [124]	Value of products sold Total (mil dol) [125]	Average per farm (dollars) [126]	Percent from: Crops [127]	Livestock and poultry products [128]	Percent of farms with sales of: $10,000 or more [129]	$100,000 or more [130]	Government payments Total ($1,000) [131]	Percent of farms [132]
Jonesboro, AR	723	6.7	738	581.6	684.0	2 311 689	3 134	359 641	549.0	560 225	99.4	0.6	60.0	44.9	25 872	68.1
Joplin, MO	494	-2.0	172	3.8	221.1	422 288	2 457	61 142	352.0	122 343	13.5	86.5	43.1	9.2	3 356	26.2
Kahului-Wailuku-Lahaina, HI	229	1.6	203	41.5	49.6	1 998 207	9 836	53 229	188.1	166 755	96.5	3.5	37.1	7.1	558	10.5
Kalamazoo-Portage, MI	319	-3.5	173	73.1	237.9	782 997	4 538	138 933	438.6	237 484	81.1	18.9	47.4	18.5	4 898	23.6
Kankakee, IL	343	-11.2	419	14.6	327.9	2 769 373	6 612	264 800	287.5	351 460	90.2	9.8	71.8	48.5	5 827	76.5
Kansas City, MO-KS	3 124	-5.1	245	D	1 916.0	749 999	3 062	83 462	785.7	61 589	68.9	31.1	41.2	10.1	34 070	44.7
Kennewick-Richland, WA	1 329	7.0	555	404.5	971.3	1 569 965	2 827	192 328	1 663.2	695 308	D	D	44.1	26.5	14 367	21.2
Killeen-Temple, TX	1 329	-0.5	274	3.7	306.5	727 280	2 658	57 979	169.6	34 950	45.8	54.2	25.2	4.0	3 614	15.2
Kingsport-Bristol-Bristol, TN-VA	569	-2.9	105	0.5	161.6	374 389	3 558	48 349	126.4	23 393	15.2	84.8	26.1	3.5	6 226	30.7
Kingston, NY	71	-5.3	147	4.2	26.1	738 835	5 042	103 237	55.9	115 019	83.0	17.0	43.0	12.6	328	10.1
Knoxville, TN	538	-6.7	96	1.6	194.1	495 626	5 174	57 244	158.2	28 176	56.8	43.2	22.7	2.2	1 294	13.0
Kokomo, IN	144	-11.1	303	D	134.5	1 924 391	6 353	182 880	140.4	294 874	81.1	18.9	68.1	37.2	2 993	67.0
La Crosse-Onalaska, WI-MN	388	-5.3	233	1.1	216.2	792 875	3 409	126 932	232.8	139 555	48.7	51.3	56.6	25.2	7 429	71.6
Lafayette, LA	761	-3.1	232	152.3	537.5	627 401	2 702	115 382	440.9	134 575	84.1	15.9	32.9	11.7	14 740	39.4
Lafayette-West Lafayette, IN	679	-0.4	431	D	638.6	2 869 720	6 657	239 864	583.0	370 363	75.3	24.7	57.4	39.8	12 438	64.2
Lake Charles, LA	573	-1.8	461	27.4	141.2	1 029 838	2 235	77 753	52.3	42 007	60.6	39.4	27.3	6.2	3 549	22.7
Lake Havasu City-Kingman, AZ	1 244	45.0	3 714	20.8	29.1	1 792 487	483	75 743	30.2	90 102	68.9	31.1	33.7	11.9	1 242	11.3
Lakeland-Winter Haven, FL	521	-5.1	216	79.9	125.1	1 182 091	5 480	64 954	350.3	145 042	90.2	9.8	48.1	18.3	419	1.4
Lancaster, PA	439	3.3	78	6.1	332.0	973 388	12 529	101 987	1 475.0	260 731	17.7	82.3	74.2	48.4	5 843	18.4
Lansing-East Lansing, MI	668	-1.8	206	7.4	549.2	837 223	4 057	126 959	513.0	158 584	63.2	36.8	46.4	19.6	9 730	43.6
Laredo, TX	2 098	13.1	3 015	2.6	25.2	3 265 045	1 083	57 487	30.3	43 476	2.8	97.2	31.2	7.0	1 169	14.1
Las Cruces, NM	660	12.0	302	76.3	93.8	540 877	1 790	75 238	351.0	160 729	47.5	52.5	23.9	8.1	1 453	9.5
Las Vegas-Henderson-Paradise, NV	16	-82.3	62	3.7	4.4	347 790	5 611	66 325	6.8	27 083	48.2	51.8	33.7	4.4	34	3.6
Lawrence, KS	211	-4.5	223	3.3	127.3	636 186	2 854	82 519	43.9	46 436	66.2	33.8	37.7	8.4	2 332	46.9
Lawton, OK	863	-0.2	537	0.8	322.6	678 021	1 263	80 981	111.8	69 573	41.7	58.3	46.7	14.1	8 694	54.8
Lebanon, PA	121	7.0	100	1.5	97.4	1 052 028	10 562	122 164	348.9	286 245	13.1	86.9	64.1	37.6	2 250	26.6
Lewiston, ID-WA	585	-6.7	952	1.3	265.7	1 245 914	1 309	136 184	101.7	165 337	87.2	12.8	44.4	26.0	7 534	54.0
Lewiston-Auburn, ME	59	16.9	128	0.8	22.0	329 181	2 564	72 955	53.8	116 266	22.1	77.9	32.8	8.0	445	15.6
Lexington-Fayette, KY	759	-6.0	161	3.1	281.9	895 506	5 577	77 863	459.8	97 273	19.6	80.4	42.7	11.0	7 009	31.4
Lima, OH	183	-2.2	203	D	163.0	1 070 715	5 284	144 872	144.1	159 393	76.2	23.8	61.7	30.3	3 593	74.4
Lincoln, NE	844	11.9	298	151.4	696.9	1 423 260	4 770	156 127	486.3	171 957	68.0	32.0	48.6	23.8	15 528	63.6
Little Rock-North Little Rock-Conway, AR	788	-2.6	223	233.1	424.9	654 503	2 936	91 716	348.0	98 485	68.6	31.4	33.2	7.8	16 332	22.1
Logan, UT-ID	531	11.5	259	137.5	278.0	718 986	2 776	105 031	249.0	121 400	24.9	75.1	44.4	16.3	5 876	39.8
Longview, TX	525	-3.6	143	1.2	98.9	371 975	2 602	49 545	139.5	37 992	18.1	81.9	22.0	2.9	634	2.3
Longview, WA	39	27.1	79	7.6	18.6	689 236	8 693	67 535	28.8	58 482	D	D	19.5	6.9	44	1.6
Los Angeles-Long Beach-Anaheim, CA	152	-22.3	95	47.7	74.7	1 534 556	16 194	50 774	351.6	218 935	94.1	5.9	35.6	12.9	290	3.4
Anaheim-Santa Ana-Irvine, CA Div 11244	60	-30.8	194	8.1	15.2	4 237 538	21 854	70 968	158.5	508 055	99.0	1.0	41.3	18.3	43	4.8
Los Angeles-Long Beach-Glendale, CA Div 31084	92	-15.5	71	39.7	59.6	882 832	12 459	45 905	193.1	149 225	90.1	9.9	34.2	11.6	247	3.1
Louisville/Jefferson County, KY-IN	1 068	-8.0	141	D	607.7	573 173	4 054	69 317	410.6	54 342	60.1	39.9	33.6	7.7	13 211	37.0
Lubbock, TX	1 533	-1.9	766	338.8	1 130.1	915 687	1 196	206 678	314.0	156 835	72.9	27.1	45.8	27.4	28 253	73.9
Lynchburg, VA	552	6.9	186	D	151.2	674 238	3 620	60 278	74.4	25 088	28.4	71.6	35.9	4.1	2 334	18.5
Macon, GA	145	-14.1	197	10.1	46.0	599 775	3 039	77 030	120.5	164 170	31.4	68.6	28.5	10.6	1 459	19.1
Madera, CA	654	-3.8	434	292.3	304.2	3 302 033	7 614	182 022	1 602.8	1 063 547	77.4	22.6	70.2	46.8	2 400	11.4
Madison, WI	1 466	-3.8	197	14.2	1 067.2	984 545	5 002	132 972	1 081.6	145 256	40.2	59.8	49.3	22.9	31 173	62.4
Manchester-Nashua, NH	48	-5.0	69	0.7	11.1	450 385	6 495	52 282	22.5	32 759	69.8	30.2	22.8	7.0	261	6.8
Manhattan, KS	628	-5.0	454	26.0	264.3	853 839	1 881	103 492	171.4	123 929	51.7	48.3	54.2	19.6	4 125	59.9
Mankato-North Mankato, MN	651	-5.6	355	1.7	588.8	2 286 660	6 445	257 171	892.1	486 398	49.3	50.7	71.0	49.7	13 782	82.1
Mansfield, OH	161	9.6	159	0.1	120.3	789 172	4 962	110 557	128.7	127 408	51.7	48.3	55.0	29.5	1 806	32.5
McAllen-Edinburg-Mission, TX	795	10.0	368	183.6	465.6	1 117 900	3 038	115 296	452.8	209 517	91.7	8.3	33.2	14.2	9 106	20.0
Medford, OR	214	-12.3	124	36.5	32.8	582 023	4 682	40 415	64.1	37 240	57.6	42.4	25.7	3.4	252	3.8
Memphis, TN-MS-AR	1 573	-0.6	400	D	1 086.1	1 072 560	2 682	131 704	661.4	168 123	D	D	32.2	13.4	26 335	44.6
Merced, CA	979	-6.0	394	468.2	522.6	3 045 778	7 737	236 454	2 967.5	1 193 694	42.9	57.1	76.0	45.7	9 528	20.2
Miami-Fort Lauderdale-West Palm Beach, FL	610	1.4	122	409.8	509.9	1 213 970	9 911	83 861	1 650.7	331 597	98.0	2.0	52.0	15.2	8 726	7.1
Fort Lauderdale-Pompano Beach-Deerfield Beach, FL Div 22744	14	65.9	24	1.8	4.3	540 185	22 916	31 886	47.4	77 099	91.2	8.8	41.0	8.6	246	2.9
Miami-Miami Beach-Kendall, FL Div 33124	81	21.3	28	45.2	64.9	699 727	25 423	47 644	604.2	204 549	98.0	2.0	58.5	16.0	6 944	8.5
West Palm Beach-Boca Raton-Delray Beach, FL Div 48424	514	-2.2	365	362.7	440.7	2 586 187	7 090	182 476	999.0	709 041	98.3	1.7	43.2	16.2	1 536	6.0
Michigan City-La Porte, IN	228	-11.0	312	54.4	209.3	1 896 432	6 084	188 253	223.1	305 215	80.5	19.5	55.7	33.8	4 036	58.4
Midland, MI	90	-1.2	161	1.0	69.5	580 838	3 600	98 339	70.1	126 285	67.9	32.1	39.1	14.1	2 310	44.3
Midland, TX	858	-6.2	899	27.9	342.0	1 097 884	1 221	116 852	37.5	39 285	78.2	21.8	21.3	8.8	7 024	48.4
Milwaukee-Waukesha-West Allis, WI	295	0.9	167	2.2	238.1	1 011 705	6 056	128 100	250.1	141 516	49.0	51.0	50.8	22.7	5 478	43.0
Minneapolis-St. Paul-Bloomington, MN	2 598	-1.6	196	105.7	2 044.9	1 015 662	5 180	136 564	2 169.8	163 748	66.3	33.7	52.7	22.9	43 747	54.6
Missoula, MT	247	-12.3	388	16.8	19.9	1 074 215	2 769	40 830	13.6	21 355	29.8	70.2	22.1	4.6	395	9.4

Table C. Metropolitan Areas — Water Use, Wholesale Trade, Retail Trade, and Real Estate

Area name	Water use, 2010		Wholesale trade,[1] 2012				Retail trade, 2012				Real estate and rental and leasing, 2012			
	Total water withdrawn (mil gal/day)	Gallons withdrawn per person per day	Number of establishments	Number of employees	Sales (mil dol)	Annual payroll (mil dol)	Number of establishments	Number of employees	Sales (mil dol)	Annual payroll (mil dol)	Number of establishments	Number of employees	Receipts (mil dol)	Annual payroll (mil dol)
	133	134	135	136	137	138	139	140	141	142	143	144	145	146
Jonesboro, AR	1 360.0	11 237	153	1 899	1 854.8	94.1	524	7 142	1 858.9	156.2	124	509	83.2	13.9
Joplin, MO	40.5	231	184	2 895	2 647.0	118.9	710	9 859	2 841.3	215.3	143	583	86.0	14.9
Kahului-Wailuku-Lahaina, HI	278.1	1 795	140	1 141	714.6	50.4	759	9 174	2 461.0	258.2	306	2 022	454.4	70.8
Kalamazoo-Portage, MI	218.7	670	287	D	D	D	1 115	14 993	3 764.0	338.3	242	2 430	239.0	73.5
Kankakee, IL	26.8	236	119	2 196	1 443.3	95.0	370	5 548	1 463.3	120.0	95	371	70.9	10.6
Kansas City, MO-KS	1 626.1	809	2 529	42 419	52 860.3	2 756.7	6 294	104 436	29 998.3	2 579.3	2 430	13 232	3 092.0	568.9
Kennewick-Richland, WA	894.8	3 532	222	2 512	2 971.9	112.3	772	11 935	3 382.4	307.4	300	1 244	220.5	37.3
Killeen-Temple, TX	80.7	199	143	2 717	3 687.0	139.5	1 093	15 406	4 328.6	344.5	350	1 640	241.7	55.4
Kingsport-Bristol-Bristol, TN-VA	929.6	3 003	275	3 317	1 816.0	121.0	1 101	15 030	3 779.9	327.2	208	741	126.5	23.1
Kingston, NY	458.2	2 511	159	1 504	810.4	71.3	733	8 606	2 324.9	211.8	195	732	116.6	22.0
Knoxville, TN	699.1	835	867	12 090	8 194.7	621.5	2 923	44 783	11 873.6	1 086.3	791	4 105	764.5	149.0
Kokomo, IN	17.5	212	62	559	512.7	31.6	328	4 927	1 193.3	104.0	71	311	50.4	8.9
La Crosse-Onalaska, WI-MN	37.3	279	137	2 724	6 239.4	119.7	491	9 017	2 027.3	185.4	125	801	101.7	20.9
Lafayette, LA	436.2	935	708	10 557	5 896.8	547.1	1 856	25 397	7 064.9	625.9	688	6 875	2 269.2	460.8
Lafayette-West Lafayette, IN	39.9	198	142	1 637	1 256.9	69.6	611	9 409	2 378.7	200.9	181	892	148.2	30.0
Lake Charles, LA	250.2	1 254	199	2 196	1 971.0	102.7	772	10 240	3 155.4	241.0	216	1 018	235.6	41.5
Lake Havasu City-Kingman, AZ	121.2	605	114	816	391.1	30.5	593	8 918	2 712.7	211.4	199	628	83.2	15.6
Lakeland-Winter Haven, FL	298.7	496	544	8 056	10 601.3	394.0	1 756	22 988	6 495.3	558.8	651	2 928	510.6	93.1
Lancaster, PA	78.2	151	582	10 776	8 764.0	496.7	1 917	29 783	6 899.6	669.6	342	2 009	396.6	79.1
Lansing-East Lansing, MI	239.1	515	327	5 044	7 143.8	236.0	1 416	20 926	5 462.7	475.9	385	2 530	349.8	88.0
Laredo, TX	43.5	174	357	2 839	2 410.1	97.0	784	12 356	3 217.6	257.8	199	692	132.4	22.0
Las Cruces, NM	397.2	1 899	102	D	D	D	496	7 916	1 965.4	167.7	209	690	116.6	18.9
Las Vegas-Henderson-Paradise, NV	486.6	249	1 630	16 747	11 597.1	958.8	5 712	95 369	27 971.7	2 531.6	2 794	17 855	3 700.3	647.4
Lawrence, KS	19.1	172	71	610	282.9	24.6	373	6 066	1 354.2	122.6	157	761	97.7	20.9
Lawton, OK	32.1	247	64	D	D	D	424	5 410	1 444.7	119.5	126	519	90.6	16.5
Lebanon, PA	14.6	109	99	2 679	3 913.7	112.7	431	6 597	1 695.7	158.6	70	309	40.5	7.8
Lewiston, ID-WA	133.2	2 188	55	613	497.2	26.3	259	3 343	968.8	87.2	60	280	37.3	7.6
Lewiston-Auburn, ME	15.3	142	102	1 236	473.9	54.6	439	6 018	1 818.1	138.5	111	376	62.9	11.6
Lexington-Fayette, KY	183.8	389	473	9 899	9 127.9	669.6	1 734	27 528	7 438.5	652.4	554	2 474	505.0	85.7
Lima, OH	34.6	325	124	2 287	1 388.8	91.6	417	6 072	1 641.5	134.3	85	376	55.2	11.0
Lincoln, NE	73.2	242	305	4 427	3 667.9	183.4	1 063	17 686	4 428.3	398.8	353	1 726	257.6	56.7
Little Rock-North Little Rock-Conway, AR	619.6	885	868	12 971	9 583.7	658.8	2 605	37 471	10 847.9	901.3	836	4 140	765.8	147.3
Logan, UT-ID	513.5	4 094	119	978	613.1	37.7	447	5 980	1 270.6	118.4	190	D	D	D
Longview, TX	1 708.9	7 972	290	3 950	2 602.1	209.8	866	11 363	3 285.3	283.8	231	1 303	427.0	65.6
Longview, WA	146.6	1 431	85	1 036	2 021.4	53.2	333	4 644	1 188.3	113.8	104	337	50.7	8.5
Los Angeles-Long Beach-Anaheim, CA	3 829.4	298	27 704	317 329	297 600.8	18 082.1	37 817	528 453	166 583.0	14 835.1	19 194	120 995	38 846.0	6 397.2
Anaheim-Santa Ana-Irvine, CA Div 11244	765.4	254	6 434	79 685	97 796.0	5 200.7	9 390	143 012	45 193.6	4 135.3	5 320	38 952	9 259.7	1 921.2
Los Angeles-Long Beach-Glendale, CA Div 31084	3 064.0	312	21 270	237 644	199 804.8	12 881.4	28 427	385 441	121 389.4	10 699.7	13 874	82 043	29 586.3	4 476.1
Louisville/Jefferson County, KY-IN	1 008.9	816	1 322	19 345	15 452.9	992.4	4 011	59 405	16 279.7	1 413.5	1 250	8 356	3 099.2	326.1
Lubbock, TX	260.9	897	389	D	D	D	1 073	16 669	4 850.9	409.5	399	D	D	D
Lynchburg, VA	47.7	189	178	2 025	1 098.8	87.6	939	13 555	3 665.7	315.0	269	773	131.2	23.3
Macon, GA	131.1	565	224	2 679	1 666.2	128.0	980	11 588	2 932.4	260.9	225	969	179.2	32.4
Madera, CA	748.7	4 963	76	815	508.9	37.8	326	3 455	1 012.9	84.3	75	336	38.4	8.5
Madison, WI	116.5	192	709	13 072	8 970.5	679.2	2 123	38 927	11 740.7	1 042.3	695	4 410	992.1	164.6
Manchester-Nashua, NH	55.1	137	537	6 822	4 749.3	470.5	1 584	26 984	7 724.7	700.9	387	2 697	565.9	123.8
Manhattan, KS	46.0	496	56	725	307.1	30.8	353	6 208	1 242.8	130.0	129	511	74.1	13.2
Mankato-North Mankato, MN	41.1	425	123	1 798	1 325.4	85.2	395	6 930	1 645.7	151.2	104	692	75.5	16.9
Mansfield, OH	17.0	137	104	1 993	939.2	78.9	438	6 528	1 501.2	139.9	102	417	49.2	9.1
McAllen-Edinburg-Mission, TX	470.2	607	841	D	D	D	2 219	33 566	9 296.8	733.9	497	2 209	445.0	61.9
Medford, OR	392.4	1 931	206	1 771	828.4	76.8	865	11 223	3 202.7	297.5	306	1 043	164.1	26.3
Memphis, TN-MS-AR	1 088.0	821	1 435	28 963	41 205.9	1 583.6	4 178	61 787	26 311.6	1 598.5	1 125	7 663	1 573.2	327.6
Merced, CA	1 494.7	5 843	112	1 635	2 260.2	71.2	528	7 497	1 959.5	173.3	152	532	79.1	14.6
Miami-Fort Lauderdale-West Palm Beach, FL	2 446.7	440	14 077	109 773	124 749.4	5 674.1	22 695	290 852	90 104.2	7 832.7	10 475	48 690	11 005.1	1 996.5
Fort Lauderdale-Pompano Beach-Deerfield Beach, FL Div 22744	1 279.1	732	3 902	33 141	33 606.6	1 781.8	7 070	97 344	32 042.9	2 675.4	3 237	17 682	3 934.9	701.7
Miami-Miami Beach-Kendall, FL Div 33124	461.0	185	8 242	61 377	78 985.4	3 003.6	10 389	123 883	38 361.2	3 252.7	4 776	19 563	4 936.4	811.0
West Palm Beach-Boca Raton-Delray Beach, FL Div 48424	706.5	535	1 933	15 255	12 157.3	888.7	5 236	69 625	19 700.1	1 904.6	2 462	11 445	2 133.8	482.9
Michigan City-La Porte, IN	44.0	395	100	1 161	694.9	46.8	457	5 845	1 367.8	116.2	84	367	95.2	10.6
Midland, MI	10.6	127	44	297	703.7	16.7	314	4 050	1 015.7	88.4	63	257	36.8	8.4
Midland, TX	73.9	521	272	D	D	D	515	7 607	3 019.3	221.5	267	1 505	491.4	79.1
Milwaukee-Waukesha-West Allis, WI	2 280.3	1 466	1 981	34 545	23 162.4	2 243.4	4 695	77 813	20 086.4	1 806.6	1 354	9 103	1 636.8	343.6
Minneapolis-St. Paul-Bloomington, MN	1 762.8	526	4 390	77 536	72 483.1	5 723.3	10 525	179 498	51 537.1	4 494.9	4 636	27 832	6 835.8	1 224.7
Missoula, MT	85.6	783	151	1 838	1 220.7	81.5	570	7 931	2 044.0	180.0	206	918	130.6	29.7

1. Merchant wholesalers, except manufacturers' sales branches and offices.

Table C. Metropolitan Areas — **Professional Services, Manufacturing, and Accommodation and Food Services**

Area name	Professional, scientific, and technical services, 2012				Manufacturing, 2012				Accommodation and food services, 2012			
	Number of establishments	Number of employees	Sales (mil dol)	Annual payroll (mil dol)	Number of establishments	Number of employees	Sales (mil dol)	Annual payroll (mil dol)	Number of establishments	Number of employees	Sales (mil dol)	Annual payroll (mil dol)
	147	148	149	150	151	152	153	154	155	156	157	158
Jonesboro, AR	188	916	129.1	47.1	120	5 910	2 325.7	245.4	248	4 784	213.7	57.5
Joplin, MO	250	D	D	D	243	11 659	4 282.8	486.5	358	6 644	297.2	81.6
Kahului-Wailuku-Lahaina, HI	390	1 381	186.4	67.0	99	997	D	41.1	499	19 943	2 307.5	625.7
Kalamazoo-Portage, MI	621	5 037	771.8	268.6	398	18 339	8 609.7	1 051.9	695	13 630	575.0	173.0
Kankakee, IL	152	735	64.1	24.5	100	4 889	4 842.8	269.7	219	3 675	160.3	47.4
Kansas City, MO-KS	6 155	69 705	13 938.8	5 014.4	1 744	74 320	40 520.9	4 025.8	3 910	82 476	4 552.6	1 254.3
Kennewick-Richland, WA	511	9 341	1 701.1	687.2	197	6 764	2 821.7	327.1	492	7 736	405.8	114.5
Killeen-Temple, TX	474	4 383	504.2	203.8	180	6 556	2 110.1	268.1	697	13 241	632.5	170.8
Kingsport-Bristol-Bristol, TN-VA	460	2 948	327.7	135.9	282	24 543	9 574.3	1 421.8	586	10 841	488.5	140.0
Kingston, NY	443	1 601	189.3	69.1	170	3 518	D	170.2	546	6 655	367.3	117.4
Knoxville, TN	1 691	21 671	2 523.0	1 399.6	727	33 148	13 060.5	1 823.5	1 507	32 820	1 566.1	466.9
Kokomo, IN	114	631	61.2	22.6	70	7 671	D	593.4	186	3 866	159.9	46.1
La Crosse-Onalaska, WI-MN	274	1 949	185.4	88.2	179	7 092	1 996.6	277.2	365	6 575	252.0	74.4
Lafayette, LA	1 761	10 784	1 848.4	631.0	582	19 339	9 405.7	1 128.7	969	19 563	1 026.7	290.3
Lafayette-West Lafayette, IN	331	2 418	345.0	108.9	161	16 598	13 028.7	935.4	446	8 493	383.2	104.9
Lake Charles, LA	432	5 212	479.4	222.9	128	8 620	44 186.6	688.2	358	10 817	984.6	210.8
Lake Havasu City-Kingman, AZ	239	931	72.4	30.8	133	2 566	D	109.5	382	5 787	256.7	74.3
Lakeland-Winter Haven, FL	1 036	6 724	768.7	300.4	401	14 200	9 822.2	681.0	788	15 188	797.9	220.1
Lancaster, PA	957	12 486	1 249.1	1 037.2	856	33 212	13 655.7	1 638.7	998	17 833	878.4	246.9
Lansing-East Lansing, MI	1 051	7 399	1 210.3	408.7	341	17 312	16 198.9	1 002.6	913	17 000	708.1	201.7
Laredo, TX	317	1 803	186.1	58.6	69	635	339.6	22.0	389	8 216	423.7	106.2
Las Cruces, NM	339	D	D	D	128	2 520	D	87.1	319	6 813	285.2	80.7
Las Vegas-Henderson-Paradise, NV	5 645	35 253	5 825.0	2 128.2	894	17 390	5 673.8	782.0	4 050	250 601	24 283.8	7 612.3
Lawrence, KS	292	D	D	D	69	3 079	1 217.3	136.1	301	6 511	261.1	72.2
Lawton, OK	168	1 143	115.7	50.2	49	3 495	1 354.6	D	234	4 927	223.2	66.8
Lebanon, PA	197	1 083	151.2	48.6	205	8 099	2 743.8	336.5	232	3 320	146.1	40.5
Lewiston, ID-WA	112	D	D	D	60	3 067	1 175.1	144.0	139	2 677	133.7	38.7
Lewiston-Auburn, ME	183	1 652	359.2	80.1	150	5 205	1 886.9	251.6	209	3 021	153.3	44.5
Lexington-Fayette, KY	1 384	12 042	1 702.3	653.5	423	25 017	17 174.3	1 286.4	1 051	23 086	1 191.8	340.1
Lima, OH	164	952	75.8	33.0	124	7 318	15 270.4	448.1	234	4 521	211.3	54.3
Lincoln, NE	871	9 241	1 313.8	464.2	255	13 208	6 540.1	653.7	702	13 936	616.8	161.3
Little Rock-North Little Rock-Conway, AR	2 012	12 058	1 911.2	627.2	540	21 045	9 263.0	990.1	1 461	29 034	1 362.2	386.9
Logan, UT-ID	385	2 538	251.4	88.6	226	10 761	4 556.5	443.1	178	3 173	130.7	35.4
Longview, TX	508	3 998	554.5	213.9	233	10 657	4 029.0	552.1	426	8 138	374.1	105.1
Longview, WA	140	830	86.5	34.9	116	5 722	3 264.5	385.6	215	2 796	124.2	39.2
Los Angeles-Long Beach-Anaheim, CA	45 444	633 648	90 371.7	35 143.8	17 461	509 552	211 129.0	28 731.8	27 439	499 255	32 015.8	8 990.4
Anaheim-Santa Ana-Irvine, CA Div 11244	14 120	112 581	24 110.2	8 899.6	4 701	150 020	47 299.4	8 879.0	7 141	143 519	9 050.6	2 599.9
Los Angeles-Long Beach-Glendale, CA Div 31084	31 324	521 067	66 261.5	26 244.3	12 760	359 532	163 829.6	19 852.8	20 298	355 736	22 965.1	6 390.6
Louisville/Jefferson County, KY-IN	3 045	26 012	3 734.3	1 286.6	1 223	65 362	37 466.2	3 253.0	2 382	56 076	2 984.5	793.9
Lubbock, TX	640	3 878	483.4	176.3	246	5 075	1 586.2	219.0	638	14 366	721.2	191.8
Lynchburg, VA	508	5 203	1 175.9	359.6	276	15 749	6 265.7	883.3	461	8 653	367.3	101.8
Macon, GA	467	2 857	365.3	128.7	154	5 041	1 729.2	234.4	470	8 864	394.7	109.9
Madera, CA	116	493	66.9	21.6	92	3 298	1 441.1	168.0	193	2 461	150.1	37.1
Madison, WI	1 917	20 780	3 515.0	1 348.2	734	31 666	12 491.6	1 595.6	1 567	29 215	1 330.4	378.2
Manchester-Nashua, NH	1 335	10 986	1 721.0	737.1	554	25 287	7 450.8	1 732.0	897	14 781	762.2	229.8
Manhattan, KS	198	D	D	D	60	1 847	472.0	93.5	201	4 325	164.5	46.5
Mankato-North Mankato, MN	189	1 540	173.9	77.6	138	7 573	4 903.6	321.6	208	4 343	170.1	46.8
Mansfield, OH	187	925	113.1	36.0	168	8 064	3 122.7	385.9	239	4 556	190.1	54.1
McAllen-Edinburg-Mission, TX	886	5 381	566.0	169.6	268	5 713	1 675.4	216.0	1 014	19 468	985.9	247.1
Medford, OR	506	D	D	D	308	5 370	1 624.6	217.4	586	7 381	382.2	112.5
Memphis, TN-MS-AR	2 112	19 494	2 687.2	1 117.7	846	34 515	26 369.2	1 846.8	2 239	55 258	3 253.0	858.2
Merced, CA	142	791	67.1	26.2	116	9 973	4 435.6	405.4	298	4 585	232.9	60.2
Miami-Fort Lauderdale-West Palm Beach, FL	28 955	142 450	26 210.5	9 220.5	4 452	63 174	16 753.9	2 987.1	11 402	234 634	16 293.0	4 445.0
Fort Lauderdale-Pompano Beach-Deerfield Beach, FL Div 22744	9 583	46 815	8 286.6	2 833.0	1 454	21 057	6 010.6	1 054.7	3 685	72 428	5 129.2	1 322.2
Miami-Miami Beach-Kendall, FL Div 33124	12 008	58 711	11 734.8	4 018.8	2 070	30 387	7 192.9	1 318.2	5 052	104 467	7 696.6	2 078.4
West Palm Beach-Boca Raton-Delray Beach, FL Div 48424	7 364	36 924	6 189.1	2 368.7	928	11 731	3 550.4	614.2	2 665	57 739	3 467.3	1 044.3
Michigan City-La Porte, IN	158	1 069	85.0	40.4	172	7 589	2 644.0	350.5	235	4 992	357.0	78.7
Midland, MI	154	785	87.9	34.9	62	6 241	3 591.1	466.1	138	2 861	136.2	40.7
Midland, TX	499	4 739	1 006.1	267.4	143	3 296	1 324.8	165.8	304	6 675	477.6	109.6
Milwaukee-Waukesha-West Allis, WI	3 841	40 983	6 746.8	2 630.0	2 465	114 114	40 901.0	6 604.8	3 179	59 849	2 856.5	780.7
Minneapolis-St. Paul-Bloomington, MN	13 160	111 963	20 342.0	8 273.1	4 641	176 842	71 530.0	10 348.0	6 596	144 111	7 830.5	2 217.4
Missoula, MT	501	2 865	325.4	137.2	102	1 351	310.6	49.1	342	6 106	317.4	84.0

Area name	Health care and social assistance, 2012				Other services, 2012				Nonemployer business, 2015		Value of residential construction authorized by building permits, 2016	
	Number of establishments	Number of employees	Receipts (mil dol)	Annual payroll (mil dol)	Number of establishments	Number of employees	Receipts (mil dol)	Annual payroll (mil dol)	Number	Receipts (mil dol)	New construction ($1,000)	Number of housing units
	159	160	161	162	163	164	165	166	167	168	169	170
Jonesboro, AR	405	9 349	958.7	378.4	151	D	D	D	9 048	419.5	105 616	1 028
Joplin, MO	474	12 922	1 236.6	588.5	288	1 496	119.0	35.0	10 344	433.9	51 782	422
Kahului-Wailuku-Lahaina, HI	393	6 138	741.5	308.2	383	2 185	238.1	62.0	16 174	788.5	151 108	567
Kalamazoo-Portage, MI	760	21 248	2 457.4	946.4	516	3 367	414.5	97.6	20 682	871.0	169 951	724
Kankakee, IL	311	7 349	753.9	294.5	180	956	100.3	25.1	6 193	214.8	18 964	86
Kansas City, MO-KS	5 421	133 626	15 085.9	5 992.9	3 361	22 120	3 219.6	701.1	142 397	6 646.3	1 884 251	10 389
Kennewick-Richland, WA	662	11 539	1 309.8	520.5	345	1 968	161.5	50.3	12 154	544.6	450 691	1 887
Killeen-Temple, TX	606	24 367	2 965.3	1 295.4	506	3 411	248.4	84.7	21 167	883.1	338 644	2 328
Kingsport-Bristol-Bristol, TN-VA	733	17 517	1 976.4	754.1	387	2 119	527.7	56.8	18 022	706.1	105 803	992
Kingston, NY	514	8 991	741.4	312.4	322	1 229	114.9	28.6	16 327	691.2	53 800	252
Knoxville, TN	1 987	53 573	5 749.5	2 129.1	1 162	8 068	755.7	251.4	60 935	2 964.3	664 218	3 637
Kokomo, IN	221	5 417	456.4	182.6	129	922	68.2	18.9	4 225	150.6	34 057	318
La Crosse-Onalaska, WI-MN	327	12 270	1 508.1	539.7	274	1 785	157.9	46.8	7 703	342.7	63 636	281
Lafayette, LA	1 533	32 257	3 120.9	1 178.7	715	5 199	674.7	168.1	41 190	1 785.9	318 524	1 698
Lafayette-West Lafayette, IN	424	11 181	1 217.2	433.2	276	1 907	218.4	49.4	11 041	478.2	121 763	627
Lake Charles, LA	521	12 330	1 209.9	457.2	244	1 617	178.0	51.1	14 099	645.2	223 938	1 563
Lake Havasu City-Kingman, AZ	478	8 222	995.0	364.2	290	1 394	110.3	29.4	10 592	461.3	133 961	683
Lakeland-Winter Haven, FL	1 048	27 066	3 015.2	1 109.8	673	3 366	328.5	94.6	41 872	1 618.1	752 640	4 567
Lancaster, PA	1 110	34 977	3 387.5	1 411.1	1 031	6 339	588.6	161.3	41 260	2 188.1	281 242	1 287
Lansing-East Lansing, MI	1 155	27 524	2 988.8	1 167.0	817	6 682	808.3	240.6	31 133	1 359.2	242 705	1 225
Laredo, TX	536	14 678	926.2	373.6	203	1 129	101.1	27.1	24 479	1 146.6	212 895	1 158
Las Cruces, NM	496	12 122	1 010.7	418.4	234	1 124	86.4	26.3	12 253	465.5	153 181	770
Las Vegas-Henderson-Paradise, NV	4 426	75 019	9 714.9	3 493.8	2 344	17 926	1 602.8	476.8	154 711	7 851.8	2 016 831	13 577
Lawrence, KS	289	6 580	545.8	211.1	181	1 423	230.7	37.2	8 004	329.5	143 555	1 395
Lawton, OK	282	6 960	709.7	273.2	141	846	70.7	21.3	5 063	219.8	18 507	100
Lebanon, PA	279	8 165	772.4	341.9	233	1 086	110.1	27.5	8 125	388.0	71 057	432
Lewiston, ID-WA	192	4 024	440.3	159.8	108	561	39.4	12.2	3 209	129.6	23 620	108
Lewiston-Auburn, ME	385	9 531	947.5	402.8	211	1 024	84.6	23.5	6 137	288.8	33 356	185
Lexington-Fayette, KY	1 524	34 868	4 154.5	1 607.9	792	5 378	821.8	163.5	35 556	1 678.2	353 999	2 732
Lima, OH	307	11 307	1 256.5	501.7	197	1 264	92.0	25.5	5 366	211.5	16 004	76
Lincoln, NE	1 007	23 965	2 418.6	963.5	705	4 286	593.7	134.2	21 942	860.9	374 904	2 384
Little Rock-North Little Rock-Conway, AR	2 067	52 656	5 908.8	2 359.2	1 178	8 198	1 001.5	238.3	50 928	2 245.8	367 900	2 327
Logan, UT-ID	373	5 431	519.3	170.7	191	D	D	D	9 455	368.1	162 618	897
Longview, TX	543	12 575	1 468.4	479.6	311	2 349	288.1	91.0	15 380	745.0	27 563	164
Longview, WA	240	5 444	567.0	232.1	148	D	D	D	4 469	182.6	65 525	308
Los Angeles-Long Beach-Anaheim, CA	40 695	651 603	87 943.5	31 496.0	20 823	146 211	17 344.3	4 317.7	1 323 907	71 793.1	7 355 806	32 114
Anaheim-Santa Ana-Irvine, CA Div 11244	10 873	152 659	20 682.2	7 379.9	4 980	35 537	3 782.2	1 039.3	NA	NA	2 445 261	11 523
Los Angeles-Long Beach-Glendale, CA Div 31084	29 822	498 944	67 261.3	24 116.1	15 843	110 674	13 562.1	3 278.3	NA	NA	4 910 545	20 591
Louisville/Jefferson County, KY-IN	3 410	86 187	9 206.9	3 559.7	1 965	16 301	1 665.5	481.2	85 248	3 855.9	815 393	5 149
Lubbock, TX	864	22 490	2 538.0	873.1	472	3 502	313.4	94.4	21 764	1 105.4	450 835	2 648
Lynchburg, VA	572	13 913	1 313.6	539.9	452	2 320	207.0	60.3	14 632	541.7	127 500	663
Macon, GA	642	16 370	1 869.5	686.3	318	1 831	220.9	58.8	18 146	618.2	45 976	236
Madera, CA	204	5 871	761.0	321.0	112	489	45.2	11.8	7 161	350.2	52 021	300
Madison, WI	1 473	49 078	5 684.6	2 239.3	1 298	9 034	1 314.3	300.0	45 196	2 195.3	900 633	4 953
Manchester-Nashua, NH	1 094	28 561	3 089.1	1 339.9	824	5 516	490.3	160.3	28 477	1 657.8	188 178	1 097
Manhattan, KS	230	4 249	391.3	142.5	172	1 252	223.3	48.7	5 122	224.0	136 282	962
Mankato-North Mankato, MN	301	11 383	823.6	416.8	186	1 230	262.3	31.3	6 242	268.6	73 408	404
Mansfield, OH	316	7 570	674.5	274.6	209	1 186	108.4	25.3	6 844	281.9	16 502	69
McAllen-Edinburg-Mission, TX	2 048	54 356	3 479.0	1 471.2	571	3 701	350.3	84.2	69 823	2 680.3	637 566	4 568
Medford, OR	674	12 116	1 443.8	510.7	315	1 836	157.3	51.0	16 786	753.1	192 114	912
Memphis, TN-MS-AR	2 948	80 010	9 324.5	3 561.1	1 557	12 365	2 119.0	414.4	108 553	4 160.9	724 436	4 354
Merced, CA	427	6 718	788.1	302.8	183	895	72.4	26.3	10 850	545.0	114 818	720
Miami-Fort Lauderdale-West Palm Beach, FL	20 622	297 739	39 497.8	13 743.7	12 231	68 020	7 193.6	1 854.5	885 524	38 524.4	4 207 477	18 742
Fort Lauderdale-Pompano Beach-Deerfield Beach, FL Div 22744	6 273	89 756	12 193.7	4 272.6	4 124	21 448	2 245.9	602.5	NA	NA	846 723	4 105
Miami-Miami Beach-Kendall, FL Div 33124	9 030	132 886	17 547.4	6 100.1	4 903	28 561	3 116.7	758.0	NA	NA	2 088 260	9 317
West Palm Beach-Boca Raton-Delray Beach, FL Div 48424	5 319	75 097	9 756.7	3 371.0	3 204	18 011	1 831.0	493.9	NA	NA	1 272 494	5 320
Michigan City-La Porte, IN	228	5 626	611.2	208.3	194	1 090	79.0	22.5	5 858	206.4	21 719	108
Midland, MI	239	6 268	682.2	242.8	147	882	113.0	23.2	4 899	192.0	26 204	201
Midland, TX	405	7 331	829.3	304.4	272	2 159	340.6	74.2	16 579	1 137.7	130 498	676
Milwaukee-Waukesha-West Allis, WI	4 732	123 973	13 694.3	5 445.8	2 736	20 368	2 267.0	636.2	89 843	4 337.4	840 118	4 055
Minneapolis-St. Paul-Bloomington, MN	9 429	270 065	26 555.5	11 497.3	6 672	51 085	5 701.2	1 543.4	264 395	12 575.8	3 346 588	14 160
Missoula, MT	489	9 292	965.9	351.1	287	1 889	258.2	56.0	9 848	453.1	90 195	930

1. Establishments subject to federal tax.

Table C. Metropolitan Areas

Government Employment and Payroll and Local Government Finances

Area name	Government employment and payroll, 2012									Local government finances, 2012				
			March payroll (percent of total)							General revenue				
												Taxes		
													Per capita[1] (dollars)	
	Full-time equivalent employees	March Payroll (dollars)	Administration, judicial, and legal	Police and corrections	Fire protection	Highways and transportation	Health and welfare	Natural resources and utilities	Education and libraries	Total (mil dol)	Inter-governmental (mil dol)	Total (mil dol)	Total	Property
	171	172	173	174	175	176	177	178	179	180	181	182	183	184
Jonesboro, AR	4 524	13 523 979	4.9	9.6	2.5	3.7	1.1	9.1	68.6	354.5	215.8	87.8	708	311
Joplin, MO	6 292	18 337 340	4.7	8.3	3.6	3.0	2.0	3.3	74.4	510.9	199.2	185.7	1 065	527
Kahului-Wailuku-Lahaina, HI..	2 328	11 762 934	19.0	23.7	16.4	6.9	6.2	25.4	0.0	252.6	23.1	224.7	1 419	1 316
Kalamazoo-Portage, MI	9 976	43 436 306	7.0	10.5	12.8	2.9	6.0	3.3	56.6	1 340.8	705.4	408.5	1 238	1 210
Kankakee, IL	4 413	16 356 166	7.8	13.5	3.6	3.7	1.5	3.4	65.4	441.9	208.0	169.2	1 496	1 433
Kansas City, MO-KS	86 196	339 122 341	5.7	9.8	5.2	3.5	13.8	6.1	54.6	9 183.3	2 533.9	4 159.3	2 040	1 219
Kennewick-Richland, WA	10 152	53 295 192	5.2	7.0	3.2	4.4	10.2	28.7	40.3	1 194.4	543.2	325.4	1 213	704
Killeen-Temple, TX	19 513	61 961 488	4.6	8.5	3.2	1.8	4.0	4.2	72.6	1 379.2	598.6	457.1	1 087	854
Kingsport-Bristol-Bristol, TN-VA	11 566	36 313 120	5.1	10.8	2.2	3.5	5.1	5.7	66.0	805.9	377.3	312.3	1 011	695
Kingston, NY	8 282	38 442 668	5.7	7.7	1.3	4.8	8.8	1.7	68.0	1 095.2	330.4	630.3	3 467	2 848
Knoxville, TN	29 145	97 687 242	5.6	9.5	2.6	3.1	10.2	13.4	54.2	2 517.0	845.0	1 010.5	1 191	718
Kokomo, IN	4 091	15 459 399	5.0	6.2	3.5	2.0	35.8	3.0	42.2	435.8	136.7	118.7	1 433	1 170
La Crosse-Onalaska, WI-MN .	5 559	21 504 753	6.0	8.2	2.4	4.3	16.8	4.2	57.0	720.4	365.8	237.4	1 755	1 630
Lafayette, LA	17 787	55 296 831	6.7	12.0	3.2	3.4	8.4	8.0	57.3	1 668.5	663.9	685.1	1 444	587
Lafayette-West Lafayette, IN .	5 636	18 225 886	7.4	11.9	4.8	5.8	2.8	5.4	60.9	552.8	259.3	207.6	1 006	798
Lake Charles, LA	9 670	30 588 485	5.1	13.5	3.3	5.8	7.9	5.3	57.2	1 055.7	360.2	475.0	2 361	1 046
Lake Havasu City-Kingman, AZ	5 613	20 393 845	13.0	13.4	11.7	4.5	2.0	5.6	47.4	538.5	183.2	229.9	1 131	849
Lakeland-Winter Haven, FL ...	22 910	75 047 946	7.9	12.5	4.2	2.1	2.6	10.6	56.6	1 844.2	710.5	644.8	1 047	726
Lancaster, PA	12 622	54 624 168	5.9	11.7	0.8	2.8	3.4	3.5	70.9	1 833.2	668.6	843.7	1 601	1 327
Lansing-East Lansing, MI	15 249	64 035 635	8.2	8.0	3.0	4.4	9.2	6.8	56.5	1 895.2	923.3	587.0	1 260	1 174
Laredo, TX	14 741	48 977 584	5.1	9.2	5.1	3.0	3.0	3.7	70.4	1 245.0	614.2	391.8	1 512	1 216
Las Cruces, NM	7 916	26 726 295	5.8	10.4	2.7	2.6	2.1	5.9	66.7	732.8	425.3	209.7	978	447
Las Vegas-Henderson-Paradise, NV	51 796	300 546 553	8.1	16.4	5.9	3.4	8.6	10.1	45.3	8 606.7	3 678.4	2 735.1	1 367	869
Lawrence, KS	4 535	18 551 008	5.6	11.2	5.0	2.9	33.2	7.9	33.4	537.2	114.0	188.6	1 671	1 239
Lawton, OK	6 503	22 717 032	3.8	5.7	3.0	2.2	36.2	3.3	45.2	523.3	171.6	106.3	802	354
Lebanon, PA	4 116	14 939 586	6.1	9.0	1.7	2.8	9.0	5.5	65.4	485.8	160.6	191.5	1 416	1 136
Lewiston, ID-WA	2 076	7 939 079	7.0	11.4	5.6	6.0	7.0	7.6	51.8	188.3	89.3	64.0	1 042	932
Lewiston-Auburn, ME	3 959	13 779 680	4.1	8.3	4.8	4.2	2.0	5.1	70.2	355.6	153.6	163.3	1 517	1 507
Lexington-Fayette, KY	16 579	58 038 313	4.2	11.6	6.9	2.1	7.1	4.3	61.5	1 418.6	398.6	746.8	1 540	758
Lima, OH	4 029	14 917 726	8.3	9.1	4.8	3.4	9.8	5.8	55.9	394.8	197.5	125.6	1 195	774
Lincoln, NE	11 413	48 128 898	5.2	7.7	3.8	4.5	4.1	11.5	61.4	1 034.8	326.0	505.1	1 628	1 186
Little Rock-North Little Rock-Conway, AR	24 915	82 533 612	5.8	10.8	5.3	3.7	2.5	8.9	61.2	2 303.6	1 228.7	601.7	838	423
Logan, UT-ID	3 888	12 693 319	7.2	7.0	2.3	3.6	11.8	5.5	59.8	338.7	155.8	113.9	888	560
Longview, TX	9 132	29 631 047	5.5	10.9	3.9	2.0	4.4	4.8	66.6	721.4	245.0	370.6	1 710	1 319
Longview, WA	3 301	15 112 407	7.8	11.6	3.0	7.2	3.7	14.2	51.3	420.9	170.2	127.1	1 246	848
Los Angeles-Long Beach-Anaheim, CA	471 707	2 757 691 350	8.8	12.1	4.7	5.2	12.5	8.6	45.7	77 422.5	34 902.2	24 415.1	1 870	1 275
Anaheim-Santa Ana-Irvine, CA Div 11244	85 251	527 595 855	5.4	11.0	4.8	3.1	7.4	5.7	58.4	14 543.9	5 867.6	5 580.4	1 806	1 406
Los Angeles-Long Beach-Glendale, CA Div 31084	386 456	2 230 095 495	9.6	12.3	4.7	5.7	13.7	9.3	42.7	62 878.6	29 034.6	18 834.7	1 891	1 234
Louisville/Jefferson County, KY-IN	45 148	162 939 795	3.7	9.1	3.7	3.4	14.2	6.3	58.2	4 084.7	1 333.6	1 583.1	1 265	787
Lubbock, TX	13 751	49 840 306	4.7	10.3	4.2	1.2	27.8	5.7	45.1	1 319.2	362.2	422.7	1 420	1 113
Lynchburg, VA	9 196	26 684 206	6.4	11.2	3.2	1.3	7.0	5.1	63.4	712.1	348.1	270.1	1 058	752
Macon, GA	9 317	31 505 415	6.5	10.3	4.0	2.8	5.6	5.3	64.2	803.6	331.4	347.0	1 491	1 002
Madera, CA	4 578	20 019 402	8.1	8.1	0.2	2.2	10.1	5.2	64.4	627.3	366.3	154.2	1 013	706
Madison, WI	23 987	100 319 066	5.9	10.2	2.5	6.5	6.7	6.3	60.2	2 887.9	993.2	1 412.8	2 276	2 136
Manchester-Nashua, NH	13 991	56 054 764	4.1	10.8	6.0	4.5	3.9	3.8	65.8	1 458.9	470.6	808.2	2 006	1 981
Manhattan, KS	3 088	9 783 062	8.5	11.2	3.9	5.6	3.6	7.1	58.8	275.9	79.3	146.5	1 497	1 108
Mankato-North Mankato, MN .	3 049	12 248 005	8.1	9.4	1.0	5.0	10.7	5.9	57.5	419.6	200.3	109.1	1 113	999
Mansfield, OH	5 091	18 513 991	8.5	9.4	5.0	4.1	11.2	8.3	52.0	473.0	237.7	163.9	1 336	864
McAllen-Edinburg-Mission, TX	39 042	129 583 687	3.7	6.7	1.7	1.6	2.9	3.9	78.6	3 159.2	1 926.2	864.1	1 071	868
Medford, OR	4 931	20 369 335	9.1	14.6	6.5	6.1	5.2	6.8	45.2	668.0	291.3	260.8	1 263	1 068
Memphis, TN-MS-AR	53 881	181 275 652	6.8	14.3	6.6	4.1	9.1	12.2	45.2	5 455.9	2 056.3	2 087.0	1 555	1 086
Merced, CA	10 959	49 202 192	6.5	7.6	1.6	1.1	10.0	6.7	63.4	1 305.5	840.8	219.3	836	680
Miami-Fort Lauderdale-West Palm Beach, FL	222 370	1 025 593 818	5.5	14.7	6.9	4.6	20.6	7.6	34.5	30 329.9	7 063.4	12 134.4	2 106	1 662
Fort Lauderdale-Pompano Beach-Deerfield Beach, FL Div 22744	73 864	331 154 408	5.1	13.2	6.2	3.7	29.6	6.0	33.6	9 918.0	2 186.8	3 161.3	1 742	1 392
Miami-Miami Beach-Kendall, FL Div 33124	102 308	498 941 928	4.9	14.9	6.0	5.9	20.8	6.6	32.3	14 058.6	3 695.7	5 524.1	2 132	1 564
West Palm Beach-Boca Raton-Delray Beach, FL Div 48424	46 198	195 497 482	7.6	16.4	10.2	2.6	5.1	13.1	41.6	6 353.4	1 180.9	3 449.0	2 542	2 211
Michigan City-La Porte, IN ...	4 264	12 639 630	5.9	11.9	4.3	3.5	3.5	6.6	63.1	369.8	180.5	137.0	1 231	1 055
Midland, MI	2 175	9 622 686	11.4	7.8	3.3	4.0	3.3	5.7	62.5	271.7	113.5	103.5	1 235	1 220
Midland, TX	7 075	27 853 270	5.2	7.7	3.9	1.9	29.9	1.6	47.9	800.8	131.1	362.9	2 393	1 787
Milwaukee-Waukesha-West Allis, WI	53 007	250 453 387	5.4	13.5	4.4	4.2	8.1	4.6	57.7	7 417.1	2 812.4	3 111.6	1 986	1 860
Minneapolis-St. Paul-Bloomington, MN	104 532	577 809 573	7.1	9.9	1.7	3.7	7.6	5.5	63.0	15 990.0	6 976.7	5 332.5	1 558	1 450
Missoula, MT	3 035	11 623 602	8.8	11.6	6.2	6.3	5.7	3.6	55.2	333.0	140.7	131.9	1 189	1 156

1. Based on the resident population estimated as of July 1 of the year shown.

Table C. Metropolitan Areas — Local Government Finances, Government Employment, and Income Taxes

Area name	Local government finances, 2012 (cont.)									Government employment, 2015			Individual income tax returns, 2014		
	Direct general expenditure							Debt outstanding							
			Percent of total for:												
	Total (mil dol)	Per capita[1] (dollars)	Education	Health and hospitals	Police protection	Public welfare	Highways	Total (mil dol)	Per capita[1] (dollars)	Federal civilian	Federal military	State and local	Number of returns	Mean Adjusted Gross income	Mean income tax
	185	186	187	188	189	190	191	192	193	194	195	196	197	198	199
Jonesboro, AR	344.4	2 776	59.5	0.3	5.9	0.1	5.2	518.7	4 182	381	537	9 019	50 540	49 381	5 492
Joplin, MO	524.5	3 009	58.0	8.8	4.8	0.2	5.1	349.6	2 005	434	628	9 053	75 550	45 948	4 748
Kahului-Wailuku-Lahaina, HI	264.1	1 668	0.0	0.0	15.8	6.0	2.7	281.6	1 779	813	1 155	9 082	78 530	53 599	6 078
Kalamazoo-Portage, MI	1 323.6	4 011	48.7	15.6	6.2	1.0	5.0	1 469.4	4 452	840	536	18 692	154 020	57 511	7 181
Kankakee, IL	442.3	3 912	52.1	0.7	6.1	0.1	5.9	327.2	2 894	237	214	6 062	50 580	50 795	5 195
Kansas City, MO-KS	8 722.0	4 278	43.2	9.9	7.0	0.6	5.4	16 793.0	8 237	27 188	11 408	123 194	982 620	66 575	9 006
Kennewick-Richland, WA	1 130.0	4 213	43.9	21.1	4.0	0.0	3.7	7 044.2	26 261	1 228	763	17 795	118 850	59 224	6 833
Killeen-Temple, TX	1 411.2	3 357	57.9	3.8	4.8	0.5	5.9	2 196.8	5 226	10 420	40 210	26 870	179 900	46 421	4 586
Kingsport-Bristol-Bristol, TN-VA	860.9	2 786	50.0	3.8	6.6	1.8	4.1	782.5	2 532	883	937	15 571	130 240	48 145	5 217
Kingston, NY	1 119.8	6 160	51.1	2.0	2.8	12.1	5.4	695.1	3 823	465	286	12 926	86 150	58 072	6 905
Knoxville, TN	2 428.1	2 862	43.0	9.6	6.5	0.1	3.1	4 983.9	5 875	5 374	2 700	52 736	377 610	58 179	7 656
Kokomo, IN	406.5	4 907	32.7	36.7	3.9	0.3	1.8	200.3	2 417	197	252	4 975	40 210	48 103	4 971
La Crosse-Onalaska, WI-MN	720.8	5 328	43.6	2.8	4.0	21.7	5.6	467.2	3 453	527	372	11 050	65 130	58 034	6 910
Lafayette, LA	1 702.8	3 589	44.6	7.6	6.9	0.4	5.4	2 036.0	4 292	1 367	2 176	24 123	214 780	63 620	9 152
Lafayette-West Lafayette, IN	486.9	2 359	51.4	0.5	5.8	0.7	6.1	413.5	2 003	540	669	24 989	87 650	53 888	6 264
Lake Charles, LA	995.9	4 950	38.4	7.2	6.5	0.4	6.8	2 332.0	11 591	543	976	13 260	89 740	57 897	7 205
Lake Havasu City-Kingman, AZ	555.1	2 730	33.9	2.7	6.9	0.1	8.7	627.7	3 087	463	448	7 167	79 020	40 480	3 781
Lakeland-Winter Haven, FL	1 992.7	3 234	48.6	3.2	8.2	1.6	5.5	2 776.3	4 506	1 065	1 238	26 233	275 310	46 114	4 850
Lancaster, PA	2 018.4	3 831	55.1	5.4	4.3	5.1	3.3	3 447.0	6 543	1 216	1 379	19 280	261 550	58 202	6 956
Lansing-East Lansing, MI	1 885.3	4 048	47.2	10.6	4.5	3.4	4.3	2 304.1	4 947	1 921	928	47 454	213 510	55 139	6 562
Laredo, TX	1 204.4	4 647	58.3	1.3	6.0	0.4	1.5	1 569.6	6 056	3 233	542	18 957	108 850	40 922	4 024
Las Cruces, NM	719.6	3 356	57.5	1.3	6.7	1.9	4.1	440.1	2 052	3 507	559	16 910	90 410	41 616	4 192
Las Vegas-Henderson-Paradise, NV	9 171.7	4 584	29.1	8.3	9.6	2.7	7.2	21 727.8	10 860	12 686	15 101	84 204	957 920	56 714	7 755
Lawrence, KS	474.7	4 206	28.6	35.1	4.9	0.0	3.3	544.9	4 828	428	469	15 406	50 280	59 019	7 364
Lawton, OK	533.8	4 027	37.6	38.9	4.3	0.0	3.4	253.8	1 915	4 081	11 432	10 812	51 720	45 496	4 212
Lebanon, PA	507.4	3 752	47.7	2.2	2.9	15.0	5.1	705.4	5 215	3 023	352	4 943	67 730	52 410	5 543
Lewiston, ID-WA	188.3	3 065	43.4	3.1	7.2	0.1	7.4	47.1	767	250	195	5 031	28 190	51 866	5 523
Lewiston-Auburn, ME	348.5	3 239	53.0	0.2	4.0	0.4	5.6	353.5	3 285	259	341	5 104	48 600	46 213	4 466
Lexington-Fayette, KY	1 363.2	2 811	49.9	3.2	5.3	0.7	2.2	2 544.8	5 247	4 451	1 569	46 068	223 010	57 773	7 307
Lima, OH	385.4	3 665	49.5	5.4	6.9	4.3	6.7	180.7	1 719	322	258	5 794	47 950	49 038	5 391
Lincoln, NE	1 130.3	3 642	53.2	1.9	4.3	0.9	6.9	2 872.1	9 255	3 274	1 132	31 262	147 980	60 238	7 191
Little Rock-North Little Rock-Conway, AR	2 292.8	3 195	53.1	2.7	6.0	0.0	4.2	3 061.0	4 265	9 664	7 441	60 709	321 860	58 752	7 251
Logan, UT-ID	308.4	2 404	52.6	4.4	6.1	0.3	5.4	194.5	1 516	372	543	11 218	50 800	51 449	4 677
Longview, TX	736.4	3 399	58.8	4.2	5.0	0.0	4.6	1 187.1	5 479	476	424	11 237	93 460	56 238	6 917
Longview, WA	424.6	4 163	38.6	3.9	5.4	0.0	4.9	609.4	5 974	226	279	5 696	44 530	52 586	5 509
Los Angeles-Long Beach-Anaheim, CA	74 228.5	5 687	36.2	9.6	7.8	8.4	3.3	106 636.6	8 170	59 140	22 586	668 221	6 036 120	70 869	10 837
Anaheim-Santa Ana-Irvine, CA Div 11244	13 915.7	4 503	41.4	2.9	7.7	7.3	4.5	22 316.3	7 222	11 271	5 151	140 943	NA	NA	NA
Los Angeles-Long Beach-Glendale, CA Div 31084	60 312.8	6 054	35.0	11.1	7.8	8.7	3.1	84 320.3	8 464	47 869	17 435	527 278	NA	NA	NA
Louisville/Jefferson County, KY-IN	4 180.4	3 341	44.5	11.9	4.0	0.3	2.5	7 079.6	5 658	8 718	4 145	67 728	608 430	57 177	7 006
Lubbock, TX	1 388.9	4 666	35.4	31.5	4.7	0.1	2.3	2 311.9	7 767	1 335	648	28 584	131 430	55 093	7 217
Lynchburg, VA	701.3	2 747	47.7	1.7	5.7	7.2	1.9	641.2	2 511	564	817	13 240	112 980	53 084	5 757
Macon, GA	816.9	3 510	46.8	7.0	6.4	0.3	2.9	577.8	2 483	1 131	622	13 374	97 680	48 985	5 491
Madera, CA	649.2	4 265	45.6	3.7	3.9	8.8	6.2	475.5	3 124	309	223	9 137	57 880	44 872	4 422
Madison, WI	2 933.1	4 725	47.0	1.8	6.0	8.3	7.1	3 254.4	5 243	5 422	1 777	81 392	321 980	69 441	9 341
Manchester-Nashua, NH	1 496.1	3 713	52.0	0.6	6.1	3.8	4.7	1 157.0	2 872	4 018	1 372	17 505	209 830	69 487	9 556
Manhattan, KS	320.7	3 239	52.2	2.1	6.0	0.0	6.6	601.2	6 146	479	393	12 705	38 190	54 192	6 026
Mankato-North Mankato, MN	409.8	4 181	36.2	5.3	4.8	5.7	13.5	455.8	4 650	284	356	8 096	45 560	59 262	7 796
Mansfield, OH	480.9	3 920	52.3	8.7	5.0	4.8	5.5	209.0	1 703	626	295	7 108	56 820	44 570	4 473
McAllen-Edinburg-Mission, TX	3 161.8	3 920	67.1	2.0	3.8	0.5	2.9	3 738.4	4 635	4 062	1 739	52 619	303 160	37 673	3 349
Medford, OR	678.0	3 285	42.6	5.3	8.6	0.0	6.1	887.0	4 297	1 834	542	8 837	96 950	51 323	5 622
Memphis, TN-MS-AR	5 764.4	4 296	46.3	6.7	8.6	0.9	2.8	6 748.2	5 030	14 037	5 838	68 274	617 970	54 668	7 082
Merced, CA	1 403.1	5 349	48.6	3.6	4.1	10.0	2.7	901.0	3 435	763	396	17 406	98 680	43 482	3 975
Miami-Fort Lauderdale-West Palm Beach, FL	31 257.3	5 424	25.8	15.2	8.8	2.5	2.0	39 629.0	6 877	33 557	14 088	268 767	2 882 710	65 631	11 131
Fort Lauderdale-Pompano Beach-Deerfield Beach, FL Div 22744	10 214.0	5 627	24.6	26.3	10.2	1.2	1.4	8 639.5	4 760	6 879	3 952	94 919	NA	NA	NA
Miami-Miami Beach-Kendall, FL Div 33124	14 468.1	5 584	25.8	12.2	7.5	3.5	2.2	23 549.3	9 089	19 917	7 407	118 473	NA	NA	NA
West Palm Beach-Boca Raton-Delray Beach, FL Div 48424	6 575.2	4 847	27.6	4.7	9.3	2.5	2.5	7 440.3	5 485	6 761	2 729	55 375	NA	NA	NA
Michigan City-La Porte, IN	330.9	2 974	53.0	1.0	4.1	0.3	2.3	311.4	2 799	171	341	6 649	51 490	49 230	5 332
Midland, MI	272.5	3 250	51.0	2.8	4.1	2.1	7.6	318.6	3 800	146	133	3 270	40 170	71 048	10 399
Midland, TX	864.5	5 700	32.3	45.1	3.2	0.0	1.2	654.6	4 316	553	336	9 024	76 990	118 358	23 801
Milwaukee-Waukesha-West Allis, WI	7 419.0	4 735	44.0	7.8	7.8	3.4	5.7	8 456.0	5 396	10 680	4 481	77 403	767 170	66 114	8 997
Minneapolis-St. Paul-Bloomington, MN	16 677.1	4 873	39.7	6.9	5.5	5.4	7.0	24 523.9	7 166	20 635	12 828	225 604	1 751 440	76 213	10 849
Missoula, MT	338.7	3 052	44.0	5.5	7.0	0.8	5.2	188.8	1 701	1 349	520	9 354	55 820	58 631	7 528

1. Based on the resident population estimated as of July 1 of the year shown.

Table C. Metropolitan Areas — **Land Area and Population**

CBSA/ DIV code[1]	Area name	Land area,[2] 2016 (sq mi)	Total persons	Rank	Per square mile	White	Black	American Indian, Alaska Native	Asian and Pacific Islander	Percent Hispanic or Latino[3]	Under 5 years	5 to 17 years	18 to 24 years	25 to 34 years	35 to 44 years	45 to 54 years
		1	2	3	4	5	6	7	8	9	10	11	12	13	14	15
33660	Mobile, AL	1 229.4	414 836	128	337.4	58.6	36.3	1.5	2.4	2.8	6.5	17.2	9.3	13.9	11.9	12.7
33700	Modesto, CA	1 496.0	541 560	102	362.0	45.0	3.3	1.3	7.6	45.6	7.2	19.9	9.6	14.4	12.5	12.3
33740	Monroe, LA	1 487.4	179 470	232	120.7	60.5	36.4	0.6	1.2	2.5	6.9	18.1	9.7	13.9	12.1	12.2
33780	Monroe, MI	549.4	149 208	278	271.6	93.2	3.1	0.9	1.0	3.5	5.3	16.6	8.0	11.5	11.7	14.6
33860	Montgomery, AL	2 713.2	373 922	142	137.8	50.0	45.1	0.7	2.6	3.1	6.4	16.8	9.4	14.1	12.9	13.1
34060	Morgantown, WV	1 008.9	138 380	293	137.2	92.0	4.1	0.6	3.3	1.9	5.3	11.9	17.8	16.8	12.0	11.4
34100	Morristown, TN	436.0	117 320	328	269.1	88.0	3.8	0.8	1.1	7.8	5.6	16.2	8.4	11.3	12.1	14.0
34580	Mount Vernon-Anacortes, WA	1 730.1	123 681	317	71.5	77.1	1.3	2.8	3.3	18.0	6.1	15.9	8.1	12.3	11.3	12.0
34620	Muncie, IN	392.1	115 603	331	294.8	89.0	8.3	0.7	1.9	2.3	5.2	13.5	19.6	11.3	10.1	11.7
34740	Muskegon, MI	500.0	173 408	239	346.8	78.7	15.6	1.6	1.1	5.6	6.2	17.3	8.6	12.8	11.9	13.1
34820	Myrtle Beach-Conway-North Myrtle Beach, NC-SC	1 983.5	449 295	118	226.5	80.3	13.2	1.1	1.6	5.6	4.8	13.2	7.0	11.3	11.0	12.5
34900	Napa, CA	748.3	142 166	290	190.0	55.0	2.6	1.1	9.8	33.9	5.3	16.0	8.8	12.3	12.5	13.5
34940	Naples-Immokalee-Marco Island, FL	1 998.8	365 136	145	182.7	64.6	7.2	0.4	1.8	27.0	4.6	13.0	6.6	9.7	9.8	11.9
34980	Nashville-Davidson—Murfreesboro—Franklin, TN	6 301.9	1 865 298	36	296.0	74.6	16.3	0.8	3.4	7.1	6.5	17.0	9.4	15.0	13.6	13.5
35100	New Bern, NC	1 514.6	126 111	312	83.3	68.5	23.0	1.1	3.3	6.5	6.1	15.1	11.4	13.0	10.5	11.1
35300	New Haven-Milford, CT	604.5	856 875	65	1 417.5	65.2	13.6	0.6	4.8	17.6	5.2	15.4	10.1	13.3	11.7	14.1
35380	New Orleans-Metairie, LA	3 202.1	1 268 883	46	396.3	53.1	35.4	0.9	3.4	8.8	6.2	16.2	8.4	15.2	12.7	13.1
35620	New York-Newark-Jersey City, NY-NJ-PA	8 294.6	20 153 634	1	2 429.7	48.0	16.7	0.5	12.1	24.3	6.1	15.7	9.0	14.7	13.1	14.0
35620	.Dutchess County-Putnam County, NY Div 20524	1 025.9	393 373	X	383.4	75.4	9.2	0.6	4.2	12.6	4.5	15.1	10.6	11.2	11.5	15.8
35620	.Nassau County-Suffolk County, NY Div 35004	1 196.6	2 854 083	X	2 385.2	65.7	9.9	0.4	7.4	18.0	5.3	16.4	9.2	11.5	12.0	15.2
35620	.Newark, NJ-PA Div 35084	2 482.8	2 507 478	X	1 009.9	53.0	20.0	0.4	8.4	19.7	5.7	17.0	8.7	12.0	13.1	15.4
35620	.New York-Jersey City-White Plains, NY-NJ Div 35614	3 589.2	14 398 700	X	4 011.7	42.8	17.7	0.5	14.0	26.7	6.3	15.4	9.0	15.9	13.4	13.4
35660	Niles-Benton Harbor, MI	567.8	154 010	265	271.2	77.3	16.0	1.2	2.6	5.3	5.9	16.3	8.4	11.5	11.3	13.3
35840	North Port-Sarasota-Bradenton, FL	1 298.9	788 457	73	607.0	79.2	7.1	0.6	2.3	12.3	4.3	12.4	6.3	9.4	9.4	12.2
35980	Norwich-New London, CT	665.1	269 801	177	405.7	78.3	7.3	1.8	5.5	10.4	5.1	14.8	10.3	13.0	11.0	14.2
36100	Ocala, FL	1 588.0	349 020	149	219.8	72.8	13.3	0.8	2.2	12.5	5.1	13.7	6.8	10.7	9.7	11.9
36140	Ocean City, NJ	252.1	94 430	363	374.6	86.7	5.2	0.5	1.5	7.6	4.9	12.9	8.1	10.5	9.1	13.0
36220	Odessa, TX	897.7	157 462	261	175.4	34.4	4.7	0.8	1.3	59.7	9.3	20.9	10.4	16.5	12.3	10.8
36260	Ogden-Clearfield, UT	7 230.0	654 417	85	90.5	83.6	1.7	0.9	3.4	12.5	8.4	22.9	9.3	14.4	13.9	10.7
36420	Oklahoma City, OK	5 511.6	1 373 211	41	249.1	69.0	12.0	6.7	4.2	13.0	7.0	17.9	10.0	15.1	12.8	12.0
36500	Olympia-Tumwater, WA	722.5	275 222	173	380.9	79.9	4.6	2.7	9.4	8.6	5.9	15.8	8.4	14.3	12.9	12.8
36540	Omaha-Council Bluffs, NE-IA	4 350.0	924 129	59	212.4	78.6	8.8	1.0	3.6	10.3	7.3	18.5	8.9	14.6	13.0	12.6
36740	Orlando-Kissimmee-Sanford, FL	3 481.3	2 441 257	23	701.2	49.8	16.7	0.6	5.3	29.5	6.0	16.2	9.6	15.2	13.4	13.5
36780	Oshkosh-Neenah, WI	434.5	169 886	245	391.0	90.6	2.7	1.0	3.3	4.0	5.5	15.2	12.0	13.2	11.8	13.5
36980	Owensboro, KY	898.5	117 959	326	131.3	91.7	5.5	0.4	1.5	2.7	6.7	17.7	8.0	12.3	11.9	13.2
37100	Oxnard-Thousand Oaks-Ventura, CA	1 843.0	849 738	67	461.1	47.9	2.2	0.8	9.0	42.5	6.1	17.4	9.6	13.2	12.4	13.8
37340	Palm Bay-Melbourne-Titusville, FL	1 015.4	579 130	95	570.3	77.2	11.1	0.9	3.4	9.9	4.8	13.7	7.3	11.0	10.1	13.7
37460	Panama City, FL	1 312.0	199 964	220	152.4	79.3	12.7	1.5	3.4	6.2	6.1	14.9	8.1	14.5	12.0	13.6
37620	Parkersburg-Vienna, WV	598.8	91 449	365	152.7	96.9	2.0	0.7	0.9	1.1	5.7	15.6	7.4	11.6	12.0	13.8
37860	Pensacola-Ferry Pass-Brent, FL	1 668.6	485 684	109	291.1	73.7	18.0	1.7	4.3	5.6	5.9	15.4	10.7	14.2	11.4	12.9
37900	Peoria, IL	2 468.8	376 246	141	152.4	84.4	10.7	0.6	2.9	3.5	6.4	17.0	8.3	12.8	12.3	12.7
37980	Philadelphia-Camden-Wilmington, PA-NJ-DE-MD	4 602.6	6 070 500	7	1 318.9	63.9	21.6	0.6	6.6	9.2	5.9	16.1	9.2	14.2	12.2	13.8
37980	.Camden, NJ Div 15804	1 342.2	1 251 764	X	932.6	67.8	17.1	0.6	5.7	10.9	5.6	16.6	8.7	13.0	12.4	14.6
37980	.Montgomery County-Bucks County-Chester County, PA Div 33874	1 837.9	1 964 436	X	1 068.8	81.4	7.5	0.4	6.7	5.7	5.4	16.5	8.4	11.7	12.1	14.7
37980	.Philadelphia, PA Div 37964	318.1	2 131 274	X	6 700.0	45.0	37.2	0.7	7.6	11.6	6.6	15.5	10.4	17.3	12.1	12.3
37980	.Wilmington, DE-MD-NJ Div 48864	1 104.4	723 026	X	654.7	65.3	22.1	0.7	5.1	8.9	5.8	16.3	9.3	14.0	12.1	14.2
38060	Phoenix-Mesa-Scottsdale, AZ	14 565.0	4 661 537	12	320.1	58.1	6.1	2.5	5.0	30.6	6.6	17.8	9.2	14.2	13.0	12.7
38220	Pine Bluff, AR	2 030.1	91 962	364	45.3	48.1	49.0	0.8	1.0	2.3	5.9	16.2	9.9	13.4	12.0	13.0
38300	Pittsburgh, PA	5 281.4	2 342 299	26	443.5	87.3	9.5	0.5	2.8	1.7	5.1	14.0	8.5	13.3	11.3	13.5
38340	Pittsfield, MA	926.9	126 903	308	136.9	90.9	4.1	0.6	2.1	4.3	4.2	13.1	9.7	10.4	10.2	14.0
38540	Pocatello, ID	1 112.5	84 377	371	75.8	86.3	1.3	3.6	2.3	8.4	7.3	19.2	10.0	15.4	12.2	10.5
38860	Portland-South Portland, ME	2 080.4	529 657	104	254.6	94.1	2.5	0.9	2.4	1.8	4.9	14.3	8.3	12.6	11.7	14.6
38900	Portland-Vancouver-Hillsboro, OR-WA	6 686.6	2 424 955	25	362.7	77.4	3.9	1.7	9.1	11.7	5.9	16.0	8.2	15.2	14.4	13.4
38940	Port St. Lucie, FL	1 115.4	465 208	111	417.1	66.8	15.4	0.6	2.3	16.6	4.9	14.1	7.0	10.6	10.3	13.0
39140	Prescott, AZ	8 123.5	225 562	198	27.8	82.3	1.1	2.3	1.7	14.4	4.3	12.4	6.6	9.1	8.7	11.3
39300	Providence-Warwick, RI-MA	1 587.0	1 614 750	38	1 017.5	78.7	6.3	0.9	3.7	12.4	5.2	14.9	10.3	13.2	11.8	14.3
39340	Provo-Orem, UT	5 395.3	603 309	92	111.8	85.1	1.0	0.9	4.1	11.4	9.8	24.4	16.7	14.1	12.5	8.3
39380	Pueblo, CO	2 386.1	165 123	254	69.2	53.7	2.3	1.4	1.3	42.8	6.0	17.1	9.3	12.7	11.6	12.3
39460	Punta Gorda, FL	681.1	178 465	234	262.0	85.8	6.2	0.7	1.9	6.9	3.1	9.4	5.2	7.8	7.4	11.2
39540	Racine, WI	332.5	195 140	223	586.9	74.2	12.5	0.8	1.7	12.9	6.2	17.4	8.4	11.9	11.9	14.3
39580	Raleigh, NC	2 117.8	1 302 946	43	615.2	63.6	20.8	0.9	6.4	10.4	6.3	18.3	9.0	14.1	14.9	14.7
39660	Rapid City, SD	7 804.5	145 661	284	18.7	85.3	2.1	9.4	1.9	4.7	6.4	16.6	8.7	13.4	11.4	11.8

1. CBSA = Core Based Statistical Area. DIV = Metropolitan Division. See Appendix A for explanation. See Appendix B for list of metropolitan areas identified by type.　2. Dry land or land partially or temporarily covered by water.　3. May be of any race.

Table C. Metropolitan Areas — **Population and Households**

Area name	Age (percent) (cont.) 55 to 64 years	65 to 74 years	75 years and over	Percent female	Total persons 2000	2010	Percent change 2000–2010	2010–2016	Components of change, 2010–2016 Births	Deaths	Net migration	Households, 2015 Number	Persons per household	Family households	Female family householder[1]	One person
	16	17	18	19	20	21	22	23	24	25	26	27	28	29	30	31
Mobile, AL	13.2	9.2	6.2	52.2	399 843	413 143	3.3	0.4	34 956	26 603	-6 253	152 938	2.65	65.0	17.9	30.2
Modesto, CA	11.2	7.5	5.3	50.6	446 997	514 451	15.1	5.3	47 899	24 893	4 109	171 960	3.10	73.4	15.4	20.4
Monroe, LA	12.6	8.4	6.2	51.9	170 053	176 505	3.8	1.7	16 017	11 033	-1 936	64 955	2.66	63.3	18.0	32.5
Monroe, MI	15.3	10.0	7.0	50.6	145 945	152 021	4.2	-1.9	9 565	8 765	-3 630	58 886	2.52	67.2	10.7	28.6
Montgomery, AL	12.7	8.6	5.9	52.2	346 528	374 541	8.1	-0.2	30 476	21 692	-9 451	144 379	2.52	66.4	18.0	29.6
Morgantown, WV	11.7	7.9	5.2	48.5	111 200	129 709	16.6	6.7	9 130	6 281	5 936	50 274	2.57	55.4	9.6	33.8
Morristown, TN	13.4	11.3	7.6	51.0	102 422	114 193	11.5	2.7	8 163	8 148	3 003	44 574	2.56	69.6	11.0	24.7
Mount Vernon-Anacortes, WA	14.4	11.9	8.0	50.5	102 979	116 901	13.5	5.8	9 048	7 096	4 506	48 056	2.49	69.4	9.6	23.8
Muncie, IN	12.0	9.2	7.3	51.7	118 769	117 671	-0.9	-1.8	7 785	7 496	-2 218	45 278	2.43	62.7	14.6	25.5
Muskegon, MI	14.3	9.4	6.5	50.2	170 200	172 188	1.2	0.7	13 168	10 455	-1 520	63 215	2.63	69.2	14.2	25.3
Myrtle Beach-Conway-North Myrtle Beach, NC-SC	16.0	16.3	7.9	51.7	269 772	376 722	39.6	19.3	25 821	26 202	70 028	174 808	2.45	66.2	10.0	27.5
Napa, CA	13.5	10.3	7.8	50.4	124 279	136 530	9.9	4.1	9 282	7 526	3 728	49 619	2.78	66.7	10.5	26.5
Naples-Immokalee-Marco Island, FL	13.4	16.0	14.9	50.9	251 377	321 520	27.9	13.6	20 150	19 195	41 092	134 906	2.62	70.4	9.4	24.6
Nashville-Davidson—Murfreesboro—Franklin, TN	12.2	7.8	4.9	51.3	1 381 287	1 670 883	21.0	11.6	146 379	84 552	130 138	686 640	2.62	66.2	12.1	26.3
New Bern, NC	13.4	11.3	8.3	49.5	114 751	126 795	10.5	-0.5	10 912	8 067	-3 892	51 013	2.37	66.5	10.9	29.4
New Haven-Milford, CT	13.8	9.1	7.1	51.8	824 008	862 462	4.7	-0.6	56 078	47 891	-12 690	323 270	2.57	61.1	13.9	32.4
New Orleans-Metairie, LA	13.6	8.8	5.7	51.6	1 337 726	1 189 860	-11.1	6.6	99 122	67 712	46 690	481 754	2.58	61.1	16.4	33.2
New York-Newark-Jersey City, NY-NJ-PA	12.7	8.3	6.4	51.6	18 944 519	19 566 471	3.3	3.0	1 564 247	892 530	-53 912	7 125 065	2.77	65.8	14.8	28.2
Dutchess County-Putnam County, NY Div 20524	15.0	9.4	6.9	50.2	375 895	397 224	5.7	-1.0	22 165	19 263	-6 401	140 500	2.66	69.4	11.4	25.9
Nassau County-Suffolk County, NY Div 35004	14.0	9.2	7.3	51.1	2 753 913	2 833 066	2.9	0.7	187 994	143 039	-18 764	918 363	3.06	74.1	11.4	22.1
Newark, NJ-PA Div 35084	13.6	8.3	6.2	51.3	2 396 333	2 469 779	3.1	1.5	173 519	114 900	-18 161	886 182	2.78	69.4	13.4	26.3
New York-Jersey City-White Plains, NY-NJ Div 35614	12.2	8.1	6.3	51.8	13 418 378	13 866 402	3.3	3.8	1 180 569	615 328	-10 586	5 180 020	2.73	63.6	15.7	29.6
Niles-Benton Harbor, MI	14.7	10.6	8.0	50.9	162 453	156 817	-3.5	-1.8	11 516	10 473	-3 714	64 279	2.33	62.1	14.4	32.6
North Port-Sarasota-Bradenton, FL	15.1	16.5	14.5	52.0	589 959	702 268	19.0	12.3	39 545	55 467	98 328	312 497	2.43	63.8	10.5	30.3
Norwich-New London, CT	14.6	9.8	7.2	49.9	259 088	274 049	5.8	-1.6	17 033	14 674	-6 043	105 376	2.46	63.6	13.3	30.5
Ocala, FL	13.7	15.9	12.6	52.0	258 916	331 303	28.0	5.3	21 139	28 809	24 049	125 227	2.67	62.1	11.1	33.0
Ocean City, NJ	16.6	14.5	10.5	51.0	102 326	97 265	-4.9	-2.9	5 772	8 147	-223	38 708	2.37	65.6	9.9	30.3
Odessa, TX	9.9	5.6	4.2	49.4	121 123	137 136	13.2	14.8	17 706	7 362	9 866	52 023	3.03	70.9	15.1	22.8
Ogden-Clearfield, UT	10.0	6.2	4.4	49.6	485 401	597 159	23.0	9.6	67 422	22 048	11 989	201 165	3.18	77.9	9.8	19.1
Oklahoma City, OK	12.0	7.8	5.4	50.7	1 095 421	1 252 991	14.4	9.6	118 701	70 256	70 628	505 074	2.62	65.0	12.5	28.7
Olympia-Tumwater, WA	13.5	10.2	6.3	51.1	207 355	252 258	21.7	9.1	19 467	12 650	15 858	105 159	2.53	65.8	10.9	27.0
Omaha-Council Bluffs, NE-IA	12.2	7.6	5.3	50.5	767 041	865 356	12.8	6.8	83 067	40 729	17 519	351 446	2.55	65.2	11.4	28.1
Orlando-Kissimmee-Sanford, FL	11.8	8.4	5.9	51.1	1 644 561	2 134 399	29.8	14.4	171 495	100 090	231 465	845 295	2.77	67.3	14.8	24.6
Oshkosh-Neenah, WI	13.3	8.6	7.0	49.6	156 763	166 994	6.5	1.7	11 721	8 933	38	69 636	2.31	60.0	9.9	31.2
Owensboro, KY	13.4	9.5	7.2	51.0	109 875	114 754	4.4	2.8	9 759	7 536	1 020	46 415	2.47	68.9	12.0	26.0
Oxnard-Thousand Oaks-Ventura, CA	12.9	8.5	6.1	50.5	753 197	823 387	9.3	3.2	66 011	33 801	-6 044	269 566	3.11	73.3	12.7	21.6
Palm Bay-Melbourne-Titusville, FL	16.0	12.6	10.6	51.2	476 230	543 378	14.1	6.6	32 066	40 945	42 960	225 682	2.49	62.7	12.1	30.2
Panama City, FL	13.7	9.9	7.0	49.4	161 549	184 715	14.3	8.3	14 923	12 101	11 819	74 276	2.60	61.5	13.4	32.2
Parkersburg-Vienna, WV	14.7	11.2	8.0	51.4	93 859	92 673	-1.3	-1.3	6 521	6 907	-651	39 349	2.33	64.2	11.8	31.0
Pensacola-Ferry Pass-Brent, FL	13.3	9.5	6.5	49.8	412 153	448 991	8.9	8.2	35 668	28 123	28 331	177 675	2.55	63.7	12.7	28.8
Peoria, IL	13.4	9.5	7.6	51.0	366 899	379 186	3.3	-0.8	30 509	23 541	-9 619	150 639	2.44	64.2	12.0	31.3
Philadelphia-Camden-Wilmington, PA-NJ-DE-MD	13.4	8.6	6.6	51.6	5 687 147	5 965 662	4.9	1.8	450 964	335 544	-4 729	2 233 752	2.65	65.2	14.5	28.6
Camden, NJ Div 15804	13.7	8.9	6.6	51.3	1 186 999	1 250 991	5.4	0.1	87 368	68 412	-17 032	452 494	2.72	68.5	14.0	26.3
Montgomery County-Bucks County-Chester County, PA Div 33874	14.5	9.4	7.5	51.1	1 781 233	1 924 285	8.0	2.1	127 018	104 904	18 040	732 646	2.62	70.2	9.4	24.6
Philadelphia, PA Div 37964	12.2	7.6	6.0	52.5	2 068 414	2 084 732	0.8	2.2	184 032	124 535	-9 102	784 807	2.63	58.1	19.7	34.3
Wilmington, DE-MD-NJ Div 48864	13.5	8.8	6.2	51.3	650 501	705 654	8.5	2.5	52 546	37 693	3 365	263 805	2.66	67.1	14.3	26.2
Phoenix-Mesa-Scottsdale, AZ	11.4	8.9	6.2	50.3	3 251 876	4 193 127	28.9	11.2	371 027	189 479	276 953	1 608 722	2.80	65.1	12.4	27.2
Pine Bluff, AR	13.6	9.5	6.6	48.7	107 341	100 258	-6.6	-8.3	7 175	6 625	-8 901	34 059	2.45	63.5	18.2	33.5
Pittsburgh, PA	15.2	10.5	8.7	51.3	2 431 087	2 356 291	-3.1	-0.6	149 579	170 176	10 846	990 355	2.31	61.5	11.0	32.4
Pittsfield, MA	16.2	12.5	9.7	51.7	134 953	131 272	-2.7	-3.3	6 891	9 057	-1 956	55 497	2.18	61.6	12.0	31.5
Pocatello, ID	11.8	8.2	5.3	50.1	75 565	82 839	9.6	1.9	8 202	4 114	-2 486	30 174	2.71	62.4	11.6	27.1
Portland-South Portland, ME	15.3	10.8	7.5	51.3	487 568	514 103	5.4	3.0	31 264	29 355	13 214	212 240	2.42	63.3	8.9	28.8
Portland-Vancouver-Hillsboro, OR-WA	12.6	8.7	5.4	50.6	1 927 881	2 226 012	15.5	8.9	174 263	102 843	124 705	901 402	2.61	63.1	10.0	27.6
Port St. Lucie, FL	14.4	13.7	12.1	51.0	319 426	424 107	32.8	9.7	26 389	29 736	42 547	173 912	2.58	64.7	10.1	29.2
Prescott, AZ	17.5	18.0	12.1	51.2	167 517	211 015	26.0	6.9	11 670	17 156	19 101	94 920	2.30	64.2	8.4	28.3
Providence-Warwick, RI-MA	13.9	9.2	7.2	51.5	1 582 997	1 601 200	1.1	0.8	103 653	92 140	3 811	622 607	2.50	62.2	14.2	30.9
Provo-Orem, UT	6.7	4.4	3.1	49.4	376 774	526 886	39.8	14.5	76 275	13 587	13 411	158 270	3.59	81.7	7.8	11.8
Pueblo, CO	13.5	10.3	7.4	50.7	141 472	159 063	12.4	3.8	11 877	10 407	4 322	61 876	2.57	65.4	13.0	28.4
Punta Gorda, FL	17.1	21.3	17.6	51.1	141 627	159 968	13.0	11.6	6 366	15 034	26 312	72 671	2.33	66.1	8.5	28.3
Racine, WI	14.4	9.0	6.6	50.6	188 831	195 428	3.5	-0.1	14 992	10 682	-4 386	74 960	2.53	68.4	11.8	26.2
Raleigh, NC	11.5	7.0	4.2	51.3	797 071	1 130 479	41.8	15.3	96 929	41 735	114 418	470 527	2.65	68.0	11.6	25.0
Rapid City, SD	14.6	10.2	6.9	49.3	120 093	134 612	12.1	8.2	12 022	6 772	5 674	58 598	2.40	63.8	7.8	31.3

1. No spouse present.

Table C. Metropolitan Areas — **Population, Vital Statistics, Health, and Crime**

Area name	Persons in group quarters, 2016	Daytime population, 2015 Number	Daytime population, 2015 Employment/residence ratio	Births, 2016 Total	Births, 2016 Rate[1]	Deaths, 2016 Number	Deaths, 2016 Rate[1]	Persons under 65 with no health insurance 2015 Number	Persons under 65 with no health insurance 2015 Percent	Medicare, 2015 Total Beneficiaries	Medicare, 2015 Enrolled in Original Medicare	Medicare, 2015 Enrolled in Medicare Advantage	Serious crimes known to police,[2] 2014 Total Number	Serious crimes known to police,[2] 2014 Total Rate[3]
	32	33	34	35	36	37	38	39	40	41	42	43	44	45
Mobile, AL	7 516	423 119	1.04	5 596	13.5	4 514	10.9	45 101	13.0	76 274	41 491	34 783	18 673	4 505
Modesto, CA	6 413	518 320	0.90	7 708	14.2	4 281	7.9	39 586	8.5	76 544	40 820	35 724	21 385	4 027
Monroe, LA	6 030	183 102	1.05	2 558	14.3	1 877	10.5	20 018	13.5	30 886	23 414	7 472	11 512	6 624
Monroe, MI	1 463	127 900	0.68	1 456	9.8	1 420	9.5	7 345	5.9	28 548	19 035	9 513	2 847	1 947
Montgomery, AL	14 818	383 913	1.05	4 902	13.1	3 607	9.6	34 248	11.2	66 587	45 332	21 255	14 790	3 999
Morgantown, WV	8 519	147 837	1.16	1 582	11.4	1 052	7.6	7 148	6.4	18 756	12 893	5 863	2 285	1 781
Morristown, TN	2 558	114 609	0.96	1 308	11.1	1 363	11.6	12 438	13.4	28 392	15 762	12 630	3 580	3 092
Mount Vernon-Anacortes, WA	1 626	123 219	1.03	1 447	11.7	1 229	9.9	9 527	9.8	26 644	18 153	8 491	4 588	3 829
Muncie, IN	8 414	118 691	1.04	1 215	10.5	1 198	10.4	9 907	11.0	23 216	18 879	4 337	3 820	3 250
Muskegon, MI	6 372	166 557	0.91	2 059	11.9	1 734	10.0	10 030	7.1	36 381	21 414	14 967	6 907	4 041
Myrtle Beach-Conway-North Myrtle Beach, NC-SC	4 582	424 752	0.96	4 214	9.4	4 702	10.5	54 510	16.6	110 836	89 759	21 077	19 514	4 754
Napa, CA	4 998	151 623	1.13	1 483	10.4	1 296	9.1	9 719	8.5	25 996	16 028	9 968	2 919	2 055
Naples-Immokalee-Marco Island, FL	4 545	365 406	1.05	3 270	9.0	3 490	9.6	57 233	23.2	85 461	66 303	19 158	5 985	1 726
Nashville-Davidson—Murfreesboro—Franklin, TN	39 585	1 856 457	1.03	24 679	13.2	14 578	7.8	179 748	11.4	261 948	150 889	111 059	56 914	3 190
New Bern, NC	5 806	122 046	0.95	1 614	12.8	1 337	10.6	11 785	12.1	28 306	25 082	3 224	3 229	2 728
New Haven-Milford, CT	29 511	831 144	0.93	8 781	10.2	7 924	9.2	49 152	7.0	144 634	98 063	46 571	24 314	3 009
New Orleans-Metairie, LA	19 848	1 289 534	1.05	16 396	12.9	11 630	9.2	148 770	13.9	202 831	90 525	112 306	46 920	3 752
New York-Newark-Jersey City, NY-NJ-PA	417 453	20 331 620	1.02	247 502	12.3	152 782	7.6	1 635 062	9.6	2 928 532	1 978 896	949 636	377 851	1 883
Dutchess County-Putnam County, NY Div 20524	22 225	NA	NA	3 497	8.9	3 329	8.5	19 089	6.0	68 507	54 534	13 973	5 582	1 418
Nassau County-Suffolk County, NY Div 35004	49 439	NA	NA	29 770	10.4	24 147	8.5	160 257	6.7	485 109	360 786	124 323	43 631	1 526
Newark, NJ-PA Div 35084	48 838	2 497 783	0.99	27 185	10.8	19 436	7.8	215 818	10.2	353 177	288 852	64 325	47 882	1 910
New York-Jersey City-White Plains, NY-NJ Div 35614	296 951	14 801 591	1.06	187 050	13.0	105 870	7.4	1 239 898	10.2	2 021 739	1 274 724	747 015	280 756	1 963
Niles-Benton Harbor, MI	3 535	154 910	1.00	1 786	11.6	1 662	10.8	10 879	8.8	36 752	23 446	13 306	3 541	2 345
North Port-Sarasota-Bradenton, FL	10 602	769 275	1.00	6 545	8.3	9 772	12.4	89 996	17.0	217 047	150 451	66 596	21 816	2 925
Norwich-New London, CT	11 503	271 523	1.00	2 676	9.9	2 465	9.1	11 860	5.5	48 825	38 704	10 121	NA	NA
Ocala, FL	8 967	334 606	0.92	3 509	10.1	4 824	13.8	39 320	16.6	103 609	60 874	42 735	8 346	2 444
Ocean City, NJ	2 613	95 753	1.02	941	10.0	1 308	13.9	7 286	10.4	25 430	22 652	2 778	3 765	3 934
Odessa, TX	2 636	161 419	1.03	3 145	20.0	1 247	7.9	30 616	21.5	18 182	14 241	3 941	7 375	4 797
Ogden-Clearfield, UT	6 059	595 913	0.84	10 799	16.5	3 646	5.6	55 091	9.6	72 190	45 114	27 076	14 042	2 243
Oklahoma City, OK	31 616	1 362 860	1.01	19 211	14.0	11 558	8.4	172 752	15.0	195 019	149 639	45 380	51 242	3 833
Olympia-Tumwater, WA	4 027	260 744	0.93	3 172	11.5	2 172	7.9	14 801	6.6	48 843	31 268	17 575	7 956	2 991
Omaha-Council Bluffs, NE-IA	18 099	918 278	1.01	13 466	14.6	6 672	7.2	63 177	8.0	130 739	100 976	29 763	31 601	3 501
Orlando-Kissimmee-Sanford, FL	45 254	2 445 235	1.05	28 849	11.8	18 051	7.4	303 633	15.1	415 874	233 404	182 470	86 516	3 746
Oshkosh-Neenah, WI	7 714	179 946	1.12	1 833	10.8	1 449	8.5	7 061	5.2	28 976	12 763	16 213	3 126	1 837
Owensboro, KY	2 751	118 396	1.01	1 583	13.4	1 238	10.5	5 721	6.0	24 956	19 477	5 479	2 956	2 527
Oxnard-Thousand Oaks-Ventura, CA	11 204	804 112	0.88	10 348	12.2	5 996	7.1	71 633	9.9	126 228	85 093	41 135	18 702	2 206
Palm Bay-Melbourne-Titusville, FL	6 570	557 364	0.96	5 317	9.2	7 040	12.2	58 601	13.5	138 722	85 688	53 034	17 253	3 098
Panama City, FL	7 319	198 854	1.01	2 462	12.3	2 081	10.4	21 945	13.8	40 194	31 646	8 548	8 401	4 335
Parkersburg-Vienna, WV	996	96 991	1.11	1 050	11.5	1 109	12.1	5 006	6.7	23 005	17 706	5 299	1 964	2 130
Pensacola-Ferry Pass-Brent, FL	26 226	465 985	0.94	5 730	11.8	4 923	10.1	46 809	12.3	91 879	63 975	27 904	16 540	3 484
Peoria, IL	8 989	380 595	1.02	4 806	12.8	3 859	10.3	15 780	5.1	70 875	49 209	21 666	9 871	2 697
Philadelphia-Camden-Wilmington, PA-NJ-DE-MD	167 751	6 028 903	0.99	71 339	11.8	56 616	9.3	382 272	7.6	984 613	685 538	299 075	168 972	2 792
Camden, NJ Div 15804	25 283	1 164 117	0.85	13 766	11.0	11 437	9.1	75 725	7.2	207 341	166 716	40 625	29 595	2 355
Montgomery County-Bucks County-Chester County, PA Div 33874	43 161	NA	NA	20 327	10.3	17 916	9.1	93 166	5.8	333 840	229 330	104 510	32 164	1 647
Philadelphia, PA Div 37964	79 191	2 178 771	1.05	28 924	13.6	20 779	9.7	175 724	9.9	328 003	186 352	141 651	82 502	3 889
Wilmington, DE-MD-NJ Div 48864	20 116	720 598	0.99	8 322	11.5	6 484	9.0	37 657	6.3	115 429	103 140	12 289	24 711	3 424
Phoenix-Mesa-Scottsdale, AZ	88 541	4 564 070	0.99	60 616	13.0	33 666	7.2	475 906	12.5	639 933	348 111	291 822	148 820	3 324
Pine Bluff, AR	9 025	94 028	0.99	1 089	11.8	1 080	11.7	6 471	9.2	19 195	14 719	4 476	4 166	4 399
Pittsburgh, PA	62 648	2 368 267	1.01	23 738	10.1	27 925	11.9	110 848	5.9	492 395	163 970	328 425	49 484	2 106
Pittsfield, MA	5 898	128 447	1.01	1 046	8.2	1 467	11.6	3 263	3.4	31 447	29 686	1 761	2 911	2 446
Pocatello, ID	2 129	81 520	0.94	1 263	15.0	653	7.7	8 107	11.5	13 694	8 782	4 912	2 131	2 540
Portland-South Portland, ME	12 795	526 095	1.00	5 070	9.6	5 022	9.5	39 470	9.3	107 033	77 037	29 996	11 106	2 127
Portland-Vancouver-Hillsboro, OR-WA	39 610	2 397 684	1.01	28 374	11.7	17 818	7.3	153 257	7.5	353 466	137 417	216 049	70 330	3 300
Port St. Lucie, FL	7 255	430 134	0.86	4 357	9.4	5 247	11.3	59 266	17.7	107 330	70 383	36 947	10 070	2 263
Prescott, AZ	4 154	216 371	0.93	1 944	8.6	2 886	12.8	20 512	13.2	64 387	44 511	19 876	NA	NA
Providence-Warwick, RI-MA	59 115	1 538 004	0.90	16 395	10.2	15 047	9.3	73 671	5.6	299 093	205 114	93 979	39 662	2 463
Provo-Orem, UT	13 542	571 720	0.95	12 347	20.5	2 343	3.9	56 211	10.6	45 717	26 756	18 961	9 684	1 692
Pueblo, CO	4 149	163 378	1.00	1 926	11.7	1 765	10.7	11 907	9.1	33 300	20 738	12 562	9 275	5 695
Punta Gorda, FL	3 227	163 981	0.85	1 044	5.8	2 658	14.9	17 535	16.8	54 788	36 946	17 842	3 208	1 918
Racine, WI	4 792	182 636	0.87	2 353	12.1	1 676	8.6	10 844	6.7	37 755	23 503	14 252	4 833	2 479
Raleigh, NC	24 298	1 264 492	0.99	15 893	12.2	7 479	5.7	117 109	10.5	157 909	106 701	51 208	19 881	1 615
Rapid City, SD	3 618	145 226	1.00	1 866	12.8	1 163	8.0	15 004	12.8	27 797	22 226	5 571	4 101	2 863

1. Per 1,000 estimated resident population. 2. Data for serious crimes have not been adjusted for underreporting; this may affect comparability between geographic areas and over time.
3. Per 100,000 population estimated by the FBI.

Table C. Metropolitan Areas — Crime, Education, Money Income, and Poverty

Area name	Serious crimes known to police, 2014 (cont.)[1] Rate[2] Violent	Property	Education — Enrollment[3] Total	Percent private	High school graduate or less	Bachelor's degree or more	Total current expenditures (mil dol)	Current expenditures per student (dollars)	Per capita income[6] (dollars)	Mean household income (dollars)	Median household income	Percent of households with income of less than $50,000	Percent of households with income of $200,000 or more	All persons	Children under 18 years	Age 65 years and older
	46	47	48	49	50	51	52	53	54	55	56	57	58	59	60	61
Mobile, AL	510	3 994	103 740	17.8	47.1	23.5	563.2	8 839	23 266	59 771	42 699	54.7	2.6	17.7	24.2	8.6
Modesto, CA	532	3 495	150 544	7.5	51.3	16.4	1 006.6	9 643	23 066	69 743	52 363	46.9	3.6	19.7	27.7	10.3
Monroe, LA	1 255	5 369	43 582	9.9	48.2	25.1	330.6	10 420	21 085	55 139	36 346	61.3	3.3	23.9	35.0	14.9
Monroe, MI	224	1 723	34 380	11.2	46.0	18.3	246.9	10 458	27 243	67 909	54 396	45.5	2.4	10.5	15.0	6.9
Montgomery, AL	393	3 607	95 565	21.9	43.6	28.0	462.7	8 230	25 688	65 358	45 636	53.0	3.8	19.6	29.4	10.3
Morgantown, WV	227	1 554	43 919	5.6	44.4	34.3	166.8	10 572	26 395	65 762	45 941	52.7	5.0	20.3	17.7	6.6
Morristown, TN	383	2 708	26 335	14.9	60.0	14.9	142.6	8 057	20 709	53 782	40 041	59.6	1.6	17.7	22.7	11.2
Mount Vernon-Anacortes, WA	206	3 622	25 479	8.6	36.8	24.4	204.5	10 784	28 459	71 459	57 122	45.0	3.5	16.0	24.1	7.7
Muncie, IN	281	2 970	33 954	8.2	46.6	23.1	158.9	9 851	20 925	52 733	40 606	58.8	1.7	23.4	33.9	6.3
Muskegon, MI	443	3 597	40 487	13.7	45.8	18.7	297.7	10 332	22 081	58 526	47 453	52.3	1.9	15.5	21.7	6.3
Myrtle Beach-Conway-North Myrtle Beach, NC-SC	426	4 328	86 030	11.8	42.0	24.9	539.6	9 940	26 262	61 721	47 379	52.5	2.7	16.1	28.5	7.2
Napa, CA	376	1 679	34 250	14.7	33.4	32.8	229.7	11 009	41 002	111 567	75 513	33.2	11.8	10.8	13.2	7.8
Naples-Immokalee-Marco Island, FL	260	1 466	67 853	16.3	39.3	35.2	455.0	10 244	40 138	101 833	62 126	38.9	9.5	14.2	24.9	6.8
Nashville-Davidson—Murfreesboro—Franklin, TN	614	2 576	456 500	19.9	38.9	33.6	2 424.2	8 800	30 911	79 665	57 985	43.1	6.0	12.7	17.4	8.4
New Bern, NC	240	2 488	27 934	15.6	39.0	23.0	149.9	8 696	25 694	60 474	45 971	55.0	2.2	13.7	22.4	7.7
New Haven-Milford, CT	333	2 676	218 714	23.9	40.8	34.3	2 123.0	17 186	33 148	83 327	61 760	40.7	7.0	13.7	20.6	8.2
New Orleans-Metairie, LA	522	3 230	312 612	27.4	42.4	28.6	1 965.6	12 063	27 767	68 409	48 343	51.1	4.1	18.0	27.7	11.8
New York-Newark-Jersey City, NY-NJ-PA	372	1 511	5 034 813	23.5	39.7	38.4	56 450.5	19 999	37 497	101 934	68 743	38.2	11.0	14.1	20.0	11.5
Dutchess County-Putnam County, NY Div 20524	175	1 243	99 392	25.2	36.8	34.2	1 204.1	20 922	35 570	95 030	76 877	32.2	7.8	9.0	11.1	5.8
Nassau County-Suffolk County, NY Div 35004	137	1 389	721 256	19.3	35.9	38.9	10 615.6	23 567	41 337	123 060	94 079	25.7	14.9	6.7	8.8	5.2
Newark, NJ-PA Div 35084	316	1 594	639 483	18.9	37.0	40.9	7 446.3	18 527	40 741	111 416	76 596	34.2	13.8	10.3	15.0	7.8
New York-Jersey City-White Plains, NY-NJ Div 35614	434	1 528	3 574 682	25.1	41.0	38.0	37 184.5	19 440	36 222	96 754	62 452	41.3	10.0	16.4	23.3	13.7
Niles-Benton Harbor, MI	390	1 955	39 053	20.8	37.7	28.9	276.6	10 920	29 466	68 931	46 649	52.5	4.1	17.0	26.1	6.7
North Port-Sarasota-Bradenton, FL	402	2 523	137 237	15.8	40.2	31.3	808.9	9 182	32 280	75 124	53 698	46.1	4.8	11.8	20.0	6.6
Norwich-New London, CT	NA	NA	62 545	22.3	39.5	33.4	637.2	17 040	34 769	84 818	65 764	38.0	5.7	11.4	20.3	5.7
Ocala, FL	415	2 028	70 382	18.0	49.6	19.7	349.9	8 309	21 487	52 323	40 050	58.8	1.6	18.8	33.5	8.9
Ocean City, NJ	239	3 694	19 208	15.8	41.8	30.7	253.7	19 900	33 892	79 746	57 116	44.2	5.3	8.7	13.8	5.7
Odessa, TX	911	3 886	46 543	7.9	52.7	16.2	236.0	7 368	27 328	81 301	65 454	38.3	5.2	11.7	15.0	5.4
Ogden-Clearfield, UT	159	2 083	200 775	8.7	33.4	30.0	885.3	6 247	25 428	78 708	65 538	35.7	3.7	8.8	10.7	6.3
Oklahoma City, OK	466	3 367	377 169	10.7	39.8	29.3	1 644.0	7 178	27 901	72 437	52 221	47.2	4.3	14.5	20.1	6.6
Olympia-Tumwater, WA	228	2 764	63 272	14.9	30.7	32.7	408.8	9 926	30 051	74 949	62 137	38.1	3.8	12.7	16.3	5.2
Omaha-Council Bluffs, NE-IA	365	3 136	246 912	19.0	32.9	34.7	1 653.2	10 926	31 260	79 771	61 024	41.3	4.9	12.3	18.3	6.8
Orlando-Kissimmee-Sanford, FL	531	3 214	615 769	16.6	37.3	29.9	2 961.5	8 280	26 254	70 292	51 077	48.8	4.2	15.0	21.8	9.3
Oshkosh-Neenah, WI	172	1 665	42 527	10.0	41.7	25.6	235.7	10 430	28 543	68 493	52 136	46.7	3.2	11.7	13.3	3.4
Owensboro, KY	129	2 398	27 584	14.7	49.7	19.5	179.8	9 047	25 719	64 436	47 751	52.0	2.9	15.3	23.1	7.1
Oxnard-Thousand Oaks-Ventura, CA	223	1 983	226 636	15.7	35.4	32.7	1 280.6	9 020	34 226	104 004	80 032	30.3	10.8	9.6	13.7	6.8
Palm Bay-Melbourne-Titusville, FL	493	2 605	121 748	16.7	37.8	28.4	575.6	8 080	28 384	67 688	50 416	49.6	3.1	13.2	21.1	7.6
Panama City, FL	500	3 835	44 905	12.5	42.2	22.4	237.8	8 223	25 194	62 509	48 066	52.1	2.6	16.0	25.3	10.3
Parkersburg-Vienna, WV	201	1 929	19 463	12.6	48.8	19.7	154.8	10 842	24 508	57 101	40 547	58.5	2.0	17.3	24.6	6.6
Pensacola-Ferry Pass-Brent, FL	503	2 981	115 492	17.0	36.9	26.2	546.4	8 198	25 943	65 554	50 560	49.2	2.5	13.1	22.3	6.2
Peoria, IL	323	2 373	91 475	20.0	39.5	27.4	664.3	11 114	30 740	75 757	56 350	43.4	4.4	11.9	17.2	6.6
Philadelphia-Camden-Wilmington, PA-NJ-DE-MD	460	2 332	1 539 024	26.0	39.7	36.0	13 171.7	15 299	34 414	89 851	65 123	39.5	8.1	13.1	18.7	8.3
Camden, NJ Div 15804	276	2 079	316 366	16.5	39.4	33.0	3 523.6	17 474	34 179	90 791	71 605	36.0	7.5	9.9	14.5	6.2
Montgomery County-Bucks County-Chester County, PA Div 33874	126	1 521	487 730	25.7	32.0	45.6	4 491.9	15 795	43 273	113 213	84 349	29.3	13.0	6.2	7.2	4.7
Philadelphia, PA Div 37964	861	3 027	549 237	34.5	47.2	29.8	3 669.9	13 529	26 958	68 661	47 220	51.8	4.6	21.7	31.9	14.2
Wilmington, DE-MD-NJ Div 48864	501	2 923	185 691	17.9	40.1	32.6	1 486.4	14 339	32 760	86 393	67 091	37.0	5.7	11.8	18.2	6.9
Phoenix-Mesa-Scottsdale, AZ	369	2 955	1 189 149	11.2	37.1	29.4	5 529.5	7 146	28 194	76 146	55 547	45.0	5.1	16.2	23.0	8.7
Pine Bluff, AR	694	3 706	22 400	13.9	56.3	14.2	153.9	10 012	18 735	48 842	36 538	63.2	1.1	25.7	41.2	10.5
Pittsburgh, PA	291	1 814	513 762	21.6	41.0	33.0	4 290.7	13 787	32 058	74 452	54 080	46.1	4.8	12.3	17.6	7.8
Pittsfield, MA	309	2 136	29 047	27.6	40.3	32.4	278.8	16 553	30 480	69 880	50 765	49.5	4.4	14.7	20.1	8.1
Pocatello, ID	223	2 317	25 607	8.4	34.7	24.3	88.6	6 442	21 107	56 585	41 530	57.0	1.5	25.3	26.6	12.2
Portland-South Portland, ME	127	2 000	113 074	16.5	33.4	39.6	940.6	13 223	33 821	81 158	62 074	39.4	4.7	9.6	11.9	6.1
Portland-Vancouver-Hillsboro, OR-WA	272	3 027	576 951	18.3	29.3	37.9	3 357.0	9 798	32 997	84 633	63 850	39.0	6.7	12.2	14.9	6.5
Port St. Lucie, FL	299	1 964	97 587	13.8	44.0	25.0	500.5	8 590	27 300	66 868	48 002	51.4	3.8	14.4	21.5	8.2
Prescott, AZ	NA	NA	43 066	16.7	34.8	26.5	185.5	7 628	26 650	61 037	48 105	51.4	2.2	15.1	21.9	6.3
Providence-Warwick, RI-MA	329	2 133	398 239	23.2	42.2	30.6	3 218.7	14 552	31 466	77 620	58 965	43.1	5.3	13.4	18.8	10.0
Provo-Orem, UT	74	1 617	227 587	22.3	24.6	37.7	798.2	5 856	22 397	81 551	65 092	36.4	4.7	12.6	12.2	6.9
Pueblo, CO	577	5 119	39 141	7.9	41.6	21.6	214.5	7 866	22 590	57 414	40 050	58.5	1.9	20.1	28.9	10.2
Punta Gorda, FL	176	1 741	25 061	13.6	48.1	21.0	148.0	9 102	28 101	62 168	45 492	55.3	3.0	11.3	20.6	6.1
Racine, WI	200	2 279	48 352	23.3	40.7	24.0	349.9	11 755	28 469	72 857	57 232	42.1	4.1	11.9	16.7	7.8
Raleigh, NC	136	1 479	348 923	15.0	28.4	44.4	1 603.4	7 837	32 970	87 155	65 778	37.7	6.8	11.6	16.0	5.7
Rapid City, SD	392	2 472	36 123	15.1	33.8	30.0	182.1	8 706	28 641	69 847	52 809	47.7	3.9	10.5	12.7	8.0

1. Data for serious crimes have not been adjusted for underreporting; this may affect comparability between geographic areas and over time.   2. Per 100,000 population estimated by the FBI.
3. All persons 3 years old and over enrolled in nursery school through college.   4. Persons 25 years old and over.   5. Elementary and secondary education expenditures.   6. Based on resident population estimated in the 2015 American Community Survey.

Table C. Metropolitan Areas — **Personal Income**

| | Personal income, 2015 | | | | | | | | | | Earnings, 2015 | | |
| | | | Per capita[1] | | | Supplements to wages and salaries; employer contributions (mil dol) | | | | | | Contributions for government social insurance (mil dol) | |
Area name	Total (mil dol)	Percent change 2014–2015	Dollars	Rank	Wages and salaries (mil dol)	Pension and insurance	Government social insurance	Proprietors' income (mil dol)	Dividends, interest, and rent (mil dol)	Personal transfer receipts (mil dol)	Total (mil dol)	From employee and self-employed	From employer
	62	63	64	65	66	67	68	69	70	71	72	73	74
Mobile, AL	14 684	3.5	35 348	338	8 181	1 262	607	1 079	2 311	3 707	11 129	721	607
Modesto, CA	21 237	6.9	39 445	237	8 473	1 754	622	2 100	3 189	4 756	12 950	714	622
Monroe, LA	6 491	4.2	36 214	316	3 161	549	204	464	1 025	1 692	4 377	245	204
Monroe, MI	6 238	4.8	41 707	187	2 059	335	153	272	805	1 305	2 819	191	153
Montgomery, AL	14 713	3.5	39 362	239	7 570	1 364	571	818	2 773	3 283	10 324	637	571
Morgantown, WV	5 442	4.1	39 383	238	3 204	590	240	340	841	1 047	4 374	265	240
Morristown, TN	3 903	4.9	33 463	364	1 722	298	122	376	500	1 123	2 518	165	122
Mount Vernon-Anacortes, WA	5 419	4.6	44 470	123	2 276	412	215	447	1 186	1 168	3 351	201	215
Muncie, IN	3 844	3.2	32 896	368	1 897	354	144	174	614	1 133	2 569	166	144
Muskegon, MI	5 979	5.1	34 604	346	2 677	457	208	290	849	1 724	3 633	240	208
Myrtle Beach-Conway-North Myrtle Beach, NC-SC	14 608	6.3	33 818	357	5 602	895	451	1 004	2 811	4 500	7 952	581	451
Napa, CA	8 759	7.6	61 483	13	4 120	810	298	1 427	2 023	1 157	6 655	356	298
Naples-Immokalee-Marco Island, FL	28 039	4.2	78 473	5	6 817	871	464	1 585	15 357	3 194	9 736	663	464
Nashville-Davidson—Murfreesboro—Franklin, TN	92 680	8.6	50 635	53	48 362	6 329	3 265	18 894	12 011	12 763	76 850	4 352	3 265
New Bern, NC	5 047	2.0	39 975	226	2 390	554	205	207	1 101	1 251	3 355	195	205
New Haven-Milford, CT	44 551	3.4	51 835	43	20 990	3 432	1 602	3 437	7 708	8 364	29 461	1 603	1 602
New Orleans-Metairie, LA	60 404	4.9	47 830	77	30 140	4 753	1 964	7 417	11 367	10 419	44 275	2 399	1 964
New York-Newark-Jersey City, NY-NJ-PA	1 303 530	3.9	64 588	11	689 238	106 113	48 117	122 538	269 697	195 229	966 007	52 055	48 117
Dutchess County-Putnam County, NY Div 20524	20 328	3.5	51 490	X	7 196	1 657	596	977	3 445	3 452	10 427	568	596
Nassau County-Suffolk County, NY Div 35004	195 181	3.5	68 175	X	76 182	14 971	6 091	14 588	40 208	26 954	111 833	5 852	6 091
Newark, NJ-PA Div 35084	173 752	4.0	69 183	X	86 286	12 287	6 078	16 988	33 047	20 319	121 638	7 015	6 078
New York-Jersey City-White Plains, NY-NJ Div 35614	914 269	3.9	63 433	X	519 574	77 199	35 352	89 984	192 997	144 504	722 109	38 619	35 352
Niles-Benton Harbor, MI	6 485	4.0	41 939	179	3 025	567	228	312	1 107	1 564	4 132	260	228
North Port-Sarasota-Bradenton, FL	38 553	5.9	50 139	57	12 866	1 832	895	2 223	14 328	8 027	17 816	1 263	895
Norwich-New London, CT	14 272	3.5	52 498	39	6 985	1 410	515	972	2 742	2 415	9 881	508	515
Ocala, FL	11 602	4.7	33 800	358	3 912	663	280	434	2 614	3 987	5 289	424	280
Ocean City, NJ	5 050	4.1	53 309	34	1 650	350	148	469	1 303	1 185	2 618	171	148
Odessa, TX	7 303	-5.0	45 806	96	4 270	541	284	1 009	801	979	6 104	311	284
Ogden-Clearfield, UT	24 564	6.4	38 212	266	10 648	2 031	859	1 347	4 172	3 371	14 885	872	859
Oklahoma City, OK	62 592	5.3	46 076	92	31 146	5 149	2 313	8 410	11 080	9 701	47 018	2 489	2 313
Olympia-Tumwater, WA	11 901	4.4	44 155	131	5 314	1 024	475	724	2 420	2 300	7 536	440	475
Omaha-Council Bluffs, NE-IA	47 178	2.0	51 543	45	24 918	3 594	1 881	6 185	8 700	6 297	36 578	2 178	1 881
Orlando-Kissimmee-Sanford, FL	92 221	7.0	38 632	255	55 464	7 573	3 825	4 864	14 761	17 902	71 727	4 421	3 825
Oshkosh-Neenah, WI	7 189	3.6	42 399	166	4 779	805	365	408	1 309	1 204	6 357	384	365
Owensboro, KY	4 658	3.6	39 657	234	2 236	379	171	340	749	1 157	3 125	196	171
Oxnard-Thousand Oaks-Ventura, CA	46 060	5.6	54 155	29	18 759	3 428	1 299	4 006	9 038	6 182	27 491	1 537	1 299
Palm Bay-Melbourne-Titusville, FL	23 014	5.4	40 511	211	10 109	1 590	720	944	4 890	5 781	13 362	899	720
Panama City, FL	7 692	5.3	38 947	248	3 604	666	273	403	1 607	1 791	4 945	306	273
Parkersburg-Vienna, WV	3 568	3.9	38 642	254	1 600	301	129	315	521	986	2 344	160	129
Pensacola-Ferry Pass-Brent, FL	18 667	4.9	39 048	246	8 039	1 510	611	869	3 794	4 240	11 029	680	611
Peoria, IL	17 061	1.3	45 132	107	9 846	1 524	695	648	3 050	3 021	12 714	728	695
Philadelphia-Camden-Wilmington, PA-NJ-DE-MD	347 032	4.0	57 173	21	173 064	28 091	13 112	35 369	61 411	57 296	249 636	14 303	13 112
Camden, NJ Div 15804	63 656	4.1	50 818	X	27 938	4 776	2 262	3 693	9 710	11 291	38 670	2 345	2 262
Montgomery County-Bucks County-Chester County, PA Div 33874	136 840	3.6	69 725	X	66 633	9 953	4 934	7 147	29 935	15 982	88 666	5 227	4 934
Philadelphia, PA Div 37964	110 472	3.5	51 832	X	57 236	9 838	4 363	22 036	15 580	23 683	93 473	5 019	4 363
Wilmington, DE-MD-NJ Div 48864	36 064	6.6	49 858	X	21 257	3 523	1 553	2 494	6 186	6 339	28 827	1 712	1 553
Phoenix-Mesa-Scottsdale, AZ	186 693	4.8	40 811	204	101 296	13 482	7 167	12 358	33 406	33 811	134 303	8 329	7 167
Pine Bluff, AR	2 940	0.1	31 377	376	1 371	252	112	192	374	946	1 928	126	112
Pittsburgh, PA	119 432	4.3	50 756	49	63 105	10 813	4 877	9 259	19 276	23 223	88 054	5 208	4 877
Pittsfield, MA	6 482	4.9	50 712	50	2 848	539	205	438	1 363	1 581	4 030	228	205
Pocatello, ID	2 792	4.4	33 344	366	1 261	243	116	164	455	652	1 784	117	116
Portland-South Portland, ME	25 918	4.2	49 246	66	13 340	2 112	1 004	1 811	4 890	4 510	18 267	1 177	1 004
Portland-Vancouver-Hillsboro, OR-WA	115 691	6.3	48 422	69	64 148	8 447	5 453	8 292	22 140	17 622	86 340	5 311	5 453
Port St. Lucie, FL	21 763	5.5	47 847	76	5 892	954	415	1 040	7 367	4 531	8 301	594	415
Prescott, AZ	7 900	5.5	35 545	331	2 383	398	175	556	2 058	2 479	3 512	279	175
Providence-Warwick, RI-MA	79 722	4.9	49 423	64	36 686	6 229	2 875	5 288	12 975	16 601	51 078	3 200	2 875
Provo-Orem, UT	20 050	7.9	34 227	353	9 658	1 508	747	1 816	3 291	2 572	13 730	799	747
Pueblo, CO	5 698	4.7	34 831	345	2 589	367	201	243	940	1 729	3 401	212	201
Punta Gorda, FL	6 534	6.2	37 745	279	1 809	288	129	339	1 882	2 194	2 565	218	129
Racine, WI	8 483	3.6	43 486	145	3 684	691	282	325	1 497	1 646	4 982	313	282
Raleigh, NC	61 655	5.4	48 411	70	32 674	4 502	2 449	3 888	10 219	7 338	43 513	2 610	2 449
Rapid City, SD	6 454	3.3	44 775	116	2 850	537	218	668	1 552	1 140	4 274	261	218

1. Based on the resident population estimated as of July 1 of the year shown.

Table C. Metropolitan Areas — Earnings, Social Security, and Housing

Area name	Earnings, 2015 (cont.) Percent by selected industries									Social Security beneficiaries, December 2015			Housing units, 2016	
	Farm	Mining	Construction	Manufacturing	Information, professional, scientific, technical services	Retail trade	Finance, insurance, real estate, rental and leasing	Health care and social assistance	Government	Number	Rate[1]	Supplemental Security Income recipients, December 2015	Total	Percent change, 2010–2016
	75	76	77	78	79	80	81	82	83	84	85	86	87	88
Mobile, AL	0.3	0.4	7.3	15.9	8.8	6.6	6.9	12.2	15.3	89 650	216	15 281	182 642	2.5
Modesto, CA	8.2	0.0	6.1	13.3	4.0	7.6	4.1	16.2	18.2	85 825	160	22 102	180 825	0.7
Monroe, LA	1.0	D	5.6	D	D	7.4	7.1	18.2	16.0	34 350	191	7 868	78 971	4.1
Monroe, MI	1.0	D	8.9	16.1	7.8	6.6	3.1	9.8	12.6	33 860	226	2 572	63 683	1.1
Montgomery, AL	1.1	0.1	4.7	12.3	D	6.1	D	11.0	29.0	77 820	208	14 560	166 419	3.0
Morgantown, WV	-0.2	1.6	7.1	9.8	D	5.4	3.0	D	26.6	21 950	159	2 783	59 704	2.3
Morristown, TN	0.4	D	D	27.6	3.0	8.0	3.1	D	13.7	30 470	261	3 570	50 814	0.6
Mount Vernon-Anacortes, WA	3.5	0.1	9.4	15.5	5.7	8.5	5.8	8.0	23.2	28 855	237	2 486	52 526	2.0
Muncie, IN	-0.3	D	4.5	11.0	5.8	8.1	6.3	19.1	22.8	25 860	223	3 086	52 425	0.1
Muskegon, MI	0.8	D	5.7	27.2	4.1	9.6	3.7	17.1	14.0	41 655	241	6 331	73 465	-0.1
Myrtle Beach-Conway-North Myrtle Beach, NC-SC	0.4	D	7.1	3.2	D	11.4	9.2	11.8	16.5	127 640	295	8 039	284 712	8.1
Napa, CA	1.9	D	8.0	22.9	6.5	5.1	5.5	9.0	14.9	26 585	187	2 362	55 531	1.4
Naples-Immokalee-Marco Island, FL	1.4	-0.3	10.7	3.1	12.6	9.0	11.1	11.6	9.9	88 625	249	4 061	210 128	6.5
Nashville-Davidson—Murfreesboro—Franklin, TN	0.1	0.2	6.4	7.5	D	6.4	D	20.8	9.7	300 985	165	32 494	761 285	8.3
New Bern, NC	1.1	0.1	3.0	7.6	D	5.4	3.0	9.1	50.1	30 015	238	3 199	58 940	2.7
New Haven-Milford, CT	0.1	0.1	6.0	8.8	10.5	6.3	6.3	15.3	15.3	161 755	188	19 858	363 122	0.3
New Orleans-Metairie, LA	0.0	6.8	6.9	7.5	10.9	D	6.4	10.4	13.7	227 670	180	44 844	557 576	2.0
New York-Newark-Jersey City, NY-NJ-PA	0.0	0.1	4.6	4.0	18.3	4.9	18.2	10.3	14.0	3 240 325	161	599 843	7 918 895	1.7
Dutchess County-Putnam County, NY Div 20524	0.0	0.2	7.3	11.6	7.3	6.6	3.5	15.8	24.8	77 355	196	6 176	157 625	0.5
Nassau County-Suffolk County, NY Div 35004	0.1	0.1	6.8	5.6	11.4	7.5	10.1	14.8	19.5	544 890	191	37 339	1 037 837	-0.1
Newark, NJ-PA Div 35084	0.0	0.1	4.7	8.8	18.1	4.6	10.4	9.4	13.8	405 630	162	50 719	986 815	1.2
New York-Jersey City-White Plains, NY-NJ Div 35614	0.0	0.0	4.2	2.9	19.5	4.5	21.0	9.7	13.0	2 212 450	154	505 609	5 736 618	2.2
Niles-Benton Harbor, MI	1.2	0.2	3.8	31.9	3.8	5.3	4.4	11.2	13.6	37 235	241	4 851	76 856	-0.1
North Port-Sarasota-Bradenton, FL	0.9	0.1	8.0	6.3	11.9	9.1	8.5	15.8	10.8	224 775	293	10 744	420 967	5.0
Norwich-New London, CT	0.5	0.0	5.2	18.1	7.7	6.0	3.0	11.3	27.8	54 575	202	4 176	121 923	0.8
Ocala, FL	-0.2	0.1	6.8	9.1	6.3	11.1	5.2	19.8	16.1	112 580	328	9 610	164 416	0.2
Ocean City, NJ	0.2	D	10.7	D	5.1	9.7	7.1	10.9	27.9	28 205	297	1 814	99 235	0.9
Odessa, TX	0.0	20.2	13.8	9.3	3.8	7.0	5.3	5.1	10.8	19 630	123	3 453	57 602	8.6
Ogden-Clearfield, UT	0.4	0.1	8.4	15.2	D	6.9	D	D	25.1	80 960	126	6 674	217 902	6.8
Oklahoma City, OK	0.3	D	6.2	5.8	D	6.2	6.7	11.6	19.7	224 225	165	27 197	569 608	5.7
Olympia-Tumwater, WA	0.9	0.0	5.3	3.1	6.3	6.3	4.9	12.7	39.3	55 735	207	5 207	113 324	4.8
Omaha-Council Bluffs, NE-IA	0.9	0.2	7.6	6.3	D	5.0	9.7	10.8	13.7	143 855	157	14 768	381 191	5.2
Orlando-Kissimmee-Sanford, FL	0.3	D	6.1	4.7	12.6	7.4	8.7	11.5	11.4	415 815	175	60 114	1 007 521	6.9
Oshkosh-Neenah, WI	0.3	D	7.1	29.1	7.2	4.8	5.6	9.6	12.5	33 535	198	2 502	75 104	2.4
Owensboro, KY	2.6	0.9	5.8	22.2	D	6.7	D	D	12.1	28 010	238	4 225	50 915	3.0
Oxnard-Thousand Oaks-Ventura, CA	3.6	0.9	5.6	15.3	10.1	7.4	8.8	9.1	17.0	134 090	158	16 475	286 864	1.8
Palm Bay-Melbourne-Titusville, FL	0.2	0.0	5.0	16.2	11.2	7.6	4.3	13.9	16.9	154 590	272	11 846	274 540	1.7
Panama City, FL	0.0	0.0	5.2	5.5	8.5	8.7	6.0	D	26.6	43 205	218	5 166	110 684	1.8
Parkersburg-Vienna, WV	-0.2	4.8	7.3	D	D	9.0	D	14.8	20.1	24 970	271	3 987	43 578	0.3
Pensacola-Ferry Pass-Brent, FL	0.2	0.1	5.4	4.4	9.0	7.3	7.6	15.1	27.8	104 170	218	12 559	209 835	4.2
Peoria, IL	0.0	D	5.5	23.8	D	5.1	D	14.0	11.5	77 955	206	7 301	166 271	1.2
Philadelphia-Camden-Wilmington, PA-NJ-DE-MD	0.1	D	D	D	D	5.2	10.2	13.0	12.6	1 108 445	183	182 428	2 462 157	1.2
Camden, NJ Div 15804	0.2	0.0	6.4	8.0	D	7.9	7.6	14.8	19.6	242 890	194	27 178	497 804	1.5
Montgomery County-Bucks County-Chester County, PA Div 33874	0.2	0.1	6.5	9.9	19.3	6.4	10.4	11.9	8.4	370 755	189	19 618	774 947	1.4
Philadelphia, PA Div 37964	0.0	D	2.8	3.8	28.2	3.0	8.4	13.5	13.4	362 535	170	121 972	896 229	0.4
Wilmington, DE-MD-NJ Div 48864	0.2	D	4.7	D	14.8	4.9	18.6	12.6	13.6	132 265	183	13 660	293 177	2.5
Phoenix-Mesa-Scottsdale, AZ	0.4	0.5	5.3	8.1	11.2	7.8	11.8	12.0	12.9	733 885	161	67 685	1 881 995	4.6
Pine Bluff, AR	5.0	D	2.9	17.3	D	5.5	D	D	29.5	21 180	226	5 290	42 139	0.5
Pittsburgh, PA	0.0	2.2	6.7	7.9	12.6	5.4	8.7	13.9	11.2	554 050	236	66 910	1 109 914	0.7
Pittsfield, MA	0.1	0.1	D	9.9	8.7	7.9	5.4	19.0	15.0	34 080	267	4 070	68 458	-0.1
Pocatello, ID	0.7	D	5.7	7.8	5.5	8.1	7.4	15.4	25.5	14 295	170	1 942	33 568	1.1
Portland-South Portland, ME	0.1	D	6.7	D	10.5	6.8	9.4	14.9	16.0	116 775	222	10 118	268 499	2.2
Portland-Vancouver-Hillsboro, OR-WA	0.6	0.1	5.9	13.6	D	5.8	6.9	D	13.2	392 330	165	44 471	972 093	5.1
Port St. Lucie, FL	1.2	D	6.9	5.2	9.0	9.9	5.8	17.5	15.4	120 605	266	8 574	218 557	1.6
Prescott, AZ	0.2	2.9	9.4	5.5	5.7	9.5	5.1	15.1	19.7	74 885	338	3 713	114 798	4.0
Providence-Warwick, RI-MA	0.1	D	D	D	8.9	6.8	7.9	14.5	16.7	337 740	209	52 278	694 657	0.1
Provo-Orem, UT	0.5	0.1	9.8	10.1	D	10.0	D	D	11.9	54 800	94	4 275	170 436	12.2
Pueblo, CO	0.2	0.2	8.0	9.4	6.4	8.1	3.4	20.5	21.5	35 720	219	6 254	70 281	1.1
Punta Gorda, FL	2.3	0.1	7.6	1.8	7.9	12.3	6.4	22.2	15.3	64 695	374	2 681	102 704	2.1
Racine, WI	0.3	0.1	5.0	34.1	3.9	5.5	4.4	12.3	14.3	41 265	212	5 485	82 367	0.3
Raleigh, NC	0.3	D	6.6	8.8	D	6.1	7.7	9.2	14.7	175 945	138	17 669	520 340	11.6
Rapid City, SD	0.4	D	8.9	4.0	D	8.1	7.1	D	23.3	31 430	218	2 376	64 409	6.3

1. Per 1,000 resident population estimated as of July 1, 2011 of the year shown.

Table C. Metropolitan Areas — **Housing, Labor Force, and Employment**

	Housing units, 2015								Civilian labor force, 2016				Civilian employment[5], 2015		
	Occupied units										Unemployment			Percent	
	Owner-occupied					Renter-occupied									
				Median owner cost as a percent of income											
Area name	Total	Percent	Median value[1]	With a mort-gage	Without a mort-gage[2]	Median rent[3]	Median rent as a percent of income	Percent with a com-puter	Total	Percent change, 2015–2016	Total	Rate[4]	Total employed	Management, professional, and related occupations	Construction, production, and related occupations
	89	90	91	92	93	94	95	96	97	98	99	100	101	102	103
Mobile, AL............................	152 938	65.4	120 500	20.7	11.8	797	32.4	77.2	185 092	0.7	12 716	6.9	174 686	34.3	26.3
Modesto, CA........................	171 960	56.5	243 500	24.2	10.4	1 025	32.9	87.2	244 500	1.2	20 845	8.5	215 825	27.3	30.5
Monroe, LA..........................	64 955	61.6	124 100	20.1	10.0	697	32.1	73.5	81 134	-0.8	4 975	6.1	71 483	34.5	22.5
Monroe, MI..........................	58 886	80.1	145 800	19.3	12.1	731	30.1	87.2	76 929	1.0	3 342	4.3	69 299	31.0	30.6
Montgomery, AL...................	144 379	63.1	138 000	19.5	10.2	819	31.9	84.4	171 000	1.1	9 704	5.7	159 169	35.8	22.2
Morgantown, WV	50 274	62.8	163 700	17.5	10.0	865	33.7	87.0	66 132	1.5	3 029	4.6	60 782	44.4	18.3
Morristown, TN....................	44 574	67.0	134 000	21.5	10.0	660	30.5	77.9	50 534	1.5	2 669	5.3	48 912	25.4	36.0
Mount Vernon-Anacortes, WA........................	48 056	66.4	255 900	23.8	12.3	952	31.8	90.4	58 138	2.6	3 945	6.8	54 890	31.0	28.1
Muncie, IN...........................	45 278	64.5	94 100	18.1	11.6	724	35.9	85.7	54 851	0.6	2 863	5.2	52 858	30.2	24.4
Muskegon, MI......................	63 215	73.3	105 400	18.5	11.8	714	30.4	83.8	77 329	0.1	4 046	5.2	72 983	26.3	30.3
Myrtle Beach-Conway-North Myrtle Beach, NC-SC	174 808	71.1	177 300	23.5	12.0	873	32.6	88.8	188 970	1.6	10 928	5.8	184 995	28.5	19.2
Napa, CA.............................	49 619	61.8	555 900	24.4	10.9	1 516	32.6	90.9	73 426	-0.7	3 127	4.3	70 701	34.6	24.2
Naples-Immokalee-Marco Island, FL........................	134 906	72.2	315 000	25.5	12.2	1 177	31.4	92.0	167 737	2.6	7 987	4.8	151 828	31.1	22.0
Nashville-Davidson—Mur-freesboro—Franklin, TN	686 640	65.7	192 200	20.7	10.0	917	28.6	88.1	972 623	3.5	36 910	3.8	927 745	38.8	20.8
New Bern, NC.......................	51 013	61.3	149 500	22.8	11.0	842	30.9	85.3	51 864	1.3	2 726	5.3	50 585	31.2	28.4
New Haven-Milford, CT	323 270	61.5	244 400	24.2	16.1	1 070	32.6	86.4	454 896	-0.1	24 872	5.5	427 933	40.1	18.0
New Orleans-Metairie, LA.....	481 754	60.2	188 300	22.4	11.1	920	33.5	82.9	598 798	-1.2	33 074	5.5	592 425	36.5	20.4
New York-Newark-Jersey City, NY-NJ-PA..............	7 125 065	50.8	414 000	26.8	16.2	1 308	32.2	87.5	10 003 261	0.1	479 667	4.8	9 795 868	41.5	15.9
Dutchess County-Putnam County, NY Div 20524 .	140 500	70.8	288 200	25.5	14.9	1 169	33.0	91.0	193 218	-0.6	7 959	4.1	190 579	39.3	16.6
Nassau County-Suffolk County, NY Div 35004 .	918 363	79.9	418 300	27.9	18.4	1 605	35.9	90.8	1 476 584	-0.1	60 887	4.1	1 428 225	41.3	16.6
Newark, NJ-PA Div 35084 ..	886 182	61.6	374 900	25.0	17.3	1 172	32.1	88.7	1 248 478	-0.7	61 483	4.9	1 250 744	42.6	16.6
New York-Jersey City-White Plains, NY-NJ Div 35614 ...	5 180 020	43.3	432 500	27.0	15.2	1 314	32.0	86.6	7 084 981	0.3	349 338	4.9	6 926 320	41.3	15.7
Niles-Benton Harbor, MI	64 279	69.0	141 200	20.1	12.2	688	28.1	83.7	73 901	0.7	3 548	4.8	70 514	33.5	24.7
North Port-Sarasota-Braden-ton, FL............................	312 497	70.6	208 100	23.0	12.2	1 056	31.7	87.6	350 959	2.5	16 020	4.6	307 210	34.6	18.9
Norwich-New London, CT.....	105 376	65.1	240 900	22.9	13.4	1 061	33.1	88.4	136 592	0.0	6 878	5.0	131 346	38.5	17.4
Ocala, FL	125 227	76.0	120 500	23.9	10.9	776	32.6	81.2	132 670	2.1	7 731	5.8	111 085	28.3	22.0
Ocean City, NJ	38 708	76.5	311 800	29.6	17.8	1 072	35.0	85.6	47 219	-2.5	4 634	9.8	41 556	37.4	19.1
Odessa, TX	52 023	68.7	126 100	18.0	10.0	1 045	23.6	84.7	75 790	-4.7	4 859	6.4	75 131	24.0	33.8
Ogden-Clearfield, UT............	201 165	74.1	216 200	21.1	10.0	886	28.0	92.9	315 053	2.6	10 800	3.4	298 430	36.6	24.1
Oklahoma City, OK	505 074	63.9	146 100	20.9	10.0	821	28.3	87.4	666 220	0.2	28 209	4.2	646 240	36.9	21.3
Olympia-Tumwater, WA........	105 159	64.4	244 800	22.2	10.3	1 044	29.8	91.5	130 653	3.9	7 604	5.8	121 109	41.8	18.5
Omaha-Council Bluffs, NE-IA.........................	351 446	65.8	155 200	20.2	11.8	835	27.4	88.2	478 556	0.4	16 125	3.4	472 752	39.2	19.7
Orlando-Kissimmee-Sanford, FL...................	845 295	59.6	176 100	23.1	12.0	1 070	33.2	90.5	1 254 826	2.9	56 756	4.5	1 147 148	36.0	16.4
Oshkosh-Neenah, WI............	69 636	64.7	144 200	21.0	12.2	695	27.1	87.3	93 042	1.7	3 435	3.7	86 222	30.9	27.2
Owensboro, KY	46 415	71.4	115 000	18.3	10.2	623	28.0	84.9	53 622	1.3	2 451	4.6	52 816	28.3	29.3
Oxnard-Thousand Oaks-Ven-tura, CA..........................	269 566	63.3	528 700	25.5	10.0	1 564	33.3	90.0	427 785	-0.1	22 149	5.2	405 614	37.7	22.3
Palm Bay-Melbourne-Titus-ville, FL..........................	225 682	70.0	158 800	22.1	11.2	976	30.3	90.1	262 026	2.3	13 574	5.2	241 881	37.7	16.6
Panama City, FL	74 276	62.1	164 900	22.5	11.6	983	30.5	87.3	93 991	0.6	4 577	4.9	87 315	32.0	19.9
Parkersburg-Vienna, WV	39 349	68.7	109 000	18.3	10.0	642	31.1	83.1	39 084	-0.7	2 283	5.8	39 401	28.2	23.9
Pensacola-Ferry Pass-Brent, FL....................................	177 675	64.3	142 700	21.8	11.0	911	28.4	89.8	216 531	2.2	10 408	4.8	209 273	32.6	19.7
Peoria, IL.............................	150 639	72.4	137 100	19.7	11.0	739	27.0	83.6	183 863	-1.2	11 930	6.5	177 396	36.2	21.4
Philadelphia-Camden-Wil-mington, PA-NJ-DE-MD.	2 233 752	67.2	240 900	23.1	14.0	1 062	31.5	87.3	3 091 549	1.1	157 425	5.1	2 945 673	42.8	16.4
Camden, NJ Div 15804	452 494	71.8	216 100	24.7	17.4	1 105	32.2	88.9	638 721	0.3	31 906	5.0	610 773	41.6	17.3
Montgomery County-Bucks County-Chester County, PA Div 33874 .	732 646	74.2	314 300	22.1	13.4	1 213	29.5	90.8	1 071 426	1.4	45 604	4.3	1 019 839	48.1	15.6
Philadelphia, PA Div 37964	784 807	57.2	168 000	23.3	13.8	962	33.2	83.4	1 003 113	1.6	62 664	6.2	956 497	38.2	16.8
Wilmington, DE-MD-NJ Div 48864	263 805	69.6	244 000	22.3	11.6	1 073	29.0	86.8	378 289	0.5	17 251	4.6	358 564	42.2	16.3
Phoenix-Mesa-Scottsdale, AZ..................................	1 608 722	60.5	219 100	21.4	10.0	986	29.4	89.0	2 238 744	2.9	102 612	4.6	2 070 696	35.4	18.8
Pine Bluff, AR	34 059	64.8	81 900	22.1	11.2	688	31.3	74.5	36 013	-0.7	1 960	5.4	34 239	29.5	33.6
Pittsburgh, PA......................	990 355	69.2	143 200	19.1	12.3	756	28.1	84.1	1 217 736	0.4	69 261	5.7	1 151 035	39.9	19.5
Pittsfield, MA.......................	55 497	65.6	209 400	22.5	13.9	821	32.1	83.6	64 477	-1.5	2 773	4.3	63 926	34.0	17.9
Pocatello, ID........................	30 174	62.5	151 500	20.6	10.0	655	28.3	90.4	42 300	0.7	1 483	3.5	34 863	31.4	24.7
Portland-South Portland, ME	212 240	70.6	245 800	22.8	13.6	958	29.2	90.3	290 509	1.9	9 009	3.1	279 601	39.9	18.5
Portland-Vancouver-Hills-boro, OR-WA..................	901 402	61.1	303 100	23.1	11.9	1 071	30.0	92.9	1 275 664	3.8	59 775	4.7	1 194 135	40.8	18.4
Port St. Lucie, FL.................	173 912	72.9	165 800	24.5	14.0	997	32.8	88.7	205 626	2.5	11 066	5.4	186 242	29.4	19.8
Prescott, AZ.........................	94 920	70.4	216 300	24.1	10.3	868	28.7	88.8	99 838	3.5	4 851	4.9	84 647	32.1	21.3
Providence-Warwick, RI-MA .	622 607	59.8	254 500	23.5	14.4	910	29.0	86.4	839 868	-0.2	42 882	5.1	802 404	37.7	19.5
Provo-Orem, UT....................	158 270	67.4	251 600	21.8	10.0	956	28.3	96.1	284 524	4.6	8 698	3.1	264 524	40.6	19.1
Pueblo, CO	61 876	63.4	148 000	22.1	11.6	752	34.1	82.9	72 966	1.5	3 543	4.9	65 558	32.4	23.1
Punta Gorda, FL	72 671	75.9	167 300	24.4	13.3	932	33.8	87.0	69 152	2.3	3 687	5.3	61 895	26.0	23.1
Racine, WI	74 960	69.8	162 000	20.8	13.0	800	32.2	85.0	99 649	0.2	5 094	5.1	95 117	31.7	28.4
Raleigh, NC..........................	470 527	64.6	225 000	20.2	10.0	971	28.3	92.9	679 703	3.6	29 426	4.3	645 308	46.0	15.9
Rapid City, SD	58 598	72.2	170 300	22.7	11.4	805	28.1	89.4	72 095	0.6	2 142	3.0	71 748	33.4	22.3

1. Specified owner-occupied units.   2. A value of 10.0 represents 10 percent or less.   3. Specified renter-occupied units.   4. Percent of civilian labor force.
5. Civilian employed persons 16 years old and over.

Table C. Metropolitan Areas — **Nonfarm Employment and Agriculture**

Area name	Private nonfarm establishments, employment and payroll, 2015									Agriculture, 2012			
	Number of establishments	Employment						Annual payroll		Farms	Percent with:		Farm operators whose principal occupation is farming (percent)
		Total	Health care and social assistance	Manufacturing	Retail trade	Finance and insurance	Professional, scientific, and technical services	Total (mil dol)	Average per employee (dollars)	Number	Fewer than 50 acres	500 acres or more	
	104	105	106	107	108	109	110	111	112	113	114	115	116
Mobile, AL	8 600	148 864	20 646	16 770	20 827	5 354	9 371	6 156	41 351	698	60.9	4.4	48.6
Modesto, CA	8 744	135 488	22 813	18 998	23 224	3 328	6 418	5 877	43 379	4 143	68.8	5.9	59.1
Monroe, LA	4 549	66 903	15 386	5 893	10 516	3 608	2 923	2 490	37 219	863	40.0	6.7	44.5
Monroe, MI	2 254	36 847	5 184	7 145	5 165	874	1 328	1 585	43 021	1 144	53.0	10.9	46.3
Montgomery, AL	7 671	129 973	20 817	17 453	18 569	4 915	6 533	5 072	39 021	1 985	33.0	15.7	47.5
Morgantown, WV	2 860	51 192	15 514	4 400	7 148	947	2 815	2 220	43 371	1 542	26.3	3.3	42.6
Morristown, TN	1 962	38 306	4 940	10 837	5 958	707	456	1 364	35 596	1 550	47.2	1.6	45.5
Mount Vernon-Anacortes, WA	3 417	39 772	6 933	6 000	7 130	1 402	1 585	1 724	43 353	1 074	73.0	4.4	48.0
Muncie, IN	2 393	39 382	9 861	4 538	6 191	2 877	1 503	1 396	35 454	610	49.5	13.3	54.8
Muskegon, MI	3 137	53 027	10 169	12 474	7 979	1 050	1 598	2 078	39 183	514	56.6	4.9	48.4
Myrtle Beach-Conway-North Myrtle Beach, NC-SC	10 873	126 884	14 648	3 908	27 284	4 194	3 921	3 951	31 142	1 192	46.0	9.2	48.9
Napa, CA	4 160	62 275	10 016	11 592	6 991	1 389	1 874	3 149	50 567	1 685	71.9	5.3	34.9
Naples-Immokalee-Marco Island, FL	11 293	118 795	17 249	3 102	21 075	3 843	5 267	4 918	41 395	319	74.0	10.3	43.9
Nashville-Davidson—Murfreesboro—Franklin, TN	41 609	797 655	131 376	68 911	92 038	47 750	42 546	39 934	50 064	13 301	39.9	4.5	41.6
New Bern, NC	2 517	30 768	7 051	3 316	5 321	906	1 898	1 143	37 149	506	41.3	17.2	61.3
New Haven-Milford, CT	19 566	335 845	73 797	30 833	42 242	12 252	15 056	16 945	50 455	695	77.3	1.2	43.0
New Orleans-Metairie, LA	30 498	496 807	72 414	26 205	64 438	19 782	33 428	23 527	47 357	1 027	65.4	7.4	45.2
New York-Newark-Jersey City, NY-NJ-PA	572 361	8 123 112	1 470 104	335 792	942 619	563 100	745 940	564 015	69 433	6 758	68.3	2.9	50.9
Dutchess County-Putnam County, NY Div 20524	NA	NA	NA	NA	NA	NA	NA	NA	NA	750	47.2	6.9	53.9
Nassau County-Suffolk County, NY Div 35004	NA	NA	NA	NA	NA	NA	NA	NA	NA	659	72.1	1.5	67.4
Newark, NJ-PA Div 35084	NA	NA	NA	NA	NA	NA	NA	NA	NA	3 169	71.7	2.1	43.4
New York-Jersey City-White Plains, NY-NJ Div 35614	NA	NA	NA	NA	NA	NA	NA	NA	NA	2 180	69.6	3.0	55.9
Niles-Benton Harbor, MI	3 543	53 404	8 894	9 147	6 987	1 386	1 952	2 369	44 361	1 063	57.9	7.0	51.0
North Port-Sarasota-Bradenton, FL	21 885	232 638	42 708	15 259	42 687	7 495	13 509	8 983	38 612	972	65.3	8.8	43.7
Norwich-New London, CT	5 805	102 909	17 185	12 546	14 605	2 111	7 863	5 096	49 524	949	64.0	1.3	48.6
Ocala, FL	6 912	80 011	16 190	6 651	16 145	1 958	3 840	2 735	34 185	3 870	76.7	2.2	49.5
Ocean City, NJ	3 810	26 513	4 730	524	6 550	1 071	1 000	1 050	39 604	152	75.7	1.3	48.0
Odessa, TX	3 717	65 095	6 827	4 619	8 418	1 442	1 481	3 230	49 626	264	70.5	14.4	28.8
Ogden-Clearfield, UT	13 364	177 240	22 751	30 764	27 669	6 637	13 022	6 922	39 053	3 150	64.5	11.0	37.7
Oklahoma City, OK	35 224	504 306	77 612	31 613	67 366	24 652	31 741	22 421	44 459	9 797	35.7	12.4	43.2
Olympia-Tumwater, WA	6 039	68 684	14 080	2 657	12 558	2 612	4 539	2 709	39 435	1 336	79.3	2.0	30.7
Omaha-Council Bluffs, NE-IA	23 116	414 460	61 792	30 890	55 335	39 592	25 199	19 477	46 995	6 055	35.4	26.4	56.8
Orlando-Kissimmee-Sanford, FL	60 881	991 947	116 861	36 835	143 045	37 889	63 533	41 278	41 613	3 123	76.1	4.8	47.9
Oshkosh-Neenah, WI	3 499	82 979	12 118	21 930	8 607	3 346	2 882	4 160	50 129	1 117	48.5	6.0	39.2
Owensboro, KY	2 612	46 639	8 158	7 722	6 512	3 295	1 850	1 835	39 339	1 600	41.6	11.8	46.0
Oxnard-Thousand Oaks-Ventura, CA	20 602	257 011	37 055	24 828	40 237	12 295	22 132	13 635	53 053	2 150	78.0	5.2	48.7
Palm Bay-Melbourne-Titusville, FL	13 648	169 860	29 105	18 282	28 570	4 861	13 435	7 288	42 905	513	80.3	5.1	38.8
Panama City, FL	4 868	65 829	9 943	4 418	12 050	1 592	4 346	2 344	35 611	149	64.4	3.4	45.0
Parkersburg-Vienna, WV	2 095	32 257	7 158	2 295	6 172	979	1 054	1 143	35 429	1 033	28.0	2.3	34.8
Pensacola-Ferry Pass-Brent, FL	9 339	126 500	24 897	5 091	20 967	7 931	8 769	4 855	38 380	1 395	64.1	5.7	42.3
Peoria, IL	8 422	165 198	29 947	16 121	19 646	5 912	6 728	8 613	52 138	3 605	32.5	22.3	52.8
Philadelphia-Camden-Wilmington, PA-NJ-DE-MD	145 816	2 563 343	475 887	169 091	309 330	174 297	202 975	144 649	56 430	6 543	65.1	3.9	54.8
Camden, NJ Div 15804	NA	NA	NA	NA	NA	NA	NA	NA	NA	1 597	72.5	3.7	51.6
Montgomery County-Bucks County-Chester County, PA Div 33874	NA	NA	NA	NA	NA	NA	NA	NA	NA	3 153	64.2	2.3	57.2
Philadelphia, PA Div 37964	NA	NA	NA	NA	NA	NA	NA	NA	NA	98	68.4	0.0	48.0
Wilmington, DE-MD-NJ Div 48864	NA	NA	NA	NA	NA	NA	NA	NA	NA	1 695	59.6	7.4	53.7
Phoenix-Mesa-Scottsdale, AZ	92 265	1 619 025	225 097	101 436	211 707	118 981	113 206	76 943	47 524	3 417	76.9	10.4	54.2
Pine Bluff, AR	1 605	22 919	4 467	5 568	3 738	880	340	810	35 330	1 032	32.0	19.6	54.9
Pittsburgh, PA	59 858	1 094 529	198 007	87 473	127 659	57 460	77 340	53 193	48 599	7 048	37.1	3.0	45.3
Pittsfield, MA	3 868	53 467	11 652	5 020	8 744	1 951	2 387	2 291	42 843	525	49.9	4.4	51.0
Pocatello, ID	1 987	24 406	5 065	1 426	4 479	2 253	1 582	767	31 417	819	46.6	16.1	42.6
Portland-South Portland, ME	17 640	231 298	46 324	21 681	34 144	14 962	12 839	10 341	44 707	1 726	56.6	2.8	50.2
Portland-Vancouver-Hillsboro, OR-WA	66 947	978 967	140 112	101 221	115 910	44 714	74 539	52 730	53 863	10 838	79.1	1.9	42.3
Port St. Lucie, FL	10 681	111 852	21 375	5 196	23 248	3 008	5 972	4 084	36 516	993	64.7	13.1	54.0
Prescott, AZ	5 741	57 307	13 011	3 387	10 725	1 154	1 698	1 960	34 206	940	69.9	13.1	64.1
Providence-Warwick, RI-MA	40 821	616 068	128 047	63 785	83 575	29 724	28 018	27 965	45 392	1 960	72.3	0.8	49.5
Provo-Orem, UT	12 438	192 435	23 531	17 927	26 129	5 213	13 376	7 671	39 863	2 815	73.2	6.1	30.3
Pueblo, CO	3 020	48 828	12 944	4 370	7 954	1 151	1 999	1 827	37 423	894	38.9	21.3	52.3
Punta Gorda, FL	3 815	37 485	8 238	516	9 117	1 076	1 452	1 236	32 980	284	61.3	12.0	51.1
Racine, WI	4 004	69 285	11 236	16 579	9 298	2 144	1 955	3 149	45 445	575	51.0	8.2	45.6
Raleigh, NC	31 493	481 122	63 838	22 900	66 489	23 255	49 825	24 145	50 185	2 500	50.5	6.7	45.9
Rapid City, SD	4 737	54 861	10 865	3 161	9 986	2 922	2 086	2 101	38 298	1 936	24.9	42.6	54.8

Table C. Metropolitan Areas — **Agriculture**

	Agriculture, 2012 (cont.)															
Area name	Land in farms					Value of land and buildings (dollars)		Value of machinery and equipment, average per farm (dollars)	Value of products sold				Percent of farms with sales of:		Government payments	
	Acreage (1,000)	Percent change, 2007–2012	Acres			Average per farm	Average per acre		Total (mil dol)	Average per farm (dollars)	Percent from:		$10,000 or more	$100,000 or more	Total ($1,000)	Percent of farms
			Average size of farm	Total irrigated (1,000)	Total cropland (1,000)						Crops	Livestock and poultry products				
	117	118	119	120	121	122	123	124	125	126	127	128	129	130	131	132
Mobile, AL	89	-21.9	127	2.8	36.6	516 701	4 062	78 354	84.7	121 289	90.7	9.3	33.2	8.5	796	12.2
Modesto, CA	768	-2.7	185	320.8	340.9	1 786 289	9 636	117 810	2 228.1	537 807	47.7	52.3	66.5	33.9	7 049	10.7
Monroe, LA	156	2.0	180	12.2	64.3	525 813	2 913	73 651	142.0	164 531	20.0	80.0	34.8	12.4	2 099	17.8
Monroe, MI	215	3.2	188	9.8	196.2	853 688	4 553	135 682	173.9	152 008	95.5	4.5	54.6	20.3	3 653	50.8
Montgomery, AL	640	2.6	322	10.1	172.7	753 146	2 337	72 061	200.1	100 782	D	D	36.2	8.4	4 011	25.6
Morgantown, WV	219	3.4	142	0.1	59.8	373 360	2 633	53 257	22.2	14 383	28.0	72.0	28.7	2.2	387	7.7
Morristown, TN	154	-9.7	100	D	65.1	510 717	5 127	57 306	59.8	38 562	26.4	73.6	27.5	3.4	754	15.3
Mount Vernon-Anacortes, WA	107	-1.8	99	19.2	66.8	752 365	7 585	118 998	272.3	253 515	73.8	26.2	29.1	12.2	1 442	11.1
Muncie, IN	175	13.5	287	0.0	160.4	1 522 762	5 300	152 951	125.6	205 836	93.2	6.8	52.1	26.9	3 980	67.4
Muskegon, MI	74	-6.8	144	9.5	49.0	741 080	5 130	95 333	76.0	147 860	61.6	38.4	38.9	15.6	658	21.8
Myrtle Beach-Conway-North Myrtle Beach, NC-SC	223	7.4	187	6.8	135.5	613 356	3 278	93 415	159.5	133 816	67.5	32.5	32.0	13.7	2 576	41.3
Napa, CA	253	13.5	150	54.6	63.0	3 278 130	21 801	85 134	536.1	318 188	97.8	2.2	74.5	34.1	85	1.1
Naples-Immokalee-Marco Island, FL	124	12.4	387	26.4	66.9	1 736 727	4 482	151 806	202.8	635 583	98.1	1.9	36.4	14.7	207	2.8
Nashville-Davidson—Murfreesboro—Franklin, TN	1 868	-3.1	140	6.1	733.8	592 188	4 217	60 620	D	D	D	D	28.9	4.6	7 865	17.8
New Bern, NC	177	-5.0	349	4.4	136.2	1 010 889	2 893	192 399	276.9	547 283	D	D	49.4	31.8	4 482	57.7
New Haven-Milford, CT	42	-7.4	61	1.3	14.1	764 679	12 561	56 881	84.6	121 755	91.7	8.3	31.9	10.1	383	7.3
New Orleans-Metairie, LA	230	-15.3	224	D	68.4	635 817	2 843	75 303	77.8	75 785	71.4	28.6	33.7	7.6	D	6.3
New York-Newark-Jersey City, NY-NJ-PA	D	D	D	D	D	D	D	D	D	D	D	D	39.5	13.2	D	9.8
Dutchess County-Putnam County, NY Div 20524	118	9.6	158	D	47.2	820 965	5 201	92 353	52.3	69 704	55.5	44.5	47.2	16.4	451	10.0
Nassau County-Suffolk County, NY Div 35004	39	8.3	59	11.9	23.5	713 168	12 158	131 416	246.1	373 389	84.3	15.7	62.4	31.1	790	6.5
Newark, NJ-PA Div 35084	235	-3.4	74	2.8	117.1	1 055 516	14 250	59 764	144.7	45 663	D	D	27.8	6.2	D	8.4
New York-Jersey City-White Plains, NY-NJ Div 35614	D	D	D	10.2	D	D	D	D	D	D	D	D	46.8	16.9	D	12.8
Niles-Benton Harbor, MI	156	-7.5	147	18.1	126.1	822 736	5 591	123 913	161.5	151 968	90.3	9.7	51.6	20.6	3 303	29.4
North Port-Sarasota-Bradenton, FL	267	-6.9	274	52.1	75.1	1 468 749	5 356	94 934	323.5	332 798	89.0	11.0	38.4	12.4	395	1.3
Norwich-New London, CT	65	2.8	69	0.8	22.8	709 299	10 330	47 891	118.3	124 690	43.2	56.8	26.9	6.7	537	9.2
Ocala, FL	321	20.6	83	13.2	69.8	776 909	9 353	37 481	188.2	48 624	23.3	76.7	27.8	8.2	483	2.1
Ocean City, NJ	7	-7.8	48	2.2	4.3	557 868	11 534	51 809	8.0	52 809	93.4	6.6	40.1	10.5	D	2.0
Odessa, TX	429	1.2	1 624	0.8	3.6	786 019	484	48 008	2.2	8 296	28.9	71.1	16.3	1.5	211	5.3
Ogden-Clearfield, UT	1 572	-11.5	499	163.5	390.3	891 628	1 787	88 691	266.5	84 616	48.0	52.0	35.1	12.3	8 138	20.8
Oklahoma City, OK	2 466	-7.5	252	31.6	839.6	492 117	1 955	64 720	451.1	46 043	32.4	67.6	32.8	6.8	13 028	25.7
Olympia-Tumwater, WA	77	-4.9	57	5.3	23.1	498 439	8 689	40 468	122.4	91 634	39.9	60.1	19.5	5.2	267	2.4
Omaha-Council Bluffs, NE-IA	2 373	9.9	392	D	2 092.0	2 376 608	6 064	217 610	1 649.3	272 378	74.2	25.8	60.6	39.0	40 234	69.0
Orlando-Kissimmee-Sanford, FL	853	-9.2	273	55.0	81.9	1 468 380	5 374	45 570	539.8	172 845	88.9	11.1	37.6	14.1	632	1.6
Oshkosh-Neenah, WI	156	-5.2	139	0.4	126.2	585 332	4 204	97 747	126.6	113 315	41.3	58.7	41.5	20.1	3 245	54.3
Owensboro, KY	414	-10.9	259	11.3	310.1	959 871	3 711	135 426	370.2	231 353	49.6	50.4	43.7	18.8	6 252	57.9
Oxnard-Thousand Oaks-Ventura, CA	281	8.5	131	87.1	101.1	2 041 990	15 621	94 136	1 440.1	669 829	99.3	0.7	65.1	24.7	154	2.0
Palm Bay-Melbourne-Titusville, FL	146	-12.3	286	13.4	19.3	1 545 698	5 414	45 433	46.0	89 651	77.2	22.8	36.8	6.6	142	2.1
Panama City, FL	15	-12.4	101	D	3.2	494 671	4 886	36 826	3.6	24 436	63.6	36.4	18.8	2.0	D	7.4
Parkersburg-Vienna, WV	126	-3.3	122	D	29.5	258 830	2 124	35 881	8.3	8 082	30.4	69.6	15.3	0.5	157	4.5
Pensacola-Ferry Pass-Brent, FL	172	13.2	123	7.1	109.7	508 622	4 120	72 795	105.3	75 502	92.7	7.3	24.9	9.5	3 971	27.7
Peoria, IL	1 288	2.9	357	D	1 149.9	2 619 353	7 332	215 209	960.8	266 524	87.7	12.3	62.8	41.4	25 748	76.4
Philadelphia-Camden-Wilmington, PA-NJ-DE-MD	653	-3.8	100	51.0	456.1	1 066 581	10 682	100 412	1 264.9	193 316	D	D	43.9	18.2	D	16.8
Camden, NJ Div 15804	146	3.6	92	24.7	89.0	960 535	10 485	93 126	204.6	128 112	95.0	5.0	39.6	14.6	2 659	12.4
Montgomery County-Bucks County-Chester County, PA Div 33874	259	-8.9	82	2.9	173.7	1 068 407	12 992	94 153	748.8	237 474	80.2	19.8	47.1	20.3	2 503	14.3
Philadelphia, PA Div 37964	5	8.4	51	0.1	1.3	797 133	15 593	51 439	10.5	107 643	98.7	1.3	36.7	7.1	D	2.0
Wilmington, DE-MD-NJ Div 48864	243	-2.4	143	23.3	192.1	1 178 678	8 232	121 753	301.0	177 561	D	D	42.4	18.3	4 693	26.5
Phoenix-Mesa-Scottsdale, AZ	1 651	7.7	483	416.5	525.1	1 606 626	3 326	134 243	1 931.2	565 178	39.5	60.5	37.0	18.4	14 937	14.7
Pine Bluff, AR	519	-0.3	503	D	421.0	1 463 373	2 912	248 855	540.5	523 758	58.2	41.8	49.1	33.6	18 108	53.1
Pittsburgh, PA	818	-6.7	116	2.4	409.7	491 395	4 235	76 477	231.1	32 792	59.1	40.9	34.4	6.1	5 514	18.6
Pittsfield, MA	62	-7.1	117	0.2	18.4	824 924	7 024	51 476	22.5	42 796	45.1	54.9	29.5	6.7	268	9.3
Pocatello, ID	295	-8.3	360	52.6	164.1	651 077	1 807	83 179	54.3	66 267	66.6	33.4	29.4	9.2	3 067	37.0
Portland-South Portland, ME	147	13.6	85	2.1	44.1	404 259	4 737	57 375	D	D	D	D	32.4	6.8	994	7.0
Portland-Vancouver-Hillsboro, OR-WA	644	-2.7	59	75.1	340.4	624 772	10 520	59 443	1 008.5	93 072	D	D	27.6	7.6	5 384	7.7
Port St. Lucie, FL	334	18.2	337	94.1	110.4	1 858 422	5 518	72 106	333.5	335 878	77.8	22.2	42.8	17.1	1 270	5.5
Prescott, AZ	825	29.0	877	7.6	10.7	1 382 518	1 576	51 250	41.6	44 285	25.5	74.5	32.2	12.0	141	3.2
Providence-Warwick, RI-MA	D	D	D	5.6	34.5	757 972	D	54 363	97.3	49 648	81.1	18.9	35.9	8.7	D	14.3
Provo-Orem, UT	586	-3.3	208	95.6	157.4	753 272	3 619	70 725	251.0	89 161	43.7	56.3	31.4	6.9	2 120	11.0
Pueblo, CO	895	-1.7	1 001	18.6	88.5	735 098	734	62 169	51.1	57 149	35.4	64.6	27.2	8.1	2 223	20.6
Punta Gorda, FL	217	30.8	765	13.7	18.4	3 875 556	5 067	65 965	103.4	364 088	91.8	8.2	38.0	13.0	92	1.8
Racine, WI	110	-8.7	191	1.9	92.6	1 042 289	5 450	127 732	94.8	164 887	77.6	22.4	50.3	21.7	1 972	50.6
Raleigh, NC	396	1.0	158	10.6	237.5	902 766	5 700	94 320	411.9	164 756	65.9	34.1	35.6	14.4	6 265	34.1
Rapid City, SD	3 730	-6.6	1 927	12.9	619.5	1 464 509	760	105 970	208.2	107 542	27.8	72.2	56.0	24.1	9 162	33.6

Area name	Water use, 2010		Wholesale trade,[1] 2012				Retail trade, 2012				Real estate and rental and leasing, 2012			
	Total water withdrawn (mil gal/day)	Gallons withdrawn per person per day	Number of establishments	Number of employees	Sales (mil dol)	Annual payroll (mil dol)	Number of establishments	Number of employees	Sales (mil dol)	Annual payroll (mil dol)	Number of establishments	Number of employees	Receipts (mil dol)	Annual payroll (mil dol)
	133	134	135	136	137	138	139	140	141	142	143	144	145	146
Mobile, AL	1 096.7	2 656	499	6 116	3 680.0	283.8	1 454	19 204	5 102.6	454.7	410	2 125	419.1	83.2
Modesto, CA	1 642.7	3 193	405	6 087	5 295.1	313.6	1 374	20 970	5 933.6	527.1	433	2 141	387.9	73.2
Monroe, LA	72.2	409	187	2 190	1 793.0	96.6	776	9 812	2 528.4	220.3	190	1 154	229.3	38.1
Monroe, MI	1 830.0	12 038	89	D	D	D	377	4 977	1 471.2	110.5	78	306	43.8	7.9
Montgomery, AL	113.7	303	360	5 844	4 361.6	272.4	1 322	17 359	4 678.9	421.7	309	2 146	377.1	72.4
Morgantown, WV	123.3	950	71	486	374.3	17.4	476	7 179	1 843.1	146.7	152	799	128.8	22.1
Morristown, TN	18.2	160	68	943	1 100.5	45.5	391	5 674	1 619.1	131.9	79	297	62.0	8.9
Mount Vernon-Anacortes, WA	45.3	388	104	1 277	793.5	58.2	553	6 801	1 999.2	186.8	158	467	81.8	14.4
Muncie, IN	15.6	132	92	894	805.8	32.1	428	6 189	1 519.9	131.9	95	447	90.7	16.5
Muskegon, MI	271.7	1 578	121	D	D	D	552	7 597	1 919.4	171.2	91	457	71.7	14.8
Myrtle Beach-Conway-North Myrtle Beach, NC-SC	1 525.6	4 050	307	2 149	971.4	87.0	2 037	25 110	6 365.9	556.0	718	5 052	591.6	151.2
Napa, CA	96.9	710	167	D	D	D	524	6 318	1 699.0	184.2	207	1 026	160.4	38.2
Naples-Immokalee-Marco Island, FL	256.9	799	306	2 417	2 306.5	163.1	1 418	18 924	5 304.1	511.0	907	2 610	546.6	109.8
Nashville-Davidson—Murfreesboro—Franklin, TN	891.7	534	1 760	32 450	48 065.9	1 851.8	6 018	85 291	23 831.1	2 149.6	1 756	10 598	2 557.2	478.8
New Bern, NC	44.8	353	91	803	1 408.6	30.5	461	4 882	1 347.4	115.1	111	376	46.1	10.7
New Haven-Milford, CT	113.5	132	922	14 185	11 237.2	821.2	2 901	41 925	11 567.5	1 100.7	673	5 378	2 008.0	220.2
New Orleans-Metairie, LA	4 541.9	3 817	1 411	19 692	33 417.9	1 064.1	4 480	57 986	16 445.2	1 503.7	1 222	7 682	1 793.8	319.7
New York-Newark-Jersey City, NY-NJ-PA	7 105.0	363	33 908	412 171	507 384.4	28 173.7	78 193	896 588	270 758.2	25 968.1	33 390	178 052	65 022.2	9 852.3
Dutchess County-Putnam County, NY Div 20524	84.5	213	315	2 814	4 858.3	181.1	1 375	17 192	4 744.9	429.7	414	1 533	280.2	53.6
Nassau County-Suffolk County, NY Div 35004	1 136.2	401	5 694	66 586	60 342.0	4 120.9	12 669	156 986	47 799.0	4 388.8	4 008	16 099	4 922.6	835.9
Newark, NJ-PA Div 35084	410.6	166	3 527	58 817	76 074.4	4 651.1	8 600	112 874	36 178.3	3 107.7	2 541	16 253	5 851.7	899.5
New York-Jersey City-White Plains, NY-NJ Div 35614	5 473.7	395	24 372	283 954	366 109.6	19 220.6	55 549	609 536	182 036.0	18 042.0	26 427	144 167	53 967.8	8 063.3
Niles-Benton Harbor, MI	2 019.0	12 875	133	D	D	D	587	6 783	1 681.1	147.2	152	614	78.3	19.5
North Port-Sarasota-Bradenton, FL	157.8	225	751	6 092	3 496.9	283.0	2 832	37 299	9 942.8	926.9	1 301	4 688	1 068.6	180.5
Norwich-New London, CT	2 249.8	8 209	150	D	D	D	1 023	14 372	3 679.3	364.3	204	765	182.6	32.0
Ocala, FL	65.4	197	277	3 157	1 719.3	143.3	1 152	14 430	4 263.6	353.9	338	1 382	211.8	41.3
Ocean City, NJ	79.6	818	60	D	D	D	669	5 803	1 639.4	166.2	218	681	148.7	26.0
Odessa, TX	60.2	439	298	4 659	3 608.8	330.5	451	7 286	2 711.7	218.7	176	1 482	604.9	101.9
Ogden-Clearfield, UT	795.6	1 332	460	5 797	4 437.8	247.6	1 708	25 217	6 975.2	593.7	726	1 965	359.1	61.2
Oklahoma City, OK	263.1	210	1 472	21 416	45 661.6	1 219.0	4 318	61 357	19 131.2	1 578.5	1 713	9 151	2 064.4	407.4
Olympia-Tumwater, WA	52.3	207	169	1 824	1 252.0	90.8	769	12 317	3 330.8	324.6	325	994	202.1	31.3
Omaha-Council Bluffs, NE-IA	1 570.7	1 815	1 139	16 116	19 466.9	866.4	2 705	51 093	14 650.4	1 227.3	1 015	6 759	1 210.3	292.0
Orlando-Kissimmee-Sanford, FL	509.9	239	2 582	28 410	24 271.6	1 413.0	8 166	124 686	37 046.0	3 002.2	3 691	27 653	6 908.9	1 046.4
Oshkosh-Neenah, WI	35.3	211	136	D	D	D	473	7 892	2 064.9	174.5	113	576	219.2	19.9
Owensboro, KY	577.6	5 034	108	1 392	1 267.3	60.1	456	6 229	1 547.9	141.1	85	591	102.2	19.5
Oxnard-Thousand Oaks-Ventura, CA	719.5	874	985	D	D	D	2 562	37 012	11 194.2	1 011.0	1 008	4 568	983.6	196.5
Palm Bay-Melbourne-Titusville, FL	251.4	463	451	3 962	1 846.5	195.7	1 955	24 885	6 527.5	606.1	642	2 056	340.7	66.7
Panama City, FL	303.6	1 644	163	1 472	522.2	63.9	857	10 636	2 805.1	256.9	291	1 460	213.3	40.8
Parkersburg-Vienna, WV	63.8	689	77	D	D	D	403	6 095	1 416.4	130.3	85	D	D	D
Pensacola-Ferry Pass-Brent, FL	337.9	753	330	2 953	1 719.6	124.7	1 477	19 315	5 356.2	468.5	489	1 781	340.3	56.9
Peoria, IL	648.5	1 710	401	6 169	4 946.2	296.2	1 290	19 211	5 010.7	456.4	312	1 335	266.4	43.7
Philadelphia-Camden-Wilmington, PA-NJ-DE-MD	5 352.0	897	6 714	103 885	112 303.8	6 892.7	19 892	297 081	85 570.3	7 755.5	5 229	36 509	13 076.4	1 908.7
Camden, NJ Div 15804	239.2	191	1 360	25 642	36 358.5	1 498.0	4 112	63 959	17 767.4	1 638.0	933	7 228	1 743.9	381.8
Montgomery County-Bucks County-Chester County, PA Div 33874	488.6	254	3 100	47 014	49 846.9	3 504.5	7 186	122 083	38 696.3	3 449.9	1 977	13 567	3 404.4	703.1
Philadelphia, PA Div 37964	1 157.1	555	1 569	23 901	18 664.2	1 509.3	6 206	74 456	18 710.1	1 767.7	1 488	11 801	2 727.4	613.2
Wilmington, DE-MD-NJ Div 48864	3 467.2	4 913	685	7 328	7 434.2	380.9	2 388	36 583	10 396.5	899.8	831	3 913	5 200.6	210.6
Phoenix-Mesa-Scottsdale, AZ	3 083.7	735	4 058	59 578	61 626.6	3 549.5	10 899	191 751	59 671.8	5 115.0	5 578	30 399	7 712.9	1 367.6
Pine Bluff, AR	576.3	5 748	65	D	D	D	329	3 719	914.8	82.4	70	229	39.7	6.6
Pittsburgh, PA	1 712.7	727	2 561	37 959	42 687.8	2 075.7	8 271	126 114	34 250.1	2 907.5	2 034	12 564	2 998.5	548.8
Pittsfield, MA	24.3	185	105	1 242	455.0	58.0	711	8 482	1 916.5	201.7	108	715	99.5	23.1
Pocatello, ID	168.1	2 029	80	D	D	D	299	4 330	1 155.3	95.7	80	221	31.5	5.2
Portland-South Portland, ME	114.0	222	622	7 227	6 787.0	367.3	2 457	32 974	8 665.6	788.1	768	3 495	647.7	132.3
Portland-Vancouver-Hillsboro, OR-WA	733.4	329	3 035	44 671	40 137.7	2 629.7	7 084	105 037	29 004.4	2 832.2	3 353	17 891	3 578.8	700.3
Port St. Lucie, FL	1 302.5	3 071	352	D	D	D	1 438	21 908	6 262.8	600.4	519	2 333	386.7	80.6
Prescott, AZ	92.3	437	163	1 385	880.4	59.1	787	9 854	2 504.3	233.3	341	941	153.0	27.7
Providence-Warwick, RI-MA	1 257.6	786	1 675	26 253	31 686.2	1 626.5	5 987	81 494	20 467.4	2 020.3	1 476	6 997	1 413.5	271.7
Provo-Orem, UT	422.2	801	377	5 832	3 148.9	300.7	1 553	22 409	6 153.9	534.7	686	1 871	339.0	53.7
Pueblo, CO	288.9	1 816	85	D	D	D	508	7 551	1 952.8	183.4	143	585	105.1	17.7
Punta Gorda, FL	58.8	367	94	D	D	D	558	8 000	2 091.3	185.9	232	680	113.1	19.1
Racine, WI	28.6	146	170	2 243	1 702.5	118.6	591	8 542	2 182.0	181.6	100	327	58.9	9.7
Raleigh, NC	153.6	136	1 212	19 573	19 650.4	1 474.6	3 838	59 857	16 847.3	1 453.3	1 439	7 825	1 764.6	407.5
Rapid City, SD	74.5	554	180	1 944	1 287.9	86.1	683	9 154	2 529.9	219.6	192	645	115.1	18.0

1. Merchant wholesalers, except manufacturers' sales branches and offices.

Table C. Metropolitan Areas — **Professional Services, Manufacturing, and Accommodation and Food Services**

Area name	Professional, scientific, and technical services, 2012				Manufacturing, 2012				Accommodation and food services, 2012			
	Number of establishments	Number of employees	Sales (mil dol)	Annual payroll (mil dol)	Number of establishments	Number of employees	Sales (mil dol)	Annual payroll (mil dol)	Number of establishments	Number of employees	Sales (mil dol)	Annual payroll (mil dol)
	147	148	149	150	151	152	153	154	155	156	157	158
Mobile, AL......................	850	9 039	1 175.1	474.0	343	16 063	10 562.7	886.3	671	13 684	617.9	167.9
Modesto, CA	649	5 111	507.5	196.0	395	19 963	11 703.6	1 007.8	813	13 611	705.7	192.6
Monroe, LA	449	2 737	379.1	125.2	136	6 067	2 438.8	286.3	310	6 524	298.1	81.5
Monroe, MI	147	828	129.9	40.6	128	6 591	2 976.5	351.3	259	4 280	179.9	49.6
Montgomery, AL..................	756	6 906	1 421.8	433.6	287	17 367	14 627.6	896.5	671	13 503	636.6	174.8
Morgantown, WV	234	2 834	405.3	124.7	78	4 133	2 181.4	273.8	317	6 165	267.1	73.8
Morristown, TN....................	110	438	48.8	14.1	144	10 205	4 224.1	418.1	178	3 065	152.3	40.6
Mount Vernon-Anacortes, WA	300	D	D	D	174	5 269	11 529.4	295.7	330	4 195	291.5	79.1
Muncie, IN...........................	163	1 522	240.5	63.4	130	4 205	1 591.3	191.2	211	4 417	172.7	49.6
Muskegon, MI......................	223	1 513	182.5	65.7	259	12 483	3 727.0	608.0	335	5 450	236.1	67.6
Myrtle Beach-Conway-North Myrtle Beach, NC-SC	866	3 696	400.6	143.7	216	4 213	2 742.7	222.8	1 489	29 339	1 897.5	499.8
Napa, CA	395	1 801	280.5	101.5	431	10 837	4 623.5	622.5	375	10 466	774.1	247.7
Naples-Immokalee-Marco Island, FL......................	1 342	4 810	784.7	270.4	197	2 722	607.5	130.0	763	19 624	1 406.5	404.2
Nashville-Davidson—Murfreesboro—Franklin, TN	3 785	38 289	6 215.8	2 520.0	1 488	61 378	28 947.4	2 916.1	3 530	76 659	4 275.8	1 250.6
New Bern, NC......................	250	1 884	220.7	97.0	85	3 535	1 308.0	164.3	234	4 207	198.3	54.1
New Haven-Milford, CT	1 907	16 222	2 461.1	1 216.8	1 151	31 792	10 818.1	1 879.2	1 969	26 342	1 487.2	411.3
New Orleans-Metairie, LA.....	3 884	31 419	5 507.7	2 078.7	742	34 170	104 969.4	2 377.1	3 217	69 067	4 502.4	1 259.1
New York-Newark-Jersey City, NY-NJ-PA..............	69 819	710 316	163 194.8	61 316.7	16 232	346 950	134 229.9	19 621.2	48 312	634 388	49 193.7	13 558.1
Dutchess County-Putnam County, NY Div 20524.	1 086	5 256	833.3	299.0	285	10 022	2 790.6	742.5	979	10 711	599.9	162.2
Nassau County-Suffolk County, NY Div 35004.	12 457	87 339	13 447.4	5 200.1	3 110	68 546	21 084.1	3 694.2	7 107	89 642	5 929.2	1 628.8
Newark, NJ-PA Div 35084..	9 067	112 684	22 364.6	9 712.9	2 448	70 600	38 127.3	4 797.5	5 475	72 580	4 728.5	1 272.8
New York-Jersey City-White Plains, NY-NJ Div 35614..................	47 209	505 037	126 549.4	46 104.7	10 389	197 783	72 228.0	10 387.1	34 751	461 455	37 936.1	10 494.2
Niles-Benton Harbor, MI	284	2 149	201.0	108.3	289	8 330	1 962.8	388.9	365	5 323	241.7	69.4
North Port-Sarasota-Bradenton, FL...........................	2 703	20 704	1 945.0	841.3	591	13 680	3 538.1	670.9	1 446	26 437	1 429.1	419.4
Norwich-New London, CT.....	529	8 100	666.1	862.0	172	12 435	4 693.7	950.2	698	28 347	3 023.8	748.7
Ocala, FL	669	3 676	415.5	157.2	178	4 806	1 471.2	212.9	437	7 369	375.2	102.5
Ocean City, NJ	214	D	D	D	66	615	98.2	21.5	903	5 888	593.0	160.0
Odessa, TX	227	1 832	205.4	80.1	251	4 756	1 706.3	265.7	261	6 150	389.0	94.0
Ogden-Clearfield, UT............	1 443	10 848	1 407.6	525.8	596	27 115	14 050.6	1 478.6	855	15 956	671.2	190.6
Oklahoma City, OK	4 132	27 776	4 052.7	1 582.9	1 050	31 032	11 209.0	1 338.6	2 685	57 866	2 741.9	749.8
Olympia-Tumwater, WA........	593	D	D	D	168	2 883	910.5	123.8	533	7 785	419.2	120.5
Omaha-Council Bluffs, NE-IA....................................	2 342	59 415	3 755.6	2 966.2	656	30 185	17 651.7	1 361.4	1 901	36 416	1 866.7	512.8
Orlando-Kissimmee-Sanford, FL......................	7 816	58 862	8 811.8	3 756.9	1 337	32 960	11 209.7	1 917.5	4 484	138 873	10 349.4	2 695.0
Oshkosh-Neenah, WI...........	247	2 575	514.5	134.8	300	23 892	11 476.5	1 321.6	367	5 963	234.6	65.3
Owensboro, KY	169	1 563	105.3	44.8	125	6 938	5 391.9	357.4	193	4 448	191.8	55.3
Oxnard-Thousand Oaks-Ventura, CA...........................	2 634	22 377	3 185.4	2 063.2	867	23 166	8 334.0	1 295.4	1 598	27 725	1 597.4	442.6
Palm Bay-Melbourne-Titusville, FL...........................	1 669	13 893	2 433.6	981.2	407	19 152	5 441.9	1 311.3	1 042	18 994	902.6	257.7
Panama City, FL..................	434	3 465	493.8	184.2	110	3 904	1 482.5	197.5	497	10 318	581.6	165.7
Parkersburg-Vienna, WV	165	D	D	D	63	2 882	D	207.9	218	D	D	D
Pensacola-Ferry Pass-Brent, FL....................................	1 063	9 010	1 234.8	486.1	229	4 433	2 552.0	262.3	747	14 767	744.0	203.9
Peoria, IL	676	6 718	865.5	374.9	331	19 563	13 708.7	1 081.5	870	15 632	778.2	212.7
Philadelphia-Camden-Wilmington, PA-NJ-DE-MD.	18 064	199 353	37 881.9	16 087.3	5 115	172 790	99 584.5	10 453.8	12 771	198 333	11 474.3	3 164.3
Camden, NJ Div 15804	3 281	D	D	D	967	34 775	D	2 101.0	2 395	36 821	1 967.4	525.4
Montgomery County-Bucks County-Chester County, PA Div 33874.	8 266	83 896	15 163.1	6 634.4	2 565	82 694	30 889.5	4 823.6	4 218	66 585	3 705.4	1 043.4
Philadelphia, PA Div 37964	4 370	59 242	12 848.3	5 152.2	1 132	35 487	27 083.4	2 173.3	4 774	69 816	4 429.8	1 218.4
Wilmington, DE-MD-NJ Div 48864......................	2 147	D	D	D	451	19 834	D	1 356.0	1 384	25 111	1 371.7	377.1
Phoenix-Mesa-Scottsdale, AZ....................................	11 812	91 918	15 658.8	5 865.3	3 000	94 061	36 827.5	5 560.6	7 121	165 154	9 456.3	2 745.4
Pine Bluff, AR	87	594	66.7	28.3	70	5 532	2 226.6	243.5	134	2 365	93.0	23.1
Pittsburgh, PA	5 871	81 204	15 404.9	5 698.3	2 506	90 107	38 416.1	4 812.4	5 374	92 549	4 548.1	1 266.2
Pittsfield, MA	338	2 688	397.7	162.8	151	5 275	1 288.9	310.7	522	7 006	418.7	124.2
Pocatello, ID	165	1 277	84.2	40.3	44	1 633	916.3	67.7	197	3 199	135.5	37.2
Portland-South Portland, ME	1 923	13 183	2 086.5	801.2	662	21 142	6 501.6	1 099.6	1 823	24 102	1 457.2	436.0
Portland-Vancouver-Hillsboro, OR-WA	8 099	68 556	9 720.6	5 233.3	3 058	D	D	D	5 743	86 242	4 870.0	1 428.9
Port St. Lucie, FL.................	1 211	5 244	685.0	246.3	296	4 883	1 709.0	237.3	724	12 867	642.0	182.8
Prescott, AZ	522	1 748	190.9	74.3	184	2 765	706.9	130.8	548	8 223	407.5	130.8
Providence-Warwick, RI-MA .	4 042	27 215	4 161.4	1 605.4	2 183	66 543	19 277.2	3 628.5	4 214	63 818	3 450.4	982.0
Provo-Orem, UT...................	1 654	16 956	1 741.7	656.2	525	15 963	6 082.1	807.2	709	13 249	577.3	161.5
Pueblo, CO	238	1 744	435.3	157.3	90	4 221	2 333.3	216.8	356	5 698	236.0	67.8
Punta Gorda, FL	381	1 295	138.5	50.5	69	402	90.4	14.6	261	4 804	219.2	61.7
Racine, WI	310	1 967	234.8	91.7	325	15 444	8 100.1	844.4	382	5 974	251.7	70.5
Raleigh, NC	4 656	41 942	7 437.7	3 117.2	738	21 629	17 865.0	1 146.8	2 415	47 908	2 436.0	675.1
Rapid City, SD	372	2 151	243.7	83.2	164	2 383	570.3	95.4	480	7 455	426.6	117.1

Table C. Metropolitan Areas — Health Care and Social Assistance, Other Services, Nonemployer Business and Residential Construction

Area name	Health care and social assistance, 2012				Other services, 2012				Nonemployer business, 2015		Value of residential construction authorized by building permits, 2016	
	Number of establishments	Number of employees	Receipts (mil dol)	Annual payroll (mil dol)	Number of establishments	Number of employees	Receipts (mil dol)	Annual payroll (mil dol)	Number	Receipts (mil dol)	New construction ($1,000)	Number of housing units
	159	160	161	162	163	164	165	166	167	168	169	170
Mobile, AL	734	21 863	2 397.2	927.8	570	3 577	334.8	96.2	30 496	1 117.8	203 382	1 195
Modesto, CA	1 075	24 257	3 635.0	1 274.8	604	3 817	371.6	118.9	27 111	1 418.2	116 156	573
Monroe, LA	661	14 936	1 407.9	504.3	243	1 568	144.3	42.1	14 105	573.4	131 423	670
Monroe, MI	282	5 347	457.9	193.6	156	727	67.6	17.0	8 299	363.4	62 555	511
Montgomery, AL	875	20 240	2 062.6	869.8	569	3 906	468.3	130.1	24 543	1 018.8	153 138	805
Morgantown, WV	295	14 178	1 582.2	569.5	177	1 316	190.7	34.3	7 058	326.1	3 052	21
Morristown, TN	230	5 680	491.1	189.8	114	526	42.4	12.9	6 669	290.2	50 679	236
Mount Vernon-Anacortes, WA	330	7 152	700.3	296.6	252	1 128	106.0	31.3	7 712	369.9	99 532	505
Muncie, IN	313	9 158	873.1	318.7	174	1 043	105.9	26.2	5 649	206.4	20 048	124
Muskegon, MI	369	11 494	982.3	483.8	250	1 315	120.8	29.6	9 379	357.4	45 718	233
Myrtle Beach-Conway-North Myrtle Beach, NC-SC	878	14 479	1 600.7	571.0	623	3 183	324.9	77.9	33 816	1 513.6	1 349 623	6 525
Napa, CA	404	10 222	1 360.7	553.3	241	1 359	127.7	40.0	11 921	730.9	69 137	212
Naples-Immokalee-Marco Island, FL	995	16 310	2 089.4	772.0	850	5 209	474.4	138.1	38 777	2 323.8	1 093 119	3 829
Nashville-Davidson—Murfreesboro—Franklin, TN	4 208	109 447	13 584.2	5 158.9	2 507	19 844	2 180.7	640.4	164 992	8 687.5	4 042 667	20 182
New Bern, NC	293	8 064	806.0	330.9	167	832	70.7	18.5	7 353	280.8	52 130	292
New Haven-Milford, CT	2 408	73 162	7 788.2	3 238.4	1 717	9 881	977.8	297.8	59 574	3 112.0	147 953	918
New Orleans-Metairie, LA	3 205	67 442	7 698.1	2 899.3	1 850	12 712	1 868.6	426.7	116 471	5 280.2	655 424	2 986
New York-Newark-Jersey City, NY-NJ-PA	60 802	1 438 772	161 273.4	66 480.3	48 848	291 897	42 605.8	10 194.7	1 861 540	103 653.2	7 227 359	43 231
Dutchess County-Putnam County, NY Div 20524	1 162	23 662	2 563.7	1 086.5	824	3 627	397.2	105.5	NA	NA	130 052	456
Nassau County-Suffolk County, NY Div 35004	10 507	207 080	23 582.4	10 013.4	8 013	40 426	4 189.4	1 107.1	NA	NA	971 820	1 796
Newark, NJ-PA Div 35084	7 795	155 717	17 765.9	7 176.8	5 410	35 343	3 614.8	1 051.8	NA	NA	892 834	7 269
New York-Jersey City-White Plains, NY-NJ Div 35614	41 338	1 052 313	117 361.3	48 203.6	34 601	212 501	34 404.4	7 930.2	NA	NA	5 232 653	33 710
Niles-Benton Harbor, MI	399	9 410	816.5	329.2	251	1 199	116.0	32.2	9 842	395.1	86 878	312
North Port-Sarasota-Bradenton, FL	2 393	40 770	4 488.5	1 669.2	1 448	7 481	648.2	176.8	71 186	3 575.8	1 814 455	8 104
Norwich-New London, CT	734	17 357	1 728.0	751.2	459	2 498	274.7	61.9	16 548	788.9	75 891	330
Ocala, FL	878	15 494	1 874.0	674.9	455	2 315	196.6	54.0	24 391	1 017.0	238 690	1 428
Ocean City, NJ	278	4 767	443.7	186.8	296	1 237	96.3	32.4	8 066	492.5	190 565	642
Odessa, TX	293	7 384	823.7	297.6	250	2 276	340.1	83.5	11 141	612.8	85 659	448
Ogden-Clearfield, UT	1 431	21 624	2 361.9	801.8	809	4 688	374.1	106.9	39 963	1 726.9	718 052	3 610
Oklahoma City, OK	4 134	76 535	9 611.3	3 270.6	2 067	13 049	1 632.8	381.5	105 556	5 150.4	1 255 766	6 740
Olympia-Tumwater, WA	790	13 079	1 584.8	619.1	483	2 769	331.1	98.1	14 707	630.2	371 772	2 081
Omaha-Council Bluffs, NE-IA	2 439	61 248	6 795.6	2 552.5	1 603	10 653	1 536.4	314.5	58 505	2 675.9	663 605	4 240
Orlando-Kissimmee-Sanford, FL	5 726	108 835	13 809.2	4 884.8	3 592	23 294	2 405.8	635.2	221 721	8 815.5	4 969 432	23 254
Oshkosh-Neenah, WI	439	13 580	1 272.0	555.0	257	2 279	221.0	68.1	8 307	383.1	101 057	411
Owensboro, KY	348	7 891	759.3	301.6	167	1 100	83.1	25.8	6 528	275.1	34 178	377
Oxnard-Thousand Oaks-Ventura, CA	2 557	32 438	3 987.6	1 434.5	1 176	7 150	763.3	188.6	67 736	3 653.3	340 979	1 609
Palm Bay-Melbourne-Titusville, FL	1 522	31 218	3 727.6	1 387.7	958	4 563	372.7	117.7	42 420	1 698.9	840 332	2 915
Panama City, FL	515	10 051	1 078.2	412.5	321	1 936	160.6	43.4	14 826	721.4	249 497	1 055
Parkersburg-Vienna, WV	287	7 169	639.4	248.5	152	D	D	D	4 412	177.3	20 812	132
Pensacola-Ferry Pass-Brent, FL	1 019	24 040	2 905.3	1 091.4	594	3 417	307.7	88.5	32 054	1 359.9	430 921	2 873
Peoria, IL	840	30 651	3 197.1	1 286.0	613	6 256	590.3	251.2	19 632	734.5	89 025	350
Philadelphia-Camden-Wilmington, PA-NJ-DE-MD	17 408	463 943	51 028.6	20 690.6	11 378	74 202	9 462.5	2 309.9	410 065	21 806.0	1 925 175	12 245
Camden, NJ Div 15804	3 439	76 614	8 247.2	3 369.2	2 200	13 271	1 065.6	334.8	NA	NA	265 100	2 105
Montgomery County-Bucks County-Chester County, PA Div 33874	6 477	145 503	15 158.5	6 213.8	4 374	28 315	4 325.0	894.6	NA	NA	836 230	4 655
Philadelphia, PA Div 37964	5 528	191 974	21 925.2	8 572.2	3 609	24 712	3 271.7	844.7	NA	NA	650 149	3 627
Wilmington, DE-MD-NJ Div 48864	1 964	49 852	5 697.8	2 535.4	1 195	7 904	800.2	235.9	NA	NA	173 696	1 858
Phoenix-Mesa-Scottsdale, AZ	11 231	207 257	24 523.2	9 574.2	5 505	43 914	4 609.6	1 279.1	316 042	15 396.1	6 432 518	28 583
Pine Bluff, AR	237	4 827	429.9	173.6	105	530	49.1	15.8	4 706	164.3	4 318	46
Pittsburgh, PA	7 942	190 828	18 711.4	7 858.7	5 155	32 089	3 524.7	897.4	144 705	6 683.4	927 317	4 403
Pittsfield, MA	438	11 415	1 091.4	488.4	278	1 675	144.1	39.5	10 183	450.2	63 551	191
Pocatello, ID	335	3 819	314.1	115.4	120	591	61.6	15.7	5 007	198.7	26 237	202
Portland-South Portland, ME	2 038	44 844	4 350.3	1 882.7	1 164	6 448	701.2	179.9	48 294	2 351.1	457 903	2 397
Portland-Vancouver-Hillsboro, OR-WA	7 272	132 399	16 118.5	6 283.0	4 277	25 065	3 122.2	806.2	174 121	8 730.1	2 981 386	14 729
Port St. Lucie, FL	1 191	18 821	2 288.4	829.9	761	3 811	330.2	96.8	40 041	1 810.6	509 322	1 937
Prescott, AZ	759	11 555	1 245.1	517.8	364	1 717	142.9	41.0	18 282	750.9	375 819	1 602
Providence-Warwick, RI-MA	4 650	123 284	11 708.9	5 129.5	3 361	18 660	1 923.7	529.5	108 621	5 062.9	450 988	2 564
Provo-Orem, UT	1 219	21 246	2 228.3	776.1	634	3 398	272.7	73.9	44 439	1 931.7	1 300 400	5 317
Pueblo, CO	419	11 404	1 063.1	458.0	238	1 222	93.1	28.2	8 177	323.3	47 774	282
Punta Gorda, FL	485	8 927	1 119.6	401.0	297	1 326	113.0	33.0	12 899	602.0	52 064	665
Racine, WI	459	10 588	764.4	335.7	317	1 839	140.4	44.5	9 535	395.1	70 010	358
Raleigh, NC	3 069	53 424	5 654.4	2 278.0	1 959	13 792	1 557.4	446.6	100 662	4 615.2	2 439 918	13 514
Rapid City, SD	408	11 766	1 318.5	509.7	334	1 801	220.7	45.4	11 009	507.6	138 682	971

1. Establishments subject to federal tax.

Table C. Metropolitan Areas — Government Employment and Payroll and Local Government Finances

Area name	Government employment and payroll, 2012									Local government finances, 2012				
	Full-time equivalent employees	March Payroll (dollars)	March payroll (percent of total)							General revenue				
			Adminis-tration, judicial, and legal	Police and corrections	Fire protection	Highways and transporta-tion	Health and welfare	Natural resources and utilities	Education and libraries	Total (mil dol)	Inter-govern-mental (mil dol)	Taxes		
												Total (mil dol)	Per capita[1] (dollars)	
													Total	Property
	171	172	173	174	175	176	177	178	179	180	181	182	183	184
Mobile, AL	15 334	47 151 677	5.5	11.5	5.1	4.9	9.2	7.3	53.7	1 405.0	626.1	561.4	1 356	491
Modesto, CA	19 446	94 702 481	5.9	8.3	2.5	1.6	11.8	9.4	58.2	2 696.4	1 547.9	554.1	1 062	825
Monroe, LA	8 044	23 625 209	7.1	11.1	3.2	2.1	4.4	5.4	65.9	699.4	335.0	289.5	1 628	585
Monroe, MI	3 882	16 268 085	7.1	8.4	1.4	3.3	1.1	4.8	72.4	475.7	225.8	166.5	1 102	1 074
Montgomery, AL	12 833	40 413 140	4.7	13.6	5.4	3.2	3.3	7.9	56.9	1 415.6	468.2	359.9	954	325
Morgantown, WV	3 679	10 784 021	6.6	6.4	2.1	3.9	3.1	7.2	67.9	282.4	117.1	109.2	814	659
Morristown, TN	3 406	10 523 184	5.5	8.9	3.2	3.2	3.1	11.3	62.6	288.5	121.7	106.7	928	541
Mount Vernon-Anacortes, WA	5 963	27 675 332	5.4	5.4	2.0	4.5	41.5	4.7	33.8	852.8	275.6	199.6	1 688	1 157
Muncie, IN	3 335	10 832 587	6.2	9.0	3.6	4.7	3.7	4.2	64.9	345.4	171.1	109.1	930	778
Muskegon, MI	5 428	21 789 876	7.5	7.4	2.5	3.3	9.1	3.1	65.4	721.5	413.6	168.4	989	913
Myrtle Beach-Conway-North Myrtle Beach, NC-SC	13 720	47 691 925	8.0	11.3	4.0	2.9	7.2	7.6	55.9	1 554.9	373.0	787.2	1 995	1 260
Napa, CA	5 012	27 819 123	11.8	13.2	3.0	2.1	9.4	6.0	49.6	811.6	274.6	367.8	2 645	2 138
Naples-Immokalee-Marco Island, FL	9 918	41 162 175	6.9	15.7	6.7	3.5	4.2	9.1	52.0	1 300.6	231.7	737.4	2 218	2 006
Nashville-Davidson—Mur-freesboro—Franklin, TN	62 367	213 611 379	6.4	10.6	4.9	2.3	11.3	9.7	53.1	5 944.5	1 864.0	2 495.0	1 445	925
New Bern, NC	6 791	24 592 380	3.3	4.8	1.6	1.2	45.2	4.1	38.0	754.9	290.2	112.7	880	654
New Haven-Milford, CT	28 448	140 929 161	3.5	10.1	6.3	2.6	2.7	5.4	68.7	3 790.8	1 443.5	2 034.2	2 358	2 333
New Orleans-Metairie, LA	43 957	168 084 037	8.4	14.9	3.0	2.9	22.4	8.9	37.2	7 012.5	2 504.9	2 443.4	1 991	986
New York-Newark-Jersey City, NY-NJ-PA	859 136	4 981 795 701	4.0	15.9	3.9	8.2	12.0	4.2	49.2	158 755.3	48 519.4	84 882.7	4 280	2 827
Dutchess County-Putnam County, NY Div 20524	15 834	82 439 707	5.8	9.6	2.2	4.0	5.7	1.6	70.0	2 303.5	678.0	1 388.4	3 498	2 873
Nassau County-Suffolk County, NY Div 35004	123 812	732 874 581	4.1	11.7	0.9	2.5	7.4	3.2	68.6	20 978.5	5 325.7	13 527.4	4 749	3 856
Newark, NJ-PA Div 35084	95 852	533 906 989	5.6	13.8	3.9	2.5	4.8	4.3	63.1	13 124.9	3 533.4	8 066.3	3 241	3 160
New York-Jersey City-White Plains, NY-NJ Div 35614	623 638	3 632 574 424	3.8	17.2	4.5	10.3	14.2	4.4	42.7	122 348.4	38 982.3	61 900.6	4 391	2 559
Niles-Benton Harbor, MI	4 813	18 604 576	9.6	10.9	2.0	2.9	2.9	4.5	64.6	601.1	301.4	200.9	1 288	1 264
North Port-Sarasota-Braden-ton, FL	26 901	101 649 100	7.7	11.2	6.0	3.4	20.0	5.4	43.7	3 172.2	626.1	1 212.8	1 684	1 368
Norwich-New London, CT	8 967	42 369 410	4.4	7.7	3.8	3.8	2.3	8.0	68.3	1 101.6	386.5	598.5	2 183	2 159
Ocala, FL	10 760	33 096 942	6.2	11.8	9.0	0.5	2.5	5.9	63.0	875.9	312.2	296.0	883	746
Ocean City, NJ	5 885	27 086 618	8.8	13.8	3.3	3.6	9.4	7.3	49.4	701.1	152.6	449.5	4 667	4 561
Odessa, TX	6 915	26 339 816	4.0	7.3	3.2	1.3	27.3	2.1	53.3	690.5	140.4	269.5	1 867	1 389
Ogden-Clearfield, UT	19 885	69 703 618	6.0	9.0	3.0	1.6	5.2	6.0	67.8	1 758.6	707.7	680.0	1 110	794
Oklahoma City, OK	43 376	150 970 463	5.1	11.2	7.5	3.0	11.2	5.1	56.1	4 132.3	1 264.1	1 725.9	1 331	666
Olympia-Tumwater, WA	7 290	36 403 899	10.9	9.6	5.9	9.3	2.0	8.9	51.8	946.4	372.7	391.6	1 516	997
Omaha-Council Bluffs, NE-IA	36 524	145 002 288	4.4	9.9	3.3	3.6	4.1	18.6	55.0	3 737.9	1 239.7	1 804.1	2 037	1 532
Orlando-Kissimmee-Sanford, FL	79 591	284 688 968	6.3	14.2	7.2	4.2	4.2	8.8	52.4	8 588.1	2 537.2	3 519.5	1 583	1 131
Oshkosh-Neenah, WI	5 300	21 156 305	4.4	11.7	4.6	5.5	11.2	7.1	54.5	697.9	338.4	249.0	1 475	1 436
Owensboro, KY	5 043	15 494 560	4.3	6.6	2.9	2.8	6.8	13.2	62.0	421.7	154.4	115.6	996	570
Oxnard-Thousand Oaks-Ven-tura, CA	27 714	159 457 912	10.1	10.8	4.6	3.0	13.0	7.6	49.2	4 630.9	2 005.3	1 379.1	1 650	1 378
Palm Bay-Melbourne-Titus-ville, FL	19 755	66 076 682	7.5	12.3	7.0	4.4	7.8	7.9	52.0	1 764.4	557.0	634.8	1 160	923
Panama City, FL	8 675	32 038 863	3.7	6.7	2.4	3.9	34.3	5.0	42.7	881.5	209.8	288.2	1 536	1 098
Parkersburg-Vienna, WV	3 144	10 362 577	4.7	5.3	2.0	2.6	2.6	6.3	74.9	235.4	113.7	77.6	838	630
Pensacola-Ferry Pass-Brent, FL	14 772	47 095 540	7.2	13.2	2.2	2.6	3.7	6.5	62.2	1 288.3	501.5	467.6	1 014	750
Peoria, IL	13 803	52 130 853	6.3	10.3	3.9	4.6	3.2	6.6	63.1	1 517.9	612.5	635.6	1 671	1 435
Philadelphia-Camden-Wilmin-gton, PA-NJ-DE-MD	205 195	1 004 418 815	6.6	13.0	2.3	7.2	5.0	5.0	59.4	31 396.9	12 075.3	14 182.1	2 356	1 683
Camden, NJ Div 15804	50 866	263 407 426	3.8	10.2	2.3	2.9	4.8	3.0	70.8	6 825.7	2 374.5	3 161.2	2 520	2 481
Montgomery County-Bucks County-Chester County, PA Div 33874	55 254	262 211 582	6.4	11.3	0.4	2.9	4.5	3.7	69.4	8 269.3	2 143.8	4 825.6	2 485	2 076
Philadelphia, PA Div 37964	78 984	387 798 667	9.0	16.8	3.9	13.9	6.0	7.3	42.1	13 846.4	6 463.2	5 279.8	2 504	1 061
Wilmington, DE-MD-NJ Div 48864	20 091	91 001 140	5.5	9.7	1.2	2.8	2.8	4.4	71.6	2 455.5	1 093.8	915.5	1 283	1 049
Phoenix-Mesa-Scottsdale, AZ	139 712	587 672 336	8.5	13.3	5.3	2.9	6.2	12.0	50.6	15 082.4	5 190.2	6 265.2	1 447	928
Pine Bluff, AR	3 495	9 830 121	6.5	12.0	3.9	3.6	1.5	2.1	68.3	261.9	169.1	57.9	594	257
Pittsburgh, PA	76 232	322 348 429	6.5	11.1	1.8	8.6	5.9	6.4	58.3	10 916.6	4 733.0	4 213.3	1 785	1 286
Pittsfield, MA	4 790	19 230 480	4.3	8.5	3.3	5.5	1.3	4.1	71.5	506.3	218.2	246.7	1 897	1 828
Pocatello, ID	2 618	8 746 568	9.9	14.1	5.7	4.5	6.0	6.6	51.4	238.0	114.9	73.0	871	828
Portland-South Portland, ME	19 117	71 307 958	5.3	8.8	5.0	4.0	3.6	6.3	65.4	1 897.9	500.0	1 074.0	2 073	2 046
Portland-Vancouver-Hillsboro, OR-WA	70 641	332 827 613	7.2	11.0	5.2	8.1	4.4	8.5	51.7	10 118.9	3 858.3	4 062.9	1 774	1 375
Port St. Lucie, FL	15 221	57 466 642	7.0	15.0	8.7	2.3	1.8	6.2	55.9	1 562.3	448.2	714.5	1 651	1 400
Prescott, AZ	6 155	23 081 009	10.4	13.4	9.4	4.0	2.1	5.5	45.2	648.3	201.2	335.8	1 579	1 029
Providence-Warwick, RI-MA	47 209	226 744 364	3.5	10.7	8.1	2.2	1.2	5.2	67.9	6 092.6	2 097.6	3 232.0	2 018	1 964
Provo-Orem, UT	14 474	53 579 798	6.4	8.0	2.5	1.5	4.8	8.4	66.6	1 615.5	670.1	586.2	1 064	722
Pueblo, CO	5 698	21 434 409	5.8	12.3	11.0	3.0	6.6	9.0	49.7	552.8	247.0	223.3	1 388	895
Punta Gorda, FL	4 654	16 650 878	13.2	15.5	8.9	5.6	2.0	7.8	45.5	559.2	101.1	264.1	1 626	1 290
Racine, WI	6 208	25 453 020	4.3	13.6	5.6	3.5	5.9	4.0	61.9	757.1	345.7	302.7	1 554	1 513
Raleigh, NC	40 839	150 997 987	3.4	8.5	3.1	3.1	10.3	5.9	61.8	4 020.3	1 569.5	1 583.3	1 332	1 007
Rapid City, SD	5 051	15 769 374	6.1	10.9	1.5	3.1	2.5	4.6	66.3	484.3	139.9	245.9	1 773	1 269

1. Based on the resident population estimated as of July 1 of the year shown.

Table C. Metropolitan Areas — Local Government Finances, Government Employment, and Income Taxes

Area name	Local government finances, 2012 (cont.) Direct general expenditure Total (mil dol)	Per capita[1] (dollars)	Percent of total for: Education	Health and hospitals	Police protection	Public welfare	Highways	Debt outstanding Total (mil dol)	Per capita[1] (dollars)	Government employment, 2015 Federal civilian	Federal military	State and local	Individual income tax returns, 2014 Number of returns	Mean Adjusted Gross income	Mean income tax
	185	186	187	188	189	190	191	192	193	194	195	196	197	198	199
Mobile, AL	1 433.8	3 464	41.2	6.0	6.8	0.5	8.3	1 386.2	3 349	2 601	2 687	23 168	176 120	48 416	5 469
Modesto, CA	2 792.3	5 352	50.1	6.9	4.9	10.2	3.4	4 496.8	8 619	830	809	27 104	216 690	50 888	5 402
Monroe, LA	748.1	4 208	53.1	2.8	5.8	0.1	2.9	495.7	2 788	517	765	11 088	75 880	51 679	6 106
Monroe, MI	515.6	3 414	53.6	6.7	3.7	0.2	9.1	557.6	3 691	228	241	5 338	73 050	56 044	6 287
Montgomery, AL	1 403.7	3 722	34.2	33.5	5.6	0.3	2.9	1 403.6	3 722	6 400	4 194	33 478	164 160	51 541	5 752
Morgantown, WV	293.9	2 191	58.5	2.3	5.1	0.3	1.8	267.7	1 996	2 101	626	16 315	55 790	59 321	7 806
Morristown, TN	294.2	2 560	53.3	1.8	5.5	4.4	4.6	336.9	2 932	278	354	5 938	48 620	43 074	4 130
Mount Vernon-Anacortes, WA	797.6	6 747	26.4	43.2	2.9	0.1	3.4	556.4	4 706	388	327	10 706	56 960	59 113	6 844
Muncie, IN	323.3	2 755	48.4	0.8	3.9	0.5	2.7	191.9	1 635	283	338	10 601	49 030	44 690	4 665
Muskegon, MI	746.4	4 386	51.2	13.2	3.2	3.6	4.5	688.6	4 046	338	295	7 254	77 840	44 649	4 587
Myrtle Beach-Conway-North Myrtle Beach, NC-SC	1 496.4	3 793	37.4	11.8	6.6	1.4	4.4	2 146.9	5 441	1 041	1 576	20 194	198 380	47 267	5 263
Napa, CA	821.7	5 909	37.5	5.9	7.5	4.2	4.0	746.0	5 365	207	208	10 216	67 710	81 667	12 460
Naples-Immokalee-Marco Island, FL	1 313.8	3 952	37.5	3.0	12.1	0.6	6.0	2 257.5	6 791	643	648	12 222	173 430	125 170	26 098
Nashville-Davidson—Murfreesboro—Franklin, TN	5 917.9	3 427	40.3	11.8	6.7	0.7	3.2	9 772.4	5 660	13 078	6 002	94 659	854 440	65 473	9 397
New Bern, NC	730.7	5 704	24.7	49.9	4.0	4.0	0.8	197.3	1 540	5 696	8 585	8 439	55 560	49 866	5 180
New Haven-Milford, CT	4 427.8	5 132	58.4	0.6	4.3	0.3	2.5	3 649.0	4 229	5 414	1 912	44 806	412 580	68 822	9 416
New Orleans-Metairie, LA	6 862.8	5 593	28.3	16.1	5.5	1.0	4.4	9 273.5	7 557	11 839	8 493	68 877	561 700	60 832	8 687
New York-Newark-Jersey City, NY-NJ-PA	155 295.2	7 831	37.1	7.8	6.1	10.2	2.3	228 317.6	11 513	112 186	43 130	1 161 009	9 822 750	88 348	15 248
Dutchess County-Putnam County, NY Div 20524	2 273.0	5 726	57.0	3.2	3.6	6.6	4.3	1 817.8	4 580	1 308	591	22 958	NA	NA	NA
Nassau County-Suffolk County, NY Div 35004	22 106.9	7 761	50.8	5.4	7.0	5.6	3.2	19 089.0	6 701	16 544	5 178	166 898	NA	NA	NA
Newark, NJ-PA Div 35084	13 275.6	5 334	50.9	2.5	6.4	2.0	2.6	11 054.8	4 442	18 457	5 275	155 230	NA	NA	NA
New York-Jersey City-White Plains, NY-NJ Div 35614	117 639.8	8 345	32.6	8.9	6.0	12.1	2.1	196 356.0	13 928	75 877	32 086	815 923	NA	NA	NA
Niles-Benton Harbor, MI	618.7	3 965	53.9	7.1	5.5	1.4	5.2	398.2	2 551	316	265	8 967	73 360	52 461	6 340
North Port-Sarasota-Bradenton, FL	3 246.3	4 509	31.7	19.9	6.6	0.3	4.4	3 286.5	4 564	1 917	1 479	24 683	365 350	71 945	11 488
Norwich-New London, CT	1 142.0	4 165	60.1	0.7	5.5	0.6	6.1	911.5	3 324	2 728	6 859	28 499	134 330	66 909	8 660
Ocala, FL	879.1	2 623	48.9	2.0	7.6	0.7	6.3	732.6	2 186	670	617	13 660	151 600	44 870	5 320
Ocean City, NJ	808.9	8 400	33.8	1.5	5.3	4.4	4.9	673.4	6 992	443	1 094	8 307	49 700	57 468	7 068
Odessa, TX	691.3	4 790	36.3	40.0	3.5	0.0	2.4	385.4	2 670	179	321	9 721	70 810	67 171	9 441
Ogden-Clearfield, UT	1 761.7	2 877	51.2	2.7	6.1	1.8	3.1	1 655.4	2 703	18 615	6 128	30 395	265 440	59 655	6 139
Oklahoma City, OK	3 850.3	2 970	45.9	9.2	8.1	0.1	5.6	3 940.9	3 039	27 573	10 700	96 003	588 380	63 339	8 668
Olympia-Tumwater, WA	952.8	3 688	42.4	5.4	4.0	0.0	7.1	917.5	3 552	863	776	36 001	127 650	59 576	6 794
Omaha-Council Bluffs, NE-IA	3 646.7	4 118	52.0	2.7	5.1	0.7	4.4	7 717.4	8 714	9 419	9 115	53 646	433 060	68 647	9 218
Orlando-Kissimmee-Sanford, FL	8 694.5	3 910	39.3	3.5	7.5	0.8	5.5	14 655.7	6 591	12 968	4 646	103 571	1 117 700	52 004	6 823
Oshkosh-Neenah, WI	708.5	4 197	35.6	2.5	5.6	20.8	8.3	688.0	4 076	407	437	11 858	82 080	57 666	6 859
Owensboro, KY	454.5	3 917	36.1	5.3	3.4	0.1	3.3	1 881.3	16 214	306	381	6 463	52 740	51 253	5 359
Oxnard-Thousand Oaks-Ventura, CA	4 471.8	5 349	38.6	13.1	7.5	4.6	3.5	3 011.8	3 603	7 173	5 059	37 115	401 040	72 570	10 045
Palm Bay-Melbourne-Titusville, FL	1 830.9	3 345	36.4	11.6	7.9	0.4	4.3	1 872.2	3 421	6 275	2 829	21 865	269 250	55 029	7 117
Panama City, FL	987.2	5 261	32.4	23.6	6.5	0.0	4.6	937.7	4 998	3 785	4 250	10 290	92 340	50 000	6 228
Parkersburg-Vienna, WV	236.3	2 554	64.2	0.1	5.1	0.0	3.8	191.5	2 070	2 305	433	4 588	41 590	50 800	5 634
Pensacola-Ferry Pass-Brent, FL	1 512.8	3 280	44.3	2.8	7.1	0.2	4.4	3 484.8	7 556	6 610	13 190	21 112	212 860	52 401	6 246
Peoria, IL	1 492.8	3 924	48.0	1.3	5.9	1.7	6.8	1 259.9	3 312	2 281	823	19 375	180 770	64 297	8 279
Philadelphia-Camden-Wilmington, PA-NJ-DE-MD	30 309.1	5 036	49.1	6.0	5.4	5.2	2.6	44 541.2	7 400	51 250	23 106	289 150	2 888 630	73 912	10 939
Camden, NJ Div 15804	6 604.3	5 265	56.5	2.6	4.4	2.8	3.3	7 416.2	5 912	7 935	7 611	72 641	NA	NA	NA
Montgomery County-Bucks County-Chester County, PA Div 33874	8 574.7	4 415	57.3	2.4	4.9	5.8	3.8	11 320.4	5 829	6 070	5 235	76 808	NA	NA	NA
Philadelphia, PA Div 37964	12 546.9	5 950	37.7	11.3	5.9	7.0	1.3	23 338.7	11 068	31 925	6 671	96 455	NA	NA	NA
Wilmington, DE-MD-NJ Div 48864	2 583.2	3 620	58.6	1.0	6.6	0.5	3.1	2 465.8	3 456	5 320	3 589	43 246	NA	NA	NA
Phoenix-Mesa-Scottsdale, AZ	15 046.5	3 475	42.0	5.1	8.3	1.5	4.0	29 018.4	6 702	21 851	13 740	212 037	1 914 200	60 744	8 062
Pine Bluff, AR	262.8	2 696	61.5	0.1	6.9	0.1	4.7	246.8	2 533	1 517	389	8 474	37 310	41 757	3 708
Pittsburgh, PA	10 894.8	4 615	46.7	6.2	3.8	6.8	3.4	20 628.3	8 738	17 864	6 519	100 362	1 190 990	63 764	8 784
Pittsfield, MA	629.4	4 841	60.3	0.5	3.2	0.3	5.9	274.5	2 111	373	309	8 129	64 490	59 048	7 365
Pocatello, ID	221.0	2 637	41.2	2.7	8.1	1.0	5.5	54.8	654	549	280	7 751	33 960	47 062	4 309
Portland-South Portland, ME	1 867.4	3 604	49.3	0.7	4.6	1.6	5.8	1 662.8	3 209	8 339	4 073	28 089	270 390	62 331	7 692
Portland-Vancouver-Hillsboro, OR-WA	9 964.4	4 352	40.1	4.1	5.7	2.0	5.7	15 721.1	6 866	17 950	6 657	121 607	1 118 280	68 156	8 915
Port St. Lucie, FL	1 660.8	3 838	40.0	3.2	8.5	1.4	5.4	2 747.3	6 349	1 000	897	17 661	208 410	66 342	10 001
Prescott, AZ	653.7	3 074	36.5	2.1	7.2	1.8	9.0	725.7	3 413	1 497	500	9 188	100 270	49 296	5 492
Providence-Warwick, RI-MA	5 907.2	3 689	56.8	0.5	6.6	0.5	2.8	4 257.8	2 659	11 627	8 367	81 772	789 140	61 673	7 949
Provo-Orem, UT	1 466.7	2 663	52.0	4.0	6.1	0.1	5.2	2 448.4	4 445	945	2 430	28 809	212 430	60 732	6 438
Pueblo, CO	566.4	3 521	40.3	1.5	6.6	5.3	3.7	456.3	2 837	1 098	436	11 341	68 330	47 110	4 778
Punta Gorda, FL	563.6	3 470	33.1	3.8	11.0	1.5	11.1	628.4	3 868	334	314	5 549	78 270	53 047	6 885
Racine, WI	764.1	3 923	45.5	3.8	9.7	5.3	7.3	710.7	3 648	346	510	8 680	95 040	57 036	6 642
Raleigh, NC	4 137.2	3 481	42.6	8.6	6.0	3.5	1.9	9 884.5	8 316	5 522	3 580	89 992	569 440	72 401	9 784
Rapid City, SD	516.0	3 719	46.0	1.5	5.8	0.4	9.0	476.3	3 433	3 079	3 829	8 110	71 830	57 691	7 209

1. Based on the resident population estimated as of July 1 of the year shown.

Table C. Metropolitan Areas — Land Area and Population

CBSA/ DIV code[1]	Area name	Land area,[2] 2016 (sq mi)	Population 2016 Total persons	Rank	Per square mile	White	Black	American Indian, Alaska Native	Asian and Pacific Islander	Percent Hispanic or Latino[3]	Under 5 years	5 to 17 years	18 to 24 years	25 to 34 years	35 to 44 years	45 to 54 years
			1	2	3	4	5	6	7	8	9	10	11	12	13	14	15
39740	Reading, PA..................	856.4	414 812	129	484.4	74.1	5.1	0.4	1.8	20.0	5.9	16.8	9.7	12.2	11.5	14.0
39820	Redding, CA	3 775.4	179 631	231	47.6	83.8	1.8	4.0	4.4	9.8	5.9	15.6	7.8	12.7	10.6	12.3
39900	Reno, NV	6 565.3	457 667	114	69.7	66.1	3.0	2.0	7.8	24.0	6.0	15.9	9.0	14.8	12.0	13.1
40060	Richmond, VA	4 576.3	1 281 708	45	280.1	59.6	31.0	0.9	4.7	5.9	5.9	16.1	9.3	14.2	12.6	14.0
40140	Riverside-San Bernardino-Ontario, CA........	27 263.6	4 527 837	13	166.1	34.9	8.0	1.0	8.1	50.5	6.9	19.3	10.3	14.3	12.7	12.7
40220	Roanoke, VA.................	1 868.7	313 698	160	167.9	80.3	14.4	0.6	2.7	3.9	5.4	15.2	8.3	12.0	11.5	13.9
40340	Rochester, MN	2 477.2	215 884	206	87.1	86.5	5.0	0.6	5.4	4.4	6.8	17.7	7.7	13.5	12.4	12.7
40380	Rochester, NY	3 266.3	1 078 879	51	330.3	78.5	12.2	0.6	3.5	7.2	5.4	15.5	10.3	13.1	11.0	13.8
40420	Rockford, IL	794.1	339 376	151	427.4	72.4	12.2	0.6	3.1	13.9	6.1	17.8	8.5	12.2	12.0	13.7
40580	Rocky Mount, NC	1 045.9	147 323	282	140.9	46.4	47.1	1.0	1.0	5.9	5.8	16.9	8.6	11.5	11.4	13.5
40660	Rome, GA	509.9	96 560	362	189.4	73.1	15.2	0.7	1.8	10.8	6.1	17.4	10.0	12.6	12.1	12.9
40900	Sacramento—Roseville—Arden-Arcade, CA	5 094.7	2 296 418	27	450.7	56.5	8.5	1.5	16.6	21.4	6.1	17.1	9.6	14.1	12.6	13.1
40980	Saginaw, MI	800.5	192 326	224	240.3	71.3	19.8	0.8	1.7	8.4	5.8	15.9	9.8	12.1	10.9	13.0
41060	St. Cloud, MN	1 751.1	195 644	222	111.7	89.6	5.7	0.7	2.6	3.0	6.5	16.8	13.9	12.9	11.3	12.3
41100	St. George, UT	2 426.9	160 245	257	66.0	86.6	0.9	1.6	2.7	10.1	6.9	20.2	8.6	11.7	11.3	9.4
41140	St. Joseph, MO-KS..........	1 655.5	126 565	309	76.5	87.6	6.6	1.1	1.6	5.2	6.0	16.0	9.2	14.0	12.4	13.1
41180	St. Louis, MO-IL.............	7 863.6	2 807 002	20	357.0	75.7	19.4	0.7	3.2	3.0	6.0	16.5	8.6	13.6	12.3	13.5
41420	Salem, OR	1 921.5	418 139	127	217.6	71.0	1.7	2.3	4.1	23.8	6.6	18.0	10.1	13.3	12.2	11.9
41500	Salinas, CA..................	3 280.6	435 232	124	132.7	32.2	3.2	0.9	7.9	58.3	7.4	18.9	10.3	14.6	12.9	12.0
41540	Salisbury, MD-DE	2 098.5	400 200	135	190.7	72.9	19.0	0.9	2.2	7.1	5.3	14.3	9.5	10.9	10.0	12.4
41620	Salt Lake City, UT	7 684.0	1 186 187	48	154.4	74.4	2.1	1.1	6.8	17.7	7.8	20.4	9.4	16.3	14.5	11.3
41660	San Angelo, TX	2 573.5	119 943	323	46.6	55.5	4.3	0.8	1.8	39.1	6.9	16.7	12.1	15.7	11.0	10.9
41700	San Antonio-New Braunfels, TX	7 312.7	2 429 609	24	332.2	35.4	7.1	0.6	3.2	55.2	7.0	18.6	10.1	14.9	13.1	12.5
41740	San Diego-Carlsbad, CA	4 206.6	3 317 749	17	788.7	48.9	5.7	1.0	14.5	33.5	6.4	15.5	10.7	16.4	13.1	12.7
41860	San Francisco-Oakland-Hayward, CA	2 477.8	4 679 166	11	1 888.4	43.5	8.5	0.8	29.5	21.9	5.6	14.5	8.0	16.2	14.4	14.1
41860	.Oakland-Hayward-Berkeley, CA Div 36084	1 461.9	2 782 831	X	1 903.6	40.6	11.2	0.9	28.0	23.7	5.9	15.9	8.5	15.0	14.2	14.1
41860	.San Francisco-Redwood City-South San Francisco, CA Div 41884.....	495.4	1 635 684	X	3 301.7	43.4	4.6	0.7	35.4	19.7	5.2	11.9	7.3	19.3	15.1	13.9
41860	.San Rafael, CA Div 42034 .	520.5	260 651	X	500.8	74.8	3.2	0.8	8.5	16.0	4.7	15.7	6.6	8.7	12.3	15.9
41940	San Jose-Sunnyvale-Santa Clara, CA	2 679.9	1 978 816	35	738.4	35.1	2.9	0.7	37.7	26.9	6.2	16.5	8.6	15.7	14.4	14.1
42020	San Luis Obispo-Paso Robles-Arroyo Grande, CA	3 300.6	282 887	166	85.7	71.6	2.2	1.3	5.3	22.3	4.8	13.2	15.4	11.5	10.6	11.5
42100	Santa Cruz-Watsonville, CA	445.2	274 673	174	617.0	60.4	1.7	1.2	6.4	33.5	5.4	14.3	15.1	12.1	11.6	12.8
42140	Santa Fe, NM	1 908.0	148 651	280	77.9	44.2	1.1	3.1	1.8	51.0	4.5	14.3	7.5	11.1	11.3	13.0
42200	Santa Maria-Santa Barbara, CA	2 735.1	446 170	119	163.1	47.1	2.4	1.0	6.9	45.1	6.5	15.9	15.8	13.3	11.2	11.3
42220	Santa Rosa, CA.............	1 575.9	503 070	107	319.2	66.6	2.3	1.6	6.0	26.6	5.1	14.9	8.4	13.1	12.2	13.4
42340	Savannah, GA	1 343.1	384 024	137	285.9	57.6	34.4	0.7	3.3	6.1	6.7	16.6	10.5	16.0	12.7	12.2
42540	Scranton—Wilkes-Barre—Hazleton, PA	1 746.4	555 225	99	317.9	86.1	3.9	0.4	2.1	8.9	5.1	14.7	8.9	12.4	11.3	13.8
42660	Seattle-Tacoma-Bellevue, WA	5 870.7	3 798 902	15	647.1	68.8	7.4	2.0	17.2	9.9	6.3	15.5	8.5	16.4	14.1	13.7
42660	.Seattle-Bellevue-Everett, WA Div 42644	4 202.2	2 937 590	X	699.1	67.6	6.8	1.8	18.9	9.6	6.1	15.1	8.3	16.8	14.4	14.0
42660	.Tacoma-Lakewood, WA Div 45104	1 668.5	861 312	X	516.2	72.9	9.4	2.7	11.2	10.6	6.8	16.9	9.3	15.3	12.7	13.0
42680	Sebastian-Vero Beach, FL ..	502.8	151 563	271	301.4	77.1	9.6	0.6	2.0	12.0	4.3	12.6	6.4	9.1	8.9	11.8
42700	Sebring, FL	1 016.6	100 917	351	99.3	69.3	10.3	0.9	1.8	19.1	4.6	12.8	6.3	9.5	8.5	10.4
43100	Sheboygan, WI	511.3	115 427	332	225.8	86.0	2.5	0.8	5.9	6.3	5.5	17.0	8.3	11.5	11.7	14.1
43300	Sherman-Denison, TX	932.8	128 235	306	137.5	78.3	6.8	2.4	1.9	13.0	6.4	17.4	8.6	12.2	11.4	12.9
43340	Shreveport-Bossier City, LA	3 188.3	441 767	121	138.6	55.2	39.9	1.0	1.8	3.8	6.9	17.4	8.7	14.3	12.2	12.1
43420	Sierra Vista-Douglas, AZ	6 164.6	125 770	313	20.4	57.7	4.8	1.6	3.4	35.0	6.1	15.9	8.6	12.5	10.8	11.3
43580	Sioux City, IA-NE-SD..........	2 936.9	169 140	247	57.6	77.7	3.6	2.0	3.0	15.8	7.2	19.0	9.4	12.2	11.9	12.4
43620	Sioux Falls, SD	2 575.7	255 729	186	99.3	88.0	5.0	2.6	2.4	4.1	7.7	18.3	8.6	15.1	13.0	12.2
43780	South Bend-Mishawaka, IN-MI..............................	948.0	320 740	156	338.3	77.9	13.3	1.1	2.7	7.8	6.3	17.2	10.5	12.6	11.6	12.7
43900	Spartanburg, SC	1 322.1	329 136	153	248.9	69.8	22.5	0.6	2.5	6.2	6.1	17.1	9.2	12.9	12.0	13.7
44060	Spokane-Spokane Valley, WA	5 641.6	556 634	98	98.7	88.4	2.8	3.1	4.1	5.3	6.1	16.1	9.5	14.1	11.7	12.5
44100	Springfield, IL	1 182.7	210 015	211	177.6	83.7	13.4	0.6	2.4	2.2	5.7	16.9	8.1	12.7	12.1	13.5
44140	Springfield, MA	1 144.3	630 283	90	550.8	70.3	7.4	0.6	3.9	19.7	5.1	15.1	14.0	12.3	10.9	13.1
44180	Springfield, MO	3 006.8	458 930	113	152.6	92.3	3.2	1.5	2.1	3.2	6.2	16.3	11.8	13.3	11.9	12.2
44220	Springfield, OH	397.5	134 786	298	339.1	86.8	10.6	0.9	1.2	3.3	6.0	16.8	8.6	11.7	10.9	13.3
44300	State College, PA	1 109.9	161 464	256	145.5	87.1	4.1	0.4	7.1	2.9	4.1	11.1	24.1	14.6	10.4	11.4
44420	Staunton-Waynesboro, VA ..	1 002.0	121 247	320	121.0	88.2	8.1	0.7	1.2	3.7	5.3	14.7	7.8	12.2	11.6	13.9
44700	Stockton-Lodi, CA	1 392.4	733 709	77	526.9	35.5	8.1	1.2	17.7	41.2	7.1	20.3	9.9	13.9	12.8	12.6
44940	Sumter, SC	665.1	107 396	340	161.5	46.9	48.2	0.9	2.1	3.8	6.9	17.5	10.2	13.9	11.1	12.4
45060	Syracuse, NY	2 384.9	656 510	84	275.3	84.0	9.4	1.2	3.7	4.1	5.5	15.8	10.9	12.7	11.0	14.0
45220	Tallahassee, FL	2 387.7	379 627	140	159.0	57.6	33.6	0.8	3.6	6.4	5.3	14.0	18.6	14.1	11.2	11.5
45300	Tampa-St. Petersburg-Clearwater, FL	2 514.6	3 032 171	18	1 205.8	65.8	12.6	0.7	4.2	18.6	5.5	14.8	7.9	13.1	12.2	13.7
45460	Terre Haute, IN...............	1 465.1	170 687	242	116.5	90.9	6.2	0.8	1.8	2.2	5.8	15.2	12.5	12.6	11.9	12.6

1. CBSA = Core Based Statistical Area. DIV = Metropolitan Division. See Appendix A for explanation. See Appendix B for list of metropolitan areas identified by type.　2. Dry land or land partially or temporarily covered by water.　3. May be of any race.

Table C. Metropolitan Areas — **Population and Households**

Area name	55 to 64 years	65 to 74 years	75 years and over	Percent female	2000	2010	2000–2010	2010–2016	Births	Deaths	Net migration	Number	Persons per household	Family households	Female family householder[1]	One person
	16	17	18	19	20	21	22	23	24	25	26	27	28	29	30	31
Reading, PA........................	13.5	9.2	7.3	50.8	373 638	411 572	10.2	0.8	30 533	23 373	-3 275	151 792	2.64	68.0	13.1	27.0
Redding, CA.......................	14.8	12.0	8.3	51.0	163 256	177 223	8.6	1.4	13 102	13 101	2 055	69 799	2.53	63.6	11.0	28.3
Reno, NV............................	13.4	10.0	5.7	49.7	342 885	425 437	24.1	7.6	33 787	22 568	20 185	174 571	2.55	61.8	12.6	28.4
Richmond, VA......................	13.4	8.9	5.7	51.7	1 055 683	1 208 096	14.4	6.1	93 029	63 191	42 927	483 127	2.56	63.8	13.5	29.4
Riverside-San Bernardino-Ontario, CA........................	11.1	7.4	5.2	50.3	3 254 821	4 224 965	29.8	7.2	382 981	177 241	93 298	1 343 526	3.27	74.0	15.4	20.7
Roanoke, VA.......................	14.6	11.3	7.9	51.6	288 309	308 665	7.1	1.6	20 788	21 094	5 218	127 273	2.38	63.9	13.2	30.3
Rochester, MN....................	13.4	8.5	7.2	50.8	184 740	206 877	12.0	4.4	18 190	9 453	94	83 418	2.52	66.7	8.0	28.3
Rochester, NY.....................	14.1	9.7	7.2	51.4	1 062 452	1 079 693	1.6	-0.1	73 193	60 133	-13 426	427 520	2.43	62.6	13.0	30.0
Rockford, IL........................	13.5	9.4	6.8	50.9	320 204	349 431	9.1	-2.9	26 286	19 525	-16 605	132 190	2.54	64.4	12.4	30.4
Rocky Mount, NC.................	14.5	10.6	7.1	52.6	143 026	152 383	6.5	-3.3	10 773	9 984	-5 927	57 450	2.52	64.0	21.2	31.0
Rome, GA...........................	12.6	9.3	6.9	51.6	90 565	96 317	6.4	0.3	7 439	6 434	-749	34 931	2.64	65.9	14.7	29.7
Sacramento—Roseville—Arden-Arcade, CA..............	12.6	8.6	6.2	51.1	1 796 857	2 149 144	19.6	6.9	172 176	103 200	76 230	809 295	2.76	66.4	13.0	26.5
Saginaw, MI........................	14.3	10.3	7.9	51.4	210 039	200 169	-4.7	-3.9	14 212	12 815	-8 997	77 211	2.42	63.2	15.6	30.8
St. Cloud, MN.....................	12.0	7.9	6.4	49.6	167 392	189 093	13.0	3.5	15 667	8 050	-941	74 617	2.49	64.3	10.3	26.0
St. George, UT....................	11.0	11.6	9.2	50.5	90 354	138 115	52.9	16.0	13 981	6 987	14 471	52 453	2.93	75.4	9.7	19.6
St. Joseph, MO-KS..............	13.3	8.9	7.0	48.4	122 336	127 329	4.1	-0.6	9 615	8 148	-2 138	46 518	2.56	66.1	11.8	25.9
St. Louis, MO-IL..................	14.0	8.9	6.7	51.5	2 675 343	2 787 759	4.2	0.7	212 784	159 370	-32 609	1 108 303	2.49	64.4	13.3	30.0
Salem, OR..........................	12.3	9.2	6.4	50.4	347 214	390 739	12.5	7.0	32 956	20 778	14 787	144 600	2.76	69.1	13.2	23.9
Salinas, CA........................	11.1	7.3	5.4	49.1	401 762	415 055	3.3	4.9	41 336	15 211	-5 343	126 904	3.27	71.1	13.7	22.0
Salisbury, MD-DE................	15.0	13.7	8.8	51.4	312 572	373 764	19.6	7.1	26 130	25 409	24 705	154 242	2.47	66.3	11.8	27.4
Salt Lake City, UT...............	10.1	6.1	4.0	49.8	939 122	1 087 799	15.8	9.0	118 171	39 297	21 068	377 058	3.07	69.7	10.6	23.3
San Angelo, TX..................	11.7	8.3	6.7	50.3	105 781	111 823	5.7	7.3	10 060	6 371	4 466	45 137	2.53	61.5	12.2	30.0
San Antonio-New Braunfels, TX...................................	11.1	7.6	5.1	50.6	1 711 703	2 142 516	25.2	13.4	202 053	99 761	180 045	791 273	2.96	68.7	14.9	26.1
San Diego-Carlsbad, CA	11.7	7.7	5.7	49.7	2 813 833	3 095 342	10.0	7.2	276 631	128 855	74 361	1 113 610	2.89	66.2	11.6	24.9
San Francisco-Oakland-Hayward, CA..........................	12.6	8.4	6.2	50.6	4 123 740	4 335 561	5.1	7.9	326 874	184 519	207 374	1 689 907	2.71	63.9	10.7	26.6
Oakland-Hayward-Berkeley, CA Div 36084........	12.5	8.2	5.7	51.0	2 392 557	2 559 461	7.0	8.7	199 205	107 049	134 214	963 824	2.83	68.9	12.1	23.4
San Francisco-Redwood City-South San Francisco, CA Div 41884	12.3	8.3	6.7	49.8	1 483 894	1 523 691	2.7	7.4	113 010	65 634	67 219	620 196	2.58	56.4	8.9	30.9
San Rafael, CA Div 42034 .	15.5	12.1	8.5	51.2	247 289	252 409	2.1	3.3	14 659	11 836	5 941	105 887	2.40	62.4	7.8	30.5
San Jose-Sunnyvale-Santa Clara, CA........................	11.6	7.2	5.6	49.5	1 735 819	1 836 941	5.8	7.7	153 159	62 768	54 514	651 352	2.98	72.2	10.1	20.4
San Luis Obispo-Paso Robles-Arroyo Grande, CA...................................	14.0	11.1	7.8	49.3	246 681	269 599	9.3	4.9	16 554	14 368	10 644	104 760	2.53	63.1	8.8	26.2
Santa Cruz-Watsonville, CA .	13.8	9.5	5.4	50.5	255 602	262 362	2.6	4.7	19 105	10 917	4 129	93 317	2.80	62.3	11.1	27.7
Santa Fe, NM.....................	16.1	14.4	7.8	51.5	129 292	144 172	11.5	3.1	8 423	6 807	2 540	60 642	2.40	60.7	13.0	33.0
Santa Maria-Santa Barbara, CA...................................	11.3	7.9	6.7	50.0	399 347	423 939	6.2	5.2	36 061	18 763	4 970	144 261	2.94	65.7	10.7	24.0
Santa Rosa, CA..................	14.7	11.1	7.1	51.1	458 614	483 880	5.5	4.0	32 093	25 136	11 677	190 662	2.59	63.3	11.7	27.9
Savannah, GA.....................	11.8	8.2	5.3	51.4	293 000	347 598	18.6	10.5	32 277	18 178	21 775	138 784	2.64	66.0	16.2	26.5
Scranton—Wilkes-Barre—Hazleton, PA....................	14.3	10.7	8.8	50.9	560 625	563 627	0.5	-1.5	35 238	43 409	717	221 200	2.43	62.2	13.3	32.0
Seattle-Tacoma-Bellevue, WA.................................	12.6	7.8	5.1	50.0	3 043 878	3 439 808	13.0	10.4	286 468	148 112	219 950	1 437 222	2.55	62.9	9.5	27.3
Seattle-Bellevue-Everett, WA Div 42644..................	12.6	7.7	5.0	49.9	2 343 058	2 644 589	12.9	11.1	215 552	109 668	187 114	1 130 166	2.52	61.9	8.8	27.6
Tacoma-Lakewood, WA Div 45104....................	12.5	8.1	5.2	50.3	700 820	795 219	13.5	8.3	70 916	38 444	32 836	307 056	2.69	66.5	12.1	26.4
Sebastian-Vero Beach, FL....	15.2	16.6	15.1	52.0	112 947	138 028	22.2	9.8	7 902	11 720	16 530	55 494	2.64	61.9	6.9	33.7
Sebring, FL.........................	13.5	17.1	17.4	51.3	87 366	98 786	13.1	2.2	5 670	9 113	5 346	41 116	2.37	66.0	7.9	29.5
Sheboygan, WI	14.7	9.6	7.5	49.7	112 646	115 510	2.5	-0.1	7 895	6 704	-1 359	47 438	2.37	67.8	8.1	27.5
Sherman-Denison, TX..........	13.7	10.1	7.1	51.1	110 595	120 864	9.3	6.1	9 535	8 538	6 176	47 538	2.59	66.7	13.4	29.2
Shreveport-Bossier City, LA .	12.9	8.9	6.6	51.8	417 796	439 811	5.3	0.4	39 952	28 111	-9 633	171 531	2.53	63.9	16.9	31.6
Sierra Vista-Douglas, AZ.....	13.4	12.2	9.0	49.0	117 755	131 356	11.6	-4.3	10 347	7 775	-8 261	50 202	2.26	68.2	14.3	27.3
Sioux City, IA-NE-SD..........	12.8	8.6	6.5	50.2	167 902	168 563	0.4	0.3	15 194	9 337	-5 000	63 198	2.56	65.8	12.3	28.2
Sioux Falls, SD	12.1	7.6	5.4	49.8	187 093	228 264	22.0	12.0	23 890	10 586	13 783	98 273	2.50	64.8	10.0	28.6
South Bend-Mishawaka, IN-MI..................................	13.4	9.1	6.7	51.1	316 663	319 215	0.8	0.5	24 951	18 963	-3 943	119 494	2.58	64.6	12.2	30.1
Spartanburg, SC	12.9	9.7	6.4	51.6	283 672	313 268	10.4	5.1	24 298	20 187	11 469	124 570	2.54	66.2	14.2	29.4
Spokane-Spokane Valley, WA.................................	13.7	9.8	6.4	50.4	469 737	527 753	12.4	5.5	40 671	30 004	17 821	215 652	2.46	63.7	11.1	29.9
Springfield, IL.....................	14.1	9.7	7.0	51.9	201 437	210 170	4.3	-0.1	15 146	12 843	-2 225	88 081	2.35	61.0	13.1	32.9
Springfield, MA...................	13.5	9.1	6.8	52.1	608 479	621 705	2.2	1.4	40 141	34 727	3 997	233 619	2.55	61.6	15.3	30.5
Springfield, MO...................	12.3	9.1	6.9	50.9	368 374	436 711	18.6	5.1	35 490	25 424	11 674	179 752	2.45	63.8	10.4	27.5
Springfield, OH...................	14.1	10.6	8.1	51.5	144 742	138 333	-4.4	-2.6	9 962	10 424	-2 946	54 232	2.45	65.9	14.3	28.1
State College, PA	11.2	7.3	5.7	47.4	135 758	154 027	13.5	4.8	8 165	5 940	5 400	56 116	2.53	56.5	7.1	28.4
Staunton-Waynesboro, VA ...	14.3	11.5	8.6	50.8	108 988	118 502	8.7	2.3	7 929	7 991	2 565	46 768	2.45	65.6	12.1	28.7
Stockton-Lodi, CA...............	11.1	7.3	5.0	50.1	563 598	685 308	21.6	7.1	63 542	32 847	16 893	223 062	3.18	74.5	15.0	20.4
Sumter, SC	12.6	8.9	6.5	51.7	104 646	107 463	2.7	-0.1	9 384	6 425	-3 103	41 017	2.56	67.4	21.4	27.0
Syracuse, NY......................	14.1	9.1	6.9	51.3	650 154	662 625	1.9	-0.9	45 538	36 480	-14 296	254 001	2.49	61.8	12.6	29.2
Tallahassee, FL	11.8	8.4	5.1	51.7	320 304	368 770	15.1	2.9	25 307	16 271	1 494	142 295	2.49	56.4	15.1	31.5
Tampa-St. Petersburg-Clearwater, FL........................	13.6	10.8	8.5	51.6	2 395 997	2 783 514	16.2	8.9	196 969	186 033	230 607	1 166 704	2.51	61.1	12.9	31.9
Terre Haute, IN...................	13.0	9.5	6.9	49.1	170 943	172 422	0.9	-1.0	12 513	11 762	-2 702	66 685	2.41	61.6	11.9	31.6

1. No spouse present.

Table C. Metropolitan Areas — Population, Vital Statistics, Health, and Crime

Area name	Persons in group quarters, 2016	Daytime population, 2015		Births, 2016		Deaths, 2016		Persons under 65 with no health insurance 2015		Medicare, 2015			Serious crimes known to police,[2] 2014 Total	
		Number	Employment/residence ratio	Total	Rate[1]	Number	Rate[1]	Number	Percent	Total Beneficiaries	Enrolled in Original Medicare	Enrolled in Medicare Advantage	Number	Rate[3]
	32	33	34	35	36	37	38	39	40	41	42	43	44	45
Reading, PA	11 795	398 889	0.92	4 879	11.8	3 821	9.2	29 080	8.6	75 804	47 843	27 961	8 699	2 102
Redding, CA	2 828	181 749	1.03	2 072	11.5	2 227	12.4	12 195	8.6	43 370	40 695	2 675	6 980	3 869
Reno, NV	5 305	451 735	1.00	5 501	12.0	3 835	8.4	46 538	12.3	75 525	51 679	23 846	12 175	2 737
Richmond, VA	35 206	1 277 318	1.01	15 126	11.8	10 666	8.3	111 294	10.5	203 537	148 922	54 615	31 483	2 507
Riverside-San Bernardino-Ontario, CA	71 464	4 243 578	0.87	62 028	13.7	31 598	7.0	397 943	10.3	560 263	200 262	360 001	130 753	2 945
Roanoke, VA	8 026	322 314	1.07	3 381	10.8	3 492	11.1	27 082	10.8	66 227	48 297	17 930	7 678	2 455
Rochester, MN	3 267	221 005	1.06	2 913	13.5	1 571	7.3	7 980	4.4	35 868	19 238	16 630	3 248	1 522
Rochester, NY	41 182	1 089 772	1.02	11 555	10.7	9 849	9.1	50 583	5.8	206 614	71 648	134 966	27 279	2 512
Rockford, IL	5 028	338 598	0.99	4 179	12.3	3 101	9.1	20 771	7.3	62 005	42 707	19 298	11 971	3 503
Rocky Mount, NC	2 827	144 954	0.95	1 632	11.1	1 662	11.3	14 830	12.4	31 713	25 393	6 320	5 053	3 437
Rome, GA	3 830	103 521	1.18	1 170	12.1	1 097	11.4	13 654	17.6	19 506	14 182	5 324	4 392	4 576
Sacramento—Roseville—Arden-Arcade, CA	37 118	2 264 550	0.99	27 776	12.1	18 301	8.0	131 750	6.9	346 711	178 656	168 055	64 748	2 886
Saginaw, MI	7 077	208 930	1.20	2 208	11.5	2 122	11.0	10 617	6.9	43 840	29 014	14 826	5 135	2 621
St. Cloud, MN	8 619	199 926	1.05	2 514	12.8	1 297	6.6	7 432	4.6	34 825	14 939	19 886	4 798	2 497
St. George, UT	1 903	156 019	1.01	2 232	13.9	1 206	7.5	20 573	16.9	30 025	21 739	8 286	2 749	1 860
St. Joseph, MO-KS	8 606	129 867	1.04	1 469	11.6	1 219	9.6	11 180	11.2	22 616	20 515	2 101	5 556	4 339
St. Louis, MO-IL	55 083	2 816 318	1.00	33 480	11.9	26 847	9.6	199 683	8.5	484 932	301 017	183 915	80 890	2 944
Salem, OR	12 397	400 199	0.94	5 332	12.8	3 552	8.5	31 504	9.4	71 254	27 801	43 453	13 696	3 387
Salinas, CA	18 190	432 415	0.99	6 452	14.8	2 630	6.0	43 444	11.9	54 495	52 638	1 857	12 410	2 857
Salisbury, MD-DE	13 850	390 060	0.97	4 229	10.6	4 510	11.3	26 380	8.8	94 001	89 258	4 743	14 174	3 642
Salt Lake City, UT	14 396	1 233 174	1.11	18 728	15.8	6 704	5.7	125 109	12.0	122 563	67 092	55 471	54 565	4 719
San Angelo, TX	5 479	119 769	0.99	1 705	14.2	1 026	8.6	17 311	17.8	20 173	15 627	4 546	4 649	3 923
San Antonio-New Braunfels, TX	50 473	2 372 211	0.99	34 143	14.1	17 457	7.2	340 113	16.6	334 425	187 149	147 276	106 461	4 578
San Diego-Carlsbad, CA	105 973	3 323 094	1.01	44 652	13.5	22 552	6.8	263 461	9.5	437 333	202 020	235 313	69 635	2 138
San Francisco-Oakland-Hayward, CA	87 118	4 703 318	1.02	53 569	11.4	32 407	6.9	242 121	6.2	651 645	337 808	313 837	177 382	3 868
Oakland-Hayward-Berkeley, CA Div 36084	46 957	2 591 122	0.86	32 803	11.8	19 042	6.8	147 034	6.2	366 274	182 352	183 922	103 858	3 825
San Francisco-Redwood City-South San Francisco, CA Div 41884	32 203	1 851 852	1.25	18 458	11.3	11 386	7.0	82 436	6.0	234 558	125 128	109 430	68 505	4 258
San Rafael, CA Div 42034	7 958	260 344	0.99	2 308	8.9	1 979	7.6	12 651	6.2	50 813	30 328	20 485	5 019	1 922
San Jose-Sunnyvale-Santa Clara, CA	30 883	2 107 199	1.14	24 549	12.4	11 266	5.7	103 652	6.1	233 096	110 635	122 461	48 692	2 497
San Luis Obispo-Paso Robles-Arroyo Grande, CA	15 800	279 974	0.99	2 666	9.4	2 414	8.5	17 356	8.0	54 334	46 703	7 631	6 860	2 453
Santa Cruz-Watsonville, CA	13 656	265 284	0.93	3 006	10.9	1 877	6.8	17 542	7.8	41 497	37 348	4 149	9 260	3 398
Santa Fe, NM	2 631	148 729	1.00	1 280	8.6	1 138	7.7	17 158	14.9	32 301	21 524	10 777	4 483	3 033
Santa Maria-Santa Barbara, CA	18 835	458 240	1.06	5 841	13.1	3 216	7.2	44 488	12.2	67 169	56 203	10 966	10 382	2 354
Santa Rosa, CA	10 396	485 952	0.93	5 084	10.1	4 359	8.7	35 290	8.7	91 408	50 969	40 439	10 404	2 079
Savannah, GA	14 511	387 977	1.05	5 361	14.0	3 135	8.2	46 370	14.7	56 087	36 418	19 669	12 589	3 387
Scranton—Wilkes-Barre—Hazleton, PA	20 339	562 683	1.02	5 572	10.0	6 971	12.6	33 799	7.7	122 492	88 648	33 844	12 814	2 294
Seattle-Tacoma-Bellevue, WA	65 412	3 778 389	1.02	47 412	12.5	26 089	6.9	218 314	6.8	500 505	305 783	194 722	163 662	4 466
Seattle-Bellevue-Everett, WA Div 42644	48 658	2 991 244	1.07	35 637	12.1	19 125	6.5	165 602	6.6	373 061	219 099	153 962	128 220	4 523
Tacoma-Lakewood, WA Div 45104	16 754	787 145	0.85	11 775	13.7	6 964	8.1	52 712	7.3	127 444	86 684	40 760	35 442	4 272
Sebastian-Vero Beach, FL	1 324	148 117	1.00	1 284	8.5	2 050	13.5	19 588	19.4	44 665	33 683	10 982	3 579	2 484
Sebring, FL	1 734	97 318	0.93	931	9.2	1 485	14.7	11 807	18.3	31 095	21 335	9 760	2 841	3 182
Sheboygan, WI	2 818	117 050	1.03	1 226	10.6	1 086	9.4	5 577	5.9	22 261	12 646	9 615	2 162	1 883
Sherman-Denison, TX	2 251	118 791	0.88	1 582	12.3	1 402	10.9	20 594	20.1	26 011	20 343	5 668	2 961	2 417
Shreveport-Bossier City, LA	10 272	448 739	1.03	6 139	13.9	4 607	10.4	48 601	13.2	77 512	61 200	16 312	17 617	3 976
Sierra Vista-Douglas, AZ	5 204	125 909	0.99	1 582	12.6	1 283	10.2	10 179	10.7	27 552	17 928	9 624	2 473	2 314
Sioux City, IA-NE-SD	3 285	165 365	1.00	2 403	14.2	1 454	8.6	12 443	8.8	29 070	22 367	6 703	4 867	2 926
Sioux Falls, SD	7 023	258 134	1.04	3 899	15.2	1 790	7.0	20 441	9.5	38 091	28 339	9 752	6 476	2 616
South Bend-Mishawaka, IN-MI	11 997	310 823	0.94	3 969	12.4	3 013	9.4	28 438	10.9	54 170	36 166	18 004	9 890	3 166
Spartanburg, SC	8 727	336 360	1.08	3 917	11.9	3 363	10.2	34 288	12.9	69 177	43 204	25 973	11 008	3 421
Spokane-Spokane Valley, WA	15 346	550 889	1.02	6 550	11.8	5 113	9.2	29 431	6.6	103 385	68 421	34 964	30 790	5 703
Springfield, IL	4 068	224 095	1.13	2 311	11.0	2 256	10.7	8 753	5.0	39 753	23 909	15 844	8 834	4 388
Springfield, MA	38 421	624 899	0.98	6 260	9.9	5 665	9.0	18 614	3.7	118 547	81 550	36 997	18 801	3 053
Springfield, MO	14 510	463 318	1.04	5 765	12.6	4 321	9.4	48 923	13.1	87 342	48 240	39 102	20 129	4 452
Springfield, OH	2 785	125 856	0.83	1 566	11.6	1 676	12.4	8 631	7.9	29 014	13 443	15 571	6 145	4 539
State College, PA	19 306	168 176	1.10	1 335	8.3	1 039	6.4	9 576	7.9	21 242	10 614	10 628	1 970	1 265
Staunton-Waynesboro, VA	4 086	113 826	0.88	1 350	11.1	1 294	10.7	10 904	11.7	26 063	21 467	4 596	2 228	1 859
Stockton-Lodi, CA	15 110	693 980	0.89	10 239	14.0	5 701	7.8	53 841	8.6	94 535	56 113	38 422	30 438	4 271
Sumter, SC	2 666	108 443	1.02	1 446	13.5	1 055	9.8	11 693	13.2	20 552	16 637	3 915	4 780	4 395
Syracuse, NY	26 590	665 991	1.02	7 091	10.8	5 912	9.0	31 670	5.9	121 914	74 305	47 609	16 807	2 536
Tallahassee, FL	22 807	383 240	1.03	4 058	10.7	2 716	7.2	37 339	12.1	53 231	26 908	26 323	16 349	4 341
Tampa-St. Petersburg-Clearwater, FL	50 479	2 964 118	0.99	32 592	10.7	32 508	10.7	345 519	14.5	593 609	290 650	302 959	88 473	3 036
Terre Haute, IN	12 236	170 877	0.98	1 984	11.6	1 854	10.9	14 297	10.8	34 051	28 990	5 061	NA	NA

1. Per 1,000 estimated resident population.   2. Data for serious crimes have not been adjusted for underreporting; this may affect comparability between geographic areas and over time.
3. Per 100,000 population estimated by the FBI.

Items 32—45

Table C. Metropolitan Areas — **Crime, Education, Money Income, and Poverty**

Area name	Serious crimes known to police, 2014 (cont.)[1] Rate[2] Violent	Property	Education — School enrollment and attainment, 2015 — Enrollment[3] Total	Percent private	Attainment[4] (percent) High school graduate or less	Bachelor's degree or more	Local government expenditures,[5] 2013–2014 Total current expenditures (mil dol)	Current expenditures per student (dollars)	Income and Poverty, 2015 Per capita income[6] (dollars)	Mean household income (dollars)	Median household income	Percent of households with income of less than $50,000	Percent of households with income of $200,000 or more	Percent below poverty level All persons	Children under 18 years	Age 65 years and older
	46	47	48	49	50	51	52	53	54	55	56	57	58	59	60	61
Reading, PA	328	1 774	102 885	18.5	50.7	24.4	896.1	13 113	28 016	73 796	56 122	43.9	3.8	12.8	20.8	8.3
Redding, CA	707	3 162	41 200	17.3	35.1	22.0	274.5	10 191	25 323	62 549	46 693	52.0	3.0	19.6	28.0	6.5
Reno, NV	374	2 363	112 285	10.0	35.8	29.6	563.1	8 521	30 180	75 135	56 611	45.1	4.7	13.6	17.6	6.3
Richmond, VA	231	2 276	313 820	18.1	36.7	35.2	1 873.1	9 582	32 423	82 209	60 713	41.5	6.5	11.8	16.5	6.7
Riverside-San Bernardino-Ontario, CA	327	2 617	1 269 874	10.7	47.1	20.1	7 417.9	8 854	23 260	73 425	56 087	44.6	4.2	17.5	25.0	9.9
Roanoke, VA	203	2 252	69 129	21.1	41.5	26.5	459.8	10 295	27 121	64 370	50 571	49.4	2.5	13.2	18.0	8.8
Rochester, MN	141	1 381	52 950	17.1	30.5	37.3	341.3	9 943	34 624	87 082	65 627	37.3	6.3	8.6	11.3	5.0
Rochester, NY	266	2 247	261 609	22.5	37.4	33.0	2 794.7	17 735	29 608	72 186	53 667	46.7	3.9	13.8	20.2	7.4
Rockford, IL	668	2 836	82 884	17.0	45.9	22.1	676.5	11 982	26 281	64 934	51 036	48.4	2.5	14.3	21.4	6.6
Rocky Mount, NC	457	2 980	32 233	13.1	50.9	16.4	205.0	8 465	22 049	54 582	37 324	61.0	2.5	22.0	32.2	16.4
Rome, GA	349	4 227	23 832	25.2	53.6	18.5	159.0	9 665	21 680	56 790	40 510	59.8	2.2	18.9	28.3	6.4
Sacramento—Roseville—Arden-Arcade, CA	411	2 475	617 636	11.3	32.7	32.2	3 285.0	9 130	30 569	82 648	62 813	40.1	6.2	15.0	19.4	8.8
Saginaw, MI	659	1 962	47 341	11.0	46.1	19.4	306.3	10 740	24 801	60 183	43 383	56.3	3.2	18.4	26.9	7.9
St. Cloud, MN	179	2 319	54 209	16.8	37.0	25.6	313.2	10 176	27 262	68 555	54 157	45.9	2.7	14.5	19.9	11.8
St. George, UT	135	1 725	44 762	12.2	34.7	26.0	223.8	7 288	25 644	72 624	54 913	43.3	4.5	13.7	19.0	4.9
St. Joseph, MO-KS	345	3 994	30 452	10.7	48.6	20.2	168.2	9 180	22 954	59 773	49 263	50.8	2.3	16.5	23.6	9.4
St. Louis, MO-IL	440	2 504	707 565	24.4	36.1	32.5	4 590.7	11 087	31 529	77 901	56 483	44.1	5.3	12.2	17.4	7.4
Salem, OR	234	3 154	106 646	16.5	40.9	23.0	684.3	8 878	24 335	67 428	52 448	47.3	2.8	16.1	24.4	5.1
Salinas, CA	422	2 435	120 257	5.9	50.5	23.3	765.5	10 262	26 495	86 090	60 494	40.4	5.9	15.3	23.1	8.1
Salisbury, MD-DE	412	3 229	90 320	11.4	45.9	25.8	732.2	13 709	28 615	71 289	54 233	45.9	3.3	12.1	17.5	5.3
Salt Lake City, UT	344	4 375	344 603	12.0	34.4	32.7	1 449.3	6 440	28 192	83 088	65 792	37.0	5.4	10.2	11.7	7.1
San Angelo, TX	294	3 628	30 481	14.9	45.7	23.5	170.5	8 668	26 490	67 626	48 441	50.8	4.7	16.4	24.1	8.1
San Antonio-New Braunfels, TX	402	4 176	651 447	13.2	42.7	26.6	3 716.9	8 541	26 209	73 771	55 083	45.3	4.5	14.6	21.1	10.0
San Diego-Carlsbad, CA	325	1 813	869 872	14.3	32.2	37.2	4 604.0	9 151	32 227	90 125	67 320	37.0	8.2	13.8	17.7	9.2
San Francisco-Oakland-Hayward, CA	498	3 370	1 124 169	18.5	27.9	47.2	5 773.9	9 923	46 511	124 194	88 518	29.6	16.6	10.6	12.2	8.2
Oakland-Hayward-Berkeley, CA Div 36084	516	3 309	707 128	14.5	30.0	43.1	3 634.8	9 178	40 042	111 540	82 196	30.8	13.6	10.9	13.4	7.0
San Francisco-Redwood City-South San Francisco, CA Div 41884	521	3 737	356 491	25.2	26.1	51.6	1 744.2	11 395	54 404	138 172	96 989	28.3	20.2	10.5	10.6	10.7
San Rafael, CA Div 42034	174	1 748	60 550	26.0	18.5	58.9	394.9	12 043	65 742	157 498	100 662	26.5	22.2	7.1	7.4	4.7
San Jose-Sunnyvale-Santa Clara, CA	250	2 247	523 840	21.5	27.9	48.7	2 808.9	9 792	46 148	136 386	101 980	24.9	20.7	8.1	8.3	7.9
San Luis Obispo-Paso Robles-Arroyo Grande, CA	421	2 032	76 496	8.5	30.2	34.1	331.9	9 552	33 301	86 082	62 648	38.8	6.8	14.9	14.6	7.0
Santa Cruz-Watsonville, CA	418	2 980	78 901	10.2	31.4	37.1	417.6	10 238	32 374	91 144	65 139	38.7	9.5	16.1	19.6	8.0
Santa Fe, NM	267	2 766	32 451	13.2	32.8	40.9	169.1	9 134	34 752	80 867	55 676	45.0	6.4	13.0	15.7	8.3
Santa Maria-Santa Barbara, CA	293	2 060	133 914	10.1	37.8	33.2	655.5	9 685	31 311	92 453	63 625	39.6	8.7	15.7	21.0	7.7
Santa Rosa, CA	364	1 715	120 516	11.5	32.1	32.8	701.5	9 890	36 254	93 407	66 674	35.3	8.5	11.1	14.6	7.7
Savannah, GA	341	3 046	107 262	21.9	37.5	28.9	513.3	8 970	26 020	67 583	51 390	48.4	3.2	16.6	22.9	6.8
Scranton—Wilkes-Barre—Hazleton, PA	229	2 065	123 801	25.9	49.3	23.3	956.0	12 586	26 524	64 045	49 670	50.2	2.8	15.2	24.2	8.1
Seattle-Tacoma-Bellevue, WA	325	4 141	881 526	17.5	28.0	41.2	5 265.7	10 275	39 152	99 442	75 331	32.7	9.8	10.2	12.3	7.8
Seattle-Bellevue-Everett, WA Div 42644	294	4 229	676 968	18.3	25.5	45.4	3 952.9	10 301	42 023	105 738	80 688	30.4	11.3	9.6	10.8	7.9
Tacoma-Lakewood, WA Div 45104	432	3 840	204 558	15.0	37.2	25.7	1 312.7	10 199	29 322	76 266	60 167	40.9	4.2	12.3	16.9	7.6
Sebastian-Vero Beach, FL	282	2 202	25 747	15.4	45.9	25.6	153.5	8 498	32 694	79 405	49 379	50.9	5.7	12.5	19.6	7.7
Sebring, FL	308	2 874	17 184	10.6	53.7	17.6	109.5	8 977	23 991	53 170	34 242	68.0	1.3	24.6	42.9	9.5
Sheboygan, WI	162	1 721	27 299	17.5	46.7	23.4	207.8	10 727	28 054	68 527	57 047	42.5	2.2	8.9	10.4	7.9
Sherman-Denison, TX	272	2 145	31 139	11.4	46.5	19.2	190.8	8 828	25 832	65 970	48 126	51.4	3.0	15.9	25.4	8.3
Shreveport-Bossier City, LA	517	3 459	105 582	12.1	47.6	22.0	803.1	10 710	24 490	61 070	43 292	55.2	3.2	21.0	32.4	9.7
Sierra Vista-Douglas, AZ	283	2 032	27 003	9.2	36.9	19.8	158.8	8 084	24 140	58 109	43 291	54.5	2.5	17.0	21.9	9.3
Sioux City, IA-NE-SD	247	2 679	41 037	17.5	48.2	21.6	342.6	11 116	26 082	66 109	52 698	46.9	3.5	13.3	17.3	6.7
Sioux Falls, SD	331	2 285	60 829	15.9	34.7	31.7	328.5	8 159	29 926	75 088	59 844	42.5	4.1	11.5	15.6	6.4
South Bend-Mishawaka, IN-MI	325	2 842	83 091	29.7	44.9	25.9	447.4	9 779	25 285	63 809	47 207	51.8	3.2	16.6	25.0	7.2
Spartanburg, SC	392	3 028	81 078	13.5	47.0	22.2	499.6	9 679	23 134	58 601	44 028	54.9	2.3	15.6	22.6	10.4
Spokane-Spokane Valley, WA	319	5 384	139 883	17.4	33.9	27.2	841.0	10 340	25 919	63 728	47 548	52.5	2.8	16.3	21.6	8.0
Springfield, IL	796	3 592	53 932	13.5	35.2	34.1	374.4	11 580	32 440	76 970	57 824	42.9	4.7	16.2	26.4	6.6
Springfield, MA	511	2 542	178 120	17.8	41.6	31.1	1 371.6	14 918	28 120	72 728	53 393	46.9	4.3	16.9	24.1	9.1
Springfield, MO	536	3 916	119 361	15.0	40.2	27.1	570.4	8 436	23 691	58 419	44 786	54.3	2.0	16.8	21.2	7.2
Springfield, OH	369	4 171	33 066	17.6	50.1	17.7	218.7	10 468	24 737	60 901	47 963	51.6	2.1	14.5	23.8	5.4
State College, PA	82	1 184	57 164	9.2	38.7	43.0	186.4	14 094	26 895	73 000	56 337	45.1	4.4	16.8	12.7	2.2
Staunton-Waynesboro, VA	146	1 713	24 638	12.0	51.1	22.9	160.9	9 660	25 046	60 756	49 834	50.1	2.5	12.9	18.0	6.4
Stockton-Lodi, CA	750	3 521	208 884	12.0	48.4	18.8	1 262.6	9 081	23 046	71 750	53 705	46.5	3.7	17.4	23.9	8.2
Sumter, SC	647	3 748	26 820	13.0	47.3	17.3	147.0	8 752	20 173	51 156	41 169	58.4	1.2	18.5	27.3	12.4
Syracuse, NY	285	2 251	171 669	22.9	38.9	31.0	1 745.5	17 061	29 123	72 625	56 371	44.4	3.6	15.0	22.3	8.0
Tallahassee, FL	679	3 662	128 637	12.7	35.2	35.3	402.5	8 273	23 995	61 080	44 295	55.8	3.1	22.4	25.3	6.4
Tampa-St. Petersburg-Clearwater, FL	372	2 664	670 268	16.0	39.4	28.9	3 443.7	8 674	28 339	68 251	48 911	50.8	4.2	14.7	20.4	10.0
Terre Haute, IN	NA	NA	43 836	14.5	48.9	21.1	238.8	9 303	21 862	54 352	40 974	58.3	2.2	17.7	21.5	10.4

1. Data for serious crimes have not been adjusted for underreporting; this may affect comparability between geographic areas and over time.   2. Per 100,000 population estimated by the FBI.   3. All persons 3 years old and over enrolled in nursery school through college.   4. Persons 25 years old and over.   5. Elementary and secondary education expenditures.   6. Based on resident population estimated in the 2015 American Community Survey.

Table C. Metropolitan Areas — **Personal Income**

Area name	Personal income, 2015										Earnings, 2015		
			Per capita[1]			Supplements to wages and salaries; employer contributions (mil dol)						Contributions for government social insurance (mil dol)	
	Total (mil dol)	Percent change 2014–2015	Dollars	Rank	Wages and salaries (mil dol)	Pension and insurance	Government social insurance	Proprietors' income (mil dol)	Dividends, interest, and rent (mil dol)	Personal transfer receipts (mil dol)	Total (mil dol)	From employee and self-employed	From employer
	62	63	64	65	66	67	68	69	70	71	72	73	74
Reading, PA..................	18 609	4.1	44 813	115	8 442	1 710	683	1 321	2 984	3 769	12 157	703	683
Redding, CA..................	7 340	6.3	40 882	201	2 771	644	204	564	1 381	2 307	4 183	268	204
Reno, NV	21 429	7.9	47 526	80	9 987	1 993	736	949	5 901	3 293	13 665	808	736
Richmond, VA	64 152	5.1	50 460	54	34 835	5 636	2 519	5 296	12 041	9 546	48 286	2 895	2 519
Riverside-San Bernardino-Ontario, CA..................	159 429	6.5	35 514	332	65 149	14 069	4 791	10 668	24 468	33 521	94 676	5 512	4 791
Roanoke, VA	13 653	4.6	43 405	149	7 377	1 240	555	833	2 641	2 847	10 005	639	555
Rochester, MN	10 454	4.2	48 881	68	6 210	823	456	825	1 674	1 572	8 314	500	456
Rochester, NY	49 852	4.5	46 076	92	25 154	5 401	2 067	3 510	7 561	10 471	36 131	1 941	2 067
Rockford, IL	13 516	3.8	39 674	233	7 050	1 234	513	574	2 050	2 816	9 370	542	513
Rocky Mount, NC	5 398	2.3	36 459	312	2 370	435	187	283	881	1 533	3 275	214	187
Rome, GA	3 383	3.6	35 054	343	1 701	284	120	291	509	912	2 397	149	120
Sacramento—Roseville—Arden-Arcade, CA.........	112 889	6.6	49 639	63	55 858	13 349	3 684	7 890	19 314	20 570	80 780	4 197	3 684
Saginaw, MI	6 849	2.8	35 429	334	3 719	618	290	391	1 045	2 111	5 018	330	290
St. Cloud, MN	8 054	3.6	41 429	192	4 574	721	360	719	1 268	1 509	6 374	379	360
St. George, UT	4 881	7.2	31 368	377	2 047	351	165	365	1 128	1 172	2 928	195	165
St. Joseph, MO-KS	4 516	1.5	35 589	329	2 438	453	178	230	698	1 097	3 299	200	178
St. Louis, MO-IL.............	137 702	3.7	48 977	67	72 915	11 348	5 241	9 297	27 451	23 207	98 802	5 859	5 241
Salem, OR	15 223	7.2	37 121	290	7 082	1 274	632	1 105	2 599	3 929	10 093	629	632
Salinas, CA	21 624	8.0	49 836	60	9 082	1 984	681	3 265	4 757	3 153	15 011	709	681
Salisbury, MD-DE...........	17 115	4.3	43 296	152	6 242	1 208	490	1 839	3 357	4 374	9 779	611	490
Salt Lake City, UT..........	51 558	6.2	44 057	135	35 239	5 531	2 684	4 879	9 555	6 338	48 332	2 790	2 684
San Angelo, TX	5 274	1.7	44 072	133	2 205	388	157	625	1 180	992	3 375	174	157
San Antonio-New Braunfels, TX	103 790	5.9	43 535	144	49 119	7 792	3 485	13 327	18 079	17 845	73 724	3 782	3 485
San Diego-Carlsbad, CA	175 859	5.2	53 298	35	92 225	17 182	6 656	12 146	37 800	25 715	128 209	7 026	6 656
San Francisco-Oakland-Hayward, CA....................	368 795	7.7	79 206	4	199 240	27 962	12 286	35 831	79 333	36 281	275 320	15 225	12 286
Oakland-Hayward-Berkeley, CA Div 36084........	176 127	8.2	63 700	X	78 782	13 055	5 395	13 449	31 870	22 133	110 681	6 212	5 395
San Francisco-Redwood City-South San Francisco, CA Div 41884	164 175	7.4	100 724	X	112 498	13 635	6 364	18 727	38 291	12 092	151 223	8 261	6 364
San Rafael, CA Div 42034 .	28 493	5.8	109 076	X	7 961	1 273	527	3 655	9 172	2 056	13 416	752	527
San Jose-Sunnyvale-Santa Clara, CA....................	161 295	7.8	81 592	3	123 593	12 255	6 595	10 686	31 993	13 151	153 129	8 686	6 595
San Luis Obispo-Paso Robles-Arroyo Grande, CA................................	14 034	6.2	49 873	59	5 384	1 250	378	1 624	3 427	2 167	8 636	487	378
Santa Cruz-Watsonville, CA .	15 697	6.0	57 257	19	5 074	1 051	357	2 217	3 412	2 048	8 698	473	357
Santa Fe, NM................	7 536	3.9	50 684	51	2 905	502	226	519	2 320	1 296	4 152	273	226
Santa Maria-Santa Barbara, CA................................	24 208	5.8	54 428	26	10 788	2 148	760	2 883	7 020	3 129	16 579	877	760
Santa Rosa, CA	26 875	7.2	53 520	33	10 648	1 990	774	3 309	6 235	4 128	16 720	968	774
Savannah, GA	15 894	5.4	41 915	180	8 189	1 360	592	914	2 832	2 861	11 054	641	592
Scranton—Wilkes-Barre—Hazleton, PA...............	23 167	3.8	41 505	190	10 795	2 253	906	1 317	3 749	5 762	15 271	929	906
Seattle-Tacoma-Bellevue, WA	227 827	4.3	61 021	14	131 826	16 797	10 865	18 720	48 807	25 674	178 208	10 200	10 865
Seattle-Bellevue-Everett, WA Div 42644...............	190 187	4.3	65 817	X	115 326	13 863	9 292	16 099	42 181	18 760	154 579	8 867	9 292
Tacoma-Lakewood, WA Div 45104....................	37 640	4.8	44 600	X	16 500	2 934	1 574	2 621	6 626	6 914	23 629	1 333	1 574
Sebastian-Vero Beach, FL....	10 055	4.9	67 978	8	2 225	320	157	573	4 701	1 672	3 274	240	157
Sebring, FL	3 179	5.2	31 949	373	986	177	72	179	668	1 213	1 413	109	72
Sheboygan, WI	5 304	1.9	45 896	95	2 858	478	221	336	1 053	855	3 892	237	221
Sherman-Denison, TX	4 916	5.5	39 181	244	1 946	301	138	351	734	1 237	2 736	160	138
Shreveport-Bossier City, LA .	20 127	3.8	45 360	102	8 399	1 525	572	3 529	3 577	4 171	14 026	733	572
Sierra Vista-Douglas, AZ	4 821	3.1	38 133	269	1 855	426	152	218	956	1 528	2 651	163	152
Sioux City, IA-NE-SD.......	7 864	5.5	46 514	88	3 869	605	294	1 038	1 384	1 270	5 806	341	294
Sioux Falls, SD	13 542	8.7	53 769	32	6 903	1 040	498	2 482	2 429	1 538	10 923	644	498
South Bend-Mishawaka, IN-MI..............................	13 560	5.2	42 362	169	5 979	945	457	1 481	2 212	2 688	8 862	540	457
Spartanburg, SC	12 338	5.5	37 954	272	6 515	1 032	497	854	2 268	2 871	8 898	582	497
Spokane-Spokane Valley, WA	21 775	4.1	39 748	231	10 884	1 736	1 009	1 277	4 171	5 073	14 906	913	1 009
Springfield, IL................	9 204	2.2	43 590	143	5 056	988	342	517	1 749	1 689	6 903	370	342
Springfield, MA..............	29 295	5.3	46 354	90	13 219	2 800	903	1 791	4 316	7 448	18 712	974	903
Springfield, MO.............	16 808	5.0	36 824	304	8 367	1 473	618	1 478	2 715	3 725	11 936	734	618
Springfield, OH..............	5 055	3.4	37 183	288	1 992	382	143	221	723	1 417	2 738	171	143
State College, PA	6 639	2.8	41 344	193	3 622	1 426	273	560	1 201	1 000	5 883	289	273
Staunton-Waynesboro, VA ...	4 809	4.8	40 000	223	1 998	375	146	349	902	1 040	2 868	189	146
Stockton-Lodi, CA	28 151	7.9	38 769	252	10 996	2 409	811	2 301	4 276	6 938	16 517	920	811
Sumter, SC	3 959	2.9	36 834	303	1 845	396	158	177	653	1 050	2 576	153	158
Syracuse, NY	29 258	4.2	44 299	129	14 674	3 470	1 220	2 080	4 295	6 213	21 444	1 131	1 220
Tallahassee, FL	14 258	3.9	37 728	280	7 477	1 583	515	756	2 672	2 669	10 331	602	515
Tampa-St. Petersburg-Clearwater, FL......................	127 958	6.1	43 008	157	64 213	9 469	4 468	7 235	24 558	27 484	85 385	5 481	4 468
Terre Haute, IN.................	5 882	1.6	34 396	350	2 784	516	214	326	936	1 639	3 841	245	214

1. Based on the resident population estimated as of July 1 of the year shown.

Table C. Metropolitan Areas — Earnings, Social Security, and Housing

Area name	Earnings, 2015 (cont.)									Social Security beneficiaries, December 2015			Housing units, 2016	
	Percent by selected industries											Supplemental Security Income recipients, December 2015		Percent change, 2010–2016
	Farm	Mining	Construction	Manufacturing	Information, professional, scientific, technical services	Retail trade	Finance, insurance, real estate, rental and leasing	Health care and social assistance	Government	Number	Rate[1]		Total	
	75	76	77	78	79	80	81	82	83	84	85	86	87	88
Reading, PA	1.2	0.1	6.9	19.1	7.2	6.0	5.3	13.8	13.5	85 440	206	10 548	164 954	0.1
Redding, CA	0.8	D	6.5	3.7	6.8	9.8	5.4	19.4	24.7	48 495	270	10 066	78 311	1.3
Reno, NV	0.1	D	8.1	7.0	D	D	D	D	17.8	82 650	184	7 139	193 367	3.5
Richmond, VA	0.0	D	D	D	11.5	5.2	11.1	11.6	18.7	228 870	180	27 650	526 515	3.8
Riverside-San Bernardino-Ontario, CA	0.5	0.3	8.2	7.3	5.2	8.0	4.4	11.6	24.3	639 490	143	135 496	1 545 677	3.0
Roanoke, VA	0.1	D	D	13.8	D	D	7.2	16.0	14.4	74 615	238	8 241	146 534	1.1
Rochester, MN	2.0	0.1	5.3	12.3	4.1	5.1	3.2	44.8	9.6	38 910	182	2 723	91 881	4.2
Rochester, NY	0.5	D	5.2	13.4	10.3	5.6	6.1	12.9	17.9	235 405	218	32 060	478 125	2.0
Rockford, IL	-0.1	D	4.4	26.8	4.6	6.6	5.5	15.3	12.9	70 250	206	7 817	145 277	-0.5
Rocky Mount, NC	1.7	0.1	5.4	22.5	D	8.5	4.2	D	17.8	35 125	238	6 482	67 280	0.2
Rome, GA	1.0	D	2.6	16.9	D	7.0	4.2	24.2	13.5	21 860	227	3 340	40 414	-0.3
Sacramento—Roseville—Arden-Arcade, CA	0.5	0.1	6.5	4.5	10.5	5.6	7.2	11.7	33.6	378 365	167	82 240	893 858	2.5
Saginaw, MI	0.3	0.2	4.5	19.2	6.2	7.3	6.0	19.0	14.2	49 135	254	8 577	87 037	0.2
St. Cloud, MN	3.1	D	9.7	14.2	5.5	7.1	5.9	17.1	14.1	33 450	172	2 784	80 470	3.0
St. George, UT	0.1	0.3	9.8	5.5	7.2	9.7	6.7	17.0	15.3	33 725	217	1 338	65 472	13.4
St. Joseph, MO-KS	-0.3	D	7.5	D	D	6.3	5.5	14.1	16.2	25 655	202	2 858	53 656	0.0
St. Louis, MO-IL	0.0	D	D	10.8	D	5.5	D	12.5	12.7	546 675	195	59 770	1 246 400	1.7
Salem, OR	2.9	D	7.1	6.7	4.8	6.8	5.2	15.3	30.0	80 110	196	8 699	155 632	2.9
Salinas, CA	13.4	0.3	4.0	2.6	5.6	5.3	4.5	7.5	24.5	60 650	140	8 977	140 813	1.3
Salisbury, MD-DE	3.8	0.0	8.1	8.2	5.2	8.9	7.8	15.6	16.5	103 360	262	7 582	243 139	1.7
Salt Lake City, UT	0.1	0.5	6.7	8.9	D	7.5	11.9	7.7	15.6	141 820	121	14 320	407 531	6.3
San Angelo, TX	1.0	8.1	D	D	D	7.3	D	D	21.6	22 000	184	2 977	49 320	4.0
San Antonio-New Braunfels, TX	0.1	6.7	6.2	4.4	9.2	6.5	11.1	10.6	20.3	379 045	159	63 359	879 480	4.9
San Diego-Carlsbad, CA	0.2	0.0	4.7	8.8	18.2	5.3	7.6	8.6	24.2	475 805	145	84 965	1 202 324	3.2
San Francisco-Oakland-Hayward, CA	0.1	D	5.1	6.2	27.3	4.8	10.6	8.2	12.9	669 620	144	137 094	1 792 109	2.9
Oakland-Hayward-Berkeley, CA Div 36084	0.1	0.2	6.7	9.5	18.0	5.6	6.3	11.7	15.5	386 665	140	78 420	1 010 485	2.8
San Francisco-Redwood City-South San Francisco, CA Div 41884	0.1	0.0	3.8	3.9	34.8	4.1	13.6	5.4	11.0	232 430	143	55 161	668 742	3.2
San Rafael, CA Div 42034	0.2	D	6.7	4.7	19.8	6.6	11.6	10.7	12.8	50 525	194	3 513	112 882	1.5
San Jose-Sunnyvale-Santa Clara, CA	0.2	D	3.4	21.4	D	3.9	5.2	6.4	6.6	237 490	121	48 177	683 465	5.2
San Luis Obispo-Paso Robles-Arroyo Grande, CA	2.2	0.2	8.5	6.5	9.1	8.7	5.6	10.9	21.6	57 130	203	4 777	120 856	3.0
Santa Cruz-Watsonville, CA	4.2	D	12.1	7.1	8.9	7.1	6.0	12.6	19.0	44 385	162	5 928	105 649	1.1
Santa Fe, NM	-0.1	0.8	4.8	1.2	10.7	8.5	7.3	14.0	29.6	34 820	236	2 681	71 869	0.8
Santa Maria-Santa Barbara, CA	4.8	1.4	4.9	7.3	13.2	6.0	6.7	10.6	20.8	71 110	160	9 090	155 953	2.0
Santa Rosa, CA	1.7	0.1	9.5	13.5	9.9	7.5	6.1	12.9	14.6	96 460	192	9 454	208 150	1.7
Savannah, GA	0.1	D	4.5	17.1	D	6.5	5.2	13.0	18.5	63 680	168	8 434	159 946	5.9
Scranton—Wilkes-Barre—Hazleton, PA	0.1	0.7	5.3	11.5	6.5	7.1	6.6	D	15.3	139 250	250	17 381	259 888	0.4
Seattle-Tacoma-Bellevue, WA	0.1	0.2	6.1	11.3	20.8	7.6	7.1	9.1	15.0	545 085	146	70 504	1 552 210	6.1
Seattle-Bellevue-Everett, WA Div 42644	0.1	0.3	5.9	12.2	23.2	7.8	7.4	8.0	12.4	400 410	139	50 638	1 213 650	6.7
Tacoma-Lakewood, WA Div 45104	0.3	0.1	7.2	5.9	4.8	6.5	5.1	16.0	32.2	144 675	172	19 866	338 560	4.1
Sebastian-Vero Beach, FL	1.6	D	5.6	4.1	13.2	9.6	8.1	16.9	10.6	48 065	325	2 505	78 628	3.0
Sebring, FL	9.1	0.0	3.9	2.4	3.8	10.6	3.7	22.5	16.8	33 525	337	2 838	54 834	-1.0
Sheboygan, WI	1.3	D	4.7	39.8	2.8	5.5	6.3	11.8	9.9	24 955	216	1 784	50 599	-0.3
Sherman-Denison, TX	0.4	1.7	8.7	15.8	4.5	8.3	7.0	18.5	13.4	27 255	217	3 031	54 973	2.3
Shreveport-Bossier City, LA	0.0	19.5	D	D	4.9	7.0	4.2	14.4	18.6	86 865	196	19 810	201 131	4.2
Sierra Vista-Douglas, AZ	2.2	0.2	4.2	1.1	8.2	5.8	2.8	7.7	50.9	31 020	245	3 086	60 873	3.1
Sioux City, IA-NE-SD	7.1	D	11.7	D	D	Retail	6.1	11.6	11.6	31 905	189	2 621	70 118	2.2
Sioux Falls, SD	1.7	D	6.6	D	D	7.2	D	D	8.6	42 715	170	3 338	105 503	10.1
South Bend-Mishawaka, IN-MI	0.1	D	5.2	15.8	8.9	5.8	5.2	D	10.0	64 065	200	6 947	141 952	0.9
Spartanburg, SC	0.2	D	6.0	24.4	D	6.5	5.1	D	16.6	74 595	230	8 334	140 501	2.7
Spokane-Spokane Valley, WA	0.4	D	6.2	7.7	7.2	7.1	8.4	D	20.6	114 395	209	16 042	239 765	4.0
Springfield, IL	-0.2	D	5.6	3.3	D	6.2	8.6	D	25.6	44 005	209	4 742	96 648	1.1
Springfield, MA	0.0	0.1	6.1	8.7	5.9	6.2	8.0	18.1	22.8	130 320	207	33 366	255 166	0.2
Springfield, MO	0.2	D	D	8.5	9.2	7.9	6.4	17.3	14.2	95 175	209	9 930	200 791	4.4
Springfield, OH	0.1	0.4	4.0	16.5	3.2	6.9	8.4	14.6	16.2	30 990	228	4 111	61 031	-0.6
State College, PA	0.1	2.4	4.4	4.7	7.8	4.5	3.9	9.7	49.5	23 680	148	1 522	65 762	3.9
Staunton-Waynesboro, VA	1.5	D	D	17.6	6.7	6.8	3.8	D	17.4	30 165	250	2 170	54 233	3.0
Stockton-Lodi, CA	5.0	0.1	5.2	8.1	4.0	7.0	4.5	12.2	22.0	107 155	148	29 502	240 582	2.9
Sumter, SC	0.3	0.0	7.0	15.5	3.7	5.9	2.9	11.2	36.3	23 195	216	4 373	47 289	2.8
Syracuse, NY	0.3	D	5.1	10.0	D	6.6	7.2	D	21.9	138 660	210	18 799	290 955	1.1
Tallahassee, FL	0.6	0.1	3.6	2.1	D	6.1	D	D	38.1	62 295	165	9 850	166 992	2.4
Tampa-St. Petersburg-Clearwater, FL	0.3	0.0	5.4	5.6	14.9	8.1	10.7	13.4	13.4	660 755	222	79 069	1 397 779	3.3
Terre Haute, IN	0.3	2.1	6.5	19.2	D	6.8	D	D	18.2	37 960	222	4 539	74 710	0.8

1. Per 1,000 resident population estimated as of July 1, 2011 of the year shown.

Table C. Metropolitan Areas — **Housing, Labor Force, and Employment**

Area name	Housing units, 2015								Civilian labor force, 2016				Civilian employment[5], 2015		
	Occupied units										Unemployment			Percent	
		Owner-occupied				Renter-occupied									
				Median owner cost as a percent of income			Median rent as a percent of income	Percent with a computer		Percent change, 2015–2016				Management, professional, and related occupations	Construction, production, and related occupations
	Total	Percent	Median value[1]	With a mort-gage	Without a mort-gage[2]	Median rent[3]			Total		Total	Rate[4]	Total employed		
	89	90	91	92	93	94	95	96	97	98	99	100	101	102	103
Reading, PA.....................	151 792	71.6	171 100	22.5	14.8	865	31.4	87.0	214 132	0.7	10 738	5.0	200 854	32.1	28.9
Redding, CA.....................	69 799	61.5	238 900	25.6	13.2	919	30.8	82.6	74 700	0.5	5 167	6.9	72 329	29.9	18.8
Reno, NV	174 571	56.0	268 100	22.9	10.0	920	28.2	90.2	232 266	1.9	11 626	5.0	221 541	32.5	18.9
Richmond, VA	483 127	64.0	219 700	21.4	10.0	1 019	30.3	87.6	663 377	1.2	27 309	4.1	637 833	40.5	17.7
Riverside-San Bernardino-Ontario, CA..................	1 343 526	60.8	299 300	26.5	12.1	1 166	34.7	88.7	1 987 394	1.6	117 180	5.9	1 858 130	28.3	26.3
Roanoke, VA	127 273	67.3	172 600	21.5	10.7	803	26.2	84.5	157 307	0.3	6 203	3.9	144 562	35.7	23.7
Rochester, MN	83 418	75.8	173 700	19.5	10.0	802	28.2	90.5	119 171	1.1	3 873	3.2	113 303	46.0	18.7
Rochester, NY	427 520	67.1	138 900	20.6	13.6	833	31.6	86.6	523 683	-0.7	24 618	4.7	522 737	39.7	19.2
Rockford, IL	132 190	67.8	122 700	21.9	12.2	729	28.1	85.4	167 952	-0.5	11 071	6.6	156 695	29.4	28.1
Rocky Mount, NC	57 450	60.7	104 700	22.9	14.0	688	32.0	76.1	66 921	0.4	4 866	7.3	64 856	27.2	30.7
Rome, GA	34 931	57.7	120 600	19.2	11.5	690	31.7	76.4	43 531	1.3	2 628	6.0	39 913	29.2	28.2
Sacramento—Roseville—Arden-Arcade, CA..........	809 295	58.6	339 900	24.1	10.6	1 109	32.4	92.2	1 073 254	1.7	55 994	5.2	1 015 471	39.7	16.8
Saginaw, MI	77 211	70.6	93 500	19.5	13.1	720	33.1	79.7	88 844	0.5	4 542	5.1	82 058	30.3	24.1
St. Cloud, MN	74 617	65.4	168 100	21.3	11.1	751	27.2	89.4	109 594	0.6	4 319	3.9	107 724	31.6	26.3
St. George, UT	52 453	66.4	231 400	23.8	10.0	936	27.1	92.4	67 474	5.6	2 493	3.7	62 786	31.3	19.8
St. Joseph, MO-KS	46 518	67.7	112 900	19.6	11.3	728	25.7	81.1	66 238	0.1	2 693	4.1	61 067	31.1	25.3
St. Louis, MO-IL	1 108 303	68.3	164 200	19.9	11.7	839	29.0	87.4	1 482 748	0.5	68 323	4.6	1 387 444	38.7	19.6
Salem, OR	144 600	60.1	205 000	22.6	11.4	817	30.1	91.3	196 681	4.0	10 060	5.1	183 850	30.1	28.2
Salinas, CA	126 904	49.1	429 100	27.0	10.3	1 290	31.7	85.0	220 414	0.8	16 662	7.6	182 151	26.8	33.2
Salisbury, MD-DE	154 242	71.4	218 200	22.9	11.6	981	31.2	86.2	185 332	1.4	10 332	5.6	173 250	32.7	23.5
Salt Lake City, UT	377 058	66.2	251 200	21.0	10.0	964	27.8	93.4	636 054	3.1	20 304	3.2	591 175	36.4	21.0
San Angelo, TX	45 137	60.7	124 000	21.4	10.7	883	31.4	80.5	54 987	-0.3	2 467	4.5	53 145	31.0	27.5
San Antonio-New Braunfels, TX	791 273	60.8	151 400	21.3	11.0	926	28.3	87.2	1 135 726	3.0	42 589	3.7	1 075 502	33.8	21.0
San Diego-Carlsbad, CA	1 113 610	52.0	485 900	26.8	11.3	1 427	33.3	91.9	1 570 422	1.0	73 468	4.7	1 552 867	40.3	16.2
San Francisco-Oakland-Hayward, CA..................	1 689 907	53.5	718 400	25.1	10.1	1 623	29.0	92.6	2 543 805	2.0	96 378	3.8	2 409 944	48.1	14.3
Oakland-Hayward-Berkeley, CA Div 36084........	963 824	57.2	606 700	24.7	10.3	1 525	30.6	92.9	1 394 371	1.7	60 169	4.3	1 372 611	46.0	16.6
San Francisco-Redwood City-South San Francisco, CA Div 41884	620 196	45.9	928 900	25.9	10.0	1 765	27.1	92.0	1 008 375	2.5	31 642	3.1	907 232	50.7	11.4
San Rafael, CA Div 42034 .	105 887	63.6	906 500	26.1	10.7	1 782	29.4	92.9	141 059	1.1	4 567	3.2	130 101	52.0	9.5
San Jose-Sunnyvale-Santa Clara, CA	651 352	56.2	823 700	24.4	10.0	1 894	28.9	94.4	1 056 315	1.7	40 636	3.8	995 869	51.4	14.6
San Luis Obispo-Paso Robles-Arroyo Grande, CA..................................	104 760	58.9	508 200	26.0	10.6	1 254	32.2	91.2	140 365	0.5	5 982	4.3	128 903	41.9	17.0
Santa Cruz-Watsonville, CA .	93 317	55.4	668 300	27.1	12.8	1 442	36.5	89.4	144 525	0.8	9 971	6.9	132 081	39.6	19.9
Santa Fe, NM...................	60 642	70.1	286 200	24.1	10.0	951	32.3	82.9	72 574	0.0	3 883	5.4	71 599	43.8	14.1
Santa Maria-Santa Barbara, CA............................	144 261	51.3	547 600	25.3	11.5	1 419	32.2	90.1	216 625	-0.5	10 846	5.0	214 133	35.3	24.9
Santa Rosa, CA	190 662	59.5	512 100	25.6	11.6	1 376	32.4	92.4	260 479	0.8	10 296	4.0	250 066	36.0	22.9
Savannah, GA	138 784	55.1	173 600	21.4	11.7	989	30.8	89.4	180 795	2.4	9 299	5.1	175 342	34.1	22.3
Scranton—Wilkes-Barre—Hazleton, PA................	221 200	67.5	132 900	20.7	14.2	753	28.4	79.7	280 486	0.3	17 175	6.1	261 710	32.8	24.1
Seattle-Tacoma-Bellevue, WA	1 437 222	59.9	361 500	22.9	11.8	1 263	28.7	93.5	2 026 229	2.7	91 023	4.5	1 903 626	44.8	18.0
Seattle-Bellevue-Everett, WA Div 42644.............	1 130 166	59.9	396 300	22.7	11.6	1 327	28.1	94.1	1 620 512	2.5	65 561	4.0	1 524 853	47.8	16.4
Tacoma-Lakewood, WA Div 45104.....................	307 056	60.2	249 600	23.6	12.2	1 062	31.3	91.3	405 717	3.4	25 462	6.3	378 773	32.8	24.4
Sebastian-Vero Beach, FL....	55 494	77.0	174 000	23.2	12.1	911	29.2	85.7	62 248	1.8	3 829	6.2	52 438	30.9	21.0
Sebring, FL	41 116	74.9	92 600	22.2	11.9	752	37.1	81.2	36 071	2.2	2 376	6.6	32 038	29.9	20.1
Sheboygan, WI	47 438	69.7	145 000	19.8	11.9	688	23.9	87.3	61 961	1.1	2 171	3.5	59 624	29.5	33.8
Sherman-Denison, TX	47 538	68.1	112 300	20.5	13.2	783	28.2	83.6	60 832	1.7	2 340	3.8	58 993	31.4	27.0
Shreveport-Bossier City, LA .	171 531	61.4	145 300	20.4	10.0	754	35.2	77.0	190 835	-2.4	12 293	6.4	184 336	31.8	23.3
Sierra Vista-Douglas, AZ	50 202	67.6	146 900	20.4	11.0	746	28.6	83.4	50 187	-0.7	3 071	6.1	39 648	30.1	18.3
Sioux City, IA-NE-SD..........	63 198	68.5	121 700	17.7	10.8	695	26.6	81.9	93 112	-0.1	3 241	3.5	82 382	30.2	30.2
Sioux Falls, SD	98 273	67.6	167 900	19.5	10.0	750	26.0	87.7	146 409	1.3	3 432	2.3	134 674	34.1	24.1
South Bend-Mishawaka, IN-MI	119 494	71.0	125 900	19.1	10.0	709	29.7	83.9	158 278	2.4	7 176	4.5	147 249	34.8	26.1
Spartanburg, SC	124 570	68.6	124 300	19.2	10.0	711	29.9	81.5	154 149	1.7	7 224	4.7	145 938	28.2	32.5
Spokane-Spokane Valley, WA	215 652	62.0	192 400	23.0	10.5	781	31.1	89.2	257 172	2.9	16 830	6.5	231 789	35.4	20.1
Springfield, IL	88 081	68.3	134 700	19.2	10.5	748	27.4	86.8	113 030	0.7	5 483	4.9	99 663	42.3	16.0
Springfield, MA	233 619	62.5	217 200	22.6	14.7	906	33.5	85.6	307 680	-0.5	14 044	4.6	304 555	37.5	17.7
Springfield, MO	179 752	61.4	137 600	19.3	10.0	711	29.3	85.5	233 110	0.6	9 285	4.0	210 655	33.8	22.1
Springfield, OH	54 232	65.5	102 100	19.5	10.8	696	27.3	84.7	63 318	-1.1	3 289	5.2	60 796	28.7	29.7
State College, PA	56 116	59.1	206 600	21.2	11.3	945	31.3	90.9	79 084	1.6	3 329	4.2	77 408	47.3	17.5
Staunton-Waynesboro, VA	46 768	65.6	186 900	21.7	10.0	827	27.6	81.9	58 893	0.9	2 210	3.8	55 230	27.9	30.2
Stockton-Lodi, CA..............	223 062	55.0	278 400	24.9	12.0	1 036	33.8	85.7	319 187	1.3	25 729	8.1	292 491	27.0	31.2
Sumter, SC	41 017	63.9	100 900	21.8	10.3	775	28.1	81.5	44 317	-0.2	2 543	5.7	44 206	26.1	31.7
Syracuse, NY....................	254 001	67.5	131 500	19.9	12.7	813	28.9	86.8	307 381	-0.9	15 090	4.9	309 687	38.1	18.8
Tallahassee, FL	142 295	56.8	160 100	23.5	10.0	904	36.7	88.8	187 828	1.6	8 870	4.7	175 785	39.5	11.7
Tampa-St. Petersburg-Clearwater, FL	1 166 704	62.9	165 600	22.8	12.1	976	31.5	87.7	1 475 815	2.5	68 344	4.6	1 350 375	37.1	17.2
Terre Haute, IN.................	66 685	63.2	87 500	17.8	10.4	677	31.2	80.8	77 531	0.2	4 240	5.5	72 906	31.0	30.6

1. Specified owner-occupied units. 2. A value of 10.0 represents 10 percent or less. 3. Specified renter-occupied units. 4. Percent of civilian labor force.
5. Civilian employed persons 16 years old and over.

Table C. Metropolitan Areas — **Nonfarm Employment and Agriculture**

Area name	Private nonfarm establishments, employment and payroll, 2015									Agriculture, 2012			
		Employment						Annual payroll		Farms			
												Percent with:	
	Number of establishments	Total	Health care and social assistance	Manufacturing	Retail trade	Finance and insurance	Professional, scientific, and technical services	Total (mil dol)	Average per employee (dollars)	Number	Fewer than 50 acres	500 acres or more	Farm operators whose principal occupation is farming (percent)
	104	105	106	107	108	109	110	111	112	113	114	115	116
Reading, PA	8 404	154 975	25 371	31 436	20 908	5 723	6 744	7 072	45 633	2 039	47.8	3.5	61.4
Redding, CA	4 141	49 163	10 429	2 058	9 647	1 892	2 263	1 877	38 174	1 544	72.9	6.1	44.9
Reno, NV	11 989	179 215	22 688	15 204	24 141	5 725	9 435	7 844	43 771	485	69.7	7.0	43.5
Richmond, VA	31 020	523 449	81 953	30 023	66 099	47 929	37 670	25 545	48 801	3 131	43.1	8.6	48.2
Riverside-San Bernardino-Ontario, CA	70 200	1 118 924	161 949	94 948	179 783	26 642	37 002	44 494	39 765	4 198	86.0	3.0	51.5
Roanoke, VA	8 063	138 842	25 823	15 621	18 371	8 090	5 659	5 667	40 819	2 094	34.0	6.6	46.1
Rochester, MN	5 172	108 519	21 567	7 734	12 899	2 247	D	5 837	53 789	4 233	29.7	14.5	53.4
Rochester, NY	24 580	443 427	81 611	53 761	58 579	15 282	26 133	19 744	44 526	4 268	38.0	9.1	61.0
Rockford, IL	7 342	133 966	21 842	33 665	16 022	3 791	5 057	5 825	43 483	1 286	47.4	13.6	47.5
Rocky Mount, NC	2 745	48 602	8 443	10 828	6 625	1 607	1 030	1 786	36 741	702	37.9	16.7	54.8
Rome, GA	1 940	34 336	7 640	6 082	4 580	759	715	1 270	36 993	559	44.4	3.6	36.5
Sacramento—Roseville—Arden-Arcade, CA	46 889	697 430	114 033	34 331	99 786	40 272	53 374	35 853	51 407	5 076	71.7	6.4	50.7
Saginaw, MI	4 300	79 117	17 254	11 127	12 716	2 741	2 448	3 075	38 867	1 318	41.0	12.1	48.9
St. Cloud, MN	5 249	97 391	19 920	15 359	13 293	4 305	2 828	4 104	42 138	4 459	24.5	8.3	54.6
St. George, UT	4 557	45 178	8 190	2 517	8 405	1 423	1 896	1 469	32 515	579	63.0	13.1	43.5
St. Joseph, MO-KS	2 996	48 349	9 174	10 875	6 471	2 026	1 058	1 950	40 323	2 838	26.1	14.6	44.1
St. Louis, MO-IL	75 922	1 223 383	192 274	107 121	145 073	64 459	84 975	60 263	49 259	11 270	35.8	13.6	43.9
Salem, OR	9 244	114 637	21 106	12 103	18 159	3 141	4 112	4 217	36 789	3 710	70.5	5.4	48.7
Salinas, CA	8 557	106 652	15 875	7 750	17 003	2 843	7 088	4 637	43 477	1 179	42.0	26.4	61.7
Salisbury, MD-DE	10 493	123 924	23 829	14 549	23 795	3 746	3 787	4 548	36 704	2 384	51.8	10.4	63.4
Salt Lake City, UT	31 772	582 047	62 802	50 248	65 343	41 689	49 050	27 873	47 889	1 106	77.0	8.0	30.1
San Angelo, TX	2 860	41 413	8 074	3 162	6 687	1 608	1 400	1 518	36 662	1 358	41.6	23.9	40.5
San Antonio-New Braunfels, TX	44 267	825 174	127 641	44 204	109 645	63 780	47 400	35 669	43 226	14 598	41.6	10.4	40.4
San Diego-Carlsbad, CA	81 710	1 239 334	162 748	100 268	154 012	52 423	135 903	66 592	53 732	5 732	91.6	0.9	47.6
San Francisco-Oakland-Hayward, CA	127 015	2 045 647	253 500	114 521	211 851	114 608	234 619	170 870	83 529	1 717	61.4	13.6	53.2
Oakland-Hayward-Berkeley, CA Div 36084	NA	NA	NA	NA	NA	NA	NA	NA	NA	1 054	67.6	9.8	50.6
San Francisco-Redwood City-South San Francisco, CA Div 41884	NA	NA	NA	NA	NA	NA	NA	NA	NA	340	62.4	6.2	56.5
San Rafael, CA Div 42034	NA	NA	NA	NA	NA	NA	NA	NA	NA	323	39.9	34.1	58.5
San Jose-Sunnyvale-Santa Clara, CA	48 731	1 010 970	107 425	87 629	88 639	26 093	130 743	110 177	108 981	1 631	66.8	12.4	56.9
San Luis Obispo-Paso Robles-Arroyo Grande, CA	8 164	91 540	15 394	6 489	14 883	2 299	4 766	3 727	40 719	2 666	55.8	12.2	47.0
Santa Cruz-Watsonville, CA	6 961	75 572	13 179	5 182	12 274	2 225	4 158	3 364	44 511	667	73.8	4.6	62.1
Santa Fe, NM	4 696	46 233	8 704	833	9 385	1 694	2 423	1 853	40 084	715	67.0	13.4	43.6
Santa Maria-Santa Barbara, CA	11 455	146 504	22 182	14 223	20 336	4 268	9 630	7 278	49 675	1 597	63.9	11.3	51.7
Santa Rosa, CA	13 746	166 604	25 550	20 322	25 726	5 456	9 216	8 170	49 038	3 579	71.3	6.0	51.3
Savannah, GA	8 884	147 128	21 638	17 700	20 544	3 142	5 647	5 977	40 628	281	50.9	9.3	43.1
Scranton—Wilkes-Barre—Hazleton, PA	13 185	236 587	46 090	27 914	32 140	10 587	9 742	9 050	38 254	1 367	32.8	2.9	44.0
Seattle-Tacoma-Bellevue, WA	101 754	1 626 232	223 048	165 211	177 939	60 278	125 562	106 896	65 732	4 753	86.4	0.6	42.5
Seattle-Bellevue-Everett, WA Div 42644	NA	NA	NA	NA	NA	NA	NA	NA	NA	3 275	86.9	0.7	40.5
Tacoma-Lakewood, WA Div 45104	NA	NA	NA	NA	NA	NA	NA	NA	NA	1 478	85.3	0.3	47.0
Sebastian-Vero Beach, FL	4 156	42 560	8 992	1 813	9 075	1 287	1 681	1 569	36 862	461	73.1	7.2	49.0
Sebring, FL	1 876	19 861	5 558	747	4 521	513	653	614	30 897	969	64.3	11.0	49.3
Sheboygan, WI	2 651	54 832	6 543	17 664	6 113	2 060	1 255	2 351	42 868	986	42.4	10.1	52.7
Sherman-Denison, TX	2 511	39 777	8 664	7 000	6 222	1 831	919	1 373	34 508	2 562	50.8	5.6	44.1
Shreveport-Bossier City, LA	9 994	156 849	32 917	9 478	24 081	4 425	6 399	6 099	38 883	2 202	45.9	7.6	49.0
Sierra Vista-Douglas, AZ	2 188	26 092	4 560	348	5 329	500	3 646	905	34 676	1 093	43.8	22.4	56.1
Sioux City, IA-NE-SD	4 415	77 546	11 837	15 051	10 173	3 166	1 587	2 952	38 072	3 644	26.2	30.3	61.9
Sioux Falls, SD	7 463	136 675	26 698	14 557	18 062	14 100	4 967	5 936	43 431	3 418	32.9	28.4	53.1
South Bend-Mishawaka, IN-MI	6 473	126 814	19 965	17 896	16 587	3 888	4 880	4 997	39 407	1 489	48.6	10.8	47.1
Spartanburg, SC	6 560	130 867	15 795	30 084	15 255	2 243	4 090	5 568	42 550	1 602	53.6	2.4	42.1
Spokane-Spokane Valley, WA	13 750	189 825	37 889	16 044	28 265	10 810	8 988	8 198	43 189	3 937	54.2	9.4	42.8
Springfield, IL	5 203	86 462	23 350	2 740	12 917	5 897	4 319	3 490	40 365	1 461	40.4	21.7	52.1
Springfield, MA	13 176	227 956	59 693	21 474	31 434	10 435	8 572	9 479	41 582	1 381	40.5	1.2	46.8
Springfield, MO	11 904	179 168	33 180	16 213	25 161	8 442	8 926	6 791	37 902	7 459	37.1	6.4	45.1
Springfield, OH	2 281	41 116	8 063	6 242	5 454	2 830	1 314	1 471	35 772	785	53.2	11.3	49.6
State College, PA	3 313	44 884	8 343	3 970	8 074	1 261	3 024	1 701	37 900	1 192	40.1	4.8	57.4
Staunton-Waynesboro, VA	2 774	39 796	8 112	5 971	6 198	975	1 003	1 418	35 638	1 706	42.3	6.2	48.8
Stockton-Lodi, CA	11 025	173 611	27 966	19 410	26 236	6 248	4 564	7 360	42 394	3 580	63.8	8.3	59.0
Sumter, SC	1 755	32 393	5 279	5 985	4 648	780	617	1 107	34 161	515	44.3	14.2	45.8
Syracuse, NY	15 352	258 000	47 473	23 854	36 570	12 248	15 357	11 115	43 081	2 176	34.1	8.5	56.1
Tallahassee, FL	8 788	110 022	20 878	2 925	19 323	4 783	10 705	4 315	39 219	1 474	59.2	5.7	39.4
Tampa-St. Petersburg-Clearwater, FL	74 726	1 080 271	175 699	54 798	151 367	77 463	94 025	48 099	44 525	4 448	78.6	3.0	51.6
Terre Haute, IN	3 514	56 795	11 177	10 364	8 755	1 457	1 247	2 037	35 864	1 732	43.6	18.7	46.1

Table C. Metropolitan Areas — **Agriculture**

	Land in farms					Value of land and buildings (dollars)		Value of machinery and equipment, average per farm (dollars)	Value of products sold				Percent of farms with sales of:		Government payments	
			Acres								Percent from:					
Area name	Acreage (1,000)	Percent change, 2007–2012	Average size of farm	Total irrigated (1,000)	Total cropland (1,000)	Average per farm	Average per acre		Total (mil dol)	Average per farm (dollars)	Crops	Live-stock and poultry products	$10,000 or more	$100,000 or more	Total ($1,000)	Percent of farms
	117	118	119	120	121	122	123	124	125	126	127	128	129	130	131	132
Reading, PA	234	5.2	115	1.6	182.3	1 015 554	8 859	120 253	528.7	259 299	42.6	57.4	58.5	30.2	3 646	28.3
Redding, CA	376	-3.7	244	38.2	36.9	682 565	2 801	36 550	65.6	42 501	36.6	63.4	26.2	4.8	420	4.6
Reno, NV	443	-8.9	913	D	D	749 691	821	52 786	D	D	D	D	27.4	6.6	75	3.9
Richmond, VA	649	-1.9	207	D	325.5	853 057	4 118	85 962	338.0	107 947	D	D	32.0	10.1	12 201	26.8
Riverside-San Bernardino-Ontario, CA	421	-51.5	100	167.7	257.1	1 084 366	10 807	78 134	1 621.2	386 179	50.1	49.9	47.9	14.7	3 038	4.5
Roanoke, VA	332	2.0	159	1.1	102.0	599 779	3 783	70 357	93.2	44 495	D	D	33.2	6.5	1 600	16.1
Rochester, MN	1 158	-7.6	274	D	906.6	1 399 848	5 117	185 604	1 111.6	262 609	59.8	40.2	63.1	35.0	23 694	71.1
Rochester, NY	927	-6.2	217	9.2	701.3	663 751	3 055	158 475	930.7	218 057	61.4	38.6	56.4	29.8	11 479	29.3
Rockford, IL	318	-1.0	247	1.4	286.5	1 617 918	6 550	156 317	205.4	159 703	83.9	16.1	48.3	27.9	8 500	57.8
Rocky Mount, NC	267	-8.9	381	11.9	181.9	1 238 600	3 253	197 288	340.4	484 865	61.8	38.2	49.1	32.2	4 184	58.5
Rome, GA	70	-17.1	126	0.8	19.6	489 283	3 898	54 420	77.0	137 828	6.9	93.1	29.3	8.6	616	19.7
Sacramento—Roseville—Arden-Arcade, CA	927	-11.5	183	343.4	457.4	1 259 225	6 892	84 057	961.8	189 475	D	D	39.7	14.6	10 256	9.9
Saginaw, MI	310	-4.5	235	2.3	274.5	896 656	3 816	144 832	243.6	184 855	91.7	8.3	55.8	27.6	6 093	71.6
St. Cloud, MN	946	5.8	212	63.5	722.7	808 127	3 808	165 913	976.0	218 883	34.3	65.7	66.3	35.3	19 180	71.8
St. George, UT	148	-15.0	256	14.8	20.2	934 487	3 656	50 485	12.6	21 843	51.1	48.9	29.2	5.5	210	7.8
St. Joseph, MO-KS	810	-14.3	285	D	576.3	947 085	3 320	103 711	265.9	93 709	82.2	17.8	51.1	17.0	14 038	67.9
St. Louis, MO-IL	2 912	-0.9	258	14.1	2 232.2	1 359 070	5 260	137 402	1 235.6	109 636	73.4	26.6	46.7	19.4	42 877	56.7
Salem, OR	431	-9.1	116	105.3	314.8	852 208	7 337	116 718	742.7	200 189	80.7	19.3	38.6	16.2	2 495	11.7
Salinas, CA	1 268	-4.5	1 076	263.8	358.3	5 263 068	4 893	396 806	2 979.7	2 527 341	98.5	1.5	59.6	35.4	635	7.0
Salisbury, MD-DE	520	-2.4	218	105.7	399.5	1 515 910	6 943	176 840	1 575.7	660 933	24.2	75.8	66.0	48.9	11 071	48.2
Salt Lake City, UT	425	18.0	384	29.8	53.7	709 106	1 845	65 829	61.9	55 974	41.1	58.9	26.7	7.1	250	4.3
San Angelo, TX	1 453	-6.1	1 070	31.8	179.0	1 146 386	1 071	85 947	138.9	102 282	24.0	76.0	29.2	9.4	6 065	25.5
San Antonio-New Braunfels, TX	3 642	3.0	249	102.6	629.7	791 780	3 174	49 698	D	D	D	55.8	22.7	3.3	11 155	13.4
San Diego-Carlsbad, CA	222	-27.1	39	45.2	68.2	694 313	17 964	34 672	726.0	126 657	89.3	10.7	42.9	9.1	451	1.7
San Francisco-Oakland-Hayward, CA	525	-3.2	305	42.7	89.8	2 135 551	6 991	67 439	D	D	D	D	48.0	16.4	1 746	6.8
Oakland-Hayward-Berkeley, CA Div 36084	305	-13.1	290	36.2	66.9	1 951 273	6 733	66 327	146.9	139 355	83.9	16.1	43.0	11.7	281	4.7
San Francisco-Redwood City-South San Francisco, CA Div 41884	48	-15.6	142	2.8	8.5	1 604 941	11 328	69 188	D	D	D	D	48.2	14.4	182	4.1
San Rafael, CA Div 42034	171	28.2	529	3.7	14.4	3 295 415	6 229	69 226	91.8	284 238	9.3	90.7	64.1	34.1	1 283	16.4
San Jose-Sunnyvale-Santa Clara, CA	834	-5.2	511	37.0	76.9	2 000 239	3 911	78 560	407.9	250 068	88.1	11.9	47.1	15.1	194	3.6
San Luis Obispo-Paso Robles-Arroyo Grande, CA	1 339	-2.2	502	81.6	255.4	2 115 410	4 212	92 222	665.0	249 431	92.9	7.1	52.2	19.1	3 488	9.0
Santa Cruz-Watsonville, CA	100	110.5	150	28.9	41.1	1 857 240	12 390	113 943	565.8	848 328	96.9	3.1	59.2	28.0	D	0.1
Santa Fe, NM	718	26.0	1 004	8.9	13.1	848 969	846	39 010	12.8	17 869	75.1	24.9	15.0	2.7	394	5.7
Santa Maria-Santa Barbara, CA	701	-3.6	439	96.7	132.3	3 233 061	7 365	125 663	1 177.9	737 581	95.8	4.2	58.8	29.4	554	1.5
Santa Rosa, CA	590	11.1	165	75.0	130.6	2 409 158	14 620	78 965	974.4	272 253	62.2	37.8	60.3	24.3	2 615	4.1
Savannah, GA	59	-8.5	212	D	23.3	629 249	2 972	99 313	D	D	105.4	D	32.0	9.6	D	25.6
Scranton—Wilkes-Barre—Hazleton, PA	162	-11.9	119	0.5	82.9	519 072	4 369	72 280	48.8	35 732	71.8	28.2	32.1	8.2	1 730	32.5
Seattle-Tacoma-Bellevue, WA	167	-3.9	35	12.3	60.3	598 066	17 015	38 276	351.2	73 883	37.3	62.7	20.9	4.7	1 507	3.5
Seattle-Bellevue-Everett, WA Div 42644	118	-6.8	36	9.5	48.7	653 085	18 191	39 507	260.2	79 461	41.2	58.8	22.3	5.4	1 411	4.4
Tacoma-Lakewood, WA Div 45104	49	3.8	33	2.8	11.5	476 152	14 222	35 548	90.9	61 524	26.3	73.7	17.9	3.0	96	1.3
Sebastian-Vero Beach, FL	162	3.3	352	57.6	54.8	1 359 020	3 856	54 672	144.9	314 419	92.2	7.8	49.7	18.4	809	4.1
Sebring, FL	490	2.9	506	61.8	84.0	1 484 852	2 937	82 911	273.4	282 121	72.6	27.4	41.4	21.4	609	2.2
Sheboygan, WI	190	-0.8	193	0.2	155.9	1 011 178	5 243	162 747	242.1	245 507	27.1	72.9	59.2	29.8	3 790	51.4
Sherman-Denison, TX	431	7.7	168	3.5	176.4	632 363	2 927	58 110	91.9	35 889	72.7	27.3	24.6	4.3	1 948	14.2
Shreveport-Bossier City, LA	438	-7.2	199	D	127.3	581 894	2 927	75 391	96.1	43 622	61.7	38.3	27.8	5.2	4 003	11.5
Sierra Vista-Douglas, AZ	917	11.2	839	65.5	123.3	1 175 308	1 401	81 234	150.0	137 235	D	D	37.6	13.3	2 594	16.9
Sioux City, IA-NE-SD	1 733	4.6	476	102.0	1 485.9	2 768 921	5 823	252 868	1 460.1	400 692	50.7	49.3	70.1	45.3	32 806	77.9
Sioux Falls, SD	1 521	2.1	445	D	1 281.2	2 132 173	4 792	221 113	781.7	228 689	59.5	40.5	61.6	35.5	22 368	70.5
South Bend-Mishawaka, IN-MI	341	-7.7	229	85.2	284.3	1 128 461	4 932	144 874	310.7	208 639	74.9	25.1	45.5	22.1	5 134	51.0
Spartanburg, SC	149	-4.0	93	2.0	46.7	380 610	4 088	39 334	49.9	31 150	43.0	57.0	20.0	2.2	1 136	9.2
Spokane-Spokane Valley, WA	1 108	-8.6	281	17.9	473.7	632 566	2 247	63 943	190.1	48 275	80.3	19.7	26.8	8.2	8 308	19.6
Springfield, IL	672	-2.2	460	5.3	615.7	3 274 998	7 122	262 928	442.9	303 152	94.0	6.0	51.0	34.3	12 337	73.8
Springfield, MA	93	3.4	67	1.7	32.6	521 085	7 767	50 067	72.8	52 742	74.9	25.1	28.8	8.6	1 162	10.7
Springfield, MO	1 216	-3.9	163	2.2	367.2	435 524	2 671	46 051	274.8	36 841	11.5	88.5	41.9	6.8	3 665	10.0
Springfield, OH	174	-1.7	222	1.6	149.8	1 141 031	5 138	147 288	145.1	184 896	80.4	19.6	45.1	23.8	2 754	47.6
State College, PA	162	9.1	136	1.1	84.9	736 207	5 416	86 739	91.6	76 830	34.3	65.7	47.2	20.0	1 985	30.3
Staunton-Waynesboro, VA	260	-9.1	152	3.3	89.6	953 997	6 256	79 364	232.1	136 059	11.9	88.1	49.1	15.1	1 677	18.2
Stockton-Lodi, CA	787	6.7	220	485.4	517.9	2 218 140	10 090	145 302	2 250.2	628 536	73.7	26.3	73.5	39.3	5 508	9.4
Sumter, SC	176	14.7	342	8.9	69.5	792 967	2 320	105 033	130.5	253 379	36.9	63.1	27.2	10.9	1 870	57.3
Syracuse, NY	432	-1.6	199	2.7	258.2	481 316	2 425	122 464	317.4	145 856	32.1	67.9	47.7	19.0	4 474	26.8
Tallahassee, FL	293	-6.7	198	7.2	46.2	899 716	4 533	43 945	108.8	73 841	D	D	25.0	4.1	761	14.9
Tampa-St. Petersburg-Clearwater, FL	449	5.2	101	35.5	116.5	824 501	8 159	47 987	482.9	108 574	75.8	24.2	31.0	8.7	1 670	2.4
Terre Haute, IN	569	-3.3	329	D	489.0	1 408 309	4 286	168 128	261.3	150 886	84.3	15.7	46.0	24.4	9 160	68.2

Table C. Metropolitan Areas — Water Use, Wholesale Trade, Retail Trade, and Real Estate

Area name	Water use, 2010		Wholesale trade,[1] 2012				Retail trade, 2012				Real estate and rental and leasing, 2012			
	Total water withdrawn (mil gal/day)	Gallons withdrawn per person per day	Number of establishments	Number of employees	Sales (mil dol)	Annual payroll (mil dol)	Number of establishments	Number of employees	Sales (mil dol)	Annual payroll (mil dol)	Number of establishments	Number of employees	Receipts (mil dol)	Annual payroll (mil dol)
	133	134	135	136	137	138	139	140	141	142	143	144	145	146
Reading, PA	57.1	139	354	6 912	4 277.4	362.2	1 256	20 219	5 719.4	494.3	246	1 249	213.0	41.4
Redding, CA	239.0	1 349	158	1 437	1 023.9	59.8	647	8 980	2 507.1	241.4	207	765	121.4	22.1
Reno, NV	134.9	317	584	8 064	6 401.9	414.6	1 411	21 644	6 173.0	580.9	672	3 245	1 049.1	124.3
Richmond, VA	1 231.6	1 019	1 349	21 390	20 135.9	1 158.4	4 251	64 627	16 923.0	1 530.7	1 288	8 019	1 667.1	345.4
Riverside-San Bernardino-Ontario, CA	1 758.7	416	4 061	55 568	49 713.0	2 646.5	9 744	160 809	49 439.3	4 142.4	3 608	16 254	3 307.2	620.1
Roanoke, VA	44.4	144	434	6 455	3 944.5	340.1	1 226	18 356	4 658.8	424.8	361	1 693	283.0	57.0
Rochester, MN	48.4	234	171	2 237	1 675.9	108.3	823	12 429	2 948.5	271.3	194	803	149.2	24.0
Rochester, NY	714.6	662	1 041	13 319	7 667.8	692.4	3 549	57 373	13 433.0	1 266.8	1 069	7 229	1 212.2	257.3
Rockford, IL	41.5	119	364	4 362	2 903.0	219.4	1 094	15 667	4 147.5	358.1	236	1 573	178.9	45.3
Rocky Mount, NC	35.9	235	128	2 404	2 899.8	109.2	551	6 475	1 606.6	140.2	126	464	73.5	14.7
Rome, GA	474.7	4 928	74	812	691.5	33.8	386	3 986	1 022.4	89.3	76	252	41.7	8.2
Sacramento—Roseville—Arden-Arcade, CA	1 708.2	795	1 768	24 256	30 299.6	1 354.9	5 715	89 921	25 231.7	2 423.6	2 832	14 883	2 682.4	598.9
Saginaw, MI	22.3	111	181	1 975	1 264.9	96.7	870	12 210	2 913.3	262.8	132	602	101.1	16.3
St. Cloud, MN	58.0	307	225	4 802	2 975.1	220.1	790	12 674	3 428.2	287.7	196	900	146.3	25.1
St. George, UT	122.2	885	149	1 284	1 514.7	47.4	574	7 375	1 900.8	168.4	306	702	95.2	18.7
St. Joseph, MO-KS	99.5	781	133	2 102	1 983.2	91.9	440	6 469	1 627.6	140.6	124	D	D	D
St. Louis, MO-IL	3 444.4	1 236	3 234	52 073	56 278.9	2 936.0	9 170	140 597	44 947.4	3 614.6	2 904	17 590	3 989.1	764.2
Salem, OR	324.1	829	293	3 958	3 290.9	187.9	1 228	17 043	4 222.9	413.9	476	2 158	289.1	61.7
Salinas, CA	545.5	1 314	346	4 574	5 775.2	278.9	1 316	16 335	4 457.4	437.2	444	1 873	436.3	69.6
Salisbury, MD-DE	311.4	833	321	3 198	3 074.0	154.2	1 959	22 278	5 698.2	523.9	562	2 528	400.9	85.4
Salt Lake City, UT	596.8	549	1 666	27 811	19 766.8	1 643.3	3 499	57 496	17 675.2	1 573.1	1 961	9 056	1 937.9	379.9
San Angelo, TX	59.6	533	115	D	D	D	422	5 980	1 823.1	150.0	134	595	92.7	16.5
San Antonio-New Braunfels, TX	1 571.4	733	1 816	D	D	D	5 984	96 472	32 018.0	2 399.0	2 102	15 075	3 359.6	662.5
San Diego-Carlsbad, CA	2 818.2	910	3 883	59 227	35 937.4	4 055.0	9 219	138 929	39 786.1	3 787.5	5 401	28 321	7 895.7	1 308.8
San Francisco-Oakland-Hayward, CA	787.0	182	5 594	81 370	73 423.7	5 831.6	13 370	195 011	63 799.7	6 071.0	6 785	40 566	14 041.3	2 383.1
Oakland-Hayward-Berkeley, CA Div 36084	557.6	218	3 119	51 504	44 467.8	3 551.0	6 703	102 866	32 748.9	3 008.4	3 226	16 093	4 354.7	794.9
San Francisco-Redwood City-South San Francisco, CA Div 41884	186.6	122	2 116	27 086	27 091.4	2 099.8	5 614	77 447	25 963.3	2 517.8	2 970	22 018	8 228.1	1 419.5
San Rafael, CA Div 42034	42.9	170	359	2 780	1 864.6	180.8	1 053	14 698	5 087.5	544.8	589	2 455	1 458.6	168.7
San Jose-Sunnyvale-Santa Clara, CA	383.7	209	2 349	84 942	92 134.3	10 863.8	5 032	85 434	40 681.9	3 247.2	2 479	12 943	4 484.6	767.8
San Luis Obispo-Paso Robles-Arroyo Grande, CA	2 579.1	9 565	289	D	D	D	1 177	13 992	3 624.0	361.5	430	1 552	278.4	52.2
Santa Cruz-Watsonville, CA	66.4	253	266	5 614	5 898.2	297.2	887	11 120	4 368.0	294.7	363	1 271	264.1	41.8
Santa Fe, NM	49.8	345	111	867	773.2	37.4	813	8 981	2 324.5	250.1	280	933	181.8	36.9
Santa Maria-Santa Barbara, CA	264.3	623	406	5 325	3 475.6	397.1	1 509	18 781	4 853.8	501.5	691	3 047	570.7	113.7
Santa Rosa, CA	259.5	536	593	8 047	4 443.2	557.8	1 768	23 032	6 016.3	655.8	679	2 824	631.1	103.4
Savannah, GA	404.3	1 163	348	4 265	6 501.3	216.0	1 407	18 108	4 967.3	427.7	445	1 954	404.7	63.4
Scranton—Wilkes-Barre—Hazleton, PA	150.5	267	569	9 845	7 916.9	425.6	2 277	32 708	11 676.8	720.0	357	1 640	353.7	57.2
Seattle-Tacoma-Bellevue, WA	658.8	192	4 652	65 726	55 450.8	4 041.0	10 862	163 846	80 843.3	5 007.9	5 996	31 037	7 372.8	1 461.3
Seattle-Bellevue-Everett, WA Div 42644	461.6	175	3 966	56 555	47 745.2	3 591.1	8 708	130 735	70 728.9	4 063.0	5 049	26 364	6 535.2	1 302.6
Tacoma-Lakewood, WA Div 45104	197.2	248	686	9 171	7 705.6	449.9	2 154	33 111	10 114.4	944.9	947	4 673	837.6	158.6
Sebastian-Vero Beach, FL	154.5	1 119	125	D	D	D	659	7 958	1 881.3	189.1	231	1 213	162.3	36.9
Sebring, FL	107.8	1 091	57	D	D	D	316	4 292	1 112.5	100.2	87	264	51.2	7.5
Sheboygan, WI	328.5	2 844	86	1 002	593.9	47.9	395	6 124	1 400.0	133.5	73	298	58.2	10.4
Sherman-Denison, TX	22.3	185	100	905	906.6	36.6	417	5 685	1 620.2	137.9	109	327	48.9	8.6
Shreveport-Bossier City, LA	206.3	469	487	7 141	6 959.9	343.2	1 641	22 553	6 759.2	557.8	462	3 206	620.0	123.9
Sierra Vista-Douglas, AZ	238.4	1 815	47	269	133.9	10.1	408	5 266	1 267.3	115.2	113	424	57.1	11.4
Sioux City, IA-NE-SD	1 055.6	6 263	242	3 529	4 024.5	168.6	652	9 729	2 409.8	203.7	143	679	87.2	18.3
Sioux Falls, SD	45.5	200	440	6 274	4 859.6	319.5	981	16 468	4 854.0	385.7	293	1 511	299.3	56.7
South Bend-Mishawaka, IN-MI	68.2	214	352	4 687	3 447.2	229.0	1 027	15 578	4 032.2	362.8	246	1 281	213.2	42.5
Spartanburg, SC	46.7	149	428	5 915	5 383.9	301.5	1 168	14 364	4 162.4	333.6	241	1 133	188.7	40.3
Spokane-Spokane Valley, WA	219.0	415	586	D	D	D	1 777	26 212	6 902.3	700.5	644	3 143	531.3	104.3
Springfield, IL	325.6	1 549	206	3 433	3 525.5	155.9	785	12 269	3 205.4	283.0	215	849	154.4	25.7
Springfield, MA	176.6	284	470	8 257	7 835.9	436.2	2 119	30 551	7 502.9	727.9	478	2 274	569.0	81.5
Springfield, MO	249.7	572	527	8 382	5 528.0	354.2	1 646	24 111	6 492.0	552.8	520	2 647	375.5	75.4
Springfield, OH	25.8	187	88	2 274	2 697.8	111.4	403	5 708	1 541.5	128.0	95	468	56.8	12.5
State College, PA	45.4	295	90	873	538.9	42.5	481	7 570	1 748.7	155.7	133	1 036	255.5	34.7
Staunton-Waynesboro, VA	46.4	391	90	1 190	438.9	52.9	465	5 926	1 528.2	134.3	134	424	45.0	11.2
Stockton-Lodi, CA	1 753.4	2 559	515	9 279	11 713.5	495.7	1 602	24 097	7 059.5	616.4	572	2 655	464.7	97.2
Sumter, SC	23.5	219	69	635	342.0	28.8	398	4 416	1 096.8	85.4	78	258	28.9	6.4
Syracuse, NY	1 098.7	1 658	685	11 688	17 632.5	597.7	2 257	36 012	8 919.9	802.6	700	4 109	704.0	159.0
Tallahassee, FL	68.0	185	285	D	D	D	1 227	17 445	4 073.0	382.0	438	2 112	295.1	62.2
Tampa-St. Petersburg-Clearwater, FL	4 151.3	1 492	3 244	40 574	34 352.8	2 027.1	9 767	136 584	39 880.0	3 530.2	3 941	17 281	3 803.9	672.2
Terre Haute, IN	1 382.6	8 019	135	D	D	D	635	8 698	2 233.2	180.8	116	570	93.5	18.9

1. Merchant wholesalers, except manufacturers' sales branches and offices.

Table C. Metropolitan Areas — Professional Services, Manufacturing, and Accommodation and Food Services

Area name	Professional, scientific, and technical services, 2012				Manufacturing, 2012				Accommodation and food services, 2012			
	Number of establishments	Number of employees	Sales (mil dol)	Annual payroll (mil dol)	Number of establishments	Number of employees	Sales (mil dol)	Annual payroll (mil dol)	Number of establishments	Number of employees	Sales (mil dol)	Annual payroll (mil dol)
	147	148	149	150	151	152	153	154	155	156	157	158
Reading, PA	703	D	D	D	498	29 439	10 905.1	1 547.9	754	12 294	548.8	155.6
Redding, CA	358	D	D	D	147	1 990	511.9	93.7	376	5 421	285.5	76.7
Reno, NV	1 625	9 036	1 435.9	540.1	448	14 065	6 444.7	843.5	987	28 209	1 870.1	583.2
Richmond, VA	3 513	32 374	5 370.9	2 052.1	889	29 624	27 862.1	1 722.4	2 516	48 940	2 419.9	696.4
Riverside-San Bernardino-Ontario, CA	5 671	33 151	4 350.9	1 587.8	3 261	88 341	32 728.6	4 043.2	6 476	128 108	8 088.9	2 150.4
Roanoke, VA	773	5 088	632.5	261.7	309	15 342	5 067.6	743.0	665	12 830	592.8	172.4
Rochester, MN	368	11 211	1 098.1	677.9	194	12 474	4 784.7	741.7	493	8 963	441.5	124.4
Rochester, NY	2 481	24 105	3 556.2	1 390.8	1 326	56 345	20 527.1	3 110.6	2 383	36 363	1 740.8	499.6
Rockford, IL	667	4 418	717.0	220.8	678	32 643	14 051.7	1 895.8	635	10 964	531.9	147.7
Rocky Mount, NC	201	1 066	109.1	42.5	119	9 582	4 213.2	455.8	244	4 714	204.8	56.0
Rome, GA	186	809	104.1	35.0	100	5 567	3 615.6	265.3	183	3 593	163.4	46.9
Sacramento—Roseville—Arden-Arcade, CA	5 860	50 049	10 506.0	3 539.0	1 348	32 798	10 949.4	1 820.9	4 221	76 566	4 851.1	1 263.4
Saginaw, MI	318	2 226	299.2	109.3	206	11 249	4 523.3	653.2	368	7 829	373.8	97.6
St. Cloud, MN	359	D	D	D	318	14 205	4 221.1	604.2	419	7 450	311.7	84.8
St. George, UT	433	D	D	D	133	1 838	415.3	76.1	307	5 140	282.3	74.4
St. Joseph, MO-KS	184	1 131	128.8	54.6	110	12 749	7 338.7	492.7	223	D	D	D
St. Louis, MO-IL	7 187	83 135	14 035.8	5 306.9	2 641	99 727	61 153.6	6 113.4	6 026	120 774	6 396.3	1 759.0
Salem, OR	781	4 222	484.6	183.1	412	10 956	2 965.0	415.7	809	12 587	746.7	203.9
Salinas, CA	806	7 448	847.3	338.0	263	6 078	2 258.9	252.3	979	17 786	1 328.8	378.0
Salisbury, MD-DE	742	D	D	D	263	12 888	5 301.6	483.0	1 263	18 991	1 296.5	358.3
Salt Lake City, UT	4 213	40 353	6 437.6	2 413.6	1 394	48 107	22 944.7	2 761.9	2 149	42 602	2 217.2	646.5
San Angelo, TX	213	1 362	159.7	58.6	102	D	1 276.3	D	231	4 761	237.4	64.7
San Antonio-New Braunfels, TX	4 713	44 402	7 158.5	2 719.4	1 207	40 835	18 863.7	1 918.7	4 448	101 868	5 687.6	1 548.8
San Diego-Carlsbad, CA	12 528	134 334	24 111.3	9 099.2	2 891	97 346	33 320.5	6 196.1	6 880	147 457	10 403.8	2 857.4
San Francisco-Oakland-Hayward, CA	19 772	214 269	59 734.6	20 918.1	3 931	110 944	80 170.9	8 312.6	12 156	197 200	14 277.7	4 118.8
Oakland-Hayward-Berkeley, CA Div 36084	8 734	87 351	19 476.4	7 526.8	2 386	78 796	D	5 592.8	5 436	79 002	4 852.4	1 340.7
San Francisco-Redwood City-South San Francisco, CA Div 41884	9 294	117 823	38 220.9	12 693.3	1 326	30 213	D	2 627.2	5 969	106 620	8 695.6	2 552.5
San Rafael, CA Div 42034	1 744	9 095	2 037.3	698.0	219	1 935	D	92.7	751	11 578	729.7	225.6
San Jose-Sunnyvale-Santa Clara, CA	8 465	125 608	30 165.3	13 558.7	2 447	103 203	42 041.7	9 264.8	4 487	73 416	4 859.1	1 349.7
San Luis Obispo-Paso Robles-Arroyo Grande, CA	868	4 914	673.1	269.5	382	6 107	2 854.0	285.7	865	14 254	824.8	229.5
Santa Cruz-Watsonville, CA	880	4 268	603.0	249.2	293	4 479	1 213.4	219.2	678	10 032	586.0	168.6
Santa Fe, NM	625	2 604	356.9	151.5	138	719	131.0	27.5	421	9 049	592.4	179.9
Santa Maria-Santa Barbara, CA	1 347	9 785	1 751.7	654.0	458	13 896	4 157.6	851.5	1 087	20 623	1 428.9	400.1
Santa Rosa, CA	1 514	9 140	1 244.4	524.0	821	19 324	6 131.7	1 085.2	1 192	17 606	1 058.7	301.8
Savannah, GA	833	6 360	692.4	274.9	208	15 862	10 027.5	1 138.9	1 033	19 741	1 097.8	296.2
Scranton—Wilkes-Barre—Hazleton, PA	1 111	8 480	925.1	352.4	581	27 852	12 229.0	1 255.8	1 390	20 178	960.9	249.9
Seattle-Tacoma-Bellevue, WA	12 651	117 190	21 306.5	9 251.6	3 584	155 814	77 904.1	9 877.4	8 964	135 680	8 755.3	2 557.9
Seattle-Bellevue-Everett, WA Div 42644	11 224	107 726	20 263.1	8 705.3	3 018	139 787	73 443.1	9 080.9	7 411	113 145	7 392.3	2 189.1
Tacoma-Lakewood, WA Div 45104	1 427	9 464	1 043.4	546.3	566	16 027	4 461.0	796.5	1 553	22 535	1 363.0	368.8
Sebastian-Vero Beach, FL	454	1 601	229.1	84.3	84	1 487	D	68.7	250	4 351	225.1	66.2
Sebring, FL	132	602	57.5	18.4	44	570	214.0	22.7	147	2 331	110.6	30.7
Sheboygan, WI	179	1 240	207.9	65.8	230	16 716	7 346.2	825.1	269	4 151	188.8	53.4
Sherman-Denison, TX	227	844	99.0	32.7	112	6 886	2 574.9	288.3	224	4 305	200.2	57.1
Shreveport-Bossier City, LA	894	5 650	756.8	265.3	294	9 906	7 610.9	533.8	821	21 991	1 491.1	349.4
Sierra Vista-Douglas, AZ	217	4 592	586.7	254.7	43	279	141.0	14.2	277	3 875	173.4	48.4
Sioux City, IA-NE-SD	306	1 520	178.5	67.1	183	15 637	10 083.3	584.0	411	6 796	312.3	86.0
Sioux Falls, SD	587	D	D	D	260	13 256	4 720.2	584.5	535	11 487	535.9	159.1
South Bend-Mishawaka, IN-MI	563	5 073	1 374.8	279.6	435	16 080	7 230.4	829.5	624	11 677	516.5	147.6
Spartanburg, SC	474	4 904	698.1	265.2	425	25 455	15 562.6	1 351.9	586	10 544	498.9	134.0
Spokane-Spokane Valley, WA	1 337	D	D	D	566	15 225	D	723.6	1 171	18 692	1 099.7	310.1
Springfield, IL	542	4 460	556.4	227.4	114	2 858	688.9	140.1	544	9 678	444.7	130.5
Springfield, MA	1 214	8 727	1 111.4	446.2	717	23 526	7 355.7	1 240.8	1 312	20 253	978.6	276.9
Springfield, MO	1 042	7 464	1 131.2	410.6	477	14 338	5 202.5	607.4	938	17 836	761.9	224.2
Springfield, OH	166	1 172	141.2	58.3	158	6 116	2 832.4	275.0	235	4 288	197.0	53.2
State College, PA	365	3 204	432.1	191.2	145	3 960	1 053.5	181.9	311	6 352	289.0	79.7
Staunton-Waynesboro, VA	187	1 469	92.3	70.3	124	6 667	2 437.0	320.0	227	3 992	183.9	52.3
Stockton-Lodi, CA	780	4 463	491.1	190.0	517	18 703	9 212.4	879.0	997	15 422	808.6	211.0
Sumter, SC	126	714	75.8	23.2	71	5 524	1 817.5	214.6	158	2 951	127.0	34.9
Syracuse, NY	1 435	14 683	2 187.0	815.3	579	23 640	10 592.6	1 283.4	1 600	24 414	1 158.4	330.5
Tallahassee, FL	1 454	D	D	D	141	2 861	D	138.7	755	D	D	D
Tampa-St. Petersburg-Clearwater, FL	10 447	85 745	12 902.8	5 325.3	2 121	51 778	18 823.8	2 583.0	5 275	100 640	6 300.5	1 646.5
Terre Haute, IN	257	1 453	145.3	54.2	174	12 457	5 125.1	604.5	385	6 822	291.4	82.5

Area name	Health care and social assistance, 2012				Other services, 2012				Nonemployer business, 2015		Value of residential construction authorized by building permits, 2016	
	Number of establishments	Number of employees	Receipts (mil dol)	Annual payroll (mil dol)	Number of establishments	Number of employees	Receipts (mil dol)	Annual payroll (mil dol)	Number	Receipts (mil dol)	New construction ($1,000)	Number of housing units
	159	160	161	162	163	164	165	166	167	168	169	170
Reading, PA	827	25 605	2 588.9	1 067.0	767	4 046	363.5	101.5	24 122	1 151.4	84 612	436
Redding, CA	634	10 525	1 324.6	469.3	296	1 658	162.7	48.2	11 869	557.8	74 158	400
Reno, NV	1 191	23 356	3 028.7	1 167.9	731	4 788	675.8	142.5	30 677	1 792.1	670 529	3 600
Richmond, VA	3 086	77 601	9 636.5	3 570.9	2 343	16 581	1 941.2	497.6	84 106	3 661.7	847 323	4 919
Riverside-San Bernardino-Ontario, CA	7 983	147 321	19 611.4	7 140.3	4 688	30 021	2 676.3	788.6	302 786	13 266.7	2 447 666	10 921
Roanoke, VA	784	24 402	2 855.7	1 119.8	644	3 814	287.1	88.7	19 065	779.6	112 405	542
Rochester, MN	549	22 061	2 524.6	908.0	368	2 406	208.4	59.1	14 392	656.6	316 223	1 737
Rochester, NY	2 645	78 759	7 020.1	3 004.4	1 691	9 959	979.4	264.8	63 347	2 864.7	370 848	2 067
Rockford, IL	738	20 948	2 479.1	953.1	601	3 558	336.6	91.8	21 220	766.5	28 021	213
Rocky Mount, NC	348	6 552	552.6	216.7	184	D	D	D	8 084	296.6	45 328	316
Rome, GA	281	8 058	1 049.2	412.6	104	831	64.9	19.5	6 891	252.9	30 055	226
Sacramento—Roseville—Arden-Arcade, CA	5 224	109 282	17 012.0	6 397.8	3 327	24 372	2 889.2	797.2	161 569	7 992.1	2 026 916	7 204
Saginaw, MI	582	17 262	1 766.5	712.8	328	1 943	161.3	45.2	10 737	406.8	40 089	281
St. Cloud, MN	497	18 050	1 736.2	799.1	438	2 932	286.2	73.2	12 910	627.8	189 045	1 107
St. George, UT	500	7 443	830.8	271.4	188	1 043	87.9	24.3	13 038	612.0	405 470	2 196
St. Joseph, MO-KS	380	8 613	902.6	367.8	208	1 294	140.0	39.2	6 445	254.7	18 308	101
St. Louis, MO-IL	8 729	185 365	18 992.4	7 415.9	4 924	33 886	3 497.5	1 037.4	183 648	8 125.4	1 643 546	7 711
Salem, OR	1 162	19 987	1 955.5	833.3	571	2 726	241.4	74.3	20 537	958.3	296 944	1 478
Salinas, CA	994	14 898	2 151.0	838.2	560	3 765	457.6	111.7	24 701	1 366.2	148 744	627
Salisbury, MD-DE	1 062	22 506	2 375.2	963.4	711	4 120	359.8	107.3	28 300	1 404.1	464 118	3 227
Salt Lake City, UT	3 025	61 712	7 734.6	2 715.1	1 930	12 970	1 348.9	402.0	84 930	4 225.8	1 616 249	8 731
San Angelo, TX	270	6 877	701.7	303.3	213	1 158	130.1	31.8	8 766	361.2	38 989	172
San Antonio-New Braunfels, TX	5 165	124 245	13 302.5	4 824.4	3 055	21 342	1 912.9	575.5	172 579	8 148.8	1 927 467	12 241
San Diego-Carlsbad, CA	8 522	151 783	21 337.8	7 872.6	5 193	41 437	4 080.6	1 179.4	268 900	13 549.9	2 223 118	10 791
San Francisco-Oakland-Hayward, CA	13 665	244 910	38 656.8	14 517.2	8 720	66 357	12 726.2	2 535.8	437 632	25 446.0	4 057 153	14 787
Oakland-Hayward-Berkeley, CA Div 36084	7 150	133 199	21 211.7	7 813.2	4 276	30 323	3 881.3	1 077.8	NA	NA	2 209 630	8 613
San Francisco-Redwood City-South San Francisco, CA Div 41884	5 398	95 851	15 342.8	5 855.6	3 801	31 495	8 261.0	1 298.0	NA	NA	1 771 560	6 062
San Rafael, CA Div 42034	1 117	15 860	2 102.3	848.3	643	4 539	583.8	160.1	NA	NA	75 963	112
San Jose-Sunnyvale-Santa Clara, CA	5 506	100 436	17 164.2	6 157.0	3 076	21 108	3 516.2	733.7	142 700	8 493.3	1 295 220	6 167
San Luis Obispo-Paso Robles-Arroyo Grande, CA	1 010	14 086	1 580.5	650.0	430	2 668	216.9	60.5	24 586	1 308.5	228 688	853
Santa Cruz-Watsonville, CA	893	12 989	1 689.9	622.3	451	2 973	328.1	98.5	25 004	1 275.9	83 703	489
Santa Fe, NM	513	8 697	961.0	384.4	335	1 892	268.6	66.4	16 363	752.4	29 198	117
Santa Maria-Santa Barbara, CA	1 360	20 279	2 637.3	949.2	725	4 544	933.5	142.1	33 871	1 940.5	199 502	842
Santa Rosa, CA	1 462	23 222	3 156.2	1 198.4	853	4 845	494.1	146.9	46 138	2 542.0	188 186	919
Savannah, GA	830	20 161	2 442.9	911.6	498	3 921	368.3	118.2	26 632	1 169.5	448 214	1 971
Scranton—Wilkes-Barre—Hazleton, PA	1 764	43 487	4 120.7	1 722.2	1 012	5 221	498.0	131.3	30 418	1 474.9	214 992	1 018
Seattle-Tacoma-Bellevue, WA	10 994	207 089	26 020.0	10 446.3	7 088	43 847	10 657.9	1 493.5	253 114	13 357.2	5 274 516	25 489
Seattle-Bellevue-Everett, WA Div 42644	9 079	163 844	20 650.8	8 327.4	5 760	35 714	9 897.2	1 252.5	NA	NA	4 366 881	21 624
Tacoma-Lakewood, WA Div 45104	1 915	43 245	5 369.3	2 118.8	1 328	8 133	760.7	241.0	NA	NA	907 635	3 865
Sebastian-Vero Beach, FL	466	7 828	886.2	333.8	280	1 395	124.5	34.6	13 700	760.1	381 844	1 018
Sebring, FL	325	5 021	576.5	194.8	134	504	37.4	9.1	5 802	238.2	32 541	128
Sheboygan, WI	299	6 483	597.2	247.8	202	992	67.4	19.5	5 705	239.4	54 961	307
Sherman-Denison, TX	381	9 105	809.1	337.4	139	834	81.0	27.5	9 582	456.3	88 659	730
Shreveport-Bossier City, LA	1 150	35 588	3 413.9	1 334.0	581	3 848	379.2	103.9	33 122	1 415.0	219 829	1 186
Sierra Vista-Douglas, AZ	273	4 896	408.9	167.4	150	684	53.1	16.1	6 628	206.3	21 936	149
Sioux City, IA-NE-SD	487	11 259	1 083.6	409.5	317	2 057	192.8	55.5	10 348	499.0	107 384	534
Sioux Falls, SD	636	24 272	2 615.5	1 082.9	478	2 699	293.8	76.5	18 977	1 032.3	458 595	3 084
South Bend-Mishawaka, IN-MI	704	18 666	2 226.8	752.1	517	3 460	318.4	91.6	18 826	756.9	97 319	405
Spartanburg, SC	613	11 037	1 165.9	495.2	443	3 072	334.2	82.5	20 142	879.1	328 611	1 921
Spokane-Spokane Valley, WA	1 598	D	D	D	888	D	D	D	32 266	1 453.5	653 545	3 764
Springfield, IL	457	20 585	2 565.9	894.3	490	3 383	422.4	126.1	12 990	495.6	87 809	426
Springfield, MA	1 596	55 768	4 697.9	2 118.5	1 110	7 289	661.2	187.6	37 081	1 759.0	130 129	585
Springfield, MO	1 095	33 457	3 330.3	1 366.5	815	5 245	457.3	131.9	33 612	1 526.5	281 811	1 977
Springfield, OH	313	10 029	912.0	334.8	212	1 363	134.3	40.5	6 681	244.8	13 160	55
State College, PA	363	7 882	767.4	316.6	249	1 471	131.7	37.0	9 780	464.7	90 561	393
Staunton-Waynesboro, VA	244	6 985	733.2	275.4	237	1 272	121.3	36.9	7 186	303.7	40 726	302
Stockton-Lodi, CA	1 361	27 052	3 447.7	1 264.8	841	5 038	445.0	135.0	36 951	1 944.5	548 046	1 998
Sumter, SC	188	5 504	471.1	184.1	130	996	77.4	27.8	6 120	215.8	38 734	273
Syracuse, NY	1 666	46 313	5 000.1	1 985.0	1 157	7 013	701.6	199.0	37 228	1 648.3	219 355	1 370
Tallahassee, FL	851	19 656	2 074.4	853.0	692	4 701	687.4	176.0	26 408	1 004.3	216 353	1 613
Tampa-St. Petersburg-Clearwater, FL	8 585	162 388	21 286.9	7 571.4	4 856	28 790	2 982.5	812.9	244 186	10 780.2	3 959 582	17 752
Terre Haute, IN	458	10 665	1 309.9	409.5	262	1 677	144.4	39.2	7 911	289.5	28 840	414

1. Establishments subject to federal tax.

Table C. Metropolitan Areas — Government Employment and Payroll and Local Government Finances

Area name	Full-time equivalent employees	March Payroll (dollars)	Administration, judicial, and legal	Police and corrections	Fire protection	Highways and transportation	Health and welfare	Natural resources and utilities	Education and libraries	Total (mil dol)	Inter-governmental (mil dol)	Total (mil dol)	Per capita¹ Total	Per capita¹ Property
	171	172	173	174	175	176	177	178	179	180	181	182	183	184
Reading, PA	14 566	69 528 665	6.1	16.3	5.1	2.6	4.7	5.3	58.7	2 039.3	792.5	835.6	2 021	1 642
Redding, CA	6 528	30 533 939	6.7	8.7	2.8	3.4	15.6	9.0	52.2	922.9	498.8	217.9	1 220	1 000
Reno, NV	13 611	57 292 494	10.4	14.1	5.7	4.2	4.2	8.4	50.4	1 736.5	755.1	608.1	1 402	1 025
Richmond, VA	47 868	168 064 481	7.1	13.2	5.2	1.8	6.2	5.1	57.6	4 453.2	1 860.0	1 873.9	1 521	1 127
Riverside-San Bernardino-Ontario, CA	137 986	750 815 862	7.1	10.8	3.0	2.2	12.9	6.4	55.7	22 872.7	12 544.1	5 769.7	1 326	1 022
Roanoke, VA	11 938	41 210 661	8.0	9.5	5.8	2.0	5.0	6.0	62.2	1 089.3	447.6	480.6	1 550	1 087
Rochester, MN	6 278	37 136 188	6.6	8.4	1.8	3.7	9.6	6.9	60.3	935.5	426.1	273.1	1 303	1 205
Rochester, NY	48 625	209 834 432	4.8	9.5	2.6	3.2	6.4	4.2	67.9	6 041.6	2 624.6	2 577.1	2 381	1 781
Rockford, IL	11 902	48 299 662	5.1	11.8	5.6	3.5	3.6	7.1	62.7	1 352.3	558.1	615.0	1 777	1 610
Rocky Mount, NC	8 741	30 617 673	3.2	6.0	2.3	1.7	32.7	6.1	46.8	725.6	291.0	136.9	903	699
Rome, GA	3 631	12 476 709	5.7	9.3	4.2	4.2	1.7	5.5	67.7	620.3	284.0	151.4	1 574	957
Sacramento—Roseville—Arden-Arcade, CA	74 788	405 371 174	6.2	12.5	5.4	3.7	8.2	11.7	48.6	11 604.0	5 395.4	3 303.5	1 504	1 115
Saginaw, MI	5 686	21 466 345	8.3	8.5	2.2	2.7	9.8	4.8	61.7	786.5	475.8	154.2	777	684
St. Cloud, MN	5 890	30 573 727	7.4	9.3	1.2	4.2	13.3	3.7	58.2	805.5	393.2	236.4	1 241	1 100
St. George, UT	4 130	14 492 173	7.3	10.1	1.7	2.6	6.5	13.4	56.5	453.7	154.1	197.8	1 366	972
St. Joseph, MO-KS	4 475	13 492 001	5.7	7.9	3.9	3.6	2.8	5.1	69.9	408.2	157.7	172.1	1 346	855
St. Louis, MO-IL	99 216	391 779 336	5.2	10.7	5.1	5.6	2.8	5.2	63.6	10 918.1	3 849.2	5 146.2	1 841	1 249
Salem, OR	13 276	58 238 836	5.8	9.3	3.5	3.1	4.0	3.9	68.1	1 449.9	756.3	442.2	1 116	1 009
Salinas, CA	16 674	95 953 296	5.6	9.2	2.7	3.8	28.8	5.1	41.4	3 062.0	1 376.2	682.3	1 599	1 199
Salisbury, MD-DE	12 705	51 865 541	5.6	9.0	1.0	1.9	3.6	5.9	70.9	1 432.6	624.3	557.2	1 459	1 077
Salt Lake City, UT	36 279	131 818 213	7.3	10.3	5.1	9.5	5.0	8.7	51.6	3 934.4	1 398.7	1 572.5	1 399	1 008
San Angelo, TX	4 541	12 163 357	8.9	16.3	6.6	1.5	3.5	6.2	55.4	335.7	127.3	150.0	1 306	1 006
San Antonio-New Braunfels, TX	94 742	356 044 474	4.4	8.7	3.2	3.7	9.8	10.5	58.5	8 697.5	3 005.2	3 729.5	1 669	1 358
San Diego-Carlsbad, CA	97 178	529 647 292	9.3	10.8	3.9	3.4	11.1	7.0	52.0	16 495.7	6 780.5	5 691.2	1 791	1 381
San Francisco-Oakland-Hayward, CA	155 343	998 941 828	7.6	12.2	5.4	11.0	17.4	9.2	35.0	32 009.2	10 425.4	11 842.8	2 658	1 820
Oakland-Hayward-Berkeley, CA Div 36084	87 214	540 452 372	5.4	11.4	5.0	8.5	17.1	9.7	40.0	17 465.2	6 071.1	5 674.3	2 154	1 538
San Francisco-Redwood City-South San Francisco, CA Div 41884	59 585	406 735 774	10.1	13.4	5.7	15.2	18.9	8.4	27.1	13 022.2	4 026.7	5 343.5	3 414	2 179
San Rafael, CA Div 42034	8 544	51 753 682	10.8	11.2	8.5	4.2	8.9	10.4	44.3	1 521.9	327.6	825.0	3 222	2 533
San Jose-Sunnyvale-Santa Clara, CA	61 998	413 816 866	7.6	10.1	4.9	4.9	20.6	6.4	42.8	13 018.5	4 094.2	4 897.7	2 585	1 941
San Luis Obispo-Paso Robles-Arroyo Grande, CA	8 194	48 094 004	7.2	11.4	2.8	2.5	6.9	6.4	57.6	1 189.7	435.4	547.8	1 994	1 615
Santa Cruz-Watsonville, CA	9 292	50 504 116	8.1	10.1	3.9	7.3	13.5	7.9	47.1	1 432.9	632.4	483.8	1 813	1 441
Santa Fe, NM	4 848	18 022 225	9.3	12.0	6.4	3.8	4.1	9.6	48.1	527.4	253.9	199.3	1 361	807
Santa Maria-Santa Barbara, CA	15 712	89 085 924	7.3	11.4	5.3	3.7	14.4	7.2	48.4	2 761.9	960.5	877.6	2 035	1 531
Santa Rosa, CA	16 072	90 178 192	9.5	12.6	3.9	2.6	12.9	7.2	47.9	2 545.8	918.8	972.6	1 978	1 555
Savannah, GA	13 962	46 151 027	10.0	13.9	3.6	3.3	6.0	6.9	53.1	1 947.0	409.1	744.0	2 056	1 229
Scranton—Wilkes-Barre—Hazleton, PA	16 712	64 672 766	7.6	11.9	3.2	3.8	5.2	5.6	61.4	1 935.2	804.6	806.0	1 430	1 072
Seattle-Tacoma-Bellevue, WA	109 144	628 710 550	8.0	10.0	6.7	11.2	9.8	13.4	38.7	18 576.7	5 896.1	7 417.8	2 088	1 239
Seattle-Bellevue-Everett, WA Div 42644	85 210	497 008 852	7.8	10.1	6.0	12.0	11.7	13.8	36.5	15 276.4	4 566.4	6 183.2	2 256	1 287
Tacoma-Lakewood, WA Div 45104	23 934	131 701 698	8.7	9.5	9.2	8.4	2.7	12.1	47.1	3 300.2	1 329.7	1 234.7	1 521	1 076
Sebastian-Vero Beach, FL	4 188	14 858 891	4.7	16.3	4.8	5.0	5.1	12.6	48.7	445.1	88.8	266.5	1 896	1 553
Sebring, FL	3 358	10 445 615	8.2	12.8	2.4	5.5	3.7	6.4	56.9	264.2	111.3	100.2	1 021	799
Sheboygan, WI	4 469	19 622 392	8.8	8.8	2.1	5.2	8.0	3.0	63.5	489.1	213.6	207.1	1 801	1 746
Sherman-Denison, TX	5 248	18 290 717	5.6	9.2	3.5	2.7	4.2	4.8	69.0	414.8	144.6	188.3	1 544	1 271
Shreveport-Bossier City, LA	18 558	60 559 700	6.4	15.5	6.0	2.9	2.1	5.0	60.8	1 909.4	657.9	985.4	2 204	997
Sierra Vista-Douglas, AZ	4 879	16 984 358	11.7	10.2	5.2	2.9	3.0	3.3	61.1	397.9	175.5	144.2	1 092	821
Sioux City, IA-NE-SD	7 016	27 062 681	5.1	8.4	2.6	4.9	5.3	5.2	67.0	775.3	326.0	295.7	1 751	1 347
Sioux Falls, SD	7 176	25 345 869	6.6	9.8	3.7	4.0	2.2	5.5	66.9	751.2	210.8	404.9	1 707	1 166
South Bend-Mishawaka, IN-MI	10 955	36 623 695	5.5	11.4	6.3	4.0	1.2	6.4	63.3	1 211.4	523.3	434.1	1 362	1 022
Spartanburg, SC	15 589	60 744 767	3.4	5.1	1.5	0.6	46.5	4.0	38.2	1 645.4	411.5	361.9	1 142	1 015
Spokane-Spokane Valley, WA	15 408	75 996 689	9.2	11.0	6.8	7.0	5.4	7.5	51.4	2 043.9	939.8	680.9	1 279	830
Springfield, IL	9 009	38 285 598	5.0	9.2	3.6	4.6	2.0	19.1	56.1	823.8	336.6	347.9	1 641	1 427
Springfield, MA	24 505	106 805 892	3.3	9.5	6.2	2.5	1.8	7.6	67.7	2 499.8	1 290.8	947.8	1 515	1 471
Springfield, MO	15 530	53 052 304	4.5	7.1	2.8	3.8	8.8	10.0	56.5	1 328.3	481.9	530.1	1 192	662
Springfield, OH	5 386	19 627 638	7.6	10.0	4.2	2.3	8.2	4.4	57.6	501.3	270.1	168.3	1 227	774
State College, PA	3 965	14 048 206	7.5	8.6	0.0	7.9	9.9	5.8	58.3	455.2	154.4	216.4	1 394	1 018
Staunton-Waynesboro, VA	4 314	12 615 495	6.6	13.2	3.6	1.7	3.9	3.8	64.6	321.2	157.8	126.3	1 064	712
Stockton-Lodi, CA	23 911	123 453 125	6.5	12.7	3.3	2.6	14.7	5.0	53.3	3 894.7	2 276.8	855.2	1 217	851
Sumter, SC	6 341	17 021 292	4.2	6.1	1.7	1.8	1.6	3.3	80.4	271.8	124.5	114.5	1 060	719
Syracuse, NY	30 026	133 886 154	3.8	8.2	2.5	4.2	6.3	4.1	69.2	3 812.8	1 691.2	1 541.0	2 332	1 687
Tallahassee, FL	14 377	48 690 908	8.9	11.4	3.1	5.3	3.7	13.3	50.6	1 358.3	476.8	458.3	1 221	865
Tampa-St. Petersburg-Clearwater, FL	98 152	350 589 348	7.0	15.7	5.6	4.0	2.8	8.5	53.8	9 943.4	3 586.7	3 926.4	1 381	1 060
Terre Haute, IN	5 719	18 131 023	7.8	8.7	4.1	4.4	5.0	5.4	63.3	562.1	284.5	168.7	978	782

1. Based on the resident population estimated as of July 1 of the year shown.

Table C. Metropolitan Areas — Local Government Finances, Government Employment, and Income Taxes

Area name	Local government finances, 2012 (cont.)									Government employment, 2015			Individual income tax returns, 2014		
	Direct general expenditure							Debt outstanding							
			Percent of total for:												
	Total (mil dol)	Per capita¹ (dollars)	Education	Health and hospitals	Police protection	Public welfare	Highways	Total (mil dol)	Per capita¹ (dollars)	Federal civilian	Federal military	State and local	Number of returns	Mean Adjusted Gross income	Mean income tax
	185	186	187	188	189	190	191	192	193	194	195	196	197	198	199
Reading, PA	2 024.3	4 896	54.5	3.4	4.1	7.2	2.8	3 478.7	8 413	915	1 064	21 503	201 400	56 873	6 724
Redding, CA	906.1	5 074	43.3	8.1	5.8	10.6	4.0	544.3	3 048	1 312	309	11 696	75 780	50 859	5 338
Reno, NV	1 700.3	3 919	35.7	1.0	6.7	4.2	3.4	4 528.8	10 439	3 554	1 291	24 361	214 490	69 803	10 910
Richmond, VA	4 393.3	3 566	45.4	3.2	6.9	3.5	2.9	4 997.3	4 056	16 868	13 376	94 514	605 130	65 850	8 583
Riverside-San Bernardino-Ontario, CA	23 480.7	5 398	39.0	11.9	6.3	7.3	4.9	24 738.9	5 687	20 445	21 690	223 926	1 810 170	50 161	4 923
Roanoke, VA	1 134.6	3 659	44.3	2.7	5.5	7.8	1.9	1 358.0	4 379	3 874	997	17 443	146 310	54 412	6 304
Rochester, MN	953.0	4 547	35.9	2.2	5.0	7.4	11.0	3 142.1	14 990	996	763	11 095	106 010	66 121	8 173
Rochester, NY	6 147.1	5 680	50.8	4.1	3.8	11.1	4.2	4 984.9	4 606	4 695	1 749	70 327	517 430	57 662	7 052
Rockford, IL	1 291.0	3 731	51.6	1.6	7.8	2.7	5.4	877.0	2 534	885	705	16 322	161 570	52 049	5 736
Rocky Mount, NC	764.0	5 037	34.6	34.0	5.2	5.1	1.5	144.7	954	377	349	10 062	65 850	42 918	4 121
Rome, GA	658.4	6 846	27.4	47.2	2.2	0.1	2.6	238.0	2 474	207	261	5 521	39 980	48 567	5 057
Sacramento—Roseville—Arden-Arcade, CA	11 753.9	5 351	35.4	5.1	5.1	7.8	5.9	20 700.4	9 424	13 817	4 196	235 875	999 130	63 751	7 888
Saginaw, MI	801.9	4 043	42.8	14.5	5.8	0.7	5.8	494.0	2 490	1 420	313	9 323	90 260	46 355	5 097
St. Cloud, MN	798.0	4 189	41.0	7.6	5.1	5.3	11.0	1 171.2	6 149	2 304	674	11 260	90 840	56 127	6 477
St. George, UT	401.3	2 771	50.1	0.8	7.7	0.0	6.0	585.2	4 041	558	647	7 552	60 380	52 798	5 488
St. Joseph, MO-KS	361.2	2 824	56.2	2.3	8.0	0.6	5.5	644.5	5 038	607	432	9 421	54 880	48 520	5 082
St. Louis, MO-IL	11 016.7	3 940	50.5	2.4	7.4	0.6	5.2	13 307.4	4 760	28 278	13 462	138 660	1 357 220	65 855	9 096
Salem, OR	1 466.0	3 699	55.7	4.1	5.3	0.2	4.7	2 202.9	5 558	1 352	1 036	38 245	173 890	51 673	5 165
Salinas, CA	2 904.3	6 806	36.5	22.7	4.6	5.4	2.6	1 444.4	3 385	5 186	5 622	26 560	194 370	58 507	6 994
Salisbury, MD-DE	1 397.6	3 660	55.9	1.9	6.1	1.0	2.5	1 055.9	2 765	1 073	1 863	22 447	182 840	52 600	6 008
Salt Lake City, UT	3 773.6	3 358	42.9	1.2	5.6	2.1	5.3	7 423.5	6 606	12 403	5 143	92 038	511 690	62 074	7 623
San Angelo, TX	359.0	3 125	52.5	3.3	5.7	0.2	2.7	590.0	5 137	1 176	3 103	7 743	53 760	62 849	9 388
San Antonio-New Braunfels, TX	8 877.6	3 974	45.3	13.6	5.3	1.8	3.0	21 467.3	9 609	34 887	34 285	130 702	1 057 600	59 714	8 127
San Diego-Carlsbad, CA	16 846.0	5 302	37.0	9.8	5.3	6.9	2.9	27 732.0	8 729	46 442	98 828	190 043	1 531 220	70 203	9 808
San Francisco-Oakland-Hayward, CA	31 954.0	7 172	25.5	16.6	5.8	5.5	3.3	56 702.8	12 726	32 596	9 062	279 028	2 271 070	113 041	20 363
Oakland-Hayward-Berkeley, CA Div 36084	18 716.4	7 105	26.5	15.3	5.6	5.5	3.2	31 762.2	12 057	13 979	5 650	146 730	NA	NA	NA
San Francisco-Redwood City-South San Francisco, CA Div 41884	11 668.6	7 455	22.7	19.9	6.1	5.8	3.5	22 636.4	14 463	17 865	2 864	117 609	NA	NA	NA
San Rafael, CA Div 42034	1 569.1	6 127	34.5	6.9	6.2	4.1	3.1	2 304.2	8 998	752	548	14 689	NA	NA	NA
San Jose-Sunnyvale-Santa Clara, CA	12 193.4	6 437	32.5	22.1	5.1	5.2	2.2	18 023.9	9 514	10 091	3 451	82 289	924 540	133 000	24 221
San Luis Obispo-Paso Robles-Arroyo Grande, CA	1 206.8	4 391	38.5	5.9	6.2	8.2	3.9	850.7	3 096	538	533	20 699	129 600	64 331	8 291
Santa Cruz-Watsonville, CA	1 415.2	5 305	36.6	6.6	6.3	8.5	2.3	1 074.8	4 029	531	397	18 204	129 940	73 672	10 667
Santa Fe, NM	578.2	3 950	45.8	1.3	6.0	2.2	3.5	916.2	6 259	950	388	16 027	75 260	68 337	10 314
Santa Maria-Santa Barbara, CA	2 786.6	6 462	32.4	18.7	5.7	6.7	3.0	1 346.9	3 123	3 618	3 123	31 536	200 020	70 510	10 208
Santa Rosa, CA	2 601.9	5 290	35.4	10.3	6.3	6.4	5.0	2 547.1	5 179	1 372	1 407	27 275	243 170	68 320	9 157
Savannah, GA	1 874.0	5 178	31.0	28.9	9.3	0.3	2.3	889.2	2 457	2 887	6 143	20 535	167 050	55 303	6 529
Scranton—Wilkes-Barre—Hazleton, PA	2 105.8	3 736	51.8	0.4	3.4	5.0	4.2	2 409.6	4 275	4 213	1 442	25 816	272 960	49 700	5 678
Seattle-Tacoma-Bellevue, WA	17 216.0	4 847	33.8	9.8	5.1	1.0	5.3	30 708.3	8 645	34 120	46 996	235 474	1 806 310	85 997	13 548
Seattle-Bellevue-Everett, WA Div 42644	13 942.5	5 088	31.5	11.7	5.0	1.1	5.2	26 143.1	9 540	22 243	13 836	190 254	NA	NA	NA
Tacoma-Lakewood, WA Div 45104	3 273.5	4 033	43.7	2.1	5.8	0.6	5.6	4 565.2	5 624	11 877	33 160	45 220	NA	NA	NA
Sebastian-Vero Beach, FL	470.0	3 343	38.2	4.8	9.4	0.8	8.2	436.2	3 103	330	269	4 673	70 520	94 952	17 433
Sebring, FL	276.6	2 818	46.6	3.7	7.8	0.6	6.0	143.0	1 457	262	180	3 736	40 520	39 928	3 883
Sheboygan, WI	492.9	4 286	55.2	3.6	5.7	6.1	8.2	375.9	3 269	200	320	5 513	58 030	56 722	6 405
Sherman-Denison, TX	423.3	3 471	54.8	3.3	5.1	0.0	6.0	717.6	5 885	331	252	6 240	55 050	52 057	5 938
Shreveport-Bossier City, LA	1 871.4	4 185	49.7	1.4	7.4	0.2	3.7	1 823.7	4 078	4 888	7 033	26 683	195 310	54 305	6 787
Sierra Vista-Douglas, AZ	407.1	3 082	44.0	3.5	12.3	4.9	7.3	161.6	1 223	5 101	4 254	6 385	52 000	46 526	4 433
Sioux City, IA-NE-SD	799.7	4 734	53.5	7.0	4.5	1.1	5.7	754.0	4 464	928	652	9 984	79 200	57 497	7 179
Sioux Falls, SD	772.0	3 254	47.6	1.5	5.3	0.5	10.0	951.0	4 008	2 646	1 489	10 649	127 780	68 756	9 963
South Bend-Mishawaka, IN-MI	1 028.2	3 227	51.4	1.7	4.7	1.1	3.4	1 041.8	3 270	944	1 023	14 692	148 200	52 700	6 325
Spartanburg, SC	1 655.8	5 223	33.7	46.8	3.0	0.4	1.0	1 083.5	3 418	561	1 262	21 786	138 900	50 383	5 464
Spokane-Spokane Valley, WA	2 096.5	3 939	45.9	6.2	5.2	0.2	4.3	1 764.2	3 315	5 022	4 222	34 887	243 980	55 830	6 688
Springfield, IL	869.8	4 103	52.8	1.5	7.5	0.9	4.5	2 540.3	11 983	1 790	465	19 377	106 090	63 272	8 205
Springfield, MA	2 618.5	4 185	57.6	0.6	4.8	0.6	3.1	1 821.1	2 910	5 215	1 727	47 644	288 710	56 740	6 852
Springfield, MO	1 305.4	2 936	50.3	8.6	6.8	0.8	6.6	1 931.0	4 343	2 424	1 537	25 998	198 530	51 228	5 970
Springfield, OH	474.6	3 459	49.3	5.8	5.9	6.2	3.3	206.0	1 502	563	345	6 435	63 770	45 120	4 379
State College, PA	453.5	2 923	51.0	2.2	3.5	7.9	6.1	486.7	3 136	459	450	47 937	59 660	63 804	8 068
Staunton-Waynesboro, VA	339.0	2 856	51.3	2.7	4.7	6.7	3.4	294.4	2 480	258	369	8 373	56 200	49 727	4 892
Stockton-Lodi, CA	3 717.2	5 291	40.5	9.2	5.9	8.8	3.5	3 309.2	4 710	3 066	1 146	37 456	293 270	53 299	5 823
Sumter, SC	256.2	2 371	55.2	1.2	7.1	0.3	2.5	245.3	2 270	1 218	5 566	5 493	46 770	39 689	3 318
Syracuse, NY	4 111.0	6 220	49.2	3.2	3.0	9.8	5.1	4 285.9	6 485	4 847	1 155	49 639	307 030	57 855	7 073
Tallahassee, FL	1 372.1	3 655	40.1	1.3	7.9	0.1	7.2	4 333.3	11 544	1 963	702	58 655	164 120	53 168	6 689
Tampa-St. Petersburg-Clearwater, FL	10 477.2	3 685	38.4	3.3	8.7	2.4	4.2	11 252.6	3 958	22 744	12 064	124 312	1 372 170	57 210	7 912
Terre Haute, IN	504.6	2 925	50.6	6.3	3.2	0.5	3.2	559.6	3 244	1 277	513	11 145	74 450	47 084	4 913

1. Based on the resident population estimated as of July 1 of the year shown.

Table C. Metropolitan Areas — **Land Area and Population**

CBSA/ DIV code[1]	Area name	Land area,[2] 2016 (sq mi)	Total persons	Rank	Per square mile	White	Black	American Indian, Alaska Native	Asian and Pacific Islander	Percent Hispanic or Latino[3]	Under 5 years	5 to 17 years	18 to 24 years	25 to 34 years	35 to 44 years	45 to 54 years
		1	2	3	4	5	6	7	8	9	10	11	12	13	14	15
45500	Texarkana, TX-AR	2 042.9	150 098	274	73.5	67.9	25.3	1.5	1.3	6.0	6.5	17.2	8.4	13.5	12.6	12.9
45540	The Villages, FL	547.6	123 996	316	226.4	86.0	7.5	0.7	1.2	5.5	2.0	5.1	3.1	5.8	5.9	6.9
45780	Toledo, OH	1 363.5	605 221	91	443.9	76.9	15.9	0.7	2.1	6.7	6.2	16.4	10.9	13.4	11.5	12.6
45820	Topeka, KS	3 232.6	233 068	194	72.1	81.1	7.9	2.5	1.8	10.0	6.3	17.7	8.1	12.1	11.4	12.8
45940	Trenton, NJ	224.4	371 023	143	1 653.4	51.7	20.6	0.5	12.0	17.1	5.7	15.9	11.4	12.6	12.8	14.3
46060	Tucson, AZ	9 187.2	1 016 206	53	110.6	54.2	4.1	3.1	3.9	36.8	5.8	15.6	12.0	12.3	11.2	11.4
46140	Tulsa, OK	6 269.7	987 201	55	157.5	71.2	9.7	12.9	3.1	9.5	6.9	18.1	8.7	13.8	12.5	12.6
46220	Tuscaloosa, AL	2 847.1	241 378	190	84.8	61.0	34.4	0.6	1.7	3.4	6.0	15.0	16.0	14.5	11.8	11.6
46340	Tyler, TX	921.5	225 290	199	244.5	61.4	18.1	0.8	2.0	19.2	7.0	17.8	9.9	13.7	11.6	11.9
46520	Urban Honolulu, HI	600.6	992 605	54	1 652.7	32.1	3.6	1.5	78.2	9.7	6.5	14.9	9.7	15.5	12.5	12.3
46540	Utica-Rome, NY	2 623.8	293 803	164	112.0	86.5	6.0	0.6	3.9	4.8	5.6	15.6	9.5	12.1	10.9	13.7
46660	Valdosta, GA	1 589.4	144 676	285	91.0	57.3	35.1	0.8	2.4	6.3	6.9	17.0	15.5	14.7	11.3	11.3
46700	Vallejo-Fairfield, CA	821.8	440 207	122	535.7	42.9	15.9	1.4	19.5	26.2	6.1	16.4	9.1	14.6	12.2	13.3
47020	Victoria, TX	1 734.1	99 984	354	57.7	47.1	6.2	0.6	1.5	45.5	6.9	18.5	9.3	13.8	11.7	11.6
47220	Vineland-Bridgeton, NJ	483.5	153 797	267	318.1	48.4	20.3	1.4	1.9	30.2	6.6	17.3	8.4	14.8	13.1	13.5
47260	Virginia Beach-Norfolk-Newport News, VA-NC	2 682.9	1 726 907	37	643.7	58.3	32.0	1.1	5.4	6.6	6.4	15.9	11.0	15.5	12.0	12.8
47300	Visalia-Porterville, CA	4 824.4	460 437	112	95.4	30.5	1.6	1.2	4.1	64.1	8.4	22.8	10.3	14.1	12.4	11.2
47380	Waco, TX	1 802.6	265 207	181	147.1	57.6	15.6	0.7	2.1	25.7	7.0	17.6	14.5	12.9	11.2	11.8
47460	Walla Walla, WA	2 138.6	64 278	379	30.1	75.0	2.4	1.6	2.8	20.4	5.6	15.6	12.6	12.4	11.1	11.8
47580	Warner Robins, GA	774.9	190 028	225	245.2	57.9	33.7	0.8	3.5	6.5	6.5	18.3	9.5	14.3	12.6	13.4
47900	Washington-Arlington-Alexandria, DC-VA-MD-WV	6 246.7	6 131 977	6	981.6	48.4	26.5	0.8	11.9	15.5	6.6	16.6	8.9	15.0	14.3	14.3
47900	.Silver Spring-Frederick-Rockville, MD Div 43524	1 153.5	1 291 454	X	1 119.6	52.7	17.6	0.6	14.7	17.2	6.3	17.1	8.2	12.8	13.5	14.6
47900	.Washington-Arlington-Alexandria, DC-VA-MD-WV Div 47894	5 093.2	4 840 523	X	950.4	47.3	28.8	0.8	11.1	15.0	6.6	16.5	9.2	15.6	14.5	14.3
47940	Waterloo-Cedar Falls, IA	1 503.1	170 015	244	113.1	86.8	8.4	0.5	2.6	3.7	6.3	15.5	14.3	12.5	11.1	11.2
48060	Watertown-Fort Drum, NY	1 268.7	114 006	336	89.9	84.4	7.3	1.0	2.7	7.2	7.8	16.4	12.5	16.7	11.6	11.1
48140	Wausau, WI	1 545.0	135 603	296	87.8	90.2	1.3	0.8	6.3	2.8	5.9	17.1	8.0	11.9	11.9	14.0
48260	Weirton-Steubenville, WV-OH	580.0	119 271	325	205.6	94.0	5.1	0.6	0.8	1.3	4.8	14.3	8.8	10.6	11.1	13.3
48300	Wenatchee, WA	4 740.4	117 665	327	24.8	68.4	0.9	1.7	1.8	29.0	6.6	18.1	8.4	12.2	11.4	11.9
48540	Wheeling, WV-OH	943.4	142 982	288	151.6	95.0	4.1	0.6	0.8	1.0	5.2	14.1	8.4	12.0	11.5	13.0
48620	Wichita, KS	5 012.1	644 672	87	128.6	75.2	8.8	2.0	4.5	12.8	7.0	18.9	9.2	13.8	12.0	12.1
48660	Wichita Falls, TX	2 619.6	150 734	273	57.5	70.6	10.0	1.4	2.7	17.4	6.4	15.9	12.7	14.4	11.1	11.6
48700	Williamsport, PA	1 228.6	115 248	333	93.8	92.7	5.8	0.6	1.0	1.9	5.7	14.9	9.1	13.3	10.8	13.1
48900	Wilmington, NC	1 063.2	282 573	167	265.8	78.3	15.0	1.0	2.0	5.7	5.2	14.5	11.5	12.9	12.6	13.1
49020	Winchester, VA-WV	1 063.1	135 238	297	127.2	84.5	6.1	0.6	2.1	8.6	5.8	16.6	8.3	12.1	12.1	14.5
49180	Winston-Salem, NC	2 008.6	662 079	83	329.6	70.0	18.6	0.8	2.2	10.1	5.7	17.0	8.9	11.8	12.0	14.4
49340	Worcester, MA-CT	2 023.5	935 781	58	462.5	80.0	5.0	0.6	5.1	11.1	5.4	16.0	10.0	12.6	12.1	15.0
49420	Yakima, WA	4 294.5	249 636	188	58.1	45.4	1.2	4.6	1.8	48.8	8.3	21.6	9.8	13.0	11.8	11.3
49620	York-Hanover, PA	904.2	443 744	120	490.8	85.6	6.7	0.5	1.9	7.2	5.7	16.6	8.2	12.3	12.0	14.5
49660	Youngstown-Warren-Boardman, OH-PA	1 702.4	544 746	101	320.0	85.0	11.9	0.7	1.1	3.3	5.2	15.2	8.6	11.1	11.0	13.2
49700	Yuba City, CA	1 234.5	171 926	240	139.3	54.1	3.8	2.6	14.4	29.3	7.4	19.3	9.5	14.5	12.0	11.9
49740	Yuma, AZ	5 514.0	205 631	215	37.3	32.9	2.3	1.4	1.8	62.8	7.3	18.1	11.6	13.5	10.7	10.6

1. CBSA = Core Based Statistical Area. DIV = Metropolitan Division. See Appendix A for explanation. See Appendix B for list of metropolitan areas identified by type. 2. Dry land or land partially or temporarily covered by water. 3. May be of any race.

Table C. Metropolitan Areas — **Population and Households**

Area name	55 to 64 years	65 to 74 years	75 years and over	Percent female	Total persons 2000	2010	Percent change 2000–2010	2010–2016	Births	Deaths	Net migration	Number	Persons per household	Family households	Female family householder[1]	One person
	16	17	18	19	20	21	22	23	24	25	26	27	28	29	30	31
Texarkana, TX-AR	12.6	9.5	6.8	50.2	143 377	149 195	4.1	0.6	12 271	9 925	-1 285	54 440	2.65	68.4	17.2	27.2
The Villages, FL	14.9	34.8	21.5	50.0	53 345	93 420	75.1	32.7	2 925	9 004	35 174	51 170	2.13	65.8	3.5	31.0
Toledo, OH.........................	13.5	8.9	6.5	51.2	618 203	610 001	-1.3	-0.8	47 016	36 356	-15 359	242 641	2.43	60.7	13.5	31.9
Topeka, KS.........................	14.3	9.9	7.5	51.1	224 551	233 868	4.1	-0.3	18 693	14 388	-4 945	93 078	2.45	63.9	9.9	31.3
Trenton, NJ........................	13.0	8.1	6.3	51.1	350 761	367 517	4.8	1.0	26 395	18 011	-4 487	127 965	2.77	68.9	14.1	26.2
Tucson, AZ.........................	12.6	10.9	8.2	50.8	843 746	980 263	16.2	3.7	74 431	56 200	16 140	395 992	2.48	60.9	12.9	30.9
Tulsa, OK...........................	12.6	8.7	6.1	50.9	859 532	937 531	9.1	5.3	83 292	57 220	23 139	380 841	2.54	67.0	12.8	26.8
Tuscaloosa, AL	11.9	7.9	5.3	51.7	203 009	230 163	13.4	4.9	17 976	13 176	6 321	84 889	2.70	64.7	15.5	29.5
Tyler, TX............................	12.1	9.0	7.0	51.7	174 706	209 721	20.0	7.4	19 123	12 502	8 634	78 380	2.77	67.9	12.4	26.2
Urban Honolulu, HI	11.9	9.0	7.6	49.6	876 156	953 207	8.8	4.1	84 327	47 150	3 708	307 703	3.12	69.9	11.8	22.9
Utica-Rome, NY	14.1	10.2	8.3	50.3	299 896	299 357	-0.2	-1.9	20 241	19 820	-5 518	114 580	2.46	62.8	12.4	31.8
Valdosta, GA......................	10.6	7.5	5.0	51.0	119 560	139 663	16.8	3.6	12 787	7 082	-1 023	48 600	2.83	59.4	15.3	33.2
Vallejo-Fairfield, CA	13.5	8.9	5.7	50.3	394 542	413 344	4.8	6.5	32 406	19 292	13 319	145 502	2.93	70.9	15.9	22.8
Victoria, TX	12.5	9.0	6.6	50.9	91 016	94 003	3.3	6.4	8 589	5 326	2 770	35 842	2.72	72.6	15.9	22.8
Vineland-Bridgeton, NJ	12.0	8.3	6.1	48.8	146 438	156 628	7.0	-1.8	13 133	9 063	-6 636	50 380	2.82	69.1	18.4	24.3
Virginia Beach-Norfolk-Newport News, VA-NC	12.5	8.2	5.7	50.8	1 580 057	1 676 817	6.1	3.0	141 554	83 695	-7 982	642 911	2.57	66.2	14.5	27.2
Visalia-Porterville, CA	9.8	6.5	4.5	50.0	368 021	442 182	20.2	4.1	48 587	18 088	-11 659	134 801	3.37	77.7	17.7	17.7
Waco, TX...........................	11.4	7.9	6.2	51.3	232 093	252 769	8.9	4.9	23 158	13 967	3 292	93 239	2.70	68.1	15.0	24.8
Walla Walla, WA	13.0	10.0	8.0	49.1	59 244	62 859	6.1	2.3	4 441	3 801	685	24 201	2.41	64.7	9.2	31.1
Warner Robins, GA..............	12.2	7.8	5.3	51.8	144 021	179 605	24.7	5.8	15 169	8 810	3 747	69 562	2.63	73.0	17.3	22.0
Washington-Arlington-Alexandria, DC-VA-MD-WV-Silver Spring-Frederick-Rockville, MD Div 43524	12.1	7.4	4.8	51.2	4 837 428	5 636 416	16.5	8.8	504 490	207 095	199 276	2 172 310	2.76	65.7	12.0	27.1
Washington-Arlington-Alexandria, DC-VA-MD-WV Div 47894..................	13.1	8.2	6.1	51.6	1 068 618	1 205 334	12.8	7.1	99 623	47 100	34 801	461 405	2.76	69.6	11.2	24.8
	11.8	7.2	4.4	51.1	3 768 810	4 431 082	17.6	9.2	404 867	159 995	164 475	1 710 905	2.76	64.6	12.3	27.8
Waterloo-Cedar Falls, IA	12.7	8.9	7.5	50.9	163 706	167 819	2.5	1.3	13 171	9 473	-1 230	66 986	2.45	62.5	9.2	29.0
Watertown-Fort Drum, NY	10.7	7.8	5.5	47.4	111 738	116 232	4.0	-1.9	13 291	5 616	-10 127	43 145	2.59	67.2	10.5	27.5
Wausau, WI........................	14.3	9.4	7.5	49.7	125 834	134 063	6.5	1.1	10 060	7 115	-1 524	54 558	2.46	67.0	8.2	26.9
Weirton-Steubenville, WV-OH.	16.1	11.7	9.3	51.2	132 008	124 455	-5.7	-4.2	7 093	10 572	-1 487	50 699	2.32	60.6	10.8	34.1
Wenatchee, WA	13.6	10.4	7.4	49.9	99 219	110 895	11.8	6.1	9 154	6 088	3 607	41 304	2.77	70.3	10.5	25.5
Wheeling, WV-OH................	15.8	11.3	8.8	50.1	153 172	147 951	-3.4	-3.4	9 283	11 721	-2 088	58 313	2.35	64.3	10.9	31.0
Wichita, KS.........................	12.9	8.1	6.1	50.5	579 839	630 919	8.8	2.2	57 142	34 790	-8 444	244 522	2.59	63.6	11.8	31.6
Wichita Falls, TX.................	12.7	8.3	6.8	48.5	151 524	151 476	0.0	-0.5	12 106	9 392	-3 525	55 562	2.44	61.7	11.4	31.0
Williamsport, PA.................	14.7	10.2	8.2	50.9	120 044	116 108	-3.3	-0.7	8 073	7 938	-905	45 751	2.41	64.3	9.4	30.0
Wilmington, NC...................	13.3	10.3	6.6	51.7	201 389	254 883	26.6	10.9	17 908	14 103	23 067	111 546	2.42	61.6	11.3	27.4
Winchester, VA-WV	13.5	10.2	6.9	50.1	102 997	128 480	24.7	5.3	9 667	7 167	4 088	48 995	2.67	67.7	12.4	25.9
Winston-Salem, NC	13.6	9.7	6.9	51.9	569 207	640 580	12.5	3.4	46 502	38 530	13 219	260 437	2.48	66.0	11.9	29.0
Worcester, MA-CT	14.1	8.7	6.3	50.6	860 054	916 822	6.6	2.1	61 409	48 517	7 071	345 269	2.60	65.4	13.1	27.5
Yakima, WA	10.8	7.8	5.6	50.0	222 581	243 237	9.3	2.6	25 949	11 838	-7 609	81 709	3.00	72.5	15.6	22.3
York-Hanover, PA	14.2	9.6	7.0	50.6	381 751	434 998	13.9	2.0	30 522	23 932	2 896	165 672	2.62	68.8	12.3	24.0
Youngstown-Warren-Boardman, OH-PA	15.4	11.1	9.2	51.1	602 964	565 799	-6.2	-3.7	35 091	43 185	-11 803	228 692	2.33	62.5	12.7	32.4
Yuba City, CA	11.6	8.0	5.8	49.8	139 149	166 891	19.9	3.0	15 723	8 251	-2 518	58 262	2.89	71.5	11.3	21.5
Yuma, AZ...........................	9.8	9.4	9.0	48.5	160 026	195 750	22.3	5.0	19 474	8 786	-1 690	71 751	2.77	73.1	13.9	22.2

1. No spouse present.

Table C. Metropolitan Areas — **Population, Vital Statistics, Health, and Crime**

Area name	Persons in group quarters, 2016	Daytime population, 2015		Births, 2016		Deaths, 2016		Persons under 65 with no health insurance 2015		Medicare, 2015			Serious crimes known to police,[2] 2014 Total	
		Number	Employ-ment/ residence ratio	Total	Rate[1]	Number	Rate[1]	Number	Percent	Total Benefici-aries	Enrolled in Original Medicare	Enrolled in Medicare Advantage	Number	Rate[3]
	32	33	34	35	36	37	38	39	40	41	42	43	44	45
Texarkana, TX-AR	7 908	152 620	1.02	1 945	13.0	1 673	11.1	16 468	13.9	29 394	22 872	6 522	6 928	4 609
The Villages, FL	8 203	126 411	1.32	501	4.0	1 742	14.0	5 463	12.0	20 255	12 511	7 744	1 302	1 178
Toledo, OH	17 608	623 076	1.06	7 478	12.4	6 013	9.9	36 927	7.4	105 813	57 011	48 802	14 235	2 496
Topeka, KS	5 051	233 262	1.00	2 864	12.3	2 339	10.0	17 406	9.1	46 306	41 869	4 437	8 687	3 748
Trenton, NJ	20 531	426 965	1.32	4 193	11.3	2 974	8.0	29 873	9.9	58 920	49 261	9 659	7 866	2 117
Tucson, AZ	25 162	1 009 877	1.00	11 778	11.6	9 795	9.6	98 124	12.2	191 101	96 906	94 195	49 303	4 894
Tulsa, OK	15 539	984 797	1.01	13 409	13.6	9 695	9.8	126 858	15.3	159 772	110 631	49 141	34 728	3 587
Tuscaloosa, AL	13 070	245 085	1.03	2 962	12.3	2 269	9.4	19 934	10.1	40 480	35 046	5 434	8 177	3 682
Tyler, TX	5 046	230 564	1.08	3 146	14.0	2 095	9.3	34 968	19.0	41 188	31 180	10 008	7 096	3 269
Urban Honolulu, HI	36 429	1 000 894	1.00	13 231	13.3	8 352	8.4	35 329	4.4	153 378	70 276	83 102	11 193	1 126
Utica-Rome, NY	14 289	293 976	0.99	3 077	10.5	3 186	10.8	14 187	6.1	62 204	38 928	23 276	6 996	2 385
Valdosta, GA	6 739	144 187	1.04	1 966	13.6	1 214	8.4	20 760	17.4	21 098	15 688	5 410	5 542	3 864
Vallejo-Fairfield, CA	11 318	390 844	0.76	5 302	12.0	3 472	7.9	21 726	6.0	64 619	35 813	28 806	15 562	3 620
Victoria, TX	1 915	101 435	1.05	1 416	14.2	907	9.1	14 715	17.7	17 849	13 412	4 437	3 321	3 352
Vineland-Bridgeton, NJ	10 782	154 941	0.99	2 053	13.3	1 443	9.4	15 749	12.7	26 997	22 864	4 133	6 931	4 397
Virginia Beach-Norfolk-Newport News, VA-NC	71 281	1 732 784	1.01	22 644	13.1	14 394	8.3	142 486	10.0	256 922	199 612	57 310	52 249	3 067
Visalia-Porterville, CA	4 808	448 650	0.93	7 575	16.5	3 119	6.8	45 247	11.2	54 396	45 924	8 472	13 301	2 895
Waco, TX	11 166	266 263	1.03	3 801	14.3	2 303	8.7	39 234	18.1	41 459	27 683	13 776	8 909	3 471
Walla Walla, WA	4 704	70 261	1.23	707	11.0	650	10.1	4 331	8.9	12 505	11 044	1 461	2 394	3 742
Warner Robins, GA	3 764	188 326	1.00	2 368	12.5	1 591	8.4	21 719	13.5	29 246	22 729	6 517	7 978	4 364
Washington-Arlington-Alexandria, DC-VA-MD-WV	105 884	6 247 796	1.05	80 905	13.2	37 019	6.0	451 419	8.5	658 216	555 415	102 801	146 420	2 430
Silver Spring-Frederick-Rockville, MD Div 43524	13 602	1 234 524	0.92	15 915	12.3	8 027	6.2	87 056	8.0	156 670	137 639	19 031	22 815	1 792
Washington-Arlington-Alexandria, DC-VA-MD-WV Div 47894	92 282	5 013 272	1.08	64 990	13.4	28 992	6.0	364 363	8.7	501 546	417 776	83 770	123 605	2 600
Waterloo-Cedar Falls, IA	7 267	175 055	1.05	2 164	12.7	1 537	9.0	8 185	6.0	31 664	27 515	4 149	4 891	2 873
Watertown-Fort Drum, NY	6 199	121 134	1.06	2 000	17.5	945	8.3	6 347	6.5	18 696	13 543	5 153	2 563	2 180
Wausau, WI	1 591	137 247	1.02	1 582	11.7	1 141	8.4	7 037	6.2	23 766	13 075	10 691	1 906	1 424
Weirton-Steubenville, WV-OH	3 367	113 645	0.85	1 147	9.6	1 716	14.4	6 472	7.0	29 767	19 794	9 973	NA	NA
Wenatchee, WA	1 121	115 088	0.98	1 474	12.5	984	8.4	9 713	10.2	22 513	17 602	4 911	2 503	2 186
Wheeling, WV-OH	6 781	149 729	1.09	1 469	10.3	1 844	12.9	7 199	6.5	31 987	17 209	14 778	2 453	1 864
Wichita, KS	11 507	646 033	1.01	8 773	13.6	5 739	8.9	69 125	12.7	101 222	81 801	19 421	26 377	4 146
Wichita Falls, TX	12 516	150 132	0.99	1 884	12.5	1 528	10.1	19 687	16.9	26 852	22 612	4 240	5 529	3 785
Williamsport, PA	5 311	118 370	1.04	1 298	11.3	1 336	11.6	6 492	7.2	24 934	16 242	8 692	2 479	2 121
Wilmington, NC	7 808	286 323	1.07	2 964	10.5	2 471	8.7	28 946	12.8	52 221	42 474	9 747	10 287	3 810
Winchester, VA-WV	2 449	131 501	0.97	1 540	11.4	1 168	8.6	12 984	11.8	24 217	20 814	3 403	3 060	2 310
Winston-Salem, NC	13 362	636 793	0.92	7 317	11.1	6 471	9.8	71 454	13.2	122 955	53 186	69 769	25 542	3 929
Worcester, MA-CT	33 857	872 958	0.86	9 684	10.3	8 183	8.7	25 670	3.3	155 799	96 230	59 569	19 400	2 289
Yakima, WA	3 495	248 383	1.00	4 113	16.5	2 033	8.1	32 748	15.5	38 458	31 028	7 430	8 831	3 549
York-Hanover, PA	8 745	408 334	0.84	4 872	11.0	3 997	9.0	25 815	7.1	81 673	51 279	30 394	8 253	1 877
Youngstown-Warren-Boardman, OH-PA	18 527	547 928	0.99	5 578	10.2	6 954	12.8	33 966	8.0	125 706	60 102	65 604	15 558	2 932
Yuba City, CA	2 016	162 561	0.87	2 502	14.6	1 359	7.9	15 011	10.3	26 588	25 257	1 331	5 111	3 006
Yuma, AZ	9 540	201 279	0.96	2 997	14.6	1 562	7.6	27 580	17.4	29 595	21 900	7 695	6 006	2 946

1. Per 1,000 estimated resident population.   2. Data for serious crimes have not been adjusted for underreporting; this may affect comparability between geographic areas and over time.
3. Per 100,000 population estimated by the FBI.

Table C. Metropolitan Areas — Crime, Education, Money Income, and Poverty

Area name	Serious crimes known to police, 2014 (cont.)[1] Rate[2] Violent	Property	Education: Enrollment[3] Total	Percent private	Attainment[4] (percent) High school graduate or less	Bachelor's degree or more	Local government expenditures,[5] 2013–2014 Total current expenditures (mil dol)	Current expenditures per student (dollars)	Income and Poverty, 2015 Per capita income[6] (dollars)	Mean household income (dollars)	Median household income	Percent of households with income of less than $50,000	Percent of households with income of $200,000 or more	Percent below poverty level All persons	Children under 18 years	Age 65 years and older
	46	47	48	49	50	51	52	53	54	55	56	57	58	59	60	61
Texarkana, TX-AR	532	4 076	34 756	8.7	51.5	14.1	240.3	8 989	21 726	56 904	38 814	59.1	2.9	19.6	26.4	8.0
The Villages, FL	188	990	10 076	22.9	38.1	33.0	72.8	8 788	33 635	69 104	51 335	48.8	3.0	8.1	22.0	5.4
Toledo, OH	586	1 910	161 688	16.7	41.5	25.5	1 120.4	10 998	26 564	64 636	47 093	51.8	3.1	17.2	24.2	7.1
Topeka, KS	364	3 383	56 686	8.8	41.1	27.4	402.6	10 406	26 614	64 686	51 674	48.0	2.4	13.3	24.2	7.1
Trenton, NJ	343	1 774	100 821	23.2	38.6	38.1	1 081.6	18 723	36 820	103 099	72 417	35.4	12.0	11.2	15.6	6.8
Tucson, AZ	443	4 451	260 533	9.5	35.6	31.1	1 149.6	7 936	26 164	64 613	47 099	52.4	3.2	18.9	28.3	8.8
Tulsa, OK	467	3 121	248 978	15.5	40.4	26.7	1 288.7	7 664	28 121	70 968	51 352	48.4	4.3	15.4	23.5	6.9
Tuscaloosa, AL	386	3 296	69 647	12.6	46.6	28.1	306.6	9 122	24 067	63 059	46 470	52.6	3.2	21.0	27.8	7.6
Tyler, TX	342	2 927	59 598	11.0	42.4	24.6	289.8	8 419	26 972	72 511	49 060	50.9	4.4	16.4	24.2	8.3
Urban Honolulu, HI	72	1 054	236 519	24.9	35.2	33.2	2 327.5	12 458	32 461	98 463	77 273	30.5	8.8	9.2	11.0	8.0
Utica-Rome, NY	269	2 116	66 394	14.8	45.8	23.1	682.5	15 644	26 702	65 700	48 935	50.6	2.9	16.5	27.6	8.3
Valdosta, GA	295	3 569	43 538	8.6	48.6	21.6	208.0	8 904	18 174	48 099	36 740	65.0	1.2	26.6	34.0	14.0
Vallejo-Fairfield, CA	491	3 129	108 571	13.9	37.0	25.7	576.9	8 725	29 672	84 403	67 443	37.5	5.6	12.1	16.4	7.1
Victoria, TX	427	2 925	24 979	13.3	46.9	21.8	153.7	9 076	26 989	73 247	56 073	45.1	3.8	12.7	16.9	9.6
Vineland-Bridgeton, NJ	511	3 886	34 623	7.7	65.2	13.5	485.7	17 611	22 425	64 461	51 315	48.5	2.2	16.9	25.1	10.9
Virginia Beach-Norfolk-Newport News, VA-NC	309	2 757	455 614	15.7	34.5	30.2	2 730.7	10 226	29 495	75 461	60 093	41.3	4.0	12.3	18.9	5.9
Visalia-Porterville, CA	414	2 481	140 867	6.9	55.2	14.2	978.7	9 681	18 625	61 617	42 413	55.7	2.7	27.6	37.0	13.1
Waco, TX	387	3 084	76 247	20.7	45.2	22.5	447.8	9 060	22 852	61 827	46 307	53.2	3.1	20.3	29.0	9.0
Walla Walla, WA	203	3 539	14 709	26.1	33.5	29.2	99.9	10 636	25 607	66 307	47 283	50.8	3.5	16.6	22.9	10.4
Warner Robins, GA	341	4 023	50 986	7.5	39.0	20.7	306.8	9 264	24 856	66 488	51 954	46.6	2.0	17.8	28.0	12.1
Washington-Arlington-Alexandria, DC-VA-MD-WV.. Silver Spring-Frederick-Rockville, MD Div 43524	317	2 113	1 611 064	21.0	28.6	49.3	12 697.8	13 817	44 677	121 072	93 294	25.2	15.1	8.3	10.6	7.0
Washington-Arlington-Alexandria, DC-VA-MD-WV Div 47894	184	1 608	339 924	21.1	25.3	54.3	2 817.9	14 681	47 323	128 504	95 519	25.4	17.1	7.5	10.6	6.4
	352	2 248	1 271 140	20.9	29.5	48.0	9 879.8	13 589	43 971	119 068	92 668	25.2	14.5	8.5	10.6	7.2
Waterloo-Cedar Falls, IA	480	2 393	48 110	15.7	39.0	29.0	311.8	11 699	28 581	70 719	52 255	47.2	3.3	12.4	13.8	6.2
Watertown-Fort Drum, NY	185	1 994	26 862	12.3	40.8	23.0	284.1	15 191	23 872	62 104	51 107	48.8	1.7	13.4	18.5	5.4
Wausau, WI	96	1 328	29 697	11.6	45.7	23.7	224.6	11 141	30 080	72 684	55 687	45.1	3.1	8.9	12.4	7.9
Weirton-Steubenville, WV-OH	NA	NA	26 753	21.7	53.5	16.5	175.6	10 688	24 083	55 103	43 452	57.3	1.0	16.0	25.7	8.9
Wenatchee, WA	118	2 068	27 292	7.9	46.8	21.6	217.7	10 398	26 036	69 094	56 319	45.0	2.8	11.4	17.0	7.0
Wheeling, WV-OH	291	1 573	29 488	15.1	45.6	22.5	208.8	11 094	26 808	64 995	47 726	52.1	3.2	11.7	13.2	7.7
Wichita, KS	531	3 615	177 029	14.1	38.4	27.7	1 087.3	9 414	26 511	67 630	51 591	47.9	3.4	14.1	20.3	9.2
Wichita Falls, TX	348	3 438	35 862	6.7	49.4	21.8	214.5	8 595	22 866	60 804	45 641	54.8	2.6	18.7	28.0	8.1
Williamsport, PA	218	1 903	23 716	19.2	53.6	22.9	221.7	13 785	25 200	62 165	51 455	48.8	2.1	15.2	25.8	7.2
Wilmington, NC	408	3 402	70 780	9.8	31.6	34.3	304.1	8 739	29 027	70 632	52 655	47.8	4.0	16.9	21.0	9.4
Winchester, VA-WV	180	2 130	32 569	18.6	46.9	26.3	222.6	10 638	27 790	72 798	60 752	40.0	3.5	13.0	20.1	12.2
Winston-Salem, NC	402	3 526	161 899	15.0	43.5	26.9	832.6	8 370	26 173	64 892	45 098	54.2	3.5	16.7	26.9	9.1
Worcester, MA-CT	419	1 870	243 148	20.4	39.9	33.3	2 037.1	14 018	32 718	85 490	65 427	38.3	7.0	11.9	15.7	9.1
Yakima, WA	244	3 305	67 763	7.7	57.0	15.7	537.7	10 201	21 769	64 372	47 223	54.0	2.4	18.8	28.0	9.6
York-Hanover, PA	206	1 671	99 971	18.9	51.8	22.7	818.4	12 189	28 544	73 339	58 409	40.8	2.7	10.7	16.0	8.5
Youngstown-Warren-Boardman, OH-PA	246	2 687	118 657	14.3	52.2	21.2	942.0	12 133	25 023	58 927	43 127	56.0	2.2	16.4	27.4	7.0
Yuba City, CA	360	2 646	47 420	9.4	44.8	15.2	313.9	8 898	23 307	66 463	51 185	48.6	2.8	20.6	30.1	9.4
Yuma, AZ	370	2 576	50 371	5.2	53.1	15.4	251.2	6 748	19 274	52 633	40 539	60.2	1.9	20.5	30.5	10.4

1. Data for serious crimes have not been adjusted for underreporting; this may affect comparability between geographic areas and over time.   2. Per 100,000 population estimated by the FBI.   3. All persons 3 years old and over enrolled in nursery school through college.   4. Persons 25 years old and over.   5. Elementary and secondary education expenditures.   6. Based on resident population estimated in the 2015 American Community Survey.

Table C. Metropolitan Areas — **Personal Income**

Area name	Personal income, 2015										Earnings, 2015		
	Total (mil dol)	Percent change 2014–2015	Per capita Dollars	Per capita Rank	Wages and salaries (mil dol)	Supplements to wages and salaries; employer contributions (mil dol) Pension and insurance	Supplements to wages and salaries; employer contributions (mil dol) Government social insurance	Proprietors' income (mil dol)	Dividends, interest, and rent (mil dol)	Personal transfer receipts (mil dol)	Total (mil dol)	Contributions for government social insurance (mil dol) From employee and self-employed	Contributions for government social insurance (mil dol) From employer
	62	63	64	65	66	67	68	69	70	71	72	73	74
Texarkana, TX-AR	5 246	4.4	35 026	344	2 450	437	182	380	861	1 396	3 449	205	182
The Villages, FL	4 638	7.2	39 012	247	1 103	203	81	156	1 304	2 024	1 543	166	81
Toledo, OH	25 503	4.0	42 087	176	14 137	2 598	1 011	1 936	3 553	5 548	19 683	1 089	1 011
Topeka, KS	9 905	2.8	42 365	168	5 041	883	395	629	1 619	2 078	6 947	431	395
Trenton, NJ	23 490	3.2	63 247	12	15 659	2 426	1 139	1 776	4 659	3 216	21 001	1 199	1 139
Tucson, AZ	38 922	2.7	38 536	259	17 163	2 981	1 251	2 263	8 442	9 586	23 659	1 525	1 251
Tulsa, OK	56 631	-1.0	57 727	18	22 042	3 285	1 659	16 508	9 356	7 531	43 494	2 013	1 659
Tuscaloosa, AL	8 499	3.6	35 424	336	4 459	783	326	563	1 477	1 935	6 131	386	326
Tyler, TX	11 197	1.1	50 224	56	4 551	683	317	3 105	1 701	1 943	8 656	419	317
Urban Honolulu, HI	52 055	4.5	52 122	41	26 894	5 852	2 204	3 558	10 605	7 342	38 509	2 173	2 204
Utica-Rome, NY	11 572	2.8	39 146	245	5 069	1 451	428	561	1 761	3 077	7 509	415	428
Valdosta, GA	4 592	3.1	32 138	371	2 248	477	167	229	808	1 117	3 121	174	167
Vallejo-Fairfield, CA	19 408	8.3	44 504	122	8 020	1 682	576	1 005	3 229	3 607	11 283	654	576
Victoria, TX	4 696	1.3	47 005	85	2 039	311	138	555	876	886	3 042	162	138
Vineland-Bridgeton, NJ	5 650	3.4	36 253	315	2 829	600	236	396	798	1 583	4 060	247	236
Virginia Beach-Norfolk-Newport News, VA-NC	80 034	4.5	46 400	89	41 403	8 515	3 303	3 208	17 060	13 193	56 429	3 175	3 303
Visalia-Porterville, CA	16 809	2.4	36 551	307	6 129	1 555	442	2 225	2 400	4 184	10 352	500	442
Waco, TX	9 702	5.3	36 917	299	4 999	818	349	843	1 467	2 169	7 010	381	349
Walla Walla, WA	2 721	6.2	42 333	170	1 196	219	110	344	539	585	1 870	97	110
Warner Robins, GA	7 120	3.7	37 841	276	3 421	828	265	250	1 282	1 481	4 763	262	265
Washington-Arlington-Alexandria, DC-VA-MD-WV	395 632	4.9	64 882	9	238 164	38 710	17 292	32 132	76 866	36 188	326 298	18 212	17 292
Silver Spring-Frederick-Rockville, MD Div 43524	93 413	5.2	72 670	X	41 321	6 417	3 001	11 787	19 510	7 728	62 526	3 503	3 001
Washington-Arlington-Alexandria, DC-VA-MD-WV Div 47894	302 219	4.8	62 802	X	196 843	32 294	14 290	20 344	57 356	28 460	263 772	14 709	14 290
Waterloo-Cedar Falls, IA	7 077	1.9	41 478	191	3 979	662	294	448	1 292	1 399	5 383	337	294
Watertown-Fort Drum, NY	5 078	0.4	43 170	154	2 661	820	254	187	952	979	3 923	178	254
Wausau, WI	5 967	2.5	43 921	138	3 324	581	256	466	956	970	4 628	277	256
Weirton-Steubenville, WV-OH	4 402	3.5	36 529	308	1 608	318	125	182	569	1 346	2 232	152	125
Wenatchee, WA	4 860	6.2	41 836	183	2 125	343	207	452	1 022	1 036	3 127	173	207
Wheeling, WV-OH	5 854	1.4	40 594	210	2 847	491	207	329	975	1 499	3 873	250	207
Wichita, KS	31 148	2.2	48 321	71	14 288	2 370	1 141	3 817	7 522	4 628	21 617	1 249	1 141
Wichita Falls, TX	6 393	-0.3	42 398	167	2 513	485	185	1 022	1 168	1 362	4 206	210	185
Williamsport, PA	4 778	2.7	41 171	195	2 410	535	195	250	774	1 099	3 389	203	195
Wilmington, NC	10 819	5.3	38 922	249	5 288	847	407	708	2 397	2 310	7 251	471	407
Winchester, VA-WV	5 680	4.4	42 436	164	2 695	458	200	390	960	966	3 744	233	200
Winston-Salem, NC	26 516	4.3	40 217	219	12 611	1 831	970	1 769	4 567	5 602	17 180	1 118	970
Worcester, MA-CT	47 102	5.6	50 348	55	20 027	3 773	1 399	2 980	6 629	8 311	28 180	1 496	1 399
Yakima, WA	9 587	3.6	38 527	260	4 122	658	408	1 114	1 628	2 365	6 301	317	408
York-Hanover, PA	19 774	4.0	44 651	118	8 301	1 630	682	975	2 966	3 734	11 588	693	682
Youngstown-Warren-Boardman, OH-PA	21 145	2.8	38 454	262	9 089	1 762	686	1 548	3 168	5 896	13 085	804	686
Yuba City, CA	6 704	7.1	39 216	241	2 318	595	175	601	1 068	1 731	3 689	199	175
Yuma, AZ	6 450	8.3	31 574	374	2 698	535	220	897	948	1 565	4 351	230	220

1. Based on the resident population estimated as of July 1 of the year shown.

Table C. Metropolitan Areas — Earnings, Social Security, and Housing

Area name	Earnings, 2015 (cont.) Percent by selected industries									Social Security beneficiaries, December 2015			Housing units, 2016	
	Farm	Mining	Construction	Manufacturing	Information, professional, scientific, technical services	Retail trade	Finance, insurance, real estate, rental and leasing	Health care and social assistance	Government	Number	Rate[1]	Supplemental Security Income recipients, December 2015	Total	Percent change, 2010–2016
	75	76	77	78	79	80	81	82	83	84	85	86	87	88
Texarkana, TX-AR	1.2	D	5.3	11.8	D	7.9	6.2	D	24.7	32 490	217	6 678	65 412	1.8
The Villages, FL	1.3	0.2	10.9	4.3	D	8.8	6.6	13.3	22.7	64 785	545	1 623	68 199	28.6
Toledo, OH	0.2	D	6.3	19.1	D	6.0	6.3	D	15.9	116 195	192	19 723	273 234	-0.1
Topeka, KS	0.1	0.6	6.6	7.0	D	5.0	D	14.5	24.3	50 755	217	5 695	104 450	0.6
Trenton, NJ	0.0	0.0	3.3	4.2	21.6	4.0	11.9	8.9	19.5	64 860	175	9 663	144 714	1.1
Tucson, AZ	0.2	1.3	4.9	9.9	9.5	6.6	6.0	14.7	25.2	208 665	207	20 275	456 551	3.5
Tulsa, OK	0.3	D	5.9	9.7	D	4.7	D	8.6	7.4	185 705	189	22 086	428 154	4.5
Tuscaloosa, AL	1.3	4.8	4.7	19.1	D	5.7	D	7.3	27.4	49 220	205	8 798	106 824	4.7
Tyler, TX	0.3	23.2	4.3	6.8	6.4	10.4	5.6	16.5	9.6	43 405	195	5 554	89 329	2.3
Urban Honolulu, HI	0.2	0.1	7.4	1.9	7.8	5.5	6.2	10.2	33.7	171 060	172	16 308	347 413	3.1
Utica-Rome, NY	0.5	0.3	4.0	9.7	6.0	6.0	6.9	15.6	32.3	70 990	241	9 835	137 077	-0.3
Valdosta, GA	1.6	D	5.7	8.3	D	D	D	D	35.0	24 895	173	5 044	59 859	4.2
Vallejo-Fairfield, CA	1.0	0.3	8.9	13.2	4.4	6.7	4.4	16.6	25.1	74 015	170	12 611	156 819	2.7
Victoria, TX	-0.1	14.2	8.3	8.8	D	7.8	D	13.5	13.4	19 140	192	2 757	40 691	4.0
Vineland-Bridgeton, NJ	1.5	0.3	6.2	14.6	D	7.3	2.9	15.5	28.5	30 570	197	5 908	56 423	1.0
Virginia Beach-Norfolk-Newport News, VA-NC	0.0	D	D	D	9.3	5.4	D	9.9	36.1	292 330	170	34 164	716 832	4.2
Visalia-Porterville, CA	15.2	0.1	3.7	8.3	3.2	6.9	3.7	6.6	24.5	63 130	138	18 954	147 518	4.1
Waco, TX	0.6	D	8.1	18.2	5.4	6.1	D	10.5	16.1	46 785	178	8 182	107 790	4.8
Walla Walla, WA	14.9	D	4.2	13.5	D	4.7	4.2	14.3	23.2	13 675	213	1 544	26 293	2.8
Warner Robins, GA	0.8	D	D	D	6.8	5.4	D	D	52.4	31 975	170	5 158	78 439	5.3
Washington-Arlington-Alexandria, DC-VA-MD-WV..	0.0	D	D	1.7	D	D	D	6.8	27.6	722 811	119	88 081	2 343 438	4.8
Silver Spring-Frederick-Rockville, MD Div 43524	0.0	D	D	3.6	21.5	D	D	9.1	20.9	168 500	131	16 173	486 460	4.4
Washington-Arlington-Alexandria, DC-VA-MD-WV Div 47894	0.0	0.0	D	1.2	27.3	3.2	5.4	6.3	29.2	554 311	116	71 908	1 856 978	5.0
Waterloo-Cedar Falls, IA	1.8	0.1	5.5	23.7	D	6.4	D	12.4	16.1	34 600	203	3 424	73 130	2.5
Watertown-Fort Drum, NY	1.1	0.1	4.0	4.5	2.6	5.9	1.9	9.7	59.3	21 570	184	2 731	59 113	2.0
Wausau, WI	2.1	0.2	5.4	22.2	5.3	7.2	9.6	15.8	11.5	27 840	205	2 026	58 725	1.7
Weirton-Steubenville, WV-OH	0.0	D	D	18.3	D	7.1	3.3	17.6	13.7	32 875	273	4 079	57 598	-1.3
Wenatchee, WA	10.4	D	6.8	5.6	5.1	7.9	3.8	14.6	21.0	24 270	209	2 030	53 233	3.4
Wheeling, WV-OH	-0.1	D	D	6.0	D	8.1	4.9	D	13.7	36 215	251	4 303	68 883	-0.9
Wichita, KS	0.5	5.1	5.9	22.5	D	5.7	6.2	11.2	12.9	115 480	180	12 647	272 442	2.1
Wichita Falls, TX	0.7	15.7	4.1	9.0	D	7.4	5.0	D	24.2	29 195	194	4 301	65 408	0.9
Williamsport, PA	0.1	6.3	7.1	15.8	5.0	6.4	4.5	15.2	18.6	27 590	238	3 299	52 694	0.4
Wilmington, NC	0.9	D	8.2	5.8	D	8.4	7.0	10.9	20.2	56 755	204	5 543	137 084	7.0
Winchester, VA-WV	0.0	D	D	13.4	D	8.6	6.9	D	18.1	27 000	202	2 378	59 158	4.0
Winston-Salem, NC	0.5	0.1	4.8	13.1	D	6.8	D	D	10.7	140 465	214	14 066	294 554	2.6
Worcester, MA-CT	0.0	D	D	13.2	9.8	6.2	6.6	15.9	17.3	173 420	186	25 173	379 980	1.1
Yakima, WA	17.5	0.1	4.2	8.0	2.9	6.5	3.3	13.2	18.2	43 390	175	7 487	86 728	1.5
York-Hanover, PA	0.1	0.3	9.1	19.5	5.5	6.3	3.9	13.7	14.2	93 000	210	8 368	181 457	1.6
Youngstown-Warren-Boardman, OH-PA	0.1	0.9	6.3	17.8	4.3	7.8	5.0	16.2	15.2	140 535	256	18 869	257 875	-0.7
Yuba City, CA	7.5	0.4	5.4	4.3	3.5	6.5	3.6	12.6	35.0	29 895	176	8 168	62 639	1.9
Yuma, AZ	14.1	0.0	4.0	2.7	4.8	7.5	3.1	10.2	29.7	34 735	171	4 363	91 314	3.9

1. Per 1,000 resident population estimated as of July 1, 2011 of the year shown.

Table C. Metropolitan Areas — Housing, Labor Force, and Employment

Area name	Housing units, 2015 — Total	Percent	Owner-occupied Median value[1]	With a mortgage	Without a mortgage[2]	Renter-occupied Median rent[3]	Median rent as a percent of income	Percent with a computer	Civilian labor force, 2016 — Total	Percent change, 2015–2016	Unemployment Total	Rate[4]	Civilian employment[5], 2015 — Total employed	Management, professional, and related occupations	Construction, production, and related occupations
	89	90	91	92	93	94	95	96	97	98	99	100	101	102	103
Texarkana, TX-AR	54 440	65.8	97 900	21.5	10.9	731	33.3	76.8	65 288	1.2	2 974	4.6	57 963	32.0	24.9
The Villages, FL	51 170	90.4	243 500	23.8	10.0	807	36.5	89.5	29 239	2.3	2 052	7.0	NA	NA	NA
Toledo, OH	242 641	62.3	118 700	19.6	12.7	695	28.5	87.1	303 491	1.0	14 666	4.8	288 198	33.7	26.5
Topeka, KS	93 078	66.9	129 200	19.9	12.5	755	27.9	84.8	120 395	0.2	4 948	4.1	109 226	35.5	24.0
Trenton, NJ	127 965	62.9	283 600	24.0	16.5	1 154	30.0	89.6	199 781	0.8	8 644	4.3	180 186	43.2	15.8
Tucson, AZ	395 992	60.8	165 900	22.0	10.3	824	30.9	89.5	472 015	1.2	23 078	4.9	429 496	35.9	17.4
Tulsa, OK	380 841	63.8	141 800	19.6	10.5	791	27.1	86.5	475 647	0.0	23 771	5.0	465 851	35.4	23.3
Tuscaloosa, AL	84 889	64.3	156 400	20.3	11.2	778	30.8	81.9	112 577	0.4	6 711	6.0	99 055	35.2	28.6
Tyler, TX	78 380	66.0	145 500	21.3	10.9	852	32.7	86.7	105 569	2.1	4 742	4.5	98 334	33.4	24.4
Urban Honolulu, HI	307 703	53.5	629 900	25.9	10.0	1 638	35.0	90.1	473 947	1.4	13 357	2.8	471 067	35.0	18.1
Utica-Rome, NY	114 580	66.8	112 200	20.3	13.0	719	30.1	83.9	129 622	-1.0	6 451	5.0	129 071	32.9	21.7
Valdosta, GA	48 600	54.6	129 800	22.2	11.3	723	32.2	84.5	63 882	1.6	3 327	5.2	54 903	30.8	23.5
Vallejo-Fairfield, CA	145 502	60.3	344 900	24.9	10.1	1 320	35.0	91.3	207 882	1.3	11 355	5.5	193 706	30.6	23.4
Victoria, TX	35 842	70.0	131 400	19.5	10.0	792	29.1	83.8	47 264	-2.8	2 555	5.4	44 562	34.9	23.4
Vineland-Bridgeton, NJ	50 380	65.3	157 300	24.7	16.5	980	33.6	77.4	67 209	-0.8	5 025	7.5	66 220	28.5	32.1
Virginia Beach-Norfolk-Newport News, VA-NC	642 911	60.5	236 900	23.8	12.0	1 106	32.8	90.4	834 737	0.2	38 337	4.6	779 180	37.5	20.2
Visalia-Porterville, CA	134 801	54.8	174 300	24.0	10.0	853	34.7	80.3	205 909	0.9	22 627	11.0	170 090	25.1	37.3
Waco, TX	93 239	59.7	119 300	22.2	12.8	813	31.0	84.6	121 920	2.8	4 881	4.0	116 676	32.8	26.6
Walla Walla, WA	24 201	64.6	193 200	22.7	11.7	825	32.8	87.0	30 622	3.0	1 747	5.7	27 562	40.4	20.6
Warner Robins, GA	69 562	62.8	132 800	20.0	10.4	851	30.0	85.8	83 020	2.5	4 657	5.6	81 293	34.5	25.8
Washington-Arlington-Alexandria, DC-VA-MD-WV Silver Spring-Frederick-Rockville, MD Div 43524	2 172 310	62.3	401 500	22.1	10.0	1 553	29.4	93.4	3 313 061	1.2	126 462	3.8	3 250 230	51.1	12.7
Washington-Arlington-Alexandria, DC-VA-MD-WV Div 43524	461 405	66.0	430 800	21.9	10.0	1 610	31.2	93.5	680 832	0.5	23 044	3.4	687 230	53.6	11.9
Washington-Arlington-Alexandria, DC-VA-MD-WV Div 47894	1 710 905	61.2	394 100	22.1	10.0	1 537	29.1	93.4	2 632 229	1.4	103 418	3.9	2 563 000	50.5	12.9
Waterloo-Cedar Falls, IA	66 986	69.9	143 400	19.1	10.5	688	28.9	85.6	90 281	-1.1	4 023	4.5	89 190	31.9	25.8
Watertown-Fort Drum, NY	43 145	55.2	155 600	20.0	11.9	909	29.1	88.8	45 877	-1.7	2 858	6.2	45 588	32.3	23.9
Wausau, WI	54 558	72.8	151 500	19.8	12.5	721	25.7	84.2	73 935	0.6	2 715	3.7	71 878	33.8	28.9
Weirton-Steubenville, WV-OH	50 699	71.2	88 000	16.8	11.3	616	28.2	80.6	51 644	-1.6	3 968	7.7	54 171	25.7	27.0
Wenatchee, WA	41 304	69.1	248 900	22.5	10.0	796	23.4	89.0	64 578	3.5	4 047	6.3	52 750	28.4	28.6
Wheeling, WV-OH	58 313	74.7	103 900	16.7	10.0	588	28.1	80.5	65 388	-0.8	4 519	6.9	61 910	33.5	24.3
Wichita, KS	244 522	65.3	127 800	20.0	11.1	751	27.5	82.8	309 339	-0.2	14 547	4.7	306 300	34.5	25.4
Wichita Falls, TX	55 562	62.3	98 300	20.9	11.4	743	27.7	83.4	63 964	-0.3	2 812	4.4	62 193	31.9	24.8
Williamsport, PA	45 751	69.2	147 500	19.8	13.4	755	30.8	82.2	59 014	-3.2	3 959	6.7	55 739	28.7	27.4
Wilmington, NC	111 546	61.8	219 400	22.5	12.9	935	29.7	87.7	143 363	2.9	6 873	4.8	129 936	37.9	19.6
Winchester, VA-WV	48 995	68.9	223 700	21.6	10.0	928	28.6	81.0	69 246	1.3	2 543	3.7	64 068	35.7	27.3
Winston-Salem, NC	260 437	65.0	145 100	20.1	10.3	725	29.2	83.3	322 137	1.4	15 467	4.8	297 528	34.8	25.9
Worcester, MA-CT	345 269	65.3	247 600	22.5	14.5	972	29.7	88.6	489 000	-0.1	20 211	4.1	468 421	39.9	18.7
Yakima, WA	81 709	64.1	163 200	22.1	11.6	764	29.9	84.1	125 794	3.3	10 055	8.0	104 851	25.3	39.4
York-Hanover, PA	165 672	73.8	168 800	22.1	13.1	890	30.6	86.1	235 131	0.9	10 967	4.7	222 498	32.7	28.1
Youngstown-Warren-Boardman, OH-PA	228 692	69.9	103 000	19.9	11.5	634	29.8	82.1	249 043	-0.9	15 896	6.4	242 168	28.9	27.6
Yuba City, CA	58 262	58.6	221 700	23.6	11.3	902	33.9	87.1	73 646	1.5	6 758	9.2	65 196	31.5	29.6
Yuma, AZ	71 751	65.3	119 400	23.3	10.0	756	29.3	78.1	94 005	0.5	17 486	18.6	72 053	27.8	30.7

1. Specified owner-occupied units. 2. A value of 10.0 represents 10 percent or less. 3. Specified renter-occupied units. 4. Percent of civilian labor force.
5. Civilian employed persons 16 years old and over.

Table C. Metropolitan Areas — **Nonfarm Employment and Agriculture**

Area name	Private nonfarm establishments, employment and payroll, 2015									Agriculture, 2012			
		Employment						Annual payroll		Farms			
												Percent with:	
	Number of establishments	Total	Health care and social assistance	Manufacturing	Retail trade	Finance and insurance	Professional, scientific, and technical services	Total (mil dol)	Average per employee (dollars)	Number	Fewer than 50 acres	500 acres or more	Farm operators whose principal occupation is farming (percent)
	104	105	106	107	108	109	110	111	112	113	114	115	116
Texarkana, TX-AR	3 069	46 653	8 674	5 812	8 345	1 769	1 968	1 624	34 815	2 592	38.7	9.6	42.6
The Villages, FL....................	1 383	20 144	4 088	1 185	3 528	650	541	717	35 590	1 367	70.1	4.0	34.7
Toledo, OH...........................	13 265	271 481	46 058	42 376	31 296	7 323	12 189	11 483	42 297	2 246	43.9	13.4	45.9
Topeka, KS	5 135	85 504	19 750	7 191	10 987	5 815	4 676	3 501	40 942	4 507	27.3	16.6	39.9
Trenton, NJ	9 664	188 908	30 894	6 284	19 849	15 418	21 524	12 428	65 788	272	71.0	2.9	46.0
Tucson, AZ	20 152	310 979	59 120	22 501	47 724	12 914	16 236	12 162	39 107	855	79.4	9.4	49.0
Tulsa, OK	24 241	403 144	59 662	57 281	49 311	16 981	22 677	18 890	46 856	9 103	39.4	11.1	37.6
Tuscaloosa, AL	4 490	80 890	12 929	15 397	10 931	1 889	2 355	3 222	39 838	1 386	33.4	11.8	44.3
Tyler, TX	5 776	91 548	22 769	6 663	13 025	4 745	4 888	3 821	41 735	2 961	54.8	3.0	45.3
Urban Honolulu, HI	21 167	355 607	52 207	9 656	48 249	16 269	17 949	15 778	44 368	999	90.6	2.1	66.3
Utica-Rome, NY	6 047	99 886	21 614	11 848	14 053	6 977	3 859	3 704	37 085	1 753	23.8	8.1	57.8
Valdosta, GA	3 050	43 020	7 952	3 723	7 061	1 200	1 303	1 340	31 155	901	43.4	13.7	47.7
Vallejo-Fairfield, CA	6 855	107 550	22 405	9 760	19 539	4 203	3 376	5 250	48 811	860	62.9	11.7	53.7
Victoria, TX	2 547	36 273	6 642	2 225	6 294	955	1 183	1 562	43 055	2 708	35.7	14.3	42.8
Vineland-Bridgeton, NJ........	2 832	44 519	9 765	7 303	7 417	1 133	1 013	1 745	39 202	583	61.7	5.3	55.2
Virginia Beach-Norfolk-Newport News, VA-NC	37 174	603 621	91 357	58 179	89 112	25 592	50 559	25 181	41 717	1 546	57.2	11.5	48.3
Visalia-Porterville, CA	6 259	94 155	15 753	12 958	16 511	2 977	2 544	3 517	37 352	4 931	61.2	8.4	58.3
Waco, TX	5 277	103 218	17 499	14 151	12 501	5 018	2 548	3 741	36 245	4 541	47.3	7.9	42.8
Walla Walla, WA	1 483	20 122	4 204	3 576	2 315	684	487	760	37 785	1 251	45.6	27.3	46.9
Warner Robins, GA..............	3 130	45 576	8 012	6 684	8 438	1 268	3 974	1 530	33 563	592	50.2	13.3	42.4
Washington-Arlington-Alexandria, DC-VA-MD-WV ..	149 805	2 559 666	310 312	48 559	276 871	99 846	520 743	164 325	64 198	9 020	55.6	5.5	44.4
Silver Spring-Frederick-Rockville, MD Div 43524	NA	NA	NA	NA	NA	NA	NA	NA	NA	1 848	54.5	5.7	46.0
Washington-Arlington-Alexandria, DC-VA-MD-WV Div 47894	NA	NA	NA	NA	NA	NA	NA	NA	NA	7 172	55.9	5.4	43.9
Waterloo-Cedar Falls, IA	4 125	81 913	18 185	14 919	10 863	3 628	3 991	3 083	37 633	2 643	33.6	21.2	53.4
Watertown-Fort Drum, NY	2 435	29 527	6 232	2 393	6 837	682	872	1 057	35 813	876	20.5	17.2	57.4
Wausau, WI	3 273	64 477	9 922	17 087	9 960	3 708	1 953	2 664	41 315	2 266	23.2	7.5	55.0
Weirton-Steubenville, WV-OH..................................	2 231	35 986	7 819	5 579	4 983	728	799	1 270	35 286	685	29.5	4.2	39.0
Wenatchee, WA	3 215	35 650	6 841	2 289	6 139	872	1 300	1 461	40 976	1 739	58.0	14.1	55.8
Wheeling, WV-OH.................	3 346	56 778	12 827	2 490	8 774	2 120	2 630	2 131	37 532	1 579	25.4	3.5	42.2
Wichita, KS	14 695	265 128	40 703	53 651	33 868	8 904	11 979	11 710	44 169	5 345	27.9	25.2	45.7
Wichita Falls, TX	3 458	47 202	11 307	4 867	7 744	1 722	1 685	1 662	35 220	2 031	24.1	25.8	42.8
Williamsport, PA..................	2 817	46 211	8 912	7 801	7 609	1 518	1 552	1 759	38 071	1 207	32.4	3.7	44.0
Wilmington, NC	8 073	99 208	17 786	5 018	16 879	3 001	6 842	4 060	40 927	385	54.3	7.0	50.1
Winchester, VA-WV	3 149	52 110	9 678	6 606	8 388	2 645	2 807	2 034	39 026	1 479	42.7	7.4	40.4
Winston-Salem, NC	13 114	231 599	40 678	28 695	29 308	11 701	8 209	10 438	45 069	4 242	53.3	2.0	47.5
Worcester, MA-CT	19 860	319 287	69 856	37 986	44 751	15 593	19 186	15 144	47 431	2 252	63.7	1.6	45.8
Yakima, WA	4 680	66 044	12 845	8 574	10 402	1 520	1 747	2 542	38 496	3 143	73.9	5.5	51.9
York-Hanover, PA.................	8 675	164 072	23 886	30 511	22 218	3 696	5 907	6 859	41 803	2 171	56.6	4.4	48.9
Youngstown-Warren-Boardman, OH-PA	12 313	197 478	41 771	35 253	29 284	5 157	6 046	7 153	36 219	2 651	38.1	4.1	46.4
Yuba City, CA	2 529	30 114	5 829	2 058	6 017	967	1 339	1 198	39 772	2 153	55.4	12.7	56.9
Yuma, AZ	2 942	41 516	7 181	3 390	8 294	1 102	1 390	1 360	32 754	562	64.4	14.4	54.8

Table C. Metropolitan Areas — **Agriculture**

Table C. Metropolitan Areas — **Agriculture**

Area name	Agriculture, 2012 (cont.)														
	Land in farms					Value of land and buildings (dollars)			Value of products sold				Percent of farms with sales of:		Government payments	
			Acres								Percent from:					
	Acreage (1,000)	Percent change, 2007–2012	Average size of farm	Total irrigated (1,000)	Total cropland (1,000)	Average per farm	Average per acre	Value of machinery and equipment, average per farm (dollars)	Total (mil dol)	Average per farm (dollars)	Crops	Live-stock and poultry products	$10,000 or more	$100,000 or more	Total ($1,000)	Percent of farms
	117	118	119	120	121	122	123	124	125	126	127	128	129	130	131	132
Texarkana, TX-AR	609	0.4	235	21.4	223.1	475 867	2 027	61 443	188.1	72 558	30.0	70.0	34.1	7.9	3 271	16.9
The Villages, FL	183	14.7	134	3.1	20.7	717 143	5 350	45 931	42.1	30 773	58.9	41.1	19.3	5.3	164	2.9
Toledo, OH	526	0.8	234	2.9	491.5	1 339 764	5 717	160 193	469.6	209 092	80.6	19.4	61.5	34.6	10 688	72.1
Topeka, KS	1 606	-4.5	356	30.4	746.2	645 650	1 812	88 309	290.6	64 475	54.1	45.9	44.2	12.8	13 372	51.5
Trenton, NJ	20	-9.1	73	1.1	12.4	1 474 301	20 310	59 195	19.7	72 533	83.1	16.9	43.0	11.0	310	14.3
Tucson, AZ	D	D	D	32.4	36.7	1 651 870	D	64 622	97.3	113 786	76.8	23.2	31.2	10.3	1 085	5.3
Tulsa, OK	2 757	-8.9	303	12.2	525.7	487 549	1 610	48 596	320.1	35 165	20.5	79.5	31.0	5.0	10 260	18.1
Tuscaloosa, AL	349	-15.0	252	D	79.8	579 205	2 299	70 007	203.4	146 773	D	D	35.1	12.3	1 801	22.9
Tyler, TX	302	0.0	102	2.5	77.1	386 589	3 786	43 300	76.8	25 934	77.5	22.5	18.6	2.6	189	1.8
Urban Honolulu, HI	69	14.5	69	10.8	22.2	1 396 597	20 171	56 908	161.5	161 650	90.0	10.0	54.6	12.7	283	6.1
Utica-Rome, NY	345	4.0	197	0.3	195.1	387 175	1 965	102 671	183.6	104 752	32.6	67.4	52.0	21.4	3 569	31.7
Valdosta, GA	268	-17.4	298	37.0	127.0	994 700	3 343	118 135	172.8	191 747	73.9	26.1	35.2	14.1	4 463	47.7
Vallejo-Fairfield, CA	407	13.6	473	130.9	169.6	2 631 010	5 558	146 770	307.4	357 463	79.0	21.0	53.1	22.7	1 911	15.7
Victoria, TX	933	-3.2	344	4.1	113.1	748 694	2 174	54 903	67.0	24 741	47.2	52.8	28.4	4.1	3 202	14.4
Vineland-Bridgeton, NJ	65	-7.1	111	19.3	49.7	889 362	8 035	130 184	170.4	292 216	97.2	2.8	50.9	22.1	520	14.9
Virginia Beach-Norfolk-Newport News, VA-NC	348	-3.4	225	5.6	D	954 757	4 240	128 940	D	D	D	D	39.2	17.0	7 172	37.0
Visalia-Porterville, CA	1 239	6.0	251	557.4	677.5	1 893 271	7 535	144 666	4 017.1	814 657	41.6	58.4	70.2	36.6	12 174	13.5
Waco, TX	936	-4.0	206	8.6	418.3	479 933	2 328	62 287	318.4	70 112	40.8	59.2	26.8	6.6	8 368	20.6
Walla Walla, WA	943	-5.3	753	95.2	750.3	1 331 341	1 767	176 191	495.1	395 756	D	D	41.5	23.7	17 645	52.1
Warner Robins, GA	145	1.2	245	33.2	89.1	763 294	3 110	139 532	129.7	219 166	72.7	27.3	30.7	14.9	2 575	34.1
Washington-Arlington-Alexandria, DC-VA-MD-WV ..	1 192	-2.8	132	D	D	1 082 771	8 191	74 808	479.4	53 150	D	D	31.3	7.8	9 447	15.6
Silver Spring-Frederick-Rockville, MD Div 43524	245	-9.2	133	2.4	172.7	1 095 421	8 262	106 409	198.8	107 576	58.6	41.4	37.6	15.7	3 896	28.8
Washington-Arlington-Alexandria, DC-VA-MD-WV Div 47894	947	-1.0	132	D	D	1 079 511	8 173	66 666	280.6	39 126	D	D	29.7	5.7	5 551	12.2
Waterloo-Cedar Falls, IA	886	5.4	335	0.8	817.5	2 653 546	7 913	260 785	921.7	348 721	69.2	30.8	66.5	46.6	23 091	81.8
Watertown-Fort Drum, NY	291	10.9	332	0.3	173.5	544 535	1 640	133 429	183.6	209 551	24.7	75.3	51.6	24.1	2 974	31.5
Wausau, WI	479	-2.4	211	6.2	320.1	616 429	2 916	136 874	391.1	172 605	24.8	75.2	61.9	32.7	6 615	48.5
Weirton-Steubenville, WV-OH	92	-2.7	134	D	33.3	354 781	2 643	67 448	9.9	14 394	44.8	55.2	27.9	3.1	D	15.5
Wenatchee, WA	890	-8.9	512	41.1	577.0	858 859	1 678	96 734	405.5	233 192	98.3	1.7	60.6	34.7	13 598	27.3
Wheeling, WV-OH	229	-10.3	145	D	69.6	403 551	2 779	56 892	26.9	17 067	24.1	75.9	25.3	2.5	798	10.6
Wichita, KS	2 856	-1.3	534	147.5	1 911.4	1 018 921	1 907	140 007	864.4	161 729	63.3	36.7	54.3	23.6	25 429	62.2
Wichita Falls, TX	1 541	2.7	759	4.8	332.0	968 725	1 277	78 397	194.6	95 797	23.0	77.0	45.3	14.2	6 647	35.8
Williamsport, PA	158	-1.2	131	0.6	79.7	559 934	4 265	73 065	72.2	59 819	53.8	46.2	41.6	13.2	2 246	39.1
Wilmington, NC	59	-11.1	152	1.8	31.7	719 145	4 720	86 745	178.9	464 691	21.8	78.2	41.3	24.4	1 612	31.2
Winchester, VA-WV	243	6.7	164	0.3	74.5	747 885	4 556	53 968	73.5	49 694	44.1	55.9	30.0	5.5	625	11.7
Winston-Salem, NC	379	-5.4	89	2.1	174.8	500 191	5 592	54 495	252.2	59 444	37.1	62.9	26.1	6.9	3 083	11.0
Worcester, MA-CT	160	-3.9	71	1.8	52.3	619 520	8 716	50 890	101.7	45 155	56.7	43.3	27.4	7.0	1 949	9.0
Yakima, WA	1 780	8.0	566	224.4	306.9	1 021 212	1 803	118 874	1 645.5	523 548	65.0	35.0	45.7	22.4	5 804	11.5
York-Hanover, PA	262	-10.4	121	0.8	195.0	910 957	7 547	87 005	234.1	107 814	62.9	37.1	45.3	16.5	2 746	22.2
Youngstown-Warren-Boardman, OH-PA	352	-2.5	133	1.2	229.7	523 104	3 940	102 994	214.6	80 935	58.1	41.9	46.8	15.9	3 340	30.7
Yuba City, CA	563	8.1	261	326.8	365.6	1 658 114	6 343	168 077	701.6	325 882	93.5	6.5	66.0	35.1	14 667	22.8
Yuma, AZ	215	2.0	382	181.4	200.1	2 758 098	7 220	372 064	985.0	1 752 685	D	D	61.7	28.5	1 815	17.1

Table C. Metropolitan Areas — Water Use, Wholesale Trade, Retail Trade, and Real Estate

Area name	Water use, 2010		Wholesale trade,[1] 2012				Retail trade, 2012				Real estate and rental and leasing, 2012			
	Total water withdrawn (mil gal/day)	Gallons withdrawn per person per day	Number of establishments	Number of employees	Sales (mil dol)	Annual payroll (mil dol)	Number of establishments	Number of employees	Sales (mil dol)	Annual payroll (mil dol)	Number of establishments	Number of employees	Receipts (mil dol)	Annual payroll (mil dol)
	133	134	135	136	137	138	139	140	141	142	143	144	145	146
Texarkana, TX-AR	136.7	917	132	1 974	2 955.7	87.5	577	7 946	2 151.3	185.7	131	589	110.1	20.1
The Villages, FL	32.0	342	45	D	D	D	217	2 840	908.8	62.1	79	176	25.6	5.7
Toledo, OH	701.5	1 150	649	9 697	7 499.0	479.7	2 001	31 636	8 224.9	732.7	547	3 285	2 664.1	183.5
Topeka, KS	47.9	205	192	2 204	1 496.3	107.9	801	10 823	2 632.3	233.1	218	946	138.5	27.3
Trenton, NJ	477.6	1 303	354	D	D	D	1 305	18 794	5 127.4	477.9	347	1 934	729.3	91.8
Tucson, AZ	305.4	312	703	6 172	3 099.3	269.6	2 770	43 642	11 377.2	1 094.8	1 250	6 042	973.5	205.5
Tulsa, OK	387.7	414	1 210	16 787	15 854.1	976.9	3 066	44 465	12 865.2	1 081.7	1 097	6 653	1 083.1	261.7
Tuscaloosa, AL	65.7	285	160	1 774	1 240.0	86.6	835	10 366	2 796.3	233.7	192	1 511	166.7	45.0
Tyler, TX	30.8	147	215	D	D	D	829	11 883	3 388.9	293.6	281	1 477	301.0	61.6
Urban Honolulu, HI	799.2	838	1 167	13 446	8 052.8	596.9	2 889	46 165	13 036.4	1 233.1	1 219	7 213	2 553.5	340.7
Utica-Rome, NY	48.2	161	205	2 626	1 249.6	116.1	1 017	13 905	3 556.1	308.4	204	799	126.9	22.4
Valdosta, GA	41.3	296	128	1 261	1 438.4	48.5	563	6 439	1 880.1	142.3	142	1 467	107.4	26.5
Vallejo-Fairfield, CA	452.8	1 095	249	4 165	2 803.7	215.6	1 060	17 610	5 106.6	469.9	381	1 629	389.2	59.2
Victoria, TX	456.6	4 858	115	1 716	1 251.0	91.8	397	5 629	1 698.7	143.3	129	1 057	604.9	59.8
Vineland-Bridgeton, NJ	58.9	375	152	3 223	2 422.4	133.6	512	7 201	2 049.0	175.0	120	471	96.2	15.8
Virginia Beach-Norfolk-Newport News, VA-NC	1 494.4	891	1 282	18 502	16 160.5	1 040.2	5 848	87 532	21 164.8	1 960.2	2 017	14 556	2 348.7	549.1
Visalia-Porterville, CA	2 600.3	5 881	325	4 564	3 890.5	191.8	1 044	14 210	3 903.5	340.6	306	1 421	249.0	40.9
Waco, TX	84.6	335	248	D	D	D	898	11 518	3 321.4	258.7	228	1 531	290.6	64.7
Walla Walla, WA	168.5	2 681	88	673	602.4	25.8	201	2 433	586.0	59.1	62	187	23.0	5.2
Warner Robins, GA	62.6	348	73	D	D	D	581	7 789	2 146.6	179.0	151	519	81.0	14.4
Washington-Arlington-Alexandria, DC-VA-MD-WV	6 238.9	1 107	3 527	49 567	57 941.8	3 388.0	16 124	264 471	74 306.7	7 157.0	6 881	53 448	15 623.8	3 069.8
Silver Spring-Frederick-Rockville, MD Div 43524	778.5	646	875	11 325	11 642.7	792.1	3 438	58 054	16 973.9	1 633.0	1 570	13 206	4 741.5	869.1
Washington-Arlington-Alexandria, DC-VA-MD-WV Div 47894	5 460.4	1 232	2 652	38 242	46 299.2	2 595.9	12 686	206 417	57 332.8	5 524.0	5 311	40 242	10 882.3	2 200.7
Waterloo-Cedar Falls, IA	43.2	257	197	3 210	2 774.7	154.0	639	10 445	2 555.7	225.1	164	706	141.0	22.9
Watertown-Fort Drum, NY	24.2	208	67	870	345.2	34.7	476	6 849	1 937.9	161.4	119	588	103.9	17.8
Wausau, WI	126.8	946	180	2 955	1 276.6	126.2	472	9 545	2 572.4	208.5	83	412	79.2	11.9
Weirton-Steubenville, WV-OH	1 825.2	14 665	71	D	D	D	372	5 013	1 195.3	105.3	67	306	35.9	8.4
Wenatchee, WA	103.7	935	127	D	D	D	477	5 701	1 434.5	146.9	145	475	63.0	13.5
Wheeling, WV-OH	623.9	4 217	126	D	D	D	585	8 547	2 283.3	189.1	117	601	84.5	16.8
Wichita, KS	185.4	294	727	9 369	9 027.7	524.5	2 115	31 655	8 362.2	740.0	650	4 202	610.9	138.1
Wichita Falls, TX	83.4	551	163	1 255	715.2	58.5	544	7 725	2 105.4	174.4	170	822	169.1	30.2
Williamsport, PA	16.0	138	108	2 110	1 271.2	82.6	503	7 404	1 878.1	154.7	89	618	120.0	24.4
Wilmington, NC	55.0	216	315	2 837	1 368.8	136.0	1 174	14 996	4 258.4	367.1	425	2 314	395.5	86.3
Winchester, VA-WV	18.9	147	129	D	D	D	537	8 118	2 358.1	195.3	127	432	90.4	14.8
Winston-Salem, NC	1 381.9	2 157	608	8 614	5 513.2	389.1	2 151	27 365	7 696.4	651.1	530	2 200	739.1	77.4
Worcester, MA-CT	316.8	346	827	12 550	7 416.0	685.2	2 928	43 798	12 212.7	1 080.8	643	2 883	651.1	124.6
Yakima, WA	608.4	2 501	234	4 373	3 335.1	198.3	713	9 575	2 560.2	246.1	249	974	132.0	26.7
York-Hanover, PA	2 641.2	6 072	359	6 685	4 340.8	301.4	1 297	21 024	5 192.4	463.9	258	1 470	263.7	51.8
Youngstown-Warren-Boardman, OH-PA	214.8	380	538	7 293	4 748.0	345.2	2 094	29 036	7 127.0	610.9	384	3 946	486.5	114.2
Yuba City, CA	983.7	5 894	96	D	D	D	414	5 557	1 459.7	136.6	134	559	68.5	14.4
Yuma, AZ	1 161.4	5 933	137	2 433	1 439.8	102.5	449	7 408	1 996.0	171.9	159	639	91.9	18.0

1. Merchant wholesalers, except manufacturers' sales branches and offices.

Area name	Professional, scientific, and technical services, 2012				Manufacturing, 2012				Accommodation and food services, 2012			
	Number of establishments	Number of employees	Sales (mil dol)	Annual payroll (mil dol)	Number of establishments	Number of employees	Sales (mil dol)	Annual payroll (mil dol)	Number of establishments	Number of employees	Sales (mil dol)	Annual payroll (mil dol)
	147	148	149	150	151	152	153	154	155	156	157	158
Texarkana, TX-AR	208	1 126	118.7	38.6	99	5 410	2 601.2	308.5	270	5 616	260.2	74.3
The Villages, FL	128	500	53.9	21.0	36	942	461.9	40.7	106	2 464	117.2	35.9
Toledo, OH	1 127	D	D	D	732	35 417	35 387.1	2 068.8	1 420	26 503	1 122.3	320.8
Topeka, KS	517	D	D	D	131	5 986	2 893.2	270.6	434	D	D	D
Trenton, NJ	1 591	21 394	5 318.1	2 127.7	246	7 070	2 220.3	378.2	812	11 894	731.4	201.0
Tucson, AZ	2 531	16 514	2 241.1	940.0	640	24 297	8 686.6	1 906.7	1 787	42 311	2 154.7	637.4
Tulsa, OK	2 808	D	D	D	1 317	52 150	24 817.4	2 774.6	1 901	37 592	1 899.4	537.9
Tuscaloosa, AL	357	2 263	328.8	102.3	172	12 576	14 491.5	745.1	418	9 331	443.6	113.5
Tyler, TX	596	4 265	689.9	244.8	189	6 739	5 066.1	318.0	405	9 236	427.1	124.3
Urban Honolulu, HI	2 399	18 234	2 895.1	1 105.4	544	9 076	D	370.8	2 355	57 486	5 273.2	1 333.0
Utica-Rome, NY	469	3 829	573.9	215.9	296	12 368	4 147.5	581.4	727	12 339	862.6	219.5
Valdosta, GA	239	1 235	144.3	51.3	103	3 263	2 683.6	142.3	322	5 907	255.2	68.6
Vallejo-Fairfield, CA	547	3 258	415.3	150.6	259	9 266	11 412.2	558.9	711	11 129	625.6	163.2
Victoria, TX	173	899	118.4	42.6	77	2 090	2 172.9	136.0	204	3 702	192.7	50.8
Vineland-Bridgeton, NJ	207	D	D	D	162	8 055	2 812.0	351.2	265	3 555	173.7	43.6
Virginia Beach-Norfolk-Newport News, VA-NC	4 187	51 649	9 454.7	3 521.0	847	54 304	15 652.6	2 873.8	3 805	74 606	3 885.1	1 062.9
Visalia-Porterville, CA	407	D	D	D	237	11 412	8 362.4	538.0	568	8 540	451.9	118.1
Waco, TX	377	2 607	337.8	140.5	240	14 284	6 478.1	682.2	502	9 682	475.4	130.6
Walla Walla, WA	117	459	46.0	17.6	137	3 450	1 773.2	159.6	147	1 998	95.8	28.4
Warner Robins, GA	312	3 445	450.1	174.3	85	5 334	2 785.0	216.8	343	6 719	310.2	80.9
Washington-Arlington-Alexandria, DC-VA-MD-WV	30 747	517 949	125 259.6	49 288.9	2 091	49 219	15 671.4	3 030.8	12 138	247 606	17 932.2	4 868.0
Silver Spring-Frederick-Rockville, MD Div 43524	6 546	80 941	15 488.5	7 179.1	544	14 259	5 408.7	974.0	2 259	39 978	2 529.6	701.8
Washington-Arlington-Alexandria, DC-VA-MD-WV Div 47894	24 201	437 008	109 771.1	42 109.9	1 547	34 961	10 262.7	2 056.8	9 879	207 628	15 402.6	4 166.1
Waterloo-Cedar Falls, IA	280	3 998	310.2	210.6	213	15 285	10 703.1	762.0	370	7 330	342.8	91.2
Watertown-Fort Drum, NY	142	1 092	115.9	45.4	66	2 247	770.5	102.6	335	4 117	198.8	57.0
Wausau, WI	225	1 943	284.9	113.9	238	14 472	4 306.0	654.1	305	4 458	180.7	51.8
Weirton-Steubenville, WV-OH	155	D	D	D	77	5 822	3 877.9	314.9	276	4 415	375.3	63.3
Wenatchee, WA	217	1 070	116.2	45.4	109	2 005	635.0	99.6	341	4 174	233.2	73.2
Wheeling, WV-OH	268	2 501	287.4	105.6	106	2 887	981.8	117.4	322	6 150	371.3	85.2
Wichita, KS	1 350	11 334	1 676.4	603.6	687	46 169	23 736.2	2 589.4	1 320	25 323	1 163.6	321.8
Wichita Falls, TX	250	1 551	212.3	72.3	142	5 114	1 434.9	238.1	286	D	D	D
Williamsport, PA	200	2 151	184.5	74.5	160	8 162	3 186.7	371.5	296	4 696	237.9	62.6
Wilmington, NC	937	5 852	1 090.5	295.5	207	5 268	2 640.9	349.5	746	13 951	673.8	185.5
Winchester, VA-WV	269	1 885	178.2	85.7	119	6 864	3 469.8	346.3	294	5 209	255.3	68.9
Winston-Salem, NC	1 288	8 118	1 077.1	446.8	671	26 926	18 915.9	1 212.5	1 133	20 985	989.5	278.5
Worcester, MA-CT	1 945	D	D	D	1 132	40 227	12 621.8	2 273.0	1 956	27 526	1 425.5	400.0
Yakima, WA	319	2 023	193.3	80.5	232	8 152	2 622.2	327.3	416	5 364	281.5	79.8
York-Hanover, PA	705	5 671	635.2	279.4	568	31 890	11 489.4	1 602.6	791	13 391	593.3	165.9
Youngstown-Warren-Boardman, OH-PA	917	5 807	560.3	218.3	730	31 925	14 956.5	1 845.3	1 140	24 546	1 101.8	309.3
Yuba City, CA	204	978	118.4	46.1	100	2 091	650.7	99.0	224	3 374	171.4	44.9
Yuma, AZ	221	1 364	132.3	68.0	68	2 084	884.3	79.8	329	5 736	307.5	76.2

Area name	Health care and social assistance, 2012				Other services, 2012				Nonemployer business, 2015		Value of residential construction authorized by building permits, 2016	
	Number of establishments	Number of employees	Receipts (mil dol)	Annual payroll (mil dol)	Number of establishments	Number of employees	Receipts (mil dol)	Annual payroll (mil dol)	Number	Receipts (mil dol)	New construction ($1,000)	Number of housing units
	159	160	161	162	163	164	165	166	167	168	169	170
Texarkana, TX-AR	370	8 528	889.6	333.1	212	1 253	110.7	32.9	8 300	364.9	20 816	129
The Villages, FL	146	2 956	381.2	123.8	64	304	22.2	6.7	6 006	251.6	308 368	1 072
Toledo, OH	1 611	45 338	4 689.0	1 918.0	1 012	6 823	597.0	174.5	35 200	1 529.9	202 449	827
Topeka, KS	609	19 147	1 803.3	791.6	449	3 859	347.5	108.9	13 051	551.7	73 924	388
Trenton, NJ	1 165	28 970	2 981.0	1 326.6	815	6 403	1 245.5	239.1	24 347	1 353.3	81 894	711
Tucson, AZ	2 777	56 539	6 617.5	2 441.8	1 483	10 691	1 008.6	281.2	64 179	2 556.9	693 032	2 466
Tulsa, OK	2 640	57 324	6 459.5	2 399.4	1 479	9 217	1 253.9	281.4	72 114	3 390.1	666 769	3 752
Tuscaloosa, AL	479	14 351	1 485.8	644.6	259	1 660	154.9	43.1	13 552	590.5	233 657	1 465
Tyler, TX	640	21 211	2 527.9	969.6	347	2 613	252.8	87.5	18 125	911.4	149 444	581
Urban Honolulu, HI	2 520	50 049	6 302.6	2 481.0	2 012	14 967	1 522.4	411.8	64 258	3 187.6	641 470	1 658
Utica-Rome, NY	724	21 377	1 820.7	801.3	501	4 229	251.1	82.6	15 435	619.5	49 400	234
Valdosta, GA	400	8 078	828.5	305.9	174	1 111	78.5	22.0	8 566	413.2	172 732	1 018
Vallejo-Fairfield, CA	861	21 490	3 241.8	1 204.0	552	3 228	326.8	102.6	23 834	990.2	251 034	944
Victoria, TX	314	6 698	684.2	276.3	158	1 175	163.1	46.9	6 809	312.1	12 935	65
Vineland-Bridgeton, NJ	417	8 593	872.1	338.7	240	1 253	97.1	27.3	5 918	277.7	14 350	134
Virginia Beach-Norfolk-Newport News, VA-NC	3 558	88 360	9 916.7	4 051.8	2 792	18 235	2 070.9	534.5	99 469	3 999.6	1 011 272	6 213
Visalia-Porterville, CA	836	15 488	1 610.2	632.1	383	2 114	219.4	60.0	20 102	979.6	266 646	1 316
Waco, TX	574	17 072	1 527.0	641.3	379	2 408	236.0	65.4	15 865	727.5	225 374	1 765
Walla Walla, WA	171	4 358	455.3	204.5	88	D	D	D	3 465	145.0	46 652	220
Warner Robins, GA	351	7 250	654.0	264.3	181	983	79.5	22.9	12 195	378.9	163 061	839
Washington-Arlington-Alexandria, DC-VA-MD-WV ..	15 282	295 912	36 062.8	14 351.2	12 704	147 087	35 947.3	8 469.9	526 235	24 307.8	4 317 156	25 687
Silver Spring-Frederick-Rockville, MD Div 43524	4 197	73 187	8 433.4	3 585.4	2 317	21 946	4 674.0	1 095.5	NA	NA	764 596	4 076
Washington-Arlington-Alexandria, DC-VA-MD-WV Div 47894	11 085	222 725	27 629.4	10 765.8	10 387	125 141	31 273.3	7 374.5	NA	NA	3 552 560	21 611
Waterloo-Cedar Falls, IA	446	12 695	1 142.7	482.3	309	1 779	161.8	43.2	9 882	441.3	95 552	551
Watertown-Fort Drum, NY	277	6 183	536.8	247.5	187	912	83.3	21.0	5 164	206.7	12 454	105
Wausau, WI	367	10 123	1 133.0	459.7	221	1 313	138.5	37.7	7 863	385.9	59 611	245
Weirton-Steubenville, WV-OH	295	7 787	682.8	262.3	179	953	64.5	18.5	5 254	185.5	9 226	35
Wenatchee, WA	285	6 275	701.9	314.4	205	720	79.7	19.0	6 250	273.4	124 555	574
Wheeling, WV-OH	521	12 959	1 076.5	427.5	291	1 936	174.3	45.2	6 826	283.9	6 711	34
Wichita, KS	1 710	42 014	4 111.4	1 693.2	983	6 533	748.0	191.4	40 305	1 792.0	365 859	2 098
Wichita Falls, TX	414	11 201	1 080.1	404.4	242	1 300	124.4	32.5	9 416	442.8	38 930	226
Williamsport, PA	287	8 233	825.8	345.7	240	1 546	152.8	35.4	6 254	281.5	20 313	93
Wilmington, NC	845	13 790	1 374.7	550.2	495	2 759	244.2	70.6	24 089	1 118.9	547 065	2 947
Winchester, VA-WV	383	8 763	1 051.5	423.6	215	1 204	101.6	30.6	8 903	390.2	166 319	882
Winston-Salem, NC	1 155	39 069	3 997.0	1 523.5	848	4 224	485.5	115.3	45 251	1 787.9	410 580	2 727
Worcester, MA-CT	2 274	67 479	6 940.7	3 070.9	1 518	8 318	808.2	227.2	58 294	2 860.9	320 758	1 623
Yakima, WA	557	12 903	1 431.4	574.7	281	1 449	130.9	34.3	9 242	429.4	102 684	422
York-Hanover, PA	924	24 161	2 604.4	1 031.9	783	5 242	651.3	139.7	25 875	1 231.5	156 288	878
Youngstown-Warren-Boardman, OH-PA	1 755	40 695	3 681.2	1 454.5	946	5 527	442.5	117.9	34 325	1 463.8	79 884	466
Yuba City, CA	329	5 566	789.3	253.2	155	724	67.1	20.7	8 862	495.0	62 750	261
Yuma, AZ	359	7 092	794.1	282.4	194	1 099	77.8	25.0	8 910	341.6	138 205	897

1. Establishments subject to federal tax.

Table C. Metropolitan Areas — Government Employment and Payroll and Local Government Finances

			Government employment and payroll, 2012							Local government finances, 2012				
			March payroll (percent of total)							General revenue				
												Taxes		
													Per capita[1] (dollars)	
Area name	Full-time equivalent employees	March Payroll (dollars)	Administration, judicial, and legal	Police and corrections	Fire protection	Highways and transportation	Health and welfare	Natural resources and utilities	Education and libraries	Total (mil dol)	Inter-governmental (mil dol)	Total (mil dol)	Total	Property
	171	172	173	174	175	176	177	178	179	180	181	182	183	184
Texarkana, TX-AR	6 292	19 132 215	5.6	9.2	3.4	2.8	3.9	5.8	68.2	458.1	217.9	156.0	1 042	715
The Villages, FL	1 509	4 669 736	4.3	3.1	1.1	6.4	1.4	4.3	72.3	251.5	43.7	105.9	1 042	834
Toledo, OH	20 923	85 663 164	9.0	10.9	7.2	4.7	9.5	5.3	52.3	2 794.2	1 171.7	1 080.1	1 774	1 098
Topeka, KS	10 897	35 463 350	4.3	10.3	3.4	3.2	2.7	5.2	70.1	954.7	354.8	369.2	1 574	1 171
Trenton, NJ	15 352	84 285 619	4.4	12.4	3.3	2.0	4.4	4.9	64.8	2 164.5	711.0	1 168.1	3 172	3 117
Tucson, AZ	31 634	115 785 276	10.5	14.5	6.6	3.5	2.2	7.1	52.9	3 257.1	1 214.5	1 427.3	1 438	1 057
Tulsa, OK	33 451	106 348 173	5.8	9.5	5.7	4.2	2.6	6.1	63.2	2 858.0	992.1	1 256.0	1 319	714
Tuscaloosa, AL	11 519	40 376 521	3.7	7.3	3.3	3.6	45.3	3.8	32.1	1 108.1	293.7	229.4	983	397
Tyler, TX	8 764	29 028 100	7.6	10.8	2.8	1.5	6.8	3.6	65.8	648.3	207.0	325.4	1 515	1 170
Urban Honolulu, HI	9 304	47 881 176	14.1	35.4	14.0	2.6	6.8	20.8	0.0	2 232.4	331.8	1 316.4	1 348	833
Utica-Rome, NY	13 622	60 609 793	5.4	11.3	5.5	6.7	5.6	4.7	59.5	1 597.5	779.4	603.1	2 024	1 388
Valdosta, GA	7 094	22 829 566	3.5	7.5	1.9	1.7	36.8	2.6	44.7	654.5	164.9	169.0	1 171	661
Vallejo-Fairfield, CA	14 386	72 410 858	7.6	13.9	3.4	2.8	9.9	7.1	53.4	1 896.3	937.5	594.6	1 413	1 051
Victoria, TX	5 691	19 191 140	4.0	10.2	2.9	1.9	29.7	3.0	47.2	483.0	112.9	173.9	1 800	1 367
Vineland-Bridgeton, NJ	7 697	36 180 326	5.2	9.1	0.8	1.2	4.3	5.3	72.5	886.9	544.0	234.1	1 483	1 435
Virginia Beach-Norfolk-Newport News, VA-NC	78 042	285 080 100	5.2	9.8	4.7	2.6	8.9	7.9	57.4	7 361.3	2 849.8	2 945.6	1 733	1 190
Visalia-Porterville, CA	21 502	97 324 423	4.7	7.2	1.7	1.1	30.4	3.5	50.1	3 132.9	1 499.7	450.9	998	665
Waco, TX	11 156	37 341 296	5.7	11.3	3.0	2.0	4.2	8.5	64.1	1 218.5	462.8	380.3	1 484	1 179
Walla Walla, WA	2 119	9 087 256	8.5	10.7	5.3	6.5	9.7	4.4	51.5	269.2	118.5	82.8	1 307	907
Warner Robins, GA	6 945	22 535 113	5.6	9.7	2.9	2.1	4.2	3.2	70.2	591.5	229.4	253.3	1 365	800
Washington-Arlington-Alexandria, DC-VA-MD-WV	238 082	1 225 240 040	6.3	10.4	4.1	8.1	7.2	5.9	54.7	35 371.1	10 257.7	19 074.9	3 255	1 833
Silver Spring-Frederick-Rockville, MD Div 43524	49 143	284 578 074	3.5	7.4	4.0	2.8	6.0	9.5	65.7	6 273.9	1 440.7	3 712.4	2 984	1 415
Washington-Arlington-Alexandria, DC-VA-MD-WV Div 47894	188 939	940 661 966	7.1	11.3	4.2	9.7	7.5	4.8	51.4	29 097.2	8 817.0	15 362.6	3 328	1 946
Waterloo-Cedar Falls, IA	5 986	22 105 854	5.2	9.3	3.5	4.9	8.6	9.6	56.3	779.9	309.2	283.0	1 677	1 331
Watertown-Fort Drum, NY	5 239	20 682 670	6.0	6.1	2.2	6.7	6.7	3.0	66.9	631.5	312.9	217.3	1 807	1 154
Wausau, WI	5 721	22 517 091	4.6	6.0	1.9	5.6	19.3	2.6	59.4	701.3	346.1	232.0	1 722	1 622
Weirton-Steubenville, WV-OH	4 496	13 800 652	7.0	10.6	2.3	5.5	8.0	7.2	56.9	422.2	201.3	126.9	1 036	755
Wenatchee, WA	4 724	22 972 485	4.8	6.6	2.1	5.8	6.9	31.1	41.1	513.2	239.9	153.9	1 361	918
Wheeling, WV-OH	5 774	18 658 082	6.6	9.0	3.0	7.2	6.7	13.1	53.0	499.7	202.4	181.6	1 241	837
Wichita, KS	24 964	87 029 872	6.0	10.7	4.3	3.5	5.1	4.4	64.0	2 420.1	936.4	884.7	1 391	1 088
Wichita Falls, TX	6 724	21 253 583	6.4	13.3	6.1	3.0	9.1	5.3	54.1	453.8	154.7	207.0	1 372	1 062
Williamsport, PA	3 615	14 906 594	7.7	7.9	1.8	4.3	2.7	6.0	68.7	451.3	198.0	155.7	1 329	953
Wilmington, NC	13 583	50 754 541	2.9	7.0	2.4	1.1	45.2	4.5	33.4	1 618.1	350.1	385.0	1 461	1 059
Winchester, VA-WV	5 411	16 715 382	6.8	13.2	4.1	1.2	2.9	3.6	66.6	418.3	170.3	190.4	1 454	1 027
Winston-Salem, NC	1 023 990	75 606 649	4.5	8.8	4.0	1.2	8.6	5.0	65.1	1 918.0	964.0	681.2	1 052	828
Worcester, MA-CT	32 279	147 826 569	3.6	7.7	4.7	3.3	1.4	4.3	74.0	3 495.3	1 632.4	1 503.7	1 628	1 589
Yakima, WA	8 019	34 900 911	7.0	10.7	3.2	2.8	3.3	5.9	66.0	970.4	601.4	232.4	941	607
York-Hanover, PA	12 293	50 416 660	6.7	12.2	1.5	2.7	6.3	3.6	64.5	1 771.5	572.5	787.5	1 799	1 467
Youngstown-Warren-Boardman, OH-PA	20 254	71 750 350	7.4	10.2	3.8	3.6	7.7	6.8	59.4	1 994.8	1 016.8	698.5	1 251	866
Yuba City, CA	6 669	32 864 622	7.3	8.3	2.0	2.2	10.3	3.3	64.0	941.7	532.4	189.6	1 129	918
Yuma, AZ	7 924	25 609 990	12.0	12.1	3.1	2.2	2.4	7.3	59.9	638.9	314.0	221.6	1 108	716

1. Based on the resident population estimated as of July 1 of the year shown.

Table C. Metropolitan Areas — Local Government Finances, Government Employment, and Income Taxes

Area name	Local government finances, 2012 (cont.)									Government employment, 2015			Individual income tax returns, 2014		
	Direct general expenditure							Debt outstanding							
			Percent of total for:												
	Total (mil dol)	Per capita[1] (dollars)	Education	Health and hospitals	Police protection	Public welfare	Highways	Total (mil dol)	Per capita[1] (dollars)	Federal civilian	Federal military	State and local	Number of returns	Mean Adjusted Gross income	Mean income tax
	185	186	187	188	189	190	191	192	193	194	195	196	197	198	199
Texarkana, TX-AR	437.3	2 921	59.2	2.4	5.9	1.0	4.9	430.1	2 873	4 310	437	9 086	62 570	47 848	5 341
The Villages, FL	263.4	2 592	27.3	1.6	6.0	0.5	7.8	594.1	5 846	1 611	203	2 962	52 270	72 195	10 493
Toledo, OH	2 631.6	4 323	42.5	7.5	6.3	6.1	4.2	2 796.0	4 593	2 142	1 624	42 744	285 340	53 252	6 267
Topeka, KS	921.3	3 928	54.3	2.2	6.2	0.2	4.0	1 441.3	6 144	3 657	1 020	23 845	110 230	52 663	5 756
Trenton, NJ	2 145.5	5 825	52.3	0.9	5.3	4.3	1.4	1 928.9	5 237	2 364	741	38 770	173 960	90 837	15 098
Tucson, AZ	3 531.8	3 559	37.0	3.1	9.1	2.7	5.3	5 788.9	5 833	12 506	8 041	67 320	434 040	54 350	6 327
Tulsa, OK	2 829.0	2 972	48.0	4.0	5.9	0.6	8.2	3 865.4	4 061	4 650	3 731	49 897	426 840	66 828	9 124
Tuscaloosa, AL	1 116.2	4 783	30.5	41.4	4.7	0.0	5.1	682.1	2 923	1 900	1 020	24 384	95 450	51 775	5 882
Tyler, TX	645.1	3 003	55.0	5.1	5.6	0.2	3.4	1 145.0	5 330	631	468	13 278	97 400	60 868	8 396
Urban Honolulu, HI	1 596.7	1 635	0.0	1.5	15.2	0.0	7.8	5 300.0	5 428	30 403	55 136	68 941	483 720	60 995	7 170
Utica-Rome, NY	1 653.0	5 546	53.3	2.7	2.8	10.6	6.2	1 633.5	5 480	2 350	501	27 768	132 510	49 107	5 157
Valdosta, GA	724.2	5 017	28.8	47.7	4.1	0.7	2.5	413.2	2 862	1 165	4 620	11 726	56 070	41 960	4 302
Vallejo-Fairfield, CA	1 873.8	4 454	35.1	6.1	9.3	7.8	4.2	1 624.0	3 860	3 765	6 808	20 558	199 140	60 907	6 714
Victoria, TX	470.7	4 872	36.4	29.6	5.8	0.0	7.0	443.6	4 591	209	207	6 825	45 640	66 537	10 064
Vineland-Bridgeton, NJ	880.4	5 580	60.1	2.7	3.8	3.4	2.5	354.4	2 246	632	294	12 698	67 710	45 541	4 300
Virginia Beach-Norfolk-Newport News, VA-NC	7 765.7	4 568	42.7	6.6	4.8	4.0	3.4	9 372.3	5 513	56 517	85 855	105 379	809 590	57 419	6 547
Visalia-Porterville, CA	3 186.6	7 050	39.0	24.4	3.2	8.0	4.7	1 380.8	3 055	1 055	690	30 131	173 730	42 428	4 129
Waco, TX	1 187.0	4 631	42.3	2.5	5.0	0.6	1.8	11 603.4	45 270	3 053	604	15 479	110 950	50 081	5 817
Walla Walla, WA	257.4	4 061	43.0	9.4	5.8	0.0	7.2	267.1	4 213	1 332	165	4 709	26 890	55 558	6 412
Warner Robins, GA	571.7	3 082	54.7	6.0	6.4	0.1	5.0	263.3	1 419	14 901	3 891	12 093	82 310	49 638	4 801
Washington-Arlington-Alexandria, DC-VA-MD-WV	35 473.9	6 053	40.6	3.4	5.3	10.4	3.3	44 210.4	7 544	380 384	65 072	324 064	3 005 260	88 133	13 440
Silver Spring-Frederick-Rockville, MD Div 43524	6 498.3	5 222	51.5	1.7	5.2	3.2	3.5	7 084.9	5 694	51 121	9 926	54 041	NA	NA	NA
Washington-Arlington-Alexandria, DC-VA-MD-WV Div 47894	28 975.7	6 277	38.1	3.8	5.3	12.0	3.3	37 125.5	8 043	329 263	55 146	270 023	NA	NA	NA
Waterloo-Cedar Falls, IA	855.9	5 072	49.6	11.0	4.2	0.3	7.5	561.2	3 325	629	641	14 035	77 090	58 416	6 615
Watertown-Fort Drum, NY	631.0	5 247	49.6	3.4	2.6	9.2	6.9	554.7	4 612	3 168	15 779	8 370	52 390	45 482	4 274
Wausau, WI	710.6	5 274	41.9	10.2	3.9	18.8	7.9	440.9	3 273	433	361	7 598	67 140	57 287	7 008
Weirton-Steubenville, WV-OH	426.7	3 482	52.1	4.9	6.0	2.5	5.9	341.9	2 790	253	412	5 367	56 210	46 829	4 869
Wenatchee, WA	488.0	4 317	47.1	12.8	4.5	0.0	5.8	1 944.4	17 202	857	314	8 046	54 670	56 728	7 023
Wheeling, WV-OH	488.4	3 335	43.9	3.2	5.0	2.6	4.4	552.7	3 775	603	509	9 124	66 940	56 668	7 404
Wichita, KS	2 506.2	3 940	49.5	4.3	5.3	0.1	5.5	6 729.7	10 580	4 880	5 286	36 592	293 550	62 189	8 027
Wichita Falls, TX	440.1	2 918	47.9	5.2	7.0	0.7	4.4	688.7	4 566	1 944	4 619	10 431	62 630	56 202	7 156
Williamsport, PA	560.5	4 783	43.8	0.0	2.2	3.1	4.4	997.6	8 514	356	293	8 957	54 980	50 198	5 465
Wilmington, NC	1 610.9	6 115	23.7	45.2	4.9	2.9	1.0	1 660.3	6 303	1 028	879	21 590	124 510	60 111	8 025
Winchester, VA-WV	404.5	3 090	60.9	0.7	5.4	3.3	1.5	564.7	4 314	1 991	466	7 307	62 000	56 977	6 472
Winston-Salem, NC	2 021.7	3 121	49.9	5.3	7.8	4.7	1.7	1 785.1	2 756	2 048	1 589	29 857	291 030	55 481	6 680
Worcester, MA-CT	3 721.4	4 029	62.3	0.4	3.9	0.2	3.5	2 671.4	2 892	3 275	2 202	56 571	446 690	66 857	8 762
Yakima, WA	1 052.2	4 260	60.9	3.2	4.2	0.8	4.9	606.3	2 455	1 245	802	16 036	107 840	47 135	5 284
York-Hanover, PA	1 790.5	4 089	47.4	3.5	3.3	9.2	2.6	2 454.1	5 605	4 136	1 306	16 010	219 430	56 561	6 387
Youngstown-Warren-Boardman, OH-PA	2 023.9	3 626	53.2	5.1	6.2	4.2	4.0	1 224.6	2 194	1 941	1 431	27 712	266 510	47 079	5 143
Yuba City, CA	962.8	5 733	49.2	5.2	4.2	8.2	2.8	640.8	3 816	1 573	4 472	9 349	66 230	47 532	4 482
Yuma, AZ	616.3	3 081	47.8	2.1	6.0	2.5	4.6	668.5	3 342	3 465	4 265	10 922	82 770	39 369	3 414

1. Based on the resident population estimated as of July 1 of the year shown.

Cities of 25,000 or More

(For explanation of symbols, see page viii)

City Highlights and Rankings

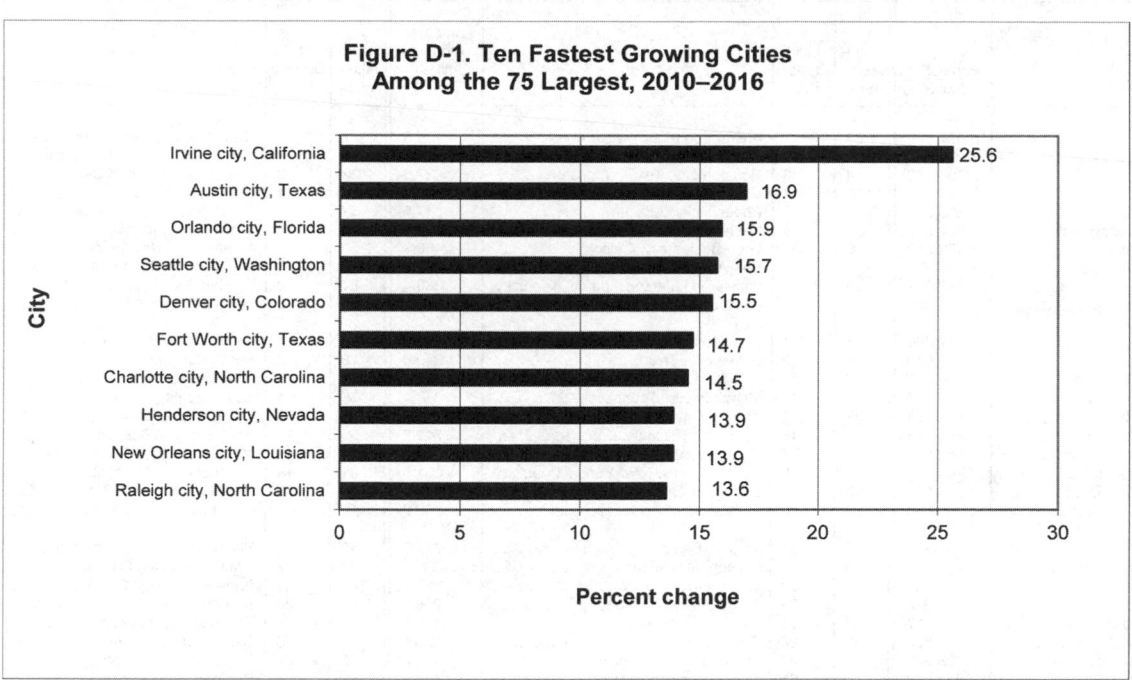

Figure D-1. Ten Fastest Growing Cities Among the 75 Largest, 2010–2016

(Percent change, by city)

- Irvine city, California: 25.6
- Austin city, Texas: 16.9
- Orlando city, Florida: 15.9
- Seattle city, Washington: 15.7
- Denver city, Colorado: 15.5
- Fort Worth city, Texas: 14.7
- Charlotte city, North Carolina: 14.5
- Henderson city, Nevada: 13.9
- New Orleans city, Louisiana: 13.9
- Raleigh city, North Carolina: 13.6

In 2016, 10 cities had more than 1 million residents, led by New York City with over 8.5 million people, Los Angeles with nearly 4.0 million people, and Chicago with 2.7 million people. California had 15 cities among the nation's 75 most populous, as well as 4 among the top 15 (Los Angeles, San Diego, San Jose, and San Francisco). Texas had 9 cities in the top 75, and also had 4 among the top 15 (Houston, San Antonio, Dallas, and Austin).

Among the largest cities, 47 had growth rates equaling 5 percent or higher from 2010 to 2016 and twenty two had growth rates exceeding 10 percent. Many of these cities were in the south. Irvine, CA had the highest growth rate at 25.6 percent. Texas had two cities in the top ten (Austin and Fort Worth), as did North Carolina (Charlotte, Raleigh). Forty-nine of the largest cities equaled or exceeded the U.S. growth rate of 4.7 percent. Among the 75 largest cities, six lost population between 2010 and 2016. Detroit lost nearly 6 percent of its population while St. Louis, Cleveland, and Toledo each lost between 2.5 and 3 percent.

New Orleans, with a 13.9 percent increase, was among the top ten cities for population growth. Though New Orleans lost 29.1 percent of its population between 2000 and 2010, it actually grew by nearly two-thirds between 2006 and 2010, after losing more than half of its population after Hurricane Katrina in 2005. It was the eighth fastest growing city from 2010 to 2016, but its 2016 population is still more than 63,000 short of its pre-Katrina total.

Among all cities of 25,000 or more, 20 cities had unemployment rates of 10 percent or more, significantly lower than six years earlier, when 555 cities had unemployment rates of 10 percent or more. Twelve of the twenty-five cities with the highest unemployment rates were located in California, three were in Michigan, two each were in Arizona, Illinois, Texas, and New Jersey while New Mexico and Louisiana each had one. Among the largest cities, Detroit, MI had the highest unemployment rate at 10.9 percent followed by Fresno, CA at 10.2 percent. Irvine, CA and Lincoln, NE had the lowest unemployment rates at 3.0 percent and 2.8 percent respectively. Among all cities, 475 had unemployment rates of 4.0 percent or lower. Three of the ten cities with the lowest unemployment rates were in North Dakota and two were in Iowa.

While the 2010 census provides updated counts of the population and basic demographic characteristics, updated information on social and economic characteristics is now obtained through the ongoing American Community Survey (ACS). For states, counties, and metropolitan areas, the official intercensal estimates are provided by age, sex, race, and Hispanic origin through the Population Estimates Program. Estimates of these demographic characteristics are not included for cities through the Population Estimates Program, but are available through the ACS. This book includes ACS 1-year estimates for 2015, including data on education, income, housing characteristics, and more.

Among the largest cities, Irvine, San Francisco, and San Jose were the top three for both median income and median housing value. Seattle, Washington, DC, and San Diego also ranked in the top ten for both median income and housing value. Plano, TX ranked fourth for median household income, but its median housing value ranked only 25th among the large cities. Los Angeles and New York ranked 7th and 8th for median housing value, but their median household incomes ranked 32nd and 25th among large cities. San Francisco tops the ranking with an estimated median housing value of $941,400. Detroit had the lowest median housing value among the large cities in 2015, at $42,600.

Among the 75 largest cities in 2015, there were five cities where 10 percent or more of residents had moved from another state or county within the previous year. This may result from population growth: Irvine, CA had one of the highest growth rates in recent years as well as one of the highest proportions of people who had moved there in the past year. Other cities have large shifts because of student or military population groups: Pittsburgh, PA lost .7 percent of its population from 2010 to 2016 but 9.1 percent of its population were new residents in 2015, reflecting the 17.7 percent of residents who were between the ages of 18 and 24, well above the 9.5 percent national average.

75 Largest Cities by 2016 Population
Selected rankings

Popu-lation rank	City (Population, 2014)	Population [col 2]	Popu-lation rank	Land area rank	City (Land area, 2016)	Land area (square miles) [col 1]	Popu-lation rank	Density rank	City (Population density, 2016)	Density (per square mile) [col 4]
1	New York city, New York	8 537 673	66	1	Anchorage municipality, Alaska	1 706.6	1	1	New York city, New York	28 317
2	Los Angeles city, California	3 976 322	12	2	Jacksonville city, Florida	747.4	13	2	San Francisco city, California	18 569
3	Chicago city, Illinois	2 704 958	4	3	Houston city, Texas	637.5	22	3	Boston city, Massachusetts	13 938
4	Houston city, Texas	2 303 482	27	4	Oklahoma City city, Oklahoma	606.3	42	4	Miami city, Florida	12 599
5	Phoenix city, Arizona	1 615 017	5	5	Phoenix city, Arizona	517.6	57	5	Santa Ana city, California	12 333
6	Philadelphia city, Pennsylvania	1 567 872	24	6	Nashville-Davidson, Tennessee	504.0	3	6	Chicago city, Illinois	11 900
7	San Antonio city, Texas	1 492 510	2	7	Los Angeles city, California	468.7	70	7	Newark city, New Jersey	11 692
8	San Diego city, California	1 406 630	7	8	San Antonio city, Texas	461.0	6	8	Philadelphia city, Pennsylvania	11 683
9	Dallas city, Texas	1 317 929	29	9	Louisville/Jefferson County, Kentucky	380.4	21	9	Washington city, District of Columbia	11 148
10	San Jose city, California	1 025 350	15	10	Indianapolis city, Indiana	366.5	39	10	Long Beach city, California	9 347
11	Austin city, Texas	947 890	16	11	Fort Worth city, Texas	342.9	2	11	Los Angeles city, California	8 484
12	Jacksonville city, Florida	880 619	9	12	Dallas city, Texas	340.9	18	12	Seattle city, Washington	8 405
13	San Francisco city, California	870 887	8	13	San Diego city, California	325.2	46	13	Minneapolis city, Minnesota	7 660
14	Columbus city, Ohio	860 090	25	14	Memphis city, Tennessee	317.4	30	14	Baltimore city, Maryland	7 598
15	Indianapolis city, Indiana	855 164	37	15	Kansas City city, Missouri	315.0	45	15	Oakland city, California	7 514
16	Fort Worth city, Texas	854 113	11	16	Austin city, Texas	312.7	56	16	Anaheim city, California	7 021
17	Charlotte city, North Carolina	842 051	17	17	Charlotte city, North Carolina	305.4	31	17	Milwaukee city, Wisconsin	6 186
18	Seattle city, Washington	704 352	1	18	New York city, New York	301.5	64	18	St. Paul city, Minnesota	5 815
19	Denver city, Colorado	693 060	60	19	Lexington-Fayette, Kentucky	283.6	55	19	Urban Honolulu CDP, Hawaii	5 815
20	El Paso city, Texas	683 080	20	20	El Paso city, Texas	256.8	10	20	San Jose city, California	5 777
21	Washington city, District of Columbia	681 170	43	21	Virginia Beach city, Virginia	244.7	63	21	Pittsburgh city, Pennsylvania	5 481
22	Boston city, Massachusetts	673 184	33	22	Tucson city, Arizona	230.8	74	22	Chula Vista city, California	5 387
23	Detroit city, Michigan	672 795	3	23	Chicago city, Illinois	227.3	35	23	Sacramento city, California	5 059
24	Nashville-Davidson, Tennessee	660 388	14	24	Columbus city, Ohio	218.5	61	24	St. Louis city, Missouri	5 023
25	Memphis city, Tennessee	652 717	47	25	Tulsa city, Oklahoma	196.8	62	25	Stockton city, California	4 977
26	Portland city, Oregon	639 863	40	26	Colorado Springs city, Colorado	195.6	51	26	Cleveland city, Ohio	4 965
27	Oklahoma City city, Oklahoma	638 367	32	27	Albuquerque city, New Mexico	188.2	23	27	Detroit city, Michigan	4 847
28	Las Vegas city, Nevada	632 912	10	28	San Jose city, California	177.5	26	28	Portland city, Oregon	4 793
29	Louisville/Jefferson County, Kentucky	616 261	58	29	Corpus Christi city, Texas	174.6	28	29	Las Vegas city, Nevada	4 709
30	Baltimore city, Maryland	614 664	49	30	New Orleans city, Louisiana	169.4	34	30	Fresno city, California	4 563
31	Milwaukee city, Wisconsin	595 047	50	31	Wichita city, Kansas	160.4	19	31	Denver city, Colorado	4 521
32	Albuquerque city, New Mexico	559 277	54	32	Aurora city, Colorado	153.5	8	32	San Diego city, California	4 325
33	Tucson city, Arizona	530 706	19	33	Denver city, Colorado	153.3	48	33	Arlington city, Texas	4 100
34	Fresno city, California	522 053	53	34	Bakersfield city, California	148.8	75	34	Irvine city, California	4 057
35	Sacramento city, California	495 234	41	35	Raleigh city, North Carolina	145.1	59	35	Riverside city, California	3 999
36	Mesa city, Arizona	484 587	23	36	Detroit city, Michigan	138.8	69	36	Plano city, Texas	3 990
37	Kansas City city, Missouri	481 420	36	37	Mesa city, Arizona	137.9	14	37	Columbus city, Ohio	3 936
38	Atlanta city, Georgia	472 522	28	38	Las Vegas city, Nevada	134.4	9	38	Dallas city, Texas	3 866
39	Long Beach city, California	470 130	6	39	Philadelphia city, Pennsylvania	134.2	65	39	Cincinnati city, Ohio	3 861
40	Colorado Springs city, Colorado	465 101	26	40	Portland city, Oregon	133.5	4	40	Houston city, Texas	3 613
41	Raleigh city, North Carolina	458 880	38	40	Atlanta city, Georgia	133.5	38	41	Atlanta city, Georgia	3 540
42	Miami city, Florida	453 579	44	42	Omaha city, Nebraska	133.2	36	42	Mesa city, Arizona	3 514
43	Virginia Beach city, Virginia	452 602	68	43	Greensboro city, North Carolina	128.3	72	43	Toledo city, Ohio	3 451
44	Omaha city, Nebraska	446 970	34	44	Fresno city, California	114.4	44	44	Omaha city, Nebraska	3 356
45	Oakland city, California	420 005	52	45	Tampa city, Florida	113.4	52	45	Tampa city, Florida	3 326
46	Minneapolis city, Minnesota	413 651	73	46	Orlando city, Florida	105.2	7	46	San Antonio city, Texas	3 238
47	Tulsa city, Oklahoma	403 090	67	47	Henderson city, Nevada	104.7	41	47	Raleigh city, North Carolina	3 163
48	Arlington city, Texas	392 772	35	48	Sacramento city, California	97.9	5	48	Phoenix city, Arizona	3 120
49	New Orleans city, Louisiana	391 495	31	49	Milwaukee city, Wisconsin	96.2	71	49	Lincoln city, Nebraska	3 044
50	Wichita city, Kansas	389 902	48	50	Arlington city, Texas	95.8	11	50	Austin city, Texas	3 031
51	Cleveland city, Ohio	385 809	71	51	Lincoln city, Nebraska	92.1	32	51	Albuquerque city, New Mexico	2 972
52	Tampa city, Florida	377 165	18	52	Seattle city, Washington	83.8	67	52	Henderson city, Nevada	2 798
53	Bakersfield city, California	376 380	59	53	Riverside city, California	81.2	17	53	Charlotte city, North Carolina	2 757
54	Aurora city, Colorado	361 710	30	54	Baltimore city, Maryland	80.9	20	54	El Paso city, Texas	2 660
55	Urban Honolulu CDP, Hawaii	351 792	72	55	Toledo city, Ohio	80.7	73	55	Orlando city, Florida	2 635
56	Anaheim city, California	351 043	51	56	Cleveland city, Ohio	77.7	53	56	Bakersfield city, California	2 529
57	Santa Ana city, California	334 217	65	57	Cincinnati city, Ohio	77.4	16	57	Fort Worth city, Texas	2 491
58	Corpus Christi city, Texas	325 733	69	58	Plano city, Texas	71.7	50	58	Wichita city, Kansas	2 431
59	Riverside city, California	324 722	75	59	Irvine city, California	65.6	40	59	Colorado Springs city, Colorado	2 378
60	Lexington-Fayette, Kentucky	318 449	61	60	St. Louis city, Missouri	62.0	15	60	Indianapolis city, Indiana	2 366
61	St. Louis city, Missouri	311 404	62	61	Stockton city, California	61.7	54	61	Aurora city, Colorado	2 356
62	Stockton city, California	307 072	21	62	Washington city, District of Columbia	61.1	49	62	New Orleans city, Louisiana	2 311
63	Pittsburgh city, Pennsylvania	303 625	55	63	Urban Honolulu CDP, Hawaii	60.5	33	63	Tucson city, Arizona	2 299
64	St. Paul city, Minnesota	302 398	45	64	Oakland city, California	55.9	68	64	Greensboro city, North Carolina	2 237
65	Cincinnati city, Ohio	298 800	63	65	Pittsburgh city, Pennsylvania	55.4	25	65	Memphis city, Tennessee	2 056
66	Anchorage municipality, Alaska	298 192	46	66	Minneapolis city, Minnesota	54.0	47	66	Tulsa city, Oklahoma	2 048
67	Henderson city, Nevada	292 969	64	67	St. Paul city, Minnesota	52.0	29	67	Louisville/Jefferson County, Kentucky	1 896
68	Greensboro city, North Carolina	287 027	39	68	Long Beach city, California	50.3	58	68	Corpus Christi city, Texas	1 866
69	Plano city, Texas	286 057	56	69	Anaheim city, California	50.0	43	69	Virginia Beach city, Virginia	1 850
70	Newark city, New Jersey	281 764	74	70	Chula Vista city, California	49.6	37	70	Kansas City city, Missouri	1 528
71	Lincoln city, Nebraska	280 364	22	71	Boston city, Massachusetts	48.3	24	71	Nashville-Davidson, Tennessee	1 388
72	Toledo city, Ohio	278 508	13	72	San Francisco city, California	46.9	12	72	Jacksonville city, Florida	1 178
73	Orlando city, Florida	277 173	42	73	Miami city, Florida	36.0	60	73	Lexington-Fayette, Kentucky	1 123
74	Chula Vista city, California	267 172	57	74	Santa Ana city, California	27.1	27	74	Oklahoma City city, Oklahoma	1 053
75	Irvine city, California	266 122	70	75	Newark city, New Jersey	24.1	66	75	Anchorage municipality, Alaska	175

75 Largest Cities by 2016 Population
Selected rankings

	Percent population change, 2010–2016				Percent White alone, 2015				Percent Black alone, 2015		
Population rank	Percent change rank	City	Percent change [col 26]	Population rank	White rank	City	Percent White [col 5]	Population rank	Black rank	City	Percent Black [col 6]
75	1	Irvine city, California	25.6	58	1	Corpus Christi city, Texas	88.9	23	1	Detroit city, Michigan	79.5
11	2	Austin city, Texas	16.9	71	2	Lincoln city, Nebraska	85.6	25	2	Memphis city, Tennessee	63.3
73	3	Orlando city, Florida	15.9	20	3	El Paso city, Texas	84.6	30	3	Baltimore city, Maryland	61.6
18	4	Seattle city, Washington	15.7	36	4	Mesa city, Arizona	84.3	49	4	New Orleans city, Louisiana	59.2
19	5	Denver city, Colorado	15.5	7	5	San Antonio city, Texas	81.9	38	5	Atlanta city, Georgia	51.9
16	6	Fort Worth city, Texas	14.7	67	6	Henderson city, Nevada	78.8	51	6	Cleveland city, Ohio	50.7
17	7	Charlotte city, North Carolina	14.5	40	7	Colorado Springs city, Colorado	77.9	70	7	Newark city, New Jersey	50.2
49	8	New Orleans city, Louisiana	13.9	26	8	Portland city, Oregon	77.7	21	8	Washington city, District of Columbia	47.4
67	8	Henderson city, Nevada	13.9	19	8	Denver city, Colorado	77.1	61	9	St. Louis city, Missouri	46.6
41	10	Raleigh city, North Carolina	13.6	44	9	Omaha city, Nebraska	77.1	6	10	Philadelphia city, Pennsylvania	42.4
42	11	Miami city, Florida	13.5	60	11	Lexington-Fayette, Kentucky	75.9	65	11	Cincinnati city, Ohio	42.2
21	12	Washington city, District of Columbia	13.2	50	12	Wichita city, Kansas	75.7	68	12	Greensboro city, North Carolina	41.4
7	13	San Antonio city, Texas	12.4	42	13	Miami city, Florida	75.1	31	13	Milwaukee city, Wisconsin	38.8
38	13	Atlanta city, Georgia	12.4	11	14	Austin city, Texas	73.3	17	14	Charlotte city, North Carolina	34.5
52	15	Tampa city, Florida	12.3	33	15	Tucson city, Arizona	72.8	3	15	Chicago city, Illinois	31.1
5	16	Phoenix city, Arizona	11.6	56	16	Anaheim city, California	71.9	12	16	Jacksonville city, Florida	31.0
40	17	Colorado Springs city, Colorado	11.4	5	17	Phoenix city, Arizona	71.6	37	17	Kansas City city, Missouri	29.7
54	17	Aurora city, Colorado	11.4	29	18	Louisville/Jefferson County, Kentucky	71.4	41	18	Raleigh city, North Carolina	29.5
27	19	Oklahoma City city, Oklahoma	10.1	53	19	Bakersfield city, California	70.5	15	19	Indianapolis city, Indiana	27.9
36	19	Mesa city, Arizona	10.1	32	20	Albuquerque city, New Mexico	70.1	14	20	Columbus city, Ohio	27.8
69	19	Plano city, Texas	10.1	18	21	Seattle city, Washington	69.1	72	21	Toledo city, Ohio	27.4
9	22	Dallas city, Texas	10.0	52	22	Tampa city, Florida	67.7	24	22	Nashville-Davidson, Tennessee	27.3
4	23	Houston city, Texas	9.7	27	23	Oklahoma City city, Oklahoma	67.5	22	23	Boston city, Massachusetts	25.3
26	24	Portland city, Oregon	9.6	43	24	Virginia Beach city, Virginia	67.2	45	24	Oakland city, California	24.9
74	25	Chula Vista city, California	9.5	69	25	Plano city, Texas	66.9	63	25	Pittsburgh city, Pennsylvania	24.3
24	26	Nashville-Davidson, Tennessee	9.4	16	26	Fort Worth city, Texas	66.2	1	26	New York city, New York	24.0
14	27	Columbus city, Ohio	9.0	74	27	Chula Vista city, California	65.3	9	27	Dallas city, Texas	23.8
22	27	Boston city, Massachusetts	9.0	63	28	Pittsburgh city, Pennsylvania	65.2	73	28	Orlando city, Florida	23.6
71	29	Lincoln city, Nebraska	8.5	59	29	Riverside city, California	65.0	52	29	Tampa city, Florida	23.4
28	30	Las Vegas city, Nevada	8.3	28	30	Las Vegas city, Nevada	64.3	48	30	Arlington city, Texas	22.9
53	30	Bakersfield city, California	8.3	8	31	San Diego city, California	63.9	29	31	Louisville/Jefferson County, Kentucky	22.5
13	32	San Francisco city, California	8.2	73	32	Orlando city, Florida	63.7	4	32	Houston city, Texas	22.3
8	33	San Diego city, California	8.1	24	33	Nashville-Davidson, Tennessee	63.5	46	33	Minneapolis city, Minnesota	19.7
46	33	Minneapolis city, Minnesota	8.1	46	34	Minneapolis city, Minnesota	63.4	43	34	Virginia Beach city, Virginia	19.6
60	35	Lexington-Fayette, Kentucky	7.7	15	35	Indianapolis city, Indiana	63.0	16	35	Fort Worth city, Texas	19.0
10	36	San Jose city, California	7.6	66	36	Anchorage municipality, Alaska	62.9	42	36	Miami city, Florida	18.9
48	37	Arlington city, Texas	7.5	47	37	Tulsa city, Oklahoma	62.8	64	37	St. Paul city, Minnesota	15.6
45	38	Oakland city, California	7.4	9	38	Dallas city, Texas	62.6	47	38	Tulsa city, Oklahoma	15.2
12	39	Jacksonville city, Florida	7.2	48	38	Arlington city, Texas	62.6	54	39	Aurora city, Colorado	14.8
59	40	Riverside city, California	6.8	72	40	Toledo city, Ohio	62.4	27	40	Oklahoma City city, Oklahoma	14.7
58	41	Corpus Christi city, Texas	6.7	54	41	Aurora city, Colorado	62.1	60	41	Lexington-Fayette, Kentucky	14.4
68	41	Greensboro city, North Carolina	6.7	14	42	Columbus city, Ohio	61.5	35	42	Sacramento city, California	13.1
35	43	Sacramento city, California	6.2	34	43	Fresno city, California	59.9	44	42	Omaha city, Nebraska	13.1
64	44	St. Paul city, Minnesota	6.1	37	44	Kansas City city, Missouri	59.8	39	44	Long Beach city, California	12.4
20	45	El Paso city, Texas	5.4	12	45	Jacksonville city, Florida	59.7	50	45	Wichita city, Kansas	11.9
62	46	Stockton city, California	5.3	64	46	St. Paul city, Minnesota	59.2	28	46	Las Vegas city, Nevada	11.6
34	47	Fresno city, California	5.2	4	47	Houston city, Texas	58.8	62	47	Stockton city, California	10.6
2	48	Los Angeles city, California	4.8	41	48	Raleigh city, North Carolina	58.6	19	48	Denver city, Colorado	9.5
37	49	Kansas City city, Missouri	4.7	39	49	Long Beach city, California	55.3	2	49	Los Angeles city, California	9.2
1	50	New York city, New York	4.4	22	50	Boston city, Massachusetts	52.7	53	50	Bakersfield city, California	8.4
56	51	Anaheim city, California	4.3	2	51	Los Angeles city, California	52.1	69	51	Plano city, Texas	7.9
15	52	Indianapolis city, Indiana	4.2	17	52	Charlotte city, North Carolina	52.0	34	52	Fresno city, California	7.7
55	52	Urban Honolulu CDP, Hawaii	4.2	65	53	Cincinnati city, Ohio	51.7	11	53	Austin city, Texas	7.6
44	54	Omaha city, Nebraska	3.5	35	54	Sacramento city, California	49.7	18	54	Seattle city, Washington	7.3
43	55	Virginia Beach city, Virginia	3.4	3	55	Chicago city, Illinois	48.4	7	55	San Antonio city, Texas	7.2
29	56	Louisville/Jefferson County, Kentucky	3.3	68	56	Greensboro city, North Carolina	48.1	5	56	Phoenix city, Arizona	7.1
57	57	Santa Ana city, California	2.9	13	57	San Francisco city, California	47.3	8	57	San Diego city, California	6.8
47	58	Tulsa city, Oklahoma	2.8	57	58	Santa Ana city, California	47.1	40	58	Colorado Springs city, Colorado	6.6
6	59	Philadelphia city, Pennsylvania	2.7	61	59	St. Louis city, Missouri	46.8	59	59	Riverside city, California	6.2
32	60	Albuquerque city, New Mexico	2.4	31	60	Milwaukee city, Wisconsin	46.1	66	59	Anchorage municipality, Alaska	6.2
66	61	Anchorage municipality, Alaska	2.2	62	61	Stockton city, California	46.0	26	61	Portland city, Oregon	5.7
50	62	Wichita city, Kansas	2.0	75	62	Irvine city, California	45.3	67	62	Henderson city, Nevada	5.3
33	63	Tucson city, Arizona	1.9	1	63	New York city, New York	42.6	13	63	San Francisco city, California	5.2
39	64	Long Beach city, California	1.7	6	64	Philadelphia city, Pennsylvania	41.9	33	64	Tucson city, Arizona	5.1
70	64	Newark city, New Jersey	1.7	38	65	Atlanta city, Georgia	40.8	74	65	Chula Vista city, California	5.0
65	66	Cincinnati city, Ohio	0.6	51	66	Cleveland city, Ohio	40.3	71	66	Lincoln city, Nebraska	4.4
3	67	Chicago city, Illinois	0.3	21	67	Washington city, District of Columbia	40.0	20	67	El Paso city, Texas	4.3
25	68	Memphis city, Tennessee	0.1	10	68	San Jose city, California	39.1	58	68	Corpus Christi city, Texas	4.2
31	69	Milwaukee city, Wisconsin	0.0	45	69	Oakland city, California	36.8	36	69	Mesa city, Arizona	3.7
63	70	Pittsburgh city, Pennsylvania	-0.7	49	70	New Orleans city, Louisiana	34.4	32	70	Albuquerque city, New Mexico	3.6
30	71	Baltimore city, Maryland	-1.0	30	71	Baltimore city, Maryland	31.0	10	71	San Jose city, California	3.1
61	72	St. Louis city, Missouri	-2.5	25	72	Memphis city, Tennessee	29.7	75	72	Irvine city, California	3.0
51	73	Cleveland city, Ohio	-2.7	70	73	Newark city, New Jersey	25.8	56	73	Anaheim city, California	2.3
72	74	Toledo city, Ohio	-3.0	55	74	Urban Honolulu CDP, Hawaii	19.0	55	74	Urban Honolulu CDP, Hawaii	1.9
23	75	Detroit city, Michigan	-5.8	23	75	Detroit city, Michigan	14.1	57	75	Santa Ana city, California	1.4

75 Largest Cities by 2016 Population
Selected rankings

Percent American Indian, Alaska Native alone, 2015				Percent Asian and Pacific Islander alone, 2015				Percent Hispanic or Latino,[1] 2015			
Population rank	American Indian, Alaska Native rank	City	Percent American Indian, Alaska Native [col 7]	Population rank	Asian and Pacific Islander rank	City	Percent Asian and Pacific Islander [col 8]	Population rank	Hispanic or Latino rank	City	Percent Hispanic or Latino [col 12]
66	1	Anchorage municipality, Alaska	6.5	55	1	Urban Honolulu CDP, Hawaii	54.9	20	1	El Paso city, Texas	79.6
47	2	Tulsa city, Oklahoma	4.7	75	2	Irvine city, California	45.3	57	2	Santa Ana city, California	78.2
32	3	Albuquerque city, New Mexico	4.4	10	3	San Jose city, California	34.9	42	3	Miami city, Florida	72.6
33	4	Tucson city, Arizona	3.3	13	4	San Francisco city, California	34.8	7	4	San Antonio city, Texas	63.8
27	5	Oklahoma City city, Oklahoma	2.9	62	5	Stockton city, California	21.8	58	5	Corpus Christi city, Texas	61.9
36	6	Mesa city, Arizona	2.2	69	6	Plano city, Texas	20.3	74	6	Chula Vista city, California	58.9
5	7	Phoenix city, Arizona	2.0	35	7	Sacramento city, California	18.3	56	7	Anaheim city, California	57.5
39	8	Long Beach city, California	1.8	64	8	St. Paul city, Minnesota	17.8	59	8	Riverside city, California	49.8
50	9	Wichita city, Kansas	1.2	8	9	San Diego city, California	16.1	34	9	Fresno city, California	49.3
34	10	Fresno city, California	1.1	74	10	Chula Vista city, California	16.0	2	10	Los Angeles city, California	48.8
19	11	Denver city, Colorado	1.0	45	11	Oakland city, California	15.3	32	11	Albuquerque city, New Mexico	48.6
53	11	Bakersfield city, California	1.0	1	12	New York city, New York	14.1	53	12	Bakersfield city, California	48.2
2	13	Los Angeles city, California	0.9	18	12	Seattle city, Washington	14.1	4	13	Houston city, Texas	44.7
46	13	Minneapolis city, Minnesota	0.9	56	14	Anaheim city, California	13.8	39	14	Long Beach city, California	43.8
57	13	Santa Ana city, California	0.9	34	15	Fresno city, California	13.3	33	15	Tucson city, Arizona	43.5
69	13	Plano city, Texas	0.9	39	16	Long Beach city, California	12.4	5	16	Phoenix city, Arizona	42.9
7	17	San Antonio city, Texas	0.8	2	17	Los Angeles city, California	11.5	9	17	Dallas city, Texas	42.3
44	17	Omaha city, Nebraska	0.8	57	18	Santa Ana city, California	10.8	62	18	Stockton city, California	41.9
45	17	Oakland city, California	0.8	66	19	Anchorage municipality, Alaska	9.7	70	19	Newark city, New Jersey	35.6
54	17	Aurora city, Colorado	0.8	22	20	Boston city, Massachusetts	9.5	16	20	Fort Worth city, Texas	35.4
59	17	Riverside city, California	0.8	26	21	Portland city, Oregon	7.9	11	21	Austin city, Texas	35.2
20	22	El Paso city, Texas	0.7	53	22	Bakersfield city, California	7.8	73	22	Orlando city, Florida	33.0
26	22	Portland city, Oregon	0.7	11	23	Austin city, Texas	7.5	28	23	Las Vegas city, Nevada	32.9
28	22	Las Vegas city, Nevada	0.7	48	24	Arlington city, Texas	7.3	10	24	San Jose city, California	32.3
35	22	Sacramento city, California	0.7	6	25	Philadelphia city, Pennsylvania	7.2	35	25	Sacramento city, California	30.6
40	22	Colorado Springs city, Colorado	0.7	67	26	Henderson city, Nevada	7.0	8	26	San Diego city, California	30.5
51	22	Cleveland city, Ohio	0.7	4	27	Houston city, Texas	6.9	19	26	Denver city, Colorado	30.5
18	28	Seattle city, Washington	0.6	28	28	Las Vegas city, Nevada	6.8	54	26	Aurora city, Colorado	30.5
31	28	Milwaukee city, Wisconsin	0.6	46	29	Minneapolis city, Minnesota	6.6	1	29	New York city, New York	29.1
67	28	Henderson city, Nevada	0.6	43	30	Virginia Beach city, Virginia	6.3	3	30	Chicago city, Illinois	28.9
71	28	Lincoln city, Nebraska	0.6	59	30	Riverside city, California	6.3	48	30	Arlington city, Texas	28.9
10	32	San Jose city, California	0.5	3	32	Chicago city, Illinois	6.2	36	32	Mesa city, Arizona	27.9
58	32	Corpus Christi city, Texas	0.5	17	33	Charlotte city, North Carolina	6.1	45	33	Oakland city, California	27.2
62	32	Stockton city, California	0.5	50	33	Wichita city, Kansas	6.1	52	34	Tampa city, Florida	25.8
64	32	St. Paul city, Minnesota	0.5	63	35	Pittsburgh city, Pennsylvania	5.9	22	35	Boston city, Massachusetts	19.5
70	32	Newark city, New Jersey	0.5	14	36	Columbus city, Ohio	5.1	27	36	Oklahoma City city, Oklahoma	18.6
1	37	New York city, New York	0.4	54	37	Aurora city, Colorado	4.8	31	37	Milwaukee city, Wisconsin	18.4
6	37	Philadelphia city, Pennsylvania	0.4	27	38	Oklahoma City city, Oklahoma	4.7	40	38	Colorado Springs city, Colorado	17.2
16	37	Fort Worth city, Texas	0.4	12	39	Jacksonville city, Florida	4.6	50	39	Wichita city, Kansas	16.7
24	37	Nashville-Davidson, Tennessee	0.4	41	40	Raleigh city, North Carolina	4.5	67	40	Henderson city, Nevada	16.5
41	37	Raleigh city, North Carolina	0.4	38	41	Atlanta city, Georgia	4.4	13	41	San Francisco city, California	15.3
48	37	Arlington city, Texas	0.4	71	42	Lincoln city, Nebraska	4.2	47	42	Tulsa city, Oklahoma	15.2
3	43	Chicago city, Illinois	0.3	16	43	Fort Worth city, Texas	4.1	69	43	Plano city, Texas	15.1
4	43	Houston city, Texas	0.3	68	44	Greensboro city, North Carolina	4.0	44	44	Omaha city, Nebraska	14.3
8	43	San Diego city, California	0.3	21	45	Washington city, District of Columbia	3.9	6	45	Philadelphia city, Pennsylvania	14.0
9	43	Dallas city, Texas	0.3	31	46	Milwaukee city, Wisconsin	3.8	17	46	Charlotte city, North Carolina	13.8
11	43	Austin city, Texas	0.3	44	47	Omaha city, Nebraska	3.5	41	47	Raleigh city, North Carolina	11.5
13	43	San Francisco city, California	0.3	47	47	Tulsa city, Oklahoma	3.5	21	48	Washington city, District of Columbi	10.6
15	43	Indianapolis city, Indiana	0.3	60	47	Lexington-Fayette, Kentucky	3.5	51	49	Cleveland city, Ohio	10.5
17	43	Charlotte city, North Carolina	0.3	19	50	Denver city, Colorado	3.4	24	50	Nashville-Davidson, Tennessee	10.3
23	43	Detroit city, Michigan	0.3	52	50	Tampa city, Florida	3.4	15	51	Indianapolis city, Indiana	9.8
37	43	Kansas City city, Missouri	0.3	5	52	Phoenix city, Arizona	3.3	26	52	Portland city, Oregon	9.7
38	43	Atlanta city, Georgia	0.3	40	52	Colorado Springs city, Colorado	3.3	37	52	Kansas City city, Missouri	9.7
72	43	Toledo city, Ohio	0.3	24	54	Nashville-Davidson, Tennessee	3.2	46	52	Minneapolis city, Minnesota	9.7
73	43	Orlando city, Florida	0.3	73	54	Orlando city, Florida	3.2	12	55	Jacksonville city, Florida	9.2
74	43	Chula Vista city, California	0.3	9	56	Dallas city, Texas	3.1	64	56	St. Paul city, Minnesota	9.1
14	57	Columbus city, Ohio	0.2	33	56	Tucson city, Arizona	3.1	66	56	Anchorage municipality, Alaska	9.1
21	57	Washington city, District of Columbia	0.2	49	56	New Orleans city, Louisiana	3.1	72	58	Toledo city, Ohio	8.4
22	57	Boston city, Massachusetts	0.2	15	59	Indianapolis city, Indiana	3.0	23	59	Detroit city, Michigan	8.0
30	57	Baltimore city, Maryland	0.2	7	60	San Antonio city, Texas	2.9	43	59	Virginia Beach city, Virginia	8.0
43	57	Virginia Beach city, Virginia	0.2	37	60	Kansas City city, Missouri	2.9	68	61	Greensboro city, North Carolina	7.8
49	57	New Orleans city, Louisiana	0.2	61	60	St. Louis city, Missouri	2.9	75	62	Irvine city, California	7.5
52	57	Tampa city, Florida	0.2	30	63	Baltimore city, Maryland	2.7	71	63	Lincoln city, Nebraska	7.3
56	57	Anaheim city, California	0.2	29	64	Louisville/Jefferson County, Kentucky	2.5	25	64	Memphis city, Tennessee	7.1
60	57	Lexington-Fayette, Kentucky	0.2	32	64	Albuquerque city, New Mexico	2.5	55	65	Urban Honolulu CDP, Hawaii	7.0
61	57	St. Louis city, Missouri	0.2	36	66	Mesa city, Arizona	2.2	60	66	Lexington-Fayette, Kentucky	6.9
65	57	Cincinnati city, Ohio	0.2	58	66	Corpus Christi city, Texas	2.2	18	67	Seattle city, Washington	6.3
68	57	Greensboro city, North Carolina	0.2	70	66	Newark city, New Jersey	2.2	49	68	New Orleans city, Louisiana	5.6
12	69	Jacksonville city, Florida	0.1	25	69	Memphis city, Tennessee	2.1	14	69	Columbus city, Ohio	5.5
29	69	Louisville/Jefferson County, Kentucky	0.1	51	69	Cleveland city, Ohio	2.1	30	70	Baltimore city, Maryland	4.8
55	69	Urban Honolulu CDP, Hawaii	0.1	65	69	Cincinnati city, Ohio	2.1	29	71	Louisville/Jefferson County, Kentucky	4.7
75	69	Irvine city, California	0.1	72	69	Toledo city, Ohio	2.1	38	72	Atlanta city, Georgia	4.0
25	73	Memphis city, Tennessee	0.0	20	73	El Paso city, Texas	1.5	61	73	St. Louis city, Missouri	3.9
42	73	Miami city, Florida	0.0	23	74	Detroit city, Michigan	1.3	65	74	Cincinnati city, Ohio	3.1
63	73	Pittsburgh city, Pennsylvania	0.0	42	75	Miami city, Florida	0.6	63	75	Pittsburgh city, Pennsylvania	3.0

75 Largest Cities by 2016 Population
Selected rankings

	Percent under 18 years old, 2015				Percent 65 years old and over, 2015				Percent high school graduate or less, 2015		
Population rank	Under 18 years old rank	City	Percent under 18 years old [col 14]	Population rank	65 years old and over rank	City	Percent 65 years old and over [col 20]	Population rank	Percent high school graduate or less rank	City	Percent high school graduate or less [col 40]
34	1	Fresno city, California	29.3	67	1	Henderson city, Nevada	19.7	57	1	Santa Ana city, California	69.4
53	2	Bakersfield city, California	29.1	55	2	Urban Honolulu CDP, Hawaii	19.1	70	2	Newark city, New Jersey	59.4
57	3	Santa Ana city, California	29.0	42	3	Miami city, Florida	17.0	42	3	Miami city, Florida	55.1
16	4	Fort Worth city, Texas	28.2	36	4	Mesa city, Arizona	16.0	51	4	Cleveland city, Ohio	53.7
62	5	Stockton city, California	27.4	13	5	San Francisco city, California	14.6	23	5	Detroit city, Michigan	52.8
20	6	El Paso city, Texas	26.9	63	5	Pittsburgh city, Pennsylvania	14.6	62	6	Stockton city, California	50.7
5	7	Phoenix city, Arizona	26.3	29	7	Louisville/Jefferson County, Kentucky	14.4	6	7	Philadelphia city, Pennsylvania	50.0
48	7	Arlington city, Texas	26.3	32	8	Albuquerque city, New Mexico	14.2	53	8	Bakersfield city, California	49.5
27	9	Oklahoma City city, Oklahoma	26.0	72	8	Toledo city, Ohio	14.2	56	9	Anaheim city, California	49.4
31	9	Milwaukee city, Wisconsin	26.0	28	10	Las Vegas city, Nevada	13.8	34	10	Fresno city, California	48.2
74	11	Chula Vista city, California	25.9	68	10	Greensboro city, North Carolina	13.8	72	10	Toledo city, Ohio	48.2
9	12	Dallas city, Texas	25.8	33	12	Tucson city, Arizona	13.7	58	12	Corpus Christi city, Texas	47.7
54	12	Aurora city, Colorado	25.8	47	13	Tulsa city, Oklahoma	13.5	25	13	Memphis city, Tennessee	46.6
4	14	Houston city, Texas	25.6	51	13	Cleveland city, Ohio	13.5	9	14	Dallas city, Texas	46.3
7	15	San Antonio city, Texas	25.4	40	15	Colorado Springs city, Colorado	13.3	31	15	Milwaukee city, Wisconsin	46.0
50	15	Wichita city, Kansas	25.4	1	16	New York city, New York	13.2	7	16	San Antonio city, Texas	45.9
23	17	Detroit city, Michigan	25.3	58	17	Corpus Christi city, Texas	12.9	59	17	Riverside city, California	45.9
25	18	Memphis city, Tennessee	24.9	50	18	Wichita city, Kansas	12.8	4	18	Houston city, Texas	45.5
15	19	Indianapolis city, Indiana	24.8	6	19	Philadelphia city, Pennsylvania	12.7	30	19	Baltimore city, Maryland	45.2
44	19	Omaha city, Nebraska	24.8	12	19	Jacksonville city, Florida	12.7	16	20	Fort Worth city, Texas	45.1
56	19	Anaheim city, California	24.8	23	19	Detroit city, Michigan	12.7	20	20	El Paso city, Texas	45.1
66	19	Anchorage municipality, Alaska	24.8	35	19	Sacramento city, California	12.7	5	22	Phoenix city, Arizona	44.5
58	23	Corpus Christi city, Texas	24.7	62	19	Stockton city, California	12.7	2	23	Los Angeles city, California	43.8
35	24	Sacramento city, California	24.6	43	24	Virginia Beach city, Virginia	12.6	28	23	Las Vegas city, Nevada	43.8
47	25	Tulsa city, Oklahoma	24.5	20	25	El Paso city, Texas	12.5	1	25	New York city, New York	43.0
28	26	Las Vegas city, Nevada	24.3	30	25	Baltimore city, Maryland	12.5	15	26	Indianapolis city, Indiana	42.7
70	26	Newark city, New Jersey	24.3	49	25	New Orleans city, Louisiana	12.5	33	27	Tucson city, Arizona	41.0
64	28	St. Paul city, Minnesota	24.2	44	28	Omaha city, Nebraska	12.4	39	28	Long Beach city, California	40.3
59	29	Riverside city, California	24.0	65	28	Cincinnati city, Ohio	12.4	50	28	Wichita city, Kansas	40.3
17	30	Charlotte city, North Carolina	23.7	37	30	Kansas City city, Missouri	12.3	27	30	Oklahoma City city, Oklahoma	40.0
36	31	Mesa city, Arizona	23.6	60	31	Lexington-Fayette, Kentucky	12.1	29	30	Louisville/Jefferson County, Kentucky	40.0
40	31	Colorado Springs city, Colorado	23.6	25	32	Memphis city, Tennessee	12.0	52	30	Tampa city, Florida	40.0
39	33	Long Beach city, California	23.4	27	32	Oklahoma City city, Oklahoma	12.0	12	33	Jacksonville city, Florida	39.8
12	34	Jacksonville city, Florida	23.3	71	34	Lincoln city, Nebraska	11.9	3	34	Chicago city, Illinois	39.5
37	34	Kansas City city, Missouri	23.3	8	35	San Diego city, California	11.8	48	35	Arlington city, Texas	39.4
69	36	Plano city, Texas	23.2	10	35	San Jose city, California	11.8	47	36	Tulsa city, Oklahoma	38.6
10	37	San Jose city, California	23.0	26	35	Portland city, Oregon	11.8	35	37	Sacramento city, California	38.5
29	38	Louisville/Jefferson County, Kentucky	22.9	38	35	Atlanta city, Georgia	11.8	54	38	Aurora city, Colorado	38.1
32	38	Albuquerque city, New Mexico	22.9	45	39	Oakland city, California	11.7	61	39	St. Louis city, Missouri	38.0
71	40	Lincoln city, Nebraska	22.8	3	40	Chicago city, Illinois	11.6	36	40	Mesa city, Arizona	37.9
43	41	Virginia Beach city, Virginia	22.6	7	40	San Antonio city, Texas	11.6	37	41	Kansas City city, Missouri	37.4
51	42	Cleveland city, Ohio	22.5	61	40	St. Louis city, Missouri	11.6	14	42	Columbus city, Ohio	37.2
14	43	Columbus city, Ohio	22.2	2	43	Los Angeles city, California	11.5	65	43	Cincinnati city, Ohio	36.9
6	44	Philadelphia city, Pennsylvania	22.1	52	43	Tampa city, Florida	11.5	55	44	Urban Honolulu CDP, Hawaii	36.8
41	44	Raleigh city, North Carolina	22.1	15	45	Indianapolis city, Indiana	11.4	74	44	Chula Vista city, California	36.5
72	46	Toledo city, Ohio	22.0	21	45	Washington city, District of Columbia	11.4	24	46	Nashville-Davidson, Tennessee	36.1
52	47	Tampa city, Florida	21.8	74	45	Chula Vista city, California	11.4	45	47	Oakland city, California	36.0
68	48	Greensboro city, North Carolina	21.7	18	48	Seattle city, Washington	11.3	49	47	New Orleans city, Louisiana	36.0
33	49	Tucson city, Arizona	21.6	39	49	Long Beach city, California	11.2	63	49	Pittsburgh city, Pennsylvania	35.7
2	50	Los Angeles city, California	21.5	69	49	Plano city, Texas	11.2	32	50	Albuquerque city, New Mexico	35.6
65	50	Cincinnati city, Ohio	21.5	19	51	Denver city, Colorado	11.1	22	51	Boston city, Massachusetts	35.2
3	52	Chicago city, Illinois	21.4	24	52	Nashville-Davidson, Tennessee	10.9	44	52	Omaha city, Nebraska	34.3
24	53	Nashville-Davidson, Tennessee	21.3	70	53	Newark city, New Jersey	10.7	64	52	St. Paul city, Minnesota	34.3
1	54	New York city, New York	21.1	22	54	Boston city, Massachusetts	10.6	10	54	San Jose city, California	34.1
30	54	Baltimore city, Maryland	21.1	5	55	Phoenix city, Arizona	10.4	73	54	Orlando city, Florida	34.1
60	56	Lexington-Fayette, Kentucky	21.0	54	55	Aurora city, Colorado	10.4	67	56	Henderson city, Nevada	33.2
11	57	Austin city, Texas	20.9	56	57	Anaheim city, California	10.3	68	57	Greensboro city, North Carolina	32.3
67	57	Henderson city, Nevada	20.9	59	58	Riverside city, California	10.2	17	58	Charlotte city, North Carolina	31.6
19	59	Denver city, Colorado	20.6	73	58	Orlando city, Florida	10.2	19	59	Denver city, Colorado	30.7
75	60	Irvine city, California	20.5	34	60	Fresno city, California	10.1	60	60	Lexington-Fayette, Kentucky	30.4
8	61	San Diego city, California	20.4	17	61	Charlotte city, North Carolina	10.0	66	61	Anchorage municipality, Alaska	29.8
49	61	New Orleans city, Louisiana	20.4	31	61	Milwaukee city, Wisconsin	10.0	38	62	Atlanta city, Georgia	29.6
45	63	Oakland city, California	20.3	75	61	Irvine city, California	10.0	43	62	Virginia Beach city, Virginia	29.6
73	63	Orlando city, Florida	20.3	14	64	Columbus city, Ohio	9.9	11	64	Austin city, Texas	28.8
61	65	St. Louis city, Missouri	20.1	64	65	St. Paul city, Minnesota	9.8	8	65	San Diego city, California	28.7
46	66	Minneapolis city, Minnesota	19.9	4	66	Houston city, Texas	9.6	71	66	Lincoln city, Nebraska	28.0
26	67	Portland city, Oregon	18.3	9	66	Dallas city, Texas	9.6	46	67	Minneapolis city, Minnesota	27.8
38	68	Atlanta city, Georgia	17.9	53	68	Bakersfield city, California	9.4	21	68	Washington city, District of Columbia	27.6
21	69	Washington city, District of Columbia	17.5	41	69	Raleigh city, North Carolina	9.3	40	69	Colorado Springs city, Colorado	27.3
42	70	Miami city, Florida	17.1	48	69	Arlington city, Texas	9.3	41	70	Raleigh city, North Carolina	25.4
22	71	Boston city, Massachusetts	16.7	16	71	Fort Worth city, Texas	9.2	13	71	San Francisco city, California	25.2
55	72	Urban Honolulu CDP, Hawaii	16.1	46	71	Minneapolis city, Minnesota	9.2	26	72	Portland city, Oregon	23.7
63	73	Pittsburgh city, Pennsylvania	15.2	66	71	Anchorage municipality, Alaska	9.2	69	73	Plano city, Texas	19.7
18	74	Seattle city, Washington	14.6	57	74	Santa Ana city, California	8.3	18	74	Seattle city, Washington	15.4
13	75	San Francisco city, California	13.4	11	75	Austin city, Texas	8.1	75	75	Irvine city, California	11.7

75 Largest Cities by 2016 Population
Selected rankings

Percent college graduates (bachelor's degree or more), 2015				Percent female-headed family households, 2015				Percent of households composed of one person, 2015			
Population rank	Percent college graduate rank	City	Percent college graduates [col 41]	Population rank	Female households rank	City	Percent female households [col 29]	Population rank	One-person household rank	City	Percent one-person households [col 30]
75	1	Irvine city, California	69.1	23	1	Detroit city, Michigan	28.4	38	1	Atlanta city, Georgia	50.3
18	2	Seattle city, Washington	62.1	70	2	Newark city, New Jersey	25.9	49	2	New Orleans city, Louisiana	45.1
21	3	Washington city, District of Columbia	56.7	25	3	Memphis city, Tennessee	24.5	61	3	St. Louis city, Missouri	44.8
13	4	San Francisco city, California	55.2	51	4	Cleveland city, Ohio	23.3	65	4	Cincinnati city, Ohio	44.7
69	5	Plano city, Texas	54.2	30	5	Baltimore city, Maryland	21.7	51	5	Cleveland city, Ohio	43.9
41	6	Raleigh city, North Carolina	49.2	6	6	Philadelphia city, Pennsylvania	21.2	63	6	Pittsburgh city, Pennsylvania	42.4
26	7	Portland city, Oregon	48.6	34	7	Fresno city, California	21.1	21	7	Washington city, District of Columbia	42.0
11	8	Austin city, Texas	48.3	31	8	Milwaukee city, Wisconsin	21.0	42	8	Miami city, Florida	41.1
38	8	Atlanta city, Georgia	48.3	73	9	Orlando city, Florida	19.7	46	8	Minneapolis city, Minnesota	41.1
46	8	Minneapolis city, Minnesota	48.3	62	10	Stockton city, California	19.0	23	10	Detroit city, Michigan	39.2
19	11	Denver city, Colorado	47.1	65	11	Cincinnati city, Ohio	18.9	15	11	Indianapolis city, Indiana	39.0
22	12	Boston city, Massachusetts	46.6	72	12	Toledo city, Ohio	18.3	72	12	Toledo city, Ohio	38.7
8	13	San Diego city, California	44.3	57	13	Santa Ana city, California	18.2	30	13	Baltimore city, Maryland	38.4
17	14	Charlotte city, North Carolina	41.9	61	13	St. Louis city, Missouri	18.2	18	14	Seattle city, Washington	37.9
60	15	Lexington-Fayette, Kentucky	41.6	1	15	New York city, New York	18.0	37	14	Kansas City city, Missouri	37.9
63	16	Pittsburgh city, Pennsylvania	41.3	74	15	Chula Vista city, California	18.0	19	16	Denver city, Colorado	37.8
10	17	San Jose city, California	40.7	4	17	Houston city, Texas	17.8	13	17	San Francisco city, California	37.5
45	18	Oakland city, California	40.0	52	18	Tampa city, Florida	17.2	22	18	Boston city, Massachusetts	37.3
64	19	St. Paul city, Minnesota	39.8	7	19	San Antonio city, Texas	17.1	6	19	Philadelphia city, Pennsylvania	36.7
40	20	Colorado Springs city, Colorado	38.3	20	19	El Paso city, Texas	17.1	31	20	Milwaukee city, Wisconsin	36.6
24	21	Nashville-Davidson, Tennessee	37.9	48	19	Arlington city, Texas	17.1	3	21	Chicago city, Illinois	36.3
71	22	Lincoln city, Nebraska	37.1	12	22	Jacksonville city, Florida	17.0	14	21	Columbus city, Ohio	36.3
1	23	New York city, New York	36.8	49	23	New Orleans city, Louisiana	16.7	52	23	Tampa city, Florida	35.8
3	24	Chicago city, Illinois	36.6	3	24	Chicago city, Illinois	16.5	50	24	Wichita city, Kansas	35.3
49	25	New Orleans city, Louisiana	36.0	42	25	Miami city, Florida	16.1	25	25	Memphis city, Tennessee	35.1
66	26	Anchorage municipality, Alaska	35.6	16	26	Fort Worth city, Texas	16.0	64	26	St. Paul city, Minnesota	35.0
52	27	Tampa city, Florida	35.5	22	26	Boston city, Massachusetts	16.0	26	27	Portland city, Oregon	34.4
73	27	Orlando city, Florida	35.5	53	26	Bakersfield city, California	16.0	70	27	Newark city, New Jersey	34.4
55	29	Urban Honolulu CDP, Hawaii	35.4	29	29	Louisville/Jefferson County, Kentucky	15.9	9	29	Dallas city, Texas	34.3
68	30	Greensboro city, North Carolina	35.2	33	30	Tucson city, Arizona	15.8	11	29	Austin city, Texas	34.3
14	31	Columbus city, Ohio	34.8	68	31	Greensboro city, North Carolina	15.6	68	29	Greensboro city, North Carolina	34.3
44	31	Omaha city, Nebraska	34.8	9	32	Dallas city, Texas	15.5	33	32	Tucson city, Arizona	34.2
61	33	St. Louis city, Missouri	34.7	56	33	Anaheim city, California	15.4	32	33	Albuquerque city, New Mexico	34.0
65	34	Cincinnati city, Ohio	34.3	58	34	Corpus Christi city, Texas	15.3	24	34	Nashville-Davidson, Tennessee	33.7
37	35	Kansas City city, Missouri	33.3	14	35	Columbus city, Ohio	15.2	47	35	Tulsa city, Oklahoma	33.5
43	36	Virginia Beach city, Virginia	32.8	59	35	Riverside city, California	15.2	44	36	Omaha city, Nebraska	33.4
2	37	Los Angeles city, California	32.6	5	37	Phoenix city, Arizona	15.1	29	37	Louisville/Jefferson County, Kentucky	33.3
32	37	Albuquerque city, New Mexico	32.6	15	37	Indianapolis city, Indiana	15.1	71	37	Lincoln city, Nebraska	33.3
9	39	Dallas city, Texas	31.8	21	37	Washington city, District of Columbia	15.1	41	39	Raleigh city, North Carolina	32.6
67	40	Henderson city, Nevada	31.3	35	37	Sacramento city, California	15.1	1	40	New York city, New York	32.5
4	41	Houston city, Texas	30.9	2	41	Los Angeles city, California	14.9	17	41	Charlotte city, North Carolina	32.4
47	42	Tulsa city, Oklahoma	30.8	39	42	Long Beach city, California	14.8	73	42	Orlando city, Florida	31.8
35	43	Sacramento city, California	30.3	47	43	Tulsa city, Oklahoma	14.6	4	43	Houston city, Texas	31.7
27	44	Oklahoma City city, Oklahoma	30.1	17	44	Charlotte city, North Carolina	14.5	45	43	Oakland city, California	31.7
29	44	Louisville/Jefferson County, Kentucky	30.1	28	45	Las Vegas city, Nevada	14.1	28	45	Las Vegas city, Nevada	31.6
30	46	Baltimore city, Maryland	29.9	45	45	Oakland city, California	14.1	55	46	Urban Honolulu CDP, Hawaii	31.5
74	47	Chula Vista city, California	29.8	66	45	Anchorage municipality, Alaska	14.1	35	47	Sacramento city, California	31.3
48	48	Arlington city, Texas	29.7	24	48	Nashville-Davidson, Tennessee	13.8	27	48	Oklahoma City city, Oklahoma	31.2
39	49	Long Beach city, California	29.5	60	49	Lexington-Fayette, Kentucky	13.7	39	49	Long Beach city, California	30.9
15	50	Indianapolis city, Indiana	29.4	27	50	Oklahoma City city, Oklahoma	13.6	60	50	Lexington-Fayette, Kentucky	30.4
54	51	Aurora city, Colorado	29.0	64	51	St. Paul city, Minnesota	13.2	2	51	Los Angeles city, California	30.1
12	52	Jacksonville city, Florida	27.7	54	52	Aurora city, Colorado	13.1	12	52	Jacksonville city, Florida	30.0
6	53	Philadelphia city, Pennsylvania	27.4	41	53	Raleigh city, North Carolina	12.9	7	53	San Antonio city, Texas	29.3
16	54	Fort Worth city, Texas	27.3	50	53	Wichita city, Kansas	12.9	40	54	Colorado Springs city, Colorado	29.1
5	55	Phoenix city, Arizona	26.6	32	55	Albuquerque city, New Mexico	12.8	67	55	Henderson city, Nevada	28.8
33	56	Tucson city, Arizona	26.5	37	55	Kansas City city, Missouri	12.8	8	56	San Diego city, California	28.7
50	57	Wichita city, Kansas	26.0	38	55	Atlanta city, Georgia	12.8	36	57	Mesa city, Arizona	28.6
42	58	Miami city, Florida	25.7	43	55	Virginia Beach city, Virginia	12.8	5	58	Phoenix city, Arizona	28.3
36	59	Mesa city, Arizona	25.2	44	59	Omaha city, Nebraska	12.4	54	59	Aurora city, Colorado	27.5
25	60	Memphis city, Tennessee	24.9	63	60	Pittsburgh city, Pennsylvania	12.2	16	60	Fort Worth city, Texas	27.3
20	61	El Paso city, Texas	24.3	36	61	Mesa city, Arizona	12.0	66	61	Anchorage municipality, Alaska	27.2
7	62	San Antonio city, Texas	24.2	55	62	Urban Honolulu CDP, Hawaii	11.8	58	62	Corpus Christi city, Texas	26.0
31	63	Milwaukee city, Wisconsin	23.9	10	63	San Jose city, California	11.7	43	63	Virginia Beach city, Virginia	25.6
56	64	Anaheim city, California	23.2	40	64	Colorado Springs city, Colorado	11.2	69	64	Plano city, Texas	25.3
28	65	Las Vegas city, Nevada	23.0	46	65	Minneapolis city, Minnesota	10.8	20	65	El Paso city, Texas	24.4
59	66	Riverside city, California	22.2	8	66	San Diego city, California	10.7	34	66	Fresno city, California	24.1
53	67	Bakersfield city, California	21.4	67	66	Henderson city, Nevada	10.7	48	67	Arlington city, Texas	24.0
58	68	Corpus Christi city, Texas	20.9	19	68	Denver city, Colorado	10.1	75	67	Irvine city, California	24.0
34	69	Fresno city, California	19.3	69	69	Plano city, Texas	10.0	62	69	Stockton city, California	22.4
62	70	Stockton city, California	17.8	26	70	Portland city, Oregon	9.4	59	70	Riverside city, California	21.6
72	71	Toledo city, Ohio	16.8	75	70	Irvine city, California	9.4	53	71	Bakersfield city, California	20.0
51	72	Cleveland city, Ohio	16.2	11	72	Austin city, Texas	9.3	10	72	San Jose city, California	19.5
70	73	Newark city, New Jersey	16.0	71	73	Lincoln city, Nebraska	9.1	56	73	Anaheim city, California	19.2
23	74	Detroit city, Michigan	14.2	13	74	San Francisco city, California	7.6	74	74	Chula Vista city, California	17.9
57	75	Santa Ana city, California	11.5	18	75	Seattle city, Washington	5.9	57	75	Santa Ana city, California	12.2

75 Largest Cities by 2016 Population
Selected rankings

Median household income, 2010–2014				Median value of owner-occupied housing units, 2010–2014				Median gross rent of renter-occupied housing units, 2010–2014			
Population rank	Median income rank	City	Median income (dollars) [col 43]	Population rank	Median value rank	City	Median value (dollars) [col 52]	Population rank	Commutes of 30 minutes or more rank	City	Percent of workers with commutes of 30 minutes or more [col 56]
75	1	Irvine city, California	$93 781	13	1	San Francisco city, California	$941 400	1	1	New York city, New York	69.7
13	2	San Francisco city, California	$92 094	75	2	Irvine city, California	$777 000	3	2	Chicago city, Illinois	60.9
10	3	San Jose city, California	$91 451	10	3	San Jose city, California	$717 100	13	3	San Francisco city, California	57.4
69	4	Plano city, Texas	$83 769	55	4	Urban Honolulu CDP, Hawaii	$641 900	70	4	Newark city, New Jersey	56.7
18	5	Seattle city, Washington	$80 349	45	5	Oakland city, California	$557 000	6	5	Philadelphia city, Pennsylvania	54.6
66	6	Anchorage municipality, Alaska	$78 662	21	6	Washington city, District of Columbia	$551 300	22	6	Boston city, Massachusetts	54.2
21	7	Washington city, District of Columbia	$75 628	2	7	Los Angeles city, California	$542 100	42	7	Miami city, Florida	52.7
8	8	San Diego city, California	$67 871	1	8	New York city, New York	$538 300	21	8	Washington city, District of Columbia	51.7
43	9	Virginia Beach city, Virginia	$67 281	18	9	Seattle city, Washington	$530 900	2	9	Los Angeles city, California	51.6
74	10	Chula Vista city, California	$66 868	8	10	San Diego city, California	$526 900	45	10	Oakland city, California	50.9
55	11	Urban Honolulu CDP, Hawaii	$64 658	39	11	Long Beach city, California	$483 700	10	11	San Jose city, California	48.2
67	12	Henderson city, Nevada	$64 035	56	12	Anaheim city, California	$482 700	74	12	Chula Vista city, California	48.1
56	13	Anaheim city, California	$63 104	22	13	Boston city, Massachusetts	$453 000	39	13	Long Beach city, California	47.2
11	14	Austin city, Texas	$62 250	74	14	Chula Vista city, California	$440 400	30	14	Baltimore city, Maryland	46.7
59	15	Riverside city, California	$61 279	57	15	Santa Ana city, California	$437 500	4	15	Houston city, Texas	45.0
53	16	Bakersfield city, California	$61 039	26	16	Portland city, Oregon	$348 300	54	16	Aurora city, Colorado	44.3
26	17	Portland city, Oregon	$60 892	59	17	Riverside city, California	$317 600	18	17	Seattle city, Washington	44.2
45	18	Oakland city, California	$58 807	19	18	Denver city, Colorado	$316 700	56	18	Anaheim city, California	42.0
54	19	Aurora city, Colorado	$58 445	66	19	Anchorage municipality, Alaska	$302 500	9	19	Dallas city, Texas	41.9
22	20	Boston city, Massachusetts	$58 263	35	20	Sacramento city, California	$287 300	48	19	Arlington city, Texas	41.9
19	21	Denver city, Colorado	$58 003	42	21	Miami city, Florida	$286 600	59	21	Riverside city, California	41.4
41	22	Raleigh city, North Carolina	$56 910	11	22	Austin city, Texas	$282 700	69	22	Plano city, Texas	40.9
40	23	Colorado Springs city, Colorado	$56 079	67	23	Henderson city, Nevada	$273 800	16	23	Fort Worth city, Texas	39.9
16	24	Fort Worth city, Texas	$55 888	43	24	Virginia Beach city, Virginia	$262 900	28	24	Las Vegas city, Nevada	39.8
1	25	New York city, New York	$55 752	69	25	Plano city, Texas	$261 800	73	25	Orlando city, Florida	39.1
39	26	Long Beach city, California	$54 971	38	26	Atlanta city, Georgia	$241 200	19	26	Denver city, Colorado	38.8
46	27	Minneapolis city, Minnesota	$54 571	3	27	Chicago city, Illinois	$238 500	17	27	Charlotte city, North Carolina	38.7
57	28	Santa Ana city, California	$54 392	53	28	Bakersfield city, California	$237 600	5	28	Phoenix city, Arizona	38.1
17	29	Charlotte city, North Carolina	$53 919	70	29	Newark city, New Jersey	$235 700	26	29	Portland city, Oregon	37.5
48	30	Arlington city, Texas	$53 487	40	30	Colorado Springs city, Colorado	$228 600	36	30	Mesa city, Arizona	37.2
35	31	Sacramento city, California	$52 151	46	31	Minneapolis city, Minnesota	$227 500	23	31	Detroit city, Michigan	36.4
2	32	Los Angeles city, California	$52 024	54	32	Aurora city, Colorado	$227 300	38	32	Atlanta city, Georgia	35.7
60	33	Lexington-Fayette, Kentucky	$51 948	41	33	Raleigh city, North Carolina	$226 500	24	33	Nashville-Davidson, Tennessee	35.6
71	34	Lincoln city, Nebraska	$51 503	62	34	Stockton city, California	$224 300	35	34	Sacramento city, California	34.9
44	35	Omaha city, Nebraska	$51 407	49	35	New Orleans city, Louisiana	$216 800	7	35	San Antonio city, Texas	34.5
24	36	Nashville-Davidson, Tennessee	$51 393	73	36	Orlando city, Florida	$214 400	12	36	Jacksonville city, Florida	34.4
58	37	Corpus Christi city, Texas	$51 255	28	37	Las Vegas city, Nevada	$209 400	55	37	Urban Honolulu CDP, Hawaii	34.1
27	38	Oklahoma City city, Oklahoma	$50 739	34	38	Fresno city, California	$203 700	62	38	Stockton city, California	33.8
3	39	Chicago city, Illinois	$50 702	5	39	Phoenix city, Arizona	$200 800	57	39	Santa Ana city, California	33.7
64	40	St. Paul city, Minnesota	$50 267	52	40	Tampa city, Florida	$189 800	11	40	Austin city, Texas	33.5
37	41	Kansas City city, Missouri	$50 259	32	41	Albuquerque city, New Mexico	$189 200	49	41	New Orleans city, Louisiana	33.0
38	42	Atlanta city, Georgia	$50 210	17	42	Charlotte city, North Carolina	$188 800	43	42	Virginia Beach city, Virginia	32.7
28	43	Las Vegas city, Nevada	$49 676	36	43	Mesa city, Arizona	$188 100	51	43	Cleveland city, Ohio	32.5
36	44	Mesa city, Arizona	$49 177	64	44	St. Paul city, Minnesota	$186 800	63	44	Pittsburgh city, Pennsylvania	32.4
7	45	San Antonio city, Texas	$48 869	24	45	Nashville-Davidson, Tennessee	$185 000	64	45	St. Paul city, Minnesota	32.2
5	46	Phoenix city, Arizona	$48 452	60	46	Lexington-Fayette, Kentucky	$170 200	61	46	St. Louis city, Missouri	31.9
12	47	Jacksonville city, Florida	$48 239	30	47	Baltimore city, Maryland	$155 600	8	47	San Diego city, California	31.3
29	48	Louisville/Jefferson County, Kentucky	$48 100	71	48	Lincoln city, Nebraska	$155 100	41	48	Raleigh city, North Carolina	30.1
4	49	Houston city, Texas	$48 064	9	49	Dallas city, Texas	$152 400	52	49	Tampa city, Florida	30.0
14	50	Columbus city, Ohio	$47 401	4	50	Houston city, Texas	$152 200	67	50	Henderson city, Nevada	29.6
32	51	Albuquerque city, New Mexico	$47 096	6	51	Philadelphia city, Pennsylvania	$150 700	29	51	Louisville/Jefferson County, Kentucky	28.9
50	52	Wichita city, Kansas	$46 894	27	52	Oklahoma City city, Oklahoma	$148 500	31	51	Milwaukee city, Wisconsin	28.9
62	53	Stockton city, California	$46 795	68	53	Greensboro city, North Carolina	$148 200	20	53	El Paso city, Texas	28.5
9	54	Dallas city, Texas	$45 918	12	54	Jacksonville city, Florida	$146 500	46	54	Minneapolis city, Minnesota	28.3
20	55	El Paso city, Texas	$45 069	29	55	Louisville/Jefferson County, Kentucky	$145 000	65	55	Cincinnati city, Ohio	28.2
68	56	Greensboro city, North Carolina	$44 934	48	56	Arlington city, Texas	$144 900	15	56	Indianapolis city, Indiana	28.1
73	57	Orlando city, Florida	$44 804	44	57	Omaha city, Nebraska	$143 200	33	57	Tucson city, Arizona	28.0
52	58	Tampa city, Florida	$44 432	33	58	Tucson city, Arizona	$139 400	75	58	Irvine city, California	27.7
30	59	Baltimore city, Maryland	$44 165	37	59	Kansas City city, Missouri	$138 400	37	59	Kansas City city, Missouri	26.8
34	60	Fresno city, California	$43 494	14	60	Columbus city, Ohio	$137 100	25	60	Memphis city, Tennessee	26.7
47	61	Tulsa city, Oklahoma	$43 322	16	61	Fort Worth city, Texas	$136 700	14	61	Columbus city, Ohio	25.1
63	62	Pittsburgh city, Pennsylvania	$41 293	47	62	Tulsa city, Oklahoma	$133 700	60	62	Lexington-Fayette, Kentucky	23.6
15	63	Indianapolis city, Indiana	$41 278	61	63	St. Louis city, Missouri	$130 800	53	63	Bakersfield city, California	23.5
6	64	Philadelphia city, Pennsylvania	$41 233	7	64	San Antonio city, Texas	$126 600	32	64	Albuquerque city, New Mexico	23.3
49	65	New Orleans city, Louisiana	$39 077	50	65	Wichita city, Kansas	$124 400	40	65	Colorado Springs city, Colorado	22.3
61	66	St. Louis city, Missouri	$38 397	58	66	Corpus Christi city, Texas	$124 300	27	66	Oklahoma City city, Oklahoma	22.2
33	67	Tucson city, Arizona	$38 155	15	67	Indianapolis city, Indiana	$123 500	34	67	Fresno city, California	21.8
31	68	Milwaukee city, Wisconsin	$37 495	65	68	Cincinnati city, Ohio	$119 000	68	68	Greensboro city, North Carolina	20.6
25	69	Memphis city, Tennessee	$36 908	20	69	El Paso city, Texas	$118 500	72	69	Toledo city, Ohio	20.3
72	70	Toledo city, Ohio	$35 289	31	70	Milwaukee city, Wisconsin	$114 000	58	70	Corpus Christi city, Texas	17.7
65	71	Cincinnati city, Ohio	$35 001	63	71	Pittsburgh city, Pennsylvania	$108 400	44	71	Omaha city, Nebraska	16.8
70	72	Newark city, New Jersey	$30 966	25	72	Memphis city, Tennessee	$94 400	66	72	Anchorage municipality, Alaska	16.5
42	73	Miami city, Florida	$29 989	72	73	Toledo city, Ohio	$78 400	47	73	Tulsa city, Oklahoma	15.2
51	74	Cleveland city, Ohio	$28 831	51	74	Cleveland city, Ohio	$66 200	71	74	Lincoln city, Nebraska	13.4
23	75	Detroit city, Michigan	$25 980	23	75	Detroit city, Michigan	$42 600	50	75	Wichita city, Kansas	12.4

75 Largest Cities by 2016 Population
Selected rankings

Percent of population below the poverty level, 2015

Population rank	Poverty rate rank	City	Poverty rate [col 46]
23	1	Detroit city, Michigan	35.5
51	2	Cleveland city, Ohio	30.6
70	3	Newark city, New Jersey	26.5
34	4	Fresno city, California	23.4
31	5	Milwaukee city, Wisconsin	23.1
42	6	Miami city, Florida	21.7
72	7	Toledo city, Ohio	21.3
65	8	Cincinnati city, Ohio	21.1
61	9	St. Louis city, Missouri	21.0
6	10	Philadelphia city, Pennsylvania	20.9
25	11	Memphis city, Tennessee	20.8
38	12	Atlanta city, Georgia	19.2
9	13	Dallas city, Texas	18.6
62	13	Stockton city, California	18.6
4	15	Houston city, Texas	18.5
33	15	Tucson city, Arizona	18.5
57	17	Santa Ana city, California	18.3
30	18	Baltimore city, Maryland	18.2
49	19	New Orleans city, Louisiana	17.5
5	20	Phoenix city, Arizona	17.3
22	21	Boston city, Massachusetts	17.0
73	21	Orlando city, Florida	17.0
52	23	Tampa city, Florida	16.9
1	24	New York city, New York	16.8
47	25	Tulsa city, Oklahoma	16.6
3	26	Chicago city, Illinois	16.5
35	27	Sacramento city, California	16.4
2	28	Los Angeles city, California	15.8
14	29	Columbus city, Ohio	15.6
45	29	Oakland city, California	15.6
64	31	St. Paul city, Minnesota	15.3
15	32	Indianapolis city, Indiana	15.2
20	33	El Paso city, Texas	14.8
63	34	Pittsburgh city, Pennsylvania	14.7
53	35	Bakersfield city, California	14.3
32	36	Albuquerque city, New Mexico	14.2
7	37	San Antonio city, Texas	14.1
21	38	Washington city, District of Columbia	14.0
58	39	Corpus Christi city, Texas	13.7
60	40	Lexington-Fayette, Kentucky	13.6
39	41	Long Beach city, California	13.5
24	42	Nashville-Davidson, Tennessee	13.1
48	43	Arlington city, Texas	12.9
46	44	Minneapolis city, Minnesota	12.8
16	45	Fort Worth city, Texas	12.7
36	45	Mesa city, Arizona	12.7
44	45	Omaha city, Nebraska	12.7
68	48	Greensboro city, North Carolina	12.6
12	49	Jacksonville city, Florida	12.5
27	49	Oklahoma City city, Oklahoma	12.5
37	51	Kansas City city, Missouri	12.4
28	52	Las Vegas city, Nevada	12.3
50	53	Wichita city, Kansas	11.9
17	54	Charlotte city, North Carolina	11.8
56	54	Anaheim city, California	11.8
29	56	Louisville/Jefferson County, Kentucky	11.5
41	57	Raleigh city, North Carolina	11.3
19	58	Denver city, Colorado	11.0
8	59	San Diego city, California	10.5
59	59	Riverside city, California	10.5
71	61	Lincoln city, Nebraska	9.9
11	62	Austin city, Texas	9.8
54	63	Aurora city, Colorado	9.1
74	63	Chula Vista city, California	9.1
26	65	Portland city, Oregon	9.0
40	66	Colorado Springs city, Colorado	8.9
75	67	Irvine city, California	8.5
13	68	San Francisco city, California	7.2
55	68	Urban Honolulu CDP, Hawaii	7.2
67	70	Henderson city, Nevada	6.9
69	71	Plano city, Texas	6.7
66	72	Anchorage municipality, Alaska	6.6
10	73	San Jose city, California	6.4
43	74	Virginia Beach city, Virginia	5.8
18	75	Seattle city, Washington	4.9

Unemployment rate, 2015

Population rank	Unemployment rate rank	City	Unemployment rate [col 64]
23	1	Detroit city, Michigan	10.9
34	2	Fresno city, California	10.2
53	3	Bakersfield city, California	9.2
62	4	Stockton city, California	8.7
70	5	Newark city, New Jersey	7.9
51	6	Cleveland city, Ohio	6.9
6	7	Philadelphia city, Pennsylvania	6.8
3	8	Chicago city, Illinois	6.5
30	9	Baltimore city, Maryland	6.3
21	10	Washington city, District of Columbia	6.0
25	10	Memphis city, Tennessee	6.0
28	10	Las Vegas city, Nevada	6.0
49	13	New Orleans city, Louisiana	5.9
74	13	Chula Vista city, California	5.9
31	15	Milwaukee city, Wisconsin	5.8
32	15	Albuquerque city, New Mexico	5.8
38	15	Atlanta city, Georgia	5.8
59	15	Riverside city, California	5.8
35	19	Sacramento city, California	5.7
39	19	Long Beach city, California	5.7
2	21	Los Angeles city, California	5.6
58	21	Corpus Christi city, Texas	5.6
72	21	Toledo city, Ohio	5.6
61	24	St. Louis city, Missouri	5.4
63	24	Pittsburgh city, Pennsylvania	5.4
67	24	Henderson city, Nevada	5.4
68	24	Greensboro city, North Carolina	5.4
42	28	Miami city, Florida	5.3
45	28	Oakland city, California	5.3
66	28	Anchorage municipality, Alaska	5.3
1	31	New York city, New York	5.2
12	32	Jacksonville city, Florida	5.1
33	32	Tucson city, Arizona	5.1
56	32	Anaheim city, California	5.1
4	35	Houston city, Texas	5.0
50	35	Wichita city, Kansas	5.0
37	37	Kansas City city, Missouri	4.9
17	38	Charlotte city, North Carolina	4.8
52	38	Tampa city, Florida	4.8
65	38	Cincinnati city, Ohio	4.8
5	41	Phoenix city, Arizona	4.7
20	41	El Paso city, Texas	4.7
57	43	Santa Ana city, California	4.6
36	44	Mesa city, Arizona	4.5
41	44	Raleigh city, North Carolina	4.5
47	44	Tulsa city, Oklahoma	4.5
8	47	San Diego city, California	4.4
15	47	Indianapolis city, Indiana	4.4
29	47	Louisville/Jefferson County, Kentucky	4.4
10	50	San Jose city, California	4.2
16	50	Fort Worth city, Texas	4.2
26	50	Portland city, Oregon	4.2
73	50	Orlando city, Florida	4.2
14	54	Columbus city, Ohio	4.1
27	55	Oklahoma City city, Oklahoma	4.0
9	56	Dallas city, Texas	3.9
43	56	Virginia Beach city, Virginia	3.9
48	56	Arlington city, Texas	3.9
7	59	San Antonio city, Texas	3.7
40	59	Colorado Springs city, Colorado	3.7
64	59	St. Paul city, Minnesota	3.7
18	62	Seattle city, Washington	3.6
24	62	Nashville-Davidson, Tennessee	3.6
69	62	Plano city, Texas	3.6
54	65	Aurora city, Colorado	3.5
60	65	Lexington-Fayette, Kentucky	3.5
22	67	Boston city, Massachusetts	3.4
46	67	Minneapolis city, Minnesota	3.4
13	69	San Francisco city, California	3.3
44	69	Omaha city, Nebraska	3.3
19	71	Denver city, Colorado	3.1
11	72	Austin city, Texas	3.0
75	72	Irvine city, California	3.0
71	74	Lincoln city, Nebraska	2.8
55		Urban Honolulu CDP, Hawaii	NA

Percent change in civilian labor force, 2014–2015

Population rank	Percent change rank	City	Percent change [col 62]
17	1	Charlotte city, North Carolina	4.1
11	2	Austin city, Texas	4.0
26	2	Portland city, Oregon	4.0
41	2	Raleigh city, North Carolina	4.0
69	5	Plano city, Texas	3.9
9	6	Dallas city, Texas	3.8
24	7	Nashville-Davidson, Tennessee	3.5
7	8	San Antonio city, Texas	3.1
38	8	Atlanta city, Georgia	3.1
20	10	El Paso city, Texas	2.9
5	11	Phoenix city, Arizona	2.8
36	11	Mesa city, Arizona	2.8
73	11	Orlando city, Florida	2.8
13	14	San Francisco city, California	2.6
18	14	Seattle city, Washington	2.6
52	16	Tampa city, Florida	2.5
15	17	Indianapolis city, Indiana	2.3
16	17	Fort Worth city, Texas	2.3
29	19	Louisville/Jefferson County, Kentucky	2.2
12	20	Jacksonville city, Florida	2.0
19	20	Denver city, Colorado	2.0
40	20	Colorado Springs city, Colorado	2.0
48	20	Arlington city, Texas	2.0
54	24	Aurora city, Colorado	1.9
42	25	Miami city, Florida	1.8
6	26	Philadelphia city, Pennsylvania	1.7
45	26	Oakland city, California	1.7
10	28	San Jose city, California	1.6
35	28	Sacramento city, California	1.6
59	28	Riverside city, California	1.6
21	31	Washington city, District of Columbia	1.5
32	31	Albuquerque city, New Mexico	1.5
60	31	Lexington-Fayette, Kentucky	1.5
14	34	Columbus city, Ohio	1.4
68	34	Greensboro city, North Carolina	1.4
4	36	Houston city, Texas	1.3
23	36	Detroit city, Michigan	1.3
37	38	Kansas City city, Missouri	1.2
62	38	Stockton city, California	1.2
25	40	Memphis city, Tennessee	1.1
33	40	Tucson city, Arizona	1.1
34	40	Fresno city, California	1.1
46	40	Minneapolis city, Minnesota	1.1
64	40	St. Paul city, Minnesota	1.1
8	45	San Diego city, California	1.0
75	45	Irvine city, California	1.0
67	47	Henderson city, Nevada	0.9
71	47	Lincoln city, Nebraska	0.9
72	47	Toledo city, Ohio	0.9
74	47	Chula Vista city, California	0.9
2	51	Los Angeles city, California	0.8
3	51	Chicago city, Illinois	0.8
28	51	Las Vegas city, Nevada	0.8
57	51	Santa Ana city, California	0.8
22	55	Boston city, Massachusetts	0.7
39	55	Long Beach city, California	0.7
56	55	Anaheim city, California	0.7
65	55	Cincinnati city, Ohio	0.7
1	59	New York city, New York	0.5
44	59	Omaha city, Nebraska	0.5
51	61	Cleveland city, Ohio	0.4
30	62	Baltimore city, Maryland	0.3
58	62	Corpus Christi city, Texas	0.3
61	64	St. Louis city, Missouri	0.2
27	65	Oklahoma City city, Oklahoma	0.1
31	65	Milwaukee city, Wisconsin	0.1
43	65	Virginia Beach city, Virginia	0.1
63	65	Pittsburgh city, Pennsylvania	0.1
47	69	Tulsa city, Oklahoma	-0.1
50	70	Wichita city, Kansas	-0.2
66	71	Anchorage municipality, Alaska	-0.3
53	72	Bakersfield city, California	-0.4
70	73	Newark city, New Jersey	-1.2
49	74	New Orleans city, Louisiana	-1.3
55		Urban Honolulu CDP, Hawaii	NA

75 Largest Cities by 2016 Population
Selected rankings

Per capita local government taxes, 2012				Per capita city government debt outstanding, 2012				Violent crime rate, 2014 (violent crimes known to police)			
Population rank	Local taxes rank	City	Local per capita taxes (dollars) [col 121]	Population rank	Debt rank	City	Debt per capita (dollars) [col 138]	Population rank	Violent crime rate rank	City	Violent crimes (per 100,000 population) [col 37]
21	1	Washington city, District of Columbia	9 344	21	1	Washington city, District of Columbia	17 761	23	1	Detroit city, Michigan	1 990
1	2	New York city, New York	5 077	38	2	Atlanta city, Georgia	16 770	25	2	Memphis city, Tennessee	1 744
13	3	San Francisco city, California	3 430	13	3	San Francisco city, California	15 759	45	3	Oakland city, California	1 685
22	4	Boston city, Massachusetts	2 844	1	4	New York city, New York	15 714	61	4	St. Louis city, Missouri	1 679
6	5	Philadelphia city, Pennsylvania	2 089	12	5	Jacksonville city, Florida	12 465	31	5	Milwaukee city, Wisconsin	1 485
30	6	Baltimore city, Maryland	1 989	23	6	Detroit city, Michigan	11 720	30	6	Baltimore city, Maryland	1 339
24	7	Nashville-Davidson, Tennessee	1 952	19	7	Denver city, Colorado	11 106	51	6	Cleveland city, Ohio	1 339
66	8	Anchorage municipality, Alaska	1 830	50	8	Wichita city, Kansas	9 003	62	8	Stockton city, California	1 331
43	9	Virginia Beach city, Virginia	1 817	46	9	Minneapolis city, Minnesota	8 754	37	9	Kansas City city, Missouri	1 258
19	10	Denver city, Colorado	1 748	24	10	Nashville-Davidson, Tennessee	7 828	15	10	Indianapolis city, Indiana	1 255
61	11	St. Louis city, Missouri	1 706	3	11	Chicago city, Illinois	7 811	38	11	Atlanta city, Georgia	1 227
37	12	Kansas City city, Missouri	1 599	15	12	Indianapolis city, Indiana	7 191	21	12	Washington city, District of Columbia	1 185
18	13	Seattle city, Washington	1 438	18	13	Seattle city, Washington	6 556	24	13	Nashville-Davidson, Tennessee	1 125
45	14	Oakland city, California	1 420	51	14	Cleveland city, Ohio	6 465	72	14	Toledo city, Ohio	1 091
65	15	Cincinnati city, Ohio	1 400	4	15	Houston city, Texas	6 459	70	15	Newark city, New Jersey	1 078
49	16	New Orleans city, Louisiana	1 349	11	16	Austin city, Texas	6 438	42	16	Miami city, Florida	1 060
38	17	Atlanta city, Georgia	1 173	9	17	Dallas city, Texas	6 389	6	17	Philadelphia city, Pennsylvania	1 021
46	18	Minneapolis city, Minnesota	1 170	7	18	San Antonio city, Texas	6 374	46	18	Minneapolis city, Minnesota	1 012
63	19	Pittsburgh city, Pennsylvania	1 166	37	19	Kansas City city, Missouri	6 347	4	19	Houston city, Texas	991
12	20	Jacksonville city, Florida	1 104	40	20	Colorado Springs city, Colorado	6 097	49	20	New Orleans city, Louisiana	974
70	21	Newark city, New Jersey	1 099	75	21	Irvine city, California	6 096	65	21	Cincinnati city, Ohio	913
23	22	Detroit city, Michigan	1 078	59	22	Riverside city, California	6 092	73	22	Orlando city, Florida	901
51	23	Cleveland city, Ohio	1 071	10	23	San Jose city, California	6 013	3	23	Chicago city, Illinois	886
15	24	Indianapolis city, Indiana	1 064	66	24	Anchorage municipality, Alaska	5 991	32	24	Albuquerque city, New Mexico	883
60	25	Lexington-Fayette, Kentucky	1 045	2	25	Los Angeles city, California	5 983	66	25	Anchorage municipality, Alaska	865
26	26	Portland city, Oregon	1 016	61	26	St. Louis city, Missouri	5 832	28	26	Las Vegas city, Nevada	841
27	27	Oklahoma City city, Oklahoma	1 003	48	27	Arlington city, Texas	5 724	47	27	Tulsa city, Oklahoma	805
2	28	Los Angeles city, California	997	45	28	Oakland city, California	5 709	63	28	Pittsburgh city, Pennsylvania	798
42	29	Miami city, Florida	976	26	29	Portland city, Oregon	5 608	13	29	San Francisco city, California	795
14	30	Columbus city, Ohio	958	5	30	Phoenix city, Arizona	5 557	27	30	Oklahoma City city, Oklahoma	774
3	31	Chicago city, Illinois	930	49	31	New Orleans city, Louisiana	5 454	50	31	Wichita city, Kansas	758
69	32	Plano city, Texas	907	56	32	Anaheim city, California	5 304	22	32	Boston city, Massachusetts	726
44	33	Omaha city, Nebraska	903	39	33	Long Beach city, California	5 095	12	33	Jacksonville city, Florida	684
73	34	Orlando city, Florida	895	6	34	Philadelphia city, Pennsylvania	4 985	9	34	Dallas city, Texas	665
4	35	Houston city, Texas	888	71	35	Lincoln city, Nebraska	4 876	64	35	St. Paul city, Minnesota	662
39	36	Long Beach city, California	877	73	36	Orlando city, Florida	4 219	58	36	Corpus Christi city, Texas	656
10	37	San Jose city, California	876	30	37	Baltimore city, Maryland	4 208	33	37	Tucson city, Arizona	653
9	38	Dallas city, Texas	872	17	38	Charlotte city, North Carolina	4 165	35	38	Sacramento city, California	615
47	39	Tulsa city, Oklahoma	862	52	39	Tampa city, Florida	3 945	18	39	Seattle city, Washington	604
8	40	San Diego city, California	838	43	40	Virginia Beach city, Virginia	3 811	19	40	Denver city, Colorado	601
17	41	Charlotte city, North Carolina	803	25	41	Memphis city, Tennessee	3 791	1	41	New York city, New York	597
25	42	Memphis city, Tennessee	789	32	42	Albuquerque city, New Mexico	3 769	29	42	Louisville/Jefferson County, Kentucky	592
16	43	Fort Worth city, Texas	783	58	43	Corpus Christi city, Texas	3 689	17	43	Charlotte city, North Carolina	590
56	44	Anaheim city, California	779	54	44	Aurora city, Colorado	3 582	52	44	Tampa city, Florida	582
52	45	Tampa city, Florida	774	36	45	Mesa city, Arizona	3 305	5	45	Phoenix city, Arizona	572
35	46	Sacramento city, California	771	60	46	Lexington-Fayette, Kentucky	3 277	44	46	Omaha city, Nebraska	561
29	47	Louisville/Jefferson County, Kentucky	753	47	47	Tulsa city, Oklahoma	3 179	14	47	Columbus city, Ohio	558
68	48	Greensboro city, North Carolina	711	14	48	Columbus city, Ohio	3 153	16	47	Fort Worth city, Texas	558
11	49	Austin city, Texas	709	65	49	Cincinnati city, Ohio	3 091	7	49	San Antonio city, Texas	539
41	50	Raleigh city, North Carolina	679	16	50	Fort Worth city, Texas	3 084	2	50	Los Angeles city, California	491
5	51	Phoenix city, Arizona	663	64	51	St. Paul city, Minnesota	2 646	39	51	Long Beach city, California	489
32	51	Albuquerque city, New Mexico	663	29	52	Louisville/Jefferson County, Kentucky	2 633	48	52	Arlington city, Texas	484
75	53	Irvine city, California	656	8	53	San Diego city, California	2 563	68	53	Greensboro city, North Carolina	477
48	54	Arlington city, Texas	644	22	54	Boston city, Massachusetts	2 454	26	54	Portland city, Oregon	473
54	55	Aurora city, Colorado	638	44	55	Omaha city, Nebraska	2 411	34	55	Fresno city, California	464
59	56	Riverside city, California	631	41	56	Raleigh city, North Carolina	2 373	36	56	Mesa city, Arizona	459
57	57	Santa Ana city, California	621	70	57	Newark city, New Jersey	2 366	53	57	Bakersfield city, California	457
72	58	Toledo city, Ohio	618	63	58	Pittsburgh city, Pennsylvania	2 300	40	58	Colorado Springs city, Colorado	456
58	59	Corpus Christi city, Texas	614	35	59	Sacramento city, California	2 286	59	59	Riverside city, California	433
64	60	St. Paul city, Minnesota	602	20	60	El Paso city, Texas	2 270	54	60	Aurora city, Colorado	407
20	61	El Paso city, Texas	572	33	61	Tucson city, Arizona	2 236	11	61	Austin city, Texas	396
62	62	Stockton city, California	544	27	62	Oklahoma City city, Oklahoma	2 199	20	62	El Paso city, Texas	393
7	63	San Antonio city, Texas	534	31	63	Milwaukee city, Wisconsin	2 181	8	63	San Diego city, California	381
33	63	Tucson city, Arizona	534	34	64	Fresno city, California	2 099	57	64	Santa Ana city, California	374
34	65	Fresno city, California	529	42	65	Miami city, Florida	2 095	71	65	Lincoln city, Nebraska	338
71	66	Lincoln city, Nebraska	516	74	66	Chula Vista city, California	2 027	60	66	Lexington-Fayette, Kentucky	337
31	67	Milwaukee city, Wisconsin	505	62	67	Stockton city, California	1 926	10	67	San Jose city, California	321
74	68	Chula Vista city, California	501	68	68	Greensboro city, North Carolina	1 603	56	68	Anaheim city, California	317
40	69	Colorado Springs city, Colorado	494	69	69	Plano city, Texas	1 293	74	69	Chula Vista city, California	235
67	70	Henderson city, Nevada	487	72	70	Toledo city, Ohio	1 260	67	70	Henderson city, Nevada	165
50	71	Wichita city, Kansas	435	67	71	Henderson city, Nevada	1 165	69	70	Plano city, Texas	165
53	72	Bakersfield city, California	417	57	72	Santa Ana city, California	1 080	41	72	Raleigh city, North Carolina	152
36	73	Mesa city, Arizona	346	28	73	Las Vegas city, Nevada	1 069	43	73	Virginia Beach city, Virginia	148
28	74	Las Vegas city, Nevada	336	53	74	Bakersfield city, California	966	75	74	Irvine city, California	49
55		Urban Honolulu CDP, Hawaii	NA	55		Urban Honolulu CDP, Hawaii	NA	55		Urban Honolulu CDP, Hawaii	NA

Selected rankings

Population rank	Property crime rate rank	(property crimes known to police) City	Property crimes (per 100,000 population) [col 38]	Population rank	Government employees rank	City	Government employees [col 108]	Population rank	Government employee payroll rank	City	Government payroll (thousands of dollars) [col 109]
		Property crime rate, 2014				**Full time equivalent local government employees, 2012**				**Local government employee payroll for March 2012**	
73	1	Orlando city, Florida	6 360	1	1	New York city, New York	404 260	1	1	New York city, New York	2 380 283 176
61	2	St. Louis city, Missouri	6 253	2	2	Los Angeles city, California	47 505	2	2	Los Angeles city, California	361 983 103
18	3	Seattle city, Washington	6 146	21	3	Washington city, District of Columbia	34 002	13	3	San Francisco city, California	217 722 943
25	4	Memphis city, Tennessee	5 995	6	4	Philadelphia city, Pennsylvania	29 409	21	4	Washington city, District of Columbia	194 813 463
33	5	Tucson city, Arizona	5 993	13	5	San Francisco city, California	28 349	3	5	Chicago city, Illinois	175 627 618
45	6	Oakland city, California	5 943	30	6	Baltimore city, Maryland	26 392	6	6	Philadelphia city, Pennsylvania	148 399 324
38	7	Atlanta city, Georgia	5 747	3	7	Chicago city, Illinois	25 630	30	7	Baltimore city, Maryland	122 552 640
65	8	Cincinnati city, Ohio	5 604	25	8	Memphis city, Tennessee	24 196	22	8	Boston city, Massachusetts	112 444 857
51	9	Cleveland city, Ohio	5 459	24	9	Nashville-Davidson, Tennessee	21 697	4	9	Houston city, Texas	99 616 057
32	10	Albuquerque city, New Mexico	5 446	4	10	Houston city, Texas	21 007	24	10	Nashville-Davidson, Tennessee	83 700 973
7	11	San Antonio city, Texas	5 418	22	11	Boston city, Massachusetts	19 230	25	11	Memphis city, Tennessee	79 305 378
13	12	San Francisco city, California	5 303	43	12	Virginia Beach city, Virginia	18 286	18	12	Seattle city, Washington	71 586 796
26	13	Portland city, Oregon	5 235	7	13	San Antonio city, Texas	15 382	7	13	San Antonio city, Texas	70 371 976
47	14	Tulsa city, Oklahoma	5 082	9	14	Dallas city, Texas	14 235	5	14	Phoenix city, Arizona	69 633 897
21	15	Washington city, District of Columbia	5 012	5	15	Phoenix city, Arizona	13 392	9	15	Dallas city, Texas	67 511 933
37	16	Kansas City city, Missouri	4 862	11	16	Austin city, Texas	12 580	11	16	Austin city, Texas	64 599 610
42	17	Miami city, Florida	4 833	23	17	Detroit city, Michigan	12 364	43	17	Virginia Beach city, Virginia	64 539 702
15	18	Indianapolis city, Indiana	4 823	15	18	Indianapolis city, Indiana	12 328	19	18	Denver city, Colorado	62 559 560
23	19	Detroit city, Michigan	4 819	19	19	Denver city, Colorado	11 914	8	19	San Diego city, California	62 476 850
46	20	Minneapolis city, Minnesota	4 728	18	20	Seattle city, Washington	10 193	23	20	Detroit city, Michigan	57 433 160
50	21	Wichita city, Kansas	4 723	12	21	Jacksonville city, Florida	10 137	66	21	Anchorage municipality, Alaska	51 971 256
30	22	Baltimore city, Maryland	4 718	66	22	Anchorage municipality, Alaska	9 819	15	22	Indianapolis city, Indiana	49 785 804
4	23	Houston city, Texas	4 694	8	23	San Diego city, California	9 425	12	23	Jacksonville city, Florida	46 960 164
31	24	Milwaukee city, Wisconsin	4 588	29	24	Louisville/Jefferson County, Kentucky	8 264	14	24	Columbus city, Ohio	42 573 757
58	25	Corpus Christi city, Texas	4 420	38	25	Atlanta city, Georgia	8 214	10	25	San Jose city, California	38 715 963
27	26	Oklahoma City city, Oklahoma	4 411	14	26	Columbus city, Ohio	8 035	40	26	Colorado Springs city, Colorado	37 084 390
62	27	Stockton city, California	4 390	17	27	Charlotte city, North Carolina	7 449	39	27	Long Beach city, California	36 050 392
44	28	Omaha city, Nebraska	4 345	51	28	Cleveland city, Ohio	7 389	26	28	Portland city, Oregon	35 556 383
14	29	Columbus city, Ohio	4 278	40	29	Colorado Springs city, Colorado	6 835	17	29	Charlotte city, North Carolina	34 348 745
49	30	New Orleans city, Louisiana	4 232	49	30	New Orleans city, Louisiana	6 570	32	30	Albuquerque city, New Mexico	33 331 138
29	31	Louisville/Jefferson County, Kentucky	4 196	16	31	Fort Worth city, Texas	6 536	51	31	Cleveland city, Ohio	33 318 506
11	32	Austin city, Texas	4 142	37	32	Kansas City city, Missouri	6 482	29	32	Louisville/Jefferson County, Kentucky	32 734 538
34	33	Fresno city, California	4 112	31	33	Milwaukee city, Wisconsin	6 455	31	33	Milwaukee city, Wisconsin	32 385 292
16	34	Fort Worth city, Texas	4 001	32	34	Albuquerque city, New Mexico	6 438	16	34	Fort Worth city, Texas	32 292 472
53	35	Bakersfield city, California	3 972	61	35	St. Louis city, Missouri	6 234	38	35	Atlanta city, Georgia	31 551 612
12	36	Jacksonville city, Florida	3 941	20	36	El Paso city, Texas	5 996	45	36	Oakland city, California	30 153 764
60	37	Lexington-Fayette, Kentucky	3 912	39	37	Long Beach city, California	5 861	35	37	Sacramento city, California	29 508 935
66	38	Anchorage municipality, Alaska	3 827	26	38	Portland city, Oregon	5 804	65	38	Cincinnati city, Ohio	26 843 252
5	39	Phoenix city, Arizona	3 724	65	39	Cincinnati city, Ohio	5 222	46	39	Minneapolis city, Minnesota	26 103 507
40	40	Colorado Springs city, Colorado	3 668	10	40	San Jose city, California	5 214	49	40	New Orleans city, Louisiana	26 033 023
24	41	Nashville-Davidson, Tennessee	3 647	46	41	Minneapolis city, Minnesota	5 068	70	41	Newark city, New Jersey	25 580 741
68	42	Greensboro city, North Carolina	3 600	33	42	Tucson city, Arizona	4 691	61	42	St. Louis city, Missouri	25 364 525
9	43	Dallas city, Texas	3 589	35	43	Sacramento city, California	4 483	27	43	Oklahoma City city, Oklahoma	24 268 820
17	44	Charlotte city, North Carolina	3 567	27	44	Oklahoma City city, Oklahoma	4 418	20	44	El Paso city, Texas	23 812 936
48	45	Arlington city, Texas	3 515	52	45	Tampa city, Florida	4 247	52	45	Tampa city, Florida	22 517 912
64	46	St. Paul city, Minnesota	3 484	63	46	Pittsburgh city, Pennsylvania	4 176	33	46	Tucson city, Arizona	21 780 237
6	47	Philadelphia city, Pennsylvania	3 388	45	47	Oakland city, California	3 940	37	47	Kansas City city, Missouri	21 087 489
19	48	Denver city, Colorado	3 367	41	48	Raleigh city, North Carolina	3 936	36	48	Mesa city, Arizona	20 622 110
71	49	Lincoln city, Nebraska	3 349	47	49	Tulsa city, Oklahoma	3 932	42	49	Miami city, Florida	18 642 774
63	50	Pittsburgh city, Pennsylvania	3 213	60	50	Lexington-Fayette, Kentucky	3 926	34	50	Fresno city, California	18 551 770
3	51	Chicago city, Illinois	3 133	70	51	Newark city, New Jersey	3 857	64	51	St. Paul city, Minnesota	18 028 194
35	52	Sacramento city, California	3 123	42	52	Miami city, Florida	3 807	28	52	Las Vegas city, Nevada	17 371 881
59	53	Riverside city, California	3 088	36	53	Mesa city, Arizona	3 616	47	53	Tulsa city, Oklahoma	16 951 552
28	54	Las Vegas city, Nevada	2 923	34	54	Fresno city, California	3 214	63	54	Pittsburgh city, Pennsylvania	16 527 485
70	55	Newark city, New Jersey	2 851	68	55	Greensboro city, North Carolina	3 098	60	55	Lexington-Fayette, Kentucky	16 180 537
54	56	Aurora city, Colorado	2 839	64	56	St. Paul city, Minnesota	3 092	41	56	Raleigh city, North Carolina	15 850 858
36	57	Mesa city, Arizona	2 800	50	57	Wichita city, Kansas	2 864	56	57	Anaheim city, California	15 281 363
39	58	Long Beach city, California	2 640	44	58	Omaha city, Nebraska	2 835	44	58	Omaha city, Nebraska	15 258 712
22	59	Boston city, Massachusetts	2 639	73	59	Orlando city, Florida	2 773	59	59	Riverside city, California	15 114 251
10	60	San Jose city, California	2 434	58	60	Corpus Christi city, Texas	2 747	73	60	Orlando city, Florida	14 180 368
52	61	Tampa city, Florida	2 428	57	61	Santa Ana city, California	2 711	67	61	Henderson city, Nevada	13 759 509
56	62	Anaheim city, California	2 362	71	62	Lincoln city, Nebraska	2 609	54	62	Aurora city, Colorado	13 742 359
43	63	Virginia Beach city, Virginia	2 187	28	63	Las Vegas city, Nevada	2 582	71	63	Lincoln city, Nebraska	13 359 820
20	64	El Paso city, Texas	2 142	54	64	Aurora city, Colorado	2 579	57	64	Santa Ana city, California	12 719 386
2	65	Los Angeles city, California	2 128	48	65	Arlington city, Texas	2 551	62	65	Stockton city, California	12 427 436
72	66	Toledo city, Ohio	2 006	59	66	Riverside city, California	2 260	50	66	Wichita city, Kansas	12 396 633
69	67	Plano city, Texas	1 983	67	67	Henderson city, Nevada	2 239	48	67	Arlington city, Texas	12 130 944
67	68	Henderson city, Nevada	1 978	56	68	Anaheim city, California	2 214	68	68	Greensboro city, North Carolina	11 503 988
8	69	San Diego city, California	1 959	72	69	Toledo city, Ohio	2 146	58	69	Corpus Christi city, Texas	10 789 288
74	70	Chula Vista city, California	1 741	69	70	Plano city, Texas	2 089	69	70	Plano city, Texas	10 395 648
57	71	Santa Ana city, California	1 719	62	71	Stockton city, California	2 010	72	71	Toledo city, Ohio	10 282 276
1	72	New York city, New York	1 602	53	72	Bakersfield city, California	1 424	53	72	Bakersfield city, California	8 316 644
75	73	Irvine city, California	1 253	74	73	Chula Vista city, California	1 114	74	73	Chula Vista city, California	7 346 424
41	74	Raleigh city, North Carolina	1 030	75	74	Irvine city, California	977	75	74	Irvine city, California	6 075 973
55		Urban Honolulu CDP, Hawaii	NA	55		Urban Honolulu CDP, Hawaii	NA	55		Urban Honolulu CDP, Hawaii	NA

Table D. Cities — **Land Area and Population**

STATE Place code	City	Land area,[1] 2016 (sq mi)	Population, 2016			Race alone[2] (percent), 2015						
			Total persons	Rank	Per square mile	White	Black or African American	American Indian, Alaska Native	Asian	Hawaiian Pacific Islander	Some other race	2 or more races[2]
		1	2	3	4	5	6	7	8	9	10	11

1. Dry land or land partially or temporarily covered by water.　2. Hispanic or Latino persons may be of any race.

Table D. Cities — **Population**

City	Percent Hispanic or Latino[1], 2015	Percent foreign born 2015	Age of population (percent), 2010-2014							Median age 2015	Percent female 2015	Population			
												Census counts		Percent change	
			Under 18 years	18 to 24 years	25 to 34 years	35 to 44 years	45 to 54 years	55 to 64 years	65 years and over			2000	2010	2000– 2010	2010– 2016
	12	13	14	15	16	17	18	19	20	21	22	23	24	25	26

1. May be of any race.

Table D. Cities — **Households, Group Quarters, Crime, and Education**

City	Households, 2015				Persons in group quarters, 2010				Serious crimes known to police,[2] 2014				Educational attainment, 2015		
		Percent				Institutional			Total	Rate[3]			Attainment[4] (percent)		
	Number	Persons per household	Female family householder[1]	One-person	Total	Total	Persons in nursing facilities	Non-institutional	Number	Rate[3]	Violent	Property	Population age 25 and older	High school graduate or less	Bachelor's degree or more
	27	28	29	30	31	32	33	34	35	36	37	38	39	40	41

1. No spouse present.　2. Data for serious crimes have not been adjusted for underreporting. This may affect comparability between geographic areas and over time.　3. Per 100,000 population estimated by the FBI.　4. Persons 25 years old and over.

Table D. Cities — **Income, Poverty, and Housing**

City	Money income, 2015					Housing units, 2010			Occupied housing units 2015				
	Households			Families						Owner-occupied		Renter-occupied	
	Median income	Percent with income of $200,000 or more	Percent with income of less than $25,000	Total Families	Percent with income below poverty	Total	Percent change, 2000– 2010	Vacant units for sale or rent[2]	Total	Percent	Median value[3] (dollars)	Percent	Median rent (dollars)
	42	43	44	45	46	47	48	49	50	51	52	53	54

1. Based on population estimated by the American Community Survey.　2. Includes units rented or sold but not occupied.　3. Specified owner-occupied units; $1,000,000 represents $1,000,000 or more　4. 50.0 represents 50 percent or more.　5. 10.0 represents 10 percent or less.

Table D. Cities — **Commuting, Computer Access, Migration, Labor Force, and Employment**

City	Commuting Percent		Computer Access[2] Percent		Migration, 2015		Civilian labor force, 2016				Civilian employment[4], 2015			
									Unemployment		Population age 16 and older		Population age 16 to 64	
	Drove alone	With Commutes of 30 minutes or more[1]	With a Computer in the house	With Internet Access	Percent who lived in the same house one year ago	Percent who lived in an other state or county one year ago	Total	Percent change, 2015–2016	Total	Rate[3]	Number	Percent in Labor Force	Number	Percent who worked full-year full-time
	55	56	57	58	59	60	61	62	63	64	65	66	67	68

1. Employed persons.   2. Households.   3. Percent of civilian labor force.   4. Persons 16 years old and over.

Table D. Cities — **Construction, Wholesale Trade, and Retail Trade**

City	Value of residential construction authorized by building permits, 2016			Wholesale trade,[1] 2012				Retail trade,[2] 2012			
	New construction ($1,000)	Number of housing units	Percent single family	Number of establish-ments	Number of employees	Sales (mil dol)	Annual payroll (mil dol)	Number of establish-ments	Number of employees	Sales (mil dol)	Annual payroll (mil dol)
	69	70	71	72	73	74	75	76	77	78	79

1. Merchant wholesalers except manufacturers' sales branches and offices.   2. Establishments with payroll.

Table D. Cities — **Real Estate, Professional Services, and Manufacturing**

City	Real estate and rental and leasing, 2012				Professional, scientific, and technical services,[1] 2012				Manufacturing, 2012			
	Number of establish-ments	Number of employees	Receipts (mil dol)	Annual payroll (mil dol)	Number of establish-ments	Number of employees	Receipts (mil dol)	Annual payroll (mil dol)	Number of establish-ments	Number of employees	Receipts (mil dol)	Annual payroll (mil dol)
	80	81	82	83	84	85	86	87	88	89	90	91

1. Establishments subject to federal tax.

Table D. Cities — **Accommodation and Food Services, Arts, Entertainment, and Recreation, and Health Care and Social Assistance**

City	Accommodation and food services, 2012				Arts, entertainment, and recreation,[1] 2012				Health care and social assistance,[1] 2012			
	Number of establish-ments	Number of employees	Sales (mil dol)	Annual payroll (mil dol)	Number of establish-ments	Number of employees	Receipts (mil dol)	Annual payroll (mil dol)	Number of establish-ments	Number of employees	Receipts (mil dol)	Annual payroll (mil dol)
	92	93	94	95	96	97	98	99	100	101	102	103

1. Establishments subject to federal tax.

Table D. Cities — **Other Services and Government Employment and Payroll**

City	Other services[1], 2012				Government employment and payroll, 2012								
						March payroll							
							Percent of total for:						
	Number of establish-ments	Number of employees	Receipts (mil dol)	Annual payroll (mil dol)	Full-time equivalent employees	Total (dollars)	Adminis-tration, judicial, and legal	Police and Corrections	Fire Protection	Highways and trans-portation	Health and welfare	Natural resources and utilities	Education and libraries
	104	105	106	107	108	109	110	111	112	113	114	115	116

1. Establishments subject to federal tax.

Table D. Cities — **City Government Finances**

City	City government finances, 2012										
	General revenue								General expenditure		
		Intergovernmental		Taxes						Per capita[1] (dollars)	
					Per capita[1] (dollars)						
	Total (mil dol)	Total (mil dol)	Percent from state government	Total (mil dol)	Total	Property	Sales and gross receipts		Total (mil dol)	Total	Capital outlays
	117	118	119	120	121	122	123		124	125	126

1. Based on population estimated as of July 1 of the year shown.

Table D. Cities — **City Government Finances**

City	City government finances, 2012 (cont.)									
	General expenditure (cont.)									
	Percent of total for:									
	Public welfare	Highways	Parking facilities	Education	Health and hospitals	Police protection	Sewerage and sanitation	Parks and recreation	Housing and community development	Interest on debt
	127	128	129	130	131	132	133	134	135	136

Table D. Cities — **City Government Finances, City Government Employment, and Climate**

City	City government finances, 2012 (cont.)			Climate[2]						
	Debt outstanding			Average daily temperature (degrees Fahrenheit)						
				Mean		Limits				
	Total (mil dol)	Per capita[1] (dollars)	Debt issued during year	January	July	January[3]	July[4]	Annual precipitation (inches)	Heating degree days	Cooling degree days
	137	138	139	140	141	142	143	144	145	146

1. Based on the population estimated as of July 1 of the year shown. 2. Represents normal values based on the 30-year period, 1971–2000. 3. Average daily minimum.
4. Average daily maximum.

Table D. Cities — Land Area and Population

STATE Place code	City	Land area,[1] 2016 (sq mi)	Total persons	Rank	Per square mile	White	Black or African American	American Indian, Alaska Native	Asian	Hawaiian Pacific Islander	Some other race	2 or more races[2]
		1	2	3	4	5	6	7	8	9	10	11
00 00000	United States............	3 532 068.7	323 127 513	X	91.5	73.1	12.7	0.8	5.4	0.2	4.8	3.1
01 00000	ALABAMA	50 646.4	4 863 300	X	96.0	68.5	26.8	0.4	1.2	0.1	1.1	1.8
01 00820	Alabaster................	25.1	32 948	1 153	1 312.7	75.0	12.7	0.7	0.3	0.1	8.4	2.8
01 03076	Auburn...................	58.8	63 118	578	1 073.4	69.2	21.3	0.1	7.9	0.0	0.4	1.1
01 05980	Bessemer................	40.5	26 511	1 383	654.6	NA	NA	NA	NA	NA	NA	NA
01 07000	Birmingham.............	146.1	212 157	104	1 452.1	23.2	72.8	0.2	0.6	0.0	2.2	1.1
01 20104	Decatur..................	54.4	55 072	680	1 012.4	71.0	24.8	0.1	1.2	0.0	0.5	2.5
01 21184	Dothan...................	89.6	68 468	515	764.2	62.6	33.3	0.4	1.1	0.2	0.3	2.1
01 24184	Enterprise...............	30.6	28 024	1 324	915.8	70.3	25.2	0.0	0.9	0.0	1.3	2.3
01 26896	Florence	26.1	39 959	948	1 531.0	NA	NA	NA	NA	NA	NA	NA
01 28696	Gadsden.................	37.3	35 837	1 063	960.8	NA	NA	NA	NA	NA	NA	NA
01 35800	Homewood	8.4	25 613	1 411	3 049.2	70.6	21.4	0.0	4.6	0.0	2.2	1.2
01 35896	Hoover	47.1	84 978	389	1 804.2	71.2	20.5	0.0	5.3	0.0	1.2	1.8
01 37000	Huntsville...............	213.4	193 079	124	904.8	62.4	31.3	0.1	2.5	0.0	1.0	2.7
01 45784	Madison	29.6	47 959	794	1 620.2	72.0	15.9	0.5	7.1	0.0	0.1	4.4
01 50000	Mobile	139.4	192 904	125	1 383.8	45.9	47.9	0.2	2.5	0.0	0.7	2.8
01 51000	Montgomery	159.8	200 022	115	1 251.7	35.1	59.6	0.1	2.3	0.0	0.8	2.1
01 57048	Opelika	59.7	29 869	1 256	500.3	NA	NA	NA	NA	NA	NA	NA
01 59472	Phenix City	28.0	37 132	1 028	1 326.1	NA	NA	NA	NA	NA	NA	NA
01 62328	Prattville................	33.4	35 606	1 073	1 066.0	72.8	21.4	0.6	1.8	0.2	0.0	3.1
01 77256	Tuscaloosa.............	61.6	99 543	306	1 616.0	53.0	42.8	0.1	2.6	0.3	0.7	0.5
01 78552	Vestavia Hills...........	20.0	34 688	1 098	1 734.4	NA	NA	NA	NA	NA	NA	NA
02 00000	ALASKA	570 638.3	741 894	X	1.3	65.2	3.5	13.7	6.4	0.9	1.7	8.6
02 03000	Anchorage..............	1 706.6	298 192	66	174.7	62.9	6.2	6.5	9.7	1.9	3.2	9.6
02 24230	Fairbanks...............	31.7	32 751	1 160	1 033.2	62.6	8.3	10.4	5.0	0.3	1.1	12.2
02 36400	Juneau	2 702.0	32 468	1 165	12.0	69.3	1.3	12.2	8.7	0.3	0.2	8.0
04 00000	ARIZONA	113 590.7	6 931 071	X	61.0	77.4	4.4	4.5	3.2	0.2	7.1	3.3
04 02830	Apache Junction............	34.8	39 954	949	1 148.1	NA	NA	NA	NA	NA	NA	NA
04 04720	Avondale	45.2	82 881	405	1 833.7	74.8	13.0	0.4	2.8	0.1	6.3	2.6
04 07940	Buckeye.................	392.3	64 629	560	164.7	75.8	10.7	2.1	1.1	0.3	6.1	4.0
04 08220	Bullhead City	59.4	39 970	947	672.9	90.5	1.7	0.5	1.4	0.1	2.6	3.2
04 10530	Casa Grande............	110.2	54 534	692	494.9	65.0	4.2	9.1	1.6	0.0	18.3	1.7
04 12000	Chandler................	64.9	247 477	84	3 813.2	76.7	4.9	1.5	11.0	0.0	2.1	3.8
04 22220	El Mirage	9.9	35 043	1 083	3 539.7	77.8	11.9	2.4	0.9	0.0	4.5	2.5
04 23620	Flagstaff................	64.7	71 459	492	1 104.5	79.0	2.5	6.4	2.6	0.3	4.7	4.5
04 23760	Florence	62.6	25 779	1 404	411.8	83.3	6.5	3.0	0.3	0.1	3.4	3.3
04 27400	Gilbert...................	68.0	237 133	93	3 487.3	82.4	2.8	1.6	6.7	0.1	3.1	3.2
04 27820	Glendale.................	59.1	245 895	86	4 160.7	80.5	5.3	0.7	5.1	0.2	3.7	4.4
04 28380	Goodyear...............	191.2	77 258	441	404.1	77.7	10.0	0.4	5.9	0.1	2.5	3.4
04 37620	Kingman	34.8	29 029	1 280	834.2	83.8	2.1	3.7	4.1	0.0	3.9	2.3
04 39370	Lake Havasu City.........	46.2	53 743	704	1 163.3	93.6	0.1	0.8	1.4	0.0	2.8	1.2
04 44270	Marana	121.0	43 474	866	359.3	78.8	3.4	0.2	7.4	0.0	4.6	5.6
04 44410	Maricopa................	41.0	46 903	818	1 144.0	67.4	11.0	1.7	4.2	0.1	9.1	6.6
04 46000	Mesa.....................	137.9	484 587	36	3 514.0	84.3	3.7	2.2	2.2	0.4	3.6	3.5
04 51600	Oro Valley	35.6	43 781	861	1 229.8	87.0	1.8	0.4	2.9	0.0	3.4	4.4
04 54050	Peoria	175.7	164 173	156	934.4	85.5	3.6	1.1	2.8	0.3	3.6	3.2
04 55000	Phoenix..................	517.6	1 615 017	5	3 120.2	71.6	7.1	2.0	3.3	0.2	12.5	3.3
04 57380	Prescott	44.9	42 513	886	946.8	92.8	0.6	1.1	2.1	0.6	0.3	2.6
04 57450	Prescott Valley...........	40.8	43 132	870	1 057.2	93.1	1.5	0.2	1.0	0.0	1.1	3.0
04 58150	Queen Creek............	29.2	35 524	1 075	1 216.6	87.6	3.6	2.1	2.0	0.1	0.7	3.9
04 62140	Sahuarita	31.5	28 794	1 291	914.1	82.3	5.3	0.4	3.9	0.0	3.5	4.5
04 63470	San Luis	34.1	32 148	1 176	942.8	84.5	0.2	0.3	0.0	0.0	14.6	0.3
04 65000	Scottsdale..............	183.9	246 645	85	1 341.2	84.7	1.6	2.2	3.9	0.3	5.1	2.2
04 66820	Sierra Vista.............	152.2	43 208	868	283.9	78.4	7.9	0.6	5.1	0.4	3.1	4.5
04 71510	Surprise	107.9	132 677	202	1 229.6	86.4	6.0	0.2	1.2	0.2	2.3	3.7
04 73000	Tempe	40.0	182 498	133	4 562.5	70.8	5.6	1.9	8.3	0.5	9.4	3.5
04 77000	Tucson...................	230.8	530 706	33	2 299.4	72.8	5.1	3.3	3.1	0.1	11.5	4.0
04 85540	Yuma	121.0	94 906	330	784.3	71.9	3.0	0.5	0.8	0.0	21.1	2.6
05 00000	ARKANSAS...............	52 035.6	2 988 248	X	57.4	77.5	15.8	0.7	1.4	0.3	2.2	2.2
05 04840	Bella Vista	45.3	28 406	1 313	627.1	NA	NA	NA	NA	NA	NA	NA
05 05290	Benton...................	22.2	35 775	1 066	1 611.5	NA	NA	NA	NA	NA	NA	NA
05 05320	Bentonville..............	31.5	47 093	814	1 495.0	82.0	4.8	0.3	10.6	0.1	1.1	1.0
05 15190	Conway..................	46.1	65 300	552	1 416.5	76.4	17.1	0.2	2.5	0.0	1.6	2.1
05 23290	Fayetteville.............	54.0	83 826	397	1 552.3	77.9	7.7	0.4	4.0	0.0	4.8	5.2
05 24550	Fort Smith...............	63.2	88 133	369	1 394.5	71.4	10.7	1.5	5.9	0.0	6.6	4.0
05 33400	Hot Springs	36.4	36 867	1 032	1 012.8	NA	NA	NA	NA	NA	NA	NA

1. Dry land or land partially or temporarily covered by water. 2. Hispanic or Latino persons may be of any race.

Table D. Cities — Population

City	Percent Hispanic or Latino[1], 2015	Percent foreign born 2015	Age of population (percent), 2010-2014							Median age 2015	Percent female 2015	Population			
			Under 18 years	18 to 24 years	25 to 34 years	35 to 44 years	45 to 54 years	55 to 64 years	65 years and over			Census counts		Percent change	
												2000	2010	2000–2010	2010–2016
	12	13	14	15	16	17	18	19	20	21	22	23	24	25	26
United States............	17.6	13.5	22.9	9.8	13.7	12.7	13.4	12.7	14.9	37.8	50.8	281 421 906	308 758 105	9.7	4.7
ALABAMA	4.0	3.5	22.8	9.6	12.9	12.6	13.3	13.2	15.7	38.7	51.6	4 447 100	4 780 131	7.5	1.7
Alabaster..................	12.1	5.4	22.7	9.8	12.7	13.3	16.7	11.4	13.4	37.9	49.8	22 619	31 066	37.3	6.1
Auburn.....................	4.3	10.2	20.1	33.4	12.2	12.9	7.0	7.7	6.7	23.9	51.3	42 987	53 393	24.2	18.2
Bessemer..................	4.6	3.3	23.1	8.5	13.4	15.7	10.7	11.9	16.7	39.7	52.9	29 672	27 467	-7.4	-3.5
Birmingham..............	4.2	3.8	20.8	11.1	17.3	11.1	12.2	13.7	13.8	35.6	52.5	242 820	212 204	-12.6	0.0
Decatur....................	7.6	6.8	23.3	7.6	14.3	11.5	13.3	13.9	16.0	38.6	53.0	53 929	55 711	3.3	-1.1
Dothan.....................	2.5	2.5	23.8	7.9	13.6	12.6	12.8	12.3	16.9	38.9	52.4	57 737	65 773	13.9	4.1
Enterprise.................	9.9	6.1	25.7	9.2	10.0	14.5	14.2	11.0	15.4	39.9	51.9	21 178	26 612	25.7	5.3
Florence...................	2.2	2.1	18.5	18.5	10.8	10.8	11.2	12.2	18.0	38.2	54.7	36 264	39 339	8.5	1.6
Gadsden...................	9.2	5.1	20.7	12.5	11.0	13.7	10.9	14.2	17.0	39.1	49.6	38 978	36 895	-5.3	-2.9
Homewood................	2.5	9.7	23.3	13.3	20.1	13.3	9.9	9.2	11.0	31.1	55.2	25 043	25 163	0.5	1.8
Hoover.....................	4.0	9.7	25.8	6.3	12.1	14.5	12.6	13.1	15.5	38.5	55.2	62 742	80 996	29.1	4.9
Huntsville.................	5.8	6.7	20.3	10.2	15.6	11.9	12.9	13.2	15.8	38.1	51.5	158 216	180 375	14.0	7.0
Madison...................	3.9	9.2	26.1	8.4	10.8	16.0	16.4	13.4	8.9	39.0	50.9	29 329	42 961	46.5	11.6
Mobile.....................	2.7	3.7	21.1	10.1	15.3	11.9	12.7	13.6	15.4	38.0	53.0	198 915	194 670	-2.1	-0.9
Montgomery..............	3.3	4.7	23.5	11.0	14.9	12.5	12.2	12.4	13.5	35.4	52.8	201 568	205 514	2.0	-2.7
Opelika....................	0.3	4.1	26.8	13.0	11.0	17.9	12.2	9.3	9.9	32.9	51.2	23 498	26 425	12.5	13.0
Phenix City...............	8.7	6.6	26.0	10.2	20.0	7.5	11.5	10.4	14.4	30.9	54.0	28 265	32 874	16.3	13.0
Prattville..................	1.5	3.4	20.2	10.8	12.6	12.4	13.3	14.2	16.6	40.7	50.7	24 303	34 001	39.9	4.7
Tuscaloosa...............	2.5	4.8	16.8	27.5	14.2	8.9	11.1	10.7	10.8	29.1	51.9	77 906	90 353	16.0	10.2
Vestavia Hills............	5.9	7.4	25.1	3.4	14.2	14.8	12.0	10.1	20.3	40.4	49.7	24 476	34 154	39.5	1.6
ALASKA	7.0	7.9	25.2	11.2	16.1	12.4	12.6	12.8	9.6	33.3	47.4	626 932	710 249	13.3	4.5
Anchorage................	9.1	11.1	24.8	11.6	17.7	12.5	12.2	12.0	9.2	32.2	48.8	260 283	291 826	12.1	2.2
Fairbanks.................	8.5	6.0	25.0	21.8	20.1	12.0	7.1	9.9	4.1	26.1	45.4	30 224	31 535	4.3	3.9
Juneau.....................	6.5	9.5	22.6	7.8	17.7	11.2	15.1	14.9	10.6	36.8	48.6	30 711	31 275	1.8	3.8
ARIZONA	30.7	13.4	23.7	9.8	13.4	12.4	12.3	11.9	16.4	37.4	50.4	5 130 632	6 392 301	24.6	8.4
Apache Junction...........	9.5	5.1	16.5	6.4	10.1	13.0	11.9	12.4	29.7	48.9	48.5	31 814	35 745	12.4	11.8
Avondale..................	43.0	10.4	32.2	10.0	17.2	12.9	11.8	8.2	7.8	29.1	52.0	35 883	76 130	112.2	8.9
Buckeye...................	30.6	10.1	29.2	7.6	17.0	13.7	13.9	8.1	10.5	33.3	47.0	6 537	50 908	678.8	27.0
Bullhead City............	21.6	7.3	15.2	9.4	9.9	7.2	12.4	17.8	28.2	53.1	50.7	33 769	39 540	17.1	1.1
Casa Grande............	44.8	11.7	25.5	8.2	10.3	10.7	12.5	12.7	20.0	39.7	53.5	25 224	48 583	92.6	12.2
Chandler..................	21.9	14.8	26.0	7.8	14.8	15.2	14.1	12.1	9.9	35.6	50.6	176 581	236 190	33.8	4.8
El Mirage.................	46.0	11.6	36.8	9.1	18.3	12.3	9.6	7.2	6.7	27.0	47.5	7 609	31 797	317.9	10.2
Flagstaff..................	19.3	6.1	18.9	33.3	12.8	10.5	8.3	8.6	7.5	23.9	52.8	52 894	66 067	24.9	8.2
Florence	37.0	16.8	8.9	10.4	22.6	17.2	13.8	12.6	14.5	38.1	28.6	17 054	25 561	49.9	0.9
Gilbert.....................	16.1	9.9	30.7	8.7	13.2	16.0	13.9	10.1	7.3	33.2	52.8	109 697	208 403	90.0	13.8
Glendale..................	34.9	18.4	25.8	10.3	14.8	12.6	13.9	11.5	11.2	34.4	51.4	218 812	226 408	3.5	8.6
Goodyear.................	27.3	14.9	24.4	7.3	11.9	16.2	14.1	11.1	15.0	38.6	53.5	18 911	65 236	245.0	18.4
Kingman...................	9.7	4.8	20.6	6.0	10.3	11.2	9.9	14.1	27.9	46.8	51.7	20 069	28 068	39.9	3.4
Lake Havasu City.........	18.2	9.9	16.1	5.0	8.8	10.2	12.8	16.7	30.3	52.7	49.8	41 938	52 531	25.3	2.3
Marana.....................	27.1	13.1	25.4	9.5	12.4	12.0	12.0	10.5	11.2	36.8	52.6	13 556	34 566	155.0	25.8
Maricopa..................	29.7	14.1	31.0	7.2	16.8	15.3	10.0	8.4	11.2	33.7	52.0	1 040	43 482	4 081.0	7.9
Mesa........................	27.9	12.2	23.6	9.6	14.6	11.9	12.2	12.0	16.0	36.9	50.2	396 375	440 134	11.0	10.1
Oro Valley	16.8	6.2	15.9	5.8	5.5	11.4	10.9	17.9	32.7	55.4	49.3	29 700	41 033	38.2	6.7
Peoria......................	24.0	8.3	26.5	8.7	12.8	11.0	12.2	13.5	15.3	36.9	53.2	108 364	154 105	42.2	6.5
Phoenix....................	42.9	19.2	26.3	10.0	15.6	14.3	12.8	10.6	10.4	33.8	49.7	1 321 045	1 447 624	9.6	11.6
Prescott....................	9.0	4.3	13.1	10.2	7.9	8.2	10.8	16.4	33.3	54.8	49.3	33 938	39 834	17.4	6.7
Prescott Valley	18.3	5.9	22.8	6.8	10.4	10.7	10.6	15.8	22.9	43.9	52.4	23 535	38 875	65.2	11.0
Queen Creek.............	17.2	8.3	38.6	6.2	8.0	15.9	12.0	9.2	10.2	33.5	51.1	4 316	26 348	510.5	34.8
Sahuarita..................	31.1	8.4	26.6	6.8	13.0	16.2	8.1	10.2	19.1	37.3	52.9	3 242	25 259	679.1	14.0
San Luis...................	97.8	50.9	32.7	15.0	12.9	12.4	13.1	9.2	4.7	27.4	48.9	15 322	27 909	82.1	15.2
Scottsdale................	10.5	11.5	15.4	6.7	13.5	11.6	15.3	13.4	24.1	46.9	51.1	202 705	217 434	7.3	13.4
Sierra Vista..............	25.9	9.4	25.8	9.6	15.9	11.1	9.6	10.5	17.4	33.9	55.9	37 775	45 268	19.8	-4.6
Surprise...................	19.7	7.7	27.4	6.1	11.8	13.4	10.3	9.9	21.1	39.4	51.0	30 848	117 517	281.0	12.9
Tempe......................	25.3	15.1	16.2	25.6	19.0	10.3	11.2	8.2	9.5	28.8	48.0	158 625	161 780	2.0	12.8
Tucson.....................	43.5	15.5	21.6	16.0	14.4	11.4	11.1	11.7	13.7	33.6	50.2	486 699	520 562	7.0	1.9
Yuma.......................	60.6	20.5	24.3	13.4	13.7	11.9	11.3	10.2	15.2	33.4	48.7	77 515	90 715	17.0	4.6
ARKANSAS..............	7.0	4.8	23.7	9.6	12.9	12.3	12.9	12.5	16.1	37.9	50.9	2 673 400	2 916 025	9.1	2.5
Bella Vista	4.6	2.7	16.4	6.5	6.4	11.7	13.9	13.2	31.9	51.2	52.5	16 582	26 507	59.9	7.2
Benton.....................	3.4	3.2	25.1	7.6	19.1	11.0	9.6	9.4	18.2	34.2	52.9	21 906	30 518	39.3	17.2
Bentonville...............	8.0	15.5	31.0	6.8	14.9	18.8	10.9	8.3	9.3	33.4	52.0	19 730	35 282	78.8	33.5
Conway....................	3.2	3.9	22.5	20.0	15.1	13.6	9.9	8.7	10.1	29.0	51.4	43 167	58 877	36.4	10.9
Fayetteville...............	6.7	7.6	19.0	25.4	18.5	11.0	8.1	7.7	10.3	27.1	49.3	58 047	73 585	26.8	13.9
Fort Smith.................	19.4	14.9	24.2	10.4	15.5	10.9	12.8	11.8	14.4	34.9	50.9	80 268	86 267	7.5	2.2
Hot Springs	4.5	4.8	19.9	7.7	11.3	7.9	13.9	17.3	22.0	46.9	55.8	35 750	36 292	1.5	1.6

1. May be of any race.

Table D. Cities — Households, Group Quarters, Crime, and Education

| City | Households, 2015 | | Percent | | Persons in group quarters, 2010 | | Institutional | | Serious crimes known to police,[2] 2014 | | | | Educational attainment, 2015 | | Attainment[4] (percent) |
| | Number | Persons per house-hold | Female family house-holder[1] | One-person | Total | Total | Persons in nursing facilities | Non-institu-tional | Number | Rate[3] | Violent | Property | Population age 25 and older | High school graduate or less | Bachelor's degree or more |
	27	28	29	30	31	32	33	34	35	36	37	38	39	40	41
United States	118 208 250	2.65	12.8	27.9	7 987 323	3 993 659	1 502 264	3 993 664	94 432 120	2 962	3 660	2 596	216 447 163	40.4	30.6
ALABAMA	1 846 390	2.57	14.7	29.9	115 816	67 004	22 995	48 812	174 821	3 605	427	3 178	3 282 252	46.2	24.2
Alabaster	11 416	2.84	8.3	22.2	300	297	293	3	670	2 122	184	1 939	22 090	32.2	32.7
Auburn	22 255	2.57	13.7	30.6	3 827	130	130	3 697	1 780	2 974	211	2 763	28 853	14.8	56.8
Bessemer	10 124	2.56	31.1	31.5	871	519	472	352	2 226	8 258	1 339	6 918	18 276	57.6	12.2
Birmingham	93 467	2.21	23.5	41.6	9 035	3 300	1 559	5 735	17 298	8 155	1 588	6 567	146 295	42.1	25.3
Decatur	23 214	2.33	19.0	32.9	966	767	246	199	2 563	4 590	201	4 390	38 205	40.0	26.2
Dothan	25 709	2.59	18.6	31.0	1 369	1 171	484	198	1 998	2 918	304	2 614	46 150	41.1	24.8
Enterprise	9 613	2.88	18.6	24.6	279	245	245	34	1 059	3 778	375	3 403	18 200	31.9	29.0
Florence	17 518	2.17	14.5	41.7	1 701	524	370	1 177	1 678	4 170	502	3 668	25 215	42.1	28.8
Gadsden	13 614	2.57	21.0	32.9	1 752	1 189	380	563	3 164	8 679	982	7 697	24 063	56.5	15.2
Homewood	10 040	2.35	20.2	30.5	1 864	18	0	1 846	1 101	4 251	259	3 992	16 306	20.5	53.0
Hoover	32 767	2.58	10.4	26.9	408	393	361	15	2 357	2 778	116	2 663	57 598	17.9	54.1
Huntsville	83 144	2.18	12.7	37.3	6 786	1 924	874	4 862	10 628	5 665	782	4 883	131 333	30.0	42.3
Madison	17 062	2.86	9.0	22.0	270	270	225	0	1 093	2 354	323	2 031	32 087	16.7	59.2
Mobile	77 701	2.40	19.4	36.8	5 598	2 632	1 196	2 966	13 091	5 223	594	4 629	133 825	42.3	28.3
Montgomery	80 655	2.41	20.7	33.0	6 879	2 967	1 005	3 912	10 071	5 031	522	4 508	131 409	39.7	31.7
Opelika	10 326	2.81	16.1	25.3	572	481	141	91	1 810	6 198	644	5 555	17 787	39.1	27.5
Phenix City	14 610	2.57	16.4	36.0	557	494	203	63	2 499	6 462	644	5 818	24 303	38.3	16.8
Prattville	13 159	2.56	9.0	24.9	398	362	181	36	1 355	3 814	228	3 586	23 600	47.6	30.4
Tuscaloosa	33 270	2.67	19.2	32.1	9 659	942	144	8 717	4 604	4 775	483	4 292	54 778	39.5	37.8
Vestavia Hills	14 319	2.38	5.3	25.9	141	138	138	3	478	1 406	65	1 341	24 402	15.2	64.0
ALASKA	250 185	2.84	11.3	26.7	26 352	6 458	1 626	19 894	25 018	3 396	636	2 760	469 523	34.6	29.7
Anchorage	104 936	2.77	14.1	27.2	8 450	2 828	1 137	5 622	14 136	4 692	865	3 827	190 006	29.8	35.6
Fairbanks	10 923	2.74	12.1	25.5	2 518	427	81	2 091	1 461	4 499	659	3 840	17 211	27.7	34.2
Juneau	12 423	2.57	9.4	27.9	887	408	57	479	1 061	3 216	573	2 643	22 782	26.5	39.4
ARIZONA	2 463 008	2.71	12.5	27.6	139 384	84 788	13 819	54 596	242 156	3 597	400	3 198	4 536 954	38.4	27.7
Apache Junction	16 690	2.27	7.9	38.7	283	120	120	163	1 323	3 549	247	3 303	29 262	41.3	18.7
Avondale	25 329	3.18	17.3	21.9	160	146	132	14	3 797	4 778	287	4 491	46 656	38.5	18.9
Buckeye	16 701	3.39	13.8	11.2	5 094	5 084	0	10	1 170	2 013	50	1 963	39 266	38.1	15.1
Bullhead City	16 880	2.33	16.6	30.7	166	96	93	70	1 684	4 281	206	4 075	29 733	59.0	10.1
Casa Grande	16 364	3.13	19.2	25.5	282	47	3	235	2 035	4 053	478	3 575	34 081	46.2	16.0
Chandler	93 639	2.78	11.0	24.7	546	136	94	410	6 109	2 421	185	2 236	172 466	23.9	43.2
El Mirage	9 087	3.73	21.2	15.6	13	0	0	13	1 071	3 216	168	3 047	18 379	50.9	16.4
Flagstaff	22 707	2.55	10.0	25.9	8 076	668	114	7 408	3 295	4 742	396	4 346	33 612	21.8	44.7
Florence	6 500	2.33	7.4	31.1	17 700	17 700	0	0	182	726	128	598	25 118	52.5	14.3
Gilbert	77 123	3.20	10.7	17.4	304	4	0	300	3 730	1 584	90	1 494	150 007	22.6	40.5
Glendale	81 948	2.89	17.0	26.4	3 257	1 000	836	2 257	13 499	5 701	389	5 312	153 520	43.7	21.3
Goodyear	25 541	2.97	10.6	16.2	3 828	3 670	164	158	1 684	2 251	148	2 102	53 953	26.9	30.1
Kingman	11 413	2.41	14.5	27.8	699	541	132	158	1 544	5 413	256	5 157	21 235	44.9	16.0
Lake Havasu City	23 767	2.25	10.6	26.0	201	151	142	50	1 197	2 263	166	2 097	42 254	48.1	13.6
Marana	14 694	2.78	7.7	15.3	520	499	0	21	1 090	2 777	51	2 726	26 901	23.7	45.1
Maricopa	13 153	3.70	9.4	17.0	0	0	0	0	738	1 613	175	1 439	29 997	39.2	21.7
Mesa	174 853	2.68	12.0	28.6	3 538	1 344	928	2 194	15 059	3 259	459	2 800	314 920	37.9	25.2
Oro Valley	19 476	2.23	5.1	25.6	68	63	42	5	665	1 592	36	1 556	34 105	21.3	47.2
Peoria	57 095	2.97	13.4	20.9	1 227	868	826	359	3 543	2 151	148	2 003	110 871	32.5	29.4
Phoenix	534 199	2.89	15.1	28.3	21 738	13 589	2 696	8 149	65 726	4 296	572	3 724	995 646	44.5	26.6
Prescott	19 424	2.02	5.0	39.9	2 008	675	474	1 333	1 370	3 342	344	2 998	32 129	22.2	38.1
Prescott Valley	16 910	2.48	13.6	24.1	209	158	118	51	1 016	2 538	220	2 318	29 707	44.3	20.4
Queen Creek	9 803	3.50	6.5	16.7	16	0	0	16	NA	NA	NA	NA	18 975	24.9	42.2
Sahuarita	9 848	2.61	7.4	23.0	63	44	44	19	402	1 478	33	1 444	17 116	23.2	33.6
San Luis	7 737	3.85	19.1	9.2	524	502	0	22	507	1 581	156	1 425	16 467	75.8	8.3
Scottsdale	108 501	2.17	6.7	38.4	1 159	686	622	473	5 663	2 469	158	2 312	184 631	18.4	55.1
Sierra Vista	17 140	2.38	14.5	25.2	3 037	233	217	2 804	1 396	3 092	171	2 922	28 004	21.8	27.6
Surprise	44 180	2.90	10.9	21.2	274	89	80	185	2 236	1 788	110	1 679	85 451	34.6	26.3
Tempe	67 325	2.44	10.5	33.7	10 188	298	280	9 890	8 843	5 208	471	4 737	102 347	23.8	43.8
Tucson	206 448	2.45	15.8	34.2	20 706	9 920	1 798	10 786	35 048	6 646	653	5 993	331 389	41.0	26.5
Yuma	34 467	2.64	15.4	25.3	5 128	3 291	308	1 837	5 223	3 397	442	2 956	58 611	46.8	18.0
ARKANSAS	1 144 663	2.53	13.1	28.4	78 931	47 287	18 532	31 644	113 261	3 818	480	3 338	1 987 819	48.7	21.8
Bella Vista	12 553	2.22	7.7	27.6	133	133	133	0	213	763	158	605	21 574	28.5	37.1
Benton	12 325	2.73	12.8	29.5	493	462	289	31	1 576	4 669	376	4 292	23 005	45.2	26.9
Bentonville	15 572	2.81	7.2	24.4	258	179	160	79	751	1 817	150	1 667	27 684	31.8	45.9
Conway	23 440	2.57	14.5	27.2	4 038	1 118	372	2 920	3 265	5 031	391	4 640	37 392	26.9	38.7
Fayetteville	33 227	2.28	9.5	36.6	6 818	1 124	405	5 694	3 799	4 733	496	4 237	46 034	21.2	48.5
Fort Smith	35 543	2.44	13.9	34.3	1 930	1 083	592	847	5 339	6 068	752	5 315	57 680	52.5	19.0
Hot Springs	16 647	2.04	14.3	46.6	1 692	1 127	578	565	NA	NA	NA	NA	25 801	42.7	20.2

1. No spouse present. 2. Data for serious crimes have not been adjusted for underreporting. This may affect comparability between geographic areas and over time. 3. Per 100,000 population estimated by the FBI. 4. Persons 25 years old and over.

Table D. Cities — Income, Poverty, and Housing

City	Money income, 2015 Households — Median income	Percent with income of $200,000 or more	Percent with income of less than $25,000	Families — Total Families	Percent with income below poverty	Housing units, 2010 — Total	Percent change, 2000–2010	Vacant units for sale or rent[2]	Occupied housing units 2015 Owner-occupied — Total	Percent	Median value[3] (dollars)	Renter-occupied — Percent	Median rent (dollars)
	42	43	44	45	46	47	48	49	50	51	52	53	54
United States............	55 775	5.8	16.8	77 530 756	10.6	131 704 730	13.6	14 988 438	118 208 250	63.0	194 500	37.0	959
ALABAMA	44 765	3.1	22.8	1 213 540	13.7	2 171 853	10.6	288 062	1 846 390	67.9	134 100	32.1	729
Alabaster	67 332	2.8	13.0	8 341	9.4	11 295	28.3	667	11 416	81.9	167 100	18.1	932
Auburn	38 867	5.1	34.0	12 500	16.8	24 646	22.7	2 535	22 255	42.5	253 100	57.5	844
Bessemer..................	28 011	2.1	31.0	6 615	18.4	12 369	-3.2	1 658	10 124	58.1	87 000	41.9	773
Birmingham	32 378	1.3	33.6	47 331	24.9	108 981	-2.9	19 599	93 467	44.0	93 000	56.0	743
Decatur.....................	39 305	2.9	23.8	14 214	24.0	24 538	2.2	1 962	23 214	59.3	136 100	40.7	616
Dothan......................	44 208	4.7	23.9	16 686	15.5	29 274	12.6	2 429	25 709	58.0	142 200	42.0	703
Enterprise.................	53 792	3.0	20.2	7 139	10.9	11 616	20.2	1 103	9 613	60.8	151 900	39.2	701
Florence	32 991	0.7	28.6	8 478	16.7	19 299	9.1	2 032	17 518	53.8	114 100	46.2	616
Gadsden	31 639	0.9	24.7	8 741	18.3	17 672	-5.9	2 501	13 614	58.8	72 900	41.2	636
Homewood	57 840	7.9	11.7	6 585	9.8	11 385	0.5	1 293	10 040	57.2	292 000	42.8	1 013
Hoover......................	77 365	9.9	7.0	23 304	3.5	35 474	31.2	2 996	32 767	70.5	277 900	29.5	1 008
Huntsville.................	46 769	4.7	21.9	46 014	13.6	84 949	15.4	7 916	83 144	57.8	175 100	42.2	745
Madison	105 916	11.7	6.3	12 888	5.4	17 203	43.1	1 092	17 062	74.6	246 300	25.4	869
Mobile......................	38 678	3.0	27.6	44 116	15.6	89 127	3.5	10 168	77 701	55.0	113 800	45.0	783
Montgomery	41 836	3.8	24.0	49 756	18.0	92 115	6.1	10 629	80 655	54.6	116 700	45.4	822
Opelika	46 111	0.8	21.2	7 453	14.2	11 751	14.4	1 228	10 326	60.0	152 100	40.0	768
Phenix City...............	32 359	1.2	30.4	8 513	22.7	15 198	15.0	1 955	13 159	43.8	143 400	56.2	759
Prattville...................	51 842	4.1	17.4	9 060	3.5	13 541	40.7	830	13 159	65.6	169 400	34.4	852
Tuscaloosa................	44 125	4.3	24.0	19 022	14.1	40 842	16.8	4 657	33 270	47.7	179 800	52.3	822
Vestavia Hills............	94 205	18.1	6.3	NA	NA	14 952	40.8	965	14 319	74.3	345 700	25.7	824
ALASKA	73 355	6.7	10.7	163 800	7.0	306 967	17.6	48 909	250 185	63.9	259 600	36.1	1 163
Anchorage.................	78 662	8.7	8.3	67 371	6.6	113 032	12.6	5 700	104 936	61.4	302 500	38.6	1 241
Fairbanks..................	52 172	5.6	13.9	7 297	6.9	13 056	5.2	1 522	10 923	28.7	220 600	71.3	1 311
Juneau......................	86 110	7.6	7.5	7 797	7.5	13 055	6.3	868	12 423	65.2	330 400	34.8	1 230
ARIZONA	51 492	4.2	17.5	1 598 414	12.5	2 844 526	29.9	463 536	2 463 008	61.9	194 300	38.1	933
Apache Junction............	40 559	0.4	26.5	9 281	7.4	22 564	-1.0	6 990	16 690	74.6	98 500	25.4	718
Avondale	54 686	0.8	13.3	17 791	14.1	27 001	136.6	3 615	25 329	45.6	181 200	54.4	1 066
Buckeye....................	61 491	1.5	9.1	14 070	6.5	18 207	NA	3 783	16 701	59.8	175 500	40.2	1 130
Bullhead City.............	35 075	1.6	21.1	10 051	9.7	23 464	27.5	6 703	16 880	57.0	108 400	43.0	692
Casa Grande.............	45 183	0.6	20.5	11 038	14.4	22 400	104.8	4 749	16 364	69.1	135 000	30.9	840
Chandler...................	75 562	6.8	9.9	64 771	7.0	94 404	41.7	7 480	93 639	62.8	273 600	37.2	1 153
El Mirage	53 940	0.7	9.5	7 115	16.3	11 326	NA	1 910	9 087	61.5	139 900	38.5	1 076
Flagstaff...................	51 616	5.8	20.9	11 890	8.2	26 254	22.5	3 418	22 707	46.2	280 300	53.8	1 144
Florence	47 332	3.0	13.3	NA	NA	5 224	60.5	1 894	6 500	74.3	119 500	25.7	877
Gilbert......................	86 045	7.7	6.1	58 968	5.0	74 907	102.2	5 535	77 123	72.3	284 800	27.7	1 323
Glendale	45 812	2.7	19.8	53 617	18.0	90 505	13.6	11 391	81 948	53.1	181 000	46.9	867
Goodyear..................	73 164	7.0	9.8	19 923	8.9	25 027	275.6	3 536	25 541	77.5	254 600	22.5	1 169
Kingman....................	45 118	1.3	20.3	7 628	4.2	12 724	48.6	1 507	11 413	67.7	151 000	32.3	780
Lake Havasu City........	45 277	2.2	16.2	15 274	8.0	32 327	40.6	9 159	23 767	66.8	220 500	33.2	854
Marana	74 611	2.2	5.4	11 721	3.9	14 726	160.3	1 653	14 694	70.8	226 300	29.2	1 197
Maricopa...................	66 591	2.2	10.5	10 308	10.1	17 240	NA	2 881	13 153	72.0	169 900	28.0	1 309
Mesa........................	49 177	3.0	17.1	111 896	12.7	201 173	14.5	35 799	174 853	58.4	188 100	41.6	892
Oro Valley	78 180	10.6	9.1	13 762	3.4	20 340	45.2	2 536	19 476	75.2	285 200	24.8	1 030
Peoria	66 308	6.0	8.5	41 443	4.7	64 818	51.9	7 361	57 095	71.8	223 000	28.2	1 116
Phoenix	48 452	4.6	19.2	336 611	17.3	590 149	19.0	75 343	534 199	50.4	200 800	49.6	922
Prescott....................	45 962	1.9	18.6	10 124	6.2	22 159	27.1	3 548	19 424	62.6	319 900	37.4	817
Prescott Valley	47 388	0.6	17.1	11 690	14.2	17 494	84.5	2 130	16 910	69.0	194 700	31.0	884
Queen Creek..............	91 767	13.1	12.3	NA	NA	8 557	NA	837	9 803	84.9	324 600	15.1	1 233
Sahuarita..................	68 558	2.4	5.9	NA	NA	10 615	NA	1 595	9 848	79.8	182 600	20.2	1 504
San Luis	31 326	0.0	26.7	7 022	24.2	6 525	95.8	572	7 737	71.9	106 300	28.1	616
Scottsdale.................	75 346	14.2	10.5	57 433	5.5	124 001	18.2	22 728	108 501	64.7	434 700	35.3	1 143
Sierra Vista...............	60 508	3.1	14.2	12 234	8.2	18 742	20.0	1 683	17 140	52.4	182 800	47.6	845
Surprise	65 688	2.1	8.0	32 802	5.2	52 586	222.5	9 314	44 180	73.6	213 900	26.4	1 187
Tempe......................	51 688	3.6	19.0	32 964	8.5	73 462	9.6	7 462	67 325	40.5	246 200	59.5	972
Tucson......................	38 155	1.3	25.7	112 532	18.5	229 762	9.5	24 372	206 448	47.5	139 400	52.5	775
Yuma........................	43 663	2.0	25.1	24 380	18.7	38 626	10.2	7 912	34 467	59.9	125 500	40.1	836
ARKANSAS..............	41 995	3.0	22.6	761 494	13.7	1 316 299	12.2	169 215	1 144 663	65.2	120 700	34.8	695
Bella Vista	53 332	6.5	10.4	NA	NA	13 241	49.2	1 512	12 553	86.8	156 400	13.2	970
Benton......................	46 062	2.9	13.8	NA	NA	12 902	38.9	1 068	12 325	68.3	135 400	31.7	670
Bentonville................	71 933	12.2	8.2	10 919	4.7	14 693	84.9	1 440	15 572	58.1	211 600	41.9	834
Conway.....................	50 705	3.2	23.2	14 073	7.5	24 402	41.2	2 003	23 440	49.5	161 300	50.5	765
Fayetteville...............	39 546	4.0	25.9	16 195	12.4	36 188	42.9	5 462	33 227	36.5	182 600	63.5	690
Fort Smith.................	33 534	2.4	28.4	21 355	26.1	37 899	7.2	3 547	35 543	51.0	116 300	49.0	621
Hot Springs	25 508	1.7	39.3	7 953	22.8	18 947	1.2	3 372	16 647	53.1	119 100	46.9	642

1. Based on population estimated by the American Community Survey.   2. Includes units rented or sold but not occupied.   3. Specified owner-occupied units; $1,000,000 represents $1,000,000 or more   4. 50.0 represents 50 percent or more.   5. 10.0 represents 10 percent or less.

Table D. Cities — Commuting, Computer Access, Migration, Labor Force, and Employment

City	Commuting Percent - Drove alone	With Commutes of 30 minutes or more [1]	Computer Access [2] Percent - With a Computer in the house	With Internet Access	Migration, 2015 - Percent who lived in the same house one year ago	Percent who lived in an other state or county one year ago	Civilian labor force, 2016 - Total	Percent change, 2015–2016	Unemployment - Total	Rate [3]	Population age 16 and older - Number	Percent in Labor Force	Population age 16 to 64 - Number	Percent who worked full-year full-time
	55	56	57	58	59	60	61	62	63	64	65	66	67	68
United States.............	80.3	37.6	86.8	76.7	85.3	6.3	158 741 900	1.1	7 729 204	4.9	256 167 758	63.1	208 435 278	49.1
ALABAMA	88.3	34.4	80.8	68.3	85.7	5.8	2 168 608	0.8	129 833	6.0	3 878 471	56.9	3 116 624	45.7
Alabaster	83.4	52.3	93.5	85.7	92.0	4.2	17 428	0.6	761	4.4	25 758	68.4	21 362	55.6
Auburn.....................	83.8	20.0	93.4	83.6	64.6	16.5	29 055	1.9	1 628	5.6	50 984	59.2	46 849	34.1
Bessemer	NA	32.9	72.7	57.0	77.0	7.7	9 914	0.4	871	8.8	21 446	54.7	16 992	35.5
Birmingham	80.6	23.5	78.8	61.0	78.8	6.0	92 491	0.5	6 588	7.1	174 713	60.9	144 984	43.3
Decatur	NA	27.2	81.2	67.4	78.1	7.3	26 355	-0.1	1 524	5.8	43 810	55.6	34 968	43.1
Dothan	90.9	20.6	81.9	71.9	85.5	4.9	29 348	0.0	1 724	5.9	53 202	58.4	41 763	47.0
Enterprise	91.8	23.7	94.4	87.8	78.7	12.4	10 702	0.3	654	6.1	21 409	62.7	17 091	54.2
Florence	86.5	17.2	80.3	56.3	80.1	12.0	18 535	0.7	1 167	6.3	33 419	51.2	26 226	37.3
Gadsden	86.4	26.4	74.0	60.4	72.8	8.8	13 963	1.4	974	7.0	29 426	54.2	23 307	43.9
Homewood	83.0	16.7	88.6	83.9	74.9	7.5	13 962	0.5	560	4.0	20 460	70.1	17 638	50.6
Hoover	89.4	33.8	95.6	86.8	80.0	10.1	44 108	0.6	1 849	4.2	65 649	70.7	52 463	58.5
Huntsville	90.4	16.8	87.8	78.7	82.1	7.0	93 014	1.5	5 083	5.5	155 178	60.9	125 298	49.6
Madison....................	94.9	19.1	96.7	90.8	90.6	5.2	23 949	1.8	1 117	4.7	38 670	65.7	34 305	50.9
Mobile	90.4	26.9	77.6	64.0	83.9	3.6	86 197	0.7	6 140	7.1	157 373	57.8	127 362	46.0
Montgomery	88.3	17.8	83.9	73.6	77.8	6.5	92 107	0.9	5 497	6.0	159 332	62.0	132 254	46.3
Opelika	NA	18.2	85.4	71.9	87.1	7.5	13 832	1.7	753	5.4	22 696	62.5	19 787	41.4
Phenix City	92.9	21.0	79.9	67.5	75.0	16.4	15 339	-0.3	815	5.3	29 251	61.5	23 787	49.7
Prattville	83.6	31.1	88.5	83.2	80.5	12.1	16 800	1.3	832	5.0	28 095	57.6	22 431	50.3
Tuscaloosa	90.3	14.0	81.5	74.0	76.9	12.9	45 276	0.5	2 996	6.6	84 180	51.0	73 520	36.3
Vestavia Hills.............	86.4	19.2	90.7	85.4	83.7	9.7	17 355	0.5	659	3.8	26 442	66.6	19 493	64.7
ALASKA	71.1	17.2	92.4	81.9	80.1	8.0	360 426	-0.6	23 806	6.6	571 393	70.5	500 385	47.3
Anchorage.................	77.7	16.5	94.0	84.6	77.5	7.8	156 112	-0.3	8 226	5.3	231 969	73.2	204 517	51.7
Fairbanks..................	73.0	4.0	96.2	78.9	70.0	16.0	12 585	-0.4	842	6.7	24 535	77.0	23 198	51.9
Juneau......................	68.6	15.0	97.7	89.7	77.9	4.6	17 162	0.6	750	4.4	26 251	74.9	22 765	53.6
ARIZONA	81.6	35.9	87.6	78.1	82.0	6.1	3 237 864	2.3	171 600	5.3	5 393 214	58.8	4 273 210	46.9
Apache Junction...........	77.6	32.6	75.5	61.8	84.8	11.4	13 914	2.5	981	7.1	32 384	44.7	21 115	45.7
Avondale	86.5	40.1	91.3	85.3	87.5	4.6	41 251	2.6	1 959	4.7	57 437	67.3	51 147	55.7
Buckeye....................	87.9	46.4	97.5	89.9	86.0	6.2	25 026	2.9	1 370	5.5	46 511	55.2	40 003	45.1
Bullhead City..............	86.4	17.4	78.7	68.7	74.6	8.4	15 951	1.8	1 102	6.9	34 072	46.8	22 969	34.2
Casa Grande..............	86.1	25.8	85.0	72.9	80.6	5.7	22 404	3.3	1 300	5.8	39 572	53.8	29 281	41.9
Chandler...................	84.0	32.1	95.2	89.5	78.5	7.1	147 909	2.9	5 766	3.9	200 978	70.4	175 148	55.9
El Mirage	86.6	49.6	92.0	83.8	91.8	2.2	15 624	2.6	784	5.0	22 553	70.5	20 265	55.0
Flagstaff....................	70.2	11.5	94.8	87.2	63.4	24.1	41 003	1.6	1 687	4.1	58 397	67.1	53 096	38.1
Florence	63.2	33.1	82.4	74.8	64.2	25.6	3 883	3.6	242	6.2	28 987	23.2	24 478	19.4
Gilbert	85.9	45.8	97.6	93.9	82.5	6.7	135 702	3.1	4 994	3.7	179 208	72.0	161 016	55.3
Glendale	80.4	42.8	84.4	73.0	81.6	4.0	117 260	2.8	5 688	4.9	185 945	62.2	159 087	47.3
Goodyear..................	85.2	47.1	98.8	95.3	90.6	4.9	37 452	2.8	1 745	4.7	62 896	58.7	51 028	51.3
Kingman	87.5	17.2	86.9	73.8	75.9	15.6	12 581	0.6	782	6.2	23 722	49.3	15 655	44.3
Lake Havasu City.........	81.9	13.2	87.3	81.2	82.9	7.6	23 135	1.1	1 408	6.1	46 630	46.9	30 384	46.3
Marana	85.3	45.9	93.3	90.0	81.8	7.6	20 995	1.3	807	3.8	31 502	63.0	23 620	51.1
Maricopa...................	79.5	64.7	95.4	89.0	81.3	15.1	24 262	3.2	1 138	4.7	35 008	61.2	29 581	47.3
Mesa........................	79.0	37.2	87.7	78.6	79.4	5.3	231 211	2.8	10 488	4.5	373 724	63.6	298 018	50.2
Oro Valley	91.4	43.4	92.0	86.4	77.4	10.8	19 033	1.4	874	4.6	37 810	48.0	23 586	47.4
Peoria	85.9	44.0	92.0	86.0	85.6	3.9	87 949	3.0	3 720	4.2	129 724	64.1	103 531	51.8
Phoenix	79.2	38.1	85.8	74.4	82.8	3.8	778 292	2.8	36 596	4.7	1 198 549	64.7	1 036 651	49.4
Prescott	86.9	20.0	88.2	78.8	80.1	10.3	17 529	3.4	948	5.4	37 527	45.5	23 572	37.8
Prescott Valley	81.0	12.5	90.2	75.2	72.8	10.3	20 368	3.6	883	4.3	33 876	50.1	24 215	39.6
Queen Creek..............	84.0	57.5	NA	NA	86.8	5.3	17 083	3.0	594	3.5	22 738	63.3	19 226	48.9
Sahuarita	85.0	46.3	97.5	91.4	86.5	2.2	11 778	1.3	525	4.5	19 638	59.2	14 724	61.2
San Luis	83.6	43.7	75.2	66.9	93.7	3.8	18 237	-4.0	7 839	43.0	23 016	52.3	21 534	24.8
Scottsdale..................	90.1	32.2	94.7	91.1	82.9	6.3	132 962	3.1	5 072	3.8	204 557	61.8	147 379	55.6
Sierra Vista	83.4	16.1	89.9	83.1	76.5	13.4	18 379	-0.7	940	5.1	33 389	59.2	25 865	56.2
Surprise....................	85.0	50.3	93.6	88.6	88.8	4.4	53 256	2.7	2 577	4.8	97 185	58.6	70 049	53.9
Tempe......................	74.7	19.6	91.9	84.5	70.0	9.3	104 369	2.9	4 426	4.2	150 313	69.5	133 595	46.6
Tucson......................	76.4	28.0	87.8	75.7	73.1	7.3	254 270	1.1	12 999	5.1	430 274	60.3	357 238	39.9
Yuma.......................	86.6	10.3	79.2	72.4	78.4	7.8	42 856	1.8	5 007	11.7	73 504	59.3	59 232	47.3
ARKANSAS...............	85.2	26.9	81.4	64.4	83.1	7.0	1 342 691	0.8	53 697	4.0	2 352 507	57.6	1 874 393	47.1
Bella Vista	91.8	32.0	94.1	75.2	86.1	8.3	11 999	3.8	430	3.6	24 209	51.1	15 290	47.8
Benton	84.5	34.9	82.6	74.2	79.9	10.2	16 317	0.7	517	3.2	26 510	64.5	20 292	58.5
Bentonville.................	86.8	14.8	91.6	62.3	83.0	7.1	23 631	3.9	639	2.7	32 600	65.0	28 466	57.9
Conway	85.7	32.2	92.2	80.0	73.7	12.3	33 096	1.0	1 186	3.6	52 660	65.3	46 088	49.8
Fayetteville................	83.5	22.0	91.9	79.7	66.4	18.7	46 129	3.6	1 300	2.8	68 448	63.1	59 894	41.5
Fort Smith.................	84.6	9.8	76.4	63.2	78.1	9.8	40 342	0.3	1 487	3.7	69 026	55.2	56 364	42.6
Hot Springs	79.8	16.0	78.8	66.3	72.0	8.9	14 023	0.2	667	4.8	29 915	53.4	22 072	32.9

1. Employed persons.   2. Households.   3. Percent of civilian labor force.   4. Persons 16 years old and over.

Table D. Cities — Construction, Wholesale Trade, and Retail Trade

City	Value of residential construction authorized by building permits, 2016			Wholesale trade,[1] 2012				Retail trade,[2] 2012			
	New construction ($1,000)	Number of housing units	Percent single family	Number of establishments	Number of employees	Sales (mil dol)	Annual payroll (mil dol)	Number of establishments	Number of employees	Sales (mil dol)	Annual payroll (mil dol)
	69	70	71	72	73	74	75	76	77	78	79
United States.............	237 101 606	1 206 642	62.2	355 983	4 880 666	5 208 023.5	287 549.6	1 062 083	14 703 529	4 219 821.9	369 001.4
ALABAMA	2 722 956	15 001	77.9	4 600	60 332	57 746.6	2 894.7	18 211	218 531	58 565.0	5 123.1
Alabaster	32 974	132	100.0	44	579	489.1	26.3	92	1 773	388.8	39.2
Auburn	146 859	527	94.3	34	217	235.5	9.0	206	3 180	779.4	70.4
Bessemer	8 349	56	100.0	58	944	417.9	52.0	194	2 746	732.0	70.4
Birmingham	88 808	606	14.9	500	9 168	7 099.9	481.8	943	12 300	3 305.9	318.1
Decatur	14 885	67	100.0	77	1 316	1 022.6	56.7	332	4 256	1 140.4	99.1
Dothan	55 920	210	97.1	148	D	D	D	501	7 114	1 990.0	173.0
Enterprise	11 747	61	100.0	11	38	13.6	1.4	155	1 802	521.3	47.9
Florence	15 003	154	49.4	49	584	209.3	22.4	302	4 139	967.8	88.7
Gadsden....................	0	0	0.0	39	351	293.5	14.5	229	3 037	731.2	60.6
Homewood	15 057	44	100.0	65	775	499.4	42.2	224	3 152	662.1	76.7
Hoover	100 533	373	100.0	80	1 134	2 347.7	102.5	384	7 578	2 425.7	200.6
Huntsville	98 328	1 763	61.9	225	3 051	3 197.3	168.8	999	14 677	3 945.3	360.9
Madison	156 745	490	100.0	52	728	426.2	39.6	131	2 356	550.6	52.7
Mobile	34 350	296	31.1	353	4 191	2 717.6	205.9	968	14 109	3 661.5	339.7
Montgomery	46 012	311	74.3	274	4 739	3 703.7	214.7	874	11 871	3 163.3	294.6
Opelika	43 591	188	95.7	32	373	261.3	18.4	206	2 732	725.2	58.3
Phenix City	10 301	59	76.3	10	D	D	D	125	1 683	413.4	36.8
Prattville...................	45 256	169	100.0	19	84	33.2	2.7	152	2 669	621.9	60.7
Tuscaloosa	182 072	1 231	24.6	77	955	638.5	48.4	475	6 821	1 782.8	149.8
Vestavia Hills............	46 180	104	100.0	39	220	213.9	14.5	156	1 659	396.1	43.3
ALASKA	369 042	1 503	68.9	638	7 734	5 216.3	440.9	2 508	33 721	10 474.3	977.4
Anchorage.................	259 216	930	77.3	336	5 228	3 147.7	296.6	860	15 253	4 966.8	462.2
Fairbanks..................	0	0	0.0	47	531	309.2	29.6	208	3 630	1 300.3	116.3
Juneau......................	25 610	153	32.7	36	265	196.9	12.8	142	1 821	491.4	53.0
ARIZONA	8 044 524	35 578	69.9	5 570	73 496	69 437.3	4 144.3	17 479	286 184	84 716.5	7 367.8
Apache Junction...........	7 106	52	100.0	11	D	D	D	90	1 591	515.0	41.0
Avondale	86 383	355	100.0	15	161	73.6	8.2	113	3 480	1 360.9	107.5
Buckeye.....................	380 979	1 521	100.0	15	106	71.4	4.9	50	597	260.8	14.1
Bullhead City	20 056	88	100.0	9	64	26.3	2.4	119	2 195	552.0	52.5
Casa Grande..............	32 771	136	100.0	25	403	196.3	17.9	190	3 440	896.6	75.4
Chandler	547 227	2 215	54.3	228	4 007	5 269.8	257.8	658	13 607	4 225.0	382.5
El Mirage...................	898	3	100.0	4	36	16.5	1.3	26	498	117.5	12.0
Flagstaff....................	92 485	469	49.3	68	554	377.7	26.2	322	5 224	1 383.9	120.5
Florence	62 447	187	100.0	1	D	D	D	12	142	39.9	3.1
Gilbert.......................	379 787	2 539	63.1	143	1 264	666.2	63.7	470	9 470	2 762.7	251.0
Glendale....................	54 625	183	94.5	118	1 188	834.2	47.7	674	12 710	3 821.3	320.8
Goodyear...................	298 492	1 128	88.1	23	D	D	D	141	3 318	788.1	74.7
Kingman	28 354	185	96.8	22	211	115.2	7.7	128	2 586	896.1	59.8
Lake Havasu City.........	62 662	326	93.9	48	223	86.2	9.0	215	2 843	914.5	71.1
Marana	180 933	596	100.0	20	108	41.2	5.1	114	2 868	865.1	73.1
Maricopa	129 916	524	100.0	7	16	4.6	0.6	26	729	213.8	16.1
Mesa.........................	708 681	2 811	75.2	292	3 313	2 705.3	168.9	1 315	22 342	5 819.7	549.5
Oro Valley	78 716	176	100.0	23	57	52.4	3.6	90	2 092	496.7	46.5
Peoria	446 742	1 636	100.0	60	289	266.3	12.7	387	8 515	2 657.7	235.0
Phoenix	1 324 082	6 972	35.6	1 853	30 877	31 193.7	1 638.2	3 712	60 797	18 448.4	1 620.7
Prescott	107 785	343	98.8	62	557	453.8	29.8	279	4 290	1 030.2	102.4
Prescott Valley	137 190	694	68.0	31	430	305.1	15.7	100	1 348	360.2	32.2
Queen Creek	433 478	1 096	100.0	7	14	5.0	0.6	50	973	227.1	20.0
Sahuarita...................	70 073	250	100.0	3	D	D	D	23	730	192.6	16.4
San Luis	28 179	193	100.0	8	233	36.1	11.0	36	591	136.0	10.2
Scottsdale..................	453 803	1 549	34.5	505	4 707	4 011.1	311.5	1 218	18 728	5 848.1	574.5
Sierra Vista...............	9 958	60	100.0	12	86	25.4	2.4	160	2 810	686.5	63.9
Surprise	173 066	623	83.9	27	401	159.2	16.0	169	4 396	1 137.0	105.7
Tempe	179 527	1 585	5.4	436	8 635	8 373.2	562.7	755	14 805	7 231.6	431.6
Tucson.......................	176 009	759	93.9	446	4 468	2 221.8	192.0	1 883	30 599	7 878.2	774.0
Yuma.........................	76 026	456	98.5	80	1 615	963.8	67.0	302	5 503	1 528.9	132.8
ARKANSAS..................	1 562 882	9 474	71.9	2 884	34 492	31 256.1	1 630.8	10 923	135 448	36 815.3	3 061.5
Bella Vista	26 301	98	100.0	12	20	21.6	0.9	25	307	60.7	5.8
Benton	34 244	186	81.7	23	138	130.1	5.6	127	1 859	659.5	46.2
Bentonville.................	204 526	908	65.4	86	1 135	1 338.4	79.1	119	2 488	1 024.2	68.7
Conway	49 226	263	76.8	57	618	460.6	27.8	284	4 730	1 246.1	100.9
Fayetteville	137 007	841	57.2	54	550	372.7	25.1	419	7 043	1 766.8	156.5
Fort Smith.................	51 179	344	33.7	171	2 184	1 605.2	98.1	521	7 161	1 767.6	157.2
Hot Springs	14 287	45	100.0	43	409	151.5	14.7	364	4 655	1 242.1	108.3

1. Merchant wholesalers except manufacturers' sales branches and offices. 2. Establishments with payroll.

Table D. Cities — Real Estate, Professional Services, and Manufacturing

City	Real estate and rental and leasing, 2012				Professional, scientific, and technical services,[1] 2012				Manufacturing, 2012			
	Number of establishments	Number of employees	Receipts (mil dol)	Annual payroll (mil dol)	Number of establishments	Number of employees	Receipts (mil dol)	Annual payroll (mil dol)	Number of establishments	Number of employees	Receipts (mil dol)	Annual payroll (mil dol)
	80	81	82	83	84	85	86	87	88	89	90	91
United States.............	354 106	1 923 770	487 655.2	85 326.0	851 542	7 997 617	1 440 060.5	566 412.5	297 191	11 214 165	5 696 729.6	593 397.0
ALABAMA	3 858	22 852	3 919.4	819.6	9 062	88 566	16 043.5	5 633.1	4 283	232 650	124 809.8	11 099.5
Alabaster......................	17	54	11.1	1.8	58	528	119.8	20.0	26	1 145	478.6	63.1
Auburn.........................	54	299	45.0	8.5	125	1 074	102.4	44.3	60	3 523	D	141.7
Bessemer.....................	27	159	26.3	6.6	72	D	D	D	41	1 549	466.6	70.1
Birmingham	281	3 076	417.2	129.1	834	D	D	D	249	10 654	4 118.4	568.2
Decatur........................	57	218	43.9	6.7	139	978	110.2	44.0	82	4 735	4 680.9	284.7
Dothan.........................	94	D	D	D	192	D	D	D	78	D	1 285.1	D
Enterprise....................	40	198	19.6	4.1	49	425	74.3	21.0	18	844		32.6
Florence......................	77	309	47.2	9.1	134	D	D	D	53	2 616	631.6	82.3
Gadsden......................	39	182	34.3	5.0	99	1 065	55.2	29.2	48	3 839	1 058.2	162.3
Homewood	59	362	70.9	17.5	157	1 291	225.2	76.1	24	1 121	564.1	55.4
Hoover.........................	95	675	274.1	36.2	281	D	D	D	25	345	49.7	13.1
Huntsville....................	311	D	D	D	999	28 634	6 933.7	2 324.3	173	13 598	6 213.8	771.4
Madison.......................	56	266	48.8	8.9	150	D	D	D	32	977		48.4
Mobile.........................	310	1 554	312.4	60.4	701	D	D	D	152	8 817	3 274.4	471.1
Montgomery................	219	1 890	339.1	64.8	575	5 871	1 258.6	386.5	172	10 902	9 125.1	528.6
Opelika........................	40	149	17.8	4.0	62	D	D	D	34	2 067		93.7
Phenix City	34	95	16.7	2.5	46	170	16.6	4.4	31	D	1 110.6	113.0
Prattville.....................	35	138	20.4	3.9	54	276	28.7	10.8	15	839	651.5	54.1
Tuscaloosa..................	124	1 192	129.1	35.8	232	1 584	260.5	78.4	53	4 454	4 234.8	221.7
Vestavia Hills..............	81	1 191	389.9	73.2	173	D	D	D	15	47		1.9
ALASKA	872	4 212	1 022.7	187.6	1 866	17 328	3 140.3	1 163.5	527	12 450	D	514.5
Anchorage...................	383	2 403	631.3	112.1	1 128	13 444	2 515.7	954.8	182	2 049	479.8	95.7
Fairbanks....................	88	468	116.2	25.1	137	D	D	D	37	239	D	10.7
Juneau........................	61	249	42.2	7.0	86	D	D	D	26	236	75.4	11.7
ARIZONA	8 089	40 479	9 329.7	1 693.2	16 112	119 843	19 041.9	7 272.6	4 269	131 941	51 243.5	8 193.2
Apache Junction...........	40	141	22.6	2.6	22	76	7.6	2.2	13	85	D	3.5
Avondale	42	118	15.7	3.1	47	197	14.8	5.4	9	29	12.9	1.5
Buckeye.......................	19	59	9.6	2.0	37	196	32.4	10.6	11	203	D	6.4
Bullhead City	52	187	20.0	4.5	45	D	D	D	6	39	D	1.3
Casa Grande................	52	198	39.6	5.6	59	D	D	D	37	1 753	1 807.3	96.5
Chandler......................	304	896	252.4	34.7	642	3 678	535.3	203.9	165	7 413	2 535.2	459.9
El Mirage.....................	10	D	D	D	7	18	2.4	0.4	13	251	74.4	12.3
Flagstaff......................	129	450	101.0	16.3	249	D	D	D	58	3 453	2 006.0	287.8
Florence	4	D	D	D	8	23	1.4	0.8	NA	NA	NA	NA
Gilbert.........................	292	787	170.2	33.4	533	D	D	D	118	1 887	338.2	84.8
Glendale......................	215	820	160.3	26.3	308	D	D	D	134	2 988	829.9	156.5
Goodyear.....................	62	136	25.4	4.4	88	480	48.3	24.1	22	1 220	384.0	58.7
Kingman	35	94	14.4	2.6	48	D	D	D	11	133	47.4	5.1
Lake Havasu City........	80	277	38.8	6.6	96	319	26.2	9.5	65	916	217.3	34.4
Marana........................	31	81	12.7	2.8	57	D	D	D	30	1 028	344.7	59.1
Maricopa.....................	15	29	4.7	0.7	38	94	6.4	4.0	11	148	D	6.4
Mesa...........................	547	2 280	456.6	72.6	1 021	5 199	668.1	255.6	245	7 319	3 353.0	583.2
Oro Valley	60	D	D	D	123	447	49.3	36.5	10	2 279	803.0	215.5
Peoria.........................	156	621	111.0	20.1	219	D	D	D	49	874	177.8	36.4
Phoenix	1 894	13 507	2 965.5	673.8	4 848	43 895	7 794.4	2 992.6	1 338	38 642	12 978.9	2 175.5
Prescott	127	254	52.5	7.3	218	D	D	D	61	1 457	404.8	76.0
Prescott Valley	36	99	21.8	4.0	42	336	43.9	21.0	31	603	149.6	24.3
Queen Creek...............	24	D	D	D	52	136	13.3	4.6	5	27	D	1.3
Sahuarita	10	17	2.7	0.4	14	34	3.1	1.2	3	D	D	D
San Luis	5	D	D	D	6	D	D	D	5	D	D	D
Scottsdale...................	983	5 713	2 175.5	276.0	1 986	D	D	D	216	7 082	4 532.5	612.3
Sierra Vista.................	60	317	42.5	9.0	103	D	D	D	11	57	7.8	1.7
Surprise......................	63	148	31.2	4.2	81	D	D	D	19	281	143.7	8.9
Tempe.........................	407	3 684	1 027.0	165.6	970	12 464	2 302.8	772.1	373	15 660	5 445.1	914.4
Tucson........................	735	3 966	628.3	129.9	1 563	10 568	1 457.1	581.5	393	6 648	1 551.5	312.7
Yuma..........................	124	513	71.6	14.0	171	D	D	D	42	1 800	785.5	71.2
ARKANSAS...............	2 802	12 867	1 922.7	409.8	5 655	31 871	4 464.9	1 549.2	2 688	153 706	62 712.9	6 290.8
Bella Vista	24	D	D	D	34	65	9.3	2.6	NA	NA	NA	NA
Benton........................	26	53	14.9	1.3	62	250	26.1	8.8	35	561	133.7	24.4
Bentonville..................	67	286	68.9	14.3	225	D	D	D	21	304	135.3	12.0
Conway	94	402	98.9	17.6	168	D	D	D	54	3 479	1 156.6	168.0
Fayetteville.................	137	2 012	133.0	52.1	364	1 850	231.9	87.0	57	4 106	1 031.7	156.0
Fort Smith...................	156	813	124.2	25.5	272	D	D	D	148	13 228	4 983.3	538.8
Hot Springs	73	302	48.2	8.4	147	D	D	D	33	800	147.3	37.0

1. Establishments subject to federal tax.

Accommodation and Food Services, Arts, Entertainment, and Recreation, and Health Care and Social Assistance

City	Accommodation and food services, 2012				Arts, entertainment, and recreation,[1] 2012				Health care and social assistance,[1] 2012			
	Number of establishments	Number of employees	Sales (mil dol)	Annual payroll (mil dol)	Number of establishments	Number of employees	Receipts (mil dol)	Annual payroll (mil dol)	Number of establishments	Number of employees	Receipts (mil dol)	Annual payroll (mil dol)
	92	93	94	95	96	97	98	99	100	101	102	103
United States............	662 489	12 007 689	708 138.6	196 103.3	99 659	1 486 462	161 690.3	50 328.5	690 525	9 542 138	1 008 744.6	409 811.9
ALABAMA	8 339	157 337	7 576.5	2 071.1	782	10 487	885.0	178.3	8 489	142 386	14 627.8	5 995.0
Alabaster	48	1 162	60.6	17.0	5	D	D	D	85	D	D	D
Auburn	198	3 581	163.3	41.4	13	D	D	D	103	D	D	D
Bessemer	95	1 734	86.8	24.2	7	89	6.5	2.0	85	D	D	D
Birmingham	564	11 239	625.3	185.7	38	570	38.8	10.9	615	12 973	1 675.5	690.7
Decatur..........................	140	2 847	134.6	38.0	10	171	6.8	2.2	217	2 511	271.7	95.3
Dothan..........................	223	4 538	209.2	56.1	18	D	D	D	257	D	D	D
Enterprise	73	1 202	58.3	14.4	9	D	D	D	75	D	D	D
Florence	129	3 445	141.4	42.9	10	D	D	D	183	3 575	406.3	142.1
Gadsden........................	90	2 203	101.3	27.6	6	D	D	D	182	5 271	564.2	244.0
Homewood	117	2 294	132.3	35.5	6	D	D	D	182	5 513	800.3	271.4
Hoover...........................	187	4 241	244.5	72.4	20	213	19.4	3.1	219	3 211	266.0	124.0
Huntsville......................	527	11 685	575.1	162.0	53	831	33.1	12.8	596	9 963	1 301.2	536.7
Madison.........................	109	1 795	93.9	24.8	11	105	3.9	1.2	110	D	D	D
Mobile...........................	488	10 868	488.5	134.3	41	1 339	25.6	7.7	469	10 192	1 150.0	515.1
Montgomery	471	9 716	462.3	127.8	28	D	D	D	539	D	D	D
Opelika	98	2 049	94.4	25.6	3	D	D	D	82	D	D	D
Phenix City....................	67	1 285	60.2	14.6	3	D	D	D	53	D	D	D
Prattville........................	85	2 148	103.2	28.2	7	D	D	D	73	D	D	D
Tuscaloosa....................	284	6 941	344.2	86.9	13	157	8.5	3.2	217	D	D	D
Vestavia Hills................	77	1 770	83.6	23.4	13	226	19.2	8.0	118	D	D	D
ALASKA	2 126	26 836	2 221.3	626.0	441	4 161	328.4	68.0	1 851	21 389	2 810.2	1 098.5
Anchorage.....................	788	14 957	1 106.2	338.1	108	D	D	D	962	12 792	1 783.5	682.5
Fairbanks......................	138	2 215	177.4	46.9	31	D	D	D	165	2 316	301.7	136.0
Juneau..........................	119	1 329	81.5	24.1	27	D	D	D	92	644	90.1	33.2
ARIZONA	11 669	251 455	13 996.6	4 030.3	1 424	33 881	3 279.3	1 088.3	15 041	184 186	20 221.1	7 974.6
Apache Junction...........	45	665	28.9	7.9	4	D	D	D	48	1 078	84.4	37.2
Avondale	86	1 658	82.7	22.2	7	D	D	D	104	1 026	109.9	35.9
Buckeye........................	46	798	35.8	9.3	4	163	5.7	2.3	16	D	D	D
Bullhead City................	85	1 091	54.2	14.5	7	167	4.0	1.5	109	2 009	285.4	97.3
Casa Grande................	114	D	D	D	7	D	D	D	144	1 810	164.5	71.2
Chandler.......................	474	10 996	559.8	181.3	63	2 325	434.4	62.7	676	7 874	833.7	289.4
El Mirage......................	11	128	7.1	1.6	NA	NA	NA	NA	6	D	D	D
Flagstaff........................	300	6 034	326.5	86.4	29	440	27.4	9.3	286	2 220	273.8	105.4
Florence	24	D	D	D	2	D	D	D	17	D	D	D
Gilbert...........................	287	6 139	297.6	85.7	48	1 045	48.7	14.8	619	5 146	520.0	191.9
Glendale........................	381	8 050	387.3	108.4	40	D	D	D	574	7 794	931.5	370.5
Goodyear......................	113	2 899	141.1	39.2	12	D	D	D	129	3 464	369.7	146.7
Kingman........................	92	1 681	74.6	21.2	5	D	D	D	103	D	D	D
Lake Havasu City..........	134	2 333	97.3	29.5	12	D	D	D	165	2 272	263.2	93.2
Marana..........................	96	2 178	121.3	36.3	14	454	19.5	9.8	44	D	D	D
Maricopa.......................	30	479	23.2	5.9	3	D	D	D	33	D	D	D
Mesa.............................	733	14 688	685.3	202.1	76	1 920	85.3	29.5	1 135	14 098	1 418.9	568.5
Oro Valley	67	1 998	87.2	30.1	14	D	D	D	117	D	D	D
Peoria...........................	243	5 889	281.9	85.8	31	480	28.5	9.0	368	4 425	462.6	214.7
Phoenix	2 493	57 339	3 479.6	992.4	295	6 038	626.0	312.8	3 435	45 960	5 433.6	2 241.6
Prescott........................	154	2 390	116.7	34.9	17	163	10.3	3.5	323	3 046	292.3	110.1
Prescott Valley	75	1 112	49.3	14.8	11	241	7.4	2.9	103	1 203	95.9	41.0
Queen Creek................	38	698	31.9	9.4	4	109	6.9	1.7	71	D	D	D
Sahuarita	19	438	15.1	4.0	2	D	D	D	19	D	D	D
San Luis	14	206	9.5	2.2	1	D	D	D	14	123	10.6	4.7
Scottsdale.....................	746	22 062	1 370.6	421.5	145	3 996	294.0	97.4	1 422	13 486	1 598.1	648.8
Sierra Vista...................	100	2 058	91.3	26.4	8	D	D	D	135	1 490	125.8	49.2
Surprise	140	3 145	151.8	42.8	11	210	10.9	4.1	165	1 110	119.2	43.1
Tempe	563	12 672	646.1	183.9	60	1 217	267.5	181.7	507	7 866	855.5	321.6
Tucson..........................	1 214	26 136	1 235.4	350.0	117	1 487	61.4	17.9	1 485	19 878	2 194.4	824.6
Yuma............................	227	4 641	254.2	64.1	14	D	D	D	273	D	D	D
ARKANSAS.............	5 473	95 854	4 307.3	1 182.5	563	5 927	499.0	104.3	5 936	86 999	8 540.6	3 495.8
Bella Vista	20	D	D	D	2	D	D	D	26	402	28.6	11.3
Benton..........................	62	1 080	51.2	13.5	9	53	1.6	0.5	80	1 254	91.3	43.5
Bentonville....................	123	2 365	111.2	30.2	10	119	8.0	2.2	99	1 121	120.3	44.2
Conway	172	4 248	177.6	48.5	11	D	D	D	206	2 682	239.8	96.7
Fayetteville...................	326	6 288	270.4	77.3	28	309	13.5	4.3	304	4 648	483.1	202.3
Fort Smith.....................	245	5 188	232.1	67.2	16	D	D	D	299	6 889	843.4	335.9
Hot Springs	194	4 178	178.1	52.6	27	D	D	D	199	2 884	369.2	142.9

1. Establishments subject to federal tax.

Table D. Cities — Other Services and Government Employment and Payroll

City	Other services[1], 2012					Government employment and payroll, 2012							
							March payroll						
							Percent of total for:						
	Number of establish-ments	Number of employees	Receipts (mil dol)	Annual payroll (mil dol)	Full-time equivalent employees	Total (dollars)	Adminis-tration, judicial, and legal	Police and Corrections	Fire Protection	Highways and trans-portation	Health and welfare	Natural resources and utilities	Education and libraries
	104	105	106	107	108	109	110	111	112	113	114	115	116
United States............	422 719	2 543 493	230 974.9	69 948.3	X	X	X	X	X	X	X	X	X
ALABAMA	5 009	31 262	3 191.9	893.0	X	X	X	X	X	X	X	X	X
Alabaster.....................	36	177	12.5	3.9	226	902 906	9.2	32.9	29.4	6.0	0.0	14.0	4.0
Auburn.........................	70	342	24.8	7.2	541	1 872 172	15.3	25.8	16.5	9.6	0.9	24.2	4.1
Bessemer.....................	45	470	67.5	19.5	570	2 109 401	7.5	25.2	23.3	0.5	0.9	32.7	1.8
Birmingham	308	3 072	292.1	97.3	4 784	19 867 336	9.5	27.6	17.4	3.5	0.9	29.6	4.1
Decatur........................	77	654	60.7	18.3	695	2 762 157	6.2	20.0	17.7	5.1	1.4	45.8	0.0
Dothan.........................	145	D	D	D	980	3 540 917	11.7	22.1	20.0	3.1	0.8	33.9	0.0
Enterprise....................	45	236	21.2	6.5	572	1 406 470	3.3	16.3	8.9	3.8	48.7	17.5	0.8
Florence	70	471	30.4	9.5	814	2 966 594	5.4	16.5	13.1	6.3	0.6	51.8	0.0
Gadsden......................	51	332	33.7	10.1	813	2 569 152	8.3	19.3	20.9	8.8	0.9	30.2	2.8
Homewood...................	63	1 403	81.3	31.4	357	1 440 394	4.5	33.6	23.3	6.7	0.0	16.2	7.0
Hoover.........................	79	450	43.0	12.5	663	3 382 691	10.6	31.1	26.9	5.3	0.7	8.2	7.7
Huntsville....................	269	2 553	476.6	101.5	2 636	11 833 638	8.9	19.0	14.5	7.2	2.2	32.4	0.0
Madison.......................	54	366	30.0	9.7	374	1 553 149	16.6	30.8	22.6	2.6	0.0	24.9	0.0
Mobile.........................	311	2 205	183.3	55.0	2 894	9 605 291	10.7	26.2	21.6	4.7	1.5	25.1	3.9
Montgomery	243	1 612	142.5	42.9	2 884	10 068 707	8.1	26.1	17.3	7.2	0.4	29.4	2.1
Opelika	49	232	22.7	6.1	355	1 405 862	10.4	27.1	19.6	3.6	0.5	35.2	2.4
Phenix City.................	46	253	19.0	6.6	795	2 466 225	53.9	13.6	9.1	2.5	0.4	18.3	0.5
Prattville.....................	44	210	18.2	5.4	328	1 108 761	10.0	29.2	32.0	3.9	0.0	16.8	0.0
Tuscaloosa..................	103	1 037	83.4	26.8	1 302	4 845 351	13.7	29.6	21.7	13.7	0.3	17.3	0.0
Vestavia Hills.............	55	493	33.3	12.2	264	1 136 169	7.5	27.3	44.1	1.9	0.0	6.9	5.2
ALASKA	882	4 807	495.9	152.7	X	X	X	X	X	X	X	X	X
Anchorage...................	400	2 688	261.8	87.3	9 819	51 971 256	4.5	7.8	6.6	5.5	1.4	9.1	63.8
Fairbanks....................	82	408	40.9	12.3	207	1 185 064	19.9	35.9	23.3	6.8	8.7	5.4	0.0
Juneau........................	45	202	18.7	5.3	1 960	10 163 476	5.6	5.4	3.1	7.4	27.2	8.1	43.2
ARIZONA	7 025	46 847	4 192.9	1 223.9	X	X	X	X	X	X	X	X	X
Apache Junction...........	31	165	25.8	8.4	234	1 013 473	20.4	42.8	0.0	10.1	7.9	13.1	5.7
Avondale	58	399	27.3	8.4	512	2 677 540	26.3	33.3	15.4	3.4	3.4	12.3	1.8
Buckeye.......................	12	37	3.0	0.8	391	1 821 664	27.3	19.8	28.2	3.6	1.6	9.5	2.0
Bullhead City	36	207	15.3	4.8	298	1 290 523	21.2	44.5	0.0	12.9	1.8	11.0	0.0
Casa Grande...............	61	361	28.4	8.8	385	1 771 597	18.0	31.5	19.5	7.8	0.7	17.0	3.4
Chandler......................	257	1 995	169.0	53.6	1 623	9 363 010	16.5	33.2	15.8	6.3	4.4	16.4	3.0
El Mirage.....................	13	58	3.7	1.3	144	789 368	14.2	35.0	17.6	4.7	0.0	9.4	0.0
Flagstaff......................	123	695	58.4	17.0	767	3 403 748	18.4	24.3	12.4	4.2	3.2	21.7	4.8
Florence	3	D	D	D	163	645 551	22.7	26.9	19.9	12.8	1.7	13.7	2.3
Gilbert.........................	212	1 299	91.0	27.5	1 117	5 590 864	15.8	33.0	20.5	2.9	0.1	18.9	0.0
Glendale......................	250	1 436	143.9	40.6	1 775	9 436 681	12.7	32.7	19.8	5.2	1.8	16.0	2.7
Goodyear.....................	48	281	17.3	5.6	482	2 715 439	27.9	20.6	25.2	2.4	0.0	14.0	0.0
Kingman......................	41	257	19.9	6.4	335	1 383 755	16.2	24.7	22.1	11.4	0.0	22.8	0.0
Lake Havasu City.........	117	416	37.7	9.5	484	2 122 419	13.0	26.9	20.4	8.0	0.0	20.7	0.0
Marana	69	387	30.7	10.5	306	1 328 433	22.4	36.4	0.0	14.2	1.2	11.8	0.0
Maricopa.....................	23	D	D	D	204	1 087 610	13.2	32.5	35.7	1.6	0.0	5.6	2.4
Mesa...........................	552	3 294	272.4	78.7	3 616	20 622 110	15.1	36.5	16.1	6.6	1.6	17.7	1.6
Oro Valley	49	327	22.6	8.3	311	1 409 218	13.9	47.7	0.0	6.6	0.8	15.0	4.3
Peoria	157	942	72.8	23.1	1 162	6 255 922	23.5	26.8	16.6	7.4	0.0	20.3	2.2
Phoenix	1 631	14 684	1 515.2	403.1	13 392	69 633 897	11.5	35.6	16.7	9.5	5.0	18.7	1.5
Prescott.......................	111	551	45.7	13.9	538	2 411 836	19.0	24.9	16.7	6.7	0.0	14.5	3.4
Prescott Valley	54	199	17.3	4.8	189	851 635	20.9	38.1	0.0	4.8	7.5	7.0	8.5
Queen Creek................	21	101	6.9	2.3	217	1 060 750	23.5	0.0	16.7	8.1	23.4	23.1	0.0
Sahuarita....................	8	91	4.3	1.9	131	644 309	29.4	41.1	0.0	11.3	0.0	7.5	0.0
San Luis......................	3	6	0.3	0.1	233	639 318	48.6	5.8	13.3	7.7	0.0	21.5	0.0
Scottsdale...................	533	3 863	294.6	94.1	2 454	13 029 893	23.6	31.2	13.0	3.8	2.1	18.0	3.7
Sierra Vista.................	47	253	19.6	6.5	380	1 580 863	16.3	28.2	17.1	6.7	1.2	17.2	2.1
Surprise	87	462	30.5	9.9	738	4 192 160	14.5	25.4	22.6	5.1	6.0	22.1	0.0
Tempe	292	2 006	188.3	62.7	1 762	9 492 774	16.0	31.6	13.1	6.2	9.5	18.8	1.5
Tucson.........................	756	4 997	423.7	128.2	4 691	21 780 237	12.6	30.8	18.8	10.4	3.2	19.2	0.0
Yuma...........................	115	709	52.0	16.5	946	3 797 070	16.5	30.3	16.4	7.6	3.3	23.1	0.0
ARKANSAS..............	3 157	17 091	1 427.6	423.7	X	X	X	X	X	X	X	X	X
Bella Vista	11	D	D	D	93	498 217	10.0	35.9	53.0	1.1	0.0	0.0	0.0
Benton.........................	48	216	21.4	5.5	270	875 166	13.5	25.7	22.5	4.2	2.4	27.6	0.0
Bentonville..................	62	475	27.9	13.7	435	1 712 143	20.1	20.9	18.7	4.1	0.0	33.1	3.1
Conway........................	100	535	40.7	11.2	474	1 540 085	12.3	31.7	27.5	7.8	0.0	17.9	0.0
Fayetteville.................	111	661	43.6	14.9	692	2 378 996	14.3	27.3	16.7	11.7	2.3	20.9	0.0
Fort Smith...................	143	751	62.0	17.6	880	3 505 049	10.2	26.1	17.9	14.1	2.6	29.1	0.0
Hot Springs	82	454	27.2	9.5	597	2 082 915	9.8	24.7	17.9	10.7	1.2	28.2	0.0

1. Establishments subject to federal tax.

Table D. Cities — City Government Finances

City	City government finances, 2012									
	General revenue							General expenditure		
	Intergovernmental			Taxes					Per capita[1] (dollars)	
					Per capita[1] (dollars)					
	Total (mil dol)	Total (mil dol)	Percent from state government	Total (mil dol)	Total	Property	Sales and gross receipts	Total (mil dol)	Total	Capital outlays
	117	118	119	120	121	122	123	124	125	126
United States.............	X	X	X	X	X	X	X	X	X	X
ALABAMA	X	X	X	X	X	X	X	X	X	X
Alabaster	27.6	0.0	**********	19.2	619	107	511	23.9	773	0
Auburn.........................	94.7	3.9	77.7	64.8	1 135	368	766	67.3	1 180	135
Bessemer.....................	51.9	5.8	81.8	34.8	1 279	240	1 039	52.4	1 924	4
Birmingham	436.4	42.3	52.9	334.4	1 583	243	985	466.4	2 207	235
Decatur.........................	174.2	68.7	100.0	61.6	1 103	209	877	202.0	3 616	209
Dothan.........................	93.4	4.5	88.0	70.5	1 046	66	980	98.8	1 467	83
Enterprise	30.6	1.8	95.9	23.0	826	157	670	32.1	1 155	209
Florence	64.7	4.1	76.8	43.9	1 107	284	821	58.6	1 477	59
Gadsden.......................	64.3	6.9	28.4	44.2	1 206	66	731	60.4	1 647	45
Homewood...................	54.6	1.8	36.5	50.5	1 996	632	1 363	51.4	2 034	100
Hoover..........................	104.2	6.8	51.4	83.0	998	121	853	95.0	1 143	78
Huntsville......................	329.0	28.2	93.3	217.9	1 186	320	866	337.4	1 836	440
Madison	51.4	5.9	79.3	34.9	777	291	451	50.2	1 117	123
Mobile..........................	353.3	20.4	65.4	248.6	1 275	83	1 192	344.5	1 767	296
Montgomery	280.1	36.3	46.1	169.8	830	151	679	218.0	1 065	80
Opelika.........................	54.6	2.4	35.3	39.9	1 425	328	810	51.4	1 834	224
Phenix City	33.7	1.9	100.0	26.0	717	165	552	36.4	1 007	213
Prattville.......................	35.5	1.0	99.2	26.5	765	71	695	28.2	814	6
Tuscaloosa....................	163.4	34.6	20.3	77.7	834	145	637	163.0	1 750	124
Vestavia Hills................	34.2	1.8	33.1	29.1	857	387	470	34.6	1 017	160
ALASKA	X	X	X	X	X	X	X	X	X	X
Anchorage....................	1 296.8	572.1	91.3	546.6	1 830	1 623	208	1 251.1	4 190	417
Fairbanks......................	42.7	11.6	100.0	21.4	659	432	227	39.7	1 220	110
Juneau..........................	316.5	94.8	75.9	83.0	2 561	1 130	1 431	302.2	9 325	1 605
ARIZONA	X	X	X	X	X	X	X	X	X	X
Apache Junction...........	26.7	11.0	100.0	11.6	316	0	316	29.2	793	0
Avondale	84.4	25.7	100.0	40.9	523	67	456	73.8	945	93
Buckeye.......................	61.1	12.9	69.2	27.9	512	172	339	48.2	882	7
Bullhead City	48.4	17.4	91.6	11.3	286	0	285	42.5	1 075	35
Casa Grande.................	70.3	17.3	83.1	29.4	586	128	458	77.3	1 541	234
Chandler.......................	333.6	72.6	90.2	151.1	617	130	487	266.6	1 089	179
El Mirage	30.1	8.5	100.0	9.5	290	94	196	33.0	1 011	114
Flagstaff.......................	130.0	35.8	90.1	54.3	801	176	624	120.0	1 768	130
Florence	23.1	8.7	80.8	6.8	254	38	210	20.6	772	122
Gilbert..........................	261.7	63.3	83.0	136.2	614	108	503	189.6	854	154
Glendale.......................	324.3	103.3	81.2	145.1	625	87	538	226.0	974	13
Goodyear......................	108.3	19.5	99.3	60.0	864	237	627	78.8	1 135	56
Kingman	39.6	14.2	100.0	12.5	439	0	439	31.4	1 108	1
Lake Havasu City..........	80.6	21.3	85.8	26.9	509	186	322	98.9	1 874	405
Marana	50.4	18.1	58.5	27.9	760	14	742	43.7	1 189	179
Maricopa.......................	36.8	14.6	100.0	19.2	428	242	187	33.5	747	45
Mesa............................	511.1	172.3	70.6	156.6	346	32	309	601.2	1 330	186
Oro Valley	29.7	10.8	100.0	15.4	373	0	373	29.9	723	49
Peoria	190.2	41.3	95.5	90.5	566	140	418	239.6	1 498	187
Phoenix	2 902.9	848.4	63.4	987.1	663	152	507	2 651.7	1 780	445
Prescott........................	74.7	16.1	77.8	30.5	761	71	684	77.2	1 928	429
Prescott Valley	38.2	14.1	87.4	14.0	357	47	310	41.2	1 051	74
Queen Creek.................	50.6	8.0	99.8	20.6	739	223	477	52.0	1 861	347
Sahuarita......................	26.6	12.6	63.4	10.0	379	11	368	22.4	852	221
San Luis	21.1	8.0	87.4	6.9	228	0	228	26.1	861	37
Scottsdale.....................	477.7	126.1	80.7	238.4	1 068	291	776	562.4	2 518	823
Sierra Vista...................	48.4	13.6	97.0	18.9	407	9	398	48.8	1 052	142
Surprise........................	112.2	31.8	91.0	40.3	332	56	276	106.8	880	55
Tempe..........................	344.4	69.4	71.3	183.5	1 097	215	883	286.8	1 715	177
Tucson..........................	736.3	277.8	53.0	280.3	534	76	458	608.5	1 159	174
Yuma............................	125.5	30.9	90.5	51.1	545	108	435	125.6	1 341	167
ARKANSAS.............	X	X	X	X	X	X	X	X	X	X
Bella Vista	12.2	6.0	28.9	3.3	122	28	94	12.1	440	15
Benton..........................	23.3	4.6	40.9	12.8	398	73	324	22.8	712	138
Bentonville....................	57.6	8.2	48.3	30.3	790	159	630	57.0	1 486	389
Conway	95.8	7.8	55.2	33.5	532	61	471	88.6	1 408	244
Fayetteville...................	107.6	24.4	45.2	48.2	626	53	572	96.7	1 256	246
Fort Smith.....................	133.9	29.8	38.6	61.3	700	146	554	126.0	1 439	456
Hot Springs	69.7	12.2	60.6	26.7	752	1	751	69.2	1 951	328

1. Based on population estimated as of July 1 of the year shown.

Table D. Cities — **City Government Finances**

City	Public welfare	Highways	Parking facilities	Education	Health and hospitals	Police protection	Sewerage and sanitation	Parks and recreation	Housing and community development	Interest on debt
	City government finances, 2012 (cont.) — General expenditure (cont.) — Percent of total for:									
	127	128	129	130	131	132	133	134	135	136
United States.............	X	X	X	X	X	X	X	X	X	X
ALABAMA	X	X	X	X	X	X	X	X	X	X
Alabaster	0.0	6.5	0.0	0.0	0.0	25.9	23.2	8.6	0.0	0.0
Auburn........................	0.0	5.6	0.0	0.0	2.5	16.6	14.8	7.9	1.4	12.2
Bessemer.....................	0.0	6.1	0.0	0.0	0.0	21.1	6.2	3.2	0.0	6.0
Birmingham	0.0	12.7	1.3	0.0	0.0	16.8	0.0	4.0	1.4	4.9
Decatur........................	0.3	5.0	0.0	53.7	2.3	6.1	12.6	3.4	0.9	1.1
Dothan........................	0.0	10.4	0.0	4.0	2.8	16.8	17.1	8.5	0.5	3.4
Enterprise	0.0	8.4	0.0	16.6	0.7	13.2	23.7	7.3	0.0	8.6
Florence	0.0	9.8	0.0	14.4	0.0	15.5	16.1	11.6	0.3	2.8
Gadsden......................	0.0	6.2	0.0	0.0	0.0	16.2	16.8	9.0	2.3	4.3
Homewood	0.1	5.6	0.0	28.6	0.0	16.9	4.9	6.2	0.0	4.2
Hoover........................	0.0	9.1	0.0	2.1	0.3	21.8	8.8	8.6	0.0	4.5
Huntsville....................	0.2	6.6	0.5	5.6	1.2	12.4	8.8	9.0	2.3	8.1
Madison	0.0	14.5	0.0	0.0	0.0	14.0	12.2	7.0	0.0	6.1
Mobile........................	0.0	7.7	2.7	0.0	0.4	12.3	20.0	8.1	0.0	6.1
Montgomery	0.0	5.6	1.7	0.0	0.0	20.0	7.3	12.6	0.1	6.6
Opelika	0.0	8.4	0.0	14.7	0.6	16.6	11.9	9.8	0.5	6.3
Phenix City..................	0.0	1.8	0.0	5.6	0.3	16.9	14.0	10.2	0.0	3.9
Prattville.....................	0.0	0.0	0.0	0.0	0.0	22.0	13.5	6.2	0.0	8.8
Tuscaloosa..................	0.1	14.2	0.3	7.9	0.1	17.4	17.1	9.0	1.4	2.3
Vestavia Hills...............	0.0	4.8	0.0	0.7	0.5	12.9	7.4	16.4	0.0	5.5
ALASKA	X	X	X	X	X	X	X	X	X	X
Anchorage...................	0.0	5.9	0.4	53.2	2.1	9.9	5.0	1.7	0.0	2.8
Fairbanks....................	0.0	33.1	0.6	0.0	0.0	15.6	0.0	0.0	0.0	0.5
Juneau........................	0.0	4.5	0.0	28.1	32.3	5.7	3.6	4.3	1.4	3.0
ARIZONA	X	X	X	X	X	X	X	X	X	X
Apache Junction............	0.0	24.4	0.0	0.0	0.0	30.0	0.0	11.6	6.9	0.0
Avondale	3.8	15.7	0.0	0.0	0.0	31.7	20.3	3.4	4.4	6.6
Buckeye......................	0.0	4.5	0.0	0.0	0.0	19.8	24.3	3.3	0.4	17.7
Bullhead City	0.0	20.8	0.0	0.0	4.2	23.1	21.7	7.4	1.4	6.7
Casa Grande................	0.0	8.0	0.0	0.0	0.0	17.5	17.4	8.7	0.9	6.8
Chandler......................	0.0	7.7	0.0	0.0	0.0	21.8	19.2	0.9	13.7	4.7
El Mirage	0.0	8.4	0.0	0.0	1.4	31.0	25.8	3.8	0.3	1.9
Flagstaff......................	0.0	14.0	0.0	0.0	0.0	13.5	14.1	0.0	12.3	3.7
Florence	0.0	8.9	3.0	0.0	0.0	25.5	11.9	4.9	4.2	6.6
Gilbert........................	0.0	20.7	0.0	0.0	0.0	19.1	13.1	5.3	0.8	8.4
Glendale......................	0.0	3.3	0.2	0.0	0.0	22.4	12.4	4.5	6.7	18.5
Goodyear.....................	0.0	2.1	0.0	0.0	0.0	16.8	9.8	9.8	5.8	13.2
Kingman	0.0	5.6	0.0	0.0	0.0	23.3	22.2	11.9	2.1	2.3
Lake Havasu City..........	0.0	6.5	0.0	0.0	0.0	11.7	38.4	6.7	0.4	10.7
Marana.......................	0.0	15.9	0.0	0.0	0.0	23.0	2.8	3.8	0.9	10.8
Maricopa.....................	0.0	3.8	0.0	0.0	0.0	20.8	0.0	6.7	29.9	3.2
Mesa..........................	0.6	10.4	0.0	0.0	0.0	26.2	11.2	7.4	3.3	6.1
Oro Valley	0.0	14.5	0.0	0.0	0.0	40.4	0.0	9.9	0.0	0.0
Peoria.........................	0.0	9.6	0.0	0.2	0.0	12.3	12.7	11.6	0.7	5.5
Phoenix.......................	0.0	6.6	0.0	0.9	0.0	17.8	11.1	7.4	7.3	10.4
Prescott.......................	0.0	26.8	0.1	0.0	0.0	16.5	17.0	7.8	0.3	3.3
Prescott Valley	0.0	10.3	0.0	0.0	0.0	20.4	14.9	3.7	0.0	11.3
Queen Creek................	0.0	6.0	0.0	0.0	0.0	3.2	8.0	12.7	1.3	8.9
Sahuarita	0.0	27.9	0.0	0.0	0.0	23.8	7.8	5.8	0.0	11.5
San Luis	0.5	5.6	0.0	0.0	0.0	14.5	18.2	0.0	0.6	24.2
Scottsdale....................	0.0	5.4	0.0	0.0	0.0	14.2	16.1	6.3	1.5	9.3
Sierra Vista..................	0.0	26.3	0.0	0.0	0.0	32.3	13.8	9.6	2.6	2.4
Surprise	0.0	14.1	0.0	0.0	0.0	19.0	11.3	12.5	5.8	4.6
Tempe........................	0.0	10.3	0.0	0.0	0.0	21.8	10.9	1.8	14.8	5.2
Tucson........................	0.0	5.0	0.0	0.0	0.0	21.9	6.7	8.0	12.2	6.0
Yuma..........................	0.0	11.8	0.0	0.0	0.6	17.9	15.0	9.1	1.2	11.1
ARKANSAS...............	X	X	X	X	X	X	X	X	X	X
Bella Vista	0.0	26.0	0.0	0.0	0.0	19.9	13.8	0.0	0.0	0.0
Benton........................	0.0	22.3	0.0	0.0	1.5	20.7	12.3	6.4	0.0	7.0
Bentonville...................	0.0	16.9	0.0	0.0	0.0	12.6	25.2	11.3	0.2	5.6
Conway	0.0	14.7	0.0	0.0	0.4	11.7	15.7	4.1	0.0	15.9
Fayetteville	0.0	11.2	1.0	0.0	1.0	16.4	26.2	5.7	0.5	5.3
Fort Smith....................	0.0	13.8	0.2	0.0	0.1	12.5	25.6	2.5	1.0	8.9
Hot Springs..................	0.0	6.7	0.2	0.0	0.9	15.8	27.9	2.4	0.4	2.1

Table D. Cities — City Government Finances, City Government Employment, and Climate

City	City government finances, 2012 (cont.) Debt outstanding Total (mil dol)	Per capita[1] (dollars)	Debt issued during year	Climate[2] Average daily temperature (degrees Fahrenheit) Mean January	July	Limits January[3]	July[4]	Annual precipitation (inches)	Heating degree days	Cooling degree days
	137	138	139	140	141	142	143	144	145	146
United States	X	X	X	X	X	X	X	X	X	X
ALABAMA	X	X	X	X	X	X	X	X	X	X
Alabaster	101.5	3 276	0.0	NA	NA	NA	NA	NA	NA	NA
Auburn	229.8	4 028	11.0	44.7	79.9	34.2	89.7	52.63	2 507	1 932
Bessemer	103.0	3 783	12.0	42.9	81.0	30.8	93.6	59.38	2 766	1 943
Birmingham	573.7	2 715	109.7	42.6	80.2	32.3	90.6	53.99	2 823	1 881
Decatur	508.8	9 106	6.5	38.9	79.2	29.1	90.3	55.31	3 469	1 609
Dothan	84.7	1 257	3.4	47.7	81.3	36.2	93.3	56.61	2 058	2 264
Enterprise	79.9	2 876	8.3	NA	NA	NA	NA	NA	NA	NA
Florence	116.3	2 932	59.9	39.9	80.2	30.7	90.6	55.80	3 236	1 789
Gadsden	75.3	2 052	5.0	40.3	79.8	29.9	90.5	56.10	3 220	1 716
Homewood	49.2	1 946	0.3	42.6	80.2	32.3	90.6	53.99	2 823	1 881
Hoover	108.5	1 306	58.5	42.9	81.0	30.8	93.6	59.38	2 766	1 943
Huntsville	774.8	4 216	13.8	39.8	79.5	30.7	89.4	57.51	3 262	1 671
Madison	75.1	1 672	13.3	46.6	81.8	35.5	92.7	54.77	2 194	2 252
Mobile	547.6	2 809	13.3	50.1	81.5	39.5	91.2	66.29	1 681	2 539
Montgomery	275.9	1 348	38.8	46.6	81.8	35.5	92.7	54.77	2 194	2 252
Opelika	162.2	5 790	70.3	NA	NA	NA	NA	NA	NA	NA
Phenix City	139.4	3 853	52.5	46.8	82.0	36.6	91.7	48.57	2 154	2 296
Prattville	61.2	1 766	5.6	NA	NA	NA	NA	NA	NA	NA
Tuscaloosa	198.6	2 132	1.3	42.9	80.4	32.5	90.8	54.99	2 787	1 893
Vestavia Hills	41.6	1 224	0.0	NA	NA	NA	NA	NA	NA	NA
ALASKA	X	X	X	X	X	X	X	X	X	X
Anchorage	1 789.0	5 991	62.0	15.8	58.4	9.3	65.3	16.08	10 470	3
Fairbanks	2.3	71	0.0	-9.7	62.4	-19.0	73.0	10.34	13 980	74
Juneau	193.0	5 956	14.8	25.7	56.8	20.7	64.3	58.33	8 574	0
ARIZONA	X	X	X	X	X	X	X	X	X	X
Apache Junction	10.8	294	0.0	52.7	89.5	40.0	104.3	12.29	1 542	3 443
Avondale	93.9	1 202	0.0	54.7	93.5	41.3	107.6	9.03	1 173	4 166
Buckeye	160.3	2 937	1.5	NA	NA	NA	NA	NA	NA	NA
Bullhead City	73.4	1 858	0.0	54.4	95.6	43.3	111.7	5.84	1 164	4 508
Casa Grande	119.9	2 388	14.4	52.4	90.4	37.3	105.1	9.22	1 572	3 554
Chandler	579.4	2 367	0.0	54.3	91.3	41.5	105.7	9.23	1 271	3 798
El Mirage	27.3	836	0.0	NA	NA	NA	NA	NA	NA	NA
Flagstaff	118.5	1 746	34.4	29.7	66.1	16.5	82.2	22.91	6 999	126
Florence	18.6	697	0.0	NA	NA	NA	NA	NA	NA	NA
Gilbert	479.5	2 159	37.9	54.3	91.3	41.5	105.7	9.23	1 271	3 798
Glendale	1 053.0	4 536	86.3	52.5	90.6	39.2	104.2	7.78	1 535	3 488
Goodyear	426.4	6 140	38.6	NA	NA	NA	NA	NA	NA	NA
Kingman	55.1	1 944	11.1	NA	NA	NA	NA	NA	NA	NA
Lake Havasu City	321.9	6 096	8.4	53.9	95.2	42.9	107.5	6.25	1 230	4 523
Marana	94.8	2 584	0.1	NA	NA	NA	NA	NA	NA	NA
Maricopa	19.3	430	0.0	NA	NA	NA	NA	NA	NA	NA
Mesa	1 494.6	3 305	352.1	54.3	91.3	41.5	105.7	9.23	1 271	3 798
Oro Valley	64.1	1 547	21.8	50.6	86.3	34.6	100.7	12.40	1 831	2 810
Peoria	511.6	3 199	51.7	54.7	93.5	41.3	107.6	9.03	1 173	4 166
Phoenix	8 278.0	5 557	760.6	54.2	92.8	43.4	104.2	8.29	1 125	4 189
Prescott	73.2	1 829	3.5	37.1	73.4	23.3	88.3	19.19	4 849	742
Prescott Valley	104.9	2 678	33.8	NA	NA	NA	NA	NA	NA	NA
Queen Creek	165.6	5 930	0.1	NA	NA	NA	NA	NA	NA	NA
Sahuarita	56.9	2 161	0.4	NA	NA	NA	NA	NA	NA	NA
San Luis	169.5	5 602	0.0	NA	NA	NA	NA	NA	NA	NA
Scottsdale	1 200.6	5 375	53.3	54.2	92.8	43.4	104.2	8.29	1 125	4 189
Sierra Vista	37.2	803	9.3	47.7	79.1	33.7	92.6	14.02	2 369	1 739
Surprise	37.0	305	0.0	54.7	93.5	41.3	107.6	9.03	1 173	4 166
Tempe	740.2	4 427	68.6	54.1	89.9	40.1	103.6	9.36	1 390	3 655
Tucson	1 174.4	2 236	152.8	54.0	88.5	41.9	100.5	12.00	1 333	3 501
Yuma	302.8	3 234	0.0	58.1	94.1	46.2	107.3	3.01	782	4 540
ARKANSAS	X	X	X	X	X	X	X	X	X	X
Bella Vista	0.0	0	0.0	NA	NA	NA	NA	NA	NA	NA
Benton	44.1	1 373	0.0	NA	NA	NA	NA	NA	NA	NA
Bentonville	97.5	2 541	0.0	NA	NA	NA	NA	NA	NA	NA
Conway	383.2	6 092	0.0	38.3	82.1	28.1	92.4	48.67	3 320	1 961
Fayetteville	139.6	1 813	0.0	34.3	78.9	24.2	89.1	46.02	4 166	1 439
Fort Smith	454.0	5 184	22.1	38.0	82.2	27.8	92.9	43.87	3 437	1 929
Hot Springs	68.3	1 925	1.0	40.2	82.2	29.6	94.3	57.69	3 133	1 993

1. Based on the population estimated as of July 1 of the year shown.   2. Represents normal values based on the 30-year period, 1971–2000.   3. Average daily minimum.
4. Average daily maximum.

Table D. Cities — **Land Area and Population**

STATE Place code	City	Land area,[1] 2016 (sq mi)	Population, 2016 Total persons	Rank	Per square mile	Race alone[2] (percent), 2015 White	Black or African American	American Indian, Alaska Native	Asian	Hawaiian Pacific Islander	Some other race	2 or more races[2]
		1	2	3	4	5	6	7	8	9	10	11
	ARKANSAS—Cont'd											
05 34750	Jacksonville	28.9	28 518	1 306	986.8	52.6	38.2	0.3	2.2	0.0	2.2	4.4
05 35710	Jonesboro	80.4	74 889	464	931.5	73.2	17.2	2.0	1.7	0.0	2.5	3.4
05 41000	Little Rock	118.7	198 541	117	1 672.6	50.7	42.5	0.0	3.7	0.0	1.4	1.6
05 50450	North Little Rock	51.8	66 278	544	1 279.5	50.4	46.0	0.8	0.1	0.0	1.5	1.1
05 53390	Paragould	31.2	28 232	1 316	904.9	NA	NA	NA	NA	NA	NA	NA
05 55310	Pine Bluff	44.6	43 841	859	983.0	NA	NA	NA	NA	NA	NA	NA
05 60410	Rogers	37.9	65 021	556	1 715.6	89.2	0.4	0.8	2.9	0.2	2.7	3.8
05 61670	Russellville	28.3	29 583	1 266	1 045.3	85.0	6.4	0.5	0.8	0.0	3.0	4.3
05 63800	Sherwood	20.8	30 657	1 228	1 473.9	73.7	19.8	1.7	2.6	0.0	0.0	2.2
05 66080	Springdale	46.5	78 557	432	1 689.4	69.4	1.9	0.3	1.5	6.5	18.6	1.7
05 68810	Texarkana	41.6	30 283	1 241	728.0	61.9	33.7	0.0	0.0	0.0	1.9	2.5
05 74540	West Memphis	28.4	25 284	1 416	890.3	31.9	64.2	0.4	0.7	0.0	0.3	2.5
06 00000	**CALIFORNIA**	155 792.7	39 250 017	X	251.9	60.9	5.8	0.7	14.2	0.4	13.5	4.5
06 00296	Adelanto	53.0	33 391	1 138	630.0	64.9	19.1	0.0	1.4	0.0	13.7	0.9
06 00562	Alameda	10.4	78 906	430	7 587.1	49.8	7.7	0.4	30.6	1.0	2.9	7.6
06 00884	Alhambra	7.6	85 474	385	11 246.6	22.6	1.8	0.0	50.6	0.3	22.5	2.2
06 00947	Aliso Viejo	6.9	51 424	743	7 452.8	71.7	3.0	0.0	14.3	0.2	3.2	7.6
06 02000	Anaheim	50.0	351 043	56	7 020.9	71.9	2.3	0.2	13.8	0.4	8.9	2.4
06 02252	Antioch	29.4	110 898	260	3 772.0	41.4	19.4	1.3	10.1	2.4	18.0	7.5
06 02364	Apple Valley	74.4	72 553	484	975.2	79.3	9.3	1.1	1.8	0.1	3.0	5.5
06 02462	Arcadia	10.9	58 523	642	5 369.1	24.5	2.6	0.0	64.3	0.0	3.6	5.1
06 03064	Atascadero	26.1	30 330	1 238	1 162.1	NA	NA	NA	NA	NA	NA	NA
06 03162	Atwater	6.1	29 270	1 273	4 798.4	50.2	4.9	0.1	3.2	0.0	35.4	6.0
06 03386	Azusa	9.7	49 628	759	5 116.3	40.1	2.9	0.5	10.7	0.0	42.3	3.3
06 03526	Bakersfield	148.8	376 380	53	2 529.4	70.5	8.4	1.0	7.8	0.2	8.9	3.2
06 03666	Baldwin Park	6.6	76 464	450	11 585.5	46.6	2.0	0.3	19.4	0.0	29.7	2.0
06 03820	Banning	23.3	31 026	1 210	1 331.6	68.4	6.5	8.2	7.5	0.0	7.5	1.9
06 04758	Beaumont	30.7	45 349	834	1 477.2	70.8	8.3	0.5	10.1	0.4	5.6	4.4
06 04870	Bell	2.5	35 864	1 062	14 345.6	NA	NA	NA	NA	NA	NA	NA
06 04982	Bellflower	6.1	77 790	434	12 752.5	27.9	15.5	0.6	12.9	0.2	40.5	2.4
06 04996	Bell Gardens	2.5	42 806	880	17 122.4	NA	NA	NA	NA	NA	NA	NA
06 05108	Belmont	4.6	27 081	1 362	5 887.2	76.4	0.6	0.3	17.6	0.0	3.7	1.5
06 05290	Benicia	12.9	28 174	1 319	2 184.0	70.8	3.3	0.5	17.6	0.2	1.8	6.0
06 06000	Berkeley	10.5	121 240	226	11 546.7	63.0	7.5	0.6	18.4	0.1	4.0	6.4
06 06308	Beverly Hills	5.7	34 687	1 099	6 085.4	80.2	1.8	0.0	10.2	0.0	3.6	4.2
06 08100	Brea	12.2	42 471	889	3 481.2	72.7	0.6	1.5	17.3	0.0	5.1	2.8
06 08142	Brentwood	14.9	60 532	608	4 062.6	62.2	10.9	0.0	11.4	0.1	8.1	7.4
06 08786	Buena Park	10.5	83 156	402	7 919.6	55.8	0.9	0.2	28.1	2.2	9.7	3.0
06 08954	Burbank	17.4	104 447	290	6 002.7	72.0	2.7	0.5	12.2	0.0	8.3	4.3
06 09066	Burlingame	4.4	30 301	1 240	6 886.6	63.0	1.1	0.0	21.0	0.2	8.2	6.6
06 09710	Calexico	8.6	40 232	939	4 678.1	NA	NA	NA	NA	NA	NA	NA
06 10046	Camarillo	19.7	67 363	530	3 419.4	83.6	1.4	0.0	7.8	0.0	2.2	5.0
06 10345	Campbell	5.9	40 939	922	6 938.8	66.3	1.6	1.7	16.6	0.3	8.5	5.1
06 11194	Carlsbad	37.7	113 952	246	3 022.6	84.6	0.5	0.5	9.0	0.2	2.3	2.9
06 11530	Carson	18.7	92 797	340	4 962.4	28.1	20.2	1.7	31.6	2.6	11.5	4.3
06 12048	Cathedral City	22.6	54 056	700	2 391.9	74.4	3.8	0.4	3.1	0.3	16.3	1.7
06 12524	Ceres	9.4	48 278	789	5 136.0	58.8	1.3	1.8	10.0	0.5	23.7	3.9
06 12552	Cerritos	8.7	50 555	752	5 810.9	20.1	8.3	0.8	61.4	0.1	4.2	5.1
06 13014	Chico	33.0	91 567	347	2 774.8	83.6	1.3	1.0	5.0	0.1	3.1	5.9
06 13210	Chino	29.7	87 776	372	2 955.4	45.0	5.1	0.6	12.8	0.2	26.5	9.9
06 13214	Chino Hills	44.7	78 822	431	1 763.4	48.1	4.1	0.9	34.4	0.2	9.0	3.3
06 13392	Chula Vista	49.6	267 172	74	5 386.5	65.3	5.0	0.3	16.0	0.5	8.5	4.4
06 13588	Citrus Heights	14.2	87 432	377	6 157.2	85.2	5.5	0.1	2.5	0.2	1.9	4.6
06 13756	Claremont	13.4	36 059	1 056	2 691.0	65.0	4.3	2.4	15.1	0.0	7.2	6.1
06 14218	Clovis	24.2	106 583	279	4 404.3	71.2	2.6	0.7	12.2	0.0	9.2	4.0
06 14260	Coachella	30.1	44 953	839	1 493.5	NA	NA	NA	NA	NA	NA	NA
06 14890	Colton	15.3	54 712	691	3 575.9	71.3	5.3	0.1	8.3	0.1	12.3	2.7
06 15044	Compton	10.0	97 550	313	9 755.0	53.8	26.3	0.3	1.6	1.0	15.5	1.5
06 16000	Concord	30.5	128 726	213	4 220.5	67.2	4.0	0.1	10.7	0.7	11.7	5.5
06 16350	Corona	39.5	166 785	153	4 222.4	68.7	5.0	0.3	11.0	0.1	10.3	4.5
06 16532	Costa Mesa	15.7	112 822	254	7 186.1	74.8	2.4	0.9	6.8	1.1	11.3	2.8
06 16742	Covina	7.0	48 549	786	6 935.6	44.5	4.0	1.3	11.0	0.0	35.2	4.0
06 17568	Culver City	5.1	39 364	966	7 718.4	61.7	9.6	0.0	13.2	0.0	7.0	8.6
06 17610	Cupertino	11.3	60 643	607	5 366.6	33.0	0.6	0.3	61.0	0.0	2.0	3.1
06 17750	Cypress	6.6	48 906	775	7 410.0	45.8	6.5	0.3	39.6	0.1	4.7	3.0
06 17918	Daly City	7.6	106 472	280	14 009.5	21.2	4.3	0.5	56.0	2.1	12.5	3.3
06 17946	Dana Point	6.5	34 012	1 116	5 232.6	78.6	0.8	0.2	3.7	0.0	14.5	2.2
06 17988	Danville	18.1	44 631	845	2 465.8	81.5	0.9	0.0	14.4	0.0	0.4	2.8
06 18100	Davis	9.9	68 111	519	6 879.9	64.3	2.0	0.1	21.7	0.1	4.5	7.2

1. Dry land or land partially or temporarily covered by water.　　2. Hispanic or Latino persons may be of any race.

Table D. Cities — **Population**

City	Percent Hispanic or Latino[1], 2015	Percent foreign born 2015	Age of population (percent), 2010-2014							Median age 2015	Percent female 2015	Population Census counts		Percent change	
			Under 18 years	18 to 24 years	25 to 34 years	35 to 44 years	45 to 54 years	55 to 64 years	65 years and over			2000	2010	2000–2010	2010–2016
	12	13	14	15	16	17	18	19	20	21	22	23	24	25	26
ARKANSAS—Cont'd															
Jacksonville	4.3	2.6	28.5	13.3	16.9	11.2	9.1	10.7	10.2	28.9	55.9	29 916	28 339	-5.3	0.6
Jonesboro	6.2	4.4	24.3	14.3	14.7	14.3	11.3	8.9	12.2	32.6	51.7	55 515	67 305	21.2	11.3
Little Rock	7.8	8.4	22.9	9.7	15.0	13.4	12.9	13.1	13.1	36.6	51.0	183 133	193 487	5.7	2.6
North Little Rock	7.3	4.2	28.9	8.5	15.6	14.2	11.4	8.5	12.9	33.6	52.4	60 433	62 369	3.2	6.3
Paragould	3.8	0.4	24.0	12.2	15.5	10.1	11.8	12.7	13.6	33.7	52.4	22 017	26 102	18.6	8.2
Pine Bluff	1.9	0.4	26.7	12.9	12.5	11.8	11.3	12.1	12.7	33.0	52.5	55 085	49 080	-10.9	-10.7
Rogers	31.3	17.6	27.3	7.3	17.3	14.6	10.8	10.9	11.7	33.8	47.4	38 829	55 920	44.0	16.3
Russellville	15.0	12.4	23.4	24.8	15.4	6.9	10.0	8.7	10.9	26.2	48.7	23 682	28 125	18.8	5.2
Sherwood	0.0	3.2	22.7	9.0	12.2	11.5	17.2	11.9	15.4	41.0	53.4	21 511	29 561	37.4	3.7
Springdale	37.5	24.8	30.4	9.9	13.7	14.0	12.7	10.2	9.2	31.8	54.2	45 798	70 759	54.5	11.0
Texarkana	4.3	1.9	25.1	8.5	14.4	13.6	9.8	12.3	16.4	35.9	52.4	26 448	29 911	13.1	1.2
West Memphis	0.0	0.5	25.1	11.6	14.0	10.8	13.3	11.2	13.9	34.4	53.1	27 666	26 247	-5.1	-3.7
CALIFORNIA	38.8	27.3	23.3	10.1	14.9	13.3	13.4	11.8	13.3	36.2	50.3	33 871 648	37 254 522	10.0	5.4
Adelanto	69.9	23.4	38.8	8.7	13.8	13.9	10.3	6.8	7.6	26.6	47.3	18 130	31 760	75.2	5.1
Alameda	10.5	24.0	19.1	6.2	14.4	15.8	16.0	13.7	14.8	41.4	52.0	72 259	73 812	2.1	6.9
Alhambra	36.7	51.9	16.2	7.7	17.8	13.8	14.2	14.9	15.3	41.0	50.7	85 804	83 096	-3.2	2.9
Aliso Viejo	16.0	20.0	24.1	7.8	16.2	17.6	15.7	10.1	8.5	36.4	53.4	40 166	48 052	19.6	7.0
Anaheim	57.5	39.1	24.8	10.7	16.4	15.0	13.4	9.4	10.3	33.6	48.8	328 014	336 440	2.6	4.3
Antioch	32.2	22.6	26.7	11.1	13.4	11.7	14.9	12.4	9.9	34.0	50.5	90 532	102 745	13.5	7.9
Apple Valley	35.9	8.0	28.9	11.3	10.7	9.5	11.0	11.5	17.1	34.3	54.5	54 239	69 139	27.5	4.9
Arcadia	10.3	49.5	21.4	6.5	10.9	12.9	15.0	14.4	18.9	44.0	56.5	53 054	56 370	6.3	3.8
Atascadero	18.0	5.5	21.8	5.4	17.6	14.0	11.2	15.1	14.9	38.2	48.1	26 411	28 304	7.2	7.2
Atwater	60.4	20.4	33.7	9.2	16.9	10.1	11.1	6.8	12.1	29.0	50.7	23 113	28 172	21.9	3.9
Azusa	66.5	26.3	19.7	20.8	16.6	9.9	13.5	9.4	9.9	29.7	53.5	44 712	46 346	3.7	7.1
Bakersfield	48.2	19.2	29.1	11.8	15.8	12.8	11.2	9.9	9.4	30.6	51.2	247 057	347 611	40.7	8.3
Baldwin Park	73.0	44.5	24.9	9.9	13.9	12.8	14.6	10.8	13.0	35.8	49.7	75 837	75 390	-0.6	1.4
Banning	43.9	17.8	24.5	8.5	15.4	8.6	7.6	10.1	25.2	36.5	53.8	23 562	29 594	25.6	4.8
Beaumont	45.1	19.9	26.4	7.9	13.5	14.1	10.9	12.6	14.6	36.4	50.2	11 384	36 874	223.9	23.0
Bell	91.1	39.1	30.6	11.2	15.7	14.1	11.9	7.4	9.1	29.3	49.5	36 664	35 477	-3.2	1.1
Bellflower	54.1	31.4	28.7	11.8	11.4	14.6	10.9	11.1	11.5	33.4	50.4	72 878	76 610	5.1	1.5
Bell Gardens	94.4	40.1	34.0	10.1	15.7	13.1	12.6	7.1	7.4	28.3	52.0	44 054	42 053	-4.5	1.8
Belmont	12.0	33.7	20.5	6.9	14.2	12.3	11.0	16.4	18.8	41.4	50.5	25 123	25 844	2.9	4.8
Benicia	10.3	16.8	20.8	5.4	10.6	10.7	14.7	16.3	21.5	47.3	52.3	26 865	26 997	0.5	4.4
Berkeley	12.8	20.7	13.0	22.4	17.8	11.8	10.8	10.1	14.1	32.5	50.3	102 743	112 489	9.5	7.8
Beverly Hills	6.6	43.6	25.0	4.5	12.7	14.1	13.9	8.9	20.9	41.2	52.1	33 784	34 102	0.9	1.7
Brea	32.9	19.3	25.7	7.8	12.6	14.7	14.7	13.5	11.0	38.6	48.6	35 410	39 189	10.7	8.4
Brentwood	19.3	16.1	26.2	8.8	10.3	11.8	17.2	10.2	15.6	39.4	50.6	23 302	51 624	121.5	17.3
Buena Park	39.5	34.1	25.9	7.8	14.9	14.6	14.1	10.1	12.6	35.7	50.0	78 282	80 613	3.0	3.2
Burbank	21.0	30.8	22.4	7.2	16.9	13.2	15.5	10.9	13.8	37.0	52.1	100 316	103 375	3.0	1.0
Burlingame	18.5	33.6	23.1	4.5	16.8	15.9	12.6	13.6	13.4	39.5	53.7	28 158	28 806	2.3	5.2
Calexico	97.1	45.7	29.6	12.4	14.7	9.7	13.3	9.0	11.2	30.2	51.7	27 109	38 573	42.3	4.3
Camarillo	23.9	14.4	22.4	7.4	12.1	12.6	9.8	13.8	21.8	40.8	52.8	57 077	65 177	14.2	3.4
Campbell	25.4	23.4	23.2	4.6	16.2	18.0	12.5	13.4	12.1	39.4	51.2	38 138	39 348	3.2	4.0
Carlsbad	11.4	15.6	22.5	7.5	11.7	12.8	15.9	12.5	17.0	42.1	51.4	78 247	105 569	34.9	7.9
Carson	35.3	36.3	19.4	9.6	14.1	11.4	15.4	13.1	17.1	40.4	53.1	89 730	91 714	2.2	1.2
Cathedral City	65.0	32.6	26.5	9.3	12.9	11.8	12.7	12.8	14.0	35.4	48.5	42 647	51 200	20.1	5.6
Ceres	60.1	29.5	30.4	9.8	17.0	12.6	10.8	10.1	9.4	30.6	50.0	34 609	45 899	32.6	5.2
Cerritos	10.8	43.7	19.9	7.6	11.7	12.4	13.4	13.8	21.3	44.0	51.2	51 488	49 047	-4.7	3.1
Chico	17.2	9.3	18.7	23.2	14.1	11.8	10.2	8.8	13.2	29.9	48.9	59 954	86 401	44.1	6.0
Chino	53.1	21.8	19.1	10.9	17.2	15.4	16.7	11.4	9.3	36.5	40.4	67 168	77 972	16.1	12.6
Chino Hills	28.8	31.6	21.3	8.4	12.0	13.4	18.0	16.0	10.8	41.9	49.4	66 787	74 799	12.0	5.4
Chula Vista	58.9	31.1	25.9	10.5	14.1	14.9	13.6	9.6	11.4	34.6	50.5	173 556	243 920	40.5	9.5
Citrus Heights	16.8	10.9	21.1	10.0	15.7	11.6	13.0	11.9	16.8	37.8	51.8	85 071	83 255	-2.1	5.0
Claremont	23.6	20.9	18.6	16.7	10.6	10.9	11.5	13.9	17.9	38.1	56.1	33 998	34 929	2.7	3.2
Clovis	22.8	12.9	24.1	8.5	14.2	12.7	13.0	12.8	14.7	37.8	49.7	68 468	95 756	39.9	11.3
Coachella	99.4	43.1	28.8	10.5	18.5	12.2	14.6	9.8	5.7	31.3	49.3	22 724	40 724	79.2	10.4
Colton	59.8	18.9	27.5	9.3	18.9	15.0	9.3	9.4	10.6	32.5	51.5	47 662	52 155	9.4	4.9
Compton	68.6	31.1	28.5	13.8	14.4	11.9	13.1	9.3	9.0	30.1	50.0	93 493	96 418	3.1	1.2
Concord	32.2	29.1	21.0	7.0	15.1	16.0	13.5	14.5	13.0	39.6	51.6	121 780	122 154	0.3	5.4
Corona	41.8	25.7	24.1	9.3	14.0	15.6	15.6	11.3	10.2	37.1	51.4	124 966	152 425	22.0	9.4
Costa Mesa	33.8	23.5	19.8	9.6	21.1	15.4	11.7	12.3	10.1	34.8	47.8	108 724	110 078	1.2	2.5
Covina	61.5	20.4	26.7	10.1	13.5	13.8	16.0	8.9	11.0	34.6	51.8	46 837	47 792	2.0	1.6
Culver City	28.4	21.9	19.0	6.6	13.8	14.6	16.6	14.1	15.3	41.9	52.7	38 816	38 904	0.2	1.2
Cupertino	4.3	50.8	29.1	4.4	7.0	19.0	18.0	9.6	12.9	40.8	51.6	50 546	58 572	15.9	3.5
Cypress	18.9	35.9	21.3	8.2	10.6	12.5	18.3	14.8	14.3	43.6	51.7	46 229	47 860	3.5	2.2
Daly City	22.8	53.1	15.9	9.7	17.2	14.0	15.8	12.9	14.5	39.7	49.5	103 621	101 148	-2.4	5.3
Dana Point	24.3	14.2	16.5	3.1	12.4	11.8	17.8	15.7	22.7	48.4	53.7	35 110	33 293	-5.2	2.2
Danville	5.2	14.0	29.5	7.2	4.3	12.6	19.2	11.8	15.4	42.3	48.9	41 715	41 849	0.3	6.6
Davis	13.4	20.7	17.1	30.7	12.6	8.8	9.8	8.5	12.6	26.3	50.5	60 308	65 636	8.8	3.8

1. May be of any race.

Table D. Cities — Households, Group Quarters, Crime, and Education

City	Households, 2015		Percent		Persons in group quarters, 2010		Institutional		Serious crimes known to police,[2] 2014		Rate[3]		Educational attainment, 2015	Attainment[4] (percent)	
	Number	Persons per house-hold	Female family house-holder[1]	One-person	Total	Total	Persons in nursing facilities	Non-institu-tional	Number	Rate[3]	Violent	Property	Population age 25 and older	High school graduate or less	Bachelor's degree or more
	27	28	29	30	31	32	33	34	35	36	37	38	39	40	41
ARKANSAS—Cont'd															
Jacksonville	9 738	2.86	18.6	21.3	847	100	98	747	1 505	5 219	728	4 491	16 658	40.6	21.1
Jonesboro	28 816	2.44	16.0	31.5	3 412	1 238	800	2 174	3 578	4 930	539	4 392	45 336	37.8	29.1
Little Rock	82 603	2.36	16.5	37.0	4 543	2 781	1 074	1 762	17 457	8 807	1 405	7 402	133 452	30.9	39.7
North Little Rock	25 116	2.62	20.6	33.2	870	638	583	232	3 277	4 889	639	4 250	41 627	46.3	24.6
Paragould	10 210	2.69	12.4	25.7	550	391	226	159	2 112	7 736	432	7 304	17 966	61.7	12.9
Pine Bluff	16 400	2.52	20.5	42.2	3 999	2 512	429	1 487	3 232	7 119	1 269	5 850	27 045	54.4	14.3
Rogers	23 631	2.65	8.5	30.0	450	312	312	138	1 998	3 270	347	2 923	41 263	43.8	34.1
Russellville	9 693	2.66	20.5	23.2	3 251	448	277	2 803	1 409	4 923	321	4 602	15 132	45.7	27.4
Sherwood	11 838	2.57	17.0	33.1	85	85	85	0	1 316	4 364	497	3 866	20 826	36.6	29.2
Springdale	26 151	3.04	10.2	19.0	830	678	577	152	NA	NA	NA	NA	48 055	55.7	22.4
Texarkana	12 169	2.57	19.6	34.7	1 468	1 251	300	217	2 041	6 797	749	6 048	21 598	54.3	16.2
West Memphis	9 253	2.48	27.4	27.7	608	505	206	103	1 841	7 257	1 435	5 822	14 822	59.2	15.8
CALIFORNIA	12 896 357	2.97	13.3	24.0	819 816	397 142	111 884	422 674	1 100 901	2 837	396	2 441	26 085 263	38.6	32.3
Adelanto	7 669	4.08	29.0	10.1	1 753	1 723	0	30	979	3 137	606	2 531	17 400	61.5	5.4
Alameda	30 710	2.52	11.2	27.5	1 496	639	639	857	1 868	2 424	188	2 236	58 780	19.4	54.5
Alhambra	29 362	2.89	14.2	22.1	614	482	455	132	1 911	2 250	198	2 052	65 048	44.7	34.7
Aliso Viejo	18 334	2.72	13.6	20.9	469	19	19	450	308	608	69	539	34 171	13.2	54.5
Anaheim	99 991	3.45	15.4	19.2	3 557	1 537	1 376	2 020	9 297	2 680	317	2 362	226 279	49.4	23.2
Antioch	33 214	3.31	18.4	18.2	664	260	229	404	5 039	4 656	784	3 872	68 754	38.3	19.5
Apple Valley	23 644	3.03	20.2	20.1	461	300	104	161	1 866	2 616	297	2 319	43 155	47.1	18.9
Arcadia	18 819	3.07	18.6	16.0	862	223	220	639	1 219	2 104	104	2 000	42 102	23.6	52.9
Atascadero	11 927	2.46	8.1	29.9	1 324	1 100	91	224	520	1 777	246	1 531	21 733	23.3	32.4
Atwater	8 766	3.32	26.4	18.3	102	71	63	31	1 206	4 164	628	3 536	16 676	54.2	12.6
Azusa	12 307	3.58	17.6	16.6	2 802	111	97	2 691	1 230	2 551	342	2 208	29 541	47.3	21.3
Bakersfield	114 383	3.23	16.0	20.0	3 395	1 301	749	2 094	16 273	4 429	457	3 972	220 726	49.5	21.4
Baldwin Park	18 541	4.13	18.0	14.4	406	318	276	88	1 561	2 029	285	1 744	50 201	65.5	13.9
Banning	10 311	2.88	15.7	29.7	1 365	1 111	177	254	747	2 433	417	2 016	20 729	54.2	14.4
Beaumont	13 764	3.16	11.0	16.2	474	211	137	263	1 045	2 529	172	2 357	28 771	44.5	21.8
Bell	8 957	4.00	19.7	14.8	579	89	89	490	935	2 593	602	1 991	21 075	76.4	7.5
Bellflower	21 729	3.58	18.6	23.0	739	340	329	399	1 916	2 462	376	2 085	46 671	50.8	19.6
Bell Gardens	9 337	4.58	26.0	6.2	424	299	299	125	818	1 898	251	1 648	24 095	78.8	6.1
Belmont	10 068	2.65	7.0	21.9	514	120	120	394	408	1 514	134	1 380	19 772	14.7	60.7
Benicia	11 244	2.50	14.0	25.7	26	0	0	26	510	1 837	94	1 743	20 790	20.1	48.2
Berkeley	46 277	2.35	6.9	37.5	12 849	419	237	12 430	5 533	4 699	366	4 333	78 172	10.0	73.1
Beverly Hills	14 786	2.36	5.0	36.3	121	0	0	121	1 182	3 398	319	3 079	24 569	14.7	66.8
Brea	14 840	2.82	12.0	19.1	69	0	0	69	1 177	2 846	128	2 718	27 883	20.1	48.2
Brentwood	19 020	3.09	14.5	13.2	146	5	5	141	1 352	2 422	183	2 239	38 349	27.1	26.5
Buena Park	23 264	3.55	16.6	16.6	814	261	242	553	2 247	2 694	260	2 434	55 156	39.0	30.8
Burbank	41 633	2.52	10.1	30.7	573	282	268	291	2 576	2 452	143	2 310	74 116	27.2	38.4
Burlingame	11 682	2.56	8.6	24.4	449	294	294	155	797	2 642	156	2 487	22 057	21.7	55.3
Calexico	9 465	4.22	21.2	17.8	100	0	0	100	1 726	4 362	243	4 119	23 217	53.8	17.6
Camarillo	24 247	2.77	9.5	27.8	496	341	227	155	1 037	1 565	109	1 456	47 454	23.7	41.2
Campbell	16 042	2.54	10.4	25.3	201	122	114	79	1 469	3 594	198	3 396	29 672	21.3	54.3
Carlsbad	42 216	2.68	11.8	20.7	915	456	451	459	1 935	1 723	182	1 541	79 397	17.7	54.8
Carson	24 956	3.70	19.9	16.3	1 303	133	49	1 170	2 455	2 644	365	2 279	66 270	43.2	26.8
Cathedral City	17 084	3.13	16.1	26.2	295	32	32	263	1 322	2 477	240	2 237	34 550	53.7	17.3
Ceres	12 915	3.66	19.3	12.9	353	60	38	293	1 729	3 686	309	3 377	28 664	61.5	7.0
Cerritos	15 354	3.24	13.0	10.1	104	18	18	86	1 611	3 231	172	3 058	36 264	18.6	52.9
Chico	34 919	2.50	8.7	26.4	3 178	587	577	2 591	3 553	4 012	384	3 628	52 528	23.1	40.1
Chino	17 610	3.62	13.8	14.6	7 064	6 900	3	164	2 002	2 453	228	2 225	59 901	49.0	17.0
Chino Hills	25 659	3.05	8.2	12.5	155	147	0	8	1 091	1 417	79	1 338	55 055	22.4	43.1
Chula Vista	79 461	3.32	18.0	17.9	1 736	1 080	538	656	5 136	1 976	235	1 741	169 025	36.5	29.8
Citrus Heights	34 610	2.49	14.4	31.4	486	182	131	304	3 080	3 592	454	3 138	60 046	36.5	18.4
Claremont	11 293	2.81	10.0	26.4	5 124	198	192	4 926	892	2 475	108	2 367	23 489	22.5	56.3
Clovis	37 621	2.76	8.8	25.4	388	258	221	130	3 280	3 257	214	3 043	70 261	29.6	29.8
Coachella	12 458	3.58	18.0	26.2	58	0	0	58	1 318	3 021	380	2 640	27 124	77.4	4.7
Colton	17 820	3.04	20.8	15.5	330	245	243	85	1 712	3 201	256	2 945	34 505	53.5	12.7
Compton	23 978	4.08	29.8	12.0	755	112	84	643	3 748	3 816	1 149	2 666	56 762	66.9	9.6
Concord	46 885	2.72	9.4	23.1	1 047	535	469	512	5 661	4 466	367	4 100	92 753	32.9	33.5
Corona	55 011	2.97	7.6	31.0	511	282	268	229	3 611	2 241	106	2 135	109 374	39.7	27.6
Costa Mesa	42 871	2.59	10.8	29.3	2 970	738	581	2 232	3 780	3 354	282	3 072	79 858	29.7	40.3
Covina	14 549	3.33	19.8	16.4	435	367	341	68	1 218	2 502	226	2 276	30 970	37.2	26.8
Culver City	16 883	2.33	11.4	36.3	311	227	227	84	1 862	4 707	427	4 279	29 573	18.6	54.6
Cupertino	20 481	2.94	4.4	16.4	337	276	258	61	1 066	1 760	66	1 694	40 262	7.5	77.2
Cypress	15 938	3.08	13.0	15.5	502	0	0	502	803	1 626	103	1 523	34 762	31.3	37.8
Daly City	32 434	3.26	13.2	18.5	681	408	397	273	1 879	1 779	184	1 595	79 292	31.6	35.6
Dana Point	14 379	2.37	7.7	26.6	241	81	77	160	534	1 559	207	1 352	27 474	17.5	41.4
Danville	14 947	2.96	7.5	17.9	243	187	183	56	456	1 044	39	1 005	28 076	9.5	71.0
Davis	24 426	2.69	7.1	26.6	2 100	277	203	1 823	1 539	2 319	127	2 193	35 312	6.3	80.0

1. No spouse present.   2. Data for serious crimes have not been adjusted for underreporting. This may affect comparability between geographic areas and over time.   3. Per 100,000 population estimated by the FBI.   4. Persons 25 years old and over.

Table D. Cities — Income, Poverty, and Housing

City	Money income, 2015					Housing units, 2010			Occupied housing units 2015				
	Households			Families					Owner-occupied			Renter-occupied	
	Median income	Percent with income of $200,000 or more	Percent with income of less than $25,000	Total Families	Percent with income below poverty	Total	Percent change, 2000–2010	Vacant units for sale or rent[2]	Total	Percent	Median value[3] (dollars)	Percent	Median rent (dollars)
	42	43	44	45	46	47	48	49	50	51	52	53	54
ARKANSAS—Cont'd													
Jacksonville	51 402	1.1	19.2	6 943	16.8	12 412	4.8	1 476	9 738	49.0	134 400	51.0	752
Jonesboro	38 094	2.2	24.2	17 501	12.9	28 321	16.5	2 210	28 816	52.3	139 000	47.7	717
Little Rock	44 251	7.0	19.5	46 612	13.6	91 288	7.5	9 270	82 603	54.4	162 000	45.6	820
North Little Rock	39 686	3.0	28.1	15 081	30.8	29 437	6.8	2 907	25 116	47.3	130 700	52.7	819
Paragould	44 505	2.2	20.0	7 179	14.2	11 070	12.9	782	10 210	55.1	128 100	44.9	669
Pine Bluff	30 161	1.8	35.2	8 982	27.9	20 923	-6.2	2 852	16 400	52.6	65 700	47.4	676
Rogers	60 044	8.5	11.9	15 245	9.5	22 022	47.9	2 347	23 631	56.4	170 100	43.6	839
Russellville	30 697	0.4	36.0	6 754	30.1	11 124	8.9	806	9 693	40.9	116 900	59.1	645
Sherwood	57 167	3.8	14.4	7 621	10.5	12 924	40.5	717	11 838	66.6	158 000	33.4	818
Springdale	48 953	4.8	11.9	20 007	14.3	25 614	50.4	2 809	26 151	54.4	151 000	45.6	705
Texarkana	32 474	2.2	27.3	7 395	22.0	13 375	13.5	1 343	12 169	53.1	104 300	46.9	768
West Memphis	31 452	1.1	27.7	5 911	23.1	10 966	-0.5	1 131	9 253	49.3	87 700	50.7	732
CALIFORNIA	64 500	8.9	14.7	8 835 906	11.3	13 680 081	12.0	1 102 583	12 896 357	53.6	449 100	46.4	1 311
Adelanto	30 416	0.6	31.4	6 596	34.6	9 086	62.6	1 277	7 669	40.7	143 900	59.3	1 007
Alameda	92 225	13.6	10.7	19 545	5.2	32 351	2.2	2 228	30 710	44.1	738 000	55.9	1 515
Alhambra	51 641	6.6	21.0	20 710	11.8	30 915	2.8	1 698	29 362	41.5	562 500	58.5	1 188
Aliso Viejo	102 763	15.7	6.1	12 893	3.4	18 867	13.6	663	18 334	57.8	604 200	42.2	1 916
Anaheim	63 104	5.2	13.1	72 712	11.8	104 237	4.7	5 943	99 991	43.5	482 700	56.5	1 392
Antioch	68 800	5.0	11.5	25 806	11.8	34 849	15.5	2 597	33 214	56.6	348 200	43.4	1 575
Apple Valley	44 498	2.9	14.4	17 783	19.3	26 117	29.5	2 519	23 644	65.2	217 500	34.8	903
Arcadia	86 909	14.0	12.0	15 306	7.9	20 686	3.5	1 094	18 819	58.4	1 057 800	41.6	1 539
Atascadero	69 916	2.1	14.5	7 529	13.8	11 505	16.8	768	11 927	56.7	400 300	43.3	1 232
Atwater	40 768	1.3	20.6	6 939	21.6	9 771	20.8	933	8 766	51.5	179 100	48.5	804
Azusa	62 392	3.8	11.6	9 196	10.8	13 386	3.6	670	12 307	55.9	362 700	44.1	1 337
Bakersfield	61 039	4.9	14.6	85 439	14.3	120 725	36.9	9 593	114 383	57.8	237 600	42.2	979
Baldwin Park	47 502	2.8	18.8	15 288	14.4	17 736	1.8	547	18 541	54.4	357 700	45.6	1 339
Banning	44 047	1.0	17.1	7 077	13.0	12 144	24.7	1 306	10 311	66.6	187 400	33.4	1 068
Beaumont	62 387	3.5	14.6	10 519	12.1	12 908	203.1	1 107	13 764	74.1	270 600	25.9	1 242
Bell	39 042	0.4	20.4	7 284	19.8	9 217	0.0	347	8 957	26.9	372 300	73.1	1 072
Bellflower	50 692	4.4	16.5	16 143	10.9	24 897	2.9	1 246	21 729	40.1	432 700	59.9	1 223
Bell Gardens	40 499	0.0	17.9	8 671	22.5	9 986	2.0	331	9 337	22.2	405 400	77.8	1 114
Belmont	122 490	25.6	5.4	7 297	2.8	11 028	3.8	453	10 068	60.1	1 210 200	39.9	1 858
Benicia	80 303	12.2	7.2	NA	NA	11 306	7.1	620	11 244	71.2	507 700	28.8	1 472
Berkeley	73 462	13.3	17.5	20 662	4.4	49 454	5.5	3 425	46 277	44.6	888 300	55.4	1 460
Beverly Hills	101 209	24.6	14.9	8 648	6.5	16 394	3.4	1 525	14 786	39.2	2	60.8	2 043
Brea	86 702	12.0	10.5	11 427	5.5	14 785	11.4	519	14 840	62.2	608 600	37.8	1 541
Brentwood	100 945	11.9	10.3	16 050	5.0	17 523	125.6	1 029	19 020	77.1	482 900	22.9	2 019
Buena Park	68 656	4.5	12.2	18 593	13.0	24 623	3.1	937	23 264	55.4	483 500	44.6	1 470
Burbank	70 816	10.1	16.8	26 210	9.0	44 309	3.4	2 369	41 633	38.6	664 700	61.4	1 528
Burlingame	101 992	23.4	10.5	8 006	8.0	13 027	1.3	666	11 682	43.0	1 627 200	57.0	1 840
Calexico	36 730	1.8	27.6	7 704	25.4	10 651	52.5	535	9 465	54.2	179 900	45.8	831
Camarillo	85 495	10.9	12.7	16 613	5.4	25 702	17.2	1 198	24 247	65.6	548 200	34.4	1 755
Campbell	108 194	16.4	5.7	10 363	4.6	16 950	3.7	787	16 042	51.2	841 600	48.8	2 028
Carlsbad	96 346	18.6	6.9	30 844	2.7	44 673	32.5	3 328	42 216	64.2	704 600	35.8	2 032
Carson	77 162	6.0	9.6	20 013	6.4	26 226	3.6	794	24 956	75.4	421 600	24.6	1 464
Cathedral City	38 231	2.6	23.7	10 888	20.4	20 995	17.9	3 948	17 084	54.7	247 400	45.3	1 095
Ceres	50 540	0.9	15.5	10 653	10.5	13 673	26.6	981	12 915	58.9	220 400	41.1	1 012
Cerritos	86 515	11.9	7.3	13 176	4.4	15 859	1.6	333	15 354	74.5	640 500	25.5	2 357
Chico	45 598	3.2	25.6	18 205	14.1	37 050	52.1	2 245	34 919	44.0	278 600	56.0	976
Chino	72 155	4.6	11.7	14 098	10.5	21 797	21.0	1 025	17 610	60.7	415 900	39.3	1 504
Chino Hills	102 890	9.9	4.2	21 126	2.8	23 617	15.8	676	25 659	76.2	590 200	23.8	2 035
Chula Vista	66 868	4.9	13.2	62 437	9.1	79 416	33.4	3 901	79 461	58.7	440 400	41.3	1 360
Citrus Heights	49 808	1.6	13.4	21 167	8.4	35 075	0.4	2 389	34 610	53.7	249 300	46.3	990
Claremont	81 839	18.7	9.1	7 432	6.8	12 156	5.0	548	11 293	64.8	637 200	35.2	1 443
Clovis	62 863	4.1	13.2	26 430	9.9	35 306	40.4	1 887	37 621	61.6	276 400	38.4	1 092
Coachella	35 551	0.7	19.3	8 991	20.3	9 903	98.8	905	12 458	64.9	172 800	35.1	884
Colton	44 923	0.4	11.6	13 827	9.7	16 350	3.6	1 379	17 820	48.7	194 000	51.3	1 044
Compton	45 676	1.0	19.5	20 385	19.0	24 523	3.1	1 461	23 978	50.4	306 200	49.6	1 098
Concord	72 114	7.0	9.0	31 012	7.6	47 125	4.8	2 847	46 885	57.9	463 700	42.1	1 367
Corona	71 291	5.9	14.2	36 132	8.5	47 174	20.2	2 224	55 011	64.1	412 200	35.9	1 405
Costa Mesa	72 128	9.2	11.8	24 494	9.6	42 120	4.3	2 174	42 871	36.1	657 100	63.9	1 645
Covina	62 010	5.1	8.5	11 298	7.5	16 576	0.9	721	14 549	48.8	449 000	51.2	1 366
Culver City	86 467	11.4	10.8	10 016	2.2	17 491	2.1	712	16 883	53.0	764 700	47.0	1 556
Cupertino	156 680	35.9	5.5	16 173	3.2	21 027	12.4	846	20 481	60.2	1 526 700	39.8	2 807
Cypress	76 299	8.7	7.1	12 656	5.2	16 068	0.3	414	15 938	60.9	560 300	39.1	1 657
Daly City	81 355	6.2	8.9	23 824	5.9	32 588	4.3	1 498	32 434	56.4	633 100	43.6	1 930
Dana Point	96 561	15.6	8.5	NA	NA	15 938	1.8	1 756	14 379	57.7	836 800	42.3	1 806
Danville	151 821	38.4	3.4	11 603	1.3	15 934	3.9	514	14 947	81.1	1 024 600	18.9	2 428
Davis	58 176	12.9	26.2	12 469	6.7	25 869	9.6	996	24 426	46.3	598 800	53.7	1 307

1. Based on population estimated by the American Community Survey.   2. Includes units rented or sold but not occupied.   3. Specified owner-occupied units; $1,000,000 represents $1,000,000 or more   4. 50.0 represents 50 percent or more.   5. 10.0 represents 10 percent or less.

City	Commuting Percent		Computer Access[2] Percent		Migration, 2015		Civilian labor force, 2016		Unemployment		Civilian employment[4], 2015 Population age 16 and older		Population age 16 to 64	
	Drove alone	With Commutes of 30 minutes or more[1]	With a Computer in the house	With Internet Access	Percent who lived in the same house one year ago	Percent who lived in an other state or county one year ago	Total	Percent change, 2015–2016	Total	Rate[3]	Number	Percent in Labor Force	Number	Percent who worked full-year full-time
	55	56	57	58	59	60	61	62	63	64	65	66	67	68
ARKANSAS—Cont'd														
Jacksonville	82.0	23.2	85.9	71.7	77.5	5.3	11 738	0.9	529	4.5	21 048	60.6	18 124	49.7
Jonesboro	82.6	10.6	91.4	80.7	76.8	8.7	36 665	2.2	1 207	3.3	58 383	63.3	49 398	45.9
Little Rock	84.2	16.0	87.8	72.2	79.5	5.8	96 612	0.8	3 405	3.5	157 319	65.4	131 463	52.4
North Little Rock	88.6	18.7	75.2	56.3	69.8	7.5	29 890	0.6	1 148	3.8	48 994	58.3	40 422	47.5
Paragould	93.2	23.9	81.7	64.5	74.1	7.2	12 488	-0.1	595	4.8	21 969	59.8	18 131	48.6
Pine Bluff	85.4	14.3	71.1	35.6	86.8	6.8	17 165	-0.9	1 093	6.4	34 153	55.4	28 484	36.1
Rogers	86.8	14.5	92.9	56.1	88.9	3.4	33 588	3.3	924	2.8	47 162	68.9	39 777	64.2
Russellville	80.6	9.1	91.1	68.6	74.2	9.3	13 619	-1.6	572	4.2	22 891	56.9	19 715	32.4
Sherwood	87.8	25.4	83.5	76.7	NA	NA	15 565	1.2	493	3.2	24 452	68.1	19 749	60.7
Springdale	82.9	16.0	89.5	61.9	88.8	6.2	38 203	3.7	1 038	2.7	58 828	64.4	51 421	55.8
Texarkana	86.7	8.6	75.5	64.5	73.2	18.6	13 924	0.9	615	4.4	25 157	57.2	19 832	45.4
West Memphis	81.4	25.6	67.4	52.8	82.3	4.3	10 671	0.5	559	5.2	17 792	55.3	14 545	40.4
CALIFORNIA	78.2	42.5	89.7	81.3	86.5	5.0	19 102 726	1.1	1 037 683	5.4	31 068 647	63.0	25 879 089	45.9
Adelanto	73.4	62.7	80.1	61.0	76.0	6.4	9 322	1.1	896	9.6	21 219	51.8	18 686	26.9
Alameda	61.6	52.2	95.4	89.5	88.3	4.8	41 776	1.9	1 524	3.6	64 837	66.7	53 168	55.0
Alhambra	84.5	53.1	89.6	81.7	89.5	3.6	45 499	1.4	1 544	3.4	73 529	60.6	60 397	50.6
Aliso Viejo	88.8	38.3	96.1	93.8	84.5	4.7	29 200	1.0	916	3.1	39 886	74.5	35 614	54.0
Anaheim	80.3	42.0	91.5	87.0	88.4	4.1	171 577	0.7	8 757	5.1	273 225	69.0	237 086	50.7
Antioch	70.9	61.8	92.0	83.3	84.6	5.5	51 401	1.4	3 163	6.2	84 415	62.1	73 524	41.6
Apple Valley	81.2	34.5	84.8	78.8	91.4	1.8	28 235	1.5	1 721	6.1	54 100	52.1	41 737	35.6
Arcadia	83.1	54.1	95.2	87.5	89.9	4.4	28 879	1.5	868	3.0	47 149	59.0	36 107	51.3
Atascadero	79.9	28.8	90.8	81.3	87.1	2.8	15 178	0.6	535	3.5	23 943	65.9	19 506	50.3
Atwater	86.7	29.8	93.9	81.6	84.0	3.5	12 294	0.5	1 421	11.6	20 351	59.7	16 818	39.5
Azusa	75.2	44.0	93.5	76.4	89.9	5.3	24 378	1.2	959	3.9	40 523	62.4	35 589	42.2
Bakersfield	84.1	23.5	86.8	79.6	86.5	3.7	178 818	-0.4	16 487	9.2	276 600	66.3	241 521	47.7
Baldwin Park	81.5	45.0	85.2	71.8	95.9	1.5	35 107	0.4	2 452	7.0	59 621	59.1	49 628	47.3
Banning	86.5	46.2	85.5	76.0	80.8	6.0	10 841	1.7	580	5.4	24 010	44.4	16 204	32.4
Beaumont	82.4	53.0	88.5	84.0	86.7	10.2	19 910	1.8	712	3.6	33 289	57.7	26 888	48.1
Bell	65.7	59.7	71.4	60.1	NA	NA	15 349	0.3	1 098	7.2	26 217	62.1	22 925	41.1
Bellflower	82.7	50.1	83.7	75.3	92.7	1.3	36 126	0.9	1 798	5.0	59 473	57.6	50 417	45.2
Bell Gardens	79.4	51.0	80.7	54.6	NA	NA	18 244	0.6	1 106	6.1	29 882	66.2	26 674	46.4
Belmont	72.1	52.9	97.5	94.7	90.3	3.7	16 543	2.5	434	2.6	21 797	63.4	16 684	53.3
Benicia	81.3	45.4	90.6	87.8	84.1	8.8	14 894	1.5	506	3.4	23 314	58.8	17 248	48.4
Berkeley	38.4	44.0	95.4	88.4	75.4	16.0	62 616	1.9	2 133	3.4	107 090	63.6	90 006	36.9
Beverly Hills	85.5	38.2	91.3	84.5	84.1	7.6	18 437	0.9	917	5.0	26 789	62.7	19 507	54.5
Brea	85.2	58.8	95.1	91.6	84.8	6.3	22 161	0.9	854	3.9	31 998	66.7	27 368	49.1
Brentwood	75.6	60.8	96.4	91.5	86.5	4.0	27 323	1.7	1 018	3.7	45 686	63.1	36 510	45.9
Buena Park	82.0	50.5	92.9	84.6	89.6	3.8	40 113	0.9	1 378	3.4	63 979	61.3	53 484	46.8
Burbank	86.2	46.8	92.9	82.4	88.0	4.9	58 056	1.1	2 484	4.3	84 504	66.3	69 965	50.7
Burlingame	70.2	42.1	94.4	89.3	82.9	8.7	18 053	2.6	421	2.3	24 512	68.5	20 417	54.7
Calexico	89.7	29.7	82.2	65.1	79.7	5.5	17 714	-1.7	4 817	27.2	29 218	57.4	24 728	33.6
Camarillo	83.4	27.9	88.3	82.8	88.8	4.3	33 823	-0.1	1 468	4.3	53 760	58.4	38 995	48.7
Campbell	85.1	43.2	96.6	88.8	84.8	2.7	25 313	1.8	687	2.7	32 585	75.6	27 613	65.7
Carlsbad	86.8	48.9	96.5	94.1	87.0	4.5	54 179	1.1	2 291	4.2	91 226	65.6	71 915	55.7
Carson	80.8	40.9	89.4	81.0	90.8	1.9	46 549	0.4	3 155	6.8	77 995	61.7	62 058	48.5
Cathedral City	87.5	17.5	82.0	73.5	92.7	3.3	25 343	1.7	1 246	4.9	41 164	57.5	33 615	39.9
Ceres	83.2	34.1	85.4	73.1	85.7	2.5	21 674	1.1	1 981	9.1	34 456	61.8	29 971	39.8
Cerritos	86.9	62.3	91.7	90.1	91.8	4.1	24 551	1.2	950	3.9	41 971	56.2	31 320	46.6
Chico	77.4	14.8	93.3	85.1	71.8	7.6	47 824	1.1	2 607	5.5	75 131	63.6	63 199	35.1
Chino	84.9	51.2	94.3	85.1	76.7	16.9	39 858	1.8	1 742	4.4	71 209	48.8	63 213	32.5
Chino Hills	87.3	64.7	96.8	92.7	88.2	6.1	42 158	1.8	1 761	4.2	64 172	67.9	55 711	47.5
Chula Vista	84.3	48.1	86.0	82.8	89.3	3.0	122 181	0.9	7 202	5.9	204 519	64.1	174 224	40.8
Citrus Heights	85.5	31.0	92.3	80.1	82.4	5.7	43 688	1.6	2 461	5.6	70 602	60.9	55 970	45.6
Claremont	73.3	36.4	94.7	87.4	81.7	9.7	16 861	0.9	839	5.0	30 333	60.0	23 849	38.9
Clovis	86.0	17.6	89.7	80.1	86.6	3.1	52 079	1.3	3 800	7.3	81 571	63.5	66 221	46.3
Coachella	86.3	21.8	74.3	53.2	NA	NA	18 821	1.2	1 767	9.4	33 217	73.3	30 685	50.1
Colton	83.5	35.5	83.1	72.2	NA	NA	24 302	1.6	1 389	5.7	41 114	62.3	35 323	47.4
Compton	74.5	45.4	80.4	64.0	91.1	1.8	39 782	0.0	3 260	8.2	73 191	62.1	64 360	40.4
Concord	70.3	52.6	93.6	88.2	87.6	5.4	66 637	1.6	3 200	4.8	103 826	68.7	87 097	50.2
Corona	81.1	55.3	89.8	85.0	90.5	3.7	81 226	1.7	3 832	4.7	129 002	67.5	112 183	50.9
Costa Mesa	84.6	29.0	89.9	84.7	85.6	4.8	65 611	0.9	2 670	4.1	93 346	73.6	81 915	54.8
Covina	79.5	51.9	94.6	85.4	86.1	4.3	24 292	0.6	1 521	6.3	37 228	68.8	31 822	52.4
Culver City	84.3	47.0	94.7	89.2	94.9	1.2	22 642	1.3	869	3.8	32 996	71.2	26 918	56.0
Cupertino	84.8	39.8	97.8	94.3	84.4	6.7	29 318	1.7	889	3.0	44 777	61.5	36 955	52.2
Cypress	87.9	55.4	96.5	88.2	89.6	4.5	24 760	1.0	676	2.7	40 893	62.7	33 836	48.2
Daly City	65.8	46.8	94.3	87.9	90.7	6.3	64 557	2.4	2 372	3.7	91 833	68.6	76 416	48.6
Dana Point	75.8	44.7	98.6	91.0	83.8	3.3	18 915	0.9	711	3.8	29 760	65.1	21 985	50.0
Danville	88.0	51.5	93.0	91.7	90.8	3.7	20 781	1.8	729	3.5	33 380	62.0	26 550	50.5
Davis	57.7	25.6	95.8	92.5	63.2	15.8	35 356	1.7	1 568	4.4	57 594	58.8	49 077	34.1

1. Employed persons. 2. Households. 3. Percent of civilian labor force. 4. Persons 16 years old and over.

Table D. Cities — Construction, Wholesale Trade, and Retail Trade

City	Value of residential construction authorized by building permits, 2016			Wholesale trade,[1] 2012				Retail trade,[2] 2012			
	New construction ($1,000)	Number of housing units	Percent single family	Number of establishments	Number of employees	Sales (mil dol)	Annual payroll (mil dol)	Number of establishments	Number of employees	Sales (mil dol)	Annual payroll (mil dol)
	69	70	71	72	73	74	75	76	77	78	79
ARKANSAS—Cont'd											
Jacksonville	4 588	39	100.0	10	84	66.9	3.8	89	1 404	396.8	36.7
Jonesboro	91 714	858	50.1	94	1 133	643.5	50.6	406	6 053	1 556.4	135.5
Little Rock	135 843	831	39.7	358	6 552	3 801.0	340.0	994	14 533	4 025.2	354.2
North Little Rock	18 474	160	48.8	196	3 234	3 898.4	185.7	417	6 092	1 557.4	138.8
Paragould	16 300	134	70.1	26	378	459.2	15.1	130	1 608	395.9	33.7
Pine Bluff	1 043	10	100.0	40	354	189.0	14.8	248	3 072	744.6	71.2
Rogers	83 741	537	76.5	60	510	619.9	30.8	297	5 130	1 162.2	114.4
Russellville	6 150	62	90.3	47	384	296.7	16.6	216	2 815	782.7	60.7
Sherwood	35 021	223	100.0	30	188	93.2	8.1	94	1 899	763.9	53.7
Springdale	77 973	314	100.0	144	1 569	1 133.8	74.0	247	3 448	1 011.1	86.8
Texarkana	6 262	42	100.0	37	D	D	D	113	1 324	416.4	29.7
West Memphis	3 053	22	100.0	38	717	1 799.2	32.4	102	1 660	617.7	35.6
CALIFORNIA	430	2	100.0	52 664	723 526	666 652.2	48 408.7	106 419	1 540 055	481 800.5	43 361.0
Adelanto	1 396	6	100.0	7	114	42.2	4.5	19	286	80.8	8.0
Alameda	19 407	90	65.6	63	2 252	2 887.1	218.6	155	1 956	492.2	54.1
Alhambra	7 801	37	62.2	234	999	476.8	31.3	233	3 923	1 636.6	116.7
Aliso Viejo	24 114	200	0.0	74	1 311	1 010.6	133.6	82	1 210	500.3	43.2
Anaheim	142 862	939	13.7	799	9 520	7 153.5	562.0	826	13 333	3 757.9	374.1
Antioch	28 089	127	33.1	23	316	276.1	18.2	216	3 781	939.3	102.9
Apple Valley	20 256	148	100.0	10	32	8.6	1.2	113	2 311	598.1	53.9
Arcadia	49 208	267	28.1	284	1 066	527.0	39.5	295	4 276	860.3	94.2
Atascadero	18 222	101	10.9	30	210	66.5	9.5	116	1 230	298.5	30.7
Atwater	505	3	100.0	8	D	D	D	74	1 314	257.5	27.3
Azusa	46 744	106	59.4	75	1 416	883.0	103.9	94	1 147	470.7	33.6
Bakersfield	370 956	1 438	93.0	274	3 933	3 693.1	216.0	960	18 130	5 263.8	454.7
Baldwin Park	5 799	28	85.7	151	860	373.8	34.0	130	2 106	535.3	52.4
Banning	0	0	0.0	11	347	72.0	10.9	58	616	176.7	16.6
Beaumont	80 438	488	92.2	9	27	3.9	0.8	57	1 297	348.8	32.0
Bell	0	0	0.0	71	1 564	1 029.1	83.9	51	458	128.5	10.8
Bellflower	10 877	47	87.2	34	226	98.4	10.3	174	1 970	551.5	53.2
Bell Gardens	436	3	100.0	39	474	178.2	18.6	79	1 127	321.2	30.9
Belmont	4 197	6	100.0	19	D	D	D	57	761	292.3	28.8
Benicia	2 396	10	100.0	66	1 134	733.7	63.0	71	844	266.6	31.0
Berkeley	55 453	357	4.5	94	1 175	565.1	82.4	497	5 449	1 341.0	164.2
Beverly Hills	91 126	39	100.0	158	778	647.5	48.2	429	5 382	2 912.3	275.0
Brea	44 454	181	75.7	263	3 865	3 321.6	215.5	321	6 133	1 260.4	134.2
Brentwood	123 462	559	100.0	14	59	18.3	2.5	142	2 263	557.2	54.7
Buena Park	20 347	74	100.0	204	3 037	2 044.9	165.9	202	3 987	1 731.1	134.4
Burbank	63 321	267	6.0	208	2 987	4 628.6	209.3	399	7 310	2 316.8	191.7
Burlingame	42 618	145	13.8	136	978	870.8	64.3	159	2 011	776.4	79.8
Calexico	178	2	0.0	58	403	416.3	11.7	136	1 997	432.4	40.7
Camarillo	45 893	236	51.3	147	2 132	1 157.4	130.2	313	5 248	1 526.8	133.7
Campbell	49 824	233	27.5	74	D	D	D	182	2 925	757.9	83.6
Carlsbad	182 133	683	40.6	292	5 465	3 115.2	354.2	485	7 796	2 649.1	215.9
Carson	4 132	18	50.0	337	6 718	5 893.4	352.1	210	4 267	1 398.5	148.4
Cathedral City	10 065	46	95.7	24	127	37.6	4.6	145	2 002	790.1	65.7
Ceres	4 200	21	100.0	22	335	281.9	16.9	89	1 606	443.7	38.5
Cerritos	19 379	197	0.0	254	5 230	5 454.5	329.6	233	7 278	2 479.9	213.9
Chico	86 242	534	52.8	84	831	399.3	40.8	419	6 368	1 790.7	165.7
Chino	142 304	570	64.9	457	5 476	3 872.9	265.8	266	4 563	1 188.9	105.8
Chino Hills	76 846	450	26.4	90	248	203.5	8.8	140	2 399	635.6	57.1
Chula Vista	176 606	1 175	7.3	299	1 793	1 406.4	77.9	616	11 228	2 744.4	273.1
Citrus Heights	3 541	15	100.0	16	58	70.0	3.3	263	4 698	1 029.7	103.2
Claremont	11 335	42	100.0	20	86	48.1	4.1	80	1 102	379.7	34.8
Clovis	301 128	1 086	100.0	47	190	189.9	9.0	267	5 059	1 496.3	130.8
Coachella	9 373	51	100.0	22	460	162.5	29.0	49	671	259.6	15.9
Colton	575	4	100.0	44	770	642.1	36.6	103	1 508	480.9	44.2
Compton	9 907	57	40.4	141	2 276	1 584.9	122.5	160	1 571	368.8	31.3
Concord	36 574	195	7.7	116	896	444.6	53.7	423	7 650	2 376.7	225.2
Corona	16 899	66	100.0	288	5 898	7 239.0	355.9	450	8 115	2 616.1	218.4
Costa Mesa	68 875	644	23.9	288	4 160	17 724.3	315.1	748	13 371	3 815.5	386.4
Covina	845	3	100.0	67	405	143.3	18.1	154	2 746	671.1	78.3
Culver City	1 573	6	50.0	110	2 279	1 690.9	200.3	287	5 510	1 660.3	154.5
Cupertino	21 717	57	100.0	71	1 507	1 092.5	107.8	121	D	D	D
Cypress	30 805	133	100.0	101	3 164	3 767.2	259.9	103	1 617	614.0	46.7
Daly City	38 999	125	82.4	35	D	D	D	193	3 738	885.4	91.3
Dana Point	51 892	44	100.0	51	232	155.8	12.7	102	1 042	340.4	27.3
Danville	13 713	17	100.0	44	173	167.2	10.3	124	1 610	548.1	45.5
Davis	52 466	261	66.3	16	256	495.9	21.3	124	2 061	466.0	50.5

1. Merchant wholesalers except manufacturers' sales branches and offices.   2. Establishments with payroll.

Table D. Cities — Real Estate, Professional Services, and Manufacturing

City	Real estate and rental and leasing, 2012				Professional, scientific, and technical services,[1] 2012				Manufacturing, 2012			
	Number of establishments	Number of employees	Receipts (mil dol)	Annual payroll (mil dol)	Number of establishments	Number of employees	Receipts (mil dol)	Annual payroll (mil dol)	Number of establishments	Number of employees	Receipts (mil dol)	Annual payroll (mil dol)
	80	81	82	83	84	85	86	87	88	89	90	91
ARKANSAS—Cont'd												
Jacksonville	44	170	24.3	4.4	34	191	14.4	5.0	23	543	D	27.2
Jonesboro	110	469	79.0	12.8	157	D	D	D	80	4 781	1 900.6	203.7
Little Rock	377	2 450	423.0	89.3	1 182	D	D	D	166	8 152	4 227.1	419.7
North Little Rock	89	440	89.0	13.4	175	1 435	172.4	62.8	62	1 978	D	93.1
Paragould	30	D	D	D	47	423	38.2	18.6	37	3 299	D	128.4
Pine Bluff	53	173	26.7	4.4	57	D	D	D	48	4 258	1 859.3	185.2
Rogers	83	322	65.1	13.2	216	1 644	275.6	87.7	53	5 462	1 753.7	217.3
Russellville	59	174	26.2	4.9	105	D	D	D	40	4 067	1 339.7	149.1
Sherwood	28	80	21.3	2.5	43	539	113.1	30.5	17	D	D	D
Springdale	74	254	39.7	7.5	135	D	D	D	101	7 619	2 375.8	265.0
Texarkana	27	D	D	D	41	D	D	D	26	2 303	D	D
West Memphis	30	168	20.0	5.0	37	D	D	D	25	815	469.3	31.6
CALIFORNIA	49 276	273 511	78 740.2	13 467.5	113 553	1 270 902	227 858.9	87 924.6	38 741	1 163 341	512 303.2	69 316.8
Adelanto	9	21	3.3	0.4	7	75	11.0	4.5	42	1 108	263.4	55.3
Alameda	95	382	65.5	13.6	234	2 323	614.3	222.1	50	3 006	1 130.2	274.0
Alhambra	117	396	66.2	15.1	220	D	D	D	76	1 252	307.3	64.9
Aliso Viejo	79	D	D	D	288	3 609	843.5	364.2	30	378	58.0	21.7
Anaheim	381	3 684	508.9	131.9	681	4 384	760.1	251.7	693	19 991	4 824.4	1 071.6
Antioch	60	266	43.1	7.5	92	600	103.3	28.6	22	235	125.9	12.2
Apple Valley	37	179	23.1	4.3	68	339	33.2	12.1	25	319	D	15.4
Arcadia	175	483	98.1	17.1	258	D	D	D	47	905	194.3	46.0
Atascadero	27	D	D	D	74	D	D	D	26	109	15.8	4.6
Atwater	12	32	4.9	0.6	10	27	3.0	1.0	13	368	D	18.9
Azusa	22	46	13.8	1.5	35	309	64.0	22.4	100	4 979	1 505.2	318.8
Bakersfield	343	1 907	335.7	69.5	798	D	D	D	143	2 541	646.2	110.3
Baldwin Park	22	119	17.8	4.2	31	143	12.0	4.6	85	1 533	285.7	63.8
Banning	29	216	38.8	6.0	14	145	9.5	3.7	22	326	72.9	14.2
Beaumont	24	77	10.2	1.7	19	45	4.4	1.7	14	361	102.3	15.9
Bell	12	D	D	D	16	405	45.4	18.2	30	1 711	657.2	85.4
Bellflower	78	249	48.7	10.7	60	317	17.0	6.3	33	254	46.8	11.2
Bell Gardens	10	36	10.0	0.9	10	153	14.6	5.2	50	863	156.7	32.5
Belmont	49	533	67.1	25.6	107	508	62.1	41.7	20	352	D	19.2
Benicia	43	187	47.1	8.7	98	580	92.2	36.8	70	2 579	7 511.9	195.5
Berkeley	198	744	175.2	40.0	605	3 646	692.1	295.7	152	3 744	D	241.1
Beverly Hills	481	2 312	1 293.7	155.3	1 017	5 275	1 681.6	538.7	57	348	33.9	9.2
Brea	97	536	118.4	26.9	288	D	D	D	152	5 251	1 292.7	254.2
Brentwood	55	173	40.2	6.8	84	280	36.7	12.6	17	232	D	12.3
Buena Park	57	218	40.3	6.9	110	960	135.1	50.1	109	3 966	1 990.3	204.1
Burbank	242	2 976	1 052.6	246.5	608	D	D	D	191	5 031	1 269.2	284.4
Burlingame	149	935	213.8	44.8	272	D	D	D	49	1 679	D	98.9
Calexico	24	104	9.3	1.8	42	112	12.2	3.4	12	265	D	20.8
Camarillo	87	608	111.7	28.3	299	2 498	601.1	181.4	134	4 292	1 636.8	230.4
Campbell	85	448	155.2	36.3	312	D	D	D	92	1 840	431.0	113.7
Carlsbad	314	1 571	330.6	74.0	894	D	D	D	160	12 711	4 983.1	1 024.6
Carson	64	625	453.8	62.4	101	970	159.8	40.6	230	9 808	15 329.4	624.3
Cathedral City	38	182	40.7	5.8	40	99	11.0	2.7	13	29	5.5	1.3
Ceres	30	110	24.6	4.0	25	311	34.0	14.1	21	391	90.1	16.8
Cerritos	79	226	56.8	9.6	188	D	D	D	88	2 532	509.8	111.1
Chico	137	769	88.0	18.4	291	D	D	D	71	1 549	568.6	65.1
Chino	78	289	66.4	11.5	148	1 068	130.1	42.1	220	5 480	1 465.1	232.5
Chino Hills	66	116	36.2	4.9	169	428	66.5	18.7	10	72	D	1.4
Chula Vista	241	987	217.4	34.8	357	D	D	D	126	4 237	1 363.4	330.2
Citrus Heights	79	408	46.7	11.6	122	1 252	128.6	50.2	12	31	3.2	1.0
Claremont	58	180	24.5	7.7	133	D	D	D	20	620	114.6	26.2
Clovis	79	276	49.5	7.6	155	894	88.8	35.3	42	2 866	D	131.0
Coachella	17	58	8.7	1.8	6	D	D	D	11	773	433.2	37.5
Colton	34	222	39.8	7.7	49	D	D	D	53	2 758	1 090.7	95.5
Compton	21	61	13.2	2.3	15	D	D	D	129	4 001	1 184.2	178.4
Concord	148	996	215.3	48.3	298	3 084	581.0	226.3	106	1 779	464.2	97.9
Corona	175	641	156.0	25.2	319	1 877	210.8	106.2	341	12 813	4 810.5	586.6
Costa Mesa	298	3 347	666.1	135.9	687	8 743	2 097.9	740.2	232	6 196	1 541.4	321.1
Covina	94	479	63.9	16.8	148	946	131.5	44.7	89	1 490	344.0	69.4
Culver City	107	1 251	229.6	59.8	424	D	D	D	53	1 612	367.4	84.7
Cupertino	104	401	256.0	28.6	444	2 980	1 111.0	417.2	35	927	382.1	90.2
Cypress	65	277	58.0	13.3	118	979	212.8	55.6	35	1 287	588.1	92.4
Daly City	54	273	136.9	13.2	69	291	25.2	8.4	20	283	D	7.2
Dana Point	78	163	34.4	7.8	168	548	113.1	46.1	24	155	37.3	7.0
Danville	103	379	148.2	26.7	223	956	185.9	66.9	11	125	D	5.1
Davis	116	619	75.6	21.2	205	D	D	D	22	627	D	32.0

1. Establishments subject to federal tax.

Table D. Cities — Accommodation and Food Services, Arts, Entertainment, and Recreation, and Health Care and Social Assistance

City	Accommodation and food services, 2012				Arts, entertainment, and recreation,[1] 2012				Health care and social assistance,[1] 2012			
	Number of establish-ments	Number of employees	Sales (mil dol)	Annual payroll (mil dol)	Number of establish-ments	Number of employees	Receipts (mil dol)	Annual payroll (mil dol)	Number of establish-ments	Number of employees	Receipts (mil dol)	Annual payroll (mil dol)
	92	93	94	95	96	97	98	99	100	101	102	103
ARKANSAS—Cont'd												
Jacksonville	61	1 010	44.9	12.3	5	D	D	D	51	D	D	D
Jonesboro	193	4 134	182.9	50.6	14	184	7.4	3.1	284	D	D	D
Little Rock	593	12 849	626.5	185.9	64	677	40.9	13.3	825	10 939	1 405.6	615.5
North Little Rock	227	4 536	213.5	63.3	20	D	D	D	212	2 659	322.4	127.2
Paragould	61	D	D	D	4	D	D	D	73	D	D	D
Pine Bluff	102	D	D	D	3	D	D	D	153	D	D	D
Rogers	145	3 735	169.7	52.0	9	174	11.6	4.9	164	D	D	D
Russellville	103	2 256	101.8	24.9	9	42	2.0	0.4	112	D	D	D
Sherwood	43	673	34.9	8.9	3	D	D	D	68	D	D	D
Springdale	134	2 345	106.4	30.2	12	D	D	D	139	3 900	446.2	171.2
Texarkana	69	D	D	D	5	D	D	D	50	D	D	D
West Memphis	68	1 158	65.6	15.7	5	D	D	D	66	D	D	D
CALIFORNIA	78 560	1 394 984	90 830.4	25 147.8	19 010	245 599	34 302.9	11 726.7	89 999	1 005 201	127 355.7	48 372.7
Adelanto	14	D	D	D	1	D	D	D	4	D	D	D
Alameda	208	2 505	145.4	38.8	28	566	281.4	169.8	182	2 115	251.2	88.4
Alhambra	196	3 107	170.3	46.8	15	D	D	D	265	2 672	292.9	102.2
Aliso Viejo	68	1 335	87.1	24.8	15	D	D	D	119	D	D	D
Anaheim	692	23 526	1 589.1	507.2	75	D	D	D	825	11 330	1 388.6	525.8
Antioch	129	1 981	105.6	29.7	13	D	D	D	210	D	D	D
Apple Valley	85	D	D	D	7	D	D	D	190	D	D	D
Arcadia	212	3 593	220.4	59.1	70	D	D	D	383	D	D	D
Atascadero	70	926	53.1	12.9	9	127	4.6	1.6	85	D	D	D
Atwater	35	532	27.7	6.5	3	69	3.6	1.0	23	D	D	D
Azusa	73	895	48.0	12.8	3	D	D	D	44	523	27.4	11.7
Bakersfield	675	12 835	713.4	189.0	59	2 198	85.8	29.3	973	11 550	1 564.5	498.1
Baldwin Park	85	1 201	74.2	18.5	2	D	D	D	77	D	D	D
Banning	46	751	41.3	10.1	NA	NA	NA	NA	41	653	93.4	23.7
Beaumont	45	629	33.1	10.0	4	D	D	D	41	D	D	D
Bell	54	580	35.7	8.8	1	D	D	D	30	279	20.7	8.9
Bellflower	117	1 294	72.6	18.7	8	170	7.6	2.4	143	D	D	D
Bell Gardens	53	669	50.4	10.7	2	D	D	D	26	526	40.3	15.0
Belmont	62	716	58.0	13.2	5	D	D	D	47	D	D	D
Benicia	60	767	40.2	10.6	6	112	8.9	1.7	51	D	D	D
Berkeley	437	6 068	383.7	114.8	62	836	131.8	27.2	401	3 197	463.0	188.7
Beverly Hills	200	8 518	782.3	248.1	857	3 764	1 868.9	804.7	1 091	5 921	1 249.2	360.7
Brea	160	4 045	232.7	69.9	18	221	20.7	4.9	158	D	D	D
Brentwood	102	1 623	88.8	23.1	10	D	D	D	98	D	D	D
Buena Park	185	2 924	183.6	46.4	13	D	D	D	161	1 619	170.0	58.5
Burbank	325	6 840	532.9	130.3	308	D	D	D	467	D	D	D
Burlingame	145	4 340	387.8	115.5	18	216	19.1	4.6	179	2 136	426.2	133.0
Calexico	53	852	44.7	11.6	2	D	D	D	16	115	12.0	4.3
Camarillo	165	3 099	173.5	47.2	21	379	23.1	7.4	236	2 256	202.5	78.3
Campbell	133	2 474	150.8	42.2	19	D	D	D	193	D	D	D
Carlsbad	251	7 216	468.8	154.5	59	2 435	246.6	49.3	290	3 598	496.5	180.1
Carson	158	2 289	144.2	34.6	17	D	D	D	146	1 327	109.9	42.4
Cathedral City	85	1 365	67.0	19.6	10	D	D	D	53	462	29.2	13.1
Ceres	58	1 188	52.0	13.4	4	54	5.6	0.7	39	345	34.5	12.9
Cerritos	146	D	D	D	10	D	D	D	196	2 163	236.9	89.7
Chico	247	4 730	213.1	60.4	23	556	19.7	6.3	374	3 766	383.8	139.8
Chino	149	2 564	127.7	36.8	26	441	22.0	7.2	190	2 297	255.9	84.2
Chino Hills	116	2 267	114.5	33.9	13	324	19.0	6.0	108	661	71.1	23.0
Chula Vista	385	6 198	357.9	96.7	35	829	66.2	15.1	506	4 450	514.8	213.8
Citrus Heights	126	2 343	113.2	32.5	18	D	D	D	148	1 507	122.3	49.4
Claremont	97	1 667	90.5	24.3	11	D	D	D	141	1 336	118.8	48.2
Clovis	197	3 352	167.2	46.2	16	D	D	D	187	D	D	D
Coachella	46	753	35.2	8.2	1	D	D	D	10	D	D	D
Colton	85	1 150	58.0	15.2	4	D	D	D	79	D	D	D
Compton	94	1 207	77.6	18.5	4	D	D	D	62	527	41.3	17.7
Concord	247	3 850	229.6	61.7	30	714	40.8	12.1	333	3 810	420.7	163.9
Corona	276	4 993	261.4	70.9	29	D	D	D	315	3 204	333.1	119.1
Costa Mesa	422	8 168	530.6	147.9	54	581	50.5	12.4	344	3 573	343.0	121.0
Covina	114	1 803	98.7	26.0	10	D	D	D	199	2 636	265.1	113.9
Culver City	183	3 434	231.9	63.6	129	626	172.6	43.9	181	5 143	367.4	142.9
Cupertino	150	2 728	168.4	45.5	15	203	12.8	3.5	184	D	D	D
Cypress	105	1 460	88.3	23.2	26	393	30.3	10.6	114	1 648	166.5	66.6
Daly City	145	2 549	165.7	42.9	11	D	D	D	241	D	D	D
Dana Point	111	3 674	299.2	94.4	21	D	D	D	97	613	66.3	23.1
Danville	96	1 576	85.1	25.8	18	330	35.2	9.5	132	1 097	114.6	45.2
Davis	182	D	D	D	17	266	9.0	3.2	118	1 483	229.0	63.5

1. Establishments subject to federal tax.

Table D. Cities — **Other Services and Government Employment and Payroll**

City	Other services[1], 2012 Number of establishments	Number of employees	Receipts (mil dol)	Annual payroll (mil dol)	Government employment and payroll, 2012 Full-time equivalent employees	March payroll Total (dollars)	Percent of total for: Administration, judicial, and legal	Police and Corrections	Fire Protection	Highways and transportation	Health and welfare	Natural resources and utilities	Education and libraries
	104	105	106	107	108	109	110	111	112	113	114	115	116
ARKANSAS—Cont'd													
Jacksonville	24	124	8.6	2.6	351	1 152 915	9.7	28.8	19.4	4.2	5.3	27.7	0.0
Jonesboro	90	653	67.9	19.3	689	2 345 837	8.5	24.7	13.3	9.8	1.2	42.4	0.0
Little Rock	291	2 215	176.7	54.2	2 851	11 721 278	7.5	27.1	19.0	8.2	12.4	20.1	0.0
North Little Rock	118	1 132	69.5	23.3	971	3 614 112	10.1	25.8	20.1	6.7	0.9	29.4	0.0
Paragould	34	D	D	D	282	995 938	7.4	13.5	10.1	7.0	0.0	34.9	2.5
Pine Bluff	56	D	D	D	430	1 262 555	9.4	40.1	30.3	11.6	2.7	0.0	0.0
Rogers	64	326	28.7	7.6	478	1 723 247	11.6	29.5	25.6	5.5	1.0	18.2	4.6
Russellville	62	350	23.9	8.9	247	826 281	6.7	26.5	27.2	7.8	0.0	20.1	0.0
Sherwood	41	196	17.8	5.0	260	794 982	19.0	40.7	0.0	5.0	4.1	26.7	0.1
Springdale	87	778	60.4	21.5	584	1 997 062	10.3	28.7	23.9	6.6	1.7	21.9	3.3
Texarkana	34	D	D	D	237	974 321	9.2	47.4	27.7	4.9	2.8	2.3	0.0
West Memphis	37	D	D	D	383	1 214 605	9.2	23.7	21.2	5.8	0.8	25.0	1.3
CALIFORNIA	46 852	299 033	29 320.9	8 446.1	X	X	X	X	X	X	X	X	X
Adelanto	5	D	D	D	122	519 045	17.9	63.0	0.0	6.8	0.0	11.6	0.0
Alameda	104	556	42.8	12.8	658	4 669 134	6.4	25.2	22.5	8.7	5.7	19.2	3.1
Alhambra	97	427	40.9	11.2	423	2 729 610	8.0	33.5	27.5	3.8	4.0	18.8	4.5
Aliso Viejo	41	D	D	D	20	114 486	83.1	0.0	0.0	0.0	0.0	16.9	0.0
Anaheim	354	2 718	252.4	74.3	2 214	15 281 363	10.2	31.2	18.4	2.6	1.6	22.9	1.9
Antioch	88	506	37.6	12.3	306	1 931 728	10.7	57.2	0.0	6.0	2.1	20.9	0.0
Apple Valley	38	261	13.8	6.6	115	584 392	38.7	9.0	0.0	3.2	20.4	28.7	0.0
Arcadia	97	448	32.9	10.0	327	2 164 149	7.3	33.8	24.4	10.7	0.9	4.2	5.7
Atascadero	31	126	12.9	3.7	131	738 888	19.1	30.8	22.5	9.0	0.0	14.3	0.0
Atwater	19	88	7.8	1.8	124	673 870	13.1	42.2	13.9	5.5	4.6	18.3	0.0
Azusa	61	287	23.1	6.8	312	2 003 992	16.2	36.1	0.0	4.3	3.4	34.3	3.5
Bakersfield	360	2 420	249.6	70.7	1 424	8 316 644	6.2	38.5	18.9	8.6	0.9	17.6	0.0
Baldwin Park	35	125	13.5	3.8	227	1 307 981	10.1	58.7	0.0	11.0	9.8	10.4	0.0
Banning	24	139	11.8	4.4	195	1 176 594	19.1	35.3	0.3	9.9	1.7	30.2	0.0
Beaumont	41	189	16.1	4.3	168	910 677	6.3	58.6	0.8	7.4	3.3	11.9	0.0
Bell	24	190	12.3	4.4	208	970 721	15.5	65.9	0.0	1.2	2.2	15.3	0.0
Bellflower	120	540	54.4	14.6	135	560 170	32.9	10.6	0.0	29.1	9.0	18.3	0.0
Bell Gardens	35	341	26.4	8.6	195	974 379	15.1	53.7	0.0	4.2	3.0	14.3	0.0
Belmont	51	D	D	D	110	851 441	1.4	33.4	0.0	4.3	7.0	30.3	0.0
Benicia	57	552	58.2	25.0	293	1 695 705	13.1	23.5	18.0	3.4	0.0	29.9	7.0
Berkeley	184	1 327	101.2	57.4	1 669	13 806 771	10.8	38.3	13.0	4.5	13.4	11.2	4.6
Beverly Hills	286	1 965	162.3	48.7	680	6 033 141	8.8	32.8	21.5	1.8	6.2	14.5	3.8
Brea	82	920	94.9	35.4	435	2 822 410	14.6	42.7	17.3	2.4	1.3	14.0	0.0
Brentwood	74	455	37.4	12.5	277	2 032 978	16.0	33.4	0.0	3.6	6.7	27.5	0.0
Buena Park	76	D	D	D	314	1 712 183	10.2	51.5	0.0	9.3	10.0	14.8	0.0
Burbank	249	2 438	233.0	94.4	1 339	10 789 444	10.5	20.6	13.7	5.7	4.5	35.6	3.0
Burlingame	116	720	62.3	18.2	257	2 033 098	7.4	25.4	24.0	8.9	0.0	20.2	9.2
Calexico	14	D	D	D	180	959 584	5.6	39.4	18.0	0.4	3.6	18.6	2.2
Camarillo	100	687	46.9	15.2	150	1 175 192	38.2	4.5	0.0	28.2	1.2	24.7	0.0
Campbell	176	1 133	97.9	32.0	194	1 441 718	19.7	44.4	0.0	5.3	0.4	13.4	0.0
Carlsbad	145	1 476	146.1	43.5	776	4 824 420	15.7	25.6	15.4	11.2	1.9	15.0	9.2
Carson	96	716	83.4	24.7	510	2 517 774	28.5	6.7	0.0	15.0	7.7	26.1	0.0
Cathedral City	80	514	39.8	11.8	175	1 230 278	13.0	52.3	30.1	4.1	0.0	0.6	0.0
Ceres	43	562	63.2	34.2	182	1 207 924	11.0	48.7	18.9	7.5	0.0	8.8	0.0
Cerritos	58	521	37.0	16.0	300	1 151 269	17.9	4.7	0.0	2.1	2.0	12.8	8.8
Chico	143	775	76.5	23.2	388	2 759 409	11.9	39.0	24.3	7.0	1.6	8.0	0.0
Chino	127	1 343	98.7	42.2	425	2 145 199	12.8	49.4	0.0	3.6	12.3	20.9	0.0
Chino Hills	55	285	14.7	4.4	182	1 001 156	45.8	0.0	0.0	13.9	0.0	34.0	0.0
Chula Vista	207	1 602	108.9	37.2	1 114	7 346 424	14.6	37.1	17.1	15.8	1.2	10.8	2.8
Citrus Heights	80	443	53.8	12.3	204	1 278 252	11.3	69.4	0.0	6.6	1.3	2.7	0.0
Claremont	34	142	8.7	2.6	169	958 849	29.8	43.5	0.0	0.0	0.0	26.7	0.0
Clovis	111	729	59.0	17.3	505	2 897 575	9.7	32.5	16.7	12.7	3.2	20.0	0.0
Coachella	13	D	D	D	79	428 436	23.4	3.0	0.0	9.0	11.1	39.1	0.0
Colton	48	489	60.2	13.4	360	2 494 835	14.1	29.0	19.7	3.6	3.4	18.7	1.8
Compton	60	552	35.1	14.2	329	1 870 002	18.8	5.9	37.1	8.5	3.7	15.6	0.0
Concord	206	1 154	132.7	40.1	443	2 858 330	14.9	60.6	0.0	9.1	1.2	10.7	0.0
Corona	219	1 374	108.4	31.0	692	4 620 304	10.2	34.8	23.7	7.6	2.3	16.8	2.3
Costa Mesa	316	1 916	167.0	46.4	499	4 282 210	13.5	43.0	28.9	5.5	1.1	5.7	0.0
Covina	104	497	48.3	13.9	187	1 234 035	14.5	55.3	0.0	3.8	3.1	11.5	0.0
Culver City	130	1 050	82.8	22.7	409	1 848 474	11.4	41.4	12.9	4.7	9.6	15.5	0.0
Cupertino	66	268	25.6	7.0	154	1 132 814	34.4	0.0	0.0	21.5	0.0	26.3	0.0
Cypress	64	663	99.0	34.4	171	1 179 800	19.6	48.1	0.0	5.4	0.0	14.5	3.3
Daly City	83	D	D	D	560	4 065 527	12.0	29.6	20.8	3.3	0.7	19.2	3.3
Dana Point	60	358	91.5	9.6	66	459 856	20.0	0.0	0.0	25.3	3.1	14.3	3.3
Danville	46	239	14.8	4.5	101	575 902	34.0	3.2	0.0	27.3	33.8	27.4	0.0
Davis	65	350	29.0	8.9	423	2 817 726	14.4	26.2	16.3	3.9	5.3	24.3	0.0

1. Establishments subject to federal tax.

Table D. Cities — City Government Finances

City	General revenue Total (mil dol)	Intergovernmental Total (mil dol)	Intergovernmental Percent from state government	Taxes Total (mil dol)	Taxes Per capita¹ (dollars) Total	Taxes Per capita¹ (dollars) Property	Taxes Per capita¹ (dollars) Sales and gross receipts	General expenditure Total (mil dol)	General expenditure Per capita¹ (dollars) Total	General expenditure Per capita¹ (dollars) Capital outlays
	117	118	119	120	121	122	123	124	125	126
ARKANSAS—Cont'd										
Jacksonville	66.7	10.5	44.6	9.9	344	27	317	75.1	2 619	339
Jonesboro	78.3	23.6	30.3	30.7	435	65	371	71.4	1 014	147
Little Rock	376.0	98.2	37.1	121.4	617	247	370	369.8	1 881	297
North Little Rock	90.5	26.5	30.0	39.2	606	159	447	97.5	1 506	165
Paragould	29.1	6.0	40.6	7.3	270	31	239	27.7	915	56
Pine Bluff	45.8	15.6	31.1	17.4	370	78	293	42.9	832	178
Rogers	66.9	18.0	35.4	33.4	565	89	476	49.1	820	49
Russellville	28.8	7.4	31.7	14.0	492	24	468	23.4	868	128
Sherwood	26.4	11.3	17.7	7.8	261	19	243	26.0	732	67
Springdale	72.7	20.3	30.2	29.9	406	72	333	53.9	879	33
Texarkana	31.4	6.9	34.8	13.5	449	104	344	26.4	1 262	139
West Memphis	33.0	8.5	26.7	13.1	507	50	458	32.5		
CALIFORNIA	X	X	X	X	X	X	X	X	X	X
Adelanto	12.0	0.9	64.5	6.2	197	83	105	18.3	586	65
Alameda	117.1	11.9	69.1	72.8	961	544	260	118.5	1 564	250
Alhambra	94.9	11.0	57.2	48.2	570	309	120	85.5	1 012	77
Aliso Viejo	19.0	1.4	100.0	14.0	283	134	120	22.2	448	112
Anaheim	697.7	119.6	21.0	267.6	779	340	436	658.5	1 917	451
Antioch	69.2	16.1	79.1	35.4	336	194	139	57.9	550	87
Apple Valley	55.7	5.3	91.3	27.5	389	258	118	55.8	790	105
Arcadia	68.8	2.9	73.3	48.5	848	441	400	64.5	1 130	99
Atascadero	31.8	7.6	92.3	15.9	555	349	188	28.1	978	301
Atwater	26.6	3.9	48.1	8.3	291	192	93	49.2	1 714	675
Azusa	58.3	7.2	30.8	36.3	767	353	363	55.0	1 161	37
Bakersfield	360.1	84.2	69.9	149.4	417	223	192	382.6	1 069	301
Baldwin Park	50.2	15.9	46.5	25.1	328	172	153	43.8	572	46
Banning	33.1	4.9	90.4	13.0	427	251	175	30.4	1 003	237
Beaumont	83.3	0.7	100.0	14.4	366	160	203	79.5	2 017	1 172
Bell	29.7	1.8	72.8	16.9	471	317	154	30.0	835	223
Bellflower	32.9	3.7	60.2	25.4	328	163	163	34.3	442	71
Bell Gardens	36.8	3.6	71.1	22.7	531	201	329	31.1	726	78
Belmont	43.6	2.2	83.1	25.6	965	712	247	44.8	1 687	160
Benicia	43.3	1.4	100.0	29.1	1 061	603	453	46.0	1 679	414
Berkeley	293.3	31.1	90.2	147.9	1 281	526	494	300.7	2 605	242
Beverly Hills	261.2	5.5	72.9	142.7	4 124	1 370	2 727	226.1	6 532	1 003
Brea	90.0	3.5	86.5	56.2	1 395	893	497	87.6	2 176	593
Brentwood	78.8	1.8	100.0	33.7	628	397	152	88.6	1 654	238
Buena Park	87.0	7.0	64.8	64.8	788	449	336	105.8	1 285	278
Burbank	265.6	36.3	55.0	147.7	1 412	849	560	282.4	2 701	443
Burlingame	72.1	2.7	100.0	42.6	1 436	445	977	70.0	2 356	686
Calexico	34.0	6.5	59.4	15.9	405	203	194	33.5	1 117	103
Camarillo	73.4	5.0	40.6	40.7	617	335	278	73.6	1 222	261
Campbell	46.2	3.4	53.9	33.2	823	390	428	49.3	1 465	160
Carlsbad	179.5	13.2	50.3	112.9	1 033	528	496	160.2		200
Carson	105.5	19.8	56.9	74.0	799	340	456	135.1	1 459	403
Cathedral City	70.1	6.3	64.9	52.7	1 002	695	304	69.7	1 324	144
Ceres	34.3	3.7	83.6	18.9	406	213	188	38.7	834	89
Cerritos	96.9	2.0	89.7	65.5	1 320	774	541	96.8	1 950	141
Chico	99.3	7.9	55.7	69.9	799	467	330	91.9	1 050	275
Chino	102.9	7.3	90.6	54.2	677	425	248	109.3	1 365	144
Chino Hills	60.2	3.8	89.2	21.6	283	154	126	65.7	861	137
Chula Vista	240.2	25.5	80.3	126.8	501	240	258	247.0	976	73
Citrus Heights	52.7	10.0	85.5	32.4	382	164	216	48.9	578	136
Claremont	35.2	1.7	82.5	23.2	653	293	356	34.7	978	122
Clovis	110.7	10.2	67.2	46.4	470	218	249	105.9	1 074	201
Coachella	37.8	11.0	71.9	18.0	421	228	167	49.1	1 150	551
Colton	50.0	6.2	92.7	27.9	524	332	190	44.1	829	84
Compton	98.6	17.9	28.9	54.6	558	319	236	114.4	1 170	108
Concord	120.0	9.6	80.8	70.7	566	241	321	128.3	1 026	86
Corona	225.6	16.4	78.9	106.2	672	397	245	219.2	1 388	272
Costa Mesa	117.6	9.7	76.3	92.1	823	381	439	111.9	1 001	113
Covina	49.3	4.1	69.9	32.6	672	369	300	49.1	1 013	132
Culver City	173.5	27.4	43.4	99.6	2 528	1 144	1 336	143.8	3 651	482
Cupertino	60.4	2.0	89.4	42.9	716	306	399	59.2	989	78
Cypress	43.8	2.7	66.2	33.4	683	409	270	44.8	917	226
Daly City	103.9	12.0	48.5	57.4	551	324	225	112.7	1 082	108
Dana Point	29.3	1.6	100.0	25.1	740	287	445	31.5	929	121
Danville	35.0	6.4	100.0	21.8	508	306	190	34.7	809	181
Davis	96.8	18.9	87.5	47.1	714	397	221	90.4	1 372	150

1. Based on population estimated as of July 1 of the year shown.

Table D. Cities — **City Government Finances**

City	City government finances, 2012 (cont.)									
	General expenditure (cont.)									
	Percent of total for:									
	Public welfare	Highways	Parking facilities	Education	Health and hospitals	Police protection	Sewerage and sanitation	Parks and recreation	Housing and community development	Interest on debt
	127	128	129	130	131	132	133	134	135	136
ARKANSAS—Cont'd										
Jacksonville	0.0	4.8	0.0	0.0	51.2	10.2	15.6	3.1	0.4	2.2
Jonesboro	0.0	12.4	0.0	0.0	1.1	17.0	17.2	3.4	0.5	15.4
Little Rock	0.0	4.7	0.2	0.0	5.8	15.0	12.9	10.2	2.6	6.0
North Little Rock	0.0	6.2	0.0	0.0	0.4	18.6	16.6	6.3	3.6	5.9
Paragould	0.2	9.6	0.0	0.0	0.5	10.6	23.1	6.0	3.6	2.5
Pine Bluff	0.5	10.5	0.0	0.0	0.1	24.5	18.2	6.0	0.0	1.9
Rogers	0.0	9.9	0.0	0.0	0.8	17.6	15.7	9.0	4.3	5.8
Russellville	0.0	20.6	0.0	0.0	1.1	18.7	18.5	6.1	0.0	0.0
Sherwood	0.0	20.6	0.0	0.0	1.0	23.1	14.0	13.5	0.0	1.2
Springdale	0.0	8.2	0.0	0.0	1.0	20.7	17.2	4.4	1.2	9.5
Texarkana	0.0	5.7	0.0	0.0	1.2	28.6	21.0	1.4	0.8	3.8
West Memphis	0.0	13.7	0.0	0.0	0.5	20.8	16.6	4.2	2.0	3.0
CALIFORNIA	X	X	X	X	X	X	X	X	X	X
Adelanto	0.0	9.8	0.0	0.0	1.4	25.8	0.0	4.3	9.3	0.0
Alameda	0.0	8.5	0.8	0.0	14.8	22.2	8.2	11.0	6.1	3.5
Alhambra	0.0	9.2	2.7	0.0	0.1	28.1	12.5	7.4	4.9	4.2
Aliso Viejo	0.0	15.3	0.0	0.0	1.0	28.2	0.0	7.9	0.5	9.0
Anaheim	0.0	8.5	0.0	0.0	0.1	16.5	8.2	12.1	18.0	10.6
Antioch	0.0	16.1	0.0	0.0	2.4	43.6	4.2	9.6	8.8	3.6
Apple Valley	0.0	8.4	0.0	0.0	2.9	19.9	23.3	8.7	11.7	5.3
Arcadia	0.0	9.9	0.0	0.0	6.9	25.6	2.2	4.2	3.1	1.5
Atascadero	0.0	7.5	0.0	0.0	0.0	21.1	6.6	9.2	20.1	4.0
Atwater	0.0	2.7	0.0	0.0	0.0	14.1	51.3	3.5	5.4	8.0
Azusa	0.0	3.3	0.0	0.0	1.2	30.7	8.1	6.3	8.1	11.6
Bakersfield	0.0	10.0	0.0	0.0	0.0	17.9	17.4	6.8	2.6	3.6
Baldwin Park	0.0	15.9	0.0	0.0	0.0	41.3	0.6	8.7	17.9	3.9
Banning	0.0	11.9	0.0	0.0	0.3	24.5	18.5	2.1	18.5	4.9
Beaumont	0.0	3.8	0.0	0.0	0.6	12.7	7.1	4.6	0.6	0.5
Bell	0.0	6.8	0.0	0.0	0.0	22.5	4.9	3.5	21.8	9.1
Bellflower	0.0	31.2	0.0	0.0	0.0	30.7	0.0	6.3	6.8	6.6
Bell Gardens	0.0	13.1	0.0	0.0	0.0	42.3	7.6	15.9	3.0	3.7
Belmont	0.0	9.5	0.0	0.0	0.0	21.4	17.5	8.4	8.9	2.3
Benicia	0.0	7.0	0.0	0.0	0.0	19.3	14.2	10.6	4.2	3.1
Berkeley	0.0	7.4	2.4	0.0	11.4	18.1	14.2	5.9	0.2	3.1
Beverly Hills	0.0	5.7	21.3	0.0	4.9	17.9	10.5	9.5	6.0	1.9
Brea	0.0	14.6	0.0	0.0	4.1	30.3	6.4	10.8	0.1	1.7
Brentwood	0.0	14.0	0.0	0.0	0.0	18.8	17.9	12.0	11.8	1.2
Buena Park	0.0	12.0	0.0	0.0	0.3	20.3	3.1	4.7	9.8	9.7
Burbank	0.0	7.2	0.3	0.0	4.6	15.9	9.3	5.7	23.0	5.3
Burlingame	0.0	24.2	2.0	0.0	0.0	13.4	14.4	8.0	14.2	5.8
Calexico	0.0	6.0	0.0	0.0	0.9	30.5	16.3	3.8	0.0	2.4
Camarillo	0.0	24.2	0.0	0.0	0.3	20.3	17.6	0.9	10.3	0.4
Campbell	0.0	13.9	0.0	0.0	0.0	26.2	0.0	12.0	6.1	5.0
Carlsbad	0.0	8.7	0.0	0.0	8.2	17.9	8.5	13.4	10.3	3.4
Carson	0.0	13.8	1.0	0.0	0.1	16.4	0.1	13.3	4.7	1.6
Cathedral City	0.0	9.7	0.0	0.0	4.2	22.1	0.6	1.4	26.3	7.1
Ceres	0.0	8.7	0.0	0.0	1.2	28.2	19.7	5.0	22.4	15.6
Cerritos	0.0	10.6	0.0	0.0	0.3	14.0	3.4	14.7	9.7	5.6
Chico	0.0	17.5	1.9	0.0	0.3	23.6	6.6	3.2	6.5	8.1
Chino	0.0	13.4	0.0	0.0	0.0	25.6	18.7	5.2	11.8	6.1
Chino Hills	0.0	20.8	0.0	0.0	0.0	17.3	14.6	6.5	15.2	6.1
Chula Vista	0.0	10.6	0.1	0.0	0.9	20.6	17.6	9.9	0.4	6.1
Citrus Heights	0.0	22.4	0.0	0.0	1.3	38.7	1.2	0.1	2.7	7.6
Claremont	0.0	12.7	0.0	0.0	0.8	28.4	15.5	9.0	14.3	2.1
Clovis	0.0	10.8	0.0	0.0	0.7	21.2	28.1	5.4	4.2	2.9
Coachella	0.0	33.0	0.0	0.0	0.4	12.4	16.2	10.2	3.1	2.4
Colton	0.0	6.2	0.0	0.0	1.3	23.1	11.2	3.9	4.8	5.7
Compton	0.0	8.3	0.0	0.0	0.0	15.0	9.0	2.9	8.2	9.8
Concord	0.0	12.7	0.0	0.0	0.0	33.4	16.2	6.9	15.0	1.3
Corona	0.0	4.4	0.1	0.0	0.5	18.5	23.8	3.9	3.5	2.3
									7.9	9.2
Costa Mesa	0.0	8.7	0.0	0.0	1.0	33.4	0.0	6.1	2.3	2.0
Covina	0.0	5.4	0.2	0.0	0.7	30.8	3.6	5.8	13.9	6.1
Culver City	0.0	5.6	0.2	0.0	3.7	19.6	11.6	4.8	13.5	6.5
Cupertino	0.0	11.9	0.0	0.0	0.3	28.1	2.6	25.6	1.8	3.2
Cypress	0.0	21.7	0.0	0.0	0.5	31.3	3.4	13.1	11.8	1.7
Daly City	0.0	10.1	0.0	0.0	0.5	24.9	20.5	8.8	1.7	0.4
Dana Point	0.0	24.9	0.0	0.0	1.0	30.4	0.0	14.2	0.0	1.4
Danville	0.0	21.8	0.0	0.0	1.0	21.0	0.0	21.4	0.4	1.5
Davis	0.0	8.9	0.0	0.0	0.0	16.4	20.0	26.2	3.7	2.4

City	City government finances, 2012 (cont.)			Climate[2]						
	Debt outstanding			Average daily temperature (degrees Fahrenheit)						
				Mean		Limits				
	Total (mil dol)	Per capita[1] (dollars)	Debt issued during year	January	July	January[3]	July[4]	Annual precipitation (inches)	Heating degree days	Cooling degree days
	137	138	139	140	141	142	143	144	145	146
ARKANSAS—Cont'd										
Jacksonville	28.9	1 008	1.9	38.2	79.9	27.4	91.1	50.56	3 470	1 699
Jonesboro	298.0	4 230	2.9	35.6	81.6	25.8	92.3	46.18	3 737	1 858
Little Rock	511.4	2 601	23.9	40.1	82.4	30.8	92.8	50.93	3 084	2 086
North Little Rock	204.0	3 152	19.6	40.1	82.4	30.8	92.8	50.93	3 084	2 086
Paragould	25.8	953	7.4	NA	NA	NA	NA	NA	NA	NA
Pine Bluff	29.1	619	9.6	40.8	82.4	31.5	92.4	52.48	2 935	2 099
Rogers	160.5	2 718	85.8	32.9	77.5	22.0	88.8	46.92	4 483	1 269
Russellville	0.0	0	0.0	NA	NA	NA	NA	NA	NA	NA
Sherwood	8.3	277	0.0	NA	NA	NA	NA	NA	NA	NA
Springdale	110.5	1 501	0.0	34.3	78.9	24.2	89.1	46.02	4 166	1 439
Texarkana	34.1	1 136	0.0	44.3	82.7	35.6	92.7	47.38	2 421	2 280
West Memphis	31.2	1 214	0.0	37.5	81.5	28.5	90.9	52.80	3 417	1 903
CALIFORNIA	X	X	X	X	X	X	X	X	X	X
Adelanto	0.0	0	0.0	NA	NA	NA	NA	NA	NA	NA
Alameda	152.6	2 014	3.6	50.9	64.9	44.7	72.7	22.94	2 400	377
Alhambra	70.5	834	0.0	56.3	75.6	42.6	89.0	18.56	1 295	1 575
Aliso Viejo	34.0	686	0.0	56.7	72.4	47.2	82.3	14.03	1 465	1 183
Anaheim	1 822.5	5 304	0.0	56.9	73.2	45.2	84.0	11.23	1 286	1 294
Antioch	41.8	397	0.0	45.7	74.4	37.8	90.7	13.33	2 714	1 179
Apple Valley	63.0	893	0.0	45.5	80.0	31.4	99.1	6.20	2 929	1 735
Arcadia	40.4	707	0.0	56.3	75.6	42.6	89.0	18.56	1 295	1 575
Atascadero	27.6	962	0.0	47.3	71.6	33.1	91.3	14.71	2 932	785
Atwater	93.3	3 253	0.0	NA	NA	NA	NA	NA	NA	NA
Azusa	235.4	4 970	0.0	54.6	73.8	41.5	88.7	16.96	1 727	1 191
Bakersfield	345.9	966	49.8	47.8	83.1	39.3	96.9	6.49	2 120	2 286
Baldwin Park	66.8	873	0.0	56.3	75.6	42.6	89.0	18.56	1 295	1 575
Banning	48.2	1 591	0.0	NA	NA	NA	NA	NA	NA	NA
Beaumont	9.6	244	0.4	NA	NA	NA	NA	NA	NA	NA
Bell	55.7	1 550	0.0	58.8	76.6	47.9	88.9	14.44	949	1 837
Bellflower	31.8	410	0.0	57.0	73.8	46.0	82.9	12.94	1 211	1 186
Bell Gardens	36.7	856	0.0	58.8	76.6	47.9	88.9	14.44	949	1 837
Belmont	38.8	1 460	0.0	48.1	69.7	36.4	88.2	28.71	2 769	569
Benicia	55.1	2 008	4.3	46.3	71.2	38.8	87.4	19.58	2 757	786
Berkeley	188.8	1 635	0.0	50.0	62.8	43.6	70.4	25.40	2 857	142
Beverly Hills	142.3	4 111	0.0	57.9	69.5	49.4	76.9	18.68	1 379	893
Brea	39.1	971	0.0	56.9	73.2	45.2	84.0	11.23	1 286	1 294
Brentwood	194.1	3 622	22.4	NA	NA	NA	NA	NA	NA	NA
Buena Park	115.5	1 403	0.0	57.0	73.8	46.0	82.9	12.94	1 211	1 186
Burbank	463.3	4 430	9.8	54.8	75.5	42.0	88.9	17.49	1 575	1 455
Burlingame	33.1	1 114	0.0	50.0	62.7	42.9	70.5	23.35	2 720	184
Calexico	2.8	71	0.0	55.8	91.4	41.3	107.0	2.96	1 080	3 952
Camarillo	90.1	1 367	7.6	55.7	66.0	45.3	74.0	13.61	1 961	389
Campbell	28.0	694	0.1	48.7	70.3	38.8	85.4	22.64	2 641	613
Carlsbad	65.0	594	0.2	54.7	67.6	45.4	72.1	11.13	2 009	505
Carson	217.3	2 347	0.0	56.3	69.4	46.2	77.6	14.79	1 526	742
Cathedral City	271.4	5 160	0.3	57.3	92.1	44.2	108.2	5.23	951	4 224
Ceres	50.3	1 083	0.0	47.2	77.7	40.1	93.6	13.12	2 358	1 570
Cerritos	153.8	3 099	0.0	57.0	73.8	46.0	82.9	12.94	1 211	1 186
Chico	163.2	1 865	0.8	44.5	76.9	35.2	93.0	26.23	2 945	1 334
Chino	211.8	2 645	12.9	54.6	73.8	41.5	88.7	16.96	1 727	1 191
Chino Hills	127.2	1 667	0.0	56.9	73.2	45.2	84.0	11.23	1 286	1 294
Chula Vista	512.8	2 027	4.0	57.3	70.1	46.1	76.1	9.95	1 321	862
Citrus Heights	28.5	337	0.0	46.9	77.7	39.2	94.8	24.61	2 532	1 528
Claremont	26.2	739	0.0	54.6	73.8	41.5	88.7	16.96	1 727	1 191
Clovis	232.4	2 358	0.0	46.0	81.4	38.4	96.6	11.23	2 447	1 963
Coachella	94.7	2 219	2.4	NA	NA	NA	NA	NA	NA	NA
Colton	96.4	1 813	0.0	54.4	79.6	41.8	96.0	16.43	1 599	1 937
Compton	73.6	752	0.0	57.0	73.8	46.0	82.9	12.94	1 211	1 186
Concord	63.7	510	0.0	46.3	71.2	38.8	87.4	19.58	2 757	786
Corona	346.1	2 191	25.3	54.7	75.9	41.5	92.0	12.00	1 599	1 534
Costa Mesa	38.8	347	0.0	55.9	67.3	48.2	71.4	11.65	1 719	543
Covina	86.2	1 779	2.3	54.6	73.8	41.5	88.7	16.96	1 727	1 191
Culver City	206.5	5 244	0.0	56.7	70.8	46.1	80.0	13.32	1 344	959
Cupertino	43.9	734	43.9	48.7	70.3	38.8	85.4	22.64	2 641	613
Cypress	8.8	181	0.0	57.0	73.8	46.0	82.9	12.94	1 211	1 186
Daly City	45.3	435	0.0	50.6	57.3	44.6	61.1	19.77	3 665	17
Dana Point	8.2	241	0.0	55.4	68.7	43.9	77.3	13.56	1 756	666
Danville	12.9	300	0.0	47.5	72.4	39.3	85.2	23.96	3 267	983
Davis	55.0	835	0.0	45.2	74.3	37.1	92.7	19.05	2 853	1 127

1. Based on the population estimated as of July 1 of the year shown.   2. Represents normal values based on the 30-year period, 1971–2000.   3. Average daily minimum.
4. Average daily maximum.

Table D. Cities — **Land Area and Population**

STATE Place code	City	Land area,[1] 2016 (sq mi)	Population, 2016 Total persons	Rank	Per square mile	Race alone[2] (percent), 2015 White	Black or African American	American Indian, Alaska Native	Asian	Hawaiian Pacific Islander	Some other race	2 or more races[2]
		1	2	3	4	5	6	7	8	9	10	11
	CALIFORNIA—Cont'd											
06 18394	Delano	14.3	52 707	719	3 685.8	74.5	4.1	1.1	10.5	0.0	8.7	1.1
06 18996	Desert Hot Springs	30.2	28 492	1 307	943.4	78.9	7.6	0.0	1.6	0.0	9.3	2.6
06 19192	Diamond Bar	14.9	56 793	660	3 811.6	24.7	3.0	0.4	58.5	0.0	6.8	6.5
06 19766	Downey	12.4	113 267	251	9 134.4	66.6	4.2	0.2	7.7	0.1	19.2	1.9
06 20018	Dublin	15.2	59 583	621	3 919.9	47.7	4.1	0.4	40.1	0.1	1.5	6.0
06 20956	East Palo Alto	2.5	29 684	1 261	11 873.6	33.0	10.4	0.9	5.0	4.3	44.6	1.7
06 21712	El Cajon	14.5	103 768	293	7 156.4	75.6	5.2	0.2	2.6	0.9	9.0	6.5
06 21782	El Centro	11.2	44 201	854	3 946.5	57.7	4.1	0.4	3.4	0.0	28.4	6.0
06 22020	Elk Grove	42.2	169 743	148	4 022.3	45.3	10.0	0.2	30.1	1.8	3.8	8.7
06 22230	El Monte	9.6	115 807	240	12 063.2	54.2	0.2	0.4	28.2	0.1	16.0	0.9
06 22300	El Paso de Robles (Paso Robles)	19.4	31 907	1 181	1 644.7	85.9	3.5	0.0	1.3	0.0	7.9	1.3
06 22678	Encinitas	18.8	63 131	577	3 358.0	88.3	1.8	0.8	4.8	0.0	1.6	2.7
06 22804	Escondido	37.1	151 613	172	4 086.6	76.7	2.9	0.9	8.4	0.3	7.2	3.7
06 23042	Eureka	9.4	27 226	1 353	2 896.4	76.1	1.6	1.0	8.8	0.0	7.1	5.4
06 23182	Fairfield	40.9	114 756	242	2 805.8	51.3	14.0	0.5	16.3	1.4	10.1	6.5
06 24638	Folsom	27.7	77 271	440	2 789.6	70.4	3.9	0.4	17.6	0.8	1.7	5.3
06 24680	Fontana	43.0	209 665	106	4 875.9	38.5	7.0	0.6	6.0	0.1	44.4	3.5
06 25338	Foster City	3.8	34 175	1 111	8 993.4	45.8	2.3	0.6	46.0	0.0	0.6	4.8
06 25380	Fountain Valley	9.1	56 529	664	6 212.0	56.5	1.4	0.9	32.3	0.1	3.5	5.3
06 26000	Fremont	77.5	233 136	96	3 008.2	25.3	2.6	0.2	57.2	1.7	7.7	5.3
06 27000	Fresno	114.4	522 053	34	4 563.4	59.9	7.7	1.1	13.3	0.2	14.4	3.2
06 28000	Fullerton	22.4	140 721	187	6 282.2	60.8	2.3	0.1	21.9	0.3	9.8	4.8
06 28168	Gardena	5.8	60 048	616	10 353.1	17.3	24.0	0.2	22.9	1.8	29.8	4.1
06 29000	Garden Grove	18.0	174 858	143	9 714.3	36.5	0.6	0.7	40.0	0.3	20.1	1.8
06 29504	Gilroy	16.1	55 069	681	3 420.4	81.2	1.2	1.2	3.2	0.0	9.6	3.5
06 30000	Glendale	30.4	200 831	112	6 606.3	70.8	1.8	0.1	19.1	0.2	5.5	2.6
06 30014	Glendora	19.4	51 851	736	2 672.7	70.6	1.8	0.4	10.0	0.4	11.1	5.8
06 30378	Goleta	7.9	30 850	1 220	3 905.1	75.9	4.6	0.2	10.0	0.4	5.9	3.0
06 31960	Hanford	16.8	55 547	674	3 306.4	74.2	4.5	1.3	7.7	1.2	8.0	3.1
06 32548	Hawthorne	6.1	88 031	370	14 431.3	25.5	23.3	0.4	8.3	0.1	40.6	1.8
06 33000	Hayward	45.5	158 937	160	3 493.1	42.8	10.6	0.6	26.2	2.1	11.6	6.2
06 33182	Hemet	27.7	84 281	392	3 042.6	77.7	7.7	1.4	3.8	0.8	5.1	3.6
06 33434	Hesperia	73.1	93 724	337	1 282.1	82.5	5.0	1.6	1.2	0.1	7.6	1.9
06 33588	Highland	18.8	54 939	684	2 922.3	65.6	12.9	1.0	6.4	0.0	10.8	3.3
06 34120	Hollister	7.3	37 833	1 008	5 182.6	82.1	0.4	1.1	2.1	0.0	8.2	6.0
06 36000	Huntington Beach	26.9	200 652	114	7 459.2	72.2	1.4	0.7	11.3	0.3	8.6	5.5
06 36056	Huntington Park	3.0	58 879	636	19 626.3	NA	NA	NA	NA	NA	NA	NA
06 36294	Imperial Beach	4.2	27 418	1 347	6 528.1	74.6	2.6	0.9	9.6	0.0	3.8	8.5
06 36448	Indio	33.2	88 488	365	2 665.3	54.0	3.3	1.1	2.4	0.0	37.1	2.1
06 36546	Inglewood	9.1	110 654	261	12 159.8	28.1	37.8	0.4	1.5	0.1	28.8	3.3
06 36770	Irvine	65.6	266 122	75	4 056.7	45.3	3.0	0.1	45.3	0.1	1.7	4.5
06 39220	Laguna Hills	6.6	31 509	1 193	4 774.1	76.6	0.0	0.0	13.0	0.1	5.2	5.0
06 39248	Laguna Niguel	14.7	65 328	550	4 444.1	79.5	0.6	1.2	10.2	0.6	2.3	5.6
06 39290	La Habra	7.4	61 664	594	8 333.0	60.4	0.5	0.7	12.2	0.0	22.4	3.8
06 39486	Lake Elsinore	38.0	64 205	567	1 689.6	52.9	2.7	0.2	5.9	0.0	30.1	8.2
06 39496	Lake Forest	16.6	83 240	401	5 014.5	67.9	2.1	0.3	16.8	0.0	7.0	6.0
06 39892	Lakewood	9.4	81 138	417	8 631.7	50.2	6.6	0.2	21.5	2.7	14.2	4.7
06 40004	La Mesa	9.1	59 948	617	6 587.7	72.1	7.0	0.5	5.2	0.0	5.7	9.6
06 40032	La Mirada	7.8	49 216	768	6 309.7	51.6	2.9	0.4	19.7	0.2	19.2	6.0
06 40130	Lancaster	94.3	160 106	159	1 697.8	65.0	20.2	0.3	4.5	0.0	5.6	4.3
06 40340	La Puente	3.5	40 377	936	11 536.3	28.9	0.3	0.6	9.2	0.9	56.5	3.7
06 40354	La Quinta	35.3	40 956	921	1 160.2	72.7	1.1	0.0	3.1	0.0	18.5	4.6
06 40830	La Verne	8.4	32 389	1 170	3 855.8	76.4	1.3	0.8	8.4	0.0	6.2	6.9
06 40886	Lawndale	2.0	33 145	1 144	16 572.5	32.1	10.0	0.0	14.3	0.0	37.4	6.3
06 41124	Lemon Grove	3.9	26 860	1 373	6 887.2	63.9	13.4	0.2	6.2	0.1	12.5	3.8
06 41474	Lincoln	20.9	47 030	815	2 250.2	81.6	2.5	0.0	6.2	0.4	7.0	2.3
06 41992	Livermore	26.9	89 115	361	3 312.8	76.8	1.6	0.3	12.4	0.1	2.0	6.7
06 42202	Lodi	13.7	64 641	559	4 718.3	71.8	2.2	0.6	7.4	0.1	10.1	7.8
06 42524	Lompoc	11.6	43 712	862	3 768.3	68.8	7.0	2.4	4.4	0.1	12.8	4.4
06 43000	Long Beach	50.3	470 130	39	9 346.5	55.3	12.4	1.8	12.4	1.1	12.7	4.4
06 43280	Los Altos	6.5	30 561	1 232	4 701.7	NA	NA	NA	NA	NA	NA	NA
06 44000	Los Angeles	468.7	3 976 322	2	8 483.7	52.1	9.2	0.9	11.5	0.2	22.8	3.4
06 44028	Los Banos	10.0	37 643	1 016	3 764.3	79.5	2.0	0.9	3.0	0.0	10.9	5.5
06 44112	Los Gatos	11.2	30 545	1 233	2 727.2	77.2	0.6	0.0	15.9	0.0	1.6	4.7
06 44574	Lynwood	4.8	71 187	497	14 830.6	66.3	6.8	0.5	1.2	0.0	23.5	1.7
06 45022	Madera	15.8	64 444	563	4 078.7	82.2	2.4	0.3	2.3	0.0	10.0	2.8
06 45400	Manhattan Beach	3.9	35 741	1 068	9 164.4	78.2	0.6	1.1	11.0	0.0	1.6	7.6
06 45484	Manteca	20.5	76 908	445	3 751.6	67.6	5.4	0.3	7.5	1.1	9.3	8.7
06 46114	Martinez	12.6	38 259	995	3 036.4	80.2	2.3	0.1	4.9	0.0	7.7	4.8
06 46492	Maywood	1.2	27 633	1 336	23 027.5	NA	NA	NA	NA	NA	NA	NA
06 46842	Menifee	46.5	88 531	364	1 903.9	66.6	5.6	0.9	5.3	0.3	14.7	6.6

1. Dry land or land partially or temporarily covered by water.   2. Hispanic or Latino persons may be of any race.

Table D. Cities — Population

City	Percent Hispanic or Latino[1], 2015	Percent foreign born 2015	Under 18 years	18 to 24 years	25 to 34 years	35 to 44 years	45 to 54 years	55 to 64 years	65 years and over	Median age 2015	Percent female 2015	Census counts 2000	Census counts 2010	Percent change 2000–2010	Percent change 2010–2016
	12	13	14	15	16	17	18	19	20	21	22	23	24	25	26
CALIFORNIA—Cont'd															
Delano	79.9	40.5	26.4	14.2	16.7	10.1	13.2	8.5	10.8	31.3	44.8	38 824	53 041	36.6	-0.6
Desert Hot Springs	58.8	27.8	26.6	12.7	13.7	13.8	13.2	9.0	10.8	32.4	48.2	16 582	27 052	63.1	5.3
Diamond Bar	18.2	45.9	22.6	7.6	12.9	12.4	14.3	13.6	16.6	41.4	54.4	56 287	55 552	-1.3	2.2
Downey	74.3	35.0	21.1	12.1	14.2	14.4	13.7	13.8	10.6	37.3	53.6	107 323	111 770	4.1	1.3
Dublin	9.1	36.1	24.9	5.5	15.1	20.3	14.2	10.6	9.5	37.9	50.7	29 973	46 036	53.6	29.4
East Palo Alto	71.6	39.6	30.5	10.7	20.0	14.1	11.5	5.2	8.0	28.3	48.5	29 506	28 155	-4.6	5.4
El Cajon	30.4	30.7	25.6	10.7	16.1	13.2	13.7	10.5	10.1	32.7	47.5	94 869	99 516	4.9	4.3
El Centro	86.6	33.0	33.8	9.3	12.1	12.0	9.2	11.4	12.1	30.5	50.2	37 835	42 595	12.6	3.8
Elk Grove	17.2	23.2	26.4	10.4	11.9	14.3	15.0	12.2	9.9	36.1	52.0	59 984	153 015	155.1	10.9
El Monte	66.4	51.1	22.1	10.7	15.2	11.8	13.4	12.7	14.0	37.3	50.4	115 965	113 481	-2.1	2.0
El Paso de Robles (Paso Robles)	38.0	17.5	24.5	12.8	12.0	11.7	15.1	12.2	11.7	35.5	51.6	24 297	29 785	22.6	7.1
Encinitas	9.8	13.7	17.3	5.6	15.4	12.7	12.1	16.0	21.0	44.3	49.8	58 014	59 519	2.6	6.1
Escondido	48.7	30.6	23.7	11.6	17.8	11.6	12.7	10.4	12.3	33.3	49.5	133 559	143 923	7.8	5.3
Eureka	11.3	6.9	19.9	6.5	15.0	18.5	10.4	13.0	16.8	37.3	49.3	26 128	27 196	4.1	0.1
Fairfield	29.2	21.7	26.1	9.8	14.7	12.5	14.1	11.6	11.2	34.7	50.8	96 178	105 375	9.6	8.9
Folsom	7.6	17.3	23.2	5.6	12.2	16.8	18.0	13.2	11.0	40.9	46.2	51 884	72 203	39.2	7.0
Fontana	75.3	29.6	31.0	11.5	15.7	14.8	13.5	7.8	5.6	29.5	51.5	128 929	196 470	52.4	6.7
Foster City	4.7	41.5	26.1	3.3	10.8	20.6	13.1	11.8	14.3	40.2	51.1	28 803	30 567	6.1	11.8
Fountain Valley	12.0	30.0	19.5	8.0	9.9	11.9	17.6	15.0	18.1	45.3	50.7	54 978	55 360	0.7	2.1
Fremont	12.7	47.1	22.3	7.5	14.9	16.9	14.5	12.6	11.4	38.3	50.7	203 413	214 079	5.2	8.9
Fresno	49.3	19.9	29.3	11.5	16.5	11.5	11.5	9.5	10.1	30.0	50.8	427 652	496 041	16.0	5.2
Fullerton	38.0	30.8	21.2	13.8	15.7	12.1	13.5	11.0	12.6	34.5	50.6	126 003	135 235	7.3	4.1
Gardena	42.1	34.7	22.7	7.0	12.1	16.0	13.6	13.8	14.9	40.2	54.2	57 746	58 829	1.9	2.1
Garden Grove	37.7	46.0	21.8	10.2	14.2	13.4	14.5	12.2	13.7	37.8	50.5	165 196	170 964	3.5	2.3
Gilroy	70.9	26.5	28.0	10.4	13.0	16.3	11.1	11.5	9.7	33.7	50.9	41 464	48 810	17.7	12.8
Glendale	15.3	55.5	16.3	7.5	16.0	13.5	14.0	16.0	16.6	42.1	51.2	194 973	191 685	-1.7	4.8
Glendora	29.8	17.1	23.0	9.5	9.9	11.1	17.2	13.0	16.4	41.9	51.4	49 415	50 065	1.3	3.6
Goleta	26.1	17.9	20.2	10.5	16.5	9.1	12.7	12.3	18.7	38.1	52.7	55 204	29 906	-45.8	3.2
Hanford	49.6	16.4	28.7	8.4	15.7	12.2	12.5	8.5	14.0	32.7	50.2	41 686	54 076	29.7	2.7
Hawthorne	56.7	36.3	25.2	9.9	17.9	14.9	13.2	10.1	8.9	33.7	50.6	84 112	84 293	0.2	4.4
Hayward	41.0	38.5	22.5	10.0	18.7	14.1	12.4	11.2	11.1	34.3	50.6	140 030	144 372	3.1	10.1
Hemet	44.6	15.9	28.3	9.4	10.2	11.1	10.4	10.4	20.2	36.8	54.0	58 812	78 679	33.8	7.1
Hesperia	57.6	17.9	31.1	11.5	14.0	11.0	12.2	10.1	9.9	29.4	53.3	62 582	90 173	44.1	3.9
Highland	46.6	19.3	26.6	11.4	13.5	12.9	12.6	12.9	10.0	34.1	51.3	44 605	53 104	19.1	3.5
Hollister	69.0	24.6	30.3	9.6	14.3	15.0	12.5	9.1	9.1	32.1	49.1	34 413	34 893	1.4	8.4
Huntington Beach	20.9	17.5	19.8	7.0	14.1	13.6	15.4	13.5	16.6	41.6	50.5	189 594	191 037	0.8	5.0
Huntington Park	96.9	46.5	28.7	13.0	12.8	14.3	13.3	9.5	8.4	30.5	50.0	61 348	58 114	-5.3	1.3
Imperial Beach	51.9	24.9	26.4	13.2	18.3	12.1	11.8	10.6	7.6	30.2	53.1	26 992	26 324	-2.5	4.2
Indio	67.2	25.8	27.3	8.5	12.9	15.2	11.0	9.7	15.5	35.9	50.0	49 116	79 116	61.1	11.8
Inglewood	54.5	30.6	24.4	10.0	15.9	13.8	12.9	10.9	12.2	34.9	52.5	112 580	109 673	-2.6	0.9
Irvine	7.5	45.3	20.5	14.2	15.9	14.0	15.0	10.3	10.0	34.6	51.2	143 072	211 906	48.1	25.6
Laguna Hills	20.3	24.1	18.0	7.9	10.4	13.8	18.0	15.7	16.3	45.0	53.2	31 178	30 258	-3.0	4.1
Laguna Niguel	14.0	19.1	20.0	6.8	10.7	10.7	16.7	18.0	17.0	45.8	54.1	61 891	62 985	1.8	3.7
La Habra	63.5	31.9	25.9	11.4	14.8	13.7	13.0	10.7	10.6	34.2	52.1	58 974	60 281	2.2	2.3
Lake Elsinore	56.5	21.6	36.0	6.8	14.6	16.1	11.7	9.5	5.2	31.4	49.0	28 928	53 425	84.7	20.2
Lake Forest	21.1	25.2	22.1	7.1	14.5	13.5	16.9	12.7	13.2	40.3	49.7	58 707	77 448	31.9	7.5
Lakewood	30.6	22.4	22.6	7.9	11.6	16.2	16.7	11.9	13.2	39.9	49.1	79 345	80 054	0.9	1.4
La Mesa	25.9	12.3	20.3	7.6	20.1	13.7	12.3	11.1	14.9	36.6	53.2	54 749	57 013	4.1	5.1
La Mirada	40.0	24.8	18.2	13.0	11.3	12.9	12.7	11.6	20.4	41.0	53.9	46 783	48 527	3.7	1.4
Lancaster	35.6	10.7	28.6	9.8	16.9	12.5	12.5	10.6	9.1	30.9	49.9	118 718	156 643	31.9	2.2
La Puente	86.8	40.0	24.3	12.5	17.8	10.7	13.8	10.4	10.6	31.1	51.9	41 063	39 816	-3.0	1.4
La Quinta	35.9	14.3	21.7	8.1	8.9	13.6	11.5	13.6	22.6	42.5	49.4	23 694	37 468	58.1	9.3
La Verne	33.6	18.6	23.3	7.0	12.1	12.1	11.8	15.0	18.8	42.2	52.3	31 638	31 062	-1.8	4.3
Lawndale	62.0	34.9	22.8	9.6	14.2	15.6	15.3	10.8	11.7	37.4	46.7	31 711	32 769	3.3	1.1
Lemon Grove	53.4	24.3	21.6	9.3	15.1	14.6	15.6	9.2	14.6	37.7	50.3	24 918	25 318	1.6	6.1
Lincoln	24.9	16.3	22.4	5.8	11.0	13.7	9.3	11.1	26.7	42.8	52.8	11 205	42 781	281.8	9.9
Livermore	22.2	15.8	25.4	6.8	14.8	13.1	14.4	14.3	11.1	36.7	52.9	73 345	81 108	10.6	9.9
Lodi	35.4	14.2	27.0	8.4	14.3	10.5	12.0	12.8	15.1	35.4	52.9	56 999	62 134	9.0	4.0
Lompoc	57.0	28.1	22.3	10.6	16.4	10.8	16.4	11.6	11.9	36.0	46.1	41 103	42 438	3.2	3.0
Long Beach	43.8	26.9	23.4	9.9	17.3	13.3	13.9	11.0	11.2	34.6	49.8	461 522	462 256	0.2	1.7
Los Altos	2.5	31.2	25.5	2.8	5.7	12.3	16.8	17.2	19.8	46.6	53.1	27 693	28 999	4.7	5.4
Los Angeles	48.8	37.4	21.5	10.8	17.7	14.3	13.3	10.8	11.5	35.0	50.7	3 694 820	3 792 584	2.6	4.8
Los Banos	70.9	28.8	34.6	10.3	11.2	17.3	10.5	6.5	9.7	28.8	51.3	25 869	35 967	39.0	4.7
Los Gatos	9.8	20.8	18.5	7.2	8.7	13.5	16.2	15.8	20.1	47.4	51.9	28 592	29 434	2.9	3.8
Lynwood	88.0	39.0	28.6	12.5	18.3	12.9	12.1	7.9	7.8	29.4	50.5	69 845	69 766	-0.1	2.0
Madera	79.0	32.8	34.4	11.7	12.5	13.6	12.4	8.0	7.5	28.1	53.6	43 207	61 416	42.1	4.9
Manhattan Beach	9.6	9.3	27.5	3.9	5.9	14.6	16.2	12.1	19.9	44.3	51.3	33 852	35 135	3.8	1.7
Manteca	41.8	18.5	28.1	8.5	13.1	13.7	15.1	10.5	10.9	35.3	50.9	49 258	67 276	36.6	14.3
Martinez	18.5	12.5	20.0	10.1	9.5	13.5	14.4	16.5	16.1	42.7	50.1	35 866	36 036	0.5	6.2
Maywood	98.8	44.0	29.4	11.8	19.6	13.7	12.1	8.8	4.7	29.1	49.8	28 083	27 395	-2.4	0.9
Menifee	34.2	14.3	27.4	7.6	12.1	11.9	11.8	12.6	16.7	37.1	50.8	NA	77 519	NA	14.2

1. May be of any race.

Table D. Cities — Households, Group Quarters, Crime, and Education

City	Households, 2015 — Number	Persons per household	Percent — Female family householder[1]	Percent — One-person	Persons in group quarters, 2010 — Total	Institutional — Total	Persons in nursing facilities	Non-institutional	Serious crimes known to police,[2] 2014 — Total — Number	Total — Rate[3]	Rate[3] — Violent	Rate[3] — Property	Population age 25 and older	High school graduate or less	Bachelor's degree or more
	27	28	29	30	31	32	33	34	35	36	37	38	39	40	41
CALIFORNIA—Cont'd															
Delano	12 708	3.65	24.8	9.5	10 897	10 719	189	178	1 701	3 257	412	2 845	31 278	71.6	7.8
Desert Hot Springs	8 634	3.26	17.3	17.5	118	0	0	118	1 328	4 728	598	4 130	17 187	63.5	9.7
Diamond Bar	17 684	3.21	16.6	13.1	129	27	22	102	771	1 361	86	1 274	39 692	18.9	57.2
Downey	32 932	3.45	22.1	14.6	683	561	534	122	3 178	2 798	247	2 550	76 268	45.7	20.2
Dublin	19 326	2.92	5.2	14.6	5 774	5 682	0	92	868	1 614	130	1 483	40 202	20.1	61.0
East Palo Alto	7 491	3.94	26.3	15.1	154	4	0	150	698	2 376	422	1 954	17 429	57.7	19.0
El Cajon	32 120	3.14	13.7	21.7	2 482	1 350	1 339	1 132	2 579	2 508	318	2 190	66 029	46.7	19.2
El Centro	10 816	4.02	21.8	20.9	816	520	98	296	2 262	5 196	384	4 813	25 009	52.7	19.4
Elk Grove	49 724	3.34	12.4	15.4	669	209	133	460	3 694	2 267	382	1 885	105 494	27.6	36.3
El Monte	31 474	3.67	15.9	18.6	1 080	763	618	317	2 546	2 191	287	1 904	78 371	69.7	13.2
El Paso de Robles (Paso Robles)	11 024	2.85	15.6	17.9	169	5	0	164	913	2 934	402	2 532	19 802	37.5	20.3
Encinitas	24 998	2.51	6.4	29.6	528	405	405	123	1 012	1 630	168	1 463	48 545	11.7	61.3
Escondido	45 676	3.27	15.3	22.0	2 119	786	657	1 333	3 538	2 361	342	2 020	98 103	42.8	23.0
Eureka	11 980	2.15	10.6	44.3	1 883	449	8	1 434	2 321	8 647	540	8 106	19 903	40.9	23.8
Fairfield	35 392	3.14	15.7	19.4	2 489	1 268	332	1 221	4 392	3 982	471	3 511	72 458	36.9	26.5
Folsom	27 044	2.62	7.8	25.3	6 960	6 772	96	188	1 384	1 887	108	1 780	54 414	21.5	52.5
Fontana	49 811	4.15	17.7	8.2	444	228	194	216	4 420	2 161	347	1 814	119 225	58.3	13.9
Foster City	12 413	2.69	4.5	16.7	109	57	57	52	380	1 157	43	1 115	23 647	9.7	71.3
Fountain Valley	19 673	2.87	8.6	20.5	437	180	160	257	1 109	1 945	151	1 794	41 292	21.6	46.1
Fremont	73 846	3.12	8.7	14.1	1 651	682	662	969	4 194	1 843	125	1 718	163 064	25.9	54.0
Fresno	163 473	3.12	21.1	24.1	8 867	4 552	1 825	4 315	23 483	4 576	464	4 112	307 534	48.2	19.3
Fullerton	46 220	2.97	13.9	22.6	3 077	759	629	2 318	3 545	2 534	242	2 292	91 548	32.8	40.3
Gardena	20 655	2.89	17.4	26.8	794	672	631	122	1 665	2 764	458	2 306	42 536	43.6	23.7
Garden Grove	47 381	3.66	15.7	15.7	1 941	707	624	1 234	3 504	1 990	231	1 759	119 295	54.3	18.9
Gilroy	14 536	3.63	16.7	11.6	806	164	128	642	1 683	3 211	376	2 835	32 806	43.4	21.9
Glendale	74 215	2.69	12.7	26.7	1 429	1 206	1 181	223	3 259	1 654	94	1 559	153 031	34.2	39.4
Glendora	17 772	2.87	14.3	20.2	765	573	519	192	1 307	2 548	129	2 419	35 144	24.3	38.0
Goleta	11 246	2.73	9.3	25.1	201	178	170	23	457	1 490	114	1 376	21 456	22.9	49.9
Hanford	18 289	3.02	14.4	23.3	899	616	296	283	2 162	3 944	556	3 387	34 980	42.9	22.3
Hawthorne	29 545	2.97	18.8	29.9	539	331	311	208	3 246	3 745	759	2 986	57 414	53.3	16.6
Hayward	46 909	3.32	18.3	16.2	2 724	770	723	1 954	5 478	3 573	395	3 178	106 912	47.6	25.5
Hemet	27 881	2.97	17.3	29.5	614	459	421	155	3 787	4 595	522	4 073	52 243	51.5	10.0
Hesperia	26 458	3.52	26.5	15.1	28	6	6	22	2 599	2 807	320	2 487	53 476	58.4	10.6
Highland	17 033	3.21	15.0	19.3	172	96	96	76	1 565	2 868	469	2 399	33 999	47.1	19.4
Hollister	10 518	3.72	15.8	13.5	115	106	102	9	634	1 715	368	1 347	23 523	50.4	14.9
Huntington Beach	75 158	2.67	8.8	24.4	890	403	391	487	4 629	2 324	196	2 128	147 750	25.3	41.8
Huntington Park	14 696	4.03	24.6	12.2	255	7	0	248	2 215	3 750	692	3 058	34 629	78.5	5.0
Imperial Beach	8 966	3.01	25.3	22.8	619	0	0	619	528	1 939	411	1 528	16 537	40.5	19.4
Indio	28 165	3.08	13.8	22.4	949	584	135	365	2 676	3 165	551	2 614	56 137	53.2	17.1
Inglewood	35 250	3.12	21.9	27.5	1 502	515	405	987	3 523	3 146	699	2 446	73 306	47.3	17.9
Irvine	91 186	2.73	9.4	24.0	6 556	588	55	5 968	3 165	1 303	49	1 253	167 677	11.7	69.1
Laguna Hills	11 755	2.66	6.8	25.6	369	136	136	233	486	1 566	145	1 421	23 531	16.5	51.9
Laguna Niguel	25 350	2.58	6.4	28.6	248	0	0	248	627	964	112	852	48 154	17.1	52.0
La Habra	18 143	3.40	19.6	17.4	340	171	167	169	1 154	1 862	169	1 693	39 003	43.1	28.8
Lake Elsinore	15 697	3.94	17.3	12.1	432	208	0	224	1 790	3 051	218	2 833	35 417	54.7	14.5
Lake Forest	29 726	2.76	11.7	22.7	515	216	216	299	786	986	130	855	58 425	22.9	46.3
Lakewood	26 001	3.13	14.0	18.6	109	0	0	109	1 939	2 383	248	2 134	56 752	34.3	30.6
La Mesa	23 583	2.51	11.8	31.8	657	533	512	124	1 792	3 037	353	2 685	43 287	29.9	32.8
La Mirada	15 193	3.06	9.4	21.5	2 857	271	271	2 586	724	1 469	181	1 289	34 115	38.4	28.1
Lancaster	47 372	3.25	20.9	21.5	8 259	6 775	486	1 484	4 552	2 842	556	2 285	99 135	44.7	15.2
La Puente	8 547	4.76	26.3	9.0	43	0	0	43	576	1 419	335	1 084	25 771	68.8	8.3
La Quinta	15 769	2.56	9.9	25.8	57	7	7	50	1 411	3 549	219	3 331	28 429	31.8	37.3
La Verne	10 973	2.91	13.7	22.3	676	175	104	501	866	2 701	143	2 557	22 795	26.2	35.6
Lawndale	9 794	3.39	16.0	22.9	175	17	0	158	555	1 665	471	1 194	22 581	54.8	16.6
Lemon Grove	8 250	3.19	9.8	24.2	346	146	129	200	641	2 434	475	1 960	18 449	41.2	19.8
Lincoln	16 745	2.77	7.1	23.6	115	85	85	30	480	1 048	37	1 011	33 343	31.6	30.9
Livermore	30 146	2.91	8.9	18.7	510	121	121	389	1 737	2 016	274	1 742	59 740	23.0	42.3
Lodi	24 390	2.62	13.2	27.0	677	490	470	187	2 385	3 750	456	3 294	41 738	44.2	17.1
Lompoc	14 222	2.87	12.1	29.7	3 656	3 557	163	99	1 007	2 299	349	1 949	29 607	51.0	10.5
Long Beach	167 660	2.78	14.8	30.9	8 277	2 956	2 370	5 321	14 742	3 129	489	2 640	316 064	40.3	29.5
Los Altos	10 822	2.81	6.5	15.6	227	193	193	34	329	1 087	23	1 064	22 020	5.7	82.9
Los Angeles	1 360 164	2.86	14.9	30.1	84 601	26 415	13 845	58 186	102 310	2 619	491	2 128	2 687 915	43.8	32.6
Los Banos	10 760	3.47	19.3	20.4	181	78	78	103	1 033	2 791	359	2 432	20 660	53.7	14.5
Los Gatos	12 189	2.48	9.8	24.9	350	258	238	92	639	2 087	75	2 012	22 802	13.5	65.3
Lynwood	15 616	4.43	26.5	8.8	2 652	2 203	370	449	1 825	2 541	558	1 983	42 431	69.8	7.4
Madera	18 797	3.39	23.4	19.2	591	173	173	418	2 101	3 309	654	2 655	34 591	64.8	9.5
Manhattan Beach	13 293	2.69	8.9	19.6	28	0	0	28	915	2 551	103	2 448	24 579	8.0	71.6
Manteca	23 005	3.25	12.7	18.7	495	345	341	150	2 276	3 115	241	2 875	47 820	50.8	14.0
Martinez	14 306	2.62	15.3	27.6	1 296	1 061	268	235	1 047	2 798	195	2 603	26 674	28.4	35.3
Maywood	6 673	4.16	21.2	6.7	119	119	119	0	338	1 214	316	898	16 418	79.5	4.0
Menifee	28 384	3.06	11.2	21.2	188	107	106	81	1 608	1 895	126	1 769	56 675	43.2	17.5

1. No spouse present. 2. Data for serious crimes have not been adjusted for underreporting. This may affect comparability between geographic areas and over time. 3. Per 100,000 population estimated by the FBI. 4. Persons 25 years old and over.

Table D. Cities — Income, Poverty, and Housing

City	Money income, 2015					Housing units, 2010			Occupied housing units 2015				
	Households			Families						Owner-occupied		Renter-occupied	
	Median income	Percent with income of $200,000 or more	Percent with income of less than $25,000	Total Families	Percent with income below poverty	Total	Percent change, 2000–2010	Vacant units for sale or rent[2]	Total	Percent	Median value[3] (dollars)	Percent	Median rent (dollars)
	42	43	44	45	46	47	48	49	50	51	52	53	54
CALIFORNIA—Cont'd													
Delano	31 838	0.6	21.1	11 397	28.6	10 713	21.0	453	12 708	55.1	165 900	44.9	776
Desert Hot Springs	33 599	0.5	28.8	6 235	29.8	10 902	55.2	2 252	8 634	41.8	145 000	58.2	870
Diamond Bar	82 829	11.6	7.7	14 983	6.6	18 455	2.8	575	17 684	74.1	630 400	25.9	1 870
Downey	69 860	6.1	9.5	26 333	7.8	35 601	2.4	1 665	32 932	52.0	518 300	48.0	1 275
Dublin	137 181	28.3	5.0	15 558	4.3	15 782	59.6	869	19 326	63.7	760 600	36.3	2 266
East Palo Alto	55 140	2.5	10.9	5 772	15.4	7 819	10.8	879	7 491	32.2	554 300	67.8	1 735
El Cajon	49 227	2.2	21.1	22 719	19.1	35 850	1.9	1 716	32 120	37.2	388 000	62.8	1 187
El Centro	41 128	1.1	26.9	8 168	23.9	14 476	17.8	1 368	10 816	49.2	168 400	50.8	781
Elk Grove	84 454	6.9	9.4	40 688	6.2	50 634	167.9	2 707	49 724	73.6	350 300	26.4	1 515
El Monte	41 632	2.0	18.2	24 142	19.3	29 069	4.8	1 255	31 474	37.9	413 600	62.1	1 148
El Paso de Robles (Paso Robles)	54 894	3.0	9.5	8 504	10.6	11 426	30.1	593	11 024	56.6	393 400	43.4	1 139
Encinitas	101 703	21.2	10.2	16 131	8.4	25 740	7.8	1 658	24 998	61.0	853 000	39.0	1 865
Escondido	54 284	3.9	13.9	32 786	12.7	48 044	6.8	2 560	45 676	49.5	384 900	50.5	1 254
Eureka	28 676	2.4	25.8	6 103	20.1	11 891	2.6	741	11 980	44.5	246 600	55.5	793
Fairfield	70 776	5.6	10.2	27 003	11.3	37 184	16.7	2 700	35 392	55.9	345 500	44.1	1 298
Folsom	105 278	15.0	6.1	18 693	3.1	26 109	45.5	1 158	27 044	68.7	466 700	31.3	1 490
Fontana	64 297	2.7	12.1	44 072	14.2	51 857	44.5	2 741	49 811	61.0	322 100	39.0	1 196
Foster City	150 016	30.6	7.5	9 369	7.3	12 458	3.7	442	12 413	59.7	1 102 800	40.3	2 721
Fountain Valley	80 384	13.2	8.4	14 938	6.4	19 164	3.7	516	19 673	69.5	672 600	30.5	1 848
Fremont	112 263	18.4	5.9	60 260	3.1	73 989	6.5	2 985	73 846	61.3	784 400	38.7	1 923
Fresno	43 494	3.2	24.0	112 431	23.4	171 288	15.0	12 939	163 473	45.7	203 700	54.3	910
Fullerton	68 801	9.7	12.6	31 363	7.0	47 869	7.0	2 478	46 220	50.9	611 300	49.1	1 411
Gardena	50 988	3.7	15.3	13 938	11.7	21 472	2.1	914	20 655	50.5	416 800	49.5	1 212
Garden Grove	58 123	5.3	16.3	36 190	16.2	47 755	2.0	1 718	47 381	50.5	472 500	49.5	1 385
Gilroy	84 452	8.8	9.2	12 126	12.2	14 854	22.1	679	14 536	54.1	541 300	45.9	1 625
Glendale	58 076	9.0	18.4	50 759	9.1	76 269	3.5	4 000	74 215	33.0	687 400	67.0	1 354
Glendora	85 066	10.9	11.8	13 767	7.4	17 778	3.5	637	17 772	67.2	499 700	32.8	1 407
Goleta	100 751	8.9	3.9	NA	NA	11 473	-43.6	570	11 246	50.1	750 700	49.9	1 781
Hanford	61 231	4.4	15.3	12 902	11.8	18 493	25.4	1 001	18 289	53.0	193 100	47.0	897
Hawthorne	41 933	2.9	20.5	18 923	18.3	29 869	1.0	1 383	29 545	26.0	465 700	74.0	1 111
Hayward	74 723	6.9	11.5	35 848	7.5	48 296	5.1	2 931	46 909	49.1	471 800	50.9	1 484
Hemet	36 334	1.5	27.4	18 431	19.8	35 305	19.8	5 213	27 881	54.2	191 900	45.8	1 024
Hesperia	46 169	1.5	20.8	20 751	21.2	29 004	36.2	2 573	26 458	55.1	191 300	44.9	1 053
Highland	60 334	5.4	15.4	13 024	17.2	16 578	10.9	1 107	17 033	66.5	248 900	33.5	891
Hollister	84 087	6.0	8.6	8 633	4.0	10 401	4.5	541	10 518	55.2	404 700	44.8	1 479
Huntington Beach	85 778	12.3	9.6	49 351	5.7	78 003	2.9	3 718	75 158	56.7	718 700	43.3	1 708
Huntington Park	37 023	0.7	19.4	12 090	22.1	15 151	-1.2	554	14 696	22.8	365 700	77.2	970
Imperial Beach	43 132	1.7	20.3	6 513	22.1	9 882	1.5	770	8 966	22.5	472 100	77.5	1 342
Indio	52 343	4.2	11.8	19 901	10.6	28 971	71.4	5 593	28 165	61.2	248 600	38.8	1 092
Inglewood	42 122	2.2	22.3	23 579	19.1	38 429	-0.5	2 040	35 250	36.1	385 900	63.9	1 135
Irvine	93 781	16.7	15.3	60 661	8.5	83 899	56.2	4 921	91 186	46.1	777 000	53.9	2 070
Laguna Hills	80 623	15.1	14.0	7 552	6.2	11 046	-2.5	577	11 755	77.6	656 900	22.4	1 780
Laguna Niguel	86 662	14.8	7.9	17 422	5.4	25 312	5.9	1 080	25 350	72.0	738 200	28.0	2 001
La Habra	66 215	6.7	9.2	14 127	10.2	19 924	2.0	947	18 143	56.1	471 600	43.9	1 416
Lake Elsinore	60 995	5.0	13.7	13 032	16.6	16 253	70.6	1 465	15 697	64.3	316 900	35.7	1 329
Lake Forest	87 084	12.8	8.8	21 112	6.7	27 088	31.6	864	29 726	66.5	590 200	33.5	1 741
Lakewood	82 027	4.9	7.6	20 231	4.5	27 470	0.7	927	26 001	69.8	475 000	30.2	1 492
La Mesa	56 287	4.1	14.8	13 355	11.3	26 167	5.1	1 655	23 583	40.7	464 400	59.3	1 341
La Mirada	78 597	7.6	12.7	11 679	3.0	15 092	1.9	411	15 193	75.6	465 000	24.4	1 337
Lancaster	49 729	3.2	23.3	35 013	20.2	51 835	24.4	4 843	47 372	52.3	221 000	47.7	1 057
La Puente	61 850	6.1	14.5	7 715	10.8	9 761	1.0	310	8 547	63.9	375 300	36.1	1 204
La Quinta	70 183	12.7	12.5	10 684	8.0	23 489	99.7	8 669	15 769	73.2	393 200	26.8	1 324
La Verne	72 397	5.3	8.8	8 187	4.8	11 686	3.5	425	10 973	69.4	531 600	30.6	1 379
Lawndale	54 754	5.6	14.4	7 395	12.9	10 151	2.8	470	9 794	34.2	429 600	65.8	1 332
Lemon Grove	59 483	0.0	11.6	5 632	6.9	8 868	1.2	434	8 250	54.3	380 800	45.7	1 093
Lincoln	79 796	5.7	12.8	12 262	8.8	17 457	322.6	978	16 745	74.4	390 600	25.6	1 597
Livermore	110 212	19.8	5.0	22 918	3.3	30 342	14.3	1 208	30 146	71.4	654 000	28.6	1 834
Lodi	48 462	3.2	16.2	16 462	12.9	23 792	11.2	1 695	24 390	52.9	271 500	47.1	969
Lompoc	42 240	3.2	20.6	9 340	12.4	14 416	5.8	1 061	14 222	44.9	263 700	55.1	981
Long Beach	54 971	5.6	16.4	100 508	13.5	176 032	2.5	12 501	167 660	39.0	483 700	61.0	1 145
Los Altos	203 013	51.5	4.3	NA	NA	11 204	4.4	459	10 822	83.9	2	16.1	2 816
Los Angeles	52 024	7.6	19.4	810 562	15.8	1 413 995	5.7	95 827	1 360 164	36.0	542 100	64.0	1 271
Los Banos	43 470	1.1	28.0	7 647	28.4	11 375	40.9	1 116	10 760	48.0	244 800	52.0	955
Los Gatos	152 014	37.3	6.9	NA	NA	13 050	5.2	695	12 189	61.5	1 525 500	38.5	1 879
Lynwood	46 241	0.9	18.6	13 684	19.5	15 277	1.8	597	15 616	41.9	347 000	58.1	1 082
Madera	41 090	1.1	22.4	15 028	28.2	17 049	34.7	1 111	18 797	48.5	201 500	51.5	913
Manhattan Beach	126 623	32.6	6.3	9 897	4.7	14 929	-1.1	891	13 293	71.8	1 786 200	28.2	2 619
Manteca	60 716	3.3	14.8	17 473	12.0	23 132	36.9	1 514	23 005	53.2	325 500	46.8	1 285
Martinez	89 871	10.6	6.2	9 780	4.1	14 976	2.3	689	14 306	64.6	518 400	35.4	1 681
Maywood	38 714	1.1	18.1	5 700	25.9	6 766	1.0	207	6 673	22.9	386 100	77.1	956
Menifee	57 204	3.6	13.9	21 012	11.1	30 269	NA	2 808	28 384	74.4	294 000	25.6	1 197

1. Based on population estimated by the American Community Survey.   2. Includes units rented or sold but not occupied.   3. Specified owner-occupied units; $1,000,000 represents $1,000,000 or more   4. 50.0 represents 50 percent or more.   5. 10.0 represents 10 percent or less.

City	Commuting — Percent: Drove alone	With Commutes of 30 minutes or more[1]	Computer Access[2] — Percent: With a Computer in the house	With Internet Access	Migration, 2015: Percent who lived in the same house one year ago	Percent who lived in an other state or county one year ago	Civilian labor force, 2016: Total	Percent change, 2015–2016	Unemployment: Total	Rate[3]	Civilian employment[4], 2015: Population age 16 and older: Number	Percent in Labor Force	Population age 16 to 64: Number	Percent who worked full-year full-time
	55	56	57	58	59	60	61	62	63	64	65	66	67	68
CALIFORNIA—Cont'd														
Delano........................	NA	14.7	52.8	49.5	90.4	8.9	19 052	-0.4	2 354	12.4	40 347	56.2	34 648	30.7
Desert Hot Springs........	89.6	36.5	77.7	63.1	83.7	4.4	11 271	1.4	813	7.2	21 089	50.4	18 017	29.0
Diamond Bar.................	88.2	54.4	94.6	90.2	88.4	4.7	29 838	1.4	992	3.3	45 951	59.0	36 478	41.3
Downey.......................	80.0	51.7	90.8	78.6	86.7	2.7	57 117	1.0	2 651	4.6	93 480	64.3	81 322	51.2
Dublin.........................	76.6	54.5	95.6	90.6	82.9	9.7	29 524	2.0	776	2.6	44 174	71.3	38 669	57.5
East Palo Alto...............	70.3	34.7	90.7	66.7	86.6	9.4	15 126	2.2	722	4.8	21 473	73.8	19 113	52.0
El Cajon......................	78.4	39.9	89.9	81.8	82.0	3.7	46 107	0.8	3 104	6.7	79 554	63.4	69 053	40.8
El Centro.....................	84.2	12.4	84.3	73.3	86.8	5.4	20 672	-1.5	4 531	21.9	30 777	53.9	25 441	32.2
Elk Grove.....................	81.8	51.6	95.9	91.8	89.0	4.0	80 050	1.8	3 289	4.1	128 002	66.3	111 499	48.7
El Monte......................	79.6	53.6	78.6	70.6	94.5	0.8	52 066	0.5	3 390	6.5	93 817	55.9	77 484	50.2
El Paso de Robles (Paso Robles)..........	85.6	22.3	90.2	87.7	84.5	2.7	16 216	0.5	775	4.8	24 478	66.4	20 784	50.9
Encinitas.....................	82.2	40.8	93.7	91.4	88.9	3.0	33 256	1.1	1 258	3.8	53 322	62.7	40 103	50.2
Escondido....................	78.0	43.1	86.9	80.5	82.6	2.9	69 355	1.0	3 251	4.7	119 094	66.9	100 424	45.1
Eureka........................	72.2	3.2	77.5	63.0	78.7	5.4	12 787	0.4	610	4.8	22 030	52.9	17 499	37.5
Fairfield......................	79.2	41.4	92.4	86.5	80.9	7.4	52 486	1.3	2 578	4.9	86 351	65.6	73 732	45.5
Folsom........................	87.2	35.8	95.3	90.9	83.3	7.1	36 166	1.9	1 251	3.5	60 754	61.6	52 355	48.2
Fontana.......................	82.7	45.0	94.0	78.5	91.4	2.0	96 189	1.5	5 968	6.2	150 800	67.0	139 137	45.1
Foster City...................	76.5	54.1	98.1	96.2	79.1	14.0	19 408	2.5	535	2.8	25 344	68.1	20 567	56.5
Fountain Valley.............	88.3	44.9	95.5	92.1	89.0	4.8	28 723	0.9	1 132	3.9	47 637	60.1	37 329	46.8
Fremont......................	77.0	57.6	94.9	91.8	91.2	5.7	118 347	1.9	3 918	3.3	186 798	64.8	160 400	55.7
Fresno........................	79.4	21.8	86.9	75.9	79.8	4.5	238 411	1.1	24 423	10.2	382 766	61.7	330 269	38.5
Fullerton.....................	81.5	41.7	94.1	88.1	81.4	9.1	70 884	0.8	3 233	4.6	114 259	65.9	96 450	44.0
Gardena......................	80.5	40.1	84.4	74.8	89.2	2.4	30 081	0.9	1 574	5.2	48 516	62.7	39 508	54.1
Garden Grove..............	81.7	41.4	90.3	82.4	90.2	1.9	83 146	0.8	4 158	5.0	141 789	63.9	117 830	45.2
Gilroy.........................	79.7	47.4	95.9	88.3	84.8	6.0	27 408	1.5	1 355	4.9	40 951	69.5	35 769	45.6
Glendale......................	82.1	43.1	83.7	79.2	89.0	3.9	101 702	0.9	5 163	5.1	171 643	62.4	138 296	44.9
Glendora.....................	83.8	50.5	93.4	86.5	89.0	4.0	25 561	1.1	1 139	4.5	41 172	63.9	32 648	44.1
Goleta........................	79.6	9.3	94.4	90.3	81.3	6.3	17 074	-0.4	507	3.0	25 176	67.4	19 378	53.2
Hanford.......................	81.5	27.0	89.2	83.3	83.0	5.3	24 402	-1.1	2 197	9.0	41 502	59.9	33 734	47.5
Hawthorne...................	79.3	45.8	88.1	73.3	90.0	1.8	44 448	1.0	2 084	4.7	68 566	66.7	60 735	45.9
Hayward......................	77.7	54.4	93.1	85.3	90.9	3.7	79 264	1.6	4 712	5.9	125 443	65.9	107 859	52.7
Hemet........................	78.5	48.2	74.9	66.1	83.0	4.2	29 167	1.3	2 453	8.4	63 299	47.0	46 349	31.1
Hesperia.....................	88.0	52.0	87.7	79.8	85.2	4.0	35 106	1.3	2 740	7.8	67 185	58.6	57 916	39.1
Highland......................	86.4	33.3	82.3	70.0	86.5	2.7	23 996	1.7	1 193	5.0	42 724	65.0	37 217	48.9
Hollister......................	82.7	48.7	90.4	85.7	90.3	5.2	18 685	1.5	1 280	6.9	28 547	72.5	24 974	46.3
Huntington Beach..........	85.5	45.3	90.9	85.9	87.1	4.0	108 878	0.9	4 215	3.9	165 642	66.9	132 193	50.5
Huntington Park............	69.8	53.6	80.7	61.0	90.0	1.7	27 115	0.4	1 881	6.9	44 542	61.7	39 577	43.2
Imperial Beach.............	71.8	34.8	94.0	80.2	79.1	5.6	12 239	0.7	888	7.3	20 814	64.2	18 734	39.0
Indio..........................	83.7	23.3	84.6	74.9	83.2	4.0	38 808	1.5	2 546	6.6	67 201	61.2	53 625	44.7
Inglewood....................	73.1	50.1	86.2	75.2	88.4	1.8	53 288	0.4	3 695	6.9	87 257	65.8	73 655	40.8
Irvine.........................	84.3	27.7	96.7	91.2	77.0	12.3	132 612	1.0	3 975	3.0	210 577	61.9	184 852	45.4
Laguna Hills.................	83.6	37.6	90.9	84.3	NA	NA	17 341	0.9	635	3.7	27 163	63.8	21 992	49.0
Laguna Niguel..............	89.9	42.2	94.7	91.0	90.1	4.0	35 098	0.9	1 289	3.7	54 536	63.8	43 317	47.3
La Habra......................	83.8	48.2	94.2	83.4	81.4	8.8	30 930	0.8	1 412	4.6	47 567	66.9	40 976	47.7
Lake Elsinore...............	74.3	63.8	93.2	85.9	83.3	7.2	27 871	1.5	1 801	6.5	43 083	63.5	39 864	41.4
Lake Forest.................	88.0	37.7	94.3	91.3	82.8	3.8	46 732	1.0	1 332	2.9	66 507	71.6	55 588	54.9
Lakewood...................	87.7	52.4	92.2	87.0	94.0	1.2	42 546	1.2	1 713	4.0	65 974	63.2	55 199	48.9
La Mesa......................	87.9	32.9	91.6	86.2	80.5	3.9	30 884	1.0	1 463	4.7	49 538	64.9	40 562	50.3
La Mirada....................	88.5	48.8	90.4	86.0	89.7	4.9	23 919	1.3	878	3.7	41 668	54.5	31 579	46.4
Lancaster....................	88.1	36.5	77.0	68.8	91.2	2.3	63 767	0.7	3 748	5.9	120 525	50.5	105 869	41.3
La Puente....................	75.9	52.4	85.5	66.9	90.4	1.1	18 955	1.0	874	4.6	31 822	64.8	27 500	49.2
La Quinta....................	88.7	26.6	91.7	84.3	85.9	5.4	18 050	1.8	688	3.8	32 633	56.2	23 478	41.2
La Verne.....................	81.3	47.9	93.9	83.5	84.8	5.7	15 845	1.2	632	4.0	26 085	58.8	19 939	44.5
Lawndale....................	79.2	41.2	89.9	77.0	NA	NA	16 667	0.9	834	5.0	26 829	63.9	22 929	45.1
Lemon Grove...............	78.7	36.9	85.6	80.8	NA	NA	12 488	0.8	770	6.2	22 034	62.1	18 138	47.6
Lincoln.......................	88.3	42.8	94.5	87.0	83.7	6.1	18 709	1.6	908	4.9	36 841	47.4	24 437	47.5
Livermore....................	84.1	44.6	95.7	92.9	90.2	2.5	47 343	2.0	1 360	2.9	68 188	70.9	58 370	55.3
Lodi...........................	79.8	31.0	87.5	77.8	85.1	4.4	29 134	1.3	2 205	7.6	48 748	62.6	39 025	48.1
Lompoc.......................	69.5	50.9	88.0	76.7	84.7	5.8	17 893	-0.6	1 173	6.6	35 160	61.5	29 919	47.1
Long Beach..................	79.1	47.2	87.9	77.4	88.9	3.0	239 009	0.7	13 738	5.7	376 218	63.6	323 059	47.7
Los Altos.....................	87.0	25.1	98.5	94.6	92.3	5.4	14 488	1.8	353	2.4	23 487	60.0	17 414	55.6
Los Angeles.................	74.1	51.6	87.7	76.0	87.5	3.3	2 033 205	0.8	113 033	5.6	3 214 644	65.8	2 756 584	46.8
Los Banos...................	78.2	42.4	89.7	66.3	91.1	3.7	15 855	0.6	1 699	10.7	26 356	57.3	22 704	37.2
Los Gatos....................	83.6	51.9	96.7	92.8	85.1	6.6	15 740	1.8	399	2.5	26 085	58.4	19 922	48.3
Lynwood.....................	74.2	56.4	86.1	77.7	89.3	1.3	28 746	0.5	1 867	6.5	53 408	62.6	47 825	41.9
Madera........................	77.5	40.3	77.8	61.0	NA	NA	26 817	2.6	2 116	7.9	44 699	65.3	39 915	39.3
Manhattan Beach..........	86.1	52.8	98.1	94.2	89.7	1.9	19 194	1.7	408	2.1	27 281	57.5	20 152	45.3
Manteca......................	78.0	45.6	89.3	83.4	88.1	3.7	35 808	1.3	2 907	8.1	57 041	60.0	48 823	41.1
Martinez......................	78.6	41.3	97.2	93.0	86.1	4.1	20 699	1.7	823	4.0	32 292	64.4	26 154	46.3
Maywood.....................	75.1	60.4	74.1	42.4	93.0	1.6	12 479	0.8	681	5.5	20 426	69.7	19 117	44.9
Menifee.......................	78.9	54.0	90.5	84.6	84.8	4.9	37 304	1.5	2 649	7.1	66 675	54.1	52 152	41.5

1. Employed persons.   2. Households.   3. Percent of civilian labor force.   4. Persons 16 years old and over.

Table D. Cities — Construction, Wholesale Trade, and Retail Trade

City	Value of residential construction authorized by building permits, 2016			Wholesale trade,[1] 2012				Retail trade,[2] 2012			
	New construction ($1,000)	Number of housing units	Percent single family	Number of establishments	Number of employees	Sales (mil dol)	Annual payroll (mil dol)	Number of establishments	Number of employees	Sales (mil dol)	Annual payroll (mil dol)
	69	70	71	72	73	74	75	76	77	78	79
CALIFORNIA—Cont'd											
Delano	7 443	34	100.0	20	180	189.0	7.9	80	1 045	277.3	26.3
Desert Hot Springs	5 690	29	100.0	1	D	D	D	40	549	144.4	13.1
Diamond Bar	4 605	9	100.0	249	634	1 359.9	29.2	113	1 062	311.6	23.4
Downey	12 832	50	88.0	97	813	338.5	37.5	275	4 421	1 163.8	107.2
Dublin	222 201	611	99.2	64	323	222.6	20.3	175	3 862	1 329.0	124.1
East Palo Alto	705	4	100.0	5	D	D	D	24	926	270.5	24.8
El Cajon	14 268	102	100.0	134	1 080	556.8	49.7	445	6 280	1 756.0	158.4
El Centro	1 373	6	100.0	53	433	294.8	15.8	200	4 172	925.9	91.7
Elk Grove	87 373	455	100.0	42	347	83.9	18.9	280	5 913	1 823.8	173.9
El Monte	24 722	128	59.4	294	1 887	808.8	71.4	274	3 254	1 676.8	111.8
El Paso de Robles (Paso Robles)	16 545	65	67.7	47	328	129.7	14.1	151	2 429	625.2	61.4
Encinitas	18 811	85	100.0	96	462	212.1	24.3	282	3 927	1 119.7	110.9
Escondido	32 161	169	47.9	132	1 165	545.8	54.2	541	9 202	2 786.0	263.2
Eureka	480	4	100.0	42	388	134.3	15.8	233	3 186	971.3	84.0
Fairfield	66 837	264	76.1	69	1 393	869.7	72.1	311	5 307	1 398.6	133.8
Folsom	45 994	156	97.4	44	374	788.8	36.4	282	5 534	1 639.5	151.0
Fontana	130 430	488	93.9	145	3 620	1 811.5	165.0	321	5 905	2 145.1	171.5
Foster City	27 768	74	0.0	60	D	D	D	31	876	305.0	25.3
Fountain Valley	4 538	8	100.0	105	1 076	657.1	60.4	221	3 205	1 298.6	88.7
Fremont	201 543	622	66.6	458	9 470	13 487.4	720.4	411	7 229	2 617.9	231.1
Fresno	320 140	1 288	78.0	514	7 741	5 459.8	388.1	1 539	22 005	5 960.2	555.9
Fullerton	19 311	99	25.3	236	2 434	2 539.6	141.5	374	5 211	1 516.4	130.8
Gardena	17 883	102	93.1	164	1 540	642.6	63.2	177	2 197	754.0	66.5
Garden Grove	5 680	16	87.5	232	2 465	1 239.7	113.3	402	5 005	1 656.2	134.7
Gilroy	130 109	774	40.3	41	D	D	D	313	5 155	1 191.9	111.9
Glendale	136 374	1 116	0.8	254	1 911	1 386.6	97.1	731	11 330	3 138.2	300.7
Glendora	58 054	218	100.0	34	362	162.9	25.1	131	2 471	688.2	64.0
Goleta	15 198	121	2.5	52	999	620.2	95.5	127	2 317	727.7	66.4
Hanford	86 079	326	100.0	26	325	191.2	18.5	168	2 905	741.6	67.5
Hawthorne	1 627	22	0.0	67	1 209	480.3	56.2	183	3 443	1 382.2	101.6
Hayward	149 003	474	100.0	457	6 380	4 546.4	386.7	399	5 840	1 765.7	162.5
Hemet	8 670	33	100.0	21	124	69.1	4.0	203	3 658	845.5	93.6
Hesperia	44 598	303	45.2	42	186	231.4	7.7	173	2 101	615.5	45.9
Highland	20 293	89	100.0	14	D	D	D	59	836	234.9	21.1
Hollister	81 023	336	98.5	20	212	72.2	10.3	88	1 192	318.2	32.5
Huntington Beach	141 429	859	3.7	403	4 714	10 353.7	291.2	556	8 069	2 505.6	233.2
Huntington Park	2 340	21	4.8	55	740	399.3	28.5	182	2 196	622.7	55.4
Imperial Beach	5 238	34	41.2	6	9	3.3	0.3	30	224	45.3	4.4
Indio	40 423	242	100.0	35	373	166.7	15.3	162	2 624	862.9	79.5
Inglewood	14 812	64	84.4	81	2 277	977.4	76.3	257	3 440	1 219.9	85.6
Irvine	924 192	4 637	31.5	986	18 431	30 339.3	1 395.5	593	9 845	4 254.4	363.2
Laguna Hills	1 285	1	100.0	94	623	282.3	41.9	186	2 324	452.6	51.3
Laguna Niguel	103 862	549	0.2	63	264	95.4	11.1	133	2 959	1 254.0	107.5
La Habra	38 493	347	3.5	72	416	247.9	22.0	173	3 158	912.1	78.9
Lake Elsinore	160 049	585	100.0	37	272	79.4	10.4	157	2 732	784.9	69.5
Lake Forest	142 909	513	100.0	187	3 004	1 741.4	213.4	205	3 212	1 068.1	116.0
Lakewood	670	3	100.0	32	142	38.9	5.3	228	4 820	1 104.4	106.2
La Mesa	9 252	100	5.0	23	192	66.6	8.5	229	3 846	1 070.3	101.9
La Mirada	0	0	0.0	125	3 047	2 257.2	185.6	88	1 375	391.9	40.2
Lancaster	50 555	247	36.8	68	867	887.2	30.5	300	4 983	1 562.3	132.5
La Puente	970	6	100.0	24	110	40.7	3.6	92	1 111	243.8	25.7
La Quinta	30 223	102	100.0	17	33	34.7	3.3	93	2 204	637.4	57.4
La Verne	8 069	15	100.0	66	691	527.1	37.9	74	1 298	355.7	27.2
Lawndale	506	3	100.0	15	111	39.2	4.8	87	774	208.4	19.2
Lemon Grove	14 319	103	2.9	9	46	16.7	2.8	77	1 227	411.6	35.5
Lincoln	71 200	217	100.0	16	151	55.5	6.3	52	975	268.0	24.8
Livermore	85 298	330	79.1	162	3 292	2 192.9	228.9	281	3 560	1 212.0	126.4
Lodi	63 331	269	70.3	39	265	639.3	14.3	209	3 353	974.6	93.3
Lompoc	1 014	7	71.4	9	51	12.6	2.2	111	1 395	371.9	35.3
Long Beach	23 472	120	18.3	318	4 469	6 962.3	284.9	957	13 033	3 783.9	334.5
Los Altos	47 780	52	100.0	17	D	D	D	102	D	D	D
Los Angeles	3 098 661	13 890	12.9	8 552	83 938	63 834.9	4 787.1	11 359	133 706	40 156.9	3 735.0
Los Banos	52 276	438	75.1	11	131	122.9	4.9	74	1 197	270.5	26.6
Los Gatos	39 769	51	100.0	28	D	D	D	176	D	D	D
Lynwood	1 680	6	100.0	39	580	312.5	28.8	118	1 386	322.3	27.6
Madera	26 365	185	100.0	22	250	213.0	14.2	173	2 163	556.1	50.7
Manhattan Beach	79 885	116	100.0	40	D	D	D	178	2 924	772.1	69.1
Manteca	119 721	593	100.0	26	393	225.1	13.9	177	3 440	824.0	85.3
Martinez	4 275	27	100.0	23	D	D	D	57	1 031	309.8	32.5
Maywood	254	1	100.0	20	432	233.0	20.4	54	472	107.1	9.3
Menifee	153 814	565	100.0	14	57	39.8	2.4	87	1 672	417.3	37.9

1. Merchant wholesalers except manufacturers' sales branches and offices.   2. Establishments with payroll.

City	Real estate and rental and leasing, 2012				Professional, scientific, and technical services,[1] 2012				Manufacturing, 2012			
	Number of establishments	Number of employees	Receipts (mil dol)	Annual payroll (mil dol)	Number of establishments	Number of employees	Receipts (mil dol)	Annual payroll (mil dol)	Number of establishments	Number of employees	Receipts (mil dol)	Annual payroll (mil dol)
	80	81	82	83	84	85	86	87	88	89	90	91
CALIFORNIA—Cont'd												
Delano	19	69	10.6	1.6	20	D	D	D	11	85	38.3	2.9
Desert Hot Springs	10	D	D	D	8	215	4.4	2.9	NA	NA	NA	NA
Diamond Bar	98	D	D	D	234	D	D	D	14	231	D	9.9
Downey	153	1 051	130.9	28.1	145	D	D	D	79	1 968	1 037.0	95.1
Dublin	55	214	73.4	10.1	190	1 452	291.3	124.2	18	1 281	509.7	118.6
East Palo Alto	20	92	48.2	4.5	19	D	D	D	6	D	D	D
El Cajon	158	625	90.8	20.7	199	2 323	151.5	60.1	162	4 472	D	242.7
El Centro	46	207	45.5	6.7	90	D	D	D	16	204	D	7.7
Elk Grove	110	427	68.7	12.9	198	D	D	D	30	532	111.0	22.4
El Monte	72	390	52.0	11.1	105	D	D	D	142	2 558	515.5	113.7
El Paso de Robles (Paso Robles)	55	178	26.8	5.3	77	273	31.3	12.1	67	2 175	524.6	101.9
Encinitas	181	428	86.5	19.1	525	1 658	350.3	110.8	41	186	48.2	10.7
Escondido	180	937	862.9	53.1	337	1 810	230.1	84.0	165	2 794	D	125.1
Eureka	61	263	46.4	8.4	103	D	D	D	29	541	109.6	19.1
Fairfield	99	406	106.4	15.0	156	D	D	D	60	2 638	1 718.9	152.8
Folsom	103	489	95.5	17.6	327	D	D	D	26	674	198.9	49.2
Fontana	88	538	131.0	25.1	89	411	34.7	10.0	105	4 084	1 574.6	197.3
Foster City	50	352	119.1	24.9	151	2 145	485.6	210.3	11	817	D	D
Fountain Valley	106	346	80.4	15.6	231	D	D	D	86	2 752	2 318.1	165.1
Fremont	240	1 052	392.8	54.1	1 047	13 204	2 603.7	1 153.9	328	18 254	5 194.0	1 594.2
Fresno	506	3 269	512.4	105.4	1 121	D	D	D	335	12 295	4 367.7	522.7
Fullerton	172	684	123.9	23.6	378	3 338	471.3	246.0	195	6 326	2 032.2	315.5
Gardena	54	332	27.1	7.8	69	364	27.2	10.6	224	4 643	891.1	222.1
Garden Grove	138	495	125.3	19.1	244	D	D	D	272	7 436	1 533.1	355.2
Gilroy	40	136	48.6	4.7	73	382	51.8	19.1	54	1 346	498.9	68.7
Glendale	310	2 740	1 391.5	162.4	888	D	D	D	198	4 473	842.3	237.4
Glendora	63	256	46.6	7.8	114	692	77.5	31.3	41	827	363.0	37.9
Goleta	52	278	43.8	9.9	158	D	D	D	109	5 347	1 857.5	408.2
Hanford	50	200	34.3	4.8	52	268	30.2	10.9	29	894	D	35.3
Hawthorne	64	427	74.0	13.7	72	514	87.5	23.5	67	3 043	D	209.5
Hayward	171	1 330	279.1	57.6	262	D	D	D	315	10 345	4 108.1	608.5
Hemet	74	345	51.8	8.1	75	333	33.7	11.6	21	748	169.0	36.2
Hesperia	54	187	31.5	5.6	51	450	30.8	8.0	53	392	55.4	16.2
Highland	20	57	10.4	1.4	24	113	16.3	3.4	9	168	D	5.8
Hollister	32	81	20.9	2.8	46	147	15.6	4.6	38	1 274	341.6	D
Huntington Beach	319	1 411	311.7	62.6	769	D	D	D	320	12 880	D	1 221.6
Huntington Park	21	104	13.7	2.4	26	240	16.0	6.1	100	2 565	441.3	99.1
Imperial Beach	20	D	D	D	21	88	9.2	2.5	NA	NA	NA	NA
Indio	45	232	38.4	7.8	73	D	D	D	25	329	48.7	13.1
Inglewood	65	939	147.2	31.8	73	D	D	D	68	2 175	D	99.3
Irvine	647	10 154	2 790.0	512.7	2 768	D	D	D	427	27 718	11 089.1	1 999.5
Laguna Hills	93	631	88.9	28.8	335	1 852	279.2	119.9	49	426	74.9	20.6
Laguna Niguel	108	446	112.4	22.8	298	872	138.3	41.2	24	209	D	12.2
La Habra	48	128	33.4	3.9	80	381	47.0	13.4	57	829	168.9	38.3
Lake Elsinore	39	103	20.6	3.6	55	235	35.7	8.0	65	790	113.3	31.5
Lake Forest	115	1 051	165.2	49.8	412	3 461	683.1	298.9	96	5 765	1 446.9	283.3
Lakewood	36	147	28.9	4.4	67	367	30.4	11.8	10	238	D	8.7
La Mesa	133	884	104.7	26.8	229	1 068	128.8	51.4	21	115	18.7	4.0
La Mirada	56	501	98.5	23.4	67	355	47.1	17.3	58	2 267	590.8	93.1
Lancaster	132	545	134.8	19.0	149	D	D	D	57	983	219.7	36.2
La Puente	19	62	10.5	2.0	15	239	32.2	16.5	13	105	9.3	2.6
La Quinta	87	190	44.5	7.5	89	339	65.4	25.8	4	6	1.1	0.3
La Verne	34	153	21.1	4.6	72	290	37.7	11.8	55	1 093	204.7	53.5
Lawndale	22	295	59.8	9.2	43	D	D	D	18	239	D	10.5
Lemon Grove	16	71	22.3	1.9	23	119	6.7	2.7	9	81	16.3	3.8
Lincoln	38	86	18.0	2.4	44	216	18.0	6.8	10	601	176.9	30.1
Livermore	99	525	173.9	24.0	204	D	D	D	132	3 690	1 339.4	234.4
Lodi	77	403	39.7	10.1	104	656	71.3	25.7	80	2 124	561.9	81.6
Lompoc	31	146	18.8	4.1	35	D	D	D	23	573	108.4	25.5
Long Beach	502	3 660	2 647.9	266.4	1 036	7 701	1 489.9	485.4	234	8 027	4 464.4	758.2
Los Altos	98	304	114.2	21.0	275	D	D	D	23	189	30.0	12.6
Los Angeles	5 948	36 498	14 628.8	2 035.5	14 376	134 211	30 105.0	10 658.0	5 034	101 103	43 502.5	4 752.3
Los Banos	23	59	8.4	1.2	18	86	7.9	3.3	9	553	D	26.3
Los Gatos	105	366	123.7	18.9	277	1 637	303.1	122.9	32	488	169.9	36.6
Lynwood	16	100	10.7	4.5	15	96	7.2	2.2	51	1 057	236.6	42.3
Madera	35	148	19.2	4.0	38	D	D	D	35	1 055	445.4	51.3
Manhattan Beach	127	430	272.3	23.1	308	1 384	312.1	121.5	19	82	D	2.9
Manteca	56	231	50.5	9.3	54	319	23.7	9.4	22	972	D	57.2
Martinez	41	171	35.4	5.8	78	D	D	D	18	907	D	111.5
Maywood	3	4	0.2	0.0	4	D	D	D	16	228	D	6.9
Menifee	50	242	36.5	6.8	52	174	13.4	3.8	16	266	61.8	11.7

1. Establishments subject to federal tax.

Table D. Cities — Accommodation and Food Services, Arts, Entertainment, and Recreation, and Health Care and Social Assistance

City	Accommodation and food services, 2012				Arts, entertainment, and recreation,[1] 2012				Health care and social assistance,[1] 2012			
	Number of establishments	Number of employees	Sales (mil dol)	Annual payroll (mil dol)	Number of establishments	Number of employees	Receipts (mil dol)	Annual payroll (mil dol)	Number of establishments	Number of employees	Receipts (mil dol)	Annual payroll (mil dol)
	92	93	94	95	96	97	98	99	100	101	102	103
CALIFORNIA—Cont'd												
Delano	43	432	23.3	5.2	2	D	D	D	66	D	D	D
Desert Hot Springs	36	353	19.2	4.8	2	D	D	D	11	61	4.0	1.5
Diamond Bar	123	1 370	75.1	23.4	6	114	7.9	2.0	165	1 273	115.1	42.3
Downey	213	4 046	247.7	66.5	12	D	D	D	278	5 105	739.3	295.8
Dublin	141	2 588	181.4	45.7	15	D	D	D	117	1 174	151.5	51.5
East Palo Alto	14	660	46.3	16.6	2	D	D	D	12	D	D	D
El Cajon	236	3 169	173.6	44.6	13	189	15.1	2.8	205	3 958	345.4	143.9
El Centro	116	1 870	97.1	25.8	5	D	D	D	121	925	100.5	38.7
Elk Grove	206	3 919	212.5	57.4	16	D	D	D	275	2 744	414.4	112.2
El Monte	164	1 488	91.3	20.8	4	D	D	D	147	1 988	157.8	60.8
El Paso de Robles (Paso Robles)	114	2 080	119.4	31.2	13	D	D	D	71	736	45.7	15.7
Encinitas	214	4 943	277.9	78.7	46	366	24.4	7.6	362	2 859	347.1	124.7
Escondido	263	4 164	233.7	60.5	24	D	D	D	313	3 443	351.6	138.1
Eureka	135	1 649	92.7	25.5	12	186	5.8	2.1	108	1 163	110.5	46.1
Fairfield	211	3 101	190.2	46.8	18	D	D	D	219	2 316	348.6	100.5
Folsom	180	3 470	169.3	49.0	22	490	21.7	6.2	231	D	D	D
Fontana	219	3 451	188.4	48.0	18	D	D	D	159	D	D	D
Foster City	59	1 120	80.5	22.4	3	D	D	D	76	D	D	D
Fountain Valley	146	2 203	128.3	34.6	21	D	D	D	377	D	D	D
Fremont	381	5 412	331.7	87.2	32	722	36.4	11.3	577	6 977	1 074.4	399.9
Fresno	927	16 854	841.3	233.1	77	2 455	94.6	31.0	1 397	17 786	2 161.5	877.0
Fullerton	323	5 151	293.1	76.7	26	399	28.0	7.4	374	D	D	D
Gardena	202	2 258	130.3	33.5	7	D	D	D	137	2 174	270.4	96.6
Garden Grove	396	6 025	389.7	98.0	23	D	D	D	456	4 760	527.1	180.1
Gilroy	127	2 168	124.6	31.7	8	D	D	D	116	D	D	D
Glendale	403	6 449	400.5	111.6	163	755	117.6	36.7	968	8 146	871.9	316.1
Glendora	88	1 402	74.6	20.7	16	D	D	D	192	D	D	D
Goleta	102	1 752	104.7	27.1	4	145	6.5	2.2	112	1 339	152.1	57.9
Hanford	91	1 597	84.0	21.8	5	109	3.3	0.6	147	1 349	140.9	50.6
Hawthorne	124	1 650	108.8	25.2	14	222	16.5	4.3	125	1 950	189.7	72.8
Hayward	297	3 731	225.0	55.7	16	308	15.4	7.9	231	4 468	704.8	308.2
Hemet	144	2 179	112.1	32.1	10	D	D	D	213	2 976	305.8	105.1
Hesperia	104	1 773	88.6	23.7	6	D	D	D	77	700	70.2	24.3
Highland	56	753	43.6	11.0	3	D	D	D	49	D	D	D
Hollister	53	645	35.5	8.8	6	D	D	D	59	D	D	D
Huntington Beach	441	8 517	534.8	151.5	67	754	58.6	12.8	609	4 641	531.3	204.7
Huntington Park	99	1 374	82.7	20.6	2	D	D	D	125	1 294	152.6	47.9
Imperial Beach	33	351	20.6	4.8	3	D	D	D	19	367	27.3	11.4
Indio	106	2 965	229.2	63.3	21	D	D	D	114	1 760	238.1	80.6
Inglewood	168	2 570	145.5	38.5	32	1 156	168.8	33.9	237	3 724	505.3	167.9
Irvine	606	14 173	907.9	244.5	234	8 490	501.7	114.6	954	8 749	1 347.3	422.5
Laguna Hills	94	1 905	103.5	30.4	9	D	D	D	334	D	D	D
Laguna Niguel	119	1 929	110.3	29.0	25	D	D	D	215	1 500	138.1	58.8
La Habra	136	1 866	102.6	28.6	5	D	D	D	99	D	D	D
Lake Elsinore	98	1 432	77.8	21.6	9	D	D	D	57	297	31.1	11.4
Lake Forest	181	2 897	173.1	46.3	27	359	26.9	7.2	189	4 891	328.9	178.3
Lakewood	156	3 191	169.1	46.4	10	205	16.5	3.7	159	2 002	319.3	106.1
La Mesa	167	3 198	172.3	52.7	13	D	D	D	322	D	D	D
La Mirada	98	1 486	85.4	21.3	10	D	D	D	104	1 392	127.6	49.9
Lancaster	205	3 762	184.0	47.1	13	D	D	D	365	5 673	790.7	256.4
La Puente	68	734	41.5	10.1	1	D	D	D	52	352	27.9	9.6
La Quinta	73	3 254	207.1	67.1	17	498	37.2	13.8	71	389	46.6	18.3
La Verne	78	1 240	64.9	18.0	12	195	12.3	3.5	62	427	37.8	13.3
Lawndale	46	610	38.0	9.2	4	11	4.2	0.8	60	294	29.4	10.6
Lemon Grove	48	643	35.3	8.8	3	38	1.3	0.5	31	622	44.5	17.3
Lincoln	50	D	D	D	7	D	D	D	71	D	D	D
Livermore	180	2 541	153.7	42.3	23	D	D	D	150	1 658	225.7	78.3
Lodi	127	1 893	98.6	26.8	9	266	12.6	3.7	176	D	D	D
Lompoc	82	1 055	62.9	16.2	2	D	D	D	57	D	D	D
Long Beach	877	16 971	984.1	276.1	94	1 467	109.3	28.3	1 053	12 915	1 473.7	546.7
Los Altos	85	1 252	84.0	26.0	14	D	D	D	136	1 133	165.0	54.6
Los Angeles	8 009	138 886	9 295.6	2 593.6	7 686	31 974	9 416.1	3 866.7	9 711	109 130	13 605.4	4 917.1
Los Banos	57	804	43.0	11.4	2	D	D	D	41	273	29.1	10.2
Los Gatos	124	2 447	145.9	46.4	16	D	D	D	296	2 222	320.7	125.2
Lynwood	79	1 053	64.6	14.9	NA	NA	NA	NA	110	D	D	D
Madera	79	1 081	57.8	13.4	6	75	3.4	0.9	105	D	D	D
Manhattan Beach	154	3 688	247.0	75.6	73	281	48.9	19.8	187	D	D	D
Manteca	117	1 839	103.7	26.1	10	323	18.4	5.9	103	D	D	D
Martinez	79	753	43.4	10.9	6	D	D	D	41	D	D	D
Maywood	39	425	24.1	6.0	NA	NA	NA	NA	22	D	D	D
Menifee	67	1 348	75.4	21.6	8	D	D	D	87	1 573	128.0	50.8

1. Establishments subject to federal tax.

Table D. Cities — Other Services and Government Employment and Payroll

City	Other services[1], 2012 Number of establish-ments	Number of employees	Receipts (mil dol)	Annual payroll (mil dol)	Government employment and payroll, 2012 Full-time equivalent employees	March payroll Total (dollars)	Percent of total for: Adminis-tration, judicial, and legal	Police and Corrections	Fire Protection	Highways and trans-portation	Health and welfare	Natural resources and utilities	Education and libraries
	104	105	106	107	108	109	110	111	112	113	114	115	116
CALIFORNIA—Cont'd													
Delano	21	58	7.4	1.3	220	881 307	8.4	41.4	0.0	13.6	3.9	30.6	0.0
Desert Hot Springs	17	47	3.1	0.8	73	440 127	17.0	60.5	0.0	11.0	10.1	1.4	0.0
Diamond Bar	54	D	D	D	72	380 697	40.0	0.0	0.0	16.5	10.9	32.6	0.0
Downey	126	702	60.2	15.2	505	3 402 608	8.6	42.0	25.6	4.8	1.5	12.4	2.5
Dublin	83	D	D	D	106	716 632	36.7	5.5	0.8	23.0	3.5	24.9	0.0
East Palo Alto	11	D	D	D	112	1 036 706	21.8	57.6	0.0	11.0	9.5	0.0	0.0
El Cajon	171	1 183	130.3	31.8	443	2 609 521	7.2	42.2	14.7	6.2	11.0	13.4	0.0
El Centro	52	239	21.3	6.3	964	4 003 786	4.7	10.9	5.9	2.3	69.2	5.8	0.5
Elk Grove	137	707	57.1	16.3	280	1 987 037	15.1	76.6	0.0	2.4	1.4	1.1	0.0
El Monte	132	434	49.1	10.7	336	2 338 846	6.8	63.2	0.0	15.0	2.5	12.4	0.0
El Paso de Robles (Paso Robles)	43	247	23.8	6.5	164	981 684	11.7	27.8	19.1	3.0	4.3	20.5	2.9
Encinitas	141	825	67.4	21.3	242	1 673 551	30.3	0.0	25.3	14.3	0.8	20.7	3.3
Escondido	225	1 215	123.8	34.8	1 133	10 074 411	16.4	29.3	13.9	7.9	0.9	24.7	3.3
Eureka	73	461	45.5	12.5	282	1 300 511	8.5	31.6	18.8	2.4	4.7	21.0	0.0
Fairfield	121	906	97.2	32.5	645	3 404 101	10.9	36.3	15.3	11.5	3.2	11.0	0.0
Folsom	97	764	50.8	16.0	483	3 244 300	14.2	23.2	21.7	8.2	0.0	28.9	1.6
Fontana	170	945	83.8	23.5	767	4 073 819	10.2	49.0	0.0	8.3	6.6	23.2	0.0
Foster City	20	D	D	D	192	1 556 154	16.6	27.7	24.1	6.3	0.0	25.3	0.0
Fountain Valley	84	562	47.6	14.9	232	1 801 733	11.7	37.6	26.9	4.9	0.9	10.1	0.0
Fremont	276	1 983	276.4	67.3	881	7 171 062	20.6	30.1	20.1	9.2	7.6	8.2	0.0
Fresno	536	3 750	381.1	106.9	3 214	18 551 770	10.2	39.0	13.4	20.0	0.0	15.9	0.0
Fullerton	185	884	110.0	26.1	676	4 122 933	7.6	39.6	18.4	6.3	5.0	12.8	3.4
Gardena	124	780	69.3	20.9	419	2 062 110	7.9	42.6	0.0	28.2	6.3	8.7	0.0
Garden Grove	216	884	78.3	21.3	657	4 420 328	10.0	44.2	22.5	0.7	7.8	7.6	0.0
Gilroy	82	713	68.2	19.1	258	1 936 702	13.1	41.6	20.3	4.9	2.7	13.4	0.0
Glendale	308	2 190	165.1	65.5	1 864	13 741 087	17.0	23.8	18.6	3.2	4.9	27.1	3.1
Glendora	78	D	D	D	321	1 582 591	10.6	43.7	0.0	11.9	6.9	19.8	7.2
Goleta	48	D	D	D	47	334 846	63.8	0.0	0.0	23.1	5.9	7.2	0.0
Hanford	43	192	17.7	4.8	259	1 321 734	9.8	38.2	13.4	8.8	0.0	24.1	0.0
Hawthorne	97	369	35.3	7.5	283	1 907 186	16.2	40.8	0.0	5.5	2.8	5.5	0.0
Hayward	202	1 576	223.3	52.6	761	6 582 512	8.9	39.0	24.1	6.2	3.7	9.7	2.7
Hemet	88	384	31.1	8.2	409	2 543 919	11.5	33.8	20.3	7.4	2.2	11.7	3.6
Hesperia	83	355	37.7	10.1	127	669 050	29.0	0.1	0.0	16.7	15.9	0.0	0.0
Highland	29	147	9.2	2.7	38	273 354	31.6	0.0	0.0	15.6	10.8	4.6	0.0
Hollister	50	D	D	D	131	912 911	12.2	25.2	24.4	4.8	4.9	18.9	0.0
Huntington Beach	309	1 944	159.4	52.3	1 071	7 579 599	14.4	34.3	23.5	5.3	1.3	14.6	2.6
Huntington Park	49	417	37.5	10.0	208	1 200 684	11.4	67.5	0.0	5.5	5.1	6.0	0.0
Imperial Beach	23	100	6.1	1.9	82	452 081	44.4	0.0	17.6	4.4	3.2	9.8	0.0
Indio	59	314	27.8	7.7	253	1 534 809	8.8	49.5	0.0	12.9	5.9	15.1	0.0
Inglewood	122	934	85.6	23.8	724	3 812 741	19.1	49.5	0.0	10.8	5.9	11.8	2.9
Irvine	293	2 511	248.1	68.7	977	6 075 973	20.0	39.1	0.0	10.5	2.9	13.8	0.0
Laguna Hills	68	390	33.7	10.7	40	246 065	39.8	0.0	0.0	13.2	20.3	26.7	0.0
Laguna Niguel	92	520	41.6	11.9	79	590 935	24.7	1.6	0.0	17.2	21.8	28.0	0.0
La Habra	95	531	47.0	10.7	325	1 702 615	11.2	45.6	0.0	0.0	0.0	11.8	0.0
Lake Elsinore	66	351	29.9	8.7	66	784 724	0.4	0.0	0.0	8.2	0.0	11.8	0.0
Lake Forest	111	695	85.9	20.7	79	477 565	58.7	1.2	0.0	5.1	13.9	21.1	0.0
Lakewood	76	D	D	D	255	1 549 892	26.5	6.5	0.0	16.3	2.1	41.0	0.0
La Mesa	106	820	54.6	17.8	283	1 642 547	12.9	41.7	20.9	5.6	2.7	10.2	0.0
La Mirada	33	141	6.3	2.0	142	702 597	25.1	9.5	0.0	0.0	9.3	25.7	0.0
Lancaster	167	864	78.2	22.3	338	1 643 288	21.1	3.3	0.0	28.3	10.6	32.5	0.0
La Puente	35	121	7.6	2.2	44	173 692	49.1	0.0	0.0	14.7	2.7	17.6	0.0
La Quinta	39	168	10.1	2.9	94	580 882	30.3	0.0	0.0	26.7	22.0	0.0	0.0
La Verne	38	215	12.2	3.4	200	1 245 972	16.1	41.5	26.1	2.8	0.0	10.1	0.0
Lawndale	65	299	25.9	6.0	72	370 627	35.6	0.0	0.0	27.9	0.0	17.4	0.0
Lemon Grove	44	150	11.9	3.3	50	320 723	14.9	0.0	50.2	14.0	7.5	6.0	0.0
Lincoln	34	D	D	D	204	1 072 286	18.7	28.4	11.2	10.5	9.3	10.6	1.8
Livermore	109	D	D	D	431	3 325 675	14.6	36.7	0.0	16.4	4.9	18.3	6.5
Lodi	100	559	54.0	15.2	481	2 698 469	10.3	27.2	16.3	7.0	1.8	29.2	2.7
Lompoc	37	D	D	D	391	1 833 592	11.8	26.5	9.3	5.4	0.4	32.9	2.7
Long Beach	514	3 723	492.5	110.7	5 861	36 050 392	7.5	28.9	14.8	19.5	6.1	12.6	1.4
Los Altos	51	D	D	D	127	885 014	8.2	40.0	0.0	11.6	3.4	17.8	0.0
Los Angeles	5 383	33 721	2 988.4	814.2	47 505	361 983 103	11.8	27.5	11.6	12.8	4.2	30.5	1.2
Los Banos	22	100	7.8	2.4	285	749 390	11.4	40.2	15.6	5.1	2.2	19.0	0.0
Los Gatos	88	419	37.6	11.5	148	1 210 153	16.6	44.9	0.0	10.6	7.2	6.5	7.5
Lynwood	52	296	21.9	5.7	230	916 329	42.8	2.5	0.0	20.8	5.6	28.3	0.0
Madera	43	202	19.6	4.9	274	1 196 996	16.2	35.6	0.0	9.9	12.2	22.5	0.0
Manhattan Beach	76	594	37.8	12.1	381	1 720 027	11.4	41.4	12.9	4.7	9.6	15.5	0.0
Manteca	76	307	28.1	6.9	345	2 165 170	13.0	35.1	16.6	6.2	1.2	25.5	0.0
Martinez	41	166	22.5	5.1	52	324 363	4.1	88.0	0.0	0.0	4.6	1.4	0.0
Maywood	27	98	6.0	1.9	18	66 828	51.7	0.0	0.0	0.0	5.9	31.7	0.0
Menifee	43	233	27.6	5.1	23	165 702	68.9	0.0	0.0	10.5	13.6	0.0	0.0

1. Establishments subject to federal tax.

Table D. Cities — City Government Finances

City	City government finances, 2012									
	General revenue							General expenditure		
	Intergovernmental			Taxes					Per capita[1] (dollars)	
					Per capita[1] (dollars)					
	Total (mil dol)	Total (mil dol)	Percent from state government	Total (mil dol)	Total	Property	Sales and gross receipts	Total (mil dol)	Total	Capital outlays
	117	118	119	120	121	122	123	124	125	126
CALIFORNIA—Cont'd										
Delano	32.5	6.6	92.1	16.4	313	163	105	31.3	597	53
Desert Hot Springs	20.2	3.1	33.2	12.4	446	214	213	27.4	988	219
Diamond Bar	24.3	2.3	77.9	16.9	300	165	128	31.6	561	189
Downey	89.0	11.9	58.4	53.0	468	227	239	98.0	866	54
Dublin	67.1	3.0	97.7	50.4	1 032	529	415	63.3	1 298	122
East Palo Alto	36.0	3.8	90.2	24.9	858	568	285	31.6	1 090	142
El Cajon	103.0	8.1	84.7	70.6	695	308	385	103.4	1 017	157
El Centro	182.9	11.7	52.8	25.2	582	256	318	173.8	4 019	507
Elk Grove	117.6	21.2	77.7	55.8	352	138	210	116.8	737	118
El Monte	92.1	16.0	67.9	64.7	561	290	268	92.7	803	118
El Paso de Robles (Paso Robles)	46.5	6.6	62.1	30.0	983	513	466	43.1	1 414	272
Encinitas	74.3	4.1	60.5	49.4	809	584	217	77.2	1 265	265
Escondido	143.3	14.3	60.1	78.5	531	315	209	135.9	919	78
Eureka	46.5	7.0	68.0	27.9	1 036	386	648	49.7	1 845	324
Fairfield	135.2	23.7	86.3	87.3	811	437	371	120.8	1 122	219
Folsom	106.2	4.7	81.7	61.5	840	482	272	106.9	1 459	214
Fontana	243.1	25.3	66.9	150.7	748	563	182	241.4	1 198	265
Foster City	51.6	1.9	100.0	38.7	1 203	920	277	53.2	1 654	65
Fountain Valley	51.8	4.2	91.1	35.6	630	394	227	53.9	954	197
Fremont	214.4	29.7	64.9	141.4	637	367	230	244.1	1 100	468
Fresno	632.4	127.3	42.9	267.5	529	240	287	528.7	1 045	197
Fullerton	151.4	23.8	80.4	79.9	576	371	202	188.8	1 362	506
Gardena	78.5	10.8	48.9	56.0	938	205	564	63.5	1 065	158
Garden Grove	143.3	12.1	44.0	78.1	448	263	183	176.5	1 012	138
Gilroy	73.7	6.7	42.5	38.7	762	281	360	72.6	1 432	389
Glendale	315.9	29.1	55.9	145.8	748	379	366	334.4	1 717	239
Glendora	41.0	5.3	97.4	28.1	553	361	190	34.8	685	69
Goleta	31.1	4.4	87.8	22.0	727	257	426	33.8	1 118	384
Hanford	41.5	3.7	86.5	19.3	355	224	123	40.0	736	127
Hawthorne	103.1	37.8	12.8	48.4	564	260	302	99.8	1 163	96
Hayward	216.5	39.7	29.1	108.3	724	336	353	190.5	1 273	255
Hemet	71.2	3.5	72.5	44.9	552	243	299	68.8	846	126
Hesperia	73.7	15.0	93.8	44.5	483	317	165	101.5	1 103	350
Highland	29.3	5.5	73.6	17.0	315	231	64	34.1	631	199
Hollister	49.1	1.4	100.0	27.1	753	551	186	40.2	1 115	356
Huntington Beach	237.1	14.8	87.5	142.7	732	378	348	245.0	1 257	137
Huntington Park	53.9	9.0	53.2	35.6	605	397	207	47.0	799	63
Imperial Beach	31.4	1.9	89.6	17.2	640	488	150	27.2	1 012	70
Indio	79.4	8.3	78.1	47.6	577	315	258	80.9	980	123
Inglewood	168.9	42.5	51.9	97.4	874	422	400	161.6	1 451	100
Irvine	221.8	16.6	67.8	150.8	656	245	405	296.0	1 289	255
Laguna Hills	26.8	8.5	93.2	16.2	524	301	209	23.6	764	235
Laguna Niguel	38.2	3.2	97.6	31.8	495	300	189	40.3	626	203
La Habra	54.3	8.3	81.6	32.0	521	283	239	52.1	847	84
Lake Elsinore	62.9	4.4	97.8	38.1	682	451	180	70.3	1 261	194
Lake Forest	48.6	4.3	66.7	38.8	491	253	234	55.1	879	338
Lakewood	58.5	5.6	92.9	38.4	474	248	223	58.2	680	68
La Mesa	60.0	3.3	82.3	42.5	729	333	392	58.2	999	181
La Mirada	53.4	5.0	48.8	36.5	744	494	247	62.4	1 271	395
Lancaster	155.7	14.4	70.0	98.7	621	395	225	158.8	999	170
La Puente	17.0	3.2	83.5	10.1	251	139	110	16.8	417	64
La Quinta	92.3	4.4	99.5	69.5	1 801	1 413	377	79.1	2 049	214
La Verne	36.0	1.3	97.5	23.8	756	457	290	35.3	1 123	55
Lawndale	21.9	4.6	43.6	15.6	470	264	205	22.6	682	195
Lemon Grove	23.6	3.5	40.3	12.9	495	317	176	23.1	888	142
Lincoln	39.4	1.9	82.7	16.0	363	218	137	39.2	887	142
Livermore	144.6	12.8	81.4	70.9	848	452	391	146.1	1 746	314
Lodi	74.4	14.8	61.1	37.4	591	232	358	65.7	1 040	203
Lompoc	49.0	7.6	70.8	20.7	479	244	198	57.4	1 329	168
Long Beach	1 850.9	195.5	44.1	411.4	877	543	331	1 760.6	3 753	846
Los Altos	38.7	1.3	98.4	24.5	820	464	333	41.7	1 397	179
Los Angeles	9 274.5	847.5	41.5	3 849.3	997	441	528	8 678.1	2 247	524
Los Banos	30.8	1.2	94.3	16.0	437	268	87	30.9	844	146
Los Gatos	39.5	1.7	100.0	30.5	1 010	550	425	44.6	1 477	382
Lynwood	48.4	7.5	65.9	33.0	465	265	191	48.6	685	116
Madera	61.9	6.4	52.4	35.7	571	205	290	58.8	939	220
Manhattan Beach	64.9	2.0	100.0	40.2	1 132	649	468	68.9	1 939	189
Manteca	96.8	11.6	80.0	40.6	571	382	177	94.8	1 335	419
Martinez	24.4	2.4	100.0	18.2	493	310	179	24.1	653	42
Maywood	11.1	1.5	55.8	8.9	321	203	117	10.0	361	22
Menifee	33.2	8.6	100.0	19.8	243	138	102	27.8	341	43

1. Based on population estimated as of July 1 of the year shown.

Table D. Cities — City Government Finances

City		City government finances, 2012 (cont.)								
		General expenditure (cont.)								
		Percent of total for:								
	Public welfare	Highways	Parking facilities	Education	Health and hospitals	Police protection	Sewerage and sanitation	Parks and recreation	Housing and community development	Interest on debt
	127	128	129	130	131	132	133	134	135	136
CALIFORNIA—Cont'd										
Delano	0.0	7.9	0.1	0.0	0.7	35.9	16.1	5.8	6.3	4.8
Desert Hot Springs	0.0	19.3	0.0	0.0	1.2	32.8	0.0	2.7	15.7	5.8
Diamond Bar	0.0	11.3	0.0	0.0	0.4	17.3	1.0	17.5	2.2	2.7
Downey	0.0	10.4	0.0	0.0	3.3	29.8	2.0	12.8	8.4	2.2
Dublin	0.0	9.9	0.0	0.0	0.9	23.6	5.1	13.7	4.2	0.4
East Palo Alto	0.0	15.7	0.0	0.0	0.0	32.7	8.2	3.9	9.5	7.2
El Cajon	0.0	7.2	0.0	0.0	4.9	29.0	15.2	4.3	14.7	2.9
El Centro	0.0	3.7	0.0	0.0	71.3	5.1	5.8	1.4	1.4	2.7
Elk Grove	0.0	20.1	0.0	0.0	0.7	26.4	11.1	0.6	15.2	3.0
El Monte	0.0	8.9	0.1	0.0	0.1	24.2	0.0	3.9	14.8	4.7
El Paso de Robles (Paso Robles)	0.0	14.0	0.0	0.0	0.0	18.5	11.1	8.4	4.2	5.6
Encinitas	0.0	11.1	0.0	0.0	1.4	14.8	5.7	11.7	3.2	0.4
Escondido	0.0	9.0	0.0	0.0	1.1	26.8	15.4	5.9	4.7	6.9
Eureka	0.0	7.4	0.3	0.0	0.2	21.6	17.7	5.2	11.4	6.1
Fairfield	0.0	22.4	0.0	0.0	0.9	26.9	0.0	8.9	8.3	6.3
Folsom	0.0	7.4	0.0	0.0	0.6	18.0	10.0	10.4	7.7	6.6
Fontana	0.0	16.0	0.0	0.0	0.0	21.8	4.9	5.1	16.6	14.1
Foster City	0.0	4.8	0.0	0.0	0.0	17.3	12.1	18.0	5.0	0.0
Fountain Valley	0.0	16.9	0.0	0.0	5.8	26.6	8.8	7.4	11.0	1.2
Fremont	0.1	18.2	0.0	0.0	4.6	27.3	2.1	6.1	8.7	3.7
Fresno	0.0	9.2	0.9	0.0	1.8	27.9	21.5	4.8	2.7	8.1
Fullerton	0.0	19.9	0.0	0.0	3.1	19.1	8.1	6.3	16.0	3.9
Gardena	0.0	12.4	0.0	0.0	3.2	33.0	1.6	5.6	7.1	2.4
Garden Grove	0.0	9.7	0.0	0.0	3.7	26.6	4.0	4.9	25.2	3.8
Gilroy	0.0	3.9	0.0	0.0	0.1	23.5	11.0	1.2	31.3	2.7
Glendale	0.0	6.5	1.9	0.0	0.2	20.8	9.9	5.1	16.0	1.2
Glendora	0.0	7.3	0.0	0.0	0.3	38.7	0.0	9.5	14.0	4.6
Goleta	0.0	35.2	0.0	0.0	1.4	19.9	0.0	7.5	6.3	2.1
Hanford	0.0	14.3	0.0	0.0	1.1	20.5	28.6	8.9	2.1	3.4
Hawthorne	0.0	13.4	0.0	0.0	0.0	30.2	0.7	1.5	12.0	4.8
Hayward	0.0	22.7	0.0	0.0	1.1	29.9	8.1	0.9	3.9	2.6
Hemet	0.0	13.6	0.0	0.0	0.3	23.8	21.6	1.1	10.9	0.9
Hesperia	0.0	18.2	0.0	0.0	1.8	12.4	0.0	0.0	33.4	8.9
Highland	0.0	33.6	0.0	0.0	3.7	20.5	0.0	3.0	9.1	8.3
Hollister	0.0	9.2	0.0	0.0	1.5	15.8	30.4	3.1	12.4	4.5
Huntington Beach	0.0	12.4	1.3	0.0	1.9	28.9	8.3	6.7	4.8	2.2
Huntington Park	0.0	8.1	1.2	0.0	5.3	33.4	0.8	4.2	12.8	4.9
Imperial Beach	0.0	9.3	0.0	0.0	0.7	26.9	16.9	5.6	13.1	5.9
Indio	0.0	11.9	0.0	0.0	5.2	25.3	0.2	5.0	15.5	8.5
Inglewood	0.0	9.8	0.2	0.0	1.6	19.3	8.5	5.2	14.3	7.4
Irvine	0.0	25.6	0.0	0.0	1.6	18.7	0.0	21.6	1.9	12.6
Laguna Hills	0.0	25.2	0.0	0.0	0.3	27.3	0.0	23.3	0.3	2.6
Laguna Niguel	0.0	23.9	0.0	0.0	0.8	23.4	0.0	17.7	0.2	0.0
La Habra	0.0	8.8	0.0	0.0	1.8	30.7	10.8	10.5	12.4	2.9
Lake Elsinore	0.0	5.0	0.0	0.0	0.7	12.7	0.0	16.1	15.7	24.3
Lake Forest	0.0	38.6	0.0	0.0	0.2	18.1	0.0	16.3	6.7	0.7
Lakewood	0.0	18.5	0.0	0.0	0.5	20.7	12.1	21.5	3.7	3.9
La Mesa	0.0	19.6	0.3	0.0	0.9	25.3	16.9	6.5	1.6	2.5
La Mirada	0.0	37.1	0.0	0.0	0.1	12.1	0.0	18.7	14.6	3.8
Lancaster	0.0	12.1	0.0	0.0	0.4	17.3	0.0	6.5	26.8	11.9
La Puente	0.0	11.0	0.0	0.0	1.7	27.8	3.9	17.2	8.0	4.3
La Quinta	0.0	10.7	0.0	0.0	0.5	15.3	0.0	8.3	24.6	17.5
La Verne	0.0	8.7	0.0	0.0	5.5	33.7	3.3	6.8	15.6	2.9
Lawndale	0.0	12.3	0.0	0.0	0.6	20.2	0.2	10.8	29.6	4.8
Lemon Grove	0.0	4.3	0.0	0.0	0.7	19.3	17.8	3.7	15.4	4.9
Lincoln	0.0	14.1	0.0	0.0	0.0	13.0	24.9	4.2	2.1	3.8
Livermore	0.0	17.3	0.0	0.0	0.4	17.7	12.7	1.7	2.3	2.6
Lodi	0.0	12.3	0.0	0.0	0.6	24.8	16.8	7.4	2.4	0.1
Lompoc	0.0	9.5	0.0	0.0	0.6	34.0	20.4	5.7	8.5	1.8
Long Beach	0.0	3.4	0.0	0.0	3.0	11.4	5.2	7.6	7.6	4.6
Los Altos	0.0	14.1	0.0	0.0	0.8	22.9	12.7	6.1	2.6	0.2
Los Angeles	0.0	8.1	0.4	0.0	2.6	19.6	8.6	4.5	4.2	6.1
Los Banos	0.0	9.9	0.0	0.0	0.3	24.6	26.0	13.3	5.1	2.8
Los Gatos	0.0	12.1	0.0	0.0	0.3	26.6	0.3	7.1	9.0	2.5
Lynwood	0.0	22.5	0.0	0.0	1.0	16.7	1.5	5.8	13.5	1.6
Madera	0.0	25.5	0.1	0.0	1.7	16.8	19.2	6.0	4.6	5.3
Manhattan Beach	0.0	10.0	4.3	0.0	4.5	30.5	9.0	13.7	0.0	1.3
Manteca	0.0	16.3	0.0	0.0	0.3	15.0	25.2	6.9	13.6	4.5
Martinez	0.0	10.7	1.3	0.0	0.0	41.2	0.0	13.9	0.1	3.6
Maywood	0.0	11.2	0.0	0.0	0.0	39.4	0.0	6.2	4.2	10.1
Menifee	0.0	9.1	0.0	0.0	1.3	31.9	0.0	0.0	6.7	0.3

City	City government finances, 2012 (cont.)			Climate[2]						
	Debt outstanding			Average daily temperature (degrees Fahrenheit)						
				Mean		Limits				
	Total (mil dol)	Per capita[1] (dollars)	Debt issued during year	January	July	January[3]	July[4]	Annual precipitation (inches)	Heating degree days	Cooling degree days
	137	138	139	140	141	142	143	144	145	146
CALIFORNIA—Cont'd										
Delano	62.8	1 196	0.0	46.6	81.1	36.5	99.0	7.34	2 434	1 990
Desert Hot Springs	12.2	440	6.2	NA	NA	NA	NA	16.96	1 727	1 191
Diamond Bar	0.0	0	12.0	54.6	73.8	41.5	88.7	12.94	1 211	1 186
Downey	63.1	558	1.5	57.0	73.8	46.0	82.9	14.82	2 755	858
Dublin	6.2	127	0.0	47.2	72.0	37.4	89.1	15.71	2 584	452
East Palo Alto	47.6	1 643	0.0	49.0	68.0	40.4	78.8	11.96	1 560	1 371
El Cajon	68.2	671	0.1	54.9	74.7	41.6	87.0	11.63	1 080	3 852
El Centro	100.3	2 320	0.0	55.8	91.4	41.3	107.0	2.96		
Elk Grove	95.6	603	0.0	46.3	75.4	38.8	92.4	17.93	2 666	1 248
El Monte	168.9	1 465	13.3	56.3	75.6	42.6	89.0	18.56	1 295	1 575
El Paso de Robles (Paso Robles)	54.4	1 784	6.4	NA	NA	NA	NA	NA	NA	NA
Encinitas	40.7	667	0.0	55.5	75.1	42.5	88.6	15.10	1 464	1 436
Escondido	191.9	1 298	11.4	55.5	75.1	42.5	88.6	15.10	1 464	1 436
Eureka	109.2	4 052	9.4	47.9	58.1	40.8	63.3	38.10	4 430	7
Fairfield	271.5	2 523	10.5	46.1	72.6	37.5	88.8	23.46	2 649	975
Folsom	237.5	3 241	15.0	46.9	77.7	39.2	94.8	24.61	2 532	1 528
Fontana	677.9	3 364	0.8	56.6	78.3	45.3	95.0	14.77	1 364	1 901
Foster City	0.0	0	0.0	48.4	68.0	39.1	80.8	20.16	2 764	422
Fountain Valley	9.7	171	0.0	58.0	72.9	46.6	87.7	13.84	1 153	1 299
Fremont	313.6	1 414	53.3	49.8	68.0	42.0	78.3	14.85	2 367	530
Fresno	1 062.2	2 099	0.0	46.0	81.4	38.4	96.6	11.23	2 447	1 963
Fullerton	195.2	1 408	0.0	56.9	73.2	45.2	84.0	11.23	1 286	1 294
Gardena	24.8	415	0.0	56.3	69.4	46.2	77.6	14.79	1 526	742
Garden Grove	179.2	1 028	6.7	58.0	72.9	46.6	87.7	13.84	1 153	1 299
Gilroy	54.9	1 083	0.0	49.7	72.0	39.4	88.3	20.60	2 278	913
Glendale	322.6	1 656	38.3	54.8	75.5	42.0	88.9	17.49	1 575	1 455
Glendora	46.8	921	0.0	54.6	73.8	41.5	88.7	16.96	1 727	1 191
Goleta	15.7	518	0.0	53.1	67.0	40.8	76.7	16.93	2 121	482
Hanford	43.0	792	0.0	44.7	79.6	35.7	95.9	8.58	2 749	1 724
Hawthorne	104.9	1 223	0.0	57.1	69.3	48.6	75.3	13.15	1 274	679
Hayward	196.8	1 315	0.0	49.7	64.6	41.7	75.2	26.30	2 810	261
Hemet	13.7	168	0.0	52.4	79.9	38.4	97.8	12.55	1 914	1 903
Hesperia	168.7	1 834	0.0	45.5	80.0	31.4	99.1	6.20	2 929	1 735
Highland	73.8	1 364	0.0	54.4	79.6	41.8	96.0	16.43	1 599	1 937
Hollister	43.7	1 213	0.0	49.5	66.6	37.8	80.9	13.61	2 724	405
Huntington Beach	257.9	1 323	36.3	55.9	67.3	48.2	71.4	11.65	1 719	543
Huntington Park	42.4	720	0.0	58.3	74.2	48.5	83.8	15.14	928	1 506
Imperial Beach	40.1	1 493	0.0	57.3	70.1	46.1	76.1	9.95	1 321	862
Indio	184.2	2 232	0.0	56.8	92.8	42.0	107.1	3.15	903	4 388
Inglewood	277.3	2 489	30.8	57.1	69.3	48.6	75.3	13.15	1 274	679
Irvine	1 400.1	6 096	270.1	54.5	72.1	41.4	83.8	13.87	1 794	1 102
Laguna Hills	15.6	507	0.0	56.7	72.4	47.2	82.3	14.03	1 465	1 183
Laguna Niguel	0.0	0	0.0	55.4	68.7	43.9	77.3	13.56	1 756	666
La Habra	55.8	908	0.0	56.9	73.2	45.2	84.0	11.23	1 286	1 294
Lake Elsinore	410.2	7 355	1.5	52.2	79.6	38.3	98.1	12.09	1 924	1 874
Lake Forest	18.8	238	11.0	56.7	72.4	47.2	82.3	14.03	1 465	1 183
Lakewood	42.5	525	0.0	57.0	73.8	46.0	82.9	12.94	1 211	1 186
La Mesa	46.3	795	0.9	57.1	73.0	45.7	83.6	13.75	1 313	1 261
La Mirada	92.9	1 893	1.9	58.8	76.6	47.9	88.9	14.44	949	1 837
Lancaster	431.7	2 716	0.0	43.9	80.8	31.0	95.5	7.40	3 241	1 733
La Puente	9.5	236	0.0	58.8	76.6	47.9	88.9	14.44	949	1 837
La Quinta	324.4	8 401	0.0	NA	NA	NA	NA	NA	NA	NA
La Verne	19.4	618	0.0	54.6	73.8	41.5	88.7	16.96	1 727	1 191
Lawndale	21.1	635	0.0	57.1	69.3	48.6	75.3	13.15	1 274	679
Lemon Grove	26.5	1 021	0.0	NA	NA	NA	NA	NA	NA	NA
Lincoln	35.5	801	0.0	NA	NA	NA	NA	NA	NA	NA
Livermore	175.1	2 093	0.0	47.2	72.0	37.4	89.1	14.82	2 755	858
Lodi	0.2	4	0.0	46.1	73.8	37.5	91.1	18.22	2 710	1 057
Lompoc	54.1	1 253	0.0	53.7	64.5	41.4	75.4	15.85	2 250	322
Long Beach	2 390.0	5 095	112.4	57.0	73.8	46.0	82.9	12.94	1 211	1 186
Los Altos	1.9	62	0.0	49.0	68.0	40.4	78.8	15.71	2 584	452
Los Angeles	23 104.2	5 983	2 268.6	58.3	74.2	48.5	83.8	15.14	928	1 506
Los Banos	28.4	774	0.0	45.9	78.1	36.8	94.6	9.95	2 570	1 547
Los Gatos	23.8	789	0.0	48.7	70.3	38.8	85.4	22.64	2 641	613
Lynwood	30.0	423	0.0	58.3	74.2	48.5	83.8	15.14	928	1 506
Madera	114.1	1 823	0.0	45.7	79.6	37.2	96.5	11.94	2 670	1 706
Manhattan Beach	37.6	1 058	0.0	57.1	69.3	48.6	75.3	13.15	1 274	679
Manteca	214.3	3 017	1.7	46.0	77.3	38.1	93.8	13.84	2 563	1 456
Martinez	29.2	790	18.7	46.3	71.2	38.8	87.4	19.58	2 757	786
Maywood	0.0	0	0.0	58.3	74.2	48.5	83.8	15.14	928	1 506
Menifee	20.0	246	20.0	NA	NA	NA	NA	NA	NA	NA

1. Based on the population estimated as of July 1 of the year shown.   2. Represents normal values based on the 30-year period, 1971–2000.   3. Average daily minimum.
4. Average daily maximum.

Table D. Cities — **Land Area and Population**

STATE Place code	City	Land area,[1] 2016 (sq mi)	Population, 2016 Total persons	Rank	Per square mile	Race alone[2] (percent), 2015 White	Black or African American	American Indian, Alaska Native	Asian	Hawaiian Pacific Islander	Some other race	2 or more races[2]
		1	2	3	4	5	6	7	8	9	10	11
	CALIFORNIA—Cont'd											
06 46870	Menlo Park	10.0	33 888	1 121	3 388.8	67.2	5.3	0.3	14.6	0.4	9.1	3.1
06 46898	Merced	23.2	82 594	407	3 560.1	47.1	5.7	1.0	10.4	0.0	30.0	5.8
06 47766	Milpitas	13.6	77 528	436	5 700.6	19.9	2.7	0.3	66.1	0.4	7.9	2.7
06 48256	Mission Viejo	17.7	96 396	317	5 446.1	79.1	1.4	0.1	10.6	0.2	3.6	5.0
06 48354	Modesto	43.0	212 175	103	4 934.3	75.4	3.5	0.8	7.5	1.1	7.6	4.1
06 48648	Monrovia	13.6	37 126	1 029	2 729.9	71.6	2.7	0.0	14.3	0.9	7.2	3.3
06 48788	Montclair	5.5	38 944	978	7 080.7	34.4	2.5	1.0	10.6	0.3	48.5	2.7
06 48816	Montebello	8.3	63 335	576	7 630.7	50.1	1.3	1.2	13.0	0.0	31.7	2.7
06 48872	Monterey	8.7	28 454	1 310	3 270.6	77.5	5.3	0.1	10.1	0.3	1.9	4.7
06 48914	Monterey Park	7.7	61 075	601	7 931.8	11.8	0.1	0.4	67.2	0.7	18.1	1.8
06 49138	Moorpark	12.6	36 481	1 045	2 895.3	81.2	0.8	0.7	7.6	0.5	4.2	5.0
06 49270	Moreno Valley	51.3	205 499	109	4 005.8	42.2	16.4	0.4	4.9	0.6	33.1	2.5
06 49278	Morgan Hill	12.8	44 155	855	3 449.6	73.7	2.8	0.4	7.4	0.4	6.2	9.0
06 49670	Mountain View	12.0	80 447	421	6 703.9	59.5	1.6	0.2	25.9	0.2	7.4	5.3
06 50076	Murrieta	33.6	111 674	257	3 323.6	64.3	6.8	0.4	11.6	0.5	9.3	7.1
06 50258	Napa	17.8	80 416	422	4 517.8	69.5	0.5	1.3	3.7	0.1	22.3	2.5
06 50398	National City	7.3	61 147	598	8 376.3	58.6	3.9	0.4	23.4	0.1	11.2	2.5
06 50916	Newark	13.9	45 810	831	3 295.7	31.7	4.8	0.5	27.8	0.5	30.5	4.1
06 51182	Newport Beach	23.8	86 688	380	3 642.4	83.1	0.2	0.3	9.2	0.1	4.2	2.7
06 51560	Norco	13.8	26 714	1 378	1 935.8	78.9	5.2	0.1	3.4	0.1	5.4	6.9
06 52526	Norwalk	9.7	106 178	283	10 946.2	42.3	4.4	0.7	14.2	0.2	35.9	2.3
06 52582	Novato	27.4	56 004	667	2 043.9	73.8	1.1	0.5	9.2	0.0	9.8	5.7
06 53000	Oakland	55.9	420 005	45	7 513.5	36.8	24.9	0.8	15.3	0.4	15.6	6.2
06 53070	Oakley	15.9	40 622	927	2 554.8	63.9	12.0	0.7	4.2	0.2	16.0	3.0
06 53322	Oceanside	41.3	175 464	141	4 248.5	74.3	5.3	0.6	8.5	0.9	4.4	5.8
06 53896	Ontario	49.9	173 212	146	3 471.2	38.6	6.5	0.6	6.9	0.1	40.7	6.6
06 53980	Orange	25.4	140 504	188	5 531.7	68.8	1.7	0.2	13.7	0.1	12.6	2.8
06 54652	Oxnard	26.9	207 906	108	7 728.8	76.9	2.5	2.1	7.5	0.5	7.2	3.2
06 54806	Pacifica	12.7	39 062	970	3 075.7	61.5	1.8	0.7	26.3	0.0	1.1	8.6
06 55156	Palmdale	106.0	157 356	161	1 484.5	43.5	15.1	1.1	5.7	0.4	29.6	4.6
06 55184	Palm Desert	26.8	52 231	727	1 948.9	85.5	2.1	0.0	4.3	0.0	5.0	3.2
06 55254	Palm Springs	94.1	47 689	801	506.8	80.9	6.4	0.2	6.3	0.1	3.8	2.2
06 55282	Palo Alto	23.9	67 024	533	2 804.4	60.4	1.2	0.1	31.5	0.0	1.5	5.3
06 55520	Paradise	18.3	26 551	1 380	1 450.9	NA	NA	NA	NA	NA	NA	NA
06 55618	Paramount	4.7	54 909	685	11 682.8	68.6	7.9	0.0	4.8	0.7	15.6	2.4
06 56000	Pasadena	23.0	142 059	185	6 176.5	51.2	9.9	0.3	14.9	0.1	20.2	3.4
06 56700	Perris	31.6	76 331	452	2 415.5	30.0	11.2	0.5	3.7	0.1	52.5	2.0
06 56784	Petaluma	14.4	60 530	609	4 203.5	79.7	1.4	0.1	5.7	0.0	7.7	5.4
06 56924	Pico Rivera	8.3	63 635	575	7 666.9	60.5	0.9	1.2	2.6	0.0	32.8	2.0
06 57456	Pittsburg	17.2	70 679	498	4 109.2	29.4	19.0	0.6	16.7	1.0	24.3	9.1
06 57526	Placentia	6.6	52 228	728	7 913.3	76.7	0.7	0.0	17.2	0.1	3.0	2.3
06 57764	Pleasant Hill	7.1	34 853	1 091	4 908.9	72.6	2.3	0.8	14.3	0.6	2.1	7.2
06 57792	Pleasanton	24.1	82 270	410	3 413.7	58.0	1.7	0.3	31.4	1.1	2.3	5.3
06 58072	Pomona	23.0	152 494	169	6 630.2	58.0	6.5	1.0	9.4	0.2	19.5	5.3
06 58240	Porterville	18.6	58 978	634	3 170.9	77.5	0.8	0.5	2.8	0.3	14.4	3.7
06 58520	Poway	39.1	50 077	756	1 280.7	78.7	1.6	3.0	9.4	0.0	3.0	4.4
06 59444	Rancho Cordova	34.9	72 326	488	2 072.4	60.3	8.5	1.1	15.0	1.4	4.9	8.8
06 59451	Rancho Cucamonga	40.0	176 534	140	4 413.4	59.9	12.3	0.6	12.3	1.3	8.8	4.7
06 59514	Rancho Palos Verdes	13.5	42 435	891	3 143.3	53.5	3.8	0.0	27.1	3.0	5.8	6.9
06 59587	Rancho Santa Margarita	12.9	48 969	774	3 796.0	72.2	5.5	0.2	12.6	0.1	4.5	4.9
06 59920	Redding	59.6	91 808	346	1 540.4	84.2	1.7	2.9	5.0	0.0	1.6	4.5
06 59962	Redlands	36.0	71 288	496	1 980.2	72.7	8.0	0.7	7.4	0.4	5.2	5.6
06 60018	Redondo Beach	6.2	67 867	522	10 946.3	71.5	1.9	0.7	13.0	0.2	4.7	8.1
06 60102	Redwood City	19.3	84 950	390	4 401.6	56.9	1.8	0.2	14.8	1.3	21.3	3.8
06 60466	Rialto	22.3	103 314	295	4 632.9	70.9	10.1	0.7	3.2	0.0	12.6	2.5
06 60620	Richmond	30.1	109 813	269	3 648.3	29.5	22.1	0.2	16.6	0.2	25.9	5.5
06 60704	Ridgecrest	20.9	28 701	1 297	1 373.3	75.6	2.7	1.3	6.4	0.9	8.8	4.2
06 62000	Riverside	81.2	324 722	59	3 999.0	65.0	6.2	0.8	6.3	0.6	15.2	5.9
06 62364	Rocklin	19.5	62 787	582	3 219.8	81.7	1.8	0.8	9.3	0.0	1.6	4.9
06 62546	Rohnert Park	7.0	42 622	883	6 088.9	76.6	3.1	0.0	4.7	0.0	8.6	7.0
06 62896	Rosemead	5.2	54 500	694	10 480.8	13.1	0.2	0.2	63.7	0.0	21.7	1.1
06 62938	Roseville	43.0	132 671	203	3 085.4	74.5	2.3	0.5	11.0	0.4	5.3	6.0
06 64000	Sacramento	97.9	495 234	35	5 058.6	49.7	13.1	0.5	18.3	1.1	10.0	7.0
06 64224	Salinas	23.6	157 218	162	6 661.8	58.2	0.9	1.1	5.7	0.1	30.8	3.3
06 65000	San Bernardino	61.5	216 239	100	3 516.1	53.5	14.3	0.9	5.1	0.5	21.2	4.5
06 65028	San Bruno	5.5	42 957	874	7 810.4	45.9	1.7	0.1	30.3	4.2	7.4	10.5
06 65042	San Buenaventura (Ventura)	21.8	109 592	270	5 027.2	83.5	0.5	0.8	3.8	0.4	6.4	4.6
06 65070	San Carlos	5.5	29 797	1 258	5 417.6	73.3	0.4	0.1	15.7	0.0	3.9	6.7
06 65084	San Clemente	18.4	65 309	551	3 549.4	85.8	0.1	0.0	3.6	0.0	5.7	4.7
06 66000	San Diego	325.2	1 406 630	8	4 325.4	63.9	6.8	0.3	16.1	0.5	7.4	5.1
06 66070	San Dimas	15.0	34 338	1 107	2 289.2	72.8	2.8	1.2	11.4	0.1	8.9	2.8

1. Dry land or land partially or temporarily covered by water.   2. Hispanic or Latino persons may be of any race.

Table D. Cities — Population

| City | Percent Hispanic or Latino[1], 2015 | Percent foreign born 2015 | Age of population (percent), 2010-2014 | | | | | | | Median age 2015 | Percent female 2015 | Population Census counts | | Percent change | |
			Under 18 years	18 to 24 years	25 to 34 years	35 to 44 years	45 to 54 years	55 to 64 years	65 years and over			2000	2010	2000–2010	2010–2016
	12	13	14	15	16	17	18	19	20	21	22	23	24	25	26
CALIFORNIA—Cont'd															
Menlo Park	16.6	28.9	24.9	7.1	12.6	15.1	16.9	9.6	13.9	37.8	49.8	30 785	32 032	4.1	5.8
Merced	53.0	19.8	31.0	12.6	14.9	11.2	11.3	8.1	10.8	29.7	51.4	63 893	78 957	23.6	4.6
Milpitas	15.2	50.8	22.2	8.6	15.1	16.5	15.2	9.6	12.7	36.8	48.3	62 698	66 815	6.6	16.0
Mission Viejo	19.5	17.8	18.4	9.8	10.9	11.0	18.2	12.8	18.9	44.9	49.7	93 102	93 112	0.0	3.5
Modesto	40.3	18.8	25.9	10.6	13.3	12.2	12.4	12.2	13.4	35.2	50.4	188 856	203 119	7.6	4.5
Monrovia	40.8	26.2	20.9	9.3	14.8	15.3	16.4	10.7	12.6	39.5	49.0	36 929	36 590	-0.9	1.5
Montclair	73.1	35.2	26.3	10.4	17.3	13.7	13.1	9.7	9.6	31.4	50.9	33 049	36 664	10.9	6.2
Montebello	78.0	38.8	20.3	12.5	18.2	13.6	13.0	10.8	11.7	34.2	50.3	62 150	62 490	0.5	1.4
Monterey	20.5	23.0	15.2	9.8	17.7	16.2	12.5	11.2	17.3	38.1	47.4	29 674	27 492	-7.4	3.5
Monterey Park	28.1	55.7	17.2	7.5	11.7	14.5	11.6	16.2	21.3	44.1	52.5	60 051	60 256	0.3	1.4
Moorpark	25.9	16.7	18.3	10.0	15.5	10.7	15.8	18.2	11.5	41.3	53.1	31 415	34 421	9.6	6.0
Moreno Valley	59.1	26.7	28.3	12.5	15.2	13.7	12.4	9.6	8.4	30.7	51.7	142 381	193 365	35.8	6.3
Morgan Hill	34.4	17.6	27.4	7.5	8.9	12.2	16.6	14.4	13.0	40.4	51.8	33 556	37 878	12.9	16.6
Mountain View	20.4	39.6	22.3	8.1	22.9	15.5	12.9	9.9	8.4	33.5	47.2	70 708	74 020	4.7	8.7
Murrieta	30.0	18.1	27.7	10.5	11.5	12.4	16.0	10.3	11.6	35.3	55.0	44 282	103 428	133.6	8.0
Napa	41.3	22.9	23.9	8.6	13.0	14.5	12.9	12.7	14.5	37.2	50.5	72 585	77 117	6.2	4.3
National City	61.0	44.6	20.5	14.0	14.1	10.8	14.3	13.9	12.4	36.3	48.6	54 260	58 560	7.9	4.4
Newark	39.2	36.8	22.4	8.4	13.0	16.4	12.5	12.3	14.8	39.1	47.5	42 471	42 573	0.2	7.6
Newport Beach	9.3	17.6	18.1	6.5	11.5	10.3	16.9	13.7	23.0	46.8	50.5	70 032	85 219	21.7	1.7
Norco	31.1	13.5	19.9	7.8	17.0	11.7	18.6	10.5	14.5	39.7	47.7	24 157	27 063	12.0	-1.3
Norwalk	71.0	36.8	23.0	12.6	14.3	13.6	13.3	13.2	9.9	35.0	50.4	103 298	105 549	2.2	0.6
Novato	16.9	17.5	17.5	9.1	9.6	10.3	15.0	18.4	20.1	47.6	53.2	47 630	51 904	9.0	7.9
Oakland	27.2	27.2	20.3	8.6	19.6	15.7	13.1	11.1	11.7	35.7	51.4	399 484	390 905	-2.1	7.4
Oakley	31.1	14.8	30.5	9.8	11.4	17.3	12.1	9.4	9.5	33.0	51.7	25 619	35 432	38.3	14.6
Oceanside	35.3	21.3	21.1	9.2	14.1	13.2	12.6	14.4	15.4	39.4	50.2	161 029	166 992	3.7	5.1
Ontario	69.1	28.4	29.1	10.9	15.3	15.8	12.3	9.1	7.4	31.0	50.3	158 007	163 921	3.7	5.7
Orange	32.8	24.5	20.6	12.9	16.5	12.1	13.9	11.9	12.0	35.0	52.2	128 821	136 432	5.9	3.0
Oxnard	74.7	38.0	28.8	11.1	16.1	13.1	12.8	8.8	9.4	31.0	50.8	170 358	197 966	16.2	5.0
Pacifica	18.5	24.1	17.6	8.6	15.2	11.6	15.0	15.8	16.1	43.0	49.7	38 390	37 295	-2.9	4.7
Palmdale	55.2	26.5	29.5	10.1	12.9	11.9	13.6	12.5	9.6	32.6	51.8	116 670	152 746	30.9	3.0
Palm Desert	25.7	22.5	15.2	6.1	9.7	9.3	7.8	14.6	37.2	56.7	51.0	41 155	48 448	17.7	7.8
Palm Springs	25.9	19.5	14.1	5.3	9.7	9.2	13.7	18.7	29.3	54.0	42.5	42 807	44 538	4.0	7.1
Palo Alto	5.2	34.9	23.7	6.2	10.8	16.7	14.7	10.3	17.6	40.2	53.0	58 598	64 409	9.9	4.1
Paradise	6.1	1.2	19.7	7.4	11.6	8.8	12.5	17.1	23.0	47.5	55.9	26 408	26 217	-0.7	1.3
Paramount	80.4	43.3	27.4	11.3	12.1	15.2	13.9	11.2	9.0	34.1	49.9	55 266	54 098	-2.1	1.5
Pasadena	37.1	28.7	19.5	8.4	17.0	15.4	13.0	11.3	15.4	37.6	52.4	133 936	137 124	2.4	3.6
Perris	72.6	31.1	33.9	13.5	14.0	14.1	13.0	6.1	5.4	26.9	44.5	36 189	68 548	89.4	11.4
Petaluma	18.3	17.4	20.9	9.2	10.5	13.6	14.6	14.7	16.4	41.9	52.1	54 548	57 941	6.2	4.5
Pico Rivera	91.2	33.2	24.2	8.2	13.9	13.1	12.7	13.2	14.6	37.0	51.5	63 428	62 948	-0.8	1.1
Pittsburg	41.2	30.3	24.4	11.3	15.5	13.4	15.1	11.4	8.9	34.5	52.0	56 769	63 259	11.4	11.7
Placentia	40.5	24.0	24.0	10.5	14.9	13.2	12.6	11.3	13.5	36.1	51.7	46 488	50 893	9.5	2.6
Pleasant Hill	16.9	16.6	21.0	9.2	15.2	14.8	12.9	12.7	14.3	38.1	51.7	32 837	33 114	0.8	5.3
Pleasanton	10.0	29.2	26.8	6.5	8.4	13.9	19.5	11.9	13.0	41.3	53.9	63 654	70 273	10.4	17.1
Pomona	71.0	35.2	25.3	13.2	15.1	14.0	12.4	9.6	10.4	32.1	51.1	149 473	149 030	-0.3	2.3
Porterville	67.3	17.7	36.2	9.1	14.3	12.5	9.4	8.3	10.2	28.9	50.2	39 615	57 287	44.6	3.0
Poway	24.8	27.2	24.6	7.0	11.5	10.4	14.6	14.9	17.1	41.3	52.1	48 044	47 806	-0.5	4.8
Rancho Cordova	19.7	24.0	24.3	8.2	19.6	13.0	13.7	9.8	11.5	33.8	50.9	55 060	64 805	17.7	11.6
Rancho Cucamonga	37.6	19.3	25.1	11.9	13.7	12.9	14.4	12.6	9.5	34.5	49.7	127 743	165 353	29.4	6.8
Rancho Palos Verdes	13.5	26.9	22.6	4.1	7.5	10.6	15.9	15.4	23.9	49.3	52.8	41 145	41 657	1.2	1.9
Rancho Santa Margarita	13.5	16.8	27.2	7.4	10.5	14.5	19.6	14.8	6.0	39.1	53.5	47 214	47 855	1.4	2.3
Redding	10.0	5.7	21.0	10.3	14.2	9.6	12.8	12.3	19.8	38.8	53.6	80 865	89 861	11.1	2.2
Redlands	27.7	12.2	23.0	11.4	14.2	11.5	11.6	13.5	14.8	36.2	52.1	63 591	68 667	8.0	3.8
Redondo Beach	13.0	19.9	18.5	4.4	15.3	15.5	19.1	14.7	12.4	43.0	48.9	63 261	66 748	5.5	1.7
Redwood City	34.0	32.4	22.5	7.2	16.4	14.6	14.6	11.9	12.8	37.1	50.0	75 402	76 802	1.9	10.6
Rialto	76.2	31.7	26.1	12.1	17.1	13.8	12.7	9.6	8.5	31.6	51.6	91 873	99 150	7.9	4.2
Richmond	41.1	38.5	21.5	9.5	18.4	13.7	12.9	11.2	12.6	35.3	52.0	99 216	103 645	4.5	6.0
Ridgecrest	21.9	11.5	29.6	6.4	14.0	15.1	13.7	10.8	10.4	35.0	48.6	24 927	27 616	10.8	3.9
Riverside	49.8	21.6	24.0	14.5	17.1	12.5	12.0	9.7	10.2	31.4	50.2	255 166	303 990	19.1	6.8
Rocklin	10.2	12.3	23.9	10.0	10.6	14.1	15.9	12.0	13.5	39.9	51.9	36 330	57 019	56.9	10.1
Rohnert Park	26.1	15.7	20.6	13.3	13.8	13.6	11.7	13.0	14.1	37.1	54.0	42 236	40 818	-3.4	4.4
Rosemead	31.3	56.1	20.2	8.8	12.3	13.4	17.6	12.3	15.4	42.6	51.5	53 505	53 771	0.5	1.4
Roseville	18.0	13.9	23.0	9.4	12.4	14.4	13.8	11.3	15.6	38.4	52.0	79 921	118 660	48.5	11.8
Sacramento	30.6	22.9	24.6	9.5	18.1	13.2	11.4	10.6	12.7	33.7	51.6	407 018	466 488	14.6	6.2
Salinas	77.0	37.3	31.2	10.3	16.3	12.0	10.9	10.4	8.8	30.4	50.6	151 060	150 498	-0.4	4.5
San Bernardino	63.0	25.5	30.7	13.2	14.8	12.0	11.6	9.4	8.4	28.5	49.7	185 401	209 961	13.2	3.0
San Bruno	26.3	35.1	17.4	8.1	15.7	14.4	15.7	14.3	14.5	39.8	52.1	40 165	41 053	2.2	4.6
San Buenaventura (Ventura)	35.1	16.4	21.7	8.1	15.8	11.9	13.2	13.9	15.4	37.7	50.8	100 916	107 231	6.3	2.2
San Carlos	9.4	21.9	20.6	5.5	8.9	15.6	15.0	15.8	18.6	44.7	52.5	27 718	28 406	2.5	4.9
San Clemente	15.9	12.4	18.6	9.4	9.8	11.9	12.6	13.8	19.1	45.2	48.0	49 936	63 482	27.1	2.9
San Diego	30.5	26.8	20.4	11.8	18.8	13.6	12.5	11.1	11.8	34.5	50.3	1 223 400	1 301 722	6.4	8.1
San Dimas	33.6	18.5	18.6	7.3	8.0	11.8	14.8	14.1	25.4	48.7	56.0	34 980	33 375	-4.6	2.9

1. May be of any race.

Table D. Cities — Households, Group Quarters, Crime, and Education

City	Households, 2015 Number (27)	Persons per household (28)	Percent Female family householder[1] (29)	Percent One-person (30)	Persons in group quarters, 2010 Total (31)	Institutional Total (32)	Institutional Persons in nursing facilities (33)	Non-institutional (34)	Serious crimes known to police,[2] 2014 Total Number (35)	Total Rate[3] (36)	Rate[3] Violent (37)	Rate[3] Property (38)	Population age 25 and older (39)	Attainment[4] (percent) High school graduate or less (40)	Attainment[4] (percent) Bachelor's degree or more (41)
CALIFORNIA—Cont'd															
Menlo Park	11 124	2.91	5.8	25.2	845	246	236	599	617	1 852	156	1 696	22 767	18.6	65.2
Merced	25 848	3.15	24.0	23.4	1 080	588	343	492	3 202	3 924	699	3 225	46 493	50.1	19.5
Milpitas	22 756	3.32	10.0	12.6	2 698	2 594	34	104	2 243	3 178	159	3 020	53 705	27.3	47.1
Mission Viejo	33 575	2.85	7.7	19.2	942	83	66	859	935	963	73	890	69 766	20.8	45.5
Modesto	70 114	2.97	15.6	24.2	2 955	1 766	1 169	1 189	10 891	5 292	864	4 428	134 303	45.9	18.3
Monrovia	12 729	2.92	14.6	25.2	156	95	76	61	765	2 055	126	1 929	26 158	29.5	33.2
Montclair	9 954	3.86	16.7	12.5	396	181	181	215	1 716	4 475	548	3 927	24 525	60.3	16.0
Montebello	19 610	3.23	16.9	24.0	400	361	350	39	1 583	2 484	210	2 273	42 966	55.7	19.5
Monterey	11 337	2.27	2.9	35.8	2 503	293	293	2 210	1 137	3 988	403	3 584	21 243	22.8	48.9
Monterey Park	20 246	3.02	12.7	19.6	230	189	186	41	1 130	1 844	148	1 695	46 237	43.8	31.6
Moorpark	12 094	2.99	10.4	14.8	0	0	0	0	316	895	110	785	25 925	22.0	42.1
Moreno Valley	52 091	3.90	18.5	12.1	554	83	27	471	6 994	3 447	288	3 159	120 971	54.9	15.0
Morgan Hill	14 418	2.95	10.2	18.7	386	222	144	164	677	1 628	156	1 472	27 984	20.7	46.4
Mountain View	32 514	2.46	8.6	30.3	265	120	107	145	1 764	2 240	198	2 042	55 960	18.6	65.9
Murrieta	33 068	3.30	15.9	17.4	429	138	56	291	1 526	1 408	63	1 345	67 869	32.6	28.8
Napa	27 905	2.84	10.1	26.0	1 237	669	343	568	1 564	1 966	313	1 653	54 331	36.0	30.1
National City	16 214	3.58	21.7	22.2	5 752	411	411	5 341	1 856	3 087	444	2 643	40 011	56.4	11.5
Newark	13 608	3.32	9.3	12.0	145	0	0	145	1 080	2 429	245	2 184	31 344	45.9	29.9
Newport Beach	36 146	2.40	7.0	29.6	402	251	221	151	1 989	2 266	124	2 142	65 667	10.3	64.1
Norco	6 676	3.54	6.0	25.3	4 397	4 322	0	75	688	2 554	171	2 384	19 003	46.8	15.1
Norwalk	27 139	3.88	19.4	13.3	1 615	1 300	474	315	2 317	2 169	296	1 873	68 995	51.9	17.1
Novato	24 155	2.27	8.4	32.4	626	177	175	449	850	1 552	146	1 406	40 740	20.5	50.1
Oakland	161 104	2.56	14.1	31.7	8 138	2 463	1 349	5 675	31 277	7 629	1 685	5 943	298 374	36.0	40.0
Oakley	11 442	3.47	11.2	15.0	103	28	6	75	514	1 323	116	1 207	23 790	33.4	18.0
Oceanside	64 200	2.72	9.9	27.6	936	134	91	802	4 636	2 663	374	2 288	122 453	34.5	28.4
Ontario	48 463	3.52	19.1	18.3	758	347	347	411	5 085	3 022	256	2 766	102 597	55.5	15.6
Orange	42 686	3.14	11.4	18.7	6 253	3 666	299	2 587	2 383	1 693	101	1 592	93 760	32.5	36.0
Oxnard	50 396	4.08	21.5	14.4	1 434	502	465	932	7 266	3 559	433	3 126	124 686	55.6	16.7
Pacifica	13 939	2.80	11.0	23.5	182	118	115	64	729	1 873	234	1 639	28 957	22.4	42.5
Palmdale	44 629	3.54	20.1	16.8	199	41	0	158	4 059	2 566	531	2 035	95 674	51.3	13.3
Palm Desert	23 788	2.17	8.9	33.6	308	210	210	98	2 318	4 548	275	4 273	40 815	30.2	35.4
Palm Springs	23 801	1.97	5.8	48.7	539	196	190	343	3 017	6 465	632	5 833	38 204	30.0	34.7
Palo Alto	26 030	2.55	9.0	26.4	583	378	323	205	1 358	2 022	88	1 934	46 870	6.7	79.9
Paradise	10 108	2.57	12.7	26.9	408	269	246	139	568	2 159	198	1 962	19 294	28.8	20.4
Paramount	14 828	3.72	14.2	15.8	310	283	283	27	1 647	2 984	433	2 551	33 956	61.5	11.9
Pasadena	52 636	2.63	11.5	30.1	3 493	1 021	890	2 472	3 863	2 752	281	2 471	102 463	26.8	49.5
Perris	15 614	4.78	21.8	9.8	240	100	71	140	2 085	2 847	246	2 602	39 425	65.2	6.9
Petaluma	23 239	2.57	11.3	27.4	724	363	363	361	1 274	2 130	334	1 796	42 222	25.0	35.4
Pico Rivera	18 381	3.47	17.8	24.6	454	415	415	39	1 635	2 556	430	2 126	43 373	63.0	9.9
Pittsburg	21 934	3.15	19.7	17.4	291	138	123	153	2 537	3 758	259	3 499	44 654	44.7	20.0
Placentia	16 475	3.16	14.3	21.1	337	84	73	253	814	1 550	156	1 394	34 405	32.3	32.2
Pleasant Hill	13 575	2.53	9.8	25.3	463	312	291	151	1 798	5 232	175	5 058	24 305	11.7	57.0
Pleasanton	27 610	2.87	8.3	18.6	456	136	129	320	1 305	1 739	81	1 657	53 012	16.7	61.9
Pomona	40 843	3.63	21.2	16.4	4 138	1 356	1 166	2 782	5 180	3 410	512	2 899	94 234	54.2	19.7
Porterville	15 538	3.53	18.6	17.6	1 147	940	931	207	1 362	2 459	285	2 174	30 663	59.1	11.1
Poway	14 844	3.34	8.8	8.9	550	266	260	284	506	1 016	141	876	34 355	28.9	41.9
Rancho Cordova	24 656	2.86	17.8	24.3	325	155	143	170	1 949	2 840	444	2 395	47 979	33.7	27.0
Rancho Cucamonga	54 106	3.18	14.3	18.5	3 124	2 988	73	136	3 951	2 288	164	2 124	110 449	29.0	31.4
Rancho Palos Verdes	15 586	2.71	5.8	23.9	340	27	27	313	496	1 163	56	1 107	31 346	14.2	63.0
Rancho Santa Margarita	17 672	2.79	9.4	18.0	2	0	0	2	230	464	54	410	32 286	15.9	55.9
Redding	36 937	2.42	12.4	31.8	2 020	882	543	1 138	4 534	4 959	667	4 292	62 932	28.7	28.1
Redlands	24 203	2.82	16.6	22.2	2 368	512	485	1 856	2 984	4 245	209	4 036	46 634	29.8	37.3
Redondo Beach	29 119	2.34	8.9	31.1	431	64	64	367	1 605	2 358	232	2 126	52 565	13.5	60.4
Redwood City	31 716	2.64	9.1	26.4	1 547	1 139	53	408	1 922	2 348	237	2 111	60 009	32.1	46.4
Rialto	26 750	3.83	17.9	13.7	447	193	153	254	2 482	2 421	320	2 101	63 642	64.9	9.4
Richmond	37 778	2.87	21.3	27.4	1 583	913	172	670	5 124	4 724	777	3 947	75 709	43.0	26.0
Ridgecrest	11 333	2.52	12.1	35.6	196	87	87	109	588	2 040	409	1 630	18 408	37.4	24.0
Riverside	92 408	3.34	15.2	21.6	11 549	2 624	1 153	8 925	11 248	3 521	433	3 088	198 255	45.9	22.2
Rocklin	21 246	2.84	10.9	23.0	637	181	176	456	1 089	1 804	83	1 721	40 473	20.9	43.7
Rohnert Park	16 755	2.53	16.6	26.5	397	6	6	391	895	2 155	385	1 770	28 011	32.0	27.7
Rosemead	14 580	3.73	17.8	11.1	413	278	208	135	1 333	2 435	269	2 166	38 995	59.7	18.3
Roseville	47 520	2.72	10.8	26.2	847	369	361	478	3 263	2 530	150	2 380	88 068	25.1	37.2
Sacramento	177 131	2.73	15.1	31.3	8 314	4 046	1 367	4 268	18 046	3 738	615	3 123	323 209	38.5	30.3
Salinas	41 925	3.72	20.7	18.3	2 465	1 807	531	658	6 224	3 967	635	3 331	92 015	62.8	13.1
San Bernardino	57 585	3.55	25.6	20.7	7 325	4 247	878	3 078	11 367	5 297	992	4 305	121 274	59.7	12.2
San Bruno	16 368	2.61	12.7	24.3	398	82	72	316	1 164	2 720	257	2 463	32 168	27.1	37.1
San Buenaventura (Ventura)	40 166	2.68	13.3	29.7	2 493	1 738	293	755	4 143	3 792	253	3 540	77 005	33.9	31.4
San Carlos	11 906	2.50	8.5	25.7	91	12	12	79	NA	NA	NA	NA	22 102	13.5	65.8
San Clemente	24 662	2.64	5.1	21.1	273	28	0	245	756	1 156	106	1 051	47 216	16.6	52.1
San Diego	497 663	2.73	10.7	28.7	51 956	7 050	2 902	44 906	32 026	2 340	381	1 959	945 996	28.7	44.3
San Dimas	12 838	2.63	13.6	31.0	540	220	128	320	700	2 062	203	1 858	25 670	29.0	36.0

1. No spouse present.   2. Data for serious crimes have not been adjusted for underreporting. This may affect comparability between geographic areas and over time.   3. Per 100,000 population estimated by the FBI.   4. Persons 25 years old and over.

Table D. Cities — Income, Poverty, and Housing

City	Money income, 2015					Housing units, 2010			Occupied housing units 2015				
	Households			Families						Owner-occupied		Renter-occupied	
	Median income	Percent with income of $200,000 or more	Percent with income of less than $25,000	Total Families	Percent with income below poverty	Total	Percent change, 2000–2010	Vacant units for sale or rent[2]	Total	Percent	Median value[3] (dollars)	Percent	Median rent (dollars)
	42	43	44	45	46	47	48	49	50	51	52	53	54
CALIFORNIA—Cont'd													
Menlo Park	134 846	35.3	10.3	7 215	6.4	13 085	2.7	738	11 124	54.1	2	45.9	2 023
Merced	34 321	2.4	30.3	18 284	29.9	27 446	27.4	2 547	25 848	40.3	204 400	59.7	873
Milpitas	102 200	16.9	8.5	18 787	4.5	19 806	14.0	622	22 756	63.0	712 000	37.0	2 013
Mission Viejo	106 104	18.6	7.6	25 434	2.8	34 228	4.0	1 020	33 575	76.8	648 600	23.2	1 916
Modesto	51 901	3.9	15.7	48 320	16.5	75 044	11.5	5 937	70 114	54.1	234 900	45.9	1 026
Monrovia	68 906	7.7	9.1	8 470	6.1	14 473	3.9	711	12 729	45.1	604 600	54.9	1 316
Montclair	55 493	1.2	6.0	8 061	9.3	9 911	8.0	388	9 954	56.4	302 700	43.6	1 325
Montebello	48 747	2.9	18.4	13 980	10.7	19 768	1.8	756	19 610	40.6	458 100	59.4	1 167
Monterey	73 523	11.0	9.8	NA	NA	13 584	1.2	1 400	11 337	35.1	754 700	64.9	1 584
Monterey Park	48 957	6.6	20.8	15 694	13.7	20 850	3.3	887	20 246	52.2	555 100	47.8	1 187
Moorpark	96 757	16.7	4.7	9 406	3.9	10 738	18.1	254	12 094	76.3	581 200	23.7	1 900
Moreno Valley	56 025	2.4	12.2	43 577	13.4	55 559	34.0	3 967	52 091	63.5	260 900	36.5	1 261
Morgan Hill	100 784	23.6	7.8	11 496	5.7	12 859	15.7	533	14 418	75.5	721 800	24.5	1 653
Mountain View	120 102	25.4	6.0	18 313	1.7	33 881	4.5	1 924	32 514	40.6	1 149 900	59.4	2 103
Murrieta	74 594	6.0	10.3	26 166	9.1	35 294	136.5	2 545	33 068	62.0	372 300	38.0	1 590
Napa	74 315	7.9	9.0	18 510	7.4	30 149	8.6	1 983	27 905	54.2	543 500	45.8	1 533
National City	44 694	2.9	23.2	11 694	19.5	16 762	8.0	1 260	16 214	32.5	345 400	67.5	980
Newark	86 410	8.1	5.9	11 019	5.0	13 414	2.0	442	13 608	68.7	610 100	31.3	1 847
Newport Beach	123 351	31.2	8.2	22 177	5.1	44 193	18.4	5 442	36 146	57.1	1 709 300	42.9	2 148
Norco	78 060	11.7	8.3	4 804	5.3	7 322	17.7	299	6 676	84.5	493 800	15.5	1 053
Norwalk	58 957	1.5	8.9	22 437	9.2	28 083	1.9	953	27 139	56.7	386 600	43.3	1 434
Novato	79 531	11.0	9.7	14 550	5.9	21 158	11.5	879	24 155	66.2	656 700	33.8	1 896
Oakland	58 807	9.5	18.2	90 804	15.6	169 710	7.7	15 919	161 104	38.9	557 000	61.1	1 240
Oakley	84 743	6.6	11.7	9 489	6.2	11 484	44.0	757	11 442	79.2	376 400	20.8	1 130
Oceanside	60 720	5.3	14.9	41 893	10.3	64 435	8.3	5 197	64 200	57.2	421 000	42.8	1 505
Ontario	57 361	1.3	15.8	36 962	14.9	47 449	5.2	2 518	48 463	49.4	335 700	50.6	1 319
Orange	83 429	10.7	9.6	30 608	7.7	45 111	8.0	1 744	42 686	56.7	614 500	43.3	1 624
Oxnard	59 830	4.0	11.5	40 430	14.7	52 772	16.8	2 975	50 396	50.5	408 400	49.5	1 405
Pacifica	102 399	12.6	4.7	9 314	2.0	14 523	1.9	556	13 939	72.0	754 300	28.0	2 081
Palmdale	52 014	2.9	20.2	35 496	15.2	46 544	25.3	3 592	44 629	65.6	235 000	34.4	1 172
Palm Desert	58 468	7.8	16.0	13 558	6.4	37 073	32.1	13 956	23 788	59.7	337 300	40.3	1 175
Palm Springs	43 390	5.4	20.8	9 594	15.0	34 794	12.3	12 048	23 801	55.5	368 600	44.5	928
Palo Alto	147 737	35.4	8.9	17 294	5.2	28 216	7.9	1 723	26 030	54.0	2	46.0	2 337
Paradise	55 232	2.7	13.6	6 760	5.1	12 981	5.4	1 088	10 108	67.2	219 700	32.8	1 014
Paramount	52 448	2.5	17.4	12 039	14.9	14 571	-0.4	690	14 828	47.4	304 700	52.6	1 211
Pasadena	77 312	13.8	15.4	31 493	10.9	59 551	10.0	4 281	52 636	43.4	693 300	56.6	1 484
Perris	55 074	4.1	11.8	13 715	20.5	17 906	70.5	1 541	15 614	59.6	229 500	40.4	1 255
Petaluma	71 607	8.0	11.5	15 132	4.2	22 736	11.8	999	23 239	64.7	556 300	35.3	1 571
Pico Rivera	50 217	1.6	16.4	13 472	10.1	17 109	1.8	543	18 381	62.0	372 100	38.0	1 189
Pittsburg	61 878	5.5	18.4	16 101	15.9	21 126	14.9	1 599	21 934	53.5	327 500	46.5	1 495
Placentia	80 107	8.2	7.7	11 972	7.4	16 872	9.4	507	16 475	65.4	597 900	34.6	1 511
Pleasant Hill	100 021	13.2	14.3	NA	NA	14 321	2.0	613	13 575	67.3	626 500	32.7	1 491
Pleasanton	134 801	28.4	6.2	21 512	2.4	26 053	8.6	808	27 610	69.0	869 900	31.0	2 095
Pomona	51 266	2.7	15.3	31 319	14.7	40 685	2.7	2 208	40 843	51.8	348 400	48.2	1 204
Porterville	34 712	0.8	29.0	12 102	29.5	16 734	31.4	1 090	15 538	47.6	176 300	52.4	852
Poway	95 455	16.1	11.3	12 508	4.7	16 715	5.6	587	14 844	70.8	625 200	29.2	1 463
Rancho Cordova	59 552	2.3	14.8	17 164	12.0	25 479	18.5	2 031	24 656	52.6	239 500	47.4	994
Rancho Cucamonga	80 720	6.5	11.1	41 741	7.3	56 618	34.1	2 235	54 106	57.3	466 400	42.7	1 684
Rancho Palos Verdes	115 532	22.8	6.5	11 417	1.6	16 179	3.3	618	15 586	80.0	1 035 900	20.0	1 988
Rancho Santa Margarita	116 156	19.8	9.0	13 481	5.4	17 260	3.7	595	17 672	71.5	640 500	28.5	1 668
Redding	45 490	2.4	22.9	22 351	12.6	38 679	14.5	2 549	36 937	52.2	253 100	47.8	947
Redlands	66 148	8.5	12.9	16 856	11.3	26 634	7.1	1 870	24 203	57.2	344 000	42.8	1 277
Redondo Beach	101 592	17.4	6.5	17 257	2.1	30 609	3.6	1 598	29 119	49.7	802 800	50.3	1 820
Redwood City	97 750	20.6	8.7	20 738	6.0	29 167	0.8	1 210	31 716	53.6	1 053 600	46.4	1 821
Rialto	52 080	0.9	16.1	22 301	14.7	27 203	5.4	2 001	26 750	61.3	280 800	38.7	1 126
Richmond	56 374	4.7	17.1	24 671	15.0	39 328	8.8	3 235	37 778	45.8	376 700	54.2	1 301
Ridgecrest	56 003	2.4	15.2	6 547	12.8	11 915	4.8	1 134	11 333	60.7	169 300	39.3	882
Riverside	61 279	4.5	13.7	66 514	10.5	98 444	14.4	6 512	92 408	54.2	317 600	45.8	1 174
Rocklin	87 450	10.8	11.7	15 185	6.0	22 010	52.4	1 210	21 246	66.2	416 100	33.8	1 379
Rohnert Park	61 680	2.0	12.8	10 399	7.0	16 551	4.6	743	16 755	55.7	377 100	44.3	1 405
Rosemead	46 837	4.3	15.5	12 418	12.5	14 805	3.4	558	14 580	47.3	513 400	52.7	1 234
Roseville	72 312	7.9	9.8	32 013	6.9	47 757	49.3	2 698	47 520	64.3	380 900	35.7	1 362
Sacramento	52 151	4.2	19.4	106 571	16.4	190 911	16.5	16 287	177 131	45.7	287 300	54.3	1 085
Salinas	52 334	2.5	15.6	32 617	18.6	42 651	7.7	2 264	41 925	41.8	340 600	58.2	1 207
San Bernardino	35 932	0.9	28.9	42 169	29.6	65 401	3.1	6 118	57 585	45.1	201 300	54.9	924
San Bruno	88 493	10.2	4.8	NA	NA	15 356	2.7	655	16 368	55.6	723 500	44.4	1 877
San Buenaventura (Ventura)	70 627	5.7	10.8	26 186	5.9	42 827	7.5	2 389	40 166	54.8	480 600	45.2	1 413
San Carlos	142 079	35.3	9.1	NA	NA	12 018	3.6	494	11 906	73.0	1 291 700	27.0	1 846
San Clemente	100 187	24.8	9.4	17 973	2.0	25 966	25.7	2 060	24 662	66.5	880 900	33.5	1 838
San Diego	67 871	9.1	14.1	294 386	10.5	516 033	9.9	32 941	497 663	45.3	526 900	54.7	1 444
San Dimas	69 668	8.4	11.9	8 468	3.4	12 506	-0.6	476	12 838	80.2	528 400	19.8	1 225

1. Based on population estimated by the American Community Survey. 2. Includes units rented or sold but not occupied. 3. Specified owner-occupied units; $1,000,000 represents $1,000,000 or more 4. 50.0 represents 50 percent or more. 5. 10.0 represents 10 percent or less.

Table D. Cities — Commuting, Computer Access, Migration, Labor Force, and Employment

City	Commuting Percent — Drove alone	Commuting Percent — With Commutes of 30 minutes or more[1]	Computer Access[2] Percent — With a Computer in the house	Computer Access[2] Percent — With Internet Access	Migration, 2015 — Percent who lived in the same house one year ago	Migration, 2015 — Percent who lived in an other state or county one year ago	Civilian labor force, 2016 — Total	Civilian labor force, 2016 — Percent change, 2015–2016	Unemployment — Total	Unemployment — Rate[3]	Population age 16 and older — Number	Population age 16 and older — Percent in Labor Force	Population age 16 to 64 — Number	Population age 16 to 64 — Percent who worked full-year full-time
	55	56	57	58	59	60	61	62	63	64	65	66	67	68
CALIFORNIA—Cont'd														
Menlo Park	72.9	41.2	96.2	88.5	79.8	14.5	18 991	2.6	449	2.4	25 730	67.9	21 095	48.3
Merced	71.0	21.7	89.6	85.1	79.9	8.3	34 689	0.7	3 430	9.9	59 098	51.7	50 166	29.4
Milpitas	82.9	42.5	94.9	91.0	86.1	5.6	40 839	1.7	1 442	3.5	61 902	62.7	52 022	51.5
Mission Viejo	89.8	42.6	94.6	92.2	86.1	4.3	50 349	0.9	1 889	3.8	81 752	65.8	63 377	50.0
Modesto	84.6	30.1	89.2	81.0	86.7	3.7	96 237	1.2	8 033	8.3	163 380	59.1	134 979	40.5
Monrovia	80.0	54.5	86.7	78.3	87.8	2.1	20 850	1.2	835	4.0	30 543	71.2	25 818	53.4
Montclair	76.0	44.2	82.7	67.4	84.9	11.4	18 623	1.7	898	4.8	30 001	60.9	26 273	47.0
Montebello	79.3	58.0	76.6	71.0	92.8	2.1	28 684	1.1	1 283	4.5	52 634	61.5	45 145	52.8
Monterey	59.2	11.5	89.1	86.1	77.0	17.1	15 588	0.9	842	5.4	24 205	67.3	19 315	58.7
Monterey Park	81.3	47.6	87.7	79.5	91.6	1.5	29 353	1.0	1 366	4.7	52 330	56.5	39 260	48.2
Moorpark	81.6	38.8	92.2	90.3	86.5	5.0	19 423	0.0	780	4.0	30 677	70.5	26 516	49.6
Moreno Valley	77.1	50.1	91.8	84.7	89.5	2.9	92 375	1.5	5 975	6.5	154 519	63.9	137 355	42.7
Morgan Hill	82.3	60.3	94.6	91.1	90.1	3.5	22 878	1.6	953	4.2	33 018	63.6	27 415	47.0
Mountain View	76.0	28.1	97.0	88.5	82.4	11.5	50 147	1.8	1 436	2.9	64 264	77.1	57 526	59.6
Murrieta	81.7	46.1	96.0	88.6	82.7	6.2	52 771	1.7	2 558	4.8	84 000	61.1	71 230	40.6
Napa	81.5	26.0	90.8	86.3	83.8	5.6	41 723	-0.7	1 883	4.5	63 073	69.0	51 431	51.8
National City	74.6	37.1	81.3	69.5	87.2	2.4	24 786	0.9	1 474	5.9	50 092	63.4	42 501	46.6
Newark	85.7	51.4	92.0	84.8	92.6	3.9	23 884	1.9	864	3.6	35 935	64.5	29 221	56.8
Newport Beach	89.4	27.5	94.8	91.4	90.0	3.8	45 577	0.9	1 507	3.3	74 168	59.2	54 122	50.8
Norco	77.8	65.5	91.6	86.5	81.7	13.6	11 362	1.7	550	4.8	21 591	51.5	17 774	40.0
Norwalk	87.1	45.6	90.9	76.1	92.8	1.2	50 504	0.8	2 711	5.4	84 506	63.5	73 888	51.5
Novato	75.8	47.2	90.6	86.0	86.4	6.5	29 661	1.1	945	3.2	46 834	62.1	35 677	48.0
Oakland	55.7	50.9	89.1	77.2	85.9	6.8	213 405	1.7	11 219	5.3	342 395	68.3	293 265	45.9
Oakley	85.4	62.4	94.1	86.5	92.5	2.1	19 171	1.5	1 061	5.5	29 450	64.0	25 667	44.8
Oceanside	83.8	40.4	92.7	85.4	82.0	5.3	82 283	1.0	3 956	4.8	144 195	63.2	117 095	47.8
Ontario	79.8	45.7	83.2	69.5	87.9	6.3	83 238	1.6	4 771	5.7	126 640	69.4	113 933	51.1
Orange	87.3	39.5	92.7	90.4	86.4	3.2	72 547	0.9	2 746	3.8	114 952	64.8	97 988	48.0
Oxnard	79.0	31.8	86.5	75.3	87.5	2.6	100 141	-0.2	5 648	5.6	153 468	66.8	133 947	45.3
Pacifica	72.8	55.7	94.6	89.3	92.0	3.4	24 229	2.5	671	2.8	33 341	66.1	27 017	49.0
Palmdale	79.1	50.7	88.5	77.8	88.7	1.3	64 071	0.3	4 526	7.1	116 380	58.0	101 246	40.5
Palm Desert	86.5	15.0	89.0	76.6	84.5	7.3	23 562	1.8	1 013	4.3	45 104	49.8	25 805	43.7
Palm Springs	86.5	24.0	89.3	80.4	82.6	7.4	22 134	1.7	1 097	5.0	41 270	52.0	27 369	38.9
Palo Alto	70.4	34.1	97.3	91.5	82.6	10.2	35 122	1.8	904	2.6	53 183	60.8	41 389	51.7
Paradise	85.3	39.4	88.8	80.5	84.2	3.3	11 240	1.1	638	5.7	22 385	52.1	16 304	41.7
Paramount	79.4	43.0	84.2	73.0	88.0	1.7	24 806	0.6	1 528	6.2	41 877	66.2	36 907	49.3
Pasadena	74.0	43.5	90.9	80.9	87.3	4.7	78 128	1.0	3 635	4.7	116 332	68.3	94 492	53.2
Perris	72.6	51.4	91.3	85.9	86.9	4.8	29 813	1.3	2 634	8.8	51 821	63.6	47 777	44.7
Petaluma	78.2	40.7	95.1	91.3	87.4	4.5	33 055	0.9	1 008	3.0	49 738	67.4	39 796	42.9
Pico Rivera	82.6	55.6	81.2	65.0	94.0	1.0	30 198	1.0	1 456	4.8	50 931	61.5	41 549	48.4
Pittsburg	69.4	62.6	94.1	88.8	84.9	4.7	33 444	1.5	1 776	5.3	54 123	65.4	47 940	43.9
Placentia	84.5	48.2	92.7	89.8	88.1	3.0	26 250	0.8	1 190	4.5	41 850	67.8	34 747	51.3
Pleasant Hill	75.3	53.5	NA	NA	88.8	5.7	18 208	1.7	671	3.7	28 274	65.0	23 308	49.9
Pleasanton	73.5	55.5	97.0	93.4	84.8	8.4	39 912	1.9	1 308	3.3	60 985	66.0	50 679	52.5
Pomona	81.2	48.9	88.4	76.0	85.9	4.5	67 433	0.7	3 959	5.9	118 860	61.9	102 906	42.1
Porterville	75.4	38.7	81.3	66.2	85.2	1.3	24 033	0.9	2 739	11.4	37 750	52.7	32 016	31.3
Poway	84.4	44.0	94.5	91.7	89.0	3.3	25 636	1.2	770	3.0	39 337	60.5	30 767	47.0
Rancho Cordova	80.9	40.9	92.7	82.7	83.3	7.2	34 028	1.6	2 016	5.9	55 001	69.9	46 811	49.4
Rancho Cucamonga	87.2	46.6	95.5	89.8	83.3	6.8	93 502	1.8	3 953	4.2	135 990	66.6	119 364	45.3
Rancho Palos Verdes	86.7	50.4	97.1	93.5	86.7	6.4	19 286	1.6	483	2.5	34 946	52.9	24 711	48.4
Rancho Santa Margarita	91.4	54.4	94.3	91.2	85.6	4.0	27 766	1.1	645	2.3	37 502	76.8	34 561	57.7
Redding	86.8	5.3	83.1	72.6	81.9	8.2	39 888	0.6	2 531	6.3	74 844	56.3	56 721	43.9
Redlands	85.6	30.8	87.9	81.0	86.9	5.5	34 437	1.9	1 131	3.3	56 380	58.2	45 833	43.4
Redondo Beach	86.1	42.8	97.2	91.9	83.9	5.2	40 580	1.4	1 300	3.2	56 565	74.5	48 110	59.4
Redwood City	78.8	41.7	92.3	86.9	86.9	6.4	49 960	2.5	1 365	2.7	68 194	67.5	57 248	51.0
Rialto	84.3	41.8	93.0	69.4	90.6	2.4	44 388	1.4	3 022	6.8	79 659	62.6	70 908	41.4
Richmond	60.4	56.4	88.1	80.9	86.4	6.2	53 509	1.6	2 735	5.1	87 943	65.2	74 066	45.1
Ridgecrest	86.1	12.7	87.8	75.2	79.4	12.5	14 100	-0.5	980	7.0	21 515	62.9	18 515	49.9
Riverside	78.0	41.4	91.3	84.6	85.3	5.8	150 145	1.6	8 698	5.8	253 708	63.2	220 682	43.5
Rocklin	86.8	41.0	94.1	88.0	83.7	9.4	30 619	1.7	1 376	4.5	49 293	66.4	41 028	50.2
Rohnert Park	82.6	32.3	96.0	91.0	82.3	6.3	23 234	0.8	953	4.1	34 260	68.1	28 294	42.8
Rosemead	84.8	51.2	90.3	81.4	95.6	0.7	25 342	0.6	1 536	6.1	45 318	59.0	36 872	47.8
Roseville	86.4	39.3	92.9	87.9	87.4	6.8	65 008	1.7	2 722	4.2	103 982	62.3	83 638	50.5
Sacramento	80.2	34.9	91.1	78.2	83.4	5.6	230 549	1.6	13 052	5.7	382 536	62.1	320 262	46.1
Salinas	73.8	26.8	79.9	71.7	89.8	2.5	79 705	0.7	6 353	8.0	112 436	64.2	98 583	39.9
San Bernardino	79.4	34.5	85.1	63.3	82.8	5.4	84 129	1.4	6 127	7.3	156 963	57.3	138 876	35.9
San Bruno	69.8	42.6	90.2	86.9	90.8	5.8	26 716	2.5	776	2.9	36 220	70.9	29 977	58.1
San Buenaventura (Ventura)	82.4	34.7	92.3	85.1	86.0	3.8	56 466	-0.2	2 960	5.2	88 549	62.3	71 703	45.4
San Carlos	83.0	39.3	91.6	88.4	92.8	5.5	17 347	2.5	514	3.0	24 344	67.0	18 766	55.9
San Clemente	84.7	46.7	92.9	86.1	84.9	3.8	31 839	0.9	1 057	3.3	54 914	66.0	42 400	48.8
San Diego	80.9	31.3	92.8	86.6	83.1	6.2	704 959	1.0	31 348	4.4	1 141 329	67.3	976 469	49.0
San Dimas	89.0	47.3	89.1	84.1	86.7	3.3	17 817	1.2	734	4.1	29 190	57.4	20 402	49.9

1. Employed persons.   2. Households.   3. Percent of civilian labor force.   4. Persons 16 years old and over.

City	Value of residential construction authorized by building permits, 2016			Wholesale trade,[1] 2012				Retail trade,[2] 2012			
	New construction ($1,000)	Number of housing units	Percent single family	Number of establish-ments	Number of employees	Sales (mil dol)	Annual payroll (mil dol)	Number of establish-ments	Number of employees	Sales (mil dol)	Annual payroll (mil dol)
	69	70	71	72	73	74	75	76	77	78	79
CALIFORNIA—Cont'd											
Menlo Park	55 297	217	23.5	33	468	410.3	40.2	122	1 502	438.2	48.9
Merced	17 771	70	100.0	37	742	1 669.5	35.7	227	3 728	945.6	89.5
Milpitas	48 782	159	65.4	143	4 902	4 031.6	568.9	307	5 295	1 132.7	119.5
Mission Viejo	10 394	32	100.0	107	576	268.8	39.3	356	6 275	1 726.5	159.4
Modesto	15 900	130	100.0	113	1 977	2 459.5	99.8	683	10 639	2 347.6	237.2
Monrovia	3 892	17	100.0	89	709	545.3	34.5	109	1 951	779.4	62.0
Montclair	15 132	61	57.4	82	593	226.0	23.9	243	4 021	1 003.5	93.6
Montebello	235	1	100.0	114	1 826	1 166.8	90.1	203	3 498	817.9	76.0
Monterey	1 266	2	100.0	36	382	1 264.0	28.0	199	2 265	464.5	59.9
Monterey Park	16 011	61	100.0	207	1 082	878.6	44.2	202	1 671	399.6	34.6
Moorpark	44 107	85	100.0	53	774	411.4	40.9	55	890	227.3	22.6
Moreno Valley	50 892	220	45.5	30	663	544.9	23.8	311	5 600	1 696.8	136.7
Morgan Hill	73 740	274	60.6	58	1 873	1 259.4	115.3	105	D	D	D
Mountain View	95 142	498	21.5	106	2 330	2 021.6	246.3	244	4 078	1 222.6	126.3
Murrieta	53 256	279	51.3	97	667	425.6	30.9	218	3 873	1 082.7	97.5
Napa	34 050	127	96.1	69	437	309.9	24.7	315	4 374	1 128.4	125.6
National City	50 133	103	10.7	87	1 198	702.7	55.7	304	5 393	1 395.9	140.2
Newark	148 064	523	52.2	61	1 443	788.0	61.8	168	2 856	684.3	69.8
Newport Beach	102 831	147	73.5	190	1 183	976.1	98.6	441	6 409	2 885.4	252.0
Norco	678	3	100.0	27	469	175.8	13.5	86	1 093	337.4	28.9
Norwalk	7 176	43	55.8	88	639	469.4	29.8	178	3 078	1 101.5	88.1
Novato	4 593	10	100.0	73	579	450.4	38.8	162	2 538	834.3	80.7
Oakland	425 618	2 136	8.9	376	4 921	3 620.2	263.0	1 014	10 458	3 029.1	311.7
Oakley	84 305	295	100.0	9	D	D	D	38	366	124.8	10.8
Oceanside	58 108	389	6.7	149	1 476	696.8	75.4	389	6 742	1 677.8	166.9
Ontario	113 965	654	68.5	681	11 341	14 205.7	557.2	579	13 650	4 833.5	378.2
Orange	20 810	146	6.8	333	3 442	4 940.7	176.7	558	7 821	2 152.9	207.9
Oxnard	84 468	592	16.2	183	3 805	5 873.6	213.8	430	6 729	2 363.1	194.0
Pacifica	4 975	13	61.5	7	D	D	D	61	699	194.3	16.8
Palmdale	36 223	169	100.0	28	128	87.5	4.2	299	6 423	1 557.0	144.8
Palm Desert	77 016	288	26.0	74	389	215.3	17.5	453	6 199	2 309.1	160.9
Palm Springs	48 602	137	100.0	35	535	309.8	27.3	184	2 480	733.1	66.8
Palo Alto	56 512	98	86.7	76	D	D	D	317	5 759	2 461.0	261.4
Paradise	5 064	18	100.0	6	D	D	D	77	791	190.8	19.4
Paramount	4 529	20	100.0	212	1 709	989.1	73.8	110	1 202	326.9	30.2
Pasadena	114 406	410	8.0	163	1 382	2 271.6	79.9	594	9 409	2 700.9	256.4
Perris	25 471	263	59.7	20	265	204.0	12.6	92	2 151	609.3	52.9
Petaluma	30 487	188	54.3	101	2 055	1 396.4	198.1	262	3 233	875.4	96.3
Pico Rivera	471	2	100.0	84	1 923	1 419.8	97.3	113	2 571	1 480.3	55.9
Pittsburg	65 005	383	39.9	32	324	185.9	19.2	99	2 084	524.4	53.0
Placentia	10 909	42	100.0	108	923	329.5	51.3	96	1 099	356.1	33.2
Pleasant Hill	2 402	6	100.0	29	172	112.4	8.8	146	2 490	607.5	56.9
Pleasanton	103 020	331	21.8	135	5 394	2 651.3	430.8	330	6 278	1 662.3	190.3
Pomona	38 325	214	35.0	301	3 224	2 099.4	139.4	293	3 308	845.7	76.5
Porterville	11 502	43	100.0	24	127	42.0	5.9	147	2 231	513.7	52.2
Poway	10 089	18	100.0	96	2 136	1 103.5	131.1	144	2 679	969.9	77.4
Rancho Cordova	95 970	326	100.0	173	2 537	1 593.6	179.2	218	3 332	929.1	91.9
Rancho Cucamonga	54 380	168	100.0	322	3 710	3 866.2	174.8	436	8 160	2 025.3	192.2
Rancho Palos Verdes	2 096	15	100.0	53	163	209.1	8.4	46	388	128.2	10.0
Rancho Santa Margarita	4 120	33	100.0	59	550	364.4	30.7	72	1 504	540.6	43.3
Redding	29 076	133	100.0	115	1 223	918.6	51.6	444	7 061	1 974.7	192.8
Redlands	7 371	48	79.2	56	495	190.5	19.2	240	4 676	2 221.1	118.9
Redondo Beach	39 932	123	100.0	64	311	156.2	15.0	274	3 969	869.7	94.8
Redwood City	92 727	529	6.0	65	1 049	1 124.1	110.9	204	4 486	1 656.7	172.2
Rialto	1 853	15	0.0	54	698	739.7	34.3	152	2 173	541.9	52.3
Richmond	16 424	81	81.5	99	1 431	1 476.7	83.3	238	3 600	1 092.5	105.9
Ridgecrest	7 995	60	100.0	4	D	D	D	82	1 246	272.4	28.2
Riverside	67 399	473	46.3	293	4 399	2 747.6	223.9	829	13 943	4 127.4	385.4
Rocklin	177 691	781	71.8	65	1 562	785.8	86.0	149	1 824	616.0	59.6
Rohnert Park	18 287	122	100.0	41	692	299.9	40.5	106	2 088	637.6	57.9
Rosemead	11 447	59	52.5	107	450	245.6	13.5	172	1 583	460.9	34.2
Roseville	252 180	920	93.7	108	1 597	1 587.0	90.0	588	13 555	4 159.6	380.2
Sacramento	331 856	1 682	60.5	488	7 125	9 800.4	381.3	1 200	18 042	4 363.3	447.7
Salinas	4 520	52	3.8	123	1 861	1 717.4	124.3	428	6 955	1 928.3	175.7
San Bernardino	11 910	96	35.4	128	2 392	2 145.2	102.9	526	8 518	2 610.4	216.6
San Bruno	19 165	83	0.0	36	798	1 046.6	96.4	149	2 508	528.7	59.6
San Buenaventura (Ventura)	31 182	248	23.0	167	1 531	762.2	83.3	517	6 814	1 824.7	183.5
San Carlos	57 037	269	5.9	103	885	488.8	52.5	142	1 828	490.1	55.9
San Clemente	54 023	104	97.1	162	1 826	810.7	119.4	204	2 501	670.2	68.7
San Diego	1 271 487	6 612	12.4	1 823	35 353	24 027.1	2 803.8	4 119	61 044	17 869.3	1 740.7
San Dimas	5 055	17	100.0	75	704	304.0	36.4	112	1 792	538.4	45.5

1. Merchant wholesalers except manufacturers' sales branches and offices.   2. Establishments with payroll.

Table D. Cities — Real Estate, Professional Services, and Manufacturing

City	Real estate and rental and leasing, 2012				Professional, scientific, and technical services,[1] 2012				Manufacturing, 2012			
	Number of establishments	Number of employees	Receipts (mil dol)	Annual payroll (mil dol)	Number of establishments	Number of employees	Receipts (mil dol)	Annual payroll (mil dol)	Number of establishments	Number of employees	Receipts (mil dol)	Annual payroll (mil dol)
	80	81	82	83	84	85	86	87	88	89	90	91
CALIFORNIA—Cont'd												
Menlo Park	84	374	119.4	18.4	336	D	D	D	56	2 390	D	199.1
Merced	69	322	48.1	10.2	84	D	D	D	28	1 234	273.9	55.5
Milpitas	72	394	207.8	18.2	265	D	D	D	157	8 969	4 539.3	968.4
Mission Viejo	161	775	177.2	37.0	469	D	D	D	51	440	275.1	26.6
Modesto	207	925	194.6	31.8	390	D	D	D	91	7 104	D	441.5
Monrovia	58	202	32.3	8.1	152	2 436	594.7	198.6	94	2 885	719.6	171.7
Montclair	32	179	97.5	13.0	25	217	12.4	5.8	85	938	121.3	31.4
Montebello	55	309	76.9	14.6	66	375	41.1	12.3	71	2 433	753.8	101.7
Monterey	88	312	64.7	10.7	238	D	D	D	44	717	116.9	37.5
Monterey Park	89	296	53.3	13.6	158	D	D	D	42	593	89.3	24.3
Moorpark	35	137	22.6	4.9	94	313	49.0	17.9	52	1 349	398.3	73.8
Moreno Valley	73	312	60.1	8.9	85	509	32.6	12.4	23	802	233.3	32.3
Morgan Hill	65	232	49.9	8.0	142	2 207	183.8	71.9	79	3 047	933.8	193.4
Mountain View	121	668	151.4	33.2	584	17 005	3 739.2	1 721.2	121	3 230	825.0	231.9
Murrieta	118	326	62.7	12.5	206	873	98.4	34.8	63	609	108.9	27.0
Napa	101	472	90.9	17.1	210	957	151.4	55.6	110	1 899	1 079.0	127.4
National City	50	288	51.0	10.6	46	473	44.5	15.9	70	1 045	D	44.2
Newark	42	132	46.2	5.3	132	1 882	561.3	168.0	67	2 348	806.2	148.0
Newport Beach	698	4 870	1 633.4	354.5	1 244	8 075	1 727.4	632.4	86	3 739	547.2	180.8
Norco	38	108	19.4	3.4	75	1 221	142.0	76.0	33	449	71.6	20.6
Norwalk	44	194	45.2	6.9	66	D	D	D	52	698	174.2	28.2
Novato	105	D	D	D	233	D	D	D	52	557	D	30.2
Oakland	482	2 716	672.7	126.2	1 414	10 188	2 035.0	834.8	333	6 555	1 744.2	314.1
Oakley	18	78	18.0	4.3	25	102	8.8	2.9	7	201	D	7.6
Oceanside	157	562	121.3	19.3	310	2 326	256.5	95.6	164	4 715	1 537.3	221.0
Ontario	182	1 205	368.5	65.3	256	D	D	D	391	11 003	4 490.4	494.1
Orange	259	1 787	400.2	84.1	713	D	D	D	287	6 122	1 980.3	301.4
Oxnard	139	694	144.8	27.4	213	D	D	D	172	6 057	3 144.4	359.9
Pacifica	28	64	12.5	2.5	72	272	30.5	9.7	9	139	D	4.1
Palmdale	102	326	51.4	8.5	95	D	D	D	35	4 686	D	D
Palm Desert	144	713	131.3	32.2	260	862	140.2	41.9	40	196	23.4	6.1
Palm Springs	123	573	120.2	20.7	191	664	110.6	32.3	27	624	242.9	23.3
Palo Alto	197	1 214	562.6	101.1	838	11 477	3 506.9	1 646.9	81	6 683	2 798.4	597.1
Paradise	25	204	30.2	4.3	34	107	9.0	2.7	16	85	D	3.3
Paramount	33	192	28.8	4.7	38	384	35.3	13.8	205	4 348	1 996.3	204.6
Pasadena	322	1 704	320.0	64.2	1 212	D	D	D	89	1 016	172.5	47.9
Perris	32	110	24.5	4.8	29	133	17.0	5.7	39	1 034	166.0	34.9
Petaluma	70	347	64.0	10.8	207	D	D	D	100	3 106	1 069.6	156.8
Pico Rivera	34	214	58.7	11.8	30	229	21.4	8.1	60	1 446	433.3	59.6
Pittsburg	25	231	75.7	11.2	49	310	27.6	12.1	40	2 175	D	149.4
Placentia	61	362	68.3	14.1	112	377	65.9	17.6	108	3 097	757.0	153.9
Pleasant Hill	46	233	67.3	15.2	135	779	143.3	53.2	17	78	D	3.3
Pleasanton	176	748	218.6	40.7	553	7 366	1 220.2	707.5	78	1 560	836.9	109.3
Pomona	76	475	141.3	21.1	112	D	D	D	212	4 462	991.4	202.3
Porterville	33	115	18.6	2.8	45	185	15.3	4.3	16	868	312.0	29.4
Poway	89	353	53.1	11.5	252	1 442	304.0	99.7	117	9 014	3 400.3	652.7
Rancho Cordova	108	532	79.7	20.4	235	D	D	D	115	4 676	1 083.4	329.7
Rancho Cucamonga	177	1 031	236.0	40.9	400	D	D	D	246	8 056	3 331.7	401.0
Rancho Palos Verdes	66	D	D	D	138	585	104.4	49.0	11	63	D	2.8
Rancho Santa Margarita	65	148	49.0	8.1	191	1 525	234.9	55.4	42	2 892	682.8	202.3
Redding	148	550	85.4	16.5	280	D	D	D	83	757	162.0	32.5
Redlands	72	293	56.3	9.5	209	1 046	152.6	48.7	58	1 140	305.6	39.5
Redondo Beach	111	309	43.9	9.7	329	D	D	D	35	183	D	5.2
Redwood City	129	628	222.9	26.3	444	7 705	2 124.6	913.7	75	1 834	660.3	107.8
Rialto	48	204	31.0	6.1	32	208	16.6	7.5	70	1 567	410.5	74.0
Richmond	72	370	107.6	14.4	139	1 720	313.7	150.6	118	3 925	11 604.0	268.8
Ridgecrest	25	141	20.6	3.7	53	1 267	142.5	65.6	4	22	D	0.5
Riverside	341	1 685	308.8	59.2	625	4 385	630.9	250.0	264	9 041	2 802.9	410.9
Rocklin	104	407	79.5	18.3	170	1 185	267.0	79.6	45	916	173.2	47.1
Rohnert Park	49	248	58.1	11.3	67	424	45.2	16.6	38	791	240.4	44.1
Rosemead	28	70	15.0	1.6	78	389	35.5	12.1	53	670	D	19.8
Roseville	238	1 902	349.5	82.7	494	8 360	3 354.9	878.1	69	1 325	296.8	77.5
Sacramento	573	3 255	622.2	160.8	1 775	16 337	3 011.6	1 134.8	322	7 890	3 149.8	404.4
Salinas	116	586	141.3	22.3	226	D	D	D	77	2 255	903.1	105.0
San Bernardino	125	514	93.1	16.8	239	D	D	D	122	2 811	929.3	118.4
San Bruno	44	156	67.8	7.6	82	1 002	379.3	116.3	13	D	D	D
San Buenaventura (Ventura)	190	1 046	207.7	39.3	467	D	D	D	157	2 717	517.2	119.4
San Carlos	55	277	74.1	14.6	205	D	D	D	90	1 460	D	88.4
San Clemente	138	386	87.7	17.1	381	D	D	D	99	1 448	314.0	72.1
San Diego	2 764	17 178	4 869.5	851.4	7 387	100 220	18 660.6	7 260.6	1 137	41 655	14 667.0	2 613.2
San Dimas	55	535	66.7	16.9	135	1 890	352.9	135.7	71	1 267	D	61.9

1. Establishments subject to federal tax.

Table D. Cities — Accommodation and Food Services, Arts, Entertainment, and Recreation, and Health Care and Social Assistance

City	Accommodation and food services, 2012				Arts, entertainment, and recreation,[1] 2012				Health care and social assistance,[1] 2012			
	Number of establish-ments	Number of employees	Sales (mil dol)	Annual payroll (mil dol)	Number of establish-ments	Number of employees	Receipts (mil dol)	Annual payroll (mil dol)	Number of establish-ments	Number of employees	Receipts (mil dol)	Annual payroll (mil dol)
	92	93	94	95	96	97	98	99	100	101	102	103
CALIFORNIA—Cont'd												
Menlo Park	104	1 790	139.2	43.6	17	D	D	D	136	988	157.7	64.5
Merced	131	2 340	107.7	28.6	11	113	7.0	1.8	245	2 514	266.6	96.1
Milpitas	282	4 613	320.4	86.0	21	D	D	D	210	2 097	351.1	107.7
Mission Viejo	193	3 372	184.2	53.7	26	D	D	D	466	D	D	D
Modesto	394	7 262	391.0	107.5	30	469	32.2	6.4	580	10 528	1 492.8	561.7
Monrovia	108	1 787	109.3	29.1	15	D	D	D	83	1 573	150.0	63.4
Montclair	83	1 650	82.2	23.8	7	D	D	D	96	1 960	168.3	59.6
Montebello	130	1 741	101.4	26.2	6	D	D	D	171	D	D	D
Monterey	212	5 518	416.3	131.8	22	D	D	D	280	D	D	D
Monterey Park	177	2 613	149.0	40.7	8	D	D	D	262	3 352	515.5	164.7
Moorpark	41	835	48.9	14.1	11	62	4.5	1.3	40	659	51.7	22.4
Moreno Valley	213	3 468	191.9	49.7	11	137	6.3	1.7	206	D	D	D
Morgan Hill	113	1 457	89.8	23.6	9	D	D	D	96	D	D	D
Mountain View	314	4 218	296.3	90.7	19	487	228.8	14.2	302	D	D	D
Murrieta	148	2 672	135.9	36.2	33	475	27.1	7.9	256	3 678	504.8	176.8
Napa	205	3 698	270.3	79.2	18	330	12.8	4.0	225	2 573	344.6	136.0
National City	169	2 512	145.8	35.9	7	D	D	D	148	2 719	229.2	83.2
Newark	162	2 273	149.0	39.7	7	D	D	D	73	D	D	D
Newport Beach	369	11 543	805.0	251.5	95	954	123.4	41.8	887	D	D	D
Norco	72	1 532	221.1	22.5	7	D	D	D	39	D	D	D
Norwalk	138	1 902	110.9	29.2	7	198	10.0	2.5	135	D	D	D
Novato	122	1 804	98.9	28.4	19	289	14.5	5.1	150	1 781	258.6	94.9
Oakland	967	13 126	833.7	237.5	66	2 500	383.9	195.8	837	10 763	1 560.7	744.1
Oakley	25	D	D	D	3	D	D	D	24	D	D	D
Oceanside	306	5 216	354.8	87.9	32	826	47.6	13.6	290	2 490	295.4	117.0
Ontario	332	6 564	383.2	104.6	19	D	D	D	186	8 280	979.2	407.1
Orange	398	6 959	424.2	114.0	36	358	25.4	5.6	597	3 719	448.7	170.8
Oxnard	282	4 397	264.2	68.2	28	414	25.9	6.5	373	D	D	D
Pacifica	67	633	43.7	11.5	6	D	D	D	47	D	D	D
Palmdale	206	4 388	228.8	62.4	12	D	D	D	176	1 715	185.6	59.5
Palm Desert	194	5 547	365.5	109.1	37	1 326	97.5	32.4	226	2 038	226.0	76.2
Palm Springs	262	6 904	411.2	124.8	27	1 116	216.2	34.6	239	4 434	735.1	243.8
Palo Alto	280	6 048	422.3	131.5	31	530	36.4	12.6	329	D	D	D
Paradise	40	D	D	D	6	D	D	D	87	D	D	D
Paramount	73	683	41.0	9.9	2	D	D	D	78	1 276	153.4	58.7
Pasadena	473	9 619	617.4	184.7	150	954	136.2	50.7	873	10 536	1 619.4	533.6
Perris	68	1 017	55.9	14.7	4	D	D	D	34	498	47.0	17.2
Petaluma	162	2 080	125.4	33.8	29	659	49.4	12.6	165	2 145	253.5	83.3
Pico Rivera	118	1 627	105.0	26.5	4	D	D	D	74	931	85.5	31.9
Pittsburg	84	1 394	73.9	19.6	4	76	3.8	1.0	65	693	54.3	24.0
Placentia	91	1 268	74.5	19.3	7	D	D	D	125	2 113	211.4	91.8
Pleasant Hill	93	1 540	106.1	28.9	14	204	10.2	4.5	114	1 550	164.1	57.1
Pleasanton	240	3 856	247.7	70.1	37	D	D	D	273	3 240	621.3	164.5
Pomona	195	2 940	169.5	48.4	12	D	D	D	272	3 383	335.7	125.5
Porterville	81	1 268	60.0	14.8	4	D	D	D	126	D	D	D
Poway	105	1 280	69.7	20.1	24	D	D	D	148	D	D	D
Rancho Cordova	144	2 383	136.5	37.8	15	D	D	D	98	3 006	767.2	253.0
Rancho Cucamonga	312	7 074	366.2	105.5	31	299	42.0	6.4	386	4 315	417.1	156.3
Rancho Palos Verdes	38	1 388	127.9	38.1	12	D	D	D	120	D	D	D
Rancho Santa Margarita	83	1 423	76.4	22.1	16	D	D	D	83	D	D	D
Redding	254	4 374	228.7	62.0	25	D	D	D	465	6 274	676.0	257.0
Redlands	174	3 257	163.8	44.1	13	194	12.7	4.7	289	3 092	466.2	151.4
Redondo Beach	212	4 099	247.5	78.7	42	D	D	D	204	1 310	193.7	70.3
Redwood City	216	2 841	205.9	55.3	30	799	45.3	13.2	273	D	D	D
Rialto	89	1 287	71.8	18.0	6	98	17.2	3.3	87	733	63.4	25.8
Richmond	123	1 053	72.7	18.7	16	D	D	D	118	2 201	345.6	138.1
Ridgecrest	60	939	45.2	12.0	6	61	1.4	0.4	56	D	D	D
Riverside	535	9 620	516.6	142.1	52	723	46.2	12.7	761	12 615	1 758.6	662.6
Rocklin	80	1 274	65.2	19.0	13	D	D	D	137	556	81.6	20.8
Rohnert Park	87	1 698	95.0	27.2	12	D	D	D	69	D	D	D
Rosemead	157	2 023	112.0	29.5	6	155	9.1	2.8	127	1 343	141.6	46.4
Roseville	365	7 478	394.2	113.6	37	766	43.4	11.9	450	D	D	D
Sacramento	1 093	20 289	1 145.7	327.5	90	2 682	303.0	111.5	1 052	15 968	2 608.6	1 092.1
Salinas	253	3 746	221.3	57.4	11	D	D	D	276	2 941	365.6	148.3
San Bernardino	342	5 741	303.7	82.1	25	D	D	D	364	5 388	522.1	207.2
San Bruno	129	1 868	119.7	33.7	9	D	D	D	104	1 117	171.6	55.4
San Buenaventura (Ventura)	327	5 534	319.0	91.8	47	731	45.3	12.4	440	4 394	516.3	195.0
San Carlos	116	1 498	104.4	27.0	15	86	7.5	1.4	94	646	67.7	25.3
San Clemente	162	2 475	136.2	36.7	34	D	D	D	201	D	D	D
San Diego	3 527	80 688	5 590.8	1 561.3	403	8 652	1 213.2	467.7	3 572	40 873	5 882.8	2 308.0
San Dimas	77	1 183	71.5	19.0	16	D	D	D	101	1 648	157.6	61.0

1. Establishments subject to federal tax.

Table D. Cities — Other Services and Government Employment and Payroll

City	Other services[1], 2012					Government employment and payroll, 2012							
							March payroll						
										Percent of total for:			
	Number of establish-ments	Number of employees	Receipts (mil dol)	Annual payroll (mil dol)	Full-time equivalent employees	Total (dollars)	Adminis-tration, judicial, and legal	Police and Corrections	Fire Protection	Highways and trans-portation	Health and welfare	Natural resources and utilities	Education and libraries
	104	105	106	107	108	109	110	111	112	113	114	115	116
CALIFORNIA—Cont'd													
Menlo Park	62	D	D	D	265	1 760 354	14.1	39.6	0.0	11.5	2.4	17.6	6.2
Merced	59	326	26.8	8.3	442	2 547 548	11.6	31.0	16.4	3.0	2.2	22.9	0.0
Milpitas	108	1 035	201.8	34.8	391	3 312 573	25.8	33.3	22.1	4.4	1.1	10.0	0.0
Mission Viejo	169	1 052	91.3	28.5	180	959 036	31.7	0.0	0.0	15.3	6.3	22.8	18.2
Modesto	237	1 355	141.6	35.1	1 217	6 592 366	14.4	32.0	18.1	7.5	1.5	23.8	0.0
Monrovia	67	392	51.0	11.7	256	1 668 764	17.2	33.0	27.7	1.5	3.1	13.2	3.5
Montclair	73	398	35.7	9.4	251	1 296 597	25.0	33.8	17.4	1.8	13.1	5.5	0.0
Montebello	81	611	42.8	10.4	486	2 561 705	6.5	30.7	19.8	32.0	1.1	6.0	0.0
Monterey	57	547	34.6	13.1	506	3 399 804	0.1	18.1	19.6	2.7	1.3	10.8	4.3
Monterey Park	81	333	32.7	7.0	327	1 888 775	11.2	36.1	23.6	5.9	0.0	17.1	5.2
Moorpark	25	126	12.5	3.2	67	465 036	35.0	0.0	0.0	14.4	20.2	30.4	0.0
Moreno Valley	121	474	34.7	10.2	743	3 360 444	15.3	2.0	2.4	17.1	12.4	15.5	1.9
Morgan Hill	68	347	34.4	9.8	182	1 516 788	12.8	39.9	0.0	2.3	1.1	25.1	0.0
Mountain View	137	800	84.5	25.9	600	5 229 873	11.3	28.6	21.6	9.3	5.2	17.2	4.4
Murrieta	142	925	70.6	22.7	339	2 066 931	19.5	46.2	23.2	0.5	0.0	6.5	3.4
Napa	119	638	58.5	17.7	431	3 308 340	12.4	30.1	19.6	7.4	8.5	18.7	0.0
National City	104	512	41.9	13.0	361	2 077 359	8.6	42.0	20.4	3.0	4.5	9.8	7.3
Newark	63	D	D	D	169	764 266	14.7	51.1	0.0	5.4	1.7	15.4	0.0
Newport Beach	205	1 435	107.2	31.2	797	6 997 470	14.3	26.3	21.3	6.9	1.1	16.5	4.6
Norco	62	303	27.3	8.0	81	317 544	33.7	2.4	2.2	9.4	11.1	25.1	0.0
Norwalk	72	363	35.5	10.3	339	1 671 145	18.7	10.3	0.0	35.5	8.6	18.6	0.0
Novato	87	853	75.5	28.5	190	1 241 125	11.4	43.9	0.0	18.8	2.5	18.0	0.0
Oakland	594	3 810	392.7	119.0	3 940	30 153 764	10.1	31.4	20.4	17.1	7.7	5.5	3.1
Oakley	23	58	7.1	1.9	26	121 823	56.5	10.1	0.0	3.7	0.0	20.3	0.0
Oceanside	178	1 117	103.6	31.0	950	5 925 758	16.2	36.9	16.2	3.6	4.4	18.2	2.3
Ontario	177	2 305	216.1	68.5	1 078	8 143 877	8.3	39.1	22.6	0.5	2.8	14.8	2.5
Orange	279	2 345	198.3	65.4	662	5 240 608	10.8	40.5	25.9	5.9	1.0	10.0	3.4
Oxnard	159	939	94.1	25.7	1 267	7 972 661	9.1	36.5	12.3	4.2	8.3	23.4	2.6
Pacifica	29	D	D	D	186	1 351 528	12.4	28.8	17.8	10.7	2.1	16.8	0.0
Palmdale	89	433	30.0	9.6	315	1 381 568	13.7	8.9	0.0	20.8	15.6	20.9	2.9
Palm Desert	117	624	45.2	14.4	122	957 854	30.8	0.0	0.0	28.3	24.5	7.0	0.0
Palm Springs	80	514	32.2	10.3	513	3 307 054	15.7	33.0	17.9	11.3	2.5	5.4	3.1
Palo Alto	104	1 104	97.7	36.6	921	7 610 093	16.4	17.4	16.0	3.9	0.9	38.7	3.0
Paradise	41	123	12.7	3.3	88	528 134	9.9	38.1	34.1	5.6	8.4	2.9	0.0
Paramount	67	609	74.6	24.1	210	830 396	17.7	15.7	0.0	19.4	8.9	20.4	0.0
Pasadena	333	2 438	363.4	87.9	1 821	13 044 662	12.2	21.1	13.6	1.9	4.8	27.1	0.2
Perris	32	156	23.1	4.6	76	396 603	36.6	0.0	0.0	22.9	32.0	8.5	0.0
Petaluma	106	599	49.6	15.6	301	2 362 449	10.3	35.7	22.9	9.0	1.1	20.1	0.0
Pico Rivera	68	535	59.8	17.1	288	1 134 401	19.4	0.0	0.0	28.7	11.6	40.3	0.0
Pittsburg	44	530	53.6	17.1	267	1 784 475	10.5	44.3	0.0	7.0	2.9	12.6	0.0
Placentia	63	401	47.0	11.9	175	1 008 861	10.4	58.5	0.0	7.4	1.7	17.6	0.0
Pleasant Hill	55	410	36.4	10.9	125	907 055	21.9	52.8	0.0	22.8	2.3	0.0	0.0
Pleasanton	135	1 000	105.4	37.9	509	4 073 003	13.7	23.1	30.7	5.5	2.2	14.7	4.4
Pomona	133	729	74.7	22.6	630	2 988 643	8.4	51.9	0.0	5.9	6.3	15.1	2.8
Porterville	35	165	14.0	5.3	323	1 445 053	12.8	29.5	14.5	7.6	0.7	28.3	2.8
Poway	88	592	49.4	15.7	291	1 821 500	20.9	0.0	28.9	10.0	4.0	27.1	0.0
Rancho Cordova	81	482	53.1	16.4	67	438 835	46.2	0.0	0.0	25.2	6.1	0.0	0.0
Rancho Cucamonga	215	1 149	89.7	27.4	639	3 536 504	13.7	0.0	32.8	6.4	4.3	31.3	5.3
Rancho Palos Verdes	20	103	5.8	1.7	69	423 058	29.0	0.0	0.0	13.7	0.0	30.2	0.0
Rancho Santa Margarita	52	288	21.8	5.6	27	142 356	100.0	0.0	0.0	0.0	0.0	0.0	0.0
Redding	185	1 012	97.6	30.5	747	5 047 088	9.6	20.1	14.2	8.9	1.6	42.2	0.0
Redlands	110	567	48.6	15.6	429	2 798 020	10.0	32.4	23.6	5.8	1.1	19.2	3.1
Redondo Beach	123	745	68.2	17.6	980	23 723 684	11.5	36.3	24.3	11.4	4.1	9.3	3.2
Redwood City	122	D	D	D	543	4 492 820	13.2	30.5	20.6	0.0	1.1	19.6	6.0
Rialto	61	322	37.7	10.1	357	2 259 378	9.8	38.9	27.3	6.1	4.1	10.2	0.0
Richmond	88	448	49.5	16.7	843	5 538 248	8.5	38.6	12.2	3.0	6.2	8.4	4.2
Ridgecrest	29	124	10.7	3.1	106	565 833	18.2	47.9	0.0	13.3	4.0	14.5	0.0
Riverside	366	2 248	213.7	58.3	2 260	15 114 251	6.2	28.2	15.6	5.5	4.5	29.8	1.6
Rocklin	72	487	38.0	11.3	287	1 697 873	10.7	35.7	20.8	8.4	6.6	17.7	0.0
Rohnert Park	55	337	34.1	9.8	176	1 106 615	17.8	57.7	0.0	0.0	1.6	22.9	0.0
Rosemead	91	245	22.4	5.1	102	521 909	25.8	14.7	0.0	10.3	10.6	24.2	0.0
Roseville	179	1 842	231.3	58.3	1 160	7 733 037	12.9	18.3	15.7	2.8	2.2	35.9	2.0
Sacramento	612	3 879	358.6	106.5	4 483	29 508 935	6.7	46.8	16.2	10.8	3.9	15.6	0.0
Salinas	164	962	110.0	28.5	553	3 536 035	7.9	43.0	21.0	11.8	4.5	3.6	5.1
San Bernardino	202	974	78.5	24.7	1 527	9 251 817	6.8	36.8	22.6	1.2	6.6	19.6	1.2
San Bruno	96	679	64.5	18.7	262	1 918 097	12.9	28.0	20.2	5.7	0.5	17.9	6.2
San Buenaventura (Ventura)	197	993	93.1	27.9	659	4 241 287	13.8	29.9	21.1	8.7	1.1	23.0	0.0
San Carlos	83	914	67.7	24.1	99	739 930	23.5	0.0	27.1	4.5	4.5	27.8	0.0
San Clemente	88	489	39.8	11.5	220	909 552	22.8	0.0	0.0	23.9	7.3	44.4	0.0
San Diego	1 994	16 826	1 333.9	457.3	9 425	62 476 850	19.9	28.7	13.9	2.4	0.3	25.5	2.3
San Dimas	50	D	D	D	106	558 552	25.6	0.0	0.0	20.9	21.8	31.7	0.0

1. Establishments subject to federal tax.

Table D. Cities — City Government Finances

City	General revenue Total (mil dol)	Intergovernmental Total (mil dol)	Percent from state government	Taxes Total (mil dol)	Per capita (dollars) Total	Property	Sales and gross receipts	General expenditure Total (mil dol)	Per capita (dollars) Total	Capital outlays
	117	118	119	120	121	122	123	124	125	126
CALIFORNIA—Cont'd										
Menlo Park	57.5	3.5	90.3	37.8	1 149	690	444	61.2	1 859	334
Merced	96.3	17.9	51.3	32.3	401	192	205	102.4	1 271	255
Milpitas	117.5	7.2	69.9	80.2	1 162	727	430	122.5	1 776	418
Mission Viejo	74.4	7.3	60.1	55.9	588	365	219	78.4	825	168
Modesto	229.0	48.3	51.3	90.4	440	167	270	226.5	1 101	147
Monrovia	51.2	2.2	84.3	38.6	1 042	714	321	56.5	1 525	198
Montclair	47.1	5.3	94.7	33.5	892	526	363	50.6	1 346	152
Montebello	97.7	20.3	71.7	57.3	904	479	394	66.8	1 053	70
Monterey	96.6	3.5	87.7	44.7	1 575	505	1 065	99.9	3 520	328
Monterey Park	60.2	3.6	69.4	41.1	674	471	200	56.7	929	44
Moorpark	30.0	1.5	80.3	17.5	500	296	187	35.7	1 021	81
Moreno Valley	147.5	17.1	68.1	88.6	446	252	192	166.7	838	157
Morgan Hill	67.3	2.7	96.6	37.9	960	628	229	61.1	1 548	436
Mountain View	174.0	5.3	63.1	102.5	1 337	778	411	183.3	2 392	549
Murrieta	80.7	26.1	46.3	39.0	366	220	142	83.1	780	255
Napa	110.6	18.2	18.2	57.4	732	363	365	117.8	1 502	144
National City	79.9	19.2	23.1	47.7	801	407	387	70.4	1 183	258
Newark	41.0	2.5	91.0	33.4	766	334	424	40.3	924	81
Newport Beach	200.4	9.9	61.5	127.8	1 472	878	579	233.0	2 684	829
Norco	33.0	2.3	44.5	21.6	787	582	187	36.0	1 314	451
Norwalk	85.6	27.5	48.8	49.4	464	166	296	67.8	637	38
Novato	49.0	2.3	100.0	35.6	669	475	189	48.6	913	211
Oakland	1 343.3	204.3	54.6	570.6	1 420	810	448	1 312.4	3 266	765
Oakley	29.3	2.8	84.6	16.7	447	271	122	25.9	696	242
Oceanside	233.9	38.0	49.7	106.3	620	416	200	212.9	1 241	113
Ontario	317.2	21.8	84.9	172.3	1 031	570	459	290.2	1 736	274
Orange	142.3	16.7	75.8	101.3	726	444	279	160.6	1 151	284
Oxnard	312.9	40.3	93.9	115.8	575	339	234	320.7	1 592	328
Pacifica	41.0	2.7	100.0	20.9	544	352	188	44.4	1 157	119
Palmdale	135.7	21.8	54.2	85.7	550	380	156	117.3	753	85
Palm Desert	168.1	3.9	64.2	125.5	2 515	1 931	574	156.3	3 132	538
Palm Springs	141.9	13.2	18.3	76.2	1 662	780	860	157.5	3 436	660
Palo Alto	217.5	3.5	57.6	84.1	1 269	530	666	250.9	3 789	623
Paradise	16.8	4.1	95.7	11.0	420	262	156	14.4	551	19
Paramount	37.4	3.7	65.3	29.9	546	300	244	36.2	660	87
Pasadena	411.2	38.8	79.2	194.6	1 402	638	686	403.1	2 905	429
Perris	49.1	3.7	86.4	26.8	376	223	151	54.9	770	150
Petaluma	90.6	5.2	59.0	46.6	792	514	263	83.8	1 424	233
Pico Rivera	61.1	23.1	28.9	26.9	422	222	200	71.3	1 118	307
Pittsburg	89.1	17.2	34.3	46.4	708	555	146	101.3	1 544	207
Placentia	41.3	4.4	89.2	26.6	512	274	225	39.0	750	113
Pleasant Hill	28.8	3.6	100.0	22.5	664	309	316	29.7	877	199
Pleasanton	134.8	6.1	84.2	81.3	1 125	737	334	130.6	1 807	174
Pomona	196.5	41.6	62.7	104.5	692	386	299	201.6	1 334	134
Porterville	49.1	8.8	73.5	21.3	387	135	246	51.3	933	177
Poway	88.7	1.8	88.7	67.5	1 375	1 096	258	85.0	1 731	191
Rancho Cordova	68.7	14.0	40.7	44.1	660	234	422	65.9	985	308
Rancho Cucamonga	230.6	19.5	59.9	162.0	950	784	163	207.7	1 218	193
Rancho Palos Verdes	29.2	1.6	88.9	24.4	577	282	294	28.5	673	66
Rancho Santa Margarita	16.9	2.4	90.6	13.9	285	143	138	17.3	354	60
Redding	182.1	39.5	29.9	57.9	638	314	302	162.8	1 795	572
Redlands	93.8	3.7	75.1	56.2	805	451	352	85.8	1 228	162
Redondo Beach	117.9	8.1	72.6	58.6	867	423	419	113.6	1 680	108
Redwood City	145.3	7.3	85.5	81.5	1 028	589	431	149.2	1 881	250
Rialto	107.1	8.8	38.5	65.0	639	365	273	111.4	1 095	208
Richmond	254.5	35.4	49.7	151.0	1 416	681	645	274.3	2 573	398
Ridgecrest	21.9	1.1	90.4	15.8	556	343	211	20.8	736	131
Riverside	410.7	63.1	60.7	197.7	631	327	295	486.0	1 551	356
Rocklin	52.5	5.7	74.5	32.4	549	319	184	53.8	911	89
Rohnert Park	59.0	3.3	100.0	32.1	780	488	289	57.7	1 402	280
Rosemead	34.4	2.8	59.2	25.5	469	313	155	32.2	592	173
Roseville	251.3	19.4	55.2	91.7	738	331	402	243.4	1 960	236
Sacramento	884.8	128.8	66.1	366.7	771	418	342	806.3	1 695	296
Salinas	117.7	16.6	57.5	82.1	532	198	333	122.6	794	103
San Bernardino	250.9	21.3	61.3	132.6	621	311	305	230.8	1 081	128
San Bruno	58.6	3.4	100.0	29.7	704	334	342	51.8	1 228	135
San Buenaventura (Ventura)	132.2	9.8	64.9	71.9	662	319	341	135.5	1 247	155
San Carlos	46.8	1.0	100.0	27.3	933	565	359	38.4	1 315	156
San Clemente	74.5	6.4	93.0	44.4	685	501	177	82.7	1 276	289
San Diego	2 616.7	370.0	40.2	1 122.2	838	439	397	2 361.5	1 763	396
San Dimas	30.5	1.5	86.2	23.3	690	367	317	33.2	982	105

1. Based on population estimated as of July 1 of the year shown.

Table D. Cities — City Government Finances

City	Public welfare	Highways	Parking facilities	Education	Health and hospitals	Police protection	Sewerage and sanitation	Parks and recreation	Housing and community development	Interest on debt
	127	128	129	130	131	132	133	134	135	136
CALIFORNIA—Cont'd										
Menlo Park	0.0	9.7	2.0	0.0	0.0	23.7	0.7	24.5	5.2	7.1
Merced	0.0	14.7	0.0	0.0	0.2	17.9	21.6	4.9	8.8	3.6
Milpitas	0.0	8.7	0.0	0.0	10.6	17.8	7.2	5.0	24.5	5.9
Mission Viejo	0.0	22.7	0.0	0.0	2.2	20.0	0.0	20.2	7.8	1.5
Modesto	0.0	11.8	0.5	0.3	0.4	20.9	16.0	9.7	4.4	2.0
Monrovia	0.0	4.3	0.0	0.0	3.4	33.5	2.0	4.6	10.1	7.2
Montclair	0.0	8.2	0.0	0.0	8.2	20.5	7.9	8.1	24.7	6.2
Montebello	0.0	6.7	0.0	0.0	0.3	27.9	5.1	15.8	5.7	8.2
Monterey	0.0	11.5	6.8	0.0	0.0	12.8	1.9	15.4	6.0	0.7
Monterey Park	0.0	6.8	0.0	0.0	1.2	26.8	11.0	5.8	9.8	4.7
Moorpark	0.0	11.6	0.0	0.0	1.1	18.2	0.9	12.0	18.3	2.7
Moreno Valley	0.0	19.1	0.0	0.0	1.3	26.1	0.0	9.0	14.2	3.7
Morgan Hill	0.0	10.4	0.0	0.0	0.0	18.6	10.0	10.1	21.8	3.2
Mountain View	0.0	4.2	0.1	0.0	0.0	16.0	15.2	21.1	2.5	1.5
Murrieta	0.0	30.4	0.0	0.0	0.0	29.4	0.0	11.0	5.8	4.3
Napa	0.0	15.7	0.4	0.0	2.6	16.9	17.1	6.9	13.2	1.1
National City	0.0	3.6	0.0	0.0	1.7	30.9	9.9	3.5	23.8	4.2
Newark	0.0	12.0	0.0	0.0	0.6	32.5	0.4	11.1	0.5	1.2
Newport Beach	0.0	13.8	0.0	0.0	2.6	17.7	1.5	10.0	0.0	3.5
Norco	0.0	9.4	0.0	0.0	5.5	12.6	18.0	6.1	16.3	12.3
Norwalk	0.0	12.1	0.7	0.0	7.3	19.7	0.0	10.0	18.0	8.9
Novato	0.0	12.8	0.0	0.0	1.2	25.4	0.0	19.0	6.7	9.6
Oakland	0.0	3.5	0.7	0.0	5.4	14.9	3.4	3.6	9.4	7.2
Oakley	0.0	20.6	0.0	0.0	0.7	28.9	0.0	14.6	12.4	5.7
Oceanside	0.0	7.9	0.8	0.0	0.1	22.7	19.9	6.2	10.5	3.6
Ontario	0.0	7.4	0.0	0.0	0.4	24.6	11.6	5.0	10.1	4.7
Orange	0.0	11.8	0.0	0.0	6.7	23.1	3.8	11.6	10.8	2.7
Oxnard	0.0	12.2	0.3	0.0	0.0	21.3	22.0	10.3	4.4	7.3
Pacifica	0.0	14.4	0.0	0.0	1.7	20.3	20.0	8.3	0.5	4.7
Palmdale	0.0	15.6	0.0	0.0	0.7	16.8	2.5	12.1	20.8	10.5
Palm Desert	0.0	10.2	0.0	0.0	2.6	10.4	0.0	10.7	38.1	11.7
Palm Springs	0.0	15.8	0.3	0.0	0.8	12.8	3.7	14.0	5.4	3.7
Palo Alto	0.0	4.4	0.1	2.9	0.3	13.8	24.8	13.4	0.2	1.9
Paradise	0.0	15.3	0.0	0.0	1.1	27.0	4.7	0.2	1.9	7.0
Paramount	0.0	18.4	0.0	0.0	0.0	29.4	0.0	12.7	10.6	4.9
Pasadena	0.0	6.9	2.7	0.0	4.4	15.8	4.9	10.1	6.4	3.9
Perris	0.0	14.3	0.0	0.0	0.8	20.1	3.8	3.3	23.1	17.7
Petaluma	0.0	9.4	0.0	0.0	1.0	18.2	19.3	5.4	15.3	10.8
Pico Rivera	0.0	35.5	0.0	0.0	0.0	14.1	0.0	10.4	18.0	0.0
Pittsburg	0.0	7.8	0.0	0.0	0.4	18.5	2.0	3.9	33.7	17.9
Placentia	0.0	16.3	0.0	0.0	0.3	28.1	8.9	5.7	6.5	3.6
Pleasant Hill	0.0	29.3	0.0	0.0	0.6	35.4	0.8	0.0	9.2	2.4
Pleasanton	0.0	10.4	0.0	0.0	0.2	18.3	10.1	17.9	1.6	2.7
Pomona	0.0	15.1	0.0	0.0	0.0	20.1	6.5	1.6	23.4	13.4
Porterville	0.0	8.0	0.1	0.0	0.2	15.8	24.2	9.3	3.5	6.2
Poway	0.0	11.2	0.0	0.0	0.4	12.3	9.1	7.3	12.9	15.2
Rancho Cordova	0.0	34.1	0.0	0.0	0.7	24.0	0.0	1.0	7.5	1.7
Rancho Cucamonga	0.0	11.8	0.0	1.1	1.4	12.6	1.6	3.3	19.8	13.7
Rancho Palos Verdes	0.0	21.5	0.0	0.0	0.7	14.0	1.6	11.5	1.2	3.6
Rancho Santa Margarita	0.0	22.7	0.0	0.0	2.1	43.6	0.0	5.7	0.0	3.1
Redding	0.0	8.9	0.0	0.0	0.4	15.2	34.2	5.3	9.1	2.7
Redlands	0.0	5.8	0.0	0.0	5.2	24.9	19.0	6.7	5.8	3.4
Redondo Beach	0.0	6.3	0.0	0.0	4.0	24.5	5.8	5.0	14.1	1.4
Redwood City	0.0	12.8	1.2	0.0	0.5	20.3	14.1	6.2	5.9	3.2
Rialto	0.0	8.0	0.0	0.4	4.0	23.1	8.6	5.0	18.0	8.2
Richmond	0.0	11.3	0.0	0.0	0.5	23.5	3.7	1.7	15.8	7.2
Ridgecrest	0.0	9.8	0.0	0.0	0.0	30.5	5.8	8.8	15.7	7.3
Riverside	0.0	11.4	1.0	0.0	0.1	18.0	8.8	5.0	13.1	6.9
Rocklin	0.0	10.2	0.0	0.0	0.0	21.7	0.0	12.6	9.7	4.8
Rohnert Park	0.0	4.3	0.0	0.0	1.7	17.8	25.1	6.1	17.1	5.0
Rosemead	0.0	5.7	0.0	0.0	0.9	20.7	0.0	7.6	18.2	4.3
Roseville	0.0	11.4	0.0	0.0	0.0	12.0	14.3	9.5	4.3	15.7
Sacramento	0.0	18.4	1.9	0.0	2.2	16.9	15.2	7.8	3.6	5.8
Salinas	0.0	8.9	1.2	0.0	3.6	33.3	3.9	3.8	3.4	1.3
San Bernardino	0.0	5.3	0.0	0.0	1.1	29.7	15.7	3.3	9.8	1.9
San Bruno	0.0	6.9	0.0	0.0	0.0	23.1	16.6	12.8	1.6	0.9
San Buenaventura (Ventura)	0.0	11.6	0.5	0.0	0.2	22.4	15.1	9.0	2.0	3.7
San Carlos	0.0	9.3	0.2	0.0	0.0	18.2	15.9	9.3	3.0	2.2
San Clemente	0.0	8.3	0.0	0.0	3.0	14.5	11.0	25.3	3.1	1.1
San Diego	0.0	9.7	0.1	0.0	0.6	12.7	12.6	9.9	19.7	6.2
San Dimas	0.0	13.5	0.1	0.0	0.4	15.5	0.1	11.6	10.1	3.7

City	City government finances, 2012 (cont.)			Climate[2]						
	Debt outstanding			Average daily temperature (degrees Fahrenheit)						
				Mean		Limits				
	Total (mil dol)	Per capita[1] (dollars)	Debt issued during year	January	July	January[3]	July[4]	Annual precipitation (inches)	Heating degree days	Cooling degree days
	137	138	139	140	141	142	143	144	145	146
CALIFORNIA—Cont'd										
Menlo Park	89.8	2 729	9.8	49.0	68.0	40.4	78.8	15.71	2 584	452
Merced	93.3	1 159	0.0	46.3	78.6	37.5	96.5	12.50	2 602	1 578
Milpitas	171.2	2 482	0.0	50.5	70.9	41.7	84.3	15.08	2 171	811
Mission Viejo	47.5	500	0.0	56.7	72.4	47.2	82.3	14.03	1 465	1 183
Modesto	441.0	2 144	52.8	47.2	77.7	40.1	93.6	13.12	2 358	1 570
Monrovia	103.5	2 796	0.0	56.1	75.3	44.3	89.4	21.09	1 398	1 558
Montclair	77.9	2 073	0.0	54.6	73.8	41.5	88.7	16.96	1 727	1 191
Montebello	88.0	1 388	0.0	58.8	76.6	47.9	88.9	14.44	949	1 837
Monterey	14.8	521	0.0	51.6	60.2	43.4	68.1	20.35	3 092	74
Monterey Park	83.1	1 363	0.0	56.3	75.6	42.6	89.0	18.56	1 295	1 575
Moorpark	27.6	788	0.0	54.7	68.3	41.2	80.7	18.41	1 911	602
Moreno Valley	91.6	461	0.0	54.2	77.4	42.0	93.5	10.67	1 674	1 697
Morgan Hill	124.6	3 156	0.0	43.5	70.7	37.5	78.2	23.73	4 566	747
Mountain View	83.5	1 090	39.4	49.0	68.0	40.4	78.8	15.71	2 584	452
Murrieta	90.8	852	0.0	52.2	79.6	38.3	98.1	12.09	1 924	1 874
Napa	95.7	1 221	0.0	47.9	68.6	39.2	82.6	26.46	2 689	529
National City	84.5	1 419	0.0	57.3	70.1	46.1	76.1	9.95	1 321	862
Newark	11.4	261	9.7	49.8	68.0	42.0	78.3	14.85	2 367	530
Newport Beach	270.0	3 110	2.6	55.9	67.3	48.2	71.4	11.65	1 719	543
Norco	136.8	4 999	0.0	NA	NA	NA	NA	NA	NA	NA
Norwalk	142.9	1 342	2.1	57.0	73.8	46.0	82.9	12.94	1 211	1 186
Novato	141.1	2 647	0.0	48.8	67.7	41.3	80.9	34.29	2 621	451
Oakland	2 294.4	5 709	429.5	50.9	64.9	44.7	72.7	22.94	2 400	377
Oakley	39.5	1 060	0.0	45.7	74.4	37.8	90.7	13.33	2 714	1 179
Oceanside	200.5	1 168	7.7	54.7	67.6	45.4	72.1	11.13	2 009	505
Ontario	212.5	1 271	0.9	54.6	73.8	41.5	88.7	16.96	1 727	1 191
Orange	107.1	768	3.0	58.0	72.9	46.6	82.7	13.84	1 153	1 299
Oxnard	484.3	2 404	9.3	55.6	65.9	45.5	72.7	15.62	1 936	403
Pacifica	52.3	1 363	0.0	49.4	62.8	42.9	71.1	20.11	2 862	142
Palmdale	251.2	1 614	2.2	46.6	81.7	34.3	97.5	7.36	2 704	1 998
Palm Desert	450.5	9 024	1.0	56.8	92.8	42.0	107.1	3.15	903	4 388
Palm Springs	165.5	3 611	68.9	57.3	92.1	44.2	108.2	5.23	951	4 224
Palo Alto	142.0	2 144	17.2	49.0	68.0	40.4	78.8	15.71	2 584	452
Paradise	14.9	568	0.0	45.7	77.8	37.7	91.7	56.20	3 145	1 464
Paramount	69.2	1 262	0.0	57.0	73.8	46.0	82.9	12.94	1 211	1 186
Pasadena	766.2	5 522	88.3	56.1	75.3	44.3	89.4	21.09	1 398	1 558
Perris	262.8	3 686	0.0	51.2	78.3	36.1	97.8	11.40	2 123	1 710
Petaluma	244.3	4 153	12.9	48.4	67.3	38.9	82.7	25.85	2 741	385
Pico Rivera	49.9	784	0.0	58.3	74.2	48.5	83.8	15.14	928	1 506
Pittsburg	474.6	7 230	0.0	45.7	74.4	37.8	90.7	13.33	2 714	1 179
Placentia	28.8	554	0.0	58.0	72.9	46.6	82.7	13.84	1 153	1 299
Pleasant Hill	21.7	641	0.0	46.3	71.2	38.8	87.4	19.58	2 757	786
Pleasanton	82.6	1 143	0.0	47.2	72.0	37.4	89.1	14.82	2 755	858
Pomona	411.1	2 721	0.0	54.6	73.8	41.5	88.7	16.96	1 727	1 191
Porterville	72.6	1 321	0.1	48.7	82.8	39.4	98.1	11.49	2 053	2 246
Poway	246.1	5 010	0.2	55.3	70.9	43.5	80.8	11.97	1 808	979
Rancho Cordova	23.3	349	0.0	48.2	77.4	41.3	93.8	19.87	2 226	1 597
Rancho Cucamonga	503.8	2 954	0.4	56.6	78.3	45.3	95.0	14.77	1 364	1 901
Rancho Palos Verdes	24.4	575	0.3	56.3	69.4	46.2	77.6	14.79	1 526	742
Rancho Santa Margarita	11.4	233	0.0	56.7	72.4	47.2	82.3	14.03	1 465	1 183
Redding	140.7	1 552	25.2	45.5	81.3	35.5	98.5	33.52	2 961	1 741
Redlands	63.1	903	0.0	52.9	78.0	40.4	94.4	13.62	1 904	1 714
Redondo Beach	53.3	789	0.0	57.1	69.3	48.6	75.3	13.15	1 274	679
Redwood City	164.1	2 069	10.0	48.4	68.0	39.1	80.8	20.16	2 764	422
Rialto	226.0	2 222	0.0	54.4	79.6	41.8	96.0	16.43	1 599	1 937
Richmond	657.3	6 165	25.9	50.0	62.7	42.9	70.5	23.35	2 720	184
Ridgecrest	40.5	1 430	0.0	NA	NA	NA	NA	NA	NA	NA
Riverside	1 908.6	6 092	61.7	55.3	78.7	42.7	94.1	10.22	1 475	1 863
Rocklin	85.0	1 439	11.8	46.9	77.7	39.2	94.8	24.61	2 532	1 528
Rohnert Park	71.7	1 743	0.0	48.7	67.6	39.5	82.2	31.01	2 694	526
Rosemead	43.5	799	0.0	56.3	75.6	42.6	89.0	18.56	1 295	1 575
Roseville	1 069.1	8 607	0.0	46.9	77.7	39.2	94.8	24.61	2 532	1 528
Sacramento	1 087.3	2 286	1.8	46.3	75.4	38.8	92.4	17.93	2 666	1 248
Salinas	42.6	276	18.0	51.2	63.2	41.3	71.3	12.91	2 770	210
San Bernardino	121.7	570	0.0	54.4	79.6	41.8	96.0	16.43	1 599	1 937
San Bruno	11.6	274	0.0	49.4	62.8	42.9	71.1	20.11	2 862	142
San Buenaventura (Ventura)	122.9	1 132	23.5	55.6	65.9	45.5	72.7	15.62	1 936	403
San Carlos	24.3	832	0.0	48.4	68.0	39.1	80.8	20.16	2 764	422
San Clemente	18.2	280	5.0	55.4	68.7	43.9	77.3	13.56	1 756	666
San Diego	3 433.7	2 563	465.2	57.8	70.9	49.7	75.8	10.77	1 063	866
San Dimas	19.7	582	0.0	54.6	73.8	41.5	88.7	16.96	1 727	1 191

1. Based on the population estimated as of July 1 of the year shown.   2. Represents normal values based on the 30-year period, 1971–2000.   3. Average daily minimum.   4. Average daily maximum.

Table D. Cities — Land Area and Population

STATE Place code	City	Land area,[1] 2016 (sq mi)	Total persons	Rank	Per square mile	White	Black or African American	American Indian, Alaska Native	Asian	Hawaiian Pacific Islander	Some other race	2 or more races[2]
		Population, 2016				Race alone[2] (percent), 2015						
		1	2	3	4	5	6	7	8	9	10	11
	CALIFORNIA—Cont'd											
06 67000	San Francisco	46.9	870 887	13	18 569.0	47.3	5.2	0.3	34.8	0.4	7.5	4.4
06 67042	San Gabriel	4.1	40 404	935	9 854.6	NA	NA	NA	NA	NA	NA	NA
06 67112	San Jacinto	25.7	47 413	807	1 844.9	68.3	9.3	2.4	1.8	0.0	11.3	6.9
06 68000	San Jose	177.5	1 025 350	10	5 776.6	39.1	3.1	0.5	34.9	0.3	17.2	4.9
06 68028	San Juan Capistrano	14.2	36 276	1 051	2 554.6	73.1	0.2	1.2	0.9	0.0	22.8	1.7
06 68084	San Leandro................	13.3	90 465	354	6 801.9	39.2	9.9	0.6	35.3	0.4	8.4	6.2
06 68154	San Luis Obispo...........	13.1	47 536	805	3 628.7	82.9	1.5	0.8	5.7	0.0	4.4	4.7
06 68196	San Marcos.................	24.4	95 261	327	3 904.1	74.3	4.3	0.2	10.4	0.9	5.6	4.4
06 68252	San Mateo...................	12.1	103 959	292	8 591.7	56.2	1.9	0.3	25.2	2.5	8.3	5.6
06 68294	San Pablo...................	2.6	30 536	1 234	11 744.6	52.5	10.1	0.4	18.2	0.2	15.7	3.0
06 68364	San Rafael	16.6	58 954	635	3 551.4	61.9	2.4	0.6	8.3	0.0	20.3	6.5
06 68378	San Ramon	18.6	75 639	456	4 066.6	43.6	2.6	0.6	46.4	0.3	0.6	6.1
06 69000	Santa Ana	27.1	334 217	57	12 332.7	47.1	1.4	0.9	10.8	0.4	37.6	1.8
06 69070	Santa Barbara	19.5	91 930	344	4 714.4	77.6	1.7	0.5	4.8	0.0	12.6	2.8
06 69084	Santa Clara	18.4	125 948	219	6 845.0	41.0	2.9	0.5	43.4	2.2	6.0	3.9
06 69088	Santa Clarita	52.8	181 972	134	3 446.4	74.4	3.7	0.5	10.9	0.0	4.9	5.5
06 69112	Santa Cruz	12.7	64 465	562	5 076.0	76.3	1.7	0.4	10.1	0.4	4.3	6.7
06 69196	Santa Maria.................	22.8	106 290	282	4 661.8	84.3	0.8	0.4	4.5	0.0	8.0	2.0
06 70000	Santa Monica	8.4	92 478	343	11 009.3	70.3	9.4	0.2	11.8	0.1	3.0	5.2
06 70042	Santa Paula	4.6	30 335	1 237	6 594.6	84.0	0.7	0.4	4.6	0.0	9.2	1.1
06 70098	Santa Rosa	41.3	175 155	142	4 241.0	72.4	2.2	1.3	5.1	0.4	10.2	8.4
06 70224	Santee.......................	16.2	57 834	648	3 570.0	83.5	1.3	0.2	6.1	0.2	3.2	5.5
06 70280	Saratoga	12.5	30 767	1 225	2 461.4	NA	NA	NA	NA	NA	NA	NA
06 70742	Seaside	9.2	34 312	1 108	3 729.6	66.8	7.2	0.0	8.0	2.6	7.9	7.5
06 72016	Simi Valley	41.5	126 327	218	3 044.0	80.6	1.0	0.4	9.5	0.0	3.8	4.8
06 72520	Soledad	4.4	25 622	1 410	5 823.2	52.8	9.8	1.4	2.1	0.1	19.3	14.5
06 73080	South Gate	7.2	95 538	325	13 269.2	56.5	1.2	0.2	0.6	0.3	39.6	1.6
06 73220	South Pasadena...........	3.4	25 913	1 401	7 621.5	62.2	1.8	0.0	23.2	0.0	5.3	7.5
06 73262	South San Francisco.....	9.2	66 980	535	7 280.4	37.4	2.5	0.0	31.8	1.7	21.6	5.0
06 73962	Stanton	3.1	38 644	985	12 465.8	55.0	0.7	2.9	26.2	1.1	11.6	2.4
06 75000	Stockton	61.7	307 072	62	4 976.9	46.0	10.6	0.5	21.8	0.4	8.8	11.7
06 75630	Suisun City	4.1	29 505	1 268	7 196.3	47.5	17.9	0.5	17.7	0.0	9.7	6.6
06 77000	Sunnyvale...................	22.0	152 771	167	6 944.1	43.5	2.2	0.0	42.8	1.5	5.9	4.2
06 78120	Temecula	37.3	113 054	253	3 030.9	70.5	3.8	0.9	9.5	0.2	8.9	6.2
06 78148	Temple City	4.0	36 365	1 048	9 091.3	21.3	1.2	0.0	53.6	1.5	20.5	1.9
06 78582	Thousand Oaks............	55.2	128 888	212	2 334.9	80.1	2.5	0.4	10.4	0.0	2.7	3.9
06 80000	Torrance.....................	20.5	147 195	176	7 180.2	48.8	3.1	0.9	32.8	1.0	6.6	6.9
06 80238	Tracy	22.1	89 274	358	4 039.5	59.9	4.5	0.5	16.6	0.5	10.3	7.8
06 80644	Tulare	20.4	62 779	583	3 077.4	80.8	5.3	1.2	2.0	0.2	7.1	3.5
06 80812	Turlock.......................	16.9	72 796	481	4 307.5	78.3	2.4	0.7	5.5	0.0	9.1	4.0
06 80854	Tustin........................	11.1	80 395	423	7 242.8	44.7	2.2	0.0	17.1	0.1	30.8	4.9
06 80994	Twentynine Palms........	59.1	26 049	1 399	440.8	76.0	8.5	4.1	1.3	0.0	3.5	6.5
06 81204	Union City...................	19.4	75 322	461	3 882.6	19.8	6.6	0.0	56.4	2.2	10.0	4.8
06 81344	Upland	15.6	76 684	448	4 915.6	56.7	6.3	0.3	9.7	0.0	22.5	4.4
06 81554	Vacaville	28.8	98 303	310	3 413.3	62.0	14.5	0.8	6.3	0.1	7.5	8.9
06 81666	Vallejo.......................	30.7	121 299	225	3 951.1	41.7	19.8	0.4	24.8	1.5	5.2	6.7
06 82590	Victorville	73.3	122 265	222	1 668.0	65.2	16.6	0.5	4.1	0.0	4.1	9.4
06 82954	Visalia.......................	37.5	131 074	208	3 495.3	79.1	1.1	0.6	6.8	0.2	8.4	3.9
06 82996	Vista.........................	18.7	101 659	301	5 436.3	79.3	4.3	0.1	5.7	0.0	6.6	3.9
06 83332	Walnut	9.0	30 047	1 250	3 338.6	19.7	3.7	0.6	62.8	0.0	10.2	3.0
06 83346	Walnut Creek	19.8	69 122	508	3 491.0	80.2	2.1	0.0	13.6	0.2	1.1	2.8
06 83542	Wasco	9.4	26 395	1 388	2 808.0	85.6	4.9	0.0	0.3	0.0	6.6	2.6
06 83668	Watsonville.................	6.7	53 796	701	8 029.3	52.0	0.0	2.4	2.0	0.0	42.5	1.1
06 84200	West Covina	16.0	107 847	277	6 740.4	40.7	2.7	0.2	27.2	0.2	24.3	4.7
06 84410	West Hollywood	1.9	36 698	1 039	19 314.7	84.0	5.4	0.0	2.1	0.3	3.6	4.5
06 84550	Westminster	10.0	91 565	348	9 156.5	37.2	1.5	0.5	48.5	0.1	8.0	4.2
06 84816	West Sacramento.........	21.5	52 981	715	2 464.2	65.0	5.3	0.3	11.3	0.4	11.9	5.8
06 85292	Whittier	14.6	86 883	378	5 950.9	53.4	1.3	0.5	3.3	0.1	38.1	3.3
06 85446	Wildomar....................	23.7	36 042	1 057	1 520.8	71.8	4.7	1.2	5.7	0.5	14.2	2.0
06 85922	Windsor	7.3	27 555	1 338	3 774.7	72.3	0.0	0.8	2.1	0.0	16.7	8.2
06 86328	Woodland	15.3	59 068	632	3 860.7	69.3	2.4	0.5	7.8	0.5	16.2	3.3
06 86832	Yorba Linda................	19.3	68 235	518	3 535.5	71.4	1.3	0.0	23.9	0.2	0.5	2.8
06 86972	Yuba City....................	14.9	66 845	538	4 486.2	66.2	1.4	0.6	19.3	0.5	4.5	7.5
06 87042	Yucaipa	28.4	53 309	709	1 877.1	89.5	1.4	0.2	3.8	0.0	2.0	3.1
08 00000	COLORADO..............	103 641.2	5 540 545	X	53.5	84.4	4.1	0.9	3.0	0.2	3.8	3.5
08 03455	Arvada.......................	38.6	117 453	236	3 042.8	90.7	1.9	1.3	1.6	0.0	1.6	2.9
08 04000	Aurora.......................	153.5	361 710	54	2 356.4	62.1	14.8	0.8	4.8	0.4	11.1	6.0
08 07850	Boulder......................	24.8	108 090	276	4 358.5	88.3	1.1	0.2	6.2	0.1	0.8	3.4
08 08675	Brighton	21.1	38 314	993	1 815.8	86.5	1.1	0.6	1.7	0.7	7.2	2.2
08 09280	Broomfield	33.0	66 529	542	2 016.0	86.5	0.9	0.1	6.9	0.0	2.5	3.2

1. Dry land or land partially or temporarily covered by water.　　2. Hispanic or Latino persons may be of any race.

Table D. Cities — **Population**

City	Percent Hispanic or Latino¹, 2015	Percent foreign born 2015	Age of population (percent), 2010-2014							Median age 2015	Percent female 2015	Population			
			Under 18 years	18 to 24 years	25 to 34 years	35 to 44 years	45 to 54 years	55 to 64 years	65 years and over			Census counts		Percent change	
												2000	2010	2000–2010	2010–2016
	12	13	14	15	16	17	18	19	20	21	22	23	24	25	26
CALIFORNIA—Cont'd															
San Francisco	15.3	34.4	13.4	7.5	23.1	15.8	13.6	11.9	14.6	38.3	49.2	776 733	805 193	3.7	8.2
San Gabriel	25.1	58.7	18.6	9.1	13.9	13.6	16.6	13.3	14.9	41.0	51.4	39 804	39 634	-0.4	1.9
San Jacinto	53.6	17.5	32.0	10.1	13.7	13.0	12.7	7.6	10.9	29.8	51.1	23 779	44 199	85.9	7.3
San Jose	32.3	39.1	23.0	9.1	15.5	14.5	14.4	11.7	11.8	36.5	49.5	894 943	952 555	6.4	7.6
San Juan Capistrano	39.2	20.4	23.6	11.3	8.9	12.3	14.2	12.5	17.3	41.2	50.8	33 826	34 706	2.6	4.5
San Leandro	29.6	37.8	19.4	8.2	14.2	12.8	14.8	13.9	16.6	41.8	52.6	79 452	84 952	6.9	6.5
San Luis Obispo	17.9	9.4	11.6	34.8	15.5	8.9	7.5	8.6	13.1	26.7	46.4	44 174	45 164	2.2	5.3
San Marcos	37.8	23.2	26.0	11.5	11.8	16.7	13.1	9.9	11.0	35.4	51.3	54 977	83 654	52.2	13.9
San Mateo	22.4	33.8	20.6	7.7	15.4	15.7	13.8	12.6	14.2	39.3	50.8	92 482	97 207	5.1	6.9
San Pablo	62.3	50.0	24.5	14.1	15.6	10.5	15.5	10.4	9.4	32.7	50.0	30 215	29 134	-3.6	4.8
San Rafael	34.0	28.0	24.3	6.5	14.5	15.9	12.6	10.7	15.5	37.6	47.5	56 063	57 717	3.0	2.1
San Ramon	7.2	39.0	30.5	4.5	7.9	19.8	17.1	10.0	10.2	39.1	48.5	44 722	71 454	59.8	5.9
Santa Ana	78.2	45.6	29.0	10.5	16.9	14.4	12.0	8.8	8.3	30.8	50.1	337 977	324 792	-3.9	2.9
Santa Barbara	33.9	21.2	16.0	14.3	16.4	12.3	10.5	11.9	18.7	37.8	50.9	92 325	88 411	-4.2	4.0
Santa Clara	17.7	41.4	18.9	10.9	19.9	16.9	11.5	10.9	11.1	35.2	49.9	102 361	116 497	13.8	8.1
Santa Clarita	31.2	22.3	22.6	10.6	12.8	13.2	15.3	12.3	13.3	38.1	50.5	151 088	176 296	16.7	3.2
Santa Cruz	21.6	15.4	12.8	32.9	12.1	9.7	10.2	10.1	12.2	28.7	49.3	54 593	59 948	9.8	7.5
Santa Maria	77.6	37.3	32.8	11.3	14.8	14.0	9.4	8.3	9.4	30.1	49.3	77 423	99 597	28.6	6.7
Santa Monica	16.1	26.2	14.5	7.2	18.4	18.7	13.3	11.7	16.2	40.6	49.9	84 084	89 742	6.7	3.0
Santa Paula	82.7	36.2	30.4	11.4	10.5	15.9	10.5	11.7	9.6	32.3	49.8	28 598	29 321	2.5	3.5
Santa Rosa	31.2	18.9	22.3	8.1	15.8	12.7	12.8	12.5	15.9	37.9	50.4	147 595	167 834	13.7	4.4
Santee	15.5	11.3	21.6	9.2	12.5	14.7	16.5	12.1	13.3	39.0	50.4	52 975	53 414	0.8	8.3
Saratoga	3.4	42.3	20.3	6.0	4.3	9.1	18.8	17.7	23.7	50.7	51.8	29 843	29 971	0.4	2.7
Seaside	45.6	28.4	25.7	10.6	15.2	14.1	12.1	10.8	11.5	32.7	48.0	31 696	33 025	4.2	3.9
Simi Valley	26.8	18.3	23.0	10.0	12.6	12.9	16.9	12.8	11.8	39.0	50.1	111 351	124 239	11.6	1.7
Soledad	63.1	31.2	20.8	10.0	22.1	15.5	19.0	7.8	4.8	33.8	31.3	11 263	25 738	128.5	-0.5
South Gate	94.7	42.1	26.9	12.1	14.2	15.1	10.9	11.9	8.8	32.5	50.5	96 375	94 417	-2.0	1.2
South Pasadena	18.0	24.9	26.5	4.3	10.6	16.5	16.3	10.5	15.4	42.3	50.2	24 292	25 619	5.5	1.1
South San Francisco	43.4	40.9	20.4	8.8	13.6	15.0	14.0	11.8	16.5	39.4	49.2	60 552	63 664	5.1	5.2
Stanton	54.4	43.7	28.5	10.4	13.9	12.1	14.3	11.5	9.2	33.3	49.9	37 403	37 827	1.1	2.2
Stockton	41.9	26.0	27.4	11.1	15.3	11.3	12.0	10.3	12.7	32.5	50.6	243 771	291 726	19.7	5.3
Suisun City	28.7	22.9	24.8	10.4	16.5	10.9	13.0	15.7	8.6	33.4	51.1	26 118	28 104	7.6	5.0
Sunnyvale	16.9	47.1	21.8	5.9	21.3	17.2	12.0	9.3	12.6	35.7	47.6	131 760	140 058	6.3	9.1
Temecula	32.4	16.9	28.0	9.1	14.0	12.2	15.5	10.2	11.0	34.2	51.4	57 716	100 173	73.6	12.9
Temple City	24.9	44.5	23.5	8.3	11.0	14.1	14.5	13.0	15.5	40.1	50.0	33 377	35 551	6.5	2.3
Thousand Oaks	20.7	19.6	22.0	8.3	8.5	11.5	17.6	13.5	18.6	44.8	49.7	117 005	126 520	8.1	1.9
Torrance	17.3	29.0	20.2	10.3	11.5	12.6	16.8	12.5	16.1	41.2	50.7	137 946	145 434	5.4	1.2
Tracy	37.7	29.2	26.3	11.5	11.5	14.8	15.9	11.2	8.8	35.5	50.4	56 929	83 353	46.4	7.1
Tulare	57.2	20.4	31.1	11.9	13.6	13.2	12.0	8.7	9.5	29.0	52.0	43 994	59 314	34.8	5.8
Turlock	32.6	20.3	27.5	7.8	13.0	15.1	12.0	10.0	14.7	36.2	54.1	55 810	68 617	22.9	6.1
Tustin	42.2	31.1	25.7	9.7	17.0	13.7	12.3	12.1	9.5	33.4	51.0	67 504	75 301	11.6	6.8
Twentynine Palms	29.1	3.0	27.1	24.8	24.2	9.2	6.8	3.2	4.7	24.1	40.5	14 764	25 048	69.7	4.0
Union City	17.7	44.0	18.8	9.1	17.7	11.6	15.1	12.6	15.0	38.5	48.2	66 869	69 524	4.0	8.3
Upland	40.3	21.7	20.3	10.0	13.4	12.7	13.1	14.1	16.2	39.7	52.6	68 393	73 732	7.8	4.0
Vacaville	24.2	10.9	24.0	9.6	15.2	13.8	12.8	12.2	12.4	35.8	48.2	88 625	92 425	4.3	6.4
Vallejo	23.9	25.2	19.8	9.9	16.4	11.0	13.7	13.7	15.5	37.8	51.9	116 760	115 940	-0.7	4.6
Victorville	49.6	18.0	31.5	9.1	16.8	11.7	12.4	8.3	10.2	30.6	50.1	64 029	115 921	81.0	5.5
Visalia	48.8	16.0	28.5	9.6	15.0	12.7	11.5	10.8	11.8	32.6	51.0	91 565	124 470	35.9	5.3
Vista	49.1	23.1	28.5	12.1	16.7	11.4	13.9	7.0	10.3	29.3	49.8	89 857	93 712	4.3	8.5
Walnut	20.4	52.1	15.4	8.8	11.2	11.5	14.8	21.3	16.9	47.9	50.3	30 004	29 172	-2.8	3.0
Walnut Creek	7.6	19.8	19.1	5.5	11.6	10.9	12.0	13.1	27.8	47.6	53.6	64 296	64 165	-0.2	7.7
Wasco	86.1	28.4	31.8	14.0	17.7	13.9	11.7	6.8	4.0	26.8	42.8	21 263	25 552	20.2	3.3
Watsonville	85.0	38.3	32.8	9.9	14.5	13.4	11.5	8.1	9.9	30.2	48.5	44 265	51 199	15.7	5.1
West Covina	54.3	34.1	20.6	9.2	14.5	13.1	14.1	13.4	15.0	39.8	52.4	105 080	106 125	1.0	1.6
West Hollywood	9.3	22.1	4.1	6.4	34.0	18.4	17.0	9.5	10.6	37.4	42.5	35 716	34 398	-3.7	6.7
Westminster	20.7	45.8	18.3	8.2	12.8	14.1	16.5	12.7	17.3	42.9	50.6	88 207	89 613	1.6	2.2
West Sacramento	31.3	25.7	24.5	9.8	14.6	14.8	11.9	11.0	13.5	35.5	52.5	31 615	48 744	54.2	8.7
Whittier	70.1	19.6	21.3	11.4	15.8	12.9	13.7	12.1	12.8	36.1	49.2	83 680	85 317	2.0	1.8
Wildomar	33.1	18.9	25.3	10.3	12.9	11.5	13.3	14.9	11.9	36.7	50.6	14 064	32 220	129.1	11.9
Windsor	33.7	13.2	20.8	9.2	13.2	12.6	17.3	12.4	14.4	40.8	47.2	22 744	26 795	17.8	2.8
Woodland	49.4	23.7	24.2	10.6	14.3	13.8	14.4	10.5	12.1	35.5	52.2	49 151	55 473	12.9	6.5
Yorba Linda	15.6	22.9	22.6	7.1	8.7	10.7	15.3	19.1	16.5	45.5	53.0	58 918	64 193	9.0	6.3
Yuba City	31.2	26.9	27.4	8.4	15.0	11.7	13.0	9.3	15.2	34.5	49.7	36 758	65 634	78.6	1.8
Yucaipa	25.9	10.1	23.8	7.4	11.8	9.6	13.1	13.7	20.6	44.0	53.2	41 207	51 371	24.7	3.8
COLORADO	21.3	9.8	23.0	9.7	15.2	13.5	13.0	12.5	13.0	36.4	49.8	4 301 261	5 029 324	16.9	10.2
Arvada	14.3	4.3	21.7	6.0	14.4	12.8	15.4	14.5	15.3	41.0	52.3	102 153	106 524	4.3	10.3
Aurora	30.5	18.3	25.8	9.6	16.0	14.0	13.6	10.5	10.4	34.2	50.4	276 393	324 684	17.5	11.4
Boulder	9.1	12.1	11.5	31.1	14.9	11.9	10.5	8.0	12.1	29.0	47.5	94 673	97 730	3.2	10.6
Brighton	43.0	14.1	26.0	9.4	17.4	15.1	13.8	5.9	12.4	32.8	44.2	20 905	33 780	61.6	13.4
Broomfield	12.4	8.2	24.4	6.5	16.0	14.7	14.3	11.7	12.4	36.8	51.2	38 272	55 866	46.0	19.1

1. May be of any race.

City	Households, 2015 Number	Persons per household	Percent Female family householder[1]	Percent One-person	Persons in group quarters, 2010 Total	Institutional Total	Institutional Persons in nursing facilities	Non-institutional	Serious crimes known to police[2] 2014 Total Number	Total Rate[3]	Rate[3] Violent	Rate[3] Property	Population age 25 and older	Attainment[4] (percent) High school graduate or less	Bachelor's degree or more
	27	28	29	30	31	32	33	34	35	36	37	38	39	40	41
CALIFORNIA—Cont'd															
San Francisco	356 916	2.37	7.6	37.5	24 264	5 362	2 942	18 902	51 854	6 098	795	5 303	683 821	25.2	55.2
San Gabriel	12 068	3.31	15.5	16.5	452	418	395	34	638	1 579	205	1 373	29 243	50.8	30.7
San Jacinto	11 922	3.91	18.5	15.3	228	59	43	169	1 976	4 276	219	4 057	27 155	52.8	10.8
San Jose	323 133	3.13	11.7	19.5	13 322	3 780	2 190	9 542	27 819	2 755	321	2 434	697 313	34.1	40.7
San Juan Capistrano	12 219	2.98	10.1	22.2	87	0	0	87	445	1 232	172	1 060	23 732	38.5	34.1
San Leandro	32 325	2.79	15.1	28.0	650	368	364	282	4 126	4 652	416	4 236	65 634	41.5	29.5
San Luis Obispo	18 252	2.52	3.2	30.2	1 182	215	206	967	1 679	3 597	514	3 083	25 383	20.1	50.1
San Marcos	29 407	3.13	14.3	20.2	844	108	108	736	1 482	1 632	216	1 416	58 107	34.8	33.2
San Mateo	38 658	2.64	12.0	29.6	1 316	341	306	975	2 174	2 130	225	1 904	74 215	24.9	51.5
San Pablo	9 525	3.14	24.2	23.1	441	373	373	68	1 403	4 703	808	3 895	18 663	65.7	10.8
San Rafael	22 612	2.53	10.3	33.2	2 119	805	497	1 314	1 857	3 132	326	2 806	40 926	30.1	51.0
San Ramon	24 569	3.09	6.9	14.8	75	23	0	52	771	1 027	31	997	49 471	13.9	66.7
Santa Ana	72 177	4.58	18.2	12.2	4 658	3 243	895	1 415	7 044	2 094	374	1 719	202 730	69.4	11.5
Santa Barbara	36 016	2.51	9.9	33.1	1 627	455	375	1 172	2 691	2 961	332	2 628	63 973	28.2	48.4
Santa Clara	43 971	2.75	8.7	24.0	3 196	336	318	2 860	3 430	2 832	134	2 698	88 652	22.9	55.3
Santa Clarita	59 863	3.02	12.3	19.5	1 410	129	111	1 281	2 744	1 326	148	1 178	121 904	32.1	33.7
Santa Cruz	21 843	2.49	8.7	32.9	8 289	379	2	7 910	3 794	5 980	826	5 154	34 849	19.1	49.6
Santa Maria	27 144	3.83	13.3	17.2	1 007	419	263	588	3 484	3 386	427	2 960	58 821	61.7	12.3
Santa Monica	45 678	2.00	5.6	47.4	2 126	827	783	1 299	3 364	3 611	363	3 248	72 955	14.4	65.3
Santa Paula	8 985	3.39	14.2	19.4	133	89	89	44	532	1 758	281	1 477	17 769	60.2	11.5
Santa Rosa	63 648	2.70	13.5	27.4	3 410	1 713	830	1 697	4 486	2 593	368	2 226	121 849	34.7	30.4
Santee	18 517	3.01	9.9	19.4	966	889	274	77	924	1 629	229	1 399	39 960	33.4	27.5
Saratoga	11 391	2.70	6.7	19.2	199	165	161	34	307	986	61	925	22 808	12.0	73.1
Seaside	10 883	3.05	8.1	24.1	1 127	0	0	1 127	623	1 814	338	1 476	22 009	49.3	17.2
Simi Valley	40 269	3.13	11.0	18.0	660	178	123	482	1 758	1 389	111	1 278	84 935	31.8	35.7
Soledad	3 451	4.59	17.8	9.5	10 103	10 103	55	0	285	1 104	205	899	17 299	62.8	7.0
South Gate	24 276	3.97	20.0	11.4	88	72	72	16	3 193	3 327	527	2 800	58 793	70.7	10.1
South Pasadena	9 843	2.64	7.0	27.8	163	155	151	8	505	1 939	115	1 824	18 100	21.4	56.3
South San Francisco	19 995	3.33	15.1	12.0	579	51	18	528	1 430	2 141	234	1 907	47 636	43.3	28.3
Stanton	11 400	3.39	16.1	20.4	350	258	240	92	808	2 083	320	1 763	23 725	56.6	13.5
Stockton	94 561	3.16	19.0	22.4	5 734	1 838	1 558	3 896	17 136	5 721	1 331	4 390	188 184	50.7	17.8
Suisun City	9 273	3.17	19.4	20.3	44	17	5	27	674	2 325	235	2 091	19 081	35.3	18.4
Sunnyvale	55 157	2.74	7.4	23.7	849	469	457	380	2 523	1 689	112	1 577	109 728	19.3	62.6
Temecula	33 487	3.34	14.3	14.9	129	8	0	121	2 635	2 433	92	2 341	70 522	31.8	29.8
Temple City	11 522	3.12	13.5	17.2	422	393	388	29	473	1 304	124	1 180	24 797	30.7	43.0
Thousand Oaks	45 593	2.79	8.1	22.9	1 742	352	348	1 390	1 727	1 337	99	1 238	90 117	21.6	49.0
Torrance	54 436	2.70	10.2	26.5	1 146	640	578	506	2 778	1 877	105	1 773	103 150	22.3	46.8
Tracy	25 423	3.42	12.7	14.0	316	247	245	69	2 391	2 810	152	2 659	54 187	37.0	28.0
Tulare	18 538	3.34	15.6	18.7	278	216	216	62	2 511	4 077	742	3 335	35 523	52.4	15.4
Turlock	25 993	2.76	13.2	24.1	1 207	520	445	687	2 882	4 071	526	3 546	46 822	43.7	26.7
Tustin	24 433	3.27	18.5	18.3	520	180	150	340	1 488	1 882	167	1 715	52 026	30.9	41.4
Twentynine Palms	8 619	2.62	8.1	23.8	3 347	0	0	3 347	363	1 400	239	1 161	12 525	32.4	18.1
Union City	21 306	3.46	10.4	12.8	518	96	75	422	1 809	2 469	283	2 186	53 707	34.2	38.4
Upland	27 427	2.77	16.7	24.9	682	377	359	305	2 335	3 081	224	2 857	53 226	33.0	29.5
Vacaville	31 103	2.90	16.5	22.0	8 022	7 989	171	33	2 855	3 015	283	2 732	64 220	37.5	20.5
Vallejo	42 429	2.83	17.4	27.8	1 663	533	483	1 130	5 911	4 946	865	4 081	85 197	38.4	24.3
Victorville	33 774	3.47	25.1	18.6	5 103	4 762	294	341	5 016	4 101	525	3 576	72 581	48.7	16.2
Visalia	41 345	3.11	16.2	21.1	1 326	720	408	606	4 280	3 331	377	2 954	80 512	42.2	21.0
Vista	28 142	3.52	13.1	18.7	2 045	1 384	588	661	2 026	2 075	348	1 727	59 863	46.0	22.8
Walnut	9 557	3.16	7.0	11.4	34	12	10	22	323	1 067	96	971	22 921	22.2	54.1
Walnut Creek	30 572	2.22	5.9	34.9	1 002	826	826	176	2 513	3 720	110	3 610	51 905	11.4	66.5
Wasco	4 489	4.61	34.4	8.5	5 720	5 710	0	10	NA	NA	NA	NA	14 234	79.8	2.6
Watsonville	13 234	4.02	21.0	18.1	528	206	201	322	1 754	3 323	502	2 821	30 729	73.5	6.6
West Covina	30 233	3.56	15.1	16.3	674	323	299	351	3 057	2 827	208	2 619	76 147	41.8	26.6
West Hollywood	21 357	1.69	2.9	57.0	109	0	0	109	1 592	4 484	752	3 732	32 417	11.4	69.9
Westminster	28 002	3.27	17.0	18.7	670	289	197	381	2 404	2 607	210	2 397	67 691	42.7	24.1
West Sacramento	19 984	2.62	13.6	33.9	338	92	82	246	1 557	3 105	522	2 582	34 632	39.7	26.7
Whittier	27 548	3.11	15.4	22.0	1 635	552	434	1 083	2 486	2 859	275	2 584	58 836	41.8	22.7
Wildomar	10 040	3.54	17.6	19.0	42	4	4	38	589	1 736	115	1 621	22 942	41.9	16.7
Windsor	9 051	3.02	12.7	16.7	51	0	0	51	340	1 243	314	929	19 230	34.5	29.1
Woodland	19 973	2.87	17.1	23.8	985	829	323	156	2 054	3 613	524	3 089	38 164	42.2	25.5
Yorba Linda	22 559	3.00	9.1	11.4	190	93	93	97	747	1 103	66	1 037	47 781	18.6	52.9
Yuba City	22 787	2.90	11.4	23.7	580	455	247	125	1 922	2 933	340	2 593	42 973	48.9	17.1
Yucaipa	19 307	2.74	10.6	28.1	554	327	242	227	1 049	1 987	134	1 852	36 685	40.6	21.2
COLORADO	2 074 735	2.57	9.7	27.2	115 878	61 591	18 079	54 287	152 064	2 839	309	2 530	3 671 853	30.5	39.2
Arvada	46 055	2.49	8.9	27.2	506	343	314	163	2 835	2 509	150	2 359	83 223	29.9	39.8
Aurora	126 466	2.82	13.1	27.5	2 556	1 850	1 145	706	11 393	3 246	407	2 839	231 628	38.1	29.0
Boulder	43 447	2.24	4.3	34.4	8 105	1 080	531	7 025	3 025	2 901	235	2 666	61 589	11.7	73.0
Brighton	10 412	3.43	8.5	16.5	1 546	1 518	197	28	1 280	3 537	370	3 167	24 016	46.2	23.4
Broomfield	25 557	2.53	7.3	26.1	282	279	207	3	1 071	1 765	51	1 714	44 959	18.0	56.1

1. No spouse present.   2. Data for serious crimes have not been adjusted for underreporting. This may affect comparability between geographic areas and over time.   3. Per 100,000 population estimated by the FBI.   4. Persons 25 years old and over.

Table D. Cities — Income, Poverty, and Housing

City	Money income, 2015 Households Median income	Percent with income of $200,000 or more	Percent with income of less than $25,000	Families Total Families	Percent with income below poverty	Housing units, 2010 Total	Percent change, 2000–2010	Vacant units for sale or rent[2]	Occupied housing units 2015 Total	Owner-occupied Percent	Median value[3] (dollars)	Renter-occupied Percent	Median rent (dollars)
	42	43	44	45	46	47	48	49	50	51	52	53	54
CALIFORNIA—Cont'd													
San Francisco	92 094	20.4	15.3	164 201	7.2	376 942	8.8	31 131	356 916	35.8	941 400	64.2	1 659
San Gabriel	51 114	3.7	14.8	9 364	8.9	13 237	3.0	695	12 068	44.6	646 500	55.4	1 298
San Jacinto	46 518	1.1	16.9	9 808	14.4	14 977	58.7	1 825	11 922	58.9	195 000	41.1	1 077
San Jose	91 451	16.3	10.5	237 820	6.4	314 038	11.5	12 672	323 133	56.6	717 100	43.4	1 757
San Juan Capistrano	72 596	15.8	11.7	8 887	7.3	11 940	5.3	546	12 219	73.4	684 500	26.6	1 514
San Leandro	59 070	5.7	11.4	20 927	7.3	32 419	3.6	1 702	32 325	53.1	473 500	46.9	1 361
San Luis Obispo	48 198	4.0	27.8	7 351	7.0	20 553	6.3	1 360	18 252	37.6	593 200	62.4	1 314
San Marcos	66 318	9.2	14.0	21 377	9.3	28 641	51.5	1 439	29 407	60.1	466 600	39.9	1 533
San Mateo	100 238	19.9	7.8	24 144	2.9	40 014	4.7	1 781	38 658	56.9	934 500	43.1	1 966
San Pablo	41 231	0.0	25.2	6 678	28.3	9 571	2.5	810	9 525	38.1	258 600	61.9	1 034
San Rafael	81 384	14.4	7.3	13 572	5.3	24 011	4.6	1 247	22 612	49.2	830 800	50.8	1 602
San Ramon	125 832	26.0	6.0	20 261	3.7	26 222	50.5	938	24 569	70.8	887 100	29.2	2 138
Santa Ana	54 392	2.9	13.8	59 997	18.3	76 896	3.3	3 722	72 177	45.1	437 500	54.9	1 359
Santa Barbara	64 414	11.7	13.4	18 500	7.1	37 820	1.7	2 371	36 016	39.7	952 600	60.3	1 555
Santa Clara	108 886	17.1	6.8	28 862	3.2	45 147	14.0	2 126	43 971	43.3	846 000	56.7	2 093
Santa Clarita	85 916	8.3	6.9	44 707	3.6	62 055	18.3	2 548	59 863	68.0	456 900	32.0	1 667
Santa Cruz	64 887	9.7	18.0	10 374	9.9	23 316	8.6	1 659	21 843	46.4	745 900	53.6	1 496
Santa Maria	52 170	1.2	13.2	20 854	19.0	28 294	24.0	1 386	27 144	46.4	302 000	53.6	1 182
Santa Monica	85 062	15.4	13.3	18 977	3.0	50 912	6.4	3 995	45 678	28.4	1 228 600	71.6	1 654
Santa Paula	51 490	3.6	17.2	6 950	16.2	8 749	4.5	402	8 985	54.9	317 700	45.1	1 065
Santa Rosa	62 329	6.0	12.4	39 348	9.1	67 396	17.2	3 806	63 648	49.7	478 800	50.3	1 377
Santee	86 950	2.8	7.1	13 874	4.4	20 048	6.6	742	18 517	71.8	407 400	28.2	1 606
Saratoga	169 666	40.9	9.0	NA	NA	11 123	4.3	389	11 391	80.9	2	19.1	2 542
Seaside	48 202	1.6	14.4	6 957	11.3	10 872	-1.2	779	10 883	43.9	405 200	56.1	1 421
Simi Valley	93 438	12.3	5.5	31 066	3.2	42 506	13.9	1 269	40 269	73.9	512 900	26.1	1 821
Soledad	63 363	0.0	3.6	2 763	10.3	3 876	52.4	212	3 451	61.3	276 900	38.7	1 191
South Gate	45 438	1.1	14.6	20 723	14.3	24 160	-0.5	882	24 276	40.2	354 000	59.8	1 047
South Pasadena	76 777	14.2	9.9	6 677	5.2	11 118	2.5	651	9 843	42.1	897 900	57.9	1 487
South San Francisco	96 822	10.2	4.9	16 145	5.1	21 814	8.2	876	19 995	64.6	699 100	35.4	1 631
Stanton	45 537	0.4	20.1	8 606	17.7	11 283	3.1	458	11 400	47.0	332 200	53.0	1 259
Stockton	46 795	2.2	20.7	67 020	18.6	99 637	21.3	9 032	94 561	48.5	224 300	51.5	943
Suisun City	66 540	1.6	10.1	6 892	6.5	9 454	16.0	536	9 273	64.8	310 000	35.2	1 600
Sunnyvale	112 217	24.5	6.7	37 110	5.8	55 791	3.8	2 407	55 157	44.7	992 400	55.3	2 127
Temecula	80 495	8.4	7.7	26 215	6.6	34 004	78.8	2 223	33 487	62.0	389 600	38.0	1 633
Temple City	60 610	4.0	10.7	9 066	6.7	12 117	3.5	511	11 522	60.8	699 900	39.2	1 258
Thousand Oaks	108 322	19.3	6.1	32 976	2.2	47 497	10.6	1 661	45 593	69.8	684 400	30.2	1 808
Torrance	79 921	11.2	10.6	37 701	6.0	58 377	4.3	2 376	54 436	54.9	713 000	45.1	1 566
Tracy	80 166	4.3	10.7	21 249	8.0	25 963	43.9	1 632	25 423	61.6	392 900	38.4	1 513
Tulare	49 853	4.0	18.4	13 965	17.2	18 863	32.6	1 143	18 538	54.7	171 200	45.3	987
Turlock	54 842	4.3	17.3	18 097	8.9	24 627	29.3	1 855	25 993	52.4	256 300	47.6	1 021
Tustin	73 800	10.4	10.8	18 193	11.0	26 476	3.9	1 273	24 433	49.7	585 200	50.3	1 624
Twentynine Palms	40 905	1.1	18.1	NA	NA	9 431	38.9	1 336	8 619	17.1	102 100	82.9	901
Union City	96 376	13.7	6.1	17 188	3.5	21 258	12.7	825	21 306	67.7	627 000	32.3	1 914
Upland	63 771	8.1	12.3	19 157	11.1	27 355	7.4	1 532	27 427	55.3	488 600	44.7	1 226
Vacaville	76 489	4.8	10.9	22 487	10.2	32 814	14.4	1 722	31 103	59.1	357 500	40.9	1 414
Vallejo	56 923	4.6	17.3	26 759	11.3	44 433	7.9	3 874	42 429	55.7	290 100	44.3	1 222
Victorville	47 693	1.6	21.8	25 815	20.9	36 655	61.8	4 097	33 774	50.7	183 800	49.3	1 178
Visalia	52 599	2.9	20.1	31 181	19.7	44 205	34.8	2 856	41 345	58.3	189 700	41.7	935
Vista	67 421	3.3	9.7	20 866	13.0	30 986	3.5	1 669	28 142	45.4	446 800	54.6	1 486
Walnut	111 579	15.8	5.8	8 255	3.4	8 753	4.3	220	9 557	90.2	723 100	9.8	2 672
Walnut Creek	91 812	16.3	5.7	17 871	2.0	32 681	3.8	2 238	30 572	64.9	711 200	35.1	1 835
Wasco	40 879	0.0	25.5	4 108	24.2	5 477	28.2	346	4 489	59.0	165 700	41.0	621
Watsonville	41 332	0.9	19.0	10 607	15.2	14 089	19.7	561	13 234	31.7	376 100	68.3	1 279
West Covina	78 140	6.0	9.4	24 368	5.8	32 705	2.2	1 109	30 233	65.3	459 500	34.7	1 476
West Hollywood	76 042	13.9	15.2	NA	NA	24 588	2.0	2 077	21 357	14.0	646 900	86.0	1 450
Westminster	55 385	6.3	21.0	21 438	15.2	27 650	2.7	1 486	28 002	52.8	553 100	47.2	1 340
West Sacramento	57 086	2.2	16.0	12 021	5.2	18 681	54.1	1 260	19 984	57.5	289 300	42.5	824
Whittier	70 256	5.5	11.3	20 019	8.8	29 591	1.9	1 318	27 548	53.6	500 000	46.4	1 254
Wildomar	70 419	5.4	7.6	7 588	12.2	10 806	128.0	814	10 040	65.9	323 300	34.1	1 330
Windsor	86 077	8.3	3.5	NA	NA	9 549	23.4	579	9 051	68.7	479 700	31.3	1 597
Woodland	58 364	4.6	12.8	14 130	11.4	19 806	15.8	1 085	19 973	53.6	327 100	46.4	1 102
Yorba Linda	121 102	23.8	4.9	19 661	4.2	22 305	14.2	729	22 559	82.6	784 600	17.4	1 881
Yuba City	48 828	1.2	17.7	16 442	16.9	23 174	66.6	1 624	22 787	51.1	234 000	48.9	860
Yucaipa	50 549	2.5	19.9	13 444	8.6	19 642	21.9	1 411	19 307	73.7	265 400	26.3	997
COLORADO	63 909	6.6	12.7	1 331 861	7.6	2 212 898	22.4	240 030	2 074 735	63.7	283 800	36.3	1 111
Arvada	69 596	7.2	9.1	30 175	6.1	44 427	12.1	1 726	46 055	70.1	303 600	29.9	1 188
Aurora	58 445	3.7	12.6	83 312	9.1	131 040	20.1	9 139	126 466	56.9	227 300	43.1	1 120
Boulder	58 547	11.9	17.2	17 688	4.1	43 479	6.6	2 177	43 447	46.8	583 600	53.2	1 394
Brighton	79 874	5.3	10.0	7 906	8.7	11 387	63.0	599	10 412	66.7	234 000	33.3	1 165
Broomfield	84 921	9.7	5.2	17 262	1.3	22 646	57.8	1 232	25 557	65.9	342 800	34.1	1 413

1. Based on population estimated by the American Community Survey. 2. Includes units rented or sold but not occupied. 3. Specified owner-occupied units; $1,000,000 represents $1,000,000 or more. 4. 50.0 represents 50 percent or more. 5. 10.0 represents 10 percent or less.

Table D. Cities — Commuting, Computer Access, Migration, Labor Force, and Employment

| | Commuting | | Computer Access[2] | | Migration, 2015 | | Civilian labor force, 2016 | | | | Civilian employment[4], 2015 | | | |
| | Percent | | Percent | | | | | | Unemployment | | Population age 16 and older | | Population age 16 to 64 | |
City	Drove alone	With Commutes of 30 minutes or more[1]	With a Computer in the house	With Internet Access	Percent who lived in the same house one year ago	Percent who lived in an other state or county one year ago	Total	Percent change, 2015–2016	Total	Rate[3]	Number	Percent in Labor Force	Number	Percent who worked full-year full-time
	55	56	57	58	59	60	61	62	63	64	65	66	67	68
CALIFORNIA—Cont'd														
San Francisco	37.6	57.4	90.7	83.8	85.4	8.3	559 788	2.6	18 206	3.3	760 939	70.2	634 261	54.7
San Gabriel	80.6	42.8	94.3	87.0	93.7	3.6	20 897	1.4	664	3.2	33 692	61.7	27 681	48.6
San Jacinto	83.1	58.0	86.3	78.2	76.0	6.7	18 487	1.2	1 680	9.1	33 232	53.5	28 136	36.2
San Jose	79.8	48.2	92.9	87.4	87.4	5.1	546 774	1.6	23 022	4.2	815 706	67.3	695 042	50.6
San Juan Capistrano	81.2	40.3	91.8	87.4	NA	NA	17 492	0.8	778	4.4	28 885	56.9	22 591	40.9
San Leandro	68.8	52.3	88.8	77.8	87.7	4.6	47 587	1.8	2 177	4.6	75 506	67.0	60 408	52.4
San Luis Obispo	61.6	18.3	92.4	86.9	62.7	14.9	25 701	0.5	1 159	4.5	42 835	59.5	36 638	32.7
San Marcos	82.6	40.3	91.5	88.0	84.1	4.5	40 589	1.1	1 485	3.7	71 298	65.4	61 051	48.0
San Mateo	71.8	44.9	93.0	89.1	82.7	8.1	63 383	2.5	1 833	2.9	84 032	70.1	69 284	55.1
San Pablo	67.2	54.3	88.3	81.2	87.0	3.6	14 044	1.3	962	6.8	23 465	66.7	20 603	40.4
San Rafael	68.8	43.6	91.5	84.4	86.3	6.9	32 889	1.1	1 110	3.4	46 304	64.3	37 126	53.4
San Ramon	81.6	49.7	98.6	96.6	85.6	11.8	39 921	1.8	1 179	3.0	55 742	65.6	47 965	54.6
Santa Ana	77.3	33.7	86.4	77.1	90.6	1.0	159 246	0.8	7 363	4.6	248 399	65.2	220 635	47.4
Santa Barbara	70.1	12.1	88.7	84.1	81.6	5.9	50 878	-0.5	2 029	4.0	78 429	69.4	61 293	52.6
Santa Clara	81.2	32.4	93.4	88.1	80.9	10.0	68 798	1.7	2 328	3.4	104 288	69.7	90 341	55.9
Santa Clarita	81.3	51.7	93.0	87.5	87.8	3.1	96 231	1.0	4 608	4.8	145 539	68.2	121 317	50.8
Santa Cruz	58.9	30.1	97.0	87.7	74.3	12.9	33 824	0.8	2 078	6.1	57 605	57.3	49 762	26.0
Santa Maria	68.1	23.5	82.8	77.0	86.3	5.3	47 893	-0.6	2 911	6.1	74 328	68.2	64 476	49.1
Santa Monica	75.0	40.8	93.4	91.1	82.8	6.0	56 157	1.1	2 492	4.4	80 790	71.6	65 702	52.7
Santa Paula	75.3	33.9	74.6	67.4	86.3	2.1	13 947	-0.3	940	6.7	22 597	66.2	19 670	48.3
Santa Rosa	82.3	23.1	92.2	83.5	86.5	4.1	89 399	0.7	3 942	4.4	139 584	65.9	111 831	48.5
Santee	89.8	36.3	94.7	90.1	85.6	2.0	29 256	1.0	1 340	4.6	46 720	66.8	39 016	51.5
Saratoga	91.3	53.2	99.0	93.7	89.8	6.5	14 649	1.8	390	2.7	26 019	53.3	18 673	48.2
Seaside	78.4	19.8	85.6	79.9	77.8	14.4	18 437	0.7	1 432	7.8	26 793	61.5	22 819	40.3
Simi Valley	84.8	49.2	90.1	88.0	91.4	3.1	68 758	-0.1	3 130	4.6	102 001	68.7	87 052	49.9
Soledad	72.0	30.5	86.2	71.3	85.4	12.6	7 740	0.5	814	10.5	20 357	34.0	19 157	23.2
South Gate	75.3	56.4	85.7	77.3	NA	NA	43 404	0.4	2 990	6.9	73 179	66.2	64 702	46.7
South Pasadena	82.9	46.5	92.1	87.6	NA	NA	14 825	1.3	546	3.7	19 818	71.9	15 802	51.0
South San Francisco	70.4	40.9	90.8	85.5	93.4	2.8	38 915	2.5	1 242	3.2	55 039	68.7	43 968	53.6
Stanton	82.0	46.2	85.1	76.6	NA	NA	18 909	0.7	1 005	5.3	28 971	66.5	25 407	45.7
Stockton	78.8	33.8	81.8	70.1	84.8	4.2	129 404	1.2	11 274	8.7	230 552	57.5	191 714	39.9
Suisun City	78.5	44.2	92.6	83.6	89.4	5.8	14 451	1.3	686	4.7	23 304	68.7	20 774	47.6
Sunnyvale	75.5	27.5	95.9	91.6	83.9	7.6	85 855	1.7	2 895	3.4	121 269	70.6	102 204	57.8
Temecula	86.3	44.1	96.3	89.3	83.6	7.3	53 145	1.8	2 315	4.4	84 157	66.7	71 835	45.7
Temple City	88.8	35.8	90.5	80.6	NA	NA	17 899	1.4	607	3.4	29 004	62.3	23 352	51.1
Thousand Oaks	88.5	38.1	94.9	92.5	90.2	4.1	66 696	-0.1	3 362	5.0	104 528	65.5	80 414	52.2
Torrance	84.4	40.5	93.2	87.8	88.1	3.8	77 952	1.3	2 834	3.6	122 542	63.3	98 690	48.9
Tracy	78.3	55.6	95.1	90.8	85.6	9.0	42 313	1.4	2 873	6.8	67 247	70.1	59 597	46.6
Tulare	88.4	27.5	77.8	70.2	88.6	2.5	28 188	1.0	2 619	9.3	45 731	56.6	39 816	43.2
Turlock	88.9	25.9	86.8	83.3	89.0	3.5	34 315	1.3	2 615	7.6	55 474	60.3	44 837	44.1
Tustin	80.3	32.5	94.5	86.0	80.0	4.4	42 836	0.9	1 603	3.7	61 967	70.6	54 318	51.6
Twentynine Palms	74.5	6.2	95.1	85.5	56.7	34.6	6 862	1.4	508	7.4	19 411	69.7	18 189	53.7
Union City	74.0	61.3	95.5	89.4	91.6	4.7	37 162	1.9	1 421	3.8	62 501	62.8	51 334	54.5
Upland	85.7	45.0	85.8	79.1	86.8	6.7	38 510	1.8	1 614	4.2	61 972	61.6	49 554	50.3
Vacaville	86.6	36.6	94.0	89.9	81.0	7.1	45 016	1.4	1 958	4.3	76 659	60.5	64 676	43.8
Vallejo	78.1	53.9	87.4	79.9	83.0	9.0	58 383	1.0	4 340	7.4	99 875	60.2	81 047	41.1
Victorville	89.1	40.8	90.9	80.7	80.3	6.0	44 855	1.5	2 747	6.1	89 452	54.4	76 997	32.8
Visalia	88.7	27.0	83.1	75.3	86.1	2.4	62 848	1.0	5 568	8.9	95 618	56.3	80 218	42.5
Vista	88.9	33.0	95.2	87.8	85.6	2.8	44 602	1.1	1 855	4.2	74 444	70.4	64 026	53.7
Walnut	85.3	58.0	98.0	96.9	NA	NA	15 784	1.3	589	3.7	26 276	62.3	21 153	48.7
Walnut Creek	75.9	47.9	94.6	89.4	82.9	8.8	34 045	1.8	1 030	3.0	57 301	54.7	38 161	52.1
Wasco	83.9	29.5	45.6	40.3	84.5	14.5	8 377	-0.4	1 143	13.6	19 166	39.9	18 115	24.6
Watsonville	70.2	30.1	70.9	63.9	NA	NA	25 537	0.6	2 272	8.9	37 550	63.8	32 267	38.1
West Covina	82.2	54.1	93.2	86.2	90.7	2.0	53 610	0.5	3 452	6.4	89 569	64.7	73 292	49.9
West Hollywood	80.2	52.4	93.4	87.4	82.9	4.8	25 908	1.1	1 122	4.3	34 915	80.6	31 077	59.0
Westminster	81.4	52.0	88.2	77.9	91.4	3.5	42 731	0.7	2 372	5.6	78 214	60.6	62 288	43.7
West Sacramento	82.0	28.4	91.3	80.6	84.4	7.5	25 805	1.4	1 736	6.7	41 201	64.3	34 087	52.2
Whittier	83.3	53.2	90.8	78.9	90.0	1.7	43 250	1.2	1 779	4.1	70 950	64.5	59 793	52.9
Wildomar	77.7	49.1	89.1	80.1	81.1	3.8	16 849	1.6	1 027	6.1	28 579	58.6	24 350	38.5
Windsor	77.5	25.3	91.2	84.8	90.5	1.9	14 058	0.9	478	3.4	22 833	67.1	18 869	48.7
Woodland	81.2	27.8	91.5	80.8	80.2	5.0	29 783	1.5	1 829	6.1	46 399	66.0	39 301	46.5
Yorba Linda	89.7	62.2	96.5	94.0	90.5	2.7	34 802	0.9	1 223	3.5	55 623	61.6	44 387	46.1
Yuba City	81.6	33.9	86.9	79.0	84.9	6.9	31 720	1.3	3 256	10.3	50 767	57.2	40 605	39.8
Yucaipa	86.1	38.8	86.8	76.0	89.1	5.0	24 946	1.6	1 450	5.8	42 388	54.4	31 385	41.9
COLORADO	82.3	35.7	91.5	83.2	81.7	9.7	2 891 046	2.0	95 813	3.3	4 333 738	68.0	3 622 166	52.0
Arvada	87.3	41.5	89.2	83.2	82.3	10.7	63 882	2.1	1 948	3.0	92 949	69.3	75 375	58.3
Aurora	82.5	44.3	91.8	82.0	81.0	9.0	184 832	1.9	6 401	3.5	275 761	70.8	238 527	53.2
Boulder	60.1	19.1	95.3	88.4	65.5	17.6	61 863	2.0	1 579	2.6	96 578	65.2	83 619	35.5
Brighton	92.4	49.3	93.0	84.8	83.8	6.1	18 313	1.9	737	4.0	28 601	66.4	23 982	51.6
Broomfield	81.2	50.6	97.6	92.3	74.2	22.2	36 455	2.3	1 071	2.9	51 324	73.7	43 256	58.9

1. Employed persons.   2. Households.   3. Percent of civilian labor force.   4. Persons 16 years old and over.

City	Value of residential construction authorized by building permits, 2016			Wholesale trade,[1] 2012				Retail trade,[2] 2012			
	New construction ($1,000)	Number of housing units	Percent single family	Number of establishments	Number of employees	Sales (mil dol)	Annual payroll (mil dol)	Number of establishments	Number of employees	Sales (mil dol)	Annual payroll (mil dol)
	69	70	71	72	73	74	75	76	77	78	79
CALIFORNIA—Cont'd											
San Francisco	1 144 467	4 087	3.0	1 066	12 056	11 121.7	850.7	3 573	43 378	14 632.7	1 455.0
San Gabriel	29 137	84	86.9	128	479	219.8	15.3	211	1 577	473.4	36.5
San Jacinto	21 938	146	100.0	13	59	27.0	2.1	50	861	214.3	22.6
San Jose	355 826	2 728	8.1	1 023	42 254	49 902.3	5 435.8	2 297	40 525	14 982.0	1 850.7
San Juan Capistrano	28 327	62	100.0	62	339	254.3	19.5	128	1 795	714.4	61.3
San Leandro	2 110	4	100.0	249	3 095	1 784.4	179.0	305	5 619	4 342.8	158.5
San Luis Obispo	23 197	93	100.0	83	1 001	442.4	42.4	365	4 892	1 390.7	134.8
San Marcos	70 450	346	23.1	133	1 494	606.3	65.6	246	4 005	1 194.8	115.7
San Mateo	64 988	225	30.2	87	839	586.3	61.8	378	6 587	1 817.9	200.3
San Pablo	5 812	23	100.0	8	30	11.4	1.0	77	947	227.9	22.5
San Rafael	17 480	38	60.5	124	1 151	763.5	73.0	344	5 031	1 757.0	185.3
San Ramon	2 567	29	6.9	98	1 095	2 125.6	86.1	117	2 015	671.5	64.0
Santa Ana	37 490	219	68.0	555	6 699	3 284.1	352.4	822	11 680	3 169.4	309.8
Santa Barbara	40 117	186	74.2	110	1 641	832.1	115.2	531	6 881	1 537.8	181.2
Santa Clara	95 507	419	16.2	378	12 811	10 163.3	1 455.7	352	5 045	2 126.5	215.2
Santa Clarita	135 853	429	100.0	198	3 225	7 495.9	181.0	535	9 774	2 781.7	257.4
Santa Cruz	35 838	165	33.9	59	1 181	594.5	70.1	255	3 098	773.2	81.7
Santa Maria	66 114	274	73.7	109	1 108	692.5	54.8	367	5 362	1 561.2	144.1
Santa Monica	34 362	61	78.7	159	1 317	675.4	71.4	682	10 986	4 981.6	451.1
Santa Paula	2 222	15	100.0	16	D	D	D	55	705	193.2	17.9
Santa Rosa	41 305	238	43.7	166	1 963	1 002.8	113.8	654	10 479	2 817.5	292.1
Santee	9 321	80	100.0	46	410	152.7	18.9	123	2 861	750.0	73.1
Saratoga	16 970	21	100.0	25	D	D	D	34	D	D	D
Seaside	0	0	0.0	13	D	D	D	98	1 427	526.3	48.7
Simi Valley	59 158	229	55.5	144	1 371	847.5	70.8	413	5 841	1 672.1	145.6
Soledad	29 228	93	100.0	7	70	55.4	4.4	27	259	79.1	6.4
South Gate	2 114	18	61.1	79	1 000	650.4	41.1	165	2 220	686.4	53.4
South Pasadena	2 083	7	100.0	36	130	159.3	7.6	56	720	196.3	19.3
South San Francisco	16 856	97	1.0	330	5 622	4 819.0	441.5	187	3 063	1 133.4	96.8
Stanton	530	2	100.0	28	D	D	D	104	1 162	386.5	30.1
Stockton	68 771	279	81.4	239	4 944	5 746.4	249.4	695	10 893	3 295.0	277.1
Suisun City	0	0	0.0	5	D	D	D	31	316	79.6	7.7
Sunnyvale	51 624	240	97.5	210	13 280	9 873.2	2 070.1	279	5 005	1 693.0	148.4
Temecula	49 801	301	53.5	150	2 522	2 074.4	101.5	439	8 208	2 541.9	214.3
Temple City	30 255	84	100.0	91	352	104.0	8.8	99	1 152	299.8	27.6
Thousand Oaks	31 846	97	62.9	158	2 474	5 097.7	275.4	545	9 016	2 880.6	267.4
Torrance	9 490	40	80.0	607	5 653	9 142.9	349.4	663	11 780	3 783.7	319.2
Tracy	115 510	290	98.6	62	1 275	2 123.1	88.6	235	3 772	1 041.6	93.5
Tulare	51 805	337	90.5	50	515	233.8	23.8	181	2 794	808.1	63.7
Turlock	9 291	45	100.0	64	696	377.1	35.5	209	3 514	956.6	86.3
Tustin	53 878	156	88.5	192	2 126	1 489.7	157.5	282	6 234	2 205.6	177.2
Twentynine Palms	87	1	100.0	4	17	9.3	0.6	31	312	75.0	7.1
Union City	628	1	100.0	139	3 705	2 980.9	306.2	107	2 198	621.1	62.9
Upland	17 326	66	100.0	120	664	276.2	25.2	240	3 685	882.0	91.3
Vacaville	98 807	337	100.0	36	332	320.6	15.6	323	5 699	1 586.2	136.8
Vallejo	10 572	39	100.0	28	794	434.0	36.2	233	3 910	1 147.5	114.0
Victorville	31 534	115	100.0	32	241	314.6	8.8	318	6 108	1 710.9	154.4
Visalia	162 433	705	87.0	126	1 321	1 749.7	69.2	396	6 664	1 873.7	166.6
Vista	31 477	100	100.0	201	3 510	1 611.1	184.4	252	4 089	1 219.6	106.9
Walnut	18 250	73	100.0	229	925	557.6	37.6	105	1 008	232.5	20.0
Walnut Creek	25 808	201	2.5	68	595	1 067.3	50.8	308	6 753	1 972.8	221.6
Wasco	12 900	129	100.0	3	D	D	D	41	426	98.5	8.5
Watsonville	8 565	93	52.7	54	1 108	941.3	57.4	146	2 398	2 233.3	65.5
West Covina	15 262	39	100.0	88	433	203.6	17.9	292	5 618	1 476.3	137.6
West Hollywood	80 195	390	3.1	103	527	222.6	29.4	331	3 472	1 179.9	115.1
Westminster	21 289	89	100.0	118	533	307.3	24.1	453	5 841	1 466.4	145.4
West Sacramento	32 644	102	100.0	140	3 579	5 481.1	185.2	124	2 110	547.8	55.1
Whittier	11 653	51	25.5	71	342	114.4	12.0	200	2 993	619.8	66.5
Wildomar	52 710	173	100.0	8	31	5.8	0.7	39	377	110.5	10.6
Windsor	5 097	19	100.0	23	441	297.5	22.1	52	1 077	263.2	30.4
Woodland	79 491	263	100.0	77	829	565.9	44.8	154	2 515	703.3	66.7
Yorba Linda	26 405	126	100.0	124	1 029	775.1	74.6	114	1 557	565.2	46.0
Yuba City	16 069	60	93.3	44	372	199.2	19.4	247	4 003	1 015.1	97.0
Yucaipa	14 818	38	100.0	15	62	22.7	2.0	89	995	271.5	24.6
COLORADO	32 308	126	91.3	5 733	75 717	77 035.0	4 762.1	18 474	245 704	67 815.2	6 508.6
Arvada	232 636	856	100.0	83	880	498.7	59.0	259	3 832	1 145.4	99.5
Aurora	494 334	2 709	49.6	230	5 173	6 512.0	258.0	908	15 374	4 095.7	376.0
Boulder	57 275	101	84.2	187	3 538	1 572.6	297.4	574	8 079	2 002.7	229.8
Brighton	83 997	460	37.4	25	462	250.7	24.9	100	2 136	683.4	52.2
Broomfield	178 540	546	95.8	52	D	D	D	261	4 606	1 000.2	101.7

1. Merchant wholesalers except manufacturers' sales branches and offices. 2. Establishments with payroll.

Table D. Cities — **Real Estate, Professional Services, and Manufacturing**

City	Real estate and rental and leasing, 2012				Professional, scientific, and technical services,[1] 2012				Manufacturing, 2012			
	Number of establishments	Number of employees	Receipts (mil dol)	Annual payroll (mil dol)	Number of establishments	Number of employees	Receipts (mil dol)	Annual payroll (mil dol)	Number of establishments	Number of employees	Receipts (mil dol)	Annual payroll (mil dol)
	80	81	82	83	84	85	86	87	88	89	90	91
CALIFORNIA—Cont'd												
San Francisco	1 828	15 000	6 000.9	1 071.1	6 233	82 644	28 932.6	8 880.3	693	7 506	D	327.6
San Gabriel	81	209	44.7	6.0	144	483	49.4	15.3	43	389	56.0	13.7
San Jacinto	22	63	13.8	1.3	15	126	8.9	4.2	30	354	45.2	12.2
San Jose	1 045	5 858	1 734.1	314.5	2 961	39 395	9 252.2	4 203.2	897	32 421	15 126.0	2 545.5
San Juan Capistrano	74	237	68.9	14.0	219	993	197.0	63.5	28	792	272.1	51.3
San Leandro	129	905	283.7	43.6	123	D	D	D	182	4 777	1 833.5	233.7
San Luis Obispo	137	693	116.7	25.1	338	D	D	D	73	1 170	219.2	52.4
San Marcos	103	377	79.4	15.8	233	D	D	D	157	4 276		204.5
San Mateo	182	789	420.2	55.7	532	D	D	D	46	601	D	36.6
San Pablo	17	59	11.9	1.6	12	95	8.0	3.1	10	50	D	2.1
San Rafael	161	794	806.7	46.0	493	D	D	D	76	632	157.8	32.1
San Ramon	131	D	D	D	523	7 408	2 010.9	642.3	27	302	D	18.1
Santa Ana	316	2 685	564.8	123.4	1 013	D	D	D	771	19 771	5 177.3	938.8
Santa Barbara	287	1 101	228.5	47.7	647	D	D	D	96	998	197.0	51.4
Santa Clara	177	1 396	691.0	107.1	920	D	D	D	508	15 935	4 524.8	1 286.2
Santa Clarita	233	1 129	228.7	48.7	511	D	D	D	231	8 930	2 137.1	549.9
Santa Cruz	87	286	75.5	8.3	283	D	D	D	90	1 324	346.2	64.2
Santa Maria	100	522	89.8	17.0	147	D	D	D	89	2 996	790.2	118.9
Santa Monica	418	3 011	1 488.6	234.2	1 162	8 835	2 052.7	791.5	88	807	172.9	38.0
Santa Paula	22	111	32.5	6.0	21	146	17.4	6.0	23	433	81.8	19.2
Santa Rosa	254	1 131	247.9	41.8	608	4 438	446.1	232.5	153	4 862	1 036.0	344.0
Santee	58	270	38.3	8.6	72	D	D	D	84	1 353	D	65.9
Saratoga	85	219	79.9	14.2	167	D	D	D	14	252	D	24.7
Seaside	12	66	11.0	2.0	18	D	D	D	10	85	3.7	1.5
Simi Valley	118	557	168.5	25.9	369	2 804	537.5	176.7	130	3 504	833.5	189.1
Soledad	12	45	5.3	1.0	4	32	1.6	0.7	4	73	D	2.8
South Gate	41	202	45.9	8.1	28	402	45.0	18.4	121	4 380	1 778.1	206.4
South Pasadena	58	D	D	D	141	D	D	D	13	86	D	3.0
South San Francisco	76	666	132.1	27.1	187	D	D	D	111	10 909	D	1 501.6
Stanton	19	84	24.1	3.2	31	D	D	D	63	702	101.6	31.4
Stockton	253	1 338	218.7	48.2	370	D	D	D	166	5 937	2 921.8	277.1
Suisun City	10	23	4.0	0.9	18	89	8.0	3.0	7	22	3.1	0.6
Sunnyvale	153	960	227.4	45.3	804	18 744	5 191.0	1 991.2	225	25 088	10 930.7	2 976.8
Temecula	184	706	142.9	26.4	368	D	D	D	125	5 024	3 482.1	298.6
Temple City	41	D	D	D	76	235	26.3	7.7	24	149	14.3	4.1
Thousand Oaks	279	971	217.6	50.5	807	D	D	D	124	3 346	1 238.8	239.2
Torrance	343	1 992	374.5	76.2	879	D	D	D	248	12 560	11 915.2	799.0
Tracy	76	181	51.3	7.4	106	D	D	D	52	2 358	1 110.0	110.2
Tulare	46	149	26.3	3.7	47	322	46.6	16.0	27	1 940	2 387.4	99.7
Turlock	58	280	33.7	7.1	74	D	D	D	71	2 986	1 675.0	122.7
Tustin	172	853	210.1	42.1	549	D	D	D	98	3 270	679.2	193.1
Twentynine Palms	11	77	17.9	2.8	15	D	D	D	NA	NA	NA	NA
Union City	40	162	39.3	7.5	109	D	D	D	81	3 879	1 033.7	226.9
Upland	102	876	99.4	49.3	209	1 306	185.3	64.5	95	981	198.4	46.1
Vacaville	106	542	123.2	18.1	114	632	67.7	26.4	44	2 425	D	138.6
Vallejo	73	300	80.3	10.0	95	D	D	D	32	356	D	16.1
Victorville	88	465	57.7	12.2	103	D	D	D	18	1 222	665.7	49.7
Visalia	131	834	120.0	25.9	245	D	D	D	67	2 417	1 355.8	121.5
Vista	138	738	172.1	27.4	230	1 448	254.4	77.5	178	7 380	2 754.2	405.5
Walnut	56	D	D	D	107	340	55.3	13.1	30	318	84.6	17.4
Walnut Creek	224	1 209	285.4	68.5	691	6 364	1 516.1	549.4	32	591	D	33.9
Wasco	14	37	6.6	1.1	4	20	2.4	0.5	6	104	D	5.8
Watsonville	60	256	46.9	8.8	72	D	D	D	57	1 381	353.8	59.3
West Covina	82	421	55.4	14.7	144	D	D	D	16	632	104.1	35.0
West Hollywood	146	820	248.1	40.6	398	2 286	623.2	201.7	36	225	31.0	8.4
Westminster	93	300	81.0	12.0	145	635	68.8	25.2	93	775	106.4	30.0
West Sacramento	77	604	123.5	25.4	83	D	D	D	64	3 118	D	165.9
Whittier	102	338	57.2	9.6	166	755	83.9	25.8	47	732	223.4	31.7
Wildomar	15	123	9.5	2.7	23	D	D	D	8	75	D	4.6
Windsor	23	160	41.9	4.6	57	335	82.2	13.8	26	570	122.3	31.5
Woodland	60	300	55.2	10.6	81	D	D	D	57	2 002	D	92.5
Yorba Linda	102	293	60.3	12.2	246	D	D	D	54	1 386	714.1	106.8
Yuba City	78	420	47.8	10.8	103	484	48.6	18.0	43	1 144	457.9	62.2
Yucaipa	45	152	21.2	4.8	59	175	19.2	5.3	20	326	39.2	12.4
COLORADO	9 295	38 706	8 482.5	1 569.6	23 761	175 448	32 686.8	12 537.0	4 898	114 632	50 447.1	6 230.1
Arvada	125	276	48.7	9.2	382	1 535	215.1	79.5	110	2 139	615.1	128.0
Aurora	298	1 233	267.5	46.2	635	D	D	D	122	2 400	644.1	118.3
Boulder	316	1 091	258.0	42.8	1 346	D	D	D	216	7 153	2 744.6	521.0
Brighton	34	114	13.8	3.3	50	D	D	D	22	697	222.2	38.9
Broomfield	96	313	77.1	11.4	323	D	D	D	82	3 087	3 918.4	188.5

1. Establishments subject to federal tax.

Accommodation and Food Services, Arts, Entertainment, and Recreation, and Health Care and Social Assistance

City	Accommodation and food services, 2012				Arts, entertainment, and recreation,[1] 2012				Health care and social assistance,[1] 2012			
	Number of establishments	Number of employees	Sales (mil dol)	Annual payroll (mil dol)	Number of establishments	Number of employees	Receipts (mil dol)	Annual payroll (mil dol)	Number of establishments	Number of employees	Receipts (mil dol)	Annual payroll (mil dol)
	92	93	94	95	96	97	98	99	100	101	102	103
CALIFORNIA—Cont'd												
San Francisco	4 059	73 417	6 142.7	1 841.6	320	6 226	1 006.9	402.9	2 413	18 874	2 647.7	1 112.5
San Gabriel	176	1 866	105.8	26.5	3	D	D	D	209	D	D	8.2
San Jacinto	40	628	27.2	6.9	NA	NA	NA	NA	31	234	22.6	8.2
San Jose	1 916	31 023	1 919.1	523.7	141	4 615	413.7	177.4	2 175	24 468	3 274.0	1 300.7
San Juan Capistrano	73	1 257	72.0	21.1	15	325	32.8	6.9	115	1 172	106.9	43.2
San Leandro	191	2 329	146.2	37.7	12	D	D	D	240	3 538	346.0	150.9
San Luis Obispo	218	4 125	220.9	62.5	12	164	6.9	2.3	302	3 655	493.7	183.6
San Marcos	169	2 973	180.6	46.5	17	D	D	D	135	1 504	166.4	68.7
San Mateo	313	4 808	325.1	89.5	29	D	D	D	417	4 045	533.1	182.6
San Pablo	60	739	38.6	9.7	1	D	D	D	29	D	D	D
San Rafael	224	2 841	163.4	47.3	63	352	83.8	17.7	235	3 214	429.2	221.2
San Ramon	148	2 324	159.8	41.1	19	520	27.8	8.6	273	2 624	416.2	140.8
Santa Ana	542	7 493	462.8	121.3	25	226	31.1	6.2	708	9 016	1 138.6	464.2
Santa Barbara	421	8 143	494.4	143.1	62	721	53.2	16.6	469	3 762	656.2	216.6
Santa Clara	400	7 151	581.1	157.9	31	2 308	382.4	216.1	211	D	D	D
Santa Clarita	327	6 766	351.4	98.9	117	1 303	86.4	30.6	468	4 669	577.5	213.6
Santa Cruz	256	4 446	253.9	74.7	24	906	59.8	21.6	173	1 586	166.8	71.0
Santa Maria	178	2 596	144.9	39.6	14	249	11.8	3.8	274	2 403	258.2	98.4
Santa Monica	454	12 289	947.7	276.5	677	1 752	660.2	254.2	841	5 314	753.0	267.1
Santa Paula	42	D	D	D	5	29	1.6	0.4	36	257	29.5	11.9
Santa Rosa	389	5 764	355.0	95.6	52	826	50.3	22.4	579	8 031	1 158.3	525.6
Santee	108	1 620	85.1	24.6	12	D	D	D	70	450	42.3	16.6
Saratoga	64	883	58.5	15.6	6	78	7.1	2.7	102	D	D	D
Seaside	71	1 005	65.6	17.6	2	D	D	D	15	D	D	D
Simi Valley	251	3 984	230.6	59.4	45	D	D	D	324	2 835	295.7	109.2
Soledad	21	D	D	D	NA	NA	NA	NA	7	42	9.1	2.3
South Gate	108	1 192	74.4	17.5	6	D	D	D	75	841	82.5	28.5
South Pasadena	61	882	45.7	13.4	39	D	D	D	106	717	73.8	27.1
South San Francisco	204	3 673	316.2	82.3	17	D	D	D	162	2 570	353.5	192.7
Stanton	82	924	52.9	13.0	6	D	D	D	31	D	D	D
Stockton	424	6 912	366.5	95.4	34	716	47.6	17.9	587	9 180	993.6	391.5
Suisun City	31	426	23.3	5.9	4	D	D	D	17	54	5.3	2.1
Sunnyvale	346	4 781	349.1	86.3	34	D	D	D	390	3 554	486.8	163.1
Temecula	281	9 653	965.6	240.6	28	697	33.3	9.3	311	2 408	227.9	86.7
Temple City	64	836	47.4	11.5	4	8	1.6	0.3	95	D	D	D
Thousand Oaks	317	6 760	378.5	109.1	96	684	71.5	26.4	1 030	6 430	1 012.7	325.7
Torrance	419	8 055	498.1	139.8	55	D	D	D	1 030	9 696	1 168.6	428.5
Tracy	137	2 191	111.1	28.9	16	D	D	D	158	D	D	D
Tulare	80	1 403	74.5	19.3	7	D	D	D	100	D	D	D
Turlock	146	2 528	128.2	35.1	14	D	D	D	154	1 477	166.6	56.7
Tustin	232	4 167	224.8	65.2	20	D	D	D	346	3 588	605.0	147.8
Twentynine Palms	49	661	48.0	9.9	3	D	D	D	116	1 019	90.2	38.7
Union City	113	1 771	95.5	26.3	7	D	D	D	116	D	D	D
Upland	145	D	D	D	23	D	D	D	346	D	D	D
Vacaville	168	3 293	173.1	48.6	16	411	22.5	5.3	167	2 305	379.6	145.5
Vallejo	167	2 623	147.9	38.4	17	1 257	78.4	21.8	214	4 353	620.0	337.9
Victorville	175	3 245	167.9	46.5	12	D	D	D	199	3 415	365.9	130.7
Visalia	234	4 245	216.8	60.7	11	293	17.9	3.9	349	3 648	417.3	160.1
Vista	171	2 150	114.0	29.2	10	288	22.6	6.6	207	2 342	240.7	88.8
Walnut	48	539	29.1	7.5	6	D	D	D	87	702	41.8	19.2
Walnut Creek	202	4 358	259.1	78.0	28	363	25.0	7.5	442	D	D	D
Wasco	28	D	D	D	1	D	D	D	13	D	D	D
Watsonville	90	1 218	72.9	17.9	6	D	D	D	139	2 047	245.2	88.9
West Covina	196	3 421	184.5	48.2	11	D	D	D	314	D	D	D
West Hollywood	229	7 741	543.1	166.4	482	D	D	D	248	1 104	177.3	57.1
Westminster	245	2 672	144.5	39.6	14	D	D	D	281	2 520	273.5	96.0
West Sacramento	91	D	D	D	9	D	D	D	67	D	D	D
Whittier	177	2 662	149.2	42.8	10	D	D	D	295	D	D	D
Wildomar	31	402	22.3	5.8	7	D	D	D	53	1 307	161.0	68.4
Windsor	52	D	D	D	5	89	4.1	1.4	37	230	17.3	6.3
Woodland	104	D	D	D	9	124	3.6	1.1	85	1 376	153.3	86.4
Yorba Linda	92	1 710	83.5	24.6	25	D	D	D	167	D	D	D
Yuba City	124	2 121	110.6	28.1	14	D	D	D	196	D	D	D
Yucaipa	55	764	39.2	10.6	11	D	D	D	83	D	D	D
COLORADO	12 744	240 484	13 617.7	3 994.6	1 950	41 585	3 048.6	1 082.5	12 701	140 738	14 693.2	6 167.1
Arvada	186	3 172	160.0	45.6	24	225	9.3	2.8	216	2 393	194.0	72.0
Aurora	577	10 728	567.1	162.5	44	760	41.5	13.5	575	7 897	607.0	279.9
Boulder	429	8 834	501.9	149.9	102	970	50.4	16.4	579	4 074	429.0	172.7
Brighton	83	1 338	72.1	19.3	7	D	D	D	76	D	D	D
Broomfield	143	2 944	169.6	54.7	20	D	D	D	135	1 542	167.0	62.6

1. Establishments subject to federal tax.

City	Other services[1], 2012				Government employment and payroll, 2012								
						March payroll							
							Percent of total for:						
	Number of establishments	Number of employees	Receipts (mil dol)	Annual payroll (mil dol)	Full-time equivalent employees	Total (dollars)	Adminis-tration, judicial, and legal	Police and Corrections	Fire Protection	Highways and trans-portation	Health and welfare	Natural resources and utilities	Education and libraries
	104	105	106	107	108	109	110	111	112	113	114	115	116
CALIFORNIA—Cont'd													
San Francisco	1 603	10 876	1 109.6	320.2	28 349	217 722 943	13.9	17.4	7.3	22.7	24.7	11.1	2.1
San Gabriel	96	408	39.5	11.3	191	1 327 334	11.3	38.5	24.6	6.9	3.8	11.2	0.0
San Jacinto	34	D	D	D	65	267 518	30.0	0.0	0.0	10.8	18.2	28.6	0.0
San Jose	1 175	6 748	929.6	202.4	5 214	38 715 963	8.8	33.1	18.0	9.9	1.0	14.9	3.3
San Juan Capistrano	48	217	27.5	7.0	115	698 016	51.1	0.6	0.0	8.3	1.4	33.4	0.0
San Leandro	163	1 027	148.8	32.8	375	2 465 492	13.1	40.7	0.0	11.7	4.5	15.4	7.2
San Luis Obispo	106	523	45.2	13.0	406	3 104 703	10.0	27.1	17.3	3.8	5.5	22.1	0.0
San Marcos	120	713	60.9	18.7	279	1 870 622	14.4	0.0	37.4	21.7	5.6	15.9	0.0
San Mateo	203	D	D	D	610	5 077 524	8.5	28.2	20.6	5.7	5.0	23.9	4.0
San Pablo	34	189	13.0	3.7	74	394 492	49.3	1.6	0.0	13.4	12.2	22.1	0.0
San Rafael	194	1 244	151.0	45.2	864	2 915 776	12.5	26.3	32.7	4.3	0.0	17.6	4.1
San Ramon	112	897	75.3	23.7	279	2 017 589	12.1	37.5	0.0	31.3	1.9	13.4	0.0
Santa Ana	390	2 175	232.8	64.4	2 711	12 719 386	0.7	3.5	1.9	0.5	0.5	0.5	0.1
Santa Barbara	186	1 179	94.1	27.8	1 156	7 284 111	11.3	26.7	14.2	12.8	3.2	19.5	2.7
Santa Clara	235	1 567	145.2	45.6	961	8 545 138	10.4	22.6	18.9	6.8	0.6	30.5	3.6
Santa Clarita	255	1 689	176.5	43.8	434	2 697 699	16.1	0.0	0.0	6.2	6.5	35.1	0.0
Santa Cruz	86	701	70.7	23.5	774	4 763 881	12.0	20.2	14.4	4.6	2.0	33.9	8.6
Santa Maria	115	781	97.3	22.6	497	2 980 086	10.3	35.8	13.6	5.8	5.2	22.7	3.8
Santa Monica	353	2 604	175.5	57.6	2 163	15 220 898	14.3	23.8	11.2	20.8	3.2	14.6	3.3
Santa Paula	27	65	7.4	1.7	110	646 323	13.8	38.3	18.1	4.2	7.2	16.1	0.0
Santa Rosa	252	1 669	155.6	51.2	1 213	8 220 156	11.3	23.5	16.6	10.0	2.3	23.5	0.0
Santee	91	554	55.8	16.7	148	1 012 079	28.3	0.6	51.2	9.9	1.2	8.9	0.0
Saratoga	30	141	14.2	3.4	58	435 826	25.2	0.0	0.0	22.5	22.1	14.1	0.0
Seaside	49	196	21.9	5.6	158	994 460	9.5	41.0	20.0	8.9	0.9	6.0	0.0
Simi Valley	155	1 140	145.1	27.9	592	3 356 138	14.7	32.1	0.0	21.1	15.4	16.6	0.0
Soledad	4	16	1.4	0.3	45	264 288	21.2	60.5	0.0	1.9	0.0	16.4	0.0
South Gate	76	242	20.4	4.9	318	1 634 468	11.2	44.3	0.0	17.0	9.3	18.2	0.0
South Pasadena	40	185	13.1	3.6	168	950 670	11.5	35.7	20.9	5.1	8.3	7.4	9.4
South San Francisco	114	1 365	141.2	47.8	497	3 574 682	9.0	29.5	25.0	5.7	0.7	17.9	6.9
Stanton	52	290	23.7	6.8	38	219 326	37.8	0.0	0.0	18.7	21.0	22.5	0.0
Stockton	289	1 996	163.5	53.9	2 010	12 427 436	7.5	55.8	14.5	0.7	2.3	9.7	2.3
Suisun City	26	82	7.1	2.2	85	454 879	15.9	38.0	4.6	17.0	8.7	8.9	0.0
Sunnyvale	167	956	108.4	37.1	870	7 456 793	9.7	27.3	18.0	7.5	4.3	20.3	3.7
Temecula	183	1 029	84.1	22.4	200	1 117 348	29.5	0.5	0.7	25.3	14.8	29.0	0.0
Temple City	57	216	18.4	4.3	75	319 507	42.5	0.0	0.0	0.0	0.0	25.4	0.0
Thousand Oaks	209	1 193	114.8	31.6	440	2 648 993	26.5	1.5	0.0	28.8	2.2	20.8	12.0
Torrance	244	1 814	167.6	51.1	1 361	10 031 057	10.8	31.2	18.3	15.1	4.3	10.6	3.4
Tracy	100	467	54.4	18.3	420	2 906 444	11.9	31.9	22.5	6.6	1.4	20.4	0.0
Tulare	53	314	42.3	11.1	347	1 781 358	7.7	33.8	16.3	2.3	3.5	23.6	2.6
Turlock	89	557	53.2	15.3	394	2 010 112	13.5	34.3	14.7	8.6	2.6	22.0	0.0
Tustin	115	974	97.2	28.4	338	2 566 292	15.4	48.7	0.0	14.6	2.0	11.4	0.0
Twentynine Palms	17	95	7.7	2.4	26	143 616	18.5	18.8	0.0	23.3	0.0	39.5	0.0
Union City	68	618	95.8	22.4	252	1 774 885	14.0	49.2	0.0	3.0	5.2	19.0	0.0
Upland	130	575	53.8	14.8	892	4 437 479	3.7	19.6	11.3	3.4	2.6	5.7	1.6
Vacaville	115	578	46.5	13.3	584	4 121 808	12.2	30.0	19.8	13.3	4.5	20.2	0.0
Vallejo	105	454	43.4	12.4	573	3 266 338	8.6	32.1	16.0	8.2	5.4	28.1	0.0
Victorville	89	506	48.5	13.3	340	1 783 174	43.6	0.0	0.0	23.9	2.4	30.1	0.0
Visalia	159	989	95.7	27.0	612	3 335 649	7.1	37.8	15.7	9.2	6.0	23.1	0.0
Vista	114	744	73.7	22.1	290	1 741 746	25.7	0.0	39.6	9.1	5.0	16.8	0.0
Walnut	49	269	24.4	7.7	52	276 966	49.6	0.0	0.0	21.7	8.9	19.8	0.0
Walnut Creek	154	2 209	191.8	80.2	389	2 700 536	16.3	37.1	0.0	5.7	0.7	23.8	0.0
Wasco	12	D	D	D	60	270 885	30.6	0.0	0.0	10.8	0.0	46.4	0.0
Watsonville	64	225	22.2	6.1	373	2 335 983	9.1	27.3	13.3	4.5	1.8	31.8	5.7
West Covina	85	472	27.2	8.0	445	2 840 481	9.7	46.0	25.6	12.3	2.3	4.1	0.0
West Hollywood	167	1 186	102.6	24.5	216	1 683 338	37.7	0.0	0.0	20.8	29.7	11.7	0.0
Westminster	142	768	59.5	22.1	290	1 903 418	13.5	58.3	0.0	6.1	4.4	8.3	0.0
West Sacramento	87	674	95.2	28.0	402	3 250 336	14.1	25.4	25.1	1.9	6.5	14.5	0.0
Whittier	107	517	43.8	12.2	478	2 572 894	10.2	44.2	0.0	4.8	6.2	21.3	5.7
Wildomar	17	D	D	D	12	48 677	78.0	0.0	0.0	0.0	0.0	0.0	0.0
Windsor	24	D	D	D	98	584 900	39.6	0.0	0.0	13.3	0.0	47.2	0.0
Woodland	72	394	32.9	9.0	304	1 839 421	7.6	32.0	20.0	4.8	13.1	16.1	2.4
Yorba Linda	77	517	47.3	14.9	130	661 872	25.1	0.0	0.0	10.0	1.5	30.7	18.9
Yuba City	80	502	45.5	14.6	299	1 719 010	11.1	33.5	26.1	7.0	0.0	20.2	0.0
Yucaipa	42	177	13.9	3.4	44	165 657	7.8	0.0	0.0	38.1	0.0	54.1	0.0
COLORADO	7 918	46 005	3 942.1	1 242.3	X	X	X	X	X	X	X	X	X
Arvada	164	824	65.2	20.3	661	3 647 076	20.5	35.5	0.0	9.8	4.4	22.2	0.0
Aurora	396	2 655	208.3	66.3	2 579	13 742 359	13.6	38.9	14.9	4.2	2.6	20.7	1.4
Boulder	215	1 177	93.8	31.3	1 108	6 200 124	15.9	23.9	11.2	6.6	1.6	26.0	4.7
Brighton	47	213	22.1	5.8	297	2 531 155	9.4	15.0	0.0	3.0	57.8	11.9	0.0
Broomfield	92	520	39.4	13.2	687	3 465 198	16.4	35.0	0.0	2.4	18.0	19.6	3.9

1. Establishments subject to federal tax.

Table D. Cities — **City Government Finances**

City	General revenue Total (mil dol) 117	Intergovernmental Total (mil dol) 118	Intergovernmental Percent from state government 119	Taxes Total (mil dol) 120	Taxes Per capita¹ Total 121	Taxes Per capita¹ Property 122	Taxes Per capita¹ Sales and gross receipts 123	General expenditure Total (mil dol) 124	General expenditure Per capita¹ Total 125	General expenditure Capital outlays 126
CALIFORNIA—Cont'd										
San Francisco	7 274.1	2 355.9	68.6	2 846.2	3 430	1 747	885	5 704.0	6 875	846
San Gabriel	37.1	3.0	81.2	25.2	626	356	258	40.2	999	177
San Jacinto	28.1	1.5	100.0	14.5	318	213	92	31.0	681	34
San Jose	1 721.1	116.7	56.0	863.4	876	456	363	1 428.0	1 449	178
San Juan Capistrano	47.2	4.4	76.8	30.4	856	577	270	40.6	1 144	265
San Leandro	123.0	8.3	72.0	88.5	1 016	465	517	121.7	1 398	127
San Luis Obispo	81.4	6.3	56.0	48.1	1 049	330	716	76.5	1 668	350
San Marcos	121.3	7.6	84.2	76.6	879	491	384	132.6	1 523	283
San Mateo	145.7	11.0	62.3	86.7	867	454	370	148.4	1 483	264
San Pablo	44.1	1.8	97.0	39.1	1 326	549	776	38.0	1 291	386
San Rafael	85.9	4.1	86.9	52.8	903	369	506	87.5	1 496	47
San Ramon	74.2	3.7	100.0	41.1	557	343	208	75.1	1 017	190
Santa Ana	440.5	127.5	23.8	205.9	621	334	285	391.8	1 181	145
Santa Barbara	246.8	36.0	63.6	102.8	1 149	512	631	228.4	2 550	530
Santa Clara	280.5	11.7	71.5	124.3	1 039	577	456	212.3	1 776	110
Santa Clarita	152.4	24.6	54.9	80.2	448	205	233	145.6	814	191
Santa Cruz	132.1	4.8	59.8	60.6	977	437	528	145.4	2 345	279
Santa Maria	117.0	16.8	78.0	58.2	574	182	391	112.6	1 111	201
Santa Monica	560.2	57.7	51.4	332.1	3 618	1 337	2 095	538.6	5 867	1 727
Santa Paula	29.3	4.2	87.4	12.9	428	275	94	23.2	771	142
Santa Rosa	262.1	24.5	59.6	119.5	702	255	435	250.3	1 470	305
Santee	44.7	2.6	60.7	34.2	616	379	155	49.1	885	180
Saratoga	20.9	1.1	97.2	15.0	490	306	160	22.6	736	169
Seaside	27.0	2.8	39.4	22.4	662	372	288	30.5	899	206
Simi Valley	96.1	10.2	52.4	62.4	497	300	194	92.5	736	103
Soledad	15.7	1.0	97.1	6.1	229	125	103	14.9	563	43
South Gate	80.6	17.7	38.8	36.7	383	216	166	67.6	707	121
South Pasadena	28.7	3.5	84.1	19.0	731	429	296	28.2	1 089	148
South San Francisco	128.4	5.4	89.0	77.6	1 179	732	371	122.6	1 863	259
Stanton	32.9	2.6	78.3	26.3	682	496	169	38.1	989	253
Stockton	381.7	98.9	79.6	161.7	544	215	325	384.7	1 293	244
Suisun City	27.1	4.4	39.6	13.1	458	385	71	30.3	1 061	113
Sunnyvale	274.8	32.4	34.0	112.9	770	377	386	274.4	1 871	145
Temecula	113.3	14.0	33.6	69.7	665	351	310	129.7	1 238	371
Temple City	15.4	1.3	81.7	11.0	305	164	133	14.2	393	12
Thousand Oaks	143.2	11.9	64.9	84.5	660	350	305	145.4	1 135	190
Torrance	261.0	41.4	39.9	155.5	1 056	365	677	234.0	1 589	332
Tracy	114.6	11.3	53.2	47.1	556	256	297	128.6	1 519	464
Tulare	97.1	4.2	71.5	38.5	632	245	375	90.8	1 492	431
Turlock	69.6	5.8	56.0	34.6	496	222	216	83.2	1 193	431
Tustin	77.0	3.6	66.8	51.5	661	437	220	77.9	1 001	98
Twentynine Palms	11.2	1.2	85.8	9.5	370	226	143	12.3	477	86
Union City	85.1	5.7	83.5	61.0	850	562	282	92.0	1 283	294
Upland	71.1	4.5	65.1	37.7	502	337	159	74.2	987	59
Vacaville	153.8	33.0	26.6	79.6	848	575	270	156.0	1 662	571
Vallejo	195.2	49.6	22.5	64.7	549	229	308	152.7	1 295	112
Victorville	115.4	9.5	68.3	53.9	448	251	195	130.1	1 082	123
Visalia	157.6	23.1	61.9	68.5	540	218	320	143.8	1 134	282
Vista	132.0	9.1	80.1	57.8	601	345	252	117.1	1 217	321
Walnut	21.5	1.3	82.0	13.1	436	322	106	20.0	668	25
Walnut Creek	70.1	2.6	97.1	45.9	699	317	354	80.4	1 224	103
Wasco	13.5	2.6	29.2	5.5	217	145	72	13.2	517	75
Watsonville	67.3	6.4	30.2	31.1	599	394	194	72.0	1 387	113
West Covina	102.2	8.7	74.3	63.9	594	395	196	91.9	854	133
West Hollywood	88.9	5.0	44.0	55.8	1 601	602	980	93.6	2 685	485
Westminster	91.7	10.4	70.7	68.6	750	538	210	114.0	1 245	487
West Sacramento	140.9	23.6	64.6	66.7	1 344	812	401	129.2	2 601	822
Whittier	79.8	8.9	72.4	41.7	483	250	231	82.4	954	94
Wildomar	9.4	3.2	100.0	5.9	177	97	62	9.3	280	7
Windsor	23.5	2.8	29.7	16.3	603	373	188	23.2	859	257
Woodland	72.5	12.3	93.9	44.7	793	310	482	78.0	1 385	376
Yorba Linda	62.1	4.6	47.2	35.0	526	382	138	79.9	1 201	263
Yuba City	54.9	5.2	89.4	33.0	508	270	193	59.0	910	163
Yucaipa	28.1	0.9	94.5	20.9	398	293	82	29.1	554	111
COLORADO	X	X	X	X	X	X	X	X	X	X
Arvada	132.6	21.2	32.5	67.8	619	84	534	119.2	1 086	160
Aurora	380.8	48.7	50.2	216.5	638	102	536	400.3	1 180	162
Boulder	219.5	16.4	84.1	150.1	1 471	286	1 185	210.4	2 063	39
Brighton	32.9	3.4	84.3	21.9	624	53	567	24.3	691	69
Broomfield	149.9	15.4	40.7	113.5	1 924	654	1 161	109.7	1 860	53

1. Based on population estimated as of July 1 of the year shown.

Table D. Cities — **City Government Finances**

City	Public welfare	Highways	Parking facilities	Education	Health and hospitals	Police protection	Sewerage and sanitation	Parks and recreation	Housing and community development	Interest on debt
	127	128	129	130	131	132	133	134	135	136
CALIFORNIA—Cont'd										
San Francisco	8.5	4.4	2.4	0.0	30.2	6.6	4.7	4.3	4.2	7.1
San Gabriel..................	0.0	12.3	0.0	0.0	0.0	30.1	0.2	11.5	3.0	0.2
San Jacinto	0.0	13.6	0.0	0.0	0.0	28.1	10.6	3.1	13.0	4.6
San Jose	0.0	6.0	0.5	0.0	0.1	17.6	18.1	6.3	3.6	18.3
San Juan Capistrano	0.0	12.0	0.0	0.0	1.3	17.5	6.8	9.2	9.6	7.7
San Leandro................	0.0	9.1	0.2	0.0	1.1	22.2	6.5	5.1	9.9	2.9
San Luis Obispo..........	0.0	16.3	3.7	0.0	0.0	20.2	13.2	9.3	2.1	2.5
San Marcos.................	0.0	12.9	0.0	0.0	3.2	11.1	0.0	7.4	24.5	11.5
San Mateo...................	0.0	10.7	1.3	0.0	1.3	19.6	17.8	9.7	2.9	4.2
San Pablo...................	0.0	22.7	0.0	0.0	0.4	36.6	0.0	6.8	8.3	9.8
San Rafael..................	0.0	8.4	3.3	0.0	6.9	21.6	0.0	11.4	2.3	2.2
San Ramon..................	0.0	11.3	0.0	0.0	0.0	21.4	0.0	20.7	7.9	7.1
Santa Ana	0.0	9.8	1.0	0.0	2.9	30.3	5.4	5.0	15.2	5.2
Santa Barbara..............	0.0	12.0	2.9	0.0	0.2	15.2	15.9	8.4	3.7	1.3
Santa Clara.................	0.0	9.0	0.6	0.0	2.0	19.7	16.4	8.4	2.4	4.7
Santa Clarita	0.0	30.6	0.0	0.0	0.1	13.0	0.3	12.7	3.7	3.5
Santa Cruz	0.0	6.8	2.2	0.0	1.0	27.5	18.8	8.9	8.5	2.8
Santa Maria	0.0	11.1	0.0	0.0	0.0	18.5	25.1	6.9	0.4	3.7
Santa Monica	0.0	6.8	0.2	0.0	3.3	13.7	7.2	9.9	25.8	2.8
Santa Paula................	0.0	10.9	0.0	0.0	0.8	23.3	14.7	14.4	4.7	6.1
Santa Rosa	0.0	11.5	1.9	0.0	0.9	17.4	23.0	7.1	3.3	7.1
Santee.......................	0.0	15.5	0.0	0.0	6.2	21.7	0.0	3.5	17.3	4.1
Saratoga....................	0.0	23.5	0.0	0.0	3.2	18.0	0.0	18.8	0.4	2.4
Seaside......................	0.0	9.8	0.0	0.0	0.6	36.9	0.0	8.6	10.5	5.0
Simi Valley	0.0	9.2	0.0	0.0	1.4	30.9	17.3	1.0	10.4	3.5
Soledad......................	0.0	13.2	0.0	0.0	1.3	25.1	31.6	3.9	2.2	2.7
South Gate.................	0.0	24.1	0.0	0.0	0.1	28.3	7.2	6.6	3.6	9.8
South Pasadena...........	0.0	13.6	0.1	0.0	1.0	25.7	4.3	10.7	1.7	0.0
South San Francisco.....	0.0	19.1	0.7	0.0	6.2	17.3	14.3	8.2	4.4	5.1
Stanton......................	0.0	6.3	0.0	0.0	0.2	22.4	1.8	5.3	35.3	8.9
Stockton.....................	0.0	9.4	0.6	0.0	0.6	24.6	11.6	5.1	6.1	5.1
Suisun City	0.0	7.8	0.0	0.0	0.0	16.2	0.0	6.2	22.0	8.1
Sunnyvale...................	0.0	8.6	0.5	0.3	0.5	11.3	28.1	8.2	2.4	1.5
Temecula....................	0.0	19.9	0.0	0.0	0.2	17.4	4.7	15.3	10.4	3.5
Temple City	0.0	9.2	1.0	0.0	1.7	23.9	0.2	13.7	6.8	1.8
Thousand Oaks............	0.0	22.4	0.0	0.0	0.5	17.9	13.0	6.9	8.4	2.8
Torrance.....................	0.0	12.5	0.0	0.0	4.5	28.2	6.5	8.3	2.8	3.0
Tracy	0.0	6.2	0.0	0.0	0.4	16.6	24.2	12.4	3.8	5.1
Tulare	0.0	20.9	0.0	0.0	1.3	13.0	23.7	3.4	6.2	11.6
Turlock......................	0.0	9.9	0.0	0.0	0.5	33.2	16.6	4.4	11.0	1.6
Tustin........................	0.0	13.4	0.0	0.0	0.0	29.4	0.0	4.0	8.8	9.1
Twentynine Palms........	0.0	17.8	0.0	0.0	5.0	25.2	0.0	13.8	5.5	4.2
Union City..................	0.0	8.6	0.0	0.0	0.6	22.1	0.8	13.1	17.7	7.7
Upland.......................	0.0	9.8	0.0	0.0	1.4	22.4	19.7	2.8	10.4	2.3
Vacaville....................	0.0	6.6	0.0	0.0	4.4	17.0	29.3	4.9	18.9	3.8
Vallejo.......................	0.0	10.3	0.0	0.0	0.4	22.0	15.1	0.9	18.2	3.0
Victorville..................	0.0	6.3	0.0	0.0	0.4	13.7	19.3	5.0	2.1	11.3
Visalia.......................	0.0	12.5	0.0	0.0	0.0	19.7	23.2	7.4	2.8	1.1
Vista	0.0	9.8	0.0	0.0	3.8	15.0	17.2	7.4	9.0	7.5
Walnut	0.0	20.0	0.0	0.0	0.6	30.8	0.0	17.0	5.4	5.1
Walnut Creek	0.0	11.1	4.4	0.0	0.0	23.7	0.0	30.1	1.5	0.3
Wasco	0.0	17.2	0.0	0.0	1.0	28.0	26.1	0.0	8.4	1.4
Watsonville.................	0.0	7.2	0.0	0.0	1.0	19.7	25.5	4.2	6.2	0.5
West Covina................	0.0	14.3	0.4	0.0	2.6	31.7	0.0	5.3	5.0	7.9
West Hollywood	0.0	10.7	3.8	0.0	7.0	16.4	2.5	5.8	5.8	3.5
Westminster	0.0	7.6	0.0	0.0	0.9	22.8	0.0	3.0	44.5	5.1
West Sacramento........	0.0	18.1	0.0	0.0	0.3	13.0	10.0	6.8	11.0	8.6
Whittier......................	0.0	9.9	0.0	0.0	0.0	33.8	13.2	11.2	4.0	4.8
Wildomar....................	0.0	21.2	0.0	0.0	2.4	22.8	0.0	0.9	0.0	0.0
Windsor......................	0.0	20.4	0.0	0.0	1.0	24.7	0.0	3.9	13.1	4.1
Woodland....................	0.0	17.7	0.0	0.0	0.0	19.0	12.1	6.1	4.4	3.6
Yorba Linda.................	0.0	25.6	0.0	0.0	0.0	14.8	6.4	14.1	10.6	6.2
Yuba City...................	0.0	6.1	0.0	0.0	0.8	23.5	22.2	5.7	6.5	1.7
Yucaipa......................	0.0	24.1	0.0	0.0	4.3	22.0	0.0	13.1	11.5	2.4
COLORADO..............	X	X	X	X	X	X	X	X	X	X
Arvada.......................	0.0	15.3	0.0	0.0	0.0	19.8	10.3	18.6	8.4	1.3
Aurora.......................	0.0	13.0	0.0	0.0	0.0	21.5	14.3	11.3	2.9	2.2
Boulder......................	0.0	17.2	3.0	0.0	0.0	21.6	5.5	19.0	9.4	2.5
Brighton.....................	0.0	11.9	0.0	0.0	0.0	22.3	16.7	14.5	0.0	7.4
Broomfield..................	10.4	8.0	0.0	0.0	1.6	14.4	5.1	12.8	0.0	12.6

City	City government finances, 2012 (cont.)			Climate[2]						
	Debt outstanding			Average daily temperature (degrees Fahrenheit)						
				Mean		Limits				
	Total (mil dol)	Per capita[1] (dollars)	Debt issued during year	January	July	January[3]	July[4]	Annual precipitation (inches)	Heating degree days	Cooling degree days
	137	138	139	140	141	142	143	144	145	146
CALIFORNIA—Cont'd										
San Francisco	13 075.2	15 759	3 426.5	52.3	61.3	46.4	68.2	22.28	2 597	163
San Gabriel	3.0	74	3.3	56.3	75.6	42.6	89.0	18.56	1 295	1 575
San Jacinto	24.5	538	0.0	NA	NA	NA	NA	NA	NA	NA
San Jose	5 924.6	6 013	690.9	50.5	70.9	41.7	84.3	15.08	2 171	811
San Juan Capistrano	68.5	1 928	0.0	55.4	68.7	43.9	77.3	13.56	1 756	666
San Leandro	78.3	899	0.0	50.0	62.8	43.6	70.4	25.40	2 857	142
San Luis Obispo	65.5	1 429	0.0	53.3	66.5	41.9	80.3	24.36	2 138	476
San Marcos	501.2	5 755	0.0	56.4	71.6	45.1	82.2	13.69	1 514	1 047
San Mateo	159.9	1 599	0.0	48.4	68.0	39.1	80.8	20.16	2 764	422
San Pablo	81.2	2 754	0.2	48.8	67.7	41.3	80.9	34.29	2 621	451
San Rafael	46.5	794	0.1	48.8	67.7	41.3	80.9	34.29	2 621	451
San Ramon	108.0	1 464	11.6	47.2	72.0	37.4	89.1	14.82	2 755	858
Santa Ana	358.1	1 080	0.0	58.0	72.9	46.6	87.7	13.84	1 153	1 299
Santa Barbara	112.5	1 257	1.5	53.1	67.0	40.8	76.7	16.93	2 121	482
Santa Clara	388.8	3 251	0.0	50.5	70.9	41.7	84.3	15.08	2 171	811
Santa Clarita	94.2	526	0.0	50.3	74.1	36.1	94.2	13.96	2 502	1 139
Santa Cruz	79.2	1 278	0.0	50.6	63.7	40.2	74.8	30.67	2 836	162
Santa Maria	66.7	658	51.7	51.6	63.5	39.3	73.5	14.01	2 783	121
Santa Monica	353.1	3 846	20.3	57.0	65.5	50.2	68.8	13.27	1 810	429
Santa Paula	69.0	2 299	0.0	54.7	68.3	41.2	80.7	18.41	1 911	602
Santa Rosa	483.1	2 836	59.1	48.7	67.6	39.5	82.2	31.01	2 694	526
Santee	52.7	950	3.0	57.1	73.0	45.7	83.6	13.75	1 313	1 261
Saratoga	12.0	391	12.0	50.5	70.9	41.7	84.3	15.08	2 171	811
Seaside	39.4	1 164	0.0	51.6	60.2	43.4	68.1	20.35	3 092	74
Simi Valley	147.8	1 177	0.0	53.7	76.0	39.5	95.0	17.79	1 822	1 485
Soledad	45.3	1 710	0.0	NA	NA	NA	NA	NA	NA	NA
South Gate	167.3	1 750	0.0	58.3	74.2	48.5	83.8	15.14	928	1 506
South Pasadena	7.3	280	0.0	NA	NA	NA	NA	NA	NA	NA
South San Francisco	146.4	2 225	0.0	49.4	62.8	42.9	71.1	20.11	2 862	142
Stanton	76.1	1 975	0.0	58.0	72.9	46.6	87.7	13.84	1 153	1 299
Stockton	572.9	1 926	0.1	46.0	77.3	38.1	93.8	13.84	2 563	1 456
Suisun City	69.5	2 431	0.5	46.1	72.6	37.5	88.8	23.46	2 649	975
Sunnyvale	125.4	855	0.0	50.5	70.9	41.7	84.3	15.08	2 171	811
Temecula	96.6	922	0.0	51.2	78.3	36.1	97.8	11.40	2 123	1 710
Temple City	6.3	174	0.0	56.3	75.6	42.6	89.0	18.56	1 295	1 575
Thousand Oaks	133.2	1 040	0.0	53.7	76.0	39.5	95.0	17.79	1 822	1 485
Torrance	148.8	1 010	0.0	56.3	69.4	46.2	77.6	14.79	1 526	742
Tracy	222.9	2 633	0.0	47.1	76.4	38.5	92.5	12.51	2 421	1 470
Tulare	200.3	3 290	0.0	45.8	79.3	37.4	93.8	11.03	2 588	1 685
Turlock	69.6	997	0.0	46.4	77.6	39.0	93.3	12.43	2 519	1 506
Tustin	193.5	2 486	8.9	54.5	72.1	41.4	83.8	13.87	1 794	1 102
Twentynine Palms	11.0	429	0.0	50.0	88.4	36.1	105.8	4.57	1 910	3 064
Union City	178.1	2 483	0.0	49.8	68.0	42.0	78.3	14.85	2 367	530
Upland	41.7	555	0.0	54.6	73.8	41.5	88.7	16.96	1 727	1 191
Vacaville	190.4	2 028	31.2	47.2	77.3	38.8	95.8	24.55	2 410	1 498
Vallejo	192.2	1 630	0.0	46.3	71.2	38.8	87.4	19.58	2 757	786
Victorville	370.9	3 084	0.0	45.5	80.0	31.4	99.1	6.20	2 929	1 735
Visalia	31.2	246	0.0	45.8	79.3	37.4	93.8	11.03	2 588	1 685
Vista	245.6	2 552	0.0	56.4	71.6	45.1	82.2	13.69	1 514	1 047
Walnut	28.7	956	0.0	54.6	73.8	41.5	88.7	16.96	1 727	1 191
Walnut Creek	4.9	74	0.2	47.5	72.4	39.3	85.2	23.96	3 267	983
Wasco	4.4	173	0.0	NA	NA	NA	NA	NA	NA	NA
Watsonville	36.2	698	0.0	49.7	62.4	38.7	72.0	23.25	3 080	123
West Covina	181.9	1 691	8.9	56.3	75.6	42.6	89.0	18.56	1 295	1 575
West Hollywood	100.2	2 875	0.0	58.3	74.2	48.5	83.8	15.14	928	1 506
Westminster	142.2	1 553	0.0	58.0	72.9	46.6	82.7	13.84	1 153	1 299
West Sacramento	368.8	7 425	94.7	46.3	75.4	38.8	92.4	17.93	2 666	1 248
Whittier	98.6	1 142	7.7	56.3	75.6	42.6	89.0	18.56	1 295	1 575
Wildomar	0.0	0	0.0	NA	NA	NA	NA	NA	NA	NA
Windsor	27.1	1 000	12.5	NA	NA	NA	NA	NA	NA	NA
Woodland	111.4	1 977	5.9	45.7	76.4	37.6	94.0	20.78	2 683	1 417
Yorba Linda	117.7	1 769	2.7	56.9	73.2	45.2	84.0	11.23	1 286	1 294
Yuba City	63.6	980	0.0	46.3	78.9	37.8	96.3	22.07	2 488	1 687
Yucaipa	35.9	684	0.0	52.9	78.0	40.4	94.4	13.62	1 904	1 714
COLORADO	X	X	X	X	X	X	X	X	X	X
Arvada	120.5	1 098	0.0	31.2	71.5	15.6	88.3	18.17	5 988	496
Aurora	1 215.3	3 582	2.6	29.2	73.4	15.2	88.0	15.81	6 128	696
Boulder	155.7	1 527	18.5	32.5	71.6	19.2	87.2	19.93	5 687	552
Brighton	76.1	2 167	0.0	NA	NA	NA	NA	NA	NA	NA
Broomfield	293.0	4 968	0.0	32.5	71.6	19.2	87.2	19.93	5 687	552

1. Based on the population estimated as of July 1 of the year shown.   2. Represents normal values based on the 30-year period, 1971–2000.   3. Average daily minimum.
4. Average daily maximum.

Table D. Cities — Land Area and Population

STATE Place code	City	Land area,[1] 2016 (sq mi)	Total persons	Rank	Per square mile	White	Black or African American	American Indian, Alaska Native	Asian	Hawaiian Pacific Islander	Some other race	2 or more races[2]
		Population, 2016				Race alone[2] (percent), 2015						
		1	2	3	4	5	6	7	8	9	10	11
	COLORADO—Cont'd											
08 12415	Castle Rock	34.1	57 666	650	1 691.1	89.0	2.1	0.7	2.3	0.9	1.4	3.6
08 12815	Centennial	29.5	109 932	268	3 726.5	86.8	3.1	0.5	5.0	0.1	1.9	2.7
08 16000	Colorado Springs	195.6	465 101	40	2 377.8	77.9	6.6	0.7	3.3	0.3	6.2	5.1
08 16495	Commerce City	35.2	54 869	686	1 558.8	84.0	4.2	0.7	1.1	0.0	4.8	4.8
08 20000	Denver	153.3	693 060	19	4 520.9	77.1	9.5	1.0	3.4	0.1	5.4	3.5
08 24785	Englewood	6.6	34 050	1 114	5 159.1	78.7	4.3	0.3	3.5	0.0	6.1	7.1
08 27425	Fort Collins	55.8	164 207	155	2 942.8	89.6	1.4	0.5	3.3	0.0	1.2	4.0
08 27865	Fountain	24.5	28 753	1 294	1 173.6	78.5	8.4	0.2	3.2	4.5	0.2	5.0
08 31660	Grand Junction	39.3	61 881	593	1 574.6	93.7	1.2	0.2	0.4	1.3	0.9	2.2
08 32155	Greeley	47.8	103 990	291	2 175.5	89.9	1.9	1.4	1.8	0.1	2.3	2.5
08 43000	Lakewood	42.9	154 393	164	3 598.9	88.1	1.2	0.5	3.8	0.0	2.8	3.6
08 45255	Littleton	12.7	46 333	827	3 648.3	88.0	2.3	1.5	4.1	0.0	1.2	2.9
08 45970	Longmont	27.4	92 858	339	3 389.0	90.6	0.9	0.9	1.9	0.0	3.1	2.7
08 46465	Loveland	34.1	76 897	446	2 255.0	93.0	1.1	0.1	1.2	0.0	1.9	2.4
08 54330	Northglenn	7.4	38 982	974	5 267.8	90.8	1.2	0.0	1.2	0.4	4.4	2.4
08 57630	Parker	21.3	51 163	746	2 402.0	86.3	2.3	0.7	6.4	0.4	0.6	3.3
08 62000	Pueblo	53.6	110 291	266	2 057.7	74.7	2.7	5.8	1.0	0.0	11.7	4.1
08 77290	Thornton	35.7	136 703	191	3 829.2	86.8	2.1	1.4	4.4	0.1	2.4	2.9
08 83835	Westminster	31.7	113 875	247	3 592.3	85.7	1.9	0.3	6.5	0.2	2.4	3.0
08 84440	Wheat Ridge	9.4	31 372	1 201	3 337.4	NA	NA	NA	NA	NA	NA	NA
09 00000	CONNECTICUT	4 842.7	3 576 452	X	738.5	76.5	10.6	0.2	4.4	0.0	5.0	3.2
09 08000	Bridgeport	16.1	145 936	180	9 064.3	42.3	32.7	0.1	4.0	0.0	14.3	6.6
09 08420	Bristol	26.4	60 147	614	2 278.3	85.2	4.4	0.2	0.9	0.0	5.5	3.8
09 18430	Danbury	41.9	84 992	388	2 028.4	61.9	8.3	0.3	7.1	0.2	17.6	4.7
09 37000	Hartford	17.4	123 243	221	7 082.9	34.5	38.0	0.8	3.0	0.0	19.6	4.1
09 46450	Meriden	23.8	59 622	620	2 505.1	80.6	9.5	0.5	3.0	0.0	4.8	1.6
09 47290	Middletown	41.0	46 544	823	1 135.2	77.0	10.0	0.0	6.2	0.0	2.4	4.4
09 47500	Milford	22.2	52 536	722	2 398.9	89.5	2.7	0.0	5.5	0.0	0.3	2.1
09 49880	Naugatuck	16.3	31 392	1 200	1 925.9	80.0	6.0	0.0	1.5	0.0	6.3	6.1
09 50370	New Britain	13.4	72 558	483	5 414.8	73.8	11.3	0.0	2.5	0.0	8.5	3.9
09 52000	New Haven	18.7	129 934	210	6 948.3	41.3	30.9	0.4	5.3	0.0	18.2	3.9
09 52280	New London	5.6	26 984	1 368	4 818.6	54.3	18.9	0.0	1.2	0.0	14.0	11.6
09 55990	Norwalk	22.9	88 438	366	3 861.9	75.4	16.6	0.1	2.9	0.0	3.3	1.7
09 56200	Norwich	28.1	39 556	958	1 407.7	64.6	12.5	0.2	7.6	0.0	0.8	14.3
09 68100	Shelton	30.6	41 334	917	1 350.8	91.0	0.9	0.0	3.5	0.0	3.0	1.7
09 73000	Stamford	37.6	129 113	211	3 433.9	64.7	16.9	0.0	7.7	0.0	7.8	3.0
09 76500	Torrington	39.8	34 646	1 101	870.5	88.7	3.4	0.0	2.0	0.0	3.9	2.0
09 80000	Waterbury	28.5	108 272	274	3 799.0	61.6	23.3	0.2	3.4	0.0	9.1	2.4
09 82800	West Haven	10.7	54 516	693	5 095.0	66.9	18.7	0.0	4.6	0.0	4.4	5.5
10 00000	DELAWARE	1 948.7	952 065	X	488.6	69.2	21.6	0.3	3.8	0.0	2.0	3.0
10 21200	Dover	23.2	37 786	1 010	1 628.7	40.5	46.6	0.3	4.6	0.0	3.4	4.6
10 50670	Newark	9.2	33 398	1 137	3 630.2	81.5	4.8	0.0	7.1	0.0	3.7	2.8
10 77580	Wilmington	10.9	71 442	493	6 554.3	31.8	60.2	0.2	1.5	0.0	4.6	1.6
11 00000	DISTRICT OF COLUMBIA	61.1	681 170	X	11 148.4	40.0	47.4	0.2	3.9	0.1	5.2	3.2
11 50000	Washington	61.1	681 170	21	11 148.4	40.0	47.4	0.2	3.9	0.1	5.2	3.2
12 00000	FLORIDA	53 638.9	20 612 439	X	384.3	75.8	16.2	0.2	2.7	0.1	2.6	2.5
12 00950	Altamonte Springs	9.0	43 492	865	4 832.4	76.5	13.6	0.0	1.8	0.0	1.6	6.4
12 01700	Apopka	32.5	49 458	764	1 521.8	69.3	13.3	1.1	5.2	0.0	9.0	2.2
12 02681	Aventura	2.7	37 724	1 013	13 971.9	92.8	3.4	0.0	0.7	0.0	1.3	1.9
12 07300	Boca Raton	29.3	96 114	319	3 280.3	84.0	4.2	0.0	2.0	0.0	1.3	2.8
12 07525	Bonita Springs	38.9	54 198	698	1 393.3	NA	NA	NA	NA	NA	NA	NA
12 07875	Boynton Beach	16.2	75 569	457	4 664.8	66.2	26.3	0.1	2.5	0.0	3.0	1.9
12 07950	Bradenton	14.3	55 687	672	3 894.2	74.9	21.2	0.0	0.4	0.0	1.2	2.3
12 10275	Cape Coral	105.6	179 804	136	1 702.7	91.9	3.9	0.1	1.3	0.0	1.3	1.5
12 11050	Casselberry	6.9	27 053	1 364	3 920.7	85.8	9.5	0.6	1.9	0.0	2.0	0.3
12 12875	Clearwater	25.9	114 361	243	4 415.5	84.1	10.2	0.0	1.9	0.4	1.2	2.1
12 12925	Clermont	14.3	33 549	1 129	2 346.1	NA	NA	NA	NA	NA	NA	NA
12 13275	Coconut Creek	11.9	59 405	622	4 992.0	78.8	13.6	0.0	3.1	0.1	1.3	3.0
12 14125	Cooper City	8.0	35 405	1 077	4 425.6	70.9	9.0	0.0	7.4	0.0	10.3	2.5
12 14250	Coral Gables	12.9	50 815	749	3 939.1	92.6	3.1	0.3	1.8	0.0	0.5	1.8
12 14400	Coral Springs	23.8	130 059	209	5 464.7	67.6	20.0	0.1	4.1	0.1	5.0	3.0
12 15968	Cutler Bay	9.8	44 707	843	4 561.9	77.9	14.2	0.2	1.4	0.0	4.6	1.8
12 16335	Dania Beach	8.1	31 422	1 197	3 879.3	74.0	17.9	0.2	0.5	0.0	6.3	1.1
12 16475	Davie	34.9	101 871	298	2 918.9	77.8	10.2	0.2	3.9	0.3	5.9	1.6
12 16525	Daytona Beach	65.1	66 645	540	1 023.7	61.8	32.3	0.1	2.9	0.0	0.5	2.3

1. Dry land or land partially or temporarily covered by water.   2. Hispanic or Latino persons may be of any race.

Table D. Cities — Population

City	Percent Hispanic or Latino[1], 2015	Percent foreign born 2015	Age of population (percent), 2010-2014							Median age 2015	Percent female 2015	Population			
												Census counts		Percent change	
			Under 18 years	18 to 24 years	25 to 34 years	35 to 44 years	45 to 54 years	55 to 64 years	65 years and over			2000	2010	2000–2010	2010–2016
	12	13	14	15	16	17	18	19	20	21	22	23	24	25	26
COLORADO—Cont'd															
Castle Rock	8.8	5.1	27.4	10.5	12.0	17.5	13.5	11.4	7.7	35.1	49.3	20 224	48 262	138.6	19.5
Centennial	7.4	8.7	22.3	7.5	11.3	12.8	13.6	16.3	16.2	42.4	51.5	NA	101 082	NA	8.8
Colorado Springs	17.2	7.7	23.6	10.7	16.1	12.8	11.7	11.9	13.3	34.8	50.6	360 890	417 480	15.7	11.4
Commerce City	44.5	15.2	34.2	7.8	15.8	15.4	10.7	10.4	5.6	31.3	50.5	20 991	45 917	118.7	19.5
Denver	30.5	16.6	20.6	8.5	22.4	15.6	11.5	10.3	11.1	34.1	50.0	554 636	599 864	8.2	15.5
Englewood	16.3	11.1	15.8	7.7	22.1	15.9	10.7	15.1	12.7	37.2	51.5	31 727	30 255	-4.6	12.5
Fort Collins	9.6	6.0	18.3	22.2	17.3	12.2	9.8	10.2	10.0	29.6	49.8	118 652	144 639	21.9	13.5
Fountain	19.6	7.9	29.3	11.0	23.7	9.3	17.6	6.4	2.7	29.3	48.7	15 197	25 993	71.0	10.6
Grand Junction	18.5	4.5	22.5	14.4	13.9	10.5	9.8	11.3	17.6	34.4	52.0	41 986	59 100	40.8	4.7
Greeley	38.9	11.4	26.5	15.8	12.5	12.6	10.0	9.7	12.9	31.0	49.7	76 930	92 894	20.8	11.9
Lakewood	22.0	9.3	19.5	9.7	16.7	12.8	11.8	14.1	15.3	37.7	50.2	144 126	142 995	-0.8	8.0
Littleton	12.6	9.1	17.7	8.5	14.6	14.8	12.4	14.6	17.4	42.0	54.2	40 340	41 651	3.2	11.2
Longmont	26.9	11.3	25.8	8.0	12.4	13.6	13.2	13.4	13.4	36.8	52.4	71 093	86 308	21.4	7.6
Loveland	18.0	4.1	25.1	7.1	14.7	12.3	10.8	12.3	17.7	37.6	50.7	50 608	66 892	32.2	15.0
Northglenn	34.2	12.1	24.6	11.5	15.9	11.5	12.8	11.9	11.9	33.7	50.8	31 575	35 769	13.3	9.0
Parker	8.8	9.1	31.2	5.1	9.2	21.1	14.6	11.4	7.3	37.3	49.7	23 558	45 297	92.3	13.0
Pueblo	52.6	3.3	22.7	10.0	14.2	11.2	12.2	12.3	17.5	37.6	49.2	102 121	106 544	4.3	3.5
Thornton	36.9	13.4	29.8	7.7	15.3	16.1	12.6	10.0	8.6	33.1	50.9	82 384	118 777	44.2	15.1
Westminster	20.6	10.0	20.0	9.1	16.2	14.0	12.1	14.7	14.0	37.8	51.5	100 940	106 160	5.2	7.3
Wheat Ridge	23.0	3.6	19.3	7.1	13.2	12.6	12.5	16.0	19.2	43.1	51.2	32 913	30 192	-8.3	3.9
CONNECTICUT	15.4	14.5	21.3	9.8	12.3	12.0	15.0	13.8	15.7	40.6	51.2	3 405 565	3 574 114	4.9	0.1
Bridgeport	40.0	30.1	23.4	12.7	15.3	13.9	13.3	11.1	10.3	34.1	51.6	139 529	144 236	3.4	1.2
Bristol	16.9	6.7	21.8	8.6	15.4	12.9	13.6	14.0	13.6	38.2	51.0	60 062	60 474	0.7	-0.5
Danbury	29.7	30.3	18.5	10.9	17.0	16.0	12.6	11.2	13.7	37.3	48.7	74 848	80 903	8.1	5.1
Hartford	45.1	23.0	23.8	16.3	16.4	12.0	11.9	9.5	10.0	31.0	53.2	121 578	124 775	2.6	-1.2
Meriden	20.1	9.8	17.9	6.3	15.7	11.6	16.2	16.2	15.9	43.5	54.1	58 244	60 855	4.5	-2.0
Middletown	9.8	12.2	20.4	16.9	12.4	10.9	12.7	14.2	12.5	35.3	52.2	43 167	47 648	10.4	-2.3
Milford	6.3	10.5	17.7	6.9	12.8	11.0	17.9	15.5	18.2	45.9	51.2	52 305	51 271	-2.0	2.5
Naugatuck	14.7	11.6	24.2	7.1	9.3	18.4	12.3	12.2	16.5	41.0	53.2	30 989	31 884	2.9	-1.5
New Britain	41.5	20.7	24.8	11.7	16.1	12.7	12.2	11.0	11.5	33.4	48.7	71 538	73 202	2.3	-0.9
New Haven	33.4	19.9	22.9	16.3	22.0	11.7	10.9	7.4	8.9	29.9	51.1	123 626	129 890	5.1	0.0
New London	29.6	12.5	20.9	22.8	9.6	12.9	11.4	11.4	11.0	30.6	51.5	25 671	27 620	7.6	-2.3
Norwalk	27.9	25.2	18.5	9.6	13.1	12.3	17.1	14.6	14.8	42.4	53.8	82 951	85 622	3.2	3.3
Norwich	14.1	9.7	20.8	9.6	17.0	14.2	14.8	10.1	13.6	36.4	50.1	36 117	40 496	12.1	-2.3
Shelton	6.7	15.5	19.3	9.2	6.4	14.7	13.9	14.5	22.0	45.2	51.5	38 101	39 559	3.8	4.5
Stamford	25.8	34.1	21.1	9.7	18.5	13.9	12.6	11.9	12.3	35.4	49.6	117 083	122 630	4.7	5.3
Torrington	14.9	15.6	20.4	6.1	15.0	14.1	13.3	14.9	16.2	42.1	47.8	35 202	36 383	3.4	-4.8
Waterbury	35.1	18.4	24.3	9.9	14.0	14.0	14.1	11.4	12.3	36.2	52.0	107 271	110 332	2.9	-1.9
West Haven	21.2	19.3	19.7	13.5	14.6	8.7	17.2	10.8	15.5	37.2	49.1	52 360	55 564	6.1	-1.9
DELAWARE	9.0	9.3	21.6	9.4	13.1	11.7	13.7	13.5	17.0	39.7	51.6	783 600	897 936	14.6	6.0
Dover	9.7	8.8	25.8	21.4	11.9	9.3	12.2	7.7	11.7	27.1	53.2	32 135	35 934	11.8	5.2
Newark	7.4	11.5	9.7	40.5	11.7	9.1	8.5	8.4	12.1	24.8	52.5	28 547	31 513	10.4	6.0
Wilmington	7.7	4.6	23.2	7.8	16.7	13.8	12.7	12.9	12.9	36.4	54.6	72 664	70 852	-2.5	0.8
DISTRICT OF COLUMBIA	10.6	14.1	17.5	12.1	22.7	14.3	11.5	10.4	11.4	33.8	52.4	572 059	601 766	5.2	13.2
Washington	10.6	14.1	17.5	12.1	22.7	14.3	11.5	10.4	11.4	33.8	52.4	572 059	601 766	5.2	13.2
FLORIDA	24.5	20.2	20.2	8.8	12.8	12.2	13.5	13.1	19.5	41.8	51.2	15 982 378	18 804 592	17.7	9.6
Altamonte Springs	26.6	12.3	19.1	5.8	18.8	16.5	14.6	9.7	15.5	38.8	53.5	41 200	41 501	0.7	4.8
Apopka	23.0	12.6	25.5	10.3	10.0	13.9	20.1	10.1	10.3	39.1	53.9	26 642	41 736	56.7	18.5
Aventura	36.6	49.7	10.1	2.2	10.7	14.0	15.1	16.4	31.6	51.9	55.1	25 267	35 762	41.5	5.5
Boca Raton	15.8	22.7	15.9	10.1	10.0	11.2	14.7	14.2	23.8	47.3	52.0	74 764	84 401	12.9	13.9
Bonita Springs	17.6	17.7	10.8	6.8	6.9	8.2	8.7	9.8	49.0	63.6	50.5	32 797	43 924	33.9	23.4
Boynton Beach	17.0	20.9	18.1	5.7	13.0	12.7	14.8	12.0	23.8	45.8	54.4	60 389	68 217	13.0	10.8
Bradenton	14.5	7.2	23.9	6.4	12.2	10.1	9.5	13.1	24.8	43.5	54.3	49 504	49 281	-0.5	13.0
Cape Coral	18.8	13.8	19.2	5.9	12.1	12.8	15.3	13.9	20.7	45.0	51.1	102 286	154 307	50.9	16.5
Casselberry	31.9	10.5	13.2	15.1	16.2	10.3	12.4	12.9	19.9	38.7	53.0	22 629	26 091	15.3	3.7
Clearwater	15.2	15.7	16.9	7.4	12.6	11.1	13.5	15.2	23.4	47.0	51.1	108 787	108 989	0.2	4.9
Clermont	25.8	6.2	25.8	5.5	15.8	11.4	10.2	9.1	22.3	37.8	56.2	9 333	28 740	207.9	16.7
Coconut Creek	19.6	20.1	21.6	8.9	15.4	13.2	14.4	11.7	14.8	37.0	52.8	43 566	52 934	21.5	12.2
Cooper City	32.1	23.7	25.7	10.5	7.5	14.3	15.9	16.4	9.7	40.4	50.8	27 939	28 545	2.2	24.0
Coral Gables	59.3	35.8	17.8	12.3	11.7	13.0	14.5	11.4	19.3	41.5	50.9	42 249	46 752	10.7	8.7
Coral Springs	31.5	29.8	27.4	8.3	11.5	14.9	15.1	12.6	10.1	37.2	51.1	117 549	121 098	3.0	7.4
Cutler Bay	48.3	31.8	26.9	9.1	12.6	16.0	12.0	11.5	11.8	36.1	49.9	NA	40 286	NA	11.0
Dania Beach	31.8	26.2	15.2	11.5	17.7	13.7	13.4	12.1	16.4	39.6	47.7	20 061	29 639	47.7	6.0
Davie	35.0	26.3	17.7	10.4	15.2	13.1	17.8	13.8	12.0	40.8	51.7	75 720	91 992	21.5	10.7
Daytona Beach	5.3	8.5	13.6	12.5	14.1	8.1	11.7	17.2	22.7	47.2	50.5	64 112	61 326	-4.3	8.7

1. May be of any race.

Table D. Cities — Households, Group Quarters, Crime, and Education

City	Households, 2015				Persons in group quarters, 2010				Serious crimes known to police,[2] 2014				Educational attainment, 2015		
			Percent			Institutional			Total		Rate[3]			Attainment[4] (percent)	
	Number	Persons per house-hold	Female family house-holder[1]	One-person	Total	Total	Persons in nursing facilities	Non-institu-tional	Number	Rate[3]	Violent	Property	Population age 25 and older	High school graduate or less	Bachelor's degree or more
	27	28	29	30	31	32	33	34	35	36	37	38	39	40	41
COLORADO—Cont'd															
Castle Rock	20 226	2.72	9.1	18.3	460	390	108	70	452	833	76	758	34 501	14.5	48.8
Centennial	40 543	2.66	5.9	21.5	1 701	1 559	307	142	1 440	1 340	132	1 208	77 042	15.3	55.6
Colorado Springs	181 690	2.48	11.2	29.1	7 629	3 467	1 657	4 162	18 348	4 124	456	3 668	299 826	27.3	38.3
Commerce City	15 231	3.50	18.6	14.7	351	191	191	160	1 832	3 610	398	3 212	31 123	53.8	17.2
Denver	287 074	2.33	10.1	37.8	15 981	6 518	2 333	9 463	26 407	3 969	601	3 367	483 833	30.7	47.1
Englewood	15 790	2.07	10.7	47.8	291	238	238	53	1 833	5 762	201	5 561	25 315	37.7	36.0
Fort Collins	62 631	2.45	7.7	25.1	7 085	1 437	514	5 648	4 104	2 665	209	2 456	95 850	18.8	54.1
Fountain	9 278	2.99	8.6	16.4	0	0	0	0	773	2 804	301	2 503	16 579	30.8	14.7
Grand Junction	24 516	2.35	12.8	31.9	2 884	1 077	395	1 807	2 820	4 702	477	4 225	38 064	31.7	37.0
Greeley	34 611	2.75	10.8	26.7	4 853	1 627	627	3 226	3 780	3 881	496	3 385	58 189	42.6	24.7
Lakewood	65 646	2.29	11.4	34.1	2 171	1 552	1 064	619	7 558	5 099	481	4 618	108 055	32.0	38.0
Littleton	20 089	2.28	11.2	33.9	491	448	313	43	1 023	2 280	89	2 191	34 237	20.1	46.5
Longmont	34 888	2.63	13.3	29.2	639	498	482	141	2 376	2 616	344	2 273	60 998	33.1	38.4
Loveland	29 515	2.53	10.5	28.1	510	416	414	94	2 121	2 927	233	2 694	50 944	28.6	36.2
Northglenn	13 193	2.95	15.5	24.0	129	129	129	0	1 130	2 981	314	2 667	25 066	45.2	19.4
Parker	17 864	2.77	8.6	16.4	28	0	0	28	677	1 370	134	1 236	31 558	14.7	57.8
Pueblo	43 203	2.44	15.2	33.1	4 045	3 050	1 444	995	7 980	7 349	819	6 530	73 644	44.8	18.4
Thornton	44 755	2.97	10.9	20.0	462	430	430	32	4 090	3 160	255	2 905	83 463	38.7	28.4
Westminster	42 844	2.63	11.3	26.4	467	448	348	19	3 528	3 147	234	2 913	80 204	32.2	37.2
Wheat Ridge	13 803	2.21	8.6	34.5	554	434	381	120	1 182	3 801	312	3 489	22 940	34.2	30.5
CONNECTICUT	1 343 703	2.59	12.7	28.5	118 152	49 370	26 371	68 782	77 592	2 157	237	1 920	2 474 718	37.2	38.3
Bridgeport	49 811	2.86	23.9	29.3	4 838	1 960	759	2 878	5 623	3 804	905	2 899	94 390	55.8	20.0
Bristol	24 430	2.45	13.2	32.4	849	637	611	212	1 580	2 608	120	2 487	42 057	44.8	29.6
Danbury	29 775	2.74	10.4	34.3	3 953	1 904	538	2 049	1 505	1 786	178	1 608	59 726	47.7	29.2
Hartford	44 867	2.59	30.5	32.3	8 951	2 194	777	6 757	6 660	5 330	1 105	4 226	74 245	60.0	16.9
Meriden	25 551	2.30	14.1	40.0	955	688	660	267	1 595	2 643	300	2 343	45 467	49.9	22.4
Middletown	17 712	2.35	15.0	36.5	3 731	998	552	2 733	940	1 989	169	1 820	29 335	35.4	37.9
Milford	20 501	2.52	10.1	29.8	472	355	344	117	1 422	2 672	66	2 606	39 195	36.5	38.8
Naugatuck	11 173	2.80	11.6	25.4	267	236	236	31	645	2 037	85	1 951	21 674	44.0	28.2
New Britain	27 834	2.52	25.0	31.2	3 194	790	557	2 404	2 439	3 347	441	2 907	46 257	56.2	20.4
New Haven	48 690	2.48	22.0	43.0	11 220	1 774	768	9 446	6 653	5 083	1 089	3 994	79 312	45.1	35.1
New London	10 611	2.15	26.1	41.6	3 713	225	225	3 488	1 012	3 677	596	3 081	15 295	55.4	18.2
Norwalk	32 467	2.70	13.7	26.5	797	461	405	336	1 864	2 113	298	1 815	63 581	40.0	40.1
Norwich	15 716	2.51	20.3	38.0	514	219	205	295	1 001	2 484	380	2 104	27 768	54.2	15.0
Shelton	15 974	2.56	11.1	24.5	502	446	442	56	414	1 001	56	946	29 502	37.6	42.9
Stamford	47 256	2.70	11.2	27.9	1 280	662	653	618	2 373	1 863	243	1 619	89 256	29.6	47.3
Torrington	14 556	2.33	7.7	36.7	838	611	559	227	681	1 922	124	1 798	25 651	48.1	21.1
Waterbury	39 441	2.71	25.7	32.4	1 938	1 149	886	789	4 999	4 566	373	4 193	71 584	61.9	13.1
West Haven	19 657	2.63	14.5	31.1	2 857	458	362	2 399	1 665	3 032	264	2 768	36 668	49.0	27.1
DELAWARE	352 595	2.61	13.8	26.6	24 413	11 673	4 591	12 740	32 476	3 471	489	2 982	652 636	40.9	30.9
Dover	12 629	2.62	18.1	31.6	3 745	569	340	3 176	2 112	5 606	637	4 969	19 835	38.7	29.2
Newark	10 140	2.60	7.8	27.6	7 128	0	0	7 128	850	2 590	317	2 273	16 835	19.8	55.2
Wilmington	28 002	2.45	29.6	37.2	3 226	2 324	531	902	4 941	6 890	1 636	5 254	49 648	49.8	25.4
DISTRICT OF COLUMBIA	281 787	2.24	15.1	42.0	40 021	7 339	3 064	32 682	42 346	6 427	1 244	5 182	472 884	27.6	56.7
Washington	281 787	2.24	15.1	42.0	40 021	7 339	3 064	32 682	40 837	6 198	1 185	5 012	472 884	27.6	56.7
FLORIDA	7 463 184	2.66	13.4	28.9	421 709	254 506	73 372	167 203	786 967	3 956	540	3 415	14 394 281	41.6	28.4
Altamonte Springs	19 027	2.24	13.5	45.2	448	444	444	4	1 503	3 553	364	3 189	32 417	28.1	36.9
Apopka	16 908	2.85	11.1	21.2	178	118	118	60	1 676	3 599	363	3 236	31 100	40.4	29.0
Aventura	19 402	1.94	7.1	44.8	96	96	96	0	2 055	5 475	202	5 272	33 028	22.4	48.0
Boca Raton	40 551	2.22	6.4	35.9	3 444	430	415	3 014	2 233	2 468	185	2 283	69 035	20.9	53.9
Bonita Springs	22 118	2.34	5.8	31.0	157	12	0	145	NA	NA	NA	NA	42 635	38.2	31.9
Boynton Beach	29 848	2.45	10.4	38.1	1 000	649	630	351	3 257	4 536	526	4 010	56 420	40.7	28.5
Bradenton	20 510	2.58	18.3	36.8	1 757	1 074	966	683	2 347	4 483	646	3 838	37 915	49.3	20.3
Cape Coral	61 251	2.85	11.1	23.3	445	350	307	95	3 513	2 082	143	1 939	131 302	46.9	22.9
Casselberry	10 511	2.56	16.2	32.3	51	12	5	39	1 235	4 635	499	4 136	19 403	30.6	26.0
Clearwater	46 240	2.40	11.1	36.5	3 584	1 011	1 000	2 573	4 924	4 473	582	3 891	85 597	35.5	28.0
Clermont	11 389	2.83	19.8	15.7	199	177	177	22	950	3 131	224	2 907	22 261	27.9	36.8
Coconut Creek	21 547	2.74	15.4	31.5	146	138	65	8	1 353	2 342	147	2 195	41 213	39.9	31.3
Cooper City	10 411	3.39	12.0	12.2	40	0	0	40	482	1 351	118	1 233	22 572	27.8	43.9
Coral Gables	18 740	2.49	5.0	40.0	4 540	1	0	4 539	2 063	4 100	151	3 949	35 730	17.5	62.6
Coral Springs	40 825	3.17	15.9	15.8	359	227	222	132	2 684	2 098	159	1 939	83 279	29.9	37.0
Cutler Bay	13 552	3.28	13.1	19.7	338	245	199	93	1 973	4 476	288	4 188	28 682	38.4	35.0
Dania Beach	12 272	2.55	18.0	30.2	329	294	87	35	1 344	4 336	494	3 842	23 063	56.0	21.3
Davie	36 504	2.72	17.3	23.7	1 355	86	50	1 269	3 464	3 534	262	3 272	72 585	35.8	36.5
Daytona Beach	30 698	2.01	11.1	43.9	5 048	1 094	1 059	3 954	4 778	7 629	1 284	6 345	47 822	40.7	25.6

1. No spouse present.   2. Data for serious crimes have not been adjusted for underreporting. This may affect comparability between geographic areas and over time.   3. Per 100,000 population estimated by the FBI.   4. Persons 25 years old and over.

Table D. Cities — Income, Poverty, and Housing

| City | Money income, 2015 | | | | | Housing units, 2010 | | | Occupied housing units 2015 | | | | |
| | Households | | | Families | | | | | | Owner-occupied | | Renter-occupied | |
	Median income	Percent with income of $200,000 or more	Percent with income of less than $25,000	Total Families	Percent with income below poverty	Total	Percent change, 2000–2010	Vacant units for sale or rent[2]	Total	Percent	Median value[3] (dollars)	Percent	Median rent (dollars)
	42	43	44	45	46	47	48	49	50	51	52	53	54
COLORADO—Cont'd													
Castle Rock	97 500	9.3	4.0	15 536	2.5	17 626	135.5	938	20 226	74.6	348 700	25.4	1 505
Centennial	96 634	12.8	6.6	29 396	2.4	38 779	NA	1 330	40 543	82.3	369 800	17.7	1 570
Colorado Springs	56 079	4.2	13.8	115 899	8.9	179 607	20.7	11 819	181 690	57.2	228 600	42.8	985
Commerce City	65 221	2.0	11.5	12 508	12.2	15 452	123.7	973	15 231	68.8	253 600	31.2	987
Denver	58 003	7.3	15.7	143 592	11.0	285 797	13.7	22 690	287 074	49.4	316 700	50.6	1 094
Englewood	47 263	0.8	19.0	6 340	13.1	15 478	4.0	1 103	15 790	48.2	262 100	51.8	1 028
Fort Collins	61 514	4.8	14.4	33 170	6.3	60 503	26.7	2 674	62 631	54.2	302 500	45.8	1 171
Fountain	60 714	0.6	7.6	7 699	6.4	9 371	80.1	647	9 278	61.2	201 700	38.8	1 316
Grand Junction	45 406	3.9	20.9	14 341	13.9	26 170	38.7	1 859	24 516	57.6	214 500	42.4	850
Greeley	54 307	3.4	17.2	22 198	10.4	36 323	25.9	2 896	34 611	59.6	194 500	40.4	861
Lakewood	60 984	4.6	13.5	36 852	7.5	65 758	5.3	3 772	65 646	58.7	305 500	41.3	1 155
Littleton	67 282	9.3	9.7	11 902	3.3	19 434	7.1	1 122	20 089	62.4	326 100	37.6	1 133
Longmont	59 333	4.6	12.5	22 414	9.1	35 008	27.6	1 756	34 888	57.1	282 800	42.9	1 083
Loveland	61 377	3.8	11.8	18 441	4.3	28 557	40.5	1 404	29 515	62.8	247 900	37.2	1 058
Northglenn	60 293	1.7	11.4	8 494	13.7	14 274	17.5	782	13 193	54.3	236 100	45.7	1 185
Parker	105 144	9.6	4.4	14 228	3.2	16 533	97.8	616	17 864	80.1	363 300	19.9	1 455
Pueblo	36 267	1.8	30.8	25 605	19.9	47 593	10.4	4 303	43 203	55.3	124 700	44.7	702
Thornton	72 697	3.3	6.9	32 847	7.5	43 230	46.6	1 871	44 755	69.5	255 500	30.5	1 346
Westminster	70 212	7.3	9.9	27 856	4.6	43 968	11.4	1 927	42 844	65.3	275 300	34.7	1 327
Wheat Ridge	50 748	4.7	12.5	7 873	5.1	14 868	-0.7	892	13 803	55.6	314 800	44.4	893
CONNECTICUT	71 346	10.3	13.5	876 188	7.4	1 487 891	7.4	116 804	1 343 703	66.2	270 900	33.8	1 108
Bridgeport	42 420	3.4	24.4	31 543	18.1	57 012	4.9	5 757	49 811	41.6	167 100	58.4	1 122
Bristol	68 465	2.3	15.8	14 178	10.4	27 011	3.4	1 691	24 430	62.5	198 600	37.5	912
Danbury	65 517	5.8	14.3	17 846	10.3	31 154	9.2	2 247	29 775	59.3	279 400	40.7	1 467
Hartford	34 240	1.2	30.9	27 777	25.9	51 822	2.3	6 698	44 867	22.3	159 200	77.7	952
Meriden	56 751	2.3	9.5	13 858	7.3	25 892	5.1	1 915	25 551	57.0	184 200	43.0	961
Middletown	66 335	6.0	12.0	9 864	5.5	21 223	7.7	1 360	17 712	56.9	224 300	43.1	1 085
Milford	80 156	8.7	9.6	12 849	5.6	23 074	5.1	1 366	20 501	76.8	309 000	23.2	1 572
Naugatuck	60 089	8.8	13.3	7 894	6.7	13 061	5.8	722	11 173	72.0	170 300	28.0	960
New Britain	40 485	1.6	28.3	17 203	24.0	31 226	0.2	3 068	27 834	40.4	162 300	59.6	927
New Haven	36 641	3.1	31.0	23 436	26.9	54 967	3.8	6 090	48 690	24.9	194 300	75.1	1 123
New London	36 893	2.0	33.4	5 717	29.7	11 840	2.4	1 467	10 611	31.8	189 800	68.2	960
Norwalk	85 052	14.0	12.0	21 771	7.7	35 415	4.9	2 198	32 467	62.4	435 900	37.6	1 576
Norwich	55 329	2.3	14.0	8 959	14.0	18 659	12.4	2 060	15 716	53.7	159 300	46.3	1 007
Shelton	81 886	8.7	12.4	11 446	3.5	16 146	9.8	821	15 974	76.6	345 500	23.4	1 374
Stamford	79 865	17.5	12.4	29 243	4.9	50 573	6.9	3 216	47 256	53.1	510 400	46.9	1 653
Torrington	56 638	0.9	15.9	8 371	10.3	16 761	3.8	1 518	14 556	62.9	147 500	37.1	898
Waterbury	37 877	1.4	30.2	24 590	22.4	47 991	2.5	5 230	39 441	43.9	129 400	56.1	913
West Haven	54 844	2.9	21.0	11 117	12.9	22 446	0.5	1 334	19 657	55.6	189 100	44.4	1 144
DELAWARE	61 255	5.2	12.9	235 385	8.7	405 885	18.3	63 588	352 595	70.8	240 200	29.2	1 049
Dover	45 722	2.4	19.0	7 555	16.5	15 024	12.5	1 253	12 629	47.3	165 400	52.7	995
Newark	54 955	6.0	17.8	NA	NA	10 475	12.5	641	10 140	61.0	264 500	39.0	1 148
Wilmington	41 035	3.6	27.7	15 344	22.3	32 820	2.1	4 205	28 002	43.5	160 300	56.5	911
DISTRICT OF COLUMBIA	75 628	14.7	16.8	125 178	14.0	296 719	8.0	30 012	281 787	39.9	551 300	60.1	1 417
Washington	75 628	14.7	16.8	125 178	14.0	296 719	8.0	30 012	281 787	39.9	551 300	60.1	1 417
FLORIDA	49 426	4.4	18.2	4 806 611	11.3	8 989 580	23.1	1 568 778	7 463 184	63.8	179 800	36.2	1 046
Altamonte Springs	47 281	1.8	14.7	9 368	14.2	22 088	9.5	2 962	19 027	40.2	145 200	59.8	1 068
Apopka	64 106	4.7	8.6	11 612	1.6	15 707	55.9	1 347	16 908	70.7	182 600	29.3	1 087
Aventura	56 018	10.9	16.7	NA	NA	26 120	30.5	8 228	19 402	66.6	321 800	33.4	1 873
Boca Raton	71 678	14.9	13.5	22 278	5.6	44 539	18.3	7 761	40 551	66.9	402 100	33.1	1 631
Bonita Springs	61 663	9.7	11.4	14 403	6.4	31 716	35.2	11 699	22 118	81.2	278 300	18.8	1 203
Boynton Beach	47 739	1.8	17.3	15 860	12.2	36 289	18.6	7 185	29 848	60.3	160 700	39.7	1 363
Bradenton	38 688	2.3	19.4	12 091	10.9	26 767	7.3	5 362	20 510	54.1	142 100	45.9	1 052
Cape Coral	51 464	2.5	15.5	43 536	9.3	78 948	72.7	18 181	61 251	67.7	189 900	32.3	1 103
Casselberry	32 615	0.6	25.3	5 958	10.7	12 708	22.5	1 278	10 511	58.7	113 700	41.3	1 055
Clearwater	46 344	3.5	20.6	25 200	8.7	59 156	4.3	11 518	46 240	58.0	173 600	42.0	984
Clermont	64 091	1.9	11.4	9 023	8.4	12 730	NA	1 514	11 389	71.4	195 700	28.6	1 290
Coconut Creek	53 128	3.4	11.2	13 478	8.8	25 926	17.1	3 172	21 547	69.4	165 700	30.6	1 425
Cooper City	100 222	13.0	3.4	8 846	4.1	9 912	7.4	284	10 411	85.6	354 000	14.4	1 709
Coral Gables	91 654	22.5	15.7	10 086	3.3	20 266	13.9	2 320	18 740	61.8	687 700	38.2	1 531
Coral Springs	70 422	7.1	10.3	32 604	10.4	45 433	10.0	3 619	40 825	57.3	318 800	42.7	1 362
Cutler Bay	64 360	3.0	13.1	9 835	5.1	14 620	NA	1 282	13 552	59.4	247 200	40.6	1 307
Dania Beach	42 017	0.8	21.2	6 759	11.6	15 671	44.1	2 794	12 272	46.6	181 400	53.4	1 191
Davie	60 959	7.2	15.0	24 566	7.1	37 306	19.6	2 991	36 504	68.2	234 400	31.8	1 315
Daytona Beach	28 593	2.1	34.3	13 525	20.5	33 920	1.6	6 606	30 698	44.9	127 400	55.1	789

1. Based on population estimated by the American Community Survey.   2. Includes units rented or sold but not occupied.   3. Specified owner-occupied units; $1,000,000 represents $1,000,000 or more   4. 50.0 represents 50 percent or more.   5. 10.0 represents 10 percent or less.

Table D. Cities — Commuting, Computer Access, Migration, Labor Force, and Employment

City	Commuting Percent — Drove alone	With Commutes of 30 minutes or more[1]	Computer Access[2] Percent — With a Computer in the house	With Internet Access	Migration, 2015 — Percent who lived in the same house one year ago	Percent who lived in an other state or county one year ago	Civilian labor force, 2016 — Total	Percent change, 2015–2016	Unemployment Total	Rate[3]	Civilian employment[4], 2015 — Population age 16 and older Number	Percent in Labor Force	Population age 16 to 64 Number	Percent who worked full-year full-time
	55	56	57	58	59	60	61	62	63	64	65	66	67	68
COLORADO—Cont'd														
Castle Rock	89.2	49.8	96.8	93.4	80.6	8.7	29 457	2.2	843	2.9	41 783	80.3	37 504	58.3
Centennial	88.5	38.8	94.9	90.4	87.4	7.5	61 625	2.0	1 879	3.0	88 155	69.0	70 394	56.8
Colorado Springs	84.3	22.3	92.0	86.2	78.1	8.2	223 267	2.0	8 179	3.7	361 358	66.9	300 643	49.4
Commerce City	82.8	44.0	91.2	73.4	87.2	7.0	26 692	2.0	1 010	3.8	37 010	69.5	33 996	47.8
Denver	78.6	38.8	89.5	80.5	80.2	11.2	384 331	2.0	12 103	3.1	552 635	70.7	477 063	55.5
Englewood	81.3	35.0	89.1	81.2	79.4	14.7	19 596	1.9	636	3.2	28 189	72.7	23 974	58.1
Fort Collins	77.1	21.4	95.0	87.4	72.6	13.2	93 834	3.4	2 522	2.7	134 672	71.6	118 546	44.0
Fountain	87.4	19.2	97.9	89.1	80.4	8.3	11 610	1.7	520	4.5	20 409	68.7	19 667	48.4
Grand Junction	83.5	10.4	86.5	78.3	75.7	9.4	29 198	0.0	1 847	6.3	48 175	60.0	37 554	39.6
Greeley	83.2	27.1	85.9	76.7	73.4	11.0	49 773	0.8	1 885	3.8	77 802	61.3	64 822	45.9
Lakewood	82.0	42.3	91.6	81.5	83.3	10.1	82 456	1.9	2 641	3.2	126 269	70.6	102 853	58.8
Littleton	80.1	43.3	94.1	85.6	82.4	12.8	24 718	2.1	752	3.0	39 307	69.1	31 245	58.1
Longmont	83.5	35.8	89.0	83.2	83.7	5.9	49 036	2.0	1 560	3.2	70 894	68.5	58 507	49.4
Loveland	86.6	30.8	93.1	85.7	84.2	8.0	40 434	3.2	1 299	3.2	58 615	64.2	45 324	52.1
Northglenn	81.1	50.0	88.9	76.9	85.6	8.7	20 849	2.0	760	3.6	30 614	74.1	25 958	56.1
Parker	87.2	43.2	99.3	95.4	85.7	9.1	28 000	2.1	785	2.8	35 184	76.2	31 549	60.0
Pueblo	85.1	20.3	79.8	57.8	81.8	7.8	46 885	1.4	2 492	5.3	87 289	54.6	68 152	38.1
Thornton	85.6	50.1	95.3	83.2	83.9	6.3	72 031	2.1	2 424	3.4	97 770	75.1	86 258	62.1
Westminster	86.3	40.8	92.0	86.3	84.1	11.3	63 599	2.1	2 071	3.3	92 679	70.1	76 876	58.0
Wheat Ridge	81.5	33.8	86.6	74.7	83.1	8.2	16 471	2.0	628	3.8	25 678	64.1	19 699	53.3
CONNECTICUT	82.4	35.7	88.5	81.6	87.5	5.1	1 891 792	0.1	96 273	5.1	2 922 877	66.7	2 357 594	49.8
Bridgeport	71.9	40.1	84.4	69.1	82.5	5.6	70 964	-0.5	5 459	7.7	116 892	67.3	101 615	41.5
Bristol	83.1	32.6	84.4	74.4	86.7	3.7	32 823	-0.4	1 879	5.7	49 630	70.0	41 388	52.5
Danbury	72.2	38.7	87.8	81.1	83.6	7.1	47 444	0.5	1 974	4.2	70 480	69.7	58 873	43.8
Hartford	60.7	33.9	79.2	62.3	80.2	5.5	53 520	-0.9	5 046	9.4	97 874	61.8	85 475	36.3
Meriden	76.3	26.4	85.5	83.1	89.7	2.5	32 016	-0.3	1 997	6.2	51 053	66.4	41 488	53.4
Middletown	80.5	29.7	87.6	82.5	82.0	11.2	25 986	-0.2	1 318	5.1	39 007	66.2	33 166	45.6
Milford	85.5	34.6	89.9	84.7	87.0	6.1	29 957	0.2	1 345	4.5	442 670	65.4	34 782	55.8
Naugatuck	94.6	48.4	81.4	74.5	NA	NA	17 269	-0.3	995	5.8	24 140	63.4	18 949	51.0
New Britain	86.6	17.6	78.8	66.5	90.7	2.7	36 475	-0.7	2 631	7.2	56 173	59.7	47 816	43.7
New Haven	55.9	27.6	83.5	73.9	80.6	6.6	64 182	-0.4	4 248	6.6	104 220	63.3	92 629	39.7
New London	63.8	13.3	79.8	70.4	70.0	9.7	12 007	-0.4	859	7.2	22 211	66.2	19 220	35.2
Norwalk	78.9	35.3	92.6	87.5	92.1	2.7	50 721	0.6	2 237	4.4	74 219	71.7	61 149	53.3
Norwich	86.4	34.5	89.0	77.4	86.8	4.5	20 265	-0.5	1 234	6.1	32 514	70.0	27 105	47.4
Shelton	86.0	34.6	86.6	83.6	87.4	3.7	22 164	0.2	1 078	4.9	34 379	65.8	25 285	51.8
Stamford	70.0	36.5	90.7	86.0	83.5	6.2	70 042	0.6	2 973	4.2	105 093	73.4	89 198	51.4
Torrington	86.0	39.7	90.0	82.7	86.0	3.8	19 403	-2.2	1 142	5.9	28 287	65.6	22 620	53.8
Waterbury	82.4	36.1	78.6	63.5	85.5	6.6	50 641	-0.9	4 096	8.1	85 925	60.1	72 565	39.1
West Haven	84.0	34.5	87.4	80.7	84.2	6.7	30 005	-0.3	1 787	6.0	44 816	63.5	36 313	42.5
DELAWARE	85.4	34.0	87.3	77.4	85.6	6.6	472 676	1.2	20 703	4.4	765 250	62.5	604 426	50.4
Dover	81.8	30.5	90.6	83.1	70.6	13.0	15 780	1.1	961	6.1	29 559	63.1	25 174	42.6
Newark	72.5	23.3	92.5	84.9	67.5	18.7	16 427	1.0	730	4.4	30 724	50.9	26 645	31.1
Wilmington	70.1	28.5	68.7	56.0	81.9	6.4	34 246	0.8	2 207	6.4	56 503	60.0	47 210	46.5
DISTRICT OF COLUMBIA	35.7	51.7	89.3	76.7	79.2	10.7	392 448	1.5	23 602	6.0	564 206	69.8	487 615	54.0
Washington	35.7	51.7	89.3	76.7	79.2	10.7	392 448	1.5	23 602	6.0	564 206	69.8	487 615	54.0
FLORIDA	84.4	40.8	87.5	77.4	83.9	7.1	9 838 935	2.3	480 364	4.9	16 640 196	58.4	12 694 963	48.3
Altamonte Springs	88.2	41.5	93.9	87.6	77.4	11.0	25 243	2.8	1 099	4.4	35 676	66.9	28 992	57.3
Apopka	86.2	47.0	86.1	79.2	93.3	4.0	25 653	3.0	1 053	4.1	38 064	68.9	33 101	53.3
Aventura	87.9	58.0	92.5	64.0	85.6	6.5	16 989	2.1	904	5.3	34 222	56.8	22 334	57.8
Boca Raton	88.3	28.1	95.0	88.1	78.4	9.4	50 447	3.2	2 108	4.2	80 628	62.1	58 401	49.1
Bonita Springs	86.1	33.6	92.2	82.9	84.3	7.8	23 345	3.1	1 041	4.5	46 626	38.7	21 306	45.9
Boynton Beach	83.6	40.0	87.1	75.1	78.9	8.9	37 585	3.0	1 870	5.0	62 052	58.4	44 468	45.2
Bradenton	89.6	31.2	83.8	66.1	75.8	12.5	25 478	2.3	1 236	4.9	43 323	50.8	29 837	45.7
Cape Coral	86.0	42.9	93.0	81.6	88.3	3.6	86 069	2.9	3 983	4.6	147 095	55.7	110 756	50.1
Casselberry	80.8	35.6	90.2	87.9	86.6	8.1	14 786	2.7	638	4.3	23 970	57.0	18 597	38.0
Clearwater	76.0	31.8	82.1	70.5	83.1	6.6	57 109	2.5	2 517	4.4	96 892	58.8	70 407	50.9
Clermont	91.3	50.6	NA	NA	71.0	17.1	15 001	2.9	706	4.7	24 560	55.7	17 336	55.1
Coconut Creek	87.6	36.5	91.0	83.7	80.6	3.4	31 935	1.7	1 353	4.2	47 441	68.8	38 649	57.9
Cooper City	86.1	34.5	95.3	92.2	92.1	1.6	19 972	1.7	753	3.8	27 495	70.1	24 059	51.5
Coral Gables	84.3	37.1	93.1	87.1	85.0	6.3	26 527	2.4	1 215	4.6	43 010	60.4	33 148	55.5
Coral Springs	83.9	46.4	96.5	90.4	86.3	5.6	71 610	1.6	3 160	4.4	100 148	69.4	87 063	48.6
Cutler Bay	78.5	70.5	92.1	83.0	90.2	1.1	23 462	2.0	1 182	5.0	34 321	65.3	29 007	52.1
Dania Beach	82.5	36.5	86.0	73.7	75.3	5.8	16 288	1.7	832	5.1	27 059	66.2	21 888	48.1
Davie	87.0	36.1	92.4	85.8	85.7	5.7	56 237	1.9	2 322	4.1	85 696	71.2	73 579	53.9
Daytona Beach	82.2	16.8	78.3	63.6	84.0	7.7	30 240	3.0	1 920	6.3	56 410	48.7	41 716	35.2

1. Employed persons.　2. Households.　3. Percent of civilian labor force.　4. Persons 16 years old and over.

Table D. Cities — Construction, Wholesale Trade, and Retail Trade

City	Value of residential construction authorized by building permits, 2016			Wholesale trade,[1] 2012				Retail trade,[2] 2012			
	New construction ($1,000)	Number of housing units	Percent single family	Number of establishments	Number of employees	Sales (mil dol)	Annual payroll (mil dol)	Number of establishments	Number of employees	Sales (mil dol)	Annual payroll (mil dol)
	69	70	71	72	73	74	75	76	77	78	79
COLORADO—Cont'd											
Castle Rock	249 757	1 251	62.0	30	D	D	D	189	2 800	698.3	61.0
Centennial	93 207	583	8.6	189	3 340	12 326.3	261.0	264	4 771	1 842.4	159.3
Colorado Springs	NA	NA	NA	325	3 638	2 062.8	210.3	1 621	24 923	6 966.7	660.4
Commerce City	122 637	522	84.7	140	2 530	1 915.3	128.8	105	1 333	468.0	39.3
Denver	1 260 086	7 842	24.1	1 175	17 997	14 625.8	1 090.1	2 282	26 469	7 111.4	725.7
Englewood	41 148	257	17.5	100	1 489	754.3	84.5	203	2 525	876.6	72.2
Fort Collins	298 313	1 874	26.0	108	D	D	D	617	9 667	2 309.8	229.5
Fountain	NA	NA	NA	3	D	D	D	37	1 021	283.6	25.7
Grand Junction	NA	NA	NA	167	1 556	706.3	70.9	477	6 718	1 749.6	171.6
Greeley	88 685	575	45.7	77	1 110	790.0	51.2	291	4 986	1 379.5	132.7
Lakewood	131 405	770	24.8	129	930	1 069.2	68.6	669	10 547	2 528.7	263.6
Littleton	97 727	727	28.7	60	901	833.2	60.7	244	4 098	1 390.7	138.9
Longmont	171 594	1 117	27.0	69	775	427.5	52.2	270	3 932	1 137.4	105.0
Loveland	125 908	572	68.5	79	1 202	484.9	57.9	320	5 233	1 401.1	123.9
Northglenn	0	0	0.0	18	201	47.2	6.8	105	1 817	584.0	62.9
Parker	150 160	689	44.8	30	228	190.4	17.6	153	2 728	837.5	71.6
Pueblo	NA	NA	NA	58	704	341.3	29.7	406	6 473	1 653.1	157.5
Thornton	311 390	1 124	74.0	29	213	116.7	16.9	189	4 625	1 326.7	126.4
Westminster	53 291	196	100.0	72	1 572	1 733.1	183.3	322	6 329	1 552.3	145.2
Wheat Ridge	10 253	34	100.0	68	680	274.3	35.3	163	2 222	659.2	63.2
CONNECTICUT	945	3	100.0	3 675	58 814	161 962.2	3 934.4	12 597	182 528	51 632.5	4 974.5
Bridgeport	5 571	69	5.8	138	D	D	D	266	3 050	900.7	93.0
Bristol	4 879	37	100.0	38	342	180.9	16.3	170	2 867	824.5	75.6
Danbury	19 899	82	69.5	109	1 316	1 349.4	85.0	454	8 144	2 283.3	221.8
Hartford	673	5	100.0	112	2 244	1 317.7	107.6	357	3 053	1 813.7	100.6
Meriden	11 116	64	1.6	38	306	165.0	15.1	228	3 081	750.7	68.0
Middletown	4 248	25	88.0	44	1 087	800.9	65.3	120	1 690	457.4	45.7
Milford	13 945	178	16.3	98	1 476	792.5	87.7	323	5 819	1 667.1	149.2
Naugatuck	1 797	8	100.0	21	480	331.4	29.1	66	1 031	320.9	28.6
New Britain	1 454	32	100.0	39	402	179.8	21.3	146	1 691	553.7	45.6
New Haven	35 747	227	3.1	74	D	D	D	322	3 135	835.6	84.8
New London	6 455	39	100.0	13	D	D	D	101	1 343	463.7	42.2
Norwalk	41 585	199	10.6	129	2 445	1 940.3	142.7	343	5 913	1 719.0	217.9
Norwich	2 733	22	9.1	20	571	381.6	38.9	125	2 053	477.6	45.9
Shelton	9 185	46	100.0	56	D	D	D	90	1 821	831.5	65.7
Stamford	160 520	720	6.9	213	5 498	109 632.9	713.5	482	6 199	1 626.0	178.9
Torrington	0	0	0.0	32	D	D	D	159	2 832	931.4	75.3
Waterbury	4 577	40	100.0	80	803	519.7	46.1	425	6 035	1 620.9	152.8
West Haven	6 770	75	10.7	60	1 248	626.2	70.0	110	1 361	351.0	35.7
DELAWARE	390 359	2 798	85.7	835	7 653	5 628.9	385.9	3 616	51 711	14 456.0	1 270.1
Dover	38 884	228	55.3	38	296	114.7	13.2	205	3 883	1 005.0	85.7
Newark	31 932	245	8.6	41	195	117.5	9.5	176	2 877	921.4	81.8
Wilmington	3 359	126	23.8	114	878	767.7	50.7	303	2 882	862.8	84.2
DISTRICT OF COLUMBIA	510 518	4 690	7.2	335	3 415	2 591.9	260.6	1 710	19 780	4 439.9	525.2
Washington	510 518	4 690	7.2	335	3 415	2 591.9	260.6	1 710	19 780	4 439.9	525.2
FLORIDA	11 938	71	100.0	27 109	252 418	252 626.6	12 867.6	71 189	947 877	273 867.1	24 033.5
Altamonte Springs	28 737	410	4.4	77	1 929	423.7	42.2	342	5 824	1 363.3	127.9
Apopka	133 065	645	57.8	67	724	226.1	26.4	155	2 058	625.8	49.2
Aventura	18 076	131	0.0	142	476	1 807.9	35.5	375	9 146	2 197.9	206.7
Boca Raton	156 639	598	24.4	379	4 030	4 550.7	313.9	652	9 944	2 534.2	293.6
Bonita Springs	250 969	786	48.6	43	525	373.7	28.1	187	2 067	484.2	48.9
Boynton Beach	62 049	720	2.8	105	828	627.9	48.3	377	5 602	1 279.4	120.7
Bradenton	99 211	764	27.2	43	288	161.6	13.6	265	3 701	1 102.0	95.9
Cape Coral	369 891	1 587	90.9	100	294	140.4	12.3	404	6 381	1 692.8	150.1
Casselberry	55 600	605	10.9	26	111	53.1	4.2	128	2 264	478.2	52.0
Clearwater	44 538	467	7.5	143	1 373	633.3	75.8	647	9 790	2 790.5	261.7
Clermont	121 263	764	63.4	21	82	58.2	2.4	147	2 818	733.0	63.3
Coconut Creek	35 453	385	24.2	58	237	221.5	12.6	153	3 213	1 345.4	118.9
Cooper City	1 329	6	100.0	39	D	D	D	81	1 450	346.6	38.9
Coral Gables	43 681	51	96.1	180	1 576	9 268.1	128.7	297	4 154	1 556.6	152.6
Coral Springs	35 039	322	15.5	239	1 345	632.7	62.3	455	7 810	2 066.6	197.0
Cutler Bay	1 925	15	100.0	28	116	26.7	3.2	165	2 223	546.1	50.3
Dania Beach	2 874	24	79.2	129	857	529.1	39.0	183	1 613	510.5	45.7
Davie	24 645	367	14.7	262	1 782	688.4	76.7	405	5 802	2 050.3	170.3
Daytona Beach	37 027	139	100.0	79	627	253.7	26.3	461	6 387	1 687.6	152.6

1. Merchant wholesalers except manufacturers' sales branches and offices.   2. Establishments with payroll.

City	Real estate and rental and leasing, 2012				Professional, scientific, and technical services,[1] 2012				Manufacturing, 2012			
	Number of establishments	Number of employees	Receipts (mil dol)	Annual payroll (mil dol)	Number of establishments	Number of employees	Receipts (mil dol)	Annual payroll (mil dol)	Number of establishments	Number of employees	Receipts (mil dol)	Annual payroll (mil dol)
	80	81	82	83	84	85	86	87	88	89	90	91
COLORADO—Cont'd												
Castle Rock	78	202	39.4	6.8	195	D	D	D	16	221	D	9.5
Centennial	250	998	354.1	53.2	695	3 802	1 019.8	274.6	69	1 750	667.5	112.4
Colorado Springs	845	2 875	545.3	102.9	1 907	D	D	D	351	8 351	2 236.8	473.5
Commerce City	48	531	114.8	20.7	43	293	229.5	19.6	87	2 851	5 446.3	164.6
Denver	1 451	9 373	2 723.8	488.3	4 273	D	D	D	759	17 032	5 343.9	761.4
Englewood	87	377	113.3	18.9	161	D	D	D	128	2 688	522.0	118.8
Fort Collins	298	1 258	173.5	40.5	877	6 219	736.6	343.1	109	5 760	3 156.6	361.8
Fountain	9	47	2.8	0.9	20	97	3.4	1.2	7	145	D	7.6
Grand Junction	195	663	143.5	26.7	365	D	D	D	93	1 938	382.8	78.8
Greeley	119	518	73.6	16.7	181	D	D	D	53	4 235	3 090.6	145.1
Lakewood	251	791	145.6	27.9	823	D	D	D	99	1 112	270.9	51.5
Littleton	89	410	52.1	12.4	346	4 994	1 110.9	517.6	32	4 492	1 698.0	414.4
Longmont	121	362	80.1	12.2	379	4 846	752.7	392.9	118	2 180	599.1	141.3
Loveland	110	577	74.2	19.1	260	1 265	144.6	54.4	99	2 619	756.9	199.0
Northglenn	31	107	18.8	3.5	59	256	22.9	8.6	26	425	100.2	19.9
Parker	71	118	30.1	4.5	220	687	102.7	36.3	27	399	D	15.2
Pueblo	108	523	83.1	15.4	185	D	D	D	54	1 733	821.0	72.1
Thornton	81	487	118.9	13.9	171	1 048	124.5	45.4	16	250	D	12.9
Westminster	157	568	114.5	20.7	378	D	D	D	53	747	270.3	42.9
Wheat Ridge	53	272	40.7	9.7	189	D	D	D	42	1 007	293.8	54.2
CONNECTICUT	3 219	19 778	5 349.5	958.4	9 176	96 768	17 863.9	8 316.7	4 350	163 847	55 160.1	10 546.2
Bridgeport	94	406	79.7	15.6	208	D	D	D	139	3 274	1 063.3	168.4
Bristol	40	151	31.1	5.5	67	302	40.4	15.8	130	2 827	663.8	148.5
Danbury	84	1 711	327.0	105.0	226	2 662	597.8	264.5	93	5 623	2 084.0	376.1
Hartford	164	1 337	270.0	66.6	392	5 588	1 361.1	488.4	68	1 013	207.6	44.6
Meriden	44	505	47.4	17.8	76	760	108.3	45.2	66	2 433	940.2	173.9
Middletown	39	248	37.7	10.2	108	D	D	D	52	3 583	2 078.3	231.1
Milford	51	D	D	D	178	2 832	268.5	104.6	151	3 305	1 532.1	214.8
Naugatuck	14	D	D	D	32	213	24.5	9.7	47	1 168	386.1	61.1
New Britain	40	184	44.2	6.2	84	D	D	D	94	2 959	758.3	165.2
New Haven	128	751	151.1	31.4	365	2 957	599.6	267.5	70	2 250	510.5	114.6
New London	24	147	24.3	5.7	96	D	D	D	15	212	D	9.0
Norwalk	95	327	81.0	15.6	340	3 538	837.7	299.1	100	1 733	404.2	120.5
Norwich	35	D	D	D	63	894	118.3	54.5	25	699	132.4	35.9
Shelton	38	605	89.0	23.4	140	1 681	394.2	141.0	64	2 951	1 302.9	191.0
Stamford	217	1 369	456.5	114.3	641	D	D	D	104	1 959	495.4	106.4
Torrington	25	102	14.1	3.6	61	463	74.5	35.4	65	1 870	422.2	92.3
Waterbury	72	293	70.0	10.1	146	D	D	D	153	3 206	956.8	157.0
West Haven	43	132	39.5	5.1	61	D	D	D	49	1 411	382.6	73.7
DELAWARE	1 111	5 402	5 471.2	264.9	2 536	D	D	D	573	26 355	22 597.4	1 393.2
Dover	75	286	50.3	10.6	159	D	D	D	19	1 518	940.3	91.7
Newark	49	192	409.9	5.4	115	D	D	D	25	932	276.4	66.4
Wilmington	204	805	1 802.6	35.2	585	D	D	D	66	999	D	53.8
DISTRICT OF COLUMBIA	1 112	10 103	3 213.9	673.7	4 831	89 224	29 796.2	10 549.2	113	1 361	309.8	61.5
Washington	1 112	10 103	3 213.9	673.7	4 831	89 224	29 796.2	10 549.2	113	1 361	309.8	61.5
FLORIDA	29 845	139 955	30 560.1	5 337.4	70 617	436 764	69 653.4	26 855.4	12 890	277 089	96 924.1	14 270.0
Altamonte Springs	109	1 328	141.9	42.8	293	1 495	158.6	57.3	40	307	45.4	11.9
Apopka	34	90	19.6	2.6	96	354	38.7	13.1	27	360	88.0	15.1
Aventura	206	737	136.8	26.3	362	944	181.4	59.5	13	149	D	4.4
Boca Raton	432	3 486	519.2	170.9	1 457	D	D	D	153	2 052	451.1	113.8
Bonita Springs	119	399	75.8	18.8	198	962	183.2	56.3	24	146	19.5	4.6
Boynton Beach	116	610	108.0	20.3	353	1 510	207.6	76.2	64	735	153.3	33.8
Bradenton	79	390	70.6	10.9	220	D	D	D	30	1 819	995.3	132.5
Cape Coral	292	534	104.5	17.6	348	D	D	D	85	548	84.2	25.4
Casselberry	46	329	40.6	10.9	89	414	34.4	11.9	26	298	39.2	12.5
Clearwater	280	1 132	166.8	39.4	694	D	D	D	97	1 674	319.0	64.9
Clermont	83	205	38.0	6.0	105	340	36.5	12.6	9	65	7.3	1.0
Coconut Creek	46	1 730	603.7	81.4	166	725	108.1	29.6	14	216	67.0	7.5
Cooper City	42	91	15.9	2.6	180	404	60.8	17.0	7	21	2.2	0.7
Coral Gables	359	1 144	331.7	54.6	1 505	D	D	D	28	447	D	25.9
Coral Springs	217	765	177.5	30.6	752	2 530	355.4	106.9	59	775	197.7	40.5
Cutler Bay	28	68	8.8	1.8	72	344	18.6	6.2	4	9	D	0.3
Dania Beach	58	301	83.0	16.7	137	D	D	D	44	696	136.0	31.9
Davie	196	604	147.1	24.9	538	D	D	D	88	1 879	924.1	130.4
Daytona Beach	143	667	137.5	25.6	312	D	D	D	63	1 532	376.6	82.0

1. Establishments subject to federal tax.

Table D. Cities — Accommodation and Food Services, Arts, Entertainment, and Recreation, and Health Care and Social Assistance

City	Accommodation and food services, 2012				Arts, entertainment, and recreation,[1] 2012				Health care and social assistance,[1] 2012			
	Number of establishments	Number of employees	Sales (mil dol)	Annual payroll (mil dol)	Number of establishments	Number of employees	Receipts (mil dol)	Annual payroll (mil dol)	Number of establishments	Number of employees	Receipts (mil dol)	Annual payroll (mil dol)
	92	93	94	95	96	97	98	99	100	101	102	103
COLORADO—Cont'd												
Castle Rock	103	1 843	88.7	26.4	16	D	D	D	107	D	D	D
Centennial	207	3 322	186.9	57.4	34	D	D	D	365	2 886	309.3	118.6
Colorado Springs	1 040	23 240	1 274.8	344.7	133	1 678	92.3	27.7	1 477	15 806	1 630.5	678.0
Commerce City	58	926	47.2	11.4	2	D	D	D	26	D	D	D
Denver	1 982	42 906	2 884.9	823.2	235	5 851	687.1	309.6	1 695	25 982	3 209.7	1 299.9
Englewood	95	1 448	75.2	21.7	8	D	D	D	206	6 422	677.3	306.6
Fort Collins	427	8 329	374.5	113.7	66	910	47.5	15.0	546	D	D	D
Fountain	45	967	37.6	9.6	1	D	D	D	22	155	15.1	5.9
Grand Junction	211	4 578	218.7	67.6	20	321	12.9	3.7	309	D	D	D
Greeley	184	3 501	157.6	47.0	23	216	6.4	2.1	222	2 645	241.0	98.5
Lakewood	378	7 456	385.9	117.3	44	641	29.8	9.3	487	7 651	747.3	321.9
Littleton	135	D	D	D	20	D	D	D	215	2 503	244.6	108.5
Longmont	187	3 623	177.6	53.6	26	167	8.5	2.1	250	2 606	228.9	107.6
Loveland	194	4 019	189.3	53.5	30	159	8.5	2.6	224	2 558	257.2	104.5
Northglenn	45	922	46.2	14.4	8	239	10.1	2.7	53	D	D	D
Parker	106	2 252	101.4	32.7	16	287	16.5	5.5	160	1 259	131.5	51.3
Pueblo	286	4 992	205.1	60.2	20	D	D	D	319	2 057	211.7	89.3
Thornton	164	3 197	178.1	48.7	23	D	D	D	155	2 827	313.2	146.7
Westminster	231	5 395	292.5	86.3	29	610	30.4	9.2	246	D	D	D
Wheat Ridge	91	1 347	68.7	20.1	16	83	5.2	1.5	168	D	D	D
CONNECTICUT	8 263	134 546	9 542.1	2 590.8	1 160	14 862	1 538.5	418.5	7 876	131 732	13 333.4	6 058.8
Bridgeport	227	2 202	148.4	36.4	23	366	29.6	6.3	217	4 554	524.5	261.5
Bristol	108	1 222	70.9	19.2	13	381	32.1	8.0	101	1 854	157.9	72.5
Danbury	211	3 531	226.6	63.2	19	226	14.3	4.5	216	D	D	D
Hartford	326	4 429	297.2	82.4	13	201	38.9	6.7	237	5 215	831.5	439.4
Meriden	116	1 292	67.8	17.0	4	D	D	D	98	1 770	163.6	80.8
Middletown	110	1 311	86.4	24.9	8	58	5.2	1.2	116	2 661	282.4	126.8
Milford	172	2 632	141.5	39.4	20	296	17.6	7.4	139	2 189	248.7	116.0
Naugatuck	51	474	23.7	5.8	3	D	D	D	36	728	49.5	25.3
New Britain	91	1 195	66.5	18.1	8	66	9.3	1.4	104	1 728	213.0	93.8
New Haven	337	4 119	284.4	75.6	24	D	D	D	269	4 257	438.6	190.6
New London	89	1 217	68.1	20.3	11	32	2.6	0.9	84	D	D	D
Norwalk	251	2 845	219.3	61.1	54	916	118.8	42.0	192	2 678	308.7	141.5
Norwich	93	D	D	D	7	D	D	D	114	2 071	199.2	89.0
Shelton	112	1 915	117.2	36.3	10	118	9.5	2.6	105	2 312	243.7	118.4
Stamford	389	5 995	451.2	133.7	52	1 193	404.4	75.7	351	4 135	495.2	221.6
Torrington	79	959	55.1	14.4	13	91	5.9	1.4	112	1 801	182.1	71.6
Waterbury	231	3 063	158.2	43.5	11	99	6.2	1.4	230	4 952	513.4	234.8
West Haven	110	1 471	86.4	22.4	4	D	D	D	59	D	D	D
DELAWARE	1 987	35 609	2 148.4	566.7	302	5 087	490.5	148.6	1 964	30 400	3 173.7	1 434.8
Dover	151	4 280	387.3	78.2	17	D	D	D	188	3 325	290.5	129.7
Newark	133	3 183	177.0	45.9	10	143	6.6	1.8	133	D	D	D
Wilmington	197	2 964	169.2	48.2	28	243	17.8	5.4	258	3 681	330.2	137.8
DISTRICT OF COLUMBIA	2 371	60 370	5 101.6	1 504.8	210	5 103	778.3	327.3	1 353	24 356	2 870.9	1 203.4
Washington	2 371	60 370	5 101.6	1 504.8	210	5 103	778.3	327.3	1 353	24 356	2 870.9	1 203.4
FLORIDA	37 118	786 082	49 817.9	13 598.2	6 594	136 273	14 212.0	4 120.2	51 567	614 004	76 785.9	27 914.4
Altamonte Springs	140	3 730	196.0	61.3	21	D	D	D	244	D	D	D
Apopka	67	D	D	D	8	131	6.8	2.5	69	658	84.0	38.9
Aventura	109	3 319	244.7	73.0	23	168	12.3	3.3	291	D	D	D
Boca Raton	362	10 342	697.3	208.7	89	728	54.8	14.7	726	6 025	893.3	349.7
Bonita Springs	116	D	D	D	31	876	58.0	19.2	115	975	135.0	47.5
Boynton Beach	197	4 235	220.6	63.8	26	D	D	D	340	D	D	D
Bradenton	134	2 396	122.9	35.8	25	191	14.9	6.3	291	7 453	892.2	318.4
Cape Coral	212	3 797	181.0	52.6	35	238	17.4	3.5	270	2 503	346.7	110.5
Casselberry	70	873	46.2	11.5	10	85	4.3	1.5	63	D	D	D
Clearwater	346	7 252	482.0	130.8	54	917	45.3	10.5	468	5 606	706.4	279.5
Clermont	91	1 932	93.6	26.1	16	D	D	D	151	D	D	D
Coconut Creek	80	1 383	69.2	18.3	21	D	D	D	101	D	D	D
Cooper City	49	687	33.2	9.0	13	D	D	D	132	D	D	D
Coral Gables	246	5 972	363.6	117.6	51	321	44.2	14.9	528	D	D	D
Coral Springs	275	4 612	264.7	71.0	75	551	40.1	9.7	469	D	D	D
Cutler Bay	66	D	D	D	8	63	3.5	0.8	64	D	D	D
Dania Beach	83	1 723	129.3	31.1	24	D	D	D	45	D	D	D
Davie	195	D	D	D	48	D	D	D	252	D	D	D
Daytona Beach	256	5 862	321.0	91.6	38	D	D	D	237	4 513	412.7	178.0

1. Establishments subject to federal tax.

Table D. Cities — Other Services and Government Employment and Payroll

City	Other services[1], 2012				Government employment and payroll, 2012								
						March payroll							
							Percent of total for:						
	Number of establishments	Number of employees	Receipts (mil dol)	Annual payroll (mil dol)	Full-time equivalent employees	Total (dollars)	Administration, judicial, and legal	Police and Corrections	Fire Protection	Highways and transportation	Health and welfare	Natural resources and utilities	Education and libraries
	104	105	106	107	108	109	110	111	112	113	114	115	116
COLORADO—Cont'd													
Castle Rock	98	511	34.5	11.9	454	2 257 316	12.3	18.0	21.0	7.0	3.2	27.7	0.0
Centennial	167	809	75.5	22.6	56	312 389	97.1	0.0	0.0	0.0	0.0	0.0	0.0
Colorado Springs	703	4 195	357.7	115.6	6 835	37 084 390	4.0	14.0	7.5	3.0	35.7	34.0	0.0
Commerce City	90	712	87.2	22.8	331	1 840 907	22.9	42.5	0.0	11.7	8.4	14.5	0.0
Denver	1 071	8 716	708.5	244.9	11 914	62 559 560	13.5	28.4	10.9	11.0	11.2	19.1	2.3
Englewood	118	799	76.5	27.1	496	2 612 051	12.2	19.8	16.5	5.4	2.5	32.9	2.4
Fort Collins	247	1 400	92.3	31.1	1 475	7 276 841	19.4	25.1	0.0	10.9	0.5	39.9	0.0
Fountain	15	61	5.4	1.2	195	852 760	16.1	9.5	14.2	2.6	3.5	38.5	0.0
Grand Junction	187	1 438	129.5	36.6	684	3 402 863	13.8	30.4	21.4	6.4	0.5	21.7	0.0
Greeley	117	634	55.5	16.1	980	4 950 974	9.9	28.6	15.1	7.5	1.4	32.8	0.0
Lakewood	250	1 404	103.2	35.4	1 014	5 146 071	18.0	47.7	0.0	3.7	1.4	18.8	0.0
Littleton	105	756	64.3	24.2	427	2 523 624	11.4	21.4	46.3	4.8	4.3	5.3	4.2
Longmont	150	783	56.9	19.1	895	4 775 325	12.8	26.4	13.8	4.3	4.2	29.7	3.4
Loveland	134	851	75.9	24.6	677	3 104 613	23.9	23.9	13.3	6.0	0.0	25.8	3.5
Northglenn	48	237	18.5	5.9	323	4 495 142	20.4	39.8	0.0	2.3	0.0	30.8	0.0
Parker	122	772	57.9	17.7	295	1 383 773	22.2	35.4	0.0	13.3	0.0	22.5	0.0
Pueblo	142	832	57.8	18.7	859	4 316 626	8.8	33.4	18.2	8.7	0.5	28.3	0.0
Thornton	101	778	51.3	20.7	842	4 836 932	20.0	27.9	10.2	10.4	4.4	24.7	0.0
Westminster	135	894	56.6	20.4	992	5 125 430	12.9	29.5	16.6	4.2	3.5	24.3	3.3
Wheat Ridge	109	562	56.1	16.5	198	835 164	27.5	56.8	0.0	15.6	0.0	0.0	0.0
CONNECTICUT	5 816	34 073	3 031.0	960.6	X	X	X	X	X	X	X	X	X
Bridgeport	153	654	68.5	19.9	4 248	23 926 290	4.5	12.4	5.7	0.9	3.3	1.9	70.6
Bristol	76	373	31.9	9.4	1 756	9 163 919	3.3	10.9	5.8	2.6	1.2	5.4	69.3
Danbury	159	986	86.8	26.3	1 817	10 016 152	3.5	11.0	8.0	3.2	1.8	2.8	68.2
Hartford	214	1 242	113.2	33.1	5 207	24 306 797	2.8	9.1	6.3	1.0	3.8	0.9	76.1
Meriden	67	388	30.1	9.1	1 673	9 260 984	3.4	12.3	8.7	1.1	3.7	5.2	65.5
Middletown	77	441	48.9	14.4	1 621	8 623 913	3.5	13.7	9.7	2.6	6.4	5.0	55.8
Milford	126	752	61.9	20.0	2 207	11 763 788	2.2	6.1	6.4	1.6	1.9	2.6	77.1
Naugatuck	36	134	12.9	3.6	976	4 533 881	3.1	10.0	5.6	1.8	1.8	2.7	73.9
New Britain	74	358	28.8	9.3	2 064	11 112 239	2.6	10.0	9.5	2.3	1.6	6.1	66.2
New Haven	170	901	83.8	27.2	4 808	23 846 140	3.9	13.4	10.0	1.1	2.8	3.0	65.4
New London	53	336	24.9	8.5	789	3 869 245	5.6	17.4	11.4	1.4	2.1	4.5	54.9
Norwalk	178	1 009	93.6	30.5	2 837	13 813 488	4.1	12.3	8.1	3.0	1.2	1.8	68.2
Norwich	59	459	28.3	10.5	984	5 092 687	3.2	11.7	7.1	3.7	4.1	20.9	47.0
Shelton	69	379	25.9	8.9	952	5 269 099	4.2	8.4	0.5	4.0	2.3	3.1	77.5
Stamford	251	1 622	134.5	42.7	3 375	22 400 736	3.9	13.4	9.4	1.1	5.3	3.3	60.5
Torrington	69	433	30.9	10.6	923	4 776 132	2.9	12.2	7.3	3.8	3.3	2.6	66.3
Waterbury	144	916	93.7	26.2	3 875	18 570 027	3.9	12.3	7.5	1.2	2.6	5.2	67.1
West Haven	74	338	35.7	10.1	1 404	6 641 617	4.9	17.7	4.6	4.7	2.6	0.6	64.8
DELAWARE	1 190	7 668	617.2	207.1	X	X	X	X	X	X	X	X	X
Dover	59	509	30.1	11.0	348	1 666 145	16.3	43.4	1.4	2.0	1.1	25.4	3.3
Newark	53	290	15.9	6.3	258	1 304 591	12.9	41.6	0.4	3.6	4.4	29.6	0.0
Wilmington	116	825	80.0	23.8	1 254	5 779 211	16.3	41.1	15.0	4.0	5.1	11.7	0.0
DISTRICT OF COLUMBIA	940	7 719	633.3	194.1	X	X	X	X	X	X	X	X	X
Washington	940	7 719	633.3	194.1	34 002	194 813 463	15.0	19.3	5.8	2.2	15.5	8.1	25.7
FLORIDA	27 843	145 010	12 202.5	3 616.4	X	X	X	X	X	X	X	X	X
Altamonte Springs	107	D	D	D	387	1 562 231	12.2	35.2	0.0	2.6	0.0	35.5	1.2
Apopka	58	268	18.9	5.7	391	1 780 824	13.9	31.5	26.1	2.1	0.0	17.9	0.0
Aventura	79	867	43.0	16.3	366	1 349 401	17.9	28.7	27.3	9.0	0.5	15.5	0.0
Boca Raton	314	1 584	114.4	35.2	1 418	6 984 386	9.9	26.8	24.4	3.6	0.1	27.8	2.2
Bonita Springs	86	306	19.6	6.8	55	213 459	44.7	0.0	0.0	0.0	0.0	11.7	0.0
Boynton Beach	159	1 102	75.5	26.0	747	4 117 701	10.9	32.9	22.3	0.2	0.5	25.1	2.4
Bradenton	83	288	22.5	6.3	434	1 525 511	8.1	37.6	20.9	3.9	0.5	24.1	0.0
Cape Coral	227	1 016	67.2	21.0	1 360	5 329 766	17.8	25.1	19.0	5.1	0.4	27.7	0.0
Casselberry	63	237	16.4	4.8	217	833 769	18.9	28.6	21.7	6.1	0.0	23.7	0.0
Clearwater	197	921	75.6	21.2	1 653	6 760 407	11.2	29.1	14.6	5.7	0.6	28.3	0.0
Clermont	64	393	27.0	9.0	262	960 550	4.5	26.8	25.5	20.2	0.0	23.0	3.3
Coconut Creek	70	365	23.8	7.0	330	1 913 611	28.0	41.4	1.7	4.0	0.0	17.4	0.0
Cooper City	48	326	25.4	9.0	138	525 375	17.6	0.0	0.0	0.0	0.0	48.0	0.0
Coral Gables	131	897	65.6	19.8	793	4 845 710	17.3	32.6	27.2	4.5	0.5	12.9	0.0
Coral Springs	235	860	68.5	19.5	845	4 451 797	13.6	41.1	25.3	2.0	0.0	11.7	0.0
Cutler Bay	37	155	13.9	4.3	47	173 292	50.2	1.3	0.0	11.8	0.0	32.6	0.0
Dania Beach	93	1 143	60.0	18.5	113	516 841	46.4	0.0	0.0	4.7	3.0	37.2	0.0
Davie	230	1 116	121.6	32.4	617	4 513 053	8.3	40.2	31.1	7.0	1.3	8.4	0.0
Daytona Beach	122	572	38.3	13.6	1 046	4 375 710	11.9	39.3	11.4	5.1	1.4	26.4	0.0

1. Establishments subject to federal tax.

Table D. Cities — **City Government Finances**

City	General revenue Total (mil dol)	Intergovernmental Total (mil dol)	Intergovernmental Percent from state government	Taxes Total (mil dol)	Taxes Per capita[1] (dollars) Total	Taxes Per capita[1] (dollars) Property	Taxes Per capita[1] (dollars) Sales and gross receipts	General expenditure Total (mil dol)	General expenditure Per capita[1] (dollars) Total	General expenditure Per capita[1] (dollars) Capital outlays
	117	118	119	120	121	122	123	124	125	126
COLORADO—Cont'd										
Castle Rock	72.3	4.3	100.0	39.3	764	86	677	61.6	1 198	135
Centennial	67.4	9.9	66.5	52.6	505	129	376	66.6	640	152
Colorado Springs	1 020.1	65.7	31.6	214.4	494	52	442	968.4	2 233	239
Commerce City	59.2	2.8	60.8	47.8	984	138	846	61.0	1 256	0
Denver	2 940.6	477.1	60.5	1 107.9	1 748	610	1 138	2 623.4	4 139	261
Englewood....................	60.4	3.3	42.3	31.3	1 002	139	864	53.0	1 698	1
Fort Collins	238.1	30.8	16.5	125.6	843	119	724	233.7	1 569	354
Fountain	12.7	1.1	60.7	10.1	374	74	300	26.4	981	22
Grand Junction	114.1	18.2	45.4	60.4	1 009	214	795	130.2	2 176	564
Greeley	114.2	13.2	62.0	60.1	630	105	514	99.4	1 042	109
Lakewood	155.5	22.9	36.1	96.4	663	105	514	144.6	994	114
Littleton	70.6	17.6	14.5	32.8	749	95	655	75.6	1 725	102
Longmont	98.1	6.6	75.4	57.7	650	161	388	98.8	1 114	42
Loveland	115.2	11.2	96.5	59.5	847	268	579	109.1	1 554	315
Northglenn	32.1	4.4	67.4	19.9	539	82	457	33.8	914	210
Parker	53.8	8.3	22.1	33.0	699	35	636	55.5	1 175	321
Pueblo	152.7	29.0	69.9	79.2	734	146	589	141.8	1 315	332
Thornton	147.1	14.0	41.5	89.2	717	95	617	134.0	1 078	204
Westminster	153.4	13.5	40.6	99.8	914	126	788	145.3	1 330	246
Wheat Ridge	30.8	2.8	58.9	23.1	752	27	726	32.0	1 043	219
CONNECTICUT	X	X	X	X	X	X	X	X	X	X
Bridgeport....................	693.1	370.2	98.3	277.5	1 888	1 865	23	743.6	5 058	849
Bristol	263.8	119.3	95.5	120.4	1 987	1 939	38	318.7	5 258	1 671
Danbury	280.7	82.5	95.8	171.7	2 074	2 030	44	248.5	3 001	199
Hartford	809.1	477.2	84.9	283.3	2 262	2 204	49	793.7	6 336	712
Meriden	212.7	85.0	99.7	110.3	1 819	1 801	2	226.8	3 739	412
Middletown	189.7	68.5	99.3	101.5	2 142	2 129	12	158.3	3 339	308
Milford........................	203.4	27.7	97.5	162.8	3 160	3 130	13	206.1	4 000	448
Naugatuck	113.1	38.6	96.7	67.3	2 115	2 091	21	123.1	3 870	120
New Britain..................	264.0	124.4	97.4	111.2	1 521	1 505	16	274.7	3 758	394
New Haven	723.5	431.0	93.9	232.5	1 776	1 722	46	1 130.4	8 633	3 741
New London	123.5	69.0	97.3	39.7	1 438	1 415	23	112.6	4 081	298
Norwalk	353.8	52.6	97.8	263.8	3 023	2 994	29	360.1	4 125	476
Norwich	159.1	79.8	97.7	64.1	1 584	1 562	13	163.0	4 029	489
Shelton	121.4	15.0	88.2	99.0	2 457	2 415	42	115.7	2 872	166
Stamford.....................	535.4	50.2	94.1	426.4	3 408	3 340	47	551.6	4 408	402
Torrington	128.3	39.4	97.2	77.2	2 158	2 136	0	121.9	3 409	87
Waterbury....................	498.1	253.0	94.0	220.5	2 006	1 989	11	626.2	5 696	845
West Haven..................	172.1	67.7	99.0	89.3	1 617	1 606	11	169.2	3 062	287
DELAWARE	X	X	X	X	X	X	X	X	X	X
Dover..........................	42.7	9.6	91.3	15.8	426	298	91	55.8	1 506	400
Newark	23.4	3.3	100.0	8.4	258	155	72	32.7	1 010	108
Wilmington...................	193.4	38.2	53.3	110.5	1 550	547	108	166.5	2 334	116
DISTRICT OF COLUMBIA...............	X	X	X	X	X	X	X	X	X	X
Washington	10 710.4	3 077.7	0.0	5 933.8	9 344	2 957	2 601	11 199.3	17 636	2 228
FLORIDA..................	X	X	X	X	X	X	X	X	X	X
Altamonte Springs........	42.8	3.7	94.1	21.6	515	214	300	30.6	731	144
Apopka	48.2	9.5	80.2	19.4	437	163	273	45.1	1 012	64
Aventura	42.7	11.2	85.4	25.0	671	315	355	38.3	1 028	79
Boca Raton	195.4	30.0	30.6	109.3	1 242	718	524	210.8	2 397	278
Bonita Springs.............	18.8	4.9	87.3	11.2	243	125	118	17.6	382	76
Boynton Beach.............	116.4	15.6	61.0	50.6	721	474	247	120.3	1 714	146
Bradenton....................	58.2	10.3	29.0	24.6	488	329	158	58.4	1 157	9
Cape Coral	245.7	47.7	80.3	92.3	572	430	143	240.6	1 492	184
Casselberry	34.0	7.5	31.2	12.8	484	228	256	41.1	1 552	195
Clearwater...................	200.9	27.4	47.6	81.7	751	363	387	194.0	1 782	189
Clermont	32.1	6.1	87.7	12.5	423	203	221	30.7	1 043	125
Coconut Creek	61.2	5.4	70.6	29.6	537	289	249	52.9	959	77
Cooper City	35.4	2.6	92.2	17.7	547	292	255	32.2	994	12
Coral Gables	158.0	11.2	62.7	97.1	1 954	1 350	604	127.4	2 564	171
Coral Springs	123.2	15.5	67.5	65.4	521	261	253	133.1	1 060	84
Cutler Bay	23.2	9.8	41.7	11.1	260	99	161	26.0	611	269
Dania Beach................	52.7	10.5	66.3	24.3	793	518	275	52.7	1 718	156
Davie..........................	104.7	13.7	53.9	70.6	738	407	331	98.2	1 027	73
Daytona Beach.............	124.9	15.8	46.5	44.7	724	392	332	118.4	1 915	146

1. Based on population estimated as of July 1 of the year shown.

Table D. Cities — City Government Finances

City	Public welfare	Highways	Parking facilities	Education	Health and hospitals	Police protection	Sewerage and sanitation	Parks and recreation	Housing and community development	Interest on debt
	127	128	129	130	131	132	133	134	135	136
COLORADO—Cont'd										
Castle Rock	0.0	16.9	0.0	0.0	0.0	12.1	16.6	16.7	0.0	4.0
Centennial	0.0	26.3	0.0	0.0	0.0	29.9	0.0	9.5	5.1	0.2
Colorado Springs	0.0	8.7	0.2	0.0	53.3	9.2	3.9	2.2	0.5	2.8
Commerce City	0.0	7.9	0.0	0.0	0.0	23.6	3.0	10.5	3.7	7.1
Denver	6.4	5.9	0.0	0.0	2.0	8.6	3.3	7.4	4.4	11.0
Englewood	0.0	6.9	0.0	0.0	0.0	19.6	18.4	14.4	2.6	5.1
Fort Collins	0.0	22.5	0.0	0.0	0.0	13.6	7.0	20.8	0.0	1.9
Fountain	0.0	4.7	0.0	0.0	0.8	19.5	0.0	3.1	0.3	0.0
Grand Junction	0.0	12.8	0.3	0.0	0.0	27.0	12.8	14.2	1.8	5.2
Greeley	0.0	6.4	0.3	0.0	0.0	27.1	11.9	13.9	4.4	3.0
Lakewood	0.0	10.8	0.0	0.0	0.9	27.9	2.2	12.3	1.2	1.7
Littleton	0.4	8.2	0.0	0.0	0.0	14.2	10.6	3.0	0.1	2.6
Longmont	0.0	1.0	0.2	0.0	0.0	22.5	18.0	19.4	5.9	2.3
Loveland	0.0	11.3	0.0	0.0	0.0	15.0	10.4	11.8	13.3	0.5
Northglenn	1.3	36.3	0.0	0.0	0.0	21.1	7.6	18.5	0.7	0.0
Parker	0.0	15.6	0.0	0.0	0.0	16.9	2.2	37.3	2.0	5.8
Pueblo	0.0	5.5	0.8	0.0	0.0	18.6	20.0	6.8	11.0	1.6
Thornton	0.0	19.8	0.0	0.0	0.0	19.1	12.4	16.7	1.5	2.1
Westminster	0.0	5.0	0.0	0.0	0.0	13.9	6.9	14.9	9.1	4.9
Wheat Ridge	0.0	14.0	0.0	0.0	0.0	32.8	6.3	20.9	0.0	0.3
CONNECTICUT	X	X	X	X	X	X	X	X	X	X
Bridgeport	0.4	1.9	0.3	44.8	0.5	12.4	5.2	0.8	1.2	5.5
Bristol	0.0	5.0	0.0	63.2	2.8	4.2	3.8	1.2	0.3	0.8
Danbury	0.2	4.2	0.5	53.7	1.2	6.5	3.4	2.5	0.2	2.4
Hartford	1.6	3.6	0.1	58.0	1.8	8.2	0.4	0.2	0.2	1.9
Meriden	0.6	1.9	0.1	57.5	1.4	5.2	4.0	0.9	8.4	1.6
Middletown	0.1	2.3	0.3	50.9	0.6	8.1	3.9	1.7	0.4	1.8
Milford	0.5	1.5	0.0	54.6	1.2	4.9	13.6	0.5	0.3	1.1
Naugatuck	0.2	2.0	0.0	56.2	0.8	4.8	6.3	1.1	0.0	3.5
New Britain	0.1	4.1	0.0	51.5	0.6	12.7	4.6	3.5	1.1	5.1
New Haven	0.0	1.2	1.6	66.9	0.3	3.3	1.0	0.5	1.0	1.6
New London	0.0	9.3	0.5	48.4	0.2	11.0	4.0	8.9	1.6	1.9
Norwalk	0.0	4.6	1.3	50.9	0.6	5.2	5.7	3.8	0.4	3.4
Norwich	1.6	10.4	0.2	52.7	0.0	7.4	10.4	1.5	1.0	0.7
Shelton	0.0	2.6	0.0	60.5	2.6	4.5	4.5	1.7	0.1	2.3
Stamford	2.7	1.6	0.6	47.9	4.0	10.2	4.2	0.6	0.6	3.4
Torrington	0.0	4.5	0.0	56.8	5.0	6.7	4.0	1.2	0.2	1.8
Waterbury	0.6	1.7	0.0	58.3	0.5	4.8	4.0	0.7	1.1	4.5
West Haven	0.2	3.3	0.0	53.9	0.9	7.6	10.9	1.1	0.5	4.1
DELAWARE	X	X	X	X	X	X	X	X	X	X
Dover	0.0	4.4	0.0	0.0	0.1	25.4	18.7	1.5	0.7	0.2
Newark	0.0	8.2	2.2	0.0	0.0	30.5	22.1	7.9	1.1	0.3
Wilmington	0.0	5.8	4.3	0.0	0.0	30.6	10.4	4.8	6.2	3.2
DISTRICT OF COLUMBIA	X	X	X	X	X	X	X	X	X	X
Washington	25.6	4.7	0.2	21.2	6.0	5.0	5.3	1.8	4.9	4.5
FLORIDA	X	X	X	X	X	X	X	X	X	X
Altamonte Springs	0.0	19.8	0.0	0.0	0.0	30.9	9.3	11.4	0.0	0.1
Apopka	0.0	5.4	0.0	0.0	8.7	26.1	18.4	5.7	0.0	1.3
Aventura	0.0	8.4	0.0	17.8	0.0	41.5	0.0	7.7	0.0	3.2
Boca Raton	0.0	5.0	0.0	0.0	0.0	17.6	14.0	17.3	0.2	1.6
Bonita Springs	0.0	31.5	0.0	0.0	1.0	9.5	0.0	12.6	1.6	7.3
Boynton Beach	0.0	1.9	0.0	0.0	0.0	21.9	20.0	8.6	0.3	2.3
Bradenton	0.0	3.5	1.4	0.0	0.0	22.9	24.5	5.3	9.3	1.9
Cape Coral	0.0	10.9	0.0	10.4	0.0	15.1	5.4	7.0	3.0	4.8
Casselberry	0.0	6.3	0.0	0.0	0.1	13.0	22.3	3.0	0.0	1.2
Clearwater	0.1	6.4	2.0	0.0	3.0	19.9	21.2	14.6	0.6	1.4
Clermont	0.0	3.8	0.0	0.0	0.0	20.7	33.3	12.1	0.0	0.5
Coconut Creek	0.0	3.4	0.0	0.0	0.0	29.3	2.2	9.1	1.0	1.9
Cooper City	0.0	2.4	0.1	0.0	0.0	31.4	17.8	9.4	0.0	0.4
Coral Gables	0.0	4.8	3.5	0.0	0.0	29.1	12.4	6.3	0.5	1.9
Coral Springs	0.0	4.5	0.0	0.0	6.2	37.8	6.6	11.4	0.0	1.5
Cutler Bay	0.0	2.3	0.0	0.0	0.0	30.8	0.0	32.3	0.0	3.8
Dania Beach	0.0	4.0	2.3	0.0	0.0	19.8	10.2	6.8	0.0	1.4
Davie	0.0	8.0	0.0	0.0	0.0	36.2	0.0	7.4	2.6	3.2
Daytona Beach	0.0	11.2	0.0	0.0	0.0	29.4	13.1	11.5	1.8	3.5

Table D. Cities — City Government Finances, City Government Employment, and Climate

City	City government finances, 2012 (cont.) Debt outstanding Total (mil dol)	Per capita[1] (dollars)	Debt issued during year	Climate[2] Average daily temperature (degrees Fahrenheit) Mean January	July	Limits January[3]	July[4]	Annual precipitation (inches)	Heating degree days	Cooling degree days
	137	138	139	140	141	142	143	144	145	146
COLORADO—Cont'd										
Castle Rock..................	110.8	2 154	0.0	NA	NA	NA	NA	NA	NA	NA
Centennial..................	2.8	27	0.0	NA	NA	NA	NA	NA	NA	NA
Colorado Springs..........	2 643.8	6 097	167.5	28.1	69.6	14.5	84.4	17.40	6 480	404
Commerce City............	182.6	3 760	0.1	NA	NA	NA	NA	NA	NA	NA
Denver......................	7 039.4	11 106	660.3	31.2	71.5	15.6	88.3	18.17	5 988	496
Englewood..................	89.9	2 879	0.3	28.2	70.2	12.7	85.8	17.06	6 773	435
Fort Collins................	216.4	1 453	11.2	28.2	71.5	14.5	86.2	13.98	6 256	524
Fountain....................	29.0	1 078	9.0	NA	NA	NA	NA	NA	NA	NA
Grand Junction............	74.2	1 241	0.0	27.4	77.5	16.8	91.9	9.06	5 489	1 098
Greeley.....................	155.4	1 629	0.0	27.8	74.0	15.6	88.7	14.22	5 980	759
Lakewood...................	74.1	509	0.0	28.2	70.2	12.7	85.8	17.06	6 773	435
Littleton...................	52.5	1 198	2.4	28.2	70.2	12.7	85.8	17.06	6 773	435
Longmont...................	86.1	971	2.5	27.1	72.2	12.0	88.9	14.15	6 415	587
Loveland...................	5.0	71	0.0	28.2	71.5	14.5	86.2	13.98	6 256	524
Northglenn.................	9.0	244	0.0	30.0	72.0	16.2	87.9	13.25	6 074	590
Parker.....................	55.9	1 184	0.0	NA	NA	NA	NA	NA	NA	NA
Pueblo.....................	144.1	1 337	15.5	30.8	77.0	14.7	93.8	12.60	5 346	997
Thornton...................	191.4	1 539	0.0	30.0	72.0	16.2	87.9	13.25	6 074	590
Westminster...............	297.6	2 724	5.2	29.2	73.4	15.2	88.0	15.81	6 128	696
Wheat Ridge...............	2.7	86	0.0	31.2	71.5	15.6	88.3	18.17	5 988	496
CONNECTICUT..............	X	X	X	X	X	X	X	X	X	X
Bridgeport.................	742.4	5 050	77.6	29.9	74.0	22.9	81.9	44.15	5 466	789
Bristol....................	95.9	1 582	23.9	23.4	70.5	12.6	83.3	51.03	6 825	395
Danbury....................	169.5	2 047	37.8	26.5	72.5	17.6	83.9	51.77	6 159	597
Hartford...................	413.5	3 301	78.1	25.9	73.6	16.3	83.8	44.29	6 121	654
Meriden....................	121.0	1 994	1.8	28.3	73.4	20.3	84.2	52.35	5 791	669
Middletown.................	145.6	3 071	0.0	29.9	74.0	22.9	81.9	44.15	5 466	789
Milford....................	167.9	3 259	24.1	29.9	74.0	22.9	81.9	44.15	5 466	789
Naugatuck..................	75.9	2 387	0.0	29.9	74.0	22.9	81.9	44.15	5 466	789
New Britain................	280.1	3 831	34.0	28.3	73.4	20.3	84.2	52.35	5 791	669
New Haven..................	585.6	4 473	50.6	25.9	72.5	16.9	82.8	52.73	6 271	558
New London.................	63.6	2 305	6.8	28.9	71.8	20.0	80.7	48.72	5 799	511
Norwalk....................	269.9	3 093	45.1	27.8	73.4	18.8	84.2	48.38	5 854	652
Norwich....................	48.2	1 190	17.7	27.6	73.2	17.3	83.8	52.78	5 916	627
Shelton....................	84.7	2 103	22.7	29.9	74.0	22.9	81.9	44.15	5 466	789
Stamford...................	448.3	3 582	64.9	28.7	73.5	19.2	85.4	52.79	5 582	692
Torrington.................	36.3	1 015	0.0	23.6	69.5	13.9	80.7	54.59	6 839	323
Waterbury..................	472.8	4 301	67.1	25.9	72.5	16.9	82.8	52.73	6 271	558
West Haven.................	122.2	2 213	51.1	25.9	72.5	16.9	82.8	52.73	6 271	558
DELAWARE...................	X	X	X	X	X	X	X	X	X	X
Dover......................	41.3	1 115	4.1	35.3	77.8	26.9	87.4	46.28	4 212	1 262
Newark.....................	13.6	418	12.7	32.5	76.4	23.5	87.6	45.35	4 746	1 047
Wilmington.................	353.0	4 950	53.2	31.5	76.6	23.7	86.0	42.81	4 888	1 125
DISTRICT OF COLUMBIA.....	X	X	X	X	X	X	X	X	X	X
Washington.................	11 278.8	17 761	1 642.8	34.9	79.2	27.3	88.3	39.35	4 055	1 531
FLORIDA....................	X	X	X	X	X	X	X	X	X	X
Altamonte Springs.........	0.0	0	0.0	58.7	81.5	47.0	91.9	51.31	799	3 017
Apopka.....................	33.4	751	0.0	58.7	81.5	47.0	91.9	51.31	799	3 017
Aventura...................	32.5	872	6.8	67.9	82.7	62.6	87.0	46.60	141	4 090
Boca Raton.................	139.0	1 580	0.0	67.2	83.3	57.8	91.8	57.27	219	4 241
Bonita Springs............	24.3	526	0.0	64.3	82.0	53.4	91.2	51.90	316	3 646
Boynton Beach.............	126.0	1 795	0.0	66.2	82.5	57.3	90.1	61.39	246	3 999
Bradenton.................	34.5	683	0.0	61.6	81.9	50.9	91.3	54.12	538	3 327
Cape Coral.................	907.6	5 629	196.0	62.7	81.3	50.3	91.3	50.07	427	3 287
Casselberry...............	20.3	766	9.1	NA	NA	NA	NA	NA	NA	NA
Clearwater.................	247.9	2 276	47.0	61.3	82.5	52.4	89.7	44.77	591	3 482
Clermont...................	19.7	668	0.0	NA	NA	NA	NA	NA	NA	NA
Coconut Creek.............	22.8	413	0.0	67.2	83.3	57.8	91.8	57.27	219	4 241
Cooper City...............	6.1	189	1.5	67.5	82.6	59.2	89.8	64.19	167	4 120
Coral Gables..............	79.3	1 596	50.7	67.9	82.7	62.6	87.0	46.60	141	4 090
Coral Springs.............	71.6	570	8.8	67.2	83.3	57.8	91.8	57.27	219	4 241
Cutler Bay.................	18.6	437	3.6	NA	NA	NA	NA	NA	NA	NA
Dania Beach...............	30.3	988	3.6	NA	NA	NA	NA	NA	NA	NA
Davie......................	144.9	1 515	20.0	66.2	82.5	57.3	90.1	61.39	246	3 999
Daytona Beach.............	154.8	2 505	36.2	57.1	81.2	44.5	91.2	57.03	954	2 819

1. Based on the population estimated as of July 1 of the year shown.   2. Represents normal values based on the 30-year period, 1971–2000.   3. Average daily minimum.
4. Average daily maximum.

Table D. Cities — Land Area and Population

STATE Place code	City	Land area,[1] 2016 (sq mi)	Population, 2016			Race alone[2] (percent), 2015						
			Total persons	Rank	Per square mile	White	Black or African American	American Indian, Alaska Native	Asian	Hawaiian Pacific Islander	Some other race	2 or more races[2]
		1	2	3	4	5	6	7	8	9	10	11
	FLORIDA—Cont'd											
12 16725	Deerfield Beach	15.1	79 764	426	5 282.4	63.8	29.8	0.1	1.3	0.1	1.9	2.9
12 16875	DeLand	18.6	31 569	1 191	1 697.3	NA	NA	NA	NA	NA	NA	NA
12 17100	Delray Beach	15.9	67 371	529	4 237.2	60.3	30.8	0.1	1.4	0.4	4.5	2.5
12 17200	Deltona	37.2	90 124	356	2 422.7	82.0	12.0	0.0	0.4	0.0	1.7	4.0
12 17935	Doral	13.9	57 947	646	4 168.8	91.3	4.1	0.0	2.4	0.0	0.8	1.4
12 18575	Dunedin	10.4	36 381	1 047	3 498.2	90.3	4.0	1.1	1.2	0.2	1.7	1.5
12 24000	Fort Lauderdale	34.6	178 752	138	5 166.2	59.4	34.0	0.1	1.8	0.1	2.2	2.4
12 24125	Fort Myers	39.8	77 146	443	1 938.3	66.1	22.7	0.0	4.3	0.0	5.2	1.7
12 24300	Fort Pierce	23.3	45 295	835	1 944.0	NA	NA	NA	NA	NA	NA	NA
12 25175	Gainesville	62.3	131 591	206	2 112.2	64.4	22.9	0.4	8.6	0.1	0.3	3.3
12 27322	Greenacres	5.9	40 013	945	6 781.9	70.4	20.0	0.4	3.5	0.0	4.0	1.7
12 28452	Hallandale Beach	4.2	39 500	959	9 404.8	80.8	15.4	0.1	1.0	0.1	1.4	1.2
12 30000	Hialeah	21.5	236 387	94	10 994.7	92.4	2.2	0.0	0.4	0.0	4.6	0.4
12 32000	Hollywood	27.3	151 998	170	5 567.7	67.9	19.8	0.2	2.4	0.1	4.6	5.0
12 32275	Homestead	15.1	67 996	520	4 503.0	70.4	24.4	0.0	0.2	0.0	2.1	3.0
12 35000	Jacksonville	747.4	880 619	12	1 178.2	59.7	31.0	0.1	4.6	0.1	1.1	3.4
12 35875	Jupiter	21.8	63 813	572	2 927.2	91.2	1.2	0.1	3.4	0.0	2.3	1.9
12 36950	Kissimmee	20.8	69 369	505	3 335.0	71.9	8.2	0.0	3.7	0.0	13.5	2.7
12 38250	Lakeland	65.9	106 420	281	1 614.9	71.1	23.0	0.2	2.8	0.0	1.4	1.6
12 39075	Lake Worth	5.9	37 812	1 009	6 408.8	80.3	13.2	1.5	2.3	0.0	1.6	1.2
12 39425	Largo	18.2	83 065	403	4 564.0	87.3	5.4	0.7	2.6	0.0	0.4	3.6
12 39525	Lauderdale Lakes	3.7	34 790	1 093	9 402.7	NA	NA	NA	NA	NA	NA	NA
12 39550	Lauderhill	8.5	71 626	491	8 426.6	13.0	79.1	0.3	1.4	0.0	2.2	4.1
12 43125	Margate	8.9	57 870	647	6 502.2	60.6	28.3	0.0	3.1	0.0	3.5	4.5
12 43975	Melbourne	37.5	81 185	416	2 164.9	78.1	12.3	0.0	5.2	0.0	0.6	3.8
12 45000	Miami	36.0	453 579	42	12 599.4	75.1	18.9	0.0	0.6	0.1	3.3	2.1
12 45025	Miami Beach	7.7	91 917	345	11 937.3	76.7	3.8	0.0	2.8	0.0	15.2	1.5
12 45060	Miami Gardens	18.2	113 058	252	6 212.0	23.2	74.9	0.0	0.2	0.0	0.6	1.0
12 45100	Miami Lakes	5.7	30 873	1 216	5 416.3	NA	NA	NA	NA	NA	NA	NA
12 45975	Miramar	29.4	138 449	190	4 709.1	41.2	46.2	0.1	7.9	0.0	2.1	2.6
12 49425	North Lauderdale	4.6	43 699	863	9 499.8	30.8	57.4	0.5	5.1	0.0	2.1	4.2
12 49450	North Miami	8.5	62 139	587	7 310.5	33.1	59.2	0.1	2.9	0.0	3.2	1.4
12 49475	North Miami Beach	4.8	43 891	857	9 144.0	49.5	41.4	0.0	2.6	0.0	4.7	1.8
12 49675	North Port	99.4	64 274	565	646.6	NA	NA	NA	NA	NA	NA	NA
12 50575	Oakland Park	7.5	44 326	851	5 910.1	58.9	22.4	0.7	6.2	0.0	2.8	9.0
12 50750	Ocala	45.9	59 253	625	1 290.9	67.4	25.2	0.0	3.6	0.0	0.7	3.1
12 51075	Ocoee	15.2	44 820	841	2 948.7	68.0	16.8	0.1	5.0	0.0	7.5	2.6
12 53000	Orlando	105.2	277 173	73	2 634.7	63.7	23.6	0.3	3.2	0.0	6.1	3.0
12 53150	Ormond Beach	32.9	42 162	895	1 281.5	92.2	3.0	0.0	1.4	0.0	2.7	0.8
12 53575	Oviedo	15.4	39 337	967	2 554.4	78.0	10.9	0.0	5.2	0.1	2.0	3.9
12 54000	Palm Bay	65.7	110 104	267	1 675.9	75.9	17.7	0.9	0.6	0.0	2.4	2.6
12 54075	Palm Beach Gardens	56.0	53 778	703	960.3	86.0	6.6	0.2	3.9	0.1	0.8	2.3
12 54200	Palm Coast	95.0	85 109	387	895.9	79.4	12.4	0.4	2.5	0.0	2.6	2.6
12 54700	Panama City	34.9	37 635	1 017	1 078.4	70.7	18.9	0.2	4.9	0.0	0.9	4.3
12 55775	Pembroke Pines	33.0	168 587	150	5 108.7	66.5	18.9	0.3	7.0	0.0	4.7	2.5
12 55925	Pensacola	22.6	53 779	702	2 379.6	59.0	32.3	0.5	1.1	0.0	0.5	6.6
12 56975	Pinellas Park	15.9	52 137	731	3 279.1	79.8	4.1	0.1	10.1	0.0	2.0	3.9
12 57425	Plantation	21.6	92 706	341	4 291.9	70.3	19.4	0.1	3.1	0.0	4.3	2.7
12 57550	Plant City	27.2	38 200	999	1 404.4	59.4	15.8	0.0	3.1	0.0	20.5	1.1
12 58050	Pompano Beach	24.0	109 393	271	4 558.0	59.9	34.2	0.4	1.0	0.0	1.4	3.0
12 58575	Port Orange	26.8	61 105	600	2 280.0	83.4	9.4	0.2	4.3	0.0	1.8	1.0
12 58715	Port St. Lucie	118.9	185 132	130	1 557.0	74.0	16.1	0.7	2.7	0.0	3.4	3.1
12 60975	Riviera Beach	8.5	34 244	1 110	4 028.7	20.3	73.6	0.0	1.9	0.0	3.7	0.6
12 62100	Royal Palm Beach	11.1	38 006	1 005	3 424.0	62.6	26.1	0.0	7.0	0.0	2.6	1.7
12 62625	St. Cloud	18.7	47 809	799	2 556.6	76.2	7.7	0.0	0.2	0.0	14.9	1.0
12 63000	St. Petersburg	61.8	260 999	79	4 223.3	67.5	24.8	0.3	3.8	0.0	1.0	2.7
12 63650	Sanford	23.1	58 605	640	2 537.0	63.6	24.8	0.4	5.2	0.0	2.8	3.2
12 64175	Sarasota	14.7	56 610	662	3 851.0	80.7	15.1	0.0	0.7	0.0	2.1	1.4
12 69700	Sunrise	16.3	93 734	336	5 750.6	56.9	35.3	0.0	3.2	0.0	2.1	2.6
12 70600	Tallahassee	100.4	190 894	126	1 901.3	57.1	34.7	0.1	4.4	0.1	0.9	2.8
12 70675	Tamarac	11.6	65 199	554	5 620.6	66.3	25.4	0.0	3.6	0.2	2.3	2.2
12 71000	Tampa	113.4	377 165	52	3 326.0	67.7	23.4	0.2	3.4	0.0	2.3	3.0
12 71900	Titusville	29.1	46 019	828	1 581.4	75.6	18.8	1.6	0.8	0.0	1.0	2.2
12 75812	Wellington	45.1	63 900	571	1 416.9	81.3	10.3	0.6	4.0	0.0	1.0	2.9
12 76582	Weston	24.9	70 015	502	2 811.8	85.8	4.7	0.1	5.5	0.1	2.4	1.5
12 76600	West Palm Beach	55.1	108 161	275	1 963.0	55.8	36.0	0.0	2.8	0.0	4.2	1.2
12 78250	Winter Garden	16.2	41 988	901	2 591.9	58.1	10.8	0.0	12.0	2.2	9.7	7.3
12 78275	Winter Haven	31.3	38 953	976	1 244.5	64.4	29.0	0.5	0.7	0.2	2.9	2.3
12 78300	Winter Park	8.7	30 208	1 245	3 472.2	83.9	6.6	0.7	3.1	0.0	3.6	2.1
12 78325	Winter Springs	14.7	35 599	1 074	2 421.7	86.3	3.9	0.3	2.3	0.0	4.7	2.5

1. Dry land or land partially or temporarily covered by water.   2. Hispanic or Latino persons may be of any race.

Table D. Cities — Population

| City | Percent Hispanic or Latino[1], 2015 | Percent foreign born 2015 | Age of population (percent), 2010-2014 | | | | | | | Median age 2015 | Percent female 2015 | Population | | | |
| | | | Under 18 years | 18 to 24 years | 25 to 34 years | 35 to 44 years | 45 to 54 years | 55 to 64 years | 65 years and over | | | Census counts | | Percent change | |
												2000	2010	2000–2010	2010–2016
	12	13	14	15	16	17	18	19	20	21	22	23	24	25	26
FLORIDA—Cont'd															
Deerfield Beach	16.0	29.6	16.5	9.8	14.3	13.9	12.1	11.3	22.1	41.4	53.4	64 583	75 018	16.2	6.3
DeLand	24.3	5.3	19.8	16.3	7.9	9.2	10.1	11.2	25.5	42.1	54.6	20 904	26 959	29.0	17.1
Delray Beach	9.7	25.1	13.5	8.2	13.3	11.1	12.1	13.6	28.2	47.9	51.4	60 020	60 601	1.0	11.2
Deltona	35.4	8.0	23.0	9.0	12.7	11.3	14.1	13.2	16.7	39.9	49.3	69 543	85 141	22.4	5.9
Doral	85.9	65.8	31.2	10.0	11.0	16.9	16.5	9.0	5.4	33.7	50.9	20 438	45 709	123.6	26.8
Dunedin	5.0	6.7	12.2	6.4	12.0	7.5	14.9	16.5	30.5	52.3	54.3	35 691	35 356	-0.9	2.9
Fort Lauderdale	15.8	26.6	19.9	5.2	15.5	12.3	15.2	14.7	17.1	42.8	47.4	152 397	165 586	8.7	8.0
Fort Myers	24.1	20.8	19.2	10.3	18.8	9.4	11.4	12.5	18.4	37.3	50.2	48 208	62 202	29.0	24.0
Fort Pierce	24.7	23.2	28.3	9.6	13.5	8.6	12.6	10.7	16.6	33.1	53.8	37 516	41 918	11.7	8.1
Gainesville	9.4	11.7	14.1	32.9	17.5	8.5	7.2	9.1	10.7	26.0	53.3	95 447	124 486	30.4	5.7
Greenacres	35.8	32.2	20.8	7.2	14.5	14.5	12.4	13.3	17.4	39.7	53.5	27 569	37 580	36.3	6.5
Hallandale Beach	37.1	43.5	18.5	6.3	9.8	15.4	13.8	12.8	23.4	45.1	52.6	34 282	37 113	8.3	6.4
Hialeah	96.0	71.8	18.4	7.7	13.2	13.9	15.9	11.1	19.7	43.0	53.0	226 419	224 687	-0.8	5.2
Hollywood	35.6	36.8	20.7	7.8	13.5	13.4	15.5	13.2	16.1	41.4	49.7	139 357	140 769	1.0	8.0
Homestead	63.0	36.7	31.0	7.5	17.4	12.7	16.0	7.7	7.8	31.4	52.8	31 909	60 523	89.7	12.3
Jacksonville	9.2	9.9	23.3	9.5	16.1	12.6	13.4	12.3	12.7	35.7	51.7	735 617	821 784	11.7	7.2
Jupiter	13.0	12.7	19.3	5.8	12.3	14.4	13.2	12.6	22.3	43.6	51.7	39 328	55 365	40.8	15.3
Kissimmee	63.8	24.4	22.3	8.9	16.6	14.9	13.6	11.9	11.7	36.7	51.9	47 814	59 536	24.5	16.5
Lakeland	15.8	11.1	22.0	11.1	13.0	10.8	10.8	13.2	19.1	38.1	54.2	78 452	97 405	24.2	9.3
Lake Worth	41.8	32.9	21.7	8.2	12.7	11.9	14.9	10.3	20.2	41.4	51.6	35 133	34 910	-0.6	8.3
Largo	11.8	12.9	17.6	5.7	14.8	11.6	14.1	13.3	22.8	45.1	52.9	69 371	79 311	14.3	4.7
Lauderdale Lakes	7.3	50.4	27.2	12.3	12.4	9.8	14.3	9.8	14.4	31.2	57.6	31 705	32 653	3.0	6.5
Lauderhill	8.5	35.6	23.2	10.4	15.1	13.3	11.6	12.0	14.4	35.7	54.2	57 585	66 954	16.3	7.0
Margate	27.5	38.1	18.4	8.2	11.6	13.8	13.6	15.6	18.8	43.4	52.9	53 909	53 284	-1.2	8.6
Melbourne	7.6	12.1	18.3	8.7	12.9	11.5	13.2	13.4	22.0	43.4	51.1	71 382	76 232	6.8	6.5
Miami	72.6	59.1	17.1	7.6	16.9	15.0	14.1	12.3	17.0	40.4	51.1	362 470	399 527	10.2	13.5
Miami Beach	51.4	54.1	14.3	5.8	16.8	16.9	15.3	13.6	17.3	42.5	47.9	87 933	87 739	-0.2	4.8
Miami Gardens	20.6	29.5	24.8	10.8	14.6	12.1	11.8	11.9	14.1	34.9	55.2	NA	107 167	NA	5.5
Miami Lakes	82.7	49.7	21.2	7.5	13.7	14.3	18.2	12.2	13.0	40.5	51.5	22 676	29 377	29.6	5.1
Miramar	34.1	41.7	25.1	8.6	14.0	15.6	16.4	9.8	10.6	36.6	51.8	72 739	122 041	67.8	13.4
North Lauderdale	29.1	47.6	27.0	8.5	16.3	15.4	10.5	12.0	10.4	33.3	51.5	32 264	41 055	27.2	6.4
North Miami	26.5	52.7	22.7	11.5	18.8	11.4	12.7	11.7	11.2	33.0	50.8	59 880	59 581	-0.5	4.3
North Miami Beach	37.0	53.0	22.1	8.4	9.7	14.5	12.4	13.7	19.2	41.2	53.2	40 786	41 534	1.8	5.7
North Port	9.7	10.3	25.0	7.4	10.0	12.5	10.3	12.8	22.0	39.2	54.1	22 797	57 333	151.5	12.1
Oakland Park	25.6	29.2	16.2	6.0	15.4	15.3	14.4	17.0	15.7	43.8	45.2	30 966	41 394	33.7	7.1
Ocala	10.8	5.9	25.3	10.9	10.7	15.1	12.3	10.2	15.5	36.1	51.3	45 943	56 425	22.8	5.0
Ocoee	27.8	20.2	29.0	8.0	15.1	11.0	15.5	12.3	9.0	34.5	51.5	24 391	35 754	46.6	25.4
Orlando	33.0	18.7	20.3	9.8	23.6	14.0	12.6	9.5	10.2	33.1	51.7	185 951	239 057	28.6	15.9
Ormond Beach	9.5	8.0	16.2	4.9	9.4	15.7	9.7	13.6	30.5	50.2	53.3	36 301	39 486	8.8	6.8
Oviedo	18.4	12.9	24.5	10.9	8.6	13.8	18.5	11.2	12.5	38.8	54.3	26 316	33 483	27.2	17.5
Palm Bay	15.6	11.2	23.6	8.1	11.9	10.8	12.9	13.2	19.5	40.7	52.0	79 413	103 203	30.0	6.7
Palm Beach Gardens	9.8	15.6	13.8	4.3	12.4	11.4	12.0	17.3	28.8	52.8	52.0	35 058	48 568	38.5	10.7
Palm Coast	10.6	11.1	19.3	7.0	8.3	11.2	11.2	13.9	29.1	48.8	51.9	32 732	75 197	129.7	13.2
Panama City	7.5	7.7	21.2	6.6	17.7	9.0	13.8	11.7	19.9	38.2	52.9	36 417	34 687	-4.8	8.5
Pembroke Pines	36.3	37.3	20.8	9.9	13.4	12.9	15.1	12.1	15.7	40.3	53.8	137 427	154 818	12.7	8.9
Pensacola	3.8	3.3	23.8	12.5	12.3	10.6	9.2	15.8	15.8	37.0	51.5	56 255	51 969	-7.6	3.5
Pinellas Park	10.2	13.7	17.5	6.0	13.1	12.8	12.9	16.6	21.0	45.4	52.4	45 658	49 287	7.9	5.8
Plantation	28.5	30.1	21.6	6.4	15.9	11.0	14.3	14.8	16.0	40.6	53.7	82 934	84 877	2.3	9.2
Plant City	35.8	15.0	29.7	8.8	12.0	17.1	11.0	10.8	10.6	34.6	48.0	29 915	34 679	15.9	10.2
Pompano Beach	21.6	30.4	19.8	7.9	12.8	12.5	13.8	12.1	21.2	42.5	47.5	78 191	99 844	27.7	9.6
Port Orange	7.7	10.8	20.0	8.9	8.7	10.5	13.3	15.2	23.4	46.9	52.9	45 823	56 602	23.5	8.0
Port St. Lucie	19.1	19.0	22.2	7.7	11.6	13.5	12.9	11.9	20.1	42.1	53.1	88 769	164 716	85.6	12.4
Riviera Beach	3.6	16.1	26.7	10.0	13.1	10.2	14.9	10.0	15.2	35.3	53.1	29 884	32 488	8.7	5.4
Royal Palm Beach	19.0	29.9	21.0	7.4	13.8	12.8	18.5	10.3	16.2	41.1	52.0	21 523	34 140	58.6	11.3
St. Cloud	37.2	12.8	31.3	4.9	18.4	12.4	10.6	9.9	12.5	31.8	52.3	20 074	37 272	85.7	28.3
St. Petersburg	8.0	11.1	18.8	8.0	14.4	13.1	14.0	14.1	17.6	41.8	52.0	248 232	245 193	-1.2	6.4
Sanford	29.7	14.8	26.7	8.2	18.7	15.9	9.5	9.9	11.0	32.3	52.9	38 291	53 715	40.3	9.1
Sarasota	16.5	16.0	13.0	10.1	12.8	9.2	12.2	16.4	26.3	49.3	52.5	52 715	52 056	-1.3	8.7
Sunrise	31.5	41.2	21.5	7.9	17.2	12.8	13.1	12.4	15.0	37.7	55.3	85 779	84 381	-1.6	11.1
Tallahassee	7.1	8.8	16.3	31.2	15.7	10.1	8.7	8.9	9.2	26.2	52.9	150 624	181 388	20.4	5.2
Tamarac	30.7	41.6	12.6	7.2	11.9	9.9	14.9	15.6	28.0	50.7	55.7	55 588	60 503	8.8	7.8
Tampa	25.8	15.9	21.8	11.0	16.7	13.8	13.6	11.6	11.5	35.3	52.4	303 447	335 713	10.6	12.3
Titusville	5.5	5.6	17.6	9.0	12.5	10.6	16.4	14.7	19.2	45.1	52.8	40 670	43 625	7.3	5.5
Wellington	23.6	23.7	24.2	8.3	9.6	10.9	20.8	11.7	14.5	42.8	52.2	38 216	56 712	48.4	12.7
Weston	52.4	44.1	30.3	8.6	7.2	15.2	17.5	9.1	12.2	38.6	52.9	49 286	65 331	32.6	7.2
West Palm Beach	24.5	28.7	18.2	9.9	15.7	13.7	12.6	12.9	17.0	39.6	53.9	82 103	100 523	22.4	7.6
Winter Garden	19.9	21.9	25.0	13.0	11.3	12.1	11.8	14.5	12.4	38.4	48.1	14 351	34 735	142.0	20.9
Winter Haven	10.6	6.3	20.4	7.1	13.6	11.3	11.6	10.5	25.5	41.8	52.3	26 487	33 874	27.9	15.0
Winter Park	10.0	11.9	17.1	8.5	11.4	9.3	14.6	16.3	22.9	46.3	51.6	24 090	27 856	15.6	8.4
Winter Springs	17.3	9.7	21.8	3.7	18.3	10.5	14.8	14.4	16.5	41.9	50.6	31 666	33 317	5.2	6.8

1. May be of any race.

Table D. Cities — Households, Group Quarters, Crime, and Education

City	Households, 2015 Number	Persons per house-hold	Female family house-holder[1]	One-person	Persons in group quarters, 2010 Total	Institutional Total	Persons in nursing facilities	Non-institu-tional	Serious crimes Total Number	Rate[3]	Violent	Property	Population age 25 and older	High school graduate or less	Bachelor's degree or more
	27	28	29	30	31	32	33	34	35	36	37	38	39	40	41
FLORIDA—Cont'd															
Deerfield Beach	31 863	2.46	14.7	35.4	1 046	863	229	183	2 442	3 100	468	2 632	58 842	42.9	28.1
DeLand	10 637	2.61	13.9	30.7	2 377	595	587	1 782	1 424	4 988	501	4 487	19 284	42.8	24.4
Delray Beach	27 741	2.35	12.6	33.5	1 114	584	539	530	3 165	4 875	665	4 210	51 878	37.3	33.7
Deltona	30 583	2.89	14.4	16.3	166	127	127	39	NA	NA	NA	NA	60 146	46.7	16.7
Doral	15 915	3.52	21.6	11.1	6	0	0	6	2 142	4 171	140	4 031	32 952	22.0	57.7
Dunedin	17 185	2.08	7.1	44.9	385	344	338	41	794	2 219	268	1 951	29 443	37.0	31.9
Fort Lauderdale	73 871	2.38	11.3	41.0	3 418	1 861	324	1 557	10 278	5 905	773	5 132	133 650	37.1	36.3
Fort Myers	28 441	2.45	14.3	37.6	3 236	2 520	598	716	2 945	4 224	1 103	3 121	52 202	46.4	26.2
Fort Pierce	15 970	2.74	18.9	30.3	577	455	314	122	2 620	6 044	1 061	4 983	27 624	60.6	13.1
Gainesville	48 617	2.33	13.6	37.5	12 493	1 796	748	10 697	5 397	4 210	637	3 573	69 025	28.9	44.6
Greenacres	14 136	2.81	14.9	31.2	51	5	5	46	1 788	4 590	680	3 909	28 581	45.9	24.0
Hallandale Beach	17 457	2.26	14.6	44.5	101	0	0	101	1 766	4 528	615	3 913	29 689	42.5	31.6
Hialeah	71 124	3.31	21.7	23.4	1 493	727	700	766	7 318	3 108	332	2 776	175 027	65.4	12.8
Hollywood	56 104	2.65	14.5	32.6	1 203	608	476	595	7 116	4 811	494	4 317	107 085	45.8	27.6
Homestead	18 924	3.48	24.5	16.3	450	227	223	223	3 825	5 890	1 327	4 563	40 953	56.3	18.4
Jacksonville	323 488	2.62	17.0	30.0	19 747	8 158	3 155	11 589	39 585	4 624	684	3 941	583 153	39.8	27.7
Jupiter	25 510	2.43	8.8	31.6	393	131	131	262	1 175	1 990	213	1 777	46 908	27.1	41.1
Kissimmee	22 823	3.01	23.2	21.7	595	317	54	278	3 261	4 895	668	4 227	47 550	46.5	17.4
Lakeland	38 975	2.56	15.6	31.3	4 126	1 140	1 094	2 986	5 738	5 657	447	5 211	69 929	47.2	25.6
Lake Worth	15 427	2.40	7.4	42.4	618	518	409	100	2 401	6 622	1 147	5 475	26 259	50.9	22.1
Largo	35 192	2.28	9.4	42.7	1 026	941	836	85	3 214	4 094	431	3 664	62 090	43.9	19.9
Lauderdale Lakes	10 546	3.52	24.1	30.9	392	387	363	5	1 771	5 148	773	4 375	21 085	70.3	6.5
Lauderhill	23 525	3.02	24.1	26.8	592	225	225	367	2 932	4 159	654	3 505	47 527	54.9	20.6
Margate	20 103	2.83	14.4	34.0	169	6	6	163	1 027	1 835	225	1 609	41 989	46.2	21.6
Melbourne	32 825	2.37	13.2	39.5	2 125	746	713	1 379	3 713	4 773	785	3 987	58 475	41.7	26.4
Miami	171 720	2.50	16.1	41.1	8 161	5 133	1 526	3 028	24 867	5 893	1 060	4 833	331 782	55.1	25.7
Miami Beach	43 400	2.10	5.9	48.5	1 026	534	473	492	10 316	11 241	973	10 268	73 773	29.1	48.1
Miami Gardens	29 814	3.75	33.7	20.7	1 367	64	11	1 303	5 260	4 681	655	4 026	72 901	56.1	11.9
Miami Lakes	10 970	2.82	12.0	34.5	28	0	0	28	688	2 230	68	2 162	22 081	24.6	38.7
Miramar	40 203	3.41	18.3	15.2	87	24	11	63	3 167	2 393	315	2 078	90 893	30.9	34.3
North Lauderdale	11 789	3.70	23.0	13.5	31	0	0	31	1 291	2 991	426	2 564	28 179	56.0	18.5
North Miami	18 018	3.39	24.4	29.4	1 640	539	539	1 101	3 383	5 501	938	4 563	41 065	52.6	22.0
North Miami Beach	14 612	2.99	26.2	29.6	236	151	148	85	1 991	4 561	843	3 718	30 565	50.1	18.9
North Port	21 937	2.83	15.5	14.2	119	100	100	19	995	1 668	173	1 495	42 141	46.2	24.6
Oakland Park	16 436	2.68	11.1	32.3	205	19	0	186	2 019	4 615	519	4 096	34 479	51.9	23.3
Ocala	21 053	2.63	16.1	40.9	3 281	2 856	922	425	3 363	5 824	623	5 201	37 090	44.6	21.4
Ocoee	13 791	3.15	14.8	20.0	287	225	225	62	1 549	3 870	345	3 525	27 491	36.8	25.0
Orlando	111 100	2.42	19.7	31.8	3 294	1 227	1 009	2 067	18 855	7 261	901	6 360	189 403	34.1	35.5
Ormond Beach	17 451	2.32	11.6	34.4	458	434	434	24	1 721	4 438	428	4 010	32 325	36.5	24.4
Oviedo	12 696	3.03	14.4	15.1	103	94	94	9	517	1 380	149	1 230	24 910	22.9	39.8
Palm Bay	38 113	2.82	18.5	23.3	430	331	320	99	2 826	2 684	570	2 114	73 689	47.6	19.6
Palm Beach Gardens	22 362	2.35	9.2	28.3	235	205	154	30	1 523	2 974	148	2 826	43 333	25.7	48.6
Palm Coast	29 739	2.76	11.2	24.2	319	282	144	37	NA	NA	NA	NA	60 489	38.3	26.0
Panama City	16 475	2.28	20.1	45.2	2 782	2 453	553	329	2 924	7 859	922	6 937	27 598	42.6	21.8
Pembroke Pines	56 409	2.94	16.3	26.2	1 397	1 187	125	210	4 052	2 465	169	2 297	115 440	33.4	37.0
Pensacola	21 841	2.41	14.5	40.2	727	284	224	443	2 763	5 226	705	4 520	33 908	31.2	32.5
Pinellas Park	21 269	2.38	10.9	39.0	1 165	510	337	655	3 156	6 285	456	5 829	39 451	51.5	18.9
Plantation	33 712	2.73	16.5	24.5	363	307	304	56	3 067	3 350	341	3 009	66 629	26.2	41.0
Plant City	12 691	2.93	14.4	22.1	185	118	118	67	1 617	4 439	464	3 975	23 008	54.2	20.9
Pompano Beach	40 375	2.55	15.0	34.5	4 267	3 680	415	587	5 437	5 152	824	4 329	77 987	51.4	21.6
Port Orange	24 164	2.47	9.9	30.0	167	118	102	49	1 168	2 036	56	1 981	42 560	42.1	21.6
Port St. Lucie	61 310	2.91	12.9	20.0	711	330	322	381	2 741	1 589	141	1 449	125 704	48.6	21.0
Riviera Beach	10 771	3.14	27.9	24.0	323	134	134	189	1 954	5 842	1 190	4 652	21 526	50.4	20.8
Royal Palm Beach	12 930	2.89	14.6	17.6	236	229	119	7	984	2 671	269	2 402	26 978	32.6	37.6
St. Cloud	13 040	3.45	10.4	18.7	448	375	349	73	1 001	2 377	325	2 052	28 921	46.0	18.4
St. Petersburg	103 788	2.42	16.0	37.6	6 607	2 719	2 364	3 888	16 319	6 508	865	5 643	187 988	35.5	33.0
Sanford	21 076	2.69	23.7	28.4	1 531	996	180	535	3 437	6 072	804	5 268	37 845	40.7	17.7
Sarasota	24 255	2.13	12.6	42.5	3 582	1 632	738	1 950	2 894	5 397	666	4 731	42 358	36.9	36.4
Sunrise	30 856	2.98	18.3	21.0	578	506	496	72	3 331	3 639	303	3 336	65 375	40.1	24.5
Tallahassee	74 162	2.38	13.0	36.5	14 623	3 231	718	11 392	10 838	5 778	937	4 841	99 740	24.0	45.6
Tamarac	29 554	2.18	13.9	39.9	261	234	234	27	1 432	2 245	277	1 967	51 901	41.3	30.3
Tampa	144 582	2.47	17.2	35.8	12 282	2 138	876	10 144	10 750	3 010	582	2 428	247 802	40.0	35.5
Titusville	20 205	2.22	14.2	38.6	473	344	344	129	1 714	3 868	603	3 266	33 325	45.4	18.5
Wellington	20 484	3.05	12.9	20.4	2	0	0	2	1 312	2 148	167	1 981	42 226	23.2	48.4
Weston	20 939	3.34	11.9	10.3	0	0	0	0	425	615	65	550	42 754	13.8	63.1
West Palm Beach	41 168	2.53	16.5	36.4	2 943	1 196	1 093	1 747	5 637	5 471	824	4 647	76 754	40.3	33.6
Winter Garden	12 439	3.20	7.8	15.2	497	483	483	14	1 276	3 318	424	2 894	25 049	37.6	36.0
Winter Haven	14 735	2.51	11.7	36.5	598	491	490	107	1 575	4 383	623	3 760	27 298	56.8	14.1
Winter Park	12 670	2.23	6.8	31.8	1 609	338	338	1 271	1 185	4 013	274	3 739	22 272	20.2	60.2
Winter Springs	12 640	2.75	9.8	26.3	31	31	0	0	432	1 270	185	1 085	25 920	25.9	39.9

1. No spouse present.   2. Data for serious crimes have not been adjusted for underreporting. This may affect comparability between geographic areas and over time.   3. Per 100,000 population estimated by the FBI.   4. Persons 25 years old and over.

Table D. Cities — Income, Poverty, and Housing

City	Money income, 2015					Housing units, 2010			Occupied housing units 2015				
	Households			Families					Owner-occupied			Renter-occupied	
	Median income	Percent with income of $200,000 or more	Percent with income of less than $25,000	Total Families	Percent with income below poverty	Total	Percent change, 2000–2010	Vacant units for sale or rent[2]	Total	Percent	Median value[3] (dollars)	Percent	Median rent (dollars)
	42	43	44	45	46	47	48	49	50	51	52	53	54
FLORIDA—Cont'd													
Deerfield Beach............	46 582	1.6	16.4	16 976	8.4	42 671	14.3	9 301	31 863	60.4	158 500	39.6	1 126
DeLand......................	40 512	3.0	22.2	6 652	15.5	12 610	35.6	1 864	10 637	54.2	175 000	45.8	924
Delray Beach............	51 551	7.0	13.3	15 666	6.7	34 156	7.9	6 963	27 741	61.4	258 000	38.6	1 405
Deltona.....................	43 661	0.5	15.3	23 871	11.3	34 089	28.4	3 866	30 583	78.9	119 800	21.1	1 026
Doral........................	72 230	3.8	14.0	13 543	18.0	17 785	89.4	2 541	15 915	44.1	362 000	55.9	1 859
Dunedin....................	47 747	4.8	22.1	7 993	2.5	21 113	5.0	3 495	17 185	62.7	186 100	37.3	999
Fort Lauderdale............	51 247	7.0	19.6	35 017	13.4	93 159	15.3	18 373	73 817	53.0	308 200	47.0	1 204
Fort Myers.................	41 586	2.7	22.0	15 370	14.1	35 138	60.9	10 170	28 441	45.1	173 700	54.9	914
Fort Pierce..................	22 781	0.5	40.4	9 523	31.6	21 357	24.1	5 507	15 970	35.9	99 900	64.1	822
Gainesville.................	34 313	1.6	31.0	22 315	17.4	57 576	43.5	6 547	48 617	41.4	143 100	58.6	840
Greenacres................	51 281	1.1	16.8	9 110	7.5	17 249	21.0	2 865	14 136	65.3	129 500	34.7	1 192
Hallandale Beach.........	36 849	3.1	24.4	8 727	16.9	27 057	7.8	8 756	17 457	53.0	160 700	47.0	1 131
Hialeah	29 095	1.1	35.8	51 131	25.9	74 067	2.6	2 862	71 124	45.6	180 400	54.4	1 059
Hollywood..................	46 091	3.8	20.0	33 976	14.5	71 070	3.9	12 632	56 104	54.9	201 200	45.1	1 100
Homestead................	41 260	1.8	20.2	14 468	24.8	23 419	111.0	4 423	18 924	32.4	171 000	67.6	1 107
Jacksonville................	48 239	3.4	18.5	201 701	12.5	366 273	18.6	43 167	323 488	56.2	146 500	43.8	963
Jupiter......................	72 476	12.5	13.7	15 768	7.5	29 825	41.7	5 905	25 510	69.9	320 700	30.1	1 471
Kissimmee.................	40 437	0.9	23.6	15 712	24.5	26 275	33.6	5 549	22 823	44.4	147 600	55.6	957
Lakeland...................	41 007	2.1	19.8	23 941	10.3	48 218	23.3	7 460	38 975	53.2	115 800	46.8	865
Lake Worth.................	36 761	1.2	30.7	7 546	13.6	16 473	3.6	3 515	15 427	54.3	168 300	45.7	941
Largo.........................	39 931	1.7	23.2	17 541	11.5	46 859	16.4	8 837	35 192	52.3	105 500	47.7	912
Lauderdale Lakes.........	29 355	0.5	32.6	7 096	29.1	15 000	4.5	3 109	10 546	55.6	114 300	44.4	1 072
Lauderhill...................	37 496	1.3	25.8	16 327	19.5	29 519	15.0	4 693	23 525	48.9	124 200	51.1	1 116
Margate.....................	45 861	1.4	20.5	12 299	4.6	24 863	0.5	3 380	20 103	69.7	160 800	30.3	1 136
Melbourne..................	43 056	1.4	19.3	17 202	9.7	38 955	15.7	4 915	32 825	55.9	135 200	44.1	902
Miami.......................	29 989	3.6	35.0	89 479	21.7	183 994	23.9	25 677	171 720	28.2	286 600	71.8	1 020
Miami Beach	50 937	13.7	21.8	18 331	9.3	67 499	13.0	20 331	43 400	41.5	460 000	58.5	1 236
Miami Gardens............	37 672	0.5	27.5	22 081	22.3	34 284	NA	2 065	29 814	58.4	157 300	41.6	1 132
Miami Lakes...............	67 539	7.4	11.5	NA	NA	10 698	18.8	445	10 970	69.5	352 500	30.5	1 299
Miramar.....................	70 133	6.0	11.9	32 513	10.2	40 294	55.6	2 874	40 203	67.2	277 500	32.8	1 460
North Lauderdale	42 574	0.3	13.9	8 435	19.5	14 709	28.1	1 732	11 789	50.7	126 100	49.3	1 353
North Miami................	40 121	2.4	25.6	12 140	20.0	22 110	-0.7	2 835	18 018	43.4	156 300	56.6	1 068
North Miami Beach	35 589	5.5	28.2	9 631	19.1	16 402	7.1	1 990	14 612	49.4	171 900	50.6	1 053
North Port..................	61 232	4.3	7.9	17 795	5.3	27 986	170.2	5 555	21 937	76.6	164 000	23.4	1 122
Oakland Park..............	42 017	2.9	17.0	8 653	16.5	20 076	38.1	2 577	16 436	48.9	178 800	51.1	1 045
Ocala........................	35 065	2.6	27.0	11 188	20.5	26 764	29.8	3 661	21 053	49.3	128 900	50.7	792
Ocoee......................	61 142	4.1	9.2	10 301	8.6	12 802	53.8	1 010	13 791	77.8	204 400	22.2	1 242
Orlando.....................	44 804	3.7	20.5	62 186	17.0	121 254	36.8	18 733	111 100	33.4	214 400	66.6	1 027
Ormond Beach............	42 652	5.1	20.3	10 619	10.6	19 576	12.8	2 514	17 451	71.6	168 100	28.4	1 060
Oviedo......................	77 337	7.7	8.0	NA	NA	11 720	28.9	595	12 696	76.9	260 800	23.1	1 583
Palm Bay...................	45 904	1.3	17.4	26 564	10.5	45 220	37.3	5 738	38 113	68.4	118 100	31.6	994
Palm Beach Gardens....	80 212	14.2	9.9	13 924	2.3	27 663	52.6	4 859	22 362	73.6	324 800	26.4	1 406
Palm Coast...............	49 629	0.6	13.1	20 645	8.2	35 058	132.0	5 253	29 739	70.5	175 200	29.5	1 130
Panama City...............	34 971	1.1	35.5	7 843	23.7	17 438	5.5	2 646	16 475	46.7	142 200	53.3	892
Pembroke Pines...........	62 404	6.1	12.8	39 820	4.6	61 703	11.6	4 830	56 409	71.0	249 500	29.0	1 471
Pensacola.................	38 822	3.3	22.8	11 503	9.4	26 848	-0.3	3 256	21 841	54.4	145 200	45.6	850
Pinellas Park...............	41 788	1.6	17.7	11 729	11.2	23 458	7.5	2 835	21 269	69.7	131 700	30.3	1 027
Plantation..................	63 702	6.6	11.9	23 629	7.2	37 587	7.1	3 397	33 712	60.5	315 100	39.5	1 589
Plant City...................	46 133	2.6	17.9	9 481	12.0	13 732	16.5	1 493	12 691	52.9	147 900	47.1	881
Pompano Beach...........	43 799	2.9	20.3	23 383	17.7	55 885	25.9	13 703	40 375	54.8	176 200	45.2	1 128
Port Orange...............	42 423	1.4	21.3	14 753	15.5	27 972	34.2	3 131	24 164	78.1	143 000	21.9	986
Port St. Lucie	53 222	2.4	15.6	45 010	9.3	70 877	92.0	9 975	61 310	77.6	158 800	22.4	1 147
Riviera Beach..............	44 017	3.6	22.2	7 651	16.2	17 124	19.4	4 744	10 771	52.0	163 100	48.0	1 131
Royal Palm Beach	70 068	6.3	12.9	NA	NA	12 854	58.1	1 298	12 930	79.2	258 000	20.8	1 609
St. Cloud...................	52 730	1.9	15.1	9 674	13.3	14 544	68.6	1 979	13 040	73.9	148 500	26.1	1 011
St. Petersburg.............	48 858	4.3	19.9	57 230	11.9	129 401	3.9	20 586	103 788	56.9	170 000	43.1	969
Sanford.....................	39 666	1.4	25.1	13 573	14.6	23 061	49.0	2 943	21 076	49.5	115 800	50.5	1 017
Sarasota....................	47 461	6.5	15.4	11 767	9.6	29 151	8.2	6 009	24 255	54.0	211 300	46.0	994
Sunrise.....................	55 957	2.1	14.6	22 113	8.9	37 609	5.5	5 116	30 856	67.4	175 600	32.6	1 321
Tallahassee................	40 000	3.4	26.9	33 076	13.2	84 248	23.2	9 433	74 162	39.3	181 600	60.7	934
Tamarac...................	39 852	0.2	20.7	15 251	9.4	32 794	10.3	4 379	29 554	70.7	133 000	29.3	1 261
Tampa......................	44 432	6.9	23.1	81 133	16.9	157 130	15.8	21 175	144 582	47.7	189 800	52.3	974
Titusville	39 231	1.0	24.5	10 519	16.1	22 729	18.2	3 712	20 205	62.6	96 800	37.4	852
Wellington..................	85 651	11.2	9.5	15 884	9.4	22 685	54.2	3 026	20 484	77.4	349 100	22.6	1 533
Weston.....................	98 963	17.4	6.9	17 778	6.0	24 394	28.9	3 174	20 939	68.8	436 400	31.2	2 199
West Palm Beach	49 935	4.3	18.2	22 917	12.0	54 179	34.1	11 267	41 168	46.6	207 500	53.4	1 106
Winter Garden.............	62 443	14.4	9.4	NA	NA	13 260	128.8	1 385	12 439	68.3	272 500	31.7	1 097
Winter Haven..............	35 561	1.4	27.9	8 760	11.9	17 037	22.3	2 714	14 735	55.1	122 100	44.9	916
Winter Park	66 285	15.6	9.1	NA	NA	13 626	18.2	1 398	12 670	70.5	395 300	29.5	915
Winter Springs............	62 186	8.6	13.1	8 766	5.7	14 052	14.3	951	12 640	75.6	211 500	24.4	1 148

1. Based on population estimated by the American Community Survey. 2. Includes units rented or sold but not occupied. 3. Specified owner-occupied units; $1,000,000 represents $1,000,000 or more 4. 50.0 represents 50 percent or more. 5. 10.0 represents 10 percent or less.

Table D. Cities — Commuting, Computer Access, Migration, Labor Force, and Employment

City	Commuting Percent		Computer Access[2] Percent		Migration, 2015		Civilian labor force, 2016				Civilian employment[4], 2015			
									Unemployment		Population age 16 and older		Population age 16 to 64	
	Drove alone	With Commutes of 30 minutes or more[1]	With a Computer in the house	With Internet Access	Percent who lived in the same house one year ago	Percent who lived in an other state or county one year ago	Total	Percent change, 2015–2016	Total	Rate[3]	Number	Percent in Labor Force	Number	Percent who worked full-year full-time
	55	56	57	58	59	60	61	62	63	64	65	66	67	68
FLORIDA—Cont'd														
Deerfield Beach............	80.9	30.9	86.9	75.0	77.3	10.1	40 099	1.7	1 865	4.7	68 049	66.6	50 418	55.2
DeLand......................	88.5	31.9	92.7	79.6	89.0	8.4	13 228	2.9	729	5.5	24 646	43.0	16 951	34.9
Delray Beach...............	81.7	27.3	86.7	78.7	76.8	8.6	35 132	3.0	1 650	4.7	58 257	60.4	39 556	51.2
Deltona......................	90.3	45.3	92.1	82.8	92.6	4.4	43 510	2.7	2 262	5.2	70 604	57.1	55 846	47.0
Doral.........................	88.1	42.7	96.3	94.2	86.8	7.7	28 718	2.2	1 307	4.6	40 542	68.0	37 535	45.4
Dunedin.....................	90.5	34.9	87.2	75.6	85.4	5.5	18 087	2.3	770	4.3	32 430	57.2	21 386	53.6
Fort Lauderdale...........	77.6	37.2	89.4	77.9	81.0	7.4	95 485	1.7	4 624	4.8	147 592	65.6	116 978	48.1
Fort Myers..................	72.1	34.5	86.1	69.2	74.3	12.2	32 512	3.0	1 614	5.0	60 679	60.2	47 029	48.6
Fort Pierce.................	73.7	30.3	77.1	57.7	87.3	7.6	18 347	2.0	1 463	8.0	33 750	54.3	26 352	40.2
Gainesville.................	71.2	16.1	88.6	79.3	66.2	16.2	65 983	2.3	3 085	4.7	113 620	55.0	99 650	34.0
Greenacres.................	79.7	48.3	88.0	76.3	81.2	5.3	21 432	3.1	933	4.4	32 438	64.0	25 540	48.4
Hallandale Beach.........	82.2	37.5	85.6	76.2	81.2	7.0	18 221	1.5	965	5.3	32 601	67.0	23 372	45.5
Hialeah......................	87.5	44.1	70.5	63.1	93.7	2.1	112 925	1.6	6 567	5.8	198 063	56.6	151 319	49.6
Hollywood..................	79.3	47.4	85.4	77.4	81.3	5.5	78 633	1.6	3 691	4.7	121 286	67.0	97 236	47.6
Homestead.................	71.6	54.6	84.9	67.8	80.4	5.4	30 228	1.9	1 784	5.9	48 538	60.2	43 319	42.0
Jacksonville................	85.0	34.4	87.1	77.5	79.9	6.5	442 617	2.0	22 616	5.1	684 614	66.0	574 448	51.8
Jupiter.......................	83.7	27.0	90.7	84.6	86.1	6.2	33 599	3.0	1 298	3.9	51 659	64.1	37 654	53.6
Kissimmee..................	89.4	38.4	78.6	69.5	83.8	7.6	36 207	2.8	1 818	5.0	56 372	63.1	48 268	48.3
Lakeland....................	80.7	23.5	81.5	61.0	78.7	6.7	45 182	2.0	2 483	5.5	84 160	55.3	64 170	47.5
Lake Worth.................	73.0	36.6	86.4	73.2	76.9	7.0	19 352	2.8	894	4.6	30 248	61.4	22 659	48.7
Largo........................	82.0	26.0	81.6	73.5	86.3	5.8	40 019	2.6	1 861	4.7	67 536	60.7	49 037	54.5
Lauderdale Lakes.........	73.0	48.1	79.8	67.0	89.3	3.7	16 937	1.8	907	5.4	26 877	62.6	21 879	35.3
Lauderhill..................	79.7	47.3	87.6	63.6	83.8	4.0	35 620	1.4	1 935	5.4	56 295	65.9	45 989	46.7
Margate.....................	85.0	44.1	81.6	70.1	82.9	3.5	29 829	1.7	1 437	4.8	48 540	67.8	37 792	48.5
Melbourne..................	82.5	22.7	86.1	79.0	85.9	6.6	37 720	2.2	1 996	5.3	67 051	57.3	49 399	51.0
Miami........................	73.1	52.7	73.8	59.6	87.7	3.8	217 313	1.8	11 538	5.3	372 847	61.0	297 850	50.4
Miami Beach...............	57.5	43.5	91.2	78.9	82.2	6.9	56 139	2.0	2 331	4.2	79 969	68.4	64 032	60.4
Miami Gardens............	83.5	54.6	77.7	64.4	89.3	3.5	52 833	1.7	3 633	6.9	87 724	56.2	71 756	42.8
Miami Lakes................	89.3	58.2	93.0	85.1	NA	NA	16 025	1.9	749	4.7	25 690	69.3	21 670	58.3
Miramar.....................	90.6	56.1	93.5	85.0	86.2	8.5	74 873	1.8	3 419	4.6	106 906	68.8	92 429	56.7
North Lauderdale.........	74.8	49.5	92.7	76.5	80.9	9.5	23 382	1.9	1 168	5.0	32 945	75.4	28 420	49.2
North Miami................	74.6	61.3	83.7	65.9	87.1	3.7	30 779	1.4	1 904	6.2	50 367	64.9	43 405	45.6
North Miami Beach	78.1	66.7	73.2	53.0	86.7	6.9	22 518	1.7	1 208	5.4	35 511	59.0	27 048	49.3
North Port..................	96.4	72.5	92.3	86.8	87.0	4.7	27 552	2.3	1 333	4.8	47 894	46.9	34 194	51.8
Oakland Park	81.2	31.6	91.7	82.5	78.3	6.7	25 732	1.7	1 143	4.4	37 795	64.7	30 838	45.9
Ocala........................	86.4	22.1	80.1	69.0	82.2	4.2	24 922	2.3	1 415	5.7	45 366	50.8	36 367	40.8
Ocoee.......................	84.2	41.5	94.1	89.1	82.6	5.3	24 669	2.9	959	3.9	32 064	68.1	28 126	55.8
Orlando.....................	83.6	39.1	92.1	82.9	75.1	9.8	158 907	2.8	6 731	4.2	220 510	72.3	192 766	53.2
Ormond Beach.............	78.8	24.0	85.7	79.6	90.6	4.4	19 168	3.3	926	4.8	35 220	52.9	22 704	44.8
Oviedo......................	88.6	55.5	94.6	91.5	90.6	3.8	21 002	3.2	837	4.0	30 560	68.0	25 751	52.8
Palm Bay....................	91.3	26.7	87.2	81.3	85.3	8.6	50 442	2.3	2 756	5.5	85 068	53.8	64 009	46.3
Palm Beach Gardens....	88.5	21.3	94.6	90.3	82.9	8.4	27 897	3.1	1 113	4.0	46 487	56.9	31 264	56.1
Palm Coast.................	89.2	37.6	90.0	82.3	87.8	9.0	35 751	3.1	1 980	5.5	68 329	49.2	44 426	46.2
Panama City................	79.2	28.4	84.1	70.8	79.1	6.0	17 361	0.5	921	5.3	30 895	58.6	23 287	43.9
Pembroke Pines............	88.6	61.5	90.2	87.3	88.4	5.2	88 882	1.9	3 886	4.4	135 557	68.2	109 351	55.8
Pensacola...................	83.4	15.4	88.0	76.6	76.5	8.6	27 364	2.3	1 133	4.1	41 953	61.7	33 521	44.2
Pinellas Park...............	86.3	22.3	84.9	71.8	85.8	5.2	25 906	2.6	1 158	4.5	43 564	59.1	32 708	55.9
Plantation	91.6	38.0	94.2	85.9	85.7	4.3	53 116	1.9	2 163	4.1	74 116	67.0	59 286	55.4
Plant City...................	86.8	42.0	88.7	74.5	82.6	7.5	19 134	2.4	840	4.4	27 751	62.9	23 796	50.2
Pompano Beach............	76.6	37.3	88.5	74.3	80.5	5.2	51 225	1.8	2 745	5.4	88 577	59.4	65 687	43.7
Port Orange................	88.7	16.8	90.8	80.5	79.9	10.4	30 321	3.4	1 391	4.6	50 472	48.1	36 476	39.8
Port St. Lucie	84.8	40.5	93.3	82.7	81.9	12.6	85 984	2.6	4 237	4.9	143 390	57.5	107 283	46.7
Riviera Beach..............	77.9	28.7	72.4	61.3	81.2	3.8	16 158	2.9	903	5.6	26 158	60.3	20 999	47.5
Royal Palm Beach	86.9	49.4	92.4	86.2	90.5	5.0	20 621	2.9	872	4.2	30 420	66.6	24 317	59.8
St. Cloud....................	81.9	50.3	87.4	81.0	85.3	7.2	22 097	2.8	1 046	4.7	33 394	63.8	27 734	50.4
St. Petersburg..............	82.8	32.8	85.1	75.8	82.4	6.9	137 712	2.6	5 910	4.3	214 354	62.4	169 156	49.5
Sanford.....................	87.9	36.8	86.5	77.7	85.3	7.5	27 522	2.8	1 500	5.5	44 207	67.2	37 794	50.7
Sarasota....................	85.5	14.8	85.0	77.3	78.6	8.1	27 465	2.8	1 201	4.4	49 078	56.1	34 596	52.0
Sunrise......................	87.3	39.8	89.0	76.2	88.5	4.8	51 134	1.7	2 364	4.6	75 300	66.7	61 398	54.3
Tallahassee.................	80.4	17.8	92.7	84.5	69.0	12.4	98 757	1.7	4 817	4.9	162 485	66.9	145 055	36.2
Tamarac.....................	84.2	43.6	85.9	72.9	80.8	3.8	33 718	1.7	1 634	4.8	57 837	57.3	39 749	47.1
Tampa.......................	83.0	30.0	86.6	76.4	80.5	7.8	192 210	2.5	9 171	4.8	298 188	64.5	255 884	48.1
Titusville	85.4	26.0	92.9	76.6	78.2	8.8	20 288	1.9	1 078	5.3	38 253	55.9	29 525	41.1
Wellington	86.2	52.3	95.7	92.8	80.7	9.5	33 548	3.0	1 349	4.0	50 225	62.6	41 159	48.6
Weston......................	85.8	46.9	97.7	96.5	83.1	9.8	35 902	2.1	1 434	4.0	50 490	64.4	41 966	49.4
West Palm Beach	85.8	25.7	83.5	70.5	81.4	7.5	57 691	3.1	2 729	4.7	88 834	63.2	70 679	47.5
Winter Garden.............	79.8	40.2	94.8	90.7	82.5	10.0	21 066	3.3	900	4.3	31 383	65.2	26 378	50.0
Winter Haven..............	88.7	28.6	82.2	59.7	84.4	5.2	15 972	2.0	1 025	6.4	30 882	49.4	21 270	42.5
Winter Park	88.0	27.6	93.6	89.7	88.1	3.5	14 527	3.1	631	4.3	25 533	59.6	18 684	52.5
Winter Springs..............	91.4	44.8	93.8	88.0	78.5	11.5	19 019	3.2	844	4.4	28 480	62.4	22 742	50.4

1. Employed persons.   2. Households.   3. Percent of civilian labor force.   4. Persons 16 years old and over.

Table D. Cities — Construction, Wholesale Trade, and Retail Trade

City	Value of residential construction authorized by building permits, 2016			Wholesale trade,[1] 2012				Retail trade,[2] 2012			
	New construction ($1,000)	Number of housing units	Percent single family	Number of establishments	Number of employees	Sales (mil dol)	Annual payroll (mil dol)	Number of establishments	Number of employees	Sales (mil dol)	Annual payroll (mil dol)
	69	70	71	72	73	74	75	76	77	78	79
FLORIDA—Cont'd											
Deerfield Beach	5 282	32	100.0	218	2 314	10 619.2	148.1	298	3 593	1 084.7	99.1
DeLand	118 304	365	99.5	45	209	116.2	10.7	175	2 527	752.9	66.0
Delray Beach	57 480	434	19.6	112	564	548.9	32.4	380	4 553	1 576.5	139.0
Deltona	30 491	101	100.0	10	D	D	D	97	1 566	368.2	35.7
Doral	152 796	938	59.5	1 540	13 960	31 206.3	805.1	445	6 595	2 137.1	195.8
Dunedin	777	3	100.0	29	265	114.0	8.9	123	1 010	233.2	25.7
Fort Lauderdale	67 943	145	85.5	571	5 787	4 332.2	299.5	1 161	12 021	4 045.3	367.8
Fort Myers	276 743	1 387	64.7	167	2 206	1 030.4	96.2	688	9 914	2 678.6	251.3
Fort Pierce	8 905	26	92.3	35	360	225.0	16.8	220	2 803	919.2	77.6
Gainesville	23 718	323	23.5	135	1 457	1 010.0	67.6	547	8 426	2 169.4	189.1
Greenacres	14 972	77	100.0	27	108	35.5	5.1	94	1 481	469.2	42.6
Hallandale Beach	5 473	28	25.0	80	429	248.2	20.4	137	1 858	437.1	44.0
Hialeah	100 802	763	50.9	515	3 886	1 380.5	132.7	1 060	10 595	2 456.0	240.2
Hollywood	144 919	451	9.3	285	2 279	1 521.9	131.5	573	6 316	1 916.1	159.0
Homestead	78 435	410	90.0	41	288	179.1	11.0	182	2 386	656.3	51.3
Jacksonville	894 173	5 517	48.5	1 075	18 668	18 797.6	1 056.4	3 011	43 471	12 498.4	1 114.5
Jupiter	94 389	218	84.9	100	669	352.8	36.1	257	2 886	673.8	77.3
Kissimmee	69 469	378	100.0	49	D	D	D	366	4 823	1 248.2	107.1
Lakeland	70 057	306	97.1	156	2 930	7 572.0	187.5	559	8 370	2 282.0	200.0
Lake Worth	6 404	39	100.0	43	331	126.8	21.2	120	888	256.9	24.5
Largo	16 598	92	68.5	102	D	D	D	330	4 311	1 033.1	112.4
Lauderdale Lakes	67 180	494	0.4	20	102	33.4	2.8	73	1 072	253.1	26.1
Lauderhill	999	12	100.0	41	D	D	D	198	1 478	364.1	37.0
Margate	0	0	0.0	62	411	354.4	17.4	171	2 476	889.2	78.1
Melbourne	84 805	257	83.3	102	1 461	820.5	80.6	464	6 067	1 626.6	155.3
Miami	973 172	3 910	2.2	1 440	8 474	7 906.8	371.9	2 398	21 175	6 476.3	551.4
Miami Beach	62 329	116	53.4	151	415	275.6	19.3	561	5 912	1 556.8	145.4
Miami Gardens	18 717	147	29.3	180	3 106	2 120.4	149.9	302	4 416	1 685.6	138.4
Miami Lakes	521	2	100.0	113	1 305	835.1	68.0	72	1 372	559.3	49.3
Miramar	17 996	79	100.0	198	2 748	2 686.5	197.4	198	3 297	1 659.5	96.3
North Lauderdale	1 488	14	100.0	7	D	D	D	70	961	241.1	24.2
North Miami	8 273	23	100.0	76	364	210.0	18.5	188	1 749	462.3	46.5
North Miami Beach	7 183	51	100.0	57	156	76.7	6.6	191	2 470	1 125.3	69.9
North Port	220 319	898	99.1	23	133	41.1	3.9	80	1 454	375.3	35.2
Oakland Park	28 987	222	64.0	114	811	360.5	49.2	252	2 047	654.6	55.5
Ocala	21 578	100	100.0	166	2 285	1 310.3	109.1	631	9 325	2 756.9	228.6
Ocoee	79 486	475	36.4	32	632	675.2	40.5	160	2 639	564.9	54.3
Orlando	401 040	1 660	44.0	634	8 653	5 585.7	443.6	1 580	27 103	8 359.0	641.1
Ormond Beach	47 254	149	100.0	44	767	287.7	31.1	195	2 299	579.6	55.4
Oviedo	114 503	501	43.9	31	D	D	D	148	2 331	405.9	44.8
Palm Bay	103 526	429	100.0	32	202	71.9	8.4	170	2 500	736.5	63.0
Palm Beach Gardens	93 824	255	73.3	68	341	138.0	14.8	348	6 747	1 555.8	167.7
Palm Coast	148 978	548	98.2	36	100	27.0	3.2	140	2 406	588.2	58.2
Panama City	21 768	59	100.0	68	765	247.4	31.0	338	4 441	1 199.2	113.9
Pembroke Pines	95 999	455	38.5	202	702	334.8	32.1	577	10 690	3 250.8	264.3
Pensacola	15 413	52	100.0	67	641	246.2	27.8	418	6 109	1 366.9	130.7
Pinellas Park	9 407	35	100.0	166	2 065	728.0	83.2	284	3 773	1 371.7	103.5
Plantation	38 256	197	11.7	120	490	277.2	31.8	348	5 590	1 724.9	134.2
Plant City	15 839	129	96.9	79	1 769	1 236.6	70.7	157	2 140	698.8	53.4
Pompano Beach	44 348	218	12.4	454	6 291	4 882.2	310.0	624	8 020	4 203.6	258.0
Port Orange	50 018	424	15.1	34	D	D	D	164	2 608	585.4	58.6
Port St. Lucie	193 410	1 259	88.5	81	489	148.1	19.5	334	8 054	2 257.6	240.5
Riviera Beach	3 768	28	35.7	102	2 211	1 640.8	133.5	106	878	354.3	29.7
Royal Palm Beach	4 625	42	0.0	32	184	124.2	7.4	154	3 525	975.5	88.3
St. Cloud	209 287	886	100.0	12	D	D	D	127	1 765	490.8	41.8
St. Petersburg	236 554	1 297	31.1	187	2 580	1 218.2	128.5	905	13 444	4 893.4	361.6
Sanford	45 490	271	32.5	88	1 374	538.6	64.0	358	5 781	1 758.4	148.0
Sarasota	109 525	430	25.3	88	651	303.2	32.0	505	5 274	1 363.5	141.3
Sunrise	120	1	100.0	262	2 458	1 729.8	140.2	544	10 882	2 776.1	241.5
Tallahassee	96 855	869	38.0	176	1 987	1 622.5	155.3	854	13 278	3 039.5	290.5
Tamarac	11 254	111	82.0	60	1 056	609.3	50.8	131	2 294	530.4	78.0
Tampa	556 827	4 262	21.9	646	9 863	9 457.0	490.2	1 878	24 934	7 449.8	673.5
Titusville	23 795	123	100.0	21	236	100.8	11.2	168	2 468	612.6	59.0
Wellington	22 133	63	30.2	78	239	386.9	12.4	243	3 279	570.2	69.5
Weston	4 555	20	100.0	279	1 712	2 552.4	102.4	134	2 210	864.1	70.8
West Palm Beach	91 524	514	37.5	146	1 663	1 282.1	90.9	535	8 040	2 939.5	248.0
Winter Garden	191 664	410	100.0	41	446	359.2	15.9	158	2 483	603.2	53.6
Winter Haven	77 017	433	100.0	45	1 427	534.7	34.0	201	2 939	801.8	72.5
Winter Park	85 696	374	28.3	52	335	233.1	16.8	232	2 936	816.0	80.3
Winter Springs	58 990	421	12.1	28	125	30.6	5.5	43	453	182.0	13.4

1. Merchant wholesalers except manufacturers' sales branches and offices.   2. Establishments with payroll.

City	Real estate and rental and leasing, 2012				Professional, scientific, and technical services,[1] 2012				Manufacturing, 2012			
	Number of establish-ments	Number of employees	Receipts (mil dol)	Annual payroll (mil dol)	Number of establish-ments	Number of employees	Receipts (mil dol)	Annual payroll (mil dol)	Number of establish-ments	Number of employees	Receipts (mil dol)	Annual payroll (mil dol)
	80	81	82	83	84	85	86	87	88	89	90	91
FLORIDA—Cont'd												
Deerfield Beach	122	846	131.8	33.0	338	2 736	400.9	136.7	107	2 166	751.5	109.1
DeLand	56	207	30.3	5.3	131	573	65.2	21.3	57	1 798	358.7	76.5
Delray Beach	152	673	85.9	19.7	467	1 971	299.1	98.3	73	585	136.6	21.5
Deltona	18	24	3.5	0.6	67	193	17.8	5.4	3	D	D	D
Doral	212	1 180	264.7	49.9	560	D	D	D	127	2 765	533.1	112.8
Dunedin	42	87	23.3	4.0	154	544	91.0	26.6	18	234	D	11.1
Fort Lauderdale	708	3 644	1 279.5	186.4	2 319	14 924	2 716.3	1 134.6	282	3 899	975.0	177.2
Fort Myers	212	1 133	239.2	40.0	486	6 661	1 451.1	576.0	93	1 720	396.6	75.2
Fort Pierce	61	221	41.6	7.7	137	D	D	D	26	495	108.8	21.3
Gainesville	201	1 076	156.0	32.4	472	2 740	317.7	130.2	86	1 558	587.6	82.4
Greenacres	22	55	23.2	2.4	96	629	52.3	17.5	4	56	D	1.4
Hallandale Beach	92	188	43.0	7.3	183	663	109.6	34.7	34	334	52.9	11.4
Hialeah	250	682	126.3	20.8	348	1 631	208.5	68.1	436	4 833	837.4	174.1
Hollywood	297	3 294	231.6	94.1	905	3 385	541.2	200.0	96	1 125	249.1	44.8
Homestead	43	141	17.7	3.4	80	344	33.6	13.4	19	221	D	8.6
Jacksonville	1 093	6 806	1 758.4	308.0	2 865	28 566	5 420.9	2 114.3	579	21 616	10 146.3	1 252.8
Jupiter	160	862	98.9	30.5	452	D	D	D	57	777	D	68.0
Kissimmee	147	584	102.0	15.8	177	811	73.7	22.8	28	125	D	4.2
Lakeland	194	1 027	197.6	34.5	357	D	D	D	82	3 922	1 614.7	155.8
Lake Worth	43	88	31.0	3.3	120	D	D	D	45	244	36.8	9.1
Largo	115	569	108.6	20.9	220	2 075	310.6	103.4	107	2 541	531.7	128.3
Lauderdale Lakes	20	282	50.3	10.1	28	D	D	D	8	32	2.3	0.6
Lauderhill	56	635	134.3	22.4	98	342	46.2	12.8	19	158	D	5.5
Margate	51	171	34.4	4.5	133	648	71.1	23.4	30	154	14.8	5.1
Melbourne	170	628	103.9	19.7	399	3 608	775.2	251.9	96	5 615	2 026.1	392.0
Miami	1 169	4 273	1 121.7	207.2	3 517	D	D	D	343	3 948	887.3	142.4
Miami Beach	457	1 556	402.9	70.2	661	D	D	D	29	99	13.4	2.9
Miami Gardens	69	266	70.9	9.7	78	335	30.7	18.5	68	1 871	338.3	79.1
Miami Lakes	85	607	137.0	28.8	270	1 165	271.1	70.2	24	2 155	578.1	148.6
Miramar	72	466	80.6	15.6	270	D	D	D	33	825	209.5	37.4
North Lauderdale	18	70	25.2	2.4	40	D	D	D	11	44	D	1.5
North Miami	90	276	54.4	9.5	158	521	84.3	25.4	27	468	51.4	17.4
North Miami Beach	72	239	34.3	9.2	213	734	97.9	31.4	23	247	D	12.8
North Port	29	50	6.0	2.0	62	137	13.0	4.1	12	247	D	9.7
Oakland Park	96	430	59.5	12.9	220	D	D	D	103	724	157.5	34.1
Ocala	171	897	130.2	27.8	383	1 854	216.2	81.0	105	3 819	1 196.5	169.6
Ocoee	30	241	37.3	8.6	92	412	38.8	12.8	13	192	D	4.7
Orlando	762	7 122	2 384.5	297.4	2 017	D	D	D	253	11 032	4 157.9	783.3
Ormond Beach	74	338	53.8	11.0	172	654	98.2	30.8	40	820	116.8	32.7
Oviedo	66	186	41.7	5.7	140	D	D	D	13	44	D	1.7
Palm Bay	54	143	24.5	4.2	99	D	D	D	39	8 936	2 317.2	672.1
Palm Beach Gardens	138	730	253.4	36.1	499	D	D	D	24	489	D	39.2
Palm Coast	98	D	D	D	128	288	42.8	12.6	21	428	D	20.4
Panama City	98	488	90.8	15.9	199	D	D	D	39	1 448	739.4	92.9
Pembroke Pines	159	506	135.3	19.8	563	1 725	276.4	78.8	46	249	44.4	9.8
Pensacola	122	590	114.5	18.9	450	D	D	D	49	766	361.0	41.0
Pinellas Park	67	263	56.7	11.4	167	D	D	D	238	7 383	2 189.6	333.8
Plantation	198	1 034	102.6	38.4	723	D	D	D	41	268	29.7	10.0
Plant City	46	146	41.2	4.9	91	D	D	D	49	1 795	748.9	76.0
Pompano Beach	228	930	191.6	35.6	471	1 768	287.0	89.9	250	5 908	1 497.3	326.0
Port Orange	94	362	53.1	10.2	120	901	112.2	36.9	18	210	28.5	7.4
Port St. Lucie	139	353	59.0	10.1	277	D	D	D	48	840	332.3	38.3
Riviera Beach	44	312	36.6	10.6	49	464	52.6	14.6	69	1 424	463.1	63.0
Royal Palm Beach	23	38	10.3	1.6	117	547	59.2	26.1	5	15	D	0.6
St. Cloud	43	132	15.4	2.8	53	163	14.0	4.5	15	163	D	7.1
St. Petersburg	347	1 614	298.8	58.1	1 158	11 396	1 508.6	594.7	148	4 906	1 377.7	262.0
Sanford	70	417	107.4	13.6	128	D	D	D	59	1 596	652.5	69.0
Sarasota	242	768	190.2	30.9	622	D	D	D	57	552	D	30.1
Sunrise	122	492	115.4	20.6	364	2 464	366.1	135.5	71	495	165.2	25.8
Tallahassee	331	1 808	256.7	54.4	1 158	D	D	D	77	1 297	382.7	66.0
Tamarac	63	250	47.5	7.7	166	553	71.6	28.5	20	370	52.6	15.1
Tampa	856	5 003	1 353.4	236.3	2 675	31 236	6 007.1	2 573.3	303	5 894	2 751.2	266.4
Titusville	35	121	19.4	3.1	95	565	76.9	27.8	37	433	43.6	15.4
Wellington	117	203	54.6	8.9	319	776	116.3	37.7	22	191	D	5.8
Weston	165	346	86.0	13.6	485	1 320	1 009.4	95.4	20	153	D	5.0
West Palm Beach	260	1 144	229.8	51.3	1 119	D	D	D	103	1 822	343.3	103.7
Winter Garden	63	199	43.3	7.2	110	377	39.9	14.1	26	470	186.1	17.1
Winter Haven	59	305	69.0	10.4	120	497	56.7	24.6	28	513	293.4	26.9
Winter Park	134	416	89.2	15.7	476	2 577	409.0	162.9	32	185	D	7.5
Winter Springs	42	D	D	D	101	230	27.4	10.9	13	82	12.8	3.0

1. Establishments subject to federal tax.

Accommodation and Food Services, Arts, Entertainment, and Recreation, and Health Care and Social Assistance

City	Accommodation and food services, 2012				Arts, entertainment, and recreation,[1] 2012				Health care and social assistance,[1] 2012			
	Number of establishments	Number of employees	Sales (mil dol)	Annual payroll (mil dol)	Number of establishments	Number of employees	Receipts (mil dol)	Annual payroll (mil dol)	Number of establishments	Number of employees	Receipts (mil dol)	Annual payroll (mil dol)
	92	93	94	95	96	97	98	99	100	101	102	103
FLORIDA—Cont'd												
Deerfield Beach	155	2 717	163.2	44.0	38	241	25.1	6.5	168	D	D	D
DeLand	94	1 414	61.1	17.5	13	123	6.2	2.2	120	1 769	166.1	69.1
Delray Beach	211	4 061	273.6	79.2	49	255	28.5	6.0	383	4 546	761.1	220.0
Deltona	40	500	25.4	5.7	7	D	D	D	84	805	65.8	24.4
Doral	228	3 851	320.6	83.4	41	D	D	D	211	1 991	219.2	60.8
Dunedin	100	1 271	62.0	16.6	10	34	2.2	0.6	116	D	D	D
Fort Lauderdale	710	20 279	1 934.4	464.8	144	962	172.8	31.6	863	12 461	1 320.6	599.4
Fort Myers	282	5 994	305.0	89.8	33	1 294	66.5	24.3	374	5 692	734.2	298.9
Fort Pierce	126	2 222	105.7	30.7	11	241	26.7	8.7	161	3 140	489.6	153.0
Gainesville	380	8 375	391.2	105.3	43	854	29.3	8.4	379	6 465	967.8	305.0
Greenacres	58	939	46.3	12.2	11	56	2.6	0.7	84	622	60.8	18.0
Hallandale Beach	85	2 230	121.5	35.0	31	D	D	D	148	D	D	D
Hialeah	347	3 876	238.1	61.1	35	180	14.7	3.0	784	9 203	1 171.2	341.0
Hollywood	330	5 683	427.6	115.8	88	1 142	170.7	30.4	544	D	D	D
Homestead	93	1 813	102.5	26.2	8	D	D	D	148	1 687	165.8	54.6
Jacksonville	1 765	33 931	1 820.0	501.7	204	4 730	435.0	228.5	2 029	D	D	D
Jupiter	151	3 307	179.7	61.8	45	1 168	82.3	31.5	326	D	D	D
Kissimmee	209	5 035	345.2	88.3	19	D	D	D	284	4 309	608.9	218.7
Lakeland	246	5 649	294.2	83.3	19	348	16.8	6.2	352	7 330	896.2	289.6
Lake Worth	63	683	38.8	11.2	15	D	D	D	73	1 043	105.6	40.2
Largo	183	2 788	146.3	39.2	30	D	D	D	242	7 076	803.8	308.4
Lauderdale Lakes	35	391	24.5	6.3	NA	NA	NA	NA	86	1 412	256.4	72.5
Lauderhill	82	944	61.7	14.2	15	D	D	D	127	D	D	D
Margate	98	D	D	D	13	168	7.8	2.5	159	2 272	365.7	109.6
Melbourne	213	4 009	194.2	58.9	27	D	D	D	408	7 860	928.5	375.3
Miami	1 267	26 462	1 914.9	527.4	207	3 993	846.1	359.3	1 679	17 673	2 388.6	733.1
Miami Beach	626	23 117	2 085.9	568.7	114	639	135.8	30.7	404	2 235	306.7	113.0
Miami Gardens	100	1 628	91.0	22.0	22	D	D	D	144	1 173	127.5	45.6
Miami Lakes	54	1 634	101.3	26.2	16	D	D	D	197	D	D	D
Miramar	118	1 660	95.1	23.5	25	D	D	D	223	1 967	419.1	91.0
North Lauderdale	28	364	20.1	5.1	6	23	15.7	1.3	44	D	D	D
North Miami	104	1 478	83.9	21.4	18	113	14.5	2.4	129	2 233	175.9	88.9
North Miami Beach	124	1 833	98.1	26.6	16	280	9.5	1.9	212	D	D	D
North Port	38	682	30.9	9.3	5	D	D	D	44	529	51.6	15.8
Oakland Park	100	1 691	90.7	26.4	14	D	D	D	149	D	D	D
Ocala	251	5 431	277.0	76.1	17	D	D	D	535	8 831	1 199.2	423.3
Ocoee	77	904	48.0	13.4	17	D	D	D	104	D	D	D
Orlando	999	26 376	1 938.1	473.7	144	16 398	2 187.0	457.1	879	11 319	1 616.4	697.7
Ormond Beach	118	2 321	112.8	33.4	28	339	19.2	6.3	226	D	D	D
Oviedo	62	1 202	54.4	15.1	14	115	5.7	1.5	123	D	D	D
Palm Bay	108	1 820	81.1	22.2	15	D	D	D	131	1 612	113.2	50.2
Palm Beach Gardens	143	4 820	235.6	85.0	40	D	D	D	319	3 706	535.7	163.4
Palm Coast	91	D	D	D	17	D	D	D	148	D	D	D
Panama City	167	3 198	158.1	45.4	18	D	D	D	294	6 840	827.5	314.0
Pembroke Pines	285	5 958	330.2	92.6	57	500	31.2	6.7	576	D	D	D
Pensacola	212	5 204	250.7	75.2	15	709	16.7	5.1	343	6 294	856.9	350.2
Pinellas Park	106	1 876	134.8	38.0	13	122	8.7	2.1	136	1 898	203.6	78.2
Plantation	188	3 356	218.5	56.0	51	405	26.1	7.4	586	6 332	923.7	328.2
Plant City	76	D	D	D	6	D	D	D	122	D	D	D
Pompano Beach	249	3 807	258.2	69.0	50	1 455	129.3	42.4	295	3 416	395.6	135.1
Port Orange	103	2 310	99.2	30.7	20	D	D	D	133	D	D	D
Port St. Lucie	204	3 628	180.6	48.3	36	D	D	D	370	5 191	645.7	223.1
Riviera Beach	39	836	62.1	13.2	10	289	18.8	5.1	41	D	D	D
Royal Palm Beach	95	1 883	101.7	28.4	14	140	6.0	2.1	121	1 020	115.9	46.0
St. Cloud	61	1 042	46.1	13.8	5	D	D	D	72	D	D	D
St. Petersburg	525	9 116	540.4	147.3	72	1 850	212.6	143.0	799	8 081	1 079.9	424.7
Sanford	119	2 238	104.8	30.3	15	D	D	D	118	1 977	292.3	101.4
Sarasota	286	6 049	377.5	110.2	41	843	33.5	11.3	449	4 964	632.8	228.5
Sunrise	187	4 135	217.4	61.9	38	D	D	D	260	3 931	557.9	269.7
Tallahassee	588	13 051	593.0	160.9	56	691	72.6	14.7	576	D	D	D
Tamarac	63	926	55.1	12.4	20	187	11.5	3.3	216	3 052	340.0	122.6
Tampa	1 087	25 033	1 655.4	420.6	152	5 489	847.6	350.2	1 345	16 190	2 907.9	955.1
Titusville	95	1 730	81.8	23.1	6	120	6.0	2.0	141	D	D	D
Wellington	105	2 479	107.4	33.3	64	D	D	D	245	D	D	D
Weston	97	2 066	122.1	35.9	26	D	D	D	258	D	D	D
West Palm Beach	356	6 424	390.8	105.9	52	1 061	115.7	33.7	543	8 828	1 360.8	428.4
Winter Garden	62	D	D	D	23	D	D	D	82	938	79.0	29.9
Winter Haven	119	1 878	90.7	26.6	12	D	D	D	163	D	D	D
Winter Park	153	3 518	183.9	59.3	38	D	D	D	307	3 291	428.3	170.9
Winter Springs	36	497	19.9	7.0	19	D	D	D	40	D	D	D

1. Establishments subject to federal tax.

Table D. Cities — Other Services and Government Employment and Payroll

City	Other services[1], 2012				Government employment and payroll, 2012								
						March payroll							
							Percent of total for:						
	Number of establish-ments	Number of employees	Receipts (mil dol)	Annual payroll (mil dol)	Full-time equivalent employees	Total (dollars)	Adminis-tration, judicial, and legal	Police and Corrections	Fire Protection	Highways and trans-portation	Health and welfare	Natural resources and utilities	Education and libraries
	104	105	106	107	108	109	110	111	112	113	114	115	116
FLORIDA—Cont'd													
Deerfield Beach	154	534	48.1	11.9	608	3 242 063	11.8	0.0	36.3	1.9	4.4	33.5	0.0
DeLand	75	321	23.6	7.6	339	1 192 527	21.8	28.4	14.3	9.1	0.0	23.5	0.0
Delray Beach	180	854	61.4	17.8	762	3 820 363	10.4	30.3	26.8	3.3	0.8	22.2	0.0
Deltona	34	111	6.8	1.9	304	1 105 426	18.7	0.0	34.0	5.8	0.9	31.1	0.0
Doral	141	1 116	195.1	39.7	269	1 347 474	13.6	55.1	0.0	6.7	0.0	8.2	0.0
Dunedin	62	216	14.1	5.4	343	1 392 549	13.9	0.0	21.1	7.5	1.6	43.2	5.9
Fort Lauderdale	617	3 575	397.5	120.8	2 346	13 506 065	10.3	32.6	25.0	0.5	4.6	19.2	0.0
Fort Myers	248	1 391	112.7	34.8	902	3 718 361	15.0	32.5	18.3	2.3	1.3	27.1	0.0
Fort Pierce	78	337	24.3	8.8	620	2 494 232	7.9	24.2	0.0	3.9	1.4	41.0	0.0
Gainesville	188	1 011	72.3	24.6	2 090	9 866 610	13.9	18.0	9.1	12.0	1.5	36.0	0.0
Greenacres	45	127	9.8	3.0	180	934 096	15.0	34.9	33.1	2.2	0.0	2.1	0.0
Hallandale Beach	98	469	33.8	11.8	437	2 597 020	14.5	36.5	23.5	4.3	3.1	15.3	0.0
Hialeah	410	1 449	138.7	34.8	1 644	7 468 317	8.8	33.3	26.1	4.7	2.0	17.7	4.4
Hollywood	256	1 597	140.4	43.2	1 340	7 260 474	10.2	35.7	23.9	4.1	2.7	17.3	0.0
Homestead	51	169	12.9	3.3	375	2 068 115	10.3	44.1	0.0	4.5	0.9	33.5	0.0
Jacksonville	1 274	7 216	656.4	208.6	10 137	46 960 164	11.8	32.9	13.5	4.4	2.3	13.0	2.0
Jupiter	154	899	68.0	26.5	368	1 870 904	18.7	37.5	0.0	8.8	0.2	23.5	0.0
Kissimmee	109	409	27.9	7.1	912	3 901 999	9.5	20.8	12.3	5.7	0.0	51.1	0.0
Lakeland	135	802	69.7	22.6	2 156	10 065 334	11.3	18.9	7.3	4.3	2.7	48.5	1.5
Lake Worth	66	303	22.4	6.9	267	1 224 227	13.4	0.0	0.0	3.3	7.0	68.8	1.3
Largo	167	822	61.4	18.5	823	3 637 673	0.0	25.8	22.2	6.2	1.2	25.5	3.2
Lauderdale Lakes	26	93	10.1	2.1	79	272 557	39.0	0.0	0.0	5.4	19.3	16.1	0.0
Lauderhill	91	328	27.4	7.0	410	2 557 908	13.6	36.5	29.7	0.9	1.2	14.4	0.0
Margate	101	343	34.4	7.5	486	2 719 607	9.8	35.2	29.2	0.0	0.8	18.8	0.0
Melbourne	173	963	67.9	26.7	870	3 653 445	13.0	26.1	21.7	11.7	0.9	24.0	0.0
Miami	815	4 921	337.4	100.8	3 807	18 642 774	9.5	38.6	27.3	0.0	1.0	10.5	0.0
Miami Beach	201	1 617	138.3	31.8	1 861	12 515 293	9.7	37.2	16.1	3.6	1.8	12.8	0.0
Miami Gardens	70	347	28.4	7.8	499	2 715 980	13.8	61.9	0.0	4.0	1.2	10.9	0.0
Miami Lakes	42	596	33.0	12.2	31	181 241	72.9	0.0	0.0	4.7	0.0	22.4	0.0
Miramar	102	488	48.4	15.7	758	4 183 683	11.9	34.2	25.2	4.0	4.9	19.8	0.0
North Lauderdale	29	148	16.0	4.7	153	612 914	14.4	0.0	35.9	6.8	9.5	24.3	0.0
North Miami	96	627	34.0	10.9	424	1 773 052	15.3	47.6	0.0	2.6	1.4	24.9	1.4
North Miami Beach	78	383	28.4	8.4	481	2 472 451	13.4	37.7	0.0	7.0	0.3	17.7	1.3
North Port	38	124	11.1	3.5	511	2 449 083	12.2	24.5	20.8	13.4	0.8	17.6	0.0
Oakland Park	163	497	61.2	13.6	238	1 116 830	16.6	0.0	36.2	5.5	0.7	31.5	2.1
Ocala	186	1 226	89.7	29.7	961	3 935 258	12.7	25.3	17.5	2.8	1.6	37.3	0.0
Ocoee	56	321	19.2	6.5	332	1 430 323	11.3	31.2	19.8	7.4	8.7	21.6	0.0
Orlando	540	4 699	341.4	120.0	2 773	14 180 368	10.1	36.7	27.1	2.9	0.6	17.8	0.0
Ormond Beach	72	368	21.4	7.0	333	1 242 053	17.4	24.9	18.0	7.1	0.0	25.6	0.0
Oviedo	54	224	14.5	4.1	281	1 140 501	10.0	30.2	24.7	5.4	5.6	24.1	0.0
Palm Bay	89	348	28.7	9.3	738	2 860 974	8.8	34.4	22.7	12.9	2.8	18.3	0.0
Palm Beach Gardens	103	689	49.4	17.3	497	2 744 921	6.6	31.5	34.9	3.9	0.0	13.0	0.0
Palm Coast	58	222	15.1	4.1	367	1 477 520	33.5	0.4	16.8	0.0	0.0	49.3	0.0
Panama City	85	526	40.6	11.7	560	1 720 128	8.5	23.2	16.5	21.6	2.5	23.8	0.0
Pembroke Pines	180	882	72.7	21.1	811	4 498 652	8.1	38.2	36.8	0.0	0.5	11.6	0.0
Pensacola	116	886	68.1	20.8	835	3 072 149	10.7	26.9	15.4	10.9	2.2	25.7	4.6
Pinellas Park	135	807	86.2	25.7	495	2 118 077	13.5	29.2	22.2	4.8	5.1	17.7	4.0
Plantation	174	912	96.6	27.0	805	3 820 829	9.6	44.3	2.6	5.4	9.5	17.4	1.1
Plant City	52	319	26.0	8.6	501	1 604 248	10.1	22.3	11.9	11.1	2.3	30.0	3.2
Pompano Beach	268	1 609	151.4	45.6	750	3 541 060	16.9	0.0	31.9	13.8	1.8	23.5	0.0
Port Orange	84	382	25.9	7.6	401	1 524 545	16.2	27.0	16.3	4.0	8.0	26.5	0.0
Port St. Lucie	151	676	48.4	14.7	947	4 712 445	20.9	40.2	0.0	10.1	2.4	19.5	0.0
Riviera Beach	67	390	47.2	14.7	471	2 072 288	16.7	31.0	21.2	5.6	2.0	15.3	1.1
Royal Palm Beach	60	401	25.2	7.5	102	467 299	20.4	0.0	0.0	30.5	0.0	29.3	0.0
St. Cloud	42	183	11.5	3.7	437	1 502 512	12.4	20.0	15.5	4.7	0.0	25.9	0.0
St. Petersburg	399	1 874	149.2	46.8	3 700	17 064 309	4.8	45.6	11.2	0.8	1.0	27.0	1.2
Sanford	99	498	30.5	11.1	571	2 356 239	8.5	26.8	18.3	14.9	0.6	25.6	0.0
Sarasota	176	1 055	66.7	21.9	650	3 097 398	13.3	41.0	0.0	3.7	1.8	26.4	0.0
Sunrise	125	556	39.2	11.0	946	5 498 554	12.5	33.9	21.2	2.4	0.9	25.6	0.0
Tallahassee	317	2 012	143.4	46.5	3 027	13 645 644	13.9	19.4	10.3	12.4	2.1	36.5	0.0
Tamarac	58	193	15.6	4.2	364	1 617 407	25.5	0.0	24.3	8.4	1.2	29.4	0.0
Tampa	787	5 615	363.3	119.3	4 247	22 517 912	11.0	35.8	17.2	4.0	2.4	25.2	0.0
Titusville	72	353	28.7	9.0	452	1 810 027	17.0	25.5	15.5	4.3	0.7	33.4	0.0
Wellington	83	454	38.0	12.5	322	1 314 469	22.1	0.0	0.0	3.5	0.0	40.8	0.0
Weston	88	469	30.5	8.7	10	117 886	74.7	0.0	0.0	0.0	0.0	25.3	0.0
West Palm Beach	237	1 177	88.5	27.3	1 355	7 409 659	10.2	30.9	19.4	4.7	1.3	25.2	2.2
Winter Garden	45	318	31.2	9.7	272	1 145 114	16.2	35.8	18.5	3.2	0.0	17.7	0.0
Winter Haven	60	247	20.2	5.6	460	1 697 693	17.7	25.5	18.1	2.2	0.0	25.4	2.8
Winter Park	115	579	36.5	12.4	506	2 395 109	10.5	24.5	19.9	4.4	0.8	35.0	0.0
Winter Springs	26	98	6.0	1.7	207	765 305	16.8	45.2	0.0	0.0	0.0	34.3	0.0

1. Establishments subject to federal tax.

Table D. Cities — City Government Finances

City	City government finances, 2012									
	General revenue							General expenditure		
		Intergovernmental		Taxes					Per capita[1] (dollars)	
					Per capita[1] (dollars)					
	Total (mil dol)	Total (mil dol)	Percent from state government	Total (mil dol)	Total	Property	Sales and gross receipts	Total (mil dol)	Total	Capital outlays
	117	118	119	120	121	122	123	124	125	126
FLORIDA—Cont'd										
Deerfield Beach............	110.6	11.2	65.6	51.7	667	441	223	119.1	1 535	67
DeLand......................	35.7	3.0	61.4	17.0	614	289	325	31.5	1 139	109
Delray Beach...............	122.1	11.8	68.8	77.5	1 240	937	301	117.6	1 882	71
Deltona.....................	54.5	13.8	48.2	29.8	348	137	212	53.3	623	113
Doral........................	55.0	5.7	60.4	41.1	848	410	438	61.9	1 277	597
Dunedin.....................	36.4	4.4	84.4	17.5	493	184	309	42.1	1 185	73
Fort Lauderdale...........	351.8	52.9	32.9	172.6	1 007	601	406	357.5	2 086	178
Fort Myers.................	148.2	15.3	59.3	61.9	943	526	416	154.4	2 352	195
Fort Pierce.................	68.9	10.3	85.1	26.0	609	360	249	79.2	1 855	305
Gainesville.................	206.3	24.2	47.3	64.4	510	212	298	208.2	1 648	273
Greenacres.................	21.6	4.0	80.4	13.4	347	173	174	20.5	533	30
Hallandale Beach.........	73.9	8.7	37.1	31.8	827	546	281	76.5	1 992	86
Hialeah.....................	219.5	58.6	43.0	103.2	442	208	234	207.3	887	63
Hollywood..................	276.4	29.3	52.2	122.9	843	565	278	276.3	1 896	231
Homestead.................	81.0	20.4	49.7	25.1	395	226	168	68.8	1 081	164
Jacksonville................	1 946.9	245.5	61.0	924.4	1 104	595	506	1 888.1	2 255	340
Jupiter......................	55.9	5.9	86.7	35.6	621	347	274	60.5	1 056	189
Kissimmee..................	69.7	20.4	62.5	27.9	438	199	239	82.5	1 296	259
Lakeland...................	186.5	38.4	30.2	50.0	502	262	240	203.7	2 048	303
Lake Worth................	47.4	10.9	39.7	14.0	389	189	201	55.1	1 538	116
Largo.......................	106.7	10.7	72.0	39.5	505	186	318	110.7	1 416	238
Lauderdale Lakes..........	26.2	4.3	77.6	11.9	352	170	182	26.8	792	44
Lauderhill..................	67.1	12.7	52.9	27.3	394	187	208	71.1	1 026	65
Margate	70.3	9.0	65.1	33.0	598	364	233	69.8	1 266	200
Melbourne..................	117.4	17.7	39.8	45.0	584	287	297	113.2	1 469	76
Miami.......................	722.3	172.2	31.3	406.9	976	638	338	740.7	1 777	262
Miami Beach	529.5	21.7	43.5	328.2	3 597	1 276	2 320	497.2	5 448	572
Miami Gardens.............	83.2	27.7	44.3	41.1	368	176	192	85.3	765	86
Miami Lakes...............	18.1	3.9	79.9	12.9	422	185	237	19.4	635	118
Miramar....................	143.9	25.7	45.7	72.6	562	324	239	135.3	1 048	75
North Lauderdale	36.7	5.7	71.1	13.9	327	169	158	33.0	775	30
North Miami................	74.3	14.3	45.8	30.1	493	287	206	78.4	1 282	99
North Miami Beach	69.4	10.5	84.8	22.9	528	290	238	79.6	1 838	147
North Port.................	74.1	8.3	65.2	22.7	389	138	251	78.1	1 339	244
Oakland Park	60.8	8.4	54.6	23.5	546	294	252	60.3	1 403	122
Ocala.......................	118.1	16.3	79.4	40.2	707	380	327	106.1	1 865	168
Ocoee......................	39.5	8.6	94.4	16.4	428	253	175	40.9	1 066	54
Orlando.....................	675.7	172.0	30.5	223.8	895	417	478	644.8	2 578	124
Ormond Beach.............	49.2	7.5	40.8	21.3	554	253	301	51.7	1 346	298
Oviedo......................	37.7	4.2	64.8	18.8	531	271	260	40.7	1 151	91
Palm Bay...................	95.5	22.5	37.8	43.8	421	236	184	96.4	925	142
Palm Beach Gardens....	72.5	6.7	77.4	55.9	1 116	914	202	73.8	1 475	130
Palm Coast................	61.9	7.9	63.6	23.7	306	196	111	75.5	974	151
Panama City................	60.3	8.8	82.6	27.9	771	279	492	64.4	1 779	119
Pembroke Pines...........	252.5	67.1	81.6	92.9	581	321	260	310.7	1 942	78
Pensacola..................	126.4	46.1	16.9	42.4	804	266	538	157.0	2 977	968
Pinellas Park	65.8	7.8	64.1	31.4	631	274	357	68.5	1 377	108
Plantation	103.5	13.9	50.3	55.4	628	333	295	108.1	1 225	75
Plant City..................	47.9	7.5	73.4	20.0	554	231	323	40.6	1 128	97
Pompano Beach...........	157.1	12.7	50.4	84.6	819	496	323	202.4	1 959	236
Port Orange...............	65.3	6.6	74.6	25.0	440	215	225	62.8	1 105	37
Port St. Lucie	168.3	26.2	39.2	71.3	422	209	214	184.5	1 092	286
Riviera Beach..............	85.9	14.2	26.9	47.7	1 438	1 016	422	92.1	2 775	315
Royal Palm Beach	21.1	5.0	54.1	11.9	338	100	237	26.3	747	203
St. Cloud...................	51.0	4.2	78.7	15.3	386	160	226	64.8	1 632	228
St. Petersburg.............	377.4	80.5	33.2	139.7	565	303	262	403.2	1 630	142
Sanford.....................	92.0	18.1	67.1	32.7	597	311	286	78.2	1 427	372
Sarasota...................	157.9	32.8	32.3	54.1	1 023	523	501	163.4	3 091	774
Sunrise.....................	184.3	17.8	52.4	62.2	698	352	347	170.9	1 920	274
Tallahassee	339.4	52.0	38.9	105.7	565	184	381	370.9	1 983	425
Tamarac	73.4	11.5	50.2	31.8	507	261	245	68.8	1 097	20
Tampa......................	643.2	135.9	37.9	270.1	774	350	424	634.2	1 817	201
Titusville	55.0	7.1	79.7	25.9	589	263	326	44.4	1 010	129
Wellington..................	61.9	10.3	59.9	28.2	481	219	261	61.6	1 048	256
Weston.....................	90.1	5.2	88.6	38.6	569	177	392	83.3	1 228	132
West Palm Beach	226.7	39.5	30.6	109.6	1 069	714	355	255.4	2 491	117
Winter Garden............	39.8	5.5	93.8	20.7	560	226	334	40.6	1 096	279
Winter Haven.............	52.2	3.8	56.0	20.8	594	282	312	58.7	1 677	299
Winter Park	63.4	8.3	60.7	29.5	1 019	622	397	65.0	2 246	474
Winter Springs.............	27.7	4.0	89.0	13.1	389	125	264	26.4	786	144

1. Based on population estimated as of July 1 of the year shown.

City	City government finances, 2012 (cont.)									
	General expenditure (cont.)									
	Percent of total for:									
	Public welfare	Highways	Parking facilities	Education	Health and hospitals	Police protection	Sewerage and sanitation	Parks and recreation	Housing and community development	Interest on debt
	127	128	129	130	131	132	133	134	135	136
FLORIDA—Cont'd										
Deerfield Beach............	2.1	2.3	1.5	0.0	0.0	18.0	25.4	5.7	0.3	1.7
DeLand.........................	0.0	8.4	0.0	0.0	0.0	21.9	18.8	9.0	1.4	1.9
Delray Beach................	0.0	3.6	0.7	0.0	0.0	25.3	3.7	15.4	1.8	2.5
Deltona........................	0.0	8.7	0.0	0.0	0.0	17.3	17.9	5.0	6.3	2.0
Doral...........................	0.0	13.4	0.0	0.0	0.0	19.6	0.0	27.0	0.0	2.4
Dunedin.......................	0.0	7.2	0.0	0.0	0.0	9.4	14.6	15.8	0.0	0.9
Fort Lauderdale............	0.0	3.4	3.0	0.0	0.0	27.5	5.4	11.4	4.4	0.7
Fort Myers...................	0.0	10.3	0.7	0.0	0.0	19.9	24.4	9.3	1.3	3.9
Fort Pierce..................	0.0	4.7	0.0	0.0	0.0	14.8	34.2	10.9	6.0	5.4
Gainesville...................	0.7	8.6	0.2	0.0	0.1	18.0	17.1	7.9	3.6	7.8
Greenacres..................	0.0	8.7	0.0	0.0	0.0	35.2	5.1	6.4	0.0	0.9
Hallandale Beach.........	1.2	1.0	0.0	0.0	0.0	25.2	20.9	3.0	3.1	1.7
Hialeah........................	0.0	4.5	0.0	0.0	0.0	23.0	17.8	7.3	2.2	2.2
Hollywood....................	0.0	2.8	2.4	0.0	0.0	25.1	19.0	7.2	1.2	3.5
Homestead..................	1.6	5.0	0.0	0.0	0.0	28.2	30.0	12.4	6.6	0.8
Jacksonville.................	2.5	7.5	0.2	0.0	3.3	15.9	10.3	4.6	0.7	8.6
Jupiter.........................	0.0	10.0	0.0	0.0	0.0	32.3	4.8	3.6	0.0	2.5
Kissimmee....................	0.0	15.8	0.0	0.0	0.0	21.3	9.0	13.5	1.1	1.6
Lakeland......................	0.0	11.1	0.4	0.0	0.0	17.3	14.6	14.0	3.0	1.7
Lake Worth..................	0.0	2.8	0.2	0.0	0.0	27.6	23.1	9.1	0.0	0.7
Largo..........................	0.0	3.0	0.0	0.0	0.0	17.3	27.9	13.2	2.4	0.4
Lauderdale Lakes.........	0.0	1.7	0.0	0.0	9.4	27.5	7.2	4.2	0.0	4.7
Lauderhill....................	0.0	1.7	0.0	0.0	6.5	22.9	6.6	4.3	3.2	4.5
Margate.......................	0.0	3.6	0.0	0.0	0.0	27.0	14.4	4.2	3.5	3.0
Melbourne....................	0.0	12.5	0.2	0.0	0.0	16.1	13.2	8.2	2.2	0.5
Miami..........................	0.2	9.5	3.7	0.0	0.0	18.5	3.2	14.9	5.4	5.4
Miami Beach................	0.4	3.6	6.2	0.0	3.2	17.9	10.5	14.6	4.3	2.3
Miami Gardens.............	0.0	6.2	0.0	0.0	0.0	36.6	0.0	14.2	6.2	5.6
Miami Lakes.................	0.0	8.4	0.0	0.0	0.0	33.7	0.0	12.1	0.0	1.3
Miramar.......................	0.0	5.5	0.0	0.0	0.0	29.7	6.2	8.7	0.9	3.6
North Lauderdale.........	0.0	3.0	0.0	0.0	0.0	26.0	17.3	11.7	2.6	1.3
North Miami.................	0.0	9.0	0.0	0.0	0.0	28.7	22.0	7.0	7.1	2.4
North Miami Beach.......	0.0	1.7	0.0	0.0	0.0	31.6	17.5	6.7	2.7	2.4
North Port....................	0.6	22.2	0.0	0.0	0.0	16.2	17.0	6.4	0.0	0.6
Oakland Park...............	0.0	6.0	0.0	0.0	0.0	20.6	19.4	7.9	0.0	1.9
Ocala..........................	0.3	12.3	0.0	0.0	0.0	20.5	21.8	6.8	1.2	1.9
Ocoee.........................	0.0	8.8	0.0	0.0	0.0	20.3	13.9	5.3	0.0	3.7
Orlando........................	0.0	6.8	2.6	0.0	1.0	19.2	13.7	12.9	1.7	7.0
Ormond Beach.............	0.0	9.6	0.0	0.0	0.0	14.8	20.0	21.6	0.0	0.6
Oviedo.........................	0.0	31.0	0.0	0.0	0.0	16.7	17.4	8.4	0.0	3.0
Palm Bay.....................	0.0	10.3	0.0	0.0	0.0	21.3	19.2	3.6	3.9	4.7
Palm Beach Gardens....	0.0	1.7	0.0	0.0	0.0	30.2	0.0	12.4	0.0	1.4
Palm Coast..................	0.0	16.0	0.0	0.0	0.0	3.5	36.5	6.2	0.0	1.3
Panama City................	0.0	8.9	0.0	0.0	0.0	14.5	8.1	9.2	1.3	0.7
Pembroke Pines...........	0.5	1.7	0.0	0.0	0.0	15.3	12.6	5.8	3.4	5.5
Pensacola....................	0.0	3.8	0.3	0.0	0.0	13.4	4.1	25.3	10.0	4.8
Pinellas Park...............	0.0	6.9	0.0	0.0	4.5	20.1	24.8	8.4	0.0	0.7
Plantation	0.0	2.8	0.0	0.0	7.5	32.2	15.5	12.9	1.7	1.6
Plant City....................	0.0	8.8	0.0	0.0	0.0	19.8	27.0	8.6	1.2	1.3
Pompano Beach...........	0.0	2.1	0.0	0.0	7.0	18.5	11.1	7.3	1.9	0.6
Port Orange.................	0.0	8.8	0.0	0.0	0.0	18.5	37.4	7.4	0.7	2.5
Port St. Lucie	0.0	24.4	0.0	0.0	0.7	19.0	7.9	6.5	2.6	16.5
Riviera Beach...............	0.2	7.4	0.0	0.0	0.0	18.1	17.9	6.3	0.2	1.0
Royal Palm Beach	0.0	11.4	0.0	0.0	0.0	27.6	0.0	26.9	0.0	0.6
St. Cloud	0.0	25.8	0.0	0.0	3.0	12.6	26.0	4.3	0.2	6.7
St. Petersburg	0.0	9.3	1.1	0.0	3.1	22.0	21.3	14.7	2.3	1.5
Sanford.......................	0.7	8.9	0.0	0.0	0.0	15.9	18.1	5.9	1.9	2.5
Sarasota......................	0.0	7.1	0.7	0.0	0.0	17.6	23.5	19.7	10.7	3.1
Sunrise........................	0.0	3.6	0.0	0.0	0.0	29.4	25.2	8.3	0.6	0.8
Tallahassee..................	0.0	15.1	0.0	0.0	0.0	13.2	31.4	5.6	1.8	2.3
Tamarac......................	0.0	6.9	0.0	0.0	0.0	17.5	11.9	5.4	1.8	1.9
Tampa.........................	0.0	8.7	2.2	0.0	0.0	23.8	21.2	8.9	5.4	4.1
Titusville	0.0	4.6	0.0	0.0	0.0	24.8	18.5	2.8	7.4	1.2
Wellington....................	0.0	15.3	0.0	0.0	0.0	12.1	9.3	6.6	0.0	1.2
Weston	0.0	0.8	0.0	0.0	0.0	12.7	18.5	6.4	1.7	0.6
West Palm Beach	0.0	4.1	1.6	0.0	0.7	18.7	24.9	7.1	2.6	4.0
Winter Garden..............	0.1	13.7	0.2	0.0	0.0	17.5	15.8	18.6	0.0	2.5
Winter Haven	1.2	4.2	2.4	0.0	0.0	17.1	25.7	14.3	0.4	3.8
Winter Park	0.0	2.8	0.0	0.0	0.0	17.7	13.9	8.8	0.0	2.4
Winter Springs..............	0.0	10.9	0.0	0.0	0.0	28.7	22.0	7.4	0.0	2.2

City	Total (mil dol) 137	Per capita[1] (dollars) 138	Debt issued during year 139	January 140	July 141	January[3] 142	July[4] 143	Annual precipitation (inches) 144	Heating degree days 145	Cooling degree days 146
FLORIDA—Cont'd										
Deerfield Beach	72.1	929	0.0	67.2	83.3	57.8	91.8	57.27	219	4 241
DeLand	33.4	1 206	9.3	NA	NA	NA	NA	NA	NA	NA
Delray Beach	86.4	1 383	5.4	66.2	82.5	57.3	90.1	61.39	246	3 999
Deltona	97.2	1 137	0.3	57.1	81.2	44.5	91.2	57.03	954	2 819
Doral	26.4	544	0.0	NA	NA	NA	NA	NA	NA	NA
Dunedin	35.3	995	0.0	60.9	82.5	50.2	91.3	52.42	623	3 414
Fort Lauderdale	587.6	3 429	67.9	67.5	82.6	59.2	89.8	64.19	167	4 120
Fort Myers	377.2	5 747	15.1	64.9	83.0	54.5	91.7	54.19	302	3 957
Fort Pierce	216.8	5 076	1.1	62.6	81.7	50.7	91.5	53.50	477	3 430
Gainesville	1 189.9	9 418	161.7	54.4	81.1	41.8	92.4	49.56	1 249	2 608
Greenacres	4.0	105	0.0	66.2	82.5	57.3	90.1	61.39	246	3 999
Hallandale Beach	31.5	819	0.0	68.1	83.7	59.6	90.9	58.53	149	4 361
Hialeah	169.3	725	81.6	67.9	82.7	62.6	87.0	46.60	141	4 090
Hollywood	379.0	2 602	4.3	67.5	82.6	59.2	89.8	64.19	167	4 120
Homestead	18.5	291	0.0	67.0	81.8	56.2	90.6	55.55	238	3 923
Jacksonville	10 439.0	12 465	630.5	54.5	82.5	42.6	92.7	51.88	1 222	2 810
Jupiter	66.9	1 167	0.0	66.2	82.5	57.3	90.1	61.39	246	3 999
Kissimmee	457.1	7 175	151.7	59.7	81.8	47.7	91.6	48.01	694	3 111
Lakeland	951.3	9 565	203.4	62.5	84.0	51.1	94.6	49.13	487	3 886
Lake Worth	74.3	2 072	6.8	65.1	81.1	52.5	91.3	58.44	273	3 438
Largo	31.5	403	14.0	61.3	82.5	52.4	89.7	44.77	591	3 482
Lauderdale Lakes	28.4	838	0.0	67.2	83.3	57.8	91.8	57.27	219	4 241
Lauderhill	118.7	1 711	18.3	67.5	82.6	59.2	89.8	64.19	167	4 120
Margate	53.5	971	0.0	67.2	83.3	57.8	91.8	57.27	219	4 241
Melbourne	132.5	1 720	1.5	60.9	81.2	50.0	90.5	48.29	595	3 186
Miami	873.2	2 095	120.6	68.1	83.7	59.6	90.9	58.53	149	4 361
Miami Beach	465.1	5 097	56.6	68.1	83.7	59.6	90.9	58.53	149	4 361
Miami Gardens	111.4	999	55.0	NA	NA	NA	NA	NA	NA	NA
Miami Lakes	7.5	246	7.3	NA	NA	NA	NA	NA	NA	NA
Miramar	182.5	1 414	0.0	68.1	83.7	59.6	90.9	58.53	149	4 361
North Lauderdale	8.6	203	0.0	67.5	82.6	59.2	89.8	64.19	167	4 120
North Miami	21.9	359	0.0	68.1	83.7	59.6	90.9	58.53	149	4 361
North Miami Beach	111.2	2 568	18.3	68.1	83.7	59.6	90.9	58.53	149	4 361
North Port	54.0	925	17.5	NA	NA	NA	NA	NA	NA	NA
Oakland Park	38.9	904	18.2	67.5	82.6	59.2	89.8	64.19	167	4 120
Ocala	201.6	3 544	13.9	58.1	81.7	45.7	92.2	49.68	902	2 971
Ocoee	54.8	1 428	2.1	NA	NA	NA	NA	NA	NA	NA
Orlando	1 055.4	4 219	67.0	60.9	82.4	49.9	92.2	48.35	580	3 428
Ormond Beach	54.1	1 408	5.6	60.9	82.4	49.9	92.2	48.35	580	3 428
Oviedo	79.7	2 256	1.3	58.7	81.5	47.0	91.9	51.31	799	3 017
Palm Bay	157.8	1 514	5.5	60.9	81.2	50.0	90.5	48.29	595	3 186
Palm Beach Gardens	25.8	515	4.4	66.2	82.5	57.3	90.1	61.39	246	3 999
Palm Coast	176.4	2 276	2.2	57.4	82.8	46.4	92.0	49.79	909	3 193
Panama City	35.5	980	0.0	50.3	80.0	38.7	89.0	64.76	1 810	2 174
Pembroke Pines	388.8	2 430	12.3	67.5	82.6	59.2	89.8	64.19	167	4 120
Pensacola	213.6	4 050	0.0	52.0	82.6	42.7	90.7	64.28	1 498	2 650
Pinellas Park	31.8	640	0.0	61.7	83.4	54.0	90.2	49.58	548	3 718
Plantation	39.9	452	2.8	67.5	82.6	59.2	89.8	64.19	167	4 120
Plant City	68.0	1 886	0.0	61.1	81.5	49.8	90.8	51.17	625	3 261
Pompano Beach	88.3	855	28.1	67.2	83.3	57.8	91.8	57.27	219	4 241
Port Orange	156.3	2 751	13.3	57.1	81.2	44.5	91.2	57.03	954	2 819
Port St. Lucie	1 015.1	6 008	42.9	64.5	81.8	54.7	89.5	59.53	315	3 600
Riviera Beach	67.2	2 025	26.5	66.2	82.5	57.3	90.1	61.39	246	3 999
Royal Palm Beach	20.5	582	20.5	NA	NA	NA	NA	NA	NA	NA
St. Cloud	123.7	3 114	57.6	NA	NA	NA	NA	NA	NA	NA
St. Petersburg	562.7	2 275	53.9	61.7	83.4	54.0	90.2	49.58	548	3 718
Sanford	79.7	1 455	6.1	58.7	81.5	47.0	91.9	51.31	799	3 017
Sarasota	156.6	2 962	30.9	61.7	83.4	54.0	90.2	49.58	548	3 718
Sunrise	298.7	3 356	9.6	67.5	82.6	59.2	89.8	64.19	167	4 120
Tallahassee	1 263.4	6 754	173.5	51.8	82.4	39.7	92.0	63.21	1 604	2 551
Tamarac	60.4	963	23.3	67.2	83.3	57.8	91.8	57.27	219	4 241
Tampa	1 377.0	3 945	202.8	61.3	82.5	52.4	89.7	44.77	591	3 482
Titusville	56.5	1 285	3.6	59.9	82.4	49.5	91.4	52.79	677	3 300
Wellington	22.8	388	0.0	66.2	82.5	57.3	90.1	61.39	246	3 999
Weston	12.6	186	0.0	67.5	82.6	59.2	89.8	64.19	167	4 120
West Palm Beach	437.5	4 267	0.0	66.2	82.5	57.3	90.1	61.39	246	3 999
Winter Garden	22.0	596	0.0	NA	NA	NA	NA	NA	NA	NA
Winter Haven	89.2	2 549	27.3	62.3	82.3	51.0	92.5	50.22	538	3 551
Winter Park	187.9	6 488	28.7	NA	NA	NA	NA	NA	NA	NA
Winter Springs	34.5	1 028	14.4	60.9	82.4	49.9	92.2	48.35	580	3 428

1. Based on the population estimated as of July 1 of the year shown.   2. Represents normal values based on the 30-year period, 1971–2000.   3. Average daily minimum.
4. Average daily maximum.

Table D. Cities — Land Area and Population

STATE Place code	City	Population, 2016 Land area,[1] 2016 (sq mi)	Total persons	Rank	Per square mile	Race alone[2] (percent), 2015 White	Black or African American	American Indian, Alaska Native	Asian	Hawaiian Pacific Islander	Some other race	2 or more races[2]
		1	2	3	4	5	6	7	8	9	10	11
13 00000	GEORGIA..............	57 594.8	10 310 371	X	179.0	59.5	31.3	0.3	3.8	0.0	2.8	2.3
13 01052	Albany	55.1	73 801	475	1 339.4	23.5	74.4	0.5	0.6	0.0	0.0	0.9
13 01696	Alpharetta	26.9	65 338	549	2 428.9	67.6	14.9	1.2	14.1	0.0	1.8	0.3
13 03436	Athens-Clarke County ...	119.2	123 371	220	1 059.9	63.1	27.1	0.0	4.1	0.2	3.1	2.3
13 04000	Atlanta	133.5	472 522	38	3 539.5	40.8	51.9	0.3	4.4	0.1	0.5	2.0
13 04200	Augusta-Richmond County	324.3	197 081	120	651.5	37.8	56.0	0.2	1.9	0.0	1.8	2.3
13 19000	Columbus	216.4	197 485	119	912.6	45.4	45.1	0.3	2.2	0.3	2.8	3.9
13 21380	Dalton	20.3	34 077	1 113	1 678.7	77.3	7.7	0.3	3.6	0.0	10.5	0.7
13 23900	Douglasville	22.5	33 252	1 142	1 477.9	36.1	57.3	0.0	3.7	0.0	1.0	1.9
13 24600	Duluth	10.1	29 331	1 271	2 904.1	46.7	36.7	0.0	14.3	0.0	1.0	1.3
13 24768	Dunwoody	13.0	48 884	777	3 760.3	NA	NA	NA	NA	NA	NA	NA
13 25720	East Point	14.7	35 471	1 076	2 413.0	11.7	80.2	0.2	3.1	0.0	4.2	0.7
13 31908	Gainesville	33.0	40 000	946	1 212.1	77.8	10.5	0.0	1.8	0.0	8.4	1.5
13 38964	Hinesville	18.1	33 577	1 128	1 855.1	45.2	45.1	0.8	4.2	0.2	1.8	2.6
13 42425	Johns Creek	30.8	83 873	396	2 723.1	56.0	12.6	0.6	27.3	0.0	0.8	2.7
13 43192	Kennesaw	9.6	33 627	1 127	3 502.8	58.6	22.2	0.2	7.4	0.0	5.9	5.7
13 44340	LaGrange	42.0	30 771	1 224	732.6	NA	NA	NA	NA	NA	NA	NA
13 45488	Lawrenceville	13.4	30 782	1 223	2 297.2	53.5	36.2	0.0	5.3	0.0	3.5	1.5
13 49008	Macon-Bibb County......	249.3	152 555	168	611.9	41.2	54.9	0.1	1.9	0.0	1.1	0.9
13 49756	Marietta	23.3	60 941	602	2 615.5	57.8	32.4	0.3	2.6	0.4	3.6	2.9
13 51670	Milton	38.5	38 411	988	997.7	NA	NA	NA	NA	NA	NA	NA
13 55020	Newnan	19.1	37 912	1 006	1 984.9	57.5	37.5	0.0	2.7	0.0	0.5	1.8
13 59724	Peachtree City	24.5	35 186	1 079	1 436.2	85.1	6.0	0.0	4.6	0.0	0.2	4.1
13 66668	Rome.......................	31.8	36 407	1 046	1 144.9	60.2	26.9	0.4	3.2	0.0	7.4	1.9
13 67284	Roswell	40.7	94 598	332	2 324.3	71.6	14.8	0.5	6.8	0.0	3.9	2.4
13 68516	Sandy Springs.............	37.7	105 703	284	2 803.8	73.5	13.6	1.0	6.9	0.0	3.3	1.7
13 69000	Savannah	103.6	146 763	179	1 416.6	37.0	54.4	0.6	3.4	0.0	1.6	3.0
13 71492	Smyrna	15.6	56 664	661	3 632.3	46.3	35.3	0.0	6.2	0.0	9.0	3.1
13 73256	Statesboro	14.8	31 419	1 198	2 122.9	47.7	45.7	0.0	2.7	0.0	1.4	2.4
13 73704	Stockbridge	13.2	28 677	1 299	2 172.5	29.3	59.5	0.0	6.2	0.0	4.0	1.1
13 78800	Valdosta	35.9	56 474	665	1 573.1	38.2	56.4	0.0	2.3	0.0	2.3	0.8
13 80508	Warner Robins	36.1	74 388	471	2 060.6	52.9	37.4	0.2	2.9	0.0	1.5	5.1
15 00000	HAWAII....................	6 422.5	1 428 557	X	222.4	26.0	2.1	0.3	37.1	9.4	0.7	24.5
15 06290	East Honolulu CDP	23.0	NA	NA	NA	30.1	0.4	0.1	45.0	3.6	0.5	20.4
15 14650	Hilo CDP	53.4	NA	NA	NA	21.0	0.6	0.1	38.4	9.3	0.5	30.0
15 22700	Kahului CDP...............	14.4	NA	NA	NA	13.9	0.6	0.0	44.7	9.1	0.4	31.4
15 23150	Kailua CDP (Honolulu County)..........	7.8	NA	NA	NA	50.6	1.8	0.2	16.9	4.0	1.2	25.3
15 28250	Kaneohe CDP	6.5	NA	NA	NA	22.5	2.4	0.0	33.3	6.9	0.9	34.0
15 51050	Mililani Town CDP........	4.0	NA	NA	NA	15.5	3.0	0.5	41.1	4.5	0.3	38.0
15 62600	Pearl City CDP............	9.1	NA	NA	NA	13.5	3.0	0.2	46.9	4.5	0.7	31.2
15 71550	Urban Honolulu CDP	60.5	351 792	55	5 814.7	19.0	1.9	0.1	54.9	6.4	0.6	17.0
15 79700	Waipahu CDP	2.7	NA	NA	NA	1.7	1.1	0.0	64.1	20.0	0.0	13.0
16 00000	IDAHO.....................	82 642.4	1 683 140	X	20.4	91.5	0.5	1.4	1.3	0.1	2.3	2.9
16 08830	Boise City.................	82.1	223 154	99	2 718.1	90.4	1.5	0.6	3.1	0.1	0.9	3.5
16 12250	Caldwell....................	22.2	53 149	713	2 394.1	84.0	0.3	3.3	1.6	0.0	7.4	3.4
16 16750	Coeur d'Alene	15.7	50 285	754	3 202.9	NA	NA	NA	NA	NA	NA	NA
16 39700	Idaho Falls	22.7	60 211	612	2 652.5	92.8	0.4	0.3	2.4	0.0	2.7	1.5
16 46540	Lewiston	17.3	32 872	1 157	1 900.1	NA	NA	NA	NA	NA	NA	NA
16 52120	Meridian	29.7	95 623	324	3 219.6	91.8	2.0	0.5	2.4	0.4	1.5	1.4
16 56260	Nampa......................	31.6	91 382	350	2 891.8	85.5	0.3	0.8	0.8	0.8	7.3	4.6
16 64090	Pocatello...................	32.5	54 746	689	1 684.5	90.8	1.1	2.2	1.7	0.5	2.0	1.6
16 64810	Post Falls	14.4	31 865	1 184	2 212.8	NA	NA	NA	NA	NA	NA	NA
16 67420	Rexburg....................	9.7	28 222	1 317	2 909.5	NA	NA	NA	NA	NA	NA	NA
16 82810	Twin Falls	18.3	48 260	791	2 637.2	91.1	0.0	1.0	4.0	0.0	1.8	2.2
17 00000	ILLINOIS..................	55 517.1	12 801 539	X	230.6	71.8	14.3	0.2	5.2	0.0	6.0	2.3
17 00243	Addison	9.8	36 902	1 031	3 765.5	77.7	1.4	0.0	8.1	0.0	8.7	4.1
17 00685	Algonquin	12.3	30 947	1 214	2 516.0	NA	NA	NA	NA	NA	NA	NA
17 01114	Alton	15.5	26 861	1 372	1 733.0	NA	NA	NA	NA	NA	NA	NA
17 02154	Arlington Heights..........	16.6	75 525	460	4 549.7	84.7	1.5	0.1	11.7	0.2	0.4	1.5
17 03012	Aurora	44.9	201 110	111	4 479.1	55.1	10.2	0.3	7.8	0.0	24.0	2.5
17 04013	Bartlett	15.8	41 178	920	2 606.2	NA	NA	NA	NA	NA	NA	NA
17 04078	Batavia	9.6	26 391	1 389	2 749.1	NA	NA	NA	NA	NA	NA	NA
17 04845	Belleville	23.2	41 906	902	1 806.3	NA	NA	NA	NA	NA	NA	NA
17 05092	Belvidere	12.1	25 070	1 421	2 071.9	NA	NA	NA	NA	NA	NA	NA
17 05573	Berwyn	3.9	55 748	671	14 294.4	52.5	4.1	0.8	1.9	0.0	38.8	1.9
17 06613	Bloomington	27.1	78 005	433	2 878.4	75.8	13.3	0.1	7.2	0.0	1.4	2.1
17 07133	Bolingbrook	24.1	74 518	467	3 092.0	53.7	16.3	0.1	12.0	0.0	14.5	3.4
17 09447	Buffalo Grove	9.5	41 346	916	4 352.2	75.3	1.8	0.0	19.8	0.0	1.2	1.9

1. Dry land or land partially or temporarily covered by water.   2. Hispanic or Latino persons may be of any race.

Table D. Cities — **Population**

City	Percent Hispanic or Latino[1], 2015	Percent foreign born 2015	Age of population (percent), 2010-2014							Median age 2015	Percent female 2015	Population			
			Under 18 years	18 to 24 years	25 to 34 years	35 to 44 years	45 to 54 years	55 to 64 years	65 years and over			Census counts		Percent change	
												2000	2010	2000–2010	2010–2016
	12	13	14	15	16	17	18	19	20	21	22	23	24	25	26
GEORGIA	9.3	10.0	24.5	10.1	13.5	13.6	13.7	11.8	12.8	36.4	51.3	8 186 453	9 688 680	18.4	6.4
Albany	2.5	1.2	24.4	14.0	13.2	11.0	12.4	12.3	12.8	33.3	55.4	76 939	77 434	0.6	-4.7
Alpharetta	7.8	21.9	29.6	6.0	9.8	13.7	21.7	12.7	6.4	38.7	48.6	34 854	57 384	64.6	13.9
Athens-Clarke County	10.7	10.5	17.4	29.4	15.2	11.0	8.6	8.7	9.7	26.5	53.2	101 489	115 453	13.8	6.9
Atlanta	4.0	6.9	17.9	13.1	21.1	14.8	11.4	10.0	11.8	33.8	51.7	416 474	420 425	0.9	12.4
Augusta-Richmond County	4.6	4.0	23.3	11.4	16.7	11.4	11.6	12.5	13.1	33.7	51.8	199 775	195 843	-2.0	0.6
Columbus	7.6	5.2	24.2	11.4	16.5	12.7	11.5	11.4	12.3	33.7	50.8	186 291	190 545	2.3	3.6
Dalton	50.5	28.8	30.1	9.5	17.0	17.1	7.4	8.2	10.7	31.5	52.8	27 912	33 108	18.6	2.9
Douglasville	4.1	10.7	22.4	6.9	15.6	14.0	15.9	13.4	11.7	38.9	48.0	20 065	30 958	54.3	7.4
Duluth	8.3	21.2	23.6	10.5	14.6	14.0	16.6	9.9	10.8	35.6	54.2	22 122	26 604	20.3	10.3
Dunwoody	10.7	29.1	28.2	4.2	15.7	18.2	14.7	7.8	11.2	35.9	47.8	32 808	46 281	41.1	5.6
East Point	5.7	6.0	22.8	8.7	17.5	13.8	16.0	10.7	10.6	35.7	53.9	39 595	33 722	-14.8	5.2
Gainesville	47.8	30.1	26.5	14.7	13.9	14.4	11.3	9.6	9.7	31.4	52.1	25 578	35 303	38.0	13.3
Hinesville	15.3	8.9	25.6	12.0	19.8	12.3	12.3	10.2	7.9	31.0	48.9	30 392	33 415	9.9	0.5
Johns Creek	7.1	34.8	28.2	8.0	9.1	16.1	16.5	12.8	9.3	39.0	51.7	NA	76 727	NA	9.3
Kennesaw	6.2	15.5	20.8	12.7	18.7	9.9	15.1	13.2	9.5	32.3	47.7	21 675	30 575	41.1	10.0
LaGrange	5.3	7.6	27.3	9.8	14.2	14.8	11.5	11.6	10.9	32.9	57.6	25 998	29 445	13.3	4.5
Lawrenceville	15.9	20.1	23.0	10.1	15.8	10.1	11.4	14.1	15.5	36.3	52.7	22 397	28 391	26.8	8.4
Macon-Bibb County	3.2	3.2	24.9	10.4	13.5	11.6	12.4	12.8	14.4	36.0	53.2	NA	155 303	NA	-1.8
Marietta	13.2	19.1	23.1	12.0	15.8	17.5	11.2	8.6	11.7	34.2	53.4	58 748	56 628	-3.6	7.6
Milton	8.1	13.3	35.0	6.5	6.4	18.8	14.9	8.9	9.4	36.2	52.0	NA	32 842	NA	17.0
Newnan	9.6	6.7	33.1	7.5	14.1	16.6	11.2	8.2	9.3	31.1	53.0	16 242	32 723	101.5	15.9
Peachtree City	9.9	10.4	25.0	9.9	7.5	16.3	16.1	12.0	13.2	39.7	49.3	31 580	34 364	8.8	2.4
Rome	18.3	11.1	26.8	11.7	12.5	12.5	13.9	10.2	12.5	33.3	50.7	34 980	36 645	4.8	-0.6
Roswell	17.9	17.5	26.7	6.2	12.0	14.9	17.0	13.4	9.9	38.8	48.5	79 334	88 337	11.3	7.1
Sandy Springs	13.0	18.8	23.1	7.7	18.6	14.0	11.1	11.6	14.0	35.4	53.9	85 781	93 822	9.4	12.7
Savannah	6.7	7.1	21.3	17.2	18.3	10.4	10.7	10.4	11.7	30.3	52.4	131 510	136 963	4.1	7.2
Smyrna	15.0	16.2	24.6	4.9	16.8	17.4	15.0	8.8	12.4	37.0	52.2	40 999	51 373	25.3	10.3
Statesboro	3.2	4.0	16.1	45.2	14.6	7.8	5.3	4.6	6.4	22.1	48.5	22 698	28 380	25.0	10.7
Stockbridge	8.5	13.0	27.7	9.3	11.5	15.5	13.9	10.6	11.5	37.1	50.6	9 853	26 350	167.4	8.8
Valdosta	4.9	3.8	21.9	19.9	15.8	9.7	10.2	9.5	13.0	28.1	54.2	43 724	54 764	25.2	3.1
Warner Robins	7.3	4.3	27.5	11.3	17.7	10.9	12.1	9.9	10.6	31.4	52.6	48 804	68 560	40.5	8.5
HAWAII	10.4	17.7	21.7	9.4	15.1	12.4	12.2	12.6	16.6	37.7	49.4	1 211 537	1 360 301	12.3	5.0
East Honolulu CDP	3.8	14.1	19.9	3.9	9.2	12.8	13.7	17.2	23.3	47.9	49.1	NA	NA	NA	NA
Hilo CDP	13.3	8.0	19.5	12.4	11.8	12.0	11.6	15.3	17.4	40.2	49.1	40 759	43 263	6.1	NA
Kahului CDP	11.5	29.0	26.1	6.8	12.7	14.4	11.4	10.2	18.5	37.5	43.2	20 146	26 337	30.7	NA
Kailua CDP (Honolulu County)	6.8	9.0	19.6	7.1	17.3	13.0	11.4	13.5	18.1	39.3	50.9	36 513	38 635	5.8	NA
Kaneohe CDP	11.8	4.3	23.1	6.2	17.3	12.6	10.6	13.1	17.0	36.7	49.3	34 970	34 597	-1.1	NA
Mililani Town CDP	13.5	7.7	23.1	8.4	13.2	14.0	9.4	11.5	20.4	37.8	47.8	28 608	27 629	-3.4	NA
Pearl City CDP	11.0	11.0	20.4	10.6	14.8	11.0	9.8	12.2	21.2	38.6	50.1	30 976	47 698	54.0	NA
Urban Honolulu CDP	7.0	28.7	16.1	9.3	16.3	12.7	13.1	13.3	19.1	41.4	49.9	NA	337 719	NA	4.2
Waipahu CDP	7.0	38.1	24.0	13.9	13.3	9.9	15.3	8.2	15.4	34.2	51.0	33 108	38 216	4.6	NA
IDAHO	12.1	5.7	26.1	9.5	13.1	12.4	12.0	12.2	14.7	35.8	50.0	1 293 953	1 567 650	21.2	7.4
Boise City	8.9	6.1	23.8	10.7	15.7	14.5	12.0	11.5	11.8	34.9	49.6	185 787	208 341	12.1	7.1
Caldwell	37.7	10.7	32.3	10.4	12.9	12.8	11.0	10.2	10.3	31.1	52.6	25 967	46 314	78.4	14.8
Coeur d'Alene	3.8	2.4	20.4	9.2	16.7	12.3	13.1	13.6	14.6	37.2	51.0	34 514	44 135	27.9	13.9
Idaho Falls	11.9	5.5	28.5	9.9	13.1	12.8	11.9	10.1	13.7	33.4	49.6	50 730	57 038	12.4	5.6
Lewiston	1.5	0.8	21.9	7.5	12.9	12.4	11.2	13.6	20.4	42.4	52.0	30 904	31 896	3.2	3.1
Meridian	7.3	8.9	27.5	5.8	11.5	14.1	13.1	11.3	16.7	38.0	52.2	34 919	76 056	117.8	25.7
Nampa	24.6	7.4	31.1	8.6	15.3	13.9	11.1	9.4	10.7	31.4	49.2	51 867	81 772	57.7	11.8
Pocatello	9.3	5.1	24.9	14.1	16.6	11.7	9.3	10.2	13.1	31.1	51.9	51 466	54 230	5.4	1.0
Post Falls	4.9	3.1	24.6	7.4	13.5	11.7	11.7	10.1	20.9	37.1	48.5	17 247	27 710	60.7	15.0
Rexburg	3.3	2.3	19.6	40.2	20.1	3.8	4.8	5.1	6.4	23.6	53.1	17 257	25 473	47.6	10.8
Twin Falls	12.6	8.4	27.2	9.9	17.9	11.8	9.4	9.5	14.3	32.0	54.4	34 469	44 323	28.6	8.9
ILLINOIS	16.9	14.2	23.0	9.6	13.8	13.0	13.6	12.8	14.2	37.7	50.9	12 419 293	12 831 574	3.3	-0.2
Addison	36.9	30.9	21.1	9.1	15.7	11.5	16.5	12.2	13.8	37.7	46.4	35 914	36 967	2.9	-0.2
Algonquin	6.1	10.1	24.0	14.3	5.2	12.1	21.7	12.4	10.4	40.6	52.9	23 276	30 049	29.1	3.0
Alton	1.2	1.1	23.2	5.3	19.3	9.4	14.2	15.0	13.5	38.0	54.7	30 496	27 918	-8.5	-3.8
Arlington Heights	3.6	19.0	19.9	5.0	11.5	12.5	15.2	15.1	20.8	45.9	51.1	76 031	75 089	-1.2	0.6
Aurora	42.5	25.0	30.6	9.2	15.3	16.0	12.7	8.5	7.7	31.7	49.9	142 990	197 947	38.4	1.6
Bartlett	8.7	19.9	22.3	7.3	13.4	14.0	16.4	15.1	11.5	39.3	49.4	36 706	41 202	12.2	-0.1
Batavia	9.4	5.1	24.5	10.8	5.8	12.9	18.0	15.6	12.4	42.2	48.6	23 866	26 162	9.6	0.9
Belleville	1.2	1.5	27.7	5.7	15.7	13.7	10.9	12.3	13.9	35.4	51.1	41 410	44 357	7.1	-5.5
Belvidere	32.8	13.5	28.6	9.1	13.9	10.0	16.3	9.1	13.0	34.1	54.1	20 820	25 585	22.9	-2.0
Berwyn	71.9	26.7	27.3	10.8	11.1	18.1	14.2	8.4	10.0	35.5	50.1	54 016	56 653	4.9	-1.6
Bloomington	4.4	9.3	22.1	11.1	16.7	13.5	11.9	12.2	12.5	35.1	51.5	64 808	76 692	18.3	1.7
Bolingbrook	23.4	21.1	27.2	10.1	13.7	15.5	13.8	10.8	9.0	33.7	49.7	56 321	73 357	30.2	1.6
Buffalo Grove	4.7	29.3	24.0	5.3	10.5	16.8	15.5	12.2	15.7	42.1	50.3	42 909	41 442	-3.4	-0.2

1. May be of any race.

Table D. Cities — Households, Group Quarters, Crime, and Education

City	Households, 2015				Persons in group quarters, 2010				Serious crimes known to police,[2] 2014				Educational attainment, 2015		
			Percent			Institutional			Total		Rate[3]			Attainment[4] (percent)	
	Number	Persons per house-hold	Female family house-holder[1]	One-person	Total	Total	Persons in nursing facilities	Non-institu-tional	Number	Rate[3]	Violent	Property	Population age 25 and older	High school graduate or less	Bachelor's degree or more
	27	28	29	30	31	32	33	34	35	36	37	38	39	40	41
GEORGIA	3 656 407	2.72	15.0	26.9	253 199	144 545	34 738	108 654	369 413	3 659	377	3 281	6 683 767	42.0	29.9
Albany	28 359	2.38	28.3	36.0	4 288	1 421	400	2 867	4 971	6 553	1 022	5 531	43 839	50.7	19.0
Alpharetta	23 300	2.73	13.0	22.5	69	57	19	12	1 292	2 035	60	1 975	40 980	12.5	67.2
Athens-Clarke County	46 029	2.44	12.7	36.2	9 183	779	348	8 404	4 164	3 427	306	3 121	65 121	33.7	44.8
Atlanta	200 503	2.15	12.8	50.3	29 484	6 756	1 626	22 728	31 691	6 975	1 227	5 747	320 178	29.6	48.3
Augusta-Richmond County	69 567	2.67	21.6	32.9	10 508	3 907	1 137	6 601	3 224	1 626	127	1 499	128 275	46.4	21.1
Columbus	73 961	2.62	17.9	33.3	7 017	3 486	898	3 531	14 479	7 004	533	6 472	129 080	42.6	24.5
Dalton	11 284	2.95	14.8	32.1	904	754	340	150	1 332	3 980	269	3 711	20 457	58.3	15.0
Douglasville	13 208	2.42	19.1	35.0	937	826	0	111	2 241	6 979	579	6 399	23 256	32.1	35.6
Duluth	11 254	2.59	16.4	25.5	34	0	0	34	624	2 163	94	2 069	19 238	26.5	46.2
Dunwoody	19 058	2.56	8.3	30.3	154	0	0	154	2 244	4 683	121	4 562	32 906	15.0	69.2
East Point	14 712	2.39	21.5	43.6	420	44	27	376	4 220	11 745	1 291	10 454	24 305	41.0	24.4
Gainesville	13 467	2.79	21.0	26.7	1 713	649	434	1 064	1 623	4 512	364	4 148	22 779	57.7	19.8
Hinesville	13 270	2.48	21.7	29.8	310	263	0	47	1 599	4 631	469	4 162	20 870	39.9	18.0
Johns Creek	26 064	3.19	6.8	14.9	0	0	0	0	622	738	33	705	53 204	15.6	65.6
Kennesaw	13 346	2.51	13.6	25.7	244	244	99	0	545	1 681	114	1 566	22 317	34.4	31.9
LaGrange	10 600	2.81	31.2	34.6	1 242	627	381	615	1 903	6 203	411	5 792	19 320	53.6	16.5
Lawrenceville	11 010	2.73	17.4	20.0	268	238	238	30	957	3 166	175	2 991	20 423	41.9	26.2
Macon-Bibb County	59 683	2.46	18.6	35.5	NA	NA	NA	NA					99 357	46.4	25.3
Marietta	23 824	2.36	16.7	35.7	1 769	758	730	1 011	2 957	4 956	508	4 448	38 323	34.1	38.6
Milton	10 981	3.42	10.6	12.1	4	0	0	4	372	1 014	19	994	21 959	16.8	64.3
Newnan	13 664	2.70	18.9	26.1	518	518	135	0	1 202	3 412	483	2 929	22 140	42.6	26.8
Peachtree City	12 592	2.79	6.9	24.5	118	118	118	0	453	1 295	29	1 266	22 961	17.9	55.6
Rome	12 759	2.72	19.3	34.3	1 606	1 409	447	197	2 442	6 806	672	6 135	22 361	53.9	20.2
Roswell	34 758	2.70	8.3	22.7	516	356	305	160	1 899	1 991	115	1 876	63 428	21.3	56.2
Sandy Springs	43 687	2.40	6.4	37.5	327	205	205	122	2 904	2 870	157	2 713	72 940	18.5	62.1
Savannah	52 331	2.57	25.0	31.5	10 014	4 499	584	5 515	9 434	3 986	392	3 594	89 699	39.3	28.0
Smyrna	23 709	2.36	14.4	29.8	279	269	112	10	1 707	3 163	287	2 876	39 558	25.8	50.2
Statesboro	10 498	2.32	26.0	18.0	4 290	266	266	4 024	1 166	3 848	271	3 578	11 887	29.2	33.5
Stockbridge	10 199	2.76	22.6	20.0	8	0	0	8	NA	NA	NA	NA	17 771	33.3	35.9
Valdosta	20 231	2.65	16.4	45.3	4 122	1 147	444	2 975	3 492	6 141	329	5 812	32 447	46.9	25.2
Warner Robins	29 451	2.50	23.3	26.8	338	223	208	115	4 853	6 610	448	6 162	45 278	34.4	19.4
HAWAII	445 936	3.11	11.7	23.4	42 880	11 306	5 198	31 574	46 977	3 309	259	3 050	985 914	36.3	31.4
East Honolulu CDP	16 464	2.80	9.8	18.9	235	160	160	75	NA	NA	NA	NA	35 372	20.9	53.1
Hilo CDP	15 286	2.78	11.4	33.0	1 648	605	575	1 043	NA	NA	NA	NA	29 934	33.5	37.3
Kahului CDP	6 860	4.19	13.1	12.7	1 740	1 296	564	444	NA	NA	NA	NA	20 288	54.1	18.1
Kailua CDP (Honolulu County)	12 466	2.92	10.7	18.5	119	30	8	89	NA	NA	NA	NA	26 867	23.7	47.5
Kaneohe CDP	10 602	3.26	11.8	21.6	643	411	411	232	NA	NA	NA	NA	24 982	34.3	34.4
Mililani Town CDP	8 606	3.35	10.2	17.5	0	0	0	0	NA	NA	NA	NA	19 748	33.6	35.0
Pearl City CDP	12 923	3.28	8.9	17.7	3 694	165	156	3 529	NA	NA	NA	NA	30 577	32.9	29.0
Urban Honolulu CDP	126 072	2.69	11.8	31.5	13 052	4 247	1 823	8 805	NA	NA	NA	NA	262 999	36.8	35.4
Waipahu CDP	8 149	4.72	15.6	16.0	910	390	369	520	NA	NA	NA	NA	24 781	50.2	18.5
IDAHO	597 421	2.72	9.4	27.2	28 951	17 076	4 820	11 875	33 784	2 067	212	1 855	1 065 982	37.4	26.0
Boise City	82 631	2.61	10.2	32.6	3 717	1 762	548	1 955	5 137	2 375	289	2 087	142 993	25.9	39.7
Caldwell	15 894	3.18	21.9	27.2	1 532	913	149	619	1 541	3 107	325	2 782	29 601	55.6	13.9
Coeur d'Alene	20 591	2.31	7.5	30.6	1 215	813	428	402	2 067	4 402	513	3 889	34 550	30.9	23.8
Idaho Falls	20 629	2.80	11.6	25.8	1 011	477	72	534	1 627	2 776	215	2 561	36 467	37.6	29.9
Lewiston	12 926	2.37	13.5	29.9	966	594	385	372	1 193	3 668	172	3 496	22 344	42.0	24.5
Meridian	35 695	2.54	5.8	34.6	307	126	103	181	1 308	1 526	89	1 437	60 530	28.7	35.2
Nampa	29 557	2.98	11.1	29.5	1 751	540	360	1 211	2 806	3 198	320	2 878	54 230	47.2	18.2
Pocatello	20 533	2.57	13.2	28.6	1 519	630	307	889	1 359	2 500	258	2 242	33 154	34.9	28.6
Post Falls	12 478	2.42	9.3	28.4	84	42	42	42	903	3 033	171	2 861	20 688	44.2	14.8
Rexburg	6 266	3.71	6.4	17.6	1 027	127	44	900	277	1 035	34	1 001	9 608	25.0	34.5
Twin Falls	17 380	2.67	12.7	25.2	897	592	314	305	1 586	3 421	255	3 167	29 872	35.0	22.1
ILLINOIS	4 794 523	2.62	12.5	29.4	301 773	159 989	81 516	141 784	315 048	2 446	370	2 076	8 661 938	38.2	32.9
Addison	12 830	2.74	7.0	32.3	112	46	0	66	677	1 806	173	1 633	24 583	49.2	23.5
Algonquin	9 571	2.96	9.2	17.4	0	0	0	0	465	1 521	59	1 462	17 518	24.6	43.0
Alton	11 267	2.34	19.0	41.1	518	356	202	162	1 383	5 093	545	4 548	19 296	44.9	14.9
Arlington Heights	32 014	2.38	6.1	28.7	723	545	538	178	786	1 031	56	975	57 808	17.8	56.6
Aurora	61 166	3.30	11.9	20.0	2 477	751	577	1 726	3 540	1 766	278	1 488	122 593	44.6	29.8
Bartlett	13 953	2.83	7.2	19.5	58	58	58	0	250	598	34	565	27 865	27.3	42.2
Batavia	10 141	2.66	11.8	22.7	157	148	148	9	408	1 543	136	1 407	17 500	21.0	48.7
Belleville	16 934	2.41	19.3	37.8	1 246	1 167	740	79	1 731	4 063	422	3 640	27 998	33.9	25.8
Belvidere	9 006	2.94	12.6	25.7	230	221	150	9	481	1 902	182	1 720	16 652	54.5	12.5
Berwyn	17 909	3.14	14.4	19.8	52	17	14	35	1 290	2 272	224	2 048	34 893	52.7	21.5
Bloomington	32 583	2.34	6.4	30.7	2 234	566	280	1 668	2 029	2 554	419	2 135	52 286	29.7	50.9
Bolingbrook	20 989	3.42	11.6	15.0	279	279	279	0	1 142	1 542	211	1 332	45 224	33.1	35.4
Buffalo Grove	15 787	2.65	8.1	21.1	118	112	112	6	299	715	24	691	29 679	13.9	65.6

1. No spouse present.   2. Data for serious crimes have not been adjusted for underreporting. This may affect comparability between geographic areas and over time.   3. Per 100,000 population estimated by the FBI.   4. Persons 25 years old and over.

Table D. Cities — Income, Poverty, and Housing

City	Money income, 2015 Households			Families		Housing units, 2010			Occupied housing units 2015 Owner-occupied			Renter-occupied	
	Median income	Percent with income of $200,000 or more	Percent with income of less than $25,000	Total Families	Percent with income below poverty	Total	Percent change, 2000–2010	Vacant units for sale or rent[2]	Total	Percent	Median value[3] (dollars)	Percent	Median rent (dollars)
	42	43	44	45	46	47	48	49	50	51	52	53	54
GEORGIA..................	51 244	4.6	18.5	2 466 415	13.0	4 088 801	24.6	503 217	3 656 407	61.8	159 300	38.2	909
Albany.......................	31 897	1.0	32.6	16 169	25.8	33 436	3.9	3 655	28 359	36.6	92 600	63.4	678
Alpharetta.................	108 510	20.8	6.6	17 026	5.5	23 029	57.2	1 287	23 300	62.2	385 700	37.8	1 313
Athens-Clarke County ...	31 141	2.3	37.0	21 173	24.4	51 068	21.2	5 654	46 029	38.6	153 400	61.4	800
Atlanta.....................	50 210	8.6	22.7	77 962	19.2	224 573	20.1	39 431	200 503	40.2	241 200	59.8	981
Augusta-Richmond County	41 190	1.7	25.4	42 862	18.7	86 331	4.9	9 407	69 567	55.1	101 700	44.9	800
Columbus..................	41 859	2.9	26.0	45 611	17.3	82 690	8.5	8 609	73 961	46.4	137 000	53.6	844
Dalton......................	39 588	4.0	20.3	7 194	13.7	13 378	29.8	2 041	11 284	42.7	121 600	57.3	664
Douglasville..............	56 935	3.9	18.1	7 881	7.9	13 163	66.4	1 536	13 208	39.8	149 900	60.2	973
Duluth......................	56 818	4.8	13.8	7 461	13.7	11 313	23.6	758	11 254	46.8	214 700	53.2	1 124
Dunwoody..................	86 036	14.8	6.0	11 704	7.6	21 671	48.4	1 727	19 058	51.8	408 200	48.2	1 447
East Point.................	40 063	0.0	22.2	6 652	22.4	17 225	11.1	3 892	14 712	37.1	115 800	62.9	894
Gainesville................	45 428	7.6	25.4	9 129	27.9	12 967	45.5	1 694	13 467	33.8	181 700	66.2	800
Hinesville.................	36 501	0.0	25.9	8 472	19.9	14 653	24.4	2 329	13 270	48.5	117 100	51.5	871
Johns Creek..............	116 210	20.5	4.0	21 439	3.1	27 744	NA	1 478	26 064	78.0	373 700	22.0	1 309
Kennesaw..................	67 616	2.0	12.1	NA	NA	12 328	40.7	915	13 346	55.2	159 000	44.8	1 129
LaGrange..................	27 218	0.4	35.8	6 844	25.4	12 846	16.7	1 603	10 600	30.3	139 800	69.7	745
Lawrenceville............	49 387	0.4	25.1	8 370	21.2	11 187	45.8	1 214	11 010	52.6	154 800	47.4	904
Macon-Bibb County.......	38 704	2.6	29.1	35 782	17.8				59 683	54.0	106 700	46.0	755
Marietta....................	51 331	5.3	16.3	13 373	9.6	26 918	6.0	3 853	23 824	39.5	242 500	60.5	962
Milton......................	110 428	26.7	4.7	NA	NA	12 328	NA	669	10 981	77.3	494 100	22.7	1 145
Newnan.....................	55 803	5.2	22.8	9 703	18.7	13 860	108.6	1 421	13 664	54.9	183 900	45.1	860
Peachtree City...........	78 585	17.2	9.7	NA	NA	13 538	17.8	812	12 592	70.8	292 200	29.2	1 194
Rome........................	35 717	2.5	28.7	7 875	25.0	15 797	9.3	1 912	12 759	42.0	124 400	58.0	680
Roswell.....................	89 088	16.4	6.1	24 640	5.7	36 344	15.8	2 399	34 758	66.4	332 700	33.6	1 115
Sandy Springs............	71 996	17.5	9.5	24 406	4.9	46 955	9.9	4 621	43 687	51.4	415 000	48.6	1 147
Savannah..................	35 827	1.9	26.6	30 519	20.1	61 883	7.6	9 338	52 331	41.2	141 300	58.8	957
Smyrna.....................	64 122	7.4	14.1	14 468	10.0	25 745	30.6	2 743	23 709	54.8	241 000	45.2	1 053
Statesboro................	24 049	0.3	42.8	5 734	36.2	11 602	25.3	1 395	10 498	19.0	117 100	81.0	727
Stockbridge..............	51 844	1.0	15.0	7 976	14.2	10 312	NA	813	10 199	56.8	121 200	43.2	1 002
Valdosta...................	25 792	1.3	36.7	8 957	27.5	22 709	19.5	2 238	20 231	35.1	130 000	64.9	711
Warner Robins	45 270	2.6	18.3	20 014	17.0	29 084	33.2	2 948	29 451	50.5	115 600	49.5	846
HAWAII.....................	73 486	7.4	11.9	309 386	6.9	519 508	12.8	64 170	445 936	56.6	566 900	43.4	1 500
East Honolulu CDP	125 602	24.6	5.9	12 855	3.2	18 774	NA	1 090	16 464	84.4	915 700	15.6	2 637
Hilo CDP	60 522	2.1	17.9	8 834	6.7	16 905	5.5	1 422	15 286	62.1	297 100	37.9	1 090
Kahului CDP...............	75 893	5.1	11.9	5 764	7.8	7 773	28.6	662	6 860	53.4	560 300	46.6	1 357
Kailua CDP (Honolulu County)	97 784	12.9	7.1	8 942	4.0	13 650	6.9	729	12 466	62.2	868 000	37.8	2 312
Kaneohe CDP	95 756	8.8	5.6	7 621	4.2	11 553	0.7	415	10 602	67.2	680 900	32.8	1 625
Mililani Town CDP........	91 997	11.1	4.5	6 865	4.0	9 272	0.0	234	8 606	75.2	596 800	24.8	1 858
Pearl City CDP............	96 982	11.9	5.2	10 292	0.8	14 622	60.5	354	12 923	65.5	657 800	34.5	1 907
Urban Honolulu CDP	64 658	7.1	14.6	73 295	7.2	143 173	NA	13 765	126 072	42.9	641 900	57.1	1 394
Waipahu CDP	71 013	8.9	10.4	6 454	6.0	8 850	10.2	467	8 149	47.6	570 700	52.4	1 269
IDAHO	48 275	2.7	18.7	400 347	10.9	667 796	26.5	88 388	597 421	69.0	176 300	31.0	770
Boise City.................	55 309	4.9	16.8	48 020	8.9	92 700	18.9	6 996	82 631	58.9	209 900	41.1	864
Caldwell....................	37 704	0.0	25.5	10 952	19.2	16 323	68.4	1 428	15 839	66.6	120 200	33.4	675
Coeur d'Alene	43 448	2.8	23.6	12 347	14.6	20 219	36.8	1 824	20 591	58.0	183 400	42.0	860
Idaho Falls................	47 623	4.4	18.5	14 219	11.9	22 977	15.9	1 774	20 629	61.8	154 400	38.2	798
Lewiston...................	52 289	1.5	18.5	8 521	8.8	14 057	5.0	733	12 926	72.1	173 200	27.9	689
Meridian....................	54 746	3.2	16.2	22 111	4.1	26 674	117.1	1 372	35 695	76.8	213 100	23.2	987
Nampa......................	40 884	0.2	20.8	18 970	11.3	30 507	56.2	2 778	29 557	65.3	132 900	34.7	771
Pocatello..................	34 238	0.8	28.7	11 862	22.0	22 404	8.3	1 572	20 533	57.7	137 900	42.3	644
Post Falls	42 912	0.0	30.0	8 064	22.8	11 150	66.7	887	12 478	73.4	175 800	26.6	780
Rexburg....................	30 007	0.8	46.3	NA	NA	7 617	69.2	438	6 266	34.7	196 700	65.3	625
Twin Falls	44 227	0.6	15.6	12 443	12.2	18 033	27.4	1 289	17 380	62.3	137 900	37.7	724
ILLINOIS	59 588	6.4	15.9	3 099 463	9.8	5 296 715	8.4	459 743	4 794 523	65.3	180 300	34.7	936
Addison	61 189	4.1	14.7	8 054	6.0	12 581	7.3	641	12 830	64.2	240 300	35.8	956
Algonquin	91 244	8.0	5.0	NA	NA	10 727	33.4	480	9 571	87.0	244 300	13.0	1 539
Alton	37 186	0.9	25.0	6 171	20.9	13 266	-4.5	1 532	11 267	62.0	80 700	38.0	792
Arlington Heights........	86 298	12.9	9.3	20 853	2.4	32 795	3.4	1 876	32 014	74.8	344 600	25.2	1 173
Aurora......................	63 355	6.5	12.1	45 387	11.8	67 273	37.5	4 709	61 166	61.9	169 400	38.1	1 095
Bartlett....................	100 485	9.5	4.1	NA	NA	14 509	17.4	436	13 953	88.8	254 800	11.2	1 405
Batavia.....................	86 473	9.9	8.6	NA	NA	10 042	13.9	488	10 141	73.8	285 600	26.2	968
Belleville	39 914	1.1	25.1	10 017	13.5	21 099	9.4	2 304	16 934	51.9	90 900	48.1	768
Belvidere..................	51 811	0.0	17.5	6 167	13.0	9 565	20.5	762	9 006	60.9	111 700	39.1	641
Berwyn	63 734	5.1	12.1	12 708	9.1	20 719	0.1	1 809	17 909	56.1	174 800	43.9	895
Bloomington	64 339	8.9	16.3	20 231	6.4	34 339	20.4	2 676	32 583	59.8	171 700	40.2	768
Bolingbrook	77 929	5.6	6.7	16 938	5.6	23 141	29.2	929	20 989	78.5	206 300	21.5	1 374
Buffalo Grove	104 632	17.0	6.7	12 039	1.8	17 034	6.9	828	15 787	77.8	318 200	22.2	1 572

1. Based on population estimated by the American Community Survey.   2. Includes units rented or sold but not occupied.   3. Specified owner-occupied units; $1,000,000 represents $1,000,000 or more   4. 50.0 represents 50 percent or more.   5. 10.0 represents 10 percent or less.

Table D. Cities — Commuting, Computer Access, Migration, Labor Force, and Employment

City	Commuting — Percent: Drove alone	With Commutes of 30 minutes or more[1]	Computer Access[2] — Percent: With a Computer in the house	With Internet Access	Migration, 2015: Percent who lived in the same house one year ago	Percent who lived in an other state or county one year ago	Civilian labor force, 2016: Total	Percent change, 2015–2016	Unemployment Total	Rate[3]	Civilian employment[4], 2015: Population age 16 and older Number	Percent in Labor Force	Population age 16 to 64 Number	Percent who worked full-year full-time
	55	56	57	58	59	60	61	62	63	64	65	66	67	68
GEORGIA.................	83.9	41.2	86.7	74.6	84.2	8.1	4 920 464	2.8	264 209	5.4	7 998 548	62.6	6 695 789	48.8
Albany	77.3	16.6	75.6	63.5	79.8	7.6	31 015	1.0	2 185	7.0	55 581	57.3	46 470	40.6
Alpharetta	91.8	40.5	95.9	92.2	85.4	8.4	34 818	3.5	1 477	4.2	46 895	75.4	42 803	56.1
Athens-Clarke County ...	74.2	14.6	87.6	73.3	71.5	15.9	58 904	3.1	3 323	5.6	103 312	59.3	91 482	34.4
Atlanta	74.8	35.7	87.4	69.1	79.9	9.8	241 781	3.1	14 022	5.8	387 266	65.5	332 549	52.0
Augusta-Richmond County ...	81.5	23.8	82.9	65.3	83.0	7.9	85 856	1.9	5 740	6.7	155 840	5 834.0	130 176	43.4
Columbus	82.1	20.7	82.9	68.1	76.7	11.8	78 724	-0.2	5 407	6.9	156 697	60.2	132 037	42.4
Dalton	0.0	14.5	81.8	70.2	80.3	5.7	14 726	1.7	908	6.2	25 375	67.3	21 767	56.7
Douglasville	81.2	48.8	92.1	82.8	79.6	12.7	16 549	3.0	955	5.8	26 842	67.0	22 977	51.2
Duluth	79.0	39.8	94.0	87.4	85.3	8.6	15 726	3.5	718	4.6	23 295	73.5	20 141	57.1
Dunwoody	82.7	40.5	95.9	90.6	86.5	7.8	26 698	3.3	1 041	3.9	36 038	72.0	30 604	60.6
East Point	62.8	48.0	83.7	65.7	77.3	6.3	16 936	2.6	1 213	7.2	28 181	70.6	24 427	52.0
Gainesville	72.3	32.0	82.5	58.6	81.1	7.3	18 122	3.5	865	4.8	29 584	61.3	25 848	50.5
Hinesville	83.5	28.3	92.9	81.4	67.2	17.1	14 686	1.1	780	5.3	25 470	65.4	22 844	47.1
Johns Creek	88.0	52.9	99.2	96.3	84.0	9.2	43 910	3.6	1 894	4.3	62 986	69.9	55 249	50.8
Kennesaw.................	77.8	53.0	94.0	89.4	81.3	7.7	19 469	3.4	850	4.4	26 948	76.5	23 747	56.6
LaGrange	84.1	27.6	77.3	62.4	89.3	4.1	15 236	2.6	901	5.9	22 880	61.3	19 533	41.3
Lawrenceville............	84.6	51.6	93.2	75.0	85.9	4.5	14 649	3.4	809	5.5	24 432	61.3	19 710	42.6
Macon-Bibb County.......	86.7	21.6	79.6	63.9	83.5	6.2	68 856	1.4	4 118	6.0	119 333	56.4	97 174	43.5
Marietta	81.2	45.7	93.5	79.1	80.0	8.2	34 190	3.3	1 598	4.7	46 197	71.2	39 267	56.2
Milton	89.7	37.3	NA	NA	82.2	11.2	19 074	3.6	819	4.3	25 587	69.1	22 050	52.0
Newnan	88.5	47.2	90.3	80.7	87.7	5.3	17 206	3.6	981	5.7	25 779	60.1	22 320	49.2
Peachtree City..............	94.4	48.6	94.6	90.7	86.6	8.2	18 103	3.5	796	4.4	27 434	63.7	22 770	44.5
Rome	89.4	21.0	74.7	66.9	76.1	9.4	15 305	1.2	960	6.3	27 394	59.3	22 838	44.1
Roswell....................	82.9	52.8	97.0	90.4	86.0	8.1	52 989	3.5	2 169	4.1	72 138	74.8	62 808	60.4
Sandy Springs............	85.8	37.8	93.8	86.7	83.8	9.6	62 729	3.5	2 594	4.1	83 950	70.5	69 220	60.3
Savannah	72.3	19.6	84.8	73.0	68.8	14.7	66 315	2.2	3 859	5.8	117 643	63.3	100 540	42.4
Smyrna....................	89.2	46.2	95.0	82.9	76.6	11.6	34 376	3.5	1 485	4.3	43 892	73.3	36 905	61.3
Statesboro................	83.3	18.1	95.6	61.8	53.1	25.9	13 959	3.0	1 026	7.4	26 354	54.7	24 390	26.0
Stockbridge	81.7	43.2	95.7	84.2	88.0	10.2	13 706	3.3	868	6.3	21 684	66.6	18 432	55.5
Valdosta	88.1	13.8	80.5	57.7	73.0	7.9	25 472	1.4	1 451	5.7	44 822	57.2	37 557	35.6
Warner Robins	93.2	22.0	82.5	70.5	78.8	8.0	32 036	2.5	1 810	5.6	55 056	68.3	47 208	55.9
HAWAII....................	70.7	42.9	89.1	82.1	85.3	5.6	685 378	1.6	20 688	3.0	1 152 884	65.5	915 731	54.5
East Honolulu CDP	77.5	66.5	95.0	91.2	89.9	1.8	NA	NA	NA	NA	38 088	62.5	27 287	54.8
Hilo CDP	79.0	16.0	81.7	76.5	88.6	2.7	NA	NA	NA	NA	36 715	57.4	29 050	42.7
Kahului CDP...............	81.2	32.9	92.4	84.2	NA	NA	NA	NA	NA	NA	23 205	62.1	17 620	49.9
Kailua CDP (Honolulu County)...	74.4	62.7	93.8	90.9	83.6	10.8	NA	NA	NA	NA	30 339	65.9	23 714	52.4
Kaneohe CDP	70.7	60.2	88.9	85.4	86.9	3.4	NA	NA	NA	NA	27 882	68.6	21 859	62.8
Mililani Town CDP........	83.1	53.6	89.5	87.7	89.5	3.7	NA	NA	NA	NA	22 953	67.0	17 061	58.6
Pearl City CDP	70.4	48.2	88.4	83.4	85.7	7.1	NA	NA	NA	NA	36 492	61.9	27 111	58.6
Urban Honolulu CDP	57.1	34.1	86.6	78.6	84.3	5.7	NA	NA	NA	NA	302 566	65.4	235 099	56.0
Waipahu CDP	52.8	64.5	88.7	81.2	90.5	2.2	NA	NA	NA	NA	31 688	64.5	25 545	52.1
IDAHO	82.1	23.3	89.2	77.2	81.6	8.1	814 571	2.2	31 137	3.8	1 270 851	62.3	1 027 587	46.6
Boise City.................	83.5	12.5	94.4	82.3	77.1	8.3	121 046	3.4	3 991	3.3	172 640	70.3	146 858	50.9
Caldwell...................	82.5	32.6	88.7	68.9	81.7	5.8	23 738	2.7	1 109	4.7	36 079	61.5	30 736	42.1
Coeur d'Alene	82.7	14.3	86.8	77.7	74.3	10.7	24 646	2.4	1 171	4.8	39 837	66.3	32 676	48.2
Idaho Falls................	76.8	18.7	91.5	82.3	78.8	10.4	28 574	2.1	952	3.3	44 575	61.1	36 489	42.0
Lewiston	87.6	9.5	85.8	75.2	80.4	6.4	17 630	1.1	563	3.2	25 501	58.8	19 053	52.5
Meridian...................	89.0	21.9	89.6	76.8	85.7	7.3	44 640	3.5	1 495	3.3	68 206	58.4	53 032	49.3
Nampa.....................	78.4	38.2	87.3	66.1	80.8	7.6	39 908	2.8	1 736	4.4	64 603	64.7	55 030	47.1
Pocatello..................	77.4	9.9	90.3	79.6	76.2	9.1	28 716	0.8	1 004	3.5	41 866	59.8	34 755	36.5
Post Falls.................	82.8	27.0	91.9	82.5	84.1	3.7	15 870	2.5	709	4.5	23 392	62.8	17 023	53.4
Rexburg...................	68.1	21.6	96.1	74.8	48.8	20.8	14 672	3.2	369	2.5	19 784	62.2	18 252	16.5
Twin Falls.................	82.4	8.2	90.6	80.6	76.3	8.9	23 476	1.9	787	3.4	35 986	69.2	29 179	46.6
ILLINOIS..................	77.0	44.0	86.3	77.0	86.8	4.8	6 539 008	0.5	384 141	5.9	10 240 058	65.2	8 411 833	49.9
Addison	86.7	39.2	85.2	75.7	82.6	4.0	19 575	0.9	1 060	5.4	28 058	74.5	23 178	55.9
Algonquin	82.4	54.2	91.7	89.5	91.7	6.5	17 158	0.8	862	5.0	22 581	71.7	19 623	46.7
Alton	90.8	28.8	76.2	67.4	89.2	4.6	11 690	0.3	884	7.6	21 445	59.7	17 811	42.2
Arlington Heights..........	80.6	44.8	92.0	85.8	89.4	4.1	41 387	1.0	1 902	4.6	63 021	65.0	46 973	59.1
Aurora.....................	85.0	41.0	91.0	86.5	86.6	5.1	102 133	0.3	5 595	5.5	147 281	72.8	131 663	55.3
Bartlett....................	86.0	55.2	93.5	88.6	NA	NA	23 533	1.0	1 145	4.9	31 356	76.1	26 784	60.3
Batavia....................	84.0	37.3	92.9	85.3	85.8	4.9	13 814	0.3	671	4.9	21 665	71.7	18 300	52.5
Belleville	84.6	39.9	83.5	71.6	83.9	3.0	22 386	1.0	1 356	6.1	31 736	65.3	25 873	55.1
Belvidere	91.6	37.6	72.8	61.6	88.6	7.3	11 720	-0.3	886	7.6	19 805	65.2	16 341	52.8
Berwyn....................	74.1	63.6	89.7	74.7	NA	NA	27 881	0.6	1 761	6.3	42 784	68.4	37 119	53.4
Bloomington	82.3	9.1	91.0	79.6	79.0	8.3	40 526	-1.5	2 047	5.1	63 124	68.9	53 300	53.1
Bolingbrook	90.1	46.4	93.3	87.4	91.9	4.3	40 426	0.8	2 235	5.5	54 661	73.6	48 168	52.9
Buffalo Grove	86.6	45.7	94.8	87.9	90.1	5.9	24 637	0.9	1 077	4.4	32 893	71.8	26 293	58.4

1. Employed persons.   2. Households.   3. Percent of civilian labor force.   4. Persons 16 years old and over.

Table D. Cities — Construction, Wholesale Trade, and Retail Trade

City	Value of residential construction authorized by building permits, 2016			Wholesale trade,[1] 2012				Retail trade,[2] 2012			
	New construction ($1,000)	Number of housing units	Percent single family	Number of establishments	Number of employees	Sales (mil dol)	Annual payroll (mil dol)	Number of establishments	Number of employees	Sales (mil dol)	Annual payroll (mil dol)
	69	70	71	72	73	74	75	76	77	78	79
GEORGIA..................	4 215	23	100.0	10 637	150 168	143 645.3	8 476.3	33 426	433 840	119 801.5	10 290.1
Albany	9 737	86	37.2	111	1 406	824.7	63.5	458	6 179	1 449.6	129.6
Alpharetta	108 066	259	100.0	161	3 714	5 088.0	345.2	372	7 362	1 931.3	170.7
Athens-Clarke County ...	22 649	119	96.6	99	1 801	1 947.0	85.0	516	6 963	1 684.2	145.6
Atlanta	1 110 084	8 031	10.6	698	11 556	9 224.9	748.9	1 875	24 977	6 088.3	633.1
Augusta-Richmond County	65 916	586	52.9	182	1 856	864.7	81.5	812	10 830	2 627.3	229.5
Columbus	75 763	384	70.3	157	1 843	1 550.1	80.6	796	11 371	2 847.8	250.2
Dalton	NA	NA	NA	108	1 489	756.2	57.6	259	2 644	678.8	59.3
Douglasville	42 665	154	100.0	20	146	65.8	7.0	253	4 228	922.8	82.2
Duluth	13 939	49	100.0	127	3 067	2 088.3	243.7	199	2 792	1 032.1	82.9
Dunwoody	40 492	87	100.0	60	978	713.5	98.7	250	5 168	916.8	106.9
East Point	7 625	64	92.2	30	640	501.8	D	90	1 196	267.7	23.2
Gainesville	117 608	971	45.4	92	D	D	D	299	3 927	1 007.8	95.0
Hinesville	38 067	143	100.0	6	D	D	D	127	1 682	402.9	35.9
Johns Creek	76 629	277	100.0	67	231	116.5	17.8	149	1 831	395.3	40.8
Kennesaw	41 255	228	23.2	80	1 153	832.4	62.3	189	3 621	840.4	78.5
LaGrange	13 326	46	100.0	32	609	287.4	18.2	184	2 600	738.7	64.3
Lawrenceville.............	17 817	81	100.0	115	1 926	1 257.1	109.0	309	3 550	882.0	81.9
Macon-Bibb County......	14 938	89	100.0	122	D	D	D	629	7 527	1 820.1	166.1
Marietta	61 909	243	100.0	275	3 494	2 618.4	199.5	447	6 196	1 976.9	173.8
Milton	49 051	216	100.0	20	147	118.9	9.7	56	916	187.9	18.3
Newnan	100 534	345	100.0	33	D	D	D	200	3 261	798.6	73.3
Peachtree City............	29 452	87	100.0	75	1 037	874.5	65.6	145	2 641	617.7	55.5
Rome	NA	NA	NA	54	693	605.1	29.3	283	3 352	840.9	76.5
Roswell....................	109 625	287	100.0	177	1 786	1 397.9	140.4	324	5 202	1 762.9	163.1
Sandy Springs............	176 931	837	24.4	147	3 515	7 647.4	330.3	252	3 933	1 342.8	131.9
Savannah..................	77 790	300	100.0	180	1 884	3 630.1	102.2	869	11 121	2 862.9	260.4
Smyrna	43 010	226	96.5	73	2 229	2 185.5	138.4	189	2 894	1 028.8	79.6
Statesboro	2 755	44	59.1	23	141	152.5	6.2	202	2 828	655.9	59.1
Stockbridge	NA	NA	NA	11	38	9.7	0.9	95	1 819	443.8	43.5
Valdosta	81 183	424	100.0	85	822	1 113.3	32.0	370	4 978	1 314.1	109.7
Warner Robins	51 513	270	100.0	22	221	71.1	7.5	291	4 392	1 107.7	98.9
HAWAII....................	365 774	978	81.0	1 561	16 686	9 608.0	724.5	4 643	68 360	18 901.7	1 835.0
East Honolulu CDP	NA	NA	NA	33	65	22.5	2.4	55	962	343.3	27.9
Hilo CDP	NA	NA	NA	71	839	328.1	31.4	228	3 849	969.6	101.6
Kahului CDP...............	NA	NA	NA	52	637	513.5	31.8	194	4 127	1 252.3	124.8
Kailua CDP (Honolulu County)......	NA	NA	NA	17	62	21.4	2.8	96	1 388	322.1	32.7
Kaneohe CDP.............	NA	NA	NA	12	19	11.5	1.0	119	1 597	481.5	46.5
Mililani Town CDP........	NA	NA	NA	9	16	2.9	0.5	34	974	253.0	25.5
Pearl City CDP............	NA	NA	NA	38	463	261.9	19.3	65	2 081	672.5	49.9
Urban Honolulu CDP	NA	NA	NA	782	9 002	5 712.8	399.8	1 851	26 485	7 684.2	748.6
Waipahu CDP	NA	NA	NA	56	790	292.5	35.1	106	2 248	866.1	76.8
IDAHO.....................	0	0	0.0	1 739	21 470	17 906.0	960.8	5 815	72 980	20 444.3	1 794.0
Boise City	270 408	1 399	48.7	376	5 188	5 866.3	287.1	916	13 392	3 485.8	335.1
Caldwell....................	72 651	537	100.0	29	299	130.4	10.6	121	1 512	430.0	38.0
Coeur d'Alene	55 376	295	89.2	50	612	398.5	26.2	309	4 575	1 433.8	118.5
Idaho Falls................	35 416	296	87.8	114	1 210	2 531.3	62.0	362	5 209	1 529.1	119.4
Lewiston	13 412	57	77.2	37	472	314.2	18.8	191	2 163	670.5	54.6
Meridian	360 530	1 569	94.4	93	2 282	1 086.7	100.6	246	4 537	1 648.6	139.2
Nampa......................	103 301	932	52.8	78	939	707.4	44.7	300	5 210	1 634.4	136.4
Pocatello...................	11 429	98	100.0	69	656	473.3	25.4	219	2 935	848.4	69.2
Post Falls	92 376	658	50.8	27	143	72.8	7.4	99	1 762	600.9	48.3
Rexburg....................	45 681	342	14.3	20	285	157.5	8.4	105	1 542	358.6	32.7
Twin Falls.................	55 755	318	78.0	75	810	336.8	31.3	314	4 308	1 122.4	102.5
ILLINOIS...................	718	5	100.0	16 036	255 531	295 457.0	15 973.3	39 947	592 942	166 634.5	14 576.1
Addison	950	3	100.0	198	3 798	2 418.5	282.6	96	1 807	709.5	72.4
Algonquin	9 635	27	100.0	23	95	69.6	7.5	158	3 492	706.1	66.4
Alton	610	2	100.0	27	284	219.5	14.5	150	2 233	500.2	51.8
Arlington Heights..........	56 018	155	81.9	151	3 104	2 632.1	263.1	203	3 354	749.7	97.9
Aurora	43 854	155	100.0	150	2 943	26 798.1	179.4	566	9 344	2 025.3	191.3
Bartlett	1 528	9	100.0	57	751	578.0	41.7	41	615	138.7	13.2
Batavia	20 202	96	16.7	78	799	539.8	49.0	90	1 634	394.1	34.5
Belleville	6 718	42	100.0	42	549	330.1	27.1	188	2 333	577.7	60.5
Belvidere	1 263	8	100.0	12	91	101.2	4.5	86	1 140	354.8	27.0
Berwyn	60	1	100.0	12	37	10.8	1.4	112	836	226.5	21.8
Bloomington	17 805	134	61.2	73	D	D	D	360	5 463	1 396.1	120.9
Bolingbrook	42 686	315	8.6	103	3 334	3 837.2	212.6	214	5 088	1 377.5	135.6
Buffalo Grove	6 453	17	100.0	122	2 672	2 796.2	181.6	128	1 340	381.3	40.2

1. Merchant wholesalers except manufacturers' sales branches and offices.   2. Establishments with payroll.

Table D. Cities — Real Estate, Professional Services, and Manufacturing

City	Real estate and rental and leasing, 2012				Professional, scientific, and technical services,[1] 2012				Manufacturing, 2012			
	Number of establish-ments	Number of employees	Receipts (mil dol)	Annual payroll (mil dol)	Number of establish-ments	Number of employees	Receipts (mil dol)	Annual payroll (mil dol)	Number of establish-ments	Number of employees	Receipts (mil dol)	Annual payroll (mil dol)
	80	81	82	83	84	85	86	87	88	89	90	91
GEORGIA..............	10 484	55 551	14 232.4	2 703.7	28 018	239 289	41 359.0	15 587.7	7 456	333 837	155 836.8	15 316.6
Albany	130	493	87.1	15.3	197	D	D	D	60	2 943	D	172.1
Alpharetta	203	1 412	723.0	90.7	847	13 182	2 303.2	1 072.3	21	412	D	27.7
Athens-Clarke County ...	190	926	140.6	27.0	300	D	D	D	78	5 115	2 004.8	229.5
Atlanta	1 121	9 940	2 333.2	660.6	3 501	52 799	12 632.0	4 945.1	295	7 404	3 609.7	356.0
Augusta-Richmond County	201	1 069	248.9	37.9	473	D	D	D	111	7 884	5 452.2	451.0
Columbus	237	1 461	258.1	55.7	346	D	D	D	122	6 977	1 937.2	297.0
Dalton	41	158	35.4	5.2	123	D	D	D	147	10 548	4 437.1	403.8
Douglasville	50	204	53.1	5.6	113	604	56.4	22.1	20	D	69.0	D
Duluth.....................	98	459	112.5	23.3	279	2 539	420.2	172.3	39	1 549	553.4	127.0
Dunwoody	123	1 450	871.4	84.1	572	6 017	1 408.3	415.3	14	54	9.2	1.8
East Point...............	33	301	93.9	11.3	51	D	D	D	24	648	348.8	32.4
Gainesville	71	254	69.6	10.5	178	D	D	D	86	8 909	4 539.2	335.2
Hinesville	41	159	23.1	4.8	41	D	D	D	4	D	D	D
Johns Creek............	99	D	D	D	580	D	D	D	14	D	D	D
Kennesaw	43	220	61.9	8.7	145	980	130.0	42.9	51	1 225	550.7	60.0
LaGrange	42	193	28.8	5.2	65	746	40.9	19.9	57	5 180	2 151.0	258.5
Lawrenceville...........	71	367	85.4	15.0	231	D	D	D	67	2 258	1 017.4	99.4
Macon-Bibb County.......	126	575	116.3	18.0	284	D	D	D	71	D	929.5	D
Marietta	186	884	174.8	41.4	557	D	D	D	109	3 408	1 129.4	161.1
Milton.....................	24	D	D	D	205	4 498	264.7	132.2	6	16	D	0.6
Newnan	68	185	39.4	6.8	92	514	49.6	22.3	31	1 019	330.9	40.1
Peachtree City..........	74	158	32.4	7.0	172	D	D	D	39	1 864	789.3	97.9
Rome.....................	61	202	33.1	6.2	146	700	85.0	31.2	61	3 069	2 196.8	142.6
Roswell..................	179	787	172.4	34.4	750	D	D	D	57	636	113.0	30.6
Sandy Springs.........	334	2 561	796.8	127.6	970	15 638	2 999.5	1 194.6	30	529	156.7	22.9
Savannah...............	246	1 266	247.7	38.9	496	D	D	D	104	3 234	1 475.3	166.2
Smyrna..................	87	297	62.2	12.4	280	8 545	575.5	275.5	40	1 132	208.7	40.4
Statesboro..............	56	266	44.6	6.7	87	D	D	D	26	1 163	359.6	43.1
Stockbridge	38	151	35.8	4.6	73	454	64.7	16.6	12	D	21.3	D
Valdosta	100	1 363	89.3	24.2	172	D	D	D	65	2 208	2 117.3	89.1
Warner Robins	79	303	50.0	7.6	158	D	D	D	25	519	D	28.4
HAWAII...................	1 919	11 369	3 411.2	483.9	3 188	20 998	3 229.4	1 225.0	796	11 440	D	465.0
East Honolulu CDP.......	49	105	18.6	4.2	110	282	33.8	12.2	3	9	1.6	0.4
Hilo CDP	80	358	59.7	9.4	98	D	D	D	46	425	D	16.8
Kahului CDP............	52	535	142.3	21.3	43	258	27.7	9.5	18	95	17.3	3.1
Kailua CDP (Honolulu County)	54	176	31.5	7.2	95	D	D	D	13	47	5.7	1.5
Kaneohe CDP	26	89	11.6	3.0	50	D	D	D	15	120	16.9	4.1
Mililani Town CDP........	6	28	3.2	0.7	17	D	D	D	NA	NA	NA	NA
Pearl City CDP............	21	101	22.5	4.4	36	224	27.6	10.3	12	171	D	6.6
Urban Honolulu CDP	825	5 335	1 834.2	255.2	1 694	14 113	2 397.4	907.6	351	5 599	1 152.7	200.0
Waipahu CDP	34	182	27.7	5.7	20	226	15.2	5.4	20	359	128.8	13.0
IDAHO....................	2 033	6 268	1 039.9	184.2	4 177	D	D	D	1 759	52 084	20 201.4	2 445.5
Boise City	452	1 905	341.1	61.6	1 150	9 739	1 465.6	588.0	216	12 584	D	855.5
Caldwell..................	36	183	17.7	4.2	49	D	D	D	53	D	579.1	63.7
Coeur d'Alene	103	404	92.6	13.1	244	2 077	149.0	74.7	63	1 116	D	47.4
Idaho Falls..............	101	366	67.8	11.7	282	D	D	D	80	1 528	472.1	54.6
Lewiston.................	35	D	D	D	77	D	D	D	27	D	D	D
Meridian..................	101	236	40.4	10.5	197	1 595	242.0	88.2	55	1 143	D	46.4
Nampa....................	77	186	21.2	4.6	141	798	73.2	31.0	78	3 627	1 102.2	140.3
Pocatello.................	69	D	D	D	138	D	D	D	33	1 499	D	61.6
Post Falls	33	91	10.5	2.3	57	275	44.3	11.2	49	1 109	320.4	44.4
Rexburg..................	46	149	22.5	2.6	58	D	D	D	18	415	55.6	13.7
Twin Falls	87	259	45.4	7.1	174	D	D	D	59	1 669	683.0	64.1
ILLINOIS................	12 035	76 794	23 649.1	3 816.1	38 540	355 434	68 675.2	27 645.3	13 868	542 004	281 037.8	28 413.7
Addison	42	347	75.6	16.6	94	455	89.2	21.9	310	5 793	1 395.5	279.1
Algonquin	23	D	D	D	111	340	48.7	17.3	23	391	84.6	20.1
Alton	34	109	15.7	3.5	63	D	D	D	22	1 105	442.7	50.3
Arlington Heights..........	96	633	105.7	32.7	488	D	D	D	71	1 902	980.2	109.7
Aurora....................	130	676	147.4	22.5	450	2 399	351.6	125.4	138	8 689	4 775.2	512.4
Bartlett	22	61	10.8	1.9	148	319	58.9	19.0	29	999	273.5	53.2
Batavia	26	100	13.6	3.2	138	D	D	D	88	3 758	1 380.5	182.1
Belleville	55	169	31.9	5.4	153	D	D	D	38	1 347	380.4	61.5
Belvidere	15	45	6.4	1.1	31	D	D	D	39	6 985	5 764.7	374.7
Berwyn	27	68	14.4	1.6	71	1 276	49.3	27.9	15	486	D	28.0
Bloomington	95	439	107.7	14.1	238	D	D	D	49	1 525	554.8	71.0
Bolingbrook	39	190	34.0	6.3	154	1 517	178.4	76.7	54	3 763	1 169.0	181.2
Buffalo Grove	47	261	56.0	11.4	313	3 419	392.2	178.1	53	3 097	1 205.8	154.6

1. Establishments subject to federal tax.

Table D. Cities — Accommodation and Food Services, Arts, Entertainment, and Recreation, and Health Care and Social Assistance

City	Accommodation and food services, 2012				Arts, entertainment, and recreation,[1] 2012				Health care and social assistance,[1] 2012			
	Number of establishments	Number of employees	Sales (mil dol)	Annual payroll (mil dol)	Number of establishments	Number of employees	Receipts (mil dol)	Annual payroll (mil dol)	Number of establishments	Number of employees	Receipts (mil dol)	Annual payroll (mil dol)
	92	93	94	95	96	97	98	99	100	101	102	103
GEORGIA	18 815	353 638	18 976.6	5 173.4	2 232	28 800	2 877.8	953.0	20 166	256 945	28 196.2	11 171.4
Albany	211	D	D	D	15	D	D	D	238	D	D	D
Alpharetta	286	6 486	342.2	98.9	33	D	D	D	389	3 667	556.5	236.2
Athens-Clarke County	342	6 927	307.6	83.9	27	354	20.5	5.5	394	D	D	D
Atlanta	1 618	42 124	3 023.4	844.6	272	3 724	871.2	309.6	1 336	17 100	2 332.0	908.9
Augusta-Richmond County	424	9 448	447.0	125.6	28	D	D	D	577	9 118	1 230.5	456.4
Columbus	442	10 453	519.3	149.2	30	427	26.0	6.5	520	6 215	649.7	261.6
Dalton	120	D	D	D	7	D	D	D	122	D	D	D
Douglasville	129	2 867	130.6	36.6	4	D	D	D	115	1 033	118.2	46.4
Duluth	144	1 624	82.0	22.3	19	D	D	D	166	D	D	D
Dunwoody	141	3 952	244.2	73.0	17	D	D	D	202	3 057	258.8	98.0
East Point	72	1 504	97.0	26.8	14	D	D	D	83	1 789	177.9	59.5
Gainesville	151	2 837	163.0	43.3	15	D	D	D	271	D	D	D
Hinesville	80	1 307	68.7	14.9	3	D	D	D	49	525	40.8	18.1
Johns Creek	137	2 100	98.6	30.2	20	557	47.0	15.0	158	D	D	D
Kennesaw	111	2 319	109.7	31.5	15	D	D	D	85	D	D	D
LaGrange	86	1 738	76.2	21.7	7	D	D	D	79	D	D	D
Lawrenceville	128	2 022	107.6	29.9	15	D	D	D	262	D	D	D
Macon-Bibb County	266	4 795	207.3	58.8	11	D	D	D	365	D	D	D
Marietta	289	4 708	264.5	74.0	24	174	19.7	3.8	392	D	D	D
Milton	44	635	34.6	9.8	17	171	13.5	3.2	28	D	D	D
Newnan	112	2 784	129.1	37.1	7	189	9.1	2.2	93	D	D	D
Peachtree City	100	2 410	112.6	35.3	20	D	D	D	119	D	D	D
Rome	138	3 070	136.6	40.0	11	D	D	D	215	D	D	D
Roswell	237	4 531	234.3	68.0	51	D	D	D	352	5 025	553.5	202.6
Sandy Springs	266	4 373	280.1	75.7	33	577	39.2	11.4	640	8 319	1 459.9	597.1
Savannah	571	12 766	759.1	203.0	40	D	D	D	486	8 390	1 182.6	453.3
Smyrna	161	2 788	152.3	41.7	19	291	13.0	4.8	208	1 508	188.3	61.4
Statesboro	124	D	D	D	4	D	D	D	148	D	D	D
Stockbridge	83	1 205	57.8	14.1	8	D	D	D	143	D	D	D
Valdosta	214	4 519	199.0	53.2	13	D	D	D	275	D	D	D
Warner Robins	157	3 608	168.4	44.7	11	234	7.1	2.4	179	D	D	D
HAWAII	3 518	98 364	9 536.7	2 536.0	398	7 327	571.1	168.2	2 794	26 788	3 180.4	1 347.2
East Honolulu CDP	65	D	D	D	12	D	D	D	64	548	56.6	19.3
Hilo CDP	146	2 239	133.8	33.2	6	D	D	D	176	2 291	225.8	99.0
Kahului CDP	84	1 703	123.3	31.2	10	D	D	D	75	704	99.2	42.4
Kailua CDP (Honolulu County)	86	1 446	81.3	20.9	9	D	D	D	113	D	D	D
Kaneohe CDP	74	1 140	76.8	17.5	12	D	D	D	81	725	78.1	31.0
Mililani Town CDP	41	1 055	60.1	15.0	3	119	8.8	1.8	19	180	19.9	10.1
Pearl City CDP	74	1 346	79.7	19.3	3	146	11.9	2.5	76	785	82.2	31.8
Urban Honolulu CDP	1 471	38 426	3 944.0	955.4	103	1 558	117.6	31.5	1 262	11 394	1 445.9	615.3
Waipahu CDP	77	1 007	64.5	15.0	3	5	0.7	0.1	86	749	74.2	28.6
IDAHO	3 564	54 257	2 680.2	726.1	573	6 755	355.9	102.6	4 271	49 613	4 281.1	1 636.4
Boise City	617	11 334	523.9	154.0	56	1 166	44.4	12.3	793	D	D	D
Caldwell	65	1 007	46.6	12.2	5	D	D	D	93	1 484	160.5	55.9
Coeur d'Alene	184	3 531	181.2	51.4	28	244	18.5	5.6	274	D	D	D
Idaho Falls	191	3 578	159.1	46.2	13	D	D	D	416	D	D	D
Lewiston	95	D	D	D	13	D	D	D	119	1 820	167.6	56.4
Meridian	178	3 513	161.9	44.2	25	439	19.6	5.9	279	D	D	D
Nampa	159	2 965	122.8	34.2	16	D	D	D	197	3 419	215.1	99.1
Pocatello	151	2 633	111.4	30.7	17	D	D	D	245	D	D	D
Post Falls	57	735	34.0	9.7	8	65	4.8	1.2	83	1 406	124.7	47.3
Rexburg	48	840	30.4	8.5	7	60	1.8	0.5	84	D	D	D
Twin Falls	140	2 486	123.3	32.4	23	D	D	D	235	D	D	D
ILLINOIS	27 117	469 870	27 937.4	7 707.1	3 564	49 286	5 591.9	1 678.3	27 624	383 980	39 270.3	16 150.8
Addison	73	D	D	D	8	D	D	D	50	969	81.3	41.9
Algonquin	82	1 821	81.9	26.2	16	D	D	D	89	733	76.2	36.1
Alton	92	1 842	85.5	26.3	11	D	D	D	92	D	D	D
Arlington Heights	148	2 732	161.0	45.4	29	274	16.7	5.1	351	D	D	D
Aurora	257	4 005	227.2	56.8	34	973	161.4	29.9	304	4 552	575.3	222.8
Bartlett	36	460	24.8	6.5	7	D	D	D	49	D	D	D
Batavia	63	1 094	50.3	15.2	5	D	D	D	57	D	D	D
Belleville	142	D	D	D	14	D	D	D	159	4 006	362.8	191.6
Belvidere	49	D	D	D	5	D	D	D	45	D	D	D
Berwyn	86	D	D	D	6	42	2.7	0.7	130	3 811	433.8	197.0
Bloomington	223	4 927	234.3	67.4	33	601	18.3	6.0	204	2 790	335.9	142.6
Bolingbrook	154	3 230	173.5	49.0	19	569	17.7	8.6	138	D	D	D
Buffalo Grove	101	1 514	92.8	28.1	14	D	D	D	172	1 506	181.5	64.6

1. Establishments subject to federal tax.

Table D. Cities — Other Services and Government Employment and Payroll

City	Other services[1], 2012				Government employment and payroll, 2012								
							March payroll						
							Percent of total for:						
	Number of establishments	Number of employees	Receipts (mil dol)	Annual payroll (mil dol)	Full-time equivalent employees	Total (dollars)	Administration, judicial, and legal	Police and Corrections	Fire Protection	Highways and transportation	Health and welfare	Natural resources and utilities	Education and libraries
	104	105	106	107	108	109	110	111	112	113	114	115	116
GEORGIA	11 682	71 989	6 311.9	1 949.9	X	X	X	X	X	X	X	X	X
Albany	113	D	D	D	1 213	4 293 454	11.1	19.0	17.2	7.2	2.0	31.0	0.0
Alpharetta	138	D	D	D	443	2 007 691	5.5	32.0	22.6	9.9	0.0	9.9	0.0
Athens-Clarke County	153	929	66.0	21.6	1 759	6 225 567	17.5	31.3	12.0	9.2	0.6	19.8	3.4
Atlanta	879	8 945	574.9	212.4	8 214	31 551 612	15.9	34.2	13.9	16.0	0.2	18.5	0.0
Augusta-Richmond County	220	1 531	148.4	44.6	2 708	8 108 733	23.7	31.7	13.0	8.3	1.7	16.6	2.0
Columbus	259	1 902	157.2	51.1	3 147	10 081 635	11.8	34.7	14.0	7.5	4.7	18.9	2.8
Dalton	57	D	D	D	692	2 865 431	2.7	12.6	11.3	8.7	0.3	61.7	0.0
Douglasville	80	369	35.4	10.7	232	792 422	15.8	53.4	0.0	14.1	0.0	8.0	0.0
Duluth	133	785	73.7	21.0	140	565 431	33.5	44.9	0.0	10.3	0.0	10.1	0.0
Dunwoody	73	435	28.6	8.8	67	294 800	23.0	77.0	0.0	0.0	0.0	0.0	0.0
East Point	38	747	41.5	13.4	535	1 898 606	17.4	33.8	15.0	2.6	0.0	22.3	0.0
Gainesville	86	398	34.2	9.9	670	2 183 927	9.3	16.9	16.0	8.4	2.2	43.8	0.0
Hinesville	39	208	14.9	4.4	201	695 457	7.4	56.2	19.8	0.0	3.5	2.5	0.0
Johns Creek	78	D	D	D	8	41 438	87.5	12.5	0.0	0.0	0.0	0.0	0.0
Kennesaw	99	963	111.3	41.3	205	735 014	16.6	34.2	0.0	9.0	2.2	24.9	0.0
LaGrange	45	D	D	D	408	1 594 338	6.9	28.0	14.4	4.1	0.7	29.6	0.0
Lawrenceville	135	767	85.7	27.2	246	987 618	20.7	41.4	0.0	4.4	0.0	30.9	0.0
Macon-Bibb County	145	839	91.3	25.4	1 169	3 501 960	8.9	33.1	34.1	4.1	1.9	14.4	0.0
Marietta	220	1 340	152.1	45.4	734	3 368 637	23.6	11.1	12.3	4.3	11.8	24.4	0.0
Milton	30	D	D	D	121	520 911	22.5	27.5	44.2	3.3	0.0	2.5	0.0
Newnan	69	308	24.4	6.4	267	989 419	6.4	31.3	19.7	8.0	0.0	19.0	0.6
Peachtree City	86	758	53.4	17.9	270	1 079 307	11.4	29.0	29.7	14.7	0.0	5.3	3.6
Rome	62	429	39.4	10.8	589	1 937 155	8.3	18.6	26.8	11.5	0.6	25.2	0.0
Roswell	200	1 408	111.7	41.6	741	2 812 794	17.5	29.3	11.9	8.4	0.0	29.5	0.0
Sandy Springs	170	D	D	D	295	1 455 396	3.8	60.7	34.3	0.0	0.0	0.0	0.0
Savannah	221	1 473	144.6	43.6	2 548	9 836 488	9.9	34.9	11.9	8.9	2.7	25.8	0.0
Smyrna	102	452	41.9	12.4	391	1 523 989	10.9	37.3	23.1	6.6	3.6	14.0	2.3
Statesboro	55	288	21.2	5.4	279	845 101	12.3	28.4	12.3	12.1	0.0	32.0	0.0
Stockbridge	38	175	12.6	3.1	68	227 107	32.1	0.0	0.0	21.8	0.0	33.5	0.0
Valdosta	92	512	31.4	8.5	574	1 813 002	8.4	32.3	17.3	9.7	3.4	24.8	0.0
Warner Robins	81	473	34.5	10.5	536	1 642 600	10.8	31.9	21.3	10.1	3.3	20.5	0.0
HAWAII	1 519	11 014	877.5	279.0	X	X	X	X	X	X	X	X	X
East Honolulu CDP	24	101	4.3	1.6	NA	NA	NA	NA	NA	NA	NA	NA	NA
Hilo CDP	68	351	30.2	8.4	NA	NA	NA	NA	NA	NA	NA	NA	NA
Kahului CDP	53	471	34.8	11.6	NA	NA	NA	NA	NA	NA	NA	NA	NA
Kailua CDP (Honolulu County)	47	196	15.1	4.7	NA	NA	NA	NA	NA	NA	NA	NA	NA
Kaneohe CDP	38	268	20.0	7.2	NA	NA	NA	NA	NA	NA	NA	NA	NA
Mililani Town CDP	15	93	5.1	2.0	NA	NA	NA	NA	NA	NA	NA	NA	NA
Pearl City CDP	43	187	21.3	6.1	NA	NA	NA	NA	NA	NA	NA	NA	NA
Urban Honolulu CDP	721	6 242	481.7	157.1	NA	NA	NA	NA	NA	NA	NA	NA	NA
Waipahu CDP	53	276	23.2	6.9	NA	NA	NA	NA	NA	NA	NA	NA	NA
IDAHO	2 055	9 826	849.8	240.9	X	X	X	X	X	X	X	X	X
Boise City	371	2 083	162.4	51.1	1 617	7 522 788	17.0	29.2	23.6	4.2	0.9	17.7	4.2
Caldwell	46	290	30.2	8.4	228	861 823	8.7	36.4	24.0	12.2	0.0	13.3	3.2
Coeur d'Alene	82	447	32.5	10.0	318	1 619 497	16.8	30.1	21.9	7.8	0.2	19.0	3.2
Idaho Falls	92	448	42.2	11.5	659	2 848 455	10.4	20.7	20.0	4.4	0.0	33.4	2.9
Lewiston	65	381	28.8	8.9	314	1 377 725	8.6	24.1	24.4	12.2	3.9	16.1	2.7
Meridian	90	556	37.4	13.7	343	1 643 338	14.3	34.7	25.5	8.1	0.0	15.4	0.0
Nampa	100	578	47.8	14.8	565	2 435 649	5.6	35.1	21.4	3.5	2.1	14.7	2.4
Pocatello	76	416	39.1	9.5	561	2 333 293	10.6	25.9	18.5	10.3	1.9	26.0	2.6
Post Falls	48	236	18.4	5.5	169	673 051	14.6	40.3	0.0	12.1	1.2	22.8	0.0
Rexburg	25	D	D	D	115	440 960	21.3	29.6	8.0	11.5	0.8	17.1	0.0
Twin Falls	87	614	50.1	14.4	284	1 088 260	9.5	36.0	16.2	11.3	4.2	14.9	5.2
ILLINOIS	18 681	117 388	10 571.7	3 334.1	X	X	X	X	X	X	X	X	X
Addison	113	775	89.8	27.4	245	1 559 535	9.6	44.1	0.0	4.2	9.2	20.0	8.6
Algonquin	66	364	22.1	7.5	143	751 901	11.3	26.1	0.0	11.5	0.3	33.9	0.0
Alton	46	251	16.2	5.6	230	1 141 005	7.5	40.6	24.3	8.2	1.8	13.2	0.0
Arlington Heights	138	912	99.9	29.3	594	3 727 355	11.4	27.0	22.6	8.1	2.6	6.6	15.0
Aurora	159	1 044	120.6	29.7	1 402	8 465 715	9.4	32.8	18.5	7.5	8.1	14.5	5.4
Bartlett	33	142	18.3	4.9	166	992 280	14.8	48.1	0.0	13.2	11.3	12.4	0.0
Batavia	55	509	52.3	18.0	160	528 428	11.6	29.4	18.9	8.0	7.5	24.3	0.0
Belleville	96	635	49.6	15.9	345	1 469 633	6.3	35.6	25.0	5.2	0.0	14.8	4.1
Belvidere	30	231	17.9	6.1	125	645 335	6.9	38.7	26.4	8.1	0.0	13.1	4.0
Berwyn	53	214	19.6	4.7	402	2 004 230	7.2	46.5	25.8	5.7	1.5	5.4	6.1
Bloomington	127	1 022	74.9	28.0	723	3 168 188	7.2	25.0	19.2	14.3	0.0	27.5	5.8
Bolingbrook	79	424	31.8	10.7	391	2 517 306	8.3	44.4	26.4	8.1	0.0	9.5	0.0
Buffalo Grove	77	463	37.9	11.1	255	1 764 688	6.4	35.2	28.3	6.6	3.6	14.2	0.0

1. Establishments subject to federal tax.

Table D. Cities — City Government Finances

City	General revenue Total (mil dol)	Intergovernmental Total (mil dol)	Intergovernmental Percent from state government	Taxes Total (mil dol)	Taxes Per capita¹ (dollars) Total	Taxes Per capita¹ (dollars) Property	Sales and gross receipts	General expenditure Total (mil dol)	General expenditure Per capita¹ (dollars) Total	Capital outlays
	117	118	119	120	121	122	123	124	125	126
GEORGIA	X	X	X	X	X	X	X	X	X	X
Albany	124.2	55.1	36.8	24.1	312	164	148	134.7	1 739	76
Alpharetta	73.1	15.6	8.8	42.0	678	393	285	72.3	1 166	291
Athens-Clarke County	206.5	69.1	26.0	71.2	598	405	191	1 567.5	3 530	1 093
Atlanta	1 789.4	282.2	8.0	521.0	1 173	704	465	341.5	1 731	350
Augusta-Richmond County	364.7	133.0	12.9	103.4	524	291	230	364.1	1 820	349
Columbus	354.1	116.0	29.3	135.0	675	498	175	82.6	2 478	515
Dalton	69.4	16.5	0.3	14.2	427	283	144	34.0	1 088	313
Douglasville	27.0	7.1	10.3	13.8	441	190	246	21.2	761	234
Duluth	24.7	9.0	7.9	11.7	419	226	192	26.5	560	185
Dunwoody	20.5	0.6	15.1	17.6	372	123	247	55.0	1 547	287
East Point	49.3	11.3	1.5	20.7	582	366	216	70.8	2 035	502
Gainesville	78.3	19.3	20.5	21.8	626	363	263	30.3	873	89
Hinesville	30.4	10.9	1.3	9.9	287	163	124	41.5	504	64
Johns Creek	48.5	16.3	1.2	29.0	352	203	148	24.9	796	112
Kennesaw	26.5	5.0	1.3	14.0	449	296	154	44.0	1 454	186
LaGrange	35.7	9.6	8.9	4.7	155	1	153	28.0	952	219
Lawrenceville	22.3	5.6	4.6	5.4	185	59	120	116.6	748	73
Macon-Bibb County	105.9	49.5	9.0	37.3	239	126	113	98.4	1 683	284
Marietta	82.2	22.8	7.9	30.6	524	231	293	20.2	577	192
Milton	21.7	4.6	14.9	15.2	433	294	139	29.9	875	209
Newnan	30.9	10.4	1.6	10.9	320	137	184	41.6	1 200	340
Peachtree City	37.7	9.3	2.0	19.4	559	360	199	61.5	1 706	503
Rome	65.6	22.8	6.9	19.0	526	247	230	94.3	1 006	196
Roswell	94.1	26.7	5.7	44.7	478	286	192	75.2	757	151
Sandy Springs	95.9	28.3	2.8	60.0	604	296	307	307.5	2 161	358
Savannah	345.6	126.6	7.8	105.1	739	418	308	52.4	994	224
Smyrna	56.3	11.1	0.4	27.0	513	327	184	31.3	1 045	125
Statesboro	31.5	5.9	3.1	9.5	316	131	185	12.9	481	83
Stockbridge	16.8	7.3	22.1	4.0	149	1	148	59.7	1 036	254
Valdosta	56.4	22.7	6.1	17.4	302	105	197	54.2	755	88
Warner Robins	55.2	4.5	3.8	28.0	390	229	159			
HAWAII	X	X	X	X	X	X	X	X	X	X
East Honolulu CDP	NA	NA	NA	NA	NA	NA	NA	NA	NA	NA
Hilo CDP	NA	NA	NA	NA	NA	NA	NA	NA	NA	NA
Kahului CDP	NA	NA	NA	NA	NA	NA	NA	NA	NA	NA
Kailua CDP (Honolulu County)	NA	NA	NA	NA	NA	NA	NA	NA	NA	NA
Kaneohe CDP	NA	NA	NA	NA	NA	NA	NA	NA	NA	NA
Mililani Town CDP	NA	NA	NA	NA	NA	NA	NA	NA	NA	NA
Pearl City CDP	NA	NA	NA	NA	NA	NA	NA	NA	NA	NA
Urban Honolulu CDP	NA	NA	NA	NA	NA	NA	NA	NA	NA	NA
Waipahu CDP	NA	NA	NA	NA	NA	NA	NA	NA	NA	NA
IDAHO	X	X	X	X	X	X	X	X	X	X
Boise City	272.0	25.8	66.8	117.7	555	507	48	267.8	1 262	173
Caldwell	38.9	8.0	82.7	14.3	300	279	21	36.7	769	225
Coeur d'Alene	48.9	9.7	58.0	22.9	502	399	102	55.8	1 224	307
Idaho Falls	69.3	13.2	98.9	29.0	500	478	22	71.2	1 228	104
Lewiston	41.1	7.7	98.7	16.4	511	463	48	40.2	1 252	159
Meridian	53.9	9.9	100.0	23.3	290	242	48	42.4	528	89
Nampa	96.5	19.8	60.9	39.9	476	446	30	87.0	1 036	141
Pocatello	63.5	14.4	48.1	27.0	493	456	37	67.9	1 239	121
Post Falls	27.0	5.7	100.0	8.8	307	307	0	21.0	732	124
Rexburg	28.6	9.7	87.9	4.9	188	131	58	28.9	1 102	434
Twin Falls	39.5	5.6	70.4	19.5	433	398	35	33.6	747	116
ILLINOIS	X	X	X	X	X	X	X	X	X	X
Addison	44.5	12.7	100.0	22.1	594	338	250	39.8	1 067	5
Algonquin	27.6	11.4	100.0	12.4	415	200	215	21.1	704	36
Alton	40.8	15.1	100.0	14.7	535	282	253	34.8	1 267	124
Arlington Heights	98.7	20.5	94.8	68.0	897	574	324	81.7	1 078	28
Aurora	238.0	71.0	89.2	134.1	671	453	211	225.1	1 127	121
Bartlett	31.0	7.0	96.0	17.3	415	315	93	29.2	703	48
Batavia	30.0	8.1	95.0	13.2	500	278	223	38.7	1 468	511
Belleville	58.9	17.0	97.2	27.8	641	477	164	95.3	2 198	622
Belvidere	21.8	7.4	92.3	8.4	331	227	105	17.2	679	20
Berwyn	69.4	14.0	73.5	38.6	679	499	163	80.9	1 425	107
Bloomington	114.7	26.3	94.5	54.8	704	308	396	104.9	1 349	122
Bolingbrook	85.6	23.0	91.1	43.5	588	210	348	83.2	1 124	65
Buffalo Grove	47.2	12.4	82.1	22.3	535	338	184	50.5	1 215	102

1. Based on population estimated as of July 1 of the year shown.

Table D. Cities — City Government Finances

	City government finances, 2012 (cont.)									
	General expenditure (cont.)									
	Percent of total for:									
City	Public welfare	Highways	Parking facilities	Education	Health and hospitals	Police protection	Sewerage and sanitation	Parks and recreation	Housing and community development	Interest on debt
	127	128	129	130	131	132	133	134	135	136
GEORGIA	X	X	X	X	X	X	X	X	X	X
Albany	0.0	4.9	0.0	0.0	0.0	11.4	15.9	5.6	5.6	1.4
Alpharetta	0.0	23.5	0.0	0.0	0.0	19.9	4.3	8.5	0.0	1.8
Athens-Clarke County	0.2	4.4	1.6	0.0	5.2	11.0	11.5	5.5	1.8	0.4
Atlanta	1.2	2.2	0.0	1.3	0.1	11.0	13.8	4.1	1.0	10.4
Augusta-Richmond County	0.2	6.6	0.1	0.0	6.2	11.7	18.1	4.9	6.5	1.3
Columbus	0.0	10.1	0.0	0.0	8.2	13.4	10.9	3.8	2.8	2.7
Dalton	0.8	5.6	0.0	0.0	0.0	10.7	27.0	11.8	0.1	2.3
Douglasville	0.0	4.7	0.0	0.0	0.0	25.3	15.3	31.6	0.8	3.5
Duluth	0.0	21.9	0.5	0.0	0.0	31.7	0.0	12.3	0.9	2.1
Dunwoody	0.0	22.3	0.0	0.0	0.0	22.3	2.5	23.3	8.6	0.3
East Point	0.0	6.9	0.0	0.0	0.0	25.4	20.7	2.7	3.3	3.1
Gainesville	4.3	4.3	0.0	0.0	0.0	12.4	22.0	12.2	0.9	2.6
Hinesville	0.0	11.7	0.0	0.0	0.0	23.7	19.6	1.5	4.0	1.6
Johns Creek	0.0	20.6	0.0	0.0	0.0	21.0	0.0	3.6	6.9	0.5
Kennesaw	0.0	17.6	0.0	0.0	0.0	21.1	7.9	9.3	2.7	4.0
LaGrange	0.0	12.7	0.0	0.0	0.5	20.4	32.2	2.5	1.6	0.5
Lawrenceville	0.0	16.5	0.0	0.0	0.0	37.1	18.1	0.0	1.5	0.0
Macon-Bibb County	0.0	2.6	0.1	0.0	0.4	20.4	8.6	5.0	5.9	1.3
Marietta	5.6	11.8	0.0	0.0	0.0	14.3	14.3	5.3	3.3	4.2
Milton	0.0	25.7	0.0	0.0	0.7	15.0	0.0	2.8	3.7	0.3
Newnan	0.0	11.4	0.0	0.0	0.2	21.1	23.1	3.7	1.2	0.0
Peachtree City	0.3	7.9	0.0	0.0	0.7	16.0	2.6	8.7	0.1	1.9
Rome	0.0	8.7	0.8	0.1	0.0	12.5	22.9	2.5	2.4	0.5
Roswell	0.0	12.1	0.0	0.0	0.0	17.7	10.8	11.8	2.1	1.2
Sandy Springs	0.0	27.3	0.0	0.0	0.0	23.0	1.9	6.3	1.1	0.3
Savannah	0.3	4.5	2.1	0.0	0.0	20.3	17.7	6.9	10.8	1.5
Smyrna	0.0	22.7	0.0	0.0	0.0	14.8	15.7	4.7	0.3	3.6
Statesboro	0.0	8.4	0.0	0.0	0.3	19.2	31.7	2.2	2.0	0.1
Stockbridge	0.0	17.1	0.0	0.0	0.0	8.4	17.0	3.3	1.1	5.7
Valdosta	0.0	12.1	0.0	0.0	0.0	21.5	25.4	2.4	1.0	0.2
Warner Robins	0.2	11.8	0.0	0.0	0.8	25.1	22.9	3.7	3.1	0.0
HAWAII	X	X	X	X	X	X	X	X	X	X
East Honolulu CDP	NA	NA	NA	NA	NA	NA	NA	NA	NA	NA
Hilo CDP	NA	NA	NA	NA	NA	NA	NA	NA	NA	NA
Kahului CDP	NA	NA	NA	NA	NA	NA	NA	NA	NA	NA
Kailua CDP (Honolulu County)	NA	NA	NA	NA	NA	NA	NA	NA	NA	NA
Kaneohe CDP	NA	NA	NA	NA	NA	NA	NA	NA	NA	NA
Mililani Town CDP	NA	NA	NA	NA	NA	NA	NA	NA	NA	NA
Pearl City CDP	NA	NA	NA	NA	NA	NA	NA	NA	NA	NA
Urban Honolulu CDP	NA	NA	NA	NA	NA	NA	NA	NA	NA	NA
Waipahu CDP	NA	NA	NA	NA	NA	NA	NA	NA	NA	NA
IDAHO	X	X	X	X	X	X	X	X	X	X
Boise City	0.0	0.9	0.0	0.0	0.0	16.9	19.6	7.6	2.4	0.6
Caldwell	0.0	10.3	0.0	0.0	0.0	19.7	16.9	5.7	0.0	1.3
Coeur d'Alene	0.0	10.0	0.3	0.0	0.0	18.0	32.7	5.5	0.2	1.6
Idaho Falls	0.0	6.6	0.0	0.0	4.4	14.1	16.6	12.8	0.0	0.1
Lewiston	0.0	13.4	0.0	0.0	0.0	15.9	27.8	7.7	3.2	0.7
Meridian	0.0	0.0	0.0	0.0	0.0	26.6	23.6	9.0	0.4	0.3
Nampa	0.0	7.3	0.1	0.0	0.6	21.3	17.3	14.0	0.9	3.1
Pocatello	0.0	9.8	0.0	0.0	4.3	16.7	12.7	5.2	1.4	1.8
Post Falls	0.0	12.2	0.0	0.0	0.0	22.6	27.3	8.3	0.0	3.4
Rexburg	0.0	9.2	0.0	0.0	0.7	6.6	16.2	20.9	2.6	1.0
Twin Falls	0.0	14.4	0.2	0.0	1.0	21.5	19.5	6.3	1.9	0.8
ILLINOIS	X	X	X	X	X	X	X	X	X	X
Addison	0.0	16.5	0.0	0.0	0.0	38.7	13.7	0.0	0.0	6.6
Algonquin	0.0	19.0	0.0	0.0	0.0	39.5	10.4	8.0	0.0	0.9
Alton	0.0	13.1	0.0	0.0	0.5	25.5	14.9	8.3	0.0	2.0
Arlington Heights	0.0	12.4	1.5	0.0	1.8	26.6	1.9	0.9	0.4	2.9
Aurora	0.0	10.8	0.6	0.0	0.4	28.0	2.2	3.8	2.0	11.6
Bartlett	0.0	16.3	0.7	0.0	0.0	37.2	10.5	8.1	0.0	7.2
Batavia	0.0	37.4	0.0	0.0	0.0	19.8	6.2	0.0	0.0	1.8
Belleville	0.0	8.5	0.0	0.0	0.0	9.1	31.1	1.7	0.0	4.9
Belvidere	0.0	14.5	0.0	0.0	0.1	33.8	11.9	1.0	0.0	2.3
Berwyn	0.3	11.0	0.1	0.0	0.0	26.6	8.8	2.9	4.0	5.8
Bloomington	0.0	5.5	0.9	0.0	0.0	14.8	15.4	16.9	0.6	2.8
Bolingbrook	0.0	14.2	0.0	0.0	0.0	22.2	9.2	11.1	0.3	10.3
Buffalo Grove	0.0	6.9	0.3	0.0	0.0	24.6	16.7	6.1	0.0	0.4

	City government finances, 2012 (cont.)			Climate[2]						
	Debt outstanding			Average daily temperature (degrees Fahrenheit)						
				Mean		Limits				
City	Total (mil dol)	Per capita[1] (dollars)	Debt issued during year	January	July	January[3]	July[4]	Annual precipitation (inches)	Heating degree days	Cooling degree days
	137	138	139	140	141	142	143	144	145	146
GEORGIA	X	X	X	X	X	X	X	X	X	X
Albany	71.8	926	16.6	47.5	81.4	35.1	92.5	53.40	2 106	2 264
Alpharetta	54.6	880	29.0	39.5	77.2	29.1	87.5	51.82	3 490	1 327
Athens-Clarke County	263.4	2 214	18.1	42.2	79.8	32.9	90.2	47.83	2 861	1 785
Atlanta	7 446.5	16 770	997.4	41.7	79.5	31.3	90.6	49.10	3 004	1 679
Augusta-Richmond County	619.6	3 141	0.0	44.8	80.8	33.1	92.0	44.58	2 525	1 986
Columbus	514.9	2 574	66.6	46.8	82.0	36.6	91.7	48.57	2 154	2 296
Dalton	51.3	1 540	0.5	39.4	78.0	28.8	89.8	53.64	3 534	1 393
Douglasville	43.7	1 399	13.4	NA	NA	NA	NA	NA	NA	NA
Duluth	10.1	363	0.0	NA	NA	NA	NA	NA	NA	NA
Dunwoody	7.3	154	5.2	NA	NA	NA	NA	NA	NA	NA
East Point	99.0	2 784	0.0	42.7	80.0	33.5	89.4	50.20	2 827	1 810
Gainesville	711.3	20 464	0.0	36.0	72.9	24.7	84.0	58.19	4 421	752
Hinesville	24.5	706	1.8	51.6	82.6	40.7	93.3	48.32	1 551	2 539
Johns Creek	3.2	39	0.2	NA	NA	NA	NA	NA	NA	NA
Kennesaw	25.6	819	0.0	NA	NA	NA	NA	NA	NA	NA
LaGrange	38.1	1 257	0.0	42.2	78.7	31.3	89.3	53.38	3 078	1 551
Lawrenceville	0.0	0	0.0	NA	NA	NA	NA	NA	NA	NA
Macon-Bibb County	46.4	298	19.4	45.5	81.1	34.5	91.8	45.00	2 364	2 115
Marietta	100.1	1 712	0.0	39.4	77.9	28.5	89.3	54.43	3 505	1 403
Milton	1.1	32	0.0	NA	NA	NA	NA	NA	NA	NA
Newnan	38.2	1 119	0.0	42.6	79.4	31.8	90.5	50.10	2 958	1 679
Peachtree City	15.8	457	0.0	39.4	77.5	29.1	87.7	56.16	3 510	1 360
Rome	63.5	1 764	0.0							
Roswell	12.2	130	1.7	39.5	77.2	29.1	87.5	51.82	3 490	1 327
Sandy Springs	2.8	29	0.0	NA	NA	NA	NA	NA	NA	NA
Savannah	184.3	1 296	0.0	49.2	82.1	38.0	92.3	49.58	1 799	2 454
Smyrna	50.4	956	0.0	42.7	80.0	33.5	89.4	50.20	2 827	1 810
Statesboro	18.7	623	0.1	NA	NA	NA	NA	NA	NA	NA
Stockbridge	17.6	656	0.4	NA	NA	NA	NA	NA	NA	NA
Valdosta	48.0	832	12.1	50.0	80.9	38.0	92.0	53.06	1 782	2 319
Warner Robins	39.6	552	31.7	45.5	81.1	34.5	91.8	45.00	2 364	2 115
HAWAII	X	X	X	X	X	X	X	X	X	X
East Honolulu CDP	NA	NA	NA	NA	NA	NA	NA	NA	NA	NA
Hilo CDP	NA	NA	NA	NA	NA	NA	NA	NA	NA	NA
Kahului CDP	NA	NA	NA	NA	NA	NA	NA	NA	NA	NA
Kailua CDP (Honolulu County)	NA	NA	NA	NA	NA	NA	NA	NA	NA	NA
Kaneohe CDP	NA	NA	NA	NA	NA	NA	NA	NA	NA	NA
Mililani Town CDP	NA	NA	NA	NA	NA	NA	NA	NA	NA	NA
Pearl City CDP	NA	NA	NA	NA	NA	NA	NA	NA	NA	NA
Urban Honolulu CDP	NA	NA	NA	NA	NA	NA	NA	NA	NA	NA
Waipahu CDP	NA	NA	NA	NA	NA	NA	NA	NA	NA	NA
IDAHO	X	X	X	X	X	X	X	X	X	X
Boise City	79.7	375	36.5	30.2	74.7	23.6	89.2	12.19	5 727	807
Caldwell	12.5	263	0.0	29.3	68.8	19.6	85.7	10.90	6 749	410
Coeur d'Alene	31.6	692	7.6	28.4	68.7	22.1	82.6	26.07	6 540	426
Idaho Falls	21.5	370	1.6	19.3	68.4	11.1	85.9	11.02	7 917	322
Lewiston	6.6	205	0.0	33.7	73.5	28.0	87.6	12.74	5 220	792
Meridian	1.3	17	1.3	29.4	71.8	22.1	89.2	9.94	5 752	579
Nampa	58.7	700	6.7	28.9	73.3	20.8	90.5	11.37	5 873	692
Pocatello	24.5	448	0.0	24.4	69.2	16.3	87.5	12.58	7 109	387
Post Falls	11.1	387	0.0	NA	NA	NA	NA	NA	NA	NA
Rexburg	14.4	549	10.0	NA	NA	NA	NA	NA	NA	NA
Twin Falls	43.5	967	0.0	28.2	72.2	19.7	87.9	9.42	6 300	587
ILLINOIS	X	X	X	X	X	X	X	X	X	X
Addison	59.7	1 602	6.8	22.0	73.3	14.3	83.5	36.27	6 498	830
Algonquin	13.6	453	0.1	NA	NA	NA	NA	NA	NA	NA
Alton	20.7	752	0.0	27.7	78.4	19.4	88.1	38.54	5 149	1 354
Arlington Heights	53.7	709	19.6	22.0	73.3	14.3	83.5	36.27	6 498	830
Aurora	553.2	2 769	9.1	20.0	72.4	10.5	84.2	38.39	6 859	661
Bartlett	54.9	1 320	13.6	19.3	72.6	10.9	83.0	37.22	6 975	679
Batavia	54.8	2 077	1.0	NA	NA	NA	NA	NA	NA	NA
Belleville	71.6	1 652	32.1	30.9	78.1	22.1	89.6	39.37	4 612	1 339
Belvidere	5.1	199	0.0	NA	NA	NA	NA	NA	NA	NA
Berwyn	97.3	1 712	7.4	25.8	75.3	17.3	86.2	40.96	5 555	1 027
Bloomington	96.3	1 238	12.7	22.4	75.2	13.7	85.6	37.45	6 190	998
Bolingbrook	272.1	3 679	5.0	23.1	74.8	14.2	86.8	37.94	6 053	942
Buffalo Grove	2.2	52	0.0	18.4	72.1	9.6	82.3	36.56	7 149	624

1. Based on the population estimated as of July 1 of the year shown.   2. Represents normal values based on the 30-year period, 1971–2000.   3. Average daily minimum.
4. Average daily maximum.

Table D. Cities — Land Area and Population

STATE Place code	City	Land area,[1] 2016 (sq mi)	Total persons	Rank	Per square mile	White	Black or African American	American Indian, Alaska Native	Asian	Hawaiian Pacific Islander	Some other race	2 or more races[2]
		1	2	3	4	5	6	7	8	9	10	11
	ILLINOIS—Cont'd											
17 09642	Burbank	4.2	28 886	1 284	6 877.6	NA	NA	NA	NA	NA	NA	NA
17 10487	Calumet City	7.2	36 732	1 036	5 101.7	NA	NA	NA	NA	NA	NA	NA
17 11163	Carbondale	17.3	26 179	1 395	1 513.2	63.7	25.7	0.0	5.6	0.0	2.2	2.8
17 11332	Carol Stream	9.1	40 069	943	4 403.2	75.0	4.8	2.9	13.7	0.0	2.7	0.8
17 11358	Carpentersville	7.9	38 291	994	4 847.0	66.6	6.5	0.2	11.3	0.0	13.1	2.3
17 12385	Champaign	22.7	86 637	381	3 816.6	65.4	17.6	0.1	12.6	0.0	2.0	2.4
17 14000	Chicago	227.3	2 704 958	3	11 900.4	48.4	31.1	0.3	6.2	0.0	11.4	2.6
17 14026	Chicago Heights	10.2	30 026	1 251	2 943.7	NA	NA	NA	NA	NA	NA	NA
17 14351	Cicero	5.9	82 992	404	14 066.4	35.5	3.2	0.8	1.0	0.0	58.1	1.5
17 15599	Collinsville	14.7	24 635	1 429	1 675.9	NA	NA	NA	NA	NA	NA	NA
17 17887	Crystal Lake	19.4	40 339	937	2 079.3	NA	NA	NA	NA	NA	NA	NA
17 18563	Danville	18.0	31 597	1 189	1 755.4	60.2	35.2	0.0	1.3	0.0	1.1	2.3
17 18823	Decatur	42.3	72 706	482	1 718.8	72.1	20.2	0.0	0.8	0.0	1.5	5.4
17 19161	DeKalb	15.3	43 194	869	2 823.1	69.1	14.9	0.2	5.3	0.0	7.9	2.5
17 19642	Des Plaines	14.3	58 141	645	4 065.8	78.1	1.4	0.2	15.4	0.1	2.2	2.6
17 20591	Downers Grove	14.5	49 473	763	3 411.9	84.5	5.1	0.1	7.4	0.0	1.9	1.1
17 22255	East St. Louis	13.9	26 922	1 370	1 936.8	NA	NA	NA	NA	NA	NA	NA
17 23074	Elgin	37.4	112 123	256	2 997.9	66.4	6.2	0.0	6.4	0.0	18.5	2.4
17 23256	Elk Grove Village	11.4	32 931	1 155	2 888.7	80.9	1.2	0.0	7.3	0.0	6.5	4.1
17 23620	Elmhurst	10.3	46 387	824	4 503.6	90.2	1.4	0.0	3.9	0.0	0.9	2.7
17 24582	Evanston	7.8	74 895	463	9 601.9	68.6	14.4	1.0	9.7	0.0	3.3	3.9
17 27884	Freeport	11.8	24 392	1 434	2 067.1	75.0	19.6	0.0	1.7	0.0	0.4	3.3
17 28326	Galesburg	17.7	30 960	1 212	1 749.2	77.0	13.7	0.8	1.7	0.0	5.5	1.4
17 29730	Glendale Heights	5.4	34 145	1 112	6 323.1	55.0	3.8	0.3	24.3	0.0	10.5	6.1
17 29756	Glen Ellyn	6.7	28 042	1 323	4 185.4	86.0	7.1	0.0	5.6	0.0	0.4	0.9
17 29938	Glenview	14.0	47 475	806	3 391.1	79.7	1.8	0.0	17.0	0.0	0.0	1.4
17 30926	Granite City	19.4	28 908	1 283	1 490.1	NA	NA	NA	NA	NA	NA	NA
17 32018	Gurnee	13.4	30 957	1 213	2 310.2	75.4	6.6	0.0	13.3	0.0	1.0	3.7
17 32746	Hanover Park	6.3	38 044	1 002	6 038.7	44.1	6.7	0.0	21.4	0.0	24.8	3.0
17 33383	Harvey	6.2	24 947	1 427	4 023.7	NA	NA	NA	NA	NA	NA	NA
17 34722	Highland Park	12.2	29 641	1 264	2 429.6	NA	NA	NA	NA	NA	NA	NA
17 35411	Hoffman Estates	20.8	51 738	739	2 487.4	56.3	3.4	0.9	26.2	0.1	10.4	2.8
17 38570	Joliet	64.4	148 262	174	2 302.2	67.9	17.4	0.0	1.1	0.0	10.5	3.0
17 38934	Kankakee	15.0	26 445	1 386	1 763.0	51.2	39.5	0.2	2.6	0.0	4.2	2.4
17 41183	Lake in the Hills	10.3	28 830	1 290	2 799.0	88.3	1.9	0.0	7.4	0.0	0.9	1.5
17 42028	Lansing	7.5	28 086	1 320	3 744.8	56.3	33.8	0.0	0.0	0.0	8.9	1.0
17 44407	Lombard	10.2	43 815	860	4 295.6	80.0	5.2	0.0	10.7	0.0	1.3	2.8
17 45694	McHenry	14.6	26 611	1 379	1 822.7	NA	NA	NA	NA	NA	NA	NA
17 48242	Melrose Park	4.2	25 229	1 418	6 006.9	NA	NA	NA	NA	NA	NA	NA
17 49867	Moline	16.6	42 250	894	2 545.2	84.3	4.0	0.4	3.1	0.0	6.3	1.9
17 51089	Mount Prospect	10.3	54 171	699	5 259.3	79.1	2.3	0.3	11.6	0.1	3.0	3.6
17 51349	Mundelein	9.5	31 475	1 195	3 313.2	80.7	2.9	0.2	10.7	0.0	3.6	2.0
17 51622	Naperville	38.7	147 122	177	3 801.6	71.8	5.4	0.1	19.6	0.0	0.6	2.5
17 53000	Niles	5.8	29 617	1 265	5 106.4	NA	NA	NA	NA	NA	NA	NA
17 53234	Normal	18.7	54 264	697	2 901.8	84.2	7.3	0.3	4.2	0.0	0.6	3.4
17 53481	Northbrook	13.2	33 421	1 136	2 531.9	NA	NA	NA	NA	NA	NA	NA
17 53559	North Chicago	8.0	29 951	1 254	3 743.9	61.3	27.8	0.0	3.1	0.0	1.9	5.9
17 54638	Oak Forest	6.0	27 792	1 331	4 632.0	NA	NA	NA	NA	NA	NA	NA
17 54820	Oak Lawn	8.6	56 257	666	6 541.5	83.4	6.5	0.0	0.9	0.0	6.7	2.5
17 54885	Oak Park	4.7	51 774	738	11 015.7	71.8	17.7	0.0	4.8	0.0	1.2	4.6
17 55249	O'Fallon	15.3	29 031	1 279	1 897.5	81.6	13.8	0.2	2.7	0.0	0.1	1.7
17 56640	Orland Park	22.0	58 862	637	2 675.5	93.1	2.3	0.0	2.4	0.0	0.1	2.0
17 56887	Oswego	14.9	34 571	1 103	2 320.2	NA	NA	NA	NA	NA	NA	NA
17 57225	Palatine	13.6	68 766	513	5 056.3	65.2	1.8	0.0	9.6	0.0	20.8	2.7
17 57875	Park Ridge	7.1	37 496	1 020	5 281.1	NA	NA	NA	NA	NA	NA	NA
17 58447	Pekin	14.9	33 038	1 148	2 217.3	NA	NA	NA	NA	NA	NA	NA
17 59000	Peoria	48.2	114 265	244	2 370.6	59.9	26.6	0.1	4.8	0.0	3.1	5.4
17 60287	Plainfield	24.4	42 933	876	1 759.5	81.4	6.5	0.0	6.7	0.0	1.1	4.4
17 62367	Quincy	15.9	40 531	931	2 549.1	90.9	4.3	0.1	1.5	0.0	0.0	3.1
17 65000	Rockford	63.5	147 651	175	2 325.2	68.7	19.6	0.7	3.2	0.0	4.3	3.4
17 65078	Rock Island	16.9	38 210	997	2 260.9	70.4	22.8	0.2	2.8	0.0	0.9	2.9
17 65442	Romeoville	19.1	39 706	954	2 078.8	52.5	15.7	0.1	7.7	0.0	22.3	1.7
17 66040	Round Lake Beach	5.1	27 776	1 332	5 446.3	82.4	9.8	1.2	1.4	0.0	1.1	4.0
17 66703	St. Charles	14.7	32 717	1 161	2 225.6	84.5	1.8	0.6	2.3	0.0	9.7	1.2
17 68003	Schaumburg	19.3	74 446	468	3 857.3	54.9	2.1	0.8	27.0	0.9	11.0	3.3
17 70122	Skokie	10.1	64 270	566	6 363.4	58.4	7.4	0.2	28.0	0.0	1.4	4.6
17 72000	Springfield	60.1	115 715	241	1 925.4	73.8	18.1	0.1	2.8	0.0	1.0	4.1
17 73157	Streamwood	7.8	40 166	940	5 149.5	52.8	5.5	0.1	14.5	0.0	23.5	3.7
17 75484	Tinley Park	16.1	56 831	659	3 529.9	88.6	4.0	0.0	2.8	0.0	2.4	2.2
17 77005	Urbana	11.8	42 014	899	3 560.5	56.6	12.6	0.4	22.4	1.0	1.3	5.6
17 77694	Vernon Hills	7.7	26 328	1 391	3 419.2	66.7	9.1	0.0	17.7	0.0	3.3	3.2

1. Dry land or land partially or temporarily covered by water.   2. Hispanic or Latino persons may be of any race.

City	Percent Hispanic or Latino[1], 2015	Percent foreign born 2015	Age of population (percent), 2010-2014							Median age 2015	Percent female 2015	Population			
												Census counts		Percent change	
			Under 18 years	18 to 24 years	25 to 34 years	35 to 44 years	45 to 54 years	55 to 64 years	65 years and over			2000	2010	2000–2010	2010–2016
	12	13	14	15	16	17	18	19	20	21	22	23	24	25	26
ILLINOIS—Cont'd															
Burbank	29.7	25.9	25.2	13.2	11.5	10.8	12.4	15.3	11.6	35.1	52.6	27 902	28 925	3.7	-0.1
Calumet City	18.1	14.1	22.4	9.1	9.8	13.6	15.9	14.3	15.0	42.5	53.9	39 071	37 116	-5.0	-1.0
Carbondale	8.0	11.4	13.3	37.9	12.7	11.8	4.7	8.7	10.9	24.5	48.2	20 681	26 426	27.8	-0.9
Carol Stream	15.7	21.2	23.5	11.3	15.3	13.8	11.3	14.6	10.3	35.0	49.5	40 438	39 729	-1.8	0.9
Carpentersville	46.2	30.1	32.0	10.8	13.4	17.2	8.6	8.7	9.4	30.5	49.1	30 586	37 691	23.2	1.6
Champaign	4.7	14.2	14.8	29.1	15.3	10.1	10.0	11.3	9.4	28.7	49.7	67 518	81 253	20.3	6.6
Chicago	28.9	21.1	21.4	10.5	19.5	14.0	12.0	10.9	11.6	34.2	51.5	2 896 016	2 695 620	-6.9	0.3
Chicago Heights	35.3	11.3	24.9	11.5	15.4	13.2	11.8	12.4	10.7	34.2	51.7	32 776	30 367	-7.3	-1.1
Cicero	91.1	40.3	30.1	14.4	13.6	16.7	11.7	7.4	6.1	28.5	48.5	85 616	84 241	-1.6	-1.5
Collinsville	0.5	0.6	20.3	7.9	13.2	16.2	14.1	12.6	15.7	39.2	50.7	24 707	25 558	3.4	-3.6
Crystal Lake	16.8	11.2	24.8	8.8	13.3	14.5	16.7	11.5	10.4	37.1	50.8	38 000	40 991	7.9	-1.6
Danville	5.1	4.2	25.1	9.9	15.0	13.1	8.5	11.2	17.2	35.0	50.6	33 904	33 019	-2.6	-4.3
Decatur	2.3	1.7	20.8	10.9	11.8	12.9	10.6	15.2	17.8	40.4	52.4	81 860	76 138	-7.0	-4.5
DeKalb	14.6	10.3	17.1	32.6	13.6	9.4	9.9	8.7	8.7	25.1	48.3	39 018	44 119	13.1	-2.1
Des Plaines	18.7	31.7	17.8	8.0	14.8	13.0	13.0	16.3	17.2	41.8	49.1	58 720	58 385	-0.6	-0.4
Downers Grove	6.1	15.0	23.3	7.2	10.7	12.9	15.8	13.8	16.3	41.0	51.6	48 724	48 874	0.3	1.2
East St. Louis	0.5	1.0	23.3	12.0	14.5	6.4	11.3	15.1	17.4	35.4	55.8	31 542	26 917	-14.7	0.0
Elgin	43.4	27.2	26.9	8.1	13.1	15.5	12.7	10.8	13.0	35.7	50.6	94 487	108 169	14.5	3.7
Elk Grove Village	13.4	21.3	20.1	7.5	12.7	14.2	16.1	15.3	14.1	42.5	49.6	34 727	33 125	-4.6	-0.6
Elmhurst	10.4	9.2	26.9	8.4	9.2	13.1	15.8	10.3	16.2	40.0	52.8	42 762	44 136	3.2	5.1
Evanston	12.0	19.9	19.5	15.2	13.3	11.7	13.1	13.0	14.0	36.8	54.8	74 239	74 485	0.3	0.6
Freeport	5.8	3.9	23.9	6.6	10.9	14.4	8.0	13.3	23.0	40.0	53.6	26 443	25 637	-3.0	-4.9
Galesburg	8.5	5.7	20.8	12.0	11.5	13.6	10.5	13.4	18.3	37.9	48.6	33 706	32 189	-4.5	-3.8
Glendale Heights	33.1	34.1	26.5	9.2	18.1	11.7	14.5	11.2	8.9	32.5	49.7	31 765	34 212	7.7	-0.2
Glen Ellyn	9.3	12.1	26.2	7.6	11.7	13.6	12.6	12.4	15.9	38.5	53.0	26 999	27 767	2.8	1.0
Glenview	3.8	22.2	26.0	4.0	8.4	11.0	15.8	14.7	20.1	45.3	50.7	41 847	44 719	6.9	6.2
Granite City	3.5	3.0	18.8	4.9	11.5	16.2	16.8	13.2	18.6	43.9	51.5	31 301	29 849	-4.6	-3.2
Gurnee	16.8	17.5	24.9	11.1	9.5	11.7	17.9	14.8	10.2	39.0	49.7	28 834	31 254	8.4	-1.0
Hanover Park	34.2	34.3	24.5	13.8	12.4	13.5	15.8	12.2	7.7	34.6	48.1	38 278	37 956	-0.8	0.2
Harvey	19.7	9.3	25.2	8.9	12.7	14.7	11.5	13.3	13.8	38.0	56.9	30 000	25 264	-15.8	-1.3
Highland Park	4.0	10.8	23.3	6.2	5.5	11.1	16.3	15.1	22.6	48.7	51.9	31 365	29 731	-5.2	-0.3
Hoffman Estates	17.7	34.1	21.6	9.3	13.9	12.8	16.6	16.0	9.8	39.8	50.7	49 495	51 886	4.8	-0.3
Joliet	30.2	14.9	29.8	10.3	12.8	16.1	12.9	9.5	8.6	33.1	52.8	106 221	147 533	38.9	0.5
Kankakee	17.8	9.3	26.1	10.1	13.9	16.2	9.9	12.2	11.5	33.9	52.4	27 491	27 562	0.3	-4.1
Lake in the Hills	10.4	10.8	27.6	10.9	10.8	17.7	15.2	10.6	7.2	36.0	51.9	23 152	29 005	25.3	-0.6
Lansing	11.7	9.7	18.7	12.4	6.2	12.4	19.0	15.5	15.7	45.1	52.3	28 332	28 351	0.1	-0.9
Lombard	10.4	13.2	19.9	10.2	14.3	12.1	13.2	15.4	14.9	38.3	51.6	42 322	43 347	2.4	1.1
McHenry	16.5	10.7	24.3	7.9	16.3	10.7	14.2	14.0	12.6	39.1	50.5	21 501	27 016	25.6	-1.5
Melrose Park	69.3	29.1	30.1	7.4	16.6	17.2	8.7	9.7	10.3	33.1	50.4	23 171	25 414	9.7	-0.7
Moline	22.7	10.5	23.8	9.9	12.8	10.8	11.1	14.4	17.3	38.2	49.7	43 768	43 481	-0.7	-2.8
Mount Prospect	16.8	28.3	25.3	6.6	14.8	14.5	13.2	10.9	14.7	37.6	49.6	56 265	54 177	-3.7	0.0
Mundelein	23.6	23.2	25.5	7.0	12.4	12.1	13.9	17.4	11.7	39.9	50.1	30 935	30 986	0.2	1.6
Naperville	3.3	20.7	26.1	8.9	9.8	15.6	16.3	12.2	11.1	38.5	51.5	128 358	142 101	10.7	3.5
Niles	13.5	49.3	19.3	5.9	14.0	12.3	14.4	10.8	23.4	43.9	50.7	30 068	29 806	-0.9	-0.6
Normal	8.2	5.3	19.7	34.9	9.8	9.3	10.0	8.1	8.1	23.2	52.3	45 386	52 540	15.8	3.3
Northbrook	0.9	16.1	23.2	3.1	5.8	9.3	16.1	13.2	29.3	50.8	53.0	33 435	33 197	-0.7	0.7
North Chicago	30.9	18.8	21.6	31.5	17.6	8.6	7.9	6.8	6.0	23.8	39.1	35 918	32 573	-9.3	-8.0
Oak Forest	11.8	11.4	24.2	9.8	11.3	12.7	17.4	10.7	13.9	38.6	50.7	28 051	27 954	-0.3	-0.6
Oak Lawn	25.0	13.0	25.3	7.0	15.1	12.1	12.8	12.5	15.2	37.2	50.3	55 245	56 690	2.6	-0.8
Oak Park	7.3	8.7	24.4	4.2	13.5	14.9	16.1	12.5	14.4	39.6	52.6	52 524	51 878	-1.2	-0.2
O'Fallon	5.2	3.4	25.3	9.8	8.6	15.2	17.3	12.2	11.6	38.9	50.3	21 910	28 674	30.9	1.2
Orland Park	4.6	11.2	21.3	6.6	8.3	8.6	14.9	19.3	21.0	49.1	54.9	51 077	56 664	10.9	3.9
Oswego	13.4	6.5	26.0	5.5	12.9	12.9	23.2	11.9	7.6	40.1	48.3	13 326	30 431	128.4	13.6
Palatine	26.9	31.4	23.6	6.1	15.6	14.7	16.3	11.4	12.3	38.0	47.3	65 479	68 551	4.7	0.3
Park Ridge	5.0	12.9	25.8	6.1	9.5	11.7	14.5	14.0	18.3	43.5	50.5	37 775	37 479	-0.8	0.0
Pekin	1.1	1.5	19.4	8.0	14.1	12.2	12.6	15.0	18.7	42.2	50.3	33 857	34 096	0.7	-3.1
Peoria	5.8	6.3	25.2	11.1	16.2	11.7	11.1	11.0	13.7	33.1	52.6	112 936	115 089	1.9	-0.7
Plainfield	10.1	8.0	31.7	8.9	11.4	16.0	15.2	10.2	6.5	33.7	51.1	13 038	39 850	205.6	7.7
Quincy	1.3	2.0	23.9	7.0	10.6	13.0	12.7	12.2	20.6	41.3	53.0	40 366	40 636	0.7	-0.3
Rockford	19.4	12.3	24.8	9.8	13.6	11.7	12.2	12.6	15.3	36.3	52.4	150 115	153 162	2.0	-3.6
Rock Island	6.4	7.0	21.0	12.9	11.9	10.7	12.0	13.9	17.7	37.8	53.4	39 684	39 005	-1.7	-2.0
Romeoville	31.3	22.1	26.6	12.6	7.8	17.0	20.0	6.0	9.9	37.2	50.2	21 153	39 621	87.3	0.2
Round Lake Beach	53.6	24.3	30.7	14.5	11.3	15.1	11.6	7.6	9.2	28.3	48.1	25 859	28 150	8.9	-1.3
St. Charles	13.6	10.3	26.4	6.7	9.5	12.5	17.3	16.7	10.9	41.0	49.3	27 896	32 305	15.8	1.3
Schaumburg	16.5	32.5	23.6	5.7	17.6	14.8	13.3	13.2	11.9	36.9	52.6	75 386	74 229	-1.5	0.3
Skokie	10.2	42.3	21.4	5.8	11.3	13.9	12.0	15.5	20.0	43.4	51.6	63 348	64 845	2.4	-0.9
Springfield	2.3	3.6	21.5	10.2	13.6	10.8	12.9	14.9	16.0	38.8	52.8	111 454	116 444	4.5	-0.6
Streamwood	30.7	34.8	21.8	6.5	12.8	17.9	16.3	13.9	10.9	40.1	46.4	36 407	39 839	9.4	0.8
Tinley Park	9.0	11.4	25.6	6.2	14.5	10.5	12.8	17.1	13.4	38.6	53.9	48 401	56 822	17.4	0.0
Urbana	5.7	23.1	14.3	34.9	19.4	9.3	8.2	6.7	7.1	25.2	48.2	36 395	41 453	13.9	1.4
Vernon Hills	8.2	29.8	27.9	5.9	11.2	18.5	15.1	9.7	11.8	38.5	49.4	20 120	25 024	24.4	5.2

1. May be of any race.

City	Households, 2015 Number	Persons per household	Female family householder[1]	One-person	Persons in group quarters, 2010 Total	Institutional Total	Persons in nursing facilities	Non-institutional	Serious crimes known to police,[2] 2014 Number	Rate[3]	Violent	Property	Population age 25 and older	High school graduate or less	Bachelor's degree or more
	27	28	29	30	31	32	33	34	35	36	37	38	39	40	41
ILLINOIS—Cont'd															
Burbank	9 250	3.24	12.1	22.1	242	186	186	56	445	1 520	150	1 370	18 624	61.3	10.8
Calumet City	14 360	2.58	29.6	34.5	24	4	0	20	1 752	4 699	515	4 184	25 375	48.8	16.7
Carbondale	9 704	2.34	10.8	44.2	3 600	359	193	3 241	1 078	4 088	523	3 565	12 886	20.4	47.9
Carol Stream	13 420	2.87	9.0	23.2	44	44	44	0	427	1 053	109	945	25 224	28.6	38.4
Carpentersville	10 559	3.65	14.9	13.9	5	0	0	5	622	1 621	86	1 535	22 052	48.7	20.7
Champaign	34 843	2.25	6.2	40.8	8 514	392	341	8 122	3 064	3 648	770	2 878	48 310	22.9	50.0
Chicago	1 053 229	2.53	16.5	36.3	60 246	27 250	14 382	32 996	109 484	4 019	886	3 133	1 851 852	39.5	36.6
Chicago Heights	10 741	2.75	21.5	29.9	644	507	502	137	1 114	3 658	653	3 004	19 259	46.2	14.0
Cicero	21 428	3.89	22.4	8.4	196	173	173	23	2 128	2 529	385	2 144	46 527	69.6	8.3
Collinsville	10 229	2.36	7.5	34.6	65	59	59	6	805	3 228	208	3 019	17 362	38.6	30.9
Crystal Lake	15 268	2.75	11.8	24.7	267	163	163	104	894	2 219	129	2 090	28 097	27.2	41.6
Danville	11 990	2.34	20.3	34.7	2 422	2 243	159	179	2 226	6 870	1 074	5 796	19 805	52.2	13.6
Decatur	31 141	2.23	17.6	38.9	3 918	1 908	1 005	2 010	2 580	3 469	477	2 992	49 723	46.6	20.7
DeKalb	14 773	2.64	15.9	30.5	6 292	363	363	5 929	1 345	3 071	409	2 663	21 772	30.7	39.5
Des Plaines	22 823	2.53	8.9	30.5	888	822	702	66	771	1 306	90	1 216	43 595	35.7	36.7
Downers Grove	19 676	2.49	5.3	32.7	548	176	153	372	683	1 370	62	1 308	34 421	21.6	47.4
East St. Louis	11 000	2.41	27.9	50.0	433	109	90	324	2 062	7 774	3 646	4 128	17 347	54.5	10.5
Elgin	36 761	2.97	12.9	21.6	1 953	1 041	699	912	2 217	2 005	199	1 806	72 164	45.3	24.2
Elk Grove Village	14 249	2.50	8.4	30.5	132	96	96	36	529	1 580	63	1 517	25 956	29.4	33.3
Elmhurst	15 183	2.85	8.2	21.4	1 298	373	373	925	526	1 146	44	1 102	28 802	21.9	54.7
Evanston	29 889	2.29	10.6	37.5	7 024	1 297	1 150	5 727	2 051	2 705	199	2 506	49 260	19.6	65.8
Freeport	10 132	2.17	16.3	34.8	754	613	468	141	686	2 756	193	2 563	15 803	44.7	16.5
Galesburg	12 277	2.24	11.4	41.7	3 771	2 468	485	1 303	1 161	3 681	400	3 282	21 208	49.2	18.9
Glendale Heights	11 126	3.20	12.7	24.2	1	0	0	1	537	1 547	78	1 469	22 953	47.5	24.8
Glen Ellyn	10 334	2.70	11.1	21.0	5	0	0	5	366	1 314	83	1 231	18 447	14.0	61.6
Glenview	16 717	2.76	8.9	19.9	642	606	606	36	404	886	39	847	32 783	16.4	66.1
Granite City	12 258	2.36	10.5	29.7	256	158	158	98	NA	NA	NA	NA	22 250	55.5	14.9
Gurnee	10 743	2.89	6.8	24.3	89	61	61	28	1 420	4 541	106	4 435	19 879	26.0	45.3
Hanover Park	11 926	3.39	10.9	14.0	0	0	0	0	378	978	106	872	24 901	46.2	28.6
Harvey	7 719	2.67	18.5	43.8	252	192	192	60	1 539	6 065	1 296	4 768	13 778	64.0	8.0
Highland Park	10 304	2.56	7.2	19.9	255	183	173	72	354	1 183	64	1 120	18 791	9.7	72.2
Hoffman Estates	17 906	2.94	7.6	17.3	435	172	172	263	608	1 158	95	1 063	36 531	28.1	46.8
Joliet	47 074	3.13	17.9	25.0	2 945	2 185	1 189	760	3 483	2 356	335	2 021	89 913	51.1	20.7
Kankakee	7 826	3.15	23.7	30.7	1 810	921	305	889	1 453	5 376	818	4 559	16 987	57.9	12.6
Lake in the Hills	9 957	2.95	18.7	16.2	0	0	0	0	157	543	59	484	18 058	30.7	34.0
Lansing	11 217	2.55	16.1	33.2	91	83	83	8	1 262	4 421	319	4 102	19 733	37.4	29.1
Lombard	17 094	2.54	12.9	29.1	502	288	288	214	908	2 062	70	1 992	30 764	24.7	46.0
McHenry	11 189	2.52	13.2	25.8	194	186	186	8	356	1 339	90	1 249	19 210	38.5	25.6
Melrose Park	8 602	3.15	19.5	23.5	52	0	0	52	413	1 617	106	1 511	16 970	60.5	13.1
Moline	18 091	2.36	15.6	38.5	322	280	280	42	1 603	3 726	363	3 364	28 601	37.6	25.7
Mount Prospect	19 302	2.90	10.2	20.5	121	0	0	121	608	1 108	44	1 064	38 149	28.0	43.4
Mundelein	10 449	2.78	10.0	19.4	203	0	0	203	277	880	57	823	19 806	30.9	44.2
Naperville	52 329	2.76	7.1	22.8	2 489	1 188	1 108	1 301	1 747	1 201	78	1 123	95 630	13.1	65.5
Niles	10 128	2.95	9.7	31.5	1 118	1 100	1 100	18	727	2 418	90	2 328	23 241	46.1	29.5
Normal	18 563	2.66	6.3	28.0	8 332	391	377	7 941	1 160	2 102	185	1 917	24 824	27.9	46.0
Northbrook	12 771	2.59	3.0	20.9	678	611	611	67	363	1 077	21	1 056	24 919	13.0	66.9
North Chicago	6 619	3.18	17.2	27.3	12 741	196	0	12 545	381	1 293	343	951	14 320	48.6	20.1
Oak Forest	10 240	2.73	12.8	28.1	43	5	5	38	362	1 281	92	1 189	18 534	40.3	29.7
Oak Lawn	19 878	2.83	12.5	29.5	493	479	479	14	1 101	1 926	157	1 769	38 444	39.2	26.4
Oak Park	22 163	2.34	8.7	38.2	383	255	224	128	1 667	3 199	198	3 001	37 318	14.4	68.5
O'Fallon	10 503	2.71	6.3	25.3	0	0	0	0	512	1 750	140	1 610	18 503	20.2	44.1
Orland Park	22 100	2.63	8.1	26.7	464	451	451	13	1 315	2 227	37	2 189	42 369	31.3	42.1
Oswego	11 265	2.90	6.1	16.4	52	47	47	5	524	1 607	80	1 528	22 430	23.8	42.6
Palatine	25 724	2.69	7.2	27.4	168	134	134	34	659	948	52	896	48 725	30.9	44.7
Park Ridge	14 005	2.58	6.0	33.0	492	434	399	58	463	1 221	32	1 189	24 955	18.3	58.2
Pekin	13 999	2.31	8.8	35.4	2 042	1 933	281	109	832	2 441	282	2 160	24 825	49.4	18.1
Peoria	47 756	2.40	16.5	37.0	3 832	1 313	1 109	2 519	5 617	4 804	649	4 155	75 537	34.9	34.0
Plainfield	11 980	3.52	15.0	15.4	109	109	109	0	357	846	76	770	25 094	24.3	49.4
Quincy	17 478	2.25	13.1	35.4	2 087	1 378	1 015	709	1 553	3 790	464	3 327	28 187	47.5	21.8
Rockford	57 858	2.52	16.6	35.7	4 179	2 881	1 728	1 298	8 306	5 553	1 245	4 307	97 648	47.1	20.9
Rock Island	15 189	2.28	15.5	35.2	2 441	685	452	1 756	1 036	2 667	409	2 258	24 815	44.1	21.7
Romeoville	12 743	3.33	13.7	23.4	1 188	0	0	1 188	679	1 713	119	1 594	26 483	44.3	27.5
Round Lake Beach	8 636	3.54	16.5	13.3	139	139	139	0	697	2 483	125	2 359	16 833	58.1	14.3
St. Charles	11 647	2.57	4.7	30.6	1 211	1 121	161	90	510	1 530	60	1 470	20 301	16.6	46.4
Schaumburg	27 763	2.72	8.0	27.9	414	374	374	40	1 943	2 589	97	2 491	53 550	26.7	45.3
Skokie	23 059	2.78	14.3	22.6	706	494	475	212	1 502	2 301	265	2 036	47 205	30.9	44.4
Springfield	51 364	2.22	16.0	38.1	3 396	1 489	831	1 907	6 783	5 791	1 065	4 725	80 461	35.0	36.2
Streamwood	12 863	3.08	9.1	16.5	288	268	160	20	705	1 743	101	1 641	28 568	40.0	29.9
Tinley Park	22 157	2.73	13.7	24.2	45	0	0	45	975	1 698	80	1 618	41 378	34.5	33.3
Urbana	14 536	2.42	7.7	41.8	7 050	781	339	6 269	1 597	3 820	311	3 509	21 464	17.8	62.2
Vernon Hills	9 264	2.67	13.0	23.6	43	43	43	0	518	2 011	35	1 976	16 434	11.7	66.8

1. No spouse present.   2. Data for serious crimes have not been adjusted for underreporting. This may affect comparability between geographic areas and over time.   3. Per 100,000 population estimated by the FBI.   4. Persons 25 years old and over.

Table D. Cities — Income, Poverty, and Housing

City	Money income, 2015 — Households			Families		Housing units, 2010			Occupied housing units 2015 — Owner-occupied			Renter-occupied	
	Median income	Percent with income of $200,000 or more	Percent with income of less than $25,000	Total Families	Percent with income below poverty	Total	Percent change, 2000–2010	Vacant units for sale or rent[2]	Total	Percent	Median value[3] (dollars)	Percent	Median rent (dollars)
	42	43	44	45	46	47	48	49	50	51	52	53	54
ILLINOIS—Cont'd													
Burbank	52 649	3.8	18.4	6 675	11.6	9 721	2.0	434	9 250	73.4	178 100	26.6	1 073
Calumet City	35 605	1.5	21.9	9 203	17.4	15 646	-1.8	1 668	14 360	48.8	100 500	51.2	962
Carbondale	25 818	3.4	45.5	3 694	19.1	12 419	12.7	1 384	9 704	33.1	127 000	66.9	658
Carol Stream	65 715	4.0	13.6	9 234	7.7	15 050	6.2	786	13 420	67.6	232 600	32.4	1 022
Carpentersville	58 804	3.7	17.6	8 781	16.8	11 583	29.6	731	10 559	67.8	169 100	32.2	961
Champaign	48 394	6.1	24.6	15 238	3.5	34 434	20.4	2 227	34 843	44.8	161 200	55.2	982
Chicago	50 702	6.7	21.8	567 570	16.5	1 194 337	3.6	148 777	1 053 229	43.8	238 500	56.2	985
Chicago Heights	39 291	1.3	26.7	6 721	28.5	11 060	-3.7	1 473	10 741	60.4	102 500	39.6	944
Cicero	44 664	0.9	14.7	18 327	18.2	24 329	-1.3	2 228	21 428	47.3	157 900	52.7	879
Collinsville	49 094	1.8	12.9	NA	NA	11 891	7.1	964	10 229	60.8	125 000	39.2	914
Crystal Lake	83 448	7.0	7.6	NA	NA	15 176	13.6	755	15 268	75.4	201 200	24.6	1 231
Danville	35 908	0.8	24.8	7 028	16.1	14 719	-1.0	1 876	11 990	50.9	64 400	49.1	652
Decatur	41 119	1.4	27.0	17 593	18.9	36 134	-3.0	3 790	31 141	60.3	81 300	39.7	632
DeKalb	36 748	1.4	29.8	7 824	23.9	16 436	21.4	1 050	14 773	40.5	146 900	59.5	900
Des Plaines	64 164	3.5	7.9	14 854	3.0	24 075	4.9	1 375	22 823	71.3	247 600	28.7	1 140
Downers Grove	83 711	12.4	11.2	12 574	0.6	20 478	4.9	1 291	19 676	73.1	345 700	26.9	1 202
East St. Louis	21 797	0.8	46.8	5 069	37.6	12 055	-6.6	1 936	11 000	44.4	53 800	55.6	513
Elgin	57 097	4.3	13.0	26 963	9.9	37 848	15.7	2 754	36 761	65.1	172 100	34.9	1 020
Elk Grove Village	81 217	5.0	5.5	NA	NA	13 905	3.3	598	14 249	76.9	256 000	23.1	1 198
Elmhurst	96 420	22.0	5.6	11 470	2.0	16 590	2.1	825	15 183	77.5	411 800	22.5	1 484
Evanston	70 969	18.6	16.3	16 081	8.4	33 181	7.7	3 134	29 889	53.4	401 000	46.6	1 253
Freeport	37 861	0.9	24.9	6 087	11.8	12 396	-0.7	1 364	10 132	53.6	73 900	46.4	625
Galesburg	35 088	1.0	28.4	6 241	10.3	14 280	1.2	1 272	12 277	58.3	74 900	41.7	635
Glendale Heights	61 368	2.5	5.2	7 762	2.2	11 864	7.3	607	11 126	62.7	169 000	37.3	1 102
Glen Ellyn	106 454	19.4	10.7	7 761	8.1	11 051	4.3	627	10 334	71.6	447 600	28.4	1 035
Glenview	100 905	26.6	8.9	13 040	7.4	17 746	12.2	963	16 717	79.2	533 100	20.8	1 708
Granite City	51 022	1.7	19.4	7 458	6.5	13 578	-3.9	1 364	12 258	67.1	85 800	32.9	620
Gurnee	93 588	11.8	5.9	7 437	3.4	12 031	11.2	495	10 743	70.3	250 600	29.7	1 357
Hanover Park	76 548	4.1	11.2	9 856	8.0	11 483	0.7	562	11 926	75.2	176 100	24.8	991
Harvey	21 825	2.1	44.7	3 933	24.3	9 805	-3.6	1 858	7 719	43.1	71 500	56.9	806
Highland Park	150 051	39.8	5.9	7 959	1.7	12 256	2.8	846	10 304	80.3	612 000	19.7	1 851
Hoffman Estates	93 683	6.8	6.0	14 296	3.1	18 970	8.5	838	17 906	75.7	272 800	24.3	1 192
Joliet	58 363	1.3	15.4	32 940	12.2	51 285	34.3	3 266	47 074	68.2	163 000	31.8	924
Kankakee	40 777	0.4	34.1	5 231	27.2	10 935	-0.1	1 289	7 826	44.0	87 300	56.0	803
Lake in the Hills	84 420	5.1	7.5	8 019	5.6	9 885	25.8	341	9 957	80.6	210 700	19.4	1 423
Lansing	51 250	1.1	16.3	7 040	14.4	11 741	0.1	784	11 217	70.7	129 300	29.3	1 007
Lombard	67 839	6.8	12.3	11 210	8.9	18 454	8.9	1 049	17 094	69.9	246 000	30.1	1 336
McHenry	66 848	6.1	8.3	NA	NA	10 741	32.1	666	11 189	69.1	168 200	30.9	1 055
Melrose Park	43 451	2.9	20.2	6 309	14.6	8 525	7.2	567	8 602	53.3	199 700	46.7	870
Moline	47 406	3.9	16.5	10 596	9.4	19 856	1.9	1 283	18 091	66.2	110 000	33.8	674
Mount Prospect	71 404	9.3	10.6	15 128	6.3	21 836	-1.1	1 272	19 302	66.1	319 300	33.9	987
Mundelein	85 227	10.7	5.4	7 935	4.7	10 992	8.3	485	10 449	77.1	244 500	22.9	1 165
Naperville	105 848	18.1	5.7	38 221	4.8	52 270	14.7	2 261	52 329	74.2	399 200	25.8	1 381
Niles	62 979	5.6	9.8	6 906	10.8	12 572	1.9	666	10 128	71.0	279 500	29.0	1 104
Normal	54 924	2.9	16.0	9 928	3.5	18 816	20.3	823	18 563	54.3	165 100	45.7	1 020
Northbrook	111 590	19.9	8.6	10 054	2.1	13 434	7.6	792	12 771	85.1	514 500	14.9	2 014
North Chicago	45 879	5.0	20.2	4 565	25.0	7 745	-7.3	1 125	6 619	30.3	105 900	69.7	1 094
Oak Forest	72 300	4.3	9.6	NA	NA	10 672	6.8	464	10 240	74.2	187 200	25.8	950
Oak Lawn	62 627	4.1	9.9	13 541	5.2	23 517	2.6	1 156	19 878	79.4	203 300	20.6	1 034
Oak Park	77 180	16.8	15.4	12 495	6.0	24 519	3.4	1 849	22 163	58.7	359 700	41.3	1 004
O'Fallon	78 968	5.0	11.2	NA	NA	11 414	32.7	667	10 503	64.6	196 600	35.4	899
Orland Park	83 687	10.1	8.6	15 604	1.8	22 443	17.6	804	22 100	89.3	282 100	10.7	1 127
Oswego	112 826	13.5	2.5	NA	NA	10 388	125.0	453	11 265	88.2	240 600	11.8	1 586
Palatine	75 997	8.5	7.5	16 967	10.1	28 621	9.2	1 745	25 724	68.8	278 000	31.2	1 106
Park Ridge	97 849	21.3	6.0	9 119	2.8	15 030	2.8	912	14 005	81.5	423 400	18.5	1 335
Pekin	51 738	1.2	11.5	8 559	8.6	14 714	5.1	894	13 999	73.5	115 100	26.5	613
Peoria	49 121	5.7	24.2	27 259	15.7	52 621	7.3	5 469	47 756	56.4	132 100	43.6	787
Plainfield	111 410	17.9	5.7	9 879	4.5	12 532	174.2	612	11 980	82.8	280 800	17.2	1 785
Quincy	40 309	2.7	21.6	10 292	15.7	18 655	3.7	1 504	17 478	63.6	109 700	36.4	546
Rockford	40 720	1.9	25.2	34 015	16.0	66 700	4.9	6 727	57 858	56.0	87 200	44.0	695
Rock Island	47 912	1.1	21.6	9 292	15.3	17 422	-0.5	1 492	15 189	64.3	96 500	35.7	760
Romeoville	68 017	2.5	9.0	9 023	6.6	12 623	71.3	636	12 743	79.4	160 900	20.6	1 567
Round Lake Beach	53 111	0.7	13.7	6 872	14.4	8 587	13.5	532	8 636	67.6	127 600	32.4	1 242
St. Charles	98 876	15.9	9.4	NA	NA	13 157	18.9	733	11 647	66.6	303 500	33.4	1 072
Schaumburg	73 537	6.3	8.8	18 973	5.0	33 610	1.6	2 071	27 763	62.9	227 200	37.1	1 334
Skokie	67 338	5.6	12.9	16 793	5.6	25 066	5.8	1 535	23 059	67.8	297 900	32.2	1 160
Springfield	52 102	5.2	20.0	28 698	16.0	55 729	3.4	5 015	51 364	60.0	129 000	40.0	745
Streamwood	80 719	5.1	9.3	10 333	3.4	13 629	10.0	595	12 863	81.0	168 900	19.0	1 816
Tinley Park	73 654	7.2	7.9	15 823	10.0	22 491	24.7	825	22 157	82.6	234 000	17.4	1 122
Urbana	37 814	4.8	31.5	5 628	7.2	19 090	25.2	2 129	14 536	40.4	155 500	59.6	795
Vernon Hills	99 519	18.3	9.3	6 787	5.1	9 956	25.2	439	9 264	69.7	336 200	30.3	1 217

1. Based on population estimated by the American Community Survey.   2. Includes units rented or sold but not occupied.   3. Specified owner-occupied units; $1,000,000 represents $1,000,000 or more   4. 50.0 represents 50 percent or more.   5. 10.0 represents 10 percent or less.

Table D. Cities — Commuting, Computer Access, Migration, Labor Force, and Employment

City	Commuting Percent — Drove alone	Commuting Percent — With Commutes of 30 minutes or more[1]	Computer Access[2] Percent — With a Computer in the house	Computer Access[2] Percent — With Internet Access	Migration, 2015 — Percent who lived in the same house one year ago	Migration, 2015 — Percent who lived in an other state or county one year ago	Civilian labor force, 2016 — Total	Civilian labor force, 2016 — Percent change, 2015–2016	Unemployment — Total	Unemployment — Rate[3]	Civilian employment[4], 2015 — Population age 16 and older — Number	Civilian employment[4], 2015 — Population age 16 and older — Percent in Labor Force	Civilian employment[4], 2015 — Population age 16 to 64 — Number	Civilian employment[4], 2015 — Population age 16 to 64 — Percent who worked full-year full-time
	55	56	57	58	59	60	61	62	63	64	65	66	67	68
ILLINOIS—Cont'd														
Burbank	85.6	55.3	84.9	79.1	NA	NA	14 351	0.6	860	6.0	24 530	60.3	21 013	39.3
Calumet City	79.7	69.2	71.2	60.4	NA	NA	16 588	0.7	1 530	9.2	29 813	57.6	24 273	42.4
Carbondale	81.2	9.3	87.8	69.1	55.5	22.4	11 930	0.2	674	5.6	23 034	61.1	20 146	19.5
Carol Stream	88.3	51.0	92.1	87.0	90.0	3.6	24 094	0.6	1 133	4.7	30 441	72.4	26 458	52.5
Carpentersville	80.2	45.7	90.2	80.6	91.8	6.3	19 248	0.2	1 342	7.0	27 345	70.0	23 729	52.4
Champaign	68.0	6.6	93.2	81.0	76.0	13.0	43 407	0.4	2 201	5.1	74 416	63.4	66 361	40.6
Chicago	51.9	60.9	82.8	71.1	84.7	3.9	1 371 326	0.8	89 209	6.5	2 200 593	66.0	1 884 431	48.8
Chicago Heights	85.6	39.7	71.1	61.7	91.5	2.9	13 142	0.0	1 172	8.9	23 625	65.0	20 383	42.3
Cicero	65.3	56.8	79.0	69.0	88.2	1.7	37 178	0.8	2 430	6.5	61 679	66.7	56 560	45.5
Collinsville	88.7	38.6	89.3	78.8	77.1	14.6	12 960	1.1	744	5.7	19 889	67.5	16 101	50.2
Crystal Lake	86.0	51.8	90.0	84.3	87.4	5.8	22 734	0.8	1 108	4.9	32 959	71.8	28 562	59.5
Danville	80.3	11.4	76.6	68.1	83.2	4.8	12 969	-1.2	1 042	8.0	23 615	50.6	18 371	36.8
Decatur	82.2	13.9	80.8	68.5	82.4	3.7	32 894	-0.7	2 398	7.3	59 282	58.0	46 288	41.8
DeKalb	75.3	28.2	90.6	83.6	60.4	19.7	22 347	0.1	1 212	5.4	36 133	63.0	32 378	34.5
Des Plaines	84.7	43.2	88.7	76.9	86.2	3.0	32 852	0.8	1 715	5.2	49 159	72.4	39 047	56.6
Downers Grove	84.4	40.7	85.6	81.6	90.9	3.7	27 533	1.0	1 206	4.4	39 786	69.7	31 701	58.7
East St. Louis	70.3	39.3	59.6	30.6	NA	NA	9 102	-0.2	919	10.1	20 600	52.6	15 926	24.1
Elgin	80.3	41.7	89.6	77.9	89.3	6.6	57 382	0.2	3 703	6.5	84 888	67.6	70 464	52.4
Elk Grove Village	88.2	49.9	90.5	84.0	NA	NA	19 354	0.7	971	5.0	29 080	71.1	24 026	62.0
Elmhurst	75.3	50.9	90.9	87.5	89.3	6.5	23 460	1.1	1 108	4.7	33 919	63.2	26 690	53.6
Evanston	52.0	48.1	92.5	86.0	82.4	6.2	39 757	0.8	1 951	4.9	62 725	63.0	52 116	46.6
Freeport	67.2	22.3	81.1	69.4	71.8	7.8	10 534	-0.6	691	6.6	17 859	64.0	12 636	46.8
Galesburg	75.6	8.2	76.5	66.2	87.9	5.0	12 967	-0.2	827	6.4	25 727	50.7	19 949	34.6
Glendale Heights	78.5	40.0	94.1	90.8	82.7	2.5	19 456	0.7	1 051	5.4	27 411	77.8	24 222	59.4
Glen Ellyn	76.6	45.6	91.1	86.1	89.2	3.1	14 322	0.7	641	4.5	21 547	64.9	17 121	50.7
Glenview	78.5	47.6	90.7	87.8	89.6	3.3	23 226	1.0	1 048	4.5	36 546	57.7	27 127	50.2
Granite City	84.3	39.0	82.3	77.5	NA	NA	13 523	1.6	1 064	7.9	24 473	65.2	19 056	51.7
Gurnee	89.0	33.9	93.9	87.1	87.8	4.9	17 386	1.0	821	4.7	24 490	72.1	21 313	52.5
Hanover Park	81.0	45.2	94.9	88.2	87.5	2.8	20 924	0.8	1 286	6.1	31 566	75.7	28 449	53.8
Harvey	76.2	43.7	66.2	53.7	NA	NA	8 407	0.4	956	11.4	16 179	53.5	13 296	35.8
Highland Park	78.5	47.4	92.5	89.3	86.5	3.7	15 206	1.1	632	4.2	21 363	64.8	15 344	55.3
Hoffman Estates	88.4	47.6	96.3	91.9	86.8	6.9	30 323	1.1	1 445	4.8	42 986	71.3	37 789	54.8
Joliet	87.0	41.8	87.2	78.9	88.2	4.2	75 273	0.8	5 552	7.4	110 577	70.4	97 649	49.8
Kankakee	78.4	27.3	78.9	66.3	87.6	6.2	11 159	-0.2	997	8.9	20 172	50.3	17 106	31.3
Lake in the Hills	94.6	56.6	98.8	96.4	82.6	14.0	16 278	0.9	837	5.1	22 498	77.5	20 373	56.5
Lansing	86.4	43.8	86.2	76.2	89.0	1.4	14 516	0.8	980	6.8	24 456	64.8	19 945	44.9
Lombard	85.3	43.6	89.6	85.2	84.0	5.9	25 231	0.8	1 169	4.6	36 460	64.7	29 890	50.1
McHenry	86.9	49.1	91.8	85.9	88.0	4.1	14 136	0.8	741	5.2	22 116	68.8	18 555	57.2
Melrose Park	83.9	47.1	88.3	65.7	87.9	2.7	12 035	0.3	733	6.1	19 565	67.1	16 777	54.2
Moline	85.7	14.8	84.7	74.5	87.9	6.1	21 901	-0.5	1 288	5.9	33 727	63.3	26 266	52.6
Mount Prospect	76.9	46.3	88.2	80.7	90.3	3.1	29 768	1.0	1 377	4.6	43 037	69.6	34 785	51.8
Mundelein	81.4	48.6	98.9	94.1	90.0	2.3	18 313	0.9	900	4.9	22 898	72.0	19 475	56.5
Naperville	80.6	54.0	95.9	92.7	86.3	8.6	78 524	1.0	3 636	4.6	113 376	69.5	97 086	53.1
Niles	80.2	48.5	83.1	80.0	94.5	1.0	13 980	0.9	729	5.2	25 492	55.7	18 216	51.7
Normal	79.2	12.1	96.1	79.8	76.4	14.4	28 561	-1.4	1 430	5.0	45 010	67.8	40 570	39.5
Northbrook	80.9	48.2	94.9	90.8	91.7	2.6	16 411	1.1	759	4.6	26 922	51.9	17 027	48.3
North Chicago	43.3	18.2	90.0	83.5	60.3	30.9	8 886	0.4	606	6.8	24 877	79.7	23 038	42.6
Oak Forest	80.6	43.1	82.7	78.9	NA	NA	15 295	0.6	876	5.7	21 862	71.5	17 964	50.4
Oak Lawn	82.9	59.5	85.4	74.6	91.7	2.2	28 922	0.8	1 679	5.8	43 924	61.5	35 315	49.1
Oak Park	62.0	67.1	91.9	83.7	89.1	4.5	29 752	0.7	1 400	4.7	40 634	70.1	33 103	55.5
O'Fallon	89.9	32.5	91.8	84.1	86.8	7.7	13 786	0.8	680	4.9	22 541	67.2	19 239	49.2
Orland Park	82.1	57.4	89.8	82.5	94.5	2.3	30 390	0.9	1 487	4.9	48 121	60.8	35 763	52.6
Oswego	87.6	58.2	NA	NA	NA	NA	18 625	1.0	901	4.8	25 815	77.6	23 322	64.4
Palatine	79.9	44.4	92.1	84.7	83.3	2.8	39 730	0.9	1 938	4.9	55 022	72.7	46 476	56.4
Park Ridge	75.9	49.3	90.2	86.0	93.1	2.4	19 743	1.3	969	4.9	28 084	64.9	21 368	59.1
Pekin	82.2	26.4	83.3	76.2	84.9	5.9	15 614	-1.4	1 124	7.2	28 126	59.4	21 731	48.9
Peoria	78.8	14.4	80.4	68.4	82.0	6.3	53 871	-1.4	3 741	6.9	90 860	62.6	74 573	47.8
Plainfield	87.3	56.7	98.5	96.1	NA	NA	22 206	0.8	1 073	4.8	30 300	73.7	27 539	57.9
Quincy	82.9	5.7	75.4	68.7	88.4	3.7	19 251	-0.5	972	5.0	31 813	63.2	23 395	54.1
Rockford	86.2	17.8	82.3	68.4	82.1	5.8	67 261	-0.6	5 181	7.7	116 255	62.0	93 414	40.2
Rock Island	78.2	13.7	82.0	70.8	79.9	5.9	18 329	-0.5	1 183	6.5	30 422	64.1	23 786	46.3
Romeoville	94.6	43.7	92.1	85.1	89.8	4.3	20 017	0.7	1 266	6.3	33 309	70.1	28 994	46.6
Round Lake Beach	84.7	70.1	91.5	86.3	NA	NA	15 077	0.7	1 104	7.3	22 662	71.2	19 831	48.4
St. Charles	92.8	46.3	92.7	86.4	90.8	2.1	18 760	0.1	802	4.3	23 214	68.7	19 899	53.0
Schaumburg	85.5	45.4	93.6	86.7	87.9	4.9	44 383	0.9	2 079	4.7	59 135	73.5	50 136	56.0
Skokie	72.3	51.6	89.9	85.6	89.0	1.8	33 130	0.9	1 635	4.9	52 699	58.9	39 713	44.6
Springfield	83.4	11.4	85.0	75.0	79.0	6.2	60 296	0.6	3 107	5.2	95 829	62.8	76 933	45.8
Streamwood	83.7	54.2	89.6	81.8	91.1	3.2	23 821	1.0	1 323	5.6	32 251	73.3	27 924	62.6
Tinley Park	81.3	57.7	95.4	89.0	92.1	4.0	32 307	0.7	1 577	4.9	46 519	69.5	38 393	51.0
Urbana	56.1	11.3	94.1	79.0	65.2	22.6	21 224	0.3	1 108	5.2	36 777	52.9	33 768	32.8
Vernon Hills	80.5	50.0	96.4	87.1	93.9	2.9	15 093	1.0	649	4.3	18 595	67.2	15 671	53.5

1. Employed persons.   2. Households.   3. Percent of civilian labor force.   4. Persons 16 years old and over.

Table D. Cities — Construction, Wholesale Trade, and Retail Trade

City	Value of residential construction authorized by building permits, 2016			Wholesale trade,[1] 2012				Retail trade,[2] 2012			
	New construction ($1,000)	Number of housing units	Percent single family	Number of establishments	Number of employees	Sales (mil dol)	Annual payroll (mil dol)	Number of establishments	Number of employees	Sales (mil dol)	Annual payroll (mil dol)
	69	70	71	72	73	74	75	76	77	78	79
ILLINOIS—Cont'd											
Burbank	1 205	9	100.0	6	25	6.3	0.6	90	1 363	370.6	25.7
Calumet City	0	0	0.0	12	D	D	D	173	2 769	550.6	57.6
Carbondale	3 580	23	47.8	10	108	32.8	4.7	157	2 760	760.2	56.4
Carol Stream	1 874	14	100.0	109	2 642	3 245.6	162.4	91	1 508	606.1	43.9
Carpentersville	0	0	0.0	14	D	D	D	52	882	251.1	19.5
Champaign	101 533	655	21.5	66	1 267	670.3	52.9	394	6 538	1 496.1	132.6
Chicago	1 365 599	9 104	6.7	2 310	37 189	33 135.0	2 291.0	7 285	85 388	22 627.3	2 221.8
Chicago Heights	0	0	0.0	37	1 028	850.8	52.8	68	758	172.0	15.8
Cicero	0	0	0.0	37	638	460.5	29.8	134	2 028	638.7	46.1
Collinsville	12 291	87	8.0	27	201	135.3	10.1	89	1 754	465.6	39.7
Crystal Lake	1 759	3	100.0	68	662	565.9	35.7	210	3 601	940.5	83.8
Danville	680	5	100.0	42	D	D	D	150	2 342	537.7	50.3
Decatur	2 265	15	100.0	83	1 104	2 699.4	56.1	296	4 330	1 204.4	106.5
DeKalb	439	2	100.0	15	D	D	D	133	2 587	508.9	50.7
Des Plaines	14 749	69	37.7	138	2 522	3 236.9	181.8	171	3 047	972.2	96.9
Downers Grove	32 871	71	97.2	113	2 190	3 356.2	202.4	227	4 336	1 393.7	112.5
East St. Louis	0	0	0.0	20	201	462.1	8.2	61	378	91.2	9.3
Elgin	32 492	175	100.0	193	3 654	3 558.4	242.5	240	3 813	1 223.6	105.5
Elk Grove Village	0	0	0.0	447	7 000	5 203.5	432.9	116	2 416	692.4	70.3
Elmhurst	55 088	128	100.0	130	3 294	1 738.7	321.0	158	2 107	726.8	65.1
Evanston	8 352	12	100.0	53	529	468.7	33.7	213	3 480	940.1	95.6
Freeport	0	0	0.0	22	161	104.1	5.8	111	1 665	380.4	36.5
Galesburg	997	7	100.0	23	362	188.5	15.0	153	3 184	717.4	70.5
Glendale Heights	0	0	0.0	66	1 605	1 089.3	101.3	68	1 459	410.3	38.7
Glen Ellyn	7 967	17	100.0	32	340	188.3	19.0	95	1 154	271.5	25.2
Glenview	48 637	116	100.0	100	1 478	1 320.7	86.2	159	3 471	1 344.4	153.0
Granite City	355	3	100.0	27	311	290.1	14.0	88	1 361	376.4	36.8
Gurnee	852	3	100.0	64	869	752.5	45.7	255	4 991	1 080.4	98.3
Hanover Park	0	0	0.0	29	1 122	1 993.0	59.8	68	872	216.5	19.1
Harvey	0	0	0.0	22	320	102.2	15.7	64	362	108.6	8.2
Highland Park	33 145	97	24.7	48	172	715.5	14.9	166	2 543	1 008.3	82.9
Hoffman Estates	6 887	30	100.0	80	1 536	1 900.4	178.6	116	2 421	792.2	78.3
Joliet	39 543	228	86.4	93	1 662	1 981.6	93.5	408	6 796	1 819.2	161.5
Kankakee	0	0	0.0	31	591	442.4	22.2	84	1 152	292.6	26.5
Lake in the Hills	3 640	16	100.0	21	D	D	D	43	708	221.3	19.9
Lansing	0	0	0.0	31	310	117.6	20.6	103	1 840	430.2	44.8
Lombard	6 153	20	100.0	106	1 333	3 230.1	72.3	239	4 273	911.9	91.9
McHenry	7 743	90	8.9	50	2 143	975.7	109.9	130	1 633	406.3	38.1
Melrose Park	0	0	0.0	59	1 157	832.9	67.1	100	2 887	931.5	73.3
Moline	3 514	44	34.1	34	D	D	D	259	4 706	1 022.6	104.8
Mount Prospect	1 545	5	100.0	81	1 167	1 546.9	87.3	162	3 666	4 621.7	110.6
Mundelein	5 205	36	100.0	69	698	552.8	45.2	110	1 413	332.5	32.4
Naperville	118 577	400	83.8	224	2 764	3 346.8	193.6	518	9 553	4 083.3	277.8
Niles	1 589	3	100.0	100	2 067	1 060.5	148.9	273	6 549	1 744.6	155.6
Normal	14 215	151	51.0	24	D	D	D	131	2 949	701.4	59.6
Northbrook	25 767	45	100.0	188	3 410	5 037.6	390.6	259	4 718	1 282.0	139.8
North Chicago	0	0	0.0	11	415	352.7	29.2	35	124	69.5	3.0
Oak Forest	135	1	100.0	21	89	40.6	3.4	59	630	184.5	14.8
Oak Lawn	3 005	14	100.0	28	89	34.9	3.0	162	3 509	1 151.6	95.4
Oak Park	37 735	290	6.9	22	46	58.3	2.3	154	2 087	860.4	62.7
O'Fallon	41 828	145	100.0	15	68	64.4	3.1	84	1 491	311.4	31.7
Orland Park	18 572	62	100.0	51	350	129.1	17.4	371	8 020	1 924.8	186.5
Oswego	11 409	50	100.0	25	117	64.1	6.6	94	2 158	463.8	44.6
Palatine	14 421	62	48.4	69	446	414.6	20.3	186	3 623	853.2	84.9
Park Ridge	26 011	60	83.3	52	191	275.6	12.6	93	1 009	340.9	32.3
Pekin	1 906	10	80.0	15	D	D	D	125	2 127	574.9	51.7
Peoria	11 819	39	100.0	150	2 501	1 151.3	116.8	502	7 845	1 927.7	188.2
Plainfield	67 091	343	41.7	28	361	318.9	29.1	97	1 781	459.8	37.4
Quincy	10 023	64	100.0	71	1 290	693.4	52.9	256	4 452	985.0	94.2
Rockford	11 457	86	100.0	187	2 468	1 826.9	122.4	551	8 326	2 140.2	193.8
Rock Island	1 390	4	100.0	64	1 280	853.6	61.3	79	969	240.6	25.4
Romeoville	4 474	21	90.5	67	1 833	5 959.8	104.7	59	1 194	330.6	23.6
Round Lake Beach	100	1	100.0	6	18	5.0	0.8	54	1 518	323.6	32.1
St. Charles	12 419	39	89.7	102	1 005	1 648.1	55.9	160	3 016	906.6	82.0
Schaumburg	5 601	37	5.4	270	4 850	6 838.8	373.8	483	11 457	2 790.9	301.5
Skokie	3 184	5	100.0	122	D	D	D	334	5 566	1 148.2	125.8
Springfield	32 465	168	44.0	130	2 845	2 386.0	122.5	586	10 451	2 625.3	242.6
Streamwood	400	1	100.0	21	83	41.8	3.7	88	1 637	374.7	37.3
Tinley Park	5 953	29	100.0	64	739	394.4	38.2	157	3 495	1 195.9	93.4
Urbana	6 968	54	63.0	27	D	D	D	83	1 532	423.9	38.8
Vernon Hills	3 917	21	100.0	68	2 464	2 447.8	174.3	214	5 361	2 085.3	149.8

1. Merchant wholesalers except manufacturers' sales branches and offices. 2. Establishments with payroll.

Items 69—79

Table D. Cities — Real Estate, Professional Services, and Manufacturing

City	Real estate and rental and leasing, 2012				Professional, scientific, and technical services,[1] 2012				Manufacturing, 2012			
	Number of establishments	Number of employees	Receipts (mil dol)	Annual payroll (mil dol)	Number of establishments	Number of employees	Receipts (mil dol)	Annual payroll (mil dol)	Number of establishments	Number of employees	Receipts (mil dol)	Annual payroll (mil dol)
	80	81	82	83	84	85	86	87	88	89	90	91
ILLINOIS—Cont'd												
Burbank	7	19	2.6	0.4	28	92	6.9	2.3	6	47	D	2.4
Calumet City	17	95	27.8	2.4	30	D	D	D	10	485	231.5	25.8
Carbondale	51	287	40.7	5.9	59	D	D	D	13	276	D	12.3
Carol Stream	36	267	56.9	10.0	90	494	86.9	25.8	95	4 421	1 452.3	237.5
Carpentersville	22	91	13.0	3.4	36	D	D	D	24	1 720	538.9	114.1
Champaign	108	1 117	307.5	45.4	245	D	D	D	55	1 692	656.3	86.6
Chicago	3 076	23 960	7 312.7	1 464.7	10 102	147 767	36 711.4	14 148.1	1 870	58 435	26 503.4	2 891.9
Chicago Heights	15	164	58.8	9.0	26	149	10.4	4.9	52	2 462	1 775.4	143.8
Cicero	14	70	16.4	2.7	36	206	15.0	4.4	70	2 847	818.5	144.4
Collinsville	26	158	27.4	6.2	83	621	69.6	28.3	11	98	D	3.6
Crystal Lake	44	197	33.9	7.5	204	763	190.2	44.2	76	2 902	770.8	138.0
Danville	31	114	16.2	2.8	59	349	40.9	15.0	48	3 425	1 654.4	180.8
Decatur	73	432	89.0	11.4	126	1 036	119.8	45.4	81	7 384	13 124.3	380.7
DeKalb	41	340	84.7	10.6	48	146	18.8	4.1	27	987	D	42.6
Des Plaines	82	1 134	1 241.2	67.9	273	D	D	D	127	5 811	1 498.2	300.7
Downers Grove	104	504	124.9	26.5	343	3 641	798.1	288.8	62	3 257	808.2	202.8
East St. Louis	14	45	15.3	1.8	13	D	D	D	11	169	61.6	8.2
Elgin	78	298	75.2	13.2	275	1 441	213.8	73.2	182	7 541	2 914.3	396.1
Elk Grove Village	59	695	109.0	32.2	179	1 872	339.1	146.4	406	13 764	3 678.1	712.1
Elmhurst	65	367	99.6	17.0	244	1 290	193.2	85.6	75	1 574	427.8	95.0
Evanston	106	443	91.9	18.5	412	D	D	D	48	1 051	255.0	51.9
Freeport	20	68	8.6	1.8	59	345	38.1	14.7	36	1 727	402.7	89.4
Galesburg	27	107	14.9	2.4	56	285	26.1	10.1	30	732	D	29.5
Glendale Heights	15	151	97.0	5.6	43	142	16.6	5.9	47	3 195	845.5	177.9
Glen Ellyn	44	278	247.0	19.2	180	484	128.6	26.7	9	D	2.3	D
Glenview	85	475	446.8	31.4	280	2 042	250.5	161.9	47	635	165.2	37.8
Granite City	30	150	19.6	4.9	32	214	26.6	10.4	30	4 619	2 895.2	320.6
Gurnee	37	175	52.1	8.6	126	488	59.5	21.2	67	2 485	890.5	140.1
Hanover Park	13	D	D	D	38	151	26.7	5.4	11	645	217.1	31.4
Harvey	9	63	19.7	3.2	8	48	2.3	1.0	22	1 384	771.4	75.1
Highland Park	61	186	88.8	10.9	232	D	D	D	24	115	12.3	3.4
Hoffman Estates	32	123	49.8	6.7	223	1 756	291.5	133.3	25	824	290.7	67.3
Joliet	83	400	66.1	14.4	235	D	D	D	73	3 592	2 050.1	225.9
Kankakee	26	75	13.1	2.6	53	D	D	D	29	1 347	1 122.5	83.6
Lake in the Hills	10	22	3.6	0.4	53	236	48.9	14.7	18	133	D	6.1
Lansing	25	95	15.1	3.8	46	169	21.1	7.6	29	1 427	348.7	60.1
Lombard	76	2 385	474.0	96.8	222	2 198	376.2	172.9	58	895	170.8	44.5
McHenry	31	D	D	D	77	D	D	D	58	1 296	242.2	60.0
Melrose Park	20	106	26.8	4.9	23	83	8.2	2.1	97	4 615	1 763.8	222.9
Moline	56	286	74.2	8.4	112	D	D	D	39	2 353	1 518.8	140.6
Mount Prospect	45	235	50.8	15.4	176	2 613	107.1	270.5	39	1 541	536.1	97.6
Mundelein	23	66	11.9	2.4	107	590	108.0	47.9	59	1 625	451.6	80.5
Naperville	207	731	212.6	33.0	1 076	D	D	D	82	1 751	570.1	88.3
Niles	46	319	45.9	11.5	89	472	65.9	22.7	55	1 914	667.9	113.0
Normal	34	256	37.5	7.9	68	D	D	D	16	1 881	D	110.0
Northbrook	152	2 172	237.2	61.1	578	D	D	D	79	2 299	514.6	113.0
North Chicago	4	29	4.8	0.8	16	D	D	D	15	6 797	2 649.0	D
Oak Forest	14	64	7.2	2.9	48	131	20.5	5.8	14	366	D	16.0
Oak Lawn	38	162	27.7	5.8	95	D	D	D	27	436	128.7	21.9
Oak Park	83	352	86.0	14.7	288	D	D	D	18	158	21.7	5.4
O'Fallon	37	143	25.6	6.3	85	1 347	224.8	91.9	11	276	143.6	10.8
Orland Park	74	201	68.1	8.1	237	1 155	156.2	64.1	33	414	146.6	18.0
Oswego	25	D	D	D	71	D	D	D	23	477	D	21.9
Palatine	72	198	39.9	7.0	349	1 385	221.4	84.5	43	1 882	566.4	85.8
Park Ridge	68	D	D	D	252	874	133.5	45.1	10	358	80.9	10.7
Pekin	20	57	9.2	1.3	41	251	21.0	9.2	30	1 003	960.8	60.6
Peoria	152	778	137.6	26.5	356	D	D	D	84	3 270	3 634.4	162.3
Plainfield	29	128	38.7	7.4	134	801	113.1	58.2	21	620	D	39.0
Quincy	50	201	30.4	5.6	116	693	66.3	25.0	45	1 744	651.1	85.8
Rockford	144	1 187	133.5	34.0	418	2 844	539.9	150.2	340	15 649	5 385.6	961.7
Rock Island	22	66	12.2	2.0	112	D	D	D	39	1 390	455.3	64.7
Romeoville	22	435	71.1	23.9	38	346	43.1	12.5	50	1 642	564.9	85.4
Round Lake Beach	9	25	5.3	0.6	20	74	5.0	2.4	7	67	D	1.9
St. Charles	79	456	262.5	22.0	213	D	D	D	93	5 614	1 569.4	280.4
Schaumburg	148	1 064	356.5	64.7	713	10 430	2 509.6	777.0	151	3 929	1 699.7	201.9
Skokie	103	670	179.7	36.8	383	D	D	D	134	5 070	1 263.7	258.2
Springfield	152	676	136.6	22.0	414	3 918	504.4	206.6	66	2 116	497.3	107.6
Streamwood	21	247	67.4	13.8	81	236	22.9	7.3	34	764	188.1	37.3
Tinley Park	35	135	46.3	4.5	140	990	136.0	48.8	38	1 063	253.5	56.4
Urbana	31	1 483	202.8	62.7	72	D	D	D	21	D	320.6	50.9
Vernon Hills	24	D	D	D	160	1 632	384.7	139.2	24	1 696	622.7	133.0

1. Establishments subject to federal tax.

Table D. Cities — Accommodation and Food Services, Arts, Entertainment, and Recreation, and Health Care and Social Assistance

City	Accommodation and food services, 2012				Arts, entertainment, and recreation,[1] 2012				Health care and social assistance,[1] 2012			
	Number of establishments	Number of employees	Sales (mil dol)	Annual payroll (mil dol)	Number of establishments	Number of employees	Receipts (mil dol)	Annual payroll (mil dol)	Number of establishments	Number of employees	Receipts (mil dol)	Annual payroll (mil dol)
	92	93	94	95	96	97	98	99	100	101	102	103
ILLINOIS—Cont'd												
Burbank	50	742	37.9	10.4	3	D	D	D	36	D	D	D
Calumet City	79	1 238	63.8	16.5	3	37	2.1	0.6	58	798	48.1	23.9
Carbondale	95	D	D	D	4	D	D	D	90	D	D	D
Carol Stream	76	991	58.0	13.5	9	62	3.5	0.8	56	456	43.3	17.0
Carpentersville	37	859	34.9	10.1	4	D	D	D	20	D	D	D
Champaign	301	6 636	298.9	82.6	23	D	D	D	155	D	D	D
Chicago	6 022	115 965	8 996.4	2 481.8	716	11 186	2 159.3	742.9	5 253	73 916	6 786.9	2 549.9
Chicago Heights	46	576	26.8	8.0	1	D	D	D	52	713	57.4	23.5
Cicero	86	1 040	64.0	16.5	5	34	3.0	0.5	60	505	41.7	14.5
Collinsville	67	1 471	64.6	18.7	9	D	D	D	50	D	D	D
Crystal Lake	120	2 615	143.7	41.2	18	106	6.5	1.3	185	2 021	186.4	82.5
Danville	87	1 544	65.9	18.9	7	55	2.8	0.8	77	1 103	96.0	44.9
Decatur	179	3 415	152.1	43.8	13	279	8.2	4.1	206	D	D	D
DeKalb	99	1 677	69.6	19.5	3	D	D	D	53	D	D	D
Des Plaines	163	2 001	135.4	30.3	14	D	D	D	211	2 857	244.0	99.0
Downers Grove	154	3 004	175.7	52.0	16	208	8.5	2.6	215	D	D	D
East St. Louis	35	D	D	D	1	D	D	D	29	D	D	D
Elgin	185	3 061	147.6	41.1	19	D	D	D	246	2 757	302.9	148.7
Elk Grove Village	114	1 739	121.7	33.6	14	D	D	D	130	D	D	D
Elmhurst	108	1 721	92.5	25.7	17	117	7.6	1.9	219	D	D	D
Evanston	238	3 779	274.7	77.2	42	393	24.7	8.6	259	4 212	630.9	389.4
Freeport	64	889	41.2	10.4	8	D	D	D	62	D	D	D
Galesburg	92	1 464	65.9	18.5	3	24	0.8	0.2	67	1 761	183.4	64.6
Glendale Heights	45	706	42.6	10.1	9	D	D	D	33	D	D	D
Glen Ellyn	61	959	51.4	13.8	9	D	D	D	92	1 095	190.8	87.2
Glenview	158	2 761	163.8	52.1	34	328	45.9	20.6	254	3 243	317.0	133.0
Granite City	67	1 011	46.0	12.7	6	D	D	D	67	D	D	D
Gurnee	136	3 217	166.2	47.8	15	D	D	D	166	1 442	196.1	77.9
Hanover Park	36	446	26.2	5.9	3	73	3.6	0.8	32	286	24.4	8.9
Harvey	40	744	41.1	12.3	NA	NA	NA	NA	42	D	D	D
Highland Park	90	1 506	91.0	28.9	30	393	19.9	9.5	155	D	D	D
Hoffman Estates	117	1 993	130.7	36.7	15	D	D	D	226	D	D	D
Joliet	235	5 812	555.9	117.0	16	277	67.5	9.0	337	4 717	581.8	230.6
Kankakee	53	D	D	D	5	D	D	D	71	D	D	D
Lake in the Hills	29	524	25.4	7.8	8	D	D	D	51	583	38.8	16.8
Lansing	62	1 206	57.9	15.9	6	D	D	D	57	504	38.4	15.2
Lombard	148	3 359	210.1	62.0	14	320	14.7	4.6	147	2 367	232.5	95.6
McHenry	83	1 267	53.3	15.2	7	55	4.6	1.2	91	D	D	D
Melrose Park	72	D	D	D	6	D	D	D	106	D	D	D
Moline	156	2 771	128.6	36.9	11	D	D	D	163	2 283	237.6	107.0
Mount Prospect	112	1 568	86.8	23.9	8	D	D	D	118	2 071	159.2	61.2
Mundelein	75	1 082	53.2	13.5	12	D	D	D	48	296	26.4	10.5
Naperville	361	7 975	472.3	129.5	58	730	82.7	29.4	589	D	D	D
Niles	135	D	D	D	9	D	D	D	147	2 732	262.6	89.7
Normal	106	2 742	132.3	36.2	10	D	D	D	74	1 254	119.4	45.5
Northbrook	96	2 082	140.2	46.3	33	D	D	D	269	3 224	294.6	125.2
North Chicago	31	390	19.8	4.9	NA	NA	NA	NA	8	D	D	D
Oak Forest	37	593	28.3	7.6	4	D	D	D	45	869	44.4	23.5
Oak Lawn	108	2 406	172.7	39.1	12	144	7.9	1.8	239	D	D	D
Oak Park	101	1 703	86.0	26.0	25	275	23.2	5.9	262	4 148	374.6	171.8
O'Fallon	69	D	D	D	8	D	D	D	69	D	D	D
Orland Park	170	4 254	207.9	61.7	20	D	D	D	293	4 528	413.6	185.3
Oswego	60	1 375	66.7	19.5	10	108	5.4	1.2	70	D	D	D
Palatine	111	1 558	80.0	22.1	18	D	D	D	134	1 711	101.3	39.2
Park Ridge	66	887	51.4	13.9	11	D	D	D	242	D	D	D
Pekin	86	1 460	62.7	17.3	9	D	D	D	68	926	65.6	30.9
Peoria	326	6 429	294.4	84.8	27	955	36.5	13.6	334	6 614	826.5	352.7
Plainfield	85	1 610	75.6	19.6	7	D	D	D	115	D	D	D
Quincy	126	2 186	98.8	28.2	11	D	D	D	97	2 168	334.1	112.8
Rockford	336	7 122	344.0	97.8	28	317	17.3	4.8	365	5 805	856.7	340.5
Rock Island	62	1 356	157.5	22.1	7	D	D	D	75	D	D	D
Romeoville	61	1 259	58.0	17.6	10	420	22.6	6.8	31	D	D	D
Round Lake Beach	31	484	31.5	8.2	7	87	5.3	1.3	26	D	D	D
St. Charles	114	2 960	140.1	44.4	17	D	D	D	149	1 471	169.2	71.4
Schaumburg	265	7 508	488.2	150.8	31	777	47.5	11.9	261	3 141	316.3	118.4
Skokie	155	3 453	232.9	63.6	22	D	D	D	346	3 873	352.6	149.3
Springfield	402	8 032	383.4	114.2	43	D	D	D	286	9 744	1 233.0	436.3
Streamwood	64	991	53.1	13.9	3	15	0.9	0.3	52	1 247	126.7	50.0
Tinley Park	130	2 621	147.9	38.4	18	216	30.4	5.9	162	2 257	259.1	86.1
Urbana	108	1 781	84.3	23.4	11	D	D	D	45	D	D	D
Vernon Hills	95	1 717	103.9	30.6	16	D	D	D	106	1 089	161.7	55.2

1. Establishments subject to federal tax.

Table D. Cities — Other Services and Government Employment and Payroll

City	Other services[1], 2012					Government employment and payroll, 2012							
						March payroll							
						Total (dollars)	Percent of total for:						
	Number of establish-ments	Number of employees	Receipts (mil dol)	Annual payroll (mil dol)	Full-time equivalent employees		Administration, judicial, and legal	Police and Corrections	Fire Protection	Highways and transportation	Health and welfare	Natural resources and utilities	Education and libraries
	104	105	106	107	108	109	110	111	112	113	114	115	116
ILLINOIS—Cont'd													
Burbank	39	134	11.1	3.7	134	786 445	7.6	47.7	28.5	12.5	0.0	0.0	0.0
Calumet City	34	108	11.2	3.2	270	1 459 484	9.0	47.4	26.2	6.4	3.6	3.2	4.2
Carbondale	42	152	13.2	3.2	243	1 024 650	20.3	36.8	14.6	7.4	0.7	17.5	0.0
Carol Stream	59	257	23.2	7.0	178	1 066 716	18.8	48.5	0.0	9.7	2.2	4.7	13.5
Carpentersville	30	124	8.9	2.6	197	1 212 358	9.8	38.1	25.5	7.4	4.7	10.2	0.0
Champaign	103	766	51.3	17.7	613	3 303 325	9.3	26.5	21.3	13.7	2.4	1.6	17.9
Chicago	3 455	21 793	1 817.1	565.1	25 630	175 627 618	2.8	74.4	7.6	3.4	2.3	5.3	1.0
Chicago Heights	40	189	15.1	5.0	294	1 453 188	3.9	43.8	28.2	5.0	0.3	9.0	5.7
Cicero	71	248	23.0	5.9	584	2 867 400	8.1	39.8	18.0	10.1	11.3	7.3	1.8
Collinsville	38	200	17.5	5.2	169	956 282	5.4	39.2	23.4	8.4	4.4	16.9	0.0
Crystal Lake	109	730	55.8	17.6	309	1 877 299	13.5	27.5	25.3	5.8	2.7	10.3	9.1
Danville	49	270	24.0	6.7	294	1 321 594	8.4	29.2	21.7	13.2	2.3	14.1	5.3
Decatur	102	865	126.6	28.1	554	2 990 379	8.4	39.2	24.9	9.4	4.8	6.5	5.6
DeKalb	43	312	15.5	5.5	198	1 271 653	11.8	36.9	32.8	11.6	1.9	5.0	0.0
Des Plaines	142	940	130.6	36.5	446	2 438 468	5.2	30.6	34.3	7.1	3.0	5.9	10.5
Downers Grove	115	1 076	103.5	31.9	390	2 164 897	16.2	30.8	26.2	1.6	2.8	10.9	8.4
East St. Louis	16	108	5.7	1.8	189	693 926	9.2	35.2	34.7	6.6	4.3	0.0	2.0
Elgin	143	1 294	139.9	49.7	718	4 472 423	10.3	39.1	24.6	3.4	0.0	18.7	0.0
Elk Grove Village	106	964	120.0	35.0	298	2 048 828	10.7	36.3	32.2	8.8	6.0	5.0	0.0
Elmhurst	94	781	68.0	22.5	587	3 047 235	10.6	25.1	12.8	8.0	0.0	13.7	21.9
Evanston	113	739	46.4	16.6	756	4 935 582	8.8	31.1	21.1	2.8	8.4	20.2	3.5
Freeport	46	195	13.7	3.9	191	868 424	5.9	37.1	28.7	6.7	0.0	12.7	3.3
Galesburg	53	D	D	D	284	1 182 039	9.7	30.8	19.6	8.9	4.7	17.2	4.2
Glendale Heights	39	299	36.2	11.3	240	1 253 066	11.8	42.0	0.0	9.8	5.4	20.6	0.0
Glen Ellyn	48	261	20.7	6.6	170	812 456	21.3	30.1	0.0	7.6	0.0	23.8	11.9
Glenview	126	726	57.9	19.6	368	2 419 770	8.4	26.3	34.2	5.3	3.0	8.4	10.8
Granite City	48	394	45.7	14.2	233	1 173 888	7.7	32.1	27.6	12.2	4.4	14.0	0.0
Gurnee	64	491	47.5	14.0	198	1 570 289	5.9	45.6	29.7	8.4	0.0	3.7	0.0
Hanover Park	34	330	19.3	6.6	207	1 331 356	9.4	44.7	23.0	7.5	3.0	8.6	0.0
Harvey	19	77	6.6	1.6	195	871 135	8.5	48.6	27.8	8.3	0.3	6.5	0.0
Highland Park	101	582	48.4	15.2	227	1 445 604	8.6	30.8	26.4	9.8	1.3	11.6	0.0
Hoffman Estates	59	416	19.3	8.7	347	2 420 731	11.8	35.1	29.9	4.6	1.4	10.1	0.0
Joliet	151	1 366	144.2	44.6	941	6 790 745	6.4	38.7	25.4	6.8	1.3	12.5	3.8
Kankakee	41	246	22.9	6.8	264	1 273 939	5.5	35.8	24.1	7.9	6.7	10.1	4.5
Lake in the Hills	43	168	14.6	4.0	131	726 848	15.2	43.1	0.0	11.6	4.1	15.1	0.0
Lansing	48	561	57.3	16.4	200	1 054 688	6.3	47.0	25.7	7.3	0.0	5.9	5.3
Lombard	107	701	75.0	22.0	289	1 794 844	9.3	33.8	26.1	6.4	0.8	8.5	8.0
McHenry	72	377	28.3	8.4	136	766 529	11.7	38.7	0.0	16.4	0.0	26.3	0.0
Melrose Park	42	D	D	D	274	1 377 728	3.3	43.1	26.6	6.0	1.7	8.5	5.6
Moline	84	478	32.8	10.5	392	2 247 548	10.9	28.1	19.6	8.6	0.7	17.4	6.2
Mount Prospect	81	458	39.5	12.0	445	2 620 859	6.5	27.8	21.6	6.5	3.5	10.4	15.1
Mundelein	71	374	31.2	9.8	167	523 415	11.5	34.6	14.6	10.6	0.0	10.8	0.0
Naperville	249	1 950	138.1	45.2	1 141	6 999 358	11.3	27.3	20.8	10.0	0.0	21.1	9.4
Niles	74	463	36.0	10.0	277	1 803 453	9.8	28.4	25.4	11.8	9.9	11.0	0.0
Normal	49	391	26.9	9.3	426	2 272 555	9.0	24.8	18.8	7.7	0.7	25.9	7.3
Northbrook	87	584	39.7	14.6	275	2 019 890	9.3	35.9	30.6	13.5	2.9	7.8	0.0
North Chicago	10	D	D	D	176	982 302	7.8	51.2	16.6	5.2	4.6	10.0	4.6
Oak Forest	38	172	15.2	3.9	137	814 381	8.2	43.6	26.4	10.5	0.1	10.0	0.0
Oak Lawn	91	709	57.2	17.9	421	2 260 980	6.9	39.4	25.9	7.3	0.7	8.8	7.3
Oak Park	100	582	47.7	14.0	450	2 566 842	9.0	37.0	19.6	5.0	4.3	3.8	10.5
O'Fallon	47	304	27.7	8.3	177	876 752	17.3	46.2	0.5	7.4	7.7	15.6	4.9
Orland Park	121	1 053	78.1	27.9	409	2 080 080	14.2	43.9	0.0	6.5	0.0	22.3	8.2
Oswego	58	331	28.0	9.2	107	609 946	20.4	64.0	0.0	0.0	0.0	15.5	0.0
Palatine	135	781	61.8	19.8	348	2 424 446	10.2	40.9	30.9	4.8	1.1	3.4	0.0
Park Ridge	61	352	31.7	10.3	255	1 549 856	7.5	29.7	26.8	7.3	4.0	6.5	14.1
Pekin	58	255	15.5	5.3	259	1 110 590	5.2	29.2	27.7	6.0	1.0	5.6	4.2
Peoria	158	3 995	358.2	183.6	831	4 963 632	9.9	36.9	26.3	5.9	1.3	5.1	5.3
Plainfield	61	426	29.8	9.2	131	858 893	12.3	62.1	0.0	9.7	0.0	13.1	0.0
Quincy	88	476	38.8	11.9	391	1 653 065	8.8	30.0	19.6	12.1	0.3	15.1	5.2
Rockford	242	1 586	154.2	43.7	1 085	6 113 597	5.6	33.3	36.5	5.3	7.4	4.8	4.2
Rock Island	50	370	31.5	9.6	372	1 377 794	14.6	16.8	10.5	8.7	9.2	29.1	7.6
Romeoville	40	474	48.6	14.5	297	1 580 154	8.8	38.4	18.0	2.8	3.6	17.7	0.0
Round Lake Beach	26	118	7.7	2.5	90	514 049	11.2	62.5	0.0	8.6	4.5	13.1	0.0
St. Charles	85	647	44.9	15.4	264	1 823 844	18.8	26.0	21.1	7.0	0.0	19.6	0.0
Schaumburg	197	1 612	162.4	51.5	536	3 458 405	11.4	32.6	25.6	5.7	7.4	8.7	0.0
Skokie	157	1 128	107.7	36.5	593	3 361 285	7.8	29.7	23.3	2.7	5.7	10.6	14.6
Springfield	184	1 494	123.1	38.3	1 621	10 142 573	6.4	16.0	12.6	5.8	1.5	56.2	1.6
Streamwood	55	288	22.7	6.3	179	1 160 444	8.6	42.2	27.2	3.9	3.6	10.8	0.0
Tinley Park	57	343	25.6	8.5	346	1 824 694	11.4	45.9	13.6	6.6	0.8	8.0	9.0
Urbana	33	193	14.3	4.6	302	1 464 071	11.1	26.0	23.5	13.2	5.3	4.2	11.9
Vernon Hills	34	373	21.8	8.8	101	697 505	10.9	66.3	0.0	16.7	0.0	0.0	0.0

1. Establishments subject to federal tax.

Table D. Cities — **City Government Finances**

City	City government finances, 2012									
	General revenue							General expenditure		
		Intergovernmental		Taxes					Per capita[1] (dollars)	
					Per capita[1] (dollars)					
	Total (mil dol)	Total (mil dol)	Percent from state government	Total (mil dol)	Total	Property	Sales and gross receipts	Total (mil dol)	Total	Capital outlays
	117	118	119	120	121	122	123	124	125	126
ILLINOIS—Cont'd										
Burbank...........	19.3	6.5	97.7	12.0	410	185	219	17.0	584	9
Calumet City...............	50.9	11.6	90.1	34.2	919	681	229	45.9	1 232	103
Carbondale............	32.4	10.9	88.9	14.1	533	69	464	31.8	1 202	47
Carol Stream	28.1	11.1	91.6	10.1	252	15	219	25.3	631	60
Carpentersville	32.2	12.8	86.2	12.7	332	234	98	36.5	955	239
Champaign............	100.8	38.9	81.8	49.4	597	285	312	101.7	1 229	343
Chicago................	6 690.6	1 758.6	65.4	2 526.4	930	327	547	7 439.1	2 740	425
Chicago Heights............	44.6	13.6	76.8	22.9	750	593	155	45.7	1 500	202
Cicero................	111.4	23.7	88.5	72.9	863	556	300	108.6	1 285	185
Collinsville	30.2	11.1	94.1	12.0	478	200	278	29.1	1 154	106
Crystal Lake	53.2	19.4	99.7	23.3	576	375	201	54.2	1 341	305
Danville................	42.4	15.6	82.1	19.3	590	227	363	42.8	1 309	210
Decatur................	75.9	32.1	85.6	34.5	458	179	279	89.1	1 182	206
DeKalb................	53.3	19.6	68.3	26.9	614	331	283	45.2	1 031	260
Des Plaines................	103.1	31.2	96.3	57.8	982	617	358	92.0	1 563	249
Downers Grove	65.8	18.9	98.8	39.1	793	447	346	58.7	1 190	157
East St. Louis...............	38.6	19.9	85.1	15.8	592	444	148	38.3	1 439	101
Elgin...............	136.9	44.5	93.0	66.3	605	479	126	125.2	1 141	155
Elk Grove Village	60.1	13.5	93.1	37.1	1 113	630	466	64.9	1 946	411
Elmhurst.....................	70.4	17.9	99.2	36.4	806	479	320	65.4	1 450	192
Evanston	123.4	24.9	70.5	64.7	858	533	298	116.5	1 544	176
Freeport.....................	29.6	13.3	99.7	8.0	317	186	130	28.8	1 144	64
Galesburg....................	39.9	19.3	93.4	14.5	455	218	236	38.4	1 207	64
Glendale Heights........	35.6	10.2	99.2	15.9	460	241	210	43.0	1 246	422
Glen Ellyn................	37.6	7.6	88.9	16.6	602	374	215	32.5	1 176	174
Glenview................	101.0	27.2	76.5	62.0	1 377	1 042	336	95.5	2 120	282
Granite City	40.9	13.0	100.0	18.6	629	472	157	45.0	1 521	211
Gurnee........................	38.2	22.9	85.8	9.6	307	0	307	34.9	1 121	11
Hanover Park	38.2	10.2	89.4	21.6	563	376	180	53.4	1 392	426
Harvey.......................	23.0	6.4	100.0	13.8	543	424	119	25.1	990	34
Highland Park...............	56.2	12.1	93.3	29.2	978	521	419	47.5	1 591	94
Hoffman Estates............	82.1	13.5	91.6	51.3	982	736	239	64.6	1 237	110
Joliet............................	202.1	70.4	93.0	72.3	488	283	198	177.8	1 199	22
Kankakee.....................	60.8	25.8	88.2	20.1	735	562	173	66.7	2 438	258
Lake in the Hills	20.2	7.5	78.9	9.1	314	217	97	18.0	620	82
Lansing.....................	33.0	8.0	94.6	18.5	649	445	203	35.4	1 241	283
Lombard	90.1	27.3	90.2	20.3	464	194	270	97.6	2 231	83
McHenry.....................	24.8	12.3	96.4	6.7	249	217	33	23.4	873	150
Melrose Park..............	43.6	13.9	98.6	23.4	918	732	185	48.9	1 914	285
Moline........................	72.2	20.2	84.2	35.3	819	413	405	74.2	1 720	148
Mount Prospect	70.6	19.0	93.5	43.9	805	533	265	70.0	1 283	142
Mundelein....................	36.2	9.6	91.1	18.0	577	372	205	32.6	1 046	94
Naperville....................	169.6	55.1	89.1	79.8	555	355	183	143.7	999	101
Niles	48.5	18.9	99.5	23.3	776	251	518	41.3	1 378	19
Normal	80.5	31.2	99.5	31.3	581	208	372	77.3	1 435	387
Northbrook..................	51.6	18.4	98.1	23.9	715	481	233	52.8	1 578	131
North Chicago	26.1	8.5	79.5	13.3	441	299	138	26.6	885	25
Oak Forest	21.4	5.3	98.7	12.5	444	315	129	20.9	744	55
Oak Lawn	62.1	19.1	99.2	28.3	496	394	96	68.1	1 194	211
Oak Park	89.0	14.1	80.8	58.0	1 115	815	268	90.4	1 737	226
O'Fallon	33.2	13.4	98.6	10.8	370	237	133	31.4	1 072	258
Orland Park.................	85.4	30.2	96.4	33.9	592	346	245	81.3	1 420	303
Oswego	21.0	9.6	98.5	6.3	198	46	152	17.5	553	6
Palatine	81.2	22.0	76.2	45.6	660	486	175	87.2	1 262	293
Park Ridge	46.1	10.0	100.0	30.9	818	523	283	47.4	1 255	36
Pekin	40.2	14.5	81.3	13.8	404	189	215	48.4	1 417	388
Peoria.........................	185.6	76.4	95.2	81.2	702	306	396	173.5	1 500	288
Plainfield.....................	34.8	10.0	90.4	14.1	348	155	193	27.5	680	54
Quincy.......................	46.5	24.3	86.8	13.5	330	59	271	36.7	898	111
Rockford......................	205.7	107.8	79.0	75.0	497	396	100	178.2	1 180	127
Rock Island	69.8	23.7	74.6	23.3	601	427	175	75.1	1 934	393
Romeoville...................	58.3	11.7	84.0	28.8	726	381	336	58.2	1 465	267
Round Lake Beach	17.9	8.1	98.7	8.5	305	231	74	22.5	802	338
St. Charles	51.7	14.2	98.9	26.8	807	424	383	54.5	1 637	225
Schaumburg................	155.0	40.4	92.8	70.0	937	341	596	138.1	1 847	106
Skokie........................	104.2	37.0	66.4	60.5	929	512	413	82.4	1 265	140
Springfield...................	137.9	49.3	90.7	68.8	587	235	353	135.8	1 159	63
Streamwood.................	29.9	8.7	93.2	15.7	390	250	135	26.2	650	57
Tinley Park	70.3	22.1	99.9	36.1	632	519	114	61.1	1 069	254
Urbana........................	47.8	17.7	62.5	22.2	531	252	279	48.4	1 159	285
Vernon Hills.................	21.2	13.2	99.1	5.7	222	0	222	18.9	740	29

1. Based on population estimated as of July 1 of the year shown.

City	Public welfare	Highways	Parking facilities	Education	Health and hospitals	Police protection	Sewerage and sanitation	Parks and recreation	Housing and community development	Interest on debt
	127	128	129	130	131	132	133	134	135	136
ILLINOIS—Cont'd										
Burbank	0.0	11.1	0.0	0.0	0.0	42.1	0.0	0.0	0.0	2.8
Calumet City	0.0	11.2	0.0	0.0	1.3	21.0	3.8	0.0	0.3	4.9
Carbondale	0.0	7.9	0.6	0.0	0.0	26.7	11.0	1.0	10.1	4.7
Carol Stream	0.0	12.8	0.0	0.0	0.0	46.9	11.5	0.0	0.0	1.4
Carpentersville	0.0	38.6	0.0	0.0	0.0	24.1	5.9	0.7	0.0	5.8
Champaign	0.3	8.8	2.1	0.0	0.0	19.0	14.5	0.0	0.8	3.1
Chicago	4.6	9.7	0.1	0.0	2.5	18.0	5.3	0.5	4.4	12.5
Chicago Heights	0.0	5.4	0.0	0.0	0.0	23.2	9.3	0.0	6.0	4.9
Cicero	0.3	10.4	0.0	0.0	1.4	22.1	4.8	0.3	1.6	5.0
Collinsville	0.0	8.9	0.0	0.0	0.6	27.3	16.9	0.0	0.0	5.9
Crystal Lake	0.0	25.3	0.0	0.0	0.2	19.8	6.0	1.9	0.0	2.7
Danville	0.0	17.2	0.0	0.0	0.0	16.9	12.9	5.0	1.7	1.3
Decatur	0.0	29.1	0.0	0.0	0.0	25.2	3.2	0.1	2.3	5.8
DeKalb	0.0	13.3	0.0	0.0	0.0	23.6	3.7	0.0	0.6	2.7
Des Plaines	0.0	20.8	0.2	0.0	0.0	21.7	6.9	0.0	0.3	2.6
Downers Grove	0.0	18.1	1.8	0.0	0.0	24.0	7.0	0.0	0.0	5.8
East St. Louis	0.0	6.6	0.0	0.0	0.0	18.9	0.4	0.0	6.8	5.2
Elgin	0.0	11.0	0.0	0.0	0.0	27.7	8.5	13.6	1.2	2.1
Elk Grove Village	0.0	19.6	0.0	0.0	0.0	23.4	3.9	0.0	0.0	5.1
Elmhurst	0.0	18.1	1.0	0.0	0.4	21.5	11.4	1.7	0.0	4.4
Evanston	1.7	7.6	6.0	0.0	2.3	18.5	5.9	10.8	6.7	7.0
Freeport	0.0	13.2	0.0	0.0	0.3	14.5	17.8	0.4	0.0	4.6
Galesburg	0.0	25.9	0.0	0.0	0.0	14.5	5.0	7.5	0.0	3.6
Glendale Heights	0.0	11.3	0.0	0.0	0.0	37.4	2.1	17.7	0.0	7.1
Glen Ellyn	0.0	21.1	0.6	0.0	0.0	22.1	17.3	8.7	0.0	1.6
Glenview	0.0	8.2	0.3	0.0	0.0	12.5	5.1	0.0	0.0	5.3
Granite City	0.0	20.6	0.0	0.0	0.0	20.0	15.5	0.0	0.0	3.9
Gurnee	0.0	13.7	0.0	0.0	0.0	33.2	3.7	0.6	0.0	1.0
Hanover Park	0.0	10.2	0.9	0.0	0.0	43.0	3.1	0.0	0.0	2.1
Harvey	0.0	17.0	0.7	0.0	0.0	22.3	4.4	0.3	0.0	8.0
Highland Park	0.0	10.3	2.4	0.0	0.0	27.0	7.1	5.1	0.0	3.1
Hoffman Estates	0.0	14.7	0.0	0.0	0.9	25.3	5.6	4.4	0.0	8.8
Joliet	0.0	9.3	0.7	0.0	0.0	20.1	10.8	4.0	1.9	1.3
Kankakee	0.0	10.0	0.0	0.0	0.0	14.5	21.2	0.0	1.5	5.0
Lake in the Hills	0.0	10.4	0.0	0.0	0.0	38.8	0.0	8.9	0.0	1.8
Lansing	0.0	15.2	0.0	0.0	0.0	25.7	5.9	0.0	0.0	2.9
Lombard	0.0	4.1	0.1	0.0	0.0	13.3	3.6	0.0	0.0	8.5
McHenry	0.0	14.9	0.0	0.0	0.0	39.0	22.4	8.5	0.0	2.9
Melrose Park	0.0	8.0	0.0	0.0	0.0	22.1	4.8	2.9	0.0	7.5
Moline	0.0	12.6	0.3	0.0	0.0	17.7	10.4	7.3	0.0	5.5
Mount Prospect	1.4	12.6	0.5	0.0	0.2	19.8	8.5	0.5	1.3	1.5
Mundelein	0.0	20.8	0.1	0.0	0.0	30.0	6.2	0.0	0.0	3.3
Naperville	0.0	19.4	0.7	0.0	0.0	24.1	7.8	5.9	0.0	3.5
Niles	0.0	16.1	0.0	0.0	0.0	31.3	5.8	3.8	0.0	1.7
Normal	0.0	7.7	0.0	0.0	0.0	14.0	6.7	12.9	0.2	5.5
Northbrook	0.0	16.7	0.3	0.0	0.0	24.8	2.5	0.0	0.0	5.0
North Chicago	0.0	8.1	0.0	0.0	0.0	30.4	1.8	0.0	1.3	5.2
Oak Forest	0.0	17.8	1.0	0.0	0.0	37.1	4.8	0.0	0.0	2.4
Oak Lawn	0.3	14.0	0.1	0.0	0.0	20.6	8.3	0.6	0.3	5.5
Oak Park	0.0	7.1	4.0	0.0	1.3	20.3	6.0	0.4	4.7	3.1
O'Fallon	0.1	13.1	0.0	0.0	0.0	15.5	10.4	15.1	0.0	9.0
Orland Park	0.0	27.8	0.4	0.0	0.0	21.1	12.3	10.6	0.0	3.0
Oswego	0.0	11.6	0.0	0.0	0.0	45.1	16.3	0.0	0.0	9.0
Palatine	0.0	7.7	0.6	0.0	0.0	41.7	6.7	0.0	0.2	6.5
Park Ridge	0.0	7.0	0.8	0.0	0.0	19.5	10.4	0.0	0.0	3.3
Pekin	0.0	9.3	0.0	0.0	0.0	17.4	28.2	0.0	1.1	3.9
Peoria	0.0	15.7	1.7	0.0	0.0	20.6	1.4	1.5	2.0	5.8
Plainfield	0.0	20.5	0.0	0.0	0.0	39.3	16.5	0.0	0.0	10.9
Quincy	0.0	11.6	0.0	0.0	0.3	22.6	10.1	1.7	2.9	2.4
Rockford	9.5	16.5	0.7	0.0	0.0	25.1	3.9	0.0	5.8	2.4
Rock Island	0.0	8.4	0.2	0.0	0.0	15.4	24.0	9.0	0.4	0.8
Romeoville	0.0	11.3	0.0	0.0	0.0	20.1	10.5	6.5	0.0	8.6
Round Lake Beach	0.0	7.7	0.0	0.0	0.0	28.5	0.0	0.6	0.0	4.2
St. Charles	0.0	20.9	0.0	0.0	1.2	19.4	13.9	0.0	0.0	9.3
Schaumburg	0.8	12.2	0.1	0.0	0.5	18.6	4.6	1.6	0.3	10.1
Skokie	0.0	10.7	0.1	0.0	1.7	19.6	5.0	2.4	1.0	3.2
Springfield	0.0	12.3	1.1	0.0	0.0	27.2	4.0	0.0	3.0	2.0
Streamwood	0.0	17.6	0.0	0.0	0.0	33.2	9.7	1.3	0.0	1.6
Tinley Park	0.0	17.1	0.9	0.0	0.0	26.6	4.6	0.0	0.0	3.6
Urbana	0.3	29.3	1.4	0.0	0.0	17.9	3.0	0.3	7.3	1.1
Vernon Hills	0.0	21.7	0.0	0.0	0.0	46.0	0.0	4.1	0.0	7.1

Table D. Cities — City Government Finances, City Government Employment, and Climate

City	City government finances, 2012 (cont.)			Climate[2]						
	Debt outstanding			Average daily temperature (degrees Fahrenheit)						
				Mean		Limits				
	Total (mil dol)	Per capita[1] (dollars)	Debt issued during year	January	July	January[3]	July[4]	Annual precipitation (inches)	Heating degree days	Cooling degree days
	137	138	139	140	141	142	143	144	145	146

City										
ILLINOIS—Cont'd										
Burbank	10.1	346	0.0	23.5	75.5	16.2	84.7	38.35	6 083	1 001
Calumet City	52.6	1 413	0.0	22.0	74.2	14.8	83.7	38.65	6 355	866
Carbondale	33.7	1 276	6.6	NA	NA	NA	NA	NA	NA	NA
Carol Stream	7.2	180	0.0	23.1	74.8	14.2	86.8	37.94	6 053	942
Carpentersville	49.4	1 295	0.0	19.3	72.6	10.9	83.0	37.22	6 975	679
Champaign	74.8	904	0.0	33.7	79.0	25.0	89.5	47.93	4 183	1 501
Chicago	21 209.6	7 811	2 295.0	25.3	75.4	18.3	84.4	38.01	5 787	994
Chicago Heights	67.7	2 223	46.7	22.0	74.2	14.8	83.7	38.65	6 355	866
Cicero	108.3	1 282	0.0	22.0	73.3	14.3	83.5	36.27	6 498	830
Collinsville	47.8	1 894	0.0	NA	NA	NA	NA	NA	NA	NA
Crystal Lake	42.4	1 049	0.0	28.6	76.3	19.0	87.2	46.96	5 168	1 112
Danville	12.0	367	4.4	25.8	75.3	17.3	86.2	40.96	5 555	1 027
Decatur	96.9	1 286	1.9	25.8	76.2	17.1	87.8	39.74	5 458	1 142
DeKalb	29.2	667	1.0	18.5	73.1	10.3	83.6	37.38	6 979	736
Des Plaines	71.7	1 218	4.0	22.0	73.3	14.3	83.5	36.27	6 498	830
Downers Grove	80.1	1 623	0.0	23.1	74.8	14.2	86.8	37.94	6 053	942
East St. Louis	25.4	954	0.0	29.1	78.6	20.0	88.7	40.33	4 826	1 378
Elgin	106.3	969	10.2	19.3	72.6	10.9	83.0	37.22	6 975	679
Elk Grove Village	52.6	1 579	0.3	22.0	73.3	14.3	83.5	36.27	6 498	830
Elmhurst	61.9	1 371	0.0	23.1	74.8	14.2	86.8	37.94	6 053	942
Evanston	237.9	3 154	19.4	22.0	72.9	13.7	83.2	36.80	6 630	702
Freeport	32.6	1 295	0.0	17.2	71.9	9.0	82.0	34.79	7 317	611
Galesburg	27.4	863	7.9	21.3	74.9	13.5	84.5	37.22	6 347	941
Glendale Heights	49.6	1 437	0.0	22.0	73.3	14.3	83.5	36.27	6 498	830
Glen Ellyn	13.3	482	0.0	21.7	74.4	12.2	85.7	38.58	6 359	888
Glenview	137.4	3 052	11.0	22.0	73.3	14.3	83.5	36.27	6 498	830
Granite City	30.0	1 015	2.2	27.7	78.4	19.4	88.1	38.54	5 149	1 354
Gurnee	16.1	518	10.0	19.9	72.2	12.1	82.2	35.50	6 955	634
Hanover Park	24.0	625	7.0	18.4	72.1	9.6	82.3	36.56	7 149	624
Harvey	50.8	2 004	0.0	22.0	74.2	14.8	83.7	38.65	6 355	866
Highland Park	44.8	1 503	4.6	22.0	72.9	13.7	83.2	36.80	6 630	702
Hoffman Estates	193.6	3 703	2.5	18.4	72.1	9.6	82.3	36.56	7 149	624
Joliet	61.9	417	12.6	21.7	73.7	13.5	84.6	36.96	6 464	809
Kankakee	78.1	2 856	8.7	21.7	74.4	12.2	85.7	38.58	6 359	888
Lake in the Hills	7.6	261	0.0	NA	NA	NA	NA	NA	NA	NA
Lansing	20.8	728	1.5	21.7	74.4	12.2	85.7	38.58	6 359	888
Lombard	219.0	5 007	0.0	23.1	74.8	14.2	86.8	37.94	6 053	942
McHenry	17.9	668	0.0	NA	NA	NA	NA	NA	NA	NA
Melrose Park	80.3	3 147	11.7	NA	NA	NA	NA	NA	NA	NA
Moline	79.9	1 853	18.2	21.8	76.4	13.3	85.1	35.10	6 179	1 100
Mount Prospect	40.7	745	9.3	22.0	73.3	14.3	83.5	36.27	6 498	830
Mundelein	21.6	693	0.0	18.4	72.1	9.6	82.3	36.56	7 149	624
Naperville	178.8	1 244	25.1	23.1	74.8	14.2	86.8	37.94	6 053	942
Niles	18.8	626	4.4	22.0	73.3	14.3	83.5	36.27	6 498	830
Normal	87.9	1 632	0.0	25.8	76.2	17.1	87.8	39.74	5 458	1 142
Northbrook	72.5	2 166	3.0	22.0	72.9	13.7	83.2	36.80	6 630	702
North Chicago	31.9	1 060	2.1	20.3	71.5	12.0	81.7	34.09	7 031	613
Oak Forest	30.0	1 067	0.0	22.0	74.2	14.8	83.7	38.65	6 355	866
Oak Lawn	87.5	1 535	9.2	23.5	75.5	16.2	84.7	38.35	6 083	1 001
Oak Park	104.7	2 013	11.4	22.0	73.3	14.3	83.5	36.27	6 498	830
O'Fallon	47.3	1 618	0.0	NA	NA	NA	NA	NA	NA	NA
Orland Park	81.7	1 427	10.0	23.5	75.5	16.2	84.7	38.35	6 083	1 001
Oswego	34.4	1 087	4.1	NA	NA	NA	NA	NA	NA	NA
Palatine	119.0	1 722	8.2	18.4	72.1	9.6	82.3	36.56	7 149	624
Park Ridge	45.7	1 210	7.5	22.0	73.3	14.3	83.5	36.27	6 498	830
Pekin	49.3	1 445	2.2	24.4	75.8	15.7	87.4	35.71	5 695	1 088
Peoria	222.0	1 920	9.4	22.5	75.1	14.3	85.7	36.03	6 097	998
Plainfield	63.7	1 575	8.4	NA	NA	NA	NA	NA	NA	NA
Quincy	20.2	494	0.0	24.9	76.8	16.0	88.0	35.63	5 707	1 117
Rockford	164.6	1 090	17.5	19.0	72.9	10.8	83.1	36.63	6 933	768
Rock Island	36.5	939	12.7	21.8	76.4	13.3	85.1	35.10	6 179	1 100
Romeoville	169.7	4 271	2.3	NA	NA	NA	NA	NA	NA	NA
Round Lake Beach	25.1	897	4.0	19.9	72.2	12.1	82.2	35.50	6 955	634
St. Charles	142.6	4 289	12.8	19.3	72.6	10.9	83.0	37.22	6 975	679
Schaumburg	302.1	4 043	23.0	18.4	72.1	9.6	82.3	36.56	7 149	624
Skokie	66.5	1 022	0.0	22.0	73.3	14.3	83.5	36.27	6 498	830
Springfield	703.4	6 000	0.3	25.1	76.3	17.1	86.5	35.56	5 596	1 165
Streamwood	10.0	249	0.0	19.3	72.6	10.9	83.0	37.22	6 975	679
Tinley Park	45.9	803	5.2	21.8	76.4	13.3	85.1	35.10	6 179	1 100
Urbana	11.4	273	0.0	20.7	73.2	12.4	83.7	34.47	6 606	774
Vernon Hills	24.7	969	9.5	NA	NA	NA	NA	NA	NA	NA

1. Based on the population estimated as of July 1 of the year shown.   2. Represents normal values based on the 30-year period, 1971–2000.   3. Average daily minimum.
4. Average daily maximum.

Table D. Cities — Land Area and Population

STATE Place code	City	Land area,[1] 2016 (sq mi)	Population, 2016 Total persons	Rank	Per square mile	Race alone[2] (percent), 2015 White	Black or African American	American Indian, Alaska Native	Asian	Hawaiian Pacific Islander	Some other race	2 or more races[2]
		1	2	3	4	5	6	7	8	9	10	11
	ILLINOIS—Cont'd											
17 79293	Waukegan	24.2	88 182	367	3 643.9	71.8	11.4	0.1	4.8	0.0	8.8	3.0
17 80060	West Chicago	15.2	27 221	1 354	1 790.9	82.5	1.0	0.0	8.3	0.0	7.0	1.2
17 81048	Wheaton	11.3	53 389	707	4 724.7	84.0	6.7	0.3	6.4	0.0	0.1	2.5
17 81087	Wheeling	8.7	38 315	992	4 404.0	73.5	2.6	0.0	15.1	0.6	6.1	2.0
17 82075	Wilmette	5.4	27 219	1 355	5 040.6	NA	NA	NA	NA	NA	NA	NA
17 83245	Woodridge	9.6	33 476	1 133	3 487.1	70.4	10.0	0.3	13.4	0.0	2.7	3.3
18 00000	INDIANA	35 826.6	6 633 053	X	185.1	84.0	9.1	0.2	2.1	0.0	2.1	2.4
18 01468	Anderson	42.7	55 130	679	1 291.1	78.8	13.5	0.0	0.2	0.0	1.2	6.2
18 05860	Bloomington	23.3	84 465	391	3 625.1	81.2	4.2	0.2	10.2	0.0	0.2	4.1
18 10342	Carmel	47.5	91 065	353	1 917.2	84.5	1.4	0.1	11.5	0.0	0.3	2.2
18 14734	Columbus	27.6	46 850	819	1 697.5	85.6	2.2	1.3	7.5	0.7	0.9	1.9
18 16138	Crown Point	17.8	29 176	1 276	1 639.1	NA	NA	NA	NA	NA	NA	NA
18 19486	East Chicago	14.1	28 418	1 311	2 015.5	20.3	39.7	0.0	0.0	0.0	37.2	2.8
18 20728	Elkhart	25.5	52 221	729	2 047.9	75.3	14.4	0.4	0.9	0.1	7.1	1.8
18 22000	Evansville	47.3	119 477	232	2 525.9	81.9	12.7	0.1	0.8	0.0	1.4	3.1
18 23278	Fishers	35.0	90 127	355	2 575.1	82.1	6.2	0.0	6.6	0.0	0.6	4.4
18 25000	Fort Wayne	110.6	264 488	76	2 391.4	74.5	14.7	0.3	4.3	0.2	0.9	4.9
18 27000	Gary	49.7	76 424	451	1 537.7	15.4	77.2	0.0	0.5	0.0	4.2	2.7
18 28386	Goshen	16.7	33 034	1 151	1 978.1	86.0	5.6	0.1	1.7	0.0	2.3	4.2
18 29898	Greenwood	27.9	56 545	663	2 026.7	NA	NA	NA	NA	NA	NA	NA
18 31000	Hammond	22.8	77 134	444	3 383.1	49.9	24.4	0.1	1.4	0.0	19.5	4.6
18 34114	Hobart	26.2	28 248	1 315	1 078.2	NA	NA	NA	NA	NA	NA	NA
18 36000	Indianapolis	366.5	855 164	15	2 365.6	63.0	27.9	0.3	3.0	0.0	3.1	2.8
18 38358	Jeffersonville	34.1	47 124	813	1 381.9	79.4	15.1	0.1	2.7	0.0	0.0	2.7
18 40392	Kokomo	36.6	57 799	649	1 579.2	84.1	9.6	0.3	1.7	0.3	0.7	3.2
18 40788	Lafayette	29.5	71 782	490	2 433.3	86.7	7.6	0.2	1.6	0.0	1.7	2.2
18 42426	Lawrence	20.1	47 866	796	2 381.4	66.0	26.8	0.0	1.2	0.0	1.5	4.5
18 46908	Marion	15.6	28 592	1 302	1 832.8	NA	NA	NA	NA	NA	NA	NA
18 48528	Merrillville	33.2	34 994	1 086	1 054.0	35.3	41.0	0.2	3.3	0.0	13.5	6.7
18 48798	Michigan City	19.7	31 157	1 208	1 581.6	NA	NA	NA	NA	NA	NA	NA
18 49932	Mishawaka	17.7	48 679	783	2 750.2	86.2	6.8	0.4	0.9	0.0	0.4	5.3
18 51876	Muncie	27.4	69 010	510	2 518.6	NA	NA	NA	NA	NA	NA	NA
18 52326	New Albany	14.9	36 670	1 040	2 461.1	85.3	9.6	0.1	0.4	0.0	1.9	2.7
18 54180	Noblesville	32.0	60 183	613	1 880.7	92.4	5.6	0.0	1.3	0.0	0.2	0.6
18 60246	Plainfield	22.6	31 409	1 199	1 389.8	81.9	7.9	0.0	4.9	0.0	4.1	1.2
18 61092	Portage	25.5	36 505	1 044	1 431.6	85.4	5.2	0.2	2.1	0.0	3.0	4.1
18 64260	Richmond	24.0	35 664	1 072	1 486.0	82.0	7.1	1.0	1.5	0.0	3.0	5.3
18 68220	Schererville	14.8	28 701	1 297	1 939.3	79.5	7.3	0.0	3.1	0.0	6.3	3.7
18 71000	South Bend	41.4	101 735	300	2 457.4	64.1	24.9	0.2	1.3	0.2	4.3	5.0
18 75428	Terre Haute	34.5	60 852	603	1 763.8	NA	NA	NA	NA	NA	NA	NA
18 78326	Valparaiso	16.2	33 104	1 146	2 043.5	95.0	1.1	0.0	1.9	0.5	0.4	1.1
18 82700	Westfield	29.7	37 221	1 027	1 253.2	90.5	3.3	0.0	4.2	0.0	0.3	1.7
18 82862	West Lafayette	13.8	45 872	830	3 324.1	65.8	3.4	0.3	26.0	0.0	1.4	3.1
19 00000	IOWA	55 856.5	3 134 693	X	56.1	90.5	3.4	0.4	2.2	0.1	1.5	1.9
19 01855	Ames	25.1	66 191	546	2 637.1	83.9	1.1	0.2	12.0	0.0	0.4	2.4
19 02305	Ankeny	29.4	58 627	638	1 994.1	NA	NA	NA	NA	NA	NA	NA
19 06355	Bettendorf	21.3	35 727	1 070	1 677.3	85.6	4.2	0.0	6.2	0.0	1.3	2.7
19 09550	Burlington	14.5	25 277	1 417	1 743.2	NA	NA	NA	NA	NA	NA	NA
19 11755	Cedar Falls	28.9	41 390	913	1 432.2	NA	NA	NA	NA	NA	NA	NA
19 12000	Cedar Rapids	70.8	131 127	207	1 852.1	85.6	5.7	0.5	2.5	0.0	0.8	5.0
19 14430	Clinton	35.2	25 719	1 408	730.7	89.2	5.6	0.1	0.5	0.0	1.0	3.5
19 16860	Council Bluffs	42.9	62 524	584	1 457.4	90.1	3.0	0.6	1.0	0.0	3.8	1.5
19 19000	Davenport	62.9	102 612	296	1 631.4	82.4	10.6	0.3	2.2	0.0	0.9	3.7
19 21000	Des Moines	88.9	215 472	102	2 423.8	76.7	10.7	1.1	6.2	0.1	1.7	3.5
19 22395	Dubuque	30.5	58 531	641	1 919.0	88.9	5.6	0.2	1.6	1.1	1.3	1.4
19 28515	Fort Dodge	16.1	24 441	1 433	1 518.1	NA	NA	NA	NA	NA	NA	NA
19 38595	Iowa City	25.9	74 398	470	2 872.5	78.5	9.2	0.3	5.7	0.5	3.2	2.5
19 49485	Marion	17.6	38 480	987	2 186.4	NA	NA	NA	NA	NA	NA	NA
19 49755	Marshalltown	19.3	27 328	1 352	1 416.0	76.7	2.2	0.1	5.2	0.0	14.2	1.5
19 50160	Mason City	27.8	27 430	1 346	986.7	NA	NA	NA	NA	NA	NA	NA
19 60465	Ottumwa	15.9	24 487	1 431	1 540.1	85.0	4.3	0.2	1.3	0.0	8.2	1.0
19 73335	Sioux City	58.4	82 872	406	1 419.0	83.8	4.1	1.6	3.6	0.3	4.9	1.6
19 79950	Urbandale	22.5	43 018	872	1 911.9	86.7	5.8	0.0	4.0	1.6	0.1	1.8
19 82425	Waterloo	61.4	67 934	521	1 106.4	73.1	16.1	0.4	2.2	0.0	6.3	1.8
19 83910	West Des Moines	46.6	64 560	561	1 385.4	84.4	3.6	0.2	7.8	0.0	1.9	2.1

1. Dry land or land partially or temporarily covered by water.   2. Hispanic or Latino persons may be of any race.

City	Percent Hispanic or Latino[1], 2015	Percent foreign born 2015	Age of population (percent), 2010-2014							Median age 2015	Percent female 2015	Population			
												Census counts		Percent change	
			Under 18 years	18 to 24 years	25 to 34 years	35 to 44 years	45 to 54 years	55 to 64 years	65 years and over			2000	2010	2000–2010	2010–2016
	12	13	14	15	16	17	18	19	20	21	22	23	24	25	26
ILLINOIS—Cont'd															
Waukegan	61.4	35.1	27.9	11.3	15.5	12.5	12.6	10.7	9.5	32.3	48.5	87 901	89 096	1.4	-1.0
West Chicago	51.3	35.6	25.0	9.4	15.7	14.6	12.9	12.6	9.7	35.0	48.1	23 469	27 200	15.9	0.1
Wheaton	4.6	10.4	21.3	11.0	12.7	10.8	12.3	17.8	14.2	40.5	49.9	55 416	52 999	-4.4	0.7
Wheeling	36.7	42.0	25.4	5.4	17.8	13.4	11.7	12.5	13.8	35.8	47.0	34 496	37 642	9.1	1.8
Wilmette	2.9	20.4	27.7	4.6	4.4	13.6	18.1	14.1	17.4	44.6	51.9	27 651	27 058	-2.1	0.6
Woodridge	10.4	20.9	23.1	9.6	12.9	11.7	14.5	17.9	10.4	37.7	50.9	30 934	32 977	6.6	1.5
INDIANA	6.6	4.9	23.9	10.2	12.7	12.4	13.3	12.9	14.6	37.5	50.9	6 080 485	6 484 136	6.6	2.3
Anderson	3.8	1.9	21.4	12.2	10.8	12.5	14.2	12.3	16.7	38.1	52.5	59 734	56 176	-6.0	-1.9
Bloomington	4.3	12.0	11.4	43.5	14.7	8.3	6.6	5.8	9.6	23.5	51.6	69 291	80 312	15.9	5.2
Carmel	3.5	10.8	27.4	7.8	8.7	14.0	16.5	14.9	10.8	39.9	51.8	37 733	79 191	109.9	15.0
Columbus	6.3	10.6	23.4	9.0	17.0	13.4	11.8	9.4	15.9	35.3	52.3	39 059	44 080	12.9	6.3
Crown Point	3.8	9.2	22.8	6.6	12.5	14.7	12.9	11.4	19.2	39.9	52.6	19 806	27 841	40.6	4.8
East Chicago	56.2	17.1	28.7	8.2	12.5	15.0	9.4	12.2	13.9	35.8	51.2	32 414	29 698	-8.4	-4.3
Elkhart	24.4	10.3	29.5	8.3	16.4	10.4	11.8	11.9	11.7	32.7	50.4	51 874	51 625	-0.5	1.2
Evansville	2.8	2.7	20.1	10.9	14.8	12.2	12.0	13.4	16.6	38.0	51.4	121 582	120 081	-1.2	-0.5
Fishers	4.0	7.1	33.4	4.0	14.1	18.1	13.9	9.4	7.1	34.5	51.0	37 835	77 248	104.2	16.7
Fort Wayne	8.2	7.4	25.9	10.2	14.3	12.4	11.7	11.8	13.6	34.7	51.6	205 727	253 700	23.3	4.3
Gary	8.1	2.4	26.3	9.2	11.0	11.8	11.8	14.7	15.2	38.1	53.6	102 746	80 314	-21.8	-4.8
Goshen	30.4	16.1	25.9	11.0	9.6	14.0	12.1	9.5	17.9	38.0	52.9	29 383	32 110	9.3	2.9
Greenwood	5.9	6.1	28.4	8.5	12.6	15.3	11.4	8.6	15.2	35.2	50.5	36 037	51 183	42.0	10.5
Hammond	32.6	11.9	22.6	11.7	14.4	11.9	14.2	12.5	12.8	36.0	49.8	83 048	80 823	-2.7	-4.6
Hobart	15.1	2.3	18.2	8.6	14.9	17.4	13.2	9.7	17.9	38.5	53.2	25 363	29 386	15.9	-3.9
Indianapolis	9.8	8.5	24.8	9.7	16.6	12.9	12.7	11.9	11.4	34.1	51.6	791 926	820 441	3.6	4.2
Jeffersonville	3.0	2.5	24.2	7.8	15.1	15.0	10.5	14.1	13.1	36.9	53.3	27 362	45 031	64.6	4.6
Kokomo	3.6	1.7	21.5	8.8	11.8	11.2	13.7	13.6	19.5	42.2	51.2	46 113	58 062	25.9	-0.5
Lafayette	12.9	8.0	22.6	13.6	15.8	12.2	10.8	11.1	13.8	33.5	51.8	56 397	68 860	22.1	4.2
Lawrence	17.0	10.7	25.4	8.2	16.2	14.7	12.6	12.9	10.0	35.1	54.7	38 915	46 003	18.2	4.0
Marion	5.6	0.7	20.0	17.7	13.2	6.7	9.9	14.9	17.6	34.4	56.7	31 320	29 920	-4.5	-4.4
Merrillville	22.1	6.4	27.0	9.2	14.8	10.7	10.9	13.8	13.8	34.5	55.3	30 560	34 971	14.4	0.1
Michigan City	5.2	1.8	22.4	7.9	16.9	11.4	12.4	12.5	16.6	37.6	49.2	32 900	31 484	-4.3	-1.0
Mishawaka	2.5	3.2	21.5	9.4	13.5	12.7	12.7	11.8	18.5	39.8	53.6	46 557	48 307	3.8	0.8
Muncie	3.6	1.5	18.9	28.3	10.8	9.3	9.4	11.0	12.3	27.4	53.4	67 430	70 203	4.1	-1.7
New Albany	4.8	1.7	21.9	9.1	16.4	12.9	12.0	11.8	15.9	37.0	53.7	37 603	36 345	-3.3	0.9
Noblesville	5.8	4.2	25.2	9.0	14.9	16.2	13.9	9.0	11.9	35.6	51.1	28 590	52 184	82.5	15.3
Plainfield	11.3	9.0	26.1	5.3	19.0	11.5	12.5	13.0	12.7	34.6	50.4	18 396	27 655	50.3	13.6
Portage	19.0	6.8	24.7	9.2	13.0	14.0	14.8	10.2	14.1	37.4	52.0	33 496	36 828	9.9	-0.9
Richmond	4.4	2.3	23.6	10.0	10.2	10.1	13.1	14.5	18.7	40.8	53.3	39 124	36 797	-5.9	-3.1
Schererville	11.4	13.1	23.7	9.0	8.3	11.8	15.1	14.6	17.4	42.1	52.9	24 851	29 247	17.7	-1.9
South Bend	15.9	8.5	28.4	10.6	16.0	12.0	10.0	11.8	11.2	32.4	51.3	107 789	101 059	-6.2	0.7
Terre Haute	1.8	2.1	18.7	19.5	13.2	10.9	11.3	11.2	15.3	33.2	48.3	59 614	60 785	2.0	0.1
Valparaiso	6.3	3.2	16.5	17.3	14.6	11.9	12.2	10.1	17.4	35.9	52.3	27 428	31 734	15.7	4.3
Westfield	4.3	7.9	28.7	8.1	13.5	14.1	13.9	11.0	10.7	34.9	52.9	9 293	30 109	224.0	23.6
West Lafayette	5.0	27.1	12.3	55.4	11.4	6.9	5.0	2.7	6.3	22.0	48.1	28 778	42 008	46.0	9.2
IOWA	5.6	4.8	23.3	10.3	12.6	11.8	12.8	13.2	16.0	38.1	50.4	2 926 324	3 046 869	4.1	2.9
Ames	3.1	13.2	13.1	44.3	14.2	6.6	6.8	6.5	8.4	23.0	48.0	50 731	59 011	16.3	12.2
Ankeny	4.3	5.1	31.7	8.3	16.7	16.3	10.3	8.9	7.8	30.7	53.5	27 117	45 582	68.1	28.6
Bettendorf	3.4	6.0	24.7	6.7	8.4	14.2	16.3	14.5	15.2	42.9	49.0	31 275	33 213	6.2	7.6
Burlington	3.2	2.1	23.6	5.9	12.1	11.7	14.3	13.4	19.0	43.2	51.2	26 839	25 625	-4.5	-1.4
Cedar Falls	0.5	2.0	18.3	27.7	12.5	9.8	7.4	9.5	14.9	28.5	55.2	36 145	39 259	8.6	5.4
Cedar Rapids	4.1	4.1	22.8	10.8	14.4	14.6	11.1	12.3	13.8	36.2	51.6	120 758	126 441	4.7	3.7
Clinton	1.4	1.0	24.7	8.5	13.4	10.5	11.4	12.8	18.7	37.9	54.1	27 772	26 885	-3.2	-4.3
Council Bluffs	9.9	7.1	22.5	10.4	13.3	11.8	13.9	12.4	15.7	39.3	50.9	58 268	62 229	6.8	0.5
Davenport	8.9	4.0	24.4	9.8	15.6	12.2	12.2	11.6	14.3	35.2	51.1	98 359	99 687	1.4	2.9
Des Moines	12.0	11.3	23.2	10.8	16.7	13.4	12.4	11.6	11.9	34.5	50.7	198 682	204 190	2.8	5.5
Dubuque	3.4	3.7	19.8	12.8	14.2	8.5	11.6	14.0	19.1	38.9	49.9	57 686	57 603	-0.1	1.6
Fort Dodge	5.1	1.4	22.7	12.4	14.1	12.2	9.3	13.0	16.3	36.0	49.2	25 136	25 206	0.3	-3.0
Iowa City	5.5	12.4	17.1	31.9	16.7	9.0	8.8	7.1	9.4	25.5	50.0	62 220	67 946	9.2	9.5
Marion	1.6	1.2	25.2	5.0	15.1	11.1	17.0	11.1	15.4	39.8	49.9	26 294	35 141	33.6	9.5
Marshalltown	29.3	20.2	25.2	9.3	11.2	12.6	12.1	10.9	18.7	37.8	48.2	26 009	27 552	5.9	-0.8
Mason City	5.8	1.9	20.1	9.5	8.8	13.1	10.7	16.0	21.7	43.8	52.7	29 172	28 079	-3.7	-2.3
Ottumwa	14.7	11.2	25.0	8.7	14.2	12.1	12.4	11.0	16.4	36.7	51.8	24 998	25 023	0.1	-2.1
Sioux City	18.8	9.0	25.4	11.5	14.6	10.6	12.3	12.4	13.4	34.3	53.1	85 013	82 686	-2.7	0.2
Urbandale	5.6	8.9	28.2	7.7	13.5	10.0	15.3	10.5	14.8	35.5	52.1	29 072	39 459	35.7	9.0
Waterloo	7.2	7.4	22.9	10.1	15.2	10.8	13.2	13.3	14.5	37.2	49.6	68 747	68 408	-0.5	-0.7
West Des Moines	7.7	14.0	21.8	6.7	21.0	16.0	10.6	12.6	11.4	35.3	51.1	46 403	56 703	22.2	13.9

1. May be of any race.

Table D. Cities — **Households, Group Quarters, Crime, and Education**

City	Households, 2015				Persons in group quarters, 2010				Serious crimes known to police,[2] 2014				Educational attainment, 2015		
			Percent			Institutional				Total		Rate[3]			Attainment[4] (percent)	
	Number	Persons per house-hold	Female family house-holder[1]	One-person	Total	Total	Persons in nursing facilities	Non-institu-tional	Number	Rate[3]	Violent	Property	Population age 25 and older	High school graduate or less	Bachelor's degree or more
	27	28	29	30	31	32	33	34	35	36	37	38	39	40	41
ILLINOIS—Cont'd															
Waukegan	29 510	2.92	17.7	27.4	2 077	1 586	842	491	2 966	3 342	439	2 903	53 716	58.8	18.4
West Chicago	7 387	3.67	9.7	11.5	333	325	325	8	371	1 342	90	1 252	18 018	52.6	24.8
Wheaton	20 004	2.54	8.2	25.5	3 379	1 395	578	1 984	398	740	52	688	36 370	14.3	61.4
Wheeling	14 050	2.67	6.9	31.1	465	461	461	4	546	1 433	118	1 315	26 350	41.5	33.4
Wilmette	9 418	2.89	3.5	17.0	126	69	69	57	362	1 320	36	1 283	18 498	7.5	80.3
Woodridge	12 416	2.68	10.9	25.0	88	86	0	2	410	1 224	110	1 113	22 512	22.1	48.2
INDIANA	2 515 143	2.56	12.0	29.1	186 923	95 336	41 158	91 587	198 875	3 015	365	2 649	4 363 573	46.1	24.9
Anderson	24 059	2.22	16.8	37.2	2 401	910	527	1 491	2 680	4 825	342	4 483	37 099	52.6	16.8
Bloomington	29 579	2.33	8.0	36.8	14 669	543	282	14 126	2 760	3 322	354	2 968	37 794	20.8	55.1
Carmel	32 675	2.71	7.3	20.2	600	579	470	21	828	946	14	932	57 737	12.4	69.8
Columbus	18 244	2.48	11.7	30.5	870	704	450	166	2 046	4 429	97	4 332	31 052	33.4	36.1
Crown Point	10 623	2.41	14.8	29.9	1 863	1 839	338	24	NA	NA	NA	NA	19 003	35.0	33.7
East Chicago	10 451	2.74	27.0	31.8	178	98	92	80	1 471	5 057	856	4 201	18 108	70.4	7.1
Elkhart	18 323	2.77	12.5	30.8	915	611	611	304	2 929	5 702	1 258	4 445	32 292	58.8	14.7
Evansville	50 419	2.25	13.7	39.8	4 727	2 103	1 194	2 624	7 506	6 236	518	5 718	81 290	50.8	20.1
Fishers	30 737	2.80	5.7	22.0	27	27	27	0	832	972	21	951	53 894	11.9	68.2
Fort Wayne	103 574	2.45	15.5	32.0	5 356	2 680	1 643	2 676	9 168	3 565	317	3 248	164 839	39.8	26.9
Gary	32 637	2.35	26.5	39.9	708	261	237	447	4 764	6 107	913	5 194	49 873	49.3	12.6
Goshen	12 535	2.65	15.5	26.8	1 467	808	411	659	1 276	3 946	111	3 835	21 872	61.0	16.5
Greenwood	21 313	2.66	11.4	24.6	481	456	405	25	2 112	3 886	351	3 535	36 089	40.0	29.9
Hammond	29 380	2.61	22.9	29.4	975	82	71	893	3 478	4 429	811	3 618	50 967	57.8	14.0
Hobart	11 203	2.64	11.0	26.6	144	1	0	143	1 823	6 422	292	6 129	21 746	51.5	23.5
Indianapolis	328 431	2.53	15.1	39.0	16 040	8 750	4 382	7 290	52 162	6 078	1 255	4 823	556 012	42.7	29.4
Jeffersonville	18 591	2.54	12.5	30.2	878	535	109	343	1 708	3 704	579	3 125	32 748	40.7	25.6
Kokomo	25 531	2.22	13.6	34.4	722	532	426	190	2 236	3 929	285	3 645	40 130	55.5	14.1
Lafayette	31 907	2.19	11.4	41.4	1 433	1 058	477	375	3 777	5 339	496	4 842	45 343	44.8	21.7
Lawrence	18 960	2.51	14.7	42.2	333	289	223	44	NA	NA	NA	NA	31 764	43.5	32.2
Marion	10 757	2.41	14.5	37.4	3 364	797	481	2 567	1 341	4 550	299	4 251	18 498	66.0	9.6
Merrillville	14 395	2.55	13.7	36.2	455	366	362	89	1 349	3 777	333	3 444	23 726	35.1	25.6
Michigan City	12 883	2.16	17.8	40.2	2 670	2 506	234	164	1 482	4 704	317	4 386	21 604	52.2	18.4
Mishawaka	21 460	2.29	10.2	39.3	1 013	212	83	801	2 458	5 128	221	4 907	34 739	45.1	25.3
Muncie	26 791	2.35	15.6	28.6	8 508	1 267	744	7 241	3 176	4 515	394	4 121	36 779	47.3	21.5
New Albany	14 962	2.34	19.5	41.3	1 008	724	429	284	2 165	5 866	244	5 622	24 917	45.3	19.0
Noblesville	22 269	2.64	15.7	20.3	661	632	316	29	NA	NA	NA	NA	39 148	33.1	36.8
Plainfield	10 753	2.63	15.0	31.0	2 615	2 595	145	20	947	3 082	179	2 903	20 331	47.7	24.0
Portage	13 334	2.75	17.4	23.6	255	233	233	22	846	2 299	163	2 136	24 383	54.9	13.3
Richmond	12 679	2.60	17.9	35.3	2 292	1 198	561	1 094	NA	NA	NA	NA	23 411	58.5	15.7
Schererville	11 321	2.53	13.2	27.9	120	63	0	57	150	518	14	504	19 378	43.1	24.9
South Bend	37 197	2.72	19.2	34.8	2 692	1 697	773	995	5 435	5 389	685	4 704	63 271	49.2	22.8
Terre Haute	24 218	2.22	12.5	41.7	8 875	4 173	589	4 702	3 210	5 255	324	4 931	38 134	49.8	22.2
Valparaiso	13 347	2.23	10.7	33.0	2 936	1 070	546	1 866	654	2 020	108	1 912	21 738	29.8	40.9
Westfield	13 210	2.90	7.8	16.8	139	99	99	40	457	1 336	105	1 230	24 303	19.9	55.1
West Lafayette	11 240	2.38	10.4	35.9	3 069	155	155	2 914	381	1 221	103	1 119	13 218	15.4	71.8
IOWA	1 247 249	2.42	9.2	29.1	98 112	43 282	26 871	54 830	73 553	2 367	273	2 094	2 074 504	40.3	26.8
Ames	25 393	2.16	6.7	27.3	7 767	294	181	7 473	1 192	1 907	120	1 787	27 692	12.3	65.2
Ankeny	19 415	2.88	12.5	17.9	663	174	146	489	748	1 409	115	1 294	34 059	24.2	44.8
Bettendorf	13 820	2.56	4.9	23.8	176	172	158	4	513	1 464	148	1 315	24 357	23.7	47.2
Burlington	10 902	2.36	11.8	33.1	495	367	235	128	1 038	4 029	633	3 396	18 414	46.9	19.8
Cedar Falls	14 751	2.44	6.1	30.7	4 574	354	354	4 220	840	2 055	122	1 932	21 657	26.1	43.8
Cedar Rapids	54 931	2.32	10.9	35.9	3 518	1 561	769	1 957	5 431	4 213	301	3 912	86 501	36.0	29.0
Clinton	10 802	2.28	15.7	34.0	713	379	347	334	1 386	5 255	626	4 629	16 945	45.2	22.7
Council Bluffs	24 879	2.42	16.4	29.7	1 908	964	440	944	4 459	7 208	548	6 660	41 997	49.9	18.4
Davenport	41 684	2.39	12.0	34.9	3 111	1 247	751	1 864	4 831	4 703	619	4 084	67 539	43.2	25.1
Des Moines	85 023	2.41	15.4	34.6	6 104	1 641	1 005	4 463	10 148	4 873	613	4 260	138 768	43.3	26.1
Dubuque	23 790	2.30	12.0	31.8	4 027	1 133	806	2 894	1 665	2 850	248	2 602	39 623	39.6	31.7
Fort Dodge	9 441	2.30	10.8	38.9	2 509	1 651	345	858	1 398	5 701	689	5 011	15 837	38.3	18.4
Iowa City	28 675	2.36	9.2	33.0	6 585	296	168	6 289	1 969	2 715	294	2 421	37 861	20.3	56.2
Marion	15 370	2.41	7.3	29.0	292	214	210	78	585	1 604	134	1 469	26 036	28.1	34.9
Marshalltown	10 683	2.58	6.9	23.5	1 190	1 040	985	150	958	3 432	552	2 880	18 559	57.7	17.3
Mason City	10 726	2.28	10.4	39.3	856	448	344	408	969	3 509	94	3 414	17 809	35.1	16.8
Ottumwa	10 259	2.35	14.2	29.7	826	371	248	455	1 147	4 626	290	4 336	16 491	45.2	16.4
Sioux City	31 015	2.57	15.4	31.5	2 565	743	437	1 822	3 479	4 224	353	3 870	52 261	51.3	21.7
Urbandale	16 885	2.60	8.6	29.6	234	230	222	4	781	1 845	198	1 646	28 310	22.2	45.8
Waterloo	27 941	2.42	15.1	33.3	1 165	687	515	478	3 336	4 880	958	3 922	45 855	44.1	25.0
West Des Moines	28 228	2.27	5.6	33.5	273	262	262	11	1 694	2 717	186	2 531	46 033	18.2	53.7

1. No spouse present.   2. Data for serious crimes have not been adjusted for underreporting. This may affect comparability between geographic areas and over time.   3. Per 100,000 population estimated by the FBI.   4. Persons 25 years old and over.

Table D. Cities — Income, Poverty, and Housing

City	Money income, 2015					Housing units, 2010			Occupied housing units 2015				
	Households			Families						Owner-occupied		Renter-occupied	
	Median income	Percent with income of $200,000 or more	Percent with income of less than $25,000	Total Families	Percent with income below poverty	Total	Percent change, 2000–2010	Vacant units for sale or rent[2]	Total	Percent	Median value[3] (dollars)	Percent	Median rent (dollars)
	42	43	44	45	46	47	48	49	50	51	52	53	54
ILLINOIS—Cont'd													
Waukegan	49 203	1.9	16.6	20 099	20.8	30 746	5.1	2 667	29 510	45.3	117 000	54.7	893
West Chicago	85 502	9.3	11.2	NA	NA	7 763	15.2	433	7 387	68.6	266 800	31.4	1 071
Wheaton	89 574	14.6	6.9	13 879	3.1	20 112	1.1	921	20 004	69.1	343 000	30.9	1 296
Wheeling	50 498	2.9	14.2	9 058	13.3	15 397	12.5	936	14 050	58.5	196 900	41.5	1 188
Wilmette	143 720	32.8	3.5	NA	NA	10 290	-0.4	548	9 418	83.1	712 400	16.9	1 552
Woodridge	80 364	7.4	10.4	8 541	6.8	13 392	14.6	746	12 416	71.4	252 600	28.6	1 225
INDIANA	50 532	3.3	17.3	1 633 695	10.2	2 795 541	10.4	293 387	2 515 143	68.2	131 000	31.8	758
Anderson	34 544	0.8	26.1	13 332	20.2	27 953	1.3	4 393	24 059	56.2	67 200	43.8	696
Bloomington	31 115	2.3	34.8	11 259	13.2	33 239	17.2	1 814	29 579	33.4	199 500	66.6	856
Carmel	108 660	27.3	5.1	24 381	3.9	30 738	117.0	1 741	32 675	78.5	318 800	21.5	1 094
Columbus	54 772	3.9	15.7	10 923	9.4	19 700	14.9	1 913	18 244	61.3	143 600	38.7	839
Crown Point	65 448	5.1	8.7	7 140	4.3	10 976	36.0	582	10 623	73.2	171 200	26.8	954
East Chicago	27 762	0.0	35.4	6 993	28.3	12 958	-2.3	2 234	10 451	50.8	64 700	49.2	651
Elkhart	36 406	1.6	26.5	11 065	24.4	22 699	4.9	3 438	18 323	50.3	90 300	49.7	765
Evansville	35 293	1.6	23.4	27 898	19.6	57 799	1.2	7 211	50 419	57.6	89 700	42.4	693
Fishers	109 397	13.8	3.7	23 043	2.6	28 511	82.0	1 293	30 737	79.4	233 500	20.6	1 148
Fort Wayne	44 977	2.6	19.7	63 839	12.8	113 541	24.9	11 956	103 574	60.8	105 900	39.2	716
Gary	30 467	0.9	35.1	19 069	23.8	39 531	-9.4	8 151	32 637	45.9	68 000	54.1	748
Goshen	39 948	0.7	18.2	8 324	15.7	12 631	12.2	1 287	12 535	52.1	110 300	47.9	687
Greenwood	66 304	3.0	11.3	14 673	4.3	21 339	33.6	1 724	21 313	50.0	144 800	50.0	890
Hammond	41 359	1.2	20.3	18 945	19.6	32 945	-3.5	2 996	29 380	63.2	86 600	36.8	851
Hobart	60 483	2.2	9.1	7 634	8.1	12 399	20.6	749	11 203	78.8	131 200	21.2	920
Indianapolis	41 278	2.6	22.2	173 377	15.2	384 414	7.6	48 228	328 431	51.8	123 500	48.2	807
Jeffersonville	49 518	1.5	12.8	11 962	5.1	19 991	60.9	1 411	18 591	68.3	130 600	31.7	810
Kokomo	41 659	1.0	24.9	15 347	18.9	23 010	3.0	3 162	25 531	60.3	78 000	39.7	635
Lafayette	41 328	0.6	23.3	15 058	15.4	31 260	22.4	2 715	31 907	44.0	106 300	56.0	737
Lawrence	47 345	0.7	17.7	10 147	14.8	19 515	19.9	1 651	18 960	65.0	123 400	35.0	755
Marion	29 785	0.0	23.8	5 721	11.6	13 715	-0.6	1 887	10 757	56.6	58 800	43.4	655
Merrillville	55 405	0.7	15.8	8 352	8.2	14 842	19.8	1 146	14 395	63.6	130 900	36.4	965
Michigan City	34 614	1.8	26.8	6 782	22.2	14 435	1.5	2 299	12 883	56.1	90 700	43.9	685
Mishawaka	40 119	1.4	22.3	11 459	10.4	24 088	11.4	2 745	21 460	53.0	102 800	47.0	682
Muncie	32 334	0.1	34.8	14 347	23.5	31 958	5.8	4 236	26 791	50.6	72 700	49.4	730
New Albany	37 448	0.4	29.9	7 947	22.3	17 315	1.5	1 740	14 962	54.0	109 200	46.0	680
Noblesville	69 350	5.3	5.6	16 516	3.7	21 121	86.3	2 041	22 269	69.9	185 800	30.1	929
Plainfield	55 329	0.9	16.7	7 360	8.8	10 386	38.3	639	10 753	67.6	153 600	32.4	946
Portage	49 660	2.3	24.7	9 248	20.6	14 807	11.1	815	13 334	62.9	139 800	37.1	865
Richmond	32 224	2.8	25.1	7 673	16.2	17 649	-0.4	2 551	12 679	60.8	97 500	39.2	606
Schererville	57 772	4.9	13.8	7 527	6.2	12 393	24.0	510	11 321	77.3	201 900	22.7	923
South Bend	36 273	0.6	24.1	22 168	22.0	46 324	0.2	6 564	37 197	59.4	79 500	40.6	711
Terre Haute	31 143	1.7	32.9	11 916	20.3	25 518	-0.3	2 873	24 218	49.5	75 300	50.5	646
Valparaiso	49 526	6.3	19.8	7 366	12.8	13 506	15.8	896	13 347	58.0	177 900	42.0	882
Westfield	88 681	15.0	9.0	NA	NA	11 209	NA	719	13 210	83.5	212 500	16.5	1 276
West Lafayette	34 106	5.8	32.7	4 099	11.8	12 591	16.5	646	11 210	38.1	188 100	61.9	867
IOWA	54 736	3.3	15.9	796 799	7.7	1 336 417	8.4	114 841	1 247 249	70.7	136 100	29.3	718
Ames	42 446	6.2	26.3	10 674	3.5	23 876	27.6	1 117	25 393	40.3	187 700	59.7	853
Ankeny	71 262	5.6	5.9	14 128	5.0	18 339	69.8	906	19 415	73.2	189 300	26.8	836
Bettendorf	75 637	9.7	8.6	9 560	1.6	14 437	10.6	756	13 820	78.3	201 600	21.7	917
Burlington	48 029	2.4	23.4	7 002	11.8	11 899	-1.0	961	10 902	73.2	95 200	26.8	707
Cedar Falls	56 546	5.6	14.9	7 964	3.0	15 477	16.4	869	14 751	65.0	176 200	35.0	738
Cedar Rapids	51 011	3.1	17.0	30 234	10.5	57 217	9.7	3 981	54 931	66.2	135 100	33.8	697
Clinton	42 010	2.1	21.4	6 119	14.1	12 202	-1.8	956	10 802	70.5	101 600	29.5	624
Council Bluffs	49 638	0.9	17.9	15 679	14.9	26 594	9.1	1 801	24 879	59.2	113 900	40.8	731
Davenport	49 745	1.4	19.8	23 966	12.1	44 087	6.6	3 467	41 684	59.3	121 500	40.7	741
Des Moines	49 072	2.8	19.1	47 872	11.6	88 729	4.3	7 360	85 023	59.7	119 500	40.3	781
Dubuque	50 807	2.2	18.4	14 673	11.7	25 029	5.1	1 523	23 790	63.3	139 600	36.7	699
Fort Dodge	37 410	3.4	26.6	5 108	9.2	11 215	0.1	940	9 441	61.5	80 800	38.5	585
Iowa City	47 593	4.2	26.9	12 682	13.8	29 270	12.4	1 613	28 675	48.1	195 600	51.9	872
Marion	65 997	4.8	7.7	10 062	6.6	15 064	37.2	956	15 370	77.2	163 300	22.8	729
Marshalltown	52 588	1.5	13.7	6 756	3.0	11 171	2.9	836	10 683	67.1	94 600	32.9	580
Mason City	45 527	2.0	29.7	5 855	13.8	13 352	2.3	986	10 726	63.4	111 300	36.6	622
Ottumwa	38 607	1.1	21.3	6 888	12.8	11 257	2.6	1 006	10 259	67.9	74 700	32.1	607
Sioux City	47 584	2.6	19.9	19 061	13.0	33 425	-1.1	1 854	31 015	61.3	106 200	38.7	707
Urbandale	72 666	7.1	10.2	10 773	5.0	16 319	37.7	723	16 885	71.1	220 800	28.9	890
Waterloo	44 153	2.5	19.9	16 884	9.1	30 723	4.2	2 116	27 941	62.0	111 700	38.0	678
West Des Moines	70 687	8.3	6.0	16 642	2.4	26 219	26.2	1 908	28 228	63.6	188 200	36.4	878

1. Based on population estimated by the American Community Survey.   2. Includes units rented or sold but not occupied.   3. Specified owner-occupied units; $1,000,000 represents $1,000,000 or more   4. 50.0 represents 50 percent or more.   5. 10.0 represents 10 percent or less.

Table D. Cities — **Commuting, Computer Access, Migration, Labor Force, and Employment**

City	Commuting Percent		Computer Access[2] Percent		Migration, 2015		Civilian labor force, 2016		Unemployment		Civilian employment[4], 2015 Population age 16 and older		Population age 16 to 64	
	Drove alone	With Commutes of 30 minutes or more[1]	With a Computer in the house	With Internet Access	Percent who lived in the same house one year ago	Percent who lived in an other state or county one year ago	Total	Percent change, 2015–2016	Total	Rate[3]	Number	Percent in Labor Force	Number	Percent who worked full-year full-time
	55	56	57	58	59	60	61	62	63	64	65	66	67	68
ILLINOIS—Cont'd														
Waukegan	79.2	40.3	89.7	83.6	80.1	5.3	45 091	0.6	3 017	6.7	65 881	72.2	57 517	52.2
West Chicago	78.9	30.5	89.0	78.3	87.4	1.7	14 440	0.5	813	5.6	21 415	71.2	18 741	52.8
Wheaton	74.0	37.1	92.6	87.4	85.0	8.9	29 174	1.0	1 312	4.5	44 283	67.6	36 659	49.9
Wheeling	83.3	32.3	92.3	82.8	82.9	3.2	22 574	0.8	1 077	4.8	29 128	64.2	23 860	51.5
Wilmette	67.0	55.6	98.2	94.3	NA	NA	12 942	0.9	566	4.4	20 702	63.6	15 931	49.5
Woodridge	87.9	53.5	92.0	85.2	88.6	4.8	20 237	1.1	945	4.7	26 452	71.6	22 973	52.8
INDIANA	86.2	30.2	85.0	73.5	84.5	6.2	3 326 893	1.7	147 087	4.4	5 215 392	63.6	4 250 068	49.8
Anderson	83.1	31.6	81.3	70.3	74.2	7.7	23 763	2.4	1 366	5.7	44 884	59.6	35 578	42.4
Bloomington	67.6	14.3	94.0	80.1	52.6	19.6	37 519	0.9	1 837	4.9	75 369	56.6	67 283	26.0
Carmel	91.2	43.9	97.5	95.0	84.7	9.6	48 422	2.8	1 521	3.1	67 694	71.1	58 100	57.3
Columbus	89.0	13.5	89.7	78.9	83.3	7.2	25 475	1.9	846	3.3	36 040	67.4	28 752	56.8
Crown Point	94.4	49.9	85.1	75.7	77.5	12.7	14 949	1.2	793	5.3	21 706	60.7	16 536	52.3
East Chicago	77.7	34.6	72.0	50.4	89.1	2.8	10 287	1.5	918	8.9	21 174	54.1	17 191	39.4
Elkhart	75.6	12.4	77.6	63.6	88.4	3.7	25 424	2.7	1 049	4.1	37 548	57.6	31 469	44.4
Evansville	87.9	17.8	83.7	68.2	83.0	6.1	59 339	0.9	2 615	4.4	96 559	61.0	77 023	50.8
Fishers	93.6	47.6	98.3	95.5	85.9	7.5	49 707	2.8	1 532	3.1	59 272	79.1	53 171	66.8
Fort Wayne	86.6	17.1	87.5	75.9	84.1	4.8	124 481	1.3	5 608	4.5	196 788	66.1	161 681	52.0
Gary	78.7	32.2	70.1	53.5	84.3	4.3	27 553	0.6	2 466	9.0	59 768	55.0	47 989	33.2
Goshen	75.8	17.9	78.8	63.8	83.0	5.8	16 783	3.1	586	3.5	27 199	63.4	20 987	52.7
Greenwood	89.5	49.2	88.6	78.5	78.5	11.5	29 336	2.4	1 085	3.7	43 195	62.5	34 488	56.1
Hammond	80.9	37.3	83.0	68.1	88.2	6.5	35 137	1.1	2 320	6.6	62 446	60.6	52 541	42.8
Hobart	92.5	41.4	90.6	84.5	88.3	4.2	15 069	0.7	1 013	6.7	24 821	63.0	19 493	50.6
Indianapolis	84.5	28.1	81.9	70.9	83.9	5.2	443 385	2.3	19 720	4.4	659 055	67.3	562 009	48.8
Jeffersonville	88.7	33.1	88.3	80.5	84.0	7.4	25 036	3.4	990	4.0	37 492	65.4	31 165	51.5
Kokomo	82.3	19.4	77.3	64.6	82.1	5.8	26 247	3.5	1 301	5.0	46 917	58.0	35 691	45.9
Lafayette	74.5	10.9	90.5	72.1	74.4	8.5	38 207	1.8	1 499	3.9	56 856	71.5	47 045	53.0
Lawrence	90.8	45.7	83.8	74.5	89.4	3.2	26 253	2.6	1 102	4.2	36 220	76.6	31 447	61.3
Marion	78.0	15.6	81.1	64.4	88.5	4.7	12 713	-2.0	704	5.5	24 188	57.3	18 957	38.7
Merrillville	92.8	43.7	86.3	80.8	87.3	3.0	17 225	1.3	1 134	6.6	28 500	66.6	23 379	48.0
Michigan City	79.9	28.0	81.6	66.2	69.2	8.8	12 950	-0.2	864	6.7	24 799	53.8	19 660	34.5
Mishawaka	86.1	20.9	78.4	68.7	85.0	5.8	25 427	2.6	1 092	4.3	40 932	61.8	31 634	44.1
Muncie	74.9	16.3	84.8	71.2	67.0	12.2	31 857	0.7	1 796	5.6	58 413	59.2	49 830	32.3
New Albany	84.1	24.7	76.9	63.2	88.6	5.3	18 822	3.0	865	4.6	28 592	63.9	22 840	51.7
Noblesville	90.0	39.3	93.3	88.1	80.7	6.5	33 279	2.8	1 083	3.3	45 862	73.7	38 797	58.8
Plainfield	91.1	25.1	87.8	80.5	82.4	6.0	15 051	2.5	580	3.9	22 840	67.6	19 088	53.1
Portage	86.8	33.8	88.4	73.9	86.0	7.9	18 074	1.4	1 108	6.1	28 730	60.5	23 519	48.7
Richmond	82.1	6.3	79.1	69.4	82.2	5.5	15 047	0.5	766	5.1	27 699	51.4	21 119	37.2
Schererville	83.5	42.3	87.8	81.7	88.2	5.3	16 227	1.4	784	4.8	23 164	62.1	18 148	48.1
South Bend	80.4	23.1	80.5	64.3	83.7	5.0	47 503	2.3	2 424	5.1	76 476	63.7	64 847	47.1
Terre Haute	80.8	13.6	80.2	67.3	68.9	13.2	25 648	0.1	1 478	5.8	51 767	55.4	42 348	31.8
Valparaiso	89.8	35.4	86.9	76.7	70.8	14.5	16 233	1.3	764	4.7	28 101	61.6	22 379	41.2
Westfield	91.4	37.3	93.4	92.4	83.1	6.6	20 436	2.9	619	3.0	28 429	74.9	24 329	54.5
West Lafayette	51.3	5.8	92.2	84.5	52.7	31.7	21 246	2.1	740	3.5	36 212	49.6	33 641	19.1
IOWA	84.4	20.1	85.7	75.5	84.3	7.0	1 700 683	-0.1	62 395	3.7	2 475 140	67.5	1 973 988	55.1
Ames	69.8	12.3	97.3	89.8	59.3	18.5	39 175	-0.6	840	2.1	57 719	62.8	52 262	29.1
Ankeny	94.4	23.8	96.9	90.2	73.1	9.5	32 580	1.1	745	2.3	40 644	78.6	36 208	59.4
Bettendorf	95.5	17.3	89.4	86.3	87.5	6.0	17 684	-1.5	628	3.6	27 929	65.8	22 537	57.2
Burlington	84.7	10.4	86.6	74.0	83.4	6.8	12 532	-1.6	662	5.3	20 367	66.1	15 405	51.0
Cedar Falls	81.5	5.2	92.0	84.8	74.0	12.0	22 438	-1.2	716	3.2	33 600	70.4	27 632	45.8
Cedar Rapids	85.1	13.3	85.5	73.2	81.6	7.1	70 985	-1.2	2 664	3.8	104 588	71.8	86 535	57.1
Clinton	84.7	14.1	77.2	70.5	82.0	9.7	12 447	-2.3	652	5.2	19 889	60.3	15 144	50.5
Council Bluffs	87.0	20.5	79.0	66.3	82.7	9.0	32 074	-0.2	1 150	3.6	49 979	64.5	40 169	55.6
Davenport	87.4	14.7	81.6	73.7	87.5	5.7	50 244	-1.5	2 551	5.1	80 162	63.1	65 534	50.6
Des Moines	81.8	14.2	86.4	72.5	78.2	7.3	110 707	0.9	4 568	4.1	166 628	71.6	141 671	54.2
Dubuque	86.9	9.1	84.7	75.0	79.9	9.0	32 822	-1.3	1 142	3.5	49 111	63.2	37 885	49.4
Fort Dodge	84.7	6.8	82.7	79.1	78.4	12.7	13 162	1.5	546	4.1	19 691	54.8	15 698	40.4
Iowa City	61.9	11.1	91.8	81.5	72.8	12.8	42 918	0.5	1 047	2.4	62 768	73.7	55 824	39.1
Marion	94.0	18.5	84.8	74.4	NA	NA	19 768	-1.0	626	3.2	28 463	68.6	22 705	65.0
Marshalltown	66.7	15.1	85.3	74.1	87.4	4.2	12 536	-0.7	687	5.5	21 768	65.7	16 477	51.3
Mason City	82.9	15.5	80.4	61.0	87.3	6.0	14 659	0.5	535	3.6	21 081	61.7	15 580	42.7
Ottumwa	70.8	9.5	78.3	65.9	80.9	7.2	12 311	-0.3	732	5.9	18 936	64.3	14 843	51.5
Sioux City	85.1	10.5	80.1	69.0	87.0	5.9	44 844	-0.5	1 609	3.6	64 505	68.2	53 416	53.9
Urbandale	92.4	11.7	95.4	88.2	80.4	7.6	25 496	1.1	647	2.5	32 896	73.0	26 357	63.2
Waterloo	84.8	13.5	82.1	70.3	83.5	7.3	34 233	-1.3	1 893	5.5	54 208	64.5	44 293	53.2
West Des Moines	90.6	10.9	94.4	85.9	81.5	11.0	38 341	1.2	969	2.5	51 490	75.7	44 176	63.2

1. Employed persons. 2. Households. 3. Percent of civilian labor force. 4. Persons 16 years old and over.

Table D. Cities — Construction, Wholesale Trade, and Retail Trade

City	Value of residential construction authorized by building permits, 2016			Wholesale trade,[1] 2012				Retail trade,[2] 2012			
	New construction ($1,000)	Number of housing units	Percent single family	Number of establishments	Number of employees	Sales (mil dol)	Annual payroll (mil dol)	Number of establishments	Number of employees	Sales (mil dol)	Annual payroll (mil dol)
	69	70	71	72	73	74	75	76	77	78	79
ILLINOIS—Cont'd											
Waukegan	1 053	5	100.0	65	1 228	1 089.5	83.7	209	3 534	1 105.5	133.6
West Chicago	978	4	100.0	61	1 725	746.3	91.4	77	1 098	360.6	32.2
Wheaton	14 396	49	100.0	50	D	D	D	176	2 564	508.7	50.3
Wheeling	18 477	151	16.6	143	2 705	1 386.7	156.5	90	1 437	387.8	41.5
Wilmette	56 618	110	31.8	33	69	103.7	4.1	98	1 255	245.6	33.2
Woodridge	19 523	81	71.6	64	2 715	1 589.2	157.6	98	2 039	526.8	51.5
INDIANA	258 232	1 338	70.0	6 460	91 474	81 173.4	4 650.5	21 601	309 552	85 858.0	7 078.7
Anderson	3 202	10	100.0	36	D	D	D	234	3 713	1 008.3	83.7
Bloomington	NA	NA	NA	40	444	172.5	22.8	386	6 729	1 480.9	132.7
Carmel	213 789	431	98.1	135	1 253	1 277.1	106.2	289	5 860	1 749.0	168.1
Columbus	NA	NA	NA	53	895	681.4	49.3	193	3 316	829.1	75.4
Crown Point	61 968	260	83.8	38	D	D	D	75	895	236.8	22.0
East Chicago	0	0	0.0	35	D	D	D	47	356	120.1	7.8
Elkhart	1 500	12	100.0	144	2 148	1 552.6	109.2	258	3 871	1 039.2	93.7
Evansville	17 636	176	54.5	219	4 224	2 315.7	264.0	730	11 717	2 871.9	268.3
Fishers	149 466	599	88.0	83	1 279	847.7	83.2	185	3 340	974.1	83.5
Fort Wayne	NA	NA	NA	412	5 926	6 481.8	278.0	1 096	18 193	4 689.3	426.8
Gary	1 503	8	100.0	44	928	661.1	43.3	173	1 321	596.3	26.9
Goshen	7 215	42	95.2	30	825	530.5	32.8	162	2 853	779.2	65.8
Greenwood	66 113	325	100.0	45	1 444	883.1	87.1	327	6 283	1 488.0	138.5
Hammond	1 057	6	100.0	81	D	D	D	196	3 401	1 185.3	79.1
Hobart	10 323	66	100.0	26	D	D	D	224	4 767	1 210.7	105.5
Indianapolis	347 911	1 899	43.8	1 210	22 417	17 495.9	1 279.5	2 725	42 887	13 502.0	1 070.3
Jeffersonville	33 276	233	78.1	49	686	899.7	38.8	120	1 524	415.4	38.2
Kokomo	32 787	310	34.8	50	498	469.3	28.2	297	4 441	1 060.7	94.2
Lafayette	14 545	115	54.8	81	1 088	600.2	46.6	416	7 125	1 844.9	158.1
Lawrence	17 919	95	100.0	45	780	664.6	40.1	120	1 957	467.6	43.6
Marion	2 200	15	100.0	21	206	95.7	7.4	176	2 595	668.9	55.6
Merrillville	6 853	51	68.6	37	D	D	D	204	3 524	1 049.1	88.4
Michigan City	2 182	9	100.0	36	448	266.0	19.3	250	3 669	736.3	67.8
Mishawaka	16 327	104	34.6	61	679	706.9	35.2	371	6 956	1 843.0	151.6
Muncie	1 808	27	63.0	53	551	381.5	19.7	355	5 605	1 266.9	117.5
New Albany	9 328	47	100.0	48	509	301.0	21.0	144	2 129	508.3	50.0
Noblesville	150 409	646	74.3	68	634	325.3	35.9	231	4 179	1 028.1	93.8
Plainfield	85 501	581	46.1	32	2 638	2 509.8	127.5	135	2 794	782.2	64.2
Portage	14 088	83	100.0	24	481	501.3	27.5	91	1 828	490.5	39.4
Richmond	8 166	80	10.0	38	352	241.7	16.5	208	3 244	850.5	72.5
Schererville	17 715	60	71.7	19	130	51.7	6.1	105	2 289	598.8	55.5
South Bend	NA	NA	NA	154	2 577	1 673.0	124.2	315	5 010	1 310.0	127.9
Terre Haute	25 047	361	6.9	77	971	395.4	37.9	330	4 709	998.1	92.0
Valparaiso	48 672	256	33.6	42	550	236.6	28.3	193	3 356	854.6	76.4
Westfield	269 793	845	82.7	30	722	804.8	55.3	85	1 872	467.8	42.5
West Lafayette	17 146	131	38.9	5	15	2.2	0.3	61	1 350	300.6	25.6
IOWA	2 660 753	14 317	57.3	4 302	58 872	62 318.3	2 841.8	12 046	174 556	44 905.6	3 865.3
Ames	88 082	569	19.3	35	204	102.0	9.8	212	4 054	937.4	86.2
Ankeny	323 181	1 569	64.5	40	1 385	1 852.5	76.7	142	3 622	1 175.9	94.1
Bettendorf	44 985	147	100.0	42	466	570.2	23.8	95	1 525	358.6	39.9
Burlington	5 550	29	51.7	24	377	939.4	17.8	114	1 524	307.2	32.6
Cedar Falls	42 327	229	65.9	48	961	646.7	49.7	154	2 884	678.7	60.5
Cedar Rapids	37 749	395	67.8	219	3 999	2 352.7	219.9	489	11 220	3 525.8	272.5
Clinton	5 735	24	25.0	22	155	188.1	5.7	127	2 161	509.2	45.4
Council Bluffs	14 095	63	100.0	67	1 010	1 416.1	50.6	236	5 340	1 462.8	116.1
Davenport	31 002	160	70.0	180	2 928	1 425.4	139.1	478	8 922	2 337.4	209.0
Des Moines	212 958	1 445	16.3	270	4 570	3 586.5	243.0	647	9 121	2 190.1	215.3
Dubuque	28 878	183	54.1	81	883	870.3	39.7	336	6 175	1 355.8	127.8
Fort Dodge	1 535	3	100.0	36	544	228.3	29.6	151	2 488	569.8	52.6
Iowa City	164 179	1 080	24.4	34	676	502.3	27.6	247	4 188	927.7	101.9
Marion	26 972	233	69.1	29	257	106.8	10.9	120	1 894	456.6	41.3
Marshalltown	7 665	46	43.5	23	346	225.9	19.4	125	1 923	405.0	41.2
Mason City	4 518	16	100.0	45	584	587.7	27.6	179	3 317	753.3	71.5
Ottumwa	85	1	100.0	24	177	281.4	7.1	119	2 164	488.7	46.0
Sioux City	34 742	220	42.7	129	2 034	1 640.3	91.5	388	6 950	1 675.3	148.6
Urbandale	50 960	159	100.0	96	1 331	1 041.5	81.9	148	2 686	1 017.6	92.9
Waterloo	17 692	148	59.5	80	1 370	961.3	60.8	300	5 413	1 274.6	120.3
West Des Moines	131 041	574	43.4	63	723	1 145.8	42.9	389	8 652	1 620.3	164.8

1. Merchant wholesalers except manufacturers' sales branches and offices. 2. Establishments with payroll.

Table D. Cities — Real Estate, Professional Services, and Manufacturing

City	Real estate and rental and leasing, 2012				Professional, scientific, and technical services,[1] 2012				Manufacturing, 2012			
	Number of establishments	Number of employees	Receipts (mil dol)	Annual payroll (mil dol)	Number of establishments	Number of employees	Receipts (mil dol)	Annual payroll (mil dol)	Number of establishments	Number of employees	Receipts (mil dol)	Annual payroll (mil dol)
	80	81	82	83	84	85	86	87	88	89	90	91
ILLINOIS—Cont'd												
Waukegan	52	239	61.7	8.2	162	D	D	D	81	4 911	1 775.3	314.4
West Chicago	19	129	44.2	8.8	78	800	255.7	58.8	94	4 848	2 358.0	245.6
Wheaton	66	209	51.0	8.1	413	D	D	D	21	440	D	11.9
Wheeling	30	116	28.1	4.2	124	976	245.8	57.2	141	7 219	2 463.4	346.7
Wilmette	38	D	D	D	174	390	77.3	26.0	11	95	13.4	3.1
Woodridge	31	303	62.1	11.4	115	924	133.2	66.7	40	1 714	481.7	77.3
INDIANA	5 729	31 715	6 547.9	1 171.7	12 780	99 322	14 627.5	5 453.3	8 141	452 513	242 763.8	23 041.3
Anderson	58	276	42.1	7.7	107	513	42.1	13.9	48	982	383.8	48.4
Bloomington	134	709	132.7	22.7	219	D	D	D	40	1 182	241.2	D
Carmel	200	1 684	1 226.0	116.1	575	3 523	604.7	250.0	61	827	D	40.4
Columbus	60	218	38.5	7.2	137	D	D	D	100	10 319	5 398.3	500.9
Crown Point	32	105	15.4	2.8	102	724	104.2	33.1	36	838	D	35.7
East Chicago	12	173	50.5	9.5	16	193	24.4	13.4	42	7 628	5 950.8	662.5
Elkhart	76	452	90.7	16.9	136	D	D	D	314	16 342	4 442.2	707.8
Evansville	178	1 359	201.9	40.1	355	D	D	D	173	7 490	2 730.9	322.8
Fishers	86	267	80.1	12.2	340	D	D	D	37	685	185.6	42.0
Fort Wayne	307	1 715	327.5	60.5	719	D	D	D	352	14 791	4 689.3	736.2
Gary	40	347	61.9	9.3	44	D	D	D	42	6 100	4 920.5	465.3
Goshen	36	126	18.2	3.3	67	397	35.4	12.0	103	14 551	4 138.7	617.4
Greenwood	67	247	68.4	7.6	121	819	94.6	30.4	41	1 175	496.5	70.8
Hammond	38	284	60.7	13.8	92	D	D	D	59	3 013	2 166.5	170.1
Hobart	22	79	14.1	2.3	44	D	D	D	19	816	D	31.4
Indianapolis	1 177	11 003	2 038.4	451.9	2 572	31 210	5 676.0	2 251.5	813	41 099	27 082.4	2 493.8
Jeffersonville	41	313	57.6	11.4	100	642	81.8	24.1	77	5 491	1 891.2	249.7
Kokomo	64	300	49.5	8.7	100	600	57.6	21.5	62	D	D	D
Lafayette	103	496	99.6	16.6	177	D	D	D	81	11 970	11 260.2	713.8
Lawrence	40	217	36.3	8.8	100	1 046	175.5	60.2	25	363	D	14.9
Marion	29	121	14.4	2.9	54	292	26.1	8.6	38	3 034	1 474.2	200.8
Merrillville	66	525	67.7	18.5	179	1 403	137.5	58.3	25	452	D	16.8
Michigan City	29	131	30.0	3.4	61	333	37.9	11.7	59	2 978	1 323.9	145.8
Mishawaka	56	374	68.2	12.6	109	D	D	D	85	2 618	1 071.2	119.6
Muncie	71	314	54.3	9.6	124	D	D	D	64	1 955	638.9	86.2
New Albany	35	133	17.1	3.6	117	D	D	D	83	4 966	1 660.8	246.4
Noblesville	57	170	50.0	6.5	182	708	90.1	32.6	46	2 056	753.2	95.0
Plainfield	30	252	25.8	8.5	51	387	47.2	16.3	21	582	205.4	24.2
Portage	30	140	24.9	5.4	40	239	24.9	10.8	20	2 252	2 221.9	151.4
Richmond	38	158	31.0	5.0	62	323	23.8	8.9	70	4 238	1 843.2	185.9
Schererville	34	201	46.0	7.4	88	D	D	D	12	374		19.1
South Bend	107	659	100.9	22.8	269	D	D	D	164	7 099	2 747.8	370.2
Terre Haute	72	414	69.8	14.9	163	1 035	102.5	38.7	74	6 131	1 922.0	300.0
Valparaiso	62	346	53.3	9.7	150	850	100.6	37.4	46	1 909	959.1	107.0
Westfield	24	131	15.0	4.0	72	234	25.1	9.7	19	1 092	234.3	44.2
West Lafayette	36	182	25.6	5.1	59	D	D	D	15	488	116.3	27.2
IOWA	2 742	12 031	2 268.3	425.9	6 169	48 261	6 396.9	2 454.9	3 598	203 722	116 668.8	10 021.2
Ames	72	364	55.3	11.2	135	D	D	D	43	3 163	2 048.5	180.0
Ankeny	58	148	31.5	4.9	91	463	55.4	23.8	27	3 429	3 100.7	185.8
Bettendorf	45	D	D	D	103	431	48.8	16.2	27	3 277	1 415.5	207.7
Burlington	25	623	110.3	24.4	45	238	25.6	8.8	26	2 687	913.6	110.1
Cedar Falls	49	224	50.1	6.5	98	2 726	150.9	151.5	43	1 523	393.3	69.6
Cedar Rapids	159	744	172.7	28.1	360	3 991	504.1	239.3	120	15 535	8 635.1	1 164.2
Clinton	26	89	14.9	2.9	47	221	17.0	6.7	30	2 803	4 090.3	156.2
Council Bluffs	70	329	51.2	8.3	103	D	D	D	39	3 878	D	167.8
Davenport	121	566	155.1	21.9	271	1 963	252.4	86.8	98	6 751	4 872.0	387.3
Des Moines	212	1 470	302.4	56.6	550	6 032	895.0	375.5	155	6 111	4 837.8	293.4
Dubuque	80	318	61.8	10.7	130	D	D	D	87	3 472	1 283.3	159.6
Fort Dodge	35	D	D	D	64	1 039	34.0	52.4	33	1 006	D	53.5
Iowa City	75	326	63.0	11.7	148	D	D	D	42	2 852	2 889.9	132.3
Marion	24	D	D	D	55	357	46.9	21.3	39	633	123.6	28.6
Marshalltown	27	D	D	D	37	306	46.3	11.9	30	4 891	D	241.9
Mason City	44	116	21.6	3.1	60	D	D	D	37	2 333	1 240.8	109.0
Ottumwa	20	86	12.2	2.9	41	D	D	D	17	D	D	D
Sioux City	83	496	61.9	12.7	176	D	D	D	77	4 428	2 997.7	172.8
Urbandale	43	245	52.4	7.0	178	1 832	517.5	150.7	35	1 403	548.8	83.4
Waterloo	83	387	67.2	10.9	114	D	D	D	98	11 343	9 231.0	577.4
West Des Moines	120	906	193.1	50.2	359	4 625	709.2	247.2	32	1 031	238.7	49.4

1. Establishments subject to federal tax.

Table D. Cities — Accommodation and Food Services, Arts, Entertainment, and Recreation, and Health Care and Social Assistance

City	Accommodation and food services, 2012				Arts, entertainment, and recreation,[1] 2012				Health care and social assistance,[1] 2012			
	Number of establish-ments	Number of employees	Sales (mil dol)	Annual payroll (mil dol)	Number of establish-ments	Number of employees	Receipts (mil dol)	Annual payroll (mil dol)	Number of establish-ments	Number of employees	Receipts (mil dol)	Annual payroll (mil dol)
	92	93	94	95	96	97	98	99	100	101	102	103
ILLINOIS—Cont'd												
Waukegan	133	1 955	117.5	30.2	13	228	14.6	3.3	102	2 622	313.1	118.7
West Chicago	46	567	27.5	7.3	8	104	6.4	1.7	39	463	43.9	15.0
Wheaton	111	1 954	95.4	29.0	19	D	D	D	173	2 236	205.0	92.6
Wheeling	57	D	D	D	3	31	1.9	0.6	69	897	57.7	26.2
Wilmette	50	D	D	D	17	D	D	D	117	1 034	80.0	32.5
Woodridge	55	965	50.5	14.1	12	231	12.5	4.0	78	443	46.8	18.2
INDIANA	13 057	255 223	13 076.6	3 432.7	1 559	23 917	3 152.7	761.2	12 360	206 531	21 191.4	8 625.9
Anderson	148	2 940	123.6	36.2	19	D	D	D	137	2 075	182.3	76.1
Bloomington	340	7 466	320.5	87.5	15	D	D	D	237	4 035	430.7	181.7
Carmel	185	3 477	180.6	55.8	53	590	40.5	11.1	391	D	D	D
Columbus	167	3 488	160.7	43.7	13	148	5.0	1.5	157	D	D	D
Crown Point	69	1 271	51.6	14.7	10	D	D	D	90	1 145	161.3	56.8
East Chicago	39	D	D	D	1	D	D	D	25	D	D	D
Elkhart	161	3 011	128.0	35.9	9	102	4.4	1.9	129	2 634	317.3	126.3
Evansville	403	9 956	511.6	133.5	39	847	67.1	10.5	405	6 878	732.3	335.7
Fishers	175	3 719	185.5	48.2	34	D	D	D	208	D	D	D
Fort Wayne	614	14 022	590.8	175.7	69	D	D	D	691	18 728	1 992.0	878.5
Gary	87	1 078	119.7	22.5	6	D	D	D	88	1 360	86.0	35.2
Goshen	88	1 742	78.3	20.9	5	D	D	D	82	1 106	106.4	53.7
Greenwood	152	4 007	177.8	52.2	13	D	D	D	159	D	D	D
Hammond	145	D	D	D	9	D	D	D	86	D	D	D
Hobart	73	1 440	66.3	18.9	12	D	D	D	58	D	D	D
Indianapolis	1 988	45 071	2 532.3	704.9	221	D	D	D	1 867	36 083	4 152.6	1 810.4
Jeffersonville	90	D	D	D	10	D	D	D	113	D	D	D
Kokomo	175	3 811	157.7	45.4	17	D	D	D	180	D	D	D
Lafayette	222	4 819	220.1	61.7	19	300	7.8	2.4	237	4 108	437.4	191.0
Lawrence	81	D	D	D	12	D	D	D	54	D	D	D
Marion	84	1 540	67.8	18.3	4	D	D	D	117	D	D	D
Merrillville	132	3 016	167.2	45.4	10	213	9.5	3.1	238	D	D	D
Michigan City	100	3 199	274.3	57.2	3	40	1.7	0.4	82	D	D	D
Mishawaka	200	4 928	221.2	62.2	17	D	D	D	153	D	D	D
Muncie	171	3 804	149.0	42.5	17	163	5.6	1.7	213	D	D	D
New Albany	85	D	D	D	8	D	D	D	146	D	D	D
Noblesville	107	2 503	119.1	34.3	21	D	D	D	128	D	D	D
Plainfield	89	1 947	96.7	26.6	7	D	D	D	46	D	D	D
Portage	81	1 687	81.6	20.3	10	D	D	D	69	976	86.3	32.1
Richmond	119	2 480	107.7	31.2	8	49	1.8	0.6	105	D	D	D
Schererville	96	2 116	88.9	27.7	6	D	D	D	81	670	59.9	25.5
South Bend	234	4 026	180.5	52.6	14	D	D	D	238	5 356	735.7	255.2
Terre Haute	231	4 616	201.8	58.6	14	D	D	D	210	3 875	484.6	171.0
Valparaiso	117	2 468	107.6	31.2	10	D	D	D	152	2 234	223.6	93.3
Westfield	63	1 494	64.3	18.4	14	D	D	D	52	D	D	D
West Lafayette	129	2 599	113.0	30.0	6	D	D	D	46	D	D	D
IOWA	7 047	115 134	5 468.7	1 466.6	993	13 165	1 305.5	255.5	5 582	78 961	7 151.2	3 356.8
Ames	195	3 976	160.9	45.2	15	308	12.5	4.4	96	1 702	217.7	103.8
Ankeny	100	2 414	109.4	31.1	13	150	6.4	2.3	88	925	74.7	32.2
Bettendorf	70	1 919	134.2	30.7	10	D	D	D	108	2 123	185.4	93.7
Burlington	80	1 689	71.7	21.2	9	D	D	D	56	D	D	D
Cedar Falls	110	2 719	94.9	30.9	15	D	D	D	70	D	D	D
Cedar Rapids	372	7 177	316.2	94.2	36	915	31.4	8.9	302	4 513	532.9	246.0
Clinton	76	1 377	93.3	20.1	7	D	D	D	65	987	85.4	33.0
Council Bluffs	159	4 908	393.2	86.2	13	D	D	D	143	D	D	D
Davenport	285	6 066	266.6	78.3	27	D	D	D	241	3 098	348.5	158.8
Des Moines	537	9 062	464.2	133.8	57	601	36.0	10.3	366	7 237	912.1	461.0
Dubuque	181	3 760	145.4	43.6	30	1 253	135.0	29.9	154	2 900	320.2	179.6
Fort Dodge	79	1 347	60.6	16.5	10	31	2.3	0.5	70	D	D	D
Iowa City	214	D	D	D	19	D	D	D	145	1 949	198.8	81.8
Marion	53	880	36.2	10.1	8	D	D	D	50	721	47.7	20.7
Marshalltown	79	1 049	43.7	11.9	4	D	D	D	36	D	D	D
Mason City	83	1 464	60.4	16.8	10	D	D	D	67	D	D	D
Ottumwa	71	1 188	46.2	13.1	9	D	D	D	63	D	D	D
Sioux City	232	D	D	D	26	D	D	D	190	2 778	287.8	121.9
Urbandale	81	1 762	88.7	23.4	19	D	D	D	73	1 189	68.9	30.2
Waterloo	169	3 684	214.3	51.0	21	179	11.7	3.4	154	2 109	227.0	109.8
West Des Moines	214	4 793	244.9	74.5	26	D	D	D	257	3 685	465.1	241.5

1. Establishments subject to federal tax.

Table D. Cities — Other Services and Government Employment and Payroll

City	Other services[1], 2012				Government employment and payroll, 2012								
					Full-time equivalent employees	March payroll	Percent of total for:						
	Number of establishments	Number of employees	Receipts (mil dol)	Annual payroll (mil dol)		Total (dollars)	Administration, judicial, and legal	Police and Corrections	Fire Protection	Highways and transportation	Health and welfare	Natural resources and utilities	Education and libraries
	104	105	106	107	108	109	110	111	112	113	114	115	116
ILLINOIS—Cont'd													
Waukegan	90	374	30.5	9.1	502	3 187 722	12.7	40.5	27.8	4.1	1.1	8.7	5.1
West Chicago	41	238	37.0	10.5	117	799 988	15.4	54.5	0.0	9.6	0.7	18.2	0.0
Wheaton	86	578	31.9	12.0	437	2 488 726	8.6	34.0	12.7	8.3	0.0	11.5	18.2
Wheeling	63	347	44.9	9.4	232	1 575 381	12.4	38.6	25.9	1.8	8.3	8.9	0.0
Wilmette	59	364	33.8	10.9	220	1 531 248	12.5	32.9	25.0	14.4	0.9	11.8	0.0
Woodridge	42	429	12.7	12.4	165	972 329	16.5	46.7	0.0	5.4	0.0	13.1	14.2
INDIANA	8 429	54 735	5 020.8	1 548.5	X	X	X	X	X	X	X	X	X
Anderson	85	519	38.8	12.0	638	2 851 826	7.5	21.3	15.8	10.2	3.5	35.9	0.0
Bloomington	117	1 148	86.0	27.5	814	3 124 701	11.6	21.8	16.1	13.9	5.2	29.9	0.0
Carmel	145	861	63.7	22.3	467	2 600 210	3.5	30.7	43.9	10.0	0.0	10.1	0.0
Columbus	72	502	46.4	13.8	432	1 650 956	6.5	22.9	26.7	7.3	1.6	34.1	0.0
Crown Point	73	560	52.3	16.4	201	804 519	8.2	32.5	18.8	9.5	0.4	23.3	0.0
East Chicago	23	128	12.0	3.5	698	2 567 542	8.3	26.6	16.1	7.5	4.7	36.8	0.0
Elkhart	102	757	71.7	22.9	536	2 197 116	9.6	30.1	28.2	10.0	0.6	18.8	0.0
Evansville	234	2 033	185.2	56.8	1 278	5 214 822	2.6	31.8	24.3	11.2	3.0	24.8	0.0
Fishers	97	503	32.5	10.3	389	1 761 025	11.8	31.1	35.0	5.2	0.0	6.0	0.0
Fort Wayne	462	3 446	282.9	96.5	2 016	8 885 678	3.7	33.2	19.0	14.2	5.3	20.6	0.0
Gary	67	396	46.9	12.4	1 123	2 786 750	11.6	16.2	20.1	6.3	10.1	27.4	0.0
Goshen	54	D	D	D	227	709 892	8.9	38.2	24.5	7.4	0.8	13.4	0.0
Greenwood	101	880	101.2	32.1	279	1 071 961	16.9	33.3	24.5	11.2	0.0	12.1	0.0
Hammond	107	762	80.9	23.2	849	3 866 970	4.7	34.3	24.6	4.0	3.3	25.4	0.0
Hobart	62	410	42.4	12.6	245	963 819	14.4	31.6	27.9	6.1	0.0	15.8	0.0
Indianapolis	1 040	10 121	1 009.7	343.3	12 328	49 785 804	10.1	20.7	10.8	4.3	40.3	12.3	0.0
Jeffersonville	66	556	87.2	16.9	348	1 320 589	10.0	25.0	25.4	9.1	2.7	26.2	0.0
Kokomo	100	D	D	D	458	1 913 705	2.4	27.7	28.3	8.2	3.0	16.6	0.0
Lafayette	147	919	77.8	25.0	727	2 921 411	4.8	26.6	23.4	22.4	1.3	19.2	0.0
Lawrence	58	217	23.6	6.3	310	1 228 922	6.9	27.5	42.0	4.8	1.5	16.4	0.0
Marion	48	255	24.2	7.2	258	851 770	12.9	39.0	29.5	14.0	1.8	2.1	0.0
Merrillville	65	497	47.3	14.9	123	450 414	14.0	61.3	1.8	18.1	0.0	2.7	0.0
Michigan City	51	258	17.2	5.5	429	1 619 412	5.6	25.8	23.0	10.4	1.1	32.5	0.0
Mishawaka	92	578	41.4	14.5	503	2 151 708	6.9	27.5	24.4	4.6	0.7	31.4	0.0
Muncie	100	658	53.2	16.5	505	1 776 621	4.8	23.6	21.0	18.0	2.0	19.4	0.0
New Albany	66	330	28.2	7.9	265	917 338	5.7	32.4	36.7	5.6	3.3	8.7	0.0
Noblesville	75	484	34.1	10.6	368	1 696 635	8.6	26.2	41.3	9.3	0.0	13.7	0.0
Plainfield	49	570	37.3	14.9	268	950 626	7.8	22.5	43.0	4.3	0.0	21.5	0.0
Portage	48	374	27.4	9.2	254	948 853	7.5	31.0	27.5	15.8	0.6	16.7	0.0
Richmond	44	180	12.4	3.9	513	1 860 795	5.6	18.1	16.9	7.3	0.0	51.7	0.0
Schererville	62	588	52.8	16.0	180	726 293	13.7	41.3	15.8	13.1	0.0	16.0	0.0
South Bend	167	1 443	141.4	42.6	1 318	5 351 987	3.8	29.1	24.4	12.9	2.3	21.5	0.0
Terre Haute	91	666	55.3	17.5	615	2 301 273	8.2	27.5	28.9	17.6	1.5	14.9	0.0
Valparaiso	87	594	43.2	16.2	288	1 148 922	5.9	21.1	26.3	6.8	0.0	39.9	0.0
Westfield	43	296	23.5	7.3	176	867 739	19.6	28.0	32.8	8.5	1.6	9.5	0.0
West Lafayette	24	197	10.2	3.7	229	856 416	6.6	32.8	21.3	4.1	5.3	24.8	0.0
IOWA	4 687	23 537	2 103.6	598.9	X	X	X	X	X	X	X	X	X
Ames	69	451	33.2	10.8	616	2 954 800	12.2	13.1	10.5	21.5	2.3	30.9	5.6
Ankeny	64	D	D	D	283	1 240 311	16.5	23.8	24.3	9.4	0.0	18.9	4.5
Bettendorf	53	297	15.9	5.6	243	1 226 060	11.1	23.4	12.3	14.0	5.9	13.4	10.5
Burlington	47	248	20.8	6.4	239	935 691	5.6	25.4	21.5	13.3	0.5	20.2	7.2
Cedar Falls	51	454	36.1	12.0	478	2 270 443	8.5	9.9	7.7	7.0	0.6	57.2	2.9
Cedar Rapids	209	1 602	138.5	47.7	1 296	6 423 374	10.4	21.6	12.8	16.4	1.8	24.1	3.3
Clinton	47	172	15.3	4.4	210	897 240	6.0	29.8	22.4	15.6	2.5	17.4	5.3
Council Bluffs	102	553	47.5	14.5	471	2 609 951	9.1	27.0	20.1	6.8	10.1	21.8	5.0
Davenport	162	1 345	100.9	34.1	906	4 276 351	9.9	26.0	20.2	14.2	1.5	17.2	5.2
Des Moines	289	2 035	156.6	53.2	1 956	10 193 831	8.0	24.9	16.0	11.6	5.0	26.6	3.2
Dubuque	124	804	67.4	20.0	645	3 046 153	13.2	22.4	16.1	21.5	5.8	14.0	4.4
Fort Dodge	36	286	34.2	9.2	118	524 670	9.2	38.3	26.4	3.8	0.0	16.1	6.2
Iowa City	90	577	45.4	14.4	20	1 762 642	14.5	13.9	9.2	13.9	4.6	17.2	6.5
Marion	47	242	23.0	6.9	184	916 685	6.3	31.1	21.9	10.4	6.4	17.3	6.7
Marshalltown	41	238	19.3	4.7	231	825 058	5.3	30.0	16.7	12.6	5.2	25.4	4.7
Mason City	58	375	29.2	9.1	326	1 435 146	5.2	16.5	11.1	10.8	8.2	18.1	25.1
Ottumwa	32	185	14.3	5.3	247	856 818	6.4	16.0	15.1	23.1	5.3	28.1	3.8
Sioux City	120	879	56.6	19.4	794	3 661 919	9.1	25.7	18.3	17.6	2.2	19.7	3.4
Urbandale	61	470	34.2	12.7	223	998 550	11.0	20.8	15.3	12.5	1.1	26.9	9.6
Waterloo	97	708	57.5	17.4	603	2 720 527	5.5	26.6	21.7	9.9	2.6	18.8	4.1
West Des Moines	89	585	36.6	14.7	435	2 294 576	8.6	23.7	13.4	9.2	16.6	19.7	4.4

1. Establishments subject to federal tax.

Table D. Cities — City Government Finances

City	City government finances, 2012									
	General revenue							General expenditure		
	Intergovernmental			Taxes					Per capita[1] (dollars)	
					Per capita[1] (dollars)					
	Total (mil dol)	Total (mil dol)	Percent from state government	Total (mil dol)	Total	Property	Sales and gross receipts	Total (mil dol)	Total	Capital outlays
	117	118	119	120	121	122	123	124	125	126
ILLINOIS—Cont'd										
Waukegan	87.3	16.1	90.5	46.7	525	307	218	72.7	819	47
West Chicago	29.0	8.4	99.1	8.9	324	172	153	28.0	1 022	227
Wheaton	56.0	12.7	96.7	32.9	616	438	167	46.6	872	33
Wheeling	45.9	10.7	93.0	29.0	765	553	212	45.1	1 188	197
Wilmette	38.5	7.6	85.0	22.4	821	509	287	38.9	1 425	199
Woodridge	30.1	9.8	82.4	14.4	434	225	199	26.2	789	18
INDIANA	X	X	X	X	X	X	X	X	X	X
Anderson	84.2	19.0	48.2	36.3	652	443	39	65.2	1 172	281
Bloomington	85.2	17.5	64.4	44.3	539	434	15	72.9	886	129
Carmel	111.9	17.9	66.3	72.8	871	597	53	93.8	1 122	60
Columbus	72.5	21.0	50.2	29.8	657	647	11	59.6	1 314	244
Crown Point	35.9	4.6	85.5	17.3	616	580	36	21.8	773	94
East Chicago	103.6	44.0	82.6	50.0	1 697	1 676	21	63.2	2 147	65
Elkhart	70.5	21.2	34.3	30.9	606	596	10	59.6	1 167	88
Evansville	183.6	54.1	55.1	68.3	568	460	15	192.0	1 598	442
Fishers	58.2	7.3	74.3	35.2	430	286	25	55.3	676	109
Fort Wayne	289.9	59.4	54.7	141.1	554	423	16	257.6	1 011	147
Gary	181.4	65.4	74.4	81.4	1 028	1 008	20	145.6	1 839	385
Goshen	35.1	9.7	53.7	14.5	454	447	7	47.8	1 498	416
Greenwood	47.0	10.2	33.2	19.8	376	365	12	34.0	645	24
Hammond	192.8	73.8	83.1	63.5	797	775	22	155.5	1 953	159
Hobart	40.0	5.7	88.9	23.0	794	772	22	36.0	1 242	112
Indianapolis	2 604.6	712.4	81.1	887.7	1 064	601	112	3 151.6	3 777	1 038
Jeffersonville	55.6	10.3	33.9	27.6	605	592	13	57.7	1 264	472
Kokomo	76.1	16.8	67.8	44.3	777	655	2	63.7	1 118	63
Lafayette	99.8	25.3	67.7	44.5	637	508	7	75.9	1 086	2
Lawrence	36.4	5.3	60.9	19.2	411	308	19	34.5	739	4
Marion	32.5	6.6	85.0	19.7	665	514	11	37.1	1 252	46
Merrillville	30.3	3.8	91.0	20.7	587	559	28	18.3	518	137
Michigan City	59.4	25.0	70.4	17.2	553	532	21	50.5	1 621	213
Mishawaka	83.6	10.9	75.5	54.8	1 142	914	13	78.3	1 630	554
Muncie	72.4	20.0	73.9	29.0	414	346	11	72.9	1 040	117
New Albany	59.3	15.9	55.8	20.6	564	548	16	50.5	1 385	371
Noblesville	84.0	18.9	89.5	45.5	823	556	66	67.7	1 226	347
Plainfield	48.8	11.2	29.1	24.9	854	718	136	35.1	1 203	268
Portage	42.2	5.4	93.6	22.3	604	531	19	46.8	1 270	181
Richmond	48.2	15.7	58.1	13.4	368	357	11	46.4	1 269	343
Schererville	33.2	3.7	90.7	21.3	734	702	32	19.4	667	73
South Bend	201.3	37.3	61.0	106.9	1 060	823	30	141.5	1 404	147
Terre Haute	82.6	28.3	35.8	31.8	519	512	8	64.3	1 051	189
Valparaiso	44.4	6.4	59.9	22.8	713	632	30	35.7	1 116	232
Westfield	33.7	3.8	75.3	18.3	572	359	56	25.9	808	40
West Lafayette	32.5	8.8	47.0	12.7	416	322	9	24.7	808	153
IOWA	X	X	X	X	X	X	X	X	X	X
Ames	250.4	24.1	59.9	29.1	475	382	93	219.0	3 578	476
Ankeny	57.6	6.0	79.4	32.3	658	584	74	69.7	1 421	618
Bettendorf	52.9	7.7	67.3	30.2	883	675	208	55.4	1 617	483
Burlington	34.5	5.6	56.2	17.9	700	447	253	35.7	1 395	364
Cedar Falls	77.7	19.4	43.0	31.2	783	598	185	81.6	2 049	977
Cedar Rapids	405.0	168.3	22.7	115.9	905	655	249	457.5	3 573	2 065
Clinton	48.5	10.4	28.4	20.3	761	562	198	67.1	2 521	1 417
Council Bluffs	118.7	29.8	38.3	61.1	983	702	281	111.9	1 801	467
Davenport	165.6	37.9	52.7	84.9	837	610	227	177.4	1 749	508
Des Moines	404.2	93.7	24.5	156.5	757	643	114	460.9	2 228	484
Dubuque	135.5	48.8	22.7	45.3	780	520	260	160.4	2 763	1 348
Fort Dodge	36.9	6.2	50.6	17.7	717	531	186	39.3	1 589	605
Iowa City	138.3	36.0	53.0	63.8	906	715	191	128.1	1 819	366
Marion	36.5	5.5	81.7	22.6	630	474	156	37.9	1 056	306
Marshalltown	34.2	10.2	31.7	16.6	595	411	184	35.1	1 262	431
Mason City	52.9	17.0	23.3	20.8	748	531	218	45.1	1 625	357
Ottumwa	40.4	7.9	63.1	16.8	679	503	177	37.3	1 505	459
Sioux City	139.6	32.9	58.3	63.3	766	553	213	143.7	1 737	477
Urbandale	41.8	4.8	80.6	29.6	721	645	76	40.8	995	315
Waterloo	115.1	25.8	46.6	59.1	865	644	221	119.5	1 749	524
West Des Moines	100.9	15.8	70.7	63.9	1 076	976	100	85.4	1 439	353

1. Based on population estimated as of July 1 of the year shown.

Table D. Cities — **City Government Finances**

City	City government finances, 2012 (cont.)									
	General expenditure (cont.)									
	Percent of total for:									
	Public welfare	Highways	Parking facilities	Education	Health and hospitals	Police protection	Sewerage and sanitation	Parks and recreation	Housing and community development	Interest on debt
	127	128	129	130	131	132	133	134	135	136
ILLINOIS—Cont'd										
Waukegan	0.0	11.3	0.5	0.0	0.0	30.6	9.2	0.0	1.6	5.9
West Chicago	0.0	15.8	0.4	0.0	0.0	30.2	28.0	0.7	0.0	2.8
Wheaton	0.0	14.4	1.4	0.0	0.0	27.1	7.8	1.1	0.0	4.7
Wheeling	0.0	15.8	0.1	0.0	0.0	27.4	4.3	0.0	0.0	7.2
Wilmette	0.0	14.4	0.8	0.0	0.6	24.7	15.4	0.0	0.0	5.9
Woodridge	0.0	11.2	0.0	0.0	0.0	36.6	9.9	0.1	0.0	4.4
INDIANA	X	X	X	X	X	X	X	X	X	X
Anderson	0.0	5.6	0.1	0.0	0.3	14.5	38.2	1.7	3.5	2.5
Bloomington	0.0	7.2	2.0	0.0	1.5	13.2	15.3	10.4	1.4	3.6
Carmel	0.0	9.2	0.0	0.0	0.0	16.1	5.8	3.9	6.8	11.8
Columbus	0.0	3.5	0.0	0.0	0.5	9.2	28.6	6.4	0.8	4.1
Crown Point	0.0	12.6	0.0	0.0	0.3	15.8	28.1	3.3	0.0	1.9
East Chicago	0.0	1.5	0.0	0.0	4.1	14.6	18.5	4.4	3.2	0.9
Elkhart	0.0	9.1	0.0	0.0	0.0	15.2	19.4	5.4	1.3	2.0
Evansville	0.0	4.5	0.1	0.0	0.4	13.7	25.8	6.1	1.4	1.4
Fishers	0.0	15.5	0.0	0.0	0.0	12.7	15.0	1.2	0.0	7.5
Fort Wayne	0.0	6.4	0.2	0.0	0.9	19.3	29.0	5.5	5.1	2.8
Gary	0.0	2.5	0.0	0.0	2.6	8.6	23.7	5.0	3.3	1.1
Goshen	0.0	13.7	1.0	0.0	0.0	8.2	27.0	2.5	1.1	7.9
Greenwood	0.0	14.9	0.0	0.0	0.0	16.9	24.3	2.9	0.0	3.6
Hammond	0.0	2.9	0.0	0.0	0.0	16.8	11.7	12.4	3.7	2.7
Hobart	0.0	12.7	0.0	0.0	0.1	10.5	26.5	4.8	0.0	0.9
Indianapolis	0.0	1.2	0.4	0.0	35.8	6.6	8.7	11.7	4.3	10.4
Jeffersonville	0.0	1.9	0.0	0.0	0.6	13.1	50.7	3.9	2.0	4.1
Kokomo	0.0	6.8	0.0	0.0	0.0	19.6	18.4	4.5	3.7	1.9
Lafayette	0.0	6.9	0.0	0.0	0.0	16.5	15.5	7.3	3.9	5.6
Lawrence	0.0	3.7	0.0	0.0	2.8	16.4	18.9	3.1	0.0	1.4
Marion	0.0	5.7	0.0	0.0	0.0	20.7	14.4	2.8	0.0	1.5
Merrillville	0.0	6.0	0.0	0.0	0.0	21.1	8.9	0.9	0.0	4.6
Michigan City	0.0	3.1	0.0	0.0	0.5	13.7	18.8	10.2	2.7	3.3
Mishawaka	0.0	3.8	0.0	0.0	1.4	11.5	26.4	3.8	0.9	3.5
Muncie	0.0	3.7	0.1	0.0	0.3	11.3	46.5	1.9	1.2	2.0
New Albany	0.0	2.5	0.9	0.0	0.8	9.6	21.0	4.4	6.5	5.0
Noblesville	0.0	5.0	0.2	0.0	0.2	11.2	32.6	4.6	0.0	13.9
Plainfield	0.0	3.4	0.0	0.0	0.0	12.1	14.0	10.2	0.0	3.2
Portage	0.0	7.4	0.0	0.0	0.2	9.3	26.6	6.0	0.0	5.4
Richmond	0.0	3.5	0.1	0.0	1.1	13.2	43.5	6.3	0.0	2.2
Schererville	0.0	8.6	0.0	0.0	0.3	23.5	39.5	5.2	0.0	2.5
South Bend	0.0	5.8	0.5	0.0	0.3	16.8	22.7	12.5	1.8	5.0
Terre Haute	0.0	7.4	0.0	0.0	0.4	14.5	16.6	4.9	14.2	3.8
Valparaiso	0.0	12.1	0.1	0.0	0.0	9.7	21.3	7.1	0.0	3.4
Westfield	0.0	6.4	0.0	0.0	0.0	16.6	19.5	1.9	0.0	6.9
West Lafayette	0.0	12.3	0.0	0.0	0.0	16.7	38.4	6.0	2.0	4.7
IOWA	X	X	X	X	X	X	X	X	X	X
Ames	0.5	2.1	0.3	0.0	72.3	3.5	4.7	2.0	0.3	2.0
Ankeny	0.4	27.0	0.0	0.0	3.9	9.7	21.2	8.8	0.0	7.2
Bettendorf	0.0	12.9	0.0	0.0	0.0	11.1	12.3	17.3	0.9	8.1
Burlington	0.0	6.6	0.2	0.0	2.2	14.7	12.6	9.1	0.0	6.4
Cedar Falls	0.0	13.0	0.2	0.0	0.3	5.2	6.7	5.8	2.0	1.5
Cedar Rapids	0.0	7.6	0.9	0.0	0.2	7.2	13.4	2.0	1.6	3.1
Clinton	0.0	10.7	0.1	0.0	2.5	7.2	48.1	3.5	1.1	3.6
Council Bluffs	0.0	3.7	0.1	0.0	2.9	13.5	11.9	3.6	1.1	1.9
Davenport	0.0	4.9	0.6	0.0	0.0	13.1	17.7	6.8	6.3	6.4
Des Moines	2.3	11.4	1.8	0.0	0.0	12.6	19.8	4.9	6.4	5.1
Dubuque	0.3	10.6	1.2	0.0	1.4	7.8	26.9	4.5	3.9	3.8
Fort Dodge	0.8	9.9	0.4	0.0	0.1	9.5	14.8	11.3	1.5	5.7
Iowa City	0.0	8.1	3.7	0.0	0.5	8.4	16.3	4.9	8.7	4.8
Marion	0.0	7.5	0.0	0.0	0.1	13.8	13.7	4.6	1.9	5.3
Marshalltown	0.1	16.2	0.1	0.0	4.0	15.0	32.3	6.4	5.1	2.3
Mason City	1.7	6.4	0.2	0.0	4.0	12.0	17.3	4.5	0.0	4.0
Ottumwa	0.3	19.9	0.0	0.0	1.4	12.0	30.9	4.9	0.0	2.4
Sioux City	0.0	5.9	1.1	0.0	0.4	12.2	17.1	8.9	5.9	5.4
Urbandale	0.0	28.4	0.0	0.0	0.1	15.2	5.4	9.9	1.4	4.5
Waterloo	0.2	14.3	0.3	0.0	1.7	13.5	9.5	5.5	7.5	3.5
West Des Moines	1.3	14.3	0.0	0.0	5.2	10.7	16.9	5.3	0.9	4.8

Table D. Cities — City Government Finances, City Government Employment, and Climate

City	City government finances, 2012 (cont.) Debt outstanding			Climate[2] Average daily temperature (degrees Fahrenheit)						
				Mean		Limits				
	Total (mil dol)	Per capita[1] (dollars)	Debt issued during year	January	July	January[3]	July[4]	Annual precipitation (inches)	Heating degree days	Cooling degree days
	137	138	139	140	141	142	143	144	145	146
ILLINOIS—Cont'd										
Waukegan	133.5	1 504	26.6	20.3	71.5	12.0	81.7	34.09	7 031	613
West Chicago	20.8	757	0.0	NA	NA	NA	NA	NA	NA	NA
Wheaton	45.4	849	0.0	23.1	74.8	14.2	86.8	37.94	6 053	942
Wheeling	84.5	2 228	8.5	18.4	72.1	9.6	82.3	36.56	7 149	624
Wilmette	76.2	2 790	14.3	22.0	73.3	14.3	83.5	36.27	6 498	830
Woodridge	24.8	746	3.3	23.1	74.8	14.2	86.8	37.94	6 053	942
INDIANA	X	X	X	X	X	X	X	X	X	X
Anderson	127.1	2 286	25.5	25.7	74.0	18.4	83.8	39.82	5 807	872
Bloomington	159.2	1 937	55.7	27.9	75.4	19.3	86.0	44.91	5 348	1 017
Carmel	367.8	4 400	0.0	25.3	74.2	17.0	84.5	42.85	5 901	873
Columbus	109.4	2 413	0.0	27.9	75.9	19.1	86.4	41.94	5 367	1 059
Crown Point	22.4	795	1.9	NA	NA	NA	NA	NA	NA	NA
East Chicago	42.0	1 427	0.0	23.7	74.0	15.3	84.8	38.13	6 055	887
Elkhart	28.7	562	0.0	22.8	72.1	14.3	83.3	38.56	6 487	663
Evansville	274.1	2 281	67.7	33.2	79.6	24.8	90.5	45.76	4 140	1 616
Fishers	131.1	1 603	33.0	25.3	74.2	17.0	84.5	42.85	5 901	873
Fort Wayne	435.4	1 708	0.0	23.6	73.4	16.1	84.3	36.55	6 205	830
Gary	85.2	1 076	21.7	22.2	73.5	13.9	83.9	38.02	6 075	826
Goshen	101.3	3 178	9.3	24.3	73.7	17.0	84.5	36.59	6 075	826
Greenwood	30.0	570	0.0	25.7	74.7	18.0	84.0	40.24	5 783	942
Hammond	112.1	1 407	0.0	22.2	73.5	13.9	83.9	38.02	6 497	776
Hobart	25.7	886	0.0	22.2	73.5	13.9	83.9	38.02	6 497	776
Indianapolis	6 001.3	7 191	2 503.6	26.5	75.4	18.5	85.6	40.95	5 521	1 042
Jeffersonville	54.0	1 182	0.0	31.3	75.8	21.4	88.5	45.47	4 829	1 079
Kokomo	32.5	570	0.0	22.8	73.0	15.0	84.1	41.54	6 368	771
Lafayette	133.7	1 913	0.0	23.0	73.5	14.3	84.5	36.90	6 206	842
Lawrence	27.5	589	0.0	25.7	74.7	18.0	84.0	40.24	5 783	942
Marion	11.4	385	0.0	24.2	73.8	16.3	84.5	39.01	6 143	819
Merrillville	22.7	644	0.2	21.1	72.7	12.1	83.6	40.04	6 642	734
Michigan City	54.0	1 733	7.8	23.4	73.0	15.7	83.1	39.70	6 294	812
Mishawaka	117.0	2 436	0.0	24.3	73.7	17.0	84.5	36.59	6 075	826
Muncie	33.5	478	0.0	24.4	72.5	15.9	83.9	41.23	6 215	717
New Albany	61.3	1 681	0.0	31.3	75.8	21.4	88.5	45.47	4 829	1 079
Noblesville	240.4	4 350	12.0	25.3	74.2	17.0	84.5	42.85	5 901	873
Plainfield	56.2	1 924	0.0	NA	NA	NA	NA	40.06	6 270	745
Portage	59.2	1 607	0.0	22.9	73.0	15.5	83.1	39.55	5 942	769
Richmond	34.6	947	0.0	25.7	73.1	17.2	84.6	NA	NA	NA
Schererville	18.2	626	0.0	NA	NA	NA	NA	NA	NA	NA
South Bend	230.5	2 286	60.5	23.4	73.0	15.7	83.1	39.70	6 294	812
Terre Haute	52.7	860	0.0	26.5	76.2	17.7	87.3	42.47	5 433	1 107
Valparaiso	56.6	1 769	9.8	22.9	73.0	15.5	83.1	40.06	6 270	745
Westfield	55.7	1 737	0.0	NA	NA	NA	NA	NA	NA	NA
West Lafayette	40.9	1 338	2.5	25.2	75.5	17.2	86.3	36.32	5 732	1 024
IOWA	X	X	X	X	X	X	X	X	X	X
Ames	127.9	2 091	71.7	18.5	73.8	9.6	84.3	34.07	6 791	830
Ankeny	178.3	3 634	21.3	18.2	74.8	8.7	85.8	33.38	6 961	881
Bettendorf	119.0	3 478	20.8	21.1	76.2	13.2	85.4	34.11	6 246	1 072
Burlington	62.6	2 447	19.5	22.8	76.3	15.1	85.4	37.94	5 948	1 095
Cedar Falls	86.6	2 177	4.4	16.1	73.6	6.3	85.0	33.15	7 348	758
Cedar Rapids	538.7	4 206	127.7	19.9	74.8	11.5	85.3	36.62	6 488	910
Clinton	83.3	3 130	29.0	20.4	74.7	12.5	85.0	35.68	6 416	915
Council Bluffs	125.8	2 024	15.1	21.1	76.2	10.4	87.7	33.25	6 323	1 057
Davenport	324.8	3 202	66.5	21.1	76.2	13.2	85.4	34.11	6 246	1 072
Des Moines	556.3	2 689	43.7	20.4	76.1	11.7	86.0	34.72	6 436	1 052
Dubuque	185.8	3 199	67.9	17.8	75.1	8.7	85.4	33.96	6 891	908
Fort Dodge	80.9	3 272	8.5	15.4	73.1	5.8	84.3	34.39	7 513	746
Iowa City	187.9	2 668	19.6	21.7	76.9	13.4	87.5	37.27	6 052	1 134
Marion	67.4	1 881	13.8	16.8	73.9	7.1	84.4	36.40	7 191	787
Marshalltown	31.2	1 121	12.4	16.8	73.9	7.1	84.4	36.40	7 191	787
Mason City	60.3	2 170	1.5	13.9	72.4	5.1	83.3	34.48	7 765	655
Ottumwa	37.1	1 498	13.2	NA	NA	NA	NA	NA	NA	NA
Sioux City	249.2	3 013	42.4	18.6	74.6	8.5	86.2	25.99	6 900	914
Urbandale	55.3	1 347	9.4	20.4	76.1	11.7	86.0	34.72	6 436	1 052
Waterloo	115.2	1 686	21.4	16.1	73.6	6.3	85.0	33.15	7 348	758
West Des Moines	136.6	2 302	44.3	20.4	76.1	11.7	86.0	34.72	6 436	1 052

1. Based on the population estimated as of July 1 of the year shown. 2. Represents normal values based on the 30-year period, 1971–2000. 3. Average daily minimum.
4. Average daily maximum.

Table D. Cities — Land Area and Population

STATE Place code	City	Land area,[1] 2016 (sq mi)	Population, 2016 Total persons	Rank	Per square mile	Race alone[2] (percent), 2015 White	Black or African American	American Indian, Alaska Native	Asian	Hawaiian Pacific Islander	Some other race	2 or more races[2]
		1	2	3	4	5	6	7	8	9	10	11
20 00000	KANSAS..................	81 758.4	2 907 289	X	35.6	84.7	5.9	0.9	2.9	0.1	2.3	3.2
20 18250	Dodge City	14.6	27 453	1 344	1 880.3	84.1	1.8	1.4	1.9	0.0	8.6	2.2
20 25325	Garden City	10.1	26 747	1 376	2 648.2	64.0	1.2	0.3	8.0	0.0	24.7	1.8
20 33625	Hutchinson	24.6	41 310	918	1 679.3	88.4	5.3	1.5	0.0	0.0	1.6	3.1
20 36000	Kansas City	124.8	151 709	171	1 215.6	59.5	24.0	0.4	4.4	0.0	7.1	4.5
20 38900	Lawrence	34.1	95 358	326	2 796.4	81.6	4.7	3.1	5.4	0.0	1.2	4.0
20 39000	Leavenworth	24.0	36 154	1 053	1 506.4	75.1	16.7	0.5	2.0	0.0	2.3	3.4
20 39075	Leawood.................	15.1	34 565	1 104	2 289.1	NA	NA	NA	NA	NA	NA	NA
20 39350	Lenexa...................	34.1	52 903	716	1 551.4	89.2	5.4	0.5	3.0	0.0	0.8	1.2
20 44250	Manhattan	19.3	54 983	683	2 848.9	80.5	5.4	0.4	5.9	0.9	2.5	4.4
20 52575	Olathe...................	60.9	135 473	193	2 224.5	85.5	5.0	0.4	3.6	0.3	1.0	4.2
20 53775	Overland Park	75.1	188 966	128	2 516.2	84.1	4.4	0.2	8.1	0.0	0.6	2.5
20 62700	Salina...................	25.3	47 336	811	1 871.0	84.6	3.1	0.9	3.5	0.0	4.7	3.2
20 64500	Shawnee.................	41.9	65 194	555	1 555.9	82.3	8.6	0.0	3.8	0.0	1.5	3.8
20 71000	Topeka..................	61.5	126 808	217	2 061.9	80.8	8.9	1.2	1.9	0.2	2.1	5.0
20 79000	Wichita..................	160.4	389 902	50	2 430.8	75.7	11.9	1.2	6.1	0.1	2.0	3.0
21 00000	KENTUCKY	39 485.2	4 436 974	X	112.4	87.4	8.0	0.2	1.3	0.1	0.9	2.1
21 08902	Bowling Green	38.3	65 234	553	1 703.2	71.6	14.5	0.1	5.9	0.3	5.5	2.1
21 17848	Covington	13.2	40 797	923	3 090.7	78.6	13.3	0.0	0.0	0.0	4.7	3.3
21 24274	Elizabethtown...........	27.2	29 906	1 255	1 099.5	73.9	13.8	0.1	3.8	0.6	0.4	7.3
21 27982	Florence	10.6	32 460	1 167	3 062.3	NA	NA	NA	NA	NA	NA	NA
21 28900	Frankfort	14.8	27 885	1 330	1 884.1	72.3	15.1	0.2	4.1	0.0	3.8	4.5
21 30700	Georgetown..............	16.6	33 440	1 135	2 014.5	NA	NA	NA	NA	NA	NA	NA
21 35866	Henderson	15.6	28 841	1 287	1 848.8	NA	NA	NA	NA	NA	NA	NA
21 37918	Hopkinsville	31.6	31 811	1 186	1 006.7	NA	NA	NA	NA	NA	NA	NA
21 40222	Jeffersontown	10.0	27 352	1 350	2 735.2	NA	NA	NA	NA	NA	NA	NA
21 46027	Lexington-Fayette........	283.6	318 449	60	1 122.9	75.9	14.4	0.2	3.5	0.0	2.4	3.5
21 48003	Louisville/Jefferson County	380.4	616 261	29	1 896.2	71.4	22.5	0.1	2.5	0.1	0.4	2.9
21 56136	Nicholasville	13.9	30 006	1 252	2 158.7	NA	NA	NA	NA	NA	NA	NA
21 58620	Owensboro	20.3	59 273	624	2 919.9	84.9	6.9	0.1	1.7	0.0	0.3	6.2
21 58836	Paducah	20.2	25 145	1 420	1 244.8	NA	NA	NA	NA	NA	NA	NA
21 65226	Richmond	22.9	34 652	1 100	1 513.2	NA	NA	NA	NA	NA	NA	NA
22 00000	LOUISIANA	43 206.7	4 681 666	X	108.4	62.4	32.2	0.5	1.7	0.0	1.1	2.1
22 00975	Alexandria	28.4	47 832	798	1 684.2	45.0	52.5	1.1	0.5	0.0	0.2	0.7
22 05000	Baton Rouge	85.9	227 715	97	2 650.9	41.8	53.4	0.2	3.1	0.0	0.9	0.7
22 08920	Bossier City	42.9	68 485	514	1 596.4	66.7	27.0	0.4	2.0	0.0	0.6	3.3
22 13960	Central	62.2	28 529	1 304	458.7	NA	NA	NA	NA	NA	NA	NA
22 36255	Houma..................	14.4	34 024	1 115	2 362.8	63.8	27.3	3.4	1.8	0.0	0.3	3.4
22 39475	Kenner..................	14.9	67 089	532	4 502.6	66.0	25.2	0.1	3.8	0.0	3.9	0.9
22 40735	Lafayette................	53.8	127 626	215	2 372.2	65.4	30.3	0.2	1.9	0.0	0.6	1.6
22 41155	Lake Charles	42.1	76 848	447	1 825.4	46.5	48.7	0.6	1.6	0.0	0.9	1.8
22 51410	Monroe	29.3	49 297	766	1 682.5	31.3	65.7	0.2	1.2	0.0	0.4	1.2
22 54035	New Iberia	11.1	30 386	1 235	2 737.5	47.4	47.6	0.0	1.3	0.0	2.1	1.7
22 55000	New Orleans	169.4	391 495	49	2 311.1	34.4	59.2	0.2	3.1	0.0	1.3	1.7
22 70000	Shreveport	107.1	194 920	122	1 820.0	39.0	56.3	0.2	1.8	0.0	0.8	1.9
22 70805	Slidell...................	14.8	28 013	1 325	1 892.8	NA	NA	NA	NA	NA	NA	NA
23 00000	MAINE	30 843.9	1 331 479	X	43.2	94.6	1.1	0.7	1.0	0.0	0.2	2.3
23 02795	Bangor..................	34.3	31 985	1 179	932.5	92.5	1.9	0.1	2.3	0.0	0.0	3.2
23 38740	Lewiston................	34.1	36 140	1 054	1 059.8	90.6	2.3	0.0	0.7	0.0	0.6	5.7
23 60545	Portland	21.5	66 937	537	3 113.3	84.5	7.5	0.1	3.0	0.0	0.1	4.8
23 71990	South Portland	12.0	25 577	1 412	2 131.4	NA	NA	NA	NA	NA	NA	NA
24 00000	MARYLAND	9 709.6	6 016 447	X	619.6	56.5	29.5	0.3	6.4	0.0	4.2	3.1
24 01600	Annapolis................	7.2	39 418	963	5 474.7	63.4	29.8	0.1	1.0	0.0	3.6	2.0
24 04000	Baltimore	80.9	614 664	30	7 597.8	31.0	61.6	0.2	2.7	0.1	1.5	2.9
24 08775	Bowie...................	19.0	58 393	643	3 073.3	37.7	51.1	0.0	6.3	0.0	0.7	4.3
24 18750	College Park............	5.6	32 275	1 173	5 763.4	54.2	20.9	0.0	15.7	0.4	4.3	4.5
24 30325	Frederick	23.0	70 060	501	3 046.1	67.7	16.8	0.2	6.9	0.0	3.9	4.5
24 31175	Gaithersburg	10.3	67 776	524	6 580.2	51.5	17.3	0.1	18.6	0.0	9.2	3.2
24 36075	Hagerstown	12.2	40 452	933	3 315.7	67.7	18.5	0.2	3.9	0.1	3.5	6.1
24 45900	Laurel	4.8	25 853	1 403	5 386.0	29.3	51.6	0.7	6.9	0.0	7.4	4.1
24 67675	Rockville	13.6	66 940	536	4 922.1	57.9	10.0	0.2	22.2	0.0	4.2	5.4
24 69925	Salisbury................	13.9	33 114	1 145	2 382.3	48.8	41.8	0.8	2.7	0.0	1.7	4.2
25 00000	MASSACHUSETTS ...	7 801.0	6 811 779	X	873.2	79.1	7.3	0.2	6.3	0.0	4.1	2.9
25 00840	Agawam Town	23.3	28 718	1 295	1 232.5	NA	NA	NA	NA	NA	NA	NA
25 02690	Attleboro................	26.8	44 434	849	1 658.0	92.3	4.2	0.0	1.7	0.0	0.1	1.7
25 03690	Barnstable Town	59.9	44 254	853	738.8	91.8	4.7	0.4	0.4	0.0	1.5	1.2

1. Dry land or land partially or temporarily covered by water. 2. Hispanic or Latino persons may be of any race.

City	Percent Hispanic or Latino[1], 2015	Percent foreign born 2015	Age of population (percent), 2010-2014							Median age 2015	Percent female 2015	Population			
												Census counts		Percent change	
			Under 18 years	18 to 24 years	25 to 34 years	35 to 44 years	45 to 54 years	55 to 64 years	65 years and over			2000	2010	2000–2010	2010–2016
	12	13	14	15	16	17	18	19	20	21	22	23	24	25	26
KANSAS...............	11.6	7.1	24.7	10.4	13.2	11.9	12.4	12.7	14.6	36.2	50.2	2 688 418	2 853 129	6.1	1.9
Dodge City	58.2	29.5	30.9	10.8	15.5	9.5	15.4	9.6	8.3	29.9	46.7	25 176	27 340	8.6	0.4
Garden City	52.1	27.7	31.6	12.9	14.9	10.3	11.2	10.8	8.3	28.9	46.4	28 451	26 731	-6.0	0.1
Hutchinson	14.4	3.2	21.9	8.4	15.8	10.5	12.3	13.1	17.9	40.0	47.8	40 787	42 192	3.4	-2.1
Kansas City	29.3	16.9	27.6	9.8	15.0	12.4	12.2	12.0	11.0	33.4	50.7	146 866	145 786	-0.7	4.1
Lawrence	6.9	9.3	17.9	27.6	15.9	10.5	10.4	7.9	9.8	27.4	51.5	80 098	87 720	9.5	8.7
Leavenworth	11.4	2.4	26.9	11.6	15.2	15.1	11.6	9.0	10.6	33.0	49.1	35 420	35 251	-0.5	2.6
Leawood......................	1.5	5.8	28.5	3.2	5.8	10.0	17.6	17.8	17.1	46.1	50.4	27 656	31 867	15.2	8.5
Lenexa........................	8.0	8.0	19.2	10.2	17.9	9.7	15.1	15.2	12.7	38.2	50.4	40 238	48 188	19.8	9.8
Manhattan	7.9	11.4	13.9	37.8	18.9	9.5	5.6	6.5	7.8	24.2	49.8	44 831	52 302	16.7	5.1
Olathe........................	12.0	8.9	30.7	9.8	11.7	15.4	13.8	9.9	8.7	33.0	51.6	92 962	125 895	35.4	7.6
Overland Park	5.4	11.5	22.7	7.8	14.7	13.6	13.2	13.0	15.0	38.2	49.9	149 080	173 325	16.3	9.0
Salina.........................	12.4	6.1	22.3	9.0	11.9	12.1	13.9	13.4	17.3	39.0	51.9	45 679	47 707	4.4	-0.8
Shawnee......................	7.5	6.4	24.2	7.8	11.0	16.5	14.4	11.5	14.6	40.1	50.3	47 996	62 209	29.6	4.8
Topeka........................	14.6	5.3	23.4	10.2	13.9	12.1	11.6	12.1	16.6	37.1	52.2	122 377	127 632	4.3	-0.6
Wichita.......................	16.7	10.3	25.4	10.6	14.6	12.1	12.5	12.1	12.8	34.6	50.7	344 284	382 417	11.1	2.0
KENTUCKY	3.3	3.6	22.8	9.6	12.7	12.7	13.6	13.3	15.2	38.8	50.9	4 041 769	4 339 344	7.4	2.2
Bowling Green..............	6.6	15.9	22.4	22.9	12.0	11.1	11.7	8.5	11.5	27.4	52.4	49 296	58 895	19.5	10.8
Covington	5.9	3.8	22.7	9.3	16.5	14.2	12.8	11.0	13.4	35.5	51.1	43 370	40 511	-6.6	0.7
Elizabethtown...............	6.4	3.3	24.8	13.9	15.5	9.3	12.4	11.8	12.4	31.6	52.9	22 542	28 581	26.8	4.6
Florence	8.9	11.0	27.0	8.4	15.4	10.4	15.8	10.8	12.2	33.9	49.1	23 551	29 990	27.3	8.2
Frankfort.....................	5.6	4.7	18.2	10.3	14.0	11.9	13.8	14.6	17.1	41.0	53.8	27 741	27 269	-1.7	2.3
Georgetown..................	2.0	2.6	26.6	11.5	13.1	15.4	13.7	9.0	10.7	34.0	50.5	18 080	29 138	61.2	14.8
Henderson	1.9	1.8	22.8	10.1	13.5	11.7	12.2	12.0	17.7	39.0	53.2	27 373	28 794	5.2	0.2
Hopkinsville..................	4.0	1.9	25.3	8.3	17.9	12.3	11.1	9.7	15.4	34.1	50.8	30 089	32 040	6.5	-0.7
Jeffersontown...............	6.6	15.8	20.4	5.9	15.8	11.7	13.1	18.1	15.1	42.1	50.7	26 633	27 019	1.4	1.2
Lexington-Fayette..........	6.9	9.1	21.0	14.4	15.4	13.6	12.0	11.4	12.1	34.4	51.0	260 512	295 805	13.5	7.7
Louisville/Jefferson County	4.7	6.2	22.9	9.3	14.3	12.6	13.4	13.0	14.4	37.5	51.5	693 604	596 332	-14.0	3.3
Nicholasville	1.4	3.3	24.7	10.7	14.6	14.7	13.2	10.6	11.5	35.0	51.2	19 680	28 041	42.5	7.0
Owensboro	1.2	2.1	25.9	9.8	13.5	11.5	11.2	11.4	16.6	35.5	55.1	54 067	57 449	6.3	3.2
Paducah	2.7	1.9	17.5	10.4	12.9	12.0	12.1	14.5	20.6	42.2	54.8	26 307	25 028	-4.9	0.5
Richmond	1.9	4.8	18.0	27.9	13.9	11.6	10.0	11.1	7.5	26.7	52.5	27 152	31 374	15.5	10.4
LOUISIANA	4.9	4.0	23.9	9.8	14.4	12.4	12.8	12.7	14.0	36.4	51.1	4 468 976	4 533 479	1.4	3.3
Alexandria	2.3	1.6	22.5	7.9	12.1	12.3	12.4	12.8	20.0	41.5	51.8	46 342	47 592	2.7	0.5
Baton Rouge	3.2	5.4	21.2	19.1	15.3	11.3	9.8	10.9	12.4	31.2	51.2	227 818	229 538	0.8	-0.8
Bossier City	8.2	4.4	23.7	12.0	18.0	11.2	10.0	11.0	14.0	32.7	50.9	56 461	61 631	9.2	11.1
Central........................	3.5	1.8	24.7	5.3	11.7	13.1	13.7	13.2	18.2	41.8	54.5	NA	26 867	NA	6.2
Houma........................	11.6	6.9	22.2	8.3	16.6	12.3	11.7	13.5	15.3	35.9	53.3	32 393	33 700	4.0	1.0
Kenner........................	26.5	18.4	22.7	10.4	14.2	11.7	12.5	13.7	14.7	36.9	49.3	70 517	66 705	-5.4	0.6
Lafayette.....................	5.1	4.2	22.9	14.2	17.5	9.2	12.3	12.4	11.6	31.7	49.9	110 257	121 194	9.9	5.3
Lake Charles	4.2	4.2	23.9	13.4	17.0	9.7	9.7	12.0	14.3	31.8	53.1	71 757	72 033	0.4	6.7
Monroe	3.4	2.4	27.9	12.3	14.5	10.1	10.1	12.5	12.6	30.9	52.9	53 107	48 906	-7.9	0.8
New Iberia	2.9	2.5	25.2	10.2	13.8	8.4	12.5	13.1	16.8	35.6	50.8	32 623	30 617	-6.1	-0.8
New Orleans	5.6	5.6	20.4	9.8	18.5	12.9	12.7	13.2	12.5	35.9	52.3	484 674	343 829	-29.1	13.9
Shreveport...................	2.6	2.9	25.2	9.5	14.9	12.4	11.9	12.0	14.1	35.2	52.7	200 145	200 410	0.1	-2.7
Slidell.........................	10.2	5.1	23.7	6.5	14.7	15.9	8.9	13.1	17.2	38.1	50.9	25 695	27 068	5.3	3.5
MAINE......................	1.5	3.4	19.2	8.4	11.4	11.5	14.8	15.8	18.8	44.6	51.0	1 274 923	1 328 364	4.2	0.2
Bangor........................	1.4	3.8	16.8	11.6	16.9	11.3	13.1	11.9	18.4	37.7	49.7	31 473	33 037	5.0	-3.2
Lewiston	2.3	5.0	18.8	12.4	10.4	10.8	13.9	13.2	20.4	43.0	54.4	35 690	36 592	2.5	-1.2
Portland......................	3.0	13.8	15.0	9.3	20.5	11.0	13.9	14.3	15.9	40.3	52.9	64 249	66 194	3.0	1.1
South Portland	1.9	7.2	17.7	12.4	14.7	11.1	17.3	15.2	11.6	39.9	52.9	23 324	25 002	7.2	2.3
MARYLAND	9.5	15.2	22.4	9.3	13.9	12.8	14.5	13.0	14.1	38.3	51.5	5 296 486	5 773 786	9.0	4.2
Annapolis....................	18.3	14.5	18.4	7.4	19.5	12.1	10.8	14.0	17.8	37.7	53.6	35 838	38 293	6.9	2.9
Baltimore	4.8	8.0	21.1	10.5	18.8	12.1	12.6	12.4	12.5	34.7	52.7	651 154	621 139	-4.6	-1.0
Bowie.........................	6.8	15.6	21.6	6.5	10.3	14.2	19.3	13.6	14.6	43.5	54.0	50 269	55 332	10.1	5.5
College Park.................	6.6	22.0	8.8	51.5	9.9	7.7	7.3	8.5	6.2	21.6	46.3	24 657	30 413	23.3	6.1
Frederick	18.8	20.5	23.4	9.7	15.5	14.7	12.6	11.8	12.2	36.1	52.3	52 767	65 290	23.7	7.3
Gaithersburg	27.8	41.7	22.5	10.2	16.1	13.8	16.6	10.4	10.4	35.7	52.2	52 613	59 905	13.9	13.1
Hagerstown	7.9	8.0	31.4	6.0	15.9	12.5	11.3	10.5	12.4	33.2	53.3	36 687	39 729	8.3	1.8
Laurel........................	14.5	29.6	26.0	11.1	17.7	14.9	13.9	10.0	6.3	32.0	52.8	19 960	24 925	24.9	3.7
Rockville	13.7	37.4	20.7	10.0	14.0	14.9	12.7	11.4	16.3	38.1	53.4	47 388	61 250	29.3	9.3
Salisbury.....................	5.1	13.1	25.1	17.7	11.9	16.7	10.2	8.7	9.8	28.9	52.0	23 743	30 506	28.5	8.5
MASSACHUSETTS ...	11.2	16.1	20.4	10.3	13.9	12.3	14.4	13.3	15.4	39.4	51.5	6 349 097	6 547 813	3.1	4.0
Agawam Town	5.2	12.8	18.8	5.7	11.6	13.2	12.9	14.3	23.4	45.3	51.2	28 144	28 438	1.0	1.0
Attleboro	4.5	9.4	23.9	6.1	12.2	13.8	15.3	13.5	15.1	40.7	51.4	42 068	43 593	3.6	1.9
Barnstable Town	7.5	16.0	18.6	7.0	9.1	12.2	15.7	15.6	21.8	47.3	52.5	47 821	45 189	-5.5	-2.1

1. May be of any race.

Table D. Cities — Households, Group Quarters, Crime, and Education

City	Households, 2015				Persons in group quarters, 2010				Serious crimes known to police,[2] 2014				Educational attainment, 2015		
			Percent			Institutional			Total		Rate[3]			Attainment[4] (percent)	
	Number	Persons per house-hold	Female family house-holder[1]	One-person	Total	Total	Persons in nursing facilities	Non-institu-tional	Number	Rate[3]	Violent	Property	Population age 25 and older	High school graduate or less	Bachelor's degree or more
	27	28	29	30	31	32	33	34	35	36	37	38	39	40	41
KANSAS	1 111 582	2.55	9.9	29.5	79 074	41 393	20 672	37 681	89 554	3 084	349	2 735	1 888 479	36.3	31.7
Dodge City	8 708	2.97	12.6	24.0	596	363	207	233	895	3 160	420	2 740	15 406	55.0	17.6
Garden City	9 099	3.17	14.7	27.5	548	231	96	317	976	3 613	611	3 003	16 312	50.0	19.4
Hutchinson	16 226	2.30	11.8	35.1	2 850	2 402	447	448	1 916	4 583	490	4 093	27 801	42.3	20.0
Kansas City	55 342	2.71	14.4	33.7	1 109	815	421	294	8 376	5 618	711	4 907	94 606	56.2	16.3
Lawrence	33 972	2.53	9.0	33.5	7 984	430	270	7 554	2 128	2 325	231	2 095	51 126	24.8	50.1
Leavenworth	11 429	2.85	18.5	24.7	4 031	3 352	72	679	1 427	3 962	694	3 268	22 106	36.1	31.7
Leawood	12 600	2.74	3.9	17.5	11	0	0	11	432	1 299	69	1 229	23 631	5.6	78.6
Lenexa	21 154	2.46	7.6	27.1	348	327	325	21	870	1 710	110	1 600	37 034	17.3	58.5
Manhattan	20 330	2.46	5.1	35.0	6 227	401	306	5 826	NA	NA	NA	NA	27 045	20.7	46.1
Olathe	44 701	2.97	9.8	19.4	1 418	789	661	629	1 847	1 385	76	1 309	79 965	23.6	47.0
Overland Park	77 006	2.41	7.4	32.2	1 343	1 215	1 040	128	3 360	1 835	179	1 656	129 737	13.8	61.5
Salina	18 713	2.33	12.1	36.8	1 435	545	377	890	2 028	4 238	403	3 835	31 052	45.5	19.7
Shawnee	24 454	2.64	11.5	22.7	406	384	384	22	1 173	1 809	163	1 646	44 278	30.9	45.5
Topeka	52 958	2.32	11.4	38.8	4 083	2 648	1 246	1 435	6 911	5 413	510	4 903	84 431	39.2	29.3
Wichita	150 497	2.56	12.9	35.3	6 420	3 555	1 666	2 865	21 240	5 481	758	4 723	249 658	40.3	26.0
KENTUCKY	1 716 168	2.50	12.7	28.5	125 870	70 779	26 044	55 091	108 506	2 459	212	2 247	2 988 790	48.4	23.3
Bowling Green	23 082	2.46	13.2	35.2	6 147	1 173	492	4 974	3 160	5 087	335	4 752	34 802	41.6	31.1
Covington	16 167	2.45	16.8	37.8	1 406	946	420	460	1 888	4 597	497	4 100	27 854	52.3	19.6
Elizabethtown	11 745	2.44	16.3	30.5	1 075	995	284	80	1 113	3 684	136	3 549	18 199	40.8	26.5
Florence	12 392	2.58	13.7	29.0	268	265	265	3	1 548	4 873	195	4 678	20 836	35.1	25.2
Frankfort	10 437	2.12	12.2	50.0	1 644	648	188	996	1 126	4 096	338	3 758	16 760	45.5	25.2
Georgetown	12 290	2.66	18.1	18.0	1 284	211	136	1 073	1 005	3 213	205	3 008	21 023	41.8	28.8
Henderson	12 246	2.34	11.2	34.1	1 162	806	262	356	1 052	3 647	236	3 412	20 167	50.0	17.1
Hopkinsville	12 279	2.45	17.2	31.8	1 425	1 204	348	221	1 133	3 465	315	3 150	21 358	44.8	18.3
Jeffersontown	10 678	2.50	4.7	34.3	351	351	351	0	675	2 489	129	2 360	19 859	29.8	38.8
Lexington-Fayette	129 088	2.34	13.7	30.4	12 804	3 996	1 092	8 808	13 251	4 249	337	3 912	203 167	30.4	41.6
Louisville/Jefferson County	245 874	2.45	15.9	33.3	14 153	8 529	4 831	5 624	32 453	4 789	592	4 196	417 075	40.4	30.1
Nicholasville	10 922	2.56	21.2	19.3	312	269	80	43	1 135	3 929	183	3 745	18 227	47.9	25.4
Owensboro	24 604	2.32	17.0	34.5	1 817	1 025	806	792	2 385	4 066	210	3 856	37 957	47.0	22.0
Paducah	11 045	2.14	13.6	41.8	1 090	1 024	510	66	1 448	5 788	324	5 464	17 938	42.3	27.1
Richmond	12 567	2.29	15.9	41.2	4 344	480	207	3 864	1 366	4 161	308	3 853	18 121	41.0	32.5
LOUISIANA	1 737 908	2.61	15.9	30.7	127 427	88 104	24 524	39 323	184 758	3 974	515	3 459	3 095 255	49.5	23.2
Alexandria	18 764	2.44	19.3	34.2	2 356	1 611	531	745	4 619	9 501	1 765	7 736	33 313	48.1	24.0
Baton Rouge	87 286	2.52	17.8	37.6	9 554	3 531	1 129	6 023	12 390	5 401	924	4 477	136 406	38.3	32.9
Bossier City	27 404	2.40	17.6	26.7	1 614	811	671	803	3 637	5 391	642	4 749	43 795	40.5	20.5
Central	10 581	2.67	7.4	18.6	59	0	0	59	NA	NA	NA	NA	19 785	47.7	29.8
Houma	13 505	2.52	15.5	30.5	212	134	114	78	1 601	4 691	618	4 073	23 828	56.9	18.0
Kenner	25 896	2.57	17.2	31.9	422	319	303	103	2 577	3 844	236	3 608	44 843	48.8	22.9
Lafayette	48 597	2.54	14.5	34.1	4 509	1 775	613	2 734	7 614	6 085	651	5 435	80 338	36.2	38.4
Lake Charles	30 987	2.36	20.6	36.2	3 149	2 018	596	1 131	3 733	5 013	690	4 323	47 654	42.4	25.3
Monroe	17 438	2.64	28.4	36.3	3 273	1 229	663	2 044	6 385	12 796	2 579	10 216	29 666	45.6	29.5
New Iberia	11 718	2.59	26.2	25.5	433	367	367	66	NA	NA	NA	NA	19 867	66.1	15.3
New Orleans	156 591	2.41	16.7	45.1	13 165	5 509	1 509	7 656	20 152	5 206	974	4 232	272 132	36.0	36.0
Shreveport	75 823	2.53	18.9	38.6	5 574	3 588	1 975	1 986	10 648	5 319	721	4 598	128 570	46.0	24.9
Slidell	10 054	2.74	17.4	23.1	315	286	286	29	1 553	5 622	300	5 321	19 498	47.3	26.4
MAINE	545 226	2.37	9.8	29.6	35 545	12 409	7 878	23 136	28 121	2 114	128	1 986	961 240	41.0	30.1
Bangor	12 917	2.34	8.7	35.6	2 690	854	561	1 836	1 733	5 318	169	5 149	23 194	36.4	27.2
Lewiston	16 001	2.11	10.9	35.9	2 117	365	344	1 752	986	2 709	231	2 478	24 897	51.9	19.7
Portland	30 487	2.13	7.0	40.2	2 613	1 065	592	1 548	2 292	3 453	238	3 215	50 620	25.9	50.0
South Portland	9 794	2.54	20.1	23.9	636	195	73	441	840	3 317	154	3 163	17 859	29.6	43.2
MARYLAND	2 177 934	2.69	14.0	27.0	138 375	66 838	28 001	71 537	176 520	2 954	446	2 508	4 102 486	35.5	38.8
Annapolis	16 138	2.41	20.4	30.4	603	143	143	460	1 143	2 946	500	2 446	29 275	37.1	42.1
Baltimore	238 400	2.51	21.7	38.4	25 199	9 951	3 793	15 248	37 766	6 057	1 339	4 718	425 261	45.2	29.9
Bowie	20 789	2.78	12.7	28.4	255	148	145	107	921	1 610	133	1 478	41 745	22.0	51.1
College Park	7 599	2.71	9.9	25.9	11 535	0	0	11 535	NA	NA	NA	NA	12 806	33.7	48.4
Frederick	27 298	2.48	14.0	29.4	1 785	803	803	982	1 845	2 743	430	2 314	46 485	34.8	37.2
Gaithersburg	24 544	2.73	11.1	25.6	547	372	366	175	NA	NA	NA	NA	45 405	27.4	52.4
Hagerstown	16 441	2.41	25.7	30.3	806	546	508	260	1 741	4 269	650	3 619	25 338	55.8	14.2
Laurel	9 909	2.63	14.0	39.5	183	0	0	183	1 068	4 115	593	3 522	16 500	27.4	49.0
Rockville	25 426	2.60	10.7	28.6	1 103	833	665	270	NA	NA	NA	NA	46 438	17.4	66.0
Salisbury	12 977	2.43	19.8	27.2	1 391	155	135	1 236	2 121	6 674	900	5 774	18 798	44.6	25.8
MASSACHUSETTS	2 559 951	2.56	12.5	28.8	238 882	74 667	43 833	164 215	151 666	2 248	391	1 857	4 706 644	34.9	41.5
Agawam Town	11 630	2.43	5.7	33.9	677	669	669	8	426	1 481	181	1 300	21 753	38.3	25.5
Attleboro	17 622	2.48	15.1	29.9	564	451	429	113	953	2 162	243	1 919	31 007	37.3	30.9
Barnstable Town	19 455	2.25	9.5	34.2	363	106	79	257	1 365	3 058	632	2 426	32 968	36.8	33.4

1. No spouse present.   2. Data for serious crimes have not been adjusted for underreporting. This may affect comparability between geographic areas and over time.   3. Per 100,000 population estimated by the FBI.   4. Persons 25 years old and over.

Table D. Cities — Income, Poverty, and Housing

City	Money income, 2015 Households Median income	Households Percent with income of $200,000 or more	Households Percent with income of less than $25,000	Families Total Families	Families Percent with income below poverty	Housing units, 2010 Total	Percent change, 2000–2010	Vacant units for sale or rent[2]	Occupied housing units 2015 Total	Owner-occupied Percent	Owner-occupied Median value[3] (dollars)	Renter-occupied Percent	Renter-occupied Median rent (dollars)
	42	43	44	45	46	47	48	49	50	51	52	53	54
KANSAS	53 906	4.2	16.0	720 780	8.4	1 233 215	9.0	121 119	1 111 582	66.4	141 200	33.6	782
Dodge City	42 436	0.6	17.0	6 417	14.7	9 378	4.3	601	8 708	55.5	105 400	44.5	838
Garden City	55 331	3.4	14.5	6 204	10.0	9 656	-1.7	585	9 099	56.8	129 800	43.2	677
Hutchinson	45 168	1.8	15.9	9 364	10.0	18 580	5.1	1 599	16 226	64.6	92 500	35.4	651
Kansas City	41 255	0.9	21.7	33 152	17.2	61 969	0.8	8 044	55 342	57.0	87 600	43.0	812
Lawrence	46 564	4.0	22.5	17 122	9.0	37 502	14.4	2 532	33 972	46.7	179 100	53.3	814
Leavenworth	57 695	4.8	21.0	8 030	16.2	13 670	5.9	1 414	11 429	49.2	109 900	50.8	860
Leawood	146 528	32.4	4.3	NA	NA	12 384	22.2	603	12 600	88.9	447 400	11.1	1 806
Lenexa	86 178	8.1	4.9	14 255	1.9	20 832	27.4	1 544	21 154	63.6	240 100	36.4	984
Manhattan	47 230	1.8	23.5	8 300	7.1	21 619	22.1	1 611	20 330	34.5	187 600	65.5	923
Olathe	80 242	7.7	7.8	33 505	4.2	46 851	40.6	2 344	44 701	69.8	207 700	30.2	912
Overland Park	81 144	9.9	8.1	47 939	2.4	76 280	21.7	4 837	77 006	66.8	249 000	33.2	1 022
Salina	40 857	2.7	23.0	10 121	15.2	20 803	6.1	1 412	18 713	59.5	118 200	40.5	724
Shawnee	88 636	7.0	9.4	18 000	5.5	24 954	30.6	1 303	24 454	70.3	218 200	29.7	946
Topeka	43 860	2.6	20.7	29 242	13.7	59 582	5.5	5 639	52 958	54.8	102 800	45.2	744
Wichita	46 894	3.1	20.0	89 192	11.9	167 310	10.0	15 492	150 497	58.8	124 400	41.2	734
KENTUCKY	45 215	2.9	22.1	1 131 839	14.0	1 927 164	10.1	207 199	1 716 168	66.3	130 000	33.7	702
Bowling Green	38 835	2.9	28.2	12 748	16.4	24 712	16.6	1 977	23 082	40.3	146 700	59.7	697
Covington	37 564	1.4	26.8	8 077	22.1	20 053	-1.9	3 020	16 167	47.6	99 300	52.4	675
Elizabethtown	41 078	1.6	23.6	7 521	18.0	12 664	26.3	953	11 745	42.3	169 600	57.7	744
Florence	47 517	5.1	25.0	8 606	14.9	13 447	31.2	954	12 392	46.7	145 000	53.3	873
Frankfort	46 142	2.2	17.6	4 554	12.5	12 938	-3.4	1 798	10 437	50.1	123 900	49.9	712
Georgetown	62 279	2.8	13.2	9 241	10.4	11 957	66.8	1 224	12 290	56.7	164 000	43.3	878
Henderson	32 254	2.3	25.3	6 859	15.5	13 171	4.0	1 080	12 246	41.0	130 300	59.0	659
Hopkinsville	38 335	0.8	26.5	8 136	17.1	14 318	7.8	1 464	12 279	48.1	112 100	51.9	710
Jeffersontown	62 270	2.9	7.3	6 210	7.9	11 800	5.5	735	10 678	66.3	164 400	33.7	889
Lexington-Fayette	51 948	4.7	20.2	76 328	13.6	135 160	16.3	12 117	129 088	51.5	170 200	48.5	816
Louisville/Jefferson County	48 100	3.7	20.5	146 522	11.5	337 616	NA	28 441	245 874	59.2	145 000	40.8	769
Nicholasville	44 918	0.5	16.8	7 946	23.5	11 405	47.0	913	10 922	56.0	142 000	44.0	694
Owensboro	37 149	2.0	24.1	14 649	14.8	26 072	7.0	1 857	24 604	60.9	94 100	39.1	625
Paducah	37 082	6.3	26.0	5 697	14.0	12 851	-2.5	1 389	11 045	57.0	113 500	43.0	553
Richmond	35 859	0.5	33.8	5 959	25.0	13 788	16.5	1 353	12 567	32.4	148 300	67.6	668
LOUISIANA	45 727	3.6	23.4	1 108 586	14.7	1 964 981	6.4	236 621	1 737 908	64.6	155 600	35.4	800
Alexandria	36 699	3.5	28.6	10 882	18.6	20 366	2.4	2 094	18 764	50.0	144 200	50.0	715
Baton Rouge	41 224	3.5	27.0	45 336	17.0	100 801	3.6	9 327	87 286	49.6	172 600	50.4	805
Bossier City	46 322	2.9	17.3	17 923	11.5	25 579	11.7	1 713	27 404	50.6	163 200	49.4	892
Central	65 987	4.8	6.5	NA	NA	10 574	NA	395	10 581	87.7	198 000	12.3	740
Houma	36 707	2.5	36.1	7 718	23.8	13 924	12.1	1 173	13 505	67.9	127 400	32.1	571
Kenner	44 647	3.3	22.6	16 798	17.0	28 076	2.5	3 232	25 896	54.3	179 200	45.7	890
Lafayette	47 830	8.5	24.5	27 750	14.0	53 356	13.9	3 912	48 597	52.4	186 100	47.6	816
Lake Charles	38 256	3.1	25.3	17 177	20.8	32 469	3.7	3 529	30 987	48.2	152 900	51.8	758
Monroe	30 062	4.1	33.2	10 572	30.1	20 570	-3.5	2 125	17 438	42.7	129 100	57.3	725
New Iberia	35 399	2.4	31.6	8 204	19.8	13 059	1.1	1 353	11 718	59.9	99 300	40.1	672
New Orleans	39 077	5.0	29.1	74 561	17.5	189 896	-11.7	47 738	156 591	46.3	216 800	53.7	947
Shreveport	38 497	3.3	26.3	43 070	17.4	88 253	1.5	7 602	75 823	52.1	141 000	47.9	744
Slidell	51 986	1.9	22.2	7 047	19.4	11 155	10.4	1 105	10 054	65.5	154 600	34.5	892
MAINE	51 494	3.1	19.0	342 926	8.9	721 830	10.7	164 611	545 226	71.0	180 300	29.0	792
Bangor	36 302	3.0	29.8	6 761	16.0	15 674	7.5	1 199	12 917	47.6	160 300	52.4	769
Lewiston	40 930	1.7	30.7	8 921	17.5	16 731	1.6	1 464	16 001	53.7	134 500	46.3	674
Portland	52 139	4.2	22.5	13 816	11.2	33 836	6.2	3 111	30 427	43.0	267 100	57.0	1 000
South Portland	65 549	3.7	21.4	6 861	13.1	11 484	11.0	607	9 794	59.0	206 400	41.0	1 200
MARYLAND	75 847	9.6	11.3	1 454 839	6.7	2 378 814	10.9	222 403	2 177 934	65.9	299 800	34.1	1 278
Annapolis	65 979	8.8	13.1	9 763	10.6	17 845	10.2	1 709	16 138	51.5	404 200	48.5	1 444
Baltimore	44 165	4.2	25.9	123 502	18.2	296 685	-1.3	46 782	238 400	44.8	155 600	55.2	981
Bowie	107 735	10.3	4.3	13 988	1.2	20 687	11.1	737	20 789	82.4	304 700	17.6	1 858
College Park	64 647	5.8	22.5	NA	NA	8 212	31.4	1 455	7 599	43.5	301 200	56.5	1 694
Frederick	62 500	4.4	10.9	16 784	9.4	27 559	25.0	2 207	27 298	54.1	254 500	45.9	1 343
Gaithersburg	85 854	11.2	8.3	16 798	4.7	23 337	13.5	1 337	24 544	54.4	356 800	45.6	1 547
Hagerstown	37 329	0.6	27.2	10 394	23.5	18 682	9.5	2 233	16 441	39.8	153 000	60.2	833
Laurel	71 417	6.9	8.1	5 414	10.2	11 397	19.4	899	9 909	46.4	263 900	53.6	1 400
Rockville	97 377	17.1	7.9	16 390	3.9	25 199	41.6	1 513	25 426	55.7	550 300	44.3	1 847
Salisbury	37 344	0.7	27.4	7 867	18.3	13 401	37.2	1 418	12 977	25.8	155 900	74.2	1 018
MASSACHUSETTS	70 628	10.0	15.0	1 613 404	7.9	2 808 254	7.1	261 179	2 559 951	61.7	352 100	38.3	1 164
Agawam Town	61 898	2.8	13.1	7 046	2.4	12 139	4.1	475	11 630	74.9	219 300	25.1	977
Attleboro	68 214	4.5	14.3	11 325	10.3	18 022	8.9	1 138	17 622	70.1	253 100	29.9	990
Barnstable Town	65 015	6.9	14.0	11 644	1.0	26 343	5.3	7 118	19 455	69.8	371 500	30.2	1 236

1. Based on population estimated by the American Community Survey.   2. Includes units rented or sold but not occupied.   3. Specified owner-occupied units; $1,000,000 represents $1,000,000 or more   4. 50.0 represents 50 percent or more.   5. 10.0 represents 10 percent or less.

Table D. Cities — Commuting, Computer Access, Migration, Labor Force, and Employment

City	Commuting		Computer Access[2]		Migration, 2015		Civilian labor force, 2016		Unemployment		Civilian employment[4], 2015			
	Percent		Percent								Population age 16 and older		Population age 16 to 64	
	Drove alone	With Commutes of 30 minutes or more[1]	With a Computer in the house	With Internet Access	Percent who lived in the same house one year ago	Percent who lived in an other state or county one year ago	Total	Percent change, 2015–2016	Total	Rate[3]	Number	Percent in Labor Force	Number	Percent who worked full-year full-time
	55	56	57	58	59	60	61	62	63	64	65	66	67	68
KANSAS	86.2	20.9	86.0	76.3	83.7	7.2	1 484 001	-0.3	61 879	4.2	2 270 108	66.3	1 844 056	53.4
Dodge City	NA	8.9	86.0	73.5	81.3	7.9	14 401	0.2	495	3.4	18 903	72.7	16 697	56.0
Garden City	81.7	8.0	86.2	76.8	84.1	6.4	14 812	0.9	476	3.2	20 507	74.7	18 066	59.3
Hutchinson	91.7	14.5	84.1	74.1	75.5	9.3	19 132	-2.1	926	4.8	32 281	63.6	25 142	57.0
Kansas City	81.2	24.9	80.7	66.1	83.6	7.7	69 862	0.4	4 041	5.8	113 802	67.0	97 214	50.5
Lawrence	79.7	24.4	92.5	85.8	72.4	15.2	52 444	0.4	1 876	3.6	78 699	67.7	69 529	43.4
Leavenworth	79.9	16.9	90.6	80.5	70.8	17.7	13 825	0.6	695	5.0	26 797	59.7	22 998	45.8
Leawood	91.9	26.0	96.2	93.7	89.1	5.0	17 293	0.7	533	3.1	25 561	64.3	19 657	52.3
Lenexa	90.7	18.7	93.5	88.4	83.6	6.6	30 384	0.5	1 016	3.3	42 939	76.0	36 297	61.3
Manhattan	78.9	10.3	91.4	83.3	66.9	19.8	30 742	-0.8	939	3.1	48 758	66.7	44 370	35.3
Olathe	88.4	27.0	94.4	90.9	84.4	4.7	75 808	0.5	2 406	3.2	97 718	74.2	86 075	56.6
Overland Park	93.3	22.3	95.5	91.4	82.0	8.4	105 456	0.6	3 596	3.4	149 556	70.2	121 545	57.9
Salina	84.1	9.0	87.4	71.9	82.5	8.5	26 194	0.1	1 024	3.9	36 042	63.8	28 195	48.8
Shawnee	92.5	20.8	92.0	85.9	86.0	7.7	35 766	0.6	1 253	3.5	51 886	72.6	42 374	58.5
Topeka	85.2	11.1	83.6	71.7	78.5	6.9	63 504	0.3	2 825	4.4	100 733	64.0	79 597	49.6
Wichita	87.3	12.4	80.5	69.7	85.4	3.5	186 579	-0.2	9 277	5.0	300 555	66.0	250 781	51.2
KENTUCKY	84.8	30.4	82.1	70.8	84.8	6.9	1 991 974	1.3	99 701	5.0	3 531 385	58.8	2 857 257	46.6
Bowling Green	79.1	15.3	83.6	75.5	72.0	15.3	30 567	2.9	1 254	4.1	51 256	59.2	43 972	35.3
Covington	78.5	25.4	79.6	64.9	79.4	8.5	18 460	1.4	906	4.9	32 356	62.8	26 852	48.2
Elizabethtown	80.3	19.2	86.3	78.0	72.0	12.1	13 812	2.2	602	4.4	22 946	63.7	19 266	43.7
Florence	0.0	29.8	91.7	82.1	75.0	11.8	15 933	1.3	726	4.6	24 492	70.1	20 574	53.5
Frankfort	84.4	24.3	85.4	76.1	83.8	13.0	13 766	0.7	574	4.2	19 282	63.1	15 277	51.2
Georgetown	89.6	24.2	92.5	81.9	77.6	9.8	16 745	1.7	669	4.0	26 161	73.1	22 516	54.3
Henderson	85.4	18.5	81.5	69.7	77.2	8.6	12 717	0.6	644	5.1	23 894	55.9	18 579	40.1
Hopkinsville	82.1	8.3	82.8	72.2	78.5	5.2	12 155	0.4	781	6.4	24 496	58.7	19 547	46.7
Jeffersontown	88.9	30.8	89.8	80.4	87.5	3.7	15 084	2.1	546	3.6	21 997	71.8	17 927	55.0
Lexington-Fayette	81.0	23.6	91.4	79.2	74.7	11.2	168 079	1.5	5 875	3.5	255 389	66.7	217 284	49.1
Louisville/Jefferson County	82.7	28.9	82.9	70.0	85.8	4.4	380 367	2.2	16 621	4.4	490 481	64.4	401 822	50.2
Nicholasville	83.8	40.6	89.4	80.8	75.6	11.0	14 566	1.4	578	4.0	22 027	67.7	18 784	44.1
Owensboro	93.6	12.7	84.4	73.5	84.3	5.6	25 943	1.2	1 230	4.7	45 127	60.1	35 298	48.7
Paducah	84.3	13.3	72.9	65.1	83.6	8.2	10 325	0.9	660	6.4	20 964	57.1	15 837	48.6
Richmond	82.4	33.8	92.3	77.6	65.7	23.5	17 080	-0.5	785	4.6	28 521	57.3	26 009	32.9
LOUISIANA	85.2	33.1	80.8	68.6	86.9	5.4	2 121 230	-1.8	129 105	6.1	3 676 681	60.1	3 023 073	47.0
Alexandria	83.9	8.7	76.4	66.6	88.3	5.3	19 779	-1.5	1 285	6.5	38 739	56.8	29 136	44.7
Baton Rouge	80.9	22.3	85.7	74.0	80.1	7.3	115 628	-1.1	6 448	5.6	185 137	64.8	156 699	42.8
Bossier City	87.3	11.8	81.4	71.8	83.9	6.5	30 212	-2.2	1 620	5.4	53 363	64.5	43 819	54.1
Central	86.5	53.4	89.6	84.7	NA	NA	15 295	-0.5	687	4.5	22 110	56.4	16 989	58.0
Houma	81.2	24.6	87.5	64.9	92.1	1.2	15 009	-7.2	1 092	7.3	27 032	58.7	21 773	48.7
Kenner	84.0	29.7	74.1	67.1	91.7	3.6	33 653	-0.9	1 727	5.1	53 117	62.8	43 249	48.7
Lafayette	85.0	21.3	85.8	78.3	79.4	9.1	60 857	-5.6	3 696	6.1	101 682	68.6	86 915	51.1
Lake Charles	83.9	10.8	81.9	67.8	79.9	7.1	39 527	3.4	1 913	4.8	59 604	62.9	48 734	46.1
Monroe	85.0	10.1	76.0	68.2	83.2	6.5	20 651	-1.0	1 446	7.0	37 415	57.8	31 184	42.0
New Iberia	79.2	23.7	75.0	59.1	88.4	2.8	11 756	-4.2	1 252	10.6	23 566	65.0	18 388	43.8
New Orleans	72.1	33.0	78.1	62.2	85.1	6.5	179 967	-1.3	10 565	5.9	317 258	63.9	268 733	46.7
Shreveport	86.6	15.8	77.4	66.6	87.2	4.4	84 975	-2.5	5 614	6.6	153 041	57.0	125 347	44.2
Slidell	89.4	45.7	94.1	85.9	84.0	6.9	12 616	-1.9	723	5.7	21 836	61.3	17 024	50.1
MAINE	84.5	31.3	86.9	77.5	85.6	5.7	690 624	1.2	26 614	3.9	1 103 834	62.2	853 266	47.7
Bangor	80.7	7.6	80.7	70.7	77.3	9.5	16 827	0.7	620	3.7	27 565	57.6	21 598	34.8
Lewiston	79.5	28.9	83.5	67.8	76.8	8.4	17 261	1.2	662	3.8	29 754	61.1	22 366	52.1
Portland	73.7	16.4	88.1	78.8	78.6	7.5	38 167	1.9	1 084	2.8	57 683	69.5	47 018	54.5
South Portland	88.1	13.5	90.7	82.3	84.7	8.4	14 499	1.9	414	2.9	21 982	70.4	19 015	47.2
MARYLAND	77.2	51.8	89.9	81.4	85.6	6.7	3 170 011	0.7	135 880	4.3	4 814 546	67.3	3 967 561	54.5
Annapolis	68.7	33.8	84.8	74.5	84.7	6.5	22 327	0.9	797	3.6	32 832	66.3	25 808	53.1
Baltimore	60.9	46.7	81.7	67.0	82.2	6.5	294 985	0.3	18 555	6.3	502 319	60.1	424 668	45.6
Bowie	81.2	65.9	94.8	92.3	86.2	7.0	33 291	1.5	1 161	3.5	47 219	73.1	38 761	63.5
College Park	49.5	36.6	95.8	81.2	68.8	24.2	14 660	1.2	796	5.4	29 981	49.9	27 969	23.5
Frederick	79.9	40.0	84.0	79.7	83.9	6.9	37 098	0.4	1 438	3.9	54 598	74.5	46 103	57.9
Gaithersburg	74.4	50.2	91.8	86.2	76.7	8.8	36 036	0.6	1 184	3.3	53 612	74.6	46 594	59.3
Hagerstown	76.5	30.8	82.2	66.6	80.9	5.3	19 808	-0.1	1 185	6.0	28 352	63.2	23 332	51.7
Laurel	78.7	55.4	94.2	85.6	81.4	8.7	15 536	1.5	611	3.9	20 086	74.5	18 430	54.1
Rockville	66.5	53.1	95.4	91.7	79.1	9.3	36 941	0.6	1 101	3.0	54 141	68.7	43 252	58.2
Salisbury	83.0	31.9	82.8	62.4	66.1	18.9	15 324	1.2	1 064	6.9	25 869	65.9	22 659	44.0
MASSACHUSETTS	73.7	45.9	89.0	82.4	87.6	5.8	3 588 610	0.2	132 783	3.7	5 578 648	67.1	4 534 422	49.6
Agawam Town	89.5	20.7	85.0	78.8	NA	NA	15 786	-0.1	603	3.8	24 180	60.8	17 427	47.7
Attleboro	83.0	54.6	91.3	82.5	NA	NA	24 061	0.2	907	3.8	34 909	70.6	28 224	54.2
Barnstable Town	91.1	21.1	90.9	82.4	89.4	4.4	23 448	0.0	1 017	4.3	37 227	60.1	27 558	53.6

1. Employed persons.   2. Households.   3. Percent of civilian labor force.   4. Persons 16 years old and over.

Table D. Cities — Construction, Wholesale Trade, and Retail Trade

City	Value of residential construction authorized by building permits, 2016			Wholesale trade,[1] 2012				Retail trade,[2] 2012			
	New construction ($1,000)	Number of housing units	Percent single family	Number of establishments	Number of employees	Sales (mil dol)	Annual payroll (mil dol)	Number of establishments	Number of employees	Sales (mil dol)	Annual payroll (mil dol)
	69	70	71	72	73	74	75	76	77	78	79
KANSAS	0	0	0.0	3 790	52 168	60 226.3	3 055.4	10 548	145 480	38 276.5	3 325.0
Dodge City	2 235	15	100.0	44	535	470.1	27.0	108	1 697	469.2	38.7
Garden City	5 043	29	93.1	27	199	227.0	9.5	149	2 259	538.9	49.9
Hutchinson	4 360	28	42.9	50	630	742.0	25.0	202	2 967	705.3	66.8
Kansas City	46 518	245	87.8	197	4 909	4 507.3	256.9	405	6 193	1 594.1	155.6
Lawrence	123 590	1 343	15.6	53	413	168.8	16.7	333	5 800	1 253.6	118.2
Leavenworth	4 503	19	100.0	9	D	D	D	110	1 589	405.0	34.5
Leawood	15 442	63	71.4	34	407	217.0	33.5	137	2 931	520.8	74.5
Lenexa	93 885	317	63.4	289	4 625	2 981.9	267.5	200	3 850	2 504.9	122.2
Manhattan	90 871	781	15.4	31	480	144.0	19.7	260	5 438	1 031.9	111.4
Olathe	218 014	790	71.1	154	3 054	3 163.4	177.9	336	6 935	2 223.4	179.6
Overland Park	247 551	1 227	35.0	248	7 767	18 445.8	776.3	739	13 517	3 011.8	310.8
Salina	8 203	42	90.5	72	898	704.3	43.4	243	3 949	1 112.7	86.1
Shawnee	46 597	175	98.3	58	805	700.8	45.9	175	3 243	761.8	72.7
Topeka	20 976	112	89.3	120	1 342	845.1	62.1	574	8 921	2 185.9	197.4
Wichita	211 151	1 346	46.4	515	7 443	7 544.6	436.2	1 477	24 136	6 284.9	572.7
KENTUCKY	74 945	556	72.1	3 690	57 630	71 745.9	3 090.3	15 224	202 615	54 870.0	4 619.2
Bowling Green	68 049	824	23.4	108	1 303	2 669.4	65.2	449	6 831	1 634.5	150.6
Covington	0	0	0.0	26	D	D	D	121	1 297	396.0	33.7
Elizabethtown	12 174	129	43.4	36	319	194.9	14.2	264	4 076	1 089.3	97.1
Florence	NA	NA	NA	40	D	D	D	295	6 297	1 571.5	138.6
Frankfort	970	7	100.0	22	D	D	D	137	1 965	476.8	42.0
Georgetown	NA	NA	NA	18	D	D	D	107	1 687	510.4	35.6
Henderson	2 690	22	54.5	34	D	D	D	152	2 089	665.2	51.4
Hopkinsville	6 807	95	35.8	50	739	958.0	28.8	169	2 369	717.7	61.0
Jeffersontown	6 432	44	81.8	163	2 822	1 782.0	150.6	145	2 960	1 005.9	85.4
Lexington-Fayette	165 709	1 365	49.1	352	7 283	4 517.8	527.7	1 192	19 820	4 994.8	466.9
Louisville/Jefferson County	331 629	2 808	38.2	1 006	15 867	13 048.4	836.7	2 659	41 294	10 964.4	1 004.0
Nicholasville	22 911	112	85.7	27	D	D	D	117	1 996	741.7	56.1
Owensboro	32 707	364	64.0	67	943	527.4	41.0	336	4 944	1 209.2	111.0
Paducah	10 262	59	49.2	72	D	D	D	320	5 310	1 415.2	120.6
Richmond	13 800	203	60.6	18	99	134.9	3.7	199	2 976	712.7	59.7
LOUISIANA	2 766 650	14 503	86.3	4 823	64 259	68 012.8	3 260.2	16 743	220 257	61 396.4	5 334.6
Alexandria	21 872	73	100.0	73	914	443.7	37.0	385	5 698	1 633.6	142.8
Baton Rouge	69 140	284	100.0	306	3 894	2 296.2	192.8	1 146	16 570	4 262.5	409.4
Bossier City	49 278	362	77.3	77	1 165	822.5	55.7	379	5 660	1 621.7	137.8
Central	34 488	175	100.0	9	33	250.0	3.7	40	867	203.6	18.8
Houma	NA	NA	NA	68	686	325.7	42.9	167	2 292	639.3	51.6
Kenner	12 842	43	95.3	113	883	385.7	48.5	266	4 356	1 554.2	130.9
Lafayette	NA	NA	NA	276	3 728	1 815.8	182.4	808	12 699	3 434.7	316.5
Lake Charles	116 076	987	36.3	72	847	764.6	33.7	442	6 000	1 812.8	143.5
Monroe	30 938	182	61.5	81	1 211	1 198.0	53.9	400	5 914	1 452.5	131.1
New Iberia	3 148	28	32.1	54	695	330.9	34.5	208	2 791	743.1	68.9
New Orleans	131 484	608	46.1	256	3 794	2 687.0	191.5	1 275	12 371	3 245.1	337.8
Shreveport	65 252	244	100.0	294	D	D	D	875	12 231	3 645.9	311.7
Slidell	4 380	24	100.0	27	158	337.9	7.3	282	4 263	1 096.7	96.6
MAINE	3 630	19	100.0	1 344	14 753	12 961.3	691.5	6 351	80 155	21 521.7	1 884.6
Bangor	2 414	10	100.0	63	849	463.0	41.9	310	6 147	1 819.4	136.7
Lewiston	8 019	44	34.1	37	657	300.1	30.0	157	1 935	710.1	46.6
Portland	24 338	150	18.7	174	2 511	1 899.3	129.6	395	4 893	1 551.1	135.3
South Portland	3 094	39	33.3	50	811	2 204.9	43.1	244	4 606	1 131.5	98.7
MARYLAND	237 170	1 293	57.4	4 768	73 369	60 734.2	4 378.5	18 179	281 678	76 379.7	7 168.5
Annapolis	6 903	40	100.0	62	404	423.4	22.4	488	7 230	1 508.1	172.2
Baltimore	184 694	943	28.3	544	8 592	7 954.3	495.2	1 839	15 747	3 647.7	379.0
Bowie	NA	NA	NA	14	168	62.8	11.9	149	3 864	884.7	82.7
College Park	NA	NA	NA	11	55	15.5	4.5	69	1 686	494.9	46.8
Frederick	89 661	625	23.4	78	844	448.2	45.2	320	5 293	1 594.9	145.0
Gaithersburg	11 916	75	92.0	76	1 339	619.5	79.4	337	6 863	2 146.6	197.4
Hagerstown	3 647	25	100.0	51	463	287.1	20.7	207	4 043	1 212.7	101.4
Laurel	4 388	16	100.0	11	195	101.4	9.1	138	2 078	542.5	48.4
Rockville	56 503	306	10.1	74	1 661	4 078.6	182.6	321	5 420	1 877.2	162.5
Salisbury	7 208	78	7.7	58	707	461.6	31.3	234	4 178	987.1	91.9
MASSACHUSETTS	3 685	24	20.8	6 619	114 195	123 904.4	8 035.1	24 311	351 598	92 915.4	9 161.7
Agawam Town	6 838	43	37.2	49	729	819.9	46.1	75	922	262.8	26.5
Attleboro	9 941	63	90.5	32	496	227.5	26.1	134	2 277	638.5	51.3
Barnstable Town	18 761	79	87.3	47	444	185.9	22.3	384	4 724	1 267.9	127.6

1. Merchant wholesalers except manufacturers' sales branches and offices.   2. Establishments with payroll.

Table D. Cities — Real Estate, Professional Services, and Manufacturing

City	Real estate and rental and leasing, 2012				Professional, scientific, and technical services,[1] 2012				Manufacturing, 2012			
	Number of establishments	Number of employees	Receipts (mil dol)	Annual payroll (mil dol)	Number of establishments	Number of employees	Receipts (mil dol)	Annual payroll (mil dol)	Number of establishments	Number of employees	Receipts (mil dol)	Annual payroll (mil dol)
	80	81	82	83	84	85	86	87	88	89	90	91
KANSAS	2 999	14 256	2 743.1	507.6	7 071	60 615	8 562.6	3 577.1	2 875	152 423	86 076.3	7 578.3
Dodge City	21	D	D	D	42	D	D	D	17	D	D	D
Garden City	26	69	13.5	2.3	54	D	D	D	12	D	D	7.6
Hutchinson	52	145	22.9	3.9	82	D	D	D	41	1 579	441.5	70.9
Kansas City	128	519	107.4	18.4	173	D	D	D	161	10 043	10 883.2	640.0
Lawrence	141	D	D	D	249	D	D	D	45	2 467	957.6	103.4
Leavenworth	25	130	39.4	3.8	73	D	D	D	17	685	178.8	28.4
Leawood	102	D	D	D	236	D	D	D	14	189	26.4	9.8
Lenexa	105	588	133.8	31.5	319	D	D	D	135	6 020	2 108.2	298.4
Manhattan	102	D	D	D	117	D	D	D	34	673	137.0	28.9
Olathe	131	585	134.3	24.4	342	1 676	199.2	77.5	100	5 995	1 402.8	337.4
Overland Park	362	2 042	672.6	98.2	1 219	D	D	D	84	2 007	667.9	95.7
Salina	59	199	48.3	6.0	101	D	D	D	55	3 944	1 128.0	159.4
Shawnee	77	306	61.9	10.1	168	929	127.9	46.9	46	1 586	D	105.0
Topeka	173	803	124.1	24.6	382	D	D	D	84	4 722	2 456.0	220.0
Wichita	478	3 607	493.4	121.0	1 002	8 827	1 463.6	506.0	442	25 801	10 181.7	1 336.6
KENTUCKY	3 534	18 250	4 845.5	637.3	8 064	62 431	7 746.8	2 799.3	3 782	213 545	129 284.4	10 140.1
Bowling Green	102	363	73.7	10.4	181	D	D	D	95	7 873	5 079.8	402.6
Covington	32	203	62.0	10.6	124	D	D	D	28	746	215.7	33.6
Elizabethtown	61	304	42.3	7.6	110	D	D	D	51	4 727	2 009.7	220.6
Florence	49	260	71.8	7.9	102	1 559	106.1	43.1	38	3 293	1 633.6	176.6
Frankfort	27	154	13.2	3.5	102	714	77.5	30.0	15	550	104.0	23.3
Georgetown	32	D	D	D	53	261	31.3	12.5	22	7 150	D	502.3
Henderson	36	D	D	D	62	364	31.7	11.1	54	2 214	1 110.0	98.3
Hopkinsville	44	124	19.1	3.1	58	D	D	D	49	4 305	D	191.7
Jeffersontown	85	586	185.4	19.1	180	3 598	284.8	154.5	93	3 786	999.1	163.6
Lexington-Fayette	431	2 128	442.3	76.6	1 067	10 048	1 438.1	560.1	224	8 005	2 922.0	351.1
Louisville/Jefferson County	926	7 168	2 895.1	289.1	2 191	21 986	3 257.7	1 129.8	718	40 666	28 642.1	2 159.3
Nicholasville	21	87	10.8	2.2	52	286	63.6	15.3	51	2 245	588.9	79.9
Owensboro	63	427	57.1	11.7	128	D	D	D	64	3 644	2 865.5	159.3
Paducah	58	252	47.8	8.1	140	D	D	D	36	D	D	
Richmond	42	150	29.2	4.2	77	D	D	D	32	1 896	D	83.4
LOUISIANA	4 500	31 298	7 486.4	1 461.4	11 669	87 367	13 417.4	4 986.5	3 308	136 327	271 191.1	8 489.3
Alexandria	98	472	76.2	15.2	202	1 325	163.5	55.0	37	1 826	753.8	99.6
Baton Rouge	339	1 827	382.5	71.7	1 144	D	D	D	185	4 968	D	343.8
Bossier City	79	508	104.5	16.1	116	D	D	D	47	1 018	D	47.8
Central	15	42	5.7	0.8	25	75	9.7	3.2	21	155	D	5.6
Houma	61	589	138.9	37.8	145	925	121.6	47.4	32	1 045	228.4	59.8
Kenner	86	622	156.8	20.9	159	1 862	349.7	122.5	54	1 074	182.8	43.0
Lafayette	334	2 352	623.9	122.8	1 009	7 293	1 312.5	444.7	129	3 831	1 042.7	171.7
Lake Charles	117	480	85.9	16.5	275	1 775	214.0	77.5	39	1 224	1 251.5	76.1
Monroe	119	811	137.7	26.1	292	D	D	D	41	1 356	455.0	66.4
New Iberia	56	311	60.9	12.3	100	400	51.5	15.9	49	1 703	566.7	100.5
New Orleans	379	2 156	411.6	79.1	1 421	D	D	D	144	6 049	4 352.7	335.6
Shreveport	285	2 266	439.8	90.1	574	D	D	D	145	4 796	3 670.1	251.9
Slidell	37	365	116.2	26.1	139	583	62.2	21.6	26	1 895	D	115.8
MAINE	1 580	6 242	1 100.4	220.6	3 457	21 188	3 061.0	1 134.1	1 650	49 238	16 044.5	2 424.3
Bangor	90	404	80.3	14.5	157	D	D	D	37	775	167.2	34.7
Lewiston	48	222	31.1	6.6	83	D	D	D	65	1 507	430.2	65.7
Portland	226	1 453	291.5	56.6	586	5 193	1 044.1	380.9	101	2 425	747.5	112.2
South Portland	48	459	93.8	16.4	101	686	96.6	37.9	33	1 452	247.9	86.6
MARYLAND	6 001	42 838	13 410.1	2 253.2	19 529	D	D	D	3 096	100 079	39 533.0	5 908.9
Annapolis	98	449	115.3	25.7	371	D	D	D	37	324	65.5	14.9
Baltimore	596	4 055	883.7	187.6	1 524	20 740	4 544.9	1 808.5	409	11 748	5 043.3	574.0
Bowie	28	170	59.1	7.0	167	D	D	D	6	19	2.6	0.7
College Park	19	77	10.8	2.5	75	D	D	D	6	101	D	4.3
Frederick	99	462	123.1	23.3	369	D	D	D	59	2 045	D	129.9
Gaithersburg	95	514	181.9	30.3	415	D	D	D	35	1 039	397.5	72.6
Hagerstown	65	251	58.6	8.6	113	1 009	111.0	43.9	61	3 335	1 870.3	199.2
Laurel	42	655	104.1	25.6	74	930	154.4	60.6	12	115	D	8.2
Rockville	131	1 785	1 087.7	198.4	861	18 500	3 927.4	1 747.3	61	1 516	348.0	107.9
Salisbury	77	478	55.7	16.0	156	D	D	D	46	2 713	882.7	109.7
MASSACHUSETTS	6 485	42 788	13 628.4	2 357.9	21 203	243 993	57 979.0	22 938.7	6 806	234 168	81 927.8	14 395.3
Agawam Town	20	77	20.6	3.4	65	707	80.2	36.0	54	2 280	779.8	112.5
Attleboro	26	115	23.8	5.4	59	342	38.7	16.0	88	3 518	926.6	223.9
Barnstable Town	70	227	72.0	9.2	201	D	D	D	46	897	215.2	51.6

1. Establishments subject to federal tax.

Table D. Cities — Accommodation and Food Services, Arts, Entertainment, and Recreation, and Health Care and Social Assistance

City	Accommodation and food services, 2012				Arts, entertainment, and recreation,[1] 2012				Health care and social assistance,[1] 2012			
	Number of establishments	Number of employees	Sales (mil dol)	Annual payroll (mil dol)	Number of establishments	Number of employees	Receipts (mil dol)	Annual payroll (mil dol)	Number of establishments	Number of employees	Receipts (mil dol)	Annual payroll (mil dol)
	92	93	94	95	96	97	98	99	100	101	102	103
KANSAS	5 943	106 850	4 873.4	1 342.9	668	9 807	615.7	170.2	5 977	93 121	9 677.8	3 955.4
Dodge City	71	D	D	D	5	D	D	D	53	981	66.9	26.7
Garden City	66	1 333	67.5	17.5	4	37	0.8	0.3	68	1 783	206.1	89.5
Hutchinson	99	1 867	82.0	23.3	1	D	D	D	103	D	D	D
Kansas City	227	4 773	254.8	69.8	24	D	D	D	224	2 798	242.1	93.0
Lawrence	270	6 211	249.2	69.3	22	327	36.2	3.7	203	D	D	D
Leavenworth	59	974	43.6	11.6	6	39	1.0	0.2	65	1 906	259.5	108.9
Leawood	73	2 185	96.2	31.7	14	D	D	D	158	4 505	700.3	214.6
Lenexa	106	1 884	94.5	28.0	18	D	D	D	144	1 402	163.2	57.6
Manhattan	168	3 912	150.0	41.4	8	D	D	D	132	D	D	D
Olathe	234	5 437	245.6	70.9	32	D	D	D	244	12 623	1 736.3	705.9
Overland Park	456	10 355	538.6	162.8	71	1 583	78.0	25.7	664	2 391	231.7	93.3
Salina	132	2 986	115.8	31.0	10	D	D	D	137	1 609	123.8	58.3
Shawnee	109	2 166	95.9	27.2	12	D	D	D	121	5 825	699.8	308.8
Topeka	330	6 636	291.1	80.0	32				358	18 132	2 250.5	883.1
Wichita	962	19 526	918.8	255.2	78	1 300	48.4	18.5	977			
KENTUCKY	7 678	156 965	7 500.1	2 083.5	931	11 322	862.3	237.6	9 449	127 446	11 985.2	5 178.2
Bowling Green	243	5 498	255.4	68.2	15	425	12.3	4.3	289	D	D	D
Covington	125	1 793	117.0	29.4	9	D	D	D	204	D	D	D
Elizabethtown	112	2 798	132.4	37.0	9	115	5.2	1.4	136	2 375	210.7	92.3
Florence	161	3 755	201.4	55.7	21	500	20.0	5.8	109	1 198	100.9	45.0
Frankfort	88	1 698	83.5	22.2	6	D	D	D	93	D	D	D
Georgetown	80	D	D	D	5	D	D	D	105	D	D	D
Henderson	81	1 388	64.2	16.5	9	D	D	D				
Hopkinsville	77	1 524	67.6	19.2	5	39	1.9	0.6	120	1 151	111.2	36.4
Jeffersontown	108	2 931	141.4	41.9	18	397	13.0	4.8	101	2 692	165.9	77.6
Lexington-Fayette	772	17 490	939.4	270.7	91	1 469	110.6	37.9	895	12 181	1 255.7	587.7
Louisville/Jefferson County	1 651	39 711	2 006.3	572.1	220	3 486	288.7	88.2	2 072	32 822	3 186.5	1 478.1
Nicholasville	53	D	D	D	9	D	D	D	67	551	35.4	17.4
Owensboro	134	3 481	150.9	44.1	13	D	D	D	235	D	D	D
Paducah	174	3 615	161.2	46.8	10	D	D	D	187	D	D	D
Richmond	113	2 762	121.8	33.3	11	D	D	D	134	1 421	115.1	50.1
LOUISIANA	9 019	193 928	11 697.9	3 110.7	1 085	18 036	2 224.7	606.4	10 240	167 792	15 869.9	6 156.9
Alexandria	165	3 114	158.9	43.1	11	D	D	D	277	5 734	754.5	262.4
Baton Rouge	699	15 983	881.3	244.6	65	1 706	232.9	31.8	746	12 755	1 183.1	497.2
Bossier City	202	7 287	643.8	129.8	23	935	126.5	17.7	153	2 187	184.1	66.4
Central	15	363	12.6	3.5	4	D	D	D	36	473	33.6	14.0
Houma	90	1 690	114.5	33.7	9	78	3.3	1.2	145	D	D	D
Kenner	184	3 718	210.3	58.3	20	D	D	D	149	1 864	186.3	74.9
Lafayette	542	12 372	689.9	202.6	50	D	D	D	756	14 701	1 619.6	624.3
Lake Charles	197	6 132	579.2	125.3	24	D	D	D	314	5 528	599.3	241.0
Monroe	167	3 761	170.7	46.2	17	310	15.7	2.3	346	5 454	463.4	179.3
New Iberia	81	D	D	D	10	D	D	D	157	D	D	D
New Orleans	1 300	35 510	2 765.4	764.7	129	3 024	367.8	140.6	628	8 481	1 013.6	371.5
Shreveport	460	12 644	750.2	196.0	43	D	D	D	687	D	D	D
Slidell	180	3 220	150.4	41.0	4	D	D	D	196	D	D	D
MAINE	3 958	49 672	2 901.3	850.8	585	4 484	368.2	96.3	3 071	41 700	3 486.8	1 613.4
Bangor	139	3 366	222.7	58.4	8	D	D	D	211	4 175	353.1	166.6
Lewiston	74	1 015	51.8	14.3	11	D	D	D	98	1 182	131.6	53.6
Portland	330	5 887	312.7	99.7	39	404	34.3	8.7	278	4 363	470.5	216.3
South Portland	124	2 729	137.4	41.5	11	D	D	D	106	1 379	150.4	64.4
MARYLAND	11 344	204 222	12 516.8	3 410.5	1 561	24 878	2 726.9	806.3	13 217	168 241	18 823.4	7 784.6
Annapolis	194	4 975	299.5	91.6	NA	NA	NA	NA	143	1 523	189.2	69.3
Baltimore	1 541	21 832	1 607.8	435.6	NA	NA	NA	NA	1 069	16 427	1 991.0	827.4
Bowie	72	1 969	110.3	30.4	NA	NA	NA	NA	188	1 744	157.8	67.7
College Park	111	1 966	116.5	30.5	NA	NA	NA	NA	29	175	16.3	7.5
Frederick	218	4 153	220.7	64.6	NA	NA	NA	NA	318	4 441	550.3	212.9
Gaithersburg	204	3 774	267.0	71.0	NA	NA	NA	NA	170	1 725	182.4	60.5
Hagerstown	127	2 416	121.7	34.9	NA	NA	NA	NA	132	1 703	199.8	82.6
Laurel	79	1 725	94.2	26.6	NA	NA	NA	NA	94	1 192	123.7	48.8
Rockville	252	4 133	278.5	76.7	NA	NA	NA	NA	278	4 285	845.6	434.3
Salisbury	143	2 552	128.3	31.6	NA	NA	NA	NA	161	2 553	311.6	133.3
MASSACHUSETTS	16 898	273 185	17 509.0	5 019.8	2 277	35 108	3 412.3	1 261.8	13 136	237 631	26 639.0	12 209.0
Agawam Town	58	618	30.0	7.9	9	D	D	D	53	1 341	109.3	47.0
Attleboro	83	D	D	D	9	102	3.7	1.9	90	2 274	169.0	83.7
Barnstable Town	196	2 834	192.1	58.4	21	136	11.2	2.6	157	2 523	267.3	130.6

1. Establishments subject to federal tax.

Table D. Cities — Other Services and Government Employment and Payroll

City	Other services[1], 2012 Number of establish-ments	Number of employees	Receipts (mil dol)	Annual payroll (mil dol)	Government employment and payroll, 2012 Full-time equivalent employees	March payroll Total (dollars)	Percent of total for: Adminis-tration, judicial, and legal	Police and Corrections	Fire Protection	Highways and trans-portation	Health and welfare	Natural resources and utilities	Education and libraries
	104	105	106	107	108	109	110	111	112	113	114	115	116
KANSAS	3 957	21 148	1 920.4	560.0	X	X	X	X	X	X	X	X	X
Dodge City	37	229	22.9	5.6	249	803 190	14.8	27.3	12.1	6.2	2.3	27.5	6.6
Garden City	35	D	D	D	310	1 086 046	12.7	30.4	12.2	6.7	0.7	30.7	0.0
Hutchinson	66	343	20.9	7.2	392	1 720 937	8.7	26.7	25.6	7.2	2.1	25.6	0.0
Kansas City	157	827	89.5	25.3	2 707	14 492 572	12.6	24.6	15.1	5.6	5.3	29.9	0.0
Lawrence	117	713	43.2	14.4	1 978	10 089 159	4.2	10.8	8.9	2.8	58.2	13.8	0.0
Leavenworth	44	255	17.7	5.7	268	973 969	12.2	33.1	20.9	8.2	4.8	17.2	0.0
Leawood	48	451	48.8	18.0	262	1 218 472	17.8	32.5	22.4	11.6	1.7	11.1	0.0
Lenexa	68	538	49.5	18.3	414	1 898 039	18.6	33.0	22.5	12.1	0.0	11.7	0.0
Manhattan	72	D	D	D	362	1 385 412	18.7	25.9	14.5	12.1	0.0	32.8	0.0
Olathe	158	1 168	93.9	28.8	826	3 674 590	18.5	24.2	20.1	14.5	5.9	17.6	0.0
Overland Park	304	1 696	122.8	39.0	899	4 414 214	19.0	34.6	19.7	16.9	2.0	8.8	0.0
Salina	87	D	D	D	484	1 858 261	10.4	24.5	13.5	13.5	0.9	23.9	0.0
Shawnee	76	534	37.2	13.3	287	1 666 597	13.6	38.1	22.0	12.0	3.3	9.1	0.0
Topeka	190	1 382	108.7	34.1	1 062	3 978 506	7.7	32.8	23.7	12.5	0.8	15.4	0.0
Wichita	560	4 092	364.5	115.2	2 864	12 396 633	10.7	30.7	28.1	11.7	1.6	15.4	2.9
									18.5	13.7	3.8		
KENTUCKY	4 793	31 452	2 830.7	850.2	X	X	X	X	X	X	X	X	X
Bowling Green	137	784	69.1	19.1	699	2 772 912	7.1	20.2	19.5	5.5	2.9	30.0	0.0
Covington	74	318	25.9	8.4	421	1 788 490	6.5	36.3	30.5	3.6	11.9	5.7	0.0
Elizabethtown	66	436	37.9	11.0	289	996 440	11.3	24.1	21.7	8.8	0.0	27.7	0.0
Florence	67	538	35.4	12.7	198	919 937	6.2	36.7	28.5	4.6	0.0	11.5	0.0
Frankfort	38	233	14.8	4.7	530	2 153 521	5.6	15.6	18.6	4.9	2.2	22.3	0.0
Georgetown	38	166	11.3	3.2	179	621 131	11.9	34.9	35.4	6.1	0.0	6.7	0.0
Henderson	41	D	D	D	454	1 639 406	10.9	14.7	13.1	5.8	6.0	45.6	0.0
Hopkinsville	39	229	21.7	5.9	398	1 517 254	6.4	20.1	21.3	2.1	5.3	33.5	0.0
Jeffersontown	78	735	118.2	28.7	108	518 932	9.2	65.9	0.0	12.9	0.0	1.6	0.0
Lexington-Fayette	393	3 062	238.3	81.6	3 926	16 180 537	10.0	31.5	18.1	5.0	11.0	15.2	1.2
Louisville/Jefferson County	1 023	8 809	890.5	254.0	8 264	32 734 538	10.3	29.9	8.6	12.9	15.7	14.6	3.0
Nicholasville	46	174	21.5	4.3	214	748 387	13.4	32.1	20.0	4.1	0.0	17.4	2.2
Owensboro	90	706	49.6	17.4	840	3 418 017	7.9	17.9	10.1	5.1	3.1	53.8	0.0
Paducah	76	584	48.2	13.4	537	2 054 380	7.5	18.4	12.7	12.4	7.8	37.6	0.0
Richmond	48	242	17.3	4.8	264	708 015	11.1	30.0	21.4	6.8	9.1	12.4	0.0
LOUISIANA	5 092	36 098	3 916.0	1 216.5	X	X	X	X	X	X	X	X	X
Alexandria	89	539	45.5	13.2	858	3 139 622	13.3	29.0	18.9	9.8	0.4	22.4	0.0
Baton Rouge	392	4 825	381.6	214.7	7 745	28 842 476	18.7	20.3	13.5	8.8	15.7	11.6	4.2
Bossier City	98	634	55.2	15.9	738	2 695 669	13.1	32.2	30.2	2.8	1.1	15.5	0.0
Central	24	115	12.9	4.0	11	24 511	92.3	7.7	0.0	0.0	0.0	0.0	0.0
Houma	57	527	77.3	29.1	2 552	9 484 779	6.9	16.5	2.3	2.5	60.4	8.0	3.4
Kenner	107	759	114.6	27.1	633	2 227 138	15.0	42.0	19.4	6.5	3.2	7.8	0.0
Lafayette	232	2 047	253.7	62.1	3 047	10 656 600	18.8	30.9	10.4	8.4	1.8	24.1	2.4
Lake Charles	98	793	74.7	23.3	1 030	3 427 311	10.3	24.5	19.4	6.9	0.4	29.2	0.0
Monroe	65	549	40.9	12.8	1 137	2 092 527	21.1	3.5	2.5	12.5	15.1	42.2	0.0
New Iberia	69	388	35.3	10.7	222	646 974	12.2	1.2	36.3	13.5	4.6	27.2	0.0
New Orleans	364	2 537	210.4	62.9	6 570	26 033 023	13.9	33.2	9.9	2.7	8.0	23.7	1.6
Shreveport	252	2 069	184.1	54.8	2 841	10 287 795	8.1	28.1	26.4	6.9	2.4	18.7	7.2
Slidell	83	392	28.4	8.2	294	1 068 129	19.4	46.5	0.0	11.4	0.0	18.5	0.0
MAINE	2 041	9 424	881.5	242.9	X	X	X	X	X	X	X	X	X
Bangor	71	499	47.6	12.4	1 172	4 803 542	4.3	9.1	8.0	17.8	2.9	5.2	50.9
Lewiston	60	355	30.1	8.5	1 063	4 275 573	4.7	10.1	8.1	4.7	0.9	4.1	64.8
Portland	167	1 005	87.6	26.5	2 667	11 280 661	5.1	9.2	9.4	4.1	13.4	3.5	50.8
South Portland	63	561	29.1	10.6	774	2 806 318	7.4	11.7	11.2	5.1	0.2	9.9	54.4
MARYLAND	7 877	57 077	5 195.8	1 677.9	X	X	X	X	X	X	X	X	X
Annapolis	153	1 410	122.6	50.1	620	3 140 557	12.6	28.5	24.6	16.2	0.0	13.6	0.0
Baltimore	682	6 054	643.0	173.9	26 392	122 552 640	6.0	16.4	7.7	3.4	7.5	8.8	48.9
Bowie	43	274	19.4	6.5	332	1 491 481	15.5	19.2	0.0	6.4	9.8	36.4	0.0
College Park	45	300	26.5	9.3	308	540 180	25.6	19.0	0.0	6.4	12.3	21.9	0.0
Frederick	147	996	81.8	25.1	560	2 537 922	10.7	39.5	0.0	8.4	5.7	23.2	0.0
Gaithersburg	133	875	110.8	28.8	303	1 564 921	28.1	25.0	0.0	16.4	6.3	21.9	0.0
Hagerstown	81	428	34.6	11.4	445	2 038 054	10.3	26.5	16.9	6.9	0.7	32.9	0.0
Laurel	51	465	33.5	12.3	197	975 036	19.1	49.9	0.0	7.4	0.0	18.1	0.0
Rockville	185	1 289	135.0	38.5	652	3 046 807	18.3	18.4	0.0	9.1	8.6	45.6	0.0
Salisbury	83	757	60.2	19.3	375	1 345 111	6.4	35.5	18.2	7.5	4.4	26.4	0.0
MASSACHUSETTS	11 154	67 531	5 985.4	1 892.2	X	X	X	X	X	X	X	X	X
Agawam Town	46	197	22.9	5.6	958	3 825 533	4.3	9.2	8.3	3.0	2.5	2.9	64.5
Attleboro	67	272	24.0	6.7	1 376	5 707 365	4.1	9.4	7.8	1.4	1.4	7.2	68.0
Barnstable Town	119	629	54.1	17.3	1 040	5 101 618	12.3	17.0	0.0	7.1	2.3	6.5	50.4

1. Establishments subject to federal tax.

Table D. Cities — City Government Finances

City	City government finances, 2012									
	General revenue							General expenditure		
		Intergovernmental		Taxes					Per capita[1] (dollars)	
					Per capita[1] (dollars)					
	Total (mil dol)	Total (mil dol)	Percent from state government	Total (mil dol)	Total	Property	Sales and gross receipts	Total (mil dol)	Total	Capital outlays
	117	118	119	120	121	122	123	124	125	126
KANSAS	X	X	X	X	X	X	X	X	X	X
Dodge City	42.1	4.4	73.2	19.0	676	272	403	61.8	2 199	497
Garden City	32.6	5.3	13.6	13.7	508	224	285	32.2	1 196	137
Hutchinson	47.8	10.1	16.6	24.0	572	287	285	36.3	867	15
Kansas City	345.7	20.8	59.0	197.9	1 342	609	724	304.9	2 068	35
Lawrence	300.0	35.4	66.1	51.1	569	251	318	265.3	2 952	315
Leavenworth	35.9	6.9	24.9	18.7	523	329	194	39.7	1 108	180
Leawood	52.4	9.2	26.4	36.5	1 121	518	604	38.2	1 173	233
Lenexa	84.1	15.1	53.5	48.4	979	537	442	101.5	2 056	664
Manhattan	75.3	14.5	19.2	38.3	675	346	329	70.4	1 243	66
Olathe	165.1	23.5	34.3	90.7	697	288	410	149.2	1 147	163
Overland Park	224.8	42.2	25.4	90.5	506	129	377	208.7	1 166	223
Salina	68.5	10.3	26.4	25.7	535	240	295	75.4	1 572	264
Shawnee	54.4	10.0	26.2	38.6	607	330	277	48.9	769	62
Topeka	206.4	27.9	31.8	106.8	835	320	515	153.6	1 201	139
Wichita	562.5	102.8	20.6	167.5	435	306	129	543.6	1 410	223
KENTUCKY	X	X	X	X	X	X	X	X	X	X
Bowling Green	98.4	10.3	24.6	55.7	916	177	90	76.0	1 251	71
Covington	71.2	13.5	27.4	40.2	989	171	268	54.8	1 350	183
Elizabethtown	45.8	8.2	36.9	25.3	863	132	141	37.6	1 280	347
Florence	43.3	5.6	79.1	28.8	928	238	150	28.8	926	346
Frankfort	67.6	2.6	55.3	25.5	937	148	100	57.0	2 091	104
Georgetown	46.6	3.3	36.0	15.8	523	64	172	38.6	1 277	68
Henderson	46.8	13.7	10.5	17.3	597	254	143	40.9	1 415	213
Hopkinsville	42.0	7.0	7.7	23.2	702	139	127	37.4	1 128	88
Jeffersontown	25.4	1.1	76.1	17.1	637	144	99	23.6	876	92
Lexington-Fayette	544.8	60.2	29.6	318.9	1 045	282	143	440.5	1 443	142
Louisville/Jefferson County	935.3	222.4	25.0	456.1	753	225	93	992.9	1 640	335
Nicholasville	20.8	2.5	72.9	13.4	473	139	110	18.1	638	35
Owensboro	98.3	27.0	14.9	35.0	602	166	123	105.2	1 812	630
Paducah	63.2	11.9	37.1	32.6	1 297	237	164	49.1	1 954	263
Richmond	34.6	1.4	35.9	20.5	631	93	132	25.5	785	137
LOUISIANA	X	X	X	X	X	X	X	X	X	X
Alexandria	82.5	13.7	28.9	53.7	1 121	153	967	92.8	1 936	198
Baton Rouge	959.1	199.4	55.2	458.1	1 992	692	1 300	1 203.6	5 233	1 750
Bossier City	108.4	8.2	55.5	71.3	1 090	181	909	129.1	1 975	823
Central	9.1	0.3	100.0	8.6	313	0	313	4.7	169	2
Houma	411.9	103.8	73.9	117.3	3 483	1 624	1 859	430.0	12 764	2 321
Kenner	77.5	40.2	21.3	22.2	332	125	207	70.3	1 050	164
Lafayette	402.4	70.2	47.1	201.1	1 631	828	803	443.4	3 597	882
Lake Charles	116.9	27.3	9.2	70.1	952	108	845	117.0	1 590	348
Monroe	129.3	28.8	34.5	77.5	1 564	218	1 346	140.8	2 843	755
New Iberia	32.2	4.6	29.3	21.4	693	131	562	42.4	1 376	297
New Orleans	1 505.1	535.6	44.1	499.4	1 349	692	647	1 604.4	4 334	1 371
Shreveport	369.6	59.6	35.0	209.5	1 037	312	725	315.2	1 560	169
Slidell	55.2	15.5	65.5	27.4	1 001	202	798	55.1	2 012	612
MAINE	X	X	X	X	X	X	X	X	X	X
Bangor	131.1	38.3	93.4	54.2	1 653	1 624	29	165.2	5 035	1 527
Lewiston	117.7	52.6	84.0	49.4	1 355	1 342	13	112.8	3 095	292
Portland	318.6	71.3	78.7	144.3	2 178	2 129	49	329.4	4 972	746
South Portland	82.8	11.7	92.5	61.0	2 430	2 411	20	82.1	3 270	347
MARYLAND	X	X	X	X	X	X	X	X	X	X
Annapolis	82.8	14.6	35.6	43.3	1 125	985	140	65.6	1 703	14
Baltimore	3 407.6	1 720.1	81.7	1 238.8	1 989	1 226	267	3 659.5	5 874	527
Bowie	46.8	10.8	16.7	27.6	491	444	47	42.1	748	0
College Park	15.3	2.1	19.1	9.8	315	239	76	14.1	451	4
Frederick	90.8	14.2	14.9	46.5	700	655	45	84.6	1 273	9
Gaithersburg	54.0	13.4	7.5	31.2	495	390	104	49.4	783	40
Hagerstown	57.3	7.1	21.8	26.1	645	527	114	50.2	1 239	16
Laurel	29.2	4.0	20.5	20.5	800	757	43	25.4	992	3
Rockville	92.8	17.8	12.0	40.8	644	553	86	94.1	1 486	5
Salisbury	51.7	5.3	32.3	22.5	725	675	49	39.7	1 279	49
MASSACHUSETTS	X	X	X	X	X	X	X	X	X	X
Agawam Town	84.8	27.5	99.5	50.0	1 745	1 720	26	102.8	3 589	65
Attleboro	126.9	47.0	97.8	61.9	1 412	1 380	32	113.5	2 593	116
Barnstable Town	177.7	41.0	87.9	109.9	2 458	2 319	139	175.2	3 917	633

1. Based on population estimated as of July 1 of the year shown.

City	City government finances, 2012 (cont.) — General expenditure (cont.) — Percent of total for:									
	Public welfare	Highways	Parking facilities	Education	Health and hospitals	Police protection	Sewerage and sanitation	Parks and recreation	Housing and community development	Interest on debt
	127	128	129	130	131	132	133	134	135	136
KANSAS	X	X	X	X	X	X	X	X	X	X
Dodge City	0.0	1.2	0.0	0.0	0.8	7.8	35.2	17.9	0.0	16.3
Garden City	0.0	11.0	0.0	0.0	0.0	19.9	11.8	14.6	0.0	1.0
Hutchinson	0.0	4.4	0.0	0.0	1.3	22.1	23.3	12.7	0.0	3.8
Kansas City	0.0	2.6	0.2	0.0	3.4	15.9	7.5	2.3	0.0	23.3
Lawrence	0.0	2.7	0.5	0.0	59.4	5.5	8.3	3.1	1.5	2.8
Leavenworth	0.0	10.0	0.0	0.0	0.0	17.1	12.8	5.5	9.0	2.9
Leawood	0.0	22.0	0.0	0.0	0.0	21.4	0.0	17.6	0.0	6.5
Lenexa	0.0	20.0	0.0	0.0	0.0	12.2	3.8	8.5	0.0	16.9
Manhattan	0.0	6.3	0.0	0.0	1.1	17.5	8.4	8.0	1.8	12.6
Olathe	0.0	15.8	0.0	0.0	0.2	13.0	15.5	3.6	0.0	9.4
Overland Park	0.0	21.1	0.0	0.0	0.0	14.4	2.5	5.2	0.0	25.8
Salina	0.0	9.2	0.0	0.0	1.6	11.2	10.5	9.0	0.0	11.5
Shawnee	0.0	12.9	0.0	0.0	0.0	24.3	6.3	9.2	5.0	18.0
Topeka	1.1	9.1	1.4	0.0	0.0	20.4	12.2	10.5	0.0	7.1
Wichita	0.0	13.4	0.0	0.0	0.7	13.7	8.7	4.9	1.5	31.2
KENTUCKY	X	X	X	X	X	X	X	X	X	X
Bowling Green	0.0	9.4	0.0	0.0	0.0	12.0	10.5	10.4	6.4	20.5
Covington	0.0	7.9	3.6	0.0	0.0	19.6	4.0	2.4	21.8	12.5
Elizabethtown	0.0	9.8	0.1	0.0	0.0	10.7	9.3	8.0	0.0	3.4
Florence	0.0	44.2	0.0	0.0	0.0	16.0	5.1	0.0	0.0	10.7
Frankfort	0.0	3.8	0.0	0.0	5.8	7.9	12.9	5.0	0.0	2.6
Georgetown	0.2	3.1	0.0	0.0	0.0	7.8	10.8	2.3	1.1	49.3
Henderson	0.0	5.4	0.0	0.0	0.0	9.2	27.0	2.5	13.3	1.8
Hopkinsville	0.7	5.7	0.0	0.0	0.0	20.8	13.6	1.2	13.7	14.5
Jeffersontown	0.0	9.1	0.0	0.0	0.0	23.5	4.4	2.6	2.8	37.7
Lexington-Fayette	2.0	2.5	0.3	0.0	3.6	10.8	15.8	4.0	1.1	4.1
Louisville/Jefferson County	1.2	6.8	7.9	5.7	3.3	10.2	1.5	5.7	6.5	9.9
Nicholasville	0.0	18.8	0.0	0.0	0.0	22.5	18.6	0.0	0.0	5.0
Owensboro	0.0	5.3	0.2	0.0	0.0	7.1	17.8	7.1	27.9	10.8
Paducah	0.0	8.5	0.0	3.6	0.0	12.3	6.2	4.9	18.9	2.5
Richmond	0.0	3.7	0.0	0.0	0.0	13.5	29.4	8.7	7.4	15.3
LOUISIANA	X	X	X	X	X	X	X	X	X	X
Alexandria	0.0	13.7	0.0	0.0	0.0	18.0	11.3	3.8	8.9	3.0
Baton Rouge	0.2	8.7	0.1	1.3	8.7	10.5	28.4	2.0	5.2	5.2
Bossier City	0.0	1.7	0.0	0.0	0.4	15.1	16.6	5.5	6.7	5.7
Central	0.4	4.9	0.0	0.0	2.1	3.8	0.0	0.0	0.0	0.0
Houma	0.0	4.2	0.0	0.0	41.2	6.3	5.5	2.3	1.7	1.6
Kenner	0.0	19.8	0.0	0.0	0.2	23.7	14.3	6.4	1.0	2.8
Lafayette	0.2	7.6	0.2	0.0	1.4	12.7	9.1	6.0	5.0	8.8
Lake Charles	0.7	13.5	0.0	0.0	0.5	14.4	17.5	8.9	13.5	3.4
Monroe	0.1	4.4	0.0	0.0	0.0	13.1	9.8	5.7	17.4	5.8
New Iberia	0.4	16.2	0.0	0.0	0.0	14.0	25.5	5.1	10.0	4.0
New Orleans	0.2	7.6	0.1	0.0	0.8	8.9	13.7	5.5	15.5	5.9
Shreveport	0.0	4.5	0.2	0.0	0.0	18.2	14.6	9.9	7.6	4.3
Slidell	0.0	11.7	0.0	0.0	0.7	14.9	13.3	2.9	10.4	1.7
MAINE	X	X	X	X	X	X	X	X	X	X
Bangor	0.0	0.0	0.4	26.4	2.3	4.8	3.0	22.8	0.9	2.0
Lewiston	0.9	3.4	0.0	49.5	0.0	5.9	6.7	0.6	1.5	5.2
Portland	7.7	5.4	0.6	30.3	1.3	4.1	8.1	2.0	1.0	5.2
South Portland	0.3	4.6	0.0	52.3	0.0	5.4	11.2	4.3	0.0	1.6
MARYLAND	X	X	X	X	X	X	X	X	X	X
Annapolis	0.0	7.2	2.3	0.0	0.0	25.6	12.0	5.3	0.0	5.0
Baltimore	0.0	5.7	0.8	38.4	3.3	10.2	6.6	1.6	2.1	1.4
Bowie	0.0	11.4	0.0	0.0	0.5	17.6	23.4	16.4	0.1	1.5
College Park	0.0	22.3	1.0	0.0	0.6	7.3	18.8	9.4	1.5	2.1
Frederick	0.0	10.8	3.8	0.0	0.0	30.2	13.3	9.7	0.6	5.8
Gaithersburg	0.0	8.4	0.0	0.0	1.2	15.6	4.7	20.3	1.6	11.6
Hagerstown	0.0	5.9	1.4	0.0	0.0	23.0	29.3	6.2	1.0	2.0
Laurel	0.0	4.9	0.0	0.0	0.0	34.6	4.6	9.1	0.2	1.9
Rockville	0.0	12.9	2.9	0.0	0.4	17.1	13.5	19.7	4.1	4.0
Salisbury	0.0	9.1	1.5	0.0	0.5	25.3	23.5	5.2	2.1	3.6
MASSACHUSETTS	X	X	X	X	X	X	X	X	X	X
Agawam Town	0.1	2.9	0.0	52.9	1.8	4.2	4.3	0.8	0.0	0.8
Attleboro	0.6	3.1	0.0	63.9	0.2	5.5	8.6	1.4	0.5	2.3
Barnstable Town	0.2	2.3	0.0	45.7	0.6	6.2	4.5	2.8	0.2	2.5

Table D. Cities — City Government Finances, City Government Employment, and Climate

	City government finances, 2012 (cont.)			Climate[2]						
	Debt outstanding			Average daily temperature (degrees Fahrenheit)						
				Mean		Limits				
City	Total (mil dol)	Per capita[1] (dollars)	Debt issued during year	January	July	January[3]	July[4]	Annual precipitation (inches)	Heating degree days	Cooling degree days
	137	138	139	140	141	142	143	144	145	146
KANSAS	X	X	X	X	X	X	X	X	X	X
Dodge City	220.7	7 857	12.2	30.1	79.8	18.7	92.8	22.35	5 037	1 481
Garden City	42.2	1 564	3.5	28.6	77.8	14.7	92.1	18.77	5 423	1 191
Hutchinson	54.3	1 294	5.6	28.5	79.9	17.0	92.7	30.32	5 146	1 454
Kansas City	1 786.2	12 115	126.8	29.1	79.0	19.9	89.4	40.17	4 847	1 406
Lawrence	287.4	3 197	46.3	29.9	80.2	20.5	90.6	39.78	4 685	1 582
Leavenworth	32.8	917	10.5	26.6	79.1	16.4	89.8	40.94	5 331	1 356
Leawood	60.6	1 863	5.3	29.1	79.0	19.9	89.4	40.17	4 847	1 406
Lenexa	280.1	5 672	46.2	29.1	79.0	19.9	89.4	40.17	4 847	1 406
Manhattan	344.8	6 084	41.3	27.8	79.9	16.1	92.5	34.80	5 120	1 465
Olathe	1 141.4	8 779	55.5	29.1	79.0	19.9	89.4	40.17	4 847	1 406
Overland Park	1 428.3	7 983	15.2	29.1	79.0	19.9	89.4	40.17	4 847	1 406
Salina	168.5	3 513	22.8	29.0	81.3	18.8	93.3	32.19	4 952	1 600
Shawnee	215.7	3 390	22.2	29.1	79.0	19.9	89.4	40.17	4 847	1 406
Topeka	364.4	2 850	72.6	27.2	78.4	17.2	89.1	35.64	5 225	1 357
Wichita	3 471.3	9 003	335.8	30.2	81.0	20.3	92.9	30.38	4 765	1 658
KENTUCKY	X	X	X	X	X	X	X	X	X	X
Bowling Green	283.6	4 667	7.1	34.2	78.5	25.4	89.2	51.63	4 243	1 413
Covington	162.2	3 993	3.6	32.0	76.1	24.1	85.9	45.91	4 713	1 154
Elizabethtown	55.2	1 880	18.5	NA	NA	NA	NA	NA	NA	NA
Florence	69.3	2 230	3.1	30.3	75.2	20.8	86.9	43.56	5 129	994
Frankfort	46.6	1 711	0.0	NA	NA	NA	NA	NA	NA	NA
Georgetown	473.4	15 642	0.0	NA	NA	NA	NA	44.77	4 374	1 344
Henderson	50.4	1 744	15.8	32.6	77.6	23.6	88.4			
Hopkinsville	170.2	5 136	12.2	33.2	78.2	24.4	88.5	50.92	4 298	1 433
Jeffersontown	160.3	5 960	0.0	33.0	78.4	24.9	87.0	44.54	4 352	1 443
Lexington-Fayette	1 000.4	3 277	37.3	31.6	75.9	22.5	86.3	46.39	4 769	1 094
Louisville/Jefferson County	1 594.3	2 633	310.5	NA	NA	NA	NA	NA	NA	NA
Nicholasville	32.1	1 130	3.5	NA	NA	NA	NA	NA	NA	NA
Owensboro	399.8	6 888	55.2	33.5	79.2	24.4	90.7	46.53	4 159	1 565
Paducah	39.7	1 583	6.6	35.2	79.9	27.2	90.8	46.04	3 893	1 635
Richmond	104.2	3 208	2.7	34.7	75.8	25.6	87.0	47.33	4 231	1 150
LOUISIANA	X	X	X	X	X	X	X	X	X	X
Alexandria	94.9	1 980	2.6	48.1	83.3	38.0	92.8	61.44	1 908	2 602
Baton Rouge	1 639.8	7 130	219.4	50.1	81.7	40.2	90.7	63.08	1 689	2 628
Bossier City	360.5	5 513	5.7	48.3	81.0	37.4	91.0	61.06	1 981	2 220
Central	0.0	0	0.0	NA	NA	NA	NA	NA	NA	NA
Houma	213.1	6 326	64.3	53.1	82.5	43.4	90.7	63.67	1 346	2 804
Kenner	61.5	919	19.6	52.6	82.7	43.4	91.1	64.16	1 417	2 773
Lafayette	1 132.6	9 186	183.7	51.3	82.2	41.6	91.2	60.54	1 531	2 671
Lake Charles	92.3	1 253	3.7	50.9	82.6	41.2	91.0	57.19	1 546	2 705
Monroe	177.3	3 581	34.9	44.6	83.0	33.5	94.1	58.04	2 399	2 311
New Iberia	38.7	1 257	24.3	51.3	82.3	41.4	91.1	60.89	1 544	2 680
New Orleans	2 018.9	5 454	51.5	52.7	82.2	43.3	90.9	65.15	1 416	2 686
Shreveport	540.8	2 676	85.6	46.4	83.4	36.5	93.3	51.30	2 251	2 405
Slidell	25.1	916	0.0	50.7	82.1	40.2	91.1	62.66	1 652	2 548
MAINE	X	X	X	X	X	X	X	X	X	X
Bangor	109.4	3 335	32.1	18.0	69.2	8.3	79.6	39.57	7 676	313
Lewiston	152.4	4 182	7.6	20.5	71.4	11.5	81.5	45.79	7 107	465
Portland	423.0	6 384	38.7	21.7	68.7	12.5	78.8	45.83	7 318	347
South Portland	50.1	1 994	30.0	NA	NA	NA	NA	NA	NA	NA
MARYLAND	X	X	X	X	X	X	X	X	X	X
Annapolis	96.8	2 513	0.0	32.8	77.5	23.8	87.7	44.78	4 695	1 162
Baltimore	2 621.6	4 208	13.3	36.8	81.7	29.4	90.6	43.59	4 720	1 147
Bowie	18.0	320	0.1	31.8	75.2	21.2	87.1	44.66	4 970	917
College Park	8.4	269	0.0	NA	NA	NA	NA	NA	NA	NA
Frederick	224.2	3 375	31.4	33.3	77.9	25.1	88.9	40.64	4 430	1 272
Gaithersburg	142.6	2 261	0.0	31.8	75.3	23.8	85.4	43.08	4 990	983
Hagerstown	66.0	1 630	7.9	29.3	75.2	20.8	86.1	39.45	5 249	902
Laurel	10.1	396	0.1	NA	NA	NA	NA	NA	NA	NA
Rockville	135.9	2 144	40.7	31.8	75.3	23.8	85.4	43.08	4 990	983
Salisbury	70.9	2 286	15.2	NA	NA	NA	NA	NA	NA	NA
MASSACHUSETTS	X	X	X	X	X	X	X	X	X	X
Agawam Town	25.0	871	6.2	NA	NA	NA	NA	NA	NA	NA
Attleboro	72.7	1 660	1.5	27.4	72.2	17.8	83.0	48.34	6 012	558
Barnstable Town	131.5	2 941	18.5	29.2	70.5	21.2	77.8	43.03	6 026	413

1. Based on the population estimated as of July 1 of the year shown.   2. Represents normal values based on the 30-year period, 1971–2000.   3. Average daily minimum.
4. Average daily maximum.

STATE Place code	City	Land area,[1] 2016 (sq mi)	Population, 2016			Race alone[2] (percent), 2015						
			Total persons	Rank	Per square mile	White	Black or African American	American Indian, Alaska Native	Asian	Hawaiian Pacific Islander	Some other race	2 or more races[2]
		1	2	3	4	5	6	7	8	9	10	11
	MASSACHUSETTS— Cont'd											
25 05595	Beverly	15.1	41 365	914	2 739.4	95.5	0.3	0.0	0.7	0.2	1.5	1.8
25 07000	Boston	48.3	673 184	22	13 937.6	52.7	25.3	0.2	9.5	0.0	7.8	4.5
25 07740	Braintree Town	13.8	37 297	1 026	2 702.7	85.8	2.7	0.0	9.3	0.0	0.3	1.9
25 09000	Brockton	21.3	95 630	323	4 489.7	40.3	43.7	0.1	2.4	0.0	10.7	2.8
25 11000	Cambridge	6.4	110 651	262	17 289.2	69.8	9.4	0.0	14.7	0.0	2.4	3.7
25 13205	Chelsea	2.2	39 699	955	18 045.0	54.2	5.0	0.0	2.8	0.0	6.4	31.7
25 13660	Chicopee	22.8	55 991	668	2 455.7	88.4	4.0	0.3	1.8	0.0	1.9	3.6
25 21990	Everett	3.4	46 340	826	13 629.4	58.9	22.3	0.0	9.2	0.0	3.6	5.9
25 23000	Fall River	33.1	88 930	363	2 686.7	81.9	3.8	0.0	1.9	0.3	6.9	5.3
25 23875	Fitchburg	27.8	40 414	934	1 453.7	83.9	4.5	0.3	3.3	0.0	4.7	3.3
25 25172	Franklin Town	26.6	33 150	1 143	1 246.2	91.2	0.7	0.0	6.1	0.0	0.2	1.8
25 26150	Gloucester	26.2	29 798	1 257	1 137.3	NA	NA	NA	NA	NA	NA	NA
25 29405	Haverhill	33.0	62 873	581	1 905.2	83.4	2.6	0.5	1.2	0.0	8.7	3.6
25 30840	Holyoke	21.3	40 280	938	1 891.1	88.7	5.4	0.5	0.4	0.2	2.5	2.4
25 34550	Lawrence	6.9	80 209	425	11 624.5	46.3	7.3	0.2	2.6	0.0	37.9	5.7
25 35075	Leominster	28.8	41 663	906	1 446.6	84.8	3.0	0.0	3.2	0.0	6.5	2.5
25 37000	Lowell	13.6	110 558	263	8 129.3	60.0	5.4	0.2	25.9	0.0	6.1	2.4
25 37490	Lynn	10.7	92 697	342	8 663.3	47.2	13.1	0.2	8.9	0.0	21.5	9.1
25 37875	Malden	5.0	60 840	604	12 168.0	51.5	19.9	0.0	23.1	0.1	0.9	4.5
25 38715	Marlborough	20.9	39 697	956	1 899.4	79.2	4.0	0.0	5.9	0.0	4.8	6.0
25 39835	Medford	8.1	57 213	654	7 063.3	77.8	7.7	0.3	9.1	0.0	1.9	3.1
25 40115	Melrose	4.7	27 928	1 328	5 942.1	NA	NA	NA	NA	NA	NA	NA
25 40710	Methuen Town	22.2	49 917	757	2 248.5	84.1	2.7	0.9	3.9	0.0	7.9	0.5
25 45000	New Bedford	20.0	95 032	329	4 751.6	64.9	7.0	0.0	1.4	0.0	22.7	4.0
25 45560	Newton	17.8	89 045	362	5 002.5	75.5	2.2	0.1	15.7	0.0	3.3	3.2
25 46330	Northampton	34.2	28 483	1 308	832.8	93.0	1.7	0.1	2.2	0.0	0.4	2.5
25 52490	Peabody	16.2	52 491	724	3 240.2	87.7	2.9	0.1	3.1	0.0	3.6	2.6
25 53960	Pittsfield	40.5	42 846	878	1 057.9	89.3	3.7	0.2	2.3	0.0	2.7	1.8
25 55745	Quincy	16.6	93 688	338	5 643.9	62.0	4.2	0.0	32.2	0.0	0.9	0.8
25 56585	Revere	5.7	53 157	712	9 325.8	80.7	4.8	0.2	6.9	0.0	4.2	3.2
25 59105	Salem	8.3	43 132	870	5 196.6	71.9	4.7	1.0	3.0	0.0	15.6	3.8
25 62535	Somerville	4.1	81 322	415	19 834.6	75.4	7.5	0.0	10.6	0.0	3.1	3.3
25 67000	Springfield	31.9	154 074	165	4 829.9	60.2	19.9	0.5	2.9	0.0	12.4	4.0
25 69170	Taunton	46.7	56 843	658	1 217.2	84.2	8.8	0.0	1.7	0.0	3.5	1.8
25 72600	Waltham	12.7	63 002	579	4 960.8	73.6	3.8	0.6	13.0	0.0	5.5	3.5
25 73440	Watertown Town	4.0	35 025	1 084	8 756.3	85.5	2.5	0.0	5.8	0.0	4.2	2.0
25 76030	Westfield	46.3	41 552	909	897.5	NA	NA	NA	NA	NA	NA	NA
25 77890	West Springfield Town	16.7	28 529	1 304	1 708.3	86.8	4.4	0.2	3.2	0.0	1.7	3.7
25 78972	Weymouth Town	16.8	55 972	669	3 331.7	86.5	5.3	0.1	4.0	0.0	1.4	2.6
25 81035	Woburn	12.6	39 452	962	3 131.1	80.9	6.1	0.0	4.7	0.0	6.3	2.1
25 82000	Worcester	37.4	184 508	131	4 933.4	69.0	13.2	0.4	7.6	0.0	6.5	3.4
26 00000	MICHIGAN	56 546.7	9 928 300	X	175.6	78.6	13.9	0.5	3.0	0.0	1.2	2.7
26 01380	Allen Park	7.0	27 214	1 356	3 887.7	NA	NA	NA	NA	NA	NA	NA
26 03000	Ann Arbor	28.1	120 782	228	4 298.3	73.5	6.6	0.9	14.4	0.1	0.7	3.8
26 05920	Battle Creek	42.6	51 534	741	1 209.7	70.8	18.8	0.7	3.0	0.3	0.5	5.9
26 06020	Bay City	10.2	33 511	1 132	3 285.4	90.2	4.1	0.4	1.0	0.0	1.2	3.0
26 12060	Burton	23.4	28 648	1 300	1 224.3	NA	NA	NA	NA	NA	NA	NA
26 21000	Dearborn	24.2	94 444	333	3 902.6	90.7	3.6	0.2	2.5	0.0	0.4	2.7
26 21020	Dearborn Heights	11.7	55 761	670	4 765.9	87.2	7.0	0.4	1.2	0.4	1.7	2.0
26 22000	Detroit	138.8	672 795	23	4 847.2	14.1	79.5	0.3	1.3	0.0	3.0	1.8
26 24120	East Lansing	13.6	48 870	778	3 593.4	76.9	5.1	0.5	11.9	0.0	1.1	4.5
26 24290	Eastpointe	5.1	32 673	1 162	6 406.5	46.9	43.9	3.3	1.2	0.0	2.7	2.0
26 27440	Farmington Hills	33.3	81 129	418	2 436.3	69.0	15.7	0.2	12.2	0.0	0.9	2.2
26 29000	Flint	33.4	97 386	315	2 915.7	41.7	52.5	0.1	0.2	0.0	0.9	4.7
26 31420	Garden City	5.9	26 719	1 377	4 528.6	94.7	2.1	1.0	0.7	0.0	0.0	1.5
26 34000	Grand Rapids	44.4	196 445	121	4 424.4	68.7	17.9	0.3	2.3	0.1	5.4	5.4
26 38640	Holland	16.7	33 543	1 130	2 008.6	86.9	3.2	1.1	3.0	0.4	2.2	3.1
26 40680	Inkster	6.3	24 462	1 432	3 882.9	NA	NA	NA	NA	NA	NA	NA
26 41420	Jackson	10.8	32 918	1 156	3 048.0	67.7	24.5	0.2	1.6	0.0	0.8	5.2
26 42160	Kalamazoo	24.7	75 984	454	3 076.3	69.5	21.2	0.5	1.7	0.0	1.3	5.9
26 42820	Kentwood	20.9	51 689	740	2 473.2	69.5	21.7	0.1	3.8	0.0	2.3	2.5
26 46000	Lansing	39.1	116 020	239	2 967.3	58.9	23.4	0.4	3.5	0.0	4.2	9.7
26 47800	Lincoln Park	5.9	36 720	1 037	6 223.7	84.2	8.1	0.7	0.3	0.0	2.3	4.5
26 49000	Livonia	35.7	94 041	334	2 634.2	91.7	4.4	0.1	2.6	0.0	0.2	1.0
26 50560	Madison Heights	7.1	30 088	1 248	4 237.7	87.4	6.1	0.7	3.2	0.0	0.0	2.5
26 53780	Midland	34.2	42 096	897	1 230.9	89.4	2.8	0.2	3.1	0.6	0.9	3.0
26 56020	Mount Pleasant	7.7	26 313	1 392	3 417.3	85.3	5.0	2.9	4.1	0.0	0.5	2.3
26 56320	Muskegon	14.2	38 349	990	2 700.6	59.5	33.6	0.6	0.0	0.0	1.2	5.1
26 59440	Novi	30.2	59 211	629	1 960.6	63.5	10.3	0.6	24.0	0.0	0.1	1.5

1. Dry land or land partially or temporarily covered by water.   2. Hispanic or Latino persons may be of any race.

Table D. Cities — Population

City	Percent Hispanic or Latino[1], 2015	Percent foreign born 2015	Age of population (percent), 2010-2014 — Under 18 years	18 to 24 years	25 to 34 years	35 to 44 years	45 to 54 years	55 to 64 years	65 years and over	Median age 2015	Percent female 2015	Census counts 2000	Census counts 2010	Percent change 2000–2010	Percent change 2010–2016
	12	13	14	15	16	17	18	19	20	21	22	23	24	25	26
MASSACHUSETTS— Cont'd															
Beverly	5.1	5.1	18.5	15.0	12.4	13.4	10.2	12.5	18.1	37.6	54.1	39 862	39 502	-0.9	4.7
Boston	19.5	28.4	16.7	14.9	24.0	12.7	11.1	9.9	10.6	31.8	51.9	589 141	617 668	4.8	9.0
Braintree Town	2.8	16.5	22.8	7.2	11.3	16.2	14.2	12.8	15.5	39.9	49.3	33 698	35 726	6.0	4.4
Brockton	11.4	28.7	23.9	10.5	15.1	12.3	13.8	12.3	12.0	35.2	51.5	94 304	93 763	-0.6	2.0
Cambridge	8.5	25.1	10.5	19.0	28.2	13.1	8.0	8.7	12.6	31.5	49.8	101 355	105 201	3.8	5.2
Chelsea	72.2	44.9	27.3	10.2	17.9	15.3	13.1	7.2	8.9	31.9	49.2	35 080	35 177	0.3	12.9
Chicopee	21.0	9.1	20.9	8.2	15.9	10.9	13.9	15.1	15.1	38.6	51.3	54 653	55 298	1.2	1.3
Everett	21.4	43.8	22.2	11.6	15.4	17.4	12.0	11.2	10.3	35.9	50.5	38 037	41 667	9.5	11.2
Fall River	10.2	16.6	18.2	9.8	17.0	12.1	15.7	13.7	13.4	39.3	51.2	91 938	88 857	-3.4	0.1
Fitchburg	24.0	9.9	25.3	12.8	13.9	12.5	11.8	10.2	13.5	34.0	51.0	39 102	40 318	3.1	0.2
Franklin Town	1.9	6.9	26.7	4.9	7.3	19.0	14.5	13.5	14.1	42.1	51.6	29 560	31 633	7.0	4.8
Gloucester	3.0	8.9	15.6	9.2	8.7	10.7	13.8	22.6	19.4	49.9	53.0	30 273	28 789	-4.9	3.5
Haverhill	22.4	8.1	24.5	5.4	15.0	14.7	15.3	12.7	12.4	37.7	49.8	58 969	60 879	3.2	3.3
Holyoke	49.1	5.7	25.3	8.3	14.1	13.1	12.7	11.4	15.2	36.3	50.2	39 838	39 880	0.1	1.0
Lawrence	78.7	36.4	26.5	12.9	16.1	11.8	13.5	9.1	10.1	30.8	53.3	72 043	76 380	6.0	5.0
Leominster	15.3	8.9	24.3	8.2	13.5	13.2	13.7	12.3	14.9	37.7	54.2	41 303	40 759	-1.3	2.2
Lowell	20.0	30.2	22.4	13.9	16.0	12.9	13.6	12.4	9.0	33.4	50.8	105 167	106 519	1.3	3.8
Lynn	36.0	32.3	24.5	10.6	15.1	15.8	11.4	11.7	10.8	34.8	51.8	89 050	90 329	1.4	2.6
Malden	5.2	41.4	19.7	7.5	21.3	13.9	12.8	10.2	14.7	36.5	51.2	56 340	59 463	5.5	3.1
Marlborough	13.2	27.4	23.3	10.2	13.1	12.2	18.0	11.1	12.0	38.0	51.3	36 255	38 499	6.2	1.9
Medford	10.2	26.1	17.9	10.4	16.8	12.0	15.5	12.3	15.2	38.0	53.7	55 765	56 164	0.7	3.5
Melrose	3.2	12.6	21.8	6.3	11.0	9.3	16.5	12.4	22.6	45.8	52.0	27 134	26 987	-0.5	5.6
Methuen Town	23.5	19.9	21.4	9.7	10.3	13.8	15.5	13.0	16.4	40.9	51.9	43 789	47 252	7.9	0.0
New Bedford	19.3	20.0	21.3	10.8	13.3	12.2	13.1	13.6	15.7	38.6	53.9	93 768	95 066	1.4	4.6
Newton	5.4	24.4	21.3	11.8	10.0	10.7	15.5	12.9	17.7	42.3	52.7	83 829	85 119	1.5	-0.2
Northampton	9.1	5.4	18.4	17.3	10.9	11.3	13.1	13.4	15.7	38.3	54.3	28 978	28 549	-1.5	2.4
Peabody	8.6	15.1	17.2	9.8	14.0	10.3	11.5	16.7	20.6	43.8	51.9	48 129	51 251	6.5	-4.2
Pittsfield	6.3	7.2	19.1	7.8	14.5	11.9	13.3	14.6	18.9	42.7	51.2	45 793	44 737	-2.3	1.5
Quincy	2.7	35.2	16.2	7.9	18.1	12.6	14.4	14.4	16.4	41.0	52.9	88 025	92 266	4.8	2.7
Revere	23.4	37.3	16.4	7.4	16.4	14.0	15.1	14.3	16.4	41.7	48.7	47 283	51 737	9.4	4.3
Salem	21.0	15.7	18.1	15.4	17.4	13.6	14.4	8.9	12.3	34.6	52.4	40 407	41 340	2.3	7.4
Somerville	10.9	27.7	9.5	15.2	34.5	13.2	9.4	8.3	10.0	31.0	48.9	77 478	75 725	-2.3	0.6
Springfield	44.8	10.5	26.5	13.7	14.3	11.1	11.3	11.2	11.9	31.8	51.6	152 082	153 195	0.7	1.7
Taunton	6.8	13.0	22.3	7.7	14.3	12.5	15.0	14.1	14.1	39.9	50.4	55 976	55 874	-0.2	3.9
Waltham	11.0	27.2	13.0	16.8	20.9	11.8	11.7	11.4	14.5	34.8	50.2	59 226	60 628	2.4	9.7
Watertown Town	11.7	19.3	18.4	5.2	20.6	15.3	12.3	14.3	13.9	38.8	54.2	32 986	31 914	-3.2	1.1
Westfield	7.1	8.6	16.0	18.6	9.6	10.9	12.9	15.8	16.2	39.3	54.2	40 072	41 094	2.6	0.5
West Springfield Town	9.1	13.4	20.7	7.6	10.7	15.0	13.7	17.1	15.1	42.6	52.9	27 899	28 391	1.8	4.1
Weymouth Town	3.0	8.4	16.8	6.9	17.3	10.3	13.4	15.3	20.1	43.2	53.5	53 988	53 762	-0.4	3.5
Woburn	1.6	21.4	17.9	8.7	17.5	15.3	10.7	17.0	12.9	39.0	47.1	37 258	38 134	2.4	1.9
Worcester	21.1	20.0	18.7	15.2	16.2	11.9	14.1	10.6	13.2	34.9	50.8	172 648	180 983	4.8	1.9
MICHIGAN	4.9	6.6	22.3	9.9	12.3	11.8	13.9	14.0	15.8	39.7	50.8	9 938 444	9 884 129	-0.5	0.4
Allen Park	10.1	4.2	19.6	9.3	13.0	11.9	12.5	17.3	16.5	41.5	52.0	29 376	28 210	-4.0	-3.5
Ann Arbor	5.0	17.7	12.3	30.8	17.8	9.0	8.4	9.2	12.5	28.1	49.8	114 024	113 961	-0.1	6.0
Battle Creek	7.0	5.0	24.4	9.3	14.5	13.1	11.5	14.1	13.1	36.5	52.2	53 364	52 346	-1.9	-1.6
Bay City	10.5	2.8	22.1	10.4	14.6	11.4	13.8	14.0	13.6	37.1	52.5	36 817	34 932	-5.1	-4.1
Burton	2.2	1.4	23.6	11.0	13.7	10.6	14.4	12.4	14.3	37.2	54.2	30 308	29 999	-1.0	-4.5
Dearborn	3.7	25.1	28.5	9.9	13.8	12.0	12.6	11.3	11.8	33.5	51.2	97 775	98 146	0.4	-3.8
Dearborn Heights	3.4	22.2	25.6	11.4	11.9	12.3	12.6	11.6	14.5	35.9	49.4	58 264	57 774	-0.8	-3.5
Detroit	8.0	5.9	25.3	10.9	14.1	11.8	12.7	12.6	12.7	34.8	52.8	951 270	713 862	-25.0	-5.8
East Lansing	4.8	14.3	8.7	62.9	8.9	4.4	2.6	4.7	7.9	21.3	51.6	46 525	48 557	4.4	0.6
Eastpointe	1.2	2.3	26.4	10.8	13.6	10.7	16.0	13.2	9.4	34.2	54.6	34 077	32 442	-4.8	0.7
Farmington Hills	2.5	22.2	22.2	6.3	13.7	12.2	13.2	14.0	18.5	42.1	53.9	82 111	79 740	-2.9	1.7
Flint	2.6	2.2	25.5	9.8	14.2	12.1	12.8	13.6	11.9	35.3	50.2	124 943	102 399	-18.0	-4.9
Garden City	5.4	5.1	20.0	12.2	13.9	14.5	14.0	13.7	11.7	38.9	45.4	30 047	27 692	-7.8	-3.5
Grand Rapids	16.0	9.8	22.7	12.6	19.3	12.6	10.1	11.2	11.5	32.1	51.0	197 800	188 114	-4.9	4.4
Holland	28.5	11.7	25.4	17.1	12.1	10.1	9.3	9.4	16.7	32.0	55.8	35 048	33 117	-5.5	1.3
Inkster	0.5	4.2	22.8	7.9	15.2	14.3	12.2	11.5	16.1	38.9	47.2	30 115	25 366	-15.8	-3.6
Jackson	4.2	1.7	31.4	9.7	15.8	14.0	10.0	10.6	8.3	31.9	50.1	36 316	33 531	-7.7	-1.8
Kalamazoo	5.4	4.6	19.7	27.5	13.7	10.7	7.6	10.4	10.3	26.4	51.1	77 145	74 262	-3.7	2.3
Kentwood	10.5	17.2	21.4	12.2	15.3	11.8	13.0	12.7	13.6	35.8	51.3	45 255	48 707	7.6	6.1
Lansing	12.5	7.3	23.2	13.6	17.7	12.1	11.4	11.1	10.8	31.4	52.4	119 128	114 299	-4.1	1.5
Lincoln Park	20.6	6.6	24.8	9.3	16.3	13.0	13.4	10.6	12.5	34.8	51.6	40 008	38 144	-4.7	-3.7
Livonia	1.9	7.6	18.0	7.7	10.9	10.1	17.6	16.5	19.1	47.4	52.1	100 545	96 942	-3.6	-3.0
Madison Heights	2.4	24.2	22.1	9.8	16.7	14.6	12.8	10.2	13.8	36.0	58.0	31 101	29 694	-4.5	1.3
Midland	3.6	6.8	19.2	9.7	14.6	10.3	12.8	15.7	17.8	41.3	51.1	41 685	41 875	0.5	0.5
Mount Pleasant	4.6	6.0	9.8	49.0	11.3	6.6	5.9	7.5	10.0	22.6	52.3	25 946	26 016	0.3	1.1
Muskegon	6.8	1.9	20.6	12.1	15.3	12.1	14.6	11.6	13.6	36.9	45.5	40 105	38 403	-4.2	-0.1
Novi	2.7	24.0	22.7	8.0	13.2	12.7	16.4	15.2	11.7	39.5	49.9	47 386	55 224	16.5	7.2

1. May be of any race.

Table D. Cities — Households, Group Quarters, Crime, and Education

City	Households, 2015				Persons in group quarters, 2010				Serious crimes known to police,[2] 2014				Educational attainment, 2015		
			Percent			Institutional			Total		Rate[3]			Attainment[4] (percent)	
	Number	Persons per house-hold	Female family house-holder[1]	One-person	Total	Total	Persons in nursing facilities	Non-institu-tional	Number	Rate[3]	Violent	Property	Population age 25 and older	High school graduate or less	Bachelor's degree or more
	27	28	29	30	31	32	33	34	35	36	37	38	39	40	41
MASSACHUSETTS— Cont'd															
Beverly	15 975	2.37	10.3	33.1	2 514	533	369	1 981	552	1 346	190	1 155	27 398	25.8	47.7
Boston	261 492	2.38	16.0	37.3	46 214	6 697	3 280	39 517	22 018	3 365	726	2 639	457 625	35.2	46.6
Braintree Town	14 052	2.63	12.3	28.3	545	524	514	21	890	2 401	237	2 164	26 253	35.7	38.4
Brockton	32 494	2.88	22.0	32.9	1 768	1 088	790	680	3 900	4 130	1 052	3 079	62 495	50.9	18.1
Cambridge	45 569	2.06	6.2	38.5	17 102	324	277	16 778	2 912	2 691	279	2 412	77 884	13.6	78.5
Chelsea	12 709	3.04	22.8	32.1	682	570	570	112	1 483	3 862	1 112	2 750	24 629	67.0	16.9
Chicopee	22 719	2.44	15.5	32.4	1 155	341	231	814	1 693	3 032	385	2 647	40 233	49.8	17.8
Everett	15 008	3.05	20.2	25.2	191	150	150	41	1 045	2 410	404	2 006	30 505	59.5	16.8
Fall River	39 495	2.21	17.3	39.7	1 735	1 071	994	664	3 229	3 632	1 167	2 464	63 848	61.7	13.5
Fitchburg	14 482	2.67	13.7	28.5	2 538	669	356	1 869	1 491	3 682	815	2 867	25 110	54.4	19.8
Franklin Town	12 673	2.53	8.3	28.0	875	79	72	796	110	335	15	320	22 679	20.4	56.4
Gloucester	13 058	2.26	9.4	31.8	450	230	216	220	331	1 118	307	810	22 383	37.8	37.7
Haverhill	24 043	2.56	15.6	31.0	1 300	671	618	629	1 839	2 940	699	2 241	43 993	37.6	30.7
Holyoke	14 968	2.63	26.7	27.9	1 385	1 086	934	299	2 643	6 552	967	5 586	27 016	52.8	20.3
Lawrence	24 885	3.17	31.0	23.6	902	542	310	360	2 897	3 706	1 094	2 612	48 622	67.9	9.7
Leominster	15 814	2.60	20.2	23.3	327	251	224	76	1 442	3 502	658	2 844	28 074	45.2	28.6
Lowell	37 880	2.80	18.6	29.2	4 346	1 112	1 101	3 234	3 399	3 098	546	2 552	70 623	54.5	22.1
Lynn	32 635	2.81	18.2	29.6	835	284	263	551	2 999	3 255	777	2 478	59 970	52.8	19.5
Malden	23 056	2.63	11.3	30.7	373	116	116	257	1 327	2 178	359	1 819	44 466	39.7	36.3
Marlborough	15 155	2.59	16.7	27.1	661	286	253	375	829	2 086	340	1 746	26 458	35.1	39.2
Medford	22 171	2.48	9.2	30.6	1 959	479	465	1 480	957	1 663	184	1 479	41 169	34.2	45.2
Melrose	12 414	2.23	8.5	40.3	267	229	223	38	296	1 059	111	948	20 128	25.3	53.8
Methuen Town	17 595	2.79	10.2	26.2	420	277	232	143	883	1 804	194	1 610	34 236	41.8	29.6
New Bedford	38 826	2.39	19.1	38.7	1 966	1 415	1 196	551	4 564	4 786	1 258	3 527	64 468	60.5	17.3
Newton	29 902	2.71	9.9	21.6	7 103	483	474	6 620	811	912	68	845	59 400	13.2	76.6
Northampton	10 515	2.36	11.0	34.9	3 156	846	527	2 310	825	2 898	464	2 435	18 363	19.5	62.8
Peabody	20 933	2.48	9.8	32.4	520	397	389	123	1 028	1 963	267	1 696	38 376	43.4	33.4
Pittsfield	19 634	2.15	17.3	33.6	1 184	894	501	290	1 539	3 506	444	3 062	31 678	44.4	24.9
Quincy	38 674	2.39	8.8	35.8	1 400	729	698	671	1 894	2 014	419	1 595	71 055	37.5	40.9
Revere	19 446	2.73	16.1	24.7	280	228	228	52	1 389	2 553	557	1 996	40 680	59.3	18.3
Salem	18 101	2.26	15.2	36.8	1 770	167	156	1 603	1 311	3 060	359	2 700	28 492	35.1	39.5
Somerville	31 837	2.43	7.1	27.4	2 269	37	22	2 232	1 437	1 801	267	1 534	60 528	25.3	60.1
Springfield	53 030	2.81	26.3	31.7	5 677	954	553	4 723	7 585	4 933	1 091	3 842	92 173	55.6	17.5
Taunton	22 184	2.53	18.1	26.8	784	574	406	210	845	1 502	371	1 130	39 747	49.8	21.4
Waltham	22 677	2.47	6.8	30.0	6 686	308	287	6 378	872	1 390	196	1 194	44 519	29.1	50.3
Watertown Town	15 001	2.28	7.4	36.3	234	104	0	130	470	1 409	93	1 316	26 224	18.9	67.2
Westfield	15 820	2.43	10.7	31.8	2 976	359	294	2 617	618	1 495	208	1 287	27 291	34.7	36.5
West Springfield Town	13 291	2.15	11.6	44.5	170	120	120	50	1 414	4 915	431	4 484	20 559	40.5	28.1
Weymouth Town	24 472	2.27	9.6	37.2	460	373	373	87	812	1 450	239	1 211	42 705	36.0	35.5
Woburn	15 154	2.59	8.0	25.7	323	238	238	85	586	1 487	180	1 307	29 008	34.3	40.8
Worcester	70 553	2.43	15.6	38.2	12 152	2 093	1 845	10 059	7 380	4 027	965	3 063	122 089	46.7	28.2
MICHIGAN	3 858 532	2.51	12.3	29.5	229 068	109 867	42 473	119 201	244 895	2 471	427	2 044	6 728 347	39.3	27.8
Allen Park	10 566	2.58	16.1	24.7	171	138	132	33	610	2 214	189	2 025	19 512	37.7	26.8
Ann Arbor	48 803	2.17	6.2	37.6	11 840	78	61	11 762	2 410	2 046	166	1 881	66 632	11.4	73.9
Battle Creek	20 828	2.42	16.4	36.7	1 399	862	228	537	2 835	4 630	786	3 845	34 236	46.5	21.3
Bay City	13 831	2.42	17.0	37.0	515	180	0	335	1 187	3 460	531	2 929	22 885	48.6	12.9
Burton	11 335	2.53	20.3	30.4	111	0	0	111	1 360	4 690	476	4 214	18 818	47.1	16.6
Dearborn	31 183	3.04	11.0	29.5	226	195	180	31	3 482	3 650	359	3 292	58 590	38.7	28.4
Dearborn Heights	19 535	2.85	11.2	30.5	602	504	344	98	1 423	2 525	380	2 145	35 344	46.8	20.5
Detroit	255 580	2.60	28.4	39.2	14 759	6 541	3 365	8 218	46 617	6 808	1 990	4 819	432 410	52.8	14.2
East Lansing	13 978	2.35	4.8	37.2	15 701	193	193	15 508	839	1 728	284	1 444	13 697	10.7	71.5
Eastpointe	11 981	2.71	24.5	29.1	21	0	0	21	1 295	3 963	826	3 137	20 526	42.8	15.3
Farmington Hills	33 505	2.41	8.1	32.2	693	319	251	374	1 085	1 328	116	1 212	58 136	20.1	52.2
Flint	40 143	2.38	25.4	37.1	3 193	988	85	2 205	5 588	5 635	1 709	3 926	63 607	52.0	11.8
Garden City	10 533	2.55	10.0	32.0	54	0	0	54	443	1 639	215	1 424	18 257	47.8	11.2
Grand Rapids	73 488	2.56	14.3	34.5	8 260	3 298	2 011	4 962	6 555	3 390	714	2 675	126 174	37.1	33.6
Holland	11 510	2.64	16.9	28.9	2 723	283	273	2 440	1 149	3 421	426	2 995	19 420	38.0	31.2
Inkster	10 038	2.42	25.7	39.3	230	18	3	212	1 070	4 324	1 229	3 096	17 078	55.3	16.2
Jackson	12 178	2.66	23.3	34.4	773	468	263	305	1 727	5 170	895	4 275	19 489	55.3	17.0
Kalamazoo	29 040	2.36	15.5	37.0	7 462	1 126	489	6 336	3 791	4 998	1 165	3 832	40 114	28.9	36.0
Kentwood	21 244	2.40	15.4	32.6	395	246	114	149	1 651	3 262	358	2 904	34 068	36.7	33.7
Lansing	47 338	2.39	16.1	40.3	1 181	273	120	908	4 865	4 271	1 119	3 153	72 028	38.9	26.0
Lincoln Park	14 378	2.57	17.1	33.8	64	13	0	51	1 428	3 846	587	3 259	24 396	60.7	8.0
Livonia	36 943	2.52	10.2	25.3	1 366	791	764	575	1 899	2 002	125	1 877	70 300	31.1	34.3
Madison Heights	11 280	2.66	13.9	31.5	156	149	149	7	779	2 566	231	2 335	20 582	56.1	17.6
Midland	17 380	2.35	11.7	30.8	1 159	489	352	670	598	1 415	118	1 297	29 918	29.4	43.3
Mount Pleasant	8 125	2.45	12.5	34.7	6 365	442	286	5 923	557	2 124	248	1 876	10 743	34.2	46.3
Muskegon	14 048	2.34	19.2	32.3	5 199	4 459	426	740	2 077	5 619	822	4 797	25 831	51.8	14.5
Novi	22 952	2.54	4.3	27.5	360	316	316	44	899	1 533	78	1 454	40 673	16.1	61.5

1. No spouse present.   2. Data for serious crimes have not been adjusted for underreporting. This may affect comparability between geographic areas and over time.   3. Per 100,000 population estimated by the FBI.   4. Persons 25 years old and over.

Table D. Cities — Income, Poverty, and Housing

City	Money income, 2015					Housing units, 2010			Occupied housing units 2015				
	Households			Families					Owner-occupied			Renter-occupied	
	Median income	Percent with income of $200,000 or more	Percent with income of less than $25,000	Total Families	Percent with income below poverty	Total	Percent change, 2000–2010	Vacant units for sale or rent[2]	Total	Percent	Median value[3] (dollars)	Percent	Median rent (dollars)
	42	43	44	45	46	47	48	49	50	51	52	53	54
MASSACHUSETTS— Cont'd													
Beverly	62 438	10.3	12.5	9 026	6.4	16 641	2.2	791	15 975	61.5	393 800	38.5	1 212
Boston	58 263	9.3	23.0	124 696	17.0	272 481	8.2	19 782	261 492	34.1	453 000	65.9	1 423
Braintree Town	85 067	9.1	12.7	NA	NA	14 302	10.7	566	14 052	69.2	397 800	30.8	1 289
Brockton	43 206	1.3	22.6	20 143	16.0	35 552	2.1	2 249	32 494	49.7	230 600	50.3	950
Cambridge	89 847	16.3	15.7	20 036	8.3	47 291	5.7	3 259	45 569	38.8	665 000	61.2	1 871
Chelsea	41 998	1.7	22.9	7 873	12.3	12 621	2.3	790	12 709	26.9	310 600	73.1	1 196
Chicopee	50 927	1.7	19.6	14 178	9.8	25 140	2.9	1 401	22 719	57.0	172 000	43.0	884
Everett	51 935	1.9	10.4	9 957	11.0	16 715	5.1	1 172	15 008	31.9	354 300	68.1	1 294
Fall River	39 547	1.9	31.3	20 230	17.1	42 750	2.1	4 293	39 495	33.2	233 000	66.8	739
Fitchburg	57 022	2.6	18.8	8 906	16.4	17 117	7.0	1 952	14 482	53.1	171 400	46.9	895
Franklin Town	112 960	20.2	5.6	NA	NA	11 394	10.3	399	12 673	76.8	405 100	23.2	1 190
Gloucester	61 127	6.1	14.4	8 188	5.7	14 557	4.3	2 071	13 058	62.9	382 500	37.1	981
Haverhill	59 854	5.1	15.6	15 029	9.3	25 657	8.1	1 507	24 043	57.6	277 400	42.4	1 064
Holyoke	43 792	3.0	30.8	9 769	27.7	16 384	1.1	1 023	14 968	45.0	188 100	55.0	821
Lawrence	36 969	0.6	30.4	16 885	23.6	27 137	6.0	1 956	24 885	31.0	254 800	69.0	1 073
Leominster	57 001	3.8	16.1	10 651	14.5	17 873	5.3	1 106	15 814	57.5	226 100	42.5	877
Lowell	47 727	1.5	23.6	23 298	15.0	41 431	5.0	2 961	37 880	38.4	242 600	61.6	1 068
Lynn	49 332	2.6	23.3	20 877	15.7	35 776	3.1	2 466	32 635	42.3	272 800	57.7	1 125
Malden	56 662	3.2	20.4	14 091	8.1	25 161	6.5	1 488	23 056	39.8	355 700	60.2	1 300
Marlborough	79 944	8.6	10.1	9 742	2.4	16 416	10.2	1 021	15 155	62.7	325 400	37.3	1 224
Medford	72 463	8.1	12.7	13 079	7.0	24 046	6.0	1 236	22 171	58.4	457 000	41.6	1 498
Melrose	73 581	9.7	8.6	NA	NA	11 751	4.5	538	12 414	66.4	457 000	33.6	1 249
Methuen Town	74 617	4.1	7.8	12 373	4.2	18 340	8.6	811	17 595	74.5	293 400	25.5	1 212
New Bedford	36 808	1.6	28.4	20 743	17.6	42 933	3.4	4 172	38 826	39.2	212 900	60.8	807
Newton	126 649	32.1	8.5	21 501	1.7	32 648	1.7	1 480	29 902	70.5	809 700	29.5	1 824
Northampton	55 293	8.0	22.6	5 402	15.1	12 728	2.6	728	10 515	55.2	342 700	44.8	1 035
Peabody	53 487	7.9	19.5	13 290	9.6	22 220	17.6	907	20 933	66.6	359 200	33.4	1 138
Pittsfield	43 527	0.9	22.1	12 043	18.5	21 487	0.6	1 834	19 634	56.8	170 700	43.2	827
Quincy	66 415	5.2	17.5	20 865	8.6	42 838	6.8	2 180	38 674	49.6	389 700	50.4	1 279
Revere	50 403	4.4	19.3	12 031	12.5	22 100	9.5	1 646	19 446	48.1	348 600	51.9	1 268
Salem	62 704	1.7	17.2	9 486	15.6	19 130	5.3	1 288	18 101	42.9	332 300	57.1	1 210
Somerville	86 012	8.9	11.6	13 989	7.8	33 720	3.8	1 615	31 837	32.4	555 500	67.6	1 696
Springfield	38 398	1.1	32.3	32 870	23.4	61 706	0.9	4 954	53 030	48.0	146 700	52.0	798
Taunton	63 401	1.6	14.6	14 924	7.5	23 896	4.3	1 564	22 184	60.8	246 600	39.2	982
Waltham	87 403	12.4	10.1	13 256	3.5	24 926	4.4	1 236	22 677	56.2	459 000	43.8	1 528
Watertown Town	95 102	11.2	10.6	7 457	8.4	15 584	3.8	875	15 001	51.7	487 300	48.3	1 771
Westfield	52 027	4.4	14.2	9 341	6.1	16 075	4.1	740	15 820	65.3	222 200	34.7	887
West Springfield Town	46 727	4.5	15.9	NA	NA	12 697	3.6	573	13 291	64.2	214 500	35.8	868
Weymouth Town	69 209	3.7	11.8	13 533	6.1	23 480	4.0	1 045	24 472	61.0	356 100	39.0	1 281
Woburn	70 613	4.7	10.0	9 708	5.8	16 309	6.0	785	15 154	60.0	381 500	40.0	1 409
Worcester	43 572	3.1	26.1	36 604	14.9	74 645	5.5	6 032	70 553	41.2	206 300	58.8	1 014
MICHIGAN	51 084	3.9	18.2	2 479 724	11.1	4 532 233	7.0	659 725	3 858 532	70.4	137 500	29.6	803
Allen Park	60 000	2.4	11.9	7 386	4.0	12 206	-0.4	626	10 566	83.7	107 300	16.3	931
Ann Arbor	55 669	7.1	19.9	21 310	6.3	49 789	5.5	2 729	48 803	42.9	277 500	57.1	1 075
Battle Creek	37 192	1.7	29.0	12 174	15.9	24 277	3.1	3 159	20 828	58.9	84 500	41.1	680
Bay City	31 973	2.0	31.9	7 251	20.8	15 923	-2.1	1 487	13 831	66.6	67 000	33.4	589
Burton	44 862	1.1	25.7	7 483	24.0	13 075	5.9	1 111	11 335	74.3	79 200	25.7	823
Dearborn	51 424	2.3	21.5	20 361	24.6	37 871	-2.8	3 529	31 183	67.6	121 700	32.4	982
Dearborn Heights	46 673	2.2	19.2	12 516	16.9	24 068	0.6	1 802	19 535	73.4	101 900	26.6	1 006
Detroit	25 980	1.0	40.7	141 284	35.5	349 170	-6.9	79 725	255 580	46.6	42 600	53.4	747
East Lansing	30 811	5.1	40.9	4 433	18.9	15 787	3.1	1 013	13 978	31.2	172 700	68.8	832
Eastpointe	46 711	0.8	19.6	7 966	13.8	13 796	-1.2	1 239	11 981	59.8	68 600	40.2	1 065
Farmington Hills	70 393	8.0	12.9	20 751	6.6	36 178	3.8	2 619	33 505	62.9	234 600	37.1	1 005
Flint	25 342	0.7	40.1	22 063	34.9	51 321	-7.5	10 849	40 143	57.1	25 900	42.9	700
Garden City	48 994	0.9	14.3	6 588	7.3	11 616	-0.9	722	10 533	80.9	88 000	19.1	937
Grand Rapids	41 857	2.0	21.8	38 921	15.7	80 619	3.4	8 493	73 488	53.8	122 000	46.2	830
Holland	53 033	3.0	17.8	7 159	11.9	13 212	5.2	1 191	11 510	59.3	134 900	40.7	781
Inkster	35 187	0.9	27.4	5 367	18.0	11 647	-3.0	1 826	10 008	47.5	42 100	52.5	811
Jackson	28 890	1.3	39.6	7 256	36.8	15 457	1.4	2 163	12 178	50.3	65 800	49.7	703
Kalamazoo	36 536	2.9	30.4	13 361	16.0	32 433	2.0	3 292	29 040	44.0	107 000	56.0	670
Kentwood	48 491	2.5	19.5	12 910	11.5	21 584	10.7	1 843	21 244	57.5	136 300	42.5	788
Lansing	37 426	0.2	24.3	22 794	22.2	54 181	1.8	5 731	47 338	50.3	75 800	49.7	738
Lincoln Park	39 639	0.6	27.8	8 924	17.1	16 530	-1.7	1 606	14 378	65.8	64 200	34.2	803
Livonia	72 061	4.4	9.6	26 146	3.3	40 401	4.5	1 687	36 943	85.1	167 200	14.9	975
Madison Heights	45 335	0.0	22.5	7 090	15.1	13 685	0.5	973	11 280	55.6	96 400	44.4	868
Midland	60 338	6.2	18.2	11 092	7.4	18 578	4.7	1 072	17 380	65.1	150 000	34.9	737
Mount Pleasant	32 493	1.3	29.5	3 568	11.0	8 981	0.8	605	8 125	38.5	131 900	61.5	733
Muskegon	32 437	1.7	31.4	8 111	23.7	16 105	0.5	2 138	14 048	49.1	80 900	50.9	654
Novi	99 046	15.3	8.9	15 642	4.2	24 226	23.2	1 968	22 952	69.3	295 700	30.7	1 157

1. Based on population estimated by the American Community Survey.   2. Includes units rented or sold but not occupied.   3. Specified owner-occupied units; $1,000,000 represents $1,000,000 or more   4. 50.0 represents 50 percent or more.   5. 10.0 represents 10 percent or less.

Table D. Cities — Commuting, Computer Access, Migration, Labor Force, and Employment

City	Commuting Percent — Drove alone	Commuting Percent — With Commutes of 30 minutes or more[1]	Computer Access[2] Percent — With a Computer in the house	Computer Access[2] Percent — With Internet Access	Migration, 2015 — Percent who lived in the same house one year ago	Migration — Percent who lived in an other state or county one year ago	Civilian labor force, 2016 — Total	Civilian labor force — Percent change, 2015–2016	Unemployment — Total	Unemployment — Rate[3]	Population age 16 and older — Number	Population age 16 and older — Percent in Labor Force	Population age 16 to 64 — Number	Population age 16 to 64 — Percent who worked full-year full-time
	55	56	57	58	59	60	61	62	63	64	65	66	67	68
MASSACHUSETTS— Cont'd														
Beverly	79.7	40.6	89.6	85.5	85.4	4.8	22 623	-0.1	727	3.2	34 387	69.0	26 947	48.3
Boston	38.6	54.2	87.8	81.2	81.1	9.6	365 197	0.7	12 312	3.4	568 577	69.2	497 706	48.0
Braintree Town	76.4	56.1	92.2	88.3	83.4	7.2	20 334	0.8	696	3.4	29 696	70.0	23 884	59.4
Brockton	77.5	47.4	86.1	78.8	83.2	7.4	46 822	-0.5	2 424	5.2	75 269	68.6	63 855	44.0
Cambridge	28.6	44.9	90.4	85.5	78.4	14.4	64 538	1.0	1 503	2.3	100 634	71.3	86 713	51.0
Chelsea	38.9	54.9	77.0	72.9	89.9	6.1	19 600	0.4	686	3.5	29 159	73.5	25 634	45.7
Chicopee	90.8	20.8	87.1	80.8	86.6	2.9	27 648	-0.6	1 359	4.9	46 261	66.1	37 683	47.4
Everett	49.3	62.8	90.0	80.2	88.4	4.9	25 465	0.4	866	3.4	37 146	73.8	32 400	48.5
Fall River	83.6	30.0	80.3	64.0	84.2	3.4	39 104	-1.1	2 544	6.5	74 121	62.2	62 208	42.7
Fitchburg	80.3	38.9	84.9	73.8	80.7	7.0	19 171	-0.3	976	5.1	31 210	66.9	25 741	49.2
Franklin Town	89.8	63.3	NA	NA	87.4	9.6	17 695	1.0	556	3.1	24 933	71.7	20 265	60.2
Gloucester	84.1	30.5	88.5	78.4	NA	NA	15 455	0.1	747	4.8	25 366	65.0	19 597	52.9
Haverhill	79.8	42.3	92.9	82.5	90.3	2.9	34 084	0.4	1 327	3.9	48 946	71.5	41 167	50.3
Holyoke	82.8	19.9	81.2	68.1	90.8	2.8	16 168	-1.0	948	5.9	31 413	54.2	25 232	41.9
Lawrence	66.3	32.6	73.6	64.6	91.6	4.4	35 634	-0.9	2 468	6.9	61 482	63.8	53 357	41.6
Leominster	79.8	37.5	91.3	83.3	NA	NA	21 800	-0.3	937	4.3	32 632	72.1	26 448	46.7
Lowell	79.7	38.3	80.5	71.5	87.4	4.9	54 407	0.6	2 597	4.8	88 524	63.3	78 595	42.7
Lynn	66.4	50.6	84.9	77.9	84.4	5.3	46 493	0.0	1 926	4.1	71 950	69.8	62 002	51.9
Malden	51.7	64.6	85.8	79.9	83.8	8.7	33 096	0.4	1 132	3.4	50 041	67.0	41 090	49.9
Marlborough	77.8	43.6	94.0	90.1	NA	NA	23 143	-0.2	730	3.2	31 700	75.7	26 919	58.2
Medford	66.1	55.1	90.4	87.4	86.0	8.2	33 251	0.8	1 014	3.0	48 193	67.6	39 470	53.2
Melrose	75.1	50.7	84.6	77.9	85.5	4.7	15 945	0.6	427	2.7	22 563	70.1	16 240	50.2
Methuen Town	88.0	46.7	90.8	87.8	86.0	4.8	26 549	0.3	1 082	4.1	40 727	72.3	32 603	54.6
New Bedford	71.1	27.5	79.0	67.3	86.9	3.5	46 443	-0.7	3 023	6.5	77 359	61.8	62 442	42.0
Newton	70.8	50.2	94.8	93.0	85.6	9.6	46 346	0.7	1 325	2.9	72 328	63.2	56 569	48.0
Northampton	67.1	29.6	89.3	83.3	80.4	7.7	15 879	-0.1	435	2.7	23 671	64.8	19 192	36.7
Peabody	81.7	35.5	82.3	74.7	91.7	4.0	28 548	0.1	993	3.5	44 582	61.1	33 772	48.4
Pittsfield	74.2	12.1	83.1	74.3	91.9	2.0	21 421	-1.8	978	4.6	35 802	66.1	27 609	48.1
Quincy	56.4	62.8	88.3	81.3	86.3	8.4	52 723	0.5	1 863	3.5	80 538	69.1	65 145	49.5
Revere	58.4	58.6	83.0	73.3	88.2	7.1	28 056	0.5	1 040	3.7	45 809	65.0	37 055	50.2
Salem	62.0	45.7	90.3	84.7	84.1	5.0	23 521	-0.2	903	3.8	36 358	73.5	31 081	48.8
Somerville	39.5	58.2	90.0	83.7	73.7	13.7	50 407	0.8	1 208	2.4	73 778	78.1	65 737	58.0
Springfield	76.8	26.8	79.4	64.0	86.3	4.1	62 722	-1.2	4 333	6.9	117 828	60.3	99 523	37.2
Taunton	86.2	48.1	87.1	79.5	88.1	5.2	29 375	-0.1	1 339	4.6	45 503	68.4	37 473	51.0
Waltham	73.7	37.3	88.8	83.5	83.2	9.1	37 123	0.8	1 056	2.8	55 864	70.7	46 659	52.3
Watertown Town	65.9	49.1	95.0	90.5	80.7	9.5	21 299	0.8	527	2.5	28 660	73.7	23 892	59.8
Westfield	89.9	39.2	89.2	83.7	87.1	7.2	20 943	-0.4	907	4.3	35 985	67.4	29 246	48.3
West Springfield Town	85.6	26.1	85.3	75.3	88.6	3.0	14 449	-0.3	604	4.2	23 335	64.3	18 998	49.4
Weymouth Town	83.6	45.8	90.3	84.4	88.5	6.6	30 322	0.6	1 177	3.9	47 284	68.1	36 048	55.3
Woburn	87.7	33.3	94.0	89.5	91.9	3.3	22 537	0.7	724	3.2	33 537	76.1	28 427	53.8
Worcester	76.6	31.2	82.6	72.5	85.6	5.9	90 469	-0.4	3 964	4.4	154 305	60.8	129 842	43.9
MICHIGAN	85.9	33.0	86.2	74.4	85.6	5.5	4 836 760	1.7	237 711	4.9	7 982 332	61.0	6 411 691	45.4
Allen Park	92.2	32.8	89.9	74.7	87.5	2.1	13 888	2.0	575	4.1	22 478	65.7	17 965	51.9
Ann Arbor	57.1	19.6	94.8	88.0	64.3	15.9	63 359	1.9	1 788	2.8	104 600	59.7	89 956	35.2
Battle Creek	84.2	15.1	78.9	69.3	76.9	5.6	23 602	0.5	1 283	5.4	40 683	59.0	33 910	41.8
Bay City	85.9	21.6	81.8	68.3	87.1	4.9	16 330	-0.3	1 105	6.8	27 442	57.5	22 814	40.7
Burton	92.3	24.1	83.3	64.5	87.0	2.4	13 409	0.8	732	5.5	22 876	55.7	18 758	35.1
Dearborn	90.1	24.8	87.4	64.6	85.8	3.2	37 958	2.0	1 580	4.2	70 435	56.7	59 167	37.5
Dearborn Heights	85.6	28.3	88.6	69.3	92.6	2.7	24 635	1.9	1 154	4.7	43 456	56.1	35 299	42.2
Detroit	71.0	36.4	74.7	48.7	84.9	3.2	245 015	1.3	26 720	10.9	524 688	53.0	438 645	30.7
East Lansing	54.5	13.0	93.3	73.9	54.0	28.8	23 835	2.3	697	2.9	44 468	52.2	40 672	14.8
Eastpointe	81.5	46.2	90.3	78.8	81.3	10.0	15 307	2.1	1 184	7.7	25 159	61.9	22 102	42.6
Farmington Hills	92.2	33.3	90.8	84.6	83.9	9.3	43 700	2.5	1 182	2.7	65 430	64.0	50 415	49.8
Flint	74.4	26.6	73.3	53.8	82.5	4.7	34 410	0.3	3 356	9.8	75 799	51.6	64 065	28.0
Garden City	92.4	32.9	92.7	76.1	NA	NA	14 525	2.0	627	4.3	22 177	60.9	19 036	44.0
Grand Rapids	76.9	18.7	86.4	76.3	76.9	7.4	102 989	2.7	4 611	4.5	154 084	68.3	131 641	46.0
Holland	79.3	13.9	84.6	75.4	78.6	9.3	17 572	2.3	653	3.7	26 331	59.0	20 711	42.6
Inkster	88.8	38.2	89.0	56.0	87.4	2.2	8 808	1.5	828	9.4	19 662	54.7	15 702	40.7
Jackson	77.9	17.9	79.3	66.3	78.3	2.9	14 162	1.5	1 102	7.8	23 696	59.3	20 936	37.5
Kalamazoo	78.0	19.2	88.4	79.4	69.5	12.7	37 436	2.2	1 820	4.9	62 621	68.5	54 753	35.5
Kentwood	84.8	22.5	87.0	79.2	80.9	7.8	30 129	2.8	957	3.2	41 726	66.8	34 766	49.5
Lansing	82.5	13.3	84.0	70.9	76.8	8.9	58 621	1.9	3 440	5.9	90 007	66.1	77 672	44.1
Lincoln Park	79.3	28.2	84.3	71.5	NA	NA	16 999	1.9	829	4.9	28 930	58.5	24 292	43.1
Livonia	91.3	32.6	91.4	83.6	92.5	2.7	51 005	2.1	1 440	2.8	80 166	64.5	62 052	52.3
Madison Heights	82.9	33.0	89.9	76.0	72.6	9.9	15 437	2.1	928	6.0	23 828	61.9	19 659	48.2
Midland	89.9	19.8	87.2	80.4	78.1	8.7	21 135	-0.5	774	3.7	34 826	62.3	27 343	47.5
Mount Pleasant	72.0	17.0	93.1	72.7	58.8	17.7	13 038	0.4	595	4.6	23 854	60.9	21 254	26.7
Muskegon	80.4	17.0	78.2	64.8	74.3	10.8	14 195	-0.3	1 248	8.8	31 030	50.6	25 792	34.0
Novi	93.1	47.1	93.8	89.7	87.7	5.8	31 914	2.5	904	2.8	46 776	67.3	39 884	55.8

1. Employed persons. 2. Households. 3. Percent of civilian labor force. 4. Persons 16 years old and over.

Table D. Cities — Construction, Wholesale Trade, and Retail Trade

City	Value of residential construction authorized by building permits, 2016			Wholesale trade,[1] 2012				Retail trade,[2] 2012			
	New construction ($1,000)	Number of housing units	Percent single family	Number of establishments	Number of employees	Sales (mil dol)	Annual payroll (mil dol)	Number of establishments	Number of employees	Sales (mil dol)	Annual payroll (mil dol)
	69	70	71	72	73	74	75	76	77	78	79
MASSACHUSETTS— Cont'd											
Beverly	12 687	29	100.0	41	274	134.9	14.2	139	2 099	690.4	75.2
Boston	826 613	3 348	1.7	517	9 559	7 074.8	716.3	2 161	28 148	7 885.6	807.6
Braintree Town	1 724	12	16.7	62	1 246	1 014.3	92.0	283	5 695	1 394.2	140.3
Brockton	10 480	82	95.1	60	1 117	2 195.0	66.9	331	4 816	1 305.4	128.6
Cambridge	45 526	192	16.1	75	2 383	1 696.9	498.0	455	6 195	1 366.5	153.5
Chelsea	355	2	100.0	83	D	D	D	95	1 884	485.7	43.8
Chicopee	4 083	24	100.0	36	1 193	1 014.4	57.3	158	2 538	728.7	63.1
Everett	12 397	111	9.0	46	1 375	1 194.3	76.1	118	1 880	451.8	43.4
Fall River	5 860	55	94.5	67	1 218	454.9	57.8	284	3 310	811.3	83.8
Fitchburg	2 845	14	100.0	34	292	146.2	13.0	114	1 234	318.6	30.9
Franklin Town	9 939	33	93.9	45	1 609	1 499.3	91.0	106	1 651	413.7	42.4
Gloucester	18 417	49	51.0	47	385	675.1	24.3	129	1 514	344.3	37.0
Haverhill	17 734	100	61.0	48	626	261.0	36.0	146	2 420	677.7	59.5
Holyoke	612	3	100.0	25	483	149.6	23.2	229	4 017	717.2	79.8
Lawrence	2 092	17	64.7	57	1 311	899.2	103.3	196	1 593	486.4	47.3
Leominster	11 692	47	87.2	45	541	290.1	30.7	234	4 584	1 004.1	91.2
Lowell	4 229	28	78.6	58	945	501.5	51.4	225	2 474	725.6	63.0
Lynn	20 128	116	38.8	38	381	402.6	21.4	221	2 345	668.2	65.5
Malden	1 253	11	100.0	36	398	295.8	23.5	133	1 280	330.2	30.2
Marlborough	3 850	27	100.0	79	1 587	1 340.6	120.7	221	3 452	800.8	76.1
Medford	1 433	13	23.1	44	789	301.8	41.7	163	2 317	692.4	61.9
Melrose	16 842	92	5.4	4	D	D	D	57	664	178.2	19.3
Methuen Town	26 828	85	100.0	33	D	D	D	110	2 240	530.3	52.5
New Bedford	1 202	13	69.2	98	1 933	1 299.7	92.6	287	3 185	792.3	71.4
Newton	52 591	167	25.7	102	1 642	1 542.7	136.1	322	4 523	1 111.1	136.8
Northampton	10 893	40	90.0	26	D	D	D	176	2 277	548.9	59.6
Peabody	4 876	20	100.0	59	1 497	5 754.2	116.6	298	5 204	1 256.0	134.2
Pittsfield	240	1	100.0	54	655	284.0	28.6	186	2 985	789.5	73.5
Quincy	12 004	105	11.4	65	1 188	592.7	97.2	234	4 022	1 113.6	107.2
Revere	4 994	33	24.2	25	D	D	D	117	1 717	422.0	35.8
Salem	2 080	12	83.3	36	274	147.9	14.3	164	2 242	469.6	51.4
Somerville	24 030	182	1.6	39	489	246.5	25.9	183	3 203	759.4	74.0
Springfield	18 924	79	100.0	105	1 487	1 386.7	90.4	468	5 777	1 384.6	134.6
Taunton	11 795	70	92.9	59	2 147	1 566.7	127.8	220	3 261	718.4	76.7
Waltham	16 659	50	60.0	94	D	D	D	232	3 100	1 041.0	97.7
Watertown Town	46 405	314	9.6	31	391	146.2	20.1	144	2 660	889.9	84.5
Westfield	4 952	23	91.3	43	1 006	1 897.0	45.0	123	1 944	450.2	43.8
West Springfield Town	2 957	14	85.7	58	830	295.0	44.8	194	3 483	1 249.9	105.2
Weymouth Town	73 793	382	17.8	51	343	386.3	19.0	198	2 472	757.5	74.1
Woburn	17 423	47	87.2	201	4 360	2 476.5	299.1	185	3 843	1 053.8	112.2
Worcester	13 285	84	100.0	178	2 454	1 098.5	118.1	564	7 853	1 991.5	198.9
MICHIGAN	0	0	0.0	9 392	132 490	115 704.9	7 474.6	34 858	441 190	119 302.0	10 527.3
Allen Park	0	0	0.0	15	145	113.7	7.8	110	1 877	387.3	37.8
Ann Arbor	9 169	25	100.0	77	452	227.3	27.9	507	8 042	1 758.5	184.5
Battle Creek	2 779	9	100.0	31	440	468.0	21.3	247	3 200	796.6	70.2
Bay City	0	0	0.0	36	614	222.7	22.1	145	1 187	251.0	27.4
Burton	10 225	62	93.5	24	723	162.7	44.1	153	2 299	505.4	52.4
Dearborn	10 069	36	100.0	140	1 314	1 896.2	82.7	539	6 554	1 568.3	147.9
Dearborn Heights	2 940	8	100.0	44	157	69.3	7.1	181	1 602	400.2	33.3
Detroit	36 149	409	6.1	409	7 378	7 269.3	430.5	2 092	11 850	3 196.3	251.5
East Lansing	842	7	100.0	8	45	29.6	3.1	85	1 293	303.8	24.7
Eastpointe	0	0	0.0	14	47	9.6	1.2	126	1 120	304.3	35.7
Farmington Hills	7 702	19	57.9	182	2 605	2 587.7	175.7	298	4 091	1 269.7	118.6
Flint	0	0	0.0	62	885	587.8	37.2	377	3 419	740.2	73.0
Garden City	160	2	100.0	12	D	D	D	103	906	326.1	27.0
Grand Rapids	184 518	1 398	4.9	218	5 550	4 778.9	303.7	545	6 140	1 672.6	164.4
Holland	2 619	14	100.0	36	373	403.2	25.1	158	2 040	571.4	47.2
Inkster	0	0	0.0	5	D	D	D	53	278	74.9	5.5
Jackson	191	1	100.0	58	1 008	615.9	47.2	173	1 735	398.3	41.7
Kalamazoo	6 453	26	76.9	86	1 218	600.9	63.3	271	2 495	586.6	64.1
Kentwood	8 138	64	78.1	128	2 727	1 345.8	152.5	284	4 399	894.9	89.8
Lansing	96 055	507	8.1	107	1 728	2 126.3	82.5	430	6 033	1 623.4	150.3
Lincoln Park	255	2	100.0	10	D	D	D	123	1 315	320.8	29.8
Livonia	8 620	36	100.0	244	3 484	4 012.5	211.0	467	7 544	1 929.3	190.0
Madison Heights	602	5	100.0	107	1 638	1 062.7	88.5	178	3 280	1 059.3	85.0
Midland	12 364	148	37.8	29	219	674.5	13.8	241	3 558	887.7	77.5
Mount Pleasant	1 789	26	23.1	24	292	227.4	10.2	114	2 381	556.0	52.0
Muskegon	3 305	19	100.0	34	808	291.0	37.8	126	1 911	518.1	48.5
Novi	34 341	184	100.0	147	2 514	4 754.7	173.2	355	6 929	1 800.8	168.0

1. Merchant wholesalers except manufacturers' sales branches and offices.   2. Establishments with payroll.

Real Estate, Professional Services, and Manufacturing

City	Real estate and rental and leasing, 2012				Professional, scientific, and technical services,[1] 2012				Manufacturing, 2012			
	Number of establishments	Number of employees	Receipts (mil dol)	Annual payroll (mil dol)	Number of establishments	Number of employees	Receipts (mil dol)	Annual payroll (mil dol)	Number of establishments	Number of employees	Receipts (mil dol)	Annual payroll (mil dol)
	80	81	82	83	84	85	86	87	88	89	90	91
MASSACHUSETTS— Cont'd												
Beverly	40	226	65.8	9.7	175	1 223	238.9	90.9	56	2 099	594.9	156.1
Boston	1 030	10 940	3 760.4	812.7	3 017	57 617	17 290.7	6 428.1	284	6 965	3 334.5	386.6
Braintree Town	73	1 395	247.5	74.4	206	D	D	D	27	1 842	450.2	140.9
Brockton	51	183	48.0	7.8	133	D	D	D	68	2 022	421.8	87.6
Cambridge	159	983	360.7	52.3	892	24 581	7 324.8	3 022.0	68	1 810	464.6	113.9
Chelsea	33	184	26.2	6.5	33	1 405	47.5	25.6	37	1 604	391.5	69.8
Chicopee	43	164	29.6	4.8	47	544	46.8	19.2	70	3 014	938.8	169.4
Everett	23	85	13.8	3.5	31	D	D	D	45	705	151.2	33.6
Fall River	75	292	51.5	11.1	149	D	D	D	133	4 419	894.1	182.1
Fitchburg	29	98	16.1	3.2	46	227	27.2	11.3	58	1 701	509.9	90.9
Franklin Town	29	123	55.0	8.3	106	944	96.4	50.7	55	3 313	4 723.8	197.9
Gloucester	28	D	D	D	83	D	D	D	47	2 248	D	171.1
Haverhill	46	263	51.1	11.6	91	621	81.2	29.0	82	2 653	719.3	132.3
Holyoke	39	316	32.4	11.8	67	D	D	D	63	1 672	353.9	82.6
Lawrence	42	220	43.9	8.8	69	D	D	D	91	4 080	813.6	189.4
Leominster	43	298	52.5	14.5	96	554	77.1	29.0	88	2 714	1 094.8	142.2
Lowell	68	315	64.8	11.6	132	D	D	D	76	3 530	1 396.0	263.6
Lynn	47	222	58.0	8.5	82	D	D	D	36	3 277	D	241.3
Malden	46	174	44.4	8.5	64	300	35.7	15.4	40	1 439	436.5	64.4
Marlborough	51	206	63.9	9.2	198	D	D	D	66	3 867	1 795.8	295.1
Medford	34	148	53.8	11.0	119	497	67.5	32.1	39	450	77.5	23.5
Melrose	20	72	25.3	3.3	75	253	35.9	14.8	9	84	D	4.4
Methuen Town	38	D	D	D	85	374	54.6	17.4	42	1 448	635.2	85.2
New Bedford	81	296	63.8	12.1	160	D	D	D	109	4 990	1 543.5	202.6
Newton	155	2 297	2 336.2	131.9	607	D	D	D	51	685	D	47.9
Northampton	36	108	218.4	3.4	125	D	D	D	27	1 072	527.1	52.0
Peabody	41	393	75.7	16.1	101	1 263	182.3	85.7	58	2 187	1 063.9	159.0
Pittsfield	40	244	27.7	7.7	133	D	D	D	51	2 555	506.3	168.8
Quincy	84	455	91.4	25.9	266	D	D	D	42	593	D	33.0
Revere	18	219	29.4	6.9	46	146	14.2	4.9	12	D	D	D
Salem	42	206	55.0	8.4	167	D	D	D	33	734	133.0	33.9
Somerville	63	267	60.7	12.9	174	D	D	D	53	1 142	375.5	80.2
Springfield	109	658	100.7	25.0	325	D	D	D	98	4 029	1 528.2	237.0
Taunton	36	109	22.0	4.0	101	1 018	163.9	62.1	49	4 336	1 714.7	436.9
Waltham	106	894	257.3	51.8	385	11 201	2 336.7	1 198.6	95	4 122	1 130.4	244.5
Watertown Town	31	183	55.0	11.5	135	D	D	D	46	1 161	363.5	89.8
Westfield	32	144	31.4	5.0	59	640	85.4	34.6	92	3 103	858.0	169.0
West Springfield Town	34	90	18.2	3.4	78	498	75.3	27.3	59	1 657	439.0	81.8
Weymouth Town	46	182	44.7	10.3	120	1 165	207.3	88.8	33	495	177.0	25.2
Woburn	84	859	163.1	50.3	302	D	D	D	131	4 341	2 050.1	347.5
Worcester	152	707	200.3	28.7	419	D	D	D	163	7 061	2 300.6	426.2
MICHIGAN	7 826	48 706	11 974.5	1 806.9	21 532	238 884	34 273.5	15 936.8	12 444	514 058	238 892.4	27 611.4
Allen Park	21	399	37.1	12.9	55	593	77.8	25.3	19	158	17.2	5.1
Ann Arbor	146	1 591	367.8	76.4	634	5 588	925.1	397.5	66	1 132	201.1	53.4
Battle Creek	42	247	38.5	7.5	93	D	D	D	57	7 973	4 180.7	449.3
Bay City	24	113	12.3	2.3	91	650	61.7	29.7	50	1 974	589.5	118.2
Burton	21	98	15.2	3.2	42	240	33.2	7.1	32	334	106.0	15.6
Dearborn	95	D	D	D	267	11 832	664.8	1 048.8	79	9 205	D	660.1
Dearborn Heights	46	D	D	D	75	257	20.1	8.3	24	172	34.3	8.4
Detroit	266	1 293	212.4	45.8	682	15 164	3 821.7	1 259.7	382	17 613	19 668.1	1 008.9
East Lansing	54	D	D	D	129	D	D	D	5	D	D	0.7
Eastpointe	13	49	6.9	1.7	31	D	D	D	14	137	17.6	4.3
Farmington Hills	168	3 544	490.9	133.8	734	D	D	D	88	1 849	495.7	106.3
Flint	67	440	64.4	15.1	134	D	D	D	70	6 444	D	486.1
Garden City	11	D	D	D	20	103	8.8	3.7	18	204	31.2	9.5
Grand Rapids	194	1 027	162.3	43.8	569	D	D	D	293	17 974	7 029.5	968.4
Holland	46	225	51.8	7.0	82	D	D	D	96	7 866	2 614.0	331.6
Inkster	13	D	D	D	11	D	D	D	14	185	37.6	9.1
Jackson	31	150	23.1	4.0	91	D	D	D	92	2 477	709.6	122.5
Kalamazoo	82	669	66.4	17.7	200	D	D	D	107	3 950	1 417.5	215.2
Kentwood	48	254	101.3	10.2	124	1 622	303.9	103.1	122	9 987	2 414.6	441.7
Lansing	94	511	84.1	20.5	240	D	D	D	90	4 856	3 904.7	289.1
Lincoln Park	11	D	D	D	26	237	17.0	6.5	15	178	D	6.3
Livonia	105	607	124.1	21.4	376	D	D	D	251	9 447	3 667.7	504.5
Madison Heights	41	489	100.2	28.3	109	2 800	341.5	147.8	156	3 674	881.6	195.9
Midland	52	242	34.2	8.1	112	D	D	D	47	5 897	3 495.9	454.0
Mount Pleasant	32	980	57.2	24.5	67	D	D	D	24	434	D	18.6
Muskegon	18	121	14.3	2.7	79	D	D	D	63	3 241	931.9	148.9
Novi	81	388	98.6	16.0	314	4 877	715.8	271.8	73	1 726	450.0	99.4

1. Establishments subject to federal tax.

Table D. Cities — Accommodation and Food Services, Arts, Entertainment, and Recreation, and Health Care and Social Assistance

City	Accommodation and food services, 2012				Arts, entertainment, and recreation,[1] 2012				Health care and social assistance,[1] 2012			
	Number of establish-ments	Number of employees	Sales (mil dol)	Annual payroll (mil dol)	Number of establish-ments	Number of employees	Receipts (mil dol)	Annual payroll (mil dol)	Number of establish-ments	Number of employees	Receipts (mil dol)	Annual payroll (mil dol)
	92	93	94	95	96	97	98	99	100	101	102	103
MASSACHUSETTS— Cont'd												
Beverly	115	D	D	D	20	D	D	D	128	D	D	D
Boston	2 276	52 474	4 409.2	1 271.2	215	D	D	D	935	18 605	3 118.9	1 413.4
Braintree Town	124	2 474	142.7	42.4	18	D	D	D	86	2 494	250.8	104.6
Brockton	153	2 206	123.9	36.4	10	166	6.5	1.8	193	5 657	650.7	302.7
Cambridge	466	9 912	784.2	227.4	46	771	164.9	19.5	226	3 649	628.1	254.3
Chelsea	71	746	46.9	11.9	2	D	D	D	35	629	48.9	22.2
Chicopee	115	1 553	79.4	22.2	5	55	4.4	1.1	45	1 055	113.9	43.4
Everett	91	D	D	D	5	109	5.6	1.7	38	D	D	D
Fall River	182	D	D	D	12	120	7.1	1.8	196	5 222	598.4	259.4
Fitchburg	83	1 145	56.0	14.9	3	D	D	D	68	1 217	113.4	45.8
Franklin Town	68	1 532	90.2	24.5	14	D	D	D	54	779	75.9	31.3
Gloucester	117	1 078	72.4	21.0	13	93	12.1	4.1	60	687	65.7	29.6
Haverhill	131	1 829	100.6	28.9	23	551	30.4	10.5	103	2 729	284.2	119.1
Holyoke	92	1 516	77.7	21.2	11	154	5.0	2.0	77	1 518	115.5	58.1
Lawrence	119	D	D	D	4	83	1.9	0.7	82	1 243	149.0	68.2
Leominster	107	2 048	93.9	28.3	16	D	D	D	91	1 667	171.2	69.6
Lowell	218	D	D	D	14	128	8.9	2.5	133	3 122	284.3	143.1
Lynn	140	D	D	D	16	74	3.8	1.2	99	2 137	142.9	73.1
Malden	95	1 129	65.6	19.1	5	D	D	D	81	3 105	759.8	393.0
Marlborough	133	2 397	139.9	39.1	17	374	22.9	6.0	77	1 549	133.4	57.5
Medford	102	1 323	95.0	24.2	12	D	D	D	94	1 788	210.8	94.1
Melrose	40	467	25.4	6.4	6	34	2.2	0.8	74	D	D	D
Methuen Town	104	1 800	96.9	27.4	11	234	10.6	3.6	92	2 434	285.6	124.6
New Bedford	216	D	D	D	17	196	10.9	3.1	137	2 981	245.8	115.8
Newton	191	4 920	381.6	109.6	47	703	86.8	41.7	354	5 904	636.5	291.6
Northampton	105	1 982	92.3	30.0	18	244	11.3	3.2	116	1 464	160.8	76.5
Peabody	141	2 605	154.7	46.5	7	20	2.1	0.4	107	2 241	326.5	148.1
Pittsfield	141	1 849	90.2	26.8	19	236	14.2	3.4	143	1 881	179.7	82.1
Quincy	241	3 168	205.7	55.1	25	252	23.6	6.8	216	5 889	618.3	243.1
Revere	96	1 142	79.0	17.9	8	D	D	D	45	D	D	D
Salem	132	1 707	116.4	31.4	18	D	D	D	101	D	D	D
Somerville	195	2 436	167.1	49.0	16	122	9.6	2.4	83	1 859	219.9	94.5
Springfield	268	4 663	236.2	65.1	15	126	10.0	2.6	301	7 082	910.0	482.5
Taunton	111	D	D	D	6	D	D	D	93	1 312	137.9	60.8
Waltham	304	3 249	244.9	68.9	23	496	33.8	7.2	135	1 854	207.3	102.0
Watertown Town	84	996	61.7	16.6	17	D	D	D	69	764	93.8	34.9
Westfield	78	1 356	61.7	18.4	9	95	3.6	1.1	67	758	74.6	33.8
West Springfield Town	105	2 119	109.8	31.3	9	D	D	D	68	1 694	109.4	58.5
Weymouth Town	102	1 520	73.7	19.1	12	D	D	D	135	D	D	D
Woburn	102	2 048	148.1	39.2	24	346	15.8	4.5	119	3 488	393.7	153.8
Worcester	441	6 201	342.0	95.4	26	420	21.3	7.0	395	12 907	1 671.6	839.6
MICHIGAN	19 491	347 337	17 962.4	4 871.7	2 706	32 268	2 881.5	1 119.9	21 447	270 655	27 434.6	11 943.9
Allen Park	68	1 258	61.4	18.3	8	D	D	D	72	752	78.4	32.4
Ann Arbor	381	8 311	467.1	131.5	37	156	10.6	3.3	307	D	D	D
Battle Creek	140	D	D	D	12	128	4.6	1.3	147	1 939	187.9	82.0
Bay City	102	1 744	59.5	19.7	15	D	D	D	104	1 410	154.2	66.0
Burton	56	1 191	53.5	14.3	8	D	D	D	83	D	D	D
Dearborn	257	4 444	236.5	67.6	18	D	D	D	368	3 186	479.1	179.2
Dearborn Heights	97	1 408	65.6	17.2	5	79	5.2	1.6	94	D	D	D
Detroit	933	20 452	2 237.3	495.8	49	2 577	500.3	295.9	668	21 711	2 848.7	1 101.4
East Lansing	121	2 411	100.0	26.3	5	28	0.9	0.3	109	2 481	410.1	139.5
Eastpointe	47	704	33.1	9.1	5	D	D	D	81	D	D	D
Farmington Hills	175	2 826	137.7	40.1	25	480	16.2	6.2	395	5 861	509.0	236.8
Flint	179	2 260	102.2	25.3	5	D	D	D	148	2 244	254.3	97.4
Garden City	46	740	28.2	7.6	2	D	D	D	73	D	D	D
Grand Rapids	408	8 881	448.6	130.1	56	1 134	38.9	11.2	393	7 651	938.5	470.8
Holland	79	1 893	78.4	24.5	5	178	5.2	1.8	106	1 892	160.2	79.9
Inkster	22	187	13.4	3.1	NA	NA	NA	NA	16	63	4.7	1.5
Jackson	96	1 480	65.6	17.9	9	D	D	D	134	1 613	206.7	111.5
Kalamazoo	210	4 849	194.0	61.6	27	397	17.4	6.2	168	2 775	310.1	160.3
Kentwood	106	2 408	117.2	32.5	16	D	D	D	99	2 708	326.4	158.6
Lansing	233	4 028	181.5	50.1	24	449	82.3	10.9	213	2 226	253.4	123.9
Lincoln Park	67	895	45.1	10.9	4	16	0.8	0.2	45	D	D	D
Livonia	259	5 903	276.8	81.4	23	D	D	D	448	4 931	510.1	217.3
Madison Heights	101	1 743	87.2	23.8	13	116	6.0	1.8	93	1 696	141.7	72.2
Midland	111	2 562	122.9	37.3	14	305	14.1	4.9	166	D	D	D
Mount Pleasant	73	D	D	D	4	D	D	D	103	D	D	D
Muskegon	72	1 276	57.1	16.1	9	201	10.7	3.5	91	D	D	D
Novi	161	3 802	205.2	60.5	20	D	D	D	227	2 509	311.6	114.5

1. Establishments subject to federal tax.

Table D. Cities — Other Services and Government Employment and Payroll

City	Other services[1], 2012 Number of establishments	Number of employees	Receipts (mil dol)	Annual payroll (mil dol)	Government employment and payroll, 2012 Full-time equivalent employees	Total (dollars)	March payroll Percent of total for: Administration, judicial, and legal	Police and Corrections	Fire Protection	Highways and transportation	Health and welfare	Natural resources and utilities	Education and libraries
	104	105	106	107	108	109	110	111	112	113	114	115	116
MASSACHUSETTS— Cont'd													
Beverly	63	329	28.7	8.5	996	4 817 626	4.0	11.2	9.0	4.5	1.8	2.6	66.3
Boston	1 253	9 009	772.9	242.2	19 230	112 444 857	3.5	18.3	12.2	2.2	8.9	3.5	49.1
Braintree Town	91	1 006	75.5	22.8	1 198	6 476 545	2.5	10.2	9.4	2.2	1.8	15.8	58.0
Brockton	146	1 021	74.7	25.7	3 168	15 359 504	2.3	8.6	7.5	1.3	0.8	2.7	75.2
Cambridge	153	1 154	107.3	39.0	5 751	29 806 492	5.4	9.0	6.6	1.8	37.9	3.3	26.6
Chelsea	36	251	36.9	7.1	1 195	6 010 338	2.8	12.8	10.5	1.7	2.0	0.7	68.2
Chicopee	72	406	28.9	9.7	1 968	9 607 115	2.4	8.9	8.8	2.2	1.0	8.2	68.6
Everett	74	439	37.2	11.3	1 148	6 059 197	2.8	14.5	12.3	1.2	2.1	1.4	63.1
Fall River	150	728	56.9	17.6	2 306	10 353 050	2.4	15.4	12.8	3.5	0.6	2.2	61.8
Fitchburg	50	241	23.4	6.3	1 151	5 547 200	3.4	9.4	7.3	2.6	1.4	5.1	70.3
Franklin Town	58	546	44.2	13.5	966	4 884 796	3.9	7.4	6.9	0.9	1.2	3.4	75.4
Gloucester	53	223	18.9	5.7	1 097	5 414 614	3.5	6.3	6.5	1.4	2.1	2.0	78.1
Haverhill	84	417	36.6	12.5	1 832	8 913 896	3.7	7.9	7.8	2.3	3.5	5.7	67.6
Holyoke	46	229	15.1	4.7	1 884	8 334 885	2.7	13.7	8.2	1.9	1.5	16.1	55.4
Lawrence	88	567	48.9	15.2	537	3 239 260	9.3	38.4	19.3	2.8	4.3	18.5	2.0
Leominster	67	278	23.7	6.4	1 158	5 702 455	3.5	8.2	8.6	2.7	4.5	1.1	71.5
Lowell	142	671	60.4	19.1	2 860	17 379 993	21.6	7.8	6.2	1.2	1.9	2.6	57.2
Lynn	98	492	40.5	12.2	3 200	15 232 790	2.0	9.3	9.0	0.6	2.4	2.0	71.9
Malden	96	609	50.6	17.0	1 385	7 796 658	4.0	11.7	8.4	1.5	2.2	1.1	67.0
Marlborough	68	703	100.0	29.9	1 155	5 341 768	2.6	10.8	7.8	2.2	2.8	3.2	68.1
Medford	110	657	57.4	19.1	1 214	5 909 654	4.2	14.6	12.9	2.3	1.5	3.3	61.4
Melrose	42	212	18.3	6.1	763	3 328 642	4.7	9.6	9.5	2.3	3.8	3.1	64.8
Methuen Town	57	326	24.1	8.9	1 087	7 336 774	2.5	10.2	7.0	2.2	1.2	5.3	71.1
New Bedford	137	787	79.6	21.8	2 769	11 838 508	3.4	15.9	8.7	0.5	2.2	2.3	64.5
Newton	178	1 202	106.0	36.3	2 832	16 441 085	4.0	8.3	7.3	3.8	2.0	4.3	68.5
Northampton	60	325	25.5	8.5	1 315	6 640 659	6.9	16.3	15.0	3.3	4.8	8.4	45.1
Peabody	116	626	68.0	15.6	1 445	6 993 068	3.9	10.1	8.5	2.0	3.4	9.6	59.9
Pittsfield	73	363	30.8	10.9	1 418	6 191 800	2.1	11.1	7.7	3.1	2.0	2.3	70.3
Quincy	182	1 019	102.2	29.6	2 107	11 341 562	3.7	14.1	12.3	2.7	1.9	3.4	58.4
Revere	76	312	30.3	7.5	1 148	6 190 389	2.9	10.4	9.9	1.4	2.2	0.9	70.9
Salem	92	548	44.5	13.3	1 293	5 566 047	3.8	10.4	7.7	2.3	1.1	2.1	70.6
Somerville	109	1 376	119.9	44.1	1 637	10 044 072	4.6	10.5	15.6	1.3	3.6	1.4	56.7
Springfield	183	1 829	123.1	43.5	6 400	28 244 315	2.7	10.9	5.2	0.8	1.6	1.8	75.7
Taunton	80	381	28.6	8.7	1 574	7 371 663	2.8	12.1	9.6	1.1	6.5	4.4	62.0
Waltham	135	747	59.8	21.5	1 543	7 799 064	4.9	13.2	11.2	3.6	1.6	2.7	59.4
Watertown Town	77	1 305	112.4	47.4	718	3 483 060	6.4	20.3	14.0	1.6	1.6	4.8	50.1
Westfield	57	288	29.1	10.3	1 493	7 020 504	2.4	7.7	7.1	1.5	0.9	11.5	68.2
West Springfield Town	63	469	44.3	12.1	976	3 909 287	3.2	12.1	9.7	5.8	0.8	0.5	65.8
Weymouth Town	110	532	44.7	13.4	1 151	5 346 322	0.0	0.0	0.0	0.0	0.0	0.0	100.0
Woburn	102	D	D	D	1 052	4 899 436	3.8	10.6	8.5	4.3	1.8	2.5	67.9
Worcester	254	1 668	157.3	46.3	5 736	34 255 682	3.1	10.9	7.3	1.4	1.6	2.9	72.6
MICHIGAN	13 062	75 714	6 509.2	1 982.4	X	X	X	X	X	X	X	X	X
Allen Park	43	278	19.6	4.6	145	695 062	17.1	36.5	23.7	3.5	2.1	12.0	1.1
Ann Arbor	148	945	71.1	25.5	1 014	4 848 561	15.1	39.8	10.1	6.4	0.3	20.8	0.0
Battle Creek	75	D	D	D	520	2 297 856	15.9	27.9	16.4	20.0	2.1	17.3	0.0
Bay City	61	390	30.3	10.7	307	1 423 139	12.6	19.6	15.4	7.2	3.8	41.4	0.0
Burton	55	260	23.3	7.6	88	380 820	19.8	42.5	6.3	13.2	3.7	10.2	0.0
Dearborn	192	864	64.3	17.4	923	3 654 827	12.9	29.4	13.1	4.0	5.7	11.8	4.5
Dearborn Heights	83	282	25.1	6.7	306	1 426 569	13.6	40.6	19.1	3.5	0.6	11.8	3.5
Detroit	609	3 355	261.9	82.4	12 364	57 433 160	8.6	36.8	19.2	8.8	3.7	16.3	1.7
East Lansing	25	167	11.3	3.3	396	1 817 436	16.7	32.0	14.5	2.5	2.2	20.9	4.6
Eastpointe	54	259	22.1	6.3	180	830 736	14.8	39.6	19.5	6.0	0.0	11.0	3.5
Farmington Hills	155	1 573	97.8	33.6	445	2 178 404	16.2	39.5	19.9	10.2	0.0	13.4	0.0
Flint	105	665	52.6	13.9	3 484	16 192 746	3.4	5.1	4.1	1.1	80.7	4.6	0.0
Garden City	51	249	19.2	5.3	125	1 093 459	18.2	37.0	20.6	11.9	0.0	10.8	1.6
Grand Rapids	229	1 640	123.7	40.7	1 502	7 515 829	14.9	31.3	17.1	6.5	4.9	18.7	5.4
Holland	60	528	48.1	16.3	501	2 186 069	19.7	18.0	6.4	11.0	2.5	31.8	8.0
Inkster	15	74	2.7	1.8	210	862 765	16.2	39.6	11.9	3.5	10.7	10.1	0.0
Jackson	55	448	37.4	11.5	317	1 468 468	14.1	26.2	16.9	10.7	9.1	20.9	0.0
Kalamazoo	135	1 028	100.7	33.6	737	3 816 582	9.9	48.7	0.0	14.8	4.0	21.7	0.0
Kentwood	68	759	66.8	26.7	223	1 105 109	17.7	43.8	20.2	4.1	0.4	7.1	0.0
Lansing	145	D	D	D	1 615	8 042 053	9.4	18.0	12.0	4.6	2.5	31.5	0.0
Lincoln Park	60	339	32.7	10.6	136	745 448	11.3	45.2	24.4	3.7	3.5	7.7	0.1
Livonia	212	1 646	201.4	50.7	675	3 250 072	15.0	29.9	18.3	6.5	2.1	12.7	4.9
Madison Heights	86	577	55.1	18.3	168	954 270	18.4	39.5	19.8	4.4	6.9	6.2	3.1
Midland	83	593	47.7	13.7	384	1 817 246	18.5	13.7	13.1	13.3	3.3	24.4	7.5
Mount Pleasant	43	302	15.7	4.7	138	584 882	17.9	28.1	11.5	10.7	3.3	20.6	0.0
Muskegon	43	230	20.5	5.8	249	1 066 412	10.8	37.4	17.3	11.3	4.4	11.2	0.0
Novi	95	941	74.1	26.9	303	1 465 600	14.7	34.8	16.3	10.0	0.9	6.5	8.2

1. Establishments subject to federal tax.

Table D. Cities — **City Government Finances**

City	City government finances, 2012									
	General revenue							General expenditure		
	Intergovernmental			Taxes					Per capita[1] (dollars)	
					Per capita[1] (dollars)					
	Total (mil dol)	Total (mil dol)	Percent from state government	Total (mil dol)	Total	Property	Sales and gross receipts	Total (mil dol)	Total	Capital outlays
	117	118	119	120	121	122	123	124	125	126
MASSACHUSETTS— Cont'd										
Beverly	134.3	32.2	93.2	84.0	2 083	2 032	50	122.1	3 027	262
Boston	3 134.7	946.2	90.8	1 822.2	2 844	2 612	231	3 160.4	4 932	468
Braintree Town	122.1	30.7	98.2	76.9	2 110	2 032	78	126.4	3 467	261
Brockton	341.1	188.9	94.9	118.0	1 255	1 218	36	341.2	3 628	290
Cambridge	1 412.6	295.2	74.5	338.8	3 195	2 843	352	1 310.4	12 357	887
Chelsea	149.1	80.2	94.0	48.9	1 320	1 254	66	146.8	3 958	166
Chicopee	183.1	93.0	88.2	72.3	1 298	1 255	43	183.1	3 289	279
Everett	159.8	65.9	97.2	88.8	2 084	2 072	12	163.2	3 832	25
Fall River	291.2	173.4	87.5	84.8	956	911	46	273.3	3 082	273
Fitchburg	133.3	69.5	95.2	44.8	1 108	1 068	40	123.9	3 067	250
Franklin Town	113.1	39.1	99.7	62.6	1 932	1 864	68	108.1	3 337	214
Gloucester	108.7	22.2	85.3	70.1	2 398	2 265	133	118.1	4 041	621
Haverhill	179.2	72.3	95.2	91.2	1 477	1 436	41	178.9	2 897	125
Holyoke	180.1	108.6	96.0	51.5	1 283	1 249	34	193.1	4 810	387
Lawrence	293.4	219.3	93.9	57.3	741	711	30	270.5	3 497	39
Leominster	137.6	72.2	98.2	57.3	1 401	1 379	22	130.9	3 200	778
Lowell	379.7	222.6	91.4	119.6	1 102	1 055	47	358.5	3 303	268
Lynn	304.3	187.6	95.4	107.6	1 179	1 155	24	313.0	3 429	13
Malden	196.5	94.6	92.6	74.5	1 234	1 215	19	199.3	3 301	386
Marlborough	132.1	30.2	96.1	91.0	2 319	2 265	54	126.8	3 229	96
Medford	142.6	31.8	91.0	94.1	1 650	1 604	46	142.2	2 492	58
Melrose	82.1	18.2	97.0	52.8	1 924	1 914	10	86.2	3 141	285
Methuen Town	133.7	50.8	97.6	70.6	1 469	1 434	35	135.9	2 829	221
New Bedford	342.6	197.7	87.3	103.4	1 091	1 041	50	319.6	3 371	394
Newton	352.9	45.9	82.2	268.4	3 076	2 977	99	348.0	3 989	200
Northampton	93.2	21.7	85.3	47.2	1 647	1 575	72	100.6	3 506	673
Peabody	155.1	38.9	89.5	98.2	1 894	1 799	95	155.3	2 995	158
Pittsfield	156.1	75.8	92.6	70.5	1 592	1 549	43	180.6	4 076	509
Quincy	303.7	68.6	83.6	184.2	1 983	1 919	64	317.7	3 420	279
Revere	167.2	86.7	75.9	74.7	1 396	1 343	53	159.6	2 981	128
Salem	150.4	51.6	89.1	76.8	1 818	1 779	39	149.1	3 528	208
Somerville	214.8	65.2	90.3	115.7	1 489	1 387	102	222.7	2 865	243
Springfield	710.6	501.8	92.6	183.4	1 192	1 136	56	702.0	4 562	459
Taunton	200.1	101.1	96.2	78.0	1 394	1 336	58	198.2	3 540	473
Waltham	215.4	26.2	94.8	161.6	2 606	2 487	119	206.3	3 326	185
Watertown Town	111.0	16.6	95.8	77.8	2 365	2 342	23	108.0	3 282	224
Westfield	141.0	61.2	91.3	63.5	1 541	1 514	27	132.3	3 207	439
West Springfield Town	111.8	41.7	97.5	63.7	2 226	2 135	90	122.2	4 273	802
Weymouth Town	149.6	43.6	97.1	86.4	1 571	1 532	40	133.5	2 426	127
Woburn	134.2	22.5	96.5	94.7	2 436	2 328	108	140.9	3 624	251
Worcester	673.9	351.9	90.1	250.3	1 373	1 328	45	681.7	3 738	461
MICHIGAN	X	X	X	X	X	X	X	X	X	X
Allen Park	38.0	4.5	94.9	19.7	707	622	85	43.2	1 545	192
Ann Arbor	205.6	39.3	54.4	89.8	775	705	70	199.0	1 717	426
Battle Creek	117.1	35.5	38.6	47.3	913	607	16	105.6	2 035	231
Bay City	52.3	16.3	64.9	12.8	371	359	12	52.6	1 522	200
Burton	18.2	5.5	93.6	4.3	148	132	16	18.3	623	116
Dearborn	175.2	29.5	56.1	86.0	888	866	22	163.2	1 685	219
Dearborn Heights	74.1	29.6	29.1	28.0	490	465	25	61.3	1 071	5
Detroit	2 146.1	681.0	63.6	750.8	1 078	381	362	2 248.4	3 227	289
East Lansing	62.4	13.1	74.3	22.1	455	428	27	63.0	1 296	67
Eastpointe	33.6	7.4	68.2	15.1	466	436	30	35.4	1 090	71
Farmington Hills	79.0	13.9	86.1	37.4	463	453	10	81.3	1 007	37
Flint	502.1	117.5	72.0	32.2	321	147	26	538.2	5 357	401
Garden City	29.5	6.1	87.6	10.9	398	370	28	24.0	874	14
Grand Rapids	321.9	89.0	37.4	121.3	637	264	15	325.6	1 709	174
Holland	45.8	12.0	77.2	16.8	504	489	15	51.4	1 542	413
Inkster	43.4	14.9	32.0	13.5	537	526	11	41.5	1 654	64
Jackson	52.5	18.8	34.8	18.5	555	325	11	61.6	1 847	294
Kalamazoo	130.6	43.5	46.0	43.7	580	555	25	121.7	1 617	207
Kentwood	37.6	7.9	86.2	20.9	420	392	28	37.4	753	60
Lansing	199.5	45.8	54.5	68.7	601	343	13	191.2	1 673	175
Lincoln Park	33.8	9.0	78.1	15.8	418	401	17	38.4	1 019	22
Livonia	124.8	25.5	60.0	56.3	586	566	21	115.2	1 199	38
Madison Heights	38.4	6.7	70.4	20.2	674	650	24	43.5	1 448	121
Midland	69.8	10.8	85.7	36.7	874	857	17	61.2	1 460	164
Mount Pleasant	19.8	5.1	79.3	8.1	309	295	14	19.6	748	41
Muskegon	40.9	9.9	74.7	17.3	468	235	33	46.3	1 248	68
Novi	64.1	7.6	98.2	31.7	557	530	26	58.8	1 034	128

1. Based on population estimated as of July 1 of the year shown.

Table D. Cities — **City Government Finances**

City					City government finances, 2012 (cont.)					
					General expenditure (cont.)					
					Percent of total for:					
	Public welfare	Highways	Parking facilities	Education	Health and hospitals	Police protection	Sewerage and sanitation	Parks and recreation	Housing and community development	Interest on debt
	127	128	129	130	131	132	133	134	135	136
MASSACHUSETTS— Cont'd										
Beverly	0.3	3.4	0.0	51.9	0.4	5.3	7.8	1.4	0.2	2.4
Boston	1.5	1.6	0.1	34.9	9.0	10.0	7.1	2.1	3.3	1.8
Braintree Town	0.2	4.6	0.0	56.1	0.2	6.0	1.8	2.0	0.0	0.6
Brockton	0.3	2.4	0.1	69.7	0.2	5.1	4.9	0.4	0.7	2.6
Cambridge	0.1	0.8	0.1	15.3	59.9	2.3	2.5	1.4	0.1	0.8
Chelsea	0.4	1.5	0.0	55.8	0.0	5.6	1.8	0.1	1.3	0.9
Chicopee	0.5	2.5	0.0	55.4	0.2	5.1	10.9	1.4	1.6	1.4
Everett	0.3	4.8	0.3	53.5	0.9	5.4	1.6	0.1	0.5	1.6
Fall River	1.1	2.7	0.1	60.7	1.7	6.0	7.2	0.5	2.1	2.7
Fitchburg	0.4	3.8	0.1	55.3	0.5	5.0	7.7	0.4	1.1	1.6
Franklin Town	0.2	3.8	0.0	62.7	0.2	4.0	5.2	0.4	0.0	1.5
Gloucester	0.3	1.0	0.0	46.4	0.3	4.3	12.1	0.2	0.8	2.6
Haverhill	0.4	2.6	0.0	57.9	0.5	4.9	6.4	0.2	0.8	1.7
Holyoke	3.6	2.3	0.1	57.6	0.3	6.1	4.9	0.6	1.3	0.8
Lawrence	0.2	1.0	0.1	69.2	0.0	4.2	3.9	0.2	0.5	1.9
Leominster	0.3	5.4	0.0	62.2	0.3	4.8	12.4	0.5	0.4	0.5
Lowell	0.3	1.5	0.8	55.4	0.5	6.0	5.9	0.7	2.2	2.0
Lynn	0.3	2.2	0.3	60.6	0.0	5.4	1.5	0.5	1.5	1.0
Malden	0.1	1.8	0.0	51.9	0.3	4.9	1.7	0.4	2.1	1.9
Marlborough	0.1	6.3	0.0	59.3	0.3	5.4	5.3	0.2	0.3	0.9
Medford	0.2	2.1	0.0	42.8	0.3	7.6	4.1	0.4	1.6	0.9
Melrose	0.5	2.1	0.0	46.0	1.6	4.2	1.7	2.4	0.1	2.2
Methuen Town	0.4	4.2	0.0	68.1	0.5	6.5	5.7	0.1	0.7	1.2
New Bedford	1.1	1.1	0.2	57.4	1.0	6.6	5.2	0.4	1.7	2.7
Newton	0.1	2.9	0.0	59.6	0.6	4.5	3.4	1.2	1.0	2.4
Northampton	0.8	3.6	0.4	37.7	1.9	16.0	5.4	0.3	2.0	2.3
Peabody	0.1	2.7	0.0	56.3	0.7	5.9	2.5	1.9	2.2	0.9
Pittsfield	0.3	5.5	0.6	46.8	0.5	4.6	5.2	1.1	1.2	1.6
Quincy	0.5	2.3	0.0	39.4	0.6	6.9	3.3	0.7	2.0	1.2
Revere	0.7	1.0	0.1	51.2	0.2	5.2	7.3	0.3	0.7	1.4
Salem	0.2	3.0	0.5	53.2	0.3	5.4	2.7	1.9	0.9	1.3
Somerville	0.2	2.5	0.0	35.0	0.5	6.5	3.8	0.4	2.1	1.0
Springfield	0.4	1.8	0.0	65.3	0.2	5.5	1.3	1.2	0.9	1.9
Taunton	4.3	2.3	0.0	50.4	0.4	5.5	8.7	0.5	0.9	1.4
Waltham	0.2	3.7	0.1	36.6	0.4	6.4	4.4	0.7	0.6	1.4
Watertown Town	0.1	3.1	0.0	42.6	0.5	6.9	4.0	0.5	0.0	1.3
Westfield	0.5	3.3	0.0	62.6	1.6	4.9	3.8	1.5	0.2	1.7
West Springfield Town	0.5	8.0	0.0	57.3	1.3	5.5	3.0	0.4	0.7	0.9
Weymouth Town	0.4	2.0	0.0	50.6	0.4	6.9	5.0	0.4	0.7	1.5
Woburn	0.3	2.9	0.0	54.1	0.4	6.0	2.5	0.5	0.0	1.5
Worcester	0.0	3.3	0.2	50.4	0.0	6.0	6.2	0.7	1.5	4.3
MICHIGAN	X	X	X	X	X	X	X	X	X	X
Allen Park	0.0	6.4	0.0	0.0	0.0	14.5	38.3	2.2	0.9	7.5
Ann Arbor	0.0	12.0	16.4	0.0	0.0	13.0	19.6	7.4	7.6	4.1
Battle Creek	0.0	15.2	1.0	0.0	0.0	14.4	15.7	5.1	11.4	2.5
Bay City	0.0	12.0	0.0	0.0	0.0	11.7	20.5	1.6	9.1	4.9
Burton	0.0	14.3	0.0	0.0	2.0	21.7	30.0	0.2	0.0	1.5
Dearborn	0.0	11.9	0.7	0.0	0.0	20.4	25.1	8.8	1.7	3.2
Dearborn Heights	0.0	9.4	0.0	0.0	0.0	18.9	29.2	1.7	1.5	3.4
Detroit	0.3	4.1	0.2	2.6	3.2	16.5	19.9	1.5	2.3	14.4
East Lansing	0.0	8.7	6.6	0.0	0.1	13.6	17.4	9.9	5.3	4.2
Eastpointe	0.0	7.5	0.0	0.0	0.0	24.2	26.9	3.0	5.4	0.5
Farmington Hills	0.0	12.0	0.0	0.0	0.0	23.0	18.5	10.0	0.4	1.0
Flint	0.0	2.0	0.0	0.0	71.4	4.3	4.8	0.9	4.2	1.0
Garden City	0.0	11.4	0.0	0.0	0.2	16.2	27.1	1.4	0.6	2.6
Grand Rapids	0.0	8.3	1.9	0.0	0.0	14.7	16.6	1.9	16.1	6.7
Holland	0.2	23.5	0.0	0.0	0.6	14.8	25.5	11.0	1.1	2.2
Inkster	0.0	5.5	0.0	0.0	0.0	15.9	18.5	2.0	23.8	3.0
Jackson	0.0	33.1	0.4	0.0	0.0	12.4	10.4	5.3	12.6	2.4
Kalamazoo	0.0	11.0	0.0	0.0	0.0	27.5	24.5	3.5	2.8	2.5
Kentwood	0.0	17.7	0.0	0.0	0.0	26.5	9.2	5.2	0.1	2.3
Lansing	0.0	9.1	3.2	0.0	0.0	16.0	13.6	7.6	1.0	5.1
Lincoln Park	0.0	8.0	0.0	0.0	0.0	21.1	23.4	1.1	2.1	1.9
Livonia	0.0	11.9	0.0	0.0	0.0	19.1	24.0	8.3	8.3	1.5
Madison Heights	0.0	12.4	0.0	0.0	0.0	20.1	32.9	1.9	4.4	0.4
Midland	0.0	14.5	0.2	0.0	0.0	11.9	18.0	11.9	1.8	1.5
Mount Pleasant	0.0	13.1	1.1	0.0	0.0	24.5	10.3	7.8	4.3	1.3
Muskegon	0.0	13.1	0.0	0.0	0.0	19.8	27.3	2.8	7.1	1.1
Novi	0.0	18.7	0.0	0.0	0.0	19.2	17.0	6.8	0.0	4.0

	City government finances, 2012 (cont.)			Climate[2]						
	Debt outstanding			Average daily temperature (degrees Fahrenheit)						
				Mean		Limits				
City	Total (mil dol)	Per capita[1] (dollars)	Debt issued during year	January	July	January[3]	July[4]	Annual precipitation (inches)	Heating degree days	Cooling degree days
	137	138	139	140	141	142	143	144	145	146
MASSACHUSETTS—Cont'd										
Beverly	89.1	2 208	0.0	28.8	72.6	20.4	82.1	45.51	5 704	582
Boston	1 572.5	2 454	245.5	29.3	73.9	22.1	82.2	42.53	5 630	777
Braintree Town	145.9	4 001	8.7	NA	NA	NA	NA	NA	NA	NA
Brockton	242.9	2 583	12.5	27.9	72.1	17.8	83.2	48.25	6 008	529
Cambridge	340.3	3 209	55.5	29.3	73.9	22.1	82.2	42.53	5 630	777
Chelsea	35.1	947	2.0	29.3	73.9	22.1	82.2	42.53	5 630	777
Chicopee	51.4	924	11.0	21.5	68.9	10.4	81.7	48.07	7 312	287
Everett	61.8	1 452	1.4	29.3	73.9	22.1	82.2	42.53	5 630	777
Fall River	271.7	3 064	39.8	28.5	74.2	20.0	83.1	50.77	5 734	740
Fitchburg	74.6	1 846	20.7	24.2	71.9	15.2	81.0	49.13	6 576	548
Franklin Town	55.4	1 710	16.4	NA	NA	NA	NA	NA	NA	NA
Gloucester	137.0	4 689	26.4	28.8	72.6	20.4	82.1	45.51	5 704	582
Haverhill	94.2	1 525	3.0	25.3	72.2	15.6	83.5	46.88	6 435	550
Holyoke	104.5	2 604	16.8	21.5	68.9	10.4	81.7	48.07	7 312	287
Lawrence	148.3	1 917	0.0	24.5	71.8	14.5	82.9	44.09	6 539	510
Leominster	58.1	1 421	13.9	24.2	71.9	15.2	81.0	49.13	6 576	548
Lowell	256.6	2 363	32.8	23.6	72.4	14.1	84.5	43.14	6 575	532
Lynn	67.5	740	0.0	29.3	73.9	22.1	82.2	42.53	5 630	777
Malden	106.3	1 761	5.1	29.3	73.9	22.1	82.2	42.53	5 630	777
Marlborough	60.4	1 537	31.1	25.9	73.4	16.2	84.0	45.87	6 060	651
Medford	45.4	795	34.5	29.3	73.9	22.1	82.2	42.53	5 630	777
Melrose	63.4	2 311	5.5	29.3	73.9	22.1	82.2	42.53	5 630	777
Methuen Town	66.0	1 374	0.5	24.5	71.8	14.5	82.9	44.09	6 539	510
New Bedford	257.5	2 716	19.6	28.5	74.2	20.0	83.1	50.77	5 734	740
Newton	217.6	2 495	9.9	25.9	73.4	16.2	84.0	45.87	6 060	651
Northampton	81.7	2 847	20.6	22.3	71.2	11.2	83.2	45.57	6 856	452
Peabody	45.3	874	10.0	28.8	72.6	20.4	82.1	45.51	5 704	582
Pittsfield	87.1	1 966	7.2	19.9	67.6	11.2	77.5	48.71	7 689	222
Quincy	211.7	2 279	14.8	26.0	71.6	18.1	81.2	51.19	6 371	558
Revere	59.8	1 117	0.2	29.3	73.9	22.1	82.2	42.53	5 630	777
Salem	62.2	1 472	6.0	28.8	72.6	20.4	82.1	45.51	5 704	582
Somerville	99.6	1 281	18.7	29.3	73.9	22.1	82.2	42.53	5 630	777
Springfield	260.5	1 693	0.0	25.7	73.7	17.2	84.9	46.16	6 104	759
Taunton	120.6	2 154	0.7	27.4	72.2	17.8	83.0	48.34	6 012	558
Waltham	106.4	1 717	23.1	25.4	71.5	15.7	82.7	46.95	6 370	485
Watertown Town	44.3	1 348	4.0	29.3	73.9	22.1	82.2	42.53	5 630	777
Westfield	98.9	2 398	0.0	21.5	68.9	10.4	81.7	48.07	7 312	287
West Springfield Town	43.5	1 522	0.0	NA	NA	NA	NA	NA	NA	NA
Weymouth Town	91.2	1 657	25.5	NA	NA	NA	NA	NA	NA	NA
Woburn	86.3	2 221	30.5	25.5	71.5	15.7	82.5	48.31	6 401	472
Worcester	657.7	3 607	57.8	23.6	70.1	15.8	79.3	49.05	6 831	371
MICHIGAN	X	X	X	X	X	X	X	X	X	X
Allen Park	85.9	3 076	3.7	24.5	73.5	17.8	83.4	32.89	6 422	736
Ann Arbor	244.9	2 113	25.9	23.4	72.6	16.6	83.0	35.35	6 503	691
Battle Creek	87.6	1 690	0.0	23.1	71.0	15.3	82.5	35.15	6 742	559
Bay City	72.6	2 101	3.7	21.0	71.5	13.8	81.5	31.25	7 106	545
Burton	12.1	411	3.5	21.3	70.6	13.3	82.0	31.61	7 005	555
Dearborn	274.1	2 831	7.6	24.7	73.7	16.1	85.7	33.58	6 224	788
Dearborn Heights	58.1	1 016	3.6	24.7	73.7	16.1	85.7	33.58	6 224	788
Detroit	8 166.1	11 720	1 166.2	24.7	73.7	16.1	85.7	33.58	6 224	788
East Lansing	60.8	1 250	0.0	21.6	70.3	13.9	82.1	31.53	7 098	558
Eastpointe	15.3	472	0.4	25.3	73.6	18.8	83.3	33.97	6 160	757
Farmington Hills	17.7	219	0.0	24.7	73.7	16.1	85.7	33.58	6 224	788
Flint	170.4	1 696	13.5	21.3	70.6	13.3	82.0	31.61	7 005	555
Garden City	50.5	1 842	12.9	24.7	73.7	16.1	85.7	33.58	6 224	788
Grand Rapids	552.9	2 902	23.4	22.4	71.4	15.6	82.3	37.13	6 896	613
Holland	47.8	1 433	12.8	24.4	71.4	17.6	82.5	36.25	6 589	611
Inkster	48.3	1 924	9.7	24.5	73.5	17.8	83.4	32.89	6 422	736
Jackson	42.3	1 268	13.0	22.2	71.3	14.7	82.7	30.67	6 873	570
Kalamazoo	453.2	6 023	117.6	24.3	73.2	17.0	84.2	37.41	6 235	773
Kentwood	20.1	405	0.0	22.4	71.4	15.6	82.3	37.13	6 896	613
Lansing	693.1	6 066	30.4	21.6	70.3	13.9	82.1	31.53	7 098	558
Lincoln Park	16.7	443	0.0	24.5	73.5	17.8	83.4	32.89	6 422	736
Livonia	52.7	549	0.0	24.7	73.7	16.1	85.7	33.58	6 224	788
Madison Heights	14.5	483	0.0	24.7	73.7	16.1	85.7	33.58	6 224	788
Midland	35.9	855	4.6	22.9	72.7	16.2	83.8	30.69	6 645	679
Mount Pleasant	13.0	496	1.5	20.7	70.6	13.5	82.2	31.57	7 329	492
Muskegon	30.6	826	6.5	23.5	69.9	17.1	80.0	32.88	6 943	487
Novi	48.0	844	0.0	22.1	71.0	14.3	81.7	29.28	6 989	550

1. Based on the population estimated as of July 1 of the year shown. 2. Represents normal values based on the 30-year period, 1971–2000. 3. Average daily minimum.
4. Average daily maximum.

STATE Place code	City	Land area,[1] 2016 (sq mi)	Total persons	Rank	Per square mile	White	Black or African American	American Indian, Alaska Native	Asian	Hawaiian Pacific Islander	Some other race	2 or more races[2]
		1	2	3	4	5	6	7	8	9	10	11
	MICHIGAN—Cont'd											
26 59920	Oak Park	5.2	29 645	1 263	5 701.0	NA	NA	NA	NA	NA	NA	NA
26 65440	Pontiac	20.0	59 698	619	2 984.9	38.1	49.8	0.3	2.4	0.2	3.5	5.6
26 65560	Portage	32.2	48 508	787	1 506.5	88.5	5.1	0.4	1.6	0.0	0.1	4.4
26 65820	Port Huron	8.1	29 231	1 275	3 608.8	80.9	7.9	0.0	1.7	0.0	0.4	9.1
26 69035	Rochester Hills	32.8	73 422	478	2 238.5	82.9	4.1	0.1	10.3	0.0	0.8	1.8
26 69800	Roseville	9.8	47 602	804	4 857.3	79.1	18.5	0.7	0.2	0.0	0.5	1.0
26 70040	Royal Oak	11.8	59 006	633	5 000.5	88.6	3.9	0.0	5.4	0.0	0.5	1.5
26 70520	Saginaw	17.1	48 984	773	2 864.6	47.4	40.1	0.2	0.3	0.0	2.5	9.5
26 70760	St. Clair Shores	11.7	59 775	618	5 109.0	90.8	6.1	0.2	0.4	0.1	0.1	2.3
26 74900	Southfield	26.3	73 100	479	2 779.5	23.6	72.0	0.1	1.7	0.0	0.3	2.3
26 74960	Southgate	6.8	29 085	1 278	4 277.2	82.8	3.4	0.9	8.3	0.0	1.2	3.4
26 76460	Sterling Heights	36.5	132 427	204	3 628.1	83.8	5.3	0.0	8.6	0.0	0.6	1.8
26 79000	Taylor	23.6	61 177	597	2 592.2	79.2	15.0	0.1	2.1	0.0	0.9	2.8
26 80700	Troy	33.5	83 641	398	2 496.7	64.5	4.9	1.4	25.5	0.0	0.2	3.6
26 84000	Warren	34.4	135 125	195	3 928.1	67.7	18.8	0.3	8.7	0.1	0.6	3.8
26 86000	Westland	20.4	81 545	414	3 997.3	72.5	19.3	0.2	5.3	0.0	1.3	1.4
26 88900	Wyandotte	5.3	24 955	1 426	4 708.5	NA	NA	NA	NA	NA	NA	NA
26 88940	Wyoming	24.6	75 567	458	3 071.8	72.2	7.9	1.5	3.7	0.0	8.2	6.6
27 00000	MINNESOTA	79 626.7	5 519 952	X	69.3	84.1	5.8	1.0	4.7	0.0	1.5	2.8
27 01486	Andover	33.9	32 461	1 166	957.6	86.7	7.9	0.4	1.1	0.0	0.1	3.7
27 01900	Apple Valley	16.9	51 957	734	3 074.4	87.2	4.9	0.1	3.5	0.0	2.2	2.2
27 06382	Blaine	33.8	62 892	580	1 860.7	82.0	5.0	0.5	8.1	0.0	0.3	4.1
27 06616	Bloomington	34.7	85 319	386	2 458.8	80.7	6.0	1.2	4.8	0.0	4.6	2.7
27 07948	Brooklyn Center	8.0	30 870	1 217	3 858.8	50.3	28.8	0.0	9.0	0.0	8.0	3.8
27 07966	Brooklyn Park	26.1	79 707	427	3 053.9	50.7	27.0	0.8	17.0	0.0	1.4	3.2
27 08794	Burnsville	24.9	61 290	596	2 461.4	74.0	12.2	0.1	5.3	0.0	1.4	7.0
27 13114	Coon Rapids	22.6	62 359	586	2 759.2	90.3	3.7	0.1	2.0	0.3	0.3	3.2
27 13456	Cottage Grove	33.6	36 029	1 058	1 072.3	84.3	5.0	1.0	6.2	0.0	0.0	3.6
27 17000	Duluth	71.8	86 293	382	1 201.9	91.2	2.4	0.9	1.5	0.2	0.1	3.8
27 17288	Eagan	31.2	66 428	543	2 129.1	74.4	9.8	0.4	8.1	0.0	1.6	5.6
27 18116	Eden Prairie	32.5	63 914	570	1 966.6	77.2	7.7	0.0	11.3	0.0	0.3	3.5
27 18188	Edina	15.5	51 350	744	3 312.9	83.6	1.6	0.1	10.3	0.0	1.7	2.7
27 22814	Fridley	10.2	27 476	1 343	2 693.7	67.6	18.4	3.5	9.2	0.0	0.0	1.4
27 31076	Inver Grove Heights	27.9	35 077	1 081	1 257.2	74.7	3.7	0.1	11.1	0.0	7.4	3.0
27 35180	Lakeville	36.1	61 938	591	1 715.7	90.3	1.6	0.0	3.3	0.0	1.7	3.2
27 39878	Mankato	19.0	41 720	905	2 195.8	88.2	4.5	0.4	2.6	0.0	0.7	3.7
27 40166	Maple Grove	32.6	69 576	504	2 134.2	NA	NA	NA	NA	NA	NA	NA
27 40382	Maplewood	17.0	40 150	941	2 361.8	74.3	7.9	0.7	12.6	0.0	1.1	3.4
27 43000	Minneapolis	54.0	413 651	46	7 660.2	63.4	19.7	0.9	6.6	0.0	4.8	4.7
27 43252	Minnetonka	26.9	52 369	726	1 946.8	89.7	1.6	0.1	5.2	0.0	1.4	2.0
27 43864	Moorhead	22.3	42 492	888	1 905.5	92.6	3.6	1.3	1.3	0.0	0.6	0.7
27 47680	Oakdale	10.9	28 073	1 321	2 575.5	73.3	8.2	0.3	12.6	0.0	1.2	4.6
27 49300	Owatonna	14.8	25 773	1 405	1 741.4	86.9	4.9	0.1	3.3	0.0	3.8	1.0
27 51730	Plymouth	32.7	77 216	442	2 361.3	82.5	8.7	0.1	6.7	0.0	0.3	1.8
27 54214	Richfield	6.7	35 949	1 060	5 365.5	74.8	10.2	0.1	7.6	0.0	2.3	5.2
27 54880	Rochester	54.6	114 011	245	2 088.1	80.8	6.8	0.6	7.9	0.1	0.9	2.8
27 55852	Roseville	13.0	35 691	1 071	2 745.5	73.6	10.4	1.1	9.8	0.0	0.7	4.4
27 56896	St. Cloud	40.0	67 641	526	1 691.0	84.0	8.2	0.6	2.6	0.0	0.9	3.7
27 57220	St. Louis Park	10.6	48 747	780	4 598.8	82.5	7.3	0.4	5.0	0.0	1.6	3.1
27 58000	St. Paul	52.0	302 398	64	5 815.3	59.2	15.6	0.5	17.8	0.0	1.7	5.1
27 58738	Savage	15.6	30 807	1 222	1 974.8	84.7	3.2	0.1	8.0	0.0	1.4	2.6
27 59350	Shakopee	28.0	40 610	928	1 450.4	73.3	6.1	0.9	9.6	0.0	3.6	6.5
27 59998	Shoreview	10.8	26 548	1 381	2 458.1	81.6	1.6	0.0	12.7	0.0	0.6	3.4
27 71032	Winona	18.9	27 139	1 358	1 435.9	93.4	2.6	0.2	2.4	0.0	0.0	1.3
27 71428	Woodbury	34.9	68 820	512	1 971.9	79.0	6.3	0.1	9.0	0.0	0.5	5.1
28 00000	MISSISSIPPI	46 923.0	2 988 726	X	63.7	58.8	37.7	0.4	1.0	0.0	0.9	1.2
28 06220	Biloxi	43.0	45 975	829	1 069.2	69.6	18.3	0.1	5.4	0.0	3.1	3.4
28 14420	Clinton	41.8	25 211	1 419	603.1	59.3	31.3	0.1	6.1	0.0	2.7	0.5
28 29180	Greenville	26.9	31 517	1 192	1 171.6	NA	NA	NA	NA	NA	NA	NA
28 29700	Gulfport	55.6	72 076	489	1 296.3	56.8	36.3	0.4	2.0	0.0	1.3	3.3
28 31020	Hattiesburg	53.2	46 926	816	882.1	42.4	53.8	0.0	1.0	0.0	0.1	2.6
28 33700	Horn Lake	16.0	27 042	1 365	1 690.1	52.1	42.6	0.0	1.9	0.0	2.9	0.5
28 36000	Jackson	111.0	169 148	149	1 523.9	16.6	81.4	0.0	0.5	0.0	1.2	0.3
28 46640	Meridian	53.7	39 113	969	728.4	33.9	62.9	0.0	1.5	0.0	0.4	1.3
28 54040	Olive Branch	36.7	36 699	1 038	1 000.0	61.1	31.4	0.4	2.2	0.0	1.9	2.9
28 55760	Pearl	25.5	26 485	1 384	1 038.6	NA	NA	NA	NA	NA	NA	NA
28 69280	Southaven	41.3	53 214	710	1 288.5	72.9	21.8	0.1	1.2	0.1	1.0	3.0
28 74840	Tupelo	64.4	38 842	982	603.1	NA	NA	NA	NA	NA	NA	NA

1. Dry land or land partially or temporarily covered by water.   2. Hispanic or Latino persons may be of any race.

Table D. Cities — Population

City	Percent Hispanic or Latino[1], 2015	Percent foreign born 2015	Age of population (percent), 2010-2014							Median age 2015	Percent female 2015	Population Census counts		Percent change	
			Under 18 years	18 to 24 years	25 to 34 years	35 to 44 years	45 to 54 years	55 to 64 years	65 years and over			2000	2010	2000–2010	2010–2016
	12	13	14	15	16	17	18	19	20	21	22	23	24	25	26
MICHIGAN—Cont'd															
Oak Park	3.9	12.1	21.5	8.1	10.1	14.8	12.0	13.7	19.9	42.9	55.0	29 793	29 319	-1.6	1.1
Pontiac	18.9	7.4	26.5	12.4	14.2	14.1	14.4	9.2	9.1	32.0	48.9	66 337	59 515	-10.3	0.3
Portage	5.9	4.6	20.9	10.9	15.5	10.2	11.3	13.8	17.4	38.8	50.3	44 897	46 287	3.1	4.8
Port Huron	5.1	3.9	23.6	13.1	13.9	10.9	14.0	10.7	13.8	34.1	52.3	32 338	30 177	-6.7	-3.1
Rochester Hills	4.6	18.7	23.1	8.3	11.2	14.8	14.1	12.7	15.8	41.2	50.5	68 825	70 995	3.2	3.4
Roseville	1.5	3.5	19.7	9.0	13.0	12.8	17.1	14.0	14.4	41.1	52.1	48 129	47 299	-1.7	0.6
Royal Oak	2.1	6.7	15.0	7.8	22.7	12.6	13.6	14.7	13.7	38.4	50.2	60 062	57 236	-4.7	3.1
Saginaw	12.5	2.2	23.0	12.1	12.4	11.3	14.5	13.2	13.5	36.7	51.3	61 799	51 507	-16.7	-4.9
St. Clair Shores	1.5	3.0	18.2	6.8	13.8	11.8	14.8	15.4	19.3	44.6	52.0	63 096	59 730	-5.3	0.1
Southfield	0.8	5.5	20.5	9.0	13.1	12.0	11.2	14.7	19.5	41.6	57.1	78 296	71 739	-8.4	1.9
Southgate	5.4	13.2	17.3	10.9	11.7	10.3	12.5	16.6	20.9	44.9	53.6	30 136	30 047	-0.3	-3.2
Sterling Heights	2.1	26.0	19.6	10.1	15.2	11.5	11.8	13.3	18.4	39.6	50.8	124 471	129 699	4.2	2.1
Taylor	5.2	4.4	25.5	6.6	14.0	12.7	13.5	12.8	15.0	37.7	50.2	65 868	63 131	-4.2	-3.1
Troy	2.9	25.2	22.5	7.1	9.5	13.4	16.9	15.1	15.5	43.3	49.1	80 959	80 980	0.0	3.3
Warren	2.4	13.9	19.9	7.7	12.2	12.0	16.6	15.4	16.3	43.2	52.7	138 247	134 056	-3.0	0.8
Westland	3.4	7.8	19.8	9.2	14.7	11.5	13.9	14.4	16.7	39.9	54.0	86 602	84 097	-2.9	-3.0
Wyandotte	4.8	1.6	21.4	8.1	13.4	14.6	14.6	14.7	13.3	38.9	50.8	28 006	25 883	-7.6	-3.6
Wyoming	20.4	11.4	29.4	7.4	17.0	11.7	13.6	11.0	9.8	32.8	52.2	69 368	72 120	4.0	4.8
MINNESOTA	5.1	8.3	23.4	9.2	13.6	12.3	13.6	13.3	14.7	37.9	50.3	4 919 479	5 303 924	7.8	4.1
Andover	2.9	6.7	30.3	8.0	9.6	12.9	18.6	9.4	11.1	36.9	51.1	26 588	30 590	15.1	6.1
Apple Valley	6.0	7.8	24.8	6.9	10.3	11.1	17.3	15.8	13.7	41.6	48.2	45 527	49 102	7.9	5.8
Blaine	4.0	11.9	26.9	7.3	13.5	15.6	12.8	13.2	10.8	36.8	51.4	44 942	57 179	27.2	10.0
Bloomington	9.3	12.4	19.8	7.6	14.3	13.9	13.0	12.8	18.6	40.9	49.9	85 172	82 893	-2.7	2.9
Brooklyn Center	17.6	20.4	30.7	7.8	14.5	13.3	12.6	9.4	11.8	33.1	53.1	29 172	30 135	3.3	2.4
Brooklyn Park	5.2	22.1	27.7	8.3	13.9	14.3	14.6	11.6	9.7	35.1	52.2	67 388	75 776	12.4	5.2
Burnsville	3.2	11.9	25.4	7.6	15.2	13.2	12.2	10.6	15.8	36.4	52.2	60 220	60 276	0.1	1.7
Coon Rapids	3.0	5.1	20.1	9.1	13.7	14.5	14.3	14.9	13.5	39.1	52.1	61 607	61 480	-0.2	1.4
Cottage Grove	4.8	7.7	27.7	7.4	14.0	14.6	13.1	13.2	9.9	35.9	50.7	30 582	34 594	13.1	4.1
Duluth	2.3	2.6	17.8	19.5	13.0	10.2	11.7	12.6	15.3	34.7	52.1	86 918	86 268	-0.7	0.0
Eagan	6.5	13.0	22.4	10.1	15.5	12.3	15.6	14.2	9.9	36.8	52.3	63 557	64 150	0.9	3.6
Eden Prairie	3.8	16.0	22.8	7.3	17.3	12.9	13.5	14.7	11.5	37.1	47.0	54 901	60 797	10.7	5.1
Edina	2.1	12.0	23.4	4.6	8.8	9.8	15.7	13.9	23.8	47.3	53.5	47 425	47 980	1.2	7.0
Fridley	7.0	16.7	22.0	9.9	14.4	11.1	13.7	13.1	15.8	38.0	47.6	27 449	27 215	-0.9	1.0
Inver Grove Heights	12.8	15.6	24.5	8.8	10.4	14.2	14.9	14.2	12.9	39.1	51.0	29 751	34 001	14.3	3.2
Lakeville	3.2	6.3	27.0	8.0	13.6	14.9	15.8	11.0	9.8	36.3	49.2	43 128	55 999	29.8	10.6
Mankato	4.6	4.9	14.1	35.4	12.7	8.0	8.0	10.1	11.8	25.3	48.6	32 427	39 717	22.5	5.0
Maple Grove	2.5	11.2	26.9	4.5	13.8	10.7	17.8	16.3	10.1	38.6	53.5	50 365	61 549	22.2	13.0
Maplewood	5.5	12.0	21.0	6.1	14.6	11.6	14.8	13.2	18.9	42.5	50.5	34 947	38 022	8.8	5.6
Minneapolis	9.7	17.2	19.9	12.7	22.7	14.2	11.6	9.6	9.2	32.4	49.7	382 618	382 603	0.0	8.1
Minnetonka	2.8	11.4	18.5	6.6	11.9	11.5	13.4	17.9	20.1	47.0	51.1	51 301	49 729	-3.1	5.3
Moorhead	4.2	5.5	19.0	21.0	15.3	11.0	8.8	10.5	14.4	31.6	51.0	32 177	39 436	22.6	7.7
Oakdale	4.1	9.0	21.7	11.4	15.7	12.2	13.8	13.0	12.1	35.7	52.1	26 653	27 365	2.7	2.6
Owatonna	8.2	5.4	24.6	9.2	11.8	11.5	11.7	14.7	16.5	39.9	51.4	22 434	25 602	14.1	0.7
Plymouth	4.3	11.6	23.3	7.2	15.0	11.9	11.8	14.7	16.0	38.4	48.6	65 894	70 585	7.1	9.4
Richfield	16.5	14.6	26.1	7.6	16.0	14.7	12.4	10.6	12.5	35.1	49.3	34 439	35 094	1.9	2.4
Rochester	5.9	15.8	24.8	8.5	16.8	12.2	12.2	10.9	14.5	35.0	51.0	85 806	106 748	24.4	6.8
Roseville	5.3	14.8	20.0	10.9	15.8	8.9	11.9	12.9	19.4	39.2	54.9	33 690	33 661	-0.1	6.0
St. Cloud	3.9	8.4	22.2	18.7	15.8	11.9	8.8	9.6	13.0	30.7	49.7	59 107	66 029	11.7	2.4
St. Louis Park	4.8	11.3	18.9	6.1	28.5	13.7	11.1	10.2	11.5	33.6	52.9	44 126	45 206	2.4	7.8
St. Paul	9.1	18.8	24.2	12.6	18.6	12.1	11.6	11.0	9.8	31.5	50.3	287 151	285 063	-0.7	6.1
Savage	6.6	8.8	27.5	7.3	13.6	15.1	15.7	12.7	8.1	36.0	47.8	21 115	26 912	27.5	14.5
Shakopee	5.9	13.0	28.8	10.3	13.6	15.2	15.7	10.0	6.4	33.3	52.3	20 568	37 072	80.2	9.5
Shoreview	6.4	12.0	24.1	3.8	13.7	11.2	17.1	18.7	11.4	42.0	53.7	25 924	25 043	-3.4	6.0
Winona	1.3	3.3	13.3	30.2	12.4	9.2	8.8	11.2	14.9	29.5	54.3	27 069	27 583	1.9	-1.6
Woodbury	4.8	14.0	27.8	5.8	12.4	15.5	15.8	11.4	11.3	37.7	52.9	46 463	61 965	33.4	11.1
MISSISSIPPI	2.9	2.4	24.3	10.4	12.5	12.9	12.6	12.6	14.7	37.0	51.6	2 844 658	2 968 103	4.3	0.7
Biloxi	14.2	11.0	23.5	12.2	13.7	11.5	14.3	13.3	11.5	36.0	49.3	50 644	44 249	-12.6	3.9
Clinton	2.4	7.1	26.6	10.4	11.3	13.6	9.4	12.7	16.1	35.8	52.6	23 347	25 215	8.0	0.0
Greenville	0.0	1.3	26.4	10.3	13.3	12.4	10.8	14.3	12.5	35.0	55.3	41 633	34 410	-17.3	-8.4
Gulfport	5.9	4.3	23.8	11.3	14.8	11.7	11.8	12.0	14.6	35.1	53.9	71 127	67 786	-4.7	6.3
Hattiesburg	3.4	4.2	19.1	24.2	16.6	10.1	8.4	9.6	12.0	28.1	53.0	44 779	45 751	2.2	2.6
Horn Lake	7.7	8.0	24.7	7.7	15.5	15.2	14.0	13.1	9.6	35.8	49.0	14 099	26 068	84.9	3.7
Jackson	1.8	1.0	26.2	12.2	16.4	10.9	11.3	12.1	11.1	31.7	53.7	184 256	173 593	-5.8	-2.6
Meridian	NA	2.3	25.0	9.5	16.8	10.2	12.2	11.4	14.9	34.2	54.6	39 968	41 149	3.0	-4.9
Olive Branch	8.2	5.5	27.1	10.4	11.3	13.8	16.1	11.5	9.9	37.0	53.6	21 054	33 486	59.0	9.6
Pearl	1.1	0.8	24.3	10.2	12.5	10.3	14.2	13.6	14.8	37.8	52.2	21 961	25 700	17.0	3.1
Southaven	4.6	2.8	28.2	9.5	11.4	14.7	12.3	9.8	14.1	35.4	54.9	28 977	48 976	69.0	8.7
Tupelo	4.0	3.6	24.4	10.2	11.9	15.5	12.3	12.0	13.7	36.2	54.0	34 211	37 688	10.2	3.1

1. May be of any race.

Table D. Cities — Households, Group Quarters, Crime, and Education

City	Households, 2015				Persons in group quarters, 2010				Serious crimes known to police,[2] 2014				Educational attainment, 2015		
			Percent			Institutional			Total		Rate[3]			Attainment[4] (percent)	
	Number	Persons per house-hold	Female family house-holder[1]	One-person	Total	Total	Persons in nursing facilities	Non-institu-tional	Number	Rate[3]	Violent	Property	Population age 25 and older	High school graduate or less	Bachelor's degree or more
	27	28	29	30	31	32	33	34	35	36	37	38	39	40	41
MICHIGAN—Cont'd															
Oak Park	11 601	2.56	18.0	34.0	58	0	0	58	655	2 185	337	1 848	20 946	33.1	26.7
Pontiac	23 547	2.45	24.1	36.3	2 563	1 586	102	977	NA	NA	NA	NA	36 602	50.4	12.8
Portage	19 816	2.42	11.9	29.4	156	111	111	45	1 573	3 289	157	3 133	32 891	26.4	43.4
Port Huron	11 864	2.44	18.7	31.1	761	235	228	526	1 066	3 658	762	2 896	18 566	50.9	12.8
Rochester Hills	27 224	2.66	5.0	23.4	1 181	507	507	674	NA	NA	NA	NA	50 360	17.7	54.5
Roseville	20 778	2.28	18.4	34.8	245	148	148	97	2 080	4 368	449	3 919	33 960	50.5	11.8
Royal Oak	28 857	2.03	5.8	44.1	404	249	225	155	672	1 132	130	1 002	45 540	18.3	54.7
Saginaw	19 696	2.44	25.8	39.1	1 693	876	346	817	2 067	4 132	1 689	2 443	32 040	58.3	8.9
St. Clair Shores	26 780	2.22	10.1	35.2	277	248	248	29	883	1 468	193	1 275	44 927	36.9	23.9
Southfield	31 613	2.27	18.3	41.5	1 189	453	451	736	2 356	3 213	280	2 934	51 578	28.7	36.1
Southgate	12 082	2.41	13.3	34.7	117	88	88	29	999	3 402	310	3 092	21 050	46.3	19.2
Sterling Heights	49 296	2.66	9.4	25.4	772	566	554	206	2 234	1 698	160	1 537	92 843	42.2	25.4
Taylor	24 061	2.53	18.3	32.3	673	540	512	133	2 142	3 481	559	2 922	41 804	58.9	12.1
Troy	32 004	2.59	6.6	25.6	310	117	117	193	1 418	1 703	61	1 641	58 606	18.3	57.9
Warren	54 688	2.45	18.7	30.8	1 248	945	945	303	4 090	3 028	478	2 550	98 031	49.0	18.9
Westland	33 719	2.41	12.6	36.8	1 034	779	548	255	2 212	2 689	364	2 326	58 278	44.4	19.7
Wyandotte	10 466	2.40	18.4	35.6	88	0	0	88	616	2 456	175	2 281	17 729	46.1	20.1
Wyoming	28 200	2.65	17.6	28.3	358	149	149	209	1 808	2 423	389	2 035	47 556	48.5	17.8
MINNESOTA	2 147 262	2.49	9.2	28.4	135 395	56 308	32 989	79 087	137 882	2 527	229	2 297	3 700 935	32.7	34.7
Andover	10 382	3.10	10.2	11.6	39	0	0	39	NA	NA	NA	NA	19 857	25.3	34.1
Apple Valley	19 700	2.58	10.0	25.1	316	198	189	118	1 084	2 148	83	2 065	34 964	25.6	47.3
Blaine	22 540	2.75	11.5	19.1	147	71	31	76	1 884	3 079	72	3 007	40 903	28.4	36.2
Bloomington	37 129	2.30	9.4	33.1	991	489	481	502	3 359	3 854	180	3 674	62 814	26.8	42.0
Brooklyn Center	10 808	2.83	13.4	31.7	182	93	86	89	1 315	4 261	324	3 937	18 944	48.6	18.0
Brooklyn Park	27 645	2.85	15.8	22.4	209	17	8	192	2 678	3 390	386	3 004	50 669	34.7	27.6
Burnsville	24 605	2.48	14.2	27.4	443	294	287	149	1 770	2 869	115	2 754	41 158	26.1	38.4
Coon Rapids	24 724	2.50	14.7	22.9	359	205	201	154	1 624	2 609	133	2 476	44 057	33.5	27.2
Cottage Grove	11 970	2.99	7.3	17.0	64	13	7	51	694	1 951	56	1 894	23 292	25.4	33.5
Duluth	35 407	2.25	10.9	35.2	6 640	1 416	924	5 224	3 959	4 598	359	4 239	54 032	30.6	37.6
Eagan	26 518	2.49	12.8	26.0	197	61	61	136	1 201	1 827	36	1 790	44 745	18.0	48.6
Eden Prairie	24 184	2.61	5.5	23.3	208	127	112	81	871	1 382	35	1 347	44 366	12.5	62.3
Edina	20 976	2.38	6.0	29.8	190	112	100	78	916	1 842	54	1 788	36 105	16.7	66.0
Fridley	10 919	2.52	10.9	27.3	131	48	48	83	1 357	4 885	245	4 640	18 865	44.0	28.9
Inver Grove Heights	12 707	2.73	11.1	26.5	193	154	140	39	748	2 171	200	1 971	23 234	31.6	31.4
Lakeville	21 612	2.80	6.3	18.7	46	14	6	32	704	1 189	42	1 147	39 450	20.2	49.5
Mankato	16 635	2.26	8.7	31.4	4 347	324	239	4 023	1 536	3 750	261	3 489	20 743	26.1	39.3
Maple Grove	25 898	2.64	8.4	22.9	50	4	4	46	1 204	1 815	35	1 780	46 885	18.0	51.5
Maplewood	15 293	2.58	8.0	27.3	1 131	800	362	331	1 976	4 904	151	4 752	29 600	37.8	28.8
Minneapolis	173 686	2.26	10.8	41.1	18 066	3 896	2 814	14 170	23 216	5 740	1 012	4 728	276 896	27.8	48.3
Minnetonka	22 886	2.24	5.8	33.9	380	292	209	88	814	1 572	46	1 526	38 688	16.8	59.5
Moorhead	14 942	2.46	6.4	32.6	3 650	344	263	3 306	897	2 259	176	2 083	24 288	29.7	37.4
Oakdale	10 902	2.55	19.8	29.9	177	7	2	170	1 262	4 528	187	4 342	18 789	32.0	31.4
Owatonna	10 019	2.42	9.2	35.9	531	321	203	210	655	2 564	141	2 423	16 375	40.3	32.2
Plymouth	30 438	2.46	7.0	23.6	1 128	730	229	398	1 113	1 487	72	1 415	52 710	16.0	56.2
Richfield	13 729	2.61	7.8	35.6	347	112	110	235	955	2 623	214	2 409	23 988	27.9	39.5
Rochester	43 018	2.55	10.0	31.2	2 615	1 760	646	855	2 428	2 173	184	1 990	74 884	25.1	45.2
Roseville	15 001	2.27	10.6	40.1	1 426	342	292	1 084	1 899	5 375	127	5 247	24 567	24.8	47.6
St. Cloud	26 037	2.41	12.0	30.3	5 615	1 690	448	3 925	2 771	4 175	393	3 782	40 281	34.5	29.2
St. Louis Park	22 311	2.13	8.9	40.3	755	633	630	122	1 369	2 855	136	2 719	36 143	14.1	60.0
St. Paul	113 148	2.58	13.2	35.0	11 438	2 351	1 608	9 087	12 357	4 147	662	3 484	190 130	34.3	39.8
Savage	10 669	2.85	8.8	13.8	6	4	0	2	624	2 147	93	2 054	19 818	25.8	40.8
Shakopee	12 480	3.12	17.3	21.1	884	843	167	41	825	2 082	144	1 938	24 339	34.2	29.8
Shoreview	10 667	2.46	9.1	30.0	204	9	0	195	306	1 168	61	1 106	19 099	17.5	58.1
Winona	10 279	2.18	7.4	37.6	4 223	376	324	3 847	97	352	91	261	14 819	35.2	32.7
Woodbury	24 783	2.72	10.4	21.3	286	161	161	125	1 213	1 823	54	1 769	45 020	18.1	60.5
MISSISSIPPI	1 104 371	2.62	18.2	28.4	91 964	55 135	16 496	36 829	95 800	3 200	278	2 921	1 952 337	47.6	20.8
Biloxi	17 668	2.41	14.0	28.4	3 065	209	158	2 856	2 936	6 523	478	6 046	29 352	41.6	26.8
Clinton	8 874	2.78	18.5	23.3	397	265	265	132	NA	NA	NA	NA	15 912	24.1	42.7
Greenville	13 366	2.53	32.5	33.1	432	370	254	62	2 450	7 443	295	7 148	21 714	52.7	17.7
Gulfport	27 744	2.54	26.7	26.9	1 984	1 222	278	762	3 706	5 161	199	4 961	46 661	44.8	20.5
Hattiesburg	18 125	2.35	22.7	38.9	3 529	832	468	2 697	2 855	5 957	198	5 758	26 398	41.1	30.9
Horn Lake	10 516	2.55	18.6	37.9	56	56	56	0	571	2 133	112	2 021	18 174	51.8	11.3
Jackson	62 092	2.65	28.7	34.6	6 035	1 419	998	4 616	11 975	6 947	924	6 023	105 366	41.1	26.9
Meridian	16 122	2.36	19.2	42.0	1 678	1 161	268	517	2 242	5 485	587	4 898	25 991	40.7	16.6
Olive Branch	12 176	2.96	12.2	19.6	0	0	0	0	1 038	2 939	255	2 684	22 532	38.9	26.9
Pearl	10 503	2.51	18.7	26.4	70	57	57	13	64	243	27	216	17 322	48.1	17.4
Southaven	18 834	2.78	17.1	24.1	264	264	264	0	1 596	3 101	272	2 829	32 730	41.9	24.2
Tupelo	14 174	2.46	18.9	32.8	895	834	471	61	NA	NA	NA	NA	23 308	40.2	26.4

1. No spouse present.   2. Data for serious crimes have not been adjusted for underreporting. This may affect comparability between geographic areas and over time.   3. Per 100,000 population estimated by the FBI.   4. Persons 25 years old and over.

Table D. Cities — Income, Poverty, and Housing

City	Money income, 2015					Housing units, 2010			Occupied housing units 2015				
	Households			Families					Owner-occupied			Renter-occupied	
	Median income	Percent with income of $200,000 or more	Percent with income of less than $25,000	Total Families	Percent with income below poverty	Total	Percent change, 2000–2010	Vacant units for sale or rent[2]	Total	Percent	Median value[3] (dollars)	Percent	Median rent (dollars)
	42	43	44	45	46	47	48	49	50	51	52	53	54
MICHIGAN—Cont'd													
Oak Park	47 136	0.4	20.5	6 748	13.7	12 782	12.4	1 063	11 601	53.3	87 600	46.7	998
Pontiac	31 536	1.0	35.9	13 187	30.6	27 084	2.8	4 864	23 547	39.3	57 200	60.7	725
Portage	51 555	4.5	15.3	13 155	8.1	20 559	8.9	1 360	19 816	63.8	148 800	36.2	755
Port Huron	35 190	0.0	32.4	6 973	21.5	13 871	-0.9	1 694	11 864	50.4	70 000	49.6	719
Rochester Hills	81 124	13.9	7.5	19 475	3.0	29 494	8.1	1 916	27 224	76.3	277 000	23.7	1 177
Roseville	40 137	0.7	21.8	12 007	13.3	21 260	3.6	1 707	20 778	58.9	72 500	41.1	865
Royal Oak	67 288	7.3	10.2	13 743	3.8	30 207	0.9	2 144	28 857	70.2	191 200	29.8	920
Saginaw	27 369	0.7	38.3	10 834	29.3	23 574	-8.1	3 775	19 696	59.6	42 200	40.4	666
St. Clair Shores	52 354	1.5	12.4	15 483	6.7	28 467	0.9	1 882	26 780	77.7	116 100	22.3	964
Southfield	50 557	2.6	17.4	16 732	4.8	35 986	0.8	4 208	31 613	46.2	136 000	53.8	1 057
Southgate	49 194	1.9	15.8	7 468	8.4	13 933	4.3	871	12 082	67.6	91 700	32.4	807
Sterling Heights	61 809	3.6	14.3	33 609	10.6	52 190	9.8	2 739	49 296	69.9	162 400	30.1	952
Taylor	40 301	2.2	23.5	15 204	20.3	26 422	2.0	2 052	24 061	61.2	77 100	38.8	803
Troy	87 447	9.8	9.9	22 763	4.0	32 907	6.6	2 204	32 004	71.2	271 800	28.8	1 040
Warren	43 379	1.0	19.0	34 941	16.9	57 938	1.2	4 496	54 688	71.3	104 500	28.7	884
Westland	45 538	1.9	18.7	17 977	13.0	39 201	3.0	3 315	33 719	60.8	105 300	39.2	823
Wyandotte	56 078	2.7	15.2	6 397	9.0	12 081	-1.8	1 090	10 466	74.9	90 900	25.1	841
Wyoming	44 047	2.2	15.7	18 237	11.5	28 983	5.4	2 013	28 200	63.6	113 600	36.4	761
MINNESOTA	63 488	5.7	13.0	1 383 950	6.3	2 347 201	13.6	259 974	2 147 262	70.9	200 000	29.1	888
Andover	90 581	5.9	8.4	8 923	6.0	10 091	23.0	280	10 382	91.3	253 000	8.7	1 397
Apple Valley	80 685	5.1	7.3	13 957	5.0	19 600	18.5	725	19 700	76.8	238 600	23.2	1 142
Blaine	80 543	7.4	5.0	17 182	4.3	21 921	35.6	844	22 540	84.2	199 600	15.8	1 115
Bloomington	67 845	4.5	9.5	21 388	5.4	37 641	1.5	1 736	37 129	65.4	230 400	34.6	1 100
Brooklyn Center	40 865	1.4	23.2	6 778	23.7	11 640	0.4	884	10 808	55.7	150 600	44.3	981
Brooklyn Park	62 164	3.5	10.0	20 659	5.7	27 841	12.1	1 612	27 645	71.0	192 200	29.0	935
Burnsville	66 340	4.3	8.7	15 992	7.8	25 759	6.2	1 476	24 605	59.9	226 200	40.1	1 084
Coon Rapids	65 912	2.9	8.4	17 222	4.4	24 462	7.3	930	24 724	74.7	189 000	25.3	1 093
Cottage Grove	96 134	4.9	4.0	NA	NA	12 102	20.8	383	11 970	80.2	227 200	19.8	1 285
Duluth	47 832	3.0	18.6	18 825	9.4	38 208	3.3	2 503	35 407	62.7	154 200	37.3	717
Eagan	78 417	11.0	9.1	17 645	2.7	26 414	8.3	1 165	26 518	66.7	260 600	33.3	1 063
Eden Prairie	101 713	20.3	7.6	16 900	3.9	25 075	19.3	1 145	24 184	69.2	343 100	30.8	1 178
Edina	91 911	20.3	12.7	13 250	5.1	22 560	4.2	1 888	20 976	76.6	425 900	23.4	1 359
Fridley	60 343	2.0	15.0	7 250	9.4	11 760	2.2	650	10 919	58.6	170 300	41.4	868
Inver Grove Heights	74 413	6.6	4.8	8 608	4.6	14 062	22.8	586	12 707	69.3	235 400	30.7	1 062
Lakeville	92 422	9.6	4.2	16 997	4.5	19 456	41.0	773	21 612	84.6	269 900	15.4	1 126
Mankato	40 632	2.3	21.3	7 258	6.2	15 784	24.0	933	16 635	50.1	161 500	49.9	751
Maple Grove	89 498	13.2	3.5	NA	NA	23 626	33.2	759	25 898	85.1	276 300	14.9	1 261
Maplewood	67 480	4.2	9.0	9 891	2.5	15 561	11.1	679	15 293	73.8	188 600	26.2	994
Minneapolis	54 571	6.8	19.3	77 095	12.8	178 287	5.7	14 747	173 686	47.1	227 500	52.9	912
Minnetonka	87 753	14.0	7.7	12 983	2.2	23 294	4.8	1 393	22 886	70.6	309 700	29.4	1 287
Moorhead	56 989	2.7	20.6	8 780	7.6	15 274	25.5	970	14 942	64.6	178 500	35.4	769
Oakdale	67 365	4.5	6.0	7 082	2.8	11 388	9.5	440	10 902	70.3	207 700	29.7	1 025
Owatonna	61 934	2.0	13.0	6 046	7.8	10 724	20.0	656	10 019	69.3	152 500	30.7	812
Plymouth	93 203	13.9	6.7	20 954	2.2	29 982	18.7	1 319	30 438	69.5	319 700	30.5	1 133
Richfield	61 387	1.9	14.1	7 723	8.9	15 735	2.5	917	13 729	61.9	196 600	38.1	904
Rochester	66 340	6.8	14.1	27 205	5.9	45 683	29.7	2 658	43 018	70.6	170 800	29.4	864
Roseville	62 569	4.7	12.9	7 658	7.5	15 490	3.8	867	15 001	61.5	233 400	38.5	928
St. Cloud	43 647	2.1	16.2	14 124	11.0	27 338	17.8	1 899	26 037	47.3	144 400	52.7	781
St. Louis Park	72 020	6.9	9.4	10 478	4.2	23 285	10.2	1 542	22 311	54.6	247 300	45.4	1 114
St. Paul	50 267	3.7	19.5	60 613	15.3	120 795	4.4	9 794	113 148	50.0	186 800	50.0	874
Savage	89 730	10.1	5.3	8 532	3.5	9 429	34.5	313	10 669	80.6	278 400	19.4	1 085
Shakopee	76 259	6.5	6.5	9 061	2.9	13 339	71.2	567	12 480	70.5	255 500	29.5	1 029
Shoreview	82 106	13.0	9.9	7 221	3.7	10 826	5.2	424	10 667	76.4	257 100	23.6	1 170
Winona	46 194	2.8	20.3	4 881	6.3	10 989	3.1	540	10 279	58.1	135 300	41.9	618
Woodbury	101 785	15.0	5.3	18 654	4.3	23 568	34.4	974	24 783	78.7	296 700	21.3	1 385
MISSISSIPPI	40 593	2.1	25.7	743 154	17.0	1 274 719	9.7	158 951	1 104 371	67.4	112 700	32.6	724
Biloxi	44 773	2.6	20.2	11 305	18.1	21 278	-3.9	4 174	17 668	41.3	164 900	58.7	831
Clinton	54 709	3.6	15.8	NA	NA	10 359	16.2	593	8 874	69.4	158 200	30.6	905
Greenville	23 970	2.4	44.3	8 362	37.5	14 561	-10.5	1 883	13 366	48.6	80 500	51.4	662
Gulfport	37 268	2.3	25.4	18 598	23.1	31 602	6.8	5 295	27 744	49.1	115 000	50.9	822
Hattiesburg	23 508	0.6	40.4	8 891	33.9	21 381	11.5	2 880	18 125	35.9	105 600	64.1	680
Horn Lake	40 704	0.4	21.2	5 863	12.0	9 705	90.4	653	10 516	58.3	96 600	41.7	933
Jackson	32 482	2.2	31.0	37 101	25.9	74 537	-1.5	10 014	62 092	53.1	92 600	46.9	790
Meridian	28 639	1.5	36.8	8 521	22.9	18 591	3.6	2 082	16 122	46.9	81 500	53.1	721
Olive Branch	71 573	4.1	4.6	9 317	3.6	12 942	60.6	864	12 176	83.4	172 600	16.6	1 010
Pearl	48 325	0.3	18.3	7 394	7.3	10 396	14.6	604	10 503	62.9	103 700	37.1	837
Southaven	58 815	1.3	15.9	13 041	6.7	19 101	66.3	1 132	18 834	63.8	147 300	36.2	1 015
Tupelo	40 376	2.1	26.4	8 842	14.2	15 371	5.0	1 769	14 174	56.6	148 400	43.4	713

1. Based on population estimated by the American Community Survey.   2. Includes units rented or sold but not occupied.   3. Specified owner-occupied units; $1,000,000 represents $1,000,000 or more   4. 50.0 represents 50 percent or more.   5. 10.0 represents 10 percent or less.

Table D. Cities — Commuting, Computer Access, Migration, Labor Force, and Employment

City	Commuting Percent		Computer Access[2] Percent		Migration, 2015		Civilian labor force, 2016				Civilian employment[4], 2015			
									Unemployment		Population age 16 and older		Population age 16 to 64	
	Drove alone	With Commutes of 30 minutes or more[1]	With a Computer in the house	With Internet Access	Percent who lived in the same house one year ago	Percent who lived in an other state or county one year ago	Total	Percent change, 2015–2016	Total	Rate[3]	Number	Percent in Labor Force	Number	Percent who worked full-year full-time
	55	56	57	58	59	60	61	62	63	64	65	66	67	68
MICHIGAN—Cont'd														
Oak Park	88.5	31.0	81.1	66.5	92.7	3.4	14 257	1.9	1 004	7.0	24 016	59.6	18 110	46.6
Pontiac	78.1	30.4	82.2	70.4	75.3	6.1	25 054	1.5	2 470	9.9	45 068	64.7	39 603	36.2
Portage	87.9	18.3	87.0	79.6	83.3	6.3	25 074	2.4	894	3.6	38 537	67.3	30 142	52.6
Port Huron	84.3	21.4	84.7	72.1	72.5	6.6	12 789	1.8	1 066	8.3	23 308	60.4	19 258	33.3
Rochester Hills	92.5	43.0	94.3	88.4	89.5	4.1	38 549	2.4	1 347	3.5	58 726	64.0	47 157	51.5
Roseville	84.9	39.5	84.9	69.3	84.8	5.7	23 094	2.2	1 572	6.8	39 615	62.5	32 766	46.7
Royal Oak	89.8	37.7	94.5	87.4	83.5	7.4	37 652	2.5	975	2.6	50 793	73.0	42 736	59.5
Saginaw	79.8	21.4	69.9	55.8	75.5	4.9	19 478	0.1	1 747	9.0	39 748	54.9	33 109	29.4
St. Clair Shores	92.9	44.3	87.0	80.8	90.5	1.9	31 040	2.4	1 590	5.1	50 508	63.6	38 977	51.9
Southfield	86.7	36.7	85.0	73.6	80.3	9.5	34 529	2.1	2 086	6.0	60 147	60.3	45 868	47.1
Southgate	84.9	43.0	83.7	74.3	84.7	3.0	15 354	2.0	579	3.8	24 806	62.2	18 696	48.3
Sterling Heights	90.2	35.4	87.5	81.7	87.1	6.1	66 120	2.4	3 337	5.0	108 554	62.0	84 288	50.7
Taylor	90.3	26.4	86.2	67.1	87.0	2.2	28 316	1.8	1 795	6.3	47 027	60.1	37 810	45.7
Troy	88.6	34.7	94.0	89.2	88.4	5.5	42 590	2.4	1 478	3.5	66 963	63.0	54 018	48.9
Warren	87.7	37.2	77.1	71.3	90.5	5.9	63 126	2.3	4 027	6.4	112 639	59.2	90 637	48.3
Westland	90.4	36.8	88.9	74.8	86.7	3.4	42 673	1.9	1 906	4.5	67 026	62.1	53 370	53.1
Wyandotte	88.0	39.1	86.7	75.4	83.8	4.0	13 117	2.0	572	4.4	20 282	64.8	16 945	43.3
Wyoming	84.2	20.7	90.1	82.9	84.1	3.2	44 328	2.8	1 631	3.7	55 351	70.8	47 941	49.1
MINNESOTA	82.7	31.8	89.2	80.0	85.2	7.2	3 001 131	0.9	117 040	3.9	4 349 038	69.9	3 544 080	53.8
Andover	90.4	48.5	95.3	89.8	91.5	1.6	18 290	1.3	593	3.2	23 681	73.5	20 113	53.3
Apple Valley	91.1	35.3	95.4	86.9	89.3	7.0	29 258	1.1	928	3.2	39 926	73.4	32 883	55.7
Blaine	84.9	40.4	92.9	88.1	90.8	4.7	35 119	1.1	1 225	3.5	46 885	74.8	40 204	59.3
Bloomington	83.8	27.4	92.4	84.5	85.4	6.8	46 362	1.1	1 636	3.5	71 398	70.5	55 311	56.9
Brooklyn Center	75.4	28.5	88.7	74.5	84.6	4.5	15 166	0.8	656	4.3	22 129	71.8	18 506	51.6
Brooklyn Park	81.0	37.1	91.3	80.8	89.9	4.8	41 559	1.1	1 638	3.9	59 360	72.6	51 679	55.7
Burnsville	84.0	34.2	93.2	82.1	87.9	4.8	35 411	1.1	1 253	3.5	47 468	73.2	37 754	61.0
Coon Rapids	85.3	41.1	92.0	84.5	85.9	7.8	34 993	1.0	1 303	3.7	50 975	73.1	42 577	59.2
Cottage Grove	86.2	43.7	97.7	86.6	92.0	2.9	19 886	1.2	687	3.5	26 799	78.5	23 252	64.1
Duluth	79.2	10.4	84.3	73.4	79.1	8.1	44 966	0.0	1 812	4.0	72 863	68.5	59 721	41.2
Eagan	85.0	34.3	96.6	88.8	87.0	8.0	39 372	1.2	1 228	3.1	53 195	78.9	46 610	62.3
Eden Prairie	88.2	29.1	96.7	92.0	81.2	7.1	35 717	1.2	1 063	3.0	50 737	73.8	43 431	56.9
Edina	83.9	27.7	91.0	86.9	88.4	5.6	24 796	1.3	768	3.1	40 032	63.0	28 123	52.3
Fridley	78.5	35.7	94.0	83.6	87.5	6.7	14 699	1.2	599	4.1	22 083	68.5	17 707	56.3
Inver Grove Heights	90.4	30.6	93.8	81.8	83.6	8.3	19 399	1.1	686	3.5	27 664	67.0	23 154	51.7
Lakeville	86.7	40.4	94.4	88.9	90.3	4.8	33 945	1.1	1 030	3.0	46 549	78.9	40 597	59.0
Mankato	81.1	10.9	88.3	80.4	74.4	16.2	25 186	1.0	771	3.1	35 802	72.8	30 971	39.3
Maple Grove	89.2	39.7	97.9	93.6	91.2	4.1	39 472	1.2	1 194	3.0	52 451	72.6	45 533	59.6
Maplewood	77.0	36.6	91.2	85.2	81.3	8.0	20 535	1.3	807	3.9	32 365	68.0	24 705	55.7
Minneapolis	63.0	28.3	91.1	79.3	76.3	9.3	232 240	1.1	7 964	3.4	336 581	75.1	298 608	49.6
Minnetonka	83.9	24.7	93.3	89.3	85.9	4.9	29 234	1.2	919	3.1	43 533	71.7	33 131	57.1
Moorhead	81.6	11.4	83.8	74.3	84.4	10.1	24 068	0.9	723	3.0	33 082	69.6	27 254	45.5
Oakdale	87.3	33.1	90.9	84.0	85.6	10.5	15 990	1.1	571	3.6	22 492	76.1	19 080	61.8
Owatonna	91.9	20.1	86.8	81.2	81.3	7.6	14 746	0.6	534	3.6	19 364	66.6	15 279	54.7
Plymouth	87.4	32.8	95.0	89.5	82.8	7.8	42 570	1.1	1 306	3.1	59 837	71.8	47 663	60.4
Richfield	79.9	28.2	89.0	80.8	84.8	5.2	19 932	1.1	629	3.2	27 661	73.4	23 121	53.7
Rochester	74.6	11.0	93.6	86.2	83.9	7.2	61 853	1.2	1 829	3.0	87 497	69.6	71 170	53.3
Roseville	80.2	22.5	86.6	76.7	86.4	9.8	18 920	1.2	612	3.2	29 822	64.5	22 914	47.4
St. Cloud	82.6	18.4	91.4	76.3	69.2	18.4	36 445	0.6	1 488	4.1	54 904	69.8	46 057	42.7
St. Louis Park	79.9	26.1	94.7	87.9	76.7	7.3	29 879	1.1	890	3.0	39 585	80.2	34 040	63.8
St. Paul	72.3	32.2	87.8	79.2	75.6	11.5	153 928	1.1	5 767	3.7	234 923	70.8	205 364	47.0
Savage	93.0	37.0	97.7	87.1	86.1	11.1	17 685	1.0	510	2.9	22 748	78.5	20 297	59.4
Shakopee	84.8	33.3	94.6	84.2	87.8	6.8	22 496	1.2	735	3.3	29 376	77.3	26 827	58.6
Shoreview	92.2	40.1	93.3	89.0	88.8	4.3	14 685	1.3	467	3.2	20 934	73.1	17 904	59.9
Winona	80.0	11.1	86.5	75.4	72.0	16.2	15 747	0.0	584	3.7	23 317	71.0	19 412	45.1
Woodbury	90.8	37.4	96.6	93.6	88.0	8.8	37 940	1.3	1 126	3.0	51 541	71.3	43 865	55.6
MISSISSIPPI	87.3	32.1	78.3	61.0	86.3	6.1	1 280 432	0.8	74 653	5.8	2 345 713	56.9	1 904 752	45.3
Biloxi	77.4	17.8	78.0	71.4	69.5	18.5	19 869	0.7	1 100	5.5	35 776	70.7	30 536	53.6
Clinton	90.4	28.4	88.6	81.9	88.6	5.2	13 269	1.6	553	4.2	19 043	61.7	14 971	50.7
Greenville	88.5	11.6	73.9	58.9	87.0	3.3	12 037	-1.1	1 034	8.6	26 208	56.5	21 930	36.7
Gulfport	88.1	25.2	78.3	68.4	78.6	9.2	29 657	0.5	1 829	6.2	56 782	58.6	46 254	43.2
Hattiesburg	74.2	13.9	83.5	62.6	74.2	18.4	21 860	1.5	1 268	5.8	38 162	60.0	32 580	32.1
Horn Lake	89.2	45.1	81.5	67.2	84.5	6.7	12 795	1.2	619	4.8	20 714	66.9	18 117	50.8
Jackson	88.7	24.8	80.2	59.9	82.2	5.3	75 950	1.4	4 368	5.8	130 083	59.8	111 161	43.9
Meridian	86.7	10.6	78.0	52.4	85.5	5.7	15 580	0.1	1 000	6.4	31 310	56.9	25 382	46.0
Olive Branch	94.8	36.2	93.7	87.0	89.5	4.8	19 039	1.7	729	3.8	27 863	74.4	24 288	55.2
Pearl	84.6	23.0	81.9	69.7	86.3	6.5	12 919	1.9	555	4.3	20 924	66.7	16 999	57.1
Southaven	89.4	27.9	87.4	76.7	83.8	6.9	26 883	1.9	1 109	4.1	39 434	66.5	32 032	54.4
Tupelo	NA	18.6	84.2	74.1	79.4	8.3	16 534	2.3	851	5.1	27 834	65.0	22 961	53.6

1. Employed persons.　2. Households.　3. Percent of civilian labor force.　4. Persons 16 years old and over.

Table D. Cities — Construction, Wholesale Trade, and Retail Trade

City	Value of residential construction authorized by building permits, 2016			Wholesale trade,[1] 2012				Retail trade,[2] 2012			
	New construction ($1,000)	Number of housing units	Percent single family	Number of establishments	Number of employees	Sales (mil dol)	Annual payroll (mil dol)	Number of establishments	Number of employees	Sales (mil dol)	Annual payroll (mil dol)
	69	70	71	72	73	74	75	76	77	78	79
MICHIGAN—Cont'd											
Oak Park	896	4	100.0	63	600	307.9	37.6	121	980	220.7	22.4
Pontiac	4 091	30	100.0	43	D	D	D	190	1 572	414.7	39.7
Portage	29 346	171	42.7	46	903	352.9	70.5	302	5 471	1 137.7	105.7
Port Huron	370	3	100.0	20	194	120.3	10.2	115	1 145	299.2	29.2
Rochester Hills	82 927	334	45.5	89	959	865.6	77.0	247	5 126	1 393.8	127.7
Roseville	290	3	100.0	45	593	670.2	34.0	250	4 380	1 170.5	99.1
Royal Oak	39 711	134	100.0	55	590	1 218.9	36.5	224	2 496	634.0	65.1
Saginaw	6 382	50	12.0	35	544	276.8	28.0	146	874	188.6	18.5
St. Clair Shores	4 653	30	100.0	38	187	95.9	9.2	174	2 098	565.5	55.8
Southfield	13 249	62	12.9	149	2 717	3 983.5	188.2	421	5 634	2 009.7	163.2
Southgate	220	4	100.0	7	D	D	D	130	2 593	740.5	64.9
Sterling Heights	32 174	156	64.7	151	1 914	845.2	111.2	449	7 490	1 976.7	186.4
Taylor	6 616	24	100.0	66	1 096	783.5	53.2	326	5 342	1 360.1	125.1
Troy	30 322	114	100.0	331	6 106	4 293.4	363.9	550	10 978	3 608.5	299.7
Warren	8 417	72	30.6	165	3 181	1 893.9	188.7	460	5 305	1 498.3	137.6
Westland	6 142	58	93.1	51	477	258.8	24.8	305	4 569	1 094.1	99.9
Wyandotte	2 014	14	85.7	14	D	D	D	86	467	127.7	11.2
Wyoming	16 123	227	21.6	166	3 842	3 083.0	206.9	257	4 053	1 114.2	115.0
MINNESOTA	127	2	100.0	6 569	108 467	104 485.1	7 170.1	19 109	288 888	78 898.2	6 857.5
Andover	27 955	103	100.0	11	36	15.8	1.4	37	601	140.2	11.3
Apple Valley	43 662	161	100.0	22	83	37.5	3.8	119	3 499	924.7	85.0
Blaine	104 375	390	82.1	72	1 059	555.4	53.8	222	4 265	966.4	92.8
Bloomington	3 062	14	100.0	193	5 005	5 106.6	355.4	522	12 250	3 007.9	330.6
Brooklyn Center	169	1	100.0	25	508	285.1	24.1	72	1 863	658.2	55.7
Brooklyn Park	34 388	139	97.1	80	1 488	1 018.1	85.7	155	3 311	979.3	87.7
Burnsville	6 622	26	100.0	159	D	D	D	333	5 998	1 506.7	163.7
Coon Rapids	5 592	21	100.0	24	331	107.0	15.7	180	4 610	1 314.0	113.7
Cottage Grove	54 425	282	34.8	11	D	D	D	48	956	236.4	21.0
Duluth	13 463	102	41.2	93	1 063	531.9	52.7	427	6 141	1 384.7	130.1
Eagan	30 177	88	100.0	143	2 815	1 679.9	184.4	163	3 258	1 040.7	81.2
Eden Prairie	16 182	50	100.0	177	2 957	5 430.6	223.2	242	5 876	2 684.5	201.2
Edina	74 709	158	69.0	129	1 086	1 118.7	75.6	299	6 044	1 173.2	135.4
Fridley	16 338	109	4.6	70	9 569	5 882.7	1 457.6	86	2 040	591.5	53.8
Inver Grove Heights	27 015	95	100.0	20	D	D	D	69	1 520	766.8	54.1
Lakeville	153 137	563	80.6	45	D	D	D	120	2 125	664.4	53.6
Mankato	35 282	221	51.1	55	980	715.9	48.6	271	5 743	1 334.6	122.3
Maple Grove	49 182	399	35.8	86	935	601.4	53.7	183	4 073	1 016.9	91.2
Maplewood	20 138	164	8.5	38	425	219.9	23.7	229	4 308	1 218.2	110.9
Minneapolis	567 278	2 908	5.8	483	7 802	6 079.5	477.3	1 123	14 533	4 070.0	397.3
Minnetonka	50 981	200	23.0	131	3 457	2 016.4	204.4	294	5 982	1 771.5	167.8
Moorhead	61 005	487	29.8	31	433	356.1	22.1	113	1 992	471.4	42.2
Oakdale	1 557	6	100.0	40	480	579.2	33.5	64	1 514	365.5	31.7
Owatonna	9 089	37	100.0	22	323	216.3	18.5	103	2 096	469.4	45.5
Plymouth	116 172	303	100.0	203	5 086	4 243.4	356.7	183	3 279	1 175.4	96.4
Richfield	1 898	6	100.0	15	285	69.5	19.1	116	2 488	3 045.5	74.6
Rochester	232 014	1 396	28.9	71	905	471.2	44.1	507	9 720	2 224.4	213.7
Roseville	43 592	210	6.2	68	1 075	796.5	59.0	304	6 393	1 200.6	130.6
St. Cloud	28 728	293	16.7	75	2 002	970.1	92.7	326	6 280	1 548.2	141.3
St. Louis Park	1 855	6	100.0	108	1 486	781.5	92.4	205	4 325	1 292.0	127.0
St. Paul	98 707	930	9.5	270	4 879	3 332.8	295.3	739	9 230	1 959.9	208.7
Savage	52 541	165	91.5	33	594	1 002.6	30.7	83	1 069	286.1	23.5
Shakopee	16 885	50	100.0	54	1 186	939.9	83.8	116	2 294	688.9	52.2
Shoreview	3 788	15	100.0	23	D	D	D	38	696	153.6	16.7
Winona	2 754	13	38.5	33	354	200.2	15.4	113	2 298	532.8	46.8
Woodbury	125 146	393	81.2	38	D	D	D	232	4 979	1 005.9	93.7
MISSISSIPPI	1 125 912	6 886	89.2	2 484	30 351	28 303.0	1 373.6	11 594	136 032	37 053.2	2 968.4
Biloxi	17 608	101	92.1	37	417	188.9	14.3	209	2 470	542.5	51.4
Clinton	9 323	38	100.0	13	96	44.1	3.6	84	960	240.7	21.9
Greenville	2 886	11	100.0	40	333	825.3	15.5	168	1 891	405.4	36.0
Gulfport	21 774	124	88.7	84	869	392.0	41.4	385	5 435	1 432.3	123.6
Hattiesburg	7 856	129	53.5	85	866	532.1	33.8	453	7 195	4 103.8	149.6
Horn Lake	6 167	67	100.0	17	D	D	D	70	1 069	266.2	24.0
Jackson	3 890	15	100.0	244	3 355	2 146.6	162.5	700	9 327	2 606.3	236.8
Meridian	1 542	12	83.3	58	1 362	1 511.3	61.2	344	4 598	1 193.9	104.4
Olive Branch	38 611	320	100.0	51	1 000	862.2	45.5	122	1 896	646.7	50.2
Pearl	5 820	29	100.0	68	1 095	777.5	59.8	115	1 947	483.3	48.5
Southaven	48 561	353	96.3	38	1 464	2 194.9	63.9	214	3 945	1 123.1	94.4
Tupelo	13 860	76	100.0	113	1 169	819.3	48.5	374	6 061	1 350.0	127.5

1. Merchant wholesalers except manufacturers' sales branches and offices.   2. Establishments with payroll.

City	Real estate and rental and leasing, 2012				Professional, scientific, and technical services,[1] 2012				Manufacturing, 2012			
	Number of establish-ments	Number of employees	Receipts (mil dol)	Annual payroll (mil dol)	Number of establish-ments	Number of employees	Receipts (mil dol)	Annual payroll (mil dol)	Number of establish-ments	Number of employees	Receipts (mil dol)	Annual payroll (mil dol)
	80	81	82	83	84	85	86	87	88	89	90	91
MICHIGAN—Cont'd												
Oak Park	30	D	D	D	39	317	71.7	23.1	45	812	154.8	42.8
Pontiac	45	221	36.5	8.3	41	370	46.4	19.0	43	984	615.6	61.1
Portage	52	1 240	93.4	41.2	139	1 131	176.4	60.9	56	6 306	D	415.8
Port Huron	23	71	10.2	1.7	66	D	D	D	45	2 633	1 562.4	130.0
Rochester Hills	48	199	31.4	6.2	250	2 652	439.3	181.0	97	4 059	1 368.3	215.9
Roseville	46	301	54.9	12.4	52	288	18.1	9.4	128	3 854	761.8	216.3
Royal Oak	65	284	39.1	11.7	289	D	D	D	66	1 118	412.6	54.1
Saginaw	20	61	10.5	1.9	81	D	D	D	57	2 770	948.9	155.1
St. Clair Shores	41	130	23.1	3.4	161	781	90.7	36.7	39	1 191	382.1	60.6
Southfield	219	3 050	707.3	151.1	731	13 009	2 655.0	1 221.5	72	3 434	D	207.9
Southgate	21	D	D	D	32	230	21.4	8.4	7	D	D	D
Sterling Heights	93	549	121.6	19.3	265	D	D	D	254	15 436	10 090.2	1 077.1
Taylor	45	312	76.9	9.5	93	D	D	D	80	2 506	817.5	133.8
Troy	152	1 427	287.5	58.2	869	16 374	2 482.5	1 139.0	251	5 912	2 053.0	308.7
Warren	99	605	130.0	25.9	192	13 153	410.5	1 111.3	320	13 623	9 322.0	847.9
Westland	52	D	D	D	64	308	35.0	11.0	67	1 690	441.3	78.6
Wyandotte	9	D	D	D	43	138	19.8	7.1	31	1 430	716.3	142.2
Wyoming	73	669	147.0	27.6	108	D	D	D	155	6 340	1 682.6	298.2
MINNESOTA	6 300	34 499	7 827.9	1 396.0	16 260	D	D	D	7 313	297 884	123 076.3	15 822.6
Andover	45	162	19.1	3.6	64	129	16.1	5.4	12	165	D	6.4
Apple Valley	53	201	46.9	5.4	162	D	D	D	13	506	D	32.0
Blaine	61	190	57.9	6.1	112	D	D	D	160	2 730	1 018.4	138.7
Bloomington	199	4 195	904.5	204.9	564	D	D	D	120	4 999	1 673.6	314.9
Brooklyn Center	32	131	30.4	5.6	60	438	76.7	30.4	26	1 719	335.2	99.3
Brooklyn Park	55	299	48.8	11.3	129	1 205	373.8	58.3	113	5 330	1 491.8	294.6
Burnsville	118	503	114.9	18.3	289	1 438	260.1	94.4	94	3 051	850.4	163.6
Coon Rapids	62	199	43.3	8.6	113	842	138.1	49.1	50	2 992	990.6	184.4
Cottage Grove	21	D	D	D	33	94	8.7	3.3	11	1 173	D	82.1
Duluth	120	657	103.9	19.7	229	D	D	D	89	2 381	D	124.9
Eagan	106	799	163.5	35.3	337	D	D	D	86	3 073	1 166.7	165.1
Eden Prairie	124	916	692.7	60.9	430	4 020	819.8	326.0	110	7 861	2 647.8	545.5
Edina	195	1 617	290.7	80.5	492	D	D	D	62	3 155	866.6	221.5
Fridley	36	D	D	D	77	302	72.0	17.1	113	5 972	1 933.4	340.2
Inver Grove Heights	27	168	19.7	4.2	84	398	60.9	24.1	27	832	321.3	40.5
Lakeville	64	122	33.5	4.6	167	523	86.0	25.8	55	2 932	760.7	133.7
Mankato	70	539	63.0	12.9	117	D	D	D	49	2 644	3 469.1	126.6
Maple Grove	86	191	43.4	7.3	275	1 183	202.1	76.0	95	6 410	1 689.4	404.0
Maplewood	43	176	29.9	4.4	93	374	47.5	14.0	24	541	183.8	26.2
Minneapolis	684	4 056	764.1	195.6	2 338	31 241	6 957.8	2 808.4	427	12 837	3 944.2	689.5
Minnetonka	140	1 091	307.6	73.9	438	D	D	D	81	4 523	2 144.7	354.0
Moorhead	30	145	16.3	3.2	48	D	D	D	21	699	D	29.4
Oakdale	27	D	D	D	87	877	157.0	64.4	28	673	151.6	31.2
Owatonna	20	235	15.2	4.4	46	158	15.3	5.1	36	4 139	D	188.5
Plymouth	137	710	405.0	39.0	500	6 498	990.9	362.5	167	10 038	3 905.4	684.6
Richfield	27	384	36.7	8.3	100	450	58.9	26.5	15	46	D	1.2
Rochester	149	676	134.6	21.4	226	D	D	D	56	7 887	2 962.0	543.3
Roseville	53	352	106.4	17.5	213	2 187	545.6	150.0	56	1 644	616.8	91.4
St. Cloud	104	478	87.5	16.4	149	D	D	D	59	4 810	1 515.6	204.2
St. Louis Park	131	2 014	235.5	66.1	370	D	D	D	64	1 517	330.8	77.5
St. Paul	349	2 485	1 113.1	125.8	868	6 532	1 088.9	446.2	225	6 867	2 018.1	380.6
Savage	41	81	24.2	3.4	109	D	D	D	42	1 165	349.1	59.2
Shakopee	44	110	30.7	3.8	120	D	D	D	43	2 790	1 493.2	194.6
Shoreview	25	D	D	D	112	340	52.2	19.4	34	1 368	400.8	92.0
Winona	33	100	15.4	1.9	61	D	D	D	65	3 317	1 069.7	162.6
Woodbury	74	D	D	D	266	1 287	179.2	68.3	22	686	279.7	42.6
MISSISSIPPI	2 374	10 235	1 709.3	334.1	4 727	30 071	4 009.1	1 443.3	2 252	132 789	66 441.6	5 919.1
Biloxi	69	279	64.1	9.7	135	D	D	D	20	265	D	8.5
Clinton	33	D	D	D	58	353	36.9	13.5	8	D	D	6.4
Greenville	35	127	17.5	4.3	57	D	D	D	23	740	526.6	35.6
Gulfport	121	598	110.4	18.6	185	D	D	D	57	1 788	D	82.3
Hattiesburg	99	424	91.7	15.3	187	D	D	D	57	2 861	825.1	105.4
Horn Lake	22	106	22.8	3.1	14	102	6.4	2.4	14	683	D	35.3
Jackson	232	1 458	313.1	65.5	552	D	D	D	103	2 717	855.6	132.7
Meridian	69	242	54.7	7.4	118	D	D	D	46	1 331	448.3	47.5
Olive Branch	19	56	13.8	2.3	40	176	15.0	5.0	54	1 854	742.3	86.4
Pearl	43	218	25.5	6.6	30	169	31.9	6.3	25	628	156.7	25.9
Southaven	40	135	42.9	5.3	75	538	57.3	14.6	15	D	142.1	D
Tupelo	77	343	64.5	11.0	162	1 025	104.0	44.4	72	3 811	1 605.0	172.4

1. Establishments subject to federal tax.

Table D. Cities — Accommodation and Food Services, Arts, Entertainment, and Recreation, and Health Care and Social Assistance

City	Accommodation and food services, 2012				Arts, entertainment, and recreation,[1] 2012				Health care and social assistance,[1] 2012			
	Number of establishments	Number of employees	Sales (mil dol)	Annual payroll (mil dol)	Number of establishments	Number of employees	Receipts (mil dol)	Annual payroll (mil dol)	Number of establishments	Number of employees	Receipts (mil dol)	Annual payroll (mil dol)
	92	93	94	95	96	97	98	99	100	101	102	103
MICHIGAN—Cont'd												
Oak Park	43	D	D	D	1	D	D	D	80	555	41.2	16.1
Pontiac	102	1 226	76.3	18.3	9	96	8.4	1.6	114	1 294	156.3	59.4
Portage	142	D	D	D	14	76	4.1	0.9	160	1 924	167.2	75.6
Port Huron	64	1 016	39.8	11.6	11	132	5.3	1.5	127	1 263	153.2	78.4
Rochester Hills	105	2 490	109.1	33.8	20	D	D	D	290	3 201	358.3	139.4
Roseville	109	2 763	116.3	33.6	9	133	4.3	1.4	102	D	D	D
Royal Oak	157	3 304	170.7	49.2	15	D	D	D	175	D	D	D
Saginaw	76	948	44.7	12.0	2	D	D	D	111	1 788	193.9	83.0
St. Clair Shores	116	D	D	D	22	D	D	D	203	D	D	D
Southfield	240	4 113	234.8	65.0	21	256	17.6	7.1	692	8 755	934.5	419.4
Southgate	92	2 179	99.8	29.7	4	D	D	D	75	835	90.1	34.6
Sterling Heights	226	4 510	191.9	55.7	27	D	D	D	349	3 546	324.1	132.3
Taylor	143	2 257	103.7	28.0	15	D	D	D	121	1 790	160.6	65.4
Troy	269	6 231	342.7	102.3	34	D	D	D	477	D	D	D
Warren	296	5 058	236.0	66.5	23	D	D	D	338	D	D	D
Westland	151	2 695	119.6	32.6	16	D	D	D	120	1 569	132.3	54.9
Wyandotte	60	604	28.1	7.7	4	D	D	D	46	D	D	D
Wyoming	128	2 271	99.7	27.0	11	D	D	D	102	D	D	D
MINNESOTA	11 345	221 859	11 722.6	3 238.0	1 927	27 308	2 355.8	917.7	11 233	189 308	15 774.4	7 258.9
Andover	19	339	15.5	4.0	6	50	2.1	0.7	43	559	40.0	16.5
Apple Valley	72	1 751	80.2	22.9	10	D	D	D	113	1 128	115.6	47.6
Blaine	109	2 569	117.6	34.4	23	D	D	D	100	1 342	135.0	48.8
Bloomington	266	8 597	540.8	163.0	25	D	D	D	221	3 751	287.0	122.0
Brooklyn Center	48	1 089	53.9	12.7	5	D	D	D	75	963	59.8	29.6
Brooklyn Park	84	1 407	61.5	17.2	17	D	D	D	102	2 753	156.1	60.5
Burnsville	129	2 756	129.5	38.5	30	560	19.8	5.8	209	D	D	D
Coon Rapids	110	2 581	128.3	36.6	15	314	17.3	4.4	127	D	D	D
Cottage Grove	32	652	27.9	8.1	5	59	2.2	0.8	44	D	D	D
Duluth	227	5 656	250.0	71.8	28	286	10.4	3.7	263	5 585	485.0	214.0
Eagan	153	3 503	216.5	51.8	16	D	D	D	164	2 756	242.0	94.3
Eden Prairie	149	3 143	165.8	49.4	31	D	D	D	147	2 642	494.2	125.1
Edina	104	2 811	161.3	46.9	26	D	D	D	365	D	D	D
Fridley	48	D	D	D	8	D	D	D	77	D	D	D
Inver Grove Heights	52	971	43.3	13.0	6	60	3.4	1.0	59	944	58.2	28.1
Lakeville	65	1 687	69.7	20.5	13	D	D	D	102	D	D	D
Mankato	140	3 421	138.6	37.9	9	171	6.6	1.5	123	2 577	231.0	109.7
Maple Grove	113	3 337	169.1	48.5	14	D	D	D	150	2 340	223.3	94.4
Maplewood	108	2 244	104.6	30.3	16	D	D	D	155	2 048	258.9	103.9
Minneapolis	1 141	27 424	1 646.9	469.0	169	2 816	501.8	258.8	818	16 746	1 296.2	670.3
Minnetonka	112	2 594	147.1	44.7	29	D	D	D	167	2 597	499.3	141.1
Moorhead	57	1 584	59.7	18.0	7	D	D	D	79	1 420	94.8	40.5
Oakdale	40	963	68.0	16.0	12	D	D	D	42	522	41.1	13.4
Owatonna	66	1 448	54.8	15.6	8	D	D	D	72	D	D	D
Plymouth	131	2 863	137.0	41.4	21	384	25.4	6.2	198	2 705	421.0	189.0
Richfield	62	1 172	66.6	20.0	6	23	1.8	0.6	76	1 832	107.1	50.3
Rochester	292	7 130	374.5	106.7	28	613	20.9	6.9	260	6 019	558.8	248.2
Roseville	118	3 330	164.7	51.5	14	D	D	D	142	3 636	299.1	147.0
St. Cloud	163	3 714	163.6	44.9	28	359	23.8	5.7	166	5 141	424.5	257.6
St. Louis Park	96	2 413	135.1	40.2	28	D	D	D	198	D	D	D
St. Paul	599	11 383	589.0	173.3	84	1 613	203.0	98.9	685	15 640	1 017.7	535.3
Savage	43	D	D	D	9	203	14.3	3.9	47	428	34.8	14.0
Shakopee	78	D	D	D	17	D	D	D	72	695	58.6	29.0
Shoreview	30	629	27.3	7.8	9	42	4.1	1.1	68	703	56.7	26.4
Winona	88	1 902	68.3	18.3	12	154	6.9	2.7	43	D	D	D
Woodbury	114	2 800	133.5	38.7	22	D	D	D	188	2 604	312.7	125.7
MISSISSIPPI	5 177	116 238	6 999.2	1 765.0	467	6 178	453.1	115.8	5 149	84 441	8 730.7	3 450.8
Biloxi	127	10 835	1 089.8	266.2	21	1 448	114.4	27.6	128	D	D	D
Clinton	56	1 270	60.0	14.3	9	D	D	D	48	834	57.9	22.5
Greenville	71	1 709	115.4	27.9	5	D	D	D	110	D	D	D
Gulfport	197	5 065	345.8	81.8	12	D	D	D	209	D	D	D
Hattiesburg	232	5 570	248.9	68.4	16	D	D	D	199	5 424	709.3	332.0
Horn Lake	52	1 260	59.3	15.3	5	D	D	D	17	D	D	D
Jackson	370	7 443	378.2	103.7	22	449	42.9	10.6	515	10 396	1 297.0	513.0
Meridian	154	3 512	168.4	44.0	8	48	2.5	0.6	169	D	D	D
Olive Branch	70	1 581	77.6	19.9	10	D	D	D	54	D	D	D
Pearl	73	1 563	86.6	21.6	5	D	D	D	31	333	42.0	12.4
Southaven	125	3 105	149.8	39.2	4	D	D	D	137	D	D	D
Tupelo	165	4 002	173.2	47.7	11	D	D	D	188	D	D	D

1. Establishments subject to federal tax.

Table D. Cities — Other Services and Government Employment and Payroll

City	Other services[1], 2012 — Number of establishments	Number of employees	Receipts (mil dol)	Annual payroll (mil dol)	Full-time equivalent employees	Government employment and payroll, 2012 — March payroll — Total (dollars)	Percent of total for: Administration, judicial, and legal	Police and Corrections	Fire Protection	Highways and transportation	Health and welfare	Natural resources and utilities	Education and libraries
	104	105	106	107	108	109	110	111	112	113	114	115	116
MICHIGAN—Cont'd													
Oak Park	34	197	21.9	6.4	185	937 924	18.6	60.3	0.0	10.5	1.9	3.7	3.3
Pontiac	58	439	46.2	13.5	430	1 925 926	17.1	26.9	21.9	5.4	1.8	16.6	1.4
Portage	89	659	53.5	16.1	226	1 051 828	15.4	37.7	18.1	12.3	4.6	4.9	0.0
Port Huron	34	193	10.0	3.1	265	1 254 174	10.2	26.7	19.4	6.8	0.5	25.3	0.0
Rochester Hills	83	472	31.1	9.7	212	1 126 747	28.0	1.5	20.1	6.3	0.0	29.2	0.0
Roseville	76	425	36.9	10.6	272	1 442 763	17.1	38.9	18.8	5.1	2.8	6.5	2.7
Royal Oak	118	650	59.8	17.3	321	1 931 268	16.4	25.4	37.1	2.0	1.2	5.2	3.3
Saginaw	45	245	21.6	5.7	613	1 804 633	11.1	28.9	17.4	6.3	2.1	29.3	0.0
St. Clair Shores	98	577	33.0	10.4	289	1 541 860	15.0	42.8	21.6	1.7	0.7	11.6	5.1
Southfield	115	631	59.1	16.2	690	3 446 012	19.1	28.8	18.1	5.7	1.0	8.4	6.3
Southgate	53	532	55.1	15.3	177	773 845	14.0	43.0	18.7	6.4	1.2	9.7	2.6
Sterling Heights	175	950	85.3	27.6	579	3 290 094	12.5	40.0	22.0	5.0	1.9	8.5	3.7
Taylor	103	974	88.6	37.0	369	1 754 345	13.6	40.4	19.0	6.4	4.2	14.1	0.3
Troy	178	1 647	169.1	58.1	515	2 464 478	14.8	42.0	3.2	8.2	0.0	17.1	6.8
Warren	214	1 570	191.9	60.4	409	1 654 082	24.5	41.8	6.8	11.2	1.1	10.9	0.0
Westland	110	720	74.4	21.5	341	1 711 074	17.2	33.4	26.3	2.7	4.2	10.7	4.8
Wyandotte	35	171	15.2	4.9	264	1 258 764	6.9	21.7	11.9	10.2	0.2	39.9	0.0
Wyoming	110	771	68.1	21.3	303	1 910 038	15.8	32.7	7.9	12.1	3.7	22.2	0.0
MINNESOTA	8 286	51 746	4 542.3	1 382.9	X	X	X	X	X	X	X	X	X
Andover	33	253	11.5	4.8	57	306 532	24.8	0.0	6.4	37.0	5.8	20.9	0.0
Apple Valley	57	492	35.1	12.2	229	1 179 963	20.1	31.5	5.2	9.3	0.0	23.8	0.0
Blaine	116	899	89.2	27.5	193	1 113 430	14.4	41.7	4.5	11.3	3.0	15.1	0.0
Bloomington	150	1 477	137.0	42.8	580	3 330 394	17.4	31.1	1.2	8.0	13.9	19.4	0.0
Brooklyn Center	20	99	4.8	1.7	190	907 979	13.2	39.3	1.8	9.0	0.9	16.1	0.0
Brooklyn Park	80	457	34.6	12.1	439	1 758 756	8.0	36.5	10.9	10.9	10.0	15.7	0.0
Burnsville	117	802	66.9	22.7	283	1 681 229	9.1	34.0	19.2	3.9	1.0	16.7	0.0
Coon Rapids	75	502	44.9	12.5	274	1 545 147	17.1	30.9	13.2	6.2	5.6	15.0	0.0
Cottage Grove	38	203	11.3	4.1	144	711 248	12.8	41.8	9.7	7.9	5.8	15.7	0.0
Duluth	124	909	75.2	20.9	1 045	5 036 775	9.3	20.6	16.0	20.5	3.8	18.3	4.0
Eagan	111	1 396	130.4	45.7	268	1 561 646	13.0	28.8	3.4	11.0	7.1	30.5	0.0
Eden Prairie	117	971	89.6	26.0	328	1 743 608	14.5	34.2	4.6	8.2	2.3	23.7	0.0
Edina	90	1 073	83.2	30.7	352	1 123 601	13.6	25.8	14.8	13.3	1.1	27.2	0.0
Fridley	46	383	32.9	12.9	159	814 545	21.9	36.8	8.3	11.3	0.0	18.0	0.0
Inver Grove Heights	43	276	24.6	8.0	165	851 190	11.3	30.5	5.7	13.8	7.8	30.9	0.0
Lakeville	77	546	41.2	13.2	211	1 082 740	14.0	36.0	3.4	11.5	2.5	18.7	0.0
Mankato	71	547	40.6	13.8	247	1 231 381	15.7	27.7	8.8	14.5	6.7	19.1	0.0
Maple Grove	104	862	68.6	24.4	296	1 469 495	14.2	34.1	4.5	6.8	2.2	24.2	0.0
Maplewood	70	359	31.7	10.1	213	1 114 986	14.1	35.4	13.8	12.7	0.3	17.3	0.0
Minneapolis	680	5 266	422.1	142.9	5 068	26 103 532	17.5	27.4	10.3	12.5	9.5	21.9	0.0
Minnetonka	96	717	40.5	15.2	278	1 451 759	17.2	30.1	6.4	12.6	6.1	22.6	0.0
Moorhead	62	311	23.5	7.3	325	1 425 672	7.7	22.3	13.7	9.6	0.7	41.4	0.0
Oakdale	34	D	D	D	111	601 791	15.3	41.9	9.3	5.0	3.9	15.6	0.0
Owatonna	52	278	35.4	7.6	211	1 033 223	2.7	19.8	4.9	11.0	1.6	48.8	5.9
Plymouth	94	765	62.7	24.2	284	1 540 683	14.5	33.6	5.5	10.0	5.3	23.7	0.0
Richfield	51	337	26.5	10.6	152	758 629	14.7	33.6	0.0	13.7	5.8	23.9	0.0
Rochester	145	1 329	90.8	32.3	902	4 970 436	6.7	22.3	13.1	9.3	0.0	38.4	6.2
Roseville	88	825	60.5	20.8	191	1 032 673	11.9	37.1	9.1	3.6	4.1	15.9	0.0
St. Cloud	98	941	91.9	28.1	476	2 084 342	8.3	31.7	16.1	9.7	5.9	21.3	0.0
St. Louis Park	109	545	35.9	12.0	270	1 697 664	10.1	28.0	11.9	8.0	13.9	19.8	0.0
St. Paul	371	2 885	226.3	78.2	3 092	18 028 194	10.8	29.1	17.9	10.0	8.1	20.1	4.0
Savage	53	500	26.3	9.9	118	627 032	15.4	38.4	2.4	14.5	0.0	16.4	0.0
Shakopee	59	314	34.7	9.9	200	1 024 903	11.0	30.0	5.6	7.6	0.0	27.1	0.0
Shoreview	19	D	D	D	99	459 573	15.0	0.0	37.1	15.7	12.0	15.7	0.0
Winona	41	230	21.4	6.2	178	771 072	9.5	27.9	14.3	9.5	3.1	24.9	4.4
Woodbury	84	800	48.3	18.2	208	1 116 340	7.1	20.7	13.8	10.0	0.0	38.6	5.6
MISSISSIPPI	2 801	15 027	1 359.2	402.3	X	X	X	X	X	X	X	X	X
Biloxi	44	285	23.6	7.4	618	2 485 229	7.2	33.9	31.9	11.2	2.3	9.3	0.0
Clinton	28	135	13.3	3.9	200	583 437	12.6	31.2	23.8	11.1	0.0	20.4	0.0
Greenville	45	366	32.0	9.5	418	1 079 087	14.6	25.9	20.6	12.0	0.0	22.1	0.0
Gulfport	102	537	46.0	14.7	2 468	12 266 312	2.9	7.1	4.8	1.2	81.1	1.5	0.0
Hattiesburg	84	551	43.3	12.9	695	1 732 465	13.4	28.5	23.1	10.4	3.7	17.8	0.0
Horn Lake	20	107	13.7	3.6	207	963 937	6.8	40.4	27.4	12.4	0.0	9.9	0.0
Jackson	192	1 476	118.0	40.1	1 879	5 259 822	12.8	36.0	22.9	4.9	6.7	16.7	0.0
Meridian	85	D	D	D	506	1 342 577	12.8	26.9	25.1	9.4	2.6	19.3	0.0
Olive Branch	48	280	22.9	6.8	339	1 161 405	13.8	24.1	23.4	3.7	6.6	20.3	0.0
Pearl	42	214	24.6	7.2	218	812 891	8.6	31.3	29.5	10.4	2.5	17.7	0.0
Southaven	52	328	24.4	8.1	376	1 251 638	8.3	38.8	36.0	1.8	0.0	15.2	0.0
Tupelo	83	809	70.2	31.0	513	1 717 455	12.7	24.9	21.1	9.8	0.0	29.0	0.0

1. Establishments subject to federal tax.

City	City government finances, 2012									
	General revenue							General expenditure		
		Intergovernmental		Taxes					Per capita[1] (dollars)	
					Per capita[1] (dollars)					
	Total (mil dol)	Total (mil dol)	Percent from state government	Total (mil dol)	Total	Property	Sales and gross receipts	Total (mil dol)	Total	Capital outlays
	117	118	119	120	121	122	123	124	125	126
MICHIGAN—Cont'd										
Oak Park	34.3	6.1	77.1	15.3	515	501	14	32.4	1 094	25
Pontiac	80.8	29.4	48.1	29.2	491	278	50	91.7	1 541	157
Portage	42.4	7.6	94.6	24.0	508	481	26	39.8	842	89
Port Huron	56.4	17.9	36.7	21.0	712	492	23	60.3	2 048	427
Rochester Hills	71.4	14.4	64.9	31.6	437	403	34	59.2	819	60
Roseville	60.4	8.9	82.4	25.0	527	511	16	53.3	1 126	43
Royal Oak	80.5	15.1	59.4	31.4	537	481	56	82.6	1 412	97
Saginaw	92.8	33.0	36.6	21.3	420	150	24	92.8	1 827	78
St. Clair Shores	68.3	10.3	86.2	32.7	546	515	32	62.0	1 037	61
Southfield	103.2	22.5	49.8	64.7	892	863	29	95.5	1 316	49
Southgate	30.9	6.3	84.0	16.4	550	533	17	30.8	1 034	2
Sterling Heights	116.0	21.5	85.9	55.5	426	408	17	126.6	970	137
Taylor	98.5	28.2	37.2	43.0	688	652	36	96.7	1 549	17
Troy	91.2	12.7	89.5	49.2	600	579	21	79.5	969	131
Warren	142.5	27.4	77.3	78.9	588	570	18	136.7	1 019	40
Westland	82.4	25.5	58.5	27.2	327	312	14	78.6	943	2
Wyandotte	44.6	7.8	56.0	16.7	656	640	16	53.7	2 107	160
Wyoming	74.0	21.7	50.6	26.8	365	333	32	64.1	874	19
MINNESOTA	X	X	X	X	X	X	X	X	X	X
Andover	22.9	1.9	92.9	12.6	406	393	12	18.3	588	147
Apple Valley	46.2	2.4	99.7	25.9	518	476	43	38.3	766	170
Blaine	45.6	3.0	81.8	23.5	396	359	37	44.2	746	172
Bloomington	120.6	11.3	85.5	69.9	812	609	203	137.2	1 595	316
Brooklyn Center	39.3	5.0	72.8	18.2	595	514	59	39.3	1 280	319
Brooklyn Park	79.5	9.0	54.3	44.0	566	543	23	69.8	898	50
Burnsville	55.1	4.0	78.6	33.5	547	501	46	54.1	885	185
Coon Rapids	50.6	4.4	75.2	28.1	453	367	86	69.6	1 124	385
Cottage Grove	32.6	4.1	86.1	13.7	391	358	32	30.2	858	186
Duluth	206.7	90.6	73.8	42.1	488	216	272	223.1	2 586	972
Eagan	55.0	3.8	90.8	28.6	442	413	29	57.4	885	201
Eden Prairie	70.0	5.2	80.2	37.9	610	555	54	67.1	1 079	147
Edina	63.6	3.2	88.7	32.5	663	592	70	63.8	1 301	290
Fridley	25.2	2.5	85.3	13.4	485	445	39	22.0	798	53
Inver Grove Heights	31.7	4.0	89.5	15.9	466	442	24	53.2	1 557	670
Lakeville	38.7	2.8	74.0	25.0	436	404	32	42.0	732	180
Mankato	77.8	20.6	42.2	21.6	539	345	195	74.6	1 863	805
Maple Grove	94.0	6.8	98.0	34.4	534	494	40	87.7	1 362	607
Maplewood	49.5	5.8	59.6	18.9	481	447	34	51.2	1 300	407
Minneapolis	1 017.5	148.8	51.2	459.8	1 170	858	312	1 439.6	3 663	222
Minnetonka	66.8	15.6	62.1	35.1	686	601	85	65.7	1 286	502
Moorhead	71.8	30.0	77.2	8.2	210	171	39	91.5	2 342	1 042
Oakdale	20.9	1.3	73.5	10.5	379	346	33	27.2	981	403
Owatonna	26.3	7.8	88.0	10.8	426	355	71	25.3	995	237
Plymouth	77.8	8.1	86.5	32.3	443	399	45	66.3	909	162
Richfield	43.3	7.0	35.4	22.3	617	560	57	42.6	1 180	117
Rochester	216.6	36.4	96.7	62.4	572	415	158	238.9	2 190	743
Roseville	33.7	3.3	86.1	17.5	506	445	61	34.0	981	217
St. Cloud	89.0	22.7	89.2	36.3	550	348	201	105.0	1 592	659
St. Louis Park	76.4	3.2	86.2	35.3	760	659	101	77.7	1 676	320
St. Paul	510.2	119.9	59.1	175.4	602	412	190	504.8	1 733	219
Savage	32.0	3.4	94.3	16.3	584	537	46	22.4	802	183
Shakopee	36.9	5.1	99.9	15.9	410	373	37	36.0	928	217
Shoreview	25.3	1.3	99.9	11.3	441	424	17	23.1	899	137
Winona	24.8	11.9	97.0	7.9	284	213	71	23.2	837	90
Woodbury	61.1	3.7	75.8	30.7	475	432	44	55.7	863	229
MISSISSIPPI	X	X	X	X	X	X	X	X	X	X
Biloxi	102.9	58.6	70.6	23.1	518	393	125	110.6	2 484	715
Clinton	22.4	8.4	97.4	8.5	332	293	39	20.7	810	145
Greenville	30.6	10.5	67.0	12.3	368	293	75	32.5	970	190
Gulfport	510.2	92.4	40.6	32.6	466	348	117	508.4	7 267	1 373
Hattiesburg	68.9	33.4	74.6	25.2	537	368	168	64.6	1 378	307
Horn Lake	18.5	4.3	95.2	7.0	264	233	31	15.9	598	35
Jackson	222.7	65.9	65.5	79.3	452	389	63	212.1	1 210	208
Meridian	43.9	15.5	100.0	18.6	456	387	69	39.7	973	158
Olive Branch	42.4	15.2	100.0	15.0	434	379	55	33.8	978	185
Pearl	24.5	10.5	91.4	6.9	263	226	37	32.5	1 241	187
Southaven	49.4	12.7	100.0	25.8	512	457	55	48.7	966	118
Tupelo	65.5	32.8	96.4	15.7	442	418	24	62.2	1 751	529

1. Based on population estimated as of July 1 of the year shown.

City	City government finances, 2012 (cont.)									
	General expenditure (cont.)									
	Percent of total for:									
	Public welfare	Highways	Parking facilities	Education	Health and hospitals	Police protection	Sewerage and sanitation	Parks and recreation	Housing and community development	Interest on debt
	127	128	129	130	131	132	133	134	135	136
MICHIGAN—Cont'd										
Oak Park	0.0	4.6	0.0	0.0	0.0	26.1	25.4	3.4	1.7	4.4
Pontiac	0.0	7.1	0.9	0.0	0.0	12.5	18.4	0.4	15.4	3.8
Portage	0.3	15.3	0.0	0.0	0.0	16.1	25.8	5.4	0.7	6.0
Port Huron	0.0	9.9	0.2	0.0	0.0	12.5	24.6	6.6	0.7	4.4
Rochester Hills	0.0	16.6	0.0	0.0	0.0	14.1	16.0	6.6	19.9	4.4
Roseville	0.0	9.7	0.0	0.0	0.0	16.0	16.0	17.9	0.0	1.7
Royal Oak	0.0	8.3	2.6	0.0	0.9	22.0	20.2	4.1	2.4	0.9
Saginaw	0.0	6.8	0.3	0.0	0.0	15.6	28.0	4.9	2.8	4.3
						19.4	19.6	0.4	17.3	1.0
St. Clair Shores	0.0	8.8	0.0	0.0	0.0	18.5	24.7	7.1	0.1	3.1
Southfield	0.0	8.3	0.0	0.0	0.0	25.8	3.3	9.2	0.8	2.2
Southgate	0.0	10.8	0.0	0.0	0.0	19.5	14.2	3.9	0.7	2.6
Sterling Heights	0.0	9.6	0.0	0.0	0.0	23.7	27.1	2.0	0.7	0.9
Taylor	0.0	6.6	0.0	0.0	0.0	13.8	11.6	3.9	20.5	5.2
Troy	0.0	17.7	0.0	0.0	0.0	27.5	18.5	11.2	0.2	3.2
Warren	0.0	10.2	0.0	0.0	0.0	25.5	15.8	5.4	3.9	3.3
Westland	0.0	7.6	0.0	0.0	0.0	18.9	22.4	3.3	2.0	0.4
Wyandotte	0.0	10.3	0.0	0.0	0.0	12.1	10.3	3.8	0.0	1.2
Wyoming	0.0	10.0	0.0	0.0	0.0	23.8	19.2	7.1	14.4	1.7
MINNESOTA	X	X	X	X	X	X	X	X	X	X
Andover	0.0	21.8	0.0	0.0	0.1	14.3	10.5	11.4	13.2	10.2
Apple Valley	0.0	23.5	0.0	0.0	0.1	20.0	12.9	18.3	1.6	4.4
Blaine	0.0	19.5	0.0	0.0	0.0	20.6	22.6	3.2	4.5	4.2
Bloomington	0.0	15.1	0.0	0.0	4.6	18.4	9.8	10.4	0.3	2.3
Brooklyn Center	0.0	19.6	0.0	0.0	0.0	18.2	16.1	7.6	5.8	2.3
Brooklyn Park	0.0	12.2	0.0	0.0	0.0	24.2	11.5	13.9	1.1	5.9
Burnsville	0.0	20.0	0.0	0.0	0.0	22.5	13.2	12.7	0.0	4.0
Coon Rapids	0.0	11.5	0.9	0.0	0.1	12.5	11.3	29.9	4.5	4.1
Cottage Grove	0.0	33.1	0.0	0.0	3.9	16.5	6.7	11.5	4.3	12.1
Duluth	0.0	10.1	0.4	0.0	0.0	13.3	14.3	13.0	4.6	4.5
Eagan	0.0	20.7	0.0	0.0	0.0	19.5	13.7	14.3	0.0	5.8
Eden Prairie	1.2	12.6	0.0	0.0	0.2	17.7	14.4	15.9	4.9	12.0
Edina	0.0	27.8	0.0	0.0	0.8	13.8	14.5	20.4	1.1	3.7
Fridley	0.0	16.8	0.0	0.0	0.0	23.9	27.0	6.0	5.6	0.1
Inver Grove Heights	0.0	24.4	0.0	0.0	0.0	10.4	20.8	20.6	1.3	4.3
Lakeville	0.0	25.3	0.0	0.0	0.0	21.3	9.7	9.7	1.2	8.8
Mankato	0.0	18.4	5.3	0.0	0.0	11.5	15.6	4.6	16.8	3.8
Maple Grove	0.0	38.8	0.0	0.0	0.0	10.9	8.6	15.2	1.5	5.0
Maplewood	0.0	30.5	0.0	0.0	0.3	15.2	9.0	8.7	0.7	17.9
Minneapolis	0.0	6.6	3.3	0.0	1.1	10.1	41.6	7.3	9.6	8.6
Minnetonka	0.0	31.5	0.0	0.0	0.5	16.6	9.2	10.9	8.2	3.8
Moorhead	0.0	11.8	0.0	0.0	0.4	8.0	8.7	5.0	1.2	11.2
Oakdale	0.0	28.1	0.0	0.0	0.0	15.5	10.8	5.0	0.0	3.0
Owatonna	0.0	25.9	0.0	0.0	0.0	16.3	14.0	13.5	3.4	3.0
Plymouth	0.0	16.9	0.0	0.0	0.0	14.7	11.2	18.8	2.0	8.3
Richfield	0.0	7.8	0.0	0.0	0.3	17.0	11.9	11.5	23.0	12.9
Rochester	0.0	14.1	1.4	0.0	0.1	8.6	5.1	7.5	0.2	27.8
Roseville	0.0	14.4	0.0	0.0	0.0	18.2	17.2	12.1	4.2	1.3
St. Cloud	0.0	11.6	1.2	0.0	0.9	15.3	22.1	22.3	1.4	4.9
St. Louis Park	0.0	9.2	0.0	0.0	0.0	9.0	10.3	10.9	1.1	25.9
St. Paul	0.0	12.4	1.3	0.0	0.7	17.5	8.3	15.6	9.7	6.3
Savage	0.0	30.8	0.0	0.0	0.0	19.3	12.0	7.6	0.9	11.4
Shakopee	0.0	22.2	0.0	0.0	0.0	18.6	16.8	12.4	0.0	13.3
Shoreview	0.0	15.7	0.0	0.0	0.0	7.9	23.0	26.0	3.7	6.4
Winona	0.0	12.5	0.0	0.0	0.5	18.9	18.0	13.8	3.7	0.8
Woodbury	0.0	22.0	2.9	0.0	3.0	20.7	11.9	11.7	3.2	3.7
MISSISSIPPI	X	X	X	X	X	X	X	X	X	X
Biloxi	1.0	7.1	0.0	0.0	0.2	13.5	15.9	12.3	0.7	2.1
Clinton	0.0	13.3	0.0	0.0	0.0	19.0	28.7	7.7	0.0	3.8
Greenville	0.4	16.8	0.0	0.0	0.9	22.4	13.5	2.6	0.0	1.1
Gulfport	0.0	5.6	0.0	0.0	72.1	4.7	4.9	3.1	2.1	1.8
Hattiesburg	0.0	16.5	0.3	0.0	1.6	16.2	16.4	6.6	2.8	2.3
Horn Lake	0.0	6.3	0.0	0.0	0.7	27.6	15.3	6.7	0.7	6.2
Jackson	0.5	9.5	0.0	0.0	0.5	15.4	16.2	6.3	0.9	4.0
Meridian	0.0	13.7	0.4	0.0	0.0	18.3	14.0	5.1	2.6	5.1
Olive Branch	0.0	10.9	0.0	0.0	2.5	22.3	22.4	4.0	0.0	5.9
Pearl	0.0	22.1	0.0	0.0	1.4	19.0	18.3	4.3	0.0	6.3
Southaven	0.0	2.9	0.0	0.0	0.6	21.9	9.2	9.5	0.0	8.5
Tupelo	0.0	24.5	0.0	0.0	0.0	16.4	11.5	9.2	0.1	4.2

Table D. Cities — City Government Finances, City Government Employment, and Climate

	City government finances, 2012 (cont.)			Climate[2]						
	Debt outstanding			Average daily temperature (degrees Fahrenheit)						
				Mean		Limits				
City	Total (mil dol)	Per capita[1] (dollars)	Debt issued during year	January	July	January[3]	July[4]	Annual precipitation (inches)	Heating degree days	Cooling degree days
	137	138	139	140	141	142	143	144	145	146
MICHIGAN—Cont'd										
Oak Park	45.1	1 521	0.0	24.7	73.7	16.1	85.7	33.58	6 224	788
Pontiac	80.8	1 357	5.6	22.9	71.9	15.9	82.3	30.03	6 680	626
Portage	90.1	1 908	15.0	24.3	73.2	17.0	84.2	37.41	6 235	773
Port Huron	122.4	4 160	21.5	22.8	72.2	15.1	81.9	31.39	6 845	626
Rochester Hills	31.9	441	5.0	22.0	70.6	13.7	82.7	35.74	7 046	523
Roseville	13.3	282	0.3	25.3	73.6	18.8	83.3	33.97	6 160	757
Royal Oak	117.8	2 013	0.0	24.7	73.7	16.1	85.7	33.58	6 224	788
Saginaw	81.9	1 612	13.5	21.4	71.2	14.9	81.9	31.61	7 099	548
St. Clair Shores	53.2	890	9.1	25.3	73.6	18.8	83.3	33.97	6 160	757
Southfield	64.8	893	0.0	24.7	73.7	16.1	85.7	33.58	6 224	788
Southgate	22.5	757	0.3	24.5	73.5	17.8	83.4	32.89	6 422	736
Sterling Heights	63.9	490	13.6	24.4	71.9	18.0	81.8	32.24	6 620	597
Taylor	147.4	2 362	1.4	24.5	73.5	17.8	83.4	32.89	6 422	736
Troy	55.0	669	0.0	22.9	71.9	15.9	82.3	30.03	6 680	626
Warren	159.2	1 186	8.8	24.7	73.7	16.1	85.7	33.58	6 224	788
Westland	12.4	149	0.8	24.6	73.9	17.6	84.7	32.80	6 167	828
Wyandotte	63.3	2 483	0.8	24.5	73.5	17.8	83.4	32.89	6 422	736
Wyoming	117.0	1 595	7.3	22.4	71.4	15.6	82.3	37.13	6 896	613
MINNESOTA	X	X	X	X	X	X	X	X	X	X
Andover	55.4	1 776	0.3	10.9	70.4	1.8	80.5	31.36	8 367	500
Apple Valley	71.3	1 426	9.2	9.2	69.4	-1.1	80.5	29.19	8 805	416
Blaine	51.9	874	1.6	10.9	70.4	1.8	80.5	31.36	8 367	500
Bloomington	158.7	1 844	27.0	13.1	73.2	4.3	83.3	29.41	7 876	699
Brooklyn Center	47.5	1 549	0.0	13.0	71.4	2.8	82.8	30.50	7 983	587
Brooklyn Park	95.6	1 229	16.1	13.0	71.4	2.8	82.8	30.50	7 983	587
Burnsville	62.7	1 026	8.4	13.8	74.0	3.4	85.8	30.44	7 549	803
Coon Rapids	87.0	1 407	9.1	13.0	71.4	2.8	82.8	30.50	7 983	587
Cottage Grove	57.0	1 618	0.0	12.0	72.1	2.5	82.6	29.95	8 032	617
Duluth	251.3	2 914	21.9	8.4	65.5	-1.2	76.3	31.00	9 724	189
Eagan	61.1	943	0.0	13.1	73.2	4.3	83.3	29.41	7 876	699
Eden Prairie	202.7	3 258	11.3	10.2	71.4	-0.3	82.2	28.82	8 429	567
Edina	119.7	2 440	15.0	13.8	74.0	3.4	85.8	30.44	7 549	803
Fridley	14.9	541	0.0	10.9	70.4	1.8	80.5	31.36	8 367	500
Inver Grove Heights	55.6	1 626	4.6	10.1	71.0	0.0	81.3	34.60	8 345	533
Lakeville	90.0	1 570	4.3	13.1	72.2	3.8	83.6	31.43	7 773	658
Mankato	117.0	2 921	4.6	12.5	72.1	2.4	83.4	33.42	8 029	650
Maple Grove	207.8	3 225	5.4	13.0	71.4	2.8	82.8	30.50	7 983	587
Maplewood	157.8	4 004	10.0	14.5	73.0	6.2	83.2	32.59	7 606	715
Minneapolis	3 439.9	8 754	233.0	13.1	73.2	4.3	83.3	29.41	7 876	699
Minnetonka	91.2	1 784	0.0	13.1	73.2	4.3	83.3	29.41	7 876	699
Moorhead	252.1	6 451	10.0	3.8	69.8	-7.1	81.5	21.56	9 628	478
Oakdale	31.2	1 124	10.6	14.5	73.0	6.2	83.2	32.59	7 606	715
Owatonna	49.7	1 954	8.3	NA	NA	NA	NA	NA	NA	NA
Plymouth	108.6	1 490	0.0	13.0	71.4	2.8	82.8	30.50	7 983	587
Richfield	105.3	2 917	11.9	13.1	73.2	4.3	83.3	29.41	7 876	699
Rochester	2 086.4	19 128	285.0	9.8	70.0	0.0	80.9	29.10	8 703	474
Roseville	20.1	581	10.0	14.5	73.0	6.2	83.2	32.59	7 606	715
St. Cloud	413.3	6 266	35.1	8.8	69.8	-1.2	81.7	27.13	8 815	443
St. Louis Park	499.7	10 778	0.0	13.0	71.4	2.8	82.8	30.50	7 983	587
St. Paul	770.7	2 646	98.7	14.5	73.0	6.2	83.2	32.59	7 606	715
Savage	84.5	3 021	10.7	NA	NA	NA	NA	NA	NA	NA
Shakopee	92.8	2 394	0.0	NA	NA	NA	NA	NA	NA	NA
Shoreview	51.1	1 990	8.6	14.5	73.0	6.2	83.2	32.59	7 606	715
Winona	7.0	254	0.0	17.6	75.8	9.2	85.3	34.20	6 839	990
Woodbury	92.0	1 427	1.5	11.5	72.1	1.9	81.9	29.92	8 104	621
MISSISSIPPI	X	X	X	X	X	X	X	X	X	X
Biloxi	68.0	1 528	0.5	50.7	81.7	43.5	88.5	64.84	1 645	2 517
Clinton	36.4	1 422	1.7	NA	NA	NA	NA	NA	NA	NA
Greenville	22.8	681	10.5	42.3	82.6	33.0	92.6	54.20	2 715	2 216
Gulfport	212.6	3 038	5.0	51.6	82.6	42.6	91.3	65.20	1 514	2 679
Hattiesburg	89.3	1 904	5.4	47.9	81.7	36.0	92.1	62.47	2 024	2 327
Horn Lake	35.8	1 350	0.0	NA	NA	NA	NA	NA	NA	NA
Jackson	322.3	1 839	62.9	45.0	81.4	35.0	91.4	55.95	2 401	2 264
Meridian	61.0	1 493	9.3	46.1	81.7	34.7	92.9	58.65	2 352	2 173
Olive Branch	57.9	1 676	15.0	NA	NA	NA	NA	NA	NA	NA
Pearl	99.8	3 814	6.4	NA	NA	NA	NA	NA	NA	NA
Southaven	96.2	1 909	8.0	37.9	80.4	27.8	90.3	55.06	3 442	1 749
Tupelo	82.1	2 311	14.6	40.4	80.6	30.5	91.4	55.86	3 086	1 884

1. Based on the population estimated as of July 1 of the year shown. 2. Represents normal values based on the 30-year period, 1971–2000. 3. Average daily minimum.
4. Average daily maximum.

Table D. Cities — **Land Area and Population**

STATE Place code	City	Land area,[1] 2016 (sq mi)	Population, 2016			Race alone[2] (percent), 2015						
			Total persons	Rank	Per square mile	White	Black or African American	American Indian, Alaska Native	Asian	Hawaiian Pacific Islander	Some other race	2 or more races[2]
		1	2	3	4	5	6	7	8	9	10	11
29 00000	MISSOURI.............	68 746.5	6 093 000	X	88.6	82.4	11.7	0.4	1.9	0.1	1.1	2.5
29 03160	Ballwin.....................	9.0	30 313	1 239	3 368.1	NA	NA	NA	NA	NA	NA	NA
29 06652	Blue Springs.................	22.4	54 431	695	2 430.0	90.3	4.0	0.2	0.8	0.0	1.1	3.6
29 11242	Cape Girardeau............	29.0	39 628	957	1 366.5	81.9	12.6	0.3	2.2	0.0	0.0	2.9
29 13600	Chesterfield................	31.8	47 659	803	1 498.7	83.2	2.0	0.1	11.6	0.0	0.2	3.0
29 15670	Columbia..................	65.0	120 612	230	1 855.6	76.6	10.8	0.4	5.8	0.3	1.6	4.6
29 24778	Florissant.................	12.6	51 776	737	4 109.2	54.1	40.3	0.2	0.8	0.1	0.0	4.6
29 27190	Gladstone.................	8.1	27 114	1 360	3 347.4	87.0	2.5	2.2	1.0	0.0	4.7	2.6
29 31276	Hazelwood..............	16.0	25 443	1 414	1 590.2	52.0	35.8	0.0	4.6	0.0	0.4	7.3
29 35000	Independence..............	77.8	117 030	237	1 504.2	82.4	7.9	0.6	0.4	0.4	6.1	2.2
29 37000	Jefferson City	36.1	43 013	873	1 191.5	75.8	18.9	0.9	1.5	0.0	0.1	2.9
29 37592	Joplin.......................	36.8	52 195	730	1 418.3	88.3	2.1	3.0	1.4	0.2	0.5	4.5
29 38000	Kansas City...............	315.0	481 420	37	1 528.3	59.8	29.7	0.3	2.9	0.1	2.4	4.5
29 39044	Kirkwood..................	9.2	27 609	1 337	3 001.0	NA	NA	NA	NA	NA	NA	NA
29 41348	Lee's Summit	63.8	96 076	320	1 505.9	85.7	7.1	0.6	2.6	0.5	1.8	1.6
29 42032	Liberty.....................	28.9	30 614	1 229	1 059.3	89.6	5.9	0.6	0.0	0.0	1.9	2.1
29 46586	Maryland Heights	21.9	27 137	1 359	1 239.1	NA	NA	NA	NA	NA	NA	NA
29 54074	O'Fallon...................	29.7	86 274	383	2 904.8	88.8	5.3	0.2	3.0	0.0	0.4	2.3
29 60788	Raytown...................	9.9	29 261	1 274	2 955.7	NA	NA	NA	NA	NA	NA	NA
29 64082	St. Charles	24.1	69 293	507	2 875.2	81.2	6.9	0.0	3.8	0.2	2.9	5.0
29 64550	St. Joseph	44.0	76 472	449	1 738.0	86.7	8.0	0.6	0.8	0.0	0.8	3.1
29 65000	St. Louis..................	62.0	311 404	61	5 022.6	46.8	46.6	0.2	2.9	0.2	0.6	2.7
29 65126	St. Peters	22.4	57 289	653	2 557.5	NA	NA	NA	NA	NA	NA	NA
29 70000	Springfield...............	82.3	167 319	152	2 033.0	88.0	4.8	0.5	2.7	0.1	0.9	3.1
29 75220	University City	5.9	34 706	1 096	5 882.4	54.9	38.5	0.2	2.9	0.0	1.6	1.9
29 78442	Wentzville................	20.1	37 395	1 023	1 860.4	90.3	2.8	0.3	3.8	0.0	0.0	2.8
29 79820	Wildwood.................	66.5	35 756	1 067	537.7	93.3	1.6	0.3	3.6	0.0	0.0	1.2
30 00000	MONTANA	145 547.0	1 042 520	X	7.2	88.9	0.5	6.3	0.9	0.1	0.7	2.6
30 06550	Billings.....................	43.7	110 323	265	2 524.6	90.3	0.9	4.4	1.0	0.0	0.6	2.8
30 08950	Bozeman..................	20.0	45 250	836	2 262.5	91.8	0.6	1.0	3.5	0.0	0.6	2.4
30 11390	Butte-Silver Bow...........	718.5	33 853	1 122	47.3	NA	NA	NA	NA	NA	NA	NA
30 32800	Great Falls................	22.9	59 178	630	2 584.2	86.7	1.1	5.3	1.1	0.0	0.8	4.9
30 35600	Helena.....................	16.5	31 169	1 207	1 889.0	NA	NA	NA	NA	NA	NA	NA
30 50200	Missoula	29.2	72 364	486	2 478.2	90.6	0.9	2.8	2.6	0.0	0.0	3.1
31 00000	NEBRASKA...............	76 823.8	1 907 116	X	24.8	88.2	4.8	0.9	2.1	0.1	1.7	2.3
31 03950	Bellevue...................	16.6	53 505	706	3 223.2	82.1	8.1	0.3	3.7	0.5	1.2	4.1
31 17670	Fremont...................	9.6	26 519	1 382	2 762.4	NA	NA	NA	NA	NA	NA	NA
31 19595	Grand Island..............	29.7	51 517	742	1 734.6	92.1	3.2	0.5	0.6	0.2	3.0	0.6
31 25055	Kearney...................	14.0	33 520	1 131	2 394.3	93.6	1.8	0.7	1.1	0.0	0.4	2.4
31 28000	Lincoln....................	92.1	280 364	71	3 044.1	85.6	4.4	0.6	4.2	0.1	1.5	3.6
31 37000	Omaha.....................	133.2	446 970	44	3 355.6	77.1	13.1	0.8	3.5	0.0	2.8	2.8
32 00000	NEVADA...................	109 780.2	2 940 058	X	26.8	67.5	8.5	1.2	8.0	0.6	9.2	5.0
32 09700	Carson City	144.7	54 742	690	378.3	86.3	0.6	2.1	3.1	0.0	4.2	3.7
32 31900	Henderson................	104.7	292 969	67	2 798.2	78.8	5.3	0.6	7.0	0.2	4.3	3.8
32 40000	Las Vegas.................	134.4	632 912	28	4 709.2	64.3	11.6	0.7	6.8	0.6	10.6	5.4
32 51800	North Las Vegas	98.0	238 702	90	2 435.7	53.7	20.4	0.5	6.0	0.6	12.6	6.2
32 60600	Reno.......................	107.3	245 255	87	2 285.7	77.3	2.2	0.6	5.8	0.8	7.4	5.9
32 68400	Sparks.....................	36.2	98 345	309	2 716.7	77.9	3.1	1.3	5.9	0.7	6.6	4.5
33 00000	NEW HAMPSHIRE.....	8 952.7	1 334 795	X	149.1	93.6	1.6	0.1	2.6	0.0	0.4	1.7
33 14200	Concord....................	64.0	42 904	877	670.4	90.1	3.6	0.1	3.5	0.0	0.0	2.8
33 18820	Dover......................	26.7	31 153	1 209	1 166.8	91.1	1.7	0.3	4.5	0.0	0.0	2.4
33 45140	Manchester................	33.1	110 506	264	3 338.5	89.0	5.8	0.1	2.9	0.0	0.3	1.8
33 50260	Nashua....................	30.8	87 882	371	2 853.3	82.7	4.1	0.0	10.9	0.0	0.8	1.4
33 65140	Rochester.................	45.1	30 345	1 236	672.8	NA	NA	NA	NA	NA	NA	NA
34 00000	NEW JERSEY..........	7 355.5	8 944 469	X	1 216.0	67.7	13.4	0.2	9.5	0.0	6.5	2.7
34 02080	Atlantic City...............	10.8	38 735	984	3 586.6	31.5	39.3	0.8	21.0	0.0	3.3	4.2
34 03580	Bayonne...................	5.8	66 238	545	11 420.3	60.5	10.2	0.0	10.2	0.6	16.7	2.0
34 05170	Bergenfield	2.9	27 647	1 335	9 533.4	44.3	7.4	0.5	26.7	0.0	17.0	4.1
34 07600	Bridgeton..................	6.2	24 997	1 424	4 031.8	55.7	31.7	0.4	0.2	0.0	8.7	3.3
34 10000	Camden....................	8.9	74 420	469	8 361.8	22.2	41.5	0.7	2.2	0.1	25.9	7.2
34 13690	Clifton.....................	11.3	85 845	384	7 596.9	57.6	9.5	1.7	6.4	0.0	22.5	2.4
34 19390	East Orange...............	3.9	64 789	558	16 612.6	3.2	86.8	0.3	0.7	0.0	6.6	2.4
34 21000	Elizabeth...................	12.3	128 640	214	10 458.5	49.4	18.3	0.4	1.9	0.0	23.8	6.2
34 21480	Englewood.................	4.9	28 455	1 309	5 807.1	45.6	26.3	0.1	12.7	0.0	10.3	5.1
34 22470	Fair Lawn	5.1	33 453	1 134	6 559.4	NA	NA	NA	NA	NA	NA	NA
34 24420	Fort Lee...................	2.5	37 577	1 018	15 030.8	44.3	2.8	0.3	48.1	0.2	3.2	1.2

1. Dry land or land partially or temporarily covered by water.   2. Hispanic or Latino persons may be of any race.

City	Percent Hispanic or Latino[1], 2015	Percent foreign born 2015	Age of population (percent), 2010-2014							Median age 2015	Percent female 2015	Population			
												Census counts		Percent change	
			Under 18 years	18 to 24 years	25 to 34 years	35 to 44 years	45 to 54 years	55 to 64 years	65 years and over			2000	2010	2000–2010	2010–2016
	12	13	14	15	16	17	18	19	20	21	22	23	24	25	26
MISSOURI................	4.0	4.0	22.9	9.8	13.1	12.1	13.3	13.3	15.6	38.4	51.0	5 595 211	5 988 928	7.0	1.7
Ballwin......................	4.6	10.5	26.1	5.4	11.6	13.4	13.7	15.9	14.0	39.5	55.6	31 283	30 389	-2.9	-0.3
Blue Springs.............	5.0	4.0	27.5	6.9	14.3	13.5	10.3	13.4	14.1	36.0	53.5	48 080	52 618	9.4	3.4
Cape Girardeau..........	2.4	4.0	17.3	20.6	11.8	10.6	13.0	11.5	15.2	35.4	53.1	35 349	38 000	7.5	4.3
Chesterfield...............	1.6	14.0	18.8	7.1	10.2	13.2	10.6	15.5	24.6	45.3	51.7	46 802	47 484	1.5	0.4
Columbia....................	4.2	9.0	18.3	26.7	18.2	9.5	10.0	9.7	7.6	26.8	52.5	84 531	109 028	29.0	10.6
Florissant..................	3.7	2.9	24.6	8.3	13.3	11.8	16.1	11.3	14.5	37.8	56.1	50 497	52 300	3.6	-1.0
Gladstone..................	9.5	5.1	17.6	7.9	18.1	10.7	8.6	16.9	20.2	41.1	50.0	26 365	25 449	-3.5	6.5
Hazelwood.................	0.6	5.8	22.3	13.0	12.1	13.7	13.7	11.6	13.5	36.1	47.6	26 206	25 700	-1.9	-1.0
Independence............	10.4	4.2	22.8	8.6	14.5	10.9	12.7	14.5	16.1	38.6	53.6	113 288	116 792	3.1	0.2
Jefferson City............	3.4	4.6	19.2	8.6	15.8	13.6	14.5	13.0	15.2	39.9	46.7	39 636	43 088	8.7	-0.2
Joplin........................	2.4	2.3	22.6	12.7	12.7	12.1	10.5	13.9	15.5	36.4	48.8	45 504	50 788	11.6	2.8
Kansas City...............	9.7	7.9	23.3	9.1	15.9	13.6	13.2	12.5	12.3	35.9	51.9	441 545	459 939	4.2	4.7
Kirkwood...................	1.9	4.5	20.9	4.2	11.3	14.2	10.0	17.4	22.0	44.4	55.4	27 324	27 540	0.8	0.3
Lee's Summit............	4.7	4.0	27.6	8.3	11.0	14.0	15.2	9.9	14.1	36.8	49.1	70 700	91 363	29.2	5.2
Liberty......................	13.1	0.3	27.6	10.0	16.0	11.6	12.7	13.1	9.0	33.4	51.5	26 232	29 155	11.1	5.0
Maryland Heights	5.7	21.1	18.8	6.4	15.5	13.0	15.6	11.1	19.5	40.6	53.5	25 756	27 473	6.7	-1.2
O'Fallon....................	3.0	3.8	27.7	7.5	13.3	15.7	14.0	10.2	11.6	36.0	50.9	46 169	79 515	72.2	8.5
Raytown....................	3.4	1.9	24.7	8.6	10.5	17.6	13.5	12.1	13.0	37.8	52.8	30 388	29 467	-3.0	-0.7
St. Charles................	5.9	7.7	20.1	13.7	16.4	10.2	11.1	14.2	14.4	34.9	53.4	60 321	66 126	9.6	4.8
St. Joseph.................	7.1	4.9	22.7	10.2	16.1	11.6	12.6	11.2	15.6	35.7	50.5	73 990	76 807	3.8	-0.4
St. Louis...................	3.9	6.9	20.1	10.3	19.5	13.1	12.4	13.1	11.6	35.0	51.5	348 189	319 381	-8.3	-2.5
St. Peters..................	3.7	3.1	22.3	7.7	14.0	14.3	15.1	13.9	12.7	37.8	50.9	51 381	52 563	2.3	9.0
Springfield................	4.3	4.7	16.9	19.1	15.3	11.1	11.4	10.1	16.2	34.1	51.4	151 580	159 446	5.2	4.9
University City	4.2	7.1	20.7	10.5	19.9	14.6	11.1	10.9	12.3	34.4	52.3	37 428	35 364	-5.5	-1.9
Wentzville..................	0.9	3.8	27.0	8.6	16.1	15.5	12.6	7.8	12.6	33.3	49.4	6 896	29 358	325.7	27.4
Wildwood...................	2.6	4.6	27.3	8.0	6.3	10.4	18.5	17.6	11.8	43.4	49.5	32 884	35 532	8.1	0.6
MONTANA	3.6	2.1	21.9	9.7	12.5	11.5	12.5	14.6	17.3	39.9	49.8	902 195	989 414	9.7	5.4
Billings......................	6.8	2.9	22.3	9.5	16.5	11.3	12.2	12.7	15.5	36.3	52.2	89 847	104 289	16.1	5.8
Bozeman...................	3.1	3.5	15.2	26.6	18.8	11.3	6.9	11.1	10.1	29.1	46.7	27 509	37 283	35.5	21.4
Butte-Silver Bow..........	4.1	3.3	20.4	11.9	9.7	11.7	13.9	14.8	17.5	41.0	50.6	34 606	33 505	-3.2	1.0
Great Falls.................	3.4	2.5	21.7	10.8	12.0	10.7	12.8	13.0	19.0	40.2	51.4	56 690	59 103	4.3	0.1
Helena......................	4.8	1.1	19.2	11.5	13.3	12.6	14.3	11.8	17.3	38.3	51.6	25 780	28 220	9.5	10.5
Missoula...................	3.5	3.9	17.3	17.6	15.3	13.7	12.4	10.4	13.4	34.7	50.7	57 053	66 868	17.2	8.2
NEBRASKA...............	10.4	6.8	24.8	10.2	13.3	12.3	12.2	12.5	14.7	36.1	50.3	1 711 263	1 826 334	6.7	4.4
Bellevue....................	15.8	8.8	24.9	14.9	10.8	11.2	12.8	12.5	13.0	34.6	48.8	44 382	51 531	16.1	3.8
Fremont....................	13.1	7.7	22.5	12.6	11.9	9.2	13.7	11.6	18.4	37.4	52.4	25 174	26 415	4.9	0.4
Grand Island.............	30.5	14.9	27.7	10.4	12.2	13.6	10.5	12.0	13.5	34.6	50.5	42 940	48 647	13.3	5.9
Kearney....................	9.1	3.3	22.3	21.8	13.9	11.5	9.5	8.9	12.0	29.3	51.6	27 431	30 942	12.8	8.3
Lincoln......................	7.3	8.3	22.8	15.9	15.0	12.5	10.7	11.2	11.9	32.3	50.0	225 581	258 472	14.6	8.5
Omaha......................	14.3	10.9	24.8	10.0	16.2	12.4	12.1	12.0	12.4	34.2	50.7	390 007	432 003	10.8	3.5
NEVADA...................	28.1	19.3	23.1	8.8	14.2	13.4	13.5	12.3	14.6	37.8	49.9	1 998 257	2 700 691	35.2	8.9
Carson City	23.4	10.2	20.6	9.1	9.2	11.9	13.8	14.9	20.4	44.2	48.9	52 457	55 274	5.4	-1.0
Henderson.................	16.5	12.5	20.9	6.3	12.1	14.4	13.0	13.7	19.7	42.5	51.2	175 381	257 248	46.7	13.9
Las Vegas.................	32.9	20.5	24.3	8.4	14.1	12.8	14.3	12.4	13.8	37.5	50.2	478 434	584 526	22.2	8.3
North Las Vegas	40.4	21.2	28.5	10.7	14.5	14.5	11.8	9.6	10.4	32.2	50.4	115 488	216 686	87.6	10.2
Reno.........................	24.8	15.4	21.6	11.0	16.2	12.4	12.0	12.1	14.7	35.7	49.3	180 480	226 050	25.2	8.5
Sparks......................	30.3	16.3	25.1	8.0	15.0	12.9	13.0	11.5	14.5	36.1	50.3	66 346	90 258	36.0	9.0
NEW HAMPSHIRE.....	3.3	6.0	19.8	9.8	11.7	11.8	15.4	15.2	16.4	42.8	50.6	1 235 786	1 316 461	6.5	1.4
Concord....................	1.2	8.4	19.5	8.9	13.2	13.7	15.1	14.4	15.2	42.3	51.4	40 687	42 698	4.9	0.5
Dover........................	2.7	10.4	19.9	12.1	20.9	10.6	12.2	9.7	14.6	33.5	55.1	26 884	29 988	11.5	3.9
Manchester................	10.9	13.2	19.9	12.0	15.2	11.8	15.5	12.0	13.6	37.3	50.2	107 006	109 574	2.4	0.9
Nashua.....................	11.9	14.4	21.6	8.0	14.8	14.4	14.2	12.5	14.4	38.3	51.2	86 605	86 492	-0.1	1.6
Rochester..................	1.1	1.9	19.4	9.8	13.0	12.7	16.0	12.8	16.2	41.4	49.9	28 461	29 778	4.6	1.9
NEW JERSEY............	19.7	22.1	22.3	8.8	12.9	13.0	14.8	13.2	15.0	39.6	51.2	8 414 350	8 791 953	4.5	1.7
Atlantic City	23.5	31.3	25.2	10.0	15.0	11.7	13.3	11.5	13.4	34.6	47.8	40 517	39 558	-2.4	-2.1
Bayonne	29.4	33.0	23.4	6.4	14.4	14.6	13.2	14.2	13.8	39.7	50.7	61 842	63 010	1.9	5.1
Bergenfield................	30.2	35.5	25.4	11.3	8.4	16.7	12.8	10.7	14.7	37.4	50.6	26 247	26 837	2.2	3.0
Bridgeton..................	48.7	23.5	27.4	10.7	22.4	12.0	13.5	7.5	6.5	29.5	42.4	22 771	25 415	11.6	-1.6
Camden.....................	54.5	14.9	32.6	11.3	15.6	12.8	9.5	9.4	8.8	27.9	52.1	79 904	77 057	-3.6	-3.4
Clifton......................	38.4	32.4	21.9	9.5	12.9	14.4	12.6	15.0	13.7	38.5	51.4	78 672	84 127	6.9	2.0
East Orange..............	9.8	23.3	23.4	10.7	15.0	14.0	13.1	11.9	11.9	35.5	53.8	69 824	64 146	-8.1	1.0
Elizabeth...................	67.0	49.2	26.5	9.4	15.5	15.4	13.7	9.8	9.7	34.2	48.9	120 568	124 969	3.7	2.9
Englewood.................	28.5	36.4	15.2	6.9	13.9	16.6	16.8	14.2	16.5	44.2	52.0	26 203	27 119	3.5	4.9
Fair Lawn..................	14.4	29.8	20.1	8.2	14.5	9.0	16.7	13.9	17.6	44.1	53.1	31 637	32 401	2.4	3.2
Fort Lee....................	13.8	58.9	15.8	7.2	11.2	15.7	14.6	16.2	19.2	45.0	52.4	35 461	35 381	-0.2	6.2

1. May be of any race.

Table D. Cities — Households, Group Quarters, Crime, and Education

City	Households, 2015				Persons in group quarters, 2010				Serious crimes known to police,[2] 2014				Educational attainment, 2015		
	Number	Persons per house-hold	Percent Female family house-holder[1]	Percent One-person	Total	Institutional Total	Persons in nursing facilities	Non-institu-tional	Total Number	Total Rate[3]	Rate[3] Violent	Rate[3] Property	Population age 25 and older	High school graduate or less	Bachelor's degree or more
	27	28	29	30	31	32	33	34	35	36	37	38	39	40	41
MISSOURI	2 374 180	2.49	11.8	29.7	174 142	93 274	44 866	80 868	203 093	3 349	443	2 906	4 097 212	42.1	27.8
Ballwin	11 294	2.71	9.9	20.6	2	0	0	2	218	714	26	688	20 954	19.8	56.5
Blue Springs	19 760	2.73	13.0	20.7	218	182	182	36	1 456	2 725	157	2 567	35 525	32.8	33.3
Cape Girardeau	15 232	2.41	7.7	42.0	3 466	789	712	2 677	2 019	5 175	579	4 596	24 510	32.9	36.9
Chesterfield	19 557	2.40	5.3	28.2	934	925	925	9	764	1 598	71	1 527	35 450	12.7	69.1
Columbia	46 380	2.37	6.6	35.9	8 804	1 146	624	7 658	4 398	3 764	351	3 413	65 566	24.5	53.9
Florissant	21 068	2.44	22.9	30.6	788	668	542	120	1 010	1 928	187	1 741	35 051	38.3	22.2
Gladstone	11 592	2.32	9.2	32.7	42	36	36	6	812	3 084	277	2 807	19 996	38.5	30.2
Hazelwood	10 528	2.42	17.0	32.3	140	0	0	140	899	3 503	273	3 230	16 592	40.5	19.5
Independence	49 848	2.33	16.2	34.6	1 225	1 048	982	177	7 058	6 016	406	5 610	80 504	49.2	19.2
Jefferson City	17 246	2.22	11.9	39.9	4 964	3 990	456	974	1 464	3 375	307	3 069	31 145	33.6	34.9
Joplin	20 010	2.46	7.8	32.4	1 988	743	653	1 245	4 226	8 327	516	7 811	31 145	38.7	27.6
Kansas City	198 129	2.35	12.8	37.9	8 812	4 192	2 499	4 620	28 668	6 120	1 258	4 862	321 405	37.4	33.3
Kirkwood	12 501	2.20	6.5	40.6	257	223	218	34	521	1 887	127	1 760	20 765	16.2	61.6
Lee's Summit	35 267	2.68	10.7	22.9	714	626	573	88	1 879	2 008	88	1 920	61 016	20.5	46.6
Liberty	10 522	2.76	9.2	30.2	1 358	585	277	773	614	2 025	211	1 814	19 008	32.0	34.9
Maryland Heights	11 732	2.28	11.6	31.0	559	522	473	37	567	2 067	222	1 845	20 465	29.9	42.3
O'Fallon	30 486	2.77	10.8	21.9	294	254	247	40	1 139	1 363	72	1 291	55 080	30.6	36.9
Raytown	11 038	2.62	22.4	28.8	559	401	395	158	1 361	4 613	400	4 213	19 619	42.6	25.5
St. Charles	27 024	2.33	10.2	34.0	4 623	917	508	3 706	1 837	2 703	184	2 519	45 542	34.3	34.1
St. Joseph	27 938	2.58	15.4	27.4	4 493	3 104	673	1 389	4 645	6 011	454	5 557	51 080	46.7	20.8
St. Louis	141 312	2.16	18.2	44.8	11 978	4 822	2 060	7 156	25 267	7 931	1 679	6 253	219 675	38.0	34.7
St. Peters	22 268	2.55	10.0	26.6	203	184	184	19	1 219	2 202	170	2 032	39 896	32.2	34.5
Springfield	73 469	2.12	11.1	36.7	10 739	3 302	1 443	7 437	14 599	8 833	1 186	7 646	106 879	38.1	28.0
University City	14 671	2.37	15.7	27.3	232	200	169	32	1 532	4 365	544	3 821	24 111	21.7	57.0
Wentzville	12 607	2.81	13.1	19.6	137	133	133	4	543	1 632	129	1 502	22 956	38.7	24.4
Wildwood	11 884	3.01	4.2	13.0	66	62	40	4	NA	NA	NA	NA	23 231	12.8	58.5
MONTANA	414 804	2.42	8.4	31.5	28 849	11 929	5 200	16 920	28 625	2 797	324	2 473	706 329	37.9	30.6
Billings	44 677	2.40	7.8	31.6	3 351	1 750	753	1 601	5 381	4 881	381	4 500	75 152	36.2	33.9
Bozeman	18 220	2.18	6.5	33.4	3 030	199	145	2 831	1 194	2 946	188	2 759	25 255	16.1	56.9
Butte-Silver Bow	13 973	2.33	8.5	45.7	998	610	276	388	1 643	4 740	355	4 385	22 648	38.7	31.3
Great Falls	25 206	2.24	12.2	34.4	1 263	798	482	465	2 738	4 602	274	4 328	39 415	43.0	26.3
Helena	13 684	2.11	10.6	37.6	1 682	432	191	1 250	1 302	4 350	535	3 816	21 201	27.8	44.8
Missoula	31 518	2.15	9.7	40.2	3 519	766	374	2 753	3 147	4 517	327	4 190	46 211	25.2	46.5
NEBRASKA	744 159	2.48	9.5	30.0	51 165	23 633	13 519	27 532	52 754	2 804	280	2 523	1 232 583	35.9	30.2
Bellevue	20 871	2.65	13.8	24.4	74	31	15	43	1 003	1 849	96	1 753	33 416	35.1	28.5
Fremont	10 146	2.44	14.5	33.5	832	468	386	364	686	2 606	220	2 386	16 544	47.8	18.9
Grand Island	18 245	2.74	16.5	28.6	1 058	781	546	277	2 354	4 616	257	4 359	31 519	50.9	18.6
Kearney	13 170	2.44	13.2	24.2	2 002	390	284	1 612	761	2 341	258	2 082	19 146	29.5	38.0
Lincoln	109 923	2.40	9.1	33.3	13 579	4 236	1 001	9 343	10 000	3 687	338	3 349	169 947	28.0	37.1
Omaha	175 123	2.47	12.4	33.4	11 183	4 676	2 002	6 507	21 511	4 906	561	4 345	289 085	34.3	34.8
NEVADA	1 042 065	2.74	13.4	28.7	36 154	25 835	5 005	10 319	92 583	3 261	636	2 625	1 968 167	42.3	23.6
Carson City	22 687	2.32	15.4	33.9	3 625	3 560	313	65	1 035	1 906	295	1 611	38 334	40.6	21.7
Henderson	111 269	2.55	10.7	28.8	1 104	787	585	317	5 875	2 143	165	1 978	207 985	33.2	31.3
Las Vegas	220 418	2.79	14.1	31.6	9 482	6 514	1 628	2 968	57 630	3 764	841	2 923	419 673	43.8	23.0
North Las Vegas	70 203	3.31	20.6	19.8	2 441	2 167	683	274	7 290	3 177	777	2 401	142 781	50.2	15.3
Reno	95 855	2.46	13.8	31.9	4 583	1 679	323	2 904	7 945	3 380	488	2 892	162 711	34.7	31.3
Sparks	36 485	2.63	14.7	28.2	321	256	256	65	2 801	2 979	327	2 653	64 266	41.4	24.1
NEW HAMPSHIRE	517 615	2.49	10.0	26.2	40 104	13 113	7 767	26 991	28 643	2 159	196	1 963	937 214	35.4	35.7
Concord	16 610	2.39	11.6	33.9	2 903	2 282	454	621	1 058	2 498	203	2 295	30 521	29.6	34.7
Dover	11 996	2.51	10.2	32.6	896	789	358	107	503	1 642	134	1 508	21 005	23.9	49.4
Manchester	44 840	2.40	12.6	30.1	2 578	1 547	662	1 031	4 691	4 243	620	3 623	74 986	43.8	29.2
Nashua	35 027	2.46	14.2	29.3	1 685	546	505	1 139	2 059	2 359	234	2 125	61 892	33.5	35.0
Rochester	12 414	2.41	7.7	27.3	240	192	181	48	1 386	4 659	407	4 253	21 249	44.3	23.5
NEW JERSEY	3 187 963	2.75	13.1	25.9	186 876	100 621	45 512	86 255	178 339	1 995	261	1 734	6 166 384	39.4	37.6
Atlantic City	15 018	2.56	24.4	38.0	802	186	186	616	2 973	7 518	1 323	6 196	25 435	58.9	14.3
Bayonne	25 200	2.62	15.3	33.3	276	0	0	276	951	1 449	226	1 224	46 525	46.6	32.9
Bergenfield	9 461	2.91	12.2	25.9	38	0	0	38	127	465	40	425	17 467	36.3	41.4
Bridgeton	6 566	3.31	29.6	23.6	4 276	4 257	0	19	1 236	4 896	1 022	3 874	15 495	72.7	3.3
Camden	24 454	3.00	43.9	28.5	3 321	2 229	290	1 092	4 395	5 716	2 016	3 700	42 761	66.0	9.5
Clifton	27 497	3.11	12.1	30.3	254	192	182	62	1 613	1 879	217	1 663	59 172	48.3	27.3
East Orange	22 433	2.85	29.7	33.9	1 235	780	716	455	1 558	2 406	707	1 699	42 775	47.9	19.4
Elizabeth	39 923	3.18	21.3	21.4	2 545	1 833	398	712	4 988	3 886	890	2 997	82 781	68.1	11.7
Englewood	10 388	2.73	13.7	25.6	164	136	136	28	588	2 125	278	1 847	22 262	37.2	45.7
Fair Lawn	11 989	2.79	14.1	22.7	187	152	152	35	356	1 073	75	998	24 112	23.9	52.2
Fort Lee	15 518	2.36	7.7	33.6	7	0	0	7	273	754	47	707	28 202	24.3	60.6

1. No spouse present.   2. Data for serious crimes have not been adjusted for underreporting. This may affect comparability between geographic areas and over time.   3. Per 100,000 population estimated by the FBI.   4. Persons 25 years old and over.

Table D. Cities — **Income, Poverty, and Housing**

City	Money income, 2015					Housing units, 2010			Occupied housing units 2015				
	Households			Families					Owner-occupied			Renter-occupied	
	Median income	Percent with income of $200,000 or more	Percent with income of less than $25,000	Total Families	Percent with income below poverty	Total	Percent change, 2000–2010	Vacant units for sale or rent[2]	Total	Percent	Median value[3] (dollars)	Percent	Median rent (dollars)
	42	43	44	45	46	47	48	49	50	51	52	53	54
MISSOURI..................	50 238	3.6	18.1	1 519 299	10.2	2 712 729	11.1	337 118	2 374 180	66.1	147 800	33.9	763
Ballwin......................	95 394	14.0	4.1	NA	NA	12 435	3.2	561	11 294	81.7	260 900	18.3	999
Blue Springs...............	62 201	5.0	10.9	14 726	11.4	20 643	16.0	1 121	19 760	73.0	152 400	27.0	798
Cape Girardeau...........	47 320	6.0	19.1	7 487	9.4	16 760	6.0	1 555	15 232	56.9	143 300	43.1	629
Chesterfield	93 536	18.5	9.6	13 348	2.3	20 393	8.5	1 169	19 557	77.4	375 800	22.6	1 098
Columbia	44 160	3.5	27.0	21 697	8.3	46 758	30.0	3 693	46 380	44.4	177 400	55.6	768
Florissant	48 449	1.3	10.3	13 935	7.0	22 632	8.0	1 385	21 068	65.2	96 800	34.8	932
Gladstone	51 830	1.6	10.0	6 933	10.7	12 148	1.8	966	11 592	67.2	130 200	32.8	760
Hazelwood..................	51 463	2.1	13.1	6 804	11.7	11 730	2.9	797	10 528	57.6	133 600	42.4	800
Independence..............	42 229	1.2	22.5	29 527	16.0	53 834	7.3	5 092	49 848	58.7	100 200	41.3	813
Jefferson City	48 847	2.5	19.3	9 144	9.3	18 852	10.9	1 574	17 246	55.4	141 500	44.6	579
Joplin.........................	40 739	2.5	18.4	11 590	13.5	23 322	9.2	2 462	20 010	57.0	128 400	43.0	772
Kansas City	50 259	3.5	19.6	105 106	12.4	221 860	9.7	29 454	198 129	54.2	138 400	45.8	833
Kirkwood.....................	76 198	13.8	10.1	7 002	2.6	12 895	4.6	1 001	12 501	73.9	275 600	26.1	894
Lee's Summit	75 020	8.4	9.2	25 512	3.6	36 679	33.9	2 250	35 267	77.3	200 300	22.7	1 004
Liberty........................	73 707	5.5	14.6	NA	NA	11 284	14.5	702	10 522	68.1	164 200	31.9	927
Maryland Heights	62 354	2.8	8.7	NA	NA	13 092	10.7	912	11 732	54.1	153 900	45.9	984
O'Fallon	74 961	4.0	5.6	22 239	2.1	29 376	84.8	1 142	30 486	79.1	201 700	20.9	993
Raytown	52 929	0.3	16.7	NA	NA	13 276	-0.2	1 172	11 038	70.7	96 900	29.3	939
St. Charles	59 006	4.4	10.7	15 993	4.2	28 590	13.4	1 875	27 024	60.2	183 700	39.8	906
St. Joseph	46 398	2.4	19.5	17 477	13.7	33 189	4.7	3 462	27 938	62.8	104 600	37.2	757
St. Louis	38 397	2.9	27.6	63 705	21.0	176 002	-0.2	33 945	141 312	42.9	130 800	57.1	767
St. Peters	72 830	4.1	6.5	NA	NA	21 717	15.5	856	22 268	77.6	169 100	22.4	886
Springfield	36 107	2.2	24.8	36 667	16.7	77 620	11.1	7 866	73 469	45.1	113 500	54.9	690
University City	52 464	9.5	14.7	8 782	12.9	18 021	3.0	1 867	14 671	48.3	279 200	51.7	998
Wentzville	71 259	2.9	11.4	9 709	8.0	10 305	NA	538	12 607	81.5	199 300	18.5	1 031
Wildwood....................	119 902	23.5	4.8	NA	NA	12 604	11.5	492	11 884	88.3	376 600	11.7	1 157
MONTANA	49 509	3.5	18.3	253 101	9.3	482 825	17.0	73 218	414 804	66.7	209 500	33.3	763
Billings.......................	58 375	3.7	14.5	26 558	6.0	46 317	18.3	2 372	44 677	62.6	208 200	37.4	849
Bozeman.....................	41 227	2.7	20.5	8 120	8.3	17 464	50.0	1 689	18 220	43.3	287 800	56.7	958
Butte-Silver Bow.........	40 692	2.8	26.9	6 473	9.8	16 717	3.3	1 785	13 973	66.4	142 400	33.6	561
Great Falls..................	41 749	3.0	21.4	14 640	12.7	26 854	6.3	1 553	25 206	60.3	166 400	39.7	649
Helena........................	48 953	2.1	18.3	7 204	17.9	13 457	11.0	677	13 684	43.2	215 300	56.8	840
Missoula.....................	37 444	3.5	24.9	15 103	9.1	30 682	22.3	1 601	31 518	48.3	239 500	51.7	771
NEBRASKA..............	54 996	3.9	15.5	469 797	8.5	796 793	10.3	75 663	744 159	65.9	141 600	34.1	750
Bellevue......................	60 234	2.2	11.1	14 635	7.5	20 591	18.0	1 449	20 871	64.3	138 600	35.7	879
Fremont......................	40 080	0.6	15.2	6 354	7.8	11 427	8.0	702	10 146	58.3	116 800	41.7	756
Grand Island...............	48 165	1.4	17.6	11 554	12.8	19 426	11.7	1 100	18 245	55.1	137 800	44.9	688
Kearney......................	52 558	3.6	17.1	7 512	6.1	12 738	15.7	537	13 170	52.4	168 600	47.6	743
Lincoln.......................	51 503	2.9	17.2	61 167	9.9	110 546	16.1	7 000	109 923	56.0	155 100	44.0	770
Omaha........................	51 407	4.7	17.2	101 638	12.7	177 518	7.1	14 891	175 123	57.6	143 200	42.4	813
NEVADA..................	52 431	3.8	15.9	659 355	10.9	1 173 814	41.9	167 564	1 042 065	54.0	221 400	46.0	980
Carson City	42 251	3.9	21.8	13 398	13.1	23 534	10.6	2 107	22 687	54.3	218 100	45.7	837
Henderson...................	64 035	6.1	12.3	72 429	6.9	113 586	59.0	12 272	111 269	63.8	273 800	36.2	1 144
Las Vegas	49 676	3.7	17.3	134 507	12.3	243 701	27.7	32 012	220 418	50.7	209 400	49.3	983
North Las Vegas	53 952	1.6	16.1	52 987	13.1	76 073	107.9	9 574	70 203	54.4	185 800	45.6	1 062
Reno..........................	50 451	3.9	17.4	52 955	10.7	102 582	28.9	11 658	95 855	45.4	269 200	54.6	877
Sparks........................	52 453	2.3	13.7	23 643	9.7	36 455	39.8	2 953	36 485	54.4	243 500	45.6	966
NEW HAMPSHIRE.....	70 303	7.3	11.4	341 473	5.0	614 754	12.4	95 781	517 615	70.9	244 500	29.1	1 017
Concord......................	61 606	4.4	15.4	9 714	5.3	18 852	11.7	1 260	16 610	55.3	211 100	44.7	1 025
Dover.........................	57 612	4.3	11.6	6 646	9.0	13 685	14.8	858	11 996	52.2	267 800	47.8	967
Manchester..................	54 596	2.5	16.3	25 942	9.3	49 288	7.4	3 522	44 840	43.0	209 200	57.0	1 064
Nashua.......................	67 441	7.1	11.8	21 622	8.1	37 168	5.0	2 124	35 027	55.8	245 200	44.2	1 142
Rochester....................	51 005	1.4	24.4	7 783	7.7	13 372	13.0	994	12 414	65.4	163 400	34.6	906
NEW JERSEY............	72 222	10.9	13.2	2 205 886	8.1	3 553 562	7.3	339 202	3 187 963	63.0	322 600	37.0	1 214
Atlantic City	28 199	2.7	37.4	8 273	31.8	20 013	-1.0	4 509	15 018	29.4	183 500	70.6	831
Bayonne......................	53 731	4.8	16.4	15 816	13.7	27 799	3.6	2 562	25 200	38.6	308 900	61.4	1 108
Bergenfield..................	72 216	10.3	15.1	6 665	7.2	9 200	0.6	348	9 461	69.5	320 400	30.5	1 070
Bridgeton....................	40 310	1.1	31.3	4 763	24.6	6 782	-0.2	517	6 566	37.9	99 800	62.1	1 097
Camden......................	25 643	0.3	39.1	16 610	39.2	28 358	-4.7	3 883	24 454	38.4	84 200	61.6	904
Clifton	64 700	4.7	14.2	18 298	5.8	31 946	2.9	1 285	27 497	60.5	331 800	39.5	1 335
East Orange	40 723	2.3	22.5	13 559	13.8	28 803	1.1	3 858	22 433	27.1	225 100	72.9	992
Elizabeth.....................	44 016	1.3	20.9	29 414	18.6	45 516	6.3	3 920	39 923	20.4	262 900	79.6	1 071
Englewood...................	77 133	14.2	7.3	7 166	12.3	10 695	11.2	638	10 388	62.9	337 100	37.1	1 553
Fair Lawn....................	95 856	15.9	11.8	NA	NA	12 266	2.2	336	11 989	72.4	393 200	27.6	1 407
Fort Lee......................	78 108	14.6	13.7	9 941	5.6	17 818	2.1	1 447	15 518	62.7	370 000	37.3	1 881

1. Based on population estimated by the American Community Survey.   2. Includes units rented or sold but not occupied.   3. Specified owner-occupied units; $1,000,000 represents $1,000,000 or more   4. 50.0 represents 50 percent or more.   5. 10.0 represents 10 percent or less.

Table D. Cities — **Commuting, Computer Access, Migration, Labor Force, and Employment**

City	Commuting Percent — Drove alone	Commuting Percent — With Commutes of 30 minutes or more[1]	Computer Access[2] Percent — With a Computer in the house	Computer Access[2] Percent — With Internet Access	Migration, 2015 — Percent who lived in the same house one year ago	Migration, 2015 — Percent who lived in an other state or county one year ago	Civilian labor force, 2016 — Total	Civilian labor force, 2016 — Percent change, 2015–2016	Civilian labor force, 2016 Unemployment — Total	Civilian labor force, 2016 Unemployment — Rate[3]	Civilian employment[4], 2015 Population age 16 and older — Number	Civilian employment[4], 2015 Population age 16 and older — Percent in Labor Force	Civilian employment[4], 2015 Population age 16 to 64 — Number	Civilian employment[4], 2015 Population age 16 to 64 — Percent who worked full-year full-time
	55	56	57	58	59	60	61	62	63	64	65	66	67	68
MISSOURI................	85.9	32.1	85.3	73.6	84.1	7.3	3 111 517	0.5	140 815	4.5	4 851 761	63.1	3 900 813	51.0
Ballwin......................	86.6	41.9	97.0	95.3	78.8	8.6	17 299	0.4	527	3.0	23 746	67.6	19 467	59.4
Blue Springs..............	86.4	34.8	92.1	79.9	84.4	5.7	31 179	1.2	1 280	4.1	40 470	70.9	32 808	56.2
Cape Girardeau..........	77.0	13.1	81.4	74.9	71.9	10.9	20 289	0.1	970	4.8	32 991	62.3	26 989	45.9
Chesterfield...............	95.3	37.2	93.4	88.1	84.7	5.5	25 264	0.4	771	3.1	39 776	60.3	28 011	53.3
Columbia...................	82.0	15.7	93.4	81.3	71.1	13.2	67 696	-0.1	2 215	3.3	99 549	66.3	90 486	43.3
Florissant..................	85.1	38.3	89.9	79.2	86.7	2.4	28 836	0.3	1 349	4.7	40 873	68.6	33 284	57.7
Gladstone..................	90.9	30.9	88.8	83.4	82.8	3.5	14 988	1.4	653	4.4	22 487	66.1	17 051	49.4
Hazelwood.................	92.2	26.2	97.1	86.7	88.7	8.0	14 151	0.4	695	4.9	20 702	67.5	17 242	57.7
Independence............	90.7	40.3	79.7	72.5	89.4	4.0	59 858	1.2	3 301	5.5	93 650	61.7	74 731	51.7
Jefferson City............	89.0	12.9	89.3	77.9	77.0	14.6	21 321	0.7	816	3.8	35 835	57.6	29 267	46.0
Joplin........................	89.2	13.6	89.0	65.5	79.8	4.6	26 337	-0.1	1 100	4.2	41 208	65.1	33 265	49.5
Kansas City...............	84.1	26.8	84.3	75.1	80.9	8.2	260 850	1.2	12 772	4.9	375 338	67.7	316 874	55.1
Kirkwood...................	90.9	24.7	91.5	84.5	89.8	4.1	16 063	0.5	484	3.0	22 415	64.9	16 310	57.4
Lee's Summit..............	92.1	39.1	93.8	88.7	91.3	3.2	55 350	1.5	1 915	3.5	71 399	70.0	57 994	60.1
Liberty......................	91.1	32.4	91.1	84.3	81.2	7.8	16 480	1.7	680	4.1	22 975	73.5	20 235	59.1
Maryland Heights........	88.4	13.8	93.3	85.9	80.8	8.1	16 493	0.3	591	3.6	23 295	68.8	17 952	58.0
O'Fallon....................	89.3	43.8	93.7	87.4	87.2	6.3	48 470	0.7	1 657	3.4	64 543	74.6	54 639	60.8
Raytown....................	92.6	29.2	87.7	80.2	90.2	3.0	15 859	0.9	915	5.8	22 790	60.7	18 971	54.7
St. Charles................	90.8	30.1	89.2	79.4	81.4	7.5	38 729	0.5	1 497	3.9	55 777	69.3	45 862	52.9
St. Joseph.................	83.1	11.3	80.5	70.4	79.7	8.2	39 467	0.0	1 662	4.2	60 478	63.2	48 614	46.7
St. Louis...................	76.4	31.9	80.9	63.3	80.8	9.4	161 050	0.2	8 686	5.4	258 110	65.2	221 635	48.8
St. Peters..................	94.0	29.4	91.9	86.2	90.1	4.1	34 404	0.5	1 180	3.4	45 362	77.9	38 130	65.3
Springfield................	83.1	12.7	82.0	68.0	72.5	12.6	87 549	0.5	3 502	4.0	142 116	60.5	115 067	44.3
University City	78.5	27.9	88.8	79.3	77.4	13.3	19 189	0.4	793	4.1	28 884	73.1	24 559	56.2
Wentzville.................	88.0	38.6	93.2	85.5	88.7	5.9	19 483	0.6	644	3.3	27 047	73.2	22 566	62.3
Wildwood..................	91.8	50.1	96.2	92.4	91.0	5.8	19 369	0.4	592	3.1	27 668	69.7	23 425	51.7
MONTANA	79.3	16.3	86.1	75.5	83.9	7.8	526 404	1.3	21 831	4.1	829 911	62.3	650 980	49.9
Billings.....................	85.2	8.0	91.6	82.7	79.9	6.9	57 652	1.2	2 036	3.5	88 134	68.3	71 073	58.4
Bozeman...................	66.5	7.5	93.9	81.3	64.9	18.1	27 789	4.6	699	2.5	37 428	72.5	33 056	41.1
Butte-Silver Bow..........	82.5	9.5	86.1	75.3	82.7	9.1	17 365	1.0	746	4.3	27 485	58.0	21 624	47.9
Great Falls................	80.3	4.4	77.7	69.9	81.5	7.0	28 515	-0.2	1 131	4.0	46 661	60.6	35 580	52.6
Helena......................	73.1	3.7	87.6	80.7	69.3	13.7	17 023	1.1	519	3.0	25 478	60.8	20 190	47.6
Missoula	74.2	10.5	90.4	79.4	81.8	8.6	39 329	1.7	1 400	3.6	59 495	69.6	50 012	44.4
NEBRASKA...............	85.3	18.8	86.7	78.2	84.0	6.9	1 011 041	0.3	32 474	3.2	1 476 487	69.4	1 197 796	56.7
Bellevue....................	86.8	20.4	92.3	87.3	82.2	7.6	27 819	0.7	891	3.2	42 861	69.0	35 659	54.0
Fremont.....................	86.0	19.2	82.3	70.6	88.3	6.4	13 652	0.0	427	3.1	20 222	65.5	15 522	53.1
Grand Island..............	79.4	13.4	80.0	73.3	81.6	8.4	26 055	-0.4	948	3.6	38 539	73.9	31 634	59.3
Kearney....................	85.7	10.1	92.6	81.0	67.6	15.2	18 768	0.1	457	2.4	27 528	73.9	23 403	49.5
Lincoln.....................	84.0	13.4	91.0	83.1	78.5	8.6	152 291	0.9	4 278	2.8	219 222	71.0	186 101	53.5
Omaha......................	85.0	16.8	85.3	78.1	82.7	6.1	228 880	0.5	7 667	3.3	345 585	69.0	290 519	54.3
NEVADA...................	80.7	32.9	89.7	79.1	80.1	6.2	1 427 114	0.9	81 106	5.7	2 292 699	63.5	1 870 587	47.6
Carson City	83.2	20.6	87.6	78.4	83.1	7.4	24 766	-0.5	1 508	6.1	44 744	58.1	33 603	50.4
Henderson.................	88.2	29.6	91.5	85.3	84.7	5.6	146 777	0.9	7 975	5.4	232 283	61.5	176 064	50.8
Las Vegas.................	81.1	39.8	89.2	76.9	79.1	5.3	298 231	0.8	17 877	6.0	487 831	62.8	401 969	46.9
North Las Vegas	83.4	43.8	92.0	78.5	79.7	6.4	107 667	0.8	6 891	6.4	175 553	63.5	151 240	46.2
Reno........................	77.9	16.8	89.0	79.5	74.1	8.1	124 508	2.0	6 180	5.0	194 472	66.5	159 038	46.1
Sparks......................	79.7	26.8	89.1	81.7	82.7	4.1	49 686	1.7	2 501	5.0	74 407	66.1	60 433	52.6
NEW HAMPSHIRE.....	86.7	38.8	91.1	84.4	86.1	6.6	748 563	0.8	21 143	2.8	1 102 089	67.8	883 732	52.9
Concord....................	86.8	28.8	85.3	80.1	86.7	4.1	22 460	0.6	550	2.4	35 124	64.8	28 649	49.7
Dover.......................	89.6	24.7	89.8	80.2	77.2	11.9	18 075	1.9	412	2.3	25 341	67.9	20 820	45.4
Manchester................	82.0	30.1	91.0	82.3	78.6	8.0	62 411	1.2	1 878	3.0	90 694	69.1	75 693	50.1
Nashua.....................	82.9	37.2	92.8	85.3	79.9	8.4	49 483	1.1	1 652	3.3	71 296	69.1	58 629	55.5
Rochester..................	89.3	34.4	84.1	77.4	84.3	4.3	17 126	1.8	434	2.5	24 791	62.3	19 911	52.1
NEW JERSEY..........	74.9	46.1	88.1	81.2	90.2	4.6	4 524 258	-0.1	224 327	5.0	7 193 921	65.2	5 850 970	50.6
Atlantic City	49.1	19.5	68.2	56.9	83.6	4.0	15 283	-4.1	1 545	10.1	29 835	60.8	24 570	36.9
Bayonne....................	53.6	61.3	84.9	77.5	92.6	4.0	33 386	-0.1	1 788	5.4	52 538	64.7	43 363	48.9
Bergenfield................	74.0	51.4	89.0	87.4	NA	NA	14 877	0.2	574	3.9	21 527	64.7	17 468	54.6
Bridgeton..................	78.5	26.0	64.7	52.8	85.0	4.8	8 346	-0.9	731	8.8	18 671	57.8	17 040	41.5
Camden....................	67.1	32.4	75.3	58.1	85.2	1.9	26 635	-0.2	2 703	10.1	53 768	56.6	47 055	36.7
Clifton......................	73.6	36.6	78.7	69.9	92.9	3.8	45 390	-0.4	2 286	5.0	70 120	61.3	58 311	51.5
East Orange...............	58.9	53.7	87.9	70.2	84.8	4.3	29 840	-1.1	2 310	7.7	51 858	66.6	44 150	43.6
Elizabeth...................	50.1	39.0	83.0	66.3	85.5	5.1	62 924	-1.2	3 915	6.2	98 355	67.5	85 838	51.7
Englewood.................	65.7	53.4	92.9	82.7	96.1	2.0	15 136	0.0	684	4.5	24 421	70.0	19 698	62.0
Fair Lawn..................	72.3	39.1	90.5	88.3	90.1	4.6	18 407	0.0	750	4.1	28 030	66.1	22 100	53.5
Fort Lee....................	58.7	60.7	90.9	83.8	92.3	3.1	19 014	0.2	614	3.2	31 526	61.4	24 490	55.3

1. Employed persons.   2. Households.   3. Percent of civilian labor force.   4. Persons 16 years old and over.

Table D. Cities — Construction, Wholesale Trade, and Retail Trade

City	Value of residential construction authorized by building permits, 2016			Wholesale trade,[1] 2012				Retail trade,[2] 2012			
	New construction ($1,000)	Number of housing units	Percent single family	Number of establishments	Number of employees	Sales (mil dol)	Annual payroll (mil dol)	Number of establishments	Number of employees	Sales (mil dol)	Annual payroll (mil dol)
	69	70	71	72	73	74	75	76	77	78	79
MISSOURI.................	120	2	100.0	6 557	96 683	91 916.4	4 978.9	21 456	302 568	90 546.6	7 278.2
Ballwin......................	4 613	13	100.0	16	49	57.5	2.5	88	1 585	644.5	47.4
Blue Springs..............	25 502	223	77.1	42	304	280.9	17.1	160	3 296	929.4	76.1
Cape Girardeau...........	14 461	91	56.0	88	1 141	655.7	47.6	299	4 617	1 240.7	101.1
Chesterfield..............	NA	NA	NA	146	2 241	1 231.8	161.8	315	5 198	1 093.6	112.9
Columbia..................	187 270	973	58.4	98	1 158	461.5	55.6	537	10 468	3 251.6	254.7
Florissant.................	400	2	100.0	18	55	27.7	2.0	176	3 083	789.0	73.0
Gladstone.................	3 365	34	100.0	16	43	19.5	1.9	82	1 845	489.2	45.3
Hazelwood.................	314	4	100.0	53	1 573	1 366.0	87.1	142	3 422	2 338.6	137.3
Independence...........	12 667	83	90.4	71	473	165.7	20.6	456	8 382	2 068.8	196.1
Jefferson City...........	12 263	93	39.8	60	2 030	915.7	58.0	258	4 881	1 191.7	110.5
Joplin......................	21 407	152	82.9	99	1 568	691.6	60.1	378	6 152	1 819.7	135.3
Kansas City..............	410 127	3 340	24.7	614	10 628	14 577.6	675.7	1 458	24 531	7 537.3	620.8
Kirkwood..................	28 968	79	100.0	35	228	105.1	13.6	128	2 693	738.1	66.5
Lee's Summit..............	135 622	527	63.2	98	1 351	799.3	72.6	290	5 326	1 337.8	126.7
Liberty.....................	17 756	319	8.5	23	235	216.3	13.1	86	1 299	300.9	31.6
Maryland Heights	0	0	0.0	235	5 339	4 493.9	360.0	117	2 674	4 687.1	107.1
O'Fallon...................	84 173	509	75.2	72	D	D	D	199	3 400	962.6	85.0
Raytown...................	449	4	100.0	22	162	69.0	9.5	92	1 528	364.0	35.7
St. Charles................	110 567	581	54.9	82	1 620	1 102.6	100.2	257	4 047	1 085.4	92.7
St. Joseph................	10 798	58	89.7	92	1 627	1 421.4	72.0	321	5 412	1 353.4	119.5
St. Louis..................	103 352	1 070	7.9	452	7 692	5 916.4	423.3	923	9 422	2 471.9	231.1
St. Peters.................	22 493	89	100.0	74	D	D	D	325	6 097	1 695.3	149.1
Springfield................	63 498	620	15.6	328	6 097	4 390.8	269.4	967	16 828	4 329.5	388.8
University City	3 088	11	100.0	23	298	226.8	20.4	86	781	156.9	18.2
Wentzville.................	191 148	775	86.1	26	D	D	D	100	2 179	583.1	58.2
Wildwood..................	NA	NA	NA	30	82	30.8	4.5	35	452	97.4	10.8
MONTANA	1 408	17	100.0	1 288	13 034	12 645.8	577.1	4 831	55 418	15 623.6	1 346.5
Billings.....................	96 719	537	97.8	236	3 832	2 734.4	190.2	618	9 047	2 761.8	240.4
Bozeman...................	132 572	738	50.5	60	549	286.0	20.8	357	5 153	1 192.1	120.8
Butte-Silver Bow..........	9 097	86	50.0	37	348	189.3	14.3	172	2 203	610.1	51.7
Great Falls................	20 399	135	35.6	92	1 011	847.3	45.7	314	4 496	1 268.2	109.5
Helena.....................	27 961	175	29.1	49	425	295.9	17.8	220	3 292	803.0	77.6
Missoula	68 786	772	28.9	104	1 372	1 023.3	63.8	476	6 831	1 677.6	153.7
NEBRASKA...............	149	5	100.0	2 720	34 409	42 619.0	1 675.4	7 279	105 953	30 470.7	2 440.4
Bellevue...................	38 566	137	97.1	15	68	28.8	4.3	110	2 318	661.9	55.4
Fremont...................	8 364	31	100.0	30	395	566.6	20.6	131	2 220	1 026.6	56.2
Grand Island..............	30 025	291	35.1	75	1 089	707.6	56.0	273	4 710	1 198.9	107.1
Kearney...................	33 061	184	55.4	46	698	816.6	34.0	190	3 245	756.9	69.9
Lincoln....................	323 310	2 166	42.8	242	3 927	2 924.6	159.2	946	16 644	4 184.1	375.6
Omaha.....................	267 877	2 564	55.7	667	10 205	12 272.0	565.0	1 634	33 150	8 083.1	793.0
NEVADA....................	62 643	162	100.0	2 501	27 649	19 841.7	1 516.2	8 135	129 977	38 234.2	3 454.1
Carson City	34 002	159	54.7	89	519	276.4	25.2	212	3 139	918.2	92.6
Henderson................	682 320	3 597	61.8	196	1 314	776.5	92.8	721	13 600	5 601.8	398.5
Las Vegas.................	463 499	2 280	63.8	431	3 801	2 620.7	222.9	1 705	29 614	8 550.0	770.5
North Las Vegas..........	119 803	938	84.6	160	2 944	2 079.2	157.1	291	6 155	1 725.4	147.9
Reno.......................	402 444	2 374	44.6	302	4 234	3 320.6	229.2	975	15 952	4 519.4	438.6
Sparks.....................	162 170	907	54.0	227	3 506	2 699.0	172.5	304	4 346	1 158.3	106.8
NEW HAMPSHIRE.....	0	0	0.0	1 543	21 140	18 029.2	1 307.9	6 127	95 660	26 018.2	2 403.6
Concord....................	7 404	40	95.0	53	934	600.2	49.4	279	5 383	1 391.2	125.3
Dover......................	15 974	80	85.0	34	445	170.6	26.2	96	1 391	339.4	38.6
Manchester................	42 296	298	47.3	192	3 297	2 037.3	253.4	464	7 470	2 173.8	198.4
Nashua.....................	34 780	246	26.0	127	1 591	1 231.6	105.3	455	9 973	2 735.4	244.2
Rochester.................	15 383	139	49.6	14	D	D	D	123	2 506	621.8	67.2
NEW JERSEY...........	34 211	739	1.1	12 760	208 830	288 467.8	14 976.8	31 722	436 299	133 665.7	12 676.0
Atlantic City	14 723	95	12.6	12	388	95.8	12.0	330	3 060	641.0	61.1
Bayonne	8 275	63	73.0	48	1 157	1 944.2	72.5	190	1 864	467.1	43.6
Bergenfield................	15 861	49	87.8	32	202	122.1	10.5	88	702	178.8	19.5
Bridgeton..................	738	9	100.0	18	249	68.3	7.1	92	842	337.1	24.3
Camden....................	13 990	94	5.3	53	1 070	711.4	56.4	211	1 129	305.5	28.3
Clifton.....................	18 327	109	24.8	181	2 492	1 275.3	140.4	281	4 593	1 260.5	121.2
East Orange..............	15 843	202	5.4	16	169	350.2	9.0	133	1 073	310.1	25.7
Elizabeth..................	20 823	629	0.2	118	3 077	2 824.0	198.0	540	6 663	1 489.2	132.4
Englewood................	31 188	194	2.1	88	1 119	577.9	65.1	163	1 915	1 037.0	93.1
Fair Lawn	2 253	14	64.3	51	376	180.0	18.7	94	1 142	482.4	42.5
Fort Lee...................	186 597	521	5.0	147	950	13 212.0	91.3	127	917	350.4	26.8

1. Merchant wholesalers except manufacturers' sales branches and offices. 2. Establishments with payroll.

City	Real estate and rental and leasing, 2012				Professional, scientific, and technical services,[1] 2012				Manufacturing, 2012			
	Number of establishments	Number of employees	Receipts (mil dol)	Annual payroll (mil dol)	Number of establishments	Number of employees	Receipts (mil dol)	Annual payroll (mil dol)	Number of establishments	Number of employees	Receipts (mil dol)	Annual payroll (mil dol)
	80	81	82	83	84	85	86	87	88	89	90	91
MISSOURI.............	6 165	33 447	6 730.0	1 297.9	13 221	136 446	24 006.6	8 518.4	6 097	243 208	111 535.4	11 920.8
Ballwin....................	22	57	11.2	2.1	66	132	15.3	6.0	7	50	D	D
Blue Springs............	69	199	31.6	5.7	110	564	65.7	25.8	35	905	196.0	41.5
Cape Girardeau.........	89	263	49.1	7.5	108	D	D	D	40	1 959	2 326.0	110.1
Chesterfield.............	129	673	162.9	27.9	394	13 252	2 523.7	849.6	57	1 345	376.0	76.5
Columbia.................	192	852	153.7	27.5	346	3 314	396.5	148.0	72	2 930	1 280.6	123.0
Florissant...............	28	170	23.7	4.5	56	318	20.4	9.0	10	49	3.1	D
Gladstone...............	48	345	35.2	11.9	75	D	D	D	7	D	D	D
Hazelwood..............	29	193	34.5	5.5	46	D	D	D	35	3 589	1 384.6	228.3
Independence...........	105	593	138.5	20.2	225	1 035	89.4	34.3	72	4 011	1 235.8	227.1
Jefferson City...........	54	207	42.2	6.3	203	D	D	D	35	2 574	2 091.7	122.0
Joplin....................	77	407	68.1	11.4	146	D	D	D	83	5 204	2 217.7	227.6
Kansas City.............	578	4 517	1 142.9	221.8	1 507	D	D	D	374	17 035	8 635.1	935.0
Kirkwood................	43	D	D	D	133	613	98.8	33.0	28	643	173.8	32.9
Lee's Summit...........	120	370	82.9	14.6	305	D	D	D	71	D	482.1	101.9
Liberty..................	35	160	25.8	3.9	114	D	D	D	22	927	D	40.6
Maryland Heights........	57	371	130.2	19.0	157	3 597	566.4	254.7	107	3 658	1 408.7	207.4
O'Fallon................	80	339	58.9	11.6	124	791	323.9	65.9	56	4 204	985.7	204.9
Raytown................	23	108	16.0	2.8	58	318	30.4	13.6	26	302	38.8	13.6
St. Charles.............	104	519	285.3	25.8	245	3 406	195.4	81.6	66	1 654	463.4	84.7
St. Joseph..............	92	323	58.8	9.8	145	D	D	D	88	D	D	474.4
St. Louis................	411	2 432	1 003.0	102.5	1 003	D	D	D	484	17 422	10 737.0	975.2
St. Peters..............	64	235	46.8	7.4	140	755	82.9	31.0	49	1 365	1 527.5	64.4
Springfield..............	342	2 232	308.2	65.4	665	D	D	D	239	10 927	4 323.9	478.9
University City..........	39	404	55.6	13.4	86	241	28.4	10.3	13	112	D	6.0
Wentzville..............	12	44	8.4	1.3	40	159	15.9	6.2	21	2 315	D	183.2
Wildwood...............	29	D	D	D	112	364	57.0	18.1	4	12	D	D
MONTANA	1 726	5 207	835.4	162.3	3 501	16 363	2 160.8	784.0	1 237	15 729	11 535.2	714.5
Billings..................	231	828	152.5	28.0	518	3 166	554.9	178.6	128	2 078	D	127.4
Bozeman................	162	420	78.0	14.0	409	1 609	218.3	81.0	79	932	223.2	38.3
Butte-Silver Bow........	47	137	15.1	3.2	107	654	73.9	30.8	35	492	D	31.5
Great Falls..............	104	296	49.0	8.2	171	D	D	D	43	832	D	40.7
Helena..................	79	265	60.0	10.0	197	1 490	191.1	76.7	38	380	D	17.1
Missoula................	158	818	113.4	27.1	415	2 625	305.0	129.2	64	573	160.4	D
NEBRASKA..............	2 001	10 068	1 732.0	388.5	4 426	74 339	5 705.2	3 628.5	1 844	92 409	57 499.2	4 002.8
Bellevue................	50	167	37.5	5.0	85	D	D	D	13	578	126.4	22.9
Fremont.................	33	167	22.7	4.1	38	152	15.7	5.8	35	1 126	990.8	45.2
Grand Island............	73	293	54.1	9.0	99	D	D	D	58	6 981	5 695.9	270.6
Kearney................	50	146	37.2	4.2	80	536	65.9	24.4	29	710	130.2	28.7
Lincoln.................	323	1 561	243.8	53.6	783	8 731	1 254.8	444.0	210	11 045	5 711.5	557.2
Omaha.................	605	5 464	926.8	248.9	1 472	54 641	3 129.5	2 713.5	381	16 879	9 325.5	718.3
NEVADA................	3 866	22 412	4 981.2	814.7	8 076	47 386	7 722.2	2 813.8	1 706	38 123	14 719.1	1 979.3
Carson City.............	111	304	51.7	9.5	292	D	D	D	122	2 798	634.0	162.7
Henderson..............	395	1 468	332.9	63.9	929	3 835	633.2	229.3	122	3 591	1 459.3	170.9
Las Vegas..............	904	5 221	900.9	202.0	2 331	13 142	2 330.1	827.8	197	2 631	896.8	127.8
North Las Vegas.........	103	630	126.9	24.9	136	D	D	D	107	3 260	856.0	139.6
Reno...................	454	2 345	523.8	86.2	1 172	7 000	1 131.1	437.9	231	7 327	3 300.4	385.2
Sparks.................	108	561	102.9	20.7	146	D	D	D	171	5 510	2 459.4	391.3
NEW HAMPSHIRE.....	1 338	7 044	1 593.1	309.7	3 794	29 853	3 910.7	1 678.8	1 851	66 636	18 895.6	3 923.8
Concord.................	66	330	74.2	13.3	224	D	D	D	63	1 332	330.9	62.2
Dover...................	35	358	42.1	10.5	103	D	D	D	44	919	141.4	44.7
Manchester..............	132	1 348	276.1	69.3	438	D	D	D	116	5 175	1 189.9	263.6
Nashua..................	109	414	94.6	17.1	324	D	D	D	117	8 970	D	801.7
Rochester...............	22	75	12.0	2.2	39	389	32.2	14.6	34	1 135	248.3	59.6
NEW JERSEY..........	8 749	53 751	17 327.6	2 813.1	29 289	305 648	58 415.3	23 862.4	7 758	230 697	108 855.0	14 094.8
Atlantic City............	47	475	111.2	15.8	68	D	D	D	6	54	D	1.0
Bayonne................	40	203	36.6	7.8	83	685	72.3	36.4	32	931	528.6	53.4
Bergenfield..............	15	24	5.6	1.2	46	154	20.4	6.1	17	158	D	7.5
Bridgeton...............	13	109	15.1	2.4	31	142	13.2	5.0	11	627	D	33.3
Camden................	37	D	D	D	49	D	D	D	47	1 487	488.4	119.5
Clifton..................	95	586	117.1	25.7	253	1 866	281.3	114.1	144	5 418	1 781.7	339.4
East Orange............	59	323	55.6	8.7	40	D	D	D	12	112	D	4.1
Elizabeth................	98	447	216.1	19.7	116	D	D	D	69	2 138	935.4	106.5
Englewood..............	67	538	192.2	31.5	117	650	136.9	44.5	54	1 240	667.7	61.3
Fair Lawn...............	35	D	D	D	197	1 219	374.1	71.3	35	1 421	529.1	93.8
Fort Lee.................	118	499	133.9	21.1	269	1 142	480.9	92.0	14	203	D	8.2

1. Establishments subject to federal tax.

City	Accommodation and food services, 2012				Arts, entertainment, and recreation,[1] 2012				Health care and social assistance,[1] 2012			
	Number of establishments	Number of employees	Sales (mil dol)	Annual payroll (mil dol)	Number of establishments	Number of employees	Receipts (mil dol)	Annual payroll (mil dol)	Number of establishments	Number of employees	Receipts (mil dol)	Annual payroll (mil dol)
	92	93	94	95	96	97	98	99	100	101	102	103
MISSOURI................	12 459	239 264	12 430.3	3 409.2	1 626	26 954	3 047.3	1 099.3	14 644	184 918	17 917.0	7 524.7
Ballwin.....................	42	774	31.8	8.9	11	D	D	D	41	D	D	D
Blue Springs.............	114	2 209	103.1	28.4	24	D	D	D	129	D	D	D
Cape Girardeau..........	123	3 435	142.1	40.4	14	134	31.8	7.6	227	3 601	404.0	160.5
Chesterfield.............	175	4 601	217.4	66.7	31	303	18.5	5.2	260	D	D	D
Columbia.................	367	8 566	354.6	99.6	38	D	D	D	436	5 081	598.8	232.3
Florissant................	108	2 211	103.2	28.2	9	179	6.5	1.8	178	2 003	180.9	83.4
Gladstone................	41	756	33.9	10.5	5	D	D	D	69	508	44.4	18.4
Hazelwood...............	69	1 138	60.5	14.5	7	D	D	D	69	616	49.4	20.5
Independence............	223	5 275	236.3	71.0	18	D	D	D	243	5 483	603.8	221.8
Jefferson City...........	152	3 034	126.0	37.8	16	D	D	D	175	3 035	336.4	152.1
Joplin....................	194	4 298	199.8	56.2	10	82	5.0	1.4	235	D	D	D
Kansas City..............	1 098	25 669	1 630.0	452.9	129	3 506	747.5	292.7	1 153	15 415	1 821.9	778.3
Kirkwood.................	65	1 509	68.4	21.0	13	84	5.9	1.9	100	700	105.4	39.1
Lee's Summit............	183	3 599	156.7	47.1	25	371	19.3	3.6	270	D	D	D
Liberty..................	63	1 380	57.8	18.0	9	89	2.7	0.8	110	D	D	D
Maryland Heights.........	94	3 434	445.0	76.8	11	D	D	D	65	2 502	451.7	108.7
O'Fallon.................	155	D	D	D	24	D	D	D	179	D	D	D
Raytown..................	47	658	29.3	8.7	4	D	D	D	47	837	44.3	18.0
St. Charles..............	209	5 808	481.2	101.0	27	D	D	D	194	2 341	235.7	101.5
St. Joseph...............	177	3 925	175.6	47.4	12	D	D	D	242	D	D	D
St. Louis................	1 036	22 069	1 255.7	371.4	81	4 971	819.6	293.0	927	11 437	1 124.3	388.0
St. Peters...............	181	3 751	163.4	47.8	27	514	18.2	6.3	231	2 273	249.7	105.0
Springfield..............	646	13 397	578.7	172.8	58	D	D	D	577	9 875	1 108.5	556.9
University City...........	82	1 295	66.4	19.4	6	D	D	D	163	1 216	57.8	24.6
Wentzville...............	73	D	D	D	4	D	D	D	75	824	63.4	28.0
Wildwood................	28	D	D	D	6	288	4.9	1.0	58	652	56.1	25.0
MONTANA................	3 458	46 251	2 420.5	649.5	899	8 346	676.6	130.3	2 545	24 420	2 508.0	1 040.9
Billings..................	346	7 362	421.5	113.8	89	847	119.0	13.9	412	5 194	686.5	303.8
Bozeman.................	190	3 550	160.6	45.5	46	715	36.9	10.1	220	1 633	174.1	72.1
Butte-Silver Bow..........	147	2 244	102.4	28.7	29	214	19.0	2.8	111	1 672	143.0	71.5
Great Falls..............	210	3 656	182.1	48.7	61	D	D	D	187	2 481	314.9	109.4
Helena...................	149	2 758	126.5	35.9	38	D	D	D	183	1 477	147.6	60.3
Missoula.................	275	5 444	282.1	75.2	60	656	56.0	9.2	341	4 181	428.3	166.2
NEBRASKA...............	4 326	70 128	3 094.5	855.4	557	7 147	471.2	110.6	4 282	57 239	5 706.7	2 397.7
Bellevue.................	104	1 961	88.7	25.9	10	D	D	D	94	D	D	D
Fremont.................	75	1 208	50.1	14.0	5	D	D	D	81	D	D	D
Grand Island.............	139	2 398	107.7	31.3	21	356	24.2	5.8	147	2 176	206.4	88.1
Kearney.................	123	2 815	107.4	30.4	12	D	D	D	123	D	D	D
Lincoln..................	635	12 813	573.3	149.5	78	2 255	138.6	36.4	761	10 250	1 055.7	489.8
Omaha..................	1 164	23 447	1 115.1	325.7	123	25 232	3 507.5	732.8	1 308	D	D	D
NEVADA.................	5 815	296 762	27 481.5	8 555.6	1 179	25 232	3 507.5	732.8	5 766	77 665	9 936.7	3 598.2
Carson City..............	159	2 740	133.4	41.2	43	1 064	94.0	27.2	198	2 390	334.4	123.6
Henderson...............	478	14 087	1 083.9	313.2	132	2 709	246.3	66.1	715	D	D	D
Las Vegas...............	1 140	40 393	2 979.2	962.3	260	4 052	877.0	165.9	1 677	23 573	3 082.1	1 070.0
North Las Vegas..........	224	7 028	515.5	157.2	27	D	D	D	195	D	D	D
Reno....................	697	21 617	1 436.8	452.8	105	1 995	139.2	39.9	815	10 429	1 415.2	595.9
Sparks..................	193	4 855	313.9	92.6	30	926	49.7	15.0	166	2 231	218.6	76.3
NEW HAMPSHIRE.....	3 606	54 047	2 942.3	890.9	536	10 803	681.9	192.0	2 775	35 400	4 001.6	1 769.7
Concord.................	120	2 629	122.9	41.6	15	227	11.6	3.5	158	2 713	340.2	176.7
Dover...................	88	1 552	78.5	23.4	7	29	2.3	0.3	111	D	D	D
Manchester..............	304	5 518	290.4	87.8	34	879	85.2	38.3	274	3 595	423.1	222.6
Nashua..................	232	4 426	224.1	68.4	28	534	27.4	7.4	270	3 480	458.1	196.6
Rochester...............	80	969	51.8	13.8	2	D	D	D	61	627	83.9	34.7
NEW JERSEY...........	20 127	291 933	19 673.6	5 386.8	2 821	39 560	3 690.4	1 238.1	23 088	297 847	32 634.9	13 027.7
Atlantic City.............	228	38 593	3 539.1	1 154.8	13	D	D	D	45	D	D	D
Bayonne.................	125	1 247	72.0	18.6	9	D	D	D	153	1 338	140.8	57.1
Bergenfield..............	42	284	18.5	4.4	2	D	D	D	64	527	47.5	16.0
Bridgeton................	41	364	17.4	4.4	NA	NA	NA	NA	28	230	20.9	9.3
Camden.................	87	723	46.7	11.5	5	D	D	D	70	2 037	176.9	98.4
Clifton..................	159	2 027	125.1	31.3	18	D	D	D	367	3 382	338.6	131.9
East Orange.............	44	593	35.2	8.0	3	D	D	D	103	1 643	123.2	52.2
Elizabeth................	249	2 725	206.5	52.3	10	D	D	D	201	2 087	165.7	69.3
Englewood...............	63	787	54.2	14.2	17	D	D	D	209	D	D	D
Fair Lawn...............	65	673	49.4	10.9	13	191	9.2	2.6	174	1 903	217.8	88.3
Fort Lee.................	116	1 113	88.2	18.7	14	37	4.5	1.2	190	D	D	D

1. Establishments subject to federal tax.

Table D. Cities — Other Services and Government Employment and Payroll

City	Other services[1], 2012 Number of establishments	Number of employees	Receipts (mil dol)	Annual payroll (mil dol)	Government employment and payroll, 2012 Full-time equivalent employees	March payroll Total (dollars)	Percent of total for: Administration, judicial, and legal	Police and Corrections	Fire Protection	Highways and transportation	Health and welfare	Natural resources and utilities	Education and libraries
	104	105	106	107	108	109	110	111	112	113	114	115	116
MISSOURI	8 441	49 408	4 235.2	1 361.6	X	X	X	X	X	X	X	X	X
Ballwin	42	351	20.0	7.0	0	0	0.0	0.0	0.0	0.0	0.0	0.0	0.0
Blue Springs	80	447	37.2	11.3	262	1 043 733	19.7	47.3	0.0	9.7	0.9	18.0	0.0
Cape Girardeau	86	502	37.7	12.2	634	1 734 259	10.2	18.8	19.9	13.6	0.0	29.9	5.9
Chesterfield	104	824	48.3	20.3	272	943 362	17.5	48.7	0.0	16.3	0.0	12.9	0.0
Columbia	211	1 418	87.7	32.1	1 462	5 497 108	19.3	10.6	11.4	6.9	6.7	33.2	0.0
Florissant	81	495	46.3	15.9	357	1 267 576	12.1	34.2	0.4	11.1	12.2	29.7	0.0
Gladstone	46	241	19.1	6.4	214	773 534	15.6	32.5	18.4	8.2	3.9	21.3	0.0
Hazelwood	38	323	41.2	10.4	195	925 216	9.7	45.0	25.1	8.3	0.5	6.9	0.0
Independence	153	825	65.0	20.0	1 064	6 218 560	8.1	26.4	15.4	4.9	2.8	41.9	0.0
Jefferson City	87	566	39.6	12.1	415	1 606 150	17.3	28.1	18.7	13.4	4.3	18.2	0.0
Joplin	111	749	48.9	16.7	548	1 718 395	9.6	29.9	20.7	11.8	6.0	12.5	4.3
Kansas City	634	4 554	358.7	119.1	6 482	21 087 489	9.4	47.9	29.2	7.6	1.6	0.9	0.0
Kirkwood	48	369	30.9	11.0	247	1 279 082	4.4	28.6	22.0	4.0	0.0	32.0	0.0
Lee's Summit	135	732	56.2	16.9	662	3 026 236	14.1	26.0	24.8	12.2	1.2	15.7	0.0
Liberty	46	301	25.2	7.0	236	903 212	17.2	26.6	21.9	6.0	2.2	21.9	0.0
Maryland Heights	44	455	39.8	16.5	213	1 068 259	19.4	51.3	0.0	8.8	0.8	12.2	0.0
O'Fallon	118	905	70.2	23.2	411	1 761 725	11.2	39.0	0.0	8.3	0.2	28.0	0.0
Raytown	48	344	41.1	11.9	163	693 572	15.3	25.3	23.0	16.1	0.7	19.6	0.0
St. Charles	132	941	76.1	24.6	509	2 509 796	9.9	33.7	23.0	9.7	0.0	13.6	0.0
St. Joseph	125	D	D	D	663	2 327 632	8.6	25.3	21.9	12.5	6.9	20.6	0.0
St. Louis	462	2 903	291.4	85.6	6 234	25 364 525	13.6	42.1	13.8	12.2	1.8	10.5	0.0
St. Peters	137	949	82.4	23.7	494	2 194 343	14.2	29.0	0.0	11.7	1.0	34.9	0.0
Springfield	408	2 992	241.6	75.3	2 692	13 095 113	4.7	15.6	8.4	9.6	2.7	34.5	0.0
University City	50	496	44.1	17.7	298	1 365 064	15.3	34.6	18.6	11.0	0.0	13.0	5.7
Wentzville	54	351	32.5	10.2	193	721 735	12.9	42.6	0.0	13.1	0.0	18.1	0.0
Wildwood	25	124	5.2	1.8	22	125 285	42.6	1.4	0.0	18.0	0.0	3.7	0.0
MONTANA	1 583	7 375	732.0	192.6	X	X	X	X	X	X	X	X	X
Billings	235	1 446	135.1	38.4	872	4 012 052	9.7	22.7	20.9	15.3	1.0	18.6	2.7
Bozeman	89	485	35.9	11.5	338	1 647 964	17.1	21.0	15.4	5.9	2.9	25.5	4.6
Butte-Silver Bow	57	228	22.8	6.3	430	1 750 790	15.7	24.3	18.9	14.2	2.0	21.6	0.0
Great Falls	87	593	44.9	14.1	488	2 209 954	12.9	30.2	16.9	10.2	6.8	19.7	3.2
Helena	67	355	29.9	8.9	301	1 298 064	13.5	27.1	14.7	7.9	4.9	23.7	0.0
Missoula	155	1 073	81.3	28.1	447	1 919 831	13.5	30.6	24.9	10.1	1.2	12.0	0.0
NEBRASKA	3 155	16 918	1 516.3	447.6	X	X	X	X	X	X	X	X	X
Bellevue	71	407	32.4	10.8	265	938 368	6.4	36.6	4.0	16.6	2.5	17.7	7.0
Fremont	51	D	D	D	278	1 259 723	10.6	16.8	8.8	6.2	0.0	47.0	2.3
Grand Island	102	D	D	D	596	2 645 689	9.6	16.2	16.0	8.3	0.3	43.9	3.6
Kearney	62	354	32.6	9.7	270	1 071 385	12.0	30.1	5.2	9.0	0.0	29.1	4.9
Lincoln	426	2 442	167.1	57.2	2 609	13 359 820	7.8	16.2	13.7	9.9	9.9	36.2	2.7
Omaha	770	6 202	489.2	176.4	2 835	15 258 712	6.3	39.2	26.1	8.5	2.6	11.0	3.8
NEVADA	2 935	20 584	1 790.5	543.2	X	X	X	X	X	X	X	X	X
Carson City	95	552	42.3	14.2	599	3 175 867	20.0	28.1	15.2	8.9	6.6	14.1	2.2
Henderson	315	2 190	175.4	53.3	2 239	13 759 509	18.4	29.3	14.7	1.2	2.0	25.6	0.0
Las Vegas	661	5 005	401.8	125.7	2 582	17 371 881	20.0	12.6	31.6	6.1	2.8	17.6	0.0
North Las Vegas	126	1 726	146.2	47.7	1 363	9 456 660	14.1	46.1	18.2	3.1	4.2	11.5	1.3
Reno	357	2 581	191.6	64.3	1 190	7 727 021	13.9	33.3	27.4	3.9	0.0	11.5	0.0
Sparks	153	958	119.1	35.2	500	2 883 097	19.7	31.5	22.6	3.6	0.0	21.4	0.0
NEW HAMPSHIRE	2 267	12 435	1 111.0	350.4	X	X	X	X	X	X	X	X	X
Concord	114	604	51.3	16.7	511	2 745 870	14.5	22.9	23.9	13.9	5.1	10.5	4.7
Dover	57	336	22.4	7.3	877	3 404 621	4.9	9.4	7.4	1.9	0.4	5.5	67.4
Manchester	216	1 767	144.0	51.4	3 353	14 363 066	3.8	12.5	9.5	7.7	2.7	7.3	55.0
Nashua	150	1 349	117.8	41.6	2 841	11 458 659	3.6	11.3	8.2	3.9	1.1	3.4	67.9
Rochester	44	232	20.0	6.0	998	3 938 623	4.0	9.1	4.3	1.9	0.5	3.1	75.7
NEW JERSEY	15 754	89 543	7 479.9	2 333.1	X	X	X	X	X	X	X	X	X
Atlantic City	50	743	49.3	16.0	1 521	8 728 573	8.1	41.3	24.3	1.3	7.3	9.0	1.9
Bayonne	110	457	28.1	8.9	2 167	12 420 526	2.7	16.8	11.4	3.3	4.4	2.0	58.3
Bergenfield	51	132	11.9	2.8	255	1 134 735	8.1	48.9	3.6	7.5	2.5	16.0	6.5
Bridgeton	22	89	9.0	2.2	17	61 842	0.0	0.0	0.0	0.0	100.0	0.0	0.0
Camden	54	388	28.9	9.9	98	380 956	0.0	0.0	0.0	0.0	100.0	0.0	0.0
Clifton	158	743	68.1	21.7	557	3 601 939	8.2	40.5	27.4	6.6	4.9	6.5	4.0
East Orange	57	D	D	D	2 832	17 819 602	3.5	12.8	6.9	1.2	5.1	2.4	67.4
Elizabeth	189	1 214	102.9	54.0	1 367	7 810 360	7.8	38.8	26.4	7.8	8.7	0.5	1.8
Englewood	86	425	36.5	11.9	885	5 644 368	2.5	19.1	9.9	1.8	4.0	3.8	56.7
Fair Lawn	82	345	40.2	12.5	256	1 498 256	15.9	40.2	1.4	5.4	2.1	22.3	7.1
Fort Lee	89	263	26.0	7.0	326	1 959 502	8.0	51.4	17.5	5.4	6.0	4.7	4.2

1. Establishments subject to federal tax.

Table D. Cities — City Government Finances

	City government finances, 2012									
	General revenue							General expenditure		
		Intergovernmental		Taxes					Per capita[1] (dollars)	
					Per capita[1] (dollars)					
City	Total (mil dol)	Total (mil dol)	Percent from state government	Total (mil dol)	Total	Property	Sales and gross receipts	Total (mil dol)	Total	Capital outlays
	117	118	119	120	121	122	123	124	125	126
MISSOURI	X	X	X	X	X	X	X	X	X	X
Ballwin	18.7	9.4	1.9	5.3	173	15	159	18.7	613	106
Blue Springs	53.1	13.3	54.5	24.5	462	193	260	57.4	1 082	459
Cape Girardeau	57.8	5.4	100.0	35.6	921	61	860	52.2	1 349	435
Chesterfield	34.7	22.0	9.0	9.6	202	20	182	34.5	723	209
Columbia	138.4	19.3	25.9	63.8	563	95	468	212.6	1 877	640
Florissant	33.1	18.3	15.6	8.4	161	11	147	32.8	626	96
Gladstone	29.7	4.2	55.7	15.5	597	132	465	27.7	1 069	194
Hazelwood	38.3	16.6	5.6	17.5	683	419	264	41.8	1 627	196
Independence	188.3	31.9	65.8	87.8	748	125	624	191.9	1 636	278
Jefferson City	59.3	4.3	100.0	36.2	838	120	718	57.9	1 340	163
Joplin	79.1	7.5	60.0	45.9	914	50	864	75.9	1 511	421
Kansas City	1 256.7	117.6	15.8	742.9	1 599	266	877	1 156.0	2 489	448
Kirkwood	31.5	7.3	39.6	15.7	568	296	272	30.7	1 115	279
Lee's Summit	126.6	6.4	34.2	72.9	788	290	499	116.7	1 263	277
Liberty	33.0	1.0	69.8	19.8	663	218	445	32.0	1 073	157
Maryland Heights	47.8	14.1	52.2	24.5	891	113	778	36.8	1 340	394
O'Fallon	65.0	5.7	97.0	39.2	478	97	381	58.2	710	117
Raytown	24.5	1.7	100.0	13.8	468	60	405	23.7	802	108
St. Charles	85.0	6.1	40.0	58.8	884	225	659	87.4	1 314	334
St. Joseph	112.7	24.2	75.0	53.0	685	173	513	85.5	1 107	153
St. Louis	986.4	175.2	99.4	544.6	1 706	233	878	1 082.7	3 391	490
St. Peters	69.7	8.7	23.6	38.5	712	244	469	72.3	1 337	393
Springfield	302.8	56.5	34.5	151.6	934	123	811	276.2	1 702	333
University City	39.5	14.2	32.7	14.1	401	174	227	40.5	1 149	172
Wentzville	32.7	2.6	11.6	20.8	663	174	488	39.1	1 245	374
Wildwood	13.3	6.4	6.0	5.9	164	64	100	11.4	318	100
MONTANA	X	X	X	X	X	X	X	X	X	X
Billings	139.3	26.8	53.7	38.1	356	286	52	121.4	1 134	258
Bozeman	47.2	7.7	100.0	17.3	446	415	31	47.1	1 218	295
Butte-Silver Bow	75.8	25.6	85.0	27.7	820	793	27	64.6	1 913	455
Great Falls	59.8	11.2	86.2	17.7	300	264	36	59.2	1 004	125
Helena	39.8	8.5	54.5	9.3	320	301	19	38.1	1 306	175
Missoula	74.2	24.8	96.6	28.9	422	381	42	74.8	1 093	151
NEBRASKA	X	X	X	X	X	X	X	X	X	X
Bellevue	47.3	5.6	93.3	31.0	589	275	302	46.0	874	117
Fremont	32.4	11.1	42.3	11.6	439	202	237	26.6	1 007	230
Grand Island	57.1	7.8	100.0	23.4	468	139	329	52.8	1 053	87
Kearney	41.2	6.7	95.0	15.3	478	83	395	40.5	1 270	296
Lincoln	295.4	84.6	29.9	137.0	516	178	338	277.5	1 045	307
Omaha	610.0	80.9	60.1	392.9	903	317	586	580.3	1 333	325
NEVADA	X	X	X	X	X	X	X	X	X	X
Carson City	111.3	36.0	61.3	38.3	701	418	283	103.8	1 902	301
Henderson	402.5	181.2	47.5	129.1	487	256	231	422.6	1 594	454
Las Vegas	801.6	407.6	63.4	200.6	336	186	150	876.8	1 470	462
North Las Vegas	281.9	110.2	80.4	84.1	377	246	131	281.1	1 260	340
Reno	315.2	72.0	57.4	121.3	526	255	271	287.2	1 245	153
Sparks	93.5	28.6	69.1	34.8	378	260	118	85.8	933	92
NEW HAMPSHIRE	X	X	X	X	X	X	X	X	X	X
Concord	62.7	3.7	75.0	39.6	931	895	36	59.6	1 402	31
Dover	105.4	21.2	95.8	64.9	2 139	2 120	18	90.6	2 982	200
Manchester	391.9	151.9	74.0	152.0	1 379	1 330	50	436.7	3 964	479
Nashua	282.0	81.9	99.2	176.1	2 033	2 010	23	264.6	3 055	177
Rochester	102.0	39.7	96.1	54.8	1 835	1 692	143	100.7	3 371	643
NEW JERSEY	X	X	X	X	X	X	X	X	X	X
Atlantic City	265.6	40.5	25.2	197.6	4 993	4 875	117	225.7	5 703	269
Bayonne	247.8	88.4	85.4	137.0	2 113	2 095	18	277.8	4 287	148
Bergenfield	32.3	2.9	94.6	28.1	1 033	1 005	28	28.7	1 057	46
Bridgeton	34.1	9.2	55.7	12.4	491	454	37	34.9	1 382	155
Camden	232.9	174.8	71.9	30.2	391	338	53	160.2	2 073	195
Clifton	115.4	15.5	73.5	84.3	990	936	54	103.5	1 216	37
East Orange	399.7	273.1	95.8	111.4	1 730	1 712	17	362.6	5 630	108
Elizabeth	263.2	59.9	65.7	151.2	1 191	1 058	134	254.8	2 007	251
Englewood	130.4	25.5	71.3	98.9	3 607	3 555	52	132.8	4 840	411
Fair Lawn	44.1	4.4	97.6	38.3	1 166	1 116	50	39.3	1 195	65
Fort Lee	75.6	8.8	24.0	61.9	1 726	1 666	61	78.8	2 198	328

1. Based on population estimated as of July 1 of the year shown.

Table D. Cities — **City Government Finances**

City	City government finances, 2012 (cont.)									
	General expenditure (cont.)									
	Percent of total for:									
	Public welfare	Highways	Parking facilities	Education	Health and hospitals	Police protection	Sewerage and sanitation	Parks and recreation	Housing and community development	Interest on debt
	127	128	129	130	131	132	133	134	135	136
MISSOURI	X	X	X	X	X	X	X	X	X	X
Ballwin	0.0	26.8	0.0	0.0	0.0	25.3	1.6	20.8	0.0	6.3
Blue Springs	0.0	4.3	0.0	0.0	0.0	16.3	33.2	7.3	0.0	6.1
Cape Girardeau	0.0	23.1	0.0	0.0	0.6	13.1	19.5	15.6	0.7	2.2
Chesterfield	0.0	20.9	0.0	0.0	0.0	22.6	0.8	28.1	0.0	8.7
Columbia	0.3	9.2	2.5	0.0	2.7	7.7	25.4	7.7	0.9	2.5
Florissant	0.0	13.2	0.0	0.0	1.9	30.6	0.5	18.0	2.8	1.4
Gladstone	0.0	11.8	0.0	0.0	0.8	18.2	17.1	13.9	1.8	5.2
Hazelwood	0.0	0.9	0.0	0.0	0.0	19.1	0.3	8.1	0.0	2.2
Independence	1.9	13.2	0.0	0.0	1.6	15.3	15.0	3.9	0.4	8.1
Jefferson City	0.0	20.0	1.2	0.0	1.0	18.7	8.8	13.4	0.7	3.2
Joplin	0.3	11.6	0.1	0.0	3.2	12.8	22.9	7.3	2.2	0.8
Kansas City	0.5	13.1	0.4	0.0	4.6	17.1	7.8	4.6	3.5	8.1
Kirkwood	0.0	5.0	0.0	0.0	0.0	21.3	10.0	12.4	0.0	1.8
Lee's Summit	0.0	15.2	0.0	0.0	0.0	15.6	11.5	6.5	1.2	3.3
Liberty	0.0	13.8	0.0	0.0	0.0	14.6	20.9	11.7	4.7	6.1
Maryland Heights	0.9	36.0	0.0	0.0	0.0	26.9	8.2	10.0	3.4	3.1
O'Fallon	0.0	16.9	0.0	0.0	0.0	20.3	13.7	13.5	0.3	7.4
Raytown	0.0	5.9	0.0	0.0	0.0	28.8	18.1	6.2	2.8	11.3
St. Charles	0.0	22.9	0.1	0.0	0.0	21.1	5.4	10.0	2.8	8.9
St. Joseph	2.1	11.2	0.4	0.0	5.5	11.2	14.3	7.0	0.6	5.9
St. Louis	0.0	2.3	0.9	0.0	3.6	23.2	1.7	2.2	1.5	8.4
St. Peters	0.0	24.8	0.0	0.0	0.7	19.4	20.1	17.9	2.7	4.6
Springfield	0.4	10.7	0.1	0.0	2.9	23.9	12.1	10.6	0.2	5.3
University City	0.0	18.3	0.5	0.0	0.0	18.1	6.7	8.2	0.9	2.0
Wentzville	0.0	14.6	0.0	0.0	0.0	18.0	37.0	7.4	3.5	5.5
Wildwood	0.0	34.1	0.0	0.0	0.0	26.6	0.1	4.4	0.0	1.4
MONTANA	X	X	X	X	X	X	X	X	X	X
Billings	0.0	16.9	1.9	0.0	0.6	16.1	21.3	3.4	2.8	1.8
Bozeman	11.0	10.4	0.8	0.0	0.0	20.0	29.4	0.9	0.2	3.2
Butte-Silver Bow	0.2	7.2	0.2	0.0	7.7	10.3	23.9	4.7	0.4	2.6
Great Falls	0.0	12.3	1.1	0.0	0.0	20.7	22.3	10.6	4.0	2.1
Helena	0.0	10.7	5.1	0.0	0.4	18.4	19.1	15.1	0.1	3.1
Missoula	0.2	13.6	1.8	0.0	1.9	17.8	14.7	6.3	1.4	3.5
NEBRASKA	X	X	X	X	X	X	X	X	X	X
Bellevue	0.0	10.3	0.0	0.0	0.0	34.9	13.4	5.1	0.4	3.6
Fremont	0.0	16.1	0.0	0.0	0.0	16.9	17.3	8.7	9.2	1.3
Grand Island	0.0	12.5	0.1	0.0	0.0	16.4	18.8	8.4	1.9	2.1
Kearney	0.0	21.9	0.1	0.0	0.0	16.5	18.4	15.8	3.0	0.7
Lincoln	2.3	19.2	1.4	0.0	4.4	12.9	12.2	4.2	3.8	1.5
Omaha	0.3	10.5	0.8	0.0	0.0	16.3	19.0	13.1	0.3	7.2
NEVADA	X	X	X	X	X	X	X	X	X	X
Carson City	2.3	10.5	0.0	0.0	4.2	15.9	10.8	10.1	1.5	9.1
Henderson	0.0	1.7	0.0	0.0	0.0	17.2	10.2	28.6	2.7	2.3
Las Vegas	0.1	6.9	0.4	0.0	0.4	14.6	13.4	11.0	2.7	3.5
North Las Vegas	0.0	13.1	0.0	0.0	0.0	26.3	10.0	10.6	2.4	3.8
Reno	0.0	9.4	0.0	0.0	0.0	18.6	14.1	3.8	6.8	15.2
Sparks	0.0	7.6	0.0	0.0	0.0	23.2	17.6	6.4	0.6	13.5
NEW HAMPSHIRE	X	X	X	X	X	X	X	X	X	X
Concord	1.8	11.5	1.5	0.0	0.3	16.9	15.6	4.2	0.0	4.5
Dover	0.9	5.5	0.4	50.9	0.0	7.9	7.8	2.6	0.3	5.1
Manchester	0.3	5.2	0.6	39.2	1.3	7.0	4.3	1.3	0.9	5.3
Nashua	0.3	2.6	0.0	55.6	0.3	6.6	7.7	1.0	0.5	4.0
Rochester	0.6	7.4	0.0	57.0	0.0	6.1	4.6	0.7	0.3	2.9
NEW JERSEY	X	X	X	X	X	X	X	X	X	X
Atlantic City	0.6	1.1	0.0	0.0	1.7	16.6	1.7	3.0	11.8	1.9
Bayonne	0.0	0.6	0.5	41.0	0.5	9.0	4.6	1.2	21.6	4.2
Bergenfield	0.0	7.1	0.0	0.0	1.5	23.3	16.4	2.7	0.0	1.9
Bridgeton	0.0	3.9	0.0	0.0	0.4	15.8	23.3	1.5	13.4	0.5
Camden	0.0	2.8	0.0	0.0	1.1	17.8	5.7	1.0	24.6	2.6
Clifton	0.1	2.8	0.0	0.0	1.0	20.0	12.8	1.5	3.1	2.4
East Orange	0.0	0.5	0.1	63.0	1.4	7.5	2.7	0.7	4.4	0.7
Elizabeth	0.0	2.3	0.8	0.0	2.2	17.0	12.9	4.9	15.8	1.7
Englewood	0.0	2.1	0.0	52.5	0.6	9.2	4.3	0.7	5.2	1.0
Fair Lawn	0.2	2.9	0.0	0.0	1.8	20.0	13.4	4.5	0.0	3.4
Fort Lee	0.3	3.2	1.7	0.0	1.8	18.2	8.2	2.4	8.3	3.6

City	City government finances, 2012 (cont.)			Climate[2]						
	Debt outstanding			Average daily temperature (degrees Fahrenheit)						
				Mean		Limits				
	Total (mil dol)	Per capita[1] (dollars)	Debt issued during year	January	July	January[3]	July[4]	Annual precipitation (inches)	Heating degree days	Cooling degree days
	137	138	139	140	141	142	143	144	145	146
MISSOURI	X	X	X	X	X	X	X	X	X	X
Ballwin	17.1	563	0.0	27.5	78.1	17.3	89.2	38.00	5 199	1 293
Blue Springs	129.0	2 432	12.5	24.6	76.6	14.9	87.2	41.18	5 623	1 137
Cape Girardeau	56.2	1 453	14.5	32.4	79.5	24.0	90.1	46.54	4 344	1 515
Chesterfield	69.9	1 467	0.0	27.5	78.1	17.3	89.2	38.00	5 199	1 293
Columbia	354.5	3 130	121.7	27.8	77.4	18.2	88.6	40.28	5 177	1 246
Florissant	22.1	421	7.2	29.6	80.2	21.2	89.8	38.75	4 758	1 561
Gladstone	41.1	1 585	0.0	29.3	81.3	20.7	90.5	35.51	4 734	1 676
Hazelwood	43.7	1 703	7.9	29.6	80.2	21.2	89.8	38.75	4 758	1 561
Independence	427.5	3 645	74.2	26.6	77.1	17.1	87.5	43.14	5 373	1 176
Jefferson City	62.3	1 443	0.0	28.2	77.9	17.7	89.4	39.59	5 158	1 261
Joplin	15.0	299	1.4	33.1	79.9	23.7	90.4	46.07	4 253	1 555
Kansas City	2 948.0	6 347	651.3	29.3	81.3	20.7	90.5	35.51	4 734	1 676
Kirkwood	23.0	833	0.0	29.6	80.2	21.2	89.8	38.75	4 758	1 561
Lee's Summit	98.3	1 064	7.9	24.6	76.6	14.9	87.2	41.18	5 623	1 137
Liberty	47.2	1 585	5.9	26.6	77.1	17.1	87.5	43.14	5 373	1 176
Maryland Heights	17.8	647	0.0	29.5	80.7	21.2	90.5	38.84	4 650	1 633
O'Fallon	231.0	2 818	8.6	28.3	79.0	19.0	90.2	38.28	5 020	1 399
Raytown	54.1	1 832	0.0	24.6	76.6	14.9	87.2	41.18	5 623	1 137
St. Charles	217.8	3 273	9.9	27.5	78.1	17.3	89.2	38.00	5 199	1 293
St. Joseph	532.1	6 888	30.2	26.4	78.7	15.9	89.9	35.24	5 345	1 339
St. Louis	1 862.1	5 832	143.8	29.5	80.7	21.2	90.5	38.84	4 650	1 633
St. Peters	126.3	2 335	11.7	28.3	79.0	19.0	90.2	38.28	5 020	1 399
Springfield	1 021.0	6 292	42.8	31.7	78.5	21.8	89.9	44.97	4 602	1 366
University City	13.5	382	6.6	29.5	80.7	21.2	90.5	38.84	4 650	1 633
Wentzville	64.6	2 058	31.8	NA	NA	NA	NA	NA	NA	NA
Wildwood	5.1	142	0.0	27.5	78.1	17.3	89.2	38.00	5 199	1 293
MONTANA	X	X	X	X	X	X	X	X	X	X
Billings	108.2	1 011	7.4	24.0	72.0	15.1	85.8	14.77	7 006	583
Bozeman	35.1	906	4.1	22.6	65.3	12.0	81.8	16.45	7 984	216
Butte-Silver Bow	42.1	1 246	15.8	17.6	62.7	5.4	79.8	12.78	9 399	127
Great Falls	39.4	668	0.9	21.7	66.2	11.3	82.0	14.89	7 828	288
Helena	45.1	1 546	0.5	20.2	67.8	9.9	83.4	11.32	7 975	277
Missoula	84.9	1 240	6.4	23.5	66.9	16.2	83.6	13.82	7 622	256
NEBRASKA	X	X	X	X	X	X	X	X	X	X
Bellevue	65.0	1 234	8.2	21.7	76.7	11.6	87.4	30.22	6 311	1 095
Fremont	38.9	1 473	4.0	21.1	76.2	10.4	87.7	29.80	6 444	1 004
Grand Island	50.6	1 010	9.3	22.4	75.8	12.2	87.1	25.89	6 385	1 027
Kearney	40.8	1 277	10.8	22.4	74.7	11.0	85.7	25.20	6 652	852
Lincoln	1 294.9	4 876	354.0	22.4	77.8	11.5	89.6	28.37	6 242	1 154
Omaha	1 049.9	2 411	111.5	21.7	76.7	11.6	87.4	30.22	6 311	1 095
NEVADA	X	X	X	X	X	X	X	X	X	X
Carson City	282.0	5 168	35.1	33.7	70.0	21.7	89.2	10.36	5 661	419
Henderson	308.8	1 165	35.1	47.0	91.2	36.8	104.1	4.49	2 239	3 214
Las Vegas	637.5	1 069	51.5	47.0	91.2	36.8	104.1	4.49	2 239	3 214
North Las Vegas	473.2	2 122	27.1	47.0	91.2	36.8	104.1	4.49	2 239	3 214
Reno	1 243.0	5 389	55.4	33.6	71.3	21.8	91.2	7.48	5 600	493
Sparks	243.8	2 649	0.0	33.6	71.3	21.8	91.2	7.48	5 600	493
NEW HAMPSHIRE	X	X	X	X	X	X	X	X	X	X
Concord	67.0	1 577	8.1	20.1	70.0	9.7	82.9	37.60	7 478	442
Dover	72.6	2 392	9.7	23.3	70.7	13.1	83.2	42.80	6 748	427
Manchester	566.8	5 145	160.3	18.8	68.4	5.2	82.1	39.82	7 742	263
Nashua	156.2	1 803	14.8	22.8	70.8	12.1	82.5	45.43	6 834	445
Rochester	80.7	2 701	11.6	23.3	70.7	13.1	83.2	42.80	6 748	427
NEW JERSEY	X	X	X	X	X	X	X	X	X	X
Atlantic City	164.0	4 143	51.6	35.2	75.2	29.0	80.6	38.37	4 480	951
Bayonne	460.2	7 102	0.0	31.3	77.2	24.4	85.2	46.25	4 843	1 220
Bergenfield	14.8	544	0.0	28.6	75.0	19.5	85.5	51.50	5 522	824
Bridgeton	15.0	593	0.0	NA	NA	NA	NA	NA	NA	NA
Camden	77.8	1 007	0.0	32.3	76.3	23.2	87.8	48.25	4 801	1 054
Clifton	71.7	842	15.7	28.6	75.0	19.5	85.5	51.50	5 522	824
East Orange	100.2	1 556	0.0	31.3	77.2	24.4	85.2	46.25	4 843	1 220
Elizabeth	124.1	978	19.1	29.6	74.5	19.8	85.7	50.94	5 450	787
Englewood	44.8	1 633	0.0	29.6	75.3	22.7	82.5	46.33	5 367	882
Fair Lawn	38.7	1 176	0.0	28.6	75.0	19.5	85.5	51.50	5 522	824
Fort Lee	62.2	1 736	14.1	29.6	75.3	22.7	82.5	46.33	5 367	882

1. Based on the population estimated as of July 1 of the year shown.   2. Represents normal values based on the 30-year period, 1971–2000.   3. Average daily minimum.
4. Average daily maximum.

Table D. Cities — **Land Area and Population**

STATE Place code	City	Land area,[1] 2016 (sq mi)	Population, 2016 Total persons	Rank	Per square mile	Race alone[2] (percent), 2015 White	Black or African American	American Indian, Alaska Native	Asian	Hawaiian Pacific Islander	Some other race	2 or more races[2]
		1	2	3	4	5	6	7	8	9	10	11
	NEW JERSEY— Cont'd											
34 25770	Garfield	2.1	31 876	1 183	15 179.0	83.7	3.2	0.7	2.8	0.0	6.8	2.9
34 28680	Hackensack	4.2	44 756	842	10 656.2	39.2	22.7	1.0	9.8	0.0	25.2	2.2
34 32250	Hoboken	1.3	54 379	696	41 830.0	79.0	5.6	0.0	9.3	0.0	3.2	2.9
34 36000	Jersey City	14.8	264 152	77	17 848.1	35.4	22.8	0.5	24.3	0.0	13.6	3.3
34 36510	Kearny	8.9	42 126	896	4 733.3	72.0	5.7	0.6	5.4	0.0	12.5	3.9
34 40350	Linden	10.7	42 457	890	3 967.9	56.0	27.8	0.1	3.0	0.0	9.4	3.6
34 41310	Long Branch	5.1	30 763	1 226	6 032.0	56.3	20.7	0.8	3.3	0.0	16.5	2.4
34 46680	Millville	42.0	28 059	1 322	668.1	71.6	19.1	0.7	2.3	0.0	2.6	3.6
34 51000	Newark	24.1	281 764	70	11 691.5	25.8	50.2	0.5	2.2	0.0	19.1	2.2
34 51210	New Brunswick	5.2	56 910	657	10 944.2	66.5	16.1	0.0	9.2	0.1	6.0	2.0
34 55950	Paramus	10.4	26 880	1 371	2 584.6	70.8	1.8	0.1	25.3	0.0	0.3	1.7
34 56550	Passaic	3.1	70 635	499	22 785.5	40.7	6.1	0.2	4.7	0.0	46.0	2.3
34 57000	Paterson	8.4	147 000	178	17 500.0	30.4	25.8	0.2	5.4	0.0	30.7	7.5
34 58200	Perth Amboy	4.7	52 499	723	11 170.0	80.8	8.2	0.0	1.3	0.0	8.0	1.7
34 59190	Plainfield	6.0	50 636	751	8 439.3	17.1	48.3	0.2	1.2	0.0	31.0	2.3
34 61530	Rahway	3.9	29 451	1 269	7 551.5	57.1	37.1	0.0	2.3	0.0	1.8	1.7
34 65790	Sayreville	15.8	44 905	840	2 842.1	64.8	11.6	0.2	18.0	0.0	2.5	2.9
34 74000	Trenton	7.6	84 056	394	11 060.0	43.4	50.6	0.1	1.4	0.0	3.1	1.3
34 74630	Union City	1.3	69 296	506	53 304.6	69.6	5.2	0.0	5.3	0.0	16.5	3.3
34 76070	Vineland	68.4	60 525	610	884.9	77.5	14.5	0.2	1.2	0.0	2.2	4.5
34 79040	Westfield	6.7	30 206	1 246	4 508.4	85.5	6.3	0.5	4.9	0.0	0.8	2.1
34 79610	West New York	1.0	53 343	708	53 343.0	53.5	5.3	0.0	6.1	0.4	29.5	5.2
35 00000	**NEW MEXICO**	121 301.5	2 081 015	X	17.2	73.4	2.3	9.3	1.4	0.1	10.1	3.4
35 01780	Alamogordo	21.4	31 283	1 203	1 461.8	83.5	5.6	1.4	1.7	0.0	5.5	2.2
35 02000	Albuquerque	188.2	559 277	32	2 971.7	70.1	3.6	4.4	2.5	0.1	14.1	5.1
35 12150	Carlsbad	29.0	28 914	1 282	997.0	90.5	2.2	0.3	0.0	0.0	3.9	3.1
35 16420	Clovis	23.6	39 373	965	1 668.3	63.8	7.5	1.4	0.4	0.8	24.1	2.1
35 25800	Farmington	34.0	41 629	907	1 224.4	63.6	0.8	29.7	0.5	0.0	3.0	2.4
35 32520	Hobbs	26.4	38 143	1 000	1 444.8	81.9	7.2	0.9	0.0	0.4	5.5	4.2
35 39380	Las Cruces	76.9	101 759	299	1 323.3	87.6	2.9	1.4	1.9	0.0	3.3	2.9
35 63460	Rio Rancho	103.5	96 028	321	927.8	74.2	3.3	3.1	1.2	0.3	13.3	4.6
35 64930	Roswell	29.9	48 184	792	1 611.5	88.3	1.5	2.0	0.9	0.0	5.1	2.2
35 70500	Santa Fe	52.2	83 875	395	1 606.8	87.2	1.1	1.6	1.2	0.0	5.4	3.5
36 00000	**NEW YORK**	47 124.9	19 745 289	X	419.0	63.8	15.6	0.4	8.4	0.0	8.9	2.9
36 01000	Albany	21.4	98 111	311	4 584.6	55.9	28.3	0.6	7.3	0.1	3.4	4.5
36 03078	Auburn	8.3	26 821	1 375	3 231.4	86.2	10.7	0.3	0.3	0.0	0.0	2.5
36 06607	Binghamton	10.5	45 672	832	4 349.7	75.4	12.9	0.2	3.0	0.1	2.1	6.3
36 11000	Buffalo	40.4	256 902	81	6 359.0	47.4	37.3	0.4	5.0	0.0	6.2	3.7
36 24229	Elmira	7.3	27 962	1 326	3 830.4	72.0	20.4	0.6	0.6	0.1	1.8	4.5
36 27485	Freeport	4.6	43 279	867	9 408.5	40.2	41.1	0.0	0.8	0.0	5.5	12.5
36 29113	Glen Cove	6.7	27 341	1 351	4 080.7	60.9	12.4	1.0	5.6	0.0	17.7	2.3
36 32402	Harrison	16.8	28 340	1 314	1 686.9	81.2	3.8	1.6	7.5	0.0	1.5	4.4
36 33139	Hempstead	3.7	55 555	673	15 014.9	12.5	44.3	0.1	1.9	0.0	37.7	3.5
36 38077	Ithaca	5.4	30 756	1 227	5 695.6	72.3	4.0	0.5	14.7	0.0	0.7	7.7
36 38264	Jamestown	8.9	29 775	1 259	3 345.5	NA	NA	NA	NA	NA	NA	NA
36 42554	Lindenhurst	3.8	27 074	1 363	7 124.7	89.0	3.5	0.0	2.8	0.0	3.4	1.3
36 43335	Long Beach	2.2	33 717	1 126	15 325.9	78.5	10.2	0.0	2.3	0.0	6.0	2.9
36 47042	Middletown	5.1	27 653	1 334	5 422.2	42.7	25.9	0.0	3.2	0.0	25.5	2.7
36 49121	Mount Vernon	4.4	68 344	516	15 532.7	18.2	71.2	0.4	2.2	0.0	6.3	1.7
36 50034	Newburgh	3.8	28 200	1 318	7 421.1	NA	NA	NA	NA	NA	NA	NA
36 50617	New Rochelle	10.4	79 557	428	7 649.7	52.8	20.4	0.0	4.9	0.1	18.4	3.4
36 51000	New York	301.5	8 537 673	1	28 317.3	42.6	24.0	0.4	14.1	0.0	15.5	3.3
36 51055	Niagara Falls	14.1	48 632	784	3 449.1	65.8	22.7	1.8	1.7	0.0	1.8	6.2
36 53682	North Tonawanda	10.1	30 607	1 230	3 030.4	NA	NA	NA	NA	NA	NA	NA
36 55530	Ossining	3.2	25 360	1 415	7 925.0	51.0	14.9	0.0	2.9	0.0	29.2	2.1
36 59223	Port Chester	2.3	29 524	1 267	12 836.5	62.5	3.9	3.0	3.0	0.2	25.3	2.2
36 59641	Poughkeepsie	5.1	30 267	1 242	5 934.7	41.5	42.9	0.3	0.9	0.1	10.2	4.1
36 63000	Rochester	35.8	208 880	107	5 834.6	47.6	41.5	1.2	3.9	0.0	2.0	3.9
36 63418	Rome	74.9	32 415	1 168	432.8	90.8	6.1	0.0	0.5	0.0	0.9	1.7
36 65255	Saratoga Springs	28.1	27 763	1 333	988.0	NA	NA	NA	NA	NA	NA	NA
36 65508	Schenectady	10.8	64 913	557	6 010.5	57.8	20.4	0.2	5.7	0.0	9.0	6.9
36 70420	Spring Valley	2.0	32 603	1 164	16 301.5	37.0	34.3	0.1	2.1	0.0	24.5	2.0
36 73000	Syracuse	25.0	143 378	183	5 735.1	58.1	28.3	0.7	5.9	0.1	2.0	5.0
36 75484	Troy	10.4	49 702	758	4 779.0	72.4	15.0	0.1	6.4	0.0	0.6	5.6
36 76540	Utica	16.8	60 652	606	3 610.2	62.6	13.2	0.4	10.8	0.7	6.2	6.1
36 76705	Valley Stream	3.5	37 673	1 015	10 763.7	44.5	25.8	0.0	18.3	0.0	8.2	3.2
36 78608	Watertown	9.0	25 900	1 402	2 877.8	NA	NA	NA	NA	NA	NA	NA
36 81677	White Plains	9.8	58 241	644	5 943.0	66.1	9.2	0.1	9.3	0.0	11.0	4.4

1. Dry land or land partially or temporarily covered by water.   2. Hispanic or Latino persons may be of any race.

City	Percent Hispanic or Latino[1], 2015	Percent foreign born 2015	Age of population (percent), 2010-2014							Median age 2015	Percent female 2015	Population			
												Census counts		Percent change	
			Under 18 years	18 to 24 years	25 to 34 years	35 to 44 years	45 to 54 years	55 to 64 years	65 years and over			2000	2010	2000–2010	2010–2016
	12	13	14	15	16	17	18	19	20	21	22	23	24	25	26
NEW JERSEY— Cont'd															
Garfield	39.4	39.6	22.3	9.2	15.1	13.2	15.9	13.7	10.5	37.6	52.6	29 786	30 489	2.4	4.5
Hackensack	41.7	42.5	17.2	7.9	18.3	14.3	13.8	12.4	15.9	40.4	52.2	42 677	43 010	0.8	4.1
Hoboken	14.9	15.5	14.4	7.3	41.1	18.1	7.6	5.5	6.0	31.1	52.2	38 577	50 006	29.6	8.7
Jersey City	30.2	41.3	20.9	8.8	21.7	16.8	12.7	9.2	9.9	34.3	50.1	240 055	247 643	3.2	6.7
Kearny	48.7	40.7	21.5	9.2	14.4	12.2	15.1	15.1	12.4	37.9	51.7	40 513	40 715	0.5	3.5
Linden	39.0	33.9	22.3	11.7	15.2	14.0	14.4	11.8	10.7	35.2	53.5	39 394	40 515	2.8	4.8
Long Branch	32.1	28.2	18.6	10.8	20.7	7.5	16.1	12.0	14.3	34.9	50.4	31 340	30 717	-2.0	0.1
Millville	24.2	5.1	30.3	5.1	12.6	11.0	12.6	19.1	9.3	36.4	53.6	26 847	28 417	5.8	-1.3
Newark	35.6	30.6	24.3	11.0	15.4	14.9	13.6	10.1	10.7	34.6	51.0	273 546	277 130	1.3	1.7
New Brunswick	55.1	36.1	20.7	28.9	18.0	10.3	10.6	5.5	6.1	25.2	54.5	48 573	54 500	12.2	4.4
Paramus	14.2	26.0	14.4	10.1	8.1	7.5	17.5	21.0	21.5	50.4	50.5	25 737	26 342	2.4	2.0
Passaic	75.5	34.0	30.6	10.8	14.9	14.0	12.1	9.3	8.3	30.4	48.6	67 861	69 790	2.8	1.2
Paterson	57.9	33.7	26.8	10.7	13.9	14.1	12.9	10.5	11.1	34.0	52.2	149 222	146 203	-2.0	0.5
Perth Amboy	85.0	38.9	29.3	12.0	15.8	13.5	12.6	8.9	7.8	29.7	49.8	47 303	50 814	7.4	3.3
Plainfield	36.9	38.0	24.4	12.8	14.0	13.4	12.8	10.8	11.9	33.8	49.2	47 829	49 699	3.9	1.9
Rahway	19.7	22.0	14.4	10.1	13.5	11.4	17.9	16.4	16.2	45.4	54.1	26 500	27 337	3.2	7.7
Sayreville	13.0	30.6	26.0	7.8	13.4	16.7	14.5	9.4	12.2	37.1	51.3	40 377	42 712	5.8	5.1
Trenton	36.3	24.3	25.4	9.2	17.6	15.3	13.8	9.6	9.0	33.3	49.4	85 403	84 937	-0.5	-1.0
Union City	76.9	58.6	20.7	10.6	17.9	15.0	15.0	10.8	10.0	35.4	48.8	67 088	66 439	-1.0	4.3
Vineland	38.9	12.9	24.2	9.3	12.6	14.4	12.0	10.3	17.2	38.1	52.0	56 271	60 738	7.9	-0.4
Westfield	8.5	13.9	31.7	3.2	4.5	12.6	23.4	11.4	13.2	43.4	49.7	29 644	30 316	2.3	-0.4
West New York	76.9	64.5	17.7	9.1	21.1	15.5	13.2	11.1	12.4	36.3	53.7	45 768	49 709	8.6	7.3
NEW MEXICO	48.0	9.4	24.0	10.0	13.1	11.8	12.3	13.0	15.9	37.4	50.4	1 819 046	2 059 198	13.2	1.1
Alamogordo	33.9	6.5	22.4	11.9	11.9	14.2	10.5	12.5	16.6	37.7	50.1	35 582	30 415	-14.5	2.9
Albuquerque	48.6	10.4	22.9	9.6	15.7	13.0	12.6	12.1	14.2	36.0	51.1	448 607	546 135	21.7	2.4
Carlsbad	51.7	6.2	31.1	10.8	13.1	13.4	10.5	8.9	12.2	30.5	48.4	25 625	26 159	2.1	10.5
Clovis	44.6	8.7	27.4	15.1	12.6	11.9	11.1	9.0	12.8	30.6	48.6	32 667	37 799	15.7	4.2
Farmington	21.2	5.3	26.8	9.2	15.1	13.5	12.7	10.0	12.6	33.7	51.7	37 844	45 965	21.5	-9.4
Hobbs	62.9	17.5	31.8	9.3	16.7	12.7	11.6	6.8	11.1	29.8	48.7	28 657	34 131	19.1	11.8
Las Cruces	59.6	11.7	24.5	14.0	14.6	12.4	9.9	9.2	15.5	32.7	52.9	74 267	97 643	31.5	4.2
Rio Rancho	41.1	5.5	25.4	8.0	13.7	12.8	13.7	13.3	13.1	38.3	49.8	51 765	87 361	68.8	9.9
Roswell	55.7	8.6	27.3	9.1	11.4	13.4	11.1	11.7	15.9	36.7	51.5	45 293	48 411	6.9	-0.5
Santa Fe	54.6	16.4	20.4	7.6	12.4	11.0	14.2	13.4	21.0	44.1	51.7	62 203	80 882	30.0	3.7
NEW YORK	18.8	22.9	21.3	9.8	14.5	12.6	13.9	12.8	15.0	38.3	51.4	18 976 457	19 378 110	2.1	1.9
Albany	9.5	12.1	14.8	21.7	16.4	11.2	12.2	10.2	13.6	32.8	51.6	95 658	97 840	2.3	0.3
Auburn	2.4	3.8	20.4	9.8	16.3	13.9	11.4	12.8	15.4	36.8	45.9	28 574	27 688	-3.1	-3.1
Binghamton	6.1	8.7	20.8	17.2	12.7	8.9	11.2	12.9	16.4	34.3	52.7	47 380	47 410	0.1	-3.7
Buffalo	11.5	9.5	23.1	12.2	17.5	10.9	12.0	12.1	12.2	33.1	51.7	292 648	261 433	-10.7	-1.7
Elmira	6.6	3.4	25.4	10.6	15.7	13.8	10.1	11.0	13.3	33.4	55.0	30 940	29 237	-5.5	-4.4
Freeport	37.9	28.3	22.6	11.0	13.8	15.5	12.3	10.8	13.9	37.0	53.5	43 783	42 848	-2.1	1.0
Glen Cove	19.1	23.9	18.2	14.0	12.2	10.7	12.2	14.0	18.7	38.9	51.8	26 622	26 952	1.2	1.4
Harrison	15.4	21.5	18.9	19.3	6.9	9.3	12.5	13.4	19.6	41.3	56.8	24 154	27 471	13.7	3.2
Hempstead	50.3	45.2	25.1	11.0	15.6	14.8	14.9	9.4	9.0	33.8	51.7	56 554	54 001	-4.5	2.9
Ithaca	5.8	17.4	4.5	58.7	13.4	4.6	6.0	6.3	6.5	21.9	50.9	29 287	30 020	2.5	2.5
Jamestown	5.8	1.9	22.5	9.2	12.8	12.6	14.8	11.6	16.4	39.8	49.7	31 730	31 160	-1.8	-4.4
Lindenhurst	23.1	14.6	22.1	10.6	15.1	6.3	15.7	17.3	12.9	40.3	47.0	27 819	27 258	-2.0	-0.7
Long Beach	14.1	14.1	15.6	6.8	16.4	10.1	11.7	18.3	21.1	46.0	54.0	35 462	33 327	-6.0	1.2
Middletown	38.8	12.2	25.1	9.8	11.2	14.9	14.6	13.0	11.4	37.4	53.1	25 388	27 905	9.9	-0.9
Mount Vernon	13.8	34.6	20.3	12.1	13.2	13.4	14.3	13.1	13.7	38.5	53.5	68 381	67 290	-1.6	1.6
Newburgh	46.9	16.6	39.5	11.2	13.1	10.7	9.2	7.8	8.4	24.8	54.2	28 259	28 905	2.3	-2.4
New Rochelle	29.5	33.8	21.4	10.2	11.3	13.6	13.9	10.8	18.8	40.6	51.3	72 182	77 061	6.8	3.2
New York	29.1	37.6	21.1	9.3	17.9	13.9	13.1	11.6	13.2	36.0	52.3	8 008 278	8 174 962	2.1	4.4
Niagara Falls	4.3	4.7	23.3	10.8	13.6	10.9	11.3	15.4	14.6	37.1	53.3	55 593	50 173	-9.7	-3.1
North Tonawanda	1.6	3.8	20.9	6.0	14.8	9.5	13.2	16.9	18.7	44.1	48.4	33 262	31 574	-5.1	-3.1
Ossining	48.4	39.7	20.2	4.7	16.8	14.5	19.4	10.8	13.5	40.3	49.8	24 010	25 069	4.4	1.2
Port Chester	64.3	44.8	21.2	12.7	15.1	16.6	13.7	10.5	10.3	35.4	47.7	27 867	28 946	3.9	2.0
Poughkeepsie	12.7	14.3	22.6	11.4	10.7	15.8	12.5	10.4	16.6	37.7	52.2	29 871	30 900	3.4	-2.0
Rochester	18.1	8.5	23.7	14.4	17.0	11.3	12.5	11.2	9.8	31.4	52.3	219 773	210 756	-4.1	-0.9
Rome	6.1	2.6	22.3	7.3	19.2	10.7	9.6	13.9	17.0	37.0	49.6	34 950	33 718	-3.5	-3.9
Saratoga Springs	5.4	5.5	17.2	16.2	16.7	13.4	10.9	10.3	15.3	34.9	51.2	26 186	26 565	1.4	4.5
Schenectady	9.1	16.8	18.5	11.8	17.2	12.7	13.7	13.2	12.9	36.7	50.4	61 821	66 132	7.0	-1.8
Spring Valley	34.1	38.3	32.6	9.4	16.0	19.0	9.2	6.7	7.1	30.3	47.8	25 464	31 350	23.1	4.0
Syracuse	9.3	12.3	21.8	18.1	16.5	10.1	10.2	10.6	12.8	30.3	51.8	147 306	145 208	-1.4	-1.3
Troy	9.1	8.0	15.7	17.7	22.6	8.5	11.9	11.7	11.9	31.4	50.7	49 170	50 129	2.0	-0.9
Utica	13.6	17.6	26.5	9.6	15.3	10.7	12.5	10.6	14.9	33.4	51.7	60 651	62 238	2.6	-2.5
Valley Stream	23.6	36.1	25.3	8.1	9.0	15.7	12.9	12.9	16.2	38.8	47.7	36 368	37 363	2.7	0.8
Watertown	9.6	4.4	20.9	13.9	17.9	10.9	13.8	10.6	11.9	32.2	47.9	26 705	26 816	0.4	-3.4
White Plains	33.4	32.1	21.5	7.9	13.7	14.8	13.2	12.1	16.8	39.2	51.2	53 077	56 853	7.1	2.4

1. May be of any race.

Table D. Cities — Households, Group Quarters, Crime, and Education

City	Households, 2015				Persons in group quarters, 2010				Serious crimes known to police,[2] 2014				Educational attainment, 2015		
			Percent			Institutional			Total		Rate[3]			Attainment[4] (percent)	
	Number	Persons per house-hold	Female family house-holder[1]	One-person	Total	Total	Persons in nursing facilities	Non-institu-tional	Number	Rate[3]	Violent	Property	Population age 25 and older	High school graduate or less	Bachelor's degree or more
	27	28	29	30	31	32	33	34	35	36	37	38	39	40	41
NEW JERSEY—Cont'd															
Garfield	11 479	2.77	22.1	23.3	32	0	0	32	721	2 295	207	2 088	21 775	53.0	19.3
Hackensack	17 910	2.42	12.0	34.6	1 301	985	172	316	732	1 647	202	1 444	33 557	43.8	38.2
Hoboken	24 895	2.10	6.6	34.5	1 574	0	0	1 574	1 182	2 218	280	1 938	42 013	14.0	80.0
Jersey City	101 755	2.57	17.9	27.4	2 843	984	914	1 859	5 621	2 162	531	1 631	185 673	39.3	43.0
Kearny	12 982	3.18	26.8	18.3	2 570	2 501	167	69	985	2 347	207	2 140	29 219	54.4	23.0
Linden	13 861	3.01	19.6	24.1	245	242	214	3	1 232	2 965	366	2 599	27 746	48.7	20.5
Long Branch	11 720	2.62	17.2	31.0	184	75	70	109	838	2 765	320	2 445	21 853	48.3	25.9
Millville	10 652	2.62	20.9	24.2	212	117	117	95	2 133	7 417	692	6 725	18 227	59.7	18.2
Newark	98 524	2.73	25.9	34.4	16 367	8 545	1 015	7 822	10 967	3 929	1 078	2 851	182 502	59.4	16.0
New Brunswick	15 247	3.19	20.3	28.5	7 745	182	147	7 563	2 000	3 559	744	2 815	28 773	66.2	16.8
Paramus	8 691	2.93	12.5	16.3	1 165	1 110	521	55	1 219	4 550	86	4 464	20 373	36.7	43.1
Passaic	19 864	3.56	16.1	29.5	458	232	224	226	1 601	2 248	651	1 596	41 683	71.4	13.7
Paterson	43 147	3.37	25.1	25.7	2 628	1 353	212	1 275	5 048	3 456	816	2 640	92 361	71.5	9.1
Perth Amboy	15 749	3.30	23.5	19.5	667	445	445	222	1 234	2 358	472	1 886	30 898	64.7	16.7
Plainfield	14 707	3.38	24.1	23.4	732	342	327	390	1 572	3 092	710	2 382	32 179	60.7	15.6
Rahway	12 029	2.44	15.9	36.4	124	109	109	15	365	1 273	181	1 092	22 288	50.9	30.3
Sayreville	15 418	2.90	13.8	20.7	200	193	193	7	501	1 115	80	1 035	29 745	43.1	32.9
Trenton	26 286	3.04	25.8	32.1	5 123	4 250	1 166	873	2 960	3 510	1 104	2 406	55 073	63.6	11.8
Union City	24 151	2.85	18.8	24.1	649	342	341	307	1 425	2 072	347	1 724	47 485	65.4	18.4
Vineland	19 806	2.96	16.6	23.6	1 491	897	593	594	2 510	4 107	437	3 670	40 426	66.1	15.8
Westfield	10 600	2.86	5.7	24.7	220	204	204	16	293	945	61	883	19 871	14.4	72.4
West New York	20 561	2.60	19.7	29.7	14	0	0	14	717	1 358	290	1 068	39 083	51.4	28.7
NEW MEXICO	761 797	2.68	13.1	30.6	42 629	25 266	5 567	17 363	86 336	4 140	597	3 542	1 377 548	42.2	26.5
Alamogordo	13 028	2.31	9.8	37.9	611	515	278	96	1 061	3 363	295	3 069	20 207	34.3	21.2
Albuquerque	221 855	2.49	12.8	34.0	7 659	2 897	1 712	4 762	35 371	6 329	883	5 446	377 467	35.6	32.6
Carlsbad	9 302	3.06	18.0	19.5	533	470	217	63	1 370	4 886	510	4 376	16 820	49.8	18.8
Clovis	13 827	2.86	14.7	36.8	597	503	188	94	2 461	6 180	362	5 819	22 964	46.2	18.5
Farmington	16 231	2.55	17.5	28.3	1 465	979	164	486	1 822	4 023	665	3 358	27 470	42.7	21.5
Hobbs	11 151	3.28	10.7	24.5	1 494	1 316	146	178	1 828	5 002	673	4 329	22 610	57.9	19.9
Las Cruces	38 641	2.58	13.6	28.4	1 610	1 186	251	424	4 909	4 807	289	4 519	62 574	38.6	28.4
Rio Rancho	32 761	2.86	10.2	25.8	197	141	141	56	1 989	2 140	188	1 951	62 671	32.9	29.2
Roswell	16 616	2.75	15.5	27.0	1 489	452	216	1 037	3 429	7 050	765	6 285	29 989	53.3	16.9
Santa Fe	34 179	2.41	14.1	38.0	1 119	270	247	849	3 261	4 630	346	4 283	60 578	33.4	41.0
NEW YORK	7 233 694	2.66	14.5	30.1	585 678	231 163	116 558	354 515	414 680	2 100	382	1 718	13 641 473	40.5	35.0
Albany	42 243	2.08	11.6	50.1	10 248	1 452	941	8 796	4 668	4 735	803	3 931	62 539	38.7	36.1
Auburn	11 735	2.08	13.3	42.5	2 328	2 139	370	189	1 078	3 947	454	3 493	18 846	40.7	21.0
Binghamton	19 527	2.27	13.2	43.1	1 262	846	458	416	2 355	5 094	664	4 430	28 536	46.3	22.6
Buffalo	109 961	2.27	21.4	41.7	9 371	2 530	1 201	6 841	15 622	6 045	1 228	4 817	167 166	46.0	23.9
Elmira	10 027	2.47	22.2	31.0	3 458	2 380	296	1 078	1 045	3 628	281	3 347	18 055	54.5	16.1
Freeport	13 485	3.17	22.8	22.6	574	354	346	220	1 000	2 313	352	1 961	28 783	48.9	29.9
Glen Cove	8 690	3.07	15.8	18.8	723	404	396	319	103	378	22	356	18 572	45.4	39.2
Harrison	8 677	2.81	11.4	26.3	4 285	0	0	4 285	135	480	21	459	17 512	32.2	47.5
Hempstead	14 706	3.72	30.9	23.9	1 306	686	678	620	1 446	2 595	863	1 732	35 470	58.8	19.3
Ithaca	9 109	2.51	2.6	42.9	7 701	179	172	7 522	1 221	3 985	144	3 842	11 342	19.9	66.1
Jamestown	12 488	2.35	13.8	38.0	1 134	399	353	735	1 510	4 927	728	4 200	20 539	49.6	15.8
Lindenhurst	9 463	2.88	10.0	30.1	29	0	0	29	NA	NA	NA	NA	18 361	46.0	24.4
Long Beach	14 598	2.23	7.9	46.7	1 094	920	822	174	339	1 009	128	881	26 026	30.2	43.0
Middletown	10 704	2.56	13.0	40.4	489	190	181	299	953	3 440	451	2 989	18 084	49.1	21.4
Mount Vernon	23 748	2.85	21.2	34.2	833	429	418	404	1 526	2 230	722	1 508	46 386	47.1	28.5
Newburgh	9 185	2.98	30.8	35.3	945	24	0	921	1 285	4 528	1 476	3 052	13 929	66.3	11.9
New Rochelle	26 875	2.85	11.5	28.5	3 277	1 256	999	2 021	1 396	1 744	229	1 516	54 572	35.5	45.6
New York	3 129 147	2.68	18.0	32.5	185 530	70 041	45 516	115 489	186 311	2 199	597	1 602	5 948 515	43.0	36.8
Niagara Falls	21 083	2.30	24.7	40.1	376	159	157	217	3 228	6 548	1 189	5 359	32 209	56.5	18.1
North Tonawanda	12 464	2.46	11.9	34.4	142	74	70	68	530	1 710	155	1 556	22 515	40.9	21.0
Ossining	9 373	2.67	15.2	32.2	1 858	1 830	102	28	266	1 045	216	829	20 128	48.2	27.7
Port Chester	9 164	3.30	15.3	21.1	465	154	154	311	563	1 908	213	1 694	20 164	57.5	24.4
Poughkeepsie	12 602	2.33	21.5	38.8	2 904	921	540	1 983	978	3 201	894	2 307	20 032	47.3	19.2
Rochester	84 946	2.36	26.0	41.0	10 200	3 657	1 960	6 543	10 643	5 060	850	4 210	129 744	49.3	21.6
Rome	13 302	2.27	14.3	36.6	2 882	2 581	462	301	658	2 017	101	1 916	22 905	49.4	19.4
Saratoga Springs	12 039	2.07	7.5	31.3	2 510	445	352	2 065	655	2 382	236	2 146	18 492	25.5	56.0
Schenectady	21 881	2.82	15.8	41.5	3 470	677	296	2 793	3 068	4 660	870	3 790	45 497	48.8	22.8
Spring Valley	9 603	3.50	24.0	21.8	216	0	0	216	524	1 608	408	1 200	19 603	59.0	16.8
Syracuse	54 231	2.39	19.6	38.9	12 782	2 332	1 523	10 450	6 927	4 793	811	3 982	86 596	46.3	29.0
Troy	19 626	2.31	14.7	42.4	4 508	493	202	4 015	2 561	5 127	759	4 368	33 266	45.8	24.6
Utica	23 583	2.47	23.7	36.6	3 076	1 171	983	1 905	2 788	4 518	653	3 865	39 027	51.7	15.7
Valley Stream	12 077	3.14	15.6	19.4	41	0	0	41	NA	NA	NA	NA	25 294	40.0	32.3
Watertown	10 677	2.44	10.1	36.1	905	667	473	238	1 449	5 173	546	4 627	17 444	44.2	21.6
White Plains	22 128	2.58	13.3	32.6	1 755	704	460	1 051	1 150	1 979	179	1 800	41 238	30.8	51.8

1. No spouse present.   2. Data for serious crimes have not been adjusted for underreporting. This may affect comparability between geographic areas and over time.   3. Per 100,000 population estimated by the FBI.   4. Persons 25 years old and over.

Table D. Cities — Income, Poverty, and Housing

City	Money income, 2015					Housing units, 2010			Occupied housing units 2015				
	Households			Families					Owner-occupied			Renter-occupied	
	Median income	Percent with income of $200,000 or more	Percent with income of less than $25,000	Total Families	Percent with income below poverty	Total	Percent change, 2000–2010	Vacant units for sale or rent[2]	Total	Percent	Median value[3] (dollars)	Percent	Median rent (dollars)
	42	43	44	45	46	47	48	49	50	51	52	53	54
NEW JERSEY— Cont'd													
Garfield	50 781	6.6	26.5	8 097	23.6	11 788	0.8	715	11 479	38.4	313 100	61.6	1 187
Hackensack	60 909	6.2	18.3	10 436	8.3	19 375	2.3	1 233	17 910	36.1	284 400	63.9	1 394
Hoboken	122 842	24.7	12.9	10 717	6.7	26 855	34.3	1 814	24 895	31.0	685 600	69.0	2 070
Jersey City	59 485	8.3	22.0	63 985	18.5	108 720	16.1	11 861	101 755	25.9	331 100	74.1	1 241
Kearny	56 310	3.1	11.5	10 027	11.3	14 180	2.2	718	12 982	42.4	284 500	57.6	1 249
Linden	67 061	2.5	9.8	9 883	5.1	15 872	2.0	963	13 861	56.6	266 400	43.4	1 201
Long Branch	50 916	9.4	17.9	7 207	13.0	14 170	1.3	2 417	11 720	43.9	317 900	56.1	1 189
Millville	48 261	4.6	20.0	7 157	14.7	11 435	7.4	787	10 652	67.1	153 400	32.9	902
Newark	30 966	1.4	34.8	58 758	26.5	109 520	9.4	14 978	98 524	20.8	235 700	79.2	978
New Brunswick	41 784	2.3	26.1	9 301	23.3	15 053	8.3	934	15 247	20.6	233 900	79.4	1 254
Paramus	113 590	11.8	4.2	NA	NA	8 915	8.6	285	8 691	88.0	527 600	12.0	1 912
Passaic	26 922	1.6	38.0	13 632	30.2	20 432	1.2	1 021	19 864	22.4	285 500	77.6	1 123
Paterson	31 552	1.8	34.9	30 089	28.0	47 946	1.6	3 617	43 147	27.1	226 300	72.9	1 079
Perth Amboy	46 291	3.2	19.6	12 154	19.4	16 556	8.7	1 137	15 749	30.2	270 500	69.8	1 178
Plainfield	57 451	3.0	18.9	10 024	17.8	16 621	2.7	1 441	14 707	50.2	226 300	49.8	1 083
Rahway	68 866	3.7	8.3	NA	NA	11 300	8.9	767	12 029	57.4	257 800	42.6	1 408
Sayreville	67 412	5.2	12.3	11 341	10.6	16 393	7.6	757	15 418	58.7	287 800	41.3	1 252
Trenton	35 041	1.4	32.5	16 221	23.6	33 035	-2.6	4 457	26 286	38.1	93 700	61.9	888
Union City	45 558	0.9	21.0	15 776	23.8	24 931	5.0	2 117	24 151	20.9	336 700	79.1	1 126
Vineland	49 592	1.5	17.4	13 486	9.7	22 661	8.1	1 211	19 806	65.1	164 800	34.9	920
Westfield	175 019	43.6	4.6	NA	NA	10 950	1.2	384	10 600	81.0	744 000	19.0	1 401
West New York	45 175	3.5	22.4	13 046	14.9	20 018	15.3	1 166	20 561	19.2	306 200	80.8	1 209
NEW MEXICO	45 382	3.0	22.6	485 404	14.8	901 388	15.5	109 993	761 797	67.5	164 800	32.5	783
Alamogordo	38 855	0.7	23.4	7 315	10.9	14 052	-11.2	1 289	13 028	61.3	115 400	38.7	722
Albuquerque	47 096	2.8	21.2	128 492	14.2	239 166	20.4	14 836	221 855	58.7	189 200	41.3	802
Carlsbad	61 438	0.4	8.7	6 855	6.1	11 243	-2.4	986	9 302	64.8	135 200	35.2	889
Clovis	35 595	3.5	27.5	8 257	24.9	15 573	8.9	1 285	13 827	54.3	108 100	45.7	722
Farmington	54 061	2.7	11.6	10 611	5.4	17 548	16.6	1 102	16 231	69.0	174 200	31.0	733
Hobbs	57 431	3.9	17.7	8 023	13.3	12 900	7.5	1 271	11 151	60.0	120 700	40.0	851
Las Cruces	40 994	2.2	23.9	24 855	18.1	42 370	33.9	2 937	38 641	51.6	154 200	48.4	742
Rio Rancho	64 475	1.8	12.4	22 965	4.0	33 964	68.3	2 072	32 761	77.0	180 900	23.0	1 271
Roswell	39 167	2.7	25.8	11 694	13.8	19 743	2.4	2 089	16 616	69.0	99 300	31.0	707
Santa Fe	53 635	5.1	15.4	18 903	8.0	37 200	22.0	5 305	34 179	62.6	271 000	37.4	970
NEW YORK	60 850	8.1	17.6	4 561 118	11.6	8 108 103	5.6	790 348	7 233 694	53.1	293 500	46.9	1 173
Albany	38 267	4.1	26.4	14 435	16.2	46 362	2.4	5 205	42 243	34.4	172 600	65.6	852
Auburn	43 615	1.2	18.6	6 010	8.1	12 639	0.0	948	11 735	46.8	101 100	53.2	690
Binghamton	29 473	0.4	36.8	8 242	22.7	23 842	-0.5	2 692	19 527	44.4	83 300	55.6	656
Buffalo	32 509	1.4	34.1	53 927	27.3	133 444	-8.3	20 908	109 961	40.2	75 800	59.8	711
Elmira	33 590	0.4	33.3	6 154	28.8	12 313	-4.5	1 322	10 027	44.0	67 000	56.0	742
Freeport	74 678	7.5	14.8	9 538	8.9	13 865	0.3	586	13 485	64.1	307 700	35.9	1 458
Glen Cove	83 952	15.1	13.3	6 400	12.0	10 352	6.3	588	8 690	47.6	519 800	52.4	1 896
Harrison	97 378	26.4	10.9	6 175	3.7	8 956	3.5	581	8 677	66.5	756 000	33.5	1 757
Hempstead	56 062	2.2	16.4	10 502	17.6	16 034	3.0	800	14 706	41.9	307 000	58.1	1 308
Ithaca	32 385	4.5	32.3	NA	NA	10 950	2.2	542	9 109	26.8	242 800	73.2	1 097
Jamestown	34 449	0.3	35.5	6 795	16.0	14 738	-1.9	1 616	12 488	49.7	63 600	50.3	574
Lindenhurst	75 163	7.0	13.4	NA	NA	9 665	4.1	349	9 463	67.0	341 600	33.0	1 366
Long Beach	74 250	10.7	12.6	6 610	6.1	16 450	2.0	1 641	14 598	53.8	441 900	46.2	1 637
Middletown	52 991	4.2	20.7	5 960	8.6	10 886	7.1	890	10 704	51.5	179 200	48.5	1 059
Mount Vernon	58 097	4.8	20.8	13 577	13.5	28 990	7.2	2 730	23 684	35.6	359 400	64.4	1 252
Newburgh	33 099	1.2	25.8	5 589	37.1	10 505	0.2	1 475	9 185	29.7	176 000	70.3	1 084
New Rochelle	76 496	13.4	13.2	18 036	6.4	29 586	9.6	1 633	26 875	48.4	571 800	51.6	1 459
New York	55 752	8.6	21.3	1 866 451	16.8	3 371 062	5.3	261 278	3 129 147	31.6	538 300	68.4	1 317
Niagara Falls	26 505	0.6	35.4	11 277	30.6	26 220	-5.8	3 617	21 083	50.9	73 100	49.1	655
North Tonawanda	49 873	2.0	13.6	7 633	5.1	14 757	2.3	753	12 464	75.6	113 000	24.4	644
Ossining	55 961	5.1	16.5	6 116	9.1	8 862	4.1	518	9 373	48.7	354 400	51.3	1 418
Port Chester	56 000	4.5	14.6	6 845	9.1	10 046	2.8	806	9 164	39.9	434 000	60.1	1 423
Poughkeepsie	38 656	1.8	29.2	6 979	19.2	13 984	6.3	1 584	12 602	34.5	193 000	65.5	1 041
Rochester	31 946	0.8	33.0	42 527	28.3	97 158	-2.7	10 131	84 946	35.4	76 900	64.6	790
Rome	40 649	1.1	22.7	7 108	23.1	14 893	-8.6	1 367	13 302	46.0	89 900	54.0	758
Saratoga Springs	72 787	7.7	9.8	NA	NA	12 936	11.7	1 624	12 039	51.7	353 000	48.3	1 204
Schenectady	46 461	1.0	20.9	11 269	13.1	30 095	-0.8	3 462	21 881	50.6	115 400	49.4	829
Spring Valley	40 042	3.0	26.9	6 835	30.2	9 374	20.2	619	9 603	28.0	241 100	72.0	1 302
Syracuse	36 457	1.8	30.3	25 578	20.7	64 356	-5.6	7 001	54 231	37.9	93 100	62.1	778
Troy	37 075	1.8	26.1	8 871	19.8	23 474	1.6	2 969	19 626	39.0	145 500	61.0	829
Utica	29 877	1.5	33.3	14 003	29.9	28 166	-3.4	3 261	23 583	43.1	87 000	56.9	674
Valley Stream	89 066	14.0	7.4	9 217	3.0	12 625	-0.6	436	12 077	79.9	378 900	20.1	1 678
Watertown	39 725	1.9	24.0	5 749	18.4	12 562	0.9	1 153	10 677	43.5	146 400	56.5	772
White Plains	74 006	14.1	18.6	13 219	11.2	24 382	13.0	1 472	22 128	52.6	536 800	47.4	1 498

1. Based on population estimated by the American Community Survey.   2. Includes units rented or sold but not occupied.   3. Specified owner-occupied units; $1,000,000 represents $1,000,000 or more   4. 50.0 represents 50 percent or more.   5. 10.0 represents 10 percent or less.

Table D. Cities — Commuting, Computer Access, Migration, Labor Force, and Employment

City	Commuting Percent		Computer Access[2] Percent		Migration, 2015		Civilian labor force, 2016		Unemployment		Civilian employment[4], 2015 Population age 16 and older		Population age 16 to 64	
	Drove alone	With Commutes of 30 minutes or more[1]	With a Computer in the house	With Internet Access	Percent who lived in the same house one year ago	Percent who lived in an other state or county one year ago	Total	Percent change, 2015–2016	Total	Rate[3]	Number	Percent in Labor Force	Number	Percent who worked full-year full-time
	55	56	57	58	59	60	61	62	63	64	65	66	67	68
NEW JERSEY— Cont'd														
Garfield	74.7	41.7	87.6	77.1	93.9	4.5	16 068	-0.3	1 082	6.7	25 607	60.3	22 262	49.1
Hackensack	72.4	41.0	84.3	81.5	88.3	4.8	24 400	-0.1	1 209	5.0	37 482	67.0	30 333	57.3
Hoboken	23.4	80.1	96.3	93.5	78.2	11.2	36 488	0.3	885	2.4	46 056	80.4	42 863	70.5
Jersey City	33.2	65.3	87.5	79.1	82.5	8.2	140 479	0.0	6 687	4.8	214 339	67.7	188 209	51.7
Kearny	66.1	48.0	92.1	82.7	91.5	5.8	20 814	-0.5	1 135	5.5	33 821	65.0	28 586	51.1
Linden	72.3	46.1	87.3	73.7	86.9	4.7	21 784	-1.0	1 255	5.8	34 207	70.4	29 715	54.8
Long Branch	70.3	33.3	88.1	77.1	90.8	5.6	16 369	0.2	794	4.9	25 681	71.2	21 249	49.5
Millville	NA	29.0	79.0	71.7	NA	NA	13 298	-1.1	981	7.4	20 251	64.6	17 626	46.8
Newark	52.3	56.7	78.8	64.1	87.2	4.2	117 053	-1.2	9 207	7.9	220 398	61.0	190 266	38.5
New Brunswick	42.8	23.2	80.9	70.9	91.0	6.2	27 170	0.5	1 197	4.4	46 267	49.4	42 810	27.6
Paramus	75.3	47.1	88.7	85.6	94.1	2.6	12 891	0.0	515	4.0	24 218	63.8	18 432	50.5
Passaic	46.9	36.0	54.7	40.5	96.1	2.8	29 843	-0.5	2 147	7.2	51 423	50.0	45 527	37.2
Paterson	66.7	32.8	63.7	56.2	97.8	1.0	62 144	-0.8	5 688	9.2	112 850	55.0	96 456	43.7
Perth Amboy	78.7	34.3	77.6	59.9	93.0	1.0	25 198	-0.6	1 960	7.8	39 225	60.1	35 102	50.5
Plainfield	56.6	53.3	82.9	71.4	88.6	6.0	27 155	-0.9	1 816	6.7	39 863	68.3	33 779	44.7
Rahway	71.1	50.1	87.4	78.9	NA	NA	14 827	-1.1	826	5.6	25 733	69.4	20 942	51.5
Sayreville	78.1	52.3	94.3	88.5	92.3	1.6	24 140	0.7	1 120	4.6	35 316	68.2	29 847	48.2
Trenton	66.9	24.6	81.5	62.2	81.2	7.4	39 178	0.3	2 818	7.2	65 464	61.7	57 845	44.0
Union City	29.0	60.9	85.6	75.3	94.3	2.8	34 904	-0.3	1 955	5.6	56 057	70.6	49 145	54.4
Vineland	89.6	26.8	77.3	67.7	92.0	2.6	28 340	-0.7	2 029	7.2	47 969	58.5	37 516	51.2
Westfield	72.8	70.5	91.7	90.6	88.1	3.7	14 244	-0.5	454	3.2	21 799	68.8	17 752	56.0
West New York	31.5	64.3	84.3	71.3	85.0	8.2	28 501	-0.3	1 351	4.7	44 732	67.8	38 094	51.6
NEW MEXICO	85.5	26.6	80.8	67.6	85.8	5.4	927 355	0.4	62 443	6.7	1 642 487	58.4	1 311 893	45.2
Alamogordo	73.1	4.5	84.5	70.6	79.2	8.1	13 222	1.6	696	5.3	24 356	57.6	19 254	50.2
Albuquerque	86.4	23.3	86.0	71.5	82.1	5.1	273 252	1.5	15 834	5.8	444 861	63.1	365 434	48.9
Carlsbad	91.3	12.9	88.5	81.5	84.9	5.6	14 078	-3.9	966	6.9	20 786	63.4	17 258	50.3
Clovis	88.0	5.8	79.7	64.2	79.9	3.9	17 190	0.1	897	5.2	30 414	59.6	25 282	37.4
Farmington	89.6	18.7	88.5	74.1	83.0	5.5	20 857	-2.9	1 619	7.8	33 024	63.3	27 611	48.6
Hobbs	90.8	12.9	79.8	68.3	91.1	4.5	14 359	-8.2	1 408	9.8	27 313	60.6	23 055	49.5
Las Cruces	84.1	18.2	84.3	75.7	85.0	6.2	46 057	1.8	2 931	6.4	79 096	58.7	63 325	42.1
Rio Rancho	88.9	49.3	87.2	80.4	85.2	7.0	43 839	1.8	2 827	6.4	73 426	63.9	61 116	49.5
Roswell	85.9	21.1	77.4	65.7	82.6	4.4	20 591	0.9	1 415	6.9	35 737	52.7	28 218	45.2
Santa Fe	85.6	17.8	85.5	80.8	86.9	5.4	42 072	-0.1	2 190	5.2	68 742	63.3	51 120	53.6
NEW YORK	54.9	50.7	86.6	77.5	89.5	4.6	9 584 450	-0.1	463 127	4.8	16 066 508	63.2	13 104 061	48.8
Albany	58.8	20.3	85.4	70.7	78.4	10.8	47 147	-0.2	2 250	4.8	85 302	64.0	71 880	44.6
Auburn	77.9	24.0	85.2	72.4	75.5	11.9	11 848	-1.5	669	5.6	22 406	62.2	18 254	42.6
Binghamton	73.8	14.8	82.1	72.1	71.2	7.9	18 325	-1.5	1 065	5.8	37 252	55.0	29 723	30.7
Buffalo	68.9	25.5	79.7	60.7	84.8	4.0	110 279	-0.9	6 992	6.3	204 410	58.7	172 833	39.8
Elmira	67.2	25.3	81.0	64.2	84.1	8.5	9 934	-3.1	734	7.4	21 997	51.9	18 233	32.6
Freeport	62.3	48.8	84.2	79.2	92.1	3.4	22 690	-0.1	1 135	5.0	34 631	63.7	28 593	51.9
Glen Cove	76.9	38.5	94.4	86.4	91.8	4.6	14 045	-0.3	550	3.9	22 944	64.8	17 823	49.9
Harrison	62.3	30.4	95.3	86.7	91.7	4.6	13 340	-0.2	599	4.5	23 437	54.3	17 888	38.7
Hempstead	57.6	53.3	91.6	73.3	94.6	1.3	27 507	-0.2	1 422	5.2	42 531	70.5	37 505	49.2
Ithaca	39.8	11.9	96.5	83.6	69.1	13.3	13 126	-0.4	620	4.7	29 607	46.0	27 614	20.2
Jamestown	80.0	12.5	84.7	66.1	90.8	1.3	12 051	-1.8	777	6.4	23 803	57.1	18 872	42.9
Lindenhurst	84.5	47.2	88.9	85.1	NA	NA	15 304	-0.1	659	4.3	22 071	69.1	18 560	49.1
Long Beach	68.3	62.3	92.6	84.6	83.7	5.2	19 539	-0.3	699	3.6	28 682	65.7	21 613	49.8
Middletown	75.5	43.2	92.2	44.3	NA	NA	13 577	-0.2	634	4.7	21 541	62.5	18 370	55.6
Mount Vernon	48.1	60.4	86.7	70.7	90.4	5.1	33 107	-0.4	1 847	5.6	55 917	65.0	46 535	48.5
Newburgh	58.7	20.5	71.0	43.2	90.0	2.5	12 162	-0.1	675	5.6	17 406	63.6	15 039	48.6
New Rochelle	56.4	47.5	90.3	80.5	90.7	4.8	38 946	-0.2	1 875	4.8	64 143	65.8	49 153	50.7
New York	22.7	69.7	85.6	75.8	90.0	4.5	4 138 533	0.5	214 445	5.2	6 933 836	63.8	5 806 325	49.0
Niagara Falls	82.5	19.8	76.3	64.0	83.8	3.8	21 408	-0.7	1 533	7.2	38 301	58.9	31 157	38.6
North Tonawanda	84.4	26.1	83.3	80.3	91.0	4.9	15 711	-0.5	788	5.0	25 240	62.6	19 484	50.9
Ossining	56.8	42.3	86.5	79.5	94.1	1.0	13 198	0.2	505	3.8	21 968	66.9	18 344	44.4
Port Chester	57.1	25.1	90.8	85.7	84.9	2.8	16 596	-0.2	563	3.4	24 533	73.9	21 400	49.6
Poughkeepsie	56.7	35.7	82.1	69.6	87.6	5.2	13 255	-0.6	690	5.2	24 437	60.4	19 386	38.2
Rochester	69.7	21.0	80.6	67.4	75.1	6.2	90 777	-0.8	5 893	6.5	165 183	62.1	144 664	36.9
Rome	89.5	22.3	86.1	76.3	79.5	12.1	13 345	-0.9	668	5.0	25 796	54.4	20 270	40.6
Saratoga Springs	90.3	28.2	96.1	89.0	81.5	13.7	13 858	-0.1	540	3.9	23 461	66.3	19 202	53.2
Schenectady	75.9	36.5	82.4	71.8	84.4	7.1	29 979	-0.3	1 577	5.3	54 357	60.0	45 934	42.3
Spring Valley	61.8	35.8	85.9	65.4	86.0	2.6	14 786	-0.1	575	3.9	23 411	71.2	21 018	42.5
Syracuse	67.6	15.3	77.7	62.0	75.9	9.3	58 104	-1.1	3 444	5.9	116 440	56.0	98 049	36.9
Troy	64.6	28.0	80.9	71.0	75.6	10.1	23 241	-0.2	1 270	5.5	42 784	62.1	36 821	42.4
Utica	77.6	16.0	78.5	64.6	80.6	5.5	23 436	-1.1	1 334	5.7	46 326	56.4	37 225	37.5
Valley Stream	66.6	64.2	86.8	79.6	95.3	2.0	19 640	-0.2	819	4.2	29 431	64.2	23 296	53.5
Watertown	78.7	9.3	85.5	75.3	70.8	7.9	10 865	-1.7	587	5.4	21 802	66.3	18 602	48.1
White Plains	62.6	33.2	93.7	85.9	84.9	8.2	31 795	0.0	1 122	3.5	46 950	68.3	37 135	50.4

1. Employed persons.   2. Households.   3. Percent of civilian labor force.   4. Persons 16 years old and over.

Table D. Cities — **Construction, Wholesale Trade, and Retail Trade**

City	Value of residential construction authorized by building permits, 2016			Wholesale trade,[1] 2012				Retail trade,[2] 2012			
	New construction ($1,000)	Number of housing units	Percent single family	Number of establish-ments	Number of employees	Sales (mil dol)	Annual payroll (mil dol)	Number of establish-ments	Number of employees	Sales (mil dol)	Annual payroll (mil dol)
	69	70	71	72	73	74	75	76	77	78	79
NEW JERSEY— Cont'd											
Garfield......................	1 559	62	12.9	42	407	223.0	18.5	81	825	213.1	20.6
Hackensack.................	2 243	38	18.4	182	1 678	1 878.3	95.9	259	3 895	1 208.7	112.4
Hoboken......................	31 521	110	0.0	48	269	396.8	14.6	164	1 297	314.1	30.6
Jersey City.................	299 222	1 494	13.8	191	4 740	12 481.7	338.8	807	2 568.1	2 568.1	241.5
Kearny........................	10 901	84	0.0	75	1 611	2 672.4	112.5	104	1 643	402.9	43.2
Linden........................	6 302	97	28.9	119	1 875	2 144.0	104.5	183	2 770	843.2	66.8
Long Branch...............	7 267	100	33.0	20	113	73.3	3.7	89	1 000	268.7	28.6
Millville......................	1 393	15	100.0	27	468	282.8	28.1	88	1 798	460.5	41.2
Newark.......................	23 967	310	1.6	335	5 162	5 373.5	322.4	913	5 918	2 173.9	173.8
New Brunswick............	38 014	218	2.3	60	839	751.1	41.8	121	736	179.5	15.9
Paramus.....................	11 842	29	86.2	112	2 436	2 254.0	277.8	618	15 076	3 833.9	364.1
Passaic.......................	3 136	34	11.8	80	768	311.9	30.2	260	2 083	541.7	49.8
Paterson.....................	6 873	71	8.5	194	2 269	1 075.2	105.3	541	3 169	849.8	74.6
Perth Amboy...............	16 251	302	1.7	34	1 109	1 079.3	85.1	208	1 281	324.3	30.8
Plainfield....................	9 115	81	1.2	25	D	D	D	125	633	210.9	17.7
Rahway.......................	969	30	10.0	67	808	1 282.7	55.6	70	651	321.8	21.9
Sayreville...................	1 424	141	3.5	57	511	562.7	31.4	104	1 185	406.6	29.1
Trenton.......................	8 002	168	0.0	49	733	745.6	37.2	242	1 285	341.6	27.9
Union City...................	8 745	81	0.0	48	203	107.7	8.7	270	1 209	340.8	27.0
Vineland.....................	4 983	51	100.0	78	1 429	1 467.9	65.5	271	3 918	1 066.4	95.1
Westfield.....................	29 510	86	100.0	23	D	D	D	131	1 394	262.4	28.2
West New York	25 906	257	0.0	33	D	D	D	213	1 141	288.9	27.1
NEW MEXICO...........	91 203	337	100.0	1 646	17 448	10 720.4	814.6	6 590	90 792	25 179.3	2 214.5
Alamogordo	NA	NA	NA	11	D	D	D	136	1 966	525.3	46.6
Albuquerque...............	219 178	1 292	70.7	700	8 712	4 784.9	429.6	1 885	31 702	9 067.4	817.5
Carlsbad.....................	25 646	277	26.4	21	148	74.1	6.9	118	1 753	476.4	44.9
Clovis.........................	15 261	102	37.3	30	297	117.0	9.6	176	2 391	596.7	54.0
Farmington	12 179	54	96.3	103	921	466.2	48.5	319	4 848	1 378.0	123.9
Hobbs.........................	44 059	237	63.7	69	877	465.5	45.0	146	2 271	749.8	57.5
Las Cruces	80 497	431	97.0	66	473	224.5	22.7	398	6 973	1 719.0	150.3
Rio Rancho	140 358	730	95.6	24	D	D	D	115	2 593	732.5	62.1
Roswell......................	19 046	200	28.0	33	336	163.5	12.4	211	2 992	863.1	69.9
Santa Fe.....................	29 198	117	100.0	81	683	606.3	29.8	714	7 979	2 063.4	225.7
NEW YORK..............	300	1	100.0	28 853	325 663	341 735.0	19 833.3	77 463	905 325	251 167.7	23 641.2
Albany........................	16 632	103	9.7	115	1 234	2 016.9	65.1	477	7 460	1 710.7	170.1
Auburn........................	5 855	30	100.0	20	209	353.0	9.3	130	2 095	501.8	45.0
Binghamton	0	0	0.0	61	658	687.6	26.4	183	2 279	563.7	48.1
Buffalo........................	68 066	311	8.7	253	3 776	2 011.9	178.1	939	10 760	1 972.0	200.0
Elmira........................	0	0	0.0	38	448	194.6	19.4	86	1 051	308.2	27.3
Freeport......................	2 177	8	100.0	75	737	348.1	31.7	192	1 963	803.0	63.3
Glen Cove	4 077	13	53.8	36	140	173.8	6.6	115	1 192	534.5	42.8
Harrison......................	26 134	75	52.0	58	1 192	4 816.8	148.3	53	423	82.1	12.0
Hempstead..................	180	1	100.0	31	297	136.8	16.5	198	1 830	893.6	56.3
Ithaca.........................	37 006	271	5.9	13	98	23.2	3.5	177	3 072	729.8	71.0
Jamestown..................	195	1	100.0	39	221	130.7	8.2	126	1 462	391.5	36.0
Lindenhurst.................	1 067	19	15.8	39	D	D	D	118	804	306.8	27.2
Long Beach	3 600	18	100.0	30	443	225.2	23.6	85	629	171.5	17.1
Middletown	16 417	68	100.0	25	247	257.0	9.5	133	2 251	591.3	51.0
Mount Vernon..............	937	11	27.3	91	1 605	896.2	71.5	227	2 427	597.7	59.4
Newburgh....................	1 255	10	100.0	47	378	849.8	15.9	114	2 067	558.2	48.1
New Rochelle...............	507	1	100.0	85	821	611.8	64.9	252	2 869	1 150.2	95.9
New York.....................	531 101	4 003	0.0	15 124	148 956	173 797.8	9 474.6	34 215	318 004	92 265.0	9 163.8
Niagara Falls	634	6	33.3	30	D	D	D	261	3 751	843.2	67.1
North Tonawanda.........	1 277	6	100.0	27	640	159.4	27.3	80	804	210.8	21.0
Ossining	0	0	0.0	14	70	102.9	4.5	78	542	156.6	16.1
Port Chester................	3 253	17	52.9	44	428	189.0	22.5	140	1 997	624.4	58.8
Poughkeepsie..............	23 000	136	0.0	23	D	D	D	158	2 246	497.8	50.0
Rochester....................	3 885	26	100.0	279	3 486	1 528.7	175.7	783	7 561	1 414.1	161.5
Rome..........................	4 983	40	62.5	20	148	56.4	6.1	134	2 050	539.5	47.8
Saratoga Springs	30 966	145	31.7	28	278	260.8	18.0	154	2 059	575.3	48.7
Schenectady................	24 276	259	1.5	34	354	306.2	15.9	203	1 642	460.5	43.9
Spring Valley...............	2 588	14	42.9	52	259	388.1	14.1	102	1 146	265.5	24.8
Syracuse.....................	29 449	279	1.4	145	2 316	1 344.5	108.7	573	7 928	1 726.2	168.5
Troy............................	4 706	42	16.7	30	D	D	D	148	1 648	487.5	44.5
Utica	0	0	0.0	63	877	636.7	41.8	180	2 547	686.9	58.7
Valley Stream..............	350	2	100.0	68	432	395.6	27.0	203	2 570	654.1	55.4
Watertown	0	0	0.0	21	290	143.2	11.7	185	3 253	858.3	71.7
White Plains	18 141	293	1.7	100	1 551	4 084.6	159.5	422	7 482	1 956.9	204.0

1. Merchant wholesalers except manufacturers' sales branches and offices.   2. Establishments with payroll.

Table D. Cities — Real Estate, Professional Services, and Manufacturing

City	Real estate and rental and leasing, 2012				Professional, scientific, and technical services,[1] 2012				Manufacturing, 2012			
	Number of establishments	Number of employees	Receipts (mil dol)	Annual payroll (mil dol)	Number of establishments	Number of employees	Receipts (mil dol)	Annual payroll (mil dol)	Number of establishments	Number of employees	Receipts (mil dol)	Annual payroll (mil dol)
	80	81	82	83	84	85	86	87	88	89	90	91
NEW JERSEY—Cont'd												
Garfield	12	110	9.9	3.2	35	183	14.2	5.1	56	576	146.0	27.2
Hackensack	126	573	206.3	27.3	425	D	D	D	83	1 190	233.2	55.4
Hoboken	81	472	108.6	17.5	209	1 148	266.1	80.8	22	184	33.9	9.7
Jersey City	233	1 129	301.2	53.8	587	D	D	D	99	2 493	857.6	101.8
Kearny	34	227	68.4	12.1	47	227	34.4	11.0	47	1 272	617.1	73.7
Linden	34	187	51.6	9.4	53	1 152	166.5	92.7	105	3 184	14 465.7	223.0
Long Branch	29	76	32.3	3.2	46	183	19.2	10.7	17	250	D	12.2
Millville	12	51	10.6	1.7	44	213	24.5	6.3	43	2 425	450.4	104.5
Newark	214	2 108	518.5	77.8	407	6 545	1 896.8	727.0	251	6 686	3 139.4	358.9
New Brunswick	46	263	166.0	12.3	130	D	D	D	52	842	381.4	46.7
Paramus	73	692	725.3	60.1	216	D	D	D	17	265	78.2	15.9
Passaic	44	124	26.7	4.2	60	360	31.9	10.3	101	1 388	226.0	55.4
Paterson	70	382	54.5	12.6	75	D	D	D	225	4 649	1 167.9	222.8
Perth Amboy	30	135	33.1	4.9	47	D	D	D	37	1 099	579.3	52.3
Plainfield	18	60	12.9	2.2	38	192	21.7	9.4	23	390	D	12.7
Rahway	20	257	35.9	14.9	29	264	29.6	15.4	40	3 169	425.3	361.1
Sayreville	20	95	22.3	3.6	103	857	120.9	64.8	32	1 262	1 031.9	87.6
Trenton	52	352	273.6	16.9	112	D	D	D	53	1 273	D	65.2
Union City	50	147	27.0	3.5	87	314	48.3	10.8	42	339	58.8	10.0
Vineland	76	276	62.5	10.6	119	D	D	D	86	3 864	1 553.6	169.0
Westfield	29	119	56.6	5.4	153	830	170.9	56.6	7	85	11.1	2.2
West New York	57	405	135.5	19.3	70	167	22.7	6.2	40	188	23.2	6.3
NEW MEXICO	2 369	9 754	1 960.4	368.7	4 634	42 423	7 376.4	2 677.8	1 389	26 731	29 102.4	1 349.2
Alamogordo	43	136	17.5	3.3	48	219	17.0	7.1	10	118	D	3.1
Albuquerque	851	4 012	782.3	141.7	2 015	D	D	D	482	10 810	D	522.8
Carlsbad	28	142	33.8	7.5	46	D	D	D	16	252	D	13.8
Clovis	57	204	30.2	5.5	68	439	36.7	14.2	17	120	D	D
Farmington	82	592	167.0	28.6	174	D	D	D	46	519	124.8	27.3
Hobbs	59	459	169.8	36.5	56	403	52.4	23.0	29	479	D	D
Las Cruces	160	563	89.5	15.5	257	D	D	D	55	948	D	30.1
Rio Rancho	58	157	35.2	6.9	100	D	D	D	29	3 562	D	235.3
Roswell	71	201	30.5	5.7	94	954	166.4	62.9	25	95	D	4.0
Santa Fe	229	847	162.7	33.7	477	D	D	D	87	456	D	18.4
NEW YORK	32 033	166 315	56 409.8	8 654.4	58 867	557 669	127 952.2	47 330.7	16 475	426 621	148 879.9	22 073.3
Albany	146	951	161.4	32.4	418	5 267	1 121.9	408.4	63	1 500	684.8	67.5
Auburn	40	121	21.6	3.1	54	D	D	D	49	2 185	858.0	115.1
Binghamton	61	245	29.4	5.9	121	D	D	D	49	1 261	603.4	55.5
Buffalo	257	2 117	240.0	61.9	662	D	D	D	321	11 225	5 260.6	600.2
Elmira	34	137	30.1	7.5	50	D	D	D	29	1 823	385.6	86.9
Freeport	38	176	24.9	6.9	119	447	66.6	20.2	77	1 736	324.3	69.5
Glen Cove	24	93	20.6	4.5	87	335	57.3	20.8	22	254	D	9.6
Harrison	80	718	256.3	48.2	186	D	D	D	7	54	6.5	1.8
Hempstead	51	275	67.0	9.0	96	D	D	D	19	221	D	11.0
Ithaca	53	372	54.2	11.4	123	D	D	D	32	397	63.9	19.9
Jamestown	26	D	D	D	64	D	D	D	62	1 733	251.3	68.4
Lindenhurst	13	54	7.2	2.0	67	221	25.6	8.5	37	368	96.7	17.4
Long Beach	49	129	42.9	5.6	102	203	31.3	9.6	6	15	2.6	0.6
Middletown	26	76	15.8	1.9	50	209	24.6	11.2	29	685	166.3	30.5
Mount Vernon	133	468	86.2	18.4	101	D	D	D	99	2 363	676.9	99.6
Newburgh	27	127	17.9	3.9	60	D	D	D	47	696	109.9	26.9
New Rochelle	202	770	265.6	32.8	228	D	D	D	46	744	159.1	41.2
New York	19 341	107 333	42 465.9	6 213.2	26 420	321 736	92 285.6	32 985.0	5 572	68 953	14 816.3	2 898.8
Niagara Falls	44	223	38.4	7.2	84	D	D	D	43	1 662	1 071.8	116.3
North Tonawanda	12	48	4.6	1.3	35	429	45.3	12.2	62	1 440	437.1	66.3
Ossining	21	60	21.5	2.4	56	228	31.7	12.4	5	D	D	D
Port Chester	40	119	33.4	5.7	61	187	27.4	9.5	33	874	130.1	36.0
Poughkeepsie	61	263	48.3	7.7	131	D	D	D	27	2 474	D	238.8
Rochester	261	2 499	291.6	92.4	639	7 429	1 143.0	421.6	417	19 217	7 492.3	1 164.8
Rome	41	152	24.5	4.6	75	D	D	D	37	1 439	957.7	75.1
Saratoga Springs	51	209	51.4	7.5	153	D	D	D	22	1 441	561.2	73.4
Schenectady	55	225	49.9	7.2	148	D	D	D	53	2 742	1 093.1	193.2
Spring Valley	65	212	37.0	5.2	71	167	74.5	32.1	20	159	29.9	6.4
Syracuse	258	2 011	311.6	91.5	473	D	D	D	111	3 772	1 656.4	181.3
Troy	45	214	42.4	6.9	110	D	D	D	32	620	88.8	24.3
Utica	52	213	27.6	4.7	135	D	D	D	68	1 708	322.2	73.4
Valley Stream	48	218	54.2	10.0	146	1 088	128.2	54.0	25	92	15.2	3.6
Watertown	43	232	46.9	6.4	57	D	D	D	15	818	D	47.7
White Plains	187	892	374.9	59.3	632	5 332	1 359.2	492.6	33	338	56.4	14.5

1. Establishments subject to federal tax.

Table D. Cities — Accommodation and Food Services, Arts, Entertainment, and Recreation, and Health Care and Social Assistance

City	Accommodation and food services, 2012				Arts, entertainment, and recreation,[1] 2012				Health care and social assistance,[1] 2012			
	Number of establishments	Number of employees	Sales (mil dol)	Annual payroll (mil dol)	Number of establishments	Number of employees	Receipts (mil dol)	Annual payroll (mil dol)	Number of establishments	Number of employees	Receipts (mil dol)	Annual payroll (mil dol)
	92	93	94	95	96	97	98	99	100	101	102	103
NEW JERSEY—Cont'd												
Garfield	43	343	28.9	7.8	1	D	D	D	29	313	13.6	6.1
Hackensack	120	D	D	D	12	D	D	D	342	D	D	D
Hoboken	219	D	D	D	24	D	D	D	125	2 091	237.4	98.6
Jersey City	471	4 941	422.5	97.5	47	484	52.6	13.9	439	6 026	521.3	210.3
Kearny	56	532	33.2	8.7	3	D	D	D	68	D	D	D
Linden	95	986	62.1	14.7	6	74	3.8	1.1	63	1 413	115.3	44.9
Long Branch	93	1 567	88.5	25.3	6	137	4.3	1.2	84	D	D	D
Millville	56	673	42.5	8.7	3	D	D	D	59	939	73.2	33.9
Newark	536	7 920	582.4	146.1	15	D	D	D	310	4 836	383.4	162.7
New Brunswick	161	2 009	127.1	35.8	4	D	D	D	80	D	D	D
Paramus	156	3 372	221.9	58.6	22	D	D	D	199	2 320	258.7	100.4
Passaic	115	674	46.1	9.7	12	100	4.7	1.4	103	D	D	D
Paterson	232	D	D	D	12	D	D	D	156	1 927	192.0	71.6
Perth Amboy	102	614	41.5	8.7	3	D	D	D	66	1 254	70.5	30.2
Plainfield	75	613	33.5	7.8	1	D	D	D	71	947	78.0	32.2
Rahway	53	524	34.2	8.4	3	D	D	D	39	D	D	D
Sayreville	82	677	37.9	9.2	10	203	15.2	5.0	50	D	D	D
Trenton	140	D	D	D	6	D	D	D	94	1 646	147.3	64.5
Union City	126	831	53.8	12.9	5	D	D	D	156	1 745	91.7	40.7
Vineland	128	2 165	98.9	26.5	7	D	D	D	164	2 173	268.1	95.2
Westfield	74	D	D	D	11	218	10.1	4.2	150	1 979	178.7	81.2
West New York	87	669	42.8	11.0	9	D	D	D	95	D	D	D
NEW MEXICO	4 177	82 601	4 349.7	1 250.4	488	10 536	1 207.2	219.7	3 970	67 477	6 071.0	2 449.7
Alamogordo	75	D	D	D	7	D	D	D	67	801	75.0	26.8
Albuquerque	1 281	29 238	1 579.0	454.3	138	D	D	D	1 468	25 832	2 659.8	1 045.2
Carlsbad	69	1 320	78.4	20.0	4	D	D	D	52	1 124	152.2	54.9
Clovis	78	1 927	77.4	21.9	7	42	1.6	0.5	94	D	D	D
Farmington	129	3 091	150.4	41.9	11	D	D	D	193	D	D	D
Hobbs	98	1 703	110.1	24.6	7	D	D	D	68	D	D	D
Las Cruces	276	6 189	262.7	72.6	18	383	9.9	2.9	379	8 409	840.8	336.9
Rio Rancho	91	2 066	90.2	26.7	15	D	D	D	122	1 646	119.9	51.6
Roswell	119	2 281	106.2	28.0	5	D	D	D	134	3 029	289.8	111.6
Santa Fe	349	7 896	532.7	158.5	58	186	28.8	8.2	362	3 454	397.5	170.6
NEW YORK	49 731	679 146	49 285.5	13 734.3	9 600	103 072	16 431.7	4 940.4	43 548	540 067	55 599.5	22 400.9
Albany	453	5 990	373.4	98.6	21	730	12.9	4.8	216	3 700	522.7	199.4
Auburn	94	1 291	54.4	15.1	11	61	3.8	1.2	101	1 097	105.3	48.2
Binghamton	171	3 078	154.7	38.0	12	D	D	D	103	1 390	167.0	74.4
Buffalo	660	11 300	510.5	158.3	44	820	185.7	95.7	363	7 108	684.7	361.8
Elmira	63	995	42.7	10.7	7	137	7.2	1.5	70	794	85.7	36.4
Freeport	95	638	48.3	12.2	20	92	18.8	2.7	109	1 395	96.8	41.3
Glen Cove	82	D	D	D	10	135	15.3	3.2	118	D	D	D
Harrison	67	D	D	D	25	197	12.4	4.6	87	D	D	D
Hempstead	121	983	63.5	14.5	5	D	D	D	115	1 342	148.1	53.1
Ithaca	203	2 774	153.0	43.5	10	67	6.9	1.8	68	669	57.7	22.6
Jamestown	72	733	37.0	8.9	10	D	D	D	55	543	54.4	18.6
Lindenhurst	80	893	52.0	12.7	8	D	D	D	52	555	46.4	18.9
Long Beach	91	1 052	61.6	17.7	11	97	8.0	1.8	94	D	D	D
Middletown	67	616	30.1	8.4	5	D	D	D	71	2 591	332.5	147.7
Mount Vernon	104	692	49.5	11.4	15	159	13.2	5.3	111	927	75.2	29.0
Newburgh	87	1 121	79.9	18.1	5	D	D	D	76	887	81.0	32.2
New Rochelle	208	1 949	139.6	37.0	35	D	D	D	234	3 089	327.0	117.8
New York	21 506	304 855	27 452.9	7 757.8	4 956	50 582	11 117.6	3 322.1	18 267	234 221	22 637.1	8 976.3
Niagara Falls	171	5 873	883.7	134.7	13	D	D	D	68	1 178	67.5	32.2
North Tonawanda	55	642	27.4	8.3	7	50	2.7	0.7	53	301	22.2	9.5
Ossining	44	417	28.0	10.4	6	31	4.9	1.4	33	337	27.3	11.1
Port Chester	98	948	70.4	20.3	8	D	D	D	39	469	77.9	30.2
Poughkeepsie	126	D	D	D	5	7	0.7	0.2	103	2 052	299.4	131.4
Rochester	570	7 114	366.7	105.5	64	1 228	62.6	20.8	264	5 172	420.6	192.5
Rome	81	D	D	D	15	66	3.3	1.0	85	1 234	94.7	41.1
Saratoga Springs	170	3 198	196.3	57.3	39	949	162.4	34.0	109	1 410	158.0	74.2
Schenectady	182	1 857	93.1	25.5	8	402	80.7	11.6	138	1 958	182.0	82.2
Spring Valley	46	D	D	D	4	D	D	D	40	509	41.2	14.9
Syracuse	386	6 146	311.3	92.3	29	162	13.8	4.3	316	4 768	625.4	249.8
Troy	146	1 747	95.0	28.2	7	D	D	D	107	1 509	139.2	62.8
Utica	158	D	D	D	8	52	2.6	0.7	143	2 547	301.7	130.7
Valley Stream	82	1 147	66.7	17.9	14	62	7.4	1.9	134	954	157.5	46.6
Watertown	105	2 206	96.5	28.7	10	50	2.6	0.7	96	1 331	140.6	63.4
White Plains	203	3 100	235.8	75.9	31	233	28.3	5.7	348	5 680	639.1	303.9

1. Establishments subject to federal tax.

Table D. Cities — Other Services and Government Employment and Payroll

City	Other services[1], 2012					Government employment and payroll, 2012							
									March payroll				
									Percent of total for:				
	Number of establish-ments	Number of employees	Receipts (mil dol)	Annual payroll (mil dol)	Full-time equivalent employees	Total (dollars)	Adminis-tration, judicial, and legal	Police and Corrections	Fire Protection	Highways and trans-portation	Health and welfare	Natural resources and utilities	Education and libraries
	104	105	106	107	108	109	110	111	112	113	114	115	116
NEW JERSEY— Cont'd													
Garfield	65	268	29.8	8.1	172	1 065 564	10.9	55.4	1.4	9.0	14.1	5.5	3.1
Hackensack	117	757	63.8	20.3	540	2 983 931	6.1	38.2	33.3	3.4	8.9	5.9	3.9
Hoboken	118	D	D	D	712	4 180 854	7.4	42.5	22.9	2.8	7.1	10.6	3.1
Jersey City	318	1 625	144.0	44.1	2 936	18 762 329	8.1	43.6	27.3	3.2	7.6	6.7	2.0
Kearny	58	241	26.5	6.9	326	2 506 387	6.0	43.9	30.5	0.2	2.6	7.9	1.8
Linden	101	647	63.6	20.9	585	3 237 694	11.7	49.9	25.1	3.6	5.9	2.5	0.8
Long Branch	52	195	11.3	3.2	338	2 021 115	9.6	41.0	10.8	0.7	12.9	21.3	3.7
Millville	32	147	9.8	3.3	210	1 102 759	14.1	44.9	6.7	4.0	8.6	14.2	0.0
Newark	425	4 834	339.5	123.8	3 857	25 580 741	14.8	36.1	19.3	0.6	13.6	10.8	2.2
New Brunswick	74	535	49.5	15.3	1 983	11 480 514	2.4	14.2	6.5	0.7	1.8	3.7	67.3
Paramus	63	494	49.3	22.3	293	1 879 108	9.0	31.6	18.6	10.8	1.2	13.4	8.4
Passaic	90	251	20.0	5.3	563	3 095 395	9.0	45.4	25.9	6.9	9.0	1.7	2.3
Paterson	183	1 164	94.0	28.2	1 472	8 450 610	6.5	42.6	30.2	1.1	8.2	5.3	1.6
Perth Amboy	89	736	67.5	23.4	401	2 317 835	10.2	44.0	15.6	5.1	10.9	6.6	1.8
Plainfield	75	266	22.3	6.6	551	3 548 125	11.6	36.0	23.0	0.9	9.8	7.5	2.9
Rahway	42	162	19.7	5.2	277	1 741 702	7.4	40.4	21.7	9.0	8.1	6.9	4.4
Sayreville	87	372	38.5	11.7	240	1 549 628	10.5	59.2	0.8	2.5	2.2	9.8	4.9
Trenton	83	359	27.6	7.6	2 747	16 968 078	3.1	14.5	9.4	0.5	3.5	5.2	60.7
Union City	105	233	17.4	4.5	2 174	11 223 072	2.5	14.9	0.8	0.1	2.4	3.3	73.7
Vineland	108	538	44.6	12.1	718	3 828 158	13.3	30.7	5.0	1.6	10.8	34.6	2.3
Westfield	83	465	40.5	11.7	238	1 357 302	9.1	33.5	21.3	15.6	9.8	5.2	5.0
West New York	75	228	17.6	4.0	1 416	9 134 998	2.4	10.3	4.4	1.4	1.5	0.3	79.2
NEW MEXICO	2 182	12 810	1 115.9	349.7	X	X	X	X	X	X	X	X	X
Alamogordo	38	202	14.8	4.1	280	741 098	18.0	39.9	1.3	4.0	10.8	22.4	3.5
Albuquerque	718	4 969	379.7	125.0	6 438	33 331 138	10.6	29.5	14.1	15.4	8.8	17.0	1.5
Carlsbad	39	195	24.0	6.2	381	1 625 310	11.0	22.8	19.6	11.1	0.7	23.8	1.9
Clovis	55	332	26.5	7.3	383	1 169 467	11.4	25.1	25.2	9.8	5.3	18.8	2.8
Farmington	116	973	105.0	36.0	882	3 555 193	11.2	22.9	12.7	4.9	2.4	35.0	4.8
Hobbs	62	571	72.3	23.8	403	1 643 293	10.3	27.3	18.4	9.1	3.7	22.7	2.5
Las Cruces	138	753	51.6	16.6	1 337	4 708 150	16.1	21.4	12.0	10.4	4.2	18.4	1.9
Rio Rancho	67	437	31.6	12.0	606	2 382 289	13.5	29.4	20.0	10.8	8.8	12.6	4.3
Roswell	46	222	19.0	5.4	548	1 751 942	8.5	26.4	20.7	10.4	1.6	25.5	3.2
Santa Fe	162	866	71.7	23.4	1 540	6 258 370	13.8	15.1	12.9	7.7	6.4	28.1	2.3
NEW YORK	34 948	168 002	14 493.2	4 209.4	X	X	X	X	X	X	X	X	X
Albany	146	825	81.6	24.9	1 455	6 784 879	6.9	38.4	23.1	4.0	10.7	16.1	0.0
Auburn	53	242	19.2	5.0	306	1 503 241	6.8	27.5	30.2	4.3	6.2	19.5	0.0
Binghamton	81	439	34.3	10.7	581	2 791 570	8.2	32.5	25.6	1.7	4.0	21.6	0.0
Buffalo	301	1 577	149.1	47.0	8 627	45 770 501	2.5	13.0	9.3	1.2	2.8	5.8	63.6
Elmira	29	155	12.6	3.8	297	1 470 047	6.0	34.4	27.9	5.6	6.2	16.6	0.0
Freeport	95	491	40.6	11.1	414	2 410 577	14.5	41.4	0.5	2.6	0.9	35.0	0.0
Glen Cove	71	259	21.8	5.5	313	2 051 266	16.9	46.0	2.4	7.0	7.0	17.7	0.0
Harrison	44	D	D	D	272	1 502 544	14.2	43.3	8.0	7.9	2.8	13.9	7.7
Hempstead	97	562	59.8	16.0	437	2 884 577	9.4	54.8	2.8	5.5	2.5	17.0	3.8
Ithaca	42	274	21.6	6.5	454	2 158 827	9.3	24.0	19.7	8.1	0.9	28.6	0.0
Jamestown	44	211	19.7	5.0	658	3 048 026	3.6	13.9	18.8	8.5	1.7	2.6	51.0
Lindenhurst	102	289	31.4	6.7	72	206 485	20.7	0.0	5.1	24.6	6.2	32.4	0.0
Long Beach	54	178	8.6	2.4	484	2 657 473	9.3	32.7	12.4	11.0	4.5	25.8	0.0
Middletown	54	376	29.6	8.9	283	1 449 586	12.4	41.3	15.8	7.3	3.0	20.2	0.0
Mount Vernon	128	768	87.4	28.0	873	4 489 959	6.4	36.3	23.8	1.9	2.2	13.5	2.9
Newburgh	62	479	52.2	12.3	258	1 411 393	6.5	44.1	27.5	10.5	1.6	9.6	0.0
New Rochelle	157	669	59.3	15.7	652	4 204 505	7.5	35.0	29.4	4.5	9.0	14.1	0.0
New York	15 271	69 456	5 597.1	1 634.2	404 260	2 380 283 176	3.2	19.0	5.4	13.7	18.1	4.4	34.0
Niagara Falls	62	323	23.2	6.3	687	3 126 887	0.0	30.2	23.2	0.0	6.6	0.0	0.0
North Tonawanda	56	153	11.3	3.0	281	1 334 637	8.0	28.4	16.0	17.6	0.8	25.8	0.0
Ossining	38	109	10.2	2.8	186	1 201 283	12.6	41.7	0.4	13.3	0.9	24.9	0.0
Port Chester	73	282	34.4	9.6	227	2 070 548	10.9	52.5	7.8	6.0	2.3	13.1	0.0
Poughkeepsie	71	288	25.8	7.1	365	2 055 377	6.9	43.5	19.1	6.3	5.4	15.8	0.0
Rochester	274	1 741	176.4	53.9	9 049	47 150 145	2.7	13.0	6.6	0.8	3.9	4.3	67.0
Rome	56	208	21.1	5.3	373	1 669 365	8.0	27.2	30.1	12.6	4.5	16.3	0.0
Saratoga Springs	49	232	18.3	5.5	349	1 565 062	9.5	32.3	19.4	23.7	4.3	7.4	0.0
Schenectady	90	526	61.4	17.3	637	3 109 293	5.4	38.3	21.7	5.1	10.0	14.6	0.0
Spring Valley	36	94	11.3	1.8	298	901 316	12.0	64.5	0.6	10.1	7.0	0.4	0.0
Syracuse	198	1 576	131.3	43.9	5 644	31 187 441	1.4	12.0	7.9	4.1	2.4	3.2	68.9
Troy	55	398	31.1	12.3	598	3 268 327	9.0	41.8	17.7	4.1	9.7	13.5	0.0
Utica	75	516	35.6	12.4	614	2 894 903	5.7	39.6	26.6	3.3	11.4	9.1	0.0
Valley Stream	116	1 253	73.5	22.6	225	1 128 453	12.8	3.8	0.6	18.2	0.6	37.3	6.6
Watertown	47	259	24.6	6.6	370	1 573 042	9.1	22.3	27.5	9.6	5.8	20.8	2.5
White Plains	141	958	83.4	26.2	1 041	6 536 682	8.4	25.5	18.2	8.2	6.7	11.5	3.6

1. Establishments subject to federal tax.

City	City government finances, 2012									
	General revenue							General expenditure		
		Intergovernmental		Taxes					Per capita[1] (dollars)	
					Per capita[1] (dollars)					
	Total (mil dol)	Total (mil dol)	Percent from state government	Total (mil dol)	Total	Property	Sales and gross receipts	Total (mil dol)	Total	Capital outlays
	117	118	119	120	121	122	123	124	125	126
NEW JERSEY—Cont'd										
Garfield	35.0	4.4	66.3	24.7	798	774	23	30.5	985	29
Hackensack	89.8	9.7	58.1	74.7	1 693	1 640	53	81.7	1 851	0
Hoboken	112.1	26.1	53.1	59.5	1 137	1 071	66	110.1	2 106	65
Jersey City	597.9	170.1	64.9	235.7	918	842	76	580.2	2 260	102
Kearny	76.1	28.2	95.1	41.5	994	966	27	71.6	1 713	127
Linden	93.5	30.9	71.2	55.1	1 345	1 310	36	93.7	2 288	123
Long Branch	71.9	21.4	25.7	37.9	1 241	1 202	40	74.6	2 445	343
Millville	50.7	12.0	68.9	21.9	765	691	74	49.8	1 738	61
Newark	845.2	438.4	36.2	305.9	1 099	784	156	860.7	3 093	368
New Brunswick	273.2	161.6	90.4	60.6	1 087	1 034	52	308.3	5 532	930
Paramus	60.6	4.7	91.3	49.5	1 859	1 738	120	49.8	1 869	77
Passaic	116.8	43.8	42.5	59.3	840	818	22	115.2	1 634	39
Paterson	273.4	94.3	64.3	140.1	959	943	17	265.5	1 818	72
Perth Amboy	99.9	23.5	45.3	58.9	1 136	1 119	17	92.3	1 780	148
Plainfield	100.9	20.9	40.2	54.9	1 089	1 063	26	102.8	2 039	6
Rahway	52.2	8.2	52.9	35.2	1 263	1 210	53	40.3	1 445	119
Sayreville	48.5	12.4	79.2	29.1	663	632	31	48.1	1 097	44
Trenton	505.3	395.0	94.6	79.2	938	887	51	482.0	5 714	70
Union City	355.1	263.5	96.4	81.0	1 184	1 161	23	313.3	4 583	154
Vineland	73.4	16.1	56.5	36.7	602	549	53	67.7	1 110	67
Westfield	37.4	4.0	79.9	29.6	967	909	57	39.3	1 283	88
West New York	209.6	134.4	93.8	51.2	986	966	20	216.0	4 160	249
NEW MEXICO	X	X	X	X	X	X	X	X	X	X
Alamogordo	41.0	11.2	83.4	17.7	560	107	454	39.0	1 236	363
Albuquerque	951.2	282.5	80.4	367.8	663	244	419	827.4	1 491	292
Carlsbad	58.1	6.7	35.3	37.8	1 412	97	1 316	48.5	1 811	487
Clovis	56.3	14.0	34.5	27.9	706	44	662	57.5	1 457	483
Farmington	92.1	35.8	11.0	27.5	600	38	562	99.0	2 161	207
Hobbs	89.8	35.4	93.8	38.4	1 098	56	1 042	69.8	1 994	1 088
Las Cruces	182.5	39.2	26.8	96.3	953	139	815	144.3	1 429	190
Rio Rancho	95.2	13.7	34.9	54.3	599	175	424	87.0	959	166
Roswell	55.1	34.8	96.0	9.3	192	110	82	56.9	1 173	255
Santa Fe	162.5	78.1	73.2	35.9	518	123	395	178.9	2 584	479
NEW YORK	X	X	X	X	X	X	X	X	X	X
Albany	252.8	90.3	28.3	61.5	625	548	77	277.7	2 820	454
Auburn	42.1	14.9	40.5	12.2	447	408	39	47.1	1 722	251
Binghamton	80.6	30.7	45.7	35.7	765	729	37	75.4	1 615	190
Buffalo	1 438.1	1 151.5	83.0	149.0	573	504	69	1 532.1	5 896	790
Elmira	41.8	23.4	53.0	11.6	398	367	31	41.7	1 427	358
Freeport	62.3	3.3	46.3	42.5	985	940	44	67.6	1 566	34
Glen Cove	53.4	17.4	54.0	30.6	1 125	1 054	71	56.1	2 063	478
Harrison	13.5	1.5	60.8	10.7	385	338	47	12.1	434	112
Hempstead	71.2	3.7	54.3	55.6	1 013	971	42	80.4	1 463	51
Ithaca	58.8	12.2	65.1	33.1	1 088	633	455	57.2	1 881	235
Jamestown	70.2	29.9	76.1	15.0	487	459	28	77.7	2 528	164
Lindenhurst	11.6	1.7	75.6	7.0	257	207	50	11.3	413	55
Long Beach	66.7	9.4	52.8	33.6	1 002	859	144	74.0	2 210	91
Middletown	41.5	13.3	24.7	19.0	681	633	47	38.9	1 397	51
Mount Vernon	96.7	15.2	70.5	70.8	1 042	724	319	104.4	1 537	169
Newburgh	57.5	23.9	52.4	21.2	742	667	74	56.9	1 989	235
New Rochelle	134.5	29.2	42.3	80.1	1 022	628	394	133.3	1 700	146
New York	85 078.0	30 398.8	83.5	42 476.1	5 077	2 176	970	81 160.8	9 701	1 196
Niagara Falls	98.1	50.3	53.9	40.9	824	581	243	127.6	2 570	657
North Tonawanda	43.9	17.1	37.3	18.6	596	510	86	41.6	1 330	104
Ossining	33.4	8.9	10.1	20.3	805	760	45	37.3	1 479	39
Port Chester	36.3	5.3	14.4	23.6	808	753	54	37.3	1 275	86
Poughkeepsie	58.3	29.4	22.7	19.2	624	566	58	54.6	1 777	206
Rochester	1 215.0	931.5	73.2	180.9	859	798	61	1 222.9	5 805	517
Rome	49.4	15.0	77.6	25.0	760	462	298	50.7	1 538	140
Saratoga Springs	48.9	5.5	67.4	32.2	1 193	719	474	43.3	1 605	81
Schenectady	89.2	31.5	44.8	29.9	453	405	48	98.0	1 484	180
Spring Valley	34.8	11.4	13.6	21.9	684	651	33	34.7	1 083	29
Syracuse	822.4	598.0	72.4	96.4	668	613	55	858.4	5 950	640
Troy	90.3	48.5	30.6	21.6	433	387	47	91.3	1 830	238
Utica	93.1	41.6	48.0	37.0	597	363	234	94.1	1 521	162
Valley Stream	33.6	2.5	57.9	27.0	716	656	60	37.3	987	118
Watertown	42.6	26.8	23.3	8.9	316	265	50	49.0	1 746	140
White Plains	165.8	12.3	50.2	108.8	1 897	862	1 035	178.6	3 112	124

1. Based on population estimated as of July 1 of the year shown.

Table D. Cities — **City Government Finances**

City	Public welfare	Highways	Parking facilities	Education	Health and hospitals	Police protection	Sewerage and sanitation	Parks and recreation	Housing and community development	Interest on debt
	127	128	129	130	131	132	133	134	135	136
NEW JERSEY— Cont'd										
Garfield	0.0	4.9	0.0	0.0	1.2	28.2	11.9	2.8	13.2	2.5
Hackensack	0.3	1.3	0.4	0.0	1.2	17.9	12.8	1.5	6.5	1.4
Hoboken	0.0	2.5	7.0	0.0	0.5	13.9	4.0	1.6	15.2	3.1
Jersey City	0.0	2.1	1.3	0.0	2.2	16.2	14.1	1.4	13.6	4.6
Kearny	0.0	7.5	0.1	0.0	1.0	20.6	13.2	0.8	0.0	3.6
Linden	0.8	2.4	0.6	0.0	0.9	15.3	6.7	2.6	6.2	1.7
Long Branch	0.0	2.4	0.0	0.0	1.1	15.9	20.9	1.9	20.8	3.0
Millville	0.0	2.0	0.0	0.0	0.0	13.2	16.0	1.1	16.4	2.3
Newark	0.3	0.7	0.4	0.2	4.3	15.3	9.7	2.5	24.4	3.2
New Brunswick	0.0	1.0	16.5	54.0	0.2	6.3	3.2	1.5	2.1	2.1
Paramus	0.1	3.7	0.0	0.0	3.0	23.8	11.3	5.3	0.0	2.7
Passaic	0.0	2.5	0.6	0.0	2.3	17.6	7.6	3.5	20.1	0.7
Paterson	0.0	3.0	1.9	0.0	4.0	17.4	9.1	2.0	10.5	1.2
Perth Amboy	0.1	2.3	0.6	0.0	0.6	15.2	8.7	1.9	19.0	3.0
Plainfield	0.0	6.3	0.0	0.0	0.6	15.9	18.4	1.4	13.0	1.7
Rahway	0.0	12.8	2.0	0.0	0.8	23.3	11.5	1.3	12.1	2.9
Sayreville	0.0	4.9	0.0	0.0	0.6	24.7	13.2	3.4	5.0	3.8
Trenton	0.0	0.8	0.8	58.2	0.5	6.3	3.8	0.3	4.5	2.6
Union City	0.0	2.3	0.7	64.8	0.6	6.4	1.9	0.7	4.1	0.9
Vineland	0.0	5.5	0.0	0.0	6.5	25.3	10.8	1.0	11.4	1.3
Westfield	0.0	5.2	0.5	0.0	2.2	16.1	8.8	2.6	0.0	1.6
West New York	0.0	1.4	0.6	65.2	0.6	5.6	1.5	0.6	5.1	1.0
NEW MEXICO	X	X	X	X	X	X	X	X	X	X
Alamogordo	3.1	26.7	0.0	0.0	0.0	16.5	10.5	11.1	3.1	3.2
Albuquerque	3.0	8.8	0.6	0.0	3.4	19.6	11.0	13.3	4.4	3.2
Carlsbad	0.0	11.5	0.0	0.0	1.6	17.0	21.2	11.8	0.0	0.8
Clovis	0.0	8.5	0.0	0.0	0.2	12.6	18.1	12.9	5.5	1.0
Farmington	0.0	12.8	0.0	0.0	1.2	15.7	9.6	13.8	1.3	0.6
Hobbs	0.0	29.3	0.0	0.0	1.5	6.2	12.9	10.4	0.0	0.0
Las Cruces	0.0	12.7	0.0	0.0	0.2	17.7	14.3	7.1	8.6	3.4
Rio Rancho	0.5	17.8	0.0	1.7	0.0	19.1	15.5	6.6	0.4	4.5
Roswell	0.0	8.7	0.0	0.0	0.0	19.1	9.7	11.3	0.0	1.5
Santa Fe	2.8	5.9	2.5	0.0	1.6	12.5	12.4	13.0	6.7	6.9
NEW YORK	X	X	X	X	X	X	X	X	X	X
Albany	0.0	5.6	0.0	0.0	0.2	17.8	5.3	1.6	23.5	17.5
Auburn	0.0	13.1	0.7	0.0	0.1	17.6	14.0	3.7	9.5	4.2
Binghamton	0.0	7.1	1.1	0.0	0.0	14.2	12.9	3.0	6.5	4.6
Buffalo	0.0	2.4	0.1	58.2	0.1	5.2	5.6	0.8	7.1	2.0
Elmira	0.0	21.6	0.6	0.0	0.5	16.9	2.2	3.1	4.9	2.6
Freeport	0.0	3.4	0.1	0.0	0.0	22.9	5.8	6.0	1.8	4.8
Glen Cove	0.0	9.1	0.0	0.0	0.6	22.5	4.1	13.1	9.0	6.4
Harrison	0.0	7.9	0.0	0.0	0.0	4.4	33.2	0.4	0.0	15.8
Hempstead	0.0	2.8	0.3	0.0	0.0	25.2	3.6	3.9	1.3	2.5
Ithaca	0.0	9.6	2.5	0.0	0.1	13.5	10.9	10.1	0.0	4.4
Jamestown	0.0	6.4	0.1	44.5	0.1	7.1	9.8	2.5	0.0	1.1
Lindenhurst	0.0	23.9	0.2	0.0	0.0	0.7	5.7	10.7	1.3	4.1
Long Beach	0.0	0.4	0.0	0.0	0.0	16.1	15.3	10.1	0.0	2.7
Middletown	0.0	5.3	0.0	0.0	0.0	19.0	11.9	6.4	5.3	3.9
Mount Vernon	0.0	2.6	0.1	0.0	0.4	19.2	7.2	5.0	2.7	3.0
Newburgh	0.0	3.7	0.2	0.0	0.1	24.8	13.6	2.8	1.7	4.8
New Rochelle	0.0	5.4	1.6	0.0	0.3	22.3	5.0	4.2	10.9	6.0
New York	15.7	1.8	0.1	27.7	10.4	6.2	5.6	1.3	5.8	5.3
Niagara Falls	0.0	16.1	0.0	0.0	0.1	14.7	2.8	4.1	5.6	2.1
North Tonawanda	0.0	12.9	0.0	0.0	0.1	13.1	15.2	4.4	0.0	1.2
Ossining	0.0	7.2	0.1	0.0	0.3	20.5	6.4	6.1	8.8	5.0
Port Chester	0.0	4.5	0.2	0.0	0.7	20.4	7.3	4.6	1.8	9.9
Poughkeepsie	0.0	9.9	0.9	0.0	0.2	23.5	8.9	1.2	1.5	3.8
Rochester	0.0	1.8	0.6	55.2	0.1	6.7	2.7	1.4	7.0	0.4
Rome	0.0	13.1	0.6	0.0	0.1	12.0	8.8	4.1	5.0	4.1
Saratoga Springs	0.0	10.1	0.2	0.0	0.1	23.1	9.2	8.2	0.6	3.2
Schenectady	0.0	7.4	0.7	0.0	0.1	16.3	15.5	2.0	4.8	6.5
Spring Valley	0.0	3.7	0.1	0.0	0.1	24.6	0.3	1.4	24.9	4.1
Syracuse	0.0	4.0	0.0	53.9	0.1	5.2	1.8	0.9	7.1	6.5
Troy	0.0	7.6	0.0	0.0	0.2	18.6	6.2	3.0	21.6	5.7
Utica	0.0	8.1	0.5	0.0	0.8	16.1	5.0	3.3	19.4	5.5
Valley Stream	0.0	15.7	0.7	0.0	0.4	0.6	12.9	12.6	0.0	5.6
Watertown	0.0	10.7	0.1	0.0	0.0	15.9	10.4	3.1	0.9	3.8
White Plains	0.0	8.2	7.1	0.0	0.0	18.6	5.2	4.4	3.7	1.8

City	City government finances, 2012 (cont.)			Climate[2]							
	Debt outstanding			Average daily temperature (degrees Fahrenheit)							
				Mean		Limits					
	Total (mil dol)	Per capita[1] (dollars)	Debt issued during year	January	July	January[3]	July[4]	Annual precipitation (inches)	Heating degree days	Cooling degree days
	137	138	139	140	141	142	143	144	145	146
NEW JERSEY—Cont'd										
Garfield	21.5	693	2.6	28.6	75.0	19.5	85.5	51.50	5 522	824
Hackensack	36.0	817	0.0	28.6	75.0	19.5	85.5	51.50	5 522	824
Hoboken	101.0	1 932	0.0	29.6	75.3	22.7	82.5	46.33	5 367	882
Jersey City	847.1	3 300	36.1	29.6	75.3	22.7	82.5	46.33	5 367	882
Kearny	83.3	1 995	9.1	31.3	77.2	24.4	85.2	46.25	4 843	1 220
Linden	46.6	1 137	15.0	28.5	74.0	18.2	85.8	51.61	5 595	757
Long Branch	70.9	2 322	0.0	31.7	74.1	22.8	82.6	48.63	5 168	750
Millville	39.9	1 390	9.2	32.7	76.3	24.1	85.9	43.20	4 835	1 009
Newark	658.6	2 366	2.2	31.3	77.2	24.4	85.2	46.25	4 843	1 220
New Brunswick	406.3	7 289	53.2	29.7	74.8	21.1	85.4	48.78	5 346	816
Paramus	39.3	1 477	0.0	28.6	75.0	19.5	85.5	51.50	5 522	824
Passaic	18.9	269	0.0	28.6	75.0	19.5	85.5	51.50	5 522	824
Paterson	119.6	819	5.1	28.6	75.0	19.5	85.5	51.50	5 522	824
Perth Amboy	91.3	1 761	13.7	29.7	74.8	21.1	85.4	48.78	5 346	816
Plainfield	48.0	952	0.1	30.0	74.9	21.5	86.6	49.63	5 266	854
Rahway	64.7	2 321	0.0	29.6	74.5	19.8	85.7	50.94	5 450	787
Sayreville	53.0	1 208	6.3	29.7	74.8	21.1	85.4	48.78	5 346	816
Trenton	390.2	4 626	34.2	30.4	75.2	21.3	86.9	48.83	5 262	903
Union City	82.9	1 213	0.0	29.6	75.3	22.7	82.5	46.33	5 367	882
Vineland	133.2	2 183	0.0	26.7	70.4	16.8	81.7	53.28	6 281	438
Westfield	20.7	675	0.0	30.0	74.9	21.5	86.6	49.63	5 266	854
West New York	52.4	1 010	0.0	29.6	75.3	22.7	82.5	46.33	5 367	882
NEW MEXICO	X	X	X	X	X	X	X	X	X	X
Alamogordo	58.7	1 859	25.6	42.2	79.7	28.9	93.0	13.20	31	1 715
Albuquerque	2 091.8	3 769	165.1	35.7	78.5	23.8	92.3	9.47	4 281	1 290
Carlsbad	40.7	1 520	8.7	42.7	81.7	27.5	95.8	14.15	2 823	2 029
Clovis	25.6	649	13.2	37.9	77.5	25.0	91.0	18.50	3 955	1 305
Farmington	1 802.6	39 348	11.1	29.8	74.9	17.9	90.7	8.39	5 508	805
Hobbs	58.7	1 677	0.0	42.9	80.1	29.1	93.5	18.15	2 849	1 842
Las Cruces	152.7	1 512	18.5	39.0	78.7	21.1	94.9	11.44	3 818	1 364
Rio Rancho	236.5	2 609	12.4	33.8	73.9	19.7	90.0	9.28	4 981	773
Roswell	18.0	371	0.0	40.0	80.8	24.4	94.8	13.34	3 332	1 814
Santa Fe	381.4	5 509	62.7	29.3	69.8	15.5	85.6	14.22	6 073	414
NEW YORK	X	X	X	X	X	X	X	X	X	X
Albany	773.1	7 851	27.8	22.2	71.1	13.3	82.2	38.60	6 860	544
Auburn	52.9	1 933	0.0	23.7	71.2	16.0	81.5	36.98	6 694	528
Binghamton	115.0	2 462	10.4	21.7	68.7	15.0	78.1	38.65	7 237	396
Buffalo	609.4	2 345	116.7	24.5	70.8	17.8	79.6	40.54	6 692	548
Elmira	36.3	1 243	8.5	23.9	70.3	15.0	82.3	34.95	6 806	446
Freeport	138.4	3 205	19.4	30.7	73.8	24.2	81.0	42.97	5 504	779
Glen Cove	81.8	3 010	11.6	31.9	74.2	25.4	82.8	46.36	5 231	839
Harrison	65.6	2 358	21.0	NA	NA	NA	NA	NA	NA	NA
Hempstead	47.9	872	0.0	31.9	74.2	25.4	82.8	46.36	5 231	839
Ithaca	76.9	2 530	0.0	22.6	68.7	13.9	80.1	36.71	7 182	312
Jamestown	36.2	1 179	4.0	22.3	69.2	14.1	80.1	45.68	7 048	389
Lindenhurst	5.9	218	0.0	30.7	73.8	24.2	81.0	42.97	5 504	779
Long Beach	54.6	1 631	2.5	31.8	74.8	24.7	82.9	42.46	4 947	949
Middletown	84.2	3 024	23.7	26.5	73.0	17.5	84.0	44.00	5 820	674
Mount Vernon	56.4	831	0.0	29.7	74.2	20.1	86.0	46.46	5 400	770
Newburgh	100.8	3 527	0.0	26.6	74.3	17.1	84.9	45.79	5 813	790
New Rochelle	141.5	1 805	20.0	29.7	74.2	20.1	86.0	46.46	5 400	770
New York	131 462.0	15 714	16 736.2	32.1	76.5	26.2	84.2	49.69	4 754	1 151
Niagara Falls	72.6	1 461	7.4	24.2	71.4	16.8	81.8	33.93	6 752	508
North Tonawanda	13.9	445	3.3	24.2	71.4	16.8	81.8	33.93	6 752	508
Ossining	25.9	1 027	2.3	NA	NA	NA	NA	NA	NA	NA
Port Chester	50.5	1 727	13.4	28.4	73.8	21.0	82.5	50.45	5 660	716
Poughkeepsie	86.8	2 825	12.4	24.5	71.9	14.7	83.6	44.12	6 438	550
Rochester	496.9	2 359	124.1	23.9	70.7	16.6	81.4	33.98	6 728	576
Rome	46.6	1 415	0.8	20.8	70.2	11.9	81.3	46.27	7 146	416
Saratoga Springs	36.7	1 362	3.4	20.9	71.2	11.6	83.0	43.31	6 904	477
Schenectady	159.7	2 417	13.3	22.2	71.1	13.3	82.2	38.60	6 860	544
Spring Valley	16.9	528	0.2	27.3	73.1	18.2	83.8	51.01	5 809	642
Syracuse	1 117.3	7 744	121.3	22.7	70.9	14.0	81.7	40.05	6 803	551
Troy	99.0	1 985	0.0	22.2	71.1	13.3	82.2	38.60	6 860	544
Utica	95.0	1 535	6.0	22.2	70.5	12.6	83.2	41.90	6 855	441
Valley Stream	28.5	756	3.5	22.2	70.5	12.6	83.2	41.90	6 855	441
Watertown	24.2	862	0.0	18.6	70.2	9.1	79.4	42.57	7 517	421
White Plains	106.6	1 858	45.7	29.7	74.2	20.1	86.0	46.46	5 400	770

1. Based on the population estimated as of July 1 of the year shown.   2. Represents normal values based on the 30-year period, 1971–2000.   3. Average daily minimum.
4. Average daily maximum.

Table D. Cities — **Land Area and Population**

STATE Place code	City	Land area,[1] 2016 (sq mi)	Total persons	Rank	Per square mile	White	Black or African American	American Indian, Alaska Native	Asian	Hawaiian Pacific Islander	Some other race	2 or more races[2]
		Population, 2016				Race alone[2] (percent), 2015						
		1	2	3	4	5	6	7	8	9	10	11
	NEW YORK—Cont'd											
36 84000	Yonkers	18.0	200 807	113	11 155.9	61.2	17.0	0.1	6.4	0.0	11.8	3.4
37 00000	**NORTH CAROLINA ...**	48 618.5	10 146 788	X	208.7	69.1	21.6	1.2	2.7	0.0	3.0	2.4
37 01520	Apex	17.3	47 349	809	2 736.9	83.5	4.4	0.2	6.9	0.0	1.7	3.3
37 02080	Asheboro	18.8	26 141	1 396	1 390.5	NA	NA	NA	NA	NA	NA	NA
37 02140	Asheville	45.5	89 121	360	1 958.7	86.8	9.2	0.3	1.7	0.0	0.4	1.6
37 09060	Burlington	29.2	52 709	718	1 805.1	54.9	26.6	0.2	4.1	0.0	11.6	2.5
37 10740	Cary	56.5	162 320	158	2 872.9	72.2	8.4	0.3	14.9	0.0	1.5	2.7
37 11800	Chapel Hill	21.2	59 246	626	2 794.6	69.1	14.8	0.5	12.8	0.1	0.9	1.9
37 12000	Charlotte	305.4	842 051	17	2 757.2	52.0	34.5	0.3	6.1	0.0	4.3	2.6
37 14100	Concord	61.7	89 891	357	1 456.9	67.9	19.5	0.1	3.6	0.0	6.2	2.7
37 19000	Durham	109.8	263 016	78	2 395.4	46.9	39.9	0.4	5.4	0.0	4.0	3.3
37 22920	Fayetteville	147.7	204 759	110	1 386.3	45.8	40.9	1.0	2.6	0.2	3.0	6.5
37 25480	Garner	15.1	28 776	1 292	1 905.7	NA	NA	NA	NA	NA	NA	NA
37 25580	Gastonia	51.6	75 536	459	1 463.9	60.8	28.6	0.5	3.1	0.0	5.4	1.7
37 26880	Goldsboro	28.5	35 792	1 064	1 255.9	41.2	49.8	0.7	2.8	0.0	0.4	5.1
37 28000	Greensboro	128.3	287 027	68	2 237.2	48.1	41.4	0.2	4.0	0.0	3.2	3.1
37 28080	Greenville	35.0	91 495	349	2 614.1	53.3	40.1	0.3	2.5	0.0	1.4	2.4
37 31060	Hickory	29.9	40 567	930	1 356.8	71.7	13.0	0.0	4.3	0.0	8.3	2.7
37 31400	High Point	55.2	111 223	259	2 014.9	49.6	33.8	0.2	8.9	0.2	3.2	4.1
37 33120	Huntersville	40.4	54 839	687	1 357.4	82.9	11.7	0.4	3.2	0.0	0.2	1.5
37 33560	Indian Trail	22.1	38 222	996	1 729.5	86.8	8.5	0.3	1.3	0.0	0.5	2.6
37 34200	Jacksonville	46.5	67 784	523	1 457.7	69.2	14.6	0.6	4.2	0.0	2.8	8.6
37 35200	Kannapolis	32.5	47 839	797	1 472.0	66.6	20.3	1.0	0.2	0.0	10.2	1.6
37 41960	Matthews	17.1	31 495	1 194	1 841.8	78.6	11.0	0.3	5.5	0.0	2.9	1.7
37 43920	Monroe	29.8	34 818	1 092	1 168.4	66.8	25.8	0.4	0.6	0.0	3.6	2.9
37 44220	Mooresville	22.1	36 543	1 043	1 653.5	80.2	10.4	0.4	7.2	0.0	0.6	1.2
37 46340	New Bern	28.3	30 101	1 247	1 063.6	NA	NA	NA	NA	NA	NA	NA
37 55000	Raleigh	145.1	458 880	41	3 162.5	58.6	29.5	0.4	4.5	0.1	4.5	2.6
37 57500	Rocky Mount	44.1	55 466	675	1 257.7	NA	NA	NA	NA	NA	NA	NA
37 58860	Salisbury	22.2	34 001	1 117	1 531.6	NA	NA	NA	NA	NA	NA	NA
37 59280	Sanford	26.7	29 128	1 277	1 090.9	NA	NA	NA	NA	NA	NA	NA
37 67420	Thomasville	16.8	27 030	1 366	1 608.9	NA	NA	NA	NA	NA	NA	NA
37 70540	Wake Forest	16.1	40 112	942	2 491.4	76.8	11.3	0.0	4.0	0.0	0.5	7.4
37 74440	Wilmington	51.6	117 525	235	2 277.6	75.8	20.0	0.2	2.2	0.1	0.5	1.2
37 74540	Wilson	30.6	49 620	760	1 621.6	40.9	48.0	3.5	1.9	0.0	5.1	0.7
37 75000	Winston-Salem	132.5	242 203	89	1 827.9	56.0	35.1	0.1	2.2	0.1	4.4	2.1
38 00000	**NORTH DAKOTA ....**	69 001.0	757 952	X	11.0	88.2	2.1	5.0	1.3	0.1	0.8	2.5
38 07200	Bismarck	33.4	72 417	485	2 168.2	90.4	2.3	4.3	1.1	0.0	0.1	1.7
38 25700	Fargo	49.3	120 762	229	2 449.5	87.3	4.6	1.3	3.2	0.0	0.8	2.8
38 32060	Grand Forks	27.0	57 339	651	2 123.7	86.3	3.4	2.4	3.2	0.4	1.7	2.6
38 53380	Minot	26.9	48 743	781	1 812.0	87.1	3.0	0.7	2.5	0.1	1.0	5.7
38 84780	West Fargo	15.6	34 858	1 090	2 234.5	NA	NA	NA	NA	NA	NA	NA
39 00000	**OHIO ....**	40 862.4	11 614 373	X	284.2	82.0	12.3	0.2	2.0	0.0	0.8	2.7
39 01000	Akron	62.0	197 633	118	3 187.6	60.9	30.0	0.3	4.1	0.0	0.1	4.6
39 03828	Barberton	9.0	26 120	1 397	2 902.2	87.5	6.6	0.0	1.1	0.0	0.4	4.3
39 04720	Beavercreek	26.4	46 376	825	1 756.7	85.6	3.2	0.2	5.9	0.0	0.4	4.8
39 07972	Bowling Green	12.6	31 588	1 190	2 507.0	85.8	6.4	0.0	2.8	0.0	1.2	3.8
39 09680	Brunswick	12.9	34 756	1 094	2 694.3	NA	NA	NA	NA	NA	NA	NA
39 12000	Canton	25.8	71 323	495	2 764.5	68.5	24.3	0.1	0.1	0.0	0.9	6.1
39 15000	Cincinnati	77.4	298 800	65	3 860.5	51.7	42.2	0.2	2.1	0.0	0.7	3.1
39 16000	Cleveland	77.7	385 809	51	4 965.4	40.3	50.7	0.7	2.1	0.1	2.9	3.3
39 16014	Cleveland Heights	8.1	44 633	844	5 510.2	49.2	43.7	0.1	4.4	0.0	0.3	2.4
39 18000	Columbus	218.5	860 090	14	3 936.3	61.5	27.8	0.2	5.1	0.0	1.6	3.8
39 19778	Cuyahoga Falls	25.6	49 206	769	1 922.1	89.4	5.8	0.0	2.3	0.0	0.4	2.1
39 21000	Dayton	55.7	140 489	189	2 522.2	57.0	36.9	0.2	1.1	0.0	0.2	4.6
39 21434	Delaware	19.0	38 643	986	2 033.8	87.6	9.1	0.0	1.8	0.1	0.0	1.3
39 22694	Dublin	24.5	45 568	833	1 859.9	73.5	3.0	1.6	18.2	0.0	1.7	2.0
39 25256	Elyria	20.6	53 715	705	2 607.5	78.5	13.4	0.5	1.4	0.0	1.3	4.9
39 25704	Euclid	10.6	47 360	808	4 467.9	39.2	56.8	0.1	1.1	0.0	0.3	2.5
39 25914	Fairborn	13.7	33 780	1 124	2 465.7	82.5	8.0	0.1	3.7	0.0	0.0	5.7
39 25970	Fairfield	20.9	42 617	884	2 039.1	NA	NA	NA	NA	NA	NA	NA
39 27048	Findlay	19.6	41 422	911	2 113.4	86.9	3.6	0.1	2.9	0.0	2.1	4.5
39 29106	Gahanna	12.4	34 956	1 088	2 819.0	79.1	14.4	0.0	2.0	0.0	2.4	2.2
39 29428	Garfield Heights	7.2	27 905	1 329	3 875.7	NA	NA	NA	NA	NA	NA	NA
39 31860	Green	32.1	25 673	1 409	799.8	NA	NA	NA	NA	NA	NA	NA
39 32592	Grove City	16.6	39 721	953	2 392.8	NA	NA	NA	NA	NA	NA	NA

1. Dry land or land partially or temporarily covered by water.   2. Hispanic or Latino persons may be of any race.

Table D. Cities — **Population**

City	Percent Hispanic or Latino[1], 2015	Percent foreign born 2015	Age of population (percent), 2010-2014							Median age 2015	Percent female 2015	Population			
												Census counts		Percent change	
			Under 18 years	18 to 24 years	25 to 34 years	35 to 44 years	45 to 54 years	55 to 64 years	65 years and over			2000	2010	2000–2010	2010–2016
	12	13	14	15	16	17	18	19	20	21	22	23	24	25	26
NEW YORK—Cont'd															
Yonkers	36.6	30.5	22.3	9.1	14.4	13.9	13.3	11.6	15.3	38.0	52.0	196 086	195 979	-0.1	2.5
NORTH CAROLINA	9.1	7.9	22.8	9.9	12.9	13.1	13.6	12.7	15.1	38.4	51.2	8 049 313	9 535 688	18.5	6.4
Apex	6.8	11.3	29.3	7.3	11.4	16.1	19.8	9.3	6.8	36.8	51.8	20 212	37 538	85.7	26.1
Asheboro	23.3	13.3	26.4	4.3	13.0	19.0	11.5	10.4	15.5	37.4	51.9	21 672	25 404	17.2	2.9
Asheville	4.7	7.5	18.1	9.5	18.5	13.0	12.6	11.5	16.8	37.9	52.4	68 889	83 344	21.0	6.9
Burlington	20.0	14.4	23.0	9.0	12.2	12.1	13.3	12.8	17.6	40.2	53.1	44 917	50 946	13.4	3.5
Cary	6.4	18.7	24.6	5.7	12.4	17.0	17.2	11.7	11.4	39.9	50.8	94 536	135 688	43.5	19.6
Chapel Hill	4.6	17.8	16.9	30.8	13.8	9.2	10.0	8.4	10.9	26.4	53.6	48 715	57 234	17.5	3.5
Charlotte	13.8	15.6	23.7	9.8	17.6	15.0	13.3	10.7	10.0	34.3	52.0	540 828	735 612	36.0	14.5
Concord	12.9	10.1	27.6	7.6	12.9	15.7	12.9	10.1	13.2	35.7	51.3	55 977	79 261	41.6	13.4
Durham	14.1	15.0	22.1	11.4	19.2	15.1	11.4	10.4	10.4	33.2	53.0	187 035	228 496	22.2	15.1
Fayetteville	12.4	6.4	24.2	14.5	18.1	10.4	10.8	10.3	11.7	30.7	50.0	121 015	200 585	65.8	2.1
Garner	11.7	8.0	21.6	12.8	11.9	12.2	17.3	12.7	11.5	37.6	53.0	17 757	25 773	45.1	11.7
Gastonia	8.9	7.7	24.7	8.1	14.4	13.0	12.6	13.2	14.0	36.9	52.3	66 277	71 735	8.2	5.3
Goldsboro	6.1	5.6	23.0	10.4	17.6	10.2	13.2	13.1	12.6	34.2	50.7	39 043	35 523	-9.0	0.8
Greensboro	7.8	9.3	21.7	11.9	15.6	12.7	12.5	11.7	13.8	35.5	53.7	223 891	268 887	20.1	6.7
Greenville	4.9	4.6	18.5	29.7	15.1	10.3	8.6	8.3	9.5	26.2	56.0	60 476	84 576	39.9	8.2
Hickory	11.3	7.9	19.1	10.4	10.5	13.1	14.2	12.5	20.3	42.7	51.7	37 222	40 061	7.6	1.3
High Point	10.4	14.9	24.5	10.8	14.0	12.5	13.4	11.2	13.6	35.5	52.9	85 839	104 411	21.6	6.5
Huntersville	6.9	6.7	33.1	4.7	13.9	20.2	12.9	8.2	7.1	34.0	50.0	24 960	46 759	87.3	17.3
Indian Trail	13.6	9.9	32.2	7.8	10.8	16.9	16.5	8.5	7.3	34.5	47.1	11 905	33 592	182.2	13.8
Jacksonville	17.7	5.5	20.7	32.3	20.6	8.7	6.7	4.9	6.2	24.2	40.6	66 715	70 145	5.1	-3.4
Kannapolis	14.4	6.7	28.4	8.9	11.1	16.6	12.7	10.8	11.5	36.0	52.6	36 910	42 602	15.4	12.3
Matthews	5.7	16.6	20.8	9.3	12.1	10.0	15.4	15.6	16.7	44.0	51.4	22 127	27 185	22.9	15.9
Monroe	22.6	13.9	24.4	10.0	13.3	14.0	12.7	11.3	14.4	36.3	51.8	26 228	32 786	25.0	6.2
Mooresville	8.7	9.8	27.7	8.7	12.5	16.6	14.2	7.7	12.6	36.1	49.5	18 823	33 566	78.3	8.9
New Bern	2.6	8.4	20.5	6.1	17.3	8.8	10.8	15.6	20.9	40.9	53.2	23 128	29 380	27.0	2.5
Raleigh	11.5	14.4	22.1	13.2	18.1	15.0	12.4	9.9	9.3	32.8	51.5	276 093	404 054	46.3	13.6
Rocky Mount	1.9	1.8	26.2	10.9	12.3	12.8	10.3	13.5	14.0	36.2	55.8	55 893	57 724	3.3	-3.9
Salisbury	9.2	6.3	16.7	11.9	13.2	14.5	12.4	12.5	18.8	40.6	52.1	26 462	33 529	26.7	1.4
Sanford	24.0	11.7	29.1	8.8	12.5	12.1	13.7	11.4	12.5	34.7	49.8	23 220	28 131	21.1	3.5
Thomasville	19.1	9.6	20.7	7.6	10.4	14.6	14.2	16.0	16.6	43.3	56.9	19 788	26 772	35.3	1.0
Wake Forest	4.8	7.8	31.9	5.5	8.4	20.3	11.6	10.0	12.3	36.6	52.5	12 588	30 102	139.1	33.3
Wilmington	5.9	6.4	18.6	17.6	13.0	12.1	11.5	12.1	15.1	35.5	54.9	75 838	106 430	40.3	10.4
Wilson	8.9	9.6	21.8	9.1	12.5	13.4	13.3	14.1	15.8	40.4	51.7	44 405	49 196	10.8	0.9
Winston-Salem	15.9	10.1	24.3	12.1	13.8	12.5	11.6	12.0	13.7	34.7	53.4	185 776	229 659	23.6	5.5
NORTH DAKOTA	3.4	3.8	22.6	12.4	15.1	11.4	11.7	12.6	14.2	34.9	48.7	642 200	672 591	4.7	12.7
Bismarck	2.4	2.9	19.0	11.0	16.3	11.9	11.5	14.3	16.0	38.0	50.6	55 532	61 325	10.4	18.1
Fargo	3.0	7.9	20.4	19.2	17.7	12.2	9.3	10.2	11.1	30.7	49.2	90 599	105 554	16.5	14.4
Grand Forks	4.6	5.8	18.6	24.0	17.1	8.8	9.5	10.7	11.4	28.0	48.8	49 321	52 919	7.3	8.4
Minot	6.8	5.3	20.1	16.0	19.2	9.6	10.6	11.0	13.4	31.3	50.7	36 567	40 967	12.0	19.0
West Fargo	1.6	7.1	25.1	8.5	16.4	11.9	13.7	12.3	12.0	35.0	50.7	14 940	25 838	72.9	34.9
OHIO	3.5	4.3	22.6	9.4	12.8	12.1	13.6	13.7	15.8	39.3	51.1	11 353 140	11 536 727	1.6	0.7
Akron	1.9	5.1	21.0	10.4	14.4	12.6	13.4	13.2	15.1	38.1	51.0	217 074	199 079	-8.3	-0.7
Barberton	4.6	5.5	24.6	8.0	18.6	9.2	11.1	13.8	14.6	33.7	53.3	27 899	26 570	-4.8	-1.7
Beavercreek	1.2	8.6	21.9	8.3	15.8	11.9	15.8	8.9	17.4	38.9	48.9	37 984	45 182	19.0	2.6
Bowling Green	3.7	4.8	10.8	45.7	9.2	7.2	8.1	8.5	10.6	22.9	53.1	29 636	30 052	1.4	5.1
Brunswick	2.2	3.0	22.7	7.3	10.7	14.9	13.5	13.7	17.2	42.2	49.2	33 388	34 278	2.7	1.4
Canton	5.0	3.1	26.3	11.2	15.5	10.4	11.8	11.8	13.0	33.4	52.0	80 806	73 053	-9.6	-2.4
Cincinnati	3.1	5.7	21.5	13.1	18.7	10.8	11.3	12.2	12.4	32.7	51.9	331 285	296 946	-10.4	0.6
Cleveland	10.5	4.9	22.5	11.0	14.9	11.5	13.0	13.5	13.5	36.0	52.0	478 403	396 697	-17.1	-2.7
Cleveland Heights	3.4	9.1	18.7	9.5	16.9	11.7	12.0	13.6	17.7	38.6	53.4	49 958	46 238	-7.4	-3.5
Columbus	5.5	11.9	22.2	11.8	20.5	13.3	11.7	10.6	9.9	32.5	51.2	711 470	788 866	10.9	9.0
Cuyahoga Falls	1.9	4.1	21.0	5.6	17.7	13.3	11.6	14.1	16.7	39.5	53.1	49 374	49 594	0.4	-0.8
Dayton	3.5	5.2	23.0	14.7	14.6	10.3	12.3	12.1	13.0	32.8	52.6	166 179	141 869	-14.6	-1.0
Delaware	1.8	2.7	26.2	11.3	12.3	15.0	12.8	10.5	11.9	35.2	51.4	25 243	34 756	37.7	11.2
Dublin	4.2	17.1	31.3	4.0	7.9	23.3	13.7	13.2	6.5	37.9	49.5	31 392	41 352	31.7	10.2
Elyria	7.1	2.9	24.7	8.4	15.2	11.0	12.8	13.6	14.3	36.1	50.9	55 953	54 539	-2.5	-1.5
Euclid	2.4	4.2	21.9	10.1	11.0	10.9	14.7	15.1	16.3	40.6	55.8	52 717	48 905	-7.2	-3.2
Fairborn	6.2	6.6	22.8	13.8	15.5	9.3	11.7	11.7	15.3	33.9	49.4	32 052	32 838	2.5	2.9
Fairfield	9.2	9.8	19.9	8.5	15.7	12.0	13.2	14.2	16.5	37.7	51.8	42 097	42 508	1.0	0.3
Findlay	8.9	4.3	20.9	11.8	14.1	11.1	12.3	11.6	18.1	39.1	53.4	38 967	41 184	5.7	0.6
Gahanna	3.3	4.7	24.1	3.3	11.7	13.7	12.8	18.5	16.0	43.0	52.1	32 636	33 233	1.8	5.2
Garfield Heights	1.8	0.8	24.2	8.9	15.9	12.8	11.7	13.0	13.4	35.7	52.6	30 734	28 849	-6.1	-3.3
Green	0.4	5.1	19.1	7.7	13.1	11.0	12.5	14.6	22.0	44.4	50.5	22 817	25 740	12.8	-0.3
Grove City	1.9	3.7	28.4	5.6	11.6	11.8	17.2	9.9	15.3	39.0	53.2	27 075	35 615	31.5	11.5

1. May be of any race.

Table D. Cities — Households, Group Quarters, Crime, and Education

City	Households, 2015				Persons in group quarters, 2010				Serious crimes known to police,[2] 2014				Educational attainment, 2015		
			Percent			Institutional			Total		Rate[3]			Attainment[4] (percent)	
	Number	Persons per house-hold	Female family house-holder[1]	One-person	Total	Total	Persons in nursing facilities	Non-institu-tional	Number	Rate[3]	Violent	Property	Population age 25 and older	High school graduate or less	Bachelor's degree or more
	27	28	29	30	31	32	33	34	35	36	37	38	39	40	41
NEW YORK—Cont'd															
Yonkers	70 902	2.80	16.0	31.6	3 286	1 099	864	2 187	2 986	1 488	487	1 001	137 787	43.1	31.5
NORTH CAROLINA	3 843 745	2.55	13.2	28.8	257 246	113 296	46 638	143 950	318 464	3 203	330	2 873	6 762 644	39.9	29.4
Apex	15 570	2.92	14.4	14.9	121	98	97	23	490	1 129	64	1 064	28 900	17.3	63.3
Asheboro	10 363	2.45	17.7	38.0	665	565	357	100	1 628	6 243	261	5 982	18 096	46.4	14.7
Asheville	39 098	2.18	8.9	45.1	4 249	2 292	1 047	1 957	4 778	5 418	568	4 850	64 114	26.8	47.7
Burlington	21 293	2.43	15.6	36.1	906	464	445	442	2 416	4 680	682	3 998	35 751	48.3	23.0
Cary	61 376	2.61	8.0	21.0	260	211	193	49	1 809	1 167	63	1 104	112 008	15.2	63.6
Chapel Hill	20 462	2.48	4.1	32.1	9 003	258	227	8 745	1 433	2 381	143	2 238	31 831	15.7	72.4
Charlotte	322 872	2.52	14.5	32.4	13 369	5 104	2 595	8 265	35 619	4 157	590	3 567	550 245	31.6	41.9
Concord	31 840	2.72	14.4	24.4	893	797	431	96	2 504	2 961	114	2 848	56 802	34.9	32.4
Durham	103 230	2.40	15.3	34.0	9 936	1 962	1 136	7 974	12 919	5 173	734	4 439	171 181	30.6	47.0
Fayetteville	76 856	2.50	18.3	33.4	8 841	1 253	689	7 588	11 563	5 632	506	5 126	123 801	32.6	26.8
Garner	11 079	2.51	15.5	24.6	284	243	232	41	1 264	4 682	189	4 493	18 414	30.3	36.4
Gastonia	27 432	2.67	17.7	28.4	1 745	1 149	691	596	4 172	5 670	658	5 013	50 054	44.5	23.0
Goldsboro	13 584	2.50	22.9	33.9	2 422	1 606	394	816	2 537	6 954	899	6 055	23 867	41.5	24.9
Greensboro	115 301	2.36	15.6	34.3	11 389	2 110	1 407	9 279	11 506	4 077	477	3 600	189 322	32.3	35.2
Greenville	35 455	2.40	18.2	36.9	5 858	760	734	5 098	4 153	4 604	519	4 085	46 946	32.0	36.8
Hickory	17 276	2.26	8.0	41.0	1 351	312	312	1 039	2 053	5 077	391	4 687	28 457	37.8	33.9
High Point	40 124	2.65	19.1	27.9	3 577	940	599	2 637	4 368	4 024	465	3 559	71 029	39.9	30.2
Huntersville	17 292	3.03	9.3	17.3	268	260	260	8	1 063	2 069	113	1 956	32 835	15.8	57.5
Indian Trail	12 789	2.90	13.0	18.4	0	0	0	0	NA	NA	NA	NA	22 223	28.7	33.0
Jacksonville	22 676	2.51	9.6	28.4	16 413	825	379	15 588	NA	NA	NA	NA	31 703	36.7	20.4
Kannapolis	16 278	2.82	17.6	21.4	330	303	278	27	1 042	2 327	179	2 148	29 008	45.0	21.4
Matthews	11 438	2.65	5.1	25.2	269	259	254	10	796	2 660	150	2 509	21 427	23.0	53.8
Monroe	12 241	2.79	16.5	19.3	379	273	248	106	1 945	5 679	455	5 223	22 705	48.3	16.7
Mooresville	12 819	2.79	11.7	28.1	372	252	252	120	1 112	3 161	225	2 936	22 917	25.3	39.1
New Bern	13 939	2.13	12.6	40.6	753	618	433	135	1 389	4 573	402	4 172	22 060	36.9	26.0
Raleigh	178 316	2.42	12.9	32.6	19 526	5 387	1 443	14 139	5 183	1 182	152	1 030	292 363	25.4	49.2
Rocky Mount	22 636	2.39	27.2	35.2	1 597	906	377	691	3 277	5 774	939	4 835	34 690	42.3	21.6
Salisbury	12 893	2.35	13.2	40.2	3 775	2 057	622	1 718	1 968	5 852	711	5 142	24 270	51.3	19.0
Sanford	10 071	2.82	18.1	36.1	858	684	289	174	1 093	3 667	265	3 402	18 115	44.8	19.5
Thomasville	12 753	2.09	11.4	44.0	390	315	275	75	1 160	4 294	374	3 920	19 460	55.1	18.6
Wake Forest	12 603	3.03	10.8	14.3	303	138	138	165	794	2 208	156	2 053	24 166	22.3	53.2
Wilmington	49 501	2.24	13.5	35.3	5 118	430	382	4 688	5 938	5 236	675	4 560	73 975	29.4	37.4
Wilson	20 394	2.36	21.3	29.2	1 534	1 003	756	531	2 166	4 355	533	3 823	34 295	45.8	25.2
Winston-Salem	93 621	2.47	14.3	34.3	9 431	2 480	1 268	6 951	14 592	6 129	712	5 417	153 249	37.3	35.5
NORTH DAKOTA	313 475	2.33	7.8	30.4	25 056	9 675	6 433	15 381	17 565	2 375	265	2 110	492 017	35.1	29.1
Bismarck	32 200	2.11	9.0	34.5	1 815	1 371	534	444	1 892	2 762	270	2 492	49 141	30.3	35.1
Fargo	52 437	2.18	10.3	36.7	4 924	1 011	678	3 913	3 478	3 006	359	2 648	72 088	28.7	36.1
Grand Forks	24 317	2.16	7.0	30.9	3 754	478	285	3 276	1 685	3 039	240	2 800	32 504	29.4	36.9
Minot	19 241	2.35	7.6	35.4	1 524	527	421	997	1 367	2 867	325	2 542	29 816	35.1	30.7
West Fargo	14 214	2.36	14.5	23.0	51	0	0	51	611	1 973	194	1 779	22 286	26.2	32.4
OHIO	4 606 655	2.45	12.8	30.3	306 266	166 042	83 019	140 224	357 558	3 084	285	2 799	7 896 470	44.0	26.8
Akron	86 078	2.24	18.2	40.8	6 133	1 981	878	4 152	10 489	5 300	690	4 610	135 622	49.8	20.7
Barberton	9 591	2.70	16.2	26.9	371	259	259	112	1 072	4 078	259	3 820	17 654	61.9	13.4
Beavercreek	18 558	2.42	7.3	22.9	278	257	257	21	1 037	2 262	55	2 208	31 513	24.1	44.4
Bowling Green	11 230	2.18	3.4	37.8	5 632	503	278	5 129	675	2 100	118	1 982	13 604	31.0	42.5
Brunswick	13 729	2.51	10.9	28.6	200	147	147	53	325	939	55	884	24 276	40.9	27.2
Canton	29 822	2.32	25.0	40.7	3 102	1 256	701	1 846	4 659	6 436	1 008	5 427	44 917	51.2	14.4
Cincinnati	137 445	2.08	18.9	44.7	14 443	4 531	2 199	9 912	19 399	6 517	913	5 604	195 344	36.9	34.3
Cleveland	167 667	2.24	23.3	43.9	13 742	6 258	3 062	7 484	26 421	6 798	1 339	5 459	257 937	53.7	16.2
Cleveland Heights	19 814	2.22	12.5	38.8	738	118	118	620	1 325	2 931	234	2 696	32 278	21.1	50.9
Columbus	344 839	2.40	15.2	36.3	21 099	6 086	3 236	15 013	40 184	4 837	558	4 278	560 012	37.2	34.8
Cuyahoga Falls	20 772	2.34	11.6	31.5	530	345	345	185	1 150	2 338	100	2 238	36 077	36.5	29.9
Dayton	56 466	2.26	21.8	39.6	9 365	2 099	773	7 266	9 238	6 450	864	5 587	87 575	47.0	18.1
Delaware	13 808	2.57	13.8	31.9	2 041	572	377	1 469	861	2 336	174	2 163	23 569	37.1	33.0
Dublin	15 838	2.85	7.0	14.5	127	127	127	0	482	1 091	18	1 073	29 268	9.3	76.9
Elyria	22 147	2.40	20.8	31.5	1 040	881	430	159	NA	NA	NA	NA	35 975	46.5	15.2
Euclid	22 783	2.07	16.6	47.5	675	489	391	186	125	261	25	236	32 413	43.8	20.1
Fairborn	14 101	2.24	15.4	39.0	275	229	229	46	1 043	3 134	144	2 990	20 529	41.5	27.8
Fairfield	17 351	2.43	9.5	27.1	506	404	384	102	1 355	3 177	230	2 947	30 602	47.6	26.3
Findlay	17 971	2.20	13.7	27.2	1 506	504	383	1 002	1 556	3 739	192	3 547	27 689	44.2	28.3
Gahanna	14 046	2.49	9.6	24.3	171	166	158	5	670	1 956	70	1 886	25 563	27.6	45.0
Garfield Heights	11 203	2.47	22.7	35.5	391	308	265	83	1 001	3 540	382	3 158	18 795	51.7	13.4
Green	10 492	2.45	9.4	28.0	141	133	130	8	NA	NA	NA	NA	18 979	37.1	37.3
Grove City	15 348	2.62	9.8	28.4	282	248	165	34	1 452	3 827	100	3 726	26 700	39.3	31.5

1. No spouse present. 2. Data for serious crimes have not been adjusted for underreporting. This may affect comparability between geographic areas and over time. 3. Per 100,000 population estimated by the FBI. 4. Persons 25 years old and over.

City	Median income (42)	Percent with income of $200,000 or more (43)	Percent with income of less than $25,000 (44)	Total Families (45)	Percent with income below poverty (46)	Total (47)	Percent change, 2000–2010 (48)	Vacant units for sale or rent[2] (49)	Total (50)	Percent (51)	Median value[3] (dollars) (52)	Percent (53)	Median rent (dollars) (54)
NEW YORK—Cont'd													
Yonkers	56 979	7.3	21.1	44 956	14.7	80 389	3.6	5 839	70 902	46.7	359 600	53.3	1 265
NORTH CAROLINA	47 830	4.0	19.5	2 506 215	11.8	4 327 528	22.8	582 373	3 843 745	63.9	160 100	36.1	827
Apex	96 774	9.5	5.9	12 492	5.8	13 922	72.9	697	15 570	73.0	282 100	27.0	1 214
Asheboro	40 401	0.7	21.6	5 938	12.2	11 158	16.7	1 278	10 363	52.7	115 300	47.3	584
Asheville	43 061	2.3	19.2	18 358	10.1	41 626	23.9	4 246	39 098	52.0	201 600	48.0	910
Burlington	34 322	0.2	24.9	12 473	18.4	23 414	19.9	2 782	21 293	53.3	121 000	46.7	732
Cary	95 374	14.4	4.8	45 367	2.7	55 303	50.1	3 512	61 376	67.8	322 200	32.2	1 085
Chapel Hill	61 415	15.9	17.6	10 675	3.3	22 254	16.6	1 690	20 462	45.5	405 300	54.5	1 075
Charlotte	53 919	7.0	15.5	188 467	11.8	319 918	38.8	30 058	322 872	52.3	188 800	47.7	978
Concord	52 834	4.5	15.1	23 176	7.6	32 130	43.1	2 993	31 840	62.6	167 900	37.4	854
Durham	52 106	5.0	19.0	56 904	13.9	103 221	27.6	9 780	103 230	47.8	193 100	52.2	929
Fayetteville	40 408	1.8	21.0	47 822	15.2	87 005	62.7	8 731	76 856	45.2	121 700	54.8	871
Garner	62 377	0.0	15.0	NA	NA	10 993	51.9	786	11 079	62.9	171 800	37.1	940
Gastonia	42 713	2.2	20.3	17 443	15.0	31 238	12.2	3 468	27 432	53.8	134 300	46.2	793
Goldsboro	33 410	1.1	31.3	8 236	21.0	16 824	2.3	1 859	13 584	37.7	133 100	62.3	741
Greensboro	44 934	3.8	19.5	66 155	12.6	124 074	25.2	12 343	115 301	50.7	148 200	49.3	801
Greenville	34 305	4.6	28.5	16 384	21.1	40 564	43.5	4 493	35 455	33.8	150 600	66.2	747
Hickory	41 134	6.2	27.8	9 303	8.2	18 719	12.0	2 105	17 276	55.1	143 300	44.9	624
High Point	40 263	3.0	24.3	26 913	19.4	46 677	29.9	5 765	40 124	51.0	146 000	49.0	795
Huntersville	94 888	11.4	6.1	13 081	2.4	18 477	87.2	1 054	17 292	77.2	269 700	22.8	1 126
Indian Trail	75 311	7.7	10.8	10 184	8.7	11 700	166.4	579	12 789	79.8	179 800	20.2	1 125
Jacksonville	41 375	0.8	16.2	14 649	10.2	21 135	15.2	1 150	22 676	34.1	140 000	65.9	943
Kannapolis	50 320	2.7	17.7	12 081	13.9	18 645	17.4	2 270	16 278	63.4	123 800	36.6	862
Matthews	77 445	11.6	11.2	8 284	3.0	11 021	33.2	495	11 438	77.0	238 300	23.0	1 069
Monroe	49 009	0.9	17.4	9 074	15.0	12 375	27.4	1 255	12 241	55.3	145 700	44.7	863
Mooresville	64 179	4.9	13.4	8 544	8.8	13 655	74.1	1 281	12 819	63.4	207 500	36.6	1 017
New Bern	42 545	1.7	21.0	7 573	5.8	14 471	31.0	1 701	13 939	47.2	156 600	52.8	807
Raleigh	56 910	6.7	13.4	101 127	11.3	176 124	45.9	13 125	178 316	51.4	226 500	48.6	970
Rocky Mount	33 741	1.4	26.1	13 383	22.1	26 953	11.1	3 856	22 636	44.7	111 200	55.3	696
Salisbury	39 480	3.4	23.3	6 702	16.3	14 626	28.5	2 059	12 893	50.4	121 000	49.6	706
Sanford	37 289	1.4	23.5	6 174	9.7	11 411	23.1	953	10 071	56.2	125 100	43.8	714
Thomasville	35 610	1.1	24.0	6 190	11.2	11 870	39.2	1 333	12 753	50.0	117 400	50.0	636
Wake Forest	87 344	7.5	8.2	10 186	4.1	11 370	123.8	849	12 603	71.5	282 000	28.5	899
Wilmington	42 232	3.9	24.7	25 937	16.1	53 400	38.3	6 452	49 501	42.5	221 200	57.5	893
Wilson	41 180	0.6	25.6	12 047	15.2	21 870	17.1	2 285	20 394	49.6	141 500	50.4	739
Winston-Salem	41 287	5.0	22.6	55 295	16.9	103 974	25.8	11 637	93 621	52.2	145 500	47.8	741
NORTH DAKOTA	60 557	5.1	14.6	188 210	6.9	317 498	9.6	36 306	313 475	61.7	180 900	38.3	775
Bismarck	57 596	5.8	15.0	17 873	7.3	28 648	18.6	1 385	32 200	60.1	225 600	39.9	824
Fargo	45 856	4.2	19.5	26 218	6.8	49 956	21.0	3 165	52 437	41.2	192 400	58.8	744
Grand Forks	47 963	3.8	20.4	12 868	11.7	23 449	12.6	1 189	24 317	40.9	202 200	59.1	821
Minot	61 921	4.0	10.7	10 788	4.2	18 744	13.7	881	19 241	59.8	216 300	40.2	922
West Fargo	69 308	6.2	9.0	NA	NA	10 760	83.8	412	14 214	62.7	215 500	37.3	820
OHIO	51 075	3.7	18.4	2 922 095	10.7	5 127 508	7.2	524 073	4 606 655	65.4	136 400	34.6	746
Akron	34 639	1.5	28.4	43 812	19.4	96 288	-1.0	12 576	86 078	50.0	80 600	50.0	674
Barberton	41 143	0.0	22.2	6 437	16.6	12 191	0.2	1 137	9 591	64.1	86 600	35.9	692
Beavercreek	71 976	6.1	9.5	13 135	5.9	19 449	31.1	1 254	18 558	66.9	174 100	33.1	1 065
Bowling Green	32 162	4.2	38.8	NA	NA	12 301	15.9	1 013	11 230	37.6	158 500	62.4	688
Brunswick	63 664	2.2	13.0	8 967	6.3	13 600	10.9	633	13 729	77.6	161 800	22.4	831
Canton	30 601	0.2	35.6	15 911	27.1	34 571	-2.6	4 866	29 822	46.3	62 700	53.7	583
Cincinnati	35 001	3.2	30.7	61 592	21.1	161 095	-2.9	27 675	137 445	38.0	119 000	62.0	658
Cleveland	28 831	0.9	37.9	82 300	30.6	207 536	-3.8	40 046	167 667	41.2	66 200	58.8	664
Cleveland Heights	55 310	4.0	19.3	10 676	7.7	22 465	2.9	2 508	19 814	55.4	130 400	44.6	868
Columbus	47 401	2.3	19.3	180 746	15.6	370 965	13.3	39 363	344 839	44.5	137 100	55.5	871
Cuyahoga Falls	54 901	1.7	18.4	12 474	11.9	23 859	4.9	1 609	20 772	63.9	118 000	36.1	811
Dayton	30 135	0.7	36.4	29 487	27.0	74 065	-4.2	15 661	56 466	46.6	65 700	53.4	632
Delaware	59 312	3.5	18.5	8 756	10.7	14 192	37.9	939	13 808	64.3	172 100	35.7	851
Dublin	129 772	26.5	4.7	12 628	2.4	15 779	31.1	795	15 838	74.1	368 100	25.9	1 258
Elyria	39 139	0.6	24.1	13 730	21.5	25 085	5.2	2 685	22 147	59.9	93 100	40.1	704
Euclid	32 557	1.1	30.6	11 157	18.7	26 037	-0.3	3 352	22 783	46.0	79 900	54.0	707
Fairborn	39 261	1.5	28.7	7 518	23.2	15 893	10.3	1 587	14 101	47.4	114 500	52.6	796
Fairfield	53 901	4.1	10.5	NA	NA	18 803	5.7	1 388	17 351	63.8	144 200	36.2	905
Findlay	50 607	2.1	15.9	11 099	8.1	19 318	12.5	1 964	17 971	58.3	131 800	41.7	775
Gahanna	73 560	9.1	9.7	9 793	5.9	13 577	9.9	540	14 046	76.6	202 500	23.4	967
Garfield Heights	39 849	0.7	26.0	6 642	18.4	13 125	1.6	1 434	11 203	63.3	69 100	36.7	843
Green	68 199	6.4	15.1	7 392	9.6	10 858	18.3	788	10 492	69.9	196 100	30.1	697
Grove City	62 107	3.9	13.2	10 430	6.9	14 720	38.2	774	15 348	64.9	168 800	35.1	943

1. Based on population estimated by the American Community Survey.   2. Includes units rented or sold but not occupied.   3. Specified owner-occupied units; $1,000,000 represents $1,000,000 or more   4. 50.0 represents 50 percent or more.   5. 10.0 represents 10 percent or less.

Table D. Cities — Commuting, Computer Access, Migration, Labor Force, and Employment

City	Commuting Percent		Computer Access[2] Percent		Migration, 2015		Civilian labor force, 2016		Unemployment		Civilian employment[4], 2015 Population age 16 and older		Population age 16 to 64	
	Drove alone	With Commutes of 30 minutes or more[1]	With a Computer in the house	With Internet Access	Percent who lived in the same house one year ago	Percent who lived in an other state or county one year ago	Total	Percent change, 2015–2016	Total	Rate[3]	Number	Percent in Labor Force	Number	Percent who worked full-year full-time
	55	56	57	58	59	60	61	62	63	64	65	66	67	68
NEW YORK—Cont'd														
Yonkers	57.8	54.1	80.9	72.4	91.5	2.7	94 946	-0.2	4 859	5.1	161 871	62.1	131 150	46.9
NORTH CAROLINA	85.7	32.5	85.1	74.1	84.4	7.2	4 875 701	2.3	246 372	5.1	8 011 388	61.9	6 495 843	48.8
Apex	94.1	32.6	95.7	92.4	82.1	8.0	24 847	4.0	914	3.7	33 803	75.5	30 705	56.3
Asheboro	NA	34.3	82.4	64.9	88.0	4.6	11 258	1.1	606	5.4	19 744	66.5	15 695	61.5
Asheville	82.7	8.2	87.4	82.3	85.8	9.6	48 596	3.7	1 898	3.9	74 078	65.7	59 224	47.3
Burlington	78.2	19.9	84.9	68.1	79.8	9.6	25 747	2.5	1 284	5.0	41 836	64.6	32 564	48.8
Cary	87.1	25.5	97.6	94.4	82.7	9.0	89 563	4.1	3 416	3.8	125 190	72.4	106 835	59.9
Chapel Hill	60.1	17.8	98.5	93.2	68.4	17.7	29 970	3.0	1 498	5.0	51 799	64.4	45 148	33.9
Charlotte	82.6	38.7	91.1	80.8	78.7	8.5	467 403	4.1	22 420	4.8	650 177	71.3	567 301	53.9
Concord	87.7	40.4	89.8	85.1	81.4	9.2	45 379	4.6	2 064	4.5	65 935	68.0	54 383	56.3
Durham	77.5	25.8	89.7	81.9	76.2	10.1	139 279	3.1	6 297	4.5	206 441	70.4	179 730	52.5
Fayetteville	81.9	19.2	88.5	76.5	76.4	11.2	76 020	2.6	5 148	6.8	157 598	65.8	134 037	49.9
Garner	88.5	43.0	92.8	77.1	75.1	8.3	15 919	4.1	690	4.3	23 241	70.6	20 021	53.1
Gastonia	82.0	32.6	87.1	70.5	84.6	6.1	36 016	3.8	2 075	5.8	57 990	63.1	47 563	51.9
Goldsboro	80.7	21.6	82.7	68.0	76.5	10.4	12 528	0.2	987	7.9	28 583	57.6	24 070	45.4
Greensboro	89.2	20.6	80.6	59.6	86.3	6.2	143 883	1.4	7 755	5.4	231 341	62.5	191 931	48.6
Greenville	86.8	16.3	87.7	69.8	68.7	18.1	47 192	1.5	2 767	5.9	74 995	66.3	66 373	39.1
Hickory	92.1	19.5	81.8	70.7	87.3	8.5	20 105	2.5	982	4.9	34 545	54.3	26 370	41.5
High Point	83.4	23.2	83.6	69.7	84.4	5.7	53 842	1.4	2 979	5.5	85 939	61.6	70 962	45.1
Huntersville	88.6	45.5	96.9	89.4	82.0	5.3	31 172	4.2	1 168	3.7	36 766	77.0	33 014	59.9
Indian Trail	92.1	45.3	94.8	91.7	89.0	6.0	19 818	4.4	833	4.2	26 147	72.3	23 459	57.4
Jacksonville	68.0	13.7	97.1	83.5	58.1	24.7	18 955	0.4	1 287	6.8	54 151	77.1	49 995	61.7
Kannapolis	83.0	38.3	86.0	80.3	87.5	9.6	22 053	3.6	1 146	5.2	34 369	66.4	29 062	52.9
Matthews	88.0	43.1	92.4	89.0	88.9	6.0	17 037	3.9	701	4.1	25 271	66.0	20 148	50.0
Monroe	80.4	40.4	90.7	84.1	90.7	4.0	17 019	3.6	841	4.9	27 124	68.6	22 133	59.1
Mooresville	94.4	38.1	93.0	78.6	78.8	11.7	19 461	3.9	947	4.9	27 545	67.6	23 009	52.5
New Bern	86.9	19.1	82.0	71.4	81.6	11.4	12 575	1.8	646	5.1	24 252	59.0	17 957	52.3
Raleigh	84.2	30.1	94.4	83.8	79.4	7.9	248 978	4.0	11 284	4.5	361 830	69.4	319 738	54.5
Rocky Mount	86.6	22.3	78.9	66.3	82.7	9.7	24 173	1.0	2 078	8.6	42 083	65.4	34 359	49.6
Salisbury	81.6	25.0	85.1	72.4	72.7	11.1	14 038	4.3	968	6.9	28 971	58.4	22 581	45.6
Sanford	NA	28.8	81.3	69.3	75.6	10.3	12 425	1.2	771	6.2	21 383	62.0	17 746	47.5
Thomasville	93.0	30.9	80.4	64.5	78.7	6.6	12 366	1.9	702	5.7	22 167	58.2	17 662	47.0
Wake Forest	87.0	52.5	89.0	85.7	84.3	6.8	19 935	4.5	815	4.1	27 745	67.2	23 019	54.0
Wilmington	83.8	11.7	86.0	79.8	76.3	10.9	61 004	3.3	2 992	4.9	95 965	62.3	78 491	40.1
Wilson	89.1	16.1	82.0	75.0	86.2	5.7	21 688	0.8	2 020	9.3	39 615	61.0	31 795	50.4
Winston-Salem	86.5	20.8	83.3	72.9	81.4	6.5	116 138	1.8	6 024	5.2	188 256	62.5	155 192	46.9
NORTH DAKOTA	85.8	13.4	86.2	76.4	81.6	9.5	416 227	0.5	13 160	3.2	603 014	70.0	495 657	56.0
Bismarck	90.8	7.6	85.5	73.3	79.9	8.4	38 769	3.9	978	2.5	57 891	70.5	46 637	63.1
Fargo	85.8	6.3	87.3	77.3	67.0	15.7	69 230	5.6	1 554	2.2	97 658	72.6	84 390	53.2
Grand Forks	84.8	5.6	87.1	76.0	72.7	15.4	32 993	5.8	738	2.2	46 947	72.8	40 514	45.8
Minot	88.4	9.8	86.6	81.8	74.8	9.8	24 769	-1.1	1 045	4.2	38 439	74.2	32 193	55.2
West Fargo	88.3	9.9	93.6	85.9	85.8	7.2	20 450	5.6	436	2.1	25 720	73.5	21 676	62.1
OHIO	86.4	30.7	85.5	76.0	84.7	5.7	5 713 088	0.4	282 298	4.9	9 295 255	63.2	7 455 701	49.3
Akron	83.7	23.6	78.6	66.6	85.7	4.3	90 673	0.0	5 292	5.8	161 285	62.0	131 522	43.9
Barberton	85.6	34.2	82.7	62.6	93.8	3.0	12 644	0.5	747	5.9	20 503	55.6	16 683	41.7
Beavercreek	93.2	21.6	94.3	86.1	87.0	10.6	22 997	0.4	872	3.8	36 834	64.5	28 989	53.6
Bowling Green	74.6	17.2	89.3	79.8	55.5	21.5	16 718	1.1	736	4.4	28 348	66.9	25 044	24.9
Brunswick	93.0	45.2	93.1	84.7	91.8	2.3	19 834	0.2	846	4.3	27 711	68.1	21 761	58.1
Canton	77.5	24.1	77.6	68.7	81.6	3.8	31 588	-0.3	2 037	6.4	54 974	67.0	45 643	42.1
Cincinnati	77.5	28.2	83.1	72.4	75.1	8.0	142 835	0.7	6 863	4.8	241 291	64.0	204 154	43.5
Cleveland	72.6	32.5	76.4	61.9	78.9	5.3	159 263	0.4	11 054	6.9	311 530	58.0	259 058	36.1
Cleveland Heights	80.1	32.3	89.8	80.2	87.6	3.3	22 809	0.2	1 061	4.7	37 305	64.7	29 364	49.6
Columbus	82.1	25.1	88.1	78.2	77.8	7.3	451 203	1.4	18 576	4.1	679 369	70.2	595 297	50.8
Cuyahoga Falls	88.5	27.3	86.4	80.8	90.3	3.4	26 376	0.0	1 219	4.6	39 792	66.3	31 570	58.3
Dayton	74.9	20.5	80.4	69.1	68.7	7.4	58 119	0.2	3 375	5.8	111 929	53.8	93 615	33.7
Delaware	87.6	47.6	91.5	82.2	81.0	7.4	20 471	1.6	804	3.9	28 962	65.2	24 469	57.5
Dublin	93.5	36.5	96.9	95.7	87.6	6.5	24 442	1.6	820	3.4	32 238	72.3	29 288	61.2
Elyria	85.2	31.5	85.5	70.2	78.7	4.0	26 986	0.5	1 629	6.0	41 946	59.5	34 255	41.6
Euclid	85.9	32.7	74.3	64.8	91.7	1.4	22 710	0.5	1 482	6.5	38 269	62.6	30 495	49.4
Fairborn	81.1	16.6	85.8	68.7	75.1	12.1	16 791	0.4	733	4.4	25 219	66.1	20 273	43.9
Fairfield	90.7	35.0	89.1	81.5	84.6	4.9	24 071	0.6	954	4.0	35 186	66.7	28 130	58.7
Findlay	86.9	13.6	89.6	81.5	79.6	10.0	21 636	1.3	835	3.9	33 936	68.8	26 503	51.6
Gahanna	92.4	23.6	95.5	92.8	80.5	6.4	19 817	1.5	719	3.6	27 828	67.6	22 197	51.6
Garfield Heights	84.0	31.3	80.9	75.6	NA	NA	13 701	0.6	866	6.3	22 209	67.0	18 434	55.4
Green	86.7	29.2	85.0	83.0	84.5	12.5	13 867	-0.1	620	4.5	21 594	65.5	15 884	51.7
Grove City	87.3	22.7	83.4	77.8	93.8	2.2	21 277	1.5	811	3.8	29 886	65.0	23 683	61.1

1. Employed persons. 2. Households. 3. Percent of civilian labor force. 4. Persons 16 years old and over.

Table D. Cities — Construction, Wholesale Trade, and Retail Trade

City	Value of residential construction authorized by building permits, 2016			Wholesale trade,[1] 2012				Retail trade,[2] 2012			
	New construction ($1,000)	Number of housing units	Percent single family	Number of establishments	Number of employees	Sales (mil dol)	Annual payroll (mil dol)	Number of establishments	Number of employees	Sales (mil dol)	Annual payroll (mil dol)
	69	70	71	72	73	74	75	76	77	78	79
NEW YORK—Cont'd											
Yonkers	63 165	295	5.8	161	1 348	852.6	72.2	657	9 473	2 708.5	250.0
NORTH CAROLINA	15 106	43	95.3	9 713	136 174	105 275.6	7 853.7	34 288	446 373	120 691.0	10 421.2
Apex	227 362	1 171	81.9	44	753	621.3	39.8	131	2 427	657.6	56.1
Asheboro	3 942	51	88.2	33	313	180.7	11.8	196	2 375	556.5	48.5
Asheville	74 444	349	82.8	155	1 477	883.6	71.4	776	11 310	2 822.0	265.2
Burlington	55 884	437	47.6	81	1 025	423.2	40.9	367	5 655	1 236.2	120.3
Cary	298 769	1 635	63.7	144	1 776	2 938.5	134.8	495	9 194	2 877.2	229.4
Chapel Hill	22 655	126	30.2	27	141	176.5	7.7	199	2 833	684.1	72.3
Charlotte	NA	NA	NA	1 540	25 446	19 884.6	1 617.4	2 600	39 240	10 901.0	960.8
Concord	NA	NA	NA	113	1 941	1 285.3	92.3	489	9 070	2 228.3	189.2
Durham	417 375	2 979	55.3	173	5 168	4 131.5	426.0	871	13 896	3 313.6	317.4
Fayetteville	49 525	296	100.0	104	2 032	663.0	79.3	825	12 882	3 625.9	311.0
Garner	13 583	82	100.0	57	1 381	1 135.3	57.4	112	1 911	490.5	42.2
Gastonia	141 856	552	89.1	86	848	328.4	34.2	378	5 774	1 341.6	125.3
Goldsboro	6 442	33	87.9	56	1 306	1 019.9	54.9	311	4 058	1 143.7	90.6
Greensboro	239 776	1 509	36.4	541	7 993	9 675.9	453.6	1 232	19 426	4 950.9	488.9
Greenville	60 001	601	34.3	70	700	350.5	35.0	421	6 355	1 589.1	141.5
Hickory	NA	NA	NA	129	4 126	3 196.1	196.6	454	6 897	1 934.2	165.6
High Point	20 355	198	69.7	298	4 852	3 737.6	268.8	410	4 792	1 347.0	114.9
Huntersville	NA	NA	NA	66	621	341.0	41.8	161	2 686	782.3	65.0
Indian Trail	NA	NA	NA	84	838	379.9	44.2	91	1 494	468.6	42.2
Jacksonville	2 733	22	72.7	26	109	73.0	4.5	340	5 936	1 691.7	141.4
Kannapolis	NA	NA	NA	25	178	118.1	8.3	158	1 596	398.1	36.6
Matthews	NA	NA	NA	53	549	204.2	31.8	170	3 135	1 099.4	85.6
Monroe	20 048	137	95.6	76	1 328	647.5	58.3	230	3 076	861.7	68.7
Mooresville	NA	NA	NA	81	690	499.8	38.7	226	3 734	1 130.1	84.1
New Bern	16 513	81	100.0	33	D	D	D	248	3 073	834.7	72.9
Raleigh	615 507	3 448	41.0	570	8 627	5 399.8	577.4	1 698	27 148	7 268.5	688.9
Rocky Mount	960	8	100.0	74	1 406	1 071.4	63.1	331	4 143	1 014.0	89.4
Salisbury	NA	NA	NA	47	945	612.8	38.8	203	2 948	832.5	70.1
Sanford	6 817	34	100.0	22	D	D	D	192	2 658	706.4	58.3
Thomasville	6 206	45	100.0	30	453	211.9	22.1	128	1 458	354.7	31.5
Wake Forest	108 470	812	62.8	26	139	96.6	7.8	87	1 725	489.2	43.6
Wilmington	NA	NA	NA	139	1 191	570.6	58.3	764	10 389	3 009.5	261.3
Wilson	12 006	54	100.0	76	742	444.0	30.7	263	3 268	899.3	76.9
Winston-Salem	114 035	896	50.6	239	3 943	2 266.4	189.6	1 008	15 129	4 067.8	365.3
NORTH DAKOTA	0	0	0.0	1 430	18 880	28 150.8	1 078.2	3 185	47 186	15 519.8	1 204.4
Bismarck	79 755	467	78.2	115	1 967	1 346.8	106.9	357	6 779	1 948.7	175.8
Fargo	199 940	1 333	35.6	251	5 114	4 124.9	288.3	518	11 065	3 299.9	266.9
Grand Forks	48 248	304	37.2	59	965	697.8	50.3	279	5 654	1 501.8	126.4
Minot	12 265	49	100.0	68	1 285	2 418.1	80.1	250	5 160	1 686.7	149.6
West Fargo	101 625	474	86.3	41	477	194.6	23.5	91	1 133	373.8	27.1
OHIO	0	0	0.0	11 744	182 791	155 426.0	9 627.2	36 531	549 152	153 554.0	13 099.3
Akron	NA	NA	NA	217	2 998	1 695.8	153.6	612	7 731	1 906.6	185.0
Barberton	810	6	100.0	22	523	113.2	17.8	71	780	171.4	15.5
Beavercreek	NA	NA	NA	23	167	327.3	9.5	216	4 600	941.1	87.2
Bowling Green	NA	NA	NA	15	116	109.0	6.5	99	1 599	368.3	34.6
Brunswick	18 026	111	100.0	48	532	238.0	27.5	93	1 759	727.5	48.8
Canton	2 133	15	100.0	89	1 263	770.9	58.2	249	3 432	823.7	73.9
Cincinnati	101 927	733	21.8	358	5 890	6 371.5	337.1	941	13 549	3 977.7	350.4
Cleveland	8 654	173	79.2	577	9 142	5 475.0	465.9	1 206	10 637	2 764.9	244.1
Cleveland Heights	2 485	8	100.0	8	43	11.8	1.6	97	1 340	294.9	32.8
Columbus	510 834	3 720	17.4	807	17 060	14 346.8	1 005.3	2 566	46 211	13 114.2	1 178.1
Cuyahoga Falls	NA	NA	NA	39	573	243.9	26.5	171	3 313	1 015.8	79.1
Dayton	4 390	38	100.0	158	3 063	12 234.4	182.6	375	3 791	870.1	88.8
Delaware	60 953	299	74.6	14	120	40.6	6.4	118	1 738	539.0	44.8
Dublin	110 249	630	23.5	88	1 426	1 730.1	115.1	118	2 215	997.6	79.5
Elyria	6 647	67	61.2	56	309	150.4	12.6	219	3 567	887.5	79.0
Euclid	0	0	0.0	34	533	206.2	25.9	84	993	235.3	22.0
Fairborn	14 894	66	100.0	11	330	338.2	17.0	78	1 061	300.0	22.6
Fairfield	3 500	18	100.0	72	1 793	1 060.2	92.0	175	3 937	1 355.5	133.3
Findlay	18 390	142	21.1	40	638	483.4	29.8	205	3 287	823.7	72.0
Gahanna	5 252	21	100.0	38	619	358.8	28.4	87	1 378	475.2	39.6
Garfield Heights	0	0	0.0	27	404	152.7	15.1	78	960	211.5	18.5
Green	NA	NA	NA	31	457	465.3	45.9	55	1 490	706.3	46.3
Grove City	63 450	408	62.7	32	869	592.4	38.9	121	3 256	1 130.1	76.0

1. Merchant wholesalers except manufacturers' sales branches and offices.   2. Establishments with payroll.

City	Real estate and rental and leasing, 2012				Professional, scientific, and technical services,[1] 2012				Manufacturing, 2012			
	Number of establishments	Number of employees	Receipts (mil dol)	Annual payroll (mil dol)	Number of establishments	Number of employees	Receipts (mil dol)	Annual payroll (mil dol)	Number of establishments	Number of employees	Receipts (mil dol)	Annual payroll (mil dol)
	80	81	82	83	84	85	86	87	88	89	90	91
NEW YORK—Cont'd												
Yonkers	363	1 099	341.3	42.1	254	D	D	D	88	2 755	984.9	141.4
NORTH CAROLINA	10 140	47 155	9 301.7	1 942.6	22 730	190 441	30 520.8	12 461.5	8 953	403 593	202 344.6	18 191.2
Apex	27	74	12.0	2.8	158	611	83.3	27.8	34	1 042	1 399.5	63.7
Asheboro	38	152	34.8	4.5	76	358	28.0	10.0	63	6 915	3 002.3	245.9
Asheville	244	785	163.3	26.3	575	D	D	D	130	4 595	983.8	224.4
Burlington	66	419	106.4	18.7	107	828	75.6	33.9	92	3 671	855.4	141.8
Cary	218	681	151.2	29.9	903	D	D	D	68	1 693	696.0	79.4
Chapel Hill	88	381	67.0	13.7	293	D	D	D	17	D	7.4	D
Charlotte	1 372	8 759	2 045.6	494.7	3 202	D	D	D	643	21 152	9 376.1	1 164.0
Concord	103	464	88.7	13.4	207	D	D	D	87	4 261	1 352.5	190.7
Durham	275	1 601	337.0	66.8	973	D	D	D	144	7 368	4 773.1	499.7
Fayetteville	264	1 622	314.8	54.9	443	D	D	D	63	2 169	616.0	109.6
Garner	33	128	39.8	4.6	76	558	63.6	21.5	22	684	611.1	39.6
Gastonia	90	546	125.8	21.3	170	D	D	D	104	5 248	1 597.3	223.9
Goldsboro	44	216	23.0	6.0	104	614	61.0	22.9	49	3 089	808.7	137.0
Greensboro	455	3 181	525.0	135.4	936	D	D	D	308	16 855	22 411.9	1 025.3
Greenville	125	546	86.3	17.7	228	D	D	D	35	424	84.9	15.1
Hickory	100	324	88.9	9.9	199	1 198	602.5	54.9	161	5 444	1 261.8	195.0
High Point	115	754	127.8	25.4	273	D	D	D	241	12 901	3 676.7	541.1
Huntersville	62	160	42.1	8.0	183	856	120.2	52.3	25	706	209.7	35.8
Indian Trail	21	55	11.9	2.1	59	174	17.3	6.4	53	830	197.3	35.3
Jacksonville	100	390	73.2	12.0	152	D	D	D	12	D	D	D
Kannapolis	33	142	18.6	4.1	56	D	D	D	28	468	101.5	22.4
Matthews	50	236	32.3	7.5	144	690	89.7	35.9	34	713	296.9	38.6
Monroe	43	135	28.6	5.4	90	422	47.5	18.4	89	6 657	2 763.7	321.8
Mooresville	64	191	45.4	7.3	147	1 618	202.9	72.6	73	2 277	825.9	109.7
New Bern	51	223	29.9	7.0	111	D	D	D	34	2 008	683.6	100.2
Raleigh	735	5 229	1 173.6	305.0	2 185	22 893	4 304.5	1 706.4	267	5 229	1 842.0	270.5
Rocky Mount	77	357	54.8	12.0	125	803	83.1	33.8	43	4 002	940.1	217.5
Salisbury	44	205	18.3	4.3	97	529	64.3	20.7	66	1 904	585.2	84.1
Sanford	38	144	26.2	5.2	66	D	D	D	44	4 754	1 224.1	195.9
Thomasville	24	D	D	D	44	141	15.6	3.5	86	2 096	642.1	79.0
Wake Forest	33	76	17.9	3.2	116	D	D	D	14	111	18.0	6.2
Wilmington	249	1 574	260.9	58.6	652	D	D	D	91	3 247	1 623.2	250.0
Wilson	65	229	41.2	5.8	97	D	D	D	59	6 692	12 784.2	334.9
Winston-Salem	293	1 575	276.0	58.3	672	D	D	D	200	8 322	4 017.0	410.7
NORTH DAKOTA	912	5 157	1 445.1	247.5	1 706	13 633	1 836.9	732.4	745	23 541	14 427.4	1 042.8
Bismarck	122	389	101.5	13.2	274	D	D	D	57	824	D	35.8
Fargo	238	1 613	286.7	62.0	411	D	D	D	126	6 087	2 601.4	278.6
Grand Forks	73	481	83.5	14.3	117	D	D	D	42	2 015	564.1	73.6
Minot	68	D	D	D	119	D	D	D	26	346	110.3	13.9
West Fargo	21	D	D	D	38	D	D	D	42	2 294	791.0	109.1
OHIO	9 932	60 966	16 132.7	2 441.8	23 851	228 728	35 259.4	13 870.3	14 482	627 124	313 630.0	33 135.4
Akron	167	1 062	182.7	40.1	449	D	D	D	269	8 672	3 477.8	461.5
Barberton	6	19	1.9	0.4	27	D	D	D	50	1 938	530.0	97.4
Beavercreek	46	176	56.2	4.8	188	D	D	D	28	D	76.3	D
Bowling Green	38	159	21.8	4.3	49	D	D	D	35	1 906	729.3	87.6
Brunswick	22	92	17.7	2.3	56	390	35.0	12.3	49	969	204.1	45.2
Canton	71	248	39.3	8.2	155	D	D	D	136	8 020	6 885.8	429.7
Cincinnati	405	2 489	609.1	120.1	1 118	19 286	3 946.0	1 410.5	363	12 881	7 058.1	760.4
Cleveland	349	3 895	816.6	177.7	1 159	17 004	3 382.2	1 318.3	805	22 075	7 794.7	1 192.0
Cleveland Heights	50	166	27.9	4.4	104	D	D	D	8	46	6.3	1.5
Columbus	904	6 933	1 893.8	317.8	2 055	D	D	D	518	19 881	9 829.7	1 036.6
Cuyahoga Falls	42	197	26.6	5.6	108	867	73.7	33.2	76	2 565	857.7	128.3
Dayton	136	713	118.0	24.4	306	D	D	D	266	9 794	2 940.7	467.6
Delaware	36	117	25.0	5.8	54	355	48.7	14.7	38	2 755	2 055.5	169.2
Dublin	75	673	434.5	29.4	369	3 381	496.2	250.6	33	1 051	404.2	58.3
Elyria	48	223	34.8	7.1	79	D	D	D	100	4 869	1 604.5	260.5
Euclid	49	355	51.3	9.7	42	361	39.4	16.1	75	5 059	1 704.4	368.8
Fairborn	35	161	23.0	4.0	76	D	D	D	12	443	85.9	22.3
Fairfield	50	299	94.5	11.8	82	D	D	D	82	3 088	880.8	140.4
Findlay	50	382	46.4	12.4	108	649	87.7	34.2	56	5 654	2 137.3	287.6
Gahanna	40	159	35.3	6.3	143	973	120.1	46.4	27	754	235.0	32.9
Garfield Heights	20	69	10.8	2.8	48	360	46.8	20.8	18	838	186.7	40.7
Green	22	176	38.5	6.0	77	958	102.9	39.9	37	1 479	458.4	66.2
Grove City	34	164	36.7	6.5	46	389	52.7	14.4	29	1 545	393.2	70.7

1. Establishments subject to federal tax.

Table D. Cities — Accommodation and Food Services, Arts, Entertainment, and Recreation, and Health Care and Social Assistance

City	Accommodation and food services, 2012				Arts, entertainment, and recreation,[1] 2012				Health care and social assistance,[1] 2012			
	Number of establishments	Number of employees	Sales (mil dol)	Annual payroll (mil dol)	Number of establishments	Number of employees	Receipts (mil dol)	Annual payroll (mil dol)	Number of establishments	Number of employees	Receipts (mil dol)	Annual payroll (mil dol)
	92	93	94	95	96	97	98	99	100	101	102	103
NEW YORK—Cont'd												
Yonkers	351	3 484	259.8	65.3	46	1 168	286.4	45.1	403	4 301	453.0	184.7
NORTH CAROLINA	19 496	358 602	18 622.3	5 040.6	2 696	37 335	3 805.3	1 167.0	19 152	292 709	27 305.8	11 432.3
Apex	90	1 635	79.2	21.5	10	D	D	D	104	D	D	D
Asheboro	102	1 875	87.1	22.8	8	D	D	D	121	D	D	D
Asheville	541	11 795	698.6	201.3	64	1 459	103.0	35.1	530	7 203	898.5	383.9
Burlington	188	4 010	175.6	50.4	16	956	57.7	17.6	208	3 755	374.2	204.6
Cary	372	7 249	386.6	114.4	56	956	57.7	17.6	471	4 842	566.0	221.9
Chapel Hill	220	4 078	221.9	63.0	29	97	12.9	4.1	209	D	D	D
Charlotte	1 888	40 752	2 413.6	659.0	231	5 691	619.8	322.6	1 739	25 574	3 149.2	1 263.4
Concord	233	6 309	337.1	89.4	46	2 034	599.3	132.0	197	3 012	361.3	155.4
Durham	645	12 968	767.1	209.7	64	731	58.8	11.4	604	8 801	935.0	342.0
Fayetteville	480	10 965	516.5	143.3	42	D	D	D	597	9 245	705.4	309.7
Garner	66	1 528	68.1	18.8	4	D	D	D	83	934	84.4	31.8
Gastonia	191	3 998	199.4	51.2	20	224	11.9	2.6	270	D	D	D
Goldsboro	144	2 625	129.6	33.4	13	128	5.8	1.4	156	2 442	232.0	104.5
Greensboro	789	16 835	856.6	237.3	72	1 183	77.5	21.7	723	12 951	1 352.5	583.9
Greenville	288	6 910	313.5	85.4	23	D	D	D	332	D	D	D
Hickory	219	4 748	210.4	59.9	12	130	7.0	2.3	237	D	D	D
High Point	229	D	D	D	20	234	18.3	2.9	235	4 742	580.3	213.0
Huntersville	99	2 246	118.5	33.8	28	703	130.4	49.4	145	D	D	D
Indian Trail	55	887	41.7	10.8	11	114	7.9	1.7	43	337	33.1	11.5
Jacksonville	219	4 593	257.1	60.9	15	203	9.4	2.8	179	D	D	D
Kannapolis	74	D	D	D	10	D	D	D	48	934	81.5	36.3
Matthews	104	2 147	103.8	28.4	22	250	19.1	4.6	129	D	D	D
Monroe	105	1 927	91.2	24.5	8	D	D	D	116	D	D	D
Mooresville	159	2 948	149.8	40.0	44	D	D	D	147	2 454	339.9	123.9
New Bern	123	2 528	108.2	30.7	15	213	8.3	2.6	147	D	D	D
Raleigh	1 145	24 150	1 237.1	348.9	135	4 102	350.3	97.6	1 291	18 328	1 959.5	866.1
Rocky Mount	146	3 442	150.4	41.8	20	D	D	D	192	3 250	310.3	125.0
Salisbury	138	2 714	123.3	34.0	13	85	5.4	1.7	157	D	D	D
Sanford	92	1 665	77.3	20.9	6	D	D	D	123	2 042	213.9	78.1
Thomasville	72	D	D	D	7	D	D	D	35	745	46.6	21.9
Wake Forest	57	1 050	47.5	14.0	17	195	9.0	2.3	93	1 027	78.7	31.8
Wilmington	440	9 326	440.1	124.0	48	544	29.8	8.0	547	8 125	895.9	369.0
Wilson	124	2 521	133.0	32.7	11	D	D	D	151	D	D	D
Winston-Salem	539	11 157	564.9	159.4	56	548	32.9	8.9	510	9 646	868.9	430.6
NORTH DAKOTA	1 935	35 698	2 045.1	521.3	259	2 153	145.3	34.2	1 235	15 038	1 809.1	775.9
Bismarck	162	4 873	236.6	69.4	23	D	D	D	196	D	D	D
Fargo	316	8 386	389.1	114.6	52	662	51.3	10.4	284	5 329	931.1	386.1
Grand Forks	174	4 076	173.4	51.4	24	D	D	D	97	D	D	D
Minot	150	3 741	203.9	56.9	19	D	D	D	102	D	D	D
West Fargo	38	D	D	D	6	D	D	D	39	D	D	D
OHIO	23 432	437 293	20 652.8	5 742.7	2 869	36 390	3 903.5	1 464.8	22 945	393 909	34 637.9	15 470.9
Akron	407	5 634	257.4	69.3	31	310	42.4	9.4	351	7 424	853.5	418.3
Barberton	46	D	D	D	3	D	D	D	75	2 196	237.1	87.3
Beavercreek	105	2 738	140.8	37.8	4	D	D	D	121	D	D	D
Bowling Green	117	2 586	89.2	23.7	10	D	D	D	75	D	D	D
Brunswick	63	1 072	50.8	13.5	9	D	D	D	51	762	51.6	27.8
Canton	170	2 652	119.8	31.6	14	123	7.4	1.6	154	3 277	373.8	185.5
Cincinnati	738	15 321	858.6	247.4	82	1 803	462.6	323.2	652	15 018	2 070.9	917.9
Cleveland	980	16 885	950.9	254.3	63	2 425	509.8	290.4	402	7 946	537.2	237.2
Cleveland Heights	80	1 005	55.6	16.3	9	51	2.1	0.6	85	1 247	77.8	38.2
Columbus	1 959	42 063	2 259.0	637.6	152	3 969	354.9	122.1	1 620	31 398	3 077.4	1 331.6
Cuyahoga Falls	119	2 339	111.2	32.1	9	D	D	D	130	2 582	252.4	100.3
Dayton	276	4 570	206.8	57.9	17	210	23.6	5.6	285	5 572	659.7	342.5
Delaware	87	1 313	62.5	17.1	8	D	D	D	92	1 626	86.5	40.9
Dublin	123	3 294	167.6	52.9	27	D	D	D	195	D	D	D
Elyria	118	2 230	96.8	26.9	8	74	2.5	1.0	115	D	D	D
Euclid	71	D	D	D	7	D	D	D	98	2 556	121.2	62.9
Fairborn	74	1 535	71.9	20.2	7	D	D	D	39	D	D	D
Fairfield	104	1 990	100.4	25.7	9	D	D	D	136	D	D	D
Findlay	147	3 530	146.5	42.1	8	51	1.6	0.4	125	D	D	D
Gahanna	104	1 861	89.4	24.3	12	D	D	D	140	2 473	261.4	110.1
Garfield Heights	46	654	29.6	7.2	4	10	0.8	0.2	62	614	63.7	33.4
Green	54	949	45.3	12.2	10	106	6.9	2.1	67	D	D	D
Grove City	110	2 387	130.7	34.8	14	D	D	D	94	1 147	128.8	47.1

1. Establishments subject to federal tax.

Table D. Cities — **Other Services and Government Employment and Payroll**

City	Other services[1], 2012 Number of establishments	Number of employees	Receipts (mil dol)	Annual payroll (mil dol)	Full-time equivalent employees	Government employment and payroll, 2012 — March payroll Total (dollars)	Percent of total for: Administration, judicial, and legal	Police and Corrections	Fire Protection	Highways and transportation	Health and welfare	Natural resources and utilities	Education and libraries
	104	105	106	107	108	109	110	111	112	113	114	115	116
NEW YORK—Cont'd													
Yonkers	305	1 248	129.1	34.1	5 538	39 341 604	3.2	17.5	10.4	1.0	2.7	6.0	58.2
NORTH CAROLINA	11 506	64 643	5 548.4	1 664.9	X	X	X	X	X	X	X	X	X
Apex	64	436	30.8	10.3	344	1 509 120	15.4	23.1	14.9	7.4	4.6	28.3	0.0
Asheboro	43	265	27.2	7.5	349	1 396 592	5.9	23.8	15.1	5.8	2.2	22.5	0.0
Asheville	214	1 148	87.1	27.3	1 057	3 889 185	9.1	23.7	24.5	5.3	3.3	19.0	0.0
Burlington	86	514	39.3	11.9	628	2 130 883	10.7	32.6	15.8	5.7	0.1	29.4	0.0
Cary	196	1 880	141.3	54.1	1 135	5 112 012	14.8	23.3	19.4	15.6	0.0	21.6	0.0
Chapel Hill	59	545	34.2	13.1	840	3 017 788	12.7	26.8	15.1	19.0	2.7	8.1	3.9
Charlotte	1 161	9 188	865.2	265.7	7 449	34 348 745	9.7	36.0	16.2	12.9	2.2	17.0	0.0
Concord	134	672	60.1	15.6	923	3 576 064	7.2	20.8	21.3	7.1	4.4	23.7	0.0
Durham	306	2 624	221.3	72.2	1 086	4 030 398	25.2	0.0	0.0	16.5	6.6	47.8	0.0
Fayetteville	256	1 445	107.3	33.2	1 960	7 748 728	4.9	24.8	14.8	6.6	0.8	30.0	0.0
Garner	52	338	30.0	8.8	177	821 893	16.4	47.7	0.0	3.4	1.0	15.0	0.0
Gastonia	122	742	51.1	16.1	935	3 494 489	15.2	23.5	14.9	10.2	1.1	28.7	0.0
Goldsboro	73	484	38.1	11.4	449	1 502 437	12.1	25.9	19.1	3.7	0.8	27.4	0.0
Greensboro	413	2 580	239.4	71.4	3 098	11 503 988	8.8	28.2	17.9	6.9	2.9	20.8	2.5
Greenville	103	692	52.0	14.4	1 347	5 208 426	6.5	18.6	12.5	6.2	2.4	34.6	0.0
Hickory	105	824	63.2	18.2	636	2 107 555	11.1	23.4	23.3	9.5	0.2	23.5	3.6
High Point	150	1 094	111.3	31.0	1 446	5 797 223	10.4	32.4	13.1	5.0	2.2	31.9	3.2
Huntersville	71	360	27.5	8.2	161	688 375	25.1	57.8	0.0	7.5	0.0	9.6	0.0
Indian Trail	60	283	24.5	6.8	48	144 392	56.2	0.0	0.0	9.0	0.0	9.0	0.0
Jacksonville	109	795	48.3	16.8	542	2 172 480	13.1	25.3	14.1	6.1	0.2	19.4	0.0
Kannapolis	48	D	D	D	289	1 109 005	13.6	30.3	23.4	4.8	0.0	27.8	0.0
Matthews	66	310	21.4	6.9	163	577 637	14.5	49.3	6.0	9.7	1.3	6.1	0.0
Monroe	82	392	37.1	11.2	511	1 971 029	15.1	20.8	15.3	6.0	0.0	37.8	0.0
Mooresville	81	506	50.3	12.2	760	1 406 044	10.4	25.8	21.5	3.5	0.0	23.4	4.8
New Bern	54	280	22.6	6.9	449	1 701 922	12.5	25.9	16.3	4.6	1.3	33.6	0.0
Raleigh	712	5 192	401.9	131.8	3 936	15 850 858	10.6	25.2	16.4	6.4	0.7	28.5	0.0
Rocky Mount	89	D	D	D	1 002	3 610 762	13.3	21.6	15.9	8.8	1.5	39.0	0.0
Salisbury	41	338	22.5	8.0	458	1 569 483	17.2	19.6	16.0	10.0	0.7	25.8	0.0
Sanford	52	284	18.9	6.3	345	1 295 948	13.5	31.2	15.8	6.0	2.5	21.9	0.0
Thomasville	45	207	22.4	5.7	377	1 184 674	5.8	27.3	23.1	5.5	0.0	20.8	0.0
Wake Forest	46	310	31.0	9.2	200	792 417	16.8	36.0	0.0	10.9	6.1	19.0	0.0
Wilmington	240	1 326	102.4	32.2	949	3 706 301	13.1	34.8	22.0	7.7	2.3	17.8	0.0
Wilson	74	D	D	D	776	2 938 961	12.7	19.6	12.6	8.5	5.3	36.1	0.0
Winston-Salem	276	1 682	131.3	43.3	2 489	8 460 457	12.1	31.4	15.9	7.1	5.7	23.1	0.0
NORTH DAKOTA	1 296	6 652	721.6	189.3	X	X	X	X	X	X	X	X	X
Bismarck	138	D	D	D	605	2 280 206	9.2	23.4	16.3	8.9	10.4	15.3	4.2
Fargo	226	1 642	138.6	44.9	836	3 889 052	10.7	22.5	14.1	18.2	12.7	15.1	3.8
Grand Forks	99	642	52.1	15.8	549	2 249 631	11.5	21.4	13.7	14.6	8.9	22.9	0.0
Minot	84	521	48.4	14.6	348	1 359 688	12.5	26.4	15.9	13.9	0.0	20.0	3.8
West Fargo	52	313	35.3	9.8	120	521 710	16.1	47.5	0.0	0.0	0.0	30.4	6.0
OHIO	15 038	99 624	8 638.0	2 607.8	X	X	X	X	X	X	X	X	X
Akron	272	1 576	104.3	34.7	1 872	8 159 087	15.0	31.5	21.9	4.1	0.5	18.7	0.0
Barberton	36	195	19.1	6.4	256	1 078 359	17.1	23.7	20.5	6.9	9.7	22.1	0.0
Beavercreek	54	443	31.1	9.3	144	794 411	6.5	49.4	0.0	17.6	4.9	14.0	0.0
Bowling Green	40	190	9.6	3.5	302	1 389 538	15.6	20.6	19.6	2.1	0.6	31.6	0.0
Brunswick	59	422	39.6	12.5	156	716 777	14.6	38.7	22.6	9.5	2.3	6.8	0.0
Canton	115	597	54.1	15.3	914	3 932 055	14.5	23.0	20.1	7.9	7.6	22.3	0.0
Cincinnati	415	3 189	264.2	77.6	5 222	26 843 252	9.4	25.7	17.7	5.4	8.4	28.9	0.0
Cleveland	546	3 780	261.7	90.6	7 389	33 318 506	12.7	29.1	13.0	9.9	7.8	25.3	0.0
Cleveland Heights	52	306	27.0	8.7	461	2 098 391	11.2	30.1	23.8	3.9	3.6	16.1	0.0
Columbus	916	8 412	668.6	217.0	8 035	42 573 757	14.7	32.2	23.9	4.3	5.7	16.8	0.0
Cuyahoga Falls	92	522	39.1	12.7	489	2 562 538	13.6	24.8	17.8	10.3	2.3	25.4	0.0
Dayton	176	1 277	133.1	38.3	1 940	9 617 585	13.2	22.8	17.4	11.8	4.6	25.3	0.0
Delaware	33	D	D	D	269	1 371 645	23.1	26.5	19.6	10.0	0.0	17.2	0.0
Dublin	34	D	D	D	836	2 882 615	15.9	35.7	0.0	4.5	15.6	11.3	0.0
Elyria	56	340	58.0	8.9	532	2 415 086	14.1	27.3	15.3	5.3	6.2	26.7	0.0
Euclid	50	149	11.5	3.3	454	1 882 329	12.3	36.1	22.3	4.1	5.6	15.3	0.0
Fairborn	38	187	15.5	4.8	222	557 607	20.8	22.1	26.3	4.5	1.3	11.4	0.0
Fairfield	82	590	60.6	17.0	340	1 631 218	20.0	30.2	17.2	8.1	0.0	22.3	0.0
Findlay	81	587	46.9	15.2	325	1 499 497	13.1	24.6	25.6	9.6	3.8	22.6	0.0
Gahanna	58	676	49.3	18.0	274	1 378 735	13.1	50.2	0.0	7.2	1.6	18.8	0.0
Garfield Heights	32	205	11.2	3.5	204	993 260	15.9	40.2	25.6	1.0	4.0	2.4	0.0
Green	41	531	92.4	27.9	131	615 958	19.2	0.0	49.5	27.4	0.0	2.9	0.0
Grove City	57	1 019	73.6	25.3	169	893 462	12.9	61.0	0.0	6.2	0.0	15.6	0.0

1. Establishments subject to federal tax.

Table D. Cities — **City Government Finances**

City	City government finances, 2012									
	General revenue							General expenditure		
		Intergovernmental		Taxes					Per capita[1] (dollars)	
					Per capita[1] (dollars)					
	Total (mil dol)	Total (mil dol)	Percent from state government	Total (mil dol)	Total	Property	Sales and gross receipts	Total (mil dol)	Total	Capital outlays
	117	118	119	120	121	122	123	124	125	126
NEW YORK—Cont'd										
Yonkers	973.8	463.3	98.2	426.2	2 146	1 487	460	967.5	4 872	267
NORTH CAROLINA ...	X	X	X	X	X	X	X	X	X	X
Apex	41.1	5.4	89.2	23.2	575	413	161	41.1	1 016	152
Asheboro	28.8	4.7	94.5	15.9	623	480	143	29.2	1 140	28
Asheville	115.3	28.1	51.3	66.5	775	542	233	121.5	1 415	244
Burlington	64.2	9.0	59.4	35.6	695	482	213	62.8	1 224	7
Cary	187.2	16.9	75.1	100.1	687	482	205	218.0	1 496	577
Chapel Hill	80.0	23.1	43.6	48.5	826	614	212	68.9	1 174	154
Charlotte	1 401.8	250.6	43.7	622.1	803	489	314	1 294.8	1 671	438
Concord	109.3	19.4	51.2	56.1	682	525	158	107.7	1 311	79
Durham	303.7	47.0	61.0	171.9	717	538	179	302.6	1 262	129
Fayetteville	208.3	50.9	51.4	95.2	472	298	174	235.1	1 166	340
Garner	26.6	2.9	28.3	20.3	760	553	207	24.8	926	110
Gastonia	81.0	9.5	71.1	46.3	636	418	218	85.6	1 176	76
Goldsboro	41.9	6.6	92.5	22.8	633	417	216	47.0	1 303	68
Greensboro	371.9	60.4	63.7	196.6	711	528	183	412.3	1 492	244
Greenville	116.0	31.1	70.0	46.0	525	360	165	107.6	1 228	125
Hickory	61.0	10.1	62.0	33.9	844	579	265	60.2	1 500	170
High Point	158.5	22.3	59.1	81.9	768	572	196	167.5	1 571	282
Huntersville	34.2	5.5	74.2	22.2	450	329	122	35.6	722	217
Indian Trail	10.0	2.4	32.5	6.4	182	142	41	7.7	220	16
Jacksonville	66.3	10.7	56.8	31.8	458	272	186	75.1	1 079	221
Kannapolis	41.5	5.6	64.3	25.1	572	425	147	48.1	1 099	338
Matthews	20.9	3.5	73.5	14.5	506	361	145	19.8	691	109
Monroe	55.3	6.6	75.2	24.8	738	578	160	69.9	2 080	827
Mooresville	65.3	6.7	75.3	35.6	1 034	845	189	71.2	2 068	563
New Bern	44.8	7.8	87.0	19.3	636	440	196	43.0	1 416	135
Raleigh	555.4	92.1	53.9	287.3	679	448	231	527.4	1 245	199
Rocky Mount	82.1	24.8	46.4	31.3	549	385	164	81.9	1 437	161
Salisbury	55.5	5.3	90.5	21.9	656	510	146	64.5	1 931	175
Sanford	35.2	4.6	61.9	18.2	628	419	210	34.4	1 189	24
Thomasville	26.0	4.5	82.6	14.1	525	395	129	26.2	973	39
Wake Forest	31.1	3.1	92.3	26.4	802	585	216	34.4	1 042	231
Wilmington	128.8	25.2	52.9	76.2	693	481	212	132.5	1 206	224
Wilson	71.8	10.0	67.7	27.6	557	410	147	70.7	1 427	69
Winston-Salem	293.3	50.8	63.3	139.2	594	431	163	303.3	1 294	272
NORTH DAKOTA	X	X	X	X	X	X	X	X	X	X
Bismarck	128.3	46.0	40.5	37.1	571	261	310	118.8	1 827	623
Fargo	237.9	83.4	99.5	72.5	658	188	465	229.3	2 080	749
Grand Forks	100.1	20.7	28.9	38.0	709	279	430	59.4	1 106	129
Minot	75.0	19.3	56.5	37.3	849	247	603	44.2	1 005	135
West Fargo	34.8	5.1	100.0	10.6	384	237	147	41.1	1 488	814
OHIO	X	X	X	X	X	X	X	X	X	X
Akron	350.3	65.6	64.3	174.5	879	131	9	337.8	1 701	101
Barberton	31.7	6.9	86.9	14.0	533	53	31	30.8	1 170	202
Beavercreek	25.7	8.8	100.0	12.8	279	249	24	26.8	583	125
Bowling Green	36.0	6.4	100.0	21.2	667	71	53	36.9	1 161	103
Brunswick	26.4	4.7	51.4	15.9	463	47	13	22.8	662	108
Canton	118.3	36.4	85.3	46.7	642	37	21	113.3	1 558	208
Cincinnati	947.1	392.8	17.6	415.4	1 400	180	74	783.9	2 641	864
Cleveland	897.0	231.8	58.8	419.1	1 071	143	124	897.7	2 294	222
Cleveland Heights	55.8	10.6	84.0	31.9	699	210	54	57.2	1 254	119
Columbus	1 434.3	260.4	47.1	776.6	958	53	57	1 353.3	1 670	431
Cuyahoga Falls	65.4	9.3	91.5	31.4	637	219	19	59.4	1 207	245
Dayton	304.4	74.9	66.0	118.0	832	117	10	297.8	2 099	314
Delaware	45.0	6.0	28.6	20.7	578	47	21	56.6	1 578	458
Dublin	103.4	5.5	100.0	74.6	1 739	85	61	90.8	2 117	497
Elyria	65.0	18.3	87.1	27.5	508	62	44	62.4	1 153	112
Euclid	62.8	10.1	90.8	28.1	581	104	4	73.1	1 514	131
Fairborn	38.1	6.6	99.9	16.6	498	73	74	37.4	1 124	168
Fairfield	52.2	6.6	100.0	29.3	686	121	80	61.3	1 438	11
Findlay	47.4	7.7	100.0	24.9	599	67	8	43.6	1 050	149
Gahanna	35.0	5.1	65.6	19.0	562	61	37	38.9	1 150	171
Garfield Heights	34.7	4.5	59.7	21.3	748	365	31	32.2	1 130	3
Green	27.4	4.6	79.0	20.6	800	59	29	25.0	969	123
Grove City	38.4	8.3	45.2	24.0	651	84	43	33.8	917	213

1. Based on population estimated as of July 1 of the year shown.

Table D. Cities — **City Government Finances**

City	City government finances, 2012 (cont.)									
	General expenditure (cont.)									
	Percent of total for:									
	Public welfare	Highways	Parking facilities	Education	Health and hospitals	Police protection	Sewerage and sanitation	Parks and recreation	Housing and community development	Interest on debt
	127	128	129	130	131	132	133	134	135	136
NEW YORK—Cont'd										
Yonkers	0.0	0.9	0.5	52.5	0.1	8.5	2.4	1.0	0.9	3.4
NORTH CAROLINA...	X	X	X	X	X	X	X	X	X	X
Apex	0.0	9.5	0.0	0.0	2.8	16.4	27.0	10.3	2.5	2.0
Asheboro..................	0.0	8.3	0.0	0.0	0.1	21.9	25.3	5.2	4.4	0.7
Asheville..................	0.0	11.4	6.4	0.0	0.1	18.3	8.4	17.4	4.6	1.0
Burlington	0.0	3.6	0.0	0.0	0.0	23.7	18.2	9.5	2.5	2.6
Cary.........................	0.0	5.6	0.0	0.0	0.0	10.3	37.2	10.3	1.6	2.8
Chapel Hill...............	0.0	7.2	2.8	0.0	0.0	17.7	7.9	9.7	8.4	3.6
Charlotte..................	0.0	9.3	0.1	0.0	0.0	19.2	21.6	2.2	6.0	10.5
Concord....................	0.0	5.4	0.0	0.0	0.0	16.5	22.1	5.5	14.1	2.4
Durham.....................	0.0	10.6	0.6	0.0	0.0	20.7	18.7	6.5	7.1	5.9
Fayetteville	0.0	4.9	1.7	0.0	0.0	18.9	35.9	6.3	3.1	2.1
Garner......................	0.0	19.6	0.0	0.0	0.0	27.7	7.0	11.0	3.5	2.1
Gastonia...................	0.0	10.5	1.2	0.0	0.0	19.9	26.7	5.9	5.3	3.9
Goldsboro.................	0.0	9.3	0.0	0.0	0.0	21.0	16.1	5.8	8.1	2.6
Greensboro...............	0.0	9.9	0.4	0.0	0.1	17.5	24.6	17.5	4.9	2.7
Greenville	0.0	8.9	0.1	0.0	0.0	22.4	22.7	8.4	5.4	2.9
Hickory	0.0	10.0	0.0	0.0	0.1	18.2	21.0	5.9	0.9	0.8
High Point................	0.0	8.3	0.2	0.0	0.1	15.8	29.1	8.4	4.3	4.7
Huntersville..............	0.0	24.6	0.0	0.0	1.1	36.8	1.5	16.6	4.1	3.6
Indian Trail	0.0	12.0	0.0	0.0	0.2	17.8	38.0	0.6	12.1	1.2
Jacksonville.............	0.0	5.6	0.0	0.0	0.0	20.5	39.6	8.4	2.4	3.8
Kannapolis................	0.0	7.6	0.0	0.0	0.0	14.6	9.5	9.7	2.7	4.1
Matthews..................	0.0	12.0	0.0	0.0	0.0	32.5	9.0	16.0	2.3	1.5
Monroe.....................	0.0	3.6	0.0	0.0	0.1	13.8	9.2	5.7	1.3	0.9
Mooresville	0.0	5.1	0.0	0.0	0.0	9.5	29.1	9.2	9.4	12.4
New Bern	0.0	7.7	0.0	0.0	0.0	30.7	26.9	5.0	4.4	3.1
Raleigh.....................	0.2	6.1	1.7	0.0	0.0	19.1	14.8	23.5	4.8	5.4
Rocky Mount.............	0.0	9.3	0.0	0.0	0.0	18.5	26.3	9.8	4.8	1.0
Salisbury..................	0.0	7.1	0.0	0.0	0.0	10.8	24.8	3.7	1.0	4.6
Sanford.....................	0.0	6.4	0.0	0.0	0.2	24.4	26.0	2.5	7.0	4.5
Thomasville..............	0.0	7.7	0.0	0.0	0.1	20.4	26.1	8.1	3.0	3.4
Wake Forest..............	0.0	17.8	0.0	0.0	0.0	19.6	7.2	10.3	0.0	2.7
Wilmington...............	0.0	10.5	2.9	0.0	0.0	20.7	15.0	8.1	1.1	7.7
Wilson......................	0.6	5.3	0.2	0.0	0.0	18.4	20.5	7.6	5.6	3.2
Winston-Salem..........	0.0	6.9	0.9	0.0	0.0	21.2	27.1	7.5	5.2	7.0
NORTH DAKOTA.......	X	X	X	X	X	X	X	X	X	X
Bismarck..................	0.0	24.2	0.9	0.0	2.1	9.9	17.2	6.8	0.7	2.1
Fargo.......................	4.1	24.0	0.3	0.0	0.0	12.3	6.2	5.9	0.9	7.6
Grand Forks	0.0	6.9	0.6	0.0	2.9	14.2	20.7	2.9	5.6	13.8
Minot.......................	0.0	12.9	0.3	0.0	0.0	16.1	18.8	4.7	0.0	1.5
West Fargo...............	0.0	39.8	0.0	0.0	0.0	11.7	25.6	0.8	0.0	9.2
OHIO	X	X	X	X	X	X	X	X	X	X
Akron	0.0	2.5	1.8	0.0	1.6	10.0	12.3	1.6	3.3	7.7
Barberton.................	0.0	7.0	0.0	0.0	0.0	16.3	30.7	3.3	3.5	1.0
Beavercreek..............	0.0	39.4	0.0	0.0	0.6	27.4	0.0	12.8	2.3	3.6
Bowling Green..............	0.0	18.5	0.0	0.0	0.2	14.7	20.9	5.0	0.0	3.1
Brunswick.................	0.0	16.1	0.0	0.0	0.4	28.0	10.3	6.3	1.3	1.4
Canton......................	0.0	11.9	0.3	0.0	5.6	18.0	15.3	1.7	0.0	0.9
Cincinnati..................	0.0	7.1	1.4	0.0	3.5	14.5	34.1	4.3	5.1	2.9
Cleveland	1.2	3.1	0.7	0.0	4.6	19.2	6.3	4.4	9.1	9.8
Cleveland Heights........	0.0	12.2	1.9	0.0	2.4	15.6	7.3	6.2	7.6	1.5
Columbus..................	0.0	9.9	0.2	0.0	2.8	18.9	20.2	10.2	2.3	6.4
Cuyahoga Falls	0.0	8.0	0.0	0.0	0.0	15.5	16.0	12.1	2.4	2.6
Dayton......................	0.8	8.7	0.0	0.0	0.0	14.5	12.3	2.9	7.3	0.8
Delaware	0.0	8.1	0.1	0.0	0.0	10.0	11.3	20.5	0.8	7.8
Dublin	0.0	5.5	0.0	0.0	0.3	11.4	6.9	18.8	0.0	2.5
Elyria	0.0	9.1	0.0	0.0	5.9	20.7	28.4	3.7	2.1	2.2
Euclid.......................	0.0	2.8	0.0	0.0	0.5	15.6	17.9	2.5	1.4	1.9
Fairborn....................	0.0	14.7	0.0	0.0	0.0	15.7	20.6	0.7	1.8	2.3
Fairfield....................	0.0	27.4	0.0	0.0	0.0	16.3	11.4	7.3	0.0	2.2
Findlay.....................	0.0	12.0	0.2	0.0	4.9	14.8	17.2	3.5	0.0	3.6
Gahanna....................	0.0	13.2	0.2	2.8	1.0	22.0	20.7	10.3	0.0	2.6
Garfield Heights	0.8	3.9	0.0	1.6	0.6	19.0	5.9	2.2	0.4	4.5
Green	0.0	27.0	0.0	0.0	3.3	7.4	0.7	5.3	0.0	7.8
Grove City	0.0	24.3	0.0	0.0	0.0	28.2	2.0	7.8	0.0	4.8

Table D. Cities — City Government Finances, City Government Employment, and Climate

| City | City government finances, 2012 (cont.) Debt outstanding | | | Climate[2] Average daily temperature (degrees Fahrenheit) | | | | | | |
| | Total (mil dol) | Per capita[1] (dollars) | Debt issued during year | Mean January | Mean July | Limits January[3] | Limits July[4] | Annual precipitation (inches) | Heating degree days | Cooling degree days |
	137	138	139	140	141	142	143	144	145	146
NEW YORK—Cont'd										
Yonkers	757.7	3 815	113.7	29.7	74.2	20.1	86.0	46.46	5 400	770
NORTH CAROLINA	X	X	X	X	X	X	X	X	X	X
Apex	63.3	1 566	35.0	NA	NA	NA	NA	NA	NA	NA
Asheboro	9.3	363	0.0	NA	NA	NA	NA	NA	NA	NA
Asheville	110.4	1 286	39.2	36.4	73.9	26.6	84.3	37.32	4 237	877
Burlington	62.0	1 208	18.4	38.7	79.3	27.6	90.6	45.08	3 588	1 489
Cary	243.8	1 672	11.3	39.5	78.7	30.1	87.9	46.49	3 431	1 456
Chapel Hill	60.5	1 030	33.5	38.5	79.4	27.8	88.6	48.04	3 650	1 491
Charlotte	3 227.6	4 165	470.5	41.7	80.3	32.1	90.1	43.51	3 162	1 681
Concord	100.3	1 221	19.4	39.4	79.2	27.9	90.3	47.30	3 463	1 540
Durham	398.4	1 661	15.6	39.7	78.8	29.6	89.1	43.05	3 465	1 521
Fayetteville	204.6	1 014	10.6	41.7	80.4	31.1	90.4	46.78	3 097	1 721
Garner	13.9	520	0.0	NA	NA	NA	NA	NA	NA	NA
Gastonia	94.3	1 295	6.0	42.0	79.9	31.7	89.9	49.19	3 009	1 701
Goldsboro	50.9	1 411	14.3	43.4	81.2	33.0	91.4	49.84	2 771	1 922
Greensboro	443.1	1 603	48.7	39.7	78.6	29.0	88.9	42.89	3 443	1 438
Greenville	143.1	1 633	4.3	42.0	78.8	31.9	88.4	49.30	3 113	1 516
Hickory	38.0	947	3.4	39.0	77.7	29.2	87.8	48.98	3 608	1 333
High Point	267.0	2 504	53.4	39.7	78.2	29.6	89.0	46.19	3 399	1 424
Huntersville	41.4	839	24.3	NA	NA	NA	NA	NA	NA	NA
Indian Trail	2.4	69	0.0	NA	NA	NA	NA	NA	NA	NA
Jacksonville	103.2	1 484	51.6	44.7	80.2	33.9	89.5	54.07	2 656	1 832
Kannapolis	67.9	1 550	17.0	39.4	79.2	27.9	90.3	47.30	3 463	1 540
Matthews	6.0	211	0.0	NA	NA	NA	NA	NA	NA	NA
Monroe	59.6	1 773	2.8	41.5	79.0	31.0	89.7	48.73	3 125	1 538
Mooresville	220.0	6 392	65.4	NA	NA	NA	NA	NA	NA	NA
New Bern	76.1	2 504	3.5	NA	NA	NA	NA	NA	NA	NA
Raleigh	1 004.7	2 373	218.5	39.1	79.4	28.1	89.9	45.70	3 514	1 550
Rocky Mount	10.0	175	2.4	41.1	79.2	30.8	89.7	46.51	3 215	1 518
Salisbury	81.1	2 426	8.3	40.2	78.7	29.5	89.5	42.86	3 356	1 466
Sanford	51.3	1 774	0.0	NA	NA	NA	NA	NA	NA	NA
Thomasville	42.9	1 594	11.3	NA	NA	NA	NA	NA	NA	NA
Wake Forest	32.8	993	6.3	NA	NA	NA	NA	NA	NA	NA
Wilmington	205.6	1 872	30.7	44.8	80.1	33.3	90.0	58.44	2 606	1 791
Wilson	113.0	2 279	12.2	40.4	79.2	29.5	90.2	47.18	3 328	1 575
Winston-Salem	727.7	3 105	38.5	39.7	78.2	29.6	89.0	46.19	3 399	1 424
NORTH DAKOTA	X	X	X	X	X	X	X	X	X	X
Bismarck	97.9	1 506	12.3	10.2	70.4	-0.6	84.5	16.84	8 802	471
Fargo	566.3	5 136	79.8	6.8	70.6	-2.3	82.2	21.19	9 092	533
Grand Forks	382.8	7 136	24.1	5.3	69.4	-4.3	81.9	19.60	9 489	420
Minot	41.8	952	7.0	7.5	68.4	-1.8	80.4	18.65	9 479	422
West Fargo	120.7	4 372	17.9	NA	NA	NA	NA	NA	NA	NA
OHIO	X	X	X	X	X	X	X	X	X	X
Akron	794.0	3 998	96.9	27.2	74.1	20.1	83.9	36.07	5 752	856
Barberton	16.6	631	0.0	29.1	73.6	20.3	85.0	39.16	5 348	813
Beavercreek	12.0	260	4.2	27.6	73.1	19.5	83.5	40.06	5 531	768
Bowling Green	24.2	761	3.4	23.1	72.9	15.2	84.2	33.18	6 492	690
Brunswick	11.1	322	0.4	25.7	71.9	18.8	81.4	38.71	6 121	702
Canton	20.1	276	0.0	25.2	71.8	17.4	82.3	38.47	6 154	678
Cincinnati	917.4	3 091	175.8	30.6	76.8	22.7	86.8	39.57	4 841	1 210
Cleveland	2 530.4	6 465	194.4	25.7	71.9	18.8	81.4	38.71	6 121	702
Cleveland Heights	18.6	407	0.0	25.7	71.9	18.8	81.4	38.71	6 121	702
Columbus	2 555.4	3 153	190.4	28.3	74.7	20.2	85.6	40.03	5 349	935
Cuyahoga Falls	55.8	1 133	3.3	29.1	73.6	20.3	85.0	39.58	5 348	813
Dayton	131.3	926	0.2	26.3	74.3	19.0	84.2	39.58	5 690	935
Delaware	89.4	2 492	2.2	25.1	73.0	16.6	84.6	37.58	6 178	739
Dublin	57.2	1 334	0.0	28.3	74.7	20.2	85.6	40.03	5 349	935
Elyria	50.5	934	13.2	27.1	73.8	19.3	85.0	38.02	5 731	818
Euclid	40.5	839	19.4	23.0	68.8	14.3	80.0	47.33	6 956	372
Fairborn	21.9	657	0.0	27.9	77.0	20.6	87.2	39.41	5 343	1 214
Fairfield	32.0	750	0.0	28.7	76.6	19.9	88.1	43.36	5 261	1 135
Findlay	18.2	439	2.7	24.5	73.6	17.4	83.5	36.91	6 194	809
Gahanna	26.3	777	5.8	28.3	75.1	20.3	85.3	38.52	5 492	951
Garfield Heights	27.3	959	0.0	25.7	71.9	18.8	81.4	38.71	6 121	702
Green	58.3	2 261	7.2	NA	NA	NA	NA	NA	NA	NA
Grove City	35.9	973	0.0	28.3	74.7	20.2	85.6	40.03	5 349	935

1. Based on the population estimated as of July 1 of the year shown. 2. Represents normal values based on the 30-year period, 1971–2000. 3. Average daily minimum.
4. Average daily maximum.

Table D. Cities — **Land Area and Population**

STATE Place code	City	Land area,[1] 2016 (sq mi)	Population, 2016 — Total persons	Rank	Per square mile	Race alone[2] (percent), 2015 — White	Black or African American	American Indian, Alaska Native	Asian	Hawaiian Pacific Islander	Some other race	2 or more races[2]
		1	2	3	4	5	6	7	8	9	10	11
	OHIO—Cont'd											
39 33012	Hamilton	21.5	62 127	588	2 889.6	83.0	9.2	1.7	1.5	1.3	0.0	3.5
39 35476	Hilliard	13.2	34 905	1 089	2 644.3	85.9	4.1	0.0	8.3	0.0	0.0	1.8
39 36610	Huber Heights	22.3	38 019	1 003	1 704.9	78.0	11.5	2.4	2.2	0.0	0.0	6.0
39 39872	Kent	9.2	30 071	1 249	3 268.6	76.3	11.1	0.1	5.3	0.0	0.9	6.2
39 40040	Kettering	18.7	55 306	678	2 957.5	90.1	3.6	0.0	3.0	0.0	0.6	2.6
39 41664	Lakewood	5.5	50 279	755	9 141.6	90.5	4.2	0.0	0.8	0.0	0.3	4.1
39 41720	Lancaster	18.9	39 848	951	2 108.4	93.7	2.4	0.0	0.9	0.0	0.0	2.9
39 43554	Lima	13.5	37 414	1 022	2 771.4	63.5	28.4	0.7	2.6	0.0	1.4	3.3
39 44856	Lorain	23.7	63 730	574	2 689.0	67.4	20.4	0.4	0.5	0.1	4.9	6.3
39 47138	Mansfield	30.9	46 678	821	1 510.6	72.8	16.1	0.4	1.1	0.0	0.4	9.2
39 47754	Marion	11.8	36 310	1 049	3 077.1	86.4	8.6	0.0	0.4	0.0	0.5	4.1
39 48188	Mason	18.6	33 037	1 149	1 776.2	NA	NA	NA	NA	NA	NA	NA
39 48244	Massillon	19.0	32 258	1 174	1 697.8	NA	NA	NA	NA	NA	NA	NA
39 48790	Medina	11.6	26 261	1 393	2 263.9	NA	NA	NA	NA	NA	NA	NA
39 49056	Mentor	27.8	46 732	820	1 681.0	NA	NA	NA	NA	NA	NA	NA
39 49840	Middletown	26.2	48 813	779	1 863.1	77.5	9.8	0.0	0.3	0.0	2.2	10.3
39 54040	Newark	20.8	49 134	772	2 362.2	NA	NA	NA	NA	NA	NA	NA
39 56882	North Olmsted	11.7	31 817	1 185	2 719.4	91.8	2.5	0.0	3.8	0.0	1.0	0.9
39 56966	North Ridgeville	23.4	32 983	1 152	1 409.5	NA	NA	NA	NA	NA	NA	NA
39 57008	North Royalton	21.3	30 247	1 243	1 420.0	NA	NA	NA	NA	NA	NA	NA
39 61000	Parma	20.0	79 425	429	3 971.3	93.5	2.0	0.4	1.1	0.0	0.9	2.1
39 66390	Reynoldsburg	11.1	37 449	1 021	3 373.8	61.5	27.1	0.1	1.2	0.4	2.6	7.1
39 67468	Riverside	9.7	24 981	1 425	2 575.4	78.5	11.1	0.1	6.9	0.0	0.7	2.8
39 70380	Sandusky	9.7	25 006	1 422	2 577.9	67.7	21.9	0.2	0.0	0.0	4.0	6.1
39 71682	Shaker Heights	6.3	27 448	1 345	4 356.8	53.8	36.8	0.4	3.5	0.0	1.0	4.4
39 74118	Springfield	25.5	59 087	631	2 317.1	73.2	16.5	0.1	0.7	0.1	2.6	6.8
39 74944	Stow	17.1	34 711	1 095	2 029.9	89.8	4.8	0.0	1.2	0.0	0.7	3.5
39 75098	Strongsville	24.6	44 631	845	1 814.3	90.9	2.2	0.2	4.3	0.0	0.2	2.2
39 77000	Toledo	80.7	278 508	72	3 451.2	62.4	27.4	0.3	2.1	0.1	2.4	5.3
39 77588	Troy	11.8	25 770	1 406	2 183.9	NA	NA	NA	NA	NA	NA	NA
39 79002	Upper Arlington	9.8	34 997	1 085	3 571.1	90.7	0.7	0.0	6.0	0.0	0.5	2.0
39 80892	Warren	16.1	39 898	950	2 478.1	NA	NA	NA	NA	NA	NA	NA
39 83342	Westerville	12.6	38 985	973	3 094.0	87.6	5.1	0.0	1.3	0.1	0.4	5.5
39 83622	Westlake	15.9	32 293	1 172	2 031.0	NA	NA	NA	NA	NA	NA	NA
39 86548	Wooster	16.6	27 023	1 367	1 627.9	88.9	3.9	1.2	2.8	0.0	1.1	2.2
39 86772	Xenia	13.0	26 238	1 394	2 018.3	NA	NA	NA	NA	NA	NA	NA
39 88000	Youngstown	34.0	64 312	564	1 891.5	47.8	46.3	0.7	0.3	0.0	1.1	3.9
39 88084	Zanesville	11.8	25 465	1 413	2 158.1	NA	NA	NA	NA	NA	NA	NA
40 00000	OKLAHOMA	68 596.4	3 923 561	X	57.2	72.6	7.3	7.3	2.0	0.1	2.8	7.9
40 04450	Bartlesville	22.8	36 647	1 042	1 607.3	79.9	3.7	5.6	2.4	0.2	1.3	6.9
40 09050	Broken Arrow	61.7	107 403	278	1 740.7	77.9	4.3	3.3	2.9	0.0	1.0	10.5
40 23200	Edmond	84.7	91 191	351	1 076.6	79.7	4.0	2.5	3.7	0.0	1.3	8.8
40 23950	Enid	74.0	51 004	747	689.2	78.0	4.0	3.4	0.9	0.0	8.1	5.6
40 41850	Lawton	81.0	94 653	331	1 168.6	57.8	21.4	4.7	3.1	0.4	1.9	10.7
40 48350	Midwest City	24.4	57 305	652	2 348.6	67.9	19.8	3.6	1.8	0.0	0.7	6.2
40 49200	Moore	21.8	61 415	595	2 817.2	75.9	7.2	2.4	2.1	0.0	1.4	11.0
40 50050	Muskogee	43.1	38 352	989	889.8	55.9	17.0	16.3	1.2	0.0	2.1	7.5
40 52500	Norman	178.8	122 180	224	683.3	80.1	3.1	2.7	4.4	0.1	1.1	8.6
40 55000	Oklahoma City	606.3	638 367	27	1 052.9	67.5	14.7	2.9	4.7	0.1	3.5	6.7
40 56650	Owasso	16.6	35 784	1 065	2 155.7	75.9	2.3	6.3	2.6	0.1	3.2	9.6
40 59850	Ponca City	18.4	24 527	1 430	1 333.0	77.6	3.1	6.1	0.1	0.0	1.3	11.8
40 66800	Shawnee	44.1	31 465	1 196	713.5	78.2	3.5	13.2	0.6	0.0	1.7	2.7
40 70300	Stillwater	29.5	49 504	762	1 678.1	79.1	4.5	4.4	7.4	0.2	0.1	4.3
40 75000	Tulsa	196.8	403 090	47	2 048.2	62.8	15.2	4.7	3.5	0.0	6.0	7.8
41 00000	OREGON	95 986.6	4 093 465	X	42.6	85.2	1.9	1.2	4.1	0.4	2.6	4.5
41 01000	Albany	17.5	53 211	711	3 040.6	91.7	0.2	0.7	1.0	0.3	3.2	2.9
41 05350	Beaverton	19.5	97 590	312	5 004.6	80.2	1.8	0.7	8.6	0.2	4.5	4.1
41 05800	Bend	33.0	91 122	352	2 761.3	92.6	0.4	0.4	1.3	0.0	1.3	4.1
41 15800	Corvallis	14.2	57 110	655	4 021.8	84.0	1.1	1.3	9.0	0.0	1.0	3.5
41 23850	Eugene	44.1	166 575	154	3 777.2	83.8	2.2	0.9	3.6	0.2	3.0	6.4
41 30550	Grants Pass	11.4	37 779	1 011	3 313.9	90.6	1.0	0.1	1.0	0.0	4.1	3.1
41 31250	Gresham	23.3	111 523	258	4 786.4	80.8	5.3	0.5	3.4	0.8	3.7	5.5
41 34100	Hillsboro	25.0	105 164	285	4 206.6	72.3	2.0	1.8	11.0	0.1	5.5	7.3
41 38500	Keizer	7.2	38 980	975	5 413.9	81.2	1.1	0.4	3.0	0.4	1.9	12.1
41 40550	Lake Oswego	10.7	38 945	977	3 639.7	89.5	0.3	0.0	4.9	0.0	2.4	2.8
41 45000	McMinnville	10.6	34 690	1 097	3 272.6	85.7	0.9	0.9	1.5	0.0	9.4	1.6
41 47000	Medford	25.8	81 636	412	3 164.2	90.8	0.4	0.4	1.3	0.4	2.5	4.2
41 55200	Oregon City	9.6	36 286	1 050	3 779.8	88.9	2.0	1.2	1.7	1.3	0.2	4.6
41 59000	Portland	133.5	639 863	26	4 793.0	77.7	5.7	0.7	7.9	0.6	1.8	5.5

1. Dry land or land partially or temporarily covered by water. 2. Hispanic or Latino persons may be of any race.

Table D. Cities — **Population**

City	Percent Hispanic or Latino[1], 2015	Percent foreign born 2015	Age of population (percent), 2010-2014							Median age 2015	Percent female 2015	Population			
												Census counts		Percent change	
			Under 18 years	18 to 24 years	25 to 34 years	35 to 44 years	45 to 54 years	55 to 64 years	65 years and over			2000	2010	2000–2010	2010–2016
	12	13	14	15	16	17	18	19	20	21	22	23	24	25	26
OHIO—Cont'd															
Hamilton	4.0	3.9	28.3	10.2	12.4	11.1	15.0	11.9	11.1	34.2	52.4	60 690	62 272	2.6	-0.2
Hilliard	2.4	8.2	27.1	5.4	14.2	13.2	14.6	14.6	10.8	36.7	51.7	24 230	28 225	16.5	23.7
Huber Heights	3.6	2.9	29.9	6.1	13.6	11.3	11.9	10.6	16.7	35.3	51.0	38 212	38 102	-0.3	-0.2
Kent	3.4	8.7	15.2	37.7	13.8	5.4	11.2	7.2	9.6	23.9	54.8	27 906	28 906	3.6	4.0
Kettering	1.6	4.7	23.3	7.8	14.9	12.6	9.5	12.6	19.2	38.1	52.2	57 502	56 161	-2.3	-1.5
Lakewood	7.4	12.6	18.0	9.8	19.9	13.7	11.8	15.0	11.8	36.3	49.3	56 646	52 131	-8.0	-3.6
Lancaster	4.6	1.4	26.5	6.7	12.8	15.4	12.2	10.2	16.3	36.9	50.5	35 335	38 762	9.7	2.8
Lima	2.8	1.3	25.3	11.0	15.0	14.0	11.5	12.0	11.2	33.9	46.7	40 081	38 639	-3.6	-3.2
Lorain	30.4	2.4	26.9	11.7	10.9	13.7	11.9	12.1	12.8	35.6	51.5	68 652	64 099	-6.6	-0.6
Mansfield	2.3	1.6	21.6	12.0	13.5	13.4	13.2	11.7	14.6	36.9	48.1	49 346	47 821	-3.1	-2.4
Marion	2.6	1.1	20.0	9.5	15.6	14.1	12.3	13.5	15.0	38.0	44.8	35 318	36 828	4.3	-1.4
Mason	0.9	12.9	26.1	8.7	8.4	14.2	15.9	11.3	15.4	42.5	52.3	22 016	30 857	40.2	7.1
Massillon	2.3	2.5	23.1	10.1	9.7	10.2	12.7	16.4	17.7	34.1	50.6	31 325	32 242	2.9	0.0
Medina	4.0	1.9	28.8	7.9	13.8	13.9	13.3	9.6	12.7	34.1	49.3	25 139	26 666	6.1	-1.5
Mentor	0.6	4.8	18.4	6.2	8.5	12.3	19.5	16.0	19.0	47.6	51.3	50 278	47 159	-6.2	-0.9
Middletown	6.0	3.7	25.7	8.3	13.8	12.6	13.1	12.5	13.9	37.3	53.7	51 605	48 678	-5.7	0.3
Newark	0.8	2.6	26.0	10.1	12.7	11.0	13.7	11.9	14.6	36.1	54.5	46 279	47 561	2.8	3.3
North Olmsted	3.9	8.0	20.2	6.5	10.7	10.7	16.4	14.8	20.6	45.8	53.3	34 113	32 713	-4.1	-2.7
North Ridgeville	2.0	2.8	20.5	6.1	13.9	15.5	10.7	11.4	21.9	41.3	48.5	22 338	29 466	31.9	11.9
North Royalton	0.4	9.4	21.9	5.4	14.3	10.2	14.8	13.4	20.1	43.2	48.3	28 648	30 444	6.3	-0.6
Parma	6.7	8.6	17.6	10.5	15.5	12.5	14.0	13.0	16.9	40.8	51.9	85 655	81 601	-4.7	-2.7
Reynoldsburg	6.1	6.7	24.0	10.6	11.5	10.9	14.8	14.9	13.3	37.7	54.0	32 069	35 911	12.0	4.3
Riverside	3.3	9.6	26.2	7.9	14.2	11.5	14.5	10.8	14.8	36.4	48.5	23 545	25 201	7.0	-0.9
Sandusky	6.5	1.2	26.0	9.4	10.8	15.3	12.1	13.0	13.2	37.1	52.6	27 844	25 919	-6.9	-3.5
Shaker Heights	3.5	7.6	26.9	8.1	11.8	14.2	13.1	14.0	12.0	37.2	57.8	29 405	28 448	-3.3	-3.5
Springfield	4.6	1.8	21.3	11.7	13.6	9.2	11.9	13.4	18.8	38.6	52.8	65 358	60 608	-7.3	-2.5
Stow	2.1	6.5	19.4	8.5	16.3	7.6	15.7	15.8	16.7	42.8	52.1	32 139	34 837	8.4	-0.4
Strongsville	3.4	9.0	20.0	6.1	8.8	11.2	14.8	17.5	21.7	47.7	51.8	43 858	44 750	2.0	-0.3
Toledo	8.4	3.3	22.0	11.0	15.6	11.0	12.6	13.6	14.2	36.1	51.6	313 619	287 206	-8.4	-3.0
Troy	1.0	1.9	27.4	10.6	10.5	14.4	12.8	11.4	12.9	35.8	53.6	21 999	25 211	14.6	2.2
Upper Arlington	3.1	8.6	26.8	4.1	9.3	14.3	14.2	16.2	15.1	42.2	50.1	33 686	33 684	0.0	3.9
Warren	3.2	1.2	23.7	10.3	13.5	10.5	12.9	13.5	15.7	38.4	48.3	46 832	41 553	-11.3	-4.0
Westerville	1.1	3.8	21.1	7.8	11.3	12.5	13.0	16.3	18.0	42.7	52.0	35 318	36 267	2.7	7.5
Westlake	1.4	8.4	22.8	5.1	9.2	14.3	14.2	11.8	22.5	44.4	51.4	31 719	32 729	3.2	-1.3
Wooster	2.0	3.8	20.2	14.6	12.7	9.0	11.0	12.6	19.9	38.1	52.7	24 811	26 179	5.5	3.2
Xenia	2.0	1.5	26.3	9.3	15.4	9.3	13.3	12.1	14.3	33.7	49.2	24 164	25 671	6.2	2.2
Youngstown	11.7	1.6	22.6	10.7	14.1	11.0	10.1	13.8	17.6	37.5	52.4	82 026	66 979	-18.3	-4.0
Zanesville	0.8	0.1	26.1	12.8	12.4	8.1	12.1	12.6	16.0	34.1	54.4	25 586	25 472	-0.4	0.0
OKLAHOMA	10.1	6.0	24.6	10.0	13.7	12.3	12.3	12.4	14.7	36.3	50.4	3 450 654	3 751 615	8.7	4.6
Bartlesville	6.5	5.0	22.4	9.5	12.9	10.5	11.7	13.1	19.8	39.9	52.2	34 748	35 752	2.9	2.5
Broken Arrow	8.5	6.4	27.4	8.6	11.8	14.2	14.5	10.9	12.6	36.8	51.5	74 859	98 843	32.0	8.7
Edmond	6.9	6.2	25.7	12.7	15.2	11.6	11.0	11.5	12.2	32.5	49.8	68 315	81 399	19.2	12.0
Enid	14.3	9.5	26.5	6.7	15.1	11.6	10.5	14.0	15.5	36.5	50.3	47 045	49 379	5.0	3.3
Lawton	14.3	6.3	24.4	14.6	18.0	13.1	9.8	10.5	9.7	31.1	47.1	92 757	96 867	4.4	-2.3
Midwest City	7.1	3.9	26.7	9.9	15.3	10.3	11.2	11.6	14.9	33.4	52.8	54 088	54 371	0.5	5.4
Moore	7.3	3.9	25.9	9.9	17.8	14.7	11.4	9.0	11.3	33.4	50.8	41 138	55 081	33.9	11.5
Muskogee	7.6	5.2	26.7	11.8	11.6	11.4	10.4	13.8	14.3	35.0	51.0	38 310	39 223	2.4	-2.2
Norman	9.8	7.2	19.5	21.1	14.8	12.9	10.5	10.2	11.0	30.9	50.6	95 694	110 925	15.9	10.1
Oklahoma City	18.6	12.7	26.0	9.1	16.1	13.3	11.7	11.8	12.0	34.1	51.0	506 132	580 004	14.6	10.1
Owasso	8.3	5.6	26.9	10.1	14.2	14.1	15.0	9.2	10.3	33.6	53.3	18 502	29 717	60.6	20.4
Ponca City	7.3	2.3	25.6	8.7	12.8	10.3	11.5	14.6	16.4	37.4	50.9	25 919	25 401	-2.0	-3.4
Shawnee	7.1	3.8	23.7	11.3	13.1	12.6	10.5	11.5	17.4	36.5	53.4	28 692	29 857	4.1	5.4
Stillwater	6.2	10.7	16.0	36.7	16.5	7.5	8.5	7.1	7.7	24.3	48.4	39 065	45 688	17.0	8.4
Tulsa	15.2	10.9	24.5	9.8	15.6	12.2	11.7	12.6	13.5	35.0	51.0	393 049	391 923	-0.3	2.8
OREGON	12.7	9.9	21.4	9.0	13.7	13.1	12.9	13.6	16.4	39.1	50.6	3 421 399	3 831 072	12.0	6.8
Albany	11.0	5.9	21.4	8.8	15.5	10.6	13.4	14.8	15.6	37.1	51.4	40 852	50 158	22.8	6.1
Beaverton	16.0	19.6	21.2	7.3	20.3	15.3	13.5	11.4	11.0	35.6	51.0	76 129	89 724	17.9	8.8
Bend	9.4	3.5	23.2	6.8	14.4	14.3	13.4	12.3	15.5	37.3	51.4	52 029	76 639	47.3	18.9
Corvallis	8.9	15.8	14.5	31.3	15.1	10.4	8.5	8.6	11.6	27.4	50.5	49 322	54 498	10.5	4.8
Eugene	10.6	8.9	18.0	19.1	14.4	12.6	9.4	11.6	14.9	33.4	51.6	137 893	156 412	13.4	6.5
Grants Pass	8.4	5.9	22.5	8.2	12.1	9.2	12.0	14.2	21.8	43.5	51.1	23 003	35 926	56.2	5.2
Gresham	21.3	16.2	24.5	8.0	13.9	14.0	13.3	12.8	13.5	36.7	51.3	90 205	105 635	17.1	5.6
Hillsboro	21.7	19.1	25.2	7.0	17.2	16.4	14.3	8.6	11.3	35.3	50.2	70 186	92 208	31.4	14.1
Keizer	13.6	8.1	30.1	5.6	14.1	14.9	9.1	10.2	16.0	35.2	52.0	32 203	36 485	13.3	6.8
Lake Oswego	6.7	8.4	22.8	6.3	8.8	13.4	13.1	18.5	17.1	44.0	52.8	35 278	36 720	4.1	6.1
McMinnville	28.3	14.3	23.6	11.8	11.6	13.1	11.2	12.0	16.7	35.9	51.2	26 499	32 187	21.5	7.8
Medford	17.9	7.8	23.4	7.8	13.5	12.3	13.8	12.6	16.6	38.6	50.4	63 154	74 943	18.7	8.9
Oregon City	2.7	4.0	22.8	7.1	15.7	17.1	12.7	9.8	14.7	37.5	50.3	25 754	32 609	26.6	11.3
Portland	9.7	13.6	18.3	8.5	19.8	16.9	12.8	11.9	11.8	36.7	50.4	529 121	583 799	10.3	9.6

1. May be of any race.

Table D. Cities — Households, Group Quarters, Crime, and Education

City	Households, 2015		Percent		Persons in group quarters, 2010	Institutional			Serious crimes known to police,[2] 2014 Total		Rate[3]		Educational attainment, 2015	Attainment[4] (percent)	
	Number	Persons per house-hold	Female family house-holder[1]	One-person	Total	Total	Persons in nursing facilities	Non-institu-tional	Number	Rate[3]	Violent	Property	Population age 25 and older	High school graduate or less	Bachelor's degree or more
	27	28	29	30	31	32	33	34	35	36	37	38	39	40	41
OHIO—Cont'd															
Hamilton	23 604	2.57	20.1	33.2	1 663	1 354	436	309	1 168	1 877	169	1 708	38 383	57.0	14.5
Hilliard	13 215	2.59	8.6	29.3	155	155	155	0	NA	NA	NA	NA	23 173	16.8	56.4
Huber Heights	14 900	2.72	14.8	18.3	184	64	64	120	1 235	3 238	197	3 042	26 055	39.6	19.9
Kent	11 100	2.23	14.3	29.6	6 067	81	81	5 986	654	2 007	233	1 774	14 046	36.0	38.2
Kettering	24 833	2.23	9.8	36.8	427	304	304	123	1 132	2 029	95	1 934	38 407	29.4	35.3
Lakewood	24 109	2.09	10.6	42.6	370	304	303	66	824	1 618	130	1 489	36 575	30.9	42.9
Lancaster	15 103	2.57	14.5	27.9	871	692	383	179	1 858	4 709	276	4 433	26 569	50.8	17.6
Lima	14 533	2.43	18.3	35.9	4 300	3 401	279	899	2 221	5 804	923	4 882	24 131	55.0	14.8
Lorain	24 989	2.52	21.5	32.2	662	444	423	218	2 876	4 521	384	4 137	39 051	52.8	11.0
Mansfield	16 819	2.40	15.3	38.4	6 594	5 881	519	713	3 421	7 414	466	6 948	31 086	54.2	14.1
Marion	13 024	2.43	14.7	33.9	5 267	5 112	363	155	1 666	4 531	286	4 246	26 266	54.3	7.6
Mason	12 142	2.66	8.3	27.8	186	76	76	110	393	1 251	35	1 216	21 304	20.2	61.4
Massillon	12 908	2.44	10.4	30.3	951	683	348	268	1 197	3 718	267	3 451	21 531	56.0	14.4
Medina	9 806	2.66	14.1	26.2	361	345	186	16	72	153	6	147	16 747	31.6	40.5
Mentor	19 402	2.40	6.0	26.0	403	381	381	22	118	251	6	245	35 359	38.9	25.8
Middletown	19 887	2.42	22.9	33.3	573	472	399	101	4 088	8 411	638	7 773	32 149	56.0	13.5
Newark	19 459	2.40	13.2	32.2	1 011	750	486	261	2 361	4 939	153	4 786	30 688	51.0	18.1
North Olmsted	13 012	2.43	12.3	31.7	323	264	264	59	NA	NA	NA	NA	23 437	41.3	24.2
North Ridgeville	13 396	2.41	5.1	29.4	225	213	213	12	237	747	35	713	23 842	38.0	31.0
North Royalton	13 200	2.28	6.6	34.3	247	226	226	21	NA	NA	NA	NA	22 039	35.9	36.2
Parma	32 577	2.42	13.5	28.8	1 063	897	792	166	1 293	1 613	85	1 528	57 484	49.1	20.0
Reynoldsburg	14 810	2.48	18.9	29.1	25	0	0	25	1 208	3 294	155	3 139	23 996	37.4	29.1
Riverside	10 508	2.38	12.2	30.5	0	0	0	0	632	2 521	203	2 318	16 453	40.7	25.9
Sandusky	10 483	2.35	25.1	39.1	579	305	240	274	1 120	4 438	289	4 149	16 279	56.8	12.9
Shaker Heights	10 710	2.57	16.7	31.5	156	119	44	37	272	978	32	945	17 991	13.1	61.7
Springfield	25 225	2.25	19.8	37.3	2 497	1 128	854	1 369	4 680	7 947	751	7 196	39 927	57.4	12.6
Stow	14 840	2.32	10.8	30.4	454	405	405	49	687	1 977	69	1 908	25 094	27.3	46.2
Strongsville	17 634	2.51	6.9	25.2	304	277	264	27	782	1 748	92	1 657	32 999	29.3	44.1
Toledo	119 100	2.29	18.3	38.7	8 475	2 987	1 239	5 488	8 708	3 097	1 091	2 006	187 416	48.2	16.8
Troy	10 117	2.52	12.3	37.6	420	263	163	157	934	3 663	161	3 502	16 032	40.9	26.4
Upper Arlington	13 275	2.62	6.7	23.8	254	254	254	0	411	1 188	12	1 176	24 145	10.2	71.4
Warren	16 850	2.24	20.0	40.2	2 517	2 302	525	215	1 838	4 528	448	4 080	26 577	58.8	12.8
Westerville	14 400	2.55	5.6	26.3	1 685	454	454	1 231	849	2 244	74	2 170	27 499	23.1	51.2
Westlake	13 418	2.35	10.3	34.6	871	830	830	41	400	1 234	37	1 197	23 375	20.2	51.7
Wooster	10 864	2.18	9.9	43.2	2 381	387	230	1 994	981	3 708	276	3 432	17 447	42.7	34.6
Xenia	10 752	2.31	22.0	34.2	925	700	312	225	893	3 444	216	3 228	16 745	56.2	20.6
Youngstown	27 542	2.22	24.2	41.8	5 831	3 929	644	1 902	3 623	5 602	660	4 942	43 094	54.9	12.1
Zanesville	10 776	2.32	20.8	35.4	582	514	290	68	1 597	6 284	405	5 878	15 579	57.2	10.3
OKLAHOMA	1 465 951	2.59	12.2	28.0	112 017	64 411	21 678	47 606	131 726	3 397	406	2 991	2 557 863	44.3	24.6
Bartlesville	15 035	2.33	12.3	28.9	658	256	145	402	1 001	2 753	228	2 524	24 318	42.6	32.1
Broken Arrow	38 613	2.77	11.9	18.6	468	466	466	2	1 864	1 782	142	1 641	68 861	30.2	29.7
Edmond	32 982	2.68	11.0	22.8	1 586	313	268	1 273	1 619	1 832	92	1 740	55 466	22.3	52.5
Enid	19 651	2.52	7.7	26.5	1 824	1 005	593	819	2 234	4 377	370	4 007	34 121	48.3	24.7
Lawton	32 083	2.72	16.5	30.6	10 143	3 772	523	6 371	5 401	5 570	921	4 649	58 933	43.6	19.7
Midwest City	22 156	2.57	14.8	31.7	285	260	235	25	2 778	4 847	323	4 524	36 314	47.3	17.9
Moore	22 105	2.72	13.1	25.6	309	179	179	130	1 603	2 708	132	2 577	38 804	36.2	28.5
Muskogee	14 794	2.51	16.6	38.2	1 353	834	430	519	1 956	5 047	1 102	3 945	23 688	52.5	18.7
Norman	45 369	2.47	11.2	31.0	6 757	1 124	566	5 633	3 435	2 864	160	2 703	71 429	27.7	40.1
Oklahoma City	239 137	2.58	13.6	31.2	12 144	6 609	2 521	5 535	32 040	5 185	774	4 411	409 659	40.0	30.1
Owasso	13 020	2.69	10.8	22.0	242	214	173	28	538	1 623	157	1 466	22 211	32.2	35.3
Ponca City	10 217	2.48	12.2	33.7	700	433	245	267	1 472	5 943	787	5 156	17 078	49.3	19.3
Shawnee	12 044	2.47	15.2	33.6	1 670	468	249	1 202	2 067	6 617	836	5 782	20 352	49.4	17.4
Stillwater	18 608	2.24	4.6	37.6	6 945	367	180	6 578	1 477	3 106	320	2 786	23 130	22.5	45.1
Tulsa	167 400	2.37	14.6	33.5	8 386	4 284	2 033	4 102	23 521	5 887	805	5 082	264 531	38.6	30.8
OREGON	1 553 205	2.54	10.3	27.9	86 642	36 612	11 491	50 030	123 529	3 111	232	2 879	2 804 461	33.3	32.2
Albany	21 537	2.38	11.6	28.8	824	560	256	264	1 717	3 309	81	3 228	36 366	34.8	27.7
Beaverton	38 899	2.46	9.2	33.5	945	460	393	485	1 648	1 745	135	1 611	69 076	23.4	46.7
Bend	36 083	2.39	9.7	28.4	578	183	157	395	2 312	2 805	144	2 661	60 875	17.4	47.2
Corvallis	22 557	2.24	8.2	34.9	4 899	116	74	4 783	1 813	3 264	131	3 133	30 248	19.1	60.5
Eugene	67 091	2.34	9.3	34.7	7 249	1 131	585	6 118	7 224	4 518	367	4 151	102 915	25.1	40.9
Grants Pass	15 936	2.26	10.8	35.2	1 051	627	355	424	2 163	6 146	372	5 774	25 695	47.1	12.4
Gresham	40 733	2.67	14.8	25.2	1 514	553	491	961	5 710	5 178	498	4 680	74 664	43.3	21.2
Hillsboro	37 588	2.68	7.7	25.6	1 528	989	220	539	2 391	2 424	189	2 236	69 370	27.1	40.0
Keizer	13 009	2.88	11.2	25.7	364	190	190	174	867	2 331	175	2 157	24 386	36.6	23.8
Lake Oswego	16 874	2.33	9.3	32.4	222	187	148	35	535	1 414	50	1 364	27 961	9.6	67.2
McMinnville	12 743	2.53	14.1	28.2	1 716	396	183	1 320	981	2 940	165	2 775	21 887	45.0	19.2
Medford	29 396	2.65	12.5	27.3	1 553	691	450	862	5 546	7 078	482	6 596	54 873	43.0	20.9
Oregon City	12 867	2.72	9.6	19.8	650	555	157	95	844	2 404	85	2 318	25 120	36.2	26.6
Portland	253 820	2.43	9.4	34.4	17 754	4 821	2 160	12 933	35 140	5 708	473	5 235	462 743	23.7	48.6

1. No spouse present.   2. Data for serious crimes have not been adjusted for underreporting. This may affect comparability between geographic areas and over time.   3. Per 100,000 population estimated by the FBI.   4. Persons 25 years old and over.

City	Median income	Percent with income of $200,000 or more	Percent with income of less than $25,000	Total Families	Percent with income below poverty	Total	Percent change, 2000–2010	Vacant units for sale or rent[2]	Total	Percent	Median value[3] (dollars)	Percent	Median rent (dollars)
		Money income, 2015				Housing units, 2010			Occupied housing units 2015				
		Households		Families					Owner-occupied			Renter-occupied	
	42	43	44	45	46	47	48	49	50	51	52	53	54
OHIO—Cont'd													
Hamilton	44 424	1.1	22.7	14 449	15.2	27 878	7.5	3 220	23 604	55.2	100 900	44.8	750
Hilliard	85 685	13.5	11.0	9 043	6.8	10 637	19.6	439	13 215	71.5	232 000	28.5	946
Huber Heights	56 363	0.3	8.8	11 080	13.1	15 875	6.2	1 155	14 900	69.9	104 800	30.1	876
Kent	34 509	1.4	37.6	NA	NA	11 174	6.8	886	11 100	39.6	142 900	60.4	818
Kettering	52 979	2.9	17.8	14 178	8.1	27 602	2.5	2 175	24 833	63.5	124 800	36.5	741
Lakewood	45 836	3.8	22.9	11 156	14.1	28 498	0.3	3 224	24 109	43.1	137 500	56.9	707
Lancaster	41 211	0.0	23.2	9 904	18.0	17 685	11.6	1 637	15 103	49.1	124 700	50.9	756
Lima	37 178	0.2	29.6	8 195	20.1	16 784	-5.0	2 563	14 533	46.6	66 800	53.4	600
Lorain	35 447	0.3	28.9	15 922	20.6	29 144	3.3	3 615	24 989	55.0	82 000	45.0	643
Mansfield	36 548	1.4	24.2	9 224	13.0	22 022	-1.4	3 326	16 819	51.1	76 100	48.9	626
Marion	32 762	1.6	27.5	7 697	15.8	15 066	2.3	2 198	13 024	50.9	70 400	49.1	656
Mason	110 008	15.8	4.0	NA	NA	11 471	41.1	455	12 142	81.7	239 400	18.3	1 180
Massillon	41 577	1.4	21.0	8 051	14.3	14 497	7.1	1 357	12 908	65.0	97 400	35.0	725
Medina	65 944	2.1	12.3	6 970	10.8	11 152	13.9	770	9 806	66.6	167 400	33.4	695
Mentor	71 627	3.1	6.2	NA	NA	20 218	4.8	1 052	19 402	85.6	165 900	14.4	1 012
Middletown	37 241	0.6	28.7	12 023	24.3	23 296	0.5	3 058	19 887	46.9	91 900	53.1	707
Newark	36 741	1.6	26.5	11 499	20.0	21 976	6.3	2 136	19 459	52.8	115 100	47.2	748
North Olmsted	57 259	2.3	15.9	8 433	7.8	14 500	3.1	855	13 012	71.9	145 100	28.1	791
North Ridgeville	62 865	4.9	7.5	8 571	1.8	12 109	41.0	609	13 396	86.3	170 600	13.7	840
North Royalton	57 363	5.9	14.8	7 737	7.1	13 710	16.6	766	13 200	76.6	191 400	23.4	870
Parma	52 093	1.4	13.2	21 501	8.5	36 608	0.5	2 119	32 577	72.1	110 400	27.9	783
Reynoldsburg	51 864	1.4	24.0	9 385	15.1	15 611	15.9	1 224	14 810	56.1	131 800	43.9	842
Riverside	47 447	1.7	15.9	6 486	16.0	11 304	8.8	1 020	10 508	55.6	92 100	44.4	766
Sandusky	33 150	0.6	28.4	5 995	25.8	13 386	0.4	2 304	10 483	45.4	80 700	54.6	685
Shaker Heights	83 938	17.9	11.7	7 139	5.4	13 318	2.5	1 478	10 710	67.3	192 600	32.7	993
Springfield	34 668	1.5	27.4	13 812	15.2	28 437	-2.9	3 978	25 225	48.0	74 000	52.0	684
Stow	62 983	3.5	10.7	NA	NA	15 141	17.8	915	14 840	64.8	171 800	35.2	893
Strongsville	80 181	8.7	7.2	12 153	2.1	18 476	9.6	817	17 634	80.9	189 400	19.1	950
Toledo	35 289	1.3	29.6	64 020	21.3	138 039	-1.3	18 309	119 100	51.5	78 400	48.5	679
Troy	40 427	3.0	21.4	5 620	11.2	11 166	17.1	813	10 117	53.0	152 400	47.0	750
Upper Arlington	116 235	22.2	3.1	9 580	0.8	14 544	0.8	790	13 275	81.4	350 500	18.6	1 191
Warren	33 143	1.3	32.6	8 914	27.8	20 384	-4.5	3 381	16 850	51.3	56 700	48.7	604
Westerville	86 582	6.2	10.9	10 140	3.8	14 467	10.1	608	14 400	74.5	219 600	25.5	1 112
Westlake	76 690	11.8	11.5	8 155	3.0	14 843	8.4	973	13 418	74.1	256 500	25.9	1 096
Wooster	42 276	2.5	23.4	5 919	14.1	11 822	10.0	1 089	10 864	56.5	135 200	43.5	646
Xenia	37 121	1.5	25.4	6 513	18.9	11 424	15.4	1 034	10 752	62.3	94 400	37.7	667
Youngstown	23 984	0.5	40.7	14 152	32.5	33 123	-10.9	6 284	27 542	51.5	42 600	48.5	609
Zanesville	27 531	0.3	39.7	5 765	27.5	12 385	5.4	1 521	10 776	35.8	80 400	64.2	628
OKLAHOMA	48 568	3.5	19.3	969 588	11.7	1 664 378	9.9	203 928	1 465 951	65.3	126 800	34.7	759
Bartlesville	50 550	3.5	16.3	9 996	10.3	16 768	4.1	1 791	15 035	65.9	116 500	34.1	779
Broken Arrow	70 242	5.4	9.0	29 534	6.5	38 013	40.2	1 872	38 613	72.5	162 300	27.5	987
Edmond	73 885	10.0	11.0	23 437	5.8	33 178	25.8	1 703	32 982	66.4	232 500	33.6	937
Enid	47 348	2.8	15.3	13 847	10.0	21 936	3.2	2 210	19 651	66.9	103 800	33.1	848
Lawton	42 635	1.1	20.9	19 835	12.4	39 409	8.2	4 508	32 083	42.8	112 200	57.2	784
Midwest City	45 073	0.7	19.1	13 519	15.6	24 723	3.9	1 997	22 156	58.5	96 400	41.5	822
Moore	55 671	1.3	13.1	14 654	8.3	21 444	34.8	998	22 105	69.4	129 100	30.6	922
Muskogee	34 431	2.1	31.4	8 715	21.6	18 055	2.8	2 351	14 794	58.5	89 200	41.5	681
Norman	54 159	5.2	16.3	26 994	10.7	47 965	15.5	3 304	45 369	53.6	180 000	46.4	848
Oklahoma City	50 739	4.3	17.7	148 537	12.5	256 930	12.6	26 697	239 137	58.2	148 500	41.8	814
Owasso	70 330	2.4	9.8	9 285	6.1	11 346	64.9	657	13 020	72.5	164 300	27.5	937
Ponca City	43 601	3.0	22.0	6 004	12.8	11 950	0.5	1 555	10 217	59.8	90 200	40.2	658
Shawnee	36 825	2.6	26.2	7 558	13.7	13 205	4.0	1 586	12 044	57.9	91 100	42.1	647
Stillwater	28 382	2.4	36.0	8 064	14.8	19 753	17.5	1 812	18 608	32.7	173 900	67.3	775
Tulsa	43 322	5.3	22.1	97 429	16.6	185 127	3.1	21 152	167 400	50.8	133 700	49.2	768
OREGON	54 148	4.7	16.7	978 396	9.9	1 675 562	15.3	156 624	1 553 205	61.1	264 100	38.9	943
Albany	49 301	2.4	15.4	13 679	10.9	20 979	20.6	1 274	21 537	52.4	184 100	47.6	816
Beaverton	56 564	5.5	15.3	21 736	8.7	39 500	21.5	2 287	38 899	48.2	333 000	51.8	1 080
Bend	52 905	7.3	13.9	22 763	10.5	36 110	60.5	4 320	36 083	58.4	331 300	41.6	986
Corvallis	48 401	4.8	25.4	10 681	9.3	23 423	12.1	1 140	22 557	41.9	266 400	58.1	890
Eugene	45 927	3.9	26.3	34 825	9.8	69 951	14.1	3 532	67 091	46.8	262 600	53.2	920
Grants Pass	41 238	1.8	26.1	9 304	14.7	15 561	57.8	1 248	15 936	51.9	191 900	48.1	867
Gresham	46 457	1.6	17.6	27 110	12.1	41 015	16.2	2 311	40 733	53.1	236 000	46.9	949
Hillsboro	72 242	5.1	9.4	24 996	7.2	35 487	30.5	2 198	37 588	51.0	276 600	49.0	1 256
Keizer	63 657	3.3	15.2	9 137	8.7	14 445	13.1	742	13 009	61.9	215 700	38.1	901
Lake Oswego	87 924	18.5	6.7	NA	NA	16 995	8.5	1 102	16 874	70.3	530 400	29.7	1 353
McMinnville	42 332	2.7	18.2	8 150	11.1	12 389	26.0	715	12 743	67.1	192 100	32.9	843
Medford	40 806	1.2	22.8	18 218	16.3	32 430	23.3	2 351	29 396	46.6	232 400	53.4	870
Oregon City	70 104	1.8	8.6	9 093	4.1	12 900	26.9	927	12 867	63.6	303 300	36.4	1 076
Portland	60 892	7.1	16.6	129 024	9.0	265 439	11.9	16 893	253 820	54.0	348 300	46.0	1 047

1. Based on population estimated by the American Community Survey.   2. Includes units rented or sold but not occupied.   3. Specified owner-occupied units; $1,000,000 represents $1,000,000 or more   4. 50.0 represents 50 percent or more.   5. 10.0 represents 10 percent or less.

Table D. Cities — Commuting, Computer Access, Migration, Labor Force, and Employment

City	Commuting Percent — Drove alone	Commuting Percent — With Commutes of 30 minutes or more[1]	Computer Access[2] Percent — With a Computer in the house	Computer Access[2] Percent — With Internet Access	Migration, 2015 — Percent who lived in the same house one year ago	Migration, 2015 — Percent who lived in an other state or county one year ago	Civilian labor force, 2016 — Total	Civilian labor force, 2016 — Percent change, 2015–2016	Unemployment — Total	Unemployment — Rate[3]	Population age 16 and older — Number	Population age 16 and older — Percent in Labor Force	Population age 16 to 64 — Number	Population age 16 to 64 — Percent who worked full-year full-time
	55	56	57	58	59	60	61	62	63	64	65	66	67	68
OHIO—Cont'd														
Hamilton	82.7	33.9	83.7	73.7	82.0	6.3	27 843	0.8	1 371	4.9	46 460	62.4	39 533	47.8
Hilliard	92.5	30.9	93.6	90.5	NA	NA	18 278	1.4	620	3.4	25 847	72.3	22 125	61.1
Huber Heights	90.5	18.5	89.5	80.8	86.8	6.1	18 075	0.3	871	4.8	30 043	64.4	23 253	51.0
Kent	70.7	19.7	96.0	80.6	75.2	16.2	16 669	0.1	786	4.7	25 619	57.1	22 755	25.0
Kettering	90.9	21.0	87.3	80.5	83.7	7.7	28 937	0.4	1 197	4.1	44 054	63.6	33 352	53.5
Lakewood	82.8	31.7	87.3	79.6	81.5	5.0	29 870	0.2	1 259	4.2	42 447	70.4	36 468	54.4
Lancaster	86.4	40.5	82.4	72.2	82.9	4.0	17 939	1.4	857	4.8	30 153	59.8	23 673	46.6
Lima	85.3	16.5	77.9	64.8	74.7	9.4	14 694	0.4	897	6.1	28 960	60.8	24 713	44.4
Lorain	80.3	26.3	79.6	61.2	78.2	4.1	27 370	0.6	2 136	7.8	47 908	61.4	39 774	42.6
Mansfield	81.7	20.4	80.7	69.7	79.5	8.8	17 750	-0.3	1 101	6.2	37 694	48.7	30 875	35.6
Marion	79.5	19.4	75.4	63.6	75.3	11.7	13 575	-0.5	774	5.7	30 285	45.6	24 707	31.8
Mason	86.8	35.8	90.5	88.6	89.5	5.4	16 637	1.1	646	3.9	26 046	65.4	21 001	53.0
Massillon	82.9	19.8	86.9	82.4	88.0	3.5	15 168	-0.5	886	5.8	25 963	62.3	20 244	46.4
Medina	86.4	41.6	87.3	80.3	86.1	8.4	13 212	0.5	598	4.5	20 026	70.8	16 679	55.3
Mentor	89.7	29.6	94.6	85.8	93.0	3.6	26 273	0.6	1 181	4.5	39 496	69.2	30 580	63.3
Middletown	85.5	36.7	81.4	66.3	74.9	7.5	20 760	0.7	1 140	5.5	37 182	58.8	30 424	42.1
Newark	84.2	26.4	85.0	72.4	78.2	5.8	23 294	1.2	1 064	4.6	37 586	62.5	30 569	46.2
North Olmsted	89.2	40.2	87.3	80.5	87.8	2.2	17 365	0.1	761	4.4	26 704	61.2	20 096	49.9
North Ridgeville	91.3	37.6	91.4	89.6	89.4	5.9	17 280	0.6	813	4.7	26 415	64.2	19 313	60.6
North Royalton	93.2	42.2	84.2	74.8	79.8	5.0	17 347	0.1	758	4.4	24 285	65.8	18 204	56.0
Parma	87.4	37.1	87.5	79.5	85.2	4.0	42 170	0.3	2 175	5.2	67 531	67.8	54 030	52.0
Reynoldsburg	82.4	34.0	88.8	83.3	75.1	9.1	20 520	1.4	833	4.1	28 932	62.8	24 050	50.5
Riverside	91.2	19.8	88.9	82.1	86.0	7.6	10 687	0.0	563	5.3	18 559	68.3	14 874	53.9
Sandusky	87.1	14.9	88.1	78.6	75.3	4.2	11 699	-0.3	704	6.0	19 356	64.2	16 020	44.9
Shaker Heights	85.0	27.7	93.0	85.2	83.9	4.8	14 148	0.2	620	4.4	20 877	68.6	17 552	52.3
Springfield	80.7	22.2	82.3	70.8	68.0	8.3	25 347	-0.8	1 492	5.9	47 941	59.4	36 721	43.4
Stow	95.2	29.7	92.1	86.1	90.5	4.9	18 601	-0.1	802	4.3	28 838	67.6	23 017	60.3
Strongsville	89.9	42.7	89.9	84.8	86.5	4.6	24 213	0.2	1 047	4.3	36 942	62.3	27 259	54.6
Toledo	84.3	20.3	83.5	66.5	76.9	6.5	129 371	0.9	7 231	5.6	224 366	61.9	184 677	43.4
Troy	88.4	26.4	87.2	80.7	78.8	4.1	13 514	0.5	568	4.2	19 487	66.6	16 139	48.7
Upper Arlington	85.2	15.3	96.2	93.3	90.4	2.5	18 201	1.4	599	3.3	26 405	67.5	21 127	59.2
Warren	90.6	19.5	76.9	61.5	86.0	5.0	14 422	-0.9	1 115	7.7	32 170	52.0	25 864	36.1
Westerville	90.2	28.3	89.5	85.5	80.9	8.4	21 460	1.5	783	3.6	31 258	67.4	24 299	59.2
Westlake	88.4	37.4	93.3	86.1	92.6	4.8	16 984	0.2	705	4.2	26 060	61.5	18 752	55.0
Wooster	78.5	14.9	82.2	74.6	76.9	6.9	13 864	1.2	542	3.9	22 044	58.9	16 710	41.0
Xenia	84.9	31.2	85.2	71.0	84.8	4.0	11 141	0.7	590	5.3	20 235	63.8	16 515	45.5
Youngstown	83.1	15.6	75.0	56.0	81.7	5.7	22 807	-1.1	1 791	7.9	51 047	54.3	39 668	35.6
Zanesville	81.5	25.2	77.9	67.4	69.0	8.7	9 796	1.7	645	6.6	19 671	54.6	15 602	35.1
OKLAHOMA	85.7	26.3	83.9	70.7	82.9	7.7	1 828 415	-0.3	89 053	4.9	3 053 371	61.3	2 477 340	50.4
Bartlesville	85.9	12.5	83.1	72.0	77.7	8.6	16 905	-2.5	749	4.4	28 583	58.7	21 497	53.0
Broken Arrow	91.1	21.8	93.7	87.3	83.4	7.4	55 943	-0.1	2 105	3.8	81 538	72.4	67 932	57.8
Edmond	88.4	29.8	95.3	88.5	82.8	8.2	46 611	0.1	1 505	3.2	69 266	68.7	58 266	52.4
Enid	87.0	11.6	85.0	74.4	82.3	5.7	23 708	-0.6	1 030	4.3	38 675	64.6	30 757	55.0
Lawton	77.4	4.9	83.4	73.6	66.5	18.6	37 037	-0.4	1 718	4.6	75 306	69.1	65 963	50.1
Midwest City	87.5	25.3	83.1	71.3	79.2	9.5	26 571	0.2	1 243	4.7	43 529	59.6	34 982	51.3
Moore	89.0	26.4	91.4	86.1	82.6	11.1	30 627	0.1	1 147	3.7	46 552	71.6	39 737	57.5
Muskogee	79.3	12.9	77.3	61.0	75.9	10.3	16 445	-0.6	799	4.9	29 343	52.6	23 849	40.9
Norman	85.4	31.2	92.7	82.9	73.5	13.7	60 977	0.1	2 133	3.5	99 276	65.6	86 099	46.5
Oklahoma City	84.7	22.2	86.4	74.3	80.2	8.2	310 767	0.1	12 391	4.0	481 395	66.4	405 623	52.9
Owasso	86.7	28.7	94.7	90.3	77.2	14.5	17 994	-0.3	643	3.6	27 182	73.0	23 533	60.9
Ponca City	87.5	13.3	80.7	61.4	76.0	11.2	10 369	-1.2	645	6.2	20 290	61.6	16 020	45.2
Shawnee	78.0	19.9	78.4	55.5	77.6	11.7	14 511	-0.1	599	4.1	24 676	57.7	19 231	44.6
Stillwater	79.5	13.3	90.3	77.4	64.5	20.5	24 055	0.3	789	3.3	42 366	55.5	38 608	32.6
Tulsa	82.8	15.2	85.4	73.8	79.9	6.5	196 794	-0.1	8 943	4.5	314 313	65.9	259 698	52.3
OREGON	76.0	31.4	90.7	81.2	82.2	7.7	2 055 114	3.9	100 293	4.9	3 268 296	61.8	2 608 518	45.2
Albany	79.8	28.0	90.8	80.9	76.4	8.5	25 195	3.6	1 344	5.3	42 705	61.9	34 597	43.7
Beaverton	71.6	41.5	94.4	87.3	78.0	11.4	54 906	4.3	2 168	3.9	78 416	69.4	67 813	49.4
Bend	85.9	7.3	95.6	87.5	78.2	8.8	48 364	6.2	1 822	3.8	69 031	67.1	55 556	48.8
Corvallis	64.9	8.2	93.4	84.5	64.6	18.1	30 048	3.3	1 179	3.9	48 356	61.0	41 875	33.8
Eugene	67.5	13.6	92.0	80.2	72.4	11.2	83 266	4.1	3 976	4.8	137 345	60.8	113 004	37.1
Grants Pass	84.2	21.9	85.4	77.1	86.3	4.7	15 461	3.8	907	5.9	29 799	55.1	21 722	46.9
Gresham	74.3	49.1	90.8	77.7	88.4	4.0	55 397	3.6	2 550	4.6	87 167	66.6	72 197	46.0
Hillsboro	75.6	33.3	95.7	79.8	82.4	8.1	55 831	4.1	2 214	4.0	79 687	67.6	68 163	52.6
Keizer	77.7	29.8	91.9	85.7	76.5	8.6	19 193	4.0	931	4.9	27 685	62.8	21 614	52.3
Lake Oswego	81.2	37.4	94.3	88.9	83.1	9.5	20 711	4.3	824	4.0	32 595	64.4	25 851	53.0
McMinnville	72.8	27.2	93.7	82.0	76.3	10.9	16 649	4.3	800	4.8	26 784	61.2	21 139	45.9
Medford	82.0	11.5	89.3	78.3	77.3	5.9	38 996	3.9	2 086	5.3	63 365	58.8	50 135	42.5
Oregon City	88.4	48.1	95.4	90.9	79.0	6.6	18 667	3.6	850	4.6	28 376	69.7	23 092	54.6
Portland	61.6	37.5	91.8	82.9	80.5	8.4	366 517	4.0	15 313	4.2	526 781	69.6	451 999	48.3

1. Employed persons. 2. Households. 3. Percent of civilian labor force. 4. Persons 16 years old and over.

Table D. Cities — Construction, Wholesale Trade, and Retail Trade

City	Value of residential construction authorized by building permits, 2016			Wholesale trade,[1] 2012				Retail trade,[2] 2012			
	New construction ($1,000)	Number of housing units	Percent single family	Number of establishments	Number of employees	Sales (mil dol)	Annual payroll (mil dol)	Number of establishments	Number of employees	Sales (mil dol)	Annual payroll (mil dol)
	69	70	71	72	73	74	75	76	77	78	79
OHIO—Cont'd											
Hamilton	4 949	30	100.0	43	800	635.4	43.1	213	3 262	733.6	69.0
Hilliard	28 379	268	26.9	51	700	448.5	36.9	85	1 405	382.8	40.2
Huber Heights	NA	NA	NA	20	394	270.8	20.8	98	2 020	476.1	41.0
Kent	1 777	9	55.6	13	D	D	D	78	1 344	404.7	34.2
Kettering	2 516	13	84.6	26	D	D	D	158	3 328	803.7	80.7
Lakewood	4 064	23	100.0	22	D	D	D	110	1 149	255.6	26.5
Lancaster	15 061	112	41.1	27	368	75.2	14.9	235	3 240	641.9	66.5
Lima	335	7	14.3	49	663	431.3	30.2	125	1 634	463.2	39.7
Lorain	13 601	160	50.6	27	786	333.4	26.3	121	1 836	361.1	39.0
Mansfield	2 215	14	14.3	56	1 001	369.2	44.1	185	2 073	465.0	50.1
Marion	74	3	100.0	18	286	403.2	12.9	112	1 762	446.2	42.3
Mason	36 385	144	100.0	51	1 783	1 023.7	132.9	105	1 864	428.8	46.5
Massillon	9 793	109	42.2	29	419	241.8	21.5	119	2 488	617.7	55.3
Medina	1 017	4	100.0	50	526	371.0	23.6	111	1 813	384.7	33.8
Mentor	27 092	129	100.0	97	944	439.1	43.2	303	5 884	1 498.9	130.9
Middletown	6 131	43	76.7	33	D	D	D	153	3 372	1 461.3	86.1
Newark	NA	NA	NA	34	514	459.8	22.8	145	1 825	498.5	41.2
North Olmsted	782	3	100.0	22	166	188.0	13.3	250	4 827	1 176.4	114.5
North Ridgeville	39 325	201	96.0	30	442	254.5	18.4	58	647	169.3	14.5
North Royalton	14 679	55	100.0	52	478	357.7	33.4	63	484	112.9	13.8
Parma	163	1	100.0	44	851	314.7	32.4	270	3 793	913.3	76.8
Reynoldsburg	6 602	62	14.5	8	D	D	D	119	2 127	1 053.8	79.5
Riverside	NA	NA	NA	9	D	D	D	57	516	144.4	11.9
Sandusky	2 234	5	100.0	31	380	220.9	16.7	101	1 277	330.6	28.8
Shaker Heights	0	0	0.0	10	20	7.1	0.9	47	494	109.2	11.9
Springfield	2 670	11	100.0	50	1 628	2 331.3	82.1	221	3 643	1 118.8	88.4
Stow	11 212	53	100.0	47	590	462.9	34.7	102	2 184	514.7	44.8
Strongsville	32 359	99	100.0	70	1 636	877.5	91.3	240	13 004	2 837.1	282.7
Toledo	2 090	20	75.0	249	3 832	2 592.8	188.6	935	13 004	2 837.1	282.7
Troy	NA	NA	NA	18	253	388.6	11.2	79	1 695	411.5	39.9
Upper Arlington	27 359	30	100.0	14	D	D	D	85	891	192.1	19.3
Warren	0	0	0.0	28	712	772.8	36.5	155	1 907	605.4	48.8
Westerville	43 167	205	53.2	52	494	190.6	21.8	108	1 683	454.8	41.0
Westlake	19 554	44	100.0	82	1 308	830.6	74.6	161	2 377	540.9	50.0
Wooster	6 390	26	84.6	36	476	552.5	19.5	165	2 606	597.9	55.4
Xenia	NA	NA	NA	14	263	285.6	12.0	79	1 259	331.7	32.5
Youngstown	NA	NA	NA	89	1 488	734.0	70.3	219	2 454	473.8	48.8
Zanesville	620	3	100.0	24	251	96.6	8.8	210	3 093	751.9	64.3
OKLAHOMA	2 155 011	12 092	75.8	3 909	50 660	71 892.9	2 718.6	13 051	168 839	50 256.2	4 055.1
Bartlesville	7 761	28	92.9	21	D	D	D	161	D	D	103.9
Broken Arrow	101 450	448	100.0	125	1 347	691.5	71.5	253	4 115	1 357.3	107.5
Edmond	138 538	400	98.5	96	D	D	D	327	4 505	1 154.8	81.6
Enid	12 191	62	100.0	58	690	1 312.1	33.5	251	3 289	894.8	112.7
Lawton	9 548	45	95.6	49	378	119.1	12.1	352	4 956	1 340.6	111.1
Midwest City	17 606	111	100.0	19	D	D	D	176	4 097	1 280.7	111.1
Moore	57 372	515	43.5	33	D	D	D	147	2 442	638.3	53.5
Muskogee	2 345	11	100.0	45	806	353.8	38.1	215	2 855	806.8	68.8
Norman	184 718	1 386	26.2	59	746	476.1	39.7	419	7 006	2 124.7	174.3
Oklahoma City	613 357	3 190	90.9	1 025	17 349	43 266.0	1 022.8	2 186	31 326	10 272.1	844.2
Owasso	43 161	190	100.0	15	D	D	D	115	2 434	618.1	50.9
Ponca City	0	0	0.0	23	157	74.9	5.5	126	1 576	431.5	37.3
Shawnee	12 150	83	75.9	29	D	D	D	191	2 675	676.9	59.0
Stillwater	49 628	355	35.5	22	158	163.5	7.5	202	3 157	739.2	66.5
Tulsa	126 544	850	51.3	770	11 810	11 596.9	716.4	1 708	26 411	7 542.2	665.1
OREGON	21 921	148	100.0	4 393	59 523	48 325.3	3 233.0	13 879	187 402	49 481.1	4 831.5
Albany	26 549	107	100.0	39	369	307.0	16.1	187	2 812	741.1	70.0
Beaverton	28 093	204	17.2	185	2 640	2 230.6	185.4	391	7 600	2 759.6	241.8
Bend	283 690	1 471	68.9	136	908	621.5	43.0	503	6 406	1 741.9	171.3
Corvallis	29 192	138	69.6	26	D	D	D	212	3 138	676.7	75.6
Eugene	119 981	747	43.4	241	3 013	1 585.8	151.3	726	10 971	2 487.2	271.9
Grants Pass	34 908	129	96.9	25	307	270.2	13.0	241	3 637	872.6	94.9
Gresham	32 960	134	82.1	55	1 615	854.4	73.4	270	3 677	1 087.3	95.5
Hillsboro	165 764	930	34.4	99	1 315	1 047.6	79.5	303	5 624	1 666.9	151.8
Keizer	16 049	67	82.1	11	25	18.9	1.4	83	1 213	255.2	24.0
Lake Oswego	77 283	294	32.0	94	1 457	781.5	136.0	126	D	D	D
McMinnville	27 217	144	57.6	20	111	68.0	5.4	144	2 005	510.0	49.7
Medford	95 196	440	77.0	112	1 139	543.6	46.9	479	7 401	1 965.9	194.4
Oregon City	47 133	151	100.0	14	163	69.3	8.4	98	1 607	448.7	39.4
Portland	708 942	4 929	16.9	1 139	20 024	20 321.0	1 195.1	2 527	32 426	8 508.3	886.3

1. Merchant wholesalers except manufacturers' sales branches and offices. 2. Establishments with payroll.

Table D. Cities — **Real Estate, Professional Services, and Manufacturing**

City	Real estate and rental and leasing, 2012				Professional, scientific, and technical services,[1] 2012				Manufacturing, 2012			
	Number of establish-ments	Number of employees	Receipts (mil dol)	Annual payroll (mil dol)	Number of establish-ments	Number of employees	Receipts (mil dol)	Annual payroll (mil dol)	Number of establish-ments	Number of employees	Receipts (mil dol)	Annual payroll (mil dol)
	80	81	82	83	84	85	86	87	88	89	90	91
OHIO—Cont'd												
Hamilton	31	165	34.3	5.3	96	D	D	D	69	1 827	509.6	115.7
Hilliard	39	256	40.3	9.1	85	778	123.9	56.4	28	1 506	436.3	73.5
Huber Heights	25	124	26.4	4.4	32	495	53.8	19.5	31	2 494	1 089.2	237.9
Kent	22	93	11.3	2.9	44	D	D	D	59	1 435	369.6	65.5
Kettering	57	197	60.6	6.9	110	D	D	D	45	1 601	D	73.3
Lakewood	58	322	63.1	12.5	116	388	49.3	20.4	33	587	204.9	30.5
Lancaster	54	215	27.1	4.3	70	D	D	D	45	2 844	864.5	145.2
Lima	29	186	18.9	5.7	73	D	D	D	37	1 724	D	123.5
Lorain	36	118	18.8	3.4	51	D	D	D	40	2 533	D	169.7
Mansfield	58	295	31.0	5.8	117	668	73.7	27.1	96	5 359	2 170.7	257.6
Marion	25	93	14.2	2.1	41	D	D	D	31	2 001	1 291.7	90.7
Mason	30	86	21.6	2.7	110	587	89.7	32.2	32	3 399	1 492.0	197.9
Massillon	24	88	19.8	3.6	44	236	21.2	8.8	60	5 519	1 962.7	218.7
Medina	30	110	24.7	4.1	109	531	55.5	23.3	61	3 036	1 320.6	144.5
Mentor	49	163	47.0	5.1	169	899	118.2	45.6	213	8 675	2 501.6	449.4
Middletown	53	219	40.4	5.9	63	579	51.3	23.3	53	4 040	D	250.4
Newark	42	158	22.9	4.0	82	D	D	D	41	2 302	688.0	103.5
North Olmsted	36	156	28.8	6.1	68	2 306	60.4	33.2	16	208	44.8	8.0
North Ridgeville	12	46	5.2	0.8	43	240	22.5	9.7	42	1 305	318.8	57.3
North Royalton	26	141	38.7	10.6	93	308	44.0	14.6	73	779	113.7	37.3
Parma	57	314	47.8	9.6	91	638	78.4	22.3	32	1 923	692.1	132.2
Reynoldsburg	39	185	42.9	6.5	74	464	40.2	15.9	15	243	D	12.1
Riverside	16	82	23.1	2.5	37	D	D	D	5	90	D	3.1
Sandusky	35	135	19.9	4.1	56	D	D	D	41	1 644	424.9	85.1
Shaker Heights	36	D	D	D	94	D	D	D	NA	NA	NA	NA
Springfield	58	324	35.3	9.3	101	D	D	D	79	2 767	793.4	127.3
Stow	38	169	31.6	4.4	100	864	96.2	42.2	47	1 336	230.6	74.1
Strongsville	53	439	89.0	16.3	121	402	51.7	17.6	72	2 434	685.3	137.3
Toledo	237	1 823	2 219.2	127.8	448	D	D	D	295	11 821	11 102.3	734.4
Troy	21	105	18.5	3.6	59	411	50.8	19.5	49	5 461	2 360.9	285.1
Upper Arlington	42	D	D	D	117	D	D	D	11	61	D	1.5
Warren	32	175	18.6	3.6	97	D	D	D	45	5 428	1 836.3	422.8
Westerville	54	D	D	D	206	2 231	328.1	141.2	34	1 218	354.1	56.2
Westlake	64	258	70.7	11.4	230	1 534	375.8	109.8	49	1 200	295.1	58.0
Wooster	31	107	22.8	3.7	76	746	91.7	33.1	36	3 603	1 406.3	188.9
Xenia	16	43	6.4	1.7	29	118	8.2	2.6	27	493	100.1	27.1
Youngstown	54	357	37.7	7.2	115	D	D	D	90	3 310	719.4	182.1
Zanesville	29	170	24.2	5.0	68	D	D	D	28	D	430.8	46.6
OKLAHOMA	4 000	21 261	4 269.6	898.0	9 428	71 303	10 915.0	4 080.1	3 610	133 064	74 295.4	6 416.0
Bartlesville	39	D	D	D	79	D	D	D	25	D	200.7	D
Broken Arrow	92	227	34.8	7.2	228	1 457	241.0	105.0	132	5 570	1 953.3	332.2
Edmond	181	642	256.3	35.0	430	2 414	312.1	106.9	38	410	78.6	15.7
Enid	72	312	50.1	10.7	107	563	78.8	27.9	50	2 172	D	78.6
Lawton	118	D	D	D	128	D	D	D	39	3 367	D	178.3
Midwest City	74	374	80.1	10.3	93	D	D	D	12	280	83.8	12.8
Moore	47	172	39.0	8.1	64	412	28.4	12.7	25	808	191.2	25.9
Muskogee	48	196	26.7	5.5	75	D	D	D	46	3 200	1 371.0	157.9
Norman	210	975	134.7	35.4	451	D	D	D	69	2 255	1 077.8	101.1
Oklahoma City	893	5 794	1 255.5	266.3	2 357	D	D	D	645	21 675	8 249.8	979.6
Owasso	40	125	20.4	4.6	83	452	38.5	13.8	23	633	D	26.1
Ponca City	27	97	18.0	3.1	67	377	43.2	17.4	34	1 373	488.9	60.8
Shawnee	33	139	21.6	3.8	83	D	D	D	30	2 564	1 032.2	118.3
Stillwater	66	263	46.1	7.3	101	D	D	D	28	946	343.2	37.1
Tulsa	715	5 522	899.2	224.1	1 871	16 400	3 016.5	1 025.7	629	22 012	11 517.9	1 180.7
OREGON	5 644	26 016	4 649.6	902.8	11 564	82 456	11 167.3	5 723.4	5 289	D	D	D
Albany	58	203	31.8	6.6	99	D	D	D	61	D	528.4	D
Beaverton	208	904	162.5	30.0	450	D	D	D	115	6 475	2 817.0	442.4
Bend	257	701	116.7	24.4	500	D	D	D	162	2 444	524.2	117.1
Corvallis	86	D	D	D	208	D	D	D	47	974	235.3	43.4
Eugene	286	1 256	197.0	36.9	673	D	D	D	263	5 512	1 384.9	254.1
Grants Pass	72	248	35.1	6.7	89	D	D	D	68	1 632	318.2	66.0
Gresham	119	445	65.2	11.1	128	D	D	D	73	4 848	1 275.2	291.1
Hillsboro	116	914	467.6	34.3	216	D	D	D	149	D	D	D
Keizer	36	218	22.4	4.3	43	207	22.7	7.9	7	46	6.2	1.5
Lake Oswego	127	627	148.0	38.3	372	3 174	583.8	237.4	36	674	D	54.2
McMinnville	35	120	15.8	2.6	86	D	D	D	63	1 915	776.4	85.2
Medford	145	642	102.9	17.5	242	D	D	D	91	1 599	380.2	66.1
Oregon City	37	109	23.2	4.1	93	D	D	D	47	586	113.8	28.0
Portland	1 221	8 268	1 479.3	357.0	3 434	29 338	5 410.0	2 066.2	978	26 432	8 768.5	1 300.8

1. Establishments subject to federal tax.

Table D. Cities — Accommodation and Food Services, Arts, Entertainment, and Recreation, and Health Care and Social Assistance

City	Accommodation and food services, 2012				Arts, entertainment, and recreation,[1] 2012				Health care and social assistance,[1] 2012			
	Number of establish-ments	Number of employees	Sales (mil dol)	Annual payroll (mil dol)	Number of establish-ments	Number of employees	Receipts (mil dol)	Annual payroll (mil dol)	Number of establish-ments	Number of employees	Receipts (mil dol)	Annual payroll (mil dol)
	92	93	94	95	96	97	98	99	100	101	102	103
OHIO—Cont'd												
Hamilton	129	2 433	124.0	31.5	6	40	3.8	0.7	111	1 417	122.6	51.6
Hilliard	70	1 572	72.2	20.5	14	224	14.1	4.6	92	D	D	D
Huber Heights	78	1 638	79.2	22.6	6	D	D	D	67	D	D	D
Kent	89	1 426	84.5	18.3	5	D	D	D	38	518	32.6	15.1
Kettering	107	D	D	D	12	413	16.7	6.3	170	D	D	D
Lakewood	115	1 820	86.4	27.6	11	79	4.3	1.0	104	1 259	97.6	40.3
Lancaster	108	2 393	99.5	29.4	10	66	4.6	0.9	146	D	D	D
Lima	77	1 196	63.9	15.8	2	D	D	D	129	2 405	308.3	168.9
Lorain	71	1 107	50.0	12.8	14	104	5.7	1.7	100	1 278	150.0	64.6
Mansfield	111	2 022	86.2	23.9	8	60	2.2	0.5	178	D	D	D
Marion	66	1 259	56.5	14.2	4	D	D	D	108	D	D	D
Mason	98	2 588	129.5	35.3	18	1 038	130.5	32.4	117	1 503	122.9	51.1
Massillon	79	1 175	54.7	14.4	2	D	D	D	70	2 249	205.4	75.4
Medina	59	1 182	50.2	14.5	6	D	D	D	75	D	D	D
Mentor	174	3 813	162.3	46.2	10	D	D	D	155	2 340	211.0	89.2
Middletown	91	2 064	96.7	26.8	6	68	2.6	0.9	117	D	D	D
Newark	97	1 672	72.0	20.0	10	D	D	D	126	3 126	271.2	124.2
North Olmsted	119	2 387	112.3	30.9	7	58	3.3	0.9	72	1 135	77.4	31.0
North Ridgeville	43	611	25.9	6.9	6	64	3.4	1.1	39	521	35.4	13.3
North Royalton	39	398	13.7	3.6	8	D	D	D	59	691	49.7	19.7
Parma	163	2 484	110.1	28.3	11	D	D	D	184	3 232	293.7	139.9
Reynoldsburg	74	D	D	D	7	47	1.9	0.6	104	D	D	D
Riverside	51	D	D	D	3	D	D	D	28	D	D	D
Sandusky	72	865	81.7	13.6	16	D	D	D	58	607	81.9	37.3
Shaker Heights	33	362	19.8	5.2	10	105	6.0	2.1	51	938	50.8	25.1
Springfield	154	3 174	149.7	40.3	12	82	3.9	1.3	188	3 381	255.6	114.1
Stow	86	1 724	78.0	21.0	19	D	D	D	63	1 145	88.2	37.7
Strongsville	122	2 951	127.8	36.6	14	192	30.1	6.8	98	1 391	125.2	54.7
Toledo	632	11 286	485.9	141.1	61	786	167.8	28.9	528	8 914	904.1	446.6
Troy	75	1 906	81.6	23.6	8	D	D	D	74	D	D	D
Upper Arlington	66	1 333	60.8	18.2	6	10	1.0	0.2	70	1 120	86.0	44.6
Warren	89	6 193	301.0	97.1	8	D	D	D	154	D	D	D
Westerville	102	D	D	D	7	D	D	D	222	3 299	342.2	164.6
Westlake	99	2 797	127.0	39.5	10	368	8.6	3.3	236	4 021	374.4	172.0
Wooster	85	1 683	75.0	21.6	5	D	D	D	91	1 529	140.0	69.5
Xenia	50	1 003	42.7	11.1	5	D	D	D	55	485	48.0	17.6
Youngstown	117	D	D	D	9	D	D	D	124	4 127	396.0	180.4
Zanesville	100	2 215	103.0	29.1	7	83	2.8	0.8	117	D	D	D
OKLAHOMA	7 403	143 561	7 121.2	1 908.3	816	22 012	2 526.6	578.2	8 868	128 437	13 382.5	4 996.4
Bartlesville	100	D	D	D	8	D	D	D	119	D	D	D
Broken Arrow	169	D	D	D	25	D	D	D	191	2 529	176.7	71.3
Edmond	202	4 394	197.9	54.0	33	D	D	D	403	3 669	450.9	150.6
Enid	120	2 183	111.9	26.6	11	69	5.8	1.0	172	2 734	250.9	88.2
Lawton	195	4 445	207.1	62.1	17	D	D	D	210	D	D	D
Midwest City	121	2 544	125.1	34.9	11	60	4.2	0.9	188	3 214	418.2	136.1
Moore	105	2 398	117.7	30.2	5	D	D	D	95	D	D	D
Muskogee	106	2 011	88.5	23.5	8	D	D	D	177	D	D	D
Norman	312	7 292	325.2	93.0	41	D	D	D	393	3 976	397.6	155.8
Oklahoma City	1 361	30 537	1 510.0	413.0	141	2 398	459.8	136.5	1 969	31 146	4 098.3	1 466.1
Owasso	76	1 812	82.7	24.2	12	D	D	D	85	D	D	D
Ponca City	54	932	45.7	11.3	3	21	0.7	0.2	81	1 264	109.1	40.3
Shawnee	98	2 180	95.0	25.3	7	D	D	D	99	1 508	120.2	55.9
Stillwater	146	3 143	134.8	36.7	8	D	D	D	98	1 494	114.9	44.2
Tulsa	1 099	D	D	D	114	D	D	D	1 387	22 659	3 105.8	1 205.0
OREGON	10 610	150 482	8 466.8	2 438.5	1 190	16 916	1 176.8	415.8	9 829	105 341	11 016.4	4 533.8
Albany	119	1 905	87.6	24.4	12	D	D	D	98	D	D	D
Beaverton	317	5 077	279.4	81.1	45	564	69.0	13.4	360	3 703	381.2	140.5
Bend	303	4 684	255.1	74.6	44	1 231	47.0	13.8	384	D	D	D
Corvallis	179	2 837	131.5	37.8	14	D	D	D	175	D	D	D
Eugene	526	8 479	417.8	124.4	44	574	25.5	6.4	586	D	D	D
Grants Pass	145	2 089	100.1	29.4	15	D	D	D	178	2 519	235.5	81.6
Gresham	221	3 294	181.5	49.0	21	374	19.7	6.3	284	3 040	247.1	100.5
Hillsboro	237	3 789	222.3	61.7	20	265	13.3	3.5	248	D	D	D
Keizer	56	D	D	D	10	117	5.6	1.9	60	D	D	D
Lake Oswego	113	1 928	111.3	33.3	19	156	10.0	3.4	186	1 643	156.1	60.1
McMinnville	86	1 138	56.6	16.1	6	D	D	D	111	D	D	D
Medford	262	4 049	204.4	59.8	26	355	23.4	5.9	303	D	D	D
Oregon City	79	1 044	55.6	15.6	7	D	D	D	105	D	D	D
Portland	2 522	38 496	2 261.7	671.0	274	3 542	436.5	185.9	1 963	D	D	D

1. Establishments subject to federal tax.

Table D. Cities — Other Services and Government Employment and Payroll

City	Other services[1], 2012				Government employment and payroll, 2012								
					Full-time equivalent employees	March payroll Total (dollars)	Percent of total for:						
	Number of establishments	Number of employees	Receipts (mil dol)	Annual payroll (mil dol)			Administration, judicial, and legal	Police and Corrections	Fire Protection	Highways and transportation	Health and welfare	Natural resources and utilities	Education and libraries
	104	105	106	107	108	109	110	111	112	113	114	115	116
OHIO—Cont'd													
Hamilton	73	417	41.3	11.8	648	3 715 041	12.3	21.8	20.8	4.6	2.2	31.0	0.0
Hilliard	43	287	30.7	9.1	138	630 071	19.0	53.4	0.0	3.8	0.0	18.6	0.0
Huber Heights	50	279	20.4	6.7	178	969 065	15.5	36.2	31.4	11.5	0.0	0.2	0.0
Kent	43	273	18.6	6.8	203	1 021 262	8.2	30.7	21.0	16.4	6.0	15.0	0.0
Kettering	72	623	28.5	9.9	489	2 337 531	21.1	27.0	15.6	13.9	0.8	14.6	0.0
Lakewood	55	417	19.5	6.9	462	2 388 158	12.9	31.2	24.7	3.8	7.9	16.6	0.0
Lancaster	61	400	36.0	11.3	414	1 841 272	17.3	24.9	20.9	5.2	0.7	29.3	0.9
Lima	52	297	19.1	5.3	375	1 604 715	20.6	25.2	20.8	9.0	2.6	21.4	0.0
Lorain	58	401	30.2	8.5	466	2 344 000	9.9	33.0	23.6	4.0	5.6	19.7	4.2
Mansfield	87	577	42.8	13.0	423	1 865 914	20.0	26.6	23.0	4.6	1.3	17.6	0.0
Marion	40	285	18.1	5.7	241	1 067 754	11.2	34.1	23.1	9.9	0.0	17.7	0.0
Mason	38	237	13.8	5.4	266	1 194 447	18.2	24.2	20.0	7.6	0.0	21.7	0.0
Massillon	54	340	31.7	10.7	321	1 362 818	15.6	16.2	16.6	5.0	6.2	34.1	0.0
Medina	63	487	36.1	11.8	221	904 261	23.8	27.5	4.7	5.0	3.8	26.8	0.0
Mentor	120	838	57.7	21.3	500	2 127 362	11.3	29.5	28.5	14.3	5.5	10.9	0.0
Middletown	62	465	41.4	13.1	404	1 752 509	12.7	30.0	25.2	6.7	4.9	15.7	0.0
Newark	56	410	27.1	10.1	384	1 681 225	15.2	30.1	24.2	8.0	3.0	18.9	0.0
North Olmsted	100	676	54.7	16.5	255	1 250 704	8.6	28.1	19.4	3.8	2.7	29.3	0.0
North Ridgeville	46	193	19.3	5.1	199	885 287	13.3	28.1	21.5	10.7	2.1	18.6	0.0
North Royalton	58	292	26.0	8.6	185	949 689	9.7	32.8	24.0	9.0	2.8	17.2	0.0
Parma	129	828	74.7	22.5	468	1 957 354	15.6	32.5	28.4	11.6	3.1	4.2	0.0
Reynoldsburg	41	229	17.2	6.2	136	685 686	14.7	61.7	0.0	5.3	1.2	11.6	0.0
Riverside	18	74	5.3	1.7	85	380 891	12.2	46.1	28.8	12.4	0.0	0.0	0.0
Sandusky	33	122	10.0	3.0	231	1 023 311	17.4	23.9	23.6	4.8	2.8	23.4	0.0
Shaker Heights	18	81	5.9	1.7	356	1 867 638	14.5	30.2	20.9	14.6	4.9	6.2	0.0
Springfield	93	634	55.9	15.3	591	2 580 272	18.3	27.7	26.1	4.8	3.8	16.2	0.0
Stow	59	406	27.2	9.1	268	1 324 714	23.7	25.9	29.3	6.1	0.7	9.3	0.0
Strongsville	74	755	53.2	18.6	365	1 769 488	7.3	33.1	24.7	16.5	5.3	11.6	0.0
Toledo	356	2 384	178.0	57.2	2 146	10 282 276	15.9	23.9	36.8	7.3	1.5	13.8	0.0
Troy	48	279	18.0	5.7	184	972 285	13.3	25.7	22.4	11.8	1.3	24.4	0.0
Upper Arlington	29	239	15.7	5.7	239	1 342 741	13.2	27.2	31.7	10.1	4.0	11.5	0.0
Warren	60	319	22.3	6.7	445	1 785 083	16.7	23.0	19.1	3.3	3.9	30.7	0.0
Westerville	63	D	D	D	484	2 542 559	12.4	27.1	26.3	4.3	0.0	26.7	0.0
Westlake	71	678	39.2	14.8	288	1 367 977	13.6	30.0	24.5	2.8	3.2	21.7	0.0
Wooster	44	291	21.3	6.8	879	3 824 028	2.0	5.4	6.8	4.2	78.8	2.8	0.0
Xenia	33	164	12.2	3.6	219	1 060 316	20.5	35.1	21.7	3.3	0.9	13.1	0.0
Youngstown	78	358	25.6	9.2	757	3 252 504	14.0	28.1	18.4	6.3	4.9	27.3	0.0
Zanesville	65	633	43.5	13.4	297	1 096 683	10.0	29.7	21.1	6.3	2.8	25.1	0.0
OKLAHOMA	4 369	26 154	2 610.1	707.1	X	X	X	X	X	X	X	X	X
Bartlesville	51	373	28.3	9.4	344	1 284 794	8.5	23.4	23.5	6.4	0.4	26.0	5.4
Broken Arrow	136	834	88.2	22.0	618	2 786 415	13.1	30.6	27.6	5.5	0.0	17.1	0.0
Edmond	157	902	68.3	20.1	688	3 323 448	15.6	22.5	27.9	6.2	1.5	21.4	0.0
Enid	91	468	48.5	11.7	477	1 757 022	12.4	27.9	23.3	7.6	2.5	18.8	2.4
Lawton	98	659	52.1	17.1	892	3 414 778	14.9	29.7	19.3	9.4	2.0	20.6	1.8
Midwest City	52	415	26.1	8.2	494	2 315 063	15.2	28.4	24.6	3.8	4.3	18.9	0.0
Moore	60	D	D	D	275	1 722 367	12.5	35.2	32.5	2.3	5.4	6.1	0.0
Muskogee	55	470	44.3	11.5	497	1 548 570	8.5	26.0	24.8	12.1	0.0	24.8	0.0
Norman	132	769	56.0	16.9	3 161	15 136 504	3.2	7.5	5.5	2.7	74.3	5.6	0.0
Oklahoma City	835	6 134	660.7	173.6	4 418	24 268 820	9.9	32.6	28.7	9.3	4.5	15.0	0.0
Owasso	44	155	13.3	3.2	219	910 478	15.5	28.5	31.9	5.8	0.7	11.3	0.0
Ponca City	34	192	19.0	4.9	400	1 441 141	9.1	18.8	20.4	7.8	0.7	35.3	2.6
Shawnee	45	248	17.3	5.3	279	1 055 211	16.1	30.3	23.8	5.8	1.6	22.2	0.0
Stillwater	58	D	D	D	1 308	5 630 416	4.6	9.5	6.8	1.6	62.0	12.2	1.1
Tulsa	686	4 968	482.3	149.2	3 932	16 951 552	11.3	27.1	20.9	14.4	1.8	12.8	0.0
OREGON	5 258	28 203	2 519.4	794.3	X	X	X	X	X	X	X	X	X
Albany	63	412	25.0	9.0	389	2 123 666	12.9	24.2	24.6	13.2	0.1	18.7	3.7
Beaverton	180	1 217	116.1	37.3	488	2 217 436	38.8	23.9	0.0	5.4	0.0	10.8	12.0
Bend	159	822	64.7	20.0	432	2 556 081	14.4	29.2	23.0	5.2	3.3	12.8	0.0
Corvallis	75	389	24.1	8.5	430	2 437 922	9.9	21.5	18.9	5.8	8.1	18.9	8.1
Eugene	251	1 832	146.3	47.3	1 983	11 796 504	9.0	18.2	12.2	8.0	1.2	26.1	3.1
Grants Pass	59	285	22.5	6.6	214	1 160 951	18.8	44.3	16.7	2.1	0.0	13.1	0.0
Gresham	117	495	40.4	13.3	515	3 198 886	13.0	29.6	21.1	3.3	0.6	22.0	0.0
Hillsboro	119	947	121.9	49.5	759	4 281 252	14.6	24.9	17.5	3.5	0.0	24.7	6.8
Keizer	34	166	11.3	3.7	89	489 891	18.6	57.2	0.0	2.5	4.8	16.6	0.0
Lake Oswego	74	318	23.2	7.1	325	1 928 696	17.6	21.1	21.4	8.6	1.3	17.6	6.5
McMinnville	40	165	12.8	4.0	252	1 307 113	16.9	18.4	16.1	4.8	2.3	34.2	4.5
Medford	125	860	71.7	26.4	452	2 575 154	14.2	34.5	21.7	15.1	0.1	9.8	0.0
Oregon City	49	254	20.5	7.5	159	835 368	19.0	32.4	0.0	14.2	0.0	19.2	5.8
Portland	1 246	8 014	781.3	237.5	5 804	35 656 383	18.1	25.5	15.0	10.2	0.9	27.3	0.0

1. Establishments subject to federal tax.

Table D. Cities — **City Government Finances**

City	City government finances, 2012									
	General revenue							General expenditure		
		Intergovernmental		Taxes					Per capita[1] (dollars)	
					Per capita[1] (dollars)					
	Total (mil dol)	Total (mil dol)	Percent from state government	Total (mil dol)	Total	Property	Sales and gross receipts	Total (mil dol)	Total	Capital outlays
	117	118	119	120	121	122	123	124	125	126
OHIO—Cont'd										
Hamilton	89.3	12.8	82.9	38.5	618	143	14	83.9	1 348	178
Hilliard	35.0	7.3	60.4	23.3	762	41	50	31.8	1 040	211
Huber Heights	30.3	5.3	52.2	16.8	442	90	32	34.7	911	258
Kent	26.7	4.8	93.2	14.4	488	94	24	31.0	1 046	271
Kettering	81.4	18.4	94.3	48.4	863	160	8	83.8	1 495	462
Lakewood	61.0	11.1	71.9	35.2	685	265	25	53.0	1 032	61
Lancaster	74.4	14.1	95.8	19.9	511	72	1	62.8	1 614	139
Lima	73.9	31.0	93.2	18.5	482	32	28	56.9	1 483	345
Lorain	67.9	22.6	96.7	25.7	402	58	34	56.8	890	61
Mansfield	55.9	12.3	51.1	27.7	588	43	15	51.8	1 101	78
Marion	39.4	10.3	100.0	13.8	375	33	10	36.5	989	43
Mason	54.1	7.0	87.3	29.3	937	192	66	56.2	1 798	343
Massillon	35.7	5.9	26.8	17.4	540	50	45	33.4	1 036	44
Medina	27.0	2.3	92.3	16.9	636	121	21	24.7	931	114
Mentor	61.5	10.0	90.4	40.5	862	94	40	59.9	1 274	0
Middletown	84.2	23.4	47.0	24.4	501	100	5	78.5	1 612	138
Newark	52.3	16.1	92.8	22.0	462	55	6	52.1	1 091	140
North Olmsted	41.3	6.2	95.2	23.4	724	285	44	35.0	1 082	136
North Ridgeville	32.6	5.0	88.6	15.8	516	189	54	29.7	972	100
North Royalton	28.1	4.2	100.0	16.8	554	150	19	25.8	852	47
Parma	80.5	21.4	100.0	48.3	599	109	29	75.6	937	31
Reynoldsburg	27.3	3.4	100.0	14.8	406	60	10	25.5	702	31
Riverside	11.8	3.1	96.7	6.6	263	93	1	11.2	447	11
Sandusky	39.2	10.7	84.2	17.6	686	79	317	32.3	1 262	169
Shaker Heights	52.5	8.5	41.5	33.5	1 195	272	23	57.7	2 057	258
Springfield	86.7	27.8	35.7	38.2	635	49	32	79.9	1 328	177
Stow	35.8	7.4	100.0	21.6	623	215	21	32.9	950	128
Strongsville	63.9	10.5	39.1	39.3	881	209	21	66.8	1 498	383
Toledo	451.3	105.2	62.6	175.0	618	42	23	399.2	1 408	377
Troy	33.3	3.4	70.1	17.1	674	74	29	30.1	1 187	140
Upper Arlington	43.7	6.5	59.0	27.9	815	255	41	52.7	1 538	476
Warren	62.9	13.4	36.4	19.8	486	36	24	56.8	1 394	127
Westerville	85.6	17.7	81.5	50.6	1 359	332	29	96.9	2 605	855
Westlake	58.8	5.1	53.1	39.7	1 222	403	54	49.3	1 518	310
Wooster	134.0	6.0	94.8	14.0	532	83	27	128.8	4 877	371
Xenia	28.5	5.5	95.4	13.4	514	62	40	28.4	1 089	214
Youngstown	104.6	20.7	41.1	54.6	826	37	116	89.8	1 358	37
Zanesville	44.9	17.1	96.5	17.8	701	46	54	34.3	1 347	67
OKLAHOMA	X	X	X	X	X	X	X	X	X	X
Bartlesville	40.2	4.0	79.0	22.5	619	96	523	44.1	1 213	354
Broken Arrow	90.6	4.1	24.8	53.9	528	119	409	91.4	896	239
Edmond	93.1	6.8	73.5	55.3	651	0	651	115.9	1 364	281
Enid	67.3	6.0	81.8	38.4	769	57	712	80.2	1 606	728
Lawton	96.6	12.3	38.3	56.7	575	41	534	92.9	943	108
Midwest City	69.8	4.9	68.6	36.3	646	46	600	62.1	1 107	89
Moore	45.7	1.5	65.9	32.5	561	58	503	41.5	717	95
Muskogee	130.4	3.3	45.2	28.4	729	5	724	134.9	3 462	322
Norman	443.4	6.4	56.7	79.6	687	68	619	422.1	3 646	294
Oklahoma City	1 107.5	90.6	50.5	601.9	1 003	139	865	835.1	1 392	272
Owasso	32.7	0.8	93.6	20.7	658	0	658	29.0	924	98
Ponca City	41.3	2.3	61.5	16.3	655	21	635	56.7	2 278	730
Shawnee	34.1	5.6	40.8	20.1	656	2	653	30.7	1 003	220
Stillwater	49.0	2.9	45.6	29.0	622	29	593	48.2	1 033	155
Tulsa	741.9	77.4	11.3	340.0	862	161	701	712.6	1 806	561
OREGON	X	X	X	X	X	X	X	X	X	X
Albany	59.2	9.0	56.9	32.7	638	505	133	56.1	1 094	127
Beaverton	79.4	16.3	57.8	44.0	475	344	131	78.1	842	126
Bend	88.7	15.0	54.7	44.0	558	331	227	81.1	1 029	162
Corvallis	71.4	12.8	43.7	35.6	647	446	202	62.4	1 135	94
Eugene	265.1	45.3	46.0	119.6	757	620	138	254.5	1 612	275
Grants Pass	36.2	6.8	64.2	20.5	589	453	136	35.8	1 028	164
Gresham	102.2	33.7	52.1	39.5	363	243	120	106.4	979	155
Hillsboro	134.5	12.8	83.8	79.4	832	541	291	124.8	1 309	91
Keizer	21.2	3.3	99.7	10.7	290	216	74	18.1	490	50
Lake Oswego	80.7	14.9	44.5	43.4	1 164	919	245	69.2	1 857	263
McMinnville	37.5	4.1	96.1	15.2	459	360	99	30.1	909	86
Medford	102.4	14.5	49.3	58.0	758	455	303	104.2	1 361	306
Oregon City	52.1	16.8	99.0	19.9	594	337	257	43.8	1 308	472
Portland	1 298.8	266.5	44.2	612.5	1 016	708	308	1 280.8	2 124	548

1. Based on population estimated as of July 1 of the year shown.

Table D. Cities — City Government Finances

City	Public welfare	Highways	Parking facilities	Education	Health and hospitals	Police protection	Sewerage and sanitation	Parks and recreation	Housing and community development	Interest on debt
	City government finances, 2012 (cont.)									
	General expenditure (cont.)									
	Percent of total for:									
	127	128	129	130	131	132	133	134	135	136
OHIO—Cont'd										
Hamilton	0.0	6.1	0.5	0.0	1.5	24.9	20.3	0.9	3.4	4.7
Hilliard	0.0	24.2	0.0	0.0	0.5	19.2	1.2	7.4	0.0	8.3
Huber Heights	0.0	13.8	0.0	0.0	0.0	17.2	7.9	12.9	4.7	5.3
Kent	0.4	5.1	0.0	0.0	3.0	20.7	13.4	5.7	2.8	0.8
Kettering	0.0	11.2	0.0	0.0	0.0	17.2	0.0	14.9	1.4	0.8
Lakewood	3.1	12.4	0.5	0.0	0.8	19.5	15.5	4.3	5.6	4.7
Lancaster	0.0	5.4	0.0	0.0	0.4	12.7	21.9	2.9	0.9	23.9
Lima	0.0	16.0	0.0	0.0	0.0	15.9	21.7	1.8	6.7	2.8
Lorain	1.5	5.3	0.0	0.0	2.1	22.9	25.4	0.6	7.9	2.8
Mansfield	0.0	13.1	0.0	1.8	0.0	16.3	8.4	0.5	3.4	0.6
Marion	0.0	8.9	0.0	0.0	1.3	18.4	33.3	2.5	0.0	2.0
Mason	0.0	17.2	0.0	0.0	0.0	10.0	9.1	17.8	0.0	7.0
Massillon	0.0	11.0	0.1	0.0	1.8	14.9	25.5	10.7	0.9	5.3
Medina	0.0	17.5	8.9	0.0	0.0	17.4	12.9	13.7	0.0	1.6
Mentor	0.0	24.6	0.0	0.0	0.0	19.1	0.0	11.9	0.8	2.7
Middletown	0.0	12.5	0.0	0.0	1.0	10.4	16.2	3.7	18.8	2.3
Newark	0.0	9.2	0.0	0.0	0.0	16.1	17.8	0.0	0.0	2.0
North Olmsted	0.9	13.9	0.0	0.0	0.0	15.9	22.0	12.1	0.5	5.6
North Ridgeville	0.0	12.1	0.0	0.0	8.5	17.4	25.4	1.3	4.6	3.6
North Royalton	0.0	20.6	0.0	0.0	0.7	23.5	21.0	1.5	2.7	1.6
Parma	0.0	5.8	0.0	0.0	0.4	40.5	0.5	5.1	11.3	1.6
Reynoldsburg	0.0	5.9	0.0	0.0	0.8	30.8	31.8	3.9	0.0	1.4
Riverside	0.0	14.6	0.0	0.0	0.0	41.2	0.0	0.4	0.0	0.8
Sandusky	0.0	8.5	0.0	0.0	0.0	15.5	25.9	1.2	2.8	6.9
Shaker Heights	0.0	7.5	0.0	0.0	1.0	20.4	8.3	8.9	8.8	1.6
Springfield	0.0	3.0	0.0	0.0	0.0	15.5	8.1	0.0	5.0	1.9
Stow	0.0	10.2	0.0	0.0	0.9	18.9	2.2	7.6	0.0	3.2
Strongsville	0.0	30.1	0.0	0.0	0.5	17.2	11.8	7.8	0.0	4.3
Toledo	0.4	8.8	0.2	0.0	3.7	23.7	22.4	1.8	3.2	5.8
Troy	0.0	7.4	0.4	0.0	1.1	12.4	14.3	12.0	6.3	2.2
Upper Arlington	0.0	34.9	0.0	0.0	0.4	13.2	6.2	6.9	2.2	3.4
Warren	0.0	8.6	0.2	0.0	1.6	12.9	18.9	4.3	7.2	1.3
Westerville	0.0	2.3	0.0	0.0	0.0	14.8	10.3	17.5	0.0	1.5
Westlake	0.0	17.5	0.0	0.0	0.0	13.8	11.8	6.6	0.0	1.6
Wooster	0.0	1.4	0.0	0.0	76.3	4.9	6.2	1.1	0.2	0.4
Xenia	0.0	1.1	0.3	0.0	0.0	19.2	20.9	0.6	1.7	1.4
Youngstown	0.0	6.3	0.1	0.0	1.5	22.0	27.0	2.7	6.8	1.8
Zanesville	0.0	10.9	0.0	0.0	1.2	22.8	24.7	2.4	0.0	3.0
OKLAHOMA	X	X	X	X	X	X	X	X	X	X
Bartlesville	0.0	15.9	0.0	0.0	0.0	12.6	20.7	12.2	2.0	1.5
Broken Arrow	0.0	7.8	0.0	0.0	0.8	18.6	18.5	7.7	0.8	5.5
Edmond	1.6	24.4	0.0	0.0	1.5	11.6	15.1	8.3	0.6	0.3
Enid	0.3	12.1	0.0	0.0	5.1	10.6	19.3	6.6	17.6	0.7
Lawton	0.0	9.4	0.0	5.7	0.9	21.2	15.2	1.3	1.1	1.4
Midwest City	0.0	8.1	0.0	0.0	0.0	23.9	12.5	4.6	7.6	6.6
Moore	0.0	14.8	0.0	0.0	0.0	23.2	14.3	3.7	3.2	1.9
Muskogee	0.0	3.1	0.0	0.0	65.8	5.4	5.9	4.1	0.6	0.1
Norman	0.0	6.6	0.0	0.0	68.5	5.5	5.8	1.8	0.4	3.1
Oklahoma City	0.0	8.8	0.7	2.5	0.9	18.5	8.3	17.3	3.5	5.8
Owasso	0.0	4.3	0.0	0.0	4.7	22.5	13.0	6.5	1.6	5.2
Ponca City	0.0	7.2	0.0	0.0	1.8	11.7	12.2	6.8	1.4	3.7
Shawnee	0.0	12.2	0.0	0.0	0.0	22.5	9.6	3.8	2.4	0.3
Stillwater	0.4	18.2	0.0	0.0	0.2	21.6	13.9	8.0	0.0	2.1
Tulsa	2.1	19.7	1.1	0.0	8.8	12.2	19.9	4.8	0.0	6.0
OREGON	X	X	X	X	X	X	X	X	X	X
Albany	0.0	7.1	0.0	0.0	3.9	21.6	16.2	10.8	0.1	1.7
Beaverton	0.0	7.6	0.0	0.0	0.0	31.5	10.8	0.2	1.1	0.8
Bend	0.0	12.0	0.8	0.0	0.0	21.4	12.9	0.0	4.1	3.6
Corvallis	0.0	5.9	0.2	0.0	0.0	20.1	18.1	9.1	2.8	3.7
Eugene	0.0	2.5	1.5	0.0	0.0	18.2	14.0	9.7	2.9	0.9
Grants Pass	0.0	8.4	0.0	0.0	0.0	30.5	11.8	5.8	3.1	1.3
Gresham	0.0	10.0	0.0	0.0	0.0	20.1	23.2	3.0	1.4	3.3
Hillsboro	0.0	8.1	0.1	0.0	0.0	20.0	22.0	13.5	1.2	2.5
Keizer	0.0	10.4	0.0	0.0	0.0	28.9	33.1	2.7	4.7	7.4
Lake Oswego	0.0	4.0	0.0	0.0	0.0	13.3	14.8	11.9	0.0	6.6
McMinnville	0.0	5.9	0.0	0.0	10.6	19.5	16.7	11.4	0.0	3.2
Medford	0.0	12.8	0.4	0.0	0.0	19.0	14.3	5.7	5.9	15.0
Oregon City	0.0	35.9	0.8	0.0	0.0	15.8	13.8	8.7	1.1	3.8
Portland	0.0	13.9	0.6	0.0	0.0	13.5	20.3	7.8	7.5	7.6

Table D. Cities — City Government Finances, City Government Employment, and Climate

	City government finances, 2012 (cont.)			Climate[2]						
	Debt outstanding			Average daily temperature (degrees Fahrenheit)						
				Mean		Limits				
City	Total (mil dol)	Per capita[1] (dollars)	Debt issued during year	January	July	January[3]	July[4]	Annual precipitation (inches)	Heating degree days	Cooling degree days
	137	138	139	140	141	142	143	144	145	146

OHIO—Cont'd										
Hamilton	315.7	5 070	50.5	28.7	76.6	19.9	88.1	43.36	5 261	1 135
Hilliard	62.6	2 046	8.0	NA	NA	NA	NA	NA	NA	NA
Huber Heights	57.3	1 501	0.6	27.9	77.0	20.6	87.2	39.41	5 343	1 214
Kent	19.1	645	0.0	27.2	74.1	20.1	83.9	36.07	5 752	856
Kettering	18.1	324	0.0	27.9	77.0	20.6	87.2	39.41	5 343	1 214
Lakewood	92.2	1 795	12.3	25.7	71.9	18.8	81.4	38.71	6 121	702
Lancaster	375.7	9 659	0.2	26.5	73.1	17.8	84.4	36.55	5 887	764
Lima	36.5	953	1.1	25.5	73.6	18.1	84.0	37.20	5 932	835
Lorain	48.2	755	6.9	27.1	73.8	19.3	85.0	38.02	5 731	818
Mansfield	9.9	210	0.4	24.3	71.0	16.2	81.8	43.24	6 364	653
Marion	44.8	1 215	0.0	24.5	72.7	16.0	83.7	38.35	6 300	703
Mason	120.3	3 846	16.6	NA	NA	NA	NA	NA	NA	NA
Massillon	22.4	697	0.1	25.2	71.8	17.4	82.3	38.47	6 154	678
Medina	45.6	1 720	0.0	23.7	71.3	16.2	82.0	38.34	6 525	558
Mentor	34.9	742	4.4	23.0	68.8	14.3	80.0	47.33	6 956	372
Middletown	241.5	4 959	0.3	27.5	74.2	18.3	86.3	39.54	5 609	879
Newark	24.5	514	2.9	25.8	72.7	17.3	83.8	41.62	6 084	687
North Olmsted	38.8	1 199	1.4	25.7	71.9	18.8	81.4	38.71	6 121	702
North Ridgeville	34.1	1 115	4.1	NA	NA	NA	NA	NA	NA	NA
North Royalton	40.3	1 328	15.0	25.7	71.9	18.8	81.4	38.71	6 121	702
Parma	37.5	465	0.0	25.7	71.9	18.8	81.4	38.71	6 121	702
Reynoldsburg	22.9	631	0.0	28.3	75.1	20.3	85.3	38.52	5 492	951
Riverside	2.0	79	0.0	NA	NA	NA	NA	NA	NA	NA
Sandusky	27.6	1 078	4.1	25.6	73.8	18.9	81.8	34.46	6 065	785
Shaker Heights	27.3	972	0.3	25.7	71.9	18.8	81.4	38.71	6 121	702
Springfield	42.8	711	0.0	26.1	73.5	18.2	83.8	37.70	5 921	796
Stow	28.9	832	0.0	27.2	74.1	20.1	83.9	36.07	5 752	856
Strongsville	60.3	1 353	10.7	25.7	71.9	18.8	81.4	38.71	6 121	702
Toledo	357.2	1 260	8.3	27.5	77.6	21.7	87.1	33.52	5 464	1 257
Troy	19.5	768	0.0	NA	NA	NA	NA	NA	NA	NA
Upper Arlington	51.9	1 515	6.0	28.3	75.1	20.3	85.3	38.52	5 492	951
Warren	33.9	832	0.0	24.0	70.2	15.3	82.4	37.80	6 678	458
Westerville	75.5	2 027	10.0	27.7	74.4	19.7	85.4	39.35	5 434	924
Westlake	43.8	1 350	7.4	27.1	73.8	19.3	85.0	38.02	5 731	818
Wooster	10.1	381	0.0	NA	NA	NA	NA	NA	NA	NA
Xenia	7.4	286	1.1	NA	NA	NA	NA	NA	NA	NA
Youngstown	32.0	483	0.0	24.9	69.9	17.4	81.0	38.02	6 451	552
Zanesville	6.6	261	0.0	24.3	68.4	16.3	78.7	36.91	6 639	373
OKLAHOMA	X	X	X	X	X	X	X	X	X	X
Bartlesville	60.7	1 673	0.0	35.4	82.2	23.7	94.5	38.99	3 743	1 894
Broken Arrow	183.9	1 802	48.4	34.8	81.3	23.5	92.9	40.46	3 917	1 746
Edmond	136.7	1 609	0.0	36.7	82.0	26.2	93.1	35.85	3 663	1 907
Enid	78.5	1 572	17.0	33.1	82.6	21.9	94.4	34.25	4 269	1 852
Lawton	141.0	1 431	38.0	38.2	84.2	26.4	95.7	31.64	3 326	2 199
Midwest City	106.7	1 901	73.2	36.7	82.0	26.2	93.1	35.85	3 663	1 907
Moore	71.4	1 232	25.2	36.7	82.0	26.2	93.1	35.85	3 663	1 907
Muskogee	44.3	1 136	5.0	36.1	82.1	25.2	93.1	43.77	3 667	1 858
Norman	372.5	3 217	23.4	35.8	82.1	23.2	93.9	41.65	3 713	1 906
Oklahoma City	1 318.9	2 199	185.3	36.7	82.0	26.2	93.1	35.85	3 663	1 907
Owasso	39.4	1 254	0.0	NA	NA	NA	NA	NA	NA	NA
Ponca City	59.4	2 385	24.9	33.8	82.9	23.8	94.1	36.41	4 053	1 964
Shawnee	23.5	767	3.5	37.3	83.0	25.5	94.5	40.87	3 460	2 024
Stillwater	38.1	817	4.6	34.5	82.3	21.9	93.6	36.71	3 899	1 881
Tulsa	1 254.1	3 179	126.1	37.4	81.9	27.1	92.2	45.10	3 413	1 905
OREGON	X	X	X	X	X	X	X	X	X	X
Albany	122.1	2 381	0.0	40.3	66.5	33.6	81.2	43.66	4 715	247
Beaverton	26.4	285	0.0	40.0	66.8	33.8	79.2	39.95	4 723	287
Bend	92.3	1 171	10.9	31.2	63.5	22.6	80.7	11.73	7 042	147
Corvallis	59.4	1 080	0.0	38.1	63.8	31.6	77.4	67.76	5 501	139
Eugene	418.2	2 649	112.5	39.8	66.2	33.0	81.5	50.90	4 786	242
Grants Pass	12.2	350	0.0	NA	NA	NA	NA	NA	NA	NA
Gresham	82.4	758	3.0	40.0	68.3	33.5	81.5	45.70	4 491	450
Hillsboro	62.2	652	0.0	40.5	67.6	35.1	80.4	38.19	4 532	323
Keizer	28.7	779	0.0	40.3	66.8	33.5	81.5	40.00	4 784	257
Lake Oswego	156.3	4 196	37.7	41.8	69.3	35.7	82.6	46.05	4 132	475
McMinnville	22.1	668	5.6	39.6	66.6	33.0	81.9	41.66	4 815	288
Medford	380.1	4 966	26.6	39.1	72.7	30.9	90.2	18.37	4 539	711
Oregon City	33.8	1 009	0.0	41.8	69.3	35.7	82.6	46.05	4 132	475
Portland	3 381.1	5 608	353.6	41.8	69.3	35.7	82.6	46.05	4 132	475

1. Based on the population estimated as of July 1 of the year shown.   2. Represents normal values based on the 30-year period, 1971–2000.   3. Average daily minimum.
4. Average daily maximum.

Table D. Cities — **Land Area and Population**

STATE Place code	City	Land area,[1] 2016 (sq mi)	Total persons	Rank	Per square mile	White	Black or African American	American Indian, Alaska Native	Asian	Hawaiian Pacific Islander	Some other race	2 or more races[2]
		1	2	3	4	5	6	7	8	9	10	11
	OREGON—Cont'd											
41 61200	Redmond	16.8	29 322	1 272	1 745.4	NA	NA	NA	NA	NA	NA	NA
41 64900	Salem	48.6	167 419	151	3 444.8	84.8	1.8	1.4	2.2	1.4	2.5	6.0
41 69600	Springfield	15.8	61 893	592	3 917.3	84.2	2.3	3.7	2.1	1.0	3.2	3.4
41 73650	Tigard	12.7	51 902	735	4 086.8	82.8	1.3	0.2	7.4	0.8	3.2	4.3
41 74950	Tualatin	8.2	27 545	1 339	3 359.1	NA	NA	NA	NA	NA	NA	NA
41 80150	West Linn	7.4	26 859	1 374	3 629.6	NA	NA	NA	NA	NA	NA	NA
42 00000	**PENNSYLVANIA**	44 742.4	12 784 227	X	285.7	81.1	11.0	0.2	3.3	0.0	1.9	2.4
42 02000	Allentown	17.5	120 443	231	6 882.5	58.3	15.7	0.3	1.9	0.4	19.4	4.0
42 02184	Altoona	9.8	44 589	847	4 549.9	90.5	2.6	0.0	0.1	0.0	2.6	4.2
42 06064	Bethel Park	11.7	31 911	1 180	2 727.4	NA	NA	NA	NA	NA	NA	NA
42 06088	Bethlehem	19.1	75 293	462	3 942.0	79.9	4.6	0.1	4.1	0.0	3.9	7.4
42 13208	Chester	4.8	33 988	1 118	7 080.8	21.5	68.1	0.1	0.5	0.0	6.0	3.9
42 21648	Easton	4.3	26 978	1 369	6 274.0	70.4	10.4	0.2	2.7	0.0	5.7	10.7
42 24000	Erie	19.1	98 593	308	5 161.9	74.1	17.2	0.2	2.5	0.0	0.8	5.1
42 32800	Harrisburg	8.1	48 904	776	6 037.5	35.3	47.5	0.5	6.2	0.2	5.8	4.5
42 33408	Hazleton	6.0	24 659	1 428	4 109.8	57.6	5.6	0.0	0.0	0.0	34.0	2.7
42 41216	Lancaster	7.2	59 218	628	8 224.7	66.0	13.4	0.0	5.1	0.0	11.3	4.2
42 42168	Lebanon	4.2	25 726	1 407	6 125.2	62.4	5.7	0.0	1.1	0.6	28.2	2.1
42 50528	Monroeville	19.7	27 953	1 327	1 418.9	81.1	8.4	0.0	6.2	0.0	0.7	3.5
42 54656	Norristown	3.5	34 370	1 105	9 820.0	30.8	42.3	0.0	3.9	0.0	15.4	7.5
42 60000	Philadelphia	134.2	1 567 872	6	11 683.1	41.9	42.4	0.4	7.2	0.1	5.3	2.7
42 61000	Pittsburgh	55.4	303 625	63	5 480.6	65.2	24.3	0.0	5.9	0.0	0.5	4.0
42 61536	Plum	28.6	27 399	1 348	958.0	NA	NA	NA	NA	NA	NA	NA
42 63624	Reading	9.9	87 575	375	8 846.0	58.4	10.8	4.7	1.0	0.1	9.4	15.7
42 69000	Scranton	25.3	77 291	439	3 055.0	83.9	6.2	0.0	5.0	0.0	1.7	3.2
42 73808	State College	4.6	41 992	900	9 128.7	80.2	5.5	0.0	10.0	0.3	0.9	3.0
42 85152	Wilkes-Barre	7.0	40 569	929	5 795.6	73.7	15.0	0.4	3.4	0.0	1.8	5.7
42 85312	Williamsport	8.7	28 834	1 288	3 314.3	80.8	13.8	0.0	2.1	0.0	1.2	2.2
42 87048	York	5.3	43 859	858	8 275.3	57.9	30.2	0.1	0.4	0.0	5.2	6.2
44 00000	**RHODE ISLAND**	1 033.9	1 056 426	X	1 021.8	80.4	6.2	0.4	3.4	0.0	6.2	3.4
44 19180	Cranston	28.3	81 034	419	2 863.4	76.9	7.0	0.4	6.4	0.0	4.4	4.9
44 22960	East Providence	13.2	47 337	810	3 586.1	84.4	4.0	0.2	3.0	0.0	1.8	6.7
44 54640	Pawtucket	8.7	71 427	494	8 210.0	63.5	19.1	0.7	2.2	0.0	10.4	4.2
44 59000	Providence	18.4	179 219	137	9 740.2	51.5	14.2	0.9	6.1	0.1	22.3	4.8
44 74300	Warwick	35.0	81 579	413	2 330.8	91.7	0.9	0.0	2.3	0.0	2.6	2.5
44 80780	Woonsocket	7.8	41 406	912	5 308.5	79.1	7.7	0.3	5.1	0.0	1.5	6.3
45 00000	**SOUTH CAROLINA**	30 062.6	4 961 119	X	165.0	67.2	27.5	0.3	1.4	0.1	1.4	2.1
45 00550	Aiken	20.9	30 937	1 215	1 480.2	NA	NA	NA	NA	NA	NA	NA
45 01360	Anderson	14.5	27 544	1 340	1 899.6	NA	NA	NA	NA	NA	NA	NA
45 13330	Charleston	109.0	134 385	198	1 232.9	75.3	21.5	0.1	1.3	0.0	0.3	1.6
45 16000	Columbia	133.5	134 309	199	1 006.1	52.6	41.4	0.0	1.9	0.3	1.2	2.6
45 25810	Florence	21.7	38 317	991	1 765.8	49.8	44.4	0.0	2.9	0.9	0.0	1.9
45 29815	Goose Creek	41.3	42 039	898	1 017.9	72.6	16.1	0.9	2.8	0.0	3.4	4.3
45 30850	Greenville	28.9	67 453	528	2 334.0	67.6	27.0	0.3	1.7	1.2	0.6	1.7
45 30985	Greer	20.9	29 000	1 281	1 387.6	66.8	17.7	0.0	11.0	0.0	0.8	3.7
45 34045	Hilton Head Island	41.4	40 500	932	978.3	87.1	8.6	0.0	0.6	0.0	2.5	1.3
45 48535	Mount Pleasant	45.1	84 170	393	1 866.3	93.0	4.4	0.2	1.7	0.0	0.0	0.7
45 49075	Myrtle Beach	23.7	32 240	1 175	1 360.3	79.6	11.8	0.8	0.7	0.0	4.7	2.4
45 50875	North Charleston	73.7	109 298	272	1 483.0	42.3	49.3	0.3	3.2	0.1	2.6	2.2
45 61405	Rock Hill	37.3	72 937	480	1 955.4	56.5	38.6	0.0	1.4	0.0	1.8	1.7
45 68290	Spartanburg	19.8	37 876	1 007	1 912.9	48.0	48.6	0.0	1.6	0.0	0.8	0.9
45 70270	Summerville	19.2	49 323	765	2 568.9	NA	NA	NA	NA	NA	NA	NA
45 70405	Sumter	32.3	40 723	924	1 260.8	45.2	50.9	0.0	1.1	0.0	1.7	1.1
46 00000	**SOUTH DAKOTA**	75 810.5	865 454	X	11.4	84.6	1.5	8.3	1.4	0.1	1.2	3.0
46 00100	Aberdeen	15.9	28 415	1 312	1 787.1	87.6	1.3	5.1	3.5	0.0	0.2	2.3
46 52980	Rapid City	54.4	74 048	473	1 361.2	82.1	0.6	8.1	2.4	0.0	0.6	6.1
46 59020	Sioux Falls	75.4	174 360	145	2 312.5	84.9	5.4	2.2	2.0	0.0	3.2	2.3
47 00000	**TENNESSEE**	41 234.8	6 651 194	X	161.3	77.7	16.8	0.3	1.6	0.0	1.4	2.1
47 03440	Bartlett	32.3	58 622	639	1 814.9	76.6	17.1	0.0	3.9	0.0	1.0	1.5
47 08280	Brentwood	41.2	42 517	885	1 032.0	NA	NA	NA	NA	NA	NA	NA
47 08540	Bristol	32.6	27 109	1 361	831.6	NA	NA	NA	NA	NA	NA	NA
47 14000	Chattanooga	143.1	177 571	139	1 240.9	62.1	31.9	0.3	2.3	0.0	0.8	2.6
47 15160	Clarksville	98.3	150 287	173	1 528.9	66.2	24.2	0.7	2.8	0.4	1.1	4.4
47 15400	Cleveland	26.9	44 271	852	1 645.8	83.7	10.6	0.2	1.7	0.0	1.3	2.5
47 16420	Collierville	36.0	49 177	770	1 366.0	70.6	15.8	0.0	7.8	0.3	1.6	4.0

1. Dry land or land partially or temporarily covered by water.   2. Hispanic or Latino persons may be of any race.

Table D. Cities — **Population**

City	Percent Hispanic or Latino[1], 2015	Percent foreign born 2015	Age of population (percent), 2010-2014							Median age 2015	Percent female 2015	Population			
			Under 18 years	18 to 24 years	25 to 34 years	35 to 44 years	45 to 54 years	55 to 64 years	65 years and over			Census counts		Percent change	
												2000	2010	2000–2010	2010–2016
	12	13	14	15	16	17	18	19	20	21	22	23	24	25	26
OREGON—Cont'd															
Redmond	11.3	5.6	26.0	6.9	14.0	9.7	12.9	10.3	20.1	40.1	51.8	13 481	26 215	94.5	11.9
Salem	24.0	12.0	24.2	11.6	13.7	13.4	12.4	11.9	12.9	35.4	50.9	136 924	154 744	13.0	8.2
Springfield	14.4	8.8	23.2	11.4	14.2	12.4	14.7	11.9	12.3	35.8	49.4	52 864	59 367	12.3	4.3
Tigard	16.0	15.6	21.0	8.4	17.1	13.3	10.7	12.5	17.0	37.0	52.6	41 223	48 198	16.9	7.7
Tualatin	15.1	11.3	25.5	6.7	14.1	15.3	12.0	14.8	11.6	38.2	52.2	22 791	26 118	14.6	5.5
West Linn	5.8	9.6	26.7	9.2	7.1	13.8	15.3	14.2	13.6	40.2	51.6	22 261	25 100	12.8	7.0
PENNSYLVANIA	6.8	6.5	21.0	9.5	12.9	11.7	13.9	14.0	17.0	40.7	51.1	12 281 054	12 702 857	3.4	0.6
Allentown	49.2	16.3	25.6	11.3	15.7	12.4	12.6	9.9	12.5	33.5	49.6	106 632	118 161	10.8	1.9
Altoona	2.7	1.2	20.8	8.3	13.3	13.7	12.9	14.7	16.3	38.8	51.6	49 523	45 984	-7.1	-3.0
Bethel Park	0.7	3.7	21.3	6.3	10.7	13.9	15.9	12.1	19.9	43.6	52.5	33 556	32 315	-3.7	-1.3
Bethlehem	31.5	8.5	19.0	16.0	14.8	10.7	11.1	11.7	16.5	35.1	51.8	71 329	75 013	5.2	0.4
Chester	12.6	6.2	21.6	15.1	14.9	10.7	12.7	12.5	12.5	33.0	48.3	36 854	33 972	-7.8	0.0
Easton	21.0	10.8	20.6	15.3	13.0	14.8	10.1	13.6	12.6	37.0	51.9	26 263	26 769	1.9	0.8
Erie	7.9	6.3	23.2	12.1	14.4	11.0	13.1	12.9	13.2	35.3	51.1	103 717	101 782	-1.9	-3.1
Harrisburg	21.1	12.3	22.9	15.0	15.3	10.5	13.3	13.8	9.2	32.5	51.4	48 950	49 528	1.2	-1.3
Hazleton	56.4	29.6	22.5	14.3	11.1	14.4	13.7	10.0	14.0	36.8	50.8	23 329	25 340	8.6	-2.7
Lancaster	33.4	12.3	23.3	13.4	16.3	12.3	14.2	9.1	11.3	33.0	47.5	56 348	59 322	5.3	-0.2
Lebanon	43.6	10.3	25.5	12.6	11.4	7.9	13.1	14.9	14.6	35.9	50.8	24 461	25 477	4.2	1.0
Monroeville	3.0	7.4	17.4	5.3	15.2	10.4	14.1	17.4	20.2	46.4	47.9	29 349	28 341	-3.4	-1.4
Norristown	23.1	15.6	28.6	11.6	17.2	12.8	8.8	10.7	10.3	30.6	54.1	31 282	34 324	9.7	0.1
Philadelphia	14.0	13.1	22.1	10.9	18.5	12.3	12.0	11.5	12.7	34.1	52.7	1 517 550	1 526 006	0.6	2.7
Pittsburgh	3.0	9.3	15.2	17.7	20.6	10.1	9.1	12.7	14.6	32.9	50.8	334 563	305 687	-8.6	-0.7
Plum	1.5	1.9	16.7	4.8	14.6	12.3	14.3	16.5	20.8	46.3	49.6	26 940	27 124	0.7	1.0
Reading	64.9	19.4	29.4	12.9	15.3	11.6	12.5	8.3	9.9	29.4	50.3	81 207	88 079	8.5	-0.6
Scranton	14.7	10.5	19.9	13.4	12.9	11.2	13.6	11.6	17.5	38.5	50.8	76 415	76 089	-0.4	1.6
State College	4.7	13.5	5.6	65.1	12.6	4.1	3.8	3.0	5.8	21.6	44.7	38 420	41 991	9.3	0.0
Wilkes-Barre	12.8	7.7	23.0	15.7	12.1	11.9	10.1	11.2	16.1	34.6	51.2	43 123	41 498	-3.8	-2.2
Williamsport	2.2	1.4	18.5	16.7	16.3	11.3	15.2	11.5	10.6	34.0	46.7	30 706	29 381	-4.3	-1.9
York	29.7	9.3	28.1	12.2	15.5	12.8	12.7	7.9	10.7	31.8	50.2	40 862	43 806	7.2	0.1
RHODE ISLAND	14.4	13.5	20.1	10.8	13.5	11.7	14.1	13.6	16.1	39.7	51.6	1 048 319	1 052 940	0.4	0.3
Cranston	12.8	13.1	20.7	8.5	14.9	12.4	12.2	14.5	16.6	39.9	52.7	79 269	80 386	1.4	0.8
East Providence	4.6	17.6	18.4	10.2	8.2	12.7	14.7	14.4	21.4	45.4	53.6	48 688	47 033	-3.4	0.6
Pawtucket	22.5	25.0	20.0	8.6	16.7	12.6	13.6	13.8	14.6	39.2	49.6	72 958	71 141	-2.5	0.4
Providence	43.5	29.9	23.3	16.9	18.1	12.3	10.9	8.9	9.6	29.9	50.3	173 618	178 038	2.5	0.7
Warwick	5.8	6.5	18.4	7.1	15.4	12.2	14.3	13.5	19.1	42.6	51.9	85 808	82 670	-3.7	-1.3
Woonsocket	15.1	10.8	21.4	8.4	18.3	12.0	13.6	11.9	14.4	37.3	53.4	43 224	41 196	-4.7	0.5
SOUTH CAROLINA	5.4	4.8	22.2	9.9	12.9	12.3	13.3	13.1	16.2	39.0	51.3	4 012 012	4 625 410	15.3	7.3
Aiken	1.6	2.0	16.2	8.1	9.2	7.4	13.8	19.0	26.3	51.1	52.5	25 337	29 566	16.7	4.6
Anderson	5.9	5.4	24.6	9.5	11.2	12.6	12.1	8.8	21.2	39.9	56.4	25 514	26 428	3.6	4.2
Charleston	2.9	4.3	16.0	13.4	20.6	12.8	10.6	12.5	14.1	35.0	52.8	96 650	120 150	24.3	11.8
Columbia	5.7	4.6	17.0	27.2	17.3	9.9	10.0	9.1	9.5	28.0	49.3	116 278	130 192	12.0	3.2
Florence	2.1	4.5	22.6	9.8	13.5	11.1	13.5	11.6	17.8	38.2	57.0	30 248	37 469	23.9	2.3
Goose Creek	6.6	7.1	22.9	15.8	19.0	12.3	8.1	9.0	12.9	30.3	51.1	29 208	36 434	24.7	15.4
Greenville	4.8	8.6	20.2	12.6	19.0	12.6	11.8	11.6	12.2	34.0	49.4	56 002	59 165	5.6	14.0
Greer	16.1	20.7	29.6	8.6	15.7	13.6	13.0	7.9	11.6	32.7	51.2	16 843	25 628	52.2	13.2
Hilton Head Island	15.1	12.1	18.5	2.2	9.2	7.3	14.3	14.5	34.0	54.5	54.1	33 862	37 096	9.6	9.2
Mount Pleasant	3.2	5.8	25.2	4.7	12.9	13.8	15.5	12.6	15.2	42.7	51.5	47 609	67 854	42.5	24.0
Myrtle Beach	12.4	11.9	21.1	6.9	14.1	12.5	13.4	15.1	16.8	40.6	51.0	22 759	27 101	19.1	19.0
North Charleston	11.6	7.9	25.7	11.7	18.9	12.7	12.1	9.9	9.0	30.7	49.4	79 641	97 632	22.6	11.9
Rock Hill	4.0	3.4	22.5	13.5	14.8	13.6	11.4	11.6	12.5	34.5	53.4	49 765	66 551	33.7	9.6
Spartanburg	5.9	2.7	22.8	13.4	12.7	10.5	12.8	11.0	16.9	36.3	54.2	39 673	36 760	-7.3	3.0
Summerville	5.2	5.8	22.9	7.6	13.8	14.0	15.0	12.7	14.0	38.4	49.5	27 752	42 605	53.5	15.8
Sumter	4.1	2.8	25.5	11.6	11.9	14.0	12.3	9.7	15.0	36.2	54.8	39 643	40 524	2.2	0.5
SOUTH DAKOTA	3.5	3.2	24.4	10.0	13.0	11.5	12.2	13.2	15.7	36.9	49.7	754 844	814 195	7.9	6.3
Aberdeen	2.4	3.1	21.0	11.1	14.3	9.8	12.9	13.9	17.1	37.2	49.6	24 658	26 096	5.8	8.9
Rapid City	4.0	3.2	22.1	9.0	15.6	9.1	11.7	14.3	18.2	39.5	50.9	59 607	68 446	14.8	8.2
Sioux Falls	5.5	7.5	24.2	9.6	16.8	13.7	11.4	12.1	12.2	34.6	49.5	123 975	153 954	24.2	13.3
TENNESSEE	5.1	5.0	22.6	9.6	13.1	12.7	13.5	13.0	15.4	38.7	51.3	5 689 283	6 346 298	11.5	4.8
Bartlett	3.2	7.4	21.7	9.9	10.8	13.3	14.7	15.2	14.4	41.2	51.2	40 543	56 920	40.4	3.0
Brentwood	3.6	7.6	30.9	5.8	4.6	15.4	16.2	13.2	14.0	41.1	50.9	23 445	37 084	58.2	14.7
Bristol	1.8	1.5	21.5	7.4	11.4	12.6	12.3	12.9	21.9	43.2	53.1	24 821	26 712	7.6	1.5
Chattanooga	6.2	6.0	20.9	12.4	14.6	11.4	13.1	12.0	15.6	36.6	52.6	155 554	170 315	9.5	4.3
Clarksville	10.7	5.5	26.1	13.6	20.9	12.7	10.4	8.9	7.5	29.7	49.7	103 455	132 908	28.5	13.1
Cleveland	10.7	5.9	19.8	17.2	12.3	12.0	12.1	12.3	14.3	35.8	52.9	37 192	41 267	11.0	7.3
Collierville	0.7	7.9	26.4	11.2	9.8	11.4	17.8	12.2	11.1	37.2	55.6	31 872	45 601	43.1	7.8

1. May be of any race.

Table D. Cities — Households, Group Quarters, Crime, and Education

City	Households, 2015 Number	Persons per household	Percent Female family householder[1]	Percent One-person	Persons in group quarters, 2010 Total	Institutional Total	Persons in nursing facilities	Non-institutional	Serious crimes known to police[2] 2014 Total Number	Rate[3]	Rate[3] Violent	Property	Population age 25 and older	Attainment[4] (percent) High school graduate or less	Bachelor's degree or more
	27	28	29	30	31	32	33	34	35	36	37	38	39	40	41
OREGON—Cont'd															
Redmond	10 086	2.82	11.2	24.4	300	181	181	119	1 076	3 880	328	3 552	19 229	46.4	19.0
Salem	58 456	2.69	14.2	27.2	8 635	5 610	639	3 025	7 583	4 680	314	4 367	105 793	38.8	25.9
Springfield	22 430	2.69	17.6	30.4	587	181	140	406	2 950	4 886	353	4 533	39 837	46.2	17.5
Tigard	20 974	2.42	13.1	27.0	347	111	78	236	1 445	2 832	149	2 683	36 163	24.5	46.1
Tualatin	10 675	2.43	9.2	36.8	87	45	45	42	787	2 906	103	2 803	17 705	17.5	44.6
West Linn	9 364	2.82	11.9	14.2	127	63	60	64	260	992	31	962	17 034	16.0	60.1
PENNSYLVANIA	4 956 037	2.50	12.3	29.2	426 113	197 112	87 775	229 001	287 180	2 246	314	1 932	8 895 727	46.0	29.7
Allentown	43 046	2.67	24.3	27.8	5 070	2 089	885	2 981	4 432	3 733	515	3 219	75 847	57.9	15.1
Altoona	19 707	2.25	14.3	32.2	1 189	452	443	737	1 049	2 297	348	1 949	32 155	58.8	19.6
Bethel Park	13 451	2.37	9.1	30.5	217	184	184	33	288	889	77	812	23 250	28.3	48.8
Bethlehem	27 723	2.46	18.6	31.4	6 265	955	882	5 310	2 034	2 711	281	2 430	48 309	42.2	28.3
Chester	11 750	2.58	31.5	34.5	3 151	1 328	143	1 823	1 699	4 989	1 536	3 453	21 585	67.0	10.9
Easton	9 865	2.38	13.9	32.0	3 087	1 093	311	1 994	713	2 627	298	2 328	17 261	45.6	23.3
Erie	40 914	2.31	19.4	35.1	5 244	1 578	715	3 666	3 046	3 034	404	2 629	64 341	54.3	20.5
Harrisburg	20 254	2.33	25.5	36.2	987	265	89	722	2 375	4 836	1 114	3 722	30 480	54.0	20.4
Hazleton	8 473	2.87	26.6	29.7	410	384	218	26	694	2 773	476	2 298	15 678	66.1	12.2
Lancaster	21 324	2.63	21.4	33.1	3 189	1 214	121	1 975	2 694	4 541	679	3 862	37 533	59.8	21.7
Lebanon	10 022	2.52	16.4	32.6	364	106	102	258	700	2 741	309	2 432	15 813	72.7	11.0
Monroeville	12 397	2.23	6.2	39.6	520	457	457	63	597	2 101	341	1 760	21 789	33.3	42.8
Norristown	11 041	3.04	28.6	24.4	947	224	224	723	1 139	3 306	746	2 560	20 591	57.4	22.8
Philadelphia	581 604	2.61	21.2	36.7	57 383	19 376	7 877	38 007	68 741	4 409	1 021	3 388	1 050 747	50.0	27.4
Pittsburgh	131 793	2.13	12.2	42.4	24 329	6 967	2 242	17 362	12 338	4 011	798	3 213	204 143	35.7	41.3
Plum	11 484	2.39	9.6	22.8	132	132	122	0	323	1 171	275	895	21 585	32.6	38.5
Reading	28 665	2.95	24.8	31.9	2 545	485	265	2 060	3 309	3 767	865	2 902	50 623	65.3	11.5
Scranton	29 947	2.39	15.3	37.9	5 472	2 380	1 444	3 092	2 318	3 060	285	2 775	51 427	53.8	20.1
State College	12 139	2.46	5.6	35.7	13 071	194	155	12 877	658	1 164	46	1 118	12 355	13.5	68.2
Wilkes-Barre	15 590	2.41	19.6	40.8	3 065	1 115	420	1 950	1 628	3 969	436	3 533	24 998	56.2	16.0
Williamsport	11 672	2.25	11.1	40.4	2 896	408	143	2 488	1 143	3 896	450	3 446	18 930	50.4	25.7
York	15 284	2.79	21.4	36.8	1 121	113	0	1 008	1 832	4 168	883	3 285	26 260	59.3	14.1
RHODE ISLAND	407 484	2.49	14.0	31.8	42 663	12 932	8 420	29 731	25 248	2 393	219	2 174	730 083	40.3	32.7
Cranston	29 917	2.56	14.7	33.7	4 523	4 004	224	519	1 703	2 105	133	1 971	57 353	40.6	32.2
East Providence	20 355	2.29	23.3	34.2	800	759	680	41	701	1 480	112	1 369	33 835	54.1	23.5
Pawtucket	29 451	2.41	18.8	39.0	524	357	335	167	2 328	3 259	291	2 967	51 063	52.5	20.4
Providence	60 644	2.72	21.1	32.3	15 086	1 200	1 152	13 886	7 793	4 362	522	3 840	107 284	48.0	30.1
Warwick	33 701	2.40	11.9	31.8	660	502	494	158	1 952	2 377	102	2 275	60 902	34.9	34.2
Woonsocket	16 481	2.47	18.8	34.0	802	568	568	234	1 336	3 247	532	2 715	29 109	53.5	18.1
SOUTH CAROLINA	1 857 768	2.56	14.6	28.9	139 154	63 765	19 020	75 389	191 269	3 958	498	3 460	3 319 832	43.1	26.8
Aiken	13 817	2.10	10.5	29.1	1 382	469	427	913	1 620	5 319	348	4 971	23 181	32.3	44.4
Anderson	10 889	2.33	18.8	37.4	1 751	716	577	1 035	2 429	8 953	992	7 962	18 019	45.3	21.6
Charleston	54 065	2.40	10.8	32.9	5 770	300	291	5 470	3 257	2 508	210	2 298	95 643	25.0	50.2
Columbia	44 858	2.32	17.1	40.1	29 919	7 777	920	22 142	8 280	6 173	772	5 401	74 381	31.9	40.7
Florence	16 250	2.31	20.3	36.0	654	389	384	265	3 128	8 242	843	7 399	25 827	38.5	29.7
Goose Creek	13 679	2.81	12.4	22.8	2 322	0	0	2 322	988	2 425	248	2 177	24 898	32.5	27.5
Greenville	27 874	2.17	12.0	42.3	5 129	1 393	208	3 736	3 397	5 486	809	4 677	43 434	30.4	46.2
Greer	12 016	2.77	13.5	29.6	272	130	130	142	903	3 279	356	2 923	20 670	43.0	25.9
Hilton Head Island	17 161	2.35	4.7	25.1	202	202	202	0	NA	NA	NA	NA	32 121	23.8	52.8
Mount Pleasant	31 982	2.53	6.3	28.6	568	544	544	24	1 502	1 958	180	1 778	57 034	16.0	64.6
Myrtle Beach	12 627	2.45	11.6	31.3	217	22	22	195	5 171	17 419	1 438	15 981	22 355	40.3	24.2
North Charleston	37 642	2.82	21.8	31.9	3 859	2 139	283	1 720	6 538	6 192	724	5 468	69 976	44.7	22.6
Rock Hill	29 906	2.29	15.9	37.2	3 005	612	442	2 393	2 733	3 918	515	3 403	45 791	40.1	29.7
Spartanburg	15 237	2.34	21.9	37.5	2 489	302	175	2 187	2 806	7 424	960	6 464	24 191	47.3	26.2
Summerville	18 767	2.58	14.5	32.8	318	251	160	67	1 773	3 788	299	3 489	33 849	36.3	30.5
Sumter	16 218	2.43	21.2	32.6	1 790	364	330	1 426	2 253	5 450	779	4 671	25 649	44.3	20.6
SOUTH DAKOTA	339 437	2.43	9.5	29.6	34 050	14 797	7 005	19 253	18 688	2 190	327	1 864	563 108	40.1	27.5
Aberdeen	11 968	2.16	9.0	41.5	1 191	433	351	758	623	2 255	279	1 976	18 518	42.8	27.6
Rapid City	30 363	2.31	6.7	36.8	2 471	1 331	491	1 140	3 140	4 393	599	3 794	50 701	32.6	32.1
Sioux Falls	69 613	2.38	11.0	31.6	6 085	3 336	982	2 749	5 694	3 403	445	2 958	113 568	34.4	33.5
TENNESSEE	2 530 260	2.55	13.6	28.0	153 472	84 371	33 041	69 101	240 295	3 669	608	3 061	4 473 487	47.1	25.7
Bartlett	20 032	2.88	9.5	17.6	703	688	244	15	1 155	1 973	268	1 705	40 057	36.7	33.4
Brentwood	13 829	3.02	3.8	12.7	349	312	275	37	376	923	47	876	26 442	8.5	76.4
Bristol	11 144	2.33	13.4	34.2	833	226	218	607	1 094	4 112	459	3 654	18 962	40.9	25.9
Chattanooga	69 963	2.40	16.4	37.3	7 562	3 067	1 212	4 495	12 697	7 278	973	6 306	117 791	46.1	26.0
Clarksville	55 418	2.64	12.5	28.1	2 921	904	419	2 017	5 255	3 633	671	2 963	90 080	37.3	26.4
Cleveland	17 017	2.41	11.4	37.5	2 703	786	430	1 917	2 960	6 862	858	6 004	27 666	45.1	21.5
Collierville	16 121	3.03	7.6	18.5	62	62	62	0	857	1 795	157	1 637	30 495	17.4	55.9

1. No spouse present.   2. Data for serious crimes have not been adjusted for underreporting. This may affect comparability between geographic areas and over time.   3. Per 100,000 population estimated by the FBI.   4. Persons 25 years old and over.

Table D. Cities — Income, Poverty, and Housing

City	Money income, 2015 Households Median income	Households Percent with income of $200,000 or more	Households Percent with income of less than $25,000	Families Total Families	Families Percent with income below poverty	Housing units, 2010 Total	Percent change, 2000–2010	Vacant units for sale or rent[2]	Occupied housing units 2015 Owner-occupied Total	Owner-occupied Percent	Owner-occupied Median value[3] (dollars)	Renter-occupied Percent	Renter-occupied Median rent (dollars)
	42	43	44	45	46	47	48	49	50	51	52	53	54
OREGON—Cont'd													
Redmond	42 744	1.0	23.8	6 563	19.9	10 965	92.8	1 018	10 086	53.2	205 400	46.8	921
Salem	49 037	3.5	19.3	37 507	11.4	61 276	14.0	3 986	58 456	52.0	203 200	48.0	812
Springfield	40 651	0.5	20.8	13 492	19.6	24 809	15.0	1 144	22 430	48.5	177 900	51.5	808
Tigard	60 308	7.3	9.6	13 511	8.9	20 068	15.4	911	20 974	53.3	344 800	46.7	1 054
Tualatin	63 481	8.9	15.7	6 367	8.5	10 528	14.2	528	10 675	55.4	359 500	44.6	1 133
West Linn	99 813	19.4	4.8	NA	NA	10 035	14.8	512	9 364	77.5	446 300	22.5	1 432
PENNSYLVANIA	55 702	5.1	16.8	3 204 295	9.1	5 567 315	6.0	548 411	4 956 037	68.7	170 600	31.3	868
Allentown	37 146	1.7	25.7	28 306	22.3	46 921	2.1	4 117	43 046	43.6	130 600	56.4	923
Altoona	38 963	1.7	27.1	12 101	18.0	21 179	-2.3	1 878	19 707	64.8	88 100	35.2	592
Bethel Park	67 971	6.9	9.9	8 864	4.9	14 311	3.2	652	13 451	75.6	177 900	24.4	922
Bethlehem	47 289	3.7	17.5	16 180	8.5	31 221	5.4	1 856	27 723	51.2	174 600	48.8	963
Chester	27 856	1.2	37.1	6 382	35.2	13 745	-8.2	2 083	11 750	36.7	68 200	63.3	728
Easton	49 157	1.1	22.6	5 601	6.9	10 356	-1.8	1 049	9 865	51.3	119 300	48.7	871
Erie	35 139	1.3	29.6	23 945	21.0	44 790	-0.4	3 877	40 914	50.3	89 000	49.7	644
Harrisburg	37 437	1.2	26.4	11 364	23.4	24 269	-0.3	3 664	20 254	35.4	78 000	64.6	839
Hazleton	47 667	0.3	20.4	5 829	11.9	11 409	-1.0	1 611	8 473	57.0	92 600	43.0	817
Lancaster	39 247	1.4	25.6	12 525	20.4	23 377	1.5	1 584	21 324	47.4	109 600	52.6	781
Lebanon	37 764	3.1	27.6	5 652	28.9	11 278	0.5	920	10 022	43.0	93 700	57.0	695
Monroeville	62 081	5.7	15.4	6 844	3.1	13 496	2.6	884	12 397	68.0	141 000	32.0	974
Norristown	46 675	3.0	23.7	7 560	20.8	13 420	-0.8	1 457	11 041	42.9	141 300	57.1	1 120
Philadelphia	41 233	3.3	27.1	319 164	20.9	670 171	1.2	70 435	581 604	52.6	150 700	47.4	952
Pittsburgh	41 293	5.0	27.4	58 367	14.7	156 165	-4.4	19 948	131 793	47.5	108 400	52.5	858
Plum	66 042	4.7	4.6	8 300	2.7	11 494	8.2	608	11 484	76.1	153 900	23.9	922
Reading	26 531	0.5	37.8	17 998	36.8	34 208	-0.3	4 229	28 665	38.2	69 100	61.8	735
Scranton	36 630	1.0	30.9	16 413	19.6	33 853	-4.2	3 784	29 947	51.9	98 800	48.1	735
State College	31 438	1.8	36.6	NA	NA	13 007	4.2	397	12 139	21.3	283 300	78.7	1 048
Wilkes-Barre	29 117	0.6	37.4	8 121	28.0	19 595	-3.4	2 721	15 590	44.8	73 100	55.2	723
Williamsport	40 657	1.3	24.9	5 958	7.7	12 864	-4.9	1 218	11 672	53.6	106 900	46.4	711
York	33 296	0.6	29.9	8 316	30.2	18 496	-0.2	2 243	15 284	40.9	74 300	59.1	771
RHODE ISLAND	58 073	5.6	18.2	250 262	10.1	463 388	5.4	49 788	407 484	59.0	241 000	41.0	938
Cranston	61 963	4.6	14.5	18 473	8.5	33 117	3.3	2 105	29 917	63.6	223 300	36.4	984
East Providence	46 693	2.3	23.1	12 260	10.0	21 440	0.6	1 239	20 355	56.7	204 300	43.3	883
Pawtucket	43 886	1.6	21.1	16 524	15.3	32 055	0.7	3 033	29 451	42.6	173 100	57.4	836
Providence	39 015	4.0	29.0	34 639	23.3	71 530	5.3	8 812	60 644	35.1	177 400	64.9	943
Warwick	74 570	4.8	11.2	21 088	1.8	37 730	1.7	2 496	33 701	71.9	203 600	28.1	1 114
Woonsocket	39 359	1.2	31.8	9 727	23.1	19 214	2.4	2 152	16 481	34.8	156 100	65.2	867
SOUTH CAROLINA	47 238	3.2	20.2	1 220 885	12.1	2 137 683	21.9	336 502	1 857 768	68.1	148 600	31.9	819
Aiken	60 905	5.7	15.5	8 988	9.2	14 162	25.3	1 389	13 817	67.7	188 000	32.3	886
Anderson	31 107	1.4	34.2	6 300	22.9	12 938	7.3	1 858	10 889	50.7	131 100	49.3	679
Charleston	61 993	7.7	13.9	29 415	5.7	59 522	34.8	7 181	54 065	54.0	293 500	46.0	1 119
Columbia	41 435	5.4	25.0	21 916	15.8	52 471	13.9	6 805	44 858	42.9	172 400	57.1	847
Florence	42 696	3.3	22.2	9 724	18.0	16 665	27.5	1 686	16 250	54.4	158 800	45.6	757
Goose Creek	59 729	1.9	12.6	9 774	11.4	13 484	42.4	1 128	13 679	65.5	170 600	34.5	1 084
Greenville	46 089	7.0	21.5	13 581	11.7	29 418	7.5	3 819	27 874	42.7	247 800	57.3	846
Greer	57 093	1.3	21.4	7 713	16.0	11 127	48.5	1 115	12 016	50.9	155 100	49.1	791
Hilton Head Island	65 636	10.1	13.5	11 844	10.9	33 306	35.0	16 771	17 161	75.8	432 200	24.2	1 084
Mount Pleasant	82 826	15.5	8.0	20 924	2.9	30 674	52.4	2 932	31 982	73.0	426 500	27.0	1 405
Myrtle Beach	34 506	4.9	23.5	7 603	19.0	23 262	59.2	11 149	12 627	49.9	186 300	50.1	886
North Charleston	40 365	1.8	23.3	22 358	16.4	42 219	25.5	5 304	37 642	43.5	160 000	56.5	940
Rock Hill	40 885	3.1	23.2	16 871	12.6	29 159	42.4	3 193	29 906	49.0	130 800	51.0	871
Spartanburg	35 777	3.4	26.2	8 824	18.9	17 516	-1.1	2 332	15 237	47.0	115 500	53.0	718
Summerville	51 144	6.3	18.7	11 724	13.7	18 557	64.9	1 691	18 767	68.4	186 800	31.6	961
Sumter	37 356	1.3	22.5	10 268	11.7	18 150	12.6	2 517	16 218	55.4	127 700	44.6	775
SOUTH DAKOTA	53 017	3.6	16.2	217 013	8.3	363 438	12.4	41 156	339 437	68.2	152 800	31.8	675
Aberdeen	42 600	2.3	13.7	6 647	9.4	12 158	8.1	740	11 968	55.5	150 800	44.5	613
Rapid City	49 702	4.4	13.7	17 688	6.1	30 254	20.4	1 668	30 363	66.0	170 400	34.0	788
Sioux Falls	53 802	4.4	16.4	42 260	9.4	66 283	28.1	4 576	69 613	62.1	166 100	37.9	745
TENNESSEE	47 275	3.7	19.9	1 675 678	12.3	2 812 133	15.3	318 581	2 530 260	65.8	150 600	34.2	785
Bartlett	82 047	5.6	9.6	15 862	8.3	20 143	43.9	687	20 032	83.5	170 600	16.5	1 115
Brentwood	146 583	37.5	2.4	11 951	1.2	12 577	58.5	407	13 829	93.4	591 000	6.6	2 009
Bristol	42 362	3.0	22.2	7 054	10.6	12 773	10.9	1 317	11 144	65.0	131 200	35.0	723
Chattanooga	40 004	2.9	25.1	38 388	15.3	79 607	10.4	8 858	69 963	49.7	151 400	50.3	764
Clarksville	46 113	1.0	15.4	35 487	10.5	54 815	36.9	5 376	55 418	50.4	145 400	49.6	915
Cleveland	40 223	4.2	26.7	9 768	18.8	17 841	8.4	1 734	17 017	41.9	167 100	58.1	732
Collierville	107 292	16.5	3.1	NA	NA	15 781	46.7	602	16 121	77.0	281 700	23.0	1 104

1. Based on population estimated by the American Community Survey.   2. Includes units rented or sold but not occupied.   3. Specified owner-occupied units; $1,000,000 represents $1,000,000 or more   4. 50.0 represents 50 percent or more.   5. 10.0 represents 10 percent or less.

Table D. Cities — Commuting, Computer Access, Migration, Labor Force, and Employment

City	Commuting Percent — Drove alone	Commuting Percent — With Commutes of 30 minutes or more[1]	Computer Access[2] Percent — With a Computer in the house	Computer Access[2] Percent — With Internet Access	Migration, 2015 — Percent who lived in the same house one year ago	Migration, 2015 — Percent who lived in an other state or county one year ago	Civilian labor force, 2016 — Total	Civilian labor force, 2016 — Percent change, 2015–2016	Unemployment — Total	Unemployment — Rate[3]	Population age 16 and older — Number	Population age 16 and older — Percent in Labor Force	Population age 16 to 64 — Number	Population age 16 to 64 — Percent who worked full-year full-time
	55	56	57	58	59	60	61	62	63	64	65	66	67	68
OREGON—Cont'd														
Redmond	90.9	19.1	92.2	80.7	77.1	8.4	12 272	6.0	623	5.1	21 400	56.9	15 628	44.4
Salem	75.8	27.0	92.8	85.3	81.2	6.7	78 961	3.9	3 984	5.0	129 839	61.8	108 652	41.7
Springfield	71.0	18.2	88.2	77.0	80.3	4.1	30 936	3.8	1 645	5.3	48 224	66.3	40 743	46.1
Tigard	77.6	37.9	94.1	82.2	82.7	8.5	29 603	4.2	1 145	3.9	41 325	68.4	32 618	50.0
Tualatin	82.0	32.6	92.8	88.8	80.8	11.9	15 106	4.1	606	4.0	20 310	67.9	17 281	49.6
West Linn	86.7	52.0	97.7	94.0	86.4	9.1	14 665	4.1	551	3.8	20 401	69.6	16 787	49.3
PENNSYLVANIA	79.7	38.2	84.6	75.8	87.7	5.0	6 471 990	0.7	351 961	5.4	10 429 005	62.5	8 247 812	50.0
Allentown	68.6	27.1	82.7	68.5	74.8	9.8	54 902	0.9	4 078	7.4	92 969	62.9	77 954	43.6
Altoona	86.1	13.2	81.1	71.2	89.6	3.3	20 668	0.0	1 217	5.9	37 421	58.0	30 036	46.4
Bethel Park	79.8	48.4	86.1	78.2	95.6	2.0	17 239	0.1	775	4.5	25 676	67.2	19 297	56.0
Bethlehem	77.5	27.7	84.6	74.6	78.8	9.8	37 298	0.9	2 164	5.8	61 586	60.8	49 307	46.6
Chester	54.8	40.7	70.7	53.6	84.6	7.6	13 385	1.0	1 182	8.8	27 723	51.2	23 478	27.6
Easton	81.7	29.9	84.4	75.9	77.1	12.8	11 981	0.9	797	6.7	21 740	55.5	18 342	47.3
Erie	73.3	14.5	83.3	71.9	82.7	4.9	45 484	-0.5	3 247	7.1	79 084	60.4	65 921	42.3
Harrisburg	66.7	20.6	82.7	62.4	75.4	12.2	21 679	0.9	1 530	7.1	39 780	65.1	35 256	47.0
Hazleton	73.3	25.4	78.4	63.0	89.6	5.1	11 609	0.0	1 068	9.2	20 267	64.9	16 799	51.7
Lancaster	65.2	21.8	83.6	62.8	79.4	6.3	27 129	1.4	1 653	6.1	47 358	62.7	40 626	43.4
Lebanon	75.3	20.8	67.0	55.9	85.1	2.8	11 664	0.2	759	6.5	19 802	60.6	16 073	50.2
Monroeville	80.5	41.3	91.8	85.2	94.2	1.7	14 720	0.3	739	5.0	23 763	61.9	18 066	54.5
Norristown	73.5	29.3	79.2	65.9	85.1	2.4	18 152	1.4	928	5.1	25 694	65.1	22 141	39.5
Philadelphia	52.8	54.6	81.6	69.5	85.9	4.9	707 571	1.7	48 148	6.8	1 256 533	60.4	1 057 362	43.2
Pittsburgh	57.7	32.4	84.3	74.2	75.7	9.1	157 648	0.1	8 447	5.4	263 136	61.4	218 744	44.5
Plum	92.2	47.1	86.2	79.9	90.6	2.5	15 042	0.2	732	4.9	23 167	65.0	17 445	59.0
Reading	63.9	36.9	78.5	68.7	82.4	5.1	34 257	0.4	2 564	7.5	64 458	64.8	55 800	34.9
Scranton	76.2	16.9	79.7	68.4	82.8	8.2	36 808	0.2	2 212	6.0	63 852	56.2	50 369	44.0
State College	29.7	9.9	95.1	72.1	46.1	30.0	16 666	1.7	865	5.2	40 073	46.5	37 619	22.4
Wilkes-Barre	70.7	13.8	77.7	61.2	81.0	6.1	18 631	0.5	1 370	7.4	32 079	55.8	25 525	30.6
Williamsport	72.4	12.2	85.9	69.4	81.4	7.1	13 845	-3.2	1 021	7.4	24 521	66.8	21 439	46.7
York	72.2	22.7	79.8	55.2	71.1	5.8	17 951	0.9	1 547	8.6	33 140	62.7	28 413	40.4
RHODE ISLAND	81.7	32.7	86.5	78.1	86.2	6.0	552 219	-0.3	29 407	5.3	870 136	64.6	699 604	48.0
Cranston	86.1	25.9	86.5	82.2	87.0	4.3	41 145	-0.3	2 150	5.2	66 605	62.3	53 123	50.0
East Providence	89.0	21.6	83.0	71.4	88.5	4.7	24 211	-0.2	1 371	5.7	39 625	57.7	29 500	50.3
Pawtucket	82.7	30.6	83.1	76.2	84.3	3.9	36 185	-0.3	2 182	6.0	58 745	66.9	48 275	47.3
Providence	65.9	26.9	84.8	73.1	77.3	8.6	86 238	-0.1	5 618	6.5	142 557	60.8	125 348	38.2
Warwick	90.5	29.2	89.8	81.9	88.7	6.3	45 764	-0.2	2 071	4.5	68 534	68.8	52 922	56.2
Woonsocket	80.0	32.5	81.7	73.5	92.9	2.5	19 081	0.0	1 384	7.3	34 392	56.2	28 435	45.5
SOUTH CAROLINA	86.2	33.8	83.4	69.9	84.8	7.1	2 297 807	1.2	111 067	4.8	3 931 185	60.1	3 137 231	48.1
Aiken	91.1	37.4	79.4	71.4	80.4	9.1	13 441	0.6	704	5.2	26 633	51.6	18 574	48.6
Anderson	79.3	15.4	78.7	58.5	76.3	7.5	11 690	0.7	578	4.9	21 684	54.8	15 895	43.7
Charleston	79.1	29.2	91.2	70.9	79.0	10.7	73 022	2.7	2 777	3.8	116 139	68.5	96 999	56.1
Columbia	67.3	12.5	87.3	73.3	66.3	21.8	60 745	0.7	3 230	5.3	113 365	65.5	100 746	37.2
Florence	86.4	17.6	81.9	73.5	82.5	5.1	18 938	0.1	936	4.9	30 459	63.9	23 649	51.6
Goose Creek	82.5	31.1	94.5	87.8	81.4	12.9	19 086	2.5	854	4.5	31 965	68.4	26 723	53.0
Greenville	82.1	14.2	86.0	75.0	76.6	11.6	34 060	1.1	1 396	4.1	52 373	69.8	44 508	52.1
Greer	80.0	32.6	84.1	71.5	78.9	12.7	14 980	1.3	556	3.7	24 844	70.1	20 952	52.6
Hilton Head Island	81.8	11.0	93.3	85.6	85.4	4.9	18 086	1.5	707	3.9	33 623	50.1	19 849	52.4
Mount Pleasant	91.9	24.8	93.5	86.7	81.4	9.3	45 019	2.8	1 477	3.3	62 892	67.2	50 511	60.0
Myrtle Beach	79.6	12.3	87.7	77.5	76.1	9.1	15 065	1.0	988	6.6	25 368	64.0	20 143	42.8
North Charleston	79.5	32.4	85.8	64.2	77.7	10.6	52 633	2.3	2 352	4.5	86 280	66.5	76 229	51.7
Rock Hill	87.6	35.6	88.5	77.1	81.6	8.7	38 048	2.3	1 934	5.1	57 025	67.4	48 059	49.7
Spartanburg	79.9	17.5	79.2	64.8	82.0	5.6	16 976	1.6	906	5.3	29 628	59.7	23 248	42.7
Summerville	88.3	49.8	86.4	77.8	79.5	13.1	23 796	2.2	1 030	4.3	38 437	62.0	31 618	55.8
Sumter	82.0	20.8	82.0	65.4	81.2	11.2	16 151	-0.4	917	5.7	31 669	61.6	25 558	50.9
SOUTH DAKOTA	85.5	14.7	85.0	75.3	82.8	8.6	453 069	0.5	12 770	2.8	671 301	68.1	536 788	56.7
Aberdeen	87.6	7.5	77.3	64.4	76.7	11.0	15 243	0.2	410	2.7	22 285	69.6	17 624	54.7
Rapid City	88.6	7.7	88.5	80.0	79.0	12.5	36 011	0.6	1 144	3.2	58 965	65.0	45 549	56.4
Sioux Falls	86.3	9.0	87.6	78.9	79.6	8.3	99 620	1.3	2 440	2.4	133 671	71.7	112 744	60.2
TENNESSEE	87.2	34.4	82.4	70.1	84.9	6.6	3 135 102	2.1	150 843	4.8	5 277 935	61.0	4 262 155	48.4
Bartlett	94.2	37.4	90.0	86.5	89.4	3.1	30 369	1.4	1 292	4.3	47 432	67.4	38 969	59.2
Brentwood	93.5	31.1	97.9	94.8	87.0	7.7	20 899	3.7	773	3.7	30 775	62.6	24 934	48.1
Bristol	87.8	24.1	86.2	78.1	86.0	4.4	11 672	1.3	671	5.7	21 457	58.7	15 618	54.9
Chattanooga	83.9	14.9	78.7	69.5	83.7	7.4	81 738	2.3	4 193	5.1	142 873	60.7	115 322	46.2
Clarksville	87.8	30.0	90.1	81.5	74.5	13.9	59 075	0.9	3 162	5.4	113 240	67.6	102 101	52.7
Cleveland	82.5	19.3	77.3	64.8	76.4	5.9	20 751	2.0	992	4.8	36 160	59.5	29 885	41.1
Collierville	93.0	40.3	95.8	90.6	89.1	2.4	24 688	1.5	934	3.8	37 770	67.5	32 320	54.7

1. Employed persons.   2. Households.   3. Percent of civilian labor force.   4. Persons 16 years old and over.

Construction, Wholesale Trade, and Retail Trade

City	New construction ($1,000)	Number of housing units	Percent single family	Number of establishments	Number of employees	Sales (mil dol)	Annual payroll (mil dol)	Number of establishments	Number of employees	Sales (mil dol)	Annual payroll (mil dol)
	Value of residential construction authorized by building permits, 2016			Wholesale trade,[1] 2012				Retail trade,[2] 2012			
	69	70	71	72	73	74	75	76	77	78	79
OREGON—Cont'd											
Redmond	60 534	279	100.0	33	206	78.9	8.4	113	1 962	532.5	50.2
Salem	140 404	792	38.1	141	1 652	1 862.8	77.8	604	9 646	2 535.4	252.4
Springfield	25 123	119	87.4	39	873	433.4	35.3	209	3 545	812.2	79.1
Tigard	147 758	656	54.3	148	2 255	2 065.8	150.7	327	7 093	1 827.1	198.3
Tualatin	12 020	45	73.3	107	1 685	785.6	90.2	109	1 837	478.3	43.0
West Linn	16 563	43	90.7	29	93	66.9	5.2	54	473	129.1	12.1
PENNSYLVANIA	0	0	0.0	12 568	195 004	191 170.1	11 203.8	43 952	643 903	178 794.9	15 330.6
Allentown	1 395	16	100.0	144	2 072	1 088.9	87.3	366	5 377	1 387.1	125.7
Altoona	480	2	100.0	47	803	355.3	36.0	248	4 693	1 095.5	94.3
Bethel Park	34 177	354	9.9	32	257	115.6	12.3	109	2 824	628.3	62.0
Bethlehem	3 982	30	93.3	59	D	D	D	214	3 511	919.0	79.5
Chester	0	0	0.0	18	163	78.1	8.3	61	340	119.5	10.6
Easton	0	0	0.0	28	D	D	D	143	1 730	423.5	39.8
Erie	170	2	100.0	110	1 629	679.5	74.2	374	5 516	1 018.6	108.5
Harrisburg	0	0	0.0	58	1 349	1 837.2	89.7	233	2 682	613.8	56.3
Hazleton	0	0	0.0	33	499	151.6	22.7	112	1 124	275.4	22.1
Lancaster	72	2	0.0	60	719	491.1	29.5	364	5 382	1 100.3	117.8
Lebanon	249	2	100.0	18	D	D	D	107	1 260	296.1	31.2
Monroeville	524	2	100.0	46	520	195.8	25.6	276	5 452	1 635.0	131.3
Norristown	0	0	0.0	43	732	456.5	38.6	92	614	134.5	16.5
Philadelphia	534 322	3 175	28.5	1 047	16 940	13 181.9	973.0	4 506	50 185	12 241.3	1 165.5
Pittsburgh	45 685	436	14.4	399	6 843	7 437.6	393.2	1 202	17 411	4 107.1	410.7
Plum	7 704	51	100.0	29	227	104.4	9.9	51	658	149.3	15.9
Reading	0	0	0.0	47	973	490.8	50.7	227	3 321	1 085.9	88.0
Scranton	102 043	450	100.0	96	1 385	963.1	62.1	340	4 493	1 127.2	102.9
State College	524	2	100.0	9	51	16.6	2.5	138	1 883	299.4	33.7
Wilkes-Barre	3 700	56	0.0	46	546	167.9	19.5	260	5 744	4 517.9	139.9
Williamsport	100	1	100.0	40	1 077	638.3	38.4	109	1 683	386.8	38.3
York	526	26	11.5	60	1 005	845.5	38.2	138	2 077	555.9	53.9
RHODE ISLAND	5 579	21	100.0	1 158	15 697	22 310.4	1 000.2	3 795	47 688	12 063.9	1 206.6
Cranston	6 288	55	100.0	129	D	D	D	288	4 488	1 135.5	124.6
East Providence	514	2	0.0	81	D	D	D	150	1 954	561.3	50.6
Pawtucket	1 445	10	60.0	64	D	D	D	176	1 604	456.3	41.9
Providence	8 929	62	17.7	184	1 942	1 475.2	102.4	646	6 835	1 448.7	156.4
Warwick	7 422	53	77.4	140	1 919	909.2	104.8	429	7 656	1 960.7	188.2
Woonsocket	1 313	13	100.0	33	D	D	D	129	1 366	328.2	35.2
SOUTH CAROLINA	5 798	39	100.0	4 337	54 949	45 520.9	2 806.2	17 586	220 438	58 093.8	4 954.6
Aiken	21 487	152	88.2	19	92	158.2	4.2	233	3 420	774.1	68.4
Anderson	9 922	72	100.0	35	253	105.4	9.3	279	4 031	819.8	84.6
Charleston	127 446	1 042	66.4	137	1 331	1 032.0	80.8	733	10 061	2 642.6	246.2
Columbia	49 847	251	100.0	206	3 094	2 469.9	181.7	657	10 186	2 631.1	231.5
Florence	NA	NA	NA	59	973	545.1	45.0	382	5 058	1 162.9	107.6
Goose Creek	36 195	210	100.0	9	D	D	D	74	1 511	387.6	34.0
Greenville	128 103	757	28.5	173	2 302	2 438.0	117.4	777	12 402	3 109.2	298.0
Greer	143 281	819	63.6	42	309	134.3	13.1	138	2 345	786.4	63.9
Hilton Head Island	66 019	118	100.0	54	188	132.4	9.7	259	2 750	645.8	67.0
Mount Pleasant	383 922	1 550	61.9	69	388	149.9	24.7	360	5 269	1 145.8	115.5
Myrtle Beach	121 469	418	94.5	82	616	281.5	26.0	683	9 822	2 163.0	206.7
North Charleston	81 240	767	67.1	219	3 399	1 876.0	177.0	580	8 363	2 269.3	203.1
Rock Hill	51 990	184	91.8	68	1 091	556.9	57.5	322	4 914	1 279.3	106.0
Spartanburg	5 202	22	100.0	63	508	352.6	26.2	355	5 853	1 418.3	130.5
Summerville	96 649	540	50.4	39	339	279.2	12.0	196	3 764	909.6	82.7
Sumter	NA	NA	NA	31	278	96.0	11.7	289	3 599	754.7	69.1
SOUTH DAKOTA	0	0	0.0	1 317	15 827	20 411.1	756.9	3 843	49 867	13 791.8	1 127.3
Aberdeen	4 906	83	100.0	42	698	1 225.2	35.3	176	2 778	751.1	70.2
Rapid City	72 052	574	32.9	139	1 600	1 109.9	69.4	475	7 691	2 110.4	183.0
Sioux Falls	362 280	2 510	42.2	324	5 257	3 108.2	267.7	751	14 515	4 340.9	342.0
TENNESSEE	5 873	32	100.0	5 828	92 537	111 718.4	4 863.3	22 615	306 078	91 641.6	7 420.3
Bartlett	47 612	205	100.0	64	1 097	755.5	62.6	124	2 019	889.8	54.7
Brentwood	69 265	175	100.0	59	785	1 413.2	49.0	175	3 254	1 076.3	102.5
Bristol	0	0	0.0	40	394	123.1	12.5	118	1 872	597.2	51.0
Chattanooga	161 624	1 173	49.2	374	4 859	2 711.5	249.6	1 123	16 813	4 359.1	419.3
Clarksville	107 297	1 044	75.5	68	952	553.2	43.2	489	7 756	1 983.0	188.4
Cleveland	20 901	165	60.6	41	D	D	D	297	4 319	1 150.0	103.0
Collierville	79 496	384	46.1	50	671	518.5	41.7	213	3 540	852.9	76.9

1. Merchant wholesalers except manufacturers' sales branches and offices. 2. Establishments with payroll.

City	Real estate and rental and leasing, 2012				Professional, scientific, and technical services,[1] 2012				Manufacturing, 2012			
	Number of establishments	Number of employees	Receipts (mil dol)	Annual payroll (mil dol)	Number of establishments	Number of employees	Receipts (mil dol)	Annual payroll (mil dol)	Number of establishments	Number of employees	Receipts (mil dol)	Annual payroll (mil dol)
	80	81	82	83	84	85	86	87	88	89	90	91
OREGON—Cont'd												
Redmond	42	164	23.8	5.5	43	D	D	D	59	951	221.6	36.9
Salem	271	1 130	173.7	40.0	494	3 110	381.0	145.7	182	5 324	1 708.8	217.6
Springfield	64	274	54.2	8.4	87	572	49.3	20.0	85	2 380	1 240.8	126.6
Tigard	121	615	219.5	27.6	362	D	D	D	93	1 716	D	D
Tualatin	59	595	125.1	23.3	107	D	D	D	121	6 893	2 103.6	410.6
West Linn	41	172	16.9	4.9	122	290	44.4	15.5	10	264	D	D
PENNSYLVANIA	9 438	58 585	13 364.0	2 617.5	29 113	310 692	54 014.0	22 242.0	13 988	543 641	231 396.2	28 057.8
Allentown	95	498	93.0	16.6	214	D	D	D	140	2 442	687.5	115.1
Altoona	41	193	30.0	6.0	87	D	D	D	45	1 006	293.8	39.6
Bethel Park	30	104	32.6	5.2	92	391	69.9	25.5	30	441	82.1	18.1
Bethlehem	62	306	167.0	13.3	176	1 009	152.0	61.7	53	3 306	1 017.5	188.3
Chester	15	D	D	D	14	D	D	D	26	1 401	929.4	99.3
Easton	21	D	D	D	87	369	59.0	15.1	26	505	233.3	22.1
Erie	66	427	61.9	15.9	196	D	D	D	148	5 832	1 842.9	298.2
Harrisburg	44	381	206.6	40.2	256	D	D	D	32	1 432	666.1	84.0
Hazleton	19	51	9.6	1.5	54	472	70.1	11.7	47	2 606	1 393.1	105.5
Lancaster	48	394	65.3	13.7	222	D	D	D	74	3 363	1 357.6	168.3
Lebanon	27	128	17.6	3.8	53	D	D	D	55	1 140	342.7	44.0
Monroeville	58	546	99.3	21.3	100	1 194	155.2	84.5	17	549	D	30.5
Norristown	29	108	36.4	3.7	94	D	D	D	16	470	D	19.6
Philadelphia	1 079	8 856	1 951.0	443.5	2 793	44 342	10 124.7	4 075.8	765	22 558	19 718.6	1 198.5
Pittsburgh	473	3 628	816.9	179.9	1 505	D	D	D	295	7 303	2 054.6	372.7
Plum	17	57	12.4	1.9	37	539	145.0	54.7	26	320	145.4	14.0
Reading	60	436	61.7	14.1	129	D	D	D	94	7 270	3 814.0	457.0
Scranton	54	333	56.8	10.3	205	D	D	D	77	2 100	660.4	91.6
State College	56	401	91.1	15.9	90	D	D	D	5	169	D	10.4
Wilkes-Barre	34	237	58.7	10.4	119	D	D	D	26	1 099	279.5	48.4
Williamsport	28	204	38.7	8.0	75	1 194	86.8	37.2	51	3 612	1 461.4	168.1
York	36	297	39.9	11.4	137	D	D	D	76	3 422	1 334.4	192.6
RHODE ISLAND	1 058	5 615	1 119.8	218.5	2 980	20 991	3 316.8	1 300.2	1 509	39 608	11 262.2	2 076.5
Cranston	66	366	67.9	14.3	222	1 893	287.4	103.5	156	4 275	1 845.9	211.8
East Providence	57	376	165.0	17.0	129	1 318	191.7	68.9	89	2 304	654.6	112.1
Pawtucket	55	311	38.2	12.4	106	D	D	D	132	3 327	733.0	169.5
Providence	208	1 126	227.9	50.4	790	D	D	D	217	3 165	628.4	135.4
Warwick	111	1 102	223.1	42.2	344	D	D	D	130	3 281	1 227.7	199.0
Woonsocket	40	131	18.0	4.5	44	262	40.2	12.7	43	853	178.8	39.5
SOUTH CAROLINA	4 692	23 189	4 334.4	825.9	9 688	79 433	12 645.3	4 789.2	3 854	207 396	99 160.8	10 082.1
Aiken	42	168	27.9	5.6	125	D	D	D	22	1 506	518.0	70.2
Anderson	47	178	34.4	4.7	133	D	D	D	50	1 956	626.4	79.9
Charleston	278	1 716	249.2	57.6	660	D	D	D	77	1 335	521.0	64.7
Columbia	227	1 594	529.1	96.6	838	D	D	D	69	1 172	D	60.3
Florence	79	398	74.6	14.9	132	D	D	D	20	1 773	1 034.8	117.6
Goose Creek	22	90	33.1	3.4	60	1 152	218.9	65.3	13	755	845.2	47.1
Greenville	243	1 308	310.1	54.5	809	D	D	D	104	3 863	1 260.2	160.8
Greer	35	146	25.9	4.9	66	334	57.7	16.7	39	849	372.9	42.0
Hilton Head Island	223	1 158	179.3	45.4	245	1 028	167.3	70.0	28	186	19.7	6.3
Mount Pleasant	183	384	93.3	15.5	415	D	D	D	35	D	D	D
Myrtle Beach	211	2 259	251.5	66.6	218	1 141	152.1	54.1	27	758	D	35.5
North Charleston	148	1 039	209.0	39.9	345	D	D	D	122	11 200	3 422.0	655.8
Rock Hill	77	319	47.2	10.9	160	D	D	D	60	2 691	1 154.2	153.3
Spartanburg	82	404	69.7	18.0	192	D	D	D	32	1 002	296.2	47.6
Summerville	67	248	43.1	8.3	116	D	D	D	27	1 055	374.8	46.2
Sumter	57	208	22.0	5.3	99	517	44.6	11.9	29	D	214.6	D
SOUTH DAKOTA	962	3 526	582.8	105.7	1 806	11 083	1 310.0	479.5	1 025	41 931	16 882.6	1 764.7
Aberdeen	55	D	D	D	67	378	47.4	16.1	31	2 351	873.4	93.8
Rapid City	141	528	92.4	15.1	270	D	D	D	93	1 766	D	74.6
Sioux Falls	236	1 231	268.4	47.6	473	4 266	497.7	210.2	147	9 836	3 126.3	436.3
TENNESSEE	5 470	30 593	6 178.4	1 220.0	10 815	D	D	D	5 823	293 646	139 960.5	14 180.5
Bartlett	35	145	109.4	4.8	104	921	103.5	41.7	34	920	260.5	44.4
Brentwood	94	D	D	D	306	D	D	D	18	173	D	6.9
Bristol	34	93	17.4	2.7	64	569	80.2	34.0	47	2 255	1 512.1	212.0
Chattanooga	290	1 898	384.3	91.1	621	6 999	979.3	362.0	323	18 889	10 598.1	1 048.6
Clarksville	137	605	100.4	18.4	157	D	D	D	45	3 378	1 142.0	159.0
Cleveland	55	254	33.6	7.2	125	786	71.4	30.7	80	5 481	4 457.4	229.6
Collierville	41	149	32.4	5.0	105	416	54.5	25.9	38	2 236	1 536.9	100.0

1. Establishments subject to federal tax.

Table D. Cities — Accommodation and Food Services, Arts, Entertainment, and Recreation, and Health Care and Social Assistance

City	Accommodation and food services, 2012				Arts, entertainment, and recreation,[1] 2012				Health care and social assistance,[1] 2012			
	Number of establishments	Number of employees	Sales (mil dol)	Annual payroll (mil dol)	Number of establishments	Number of employees	Receipts (mil dol)	Annual payroll (mil dol)	Number of establishments	Number of employees	Receipts (mil dol)	Annual payroll (mil dol)
	92	93	94	95	96	97	98	99	100	101	102	103
OREGON—Cont'd												
Redmond	93	1 231	64.1	18.9	5	D	D	D	80	D	D	D
Salem	405	6 360	318.8	92.9	30	515	29.4	8.7	502	6 639	715.7	304.0
Springfield	168	2 503	136.0	36.9	20	D	D	D	147	D	D	D
Tigard	167	2 707	155.8	44.5	15	D	D	D	200	2 120	229.1	90.6
Tualatin	80	1 542	78.3	23.3	11	D	D	D	126	1 520	216.2	83.7
West Linn	45	645	34.3	10.2	11	69	2.9	0.7	92	D	D	D
PENNSYLVANIA	27 646	439 159	23 504.2	6 377.4	3 117	67 396	6 763.8	2 052.6	27 983	433 818	43 779.7	19 364.3
Allentown	255	3 394	173.8	50.0	18	184	25.4	5.1	283	4 491	471.4	222.0
Altoona	137	2 176	97.5	27.2	9	D	D	D	157	2 596	276.1	123.2
Bethel Park	65	1 589	63.9	19.8	10	D	D	D	110	1 593	127.4	59.1
Bethlehem	217	4 921	636.2	121.2	9	D	D	D	186	2 369	251.4	124.0
Chester	40	D	D	D	3	D	D	D	44	1 671	222.3	122.8
Easton	110	1 447	71.7	19.1	4	D	D	D	58	653	46.2	22.0
Erie	222	3 551	151.0	40.4	29	D	D	D	285	5 043	619.6	320.3
Harrisburg	183	2 537	136.0	35.5	12	D	D	D	97	1 657	184.2	81.9
Hazleton	60	553	25.4	6.4	4	D	D	D	84	1 485	122.1	50.1
Lancaster	162	2 948	174.5	51.3	12	D	D	D	138	D	D	D
Lebanon	58	609	28.1	6.9	4	43	3.1	0.8	66	D	D	D
Monroeville	128	2 852	150.0	40.8	11	190	5.1	2.3	193	3 252	412.6	162.2
Norristown	59	D	D	D	5	1	0.5	0.1	71	787	84.8	43.2
Philadelphia	3 669	53 533	3 551.7	982.4	208	13 373	1 333.2	697.1	2 647	47 119	5 255.8	2 270.4
Pittsburgh	1 234	22 377	1 306.2	375.3	92	D	D	D	963	19 796	2 162.6	1 330.0
Plum	36	527	24.5	6.9	8	D	D	D	20	112	6.8	3.0
Reading	149	1 822	98.4	24.9	7	236	13.1	5.0	99	2 195	189.6	82.5
Scranton	217	2 965	136.3	35.6	17	367	18.8	4.6	227	5 785	719.2	314.6
State College	135	3 042	126.0	34.8	7	70	5.4	1.5	90	D	D	D
Wilkes-Barre	126	2 784	133.9	37.5	7	D	D	D	111	3 579	442.0	167.6
Williamsport	101	1 570	90.5	24.1	6	44	4.7	1.0	83	1 902	166.3	109.0
York	113	1 581	76.0	22.3	6	D	D	D	57	D	D	D
RHODE ISLAND	2 973	44 063	2 481.3	705.9	406	6 108	593.5	150.4	2 470	35 597	3 467.0	1 535.8
Cranston	182	D	D	D	28	D	D	D	231	2 679	227.2	111.4
East Providence	114	1 746	82.6	21.8	20	D	D	D	141	2 850	305.9	155.3
Pawtucket	139	1 384	74.6	20.0	16	129	16.1	5.1	136	2 049	180.2	81.1
Providence	566	9 893	584.0	169.8	35	1 396	85.4	23.1	415	5 910	770.3	358.2
Warwick	248	4 910	262.4	74.2	31	357	24.5	6.8	303	4 416	385.9	170.1
Woonsocket	93	1 218	57.8	15.7	4	52	2.2	0.6	75	2 245	236.0	95.3
SOUTH CAROLINA	9 828	185 282	9 763.8	2 650.5	1 226	17 936	1 471.4	318.4	8 346	132 360	13 822.7	5 385.0
Aiken	134	3 030	118.0	34.6	19	311	17.8	6.3	153	3 760	381.8	139.0
Anderson	165	3 355	147.6	42.8	10	31	1.2	0.4	162	D	D	D
Charleston	517	11 876	786.3	216.0	67	722	63.0	13.2	423	4 151	582.4	230.9
Columbia	505	11 042	560.3	153.4	30	D	D	D	447	7 578	925.6	362.0
Florence	192	3 845	192.1	51.2	11	264	6.4	3.5	230	D	D	D
Goose Creek	69	1 254	57.0	15.1	6	121	4.0	1.3	44	D	D	D
Greenville	448	10 151	539.9	148.8	50	743	34.0	10.5	436	6 515	671.2	316.3
Greer	74	1 172	55.8	15.5	8	D	D	D	79	949	79.1	32.7
Hilton Head Island	226	5 252	388.2	111.7	53	1 045	73.5	20.5	149	1 681	275.2	72.5
Mount Pleasant	220	4 417	229.8	62.5	39	516	25.3	7.8	316	4 075	548.0	169.8
Myrtle Beach	546	13 643	869.7	232.6	78	1 575	151.3	34.2	219	2 882	566.6	167.6
North Charleston	322	6 364	364.7	92.2	14	1 218	19.2	6.3	282	6 172	858.2	285.2
Rock Hill	196	4 123	200.9	52.8	9	52	4.6	1.0	231	5 653	666.2	221.2
Spartanburg	200	4 453	213.9	61.2	13	D	D	D	168	3 712	492.0	227.8
Summerville	146	2 968	134.8	39.0	11	D	D	D	133	D	D	D
Sumter	128	2 635	112.9	31.4	4	68	3.1	1.3	144	2 705	239.6	100.7
SOUTH DAKOTA	2 363	37 974	1 873.7	514.2	526	4 636	352.8	73.0	1 544	20 514	2 023.2	829.8
Aberdeen	90	1 833	77.5	22.9	22	121	14.3	1.8	81	D	D	D
Rapid City	247	5 808	296.8	84.8	66	D	D	D	265	3 417	424.3	155.5
Sioux Falls	409	10 412	491.0	147.6	118	D	D	D	358	6 363	680.4	300.1
TENNESSEE	12 004	241 348	12 499.0	3 546.5	1 931	20 971	2 793.2	934.8	12 286	220 313	24 541.3	9 564.0
Bartlett	84	1 282	62.5	15.3	10	D	D	D	115	2 716	316.5	97.5
Brentwood	92	1 834	107.5	27.5	55	500	59.6	22.7	220	3 698	460.8	224.1
Bristol	83	1 431	58.5	16.3	11	D	D	D	114	D	D	D
Chattanooga	651	14 791	763.5	220.8	63	1 040	59.8	17.2	661	11 426	1 520.4	604.5
Clarksville	319	5 879	285.5	77.3	14	D	D	D	281	4 771	469.8	173.3
Cleveland	163	D	D	D	8	167	5.9	2.3	169	D	D	D
Collierville	97	2 332	105.5	30.6	12	D	D	D	103	D	D	D

1. Establishments subject to federal tax.

Table D. Cities — Other Services and Government Employment and Payroll

	Other services[1], 2012				Government employment and payroll, 2012								
City						March payroll							
							Percent of total for:						
	Number of establish-ments	Number of employees	Receipts (mil dol)	Annual payroll (mil dol)	Full-time equivalent employees	Total (dollars)	Adminis-tration, judicial, and legal	Police and Corrections	Fire Protection	Highways and trans-portation	Health and welfare	Natural resources and utilities	Education and libraries
	104	105	106	107	108	109	110	111	112	113	114	115	116
OREGON—Cont'd													
Redmond	41	161	19.9	5.4	145	696 980	14.3	31.9	0.0	20.4	5.5	20.4	0.0
Salem	221	1 161	86.8	28.8	1 201	6 557 144	12.3	26.5	18.4	2.9	8.3	17.5	2.8
Springfield	79	375	36.9	11.1	535	3 245 769	12.3	22.4	20.4	10.8	4.0	18.1	2.0
Tigard	107	696	75.5	25.0	286	1 551 160	26.2	36.8	0.0	7.7	0.0	11.2	12.8
Tualatin	79	509	42.7	13.8	147	818 379	22.2	35.7	0.0	9.0	1.8	13.6	10.1
West Linn	37	171	8.2	3.3	104	541 464	20.2	40.2	0.0	4.2	0.0	22.8	12.6
PENNSYLVANIA	20 247	114 850	10 517.4	3 078.9	X	X	X	X	X	X	X	X	X
Allentown	196	1 384	115.2	37.0	870	4 561 766	8.4	33.3	19.8	5.0	8.9	19.7	0.0
Altoona	104	579	37.6	12.7	242	1 031 472	8.7	39.4	29.9	15.7	4.9	1.4	0.0
Bethel Park	80	610	37.9	13.3	127	577 790	11.9	56.2	0.0	16.0	0.0	15.3	0.0
Bethlehem	103	892	72.1	26.8	680	3 090 583	7.7	30.1	17.3	3.5	8.2	18.8	0.0
Chester	33	214	16.3	4.7	305	1 818 516	31.3	36.7	17.7	3.5	2.3	3.4	0.0
Easton	51	249	21.3	6.6	246	1 153 107	13.0	32.8	24.1	5.8	1.5	12.2	0.0
Erie	158	727	55.7	16.7	656	3 187 505	6.2	34.9	25.5	9.0	2.8	15.7	0.0
Harrisburg	73	320	28.9	9.4	534	2 458 452	13.1	41.4	17.4	3.7	6.0	16.7	0.0
Hazleton	40	119	9.2	2.8	93	424 630	10.3	46.4	20.8	13.6	6.5	0.6	0.0
Lancaster	94	499	32.6	11.6	519	2 372 327	5.8	43.9	17.4	3.9	3.7	21.3	0.0
Lebanon	51	208	18.1	5.2	153	662 861	5.0	39.2	17.2	5.8	2.6	30.3	0.0
Monroeville	82	503	30.5	10.6	148	872 947	9.5	53.2	0.0	15.7	2.8	6.5	6.5
Norristown	43	188	24.6	7.4	170	899 425	10.6	61.2	15.6	6.4	0.0	0.7	0.0
Philadelphia	1 947	10 726	869.3	257.8	29 409	148 399 324	18.0	39.0	9.6	3.4	11.1	15.4	1.7
Pittsburgh	589	4 360	396.7	123.0	4 176	16 527 485	9.4	38.3	25.1	11.2	8.9	5.4	0.0
Plum	40	182	17.4	4.7	67	358 089	66.3	0.0	0.0	0.0	0.0	0.0	0.0
Reading	80	473	47.4	14.7	730	12 558 088	5.8	44.6	24.9	0.6	5.6	13.5	1.3
Scranton	123	595	42.9	12.5	484	2 233 185	4.0	40.2	30.7	5.1	1.7	7.2	6.5
State College	41	285	15.2	6.1	165	866 140	14.2	48.6	0.0	13.8	4.0	4.8	0.0
Wilkes-Barre	70	349	30.5	8.2	284	1 342 714	13.0	34.7	27.3	0.0	8.1	12.4	0.0
Williamsport	51	390	28.4	8.2	201	913 971	5.1	32.7	21.3	35.2	1.9	3.5	0.0
York	54	510	48.9	14.2	379	1 772 634	9.4	43.1	18.8	1.0	6.2	13.8	0.0
RHODE ISLAND	1 838	9 862	884.8	273.4	X	X	X	X	X	X	X	X	X
Cranston	157	971	86.9	28.6	2 144	11 389 033	1.9	8.5	6.8	1.5	0.6	0.6	78.6
East Providence	91	431	50.1	14.8	1 234	5 386 925	3.6	8.7	7.8	3.2	0.6	4.6	71.2
Pawtucket	106	623	61.0	18.7	1 817	9 164 839	2.7	8.8	7.2	0.8	1.4	4.4	72.6
Providence	290	1 961	165.9	50.3	5 219	27 174 708	5.3	17.6	13.9	1.5	0.0	6.7	54.9
Warwick	173	1 135	94.7	30.2	2 400	12 798 555	2.8	10.0	12.2	1.9	0.5	3.3	67.2
Woonsocket	60	274	30.1	8.6	1 167	6 516 930	2.3	7.1	7.8	1.5	0.3	1.7	77.9
SOUTH CAROLINA	5 482	34 926	3 006.7	1 000.9	X	X	X	X	X	X	X	X	X
Aiken	48	279	21.0	6.0	346	1 255 386	18.9	27.9	10.5	14.5	0.0	24.7	0.0
Anderson	67	428	30.2	9.8	420	924 851	13.0	31.8	14.8	8.6	2.0	25.1	0.0
Charleston	187	1 286	81.0	28.8	2 045	7 787 974	9.2	27.1	16.5	1.2	1.0	37.8	0.0
Columbia	179	1 789	129.9	41.8	2 261	7 098 669	11.6	20.9	23.5	2.0	2.7	24.7	0.0
Florence	64	571	35.9	10.4	510	1 554 745	9.4	29.2	16.4	5.2	3.3	35.0	0.0
Goose Creek	42	220	15.4	4.7	271	928 636	14.9	34.9	20.4	3.8	0.0	23.9	0.0
Greenville	208	1 367	89.8	31.4	1 049	3 701 819	9.4	20.4	14.8	5.7	1.5	42.0	0.0
Greer	41	195	15.1	4.9	189	659 763	25.5	37.5	20.6	2.5	0.0	13.8	0.0
Hilton Head Island	97	396	33.3	11.0	242	1 283 504	30.6	0.0	57.1	4.6	0.0	0.5	0.0
Mount Pleasant	120	838	59.9	22.1	569	1 912 550	16.4	33.5	20.8	2.0	0.8	24.2	0.0
Myrtle Beach	122	653	47.9	15.1	889	3 176 078	16.3	31.5	18.5	3.8	0.5	25.7	1.3
North Charleston	192	1 544	152.2	49.9	1 049	3 596 992	11.5	39.1	21.3	5.5	0.4	16.7	0.0
Rock Hill	89	787	71.8	22.4	836	2 857 047	21.2	21.2	14.2	3.9	6.3	29.3	0.0
Spartanburg	90	737	58.3	15.4	616	2 210 757	10.5	25.6	11.1	4.0	2.5	41.1	0.0
Summerville	91	560	40.0	14.3	357	1 158 866	7.9	29.3	23.7	1.9	0.0	33.0	0.0
Sumter	73	D	D	D	550	1 497 205	11.8	29.7	18.8	1.8	1.1	29.5	0.0
SOUTH DAKOTA	1 363	6 155	578.2	152.9	X	X	X	X	X	X	X	X	X
Aberdeen	43	198	16.7	4.5	287	1 030 395	10.5	20.7	18.3	13.5	0.0	31.3	4.3
Rapid City	176	1 034	84.9	26.0	868	1 798 797	7.6	17.7	12.4	6.9	0.0	24.6	3.9
Sioux Falls	265	1 851	149.3	47.4	1 148	5 118 747	9.5	24.6	18.4	10.7	7.0	21.1	5.6
TENNESSEE	6 521	44 354	3 896.0	1 201.1	X	X	X	X	X	X	X	X	X
Bartlett	62	614	45.6	14.5	511	2 039 502	14.7	30.7	21.1	6.5	0.0	20.1	0.0
Brentwood	58	427	38.4	11.5	256	1 094 815	19.4	23.6	26.3	6.2	0.0	13.8	5.5
Bristol	47	307	29.4	9.1	919	3 282 369	4.6	12.4	6.6	3.8	0.6	7.7	61.5
Chattanooga	346	2 676	264.2	76.0	3 133	11 941 830	7.9	16.8	12.6	11.2	5.0	42.3	2.0
Clarksville	164	931	71.3	19.9	1 114	3 666 316	6.5	29.4	19.3	13.3	0.6	26.7	0.0
Cleveland	64	748	59.6	18.9	1 030	3 567 674	2.1	10.1	17.6	4.9	1.2	2.8	59.7
Collierville	58	525	30.7	11.5	435	1 694 955	11.6	31.7	20.1	7.3	1.0	19.2	0.0

1. Establishments subject to federal tax.

City	City government finances, 2012									
	General revenue							General expenditure		
		Intergovernmental		Taxes					Per capita[1] (dollars)	
					Per capita[1] (dollars)					
	Total (mil dol)	Total (mil dol)	Percent from state government	Total (mil dol)	Total	Property	Sales and gross receipts	Total (mil dol)	Total	Capital outlays
	117	118	119	120	121	122	123	124	125	126
OREGON—Cont'd										
Redmond	35.3	5.9	60.8	13.4	502	328	174	32.9	1 229	258
Salem	251.3	76.0	63.8	101.3	642	489	153	240.9	1 527	209
Springfield	103.6	9.1	99.1	32.9	549	452	97	90.7	1 514	262
Tigard	45.1	9.8	49.5	26.0	522	305	217	43.3	870	90
Tualatin	29.9	5.6	64.3	13.3	498	310	188	27.4	1 025	191
West Linn	24.0	5.0	70.0	11.3	439	271	168	22.2	865	100
PENNSYLVANIA	X	X	X	X	X	X	X	X	X	X
Allentown	129.2	30.4	47.0	56.8	477	247	115	175.0	1 471	88
Altoona	29.3	7.5	47.2	17.6	381	194	73	27.1	587	40
Bethel Park	24.5	2.7	71.8	13.8	427	131	46	25.6	790	60
Bethlehem	101.1	27.5	100.0	47.5	632	280	117	89.6	1 193	0
Chester	47.9	12.2	79.6	19.2	563	252	84	45.6	1 340	83
Easton	52.4	14.3	75.3	14.8	546	331	69	53.4	1 967	129
Erie	113.3	23.8	46.1	46.9	464	337	53	105.0	1 039	74
Harrisburg	93.9	6.2	90.0	30.4	616	345	171	78.7	1 595	121
Hazleton	18.6	7.2	55.0	8.3	329	113	39	13.3	528	65
Lancaster	69.1	11.7	71.8	31.0	522	384	54	87.4	1 472	261
Lebanon	21.7	10.2	34.6	8.3	325	116	37	26.5	1 036	259
Monroeville	23.1	1.7	95.3	19.7	695	159	284	30.1	1 058	116
Norristown	28.2	3.4	47.9	21.6	627	320	95	30.2	875	85
Philadelphia	6 411.8	2 254.7	74.3	3 239.1	2 089	323	474	5 483.2	3 537	209
Pittsburgh	607.0	163.6	87.2	357.2	1 166	443	419	548.9	1 791	25
Plum	13.3	1.8	85.5	9.6	352	192	32	13.6	498	25
Reading	139.8	30.8	89.3	42.9	488	220	111	135.9	1 543	96
Scranton	67.6	10.7	95.5	45.2	593	179	69	70.2	923	3
State College	36.3	5.5	55.6	11.4	272	114	42	35.4	843	78
Wilkes-Barre	52.9	20.4	46.2	24.1	583	208	78	57.3	1 386	201
Williamsport	41.3	20.3	45.8	15.5	526	329	123	30.5	1 035	151
York	68.7	9.7	51.4	24.7	566	395	110	63.2	1 448	39
RHODE ISLAND	X	X	X	X	X	X	X	X	X	X
Cranston	282.2	60.2	92.5	187.4	2 322	2 290	32	256.9	3 184	42
East Providence	148.4	43.6	95.5	91.6	1 942	1 918	24	155.3	3 292	150
Pawtucket	197.7	91.3	77.8	95.5	1 339	1 328	10	192.3	2 697	24
Providence	747.8	292.1	91.6	325.5	1 822	1 765	57	715.3	4 004	160
Warwick	318.8	59.3	98.4	219.5	2 682	2 607	74	303.4	3 707	110
Woonsocket	147.2	67.5	95.5	57.6	1 401	1 352	50	147.3	3 584	80
SOUTH CAROLINA	X	X	X	X	X	X	X	X	X	X
Aiken	42.7	5.6	22.9	23.7	790	330	460	40.3	1 341	206
Anderson	40.2	4.0	38.2	19.7	735	460	275	43.2	1 613	63
Charleston	207.6	27.8	72.1	132.3	1 053	446	607	178.8	1 424	222
Columbia	222.0	28.7	56.5	95.1	721	383	339	189.3	1 435	255
Florence	47.5	3.6	40.8	22.6	603	96	506	40.8	1 086	63
Goose Creek	19.6	0.7	100.0	11.6	298	47	251	20.5	528	67
Greenville	95.3	5.9	100.0	64.6	1 066	598	468	99.6	1 643	290
Greer	28.9	2.8	31.9	15.7	593	370	223	45.5	1 711	36
Hilton Head Island	89.1	35.5	16.2	48.4	1 261	625	586	94.8	2 471	1 299
Mount Pleasant	114.5	34.1	60.2	59.9	833	385	448	106.8	1 486	667
Myrtle Beach	161.3	12.2	83.8	82.5	2 918	878	2 040	123.3	4 360	375
North Charleston	122.2	14.2	23.7	93.4	915	471	408	119.1	1 168	208
Rock Hill	88.3	12.8	15.4	35.8	525	351	174	102.2	1 502	271
Spartanburg	53.3	13.1	6.6	33.4	895	449	446	42.1	1 130	160
Summerville	29.5	3.1	88.8	21.9	494	238	255	26.9	608	53
Sumter	43.8	6.9	24.7	24.0	587	218	369	40.1	980	178
SOUTH DAKOTA	X	X	X	X	X	X	X	X	X	X
Aberdeen	39.6	5.1	70.4	24.2	900	292	609	38.1	1 414	18
Rapid City	138.0	19.9	85.8	75.4	1 077	309	768	126.9	1 813	706
Sioux Falls	226.3	20.3	62.2	149.5	933	282	651	225.7	1 408	474
TENNESSEE	X	X	X	X	X	X	X	X	X	X
Bartlett	55.6	18.3	51.6	21.0	361	305	56	47.7	820	25
Brentwood	49.5	19.7	38.7	18.1	463	278	185	45.0	1 153	330
Bristol	75.0	35.6	60.9	26.6	999	899	101	74.6	2 797	336
Chattanooga	485.4	165.9	19.7	139.3	809	668	141	396.3	2 300	197
Clarksville	137.4	38.8	51.1	37.5	262	197	65	103.9	725	103
Cleveland	109.5	65.6	56.3	19.7	464	400	64	96.6	2 278	237
Collierville	56.6	15.9	37.4	25.4	547	460	87	51.4	1 107	164

1. Based on population estimated as of July 1 of the year shown.

Table D. Cities — **City Government Finances**

	City government finances, 2012 (cont.)									
	General expenditure (cont.)									
	Percent of total for:									
City	Public welfare	Highways	Parking facilities	Education	Health and hospitals	Police protection	Sewerage and sanitation	Parks and recreation	Housing and community development	Interest on debt
	127	128	129	130	131	132	133	134	135	136
OREGON—Cont'd										
Redmond	0.0	21.1	0.0	0.0	0.0	15.5	10.0	8.1	3.5	10.2
Salem	0.0	14.5	0.7	0.0	0.5	13.9	12.1	3.7	13.0	8.7
Springfield	0.0	5.4	0.0	0.0	5.6	16.9	38.3	0.0	1.1	4.0
Tigard	0.3	7.7	0.0	0.0	0.0	32.1	6.0	8.9	0.0	3.8
Tualatin	0.0	6.8	0.1	0.0	0.0	16.5	24.6	7.3	13.2	1.4
West Linn	0.0	8.3	0.0	0.0	0.0	26.6	11.1	13.8	0.0	1.9
PENNSYLVANIA	X	X	X	X	X	X	X	X	X	X
Allentown	0.0	8.9	0.0	0.0	3.5	18.4	23.6	4.4	6.1	2.8
Altoona	0.0	14.2	0.0	0.0	0.0	19.2	3.2	1.2	0.4	4.1
Bethel Park	0.0	22.7	0.0	0.0	0.0	23.6	35.2	3.1	0.5	0.9
Bethlehem	0.0	9.0	0.0	0.0	4.0	14.3	14.7	6.1	3.7	7.6
Chester	0.0	7.2	0.0	0.0	1.1	32.8	3.0	11.5	2.2	2.3
Easton	0.0	6.5	0.4	0.0	0.1	15.5	18.0	5.8	18.7	5.4
Erie	0.0	11.3	0.0	0.0	0.0	14.0	14.2	2.1	11.8	7.3
Harrisburg	0.0	7.4	0.0	0.0	0.2	24.9	23.4	3.9	8.6	3.8
Hazleton	0.0	13.4	0.0	0.0	1.1	27.9	2.4	0.8	7.7	3.1
Lancaster	0.0	5.5	0.0	0.0	0.0	20.9	23.8	6.2	5.6	9.3
Lebanon	0.0	53.3	0.1	0.0	0.7	15.7	0.8	1.4	6.1	0.1
Monroeville	0.0	20.1	0.0	0.0	0.3	34.5	4.7	6.1	1.2	3.1
Norristown	0.0	15.4	0.0	0.0	1.6	24.2	5.2	2.1	0.0	4.5
Philadelphia	10.4	2.1	0.0	1.4	24.8	11.1	7.0	1.5	3.5	3.9
Pittsburgh	0.0	0.6	0.0	0.0	2.5	14.1	2.8	3.0	16.9	6.6
Plum	0.0	28.0	0.0	0.0	0.0	29.8	11.8	0.2	0.0	4.0
Reading	0.0	8.0	0.0	0.0	2.7	20.8	21.1	2.8	14.3	8.1
Scranton	0.0	4.2	3.7	0.0	2.3	23.1	4.8	1.1	0.2	11.1
State College	0.0	15.4	4.9	0.0	0.9	24.5	27.4	3.1	3.2	2.6
Wilkes-Barre	0.0	23.8	0.5	0.0	4.6	16.0	7.5	7.7	7.2	7.7
Williamsport	0.0	28.5	0.0	0.0	0.0	21.9	14.1	2.4	3.5	1.1
York	0.0	6.2	0.9	0.0	3.2	15.4	23.5	4.9	6.1	8.0
RHODE ISLAND	X	X	X	X	X	X	X	X	X	X
Cranston	0.0	6.7	0.0	55.8	1.1	9.1	6.7	0.9	0.6	2.1
East Providence	0.0	3.8	0.0	57.0	0.3	7.9	7.4	1.5	0.8	1.9
Pawtucket	0.0	1.0	0.0	62.2	0.0	8.3	1.9	0.8	1.8	1.1
Providence	0.0	1.4	0.0	53.6	0.0	11.5	1.4	1.2	2.1	5.7
Warwick	0.4	2.3	0.0	56.7	0.1	6.4	4.3	0.7	0.4	1.6
Woonsocket	0.2	1.6	0.0	53.4	0.1	6.0	10.2	0.1	1.1	8.0
SOUTH CAROLINA	X	X	X	X	X	X	X	X	X	X
Aiken	0.0	7.0	0.0	0.0	0.0	22.5	13.8	12.3	1.7	0.1
Anderson	0.0	8.9	1.2	0.0	0.0	14.1	22.7	7.2	3.6	9.8
Charleston	0.4	3.1	5.1	0.0	0.0	22.4	4.6	13.3	3.8	1.7
Columbia	0.0	4.0	1.7	0.0	0.7	13.1	43.5	7.0	3.2	2.4
Florence	0.0	6.9	0.0	0.0	0.1	23.0	19.5	15.0	6.8	1.0
Goose Creek	0.0	12.8	0.0	0.0	0.0	27.9	5.4	24.9	0.0	0.3
Greenville	0.0	7.1	3.2	0.0	0.5	18.3	13.4	14.0	4.6	2.4
Greer	0.0	2.8	0.0	0.0	0.0	10.2	60.8	3.3	1.8	7.7
Hilton Head Island	0.0	1.9	0.0	0.0	0.0	6.5	2.0	0.0	30.1	4.5
Mount Pleasant	0.0	41.5	0.0	0.0	0.0	10.2	14.4	4.9	1.7	4.1
Myrtle Beach	0.0	3.8	1.5	0.0	0.0	16.0	11.8	19.5	3.8	7.6
North Charleston	0.0	4.5	0.5	0.0	0.0	25.1	8.9	5.1	1.0	5.2
Rock Hill	0.0	2.7	0.0	0.0	0.0	13.2	22.9	12.5	2.9	3.6
Spartanburg	0.0	6.2	2.3	0.0	0.0	22.3	4.7	7.7	4.1	5.1
Summerville	0.0	11.9	0.0	0.0	0.0	23.8	8.6	7.7	0.1	1.8
Sumter	0.0	1.7	0.0	0.0	0.0	23.3	16.2	12.9	8.3	0.8
SOUTH DAKOTA	X	X	X	X	X	X	X	X	X	X
Aberdeen	0.0	29.4	0.0	0.0	3.2	9.7	7.1	15.7	0.0	2.8
Rapid City	0.6	19.1	0.5	0.0	2.8	10.2	14.4	12.7	1.8	3.0
Sioux Falls	0.0	19.1	0.9	0.0	4.2	12.3	22.3	14.2	2.2	3.2
TENNESSEE	X	X	X	X	X	X	X	X	X	X
Bartlett	0.7	8.5	0.0	0.0	5.6	26.6	15.0	11.0	0.0	2.2
Brentwood	0.0	19.3	0.0	0.5	0.2	13.3	16.6	5.6	0.0	3.8
Bristol	0.0	4.9	0.0	54.1	0.0	9.0	9.0	5.1	0.9	1.0
Chattanooga	3.7	5.6	0.4	0.0	0.6	13.8	18.8	6.1	2.6	4.4
Clarksville	0.0	10.6	0.3	0.0	0.0	22.6	26.1	6.1	1.6	6.6
Cleveland	0.0	6.0	0.0	47.1	0.6	9.4	11.6	2.5	1.3	2.9
Collierville	0.7	12.6	0.0	0.0	1.6	20.1	14.9	7.5	0.0	2.6

Table D. Cities — City Government Finances, City Government Employment, and Climate

City	City government finances, 2012 (cont.) Debt outstanding Total (mil dol)	Per capita[1] (dollars)	Debt issued during year	Climate[2] Average daily temperature (degrees Fahrenheit) Mean January	July	Limits January[3]	July[4]	Annual precipitation (inches)	Heating degree days	Cooling degree days
	137	138	139	140	141	142	143	144	145	146
OREGON—Cont'd										
Redmond	73.6	2 750	12.3	NA	NA	NA	NA	NA	NA	NA
Salem	711.5	4 509	94.7	40.3	66.8	33.5	81.5	40.00	4 784	257
Springfield	151.8	2 534	3.8	39.8	66.2	33.0	81.5	50.90	4 786	242
Tigard	131.8	2 649	100.1	40.0	66.8	33.8	79.2	39.95	4 723	287
Tualatin	14.5	544	0.0	NA	NA	NA	NA	NA	NA	NA
West Linn	21.7	847	8.5	NA	NA	NA	NA	NA	NA	NA
PENNSYLVANIA	X	X	X	X	X	X	X	X	X	X
Allentown	119.4	1 003	11.6	27.1	73.3	19.1	83.9	45.17	5 830	787
Altoona	38.9	844	1.0	26.5	71.1	18.2	81.9	42.69	6 055	546
Bethel Park	4.8	147	0.0	28.6	73.1	19.8	84.5	37.78	5 727	709
Bethlehem	228.4	3 041	27.6	27.1	73.3	19.1	83.9	45.17	5 830	787
Chester	8.1	239	0.0	33.7	78.7	27.9	87.5	40.66	4 469	1 333
Easton	33.9	1 250	7.7	27.1	73.3	19.1	83.9	45.17	5 830	787
Erie	189.6	1 876	47.4	26.9	72.1	20.3	80.4	42.77	6 243	620
Harrisburg	110.0	2 230	0.0	30.3	75.9	23.1	85.7	41.45	5 201	955
Hazleton	11.6	460	5.6	NA	NA	NA	NA	NA	NA	NA
Lancaster	221.6	3 732	38.9	29.1	74.4	20.7	84.7	43.47	5 448	809
Lebanon	0.3	12	0.0	NA	NA	NA	NA	NA	NA	NA
Monroeville	30.2	1 064	7.5	28.6	73.1	19.8	84.5	37.78	5 727	709
Norristown	23.9	694	0.0	30.2	75.1	20.4	86.6	43.87	5 174	884
Philadelphia	7 729.2	4 985	667.1	32.3	77.6	25.5	85.5	42.05	4 759	1 235
Pittsburgh	704.7	2 300	0.0	27.5	72.6	19.9	82.7	37.85	5 829	726
Plum	50.0	1 825	11.3	28.6	73.1	19.8	84.5	37.78	5 727	709
Reading	256.9	2 918	24.4	27.1	73.6	19.1	83.8	45.28	5 876	723
Scranton	61.9	814	0.0	26.3	72.1	18.5	82.6	37.56	6 234	611
State College	28.2	673	0.0	25.4	71.2	18.3	80.7	39.76	6 345	538
Wilkes-Barre	73.4	1 775	9.2	21.5	67.7	13.2	77.4	47.89	7 466	234
Williamsport	5.4	183	2.3	25.5	72.4	17.9	83.2	41.59	6 063	709
York	128.7	2 949	22.1	30.0	74.6	20.9	86.5	43.00	5 233	862
RHODE ISLAND	X	X	X	X	X	X	X	X	X	X
Cranston	88.4	1 096	19.4	28.7	73.3	20.3	82.6	46.45	5 754	714
East Providence	75.2	1 595	23.3	28.7	73.3	20.3	82.6	46.45	5 754	714
Pawtucket	159.7	2 239	9.4	28.7	73.3	20.3	82.6	46.45	5 754	714
Providence	735.9	4 120	5.4	28.7	73.3	20.3	82.6	46.45	5 754	714
Warwick	170.1	2 078	2.4	28.7	73.3	20.3	82.6	46.45	5 754	714
Woonsocket	202.3	4 921	1.0	25.4	72.3	13.3	84.3	48.75	6 302	534
SOUTH CAROLINA	X	X	X	X	X	X	X	X	X	X
Aiken	2.8	92	0.0	45.6	81.7	33.4	93.7	52.43	2 413	2 081
Anderson	125.4	4 687	53.2	41.7	79.7	31.3	90.5	46.67	3 087	1 700
Charleston	74.3	592	0.0	49.8	82.8	42.4	88.5	46.39	1 755	2 473
Columbia	505.3	3 832	205.7	47.3	83.6	36.5	95.2	47.14	2 044	2 475
Florence	139.9	3 725	7.4	45.0	81.2	35.2	90.7	44.76	2 523	2 029
Goose Creek	1.4	36	0.0	47.9	81.7	36.9	90.9	51.53	2 005	2 306
Greenville	94.3	1 556	17.3	40.8	78.8	31.4	88.8	50.24	3 272	1 526
Greer	93.7	3 527	1.7	NA	NA	NA	NA	NA	NA	NA
Hilton Head Island	127.7	3 326	46.9	47.9	80.5	37.3	88.2	52.52	2 128	2 012
Mount Pleasant	99.4	1 383	0.0	47.1	81.1	37.5	88.5	49.38	2 260	2 124
Myrtle Beach	216.4	7 653	27.5	NA	NA	NA	NA	NA	NA	NA
North Charleston	186.0	1 823	52.5	47.9	81.7	36.9	90.9	51.53	2 005	2 306
Rock Hill	186.9	2 745	54.5	42.2	80.1	32.5	90.1	48.32	2 934	1 721
Spartanburg	205.6	5 518	0.0	42.1	79.3	30.1	91.1	49.95	3 080	1 591
Summerville	7.9	179	0.0	49.1	81.8	38.0	91.8	48.24	1 907	2 251
Sumter	45.0	1 100	4.2	44.9	80.7	33.6	91.8	48.65	2 577	1 913
SOUTH DAKOTA	X	X	X	X	X	X	X	X	X	X
Aberdeen	63.9	2 375	5.3	NA	NA	NA	NA	NA	NA	NA
Rapid City	113.7	1 624	24.2	22.3	70.2	10.3	82.7	18.45	7 623	480
Sioux Falls	307.2	1 916	24.4	14.0	73.0	2.9	85.6	24.69	7 812	747
TENNESSEE	X	X	X	X	X	X	X	X	X	X
Bartlett	40.8	701	9.5	37.3	79.6	27.3	89.9	55.09	3 665	1 635
Brentwood	29.8	765	16.6	NA	NA	NA	NA	NA	NA	NA
Bristol	50.2	1 884	3.1	NA	NA	NA	NA	NA	NA	NA
Chattanooga	733.3	4 256	51.6	39.4	79.6	29.9	89.8	54.52	3 427	1 608
Clarksville	870.1	6 075	29.2	35.2	79.0	25.0	90.4	51.78	4 058	1 512
Cleveland	130.0	3 067	3.1	38.0	77.5	27.7	88.5	55.42	3 782	1 333
Collierville	60.9	1 313	5.0	37.9	81.1	28.2	91.1	53.63	3 491	1 838

1. Based on the population estimated as of July 1 of the year shown. 2. Represents normal values based on the 30-year period, 1971–2000. 3. Average daily minimum.
4. Average daily maximum.

Table D. Cities — **Land Area and Population**

STATE Place code	City	Land area,[1] 2016 (sq mi)	Population, 2016 Total persons	Rank	Per square mile	Race alone[2] (percent), 2015 White	Black or African American	American Indian, Alaska Native	Asian	Hawaiian Pacific Islander	Some other race	2 or more races[2]
		1	2	3	4	5	6	7	8	9	10	11
	TENNESSEE— Cont'd											
47 16540	Columbia	31.9	37 540	1 019	1 176.8	75.2	20.2	0.0	0.7	0.0	1.9	2.0
47 16920	Cookeville	35.3	32 622	1 163	924.1	88.5	4.7	0.3	2.5	0.0	1.1	2.9
47 27740	Franklin	41.5	74 794	465	1 802.3	83.1	10.3	0.0	4.6	0.0	0.2	1.8
47 28540	Gallatin	31.6	35 734	1 069	1 130.8	79.2	14.8	0.0	0.4	0.4	2.5	2.8
47 28960	Germantown	20.0	39 056	972	1 952.8	89.7	2.7	0.2	6.3	0.0	0.1	0.9
47 33280	Hendersonville	31.4	57 050	656	1 816.9	82.9	6.8	0.4	2.3	0.0	4.0	3.7
47 37640	Jackson	58.5	67 005	534	1 145.4	51.6	43.9	0.0	1.2	0.0	1.0	2.2
47 38320	Johnson City	43.0	66 677	539	1 550.6	86.7	6.2	0.1	2.4	0.0	0.8	3.8
47 39560	Kingsport	53.5	52 806	717	987.0	89.7	4.6	0.1	0.4	0.1	1.6	3.4
47 40000	Knoxville	98.5	186 239	129	1 890.8	75.9	17.0	0.2	1.7	0.3	1.6	3.3
47 41200	La Vergne	25.0	35 071	1 082	1 402.8	NA	NA	NA	NA	NA	NA	NA
47 41520	Lebanon	38.4	31 317	1 202	815.5	83.5	11.9	1.5	1.5	0.0	0.8	0.9
47 46380	Maryville	16.9	28 703	1 296	1 698.4	NA	NA	NA	NA	NA	NA	NA
47 48000	Memphis	317.4	652 717	25	2 056.4	29.7	63.3	0.0	2.1	0.1	3.1	1.7
47 50280	Morristown	27.4	29 663	1 262	1 082.6	72.7	11.2	0.0	0.0	0.2	12.0	4.0
47 51560	Murfreesboro	55.9	131 947	205	2 360.4	72.7	15.0	0.1	4.6	0.0	2.8	4.7
47 52004	Nashville-Davidson	504.0	660 388	24	1 387.7	63.5	27.3	0.4	3.2	0.0	2.7	2.8
47 55120	Oak Ridge	85.3	29 350	1 270	344.1	81.2	7.7	0.8	2.5	0.0	3.6	4.2
47 69420	Smyrna	29.9	48 596	785	1 625.3	76.7	13.8	0.3	6.5	0.0	0.5	2.3
47 70580	Spring Hill	27.1	37 731	1 012	1 392.3	NA	NA	NA	NA	NA	NA	NA
48 00000	**TEXAS**	261 249.7	27 862 596	X	106.7	74.9	12.0	0.5	4.5	0.1	5.4	2.5
48 01000	Abilene	106.7	122 225	223	1 145.5	72.5	10.2	0.8	1.3	0.0	11.5	3.7
48 01924	Allen	26.4	99 179	307	3 756.8	68.7	12.4	0.2	15.1	0.0	1.0	2.6
48 03000	Amarillo	101.4	199 582	116	1 968.3	83.9	5.4	0.5	4.0	0.3	2.1	3.8
48 04000	Arlington	95.8	392 772	48	4 099.9	62.6	22.9	0.4	7.3	0.1	4.3	2.4
48 05000	Austin	312.7	947 890	11	3 031.3	73.3	7.6	0.3	7.5	0.0	8.3	2.9
48 06128	Baytown	38.6	75 992	453	1 968.7	60.9	20.7	0.6	3.2	0.0	10.1	4.5
48 07000	Beaumont	82.1	118 299	233	1 440.9	44.6	48.7	0.5	2.9	0.0	2.1	1.2
48 07132	Bedford	10.0	49 528	761	4 952.8	80.9	7.9	0.5	2.9	1.1	2.6	4.1
48 08236	Big Spring	19.1	28 532	1 303	1 493.8	NA	NA	NA	NA	NA	NA	NA
48 10768	Brownsville	132.5	183 823	132	1 387.3	94.1	0.6	0.5	0.3	0.0	3.4	1.1
48 10912	Bryan	45.5	83 260	400	1 829.9	68.3	12.7	0.5	2.9	0.0	10.3	5.2
48 11428	Burleson	26.3	45 016	838	1 711.6	NA	NA	NA	NA	NA	NA	NA
48 13024	Carrollton	36.3	133 351	201	3 673.6	75.1	7.2	0.1	13.0	0.0	2.0	2.5
48 13492	Cedar Hill	35.9	48 343	788	1 346.6	40.3	50.0	0.1	3.7	0.1	2.8	3.0
48 13552	Cedar Park	23.7	68 918	511	2 907.9	83.7	4.3	0.2	6.5	0.0	1.2	4.2
48 15364	Cleburne	34.9	30 223	1 244	866.0	NA	NA	NA	NA	NA	NA	NA
48 15976	College Station	51.0	112 141	255	2 198.8	77.0	9.9	0.0	9.2	0.0	2.0	1.8
48 16432	Conroe	69.6	82 286	409	1 182.3	83.1	9.4	0.8	3.1	0.0	2.4	1.2
48 16612	Coppell	14.4	41 360	915	2 872.2	73.1	2.1	0.0	21.9	0.0	0.9	1.9
48 16624	Copperas Cove	18.0	32 808	1 159	1 822.7	66.1	12.1	0.5	3.2	7.2	0.6	10.3
48 17000	Corpus Christi	174.6	325 733	58	1 865.6	88.9	4.2	0.5	2.2	0.0	2.4	1.6
48 19000	Dallas	340.9	1 317 929	9	3 866.0	62.6	23.8	0.3	3.1	0.0	7.7	2.5
48 19624	Deer Park	10.5	33 782	1 123	3 217.3	81.7	7.2	2.8	1.4	0.0	1.7	5.1
48 19792	Del Rio	20.3	35 998	1 059	1 773.3	NA	NA	NA	NA	NA	NA	NA
48 19972	Denton	93.4	133 808	200	1 432.6	79.1	11.6	0.4	4.6	0.0	2.2	2.2
48 20092	DeSoto	21.6	52 599	721	2 435.1	NA	NA	NA	NA	NA	NA	NA
48 21628	Duncanville	11.2	39 457	960	3 522.9	50.8	42.3	0.0	0.5	0.0	3.8	2.5
48 21892	Eagle Pass	9.6	28 834	1 288	3 003.5	NA	NA	NA	NA	NA	NA	NA
48 22660	Edinburg	40.1	87 650	374	2 185.8	90.2	0.8	1.1	0.7	0.0	5.4	1.7
48 24000	El Paso	256.8	683 080	20	2 660.0	84.6	4.3	0.7	1.5	0.0	6.9	2.0
48 24768	Euless	16.2	54 769	688	3 380.8	69.2	7.4	0.8	11.6	1.2	6.8	3.1
48 25452	Farmers Branch	11.8	34 988	1 087	2 965.1	62.0	6.4	1.3	5.8	0.0	16.8	7.7
48 26232	Flower Mound	41.9	73 547	477	1 755.3	83.2	4.2	0.4	8.2	0.0	0.6	3.4
48 27000	Fort Worth	342.9	854 113	16	2 490.9	66.2	19.0	0.4	4.1	0.0	7.4	2.8
48 27648	Friendswood	20.7	39 396	964	1 903.2	86.1	3.3	0.4	4.8	0.0	1.3	4.1
48 27684	Frisco	67.7	163 656	157	2 417.4	69.6	5.8	0.7	18.4	0.0	1.9	3.6
48 28068	Galveston	41.2	50 550	753	1 226.9	69.3	21.7	0.5	3.6	0.1	1.3	3.5
48 29000	Garland	57.0	234 943	95	4 121.8	62.9	15.5	0.5	10.2	0.1	7.6	3.3
48 29336	Georgetown	52.1	67 140	531	1 288.7	93.2	2.8	0.0	1.8	0.0	1.0	1.2
48 30464	Grand Prairie	72.3	190 682	127	2 637.4	58.9	27.5	0.4	5.6	0.1	4.9	2.6
48 30644	Grapevine	32.0	51 971	733	1 624.1	75.8	8.2	0.7	8.0	0.0	4.1	3.2
48 30920	Greenville	32.8	27 172	1 357	828.4	NA	NA	NA	NA	NA	NA	NA
48 31928	Haltom City	12.3	44 361	850	3 606.6	78.6	2.2	0.7	9.0	0.4	6.4	2.7
48 32312	Harker Heights	15.4	29 757	1 260	1 932.3	64.4	15.9	1.0	4.8	0.0	2.6	11.4
48 32372	Harlingen	40.0	65 539	548	1 638.5	NA	NA	NA	NA	NA	NA	NA
48 35000	Houston	637.5	2 303 482	4	3 613.3	58.8	22.3	0.3	6.9	0.0	9.8	1.9
48 35528	Huntsville	35.8	41 208	919	1 151.1	NA	NA	NA	NA	NA	NA	NA
48 35576	Hurst	10.0	39 160	968	3 916.0	87.5	4.9	1.7	0.6	0.0	4.2	1.1

1. Dry land or land partially or temporarily covered by water.　　2. Hispanic or Latino persons may be of any race.

Table D. Cities — **Population**

| City | Percent Hispanic or Latino[1], 2015 | Percent foreign born 2015 | Age of population (percent), 2010-2014 | | | | | | | Median age 2015 | Percent female 2015 | Population — Census counts | | Population — Percent change | |
| | | | Under 18 years | 18 to 24 years | 25 to 34 years | 35 to 44 years | 45 to 54 years | 55 to 64 years | 65 years and over | | | 2000 | 2010 | 2000–2010 | 2010–2016 |
	12	13	14	15	16	17	18	19	20	21	22	23	24	25	26
TENNESSEE—Cont'd															
Columbia	6.8	2.8	26.4	6.2	15.0	14.6	12.0	12.3	13.6	36.2	51.2	33 055	34 638	4.8	8.4
Cookeville	7.4	9.1	19.3	25.4	12.8	9.0	9.9	9.1	14.5	29.2	49.9	23 923	31 133	30.1	4.8
Franklin	6.8	9.5	27.4	7.2	10.7	15.7	16.5	11.3	11.1	38.3	51.8	41 842	62 594	49.6	19.5
Gallatin	7.0	3.3	20.5	10.7	10.6	14.3	13.4	13.7	16.7	41.4	55.2	23 230	30 338	30.6	17.8
Germantown	1.0	7.4	23.7	5.9	5.2	14.1	10.8	17.1	23.2	47.2	49.8	37 348	38 833	4.0	0.6
Hendersonville	6.6	6.4	22.9	7.8	11.5	12.9	17.6	12.6	14.8	41.3	52.8	40 620	51 317	26.3	11.2
Jackson	5.1	3.1	23.4	11.8	14.5	12.9	13.3	11.2	12.9	35.3	55.2	59 643	66 871	12.1	0.2
Johnson City	1.7	4.4	18.3	16.1	13.0	10.7	12.0	12.4	17.4	38.2	52.5	55 469	63 488	14.5	5.0
Kingsport	4.6	2.4	19.1	7.3	14.0	10.0	12.2	15.2	22.0	44.4	52.9	44 905	52 792	17.6	0.0
Knoxville	4.7	5.6	18.0	18.2	16.6	12.1	11.4	11.2	12.4	33.1	51.4	173 890	178 430	2.6	4.4
La Vergne	23.4	16.6	34.8	7.8	13.6	15.1	15.0	6.4	7.3	31.4	47.2	18 687	32 597	74.4	7.6
Lebanon	4.8	3.6	23.7	9.2	14.4	10.3	11.3	15.9	15.2	36.9	56.3	20 235	26 135	29.2	19.8
Maryville	5.9	4.7	26.8	8.7	11.6	10.4	12.7	12.0	17.8	36.9	52.4	23 120	27 412	18.6	4.7
Memphis	7.1	6.6	24.9	10.7	15.6	12.2	12.2	12.4	12.0	34.1	52.4	650 100	651 836	0.3	0.1
Morristown	21.4	10.0	24.9	7.3	14.6	11.7	11.1	15.8	14.6	36.9	51.9	24 965	29 003	16.2	2.3
Murfreesboro	7.0	7.1	21.9	18.1	16.3	14.0	10.9	10.2	8.6	30.2	51.9	68 816	109 095	58.5	20.9
Nashville-Davidson	10.3	13.5	21.3	10.4	19.5	13.8	12.5	11.5	10.9	34.1	52.0	569 891	603 445	5.9	9.4
Oak Ridge	4.3	7.3	17.8	8.4	14.0	11.1	12.2	17.6	18.8	44.3	54.6	27 387	29 314	7.0	0.1
Smyrna	5.2	8.6	25.1	9.1	12.9	15.2	15.2	13.3	9.2	36.7	50.7	25 569	40 357	57.8	20.4
Spring Hill	9.9	12.3	33.7	9.5	11.3	19.1	13.9	7.6	4.8	31.3	50.9	7 715	29 056	276.6	29.9
TEXAS	38.9	17.0	26.2	10.1	14.5	13.6	12.7	11.1	11.7	34.4	50.4	20 851 820	25 146 100	20.6	10.8
Abilene	26.4	6.5	23.1	16.5	15.9	11.4	9.9	10.3	12.9	31.3	48.2	115 930	117 463	1.3	4.1
Allen	10.8	20.0	28.6	7.9	10.9	16.4	16.3	12.0	7.9	37.2	47.7	43 554	84 275	93.5	17.7
Amarillo	32.8	10.6	27.7	9.4	14.6	13.1	11.6	11.9	11.7	33.8	50.2	173 627	190 666	9.8	4.7
Arlington	28.9	20.4	26.3	11.1	16.5	13.9	13.0	10.0	9.3	32.6	50.8	332 969	365 399	9.7	7.5
Austin	35.2	19.5	20.9	10.9	22.7	16.0	11.7	9.8	8.1	32.7	48.9	656 562	811 045	23.5	16.9
Baytown	42.0	17.5	25.1	11.8	16.6	9.4	12.5	12.4	12.1	32.9	49.7	66 430	71 709	7.9	6.0
Beaumont	15.9	8.9	26.7	11.8	15.3	11.1	10.8	10.7	13.5	31.6	51.5	113 866	117 265	3.0	0.9
Bedford	11.5	6.6	21.7	8.6	15.3	11.9	14.2	13.2	15.1	38.1	52.3	47 152	46 994	-0.3	5.4
Big Spring	47.7	15.4	26.1	12.7	15.4	16.5	9.0	10.4	9.9	33.3	41.7	25 233	27 282	8.1	4.6
Brownsville	92.5	29.0	31.7	11.3	12.7	12.9	11.1	9.1	11.2	30.6	52.3	139 722	175 030	25.3	5.0
Bryan	36.1	14.6	23.3	16.0	21.4	11.2	9.6	9.5	9.1	29.4	49.1	65 660	76 227	16.1	9.2
Burleson	11.1	2.2	27.8	7.3	14.4	16.2	10.9	8.7	14.8	35.2	53.2	20 976	36 729	75.1	22.6
Carrollton	35.2	26.5	24.8	9.1	13.6	14.6	15.3	12.5	10.1	36.9	49.7	109 576	119 093	8.7	12.0
Cedar Hill	26.6	10.8	29.1	7.9	11.8	14.8	13.8	12.5	10.1	35.5	50.0	32 093	45 028	40.3	7.4
Cedar Park	18.3	8.0	32.4	5.7	13.3	20.1	13.3	8.0	7.2	34.4	51.8	26 049	51 731	98.6	33.2
Cleburne	31.8	10.6	25.8	12.8	10.1	13.6	10.7	13.2	13.7	35.6	50.1	26 005	29 637	14.0	2.0
College Station	16.5	15.0	16.3	40.4	13.3	10.3	7.1	6.2	6.4	22.9	49.8	67 890	94 221	38.8	19.0
Conroe	34.8	20.2	26.0	12.6	17.9	14.1	10.1	8.1	11.2	31.5	49.1	36 811	64 930	76.4	26.7
Coppell	9.9	20.2	30.5	3.6	8.8	18.0	17.0	14.6	7.5	39.0	52.6	29 592	32 161	8.7	7.0
Copperas Cove	18.0	11.0	26.5	10.0	20.3	10.7	10.2	10.9	11.3	35.0	50.5				2.0
Corpus Christi	61.9	9.5	24.7	10.5	14.8	12.7	11.9	12.5	12.9	32.6	50.8	277 454	305 269	10.0	6.7
Dallas	42.3	25.1	25.8	10.0	18.2	13.7	12.6	10.1	9.6	32.6	50.8	1 188 580	1 197 824	0.8	10.0
Deer Park	37.6	9.0	27.9	13.8	14.1	13.7	8.9	11.9	9.6	30.8	48.6	28 520	32 010	12.2	5.5
Del Rio	83.0	22.0	28.3	10.0	12.1	12.7	10.8	8.7	17.4	34.8	45.3	33 867	35 926	6.1	0.2
Denton	22.4	14.1	19.8	22.6	17.4	9.4	9.4	9.4	11.9	28.7	52.3	80 537	116 291	44.4	15.1
DeSoto	18.6	11.4	25.1	5.8	11.4	17.2	14.9	12.7	12.9	39.9	52.7	37 646	49 043	30.3	7.3
Duncanville	33.7	12.7	28.4	9.9	12.5	11.7	11.9	13.2	12.5	34.1	50.6	36 081	38 533	6.8	2.4
Eagle Pass	92.1	33.5	30.6	10.7	13.4	11.3	8.3	7.0	18.6	30.8	51.8	22 413	26 242	17.1	9.9
Edinburg	88.4	19.6	32.7	11.0	17.2	12.0	10.3	8.9	8.0	29.3	53.3	48 465	76 367	57.6	14.8
El Paso	79.6	23.4	26.9	11.1	14.3	12.5	12.2	10.4	12.5	33.1	51.1	563 662	648 054	15.0	5.4
Euless	26.6	20.9	25.5	8.9	18.0	13.3	15.5	9.3	9.6	33.7	51.5	46 005	51 280	11.5	6.8
Farmers Branch	49.5	26.6	21.4	12.0	14.6	15.6	15.4	9.5	11.5	36.0	53.2	27 508	28 616	4.0	22.3
Flower Mound	8.7	9.7	27.8	7.1	7.7	15.7	21.3	12.9	7.5	40.2	50.4	50 702	64 678	27.6	13.7
Fort Worth	35.4	17.1	28.2	9.8	15.8	13.7	12.9	10.3	9.2	32.6	50.5	534 694	744 973	39.3	14.7
Friendswood	12.9	7.1	29.6	3.7	8.9	14.4	15.4	14.0	14.0	41.5	53.1	29 037	35 894	23.6	9.8
Frisco	11.1	20.0	32.6	5.8	8.9	19.9	17.1	7.8	7.9	37.2	52.1	33 714	117 062	247.2	39.8
Galveston	30.5	12.3	18.2	14.0	16.2	9.9	13.9	15.1	12.7	35.7	50.1	57 247	47 743	-16.6	5.9
Garland	38.4	26.6	26.9	9.5	14.3	13.1	13.5	11.7	11.0	34.5	50.8	215 768	226 861	5.1	3.6
Georgetown	17.0	7.7	18.4	5.5	10.1	11.8	11.7	12.8	29.7	48.6	53.9	28 339	47 466	67.5	41.4
Grand Prairie	45.6	23.9	27.9	10.3	14.2	15.9	13.8	9.7	8.2	33.1	51.6	127 427	175 484	37.7	8.7
Grapevine	25.4	16.6	23.2	11.1	10.8	14.6	13.6	15.9	10.8	39.8	50.7	42 059	46 334	10.2	12.2
Greenville	24.9	11.5	30.3	12.4	18.2	9.0	11.3	6.9	12.0	28.1	51.9	23 960	25 553	6.6	6.3
Haltom City	45.9	22.5	30.0	6.8	17.9	16.5	10.1	8.1	10.6	32.7	51.8	39 018	42 389	8.6	4.7
Harker Heights	20.3	9.6	27.6	9.4	14.4	14.5	14.0	8.5	12.0	33.8	50.3	17 308	26 715	54.4	11.4
Harlingen	78.6	15.8	32.4	9.9	14.0	11.0	10.5	9.2	13.0	30.1	50.0	57 564	64 908	12.8	1.0
Houston	44.7	30.3	25.6	10.4	18.1	14.2	11.9	10.1	9.6	32.6	50.0	1 953 631	2 100 277	7.5	9.7
Huntsville	16.6	9.8	12.0	29.9	12.6	14.0	13.7	11.7	6.1	31.4	37.9	35 078	38 550	9.9	6.9
Hurst	22.0	10.7	24.3	7.6	12.6	14.0	14.3	11.3	15.9	40.4	54.3	36 273	37 335	2.9	4.9

1. May be of any race.

Table D. Cities — Households, Group Quarters, Crime, and Education

City	Households, 2015 Number (27)	Persons per house-hold (28)	Percent Female family house-holder[1] (29)	Percent One-person (30)	Persons in group quarters, 2010 Total (31)	Institutional Total (32)	Persons in nursing facilities (33)	Non-institu-tional (34)	Serious crimes known to police,[2] 2014 Total Number (35)	Total Rate[3] (36)	Rate[3] Violent (37)	Rate[3] Property (38)	Population age 25 and older (39)	High school graduate or less (40)	Bachelor's degree or more (41)
TENNESSEE—Cont'd															
Columbia	14 855	2.41	19.1	27.9	863	795	462	68	1 452	4 060	624	3 437	24 816	52.5	16.0
Cookeville	12 443	2.35	19.3	26.7	2 410	431	201	1 979	1 525	4 879	400	4 479	17 753	47.4	29.1
Franklin	26 510	2.73	10.8	18.2	795	792	491	3	1 101	1 562	139	1 423	47 461	18.9	57.7
Gallatin	12 928	2.57	13.3	29.7	890	870	308	20	570	1 740	317	1 423	23 615	47.4	26.1
Germantown	15 274	2.57	7.1	21.1	43	43	43	0	480	1 215	81	1 134	27 624	11.9	67.9
Hendersonville	21 332	2.62	10.7	29.9	139	128	128	11	853	1 559	181	1 378	38 837	32.3	37.4
Jackson	25 199	2.52	19.4	27.8	4 297	1 456	557	2 841	3 802	5 602	1 083	4 519	43 393	41.8	30.1
Johnson City	28 201	2.18	12.8	34.9	3 936	750	626	3 186	2 611	3 984	366	3 618	42 860	33.4	40.3
Kingsport	22 614	2.26	13.2	39.0	887	744	660	143	2 957	5 578	604	4 975	38 356	46.6	26.3
Knoxville	79 736	2.21	15.3	39.3	10 048	1 723	1 287	8 325	13 656	7 407	875	6 532	118 114	40.2	29.2
La Vergne	9 710	3.58	23.5	16.1	5	0	0	5	768	2 231	502	1 728	19 960	54.3	13.5
Lebanon	11 220	2.58	20.4	26.0	1 101	609	375	492	1 175	4 057	763	3 294	20 296	50.7	26.2
Maryville	10 121	2.63	13.6	25.7	1 644	886	529	758	706	2 511	135	2 376	18 349	36.6	33.3
Memphis	250 324	2.55	24.5	35.1	16 536	10 165	2 710	6 371	50 683	7 739	1 744	5 995	422 148	46.6	24.9
Morristown	11 833	2.43	12.5	29.0	903	763	487	140	1 666	5 666	653	5 013	19 987	65.6	11.4
Murfreesboro	46 882	2.60	11.4	26.3	4 434	1 348	458	3 086	4 630	3 891	535	3 355	75 570	32.6	39.5
Nashville-Davidson	265 002	2.39	13.8	33.7	25 870	9 226	2 169	16 644	30 909	4 772	1 125	3 647	446 641	36.1	37.9
Oak Ridge	12 954	2.20	11.3	39.7	483	226	218	257	NA	NA	NA	NA	21 252	37.9	37.7
Smyrna	16 793	2.76	15.5	22.8	365	353	215	12	1 290	2 944	331	2 613	30 687	39.0	22.8
Spring Hill	11 396	3.27	8.9	10.3	47	30	0	17	376	1 123	111	1 013	21 202	22.4	38.5
TEXAS	9 421 412	2.85	14.0	25.3	581 139	375 392	94 278	205 747	923 348	3 425	406	3 019	17 472 861	42.9	28.4
Abilene	42 507	2.64	13.9	29.8	9 592	5 306	816	4 286	5 915	4 901	473	4 428	76 081	46.3	20.8
Allen	32 204	3.04	10.0	12.2	171	171	164	0	1 201	1 279	78	1 201	62 303	19.8	51.8
Amarillo	74 766	2.64	15.2	30.5	1 881	1 419	1 019	462	10 742	5 433	684	4 749	125 621	40.8	23.4
Arlington	132 835	2.89	17.1	24.0	3 132	1 061	1 053	2 071	15 316	3 999	484	3 515	242 995	39.4	29.7
Austin	364 893	2.50	9.3	34.3	20 261	4 199	1 869	16 062	41 025	4 539	396	4 142	635 470	28.8	48.3
Baytown	28 893	2.59	15.2	32.9	601	507	507	94	3 398	4 456	316	4 140	47 581	46.9	16.2
Beaumont	46 133	2.47	18.4	34.5	5 133	2 634	513	2 499	6 580	5 581	891	4 690	72 582	45.0	23.5
Bedford	20 274	2.41	11.9	31.5	331	325	287	6	1 540	3 144	457	2 687	34 405	26.5	34.9
Big Spring	7 436	3.21	16.4	31.0	6 080	5 768	280	312	1 549	5 466	762	4 704	17 898	59.9	8.7
Brownsville	52 309	3.48	21.1	15.2	1 637	963	671	674	8 063	4 396	304	4 091	104 842	58.6	16.1
Bryan	30 599	2.55	14.4	29.5	3 097	2 822	361	275	2 859	3 607	426	3 180	49 886	41.2	30.2
Burleson	14 839	2.99	13.8	15.7	108	108	108	0	983	2 355	165	2 190	28 923	36.8	25.3
Carrollton	47 577	2.78	11.7	23.7	376	350	350	26	2 950	2 294	129	2 165	87 979	37.9	36.3
Cedar Hill	15 941	2.98	20.5	21.1	293	171	171	122	1 532	3 256	198	3 058	30 260	34.6	27.6
Cedar Park	21 212	3.05	11.8	17.1	137	107	107	30	1 032	1 621	105	1 515	40 140	20.8	45.8
Cleburne	10 459	2.78	14.4	25.0	876	794	316	82	1 079	3 629	256	3 373	18 433	49.8	24.1
College Station	38 409	2.52	7.8	30.9	10 347	201	201	10 146	2 534	2 497	188	2 309	46 725	20.5	54.5
Conroe	25 298	2.65	13.3	33.6	2 263	2 088	291	175	2 463	3 822	321	3 501	42 111	47.1	27.1
Coppell	14 855	2.78	7.9	19.1	3	0	0	3	518	1 271	56	1 215	27 173	10.8	68.2
Copperas Cove	13 343	2.46	15.6	25.2	284	174	174	110	1 069	3 204	336	2 868	20 994	32.8	15.2
Corpus Christi	117 609	2.69	15.3	26.0	5 640	3 199	1 344	2 441	16 204	5 076	656	4 420	210 127	47.7	20.9
Dallas	495 362	2.59	15.5	34.3	18 725	12 739	3 693	5 986	54 126	4 254	665	3 589	834 619	46.3	31.8
Deer Park	10 088	3.34	14.1	11.7	109	87	87	22	730	2 178	137	2 040	19 719	38.1	21.2
Del Rio	9 917	3.46	17.0	21.6	1 373	1 347	203	26	975	2 742	135	2 607	21 986	61.7	17.3
Denton	45 529	2.66	11.9	25.0	8 976	1 646	391	7 330	3 388	2 705	270	2 435	75 414	31.4	35.8
DeSoto	19 935	2.61	10.1	29.0	304	275	275	29	1 920	3 690	282	3 407	36 268	32.2	32.8
Duncanville	13 588	2.92	29.0	21.9	176	165	165	11	1 531	3 841	314	3 527	24 601	43.1	20.0
Eagle Pass	8 481	3.37	27.4	21.5	342	311	59	31	875	3 121	128	2 993	16 883	55.8	9.2
Edinburg	25 073	3.31	19.6	23.0	4 072	3 008	169	1 064	4 716	5 727	359	5 367	47 626	47.1	26.1
El Paso	222 557	3.03	17.1	24.4	9 414	5 777	1 482	3 637	17 241	2 534	393	2 142	422 146	45.1	24.3
Euless	20 681	2.62	14.0	28.7	109	99	99	10	1 313	2 446	119	2 327	35 597	30.7	37.1
Farmers Branch	12 052	2.70	17.2	26.0	103	0	0	103	1 000	3 079	188	2 891	21 769	39.3	34.1
Flower Mound	23 575	3.01	9.7	12.3	159	155	110	4	691	993	55	939	46 194	13.9	61.0
Fort Worth	285 173	2.88	16.0	27.3	13 977	8 117	2 410	5 860	36 693	4 559	558	4 001	518 807	45.1	27.3
Friendswood	13 008	3.03	6.7	15.1	207	201	201	6	350	921	55	866	26 456	22.5	45.0
Frisco	50 480	3.05	7.6	16.9	225	225	225	0	2 653	1 869	83	1 786	95 043	13.6	60.3
Galveston	20 022	2.34	19.3	34.7	2 477	1 261	86	1 216	2 310	4 718	523	4 195	34 009	43.1	26.6
Garland	75 582	3.12	16.0	21.0	567	478	463	89	8 339	3 527	272	3 255	150 569	47.2	22.8
Georgetown	24 956	2.47	5.9	25.4	2 499	1 436	389	1 063	785	1 382	118	1 264	48 502	26.9	39.0
Grand Prairie	58 919	3.18	17.0	20.8	257	188	188	69	5 117	2 762	260	2 502	116 126	46.4	24.1
Grapevine	19 290	2.65	13.3	26.3	242	226	226	16	1 265	2 474	121	2 353	33 758	21.8	44.1
Greenville	9 278	2.78	13.8	36.6	678	604	316	74	1 336	5 142	550	4 591	15 204	50.2	20.5
Haltom City	14 114	3.12	16.5	26.4	96	96	96	0	1 314	2 996	246	2 750	27 972	50.6	13.8
Harker Heights	10 004	2.89	15.1	19.2	166	166	166	0	886	3 111	267	2 844	18 361	21.5	38.3
Harlingen	21 447	3.00	19.0	25.4	1 070	457	415	613	2 205	3 351	222	3 129	37 970	51.9	15.8
Houston	849 974	2.66	17.8	31.7	37 071	18 243	4 778	18 828	126 205	5 685	991	4 694	1 471 908	45.5	30.9
Huntsville	12 384	2.30	12.1	32.4	11 239	8 489	190	2 750	1 167	2 913	527	2 386	23 772	50.5	26.3
Hurst	14 088	2.75	15.6	25.2	245	239	224	6	1 848	4 774	369	4 405	26 580	39.9	28.4

1. No spouse present. 2. Data for serious crimes have not been adjusted for underreporting. This may affect comparability between geographic areas and over time. 3. Per 100,000 population estimated by the FBI. 4. Persons 25 years old and over.

Table D. Cities — Income, Poverty, and Housing

City	Money income, 2015					Housing units, 2010			Occupied housing units 2015				
	Households			Families						Owner-occupied		Renter-occupied	
	Median income	Percent with income of $200,000 or more	Percent with income of less than $25,000	Total Families	Percent with income below poverty	Total	Percent change, 2000–2010	Vacant units for sale or rent[2]	Total	Percent	Median value[3] (dollars)	Percent	Median rent (dollars)
	42	43	44	45	46	47	48	49	50	51	52	53	54
TENNESSEE—Cont'd													
Columbia	45 180	1.1	21.3	9 730	18.4	15 906	10.7	1 894	14 855	48.9	119 400	51.1	729
Cookeville	31 174	4.2	30.2	7 643	18.3	13 706	26.9	1 235	12 443	43.8	170 300	56.2	720
Franklin	91 786	13.5	8.3	19 809	4.7	25 586	48.6	1 546	26 510	61.6	347 700	38.4	1 271
Gallatin	57 075	3.6	17.3	8 077	11.3	13 093	35.8	1 222	12 928	64.7	160 500	35.3	907
Germantown	100 497	15.6	5.6	11 813	2.7	15 536	13.4	626	15 274	85.7	300 500	14.3	1 187
Hendersonville	60 994	4.6	7.6	13 981	3.7	21 543	30.6	1 432	21 332	64.8	233 200	35.2	1 101
Jackson	43 876	4.9	21.0	16 622	14.4	28 052	9.8	2 861	25 199	54.0	128 800	46.0	862
Johnson City	40 481	4.4	26.9	16 184	13.4	30 583	19.5	3 566	28 201	55.7	163 100	44.3	714
Kingsport	36 904	3.8	27.1	13 147	16.0	23 784	9.0	2 495	22 614	60.7	134 000	39.3	613
Knoxville	37 200	2.2	25.5	39 624	18.8	88 009	3.7	9 961	79 736	45.0	125 900	55.0	772
La Vergne	55 179	3.7	10.4	7 642	9.7	11 612	66.3	696	9 710	70.7	124 200	29.3	1 112
Lebanon	48 067	5.1	12.4	7 894	8.7	11 030	26.1	900	11 220	59.2	181 600	40.8	777
Maryville	52 217	4.0	12.1	7 190	6.8	11 629	19.1	917	10 121	73.6	187 000	26.4	806
Memphis	36 908	2.7	26.4	146 262	20.8	291 883	7.4	41 539	250 324	47.0	94 400	53.0	826
Morristown	28 767	0.5	35.3	7 806	23.6	12 705	15.2	1 293	11 833	47.7	100 000	52.3	678
Murfreesboro	52 266	4.7	16.4	28 495	7.7	45 500	57.2	3 560	46 882	50.3	191 300	49.7	911
Nashville-Davidson	51 393	4.9	17.3	147 842	13.1	283 978	12.3	24 479	265 002	53.9	185 000	46.1	921
Oak Ridge	43 929	4.5	23.1	7 309	11.6	14 494	8.0	1 722	12 954	59.6	136 200	40.4	653
Smyrna	58 270	0.0	12.5	11 859	6.1	15 787	57.9	980	16 793	68.0	157 100	32.0	853
Spring Hill	79 046	7.9	6.2	NA	NA	10 569	NA	708	11 396	77.2	230 600	22.8	1 564
TEXAS	55 653	6.0	16.2	6 520 909	12.2	9 977 436	22.3	1 054 503	9 421 412	61.1	152 000	38.9	932
Abilene	44 176	2.7	18.1	26 227	11.3	47 783	4.8	4 171	42 507	54.6	113 400	45.4	812
Allen	100 167	12.3	4.4	26 495	2.7	28 877	89.4	1 007	32 204	74.4	262 900	25.6	1 346
Amarillo	50 192	2.9	17.4	48 183	13.9	80 298	11.0	6 380	74 766	60.5	122 100	39.5	789
Arlington	53 487	4.1	15.4	92 746	12.9	144 805	10.7	11 733	132 835	52.9	144 900	47.1	964
Austin	62 250	8.5	12.8	189 124	9.8	354 241	28.1	29 349	364 893	44.4	282 500	55.6	1 139
Baytown	51 791	4.6	20.7	18 441	13.2	28 998	10.2	4 043	28 893	55.5	102 500	44.5	767
Beaumont	47 570	3.2	20.9	27 862	12.2	50 689	3.8	5 041	46 133	53.4	99 300	46.6	843
Bedford	68 902	4.3	7.8	12 691	1.8	22 301	5.5	1 285	20 274	58.4	176 300	41.6	972
Big Spring	44 927	3.0	27.2	4 860	20.2	9 640	-2.4	1 373	7 436	52.9	85 700	47.1	899
Brownsville	34 050	2.5	29.8	43 269	29.9	53 936	28.8	4 065	52 309	62.0	85 100	38.0	647
Bryan	44 486	2.7	19.5	17 478	16.0	30 582	18.6	2 857	30 599	45.7	134 500	54.3	845
Burleson	72 113	6.5	10.6	12 429	6.2	13 591	74.5	703	14 839	69.8	150 900	30.2	1 107
Carrollton	67 365	7.0	9.2	33 654	9.7	45 508	12.3	2 209	47 577	59.0	193 400	41.0	1 088
Cedar Hill	65 619	2.6	11.1	11 396	8.3	16 338	47.0	832	15 941	67.9	136 900	32.1	1 230
Cedar Park	90 762	8.0	3.4	16 234	2.1	18 726	108.8	909	21 212	65.3	242 400	34.7	1 194
Cleburne	57 704	2.4	19.7	7 621	8.8	11 418	14.5	979	10 459	54.4	93 100	45.6	872
College Station	37 478	4.1	28.2	17 910	9.7	37 226	43.1	2 189	38 409	37.9	203 500	62.1	903
Conroe	50 112	4.4	15.2	15 467	11.2	22 215	54.5	2 198	25 298	46.3	158 200	53.7	897
Coppell	103 082	21.1	5.9	11 559	5.8	14 343	14.2	537	14 855	72.3	328 800	27.7	1 285
Copperas Cove	47 048	4.4	18.9	9 295	15.2	13 094	16.7	1 236	13 343	49.8	110 500	50.2	829
Corpus Christi	51 255	3.6	19.3	78 150	13.7	125 469	16.3	12 674	117 609	53.7	124 300	46.3	931
Dallas	45 918	7.0	20.0	284 275	18.6	516 639	6.7	58 582	495 362	41.4	152 400	58.6	903
Deer Park	67 554	2.2	10.4	8 550	12.6	11 742	18.6	609	10 088	75.1	138 200	24.9	1 077
Del Rio	48 504	2.3	24.0	7 312	26.2	12 958	9.5	1 359	9 917	63.5	105 000	36.5	647
Denton	52 023	2.6	17.3	26 716	8.8	46 211	41.1	3 576	45 529	47.8	170 900	52.2	935
DeSoto	67 974	2.3	14.9	13 300	7.2	19 488	38.1	1 278	19 935	66.1	154 900	33.9	998
Duncanville	48 140	1.1	13.9	10 489	12.4	14 011	5.6	731	13 588	59.0	114 100	41.0	1 027
Eagle Pass	36 952	0.3	27.8	6 438	21.5	9 019	17.6	747	8 481	59.9	130 600	40.1	579
Edinburg	41 004	1.7	23.8	17 894	25.6	25 167	57.8	2 068	25 073	56.8	106 700	43.2	690
El Paso	45 069	1.7	21.2	160 679	14.8	227 605	17.5	10 711	222 557	59.1	118 500	40.9	752
Euless	55 359	4.0	10.1	13 164	8.5	23 447	16.8	1 916	20 681	48.7	164 000	51.3	1 000
Farmers Branch	67 788	4.7	11.7	8 176	9.4	11 549	13.0	752	12 052	53.3	152 900	46.7	1 171
Flower Mound	120 084	17.4	3.3	20 137	2.6	21 570	27.1	559	23 575	85.3	309 600	14.7	1 651
Fort Worth	55 888	4.4	16.4	190 765	12.7	291 086	37.8	28 434	285 173	56.3	136 700	43.7	936
Friendswood	116 265	27.8	4.0	NA	NA	13 254	28.3	528	13 008	84.3	245 100	15.7	1 076
Frisco	123 055	20.3	3.4	40 605	1.6	42 306	209.0	2 405	50 480	78.0	332 100	22.0	1 355
Galveston	40 836	3.1	27.8	11 102	15.9	32 368	8.0	12 425	20 022	43.3	156 800	56.7	887
Garland	55 725	2.4	13.5	56 539	12.7	80 834	7.4	5 138	75 582	61.7	128 700	38.3	1 020
Georgetown	70 000	5.9	8.9	17 137	2.8	20 037	81.6	1 207	24 956	76.0	239 900	24.0	1 000
Grand Prairie	60 838	3.7	12.3	44 326	11.3	62 424	34.9	4 253	58 919	61.7	136 100	38.3	996
Grapevine	81 764	10.8	3.8	13 172	3.5	19 685	19.2	1 183	19 290	55.6	279 700	44.4	1 227
Greenville	33 977	0.0	18.6	5 596	22.7	10 838	9.3	1 122	9 278	50.1	76 200	49.9	751
Haltom City	51 131	1.4	15.1	9 292	11.1	16 626	5.0	1 357	14 114	54.5	92 600	45.5	895
Harker Heights	68 716	3.0	15.1	7 637	10.5	10 347	51.2	859	10 004	65.8	198 400	34.2	782
Harlingen	35 810	2.4	30.0	14 675	25.5	25 585	10.1	3 940	21 447	53.3	86 400	46.7	669
Houston	48 064	6.9	20.0	525 369	18.5	892 646	14.1	110 003	849 974	41.4	152 200	58.6	923
Huntsville	36 787	1.5	25.1	NA	NA	12 853	12.7	1 062	12 384	33.3	140 300	66.7	763
Hurst	55 845	4.8	13.9	10 006	7.5	15 761	6.8	1 109	14 088	63.0	152 500	37.0	877

1. Based on population estimated by the American Community Survey.   2. Includes units rented or sold but not occupied.   3. Specified owner-occupied units; $1,000,000 represents $1,000,000 or more   4. 50.0 represents 50 percent or more.   5. 10.0 represents 10 percent or less.

Table D. Cities — Commuting, Computer Access, Migration, Labor Force, and Employment

City	Commuting (Percent)		Computer Access[2] (Percent)		Migration, 2015		Civilian labor force, 2016		Unemployment		Civilian employment[4], 2015			
											Population age 16 and older		Population age 16 to 64	
	Drove alone	With Commutes of 30 minutes or more[1]	With a Computer in the house	With Internet Access	Percent who lived in the same house one year ago	Percent who lived in an other state or county one year ago	Total	Percent change, 2015–2016	Total	Rate[3]	Number	Percent in Labor Force	Number	Percent who worked full-year full-time
	55	56	57	58	59	60	61	62	63	64	65	66	67	68
TENNESSEE— Cont'd														
Columbia	88.4	35.8	91.1	74.4	71.8	13.1	16 906	3.0	791	4.7	28 416	57.3	23 422	44.7
Cookeville	85.9	21.6	80.1	68.1	76.0	10.5	13 549	2.4	738	5.4	26 750	51.7	22 091	38.6
Franklin	87.1	38.2	93.2	86.2	77.3	11.7	40 475	3.7	1 342	3.3	55 031	72.1	46 934	56.2
Gallatin	92.1	35.8	80.7	76.7	79.6	11.1	17 452	3.5	749	4.3	28 069	59.7	22 329	54.3
Germantown	92.1	27.1	95.3	91.3	86.3	4.3	19 612	1.6	735	3.7	30 977	60.7	21 855	51.2
Hendersonville	92.5	49.0	86.7	81.6	81.3	11.9	30 632	3.6	1 125	3.7	45 059	70.0	36 746	55.6
Jackson	84.2	13.2	81.3	65.2	88.7	4.5	31 461	2.3	1 659	5.3	52 675	63.6	44 013	47.8
Johnson City	90.6	13.7	88.5	82.7	80.8	9.2	30 916	0.7	1 502	4.9	55 201	57.2	43 810	44.8
Kingsport	86.5	19.1	83.3	66.1	84.6	5.0	22 620	0.9	1 226	5.4	43 198	51.7	31 697	39.5
Knoxville	84.5	20.9	84.1	67.6	72.2	10.4	94 839	1.9	4 291	4.5	155 409	66.4	132 376	46.9
La Vergne	87.1	58.3	96.4	84.7	89.8	5.4	18 248	3.3	707	3.9	23 830	71.8	21 302	57.8
Lebanon	92.1	26.8	81.1	71.6	79.8	7.0	14 038	3.5	658	4.7	23 357	64.1	18 768	53.1
Maryville	NA	32.3	88.4	79.5	87.5	7.6	13 429	1.7	576	4.3	22 019	57.9	16 948	43.8
Memphis	83.7	26.7	76.3	62.0	82.6	4.2	290 888	1.1	17 358	6.0	508 945	63.7	430 172	45.7
Morristown	85.2	29.0	74.5	60.4	86.1	3.7	11 332	1.3	655	5.8	22 784	58.4	18 479	42.4
Murfreesboro	85.1	33.4	91.8	79.5	71.9	15.1	69 445	3.6	2 717	3.9	101 121	70.6	90 337	49.7
Nashville-Davidson	82.6	35.6	88.5	74.9	81.2	7.0	377 213	3.5	13 710	3.6	526 116	70.5	454 798	54.0
Oak Ridge	90.9	32.1	80.6	74.7	81.1	14.1	14 109	2.0	643	4.6	24 637	62.0	19 227	41.9
Smyrna	85.0	43.3	91.4	81.0	84.4	9.3	25 061	3.5	934	3.7	36 126	74.0	31 850	60.3
Spring Hill	92.9	61.8	NA	NA	NA	NA	19 175	3.5	662	3.5	26 189	74.3	24 383	51.3
TEXAS	84.5	38.6	86.7	74.2	83.9	6.8	13 284 623	1.8	612 822	4.6	21 043 248	64.3	17 821 741	51.2
Abilene	86.1	6.5	86.1	67.2	76.5	10.5	53 887	0.1	2 071	3.8	99 648	61.5	83 350	50.0
Allen	87.3	46.9	97.4	94.0	89.1	5.7	54 079	4.0	1 811	3.3	73 187	74.2	65 456	59.2
Amarillo	84.0	11.4	85.8	72.6	82.1	7.2	100 932	1.3	3 142	3.1	149 225	68.4	125 781	56.5
Arlington	85.9	41.9	92.4	80.3	80.7	8.3	204 072	2.0	7 915	3.9	299 334	68.2	263 396	53.5
Austin	79.9	33.5	91.8	81.6	79.3	8.7	556 712	4.0	16 931	3.0	754 228	73.4	679 085	57.0
Baytown	83.6	30.2	84.1	67.9	72.1	12.0	33 632	2.3	2 857	8.5	58 323	67.6	49 167	52.5
Beaumont	93.7	17.6	71.1	60.0	83.6	4.7	51 445	-0.6	3 186	6.2	89 764	60.7	73 761	48.4
Bedford	89.7	41.6	94.1	87.2	75.7	7.9	28 806	2.3	1 109	3.8	39 527	72.1	32 076	62.8
Big Spring	NA	16.4	81.1	61.4	76.5	15.6	9 600	-0.9	588	6.1	22 680	48.6	19 787	36.7
Brownsville	85.4	19.3	65.8	48.8	90.6	1.9	75 663	2.9	5 892	7.8	131 852	55.8	111 310	42.1
Bryan	80.8	13.4	87.2	81.6	72.3	12.3	41 317	2.0	1 465	3.5	64 829	64.1	57 363	48.2
Burleson	95.1	48.5	90.2	80.9	84.3	7.6	22 710	2.4	856	3.8	32 802	63.2	26 230	55.7
Carrollton	86.6	35.9	96.4	83.2	83.2	8.3	79 034	4.0	2 733	3.5	104 102	71.3	90 618	57.2
Cedar Hill	91.0	60.6	94.1	86.6	88.8	3.2	26 589	3.9	1 224	4.6	36 210	65.4	31 363	55.2
Cedar Park	90.5	46.4	96.4	93.2	80.3	12.7	36 012	4.3	1 199	3.3	45 142	75.5	40 452	66.1
Cleburne	89.8	33.5	87.9	78.4	84.6	4.1	13 235	2.0	616	4.7	23 226	55.7	19 110	46.9
College Station	80.1	8.3	95.0	79.2	61.4	22.0	55 788	2.1	1 875	3.4	91 765	60.4	84 819	34.1
Conroe	81.8	38.8	90.4	83.5	82.5	5.7	33 137	2.0	1 708	5.2	52 574	68.1	44 890	48.2
Coppell	88.1	39.0	98.5	94.1	86.3	6.8	23 483	4.0	841	3.6	30 393	70.2	27 310	56.9
Copperas Cove	81.0	30.8	90.6	81.5	75.2	15.6	13 298	3.9	583	4.4	25 239	68.7	21 498	56.0
Corpus Christi	85.0	17.7	85.5	73.5	78.1	8.7	150 142	0.3	8 394	5.6	253 798	64.0	211 945	51.3
Dallas	80.2	41.9	82.5	67.5	82.4	6.0	660 881	3.8	26 095	3.9	994 203	67.5	869 984	54.1
Deer Park	87.6	33.4	93.8	86.6	76.9	7.8	16 877	1.2	878	5.2	25 672	69.1	22 420	48.7
Del Rio	80.1	9.7	80.0	71.2	76.2	7.8	14 830	2.6	978	6.6	26 977	55.0	20 774	43.2
Denton	81.7	28.9	90.2	76.9	71.3	13.2	71 085	4.1	2 449	3.4	108 003	66.0	92 364	44.7
DeSoto	92.4	56.4	92.9	77.4	84.0	3.2	27 947	3.9	1 452	5.2	40 982	71.3	34 198	63.9
Duncanville	92.8	54.1	89.5	73.5	88.2	3.2	20 333	3.3	868	4.3	29 734	64.6	24 739	53.2
Eagle Pass	NA	15.3	73.5	58.9	87.7	2.5	12 874	3.8	1 713	13.3	20 931	55.2	15 566	41.5
Edinburg	83.4	26.0	84.7	69.1	87.9	3.3	38 392	2.6	2 260	5.9	60 476	65.6	53 756	43.9
El Paso	82.6	28.5	80.9	68.4	85.1	5.0	292 696	2.9	13 770	4.7	518 349	62.0	433 307	47.9
Euless	85.3	33.1	96.5	87.1	79.1	10.2	30 494	2.2	1 158	3.8	41 418	75.1	36 216	61.2
Farmers Branch	86.5	28.6	92.5	78.3	86.0	5.0	17 511	4.0	664	3.8	26 308	76.1	22 551	56.4
Flower Mound	92.4	50.5	97.2	95.3	87.8	8.9	39 600	3.9	1 276	3.2	54 333	73.0	49 026	56.0
Fort Worth	84.2	39.9	87.6	71.6	82.6	5.4	401 327	2.3	16 764	4.2	624 965	67.2	548 096	52.6
Friendswood	86.5	57.8	93.3	91.1	91.4	5.1	19 504	1.2	871	4.5	29 397	68.2	23 857	60.4
Frisco	90.5	50.8	98.3	95.5	86.3	9.9	85 146	4.5	2 848	3.3	110 136	71.6	97 964	59.6
Galveston	71.1	19.9	84.2	70.0	78.2	9.9	23 872	0.7	1 227	5.1	42 012	59.5	35 650	42.5
Garland	80.1	47.1	92.4	80.9	86.3	4.4	122 764	3.6	4 728	3.9	178 968	70.6	152 841	52.6
Georgetown	87.3	45.6	89.3	84.2	89.1	5.1	26 413	4.1	1 047	4.0	53 570	52.3	34 625	51.5
Grand Prairie	85.0	46.4	84.4	74.1	90.8	5.3	96 139	3.3	3 895	4.1	142 048	72.7	126 561	55.5
Grapevine	91.2	33.2	96.8	91.0	79.5	11.9	30 586	2.3	1 021	3.3	40 903	75.3	35 355	60.9
Greenville	82.0	23.7	90.4	72.0	75.3	9.2	11 013	3.4	510	4.6	18 849	63.3	15 663	50.8
Haltom City	88.2	33.4	88.9	68.6	77.1	11.8	22 019	1.7	844	3.8	32 081	70.0	27 398	56.3
Harker Heights	84.5	21.2	86.4	78.8	83.9	10.1	12 214	3.6	546	4.5	22 050	72.5	18 552	39.9
Harlingen	89.7	16.1	72.8	60.4	85.6	5.6	24 545	2.2	1 500	6.1	46 288	57.1	37 723	45.3
Houston	80.1	45.0	83.8	70.5	80.8	6.6	1 150 095	1.3	57 219	5.0	1 771 334	68.1	1 549 541	52.6
Huntsville	73.6	25.0	96.8	76.9	70.2	19.3	11 798	3.4	679	5.8	36 150	44.6	33 663	32.5
Hurst	87.6	43.9	91.6	78.7	84.0	5.2	20 126	2.1	804	4.0	30 288	69.1	24 073	57.0

1. Employed persons.   2. Households.   3. Percent of civilian labor force.   4. Persons 16 years old and over.

City	New construction ($1,000) [69]	Number of housing units [70]	Percent single family [71]	Number of establishments [72]	Number of employees [73]	Sales (mil dol) [74]	Annual payroll (mil dol) [75]	Number of establishments [76]	Number of employees [77]	Sales (mil dol) [78]	Annual payroll (mil dol) [79]
TENNESSEE—Cont'd											
Columbia	25 608	315	91.1	39	496	223.7	30.5	221	2 817	845.7	69.4
Cookeville	54 361	452	42.5	50	887	260.9	35.3	274	4 064	1 040.3	88.8
Franklin	371 591	1 658	53.0	134	1 764	8 777.6	126.9	477	8 372	2 529.1	225.5
Gallatin	144 930	699	78.8	37	530	497.6	26.2	144	2 057	620.6	54.0
Germantown	NA	NA	NA	33	D	D	D	140	1 977	349.6	39.7
Hendersonville	52 497	279	100.0	50	D	D	D	198	2 898	686.8	66.5
Jackson	30 847	167	100.0	117	1 383	688.7	61.0	426	6 689	1 806.3	155.1
Johnson City	22 460	148	64.9	93	1 048	664.6	41.7	436	7 306	1 780.5	155.2
Kingsport	50 197	645	13.6	75	904	642.3	38.8	337	5 487	1 293.3	119.1
Knoxville	121 629	849	37.8	411	5 879	3 451.0	312.1	1 326	22 849	6 049.5	553.2
La Vergne	11 162	63	100.0	74	4 419	12 983.0	187.8	61	667	261.9	18.8
Lebanon	72 560	396	80.3	42	1 219	891.1	66.2	213	2 781	782.1	67.1
Maryville	25 027	150	100.0	29	271	793.8	13.6	174	2 749	605.8	57.1
Memphis	NA	NA	NA	980	20 551	28 725.9	1 109.3	2 365	35 878	18 848.9	999.6
Morristown	5 716	41	100.0	42	D	D	D	248	3 728	961.9	90.9
Murfreesboro	298 382	1 639	77.1	88	925	706.0	48.5	554	8 860	2 448.0	197.9
Nashville-Davidson	1 574 313	9 463	39.2	923	17 595	17 607.0	1 115.0	2 575	37 506	10 138.3	989.0
Oak Ridge	5 504	25	100.0	21	D	D	D	107	1 720	397.7	37.9
Smyrna	56 458	423	87.5	31	831	1 062.2	40.8	149	2 386	592.6	54.0
Spring Hill	160 867	708	100.0	11	423	184.9	14.1	64	1 105	256.0	23.6
TEXAS	29 242 398	165 853	64.2	27 752	408 692	691 242.6	24 826.1	78 281	1 150 148	356 116.4	28 835.5
Abilene	55 091	302	97.4	131	1 619	1 861.9	79.7	533	7 619	2 087.4	181.6
Allen	148 035	690	64.8	58	D	D	D	281	5 344	1 113.8	105.1
Amarillo	158 078	639	97.8	216	3 356	2 985.1	174.7	841	12 920	4 067.9	311.0
Arlington	142 564	997	28.4	333	5 752	4 034.0	317.8	1 147	17 817	5 419.7	452.1
Austin	1 297 507	8 903	41.6	942	19 901	55 702.0	1 417.1	3 091	49 905	14 738.2	1 363.0
Baytown	45 017	293	100.0	41	460	164.0	19.0	276	4 460	1 572.2	105.0
Beaumont	43 072	320	48.8	180	2 151	1 889.9	117.4	611	9 166	2 511.7	234.4
Bedford	3 345	13	100.0	33	211	113.2	15.0	119	1 747	556.4	46.5
Big Spring	2 733	21	100.0	21	D	D	D	99	1 309	383.9	30.9
Brownsville	84 366	572	99.3	175	1 681	891.1	53.2	563	8 869	2 169.6	181.8
Bryan	113 504	869	45.1	83	1 126	864.9	58.7	299	3 842	1 271.3	93.6
Burleson	78 766	340	100.0	22	138	52.2	5.2	154	3 015	885.6	73.7
Carrollton	191 748	1 020	30.2	394	6 422	5 487.6	365.5	406	4 850	2 173.2	156.5
Cedar Hill	18 812	67	100.0	12	94	65.0	4.7	146	3 056	602.7	57.9
Cedar Park	172 323	946	56.6	44	D	D	D	232	3 735	835.7	75.7
Cleburne	7 332	51	84.3	35	498	315.7	25.1	155	2 084	584.0	51.3
College Station	254 259	1 900	38.7	34	344	235.6	15.6	309	5 876	1 375.4	111.6
Conroe	188 331	1 068	57.9	111	1 352	5 498.0	69.0	382	6 345	2 214.1	171.2
Coppell	53 289	141	100.0	70	2 125	1 442.5	167.5	75	1 605	713.9	59.3
Copperas Cove	20 594	149	93.3	1	D	D	D	70	1 004	278.4	21.5
Corpus Christi	208 666	1 138	97.8	326	4 376	4 143.7	229.2	1 043	16 278	4 939.2	401.2
Dallas	1 202 572	10 337	15.9	1 934	28 244	22 578.0	1 572.1	4 022	57 240	16 889.0	1 603.9
Deer Park	14 565	55	100.0	40	898	466.1	61.6	57	1 014	283.4	22.7
Del Rio	8 189	63	100.0	21	D	D	D	142	1 984	573.3	43.6
Denton	200 142	871	65.3	93	1 231	1 208.9	51.8	399	6 463	1 802.7	149.9
DeSoto	54 711	241	100.0	25	368	220.3	22.3	80	1 395	410.9	34.7
Duncanville	3 233	13	100.0	16	D	D	D	130	1 521	558.9	44.0
Eagle Pass	9 682	76	84.2	38	D	D	D	150	2 425	565.9	47.7
Edinburg	151 885	1 230	33.7	73	1 425	688.7	46.3	216	3 856	1 371.8	91.3
El Paso	622 297	2 843	70.8	884	9 548	6 348.6	404.9	2 064	32 405	8 445.4	706.3
Euless	76 268	185	100.0	48	418	306.6	25.7	135	1 595	641.0	46.0
Farmers Branch	93 615	843	3.0	207	5 093	3 422.1	356.4	150	2 360	772.0	79.2
Flower Mound	292 176	1 067	37.2	58	698	790.8	40.4	153	2 668	625.3	60.6
Fort Worth	988 732	7 408	46.7	696	16 814	17 624.0	1 062.3	2 047	31 491	10 333.5	866.2
Friendswood	67 309	173	100.0	15	D	D	D	96	1 743	480.3	37.4
Frisco	876 669	5 071	43.5	96	D	D	D	437	9 421	2 468.7	229.1
Galveston	44 924	154	100.0	36	D	D	D	208	2 523	615.4	55.4
Garland	143 690	1 048	24.2	184	2 917	1 771.9	143.2	608	9 210	2 725.4	226.9
Georgetown	208 704	1 336	51.1	33	D	D	D	190	3 460	1 234.9	95.6
Grand Prairie	133 159	807	48.6	267	5 982	5 073.0	337.2	343	5 605	2 050.9	146.2
Grapevine	90 648	770	11.3	93	1 933	1 902.9	109.6	315	4 979	1 563.4	128.1
Greenville	19 805	142	100.0	23	249	275.3	9.1	139	2 206	636.5	65.5
Haltom City	1 713	16	100.0	96	1 072	473.3	51.8	144	1 370	509.3	40.0
Harker Heights	49 585	293	50.2	4	24	7.6	0.8	58	1 136	296.4	23.4
Harlingen	22 770	219	74.9	75	738	585.5	27.3	298	4 835	1 183.7	111.2
Houston	1 609 559	9 498	43.9	4 501	77 057	322 772.6	5 461.8	8 592	130 540	41 589.4	3 488.6
Huntsville	9 072	43	100.0	22	D	D	D	138	2 258	696.9	48.1
Hurst	3 169	15	46.7	37	234	154.5	11.8	282	5 108	1 292.0	117.4

1. Merchant wholesalers except manufacturers' sales branches and offices.   2. Establishments with payroll.

Table D. Cities — Real Estate, Professional Services, and Manufacturing

City	Real estate and rental and leasing, 2012				Professional, scientific, and technical services,[1] 2012				Manufacturing, 2012			
	Number of establishments	Number of employees	Receipts (mil dol)	Annual payroll (mil dol)	Number of establishments	Number of employees	Receipts (mil dol)	Annual payroll (mil dol)	Number of establishments	Number of employees	Receipts (mil dol)	Annual payroll (mil dol)
	80	81	82	83	84	85	86	87	88	89	90	91
TENNESSEE— Cont'd												
Columbia	50	175	29.4	4.6	70	D	D	D	40	856	187.7	38.2
Cookeville	54	156	31.0	4.2	114	D	D	D	76	2 976	912.5	119.6
Franklin	120	753	357.2	45.0	373	3 940	700.5	271.3	68	1 770	474.7	74.7
Gallatin	38	456	83.3	30.3	53	D	D	D	61	2 257	985.0	92.1
Germantown	42	D	D	D	115	418	67.3	24.9	9	D	3.6	D
Hendersonville	68	251	51.2	8.8	120	D	D	D	48	810	147.5	37.5
Jackson	90	431	68.9	14.1	157	D	D	D	77	7 033	3 426.0	317.7
Johnson City	99	494	80.6	15.0	170	D	D	D	74	3 902	1 278.7	149.8
Kingsport	59	264	46.2	8.5	143	966	104.2	41.9	38	10 628	D	D
Knoxville	396	2 635	470.7	97.2	719	D	D	D	208	D	2 070.7	D
La Vergne	17	136	33.7	6.9	18	233	15.2	15.6	46	3 289	D	167.8
Lebanon	58	228	57.3	9.1	86	D	D	D	47	2 115	1 015.7	111.6
Maryville	32	88	19.0	2.5	97	D	D	D	31	3 037	2 235.1	173.7
Memphis	745	5 964	1 152.7	263.4	1 305	D	D	D	450	18 847	18 372.5	1 096.2
Morristown	49	162	32.5	4.5	60	D	D	D	84	8 441	3 203.3	350.6
Murfreesboro	134	715	238.3	31.7	226	D	D	D	99	5 030	2 935.5	226.9
Nashville-Davidson	897	6 348	1 410.7	284.0	1 922	24 110	4 015.2	1 637.4	552	18 154	7 319.4	851.8
Oak Ridge	42	152	31.4	5.8	143	D	D	D	44	5 527	1 166.0	445.1
Smyrna	26	111	31.0	4.5	53	650	88.2	43.0	31	6 099	7 170.4	405.2
Spring Hill	18	64	16.5	2.9	27	89	12.5	3.4	9	D	D	D
TEXAS	26 639	169 941	38 757.4	7 751.8	62 085	632 486	120 954.5	46 783.6	19 782	767 024	702 603.1	42 529.8
Abilene	162	881	149.9	27.0	255	D	D	D	83	1 991	898.3	84.5
Allen	77	413	84.0	17.6	280	1 169	204.3	83.0	27	987	334.1	64.8
Amarillo	272	1 247	244.3	42.2	463	D	D	D	159	12 263	D	755.5
Arlington	379	1 915	398.2	74.6	736	D	D	D	224	9 679	15 060.3	518.9
Austin	1 548	10 167	2 332.9	520.7	4 826	56 872	11 692.9	4 737.1	616	20 866	11 413.4	1 356.9
Baytown	79	444	84.3	17.5	97	2 249	182.6	303.9	55	5 545	D	545.5
Beaumont	176	1 179	231.5	49.4	370	4 918	871.7	338.4	103	4 671	D	349.7
Bedford	55	209	46.8	9.2	162	805	100.1	37.5	13	111	11.2	4.0
Big Spring	37	146	29.4	4.3	34	169	16.5	6.3	16	495	D	33.4
Brownsville	142	537	63.8	13.2	263	D	D	D	103	2 705	1 215.2	123.5
Bryan	92	558	75.5	16.4	189	D	D	D	69	3 967	928.5	149.1
Burleson	32	106	21.7	3.5	77	321	37.4	9.5	32	920	178.9	38.8
Carrollton	143	1 629	302.6	85.9	407	3 355	571.1	209.8	187	11 424	3 739.1	564.1
Cedar Hill	23	69	14.7	1.6	55	D	D	D	27	782	151.6	27.9
Cedar Park	65	185	68.5	6.1	155	912	142.0	51.6	39	1 200	384.8	75.0
Cleburne	37	120	21.7	3.8	72	434	40.1	18.2	32	1 433	599.9	75.8
College Station	120	638	132.9	20.1	165	D	D	D	13	241	D	13.6
Conroe	83	578	111.4	26.6	203	D	D	D	104	3 733	1 763.5	194.3
Coppell	47	482	113.4	25.0	208	2 604	562.9	231.0	35	1 485	297.0	66.8
Copperas Cove	29	D	D	D	31	138	10.6	3.8	4	7	D	D
Corpus Christi	370	2 602	623.1	121.9	786	5 700	840.3	306.1	168	5 412	D	357.1
Dallas	2 162	20 336	4 905.7	1 160.5	5 407	67 331	14 598.6	5 688.9	1 125	42 824	17 731.3	2 126.8
Deer Park	32	421	104.1	22.0	51	1 007	175.6	55.4	41	4 605	28 034.8	485.4
Del Rio	32	114	16.5	2.7	37	D	D	D	15	176	D	5.0
Denton	149	585	125.7	19.9	260	D	D	D	93	5 210	4 794.0	277.2
DeSoto	39	162	31.9	5.6	48	199	16.9	6.8	27	733	120.5	39.8
Duncanville	38	173	19.2	5.5	54	196	21.3	8.4	22	1 137	223.0	39.0
Eagle Pass	26	71	12.5	1.9	36	D	D	D	14	339	49.0	9.0
Edinburg	60	205	41.5	6.1	148	D	D	D	29	625	215.0	22.9
El Paso	671	2 969	548.7	101.9	1 119	D	D	D	432	11 607	13 170.8	487.1
Euless	40	267	50.6	8.9	86	D	D	D	37	832	197.2	39.3
Farmers Branch	70	929	144.0	47.3	308	4 575	1 077.9	470.0	80	2 707	910.5	117.6
Flower Mound	66	400	66.6	17.0	271	D	D	D	20	636	212.3	36.7
Fort Worth	704	4 977	1 106.6	228.7	1 652	D	D	D	645	39 747	D	2 369.4
Friendswood	44	314	23.4	8.1	128	447	58.6	21.0	16	175	D	7.2
Frisco	135	672	165.1	27.0	552	4 343	778.7	263.7	36	533	233.7	29.2
Galveston	75	403	76.2	15.5	106	D	D	D	29	948	D	48.9
Garland	173	1 113	183.7	33.5	280	3 620	463.2	299.6	264	9 585	5 396.6	427.2
Georgetown	63	228	62.7	13.0	161	616	86.9	30.9	48	1 541	344.6	63.4
Grand Prairie	126	1 945	355.9	83.2	169	1 299	174.6	65.1	181	12 084	4 512.7	758.4
Grapevine	77	785	328.6	40.5	219	1 265	198.4	76.2	43	1 942	D	95.9
Greenville	38	115	20.4	3.3	47	281	49.8	10.4	39	6 681	2 783.6	523.9
Haltom City	38	350	82.6	19.8	56	687	53.9	22.5	90	2 612	684.3	107.5
Harker Heights	32	127	18.7	4.0	28	138	9.6	3.5	4	23	2.6	D
Harlingen	97	443	80.5	9.8	146	D	D	D	49	903	D	40.8
Houston	3 435	28 791	7 005.4	1 456.0	9 252	158 979	38 304.1	14 658.9	2 436	86 899	53 787.1	4 791.2
Huntsville	48	175	42.9	6.1	68	393	27.6	9.8	17	347	D	21.3
Hurst	52	240	72.6	8.6	167	1 037	134.3	59.3	31	467	127.0	22.8

1. Establishments subject to federal tax.

Table D. Cities — Accommodation and Food Services, Arts, Entertainment, and Recreation, and Health Care and Social Assistance

City	Accommodation and food services, 2012				Arts, entertainment, and recreation,[1] 2012				Health care and social assistance,[1] 2012			
	Number of establishments	Number of employees	Sales (mil dol)	Annual payroll (mil dol)	Number of establishments	Number of employees	Receipts (mil dol)	Annual payroll (mil dol)	Number of establishments	Number of employees	Receipts (mil dol)	Annual payroll (mil dol)
	92	93	94	95	96	97	98	99	100	101	102	103
TENNESSEE— Cont'd												
Columbia	101	1 771	81.2	22.3	7	D	D	D	136	D	D	D
Cookeville	137	D	D	D	10	D	D	D	173	D	D	D
Franklin	281	6 519	337.0	97.6	95	D	D	D	285	4 901	744.3	269.8
Gallatin	58	905	44.3	12.2	6	D	D	D	84	D	D	D
Germantown	70	1 454	82.7	22.4	13	130	5.8	1.9	191	D	D	D
Hendersonville	112	2 638	113.7	34.6	26	D	D	D	142	2 039	249.7	85.2
Jackson	210	4 703	220.3	62.4	17	D	D	D	261	D	D	D
Johnson City	239	5 668	249.2	72.7	16	D	D	D	252	D	D	D
Kingsport	193	4 387	199.6	58.9	19	D	D	D	228	3 761	503.7	220.1
Knoxville	714	17 958	865.1	267.4	47	548	34.6	9.6	755	16 303	2 046.1	772.1
La Vergne	29	412	20.6	5.3	NA	NA	NA	NA	15	143	7.3	3.6
Lebanon	108	2 239	98.8	28.6	8	D	D	D	136	2 476	294.2	114.8
Maryville	94	1 644	75.5	22.0	13	D	D	D	140	1 629	171.3	82.1
Memphis	1 243	28 822	1 503.9	425.7	82	1 976	210.8	102.7	1 415	26 987	2 964.4	1 216.1
Morristown	106	D	D	D	9	D	D	D	123	2 306	227.8	96.0
Murfreesboro	314	7 922	356.0	105.3	21	D	D	D	327	6 004	576.4	262.1
Nashville-Davidson	1 714	40 106	2 573.8	759.3	665	4 720	1 476.9	524.5	1 467	30 924	4 176.2	1 568.7
Oak Ridge	74	1 604	76.3	21.4	6	101	4.6	1.6	101	D	D	D
Smyrna	109	2 367	112.1	32.0	6	D	D	D	117	D	D	D
Spring Hill	57	1 188	45.9	14.2	9	19	3.6	0.5	35	D	D	D
TEXAS	48 721	976 390	54 480.8	14 743.8	4 966	83 587	7 770.7	2 523.6	55 176	945 659	93 988.1	36 493.1
Abilene	284	D	D	D	34	258	21.1	4.0	316	7 710	657.8	271.4
Allen	170	3 771	194.3	56.4	24	462	25.4	8.1	259	D	D	D
Amarillo	500	10 147	514.1	139.7	52	687	38.7	11.3	567	10 579	1 228.0	437.8
Arlington	684	15 492	910.8	233.2	67	3 881	616.2	255.2	865	15 821	1 542.7	638.3
Austin	2 517	55 702	3 474.7	962.5	317	4 559	468.8	144.0	2 329	37 842	4 746.7	1 859.6
Baytown	174	3 836	193.7	52.2	12	D	D	D	213	D	D	D
Beaumont	283	6 727	320.7	88.3	35	D	D	D	501	D	D	D
Bedford	93	1 993	98.5	27.8	9	D	D	D	191	D	D	D
Big Spring	71	1 057	61.0	13.8	3	D	D	D	57	D	D	D
Brownsville	299	5 246	244.3	65.5	26	D	D	D	418	13 860	789.1	346.9
Bryan	139	2 436	115.0	32.5	13	D	D	D	186	2 546	275.6	118.1
Burleson	105	2 511	112.7	31.4	8	D	D	D	95	1 020	82.2	34.5
Carrollton	244	3 204	187.6	49.4	27	D	D	D	328	3 721	410.7	148.7
Cedar Hill	86	2 068	97.8	25.6	6	D	D	D	79	1 220	84.9	30.5
Cedar Park	137	2 517	119.2	31.5	20	D	D	D	163	D	D	D
Cleburne	81	1 365	63.3	18.1	7	68	3.7	0.6	99	D	D	D
College Station	287	6 966	327.7	88.0	21	330	14.7	5.0	136	D	D	D
Conroe	164	3 450	175.2	48.5	10	125	11.6	1.4	200	D	D	D
Coppell	73	1 538	93.3	22.2	9	159	6.8	2.3	106	D	D	D
Copperas Cove	50	934	42.1	10.8	3	D	D	D	27	426	22.3	10.3
Corpus Christi	749	15 806	825.4	223.7	57	D	D	D	907	17 743	1 577.5	620.5
Dallas	2 687	59 649	3 851.5	1 087.3	283	4 840	477.0	208.1	3 535	56 873	8 201.1	3 427.0
Deer Park	44	769	46.6	11.2	2	D	D	D	45	D	D	D
Del Rio	87	1 613	76.2	19.5	7	41	1.1	0.5	84	D	D	D
Denton	283	5 961	277.1	75.9	20	291	15.1	4.0	390	6 232	770.2	285.0
DeSoto	60	1 240	63.9	17.8	5	89	5.7	2.1	165	3 622	236.3	105.8
Duncanville	60	1 406	69.0	19.1	5	101	5.7	1.5	101	2 187	105.2	47.1
Eagle Pass	65	D	D	D	7	D	D	D	81	D	D	D
Edinburg	120	1 970	102.3	25.9	12	D	D	D	331	9 143	433.5	212.2
El Paso	1 362	27 187	1 310.8	354.0	89	D	D	D	1 300	26 860	2 875.1	1 005.3
Euless	89	1 538	76.0	20.2	5	D	D	D	77	D	D	D
Farmers Branch	99	1 493	83.9	25.9	6	D	D	D	136	2 292	285.2	112.7
Flower Mound	118	2 866	157.4	42.2	23	411	26.0	7.3	178	1 971	257.9	91.6
Fort Worth	1 288	28 324	1 609.5	440.5	134	2 108	225.1	46.6	1 602	24 161	2 738.6	1 078.8
Friendswood	70	1 121	55.0	14.1	11	D	D	D	111	D	D	D
Frisco	254	6 182	360.8	100.4	41	1 555	148.3	83.1	394	D	D	D
Galveston	212	6 605	391.2	110.0	22	480	35.2	7.9	85	D	D	D
Garland	309	5 540	286.8	79.7	31	504	40.5	9.4	414	7 134	439.2	187.8
Georgetown	103	2 188	109.6	30.5	14	D	D	D	152	2 278	225.8	90.9
Grand Prairie	216	3 855	221.9	54.6	21	D	D	D	234	2 519	181.0	66.5
Grapevine	175	7 278	628.9	152.0	17	379	26.3	5.7	186	D	D	D
Greenville	68	1 304	65.2	17.1	4	D	D	D	110	D	D	D
Haltom City	72	735	37.6	9.0	7	49	4.1	0.5	35	D	D	D
Harker Heights	63	951	37.1	10.2	15	D	D	D	34	D	D	D
Harlingen	170	3 749	203.8	57.5	16	D	D	D	334	11 017	834.5	354.0
Houston	5 645	122 643	7 746.6	2 082.8	442	10 362	1 681.5	523.7	6 526	105 192	11 479.2	4 372.6
Huntsville	94	D	D	D	3	D	D	D	78	D	D	D
Hurst	103	2 129	126.6	32.5	14	182	9.7	2.5	130	D	D	D

1. Establishments subject to federal tax.

Table D. Cities — Other Services and Government Employment and Payroll

City	Other services[1], 2012				Government employment and payroll, 2012								
					Full-time equivalent employees	March payroll							
						Total (dollars)	Percent of total for:						
	Number of establishments	Number of employees	Receipts (mil dol)	Annual payroll (mil dol)			Administration, judicial, and legal	Police and Corrections	Fire Protection	Highways and transportation	Health and welfare	Natural resources and utilities	Education and libraries
	104	105	106	107	108	109	110	111	112	113	114	115	116
TENNESSEE—Cont'd													
Columbia	57	381	30.1	9.6	492	1 828 149	7.0	18.8	18.5	8.4	0.0	42.6	0.0
Cookeville	80	413	34.4	9.2	2 260	9 757 664	1.2	3.6	1.9	1.3	85.3	5.8	0.0
Franklin	133	1 096	75.2	26.9	635	2 507 514	14.1	24.5	24.1	7.9	2.9	21.9	0.0
Gallatin	46	230	20.9	6.9	429	1 515 188	8.8	22.7	17.5	5.7	0.0	40.3	0.0
Germantown	51	506	24.7	9.6	286	1 166 262	0.4	46.4	32.0	8.9	0.0	6.3	0.0
Hendersonville	78	421	27.5	8.9	317	1 225 951	9.7	37.8	33.9	3.9	0.0	5.6	0.0
Jackson	91	D	D	D	732	2 706 306	10.3	39.0	26.4	6.9	0.2	15.5	0.0
Johnson City	104	D	D	D	2 069	7 207 080	4.3	9.1	5.7	7.6	0.0	24.2	46.3
Kingsport	83	531	48.6	15.0	2 088	7 112 728	4.6	8.2	5.7	3.4	0.1	9.0	66.2
Knoxville	392	3 196	242.1	83.5	2 544	10 707 196	7.3	20.0	11.8	5.2	1.3	49.6	0.0
La Vergne	24	794	124.4	25.1	165	495 446	15.9	42.8	0.0	4.2	0.0	26.3	4.3
Lebanon	56	657	63.8	20.5	337	1 064 568	9.9	34.9	13.8	8.3	1.8	27.1	0.0
Maryville	50	266	19.8	6.8	929	3 586 065	5.2	6.5	5.0	4.0	0.0	15.5	63.0
Memphis	712	5 678	522.2	172.5	24 196	79 305 378	2.0	15.7	10.1	4.9	0.8	25.5	40.2
Morristown	49	245	21.5	6.7	417	1 625 386	6.0	20.1	18.2	6.1	0.3	38.5	0.0
Murfreesboro	167	1 164	91.2	29.6	2 265	7 333 077	3.8	13.4	9.7	3.3	0.2	20.3	45.7
Nashville-Davidson	868	8 126	726.0	233.6	21 697	83 700 973	6.4	13.3	7.5	1.1	9.0	11.1	49.9
Oak Ridge	44	D	D	D	1 132	4 632 934	5.5	7.1	8.2	4.8	1.0	10.3	62.3
Smyrna	46	442	34.2	16.1	426	1 763 154	14.1	27.9	24.5	2.1	0.0	27.9	0.0
Spring Hill	26	136	10.8	3.2	153	514 319	5.2	29.3	24.9	4.9	0.0	23.4	4.4
TEXAS	28 255	216 219	21 861.4	6 765.6	X	X	X	X	X	X	X	X	X
Abilene	162	1 407	104.9	34.0	1 115	4 154 689	10.5	32.0	23.1	4.8	5.7	16.9	2.3
Allen	81	693	53.5	17.3	662	2 925 255	11.5	28.9	20.0	3.9	2.3	27.3	4.5
Amarillo	296	2 035	192.1	55.1	2 117	7 521 677	9.3	27.1	24.7	8.3	4.8	19.1	2.1
Arlington	374	2 410	207.6	61.6	2 551	12 130 944	13.1	38.1	20.5	5.1	4.7	13.8	2.7
Austin	1 319	11 317	1 060.8	331.5	12 580	64 599 610	10.4	24.1	13.4	7.1	8.1	30.6	1.9
Baytown	87	779	71.7	24.8	748	3 193 832	12.8	28.9	19.0	2.5	7.2	18.6	3.5
Beaumont	178	1 744	180.5	55.1	1 387	7 544 738	11.5	29.5	22.1	6.9	9.1	14.8	1.6
Bedford	55	334	28.4	8.5	396	1 910 062	12.2	44.6	25.8	2.3	0.9	11.0	3.3
Big Spring	28	D	D	D	255	860 648	10.2	23.3	19.7	6.6	10.8	21.6	0.0
Brownsville	98	498	35.4	11.2	1 660	6 576 268	6.3	28.3	16.9	10.1	3.1	22.4	2.2
Bryan	120	727	64.4	18.2	926	4 516 110	3.1	19.6	11.5	1.8	0.7	38.5	3.0
Burleson	66	364	26.8	8.7	314	1 837 857	11.3	27.1	16.3	3.9	5.4	20.8	2.6
Carrollton	168	1 866	164.0	66.9	750	3 791 660	11.3	30.8	28.1	4.7	3.6	12.4	3.2
Cedar Hill	35	227	19.1	5.7	345	1 415 937	9.4	29.5	24.7	6.8	4.1	17.5	2.3
Cedar Park	105	720	53.2	19.3	366	1 608 634	12.6	30.9	18.4	2.3	0.5	20.7	3.2
Cleburne	51	317	28.3	8.6	331	1 384 254	10.9	25.9	23.1	7.1	3.7	23.7	1.6
College Station	75	549	34.1	11.0	818	3 487 614	20.0	22.9	18.5	6.9	0.0	27.4	0.0
Conroe	104	679	59.5	17.1	506	2 148 894	13.0	28.8	20.3	9.4	1.3	18.9	0.0
Coppell	48	964	119.8	36.7	374	2 007 729	18.0	24.0	25.7	6.8	0.9	15.3	4.2
Copperas Cove	42	228	21.2	5.7	265	875 963	7.7	30.2	19.1	1.6	1.2	17.4	2.0
Corpus Christi	358	3 496	346.7	116.1	2 747	10 789 288	5.1	28.6	19.2	4.2	3.3	21.1	1.6
Dallas	1 450	12 565	1 440.8	409.3	14 235	67 511 933	7.3	31.8	17.3	19.3	4.4	14.9	1.2
Deer Park	58	906	130.9	49.5	328	1 382 968	18.7	32.7	5.3	2.7	0.0	31.9	2.9
Del Rio	32	D	D	D	479	1 348 047	13.5	25.7	21.8	5.8	8.4	17.9	0.0
Denton	150	972	89.5	27.1	1 265	6 238 827	15.5	19.1	17.6	2.9	1.6	38.3	2.8
DeSoto	39	154	15.1	4.3	317	1 509 174	9.4	33.2	25.8	4.2	5.1	12.0	3.0
Duncanville	63	321	32.4	8.9	262	1 180 545	13.5	32.0	24.0	4.8	0.9	15.2	3.2
Eagle Pass	29	126	7.5	2.1	351	916 457	7.8	31.5	17.9	15.9	3.9	20.4	1.6
Edinburg	69	313	21.9	6.5	687	2 190 991	12.2	35.3	5.2	5.7	1.0	33.1	3.3
El Paso	714	4 354	334.6	101.8	5 996	23 812 936	7.0	28.9	21.6	16.9	1.0	12.9	2.2
Euless	59	D	D	D	434	2 144 456	12.6	34.2	21.4	3.9	1.0	17.4	4.5
Farmers Branch	53	615	61.6	17.3	372	1 986 448	11.5	30.7	24.2	3.4	5.2	21.2	0.0
Flower Mound	88	931	73.4	25.9	440	1 883 026	25.4	26.1	22.5	3.5	4.1	11.7	3.5
Fort Worth	700	6 296	605.7	172.5	6 536	32 292 472	9.5	36.9	20.2	4.1	1.8	17.7	2.4
Friendswood	57	303	22.4	7.9	194	961 732	21.4	48.5	0.4	6.3	7.0	10.9	5.4
Frisco	142	1 037	80.7	26.6	594	2 715 180	9.9	30.4	23.9	5.3	1.2	19.8	3.8
Galveston	64	301	25.2	8.2	808	3 423 101	7.9	29.1	17.6	21.5	3.7	16.9	0.0
Garland	230	1 159	100.6	32.4	1 920	9 882 194	9.5	22.2	17.3	5.1	4.8	30.5	2.2
Georgetown	75	446	37.7	12.4	540	2 310 226	14.5	21.6	17.8	5.7	3.2	24.6	2.8
Grand Prairie	143	1 111	98.2	32.3	1 169	5 599 824	10.7	29.3	27.8	5.1	5.9	13.3	1.6
Grapevine	69	662	56.1	18.8	572	2 942 808	10.6	24.3	22.7	7.0	1.2	13.7	2.9
Greenville	36	211	16.2	5.5	403	1 671 286	7.6	21.2	16.8	3.9	1.7	41.0	1.8
Haltom City	65	D	D	D	281	1 111 357	13.5	36.6	17.0	6.0	1.5	13.9	4.9
Harker Heights	32	151	9.1	2.7	218	830 939	17.0	29.4	23.6	4.0	1.0	16.2	3.2
Harlingen	91	501	34.2	10.3	751	2 448 262	8.2	27.6	19.8	7.2	2.5	27.1	1.8
Houston	3 244	31 771	3 283.0	1 045.9	21 007	99 616 057	8.7	36.5	20.9	7.6	4.6	8.9	1.5
Huntsville	41	244	21.2	5.3	308	1 115 825	24.2	27.0	5.3	6.6	0.0	23.7	2.4
Hurst	71	450	31.1	10.3	371	1 783 347	13.7	36.1	21.5	5.6	0.0	15.6	6.0

1. Establishments subject to federal tax.

Table D. Cities — City Government Finances

City	General revenue Total (mil dol)	Intergovernmental Total (mil dol)	Intergovernmental Percent from state government	Taxes Total (mil dol)	Taxes Per capita[1] (dollars) Total	Taxes Per capita[1] (dollars) Property	Sales and gross receipts	General expenditure Total (mil dol)	General expenditure Per capita[1] (dollars) Total	Capital outlays
	117	118	119	120	121	122	123	124	125	126
TENNESSEE— Cont'd										
Columbia	41.4	15.4	53.0	12.6	360	269	88	40.7	1 166	252
Cookeville	277.1	19.0	22.5	9.4	303	201	101	277.4	8 954	919
Franklin	87.6	39.1	37.2	24.4	368	176	192	85.2	1 285	230
Gallatin	34.4	11.7	42.9	11.9	376	302	74	33.1	1 045	154
Germantown	61.8	21.1	73.1	24.7	627	570	58	65.4	1 661	429
Hendersonville	35.8	16.0	45.5	13.8	260	194	66	34.8	655	51
Jackson	87.7	28.3	31.7	40.9	609	491	118	83.5	1 243	137
Johnson City	163.0	78.4	55.6	47.4	732	608	124	167.9	2 594	204
Kingsport	166.0	83.1	48.9	57.0	1 080	915	166	164.5	3 118	644
Knoxville	351.6	81.3	38.7	163.6	898	585	313	318.2	1 747	425
La Vergne	25.4	7.8	50.3	10.3	306	225	80	18.7	553	55
Lebanon	28.1	13.4	31.2	6.1	218	112	106	31.0	1 113	106
Maryville	74.6	37.7	68.6	28.4	1 027	932	95	71.2	2 571	85
Memphis	2 270.7	1 329.3	61.2	520.3	789	551	237	2 276.9	3 451	425
Morristown	51.1	16.0	22.3	12.8	440	314	127	46.1	1 582	230
Murfreesboro	157.1	75.8	58.2	48.0	422	310	112	168.1	1 476	135
Nashville-Davidson	2 398.7	624.4	98.0	1 220.6	1 952	1 260	691	2 431.3	3 888	403
Oak Ridge	134.1	83.4	33.6	34.7	1 182	710	463	107.5	3 666	210
Smyrna	53.2	16.9	24.7	11.2	269	186	83	50.3	1 205	109
Spring Hill	19.8	7.0	49.1	5.7	182	127	55	26.7	857	343
TEXAS	X	X	X	X	X	X	X	X	X	X
Abilene	137.0	15.0	30.9	83.5	697	279	418	116.5	972	130
Allen	117.2	4.4	12.3	78.6	873	457	416	125.1	1 390	272
Amarillo	243.2	33.1	39.3	120.2	614	172	442	262.0	1 339	339
Arlington	460.5	35.2	25.8	242.5	644	301	343	480.0	1 275	145
Austin	1 410.8	92.8	27.1	613.6	709	410	298	1 511.5	1 746	382
Baytown	105.9	8.6	14.0	43.5	589	251	339	126.1	1 710	339
Beaumont	168.9	28.1	23.8	91.4	782	377	405	178.4	1 526	395
Bedford	41.1	0.8	100.0	27.1	562	290	272	42.9	889	121
Big Spring	26.6	1.5	86.7	14.4	521	200	321	29.9	1 081	134
Brownsville	224.1	50.4	11.0	74.7	415	197	218	175.9	976	181
Bryan	85.5	6.5	55.6	40.7	522	297	225	96.3	1 235	236
Burleson	54.3	0.2	84.0	35.0	897	409	488	43.5	1 115	101
Carrollton	128.2	6.2	86.1	88.8	708	435	273	119.3	951	184
Cedar Hill	54.5	2.8	12.5	34.8	748	403	345	54.1	1 163	158
Cedar Park	71.9	5.6	100.0	42.4	732	349	383	67.0	1 156	349
Cleburne	51.2	3.4	11.5	26.3	884	463	421	43.9	1 472	106
College Station	94.1	3.3	25.7	53.8	549	255	294	101.4	1 036	172
Conroe	70.6	1.0	16.8	50.6	824	235	589	74.4	1 211	375
Coppell	72.0	0.3	100.0	58.2	1 451	828	624	65.6	1 638	306
Copperas Cove	25.8	0.6	100.0	14.2	425	258	167	389.3	1 246	1 475
Corpus Christi	357.9	29.6	42.3	191.7	614	280	333	389.3	1 246	290
Dallas	2 544.8	172.7	56.8	1 084.4	872	545	327	2 543.0	2 045	435
Deer Park	42.3	0.3	34.3	19.4	585	370	215	36.3	1 097	77
Del Rio	34.7	4.3	47.7	15.1	418	189	229	37.0	1 026	201
Denton	169.7	11.5	79.7	94.5	765	357	408	149.1	1 207	175
DeSoto	50.0	1.3	100.0	32.7	640	413	227	48.8	954	113
Duncanville	37.1	1.0	60.3	22.7	573	320	253	42.9	1 085	220
Eagle Pass	32.1	2.3	62.3	10.6	387	159	228	32.6	1 184	237
Edinburg	72.5	6.4	81.8	40.8	518	269	249	71.1	903	197
El Paso	743.5	92.0	24.8	386.6	572	287	285	621.6	920	181
Euless	66.2	1.7	13.5	42.6	806	223	583	61.4	1 162	109
Farmers Branch	55.4	0.8	73.5	41.0	1 395	732	663	53.3	1 813	185
Flower Mound	74.2	2.2	6.5	54.3	800	457	343	76.4	1 125	247
Fort Worth	1 108.5	81.2	53.9	609.6	783	466	317	1 116.7	1 434	341
Friendswood	32.1	3.1	8.8	20.8	562	394	168	35.6	963	285
Frisco	214.9	32.8	2.5	125.6	977	507	469	202.2	1 572	466
Galveston	180.4	62.3	54.6	58.9	1 217	502	716	182.3	3 769	1 529
Garland	228.5	19.9	12.3	106.8	457	312	145	234.9	1 004	127
Georgetown	65.1	3.9	87.5	35.5	675	289	386	70.7	1 345	298
Grand Prairie	252.2	40.5	30.9	131.5	723	393	330	217.4	1 195	147
Grapevine	125.9	3.7	100.0	94.8	1 953	609	1 344	92.9	1 916	312
Greenville	39.6	2.4	41.3	19.8	762	371	392	43.8	1 690	468
Haltom City	42.3	2.2	23.7	24.5	565	230	336	38.1	878	131
Harker Heights	24.0	0.5	27.3	15.5	558	324	234	26.5	951	239
Harlingen	87.2	13.1	29.3	40.5	615	250	365	112.2	1 703	650
Houston	3 667.9	315.0	27.9	1 921.4	888	474	414	3 697.9	1 708	274
Huntsville	32.1	1.0	50.9	14.9	376	122	253	30.5	766	52
Hurst	51.1	2.4	26.0	34.8	911	328	583	49.1	1 285	225

1. Based on population estimated as of July 1 of the year shown.

Table D. Cities — City Government Finances

City	City government finances, 2012 (cont.)									
	General expenditure (cont.)									
	Percent of total for:									
	Public welfare	Highways	Parking facilities	Education	Health and hospitals	Police protection	Sewerage and sanitation	Parks and recreation	Housing and community development	Interest on debt
	127	128	129	130	131	132	133	134	135	136
TENNESSEE— Cont'd										
Columbia	0.0	10.7	0.0	0.0	0.0	16.5	23.4	4.1	0.0	2.9
Cookeville	0.0	1.2	0.0	0.0	84.6	2.6	1.6	1.0	0.0	1.2
Franklin	0.0	10.0	0.0	0.0	0.0	16.6	17.5	4.0	0.2	6.0
Gallatin	0.0	5.6	0.0	0.0	0.4	19.4	17.8	11.9	0.0	1.4
Germantown	0.0	27.4	0.0	0.0	0.5	17.1	10.4	14.4	0.0	1.4
Hendersonville	0.0	12.3	0.0	0.0	0.0	27.4	13.2	7.3	2.9	1.2
Jackson	0.0	14.0	0.0	0.0	0.2	25.1	12.3	11.3	3.2	3.2
Johnson City	0.5	5.3	0.0	40.8	0.0	8.8	12.9	8.4	0.3	4.0
Kingsport	0.0	3.2	0.0	40.7	0.0	7.2	9.4	4.1	0.3	3.0
Knoxville	0.0	3.1	0.3	0.0	0.0	15.7	31.2	5.9	3.8	8.0
La Vergne	0.7	9.0	0.0	0.1	0.1	30.0	21.7	6.8	0.0	2.9
Lebanon	0.0	8.4	0.0	0.0	0.0	25.7	25.8	7.6	0.0	1.0
Maryville	0.0	3.8	0.0	66.8	0.3	6.3	5.5	2.0	0.0	3.6
Memphis	0.0	1.2	0.0	52.3	0.0	9.9	4.8	1.6	6.4	4.4
Morristown	0.6	10.0	0.0	0.0	0.0	15.5	27.8	3.8	1.6	1.5
Murfreesboro	0.1	11.1	0.1	38.8	0.0	13.6	8.2	6.7	0.8	2.6
Nashville-Davidson	1.3	1.6	0.0	34.8	9.5	8.0	6.5	3.3	0.0	7.0
Oak Ridge	0.0	2.3	0.0	52.8	0.0	6.5	10.1	3.7	0.6	3.4
Smyrna	0.5	5.1	0.0	0.0	0.0	18.7	11.2	12.4	0.3	2.6
Spring Hill	0.0	9.8	0.0	0.0	0.0	14.6	51.6	2.8	0.0	0.9
TEXAS	X	X	X	X	X	X	X	X	X	X
Abilene	0.0	7.3	0.0	0.0	3.8	18.8	16.3	6.3	1.0	2.9
Allen	0.0	4.2	0.0	0.0	0.2	15.6	11.7	22.6	1.0	5.9
Amarillo	0.0	6.1	0.0	0.0	6.0	13.9	17.9	6.7	4.4	2.1
Arlington	0.1	9.3	0.0	0.0	0.9	17.6	13.8	7.7	1.1	26.6
Austin	0.0	7.5	0.0	0.0	6.9	17.8	18.1	8.2	3.3	5.9
Baytown	0.0	9.2	0.0	0.0	3.4	15.7	9.1	9.2	2.3	5.4
Beaumont	0.0	21.9	0.0	0.0	5.1	21.4	8.4	9.5	1.2	4.0
Bedford	0.0	4.8	0.0	0.0	0.8	24.7	12.9	6.3	0.0	5.0
Big Spring	0.0	5.1	0.0	0.0	7.7	15.7	16.2	15.7	0.0	2.1
Brownsville	1.3	7.1	0.3	0.0	1.0	18.2	22.3	5.7	1.0	5.9
Bryan	0.0	9.9	0.0	0.0	0.0	16.0	19.2	3.8	1.3	6.5
Burleson	0.0	9.7	0.0	0.0	1.7	16.8	16.6	12.8	0.0	9.0
Carrollton	0.0	12.5	0.0	0.0	2.0	17.5	10.3	7.8	2.6	6.3
Cedar Hill	0.1	6.3	0.0	0.0	0.3	19.0	15.2	8.6	0.0	7.0
Cedar Park	0.0	19.4	0.0	0.0	0.4	11.4	13.6	7.0	0.0	10.8
Cleburne	0.0	5.5	0.0	0.0	1.7	16.6	19.7	9.4	3.6	4.0
College Station	0.0	15.6	1.2	0.0	0.0	13.7	18.3	9.5	1.4	5.1
Conroe	0.0	11.1	0.0	0.0	0.0	18.9	12.0	15.3	0.4	6.4
Coppell	0.0	7.8	0.0	0.0	0.5	14.6	6.7	17.0	0.0	5.6
Copperas Cove	0.0	63.3	0.0	0.0	0.5	6.3	7.5	2.6	0.0	4.4
Corpus Christi	0.0	10.6	0.1	0.0	1.8	18.9	23.2	9.8	3.9	3.6
Dallas	0.7	5.5	0.0	0.0	1.0	14.0	11.3	7.1	1.9	16.7
Deer Park	0.0	3.7	0.0	0.0	0.6	17.6	14.8	15.5	0.0	4.5
Del Rio	3.2	16.9	0.0	0.0	1.4	17.0	15.7	4.1	0.0	4.6
Denton	0.0	8.4	0.0	0.0	0.6	14.7	25.1	9.1	1.2	4.9
DeSoto	0.0	7.2	0.0	0.0	1.1	16.2	19.1	6.8	0.0	10.7
Duncanville	0.0	7.7	0.0	0.0	0.7	17.1	17.5	22.4	0.0	2.2
Eagle Pass	0.0	20.2	0.0	0.0	0.2	16.0	19.6	9.2	0.0	4.5
Edinburg	0.0	4.6	0.0	0.0	2.0	17.8	26.4	14.6	1.5	3.2
El Paso	0.4	3.1	0.0	0.0	3.3	18.8	16.2	4.6	2.2	8.5
Euless	0.0	6.2	0.0	0.0	0.5	16.4	4.4	12.4	0.1	3.2
Farmers Branch	0.0	11.0	0.0	0.0	1.5	20.8	10.8	13.5	0.0	2.3
Flower Mound	0.2	27.9	0.0	0.0	1.1	16.1	10.1	9.8	0.1	4.3
Fort Worth	0.0	9.2	0.3	0.0	1.3	21.0	19.0	7.6	3.1	5.7
Friendswood	0.0	4.5	0.0	0.0	3.2	21.8	12.3	5.4	1.7	2.4
Frisco	0.0	14.8	0.0	4.9	0.6	9.4	9.2	9.5	0.2	12.3
Galveston	0.0	12.7	0.0	0.0	0.3	9.8	11.8	9.1	14.0	5.5
Garland	0.0	6.6	0.0	0.0	1.3	19.5	18.2	8.0	6.9	6.4
Georgetown	0.0	19.8	0.0	0.0	0.9	12.7	17.5	8.6	0.0	5.3
Grand Prairie	0.0	8.1	0.0	0.0	0.7	16.1	13.9	10.7	14.8	6.4
Grapevine	0.0	8.5	0.0	0.0	0.0	14.9	6.7	16.5	0.0	4.9
Greenville	0.0	8.7	0.0	0.0	0.0	15.0	24.1	3.8	3.9	3.5
Haltom City	0.0	7.6	0.0	0.0	0.9	19.6	15.2	2.7	0.0	5.1
Harker Heights	0.0	3.6	0.0	0.0	0.0	18.2	17.1	6.8	0.0	4.4
Harlingen	0.0	5.5	0.0	0.0	0.6	11.9	13.7	4.7	0.7	3.1
Houston	0.0	10.0	0.2	0.0	3.0	16.1	6.5	2.7	2.5	13.3
Huntsville	0.0	8.0	0.0	0.0	1.5	17.2	34.7	4.6	0.0	4.1
Hurst	0.0	11.9	0.0	0.0	2.5	22.9	10.3	15.1	0.0	3.7

Table D. Cities — **City Government Finances, City Government Employment, and Climate**

City	City government finances, 2012 (cont.)			Climate[2]						
	Debt outstanding			Average daily temperature (degrees Fahrenheit)						
				Mean		Limits				
	Total (mil dol)	Per capita[1] (dollars)	Debt issued during year	January	July	January[3]	July[4]	Annual precipitation (inches)	Heating degree days	Cooling degree days
	137	138	139	140	141	142	143	144	145	146
TENNESSEE—Cont'd										
Columbia	73.5	2 105	17.0	35.6	77.2	25.0	88.5	56.13	4 183	1 267
Cookeville	143.9	4 643	5.1	NA	NA	NA	NA	NA	NA	NA
Franklin	172.8	2 606	19.4	35.1	77.4	25.2	88.9	54.33	4 199	1 294
Gallatin	47.2	1 492	8.7	NA	NA	NA	NA	NA	NA	NA
Germantown	32.1	815	6.0	37.9	81.1	28.2	91.1	53.63	3 491	1 838
Hendersonville	11.8	222	0.3	36.8	79.1	27.9	88.7	48.11	3 677	1 652
Jackson	119.1	1 772	10.0	37.1	79.6	28.2	89.4	54.86	3 649	1 648
Johnson City	422.8	6 531	15.0	34.2	74.2	24.3	84.8	41.33	4 445	956
Kingsport	225.1	4 268	41.5	35.6	76.2	26.2	86.9	44.44	4 178	1 139
Knoxville	920.7	5 055	198.0	38.5	78.7	30.3	88.2	48.22	3 531	1 527
La Vergne	25.9	769	1.0	NA	NA	NA	NA	NA	NA	NA
Lebanon	61.0	2 191	5.9	NA	NA	NA	NA	NA	NA	NA
Maryville	130.5	4 709	0.0	NA	NA	NA	NA	NA	NA	NA
Memphis	2 500.9	3 791	107.2	39.9	82.5	31.3	92.1	54.65	3 041	2 187
Morristown	126.8	4 355	37.3	NA	NA	NA	NA	NA	NA	NA
Murfreesboro	318.3	2 795	1.6	35.4	78.1	25.3	89.1	54.98	4 107	1 388
Nashville-Davidson	4 895.0	7 828	800.3	36.8	79.1	27.9	88.7	48.11	3 677	1 652
Oak Ridge	170.4	5 812	11.1	36.6	77.3	27.2	88.1	55.05	3 993	1 301
Smyrna	71.6	1 717	2.4	36.8	79.1	27.9	88.7	48.11	3 677	1 652
Spring Hill	21.6	692	10.8	NA	NA	NA	NA	NA	NA	NA
TEXAS	X	X	X	X	X	X	X	X	X	X
Abilene	132.7	1 106	22.6	43.5	83.5	31.8	94.8	23.78	2 659	2 386
Allen	179.7	1 997	8.8	41.8	82.4	31.1	92.7	41.01	2 843	2 060
Amarillo	366.9	1 876	40.4	35.8	78.2	22.6	91.0	19.71	4 318	1 344
Arlington	2 154.5	5 724	564.5	44.1	85.0	34.0	95.4	34.73	2 370	2 568
Austin	5 572.8	6 438	681.1	50.2	84.2	40.0	95.0	33.65	1 648	2 974
Baytown	189.8	2 575	22.4	51.6	83.6	41.9	91.6	53.75	1 471	2 841
Beaumont	353.3	3 022	53.2	51.1	83.1	41.1	92.7	57.38	1 548	2 734
Bedford	61.2	1 268	14.8	44.1	85.0	34.0	95.4	34.73	2 370	2 568
Big Spring	23.3	843	0.0	42.7	82.7	29.6	94.3	20.12	2 724	2 243
Brownsville	528.4	2 931	23.6	59.6	83.9	50.5	92.4	27.55	644	3 874
Bryan	362.9	4 655	34.6	50.2	84.6	39.8	95.6	39.67	1 616	2 938
Burleson	130.3	3 340	17.8	NA	NA	NA	NA	NA	NA	NA
Carrollton	168.5	1 343	0.0	44.1	85.0	34.0	95.4	34.73	2 370	2 568
Cedar Hill	156.9	3 375	18.0	43.7	84.3	33.2	94.9	34.54	2 437	2 508
Cedar Park	214.5	3 700	8.4	47.2	83.8	35.1	95.7	36.42	1 998	2 584
Cleburne	132.4	4 443	26.5	45.9	84.5	34.0	97.0	36.25	2 158	2 604
College Station	242.2	2 475	47.0	50.2	84.6	39.8	95.6	39.67	1 616	2 938
Conroe	196.2	3 194	37.9	50.3	83.7	40.0	94.3	49.32	1 647	2 793
Coppell	93.5	2 332	21.3	44.1	85.0	34.0	95.4	34.73	2 370	2 568
Copperas Cove	98.1	2 937	52.5	46.0	83.5	34.0	95.3	32.88	2 190	2 477
Corpus Christi	1 152.6	3 689	80.5	56.1	83.8	46.2	93.2	32.26	950	3 497
Dallas	7 943.6	6 389	1 246.4	45.9	86.5	36.4	96.1	37.05	2 219	2 878
Deer Park	44.9	1 359	0.0	54.3	84.5	45.2	93.6	53.96	1 174	3 119
Del Rio	64.8	1 795	0.1	51.3	85.3	39.7	96.2	18.80	1 417	3 226
Denton	501.7	4 062	45.1	42.7	83.6	32.0	94.1	37.79	2 650	2 269
DeSoto	130.8	2 556	20.2	46.0	84.6	35.0	96.0	38.81	2 130	2 608
Duncanville	19.1	483	6.9	45.9	86.5	36.4	96.1	37.05	2 219	2 878
Eagle Pass	61.2	2 224	14.7	NA	NA	NA	NA	NA	NA	NA
Edinburg	98.1	1 246	24.2	58.7	85.1	48.2	95.5	22.61	719	3 898
El Paso	1 534.1	2 270	166.5	45.1	83.3	32.9	94.5	9.43	2 543	2 254
Euless	51.8	980	9.6	44.1	85.0	34.0	95.4	34.73	2 370	2 568
Farmers Branch	24.3	827	0.0	45.9	86.5	36.4	96.1	37.05	2 219	2 878
Flower Mound	129.5	1 908	3.6	44.1	85.0	34.0	95.4	34.73	2 370	2 568
Fort Worth	2 401.8	3 084	394.8	43.3	84.5	31.4	96.6	34.01	2 509	2 466
Friendswood	66.6	1 804	17.5	54.3	84.5	45.2	93.6	53.96	1 174	3 179
Frisco	640.8	4 982	148.2	41.8	82.4	31.1	92.7	41.01	2 843	2 060
Galveston	316.3	6 539	9.9	55.8	84.3	49.7	88.7	43.84	1 008	3 268
Garland	905.7	3 873	152.4	45.9	86.5	36.4	96.1	37.05	2 219	2 878
Georgetown	168.4	3 205	21.7	47.2	83.8	35.1	95.7	36.42	1 998	2 584
Grand Prairie	447.1	2 458	34.9	44.1	85.0	34.0	95.4	34.73	2 370	2 568
Grapevine	142.7	2 942	0.0	42.4	84.0	30.8	95.5	34.66	2 649	2 340
Greenville	148.3	5 723	11.5	NA	NA	NA	NA	NA	NA	NA
Haltom City	60.4	1 392	15.4	43.0	84.1	31.4	95.7	34.12	2 608	2 358
Harker Heights	50.6	1 819	8.0	NA	NA	NA	NA	NA	NA	NA
Harlingen	118.7	1 803	50.3	58.6	84.4	48.4	94.5	28.13	737	3 736
Houston	13 983.7	6 459	2 478.6	54.3	84.5	45.2	93.6	53.96	1 174	3 179
Huntsville	38.9	977	5.0	48.5	83.2	39.0	93.8	48.51	1 835	2 600
Hurst	57.6	1 508	9.1	44.1	85.0	34.0	95.4	34.73	2 370	2 568

1. Based on the population estimated as of July 1 of the year shown.   2. Represents normal values based on the 30-year period, 1971–2000.   3. Average daily minimum.
4. Average daily maximum.

Table D. Cities — **Land Area and Population**

STATE Place code	City	Land area,[1] 2016 (sq mi)	Population, 2016 Total persons	Rank	Per square mile	Race alone[2] (percent), 2015 White	Black or African American	American Indian, Alaska Native	Asian	Hawaiian Pacific Islander	Some other race	2 or more races[2]
		1	2	3	4	5	6	7	8	9	10	11
	TEXAS—Cont'd											
48 37000	Irving	67.0	238 289	91	3 556.6	54.1	11.8	0.6	19.6	0.4	10.8	2.7
48 38632	Keller	18.5	46 646	822	2 521.4	87.3	1.5	0.8	5.8	0.0	1.2	3.3
48 39148	Killeen	53.5	143 400	182	2 680.4	48.4	35.0	0.4	3.7	1.5	4.3	6.7
48 39352	Kingsville	13.8	26 071	1 398	1 889.2	86.0	4.4	0.3	1.4	0.0	6.0	1.8
48 39952	Kyle	19.6	39 060	971	1 992.9	81.0	7.5	1.1	1.9	0.0	5.3	3.2
48 40588	Lake Jackson	19.5	27 529	1 341	1 411.7	89.5	2.7	0.0	3.3	0.0	2.3	2.2
48 41212	Lancaster	33.2	38 867	980	1 170.7	NA	NA	0.0	NA	0.0	NA	NA
48 41440	La Porte	18.6	35 086	1 080	1 886.3	84.9	6.3	0.2	1.4	0.0	4.7	2.4
48 41464	Laredo	101.1	257 156	80	2 543.6	95.6	0.2	0.3	0.7	0.0	2.4	0.7
48 41980	League City	51.2	102 010	297	1 992.4	85.5	3.7	0.2	4.3	0.0	1.3	5.1
48 42016	Leander	29.6	42 761	882	1 444.6	85.4	4.3	0.0	3.3	0.0	1.1	5.8
48 42508	Lewisville	36.7	104 659	289	2 851.7	64.2	14.7	0.4	11.3	0.0	6.3	3.0
48 43012	Little Elm	17.3	42 504	887	2 456.9	60.4	15.3	0.3	1.4	0.0	19.1	3.4
48 43888	Longview	55.7	82 055	411	1 473.2	72.7	22.6	0.0	1.7	0.0	0.6	2.4
48 45000	Lubbock	124.6	252 506	83	2 026.5	80.6	7.4	1.5	2.6	0.0	4.5	3.4
48 45072	Lufkin	34.2	36 159	1 052	1 057.3	67.2	24.1	0.1	2.2	0.0	2.1	4.4
48 45384	McAllen	58.4	142 212	184	2 435.1	75.7	2.2	0.1	3.7	0.1	17.0	1.2
48 45744	McKinney	63.0	172 298	147	2 734.9	77.5	9.7	0.9	7.4	0.2	2.4	2.0
48 46452	Mansfield	36.6	65 631	547	1 793.2	67.1	17.6	0.5	5.4	0.2	4.3	4.8
48 47892	Mesquite	47.2	143 736	181	3 045.3	65.3	24.5	1.2	2.5	0.0	3.4	3.1
48 48072	Midland	74.4	134 610	196	1 809.3	85.1	6.8	0.2	1.8	0.0	3.8	2.2
48 48768	Mission	35.5	83 563	399	2 353.9	NA	NA	NA	NA	NA	NA	NA
48 48804	Missouri City	28.8	74 561	466	2 588.9	27.2	38.8	0.1	23.7	0.6	7.7	1.8
48 50256	Nacogdoches	27.4	33 932	1 119	1 238.4	NA	NA	NA	NA	NA	NA	NA
48 50820	New Braunfels	45.0	73 959	474	1 643.5	88.4	3.8	0.3	1.5	0.0	3.0	3.0
48 52356	North Richland Hills	18.1	69 798	503	3 856.2	81.7	6.5	0.6	6.8	1.4	0.1	3.0
48 53388	Odessa	45.2	117 871	234	2 607.8	86.9	4.5	0.2	1.5	0.0	3.8	3.1
48 55080	Paris	36.4	25 005	1 423	687.0	NA	NA	NA	NA	NA	NA	NA
48 56000	Pasadena	43.5	153 351	166	3 525.3	89.9	3.3	1.0	1.0	0.0	3.5	1.2
48 56348	Pearland	46.3	113 570	249	2 452.9	63.4	20.0	0.7	11.9	0.0	1.6	2.4
48 57176	Pflugerville	22.8	59 245	627	2 598.5	65.9	18.6	0.2	6.5	0.1	3.9	4.7
48 57200	Pharr	23.6	77 320	438	3 276.3	NA	NA	NA	NA	NA	NA	NA
48 58016	Plano	71.7	286 057	69	3 989.6	66.9	7.9	0.9	20.3	0.1	1.6	2.2
48 58820	Port Arthur	76.9	55 427	676	720.8	50.0	38.9	0.2	5.6	0.0	2.1	3.2
48 61796	Richardson	28.6	113 347	250	3 963.2	66.3	11.2	0.4	17.4	0.0	2.0	2.6
48 62828	Rockwall	29.3	43 586	864	1 487.6	84.0	7.9	1.3	3.2	0.0	0.9	2.8
48 63284	Rosenberg	33.1	36 937	1 030	1 115.9	76.0	13.0	0.0	0.9	0.0	6.5	3.7
48 63500	Round Rock	35.6	120 892	227	3 395.8	75.4	9.4	0.5	7.1	0.0	3.1	4.4
48 63572	Rowlett	20.9	61 999	589	2 966.5	75.9	16.2	0.5	5.3	0.0	0.5	1.6
48 64472	San Angelo	59.9	100 702	303	1 681.2	84.8	5.7	0.2	1.6	0.2	5.8	1.6
48 65000	San Antonio	461.0	1 492 510	7	3 237.5	81.9	7.2	0.8	2.9	0.1	4.3	2.7
48 65516	San Juan	11.4	36 663	1 041	3 216.1	NA	NA	NA	NA	NA	NA	NA
48 65600	San Marcos	34.1	61 980	590	1 817.6	81.6	6.8	0.5	2.2	0.0	6.7	2.2
48 66128	Schertz	31.9	39 453	961	1 236.8	62.2	11.5	0.4	3.5	0.0	16.2	6.3
48 66644	Seguin	37.1	28 614	1 301	771.3	NA	NA	NA	NA	NA	NA	NA
48 67496	Sherman	44.0	41 567	908	944.7	79.3	12.6	0.7	0.4	0.0	3.0	4.0
48 68636	Socorro	22.0	33 277	1 141	1 512.6	89.8	0.4	1.4	0.0	0.0	7.9	0.5
48 69032	Southlake	21.8	30 991	1 211	1 421.6	85.6	3.0	0.0	7.5	0.0	0.0	3.8
48 70808	Sugar Land	33.6	88 177	368	2 624.3	49.4	9.7	0.1	37.5	0.0	2.1	1.2
48 72176	Temple	70.1	73 600	476	1 049.9	71.0	18.5	0.2	1.6	0.1	3.3	5.3
48 72368	Texarkana	29.1	37 679	1 014	1 294.8	NA	NA	NA	NA	NA	NA	NA
48 72392	Texas City	64.3	48 262	790	750.6	65.4	26.6	0.2	0.9	0.0	3.4	3.6
48 72530	The Colony	14.0	42 408	892	3 029.1	NA	NA	NA	NA	NA	NA	NA
48 74144	Tyler	56.6	104 798	287	1 851.6	68.9	24.4	0.5	2.1	0.0	2.5	1.6
48 75428	Victoria	37.0	67 670	525	1 828.9	84.5	6.7	0.1	1.6	0.0	4.2	3.0
48 76000	Waco	89.0	134 432	197	1 510.5	71.2	21.6	0.2	2.9	0.0	2.0	2.2
48 76816	Waxahachie	47.6	34 345	1 106	721.5	79.2	13.6	0.1	1.0	0.0	4.1	2.1
48 76864	Weatherford	26.0	29 969	1 253	1 152.7	88.2	3.3	0.2	0.1	0.0	6.0	2.3
48 77272	Weslaco	18.9	40 033	944	2 118.1	NA	NA	NA	NA	NA	NA	NA
48 79000	Wichita Falls	72.2	104 724	288	1 450.5	76.2	12.1	0.8	3.1	0.0	4.5	3.3
48 80356	Wylie	21.4	47 701	800	2 229.0	66.7	23.1	0.2	4.5	0.0	2.3	3.2
49 00000	UTAH	82 195.6	3 051 217	X	37.1	87.2	1.2	1.2	2.3	0.8	4.5	2.9
49 01310	American Fork	10.1	28 770	1 293	2 848.5	NA	NA	NA	NA	NA	NA	NA
49 07690	Bountiful	13.2	44 078	856	3 339.2	93.4	0.4	0.4	1.3	0.4	2.3	1.8
49 11320	Cedar City	35.9	31 223	1 205	869.7	NA	NA	NA	NA	NA	NA	NA
49 13850	Clearfield	7.7	30 855	1 218	4 007.1	76.3	3.7	0.5	1.6	0.4	12.8	4.6
49 16270	Cottonwood Heights	9.2	34 285	1 109	3 726.6	NA	NA	NA	NA	NA	NA	NA
49 20120	Draper	30.1	47 328	812	1 572.4	88.6	1.0	1.4	5.8	0.4	0.2	2.6
49 36070	Holladay	8.5	30 831	1 221	3 627.2	NA	NA	NA	NA	NA	NA	NA

1. Dry land or land partially or temporarily covered by water. 2. Hispanic or Latino persons may be of any race.

Table D. Cities — **Population**

| City | Percent Hispanic or Latino[1], 2015 | Percent foreign born 2015 | Age of population (percent), 2010-2014 | | | | | | | Median age 2015 | Percent female 2015 | Population Census counts | | Percent change | |
| | | | Under 18 years | 18 to 24 years | 25 to 34 years | 35 to 44 years | 45 to 54 years | 55 to 64 years | 65 years and over | | | 2000 | 2010 | 2000–2010 | 2010–2016 |
	12	13	14	15	16	17	18	19	20	21	22	23	24	25	26
TEXAS—Cont'd															
Irving	41.4	36.7	26.8	10.2	18.8	16.2	12.3	9.0	6.7	32.3	50.5	191 615	216 285	12.9	10.2
Keller	6.2	10.2	30.4	4.4	7.6	16.5	16.1	10.3	14.8	40.2	50.7	27 345	39 627	44.9	17.7
Killeen	23.2	11.2	30.7	11.2	20.5	13.2	11.0	6.9	6.4	29.2	50.7	86 911	127 913	47.2	12.1
Kingsville	71.5	2.1	29.0	21.7	11.2	13.1	5.1	8.1	11.9	24.6	47.8	25 575	26 213	2.5	-0.5
Kyle	41.7	10.2	29.9	8.8	18.7	17.6	12.3	6.6	6.1	30.4	48.9	5 314	28 021	427.3	39.4
Lake Jackson	20.2	11.2	25.6	7.7	15.0	13.0	9.7	14.5	14.5	36.1	50.1	26 386	26 830	1.7	2.6
Lancaster	21.7	6.8	30.1	12.3	13.0	10.7	17.9	9.0	7.0	29.8	53.1	25 894	36 665	41.6	6.0
La Porte	22.8	8.5	22.0	8.2	13.3	14.7	14.3	17.7	9.7	38.7	48.7	31 880	33 806	6.0	3.8
Laredo	95.1	26.8	33.3	11.6	13.1	13.3	11.2	8.6	8.9	28.8	51.4	176 576	236 057	33.7	8.9
League City	15.1	8.5	23.4	9.5	14.5	14.9	14.5	11.7	11.3	35.9	49.8	45 444	83 563	83.9	22.1
Leander	25.9	10.9	30.2	8.3	16.2	16.9	12.7	9.2	6.5	33.2	50.5	7 596	26 452	248.2	61.7
Lewisville	30.3	23.7	27.4	8.5	19.7	15.9	13.2	7.8	7.4	31.6	49.6	77 737	95 387	22.7	9.7
Little Elm	31.9	18.8	29.4	4.7	22.5	18.0	9.9	9.9	5.6	32.1	52.5	3 646	25 877	609.7	64.3
Longview	21.6	10.8	24.2	10.6	13.5	12.3	12.7	12.0	14.7	36.8	50.9	73 344	80 425	9.7	2.0
Lubbock	36.4	5.7	23.7	19.2	15.4	10.7	9.5	9.9	11.5	29.2	50.9	199 564	229 495	15.0	10.0
Lufkin	24.2	10.0	27.8	6.3	15.9	14.3	7.2	11.2	17.3	35.0	51.5	32 709	35 106	7.3	3.0
McAllen	81.2	26.9	28.4	11.4	12.8	13.6	10.8	9.6	13.5	32.3	51.3	106 414	130 463	22.6	9.0
McKinney	19.5	15.8	29.6	7.0	12.3	18.9	14.3	8.5	9.3	35.6	52.5	54 369	131 055	141.0	31.5
Mansfield	12.6	10.1	27.6	6.9	12.3	16.8	15.0	10.7	10.6	37.9	53.4	28 031	56 358	101.1	16.5
Mesquite	39.1	18.4	27.2	10.7	12.8	12.3	12.9	11.9	12.2	34.6	52.3	124 523	139 518	12.0	3.0
Midland	44.1	12.8	26.7	11.0	16.5	12.7	11.9	11.0	10.2	32.1	49.9	94 996	111 196	17.1	21.1
Mission	88.1	27.1	33.3	11.1	7.8	17.4	12.2	7.6	10.6	32.9	51.3	45 408	77 667	71.0	7.6
Missouri City	13.9	25.9	23.9	8.0	14.8	14.8	11.8	17.0	9.8	37.2	51.3	52 913	66 824	26.3	11.6
Nacogdoches	10.6	6.8	19.8	30.4	11.9	10.3	8.5	9.2	9.8	24.9	52.5	29 914	32 918	10.0	3.1
New Braunfels	32.2	7.7	25.9	9.2	13.4	15.3	13.0	8.3	14.9	37.0	52.7	36 494	57 729	58.2	28.1
North Richland Hills	14.7	11.3	22.8	7.8	12.1	12.1	12.6	16.2	16.5	39.9	49.1	55 635	63 343	13.9	10.2
Odessa	53.4	13.3	28.8	11.3	16.4	12.6	10.5	9.8	10.7	31.2	48.6	90 943	99 876	9.8	18.0
Paris	9.0	5.2	26.1	8.6	14.6	11.1	12.7	8.7	18.1	35.6	52.0	25 898	25 163	-2.8	-0.6
Pasadena	68.8	24.8	30.6	8.5	16.1	12.9	12.4	9.6	10.0	31.5	48.7	141 674	149 285	5.4	2.7
Pearland	23.7	15.1	27.8	6.4	18.4	16.4	11.2	11.4	8.3	33.9	53.1	37 640	89 910	138.9	26.3
Pflugerville	28.5	13.4	28.2	9.1	9.4	16.1	19.7	11.2	6.3	36.8	52.3	16 335	48 366	196.1	22.5
Pharr	95.4	33.4	37.4	9.8	12.4	14.0	8.6	7.0	11.0	26.9	54.0	46 660	70 467	51.0	9.7
Plano	15.1	26.1	23.2	9.0	13.0	14.3	16.5	12.7	11.2	38.1	51.1	222 030	259 857	17.0	10.1
Port Arthur	32.8	26.6	26.9	10.8	14.5	14.5	12.2	10.9	10.2	33.6	51.6	57 755	54 376	-5.9	1.9
Richardson	14.2	26.7	22.3	9.9	16.7	12.7	13.9	10.5	13.9	35.5	50.7	91 802	99 228	8.1	14.2
Rockwall	14.1	8.1	26.0	6.6	13.7	15.4	14.0	11.1	13.3	39.0	52.6	17 976	37 558	108.9	16.0
Rosenberg	66.5	21.8	30.4	10.1	13.8	14.6	11.6	10.7	8.8	31.3	51.0	24 043	31 876	32.6	15.9
Round Rock	32.1	15.7	27.4	10.2	12.6	16.9	16.4	8.8	7.7	34.9	51.1	61 136	100 001	63.6	20.9
Rowlett	24.2	14.4	25.1	9.1	10.8	13.8	14.3	14.8	12.0	38.0	49.1	44 503	56 242	26.4	10.2
San Angelo	42.3	7.8	23.4	13.9	16.4	10.6	10.5	11.3	13.8	32.8	50.5	88 439	93 227	5.4	8.0
San Antonio	63.8	14.2	25.4	11.1	16.3	13.6	12.1	10.6	11.6	33.1	50.9	1 144 646	1 327 538	16.0	12.4
San Juan	97.9	30.6	34.9	10.3	14.5	13.9	9.3	7.0	10.2	29.1	50.4	26 229	33 856	29.1	8.3
San Marcos	41.1	8.1	15.5	37.3	17.9	7.6	7.1	4.9	9.7	23.9	51.7	34 733	45 145	30.0	37.3
Schertz	34.6	8.4	26.6	8.4	13.3	11.3	15.6	10.4	14.4	36.1	48.6	22 011	25 601	16.3	11.8
Seguin	56.3	7.1	24.4	11.3	17.0	9.4	10.8	10.9	16.3	35.0	51.0	35 082	38 340	9.3	8.4
Sherman	21.1	11.0	26.7	9.4	13.9	15.0	8.1	11.2	15.6	35.0	51.0	27 152	32 037	18.0	3.9
Socorro	96.4	35.2	27.0	17.4	13.2	8.6	11.1	11.3	11.4	30.1	53.8	21 519	26 575	23.5	16.6
Southlake	4.6	9.1	34.3	4.6	3.3	13.4	21.4	12.8	10.3	42.3	49.6				
Sugar Land	8.9	35.4	21.8	8.9	11.0	10.8	16.8	17.0	13.7	42.1	50.2	63 328	78 595	24.1	12.2
Temple	29.6	5.5	26.5	8.2	17.6	12.5	10.7	10.7	13.8	33.6	53.6	54 514	66 275	21.6	11.1
Texarkana	9.2	3.3	30.5	8.3	15.2	10.8	12.9	11.3	10.9	32.2	51.0	34 782	36 409	4.7	3.5
Texas City	27.0	8.0	25.8	6.7	11.8	17.2	11.5	13.2	13.8	39.1	52.0	41 521	45 091	8.6	7.0
The Colony	18.4	11.2	21.3	8.8	20.0	15.3	14.6	11.2	8.8	34.9	53.1	26 531	36 308	36.9	16.8
Tyler	20.8	7.9	22.5	14.8	13.7	11.0	11.4	11.5	15.3	33.9	51.4	83 650	96 887	15.8	8.2
Victoria	50.9	6.6	24.7	10.1	13.7	13.4	11.2	11.6	15.3	35.8	52.2	60 603	62 614	3.3	8.1
Waco	30.7	10.8	23.9	19.4	13.2	11.0	9.7	10.0	12.8	29.3	52.1	113 726	124 810	9.7	7.7
Waxahachie	24.2	7.6	24.5	12.4	16.1	12.9	13.5	8.6	12.0	33.4	53.3	21 426	29 603	38.2	16.0
Weatherford	12.1	5.6	26.3	7.7	11.4	13.4	11.8	13.2	16.2	37.6	55.3	19 000	25 657	35.0	16.8
Weslaco	88.1	12.2	38.0	4.3	14.9	8.7	7.8	11.9	14.3	28.1	49.5	26 935	36 847	36.8	8.6
Wichita Falls	22.0	9.4	21.4	16.0	14.3	12.5	11.5	12.5	11.9	34.0	46.7	104 197	104 724	0.5	0.0
Wylie	13.9	11.2	27.0	7.0	13.7	15.9	14.7	7.6	14.0	36.9	50.2	15 132	41 411	173.7	15.2
UTAH	13.7	8.2	30.5	11.4	14.7	13.4	10.3	9.5	10.3	30.6	49.7	2 233 169	2 763 888	23.8	10.4
American Fork	5.2	5.4	33.1	12.2	11.3	13.1	8.3	11.5	10.6	28.4	46.3	21 941	26 527	20.9	8.5
Bountiful	6.2	4.7	25.5	8.1	15.9	10.6	7.9	10.7	21.1	35.4	50.6	41 301	42 593	3.1	3.5
Cedar City	7.6	2.8	25.9	20.7	12.2	11.8	9.4	7.6	12.4	27.0	49.9	20 527	28 867	40.6	8.2
Clearfield	25.3	9.9	36.7	12.0	16.2	16.6	6.9	4.9	6.6	26.5	50.5	25 974	29 921	15.2	3.1
Cottonwood Heights	4.9	6.5	22.7	9.0	16.6	11.9	11.2	12.7	15.8	35.5	49.1	27 569	33 585	21.8	2.1
Draper	6.0	6.6	35.2	8.4	12.0	17.8	13.2	7.2	6.2	30.5	47.9	25 220	42 272	67.6	12.0
Holladay	8.6	3.8	28.2	5.4	15.2	10.4	12.7	11.1	17.1	35.7	49.8	14 561	30 127	106.9	2.3

1. May be of any race.

Table D. Cities — Households, Group Quarters, Crime, and Education

City	Households, 2015				Persons in group quarters, 2010				Serious crimes known to police,[2] 2014				Educational attainment, 2015		
			Percent			Institutional			Total		Rate[3]			Attainment[4] (percent)	
	Number	Persons per house-hold	Female family house-holder[1]	One-person	Total	Total	Persons in nursing facilities	Non-institu-tional	Number	Rate[3]	Violent	Property	Population age 25 and older	High school graduate or less	Bachelor's degree or more
	27	28	29	30	31	32	33	34	35	36	37	38	39	40	41
TEXAS—Cont'd															
Irving	84 684	2.78	11.9	29.4	873	393	393	480	6 803	2 936	221	2 715	148 941	40.2	35.4
Keller	14 670	3.10	6.8	14.4	251	251	251	0	398	911	55	856	29 810	15.8	58.3
Killeen	51 766	2.72	18.6	24.9	179	97	60	82	5 549	3 986	608	3 378	81 730	37.9	20.7
Kingsville	7 180	3.07	26.8	32.5	1 791	293	173	1 498	1 168	4 436	725	3 711	11 735	51.9	28.3
Kyle	10 604	3.32	12.4	15.7	391	388	0	3	584	1 789	205	1 584	21 916	32.7	30.6
Lake Jackson	11 329	2.42	11.4	25.3	57	56	56	1	570	2 070	127	1 943	18 352	21.1	41.3
Lancaster	13 051	2.94	29.7	18.8	360	359	359	1	1 387	3 612	276	3 336	22 364	42.6	15.5
La Porte	12 979	2.70	9.1	22.2	64	46	46	18	654	1 877	201	1 676	24 515	42.6	18.0
Laredo	69 026	3.66	21.4	18.4	3 479	2 014	367	1 465	10 663	4 248	389	3 859	141 051	60.2	17.8
League City	35 997	2.72	9.0	18.4	471	471	368	0	1 905	2 053	106	1 947	65 946	19.4	47.3
Leander	10 957	3.36	10.5	18.9	0	0	0	0	403	1 217	115	1 102	22 605	22.5	43.4
Lewisville	37 593	2.78	14.8	29.4	399	286	264	113	2 806	2 739	196	2 543	67 117	34.6	33.0
Little Elm	12 680	3.02	12.0	18.7	0	0	0	0	330	954	118	835	25 258	28.7	35.7
Longview	30 457	2.55	15.3	29.5	3 690	1 913	767	1 777	3 982	4 876	460	4 416	53 183	47.2	20.4
Lubbock	91 196	2.61	15.4	30.4	9 933	2 400	1 214	7 533	12 701	5 252	862	4 390	142 247	42.5	26.8
Lufkin	12 649	2.77	20.0	29.5	1 239	823	536	416	2 173	5 982	432	5 550	23 941	46.8	19.3
McAllen	43 578	3.19	17.5	21.5	1 110	899	890	211	5 128	3 713	131	3 582	84 494	46.8	27.9
McKinney	55 575	2.91	12.1	21.9	2 192	1 454	439	738	3 071	2 010	147	1 863	103 183	25.5	47.2
Mansfield	22 293	2.90	13.7	19.0	363	355	159	8	991	1 600	95	1 505	42 606	21.5	42.0
Mesquite	48 835	2.96	22.6	22.3	663	644	644	19	6 278	4 348	299	4 049	90 157	51.8	17.3
Midland	47 237	2.78	9.8	26.0	1 567	684	362	883	3 673	2 884	320	2 565	82 837	39.1	28.1
Mission	23 669	3.51	16.1	11.3	179	162	162	17	2 500	3 054	116	2 938	46 322	50.1	27.3
Missouri City	23 582	3.03	14.6	19.5	180	138	138	42	1 288	1 818	178	1 640	48 865	22.9	47.4
Nacogdoches	12 326	2.33	13.6	35.6	5 025	632	428	4 393	1 331	3 904	323	3 581	16 871	37.0	33.7
New Braunfels	24 211	2.85	10.1	22.2	940	666	411	274	2 283	3 533	282	3 251	45 398	37.5	33.5
North Richland Hills	26 068	2.64	11.6	27.1	294	267	267	27	1 662	2 433	176	2 257	48 065	32.0	27.3
Odessa	40 198	2.92	15.3	24.9	2 143	1 285	437	858	5 285	4 652	940	3 712	71 357	48.4	19.5
Paris	9 536	2.54	23.1	31.1	614	406	258	208	1 226	4 935	559	4 375	16 179	59.8	12.0
Pasadena	51 820	2.95	15.9	24.5	884	737	547	147	5 221	3 400	385	3 016	93 706	59.9	13.8
Pearland	37 073	3.00	6.8	24.5	318	312	299	6	2 228	2 173	156	2 017	73 433	21.8	48.6
Pflugerville	18 691	3.03	4.7	24.2	183	131	131	52	913	1 657	111	1 546	35 708	31.0	35.7
Pharr	20 839	3.67	28.3	14.1	19	15	0	4	2 676	3 589	390	3 199	40 465	63.6	9.5
Plano	106 610	2.65	10.0	25.3	859	791	733	68	5 967	2 148	165	1 983	192 070	19.7	54.2
Port Arthur	19 649	2.78	19.6	28.0	687	515	501	172	2 472	4 563	629	3 933	34 494	63.0	11.6
Richardson	38 816	2.83	7.1	20.3	931	517	501	414	2 584	2 444	169	2 274	75 082	21.6	53.2
Rockwall	14 796	2.85	7.2	22.7	325	325	158	0	802	1 924	98	1 825	28 698	23.8	40.0
Rosenberg	11 533	3.06	19.9	23.3	134	129	129	5	817	2 432	274	2 158	21 130	63.5	13.2
Round Rock	36 819	3.13	13.6	22.3	454	398	251	56	2 329	2 076	125	1 951	72 324	28.5	36.2
Rowlett	20 192	2.86	11.3	15.2	335	335	334	0	878	1 502	127	1 375	38 266	30.6	33.8
San Angelo	37 817	2.50	12.6	32.1	4 858	788	365	4 070	4 191	4 256	332	3 924	63 027	45.9	23.4
San Antonio	494 344	2.93	17.1	29.3	27 800	11 979	5 617	15 821	85 096	5 957	539	5 418	934 535	45.9	24.2
San Juan	8 978	4.05	22.3	11.6	121	112	112	9	1 335	3 710	542	3 168	20 051	63.6	12.5
San Marcos	23 320	2.37	10.0	38.4	6 202	729	300	5 473	1 933	3 414	318	3 096	29 145	41.1	30.8
Schertz	12 611	3.01	10.3	19.6	188	188	188	0	719	1 945	176	1 769	24 829	32.4	34.3
Seguin	10 347	2.53	16.5	29.8	1 644	881	396	763	1 083	4 007	351	3 655	17 929	51.8	18.0
Sherman	14 861	2.63	16.7	33.3	1 368	509	285	859	1 292	3 269	359	2 910	25 982	50.3	17.6
Socorro	8 328	3.98	23.4	10.2	25	0	0	25	427	1 309	129	1 180	18 456	72.5	5.8
Southlake	8 906	3.32	2.2	5.9	0	0	0	0	421	1 470	24	1 446	18 054	6.6	69.8
Sugar Land	29 712	2.95	9.7	15.3	1 413	1 245	313	168	1 499	1 762	116	1 646	61 033	17.6	59.9
Temple	27 319	2.59	14.9	31.6	1 613	989	908	624	2 630	3 702	251	3 451	47 259	38.0	26.7
Texarkana	12 547	2.88	26.0	24.8	1 641	1 469	554	172	2 718	7 212	862	6 350	22 820	46.4	17.2
Texas City	17 525	2.65	18.6	24.8	937	916	470	21	1 802	3 894	324	3 570	32 111	51.1	14.3
The Colony	16 844	2.48	13.6	26.2	0	0	0	0	439	1 091	134	957	29 186	29.9	34.1
Tyler	38 326	2.59	13.5	34.4	3 647	1 709	893	1 938	4 557	4 513	463	4 051	65 080	37.6	29.1
Victoria	24 575	2.70	13.0	24.7	1 324	1 053	478	271	2 649	4 030	516	3 515	44 099	47.3	23.7
Waco	48 448	2.57	17.9	30.3	8 019	3 026	1 488	4 993	5 585	4 298	443	3 855	75 120	44.0	24.7
Waxahachie	12 616	2.54	14.1	23.8	1 209	715	232	494	1 013	3 160	90	3 070	21 061	39.9	26.7
Weatherford	10 387	2.65	19.5	23.9	1 077	845	450	232	740	2 698	171	2 527	18 962	42.9	22.7
Weslaco	12 046	3.23	23.4	26.6	637	590	488	47	3 105	8 289	1 207	7 083	22 790	47.5	21.0
Wichita Falls	37 173	2.41	12.2	34.6	11 889	5 334	1 072	6 555	4 684	4 463	406	4 057	65 528	48.2	22.9
Wylie	15 103	3.04	8.4	20.3	155	155	155	0	548	1 209	108	1 101	30 353	28.8	32.1
UTAH	930 980	3.17	9.5	19.8	46 152	22 161	5 854	23 991	91 057	3 094	216	2 878	1 741 949	32.7	31.8
American Fork	8 301	3.38	9.3	10.5	283	72	62	211	842	2 192	55	2 137	15 506	23.3	36.6
Bountiful	14 822	2.93	12.0	19.8	330	318	318	12	884	2 050	90	1 960	29 032	24.8	43.1
Cedar City	9 876	2.79	9.1	22.9	986	259	83	727	845	2 892	267	2 625	15 020	32.2	39.2
Clearfield	8 469	3.57	17.1	17.2	1 263	144	96	1 119	686	2 247	128	2 119	15 720	41.8	20.9
Cottonwood Heights	13 083	2.62	8.8	29.2	14	0	0	14	801	2 326	122	2 204	23 471	22.1	44.4
Draper	12 042	3.76	9.6	4.9	3 960	3 960	71	0	1 221	2 653	156	2 496	27 118	17.3	53.3
Holladay	10 121	3.03	11.3	24.2	166	160	160	6	NA	NA	NA	NA	20 523	20.8	53.5

1. No spouse present.   2. Data for serious crimes have not been adjusted for underreporting. This may affect comparability between geographic areas and over time.   3. Per 100,000 population estimated by the FBI.   4. Persons 25 years old and over.

Table D. Cities — Income, Poverty, and Housing

City	Money income, 2015 Households Median income	Percent with income of $200,000 or more	Percent with income of less than $25,000	Families Total Families	Percent with income below poverty	Housing units, 2010 Total	Percent change, 2000–2010	Vacant units for sale or rent[2]	Occupied housing units 2015 Owner-occupied Total	Percent	Median value[3] (dollars)	Renter-occupied Percent	Median rent (dollars)
	42	43	44	45	46	47	48	49	50	51	52	53	54
TEXAS—Cont'd													
Irving	56 846	4.0	10.7	54 258	11.5	91 128	13.5	8 590	84 684	37.3	146 800	62.7	977
Keller	127 172	31.5	6.0	12 420	1.4	14 051	52.9	537	14 670	81.6	335 500	18.4	1 163
Killeen	44 716	0.9	19.0	37 441	12.0	53 913	52.8	5 861	51 766	44.0	117 300	56.0	884
Kingsville	33 900	1.4	35.5	4 398	35.7	10 354	-0.6	1 259	7 180	50.4	85 800	49.6	679
Kyle	75 199	1.6	4.6	NA	NA	9 226	NA	467	10 604	71.3	166 600	28.7	1 420
Lake Jackson	87 936	7.9	10.8	7 867	6.8	11 149	6.3	830	11 329	67.6	165 300	32.4	1 147
Lancaster	56 730	1.6	16.1	10 422	15.9	13 622	41.7	1 102	13 051	55.9	108 000	44.1	940
La Porte	68 487	2.2	11.8	NA	NA	12 875	10.2	985	12 979	74.7	128 600	25.3	953
Laredo	40 660	3.4	26.3	53 560	25.7	68 610	36.2	5 065	69 026	61.8	118 900	38.2	782
League City	111 819	13.6	6.0	26 868	5.5	32 119	86.3	1 927	35 997	81.0	219 200	19.0	1 348
Leander	86 771	4.6	2.9	NA	NA	8 949	NA	392	10 957	79.4	196 000	20.6	1 679
Lewisville	56 254	2.2	9.5	24 320	9.8	39 967	26.0	2 471	37 593	42.1	157 800	57.9	1 085
Little Elm	80 108	4.5	7.0	NA	NA	8 581	NA	421	12 680	73.2	196 900	26.8	1 356
Longview	44 969	3.3	18.4	19 298	14.5	32 751	6.8	2 189	30 457	55.9	129 900	44.1	792
Lubbock	45 551	3.1	19.9	53 381	13.7	95 926	14.2	7 420	91 196	49.5	126 900	50.5	853
Lufkin	43 509	4.0	25.7	8 620	23.6	14 183	5.9	1 255	12 649	48.6	107 000	51.4	906
McAllen	45 186	6.0	24.2	32 739	21.4	45 862	21.0	4 289	43 578	62.2	118 700	37.8	736
McKinney	83 317	9.5	7.9	41 838	4.3	47 915	146.7	3 562	55 575	67.8	254 000	32.2	1 221
Mansfield	88 549	12.3	5.7	17 803	2.9	19 106	103.0	801	22 293	75.6	217 300	24.4	1 254
Mesquite	47 518	1.3	17.9	35 059	13.3	51 952	11.9	3 562	48 835	59.4	118 200	40.6	904
Midland	80 700	11.3	9.8	32 024	4.5	44 708	12.3	2 821	47 237	68.5	199 500	31.5	1 199
Mission	47 205	7.5	19.3	20 689	19.7	27 291	54.0	4 174	23 669	66.0	100 800	34.0	875
Missouri City	92 696	11.5	6.1	18 218	3.5	23 374	34.0	998	23 582	79.4	178 400	20.6	1 657
Nacogdoches	35 160	6.7	34.9	6 512	21.3	13 635	10.3	1 493	12 326	33.6	134 600	66.4	762
New Braunfels	61 330	5.4	8.6	17 426	6.9	23 381	55.7	2 122	24 211	63.4	184 200	36.6	1 029
North Richland Hills	61 498	5.2	8.0	18 028	5.6	26 395	22.8	1 541	26 068	61.2	163 300	38.8	993
Odessa	66 585	6.1	12.6	27 884	9.6	39 806	4.8	3 198	40 198	63.3	138 500	36.7	1 077
Paris	26 925	2.2	34.0	6 012	22.8	11 883	1.0	1 577	9 536	50.0	69 400	50.0	713
Pasadena	50 236	1.6	14.8	36 369	14.0	53 899	6.9	5 428	51 820	49.1	111 200	50.9	847
Pearland	97 209	13.7	5.0	25 555	1.7	33 169	138.7	1 947	37 073	69.1	207 800	30.9	1 348
Pflugerville	83 080	6.6	6.4	13 727	3.1	16 418	209.9	629	18 691	76.6	202 100	23.4	1 350
Pharr	33 269	1.2	30.4	17 770	27.1	22 796	37.4	3 097	20 839	63.2	66 800	36.8	756
Plano	83 769	11.6	9.3	74 971	6.7	103 672	20.4	4 541	106 610	59.8	261 800	40.2	1 223
Port Arthur	34 871	1.3	25.6	13 532	17.6	23 577	-4.6	3 394	19 649	55.5	65 400	44.5	724
Richardson	80 398	9.9	8.8	28 355	5.3	40 630	11.7	1 916	38 816	60.7	226 000	39.3	1 273
Rockwall	87 420	11.1	6.7	NA	NA	13 957	96.1	745	14 796	67.6	233 800	32.4	1 263
Rosenberg	50 996	5.0	17.5	8 448	11.5	11 162	32.2	999	11 533	50.6	102 700	49.4	937
Round Rock	75 974	5.9	6.0	25 643	5.7	37 223	71.9	2 173	36 819	61.7	205 100	38.3	1 109
Rowlett	86 686	8.4	6.2	16 382	4.0	18 969	30.1	598	20 192	78.7	171 800	21.3	1 359
San Angelo	46 353	4.6	18.7	22 427	11.7	39 548	4.8	3 431	37 817	55.8	124 700	44.2	884
San Antonio	48 869	3.3	19.2	319 811	14.1	524 246	21.0	44 604	494 344	51.8	126 600	48.2	901
San Juan	31 949	2.3	27.9	7 832	36.5	9 740	25.8	858	8 978	74.0	93 300	26.0	725
San Marcos	35 150	1.1	31.8	8 904	24.2	18 179	36.8	1 148	23 320	28.6	160 800	71.4	953
Schertz	77 608	3.6	9.9	9 459	3.9	12 047	74.5	668	12 611	70.5	176 900	29.5	1 148
Seguin	45 480	1.6	23.8	6 974	19.0	9 714	18.7	920	10 347	55.3	106 400	44.7	900
Sherman	41 375	1.8	22.0	9 138	17.8	16 404	10.0	1 599	14 861	49.9	118 800	50.1	824
Socorro	33 438	0.0	25.1	7 400	23.3	9 313	28.0	521	8 328	78.0	84 500	22.0	762
Southlake	226 662	58.7	3.6	NA	NA	8 494	28.7	301	8 906	98.1	641 300	1.9	0
Sugar Land	111 124	23.5	6.2	24 789	4.3	27 727	31.0	1 018	29 712	79.7	288 700	20.3	1 621
Temple	44 749	3.8	21.2	16 663	19.1	28 422	21.2	2 309	27 319	46.5	133 900	53.5	807
Texarkana	39 679	4.2	26.7	9 014	18.1	16 115	6.5	1 693	12 547	56.1	109 900	43.9	766
Texas City	43 152	6.7	21.4	11 727	18.3	18 773	12.6	2 145	17 525	56.6	101 300	43.4	841
The Colony	81 190	2.3	4.4	10 793	5.8	14 052	59.0	884	16 844	55.2	186 500	44.8	1 198
Tyler	43 222	5.5	18.9	22 426	13.4	41 742	17.4	3 846	38 326	51.5	151 300	48.5	853
Victoria	53 779	4.9	13.7	17 414	10.9	25 660	6.1	2 239	24 575	62.6	131 600	37.4	823
Waco	36 792	2.9	27.0	29 490	16.1	51 452	12.2	5 050	48 448	47.6	114 100	52.4	781
Waxahachie	55 479	5.0	14.1	8 570	17.2	11 554	47.0	1 097	12 616	49.0	147 300	51.0	982
Weatherford	61 616	2.1	13.2	7 901	12.9	10 853	31.3	1 083	10 387	59.8	141 700	40.2	987
Weslaco	35 506	0.7	30.0	8 606	24.3	14 394	41.0	3 182	12 046	64.3	78 200	35.7	591
Wichita Falls	44 448	2.4	21.5	21 585	15.3	43 632	4.3	5 178	37 173	55.6	102 700	44.4	741
Wylie	75 099	1.5	8.7	11 698	5.3	13 840	162.5	603	15 103	85.2	172 600	14.8	1 510
UTAH	62 912	4.7	11.5	693 181	8.3	979 709	27.5	102 017	930 980	68.9	234 600	31.1	925
American Fork	61 452	3.1	9.6	NA	NA	7 598	24.2	324	8 301	82.1	233 300	17.9	917
Bountiful	65 060	6.5	11.1	11 568	5.6	15 193	10.1	689	14 822	77.4	255 800	22.6	970
Cedar City	41 587	2.9	17.1	7 242	14.4	10 860	52.2	1 391	9 876	61.5	179 700	38.5	664
Clearfield	55 680	0.0	12.9	6 818	11.0	10 062	19.7	701	8 469	56.2	159 500	43.8	1 059
Cottonwood Heights	89 103	10.6	5.7	NA	NA	13 194	33.2	735	13 083	69.5	352 300	30.5	1 184
Draper	106 597	15.5	5.7	10 795	4.8	12 125	84.3	581	12 042	82.0	411 800	18.0	1 231
Holladay	79 583	14.2	6.3	NA	NA	10 537	99.0	610	10 121	73.7	365 300	26.3	980

1. Based on population estimated by the American Community Survey.   2. Includes units rented or sold but not occupied.   3. Specified owner-occupied units; $1,000,000 represents $1,000,000 or more   4. 50.0 represents 50 percent or more.   5. 10.0 represents 10 percent or less.

Table D. Cities — Commuting, Computer Access, Migration, Labor Force, and Employment

City	Commuting Percent — Drove alone	With Commutes of 30 minutes or more[1]	Computer Access[2] Percent — With a Computer in the house	With Internet Access	Migration, 2015 — Percent who lived in the same house one year ago	Percent who lived in an other state or county one year ago	Civilian labor force, 2016 — Total	Percent change, 2015–2016	Unemployment — Total	Rate[3]	Civilian employment[4], 2015 — Population age 16 and older — Number	Percent in Labor Force	Population age 16 to 64 — Number	Percent who worked full-year full-time
	55	56	57	58	59	60	61	62	63	64	65	66	67	68
TEXAS—Cont'd														
Irving..................	81.6	33.0	92.6	76.5	79.4	10.1	128 833	3.8	4 647	3.6	178 158	73.9	162 379	59.1
Keller..................	91.2	47.1	98.8	94.8	87.6	6.4	23 303	2.2	792	3.4	33 651	65.3	26 900	57.2
Killeen................	86.1	21.3	88.8	77.0	71.2	14.1	55 662	4.0	2 797	5.0	100 960	68.5	91 980	49.6
Kingsville............	74.3	17.3	79.8	65.3	74.3	8.6	11 482	-1.6	811	7.1	17 557	64.8	14 732	39.6
Kyle....................	88.2	40.9	90.4	86.6	83.5	10.4	18 870	4.8	624	3.3	25 762	75.0	23 596	60.4
Lake Jackson	91.6	15.8	90.8	82.6	82.9	10.6	13 729	1.1	663	4.8	21 412	71.0	17 429	56.4
Lancaster............	82.3	53.9	91.3	74.2	84.6	2.6	18 563	4.0	1 086	5.9	28 559	73.5	25 833	55.4
La Porte..............	90.0	40.8	89.7	78.7	NA	NA	18 461	1.5	1 034	5.6	28 248	65.6	24 824	50.8
Laredo................	85.1	22.4	71.1	57.7	89.9	1.3	108 584	2.2	5 246	4.8	180 657	60.0	157 822	45.3
League City.........	84.1	47.8	98.6	92.0	86.7	8.9	53 741	1.0	2 233	4.2	77 695	71.7	66 538	57.5
Leander..............	89.8	57.3	95.7	93.8	80.6	11.0	19 727	4.5	649	3.3	26 882	74.0	24 483	56.3
Lewisville............	86.1	43.5	93.8	85.8	73.8	11.4	63 440	4.1	2 156	3.4	79 428	75.5	71 683	60.5
Little Elm...........	95.2	62.6	98.7	90.3	77.0	13.6	19 887	5.2	753	3.8	27 641	82.3	25 494	65.8
Longview............	88.8	15.3	86.7	65.6	80.1	5.9	38 251	-1.3	2 277	6.0	63 783	61.7	51 822	47.9
Lubbock..............	79.0	13.2	87.4	72.5	71.3	9.6	128 609	2.6	4 375	3.4	195 687	63.6	166 935	46.7
Lufkin.................	73.9	12.1	83.9	70.8	82.1	8.4	15 383	-1.4	900	5.9	26 732	54.1	20 437	40.4
McAllen...............	79.7	18.1	87.0	65.5	86.1	4.9	63 608	2.2	3 442	5.4	105 042	60.7	86 143	44.9
McKinney............	92.0	46.0	95.0	85.3	85.6	7.1	86 063	4.2	3 159	3.7	120 573	67.7	105 380	58.5
Mansfield............	92.2	52.9	97.3	92.7	85.8	5.5	33 805	2.3	1 186	3.5	50 257	71.2	43 354	58.2
Mesquite............	81.4	54.0	90.0	80.2	80.4	4.9	76 114	3.7	3 032	4.0	109 765	66.9	92 017	47.1
Midland..............	88.8	15.6	92.2	81.3	81.6	8.4	69 710	-3.9	3 051	4.4	100 572	71.6	87 054	59.3
Mission..............	88.9	18.9	83.8	70.1	89.4	3.5	33 567	3.0	2 476	7.4	58 640	57.4	49 777	44.0
Missouri City.......	90.1	58.2	98.4	95.6	90.3	5.8	39 333	1.3	2 046	5.2	56 891	71.3	49 885	55.5
Nacogdoches	79.2	20.0	91.5	83.6	63.6	15.4	14 693	2.2	696	4.7	27 943	61.9	24 617	37.6
New Braunfels......	84.8	33.6	89.3	82.2	83.6	12.1	35 958	3.7	1 259	3.5	54 113	65.2	43 684	52.2
North Richland Hills	87.3	37.8	94.6	82.1	82.7	6.0	38 352	2.1	1 356	3.5	54 385	67.6	42 937	56.4
Odessa...............	86.2	20.8	84.5	79.2	78.2	8.2	58 053	-4.7	3 429	5.9	88 459	68.4	75 752	51.6
Paris...................	83.1	3.4	67.2	54.0	75.3	6.7	11 198	5.1	567	5.1	18 819	51.4	14 323	42.9
Pasadena............	84.2	41.2	86.9	78.2	76.5	5.2	68 002	1.3	4 305	6.3	111 303	64.3	95 881	53.0
Pearland.............	94.1	56.7	95.2	89.2	93.2	4.6	58 874	1.2	2 395	4.1	82 756	75.3	73 477	65.9
Pflugerville..........	91.3	42.3	97.5	93.6	90.5	3.9	32 206	4.6	1 129	3.5	43 074	72.0	39 486	54.3
Pharr.................	91.5	11.7	65.3	55.5	96.7	0.7	29 599	3.3	2 464	8.3	50 173	55.8	41 789	40.5
Plano..................	89.6	40.9	96.1	91.2	88.6	6.6	159 494	3.9	5 671	3.6	225 838	69.8	193 990	59.2
Port Arthur..........	93.7	28.5	58.3	46.6	90.7	2.4	22 272	-0.4	2 252	10.1	41 854	57.0	36 234	43.2
Richardson..........	84.9	34.6	95.3	89.8	80.3	10.5	60 541	3.9	2 160	3.6	88 211	66.9	72 768	54.9
Rockwall.............	91.1	61.1	97.4	91.5	86.8	7.0	21 899	4.0	792	3.6	32 734	67.5	27 093	56.8
Rosenberg...........	83.9	39.3	94.3	70.2	83.1	2.0	16 979	1.4	854	5.0	25 377	65.2	22 250	48.1
Round Rock.........	87.8	36.9	95.9	89.3	81.0	9.4	63 044	4.0	2 059	3.3	88 919	74.1	80 031	58.4
Rowlett...............	84.5	52.3	98.1	90.3	89.5	6.8	33 643	3.7	1 235	3.7	44 993	75.4	38 000	63.2
San Angelo..........	84.0	10.7	79.9	71.1	83.7	9.3	45 515	-0.3	2 064	4.5	78 897	61.1	65 010	48.3
San Antonio.........	83.4	34.5	85.3	71.0	80.5	5.0	698 893	3.1	25 678	3.7	1 138 854	63.3	967 895	50.1
San Juan.............	86.0	16.8	70.5	54.3	NA	NA	14 920	3.8	1 367	9.2	24 895	56.9	21 166	44.2
San Marcos.........	83.4	24.5	87.4	65.9	65.5	23.6	31 245	4.0	1 127	3.6	53 664	66.2	47 662	39.9
Schertz..............	93.0	45.4	94.4	90.3	88.7	8.0	18 076	3.6	682	3.8	29 167	62.9	23 673	59.0
Seguin................	NA	16.5	76.7	71.2	87.9	4.1	12 770	3.3	503	3.9	21 648	59.2	17 117	53.7
Sherman.............	81.3	25.7	80.0	66.8	71.0	12.0	19 371	1.9	761	3.9	31 164	64.3	24 807	50.7
Socorro..............	78.3	51.7	81.2	53.1	NA	NA	13 652	3.4	792	5.8	24 874	55.4	21 087	41.1
Southlake............	95.2	37.1	NA	NA	94.3	3.3	13 913	2.2	497	3.6	21 026	61.5	17 971	48.4
Sugar Land..........	87.9	51.1	96.0	91.5	87.4	6.6	45 720	1.8	2 148	4.7	72 007	65.1	59 976	52.9
Temple...............	84.0	21.8	83.0	69.5	67.0	18.7	34 789	3.9	1 304	3.7	54 436	65.0	44 423	51.9
Texarkana...........	88.1	8.2	72.8	64.0	81.3	8.5	15 557	1.4	738	4.7	27 087	58.8	23 023	40.6
Texas City...........	78.4	29.2	79.9	65.5	84.2	4.8	21 283	1.4	1 493	7.0	36 388	60.7	29 834	43.4
The Colony..........	87.7	57.8	97.8	87.5	82.1	8.3	26 640	4.1	940	3.5	33 914	80.8	30 255	63.6
Tyler..................	88.3	24.8	86.8	77.1	85.4	7.5	50 513	2.2	2 196	4.3	82 549	60.7	66 731	48.7
Victoria..............	84.3	13.4	83.7	71.7	78.8	6.2	31 830	-2.8	1 697	5.3	52 394	65.5	42 081	51.2
Waco.................	82.6	13.7	82.9	64.4	79.6	9.1	58 748	2.9	2 498	4.3	103 417	58.4	86 473	42.2
Waxahachie..........	85.3	27.1	91.7	68.4	77.1	6.6	16 940	4.0	631	3.7	25 888	68.4	21 876	56.8
Weatherford.........	88.0	35.0	90.7	82.2	78.0	12.0	12 873	2.3	565	4.4	22 124	63.1	17 473	49.5
Weslaco..............	86.9	29.1	80.6	65.7	NA	NA	15 155	3.7	1 235	8.1	25 581	56.4	19 925	47.2
Wichita Falls........	79.6	5.6	82.0	64.5	79.6	10.6	42 666	-0.2	1 879	4.4	84 821	59.3	72 382	42.8
Wylie.................	95.8	63.2	96.3	89.6	91.6	6.8	25 587	4.1	887	3.5	35 812	71.0	29 377	64.8
UTAH..................	80.3	25.3	93.2	83.4	82.6	7.1	1 511 465	3.1	51 762	3.4	2 180 281	67.7	1 872 439	48.1
American Fork........	83.6	22.5	98.4	90.7	85.2	2.9	13 067	4.5	432	3.3	20 053	63.3	17 041	43.6
Bountiful	82.0	27.3	89.7	81.5	86.6	4.0	20 648	2.7	685	3.3	33 218	60.6	23 977	51.3
Cedar City	69.1	10.3	96.6	86.7	76.0	14.7	13 768	5.4	607	4.4	21 810	62.6	18 324	39.4
Clearfield............	87.2	30.3	88.3	76.3	78.9	11.8	14 180	2.5	547	3.9	20 453	66.3	18 420	44.7
Cottonwood Heights	85.0	23.3	95.7	89.6	83.4	6.5	19 895	3.1	608	3.1	27 159	70.4	21 715	57.7
Draper................	85.7	33.9	97.8	85.0	84.2	6.5	22 216	3.2	696	3.1	33 024	64.8	30 037	41.8
Holladay	87.8	16.1	94.5	89.7	84.1	9.6	15 874	3.1	476	3.0	22 940	66.5	17 658	56.7

1. Employed persons.　　2. Households.　　3. Percent of civilian labor force.　　4. Persons 16 years old and over.

City	Value of residential construction authorized by building permits, 2016			Wholesale trade,[1] 2012				Retail trade,[2] 2012			
	New construction ($1,000)	Number of housing units	Percent single family	Number of establishments	Number of employees	Sales (mil dol)	Annual payroll (mil dol)	Number of establishments	Number of employees	Sales (mil dol)	Annual payroll (mil dol)
	69	70	71	72	73	74	75	76	77	78	79
TEXAS—Cont'd											
Irving	240 853	640	97.7	356	11 506	13 262.4	880.3	606	11 927	4 776.3	357.3
Keller	55 977	138	100.0	26	93	84.4	4.7	104	1 435	420.6	32.8
Killeen	111 085	810	85.4	22	D	D	D	402	6 119	1 679.6	138.6
Kingsville	1 471	9	100.0	4	D	D	D	100	1 397	494.1	32.1
Kyle	99 608	1 046	55.1	8	D	D	D	47	997	290.2	22.3
Lake Jackson	18 335	72	100.0	12	63	27.8	5.8	111	2 489	604.1	54.6
Lancaster	28 418	134	100.0	18	D	D	D	63	995	235.8	21.5
La Porte	8 154	64	100.0	50	833	392.3	45.3	70	508	217.3	14.1
Laredo	212 895	1 158	81.6	356	D	D	D	782	D	D	D
League City	208 883	987	96.8	47	D	D	D	181	3 492	1 319.5	103.4
Leander	540 448	1 806	85.9	9	D	D	D	36	807	246.9	18.7
Lewisville	122 415	622	62.7	105	2 322	1 992.2	147.4	411	7 286	2 343.5	193.5
Little Elm	360 748	1 081	100.0	8	D	D	D	31	585	177.9	12.9
Longview	22 700	128	100.0	170	2 233	1 211.0	114.1	508	7 547	2 082.8	192.5
Lubbock	414 458	2 406	49.6	317	4 844	4 623.3	239.3	946	15 727	4 583.3	388.0
Lufkin	7 169	46	100.0	47	684	310.6	30.4	271	4 094	1 148.9	100.2
McAllen	113 719	623	72.2	348	3 131	2 539.6	124.1	870	14 085	3 716.8	301.9
McKinney	857 677	3 495	63.2	93	771	705.9	43.3	330	6 634	2 507.3	187.9
Mansfield	177 055	838	44.2	65	1 523	681.2	70.7	141	2 807	785.5	61.8
Mesquite	6 969	34	100.0	63	674	656.6	34.7	431	7 326	2 015.8	180.2
Midland	129 864	672	94.0	164	2 436	2 268.9	136.4	453	7 059	2 661.1	201.3
Mission	35 522	359	78.3	68	410	205.9	12.7	231	3 721	1 110.8	85.5
Missouri City	83 974	367	89.6	52	316	225.2	16.6	147	2 936	757.1	60.7
Nacogdoches	3 663	28	85.7	34	D	D	D	210	2 763	824.0	66.9
New Braunfels	357 454	2 256	48.0	58	D	D	D	276	4 435	1 585.3	125.1
North Richland Hills	61 056	236	100.0	29	188	82.9	9.7	150	3 641	1 423.3	108.1
Odessa	85 659	448	100.0	184	2 717	1 951.1	189.8	401	6 849	2 658.0	208.0
Paris	2 888	30	46.7	34	D	D	D	178	2 252	628.8	53.7
Pasadena	12 103	100	100.0	137	1 665	979.4	92.2	440	6 288	1 733.4	146.8
Pearland	293 601	1 201	100.0	59	481	302.0	23.9	262	5 120	1 244.6	111.1
Pflugerville	142 443	1 466	31.8	41	511	243.6	29.2	86	1 515	416.4	35.3
Pharr	53 960	616	29.7	142	1 208	876.6	51.4	179	2 374	622.6	62.7
Plano	172 929	811	60.5	420	7 367	4 626.3	589.3	1 064	20 770	7 683.0	624.0
Port Arthur	17 307	78	100.0	24	D	D	D	187	3 169	865.8	71.9
Richardson	197 040	1 506	5.2	220	8 348	31 123.6	713.3	353	4 650	1 846.0	154.0
Rockwall	77 341	326	100.0	41	D	D	D	202	3 754	1 268.6	97.4
Rosenberg	88 612	394	100.0	23	498	260.2	26.9	161	2 925	954.5	75.2
Round Rock	132 687	751	60.3	104	D	D	D	398	8 410	4 317.2	253.1
Rowlett	70 613	269	100.0	33	123	63.4	5.9	92	1 508	409.1	36.6
San Angelo	38 989	172	100.0	94	853	407.1	45.4	398	5 806	1 771.6	145.5
San Antonio	777 996	6 363	33.8	1 287	D	D	D	4 211	72 437	23 870.2	1 785.6
San Juan	6 953	93	95.7	15	D	D	D	60	887	311.7	23.2
San Marcos	51 825	352	100.0	26	D	D	D	405	7 099	1 501.9	128.8
Schertz	66 161	264	100.0	56	D	D	D	50	1 220	362.5	24.4
Seguin	46 194	252	100.0	25	D	D	D	139	1 826	516.0	45.2
Sherman	19 003	145	69.7	47	425	653.6	17.9	207	3 645	1 048.3	86.8
Socorro	7 586	79	92.4	14	140	148.7	6.1	58	695	219.3	13.8
Southlake	139 069	199	100.0	59	591	528.1	40.5	229	5 140	1 760.0	142.1
Sugar Land	106 619	513	31.6	164	1 983	3 499.2	101.2	475	8 226	2 057.7	173.9
Temple	90 678	579	95.5	59	1 974	3 323.9	110.3	286	4 130	1 179.3	95.8
Texarkana	10 928	32	100.0	57	742	2 243.1	30.4	309	5 041	1 276.2	120.7
Texas City	31 700	188	100.0	28	211	113.5	12.0	186	1 575	517.8	49.6
The Colony	76 466	198	100.0	17	D	D	D	69	987	282.7	23.2
Tyler	122 566	398	76.6	114	1 433	533.3	66.2	632	9 824	2 734.3	243.4
Victoria	12 785	62	100.0	82	1 085	557.4	58.6	353	5 240	1 563.4	134.0
Waco	181 138	1 525	26.8	130	2 062	1 025.9	88.1	589	7 888	2 154.0	176.1
Waxahachie	79 068	424	100.0	31	D	D	D	138	2 364	623.9	53.6
Weatherford	41 769	209	97.6	25	274	362.1	10.5	198	3 255	1 372.8	96.3
Weslaco	19 847	227	82.4	37	417	228.7	13.5	160	2 807	818.9	63.1
Wichita Falls	28 436	161	44.1	116	981	508.4	46.0	434	6 851	1 830.0	154.1
Wylie	102 077	414	100.0	14	D	D	D	62	1 258	340.1	30.4
UTAH	5 797	48	100.0	3 015	43 523	30 927.9	2 364.4	9 095	133 535	38 024.5	3 334.9
American Fork	57 478	276	62.0	28	439	166.3	17.1	137	2 331	737.3	56.8
Bountiful	12 322	34	79.4	42	263	209.0	14.9	146	1 951	614.2	49.5
Cedar City	45 146	220	71.4	24	183	140.2	7.3	140	1 698	505.3	39.8
Clearfield	14 742	172	28.5	21	302	360.7	12.2	58	549	136.4	11.3
Cottonwood Heights	17 152	33	93.9	41	914	513.9	135.6	70	1 589	1 291.6	68.7
Draper	78 611	301	79.7	51	772	303.2	47.8	186	3 580	1 289.4	117.5
Holladay	21 477	64	50.0	25	189	47.0	6.5	75	784	122.9	15.3

1. Merchant wholesalers except manufacturers' sales branches and offices. 2. Establishments with payroll.

Table D. Cities — Real Estate, Professional Services, and Manufacturing

City	Real estate and rental and leasing, 2012				Professional, scientific, and technical services,[1] 2012				Manufacturing, 2012			
	Number of establishments	Number of employees	Receipts (mil dol)	Annual payroll (mil dol)	Number of establishments	Number of employees	Receipts (mil dol)	Annual payroll (mil dol)	Number of establishments	Number of employees	Receipts (mil dol)	Annual payroll (mil dol)
	80	81	82	83	84	85	86	87	88	89	90	91
TEXAS—Cont'd												
Irving	339	4 857	1 213.8	191.9	1 008	D	D	D	160	6 926	3 150.8	425.8
Keller	35	219	78.0	9.7	152	562	116.2	28.5	17	87	16.4	3.7
Killeen	144	580	88.7	19.5	105	1 036	114.2	42.8	15	94	16.0	3.5
Kingsville	26	D	D	D	29	160	13.9	3.5	13	D	D	D
Kyle	13	16	5.9	0.6	12	34	3.2	0.8	7	353	D	20.9
Lake Jackson	21	113	28.2	4.2	46	D	D	D	3	10	D	0.7
Lancaster	20	75	17.6	3.2	17	D	D	D	24	949	341.2	37.1
La Porte	38	469	146.7	27.1	55	1 954	348.4	145.0	39	2 483	4 902.1	214.8
Laredo	199	692	132.4	22.0	316	D	D	D	68	D	D	D
League City	60	182	34.9	6.6	175	1 646	189.3	79.6	26	113	D	5.8
Leander	14	36	6.3	1.0	36	D	D	D	17	174	D	8.6
Lewisville	112	551	139.1	19.7	215	D	D	D	99	2 046	462.9	93.5
Little Elm	7	23	3.1	0.7	26	64	6.6	2.4	7	188	D	D
Longview	149	792	175.3	33.3	313	2 706	390.9	157.3	120	8 520	4 525.5	450.7
Lubbock	367	1 524	263.7	48.2	573	3 620	441.8	164.5	197	4 181	1 348.7	177.3
Lufkin	67	299	48.1	9.5	121	642	77.4	29.0	43	3 980	1 126.2	144.2
McAllen	206	810	213.5	27.2	455	D	D	D	96	2 207	729.1	100.2
McKinney	121	1 027	144.3	33.5	348	D	D	D	70	5 938	4 106.2	469.4
Mansfield	39	140	33.6	6.6	116	545	64.2	24.1	82	2 745	1 053.8	132.4
Mesquite	97	413	84.6	12.7	106	764	62.1	23.1	66	2 300	1 044.8	109.1
Midland	225	1 243	347.7	62.0	445	D	D	D	77	D	393.9	D
Mission	55	219	36.2	6.1	75	438	47.6	17.6	26	312	65.3	8.6
Missouri City	41	93	17.5	3.7	131	D	D	D	26	550	134.5	26.6
Nacogdoches	49	154	27.8	4.1	78	D	D	D	43	3 753	1 244.6	109.5
New Braunfels	101	423	63.9	11.7	153	670	74.9	25.1	60	2 039	587.1	86.6
North Richland Hills	66	280	42.8	9.3	141	D	D	D	20	1 003	409.0	44.1
Odessa	136	815	318.2	40.4	180	D	D	D	122	2 282	780.5	128.0
Paris	43	152	20.0	3.5	46	D	D	D	35	2 757	1 905.5	148.0
Pasadena	128	762	165.0	28.1	157	D	D	D	102	4 633	10 180.0	344.0
Pearland	86	418	104.1	16.1	189	D	D	D	62	1 502	D	81.1
Pflugerville	17	59	14.4	2.2	59	185	16.0	6.4	19	389	78.4	26.2
Pharr	41	264	37.9	6.8	60	770	34.2	14.3	25	333	95.0	12.4
Plano	398	3 742	744.5	192.9	1 492	D	D	D	150	4 601	1 698.4	277.0
Port Arthur	35	282	49.1	10.7	48	471	42.4	19.7	40	4 687	D	447.9
Richardson	172	756	194.7	32.3	682	9 109	2 070.8	693.6	138	7 059	2 336.5	546.5
Rockwall	52	D	D	D	155	D	D	D	41	936	241.2	48.1
Rosenberg	36	123	34.0	4.5	38	D	D	D	22	823	583.8	42.7
Round Rock	119	402	100.1	14.8	311	1 693	252.5	100.6	77	2 828	923.9	159.5
Rowlett	25	52	9.9	1.6	76	502	41.5	11.9	42	592	D	22.5
San Angelo	127	D	D	D	192	D	D	D	88	3 166	1 205.4	123.9
San Antonio	1 500	10 878	2 522.4	478.0	3 338	33 837	5 854.7	2 108.0	742	27 947	14 068.1	1 370.4
San Juan	10	38	3.4	1.4	12	46	4.4	0.9	9	99	D	2.1
San Marcos	75	338	87.0	9.8	96	823	54.9	19.6	40	D	687.6	D
Schertz	27	D	D	D	31	275	29.9	8.7	25	773	165.8	25.2
Seguin	34	192	36.9	7.6	49	198	16.6	6.5	48	3 995	2 029.9	180.9
Sherman	50	178	29.5	4.9	114	395	50.0	17.5	46	4 317	D	191.4
Socorro	8	33	10.2	1.2	7	41	1.7	0.5	14	79	16.7	2.2
Southlake	92	599	98.4	25.3	229	1 624	250.9	81.1	28	295	81.4	14.1
Sugar Land	167	483	155.5	20.7	521	4 603	724.3	604.4	57	3 099	1 374.8	159.4
Temple	80	409	65.1	12.8	117	D	D	D	59	4 222	1 611.1	180.0
Texarkana	78	385	79.6	15.3	123	D	D	D	26	814	276.8	36.9
Texas City	34	281	66.9	11.7	43	D	D	D	25	4 126	40 766.1	498.9
The Colony	17	177	41.1	4.0	51	276	36.3	10.4	NA	NA	NA	NA
Tyler	208	953	217.8	39.9	458	D	D	D	88	4 002	4 317.4	201.7
Victoria	110	714	492.3	39.4	142	D	D	D	55	1 062	D	D
Waco	162	1 293	245.6	55.7	272	D	D	D	134	12 060	5 828.2	576.4
Waxahachie	46	149	31.1	4.7	63	D	D	D	54	3 534	1 293.8	154.3
Weatherford	37	174	24.8	5.4	86	D	D	D	31	825	177.4	40.7
Weslaco	49	201	35.0	4.1	59	D	D	D	12	92	11.7	4.3
Wichita Falls	153	759	153.6	28.2	208	D	D	D	97	3 045	724.1	148.2
Wylie	17	54	11.1	1.6	49	153	14.8	6.1	32	1 788	653.8	75.9
UTAH	4 446	16 197	3 226.1	604.8	8 961	75 648	10 415.5	3 860.6	3 163	108 264	50 046.4	5 762.6
American Fork	60	167	27.7	5.1	118	1 593	235.8	76.3	27	591	D	31.7
Bountiful	81	170	19.1	6.0	192	D	D	D	42	797	1 594.5	52.5
Cedar City	57	140	26.1	4.5	83	385	54.8	14.5	57	1 212	639.8	51.5
Clearfield	25	102	31.3	3.3	59	1 259	142.0	70.8	47	5 724	1 740.4	267.2
Cottonwood Heights	232	745	127.3	30.7	210	1 225	192.1	76.0	23	250	D	14.9
Draper	104	334	55.2	12.8	245	1 348	180.2	73.3	41	1 216	362.4	69.8
Holladay	80	D	D	D	159	D	D	D	11	445	D	22.1

1. Establishments subject to federal tax.

Table D. Cities — Accommodation and Food Services, Arts, Entertainment, and Recreation, and Health Care and Social Assistance

City	Accommodation and food services, 2012				Arts, entertainment, and recreation,[1] 2012				Health care and social assistance,[1] 2012			
	Number of establish-ments	Number of employees	Sales (mil dol)	Annual payroll (mil dol)	Number of establish-ments	Number of employees	Receipts (mil dol)	Annual payroll (mil dol)	Number of establish-ments	Number of employees	Receipts (mil dol)	Annual payroll (mil dol)
	92	93	94	95	96	97	98	99	100	101	102	103
TEXAS—Cont'd												
Irving....................	545	11 557	795.8	219.0	41	882	308.9	194.8	524	9 189	1 018.6	422.2
Keller.....................	81	1 232	64.1	17.2	10	D	D	D	116	D	D	D
Killeen...................	248	5 406	275.3	73.2	20	D	D	D	162	D	D	D
Kingsville	70	D	D	D	4	27	1.9	0.7	49	D	D	D
Kyle.......................	39	461	26.7	7.0	5	D	D	D	42	D	D	D
Lake Jackson	58	1 421	67.1	18.7	6	180	4.8	2.3	127	D	D	D
Lancaster..............	32	646	34.6	10.3	2	D	D	D	42	882	44.4	19.0
La Porte	68	1 241	60.2	17.1	4	4	0.1	0.1	39	D	D	D
Laredo	388	D	D	D	29	D	D	D	495	D	D	D
League City	121	2 047	101.4	28.6	19	D	D	D	147	D	D	D
Leander	27	405	20.0	5.0	4	D	D	D	37	D	D	D
Lewisville	232	4 707	268.4	69.0	29	D	D	D	235	4 569	466.8	185.6
Little Elm	23	D	D	D	4	85	4.4	1.3	18	160	9.8	3.7
Longview	239	5 463	255.8	71.5	18	233	14.7	4.0	330	D	D	D
Lubbock.................	597	13 817	697.7	186.1	56	966	44.5	14.4	681	12 591	1 244.5	475.9
Lufkin....................	122	2 852	129.3	36.8	11	84	4.1	1.0	206	4 992	368.7	159.6
McAllen.................	402	8 909	434.2	116.1	27	298	31.6	5.0	737	15 849	1 434.3	538.1
McKinney...............	229	4 652	233.6	66.7	28	756	34.3	12.7	340	5 253	601.0	220.2
Mansfield...............	118	D	D	D	16	D	D	D	177	1 699	177.1	68.4
Mesquite...............	217	5 218	270.6	75.1	22	324	22.3	4.3	309	D	D	D
Midland.................	279	6 352	431.1	102.8	24	D	D	D	319	D	D	D
Mission.................	135	2 294	119.2	28.9	11	239	10.1	3.2	262	D	D	D
Missouri City.........	101	1 540	82.2	20.4	10	D	D	D	163	1 529	104.2	40.9
Nacogdoches	105	2 457	96.1	27.0	9	D	D	D	172	2 233	248.4	76.5
New Braunfels.............	228	4 685	247.9	66.5	27	D	D	D	214	D	D	D
North Richland Hills	127	2 539	118.8	33.0	20	D	D	D	129	2 717	342.9	117.9
Odessa..................	230	5 893	377.8	90.6	23	239	15.9	2.6	273	5 379	633.2	215.6
Paris	93	1 462	67.5	18.9	8	D	D	D	153	3 443	310.7	115.6
Pasadena	202	3 882	206.4	54.8	10	D	D	D	307	6 675	807.2	289.9
Pearland	180	4 226	212.0	58.5	15	D	D	D	242	2 374	209.8	83.3
Pflugerville	61	1 266	61.4	17.6	7	100	6.1	1.7	59	D	D	D
Pharr....................	92	1 721	102.4	22.5	10	95	5.8	1.3	141	3 312	128.5	68.5
Plano	681	14 581	846.9	241.8	63	1 334	112.0	25.0	1 326	16 372	2 368.0	869.3
Port Arthur............	102	1 890	86.4	24.4	8	D	D	D	111	D	D	D
Richardson	322	5 202	307.9	82.9	31	427	31.0	10.6	479	5 290	475.4	182.8
Rockwall................	124	3 006	154.6	46.0	16	D	D	D	168	2 085	270.0	90.3
Rosenberg..............	92	1 713	89.5	25.8	2	D	D	D	52	D	D	D
Round Rock	278	6 112	340.4	92.7	29	D	D	D	288	D	D	D
Rowlett..................	70	990	49.9	14.0	9	D	D	D	100	1 983	246.4	72.1
San Angelo.................	210	4 220	211.7	57.1	22	264	15.8	3.7	225	3 970	425.1	200.0
San Antonio...............	3 209	79 964	4 616.3	1 242.7	255	D	D	D	3 448	74 255	8 556.3	3 003.7
San Juan...............	28	363	19.3	4.6	3	D	D	D	52	942	37.0	17.6
San Marcos	212	4 456	215.6	59.6	6	D	D	D	119	D	D	D
Schertz..................	58	1 287	62.4	17.5	4	D	D	D	44	681	61.7	24.3
Seguin...................	81	1 368	73.6	17.3	5	D	D	D	89	D	D	D
Sherman................	102	2 593	124.4	35.3	13	171	6.6	1.6	208	4 944	426.2	184.1
Socorro	24	263	12.7	3.0	1	D	D	D	12	303	7.1	3.8
Southlake	111	D	D	D	21	D	D	D	193	2 328	300.7	102.7
Sugar Land.............	328	7 038	377.8	109.4	27	772	63.8	17.7	563	D	D	D
Temple	170	3 451	159.8	44.4	17	136	8.5	2.0	157	D	D	D
Texarkana..............	134	3 369	158.4	46.2	18	169	6.4	2.4	215	4 013	462.8	181.8
Texas City	74	1 229	55.7	15.6	3	D	D	D	92	2 400	223.0	86.3
The Colony............	47	1 083	50.1	14.3	10	136	11.6	2.8	47	D	D	D
Tyler.....................	310	7 298	339.0	97.3	33	D	D	D	465	11 350	1 145.8	482.2
Victoria.................	176	3 538	182.8	48.4	27	D	D	D	254	D	D	D
Waco.....................	350	7 672	380.5	106.7	29	338	20.8	5.4	317	6 697	512.1	245.1
Waxahachie.............	80	1 902	85.0	25.3	3	D	D	D	86	D	D	D
Weatherford.............	116	2 114	98.8	28.6	6	D	D	D	128	1 988	207.2	79.7
Weslaco.................	84	1 781	86.0	21.4	10	D	D	D	174	D	D	D
Wichita Falls...........	236	5 370	249.6	76.2	20	D	D	D	305	5 113	540.1	185.9
Wylie.....................	42	D	D	D	5	42	3.6	0.8	50	D	D	D
UTAH...................	5 108	95 933	4 789.3	1 362.9	790	17 988	982.5	330.3	6 601	77 036	8 253.6	3 016.8
American Fork..............	82	1 558	69.8	18.5	7	D	D	D	129	D	D	D
Bountiful	69	D	D	D	10	D	D	D	209	D	D	D
Cedar City	82	1 224	57.5	14.8	9	D	D	D	117	D	D	D
Clearfield	32	611	23.0	6.5	5	D	D	D	44	D	D	D
Cottonwood Heights......	54	799	43.5	11.6	13	D	D	D	120	D	D	D
Draper	94	1 494	72.3	21.8	15	D	D	D	132	997	104.1	37.5
Holladay	51	578	30.2	8.2	11	D	D	D	96	972	85.2	33.2

1. Establishments subject to federal tax.

Table D. Cities — Other Services and Government Employment and Payroll

City	Other services[1], 2012					Government employment and payroll, 2012							
							March payroll						
							Percent of total for:						
	Number of establishments	Number of employees	Receipts (mil dol)	Annual payroll (mil dol)	Full-time equivalent employees	Total (dollars)	Administration, judicial, and legal	Police and Corrections	Fire Protection	Highways and transportation	Health and welfare	Natural resources and utilities	Education and libraries
	104	105	106	107	108	109	110	111	112	113	114	115	116
TEXAS—Cont'd													
Irving	239	2 926	307.3	114.7	1 743	8 046 007	11.8	31.8	18.7	7.1	2.9	19.2	3.6
Keller	55	377	31.5	9.8	322	1 442 647	19.7	27.3	24.3	2.1	4.2	18.4	3.8
Killeen	150	974	79.5	24.9	1 394	4 447 306	9.5	31.5	19.2	10.2	0.6	25.4	2.0
Kingsville	31	D	D	D	241	740 345	13.5	34.2	17.7	5.2	3.4	18.4	2.6
Kyle	18	91	7.2	2.0	143	570 004	14.8	39.7	0.0	1.7	5.7	18.1	3.7
Lake Jackson	28	191	12.6	4.6	223	1 137 302	14.0	31.7	0.5	2.3	1.6	37.2	0.0
Lancaster	24	150	17.5	5.4	197	872 132	6.8	31.3	33.7	2.6	3.3	16.0	2.4
La Porte	42	5 934	655.6	342.7	386	1 606 505	14.9	33.6	6.2	5.1	7.8	22.0	0.0
Laredo	175	975	90.0	24.7	2 366	9 931 436	6.8	30.9	24.7	11.9	8.6	14.4	1.1
League City	93	670	50.8	15.5	495	2 096 779	14.9	38.2	2.0	7.5	5.2	20.9	5.0
Leander	26	146	11.5	3.6	176	773 154	15.8	34.3	18.9	9.2	0.8	16.9	0.0
Lewisville	150	1 053	116.4	32.6	702	3 410 758	13.2	32.7	24.8	4.3	1.7	15.0	2.1
Little Elm	12	44	4.1	1.4	174	691 106	17.2	23.6	29.0	9.8	0.8	13.6	2.1
Longview	155	1 278	152.8	44.8	813	3 225 874	7.0	26.2	26.9	3.4	3.3	21.3	2.7
Lubbock	338	2 485	217.7	69.3	2 120	8 958 861	10.0	27.2	23.3	4.5	2.1	29.5	1.5
Lufkin	75	615	135.8	27.5	429	1 543 350	10.3	27.6	23.6	6.7	2.2	23.4	1.9
McAllen	145	1 046	142.4	30.6	1 664	5 174 843	11.6	30.2	15.6	10.8	1.0	24.6	3.0
McKinney	132	1 023	89.8	27.9	813	4 047 327	14.6	26.8	24.0	4.8	0.1	11.7	2.8
Mansfield	67	D	D	D	451	2 111 359	10.1	41.1	18.9	1.8	1.4	11.7	1.5
Mesquite	122	946	102.3	28.3	1 105	5 253 222	10.9	34.0	25.7	3.7	4.0	15.6	2.0
Midland	157	D	D	D	894	4 038 726	12.2	27.1	26.9	7.2	3.1	13.6	0.5
Mission	72	434	36.4	9.7	597	1 943 490	10.4	37.6	17.4	3.6	1.5	22.5	3.1
Missouri City	68	415	28.1	9.5	283	1 318 714	9.4	42.4	22.9	9.3	0.0	4.5	0.0
Nacogdoches	49	298	23.9	7.2	302	1 195 157	10.1	30.1	23.9	1.7	1.3	26.6	1.9
New Braunfels	105	1 334	54.3	37.3	732	3 498 442	7.2	20.5	22.3	4.6	3.6	21.9	2.5
North Richland Hills	73	459	48.3	13.6	574	2 442 427	13.2	35.1	19.1	9.2	9.3	9.3	4.0
Odessa	149	1 399	178.1	47.0	873	3 249 214	13.9	28.3	26.0	7.1	3.0	16.3	0.0
Paris	58	301	28.1	7.8	203	911 303	16.1	38.4	1.6	2.6	5.8	17.2	7.9
Pasadena	135	1 402	179.6	68.1	960	4 082 891	10.8	48.1	2.1	4.7	5.5	18.7	2.8
Pearland	129	906	77.4	25.7	598	2 337 139	14.4	37.4	8.4	4.4	15.8	16.8	0.0
Pflugerville	51	308	28.6	10.5	253	1 010 931	16.1	44.8	0.0	8.0	1.3	21.6	3.5
Pharr	52	340	29.9	8.1	558	1 780 708	10.5	35.0	15.9	8.1	1.9	18.2	3.4
Plano	419	3 683	759.6	161.0	2 089	10 395 648	9.8	32.0	22.2	2.2	0.0	14.1	5.2
Port Arthur	36	162	11.7	3.2	668	2 985 904	7.8	28.2	20.4	6.1	9.3	23.9	1.7
Richardson	146	1 302	141.4	44.2	1 085	4 745 385	14.8	25.0	17.8	5.0	3.3	20.5	3.5
Rockwall	55	559	27.7	10.4	286	1 221 546	32.3	33.7	9.6	3.1	0.0	16.3	0.0
Rosenberg	53	230	30.8	8.3	213	967 179	15.7	34.7	16.7	5.1	5.0	18.2	0.0
Round Rock	147	1 405	151.8	46.8	471	2 565 694	21.2	46.9	28.7	0.0	0.0	0.7	2.5
Rowlett	74	396	34.4	11.4	332	1 590 040	18.8	30.9	25.7	4.7	2.6	10.7	1.9
San Angelo	161	867	85.1	23.1	915	3 145 374	16.7	27.8	25.3	3.8	3.2	19.2	0.0
San Antonio	1 694	12 508	1 000.7	326.7	15 382	70 371 976	6.9	20.9	12.5	5.3	3.5	46.3	2.1
San Juan	14	D	D	D	204	595 583	10.6	35.0	12.1	4.4	4.5	31.9	0.4
San Marcos	73	D	D	D	528	2 976 832	13.7	28.7	14.8	4.1	4.9	21.3	2.7
Schertz	36	342	28.5	9.8	292	1 152 930	17.4	24.7	12.8	2.8	16.4	9.2	3.8
Seguin	47	323	25.3	7.7	907	3 729 350	5.2	8.3	6.1	1.8	68.5	7.0	0.7
Sherman	43	375	37.8	16.0	387	1 528 362	13.7	25.7	23.1	4.3	3.0	22.7	2.2
Socorro	24	112	8.0	1.6	92	274 728	24.8	59.5	0.0	13.4	2.2	0.0	0.0
Southlake	68	D	D	D	274	1 309 065	24.1	24.8	21.4	7.0	0.0	20.0	2.7
Sugar Land	128	947	72.3	23.2	631	3 018 681	23.4	31.1	19.1	10.0	1.3	10.4	0.0
Temple	104	933	55.9	26.2	731	2 585 537	12.4	26.7	22.3	6.4	2.4	25.4	2.6
Texarkana	91	661	56.2	17.8	562	2 018 866	13.1	24.0	17.3	8.1	4.9	29.4	1.7
Texas City	38	241	27.2	9.5	481	1 954 986	8.1	29.3	20.9	5.9	1.6	25.9	2.0
The Colony	32	157	11.7	3.1	311	1 270 659	11.9	29.0	21.2	3.8	7.3	20.1	4.5
Tyler	170	1 478	125.2	57.0	778	3 106 473	9.1	34.9	25.5	3.1	3.1	18.2	1.7
Victoria	103	D	D	D	566	2 159 618	10.1	31.7	22.5	6.4	0.0	22.4	3.2
Waco	177	1 205	90.1	28.9	1 507	5 739 695	9.4	29.8	17.3	5.4	5.9	25.5	2.4
Waxahachie	42	262	29.4	6.8	264	1 145 356	12.3	28.0	25.5	3.4	3.0	21.1	0.0
Weatherford	63	579	42.4	15.3	345	1 550 071	17.4	23.4	20.0	5.7	2.6	21.9	3.2
Weslaco	45	347	28.5	7.3	368	1 252 682	6.2	31.0	27.7	5.1	2.2	17.8	3.2
Wichita Falls	142	835	70.0	20.7	1 213	4 712 736	7.8	25.5	27.3	8.3	5.3	16.8	1.2
Wylie	33	172	13.3	4.5	191	622 464	4.4	29.0	33.5	4.3	0.0	22.4	6.3
UTAH	3 631	21 705	1 875.3	549.2	X	X	X	X	X	X	X	X	X
American Fork	55	448	23.4	5.8	215	711 482	13.8	21.8	14.3	3.1	1.3	25.9	5.2
Bountiful	72	572	38.0	11.3	195	922 673	14.7	32.2	0.0	14.9	0.0	37.8	0.0
Cedar City	43	174	14.8	3.9	172	568 537	11.0	28.7	7.6	11.9	1.2	27.7	2.2
Clearfield	34	194	11.7	4.6	150	543 342	19.4	32.7	17.0	4.0	0.9	22.9	0.0
Cottonwood Heights	25	150	5.7	1.9	68	323 642	24.8	70.5	0.0	4.6	0.0	0.0	0.0
Draper	78	494	43.8	10.8	152	605 204	26.7	28.9	0.0	17.1	3.4	14.1	0.0
Holladay	40	158	11.1	3.1	18	69 533	64.5	0.0	0.0	0.0	22.6	12.9	0.0

1. Establishments subject to federal tax.

Table D. Cities — **City Government Finances**

City	General revenue Total (mil dol)	Intergovernmental Total (mil dol)	Intergovernmental Percent from state government	Taxes Total (mil dol)	Taxes Per capita[1] (dollars) Total	Taxes Per capita[1] (dollars) Property	Taxes Sales and gross receipts	General expenditure Total (mil dol)	General expenditure Per capita[1] (dollars) Total	General expenditure Capital outlays
	117	118	119	120	121	122	123	124	125	126
TEXAS—Cont'd										
Irving	281.4	21.9	71.5	189.3	839	427	411	289.2	1 281	200
Keller	52.3	5.6	60.6	32.1	765	471	294	46.9	1 117	201
Killeen	120.2	5.4	5.6	62.9	466	248	219	125.1	928	204
Kingsville	22.9	0.6	12.6	12.2	464	228	236	21.7	825	89
Kyle	18.5	1.7	25.7	10.7	346	201	145	21.9	709	200
Lake Jackson	29.0	0.4	54.4	14.7	543	207	335	25.6	942	152
Lancaster	48.5	11.5	23.8	24.6	649	359	290	46.9	1 238	111
La Porte	56.7	0.9	100.0	26.5	769	497	272	48.6	1 407	246
Laredo	394.6	81.6	35.0	126.6	516	281	235	350.9	1 429	400
League City	86.5	3.8	100.0	58.1	658	411	247	73.3	829	130
Leander	26.5	2.2	9.7	17.9	606	377	229	29.0	981	234
Lewisville	95.9	2.2	49.8	62.5	628	286	342	100.9	1 013	207
Little Elm	30.5	4.2	98.1	18.2	629	354	275	39.3	1 357	641
Longview	103.8	12.8	28.3	64.9	798	306	492	94.8	1 166	149
Lubbock	270.7	38.4	30.0	127.0	538	245	293	310.3	1 313	386
Lufkin	50.9	0.7	59.9	25.8	716	272	443	52.9	1 468	203
McAllen	185.3	20.0	21.5	98.4	727	242	485	201.4	1 488	430
McKinney	171.7	14.0	23.8	109.6	764	437	327	184.3	1 284	234
Mansfield	76.9	0.3	100.0	53.1	894	514	381	67.5	1 136	167
Mesquite	149.0	15.9	19.4	81.9	571	255	316	164.5	1 147	212
Midland	147.3	7.4	38.3	94.6	790	273	516	126.0	1 052	145
Mission	73.0	7.2	12.2	38.7	478	266	212	68.7	850	112
Missouri City	57.5	9.1	36.1	36.0	524	363	161	66.1	963	354
Nacogdoches	37.5	1.3	98.2	17.4	514	223	291	34.0	1 005	86
New Braunfels	75.8	2.4	48.3	46.1	754	263	491	79.1	1 294	279
North Richland Hills	83.8	11.2	100.0	46.1	705	344	361	93.1	1 424	490
Odessa	103.9	3.9	38.2	61.7	580	196	384	93.2	877	116
Paris	30.9	2.2	100.0	18.1	722	303	419	29.3	1 166	79
Pasadena	146.5	20.4	12.6	75.9	497	217	280	138.9	910	167
Pearland	113.9	0.6	58.8	76.6	794	500	295	118.6	1 230	308
Pflugerville	42.9	1.9	93.4	26.5	509	326	184	44.6	858	248
Pharr	63.4	5.8	5.1	30.9	422	211	211	59.7	815	150
Plano	386.2	19.2	55.2	247.7	907	528	380	338.6	1 240	181
Port Arthur	104.3	23.2	53.0	35.6	652	306	346	92.8	1 701	263
Richardson	156.9	3.8	94.5	105.8	1 020	591	428	174.7	1 684	269
Rockwall	44.0	0.7	30.2	36.4	910	434	476	49.9	1 249	367
Rosenberg	36.1	5.0	24.6	21.6	665	231	434	29.5	906	207
Round Rock	146.3	3.6	66.0	112.0	1 050	315	735	119.5	1 120	243
Rowlett	58.1	2.1	65.8	33.9	587	420	167	55.7	965	142
San Angelo	93.6	7.0	10.4	55.3	575	299	276	98.6	1 026	216
San Antonio	1 748.6	300.5	51.3	740.3	534	275	253	1 743.3	1 258	188
San Juan	18.0	1.1	32.3	9.7	275	168	107	18.5	524	97
San Marcos	67.7	3.7	100.0	38.5	769	285	485	82.3	1 643	440
Schertz	37.4	1.3	65.0	21.3	611	306	305	31.5	902	81
Seguin	116.5	6.1	85.0	13.9	529	240	289	116.4	4 428	511
Sherman	47.8	2.7	3.7	27.5	704	182	522	48.9	1 254	120
Socorro	7.7	0.5	0.0	6.1	185	124	61	9.8	298	92
Southlake	68.2	0.6	38.4	54.7	1 972	1 139	834	66.5	2 398	864
Sugar Land	160.2	31.2	93.8	77.6	948	347	601	161.5	1 972	729
Temple	85.5	3.7	93.7	46.0	666	317	349	91.2	1 319	299
Texarkana	47.9	0.8	78.3	31.7	853	368	485	49.1	1 322	277
Texas City	68.4	8.3	43.2	43.1	944	451	493	58.5	1 280	147
The Colony	38.4	2.1	73.4	25.5	652	384	268	46.1	1 181	397
Tyler	128.9	15.0	13.7	61.9	623	142	481	120.1	1 209	168
Victoria	78.7	5.7	39.9	49.8	773	320	453	89.3	1 386	576
Waco	359.0	127.8	9.2	97.3	762	414	348	344.8	2 700	343
Waxahachie	40.4	0.2	100.0	28.8	928	477	451	33.9	1 090	82
Weatherford	34.6	3.2	80.9	20.7	782	306	475	43.0	1 627	441
Weslaco	37.6	0.7	25.3	22.1	599	267	332	35.9	972	114
Wichita Falls	120.3	13.6	34.0	66.3	633	276	357	114.0	1 088	129
Wylie	43.1	1.6	92.9	30.5	688	467	221	53.2	1 199	374
UTAH	X	X	X	X	X	X	X	X	X	X
American Fork	30.4	2.8	100.0	13.6	497	205	291	29.8	1 092	170
Bountiful	25.9	3.0	48.4	13.7	320	93	227	21.6	504	27
Cedar City	26.1	3.3	64.2	13.5	465	185	280	21.4	736	103
Clearfield	27.3	4.4	91.5	11.8	387	164	223	21.4	704	59
Cottonwood Heights	14.9	1.2	96.8	12.7	374	206	168	16.8	494	109
Draper	36.2	2.5	98.9	24.0	544	247	297	32.8	742	114
Holladay	17.7	2.0	70.1	11.7	434	197	236	15.0	555	0

1. Based on population estimated as of July 1 of the year shown.

City	Public welfare	Highways	Parking facilities	Education	Health and hospitals	Police protection	Sewerage and sanitation	Parks and recreation	Housing and community development	Interest on debt
					City government finances, 2012 (cont.)					
					General expenditure (cont.)					
					Percent of total for:					
	127	128	129	130	131	132	133	134	135	136
TEXAS—Cont'd										
Irving	0.0	6.3	0.0	0.0	0.3	18.5	10.7	16.0	1.7	6.2
Keller	0.0	17.7	0.0	0.0	0.0	17.1	7.0	11.8	0.0	10.1
Killeen	0.2	9.1	0.0	0.0	0.4	19.5	23.3	5.7	0.3	4.1
Kingsville	0.0	9.8	0.0	0.0	1.5	31.1	19.6	0.9	0.0	1.3
Kyle	0.0	2.5	0.0	0.0	0.7	17.1	24.0	10.5	0.0	11.7
Lake Jackson	0.0	11.4	0.0	0.0	3.4	18.2	19.4	20.7	0.0	5.0
Lancaster	0.0	1.7	0.0	0.0	0.3	12.2	16.8	4.5	18.4	8.3
La Porte	0.0	8.4	0.0	0.0	0.0	21.8	10.5	11.3	0.0	3.9
Laredo	0.2	2.1	0.4	0.0	4.1	15.0	11.2	3.3	3.8	5.2
League City	0.0	10.6	0.0	0.0	3.9	20.7	11.4	6.2	0.2	5.1
Leander	0.0	21.6	0.0	0.0	0.6	14.8	12.0	7.8	0.0	17.7
Lewisville	0.0	16.6	0.0	0.0	1.2	21.6	6.1	10.4	2.2	6.4
Little Elm	0.0	4.0	0.0	0.0	0.3	8.7	13.3	2.7	0.0	4.5
Longview	0.0	10.3	0.0	0.0	1.5	21.3	12.6	8.8	7.2	2.4
Lubbock	0.0	7.3	0.0	0.0	1.8	16.3	18.4	5.2	1.4	10.2
Lufkin	0.0	14.7	0.0	0.0	1.2	15.2	18.1	7.6	0.3	13.8
McAllen	0.6	11.5	0.4	0.0	0.8	16.5	22.1	10.4	1.7	2.6
McKinney	0.0	8.4	0.0	0.0	0.8	10.9	11.9	6.8	0.3	6.0
Mansfield	0.0	9.9	0.0	0.0	0.6	14.5	12.1	8.2	0.0	8.1
Mesquite	0.0	6.4	0.0	0.0	0.8	18.5	13.6	7.0	8.4	4.2
Midland	0.0	5.4	0.0	0.0	3.3	17.0	15.9	13.4	0.6	2.3
Mission	0.0	8.3	0.0	0.0	0.5	20.0	10.6	12.1	1.7	18.9
Missouri City	0.0	12.6	0.0	0.0	0.3	16.3	9.7	12.1	0.5	7.8
Nacogdoches	0.0	4.3	0.0	0.0	0.0	20.6	28.3	4.4	0.0	1.2
New Braunfels	0.0	16.3	0.0	0.0	0.9	17.7	16.5	7.8	0.3	6.0
North Richland Hills	0.0	7.5	0.0	0.0	0.9	17.6	8.3	14.6	0.0	2.6
Odessa	0.1	14.4	0.0	0.0	0.7	18.6	16.0	6.7	2.6	1.6
Paris	0.0	12.8	0.0	0.0	10.9	19.7	12.9	3.9	4.1	2.1
Pasadena	0.3	19.6	0.0	0.0	2.5	30.9	13.9	6.5	7.8	3.5
Pearland	0.0	21.9	0.0	0.0	3.6	13.1	14.4	6.1	0.0	12.2
Pflugerville	0.0	14.9	0.0	0.0	0.0	22.4	18.1	6.3	0.0	7.6
Pharr	0.0	17.9	0.0	0.0	3.4	23.5	9.1	9.1	2.3	3.4
Plano	0.0	5.1	0.0	0.0	1.0	16.3	18.5	12.9	0.8	4.2
Port Arthur	2.1	10.7	0.0	0.0	3.3	19.4	20.8	2.7	3.2	3.5
Richardson	0.0	11.9	0.0	0.0	1.1	13.7	17.6	8.7	0.0	6.6
Rockwall	0.0	20.4	0.0	0.0	1.1	16.8	11.8	16.8	0.0	11.1
Rosenberg	0.0	19.1	0.0	0.0	0.8	23.4	17.4	3.5	0.0	6.0
Round Rock	0.0	13.0	0.0	0.0	0.7	19.5	9.2	7.3	0.4	5.1
Rowlett	0.0	13.1	0.0	0.0	1.6	18.1	14.7	6.6	0.0	6.4
San Angelo	0.0	7.5	0.0	0.0	3.5	15.8	10.8	5.9	3.1	4.7
San Antonio	7.8	6.4	0.3	0.0	1.9	17.7	19.6	7.8	2.9	1.6
San Juan	0.0	7.7	0.0	0.0	0.0	18.3	23.7	7.5	0.0	4.2
San Marcos	0.0	3.2	0.0	0.0	2.0	17.4	16.7	3.5	0.8	8.8
Schertz	0.0	7.2	0.0	0.0	12.4	14.7	16.9	4.0	0.0	6.6
Seguin	0.0	2.2	0.0	0.0	64.9	4.6	5.0	2.7	0.0	6.7
Sherman	0.1	14.6	0.0	0.0	1.2	15.7	18.0	4.8	0.6	2.0
Socorro	0.0	16.3	0.0	0.0	4.1	19.1	0.0	1.1	2.7	3.8
Southlake	0.0	16.1	0.0	0.0	0.0	12.5	7.7	19.6	0.0	8.2
Sugar Land	0.0	21.1	0.0	0.0	0.4	10.2	11.7	4.0	0.2	5.9
Temple	0.0	5.4	0.0	0.0	0.9	17.8	21.2	9.8	0.0	5.0
Texarkana	0.0	16.5	0.0	0.0	1.7	19.3	24.5	4.0	0.9	4.9
Texas City	0.0	17.5	0.0	0.0	0.7	18.1	12.1	12.9	0.8	4.6
The Colony	0.0	20.7	0.0	0.0	0.0	26.6	8.9	7.9	0.0	5.3
Tyler	0.0	11.3	0.0	0.0	0.0	18.5	17.1	3.5	6.7	14.7
Victoria	0.0	29.4	0.0	0.0	0.0	15.1	11.6	3.8	1.2	5.0
Waco	0.0	2.2	0.0	0.0	2.2	10.3	12.3	7.5	1.0	48.3
Waxahachie	0.0	7.3	0.0	0.0	2.2	18.4	13.9	8.1	0.0	10.0
Weatherford	0.0	29.0	0.0	0.0	0.1	15.8	13.4	5.2	0.0	6.7
Weslaco	0.0	3.7	0.0	0.0	1.2	15.5	23.6	1.3	0.0	10.1
Wichita Falls	0.0	8.9	0.0	0.0	4.1	17.6	17.4	5.8	5.2	1.7
Wylie	0.0	21.8	0.0	0.0	0.5	9.5	11.2	16.0	0.0	9.1
UTAH	X	X	X	X	X	X	X	X	X	X
American Fork	0.0	15.1	0.0	0.0	4.9	14.4	17.4	12.8	0.9	3.0
Bountiful	0.0	19.3	0.0	0.0	0.0	26.9	15.0	11.0	3.2	0.7
Cedar City	0.0	17.1	0.0	0.0	0.0	18.7	14.8	18.3	3.1	4.1
Clearfield	0.0	8.5	0.0	0.0	0.0	19.0	14.3	16.1	2.4	4.6
Cottonwood Heights	0.0	31.0	0.0	0.0	0.0	0.9	1.2	1.1	0.0	0.0
Draper	0.0	22.1	0.0	0.0	0.6	12.1	7.5	9.8	9.4	3.2
Holladay	0.0	9.9	0.0	0.0	0.0	21.1	1.5	5.1	20.2	6.0

City	City government finances, 2012 (cont.)			Climate[2]						
	Debt outstanding			Average daily temperature (degrees Fahrenheit)						
				Mean		Limits				
	Total (mil dol)	Per capita[1] (dollars)	Debt issued during year	January	July	January[3]	July[4]	Annual precipitation (inches)	Heating degree days	Cooling degree days
	137	138	139	140	141	142	143	144	145	146
TEXAS—Cont'd										
Irving	567.8	2 515	137.2	45.9	86.5	36.4	96.1	37.05	2 219	2 878
Keller	128.2	3 054	0.0	43.0	84.1	31.4	95.7	34.12	2 608	2 358
Killeen	238.9	1 773	75.1	46.0	83.5	34.0	95.3	32.88	2 190	2 477
Kingsville	28.3	1 072	10.0	55.9	84.3	43.4	95.5	29.03	1 001	3 404
Kyle	69.4	2 246	7.7	NA	NA	NA	NA	NA	NA	NA
Lake Jackson	42.1	1 549	0.0	54.0	83.7	45.4	90.2	50.66	1 234	3 003
Lancaster	96.3	2 540	0.0	44.4	84.0	33.3	95.7	38.69	2 380	2 452
La Porte	45.1	1 307	0.0	51.6	83.6	41.9	91.6	53.75	1 471	2 841
Laredo	576.1	2 347	109.7	55.6	88.5	43.7	101.6	21.53	931	4 213
League City	210.1	2 379	39.8	52.7	82.7	43.1	91.2	51.73	1 365	2 815
Leander	176.0	5 952	0.0	NA	NA	NA	NA	NA	NA	NA
Lewisville	244.1	2 452	15.1	42.7	83.6	32.0	94.1	37.79	2 650	2 269
Little Elm	74.2	2 564	0.0	NA	NA	NA	NA	NA	NA	NA
Longview	160.6	1 975	39.2	45.4	83.4	33.7	94.5	49.06	2 319	2 355
Lubbock	1 342.1	5 681	257.0	38.1	79.8	24.4	91.9	18.69	3 508	1 769
Lufkin	179.5	4 983	21.3	48.6	82.6	37.9	93.5	46.62	1 900	2 480
McAllen	182.6	1 349	18.6	58.7	85.1	48.2	95.5	22.61	719	3 898
McKinney	313.4	2 184	16.9	41.8	82.4	31.1	92.7	41.01	2 843	2 060
Mansfield	183.2	3 084	26.8	43.7	84.3	33.2	94.9	34.54	2 437	2 508
Mesquite	242.0	1 687	42.9	45.9	86.5	36.4	96.1	37.05	2 219	2 878
Midland	125.3	1 046	6.0	44.5	81.8	29.5	95.6	14.84	2 479	2 241
Mission	387.2	4 787	51.7	58.8	86.3	47.5	97.7	22.13	740	4 128
Missouri City	174.1	2 535	5.1	51.8	84.1	41.6	93.7	49.34	1 475	2 950
Nacogdoches	62.8	1 856	1.7	46.5	83.9	36.4	93.5	48.36	2 150	2 555
New Braunfels	122.5	2 004	19.1	48.6	82.7	35.5	94.7	35.74	1 840	2 545
North Richland Hills	95.6	1 463	9.4	44.1	85.0	34.0	95.4	34.73	2 370	2 568
Odessa	124.0	1 168	0.0	43.2	81.7	29.6	94.3	14.80	2 716	2 139
Paris	25.2	1 004	0.0	40.6	83.1	29.9	94.3	47.82	2 972	2 197
Pasadena	223.9	1 467	34.6	54.3	84.5	45.2	93.6	53.96	1 174	3 179
Pearland	497.5	5 162	21.5	54.3	84.5	45.2	93.6	53.96	1 174	3 179
Pflugerville	167.6	3 224	21.9	NA	NA	NA	NA	NA	NA	NA
Pharr	103.3	1 410	2.2	60.1	85.9	50.3	96.1	22.96	624	4 181
Plano	352.8	1 293	21.4	44.1	85.0	34.0	95.4	34.73	2 370	2 568
Port Arthur	88.1	1 615	9.5	52.2	82.7	42.9	91.6	59.89	1 447	2 823
Richardson	311.9	3 007	21.2	45.9	86.5	36.4	96.1	37.05	2 219	2 878
Rockwall	163.4	4 091	17.3	NA	NA	NA	NA	NA	NA	NA
Rosenberg	52.3	1 608	15.4	NA	NA	NA	NA	NA	NA	NA
Round Rock	260.2	2 439	16.1	47.2	83.8	35.1	95.7	36.42	1 998	2 584
Rowlett	119.6	2 070	9.2	42.1	82.8	30.8	94.2	40.06	2 710	2 212
San Angelo	234.6	2 440	163.8	44.9	82.4	31.8	94.4	20.91	2 396	2 383
San Antonio	8 830.9	6 374	589.4	50.3	84.3	38.6	94.6	32.92	1 573	3 038
San Juan	24.6	697	5.9	60.1	85.9	50.3	96.1	22.96	624	4 181
San Marcos	264.7	5 283	17.2	49.9	84.4	38.6	95.1	37.19	1 629	2 913
Schertz	73.9	2 118	13.8	NA	NA	NA	NA	NA	NA	NA
Seguin	172.6	6 568	18.6	NA	NA	NA	NA	NA	NA	NA
Sherman	23.5	602	0.0	41.5	82.8	32.2	92.7	42.04	2 850	2 137
Socorro	12.3	374	8.1	44.9	83.6	29.2	98.7	9.71	2 557	2 372
Southlake	179.6	6 478	11.1	NA	NA	NA	NA	NA	NA	NA
Sugar Land	363.3	4 437	130.2	51.8	84.1	41.6	93.7	49.34	1 475	2 950
Temple	177.8	2 572	24.1	46.1	83.7	34.9	95.0	35.81	2 191	2 551
Texarkana	69.8	1 880	0.0	41.6	82.6	30.7	93.1	51.24	2 893	2 138
Texas City	91.3	1 997	31.9	55.8	84.3	49.7	88.7	43.84	1 008	3 268
The Colony	97.6	2 499	7.6	42.7	83.6	32.0	94.1	37.79	2 650	2 269
Tyler	428.2	4 307	9.4	47.5	83.4	37.7	93.6	45.27	1 958	2 521
Victoria	179.1	2 780	9.7	53.2	84.2	43.6	93.4	40.10	1 248	3 203
Waco	8 413.1	65 880	7.3	46.1	85.4	35.1	96.7	33.34	2 164	2 840
Waxahachie	170.0	5 475	0.0	NA	NA	NA	NA	NA	NA	NA
Weatherford	117.6	4 447	33.5	NA	NA	NA	NA	NA	NA	NA
Weslaco	115.6	3 134	11.5	58.6	84.5	47.7	95.4	25.37	755	3 791
Wichita Falls	168.4	1 607	0.0	40.5	84.8	28.9	97.2	28.83	3 024	2 396
Wylie	119.8	2 699	5.4	NA	NA	NA	NA	NA	NA	NA
UTAH	X	X	X	X	X	X	X	X	X	X
American Fork	62.3	2 284	1.7	NA	NA	NA	NA	NA	NA	NA
Bountiful	18.1	421	0.0	29.1	75.8	21.6	88.4	22.40	5 937	861
Cedar City	21.1	725	0.0	NA	NA	NA	NA	NA	NA	NA
Clearfield	24.6	809	0.0	27.6	74.2	18.6	89.9	20.75	6 142	746
Cottonwood Heights	0.0	0	0.0	NA	NA	NA	NA	NA	NA	NA
Draper	33.1	749	0.0	31.6	78.0	22.0	95.3	15.76	5 251	1 172
Holladay	20.8	770	9.2	NA	NA	NA	NA	NA	NA	NA

1. Based on the population estimated as of July 1 of the year shown.   2. Represents normal values based on the 30-year period, 1971–2000.   3. Average daily minimum.
4. Average daily maximum.

Table D. Cities — Land Area and Population

STATE Place code	City	Land area,[1] 2016 (sq mi)	Total persons	Rank	Per square mile	White	Black or African American	American Indian, Alaska Native	Asian	Hawaiian Pacific Islander	Some other race	2 or more races[2]
		1	2	3	4	5	6	7	8	9	10	11
	UTAH—Cont'd											
49 40360	Kaysville	10.5	31 243	1 204	2 975.5	NA	NA	NA	NA	NA	NA	NA
49 43660	Layton	22.1	75 655	455	3 423.3	83.9	1.5	0.2	2.2	1.1	6.4	4.7
49 44320	Lehi	27.6	61 130	599	2 214.9	92.1	0.4	0.3	1.3	0.7	0.8	4.5
49 45860	Logan	17.6	50 676	750	2 879.3	84.3	0.8	0.3	4.0	0.4	7.0	3.2
49 49710	Midvale	5.9	33 035	1 150	5 599.2	78.5	3.6	0.4	4.7	0.0	10.1	2.8
49 53230	Murray	12.3	49 230	767	4 002.4	89.5	1.8	0.6	1.2	0.2	1.5	5.2
49 55980	Ogden	27.3	86 701	379	3 175.9	83.9	1.8	0.7	1.4	0.1	7.8	4.2
49 57300	Orem	18.5	97 499	314	5 270.2	87.4	0.8	0.3	2.3	1.2	4.3	3.7
49 60930	Pleasant Grove	9.1	38 756	983	4 258.9	91.1	1.6	1.1	3.7	0.3	0.4	1.8
49 62470	Provo	41.7	116 868	238	2 802.6	90.0	0.4	0.5	1.7	1.0	2.0	4.3
49 64340	Riverton	12.6	42 838	879	3 399.8	NA	NA	NA	NA	NA	NA	NA
49 65110	Roy	7.8	38 201	998	4 897.6	81.5	1.1	1.4	2.7	0.0	5.8	7.6
49 65330	St. George	76.3	82 318	408	1 078.9	86.9	1.5	1.7	0.7	0.8	5.3	3.1
49 67000	Salt Lake City	111.2	193 744	123	1 742.3	75.4	2.4	1.1	5.4	1.4	11.6	2.8
49 67440	Sandy	23.6	95 836	322	4 060.8	87.9	0.4	0.2	4.3	0.4	3.4	3.4
49 70850	South Jordan	22.2	69 034	509	3 109.6	87.2	2.9	0.2	2.7	1.5	4.1	1.4
49 71290	Spanish Fork	16.0	38 861	981	2 428.8	NA	NA	NA	NA	NA	NA	NA
49 72280	Springville	14.3	33 044	1 147	2 310.8	NA	NA	NA	NA	NA	NA	NA
49 75360	Taylorsville	10.9	60 436	611	5 544.6	80.0	2.2	0.7	3.0	0.1	10.1	3.8
49 76680	Tooele	24.1	33 762	1 125	1 400.9	92.8	0.5	0.0	0.2	0.0	3.1	3.3
49 82950	West Jordan	32.3	113 699	248	3 520.1	86.9	2.3	0.5	2.5	0.3	4.9	2.7
49 83470	West Valley City	35.5	136 574	192	3 847.2	62.0	2.1	2.3	6.4	4.3	18.7	4.2
50 00000	VERMONT	9 217.6	624 594	X	67.8	94.7	1.3	0.4	1.4	0.1	0.3	1.8
50 10675	Burlington	10.3	42 260	893	4 102.9	85.5	5.3	0.2	5.9	0.0	0.1	3.0
51 00000	VIRGINIA	39 481.8	8 411 808	X	213.1	68.2	19.2	0.3	6.3	0.1	2.4	3.5
51 01000	Alexandria	15.0	155 810	163	10 387.3	63.4	20.5	0.2	6.6	0.0	2.6	6.7
51 07784	Blacksburg	19.9	45 038	837	2 263.2	77.1	6.0	0.1	12.3	0.0	2.4	2.1
51 14968	Charlottesville	10.2	46 912	817	4 599.2	70.6	18.2	0.0	7.0	0.3	0.1	3.7
51 16000	Chesapeake	338.5	237 940	92	702.9	61.4	29.9	0.2	3.6	0.1	1.7	3.0
51 21344	Danville	42.9	41 898	903	976.6	46.4	49.9	0.1	1.1	0.0	1.3	1.2
51 35000	Hampton	51.5	135 410	194	2 629.3	42.9	49.1	0.6	2.5	0.1	1.3	3.5
51 35624	Harrisonburg	17.3	53 078	714	3 068.1	85.1	5.7	0.0	4.8	0.0	0.6	3.9
51 44984	Leesburg	12.4	52 607	720	4 242.5	78.2	5.2	0.1	6.7	0.0	6.4	3.4
51 47672	Lynchburg	49.1	80 212	424	1 633.6	65.2	28.5	0.3	2.9	0.0	0.7	2.4
51 48952	Manassas	9.9	41 483	910	4 190.2	64.6	11.3	1.0	5.4	0.6	13.5	3.5
51 56000	Newport News	69.1	181 825	135	2 631.3	48.7	40.3	0.2	3.6	0.2	2.6	4.4
51 57000	Norfolk	53.3	245 115	88	4 598.8	48.9	41.6	0.6	3.9	0.1	1.5	3.5
51 61832	Petersburg	22.9	31 882	1 182	1 392.2	NA	NA	NA	NA	NA	NA	NA
51 64000	Portsmouth	33.3	95 252	328	2 860.4	41.3	52.5	0.5	0.6	0.0	1.0	4.0
51 67000	Richmond	59.8	223 170	98	3 731.9	44.9	47.5	1.0	2.2	0.1	0.8	3.6
51 68000	Roanoke	42.5	99 660	304	2 344.9	65.0	27.5	0.0	2.7	0.0	0.7	4.1
51 76432	Suffolk	399.2	89 273	359	223.6	52.0	42.9	0.5	2.1	0.0	0.7	1.8
51 82000	Virginia Beach	244.7	452 602	43	1 849.6	67.2	19.6	0.2	6.3	0.1	1.3	5.3
51 86720	Winchester	9.2	27 516	1 342	2 990.9	82.3	8.9	0.2	3.0	0.0	0.9	4.8
53 00000	WASHINGTON	66 453.4	7 288 000	X	109.7	76.9	3.7	1.3	7.9	0.6	4.0	5.5
53 03180	Auburn	29.7	77 472	437	2 608.5	68.7	2.9	1.3	11.9	0.7	5.6	8.9
53 05210	Bellevue	33.5	141 400	186	4 220.9	54.3	2.2	0.3	34.3	0.2	3.6	5.1
53 05280	Bellingham	27.7	87 574	376	3 161.5	82.5	1.1	1.8	7.0	0.5	2.4	4.8
53 07380	Bothell	13.7	44 546	848	3 251.5	71.0	2.8	0.8	11.2	0.0	4.7	9.5
53 07695	Bremerton	28.4	40 675	925	1 432.2	73.0	4.8	0.7	4.0	0.0	3.6	13.3
53 08850	Burien	10.1	50 997	748	5 049.2	54.8	8.0	1.3	13.2	2.0	13.2	7.5
53 17635	Des Moines	6.5	31 172	1 206	4 795.7	58.0	7.7	0.0	14.1	1.3	11.2	7.8
53 20750	Edmonds	8.9	41 840	904	4 701.1	81.1	1.5	0.9	4.7	0.0	3.2	8.6
53 22640	Everett	33.3	109 043	273	3 274.6	75.4	3.9	1.0	7.5	1.8	3.4	6.9
53 23515	Federal Way	22.3	96 757	316	4 338.9	56.9	13.4	0.4	13.8	3.7	4.7	7.2
53 33805	Issaquah	12.1	37 322	1 025	3 084.5	NA	NA	NA	NA	NA	NA	NA
53 35275	Kennewick	27.4	80 454	420	2 936.3	75.4	0.3	0.4	1.7	0.1	13.6	8.5
53 35415	Kent	33.7	127 514	216	3 783.8	49.6	13.3	1.3	18.9	1.2	10.2	5.6
53 35940	Kirkland	17.8	87 701	373	4 927.0	76.9	0.9	0.2	14.5	0.3	2.8	4.3
53 36745	Lacey	16.2	47 688	802	2 943.7	66.6	6.2	2.7	9.9	4.3	1.9	8.4
53 37900	Lake Stevens	8.9	31 679	1 188	3 559.4	NA	NA	NA	NA	NA	NA	NA
53 38038	Lakewood	17.2	60 665	605	3 527.0	52.0	15.6	1.3	9.6	2.8	10.7	8.0
53 40245	Longview	14.9	37 337	1 024	2 505.8	88.3	0.1	1.6	2.7	0.0	2.4	4.9
53 40840	Lynnwood	7.9	38 092	1 001	4 821.8	64.6	9.5	0.1	13.7	0.0	5.7	6.3
53 43955	Marysville	20.7	67 626	527	3 267.0	81.4	0.9	0.7	6.2	0.3	2.6	7.9
53 47560	Mount Vernon	12.2	34 590	1 102	2 835.2	66.4	2.5	2.3	4.2	0.6	21.1	3.0
53 51300	Olympia	18.2	51 202	745	2 813.3	83.8	3.8	0.2	7.2	0.0	1.1	3.9

1. Dry land or land partially or temporarily covered by water.   2. Hispanic or Latino persons may be of any race.

Table D. Cities — **Population**

City	Percent Hispanic or Latino¹, 2015	Percent foreign born 2015	Age of population (percent), 2010-2014							Median age 2015	Percent female 2015	Population Census counts 2000	Census counts 2010	Percent change 2000–2010	Percent change 2010–2016
			Under 18 years	18 to 24 years	25 to 34 years	35 to 44 years	45 to 54 years	55 to 64 years	65 years and over						
	12	13	14	15	16	17	18	19	20	21	22	23	24	25	26
UTAH—Cont'd															
Kaysville	3.7	1.9	38.7	10.1	11.1	12.3	12.3	7.8	7.7	26.3	49.1	20 351	27 585	35.5	13.3
Layton	13.7	5.8	31.5	11.3	15.9	15.1	7.5	10.7	7.9	29.5	49.1	58 474	67 529	15.5	12.0
Lehi	7.3	4.1	45.9	6.9	16.5	15.6	7.2	3.9	4.0	20.8	48.7	19 028	47 772	151.1	28.0
Logan	15.9	10.5	24.4	28.6	19.0	9.9	5.1	5.3	7.7	24.2	51.4	42 670	48 210	13.0	5.1
Midvale	26.0	13.0	31.9	6.1	25.7	16.6	8.1	3.9	7.6	29.7	52.1	27 029	27 982	3.5	18.1
Murray	14.4	7.0	21.3	12.0	18.0	10.8	11.2	11.1	15.6	34.2	54.3	34 024	46 743	37.4	5.3
Ogden	33.1	15.0	25.7	12.9	18.2	12.1	11.7	9.6	9.9	31.3	48.1	77 226	82 836	7.3	4.7
Orem	19.4	13.6	29.6	18.1	15.6	10.7	7.9	8.2	10.0	26.1	48.4	84 324	88 329	4.7	10.4
Pleasant Grove	5.4	5.2	35.1	12.1	12.3	12.5	9.1	7.8	11.0	27.2	51.8	23 468	33 555	43.0	15.5
Provo	14.5	9.5	23.0	36.0	17.3	8.4	5.6	4.3	5.4	23.6	51.2	105 166	112 493	7.0	3.9
Riverton	10.8	0.5	38.4	6.2	9.7	18.7	9.3	11.2	6.4	32.1	48.8	25 011	38 841	55.3	10.3
Roy	15.9	6.5	34.6	8.5	16.3	12.8	8.6	11.6	7.6	29.9	50.4	32 885	36 857	12.1	3.6
St. George	13.5	6.0	24.2	12.4	10.8	10.8	8.9	11.9	21.0	37.3	51.7	49 663	72 763	46.5	13.1
Salt Lake City	21.1	16.7	19.8	13.4	22.1	12.6	10.7	9.9	11.6	32.1	48.9	181 743	186 439	2.6	3.9
Sandy	7.3	7.1	28.4	9.0	12.9	14.3	11.5	13.9	10.0	34.6	49.9	88 418	89 299	1.0	7.3
South Jordan	7.0	9.2	32.9	7.1	10.7	17.5	12.2	9.9	9.8	33.8	49.5	29 437	50 473	71.5	36.8
Spanish Fork	10.7	5.4	36.7	12.6	11.8	16.4	10.3	6.3	5.9	25.5	47.2	20 246	34 744	71.6	11.8
Springville	18.4	5.6	40.4	10.0	13.7	13.6	7.2	6.3	8.7	24.8	53.0	20 424	29 582	44.8	11.7
Taylorsville	23.3	10.7	27.0	9.8	13.8	15.5	11.4	10.8	11.8	34.3	51.4	57 439	58 686	2.2	3.0
Tooele	14.8	4.6	29.1	11.0	16.6	13.5	11.6	8.8	9.4	31.6	50.9	22 502	31 605	40.5	6.8
West Jordan	19.0	10.3	32.2	9.0	15.9	14.4	12.8	9.8	5.8	30.8	48.3	68 336	103 609	51.6	9.7
West Valley City	32.4	22.5	29.7	10.7	16.5	13.5	10.8	10.1	8.8	30.7	49.9	108 896	129 475	18.9	5.5
VERMONT	1.7	4.5	19.2	10.7	11.3	11.2	14.4	15.6	17.6	43.1	50.7	608 827	625 741	2.8	-0.2
Burlington	2.5	13.3	9.5	35.4	14.7	10.4	9.3	7.8	12.9	27.8	51.8	38 889	42 417	9.1	-0.4
VIRGINIA	9.0	12.2	22.3	9.9	14.0	13.1	14.0	12.6	14.2	37.8	50.8	7 078 515	8 001 041	13.0	5.1
Alexandria	16.7	28.7	17.9	5.9	22.6	18.9	13.2	11.0	10.4	36.6	51.2	128 283	140 006	9.1	11.3
Blacksburg	4.3	14.7	8.8	52.5	15.9	6.5	8.3	2.3	5.8	22.7	48.2	39 573	42 607	7.7	5.7
Charlottesville	5.0	10.3	14.5	21.5	23.0	10.6	10.8	9.5	10.0	29.4	50.0	45 049	43 435	-3.6	8.0
Chesapeake	5.5	5.9	24.2	9.0	14.4	13.3	14.1	12.6	12.3	36.7	51.2	199 184	222 306	11.6	7.0
Danville	3.8	3.9	22.2	8.5	12.9	11.1	11.3	14.2	19.9	39.4	53.3	48 411	43 059	-11.1	-2.7
Hampton	5.5	4.5	21.1	12.2	16.0	11.0	12.6	12.9	14.2	35.5	51.5	146 437	137 384	-6.2	-1.4
Harrisonburg	18.6	17.5	16.0	35.4	12.9	11.1	9.2	7.3	8.0	23.9	53.1	40 468	48 907	20.9	8.5
Leesburg	18.0	23.3	24.7	11.0	12.9	16.1	17.5	8.9	8.9	36.2	52.5	28 311	42 616	50.5	23.4
Lynchburg	3.4	5.5	19.4	24.2	13.9	8.8	9.6	10.2	13.9	28.7	51.6	65 269	75 608	15.8	6.1
Manassas	37.6	28.3	29.7	8.6	14.3	17.0	11.9	8.4	10.1	32.8	52.8	35 135	37 839	7.7	9.6
Newport News	8.7	6.9	23.4	13.2	16.7	11.4	12.1	11.2	12.0	32.8	51.5	180 150	181 039	0.5	0.4
Norfolk	7.6	6.8	20.2	18.6	18.8	10.9	11.0	10.4	10.2	30.2	47.7	234 403	242 823	3.6	0.9
Petersburg	4.6	2.0	20.7	13.3	14.2	8.3	14.2	14.0	15.3	38.0	54.6	33 740	32 436	-3.9	-1.7
Portsmouth	4.0	1.9	24.0	10.9	16.6	11.0	11.5	12.3	13.8	33.6	52.3	100 565	95 527	-5.0	-0.3
Richmond	6.5	7.1	18.2	13.7	20.9	11.7	11.7	12.2	11.5	33.6	52.4	197 790	204 142	3.2	9.3
Roanoke	6.1	7.4	21.7	8.8	15.8	12.6	12.6	13.2	15.3	36.9	52.7	94 911	96 919	2.1	2.8
Suffolk	4.0	3.2	24.6	9.2	12.7	12.8	14.8	12.4	13.6	38.2	51.2	63 677	84 570	32.8	5.6
Virginia Beach	8.0	8.5	22.6	10.1	16.8	12.9	13.3	11.8	12.6	35.4	50.8	425 257	437 907	3.0	3.4
Winchester	20.7	15.1	22.2	15.3	10.2	10.5	17.6	9.5	14.7	38.2	52.2	23 585	26 201	11.1	5.0
WASHINGTON	12.4	13.7	22.5	9.3	14.6	12.9	13.2	12.9	14.5	37.5	50.0	5 894 121	6 724 545	14.1	8.4
Auburn	14.1	19.4	21.9	11.8	12.7	13.0	14.3	13.5	12.8	37.1	51.9	40 314	70 172	74.1	10.4
Bellevue	8.7	39.1	20.2	7.3	19.2	13.5	14.7	10.7	14.4	37.4	49.4	109 569	127 887	16.7	10.6
Bellingham	8.2	10.2	15.4	24.2	16.2	10.0	8.4	10.7	15.2	30.7	51.5	67 171	81 266	21.0	7.8
Bothell	12.6	18.0	23.2	10.6	16.7	14.6	14.5	9.7	10.7	34.7	50.7	30 150	39 867	32.2	11.7
Bremerton	10.4	6.0	17.1	18.4	17.4	9.6	12.9	9.2	15.4	31.8	46.7	37 259	37 796	1.4	7.6
Burien	23.5	25.1	25.3	8.8	11.6	15.9	14.6	12.2	11.6	37.3	50.2	31 881	48 072	50.8	6.1
Des Moines	20.0	21.5	20.5	7.7	17.0	9.5	16.1	12.6	16.5	41.6	51.0	29 267	29 673	1.4	5.1
Edmonds	6.1	11.9	15.6	9.6	12.1	14.0	12.6	15.2	21.0	44.1	50.7	39 515	39 698	0.5	5.4
Everett	14.7	18.1	20.8	9.9	15.7	14.2	13.7	12.3	13.5	37.0	48.0	91 488	103 027	12.6	5.8
Federal Way	14.8	19.5	22.8	8.9	16.1	12.0	14.9	12.0	13.3	36.4	48.4	83 259	89 306	7.3	8.3
Issaquah	3.8	23.2	26.6	6.5	14.2	18.6	14.9	8.4	10.9	36.4	51.5	11 212	30 440	171.5	22.6
Kennewick	24.6	10.6	28.6	10.5	15.1	13.2	10.8	10.5	11.2	32.0	51.2	54 693	73 981	35.3	8.7
Kent	17.3	30.1	24.7	10.8	17.5	13.4	12.2	11.4	10.0	33.4	51.3	79 524	118 593	49.1	7.5
Kirkland	7.7	21.3	18.4	5.9	16.5	17.0	14.1	13.1	15.0	40.8	51.7	45 054	80 585	78.9	8.8
Lacey	14.1	10.7	25.0	10.5	15.0	12.4	10.6	9.5	17.1	34.7	53.7	31 226	42 398	35.8	12.5
Lake Stevens	13.9	9.0	24.4	11.0	16.7	14.2	16.3	10.9	6.5	33.8	51.8	6 361	28 060	341.1	12.9
Lakewood	19.1	16.8	25.0	7.9	19.8	11.6	11.3	11.7	12.7	33.0	48.1	58 211	58 163	-0.1	4.3
Longview	12.2	7.6	18.7	10.1	11.8	11.4	12.6	14.0	21.4	42.9	50.4	34 660	36 836	6.3	1.4
Lynnwood	14.0	28.4	20.9	8.8	13.3	15.5	15.2	12.1	14.2	39.7	52.3	33 847	35 845	5.9	6.3
Marysville	10.7	11.6	24.8	10.7	17.5	13.5	12.1	11.6	9.8	33.2	49.9	25 315	60 026	137.1	12.7
Mount Vernon	34.4	21.3	26.8	8.8	15.6	11.4	11.2	8.2	17.9	33.9	51.4	26 232	31 716	20.9	9.1
Olympia	6.9	9.8	19.2	9.4	14.1	15.4	13.8	12.5	15.6	39.9	50.1	42 514	46 880	10.3	9.2

1. May be of any race.

Table D. Cities — Households, Group Quarters, Crime, and Education

City	Households, 2015				Persons in group quarters, 2010				Serious crimes known to police[2] 2014				Educational attainment, 2015		
			Percent			Institutional			Total		Rate[3]			Attainment[4] (percent)	
	Number	Persons per house-hold	Female family house-holder[1]	One-person	Total	Total	Persons in nursing facilities	Non-institu-tional	Number	Rate[3]	Violent	Property	Population age 25 and older	High school graduate or less	Bachelor's degree or more
	27	28	29	30	31	32	33	34	35	36	37	38	39	40	41
UTAH—Cont'd															
Kaysville	7 860	3.88	10.4	6.9	24	0	0	24	210	719	51	667	15 605	21.5	45.1
Layton	22 883	3.24	11.0	16.5	44	26	0	18	1 596	2 228	123	2 105	42 409	28.3	29.5
Lehi	14 056	4.16	7.1	6.6	107	16	16	91	749	1 336	68	1 268	27 597	18.3	42.9
Logan	16 492	2.88	8.3	22.4	3 529	502	160	3 027	819	1 670	71	1 598	23 650	32.8	32.4
Midvale	12 455	2.61	12.5	31.3	85	10	0	75	NA	NA	NA	NA	20 201	36.7	31.6
Murray	18 517	2.65	12.0	29.2	175	124	97	51	2 644	5 387	454	4 932	32 877	32.4	29.1
Ogden	30 954	2.68	13.9	32.5	2 061	1 421	260	640	4 169	4 930	538	4 392	52 503	48.7	19.0
Orem	27 922	3.26	9.1	18.6	1 790	461	301	1 329	1 992	2 156	43	2 112	49 415	25.9	35.4
Pleasant Grove	11 231	3.38	9.3	18.2	51	42	42	9	275	779	42	736	20 071	25.2	34.6
Provo	31 821	3.28	7.0	11.0	10 353	1 037	223	9 316	2 388	2 038	131	1 907	47 279	21.4	43.3
Riverton	10 967	3.81	3.4	12.0	45	14	14	31	NA	NA	NA	NA	23 190	24.0	31.7
Roy	11 355	3.33	11.8	16.8	124	115	93	9	806	2 125	111	2 015	21 594	43.6	20.5
St. George	28 196	2.81	10.0	21.8	1 053	648	303	405	1 631	2 095	145	1 950	50 849	35.0	26.7
Salt Lake City	79 031	2.38	10.1	36.5	4 795	822	539	3 973	17 728	9 216	755	8 461	128 718	29.8	44.4
Sandy	28 926	3.22	8.6	17.2	365	287	287	78	2 714	2 987	175	2 812	58 531	27.1	38.9
South Jordan	18 458	3.61	7.2	14.8	7	7	7	0	1 424	2 312	78	2 234	40 002	20.3	43.1
Spanish Fork	9 762	3.74	5.2	10.7	832	813	27	19	497	1 327	24	1 303	19 234	33.8	27.8
Springville	9 068	3.54	10.8	18.1	119	119	55	0	650	2 057	108	1 950	16 004	25.9	37.9
Taylorsville	20 023	3.01	12.1	26.2	112	82	82	30	NA	NA	NA	NA	38 251	40.4	23.6
Tooele	10 879	3.02	7.1	23.2	243	237	103	6	1 469	4 520	314	4 206	19 870	38.5	22.6
West Jordan	32 234	3.46	10.8	15.4	502	394	162	108	2 288	2 050	191	1 859	65 801	37.4	24.0
West Valley City	35 654	3.81	15.3	14.0	193	158	77	35	6 620	4 919	473	4 446	81 210	55.7	13.7
VERMONT	254 865	2.36	7.9	30.3	25 329	5 571	3 588	19 758	10 173	1 624	99	1 524	438 654	37.3	36.9
Burlington	16 947	2.10	6.6	36.1	7 060	539	476	6 521	1 455	3 444	137	3 306	23 410	25.3	56.0
VIRGINIA	3 106 895	2.62	11.9	27.1	239 834	101 333	30 324	138 501	177 060	2 127	196	1 930	5 685 318	35.7	37.0
Alexandria	69 008	2.20	10.4	39.3	1 827	974	506	853	3 263	2 160	185	1 975	116 855	21.5	59.8
Blacksburg	14 648	2.43	8.3	28.7	8 718	150	134	8 568	424	967	73	894	17 134	17.3	69.9
Charlottesville	18 631	2.35	9.8	34.9	2 438	228	167	2 210	1 550	3 477	431	3 047	29 789	26.4	49.6
Chesapeake	83 593	2.73	15.3	20.9	3 721	3 258	650	463	7 428	3 195	430	2 765	157 207	31.7	31.8
Danville	18 705	2.16	18.6	40.6	1 483	987	558	496	1 965	4 577	447	4 129	29 184	52.2	18.2
Hampton	53 132	2.48	17.3	31.8	4 454	902	516	3 552	4 790	3 507	256	3 251	91 099	36.4	24.8
Harrisonburg	17 282	2.61	9.5	30.3	7 583	681	378	6 902	1 257	2 416	198	2 218	25 526	38.3	39.4
Leesburg	17 300	2.94	7.2	18.4	256	247	247	9	788	1 611	121	1 490	32 964	27.0	51.5
Lynchburg	27 864	2.48	17.6	29.3	10 198	1 534	863	8 664	2 372	3 016	472	2 545	45 037	39.0	33.0
Manassas	12 316	3.39	5.1	18.7	46	0	0	46	866	2 031	326	1 705	25 757	50.2	25.8
Newport News	70 546	2.46	17.2	32.3	7 499	1 555	633	5 944	6 334	3 473	429	3 044	115 693	36.8	24.6
Norfolk	87 819	2.51	17.9	34.0	32 780	2 746	924	30 034	10 981	4 444	520	3 924	150 965	41.2	26.6
Petersburg	13 728	2.30	19.2	42.2	1 058	587	273	471	1 036	3 183	593	2 590	21 426	59.0	17.2
Portsmouth	36 654	2.54	18.9	34.9	3 416	2 541	454	875	5 451	5 653	610	5 043	62 610	42.5	23.6
Richmond	91 396	2.29	15.9	43.7	12 725	2 884	1 312	9 841	NA	NA	NA	NA	150 042	37.6	37.7
Roanoke	41 501	2.35	17.9	36.9	2 126	1 083	517	1 043	4 476	4 524	344	4 180	69 434	48.2	21.7
Suffolk	32 232	2.72	18.7	20.6	1 128	1 029	267	99	2 485	2 890	272	2 618	58 380	41.0	27.7
Virginia Beach	169 097	2.61	12.8	25.6	9 253	2 961	1 520	6 292	10 532	2 335	148	2 187	305 033	29.6	32.8
Winchester	9 644	2.72	12.6	34.7	976	157	125	819	1 171	4 261	313	3 948	17 055	38.7	35.2
WASHINGTON	2 728 573	2.58	10.0	27.0	139 375	57 844	22 156	81 531	281 842	3 991	285	3 706	4 889 314	32.2	34.2
Auburn	27 829	2.73	11.7	24.3	668	289	228	379	4 900	6 446	397	6 048	50 842	42.7	25.1
Bellevue	56 937	2.43	7.4	27.6	1 110	154	154	956	4 750	3 507	106	3 401	101 300	14.1	65.6
Bellingham	32 933	2.44	10.2	34.8	5 172	1 065	570	4 107	4 934	5 941	270	5 671	51 443	24.9	41.1
Bothell	17 173	2.65	14.9	24.9	321	188	188	133	1 130	3 131	72	3 059	30 682	25.1	44.0
Bremerton	15 633	2.34	10.6	37.3	4 255	428	350	3 827	2 025	5 145	528	4 616	25 494	27.2	24.2
Burien	17 802	2.81	13.3	23.0	300	209	119	91	2 632	5 234	511	4 723	33 243	47.0	22.7
Des Moines	12 010	2.55	12.4	22.9	596	382	382	214	1 274	4 120	388	3 731	22 391	36.6	25.0
Edmonds	17 219	2.38	12.1	29.2	476	220	220	256	1 231	3 004	134	2 870	30 986	25.7	49.2
Everett	44 510	2.36	12.3	34.5	4 145	1 706	404	2 439	7 311	6 903	344	6 559	74 884	39.7	22.1
Federal Way	35 244	2.68	14.1	24.5	831	445	421	386	5 944	6 354	386	5 968	65 043	35.4	25.1
Issaquah	14 409	2.49	10.0	25.3	443	242	242	201	1 103	3 209	52	3 157	24 148	11.6	65.2
Kennewick	27 849	2.78	13.4	23.6	1 081	930	200	151	2 617	3 382	246	3 136	48 072	35.6	22.4
Kent	40 844	3.06	13.6	20.9	1 390	888	86	502	6 634	5 272	288	4 984	81 880	41.2	23.1
Kirkland	37 497	2.30	5.6	30.3	630	175	150	455	2 122	2 486	100	2 387	66 021	16.8	58.3
Lacey	17 589	2.59	15.0	25.7	998	207	204	791	1 507	3 310	182	3 128	29 917	24.2	33.0
Lake Stevens	10 351	2.98	12.3	14.6	29	5	5	24	830	2 731	165	2 567	19 947	32.1	29.5
Lakewood	21 932	2.68	16.6	30.3	1 268	992	152	276	2 860	4 822	644	4 178	40 143	40.2	19.2
Longview	15 270	2.34	12.9	35.7	962	769	389	193	2 453	6 728	365	6 363	26 209	45.8	18.0
Lynnwood	13 950	2.60	15.8	26.1	618	237	195	381	2 654	7 245	273	6 972	26 015	33.2	29.9
Marysville	23 790	2.79	6.6	22.8	600	225	191	375	2 897	4 522	175	4 347	43 083	37.0	21.4
Mount Vernon	12 475	2.67	11.5	24.3	639	399	173	240	1 595	4 862	265	4 597	21 928	39.0	25.4
Olympia	21 734	2.25	13.1	36.7	1 283	942	415	341	2 389	4 899	410	4 489	35 913	26.8	39.7

1. No spouse present.   2. Data for serious crimes have not been adjusted for underreporting. This may affect comparability between geographic areas and over time.   3. Per 100,000 population estimated by the FBI.   4. Persons 25 years old and over.

Table D. Cities — Income, Poverty, and Housing

City	Money income, 2015					Housing units, 2010			Occupied housing units 2015				
	Households			Families						Owner-occupied		Renter-occupied	
	Median income	Percent with income of $200,000 or more	Percent with income of less than $25,000	Total Families	Percent with income below poverty	Total	Percent change, 2000–2010	Vacant units for sale or rent[2]	Total	Percent	Median value[3] (dollars)	Percent	Median rent (dollars)
	42	43	44	45	46	47	48	49	50	51	52	53	54
UTAH—Cont'd													
Kaysville	89 892	6.5	3.7	NA	NA	7 700	35.3	176	7 860	91.6	288 300	8.4	963
Layton	73 242	3.3	7.9	18 573	9.3	22 356	16.8	981	22 883	69.9	220 000	30.1	963
Lehi	82 417	3.9	5.3	12 797	6.5	13 064	146.5	662	14 056	80.7	286 600	19.3	1 339
Logan	34 226	1.9	23.1	10 312	23.5	16 790	14.0	962	16 492	39.3	173 600	60.7	667
Midvale	51 125	1.3	13.3	7 496	7.1	11 764	9.6	851	12 455	43.4	218 600	56.6	1 036
Murray	62 364	3.7	11.6	11 785	7.0	19 181	44.1	955	18 517	66.5	257 100	33.5	976
Ogden	42 460	2.0	22.7	18 279	15.8	32 482	9.1	2 851	30 954	54.0	134 900	46.0	723
Orem	55 581	5.1	12.9	21 058	12.3	26 970	11.6	1 154	27 922	58.5	229 000	41.5	944
Pleasant Grove	62 096	2.5	13.3	NA	NA	9 841	55.1	460	11 231	61.2	259 200	38.8	1 025
Provo	46 388	3.5	20.8	22 583	17.9	33 212	9.2	1 688	31 821	40.6	227 600	59.4	790
Riverton	103 296	4.5	2.1	NA	NA	10 810	63.9	350	10 967	95.0	294 600	5.0	953
Roy	64 699	2.1	8.5	9 025	11.3	12 599	14.3	425	11 355	80.7	153 200	19.3	1 042
St. George	55 094	4.3	12.9	20 514	9.1	32 089	52.2	6 569	28 196	62.9	229 400	37.1	939
Salt Lake City	48 761	7.0	18.8	39 433	11.3	80 724	4.8	6 211	79 031	47.2	262 400	52.8	840
Sandy	81 581	6.7	6.8	22 517	5.0	29 501	10.8	1 205	28 926	74.2	315 800	25.8	1 168
South Jordan	99 681	11.1	4.0	NA	NA	14 943	92.5	610	18 458	76.3	354 000	23.7	1 395
Spanish Fork	69 672	3.4	10.0	8 341	7.0	9 440	62.3	371	9 762	71.8	223 400	28.2	1 199
Springville	60 316	2.1	10.4	6 999	9.2	8 927	42.7	396	9 068	72.7	204 000	27.3	1 022
Taylorsville	53 512	3.0	12.9	13 768	6.5	20 671	7.8	910	20 023	70.0	193 600	30.0	942
Tooele	62 138	1.2	9.1	7 826	3.9	10 646	33.6	687	10 879	74.0	163 800	26.0	952
West Jordan	68 928	3.3	6.0	26 006	6.4	31 366	60.2	1 517	32 234	74.2	239 500	25.8	1 133
West Valley City	57 111	1.7	11.5	27 813	12.9	38 978	16.4	1 839	35 654	67.2	178 400	32.8	953
VERMONT	56 990	4.2	15.6	152 379	5.8	322 539	9.6	66 097	254 865	70.7	223 700	29.3	923
Burlington	48 255	2.9	21.9	6 282	10.0	16 897	3.1	778	16 947	36.7	281 400	63.3	1 112
VIRGINIA	66 262	8.4	13.4	2 054 857	7.8	3 364 939	15.9	308 881	3 106 895	65.0	257 800	35.0	1 144
Alexandria	90 056	14.9	8.1	34 649	6.1	72 376	12.6	4 294	69 008	42.0	541 700	58.0	1 627
Blacksburg	40 133	3.6	33.1	NA	NA	15 342	12.5	887	14 648	24.5	297 100	75.5	1 076
Charlottesville	61 775	10.6	16.0	7 791	3.9	19 189	9.1	1 411	18 631	46.7	292 300	53.3	1 104
Chesapeake	67 491	5.0	8.8	62 739	7.9	83 196	14.5	3 622	83 593	67.9	259 200	32.1	1 218
Danville	32 966	1.8	29.9	10 156	15.7	22 438	-2.9	3 607	18 705	51.4	87 900	48.6	620
Hampton	51 867	2.1	19.0	32 109	12.4	59 566	3.9	4 535	53 132	56.0	183 700	44.0	1 053
Harrisonburg	40 520	2.7	22.0	8 051	14.6	17 444	27.4	1 456	17 282	37.4	219 600	62.6	768
Leesburg	112 673	19.0	9.2	12 861	3.0	15 119	41.7	678	17 300	74.7	391 500	25.3	1 477
Lynchburg	39 374	3.1	23.6	17 162	20.7	31 992	15.7	3 516	27 864	48.1	156 100	51.9	817
Manassas	73 682	3.5	9.8	9 424	7.7	13 123	8.3	596	12 316	60.3	316 200	39.7	1 485
Newport News	48 630	2.8	19.0	42 760	13.1	76 198	2.8	5 534	70 546	46.9	196 400	53.1	952
Norfolk	45 996	3.3	21.4	49 634	16.1	95 018	0.6	8 533	87 819	44.3	204 800	55.7	987
Petersburg	29 782	0.8	30.5	6 381	27.0	16 326	2.3	2 692	13 728	39.3	109 400	60.7	842
Portsmouth	49 242	1.6	21.9	21 198	14.4	40 806	-1.9	3 482	36 654	53.2	162 300	46.8	990
Richmond	39 906	5.2	27.5	40 310	17.0	98 349	6.6	11 198	91 396	40.2	199 900	59.8	927
Roanoke	39 835	2.2	26.3	22 183	21.0	47 453	4.9	4 741	41 501	50.5	134 100	49.5	759
Suffolk	61 203	4.2	16.1	24 202	11.7	33 035	33.7	2 167	32 232	67.5	234 200	32.5	995
Virginia Beach	67 281	4.7	8.9	113 342	5.8	177 879	9.6	12 790	169 097	62.6	262 900	37.4	1 258
Winchester	52 496	5.7	19.2	5 068	9.1	11 872	12.1	1 265	9 644	39.2	235 100	60.8	1 040
WASHINGTON	64 129	6.8	13.3	1 760 593	7.9	2 885 677	17.7	265 601	2 728 573	62.4	284 000	37.6	1 080
Auburn	70 602	6.2	8.0	18 642	6.3	27 834	66.3	1 776	27 829	63.3	275 200	36.7	1 089
Bellevue	98 804	18.9	10.4	35 401	5.3	55 551	15.0	5 196	56 937	53.3	645 300	46.7	1 693
Bellingham	49 245	2.8	21.5	15 549	7.5	36 760	24.9	2 089	32 933	48.9	297 900	51.1	910
Bothell	80 075	10.0	9.4	11 585	4.6	14 255	15.3	758	17 173	64.2	391 900	35.8	1 493
Bremerton	51 066	1.3	16.0	8 502	5.0	17 273	3.9	2 341	15 633	40.2	182 000	59.8	885
Burien	56 290	4.5	11.8	12 530	13.6	14 322	2.1	1 069	17 802	57.9	308 100	42.1	1 075
Des Moines	66 502	4.7	10.6	8 639	10.5	12 588	6.2	924	12 010	63.0	290 500	37.0	1 270
Edmonds	77 453	11.3	7.6	10 093	2.8	18 378	4.9	997	17 219	69.8	434 500	30.2	1 236
Everett	51 755	3.8	16.2	24 161	9.6	44 609	15.6	3 297	44 510	45.4	263 200	54.6	1 033
Federal Way	62 174	3.0	15.2	23 625	10.0	35 444	8.8	2 256	35 244	62.8	274 700	37.2	1 067
Issaquah	91 964	11.8	5.0	9 870	4.5	13 914	173.6	1 073	14 409	66.0	459 100	34.0	1 756
Kennewick	52 202	1.5	18.0	19 102	15.6	28 507	29.3	1 241	27 849	60.6	181 900	39.4	782
Kent	66 790	6.3	10.2	29 162	8.5	36 424	12.0	2 380	40 844	56.7	282 300	43.3	1 178
Kirkland	102 420	17.1	7.2	23 334	3.6	24 345	11.0	1 900	37 497	65.8	529 200	34.2	1 620
Lacey	59 727	1.0	10.6	12 304	11.4	18 493	41.4	1 544	17 589	52.9	233 400	47.1	1 123
Lake Stevens	92 227	6.1	4.8	7 823	6.0	10 414	NA	604	10 351	73.0	295 600	27.0	1 553
Lakewood	45 232	1.9	18.3	13 950	16.8	26 548	4.7	2 479	21 932	45.7	218 500	54.3	902
Longview	40 810	2.4	25.4	8 295	20.9	16 380	7.7	1 099	15 270	54.3	157 700	45.7	801
Lynnwood	58 491	2.5	20.5	8 395	17.0	14 939	8.5	832	13 950	50.4	338 800	49.6	1 133
Marysville	75 120	1.6	10.7	16 113	6.6	22 363	130.6	1 144	23 790	61.8	251 300	38.2	1 255
Mount Vernon	48 516	0.7	16.4	9 063	14.4	12 058	24.0	716	12 475	61.6	212 500	38.4	804
Olympia	53 761	3.7	19.1	11 479	9.9	22 086	12.1	1 325	21 734	45.8	255 500	54.2	974

1. Based on population estimated by the American Community Survey.   2. Includes units rented or sold but not occupied.   3. Specified owner-occupied units; $1,000,000 represents $1,000,000 or more   4. 50.0 represents 50 percent or more.   5. 10.0 represents 10 percent or less.

Table D. Cities — Commuting, Computer Access, Migration, Labor Force, and Employment

| | Commuting | | Computer Access[2] | | Migration, 2015 | | Civilian labor force, 2016 | | | | Civilian employment[4], 2015 | | | |
| | Percent | | Percent | | | | | | Unemployment | | Population age 16 and older | | Population age 16 to 64 | |
City	Drove alone	With Commutes of 30 minutes or more[1]	With a Computer in the house	With Internet Access	Percent who lived in the same house one year ago	Percent who lived in an other state or county one year ago	Total	Percent change, 2015–2016	Total	Rate[3]	Number	Percent in Labor Force	Number	Percent who worked full-year full-time
	55	56	57	58	59	60	61	62	63	64	65	66	67	68
UTAH—Cont'd														
Kaysville	82.9	31.6	NA	NA	89.0	5.6	14 055	2.7	407	2.9	19 544	70.5	17 194	49.9
Layton	80.0	28.9	95.1	88.5	80.0	10.2	37 522	2.5	1 220	3.3	53 114	72.5	47 249	48.0
Lehi	80.9	32.8	98.3	92.2	85.5	6.7	25 231	4.6	743	2.9	33 686	69.3	31 360	45.8
Logan	72.3	12.3	91.3	77.1	68.2	15.8	27 577	2.0	857	3.1	39 198	66.3	35 309	34.5
Midvale	77.5	16.7	95.6	78.8	92.2	2.6	19 808	2.8	622	3.1	22 716	78.3	20 228	65.8
Murray	78.2	20.5	93.3	80.6	85.5	4.1	29 207	3.0	926	3.2	39 968	70.2	32 294	52.6
Ogden	81.2	18.5	87.9	68.9	75.4	8.0	40 814	2.6	1 830	4.5	64 802	65.7	56 347	50.1
Orem	81.2	15.0	94.0	83.7	77.3	7.3	48 605	4.7	1 486	3.1	68 793	66.7	59 358	42.6
Pleasant Grove	82.8	28.9	96.3	78.8	87.0	5.7	18 547	4.7	555	3.0	25 994	66.9	21 822	41.6
Provo	67.2	13.6	96.7	75.5	61.3	17.7	64 904	4.7	1 900	2.9	91 153	70.3	84 910	28.8
Riverton	87.9	35.7	96.5	80.7	94.2	3.6	22 976	3.3	654	2.8	27 401	74.1	24 713	55.6
Roy	85.3	20.7	94.4	88.5	85.8	7.8	18 783	2.5	744	4.0	26 662	66.0	23 769	45.2
St. George	82.6	7.0	92.9	85.5	83.1	6.8	34 927	5.7	1 259	3.6	63 065	55.8	46 258	41.7
Salt Lake City	71.2	18.5	92.3	79.6	75.4	8.7	110 607	3.1	3 395	3.1	157 759	70.5	135 434	52.4
Sandy	83.4	27.4	93.2	84.4	85.8	4.1	52 301	3.1	1 602	3.1	69 739	70.3	60 422	51.5
South Jordan	82.0	41.3	98.4	85.8	88.4	6.1	33 961	3.1	1 026	3.0	47 336	72.0	40 828	53.4
Spanish Fork	83.0	18.4	94.2	90.0	80.8	7.3	17 020	4.7	551	3.2	25 538	66.5	23 290	44.4
Springville	84.3	21.5	94.8	86.4	82.4	3.8	15 862	4.6	480	3.0	20 468	64.9	17 670	43.9
Taylorsville	76.9	24.9	89.4	80.9	87.7	4.0	34 117	3.1	1 146	3.4	45 578	71.5	38 462	55.0
Tooele	76.4	53.9	93.6	85.1	81.5	7.7	16 139	3.1	677	4.2	24 427	68.7	21 298	57.2
West Jordan	81.5	31.9	94.7	87.8	87.2	3.4	61 459	3.1	1 926	3.1	79 865	75.0	73 328	55.0
West Valley City	78.0	25.7	92.1	83.3	80.9	6.6	70 823	3.0	2 447	3.5	100 293	71.1	88 315	52.8
VERMONT	81.9	30.1	87.0	79.1	85.9	6.5	344 892	-0.2	11 252	3.3	521 616	65.4	411 532	50.7
Burlington	57.4	17.2	88.7	82.0	66.7	15.6	24 116	0.4	633	2.6	39 185	65.7	33 706	38.0
VIRGINIA	81.3	41.4	88.2	78.7	83.9	9.3	4 240 403	0.7	170 143	4.0	6 721 590	66.0	5 534 146	52.9
Alexandria	60.5	52.6	94.8	87.8	76.3	15.6	95 389	1.4	2 740	2.9	127 843	79.2	111 928	63.4
Blacksburg	65.4	15.1	98.6	92.8	53.5	24.9	20 423	0.1	1 012	5.0	40 936	50.3	38 384	24.7
Charlottesville	60.3	19.4	92.0	83.3	73.3	21.2	24 830	0.9	831	3.3	40 416	69.0	35 743	47.9
Chesapeake	89.9	43.2	91.8	86.0	84.8	11.7	116 459	0.3	4 973	4.3	185 571	66.0	156 617	53.9
Danville	86.2	14.5	70.8	59.5	88.3	4.7	19 036	-0.3	1 144	6.0	33 952	58.5	25 588	44.3
Hampton	84.3	26.2	89.5	78.3	76.9	12.7	64 276	0.1	3 614	5.6	110 700	63.5	91 273	48.3
Harrisonburg	68.3	13.5	88.3	69.1	70.9	17.5	24 269	1.7	1 142	4.7	44 655	58.2	40 433	35.9
Leesburg	79.0	47.6	96.7	93.2	86.3	5.8	27 678	1.5	857	3.1	40 271	79.5	35 695	65.3
Lynchburg	76.8	12.0	77.9	64.9	81.9	9.2	35 374	-0.6	1 825	5.2	66 333	54.7	55 234	34.8
Manassas	84.7	52.0	89.4	77.9	84.1	10.5	21 834	1.2	776	3.6	30 620	69.1	26 409	56.9
Newport News	80.4	30.9	90.1	78.4	78.2	12.5	88 891	0.2	4 516	5.1	143 372	67.0	121 443	49.3
Norfolk	79.6	27.4	88.9	79.4	72.1	16.3	110 644	0.2	5 794	5.2	201 442	67.6	176 217	53.8
Petersburg	74.9	27.4	71.1	47.5	74.6	9.5	13 509	0.2	1 033	7.6	26 663	62.2	21 697	43.0
Portsmouth	84.3	28.4	84.1	70.2	81.5	11.2	44 370	0.4	2 688	6.1	75 328	65.5	62 088	48.0
Richmond	73.3	25.4	84.2	70.6	72.1	14.0	113 825	1.1	5 226	4.6	184 118	65.7	158 778	44.8
Roanoke	82.7	33.5	83.5	67.5	76.0	9.7	48 994	0.3	2 085	4.3	79 986	61.7	64 720	47.8
Suffolk	89.6	48.1	88.8	72.4	85.2	7.5	42 341	0.2	1 983	4.7	68 689	65.2	56 735	51.9
Virginia Beach	86.3	32.7	92.8	84.8	81.2	8.8	228 787	0.1	9 012	3.9	362 302	70.7	305 046	56.6
Winchester	70.7	37.4	79.6	68.7	77.3	17.7	14 289	0.7	563	3.9	21 703	64.8	17 696	45.1
WASHINGTON	76.8	38.6	91.4	84.0	81.5	7.5	3 643 881	2.8	198 001	5.4	5 741 873	63.7	4 705 247	48.5
Auburn	80.1	45.9	94.3	89.9	86.5	3.9	39 549	2.6	1 726	4.4	61 784	64.9	51 948	53.8
Bellevue	70.4	32.9	97.3	93.2	79.3	8.4	77 754	2.6	2 778	3.6	113 850	66.9	93 679	52.8
Bellingham	70.2	16.3	93.7	87.5	70.6	10.7	45 042	3.4	2 587	5.7	73 901	63.8	60 966	37.9
Bothell	79.2	51.3	94.8	86.8	81.2	11.1	24 166	2.6	939	3.9	36 434	69.8	31 459	54.5
Bremerton	58.1	23.8	88.0	79.2	75.7	14.0	16 516	2.5	1 174	7.1	33 710	63.7	27 608	53.9
Burien	73.8	35.3	92.1	85.8	86.3	3.3	26 665	2.5	1 064	4.0	38 857	67.3	32 997	47.5
Des Moines	88.6	41.1	95.4	89.7	82.9	3.5	16 472	2.4	773	4.7	25 704	67.1	20 559	49.7
Edmonds	79.3	52.4	95.3	89.2	84.4	6.5	22 699	2.7	931	4.1	35 919	67.7	27 239	53.4
Everett	72.3	36.7	88.1	82.3	74.6	8.1	55 486	2.4	2 666	4.8	89 099	65.6	74 548	48.8
Federal Way	77.5	51.1	91.6	85.4	85.0	4.8	49 276	2.4	2 243	4.6	76 948	66.5	64 295	47.3
Issaquah	78.1	49.6	98.9	92.7	82.4	7.4	20 218	2.7	695	3.4	27 654	70.8	23 727	54.2
Kennewick	81.8	26.5	85.6	78.3	79.6	5.0	39 167	3.1	2 531	6.5	58 845	64.3	49 981	47.2
Kent	74.9	50.5	93.0	87.9	76.9	9.6	64 753	2.3	2 948	4.6	99 862	67.2	87 166	49.1
Kirkland	75.9	49.2	96.4	92.1	84.4	5.7	51 822	2.7	1 773	3.4	73 033	68.3	59 956	56.2
Lacey	82.6	30.6	94.0	87.0	71.8	17.0	19 983	4.0	1 285	6.4	36 040	59.0	28 103	48.8
Lake Stevens	79.9	53.0	97.3	91.3	80.3	3.6	15 981	2.6	448	2.8	24 438	69.3	22 440	55.7
Lakewood	80.8	42.6	89.4	72.6	77.2	11.2	25 790	3.6	1 729	6.7	45 787	64.8	38 182	46.9
Longview	81.8	20.8	83.4	69.8	73.2	8.7	15 194	1.8	1 160	7.6	30 531	50.9	22 661	36.4
Lynnwood	71.5	45.4	90.6	81.3	83.9	6.4	19 710	2.6	913	4.6	29 754	66.5	24 485	54.4
Marysville	82.3	45.0	92.5	87.7	79.7	6.6	33 960	2.7	1 296	3.8	52 094	70.6	45 542	52.7
Mount Vernon	78.8	34.7	91.2	85.1	83.6	7.5	15 115	2.4	1 043	6.9	25 745	64.0	19 644	46.6
Olympia	75.7	21.5	93.0	81.1	75.4	12.7	26 491	4.3	1 460	5.5	41 984	57.4	34 131	44.9

1. Employed persons. 2. Households. 3. Percent of civilian labor force. 4. Persons 16 years old and over.

Table D. Cities — Construction, Wholesale Trade, and Retail Trade

City	Value of residential construction authorized by building permits, 2016			Wholesale trade,[1] 2012				Retail trade,[2] 2012			
	New construction ($1,000)	Number of housing units	Percent single family	Number of establish-ments	Number of employees	Sales (mil dol)	Annual payroll (mil dol)	Number of establish-ments	Number of employees	Sales (mil dol)	Annual payroll (mil dol)
	69	70	71	72	73	74	75	76	77	78	79
UTAH—Cont'd											
Kaysville	58 332	170	100.0	22	269	117.4	11.7	62	707	169.1	17.7
Layton	70 321	317	76.3	47	321	117.8	10.7	295	4 761	1 123.0	106.0
Lehi	173 958	616	100.0	22	303	180.4	15.0	144	2 159	637.8	63.4
Logan	19 306	124	74.2	67	606	435.2	23.7	248	3 710	725.7	71.2
Midvale	41 168	207	8.2	48	604	354.9	25.5	149	2 153	554.8	53.1
Murray	41 836	227	22.9	109	1 032	520.2	54.1	353	5 656	1 921.1	161.3
Ogden	16 158	123	49.6	100	1 412	949.3	67.5	344	3 839	1 121.8	93.9
Orem	76 389	354	32.5	102	1 421	658.4	62.1	451	7 296	1 843.7	165.6
Pleasant Grove	33 515	124	91.9	19	75	28.7	2.6	65	675	219.9	21.0
Provo	60 917	259	71.8	55	1 506	1 153.2	99.6	317	4 334	1 205.9	98.9
Riverton	75 590	298	65.8	21	76	42.2	2.7	68	1 184	261.9	25.9
Roy	13 395	176	16.5	7	D	D	D	72	906	236.3	19.3
St. George	145 825	902	88.2	106	D	D	D	425	5 477	1 468.9	126.9
Salt Lake City	403 258	3 265	2.8	603	12 541	10 292.8	748.3	918	14 096	4 071.1	374.7
Sandy	34 370	231	23.8	130	1 173	847.6	59.8	382	6 580	2 199.2	187.0
South Jordan	226 812	869	98.4	38	1 231	900.5	73.8	112	2 249	662.1	55.5
Spanish Fork	70 586	291	93.5	19	186	106.2	7.3	88	1 077	204.4	19.6
Springville	27 431	115	73.9	25	639	228.5	25.2	74	1 095	301.6	23.9
Taylorsville	8 204	33	93.9	18	76	41.8	2.9	101	1 695	375.1	36.2
Tooele	17 581	131	98.5	7	D	D	D	75	1 334	361.7	31.4
West Jordan	108 825	445	86.5	76	1 201	1 118.5	66.9	207	3 971	945.0	84.5
West Valley City	21 798	171	97.7	143	2 669	1 906.8	143.3	280	5 549	1 457.0	157.9
VERMONT	1 230	5	100.0	696	9 464	6 450.1	464.4	3 509	38 910	9 933.8	967.1
Burlington	2 238	40	2.5	48	539	327.8	37.4	224	3 271	610.2	75.9
VIRGINIA	187 279	708	73.6	6 232	88 353	86 613.6	4 983.1	27 415	410 918	110 002.4	10 007.9
Alexandria	84 900	621	23.3	82	1 139	502.8	61.6	480	7 180	2 416.0	222.6
Blacksburg	27 794	216	61.1	14	D	D	D	97	1 363	284.4	22.3
Charlottesville	34 689	197	39.6	48	513	183.3	23.7	331	3 925	747.9	82.8
Chesapeake	297 574	1 065	91.7	239	3 447	2 225.2	169.7	789	15 088	4 114.9	336.7
Danville	660	5	100.0	50	545	285.2	24.5	306	4 165	965.0	87.2
Hampton	9 214	149	100.0	71	886	344.7	39.3	436	6 791	1 512.5	148.3
Harrisonburg	24 849	151	84.1	57	1 006	405.9	43.2	334	5 664	1 519.8	144.6
Leesburg	NA	NA	NA	27	366	172.4	19.0	266	5 403	1 388.7	124.5
Lynchburg	16 471	154	39.0	69	877	509.0	39.0	385	7 371	1 995.2	178.2
Manassas	20 436	145	100.0	41	D	D	D	194	2 778	895.3	86.1
Newport News	15 601	232	51.7	110	1 438	851.3	72.7	686	9 879	2 480.8	229.7
Norfolk	78 709	1 045	36.2	209	3 287	3 195.3	161.6	867	12 440	2 683.2	281.6
Petersburg	3 768	77	14.3	21	570	560.1	16.2	145	1 426	334.5	33.0
Portsmouth	15 135	124	98.4	48	688	249.5	32.0	273	3 081	699.5	71.1
Richmond	72 308	510	54.9	269	3 767	3 288.5	201.3	808	8 666	1 955.2	206.1
Roanoke	21 281	153	9.8	180	2 727	1 398.0	130.3	535	9 912	2 461.0	230.1
Suffolk	73 334	707	55.9	54	961	666.0	49.8	226	3 536	958.9	79.1
Virginia Beach	219 498	1 583	48.5	391	6 893	8 187.6	477.1	1 500	22 723	5 671.5	521.6
Winchester	6 584	30	83.3	39	677	286.8	26.1	283	4 126	888.5	94.4
WASHINGTON	9 116 339	44 077	51.0	7 733	103 307	83 313.4	5 789.8	21 588	307 089	118 924.0	8 722.5
Auburn	95 954	534	43.1	174	3 739	4 631.5	198.0	281	4 676	1 475.0	140.8
Bellevue	302 630	1 587	15.0	324	4 333	5 128.3	368.3	673	12 225	4 113.9	412.6
Bellingham	80 700	527	37.0	147	D	D	D	532	8 805	2 243.5	206.9
Bothell	114 716	609	24.5	63	1 357	1 465.7	112.4	100	1 451	363.3	41.6
Bremerton	34 045	251	38.2	27	191	83.1	9.6	134	1 704	572.5	55.8
Burien	52 703	258	30.2	23	138	33.0	4.7	163	2 013	573.1	58.3
Des Moines	11 645	39	56.4	15	116	91.7	10.1	38	360	93.3	10.2
Edmonds	30 767	126	42.9	39	201	177.8	12.4	133	1 449	448.2	43.9
Everett	51 653	228	80.3	134	2 108	1 355.6	129.1	449	6 782	2 023.4	194.6
Federal Way	20 219	63	58.7	54	450	250.1	22.5	257	4 441	1 184.1	118.0
Issaquah	68 967	157	80.9	44	272	372.7	17.3	136	3 108	2 801.7	110.1
Kennewick	94 778	401	82.0	67	659	927.9	31.5	378	6 113	1 620.4	148.4
Kent	84 983	409	48.7	430	8 772	6 803.7	509.9	340	4 711	1 447.2	137.9
Kirkland	179 160	542	57.6	104	1 023	656.4	81.0	216	4 128	1 776.8	148.9
Lacey	151 119	879	38.1	23	493	421.0	24.6	148	3 567	869.8	92.1
Lake Stevens	103 357	370	100.0	6	40	15.9	1.2	45	848	219.2	20.3
Lakewood	9 531	33	87.9	67	834	1 407.2	41.8	227	2 725	701.2	69.7
Longview	7 299	50	30.0	39	637	712.5	30.9	175	3 043	796.3	78.7
Lynnwood	5 158	14	100.0	95	794	407.1	44.8	425	7 823	2 042.0	210.1
Marysville	56 311	335	36.1	34	236	117.4	12.5	172	3 450	933.4	88.4
Mount Vernon	23 658	144	100.0	32	385	219.6	18.1	135	2 017	491.7	53.0
Olympia	57 008	306	60.5	39	390	461.9	24.3	367	5 515	1 396.7	142.3

1. Merchant wholesalers except manufacturers' sales branches and offices.   2. Establishments with payroll.

Table D. Cities — Real Estate, Professional Services, and Manufacturing

City	Real estate and rental and leasing, 2012				Professional, scientific, and technical services,[1] 2012				Manufacturing, 2012			
	Number of establish-ments	Number of employees	Receipts (mil dol)	Annual payroll (mil dol)	Number of establish-ments	Number of employees	Receipts (mil dol)	Annual payroll (mil dol)	Number of establish-ments	Number of employees	Receipts (mil dol)	Annual payroll (mil dol)
	80	81	82	83	84	85	86	87	88	89	90	91
UTAH—Cont'd												
Kaysville	36	77	11.5	2.4	90	647	74.6	35.3	15	180	37.4	7.1
Layton	111	313	69.3	9.9	177	D	D	D	43	870	372.5	39.8
Lehi	58	70	17.2	3.3	173	D	D	D	32	518	198.1	27.0
Logan	108	396	57.3	14.3	179	D	D	D	112	7 049	2 431.3	301.9
Midvale	69	468	105.0	25.5	92	D	D	D	34	435	D	18.9
Murray	134	1 271	154.0	51.4	300	2 624	380.0	136.7	118	1 590	320.6	65.0
Ogden	100	413	51.5	10.6	245	D	D	D	134	7 939	3 135.1	383.0
Orem	185	566	108.3	15.8	358	7 806	401.3	195.9	122	2 729	780.8	124.9
Pleasant Grove	48	98	13.9	3.4	99	670	83.9	32.6	30	238	D	9.1
Provo	120	569	85.7	13.1	346	D	D	D	81	1 908	376.7	96.3
Riverton	41	95	15.9	2.7	89	191	14.6	4.9	8	D	D	0.7
Roy	19	54	5.6	1.0	29	249	16.2	8.5	17	65	8.1	D
St. George	218	541	77.1	14.8	324	D	D	D	87	1 376	322.3	55.1
Salt Lake City	528	3 093	878.2	142.4	1 434	16 666	3 114.5	1 238.7	457	24 316	11 969.2	1 556.7
Sandy	202	654	157.6	28.0	443	2 500	324.0	131.8	103	2 619	891.9	137.8
South Jordan	93	253	42.3	10.3	230	1 478	223.0	60.7	23	D	D	D
Spanish Fork	29	60	12.7	2.1	80	381	36.1	9.2	39	1 771	671.8	94.5
Springville	19	21	2.9	0.6	66	320	29.0	10.5	46	3 092	1 538.7	143.1
Taylorsville	48	157	20.9	4.6	85	D	D	D	17	601	85.8	26.6
Tooele	19	61	8.5	1.3	32	165	13.4	6.1	19	729	343.7	D
West Jordan	82	181	30.4	5.2	153	D	D	D	106	2 439	895.2	116.7
West Valley City	73	525	111.5	24.5	118	D	D	D	156	4 762	2 397.5	240.5
VERMONT	741	3 092	509.9	103.6	2 093	15 781	1 762.8	730.9	1 013	31 487	9 315.5	1 594.3
Burlington	61	347	91.9	15.5	267	D	D	D	24	613	192.2	30.9
VIRGINIA	8 862	54 246	11 758.9	2 378.3	29 176	416 651	90 042.2	35 093.6	5 101	228 197	96 389.9	11 586.1
Alexandria	240	1 475	524.1	76.6	1 228	16 537	3 436.0	1 497.8	72	1 332	273.0	57.9
Blacksburg	50	393	73.4	14.9	153	D	D	D	20	1 473	514.6	99.8
Charlottesville	99	502	107.6	19.7	316	D	D	D	46	455	98.7	21.6
Chesapeake	273	1 227	291.6	52.9	509	7 649	1 029.3	412.6	130	3 965	1 504.2	211.6
Danville	64	339	48.7	9.1	72	D	D	D	46	4 635	1 703.0	223.7
Hampton	114	750	117.3	23.7	273	D	D	D	68	2 189	508.3	114.9
Harrisonburg	72	351	75.9	10.9	137	D	D	D	46	2 556	832.6	99.4
Leesburg	64	288	136.2	14.5	302	D	D	D	11	347	D	D
Lynchburg	109	447	79.9	14.5	199	D	D	D	83	8 339	2 749.6	504.3
Manassas	52	229	64.0	11.4	212	D	D	D	32	4 012	1 365.7	366.4
Newport News	254	1 672	276.5	60.3	361	D	D	D	91	26 503	5 578.9	1 558.5
Norfolk	291	2 496	430.8	127.7	700	D	D	D	130	6 866	1 812.5	328.2
Petersburg	32	223	27.2	5.8	34	D	D	D	28	1 646	D	91.0
Portsmouth	71	332	52.6	9.7	144	D	D	D	56	2 196	447.1	97.6
Richmond	258	1 539	304.3	67.1	844	10 249	2 511.6	888.8	187	5 882	16 885.9	386.3
Roanoke	155	950	141.8	31.0	326	D	D	D	100	3 869	1 629.7	174.8
Suffolk	67	243	37.5	8.1	121	D	D	D	46	1 996	1 521.0	103.6
Virginia Beach	649	6 165	902.5	210.7	1 391	17 195	3 883.4	1 188.8	207	5 616	1 954.2	255.1
Winchester	59	260	56.4	8.0	130	D	D	D	23	2 197	866.2	117.6
WASHINGTON	9 913	45 209	9 695.5	1 895.1	19 882	D	D	D	6 992	248 192	131 530.6	14 461.8
Auburn	86	344	96.7	13.9	120	D	D	D	159	9 859	1 243.4	582.4
Bellevue	517	3 594	974.9	195.2	1 260	14 873	2 735.3	1 204.9	115	1 733	621.1	87.9
Bellingham	199	847	193.4	27.6	432	D	D	D	126	3 061	D	129.2
Bothell	75	269	75.9	9.9	201	D	D	D	38	3 273	1 724.1	260.6
Bremerton	67	218	38.4	6.6	83	D	D	D	21	578	D	27.2
Burien	72	226	38.4	6.5	95	477	40.2	15.8	28	82	D	2.8
Des Moines	16	36	6.0	1.1	32	106	9.0	3.5	6	18	3.2	0.8
Edmonds	76	205	46.1	10.6	174	755	109.3	45.1	19	214	D	9.2
Everett	168	1 056	172.8	36.9	312	D	D	D	134	43 136	D	3 324.1
Federal Way	101	442	92.4	15.2	167	1 491	176.7	97.4	25	347	D	12.5
Issaquah	77	311	89.4	14.5	189	1 046	145.5	96.2	27	1 407	505.4	96.3
Kennewick	117	683	123.7	19.6	202	D	D	D	45	714	293.9	37.4
Kent	155	866	200.1	36.9	217	1 766	282.1	127.2	247	14 012	7 642.4	924.1
Kirkland	182	867	643.3	64.0	457	D	D	D	50	668	146.4	34.4
Lacey	54	210	45.1	6.0	74	2 388	319.2	147.8	17	415	D	19.8
Lake Stevens	30	D	D	D	20	69	7.1	2.5	12	D	5.4	D
Lakewood	102	445	85.3	12.9	111	544	55.3	21.0	36	585	D	24.6
Longview	55	208	34.2	5.8	83	D	D	D	37	2 469	1 391.6	203.7
Lynnwood	90	307	99.0	13.1	155	D	D	D	48	675	213.4	31.0
Marysville	63	218	67.8	9.8	60	336	31.8	8.4	55	1 672	340.2	68.8
Mount Vernon	56	143	24.1	4.4	117	512	64.3	22.6	32	673	328.2	26.9
Olympia	114	428	88.3	14.2	280	1 524	210.6	88.8	32	514	205.9	24.6

1. Establishments subject to federal tax.

Table D. Cities — Accommodation and Food Services, Arts, Entertainment, and Recreation, and Health Care and Social Assistance

City	Accommodation and food services, 2012				Arts, entertainment, and recreation,[1] 2012				Health care and social assistance,[1] 2012			
	Number of establish-ments	Number of employees	Sales (mil dol)	Annual payroll (mil dol)	Number of establish-ments	Number of employees	Receipts (mil dol)	Annual payroll (mil dol)	Number of establish-ments	Number of employees	Receipts (mil dol)	Annual payroll (mil dol)
	92	93	94	95	96	97	98	99	100	101	102	103
UTAH—Cont'd												
Kaysville	16	354	11.4	3.4	6	239	14.9	3.3	52	D	D	D
Layton	149	3 414	138.2	40.9	19	D	D	D	156	2 734	304.0	116.0
Lehi	50	1 117	48.2	12.4	17	D	D	D	62	D	D	D
Logan	120	2 287	98.7	26.6	19	244	10.7	1.9	175	D	D	D
Midvale	94	1 572	73.1	21.6	6	D	D	D	53	D	D	D
Murray	113	2 538	120.0	40.6	13	D	D	D	298	D	D	D
Ogden	184	3 206	124.0	36.2	14	D	D	D	270	D	D	D
Orem	152	3 262	148.0	43.6	43	D	D	D	238	4 058	391.5	134.5
Pleasant Grove	29	280	12.9	3.1	11	35	4.6	0.8	60	D	D	D
Provo	186	3 335	143.9	40.6	32	387	25.6	7.2	285	D	D	D
Riverton	48	758	32.8	9.6	5	10	0.8	0.2	79	D	D	D
Roy	40	661	29.6	7.4	5	55	1.5	0.6	53	D	D	D
St. George	216	3 957	197.1	55.1	30	393	13.9	4.6	383	D	D	D
Salt Lake City	735	16 057	961.6	277.0	77	1 617	227.7	90.4	587	5 979	775.9	270.9
Sandy	188	3 696	173.1	49.7	28	D	D	D	272	D	D	D
South Jordan	68	1 569	65.6	20.3	13	D	D	D	123	D	D	D
Spanish Fork	40	664	28.4	7.4	7	D	D	D	59	644	44.7	15.2
Springville	39	D	D	D	7	26	1.6	0.3	63	D	D	D
Taylorsville	83	1 618	80.8	21.1	11	D	D	D	100	1 045	93.1	34.5
Tooele	45	755	33.8	8.9	6	60	3.3	1.1	58	D	D	D
West Jordan	116	2 362	125.2	32.2	13	D	D	D	170	2 883	365.1	92.4
West Valley City	179	2 987	161.6	43.4	18	D	D	D	101	D	D	D
VERMONT	1 920	31 365	1 564.3	494.0	286	5 468	233.6	73.7	1 370	14 976	1 297.2	578.2
Burlington	151	2 846	172.1	51.6	12	107	7.2	2.0	96	1 655	135.2	70.7
VIRGINIA	16 832	320 514	17 795.9	4 908.6	1 970	35 718	2 993.0	875.7	16 070	236 459	25 556.4	10 868.1
Alexandria	387	8 051	647.5	180.7	41	606	45.8	15.2	343	3 739	466.5	194.6
Blacksburg	100	2 054	91.4	25.1	7	D	D	D	93	1 512	197.5	73.2
Charlottesville	293	5 199	293.3	75.9	25	D	D	D	121	D	D	D
Chesapeake	466	10 267	447.6	121.1	42	D	D	D	456	6 275	637.4	290.0
Danville	139	2 850	120.4	33.6	11	D	D	D	175	3 730	374.9	152.4
Hampton	250	5 380	249.0	72.2	23	D	D	D	217	3 137	322.2	134.7
Harrisonburg	186	4 468	216.0	58.8	11	D	D	D	128	2 006	163.9	75.6
Leesburg	118	2 305	135.4	37.9	11	D	D	D	166	1 736	209.9	92.8
Lynchburg	215	5 071	216.4	61.0	21	243	10.2	3.1	205	D	D	D
Manassas	109	1 587	91.4	24.7	10	116	4.8	1.4	157	D	D	D
Newport News	386	6 621	323.8	87.6	28	D	D	D	327	6 977	693.3	380.1
Norfolk	593	11 264	547.1	148.4	41	504	37.2	10.7	422	6 733	776.7	359.3
Petersburg	79	885	39.1	10.2	6	D	D	D	103	3 619	364.2	135.7
Portsmouth	172	2 624	107.1	29.3	17	119	10.7	2.2	166	3 362	274.4	117.8
Richmond	618	11 470	576.5	184.1	53	896	52.7	10.8	441	11 147	1 922.8	628.0
Roanoke	320	6 509	308.1	94.4	17	188	7.9	2.6	228	4 017	462.5	191.5
Suffolk	147	2 477	122.9	30.6	12	D	D	D	155	2 625	273.4	125.1
Virginia Beach	1 153	21 910	1 202.7	324.3	153	1 714	129.4	31.6	919	12 464	1 177.1	571.3
Winchester	130	2 518	119.1	33.1	12	D	D	D	226	D	D	D
WASHINGTON	16 333	234 145	14 297.3	4 159.7	2 029	41 184	4 079.6	1 177.3	16 888	194 136	20 414.0	8 703.2
Auburn	145	1 859	107.0	30.9	28	D	D	D	163	2 421	232.0	100.8
Bellevue	432	8 993	618.4	184.7	63	1 856	151.9	47.0	887	8 423	958.7	398.7
Bellingham	325	5 589	277.4	84.5	50	434	20.2	6.1	423	4 236	422.2	171.3
Bothell	140	1 982	120.6	32.9	7	D	D	D	152	1 457	128.3	50.7
Bremerton	108	1 440	88.2	22.7	6	76	2.2	0.9	110	2 072	208.8	76.9
Burien	103	1 221	61.3	17.6	11	D	D	D	182	1 404	166.8	67.1
Des Moines	55	744	42.8	12.0	2	D	D	D	55	475	34.1	14.8
Edmonds	113	1 426	83.1	23.3	11	346	20.8	6.3	210	D	D	D
Everett	343	4 457	265.2	72.9	27	364	18.6	6.4	362	5 867	622.3	298.1
Federal Way	221	3 085	182.5	51.8	16	325	14.1	6.6	320	4 356	425.8	144.9
Issaquah	109	1 729	107.2	31.5	8	260	12.5	4.3	246	3 243	314.4	114.6
Kennewick	195	3 554	183.4	51.8	17	575	22.9	8.5	283	2 592	199.0	79.1
Kent	272	3 198	179.9	50.2	21	308	22.3	8.6	324	D	D	D
Kirkland	191	2 958	187.3	57.6	44	801	33.4	12.5	114	D	D	D
Lacey	122	1 852	101.8	28.7	11	D	D	D	39	276	28.1	10.4
Lake Stevens	42	621	39.4	9.0	4	145	3.7	1.0	192	2 524	199.3	92.3
Lakewood	179	2 433	132.6	35.9	16	599	28.9	13.6	131	1 795	161.7	68.4
Longview	104	1 490	63.4	19.3	12	D	D	D	193	2 322	158.2	62.4
Lynnwood	204	3 092	189.1	53.0	9	D	D	D	118	1 282	114.0	49.3
Marysville	104	1 365	81.6	21.4	8	D	D	D	114	D	D	D
Mount Vernon	83	915	52.0	14.4	6	167	6.6	2.4	400	4 538	594.5	232.9
Olympia	215	3 316	166.4	52.7	12	152	7.7	2.3				

1. Establishments subject to federal tax.

Table D. Cities — Other Services and Government Employment and Payroll

City	Other services[1], 2012				Government employment and payroll, 2012								
						March payroll							
							Percent of total for:						
	Number of establishments	Number of employees	Receipts (mil dol)	Annual payroll (mil dol)	Full-time equivalent employees	Total (dollars)	Administration, judicial, and legal	Police and Corrections	Fire Protection	Highways and transportation	Health and welfare	Natural resources and utilities	Education and libraries
	104	105	106	107	108	109	110	111	112	113	114	115	116
UTAH—Cont'd													
Kaysville	27	134	9.5	2.7	134	462 338	10.8	22.9	9.0	7.6	0.0	39.1	0.0
Layton	108	729	48.9	13.9	349	1 449 599	18.3	33.6	21.9	4.9	0.0	21.4	0.0
Lehi	36	203	13.8	4.1	336	1 214 483	12.5	20.4	13.7	4.2	0.0	36.3	4.1
Logan	86	509	36.2	11.4	471	1 727 277	13.4	20.5	14.4	3.6	0.0	36.1	3.5
Midvale	60	338	31.1	8.2	75	305 262	65.6	0.0	0.0	6.5	2.9	20.3	0.0
Murray	138	886	86.2	27.3	431	1 925 114	16.4	23.1	16.8	2.6	0.0	30.9	3.1
Ogden	134	957	76.3	22.7	634	2 507 571	18.7	28.7	20.1	7.0	5.2	16.9	0.0
Orem	137	740	53.8	15.5	516	2 194 808	19.2	27.2	17.2	4.8	2.4	19.7	7.3
Pleasant Grove	38	138	13.3	3.4	245	686 046	17.4	27.3	9.0	3.6	2.6	26.1	8.0
Provo	118	749	59.2	17.7	702	2 815 201	17.2	23.0	14.4	5.6	1.8	29.5	4.4
Riverton	36	173	15.0	3.8	91	415 613	39.8	2.6	0.0	25.0	0.6	22.8	0.0
Roy	38	172	11.7	3.2	176	633 604	20.3	31.4	22.5	4.2	0.0	16.1	0.0
St. George	118	695	59.3	16.2	700	2 450 568	9.2	24.3	5.4	10.7	2.4	44.2	0.0
Salt Lake City	459	4 071	340.1	115.3	2 853	13 446 478	15.0	21.7	15.0	20.9	2.4	14.9	4.1
Sandy	118	785	56.3	19.2	496	2 122 916	21.0	24.1	15.6	9.8	7.5	20.1	0.0
South Jordan	52	295	22.6	6.9	333	1 224 842	20.3	19.7	17.6	6.1	2.9	18.3	0.0
Spanish Fork	38	236	17.2	5.4	215	776 827	12.0	18.4	0.0	6.4	4.3	34.7	2.8
Springville	33	124	10.2	2.2	213	858 647	17.7	20.4	1.6	8.5	0.6	42.5	4.7
Taylorsville	37	220	19.4	5.4	122	499 977	35.5	62.2	0.0	0.0	0.4	0.3	0.0
Tooele	33	D	D	D	184	603 981	20.7	27.5	3.3	5.6	6.8	29.9	3.6
West Jordan	93	670	67.8	22.8	409	1 901 684	7.2	32.4	23.5	4.1	0.0	8.0	0.0
West Valley City	123	642	71.8	20.9	699	2 859 122	17.7	37.1	17.3	7.1	8.8	9.1	0.0
VERMONT	1 057	4 255	398.4	109.0	X	X	X	X	X	X	X	X	X
Burlington	65	361	25.2	9.7	741	3 858 642	9.5	18.3	12.6	11.2	3.0	32.5	2.0
VIRGINIA	11 654	76 041	6 881.1	2 289.3	X	X	X	X	X	X	X	X	X
Alexandria	241	2 374	213.3	75.6	5 221	27 072 935	10.0	12.5	7.7	2.6	12.6	6.5	44.7
Blacksburg	45	D	D	D	360	1 254 541	15.3	27.9	0.6	24.0	1.6	12.0	0.0
Charlottesville	100	817	69.3	23.2	2 140	8 097 522	10.3	6.1	3.5	6.3	5.6	8.0	55.6
Chesapeake	361	2 768	291.0	89.0	9 069	32 784 817	5.1	11.5	6.3	2.1	5.7	4.5	62.1
Danville	84	466	34.2	8.7	2 451	7 816 325	9.2	11.3	5.7	3.0	5.2	9.6	51.6
Hampton	153	854	66.1	21.4	6 070	20 036 058	6.9	11.2	6.1	1.0	5.7	6.3	61.8
Harrisonburg	101	595	47.0	15.8	1 474	5 157 943	4.1	7.6	6.7	5.8	0.3	15.0	53.6
Leesburg	78	478	39.0	13.4	378	1 973 445	18.8	28.6	0.0	10.5	0.0	34.5	1.1
Lynchburg	130	929	73.3	24.1	3 057	9 313 489	8.7	9.6	8.0	2.9	8.1	7.5	52.5
Manassas	121	713	75.6	20.4	1 551	7 149 920	5.0	8.7	4.1	2.5	3.1	8.0	67.1
Newport News	251	1 757	157.4	53.0	8 390	34 469 339	6.2	10.2	4.6	1.3	4.5	9.2	63.2
Norfolk	287	2 254	192.7	73.6	11 723	42 393 144	6.3	13.5	5.5	3.7	10.1	7.2	51.8
Petersburg	63	508	33.1	13.2	1 422	4 584 024	6.0	20.2	8.9	4.5	6.2	4.0	47.4
Portsmouth	128	1 019	117.8	35.7	4 082	15 197 404	6.6	10.7	7.0	0.8	8.6	5.3	58.8
Richmond	370	2 708	213.2	75.5	8 746	33 243 527	9.0	18.5	6.0	1.8	8.7	7.9	42.5
Roanoke	207	1 415	111.5	37.8	3 839	13 972 707	8.1	12.9	8.3	1.7	8.0	2.4	56.6
Suffolk	84	551	35.7	12.1	3 545	11 901 204	10.3	7.7	9.6	2.9	3.6	6.8	58.2
Virginia Beach	724	4 164	320.0	99.7	18 286	64 539 702	3.7	9.5	3.6	0.3	6.6	7.3	60.5
Winchester	69	422	29.0	9.2	1 441	5 056 458	6.8	23.0	6.6	2.0	4.0	7.0	48.8
WASHINGTON	9 852	54 069	4 710.4	1 503.1	X	X	X	X	X	X	X	X	X
Auburn	143	808	83.2	28.8	428	2 532 346	24.2	34.3	0.0	15.0	4.6	18.9	0.0
Bellevue	332	2 177	173.9	64.4	1 278	8 997 838	17.4	19.2	22.6	7.6	8.6	23.3	0.0
Bellingham	201	1 185	106.1	34.2	813	4 462 504	14.2	23.4	26.3	8.6	0.9	16.4	3.3
Bothell	64	407	39.1	10.4	290	2 203 744	15.3	29.0	30.7	8.0	5.8	5.8	0.0
Bremerton	60	300	27.1	8.7	363	2 283 752	11.7	25.1	21.9	5.4	0.6	29.5	0.0
Burien	98	471	39.1	11.3	70	380 590	32.7	0.0	0.0	22.6	20.3	22.5	0.0
Des Moines	23	D	D	D	130	840 420	26.3	37.5	0.0	7.8	4.0	18.8	0.0
Edmonds	59	325	27.2	9.0	206	1 296 656	16.1	35.4	0.0	8.9	4.8	28.4	0.0
Everett	192	1 194	118.6	38.2	1 193	7 513 828	9.0	22.1	21.2	14.6	2.1	22.6	3.2
Federal Way	136	668	49.6	16.5	338	1 899 108	20.8	52.5	0.0	7.2	0.0	15.6	0.0
Issaquah	76	D	D	D	241	1 458 971	48.2	24.1	0.0	5.7	0.0	22.0	0.0
Kennewick	114	736	52.9	17.4	365	2 339 914	19.2	32.4	27.2	7.2	0.0	14.0	0.0
Kent	221	1 354	135.1	42.8	659	3 957 128	25.4	33.2	0.0	11.4	1.3	24.6	0.0
Kirkland	151	703	57.2	18.9	575	3 364 380	21.8	25.2	24.8	2.6	0.0	12.1	0.0
Lacey	71	423	34.4	11.2	244	1 204 776	6.5	40.8	0.0	5.7	7.4	37.2	0.0
Lake Stevens	27	111	6.8	2.1	60	371 914	10.4	53.2	0.0	21.3	10.4	0.0	0.0
Lakewood	130	607	54.2	18.0	252	1 631 866	29.1	53.0	0.0	11.9	1.0	3.8	0.0
Longview	72	459	34.1	10.9	291	1 531 626	13.5	28.3	20.6	13.2	0.0	18.9	5.5
Lynnwood	134	974	87.8	27.1	514	3 172 400	18.5	30.1	20.2	2.4	0.0	17.3	0.0
Marysville	103	496	52.8	13.3	244	1 573 886	23.0	37.9	0.0	9.3	0.0	24.8	0.0
Mount Vernon	55	271	22.6	7.3	209	1 138 810	14.6	30.5	21.7	3.5	0.0	18.1	5.0
Olympia	130	638	50.1	16.9	524	3 201 082	31.0	21.7	21.0	4.7	0.3	21.2	0.0

1. Establishments subject to federal tax.

Table D. Cities — City Government Finances

City	City government finances, 2012									
	General revenue							General expenditure		
		Intergovernmental		Taxes					Per capita¹ (dollars)	
					Per capita¹ (dollars)					
	Total (mil dol)	Total (mil dol)	Percent from state government	Total (mil dol)	Total	Property	Sales and gross receipts	Total (mil dol)	Total	Capital outlays
	117	118	119	120	121	122	123	124	125	126
UTAH—Cont'd										
Kaysville	15.6	1.7	75.8	6.7	236	50	186	10.3	364	62
Layton	45.3	3.8	61.6	25.7	375	112	263	40.3	587	14
Lehi	47.8	1.8	100.0	28.4	552	308	244	36.9	718	82
Logan	58.6	7.2	21.6	20.1	408	111	297	49.7	1 011	194
Midvale	17.3	1.8	50.9	11.1	368	138	230	17.2	568	9
Murray	52.5	4.5	36.2	29.2	604	209	395	48.5	1 005	89
Ogden	102.4	13.2	30.0	48.5	578	280	298	114.7	1 367	205
Orem	78.3	6.3	49.6	38.7	427	131	296	65.7	725	49
Pleasant Grove	23.6	2.0	81.2	9.0	261	99	162	21.4	621	39
Provo	87.3	11.8	35.6	39.2	339	125	214	98.1	850	250
Riverton	19.6	1.5	82.4	10.7	264	47	217	34.9	864	199
Roy	21.0	1.5	77.3	10.5	279	86	193	16.4	436	23
St. George	76.3	3.8	65.5	38.0	504	165	340	76.8	1 020	221
Salt Lake City	529.4	30.7	31.4	201.1	1 062	642	419	382.9	2 021	145
Sandy	79.3	5.3	56.3	44.9	502	168	334	64.8	724	74
South Jordan	55.2	2.4	79.1	34.3	614	349	265	50.1	895	75
Spanish Fork	37.6	1.4	82.8	10.0	277	75	202	31.9	880	170
Springville	25.9	1.1	90.9	10.0	325	103	223	30.3	989	165
Taylorsville	24.7	2.8	76.1	17.3	287	79	208	28.5	473	69
Tooele	20.4	1.8	85.9	11.5	358	130	227	20.7	645	92
West Jordan	65.0	6.3	62.5	35.7	329	119	210	59.0	544	60
West Valley City	134.8	12.6	33.4	67.2	507	262	245	154.8	1 168	359
VERMONT	X	X	X	X	X	X	X	X	X	X
Burlington	110.0	17.7	38.0	38.4	908	674	234	92.8	2 192	417
VIRGINIA	X	X	X	X	X	X	X	X	X	X
Alexandria	694.5	112.0	62.0	498.6	3 394	2 493	843	697.3	4 746	514
Blacksburg	40.4	14.5	48.6	16.4	382	130	252	36.6	855	218
Charlottesville	233.9	98.5	67.6	93.0	2 089	1 298	743	229.9	5 163	617
Chesapeake	886.7	369.8	97.8	422.6	1 852	1 303	538	865.4	3 792	475
Danville	173.3	85.4	95.4	50.7	1 186	638	544	179.2	4 189	318
Hampton	525.3	220.7	90.2	218.7	1 599	1 068	519	516.8	3 777	217
Harrisonburg	165.0	51.6	74.2	63.4	1 238	628	603	166.3	3 246	275
Leesburg	59.3	13.1	95.3	31.9	693	279	414	58.7	1 273	249
Lynchburg	266.8	110.8	87.0	117.5	1 510	897	597	268.3	3 449	589
Manassas	181.8	62.5	84.3	83.5	2 049	1 559	467	169.8	4 168	200
Newport News	774.9	330.7	85.5	322.2	1 785	1 271	515	806.2	4 467	333
Norfolk	1 105.0	447.5	74.8	416.3	1 691	1 027	664	1 153.5	4 686	548
Petersburg	125.4	70.3	87.3	45.2	1 406	1 038	357	129.9	4 039	140
Portsmouth	430.0	216.4	85.2	161.2	1 669	1 218	439	514.7	5 331	1 170
Richmond	1 063.0	471.0	79.9	412.6	1 951	1 242	709	1 029.3	4 866	638
Roanoke	385.6	172.3	96.1	172.9	1 766	1 081	685	378.3	3 865	222
Suffolk	304.8	145.8	82.7	134.3	1 577	1 160	411	324.3	3 808	436
Virginia Beach	1 602.6	600.6	84.2	810.1	1 817	1 221	583	1 799.1	4 036	628
Winchester	116.1	39.1	89.9	61.6	2 267	1 283	983	112.7	4 147	231
WASHINGTON	X	X	X	X	X	X	X	X	X	X
Auburn	109.0	17.7	41.8	43.9	598	200	378	107.6	1 464	393
Bellevue	284.5	33.1	23.5	153.0	1 157	275	833	257.3	1 947	276
Bellingham	120.9	15.0	39.1	67.7	825	212	593	118.7	1 446	280
Bothell	54.5	14.0	63.8	29.4	848	273	531	61.1	1 763	521
Bremerton	57.7	6.4	49.1	25.4	646	218	419	58.3	1 484	236
Burien	28.1	4.7	75.2	18.7	378	142	222	34.9	705	215
Des Moines	29.2	4.6	73.5	12.6	412	142	257	26.8	881	214
Edmonds	45.6	4.4	75.7	28.0	693	332	334	42.6	1 054	137
Everett	182.2	16.6	67.5	108.1	1 033	367	650	170.4	1 629	324
Federal Way	65.3	12.0	93.7	40.0	435	107	311	59.1	643	167
Issaquah	59.7	10.5	71.1	31.0	949	250	650	53.3	1 633	344
Kennewick	68.6	6.5	69.3	41.7	550	142	391	69.4	914	179
Kent	137.7	20.6	82.9	62.9	511	157	335	140.6	1 143	354
Kirkland	106.7	9.7	53.2	61.0	731	262	428	105.7	1 267	159
Lacey	56.2	9.1	68.1	26.8	611	136	454	60.0	1 365	347
Lake Stevens	14.7	2.9	47.3	9.7	333	139	178	9.2	318	2
Lakewood	45.5	9.7	66.3	28.3	480	104	367	49.0	831	168
Longview	58.1	10.3	61.4	25.0	685	222	460	58.2	1 593	375
Lynnwood	66.8	5.6	76.9	38.6	1 065	319	731	58.4	1 610	230
Marysville	60.6	3.7	74.9	30.1	483	246	222	58.8	943	114
Mount Vernon	38.0	3.3	70.9	17.8	552	222	318	33.3	1 033	107
Olympia	99.6	9.9	54.8	50.0	1 045	267	761	116.3	2 434	673

1. Based on population estimated as of July 1 of the year shown.

City	City government finances, 2012 (cont.)									
	General expenditure (cont.)									
	Percent of total for:									
	Public welfare	Highways	Parking facilities	Education	Health and hospitals	Police protection	Sewerage and sanitation	Parks and recreation	Housing and community development	Interest on debt
	127	128	129	130	131	132	133	134	135	136
UTAH—Cont'd										
Kaysville	0.0	10.3	0.0	0.0	0.0	7.6	51.5	11.5	0.0	0.4
Layton	0.0	16.8	0.0	0.0	0.0	26.0	19.4	9.8	1.1	0.5
Lehi	0.0	39.4	0.0	0.0	0.0	13.0	21.2	1.1	0.0	4.8
Logan	0.0	14.4	0.0	0.0	0.0	16.5	26.1	11.6	5.4	0.7
Midvale	0.0	9.4	0.0	0.0	0.0	30.1	15.3	2.0	3.5	7.1
Murray	0.0	15.6	0.0	0.0	0.0	19.8	13.0	13.4	2.1	1.2
Ogden	0.0	4.7	0.0	0.0	0.0	14.8	16.3	5.7	17.8	2.5
Orem	0.0	11.1	0.0	0.0	0.0	20.7	17.2	10.0	3.7	2.9
Pleasant Grove	0.0	3.1	0.0	0.0	0.0	20.0	22.6	14.2	0.0	8.8
Provo	0.0	10.5	0.0	0.0	0.0	15.5	9.1	27.2	5.6	4.5
Riverton	0.0	25.5	0.0	0.0	0.0	7.2	8.5	5.8	2.0	36.7
Roy	0.0	7.7	0.0	0.0	0.0	26.4	11.6	13.2	2.1	0.2
St. George	0.0	18.8	0.0	0.0	0.0	16.5	19.8	18.3	1.4	6.6
Salt Lake City	0.0	10.9	0.0	0.0	0.0	14.9	5.8	5.6	9.0	3.8
Sandy	0.0	7.4	0.0	0.0	0.0	18.4	13.6	11.7	1.0	5.4
South Jordan	0.0	14.1	0.0	0.0	0.0	10.9	6.1	12.5	9.7	3.6
Spanish Fork	0.0	10.9	0.0	0.0	0.0	11.9	16.0	20.8	0.0	2.7
Springville	0.0	7.8	0.0	0.0	0.9	12.7	15.8	12.5	0.0	5.5
Taylorsville	0.0	10.3	0.0	0.0	0.0	27.4	1.8	1.8	4.8	1.3
Tooele	0.0	12.0	0.0	0.0	0.0	16.2	9.4	17.6	12.8	5.1
West Jordan	0.0	17.8	0.0	0.0	0.0	22.3	18.1	4.0	3.7	2.0
West Valley City	0.0	7.4	0.0	0.0	1.1	13.1	5.3	16.7	25.5	4.1
VERMONT	X	X	X	X	X	X	X	X	X	X
Burlington	0.0	9.2	5.2	0.0	0.0	11.3	8.3	8.8	5.6	3.9
VIRGINIA	X	X	X	X	X	X	X	X	X	X
Alexandria	6.3	3.7	0.0	34.5	6.0	9.6	6.1	3.7	2.0	2.8
Blacksburg	0.0	22.9	0.0	0.0	1.6	19.2	16.1	5.9	6.9	2.2
Charlottesville	11.0	6.3	0.1	31.0	8.0	7.1	5.8	5.3	2.3	1.6
Chesapeake	3.3	5.6	0.0	54.2	3.3	4.6	3.4	2.3	0.4	2.3
Danville	4.2	5.7	0.0	41.3	2.3	5.5	6.6	2.2	2.3	1.7
Hampton	5.7	1.3	0.1	45.5	0.8	5.2	4.9	6.8	8.5	3.2
Harrisonburg	1.8	11.3	0.1	38.9	0.7	4.7	9.4	3.1	0.3	18.0
Leesburg	0.0	9.2	0.0	0.0	0.0	19.2	10.4	11.6	0.0	4.3
Lynchburg	7.1	2.8	0.1	35.8	0.7	6.4	15.5	2.2	2.9	2.8
Manassas	0.7	6.2	0.1	54.0	2.2	7.8	7.8	0.2	2.3	3.2
Newport News	5.1	3.9	0.0	42.3	8.5	5.7	4.8	3.1	5.8	3.6
Norfolk	6.6	4.6	1.0	36.0	3.2	5.9	5.3	4.1	9.5	3.1
Petersburg	11.4	4.7	0.0	40.0	1.0	9.0	4.0	1.3	1.0	1.0
Portsmouth	5.0	1.3	0.2	33.2	2.1	6.8	5.2	2.1	6.8	2.7
Richmond	1.6	2.7	0.0	31.6	4.5	8.9	10.5	2.5	9.1	0.8
Roanoke	15.3	3.5	0.4	39.4	0.9	6.1	2.2	2.5	6.6	3.1
Suffolk	4.4	6.8	0.0	45.2	0.2	6.3	2.0	1.6	1.2	2.8
Virginia Beach	3.8	4.8	0.1	46.8	3.0	5.0	7.1	5.9	1.4	3.0
Winchester	6.4	5.0	0.8	43.4	1.0	6.4	10.1	2.6	1.9	4.9
WASHINGTON	X	X	X	X	X	X	X	X	X	X
Auburn	0.0	19.6	0.0	0.0	0.5	15.0	33.6	9.0	0.2	2.2
Bellevue	0.0	15.0	0.0	0.0	6.3	11.9	18.4	15.2	5.3	2.8
Bellingham	0.0	10.0	1.2	0.0	7.0	13.4	14.1	16.3	1.8	1.6
Bothell	0.0	30.3	0.0	0.0	0.2	16.3	12.8	2.0	1.6	0.9
Bremerton	0.0	5.7	0.8	0.0	4.2	18.7	14.8	21.3	1.8	3.3
Burien	0.0	31.7	0.0	0.0	3.0	27.1	2.7	8.9	2.0	2.6
Des Moines	0.1	19.9	0.0	0.0	0.8	24.9	4.7	24.1	0.0	1.4
Edmonds	0.0	7.5	0.0	0.0	0.1	18.8	16.6	11.8	0.0	2.5
Everett	0.2	7.5	0.1	0.0	4.4	15.4	24.4	7.7	1.3	4.0
Federal Way	0.2	28.9	0.0	0.0	1.1	27.6	4.7	10.0	2.0	1.0
Issaquah	0.0	14.9	0.0	0.0	0.0	8.3	20.1	9.3	2.9	3.0
Kennewick	0.0	11.4	0.0	0.0	5.3	18.7	4.5	20.4	0.8	2.9
Kent	0.2	5.1	0.0	0.0	1.2	15.6	40.1	11.7	2.0	3.1
Kirkland	0.0	10.8	0.1	0.0	0.7	17.1	22.2	8.0	0.0	2.1
Lacey	0.0	19.2	0.0	0.0	2.9	14.1	25.7	13.0	0.0	1.6
Lake Stevens	0.2	13.5	0.0	0.0	0.4	40.6	12.7	1.9	2.0	3.5
Lakewood	1.0	17.8	0.0	0.0	0.6	40.2	7.5	3.3	4.9	0.3
Longview	0.2	8.3	0.0	0.0	0.0	15.9	40.1	5.9	2.7	1.2
Lynnwood	0.0	8.5	0.0	0.0	7.2	19.4	9.5	17.2	1.2	1.4
Marysville	0.0	17.7	0.0	0.0	4.9	14.4	17.3	5.1	0.0	5.8
Mount Vernon	0.0	9.6	0.0	0.0	0.5	19.0	29.6	4.4	0.0	2.1
Olympia	0.0	6.3	0.0	0.0	1.9	9.4	24.8	12.3	0.4	3.4

Table D. Cities — City Government Finances, City Government Employment, and Climate

| City | City government finances, 2012 (cont.) Debt outstanding | | | Climate[2] Average daily temperature (degrees Fahrenheit) | | | | | | |
| | Total (mil dol) | Per capita[1] (dollars) | Debt issued during year | Mean January | Mean July | Limits January[3] | Limits July[4] | Annual precipitation (inches) | Heating degree days | Cooling degree days |
	137	138	139	140	141	142	143	144	145	146
UTAH—Cont'd										
Kaysville	2.6	91	0.0	NA	NA	NA	NA	NA	NA	NA
Layton	4.9	71	0.0	27.6	74.2	18.6	89.9	20.75	6 142	746
Lehi	97.2	1 889	0.7	NA	NA	NA	NA	NA	NA	NA
Logan	43.8	891	0.0	21.8	71.6	12.7	88.3	17.86	7 174	522
Midvale	50.8	1 678	1.5	30.4	78.5	22.1	90.9	26.19	5 441	1 197
Murray	36.9	765	6.1	29.2	77.0	21.3	90.6	16.50	5 631	1 066
Ogden	115.6	1 378	7.1	28.1	76.6	20.1	90.0	23.67	5 868	980
Orem	67.1	740	4.3	28.6	76.5	20.3	92.3	12.84	5 564	1 016
Pleasant Grove	62.2	1 801	22.8	NA	NA	NA	NA	NA	NA	NA
Provo	115.1	997	34.5	30.9	76.9	22.5	93.4	20.13	5 264	1 028
Riverton	482.2	11 921	4.6	31.6	78.0	22.0	95.3	15.76	5 251	1 172
Roy	7.2	193	0.6	27.6	74.2	18.6	89.9	20.75	6 142	746
St. George	157.4	2 090	6.1	41.8	86.3	28.9	102.8	8.77	3 103	2 471
Salt Lake City	393.2	2 075	81.7	32.0	78.1	25.4	89.0	17.75	5 095	1 190
Sandy	93.6	1 045	8.3	30.4	78.5	22.1	90.9	26.19	5 441	1 197
South Jordan	71.6	1 279	6.9	31.6	78.0	22.0	95.3	15.76	5 251	1 172
Spanish Fork	24.7	681	0.0	NA	NA	NA	NA	NA	NA	NA
Springville	37.6	1 229	0.0	NA	NA	NA	NA	NA	NA	NA
Taylorsville	10.9	182	0.7	29.2	77.0	21.3	90.6	16.50	5 631	1 066
Tooele	36.8	1 147	15.2	NA	NA	NA	NA	NA	NA	NA
West Jordan	23.2	214	3.3	30.4	78.5	22.1	90.9	26.19	5 441	1 197
West Valley City	149.0	1 125	33.1	29.2	77.0	21.3	90.6	16.50	5 631	1 066
VERMONT	X	X	X	X	X	X	X	X	X	X
Burlington	192.6	4 550	24.3	18.0	70.6	9.3	81.4	36.05	7 665	489
VIRGINIA	X	X	X	X	X	X	X	X	X	X
Alexandria	580.7	3 952	133.6	34.9	79.2	27.3	88.3	39.35	4 055	1 531
Blacksburg	23.1	541	9.5	30.9	71.1	20.6	82.5	42.63	5 559	533
Charlottesville	117.7	2 645	34.1	35.5	76.9	26.2	88.0	48.87	4 103	1 212
Chesapeake	635.5	2 785	137.5	40.1	79.1	32.3	86.8	45.74	3 368	1 612
Danville	152.0	3 554	3.9	36.6	78.8	25.8	90.0	44.98	3 970	1 418
Hampton	359.9	2 630	78.5	39.4	78.5	32.0	85.2	47.90	3 535	1 432
Harrisonburg	500.6	9 773	28.6	30.5	73.5	20.4	85.3	36.12	5 333	758
Leesburg	126.9	2 753	33.9	31.5	75.2	20.8	87.1	43.21	5 031	911
Lynchburg	330.4	4 247	7.0	34.5	75.1	24.5	86.4	43.31	4 354	1 075
Manassas	130.5	3 202	0.0	31.7	75.7	21.9	87.4	41.80	4 925	1 075
Newport News	797.6	4 419	228.9	41.2	80.3	33.8	87.9	43.53	3 179	1 682
Norfolk	1 752.2	7 119	414.1	40.1	79.1	32.3	86.8	45.26	3 334	1 619
Petersburg	34.6	1 076	1.5	39.7	79.6	29.2	91.0	45.74	3 368	1 612
Portsmouth	519.2	5 378	88.9	40.1	79.1	32.3	86.8	45.74	3 368	1 612
Richmond	1 340.2	6 336	260.0	36.4	77.9	27.6	87.5	43.91	3 919	1 435
Roanoke	544.5	5 563	52.3	35.8	76.2	26.6	87.5	42.49	4 284	1 134
Suffolk	538.4	6 320	114.6	39.6	78.5	30.3	88.1	48.71	3 467	1 427
Virginia Beach	1 698.8	3 811	173.0	40.7	78.8	32.2	86.9	44.50	3 336	1 482
Winchester	201.0	7 395	51.9	NA	NA	NA	NA	NA	NA	NA
WASHINGTON	X	X	X	X	X	X	X	X	X	X
Auburn	68.3	929	0.0	40.8	66.4	34.6	77.4	39.59	4 624	219
Bellevue	176.9	1 338	0.0	41.5	65.5	36.0	74.5	38.25	4 615	192
Bellingham	92.2	1 124	49.1	40.5	63.3	34.8	72.5	34.84	4 980	68
Bothell	43.3	1 251	30.0	40.8	65.2	35.2	75.0	35.96	4 756	174
Bremerton	75.6	1 923	12.7	40.1	64.6	34.7	75.2	53.96	4 994	158
Burien	33.0	667	8.6	40.9	65.3	35.9	75.3	37.07	4 797	173
Des Moines	14.4	471	2.0	40.9	65.3	35.9	75.3	37.07	4 797	173
Edmonds	37.6	929	13.8	40.8	65.2	35.2	75.0	35.96	4 756	174
Everett	252.3	2 410	52.2	39.7	63.6	33.6	73.0	37.54	5 199	121
Federal Way	13.7	149	0.0	41.0	65.6	35.1	76.1	38.95	4 650	167
Issaquah	38.5	1 180	5.4	NA	NA	NA	NA	NA	NA	NA
Kennewick	63.3	834	5.4	34.2	75.2	28.0	89.3	8.01	4 731	909
Kent	164.6	1 338	0.0	40.8	66.4	34.6	77.4	39.59	4 624	219
Kirkland	53.5	641	8.3	40.8	65.2	35.2	75.0	35.96	4 756	174
Lacey	24.6	561	1.6	38.1	62.8	31.8	76.1	50.79	5 531	97
Lake Stevens	22.3	768	0.0	NA	NA	NA	NA	NA	NA	NA
Lakewood	12.0	203	1.3	41.0	65.6	35.1	76.1	38.95	4 650	167
Longview	34.6	948	15.4	39.9	64.5	33.8	76.5	48.02	4 900	148
Lynnwood	46.2	1 274	6.4	40.8	65.2	35.2	75.0	35.96	4 756	174
Marysville	92.8	1 487	4.8	39.7	63.6	33.6	73.0	37.54	5 199	121
Mount Vernon	37.4	1 161	0.0	39.9	62.3	34.1	73.0	32.70	5 197	47
Olympia	95.1	1 989	3.4	38.1	62.8	31.8	76.1	50.79	5 531	97

1. Based on the population estimated as of July 1 of the year shown.   2. Represents normal values based on the 30-year period, 1971–2000.   3. Average daily minimum.
4. Average daily maximum.

Items 137—146

Table D. Cities — Land Area and Population

STATE Place code	City	Land area,[1] 2016 (sq mi)	Total persons	Rank	Per square mile	White	Black or African American	American Indian, Alaska Native	Asian	Hawaiian Pacific Islander	Some other race	2 or more races[2]
		1	2	3	4	5	6	7	8	9	10	11
	WASHINGTON— Cont'd											
53 53545	Pasco	32.3	70 579	500	2 185.1	77.6	2.3	0.1	2.4	0.0	12.9	4.6
53 56625	Pullman	10.5	33 282	1 140	3 169.7	76.9	3.2	0.0	10.2	0.6	2.9	6.3
53 56695	Puyallup	14.1	40 640	926	2 882.3	84.3	1.9	0.8	5.1	0.0	1.1	6.7
53 57535	Redmond	16.5	62 458	585	3 785.3	59.6	1.0	0.0	32.4	0.0	3.0	4.0
53 57745	Renton	23.4	100 953	302	4 314.2	53.1	10.0	0.4	19.4	1.1	9.8	6.2
53 58235	Richland	38.8	54 989	682	1 417.2	84.2	0.9	1.0	4.3	0.0	6.3	3.3
53 61115	Sammamish	20.4	63 773	573	3 126.1	64.5	0.6	0.0	30.2	0.0	0.4	4.3
53 62288	SeaTac	10.0	28 873	1 286	2 887.3	46.5	21.0	1.0	13.5	8.7	3.6	5.8
53 63000	Seattle	83.8	704 352	18	8 405.2	69.1	7.3	0.6	14.1	0.2	2.4	6.2
53 63960	Shoreline	11.7	55 333	677	4 729.3	72.9	6.5	1.0	10.2	0.1	2.6	6.8
53 67000	Spokane	68.7	215 973	101	3 143.7	85.8	2.1	1.6	2.6	0.8	1.5	5.6
53 67167	Spokane Valley	37.7	96 340	318	2 555.4	92.9	0.7	1.0	0.9	0.3	1.0	3.1
53 70000	Tacoma	49.7	211 277	105	4 251.0	65.2	10.7	0.6	10.1	0.8	4.4	8.2
53 73465	University Place	8.4	33 288	1 139	3 962.9	67.5	8.0	0.8	9.7	0.0	3.8	10.1
53 74060	Vancouver	46.9	174 826	144	3 727.6	81.7	2.5	0.7	4.5	0.7	3.9	6.0
53 75775	Walla Walla	12.8	32 132	1 178	2 510.3	84.1	1.5	0.0	2.3	0.0	6.3	5.8
53 77105	Wenatchee	8.0	33 921	1 120	4 240.1	NA	NA	NA	NA	NA	NA	NA
53 80010	Yakima	27.8	93 986	335	3 380.8	81.8	0.8	1.5	1.3	0.0	11.8	3.0
54 00000	WEST VIRGINIA	24 040.9	1 831 102	X	76.2	93.4	3.9	0.1	0.8	0.0	0.2	1.6
54 14600	Charleston	31.5	49 138	771	1 559.9	78.3	16.1	0.0	1.8	0.0	0.0	3.8
54 39460	Huntington	16.2	48 113	793	2 969.9	86.1	8.1	0.6	1.7	0.0	0.1	3.4
54 55756	Morgantown	10.0	30 855	1 218	3 085.5	90.0	4.3	0.6	3.7	0.0	0.1	1.3
54 62140	Parkersburg	11.8	30 601	1 231	2 593.3	NA	NA	NA	NA	NA	NA	NA
54 86452	Wheeling	13.8	27 375	1 349	1 983.7	90.0	7.4	0.0	1.3	0.0	0.3	1.0
55 00000	WISCONSIN	54 159.9	5 778 708	X	106.7	86.0	6.3	0.9	2.7	0.0	1.8	2.3
55 02375	Appleton	24.5	74 370	472	3 035.5	83.7	3.2	0.9	6.7	0.1	3.1	2.3
55 06500	Beloit	17.3	36 757	1 035	2 124.7	79.3	9.7	0.7	0.9	0.0	3.1	6.3
55 10025	Brookfield	27.3	38 016	1 004	1 392.5	NA	NA	NA	NA	NA	NA	NA
55 22300	Eau Claire	32.5	68 339	517	2 102.7	91.2	0.7	0.7	6.2	0.1	0.0	1.1
55 25950	Fitchburg	34.9	28 875	1 285	827.4	71.1	10.5	0.0	7.1	0.0	6.2	5.2
55 26275	Fond du Lac	18.9	42 951	875	2 272.5	92.9	1.5	0.6	1.0	0.0	0.9	3.1
55 27300	Franklin	34.6	36 131	1 055	1 044.2	86.2	4.9	0.2	6.1	0.0	1.0	1.5
55 31000	Green Bay	45.4	105 139	286	2 315.8	73.8	3.5	4.1	4.2	0.0	8.5	5.8
55 31175	Greenfield	11.5	36 858	1 033	3 205.0	85.3	5.3	0.8	4.3	0.0	1.4	2.8
55 37825	Janesville	33.8	64 159	568	1 898.2	91.5	1.8	0.6	1.7	0.0	0.3	4.1
55 39225	Kenosha	27.8	99 631	305	3 583.8	82.4	10.2	0.6	2.0	0.0	2.1	2.6
55 40775	La Crosse	21.8	52 109	732	2 390.3	90.9	1.4	0.3	6.0	0.0	0.0	1.4
55 48000	Madison	77.0	252 551	82	3 279.9	78.5	6.7	0.3	8.3	0.0	2.4	3.7
55 48500	Manitowoc	17.8	32 936	1 154	1 850.3	NA	NA	NA	NA	NA	NA	NA
55 51000	Menomonee Falls	32.9	36 769	1 034	1 117.6	90.4	2.2	0.1	5.1	0.0	0.2	2.0
55 53000	Milwaukee	96.2	595 047	31	6 185.5	46.1	38.8	0.6	3.8	0.0	6.8	3.8
55 54875	Mount Pleasant	33.7	26 360	1 390	782.2	NA	NA	NA	NA	NA	NA	NA
55 55750	Neenah	9.2	25 914	1 400	2 816.7	NA	NA	NA	NA	NA	NA	NA
55 56375	New Berlin	36.5	39 803	952	1 090.5	NA	NA	NA	NA	NA	NA	NA
55 58800	Oak Creek	28.5	35 881	1 061	1 259.0	80.0	2.9	1.5	14.0	0.0	0.6	1.0
55 60500	Oshkosh	26.8	66 579	541	2 484.3	89.8	3.8	0.2	4.8	0.0	0.7	0.7
55 66000	Racine	15.5	77 571	435	5 004.6	62.5	22.8	0.1	0.9	0.0	7.9	5.8
55 72975	Sheboygan	14.4	48 686	782	3 381.0	81.3	2.1	0.2	11.8	0.0	1.4	3.3
55 77200	Stevens Point	17.2	26 423	1 387	1 536.2	89.2	1.2	0.2	6.6	0.0	1.5	1.3
55 78600	Sun Prairie	12.0	32 820	1 158	2 735.0	83.3	7.8	0.1	5.7	0.2	0.2	2.7
55 78650	Superior	36.7	26 475	1 385	721.4	93.7	0.5	2.2	1.4	0.0	0.7	1.5
55 84250	Waukesha	25.4	72 363	487	2 848.9	89.4	1.7	0.2	2.4	0.2	2.7	3.3
55 84475	Wausau	18.9	38 872	979	2 056.7	88.9	0.8	0.5	7.4	0.3	0.3	1.9
55 84675	Wauwatosa	13.2	47 945	795	3 632.2	85.3	6.2	0.5	3.7	0.0	0.9	3.4
55 85300	West Allis	11.4	60 087	615	5 270.8	86.0	6.0	0.4	3.2	0.0	2.0	2.4
55 85350	West Bend	15.1	31 702	1 187	2 099.5	NA	NA	NA	NA	NA	NA	NA
56 00000	WYOMING	97 091.2	585 501	X	6.0	91.5	0.8	2.2	0.8	0.0	1.8	2.8
56 13150	Casper	26.5	59 324	623	2 238.6	NA	NA	NA	NA	NA	NA	NA
56 13900	Cheyenne	27.0	64 019	569	2 371.1	88.5	3.3	1.3	1.4	0.2	1.9	3.4
56 31855	Gillette	21.7	32 398	1 169	1 493.0	NA	NA	NA	NA	NA	NA	NA
56 45050	Laramie	18.2	32 382	1 171	1 779.2	89.3	1.4	1.3	2.2	0.1	2.4	3.3

1. Dry land or land partially or temporarily covered by water.   2. Hispanic or Latino persons may be of any race.

Table D. Cities — Population

City	Percent Hispanic or Latino[1], 2015	Percent foreign born 2015	Age of population (percent), 2010-2014							Median age 2015	Percent female 2015	Population			
			Under 18 years	18 to 24 years	25 to 34 years	35 to 44 years	45 to 54 years	55 to 64 years	65 years and over			Census counts		Percent change	
												2000	2010	2000–2010	2010–2016
	12	13	14	15	16	17	18	19	20	21	22	23	24	25	26
WASHINGTON— Cont'd															
Pasco	57.1	23.9	34.5	11.2	13.4	15.1	10.2	8.5	7.2	28.6	48.2	32 066	61 086	90.5	15.5
Pullman	6.9	12.1	14.4	49.0	15.4	8.2	5.6	3.3	4.2	22.2	51.5	24 675	29 821	20.9	11.6
Puyallup	6.2	6.2	20.3	7.8	15.2	12.6	13.4	15.9	14.7	39.6	50.4	33 011	37 222	12.8	9.2
Redmond	6.4	39.6	24.3	5.6	20.5	17.6	11.4	9.0	11.5	34.8	49.7	45 256	54 315	20.0	15.0
Renton	15.4	28.9	25.2	7.0	15.4	17.1	14.3	10.6	10.3	36.3	47.4	50 052	91 900	83.6	9.9
Richland	14.4	8.4	23.4	8.1	13.3	9.5	13.3	12.7	19.6	39.4	50.5	38 708	48 111	24.3	14.3
Sammamish	4.4	27.8	28.9	5.2	10.0	18.2	18.7	11.7	7.4	38.5	49.5	34 104	57 441	68.4	11.0
SeaTac	17.5	37.5	22.3	10.6	12.8	17.1	12.1	9.1	15.9	37.5	50.7	25 496	26 909	5.5	7.3
Seattle	6.3	17.5	14.6	11.4	23.1	15.4	12.7	11.6	11.3	35.5	49.5	563 374	608 659	8.0	15.7
Shoreline	9.8	17.4	20.0	5.4	13.4	14.4	14.5	15.4	16.9	42.5	51.5	53 025	53 031	0.0	4.3
Spokane	6.3	6.2	21.5	9.9	16.6	12.1	12.1	12.6	15.3	36.6	51.8	195 629	209 437	7.1	3.1
Spokane Valley	5.4	4.4	24.4	7.3	17.2	10.8	12.7	12.4	15.2	36.0	47.4	NA	89 743	NA	7.4
Tacoma	12.4	15.3	20.2	10.2	15.8	13.0	13.3	13.2	14.4	37.7	51.5	193 556	198 397	2.5	6.5
University Place	7.1	12.2	24.5	11.9	10.5	11.4	13.6	13.7	14.4	37.3	51.1	29 933	31 146	4.1	6.9
Vancouver	13.4	12.6	24.0	8.8	14.6	13.3	12.3	12.4	14.7	37.2	52.0	143 560	162 491	13.2	7.6
Walla Walla	26.1	12.5	19.3	14.6	15.7	10.5	13.5	9.5	16.9	35.3	49.8	29 686	31 731	6.9	1.3
Wenatchee	26.5	11.3	26.0	8.4	12.1	12.7	12.0	12.8	16.0	36.1	54.5	27 856	32 215	15.6	5.3
Yakima	47.1	16.8	27.4	11.1	13.6	10.7	12.1	9.9	15.1	34.0	51.8	71 845	91 281	27.1	3.0
WEST VIRGINIA	1.4	1.6	20.6	8.9	11.8	12.5	13.4	14.6	18.2	42.2	50.7	1 808 344	1 853 011	2.5	-1.2
Charleston	1.8	3.5	22.9	7.6	13.4	14.5	11.9	13.9	15.8	38.8	50.3	53 421	51 340	-3.9	-4.3
Huntington	2.8	1.9	19.1	20.0	13.9	11.8	11.3	10.7	13.1	32.4	51.1	51 475	49 206	-4.4	-2.2
Morgantown	2.6	4.9	10.7	36.7	17.2	10.4	7.8	6.1	11.1	25.7	45.3	26 809	28 630	6.8	7.8
Parkersburg	1.0	1.0	19.8	8.3	10.9	12.5	15.5	14.8	18.2	43.4	53.0	33 099	31 369	-5.2	-2.4
Wheeling	1.4	2.4	19.0	7.0	10.7	13.9	11.7	14.9	22.8	44.5	54.9	31 419	28 459	-9.4	-3.8
WISCONSIN	6.6	4.8	22.4	9.7	12.6	12.1	13.8	13.8	15.6	39.4	50.3	5 363 675	5 687 289	6.0	1.6
Appleton	6.8	5.9	23.8	10.1	15.5	11.8	12.9	12.3	13.6	35.6	50.5	70 087	72 625	3.6	2.4
Beloit	13.9	6.7	26.5	12.9	11.8	10.6	10.8	13.4	14.0	34.2	51.8	35 775	37 005	3.4	-0.7
Brookfield	4.8	11.4	22.8	5.3	7.0	9.5	15.5	16.4	23.5	48.8	54.0	38 649	37 912	-1.9	0.3
Eau Claire	2.2	4.2	18.1	21.4	15.5	9.9	11.3	10.4	13.3	32.0	52.1	61 704	66 208	7.3	3.2
Fitchburg	17.9	13.5	22.4	10.1	18.7	16.1	10.2	12.1	10.3	34.4	50.7	20 501	25 163	22.7	14.8
Fond du Lac	8.5	2.5	22.2	9.9	13.9	14.0	12.3	10.3	17.4	39.1	51.3	42 203	43 042	2.0	-0.2
Franklin	5.0	7.2	17.9	5.8	10.3	12.7	14.7	17.6	21.0	46.8	50.5	29 494	35 456	20.2	1.9
Green Bay	16.0	9.3	24.8	12.0	16.1	12.5	10.7	11.0	12.9	32.9	50.1	102 313	103 913	1.6	1.2
Greenfield	10.3	7.6	23.9	5.7	15.9	13.0	9.8	12.8	19.0	37.7	49.9	35 476	36 747	3.6	0.3
Janesville	8.1	2.2	22.6	5.8	15.3	12.7	15.6	12.9	15.1	38.9	50.1	59 498	63 621	6.9	0.8
Kenosha	18.8	7.5	25.6	10.2	12.4	14.1	13.1	12.3	12.4	36.3	50.6	90 352	99 271	9.9	0.4
La Crosse	1.6	3.1	10.2	31.8	15.1	7.4	8.6	12.2	14.6	28.8	51.6	51 818	51 329	-0.9	1.5
Madison	7.9	12.1	17.2	21.3	19.1	12.0	9.9	9.6	11.0	30.7	50.8	208 054	233 084	12.0	8.4
Manitowoc	4.9	4.8	22.3	6.9	11.2	14.8	11.4	14.0	19.4	41.7	52.8	34 053	33 745	-0.9	-2.4
Menomonee Falls	2.6	6.1	20.8	6.1	11.9	10.7	15.8	17.3	17.5	45.4	53.6	32 647	35 623	9.1	3.2
Milwaukee	18.4	9.7	26.0	12.1	16.8	12.7	11.8	10.5	10.0	31.6	52.3	596 974	594 775	-0.4	0.0
Mount Pleasant	4.9	3.0	21.1	9.0	8.4	10.9	13.2	13.1	24.4	45.5	54.1	NA	26 197	NA	0.6
Neenah	7.4	3.8	25.2	8.1	13.6	15.5	13.6	12.7	11.2	36.3	50.6	24 507	25 504	4.1	1.6
New Berlin	2.1	5.2	20.4	5.4	13.7	12.2	11.8	16.6	19.8	43.7	51.5	38 220	39 584	3.6	0.6
Oak Creek	7.4	9.8	20.9	8.1	16.9	11.6	13.0	13.8	15.6	38.7	44.8	28 456	34 452	21.1	4.1
Oshkosh	3.0	3.5	19.2	18.8	14.7	12.2	11.8	9.6	13.6	33.0	50.6	62 916	66 165	5.2	0.6
Racine	23.4	5.7	27.4	9.2	15.0	11.3	12.7	12.8	11.6	33.7	49.4	81 855	78 860	-3.7	-1.6
Sheboygan	10.6	10.8	24.1	7.9	14.4	12.9	12.0	13.3	15.4	38.6	50.1	50 792	49 293	-3.0	-1.2
Stevens Point	4.2	4.0	14.0	33.0	10.9	8.6	9.6	10.0	13.8	27.0	47.9	24 551	26 703	8.8	-1.0
Sun Prairie	5.2	8.5	21.5	8.8	15.0	14.4	12.0	13.7	14.5	38.2	51.3	20 369	29 537	45.0	11.1
Superior	2.1	2.1	19.4	11.4	14.7	10.4	13.4	13.1	17.6	38.4	51.8	27 368	27 245	-0.4	-2.8
Waukesha	13.5	6.9	21.0	12.7	15.3	13.9	13.2	12.0	11.9	35.8	49.6	64 825	71 158	9.8	1.7
Wausau	1.6	5.0	20.0	8.1	13.4	10.1	13.8	16.1	18.5	43.4	49.3	38 426	39 119	1.8	-0.6
Wauwatosa	2.1	3.1	24.8	5.2	20.6	15.1	9.7	11.9	12.7	34.5	50.3	47 271	46 449	-1.7	3.2
West Allis	13.5	8.4	20.2	6.8	17.8	13.1	13.3	14.6	14.3	38.8	51.8	61 254	60 418	-1.4	-0.5
West Bend	1.8	1.8	22.6	8.2	11.2	15.0	15.1	11.9	16.1	40.3	49.6	28 152	31 200	10.8	1.6
WYOMING	9.9	3.8	23.8	9.9	14.1	12.3	11.9	13.9	14.1	36.5	49.7	493 782	563 767	14.2	3.9
Casper	10.1	4.5	26.5	10.3	14.3	12.0	13.3	11.6	11.9	33.8	51.6	49 644	55 317	11.4	7.2
Cheyenne	11.3	2.2	22.3	10.1	14.5	11.1	11.1	14.8	16.1	38.0	50.1	53 011	59 657	12.5	7.3
Gillette	11.7	6.0	27.0	12.2	15.7	14.2	12.3	11.5	7.1	30.6	47.7	19 646	29 819	51.8	8.6
Laramie	9.8	6.5	15.8	32.8	17.4	9.9	7.4	8.8	8.0	25.8	49.2	27 204	30 815	13.3	5.1

1. May be of any race.

Table D. Cities — Households, Group Quarters, Crime, and Education

City	Households, 2015				Persons in group quarters, 2010				Serious crimes known to police,[2] 2014				Educational attainment, 2015		
			Percent			Institutional			Total		Rate[3]			Attainment[4] (percent)	
	Number	Persons per house-hold	Female family house-holder[1]	One-person	Total	Total	Persons in nursing facilities	Non-institu-tional	Number	Rate[3]	Violent	Property	Population age 25 and older	High school graduate or less	Bachelor's degree or more
	27	28	29	30	31	32	33	34	35	36	37	38	39	40	41
WASHINGTON—Cont'd															
Pasco	19 606	3.45	18.3	17.2	385	276	98	109	1 657	2 397	255	2 143	36 996	53.9	18.9
Pullman	10 388	2.56	4.1	35.2	5 788	18	18	5 770	550	1 729	211	1 518	12 078	9.5	69.1
Puyallup	16 425	2.37	16.9	30.6	710	443	403	267	2 901	7 435	282	7 153	28 510	37.8	26.0
Redmond	23 533	2.56	3.9	25.1	274	171	171	103	1 788	3 066	57	3 010	42 472	11.7	71.1
Renton	38 732	2.57	11.6	28.5	685	263	191	422	5 459	5 557	233	5 324	67 963	29.9	37.8
Richland	21 662	2.49	8.9	24.1	285	163	163	122	1 307	2 446	170	2 275	37 185	25.2	46.7
Sammamish	17 720	2.94	5.2	8.0	99	0	0	99	394	772	16	757	34 436	7.6	73.5
SeaTac	9 868	2.76	12.2	29.6	1 014	905	74	109	1 682	5 985	637	5 348	18 935	42.6	21.3
Seattle	311 038	2.13	5.9	37.9	24 925	4 904	2 588	20 021	44 776	6 749	604	6 146	506 840	15.4	62.1
Shoreline	21 853	2.45	9.4	26.5	1 415	581	578	834	1 778	3 221	170	3 050	41 399	25.6	43.3
Spokane	87 867	2.34	11.0	35.6	6 949	1 972	1 236	4 977	19 218	9 107	548	8 559	146 320	31.9	30.3
Spokane Valley	39 322	2.39	11.7	32.7	802	439	418	363	5 542	6 065	325	5 740	64 806	38.1	21.8
Tacoma	81 647	2.48	11.5	36.2	6 693	4 084	1 392	2 609	14 412	7 040	798	6 242	144 640	39.5	28.0
University Place	12 296	2.65	12.7	27.1	206	118	118	88	785	2 433	214	2 219	20 891	20.7	35.6
Vancouver	68 513	2.49	12.2	32.6	2 056	1 192	429	864	5 840	3 462	344	3 118	116 188	35.1	27.9
Walla Walla	12 457	2.23	11.0	40.5	3 651	2 600	190	1 051	1 668	5 240	330	4 910	21 298	36.1	24.6
Wenatchee	11 948	2.75	10.1	35.4	582	402	88	180	1 220	3 717	192	3 525	22 064	48.6	18.0
Yakima	33 290	2.74	17.2	29.5	2 448	1 841	650	607	5 042	5 383	438	4 945	57 609	50.5	19.1
WEST VIRGINIA	734 536	2.44	11.5	30.3	49 382	28 323	9 748	21 059	43 236	2 337	302	2 035	1 300 347	54.7	19.6
Charleston	21 948	2.16	15.1	39.0	1 940	675	220	1 265	3 985	7 861	1 243	6 618	34 563	33.2	40.7
Huntington	19 944	2.30	14.5	41.3	3 012	676	412	2 336	0	0	0	0	29 872	37.1	28.9
Morgantown	10 147	2.50	8.0	41.6	5 636	86	19	5 550	894	2 874	260	2 614	16 149	26.2	53.4
Parkersburg	13 984	2.18	17.0	38.4	547	341	326	206	1 160	3 725	286	3 439	22 280	51.4	17.4
Wheeling	11 932	2.10	11.2	39.3	1 436	523	413	913	929	3 331	782	2 549	19 497	40.0	31.8
WISCONSIN	2 319 538	2.42	9.8	29.1	150 214	74 295	33 808	75 919	136 952	2 379	290	2 088	3 918 997	39.8	28.4
Appleton	29 201	2.49	12.2	31.3	2 429	864	487	1 565	1 603	2 171	269	1 901	49 729	37.0	31.6
Beloit	14 226	2.48	20.6	33.5	1 553	242	242	1 311	1 388	3 764	404	3 360	22 376	54.9	16.9
Brookfield	15 265	2.46	8.5	25.6	513	460	460	53	1 034	2 720	58	2 662	27 343	21.5	56.3
Eau Claire	26 475	2.40	6.1	36.0	4 536	613	256	3 923	1 837	2 704	162	2 542	40 782	27.9	33.4
Fitchburg	11 361	2.39	9.0	27.7	822	815	0	7	486	1 822	277	1 544	18 877	27.8	44.1
Fond du Lac	17 188	2.37	11.4	32.9	2 087	1 481	480	606	1 344	3 129	328	2 801	29 135	44.8	24.3
Franklin	14 870	2.28	5.2	30.6	1 982	1 908	42	74	788	2 158	55	2 103	27 645	27.5	41.9
Green Bay	42 864	2.37	13.6	35.8	3 206	1 362	617	1 844	2 836	2 701	497	2 204	66 537	43.7	24.7
Greenfield	15 355	2.40	9.4	35.9	821	728	728	93	1 015	2 724	150	2 574	26 308	38.5	27.6
Janesville	26 565	2.38	9.2	26.1	930	756	309	174	2 238	3 503	254	3 250	45 924	46.9	23.3
Kenosha	37 852	2.55	15.1	31.3	3 488	1 620	736	1 868	2 701	2 700	288	2 412	64 153	43.4	22.3
La Crosse	21 479	2.21	5.8	37.6	4 681	827	540	3 854	1 638	3 177	202	2 975	30 327	31.5	35.2
Madison	105 922	2.23	8.7	33.6	10 740	2 171	1 173	8 569	7 835	3 188	344	2 844	153 194	21.4	55.0
Manitowoc	14 786	2.17	8.5	37.4	956	532	524	424	1 003	3 017	223	2 794	23 387	44.8	20.8
Menomonee Falls	15 107	2.38	6.4	30.5	217	202	202	15	451	1 253	22	1 231	26 409	34.2	42.0
Milwaukee	232 104	2.51	21.0	36.6	18 401	5 302	2 512	13 099	36 461	6 073	1 485	4 588	371 229	46.0	23.9
Mount Pleasant	10 920	2.38	12.2	27.7	290	268	265	22	811	3 092	61	3 031	18 354	35.6	31.8
Neenah	10 665	2.40	11.6	30.1	277	233	211	44	514	1 978	142	1 835	17 181	34.2	34.2
New Berlin	16 534	2.40	5.0	24.9	161	125	125	36	NA	NA	NA	NA	29 530	23.8	42.8
Oak Creek	13 988	2.51	6.0	28.1	125	0	0	125	1 015	2 889	125	2 763	25 029	42.0	27.5
Oshkosh	25 719	2.30	12.1	35.4	7 520	4 056	974	3 464	1 588	2 371	233	2 139	41 234	45.2	22.7
Racine	29 796	2.56	18.6	30.1	1 548	1 276	152	272	3 040	3 895	406	3 488	49 240	46.3	17.7
Sheboygan	20 346	2.36	10.9	31.3	953	766	472	187	1 422	2 926	317	2 609	33 189	53.5	20.3
Stevens Point	10 058	2.33	6.7	33.7	3 330	178	94	3 152	595	2 231	158	2 074	14 095	33.2	38.1
Sun Prairie	13 896	2.32	9.7	34.9	102	82	82	20	767	2 455	90	2 366	22 566	24.8	40.3
Superior	11 626	2.21	14.3	33.0	1 191	393	234	798	1 813	6 771	276	6 494	18 531	42.7	18.5
Waukesha	29 349	2.35	9.7	31.2	2 911	892	228	2 019	1 296	1 823	129	1 694	47 752	31.9	35.9
Wausau	17 071	2.23	10.3	34.3	1 100	820	526	280	851	2 162	221	1 941	28 099	39.9	27.5
Wauwatosa	19 042	2.46	8.1	33.8	871	732	615	139	1 604	3 391	159	3 232	33 305	18.4	57.4
West Allis	27 176	2.20	11.4	40.3	829	591	583	238	2 936	4 832	360	4 471	44 286	41.7	24.5
West Bend	13 456	2.32	6.1	31.5	530	429	215	101	955	3 018	164	2 853	21 953	41.7	26.9
WYOMING	228 937	2.50	7.2	29.9	13 712	6 701	2 450	7 011	12 619	2 160	195	1 965	388 747	36.6	26.2
Casper	24 109	2.49	9.6	35.7	1 125	548	483	577	1 716	2 824	138	2 685	38 694	37.3	24.0
Cheyenne	26 245	2.37	13.0	33.0	865	636	330	229	1 884	2 983	141	2 842	42 825	31.2	28.7
Gillette	12 010	2.74	8.7	32.2	422	260	123	162	1 008	3 123	158	2 965	20 296	39.8	18.6
Laramie	13 718	2.22	4.3	36.5	2 176	78	70	2 098	753	2 350	150	2 201	16 761	16.6	48.9

1. No spouse present.   2. Data for serious crimes have not been adjusted for underreporting. This may affect comparability between geographic areas and over time.   3. Per 100,000 population estimated by the FBI.   4. Persons 25 years old and over.

City	Money income, 2015 Households			Families		Housing units, 2010			Occupied housing units 2015 Owner-occupied			Renter-occupied	
	Median income	Percent with income of $200,000 or more	Percent with income of less than $25,000	Total Families	Percent with income below poverty	Total	Percent change, 2000–2010	Vacant units for sale or rent[2]	Total	Percent	Median value[3] (dollars)	Percent	Median rent (dollars)
	42	43	44	45	46	47	48	49	50	51	52	53	54
WASHINGTON— Cont'd													
Pasco	60 054	4.4	12.8	15 371	11.7	18 782	81.7	799	19 606	67.6	173 500	32.4	844
Pullman	27 331	1.5	29.5	NA	NA	11 966	27.4	937	10 388	26.8	235 400	73.2	682
Puyallup	59 393	5.1	15.9	9 655	11.8	16 171	20.8	1 221	16 425	53.2	264 900	46.8	1 080
Redmond	114 232	22.6	5.9	15 707	4.5	24 177	19.1	1 627	23 533	54.1	580 900	45.9	1 630
Renton	68 656	7.4	11.1	23 849	9.0	38 930	71.5	2 921	38 732	52.6	328 800	47.4	1 340
Richland	65 415	6.7	8.9	15 265	11.1	20 876	26.9	1 169	21 662	64.9	223 000	35.1	896
Sammamish	155 974	34.3	3.8	15 814	2.6	15 736	34.7	582	17 720	86.4	718 300	13.6	1 991
SeaTac	48 913	5.2	12.3	NA	NA	10 360	3.3	827	9 868	50.7	267 600	49.3	1 045
Seattle	80 349	13.0	12.5	139 973	4.9	308 516	14.0	25 006	311 038	46.6	530 900	53.4	1 356
Shoreline	81 232	6.6	8.8	14 003	3.5	22 787	6.8	1 226	21 853	61.3	386 200	38.7	1 356
Spokane	44 350	2.5	21.2	50 019	12.5	94 291	7.0	7 020	87 867	54.6	164 700	45.4	740
Spokane Valley	43 296	1.1	18.3	23 928	12.8	38 851	NA	2 293	39 322	56.1	171 500	43.9	839
Tacoma	52 437	3.2	18.4	45 005	12.2	85 786	5.9	7 245	81 647	49.3	218 900	50.7	987
University Place	60 146	4.8	14.2	8 024	8.9	13 573	6.8	754	12 296	54.4	314 400	45.6	1 015
Vancouver	51 988	3.6	13.7	40 038	8.1	70 005	16.6	4 314	68 513	48.8	227 700	51.2	1 026
Walla Walla	42 645	2.9	21.5	6 936	8.7	12 514	9.3	977	12 457	53.4	178 100	46.6	792
Wenatchee	49 715	3.3	20.8	NA	NA	13 175	14.6	796	11 948	59.1	225 000	40.9	793
Yakima	44 050	2.4	19.8	21 854	17.3	34 829	21.2	1 755	33 290	56.7	158 200	43.3	769
WEST VIRGINIA	42 019	2.2	23.4	471 947	13.5	881 917	4.4	118 086	734 536	72.3	112 100	27.7	675
Charleston	44 280	6.0	23.5	12 270	12.8	26 205	-3.2	2 752	21 948	54.3	145 000	45.7	702
Huntington	29 198	2.4	35.8	9 077	20.9	25 146	-3.0	3 372	19 944	49.5	90 800	50.5	641
Morgantown	41 384	5.4	28.9	NA	NA	12 664	7.2	963	10 147	45.6	176 900	54.4	1 013
Parkersburg	31 437	0.7	32.0	7 898	21.7	15 562	-3.2	1 755	13 984	59.5	88 700	40.5	624
Wheeling	44 380	4.4	25.1	6 517	9.4	14 661	-6.2	1 845	11 932	65.6	105 000	34.4	613
WISCONSIN	55 638	3.7	14.9	1 469 666	7.9	2 624 358	13.1	344 590	2 319 538	66.8	168 300	33.2	792
Appleton	49 405	2.6	13.9	18 546	10.6	30 348	9.7	1 474	29 201	66.6	137 700	33.4	776
Beloit	43 574	1.4	21.6	8 492	23.0	15 177	6.5	1 396	14 226	57.7	84 400	42.3	700
Brookfield	92 389	19.4	7.2	10 831	2.5	15 317	7.5	741	15 265	86.7	290 900	13.3	1 402
Eau Claire	48 631	2.3	16.3	13 659	8.0	28 134	13.7	1 331	26 475	59.5	138 600	40.5	762
Fitchburg	61 247	8.7	8.4	6 440	3.8	10 668	23.2	713	11 361	47.8	303 400	52.2	913
Fond du Lac	50 660	2.7	18.1	10 425	9.0	19 181	9.2	1 239	17 188	64.1	120 800	35.9	634
Franklin	75 302	8.4	10.5	9 926	2.6	14 356	31.0	714	14 870	78.6	227 200	21.4	1 014
Green Bay	41 811	1.7	20.9	24 267	12.0	45 241	4.8	2 997	42 864	55.1	125 400	44.9	652
Greenfield	51 382	1.0	13.2	8 568	6.3	17 790	9.9	930	15 355	56.6	175 400	43.4	895
Janesville	55 876	3.6	15.5	16 800	13.4	27 996	11.7	2 168	26 565	67.3	133 000	32.7	772
Kenosha	48 235	1.5	17.3	23 209	14.6	40 643	12.4	3 267	37 852	57.6	141 100	42.4	778
La Crosse	39 004	2.7	21.1	9 066	5.1	22 628	1.9	1 200	21 479	48.0	129 900	52.0	711
Madison	57 690	4.7	14.2	49 646	6.6	108 843	17.9	6 327	105 922	46.1	222 800	53.9	981
Manitowoc	38 823	0.5	21.4	8 432	16.5	15 955	6.4	1 332	14 786	63.0	109 200	37.0	608
Menomonee Falls	71 707	9.1	6.2	9 999	1.6	15 142	15.1	575	15 107	75.6	227 900	24.4	989
Milwaukee	37 495	1.5	26.6	124 229	23.1	255 569	2.5	25 348	232 104	40.5	114 000	59.5	802
Mount Pleasant	59 557	4.3	10.6	7 544	4.4	11 827	NA	691	10 920	74.9	179 400	25.1	799
Neenah	60 337	3.1	11.8	6 546	6.6	11 313	11.2	619	10 665	68.9	130 100	31.1	674
New Berlin	78 020	6.9	7.9	11 769	2.4	16 829	12.7	537	16 534	76.0	239 200	24.0	1 156
Oak Creek	66 913	2.1	6.8	9 171	2.5	14 754	24.0	690	13 988	58.7	227 900	41.3	1 019
Oshkosh	44 689	0.9	18.6	13 497	10.2	28 179	11.1	2 041	25 719	52.1	122 900	47.9	715
Racine	42 472	2.0	20.3	19 216	18.9	33 887	1.3	3 357	29 796	53.7	98 900	46.3	774
Sheboygan	46 525	0.5	19.8	12 617	10.4	22 339	2.4	2 031	20 346	58.7	103 600	41.3	659
Stevens Point	44 107	3.6	25.9	4 888	6.6	11 220	15.0	622	10 058	52.6	133 600	47.4	678
Sun Prairie	63 274	2.1	6.3	NA	NA	12 413	53.0	777	13 896	56.1	217 400	43.9	948
Superior	40 104	2.1	22.0	6 737	16.5	12 328	1.0	658	11 626	56.3	114 600	43.7	696
Waukesha	60 734	3.6	14.2	17 300	6.2	29 843	11.1	1 548	29 349	53.4	197 900	46.6	851
Wausau	47 051	3.5	16.2	9 923	4.2	18 154	8.8	1 667	17 071	61.7	117 400	38.3	696
Wauwatosa	71 350	7.6	11.9	10 723	2.6	21 520	2.9	1 085	19 042	60.7	224 400	39.3	1 060
West Allis	48 565	0.8	20.6	14 538	10.5	29 353	2.2	1 899	27 176	51.3	139 700	48.7	760
West Bend	59 350	2.7	11.2	8 072	1.9	13 546	13.7	777	13 456	65.4	167 200	34.6	776
WYOMING	60 214	3.4	13.9	145 470	6.7	261 868	17.0	34 989	228 937	68.0	212 500	32.0	815
Casper	53 936	3.4	13.9	13 830	8.9	24 536	11.6	1 742	24 109	55.9	197 900	44.1	804
Cheyenne	59 211	4.0	16.3	15 345	9.1	27 283	14.6	1 726	26 245	61.9	193 800	38.1	918
Gillette	77 143	2.8	8.6	7 622	5.5	12 153	52.3	1 178	12 010	59.1	218 600	40.9	1 046
Laramie	41 875	1.7	25.4	6 229	6.8	14 307	19.2	913	13 718	41.9	219 900	58.1	762

1.   Based on population estimated by the American Community Survey.   2.   Includes units rented or sold but not occupied.   3.   Specified owner-occupied units; $1,000,000 represents $1,000,000 or more   4.   50.0 represents 50 percent or more.   5.   10.0 represents 10 percent or less.

Table D. Cities — Commuting, Computer Access, Migration, Labor Force, and Employment

City	Commuting Percent — Drove alone	With Commutes of 30 minutes or more[1]	Computer Access Percent — With a Computer in the house	With Internet Access	Migration, 2015 — Percent who lived in the same house one year ago	Percent who lived in an other state or county one year ago	Civilian labor force, 2016 — Total	Percent change, 2015–2016	Unemployment — Total	Rate[3]	Civilian employment[4], 2015 — Population age 16 and older — Number	Percent in Labor Force	Population age 16 to 64 — Number	Percent who worked full-year full-time
	55	56	57	58	59	60	61	62	63	64	65	66	67	68
WASHINGTON— Cont'd														
Pasco	90.7	14.7	84.2	74.0	77.3	10.5	31 879	2.6	2 517	7.9	46 999	68.0	42 108	49.8
Pullman	51.1	1.2	95.6	78.9	45.4	36.4	15 812	1.5	840	5.3	28 568	63.7	27 177	28.4
Puyallup	83.1	47.8	88.5	79.9	82.1	7.1	21 055	3.7	1 274	6.1	32 374	61.9	26 530	51.7
Redmond	71.3	27.3	96.4	94.5	78.4	12.1	35 338	2.6	1 231	3.5	46 572	70.6	39 613	57.8
Renton	80.1	56.3	94.2	89.3	82.6	4.4	57 071	2.5	2 093	3.7	77 648	68.9	67 298	54.1
Richland	79.1	23.4	93.0	85.3	78.6	10.3	27 358	3.2	1 580	5.8	43 151	60.1	32 500	49.3
Sammamish	77.7	61.7	99.5	96.6	89.0	5.7	26 793	2.6	966	3.6	39 020	67.4	35 168	51.4
SeaTac	79.9	36.9	89.4	83.1	83.7	4.8	14 399	2.2	685	4.8	22 720	64.1	18 222	49.3
Seattle	52.1	44.2	93.7	86.7	76.1	8.7	431 926	2.6	15 592	3.6	593 729	73.5	516 293	54.8
Shoreline	68.7	59.7	93.8	87.0	76.7	10.7	30 113	2.6	1 200	4.0	45 476	69.2	36 113	52.0
Spokane	81.4	20.7	88.2	79.7	78.7	8.0	102 122	3.0	6 656	6.5	172 362	58.9	139 714	41.2
Spokane Valley	84.2	17.7	89.6	83.1	81.8	6.3	47 012	2.8	3 021	6.4	73 538	60.9	59 158	49.8
Tacoma	79.5	40.2	89.7	76.8	80.9	7.9	101 365	3.4	6 708	6.6	171 133	61.4	141 242	46.5
University Place	86.6	41.0	94.7	90.1	79.4	9.7	16 555	3.5	870	5.3	26 176	61.0	21 445	44.3
Vancouver	81.7	33.0	91.8	82.3	78.1	8.4	84 197	2.8	5 360	6.4	135 831	64.1	110 487	49.3
Walla Walla	73.8	8.1	87.3	78.2	74.3	11.4	14 433	3.1	898	6.2	26 625	55.6	21 180	38.4
Wenatchee	82.9	8.2	83.5	70.4	79.7	13.6	19 056	3.3	1 192	6.3	25 886	58.3	20 499	49.6
Yakima	78.2	13.1	82.8	66.7	81.1	5.4	46 762	3.4	3 218	6.9	70 557	61.8	56 379	47.4
WEST VIRGINIA	85.5	33.2	79.6	69.5	88.3	5.4	783 470	0.0	47 043	6.0	1 508 224	52.9	1 171 863	43.2
Charleston	80.6	15.3	82.5	72.6	84.5	7.4	23 329	-1.0	1 156	5.0	39 572	60.1	31 713	48.7
Huntington	72.0	16.6	80.9	68.7	74.2	10.8	20 076	0.1	1 028	5.1	40 714	51.6	34 262	32.4
Morgantown	70.8	14.0	88.9	83.4	67.0	22.5	14 319	1.1	700	4.9	28 233	49.1	24 822	33.0
Parkersburg	75.6	18.8	80.3	68.2	84.7	5.4	12 473	-0.9	781	6.3	25 564	54.8	19 939	37.9
Wheeling	85.9	17.3	79.6	68.5	94.3	3.2	12 692	-0.2	751	5.9	21 961	55.5	15 950	50.4
WISCONSIN	84.7	27.2	86.4	77.1	85.7	5.7	3 120 229	0.8	129 196	4.1	4 627 790	66.9	3 727 027	52.9
Appleton	87.6	12.8	91.1	82.9	88.9	5.8	40 605	1.7	1 529	3.8	59 639	68.4	49 436	48.4
Beloit	73.9	31.8	80.8	57.1	79.1	5.6	17 264	0.8	966	5.6	27 629	60.3	22 458	41.8
Brookfield	95.4	28.6	89.9	87.2	87.9	6.9	19 417	1.0	718	3.7	30 820	62.4	21 885	55.3
Eau Claire	86.1	12.0	85.4	80.0	74.1	12.8	39 904	0.8	1 378	3.5	56 630	69.7	47 659	49.5
Fitchburg	81.1	30.4	94.4	86.4	79.4	8.1	16 111	1.6	445	2.8	21 944	76.3	19 050	59.6
Fond du Lac	86.4	18.1	84.5	77.6	88.1	5.7	23 012	0.1	877	3.8	34 100	65.8	26 654	51.0
Franklin	90.8	39.2	92.3	84.0	83.7	6.5	18 474	0.5	719	3.9	30 374	55.9	22 760	50.6
Green Bay	85.8	14.4	86.8	77.4	81.2	4.5	54 920	0.9	2 265	4.1	81 142	68.9	67 575	51.1
Greenfield	87.8	30.4	84.0	77.6	86.8	5.7	20 111	0.8	882	4.4	29 239	60.4	22 128	55.8
Janesville	88.0	25.8	90.7	70.2	83.9	4.0	33 486	1.1	1 493	4.5	51 302	69.7	41 627	54.3
Kenosha	83.6	28.1	89.0	78.6	82.0	6.5	50 235	0.9	2 634	5.2	76 859	66.9	64 518	51.7
La Crosse	75.9	10.4	84.9	76.9	66.7	15.5	30 145	1.4	1 200	4.0	47 440	68.0	39 788	43.0
Madison	67.7	18.7	93.9	84.3	71.1	10.3	154 289	1.8	4 424	2.9	211 046	72.8	183 641	48.4
Manitowoc	87.7	14.8	83.7	66.5	87.8	3.0	16 330	-0.2	796	4.9	26 466	61.1	20 056	52.8
Menomonee Falls	93.4	25.1	90.4	86.9	86.7	7.3	20 016	0.9	717	3.6	29 458	70.9	23 148	62.6
Milwaukee	74.0	28.9	80.6	68.2	81.5	4.6	282 699	0.1	16 361	5.8	459 913	65.5	399 711	45.3
Mount Pleasant	85.1	24.5	82.0	74.6	NA	NA	14 201	0.3	640	4.5	21 481	59.4	15 079	50.8
Neenah	90.5	10.1	85.8	80.9	89.4	3.9	14 167	1.8	529	3.7	19 930	71.9	17 054	56.1
New Berlin	94.2	32.4	87.9	85.6	90.8	4.6	22 036	0.9	814	3.7	32 560	65.3	24 685	59.5
Oak Creek	90.3	31.9	91.5	85.5	86.6	3.8	20 497	0.6	768	3.7	28 417	69.8	22 903	53.1
Oshkosh	86.7	16.5	86.7	74.9	81.8	8.6	35 318	1.5	1 353	3.8	55 861	60.5	46 794	43.6
Racine	77.6	26.6	79.9	65.9	84.1	1.8	35 998	0.0	2 289	6.4	58 384	66.2	49 383	46.4
Sheboygan	81.5	14.1	83.7	73.9	86.3	3.0	25 389	1.1	989	3.9	38 225	65.8	30 722	51.1
Stevens Point	73.4	16.8	92.9	89.7	68.7	12.5	15 060	0.1	586	3.9	23 067	68.5	19 390	41.0
Sun Prairie	93.7	21.8	94.1	85.7	84.8	8.0	19 496	1.8	580	3.0	26 200	72.0	21 502	54.6
Superior	83.7	13.3	84.1	66.4	82.3	7.1	14 756	0.5	689	4.7	22 260	61.1	17 556	43.8
Waukesha	82.6	27.1	86.7	81.7	88.8	5.6	41 947	0.6	1 548	3.7	59 000	71.1	50 440	51.3
Wausau	85.7	8.4	83.9	73.9	86.2	6.5	19 892	0.5	781	3.9	32 341	67.2	25 105	55.7
Wauwatosa	86.5	19.3	87.2	81.8	89.1	3.1	27 350	0.9	970	3.5	36 664	71.7	30 639	59.9
West Allis	82.8	24.8	82.8	70.3	88.1	3.2	34 039	0.5	1 703	5.0	49 024	66.8	40 385	57.9
West Bend	84.3	37.4	80.2	74.4	88.7	5.2	17 159	0.7	634	3.7	25 442	69.3	20 337	59.4
WYOMING	80.7	17.7	89.8	78.5	82.0	9.6	302 331	-0.9	15 958	5.3	460 730	67.8	378 183	54.0
Casper	89.2	9.2	87.3	78.1	82.7	8.8	30 483	-4.2	2 097	6.9	46 121	69.3	38 809	52.3
Cheyenne	85.1	8.2	88.7	80.7	76.6	10.8	31 942	0.2	1 345	4.2	51 388	68.3	41 210	60.8
Gillette	78.2	16.8	94.6	86.0	75.1	18.4	16 060	-4.6	1 223	7.6	25 132	73.9	22 748	58.7
Laramie	71.0	7.1	92.9	80.0	65.3	19.6	17 681	1.8	529	3.0	27 808	75.5	25 202	42.5

1. Employed persons.   2. Households.   3. Percent of civilian labor force.   4. Persons 16 years old and over.

Table D. Cities — Construction, Wholesale Trade, and Retail Trade

City	Value of residential construction authorized by building permits, 2016			Wholesale trade,[1] 2012				Retail trade,[2] 2012			
	New construction ($1,000)	Number of housing units	Percent single family	Number of establish-ments	Number of employees	Sales (mil dol)	Annual payroll (mil dol)	Number of establish-ments	Number of employees	Sales (mil dol)	Annual payroll (mil dol)
	69	70	71	72	73	74	75	76	77	78	79
WASHINGTON— Cont'd											
Pasco	100 587	421	91.9	77	939	595.5	46.6	157	2 051	722.8	67.7
Pullman	31 153	176	34.1	11	177	182.1	9.0	51	1 027	222.7	20.4
Puyallup	39 143	139	94.2	39	652	343.0	27.6	239	5 078	1 686.5	152.9
Redmond	141 608	917	20.3	173	3 101	4 143.8	257.7	251	3 923	947.4	105.4
Renton	81 831	207	96.1	110	3 308	2 769.4	197.3	264	5 284	1 831.9	165.6
Richland	112 586	527	51.4	19	186	192.6	7.6	143	2 531	680.0	60.7
Sammamish	148 418	385	75.1	31	52	46.8	2.9	47	413	129.3	12.6
SeaTac	21 651	64	100.0	19	177	146.3	10.2	71	943	213.9	18.1
Seattle	1 459 645	9 999	8.0	1 093	16 045	12 790.5	1 049.7	2 530	34 652	40 037.9	1 230.2
Shoreline	63 527	369	20.6	33	135	57.2	5.6	121	2 364	835.7	75.9
Spokane	141 465	836	44.1	249	3 330	1 686.8	158.8	862	13 166	3 132.8	341.2
Spokane Valley	101 688	807	22.4	202	2 963	1 772.5	140.6	476	7 626	1 987.3	207.5
Tacoma	95 178	617	19.9	210	2 967	2 750.1	151.2	744	11 177	3 036.6	314.9
University Place	17 875	60	100.0	12	75	49.4	4.1	51	728	154.9	19.8
Vancouver	58 640	716	44.6	185	2 441	2 580.9	139.4	555	10 131	2 863.9	278.6
Walla Walla	21 710	101	84.2	54	483	437.5	18.3	150	1 667	386.1	40.7
Wenatchee	18 048	70	100.0	52	587	710.1	27.7	185	2 635	615.3	68.3
Yakima	30 985	137	100.0	108	2 196	1 875.8	100.9	346	5 078	1 334.7	134.8
WEST VIRGINIA	302	8	100.0	1 334	16 906	14 295.4	761.9	6 393	85 305	22 637.9	1 908.5
Charleston	1 433	7	100.0	121	1 588	1 059.8	78.1	358	5 805	1 495.4	134.6
Huntington	200	2	0.0	73	1 250	511.6	62.2	211	2 788	670.4	66.6
Morgantown	2 092	13	84.6	26	142	47.8	5.3	260	4 385	1 081.4	86.6
Parkersburg	4 372	35	100.0	40	338	134.5	12.1	203	3 074	791.4	68.8
Wheeling	4 217	21	23.8	62	D	D	D	142	1 690	380.3	37.4
WISCONSIN	1 805	6	100.0	5 990	97 040	77 066.9	5 253.6	19 272	296 956	78 201.8	6 835.0
Appleton	25 785	93	57.0	98	1 432	5 759.6	66.1	291	4 865	1 306.6	111.5
Beloit	1 493	12	83.3	19	456	292.8	25.0	115	1 756	481.9	40.3
Brookfield	27 429	67	100.0	108	1 733	686.6	105.7	301	5 576	1 022.7	117.4
Eau Claire	41 531	277	27.1	79	1 509	961.9	64.8	340	6 565	1 419.6	131.8
Fitchburg	45 091	388	10.6	25	967	1 149.6	59.0	58	614	173.3	16.1
Fond du Lac	11 867	67	50.7	41	812	610.4	46.3	211	3 688	959.5	81.9
Franklin	13 791	40	95.0	35	402	292.7	23.6	75	2 107	614.6	52.0
Green Bay	28 005	111	100.0	106	2 190	1 714.9	122.4	340	5 909	1 595.9	134.6
Greenfield	8 873	54	25.9	14	192	128.7	7.3	149	3 100	932.8	80.5
Janesville	16 683	91	100.0	75	1 941	1 843.2	96.1	276	5 678	1 422.0	144.0
Kenosha	16 692	369	6.2	56	763	769.3	42.7	295	5 162	1 369.5	114.4
La Crosse	4 830	24	83.3	61	1 690	2 434.7	78.4	251	4 879	976.7	97.7
Madison	382 777	2 381	14.3	270	4 849	2 859.6	252.1	972	17 918	4 804.9	409.1
Manitowoc	4 796	30	46.7	27	461	211.0	23.9	146	2 436	555.8	53.0
Menomonee Falls	60 767	331	36.6	89	1 425	651.3	89.4	126	2 741	700.4	63.1
Milwaukee	142 036	1 051	3.3	485	11 513	8 694.3	908.5	1 368	15 652	3 894.9	360.3
Mount Pleasant	15 197	57	100.0	21	346	145.5	14.4	64	1 331	441.7	31.9
Neenah	9 716	52	88.5	24	278	252.6	13.1	82	1 520	436.6	34.5
New Berlin	8 868	22	81.8	119	2 332	1 178.0	137.1	96	2 375	579.0	64.6
Oak Creek	36 413	226	14.2	32	1 429	891.0	89.5	80	2 059	718.9	43.7
Oshkosh	14 332	95	14.7	50	1 198	517.4	48.5	250	4 856	1 205.0	107.7
Racine	540	3	100.0	42	448	225.6	22.3	281	3 410	622.1	61.4
Sheboygan	1 539	8	100.0	41	451	304.5	18.9	197	3 362	758.9	74.1
Stevens Point	NA	NA	NA	32	332	270.7	14.4	120	2 003	470.3	39.3
Sun Prairie	NA	NA	NA	33	822	362.4	38.0	70	1 155	305.8	25.6
Superior	NA	NA	NA	39	669	817.8	31.9	113	1 835	541.2	45.8
Waukesha	NA	NA	NA	115	2 148	1 126.3	119.0	213	4 314	1 601.4	120.4
Wausau	NA	NA	NA	44	817	375.7	36.8	187	4 576	1 239.9	101.2
Wauwatosa	NA	NA	NA	56	1 033	652.0	55.5	293	5 436	1 107.9	113.4
West Allis	NA	NA	NA	107	1 830	975.2	99.4	243	4 249	1 154.4	102.4
West Bend	NA	NA	NA	25	201	93.9	8.1	120	2 163	553.4	46.4
WYOMING	570 418	1 727	89.7	709	7 003	5 597.9	398.7	2 681	30 088	9 446.0	796.0
Casper	17 418	71	88.7	80	841	1 414.8	51.5	299	4 299	1 244.2	116.3
Cheyenne	42 357	237	81.9	93	782	336.4	52.5	321	4 632	1 561.0	112.7
Gillette	6 986	18	100.0	49	813	462.8	41.3	160	2 202	757.5	62.0
Laramie	10 781	88	68.2	19	95	127.6	4.0	131	1 671	470.8	35.7

1. Merchant wholesalers except manufacturers' sales branches and offices. 2. Establishments with payroll.

Table D. Cities — Real Estate, Professional Services, and Manufacturing

City	Real estate and rental and leasing, 2012				Professional, scientific, and technical services,[1] 2012				Manufacturing, 2012			
	Number of establishments	Number of employees	Receipts (mil dol)	Annual payroll (mil dol)	Number of establishments	Number of employees	Receipts (mil dol)	Annual payroll (mil dol)	Number of establishments	Number of employees	Receipts (mil dol)	Annual payroll (mil dol)
	80	81	82	83	84	85	86	87	88	89	90	91
WASHINGTON—Cont'd												
Pasco	46	224	39.2	6.8	61	369	37.2	16.4	37	D	D	59.8
Pullman	40	180	19.4	4.4	36	304	40.0	17.3	12	D	D	D
Puyallup	86	417	83.6	13.0	119	627	65.7	26.1	43	954	240.9	43.2
Redmond	128	1 207	288.5	71.4	385	D	D	D	127	6 634	3 469.5	443.1
Renton	115	610	212.1	29.7	208	2 109	213.2	103.7	71	13 466	D	994.5
Richland	89	268	46.3	9.2	181	D	D	D	39	1 839	D	119.8
Sammamish	41	D	D	D	197	405	85.7	26.5	6	14	2.5	0.6
SeaTac	40	312	71.5	11.6	17	243	32.8	13.3	15	130	D	6.0
Seattle	1 966	11 652	2 431.3	587.9	4 631	50 113	10 321.5	4 432.8	859	20 323	5 200.2	1 054.2
Shoreline	70	282	64.4	11.6	113	D	D	D	17	147	29.9	5.9
Spokane	281	1 580	283.9	57.9	741	D	D	D	200	4 292	1 101.4	202.5
Spokane Valley	147	814	146.0	26.8	189	1 245	123.8	51.5	189	6 500	2 048.1	324.3
Tacoma	297	1 748	304.2	64.2	504	D	D	D	194	6 347	1 923.4	338.4
University Place	55	D	D	D	66	251	29.2	11.6	17	87	D	2.9
Vancouver	273	1 384	225.1	51.1	570	D	D	D	182	6 379	2 585.4	336.6
Walla Walla	42	128	17.4	4.0	79	356	36.7	14.4	83	1 043	221.4	46.9
Wenatchee	61	211	32.7	5.9	101	D	D	D	23	401	71.9	14.9
Yakima	146	587	81.6	16.1	211	D	D	D	99	2 981	838.8	122.6
WEST VIRGINIA	1 405	6 011	1 255.8	203.8	2 918	23 115	2 804.7	1 053.4	1 245	48 686	24 553.1	2 603.9
Charleston	135	663	154.9	22.9	385	D	D	D	39	528	148.4	22.8
Huntington	74	259	50.9	9.4	135	D	D	D	52	3 170	1 697.1	206.5
Morgantown	79	435	64.2	10.7	126	D	D	D	22	446	D	23.3
Parkersburg	53	239	52.6	7.4	89	D	D	D	25	657	134.7	26.1
Wheeling	49	D	D	D	136	D	D	D	37	D	D	D
WISCONSIN	4 509	23 762	4 358.9	801.1	11 253	98 507	15 028.9	5 701.2	8 995	436 777	177 728.9	21 879.3
Appleton	60	D	D	D	193	1 791	315.2	106.8	104	7 600	D	409.2
Beloit	17	88	66.4	4.6	38	212	20.4	9.2	52	2 599	1 801.2	132.8
Brookfield	94	1 075	88.2	31.8	306	3 589	744.8	278.8	56	1 544	368.5	79.4
Eau Claire	94	462	72.5	14.0	145	1 527	188.2	78.6	79	3 823	1 148.1	170.4
Fitchburg	42	247	46.1	7.9	85	556	90.6	34.8	30	3 154	1 287.1	205.2
Fond du Lac	31	144	25.7	3.7	91	1 050	125.8	63.4	72	4 252	1 894.6	202.1
Franklin	25	127	25.8	3.3	58	424	80.7	23.0	52	3 383	1 221.8	176.4
Green Bay	94	610	93.9	21.6	226	D	D	D	130	10 215	6 399.1	513.4
Greenfield	38	182	31.6	6.8	80	589	63.7	26.0	17	106	D	4.8
Janesville	53	260	74.1	12.6	107	624	70.8	24.5	82	3 985	1 600.9	187.1
Kenosha	67	289	44.5	7.3	125	816	73.3	33.0	99	2 044	738.6	95.7
La Crosse	74	475	70.7	12.9	171	D	D	D	93	4 666	1 527.4	195.8
Madison	369	2 871	759.2	115.5	1 019	13 787	2 399.8	978.8	182	8 788	2 798.2	467.9
Manitowoc	19	D	D	D	58	453	68.2	16.7	75	6 299	1 804.1	295.0
Menomonee Falls	20	260	33.5	14.7	91	1 294	253.1	76.0	176	8 361	3 503.9	464.3
Milwaukee	460	3 036	618.5	127.5	1 091	D	D	D	540	22 779	8 678.9	1 199.8
Mount Pleasant	20	80	9.6	2.8	50	387	38.9	19.2	35	2 073	3 299.8	155.3
Neenah	17	142	151.8	6.5	51	476	60.8	31.5	60	5 008	2 079.0	262.2
New Berlin	27	263	44.5	7.7	109	2 193	348.9	102.6	130	6 222	2 305.6	359.7
Oak Creek	38	405	92.1	16.3	35	414	32.6	12.5	55	3 412	1 390.3	196.4
Oshkosh	53	306	43.0	8.3	100	D	D	D	115	11 025	6 369.1	607.7
Racine	37	121	31.0	3.8	118	D	D	D	143	4 602	1 264.5	245.5
Sheboygan	31	181	41.8	8.1	94	D	D	D	89	6 676	2 068.9	311.6
Stevens Point	19	D	D	D	57	635	57.0	23.5	30	1 791	570.9	73.8
Sun Prairie	25	70	13.3	2.1	60	404	50.5	20.4	29	1 020	283.2	48.2
Superior	34	106	14.5	2.4	55	323	35.1	14.3	40	1 200	D	77.6
Waukesha	56	321	69.7	10.8	188	1 794	285.7	100.4	142	9 474	4 144.2	668.2
Wausau	39	D	D	D	130	D	D	D	64	4 486	1 177.6	184.4
Wauwatosa	45	268	89.0	13.0	236	D	D	D	51	3 718	1 267.0	356.5
West Allis	43	293	77.6	14.4	86	925	100.6	52.4	92	3 448	743.0	196.1
West Bend	18	D	D	D	49	D	D	D	52	1 779	409.9	79.6
WYOMING	1 076	4 546	1 259.1	215.6	2 132	D	D	D	553	10 094	10 783.8	630.6
Casper	124	649	182.3	31.4	216	1 146	166.8	64.1	27	471	91.8	25.8
Cheyenne	112	390	89.7	14.4	414	D	D	D	51	1 132	2 542.4	75.4
Gillette	61	265	72.1	9.9	94	D	D	D	27	482	D	30.7
Laramie	50	132	20.2	3.0	95	D	D	D	21	141	D	5.5

1. Establishments subject to federal tax.

Accommodation and Food Services, Arts, Entertainment, and Recreation, and Health Care and Social Assistance

City	Accommodation and food services, 2012				Arts, entertainment, and recreation,[1] 2012				Health care and social assistance,[1] 2012			
	Number of establish-ments	Number of employees	Sales (mil dol)	Annual payroll (mil dol)	Number of establish-ments	Number of employees	Receipts (mil dol)	Annual payroll (mil dol)	Number of establish-ments	Number of employees	Receipts (mil dol)	Annual payroll (mil dol)
	92	93	94	95	96	97	98	99	100	101	102	103
WASHINGTON—Cont'd												
Pasco	88	1 288	71.1	19.4	10	D	D	D	82	712	67.0	23.5
Pullman	103	1 302	55.6	15.4	4	93	5.0	1.8	58	D	D	D
Puyallup	151	2 421	134.5	41.0	11	149	7.2	2.1	186	D	D	D
Redmond	244	4 597	340.1	100.7	32	D	D	D	210	2 496	242.3	95.7
Renton	241	3 787	253.7	71.3	19	D	D	D	293	3 016	379.9	154.7
Richland	127	2 055	108.4	31.6	13	460	16.3	6.3	213	2 156	238.8	113.7
Sammamish	30	488	26.5	7.7	17	D	D	D	67	452	49.3	20.3
SeaTac	96	2 996	251.0	72.1	2	D	D	D	29	860	20.9	11.6
Seattle	2 823	45 976	3 164.1	970.4	323	4 218	540.3	224.9	2 101	24 068	3 408.6	1 564.3
Shoreline	100	1 054	55.9	15.9	21	698	31.6	10.1	181	1 928	148.4	64.8
Spokane	601	10 256	549.0	165.9	58	883	47.7	12.4	722	13 373	1 618.3	684.5
Spokane Valley	216	3 468	180.3	51.5	23	D	D	D	305	5 354	479.1	203.9
Tacoma	501	7 220	387.9	118.9	45	1 749	231.4	53.3	561	8 906	951.2	503.6
University Place	41	459	25.8	7.3	7	89	4.9	1.1	87	D	D	D
Vancouver	428	6 939	364.3	111.0	38	578	31.7	9.0	514	7 399	755.8	370.4
Walla Walla	114	1 746	83.9	25.4	12	77	4.2	1.7	96	D	D	D
Wenatchee	112	1 622	84.5	25.0	9	74	4.4	1.2	120	D	D	D
Yakima	239	3 527	183.5	53.1	20	491	18.5	7.1	291	4 885	631.0	234.6
WEST VIRGINIA	3 629	66 302	4 036.3	975.9	631	6 055	550.1	98.9	3 734	57 400	5 125.5	2 107.5
Charleston	225	4 651	253.2	69.2	20	267	22.8	5.6	318	4 136	555.2	230.6
Huntington	172	2 964	141.0	38.8	18	D	D	D	176	3 266	356.7	167.6
Morgantown	207	4 596	190.5	52.1	23	182	10.0	2.7	89	D	D	D
Parkersburg	130	2 121	97.5	29.0	21	D	D	D	158	1 922	235.2	94.9
Wheeling	103	2 033	181.0	33.4	27	D	D	D	152	D	D	D
WISCONSIN	14 137	221 567	10 303.3	2 764.3	1 966	28 433	2 548.1	826.1	11 460	175 153	16 357.2	7 784.6
Appleton	211	4 363	168.4	47.9	12	262	8.6	2.9	209	3 503	485.0	217.5
Beloit	90	1 338	63.4	17.0	5	D	D	D	43	D	D	D
Brookfield	124	3 114	159.0	44.7	22	358	14.6	5.7	306	D	D	D
Eau Claire	229	D	D	D	26	411	25.7	5.0	217	5 434	656.6	349.8
Fitchburg	43	930	42.0	12.0	15	D	D	D	35	D	D	D
Fond du Lac	125	2 424	86.8	25.7	18	200	21.7	3.5	139	D	D	D
Franklin	60	768	43.4	10.9	11	D	D	D	91	D	D	D
Green Bay	272	5 414	234.0	68.2	23	D	D	D	204	4 567	663.1	285.6
Greenfield	72	D	D	D	17	D	D	D	134	3 258	279.4	127.6
Janesville	162	3 046	132.5	37.4	15	197	9.0	2.7	104	D	D	D
Kenosha	235	3 801	160.5	45.2	22	D	D	D	282	3 366	297.5	140.4
La Crosse	222	3 923	155.1	45.9	24	D	D	D	100	1 197	86.8	36.7
Madison	743	15 474	718.3	209.5	73	1 144	96.4	19.6	443	10 016	1 248.6	619.4
Manitowoc	86	1 544	57.0	16.8	10	94	9.3	1.6	90	D	D	D
Menomonee Falls	66	1 248	56.4	15.1	11	D	D	D	68	D	D	D
Milwaukee	1 106	D	D	D	87	D	D	D	1 135	18 188	1 518.5	812.0
Mount Pleasant	56	1 290	57.7	16.9	6	D	D	D	82	886	83.4	37.3
Neenah	70	1 153	48.7	13.4	10	D	D	D	85	1 134	170.1	69.1
New Berlin	65	1 345	56.6	15.0	16	D	D	D	84	1 074	99.6	47.1
Oak Creek	68	1 366	75.1	18.9	13	D	D	D	53	580	45.6	19.9
Oshkosh	187	3 495	136.7	39.0	16	147	7.1	2.1	142	2 244	240.8	121.8
Racine	161	D	D	D	29	190	13.5	3.2	139	1 401	91.3	43.1
Sheboygan	132	1 976	79.9	21.5	9	110	5.6	1.5	155	3 073	286.6	143.0
Stevens Point	112	1 748	69.1	18.9	10	D	D	D	81	D	D	D
Sun Prairie	50	844	36.4	9.5	7	D	D	D	52	761	65.7	30.0
Superior	107	1 625	60.4	16.8	13	D	D	D	46	963	50.5	22.5
Waukesha	153	3 185	142.4	42.7	22	321	11.9	3.3	193	2 607	288.5	147.1
Wausau	111	1 690	73.6	21.1	14	137	5.1	1.9	164	D	D	D
Wauwatosa	142	3 107	158.9	47.0	13	D	D	D	329	5 474	602.4	307.0
West Allis	159	D	D	D	13	250	10.5	3.2	159	3 183	277.0	141.5
West Bend	66	1 326	52.2	14.2	11	D	D	D	98	1 085	79.5	33.4
WYOMING	1 799	27 580	1 644.8	468.7	317	2 922	168.9	57.1	1 457	13 706	1 486.2	607.7
Casper	158	3 224	170.2	49.2	17	D	D	D	239	D	D	D
Cheyenne	176	3 518	200.9	53.0	11	D	D	D	237	2 779	258.7	113.1
Gillette	94	1 529	86.2	24.3	8	81	2.7	1.1	80	D	D	D
Laramie	103	1 976	73.8	22.0	9	62	1.7	0.5	99	D	D	D

1. Establishments subject to federal tax.

Table D. Cities — Other Services and Government Employment and Payroll

City	Other services[1], 2012 — Number of establishments	Number of employees	Receipts (mil dol)	Annual payroll (mil dol)	Government employment and payroll, 2012 — March payroll — Full-time equivalent employees	Total (dollars)	Percent of total for: Administration, judicial, and legal	Police and Corrections	Fire Protection	Highways and transportation	Health and welfare	Natural resources and utilities	Education and libraries
	104	105	106	107	108	109	110	111	112	113	114	115	116
WASHINGTON—Cont'd													
Pasco	63	308	34.5	8.6	285	1 601 010	14.1	30.2	22.2	7.6	4.6	21.0	0.0
Pullman	25	D	D	D	232	989 864	6.3	23.6	22.8	32.0	0.0	11.6	3.7
Puyallup	85	763	64.8	21.2	469	3 001 181	14.9	30.0	21.9	6.7	0.0	16.4	3.2
Redmond	130	892	98.9	30.0	679	4 387 058	20.9	18.6	29.5	4.1	1.4	18.8	0.0
Renton	148	854	76.7	27.0	825	5 336 014	10.3	32.9	23.1	6.5	6.4	17.5	0.0
Richland	68	522	42.4	14.8	499	3 031 486	16.6	16.7	14.9	6.2	1.1	33.3	2.9
Sammamish	31	180	11.4	4.1	85	514 186	26.6	1.0	0.0	28.1	16.1	22.8	0.0
SeaTac	48	687	63.2	17.1	162	1 068 652	30.3	0.6	37.3	13.7	1.2	5.9	0.0
Seattle	1 302	8 892	755.8	250.0	10 193	71 586 796	7.4	21.3	13.4	5.8	3.3	38.0	3.4
Shoreline	63	326	25.3	7.4	222	1 123 950	28.0	39.9	0.0	5.5	0.6	22.6	0.0
Spokane	349	2 163	171.0	52.9	2 161	12 463 086	15.6	21.9	20.6	8.3	0.4	26.4	3.2
Spokane Valley	177	1 222	110.3	35.5	92	466 469	31.8	0.0	0.0	24.5	34.4	9.2	0.0
Tacoma	330	2 444	223.1	75.5	3 458	23 314 293	11.1	13.2	14.4	8.2	0.5	43.6	2.1
University Place	46	293	20.0	7.5	48	264 084	30.6	4.5	0.0	30.0	14.8	9.6	0.0
Vancouver	300	1 562	120.8	37.4	1 018	5 857 054	12.9	26.3	24.0	6.1	0.0	21.4	0.0
Walla Walla	42	240	16.7	6.0	251	1 313 753	15.6	33.8	26.5	0.9	0.3	16.4	3.3
Wenatchee	65	228	21.7	6.0	185	996 105	13.5	30.6	19.2	10.0	2.0	19.4	0.0
Yakima	140	736	62.9	17.7	615	3 330 932	12.9	39.5	16.4	10.4	0.9	18.9	0.0
WEST VIRGINIA	2 003	12 728	1 246.8	343.2	X	X	X	X	X	X	X	X	X
Charleston	110	979	56.3	17.8	826	2 940 542	13.0	28.6	24.9	0.8	1.4	16.3	0.0
Huntington	67	434	39.9	11.4	338	1 166 129	8.3	42.3	27.9	4.5	2.5	8.5	0.0
Morgantown	56	D	D	D	442	1 584 824	7.6	19.5	12.7	10.7	0.3	38.5	4.0
Parkersburg	64	446	33.0	10.3	347	1 079 226	8.0	24.0	18.5	10.1	1.5	34.7	0.0
Wheeling	66	715	76.6	19.2	828	2 250 153	5.6	14.0	15.9	7.2	0.0	55.8	0.0
WISCONSIN	8 338	47 662	4 015.9	1 242.4	X	X	X	X	X	X	X	X	X
Appleton	127	972	89.6	27.8	663	3 090 024	10.6	24.2	16.9	8.2	4.8	15.8	6.5
Beloit	48	195	14.1	4.2	368	1 795 646	10.7	25.3	19.5	14.3	3.6	17.7	4.9
Brookfield	101	1 064	92.4	31.2	333	1 844 609	12.7	28.6	21.1	12.3	0.0	14.9	6.1
Eau Claire	125	901	62.1	19.6	608	2 643 962	9.0	24.0	17.4	10.5	10.6	15.3	5.6
Fitchburg	30	289	28.3	9.4	168	745 550	17.6	38.6	15.3	7.5	2.7	10.2	0.8
Fond du Lac	89	610	40.0	14.2	344	1 652 329	8.9	25.7	21.9	14.0	1.9	15.0	6.8
Franklin	47	329	29.9	10.1	218	1 131 749	9.5	36.1	24.9	12.6	2.8	4.7	5.0
Green Bay	146	913	67.4	21.0	860	4 043 340	7.5	30.8	25.6	11.5	1.1	19.5	0.0
Greenfield	65	456	26.6	10.5	217	1 158 811	11.1	38.6	26.7	12.0	3.2	3.7	3.2
Janesville	99	626	36.7	12.8	482	2 513 217	10.6	24.7	21.6	15.6	3.3	16.1	7.3
Kenosha	147	915	66.9	20.6	811	3 859 872	5.8	28.1	22.1	10.6	2.7	18.1	7.7
La Crosse	93	681	44.6	17.3	567	2 357 551	9.7	24.1	19.2	17.7	2.0	14.4	9.6
Madison	349	2 839	212.6	76.1	3 036	14 945 308	10.6	21.2	12.9	22.9	2.3	18.7	5.5
Manitowoc	55	273	19.5	5.7	355	1 875 536	6.3	20.8	18.2	15.1	0.0	32.1	5.9
Menomonee Falls	63	563	52.2	15.9	252	1 124 295	9.0	39.6	11.5	12.7	2.5	9.8	5.9
Milwaukee	623	4 127	367.3	126.6	6 455	32 385 292	9.5	39.7	17.4	3.2	7.3	12.0	3.2
Mount Pleasant	34	232	17.6	5.4	206	856 388	12.7	34.6	41.4	6.6	0.0	4.6	0.0
Neenah	49	366	27.3	10.1	272	1 262 394	8.6	24.1	29.0	10.9	5.7	15.3	6.4
New Berlin	69	664	69.6	27.6	254	1 283 876	12.9	39.3	15.4	12.5	0.0	11.2	4.4
Oak Creek	42	439	49.7	12.3	266	1 412 700	9.6	31.2	21.6	13.5	2.3	15.7	2.7
Oshkosh	80	687	53.0	18.2	576	2 558 304	7.2	22.6	21.9	15.9	6.5	17.9	5.9
Racine	110	731	40.6	14.4	815	4 196 517	6.8	33.8	20.0	8.7	5.3	19.5	3.6
Sheboygan	83	518	26.7	9.1	431	1 929 836	9.1	27.3	17.8	18.6	2.9	13.8	7.8
Stevens Point	54	298	29.0	8.2	194	851 692	9.1	29.9	22.2	24.4	3.2	11.3	0.0
Sun Prairie	35	202	18.0	4.1	223	1 003 694	14.5	33.1	0.0	9.8	7.1	24.8	7.1
Superior	53	351	28.1	9.0	255	1 159 999	11.2	29.7	15.8	11.8	0.7	18.3	5.6
Waukesha	117	872	73.3	23.8	566	2 950 957	10.7	28.4	19.7	16.3	0.3	16.6	5.6
Wausau	55	328	31.9	9.2	306	1 383 873	11.0	27.3	21.3	24.5	3.8	8.0	0.0
Wauwatosa	68	639	52.4	18.0	414	2 166 975	10.9	28.6	27.5	10.0	3.1	9.0	5.3
West Allis	114	604	68.2	17.0	541	2 746 980	10.4	30.7	21.8	7.9	7.6	15.5	3.5
West Bend	76	464	30.9	10.2	261	1 244 682	11.9	33.2	19.5	9.0	0.0	16.8	5.0
WYOMING	998	5 095	660.2	169.6	X	X	X	X	X	X	X	X	X
Casper	106	687	82.8	22.0	563	2 490 135	12.1	24.0	15.7	5.9	2.6	30.8	0.0
Cheyenne	102	561	47.1	14.6	655	2 479 867	12.4	24.6	20.1	11.9	5.3	17.8	0.0
Gillette	77	512	63.1	17.6	278	1 359 171	21.1	29.1	0.0	9.2	3.7	24.3	0.0
Laramie	56	D	D	D	282	1 207 422	11.8	25.1	22.5	5.3	8.5	26.7	0.0

1. Establishments subject to federal tax.

Table D. Cities — City Government Finances

City	City government finances, 2012									
	General revenue							General expenditure		
		Intergovernmental		Taxes					Per capita[1] (dollars)	
					Per capita[1] (dollars)					
	Total (mil dol)	Total (mil dol)	Percent from state government	Total (mil dol)	Total	Property	Sales and gross receipts	Total (mil dol)	Total	Capital outlays
	117	118	119	120	121	122	123	124	125	126
WASHINGTON— Cont'd										
Pasco	56.3	7.4	83.9	27.7	414	100	307	43.0	644	84
Pullman	28.8	6.2	79.9	14.1	450	166	280	23.2	740	102
Puyallup	56.2	6.0	83.5	28.9	756	220	514	45.2	1 184	149
Redmond	132.9	19.1	27.4	73.4	1 298	388	860	135.8	2 399	780
Renton	182.1	40.0	23.2	80.9	844	338	484	161.6	1 687	421
Richland	85.1	16.9	69.5	35.1	682	273	382	81.3	1 579	382
Sammamish	38.6	2.0	89.9	31.3	638	438	144	30.6	623	115
SeaTac	44.1	5.0	93.3	33.9	1 224	437	770	38.5	1 392	195
Seattle	1 849.1	193.2	68.5	913.5	1 438	626	809	1 658.2	2 611	430
Shoreline	64.6	27.8	75.5	28.7	527	212	300	61.5	1 129	532
Spokane	360.6	46.8	62.8	134.2	641	291	339	346.3	1 653	310
Spokane Valley	47.6	9.5	74.7	34.3	379	118	250	44.6	492	104
Tacoma	497.4	82.6	61.5	160.2	792	300	477	525.2	2 597	668
University Place	20.3	3.7	81.0	12.2	386	120	255	19.2	607	164
Vancouver	216.2	36.9	48.3	102.8	622	244	361	188.0	1 138	228
Walla Walla	47.0	7.8	77.4	16.3	512	186	320	48.0	1 505	391
Wenatchee	35.6	3.6	70.5	20.4	627	183	433	31.6	972	109
Yakima	108.8	28.2	59.7	50.2	539	163	367	101.0	1 085	250
WEST VIRGINIA	X	X	X	X	X	X	X	X	X	X
Charleston	119.9	8.4	43.3	74.5	1 461	237	1 224	118.2	2 318	327
Huntington	66.4	5.5	20.3	27.6	561	105	408	69.9	1 422	172
Morgantown	47.5	3.6	18.6	18.2	602	114	488	57.9	1 916	338
Parkersburg	38.3	2.2	14.9	16.0	512	159	345	37.9	1 214	142
Wheeling	68.9	4.3	9.3	21.9	776	214	556	77.9	2 759	267
WISCONSIN	X	X	X	X	X	X	X	X	X	X
Appleton	105.8	35.3	66.9	40.0	547	511	29	95.4	1 306	185
Beloit	62.8	26.8	88.2	19.9	542	506	31	62.9	1 709	281
Brookfield	58.1	9.5	75.4	37.1	977	878	98	58.2	1 531	164
Eau Claire	86.2	27.3	65.5	36.1	536	481	48	88.9	1 320	274
Fitchburg	30.2	5.5	88.9	18.6	718	696	22	39.3	1 517	661
Fond du Lac	60.5	20.6	71.8	21.1	490	445	41	63.0	1 465	223
Franklin	41.4	6.9	92.4	26.8	747	678	68	36.9	1 030	91
Green Bay	138.7	46.3	79.3	53.7	512	485	22	133.7	1 276	218
Greenfield	36.7	6.5	88.9	20.6	556	518	38	41.0	1 106	190
Janesville	81.1	21.4	60.8	31.0	488	455	30	86.4	1 359	476
Kenosha	136.7	40.5	74.7	66.5	666	635	29	121.2	1 213	141
La Crosse	96.0	32.3	81.3	41.7	801	727	63	83.2	1 597	241
Madison	476.1	163.1	64.2	192.4	802	725	69	469.3	1 956	262
Manitowoc	48.5	17.0	90.1	15.7	469	434	32	54.5	1 630	246
Menomonee Falls	46.2	6.0	94.8	25.0	698	656	42	54.6	1 523	188
Milwaukee	1 070.1	483.1	64.8	302.6	505	483	22	1 000.4	1 671	211
Mount Pleasant	34.1	6.0	62.3	15.7	601	545	49	36.3	1 387	0
Neenah	34.2	7.5	78.2	17.5	681	647	32	35.3	1 374	110
New Berlin	42.8	4.9	98.3	23.5	591	549	41	43.8	1 103	116
Oak Creek	39.6	9.3	95.7	20.6	591	532	53	40.8	1 169	139
Oshkosh	88.9	26.0	83.5	36.9	554	503	47	92.9	1 393	336
Racine	138.3	56.9	78.9	49.1	627	593	33	139.8	1 787	186
Sheboygan	64.8	24.2	81.4	26.8	549	494	49	58.7	1 204	114
Stevens Point	34.5	13.5	80.1	14.0	519	471	42	34.2	1 272	140
Sun Prairie	36.3	6.6	89.6	21.4	700	647	49	33.4	1 092	159
Superior	47.8	19.7	86.8	13.1	488	414	69	43.1	1 604	221
Waukesha	94.8	23.2	75.8	53.6	753	709	40	92.3	1 297	257
Wausau	59.2	21.8	72.8	26.1	667	628	35	52.5	1 340	306
Wauwatosa	76.5	14.7	62.5	41.9	891	830	51	68.2	1 451	107
West Allis	89.6	27.7	67.2	39.6	652	626	24	88.3	1 455	97
West Bend	37.8	8.6	79.5	22.6	714	667	45	36.4	1 152	223
WYOMING	X	X	X	X	X	X	X	X	X	X
Casper	90.9	48.4	57.4	10.7	185	79	91	91.8	1 586	372
Cheyenne	102.2	45.4	60.0	14.2	231	86	144	84.7	1 372	240
Gillette	102.0	79.8	46.5	4.1	129	81	48	73.4	2 334	563
Laramie	40.4	21.5	68.2	5.1	162	66	95	47.7	1 503	636

1. Based on population estimated as of July 1 of the year shown.

City	City government finances, 2012 (cont.)									
	General expenditure (cont.)									
	Percent of total for:									
	Public welfare	Highways	Parking facilities	Education	Health and hospitals	Police protection	Sewerage and sanitation	Parks and recreation	Housing and community development	Interest on debt
	127	128	129	130	131	132	133	134	135	136
WASHINGTON—Cont'd										
Pasco	0.0	12.0	0.0	0.0	5.4	17.4	11.1	11.5	2.3	5.8
Pullman	0.0	11.6	0.0	0.0	6.2	18.7	14.9	9.3	0.0	0.8
Puyallup	0.0	14.1	0.0	0.0	0.3	25.3	23.3	8.8	1.9	6.7
Redmond	0.1	20.2	0.0	0.0	3.2	9.2	16.1	13.1	0.8	2.8
Renton	0.0	13.1	0.0	0.0	0.2	11.9	18.6	6.2	1.5	5.1
Richland	0.0	12.0	0.0	0.0	3.2	11.2	16.4	9.6	5.1	3.3
Sammamish	0.0	22.0	0.0	0.0	0.5	13.9	5.2	17.5	3.3	0.4
SeaTac	0.0	17.5	0.0	0.0	0.0	22.5	3.5	7.6	3.2	0.3
Seattle	6.2	11.8	0.5	0.3	1.1	10.5	29.3	9.1	1.8	4.1
Shoreline	0.0	46.6	0.0	0.0	0.0	16.3	3.4	7.7	2.4	3.0
Spokane	1.1	10.6	0.1	0.0	0.1	12.3	34.0	5.6	2.9	2.6
Spokane Valley	0.0	29.1	0.0	0.0	0.7	37.4	3.1	8.3	3.7	0.9
Tacoma	1.2	12.1	1.0	0.0	2.6	11.0	24.3	5.6	2.6	4.8
University Place	0.0	26.2	0.0	0.0	0.9	17.4	7.1	4.1	4.1	14.1
Vancouver	0.0	18.7	0.7	0.0	0.1	13.2	12.4	8.6	1.9	4.8
Walla Walla	0.0	9.6	0.0	0.0	5.4	12.5	19.2	5.1	0.0	3.1
Wenatchee	0.0	8.3	0.0	0.0	0.6	18.3	19.6	9.2	4.5	4.1
Yakima	0.0	18.3	0.0	0.0	0.4	19.6	13.4	5.3	3.1	2.2
WEST VIRGINIA	X	X	X	X	X	X	X	X	X	X
Charleston	0.0	12.8	2.4	0.0	0.0	18.6	20.7	8.7	3.5	3.1
Huntington	1.1	3.4	1.2	0.0	0.5	17.3	19.7	5.0	6.2	1.0
Morgantown	0.0	7.3	3.3	0.0	0.1	10.7	27.2	11.8	9.3	1.9
Parkersburg	0.1	17.9	0.6	0.0	0.0	14.6	24.6	1.3	3.6	0.4
Wheeling	0.3	8.2	0.9	0.0	0.0	10.7	13.4	47.9	2.8	1.1
WISCONSIN	X	X	X	X	X	X	X	X	X	X
Appleton	0.5	20.7	1.8	0.0	1.3	17.2	14.6	5.8	1.5	8.6
Beloit	0.0	15.7	0.0	0.0	2.0	18.6	18.7	5.0	1.7	7.4
Brookfield	0.0	16.4	0.0	0.0	5.1	16.4	24.7	6.6	0.0	4.2
Eau Claire	0.0	26.3	0.5	0.0	7.7	17.5	7.2	8.4	1.3	5.0
Fitchburg	0.0	15.1	0.0	0.0	1.4	15.9	6.7	4.4	0.0	3.0
Fond du Lac	0.0	15.2	1.0	0.0	7.9	15.6	15.7	3.3	5.5	12.5
Franklin	0.0	12.4	0.0	0.0	6.0	25.2	13.8	0.9	1.9	3.9
Green Bay	0.0	15.6	1.6	0.0	0.1	19.6	17.1	7.5	0.1	7.7
Greenfield	0.0	24.5	0.0	0.0	6.1	25.0	12.3	4.7	0.0	3.4
Janesville	1.0	12.8	0.1	0.0	3.5	15.3	28.2	6.8	4.9	2.7
Kenosha	0.0	15.3	0.0	0.0	8.7	23.0	12.6	7.0	3.3	5.4
La Crosse	0.1	15.0	1.9	0.1	0.2	14.5	10.0	13.5	2.4	5.6
Madison	0.0	12.8	1.8	0.0	2.2	14.5	7.9	12.6	8.8	4.6
Manitowoc	0.0	15.2	0.1	0.0	0.4	14.2	10.4	6.0	0.2	12.4
Menomonee Falls	0.0	15.5	0.0	0.0	0.2	16.2	20.2	2.6	0.0	7.8
Milwaukee	0.0	12.7	2.5	0.0	2.4	25.6	14.5	0.3	4.2	5.0
Mount Pleasant	0.0	17.1	0.0	0.0	4.2	20.6	21.1	0.8	0.0	5.8
Neenah	0.0	16.2	0.6	0.0	1.9	17.0	13.8	6.1	0.8	10.8
New Berlin	0.0	19.7	0.0	0.0	2.8	23.9	21.2	4.8	0.0	3.7
Oak Creek	0.0	19.5	0.0	0.0	14.6	24.8	12.2	3.6	0.0	2.2
Oshkosh	0.0	23.8	0.5	0.0	2.4	13.2	11.8	12.9	0.0	8.2
Racine	0.0	14.3	1.2	0.0	5.6	23.4	15.4	8.0	2.0	7.2
Sheboygan	0.0	14.8	0.7	0.0	0.9	20.3	13.9	5.4	6.3	5.0
Stevens Point	0.0	23.7	0.0	0.0	4.9	16.2	9.8	7.6	0.0	4.2
Sun Prairie	0.0	21.7	0.0	0.0	4.2	20.7	12.6	6.0	0.0	10.6
Superior	0.0	18.0	0.0	0.0	0.4	17.5	22.0	4.7	2.4	3.9
Waukesha	0.0	16.2	0.8	0.0	2.6	18.4	16.2	9.4	0.3	5.9
Wausau	0.0	21.0	3.6	0.0	5.0	16.8	11.2	7.1	1.6	3.1
Wauwatosa	0.0	13.3	0.0	0.0	8.5	23.5	12.9	2.4	2.5	4.8
West Allis	0.0	15.5	0.1	0.0	4.5	22.8	11.5	0.5	5.7	4.1
West Bend	0.0	15.4	0.3	0.0	1.8	22.0	12.1	9.0	0.5	10.6
WYOMING	X	X	X	X	X	X	X	X	X	X
Casper	2.2	10.7	0.0	0.0	1.5	13.9	20.6	12.8	0.5	0.4
Cheyenne	1.4	15.7	0.8	0.0	2.2	15.2	14.6	13.7	0.4	1.9
Gillette	0.0	29.3	0.0	0.0	0.8	10.9	11.6	5.5	1.5	0.5
Laramie	0.0	22.8	0.0	0.0	3.0	15.4	15.8	9.0	1.0	1.4

Table D. Cities — City Government Finances, City Government Employment, and Climate

City	City government finances, 2012 (cont.) Debt outstanding Total (mil dol)	Per capita[1] (dollars)	Debt issued during year	Climate[2] Average daily temperature (degrees Fahrenheit) Mean January	July	Limits January[3]	July[4]	Annual precipitation (inches)	Heating degree days	Cooling degree days
	137	138	139	140	141	142	143	144	145	146
WASHINGTON—Cont'd										
Pasco	48.6	727	4.2	34.2	75.2	28.0	89.3	8.01	4 731	909
Pullman	7.0	224	0.3	NA	NA	NA	NA	NA	NA	NA
Puyallup	75.3	1 972	2.6	39.9	64.9	32.9	77.8	40.51	4 991	153
Redmond	82.8	1 463	8.0	25.1	55.0	20.0	65.0	82.86	9 630	12
Renton	184.1	1 921	26.1	40.9	65.3	35.9	75.3	37.07	4 797	173
Richland	147.2	2 861	0.3	33.0	73.2	26.0	87.9	7.55	5 133	739
Sammamish	7.7	157	0.0	40.8	65.2	35.2	75.0	35.96	4 756	174
SeaTac	5.8	208	0.0	40.9	65.3	35.9	75.3	37.07	4 797	173
Seattle	4 163.6	6 556	431.3	41.5	65.5	36.0	74.5	38.25	4 615	192
Shoreline	38.3	704	0.0	40.8	65.2	35.2	75.0	35.96	4 756	174
Spokane	189.9	906	0.0	27.3	68.6	21.7	82.5	16.67	6 820	394
Spokane Valley	7.9	88	0.0	NA	NA	NA	NA	NA	NA	NA
Tacoma	1 587.6	7 849	58.5	41.0	65.6	35.1	76.1	38.95	4 650	167
University Place	55.9	1 770	5.9	41.0	65.6	35.1	76.1	38.95	4 650	167
Vancouver	263.9	1 597	10.6	39.0	65.4	32.4	77.3	41.92	4 990	197
Walla Walla	62.5	1 959	0.0	34.7	75.3	28.8	89.9	20.88	4 882	957
Wenatchee	42.9	1 318	18.9	29.2	74.4	23.2	87.8	9.12	5 533	832
Yakima	60.7	653	2.8	29.1	69.1	20.5	87.2	8.26	6 104	431
WEST VIRGINIA	X	X	X	X	X	X	X	X	X	X
Charleston	118.0	2 315	9.2	33.4	73.9	24.2	84.9	44.05	4 644	978
Huntington	44.1	897	2.3	32.1	76.3	23.5	87.1	41.74	4 737	1 128
Morgantown	120.1	3 972	3.8	30.8	73.5	22.3	83.4	43.30	5 174	815
Parkersburg	67.9	2 176	4.9	30.7	75.4	22.3	85.8	40.69	5 091	1 038
Wheeling	49.6	1 759	8.3	29.6	74.8	21.4	85.2	40.34	5 313	926
WISCONSIN	X	X	X	X	X	X	X	X	X	X
Appleton	159.0	2 176	6.9	16.0	71.6	7.8	81.4	30.16	7 721	572
Beloit	93.8	2 547	28.1	19.1	72.4	11.6	82.5	35.25	6 969	664
Brookfield	66.3	1 745	9.1	20.0	74.3	11.5	85.1	32.09	6 886	791
Eau Claire	99.4	1 476	8.5	11.9	71.4	2.5	82.6	32.12	8 196	554
Fitchburg	29.6	1 143	6.6	NA	NA	NA	NA	NA	NA	NA
Fond du Lac	203.2	4 724	19.8	16.6	71.8	9.1	81.1	30.15	7 534	586
Franklin	32.5	906	0.0	20.7	72.0	13.4	81.1	34.81	7 087	616
Green Bay	209.5	1 998	5.7	15.6	69.9	7.1	81.2	29.19	7 963	463
Greenfield	32.8	886	7.3	19.9	73.8	12.7	81.9	33.86	6 847	764
Janesville	106.9	1 682	22.1	17.7	72.1	8.6	83.8	32.78	7 238	629
Kenosha	179.5	1 797	26.2	20.8	71.3	13.2	78.7	34.74	6 999	549
La Crosse	98.7	1 894	17.8	15.9	74.0	6.3	85.2	32.36	7 340	775
Madison	526.8	2 195	99.4	17.3	71.6	9.3	82.1	32.95	7 493	582
Manitowoc	154.4	4 618	11.6	18.7	69.9	10.8	79.6	30.49	7 563	425
Menomonee Falls	94.1	2 625	18.0	16.5	69.3	8.1	80.2	33.45	7 832	407
Milwaukee	1 306.0	2 181	454.0	20.0	74.3	11.5	85.1	32.09	6 886	791
Mount Pleasant	47.2	1 806	5.6	NA	NA	NA	NA	NA	NA	NA
Neenah	75.6	2 939	5.0	NA	NA	NA	NA	NA	NA	NA
New Berlin	45.0	1 133	6.4	19.9	73.8	12.7	81.9	33.86	6 847	764
Oak Creek	112.6	3 230	18.5	20.7	72.0	13.4	81.1	34.81	7 087	616
Oshkosh	221.7	3 326	42.5	16.1	72.0	7.8	81.8	31.57	7 639	591
Racine	233.6	2 986	30.0	20.7	71.3	13.3	78.6	35.35	7 032	567
Sheboygan	62.5	1 281	1.4	20.9	71.4	13.2	81.4	31.90	7 056	559
Stevens Point	44.4	1 651	18.4	NA	NA	NA	NA	NA	NA	NA
Sun Prairie	70.0	2 289	0.0	NA	NA	NA	NA	NA	NA	NA
Superior	54.2	2 019	18.4	12.1	66.6	3.4	76.2	30.78	9 006	241
Waukesha	127.7	1 793	19.3	19.5	73.8	11.4	84.2	34.64	6 893	784
Wausau	50.1	1 279	7.7	13.0	70.1	3.6	80.8	33.36	8 237	464
Wauwatosa	100.8	2 142	19.5	20.0	74.3	11.5	85.1	32.09	6 886	791
West Allis	78.5	1 294	5.9	19.9	73.8	12.7	81.9	33.86	6 847	764
West Bend	79.7	2 525	6.8	18.4	70.6	10.7	81.3	32.85	7 371	502
WYOMING	X	X	X	X	X	X	X	X	X	X
Casper	19.5	338	0.1	22.3	70.0	12.2	86.8	13.03	7 571	428
Cheyenne	86.1	1 395	14.1	25.9	67.7	14.8	81.9	15.45	7 388	273
Gillette	91.7	2 916	2.2	NA	NA	NA	NA	NA	NA	NA
Laramie	44.3	1 394	0.5	20.3	62.9	7.8	79.4	11.19	9 233	75

4. Based on city population estimated as of July 1 of the year shown.   2. Represents normal values based on the 30-year period, 1971–2000.   3. Average daily minimum.

PART E.

Congressional Districts of the 115th Congress

(For explanation of symbols, see page viii)

Congressional District Highlights and Rankings

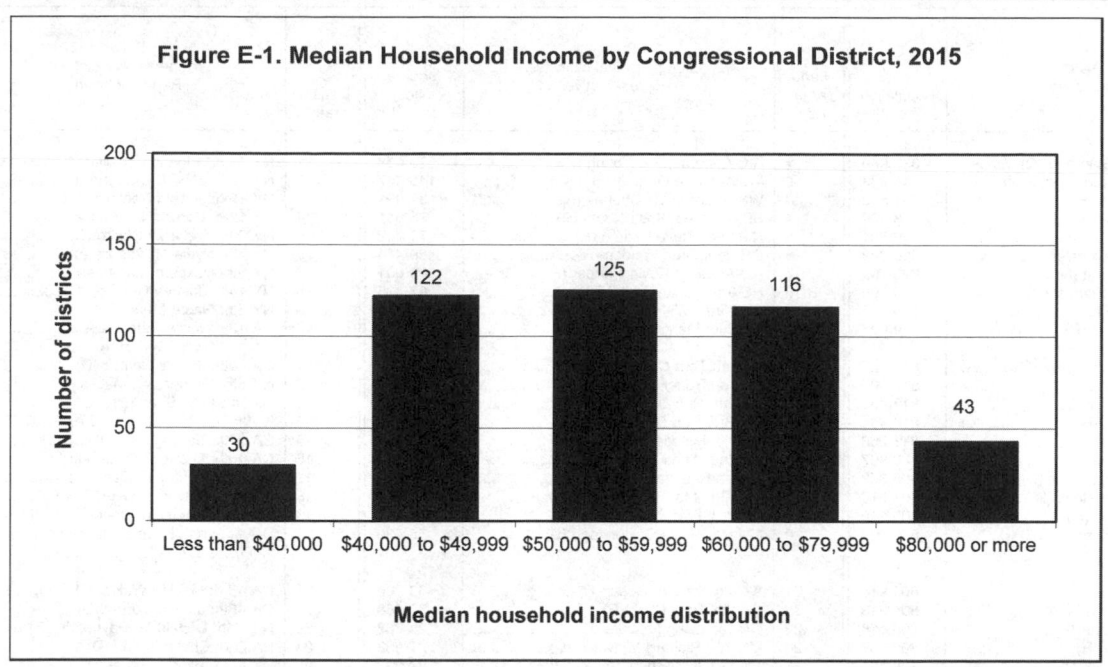

Figure E-1. Median Household Income by Congressional District, 2015

Every 10 years, the Census Bureau conducts a count to reapportion the seats in the U.S. House of Representatives. The House's 435 seats are divided among the 50 states. (The District of Columbia has no representative in Congress, although it has a nonvoting delegate.) The seats are reapportioned according to the population measured on April 1 of the census year in order to account for population changes among the states over the previous decade. The number of districts within a state may change after each decennial census, and the districts' boundaries may change more than once during a decade. The 115th Congress which convened in 2017 was the third to reflect the new boundaries based on the 2010 census. The Representatives of the 115th Congress are listed. Most of the data in Table E have been collected or updated for the 115th congress, but some sources were collected for the 114th congress or earlier. Boundary changes between the 114th and 115th congresses occurred in Florida, Minnesota, North Carolina, and Virginia.

As the state with the largest population, California had the most representatives with 53. Texas (36) and New York (27) were second and third largest, respectively. There were 7 states with just 1 representative: Alaska, Delaware, Montana, North Dakota, South Dakota, Vermont, and Wyoming. These states' representatives were considered 'At Large,' as they represented an entire state instead of a specific congressional district within the state.

Because the number of representatives is limited to 435, states with larger population growth add seats, while states with little or no growth lose seats. When the 113th Congress convened in January 2013, eight states had more representatives in congress and 10 states had fewer. Based on the 2010 census, Texas gained 4 seats, Florida gained 2, while Washington, Nevada, Utah, Arizona, Georgia, and South Carolina each gained one seat. New York and Ohio each lost two seats, while Massachusetts, New Jersey, Pennsylvania, Michigan, Illinois, Iowa, Missouri, and Louisiana each lost a seat.

As each decade progresses, population shifts alter the size of districts, leading up to the reapportionment of the next census. After the 2000 census, the population of each congressional

district was about 645,000. Based on the 2015 population estimates, the new congressional districts average over 737,000 people. Montana's at-large congressional district had over a million people, while Delaware and South Dakota also had at-large seats with above average populations. Texas' 22nd district is the largest apportioned congressional district in the United States with a population over 861,570 in 2015. Rhode Island's two congressional districts have the smallest populations at 532,557 and 523,741. Congressional districts in Nebraska and West Virginia also have smaller populations. For years, Louisiana's 2nd district was the least populous congressional district in the nation due to outmigration after Hurricane Katrina.

While most of the congressional districts had about the same population size, they varied widely in other characteristics. In Colorado's 2nd district, 96.4 percent of the residents were high school graduates, compared with just 52.6 percent in California's 40th district and 57.6 percent in Texas's 33rd district. California's 21st district and Texas's 29th district had the lowest proportion of college graduates, with only 9.1 percent of their residents holding a bachelor's degree, followed by California's 40th district at 9.5 percent, Texas's 33rd district at 10.4 percent, and California's 16th district at 12.1 percent. In New York's 12th district, 71.5 percent of residents were college graduates.

The highest unemployment rates were found in Michigan's 13th district at 14.6 percent and Illinois's 2nd district at 14.5 percent. Three districts from California, two districts each from Illinois and Michigan along with one district each from Mississippi, Florida, and Ohio ranked among the 10 highest. Sixty-nine congressional districts had 20 percent or more of their populations living in poverty. New York's 15th district had the highest poverty rate in the nation at 38.1 percent and the lowest median household income at $26,047 in 2015. In California's 18th district, the median household income was $120,089, the highest in the nation. Sixty-four congressional districts had median household incomes exceeding $75,000 per year, while thirty districts had median household incomes below $40,000. The U.S. median household income in 2015 was $55,775.

Congressional Districts of the 115th Congress of the United States
Selected Rankings

Population, 2015			Land area, 2016			Population density, 2015		
Popu-lation rank	State congressional district Representative	Population [col 2]	Land area rank	State congressional district Representative	Land area (square miles) [col 1]	Density rank	State congressional district Representative	Population density (per square mile) [col 3]
1	MT At-Large Greg Gianforte (R)	1 032 949	1	AK: At-Large Don Young (R)	570 638	1	NY 13th: Adriano Espaillat (D)	77 791
2	DE At-Large: Lisa Blunt Rochester (D)	945 934	2	MT At-Large Greg Gianforte (R)	145 547	2	NY 15th: José E. Serrano (D)	52 528
3	TX 22nd: Pete Olson (R)	861 570	3	WY At-Large Liz Cheney (R)	97 091	3	NY 10th: Jerrold Nadler (D)	51 853
4	SD At-Large: Kristi Noem (R)	858 469	4	SD At-Large: Kristi Noem (R)	75 811	4	NY 12th: Carolyn B. Maloney (D)	49 618
5	ID 1st: Raul Labrador (R)	849 601	5	NM 2nd: Steve Pearce (R)	71 742	5	NY 9th: Yvette D. Clarke (D)	48 834
6	NC 9th: Robert Pittenger (R)	828 929	6	OR 2nd: Greg Walden (R)	69 444	6	NY 7th: Nydia M. Velázquez (D)	46 669
7	TX 35th: Lloyd Doggett (D)	823 909	7	ND-At Large Kevin Cramer (R)	69 001	7	NY 8th: Hakeem S. Jeffries (D)	26 674
8	OR 1st: Suzanne Bonamici (D)	820 305	8	NE 3rd: Adrian Smith (R)	67 435	8	NY 14th: Joseph Crowley (D)	25 318
9	FL 9th: Darren Soto (D)	819 676	9	TX 23rd: Will Hurd (R)	58 058	9	NY 6th: Grace Meng (D)	24 990
10	TX 3rd: Sam Johnson (R)	819 626	10	NV 2nd: Mark E. Amodei (R)	55 829	10	CA 12th:Nancy Pelosi (D)	19 208
11	TX 26th: Michael C. Burgess (R)	818 125	11	AZ 1st: Tom O'Halleran (D)	55 037	11	CA 34th: Jimmy Gomez (D)	15 422
12	OR 3rd: Earl Blumenauer (D)	815 909	12	KS 1st: Roger W. Marshall (R)	52 542	12	NY 5th: Gregory W. Meeks (D)	15 015
13	OR 5th: Kurt Schrader (D)	813 436	13	NV 4th: Ruben J. Kihuen (D)	50 997	13	NJ 8th: Albio Sires (D)	14 033
14	IA 3rd: David Young (R)	812 464	14	NM 3rd: Ben Ray Luján (D)	44 959	14	IL 4th:Luis V. Gutierrez (D)	13 510
15	NC 4th: David E. Price (D)	811 063	15	ID 2nd: Michael K. Simpson (R)	43 224	15	CA 37th: Karen Bass (D)	13 079
16	OK 5th: Steve Russell (R)	809 997	16	UT 2nd: Chris Stewart (R)	40 015	16	CA 40th: Lucille Roybal-Allard (D)	12 499
17	VA 8th Donald S. Beyer, Jr. (D)	808 352	17	ID 1st: Raul Labrador (R)	39 418	17	MA 7th: Michael E. Capuano (D)	12 398
18	VA10th Barbara Comstock (R)	807 670	18	TX 13th: Mac Thornberry (R)	38 350	18	IL 7th: Danny K. Davis (D)	11 571
19	LA 1st: Steve Scalise (R)	806 140	19	OK 3rd: Frank D. Lucas (R)	34 117	19	NY 11th: Daniel M. Donovan Jr. (R)	11 000
20	ID 2nd: Michael K. Simpson (R)	805 329	20	MN 6th: Collin C. Peterson (D)	33 430	20	DC At Large: Eleanor Holmes Norton (D)	10 994
21	TX 31st: John R. Carter (R)	804 974	21	AZ 4th: Paul A. Gosar (R)	33 200	21	CA 43rd: Maxine Waters (D)	10 334
22	GA 7th: Robert Woodall (R)	804 318	22	CA 8th: Paul Cook (R)	32 868	22	CA 46th: J. Luis Correa (D)	10 300
23	CO 1st: Diana DeGette (D)	803 636	23	CA 1st: Doug LaMalfa (R)	28 088	23	NJ 10th: Donald M. Payne, Jr. (D)	10 084
24	TX 8th: Kevin Brady (R)	802 187	24	MN 7th: Richard M. Nolan (D)	27 908	24	PA 2nd: Chaka Fattah (D)	9 784
25	OR 2nd: Greg Walden (R)	798 161	25	TX 11th K. Michael Conaway (R)	27 833	25	NY 16th: Eliot L. Engel (D)	9 553
26	NC 2nd: George Holding (R)	796 200	26	ME 2nd: Bruce Poliquin (R)	27 558	26	PA 1st: Robert A. Brady (D)	9 238
27	CO 6th: Mike Coffman (R)	796 156	27	TX 19th: Jodey C. Arrington (R)	25 836	27	CA 44th: Nanette Diaz Barragan (D)	8 973
28	NC 12th: Alma S. Adams (D)	793 964	28	MI 1st: Jack Bergman (R)	25 028	28	NJ 9th: Bill Pascrell, Jr. (D)	7 983
29	TX 10th: Michael T. McCaul (R)	792 770	29	WI 7th: Sean P. Duffy (R)	23 039	29	CA 29th: Tony Cárdenas (D)	7 829
30	OK 1st: Jim Bridenstine (R)	792 694	30	IA 4th: Steve King (R)	22 756	30	CA 13th:Barbara Lee (D)	7 811
31	NC 13th: Ted Budd (R)	791 492	31	AR 2nd: Bruce Westerman (R)	22 339	31	IL 5th: Michael Quigley (D)	7 696
32	LA 2nd: Cedric Richmond (D)	791 393	32	OK 2nd: Markwayne Mullin (R)	20 996	32	FL 24th: Frederica S. Wilson (D)	7 283
33	NY 13th: Adriano Espaillat (D)	790 434	33	UT 3rd: Vacant	20 074	33	CA 38th: Linda T. Sánchez (D)	7 153
34	AZ 5th: Andy Biggs (R)	789 400	34	MO 8th: Jason T. Smith (R)	19 901	34	IL 9th: Janice D. Schakowsky (D)	6 854
35	TX 12th: Kay Granger (R)	788 381	35	UT 1st: Rob Bishop (R)	19 557	35	NV 1st: Dina Titus (D)	6 731
36	FL 10th: Val Butler Demings (D)	788 192	36	AR 1st: Eric A. "Rick" Crawford (R)	19 319	36	FL 27th: Ileana Ros-Lehtinen (R)	6 633
37	CO 4th: Ken Buck (R)	787 940	37	WA 4th: Dan Newsome (R)	19 246	37	NY 4th: Kathleen M. Rice (D)	6 523
38	LA 6th: Garret Graves (R)	785 840	38	MO 6th: Sam Graves (R)	18 199	38	CA 32nd: Grace F. Napolitano (D)	5 899
39	NC 7th: David Rouzer (R)	785 124	39	OR 4th: Peter A. DeFazio (D)	17 272	39	CA 53rd: Susan A. Davis (D)	5 733
40	AR 2nd: Steve Womack (R)	782 717	40	AZ 3rd: Raul M. Grijalva (D)	15 688	40	CA 30th: Brad Sherman (D)	5 672
41	TX 9th: Al Green (D)	782 554	41	MS 2nd: Bennie G. Thompson (D)	15 552	41	WI 4th: Gwen Moore (D)	5 581
42	LA 3rd: Clay Higgins (R)	782 417	42	WA 5th: Cathy McMorris Rodgers (R)	15 473	42	VA 8th Donald S. Beyer, Jr. (D)	5 416
43	CO: 2nd: Jared Polis (D)	782 278	43	NY 21st: Elise M. Stefanik (R)	15 114	43	MN 5th: Keith Ellison (D)	5 214
44	OR 4th: Peter A. DeFazio (D)	781 166	44	IL 15th: John Shimkus (R)	14 696	44	WA 7th: Pramila Jayapal (D)	5 181
45	TX 24th: Kenny Marchant (R)	779 968	45	LA 5th: Ralph Lee Abraham (R)	14 453	45	CA 48th: Dana Rohrabacher (R)	4 976
46	NY 5th: Gregory W. Meeks (D)	779 896	46	MO 4th: Vicky Hartzler (R)	14 406	46	TX 7th: John Abney Culberson (R)	4 798
47	OK 3rd: Frank D. Lucas (R)	779 713	47	KS 4th: Ron Estes (R)	14 315	47	TX 9th: Al Green (D)	4 722
48	VA 7th Dave Brat (R)	778 480	48	KS 2nd: Lynn Jenkins (R)	14 144	48	AZ 9th: Kyrsten Sinema (D)	4 721
49	IA 2nd: David Loebsack (D)	778 329	49	CA 2nd:Jared Huffman (D)	12 952	49	PA 13th: Brendan F. Boyle (D)	4 699
50	OK 4th: Tom Cole (R)	778 004	50	CA 4th:Tom McClintock (R)	12 837	50	CA 35th Norma J. Torres (D)	4 380
51	CO 7th: Ed Perlmutter (D)	777 970	51	MS 3rd: Gregg Harper (R)	12 754	51	FL 22nd: Theodore E. Deutch (D)	4 366
52	TX 7th: John Abney Culberson (R)	777 640	52	LA 4th: Mike Johnson (R)	12 436	52	CA 6th: Doris O. Matsui (D)	4 288
53	MA 7th: Michael E. Capuano (D)	777 588	53	IA 2nd: David Loebsack (D)	12 262	53	CO 1st: Diana DeGette (D)	4 231
54	AZ 9th: Kyrsten Sinema (D)	777 123	54	KY 1st: James Comer (R)	12 082	54	VA11th Gerald E. Connolly (D)	4 179
55	FL 26th: Carlos Curbelo (R)	776 959	55	IA 1st: Rod Blum (R)	12 049	55	CA 17th: Ro Khanna (D)	4 102
56	CA 53rd: Susan A. Davis (D)	776 583	56	MN 1st: Timothy J. Walz (D)	11 974	56	TX 29th: Gene Green (D)	4 057
57	MO 3rd: Blaine Luetkemeyer (R)	774 899	57	KY 5th: Harold Rogers (R)	11 234	57	TX 32nd: Pete Sessions (R)	4 002
58	TX 20th: Joaquin Castro (D)	774 521	58	WI 3rd: Ron Kind (D)	11 112	58	NY 2nd: Peter T. King (R)	3 968
59	FL 19th: Francis Rooney (R)	774 346	59	PA 7th: Brian P. Fitzpatrick (R)	11 004	59	WA 9th: Adam Smith (D)	3 967
60	VA11th Gerald E. Connolly (D)	773 973	60	PA 5th: Glenn Thompson (R)	10 711	60	FL 13th: Charlie Crist (D)	3 942
61	CA 42nd: Ken Calvert (R)	772 860	61	MS 1st: Trent Kelly (R)	10 573	61	MI 9th: Sander M. Levin (D)	3 908
62	IA 1st: Rod Blum (R)	771 888	62	IL 18th: Darin LaHood (R)	10 516	62	FL 23rd: Debbie Wasserman Schultz (D)	3 907
63	CA 15th: Eric Swalwell (D)	771 800	63	AL 7th: Terri A. Sewell (D)	10 156	63	TX 20th: Joaquin Castro (D)	3 879
64	CA 45th: Mimi Walters (R)	771 550	64	AL 2nd: Martha Roby (R)	10 142	64	AZ 7th: Ruben Gallego (D)	3 756
65	TX 21st: Lamar Smith (R)	771 369	65	TX 4th: John Ratcliffe (R)	10 130	65	MI 14th: Brenda L. Lawrence (D)	3 745
66	VA 1st Robert J. Wittman (R)	771 237	66	VA 5th Thomas A. Garrett Jr. (R)	10 030	66	MI 13th: John Conyers Jr. (D)	3 674
67	CA 30th: Brad Sherman (D)	771 108	67	CA 23rd: Kevin McCarthy (R)	9 898	67	CA 39th: Edward R. Royce (R)	3 578
68	CO 5th: Doug Lamborn (R)	770 782	68	OK 4th: Tom Cole (R)	9 777	68	NJ 6th: Frank Pallone Jr. (D)	3 501
69	MO 7th: Bill Long (R)	770 073	69	WV 3rd: Evan H. Jenkins (R)	9 746	69	TX 33rd: Marc A. Veasey (D)	3 492
70	NY 8th: Hakeem S. Jeffries (D)	769 795	70	GA 2nd: Sanford D. Bishop Jr. (D)	9 626	70	IL 8th: Raja Krishnamoorthi (D)	3 455
71	AZ 7th: Ruben Gallego (D)	769 597	71	TX 28th: Henry Cuellar (D)	9 379	71	CA 31st: Pete Aguilar (D)	3 384
72	AZ 8th: Trent Franks (R)	767 981	72	VT At-Large: Peter Welch (D)	9 218	72	HI 1st: Colleen Hanabusa (D)	3 376
73	FL 20th: Alcee L. Hastings (D)	767 766	73	TN 7th: Marsha Blackburn (R)	9 160	73	OH 3rd: Joyce Beatty (D)	3 365
74	MO 2nd: Ann Wagner (R)	767 531	74	TX 27th: Blake Farenthold (R)	9 121	74	PA 14th: Michael F. Doyle (D)	3 342
75	NJ 8th: Albio Sires (D)	767 452	75	WA 3rd Jaime Herrera Beutler (R)	9 116	75	CA 47th: Alan S. Lowenthal (D)	3 322

Congressional Districts of the 115th Congress of the United States
Selected Rankings

	Percent Non-Hispanic White alone, 2015			Percent Black alone, 2015			Percent American Indian, Alaska Native alone, 2015	
Non-Hispanic White alone rank	State congressional district Representative	Percent white [col 11]	Black rank	State congressional district Representative	Percent black [col 5]	American Indian Alaska Native rank	State congressional district Representative	Percent American Indian Alaska Native [col 6]
1	KY 5th: Harold Rogers (R)	96.0	1	MS 2nd: Bennie G. Thompson (D)	66.3	1	AZ 1st: Tom O'Halleran (D)	23.4
2	OH 6th: Bill Johnson (R)	94.4	2	TN 9th: Steve Cohen (D)	65.2	2	NM 3rd: Ben Ray Luján (D)	18.2
3	ME 2nd: Bruce Poliquin (R)	94.0	3	AL 7th: Terri A. Sewell (D)	63.6	3	OK 2nd: Markwayne Mullin (R)	16.3
4	WV 1st: David McKinley (R)	93.5	4	LA 2nd: Cedric Richmond (D)	60.5	4	AK: At-Large Don Young (R)	13.7
5	VT At-Large: Peter Welch (D)	93.4	5	GA 4th: Henry C. "Hank" Johnson Jr. (D)	59.4	5	SD At-Large: Kristi Noem (R)	8.3
6	ME 1st: Chellie Pingree (D)	93.2	6	GA 13th: David Scott (D)	58.4	6	NC 8th: Richard Hudson (R)	7.1
7	WV 3rd: Evan H. Jenkins (R)	93.1	7	GA 5th: John Lewis (D)	57.8	7	MT At-Large Greg Gianforte (R)	6.3
8	PA 9th: Bill Shuster (R)	92.7	8	PA 2nd: Chaka Fattah (D)	57.6	8	OK 3rd: Frank D. Lucas (R)	6.1
9	PA 18th: Tim Murphy (R)	92.6	8	SC 6th: James E. Clyburn (D)	57.6	9	NM 2nd: Steve Pearce (R)	5.4
10	NY 27th: Chris Collins(R)	92.3	10	VA 3rd Robert C. "Bobby" Scott (D)	57.1	9	OK 1st: Jim Bridenstine (R)	5.4
11	PA 5th: Glenn Thompson (R)	92.2	11	IL 2nd: Robin L. Kelly (D)	56.5	11	ND-At Large Kevin Cramer (R)	5.0
11	WI 3rd: Ron Kind (D)	92.2	12	MI 14th: Brenda L. Lawrence (D)	56.1	12	OK 4th: Tom Cole (R)	4.9
13	MN 7th: Richard M. Nolan (D)	91.9	13	MI 13th: John Conyers Jr. (D)	55.5	13	AZ 3rd: Raul M. Grijalva (D)	4.8
13	PA 12th: Keith J. Rothfus (R)	91.9	14	FL 24th: Frederica S. Wilson (D)	55.2	14	OK 5th: Steve Russell (R)	4.4
15	IN 6th: Luke Messer (R)	91.8	15	MD 7th: Elijah E. Cummings (D)	54.0	15	NM 1st: Michelle Lujan Grisham (D)	4.3
15	OH 16th: James B. Renacci (R)	91.8	16	FL 20th: Alcee L. Hastings (D)	53.7	16	AZ 7th: Ruben Gallego (D)	2.9
15	WI 7th: Sean P. Duffy (R)	91.8	17	MD 4th: Anthony G. Brown (D)	52.9	16	MN 6th: Collin C. Peterson (D)	2.9
18	TN 1st: David P. Roe (R)	91.6	18	NY 8th: Hakeem S. Jeffries (D)	52.7	18	AZ 9th: Kyrsten Sinema (D)	2.7
19	MI 4th: John L. Moolenar (R)	91.4	18	OH 11th: Marcia L. Fudge (D)	52.7	19	MI 1st: Jack Bergman (R)	2.6
20	MO 3rd: Blaine Luetkemeyer (R)	91.3	20	GA 2nd: Sanford D. Bishop Jr. (D)	52.6	20	MN 7th: Richard M. Nolan (D)	2.4
21	OH 7th: Bob Gibbs (R)	91.1	21	NC 1st: G. K. Butterfield (D)	52.4	20	WI 8th: Mike Gallagher (R)	2.4
22	IL 15th: John Shimkus (R)	91.0	22	IL 1st: Bobby L. Rush (D)	51.0	22	CA 1st: Doug LaMalfa (R)	2.3
22	MI 1st: Jack Bergman (R)	91.0	23	NJ 10th: Donald M. Payne, Jr. (D)	50.3	22	WA 4th: Dan Newsome (D)	2.3
22	NH 1st: Carol Shea Porter (R)	91.0	24	NY 9th: Yvette D. Clarke (D)	49.7	24	CA 2nd:Jared Huffman (D)	2.2
25	NH 2nd: Ann M. Kuster (D)	90.8	25	FL 5th: Al Lawson Jr. (D)	49.6	24	CO 3rd: Scott R. Tipton (R)	2.2
26	IN 8th: Larry Bucshon (R)	90.7	26	NC 12th: Alma S. Adams (D)	49.4	24	OR 2nd: Greg Walden (R)	2.2
26	MO 8th: Jason T. Smith (R)	90.7	27	NY 5th: Gregory W. Meeks (D)	49.3	24	WY At-Large Liz Cheney (R)	2.2
26	NY 21st: Elise M. Stefanik (R)	90.7	28	MO 1st: William Lacy Clay (D)	49.2	28	WA 6th: Derek Kilmer (D)	2.1
29	WV 2nd: Alexander X. Mooney (R)	90.4	29	IL 7th: Danny K. Davis (D)	48.9	29	NV 2nd: Mark E. Amodei (R)	2.0
30	KY 4th: Thomas Massie (R)	90.1	30	DC At Large: Eleanor Holmes Norton (D)	47.4	30	AZ 4th: Paul A. Gosar (R)	1.9
30	PA 3rd: Mike Kelly (R)	90.1	31	TX 30th: Eddie Bernice Johnson (D)	43.6	30	NC 7th: David Rouzer (R)	1.9
32	MI 10th: Paul Mitchell (R)	90.0	32	TX 9th: Al Green (D)	38.0	30	WI 7th: Sean P. Duffy (R)	1.9
32	MN 5th: Tom Emmer (R)	90.0	33	MD 5th: Steny H. Hoyer (D)	37.6	33	AZ 6th: David Schweikert (R)	1.8
34	PA 10th: Tom Marino (R)	89.9	34	TX 18th: Sheila Jackson-Lee (D)	36.4	34	NC 11th: Mark Meadows (R)	1.7
35	WI 6th: Glen Grothman(R)	89.6	35	LA 5th: Ralph Lee Abraham (R)	36.1	34	UT 3rd: Vacant	1.7
36	IN 9th: Trey Hollingsworth (R)	89.4	36	NC 12th: Rick W. Allen (R)	35.0	36	CA 44th: Nanette Diaz Barragan (D)	1.6
36	OH 14th: David P. Joyce (R)	89.4	37	PA 1st: Robert A. Brady (D)	34.9	36	ID 1st: Raul Labrador (R)	1.6
38	IL 18th: Darin LaHood (R)	89.3	38	MD 2nd: C. A. Dutch Ruppersberger (D)	34.4	36	KS 2nd: Lynn Jenkins (R)	1.6
38	MN 6th: Collin C. Peterson (D)	89.3	38	MS 3rd: Gregg Harper (R)	34.4	36	WA 5th: Cathy McMorris Rodgers (R)	1.6
40	VA 9th Morgan Griffith (R)	89.2	40	LA 4th: Mike Johnson (R)	34.2	36	WA 10th: Denny Heck (D)	1.6
41	OH 5th: Robert E. Latta (R)	89.1	41	WI 4th: Gwen Moore (D)	33.4	41	CA 34th: Jimmy Gomez (D)	1.5
42	IA 1st: Rod Blum (R)	88.9	42	NY 16th: Eliot L. Engel (D)	33.1	41	CA 47th: Alan S. Lowenthal (D)	1.5
43	OH 15th: Steve Stivers (R)	88.7	43	OH 3rd: Joyce Beatty (D)	32.7	43	AZ 5th: Andy Biggs (R)	1.4
44	TN 6th: Diane Black (R)	88.5	44	AL 2nd: Martha Roby (R)	31.8	44	CA 8th: Paul Cook (R)	1.3
45	IA 4th: Steve King (R)	88.3	45	NC 4th: David E. Price (R)	31.7	44	OR 4th: Peter A. DeFazio (R)	1.3
45	MO 7th: Bill Long (R)	88.3	46	VA 4th A. Donald McEachin (R)	31.4	46	CA 21st: David G. Valadao (R)	1.2
47	NY 23rd: Tom Reed (R)	88.2	47	NY 15th: José E. Serrano (D)	31.0	46	CA 36th: Raul Ruiz (D)	1.2
48	MO 6th: Sam Graves (R)	88.1	48	GA 8th: Austin Scott (D)	29.8	46	ID 2nd: Michael K. Simpson (R)	1.2
49	MI 7th: Tim Walberg (R)	88.0	49	GA 1st: Earl L. "Buddy" Carter (R)	29.4	46	NE 1st: Jeff Fortenberry (R)	1.2
50	OH 4th: Jim Jordan (R)	87.9	50	IN 7th: André Carson (D)	29.1	46	NV 1st: Dina Titus (D)	1.2
51	KY 1st: James Comer (R)	87.6	51	NY 13th: Adriano Espaillat (D)	28.8	46	NC 1st: G. K. Butterfield (D)	1.2
51	NY 22nd: Claudia Tenney (R)	87.6	52	AL 1st: Bradley Byrne (R)	28.3	46	UT 2nd: Chris Stewart (R)	1.2
53	WI 5th: F. James Sensenbrenner Jr. (R)	87.4	53	SC 5th: Ralph Norman (R)	28.1	46	WA 2nd Rick Larsen (R)	1.2
54	KY 2nd: Brett Guthrie (R)	87.3	54	SC 7th: Tom Rice (R)	28.0	54	AL 1st: Bradley Byrne (R)	1.1
55	MO 2nd: Ann Wagner (R)	87.2	55	MS 1st: Trent Kelly (R)	27.7	54	AR 2nd: Steve Womack (R)	1.1
55	WI 8th: Mike Gallagher (R)	87.2	56	MA 7th: Michael E. Capuano (D)	26.5	54	KS 4th: Ron Estes (R)	1.1
57	MN 1st: Timothy J. Walz (D)	86.6	57	FL 14th: Kathy Castor (D)	26.4	54	LA 1st: Steve Scalise (R)	1.1
57	MT At-Large Greg Gianforte (R)	86.6	58	GA 8th: Jody B. Hice (R)	25.7	54	OR 5th: Kurt Schrader (D)	1.1
59	MA 9th: William R. Keating (D)	86.5	59	AL 3rd: Mike Rogers (R)	25.3	54	TX 20th: Joaquin Castro (D)	1.1
59	MO 4th: Vicky Hartzler (R)	86.5	60	FL 2nd: Neal P. Dunn (R)	25.0	54	UT 1st: Rob Bishop (R)	1.1
61	OH 8th: Warren Davidson (R)	86.3	61	LA 3rd: Clay Higgins (R)	24.4	54	WA 1st Suzan K. DelBene (D)	1.1
61	OH 12th: Patrick J. Tiberi (R)	86.3	61	TN 5th: Jim Cooper (D)	24.4	62	CA 16th:Jim Costa (D)	1.0
63	NC 11th: Mark Meadows (R)	86.2	63	LA 6th: Garret Graves (R)	24.2	62	CA 26th: Julia Brownley (D)	1.0
63	TN 2nd: John J. Duncan Jr. (R)	86.2	64	GA 3rd: A. Drew Ferguson (R)	24.1	62	CA 50th: Duncan Hunter (R)	1.0
65	OH 2nd: Brad R. Wenstrup (R)	86.0	65	MS 4th: Steven Palazzo (R)	23.8	62	ME 2nd: Bruce Poliquin (R)	1.0
66	IA 2nd: David Loebsack (D)	85.9	66	CA 37th: Karen Bass (D)	23.7	62	TX 4th: John Ratcliffe (R)	1.0
66	ND-At Large Kevin Cramer (R)	85.9	67	SC 2nd: Joe Wilson (R)	23.6	62	TX 19th: Jodey C. Arrington (R)	1.0
68	IN 4th: Todd Rokita (R)	85.6	68	AR 2nd: J. French Hill (R)	22.6	68	AZ 2nd: Martha McSally (R)	0.9
68	PA 11th: Lou Barletta (R)	85.6	68	CA 43rd: Maxine Waters (D)	22.6	68	CA 3rd: John Garamendi (D)	0.9
70	NE 3rd: Adrian Smith (R)	85.2	70	OH 1st: Steve Chabot (R)	22.1	68	CO 1st: Diana DeGette (D)	0.9
71	NY 19th: John J. Faso (R)	84.9	71	VA 2nd Scott Taylor (R)	22.0	68	CO 7th: Ed Perlmutter (D)	0.9
72	PA 8th: Michael G. Fitzpatrick (R)	84.8	72	MO 5th: Emanuel Cleaver (D)	21.9	68	GA 6th: Karen Handell (R)	0.9
73	ID 1st: Raul Labrador (R)	84.1	73	DE At-Large: Lisa Blunt Rochester (D)	21.6	68	MI 4th: John L. Moolenar (R)	0.9
73	IA 3rd: David Young (R)	84.1	74	KY 3rd: John A. Yarmuth (D)	21.3	68	MS 3rd: Gregg Harper (R)	0.9
73	MA 4th:Joseph P. Kennedy III (D)	84.1	75	PA 14th: Michael F. Doyle (D)	21.1	68	MO 7th: Bill Long (R)	0.9

Congressional Districts of the 115th Congress of the United States
Selected Rankings

Percent Asian or Pacific Islander alone, 2014			Percent Hispanic or Latino,[1] 2014			Percent foreign born, 2014		
Asian or Pacific Islander rank	State congressional district Representative	Percent Asian or Pacific Islander [col 7]	Hispanic rank	State congressional district Representative	Percent Hispanic [col 10]	Foreign-born rank	State congressional district Representative	Percent foreign born [col 13]
1	HI 1st: Colleen Hanabusa (D)	56.5	1	CA 40th: Lucille Roybal-Allard (D)	87.6	1	FL 27th: Ileana Ros-Lehtinen (R)	55.2
2	CA 17th: Ro Khanna (D)	54.0	2	TX 34th: Filemon Vela (D)	83.0	2	FL 25th: Mario Diaz-Balart (R)	52.0
3	NY 6th: Grace Meng (D)	40.4	3	TX 15th: Vicente Gonzalez (D)	80.6	2	NY 6th: Grace Meng (D)	52.0
4	CA 27th: Judy Chu (D)	38.4	4	TX 16th: Beto O'Rourke (D)	79.5	4	CA 17th: Ro Khanna (D)	48.0
5	HI 2nd: Tulsi Gabbard (D)	36.8	5	TX 28th: Henry Cuellar (D)	78.2	5	FL 26th: Carlos Curbelo (R)	47.5
6	CA 14th:Jackie Speier (D)	35.3	6	TX 29th: Gene Green (D)	77.3	6	NY 14th: Joseph Crowley (D)	45.9
7	CA 15th: Eric Swalwell (D)	34.9	7	FL 27th: Ileana Ros-Lehtinen (R)	75.4	7	CA 34th: Jimmy Gomez (D)	45.8
8	CA 12th:Nancy Pelosi (D)	33.0	8	CA 21st: David G. Valadao (R)	74.7	8	NJ 8th: Albio Sires (D)	43.8
9	CA 39th: Edward R. Royce (R)	31.1	9	CA 35th Norma J. Torres (D)	71.5	9	CA 29th: Tony Cárdenas (D)	42.9
10	CA 19th: Zoe Lofgren (D)	27.5	10	FL 25th: Mario Diaz-Balart (R)	70.9	10	NY 5th: Gregory W. Meeks (D)	42.8
11	CA 45th: Mimi Walters (R)	24.7	11	CA 51st: Juan Vargas (D)	70.6	11	CA 46th: J. Luis Correa (D)	41.4
12	WA 9th: Adam Smith (D)	23.8	12	IL 4th:Luis V. Gutierrez (D)	70.1	12	CA 40th: Lucille Roybal-Allard (D)	41.2
13	CA 18th: Anna G. Eshoo (D)	23.0	13	FL 26th: Carlos Curbelo (R)	69.7	13	FL 24th: Frederica S. Wilson (D)	40.8
13	CA 47th: Alan S. Lowenthal (D)	23.0	13	TX 23rd: Will Hurd (R)	69.7	14	NY 9th: Yvette D. Clarke (D)	40.5
15	CA 13th:Barbara Lee (D)	20.8	15	CA 44th: Nanette Diaz Barragan (D)	69.4	15	CA 28th: Adam B. Schiff (D)	39.8
16	CA 34th: Jimmy Gomez (D)	19.7	16	CA 29th: Tony Cárdenas (D)	68.8	16	CA 27th: Judy Chu (D)	39.2
17	CA 52nd: Scott H. Peters (D)	19.6	17	TX 20th: Joaquin Castro (D)	67.8	17	FL 23rd: Debbie Wasserman Schultz (D)	38.7
17	NY 10th: Jerrold Nadler (D)	19.6	18	CA 46th: J. Luis Correa (D)	67.3	18	CA 14th:Jackie Speier (D)	37.9
19	NJ 6th: Frank Pallone Jr. (D)	19.0	19	TX 33rd: Marc A. Veasey (D)	67.0	19	NY 7th: Nydia M. Velázquez (D)	37.0
20	CA 48th: Dana Rohrabacher (R)	18.7	20	NY 15th: José E. Serrano (D)	66.0	20	NY 15th: José E. Serrano (D)	36.3
21	NY 7th: Nydia M. Velázquez (D)	18.6	21	CA 34th: Jimmy Gomez (D)	64.2	21	NY 13th: Adriano Espaillat (D)	36.0
22	VA11th Gerald E. Connolly (D)	18.3	22	CA 32nd: Grace F. Napolitano (D)	63.4	22	CA 19th: Zoe Lofgren (D)	35.8
23	TX 22nd: Pete Olson (R)	18.1	23	TX 35th: Lloyd Doggett (D)	63.1	23	NJ 9th: Bill Pascrell, Jr. (D)	35.6
24	NY 14th: Joseph Crowley (D)	17.8	24	AZ 7th: Ruben Gallego (D)	62.8	24	CA 51st: Juan Vargas (D)	35.3
25	CA 7th: Ami Bera (D)	17.2	25	CA 38th: Linda T. Sánchez (D)	62.5	25	TX 9th: Al Green (D)	35.2
26	CA 32nd: Grace F. Napolitano (D)	17.1	26	CA 16th:Jim Costa (D)	60.4	26	CA 32nd: Grace F. Napolitano (D)	35.0
27	CA 6th: Doris O. Matsui (D)	16.6	27	AZ 3rd: Raul M. Grijalva (D)	60.0	27	FL 20th: Alcee L. Hastings (D)	34.8
28	NJ 12th: Bonnie Watson Coleman (D)	16.5	28	CA 41st: Mark Takano (D)	58.0	28	CA 15th: Eric Swalwell (D)	34.3
29	CA 38th: Linda T. Sánchez (D)	15.7	29	NJ 8th: Albio Sires (D)	55.0	29	CA 44th: Nanette Diaz Barragan (D)	34.2
29	NY 3rd: Thomas R. Souzzi (D)	15.7	30	NY 13th: Adriano Espaillat (D)	54.4	30	CA 30th: Brad Sherman (D)	34.1
31	TX 3rd: Sam Johnson (R)	15.0	31	NM 2nd: Steve Pearce (R)	53.8	31	NY 8th: Hakeem S. Jeffries (D)	34.0
32	CA 9th:Jerry McNerney (D)	14.9	32	CA 20th: Jimmy Panetta (D)	52.9	32	IL 4th:Luis V. Gutierrez (D)	33.9
33	CA 33rd:Ted Lieu (D)	14.7	33	TX 27th: Blake Farenthold (R)	52.5	33	CA 12th:Nancy Pelosi (D)	33.5
34	NV 3rd: Jacky Rosen (D)	14.4	34	CA 31st: Pete Aguilar (D)	51.8	33	TX 33rd: Marc A. Veasey (D)	33.5
35	CA 11th:Mark Desaulnier (D)	14.3	35	CA 36th: Raul Ruiz (D)	49.8	35	CA 39th: Edward R. Royce (R)	33.4
35	NY 12th: Carolyn B. Maloney (D)	14.3	36	NM 1st: Michelle Lujan Grisham (D)	49.4	36	TX 29th: Gene Green (D)	33.2
37	VA10th Barbara Comstock (R)	14.2	37	FL 9th: Darren Soto (D)	48.7	37	MA 7th: Michael E. Capuano (D)	32.4
38	IL 8th: Raja Krishnamoorthi (D)	14.1	38	CA 43rd: Maxine Waters (D)	48.3	38	NY 10th: Jerrold Nadler (D)	32.2
38	NJ 9th: Bill Pascrell Jr. (D)	14.1	39	NY 14th: Joseph Crowley (D)	47.5	39	CA 37th: Karen Bass (D)	32.1
40	NY 5th: Gregory W. Meeks (D)	13.8	40	CA 22nd: Devin Nunes (R)	46.7	39	NV 1st: Dina Titus (D)	32.1
40	NY 11th: Daniel M. Donovan Jr. (R)	13.8	40	NV 1st: Dina Titus (D)	46.7	41	CA 38th: Linda T. Sánchez (D)	31.0
40	TX 24th: Kenny Marchant (R)	13.8	42	CA 26th: Julia Brownley (D)	45.0	41	CA 43rd: Maxine Waters (D)	31.0
43	CA 28th: Adam B. Schiff (D)	13.7	43	CA 10th: Jeff Denham (R)	42.7	41	CA 47th: Alan S. Lowenthal (D)	31.0
44	CA 30th: Brad Sherman (D)	13.4	43	TX 18th: Sheila Jackson-Lee (D)	42.7	41	VA11th Gerald E. Connolly (D)	31.0
44	CA 53rd: Susan A. Davis (D)	13.4	45	CA 19th: Zoe Lofgren (D)	41.3	45	NY 16th: Eliot L. Engel (D)	30.8
44	IL 9th: Janice D. Schakowsky (D)	13.4	46	NM 3rd: Ben Ray Luján (D)	40.8	46	CA 35th Norma J. Torres (D)	30.4
47	CA 43rd: Maxine Waters (D)	13.2	47	NY 7th: Nydia M. Velázquez (D)	40.5	46	TX 7th: John Abney Culberson (R)	30.4
48	GA 7th: Robert Woodall (R)	13.1	48	FL 23rd: Debbie Wasserman Schultz (D)	39.7	48	CA 45th: Mimi Walters (R)	30.3
49	CA 46th: J. Luis Correa (D)	12.4	49	CA 8th: Paul Cook (R)	39.2	48	NY 11th: Daniel M. Donovan Jr. (R)	30.3
50	CA 5th: Mike Thompson (D)	12.3	50	TX 30th: Eddie Bernice Johnson (D)	39.1	50	VA 8th Donald S. Beyer, Jr. (D)	30.2
51	MN 4th: Betty McCollum (D)	12.1	51	WA 4th: Dan Newsome (R)	38.4	51	CA 21st: David G. Valadao (R)	29.6
51	TX 9th: Al Green (D)	12.1	52	CA 42nd: Ken Calvert (R)	38.3	51	IL 8th: Raja Krishnamoorthi (D)	29.6
53	VA 8th Donald S. Beyer, Jr. (D)	11.9	52	TX 11th K. Michael Conaway (R)	38.3	53	NJ 10th: Donald M. Payne, Jr. (D)	29.5
54	WA 7th: Pramila Jayapal (D)	11.6	54	CA 37th: Karen Bass (D)	38.1	54	CA 18th: Anna G. Eshoo (D)	28.8
55	CA 3rd: John Garamendi (D)	11.4	54	CA 42nd: Ken Calvert (R)	38.1	55	WA 9th: Adam Smith (D)	28.7
56	GA 6th: Karen Handell (D)	11.1	56	CA 23rd: Kevin McCarthy (R)	37.7	56	NJ 6th: Frank Pallone Jr. (D)	28.2
57	MD 6th: John K. Delaney (D)	11.0	57	CA 9th:Jerry McNerney (D)	37.6	57	NJ 12th: Bonnie Watson Coleman (D)	27.9
57	MA 5th: Katherine Clark (D)	11.0	58	CA 25th: Stephen Knight (R)	37.2	58	NY 12th: Carolyn B. Maloney (D)	27.7
59	CA 42nd: Ken Calvert (R)	10.5	59	NJ 9th: Bill Pascrell, Jr. (D)	36.5	59	IL 9th: Janice D. Schakowsky (D)	27.6
59	IL 10th: Bradley Scott Schneider (D)	10.5	59	TX 19th: Jodey C. Arrington (R)	36.5	60	CA 20th: Jimmy Panetta (D)	27.1
61	NJ 7th: Leonard Lance (R)	10.3	61	CA 47th: Alan S. Lowenthal (D)	36.3	61	CA 13th:Barbara Lee (D)	27.0
61	TX 7th: John Abney Culberson (R)	10.3	62	CA 24th: Salud O. Carbajal (D)	36.0	62	CA 11th:Mark Desaulnier (D)	26.4
61	WA 1st Suzan K. DelBene (D)	10.3	63	CA 39th: Edward R. Royce (R)	34.9	63	FL 22nd: Theodore E. Deutch (D)	26.0
64	NJ 5th: Josh Gottheimer (R)	10.2	64	CA 53rd: Susan A. Davis (D)	34.2	64	TX 22nd: Pete Olson (R)	25.7
65	MA 7th: Michael E. Capuano (D)	10.1	65	IL 3rd: Daniel Lipinski (D)	33.0	65	CA 16th:Jim Costa (D)	25.6
65	MI 11th: David A.Trott (R)	10.1	66	FL 24th: Frederica S. Wilson (D)	32.4	65	FL 21st: Lois Frankel (D)	25.6
67	CA 16th:Jim Costa (D)	10.0	67	CA 50th: Duncan Hunter (R)	31.4	67	CA 48th: Dana Rohrabacher (R)	25.2
67	CA 37th: Karen Bass (D)	10.0	68	TX 7th: John Abney Culberson (R)	31.1	67	GA 7th: Robert Woodall (R)	25.2
69	MD 8th: Jamie Raskin (D)	9.8	69	TX 2nd: Ted Poe (R)	30.1	69	AZ 7th: Ruben Gallego (D)	24.8
70	NJ 11th: Rodney P. Frelinghuysen (R)	9.7	70	CA 3rd: John Garamendi (D)	30.0	70	CA 52nd: Scott H. Peters (D)	24.7
71	WA 8th: David G. Reichert (R)	9.6	71	FL 14th: Kathy Castor (D)	29.6	71	CA 41st: Mark Takano (D)	24.4
72	NV 1st: Dina Titus (D)	9.3	72	CA 6th: Doris O. Matsui (D)	29.5	72	CA 26th: Julia Brownley (D)	24.2
72	PA 13th: Brendan F. Boyle (D)	9.3	73	AZ 9th: Kyrsten Sinema (D)	29.3	73	MD 8th: Jamie Raskin (D)	24.1
74	CA 25th: Stephen Knight (R)	9.2	74	CA 30th: Brad Sherman (D)	28.9	74	IL 10th: Bradley Scott Schneider (D)	23.9
74	CA 51st: Juan Vargas (D)	9.2	74	TX 10th: Michael T. McCaul (R)	28.9	75	MA 5th: Katherine Clark (D)	23.6

Congressional Districts of the 115th Congress of the United States
Selected Rankings

Percent under 18 years old, 2015			Percent 65 years old and over, 2015			Percent college graduates (bachelor's degree or more), 2015		
Under 18 years old rank	State congressional district Representative	Percent under 18 years old [col 15 and 16]	65 years old and over rank	State congressional district Representative	Percent 65 years old and over [col 22 and 23]	College graduates rank	State congressional district Representative	Percent college graduates [col 27]
1	TX 33rd: Marc A. Veasey (D)	31.6	1	FL 11th: Daniel Webster (R)	33.9	1	NY 12th: Carolyn B. Maloney (D)	71.5
2	TX 29th: Gene Green (D)	31.5	2	FL 16th: Vern Buchanan (R)	30.6	2	CA 33rd:Ted Lieu (D)	62.4
2	UT 3rd: Vacant	31.5	3	FL 19th: Francis Rooney (R)	29.5	3	CA 18th: Anna G. Eshoo (D)	61.1
4	UT 4th: Mia B. Love (R)	31.3	4	FL 17th: Thomas J. Rooney (R)	27.3	4	NY 10th: Jerrold Nadler (D)	60.3
5	CA 21st: David G. Valadao (R)	31.2	5	AZ 4th: Paul A. Gosar (R)	26.6	5	VA 8th:Donald S. Beyer, Jr. (D)	59.6
5	UT 1st: Rob Bishop (R)	31.2	6	FL 18th: Brian J. Mast (R)	24.6	6	GA 6th: Karen Handell (R)	59.5
7	TX 15th: Vicente Gonzalez (D)	31.1	7	FL 8th: Bill Posey (R)	24.4	7	WA 7th: Pramila Jayapal (D)	59.4
7	TX 28th: Henry Cuellar (D)	31.1	8	FL 13th: Charlie Crist (D)	24.0	8	CA 52nd: Scott H. Peters (D)	57.5
9	CA 16th:Jim Costa (D)	31.0	9	FL 6th: Ron DeSantis (R)	23.8	9	DC At Large: Eleanor Holmes Norton (D)	56.7
10	AZ 7th: Ruben Gallego (D)	30.5	10	FL 22nd: Theodore E. Deutch (D)	23.1	10	CA 12th:Nancy Pelosi (D)	56.6
11	TX 34th: Filemon Vela (D)	30.0	11	FL 21st: Lois Frankel (D)	22.2	11	MA 5th: Katherine Clark (D)	55.9
12	WA 4th: Dan Newsome (R)	29.2	12	FL 12th: Gus M. Bilirakis (R)	21.7	12	CA 17th: Ro Khanna (D)	55.1
13	CA 40th: Lucille Roybal-Allard (D)	28.6	12	MI 1st: Jack Bergman (R)	21.7	13	CA 45th: Mimi Walters (R)	54.7
14	GA 7th: Robert Woodall (R)	28.3	14	NC 11th: Mark Meadows (R)	21.3	13	VA10th Barbara Comstock (R)	54.7
14	TX 23rd: Will Hurd (R)	28.3	15	AZ 8th: Trent Franks (R)	21.0	13	VA11th Gerald E. Connolly (D)	54.7
16	CA 23rd: Kevin McCarthy (R)	28.2	16	MA 9th: William R. Keating (D)	20.8	16	CO: 2nd: Jared Polis (D)	54.6
17	NY 15th: José E. Serrano (D)	28.0	17	AZ 2nd:Martha McSally (R)	20.6	17	MD 8th: Jamie Raskin (D)	53.9
17	TX 22nd: Pete Olson (R)	28.0	18	CA 4th:Tom McClintock (R)	20.4	18	TX 3rd: Sam Johnson (R)	52.6
19	TX 30th: Eddie Bernice Johnson (D)	27.9	19	CA 36th: Raul Ruiz (D)	20.1	19	NJ 7th: Leonard Lance (R)	52.2
20	AZ 3rd: Raul M. Grijalva (D)	27.8	20	CA 1st: Doug LaMalfa (R)	20.0	20	IL 5th: Michael Quigley (D)	52.0
20	UT 2nd: Chris Stewart (R)	27.8	21	OR 4th: Peter A. DeFazio (D)	19.8	20	NJ 11th: Rodney P. Frelinghuysen (R)	52.0
22	TX 16th: Beto O'Rourke (D)	27.6	21	PA 12th: Keith J. Rothfus (R)	19.8	22	NY 3rd: Thomas R. Souzzi (D)	51.8
23	TX 26th: Michael C. Burgess (R)	27.4	23	OR 2nd: Greg Walden (R)	19.5	23	IL 9th: Janice D. Schakowsky (D)	51.4
24	CA 9th:Jerry McNerney (D)	27.3	23	PA 9th: Bill Shuster (R)	19.5	24	MA 4th:Joseph P. Kennedy III (D)	49.9
25	CA 35th Norma J. Torres (D)	27.2	25	WA 6th: Derek Kilmer (D)	19.4	25	IL 6th: Peter J. Roskam (R)	49.5
26	CA 10th: Jeff Denham (R)	27.1	26	SC 7th: Tom Rice (R)	19.3	25	NC 9th: Robert Pittenger (R)	49.5
26	CA 22nd: Devin Nunes (R)	27.1	26	TN 1st: David P. Roe (R)	19.3	27	CT 4th: James A. Himes (D)	48.6
26	ID 2nd: Michael K. Simpson (R)	27.1	28	OH 16th: James B. Renacci (R)	19.1	27	TX 7th: John Abney Culberson (R)	48.6
29	CA 8th: Paul Cook (R)	27.0	29	MN 6th: Collin C. Peterson (D)	19.0	29	MN 3rd: Erik Paulsen (R)	48.0
29	CA 42nd: Ken Calvert (R)	27.0	29	MN 7th: Richard M. Nolan (D)	19.0	30	CA 13th:Barbara Lee (D)	47.5
29	CA 44th: Nanette Diaz Barragan (D)	27.0	29	NY 3rd: Thomas R. Souzzi (D)	19.0	31	MD 3rd: John P. Sarbanes (D)	47.3
32	GA 13th: David Scott (D)	26.9	29	WI 7th: Sean P. Duffy (R)	19.0	32	MO 2nd: Ann Wagner (R)	47.2
32	TX 31st: John R. Carter (R)	26.9	33	CA 2nd:Jared Huffman (D)	18.9	33	KS 3rd: Kevin Yoder (R)	47.0
32	VA10th Barbara Comstock (R)	26.9	33	ME 2nd: Bruce Poliquin (R)	18.9	34	CO 1st: Diana DeGette (D)	46.7
35	IL 11th: Bill Foster (D)	26.7	33	NJ 3rd: Thomas MacAuthur (R)	18.9	35	NJ 5th: Josh Gottheimer (D)	46.1
35	TX 3rd: Sam Johnson (R)	26.7	33	PA 10th: Tom Marino (R)	18.9	36	MI 11th: David A.Trott (R)	46.0
35	TX 20th: Joaquin Castro (D)	26.7	33	PA 18th: Tim Murphy (R)	18.9	37	MA 8th: Stephen F. Lynch (D)	45.3
38	CA 41st: Mark Takano (D)	26.6	33	WV 3rd: Evan H. Jenkins (R)	18.9	38	CA 28th: Adam B. Schiff (D)	45.1
39	CA 31st: Pete Aguilar (D)	26.5	39	VA 5th Thomas A. Garrett Jr. (R)	18.8	38	MN 5th: Keith Ellison (D)	45.1
39	CA 46th: J. Luis Correa (D)	26.5	40	OH 6th: Bill Johnson (R)	18.7	40	CA 14th:Jackie Speier (D)	44.9
41	NE 2nd: Don Bacon (D)	26.4	40	VA 9th Morgan Griffith (R)	18.7	41	TX 22nd: Pete Olson (R)	44.7
41	TX 7th: John Abney Culberson (R)	26.4	42	ME 1st: Chellie Pingree (D)	18.6	41	TX 24th: Kenny Marchant (R)	44.7
43	TX 9th: Al Green (D)	26.3	43	AZ 6th: David Schweikert (R)	18.5	43	TX 21st: Lamar Smith (R)	44.6
43	TX 18th: Sheila Jackson-Lee (D)	26.3	43	NE 3rd: Adrian Smith (R)	18.5	44	NY 17th: Nita M. Lowey (D)	44.4
45	CA 51st: Juan Vargas (D)	26.1	43	NY 19th: John J. Faso (R)	18.5	45	CA 48th: Dana Rohrabacher (R)	44.3
45	GA 6th: Karen Handell (R)	26.1	46	OH 14th: David P. Joyce (R)	18.4	45	IL 10th: Bradley Scott Schneider (D)	44.3
47	CO 4th: Ken Buck (R)	26.0	46	PA 11th: Lou Barletta (R)	18.4	47	IN 5th: Susan W. Brooks (R)	44.0
47	IL 4th:Luis V. Gutierrez (D)	26.0	46	PA 17th: Matt Cartwright (D)	18.4	48	CA 15th: Eric Swalwell (D)	43.6
47	TX 6th: Joe Barton (R)	26.0	49	AR 2nd: Bruce Westerman (R)	18.2	49	CA 49th: Darrell E. Issa (R)	43.5
50	AZ 5th: Andy Biggs (R)	25.9	49	PA 3rd: Mike Kelly (R)	18.2	50	NJ 12th: Bonnie Watson Coleman (D)	43.3
50	IN 7th: André Carson (D)	25.9	51	MI 4th: John L. Moolenar (R)	17.9	51	MN 4th: Betty McCollum (D)	43.2
50	KS 4th: Ron Estes (R)	25.9	51	OK 2nd: Markwayne Mullin (R)	17.9	52	WA 1st Suzan K. DelBene (D)	43.1
50	TX 10th: Michael T. McCaul (R)	25.9	51	TN 3rd: Chuck Fleischmann (R)	17.9	53	CA 11th:Mark Desaulnier (D)	43.0
54	GA 4th: Henry C. "Hank" Johnson Jr. (D)	25.8	51	WV 1st: David McKinley (R)	17.9	53	TX 32nd: Pete Sessions (R)	43.0
54	IN 3rd: Jim Banks (R)	25.8	55	FL 10th: Val Butler Demings (D)	17.8	55	CA 30th: Brad Sherman (D)	42.7
54	KS 3rd: Kevin Yoder (R)	25.8	55	IA 4th: Steve King (R)	17.8	56	PA 6th: Ryan A. Costello (R)	42.5
54	MN 5th: Tom Emmer (R)	25.8	55	MD 1st: Andrew Harris (R)	17.8	57	MA 6th: Seth Moulton (D)	42.4
54	TX 35th: Lloyd Doggett (D)	25.8	55	NJ 2nd: Frank A. LoBiondo (R)	17.8	57	PA 7th: Patrick Meehan (R)	42.4
59	CA 25th: Stephen Knight (R)	25.7	55	NJ 4th: Christopher H. Smith (R)	17.8	59	MA 7th: Michael E. Capuano (D)	42.2
59	MS 2nd: Bennie G. Thompson (D)	25.7	55	NY 27th: Chris Collins(R)	17.8	60	AZ 6th: David Schweikert (R)	42.0
59	OK 5th: Steve Russell (R)	25.7	55	PA 5th: Glenn Thompson (R)	17.8	61	CA 27th: Judy Chu (D)	41.8
59	TX 5th: Jeb Hensarling (R)	25.7	55	WV 2nd: Alexander X. Mooney (R)	17.8	61	NC 4th: David E. Price (D)	41.8
63	CO 6th: Mike Coffman (R)	25.6	63	IL 15th: John Shimkus (R)	17.7	63	TX 26th: Michael C. Burgess (R)	41.6
63	NV 4th: Ruben J. Kihuen (D)	25.6	63	NC 7th: David Rouzer (R)	17.7	64	NC 13th: Ted Budd (R)	41.3
63	NM 2nd: Steve Pearce (R)	25.6	65	GA 9th: Doug Collins (R)	17.6	64	WA 9th: Adam Smith (D)	41.3
63	NC 2nd: George Holding (R)	25.6	65	IL 17th: Cheri Bustos (D)	17.6	66	GA 11th: Barry Loudermilk (R)	41.2
63	NC 9th: Robert Pittenger (R)	25.6	65	KY 1st: James Comer (R)	17.6	67	CA 39th: Edward R. Royce (R)	41.1
68	IL 14th: Randy Hultgren (R)	25.5	65	NY 22nd: Claudia Tenney (R)	17.6	67	CO 6th: Mike Coffman (R)	41.1
68	TN 9th: Steve Cohen (D)	25.5	65	OH 13th: Tim Ryan (D)	17.6	67	VA 7th Dave Brat (R)	41.1
70	WI 4th: Gwen Moore (D)	25.4	65	PA 7th: Patrick Meehan (R)	17.6	70	MD 6th: John K. Delaney (D)	41.0
71	OK 1st: Jim Bridenstine (R)	25.3	71	MO 2nd: Ann Wagner (R)	17.5	71	CA 2nd:Jared Huffman (D)	40.7
71	TX 12th: Kay Granger (R)	25.3	71	NC 10th: Patrick T. McHenry (R)	17.5	71	NY 4th: Kathleen M. Rice (D)	40.7
71	TX 27th: Blake Farenthold (R)	25.3	71	OH 7th: Bob Gibbs (R)	17.5	73	GA 5th: John Lewis (D)	40.6
74	AK: At-Large Don Young (R)	25.2	71	SC 3rd: Jeff Duncan (R)	17.5	73	IL 7th: Danny K. Davis (D)	40.6
74	TX 11th K. Michael Conaway (R)	25.2	71	VT At-Large: Peter Welch (D)	17.5	75	OR 1st: Suzanne Bonamici (D)	40.4

Congressional Districts of the 115th Congress of the United States
Selected Rankings

Median value rank	Median value of owner-occupied housing units, 2015 — State congressional district Representative	Median value (dollars) [col 43]	Female householder rank	Percent female-headed family households, 2015 — State congressional district Representative	Percent with female householder [col 32]	One-person household rank	Percent of households with one person, 2015 — State congressional district Representative	Percent one-person households [col 33]
1	CA 18th: Anna G. Eshoo (D)	1 139 900	1	NY 15th: José E. Serrano (D)	34.2	1	NY 12th: Carolyn B. Maloney (D)	48.4
2	CA 33rd:Ted Lieu (D).	1 063 700	2	NY 13th: Adriano Espaillat (D)	26.7	2	GA 5th: John Lewis (D)	45.5
3	CA 12th:Nancy Pelosi (D)	952 800	3	MS 2nd: Bennie G. Thompson (D)	26.2	3	NY 10th: Jerrold Nadler (D)	43.6
4	NY 10th: Jerrold Nadler (D)	877 700	4	TN 9th: Steve Cohen (D)	24.7	4	DC At Large: Eleanor Holmes Norton (D)	42.0
5	CA 14th:Jackie Speier (D)	863 400	5	CA 44th: Nanette Diaz Barragan (D)	24.5	5	IL 7th: Danny K. Davis (D)	41.3
6	NY 12th: Carolyn B. Maloney (D)	857 600	6	NY 8th: Hakeem S. Jeffries (D)	24.4	6	OH 11th: Marcia L. Fudge (D)	40.8
7	CA 17th: Ro Khanna (D)	816 100	7	NY 5th: Gregory W. Meeks (D)	23.9	7	PA 14th: Michael F. Doyle (D)	40.7
8	CA 28th: Adam B. Schiff (D)	720 400	8	FL 5th: Al Lawson Jr. (D)	23.8	8	PA 2nd: Chaka Fattah (D)	39.8
9	CA 48th: Dana Rohrabacher (R)	705 300	8	MI 13th: John Conyers Jr. (D)	23.8	9	CA 12th:Nancy Pelosi (D)	39.4
10	CA 15th: Eric Swalwell (D)	669 000	10	IL 2nd: Robin L. Kelly (D)	23.6	9	IN 7th: André Carson (D)	39.4
11	CA 45th: Mimi Walters (R)	667 600	11	AL 7th: Terri A. Sewell (D)	23.4	11	FL 13th: Charlie Crist (D)	39.2
12	NY 7th: Nydia M. Velázquez (D)	663 000	12	FL 24th: Frederica S. Wilson (D)	23.2	12	MN 5th: Keith Ellison (D)	38.5
13	CA 19th: Zoe Lofgren (D)	657 500	13	NJ 10th: Donald M. Payne, Jr. (D)	23.0	13	MO 1st: William Lacy Clay (D)	38.0
14	CA 27th: Judy Chu (D)	654 300	14	CA 40th: Lucille Roybal-Allard (D)	22.2	14	FL 22nd: Theodore E. Deutch (D)	37.4
15	CA 49th: Darrell E. Issa (R)	650 700	15	PA 1st: Robert A. Brady (D)	22.1	14	NY 26th: Brian Higgins (D)	37.4
16	CA 52nd: Scott H. Peters (D)	640 200	16	TX 18th: Sheila Jackson-Lee (D)	22.0	16	VA 3rd Robert C. "Bobby" Scott (D)	37.0
17	CA 13th:Barbara Lee (D)	638 700	17	NY 9th: Yvette D. Clarke (D)	21.6	17	LA 2nd: Cedric Richmond (D)	36.8
18	HI 1st: Colleen Hanabusa (D)	626 500	17	TX 9th: Al Green (D)	21.6	18	CO 1st: Diana DeGette (D)	36.5
19	CA 37th: Karen Bass (D)	620 700	19	GA 4th: Henry C. "Hank" Johnson Jr. (D)	21.5	18	WI 4th: Gwen Moore (D)	36.5
20	CA 30th: Brad Sherman (D)	614 100	20	IL 1st: Bobby L. Rush (D)	21.4	20	CA 37th: Karen Bass (D)	36.4
21	CA 39th: Edward R. Royce (R)	611 300	20	PA 2nd: Chaka Fattah (D)	21.4	21	MI 13th: John Conyers Jr. (D)	36.3
22	NY 9th: Yvette D. Clarke (D)	582 700	22	FL 20th: Alcee L. Hastings (D)	21.3	21	NY 20th: Paul Tonko (D)	36.3
23	CA 11th:Mark Desaulnier (D)	580 000	23	SC 6th: James E. Clyburn (D)	21.2	21	WA 7th: Pramila Jayapal (D)	36.3
24	NY 3rd: Thomas R. Souzzi (D)	575 600	23	TX 30th: Eddie Bernice Johnson (D)	21.2	24	MI 14th: Brenda L. Lawrence (D)	36.2
25	CA 2nd:Jared Huffman (D)	560 800	25	CA 16th:Jim Costa (D)	21.1	25	MO 5th: Emanuel Cleaver (D)	35.4
26	NY 6th: Grace Meng (D)	559 000	26	NC 1st: G. K. Butterfield (D)	20.9	25	NY 13th: Adriano Espaillat (D)	35.4
27	DC At Large: Eleanor Holmes Norton (D)	551 300	27	CA 51st: Juan Vargas (D)	20.8	27	AL 7th: Terri A. Sewell (D)	35.1
28	CA 26th: Julia Brownley (D)	532 300	28	GA 2nd: Sanford D. Bishop Jr. (D)	20.7	28	CA 28th: Adam B. Schiff (D)	34.9
29	NY 8th: Hakeem S. Jeffries (D)	530 700	28	TX 29th: Gene Green (D)	20.7	29	MA 7th: Michael E. Capuano (D)	34.7
30	VA 8th Donald S. Beyer, Jr. (D)	526 300	30	CA 21st: David G. Valadao (R)	20.5	30	OH 9th: Marcy Kaptur (D)	34.6
31	CA 24th: Salud O. Carbajal (D)	524 700	31	LA 2nd: Cedric Richmond (D)	20.4	30	SC 6th: James E. Clyburn (D)	34.6
32	CA 47th: Alan S. Lowenthal (D)	515 800	31	MO 1st: William Lacy Clay (D)	20.4	32	FL 14th: Kathy Castor (D)	34.5
33	HI 2nd: Tulsi Gabbard (D)	502 100	31	OH 11th: Marcia L. Fudge (D)	20.4	33	TN 9th: Steve Cohen (D)	34.4
34	CA 34th: Jimmy Gomez (D)	501 900	34	TX 33rd: Marc A. Veasey (D)	20.3	34	AZ 9th: Kyrsten Sinema (D)	34.3
35	CA 20th: Jimmy Panetta (D)	495 300	35	MI 14th: Brenda L. Lawrence (D)	20.0	35	IL 9th: Janice D. Schakowsky (D)	34.2
36	WA 7th: Pramila Jayapal (D)	495 200	36	CA 43rd:Maxine Waters (D)	19.8	35	OH 3rd: Joyce Beatty (D)	34.2
37	CT 4th: James A. Himes (D)	489 400	37	AZ 7th: Ruben Gallego (D)	19.6	37	CA 33rd:Ted Lieu (D)	34.1
38	NY 11th: Daniel M. Donovan Jr. (R)	486 700	37	MD 7th: Elijah E. Cummings (D)	19.6	38	IL 1st: Bobby L. Rush (D)	34.0
39	NY 14th: Joseph Crowley (D)	480 300	39	VA 3rd Robert C. "Bobby" Scott (D)	19.5	39	IL 5th: Michael Quigley (D)	33.9
40	MA 5th: Katherine Clark (D)	475 900	40	CA 31st: Pete Aguilar (D)	19.4	39	KY 3rd: John A. Yarmuth (D)	33.9
41	VA10th Barbara Comstock (R)	472 000	41	TX 15th: Vicente Gonzalez (D)	19.1	41	OH 13th: Tim Ryan (D)	33.8
42	VA11th Gerald E. Connolly (D)	463 600	41	TX 34th: Filemon Vela (D)	19.1	42	IL 13th: Rodney Davis (R)	33.6
43	CA 53rd: Susan A. Davis (D)	461 600	43	NC 12th: Alma S. Adams (D)	19.0	42	MI 9th: Sander M. Levin (D)	33.6
44	NY 17th: Nita M. Lowey (D)	460 900	44	FL 14th: Kathy Castor (D)	18.9	42	VA 8th Donald S. Beyer, Jr. (D)	33.6
45	CA 46th: J. Luis Correa (D)	453 300	44	TX 28th: Henry Cuellar (D)	18.9	45	NV 1st: Dina Titus (D)	33.5
46	CA 38th: Linda T. Sánchez (D)	450 500	46	GA 13th: David Scott (D)	18.8	46	NC 12th: Alma S. Adams (D)	33.4
47	CA 43rd:Maxine Waters (D)	447 400	47	WI 4th: Gwen Moore (D)	18.6	47	AZ 2nd: Martha McSally (R)	33.3
48	NY 4th: Kathleen M. Rice (D)	442 300	48	AZ 3rd: Raul M. Grijalva (D)	18.4	48	PA 1st: Robert A. Brady (D)	33.2
49	CA 5th: Mike Thompson (D)	437 200	48	CA 35th Norma J. Torres (D)	18.4	49	NM 1st: Michelle Lujan Grisham (D)	33.1
50	NY 16th: Eliot L. Engel (D)	435 500	50	FL 25th: Mario Diaz-Balart (R)	18.3	50	IL 17th: Cheri Bustos (D)	33.0
51	NJ 11th: Rodney P. Frelinghuysen (R)	431 700	50	LA 5th: Ralph Lee Abraham (R)	18.3	51	NC 4th: David E. Price (D)	32.9
52	MD 8th: Jamie Raskin (D)	431 600	52	IL 7th: Danny K. Davis (D)	18.2	51	TX 21st: Lamar Smith (R)	32.9
53	CA 50th: Duncan Hunter (R)	431 000	53	OH 3rd: Joyce Beatty (D)	17.9	53	NC 1st: G. K. Butterfield (D)	32.8
54	NJ 7th: Leonard Lance (R)	429 800	54	MD 4th: Anthony G. Brown (D)	17.7	53	RI 1st: David Cicilline (D)	32.8
55	NY 13th: Adriano Espaillat (D)	429 600	54	NY 16th: Eliot L. Engel (D)	17.7	55	IL 2nd: Robin L. Kelly (D)	32.7
56	MA 7th: Michael E. Capuano (D)	426 500	56	FL 26th: Carlos Curbelo (R)	17.6	55	MD 7th: Elijah E. Cummings (D)	32.7
57	CA 32nd: Grace F. Napolitano (D)	422 000	56	TX 35th: Lloyd Doggett (D)	17.6	57	TN 5th: Jim Cooper (D)	32.6
58	NY 5th: Gregory W. Meeks (D)	419 100	58	GA 12th: Rick W. Allen (R)	17.5	58	CT 3rd: Rosa L. DeLauro (D)	32.4
59	CA 25th: Stephen Knight (R)	413 100	59	TX 20th: Joaquin Castro (D)	17.3	58	FL 24th: Frederica S. Wilson (D)	32.4
60	CA 29th: Tony Cárdenas (D)	412 800	60	CA 34th: Jimmy Gomez (D)	17.2	60	IL 12th: Mike Bost (R)	32.3
61	NJ 5th: Josh Gottheimer (R)	407 400	61	NY 7th: Nydia M. Velázquez (D)	17.1	61	FL 23rd: Debbie Wasserman Schultz (D).	32.2
62	MA 6th: Seth Moulton (D)	405 200	62	IL 4th:Luis V. Gutierrez (D)	17.0	61	GA 2nd: Sanford D. Bishop Jr. (D)	32.2
63	WA 1st Suzan K. DelBene (D)	399 100	63	NJ 8th: Albio Sires (D)	16.9	63	CA 13th:Barbara Lee (D)	31.9
64	MA 8th: Stephen F. Lynch (D)	390 900	63	NY 14th: Joseph Crowley (D)	16.9	63	FL 2nd: Neal P. Dunn (R)	31.9
65	CA 40th: Lucille Roybal-Allard (D)	388 100	65	CA 8th: Paul Cook (R)	16.7	65	OH 10th: Michael R. Turner (R)	31.8
66	MA 4th:Joseph P. Kennedy III (D)	381 100	65	OH 9th: Marcy Kaptur (D)	16.7	66	AL 1st: Bradley Byrne (R)	31.7
67	NY 1st: Lee M. Zeldin (R)	376 200	67	FL 27th: Ileana Ros-Lehtinen (R)	16.6	66	MI 12th: Debbie Dingell (D)	31.7
68	CA 4th:Tom McClintock (R)	374 800	67	IN 7th: André Carson (D)	16.6	68	FL 11th: Daniel Webster (R)	31.6
69	CA 42nd: Ken Calvert (R)	374 400	67	MA 7th: Michael E. Capuano (D)	16.6	68	LA 4th: Mike Johnson (R)	31.6
70	WA 9th: Adam Smith (D)	369 700	70	CA 29th: Tony Cárdenas (D)	16.5	70	MT At-Large Greg Gianforte (R)	31.5
71	NY 2nd: Peter T. King (R)	363 800	70	GA 1st: Earl L. "Buddy" Carter (R)	16.5	71	CA 34th: Jimmy Gomez (D)	31.4
72	NY 15th: José E. Serrano (D)	363 000	70	TX 16th: Beto O'Rourke (D)	16.5	71	MI 5th: Daniel T. Kildee (D)	31.4
73	CO: 2nd: Jared Polis (D)	361 600	73	AL 2nd: Martha Roby (R)	16.4	71	WV 3rd: Evan H. Jenkins (R)	31.4
74	NJ 9th: Bill Pascrell, Jr. (D)	355 600	73	CA 32nd: Grace F. Napolitano (D)	16.4	74	NY 25th: Louise McIntosh Slaughter (D)	31.2
75	NJ 4th: Christopher H. Smith (R)	354 300	73	CA 41st: Mark Takano (D)	16.4	74	OH 2nd: Brad R. Wenstrup (R)	31.2

Congressional Districts of the 115th Congress of the United States
Selected Rankings

	Median household income, 2015			Percent of persons below 65 years with no health insurance, 2015			Percent of persons below the poverty level, 2015	
Median income rank	State congressional district Representative	Median income (dollars) [col 47]	No health inurance rank	State congressional district Representative	Percent with no health insurance [col 59]	Poverty rate rank	State congressional district Representative	Poverty rate [col 49]
1	CA 18th: Anna G. Eshoo (D)	120 089	1	TX 33rd: Marc A. Veasey (D)	33.6	1	NY 15th: José E. Serrano (D)	38.1
2	VA10th Barbara Comstock (R)	114 793	2	TX 29th: Gene Green (D)	32.2	2	AZ 7th: Ruben Gallego (D)	32.5
3	CA 17th: Ro Khanna (D)	111 024	3	TX 15th: Vicente Gonzalez (D)	29.9	3	MI 13th: John Conyers Jr. (D)	32.2
4	VA11th Gerald E. Connolly (D)	105 031	4	TX 34th: Filemon Vela (D)	28.3	4	CA 16th:Jim Costa (D)	30.8
5	NY 3rd: Thomas R. Souzzi (D)	102 602	5	TX 28th: Henry Cuellar (D)	27.1	5	CA 21st: David G. Valadao (R)	30.2
6	NJ 11th: Rodney P. Frelinghuysen (R)	102 205	6	TX 9th: Al Green (D)	24.8	5	MS 2nd: Bennie G. Thompson (D)	30.2
7	NJ 7th: Leonard Lance (R)	101 746	7	TX 18th: Sheila Jackson-Lee (D)	23.6	7	TX 34th: Filemon Vela (D)	29.4
8	VA 8th Donald S. Beyer, Jr. (D)	100 644	8	TX 5th: Jeb Hensarling (R)	23.1	8	KY 5th: Harold Rogers (R)	28.9
9	CA 15th: Eric Swalwell (D)	100 634	9	FL 24th: Frederica S. Wilson (D)	23.0	9	AL 7th: Terri A. Sewell (D)	28.2
10	CA 14th:Jackie Speier (D)	98 129	9	TX 35th: Lloyd Doggett (D)	23.0	10	GA 2nd: Sanford D. Bishop Jr. (D)	27.7
11	NY 4th: Kathleen M. Rice (D)	97 111	11	TX 30th: Eddie Bernice Johnson (D)	22.8	10	NY 13th: Adriano Espaillat (D)	27.7
12	CA 33rd:Ted Lieu (D)	97 074	12	NV 1st: Dina Titus (D)	21.8	10	PA 2nd: Chaka Fattah (D)	27.7
13	NJ 5th: Josh Gottheimer (R)	96 349	13	FL 20th: Alcee L. Hastings (D)	21.7	13	TX 15th: Vicente Gonzalez (D)	27.5
14	MD 8th: Jamie Raskin (D)	95 314	13	FL 27th: Ileana Ros-Lehtinen (R)	21.7	14	NY 7th: Nydia M. Velázquez (D)	27.2
15	TX 22nd: Pete Olson (R)	95 048	15	TX 16th: Beto O'Rourke (D)	21.5	15	CA 34th: Jimmy Gomez (D)	26.6
16	NY 12th: Carolyn B. Maloney (D)	93 649	16	TX 1st: Louie Gohmert (R)	21.2	16	OH 11th: Marcia L. Fudge (D)	26.4
17	IL 6th: Peter J. Roskam (R)	93 474	17	CA 34th: Jimmy Gomez (D)	20.5	17	TX 28th: Henry Cuellar (D)	25.6
18	CA 45th: Mimi Walters (R)	93 374	17	OK 2nd: Markwayne Mullin (R)	20.5	18	NC 1st: G. K. Butterfield (D)	25.5
19	CA 12th:Nancy Pelosi (D)	93 122	19	AZ 7th: Ruben Gallego (D)	20.4	18	TX 29th: Gene Green (D)	25.5
20	MD 5th: Steny H. Hoyer (D)	91 820	19	TX 11th K. Michael Conaway (R)	20.4	20	MI 14th: Brenda L. Lawrence (D)	25.2
21	MA 4th:Joseph P. Kennedy III (D)	90 913	21	FL 25th: Mario Diaz-Balart (R)	20.2	20	SC 6th: James E. Clyburn (D)	25.2
22	NY 17th: Nita M. Lowey (D)	89 905	22	IL 4th:Luis V. Gutierrez (D)	19.5	22	TX 33rd: Marc A. Veasey (D)	24.8
23	NY 2nd: Peter T. King (R)	89 668	22	TX 14th: Randy K. Weber, Sr. (R)	19.5	23	CA 51st: Juan Vargas (D)	24.7
24	CT 4th: James A. Himes (D)	89 085	22	TX 27th: Blake Farenthold (R)	19.5	23	LA 5th: Ralph Lee Abraham (R)	24.7
25	NY 1st: Lee M. Zeldin (R)	86 645	25	FL 19th: Francis Rooney (R)	19.4	23	TN 9th: Steve Cohen (D)	24.7
26	TX 3rd: Sam Johnson (R)	86 565	25	FL 26th: Carlos Curbelo (R)	19.4	26	FL 5th: Al Lawson Jr. (D)	24.3
27	WA 1st Suzan K. DelBene (D)	86 349	27	NJ 8th: Albio Sires (D)	18.8	27	FL 24th: Frederica S. Wilson (D)	24.1
28	MA 5th: Katherine Clark (D)	86 183	27	TX 23rd: Will Hurd (R)	18.8	27	TX 30th: Eddie Bernice Johnson (D)	24.1
29	IL 14th: Randy Hultgren (R)	86 050	29	CA 40th: Lucille Roybal-Allard (D)	18.7	27	WI 4th: Gwen Moore (D)	24.1
30	CA 19th: Zoe Lofgren (D)	85 536	29	TX 13th: Mac Thornberry (R)	18.7	30	CA 40th: Lucille Roybal-Allard (D)	23.9
31	CA 52nd: Scott H. Peters (D)	84 479	31	TX 4th: John Ratcliffe (R)	18.6	30	LA 2nd: Cedric Richmond (D)	23.9
32	PA 7th: Patrick Meehan (R)	84 406	31	TX 19th: Jodey C. Arrington (R)	18.6	32	IN 7th: André Carson (D)	23.8
33	GA 6th: Karen Handell (R)	83 844	33	FL 22nd: Theodore E. Deutch (D)	18.4	33	NV 1st: Dina Titus (D)	23.6
34	CA 48th: Dana Rohrabacher (R)	83 001	33	GA 9th: Doug Collins (R)	18.4	33	NC 12th: Alma S. Adams (D)	23.6
35	NY 10th: Jerrold Nadler (D)	81 834	35	FL 5th: Al Lawson Jr. (D)	18.3	33	TX 18th: Sheila Jackson-Lee (D)	23.6
36	MN 3rd: Erik Paulsen (R)	81 788	36	CA 46th: J. Luis Correa (D)	18.1	36	AZ 3rd: Raul M. Grijalva (D)	23.4
37	CA 49th: Darrell E. Issa (R)	81 611	36	FL 17th: Thomas J. Rooney (R)	18.1	37	IL 7th: Danny K. Davis (D)	23.3
38	MD 3rd: John P. Sarbanes (D)	81 231	36	TX 32nd: Pete Sessions (R)	18.1	38	OH 3rd: Joyce Beatty (D)	23.2
39	CA 39th: Edward R. Royce (R)	81 183	39	TX 36th: Brian Babin (R)	18.0	39	PA 1st: Robert A. Brady (D)	22.9
40	MA 6th: Seth Moulton (D)	80 638	40	GA 4th: Henry C. "Hank" Johnson Jr. (D)	17.8	40	FL 20th: Alcee L. Hastings (D)	22.8
41	PA 6th: Ryan A. Costello (R)	80 129	41	GA 2nd: Sanford D. Bishop Jr. (D)	17.7	41	NM 2nd: Steve Pearce (R)	22.5
42	WA 7th: Pramila Jayapal (D)	80 119	41	NC 12th: Alma S. Adams (D)	17.7	42	VA 3rd Robert C. "Bobby" Scott (D)	22.4
43	PA 8th: Michael G. Fitzpatrick (R)	80 032	41	TX 20th: Joaquin Castro (D)	17.7	43	LA 4th: Mike Johnson (R)	22.1
44	MA 8th: Stephen F. Lynch (D)	79 789	44	MS 4th: Steven Palazzo (R)	17.4	43	WV 3rd: Evan H. Jenkins (R)	22.1
45	TX 26th: Michael C. Burgess (R)	79 738	45	OK 5th: Steve Russell (R)	17.3	45	NY 8th: Hakeem S. Jeffries (D)	22.0
46	CA 11th:Mark Desaulnier (D)	79 622	46	FL 16th: Vern Buchanan (R)	17.1	46	CA 8th: Paul Cook (R)	21.8
47	NY 18th: Sean Patrick Maloney (D)	79 540	46	GA 13th: David Scott (D)	17.1	46	GA 12th: Rick W. Allen (R)	21.8
48	NJ 12th: Bonnie Watson Coleman (D)	78 982	46	TN 9th: Steve Cohen (D)	17.1	48	AR 2nd: Bruce Westerman (R)	21.7
49	NJ 4th: Christopher H. Smith (R)	78 467	49	FL 9th: Darren Soto (D)	17.0	48	GA 8th: Austin Scott (R)	21.7
50	MD 4th: Anthony G. Brown (D)	78 412	50	GA 1st: Earl L. "Buddy" Carter (R)	16.9	50	GA 5th: John Lewis (D)	21.3
51	CA 26th: Julia Brownley (D)	77 744	51	GA 12th: Rick W. Allen (R)	16.8	51	MS 4th: Steven Palazzo (R)	21.2
52	VA 1st Robert J. Wittman (R)	77 593	51	NC 1st: G. K. Butterfield (D)	16.8	52	CA 29th: Tony Cárdenas (D)	21.1
53	MO 2nd: Ann Wagner (R)	77 477	53	LA 5th: Ralph Lee Abraham (R)	16.5	52	CA 44th: Nanette Diaz Barragan (D)	21.1
54	WA 8th: David G. Reichert (R)	77 320	53	TX 7th: John Abney Culberson (R)	16.5	54	AZ 1st: Tom O'Halleran (D)	20.8
55	MI 11th: David A.Trott (R)	77 183	55	AK: At-Large Don Young (R)	16.4	54	CA 6th: Doris O. Matsui (D)	20.8
56	HI 1st: Colleen Hanabusa (D)	77 156	55	GA 8th: Austin Scott (R)	16.4	54	NY 26th: Brian Higgins (D)	20.8
57	MN 2nd: Jason Lewis (R)	77 122	57	FL 14th: Kathy Castor (D)	16.2	54	TX 35th: Lloyd Doggett (D)	20.8
58	IL 10th: Bradley Scott Schneider (D)	77 031	58	NY 14th: Joseph Crowley (D)	16.0	58	CA 36th: Raul Ruiz (D)	20.7
59	IL 5th: Michael Quigley (D)	76 963	59	GA 7th: Robert Woodall (R)	15.9	58	CA 43rd: Maxine Waters (D)	20.7
60	NC 9th: Robert Pittenger (R)	76 101	60	NJ 10th: Donald M. Payne, Jr. (D)	15.8	58	OH 9th: Marcy Kaptur (D)	20.7
61	CA 30th: Brad Sherman (D)	75 853	60	OK 1st: Jim Bridenstine (R)	15.8	61	AR 1st: Eric A. "Rick" Crawford (R)	20.5
62	CA 25th: Stephen Knight (R)	75 732	62	TX 12th: Kay Granger (R)	15.7	61	IL 4th:Luis V. Gutierrez (D)	20.5
63	DC At Large: Eleanor Holmes Norton (D)	75 628	63	AZ 3rd: Raul M. Grijalva (D)	15.6	63	FL 14th: Kathy Castor (D)	20.4
64	NJ 6th: Frank Pallone Jr. (D)	75 203	63	SC 7th: Tom Rice (R)	15.6	63	MO 1st: William Lacy Clay (D)	20.4
65	VA 7th Dave Brat (R)	74 889	65	TX 6th: Joe Barton (R)	15.4	65	FL 2nd: Neal P. Dunn (R)	20.2
66	CO 6th: Mike Coffman (R)	74 430	66	GA 5th: John Lewis (D)	15.3	66	MI 5th: Daniel T. Kildee (D)	20.1
67	TX 2nd: Ted Poe (R)	74 246	66	TX 2nd: Ted Poe (R)	15.3	67	IL 2nd: Robin L. Kelly (D)	20.0
68	MD 6th: John K. Delaney (D)	73 641	66	TX 17th: Bill Flores (R)	15.3	67	NM 1st: Michelle Lujan Grisham (D)	20.0
69	AK: At-Large Don Young (R)	73 355	69	FL 23rd: Debbie Wasserman Schultz (D)	15.1	67	TX 9th: Al Green (D)	20.0
70	MN 5th: Tom Emmer (R)	73 227	69	LA 2nd: Cedric Richmond (D)	15.1	70	CA 22nd: Devin Nunes (R)	19.9
71	MA 3rd: Niki Tsongas (D)	72 570	69	SC 6th: James E. Clyburn (D)	15.1	71	OK 2nd: Markwayne Mullin (R)	19.8
72	CA 42nd: Ken Calvert (R)	72 536	69	TX 8th: Kevin Brady (R)	15.1	72	AL 2nd: Martha Roby (R)	19.7
73	CO: 2nd: Jared Polis (D)	72 468	73	LA 4th: Mike Johnson (R)	15.0	72	AL 4th: Robert B. Aderholt (R)	19.7
74	CO 4th: Ken Buck (R)	72 390	73	MS 2nd: Bennie G. Thompson (D)	15.0	74	AL 3rd: Mike Rogers (R)	19.6
75	WA 9th: Adam Smith (D)	71 947	75	FL 11th: Daniel Webster (R)	14.9	75	CA 31st: Pete Aguilar (D)	19.5

Table E. Congressional Districts 115th Congress — **Land Area and Population Characteristics**

STATE District	Representative, 115th Congress	Land area,[1] 2016 (sq. mi)	Total persons	Per square mile	Percent — Race alone — White	Black	American Indian, Alaska Native	Asian and Pacific Islander	Some other race	Two or more races	Hispanic or Latino[2]	Non-Hispanic White alone	Female	Foreign-born	Born in state of residence
		1	2	3	4	5	6	7	8	9	10	11	12	13	14

1. Dry land or land partially or temporarily covered by water.   2. May be of any race.

Table E. Congressional Districts 115th Congress — **Age and Education**

STATE District	Population and population characteristics, 2015 (cont.) — Age (percent) — Under 5 years	5 to 17 years	18 to 24 years	25 to 34 years	35 to 44 years	45 to 54 years	55 to 64 years	65 to 74 years	75 years and over	Median age	Education, 2015 — Total Enrollment[1]	Attainment[2] (percent) — High school graduate or more	Bachelor's degree or more
	15	16	17	18	19	20	21	22	23	24	25	26	27

1. All persons 3 years old and over enrolled in nursery school through college and graduate or professional school.   2. Persons 25 years old and over.

Table E. Congressional Districts 115th Congress — **Households and Group Quarters**

STATE District	Households, 2015 — Number	Average household size	Family households (percent)	Married-couple family (percent)	Female family householder[1]	One person households (percent)	Group quarters, 2010 — Total in group quarters, 2015	Percent 65 years and over	Persons in correctional institutions	Persons in nursing facilities	Persons in college dormitories	Persons in military quarters
	28	29	30	31	32	33	34	35	36	37	38	39

1. No spouse present.

Table E. Congressional Districts 115th Congress — **Housing and Money Income**

STATE District	Housing units, 2015 — Total	Occupied units as a percent of all units	Occupied units — Owner-occupied — Owner-occupied units as a percent of occupied units	Median value[1] (dollars)	Percent valued at $500,000 or more	Renter-occupied — Median rent[2]	Money income, 2015 — Per capita income (dollars)	Households — Median income (dollars)	Percent with income of $100,000 or more
	40	41	42	43	44	45	46	47	48

1. Specified owner-occupied units; $1,000,000 represents $1,000,000 or more.   2. Specified renter-occupied units.

1184

Table E. Congressional Districts 115th Congress — **Poverty, Labor Force, Employment, and Social Security**

STATE District	Poverty, 2015			Civilian labor force, 2015			Civilian employment,[2] 2015					Social Security beneficiaries, December 2015		
					Unemployment			Percent						
	Persons below poverty level (percent)	Families below poverty level (percent)	Percent of households receiving food stamps in past 12 months	Total	Total	Rate[1]	Total	Management, business, science and arts occupations	Service, sales, and office	Construction and production	Persons under age 65 with no health insurance, 2015 (percent)	Number	Rate[3]	Supplemental Security Income recipients, December 2015
	49	50	51	52	53	54	55	56	57	58	59	60	61	62

1. Percent of civilian labor force.　　2. Persons 16 years old and over.　　3. Per 1,000 resident population estimated in the 2014 American Community Survey.

Table E. Congressional Districts 115th Congress — **Agriculture**

STATE District	Agriculture, 2012									
	Land in farms				Value of products sold				Government payments	
	Number of farms	Acres	Average size of farm (acres)	Irrigated land (acres)	Total ($1,000)	Average per farm (dollars)	Percent from crops	Percent from livestock and poultry products	Total ($1,000)	Average per farm receiving payments (dollars)
	63	64	65	66	67	68	69	70	71	72

Table E. Congressional Districts 115th Congress — **Nonfarm Employment and Payroll**

STATE District	Private nonfarm employment and payroll, 2015												
	Number of establishments	Employment										Annual payroll	
			Percent by selected industries										
		Total	Manufacturing	Construction	Wholesale trade	Retail trade	Health care and social assistance	Finance and Insurance	Real estate and rental and leasing	Professional, scientific, and technical services	Information	Total (mil dol)	Average per employee dollars
	73	74	75	76	77	78	79	80	81	82	83	84	85

STATE District	Representative, 115th Congress	Land area,[1] 2016 (sq. mi)	Population and population characteristics, 2015: Total persons	Per square mile	Percent: Race alone: White	Black	American Indian, Alaska Native	Asian and Pacific Islander	Some other race	Two or more races	Hispanic or Latino[2]	Non-Hispanic White alone	Female	Foreign-born	Born in state of residence
		1	2	3	4	5	6	7	8	9	10	11	12	13	14
UNITED STATES....		3 532 068.7	321 418 821	91.0	73.1	12.7	0.8	5.5	4.8	3.1	17.6	61.5	50.8	13.5	58.5
ALABAMA		50 646.4	4 858 979	95.9	68.5	26.8	0.4	1.3	1.1	1.8	4.0	65.9	51.6	3.5	70.1
District 1	Bradley Byrne (R)	6 066.8	706 302	116.4	67.1	28.3	1.1	1.3	0.8	1.5	3.0	65.0	51.5	2.6	68.5
District 2	Martha Roby (R)	10 141.7	686 622	67.7	64.3	31.8	0.2	1.0	0.7	2.0	3.0	62.2	52.0	2.8	70.8
District 3	Mike Rogers (R)	7 544.1	703 986	93.3	70.0	25.3	0.2	1.5	0.8	2.2	3.0	68.1	51.0	3.1	65.0
District 4	Robert B. Aderholt (R)	8 889.2	684 685	77.0	88.3	7.2	0.5	0.8	1.3	1.9	6.3	83.9	51.2	3.8	75.2
District 5	Mo Brooks (R)	3 677.4	708 972	192.8	76.8	17.5	0.5	1.7	0.8	2.7	5.1	72.8	50.9	4.5	61.7
District 6	Gary J. Palmer (R)	4 171.3	700 691	168.0	79.0	15.5	0.2	1.9	1.9	1.5	4.2	76.8	52.2	4.7	70.5
District 7	Terri A. Sewell (D)	10 156.1	667 721	65.7	32.8	63.6	0.1	0.9	1.6	0.9	3.2	31.4	52.3	3.0	79.5
ALASKA		570 638.3	738 432	1.3	65.2	3.5	13.7	7.3	1.7	8.6	7.0	61.3	47.4	7.9	41.8
At Large....................	Don Young (R)	570 638.3	738 432	1.3	65.2	3.5	13.7	7.3	1.7	8.6	7.0	61.3	47.4	7.9	41.8
ARIZONA		113 590.7	6 828 065	60.1	77.4	4.4	4.5	3.4	7.1	3.3	30.7	55.7	50.4	13.4	39.2
District 1	Tom O' Halleran (D)	55 037.3	759 663	13.8	63.5	2.5	23.4	1.8	5.3	3.4	22.9	48.3	50.2	6.7	52.3
District 2	Martha McSally (R)	7 837.3	713 631	91.1	82.2	4.2	0.9	3.3	5.6	3.8	27.8	62.0	50.8	11.5	36.2
District 3	Raul M. Grijalva (D)	15 688.3	761 488	48.5	70.0	4.9	4.8	1.8	15.4	3.1	60.0	29.1	50.3	20.8	47.5
District 4	Paul A. Gosar (R)	33 200.0	739 374	22.3	89.2	1.6	1.9	1.2	3.2	2.9	18.1	75.6	49.3	7.5	27.0
District 5	Andy Biggs (R)	293.5	789 400	2 689.9	84.6	3.3	1.4	5.4	2.3	2.9	17.2	70.6	51.2	10.2	37.2
District 6	David Schweikert (R)	625	749 808	1 199.8	83.9	3.2	1.8	5.1	3.2	2.8	18.2	69.8	50.2	13.9	31.7
District 7	Ruben Gallego (D)	204.9	769 597	3 756.4	61.5	10.2	2.9	2.5	19.7	3.3	62.8	21.5	49.6	24.8	47.7
District 8	Trent Franks (R)	539.9	767 981	1 422.5	85.2	4.8	0.7	3.6	2.4	3.3	19.7	69.1	52.2	10.0	33.7
District 9	Kyrsten Sinema (D)	164.6	777 123	4 721.2	77.2	4.9	2.7	5.2	6.1	3.9	29.3	56.1	49.7	14.6	39.2
ARKANSAS............		52 035.6	2 978 204	57.2	77.5	15.8	0.7	1.7	2.2	2.2	7.0	73.0	50.9	4.8	61.7
District 1	Eric A. "Rick" Crawford (R)	19 319.1	722 402	37.4	77.8	18.2	0.6	0.5	1.1	1.8	3.1	76.1	50.1	1.6	66.6
District 2	J. French Hill (R)	4 978.7	761 348	152.9	72.4	22.6	0.4	1.7	1.0	1.9	5.0	68.6	51.7	4.2	65.5
District 3	Steve Womack (R)	5 399.1	782 717	145.0	84.5	3.3	1.1	3.7	4.3	3.1	13.7	75.5	50.7	9.7	50.1
District 4	Bruce Westerman (R)	22 338.7	711 737	31.9	74.9	19.7	0.7	0.6	2.3	1.8	5.6	71.9	50.9	3.2	65.5
CALIFORNIA..........		155 792.7	39 144 818	251.3	60.9	5.8	0.7	14.6	13.5	4.5	38.8	37.8	50.3	27.3	54.8
District 1	Doug LaMalfa (R)	28 088.3	710 344	25.3	86.2	1.4	2.3	3.1	2.5	4.5	13.1	77.3	49.9	6.3	69.9
District 2	Jared Huffman (D)	12 952.3	720 346	55.6	79.6	1.6	2.2	4.3	7.3	5.1	17.7	70.9	50.7	12.9	59.3
District 3	John Garamendi (D)	6 183.8	731 775	118.3	65.7	6.3	0.9	11.4	9.4	6.2	30.0	47.4	49.6	18.7	60.6
District 4	Tom McClintock (R)	12 836.9	722 313	56.3	85.1	1.6	0.8	5.0	2.8	4.7	13.2	76.2	50.3	9.0	65.6
District 5	Mike Thompson (D)	1 730.8	733 412	423.7	64.3	5.8	0.8	12.3	10.6	6.2	27.9	49.6	51.1	21.2	59.1
District 6	Doris O. Matsui (D)	175.1	750 843	4 288.0	54.0	12.1	0.7	16.6	9.7	6.9	29.5	36.6	51.4	23.5	59.5
District 7	Ami Bera (D)	548.8	739 069	1 346.7	64.5	7.6	0.5	17.2	3.4	6.7	15.9	54.6	51.2	18.2	61.4
District 8	Paul Cook (R)	32 867.7	716 399	21.8	78.1	8.0	1.3	3.2	4.9	4.5	39.2	46.1	50.6	13.6	64.4
District 9	Jerry McNerney (D)	1 252.9	746 779	596.0	56.0	8.9	0.6	14.9	9.8	9.9	37.6	35.2	50.3	22.5	64.1
District 10	Jeff Denham (R)	1 820.3	739 784	406.4	73.3	3.2	0.6	7.7	9.8	5.3	42.7	42.9	50.4	21.1	65.5
District 11	Mark Desaulnier (D)	493.2	752 786	1 526.4	58.8	8.5	0.5	14.3	12.4	5.5	27.2	46.1	51.4	26.4	52.6
District 12	Nancy Pelosi (D)	39.0	749 688	19 208.0	49.7	5.3	0.4	33.0	7.1	4.5	14.9	43.3	49.1	33.5	38.5
District 13	Barbara Lee (D)	96.8	755 776	7 811.2	43.7	17.4	0.7	20.8	10.9	6.6	22.4	35.0	51.3	27.0	48.6
District 14	Jackie Speier (D)	259.6	757 062	2 916.1	44.8	2.9	0.3	35.3	11.8	5.0	24.3	34.1	50.6	37.9	46.5
District 15	Eric Swalwell (D)	599.9	771 800	1 286.5	45.8	6.0	0.7	34.9	6.5	6.0	22.2	32.6	50.7	34.3	51.1
District 16	Jim Costa (D)	2 839.7	740 625	260.8	60.3	5.2	1.0	10.0	19.6	3.9	60.4	22.3	50.2	25.6	64.7
District 17	Ro Khanna (D)	185.4	760 444	4 101.9	31.0	2.5	0.3	54.0	8.4	3.8	16.2	24.7	49.3	48.0	38.8
District 18	Anna G. Eshoo (D)	696.1	738 774	1 061.3	63.8	1.8	0.2	23.0	6.2	5.0	15.9	55.1	50.8	28.8	47.6
District 19	Zoe Lofgren (D)	915.9	765 143	835.4	43.3	2.9	0.6	27.5	20.7	5.0	41.3	25.2	49.4	35.8	50.6
District 20	Jimmy Panetta (D)	4 874.2	733 752	150.5	70.4	1.7	0.8	5.5	17.0	4.6	52.9	36.8	49.5	27.1	56.7
District 21	David G. Valadao (R)	6 729.9	716 371	106.4	73.3	3.8	1.2	3.4	16.0	2.3	74.7	17.0	47.4	29.6	61.4
District 22	Devin Nunes (R)	1 165.2	741 313	636.2	73.5	3.4	0.7	7.7	11.2	3.5	46.7	40.1	50.7	17.3	69.1
District 23	Kevin McCarthy (R)	9 898.1	738 690	74.6	75.9	7.1	0.7	5.6	6.8	4.0	37.7	47.1	48.9	13.5	69.9
District 24	Salud O. Carbajal (D)	6 885.4	736 757	107.0	81.1	2.0	0.7	5.0	7.5	3.6	36.0	54.7	49.7	17.8	59.1
District 25	Stephen Knight (R)	1 690.7	720 316	426.1	65.5	8.3	0.5	9.2	11.2	5.2	37.2	42.8	50.1	20.9	62.7
District 26	Julia Brownley (D)	939.1	725 084	772.1	80.7	1.8	1.0	7.3	5.3	3.9	45.0	43.6	50.7	24.2	56.7
District 27	Judy Chu (D)	699.9	733 239	1 047.7	38.4	4.8	0.3	38.4	14.7	3.4	27.9	26.4	52.2	39.2	46.6
District 28	Adam B. Schiff (D)	218.5	714 897	3 272.5	67.4	3.0	0.3	13.7	11.7	3.9	24.2	56.2	50.2	39.8	37.4
District 29	Tony Cárdenas (D)	92.0	720 532	7 829.0	56.0	3.9	0.5	7.8	29.7	2.2	68.8	18.4	50.1	42.9	47.1
District 30	Brad Sherman (D)	135.9	771 108	5 672.1	65.1	4.3	0.3	13.4	12.7	4.1	28.9	49.9	51.1	34.1	44.8
District 31	Pete Aguilar (D)	218.2	738 482	3 383.7	61.5	10.9	0.5	8.7	13.9	4.4	51.8	27.1	50.6	22.3	63.5
District 32	Grace F. Napolitano (D)	124.2	732 927	5 899.4	49.2	1.9	0.6	17.1	28.0	3.2	63.4	16.3	51.3	35.0	57.1
District 33	Ted Lieu (D)	288.6	718 273	2 488.9	71.8	3.7	0.4	14.7	4.0	5.4	13.0	63.8	51.4	23.4	46.8
District 34	Jimmy Gomez (D)	47.7	735 150	15 422.3	40.6	4.7	1.5	19.7	30.6	2.8	64.2	10.3	49.5	45.8	44.2
District 35	Norma J. Torres (D)	168.9	739 819	4 380.5	45.3	6.2	0.7	7.2	35.5	5.0	71.5	13.0	49.5	30.4	61.1
District 36	Raul Ruiz (D)	5 912.4	750 645	127.0	69.4	4.8	1.2	3.4	18.2	3.0	49.8	40.2	49.8	22.1	55.0
District 37	Karen Bass (D)	55.3	722 781	13 078.9	41.5	23.7	0.7	10.0	20.2	4.0	38.1	25.2	51.4	32.1	47.1
District 38	Linda T. Sánchez (D)	101.4	725 433	7 153.4	45.2	3.9	0.8	15.7	31.3	3.2	62.5	16.4	50.2	31.0	59.9
District 39	Edward R. Royce (R)	204.4	731 324	3 578.0	53.6	1.7	0.4	31.1	9.7	3.5	34.9	30.0	50.8	33.4	53.2
District 40	Lucille Roybal-Allard (D)	57.7	721 037	12 499.1	60.4	4.8	0.5	2.6	30.1	1.5	87.6	4.9	50.5	41.2	54.0
District 41	Mark Takano (D)	316.6	745 630	2 354.9	52.9	9.3	0.6	5.5	27.7	4.0	58.0	25.1	50.0	24.4	62.2
District 42	Ken Calvert (R)	935.9	772 860	825.8	65.4	5.3	0.5	10.5	13.0	5.4	38.1	42.8	50.9	20.7	60.1
District 43	Maxine Waters (D)	72.0	744 444	10 333.9	32.1	22.6	0.4	13.2	27.7	3.9	48.3	13.5	51.5	31.0	54.7
District 44	Nanette Diaz Barragan (D)	79.4	712 204	8 973.3	46.3	15.1	1.6	7.6	26.3	3.0	69.4	6.8	51.0	34.2	57.2
District 45	Mimi Walters (R)	330.5	771 550	2 334.7	61.8	2.3	0.1	24.7	6.4	4.8	17.9	51.3	51.2	30.3	47.4
District 46	J. Luis Correa (D)	71.7	738 410	10 300.2	59.6	1.9	0.5	12.4	23.7	1.8	67.3	17.5	49.6	41.4	50.4
District 47	Alan S. Lowenthal (D)	216.3	718 339	3 321.5	55.0	7.1	1.5	23.0	9.2	4.1	36.3	30.6	50.4	31.0	53.5
District 48	Dana Rohrabacher (R)	145.5	724 082	4 976.1	67.3	1.3	0.6	18.7	7.9	4.2	20.3	56.3	50.8	25.2	52.0
District 49	Darrell E. Issa (R)	553.1	735 828	1 330.3	80.5	2.6	0.5	7.3	5.3	3.9	25.8	61.5	49.1	17.3	50.4
District 50	Duncan Hunter (R)	2 787.4	753 486	270.3	78.1	2.5	1.0	6.7	6.8	4.9	31.4	55.6	50.0	20.1	54.3
District 51	Juan Vargas (D)	4 791.6	724 812	151.3	64.0	6.1	0.7	9.2	16.6	3.4	70.6	13.1	50.1	35.3	51.0
District 52	Scott H. Peters (D)	267.0	755 498	2 829.6	69.1	2.9	0.3	19.6	2.4	5.6	15.7	57.5	49.8	24.7	41.7
District 53	Susan A. Davis (D)	135.4	776 583	5 733.4	64.4	9.3	0.4	13.4	6.7	5.8	34.2	39.3	49.9	22.5	50.5

1. Dry land or land partially or temporarily covered by water. 2. May be of any race.

Table E. Congressional Districts 115th Congress — Age and Education

STATE District	Population and population characteristics, 2015 (cont.) Age (percent)											Education, 2015	
													Attainment[2] (percent)
	Under 5 years	5 to 17 years	18 to 24 years	25 to 34 years	35 to 44 years	45 to 54 years	55 to 64 years	65 to 74 years	75 years and over	Median age	Total Enrollment[1]	High school graduate or more	Bachelor's degree or more
	15	16	17	18	19	20	21	22	23	24	25	26	27
UNITED STATES	6.2	16.7	9.8	13.6	12.7	13.4	12.7	8.6	6.2	37.8	81 618 288	87.1	30.6
ALABAMA	5.9	16.9	9.6	12.8	12.6	13.3	13.2	9.3	6.4	38.7	1 191 243	84.9	24.2
District 1	5.8	17.5	8.8	12.8	12.2	13.0	13.4	9.9	6.4	39.4	169 114	86.1	23.9
District 2	5.9	17.4	9.5	13.4	12.7	12.9	12.7	9.3	6.5	38.0	166 983	83.5	21.4
District 3	5.7	16.5	11.3	12.2	12.8	13.1	13.1	9.2	6.2	38.5	180 759	83.3	20.8
District 4	6.0	17.1	8.2	12.0	12.4	13.5	13.4	10.2	7.1	40.5	151 742	80.3	16.1
District 5	5.7	16.5	9.2	12.6	12.3	14.8	13.3	8.9	6.5	39.8	172 726	87.4	31.3
District 6	6.1	17.5	8.1	12.9	13.9	13.6	12.8	8.7	6.4	38.5	173 512	89.7	35.3
District 7	5.8	16.3	12.5	14.1	12.0	11.5	13.5	8.5	5.8	36.0	176 407	83.4	19.5
ALASKA	7.4	17.8	11.2	16.1	12.4	12.6	12.9	6.5	3.1	33.3	189 880	92.6	29.7
At Large	7.4	17.8	11.2	16.1	12.4	12.6	12.9	6.5	3.1	33.3	189 880	92.6	29.7
ARIZONA	6.3	17.4	9.8	13.4	12.4	12.3	11.9	9.5	6.8	37.4	1 739 821	86.1	27.7
District 1	6.4	18.0	10.7	12.6	11.9	10.9	12.5	10.4	6.6	36.6	201 082	86.2	23.2
District 2	5.4	14.7	10.4	12.2	10.7	12.1	13.6	11.7	8.9	41.7	165 136	90.4	33.0
District 3	7.7	20.1	12.7	14.9	12.6	11.5	9.8	6.3	4.4	31.1	223 059	75.3	15.6
District 4	5.0	14.4	7.0	10.0	10.3	11.9	14.7	15.6	11.0	47.9	145 110	86.7	18.6
District 5	6.4	19.5	7.9	11.6	13.6	13.3	11.8	9.2	6.6	38.6	211 758	92.7	35.1
District 6	5.5	15.0	7.4	13.3	12.7	14.6	13.2	10.7	7.8	42.2	166 169	90.6	42.0
District 7	8.5	22.0	11.5	16.3	14.1	11.1	8.7	4.9	2.9	29.9	219 254	68.1	13.8
District 8	5.8	17.1	7.8	11.5	11.9	12.8	12.2	11.7	9.3	41.7	188 121	92.2	27.7
District 9	5.9	15.9	12.8	18.0	13.4	12.9	11.1	6.1	4.3	33.3	220 132	88.7	36.9
ARKANSAS	6.3	17.4	9.6	12.9	12.3	12.9	12.6	9.4	6.7	37.9	742 104	85.4	21.8
District 1	6.0	17.2	8.4	12.3	12.5	13.0	13.2	10.1	7.3	40.0	171 893	84.0	15.4
District 2	6.6	17.0	10.0	14.1	12.6	12.8	12.2	8.7	6.1	36.5	194 932	88.2	29.0
District 3	6.9	18.2	10.6	14.2	12.4	12.5	11.3	8.4	5.7	35.1	210 055	85.2	26.5
District 4	5.8	17.1	9.1	11.0	11.8	13.3	13.6	10.5	7.7	41.2	165 224	84.1	15.9
CALIFORNIA	6.4	16.9	10.1	14.9	13.3	13.4	11.8	7.6	5.6	36.2	10 484 707	82.2	32.3
District 1	5.3	14.9	9.9	12.0	10.3	12.2	15.3	11.6	8.4	42.4	174 186	89.9	24.2
District 2	4.9	15.0	8.3	11.3	12.3	14.0	15.3	11.5	7.4	43.5	169 587	89.6	40.7
District 3	6.2	18.1	12.3	13.8	11.9	12.5	11.8	8.0	5.4	34.7	218 462	84.3	24.9
District 4	4.5	15.8	7.7	10.4	11.8	14.3	15.3	12.1	8.3	44.9	163 431	92.6	32.0
District 5	5.9	15.0	9.0	13.6	12.5	13.3	14.1	10.0	6.7	39.8	174 437	86.6	30.3
District 6	7.3	17.7	9.8	17.1	13.1	11.7	11.1	7.3	4.9	33.9	202 875	83.4	26.6
District 7	6.1	16.9	8.7	13.9	12.8	14.2	13.1	8.0	6.2	38.5	193 901	90.8	33.4
District 8	7.3	19.7	10.4	13.5	10.9	12.4	11.9	8.6	5.3	34.1	191 798	82.6	17.4
District 9	7.0	20.3	10.0	13.7	12.4	12.9	11.1	7.4	5.1	34.4	211 796	80.3	19.1
District 10	6.9	20.2	9.9	13.5	13.0	13.4	11.3	6.9	5.1	34.7	211 525	78.9	17.9
District 11	6.0	16.3	8.5	13.2	12.9	14.4	13.3	8.8	6.6	39.8	186 134	87.9	43.0
District 12	4.6	8.5	6.5	24.1	16.4	13.8	11.6	7.8	6.8	38.3	136 330	87.8	56.6
District 13	5.4	13.5	10.3	18.0	14.7	13.4	11.6	7.9	5.3	36.8	197 092	84.7	47.5
District 14	5.7	14.2	8.7	15.0	14.2	14.1	13.3	8.4	6.5	39.5	189 561	87.5	44.9
District 15	6.8	17.7	7.2	13.9	15.3	14.5	12.4	7.1	5.0	37.9	198 370	89.8	43.6
District 16	8.7	22.3	11.3	15.1	12.3	11.5	9.4	5.7	3.9	30.0	227 213	66.4	12.1
District 17	6.0	15.2	8.2	17.3	16.1	13.9	11.1	6.6	5.5	36.8	185 257	91.2	55.1
District 18	6.1	16.6	7.7	13.2	14.1	15.2	12.6	7.8	6.6	39.6	194 762	93.0	61.1
District 19	6.6	16.9	9.8	14.2	14.3	14.6	11.9	7.1	4.8	36.8	209 126	80.5	34.2
District 20	7.0	17.5	12.3	14.1	12.4	12.2	11.7	7.5	5.3	34.4	209 916	73.2	26.1
District 21	9.0	22.2	11.5	15.5	13.2	11.1	8.9	5.0	3.6	29.6	215 428	58.6	9.1
District 22	7.8	19.3	11.1	14.7	11.9	12.2	10.6	7.1	5.3	32.8	218 217	81.0	23.5
District 23	7.1	21.1	9.6	14.5	12.5	12.2	11.4	7.0	4.6	33.3	213 155	82.7	20.5
District 24	5.8	14.8	15.7	12.7	11.0	11.8	12.4	8.9	6.9	35.8	212 938	84.3	33.6
District 25	7.1	18.6	10.1	12.7	12.9	15.1	12.1	6.7	4.6	36.0	207 276	85.5	27.0
District 26	6.4	17.7	9.8	13.1	12.4	13.6	12.7	8.2	6.2	37.3	193 278	81.7	32.4
District 27	5.3	14.6	8.0	13.4	13.7	14.4	13.6	9.3	7.5	41.4	186 229	85.7	41.8
District 28	4.7	11.1	7.7	19.8	15.1	15.1	13.6	7.7	6.6	39.5	146 987	87.9	45.1
District 29	7.0	17.3	10.5	17.2	14.4	12.8	10.8	5.8	4.3	33.8	194 355	68.7	19.7
District 30	5.7	14.1	8.9	16.1	14.4	14.6	12.0	7.9	6.3	38.6	190 712	88.8	42.7
District 31	7.4	19.1	11.9	15.6	12.9	12.2	10.7	5.9	4.1	32.3	216 847	80.2	22.2
District 32	6.0	16.6	10.8	14.7	12.5	13.9	11.8	7.8	5.9	36.6	198 934	74.2	20.2
District 33	4.9	14.3	9.4	13.4	13.7	15.2	12.5	9.1	7.5	40.8	185 093	95.9	62.4
District 34	6.2	15.3	10.8	19.2	15.0	12.6	10.3	6.0	4.7	34.2	190 959	64.9	24.1
District 35	7.3	19.9	11.8	15.7	14.7	13.3	9.3	5.0	3.1	31.6	221 454	69.6	14.9
District 36	5.8	18.2	8.4	12.2	12.0	11.6	11.7	10.9	9.2	39.6	185 073	79.0	19.6
District 37	6.1	13.3	11.8	18.4	14.1	13.0	11.1	6.5	5.6	35.2	187 497	80.2	37.7
District 38	6.1	16.7	10.7	13.8	14.1	13.2	12.0	7.5	5.9	36.9	198 111	79.6	22.3
District 39	5.7	16.3	9.7	13.4	12.6	14.7	13.4	8.1	6.3	39.2	202 882	88.2	41.1
District 40	7.8	20.8	11.9	15.1	14.5	12.2	9.8	4.7	3.2	30.8	224 323	52.6	9.5
District 41	7.1	19.5	13.7	15.6	12.7	12.7	9.6	5.8	3.7	30.9	227 626	74.4	17.0
District 42	7.1	19.9	8.8	13.2	13.6	14.3	11.6	6.6	4.8	35.8	220 481	85.9	24.1
District 43	7.3	17.3	10.5	15.3	14.1	13.4	10.6	6.6	4.8	34.7	207 159	77.6	24.0
District 44	7.6	19.4	11.8	14.8	12.7	13.4	10.1	5.8	4.2	32.3	204 939	63.9	13.4
District 45	5.7	15.4	10.3	13.1	12.8	15.6	12.7	8.1	6.0	39.5	213 349	93.5	54.7
District 46	7.3	19.2	11.3	17.2	14.6	12.8	8.5	5.2	3.9	31.7	218 829	64.8	16.8
District 47	6.3	16.0	9.5	15.4	13.3	14.8	11.8	7.5	5.3	37.1	194 538	80.5	30.2
District 48	4.9	14.7	7.6	13.9	12.9	15.0	14.4	9.5	7.2	42.0	169 809	89.6	44.3
District 49	6.3	16.2	10.9	13.5	12.4	13.0	12.6	8.5	6.5	37.8	179 725	90.9	43.5
District 50	6.8	17.3	9.4	13.9	12.6	13.7	12.3	8.2	5.6	36.9	196 343	86.5	27.7
District 51	7.8	18.3	12.1	15.1	12.1	12.6	10.5	6.3	5.1	32.5	200 827	68.0	13.6
District 52	5.5	14.1	10.8	17.7	13.8	13.1	11.5	7.7	5.7	36.3	205 890	94.7	57.5
District 53	6.4	14.2	10.7	18.7	14.3	12.7	11.0	6.6	5.4	35.0	209 685	88.3	36.7

1. All persons 3 years old and over enrolled in nursery school through college and graduate or professional school. 2. Persons 25 years old and over.

Table E. Congressional Districts 115th Congress — Households and Group Quarters

STATE District	Households, 2015						Group quarters, 2010					
	Number	Average household size	Family households (percent)	Married-couple family (percent)	Female family householder[1]	One person households (percent)	Total in group quarters, 2015	Percent 65 years and over	Persons in correctional institutions	Persons in nursing facilities	Persons in college dormitories	Persons in military quarters
	28	29	30	31	32	33	34	35	36	37	38	39
UNITED STATES	118 208 250	2.65	65.6	48.0	12.8	27.9	8 070 896	18.3	2 263 602	1 502 264	2 521 090	338 191
ALABAMA	1 846 390	2.57	65.7	46.8	14.7	29.9	119 599	18.7	41 177	22 995	36 341	2 152
District 1	256 397	2.69	63.9	45.3	14.7	31.7	15 909	19.1	5 651	2 671	2 579	0
District 2	258 887	2.58	66.2	45.7	16.4	30.0	19 473	15.4	13 081	3 727	3 107	1 274
District 3	268 218	2.55	66.0	46.9	14.0	29.8	19 716	15.9	7 014	3 016	6 949	0
District 4	260 023	2.60	69.8	53.1	12.5	26.9	7 975	39.0	2 922	3 652	791	0
District 5	279 670	2.47	65.7	50.5	11.7	29.2	17 074	17.5	5 087	2 879	5 347	823
District 6	265 880	2.59	69.0	54.7	10.8	27.1	12 359	23.8	4 884	2 733	2 830	0
District 7	257 315	2.49	59.4	30.7	23.4	35.1	27 093	15.1	2 538	4 317	14 738	55
ALASKA	250 185	2.84	65.5	48.1	11.3	26.7	27 941	5.9	4 206	1 626	1 872	5 055
At Large	250 185	2.84	65.5	48.1	11.3	26.7	27 941	5.9	4 206	1 626	1 872	5 055
ARIZONA	2 463 008	2.71	64.9	46.8	12.5	27.6	154 682	12.2	67 767	13 819	27 987	5 172
District 1	246 360	2.95	69.1	50.3	13.1	24.8	33 950	4.2	15 071	816	7 630	0
District 2	300 061	2.30	59.0	42.8	11.6	33.3	24 915	19.9	7 538	2 914	118	3 352
District 3	236 952	3.10	71.8	46.1	18.4	21.1	25 888	5.3	11 711	863	6 913	0
District 4	291 983	2.44	66.0	52.2	9.3	27.2	25 689	6.9	19 869	1 431	1 213	1 164
District 5	275 268	2.86	71.1	57.9	8.7	23.2	3 240	55.3	11	859	346	0
District 6	303 376	2.46	61.3	46.5	10.0	31.0	4 862	53.4	10	1 594	274	0
District 7	229 608	3.31	65.3	36.6	19.6	26.7	10 390	5.2	8 915	840	1 162	0
District 8	276 097	2.74	69.8	53.6	11.5	23.7	10 319	30.5	4 624	2 809	861	656
District 9	303 303	2.51	54.1	35.4	12.8	34.3	15 429	12.2	18	1 693	9 470	0
ARKANSAS	1 144 663	2.53	66.5	49.0	13.1	28.4	84 027	21.7	25 844	18 532	24 144	619
District 1	280 712	2.47	67.4	48.0	14.7	28.2	28 126	20.6	15 495	5 770	2 669	0
District 2	293 408	2.54	63.7	45.7	14.2	30.3	16 893	20.1	3 461	3 521	6 184	616
District 3	293 570	2.61	67.6	52.9	10.1	26.4	17 668	21.3	1 599	3 663	9 499	0
District 4	276 973	2.49	67.5	49.5	13.6	28.7	21 340	24.7	5 289	5 578	5 792	3
CALIFORNIA	12 896 357	2.97	68.5	49.2	13.3	24.0	820 994	15.4	256 807	111 884	172 843	57 628
District 1	275 121	2.50	62.3	47.5	9.8	28.6	23 830	14.1	11 908	2 834	2 728	5
District 2	284 074	2.46	61.6	47.5	9.1	30.2	20 651	13.5	9 975	2 246	2 645	393
District 3	243 040	2.92	69.6	50.5	13.5	22.1	22 598	9.1	12 154	1 728	4 981	1 321
District 4	270 416	2.62	69.4	56.6	8.4	24.8	13 773	15.3	8 633	1 677	458	0
District 5	266 275	2.71	65.3	46.3	13.4	26.7	12 842	22.6	1 940	3 657	3 581	0
District 6	269 672	2.75	61.3	38.0	15.9	30.5	9 207	19.4	2 254	1 789	1 493	0
District 7	261 331	2.78	69.0	51.0	13.4	25.4	12 402	23.1	6 682	1 704	22	0
District 8	234 636	2.98	71.2	47.3	16.7	23.1	16 390	10.8	6 717	1 325	117	4 748
District 9	231 471	3.17	75.2	53.1	15.4	19.5	13 469	21.5	1 358	2 403	2 194	0
District 10	232 423	3.14	74.7	52.6	14.5	19.8	9 089	24.1	4 848	2 580	584	0
District 11	272 027	2.74	68.4	51.1	12.3	24.1	8 396	35.3	865	3 004	1 568	0
District 12	322 938	2.27	43.7	33.5	7.0	39.4	16 598	18.3	1 573	2 810	5 993	0
District 13	290 264	2.53	56.3	38.7	12.4	31.9	20 901	13.2	1 044	2 600	11 927	661
District 14	253 897	2.94	70.2	52.8	11.5	21.6	10 824	29.2	1 090	1 939	2 487	0
District 15	245 957	3.10	77.6	60.9	11.6	17.0	8 448	23.6	5 669	2 136	1 076	0
District 16	210 503	3.41	74.8	45.3	21.1	20.0	21 836	11.0	12 113	2 113	1 443	0
District 17	252 032	2.97	74.7	62.1	8.2	18.4	10 978	20.8	2 564	1 666	2 592	0
District 18	270 411	2.67	68.3	56.4	8.7	23.4	16 258	24.9	4	2 889	6 712	5
District 19	230 476	3.26	75.0	55.5	12.5	18.5	13 341	11.7	1 448	916	3 356	0
District 20	223 401	3.14	68.7	48.7	13.1	23.5	31 222	8.9	11 516	2 072	8 411	2 504
District 21	186 898	3.62	79.9	51.1	20.5	15.2	40 652	4.1	44 549	1 252	239	2 038
District 22	242 617	3.02	72.6	49.4	16.0	21.8	7 932	28.5	1 349	1 709	1 566	0
District 23	238 176	3.01	72.6	51.0	14.4	22.1	20 908	9.1	17 160	2 293	560	329
District 24	253 465	2.76	64.4	49.7	10.0	25.2	36 386	7.2	11 387	1 805	15 714	475
District 25	219 870	3.23	77.2	57.1	14.4	18.1	10 525	5.7	7 129	251	1 775	0
District 26	229 575	3.11	72.9	55.1	13.0	22.1	10 500	18.2	1 535	1 644	2 316	1 349
District 27	242 888	2.96	72.4	52.9	13.2	21.9	13 734	25.4	331	3 659	5 809	0
District 28	293 554	2.40	53.1	38.6	10.2	34.9	10 319	32.8	183	3 356	647	0
District 29	207 550	3.44	71.0	46.4	16.5	21.2	6 106	35.7	307	2 842	151	0
District 30	276 708	2.75	64.1	46.6	11.8	26.3	10 338	41.0	20	2 996	2 746	0
District 31	221 071	3.23	73.6	46.3	19.4	20.9	23 725	15.4	5 464	2 391	2 739	0
District 32	197 553	3.65	78.2	52.9	16.4	17.7	12 282	29.1	74	2 895	3 298	0
District 33	295 234	2.36	56.3	45.3	7.2	34.1	20 821	11.2	98	1 851	14 107	0
District 34	245 781	2.90	58.6	33.5	17.2	31.4	23 253	11.7	8 722	3 270	2 438	0
District 35	188 052	3.78	80.9	53.5	18.4	14.2	29 107	11.5	6 996	2 041	1 948	0
District 36	261 393	2.82	65.0	46.8	12.9	28.2	13 007	16.9	9 107	1 504	70	0
District 37	274 696	2.57	53.4	32.9	14.3	36.4	16 240	14.0	155	2 263	7 976	0
District 38	208 115	3.44	77.6	54.8	15.9	18.5	9 437	26.5	156	2 794	3 305	0
District 39	229 743	3.15	78.6	60.3	13.0	16.5	7 391	26.5	2	1 230	2 630	0
District 40	178 570	4.02	82.7	49.0	22.2	13.3	2 839	37.5	7	1 571	5	0
District 41	196 677	3.71	78.1	54.0	16.4	16.9	15 648	11.9	1 171	1 826	7 379	0
District 42	229 332	3.35	76.2	59.3	11.6	20.0	5 111	10.4	5 652	440	161	0
District 43	235 120	3.12	68.9	41.9	19.8	24.6	10 096	27.0	120	2 478	3 293	0
District 44	186 730	3.77	78.9	44.5	24.5	17.4	8 157	16.1	2 843	1 687	587	20
District 45	269 949	2.81	71.0	56.6	9.8	22.2	13 324	22.2	534	789	5 705	0
District 46	184 493	3.91	75.2	51.2	16.3	16.9	17 210	19.0	4 906	2 887	1 967	0
District 47	245 709	2.88	64.6	44.7	14.0	27.1	10 368	31.5	235	2 931	2 040	2
District 48	266 822	2.69	65.6	51.0	9.6	26.1	5 925	30.5	13	1 555	1 249	14
District 49	254 731	2.80	70.7	55.8	9.3	22.7	23 403	6.5	782	1 612	7 910	16 563
District 50	243 200	3.06	72.4	55.1	11.5	20.9	9 776	26.3	889	1 975	757	0
District 51	198 884	3.50	74.4	46.0	20.8	20.9	29 340	4.0	17 756	1 059	0	11 846
District 52	282 286	2.60	59.1	48.6	7.0	29.6	20 924	8.6	2 774	1 881	4 151	15 213
District 53	270 550	2.82	62.3	44.9	12.4	25.7	13 157	28.3	46	3 059	3 237	142

1. No spouse present.

Table E. Congressional Districts 115th Congress — Housing and Money Income

STATE District	Housing units, 2015						Money income, 2015		
		Occupied units						Households	
			Owner-occupied			Renter-occupied			
	Total	Occupied units as a percent of all units	Owner-occupied units as a percent of occupied units	Median value[1] (dollars)	Percent valued at $500,000 or more	Median rent[2]	Per capita income (dollars)	Median income (dollars)	Percent with income of $100,000 or more
	40	41	42	43	44	45	46	47	48
UNITED STATES.............	134 793 665	87.7	63.0	194 500	12.5	959	29 979	55 775	24.8
ALABAMA......................	2 218 391	83.2	67.9	134 100	3.9	729	24 769	44 765	17.3
District 1.........................	331 436	77.4	67.9	133 500	4.4	797	24 020	44 535	17.1
District 2.........................	314 366	82.4	65.1	123 900	2.5	720	23 607	42 395	15.6
District 3.........................	323 979	82.8	67.6	124 700	2.9	724	22 760	42 171	14.8
District 4.........................	313 403	83.0	73.1	109 800	3.5	608	21 977	39 608	12.6
District 5.........................	313 006	89.3	69.6	151 300	3.5	694	28 641	51 531	22.1
District 6.........................	297 166	89.5	75.2	179 000	7.3	894	32 237	61 524	26.6
District 7.........................	325 035	79.2	56.4	98 700	2.1	704	19 789	33 928	11.5
ALASKA........................	309 453	80.8	63.9	259 600	7.9	1 163	34 352	73 355	34.0
At Large	309 453	80.8	63.9	259 600	7.9	1 163	34 352	73 355	34.0
ARIZONA......................	2 929 173	84.1	61.9	194 300	8.4	933	26 721	51 492	20.8
District 1.........................	334 469	73.7	69.3	161 900	6.4	908	22 001	48 892	17.5
District 2.........................	346 231	86.7	60.5	170 200	7.2	809	28 373	48 095	17.6
District 3.........................	266 948	88.8	58.6	133 700	2.1	882	17 795	42 953	12.2
District 4.........................	389 247	75.0	72.3	167 800	4.2	856	24 216	46 467	14.5
District 5.........................	320 753	85.8	72.2	249 800	8.0	1 145	31 758	69 784	32.2
District 6.........................	352 845	86.0	62.3	323 900	26.6	1 051	40 907	63 495	31.2
District 7.........................	262 919	87.3	41.9	132 500	2.1	835	16 405	35 243	11.4
District 8.........................	316 491	87.2	71.7	214 500	4.5	1 119	28 424	60 858	23.7
District 9.........................	339 270	89.4	46.4	240 100	11.3	915	30 678	51 435	23.1
ARKANSAS..................	1 347 598	84.9	65.2	120 700	3.2	695	23 589	41 995	14.8
District 1.........................	338 995	82.8	65.2	102 600	2.2	627	20 797	36 882	11.2
District 2.........................	337 058	87.0	62.9	144 800	4.3	797	26 669	47 118	18.9
District 3.........................	328 207	89.4	62.5	144 200	4.3	715	25 214	46 740	17.0
District 4.........................	343 338	80.7	70.4	93 600	2.2	643	21 341	37 728	11.7
CALIFORNIA................	13 988 399	92.2	53.6	449 100	43.2	1 311	31 587	64 500	31.6
District 1.........................	324 602	84.8	63.5	255 200	11.8	934	25 409	46 091	18.7
District 2.........................	319 963	88.8	61.4	560 800	55.3	1 301	43 380	65 414	33.2
District 3.........................	264 020	92.1	57.9	301 100	16.6	1 118	26 802	57 401	26.3
District 4.........................	357 319	75.7	72.6	374 800	26.9	1 183	35 642	70 582	34.9
District 5.........................	289 748	91.9	60.2	437 200	37.6	1 356	34 391	67 197	30.8
District 6.........................	288 938	93.3	45.5	266 600	10.0	1 017	24 586	49 523	20.0
District 7.........................	274 290	95.3	62.4	333 600	17.4	1 126	31 951	70 131	32.2
District 8.........................	309 814	75.7	60.6	201 900	6.2	980	21 200	46 468	17.0
District 9.........................	247 402	93.6	59.4	298 900	16.4	1 032	24 991	57 509	26.9
District 10.......................	243 616	95.4	57.2	272 500	9.2	1 088	23 735	56 368	23.3
District 11.......................	284 123	95.7	61.0	580 000	57.1	1 471	42 736	79 622	40.4
District 12.......................	353 837	91.3	33.6	952 800	90.4	1 640	60 952	93 122	47.7
District 13.......................	305 149	95.1	42.9	638 700	64.0	1 361	38 732	66 046	34.1
District 14.......................	265 660	95.6	58.4	863 400	88.7	1 910	44 761	98 129	49.3
District 15.......................	253 730	96.9	63.6	669 000	73.7	1 738	40 650	100 634	50.5
District 16.......................	225 040	93.5	47.1	182 700	5.8	868	16 577	39 211	12.9
District 17.......................	262 642	96.0	53.3	816 100	86.1	2 126	45 492	111 024	55.6
District 18.......................	287 664	94.0	59.9	1 139 900	91.4	1 883	63 631	120 089	57.4
District 19.......................	237 104	97.2	59.6	657 500	74.3	1 662	35 389	85 536	43.5
District 20.......................	246 545	90.6	50.0	495 300	49.3	1 359	27 273	61 507	28.0
District 21.......................	199 302	93.8	48.7	163 300	3.2	821	15 305	37 970	12.4
District 22.......................	256 905	94.4	57.8	232 600	7.6	959	24 580	53 886	24.4
District 23.......................	268 691	88.6	59.4	227 700	6.5	954	25 554	59 341	26.0
District 24.......................	280 596	90.3	53.9	524 700	52.2	1 366	32 124	63 199	31.0
District 25.......................	232 327	94.6	68.0	413 100	34.1	1 397	29 808	75 732	36.3
District 26.......................	244 144	94.0	62.2	532 300	54.1	1 536	33 820	77 744	38.6
District 27.......................	264 391	91.9	54.6	654 300	74.9	1 349	34 331	71 343	36.5
District 28.......................	316 477	92.8	33.2	720 400	77.1	1 358	41 108	61 405	31.9
District 29.......................	215 445	96.3	40.2	412 800	23.6	1 208	19 967	47 608	19.3
District 30.......................	290 638	95.2	50.4	614 100	65.9	1 529	39 832	75 853	38.6
District 31.......................	233 846	94.5	51.4	313 000	16.3	1 177	22 112	54 453	22.3
District 32.......................	206 561	95.6	59.7	422 000	28.7	1 310	22 231	61 756	26.8
District 33.......................	326 075	90.5	49.8	1 063 700	88.7	1 888	63 899	97 074	49.1
District 34.......................	264 458	92.9	20.7	501 900	50.2	1 071	21 241	38 326	15.0
District 35.......................	195 375	96.3	54.8	323 700	8.9	1 228	18 488	56 215	20.4
District 36.......................	343 915	76.0	62.2	244 000	14.0	1 005	25 175	46 471	17.9
District 37.......................	291 919	94.1	34.7	620 700	60.3	1 311	32 212	51 114	24.9
District 38.......................	217 976	95.5	58.3	450 500	35.0	1 315	24 133	62 697	27.4
District 39.......................	239 405	96.0	65.9	611 300	68.5	1 564	33 268	81 183	39.6
District 40.......................	187 544	95.2	34.5	388 100	24.1	1 072	15 269	42 497	14.6
District 41.......................	213 134	92.3	59.4	287 000	8.2	1 189	20 878	58 592	22.4
District 42.......................	240 715	95.3	69.9	374 400	19.4	1 468	27 328	72 536	33.5
District 43.......................	248 687	94.5	41.8	447 400	37.5	1 215	23 786	50 885	22.4
District 44.......................	195 277	95.6	47.4	352 900	14.9	1 092	17 951	49 037	18.5
District 45.......................	285 147	94.7	64.1	667 600	74.3	1 897	43 493	93 374	47.4
District 46.......................	191 583	96.3	40.4	453 300	35.1	1 389	19 779	57 583	24.1
District 47.......................	258 076	95.2	45.3	515 800	52.3	1 235	28 885	59 744	28.3
District 48.......................	286 794	93.0	56.6	705 300	76.0	1 762	45 269	83 001	42.2
District 49.......................	278 364	91.5	59.1	650 700	66.1	1 723	40 709	81 611	40.8
District 50.......................	259 876	93.6	62.7	431 000	34.5	1 327	28 657	66 103	32.3
District 51.......................	222 808	89.3	42.2	296 300	6.9	1 015	16 707	41 085	13.8
District 52.......................	305 081	92.5	51.7	640 200	69.4	1 750	43 299	84 479	41.7
District 53.......................	285 661	94.7	48.6	461 600	40.9	1 373	31 240	66 917	29.8

1. Specified owner-occupied units; $1,000,000 represents $1,000,000 or more.   2. Specified renter-occupied units.

Table E. Congressional Districts 115th Congress — **Poverty, Labor Force, Employment, and Social Security**

STATE District	Poverty, 2015: Persons below poverty level (percent)	Poverty, 2015: Families below poverty level (percent)	Poverty, 2015: Percent of households receiving food stamps in past 12 months	Civilian labor force, 2015: Total	Civilian labor force, 2015: Unemployment: Total	Civilian labor force, 2015: Unemployment: Rate[1]	Civilian employment,[2] 2015: Total	Civilian employment,[2] 2015: Percent: Management, business, science and arts occupations	Civilian employment,[2] 2015: Percent: Service, sales, and office	Civilian employment,[2] 2015: Percent: Construction and production	Persons under age 65 with no health insurance, 2015 (percent)	Social Security beneficiaries, December 2015: Number	Social Security beneficiaries, December 2015: Rate[3]	Supplemental Security Income recipients, December 2015
	49	50	51	52	53	54	55	56	57	58	59	60	61	62
UNITED STATES	14.7	10.6	12.8	160 652 483	10 117 710	6.3	150 534 773	37.1	41.6	21.3	10.9	58 444 059	181.8	8 308 531
ALABAMA	18.5	13.7	15.5	2 197 662	157 544	7.2	2 040 118	33.9	39.9	26.1	11.9	1 108 543	228.1	170 844
District 1	17.4	13.0	16.0	310 739	21 960	7.1	288 779	32.8	42.7	24.5	12.9	163 246	231.1	22 650
District 2	19.7	15.0	17.2	304 022	24 012	7.9	280 010	32.0	41.3	26.7	12.4	157 700	229.7	27 846
District 3	19.6	14.5	17.0	317 680	22 640	7.1	295 040	32.5	38.6	28.9	11.0	162 338	230.6	23 490
District 4	19.7	14.7	15.6	287 948	17 149	6.0	270 799	27.6	37.4	35.0	12.5	180 647	263.8	25 419
District 5	15.2	11.5	12.0	336 883	24 106	7.2	312 777	39.6	38.1	22.4	11.8	146 999	207.3	16 781
District 6	10.3	7.2	8.3	347 985	17 731	5.1	330 254	41.6	38.6	19.8	9.3	140 496	200.5	11 599
District 7	28.2	21.7	22.9	292 405	29 946	10.2	262 459	29.2	43.5	27.3	13.7	157 117	235.3	43 059
ALASKA	10.3	7.0	10.8	385 165	30 399	7.9	354 766	36.4	40.4	23.2	16.4	91 960	124.5	12 515
At Large	10.3	7.0	10.8	385 165	30 399	7.9	354 766	36.4	40.4	23.2	16.4	91 960	124.5	12 515
ARIZONA	17.4	12.5	13.0	3 153 950	216 440	6.9	2 937 510	34.6	46.1	19.3	12.8	1 241 101	181.8	119 715
District 1	20.8	14.7	15.4	305 635	32 484	10.6	273 151	32.1	46.6	21.3	13.6	145 394	191.4	18 306
District 2	16.1	11.2	13.1	318 213	22 848	7.2	295 365	38.4	45.8	15.8	9.7	164 660	230.7	13 816
District 3	23.4	19.2	23.2	347 139	33 149	9.5	313 990	24.7	49.2	26.0	15.6	107 810	141.6	18 640
District 4	14.1	8.6	12.0	280 245	22 166	7.9	258 079	29.4	48.2	22.4	12.9	204 198	276.2	11 727
District 5	8.6	6.2	6.2	388 466	16 311	4.2	372 155	40.9	43.5	15.7	8.7	128 296	162.5	6 711
District 6	13.1	8.7	7.6	382 966	19 765	5.2	363 201	44.1	43.2	12.7	10.8	138 527	184.7	8 194
District 7	32.5	28.7	26.4	344 473	26 262	7.6	318 211	20.6	49.1	30.2	20.4	81 511	105.9	23 490
District 8	9.0	6.3	7.2	351 259	20 014	5.7	331 245	35.7	46.8	17.5	8.6	169 390	220.6	8 397
District 9	18.9	13.1	10.9	435 554	23 441	5.4	412 113	40.1	44.0	15.8	13.1	101 315	130.4	10 434
ARKANSAS	19.1	13.7	13.7	1 349 814	78 751	5.8	1 271 063	32.1	40.4	27.5	11.1	679 689	228.2	110 053
District 1	20.5	14.6	17.9	304 923	19 886	6.5	285 037	27.9	40.7	31.4	10.3	184 970	256.0	35 167
District 2	17.9	12.4	12.1	363 512	19 554	5.4	343 958	37.2	41.1	21.7	10.7	156 920	206.1	26 491
District 3	16.6	12.2	9.8	369 954	16 228	4.4	353 726	33.9	39.8	26.3	11.3	151 760	193.9	17 817
District 4	21.7	15.8	15.3	311 425	23 083	7.4	288 342	28.1	40.0	31.9	12.3	186 039	261.4	30 578
CALIFORNIA	15.3	11.3	9.7	19 463 807	1 418 357	7.3	18 045 450	37.7	41.7	20.6	9.7	5 651 601	144.4	1 292 302
District 1	19.3	12.7	10.6	305 423	24 047	7.9	281 376	32.7	47.1	20.2	8.9	179 970	253.4	32 126
District 2	12.5	7.3	7.4	359 782	21 549	6.0	338 233	42.3	40.7	17.0	8.0	148 831	206.6	18 873
District 3	17.2	12.8	10.6	337 481	30 479	9.0	307 002	33.4	41.8	24.9	8.6	121 472	166.0	23 237
District 4	9.5	6.0	6.5	329 241	25 003	7.6	304 238	41.8	42.2	16.1	6.3	164 031	227.1	13 112
District 5	11.7	7.8	8.4	379 155	23 017	6.1	356 138	34.2	43.3	22.5	7.0	136 751	186.5	17 768
District 6	20.8	16.8	16.4	361 322	29 832	8.3	331 490	34.3	47.2	18.5	8.3	109 359	145.6	45 399
District 7	12.6	8.7	9.3	368 111	30 731	8.3	337 380	42.3	42.3	15.4	5.4	121 605	164.5	23 162
District 8	21.8	17.2	18.0	295 485	36 036	12.2	259 449	28.5	45.8	25.8	8.8	122 722	171.3	28 423
District 9	16.5	13.2	15.3	337 373	33 789	10.0	303 584	28.4	41.9	29.7	7.4	113 695	152.2	29 829
District 10	17.6	13.5	14.8	341 425	37 352	10.9	304 073	27.8	42.5	29.7	7.1	113 472	153.4	26 040
District 11	11.3	8.3	7.2	386 713	26 371	6.8	360 342	43.8	39.6	16.6	7.2	123 470	164.0	20 658
District 12	11.9	7.1	5.4	469 101	22 369	4.8	446 732	56.2	34.8	8.9	5.1	103 546	138.1	39 020
District 13	16.5	11.3	8.4	420 372	26 548	6.3	393 824	48.6	36.5	14.9	7.3	103 284	136.7	33 146
District 14	9.5	5.4	4.8	423 582	23 759	5.6	399 823	43.6	42.2	14.2	5.5	111 219	146.9	15 044
District 15	7.3	4.8	5.6	401 365	17 577	4.4	383 788	47.2	35.4	17.4	4.0	93 552	121.2	15 945
District 16	30.8	27.1	26.9	307 104	35 624	11.6	271 480	21.0	42.3	36.7	12.1	92 282	124.6	38 376
District 17	6.8	4.7	3.3	408 014	20 800	5.1	387 214	57.6	30.1	12.3	3.8	81 385	107.0	14 898
District 18	7.1	3.8	2.7	392 035	14 430	3.7	377 605	61.6	29.7	8.6	4.6	102 726	139.0	11 506
District 19	9.8	6.9	8.1	404 498	25 284	6.3	379 214	39.0	40.7	20.3	6.8	89 392	116.8	26 094
District 20	15.3	10.7	8.4	342 877	20 526	6.0	322 351	29.5	40.8	29.7	10.5	107 015	145.8	15 268
District 21	30.2	26.6	24.9	293 958	36 440	12.4	257 518	16.8	36.5	46.6	13.0	78 219	109.2	26 324
District 22	19.9	16.1	16.1	342 087	27 301	8.0	314 786	33.3	42.0	24.7	8.4	108 115	145.8	26 425
District 23	17.7	14.1	13.1	321 168	27 492	8.6	293 676	32.9	39.3	27.7	6.6	112 244	152.0	26 961
District 24	15.5	9.1	7.0	369 513	21 030	5.7	348 483	37.8	40.3	22.0	11.1	130 105	176.6	13 910
District 25	12.3	9.2	7.7	344 350	25 422	7.4	318 928	39.1	41.9	19.0	8.2	95 619	132.7	22 727
District 26	10.2	7.4	8.4	366 009	25 986	7.1	340 023	36.7	40.1	23.2	10.9	115 261	159.0	14 565
District 27	13.0	9.8	4.8	374 439	21 027	5.6	353 412	45.9	40.2	14.0	8.1	110 188	150.3	29 741
District 28	13.9	9.6	5.5	419 828	27 799	6.6	392 029	49.3	39.2	11.5	11.3	89 587	125.3	44 915
District 29	21.1	18.0	12.3	373 289	28 042	7.5	345 247	26.1	47.4	26.5	14.8	76 045	105.5	33 282
District 30	10.6	6.8	4.7	429 426	25 799	6.0	403 627	48.0	39.5	12.5	10.0	107 253	139.1	22 137
District 31	19.5	15.6	16.7	346 155	28 515	8.2	317 640	29.7	45.2	25.1	9.6	92 060	124.7	28 304
District 32	13.0	10.2	8.4	363 432	27 298	7.5	336 134	27.4	45.8	26.8	13.4	100 323	136.9	27 198
District 33	9.0	4.1	2.0	387 142	21 929	5.7	365 213	61.2	32.6	6.3	5.2	113 444	157.9	11 922
District 34	26.6	21.5	13.6	384 581	30 250	7.9	354 331	29.6	46.1	24.4	20.5	76 606	104.2	43 969
District 35	17.5	14.5	16.4	355 536	32 134	9.0	323 402	22.1	44.7	33.2	12.8	76 660	103.6	22 790
District 36	20.7	15.9	11.2	313 633	32 933	10.5	280 700	24.8	52.6	22.6	12.8	156 932	209.1	23 835
District 37	19.5	14.5	10.1	392 731	30 687	7.8	362 044	41.5	42.1	16.4	14.2	92 349	127.8	30 564
District 38	11.0	8.6	7.7	352 289	22 372	6.4	329 917	30.1	45.5	24.4	11.7	107 218	147.8	26 778
District 39	9.5	6.4	5.7	374 274	24 777	6.6	349 497	43.5	41.0	15.5	8.3	102 304	139.9	16 667
District 40	23.9	20.9	19.5	340 543	29 217	8.6	311 326	16.3	46.0	37.7	18.7	68 600	95.1	26 389
District 41	17.4	13.5	12.8	360 327	35 007	9.7	325 320	23.8	43.5	32.7	12.8	85 800	115.1	25 041
District 42	11.9	9.1	8.5	365 902	33 226	9.1	332 676	35.3	42.9	21.8	8.7	102 104	132.1	11 924
District 43	20.7	16.9	12.4	370 745	28 588	7.7	342 157	30.1	47.8	22.1	14.2	92 811	124.7	32 847
District 44	21.1	17.9	17.9	339 954	32 849	9.7	307 105	20.3	45.6	34.0	14.3	84 323	118.4	36 104
District 45	10.4	6.4	3.1	405 594	20 953	5.2	384 641	53.8	36.4	9.8	6.5	105 530	136.8	9 827
District 46	18.3	14.8	14.3	377 497	22 222	5.9	355 275	22.5	47.2	30.3	18.1	73 332	99.3	27 307
District 47	17.1	12.6	9.9	364 578	20 510	5.6	344 068	36.8	42.6	20.6	10.1	94 983	132.2	33 512
District 48	10.6	7.1	5.1	388 561	19 560	5.0	369 001	46.1	40.4	13.5	7.7	118 815	164.1	10 458
District 49	9.9	6.4	4.4	366 209	19 857	5.4	346 352	43.6	41.0	15.4	9.1	110 534	150.2	8 507
District 50	12.1	9.3	9.2	371 039	25 356	6.8	345 683	32.9	46.5	20.6	10.0	117 284	155.7	15 939
District 51	24.7	22.2	19.6	316 805	36 567	11.5	280 238	20.4	54.7	24.8	14.3	110 092	151.9	39 148
District 52	9.9	4.6	3.1	403 651	20 596	5.1	383 055	55.1	36.5	8.3	6.1	105 244	139.3	14 307
District 53	12.6	8.6	7.7	418 103	31 493	7.5	386 610	42.1	43.2	14.7	9.6	101 838	131.1	20 054

1. Percent of civilian labor force. 2. Persons 16 years old and over. 3. Per 1,000 resident population estimated in the 2014 American Community Survey.

Table E. Congressional Districts 115th Congress — **Agriculture**

STATE District	Agriculture, 2012									
	Land in farms				Value of products sold				Government payments	
	Number of farms	Acres	Average size of farm (acres)	Irrigated land (acres)	Total ($1,000)	Average per farm (dollars)	Percent from crops	Percent from livestock and poultry products	Total ($1,000)	Average per farm receiving payments (dollars)
	63	64	65	66	67	68	69	70	71	72
UNITED STATES	2 109 303	914 527 657	434	55 822 231	394 644 481	187 097	53.8	46.2	8 053 346	9 925
ALABAMA	43 223	8 902 654	206	113 008	5 571 173	128 894	23.6	76.4	88 145	6 802
District 1	3 041	621 188	204	11 518	337 273	110 909	78.6	21.4	9 284	10 125
District 2	8 890	2 339 433	263	40 808	1 477 342	166 180	24.7	75.3	29 691	6 929
District 3	5 244	1 101 850	210	15 725	685 901	130 797	22.0	78.0	7 690	7 180
District 4	12 450	1 691 155	136	11 693	1 879 383	150 954	9.7	90.3	15 683	5 528
District 5	6 283	1 043 516	166	19 334	507 359	80 751	46.8	53.2	12 988	6 559
District 6	2 759	414 441	150	2 353	211 764	76 754	16.5	83.5	2 073	5 498
District 7	4 556	1 691 071	371	11 577	472 151	103 633	16.9	83.1	10 736	7 201
ALASKA	762	833 861	1 094	2 451	58 925	77 329	42.2	57.8	2 432	12 472
At Large	762	833 861	1 094	2 451	58 925	77 329	42.2	57.8	2 432	12 473
ARIZONA	20 005	26 249 195	1 312	880 613	3 732 113	186 559	55.6	44.4	31 329	10 245
District 1	13 505	20 238 604	1 499	274 134	1 189 607	88 086	41.3	58.7	15 323	6 574
District 2	1 452	981 592	676	67 103	170 117	117 161	D	D	2 662	13 513
District 3	1 467	3 206 653	2 186	220 098	1 051 870	717 021	57.8	42.2	5 901	23 892
District 4	1 851	1 618 174	874	236 656	927 038	500 831	65.5	34.5	4 673	26 551
District 5	559	39 587	71	22 692	123 985	221 798	26.0	74.0	945	26 995
District 6	459	105 916	231	16 105	77 337	168 490	D	D	295	12 303
District 7	173	D	D	22 562	110 396	638 125	D	D	911	70 065
District 8	455	D	D	16 399	60 936	133 925	70.4	29.6	541	18 664
District 9	84	7 562	90	4 864	20 827	247 937	95.6	4.4	78	12 964
ARKANSAS	45 071	13 810 786	306	4 803 902	9 775 758	216 897	49.5	50.5	262 967	20 013
District 1	14 422	7 829 889	543	4 372 332	4 886 232	338 804	87.6	12.4	213 501	29 087
District 2	5 715	1 031 106	180	81 263	377 217	66 005	25.3	74.7	10 237	9 418
District 3	9 735	1 617 495	166	9 975	1 696 333	174 251	2.7	97.3	12 498	6 975
District 4	15 199	3 332 296	219	340 332	2 815 976	185 274	14.7	85.3	26 731	9 151
CALIFORNIA	77 857	25 569 001	328	7 861 964	42 627 472	547 510	71.2	28.8	146 919	19 349
District 1	8 970	3 605 203	402	823 662	1 598 258	178 178	80.2	19.8	20 753	19 414
District 2	5 047	2 066 839	410	103 785	1 213 224	240 385	57.7	42.3	5 084	16 453
District 3	6 350	2 502 923	394	1 126 206	2 636 257	415 159	91.0	9.0	44 654	27 770
District 4	5 257	1 451 586	276	204 969	866 959	164 915	81.3	18.7	3 025	15 672
District 5	3 592	544 785	152	92 050	851 570	237 074	89.4	10.6	1 043	10 032
District 6	171	23 658	138	9 578	16 301	95 328	89.6	10.4	240	21 799
District 7	814	154 475	190	34 153	158 078	194 199	55.6	44.4	846	14 582
District 8	1 016	451 523	444	63 093	298 555	293 853	16.4	83.6	379	17 209
District 9	3 238	689 573	213	404 975	1 895 907	585 518	74.5	25.5	4 447	15 548
District 10	4 768	895 191	188	411 475	2 605 175	546 387	51.5	48.5	8 320	16 030
District 11	327	112 764	345	18 602	54 849	167 734	78.3	21.7	219	10 418
District 12	X	X	X	X	X	X	X	X	X	X
District 13	32	D	D	25	1 386	43 320	34.8	65.2	4	1 300
District 14	180	24 402	136	1 370	59 526	330 702	97.6	2.4	116	12 909
District 15	395	122 196	309	8 413	47 578	120 450	83.5	16.5	44	2 921
District 16	4 025	1 389 192	345	718 961	4 429 651	1 100 534	52.4	47.6	11 620	17 396
District 17	74	13 886	188	993	10 881	147 042	93.7	6.3	4	1 466
District 18	523	80 723	154	10 387	186 955	357 466	96.2	3.8	66	13 263
District 19	736	204 524	278	10 694	176 147	239 330	95.6	4.4	6	802
District 20	2 323	1 938 924	835	309 691	3 603 918	1 551 407	97.3	2.7	822	6 273
District 21	5 300	2 806 804	530	1 670 398	9 238 009	1 743 021	61.6	38.4	22 328	21 449
District 22	3 817	673 040	176	413 405	2 735 381	716 631	50.6	49.4	8 027	19 158
District 23	3 373	2 214 121	656	465 834	2 351 633	697 193	84.5	15.5	4 352	13 068
District 24	4 487	2 092 601	466	195 967	2 176 789	485 132	95.4	4.6	4 079	15 162
District 25	505	58 321	115	29 580	80 815	160 030	D	D	186	5 806
District 26	1 885	231 273	123	69 082	1 105 491	586 467	99.5	0.5	134	3 612
District 27	154	4 357	28	1 448	24 375	158 280	99.0	1.0	7	1 167
District 28	133	3 668	28	46	1 907	14 339	33.0	67.0	47	15 759
District 29	59	1 703	29	245	8 994	152 438	99.1	0.9	0	0
District 30	51	2 077	41	592	3 853	75 553	95.5	4.5	8	2 733
District 31	181	3 547	20	2 222	5 777	31 918	96.2	3.8	10	3 386
District 32	58	767	13	128	13 127	226 320	99.9	0.1	0	0
District 33	133	8 247	62	1 982	6 266	47 110	93.0	7.0	D	D
District 34	X	X	X	X	X	X	X	X	X	X
District 35	195	7 032	36	1 442	311 590	1 597 900	7.8	92.2	569	21 901
District 36	1 148	201 280	175	111 349	734 534	639 838	78.6	21.4	1 447	16 439
District 37	23	448	19	439	2 725	118 471	D	D	0	0
District 38	30	1 770	59	108	6 575	219 161	100.0	0.0	0	0
District 39	115	1 527	13	657	9 804	85 251	96.0	4.0	D	D
District 40	16	128	8	95	1 450	90 631	D	D	0	0
District 41	426	30 431	71	8 036	43 767	102 739	D	D	181	9 037
District 42	1 314	106 046	81	20 049	225 256	171 428	41.9	58.1	548	18 880
District 43	46	712	15	132	8 896	193 384	99.4	0.6	0	0
District 44	56	521	9	152	13 299	237 477	0.0	0.0	0	0
District 45	114	48 582	426	5 163	96 549	846 923	98.7	1.3	10	1 615
District 46	41	1 137	28	111	5 239	127 776	99.1	0.9	24	7 942
District 47	43	D	D	944	3 623	84 263	96.6	3.4	D	D
District 48	37	3 114	84	1 638	39 131	1 057 588	D	D	D	D
District 49	935	D	D	6 737	137 991	147 584	81.4	18.6	71	4 730
District 50	4 302	160 752	37	36 291	529 777	123 147	90.8	9.2	388	4 844
District 51	721	557 584	773	462 112	1 955 250	2 711 858	70.3	29.7	2 789	21 790
District 52	227	6 597	29	2 203	31 502	138 777	98.3	1.7	D	D
District 53	84	1 594	19	290	6 909	82 246	99.2	0.8	0	0

Table E. Congressional Districts 115th Congress — Nonfarm Employment and Payroll

Private nonfarm employment and payroll, 2015

STATE District	Number of establish-ments	Total	Manufact-uring	Construc-tion	Wholesale trade	Retail trade	Health care and social assistance	Finance and Insurance	Real estate and rental and leasing	Professio-nal, scientific, and technical services	Information	Total (mil dol)	Average per employee dollars
												Annual payroll	
	73	74	75	76	77	78	79	80	81	82	83	84	85
UNITED STATES	7 663 938	124 085 947	9.4	4.8	4.9	12.7	15.5	4.9	1.7	7.1	2.7	6 253 488	50 396
ALABAMA	98 540	1 634 391	15.2	4.8	4.4	14.2	14.8	4.2	1.4	5.9	2.0	67 370	41 220
District 1	15 377	232 247	12.5	6.7	4.2	16.5	13.3	3.3	2.0	5.0	1.7	9 089	39 133
District 2	14 324	216 671	12.8	4.1	4.9	16.2	16.6	3.2	1.4	4.5	1.6	8 052	37 161
District 3	11 218	168 831	22.1	4.1	3.4	15.8	15.5	2.7	1.2	2.7	1.2	5 830	34 532
District 4	12 399	182 407	26.9	3.7	3.4	15.0	16.3	3.2	1.0	2.0	1.1	6 376	34 955
District 5	14 934	252 035	15.5	4.2	3.6	14.3	15.1	2.6	1.1	15.5	2.2	11 255	44 655
District 6	15 992	249 998	6.8	6.0	4.8	16.1	12.0	8.5	1.5	5.0	4.4	11 747	46 990
District 7	13 836	287 438	17.0	5.0	5.8	9.8	17.6	5.3	1.9	3.8	1.7	13 578	47 237
ALASKA	20 907	267 999	4.6	6.9	3.4	13.1	18.4	2.7	1.7	7.0	2.5	15 643	58 371
At Large	20 907	267 999	4.6	6.9	3.4	13.1	18.4	2.7	1.7	7.0	2.5	15 643	58 371
ARIZONA	136 352	2 295 186	6.1	5.8	4.0	13.7	14.8	6.1	2.0	6.3	2.1	102 671	44 733
District 1	11 574	159 347	9.6	4.3	2.0	17.9	17.0	1.7	1.4	2.8	1.4	6 219	39 030
District 2	15 551	211 918	2.8	4.7	1.4	18.1	20.2	5.0	2.2	7.3	1.6	7 715	36 408
District 3	9 716	164 198	9.7	6.5	5.0	14.2	18.0	2.2	1.4	3.2	2.3	6 504	39 608
District 4	12 508	139 021	6.7	6.5	3.0	21.1	19.0	2.1	1.6	2.7	1.3	4 572	32 886
District 5	13 786	178 001	7.7	8.1	2.1	19.8	15.7	4.5	1.9	5.6	1.6	7 115	39 972
District 6	24 447	376 190	3.4	6.5	2.7	12.2	12.1	10.9	2.5	7.4	3.8	19 451	51 706
District 7	13 856	378 440	9.9	6.7	9.3	7.6	12.5	6.0	1.5	4.7	1.3	18 983	50 162
District 8	11 238	144 864	3.2	6.0	1.7	23.8	22.1	2.9	1.9	3.5	0.8	5 008	34 569
District 9	23 073	457 181	5.6	5.1	4.5	10.9	13.0	9.1	2.7	11.1	3.1	23 380	51 139
ARKANSAS	65 175	1 003 113	15.5	4.3	4.4	14.3	16.8	3.6	1.2	3.7	2.5	39 451	39 329
District 1	13 851	189 011	20.0	3.6	4.8	16.8	19.8	3.0	1.1	2.0	3.4	6 257	33 105
District 2	18 804	292 635	7.5	5.1	5.2	14.1	19.5	5.3	1.5	4.8	4.0	12 149	41 515
District 3	18 347	312 589	16.3	4.1	4.4	13.2	13.4	2.8	1.2	4.5	1.5	14 080	45 042
District 4	13 836	188 158	23.7	4.6	2.6	15.4	16.9	3.2	1.2	2.4	0.9	6 417	34 105
CALIFORNIA	908 120	14 325 377	8.1	4.8	6.0	11.8	13.1	4.1	2.0	8.8	4.8	856 954	59 821
District 1	15 382	169 517	7.5	5.6	3.2	18.3	21.7	3.5	1.7	4.4	1.4	6 480	38 226
District 2	21 691	223 076	7.8	5.9	4.3	16.1	15.9	4.0	2.3	6.8	2.9	11 417	51 181
District 3	11 659	162 731	9.5	6.4	5.4	17.8	17.3	3.1	1.8	3.9	1.5	7 141	43 880
District 4	18 269	218 205	4.1	7.5	2.6	16.0	14.2	6.0	2.7	7.8	2.1	10 729	49 170
District 5	16 941	232 744	12.3	6.9	4.1	14.8	17.7	3.1	1.6	4.5	1.2	11 959	51 382
District 6	15 264	258 004	4.7	6.0	5.9	12.2	18.6	3.5	2.3	7.6	2.6	13 035	50 523
District 7	13 388	202 729	4.9	6.3	5.5	15.5	16.3	8.8	1.8	7.3	3.0	11 016	54 337
District 8	9 178	113 138	4.6	5.7	1.4	19.7	17.3	2.0	2.3	3.5	1.3	3 918	34 631
District 9	10 652	158 636	9.1	6.7	5.6	15.2	18.0	3.9	1.6	2.8	1.0	7 077	44 614
District 10	11 968	184 057	13.6	5.5	6.0	17.4	15.3	2.2	1.7	4.1	0.9	7 939	43 135
District 11	16 743	221 811	4.3	6.7	3.4	15.6	17.7	8.0	2.1	7.5	2.1	13 182	59 427
District 12	32 407	596 285	1.3	3.1	2.3	7.4	10.2	8.4	2.5	16.6	10.8	58 704	98 449
District 13	18 969	295 428	6.5	5.5	5.1	10.2	17.0	3.1	1.8	8.1	4.0	19 021	64 385
District 14	19 314	356 813	6.4	4.2	7.2	9.8	8.8	3.9	2.0	9.5	12.7	39 397	110 413
District 15	16 709	278 582	8.2	6.8	9.9	11.2	11.4	3.7	1.7	11.1	5.8	20 557	73 793
District 16	9 011	146 588	15.6	5.0	6.9	13.8	18.9	1.8	1.5	2.6	1.9	5 968	40 716
District 17	21 083	546 765	15.2	4.2	14.6	6.1	6.0	1.9	1.0	13.9	7.3	64 850	118 607
District 18	22 085	387 806	3.4	3.1	3.2	10.4	17.0	3.2	1.5	13.4	15.1	42 756	110 252
District 19	13 762	205 961	6.9	8.0	5.2	11.4	10.6	4.7	1.9	10.6	4.9	12 724	61 781
District 20	16 237	195 929	7.9	4.9	5.7	17.3	15.9	2.5	1.7	5.6	1.4	8 465	43 203
District 21	6 806	104 215	17.6	4.7	9.2	19.0	11.5	1.3	1.5	1.6	0.6	4 014	38 512
District 22	14 134	206 140	7.6	5.5	3.9	18.1	17.6	4.7	2.0	4.5	1.1	7 893	38 290
District 23	12 104	186 985	4.3	7.2	4.0	14.2	19.0	3.4	2.0	6.3	1.6	7 995	42 756
District 24	20 111	243 093	8.5	6.1	3.5	14.7	15.6	2.8	2.1	6.1	3.7	11 279	46 400
District 25	12 083	159 576	9.8	5.8	4.3	17.7	12.6	3.3	1.7	6.9	2.1	6 564	41 133
District 26	18 682	243 089	9.7	5.0	6.1	15.3	13.7	5.3	1.9	9.2	2.4	13 652	56 159
District 27	21 576	254 257	2.4	2.2	3.1	12.6	18.6	7.1	1.9	9.9	1.8	12 303	48 388
District 28	24 645	499 895	4.4	1.6	1.6	7.3	11.2	1.7	1.7	25.3	10.1	25 386	50 782
District 29	11 994	167 001	15.5	7.0	8.3	13.4	19.2	1.6	2.5	3.5	1.8	7 681	45 992
District 30	29 901	395 057	4.7	3.1	2.9	10.1	12.5	6.6	2.3	10.3	18.9	19 678	49 810
District 31	12 814	239 343	8.1	5.0	5.4	13.4	20.5	3.3	1.4	3.8	1.8	10 017	41 851
District 32	15 029	244 466	16.4	4.6	10.0	13.6	13.6	3.2	1.4	4.5	1.2	10 909	44 622
District 33	40 241	495 669	6.0	1.7	2.9	10.8	11.4	4.5	3.1	14.2	9.9	37 094	74 836
District 34	23 451	334 849	7.5	1.5	10.3	7.7	14.8	8.0	2.3	9.9	2.0	20 320	60 684
District 35	13 331	261 350	12.2	6.5	11.6	13.2	11.0	1.8	1.2	2.0	1.2	11 521	44 082
District 36	12 211	165 276	3.0	6.5	1.9	20.4	16.0	1.8	2.7	2.5	1.4	5 657	34 229
District 37	20 940	313 618	3.1	1.6	3.1	8.2	9.6	3.3	2.6	9.5	24.6	18 808	59 970
District 38	14 642	236 983	13.5	5.4	14.4	13.7	13.9	2.5	1.6	3.3	1.4	10 458	44 131
District 39	19 164	248 499	10.4	7.9	11.3	12.4	8.5	6.0	1.7	5.8	1.3	11 329	45 589
District 40	11 278	215 690	21.9	2.2	16.9	11.0	11.2	1.2	1.1	1.8	0.8	9 214	42 717
District 41	9 883	178 910	8.6	7.9	5.8	15.1	15.6	2.3	1.4	3.2	1.3	7 147	39 948
District 42	11 455	151 040	12.1	14.9	5.9	15.9	11.3	1.9	1.6	4.7	1.1	6 183	40 933
District 43	15 045	285 436	11.3	2.8	6.5	10.0	12.6	2.2	2.4	5.9	2.0	14 504	50 814
District 44	8 690	162 591	21.0	5.8	12.2	10.7	8.5	1.0	1.4	1.8	1.0	7 611	46 813
District 45	25 344	400 922	10.5	5.0	8.3	8.6	9.1	8.1	4.5	12.9	4.7	27 911	69 616
District 46	17 744	391 479	10.9	6.7	5.7	7.9	12.9	4.7	1.9	4.8	1.3	17 942	45 831
District 47	15 730	243 630	8.0	5.4	4.7	11.9	15.3	4.4	1.8	5.6	1.8	12 099	49 662
District 48	24 826	321 044	8.1	4.3	5.5	14.0	11.9	6.5	3.9	11.5	1.4	19 179	59 739
District 49	21 302	270 582	11.6	5.3	6.5	12.8	13.1	2.3	2.0	11.7	2.4	14 957	55 276
District 50	15 877	195 372	7.1	11.6	3.5	18.0	11.3	1.9	1.8	3.7	1.0	7 619	38 995
District 51	10 208	141 244	12.0	3.9	6.6	23.7	14.0	2.5	1.6	3.0	1.5	5 151	36 468
District 52	29 166	529 811	7.8	4.3	6.5	8.7	6.9	6.2	2.5	15.7	4.1	33 919	64 021
District 53	15 971	231 355	3.0	4.7	1.9	13.1	27.6	4.1	2.5	6.6	0.9	10 193	44 059

1. Specified owner-occupied units; $1,000,000 represents $1,000,000 or more.   2. Specified renter-occupied units.

Table E. Congressional Districts 115th Congress — **Land Area and Population Characteristics**

STATE District	Representative, 115th Congress	Land area,[1] 2016 (sq. mi)	Total persons	Per square mile	White	Black	American Indian, Alaska Native	Asian and Pacific Islander	Some other race	Two or more races	Hispanic or Latino[2]	Non-Hispanic White alone	Female	Foreign-born	Born in state of residence
		1	2	3	4	5	6	7	8	9	10	11	12	13	14
COLORADO............		103 641.2	5 456 574	52.6	84.4	4.1	0.9	3.2	3.8	3.5	21.3	68.5	49.8	9.8	42.7
District 1	Diana DeGette (D)	190.0	803 636	4 230.6	78.8	8.3	0.9	3.4	5.0	3.6	27.6	57.6	50.0	15.0	41.8
District 2	Jared Polis (D)	7 535.7	782 278	103.8	91.0	0.8	0.3	3.6	1.3	2.9	10.5	82.5	49.3	7.3	35.1
District 3	Scott R. Tipton (R)	49 730.4	737 812	14.8	88.6	1.2	2.2	1.0	4.5	2.5	24.6	70.6	49.6	6.1	48.2
District 4	Ken Buck (R)	38 103.2	787 940	20.7	90.8	1.3	0.8	2.2	2.1	2.8	21.8	72.3	49.6	8.2	47.7
District 5	Doug Lamborn (R)	7 265.8	770 782	106.1	80.9	6.2	0.6	3.0	4.5	4.8	15.8	71.3	48.8	6.8	33.8
District 6	Mike Coffman (R)	474.0	796 156	1 679.8	74.1	8.8	0.6	5.4	6.4	4.7	20.6	61.8	50.7	14.2	41.6
District 7	Ed Perlmutter (D)	342.2	777 970	2 273.2	87.4	1.9	0.9	3.3	3.1	3.4	28.4	63.7	50.3	10.8	50.9
CONNECTICUT		4 842.7	3 590 886	741.5	76.5	10.6	0.2	4.4	5.0	3.2	15.4	67.9	51.2	14.5	55.3
District 1	John B. Larson (D)	675.4	711 436	1 053.4	70.0	15.6	0.4	4.8	5.9	3.3	15.8	62.2	52.0	16.0	58.0
District 2	Joe Courtney (D)	1 988.1	709 647	356.9	85.4	4.2	0.4	3.2	2.6	4.2	8.7	81.2	49.7	6.9	57.1
District 3	Rosa L. DeLauro (D)	470.3	720 493	1 531.9	73.0	13.2	0.2	4.6	5.9	3.0	16.0	64.6	51.8	13.1	62.2
District 4	James A. Himes (D)	460.8	736 742	1 599.0	72.9	13.0	0.1	5.4	5.3	3.3	19.4	61.2	51.6	22.1	43.7
District 5	Elizabeth H. Esty (D)	1 248.2	712 568	570.9	81.5	6.9	0.2	3.8	5.3	2.4	17.1	70.9	50.9	14.0	55.8
DELAWARE		1 948.7	945 934	485.4	69.2	21.6	0.3	3.9	2.0	3.0	9.0	63.0	51.6	9.3	45.6
At Large....................	Lisa Blunt Rochester (D)	1 948.7	945 934	485.4	69.2	21.6	0.3	3.9	2.0	3.0	9.0	63.0	51.6	9.3	45.6
DISTRICT OF COLUMBIA...........		61.1	672 228	10 994.0	40.0	47.4	0.2	3.9	5.2	3.2	10.6	36.0	52.4	14.1	35.8
Delegate District (At Large)	Eleanor Holmes Norton (D)	61.1	672 228	10 994.0	40.0	47.4	0.2	3.9	5.2	3.2	10.6	36.0	52.4	14.1	35.8
FLORIDA................		53 638.9	20 271 272	377.9	75.8	16.2	0.2	2.7	2.6	2.5	24.5	55.1	51.2	20.2	35.9
District 1	Matt Gaetz (R)	4 017.0	750 928	186.9	77.1	13.1	0.3	2.3	1.9	5.2	6.3	73.5	49.4	5.2	39.6
District 2	Neal P. Dunn (R)	11 003.7	718 173	65.3	69.3	25.0	0.4	2.1	0.6	2.6	5.9	64.6	49.7	5.6	55.2
District 3	Ted S. Yoho ®	3 564.5	721 105	202.3	78.9	13.7	0.3	3.4	0.9	2.8	8.5	72.2	50.3	7.2	52.0
District 4	John H. Rutherford (R)	1 569.6	740 304	471.7	75.7	15.0	0.1	4.8	1.1	3.3	8.4	69.2	51.1	9.7	45.3
District 5	Al Lawson (D)	3 817.6	743 735	194.8	41.5	49.6	0.3	2.6	3.5	2.6	14.3	31.5	52.0	13.4	53.1
District 6	Ron DeSantis (R)	2 171.4	755 981	348.1	84.7	9.6	0.2	2.4	1.2	1.7	7.8	78.7	51.3	7.6	34.5
District 7	Stephanie N. Murphy (D)	392.9	738 367	1 879.4	80.7	10.2	0.2	3.7	2.3	2.9	21.4	63.0	51.1	11.6	38.3
District 8	Bill Posey (R)	1 751.7	730 746	417.2	84.1	9.7	0.3	2.2	1.0	2.6	10.1	75.6	51.5	8.6	33.9
District 9	Darren Soto (D)	2 311.9	819 676	354.5	73.4	11.5	0.2	4.2	7.5	3.1	48.7	34.4	51.1	21.1	26.0
District 10	Val Butler Demings (D)	436.7	788 192	1 804.9	75.3	12.5	0.2	4.6	4.4	3.1	19.3	61.1	50.8	14.5	35.0
District 11	Daniel Webster (R)	2 389.9	740 907	310.0	87.3	8.1	0.2	1.5	1.1	1.8	9.9	79.0	51.4	6.4	31.2
District 12	Gus M. Bilirakis (R)	859.4	747 779	870.2	87.9	5.3	0.4	2.9	1.1	2.4	13.7	76.3	51.9	10.4	32.2
District 13	Charlie Crist (D)	181.8	716 429	3 941.7	86.7	5.5	0.3	4.0	0.9	2.5	10.1	78.2	51.8	13.1	30.1
District 14	Kathy Castor (D)	275.9	765 377	2 774.1	61.9	26.4	0.4	2.5	5.4	3.4	29.6	39.9	51.5	17.5	42.1
District 15	Dennis A. Ross (R)	1 087.4	728 456	669.9	75.6	13.1	0.2	4.6	3.6	2.9	18.0	62.4	51.0	12.0	45.6
District 16	Vern Buchanan (R)	1 293.4	764 808	591.3	89.1	7.0	0.1	1.8	0.7	1.5	12.2	77.9	52.2	11.9	27.1
District 17	Thomas J. Rooney (R)	5 573.1	747 648	134.2	82.6	9.8	0.3	1.3	3.8	2.2	17.6	69.6	50.2	11.6	37.9
District 18	Brian J. Mast (R)	1 513.0	748 028	494.4	80.2	13.1	0.4	2.6	2.0	1.8	14.9	68.0	51.5	15.5	32.1
District 19	Francis Rooney (R)	750.0	774 346	1 032.5	86.7	8.0	0.1	1.6	1.9	1.8	20.2	69.1	51.2	17.3	23.7
District 20	Alcee L. Hastings (D)	2 159.9	767 766	355.5	38.8	53.7	0.3	1.9	2.7	2.6	21.8	21.2	51.2	34.8	39.8
District 21	Lois Frankel (D)	257.1	758 192	2 948.7	77.4	13.7	0.2	3.0	3.1	2.7	23.5	57.6	52.6	25.6	26.7
District 22	Theodore E. Deutch (D)	167.3	730 302	4 366.2	79.6	11.5	0.2	2.4	3.6	2.7	23.6	61.0	50.7	26.0	26.6
District 23	Debbie Wasserman Schultz (D)	188.1	734 951	3 906.6	75.5	11.7	0.2	4.1	5.9	2.6	39.7	43.4	51.1	38.7	30.4
District 24	Frederica S. Wilson (D)	102.4	745 862	7 283.2	37.5	55.2	0.1	2.0	3.5	1.8	32.4	11.8	52.2	40.8	42.9
District 25	Mario Diaz-Balart (R)	3 505.5	765 164	218.3	87.1	6.2	0.3	2.1	3.2	1.1	70.9	21.2	51.2	52.0	27.7
District 26	Carlos Curbelo (R)	2 184.5	776 959	355.7	85.2	10.3	0.1	1.8	1.3	1.4	69.7	18.7	51.0	47.5	34.0
District 27	Ileana Ros-Lehtinen (R)	113.2	751 091	6 632.7	86.2	8.7	0.1	1.6	1.5	1.9	75.4	15.1	51.4	55.2	30.4
GEORGIA................		57 594.8	10 214 860	177.4	59.5	31.3	0.3	3.8	2.8	2.3	9.3	53.7	51.3	10.0	54.9
District 1	Earl L. "Buddy" Carter (R)	8 062.4	724 348	89.8	63.5	29.4	0.6	2.2	1.3	3.1	6.2	59.4	50.4	5.1	54.9
District 2	Sanford D. Bishop Jr. (D)	9 626.3	683 888	71.0	42.3	52.6	0.2	1.1	1.9	1.8	5.2	39.9	51.2	3.4	71.3
District 3	A. Drew Ferguson IV (R)	3 836.2	723 259	188.5	70.2	24.1	0.2	1.6	1.2	2.6	5.4	66.6	51.0	5.1	61.1
District 4	Henry C. "Hank" Johnson Jr. (D)	496.7	746 519	1 503.1	30.6	59.4	0.1	4.8	2.8	2.2	9.7	24.6	52.9	16.6	47.0
District 5	John Lewis (D)	265.0	736 978	2 781.5	33.3	57.8	0.4	4.6	1.8	2.1	6.3	29.3	52.5	8.6	54.1
District 6	Karen Handel (R)	298.9	729 643	2 440.9	69.8	13.2	0.9	11.1	2.7	2.3	13.2	60.5	50.1	21.3	32.1
District 7	Robert Woodall (R)	392.6	804 318	2 048.6	56.9	20.6	0.3	13.1	6.1	3.0	18.3	45.6	50.9	25.2	36.4
District 8	Austin Scott (R)	8 716.7	702 584	80.6	64.3	29.8	0.2	1.8	1.8	2.1	6.6	60.3	51.6	4.6	69.2
District 9	Doug Collins (R)	5 211.2	719 802	138.1	86.7	7.4	0.2	1.3	2.9	1.5	12.5	77.0	50.9	8.4	60.7
District 10	Jody B. Hice (R)	7 094.5	726 265	102.4	69.0	25.7	0.1	1.8	1.3	2.1	5.4	65.2	51.0	5.4	64.2
District 11	Barry Loudermilk (R)	1 070.7	744 746	695.6	73.3	15.9	0.3	3.8	4.1	2.6	10.5	67.6	51.2	12.5	44.0
District 12	Rick W. Allen (R)	8 186.1	713 146	87.1	58.7	35.0	0.2	1.5	2.3	2.2	6.2	55.3	50.8	3.8	68.0
District 13	David Scott (D)	714.2	755 256	1 057.4	32.5	58.4	0.0	2.4	4.7	2.0	12.0	26.5	52.6	11.1	50.5
District 14	Tom Graves (R)	3 623.3	704 108	194.3	84.2	8.6	0.2	1.3	3.3	2.3	11.3	76.7	51.0	6.4	59.4
HAWAII..................		6 422.5	1 431 603	222.9	26.0	2.1	0.3	46.5	0.7	24.5	10.4	22.8	49.4	17.7	53.0
District 1	Colleen Hanabusa (D)	209.0	705 773	3 376.10	19.0	2.4	0.1	56.5	0.6	21.3	8.4	16.8	49.2	22.8	51.6
District 2	Tulsi Gabbard (D)	6 213.4	725 830	116.8	32.8	1.7	0.4	36.8	0.8	27.5	12.3	28.6	49.6	12.7	54.5
IDAHO...................		82 642.4	1 654 930	20.0	91.5	0.5	1.4	1.4	2.3	2.9	12.1	82.6	50.0	5.7	48.0
District 1	Raul Labrador (R)	39 418.4	849 601	21.6	91.6	0.4	1.6	1.2	2.0	3.2	10.5	84.1	49.9	4.7	44.5
District 2	Michael K. Simpson (R)	43 224.0	805 329	18.6	91.4	0.6	1.2	1.6	2.5	2.6	13.7	81.0	50.2	6.7	51.7
ILLINOIS................		55 517.1	12 859 995	231.6	71.8	14.3	0.2	5.3	6.0	2.3	16.9	61.8	50.9	14.2	67.2
District 1	Bobby L. Rush (D)	258.4	717 447	2 776.2	40.8	51.0	0.3	1.8	3.9	2.2	9.9	35.6	53.7	7.9	75.7
District 2	Robin L. Kelly (D)	1 080.7	702 674	650.2	36.9	56.5	0.1	0.8	4.1	1.6	13.3	28.5	53.0	7.6	74.7

1. Dry land or land partially or temporarily covered by water.   2. May be of any race.

Table E. Congressional Districts 115th Congress — **Age and Education**

STATE District	Population and population characteristics, 2015 (cont.)											Education, 2015		
	Age (percent)												Attainment[2] (percent)	
	Under 5 years	5 to 17 years	18 to 24 years	25 to 34 years	35 to 44 years	45 to 54 years	55 to 64 years	65 to 74 years	75 years and over	Median age		Total Enrollment[1]	High school graduate or more	Bachelor's degree or more
	15	16	17	18	19	20	21	22	23	24		25	26	27
COLORADO	6.1	16.9	9.7	15.2	13.5	13.1	12.6	8.0	5.1	36.4		1 395 429	91.2	39.2
District 1	6.5	14.0	8.4	21.5	15.4	11.7	11.2	6.7	4.5	34.7		181 484	87.2	46.7
District 2	4.6	15.1	13.4	14.0	12.9	13.5	13.4	8.5	4.9	37.3		219 522	96.4	54.6
District 3	5.5	16.7	9.0	13.2	12.0	12.3	14.5	10.4	6.4	39.0		173 981	89.7	30.2
District 4	6.6	19.4	8.4	12.8	13.9	13.6	12.7	7.9	4.8	36.9		211 818	90.7	34.0
District 5	6.5	17.2	11.0	14.8	12.3	12.9	12.2	8.2	4.9	35.3		207 100	94.2	34.8
District 6	6.4	19.2	8.6	13.9	14.5	14.3	11.5	7.2	4.4	36.3		215 046	92.2	41.1
District 7	6.5	17.0	8.9	15.7	13.6	12.9	12.5	7.5	5.4	36.1		186 478	88.3	32.1
CONNECTICUT	5.2	16.0	9.8	12.3	12.0	15.0	13.9	8.8	7.0	40.6		913 807	90.2	38.3
District 1	5.1	15.6	9.0	13.2	12.3	14.8	13.5	9.0	7.6	41.0		175 066	89.0	36.7
District 2	4.7	14.8	11.5	11.9	11.4	14.8	14.6	9.3	6.8	41.4		177 071	91.9	34.9
District 3	5.1	15.3	11.1	13.6	11.7	14.4	13.2	8.7	6.9	39.0		188 129	90.5	35.9
District 4	5.7	18.0	9.3	11.2	12.7	15.5	13.1	7.9	6.5	39.7		199 943	90.4	48.6
District 5	5.2	16.6	8.2	11.8	12.2	15.1	15.0	9.0	6.9	41.8		173 598	89.2	35.6
DELAWARE	5.9	15.7	9.4	13.2	11.7	13.7	13.5	10.2	6.9	39.7		233 348	88.9	30.9
At Large	5.9	15.7	9.4	13.2	11.7	13.7	13.5	10.2	6.9	39.7		233 348	88.9	30.9
DISTRICT OF COLUMBIA	6.4	11.1	12.1	22.7	14.3	11.5	10.4	6.5	4.8	33.8		166 940	89.8	56.7
Delegate District (At Large) ..	6.4	11.1	12.1	22.7	14.3	11.5	10.4	6.5	4.8	33.8		166 940	89.8	56.7
FLORIDA	5.4	14.9	8.8	12.8	12.1	13.5	13.1	10.8	8.6	41.8		4 706 933	87.6	28.4
District 1	6.0	15.2	10.2	14.4	11.3	13.4	13.1	9.8	6.7	38.5		174 434	90.4	26.8
District 2	5.3	14.4	14.1	13.8	12.1	12.6	12.6	8.7	6.1	36.5		202 215	87.3	26.6
District 3	5.5	15.2	12.9	12.7	11.8	12.2	12.6	10.2	7.0	37.9		194 418	88.3	25.8
District 4	5.8	14.9	9.2	15.7	12.8	13.6	13.1	9.0	5.6	38.1		173 497	91.5	32.5
District 5	7.1	18.0	10.5	15.5	12.7	12.7	11.6	6.9	4.9	34.1		196 053	82.4	17.4
District 6	4.4	14.2	7.9	10.4	10.7	13.7	14.9	13.7	10.1	46.9		166 522	91.6	29.2
District 7	5.0	15.0	11.7	13.6	12.5	14.0	12.9	8.8	6.4	38.7		201 351	93.3	34.6
District 8	4.5	13.6	7.8	10.3	10.1	13.7	15.6	13.0	11.4	48.3		150 478	91.3	27.8
District 9	6.2	18.1	9.1	15.5	15.2	13.6	9.9	7.4	5.0	35.5		216 816	87.5	24.7
District 10	5.9	15.8	8.0	14.4	12.6	13.0	12.5	10.4	7.4	39.9		180 212	89.7	30.3
District 11	4.2	11.8	6.4	8.7	9.4	11.5	14.3	19.2	14.7	53.5		131 577	89.0	20.8
District 12	4.9	15.8	7.2	10.3	11.8	14.8	13.4	12.0	9.7	45.0		166 367	90.6	28.8
District 13	4.6	11.6	6.5	11.9	11.1	14.3	16.0	12.8	11.2	48.3		127 730	91.0	28.7
District 14	6.4	16.0	9.1	16.7	14.0	13.3	11.9	7.3	5.3	36.1		184 175	85.8	28.8
District 15	5.8	17.0	10.5	13.4	12.3	13.0	13.0	8.9	6.1	37.7		191 320	88.2	29.2
District 16	4.3	12.5	6.6	9.1	9.5	12.4	14.9	16.2	14.4	51.9		136 618	90.7	31.3
District 17	4.9	14.4	7.4	9.7	10.2	12.5	13.6	14.8	12.5	47.8		149 170	84.6	19.2
District 18	4.9	14.1	6.9	10.6	11.4	13.3	14.1	12.9	11.7	46.9		159 563	89.0	30.6
District 19	4.4	12.6	6.7	10.4	10.2	12.0	14.3	16.3	13.2	50.3		144 363	88.2	31.0
District 20	7.1	15.8	9.4	15.6	12.4	13.0	12.4	7.8	6.6	36.8		192 268	79.7	19.6
District 21	5.3	16.1	7.5	10.5	12.2	13.5	12.8	10.9	11.3	43.7		187 541	92.0	37.9
District 22	4.7	12.0	6.8	13.1	11.8	14.7	13.8	11.5	11.6	46.1		143 050	89.6	38.9
District 23	5.0	14.9	8.1	12.9	14.2	15.2	13.3	9.0	7.4	41.7		180 832	90.6	39.4
District 24	6.3	16.0	9.8	15.6	13.8	13.4	12.0	7.2	5.8	36.5		193 320	78.8	22.5
District 25	5.8	15.8	8.7	12.3	13.7	15.2	11.2	9.5	7.9	40.7		185 990	80.0	26.6
District 26	5.8	15.0	9.3	14.2	13.9	15.7	11.5	8.1	6.5	39.8		198 821	83.5	26.9
District 27	5.9	14.2	8.3	13.7	13.7	15.1	11.8	8.7	8.5	41.1		178 232	79.4	29.9
GEORGIA	6.4	18.2	10.1	13.6	13.6	13.7	11.8	7.9	4.8	36.4		2 760 000	86.1	29.9
District 1	6.9	16.7	10.7	14.9	12.3	12.4	12.1	8.4	5.5	35.7		186 645	87.3	24.3
District 2	6.6	17.5	11.1	13.4	12.2	12.3	12.8	8.3	5.8	36.2		187 588	81.7	17.9
District 3	5.5	18.4	10.2	11.7	13.6	13.9	12.1	9.3	5.4	37.8		191 472	87.1	25.8
District 4	7.0	18.8	9.3	14.1	13.8	14.3	12.5	6.7	3.5	35.5		207 480	86.8	30.5
District 5	5.8	13.9	12.7	19.8	14.8	11.9	10.0	6.8	4.3	33.7		198 544	87.6	40.6
District 6	7.0	19.1	6.9	13.2	15.3	15.4	12.1	7.0	4.2	37.6		192 428	93.2	59.5
District 7	6.7	21.6	8.7	12.9	15.6	14.8	10.7	6.0	3.2	35.1		239 154	89.0	40.0
District 8	6.4	17.8	10.5	12.8	12.8	13.1	11.8	8.8	5.9	36.8		186 307	83.6	19.9
District 9	6.0	17.1	8.8	11.2	12.6	13.7	13.1	11.0	6.6	40.9		170 094	82.7	23.0
District 10	5.3	18.2	13.0	11.7	12.4	13.9	11.8	8.6	5.1	36.4		215 138	85.2	25.0
District 11	6.1	17.9	9.6	14.0	14.4	14.6	11.7	7.7	4.0	36.6		203 367	89.8	41.2
District 12	6.5	17.7	11.4	14.1	12.7	12.4	11.9	8.0	5.2	35.2		188 629	82.7	20.8
District 13	7.2	19.7	9.0	13.2	14.3	14.7	11.5	6.4	3.9	35.6		208 996	88.1	29.3
District 14	5.9	19.0	9.4	12.5	13.1	14.0	11.9	8.4	5.5	37.4		184 158	79.9	17.0
HAWAII	6.4	15.3	9.4	15.1	12.4	12.2	12.6	9.4	7.2	37.7		330 445	90.9	31.4
District 1	5.8	14.0	9.3	15.9	12.8	12.9	11.9	9.1	8.0	38.6		161 053	90.0	34.3
District 2	7.1	16.6	9.4	14.3	11.9	11.4	13.1	9.6	6.3	36.9		169 392	91.8	28.3
IDAHO	6.8	19.3	9.5	13.1	12.4	12.0	12.2	8.8	5.9	35.8		439 310	90.0	26.0
District 1	6.1	19.0	8.8	12.0	12.4	12.7	13.0	9.8	6.2	37.9		216 506	90.5	24.7
District 2	7.4	19.7	10.2	14.3	12.3	11.3	11.4	7.8	5.6	33.7		222 804	89.4	27.4
ILLINOIS	6.1	17.0	9.6	13.8	13.0	13.6	12.8	8.1	6.1	37.7		3 325 495	88.6	32.9
District 1	6.3	17.2	10.3	12.5	11.7	13.2	14.0	8.3	6.4	38.0		193 608	88.6	26.9
District 2	5.7	18.1	9.7	12.4	12.2	14.1	13.3	7.9	6.6	38.3		189 757	88.1	22.0

1. All persons 3 years old and over enrolled in nursery school through college and graduate or professional school.   2. Persons 25 years old and over.

STATE District	Households, 2015						Group quarters, 2010					
	Number	Average household size	Family households (percent)	Married-couple family (percent)	Female family householder[1]	One person households (percent)	Total in group quarters, 2015	Percent 65 years and over	Persons in correctional institutions	Persons in nursing facilities	Persons in college dormitories	Persons in military quarters
	28	29	30	31	32	33	34	35	36	37	38	39
COLORADO	2 074 735	2.57	64.2	50.0	9.7	27.2	115 746	14.3	40 568	18 079	29 952	10 945
District 1	336 813	2.34	51.7	36.2	10.1	36.5	15 545	12.3	3 960	2 592	4 940	0
District 2	306 176	2.49	60.8	51.2	6.5	25.4	21 031	11.6	1 634	2 213	11 841	0
District 3	284 041	2.54	63.4	49.2	10.0	28.9	16 542	20.4	3 982	3 460	5 041	0
District 4	284 522	2.71	72.7	59.2	9.1	21.7	17 926	12.8	13 075	2 577	3 993	0
District 5	289 241	2.57	68.7	54.2	10.2	25.6	28 371	6.9	12 094	2 245	2 580	10 678
District 6	283 137	2.79	70.2	54.6	10.6	23.8	6 446	32.7	3 009	2 128	0	267
District 7	290 805	2.64	64.4	48.0	11.4	27.1	9 885	28.1	2 814	2 864	1 557	0
CONNECTICUT	1 343 703	2.59	65.2	48.2	12.7	28.5	116 932	20.9	20 059	26 371	48 537	3 977
District 1	278 568	2.49	64.2	45.9	13.7	29.2	17 320	33.0	1 335	6 778	5 649	0
District 2	269 220	2.49	65.8	50.4	11.3	27.2	40 600	10.7	12 975	4 306	16 779	3 977
District 3	269 917	2.57	60.7	42.5	13.3	32.4	27 615	17.9	902	5 257	16 566	0
District 4	257 674	2.8	69.7	53.3	12.5	24.3	14 109	31.6	1 159	4 719	5 030	0
District 5	268 324	2.59	65.9	49.1	12.7	28.9	17 288	28.1	3 688	5 311	4 513	0
DELAWARE	352 595	2.61	66.8	48.3	13.8	26.6	25 583	16.8	6 457	4 591	10 184	283
At Large	352 595	2.61	66.8	48.3	13.8	26.6	25 583	16.8	6 457	4 591	10 184	283
DISTRICT OF COLUMBIA	281 787	2.24	44.4	25.5	15.1	42.0	40 209	7.8	3 598	3 064	24 087	1 504
Delegate District (At Large) ..	281 787	2.24	44.4	25.5	15.1	42.0	40 209	7.8	3 598	3 064	24 087	1 504
FLORIDA	7 463 184	2.66	64.4	46.2	13.4	28.9	430 649	17.5	167 453	73 372	85 243	14 612
District 1	284 944	2.52	63.8	47.2	12.0	29.3	33 139	8.8	10 881	2 652	4 832	8 580
District 2	263 789	2.53	59.2	40.8	14.1	31.9	50 272	6.9	32 671	3 280	10 370	513
District 3	256 401	2.65	66.8	50.0	12.0	26.7	42 246	9.3	21 156	3 439	9 235	0
District 4	281 685	2.57	63.3	47.2	12.3	28.3	15 824	18.0	2 597	2 852	2 776	4 662
District 5	264 825	2.74	63.8	34.3	23.8	29.3	17 562	10.6	10 195	2 281	1 357	0
District 6	299 860	2.48	62.8	48.8	10.0	30.0	12 699	20.3	4 351	3 572	5 748	4
District 7	266 444	2.68	66.3	49.1	12.3	25.8	23 778	15.3	757	3 056	13 306	0
District 8	287 064	2.52	62.7	47.5	11.2	30.8	7 389	27.2	3 105	2 612	1 259	182
District 9	264 789	3.07	71.3	49.8	15.7	20.1	7 212	24.1	3 819	1 838	245	0
District 10	296 949	2.63	67.5	49.2	12.9	25.7	8 254	16.2	3 929	2 605	315	0
District 11	294 002	2.44	63.8	50.4	9.8	31.6	22 263	15.3	16 221	2 953	312	0
District 12	290 195	2.55	65.4	50.5	10.8	28.5	8 564	40.5	1 981	2 902	1 050	0
District 13	307 481	2.29	53.4	39.7	10.0	39.2	12 641	35.3	3 506	5 478	1 751	0
District 14	297 271	2.53	57.1	32.6	18.9	34.5	13 498	18.8	3 483	3 007	3 375	324
District 15	259 029	2.76	68.3	50.7	12.8	24.8	13 978	15.6	854	2 303	7 847	0
District 16	311 188	2.43	63.8	50.1	10.5	30.3	9 998	38.1	2 011	3 857	1 569	0
District 17	275 425	2.63	68.7	54.3	10.4	25.5	22 275	15.9	12 761	3 312	606	0
District 18	289 741	2.55	64.8	50.6	9.9	29.0	8 160	25.5	3 930	1 838	339	2
District 19	303 535	2.51	64.7	52.2	8.6	29.7	12 090	26.8	2 727	2 860	2 688	9
District 20	249 312	3.00	64.4	36.2	21.3	27.9	20 085	18.4	10 719	3 611	214	0
District 21	279 199	2.71	69.3	52.5	11.9	26.7	2 313	52.8	619	1 396	19	0
District 22	311 737	2.31	53.2	39.3	9.4	37.4	10 364	29.7	1 291	3 658	3 672	0
District 23	279 979	2.61	61.1	43.7	12.9	32.2	4 623	23.7	938	1 239	1 463	59
District 24	243 955	2.99	62.4	32.8	23.2	32.4	16 149	21.9	3 004	2 733	3 132	0
District 25	230 199	3.28	77.7	53.2	18.3	17.9	9 667	12.7	5 752	717	596	0
District 26	221 403	3.44	76.4	52.8	17.6	17.3	15 476	17.9	4 186	1 100	2 657	277
District 27	252 783	2.93	65.0	40.8	16.6	28.6	10 130	24.6	9	2 221	4 510	0
GEORGIA	3 656 407	2.72	67.5	47.9	15.0	26.9	260 364	12.5	104 012	34 738	72 288	16 072
District 1	270 110	2.58	68.6	47.2	16.5	25.5	26 152	10.4	10 733	3 028	5 798	5 069
District 2	249 232	2.59	63.5	37.8	20.7	32.2	38 379	8.4	17 145	3 559	7 343	5 167
District 3	258 762	2.75	71.0	53.2	14.0	24.7	11 430	20.6	4 777	2 837	4 020	64
District 4	257 062	2.88	68.4	41.5	21.5	25.4	6 714	17.9	4 367	1 472	653	0
District 5	299 161	2.32	44.2	24.3	15.7	45.5	41 542	5.3	6 731	2 500	22 635	78
District 6	272 191	2.67	67.1	54.3	8.5	26.8	3 012	49.0	89	1 109	620	0
District 7	256 992	3.11	76.6	59.1	13.3	18.7	5 415	18.9	4 093	1 167	0	0
District 8	253 727	2.68	67.4	47.5	16.2	27.8	23 089	13.4	13 355	4 044	5 390	401
District 9	257 730	2.74	73.4	58.3	10.5	22.9	13 245	17.7	4 824	2 514	4 115	44
District 10	252 039	2.78	68.7	51.8	13.1	24.6	26 214	12.0	10 678	2 840	9 699	74
District 11	275 721	2.66	68.7	54.0	10.9	24.7	11 255	14.1	3 520	1 539	4 296	36
District 12	246 405	2.75	67.7	46.6	17.5	26.3	35 730	10.7	15 029	3 980	5 294	5 139
District 13	258 487	2.90	70.3	45.3	18.8	25.2	5 611	21.4	3 437	1 322	0	0
District 14	248 788	2.78	72.3	52.3	13.4	23.6	12 576	21.5	5 234	2 827	2 425	0
HAWAII	445 936	3.11	69.4	52.1	11.7	23.4	44 033	12.2	5 673	5 198	7 540	12 551
District 1	228 751	2.98	67.3	50.7	11.5	25.3	23 971	13.3	3 581	2 672	4 641	5 332
District 2	217 185	3.25	71.6	53.6	11.9	21.4	20 062	10.9	2 092	2 526	2 899	7 219
IDAHO	597 421	2.72	67.0	53.7	9.4	27.2	30 374	16.9	11 275	4 820	7 223	466
District 1	313 548	2.65	66.5	53.5	9.6	28.2	18 109	15.4	7 951	2 375	4 359	0
District 2	283 873	2.79	67.5	53.9	9.2	26.0	12 265	19.2	3 324	2 445	2 864	466
ILLINOIS	4 794 523	2.62	64.6	47.7	12.5	29.4	299 694	22.6	70 828	81 516	92 960	12 483
District 1	265 639	2.66	61.7	34.9	21.4	34.0	12 168	21.7	0	4 063	5 957	0
District 2	256 770	2.69	63.3	35.0	23.6	32.7	11 869	31.1	685	5 037	2 054	0

1. No spouse present.

STATE District	Total	Occupied units as a percent of all units	Owner-occupied units as a percent of occupied units	Median value[1] (dollars)	Percent valued at $500,000 or more	Median rent[2]	Per capita income (dollars)	Median income (dollars)	Percent with income of $100,000 or more
	40	41	42	43	44	45	46	47	48
COLORADO	2 309 122	89.8	63.7	283 800	16.0	1 111	33 563	63 909	29.3
District 1	356 159	94.6	52.1	317 600	21.6	1 104	37 915	60 576	28.7
District 2	368 921	83.0	66.2	361 600	28.2	1 252	39 443	72 468	34.4
District 3	361 667	78.5	66.2	213 700	14.0	862	27 275	50 010	19.4
District 4	304 984	93.3	70.8	279 400	14.4	1 030	33 581	72 390	33.3
District 5	320 702	90.2	63.2	231 600	8.9	1 030	29 117	58 882	25.9
District 6	294 152	96.3	66.0	310 800	15.0	1 222	35 778	74 430	36.0
District 7	302 537	96.1	63.8	277 900	9.0	1 184	31 237	62 330	27.0
CONNECTICUT	1 496 056	89.8	66.2	270 900	16.5	1 108	39 430	71 346	35.6
District 1	304 510	91.5	64.8	234 500	6.3	1 032	36 369	69 959	32.5
District 2	303 636	88.7	71.3	245 200	9.2	1 055	36 547	71 670	35.3
District 3	299 342	90.2	62.3	249 000	8.3	1 120	33 324	63 315	31.2
District 4	282 761	91.1	65.4	489 400	48.6	1 422	53 862	89 085	45.1
District 5	305 807	87.7	67.0	266 800	11.9	1 015	36 610	68 810	34.1
DELAWARE	421 734	83.6	70.8	240 200	7.2	1 049	31 441	61 255	25.8
At Large	421 734	83.6	70.8	240 200	7.2	1 049	31 441	61 255	25.8
DISTRICT OF COLUMBIA	309 596	91.0	39.9	551 300	54.9	1 417	50 187	75 628	39.3
Delegate District (At Large)	309 596	91.0	39.9	551 300	54.9	1 417	50 187	75 628	39.3
FLORIDA	9 210 287	81.0	63.8	179 800	8.9	1 046	27 697	49 426	19.7
District 1	357 452	79.7	64.2	158 500	6.5	947	27 178	51 094	18.6
District 2	341 401	77.3	61.4	150 600	3.4	892	23 106	44 216	15.6
District 3	306 341	83.7	67.3	144 100	3.3	863	24 309	49 270	18.0
District 4	323 371	87.1	63.1	174 600	7.1	1 066	31 555	57 040	22.7
District 5	315 832	83.8	48.5	104 500	3.0	877	18 460	35 116	9.4
District 6	373 782	80.2	71.4	180 900	8.0	970	29 793	47 713	20.1
District 7	304 735	87.4	65.4	180 600	7.3	1 114	29 396	54 667	22.7
District 8	357 131	80.4	71.5	161 500	6.3	965	29 166	50 070	18.3
District 9	326 128	81.2	57.5	166 400	2.6	1 105	21 251	47 075	16.7
District 10	347 176	85.5	65.9	177 800	8.1	1 070	29 298	53 473	21.2
District 11	372 904	78.8	79.4	139 300	3.8	803	24 426	42 548	12.9
District 12	346 927	83.6	69.3	171 000	5.5	1 009	29 457	51 402	21.7
District 13	389 775	78.9	65.7	165 400	7.7	975	31 600	47 579	19.0
District 14	338 626	87.8	47.9	157 900	8.8	959	25 582	42 654	16.5
District 15	296 429	87.4	65.2	164 200	3.5	931	26 046	51 598	20.7
District 16	412 881	75.4	70.5	207 500	11.3	1 056	32 267	53 624	22.0
District 17	361 772	76.1	73.2	139 600	3.4	882	24 091	44 088	15.1
District 18	363 711	79.7	73.3	214 200	12.1	1 118	33 591	55 117	24.1
District 19	459 395	66.1	69.9	232 900	17.8	1 059	34 631	53 878	22.5
District 20	295 098	84.5	52.8	139 300	1.5	1 095	18 617	39 569	11.4
District 21	333 474	83.7	72.6	249 100	11.4	1 370	34 037	61 409	29.7
District 22	403 449	77.3	61.5	281 900	20.7	1 322	39 678	56 090	25.5
District 23	384 352	72.8	59.8	278 900	20.5	1 324	36 728	56 643	27.1
District 24	286 528	85.1	45.9	179 100	9.6	1 068	20 764	38 016	13.6
District 25	269 472	85.4	61.3	239 200	9.1	1 244	23 054	50 118	21.1
District 26	257 195	86.1	64.3	270 200	11.0	1 306	22 866	52 112	22.6
District 27	284 950	88.7	44.6	302 200	28.3	1 107	27 787	42 237	20.2
GEORGIA	4 182 228	87.4	61.8	159 300	6.5	909	26 810	51 244	21.7
District 1	316 499	85.3	58.5	147 200	5.4	925	24 325	45 796	17.3
District 2	299 756	83.1	53.4	99 200	1.8	700	19 723	35 347	11.5
District 3	288 494	89.7	66.7	163 200	3.9	878	26 114	52 584	21.4
District 4	282 158	91.1	58.4	142 200	2.1	977	23 408	50 668	19.0
District 5	356 690	83.9	42.5	169 900	14.4	963	31 728	48 017	20.8
District 6	293 795	92.6	63.9	339 200	22.1	1 175	44 731	83 844	42.6
District 7	268 515	95.7	65.4	217 800	7.5	1 107	29 027	69 201	31.8
District 8	297 825	85.2	64.7	115 700	3.1	757	22 608	42 582	15.6
District 9	321 609	80.1	71.8	166 100	5.5	791	24 561	48 837	18.2
District 10	294 440	85.6	66.4	158 100	4.9	792	24 281	49 033	20.6
District 11	297 883	92.6	64.1	220 200	12.5	1 043	35 842	69 662	31.9
District 12	298 145	82.6	63.3	110 500	2.2	736	21 548	42 336	15.2
District 13	286 414	90.2	61.3	134 900	2.5	949	23 555	52 761	19.7
District 14	280 005	88.9	68.6	130 400	2.0	707	22 688	46 378	15.9
HAWAII	532 413	83.8	56.6	566 900	58.2	1 500	31 052	73 486	34.7
District 1	257 392	88.9	52.8	626 500	66.8	1 552	33 638	77 156	37.6
District 2	275 021	79.0	60.6	502 100	50.2	1 446	28 538	70 420	31.6
IDAHO	692 482	86.3	69.0	176 300	4.7	770	24 273	48 216	17.5
District 1	360 322	87.0	71.7	185 300	4.3	792	24 235	48 275	17.5
District 2	332 160	85.5	65.9	167 300	5.2	756	24 312	48 363	17.5
ILLINOIS	5 317 618	90.2	65.3	180 300	8.4	936	31 867	59 588	27.2
District 1	302 682	87.8	59.1	179 300	3.5	907	25 777	48 295	20.9
District 2	300 135	85.6	60.4	121 900	1.3	890	23 619	44 353	17.3

1. Specified owner-occupied units; $1,000,000 represents $1,000,000 or more.   2. Specified renter-occupied units.

STATE District	Poverty, 2015			Civilian labor force, 2015	Unemployment		Civilian employment,[2] 2015	Percent			Persons under age 65 with no health insurance, 2015 (percent)	Social Security beneficiaries, December 2015		Supplemental Security Income recipients, December 2015
	Persons below poverty level (percent)	Families below poverty level (percent)	Percent of households receiving food stamps in past 12 months	Total	Total	Rate[1]	Total	Manage-ment, business, science and arts occupa-tions	Service, sales, and office	Con-struction and production		Number	Rate[3]	
	49	50	51	52	53	54	55	56	57	58	59	60	61	62
COLORADO	11.5	7.6	8.4	2 916 718	151 603	5.2	2 765 115	41.2	40.6	18.3	9.2	813 266	149.0	72 806
District 1	14.6	10.0	9.1	461 728	22 768	4.9	438 960	45.7	37.7	16.6	11.6	102 815	127.9	15 774
District 2	10.7	4.2	4.6	448 439	19 988	4.5	428 451	48.3	37.9	13.8	6.5	112 904	144.3	4 729
District 3	15.3	11.2	12.1	368 262	26 219	7.1	342 043	34.2	42.7	23.1	13.5	144 294	195.6	13 975
District 4	9.6	6.3	8.2	407 957	19 295	4.7	388 662	39.8	39.1	21.1	6.1	115 995	147.2	8 972
District 5	10.7	7.8	11.0	368 189	23 537	6.4	344 652	38.6	44.0	17.4	8.5	124 161	161.1	10 662
District 6	8.4	6.1	6.4	434 287	19 599	4.5	414 688	42.1	41.1	16.8	8.8	98 448	123.7	9 002
District 7	11.3	8.0	7.4	427 856	20 197	4.7	407 659	37.1	42.5	20.4	9.4	114 649	147.4	9 692
CONNECTICUT	10.5	7.4	12.6	1 941 592	134 494	6.9	1 807 098	42.4	40.6	17.0	6.9	659 238	183.6	63 736
District 1	10.7	8.0	14.9	389 065	27 202	7.0	361 863	43.5	40.0	16.5	5.6	139 357	195.9	16 761
District 2	9.0	5.9	10.8	386 333	23 846	6.2	362 487	40.4	41.6	18.0	4.3	138 107	194.6	8 380
District 3	12.7	8.7	13.2	392 471	26 793	6.8	365 678	40.9	41.4	17.8	6.5	133 076	184.7	14 073
District 4	9.0	6.5	10.0	394 089	30 241	7.7	363 848	47.1	39.8	13.1	10.2	114 218	155.0	10 302
District 5	11.3	8.2	14.1	379 634	26 412	7.0	353 222	40.2	40.2	19.6	7.8	134 480	188.7	14 220
DELAWARE	12.4	8.7	13.0	475 209	27 693	5.8	447 516	40.0	42.3	17.8	6.8	196 651	207.9	16 880
At Large	12.4	8.7	13.0	475 209	27 693	5.8	447 516	40.0	42.3	17.8	6.8	196 651	207.9	16 880
DISTRICT OF COLUMBIA	17.3	14.0	15.3	389 414	28 235	7.3	361 179	61.8	32.7	5.5	4.2	80 546	119.8	26 886
Delegate District (At Large) ..	17.3	14.0	15.3	389 414	28 235	7.3	361 179	61.8	32.7	5.5	4.2	80 546	119.8	26 886
FLORIDA	15.7	11.3	14.9	9 668 285	678 064	7.0	8 990 221	34.5	47.1	18.4	16.2	4 334 337	213.8	571 293
District 1	12.8	8.3	12.0	351 037	25 541	7.3	325 496	33.8	47.4	18.8	13.2	161 191	214.7	17 000
District 2	20.2	12.2	15.9	337 415	28 061	8.3	309 354	35.9	48.2	16.0	13.2	139 510	194.3	20 669
District 3	18.7	13.0	14.8	314 753	25 702	8.2	289 051	37.4	42.9	19.6	13.6	156 181	216.6	16 822
District 4	10.4	7.0	9.8	383 054	19 770	5.2	363 284	39.5	43.3	17.1	11.7	130 935	176.9	15 487
District 5	24.3	20.5	28.4	369 408	38 478	10.4	330 930	26.1	51.2	22.7	18.3	133 894	180.0	32 607
District 6	15.2	10.5	12.4	327 322	22 045	6.7	305 277	36.8	45.8	17.4	13.9	209 642	277.3	14 570
District 7	12.4	7.2	9.8	377 366	24 366	6.5	353 000	42.3	43.9	13.7	12.4	132 350	179.2	12 521
District 8	13.1	9.1	10.1	324 061	22 024	6.8	302 037	36.2	46.3	17.6	14.7	205 466	281.2	14 838
District 9	17.6	14.8	18.9	407 354	24 955	6.1	382 399	29.9	51.6	18.5	17.0	133 014	162.3	23 792
District 10	13.1	10.2	12.9	385 097	21 854	5.7	363 243	38.7	46.3	14.9	13.5	164 612	208.8	18 620
District 11	15.8	10.3	13.8	257 155	23 995	9.3	233 160	28.9	49.5	21.6	14.9	278 828	376.3	17 750
District 12	12.3	8.1	12.5	345 368	21 902	6.3	323 466	39.2	44.5	16.2	12.7	183 387	245.2	14 142
District 13	13.3	8.5	11.0	358 841	18 873	5.3	339 968	36.4	46.7	16.9	14.3	183 849	256.6	14 899
District 14	20.4	16.7	22.9	394 003	32 826	8.3	361 177	35.7	46.3	18.0	16.2	130 735	170.8	34 473
District 15	14.5	9.7	12.8	354 474	23 554	6.6	330 920	36.4	45.1	18.5	13.0	138 098	189.6	19 053
District 16	11.8	7.2	8.3	326 087	21 331	6.5	304 756	34.7	46.6	18.7	17.1	223 767	292.6	10 671
District 17	15.8	10.8	13.6	299 308	22 053	7.4	277 255	27.8	46.4	25.8	18.1	209 906	280.8	15 236
District 18	12.2	8.1	9.0	349 741	19 871	5.7	329 870	34.1	48.7	17.2	14.6	185 867	248.5	12 059
District 19	15.0	9.8	9.6	330 547	21 074	6.4	309 473	31.5	49.1	19.3	19.4	207 542	268.0	12 269
District 20	22.8	18.5	24.5	394 621	46 193	11.7	348 428	23.7	53.7	22.6	21.7	122 327	159.3	25 381
District 21	9.7	7.6	9.0	374 654	24 829	6.6	349 825	39.1	46.3	14.6	14.9	163 726	215.9	9 479
District 22	13.4	9.0	9.0	385 957	25 221	6.5	360 736	39.5	44.1	16.4	18.4	154 976	212.2	14 967
District 23	11.9	8.5	12.0	404 843	23 337	5.8	381 506	39.6	45.3	15.0	15.1	117 441	159.8	15 342
District 24	24.1	19.6	26.9	369 878	34 747	9.4	335 131	28.6	52.4	19.0	23.0	109 015	146.2	46 043
District 25	18.8	15.4	24.5	373 055	20 966	5.6	352 089	29.6	45.9	24.5	20.2	119 282	155.9	34 813
District 26	15.4	12.6	19.8	393 343	21 077	5.4	372 266	32.5	49.6	17.9	19.4	118 576	152.6	33 420
District 27	19.3	15.1	28.0	379 543	23 419	6.2	356 124	33.3	44.7	22.0	21.7	120 220	160.1	54 370
GEORGIA	17.0	13.0	14.7	4 957 832	352 199	7.1	4 605 633	36.4	40.7	22.9	15.7	1 714 145	167.8	258 401
District 1	19.3	15.5	16.3	332 285	26 464	8.0	305 821	32.3	44.0	23.8	16.9	129 188	178.4	18 023
District 2	27.7	21.5	23.7	287 027	32 432	11.3	254 595	30.5	42.0	27.5	17.7	139 665	204.2	32 420
District 3	14.9	11.1	14.3	340 840	27 182	8.0	313 658	33.5	39.7	26.8	14.0	139 925	193.5	18 183
District 4	18.2	15.0	17.3	387 237	34 525	8.9	352 712	33.5	43.8	22.7	17.8	106 744	143.0	21 635
District 5	21.3	17.3	17.2	402 426	33 093	8.2	369 333	45.1	39.3	15.6	15.3	100 394	136.2	26 702
District 6	8.6	5.4	4.9	401 109	20 807	5.2	380 302	54.7	34.0	11.3	11.8	90 624	124.2	5 437
District 7	10.7	8.8	8.8	417 043	24 249	5.8	392 794	41.3	39.7	19.0	15.9	84 959	105.6	9 064
District 8	21.7	16.8	16.6	310 070	24 405	7.9	285 665	32.5	40.3	27.1	16.4	137 497	195.7	23 776
District 9	16.3	11.6	14.1	322 358	16 586	5.1	305 772	30.9	40.2	28.9	18.4	162 499	225.8	15 393
District 10	18.5	12.5	14.2	332 209	20 933	6.3	311 276	33.1	43.6	23.4	14.3	136 464	187.9	18 623
District 11	10.2	7.6	8.8	401 426	19 717	4.9	381 709	42.2	40.3	17.4	13.4	105 611	141.8	9 951
District 12	21.8	15.9	18.7	303 215	22 401	7.4	280 814	31.4	41.6	27.0	16.8	133 062	186.6	24 133
District 13	17.0	14.6	17.8	384 337	31 387	8.2	352 950	31.8	42.9	25.3	17.1	107 962	142.9	17 725
District 14	15.1	12.4	13.5	336 250	18 018	5.4	318 232	27.1	40.0	32.9	14.8	139 551	198.2	17 336
HAWAII	10.6	6.9	11.5	710 239	35 025	4.9	675 214	33.6	47.7	18.6	4.7	256 912	179.5	24 778
District 1	8.4	5.1	9.3	365 589	14 627	4.0	350 962	34.9	47.8	17.2	4.4	127 985	181.3	12 036
District 2	12.7	8.6	13.9	344 650	20 398	5.9	324 252	32.3	47.6	20.2	4.9	128 927	177.6	12 742
IDAHO	15.1	10.9	11.5	786 377	42 149	5.4	744 228	33.7	42.1	24.3	12.9	315 571	190.7	30 774
District 1	14.8	10.2	12.0	394 169	23 451	5.9	370 718	33.2	43.2	23.6	12.2	174 109	204.9	15 465
District 2	15.5	11.8	10.9	392 208	18 698	4.8	373 510	34.1	41.0	24.9	13.6	141 462	175.7	15 309
ILLINOIS	13.6	9.8	13.5	6 657 355	460 831	6.9	6 196 524	37.5	41.2	21.3	8.1	2 174 883	169.1	274 621
District 1	18.7	14.6	21.5	344 400	44 705	13.0	299 695	34.4	45.9	19.7	7.9	124 489	173.5	25 822
District 2	20.0	16.4	22.4	339 449	49 354	14.5	290 095	30.7	45.3	24.0	9.7	130 798	186.1	29 115

1. Percent of civilian labor force.   2. Persons 16 years old and over.   3. Per 1,000 resident population estimated in the 2014 American Community Survey.

Table E. Congressional Districts 115th Congress — **Agriculture**

STATE District										
		Land in farms			Value of products sold				Government payments	
	Number of farms	Acres	Average size of farm (acres)	Irrigated land (acres)	Total ($1,000)	Average per farm (dollars)	Percent from crops	Percent from livestock and poultry products	Total ($1,000)	Average per farm receiving payments (dollars)
	63	64	65	66	67	68	69	70	71	72
COLORADO....................	36 180	31 886 676	881	2 516 785	7 780 874	215 060	31.3	68.7	165 576	14 897
District 1	24	1 065	44	74	D	D	D	D	0	0
District 2	3 055	926 007	303	116 782	177 941	58 246	47.7	52.3	1 675	5 511
District 3	13 954	8 837 850	633	1 062 127	970 501	69 550	53.5	46.5	18 852	8 360
District 4	15 949	20 596 438	1 291	1 293 158	6 460 512	405 073	26.6	73.4	141 885	17 318
District 5	2 520	1 237 551	491	36 488	83 271	33 044	0.0	0.0	1 745	7 897
District 6	357	220 448	618	4 345	D	D	D	D	1 001	9 351
District 7	321	67 317	210	3 811	40 961	127 603	91.2	8.8	D	D
CONNECTICUT................	5 977	436 539	73	9 272	550 620	92 123	70.7	29.3	4 841	9 328
District 1	826	46 562	56	4 128	106 344	128 745	96.7	3.3	325	5 908
District 2	2 762	200 857	73	3 001	272 398	98 624	57.4	42.6	2 729	10 579
District 3	579	35 645	62	1 080	34 176	59 026	78.6	21.4	238	5 409
District 4	348	53 930	155	319	30 068	86 401	55.1	44.9	78	6 487
District 5	1 462	99 545	68	744	107 634	73 621	80.5	19.5	1 471	9 808
DELAWARE......................	2 451	508 652	208	127 272	1 274 014	519 794	33.7	66.3	9 677	10 553
At Large	2 451	508 652	208	127 272	1 274 014	519 794	33.7	66.3	9 677	10 553
DISTRICT OF COLUMBIA	X	X	X	X	X	X	X	X	X	X
Delegate District (At Large) ..	X	X	X	X	X	X	X	X	X	X
FLORIDA..........................	47 740	9 548 342	200	1 493 320	7 701 532	161 322	77.5	22.5	40 164	10 158
District 1	3 181	469 042	147	9 215	169 985	53 438	74.9	25.1	6 426	7 377
District 2	4 105	794 768	194	33 990	256 516	62 489	75.0	25.0	5 840	5 720
District 3	8 862	1 290 144	146	107 825	975 689	110 098	34.1	65.9	6 700	7 718
District 4	1 114	95 293	86	781	31 667	28 426	29.1	70.9	242	6 916
District 5	1 419	112 887	80	5 257	243 410	171 536	89.5	10.5	183	5 709
District 6	1 811	228 498	126	29 595	233 438	128 900	93.7	6.3	1 729	12 264
District 7	473	33 415	71	4 545	59 629	126 065	96.9	3.1	43	4 825
District 8	1 122	399 784	356	73 129	203 360	181 248	85.8	14.2	959	29 963
District 9	578	578 346	1 001	32 362	130 432	225 662	67.3	32.7	328	19 265
District 10	2 017	221 769	110	26 061	198 780	98 552	94.9	5.1	366	14 635
District 11	4 978	441 454	89	14 700	170 324	34 215	45.3	54.7	881	8 476
District 12	1 298	182 782	141	7 371	82 447	63 519	45.0	55.0	427	12 948
District 13	87	847	10	101	1 856	21 332	89.1	10.9	D	D
District 14	232	56 265	243	2 466	57 548	248 052	67.4	32.6	D	D
District 15	2 141	222 673	104	19 924	237 271	110 823	82.9	17.1	569	12 116
District 16	670	141 262	211	9 799	90 251	134 703	84.6	15.4	394	39 408
District 17	6 479	2 668 107	412	382 609	1 799 624	277 763	73.4	26.6	4 283	17 132
District 18	1 341	462 571	345	169 758	540 342	402 940	85.8	14.2	1 316	18 533
District 19	480	48 914	102	11 239	73 268	152 643	96.4	3.6	31	3 924
District 20	674	563 547	836	336 357	791 626	1 174 519	98.0	2.0	1 483	23 917
District 21	554	57 082	103	35 053	223 947	404 237	96.2	3.8	547	20 272
District 22	133	2 812	21	355	8 918	67 056	81.5	18.5	46	5 072
District 23	432	6 315	15	1 372	27 072	62 667	88.8	11.2	52	17 176
District 24	40	1 870	47	53	518	12 949	68.9	31.1	D	D
District 25	695	390 142	561	134 835	486 358	699 796	97.0	3.0	344	14 964
District 26	2 382	59 843	25	35 808	551 229	231 415	96.3	3.7	6 009	27 691
District 27	442	17 910	41	8 760	56 027	126 758	97.9	2.1	876	31 299
GEORGIA	42 257	9 620 836	228	1 125 355	9 255 125	219 020	39.7	60.3	142 322	9 793
District 1	2 069	417 353	202	37 955	290 617	140 462	58.1	41.9	4 870	7 356
District 2	5 559	2 470 948	444	D	1 887 305	339 504	70.0	30.0	49 436	14 669
District 3	3 475	447 816	129	6 652	357 673	102 928	12.5	87.5	1 939	4 683
District 4	248	18 707	75	45	2 149	8 664	52.8	47.2	20	997
District 5	30	2 801	93	D	211	7 025	90.0	10.0	12	2 007
District 6	105	7 064	67	245	1 378	13 119	60.5	39.5	28	3 540
District 7	209	13 328	64	81	10 188	48 748	72.3	27.7	37	2 651
District 8	6 419	2 068 738	322	343 268	1 501 791	233 960	71.7	28.3	40 267	11 375
District 9	7 080	666 984	94	4 291	2 135 687	301 651	2.4	97.6	4 110	4 160
District 10	5 566	1 082 225	194	39 355	784 526	140 950	22.5	77.5	9 360	6 138
District 11	936	88 216	94	2 474	140 080	149 658	15.8	84.2	1 056	9 183
District 12	6 035	1 793 019	297	163 770	1 211 704	200 779	61.3	38.7	26 685	8 290
District 13	342	24 390	71	279	5 701	16 671	70.3	29.7	128	3 464
District 14	4 184	519 247	124	4 551	926 116	221 347	5.7	94.3	4 374	7 112
HAWAII	7 000	1 129 317	161	81 813	661 347	94 478	81.5	18.5	5 228	8 325
District 1	291	21 133	73	3 760	28 230	97 009	82.6	17.4	101	5 617
District 2	6 709	1 108 184	165	78 053	633 117	94 368	81.4	18.6	5 127	8 405
IDAHO..............................	24 816	11 760 109	474	3 365 292	7 801 446	314 372	44.1	55.9	99 789	10 673
District 1	11 404	4 227 137	371	612 775	1 790 850	157 037	48.6	51.4	33 991	9 847
District 2	13 412	7 532 972	562	2 752 517	6 010 597	448 151	42.8	57.2	65 798	11 156
ILLINOIS	75 087	26 937 721	359	522 479	17 187 052	228 895	82.3	17.7	553 300	9 829
District 1	191	66 255	347	387	47 865	250 604	91.7	8.3	923	10 487
District 2	1 204	451 866	375	14 622	367 131	304 926	90.6	9.4	7 554	8 898

Table E. Congressional Districts 115th Congress — Nonfarm Employment and Payroll

Private nonfarm employment and payroll, 2015

STATE District	Number of establishments	Total	Manufacturing	Construction	Wholesale trade	Retail trade	Health care and social assistance	Finance and Insurance	Real estate and rental and leasing	Professional, scientific, and technical services	Information	Total (mil dol)	Average per employee dollars
	73	74	75	76	77	78	79	80	81	82	83	84	85
COLORADO	161 737	2 253 795	5.4	6.4	4.4	12.1	13.0	4.7	1.9	8.5	3.6	117 540	52 152
District 1	28 915	485 005	4.2	4.9	5.1	8.3	13.0	5.5	2.4	9.6	3.0	28 460	58 680
District 2	29 323	354 047	8.8	5.1	4.8	12.9	11.5	3.2	2.2	12.2	3.7	19 425	54 865
District 3	25 375	247 105	4.5	8.8	3.2	15.5	17.1	2.9	2.7	4.4	1.7	9 587	38 799
District 4	19 243	235 841	9.4	9.5	4.0	15.7	12.5	4.4	1.3	6.4	4.1	11 549	48 968
District 5	19 200	246 254	4.9	5.5	2.6	14.3	15.9	4.5	1.8	8.5	4.0	10 596	43 030
District 6	19 856	309 840	2.5	5.8	6.0	12.2	14.5	8.2	1.6	8.3	7.5	18 055	58 271
District 7	19 167	264 104	6.4	10.4	5.2	14.4	12.6	3.9	1.8	7.9	2.1	12 251	46 387
CONNECTICUT	89 232	1 503 102	9.9	3.6	4.9	12.3	18.5	8.1	1.3	7.2	2.7	92 555	61 576
District 1	18 424	361 306	10.8	4.2	4.9	11.0	18.3	11.3	1.2	6.3	3.2	21 895	60 600
District 2	14 280	214 841	12.4	3.5	3.9	16.1	17.5	3.3	0.9	5.6	1.7	9 668	45 002
District 3	16 471	306 934	12.7	3.9	4.9	11.3	20.8	3.5	1.4	4.5	2.1	15 786	51 430
District 4	21 934	330 175	4.3	2.5	6.4	10.7	15.2	13.4	1.4	9.6	3.9	29 883	90 508
District 5	17 644	263 075	11.6	4.5	3.5	15.2	22.7	5.7	1.7	5.0	2.2	13 805	52 475
DELAWARE	24 852	397 385	6.6	4.9	3.9	13.9	16.7	10.8	1.5	7.9	1.7	21 305	53 614
At Large	24 852	397 385	6.6	4.9	3.9	13.9	16.7	10.8	1.5	7.9	1.7	21 305	53 614
DISTRICT OF COLUMBIA	22 553	513 002	0.2	1.8	0.9	4.3	13.0	3.3	2.2	19.6	4.7	38 446	74 943
Delegate District (At Large)	22 553	513 002	0.2	1.8	0.9	4.3	13.0	3.3	2.2	19.6	4.7	38 446	74 943
FLORIDA	532 830	7 777 990	3.8	4.7	4.0	13.8	13.5	4.4	2.1	6.3	2.1	337 075	43 337
District 1	16 677	204 902	3.5	6.4	2.6	18.4	17.4	5.1	2.3	7.6	1.3	7 680	37 479
District 2	14 642	171 671	6.7	5.0	3.2	18.5	17.7	3.5	2.1	7.1	4.3	6 271	36 529
District 3	16 248	211 256	5.9	4.9	3.1	17.9	24.4	3.4	1.9	5.4	1.9	7 735	36 613
District 4	23 280	341 132	4.5	4.9	4.5	13.0	14.1	11.1	1.8	6.5	1.8	15 804	46 328
District 5	14 384	225 407	5.6	7.0	5.0	15.3	15.1	5.4	1.8	5.5	3.1	9 681	42 947
District 6	16 609	176 971	5.7	6.4	2.7	18.7	19.2	3.3	2.3	4.6	1.9	6 094	34 433
District 7	23 651	336 635	2.7	5.8	2.7	13.6	15.2	7.5	2.0	9.6	3.9	15 929	47 319
District 8	17 996	212 400	9.5	5.6	2.5	17.8	18.0	2.9	1.7	6.8	1.6	8 780	41 337
District 9	12 864	186 465	5.6	5.3	2.6	17.1	13.7	3.8	4.1	2.9	1.6	6 840	36 681
District 10	21 856	454 769	4.2	4.1	4.6	13.3	7.3	1.9	4.1	5.6	2.0	18 332	40 312
District 11	11 972	134 581	4.1	7.4	1.9	21.2	24.5	2.4	2.0	4.2	1.9	4 486	33 332
District 12	16 275	169 210	4.3	6.4	2.6	19.9	20.4	4.5	1.8	8.0	1.3	5 936	35 081
District 13	20 673	297 458	8.2	4.1	4.2	13.2	18.9	6.3	2.1	6.7	3.2	13 201	44 380
District 14	23 953	413 625	3.1	4.1	4.7	10.3	14.0	9.4	2.2	11.6	3.5	21 138	51 105
District 15	15 728	255 136	6.0	7.0	6.5	15.0	13.1	6.5	1.9	5.5	3.1	10 195	39 958
District 16	20 468	220 407	5.9	6.6	3.6	18.0	18.6	3.5	2.5	5.7	1.5	8 551	38 795
District 17	13 415	135 133	6.5	7.7	2.7	21.1	20.6	2.9	1.8	4.1	0.9	4 642	34 349
District 18	20 992	213 491	3.5	5.7	3.1	18.4	16.6	3.3	2.1	7.3	1.8	9 207	43 125
District 19	24 805	287 169	2.5	9.3	2.9	19.3	16.1	3.0	2.8	5.4	2.1	11 457	39 895
District 20	17 075	253 701	5.4	6.3	8.5	13.5	15.1	3.7	2.1	6.7	5.1	11 784	46 449
District 21	21 441	196 716	1.8	5.2	2.5	18.0	19.0	3.3	2.4	7.0	1.5	8 224	41 805
District 22	32 598	336 756	3.1	5.0	5.5	14.8	11.8	5.5	2.9	9.9	2.4	16 668	49 495
District 23	25 883	290 553	1.9	3.4	4.4	21.8	12.9	4.4	3.3	6.5	2.5	12 729	43 809
District 24	16 047	203 396	5.1	3.4	8.8	13.6	23.2	2.9	1.6	4.4	1.9	9 112	44 802
District 25	25 572	327 220	5.8	5.4	13.0	13.1	8.6	3.8	2.3	4.2	3.4	14 718	44 978
District 26	14 744	127 774	2.4	5.8	5.8	21.1	14.1	4.2	2.6	4.6	1.3	4 359	34 117
District 27	31 919	349 670	0.8	2.3	2.4	14.0	15.5	7.4	2.7	11.8	1.8	18 892	54 029
GEORGIA	224 593	3 692 490	9.9	4.5		12.7	13.0	4.7	1.6	6.8	3.2	174 839	47 350
District 1	15 521	227 013	11.9	4.2	3.6	15.6	14.8	2.4	1.5	3.8	1.2	8 734	38 474
District 2	12 943	200 550	13.5	3.6	5.0	14.1	18.5	9.5	1.3	4.1	1.4	7 861	39 196
District 3	14 518	216 296	16.5	5.0	4.1	16.3	15.2	3.7	1.1	2.8	1.7	7 984	36 913
District 4	10 955	146 650	11.8	8.2	5.3	17.1	14.9	2.1	1.8	4.3	2.0	5 629	38 384
District 5	21 713	516 714	3.6	2.8	4.3	6.8	11.8	4.2	2.2	9.1	4.6	31 770	61 485
District 6	28 100	459 039	2.0	2.7	5.6	9.4	10.7	9.5	2.0	14.2	8.9	30 961	67 447
District 7	24 240	355 091	7.9	7.0	11.0	13.5	8.7	4.6	1.5	8.6	4.7	17 910	50 438
District 8	13 277	182 607	13.5	3.8	4.1	17.0	18.2	3.7	1.2	4.1	1.1	6 112	33 470
District 9	14 383	192 288	24.8	5.0	4.3	15.7	13.7	2.7	0.8	2.6	1.1	7 209	37 491
District 10	12 841	153 088	12.4	5.2	3.8	17.4	15.9	2.8	1.6	3.5	1.2	5 247	34 277
District 11	20 722	350 076	7.0	6.5	8.1	12.0	9.7	6.2	2.4	8.7	3.1	19 769	56 472
District 12	13 078	210 009	12.4	4.3	3.6	15.5	20.9	2.7	1.2	5.9	1.6	7 989	38 041
District 13	11 030	169 472	6.3	6.0	7.4	18.0	16.0	2.4	2.5	2.5	1.3	6 636	39 159
District 14	10 503	171 734	29.1	3.6	5.0	14.5	12.8	2.0	0.8	2.6	1.2	6 231	36 284
HAWAII	31 915	523 677	2.4	5.6	3.6	13.7	13.3	3.6	2.4	4.3	1.5	22 068	42 141
District 1	17 990	316 823	2.9	6.4	4.5	13.1	14.0	4.9	2.4	5.0	1.9	14 456	45 629
District 2	13 739	181 204	1.8	5.0	2.3	16.6	14.0	1.7	2.9	3.4	1.0	6 669	36 801
IDAHO	44 757	546 524	10.6	6.4	5.5	15.1	16.3	4.0	1.3	6.0	2.2	21 120	38 644
District 1	21 074	231 794	11.9	8.6	4.8	16.3	15.6	4.2	1.3	4.4	2.4	8 447	36 442
District 2	23 395	303 201	10.0	4.9	6.0	14.7	17.4	3.8	1.3	7.4	2.1	12 309	40 596
ILLINOIS	318 266	5 427 549	10.0	3.7	5.8	11.6	14.7	6.2	1.4	7.4	2.3	289 184	53 281
District 1	11 882	187 223	6.2	4.3	3.9	16.9	20.3	2.5	1.4	2.8	1.0	7 738	41 329
District 2	10 227	166 246	17.3	4.4	5.5	13.6	21.5	2.3	1.2	2.4	1.7	6 845	41 172

1. Specified owner-occupied units; $1,000,000 represents $1,000,000 or more.   2. Specified renter-occupied units.

Table E. Congressional Districts 115th Congress — Land Area and Population Characteristics

Population and population characteristics, 2015 — Percent

STATE District	Representative, 115th Congress	Land area,[1] 2016 (sq. mi)	Total persons	Per square mile	Race alone: White	Black	American Indian, Alaska Native	Asian and Pacific Islander	Some other race	Two or more races	Hispanic or Latino[2]	Non-Hispanic White alone	Female	Foreign-born	Born in state of residence
		1	2	3	4	5	6	7	8	9	10	11	12	13	14
ILLINOIS—Cont'd															
District 3	Daniel Lipinski (D)	237.1	727 484	3 068.4	72.8	5.1	0.3	4.1	15.4	2.4	33.0	56.7	51.0	20.7	70.7
District 4	Luis V. Gutierrez (D)	52.4	708 172	13 509.6	59.4	4.2	0.6	3.6	30.0	2.2	70.1	21.9	49.7	33.9	53.6
District 5	Michael Quigley (D)	95.6	735 985	7 696.2	82.3	3.1	0.3	6.3	4.8	3.2	20.3	68.0	50.8	21.6	54.8
District 6	Peter J. Roskam (R)	378.9	726 447	1 917.4	83.4	3.0	0.2	8.8	2.5	2.1	11.9	74.6	50.7	15.3	65.7
District 7	Danny K. Davis (D)	62.3	721 321	11 571.3	35.3	48.9	0.2	7.8	6.1	1.8	14.1	28.1	52.5	13.7	62.2
District 8	Raja Krishnamoorthi (D)	205.6	710 467	3 455.3	65.6	4.6	0.3	14.1	12.4	3.0	27.8	51.3	49.8	29.6	58.2
District 9	Janice D. Schakowsky (D)	105.4	722 268	6 853.7	72.3	8.6	0.2	13.4	2.4	3.1	11.3	64.0	50.8	27.6	52.5
District 10	Bradley Scott Schneider (D)	300.0	714 251	2 380.8	76.7	7.1	0.1	10.5	3.1	2.5	22.5	58.1	50.1	23.9	57.2
District 11	Bill Foster (D)	280.9	729 611	2 597.5	65.8	11.1	0.2	7.5	12.8	2.6	27.2	52.5	51.2	20.1	66.7
District 12	Mike Bost (R)	5 008.3	699 369	139.6	78.5	17.2	0.3	1.2	0.6	2.2	3.3	76.2	50.9	2.7	69.0
District 13	Rodney Davis (R)	5 793.6	706 596	122.0	80.5	11.3	0.1	4.1	0.9	3.0	3.1	78.7	51.1	5.1	74.2
District 14	Randy Hultgren (R)	1 597.6	728 436	456.0	87.6	3.4	0.0	4.8	2.5	1.8	11.3	79.5	50.4	9.0	72.3
District 15	John Shimkus (R)	14 695.9	703 653	47.9	93.1	4.5	0.1	0.6	0.4	1.2	2.8	91.0	50.1	1.7	75.7
District 16	Adam Kinzinger (R)	7 917.4	701 275	88.6	89.4	4.0	0.3	1.4	3.0	1.8	9.5	83.3	50.2	5.4	77.6
District 17	Cheri Bustos (D)	6 930.9	691 375	99.8	82.1	11.8	0.2	1.3	2.2	2.5	9.2	75.8	50.7	5.0	72.7
District 18	Darin LaHood (R)	10 516.1	713 164	67.8	91.1	3.5	0.2	2.5	0.7	2.0	2.8	89.3	50.4	3.6	77.1
INDIANA		35 826.6	6 619 680	184.8	84.0	9.1	0.2	2.1	2.1	2.4	6.6	79.9	50.9	4.9	68.4
District 1	Peter J. Visclosky (D)	1 156.9	716 495	619.3	69.6	18.7	0.2	1.5	7.1	2.9	15.1	62.9	51.0	6.1	58.3
District 2	Jackie Walorski (R)	3 958.7	725 415	183.2	86.5	6.7	0.3	1.6	2.4	2.5	9.4	80.0	50.5	5.3	68.8
District 3	Jim Banks (R)	4 180.2	735 864	176.0	87.9	5.8	0.3	2.1	1.0	2.9	6.1	83.3	51.0	4.2	72.0
District 4	Todd Rokita (R)	6 352.5	747 601	117.7	89.3	3.7	0.3	2.9	2.1	1.8	6.0	85.6	50.0	5.9	70.4
District 5	Susan W. Brooks (R)	1 924.8	760 212	395.0	84.6	8.5	0.1	3.3	0.8	2.7	4.4	81.3	51.4	5.2	65.2
District 6	Luke Messer (R)	6 206.9	721 380	116.2	93.2	2.7	0.3	1.5	0.7	1.6	2.4	91.8	50.9	2.2	72.0
District 7	André Carson (D)	303.9	749 776	2 467.0	61.6	29.1	0.3	3.0	3.2	2.8	10.8	54.3	51.7	9.0	69.0
District 8	Larry Bucshon (R)	7 255.9	720 955	99.4	92.0	4.0	0.2	1.0	0.8	2.1	2.2	90.7	50.2	2.1	75.9
District 9	Trey Hollingsworth (R)	4 486.8	741 982	165.4	91.4	2.9	0.3	2.3	1.1	2.0	3.3	89.4	51.0	3.5	64.4
IOWA		55 856.5	3 123 899	55.9	90.5	3.4	0.4	2.3	1.5	1.9	5.6	86.8	50.4	4.8	71.1
District 1	Rod Blum (R)	12 048.8	771 888	64.1	90.8	3.7	0.4	1.5	1.6	2.0	3.7	88.9	50.4	3.3	75.6
District 2	David Loebsack (D)	12 261.9	778 329	63.5	89.8	4.0	0.1	2.4	1.4	2.2	5.5	85.9	50.3	4.7	68.9
District 3	David Young (R)	8 789.7	812 464	92.4	89.1	4.2	0.5	3.1	1.2	2.0	6.7	84.1	50.8	6.6	67.7
District 4	Steve King (R)	22 756.0	761 218	33.5	92.4	1.7	0.5	2.1	1.9	1.4	6.4	88.3	50.2	4.4	72.4
KANSAS		81 758.4	2 911 641	35.6	84.7	5.9	0.9	3.0	2.3	3.2	11.6	76.4	50.2	7.1	58.6
District 1	Roger W. Marshall (R)	52 542.2	715 330	13.6	87.1	3.0	0.7	1.9	4.7	2.6	15.8	76.9	49.1	8.3	61.9
District 2	Lynn Jenkins (R)	14 143.6	715 752	50.6	87.4	4.4	1.6	1.6	1.0	3.9	6.7	82.5	50.8	3.2	63.3
District 3	Kevin Yoder (R)	757.3	755 396	997.5	81.1	8.6	0.3	4.6	2.1	3.3	11.7	72.4	50.8	9.8	44.5
District 4	Ron Estes (R)	14 315.4	725 163	50.7	83.3	7.5	1.1	3.6	1.5	3.0	12.0	73.9	50.1	6.8	65.5
KENTUCKY		39 485.2	4 425 092	112.1	87.4	8.0	0.2	1.4	0.9	2.1	3.3	85.2	50.9	3.6	69.6
District 1	James Comer (R)	12 082.3	723 466	59.9	89.5	7.3	0.2	0.6	0.4	2.0	2.7	87.6	50.8	1.9	68.0
District 2	Brett Guthrie (R)	7 177.9	747 645	104.2	89.1	5.6	0.2	1.5	1.1	2.4	3.1	87.3	51.0	3.1	72.2
District 3	John A. Yarmuth (D)	319.4	742 828	2 325.6	72.3	21.3	0.2	2.6	0.7	2.9	5.0	68.3	51.8	6.8	68.4
District 4	Thomas Massie (R)	4 376.3	750 449	171.5	92.3	3.5	0.1	1.3	1.0	1.8	3.4	90.1	50.1	3.1	61.6
District 5	Harold Rogers (R)	11 233.8	707 534	63.0	96.8	1.5	0.2	0.4	0.2	0.9	1.1	96.0	50.1	0.7	78.7
District 6	Garland "Andy" Barr (R)	4 295.4	753 170	175.3	84.6	8.8	0.2	2.0	1.6	2.7	4.5	82.1	51.3	5.4	68.9
LOUISIANA		43 206.7	4 670 724	108.1	62.4	32.2	0.5	1.8	1.1	2.1	4.9	59.0	51.1	4.0	78.3
District 1	Steve Scalise (R)	4 030.8	806 140	200.0	79.3	14.1	1.1	2.1	1.2	2.3	8.7	72.1	51.5	6.6	73.6
District 2	Cedric Richmond (D)	1 268.4	791 393	623.9	32.5	60.5	0.2	3.1	1.7	2.0	6.3	28.8	52.0	6.2	78.5
District 3	Clay Higgins (R)	6 984.2	782 417	112.0	70.4	24.4	0.4	1.6	0.9	2.3	3.8	67.6	51.1	3.0	83.1
District 4	Mike Johnson (R)	12 436.2	758 913	61.0	60.8	34.2	0.7	1.1	0.9	2.4	3.7	58.6	50.5	2.3	74.7
District 5	Ralph Lee Abraham (R)	14 453.3	746 021	51.6	61.6	36.1	0.2	0.4	0.5	1.1	2.3	60.0	49.9	1.4	82.2
District 6	Garret Graves (R)	4 033.9	785 840	194.8	69.6	24.2	0.2	2.2	1.4	2.4	4.3	66.8	51.3	4.0	78.0
MAINE		30 843.9	1 329 328	43.1	94.6	1.1	0.7	1.0	0.2	2.3	1.5	93.6	51.0	3.4	64.1
District 1	Chellie Pingree (D)	3 286.3	672 009	204.5	94.3	1.4	0.4	1.4	0.2	2.3	1.7	93.2	51.3	4.2	57.8
District 2	Bruce Poliquin (R)	27 557.5	657 319	23.9	95.0	0.8	1.0	0.7	0.2	2.3	1.4	94.0	50.8	2.5	70.5
MARYLAND		9 709.6	6 006 401	618.6	56.5	29.5	0.3	6.5	4.2	3.1	9.5	51.9	51.5	15.2	47.2
District 1	Andrew Harris (R)	3 977.1	725 499	182.4	82.9	11.7	0.2	2.3	0.7	2.2	3.8	80.0	50.8	5.1	61.4
District 2	C. A. Dutch Ruppersberger (D)	348.6	763 156	2 189.0	55.4	34.4	0.3	5.2	1.4	3.1	7.0	50.7	52.2	12.1	61.8
District 3	John P. Sarbanes (D)	304.5	758 683	2 491.9	65.1	19.9	0.2	8.0	3.1	3.6	9.3	59.8	51.8	16.3	48.4
District 4	Anthoney G. Brown (D)	297.8	745 629	2 503.6	29.0	52.9	0.3	3.5	11.7	2.6	15.4	26.4	51.9	19.5	29.2
District 5	Steny H. Hoyer (D)	1 481.6	760 734	513.5	49.8	37.6	0.2	4.2	4.3	3.8	8.7	46.0	51.1	11.9	38.1
District 6	John K. Delaney (D)	1 952.2	761 921	390.3	68.3	13.8	0.2	11.0	3.4	3.4	13.2	59.1	50.4	21.1	44.1
District 7	Elijah E. Cummings (D)	488.2	729 001	1 493.1	34.9	54.0	0.2	7.4	0.9	2.6	3.4	32.8	52.2	10.6	62.6
District 8	Jamie Raskin (D)	859.5	761 778	886.3	66.4	12.1	0.4	9.8	7.7	3.5	15.0	60.1	51.7	24.1	33.3
MASSACHUSETTS		7 801.0	6 794 422	871.0	79.1	7.3	0.2	6.4	4.1	2.9	11.2	73.0	51.5	16.1	61.6
District 1	Richard E. Neal (D)	2 350.2	736 190	313.2	85.2	6.3	0.3	2.0	3.8	2.5	17.5	72.8	51.8	7.8	65.9
District 2	James P. McGovern (D)	1 627.9	744 886	457.6	84.0	5.3	0.2	5.3	2.7	2.4	9.3	78.1	51.1	11.4	65.6
District 3	Niki Tsongas (D)	757.6	754 068	995.4	77.9	3.4	0.2	8.7	7.2	2.7	18.9	67.6	50.6	17.4	61.0
District 4	Joseph P. Kennedy III (D)	668.2	750 331	1 122.8	87.0	2.9	0.0	5.9	2.0	2.2	4.8	84.1	51.4	13.0	60.6
District 5	Katherine Clark (D)	265.1	765 922	2 889.3	78.1	4.9	0.2	11.0	2.7	3.1	8.3	72.6	51.7	23.6	53.6
District 6	Seth Moulton (D)	526.7	761 166	1 445.1	85.4	3.4	0.2	4.1	4.3	2.6	8.6	82.1	51.6	12.3	70.4
District 7	Michael E. Capuano (D)	62.7	777 588	12 398.2	50.1	26.5	0.2	10.1	7.0	6.1	21.9	40.5	51.5	32.4	42.4
District 8	Stephen F. Lynch (D)	326.4	764 789	2 343.3	77.1	9.6	0.1	7.9	2.2	2.2	5.9	73.9	51.9	16.8	65.1
District 9	William R. Keating (D)	1 216.1	739 482	608.1	88.3	3.1	0.1	1.8	4.3	2.4	5.0	86.5	51.6	9.6	71.0

1. Dry land or land partially or temporarily covered by water.   2. May be of any race.

Table E. Congressional Districts 115th Congress — **Age and Education**

STATE District	Population and population characteristics, 2015 (cont.)										Education, 2015		
	Age (percent)											Attainment[2] (percent)	
	Under 5 years	5 to 17 years	18 to 24 years	25 to 34 years	35 to 44 years	45 to 54 years	55 to 64 years	65 to 74 years	75 years and over	Median age	Total Enrollment[1]	High school graduate or more	Bachelor's degree or more
	15	16	17	18	19	20	21	22	23	24	25	26	27
ILLINOIS—Cont'd													
District 3	6.5	18.5	9.3	12.8	13.1	13.8	12.6	7.4	6.0	37.2	195 935	85.9	26.2
District 4	7.4	18.6	10.5	18.2	15.0	12.1	9.4	5.3	3.5	32.2	195 376	72.2	23.4
District 5	6.5	12.8	8.1	22.2	15.2	12.1	10.4	7.0	5.6	35.2	160 386	91.1	52.0
District 6	5.2	18.4	8.3	11.2	12.5	15.3	14.8	8.6	5.6	40.7	196 768	94.4	49.5
District 7	5.9	14.1	11.4	19.7	13.6	12.1	11.1	7.6	4.6	34.3	179 955	85.9	40.6
District 8	6.7	16.6	8.6	14.6	14.0	14.5	12.6	7.1	5.2	37.4	174 905	84.6	33.3
District 9	5.7	14.4	8.0	15.0	13.0	13.9	14.0	8.7	7.4	40.2	174 259	90.6	51.4
District 10	6.3	18.8	9.5	11.9	12.9	14.2	12.7	7.6	6.2	37.9	190 083	89.3	44.3
District 11	6.5	20.2	9.6	13.4	14.5	14.0	10.8	6.8	4.3	35.3	206 206	86.1	33.4
District 12	5.9	16.4	9.1	13.2	12.2	13.8	13.6	8.8	7.1	39.1	172 348	89.9	22.5
District 13	5.3	14.8	15.3	12.4	11.9	11.8	13.0	8.5	7.0	36.5	210 258	91.9	30.8
District 14	6.0	19.5	8.7	10.4	14.1	16.2	12.8	7.9	4.4	39.1	200 003	94.1	40.0
District 15	6.0	16.6	9.2	12.3	11.8	12.8	13.7	9.6	8.1	39.9	163 976	89.0	19.0
District 16	5.5	17.2	9.3	11.6	11.8	14.0	13.8	9.2	7.4	40.2	176 713	89.7	21.7
District 17	5.6	16.6	9.6	11.9	11.9	12.9	13.9	9.9	7.7	40.1	164 322	87.4	18.4
District 18	6.0	16.7	8.9	12.2	12.1	13.4	13.5	9.6	7.7	39.9	180 637	93.3	32.0
INDIANA	6.3	17.6	10.2	12.7	12.5	13.2	12.9	8.4	6.2	37.5	1 693 308	88.2	24.9
District 1	6.1	17.5	9.1	12.3	12.9	13.4	13.6	8.7	6.4	38.7	182 092	88.8	22.7
District 2	6.5	18.4	9.7	12.3	12.2	12.7	13.0	8.6	6.6	37.5	180 452	84.9	21.0
District 3	6.9	18.9	9.3	12.3	12.2	12.9	12.9	8.3	6.1	36.8	183 428	87.5	22.4
District 4	6.1	17.0	12.9	12.2	12.1	12.9	12.7	8.0	6.1	36.3	204 170	90.4	25.8
District 5	6.4	18.1	8.0	13.4	13.4	14.0	13.1	7.8	5.9	37.9	196 184	92.8	44.0
District 6	5.8	16.6	10.6	11.0	11.9	14.2	13.4	9.5	7.0	40.4	176 206	88.7	19.8
District 7	7.6	18.3	10.2	16.0	13.0	12.9	11.1	6.3	4.6	33.4	199 271	82.2	22.2
District 8	5.9	16.4	10.1	12.1	12.0	13.3	13.7	9.4	7.1	39.6	171 517	88.1	19.7
District 9	5.6	16.6	12.0	12.7	12.2	13.1	12.9	8.9	6.0	37.3	199 988	90.2	25.8
IOWA	6.2	17.1	10.3	12.5	11.8	12.8	13.2	8.6	7.4	38.1	809 269	91.7	26.8
District 1	6.1	17.0	10.3	12.1	11.5	12.9	13.4	8.9	7.8	38.9	198 837	92.3	25.6
District 2	6.2	16.6	10.7	12.7	11.7	12.7	13.3	8.8	7.3	38.1	201 457	92.0	26.2
District 3	6.8	18.2	8.5	13.9	13.1	13.3	12.4	7.7	6.0	36.7	208 138	91.3	31.3
District 4	6.0	16.5	11.7	11.4	10.6	12.2	13.7	8.9	8.9	38.9	200 837	91.4	24.0
KANSAS	6.8	18.0	10.4	13.2	11.9	12.4	12.6	8.1	6.6	36.2	783 366	90.3	31.7
District 1	7.0	17.0	12.3	13.3	10.9	11.6	12.4	8.1	7.3	35.3	191 783	87.8	23.7
District 2	6.2	16.9	12.0	12.1	11.3	12.4	13.0	8.9	7.1	37.1	193 767	91.0	27.7
District 3	6.9	18.9	8.3	13.8	13.6	13.4	12.2	7.4	5.3	36.5	201 650	92.5	47.0
District 4	7.0	18.9	9.1	13.5	11.8	12.3	12.9	8.0	6.5	36.1	196 166	89.5	27.3
KENTUCKY	6.2	16.6	9.6	12.7	12.8	13.6	13.3	9.1	6.1	38.8	1 062 437	85.1	23.3
District 1	6.3	16.2	9.8	11.7	11.6	13.1	13.7	10.4	7.2	40.1	160 001	84.4	16.9
District 2	6.1	17.3	10.0	12.1	12.7	13.9	12.9	9.0	6.1	38.5	186 980	85.4	19.8
District 3	6.4	16.0	8.9	14.6	12.6	13.4	13.3	8.4	6.3	38.0	179 705	90.1	32.7
District 4	6.2	18.0	8.4	12.5	13.3	14.1	13.3	8.6	5.7	38.6	185 161	88.3	26.5
District 5	5.9	16.3	8.7	11.7	13.0	13.7	14.0	10.2	6.4	40.9	155 204	75.7	13.2
District 6	6.1	16.1	11.9	13.3	13.2	13.5	12.4	8.1	5.5	36.9	195 386	86.7	30.1
LOUISIANA	6.5	17.4	9.8	14.3	12.3	12.7	12.8	8.3	5.8	36.4	1 174 717	84.6	23.2
District 1	6.1	16.8	8.8	14.2	12.1	13.6	13.4	8.7	6.3	38.1	204 619	87.4	29.4
District 2	6.5	16.6	10.1	16.0	12.7	12.8	13.0	7.5	5.0	35.6	198 792	81.9	22.8
District 3	6.8	18.2	9.4	14.6	12.1	13.0	12.7	7.7	5.7	35.7	194 851	83.1	20.2
District 4	6.9	17.7	9.7	13.7	12.4	12.0	12.5	8.6	6.5	36.5	183 638	84.7	19.3
District 5	6.6	17.4	9.6	13.2	12.6	12.7	12.7	8.8	6.4	37.3	179 792	81.1	17.6
District 6	6.3	17.7	11.3	14.4	12.4	12.7	12.1	8.1	5.0	35.2	213 025	89.1	29.3
MAINE	4.8	14.5	8.4	11.4	11.5	14.7	15.8	11.0	7.8	44.6	289 749	91.7	30.1
District 1	4.6	14.5	8.5	11.4	11.8	14.8	15.6	10.8	7.8	44.5	143 054	93.8	37.3
District 2	5.0	14.5	8.3	11.5	11.2	14.6	16.0	11.2	7.7	44.6	146 695	89.6	22.8
MARYLAND	6.1	16.4	9.3	13.8	12.8	14.5	13.0	8.3	5.9	38.3	1 565 730	89.6	38.8
District 1	5.0	16.5	9.4	11.0	11.3	15.0	14.2	10.3	7.5	42.4	178 945	90.5	31.0
District 2	6.7	16.5	9.4	15.1	12.9	14.1	12.8	7.5	4.9	36.3	198 120	88.4	31.1
District 3	6.6	14.7	8.8	17.0	13.5	12.3	12.4	8.3	6.4	36.7	194 875	90.9	47.3
District 4	6.8	16.6	8.5	15.2	13.3	14.7	12.1	8.1	4.5	36.8	187 367	86.9	33.0
District 5	5.6	16.9	10.8	12.7	12.8	15.5	13.4	7.3	4.8	38.2	215 706	91.4	34.9
District 6	6.2	17.6	8.9	12.6	13.2	15.0	12.8	8.1	5.8	38.4	200 719	89.5	41.0
District 7	5.5	15.9	9.8	14.7	11.9	14.1	13.5	8.5	6.2	38.3	196 783	88.7	37.0
District 8	6.3	16.0	8.3	12.8	13.5	14.8	13.2	8.4	6.7	40.0	193 215	90.6	53.9
MASSACHUSETTS	5.4	15.0	10.3	13.8	12.3	14.4	13.3	8.7	6.7	39.4	1 732 925	90.2	41.5
District 1	5.3	15.5	10.7	12.0	11.5	14.2	14.2	9.3	7.3	41.0	182 700	88.0	29.1
District 2	4.7	15.4	12.5	12.5	12.1	14.7	13.5	8.4	6.3	39.1	209 415	90.2	36.7
District 3	6.1	17.0	9.3	12.4	12.8	15.5	13.8	7.5	5.5	39.0	195 100	88.6	37.4
District 4	5.4	17.4	9.2	11.2	12.5	15.3	13.6	9.2	6.3	40.9	204 911	92.8	49.9
District 5	6.0	13.9	9.0	14.9	13.7	14.3	12.7	8.5	7.1	39.5	190 017	93.2	55.9
District 6	5.3	15.8	9.0	11.7	11.9	15.0	14.3	9.4	7.5	42.1	183 502	92.5	42.4
District 7	5.4	11.4	16.1	23.2	12.8	10.9	9.8	6.1	4.4	31.7	224 868	84.1	42.2
District 8	5.6	14.5	8.1	16.4	12.7	14.4	13.1	8.0	7.1	39.0	178 255	92.6	45.3
District 9	4.6	14.5	8.7	9.9	11.2	15.0	15.2	11.9	8.9	45.6	164 157	89.9	33.1

1. All persons 3 years old and over enrolled in nursery school through college and graduate or professional school.   2. Persons 25 years old and over.

Table E. Congressional Districts 115th Congress — **Households and Group Quarters**

STATE District	Households, 2015 Number	Average household size	Family households (percent)	Married-couple family (percent)	Female family householder[1]	One person households (percent)	Total in group quarters, 2015	Percent 65 years and over	Persons in correctional institutions	Persons in nursing facilities	Persons in college dormitories	Persons in military quarters
	28	29	30	31	32	33	34	35	36	37	38	39
ILLINOIS—Cont'd												
District 3	244 331	2.93	70.9	53.0	12.3	24.5	11 127	30.2	3 160	3 740	1 890	0
District 4	224 870	3.14	68.0	42.7	17.0	22.7	3 141	34.4	1	1 268	285	0
District 5	300 085	2.42	54.0	42.6	8.3	33.9	11 093	32.7	0	3 882	4 823	0
District 6	262 604	2.73	72.1	60.6	8.3	23.8	9 023	36.8	786	4 034	3 517	0
District 7	293 365	2.37	50.0	27.8	18.2	41.3	26 425	6.3	11 612	3 240	7 992	16
District 8	248 243	2.84	70.0	54.8	10.5	24.9	4 847	45.7	0	2 564	744	0
District 9	288 843	2.42	58.3	46.4	8.6	34.2	22 209	27.4	31	8 543	8 803	0
District 10	246 829	2.81	73.2	57.9	10.9	22.9	19 738	19.5	704	5 665	2 088	12 155
District 11	243 200	2.97	70.6	54.3	11.6	24.3	6 665	33.9	1 085	2 891	1 495	0
District 12	272 726	2.48	62.5	45.3	12.6	32.3	22 684	22.6	10 700	5 209	3 332	307
District 13	283 286	2.35	58.6	43.0	11.8	33.6	40 769	12.5	5 125	5 481	27 454	0
District 14	252 094	2.87	76.3	63.7	9.1	19.2	5 001	33.0	1 364	1 562	158	0
District 15	275 717	2.45	66.2	51.8	10.1	29.6	26 868	23.2	12 642	6 376	3 900	0
District 16	273 120	2.50	66.9	51.9	10.2	27.6	18 630	26.0	6 821	5 619	6 178	0
District 17	280 510	2.38	61.6	43.1	13.6	33.0	24 234	21.2	8 864	5 921	5 835	0
District 18	282 291	2.44	66.1	54.1	8.4	29.0	23 203	27.7	7 248	6 421	6 455	5
INDIANA	2 515 143	2.56	65.0	48.3	12.0	29.1	188 505	20.5	48 694	41 158	75 434	228
District 1	271 870	2.57	66.5	45.1	16.1	28.6	17 161	19.0	7 380	3 116	3 194	0
District 2	264 570	2.66	66.5	50.6	10.8	28.1	21 751	20.0	5 936	4 482	8 659	0
District 3	279 150	2.59	68.2	52.4	11.0	26.9	13 222	33.2	2 229	4 852	3 948	0
District 4	282 271	2.54	65.6	50.5	10.4	27.4	30 886	15.3	7 233	4 934	15 651	0
District 5	296 073	2.52	66.2	52.7	10.3	28.6	15 492	25.1	4 416	4 444	5 257	0
District 6	276 681	2.53	67.6	51.4	11.4	26.1	21 535	23.8	5 096	5 532	8 541	178
District 7	284 356	2.58	52.6	30.7	16.6	39.4	15 097	18.3	3 216	3 152	5 162	0
District 8	280 116	2.47	65.4	50.6	10.7	29.4	28 861	19.4	10 561	5 980	10 509	50
District 9	280 056	2.56	66.2	50.4	10.7	26.8	24 500	17.9	2 627	4 666	14 513	0
IOWA	1 247 249	2.42	63.9	50.4	9.2	29.1	100 975	26.1	13 309	26 871	44 574	3
District 1	308 341	2.42	64.5	51.4	8.9	28.4	26 337	26.1	2 415	7 519	13 934	3
District 2	310 109	2.43	63.2	49.6	8.9	29.4	25 006	21.8	5 185	5 702	11 804	0
District 3	319 597	2.49	65.0	49.8	10.7	28.5	17 223	27.7	3 690	5 218	5 248	0
District 4	309 202	2.36	62.9	50.7	8.4	30.0	32 409	29.1	2 019	8 432	13 588	0
KANSAS	1 111 582	2.55	64.8	50.4	9.9	29.5	79 014	24.4	18 009	20 672	27 754	3 943
District 1	274 819	2.50	63.9	51.1	8.7	29.2	28 826	23.2	5 306	7 084	10 873	3 425
District 2	275 064	2.49	63.9	50.0	9.5	30.2	29 485	17.4	7 436	5 478	12 652	192
District 3	285 639	2.62	67.1	53.0	9.9	27.7	6 200	49.6	1 355	3 598	544	0
District 4	276 060	2.57	64.3	47.5	11.4	31.0	14 503	29.4	3 912	4 512	3 685	326
KENTUCKY	1 716 168	2.50	66.0	48.3	12.7	28.5	128 838	19.2	41 122	26 044	36 340	5 856
District 1	277 984	2.51	66.3	50.9	10.8	29.4	26 297	20.4	7 869	5 548	4 101	3 843
District 2	285 680	2.54	69.3	52.5	11.5	25.8	21 637	21.3	4 501	4 378	7 527	2 013
District 3	300 937	2.42	59.1	39.5	14.8	33.9	14 538	30.7	2 662	4 723	3 307	0
District 4	275 073	2.67	69.3	52.8	11.6	25.7	17 056	21.9	9 255	3 657	1 768	0
District 5	277 933	2.46	68.5	49.5	13.8	27.5	24 950	15.1	12 451	4 570	5 039	0
District 6	298 561	2.44	63.8	45.2	13.5	28.1	24 360	12.1	4 384	3 168	14 598	0
LOUISIANA	1 737 908	2.61	63.8	43.0	15.9	30.7	128 384	16.7	60 804	24 524	24 891	2 861
District 1	302 994	2.61	65.7	47.5	13.6	28.5	13 874	24.4	1 182	2 957	5 469	57
District 2	296 445	2.60	57.2	31.0	20.4	36.8	19 564	12.0	11 687	3 058	4 007	138
District 3	295 018	2.61	65.8	46.1	15.3	28.1	13 215	26.9	4 329	4 273	2 935	0
District 4	284 937	2.58	64.2	43.9	15.6	31.6	22 631	18.4	13 410	5 425	2 390	2 524
District 5	268 071	2.60	64.8	41.8	18.3	30.9	48 011	11.6	28 559	5 925	6 333	142
District 6	290 443	2.67	65.1	47.4	12.3	28.3	11 089	23.4	1 637	2 886	3 757	0
MAINE	545 226	2.37	62.9	48.5	9.8	29.6	35 797	22.5	3 679	7 878	17 251	131
District 1	275 690	2.37	62.5	48.4	10.0	29.8	17 250	24.5	2 708	4 128	7 433	119
District 2	269 536	2.37	63.3	48.6	9.7	29.4	18 547	20.4	971	3 750	9 818	12
MARYLAND	2 177 934	2.69	66.8	47.9	14.0	27.0	140 256	19.4	35 832	28 001	48 141	7 534
District 1	270 237	2.62	70.3	54.5	10.8	23.8	18 249	20.6	5 648	3 465	5 803	7
District 2	281 300	2.64	65.1	43.3	15.9	28.5	20 136	17.1	7 411	3 533	3 971	2 113
District 3	286 542	2.58	62.5	46.3	11.9	29.4	18 567	19.9	583	3 399	6 910	4 515
District 4	258 921	2.86	67.0	42.4	17.7	27.7	5 061	42.2	1 149	2 597	410	115
District 5	257 965	2.87	71.9	53.1	14.8	22.8	21 293	11.8	1 111	2 598	14 602	387
District 6	271 377	2.73	71.0	54.2	12.2	23.4	21 661	17.6	12 569	3 716	2 766	93
District 7	270 399	2.61	60.2	35.9	19.6	32.7	24 178	14.8	6 305	4 677	10 895	0
District 8	281 193	2.67	66.9	53.4	9.3	27.1	11 111	37.8	1 056	4 016	2 784	304
MASSACHUSETTS	2 559 951	2.56	63.0	46.4	12.5	28.8	252 083	17.7	24 683	43 833	135 773	498
District 1	284 740	2.50	63.1	43.3	14.6	30.1	25 466	20.9	1 897	5 855	13 226	0
District 2	275 880	2.54	62.7	45.9	13.0	28.5	44 435	13.9	1 576	5 572	26 184	0
District 3	268 558	2.74	68.6	49.8	14.2	25.2	19 001	19.7	6 829	3 823	4 944	0
District 4	273 403	2.65	68.8	54.7	10.9	24.1	27 111	19.7	2 520	4 914	15 480	0
District 5	291 531	2.53	63.5	51.2	8.6	28.5	28 303	16.5	771	4 440	18 907	25
District 6	282 437	2.63	67.5	53.2	10.6	26.8	19 567	28.9	2 014	4 919	5 965	113
District 7	290 611	2.49	50.3	28.1	16.6	34.7	55 372	4.7	1 895	2 728	42 309	73
District 8	295 219	2.53	59.8	44.4	11.7	31.1	17 043	35.8	3 879	6 322	3 522	261
District 9	297 572	2.43	63.7	48.0	12.1	29.8	15 785	30.2	3 302	5 260	5 236	26

1. No spouse present.

Table E. Congressional Districts 115th Congress — **Housing and Money Income**

STATE District		Housing units, 2015					Money income, 2015		
		Occupied units						Households	
			Owner-occupied			Renter-occupied			
	Total	Occupied units as a percent of all units	Owner-occupied units as a percent of occupied units	Median value[1] (dollars)	Percent valued at $500,000 or more	Median rent[2]	Per capita income (dollars)	Median income (dollars)	Percent with income of $100,000 or more
	40	41	42	43	44	45	46	47	48
ILLINOIS—Cont'd									
District 3	259 477	94.2	72.9	213 600	6.6	940	28 797	61 772	28.6
District 4	250 186	89.9	45.0	213 300	5.5	922	21 166	46 805	17.4
District 5	324 657	92.4	54.8	337 500	26.6	1 209	46 576	76 963	38.4
District 6	277 200	94.7	78.6	311 200	20.2	1 185	44 496	93 474	47.5
District 7	342 523	85.6	41.4	259 700	19.2	1 055	37 439	51 346	27.8
District 8	264 729	93.8	65.7	213 800	4.4	1 124	29 766	67 079	29.1
District 9	313 969	92.0	59.1	329 000	22.6	1 035	41 421	66 202	33.6
District 10	266 828	92.5	68.5	263 000	22.3	1 111	40 838	77 031	38.7
District 11	260 299	93.4	69.2	197 600	6.0	1 138	30 516	67 065	32.4
District 12	320 788	85.0	68.0	101 300	1.6	722	25 957	46 803	17.7
District 13	320 899	88.3	64.8	122 000	2.2	774	27 950	50 211	19.7
District 14	268 473	93.9	80.1	242 400	7.4	1 129	37 702	86 050	42.2
District 15	313 756	87.9	73.4	98 800	1.4	628	25 275	49 136	17.3
District 16	299 812	91.1	72.2	135 800	2.1	777	27 964	56 180	22.0
District 17	319 916	87.7	68.4	99 000	1.4	648	24 348	45 731	14.0
District 18	311 289	90.7	75.3	145 300	2.1	724	32 360	61 544	25.9
INDIANA	2 841 450	88.5	68.2	131 000	2.9	758	26 396	50 532	18.9
District 1	304 814	89.2	70.1	147 100	2.8	841	26 484	52 256	21.0
District 2	307 854	85.9	70.6	122 000	2.2	705	24 101	48 654	15.7
District 3	315 202	88.6	71.7	123 600	2.8	697	25 849	50 690	16.6
District 4	311 328	90.7	68.6	130 700	1.7	753	26 679	54 897	20.7
District 5	324 250	91.3	71.2	179 000	7.6	867	36 845	65 165	31.2
District 6	313 400	88.3	73.0	122 000	2.2	715	25 047	50 588	17.0
District 7	331 483	85.8	50.3	107 400	2.2	784	21 112	37 939	11.3
District 8	317 723	88.2	69.7	112 600	1.8	670	24 708	47 134	15.4
District 9	315 396	88.8	68.8	141 100	2.7	777	26 400	52 041	20.0
IOWA	1 369 379	91.1	70.7	136 100	2.8	718	28 628	54 736	20.3
District 1	338 219	91.2	73.6	141 700	2.8	663	28 738	55 645	20.7
District 2	340 003	91.2	70.0	132 300	2.6	730	27 587	52 166	19.0
District 3	343 512	93.0	68.8	154 200	3.6	793	31 147	59 433	24.2
District 4	347 645	88.9	70.4	113 500	2.4	661	26 891	51 259	17.3
KANSAS	1 253 889	88.7	66.4	141 200	3.3	782	28 852	53 906	22.2
District 1	317 901	86.4	66.2	110 200	1.5	725	24 977	48 559	16.0
District 2	316 407	86.9	65.9	126 400	1.6	723	26 024	50 087	17.7
District 3	307 551	92.9	67.5	202 200	7.9	921	37 650	71 742	34.7
District 4	312 030	88.5	66.0	123 000	2.1	741	26 301	51 427	19.8
KENTUCKY	1 957 133	87.7	66.3	130 000	3.2	702	25 082	45 215	16.6
District 1	333 545	83.3	69.1	105 800	2.1	630	22 333	40 358	12.8
District 2	322 229	88.7	68.7	132 500	2.3	682	23 898	46 401	15.3
District 3	335 297	89.8	60.1	151 900	4.3	789	29 224	50 450	19.8
District 4	307 227	89.5	70.4	158 100	4.8	764	28 964	55 744	24.1
District 5	327 064	85.0	71.6	79 000	1.4	558	18 045	31 339	8.5
District 6	331 771	90.0	59.1	151 400	4.1	741	27 554	49 531	18.6
LOUISIANA	2 024 737	85.8	64.6	155 600	4.2	800	25 456	45 727	19.6
District 1	337 321	89.8	67.5	192 200	6.6	896	29 863	54 677	24.4
District 2	355 546	83.4	52.8	155 900	4.8	871	22 328	37 856	14.4
District 3	332 809	88.6	68.2	138 600	3.7	733	26 527	46 766	20.6
District 4	344 708	82.7	62.9	124 800	2.4	731	22 645	40 689	15.1
District 5	327 548	81.8	62.9	110 300	2.1	653	20 362	35 321	13.7
District 6	326 805	88.9	73.1	182 300	5.0	915	30 570	60 440	28.6
MAINE	729 392	74.8	71.0	180 300	5.5	792	28 437	51 494	18.9
District 1	351 397	78.5	70.0	231 900	8.6	889	32 447	59 452	23.6
District 2	377 995	71.3	72.1	138 100	2.5	701	24 337	44 560	14.1
MARYLAND	2 434 465	89.5	65.9	299 800	18.8	1 278	37 522	75 847	37.1
District 1	336 720	80.3	74.7	273 400	10.9	1 014	33 778	69 824	32.5
District 2	309 159	91.0	60.3	228 100	6.0	1 188	30 804	62 278	27.6
District 3	308 871	92.8	65.0	316 700	20.8	1 394	41 240	81 231	40.2
District 4	281 337	92.0	62.1	295 100	15.3	1 357	35 788	78 412	37.1
District 5	280 728	91.9	76.2	303 800	12.3	1 511	38 091	91 820	45.5
District 6	297 665	91.2	68.4	299 100	24.1	1 259	37 480	73 641	37.6
District 7	323 901	83.5	55.1	261 100	23.0	1 044	33 538	59 026	28.9
District 8	296 084	95.0	66.3	431 600	38.1	1 622	49 101	95 314	47.9
MASSACHUSETTS	2 845 805	90.0	61.7	352 100	25.3	1 164	38 130	70 628	35.5
District 1	318 947	89.3	64.2	210 200	5.1	868	29 193	53 918	23.6
District 2	301 526	91.5	62.9	260 800	8.8	1 013	32 123	62 448	29.5
District 3	288 408	93.1	63.8	321 900	20.0	1 085	35 516	72 570	37.1
District 4	288 163	94.9	70.8	381 100	34.3	1 221	46 817	90 913	45.9
District 5	309 691	94.1	60.3	475 900	45.3	1 472	46 538	86 183	43.4
District 6	302 576	93.3	70.0	405 200	31.4	1 195	40 554	80 638	41.0
District 7	315 199	92.2	33.2	426 500	36.4	1 411	34 207	56 719	29.8
District 8	314 864	93.8	60.6	390 900	28.9	1 329	41 668	79 789	39.5
District 9	406 431	73.2	70.4	343 000	22.0	927	36 190	63 532	30.4

1. Specified owner-occupied units; $1,000,000 represents $1,000,000 or more. 2. Specified renter-occupied units.

STATE District	Poverty, 2015			Civilian labor force, 2015			Civilian employment,[2] 2015					Social Security beneficiaries, December 2015		
					Unemployment			Percent						
	Persons below poverty level (percent)	Families below poverty level (percent)	Percent of households receiving food stamps in past 12 months	Total	Total	Rate[1]	Total	Manage-ment, business, science and arts occupa-tions	Service, sales, and office	Con-struction and production	Persons under age 65 with no health insurance, 2015 (percent)	Number	Rate[3]	Supple-mental Security Income recipients, December 2015
	49	50	51	52	53	54	55	56	57	58	59	60	61	62
ILLINOIS—Cont'd														
District 3	11.0	8.0	12.1	365 828	24 566	6.7	341 262	31.2	43.4	25.4	10.1	115 252	158.4	12 626
District 4	20.5	17.6	21.6	370 157	26 354	7.1	343 803	25.8	45.8	28.4	19.5	75 650	106.8	19 066
District 5	9.2	6.5	7.4	443 693	20 508	4.6	423 185	50.0	36.3	13.8	7.3	96 493	131.1	12 430
District 6	6.5	4.9	4.7	396 909	17 629	4.4	379 280	48.0	37.9	14.1	5.3	111 455	153.4	4 399
District 7	23.3	17.7	22.0	374 433	39 016	10.4	335 417	46.1	39.9	13.9	9.1	99 269	137.6	34 746
District 8	8.3	6.5	9.3	402 629	21 844	5.4	380 785	33.6	43.2	23.2	10.0	102 489	144.3	8 691
District 9	13.0	8.4	10.6	381 737	20 871	5.5	360 866	48.6	37.9	13.4	8.1	122 339	169.4	19 413
District 10	10.2	8.1	10.2	369 864	20 685	5.6	349 179	41.8	39.9	18.3	9.9	107 317	150.3	9 657
District 11	11.5	8.7	11.9	390 717	20 761	5.3	369 956	35.5	41.4	23.1	8.8	96 897	132.8	8 275
District 12	16.5	11.6	16.3	333 006	26 937	8.1	306 069	33.9	41.7	24.4	6.4	145 114	207.5	20 528
District 13	18.6	10.9	13.9	349 429	21 576	6.2	327 853	39.4	40.9	19.6	5.4	135 896	192.3	15 494
District 14	6.3	4.6	6.0	397 208	16 543	4.2	380 665	41.0	39.2	19.8	4.8	110 049	151.1	4 488
District 15	13.6	9.9	14.1	336 904	19 648	5.8	317 256	29.6	40.4	30.0	5.9	155 173	220.5	14 390
District 16	12.4	8.6	12.8	357 323	25 361	7.1	331 962	30.7	40.9	28.4	5.9	144 857	206.6	8 458
District 17	16.0	11.4	18.1	340 428	26 967	7.9	313 461	26.4	44.0	29.6	6.4	154 673	223.7	18 669
District 18	9.7	6.4	9.1	363 241	17 506	4.8	345 735	40.0	40.3	19.8	4.1	146 673	205.7	8 354
INDIANA	14.5	10.2	11.5	3 312 603	192 637	5.8	3 119 966	32.9	39.3	27.8	11.2	1 301 948	196.7	128 781
District 1	15.8	12.2	15.0	344 225	27 986	8.1	316 239	31.1	40.8	28.2	10.1	143 422	200.2	16 407
District 2	14.8	10.5	11.4	346 985	18 502	5.3	328 483	30.1	36.7	33.2	13.0	144 688	199.5	13 290
District 3	12.2	8.1	9.7	368 991	17 514	4.7	351 477	30.3	37.0	32.7	13.6	144 344	196.2	12 889
District 4	12.3	7.8	9.3	384 117	18 836	4.9	365 281	33.2	37.3	29.5	10.2	141 221	188.9	10 109
District 5	9.2	6.9	7.3	409 137	17 608	4.3	391 529	45.0	39.2	15.8	8.3	134 230	176.6	9 845
District 6	14.1	10.1	11.0	355 407	19 279	5.4	336 128	29.9	39.1	31.0	10.2	163 910	227.2	14 802
District 7	23.8	18.0	19.4	378 374	34 587	9.1	343 787	29.1	45.0	25.8	14.5	121 818	162.5	24 020
District 8	15.3	11.2	12.3	352 129	18 020	5.1	334 109	29.7	39.0	31.3	9.9	157 790	218.9	14 946
District 9	13.5	8.7	8.6	373 238	20 305	5.4	352 933	35.2	39.9	24.9	10.3	150 525	202.9	12 473
IOWA	12.2	7.7	11.3	1 669 321	69 428	4.2	1 599 893	34.4	39.0	26.6	5.9	622 906	199.4	51 059
District 1	11.1	6.7	10.0	414 572	14 523	3.5	400 049	33.6	38.8	27.6	6.0	161 147	208.8	12 740
District 2	13.6	8.6	12.0	409 660	19 437	4.7	390 223	33.2	38.9	27.9	6.3	156 320	200.8	15 109
District 3	11.4	7.7	13.1	443 132	20 650	4.7	422 482	37.6	40.0	22.5	5.5	141 569	174.2	13 117
District 4	12.7	7.7	10.0	401 957	14 818	3.7	387 139	33.1	38.2	28.7	5.9	163 870	215.3	10 093
KANSAS	13.0	8.4	8.5	1 486 201	69 132	4.7	1 417 069	37.3	39.1	23.6	10.6	528 174	181.4	48 360
District 1	13.7	8.9	7.7	359 365	17 405	4.8	341 960	32.9	38.7	28.3	11.0	133 828	187.1	9 868
District 2	16.0	9.7	9.9	355 789	18 282	5.1	337 507	36.2	39.0	24.8	8.8	146 280	204.4	15 011
District 3	8.8	5.9	6.2	411 205	17 167	4.2	394 038	44.9	38.7	16.4	8.7	113 359	150.1	9 273
District 4	13.9	9.4	10.1	359 842	16 278	4.5	343 564	34.1	39.9	26.0	14.1	134 707	185.8	14 208
KENTUCKY	18.5	14.0	16.5	2 062 779	133 812	6.5	1 928 967	33.2	40.5	26.3	7.0	963 497	217.7	184 103
District 1	18.6	13.0	16.2	310 987	19 506	6.3	291 481	28.1	39.7	32.2	8.2	177 139	244.8	28 995
District 2	16.3	11.9	15.7	353 488	23 275	6.6	330 213	28.4	39.8	31.8	6.2	160 973	215.3	24 199
District 3	15.4	10.8	14.4	388 662	23 751	6.1	364 911	38.3	39.6	22.0	6.1	144 912	195.1	25 343
District 4	13.5	10.0	12.0	371 365	19 269	5.2	352 096	36.7	39.7	23.7	7.0	141 783	188.9	18 815
District 5	28.9	24.0	26.9	254 377	25 520	10.0	228 857	29.3	42.7	28.0	6.7	194 152	274.4	62 878
District 6	19.1	14.2	14.3	383 900	22 491	5.9	361 409	35.8	41.8	22.4	7.9	144 538	191.9	23 873
LOUISIANA	19.6	14.7	14.9	2 193 370	155 558	7.1	2 037 812	33.7	42.7	23.6	13.8	868 017	185.8	178 954
District 1	15.6	12.0	10.6	403 859	23 412	5.8	380 447	36.5	43.0	20.5	13.3	149 094	184.9	19 276
District 2	23.9	19.2	20.0	386 993	35 872	9.3	351 121	31.6	44.7	23.7	15.1	138 331	174.8	41 917
District 3	18.7	13.9	13.5	378 836	27 316	7.2	351 520	31.7	42.8	25.6	13.9	143 951	184.0	25 644
District 4	22.1	16.3	17.0	316 400	23 483	7.4	292 917	31.3	42.1	26.6	15.0	150 830	198.7	32 769
District 5	24.7	19.9	18.5	306 195	25 235	8.2	280 960	30.3	45.3	24.4	16.5	155 245	208.1	39 914
District 6	13.3	8.0	10.2	401 087	20 240	5.0	380 847	38.9	39.1	22.0	9.5	130 566	166.1	19 434
MAINE	13.4	8.9	15.8	685 216	36 802	5.4	648 414	36.5	41.5	21.9	10.3	329 559	247.9	37 328
District 1	10.3	7.0	12.3	363 646	16 100	4.4	347 546	39.6	41.4	19.1	9.4	160 373	238.6	14 769
District 2	16.4	10.8	19.5	321 570	20 702	6.4	300 868	33.0	41.8	25.2	11.1	169 186	257.4	22 559
MARYLAND	9.7	6.7	11.2	3 207 268	175 802	5.5	3 031 466	44.7	39.5	15.8	7.5	952 251	158.5	120 254
District 1	9.4	6.2	11.0	376 062	19 706	5.2	356 356	38.5	41.7	19.7	4.9	154 528	213.0	11 531
District 2	11.6	8.1	13.9	396 402	22 746	5.7	373 656	40.1	42.9	17.0	7.4	122 879	161.0	17 253
District 3	7.9	5.4	8.8	417 663	22 645	5.4	395 018	50.4	36.6	13.0	6.9	114 932	151.5	16 346
District 4	8.8	6.3	10.2	418 903	23 474	5.6	395 429	38.4	43.3	18.4	11.6	99 949	134.0	11 193
District 5	6.7	5.0	8.6	413 010	19 309	4.7	393 701	43.9	39.8	16.3	6.1	105 427	138.6	9 467
District 6	9.2	6.3	11.0	396 208	17 885	4.5	378 323	46.0	38.2	15.9	7.7	115 980	152.2	13 652
District 7	16.7	11.6	19.8	360 279	30 347	8.4	329 932	45.4	40.6	14.0	7.0	126 188	173.1	32 876
District 8	7.9	5.4	6.1	428 741	19 690	4.6	409 051	53.7	33.9	12.4	8.0	112 368	147.5	7 936
MASSACHUSETTS	11.5	7.9	12.2	3 739 683	217 480	5.8	3 522 203	44.9	39.6	15.5	3.3	1 236 248	182.0	188 207
District 1	14.9	11.2	18.0	380 708	26 176	6.9	354 532	35.1	45.4	19.5	3.7	164 216	223.1	37 288
District 2	13.8	8.5	12.6	402 443	26 289	6.5	376 154	42.6	40.4	17.0	2.5	134 266	180.3	20 414
District 3	11.3	7.7	12.8	403 902	23 798	5.9	380 104	43.0	38.9	18.1	3.5	129 133	171.2	24 277
District 4	7.0	4.4	7.6	406 561	21 741	5.3	384 820	52.0	34.4	13.6	2.4	130 568	174.0	11 259
District 5	7.8	5.0	7.0	437 782	17 010	3.9	420 772	54.0	34.5	11.4	3.1	120 769	157.7	11 834
District 6	8.5	6.1	10.3	418 130	21 134	5.1	396 996	45.9	39.4	14.7	2.7	145 885	191.7	14 120
District 7	19.0	15.6	18.9	462 392	31 113	6.7	431 279	45.7	41.6	12.7	5.1	91 204	117.3	34 007
District 8	10.6	7.4	10.5	439 625	24 923	5.7	414 702	47.8	38.8	13.4	2.2	134 801	176.3	16 116
District 9	10.7	7.6	12.0	388 140	25 296	6.5	362 844	35.4	44.0	20.6	3.9	185 406	250.7	18 892

1. Percent of civilian labor force.   2. Persons 16 years old and over.   3. Per 1,000 resident population estimated in the 2014 American Community Survey.

Table E. Congressional Districts 115th Congress — **Agriculture**

STATE District	Agriculture, 2012									
	Land in farms				Value of products sold				Government payments	
	Number of farms	Acres	Average size of farm (acres)	Irrigated land (acres)	Total ($1,000)	Average per farm (dollars)	Percent from crops	Percent from livestock and poultry products	Total ($1,000)	Average per farm receiving payments (dollars)
	63	64	65	66	67	68	69	70	71	72
ILLINOIS—Cont'd										
District 3	97	13 188	136	326	8 734	90 045	0.0	0.0	212	8 140
District 4	X	X	X	X	X	X	X	X	X	X
District 5	21	349	17	D	D	D	D	D	D	D
District 6	187	17 561	94	462	30 306	162 064	95.9	4.1	420	9 765
District 7	X	X	X	X	X	X	X	X	X	X
District 8	21	4 457	212	D	3 655	174 060	99.7	0.3	D	D
District 9	X	X	X	X	X	X	X	X	X	X
District 10	141	8 223	58	407	13 357	94 727	95.6	4.4	126	8 421
District 11	131	31 383	240	D	23 965	182 943	95.8	4.2	559	9 172
District 12	6 959	1 905 115	274	15 491	688 176	98 890	85.7	14.3	29 651	6 488
District 13	7 760	2 974 971	383	13 854	1 842 362	237 418	88.1	11.9	53 882	9 103
District 14	2 132	625 197	293	18 015	560 569	262 931	83.2	16.8	13 128	13 274
District 15	22 203	7 559 605	340	102 777	3 613 564	162 751	78.7	21.3	155 644	8 968
District 16	10 468	4 292 328	410	48 782	3 466 237	331 127	84.7	15.3	92 879	11 381
District 17	9 730	3 458 529	355	118 763	2 861 291	294 069	75.5	24.5	85 811	11 696
District 18	13 826	5 528 495	400	187 608	3 658 219	264 590	84.0	16.0	112 453	10 343
INDIANA	58 695	14 720 396	251	437 445	11 210 818	191 001	67.2	32.8	267 287	8 331
District 1	1 212	348 046	287	38 398	300 726	248 123	D	D	6 174	9 572
District 2	7 547	1 747 268	232	183 555	1 685 428	223 324	61.1	38.9	32 668	8 128
District 3	11 801	1 957 311	166	53 255	1 877 293	159 079	54.8	45.2	38 957	6 794
District 4	8 570	3 273 095	382	47 054	2 697 593	314 772	72.4	27.6	59 486	10 747
District 5	2 682	803 313	300	5 904	690 258	257 367	89.1	10.9	13 671	8 507
District 6	10 531	2 532 278	240	20 206	1 686 224	160 120	69.8	30.2	50 568	8 006
District 7	185	17 001	92	163	26 173	141 475	D	D	201	6 708
District 8	9 529	2 812 457	295	79 188	1 677 310	176 022	65.2	34.8	45 753	8 707
District 9	6 638	1 229 627	185	9 722	569 814	85 841	61.2	38.8	19 809	6 733
IOWA	88 637	30 622 731	345	171 656	30 821 532	347 728	56.3	43.7	782 290	11 262
District 1	22 478	6 620 256	295	D	6 557 733	291 740	57.8	42.2	197 364	10 957
District 2	20 546	5 960 872	290	24 598	4 317 514	210 139	60.7	39.3	168 748	11 138
District 3	12 191	4 565 364	374	D	2 960 578	242 849	69.2	30.8	94 951	10 699
District 4	33 422	13 476 239	403	125 421	16 980 000	508 219	52.5	47.6	321 228	11 713
KANSAS	61 773	46 137 295	747	2 881 292	18 460 564	298 845	37.8	62.2	442 090	10 426
District 1	30 489	30 369 854	996	2 320 029	14 300 000	469 295	32.3	67.8	306 513	12 602
District 2	19 808	7 356 986	371	50 780	1 835 532	92 666	60.9	39.1	69 467	6 390
District 3	1 013	195 215	193	2 877	47 298	46 691	73.0	27.0	1 567	5 458
District 4	10 463	8 215 240	785	507 606	2 269 393	216 897	53.7	46.3	64 543	9 324
KENTUCKY	77 064	13 049 347	169	73 573	5 067 334	65 755	45.0	55.0	169 821	5 087
District 1	22 897	4 970 288	217	46 542	2 738 196	119 588	47.8	52.2	88 556	6 975
District 2	19 734	3 055 139	155	14 508	1 059 346	53 681	48.6	51.4	44 239	5 052
District 3	223	13 572	61	101	5 973	26 784	82.2	17.8	184	4 611
District 4	11 411	1 595 512	140	6 248	311 349	27 285	62.8	37.2	13 820	3 421
District 5	11 144	1 522 271	137	1 494	277 300	24 883	32.6	67.4	8 668	2 468
District 6	11 655	1 892 565	162	4 680	675 171	57 930	24.4	75.6	14 353	3 310
LOUISIANA	28 093	7 900 864	281	1 092 881	3 809 401	135 600	73.1	26.9	138 164	14 625
District 1	1 386	376 150	271	1 242	101 752	73 414	48.0	52.0	291	4 037
District 2	404	234 199	580	1 175	103 689	256 656	95.7	4.3	277	6 915
District 3	5 363	1 709 327	319	246 622	646 950	120 632	83.8	16.2	23 708	11 824
District 4	7 545	1 535 386	203	104 062	737 447	97 740	29.8	70.2	19 192	11 980
District 5	11 106	3 503 066	315	730 933	1 891 903	170 350	84.7	15.3	90 840	16 970
District 6	2 289	542 736	237	8 847	327 660	143 146	83.0	17.0	3 857	10 285
MAINE	8 173	1 454 104	178	30 887	763 062	93 364	62.1	37.9	10 162	7 629
District 1	2 650	234 530	89	2 884	91 532	34 540	66.5	33.5	1 525	6 809
District 2	5 523	1 219 574	221	28 003	671 531	121 588	61.5	38.5	8 637	7 795
MARYLAND	12 256	2 030 745	166	104 910	2 271 397	185 329	46.3	53.7	36 024	7 784
District 1	5 451	1 180 832	217	97 880	1 731 665	317 678	41.3	58.7	25 698	8 696
District 2	115	7 376	64	182	5 909	51 381	89.3	10.7	304	17 878
District 3	204	20 466	100	112	27 937	136 945	86.8	13.2	118	7 345
District 4	114	7 095	62	628	11 343	99 500	98.2	1.8	38	2 916
District 5	1 850	198 919	108	1 755	70 566	38 144	87.3	12.7	2 074	5 171
District 6	2 360	341 624	145	1 644	199 544	84 552	49.6	50.4	3 123	5 385
District 7	604	69 173	115	305	53 048	87 827	D	D	673	5 342
District 8	1 558	205 260	132	2 404	171 386	110 004	D	D	3 997	7 686
MASSACHUSETTS	7 755	523 517	68	23 433	492 211	63 470	77.8	22.2	8 124	10 415
District 1	2 043	189 425	93	1 513	72 106	35 294	56.3	43.7	2 293	10 059
District 2	1 832	142 899	78	3 554	125 634	68 578	75.5	24.5	1 671	8 033
District 3	936	37 576	40	1 304	40 736	43 522	71.8	28.2	565	8 972
District 4	750	33 528	45	2 149	41 671	55 562	88.0	12.0	467	6 578
District 5	196	6 332	32	700	43 367	221 262	99.3	0.7	D	D
District 6	464	18 673	40	464	20 476	44 129	74.9	25.1	174	9 141
District 7	23	282	12	30	164	7 113	86.0	13.4	D	D
District 8	162	5 471	34	612	9 196	56 763	66.6	33.4	120	7 031
District 9	1 349	89 331	66	13 107	138 861	102 936	84.1	15.9	2 740	18 269

Table E. Congressional Districts 115th Congress — Nonfarm Employment and Payroll

Private nonfarm employment and payroll, 2015

STATE District	Number of establishments	Employment Total	Percent by selected industries Manufacturing	Construction	Wholesale trade	Retail trade	Health care and social assistance	Finance and Insurance	Real estate and rental and leasing	Professional, scientific, and technical services	Information	Annual payroll Total (mil dol)	Average per employee dollars
	73	74	75	76	77	78	79	80	81	82	83	84	85
ILLINOIS—Cont'd													
District 3	15 412	223 309	12.3	5.6	4.9	13.8	14.6	2.6	1.2	4.7	0.9	9 985	44 716
District 4	10 841	139 687	14.0	3.3	8.0	16.6	15.5	2.6	1.1	3.2	1.0	5 421	38 811
District 5	23 168	379 412	7.7	4.0	5.2	10.8	13.0	3.5	2.4	5.4	2.2	19 227	50 677
District 6	25 085	378 661	9.1	4.2	6.4	12.3	13.0	7.3	1.4	7.6	2.6	20 966	55 369
District 7	29 796	798 226	2.7	1.5	2.7	4.9	13.0	16.1	2.0	17.8	5.4	64 905	81 312
District 8	23 671	436 313	12.8	5.3	11.3	10.1	8.0	4.6	1.6	6.9	2.9	24 787	56 811
District 9	20 371	284 880	6.6	2.5	4.8	12.2	24.5	2.8	1.9	6.0	2.1	14 689	51 560
District 10	21 355	364 038	10.7	3.1	12.1	10.5	12.2	6.7	1.1	11.4	1.2	28 173	77 391
District 11	16 205	283 140	9.9	3.6	7.8	14.8	13.4	3.1	1.3	4.8	2.5	13 141	46 411
District 12	14 758	218 417	12.2	4.7	3.5	16.0	19.5	3.1	1.1	4.5	1.1	8 388	38 406
District 13	15 605	243 623	7.2	4.6	4.1	14.2	22.3	4.3	1.7	4.3	2.4	9 418	38 658
District 14	17 384	188 940	14.6	6.7	5.9	17.1	11.7	2.9	1.1	5.4	1.1	8 009	42 387
District 15	15 421	201 170	19.7	4.3	5.5	13.4	18.3	3.6	1.0	2.3	1.3	7 413	36 851
District 16	15 219	220 945	19.9	3.5	4.7	14.9	15.5	3.5	1.1	3.5	1.2	9 336	42 253
District 17	14 979	272 058	15.9	3.2	3.9	11.3	18.3	3.4	0.8	3.8	1.4	13 552	49 814
District 18	16 103	258 150	10.9	4.3	6.4	15.8	13.8	12.2	0.9	3.4	1.3	10 998	42 605
INDIANA	145 116	2 660 503	18.4	4.4	4.9	11.9	15.7	3.7	1.2	4.2	1.6	113 315	42 592
District 1	14 731	242 092	15.6	5.7	3.4	15.1	18.6	2.2	1.2	3.3	1.0	10 304	42 561
District 2	15 628	311 487	32.7	3.3	4.8	10.7	13.0	2.5	0.9	2.5	1.2	12 570	40 355
District 3	17 355	316 415	27.4	3.8	5.4	11.7	15.5	3.6	1.0	2.6	1.4	13 012	41 122
District 4	14 927	247 952	22.8	4.4	4.0	14.8	14.7	2.2	1.0	2.5	1.0	9 550	38 515
District 5	21 349	376 043	6.3	4.1	4.7	11.7	16.4	7.3	1.8	8.1	2.7	17 788	47 303
District 6	14 223	233 506	22.4	3.8	3.1	12.7	17.0	3.2	0.8	3.6	0.9	9 092	38 936
District 7	15 002	343 470	9.1	5.2	5.6	8.5	17.0	4.2	1.9	7.0	2.9	17 124	49 855
District 8	16 181	276 241	20.1	5.8	4.7	12.9	17.4	3.1	1.0	3.2	1.4	11 336	41 037
District 9	15 130	232 889	18.4	5.0	3.7	15.3	17.0	3.0	1.2	3.2	1.3	8 529	36 624
IOWA	80 952	1 338 418	15.8	4.8	5.1	13.8	16.4	7.0	1.0	4.1	2.3	55 080	41 153
District 1	19 577	349 195	18.5	4.4	4.6	13.4	16.2	6.2	0.8	4.1	2.3	14 205	40 678
District 2	18 806	313 490	20.0	4.9	4.0	14.3	18.0	3.2	0.9	3.7	2.0	12 299	39 234
District 3	20 172	367 959	8.3	4.8	5.1	13.8	14.7	13.7	1.3	5.2	2.8	17 044	46 321
District 4	22 041	286 050	18.8	5.4	6.8	14.7	18.3	3.7	0.8	3.1	2.0	10 598	37 049
KANSAS	74 526	1 189 876	14.0	5.3	5.3	12.6	16.3	5.1	1.3	5.4	2.9	51 260	43 080
District 1	20 138	244 531	17.0	4.9	5.8	15.1	18.1	3.9	1.0	3.1	1.8	8 350	34 146
District 2	15 914	233 966	13.9	6.0	3.1	13.4	20.8	4.6	1.1	4.1	2.9	8 557	36 573
District 3	21 056	399 557	8.6	5.1	6.9	11.2	13.4	7.4	1.5	8.0	4.5	20 946	52 423
District 4	16 974	287 707	20.3	5.9	4.1	12.9	15.7	3.4	1.3	4.3	1.8	12 475	43 360
KENTUCKY	91 845	1 579 477	14.7	4.2	4.6	13.1	16.0	4.7	1.1	4.6	2.3	63 741	40 356
District 1	14 376	217 235	23.2	4.0	3.7	14.5	15.9	3.5	0.9	2.7	1.2	7 863	36 197
District 2	14 625	229 605	19.7	4.5	2.9	14.0	16.3	3.7	1.1	3.1	2.9	8 281	36 064
District 3	19 354	412 801	10.4	4.1	4.9	10.6	15.7	7.0	1.3	5.6	2.1	19 881	48 160
District 4	14 234	240 159	14.3	4.1	5.9	13.4	14.0	5.3	1.2	3.7	1.2	10 017	41 710
District 5	11 848	161 299	10.5	2.8	3.5	18.1	22.0	3.5	0.9	3.6	4.6	5 221	32 370
District 6	16 951	280 770	15.0	5.0	4.8	13.9	16.6	3.0	1.2	6.1	2.8	11 526	41 050
LOUISIANA	105 575	1 724 973	7.3	8.0	4.5	13.8	16.8	3.7	1.8	6.1	1.5	76 685	44 456
District 1	21 006	320 713	5.8	5.9	5.4	14.8	17.4	4.5	2.2	5.2	1.4	14 842	46 277
District 2	15 688	294 953	8.9	5.6	3.6	10.6	12.5	3.6	1.6	7.5	1.3	14 734	49 955
District 3	19 853	301 403	9.5	6.4	5.6	14.1	16.8	2.7	3.0	5.8	1.3	13 413	44 501
District 4	15 041	218 177	8.4	6.4	4.6	15.6	21.0	3.2	1.6	3.9	1.6	8 272	37 912
District 5	15 228	209 785	8.1	5.0	4.0	16.6	26.3	4.2	1.4	3.7	2.9	7 404	35 293
District 6	18 252	325 892	5.1	17.9	4.2	14.8	13.8	4.1	1.4	7.3	1.4	15 070	46 243
MAINE	40 801	500 549	10.1	4.7	3.5	16.4	21.9	5.4	1.3	4.6	2.2	20 413	40 782
District 1	23 151	292 515	9.0	4.6	3.5	15.7	21.6	5.8	1.4	5.2	2.3	12 616	43 128
District 2	17 382	205 095	11.7	4.9	3.3	17.8	22.6	4.5	1.1	3.4	2.2	7 584	36 977
MARYLAND	137 204	2 239 817	4.4	6.4	3.9	13.0	16.4	4.5	2.0	12.2	2.3	118 497	52 905
District 1	17 772	194 743	9.1	7.1	3.8	17.6	18.0	2.9	1.4	4.4	1.1	7 579	38 919
District 2	16 161	329 457	8.5	6.7	6.9	13.9	11.3	4.1	1.8	12.1	1.9	17 709	53 752
District 3	20 907	375 435	3.1	5.1	4.4	11.7	15.9	4.3	2.0	12.5	3.2	20 665	55 043
District 4	12 556	191 803	2.2	8.5	4.3	16.4	14.8	2.5	2.6	9.8	2.0	8 359	43 582
District 5	14 023	207 028	2.1	12.2	3.4	15.7	14.1	2.1	2.2	15.7	1.6	9 820	47 433
District 6	18 667	287 158	6.6	6.2	3.5	15.3	14.5	5.5	1.6	12.1	2.7	14 021	48 827
District 7	15 511	293 327	2.1	2.9	2.2	9.0	26.9	6.8	2.2	10.9	1.8	17 520	59 730
District 8	21 065	321 593	2.1	6.4	2.0	10.0	17.3	5.4	2.3	15.9	3.0	20 094	62 483
MASSACHUSETTS	175 225	3 167 329	7.0	3.9	4.4	11.6	19.6	5.8	1.5	8.7	3.6	198 027	62 522
District 1	16 115	249 573	11.0	4.1	3.5	14.6	22.1	4.7	1.2	3.9	1.5	10 765	43 135
District 2	16 590	284 809	9.2	3.5	4.3	13.8	25.0	5.1	1.0	5.8	1.4	12 800	44 944
District 3	16 179	272 355	15.1	4.2	6.6	10.8	18.3	3.7	0.9	10.0	3.6	17 078	62 704
District 4	20 676	328 712	8.4	3.7	6.9	14.1	16.6	3.9	1.7	6.7	2.7	19 064	57 997
District 5	20 824	386 671	4.3	3.9	3.8	9.7	14.6	4.1	1.3	11.5	6.2	26 981	69 777
District 6	21 026	346 668	10.9	5.1	5.1	14.0	18.7	3.4	1.2	8.3	5.4	20 708	59 680
District 7	16 733	486 329	2.0	1.9	2.8	7.0	21.5	6.0	2.0	10.7	3.9	38 102	78 346
District 8	24 135	521 925	3.6	4.3	3.8	9.4	21.1	13.0	2.0	11.5	4.1	38 458	73 685
District 9	22 348	243 241	6.8	6.4	3.8	18.4	20.9	2.9	1.4	5.0	1.4	11 089	45 588

1. Specified owner-occupied units; $1,000,000 represents $1,000,000 or more.   2. Specified renter-occupied units.

Table E. Congressional Districts 115th Congress — **Land Area and Population Characteristics**

STATE District	Representative, 115th Congress	Land area,[1] 2016 (sq. mi)	Total persons	Per square mile	White	Black	American Indian, Alaska Native	Asian and Pacific Islander	Some other race	Two or more races	Hispanic or Latino[2]	Non-Hispanic White alone	Female	Foreign-born	Born in state of residence
		1	2	3	4	5	6	7	8	9	10	11	12	13	14
MICHIGAN		56 546.7	9 922 576	175.5	78.6	13.9	0.5	3.0	1.2	2.7	4.9	75.4	50.8	6.6	76.6
District 1	Jack Bergman (R)	25 028.4	700 136	28.0	92.1	1.7	2.6	0.7	0.4	2.5	2.0	91.0	49.1	1.9	79.1
District 2	Bill Huizenga (R)	3 284.7	731 188	222.6	84.6	6.6	0.6	2.1	3.0	3.1	9.3	79.1	50.8	5.9	78.4
District 3	Justin Amash (R)	2 629.6	730 423	277.8	83.9	8.2	0.4	2.1	1.9	3.5	7.3	79.5	50.2	5.3	79.3
District 4	John L. Moolenar (R)	8 458.2	701 635	83.0	93.9	1.4	0.9	1.1	0.4	1.8	3.3	91.4	49.9	2.3	85.2
District 5	Daniel T. Kildee (D)	2 348.9	682 716	290.7	77.5	16.8	0.2	1.0	0.8	3.6	4.7	74.2	51.7	2.3	83.8
District 6	Fred Upton (R)	3 547.6	713 644	201.2	84.4	8.4	0.4	1.5	1.5	3.8	6.0	80.9	50.7	4.5	69.7
District 7	Tim Walberg (R)	4 227.8	697 627	165.0	91.0	4.4	0.4	1.1	0.9	2.3	4.3	88.0	49.9	2.3	73.9
District 8	Mike Bishop (R)	1 503.1	728 781	484.9	85.7	5.3	0.2	4.3	1.2	3.3	4.8	82.9	50.8	7.2	75.0
District 9	Sander M. Levin (D)	183.7	717 641	3 907.6	79.2	13.4	0.4	4.2	0.5	2.4	2.2	77.4	51.6	11.1	76.9
District 10	Paul Mitchell (R)	4 142.1	715 535	172.7	92.5	2.7	0.1	1.8	0.4	2.4	3.3	90.0	50.6	6.1	83.4
District 11	David A.Trott (R)	419.1	720 585	1 719.4	80.2	6.1	0.5	10.1	1.0	2.1	3.6	77.7	50.8	13.6	70.5
District 12	Debbie Dingell (D)	403.1	708 020	1 756.3	79.5	10.5	0.3	5.6	0.8	3.3	5.8	75.3	51.1	11.3	69.3
District 13	John Conyers Jr. (D)	184.9	679 235	3 674.3	38.2	55.5	0.3	1.4	2.9	1.8	7.1	34.1	52.5	7.1	76.9
District 14	Brenda L. Lawrence (D)	185.7	695 410	3 745.2	35.2	56.1	0.2	4.6	1.4	2.4	4.8	32.0	52.5	10.7	71.0
MINNESOTA		79 626.7	5 489 594	68.9	84.1	5.8	1.0	4.7	1.5	2.8	5.1	80.9	50.3	8.3	67.7
District 1	Timothy J. Walz (D)	11 974.4	668 741	55.8	91.0	2.7	0.4	2.9	1.4	1.6	6.2	86.6	49.8	6.5	67.8
District 2	Jason Lewis (R)	2 438.0	695 029	285.1	84.8	4.1	0.5	4.7	2.4	3.5	5.8	82.1	50.8	8.1	67.6
District 3	Erik Paulsen (R)	527.1	700 121	1 328.4	81.7	7.3	0.3	7.0	1.2	2.4	4.3	78.8	50.8	11.8	62.3
District 4	Betty McCollum (D)	332.6	704 158	2 117.1	72.2	10.0	0.5	12.1	1.2	4.1	6.7	67.6	51.2	13.8	60.6
District 5	Keith Ellison (D)	135.7	707 578	5 214.4	67.6	17.0	0.8	6.5	3.8	4.4	9.3	62.8	50.5	15.6	54.2
District 6	Tom Emmer (R)	2 881.7	687 034	238.4	91.5	2.4	0.4	2.4	0.8	2.5	2.7	90.0	49.6	5.0	78.0
District 7	Collin C. Peterson (D)	33 429.7	663 263	19.8	92.3	1.3	2.9	1.0	1.0	1.4	4.2	89.3	50.0	3.1	72.9
District 8	Richard M. Nolan (D)	27 907.6	663 670	23.8	93.0	1.0	2.4	0.7	0.2	2.6	1.7	91.9	49.4	1.7	79.4
MISSISSIPPI		46 923.0	2 992 333	63.8	58.8	37.7	0.4	1.0	0.9	1.2	2.9	57.0	51.6	2.4	71.5
District 1	Trent Kelly (R)	10 572.9	758 765	71.8	69.2	27.7	0.1	0.7	1.0	1.4	3.3	67.2	51.9	2.3	63.9
District 2	Bennie G. Thompson (D)	15 551.6	724 075	46.6	31.3	66.3	0.2	0.7	0.9	0.5	1.9	30.3	52.4	1.6	83.7
District 3	Gregg Harper (R)	12 754.0	745 475	58.5	62.1	34.4	0.9	1.2	0.5	0.8	2.1	60.5	51.2	2.5	76.0
District 4	Steven Palazzo (R)	8 044.5	764 018	95.0	71.2	23.8	0.3	1.6	1.2	2.0	4.1	68.6	51.0	3.3	63.2
MISSOURI.............		68 746.5	6 083 672	88.5	82.4	11.7	0.4	2.0	1.1	2.5	4.0	79.9	51.0	4.0	66.1
District 1	William Lacy Clay (D)	225.3	736 055	3 266.4	43.8	49.2	0.1	3.2	0.6	3.1	3.6	41.2	53.2	6.3	68.9
District 2	Ann Wagner (R)	465.8	767 531	1 647.7	89.0	3.7	0.2	4.4	0.7	2.0	2.6	87.2	51.2	6.7	65.7
District 3	Blaine Luetkemeyer (R)	6 851.5	774 899	113.1	92.9	3.4	0.3	1.2	0.4	1.8	2.2	91.3	50.2	2.4	74.8
District 4	Vicky Hartzler (R)	14 406.0	762 763	52.9	88.8	5.3	0.5	1.6	1.0	2.9	3.8	86.5	49.8	3.1	63.2
District 5	Emanuel Cleaver (D)	2 425.3	757 920	312.5	68.5	21.9	0.5	2.3	3.9	3.0	8.9	64.0	51.6	6.1	60.8
District 6	Sam Graves (R)	18 198.5	765 667	42.1	90.8	4.6	0.4	1.1	0.6	2.5	3.9	88.1	50.5	2.7	64.9
District 7	Bill Long (R)	6 272.8	770 073	122.8	91.8	1.8	0.9	1.5	1.2	2.7	5.0	88.3	51.2	3.5	57.7
District 8	Jason T. Smith (R)	19 901.1	748 764	37.6	92.0	5.1	0.4	0.6	0.2	1.8	1.7	90.7	50.1	1.3	73.3
MONTANA		145 547.0	1 032 949	7.1	88.9	0.5	6.3	1.0	0.7	2.6	3.6	86.6	49.8	2.1	54.3
At Large	Greg Gianforte (R)	145 547.0	1 032 949	7.1	88.9	0.5	6.3	1.0	0.7	2.6	3.6	86.6	49.8	2.1	54.3
NEBRASKA............		76 823.8	1 896 190	24.7	88.2	4.8	0.9	2.2	1.7	2.3	10.4	80.1	50.3	6.8	64.9
District 1	Jeff Fortenberry (R)	8 879.0	638 320	71.9	89.2	3.1	1.2	2.5	1.3	2.7	9.1	82.2	49.9	6.8	65.6
District 2	Don Bacon (R)	509.8	652 870	1 280.7	81.5	9.8	0.7	3.2	2.1	2.7	11.0	73.2	50.6	8.5	60.5
District 3	Adrian Smith (R)	67 435.0	605 000	9.0	94.3	1.1	0.8	0.7	1.6	1.5	11.1	85.2	50.3	4.9	69.0
NEVADA.................		109 780.2	2 890 845	26.3	67.5	8.5	1.2	8.6	9.2	5.0	28.1	50.5	49.9	19.3	25.8
District 1	Dina Titus (D)	104.5	703 299	6 730.8	54.1	10.3	1.2	9.3	20.4	4.8	46.7	30.7	49.0	32.1	23.9
District 2	Mark E. Amodei (R)	55 589.2	706 464	12.7	82.0	1.8	2.0	4.2	5.5	4.4	22.4	66.5	49.6	12.2	30.9
District 3	Jacky Rosen (D)	2 848.9	758 676	266.3	68.3	7.3	0.6	14.4	4.2	5.2	16.5	57.3	50.7	17.7	21.6
District 4	Ruben J. Kihuen (D)	50 997.4	722 406	14.2	65.7	14.6	0.9	6.4	7.0	5.4	27.9	47.1	50.4	15.5	26.9
NEW HAMPSHIRE..		8 952.7	1 330 608	148.6	93.6	1.6	0.1	2.6	0.4	1.7	3.3	90.9	50.6	6.0	42.1
District 1	Carol Shea-Porter (D)	2 464.5	671 640	272.5	93.9	1.8	0.0	1.8	0.6	1.7	3.7	91.0	50.9	6.1	41.0
District 2	Ann M. Kuster (D)	6 488.2	658 968	101.6	93.3	1.3	0.2	3.3	0.2	1.6	3.0	90.8	50.2	6.0	43.2
NEW JERSEY........		7 355.5	8 958 013	1 217.9	67.7	13.4	0.2	9.5	6.5	2.7	19.7	56.0	51.2	22.1	52.6
District 1	Donald Norcross (D)	350.2	738 908	2 109.9	67.4	16.5	0.1	5.4	6.7	3.9	13.0	62.7	51.9	10.0	54.7
District 2	Frank A. LoBiondo (R)	2 095.3	721 093	344.2	76.8	12.2	0.2	4.2	3.2	3.4	16.1	65.7	50.7	10.9	59.1
District 3	Thomas MacArthur (R)	898.2	735 336	818.7	80.1	10.9	0.1	3.7	1.9	3.2	8.0	75.5	50.9	7.9	61.2
District 4	Christopher H. Smith (R)	691.2	742 131	1 073.7	85.0	6.4	0.1	4.5	2.3	1.7	10.4	77.4	51.5	12.7	58.9
District 5	Josh Gottheimer (D)	991.6	743 424	749.7	78.6	5.2	0.2	10.2	4.0	1.8	12.7	70.8	51.0	19.6	52.7
District 6	Frank Pallone Jr. (D)	215.3	753 711	3 501.0	63.5	10.8	0.2	19.0	4.0	2.5	21.5	47.4	50.6	28.2	50.9
District 7	Leonard Lance (R)	970.0	743 127	766.1	79.4	4.3	0.1	10.3	3.7	2.2	11.4	72.2	50.9	18.8	56.6
District 8	Albio Sires (D)	54.7	767 452	14 032.5	56.2	10.6	0.4	8.5	20.3	4.0	55.0	25.1	50.0	43.8	37.6
District 9	Bill Pascrell, Jr. (D)	95.3	760 840	7 983.0	53.8	13.0	0.4	14.1	16.0	3.4	36.5	38.3	51.2	35.6	45.7
District 10	Donald M. Payne, Jr. (D)	75.8	764 684	10 083.7	30.3	50.3	0.1	7.6	9.4	2.3	20.8	20.3	52.2	29.5	49.1
District 11	Rodney P. Frelinghuysen (R)	505.9	735 657	1 454.2	82.4	3.9	0.0	9.7	1.6	2.3	11.5	73.5	51.6	18.1	59.0
District 12	Bonnie Watson Coleman (D)	412.1	751 650	1 824.0	58.7	18.2	0.1	16.5	4.5	1.8	17.1	47.1	51.4	27.9	46.4
NEW MEXICO.........		121 301.5	2 085 109	17.2	73.4	2.3	9.3	1.5	10.1	3.4	48.0	38.3	50.4	9.4	53.3
District 1	Michelle Lujan Grisham (D)	4 600.5	690 571	150.1	71.6	2.9	4.3	2.3	14.2	4.7	49.4	40.1	50.8	11.2	51.9
District 2	Steve Pearce (R)	71 742.1	703 727	9.8	84.0	2.0	5.4	0.8	5.5	2.2	53.8	37.3	49.9	10.6	50.5

1. Dry land or land partially or temporarily covered by water.   2. May be of any race.

Items 1—14

Table E. Congressional Districts 115th Congress — **Age and Education**

	Population and population characteristics, 2015 (cont.)											Education, 2015		
	Age (percent)												Attainment[2] (percent)	
STATE District	Under 5 years	5 to 17 years	18 to 24 years	25 to 34 years	35 to 44 years	45 to 54 years	55 to 64 years	65 to 74 years	75 years and over	Median age	Total Enrollment[1]	High school graduate or more	Bachelor's degree or more
	15	16	17	18	19	20	21	22	23	24	25	26	27
MICHIGAN	5.8	16.5	9.9	12.3	11.8	13.9	14.0	9.1	6.7	39.7	2 495 741	90.1	27.8
District 1	4.6	14.2	8.9	10.4	10.4	13.5	16.4	12.5	9.2	46.4	143 419	91.9	24.9
District 2	6.7	17.6	10.7	12.8	11.5	13.3	12.6	8.7	6.2	37.0	186 221	89.7	25.1
District 3	6.3	18.0	9.3	13.8	12.3	13.3	13.1	7.8	6.0	36.9	189 278	90.6	30.2
District 4	5.2	15.6	11.4	11.2	10.7	13.8	14.4	10.3	7.6	41.0	175 846	90.2	20.7
District 5	5.7	16.6	8.8	11.8	11.9	13.5	14.6	9.8	7.5	41.1	161 213	89.3	19.5
District 6	5.9	17.0	11.0	12.0	11.5	13.1	13.7	9.3	6.6	38.8	190 864	91.0	28.1
District 7	5.4	16.5	8.7	11.2	12.0	14.6	14.9	9.7	6.9	42.0	163 292	91.2	23.4
District 8	5.0	16.7	12.8	11.4	11.9	14.4	13.8	8.6	5.3	38.5	212 285	94.1	39.0
District 9	5.6	14.5	8.1	14.3	12.2	14.5	14.2	9.1	7.4	41.1	156 429	89.3	28.8
District 10	5.2	17.4	8.0	10.7	12.4	15.1	14.5	9.7	6.8	42.3	171 326	90.8	22.8
District 11	5.6	16.8	7.6	12.1	12.6	16.3	14.3	8.5	6.2	41.1	181 273	94.6	46.0
District 12	6.0	15.2	13.8	13.7	12.1	12.8	12.7	7.9	5.8	35.9	208 824	89.4	34.3
District 13	6.8	17.6	10.4	13.6	11.9	13.2	13.1	7.9	5.5	36.2	179 499	81.8	15.3
District 14	6.6	17.1	9.5	13.1	12.3	12.8	13.3	8.6	6.6	38.0	175 972	87.0	29.7
MINNESOTA	6.4	17.0	9.2	13.6	12.3	13.6	13.3	8.2	6.5	37.9	1 382 373	92.8	34.7
District 1	6.3	16.6	10.8	12.1	11.3	12.8	13.6	8.6	7.8	38.4	171 862	92.2	28.2
District 2	6.6	18.5	8.6	12.5	13.3	14.8	13.0	7.5	5.1	37.7	181 199	94.9	37.8
District 3	6.8	16.8	7.1	13.0	12.4	14.8	14.8	8.0	6.3	39.8	166 556	95.6	48.0
District 4	6.9	17.0	9.6	15.5	12.2	12.9	12.6	7.6	5.8	35.7	189 199	91.7	43.2
District 5	6.6	14.6	10.6	20.1	13.9	12.0	10.8	6.5	5.1	34.0	183 975	89.4	45.1
District 6	6.4	19.4	9.2	12.5	13.4	15.0	12.2	7.3	4.5	37.0	186 097	94.3	29.3
District 7	6.1	17.1	9.1	11.1	10.7	12.5	14.2	9.7	9.3	41.0	155 515	91.4	21.6
District 8	5.4	15.8	8.7	11.2	10.9	13.6	15.3	10.8	8.2	43.2	147 970	92.7	22.3
MISSISSIPPI	6.3	18.0	10.4	12.5	12.9	12.6	12.6	8.7	5.9	37.0	796 722	83.5	20.8
District 1	6.0	18.1	10.6	11.5	13.0	13.2	12.3	9.0	6.1	37.7	200 685	82.7	19.9
District 2	7.0	18.7	10.4	13.1	12.8	11.7	12.6	8.1	5.6	35.6	199 230	80.4	17.7
District 3	5.9	17.6	10.5	12.7	12.9	12.3	12.9	8.8	6.4	37.4	199 209	86.0	25.2
District 4	6.4	17.6	10.2	12.7	12.8	13.0	12.5	9.0	5.9	37.1	197 598	84.6	20.4
MISSOURI	6.2	16.8	9.8	13.1	12.1	13.3	13.3	8.9	6.7	38.4	1 511 239	88.9	27.8
District 1	6.7	15.4	10.6	16.6	12.8	12.3	12.7	7.5	5.4	35.4	190 946	87.9	30.5
District 2	5.3	16.5	7.4	11.9	11.7	14.6	15.1	9.3	8.2	42.7	189 636	94.8	47.2
District 3	6.2	17.4	9.1	12.2	12.2	14.1	13.6	9.2	6.1	39.1	188 382	90.0	24.5
District 4	6.0	16.4	12.8	12.9	11.4	12.5	12.5	8.8	6.6	36.6	204 933	88.3	25.2
District 5	6.6	16.3	9.0	15.1	12.5	12.9	13.0	8.1	6.4	36.9	175 268	88.2	27.2
District 6	6.2	17.8	9.5	12.2	12.3	13.6	13.0	8.8	6.5	38.5	190 117	90.7	27.3
District 7	6.1	16.9	10.9	12.6	11.7	12.4	12.6	9.4	7.2	37.7	193 235	88.9	24.0
District 8	6.1	17.1	8.8	11.4	11.5	13.6	14.0	9.7	7.7	40.5	178 722	82.2	15.6
MONTANA	5.8	16.1	9.7	12.5	11.5	12.5	14.6	10.2	7.1	39.9	233 966	93.5	30.6
At Large	5.8	16.1	9.7	12.5	11.5	12.5	14.6	10.2	7.1	39.9	233 966	93.5	30.6
NEBRASKA	6.9	17.9	10.2	13.3	12.2	12.2	12.6	8.1	6.7	36.1	505 827	91.0	30.2
District 1	6.8	17.6	12.3	13.1	11.7	11.9	12.2	8.1	6.3	35.2	180 035	91.7	29.9
District 2	7.5	18.9	8.8	15.6	13.8	12.5	11.5	6.8	4.7	34.5	179 102	91.4	38.5
District 3	6.3	17.3	9.4	11.2	11.2	12.0	14.0	9.4	9.1	39.9	146 690	89.9	21.9
NEVADA	6.1	17.0	8.8	14.3	13.4	13.6	12.3	9.2	5.5	37.8	699 775	85.6	23.6
District 1	6.2	16.6	10.3	14.6	13.9	14.2	12.1	7.5	4.8	36.7	159 868	75.7	15.4
District 2	5.9	16.4	8.8	13.2	12.1	13.7	13.9	10.3	5.8	39.4	169 138	86.8	26.0
District 3	5.8	16.1	7.5	15.1	15.3	13.1	11.8	9.6	5.8	38.7	179 065	93.0	31.8
District 4	6.6	19.0	8.7	14.1	12.4	13.1	11.4	9.2	5.5	36.3	191 704	85.8	19.8
NEW HAMPSHIRE	4.8	15.0	9.8	11.7	11.7	15.5	15.2	9.7	6.7	42.8	314 478	93.1	35.7
District 1	4.9	14.7	10.4	11.6	11.6	15.7	14.8	9.5	6.5	42.5	160 847	93.3	36.3
District 2	4.6	15.2	9.2	11.7	11.9	15.1	15.5	10.0	6.8	43.2	153 631	92.9	35.1
NEW JERSEY	5.9	16.4	8.8	12.9	13.0	14.8	13.1	8.4	6.5	39.6	2 246 090	89.1	37.6
District 1	6.0	16.8	9.0	13.5	12.8	14.3	13.2	8.2	6.1	39.0	187 581	89.8	30.9
District 2	5.6	15.7	8.3	11.9	12.0	14.2	14.3	10.2	7.6	42.3	164 745	86.1	25.3
District 3	5.2	15.3	8.3	11.4	11.5	15.0	14.3	10.3	8.6	43.7	170 619	92.9	32.3
District 4	6.4	18.2	8.1	10.8	11.2	13.9	13.7	9.5	8.3	41.2	197 741	92.5	38.7
District 5	5.1	17.2	8.3	10.3	12.6	16.0	14.1	9.2	7.2	42.6	183 011	92.8	46.1
District 6	6.2	15.9	10.8	14.5	13.2	14.9	11.9	7.5	5.1	36.9	204 581	87.8	38.5
District 7	4.8	18.2	7.9	9.8	12.5	17.5	14.5	8.3	6.4	42.6	190 553	94.5	52.2
District 8	7.9	14.1	8.7	20.0	15.6	13.4	10.3	5.7	4.4	34.6	175 755	79.1	31.9
District 9	6.2	16.0	9.5	13.6	14.0	13.8	12.9	8.0	6.1	38.1	188 552	84.9	32.1
District 10	6.4	16.4	10.4	15.3	14.3	13.7	11.8	7.0	4.7	36.0	202 868	84.9	27.8
District 11	5.2	16.7	8.0	10.6	12.3	16.2	14.0	9.1	7.7	43.1	186 647	94.4	52.0
District 12	5.9	16.5	9.0	12.0	14.1	14.5	13.2	8.3	6.6	39.5	193 437	89.4	43.3
NEW MEXICO	6.4	17.5	10.0	13.1	11.8	12.4	13.0	9.4	6.5	37.4	545 265	84.6	26.5
District 1	5.7	16.0	9.7	14.6	12.3	13.0	13.5	8.9	6.2	37.7	177 805	86.9	31.6
District 2	7.3	18.3	10.9	12.2	11.5	11.3	12.2	9.4	6.7	36.2	188 397	81.0	20.1

1. All persons 3 years old and over enrolled in nursery school through college and graduate or professional school. 2. Persons 25 years old and over.

Table E. Congressional Districts 115th Congress — Households and Group Quarters

STATE District	Number	Average household size	Family households (percent)	Married-couple family (percent)	Female family householder[1]	One person households (percent)	Total in group quarters, 2015	Percent 65 years and over	Persons in correctional institutions	Persons in nursing facilities	Persons in college dormitories	Persons in military quarters
	28	29	30	31	32	33	34	35	36	37	38	39
MICHIGAN	3 858 532	2.51	64.3	47.2	12.3	29.5	227 185	19.8	62 083	42 473	78 033	214
District 1	289 509	2.33	63.1	50.6	8.4	30.9	26 460	20.2	12 990	4 884	5 714	129
District 2	270 589	2.63	68.9	52.4	11.8	24.8	19 995	17.4	5 021	2 948	6 414	0
District 3	273 074	2.61	66.2	50.0	11.2	26.8	17 671	18.1	7 012	3 695	5 151	82
District 4	268 340	2.51	66.2	51.6	10.1	27.0	27 538	13.6	9 024	3 606	13 524	0
District 5	277 003	2.43	62.5	42.9	15.0	31.4	9 495	33.6	1 630	3 103	1 303	3
District 6	279 199	2.50	64.7	48.4	11.8	28.5	16 581	22.3	1 476	3 141	6 864	0
District 7	265 607	2.53	66.8	52.5	9.9	28.3	24 469	15.0	14 438	2 638	4 594	0
District 8	277 217	2.55	66.6	52.4	9.5	25.7	21 278	10.0	988	1 873	16 015	0
District 9	298 469	2.38	60.2	42.6	12.6	33.6	6 297	50.7	1 143	3 267	0	0
District 10	276 435	2.56	69.7	56.2	9.4	25.5	9 034	36.3	3 120	2 375	0	0
District 11	280 995	2.54	69.3	57.4	8.1	25.7	6 211	45.5	183	2 598	1 581	0
District 12	274 068	2.51	59.4	42.9	11.9	31.7	20 404	11.9	387	2 155	13 873	0
District 13	258 660	2.59	57.7	27.3	23.8	36.3	10 067	21.2	114	2 806	2 287	0
District 14	269 367	2.54	58.5	32.6	20.0	36.2	11 685	23.4	4 557	3 384	713	0
MINNESOTA	2 147 262	2.49	64.5	50.8	9.2	28.4	133 971	24.9	20 397	32 989	50 444	0
District 1	262 815	2.45	64.2	51.7	8.2	28.9	23 565	23.9	4 808	5 137	9 723	0
District 2	258 064	2.65	70.9	56.2	10.2	23.3	11 310	25.8	1 042	2 781	4 486	0
District 3	274 149	2.54	68.4	56.4	8.5	25.4	5 030	38.8	551	1 864	644	0
District 4	267 996	2.56	61.5	45.7	11.0	30.6	18 971	16.8	3 286	3 540	9 958	0
District 5	296 531	2.31	49.3	35.0	10.5	38.5	21 651	20.9	876	5 425	8 740	0
District 6	249 007	2.70	73.7	59.1	9.1	19.7	14 543	19.1	3 328	2 246	5 885	0
District 7	267 158	2.41	65.2	53.6	7.4	30.0	18 328	40.1	1 022	7 051	6 518	0
District 8	271 542	2.37	64.7	51.3	8.4	28.8	20 573	25.9	5 484	4 945	4 490	0
MISSISSIPPI	1 104 371	2.62	67.3	43.9	18.2	28.4	93 979	16.0	34 273	16 496	26 472	3 938
District 1	283 891	2.61	68.7	48.1	15.8	26.8	17 939	22.9	2 943	4 381	7 786	0
District 2	259 082	2.67	66.5	35.1	26.2	30.2	31 451	11.7	14 994	4 226	8 476	8
District 3	279 489	2.58	66.5	45.8	15.6	29.8	25 441	18.4	9 560	4 625	5 828	601
District 4	281 909	2.64	67.4	45.9	16.0	27.0	19 148	14.6	6 776	3 264	4 382	3 329
MISSOURI	2 374 180	2.49	64.0	47.9	11.8	29.7	174 938	22.7	41 956	44 866	52 869	10 217
District 1	307 139	2.33	54.6	29.8	20.4	38.0	19 017	17.6	1 344	4 741	9 050	0
District 2	301 963	2.50	67.9	55.7	8.5	27.2	11 438	55.7	2 300	7 231	1 046	0
District 3	286 397	2.64	69.6	54.3	10.2	26.0	19 066	19.1	6 107	3 662	5 666	0
District 4	286 431	2.54	64.3	52.1	8.6	28.4	36 202	13.4	6 015	5 555	11 262	10 217
District 5	313 815	2.37	57.1	37.5	14.6	35.4	14 045	31.8	1 420	5 172	2 626	0
District 6	288 545	2.55	67.3	53.3	9.9	26.4	29 147	20.5	11 433	6 573	8 326	0
District 7	302 451	2.48	65.8	51.3	10.2	27.0	20 377	22.7	2 358	4 919	9 841	0
District 8	287 439	2.52	66.3	50.7	11.4	28.3	25 646	23.9	10 979	7 013	5 052	0
MONTANA	414 804	2.42	61.0	48.9	8.4	31.5	28 867	19.2	5 338	5 200	8 332	678
At Large	414 804	2.42	61.0	48.9	8.4	31.5	28 867	19.2	5 338	5 200	8 332	678
NEBRASKA	744 159	2.48	63.1	49.6	9.5	30.0	52 377	24.4	8 084	13 519	22 073	443
District 1	248 175	2.49	62.5	49.6	8.7	30.0	19 535	19.1	3 362	4 124	10 719	443
District 2	249 547	2.56	63.4	48.0	11.5	29.0	13 566	17.6	2 325	2 632	4 750	0
District 3	246 437	2.38	63.4	51.3	8.3	31.0	19 276	35.5	2 397	6 763	6 604	0
NEVADA	1 042 065	2.74	63.3	43.8	13.4	28.7	36 736	15.2	19 891	5 005	3 336	1 022
District 1	245 491	2.83	57.0	33.7	15.6	33.5	9 289	11.3	4 771	954	1 211	0
District 2	271 672	2.56	63.3	46.5	11.8	27.8	12 100	12.8	6 685	1 334	2 125	166
District 3	281 502	2.69	64.2	46.9	11.2	27.7	2 420	58.1	352	1 044	0	0
District 4	243 400	2.91	68.6	47.5	15.3	25.8	12 927	14.2	8 083	1 673	0	856
NEW HAMPSHIRE	517 615	2.49	66.0	52.0	10.0	26.2	41 762	19.5	4 851	7 767	22 820	454
District 1	261 769	2.49	66.6	51.4	10.0	24.2	19 085	21.5	1 640	3 963	10 357	454
District 2	255 846	2.49	65.3	52.6	9.9	28.2	22 677	17.9	3 211	3 804	12 463	0
NEW JERSEY	3 187 963	2.75	69.2	51.2	13.1	25.9	186 013	23.7	44 468	45 512	55 483	1 452
District 1	268 186	2.71	67.6	46.7	16.2	27.0	11 046	33.0	2 221	3 995	2 424	0
District 2	265 326	2.62	67.4	49.0	13.2	27.2	25 152	17.9	11 704	4 360	2 376	768
District 3	276 418	2.60	69.0	53.2	11.0	26.4	15 300	26.5	6 383	4 169	0	360
District 4	268 362	2.74	69.6	56.0	10.3	26.4	7 801	50.3	1 319	4 614	1 306	254
District 5	261 487	2.79	73.3	60.5	9.3	23.0	13 604	39.2	1 041	5 005	4 364	0
District 6	250 016	2.89	72.5	54.9	12.8	22.9	30 628	12.3	2 976	3 169	15 266	70
District 7	265 736	2.76	72.8	61.0	8.3	23.5	10 637	37.9	2 789	3 543	129	0
District 8	278 454	2.73	62.9	38.2	16.9	27.3	7 665	22.0	3 043	2 492	1 409	0
District 9	259 420	2.91	69.0	48.4	14.9	26.5	5 279	26.3	1 068	1 145	468	0
District 10	272 446	2.73	64.3	34.5	23.0	31.0	20 340	11.0	7 245	2 896	6 771	0
District 11	261 271	2.75	71.4	59.5	8.5	24.9	16 186	30.3	411	5 741	9 278	0
District 12	260 841	2.80	71.2	54.0	12.4	24.1	22 375	16.9	4 268	4 383	11 692	0
NEW MEXICO	761 797	2.68	63.7	44.9	13.1	30.6	43 082	14.3	17 907	5 567	8 478	1 789
District 1	269 810	2.52	59.4	41.6	11.8	33.1	10 179	15.9	4 489	1 768	2 750	530
District 2	243 825	2.80	68.4	49.1	13.3	27.2	19 988	11.7	9 874	2 334	3 613	815

1. No spouse present.

STATE District		Housing units, 2015						Money income, 2015		
			Occupied units						Households	
				Owner-occupied			Renter-occupied			
	Total	Occupied units as a percent of all units	Owner-occupied units as a percent of occupied units	Median value[1] (dollars)	Percent valued at $500,000 or more	Median rent[2]	Per capita income (dollars)	Median income (dollars)	Percent with income of $100,000 or more
	40	41	42	43	44	45	46	47	48
MICHIGAN	4 550 324	84.8	70.4	137 500	3.6	803	27 865	51 084	20.5
District 1	444 180	65.2	77.9	127 400	4.8	674	25 822	45 684	14.4
District 2	315 625	85.7	73.2	138 000	2.2	749	25 400	51 681	17.7
District 3	295 928	92.3	72.2	142 800	3.1	787	27 653	53 861	20.7
District 4	344 859	77.8	76.5	117 100	1.8	709	25 085	47 461	16.2
District 5	329 343	84.1	71.2	91 400	1.2	709	23 248	42 390	13.0
District 6	326 289	85.6	70.9	142 100	3.9	700	27 596	50 511	18.8
District 7	303 492	87.5	76.2	143 600	2.7	743	27 700	53 887	21.2
District 8	298 006	93.0	73.0	196 900	5.1	862	33 371	65 400	30.1
District 9	320 396	93.2	68.8	133 100	3.9	891	30 751	52 455	21.3
District 10	309 689	89.3	79.2	165 000	2.6	826	29 187	58 068	25.0
District 11	299 461	93.8	74.7	222 200	8.3	998	40 032	77 183	37.6
District 12	300 340	91.3	63.1	131 500	4.4	906	29 317	54 212	22.8
District 13	333 703	77.5	53.5	63 100	0.6	770	18 141	31 789	8.7
District 14	329 013	81.9	54.3	105 700	4.9	860	25 826	40 785	18.2
MINNESOTA	2 397 081	89.6	70.9	200 000	6.5	888	33 425	63 488	28.0
District 1	286 374	91.8	74.2	156 700	3.1	720	29 546	57 189	21.7
District 2	268 718	96.0	75.4	236 700	6.2	1 008	35 625	77 122	35.5
District 3	286 067	95.8	73.7	273 600	14.9	1 113	44 361	81 788	40.6
District 4	281 527	95.2	63.7	225 500	7.3	934	33 524	63 638	30.2
District 5	313 425	94.6	52.8	212 500	9.2	943	35 150	56 752	26.1
District 6	262 170	95.0	77.1	210 300	4.4	873	32 438	73 227	32.4
District 7	328 305	81.4	75.6	149 700	3.9	660	28 301	54 481	19.3
District 8	370 495	73.3	77.4	163 300	3.6	699	27 695	52 179	18.4
MISSISSIPPI	1 300 932	84.9	67.4	112 700	2.0	724	21 291	40 593	14.0
District 1	325 089	87.3	70.3	116 900	1.5	710	22 341	43 910	14.5
District 2	309 895	83.6	61.4	88 600	1.7	673	17 575	32 152	9.7
District 3	328 304	85.1	71.1	121 600	2.5	739	23 407	42 817	17.4
District 4	337 644	83.5	66.2	122 200	2.3	773	21 705	42 383	13.9
MISSOURI	2 746 644	86.4	66.1	147 800	4.0	763	27 384	50 238	19.6
District 1	369 242	83.2	50.1	110 100	3.4	824	25 724	42 145	15.2
District 2	316 326	95.5	78.3	225 000	10.7	945	42 640	77 477	38.0
District 3	340 270	84.2	74.4	166 700	3.5	760	27 629	57 578	22.2
District 4	343 832	83.3	66.2	139 900	3.1	726	23 379	45 735	16.3
District 5	355 037	88.4	58.0	119 500	2.3	813	27 023	46 396	16.2
District 6	330 222	87.4	71.0	149 300	3.2	716	27 255	56 422	22.1
District 7	351 947	85.9	62.9	132 100	2.5	714	23 636	43 823	13.8
District 8	339 768	84.6	69.5	115 000	1.7	607	21 558	40 327	12.6
MONTANA	494 222	83.9	66.7	209 500	8.4	763	27 735	49 509	18.2
At Large	494 222	83.9	66.7	209 500	8.4	763	27 735	49 509	18.2
NEBRASKA	820 925	90.6	65.9	141 600	2.8	750	29 000	54 996	22.2
District 1	268 275	92.5	64.7	147 100	2.3	752	27 860	54 647	20.8
District 2	267 845	93.2	63.8	159 700	4.1	846	32 308	61 607	28.2
District 3	284 805	86.5	69.3	108 700	2.2	636	26 633	50 009	17.5
NEVADA	1 209 864	86.1	54.0	221 400	7.9	980	27 220	52 431	20.5
District 1	301 570	81.4	39.5	152 500	3.6	862	20 194	37 299	10.3
District 2	300 166	90.5	58.9	242 900	10.2	915	29 462	56 823	22.8
District 3	326 584	86.2	57.5	269 900	11.3	1 184	34 116	64 914	27.7
District 4	281 544	86.5	59.3	198 600	4.6	1 035	24 624	54 731	19.8
NEW HAMPSHIRE	622 604	83.1	70.9	244 500	7.6	1 017	35 925	70 303	32.4
District 1	314 689	83.2	69.1	249 800	8.4	1 059	36 085	71 858	33.6
District 2	307 915	83.1	72.6	239 200	6.9	972	35 762	68 252	31.2
NEW JERSEY	3 593 722	88.7	63.0	322 600	21.6	1 214	37 245	72 222	36.6
District 1	294 999	90.9	68.1	196 500	3.4	1 039	31 957	67 318	31.1
District 2	386 122	68.7	72.7	219 200	9.7	1 059	30 736	59 105	27.6
District 3	318 717	86.7	78.4	258 600	8.5	1 291	36 164	71 196	34.3
District 4	296 891	90.4	74.5	354 300	26.2	1 263	39 401	78 467	39.6
District 5	280 654	93.2	74.7	407 400	35.2	1 359	46 988	96 349	48.8
District 6	272 970	91.6	60.1	328 600	16.1	1 298	34 259	75 203	37.7
District 7	279 537	95.1	76.5	429 800	39.0	1 336	51 734	101 746	51.4
District 8	303 727	91.7	26.6	326 500	19.8	1 199	30 404	55 090	26.7
District 9	285 394	90.9	48.2	355 600	23.1	1 266	30 458	60 867	30.5
District 10	308 410	88.3	36.7	276 100	12.9	1 078	26 686	47 184	21.5
District 11	279 509	93.5	76.3	431 700	36.0	1 425	50 529	102 205	51.5
District 12	286 792	91.0	65.1	340 700	22.3	1 269	38 242	78 982	39.1
NEW MEXICO	914 979	83.3	67.5	164 100	5.7	783	24 388	45 382	17.9
District 1	300 598	89.8	63.1	187 400	5.6	790	27 191	47 199	19.7
District 2	304 459	80.1	68.8	122 900	2.7	726	20 648	41 232	14.0

1. Specified owner-occupied units; $1,000,000 represents $1,000,000 or more.   2. Specified renter-occupied units.

Table E. Congressional Districts 115th Congress — Poverty, Labor Force, Employment, and Social Security

STATE District	Poverty, 2015 Persons below poverty level (percent)	Families below poverty level (percent)	Percent of households receiving food stamps in past 12 months	Civilian labor force, 2015 Total	Unemployment Total	Rate[1]	Civilian employment,[2] 2015 Total	Percent Management, business, science and arts occupations	Service, sales, and office	Construction and production	Persons under age 65 with no health insurance, 2015 (percent)	Social Security beneficiaries, December 2015 Number	Rate[3]	Supplemental Security Income recipients, December 2015
	49	50	51	52	53	54	55	56	57	58	59	60	61	62
MICHIGAN	15.8	11.1	15.0	4 862 037	349 396	7.2	4 512 641	35.2	40.9	23.9	7.1	2 141 824	215.9	275 866
District 1	13.8	9.0	12.6	319 372	21 543	6.7	297 829	31.9	44.8	23.3	8.0	202 333	289.0	15 307
District 2	12.9	9.2	13.3	364 552	19 665	5.4	344 887	29.8	40.0	30.1	6.4	150 755	206.2	15 947
District 3	14.6	9.8	13.7	374 173	23 145	6.2	351 028	33.8	39.5	26.7	6.6	140 063	191.8	18 062
District 4	16.3	10.3	13.9	327 003	21 458	6.6	305 545	31.3	40.6	28.1	8.1	173 861	247.8	16 620
District 5	20.1	15.0	20.9	312 169	29 789	9.5	282 380	29.3	44.9	25.8	6.7	173 883	254.7	29 713
District 6	15.1	10.0	13.6	362 274	23 809	6.6	338 465	34.0	39.6	26.3	7.5	154 356	216.3	17 342
District 7	12.8	8.5	11.8	333 033	17 943	5.4	315 090	32.4	40.2	27.5	6.1	160 677	230.3	13 586
District 8	12.1	7.4	8.6	383 602	22 749	5.9	360 853	42.3	40.1	17.6	6.1	130 815	179.5	11 535
District 9	13.2	10.7	14.4	370 538	24 711	6.7	345 827	37.6	40.8	21.6	6.7	151 286	210.8	19 585
District 10	10.2	7.5	10.8	356 800	21 329	6.0	335 471	33.9	40.4	25.7	7.0	158 675	221.8	12 677
District 11	6.6	4.6	5.4	387 234	16 359	4.2	370 875	49.1	36.0	14.9	5.3	135 646	188.2	7 925
District 12	17.1	11.0	12.8	356 136	23 001	6.5	333 135	40.3	39.0	20.7	6.6	133 753	188.9	16 579
District 13	32.2	27.4	33.4	293 674	42 767	14.6	250 907	23.8	46.7	29.5	9.9	133 990	197.3	41 914
District 14	25.2	20.2	26.9	321 477	41 128	12.8	280 349	37.3	44.0	18.7	9.1	141 731	203.8	39 074
MINNESOTA	10.2	6.3	8.7	3 039 536	126 360	4.2	2 913 176	40.2	38.6	21.2	5.2	979 776	178.5	94 146
District 1	11.1	5.9	7.4	369 454	14 593	3.9	354 861	36.8	37.0	26.2	5.1	133 212	199.2	9 087
District 2	6.9	4.5	5.8	396 998	14 621	3.7	382 377	40.5	38.9	20.6	4.4	105 456	151.7	6 959
District 3	5.4	3.5	6.1	399 561	14 804	3.7	384 757	47.8	38.6	13.6	4.3	114 870	164.1	7 133
District 4	12.8	8.6	11.1	384 014	19 415	5.1	364 599	45.2	38.8	16.0	5.8	111 310	158.1	18 199
District 5	15.7	10.5	13.3	420 430	20 999	5.0	399 431	47.4	37.8	14.8	7.3	95 802	135.4	22 677
District 6	7.7	4.9	7.6	387 672	15 233	3.9	372 439	36.3	39.0	24.7	3.6	105 821	154.0	6 864
District 7	10.7	6.7	8.6	347 918	11 358	3.3	336 560	33.0	37.2	29.8	6.2	150 167	226.4	10 348
District 8	11.4	7.2	9.0	333 489	15 337	4.6	318 152	31.8	42.0	26.2	5.0	163 138	245.8	12 879
MISSISSIPPI	22.0	17.0	18.2	1 324 308	117 629	8.9	1 206 679	30.8	41.2	28.1	14.8	647 420	216.4	123 207
District 1	17.9	13.0	16.1	348 769	26 993	7.7	321 776	29.3	39.6	31.1	13.0	168 373	221.9	25 130
District 2	30.2	24.9	25.7	297 888	35 209	11.8	262 679	27.6	44.0	28.4	15.0	159 507	220.3	46 529
District 3	19.1	14.0	14.2	338 931	23 616	7.0	315 315	35.5	39.1	25.4	13.9	158 788	213.0	27 189
District 4	21.2	16.8	17.4	338 720	31 811	9.4	306 909	30.2	42.5	27.4	17.4	160 752	210.4	24 359
MISSOURI	14.8	10.2	12.1	3 042 538	162 229	5.3	2 880 309	35.4	42.0	22.6	11.4	1 258 256	206.8	140 271
District 1	20.4	16.2	19.7	392 051	34 208	8.7	357 843	36.6	45.3	18.2	11.9	134 600	182.9	29 888
District 2	5.2	3.4	3.7	414 443	14 043	3.4	400 400	48.0	39.2	12.8	5.4	151 495	197.4	5 906
District 3	10.8	6.7	9.1	398 503	17 041	4.3	381 462	32.3	41.2	26.5	9.7	158 832	205.0	10 620
District 4	17.5	10.7	11.4	354 095	20 068	5.7	334 027	34.4	40.9	24.7	11.9	158 411	207.7	15 549
District 5	17.7	12.9	14.0	389 936	19 494	5.0	370 442	33.1	44.5	22.4	14.2	146 268	193.0	19 481
District 6	12.5	8.5	8.9	386 114	18 016	4.7	368 098	35.3	40.3	24.4	10.3	149 699	195.5	12 150
District 7	16.1	11.0	11.5	374 575	17 804	4.8	356 771	32.1	43.7	24.2	14.8	173 270	225.0	17 782
District 8	19.2	13.8	18.2	332 821	21 555	6.5	311 266	29.0	41.1	29.8	13.4	185 681	248.0	28 895
MONTANA	14.6	9.3	9.1	513 209	23 334	4.5	489 875	38.1	40.0	21.9	14.0	217 758	210.8	18 312
At Large	14.6	9.3	9.1	513 209	23 334	4.5	489 875	38.1	40.0	21.9	14.0	217 758	210.8	18 312
NEBRASKA	12.6	8.5	8.7	1 019 543	32 754	3.2	986 789	36.6	40.0	23.4	9.5	330 309	174.2	27 909
District 1	12.3	7.9	8.6	346 031	11 044	3.2	334 987	35.7	39.6	24.6	9.5	107 404	168.3	8 496
District 2	12.9	9.4	9.3	353 691	12 390	3.5	341 301	41.6	41.3	17.1	8.4	94 704	145.1	10 764
District 3	12.4	8.2	8.0	319 821	9 320	2.9	310 501	32.0	39.0	29.0	10.9	128 201	211.9	8 649
NEVADA	14.7	10.9	13.1	1 446 814	115 018	7.9	1 331 796	27.4	53.7	19.0	14.0	492 121	170.2	53 440
District 1	23.6	19.6	21.6	355 790	37 105	10.4	318 685	17.2	61.1	21.7	21.8	106 480	151.4	17 747
District 2	13.4	8.8	12.2	357 542	23 375	6.5	334 167	30.2	47.6	22.2	11.5	136 863	193.7	10 638
District 3	8.7	6.6	6.2	401 894	25 798	6.4	376 096	33.2	53.5	13.3	9.0	125 521	165.4	8 683
District 4	13.5	10.6	13.6	331 588	28 740	8.7	302 848	27.7	52.8	19.5	13.7	123 257	170.6	16 372
NEW HAMPSHIRE	8.2	5.0	7.8	744 971	31 658	4.2	713 313	40.1	39.6	20.2	7.5	288 891	217.1	19 588
District 1	7.8	4.5	7.8	383 113	17 429	4.5	365 684	40.1	40.0	19.9	8.1	142 355	212.0	9 941
District 2	8.6	5.6	7.7	361 858	14 229	3.9	347 629	40.1	39.2	20.6	6.8	146 536	222.4	9 647
NEW JERSEY	10.8	8.1	9.4	4 684 036	309 500	6.6	4 374 536	41.3	40.8	17.9	10.0	1 583 456	176.8	182 247
District 1	11.8	9.2	11.3	391 357	30 662	7.8	360 695	39.5	42.7	17.8	7.7	141 272	191.2	20 309
District 2	12.3	8.4	11.9	358 935	29 276	8.2	329 659	33.7	44.3	22.0	9.8	162 909	225.9	18 134
District 3	8.0	5.7	6.1	379 090	27 851	7.3	351 239	39.3	42.8	17.9	6.2	170 361	231.7	9 788
District 4	8.8	5.7	6.8	363 296	17 991	5.0	345 305	41.5	42.9	15.6	8.3	156 802	211.3	9 057
District 5	5.4	3.5	4.5	402 332	18 819	4.7	383 513	46.8	37.9	15.2	6.2	134 101	180.4	8 194
District 6	9.7	7.4	7.7	387 174	22 653	5.9	364 521	41.6	39.9	18.5	10.0	114 106	151.4	12 679
District 7	4.8	3.5	3.9	406 217	20 521	5.1	385 696	50.0	37.0	13.0	5.8	122 232	164.5	6 084
District 8	18.5	15.1	16.8	430 237	33 576	7.8	396 661	34.0	41.3	24.7	18.8	90 078	117.4	25 422
District 9	15.6	12.5	16.3	372 628	17 622	4.7	355 006	35.6	40.5	23.9	14.3	119 869	157.5	19 524
District 10	19.2	16.9	18.3	398 725	46 436	11.6	352 289	32.2	46.7	21.1	15.8	108 084	141.3	31 353
District 11	4.6	3.2	3.1	401 819	17 553	4.4	384 266	52.4	37.0	10.6	5.2	136 586	185.7	6 638
District 12	9.9	7.3	6.0	392 226	26 540	6.8	365 686	46.9	38.1	15.0	9.9	127 056	169.0	15 065
NEW MEXICO	20.4	14.8	17.5	950 312	70 505	7.4	879 807	34.5	45.4	20.1	12.8	408 931	196.1	64 175
District 1	20.0	14.3	16.8	336 565	21 656	6.4	314 909	39.0	44.3	16.7	12.0	130 996	189.7	19 209
District 2	22.5	17.2	20.4	296 527	23 561	7.9	272 966	27.6	46.9	25.5	12.4	139 954	198.9	23 719

1. Percent of civilian labor force. 2. Persons 16 years old and over. 3. Per 1,000 resident population estimated in the 2014 American Community Survey.

STATE District	Agriculture, 2012									
	Land in farms				Value of products sold				Government payments	
	Number of farms	Acres	Average size of farm (acres)	Irrigated land (acres)	Total ($1,000)	Average per farm (dollars)	Percent from crops	Percent from livestock and poultry products	Total ($1,000)	Average per farm receiving payments (dollars)
	63	64	65	66	67	68	69	70	71	72
MICHIGAN	52 194	9 948 564	191	592 243	8 678 050	166 265	63.5	36.5	155 919	7 567
District 1	7 028	1 174 716	167	17 529	304 476	43 323	55.8	44.2	12 542	7 241
District 2	3 913	596 787	153	48 685	927 761	237 097	58.1	41.9	7 836	8 257
District 3	4 328	804 218	186	32 235	865 263	199 922	45.6	54.4	13 587	7 922
District 4	10 328	2 076 879	201	100 624	1 711 590	165 723	58.5	41.5	29 973	6 191
District 5	2 837	598 773	211	9 459	462 461	163 011	87.4	12.6	9 239	6 103
District 6	6 072	1 155 210	190	289 103	1 603 431	264 070	63.2	36.8	18 373	9 379
District 7	8 650	1 623 909	188	76 959	991 129	114 581	77.1	22.9	34 636	8 108
District 8	2 057	316 696	154	3 079	200 689	97 564	76.9	23.1	4 270	10 363
District 9	26	D	D	13	1 700	65 380	94.0	6.0	D	D
District 10	6 328	1 559 304	246	13 305	1 561 544	246 767	65.2	34.8	25 149	8 030
District 11	191	8 146	43	513	13 673	71 587	94.7	5.3	21	1 935
District 12	379	30 066	79	562	30 614	80 777	98.6	1.4	282	4 780
District 13	44	2 399	55	173	3 605	81 921	99.6	0.4	6	1 443
District 14	13	D	D	4	115	8 857	100.0	0.0	D	D
MINNESOTA	74 542	26 035 838	349	524 016	21 280 184	285 479	65.2	34.8	467 867	8 962
District 1	19 041	6 309 496	331	22 341	7 132 552	374 589	58.9	41.1	133 151	8 920
District 2	4 642	1 121 134	242	58 464	1 146 580	247 001	62.6	37.4	21 757	7 489
District 3	699	78 393	112	625	65 380	93 534	81.2	18.8	1 223	4 703
District 4	372	34 196	92	1 069	37 456	100 689	92.5	7.5	448	4 766
District 5	32	1 477	46	26	4 610	144 055	99.7	0.3	9	2 266
District 6	5 739	1 084 584	189	69 319	939 820	163 760	57.5	42.5	18 404	5 481
District 7	33 431	15 157 479	453	276 423	11 010 000	329 444	71.8	28.3	276 140	10 362
District 8	10 586	2 249 079	212	95 749	940 152	88 811	45.7	54.3	16 736	4 177
MISSISSIPPI	38 076	10 931 080	287	1 651 978	6 441 025	169 162	46.2	53.8	181 205	10 983
District 1	10 989	2 650 855	241	41 049	785 235	71 456	59.0	41.0	32 055	5 487
District 2	10 256	5 182 018	505	1 580 386	2 848 319	277 722	79.4	20.6	124 539	19 898
District 3	10 656	2 250 486	211	25 717	2 096 730	196 765	7.7	92.3	17 972	5 567
District 4	6 175	847 721	137	4 826	710 741	115 100	12.0	88.0	6 640	5 680
MISSOURI	99 171	28 266 137	285	1 180 886	9 164 886	92 415	49.8	50.2	323 953	7 834
District 1	60	6 587	110	218	3 893	64 882	92.6	7.4	62	3 422
District 2	209	28 798	138	300	17 733	84 847	98.2	1.8	285	6 059
District 3	11 580	2 688 776	232	19 373	684 080	59 074	41.2	58.8	19 580	4 688
District 4	23 699	6 461 439	273	50 614	1 917 653	80 917	37.2	62.8	54 640	6 422
District 5	3 727	1 121 876	301	13 153	444 240	119 195	75.8	24.2	14 699	6 789
District 6	27 780	9 406 377	339	66 257	2 807 585	101 065	60.0	40.0	160 256	8 483
District 7	12 894	2 269 377	176	11 727	1 301 247	100 919	7.6	92.4	9 439	4 762
District 8	19 222	6 282 907	327	1 019 244	1 988 454	103 447	72.0	28.0	64 993	11 677
MONTANA	28 008	59 758 917	2 134	1 903 019	4 230 083	151 031	53.3	46.7	209 846	16 865
At Large	28 008	59 758 917	2 134	1 903 019	4 230 083	151 031	53.3	46.7	209 846	16 865
NEBRASKA	49 969	45 331 783	907	8 296 573	23 068 756	461 661	49.3	50.7	392 428	11 436
District 1	13 381	5 484 143	410	1 187 864	5 270 537	393 882	46.5	53.5	90 779	9 562
District 2	738	169 478	230	28 590	115 796	156 905	83.2	16.8	2 519	6 845
District 3	35 850	39 678 162	1 107	7 080 119	17 680 000	493 234	49.9	50.1	299 130	12 232
NEVADA	4 137	5 913 761	1 429	687 790	764 144	184 710	47.9	52.1	3 253	9 568
District 1	X	X	X	X	X	X	X	X	X	X
District 2	2 991	5 105 484	1 707	528 164	552 567	184 743	49.0	51.0	2 568	9 303
District 3	66	6 105	93	D	D	D	D	D	D	D
District 4	1 074	802 153	747	159 045	210 323	195 831	44.9	55.1	D	D
NEW HAMPSHIRE	4 391	474 065	108	2 630	190 907	43 477	52.8	47.2	3 472	7 435
District 1	1 576	118 543	75	1 011	42 022	26 664	58.4	41.6	1 110	7 761
District 2	2 815	355 522	126	1 619	148 885	52 890	51.2	48.8	2 362	7 290
NEW JERSEY	9 071	715 057	79	88 376	1 006 936	111 006	88.5	11.5	7 596	7 332
District 1	357	21 147	59	5 235	39 064	109 422	96.3	3.7	226	8 707
District 2	2 409	235 314	98	57 342	482 153	200 147	93.7	6.3	2 652	7 245
District 3	860	94 990	110	13 112	101 201	117 676	95.4	4.6	1 939	17 315
District 4	906	45 690	50	4 542	93 422	103 115	82.2	17.8	296	4 479
District 5	1 571	109 563	70	1 993	97 306	61 939	58.1	41.9	884	5 357
District 6	122	6 224	51	606	12 143	99 531	79.7	20.3	5	752
District 7	2 154	155 495	72	2 042	114 738	53 267	86.0	14.0	1 142	4 989
District 8	X	X	X	X	X	X	X	X	X	X
District 9	11	D	D	D	D	D	D	D	D	D
District 10	X	X	X	X	X	X	X	X	X	X
District 11	264	11 276	43	286	24 624	93 272	D	D	5	1 176
District 12	416	35 112	84	3 207	41 520	99 808	92.7	7.3	447	7 320
NEW MEXICO	24 721	43 201 023	1 748	680 318	2 550 147	103 157	24.2	75.8	70 588	12 830
District 1	1 868	2 249 327	1 204	33 967	73 029	39 095	44.7	55.3	3 559	14 829
District 2	10 130	21 702 074	2 142	369 030	1 599 576	157 905	27.4	72.6	37 277	16 257

Table E. Congressional Districts 115th Congress — **Nonfarm Employment and Payroll**

Private nonfarm employment and payroll, 2015

STATE District	Number of establish-ments	Employment								Professio-nal, scientific, and technical services		Annual payroll	
			Percent by selected industries										
		Total	Manufact-uring	Construc-tion	Wholesale trade	Retail trade	Health care and social assistance	Finance and Insurance	Real estate and rental and leasing		Information	Total (mil dol)	Average per employee dollars
	73	74	75	76	77	78	79	80	81	82	83	84	85
MICHIGAN	219 627	3 725 280	15.2	3.5	4.7	12.5	16.1	4.1	1.4	7.1	1.9	174 874	46 943
District 1	19 613	207 722	13.1	5.5	3.0	17.8	20.0	3.7	1.2	3.3	1.5	7 733	37 229
District 2	16 309	308 107	27.0	3.8	6.4	12.9	10.8	2.5	1.2	3.3	0.9	12 705	41 234
District 3	15 561	306 448	19.3	3.6	6.3	8.9	16.8	4.6	1.1	4.5	1.7	13 820	45 097
District 4	13 743	186 742	16.7	4.7	3.6	17.6	16.5	3.5	1.5	2.3	1.3	7 267	38 917
District 5	13 682	211 943	12.1	3.4	4.2	15.7	23.6	3.1	1.2	3.4	1.5	8 438	39 813
District 6	14 418	229 008	21.7	3.8	4.2	13.1	15.6	3.6	1.5	4.0	1.0	10 018	43 745
District 7	12 547	198 618	21.9	3.4	3.5	13.8	14.4	3.9	0.9	4.5	1.8	8 392	42 254
District 8	15 794	218 396	11.9	4.5	3.4	15.2	17.6	6.2	1.5	6.1	1.6	9 167	41 972
District 9	17 510	268 424	15.7	3.3	4.7	12.7	19.3	2.8	2.5	9.7	2.0	12 884	47 999
District 10	14 691	203 021	26.4	5.3	3.1	16.0	12.9	2.2	0.9	7.2	0.7	8 529	42 012
District 11	23 820	453 544	9.7	3.5	7.3	12.4	11.3	4.8	1.3	14.6	2.7	26 495	58 417
District 12	15 264	290 233	11.7	2.4	4.5	13.4	20.3	3.4	1.3	8.1	2.6	15 667	53 979
District 13	9 949	201 538	14.1	2.6	4.5	9.0	22.9	1.2	1.2	2.6	1.3	9 838	48 816
District 14	16 104	326 210	6.0	2.8	4.5	7.6	16.9	9.2	2.3	12.0	4.2	20 292	62 206
MINNESOTA	148 666	2 612 314	11.7	4.4	5.2	11.5	17.3	5.8	1.5	6.9	2.2	133 093	50 948
District 1	16 873	293 201	17.1	3.8	3.4	13.2	19.6	3.2	0.9	12.8	2.1	12 885	43 946
District 2	16 762	268 095	12.5	5.1	5.5	12.9	13.5	5.0	1.3	4.6	3.3	12 728	47 475
District 3	23 292	452 974	13.2	4.0	7.6	11.8	10.6	7.4	2.7	8.8	2.4	27 036	59 685
District 4	17 490	361 601	7.7	3.5	4.4	10.2	19.4	6.7	1.4	5.0	2.5	19 282	53 323
District 5	20 812	521 476	6.1	2.8	5.0	6.5	18.7	8.9	1.6	9.0	2.5	32 587	62 490
District 6	16 422	221 170	15.7	8.8	4.8	15.0	17.0	3.1	1.1	3.2	1.3	9 228	41 725
District 7	19 246	240 103	19.5	5.3	6.3	15.0	21.7	3.4	0.6	2.6	1.4	8 711	36 279
District 8	17 209	213 230	9.3	5.3	2.7	15.9	24.8	3.6	1.1	3.6	1.4	8 134	38 147
MISSISSIPPI	58 662	926 391	15.2	4.7	4.0	15.4	17.6	3.6	1.1	3.3	1.5	33 948	36 646
District 1	14 247	224 475	22.1	3.5	4.7	15.7	14.5	3.0	0.9	2.4	1.0	7 774	34 633
District 2	12 650	191 121	15.8	4.6	4.0	15.4	18.1	2.9	1.0	2.3	1.5	6 663	34 861
District 3	17 218	262 764	10.5	4.7	4.7	15.4	20.2	5.1	1.4	4.4	2.2	10 156	38 652
District 4	14 223	226 418	14.9	6.1	2.4	16.6	17.3	3.0	1.2	3.9	1.3	8 753	38 657
MISSOURI	158 191	2 442 316	10.6	4.7	5.1	12.9	16.8	5.3	1.5	6.4	2.3	109 136	44 685
District 1	23 894	422 194	10.7	4.3	6.4	7.1	15.0	4.2	1.4	6.0	2.1	23 040	54 571
District 2	24 825	439 517	4.1	4.4	4.0	12.9	16.2	8.0	1.8	9.6	3.1	23 341	53 106
District 3	17 543	226 946	14.6	7.1	4.9	16.3	14.1	3.4	1.2	4.6	1.9	8 559	37 715
District 4	16 353	201 481	12.7	4.8	3.2	18.1	20.3	5.9	1.2	4.0	1.5	6 702	33 261
District 5	21 009	394 814	9.7	5.2	7.0	10.6	16.1	6.3	1.5	10.2	3.1	20 306	51 433
District 6	16 382	211 039	14.2	5.0	4.4	16.5	17.1	4.1	1.5	3.5	1.6	7 769	36 812
District 7	19 304	297 236	12.6	3.7	5.3	14.6	17.1	3.7	1.9	4.3	2.3	10 924	36 750
District 8	18 331	207 917	15.6	4.1	4.3	16.7	25.2	3.6	1.2	2.5	1.4	6 700	32 226
MONTANA	37 270	375 041	4.8	6.6	4.4	16.0	18.1	4.5	1.5	5.3	2.3	14 227	37 935
At Large	37 270	375 041	4.8	6.6	4.4	16.0	18.1	4.5	1.5	5.3	2.3	14 227	37 935
NEBRASKA	53 719	870 279	10.7	5.1	4.9	13.0	14.4	7.2	1.2	11.4	2.4	36 968	42 478
District 1	16 706	237 617	13.9	6.0	4.2	14.6	16.5	6.2	1.2	5.5	2.6	9 222	38 810
District 2	17 772	346 475	6.5	5.5	5.1	12.5	14.5	10.8	1.9	6.3	3.3	17 028	49 145
District 3	18 930	208 714	17.9	5.5	6.7	16.8	17.0	4.6	0.7	2.5	1.5	7 216	34 576
NEVADA	63 383	1 129 965	3.8	5.8	3.1	13.0	10.0	3.1	2.6	5.2	1.5	46 596	41 236
District 1	18 368	419 292	1.2	4.1	1.8	11.5	9.7	1.9	2.6	4.0	0.8	16 308	38 893
District 2	18 398	261 384	8.7	6.1	4.8	13.6	11.9	3.0	1.9	4.9	1.8	11 589	44 337
District 3	17 028	279 574	3.3	6.9	2.8	14.3	8.3	5.1	3.5	7.4	1.7	11 827	42 304
District 4	9 198	140 516	3.6	9.1	4.2	16.3	12.5	3.0	2.1	5.2	2.3	5 584	39 739
NEW HAMPSHIRE	37 669	576 424	11.7	4.2	4.3	17.2	15.6	4.8	1.2	5.3	2.4	28 076	48 708
District 1	19 548	283 759	10.1	4.5	4.3	17.4	15.5	6.5	1.5	5.6	2.8	13 862	48 851
District 2	17 758	263 728	14.7	4.4	4.1	18.8	17.4	3.0	1.1	4.4	2.2	12 537	47 539
NEW JERSEY	230 961	3 558 619	6.1	4.1	7.2	13.0	16.0	5.4	1.6	9.0	2.5	209 072	58 751
District 1	15 897	244 400	7.3	4.8	6.0	16.5	21.4	2.4	1.5	6.4	1.8	11 262	46 080
District 2	17 235	225 441	6.5	5.9	5.0	16.7	18.0	2.6	1.5	3.8	1.1	9 026	40 037
District 3	16 696	244 547	5.5	4.3	5.0	16.8	19.4	8.2	1.8	7.2	1.8	11 802	48 259
District 4	21 208	280 789	5.3	6.1	3.9	16.4	19.0	4.1	2.0	8.1	3.4	13 270	47 261
District 5	23 293	306 009	5.4	4.1	7.5	15.9	20.2	3.6	1.3	7.2	2.0	17 231	56 310
District 6	18 727	301 873	5.8	4.1	9.0	11.3	14.9	3.6	1.7	14.3	2.5	17 961	59 498
District 7	23 627	367 198	7.2	4.3	5.6	13.6	15.5	5.2	1.3	10.6	4.4	27 363	74 519
District 8	15 152	238 159	5.7	3.4	6.5	11.4	14.0	15.6	1.5	4.2	2.3	15 688	65 870
District 9	20 874	291 578	10.1	4.9	11.6	11.9	13.8	2.7	2.4	6.4	2.9	16 471	56 490
District 10	13 349	194 347	5.9	3.3	5.4	10.4	19.1	4.6	2.3	5.6	2.0	11 277	58 027
District 11	25 444	416 784	5.6	3.7	8.3	11.6	13.5	6.9	1.7	13.9	2.2	29 735	71 343
District 12	18 754	327 382	5.8	2.7	10.7	10.0	13.3	6.5	1.1	13.4	2.4	21 661	66 164
NEW MEXICO	43 793	626 284	4.2	6.1	3.4	15.4	19.1	3.6	1.6	(S)	1.8	25 145	40 150
District 1	16 263	264 361	4.7	6.4	4.3	14.1	19.1	4.2	1.6	(S)	2.5	11 196	42 350
District 2	12 863	171 641	3.9	7.2	2.8	16.9	19.9	2.9	1.9	4.4	1.0	6 263	36 490

1. Specified owner-occupied units; $1,000,000 represents $1,000,000 or more.   2. Specified renter-occupied units.

Table E. Congressional Districts 115th Congress — Land Area and Population Characteristics

STATE District	Representative, 115th Congress	Land area,[1] 2016 (sq. mi)	Total persons	Per square mile	White	Black	American Indian, Alaska Native	Asian and Pacific Islander	Some other race	Two or more races	Hispanic or Latino[2]	Non-Hispanic White alone	Female	Foreign-born	Born in state of residence
		1	2	3	4	5	6	7	8	9	10	11	12	13	14
NEW MEXICO—Cont'd															
District 3	Ben Ray Luján (D)	44 958.9	690 811	15.4	64.4	2.0	18.2	1.3	10.9	3.2	40.8	37.4	50.4	6.5	57.5
NEW YORK		47 124.9	19 795 791	420.1	63.8	15.6	0.4	8.5	8.9	2.9	18.8	55.8	51.4	22.9	63.1
District 1	Lee M. Zeldin (R)	650.0	726 589	1 117.8	86.7	5.6	0.2	3.7	2.0	1.8	14.8	74.9	50.2	12.2	78.6
District 2	Peter T. King (R)	181.7	721 038	3 968.3	76.2	9.6	0.1	4.0	6.3	3.7	22.8	62.5	51.1	18.6	74.1
District 3	Thomas R. Souzzi (D)	254.9	721 764	2 831.0	75.1	3.2	0.2	15.7	4.0	1.8	10.3	68.9	51.9	22.0	70.4
District 4	Kathleen M. Rice (D)	110.9	723 380	6 523.2	64.9	15.3	0.2	6.7	9.4	3.4	20.7	56.2	51.3	22.8	70.0
District 5	Gregory W. Meeks (D)	51.9	779 896	15 015.3	17.7	49.3	0.3	13.8	14.8	4.1	21.1	10.4	52.1	42.8	49.1
District 6	Grace Meng (D)	29.8	744 562	24 990.3	44.4	4.3	0.3	40.4	7.2	3.3	18.6	34.3	52.3	52.0	42.1
District 7	Nydia M. Velázquez (D)	16.1	753 292	46 669.5	49.3	10.2	0.5	18.6	18.0	3.4	40.5	31.0	50.0	37.0	46.6
District 8	Hakeem S. Jeffries (D)	28.9	769 795	26 674.3	31.0	52.7	0.3	6.1	7.7	2.3	17.9	23.8	54.6	34.0	52.6
District 9	Yvette D. Clarke (D)	15.5	759 225	48 834.2	34.9	49.7	0.2	6.8	5.9	2.4	12.4	31.2	54.0	40.5	46.2
District 10	Jerrold Nadler (D)	14	728 323	51 852.7	67.5	4.6	0.5	19.6	5.1	2.6	12.2	61.2	51.9	32.2	43.3
District 11	Daniel M. Donovan Jr. (R)	65.6	721 433	11 000.5	71.2	7.9	0.3	13.8	4.4	2.3	17.1	60.2	51.7	30.3	62.4
District 12	Carolyn B. Maloney (D)	14.8	733 946	49 617.8	73.1	4.9	0.2	14.3	4.0	3.5	13.6	64.9	51.9	27.7	41.3
District 13	Adriano Espaillat (D)	10.2	790 434	77 791.0	27.8	28.8	0.5	4.4	32.2	6.4	54.4	14.8	52.7	36.0	47.1
District 14	Joseph Crowley (D)	28.5	720 690	25 317.6	44.0	10.9	0.7	17.8	23.5	3.1	47.5	23.0	50.0	45.9	44.7
District 15	José E. Serrano (D)	14.5	762 550	52 528.1	14.2	31.0	0.5	1.7	49.7	2.9	66.0	3.1	53.2	36.3	51.5
District 16	Eliot L. Engel (D)	78.4	748 723	9 553.0	48.1	33.1	0.4	5.1	9.9	3.4	24.8	37.3	52.5	30.8	54.8
District 17	Nita M. Lowey (D)	382.5	742 551	1 941.1	69.6	10.5	0.3	6.3	10.0	3.2	22.2	59.6	50.8	23.3	63.2
District 18	Sean Patrick Maloney (D)	1 354.1	720 268	531.9	76.1	10.0	0.3	3.1	7.6	2.9	16.4	68.6	50.2	10.6	72.1
District 19	John J. Faso (R)	7 937.1	705 044	88.8	89.2	4.4	0.2	1.7	1.9	2.6	7.3	84.9	49.9	6.0	76.0
District 20	Paul Tonko (D)	1 231.4	727 216	590.6	79.9	8.9	0.1	5.3	2.1	3.7	6.3	76.3	51.1	8.8	75.8
District 21	Elise M. Stefanik (R)	15 113.9	710 842	47.0	92.6	3.2	0.4	1.0	0.8	2.0	3.3	90.7	48.6	3.2	76.6
District 22	Claudia Tenney (R)	5 077.4	711 391	140.1	89.6	3.9	0.2	2.9	1.0	2.4	3.7	87.6	50.3	4.9	80.7
District 23	Tom Reed (R)	7 371.7	708 372	96.1	90.7	3.0	0.6	2.6	1.0	2.1	3.7	88.2	50.5	4.1	74.6
District 24	John Katko (R)	2 388.6	708 959	296.8	84.7	8.4	0.5	2.8	1.0	2.8	4.4	81.7	50.9	6.2	79.1
District 25	Louise McIntosh Slaughter (D)	510.2	722 956	1 417.0	75.4	16.2	0.5	4.0	1.5	2.3	8.6	70.1	51.8	9.2	73.9
District 26	Brian Higgins (D)	219.1	714 758	3 261.7	70.9	18.5	0.4	4.1	3.2	2.9	6.5	68.4	52.1	8.1	79.4
District 27	Chris Collins (R)	3 973.1	717 794	180.7	93.9	2.5	0.5	1.1	0.7	1.3	2.5	92.3	50.0	3.6	85.6
NORTH CAROLINA		48 618.5	10 042 802	206.6	69.1	21.6	1.2	2.7	3.0	2.4	9.1	63.6	51.2	7.9	57.1
District 1	G. K. Butterfield (D)	5 872.7	728 488	124.0	40.0	52.4	1.2	1.7	2.0	2.7	8.8	34.7	52.8	6.6	67.9
District 2	George Holding (R)	2 698.2	796 200	295.1	70.6	16.6	0.9	4.1	4.2	3.2	11.3	64.5	51.1	9.0	50.9
District 3	Walter B. Jones (R)	7 216.0	756 975	104.9	74.3	18.7	0.5	1.4	2.0	3.1	7.0	70.2	49.9	4.1	51.8
District 4	David E. Price (D)	732.3	811 063	1 107.5	54.5	31.7	0.6	6.2	4.2	2.9	12.1	47.6	51.0	14.4	47.7
District 5	Virginia Foxx (R)	3 969.3	755 211	190.3	80.2	12.9	0.3	1.9	3.1	1.5	8.8	74.9	51.0	6.3	63.6
District 6	Mark Walker (R)	3 910.4	753 560	192.7	76.8	16.1	0.3	2.3	1.9	2.6	6.1	73.2	51.1	5.8	63.1
District 7	David Rouzer (R)	5 944.4	785 124	132.1	75.9	16.7	1.9	0.8	2.6	2.2	10.2	68.9	50.7	6.6	60.3
District 8	Richard Hudson (R)	2 954.0	750 103	253.9	66.1	20.0	7.1	0.9	3.9	2.0	9.4	61.3	50.9	6.2	67.2
District 9	Robert Pittenger (R)	3 874.2	828 929	214.0	77.5	13.3	0.3	4.7	2.0	2.1	8.9	70.7	52.2	11.1	39.3
District 10	Patrick T. McHenry (R)	2 589.9	751 909	290.3	81.6	11.8	0.3	1.6	2.9	1.9	6.3	78.4	51.2	5.0	65.7
District 11	Mark Meadows (R)	6 605.2	739 784	112.0	89.9	3.2	1.7	1.3	2.4	1.5	6.0	86.2	51.2	4.9	61.0
District 12	Alma S. Adams (D)	420.1	793 964	1 890.1	37.5	49.4	0.4	5.2	4.5	3.0	14.0	28.7	51.9	13.6	54.4
District 13	Ted Budd(R)	1 831.8	791 492	432.1	73.3	18.4	0.2	2.5	3.1	2.5	8.4	68.7	51.2	7.8	53.4
NORTH DAKOTA		69 001.0	756 928	11.0	88.2	2.1	5.0	1.4	0.8	2.5	3.4	85.9	48.7	3.8	63.7
At Large	Kevin Cramer (R)	69 001.0	756 928	11.0	88.2	2.1	5.0	1.4	0.8	2.5	3.4	85.9	48.7	3.8	63.7
OHIO		40 862.4	11 613 423	284.2	82.0	12.3	0.2	2.1	0.8	2.7	3.5	79.7	51.1	4.3	75.2
District 1	Steve Chabot (R)	687.0	729 977	1 062.6	71.3	22.1	0.1	3.2	0.8	2.6	2.7	69.4	51.3	5.3	73.3
District 2	Brad R. Wenstrup (R)	3 221.7	730 725	226.8	87.3	8.3	0.2	1.3	0.5	2.3	2.2	86.0	51.2	2.9	74.1
District 3	Joyce Beatty (D)	228.0	767 295	3 364.7	57.3	32.7	0.2	3.6	2.0	4.3	6.6	53.2	51.8	11.4	66.5
District 4	Jim Jordan (R)	4 664.8	713 302	152.9	90.5	5.3	0.3	1.0	0.6	2.2	3.7	87.9	50.3	1.8	82.2
District 5	Robert E. Latta (R)	5 626.4	721 478	128.2	92.0	2.7	0.1	1.3	1.5	2.4	5.2	89.1	51.2	2.4	79.4
District 6	Bill Johnson (R)	7 214.7	699 217	96.9	94.9	2.4	0.2	0.4	0.3	1.7	1.0	94.4	50.4	1.1	69.5
District 7	Bob Gibbs (R)	3 864.8	745 591	192.9	92.6	3.9	0.1	0.7	0.3	2.4	2.1	91.1	50.9	1.8	83.5
District 8	Warren Davidson (R)	2 450.6	727 589	296.9	88.5	5.7	0.2	2.1	0.8	2.6	3.4	86.3	51.1	3.6	74.4
District 9	Marcy Kaptur (D)	464.6	709 752	1 527.6	73.8	17.3	0.4	1.4	2.7	4.3	10.6	67.9	51.2	4.6	76.2
District 10	Michael R. Turner (R)	1 129.8	720 041	637.3	77.2	16.4	0.2	2.1	0.6	3.4	2.7	75.2	51.4	4.7	68.4
District 11	Marcia L. Fudge (D)	244.5	704 489	2 881.0	40.1	52.7	0.4	2.7	1.2	3.1	4.5	37.6	53.0	5.3	73.1
District 12	Patrick J. Tiberi (R)	2 272.0	765 297	336.8	87.9	4.7	0.2	3.7	0.7	2.9	2.1	86.3	50.1	4.8	73.9
District 13	Tim Ryan (D)	894.3	709 977	793.9	83.5	11.6	0.2	1.7	0.4	2.6	3.3	81.3	51.6	3.6	77.6
District 14	David P. Joyce (R)	1 954.9	716 084	366.3	91.3	4.4	0.1	2.0	0.3	1.9	2.6	89.4	51.1	5.4	76.7
District 15	Steve Stivers (R)	4 738.9	747 491	157.7	90.2	4.1	0.1	3.1	0.4	2.2	2.0	88.7	49.5	4.9	76.2
District 16	James B. Renacci (R)	1 205.4	705 118	585.0	93.3	2.2	0.2	2.3	0.4	1.5	2.1	91.8	50.8	5.4	78.3
OKLAHOMA		68 596.4	3 911 338	57.0	72.6	7.3	7.3	2.1	2.8	7.9	10.1	66.4	50.4	6.0	60.6
District 1	Jim Bridenstine (R)	1 631.7	792 694	485.8	71.1	8.8	5.4	2.7	3.6	8.4	10.9	65.0	51.2	7.7	58.1
District 2	Markwayne Mullin (R)	20 996.3	750 930	35.8	66.6	3.6	16.3	0.7	1.6	11.1	5.1	64.4	50.3	2.1	61.1
District 3	Frank D. Lucas (R)	34 117.2	779 713	22.9	79.4	3.8	6.1	1.4	3.5	5.8	9.8	74.2	49.4	4.9	63.6
District 4	Tom Cole (R)	9 777.3	778 004	79.6	76.2	6.5	4.9	2.4	1.9	8.0	8.4	71.2	49.7	4.4	61.2
District 5	Steve Russell (R)	2 073.9	809 997	390.6	69.4	13.5	4.4	3.2	3.1	6.5	16.1	57.6	51.3	10.6	59.3
OREGON		95 986.6	4 028 977	42.0	85.3	1.9	1.2	4.4	2.6	4.5	12.7	76.5	50.6	9.9	45.9
District 1	Suzanne Bonamici (D)	3 006.5	820 305	272.8	81.4	1.7	0.8	7.9	3.7	4.6	14.5	71.8	50.6	14.1	42.6
District 2	Greg Walden (R)	69 444.4	798 161	11.5	90.0	0.7	2.2	1.1	2.6	3.4	13.5	80.3	50.1	5.9	44.2

1. Dry land or land partially or temporarily covered by water.   2. May be of any race.

Table E. Congressional Districts 115th Congress — **Age and Education**

STATE District	Population and population characteristics, 2015 (cont.)											Education, 2015		
	Age (percent)												Attainment[2] (percent)	
	Under 5 years	5 to 17 years	18 to 24 years	25 to 34 years	35 to 44 years	45 to 54 years	55 to 64 years	65 to 74 years	75 years and over	Median age	Total Enrollment[1]	High school graduate or more	Bachelor's degree or more
	15	16	17	18	19	20	21	22	23	24	25	26	27
NEW MEXICO—Cont'd													
District 3	6.3	18.2	9.3	12.4	11.7	12.8	13.3	9.9	6.3	38.5	179 063	85.8	27.4
NEW YORK	6.0	15.3	9.8	14.5	12.7	14.0	12.8	8.4	6.6	38.3	4 878 140	86.0	35.0
District 1	4.8	16.3	9.7	10.5	12.5	15.9	13.6	9.8	6.8	42.1	182 233	91.9	34.3
District 2	5.7	15.6	9.9	13.1	12.0	16.1	13.2	7.6	6.7	39.8	179 040	88.0	30.0
District 3	5.0	16.5	7.7	9.8	11.5	15.7	14.7	10.0	9.0	44.7	177 000	93.2	51.8
District 4	6.1	16.5	9.0	12.2	12.7	14.0	13.5	8.9	7.1	39.8	181 858	89.1	40.7
District 5	6.3	16.1	10.1	15.2	12.4	14.3	13.1	7.3	5.2	36.7	205 866	80.3	24.3
District 6	6.4	13.1	7.3	15.1	14.4	14.5	13.1	8.6	7.4	40.5	168 987	83.8	36.2
District 7	7.8	16.3	9.7	19.3	15.2	11.6	9.5	5.9	4.6	33.1	192 557	72.1	33.0
District 8	6.8	15.2	9.9	17.1	12.6	13.1	12.3	7.1	5.8	35.6	195 831	83.0	30.9
District 9	6.7	15.7	8.9	16.9	14.0	13.1	11.6	7.6	5.7	36.0	194 011	85.2	37.3
District 10	6.8	12.2	8.9	20.2	14.5	11.9	11.4	8.2	5.9	36.0	162 478	87.1	60.3
District 11	6.5	15.0	8.1	14.9	12.9	13.8	13.4	8.9	6.5	39.3	170 405	86.9	34.4
District 12	4.6	7.3	8.7	25.9	16.3	12.2	10.4	8.2	6.5	36.6	127 635	93.4	71.5
District 13	6.9	14.0	10.0	20.9	13.1	13.0	11.2	6.1	4.9	33.9	194 942	73.3	31.5
District 14	6.4	14.3	9.2	17.0	15.7	13.5	11.2	7.0	5.7	37.0	169 962	75.5	25.6
District 15	8.0	20.0	12.0	16.4	12.0	12.8	9.4	5.7	3.8	30.7	230 937	63.9	13.9
District 16	6.4	16.4	9.4	11.7	13.5	14.3	12.1	8.4	7.7	39.7	191 014	84.9	38.7
District 17	6.2	18.1	9.0	11.7	11.9	14.3	13.4	8.3	7.1	39.1	206 452	87.0	44.4
District 18	5.4	18.1	10.4	10.8	12.1	15.8	13.1	8.3	6.0	39.4	193 710	91.1	34.6
District 19	4.8	14.5	10.1	10.7	11.1	15.1	15.4	10.9	7.6	44.1	158 512	89.6	28.3
District 20	5.3	14.5	12.0	13.3	12.0	13.6	13.4	8.9	7.0	38.9	189 426	91.8	36.4
District 21	5.9	15.0	10.4	12.2	11.8	14.5	13.9	9.5	6.8	40.8	155 963	89.1	22.6
District 22	5.2	15.4	11.5	11.5	10.7	14.0	14.1	9.7	7.9	41.3	173 740	89.5	23.4
District 23	5.3	14.9	12.7	11.6	10.6	13.4	14.2	9.8	7.4	40.3	178 157	90.1	26.3
District 24	5.5	16.0	10.5	12.7	11.2	14.3	14.0	8.9	6.9	39.9	178 750	90.1	30.5
District 25	5.7	15.4	10.6	14.0	11.3	13.6	13.4	8.9	7.0	38.5	179 887	89.5	36.3
District 26	6.0	15.2	10.7	15.1	10.6	12.5	13.5	8.4	7.8	37.7	179 755	88.6	29.8
District 27	4.7	15.2	8.5	10.9	11.7	15.9	15.4	10.4	7.4	44.3	159 032	92.2	29.3
NORTH CAROLINA	6.0	16.8	9.9	12.9	13.0	13.6	12.7	9.0	6.1	38.4	2 507 958	86.6	29.4
District 1	6.1	16.3	11.0	13.5	11.6	12.6	13.1	8.9	6.7	37.6	184 757	80.1	20.7
District 2	7.3	18.3	8.7	13.1	14.3	13.6	11.3	7.9	5.5	36.7	207 425	87.3	31.0
District 3	6.3	14.9	15.4	13.3	11.2	11.6	12.2	9.1	6.1	35.1	198 956	89.9	24.5
District 4	6.8	15.1	13.9	18.1	12.9	12.0	10.4	6.5	4.2	32.5	236 521	89.1	41.8
District 5	5.1	15.9	10.4	11.3	12.6	14.0	13.6	10.0	7.0	41.0	186 708	85.5	26.8
District 6	4.8	15.9	9.2	11.1	12.6	14.9	14.3	10.0	7.2	42.8	175 788	87.5	29.9
District 7	5.4	17.1	7.9	11.3	13.1	13.7	13.7	11.3	6.4	41.6	181 651	85.3	24.1
District 8	6.0	18.2	9.1	11.7	13.4	13.7	12.4	9.5	6.1	39.2	183 098	83.0	18.0
District 9	6.7	18.9	7.2	12.9	15.1	15.1	12.0	7.3	4.7	37.7	215 998	93.8	49.5
District 10	5.5	16.0	8.6	12.1	12.3	14.4	13.5	10.5	7.0	41.4	164 485	84.4	23.2
District 11	4.6	14.6	8.3	10.5	11.9	13.8	15.2	12.3	9.0	45.2	151 514	85.2	23.4
District 12	7.0	17.7	11.8	17.1	14.0	12.4	9.9	6.1	3.9	32.8	214 157	82.2	25.6
District 13	5.6	19.4	7.0	11.5	14.5	15.0	13.4	8.5	5.2	39.7	206 900	91.0	41.3
NORTH DAKOTA	6.9	15.7	12.4	15.1	11.5	11.7	12.6	7.4	6.7	34.9	181 102	92.5	29.1
At Large	6.9	15.7	12.4	15.1	11.5	11.7	12.6	7.4	6.7	34.9	181 102	92.5	29.1
OHIO	5.9	16.7	9.4	12.8	12.1	13.5	13.7	9.0	6.9	39.3	2 879 469	89.7	26.8
District 1	6.2	18.2	9.7	13.1	12.3	14.2	12.9	7.7	5.8	37.5	204 322	91.3	34.2
District 2	6.2	16.8	7.9	13.7	12.3	13.3	13.8	9.1	6.9	39.4	169 624	89.7	30.5
District 3	7.7	16.7	11.6	18.1	12.9	12.0	11.0	6.0	3.9	32.5	212 424	87.4	27.2
District 4	6.0	16.8	9.0	11.7	11.9	13.6	14.7	9.3	7.0	40.7	169 464	89.8	17.0
District 5	5.8	17.2	10.1	12.0	11.8	12.9	13.7	9.3	7.3	39.5	186 808	92.5	25.2
District 6	5.2	15.5	8.1	10.9	12.0	13.9	15.6	10.5	8.2	43.7	146 816	87.7	15.8
District 7	6.0	17.8	8.6	11.2	11.9	13.0	14.0	10.1	7.4	40.6	176 587	87.5	19.5
District 8	5.9	17.9	10.2	11.5	12.1	13.7	13.3	8.9	6.7	38.8	187 211	88.6	23.7
District 9	5.8	16.3	10.1	13.7	12.1	13.8	14.0	8.1	6.2	38.3	172 305	86.4	21.6
District 10	6.0	16.1	10.1	13.1	11.1	13.2	13.5	9.3	7.6	39.0	184 155	90.7	29.1
District 11	6.2	16.2	10.3	13.5	11.7	12.5	14.2	8.5	7.0	38.2	182 679	85.8	26.0
District 12	6.0	17.6	8.9	13.1	14.1	14.0	12.4	8.3	5.7	37.8	204 055	93.1	40.0
District 13	5.5	14.7	10.2	13.4	11.3	12.7	14.2	9.6	8.0	40.5	169 539	89.6	21.4
District 14	5.1	16.7	7.8	10.4	10.8	15.5	15.3	10.6	7.8	44.3	158 529	91.9	33.5
District 15	5.7	16.8	9.2	14.2	12.6	14.1	13.1	8.3	5.9	37.9	191 090	90.1	30.8
District 16	5.4	15.9	7.9	11.0	11.7	14.6	14.2	10.4	8.7	43.6	163 861	92.8	32.3
OKLAHOMA	6.7	17.8	10.0	13.8	12.3	12.3	12.4	8.5	6.2	36.3	1 025 729	87.3	24.6
District 1	7.1	18.2	9.0	14.1	12.6	12.7	12.5	7.9	5.9	36.1	203 375	89.6	29.4
District 2	6.1	17.7	9.1	11.7	11.6	12.7	13.1	10.5	7.4	39.8	181 712	84.3	17.3
District 3	6.3	18.2	10.9	13.1	11.7	12.2	12.6	8.7	6.4	36.4	209 037	87.2	22.1
District 4	6.3	17.1	11.8	14.0	12.7	12.1	12.0	8.1	5.8	35.5	216 768	89.6	24.1
District 5	7.8	17.9	9.4	15.4	12.7	11.9	11.9	7.5	5.5	34.6	214 837	85.8	29.9
OREGON	5.7	15.7	9.0	13.7	13.1	12.8	13.6	9.8	6.5	39.1	950 559	90.0	32.2
District 1	5.9	17.0	8.2	15.0	14.2	13.5	12.6	8.4	5.1	37.5	200 785	91.2	40.4
District 2	5.9	16.0	8.1	11.8	11.6	12.5	14.7	11.5	8.0	42.1	175 201	89.5	24.0

1. All persons 3 years old and over enrolled in nursery school through college and graduate or professional school.   2. Persons 25 years old and over.

STATE District		Households, 2015						Group quarters, 2010				
	Number	Average household size	Family households (percent)	Married-couple family (percent)	Female family householder[1]	One person households (percent)	Total in group quarters, 2015	Percent 65 years and over	Persons in correctional institutions	Persons in nursing facilities	Persons in college dormitories	Persons in military quarters
	28	29	30	31	32	33	34	35	36	37	38	39
NEW MEXICO—Cont'd												
District 3	248 162	2.73	63.8	44.3	14.2	31.1	12 915	17.2	3 544	1 465	2 115	444
NEW YORK	7 233 694	2.66	63.1	43.6	14.5	30.1	574 606	19.7	95 306	116 558	218 960	8 100
District 1	246 721	2.85	70.6	56.1	10.5	25.2	22 969	20.6	1 648	4 504	9 203	6
District 2	216 567	3.30	73.8	55.1	13.7	22.0	6 856	46.7	6	2 952	720	4
District 3	245 962	2.88	75.2	63.7	8.3	21.4	12 689	41.2	10	5 607	3 982	4
District 4	230 222	3.09	74.9	57.9	12.0	21.9	11 804	28.5	1 657	4 200	4 748	0
District 5	221 213	3.46	76.7	45.0	23.9	19.3	14 911	30.2	234	5 713	2 367	0
District 6	265 193	2.78	67.6	49.8	12.7	27.3	6 465	62.0	17	4 179	812	0
District 7	251 708	2.94	62.0	39.1	17.1	26.5	13 940	12.2	3 636	1 600	1 803	0
District 8	278 959	2.70	61.8	30.8	24.4	31.1	16 759	26.0	256	4 120	2 056	0
District 9	281 787	2.66	61.5	34.5	21.6	30.3	8 808	27.0	0	2 585	611	0
District 10	311 921	2.27	45.7	36.2	6.8	43.6	21 061	10.2	165	2 076	16 711	0
District 11	259 983	2.74	71.8	52.4	13.9	24.4	8 481	36.4	924	3 540	1 457	60
District 12	364 088	1.94	37.3	29.3	5.8	48.4	26 968	10.4	414	3 896	16 755	0
District 13	285 665	2.72	55.3	22.2	26.7	35.4	13 943	29.6	334	5 101	1 924	0
District 14	242 909	2.90	64.9	39.7	16.9	28.2	16 256	21.9	11 095	5 195	2 355	0
District 15	253 192	2.94	66.4	23.8	34.2	29.4	17 889	8.9	981	2 145	2 352	0
District 16	261 213	2.80	65.2	41.7	17.7	30.6	16 307	41.8	0	7 221	5 113	0
District 17	245 245	2.94	72.2	56.7	11.1	23.4	21 670	23.3	3 245	4 756	8 571	0
District 18	246 323	2.81	69.3	53.8	11.6	26.0	27 379	14.3	8 143	3 627	7 046	4 409
District 19	269 443	2.47	64.4	49.8	9.6	29.1	39 644	13.1	9 986	4 771	12 644	3
District 20	283 768	2.45	56.0	41.4	10.4	36.3	31 439	16.3	1 298	4 651	18 920	0
District 21	272 287	2.46	65.3	49.1	11.1	27.7	40 764	10.4	18 001	3 692	11 032	3 614
District 22	275 235	2.46	62.4	45.2	11.1	30.1	33 213	18.0	6 104	6 243	17 830	0
District 23	275 077	2.42	61.6	46.2	10.8	30.7	41 605	13.9	6 988	5 257	23 896	0
District 24	276 624	2.45	61.2	43.8	12.7	30.3	29 963	17.7	4 484	4 882	14 806	0
District 25	288 441	2.42	61.3	42.3	14.6	31.2	25 995	20.7	1 499	4 931	14 361	0
District 26	301 958	2.30	54.9	35.3	16.2	37.4	20 137	20.0	926	3 778	11 661	0
District 27	281 990	2.45	67.1	54.0	9.3	27.0	26 691	20.3	13 255	5 336	5 224	0
NORTH CAROLINA	3 843 745	2.55	65.2	47.6	13.2	28.8	252 683	16.6	61 680	46 638	89 795	26 326
District 1	283 132	2.46	60.8	34.9	20.9	32.8	30 871	15.6	13 922	6 285	10 496	594
District 2	290 173	2.69	69.0	52.0	13.0	26.8	14 608	21.8	1 132	3 214	1 773	5 949
District 3	288 496	2.51	65.1	48.2	12.8	27.4	31 839	6.2	6 616	2 817	8 725	19 749
District 4	317 195	2.44	56.8	39.0	13.5	32.9	36 268	7.0	5 518	2 406	22 784	0
District 5	299 365	2.46	64.7	49.6	10.5	29.4	19 490	18.3	2 268	3 598	10 492	0
District 6	298 146	2.46	65.2	49.9	11.2	30.0	20 258	23.6	2 493	3 811	6 738	0
District 7	297 420	2.60	67.5	50.2	12.5	28.0	11 055	29.2	5 511	3 495	9	33
District 8	274 863	2.67	70.5	49.4	15.3	25.4	16 977	17.1	8 325	3 469	3 449	0
District 9	308 973	2.66	68.7	55.4	9.9	25.3	5 581	45.8	50	2 736	2 155	1
District 10	288 451	2.56	65.3	48.7	12.1	29.5	14 280	30.8	2 503	4 741	4 033	0
District 11	302 408	2.38	65.3	51.1	10.3	29.9	19 157	23.1	5 915	4 622	4 965	0
District 12	300 233	2.56	57.4	33.5	19.0	33.4	25 201	10.1	4 648	3 049	13 560	0
District 13	294 890	2.66	72.1	57.0	11.2	23.1	7 098	28.6	2 779	2 395	616	0
NORTH DAKOTA	313 475	2.33	60.0	47.9	7.8	30.4	26 601	25.3	2 489	6 433	10 570	1 380
At Large	313 475	2.33	60.0	47.9	7.8	30.4	26 601	25.3	2 489	6 433	10 570	1 380
OHIO	4 606 655	2.45	63.4	46.1	12.8	30.3	312 145	25.3	76 590	83 019	106 042	571
District 1	286 903	2.47	63.0	44.9	14.8	30.7	21 418	17.7	6 431	4 486	7 060	0
District 2	293 990	2.45	62.1	45.5	11.9	31.2	10 463	55.0	880	5 887	712	0
District 3	298 494	2.50	55.9	32.0	17.9	34.2	22 179	10.7	2 353	2 793	11 851	0
District 4	277 195	2.47	67.0	50.1	12.5	27.4	27 607	17.6	15 892	5 563	5 261	0
District 5	285 097	2.47	66.2	51.9	9.9	27.2	18 712	31.9	971	6 014	8 367	0
District 6	278 729	2.43	66.0	50.6	10.8	29.1	22 580	30.8	9 881	6 354	3 595	0
District 7	284 239	2.57	66.5	51.4	10.5	27.5	14 888	35.8	795	6 223	5 129	0
District 8	272 766	2.60	67.9	51.5	11.8	25.9	17 061	24.8	1 369	4 682	8 537	0
District 9	293 232	2.37	58.1	35.6	16.7	34.6	13 880	26.5	1 894	4 930	5 512	0
District 10	299 455	2.31	61.5	43.1	13.7	31.8	27 286	21.5	1 997	5 845	12 267	547
District 11	301 051	2.26	53.6	28.7	20.4	40.8	23 797	21.5	3 906	6 243	7 446	0
District 12	288 067	2.59	68.6	55.0	10.1	24.8	18 391	19.4	6 071	3 929	6 352	0
District 13	298 474	2.31	59.1	39.9	13.6	33.8	19 418	20.6	5 134	5 394	10 204	0
District 14	283 208	2.49	68.8	55.0	9.8	26.4	11 743	40.5	2 076	5 260	1 338	24
District 15	282 495	2.53	66.8	52.3	9.9	27.1	31 609	11.1	16 670	3 476	9 591	0
District 16	283 260	2.45	65.5	53.0	8.7	30.0	11 113	51.7	270	5 940	2 820	0
OKLAHOMA	1 465 951	2.59	66.1	48.7	12.2	28.0	109 973	24.0	40 562	21 678	30 148	7 203
District 1	312 581	2.51	65.9	47.4	13.1	27.5	9 039	28.8	2 371	3 656	2 981	0
District 2	279 501	2.60	68.2	50.6	12.6	27.4	23 687	19.9	9 915	5 506	4 623	0
District 3	279 580	2.68	68.4	53.1	9.9	26.2	30 299	13.8	15 091	4 818	10 089	463
District 4	284 909	2.63	66.1	49.8	11.1	27.6	28 357	12.1	7 991	3 797	7 490	6 740
District 5	309 380	2.56	62.5	43.1	13.9	31.2	18 591	18.8	5 194	3 901	4 965	0
OREGON	1 553 205	2.54	63.0	48.3	10.3	27.9	86 962	18.0	22 203	11 491	23 704	178
District 1	308 174	2.62	64.4	50.8	9.4	27.4	14 334	20.7	4 641	1 964	3 338	127
District 2	311 030	2.50	65.1	50.1	10.7	27.1	21 020	19.0	8 762	2 660	1 775	13

1. No spouse present.

STATE District	Housing units, 2015						Money income, 2015		
		Occupied units						Households	
			Owner-occupied			Renter-occupied			
	Total	Occupied units as a percent of all units	Owner-occupied units as a percent of occupied units	Median value[1] (dollars)	Percent valued at $500,000 or more	Median rent[2]	Per capita income (dollars)	Median income (dollars)	Percent with income of $100,000 or more
	40	41	42	43	44	45	46	47	48
NEW MEXICO—Cont'd									
District 3	309 922	80.1	70.9	177 000	8.6	843	25 396	48 061	19.8
NEW YORK	8 207 161	88.1	53.1	293 500	25.1	1 173	34 297	60 850	29.6
District 1	310 953	79.3	79.9	376 200	25.6	1 591	39 851	86 645	43.2
District 2	235 923	91.8	80.2	363 800	14.2	1 533	34 604	89 668	44.6
District 3	268 352	91.7	80.8	575 600	59.3	1 794	51 565	102 602	52.1
District 4	245 624	93.7	76.8	442 300	36.2	1 517	40 051	97 111	48.9
District 5	239 310	92.4	55.8	419 100	24.6	1 302	25 327	65 012	29.8
District 6	290 190	91.4	44.6	559 000	58.0	1 463	30 155	59 696	27.8
District 7	273 338	92.1	21.9	663 000	67.0	1 281	29 285	49 420	25.5
District 8	311 598	89.5	31.8	530 700	53.9	1 157	26 653	47 220	23.3
District 9	303 759	92.8	28.5	582 700	59.3	1 263	29 948	51 148	24.5
District 10	361 126	86.4	30.3	877 700	80.9	1 713	65 227	81 834	44.0
District 11	279 355	93.1	58.0	486 700	47.3	1 273	30 930	66 344	32.3
District 12	430 694	84.5	28.5	857 600	78.2	2 016	82 163	93 649	48.2
District 13	306 558	93.2	9.4	429 600	39.3	1 127	23 906	39 258	16.6
District 14	264 250	91.9	31.3	480 300	47.2	1 389	24 582	52 346	21.2
District 15	267 658	94.6	8.9	363 000	17.0	1 026	14 482	26 047	6.9
District 16	283 211	92.2	48.9	435 500	41.7	1 265	40 393	66 325	34.7
District 17	262 202	93.5	65.4	460 900	42.5	1 440	42 651	89 905	45.7
District 18	273 901	89.9	69.4	296 500	15.0	1 188	37 527	79 540	39.1
District 19	360 528	74.7	72.2	198 100	6.4	894	30 029	58 298	24.8
District 20	328 441	86.4	60.0	202 100	4.6	914	33 184	61 393	27.3
District 21	370 282	73.5	70.1	135 900	3.5	814	25 475	51 580	18.3
District 22	320 029	86.0	68.3	113 000	1.8	708	26 315	50 416	18.8
District 23	338 976	81.1	68.9	102 000	2.2	725	25 968	49 592	18.2
District 24	314 991	87.8	66.8	131 100	2.6	793	29 094	55 014	22.4
District 25	314 407	91.7	63.5	142 800	1.6	855	29 857	53 594	22.8
District 26	340 322	88.7	58.3	116 900	1.9	731	26 630	45 106	17.2
District 27	311 183	90.6	76.5	149 300	2.1	741	31 808	62 566	26.5
NORTH CAROLINA	4 491 090	85.6	63.9	160 100	6.0	827	26 801	47 830	19.1
District 1	339 419	83.4	52.6	111 200	2.3	757	20 382	35 148	10.6
District 2	328 171	88.4	65.6	165 200	5.7	880	27 122	52 471	22.3
District 3	376 709	76.6	61.3	159 500	4.8	869	24 684	45 716	16.2
District 4	349 104	90.9	50.3	181 500	8.5	912	29 439	49 423	21.3
District 5	354 572	84.4	67.4	152 200	4.4	715	25 932	44 817	16.6
District 6	334 219	89.2	69.7	159 900	4.2	773	28 688	49 111	20.0
District 7	372 643	79.8	71.6	158 500	5.3	788	25 368	47 426	18.3
District 8	311 915	88.1	66.8	125 700	2.9	725	21 562	43 792	14.2
District 9	328 526	94.0	71.6	251 800	15.7	1 107	40 046	76 101	37.7
District 10	335 810	85.9	67.3	140 800	5.7	721	23 960	42 154	14.8
District 11	396 610	76.2	70.7	155 700	5.0	671	23 978	42 079	12.7
District 12	341 563	87.9	43.1	123 300	2.1	846	21 612	37 980	11.8
District 13	321 829	91.6	72.7	216 700	7.9	951	33 796	67 118	31.1
NORTH DAKOTA	362 889	86.4	61.7	180 900	3.8	775	34 063	60 557	26.9
At Large	362 889	86.4	61.7	180 900	3.8	775	34 063	60 557	26.9
OHIO	5 156 546	89.3	65.4	136 400	2.9	746	28 001	51 075	20.4
District 1	321 377	89.3	61.8	155 100	5.2	725	30 604	55 059	25.2
District 2	325 486	90.3	64.7	149 100	4.8	746	29 966	52 371	21.9
District 3	336 066	88.8	44.8	117 500	2.0	831	22 844	42 601	14.0
District 4	307 536	90.1	69.6	122 800	1.8	668	25 298	50 627	17.4
District 5	309 000	92.3	72.9	133 200	1.4	712	28 393	56 098	21.4
District 6	320 727	86.9	73.4	108 100	2.0	634	24 047	43 964	14.1
District 7	310 481	91.5	72.1	135 700	2.1	695	25 548	51 132	18.9
District 8	302 189	90.3	69.3	142 800	2.4	758	26 926	54 069	21.4
District 9	349 542	83.9	57.9	96 900	1.8	694	24 008	41 379	14.0
District 10	334 244	89.6	61.9	122 000	1.7	749	27 389	49 490	19.1
District 11	369 619	81.4	48.2	90 800	3.8	711	24 685	35 624	13.4
District 12	311 791	92.4	70.4	193 200	6.1	898	35 683	69 056	31.6
District 13	338 842	88.1	63.7	98 100	1.0	683	24 729	42 019	13.6
District 14	306 939	92.3	76.1	173 700	4.2	850	34 742	64 775	29.4
District 15	311 559	90.7	67.8	161 300	3.4	858	29 821	60 009	25.2
District 16	301 148	94.1	75.1	161 000	2.7	786	32 970	61 330	26.8
OKLAHOMA	1 711 515	85.7	65.3	126 800	3.1	759	25 762	48 568	18.3
District 1	344 498	90.7	61.4	147 700	3.9	806	29 204	52 054	21.5
District 2	352 831	79.2	71.2	99 500	2.6	634	21 419	41 197	13.0
District 3	335 376	83.4	69.5	114 000	2.0	726	24 514	48 571	17.8
District 4	329 642	86.4	66.3	133 500	2.2	789	25 524	51 990	19.3
District 5	349 168	88.6	59.4	139 000	4.6	799	27 849	48 426	19.6
OREGON	1 718 509	90.4	61.1	264 100	12.7	943	29 117	54 148	22.4
District 1	332 527	92.7	61.1	308 300	16.2	1 085	34 531	66 349	30.6
District 2	361 682	86.0	63.1	217 700	10.4	842	25 341	46 793	15.9

1. Specified owner-occupied units; $1,000,000 represents $1,000,000 or more.   2. Specified renter-occupied units.

Table E. Congressional Districts 115th Congress — Poverty, Labor Force, Employment, and Social Security

STATE District	Poverty, 2015			Civilian labor force, 2015			Civilian employment,[2] 2015				Persons under age 65 with no health insurance, 2015 (percent)	Social Security beneficiaries, December 2015		Supplemental Security Income recipients, December 2015
					Unemployment			Percent						
	Persons below poverty level (percent)	Families below poverty level (percent)	Percent of households receiving food stamps in past 12 months	Total	Total	Rate[1]	Total	Management, business, science and arts occupations	Service, sales, and office	Construction and production		Number	Rate[3]	
	49	50	51	52	53	54	55	56	57	58	59	60	61	62
NEW MEXICO—Cont'd														
District 3	18.8	13.0	15.4	317 220	25 288	8.0	291 932	36.1	45.2	18.7	14.0	137 981	199.7	21 247
NEW YORK	15.4	11.6	15.3	10 128 222	654 885	6.5	9 473 337	39.9	43.5	16.6	8.1	3 513 125	177.5	648 707
District 1	8.3	4.8	6.3	373 761	17 633	4.7	356 128	40.0	42.1	17.9	6.6	147 635	203.2	9 789
District 2	6.5	4.1	6.7	392 212	21 659	5.5	370 553	34.7	45.1	20.2	7.0	131 835	182.8	9 929
District 3	5.6	4.1	4.1	363 014	15 982	4.4	347 032	50.5	37.2	12.3	5.0	145 635	201.8	7 353
District 4	6.6	4.9	5.4	384 118	18 583	4.8	365 535	42.4	42.6	15.1	7.3	134 832	186.4	10 300
District 5	12.1	10.0	17.0	409 052	37 570	9.2	371 482	27.6	51.5	21.0	10.6	104 956	134.6	27 371
District 6	13.3	10.7	10.6	381 284	22 688	6.0	358 596	38.8	45.3	16.0	13.4	114 133	153.3	22 523
District 7	27.2	24.2	26.2	377 640	24 567	6.5	353 073	38.5	45.0	16.5	12.9	85 085	113.0	34 567
District 8	22.0	18.3	25.5	384 622	35 371	9.2	349 251	38.0	47.0	15.0	8.8	107 759	140.0	52 504
District 9	19.2	15.7	20.9	392 404	28 486	7.3	363 918	41.4	45.5	13.1	9.7	98 900	130.3	35 521
District 10	17.4	13.5	12.2	405 890	21 542	5.3	384 348	59.4	32.7	7.8	6.5	101 237	139.0	22 373
District 11	14.8	12.0	14.8	343 921	20 748	6.0	323 173	40.4	42.2	17.3	7.7	128 301	177.8	28 847
District 12	11.3	6.9	5.8	469 419	19 928	4.2	449 491	67.0	28.2	4.8	6.9	105 687	144.0	14 542
District 13	27.7	24.7	31.7	414 887	43 969	10.6	370 918	34.8	50.6	14.6	11.6	106 404	134.6	64 076
District 14	17.2	14.2	17.0	375 728	24 627	6.6	351 101	29.4	49.5	21.1	16.0	94 190	130.7	19 831
District 15	38.1	36.0	46.6	325 815	36 804	11.3	289 011	19.6	61.3	19.2	12.2	90 222	118.3	66 457
District 16	13.7	10.3	14.6	381 428	28 690	7.5	352 738	41.6	44.8	13.6	8.7	124 888	166.8	22 225
District 17	10.6	7.3	8.9	384 646	23 556	6.1	361 090	46.7	40.5	12.8	8.6	127 186	171.3	10 187
District 18	10.1	6.7	9.5	356 699	21 211	5.9	335 488	39.2	44.2	16.6	5.2	130 660	181.4	11 535
District 19	13.7	8.9	10.9	346 510	20 982	6.1	325 528	36.5	41.8	21.7	6.7	163 608	232.1	15 331
District 20	11.3	7.3	11.5	386 026	21 090	5.5	364 936	42.8	43.0	14.2	5.1	147 776	203.2	18 780
District 21	14.0	9.6	14.6	333 209	20 709	6.2	312 500	31.4	44.6	24.1	6.6	165 909	233.4	19 572
District 22	15.9	10.4	16.6	341 668	22 298	6.5	319 370	34.3	43.6	22.0	6.2	164 881	231.8	21 608
District 23	15.8	9.8	14.5	338 993	20 685	6.1	318 308	35.2	41.6	23.2	7.4	163 561	230.9	19 661
District 24	14.6	9.8	14.3	359 462	23 750	6.6	335 712	38.5	42.4	19.2	5.8	152 853	215.6	20 360
District 25	15.1	10.7	16.0	379 323	25 513	6.7	353 810	41.0	42.1	16.9	5.0	151 816	210.0	25 016
District 26	20.8	15.4	21.5	354 463	19 927	5.6	334 536	36.5	46.3	17.3	4.5	156 844	219.4	28 239
District 27	9.2	5.8	9.1	372 028	16 317	4.4	355 711	37.1	40.6	22.2	4.8	166 332	231.7	10 210
NORTH CAROLINA	16.4	11.8	14.2	4 886 759	335 787	6.9	4 550 972	36.6	40.1	23.3	13.1	1 984 962	197.7	235 704
District 1	25.5	20.9	25.1	336 786	30 709	9.1	306 077	30.2	42.6	27.2	16.8	163 421	224.3	38 512
District 2	14.6	10.1	11.7	367 001	25 551	7.0	341 450	39.4	37.5	23.0	12.8	141 495	177.7	15 434
District 3	17.0	11.1	12.9	348 457	31 903	9.2	316 554	31.5	46.2	22.3	12.9	149 317	197.3	16 988
District 4	18.9	13.5	13.6	429 519	25 637	6.0	403 882	42.6	40.3	17.1	13.2	111 289	137.2	16 982
District 5	17.2	11.6	11.5	367 066	25 589	7.0	341 477	34.4	40.3	25.3	12.8	166 487	220.5	14 129
District 6	13.6	9.4	11.3	374 313	21 272	5.7	353 041	38.4	39.1	22.5	10.9	168 695	223.9	14 274
District 7	16.5	11.5	14.8	363 947	22 854	6.3	341 093	33.5	40.6	25.9	14.3	178 400	227.2	19 543
District 8	18.4	13.5	18.1	347 483	26 355	7.6	321 128	30.3	38.7	31.0	14.0	156 654	208.8	22 028
District 9	8.1	5.4	6.2	446 201	22 192	5.0	424 009	48.1	38.0	13.9	8.4	117 285	141.5	6 617
District 10	16.5	12.4	16.5	353 670	26 799	7.6	326 871	31.2	40.0	28.8	13.8	174 684	232.3	19 794
District 11	15.9	11.1	14.8	333 374	18 620	5.6	314 754	32.9	38.3	28.8	14.8	206 035	278.5	16 875
District 12	23.6	19.7	20.9	410 942	37 571	9.1	373 371	30.8	43.6	25.6	17.7	117 433	147.9	25 585
District 13	9.2	6.2	8.7	408 000	20 735	5.1	387 265	45.4	37.0	17.6	8.2	133 767	169.0	8 943
NORTH DAKOTA	11.0	6.9	6.9	415 475	10 886	2.6	404 589	35.3	38.8	26.0	8.9	125 786	166.2	8 198
At Large	11.0	6.9	6.9	415 475	10 886	2.6	404 589	35.3	38.8	26.0	8.9	125 786	166.2	8 198
OHIO	14.8	10.7	14.3	5 863 639	373 897	6.4	5 489 742	35.7	40.6	23.6	7.6	2 290 813	197.3	312 351
District 1	14.7	10.2	13.0	374 913	25 701	6.9	349 212	41.6	40.9	17.5	6.1	125 717	172.2	20 262
District 2	13.8	10.4	13.1	361 630	19 092	5.3	342 538	38.6	40.1	21.3	7.5	145 161	198.7	21 668
District 3	23.2	18.5	20.4	408 963	31 433	7.7	377 530	33.2	45.7	21.0	11.8	103 719	135.2	29 462
District 4	13.6	10.3	13.4	352 884	21 177	6.0	331 707	28.0	36.7	35.2	6.1	150 528	211.0	15 068
District 5	10.5	6.4	9.4	376 355	17 785	4.7	358 570	33.8	35.7	30.5	6.1	148 118	205.3	10 799
District 6	16.5	12.8	16.5	317 556	21 320	6.7	296 236	27.8	42.2	30.1	7.9	170 360	243.6	24 862
District 7	12.8	8.7	12.2	375 833	20 345	5.4	355 488	30.1	40.3	29.6	10.7	154 380	207.1	13 649
District 8	13.6	8.9	12.5	363 729	20 616	5.7	343 113	34.5	39.5	26.1	7.0	143 534	197.3	14 871
District 9	20.7	16.4	21.7	361 014	32 186	8.9	328 828	30.1	44.7	25.2	8.0	141 337	199.1	31 212
District 10	17.0	12.8	15.8	356 427	25 893	7.3	330 534	37.9	41.0	21.1	7.5	146 266	203.1	19 669
District 11	26.4	21.3	26.1	338 985	41 912	12.4	297 073	36.7	45.1	18.2	8.0	136 456	193.7	41 355
District 12	9.7	6.2	9.3	404 034	19 236	4.8	384 798	46.6	37.9	15.5	5.3	129 911	169.8	13 031
District 13	18.0	13.4	17.4	353 372	25 673	7.3	327 699	29.9	44.6	25.5	8.3	160 146	225.6	25 114
District 14	8.1	5.3	7.7	373 343	16 757	4.5	356 586	40.0	39.0	21.0	7.6	152 475	212.9	9 996
District 15	11.6	8.1	12.8	370 406	19 139	5.2	351 267	40.7	38.7	20.6	6.3	130 075	174.0	13 777
District 16	7.3	5.4	6.7	374 195	15 632	4.2	358 563	39.3	39.1	21.6	7.4	152 630	216.5	7 556
OKLAHOMA	16.1	11.7	13.0	1 854 533	101 088	5.5	1 753 445	33.6	41.8	24.6	16.2	758 912	194.0	96 921
District 1	15.3	11.8	12.2	409 878	22 977	5.6	386 901	36.9	41.8	21.2	15.8	143 212	180.7	17 518
District 2	19.8	15.3	18.0	313 586	20 580	6.6	293 006	28.2	42.6	29.2	20.5	183 104	243.8	27 691
District 3	15.9	10.7	10.4	356 206	18 422	5.2	337 784	30.5	40.4	29.0	14.5	151 279	194.0	14 540
District 4	12.6	8.6	10.5	377 997	19 969	5.3	358 028	36.2	40.5	23.3	13.1	144 679	186.0	16 036
District 5	16.9	12.3	14.1	396 866	19 140	4.8	377 726	34.6	43.4	21.9	17.3	136 638	168.7	21 136
OREGON	15.4	9.9	18.6	2 018 994	137 739	6.8	1 881 255	37.7	41.4	20.9	8.3	818 228	203.1	86 153
District 1	11.0	7.0	13.0	430 340	24 810	5.8	405 530	43.3	40.2	16.6	7.7	131 963	160.9	11 902
District 2	18.2	12.8	21.4	368 129	28 049	7.6	340 080	32.1	42.8	25.1	9.9	196 044	245.6	17 936

1. Percent of civilian labor force.   2. Persons 16 years old and over.   3. Per 1,000 resident population estimated in the 2014 American Community Survey.

Table E. Congressional Districts 115th Congress — **Agriculture**

STATE District	Agriculture, 2012									
	Land in farms				Value of products sold				Government payments	
	Number of farms	Acres	Average size of farm (acres)	Irrigated land (acres)	Total ($1,000)	Average per farm (dollars)	Percent from crops	Percent from livestock and poultry products	Total ($1,000)	Average per farm receiving payments (dollars)
	63	64	65	66	67	68	69	70	71	72
NEW MEXICO—Cont'd										
District 3	12 723	19 249 622	1 513	277 321	877 541	68 973	16.6	83.4	29 752	10 021
NEW YORK	35 537	7 183 576	202	59 807	5 415 125	152 380	41.5	58.5	74 511	7 955
District 1	499	27 475	55	8 672	196 009	392 803	83.0	17.0	605	15 508
District 2	39	1 088	28	265	4 469	114 580	98.0	2.0	D	D
District 3	112	10 121	90	2 954	45 149	403 114	88.6	11.4	185	61 793
District 4	10	20	2	14	492	49 170	D	D	0	0
District 5	X	X	X	X	X	X	X	X	X	X
District 6	X	X	X	X	X	X	X	X	X	X
District 7	X	X	X	X	X	X	X	X	X	X
District 8	X	X	X	X	X	X	X	X	X	X
District 9	X	X	X	X	X	X	X	X	X	X
District 10	X	X	X	X	X	X	X	X	X	X
District 11	X	X	X	X	X	X	X	X	X	X
District 12	X	X	X	X	X	X	X	X	X	X
District 13	X	X	X	X	X	X	X	X	X	X
District 14	X	X	X	X	X	X	X	X	X	X
District 15	X	X	X	X	X	X	X	X	X	X
District 16	10	1 017	102	9	828	82 774	91.8	8.2	0	0
District 17	70	2 001	29	113	6 584	94 053	62.7	37.3	D	D
District 18	871	110 109	126	3 066	113 514	130 326	71.9	28.1	2 102	10 778
District 19	5 314	957 846	180	8 894	462 961	87 121	44.3	55.7	8 095	6 581
District 20	1 181	161 612	137	804	113 423	96 040	44.2	55.8	1 111	5 142
District 21	6 108	1 496 682	245	2 668	977 396	160 019	23.1	76.9	15 284	9 983
District 22	4 770	941 790	197	2 123	493 919	103 547	26.9	73.1	10 122	7 174
District 23	8 716	1 667 821	191	5 848	1 054 998	121 042	39.1	60.9	14 867	6 541
District 24	2 712	603 589	223	3 754	667 658	246 187	46.4	53.6	6 666	8 199
District 25	364	56 344	155	810	47 235	129 766	88.4	11.6	760	9 266
District 26	58	10 225	176	38	8 791	151 564	99.2	0.8	D	D
District 27	4 674	1 135 393	243	19 756	1 218 619	260 723	46.4	53.6	14 616	9 351
NORTH CAROLINA	50 218	8 414 756	168	174 526	12 588 142	250 670	34.2	65.8	120 129	8 332
District 1	3 457	1 267 552	367	37 421	1 411 910	408 421	48.5	51.5	29 500	13 176
District 2	4 319	540 316	125	9 955	794 538	183 963	20.7	79.3	6 417	7 902
District 3	3 115	1 258 856	404	23 466	1 667 112	535 188	52.2	47.8	25 085	13 663
District 4	1 051	113 099	108	2 044	117 955	112 231	33.8	66.2	1 419	5 609
District 5	7 523	782 829	104	3 009	863 937	114 839	22.6	77.4	4 295	3 873
District 6	6 051	744 474	123	12 316	442 156	73 072	44.1	55.9	6 752	4 271
District 7	5 330	1 205 092	226	46 178	3 720 633	698 055	21.0	79.0	19 390	8 106
District 8	5 065	901 322	178	11 176	1 694 602	334 571	21.9	78.1	9 344	7 205
District 9	1 068	128 936	121	1 065	282 689	264 690	68.8	31.2	819	7 805
District 10	4 082	385 987	95	1 696	307 645	75 366	22.2	77.8	2 462	3 558
District 11	6 428	461 764	72	8 510	305 338	47 501	65.3	34.7	6 241	6 125
District 12	483	49 775	103	918	36 733	76 052	71.7	28.3	289	3 849
District 13	2 246	574 754	256	16 772	942 895	419 811	54.3	45.7	8 114	8 058
NORTH DAKOTA	30 961	39 262 613	1 268	218 407	10 950 680	353 693	88.3	11.7	381 710	15 398
At Large	30 961	39 262 613	1 268	218 407	10 950 000	353 693	88.3	11.7	381 710	15 398
OHIO	75 462	13 960 604	185	46 569	10 064 085	133 366	65.6	34.4	228 858	6 603
District 1	1 200	124 692	104	970	80 571	67 142	89.9	10.1	1 194	4 593
District 2	6 107	983 627	161	1 478	373 277	61 123	82.8	17.2	17 161	5 529
District 3	92	16 593	180	144	19 539	212 376	94.4	5.6	120	4 435
District 4	9 348	2 307 012	247	6 343	1 844 009	197 262	76.8	23.2	45 190	6 949
District 5	10 792	2 847 931	264	6 809	2 386 632	221 148	70.5	29.5	61 441	7 107
District 6	11 766	1 584 934	135	4 365	426 139	36 218	46.0	54.0	10 048	4 426
District 7	9 520	1 354 995	142	6 634	1 072 386	112 646	50.5	49.5	15 873	5 529
District 8	6 055	1 174 229	194	5 577	1 371 101	226 441	43.7	56.3	23 599	6 752
District 9	506	76 485	151	1 354	82 288	162 624	97.9	2.1	1 493	4 993
District 10	1 898	378 015	199	1 868	254 837	134 266	86.2	13.8	6 374	6 612
District 11	81	2 497	31	197	3 575	44 131	94.0	6.0	37	7 391
District 12	4 307	712 235	165	1 331	536 943	124 668	67.4	32.6	9 618	6 438
District 13	1 038	107 448	104	184	57 947	55 825	69.0	31.0	962	4 413
District 14	3 053	342 898	112	2 734	265 078	86 825	77.1	22.9	2 865	4 783
District 15	6 879	1 598 791	232	5 392	850 104	123 580	83.2	16.8	27 660	8 745
District 16	2 820	348 222	123	1 189	439 660	155 908	32.6	67.4	5 223	7 048
OKLAHOMA	80 245	34 356 110	428	479 750	7 129 584	88 848	26.3	73.7	256 845	8 634
District 1	3 160	575 332	182	D	99 709	31 553	42.0	58.0	2 618	4 392
District 2	29 692	8 013 419	270	38 897	2 053 254	69 152	16.2	83.8	37 636	5 317
District 3	30 326	19 992 205	659	395 097	4 172 753	137 597	30.6	69.4	182 507	10 572
District 4	13 283	5 059 287	381	33 614	711 085	53 533	28.0	72.0	31 371	7 483
District 5	3 784	715 867	189	D	92 783	24 520	28.2	71.8	2 714	4 391
OREGON	35 439	16 301 578	460	1 629 735	4 883 674	137 805	66.5	33.5	85 840	16 054
District 1	4 759	400 597	84	46 715	584 568	122 834	84.9	15.1	4 343	6 861
District 2	13 284	13 924 323	1 048	1 349 942	2 419 047	182 102	58.7	41.3	72 580	21 038

Private nonfarm employment and payroll, 2015

STATE District	Number of establish-ments	Total	Manufact-uring	Construc-tion	Wholesale trade	Retail trade	Health care and social assistance	Finance and Insurance	Real estate and rental and leasing	Professio-nal, scientific, and technical services	Information	Total (mil dol)	Average per employee dollars
	73	74	75	76	77	78	79	80	81	82	83	84	85
NEW MEXICO—Cont'd													
District 3	14 360	177 108	3.9	5.0	2.5	17.2	19.8	3.2	1.5	8.8	1.6	7 150	40 372
NEW YORK	540 298	7 998 994	5.3	4.2	4.6	11.7	18.7	6.7	2.2	8.1	3.5	513 083	64 143
District 1	22 822	234 234	8.3	7.7	6.0	17.3	20.6	2.9	1.1	7.0	1.6	12 420	53 024
District 2	20 540	245 350	11.4	9.2	8.8	14.3	15.8	2.4	1.4	5.7	2.2	11 331	46 181
District 3	29 632	380 744	3.2	4.2	6.8	10.8	21.9	7.1	2.0	9.0	3.4	23 994	63 020
District 4	24 473	265 713	3.5	5.5	3.7	15.5	19.6	5.7	1.6	8.9	1.7	12 811	48 214
District 5	11 068	152 690	1.9	5.3	2.4	12.3	18.6	1.1	2.0	2.2	0.8	6 683	43 769
District 6	18 350	171 117	2.6	6.6	3.3	14.2	37.8	3.5	2.7	3.8	1.4	6 775	39 591
District 7	21 862	210 008	5.3	6.7	6.6	11.3	22.7	3.7	2.9	5.1	2.5	8 943	42 582
District 8	11 264	133 517	3.2	3.0	4.1	15.8	28.2	2.6	2.6	2.6	1.9	5 210	39 019
District 9	12 596	118 291	1.0	2.6	1.8	13.7	44.1	1.4	3.2	3.2	2.1	4 592	38 817
District 10	40 406	783 690	1.5	1.9	3.3	7.2	13.1	13.9	2.8	12.3	6.9	73 088	93 262
District 11	15 997	152 306	1.1	6.7	2.1	16.5	35.7	2.4	1.7	3.7	1.6	5 996	39 366
District 12	70 774	1 506 062	1.3	2.6	5.3	6.6	9.1	13.0	3.3	14.6	7.6	170 282	113 064
District 13	9 888	142 612	0.3	1.4	0.5	10.4	50.0	1.2	3.6	2.0	1.4	7 803	54 716
District 14	12 245	146 140	3.5	9.6	5.1	11.7	24.4	2.2	2.6	1.9	2.0	6 824	46 698
District 15	9 084	123 074	3.9	4.7	8.4	13.9	31.8	1.1	3.8	1.9	1.3	5 270	42 822
District 16	16 203	174 457	3.8	8.2	2.7	16.9	23.4	2.3	3.7	3.3	2.1	8 065	46 228
District 17	26 008	335 386	4.0	5.2	5.6	11.8	21.3	5.6	2.0	7.6	2.5	22 507	67 107
District 18	19 098	224 294	6.3	4.5	5.1	17.6	19.7	2.7	1.4	7.8	2.3	10 124	45 138
District 19	16 708	163 003	8.2	5.3	3.5	17.6	22.9	3.5	1.3	3.2	1.6	6 005	36 837
District 20	18 924	329 158	7.0	4.3	4.2	13.3	19.8	5.8	1.4	8.5	2.8	15 347	46 624
District 21	15 497	179 106	11.5	4.6	3.0	20.3	20.9	2.5	1.1	2.9	2.0	6 586	36 771
District 22	14 289	223 525	13.2	3.0	3.9	14.9	20.4	4.9	0.9	4.4	2.1	8 393	37 548
District 23	14 618	224 368	15.5	3.3	2.7	15.0	17.9	2.5	1.2	3.0	1.5	8 299	36 989
District 24	16 534	275 488	10.9	4.2	5.6	14.2	18.5	4.6	1.6	5.7	1.9	11 863	43 061
District 25	16 990	345 751	10.0	3.3	4.4	11.9	18.9	3.7	1.7	6.6	3.0	15 542	44 951
District 26	17 605	351 068	8.5	3.0	5.0	12.1	18.9	7.7	1.6	7.7	1.8	15 333	43 676
District 27	16 050	206 842	17.5	5.6	5.0	18.3	15.4	2.8	1.1	3.3	1.2	8 652	41 828
NORTH CAROLINA	223 209	3 670 284	11.6	4.8	4.9	13.1	15.5	4.8	1.4	5.8	2.2	164 936	44 938
District 1	14 000	251 674	12.6	3.9	2.6	12.0	22.8	4.0	1.1	4.5	1.7	10 566	41 983
District 2	14 918	182 588	13.0	7.3	5.1	16.2	14.6	2.5	1.1	4.7	2.0	7 057	38 652
District 3	15 768	182 392	10.0	6.2	2.7	19.7	16.5	3.4	2.3	3.9	1.2	5 979	32 781
District 4	24 591	461 441	3.6	4.6	6.6	11.8	14.1	5.6	1.8	14.0	5.4	26 743	57 956
District 5	15 906	268 045	12.2	5.6	3.4	13.6	17.5	4.8	1.2	3.3	1.2	11 686	43 597
District 6	13 409	195 248	24.1	5.6	4.6	14.4	16.1	2.3	0.8	2.4	1.7	7 177	36 756
District 7	16 457	206 090	12.1	5.7	4.1	17.9	18.1	3.1	1.7	4.5	2.1	7 649	37 115
District 8	13 777	198 756	10.6	5.1	2.9	18.2	20.3	2.1	1.3	3.7	1.2	6 923	34 834
District 9	16 603	238 436	14.8	5.4	4.5	14.5	13.8	6.3	1.2	5.4	1.5	10 525	44 143
District 10	17 893	272 684	19.4	3.8	4.5	14.4	20.0	2.0	1.0	2.9	1.2	10 525	38 596
District 11	15 751	195 331	20.9	5.6	3.8	16.5	16.7	2.3	1.1	2.5	1.1	6 718	34 395
District 12	23 305	493 300	5.1	4.3	7.3	9.1	11.5	11.7	1.8	8.2	3.1	30 069	60 954
District 13	20 132	365 336	14.6	4.0	6.3	11.8	14.9	4.1	1.4	4.2	1.6	15 946	43 648
NORTH DAKOTA	24 848	365 893	6.9	7.0	6.6	14.2	16.2	5.0	1.6	4.4	1.9	17 185	46 967
At Large	24 848	365 893	6.9	7.0	6.6	14.2	16.2	5.0	1.6	4.4	1.9	17 185	46 967
OHIO	251 668	4 719 985	14.1	3.8	5.0	12.0	17.5	5.1	1.4	5.3	1.8	213 161	45 161
District 1	16 687	389 726	9.1	4.2	5.9	9.5	18.8	6.5	1.4	7.4	2.7	22 438	57 574
District 2	15 758	264 932	10.2	4.3	5.3	14.4	16.7	5.9	1.5	8.1	2.3	11 994	45 273
District 3	14 976	363 369	6.1	3.8	5.0	10.8	18.6	8.5	1.9	6.0	1.9	18 242	50 202
District 4	14 496	268 884	28.9	3.8	4.4	11.8	15.9	2.1	0.7	3.7	1.0	11 074	41 186
District 5	16 253	304 696	21.7	3.6	3.6	12.5	13.8	3.0	1.1	4.0	1.0	11 928	39 146
District 6	12 985	178 658	14.8	5.4	4.0	15.0	21.3	2.7	1.0	2.5	0.9	6 382	35 720
District 7	14 315	220 170	23.0	5.7	4.5	14.3	17.2	2.5	0.8	2.5	1.0	8 291	37 657
District 8	13 718	239 700	19.7	4.4	7.4	13.4	14.4	5.1	1.0	2.7	0.9	9 722	40 557
District 9	13 408	245 781	17.5	3.4	4.6	11.5	17.8	3.3	1.6	3.1	1.7	10 836	44 087
District 10	15 022	290 568	11.2	3.4	3.9	13.0	20.2	3.8	1.5	8.3	3.4	12 979	44 666
District 11	18 593	419 129	8.3	3.0	4.8	6.9	27.4	5.9	2.2	7.5	1.7	22 505	53 695
District 12	17 058	317 126	8.4	3.5	3.0	11.3	18.1	11.1	1.1	5.9	2.6	15 647	49 340
District 13	14 940	253 239	17.4	4.3	4.9	15.5	18.1	2.0	1.4	3.6	1.4	9 745	38 482
District 14	20 458	331 053	19.1	3.6	7.9	11.6	12.2	6.5	1.9	5.3	1.4	15 905	48 043
District 15	13 893	223 984	11.9	3.6	5.3	15.8	14.8	3.8	1.4	5.1	2.5	8 913	39 791
District 16	18 313	290 238	13.9	4.0	5.2	15.9	16.8	4.3	1.3	4.6	1.9	11 838	40 787
OKLAHOMA	93 093	1 370 988	10.3	5.2	4.4	13.4	15.6	4.3	1.7	5.2	2.1	59 125	43 126
District 1	21 417	375 824	12.6	5.0	5.0	11.9	14.8	4.3	2.0	6.0	3.4	18 086	48 122
District 2	13 066	162 732	14.9	4.6	3.2	16.5	23.3	3.8	1.0	2.5	1.1	5 450	33 488
District 3	17 396	200 544	12.9	7.2	4.4	15.4	13.0	3.7	1.9	3.4	1.4	7 709	38 442
District 4	16 693	212 117	9.0	5.3	2.8	16.7	17.5	3.9	1.9	5.0	1.5	7 581	35 741
District 5	24 083	380 144	6.4	5.0	5.3	12.0	15.2	5.3	1.8	6.4	2.3	17 916	47 130
OREGON	112 393	1 498 727	10.7	5.3	5.5	13.5	15.7	4.0	1.9	6.1	2.4	71 007	47 378
District 1	22 769	359 902	12.4	5.3	7.9	12.2	12.0	4.0	1.9	7.8	3.4	21 646	60 143
District 2	23 068	244 444	10.8	5.5	3.5	17.3	18.3	3.0	1.6	3.7	1.8	8 937	36 559

1. Specified owner-occupied units; $1,000,000 represents $1,000,000 or more.   2. Specified renter-occupied units.

Table E. Congressional Districts 115th Congress — Land Area and Population Characteristics

STATE District	Representative, 115th Congress	Land area,[1] 2016 (sq. mi)	Total persons	Per square mile	White	Black	American Indian, Alaska Native	Asian and Pacific Islander	Some other race	Two or more races	Hispanic or Latino[2]	Non-Hispanic White alone	Female	Foreign-born	Born in state of residence
		1	2	3	4	5	6	7	8	9	10	11	12	13	14
OREGON—Cont'd															
District 3	Earl Blumenauer (D)	1 074.5	815 909	759.4	79.5	5.1	0.8	7.6	2.0	5.0	11.2	71.4	50.4	13.3	43.7
District 4	Peter A. DeFazio (D)	17 272.2	781 166	45.2	88.9	1.0	1.3	2.4	1.8	4.5	7.7	84.0	50.8	5.9	46.6
District 5	Kurt Schrader (D)	5 189.1	813 436	156.8	86.6	1.0	1.1	3.1	3.1	5.1	16.4	75.6	50.9	9.9	52.4
PENNSYLVANIA		44 742.4	12 802 503	286.1	81.1	11.0	0.2	3.3	1.9	2.4	6.8	77.3	51.1	6.5	72.9
District 1	Robert A. Brady (D)	78.0	720 611	9 237.9	48.4	34.9	0.3	7.6	5.6	3.1	17.2	39.5	52.1	12.5	67.6
District 2	Dwight Evans (D)	74.1	725 418	9 784.2	32.0	57.6	0.5	5.1	2.2	2.5	6.2	29.3	53.9	8.3	66.9
District 3	Mike Kelly (R)	3 850.8	701 892	182.3	91.6	4.5	0.1	0.9	0.3	2.5	2.3	90.1	50.7	2.3	82.0
District 4	Scott Perry (R)	1 517.9	724 891	477.6	85.3	7.8	0.2	2.6	1.7	2.4	7.2	80.8	50.7	5.1	66.4
District 5	Glenn Thompson (R)	10 711.4	699 108	65.3	93.3	2.7	0.1	1.9	0.4	1.5	1.9	92.2	48.9	3.3	79.5
District 6	Ryan A. Costello (R)	860.5	720 652	837.5	86.1	4.5	0.2	5.3	2.2	1.8	6.0	82.9	50.9	7.5	71.9
District 7	Patrick Meehan (R)	862.5	709 623	822.7	86.5	5.3	0.1	5.1	1.0	2.0	3.9	83.9	51.1	8.3	72.6
District 8	Michael G. Fitzpatrick (R)	707.0	707 083	1 000.1	88.0	3.9	0.2	4.8	1.4	1.7	5.0	84.8	50.9	8.9	66.5
District 9	Bill Shuster (R)	5 730.1	696 545	121.6	94.2	2.8	0.0	0.6	0.4	1.9	2.2	92.7	50.6	1.6	80.2
District 10	Tom Marino (R)	8 377.6	705 602	84.2	92.8	3.7	0.2	1.0	0.8	1.6	4.0	89.9	49.8	3.3	68.4
District 11	Lou Barletta (R)	3 356.2	704 916	210.0	88.7	5.5	0.2	1.3	2.0	2.3	6.2	85.6	50.7	4.5	77.8
District 12	Keith J. Rothfus (R)	2 163.1	700 339	323.8	93.1	3.2	0.1	1.7	0.2	1.7	1.7	91.9	51.1	2.8	83.4
District 13	Brendan F. Boyle (D)	155.2	729 101	4 698.8	63.2	19.1	0.2	9.3	5.5	2.7	11.5	58.0	51.9	17.7	67.8
District 14	Michael F. Doyle (D)	209.3	699 463	3 342.1	71.2	21.1	0.1	3.4	0.6	3.7	2.2	69.8	51.6	5.7	77.6
District 15	Charles W. Dent (R)	1 285.2	728 044	566.5	84.4	4.7	0.2	2.9	4.8	2.9	15.7	75.5	50.7	8.0	66.6
District 16	Joseph R. Pitts (R)	997.7	732 595	734.3	83.0	6.7	0.7	1.7	3.5	4.3	18.3	72.2	51.0	7.3	69.8
District 17	Matt Cartwright (D)	1 732.9	686 892	396.4	87.4	6.2	0.1	1.9	1.7	2.6	8.5	82.1	51.2	5.9	68.0
District 18	Tim Murphy (R)	2 072.8	709 728	342.4	93.6	2.1	0.1	2.0	0.2	2.1	1.4	92.6	51.5	3.9	81.0
RHODE ISLAND		1 033.9	1 056 298	1 021.6	80.4	6.2	0.4	3.4	6.2	3.4	14.4	73.4	51.6	13.5	63.7
District 1	David Cicilline (D)	268.6	532 557	1 982.8	77.8	8.5	0.4	3.6	6.0	3.8	16.3	68.5	51.5	16.8	49.8
District 2	James R. Langevin (D)	765.4	523 741	684.3	83.0	3.9	0.5	3.2	6.4	3.1	12.5	78.4	51.6	10.1	63.6
SOUTH CAROLINA		30 062.6	4 896 146	162.9	67.2	27.5	0.3	1.5	1.4	2.1	5.4	63.7	51.3	4.8	57.7
District 1	Mark Sanford (R)	1 547.9	751 679	485.6	74.2	19.7	0.3	1.9	1.9	2.0	6.2	70.3	51.2	6.0	42.5
District 2	Joe Wilson (R)	3 022.4	701 799	232.2	70.5	23.6	0.2	2.0	1.2	2.5	5.4	67.0	50.9	4.5	54.1
District 3	Jeff Duncan (R)	5 268.3	680 819	129.2	77.1	17.9	0.2	0.6	1.8	2.3	5.2	74.1	50.8	3.3	65.1
District 4	Trey Gowdy (R)	1 299.3	709 631	546.2	74.2	19.3	0.2	2.7	1.4	2.2	7.7	68.5	51.3	8.5	57.3
District 5	Ralph Norman (R)	5 505.7	693 302	125.9	67.8	28.1	0.4	1.2	0.9	1.6	3.7	65.3	51.5	3.2	59.3
District 6	James E. Clyburn (D)	8 064.3	661 521	82.0	37.6	57.6	0.2	1.0	1.1	2.4	5.0	34.5	51.7	3.4	69.8
District 7	Tom Rice (R)	5 354.7	697 395	130.2	67.2	28.0	0.6	1.0	1.5	1.8	4.3	64.5	51.5	4.1	57.8
SOUTH DAKOTA		75 810.5	858 469	11.3	84.6	1.5	8.3	1.5	1.2	3.0	3.5	82.8	49.7	3.2	64.9
At Large	Kristi Noem (R)	75 810.5	858 469	11.3	84.6	1.5	8.3	1.5	1.2	3.0	3.5	82.8	49.7	3.2	64.9
TENNESSEE		41 234.8	6 600 299	160.1	77.7	16.8	0.3	1.7	1.4	2.1	5.1	74.2	51.3	5.0	60.1
District 1	David P. Roe (R)	4 141.9	712 033	171.9	93.6	2.6	0.4	0.6	1.1	1.7	3.5	91.6	51.0	2.5	61.2
District 2	John J. Duncan Jr. (R)	2 321.6	732 112	315.3	89.1	6.0	0.2	1.6	0.8	2.3	3.9	86.2	51.5	4.3	58.5
District 3	Chuck Fleischmann (R)	4 570.4	726 420	158.9	85.1	10.7	0.4	1.2	0.7	1.9	3.8	82.1	51.5	3.4	63.5
District 4	Scott DesJarlais (R)	5 984.7	755 381	126.2	84.9	8.8	0.2	1.7	1.5	2.9	6.0	80.7	50.6	4.9	60.7
District 5	Jim Cooper (D)	1 248.4	759 800	608.6	67.0	24.4	0.4	2.9	2.5	2.8	9.2	60.1	51.8	12.0	52.6
District 6	Diane Black (R)	6 474.9	745 077	115.1	91.2	4.3	0.4	0.9	1.3	2.0	4.1	88.5	50.8	3.8	61.4
District 7	Marsha Blackburn (R)	9 160.3	753 850	82.3	84.5	10.5	0.3	2.1	0.4	2.1	4.9	80.5	50.4	4.1	53.3
District 8	David Kustoff (R)	6 848.9	709 747	103.6	74.5	20.5	0.3	2.0	0.9	1.7	2.7	72.7	51.6	3.4	66.4
District 9	Steve Cohen (D)	483.7	705 879	1 459.2	27.9	65.2	0.1	2.0	3.1	1.8	7.2	24.3	52.6	6.5	64.3
TEXAS		261 249.7	27 469 114	105.1	74.9	12.0	0.5	4.6	5.4	2.5	38.9	42.9	50.4	17.0	59.7
District 1	Louie Gohmert (R)	7 868.6	715 761	91.0	77.6	18.0	0.2	1.1	1.5	1.7	17.1	62.5	51.0	6.8	72.0
District 2	Ted Poe (R)	308.8	753 863	2 441.5	67.2	11.7	0.4	8.0	9.9	2.7	30.1	48.1	50.0	21.1	49.0
District 3	Sam Johnson (R)	481.0	819 626	1 704.2	70.3	8.8	0.8	15.0	2.3	2.8	15.2	58.5	50.9	21.5	41.7
District 4	John Ratcliffe (R)	10 130.4	725 212	71.6	80.3	10.6	1.0	0.9	4.4	2.8	13.5	71.9	50.6	6.1	68.1
District 5	Jeb Hensarling (R)	5 044.2	743 878	147.5	74.7	15.5	0.3	2.1	5.3	2.1	27.7	53.3	49.2	15.3	65.0
District 6	Joe Barton (R)	2 148.5	742 999	345.8	65.6	20.7	0.8	5.1	4.8	3.1	22.2	50.2	51.7	12.7	58.7
District 7	John Abney Culberson (R)	162.1	777 640	4 798.5	69.5	12.2	0.1	10.3	5.2	2.7	31.1	44.7	50.0	30.4	44.2
District 8	Kevin Brady (R)	6 054.1	802 187	132.5	81.2	7.9	0.6	2.9	3.5	3.8	21.6	64.9	49.1	11.8	60.1
District 9	Al Green (D)	165.7	782 554	4 722.2	36.3	38.0	0.3	12.1	12.0	1.3	38.3	10.9	51.2	35.2	48.1
District 10	Michael T. McCaul (R)	5 071.6	792 770	156.3	73.7	11.2	0.3	5.7	6.5	2.5	28.9	52.5	50.7	17.4	56.1
District 11	K. Michael Conaway (R)	27 832.6	761 153	27.3	88.6	3.7	0.3	1.1	4.0	2.3	38.3	55.5	49.5	9.5	70.6
District 12	Kay Granger (R)	1 441.2	788 381	547.0	80.5	8.4	0.6	4.2	3.4	2.8	21.9	63.4	51.7	10.0	59.9
District 13	Mac Thornberry (R)	38 349.5	707 365	18.4	86.0	5.3	0.8	2.3	2.7	3.0	26.5	63.8	49.1	9.2	66.7
District 14	Randy K. Weber Sr. (R)	2 442.1	739 877	303.0	71.5	19.8	0.3	2.7	3.1	2.6	24.3	51.4	49.2	10.5	66.1
District 15	Vicente Gonzalez (D)	7 804.1	766 342	98.2	82.9	2.1	0.3	1.1	12.2	1.4	80.6	15.9	50.5	22.8	64.5
District 16	Beto O' Rourke (D)	710.8	741 162	1 042.6	84.0	4.2	0.7	1.4	7.6	2.1	79.5	14.2	50.6	23.5	57.3
District 17	Bill Flores (R)	7 651.1	750 140	98.0	75.3	13.3	0.5	5.1	3.2	2.7	24.8	55.5	50.4	12.2	67.2
District 18	Sheila Jackson-Lee (D)	235.3	764 622	3 249.9	49.9	36.4	0.4	3.9	7.7	1.7	42.7	16.2	50.6	22.0	59.2
District 19	Jodey C. Arrington (R)	25 835.7	725 517	28.1	82.8	6.0	1.0	1.3	5.9	3.0	36.5	54.3	49.3	7.4	72.4
District 20	Joaquin Castro (D)	199.7	774 521	3 878.6	82.6	6.0	1.1	3.1	4.0	3.1	62.8	21.9	51.3	14.1	65.6
District 21	Lamar Smith (R)	5 920.9	771 369	130.3	85.6	4.1	0.3	3.8	2.9	3.2	25.0	61.7	50.3	9.8	57.5
District 22	Pete Olson (R)	1 033.8	861 570	833.4	60.5	13.9	0.4	18.1	3.9	3.2	25.0	41.3	51.2	25.7	49.6
District 23	Will Hurd (R)	58 058.2	747 732	12.9	84.7	3.2	0.7	1.9	8.5	1.4	69.7	24.7	49.7	16.8	64.9
District 24	Kenny Marchant (R)	262.8	779 968	2 967.8	65.9	10.4	0.5	13.8	6.0	3.4	24.6	48.4	51.2	23.5	45.4
District 25	Roger Williams (R)	7 622.6	762 034	100.0	84.1	7.1	0.4	3.2	1.9	3.2	17.6	69.5	51.1	7.7	57.4

1. Dry land or land partially or temporarily covered by water. 2. May be of any race.

STATE District	Population and population characteristics, 2015 (cont.)											Education, 2015	
	Age (percent)											Attainment[2] (percent)	
	Under 5 years	5 to 17 years	18 to 24 years	25 to 34 years	35 to 44 years	45 to 54 years	55 to 64 years	65 to 74 years	75 years and over	Median age	Total Enrollment[1]	High school graduate or more	Bachelor's degree or more
	15	16	17	18	19	20	21	22	23	24	25	26	27
OREGON—Cont'd													
District 3	5.9	14.0	8.4	17.3	15.9	13.4	12.5	7.8	4.8	37.3	187 991	89.8	39.9
District 4	4.9	14.1	11.5	12.0	11.4	11.9	14.5	11.7	8.1	41.1	186 139	90.1	25.9
District 5	5.9	17.3	9.0	12.5	12.2	12.9	13.6	9.8	6.7	38.9	200 443	89.7	29.9
PENNSYLVANIA	5.6	15.4	9.5	12.9	11.7	13.9	14.0	9.3	7.6	40.7	2 999 437	89.7	29.7
District 1	7.1	16.6	9.4	18.8	13.6	12.6	11.1	6.3	4.5	33.8	180 439	82.9	26.0
District 2	6.1	13.6	13.3	18.0	10.7	11.6	12.2	8.3	6.2	34.3	201 738	86.3	35.6
District 3	5.4	15.6	9.2	11.3	11.5	14.2	14.8	9.9	8.3	42.8	155 357	90.5	25.1
District 4	5.4	16.5	9.0	12.2	11.9	14.7	13.6	9.4	7.2	41.0	168 034	89.4	25.5
District 5	4.8	13.5	13.4	12.1	10.9	13.1	14.3	9.8	8.0	40.7	169 617	90.8	23.8
District 6	5.4	16.5	8.8	11.5	12.4	15.6	13.9	8.9	7.1	41.7	175 825	92.9	42.5
District 7	5.4	16.2	8.7	11.1	11.5	14.6	14.7	9.6	8.0	42.8	172 131	92.7	42.4
District 8	5.0	16.4	8.0	10.7	11.9	15.7	15.1	9.6	7.6	43.7	166 396	93.3	39.1
District 9	5.1	15.1	9.3	11.2	11.3	13.7	14.7	10.7	8.8	43.4	150 459	88.7	18.4
District 10	5.2	15.3	9.1	11.3	10.9	14.6	14.9	10.7	8.2	43.7	147 604	87.9	21.3
District 11	5.5	14.6	9.5	11.7	12.1	14.0	14.4	10.3	8.1	42.3	152 572	89.6	22.8
District 12	5.3	14.8	7.1	11.4	11.3	14.5	15.9	10.4	9.4	45.1	146 360	93.2	32.4
District 13	7.1	16.3	8.6	14.9	12.6	12.7	12.8	7.8	7.3	37.3	179 724	88.0	34.3
District 14	5.4	11.7	11.5	17.3	10.6	11.5	14.5	9.4	8.0	38.6	162 114	91.9	32.9
District 15	5.6	16.7	9.7	12.1	11.9	14.0	13.5	9.2	7.3	40.3	177 646	88.8	28.6
District 16	6.9	18.1	9.7	12.9	11.8	13.1	11.9	8.4	7.2	37.0	184 360	84.3	25.6
District 17	4.9	15.0	9.0	11.9	11.9	14.4	14.4	10.1	8.3	43.0	154 188	88.6	21.7
District 18	4.9	15.3	7.4	11.4	12.2	14.8	14.9	10.3	8.6	44.1	154 873	94.0	35.4
RHODE ISLAND	5.1	14.9	10.8	13.5	11.7	14.1	13.6	9.0	7.1	39.7	262 347	87.7	32.7
District 1	5.5	14.7	11.0	14.4	11.7	13.8	12.8	8.7	7.4	38.8	133 697	86.2	32.7
District 2	4.8	15.2	10.6	12.7	11.6	14.4	14.5	9.3	7.0	40.8	128 650	89.1	32.7
SOUTH CAROLINA	5.9	16.3	9.9	12.9	12.3	13.3	13.2	10.0	6.2	39.0	1 198 207	86.3	26.8
District 1	6.3	15.8	8.5	14.8	12.5	12.4	12.8	10.7	6.0	38.3	178 287	93.1	39.6
District 2	5.8	17.1	10.4	12.7	12.9	13.5	12.8	9.2	5.6	38.4	177 332	89.4	33.5
District 3	5.6	16.0	10.5	11.0	12.0	13.9	13.6	10.6	6.9	41.1	167 084	83.5	19.8
District 4	6.4	17.1	9.7	13.2	12.5	13.8	12.2	8.9	6.0	37.7	177 522	84.8	30.2
District 5	5.8	17.2	9.2	11.8	12.6	14.2	13.2	9.8	6.1	39.8	163 692	84.6	23.1
District 6	5.7	15.9	13.3	14.6	11.0	12.5	12.7	8.5	5.7	35.4	178 395	83.0	19.2
District 7	5.4	15.4	8.2	12.0	12.1	13.0	14.5	12.4	6.9	42.3	155 895	84.9	20.6
SOUTH DAKOTA	6.9	17.5	10.0	13.1	11.5	12.2	13.2	8.5	7.2	36.9	212 152	91.1	27.5
At Large	6.9	17.5	10.0	13.1	11.5	12.2	13.2	8.5	7.2	36.9	212 152	91.1	27.5
TENNESSEE	6.0	16.6	9.6	13.2	12.7	13.6	13.0	9.2	6.1	38.7	1 565 318	86.1	25.7
District 1	5.0	14.9	8.8	11.1	12.5	14.1	14.2	11.5	7.8	43.2	149 205	83.2	19.2
District 2	5.4	15.6	10.7	12.3	12.2	13.5	13.2	10.0	7.0	39.9	175 254	88.6	29.9
District 3	5.5	15.5	8.7	12.4	12.3	13.8	13.8	10.7	7.2	41.7	152 891	83.6	22.5
District 4	6.1	17.3	10.6	12.4	13.3	13.6	12.6	8.6	5.5	37.7	185 438	85.0	21.6
District 5	6.8	14.7	10.2	18.4	13.8	12.8	11.8	6.7	4.7	34.9	176 125	87.7	36.4
District 6	5.7	17.1	8.7	11.5	12.2	14.1	13.5	10.7	6.7	40.9	172 051	85.9	21.6
District 7	6.3	18.6	8.9	12.9	13.4	13.7	12.2	8.5	5.5	37.4	194 963	88.4	28.4
District 8	5.4	18.1	9.1	11.3	12.2	14.0	13.5	9.7	6.7	40.2	179 407	87.6	28.5
District 9	8.0	17.5	10.5	15.6	12.9	12.2	12.2	6.6	4.6	33.9	179 984	84.5	23.2
TEXAS	7.2	19.1	10.1	14.5	13.5	12.7	11.1	7.0	4.7	34.4	7 540 957	82.4	28.4
District 1	6.8	17.9	10.3	12.5	11.9	12.2	12.6	9.0	6.8	37.3	184 259	82.2	20.3
District 2	6.2	17.4	9.5	16.0	14.6	12.8	13.0	6.8	3.7	35.6	196 630	88.1	40.1
District 3	6.2	20.5	8.2	12.7	16.3	15.6	10.8	6.2	3.7	36.7	234 077	93.3	52.6
District 4	6.3	18.2	8.7	11.9	12.5	13.1	12.9	9.9	6.6	39.1	175 226	85.8	19.5
District 5	7.0	18.7	9.4	13.4	13.3	13.3	11.6	7.7	5.5	36.0	190 144	79.7	20.0
District 6	6.8	19.2	10.0	14.2	13.7	14.2	11.1	6.8	4.2	34.9	212 412	87.3	29.8
District 7	8.0	18.4	7.4	16.7	15.3	12.8	10.8	6.4	4.2	34.7	202 012	89.0	48.6
District 8	6.6	18.5	9.6	12.7	13.4	13.9	12.3	8.4	4.5	36.7	203 653	85.5	29.6
District 9	7.9	18.4	10.9	17.2	14.3	11.8	10.3	5.8	3.1	32.4	218 152	77.8	25.1
District 10	6.4	19.5	7.9	15.1	14.6	13.8	11.6	6.6	4.6	35.8	220 431	86.9	38.3
District 11	7.2	18.0	10.4	14.2	11.0	12.0	11.9	8.7	6.7	35.3	186 413	82.1	21.0
District 12	6.8	18.5	9.3	14.3	13.2	13.5	11.9	7.4	5.1	35.8	203 921	88.3	30.1
District 13	6.8	18.2	10.3	13.2	12.4	12.6	12.3	7.9	6.3	36.2	181 680	82.7	20.5
District 14	6.0	18.5	9.2	13.2	13.6	13.6	12.7	7.9	5.4	37.1	189 921	84.9	24.2
District 15	8.7	22.4	10.9	13.8	13.0	11.2	9.2	6.0	4.8	30.7	238 358	68.4	18.7
District 16	8.1	19.5	11.3	14.8	12.6	11.9	10.1	6.4	5.4	32.3	229 168	79.8	24.3
District 17	6.7	16.4	15.7	14.7	12.3	11.9	10.6	7.0	4.9	32.5	230 233	86.4	30.7
District 18	7.8	18.5	10.7	16.9	14.1	12.7	10.2	5.6	3.4	32.3	212 450	75.1	21.0
District 19	7.2	17.9	14.0	13.9	11.4	10.9	11.0	7.5	5.9	32.7	206 489	82.2	20.5
District 20	7.3	19.4	12.1	16.0	13.8	11.7	9.8	6.0	4.1	31.6	228 669	80.8	23.3
District 21	5.2	14.6	10.4	15.7	12.7	12.8	13.0	8.8	6.6	38.1	188 772	92.4	44.6
District 22	7.4	20.6	8.4	13.1	15.4	13.8	11.4	6.3	3.6	35.3	257 329	90.7	44.7
District 23	7.3	21.0	10.5	13.5	12.9	11.6	10.5	7.9	5.0	33.1	214 361	75.7	21.1
District 24	6.9	17.2	8.3	16.6	14.9	14.4	11.5	6.3	3.7	35.6	201 342	90.3	44.7
District 25	5.9	18.0	10.1	13.3	14.2	13.4	12.1	7.7	5.3	36.9	206 215	90.1	37.0

1. All persons 3 years old and over enrolled in nursery school through college and graduate or professional school.   2. Persons 25 years old and over.

Table E. Congressional Districts 115th Congress — Households and Group Quarters

STATE District	Households, 2015						Group quarters, 2010					
	Number	Average household size	Family households (percent)	Married-couple family (percent)	Female family householder[1]	One person households (percent)	Total in group quarters, 2015	Percent 65 years and over	Persons in correctional institutions	Persons in nursing facilities	Persons in college dormitories	Persons in military quarters
	28	29	30	31	32	33	34	35	36	37	38	39
OREGON—Cont'd												
District 3	314 464	2.54	57.0	42.6	10.5	30.4	18 151	15.5	2 065	2 399	6 604	0
District 4	317 272	2.41	61.5	46.3	10.2	29.0	17 899	16.5	1 354	2 067	8 825	21
District 5	302 265	2.64	67.2	51.8	10.8	25.6	15 558	19.1	5 381	2 401	3 162	17
PENNSYLVANIA	4 956 037	2.50	64.7	47.8	12.3	29.2	430 357	21.0	97 820	87 775	177 332	259
District 1	262 548	2.68	58.1	30.1	22.1	33.2	17 627	9.2	10 896	2 024	7 108	14
District 2	280 331	2.46	50.6	23.8	21.4	39.8	36 256	13.8	680	4 909	23 446	0
District 3	280 874	2.40	67.3	50.1	12.1	27.9	27 681	19.5	6 328	5 188	11 315	11
District 4	276 101	2.55	67.7	50.7	12.1	25.9	22 045	20.4	6 485	3 922	7 205	37
District 5	270 136	2.40	63.3	49.7	9.4	29.4	49 925	11.4	14 533	5 088	23 276	0
District 6	272 195	2.58	68.6	56.5	8.4	25.4	19 232	24.0	3 336	4 461	7 424	0
District 7	257 416	2.66	71.5	58.5	9.3	24.2	23 952	21.2	5 890	5 118	10 160	0
District 8	265 273	2.63	71.2	57.9	9.6	24.3	10 479	46.3	1 039	4 098	1 569	0
District 9	278 585	2.42	66.1	50.9	10.9	28.0	22 313	23.8	6 117	5 134	8 771	0
District 10	268 635	2.52	67.9	53.9	8.7	26.5	29 105	15.5	11 878	4 486	10 876	0
District 11	282 386	2.39	64.6	47.9	12.2	30.1	28 893	22.1	7 333	6 231	9 991	6
District 12	287 314	2.38	66.0	52.2	9.6	29.5	16 773	32.7	4 480	4 694	3 073	6
District 13	267 087	2.69	64.9	45.2	14.5	30.0	11 953	57.8	2	6 384	1 329	121
District 14	313 503	2.14	50.2	32.8	13.1	40.7	27 862	15.0	4 663	4 194	15 905	0
District 15	273 750	2.57	68.8	50.6	12.6	25.3	24 420	21.1	1 424	5 210	13 039	63
District 16	264 427	2.70	69.7	51.1	13.3	24.2	19 208	27.5	1 132	5 327	9 156	0
District 17	264 661	2.50	64.1	47.1	12.4	29.5	25 028	25.7	7 876	6 346	7 783	1
District 18	290 815	2.38	65.9	53.1	9.5	29.2	17 605	30.3	3 728	4 961	5 906	0
RHODE ISLAND	407 484	2.49	61.4	42.9	14.0	31.8	41 638	18.5	3 783	8 420	24 687	1 385
District 1	206 409	2.48	60.5	40.0	16.0	32.8	21 089	21.3	350	4 996	13 035	1 385
District 2	201 075	2.50	62.3	46.0	11.9	30.8	20 549	15.5	3 433	3 424	11 652	0
SOUTH CAROLINA	1 857 768	2.56	65.7	46.7	14.6	28.9	136 532	13.0	41 649	19 020	46 463	19 413
District 1	283 863	2.61	66.8	50.9	11.0	26.7	9 849	15.4	531	1 662	2 560	4 436
District 2	263 691	2.59	67.4	50.2	13.1	27.5	19 380	12.8	1 458	2 391	823	11 567
District 3	257 805	2.56	67.4	48.7	14.2	27.5	21 333	14.3	7 044	3 116	9 817	0
District 4	270 447	2.56	64.9	47.7	13.0	29.6	17 779	14.5	3 776	2 832	9 668	0
District 5	264 794	2.57	67.1	46.7	15.9	28.9	12 593	20.0	5 318	2 792	3 289	611
District 6	240 849	2.57	59.3	33.7	21.2	34.6	43 354	6.5	18 400	3 087	17 383	2 799
District 7	276 319	2.48	66.6	47.4	14.9	28.1	12 244	22.4	5 122	3 140	2 923	0
SOUTH DAKOTA	339 437	2.43	63.9	50.2	9.5	29.6	34 019	21.1	6 327	7 005	10 248	597
At Large	339 437	2.43	63.9	50.2	9.5	29.6	34 019	21.1	6 327	7 005	10 248	597
TENNESSEE	2 530 260	2.55	66.2	47.9	13.6	28.0	153 726	19.8	46 957	33 041	53 136	1 544
District 1	288 863	2.41	66.0	48.8	11.9	29.4	16 629	26.7	4 577	4 466	4 176	0
District 2	290 345	2.46	64.5	49.6	11.4	29.1	17 198	19.1	1 901	3 686	10 443	0
District 3	280 143	2.53	66.4	49.2	12.4	28.8	18 903	23.8	4 913	4 071	4 884	3
District 4	279 183	2.65	69.7	51.5	12.3	24.2	15 314	21.1	3 301	3 584	6 619	0
District 5	304 071	2.43	57.8	39.6	13.6	32.6	21 200	9.0	6 769	2 588	13 660	0
District 6	283 217	2.59	70.2	54.1	11.7	25.0	11 099	36.4	2 385	3 730	2 283	0
District 7	274 422	2.68	71.7	55.9	11.5	23.8	17 149	21.2	8 311	3 918	2 350	1 250
District 8	263 221	2.62	71.2	53.5	13.1	24.6	18 889	21.3	7 494	4 158	4 748	10
District 9	266 795	2.58	59.5	29.4	24.7	34.4	17 345	14.0	7 306	2 840	3 973	281
TEXAS	9 421 412	2.85	69.2	50.0	14.0	25.3	600 329	14.9	267 405	94 278	119 834	35 260
District 1	252 252	2.73	68.7	50.3	13.7	26.5	26 876	17.3	8 132	5 093	9 123	0
District 2	278 068	2.68	68.6	50.6	12.5	25.5	8 969	18.4	2 441	1 873	2 921	0
District 3	292 431	2.79	73.8	60.3	9.7	21.9	2 450	31.9	1 061	1 326	387	0
District 4	259 288	2.73	71.3	54.2	12.3	24.8	17 363	25.8	8 850	5 078	2 237	0
District 5	251 986	2.86	68.5	47.6	14.4	26.2	23 599	14.9	17 768	3 964	938	0
District 6	255 499	2.88	73.1	53.2	14.1	22.2	7 520	32.8	689	2 419	2 137	0
District 7	300 026	2.59	65.0	49.8	11.5	30.5	1 583	58.1	3	774	5	0
District 8	270 735	2.84	71.5	56.5	11.1	23.8	33 081	8.5	23 107	2 021	2 615	0
District 9	267 279	2.92	69.0	40.4	21.6	26.3	3 053	32.7	154	1 629	1 520	0
District 10	283 464	2.74	66.9	54.0	9.5	26.5	15 059	25.7	2 453	3 156	4 344	0
District 11	269 037	2.75	66.9	51.5	10.9	27.1	21 919	18.3	9 050	3 721	3 615	1 924
District 12	282 312	2.74	68.6	50.9	13.1	26.3	14 978	20.3	5 807	3 540	3 405	202
District 13	257 511	2.61	66.8	50.4	11.8	28.2	35 631	11.8	17 511	4 208	2 479	5 487
District 14	267 407	2.64	68.1	48.8	14.4	26.6	33 542	9.5	22 748	2 861	2 869	40
District 15	214 345	3.50	79.4	54.8	19.1	17.9	16 325	14.6	8 632	2 035	1 514	0
District 16	235 672	3.08	72.9	50.4	16.5	23.8	14 970	9.8	6 076	1 482	491	5 683
District 17	274 547	2.62	62.6	46.2	12.0	27.7	29 780	11.1	8 355	3 792	14 831	0
District 18	268 114	2.77	64.0	35.0	22.0	28.9	22 566	3.8	12 624	783	5 661	0
District 19	251 761	2.72	65.4	46.4	13.2	27.6	41 924	10.0	19 845	4 073	10 748	621
District 20	250 022	3.05	66.6	43.5	17.3	27.2	11 942	11.9	4	2 081	4 846	9 322
District 21	309 497	2.44	58.9	46.7	9.0	32.9	16 026	19.9	600	4 024	7 505	3 793
District 22	274 785	3.11	78.5	63.1	11.3	17.6	6 556	21.6	4 494	1 409	4	0
District 23	221 835	3.28	75.9	56.3	14.5	20.4	19 871	7.6	16 613	1 566	193	877
District 24	305 157	2.55	62.8	46.4	11.3	30.6	3 232	65.8	53	1 913	480	0
District 25	267 588	2.72	70.8	56.6	9.9	22.9	34 388	9.6	11 967	3 274	10 926	2 822

1. No spouse present.

Table E. Congressional Districts 115th Congress — **Housing and Money Income**

STATE District		Housing units, 2015					Money income, 2015		
		Occupied units						Households	
			Owner-occupied			Renter-occupied			
	Total	Occupied units as a percent of all units	Owner-occupied units as a percent of occupied units	Median value[1] (dollars)	Percent valued at $500,000 or more	Median rent[2]	Per capita income (dollars)	Median income (dollars)	Percent with income of $100,000 or more
	40	41	42	43	44	45	46	47	48
OREGON—Cont'd									
District 3	340 812	92.3	57.9	313 400	17.5	1 024	30 795	58 809	24.9
District 4	347 372	91.3	60.2	219 800	7.5	840	25 283	44 747	15.9
District 5	336 116	89.9	63.3	259 700	12.4	931	29 364	58 466	24.8
PENNSYLVANIA	5 603 051	88.5	68.7	170 600	6.0	868	30 384	55 702	23.8
District 1	300 762	87.3	55.8	140 300	5.9	993	25 479	45 968	19.0
District 2	333 211	84.1	49.7	153 700	13.6	933	28 835	40 244	19.2
District 3	317 890	88.4	71.4	126 700	2.8	680	26 594	50 231	18.8
District 4	302 564	91.3	71.3	173 500	3.0	890	29 178	58 510	23.4
District 5	342 111	79.0	70.1	117 200	3.0	714	25 413	48 610	16.5
District 6	286 021	95.2	75.6	253 900	13.5	1 140	40 662	80 129	38.0
District 7	272 204	94.6	78.7	292 700	16.1	1 159	41 632	84 406	41.9
District 8	279 444	94.9	75.1	315 600	15.9	1 174	41 032	80 032	39.7
District 9	318 557	87.5	73.3	121 200	2.2	685	25 035	47 413	15.8
District 10	346 991	77.4	74.4	160 600	3.3	748	26 358	53 520	19.0
District 11	322 010	87.7	70.5	154 000	2.2	791	27 218	52 367	19.2
District 12	319 833	89.8	76.7	148 400	4.0	709	32 515	57 186	24.1
District 13	288 581	92.6	63.3	223 200	5.7	1 026	30 297	57 367	27.0
District 14	363 522	86.2	54.4	96 800	2.7	773	28 522	43 763	16.5
District 15	291 253	94.0	68.6	197 000	4.2	965	30 173	58 867	24.6
District 16	281 829	93.8	64.5	191 300	5.4	915	26 925	55 802	21.1
District 17	319 469	82.8	70.0	136 800	1.8	778	25 595	50 329	18.3
District 18	316 799	91.8	75.3	165 400	3.7	768	35 168	62 254	27.8
RHODE ISLAND	462 555	88.1	59.0	241 000	10.3	938	31 888	58 073	26.6
District 1	232 043	89.0	52.9	240 900	12.1	900	31 382	51 966	24.7
District 2	230 512	87.2	65.4	241 100	8.8	988	32 403	64 118	28.5
SOUTH CAROLINA	2 210 150	84.1	68.1	148 600	6.1	819	25 627	47 238	17.5
District 1	344 619	82.4	69.2	236 500	16.0	1 092	33 707	61 907	26.7
District 2	296 879	88.8	71.5	153 500	5.0	864	28 777	56 454	22.6
District 3	304 864	84.6	70.8	130 400	4.0	698	22 619	43 034	14.2
District 4	295 914	91.4	65.3	150 000	5.0	785	26 087	50 015	18.9
District 5	300 165	88.2	72.4	135 300	3.6	780	24 181	45 802	16.1
District 6	292 572	82.3	57.4	105 200	4.0	787	19 273	34 566	9.4
District 7	375 137	73.7	69.2	136 100	3.8	769	23 681	41 473	13.3
SOUTH DAKOTA	380 307	89.3	68.2	152 800	3.7	675	27 624	53 017	18.9
At Large	380 307	89.3	68.2	152 800	3.7	675	27 624	53 017	18.9
TENNESSEE	2 892 407	87.5	65.8	150 600	5.1	785	26 216	47 275	18.0
District 1	347 403	83.1	68.7	132 000	3.0	643	22 963	39 081	12.0
District 2	327 053	88.8	67.6	164 600	5.9	768	27 653	49 841	18.8
District 3	327 350	85.6	67.2	141 600	4.2	709	24 960	43 526	17.4
District 4	309 265	90.3	67.5	147 900	3.3	762	24 464	49 312	16.9
District 5	332 158	91.5	56.6	181 700	8.8	915	30 577	51 554	20.2
District 6	317 235	89.3	74.1	160 900	3.8	752	25 055	47 227	17.3
District 7	316 514	86.7	71.5	161 300	9.7	816	28 815	53 238	23.1
District 8	296 507	88.8	72.0	153 400	4.8	748	29 633	55 100	24.2
District 9	318 922	83.7	47.5	95 900	1.6	836	21 498	37 388	12.4
TEXAS	10 588 236	89.0	61.1	152 000	6.2	932	28 210	55 653	24.9
District 1	304 023	83.0	65.9	121 700	2.6	792	24 642	46 537	18.2
District 2	295 703	94.0	60.6	190 200	9.0	1 134	39 077	74 246	36.9
District 3	305 681	95.7	64.4	271 100	9.7	1 200	40 678	86 565	43.2
District 4	305 613	84.8	71.6	121 200	3.4	765	25 580	47 850	20.4
District 5	290 387	86.8	62.4	120 500	4.1	818	23 358	46 900	18.0
District 6	279 271	91.5	64.3	152 300	2.0	1 010	28 665	62 290	27.2
District 7	327 041	91.7	52.4	236 800	25.3	1 127	46 102	71 337	36.4
District 8	306 669	88.3	69.9	177 100	9.8	1 005	32 233	64 196	32.0
District 9	292 245	91.5	44.9	120 200	1.5	898	21 151	43 572	15.9
District 10	312 973	90.6	66.0	210 200	13.1	1 082	36 391	70 494	34.2
District 11	329 415	81.7	69.8	132 900	4.6	913	28 659	56 334	24.7
District 12	311 837	90.5	62.6	151 900	5.1	975	31 645	62 274	26.8
District 13	305 206	84.4	66.0	110 200	2.7	753	24 756	49 281	18.6
District 14	314 459	85.0	65.1	144 100	2.9	865	29 912	57 520	27.1
District 15	251 456	85.2	69.2	92 900	1.7	741	17 742	41 993	16.5
District 16	262 387	89.8	59.8	119 000	1.2	760	20 124	45 316	15.3
District 17	313 482	87.6	55.6	153 200	3.0	921	26 050	51 024	20.4
District 18	298 496	89.8	44.1	116 900	6.0	881	22 826	43 100	16.3
District 19	297 842	84.5	61.0	100 000	2.0	793	23 317	47 305	16.9
District 20	270 247	92.5	54.2	126 600	1.0	890	22 397	49 404	16.9
District 21	350 820	88.2	58.2	249 500	13.7	1 098	37 659	65 254	29.6
District 22	289 056	95.1	72.5	238 400	8.0	1 229	38 436	95 048	47.6
District 23	260 481	85.2	72.7	114 600	4.6	822	24 300	53 917	25.0
District 24	325 429	93.8	49.3	230 800	13.6	1 054	39 969	68 161	32.7
District 25	306 430	87.3	68.1	212 700	16.1	1 026	34 339	65 706	31.2

1. Specified owner-occupied units; $1,000,000 represents $1,000,000 or more.   2. Specified renter-occupied units.

Table E. Congressional Districts 115th Congress — Poverty, Labor Force, Employment, and Social Security

STATE District	Poverty, 2015 — Persons below poverty level (percent)	Families below poverty level (percent)	Percent of households receiving food stamps in past 12 months	Civilian labor force, 2015 — Total	Unemployment Total	Rate[1]	Civilian employment[2] 2015 — Total	Percent — Management, business, science and arts occupations	Service, sales, and office	Construction and production	Persons under age 65 with no health insurance, 2015 (percent)	Social Security beneficiaries, December 2015 — Number	Rate[3]	Supplemental Security Income recipients, December 2015
	49	50	51	52	53	54	55	56	57	58	59	60	61	62
OREGON—Cont'd														
District 3	15.5	9.5	19.9	455 786	30 201	6.6	425 585	42.6	40.1	17.3	7.9	126 247	154.7	20 578
District 4	19.1	11.5	21.1	362 317	29 272	8.1	333 045	35.1	41.5	23.5	8.9	197 371	252.7	20 903
District 5	13.2	8.5	17.5	402 422	25 407	6.3	377 015	33.8	42.8	23.4	7.4	166 603	204.8	14 834
PENNSYLVANIA	13.2	9.1	13.3	6 518 212	408 542	6.3	6 109 670	37.4	40.7	21.9	7.5	2 744 424	214.4	368 212
District 1	22.9	19.3	24.8	363 537	37 277	10.3	326 260	35.2	45.8	19.0	11.2	110 224	153.0	39 852
District 2	27.7	21.1	25.4	343 992	35 431	10.3	308 561	45.4	43.4	11.3	9.0	127 315	175.5	51 384
District 3	14.9	11.0	16.2	338 530	19 994	5.9	318 536	32.3	41.7	26.1	6.9	169 788	241.9	23 207
District 4	10.2	7.5	11.3	382 072	19 604	5.1	362 468	34.4	40.0	25.6	7.1	151 147	208.5	13 685
District 5	14.6	8.6	12.9	332 175	20 101	6.1	312 074	33.9	37.9	28.2	6.8	163 049	233.2	17 561
District 6	6.7	4.2	5.5	394 144	17 842	4.5	376 302	46.6	36.3	17.1	5.1	136 662	189.6	7 408
District 7	5.8	3.6	4.8	376 668	17 846	4.7	358 822	47.2	37.0	15.8	6.3	139 773	197.0	5 797
District 8	6.0	4.0	5.6	389 853	20 291	5.2	369 562	43.1	38.5	18.4	5.5	144 687	204.6	7 741
District 9	14.9	10.4	14.5	328 894	21 626	6.6	307 268	29.5	41.4	29.1	8.4	174 388	250.4	24 226
District 10	12.6	8.2	12.0	342 412	17 934	5.2	324 478	30.1	40.8	29.1	9.3	170 006	240.9	14 804
District 11	11.8	7.9	11.9	353 390	18 755	5.3	334 635	32.6	42.7	24.7	6.3	165 124	234.2	16 547
District 12	10.2	7.1	10.6	354 925	18 681	5.3	336 244	41.2	38.0	20.8	4.7	175 895	251.2	16 954
District 13	14.5	11.1	15.6	375 999	29 051	7.7	346 948	38.5	42.3	19.2	9.6	128 224	175.9	31 451
District 14	18.0	11.8	18.7	371 057	24 835	6.7	346 222	40.0	44.0	16.1	7.7	152 206	217.6	29 513
District 15	10.8	7.8	11.3	382 061	19 858	5.2	362 203	35.2	41.8	23.1	7.4	154 678	212.5	16 483
District 16	13.5	9.8	13.2	379 457	25 105	6.6	354 352	32.1	39.7	28.2	11.6	142 970	195.2	18 854
District 17	13.3	9.3	14.6	337 392	25 728	7.6	311 664	31.8	42.8	25.4	7.9	167 776	244.3	19 841
District 18	8.6	5.6	9.1	371 654	18 583	5.0	353 071	40.9	40.1	19.0	4.3	170 512	240.2	12 904
RHODE ISLAND	13.9	10.1	16.2	559 733	34 758	6.2	524 975	38.2	43.3	18.4	6.7	217 881	206.3	33 114
District 1	15.8	11.7	19.1	273 705	15 550	5.7	258 155	38.7	42.9	18.3	7.4	107 791	202.4	18 438
District 2	11.9	8.5	13.3	286 028	19 208	6.7	266 820	37.7	43.7	18.5	6.0	110 090	210.2	14 676
SOUTH CAROLINA	16.6	12.1	14.4	2 336 291	170 589	7.3	2 165 702	33.8	42.5	23.6	12.9	1 066 150	217.8	118 080
District 1	11.1	7.4	7.7	377 798	18 234	4.8	359 564	40.0	41.6	18.4	11.4	145 744	193.9	8 878
District 2	13.9	10.2	12.7	352 119	25 223	7.2	326 896	40.5	40.4	19.1	10.2	133 888	190.8	12 278
District 3	18.0	12.7	15.1	311 081	21 874	7.0	289 207	30.2	40.7	29.1	13.6	164 345	241.4	15 208
District 4	14.2	10.6	11.6	350 253	22 075	6.3	328 178	34.6	40.9	24.5	13.8	145 231	204.7	15 692
District 5	16.4	11.1	13.8	326 738	24 884	7.6	301 854	30.9	41.5	27.6	11.0	152 107	219.4	17 440
District 6	25.2	20.0	23.5	302 539	30 982	10.2	271 557	27.4	46.6	26.0	15.1	140 753	212.8	26 986
District 7	19.1	14.6	17.4	315 763	27 317	8.7	288 446	30.4	47.0	22.6	15.6	184 082	264.0	21 598
SOUTH DAKOTA	13.7	8.3	10.6	454 996	18 144	4.0	436 852	33.8	40.9	25.3	12.0	168 626	196.4	14 834
At Large	13.7	8.3	10.6	454 996	18 144	4.0	436 852	33.8	40.9	25.3	12.0	168 626	196.4	14 834
TENNESSEE	16.7	12.3	16.0	3 198 285	199 471	6.2	2 998 814	34.3	41.1	24.6	12.0	1 392 164	210.9	181 992
District 1	18.9	14.4	17.7	325 546	20 564	6.3	304 982	30.5	43.6	25.8	13.8	195 803	275.0	22 988
District 2	15.2	10.1	13.8	365 312	19 968	5.5	345 344	36.7	42.0	21.3	10.8	162 971	222.6	18 639
District 3	18.8	13.8	17.6	335 274	24 268	7.2	311 006	32.8	41.9	25.4	11.3	173 086	238.3	22 309
District 4	15.2	11.2	15.1	371 153	22 337	6.0	348 816	31.2	40.0	28.8	11.3	152 387	201.7	17 446
District 5	16.9	12.9	14.9	420 563	20 923	5.0	399 640	39.2	40.4	20.3	13.8	115 817	152.4	17 454
District 6	13.7	10.6	14.0	352 918	18 528	5.2	334 390	32.7	40.6	26.7	11.5	174 782	234.6	17 058
District 7	13.6	9.3	13.2	340 129	21 559	6.3	318 570	37.9	39.0	23.1	9.2	148 473	197.0	15 795
District 8	14.2	10.7	14.4	334 622	16 396	4.9	318 226	37.6	39.0	23.4	9.4	154 927	218.3	18 247
District 9	24.7	19.4	24.1	352 768	34 928	9.9	317 840	28.9	43.9	27.2	17.1	113 918	161.4	32 056
TEXAS	15.9	12.2	12.5	13 437 133	743 232	5.5	12 693 901	35.3	41.6	23.1	19.1	3 928 648	143.0	666 218
District 1	18.2	13.6	14.4	319 207	21 121	6.6	298 086	30.4	41.7	27.8	21.2	145 688	203.5	21 546
District 2	10.3	8.4	6.1	416 793	18 419	4.4	398 374	43.3	37.9	18.8	15.3	89 417	118.6	11 722
District 3	6.5	4.7	4.0	441 842	16 256	3.7	425 586	53.3	36.4	10.4	10.4	86 645	105.7	7 248
District 4	15.8	12.0	13.4	331 490	21 055	6.4	310 435	32.3	42.1	25.6	18.6	151 701	209.2	20 104
District 5	17.6	13.8	14.8	347 987	20 056	5.8	327 931	28.0	44.8	27.2	23.1	123 450	166.0	16 777
District 6	11.4	8.3	10.4	390 540	18 852	4.8	371 688	36.6	41.2	22.2	15.4	104 452	140.6	12 293
District 7	12.1	10.3	7.0	415 685	19 372	4.7	396 313	46.8	37.5	15.7	16.5	80 313	103.3	9 760
District 8	11.3	8.0	7.0	368 950	19 129	5.2	349 821	39.9	38.4	21.7	15.1	122 398	152.6	13 099
District 9	20.0	17.2	17.5	414 939	27 834	6.7	387 105	27.9	47.4	24.7	24.8	83 304	106.5	26 939
District 10	10.1	6.9	7.3	417 851	18 588	4.4	399 263	41.4	38.9	19.7	13.9	105 437	133.0	11 160
District 11	12.9	9.0	9.5	358 867	15 067	4.2	343 800	29.6	40.7	29.8	20.4	137 426	180.5	16 340
District 12	11.5	8.4	9.9	403 976	25 372	6.3	378 604	37.1	41.2	21.8	15.7	114 280	145.0	12 840
District 13	15.7	12.2	12.2	330 063	15 153	4.6	314 910	30.4	40.9	28.7	18.7	125 633	177.6	13 755
District 14	14.7	10.8	11.1	350 149	24 232	6.9	325 917	36.6	38.7	24.7	19.5	123 404	166.8	19 103
District 15	27.5	23.0	25.5	326 049	25 058	7.7	300 991	27.9	46.7	25.4	29.9	102 022	133.1	32 800
District 16	18.5	14.6	20.9	327 921	20 524	6.3	307 397	30.4	48.5	21.1	21.5	109 299	147.5	26 454
District 17	18.0	10.9	9.4	374 655	16 858	4.5	357 797	38.9	39.5	21.6	15.3	108 680	144.9	16 873
District 18	23.6	20.9	19.0	378 606	26 556	7.0	352 050	28.2	42.9	28.9	23.6	92 379	120.8	28 694
District 19	17.3	11.8	12.8	337 044	15 186	4.5	321 858	30.9	43.0	26.1	18.6	119 988	165.4	17 262
District 20	17.8	13.7	15.2	372 008	22 959	6.2	349 049	32.7	46.2	21.2	17.7	109 648	141.6	23 484
District 21	8.9	4.8	5.0	406 756	17 723	4.4	389 033	45.8	41.0	13.2	12.8	132 459	171.7	12 066
District 22	6.8	4.9	5.4	439 030	16 034	3.7	422 996	49.8	34.8	15.5	11.0	89 204	103.5	10 420
District 23	17.5	14.4	17.7	325 978	23 214	7.1	302 764	29.4	44.1	26.5	18.8	120 639	161.3	23 734
District 24	9.0	7.1	6.4	449 784	15 292	3.4	434 492	44.4	39.2	16.4	14.4	85 025	109.0	7 120
District 25	11.1	7.6	8.6	363 750	16 272	4.5	347 478	42.8	37.4	19.8	13.4	120 469	158.1	10 994

1. Percent of civilian labor force.   2. Persons 16 years old and over.   3. Per 1,000 resident population estimated in the 2014 American Community Survey.

Table E. Congressional Districts 115th Congress — **Agriculture**

STATE District	Agriculture, 2012									
	Land in farms				Value of products sold				Government payments	
	Number of farms	Acres	Average size of farm (acres)	Irrigated land (acres)	Total ($1,000)	Average per farm (dollars)	Percent from crops	Percent from livestock and poultry products	Total ($1,000)	Average per farm receiving payments (dollars)
	63	64	65	66	67	68	69	70	71	72
OREGON—Cont'd										
District 3	2 500	86 297	35	12 384	210 983	84 393	85.5	14.5	448	6 395
District 4	8 820	1 301 199	148	95 961	646 366	73 284	67.3	32.7	3 986	7 157
District 5	6 076	589 162	97	124 733	1 022 711	168 320	70.1	29.9	4 483	7 038
PENNSYLVANIA	59 309	7 704 444	130	38 990	7 400 781	124 783	37.6	62.4	86 359	5 395
District 1	X	X	X	X	X	X	X	X	X	X
District 2	17	548	32	17	330	19 408	90.6	9.4	0	0
District 3	5 489	808 725	147	1 426	353 468	64 396	55.9	44.1	7 271	4 835
District 4	3 470	442 692	128	3 131	445 123	128 277	60.2	39.8	4 659	5 508
District 5	7 119	1 025 582	144	3 772	448 440	62 992	39.2	60.8	10 295	5 589
District 6	1 821	161 792	89	1 708	433 872	238 260	45.4	54.6	2 446	7 109
District 7	2 521	214 656	85	2 080	682 479	270 718	64.7	35.3	2 325	5 033
District 8	1 048	75 181	72	922	74 095	70 701	74.0	26.0	D	D
District 9	7 608	1 178 741	155	5 850	886 733	116 553	27.1	72.9	12 005	5 333
District 10	10 157	1 530 318	151	3 931	1 036 895	102 087	22.8	77.2	21 819	6 165
District 11	5 191	681 540	131	3 494	535 209	103 103	42.4	57.6	8 608	4 435
District 12	2 312	289 072	125	639	128 146	55 427	44.2	55.8	2 453	4 576
District 13	60	1 550	26	74	2 026	33 774	97.6	2.4	D	D
District 14	52	3 737	72	14	679	13 064	86.6	13.4	D	D
District 15	2 654	327 761	123	2 862	600 645	226 317	27.8	72.2	4 326	5 769
District 16	5 054	416 310	82	6 010	1 498 795	296 556	25.2	74.8	5 716	6 226
District 17	1 388	170 812	123	1 943	198 442	142 969	51.0	49.0	2 205	4 641
District 18	3 340	375 166	112	1 112	74 892	22 423	53.2	46.8	1 538	3 395
RHODE ISLAND	1 243	69 589	56	3 954	59 652	47 990	82.1	17.9	2 345	12 342
District 1	344	15 923	46	647	19 582	56 923	80.6	19.4	875	13 059
District 2	899	53 666	60	3 307	40 070	44 572	82.9	17.1	1 470	11 955
SOUTH CAROLINA	25 266	4 971 244	197	159 239	3 040 069	120 323	42.6	57.4	46 616	6 867
District 1	544	82 106	151	4 774	39 179	72 021	95.4	4.6	310	4 996
District 2	3 158	453 236	144	24 868	388 653	123 069	30.6	69.4	3 820	5 343
District 3	6 630	878 661	133	14 298	540 476	81 520	19.8	80.2	5 673	6 107
District 4	1 912	135 628	71	2 756	42 760	22 364	61.8	38.2	898	7 240
District 5	4 848	858 012	177	17 565	683 746	141 037	26.1	73.9	6 325	6 164
District 6	4 690	1 601 949	342	74 041	713 033	152 033	67.5	32.5	16 616	7 434
District 7	3 484	961 652	276	20 937	632 221	181 464	54.3	45.7	12 974	7 645
SOUTH DAKOTA	31 989	43 257 079	1 352	378 678	10 170 227	317 929	59.7	40.3	283 797	12 451
At Large	31 989	43 257 079	1 352	378 678	10 170 000	317 929	59.7	40.3	283 797	12 451
TENNESSEE	68 050	10 867 812	160	146 442	3 611 037	53 064	57.8	42.2	67 665	4 184
District 1	9 853	905 084	92	D	255 474	25 929	24.2	75.8	3 479	1 706
District 2	5 214	522 807	100	1 856	168 328	32 284	54.7	45.3	1 492	1 565
District 3	5 665	627 645	111	826	240 743	42 497	9.6	90.4	1 616	2 726
District 4	10 696	1 649 872	154	14 838	625 877	58 515	35.3	64.7	5 744	3 258
District 5	1 918	237 050	124	881	35 345	18 428	64.2	35.8	335	1 573
District 6	13 698	1 963 227	143	7 539	601 843	43 937	53.2	46.8	9 216	3 391
District 7	13 249	2 330 708	176	10 200	433 743	32 738	58.1	41.9	11 722	3 232
District 8	7 529	2 581 642	343	103 713	1 227 122	162 986	87.4	12.6	33 653	7 990
District 9	228	49 777	218	D	22 562	98 957	95.9	4.1	408	7 425
TEXAS	248 809	130 153 438	523	4 489 163	25 375 581	101 988	29.0	71.0	643 993	12 293
District 1	12 033	1 894 203	157	7 229	1 248 621	103 766	9.3	90.7	2 219	5 604
District 2	277	26 687	96	696	24 812	89 575	93.6	6.4	135	8 991
District 3	1 239	181 470	146	1 483	49 687	40 103	63.7	36.3	1 063	10 738
District 4	23 397	4 272 976	183	35 066	1 185 301	50 660	25.1	74.9	18 210	6 358
District 5	12 498	1 955 349	156	9 102	447 708	35 822	44.0	56.0	3 504	8 505
District 6	5 164	1 029 961	199	1 486	161 229	31 222	63.1	36.9	5 425	6 082
District 7	145	22 255	153	613	1 872	12 911	64.6	35.5	237	9 112
District 8	9 297	2 007 965	216	12 705	286 726	30 841	39.9	60.1	4 791	7 557
District 9	138	14 387	104	19	1 778	12 886	62.3	37.7	98	6 540
District 10	14 453	2 579 215	178	39 297	388 941	26 911	48.1	51.9	12 664	6 758
District 11	21 093	15 735 425	746	231 436	1 140 013	54 047	30.5	69.5	71 961	11 722
District 12	5 466	663 119	121	2 653	92 035	16 838	24.2	75.8	459	2 871
District 13	20 372	22 410 589	1 100	1 321 922	8 593 468	421 827	16.1	83.9	142 997	14 697
District 14	3 818	1 023 671	268	43 308	144 002	37 717	57.4	42.6	9 058	19 231
District 15	8 704	4 303 286	494	154 612	506 516	58 193	67.4	32.6	17 789	9 165
District 16	370	120 411	325	10 427	23 588	63 753	94.9	5.1	409	14 114
District 17	16 124	4 032 650	250	59 093	1 003 696	62 249	27.5	72.5	21 247	9 123
District 18	119	4 478	38	28	3 789	31 843	10.5	89.5	20	4 904
District 19	15 781	14 714 801	932	1 783 134	5 205 921	329 885	27.7	72.3	191 903	17 292
District 20	221	18 965	86	770	1 394	6 306	62.3	37.6	35	2 345
District 21	7 738	2 997 190	387	7 650	103 517	13 378	30.3	69.7	4 697	5 820
District 22	1 965	414 170	211	12 771	128 234	65 259	86.2	13.8	4 359	10 209
District 23	9 377	28 460 973	3 035	314 787	966 721	103 095	51.4	48.6	35 825	16 647
District 24	158	10 534	67	93	3 807	24 094	92.4	7.6	61	8 648
District 25	13 361	3 908 812	293	11 239	538 906	40 334	39.2	60.8	9 765	5 694

Private nonfarm employment and payroll, 2015

STATE District	Number of establish-ments	Employment Total	Percent by selected industries Manufact-uring	Construc-tion	Wholesale trade	Retail trade	Health care and social assistance	Finance and Insurance	Real estate and rental and leasing	Professio-nal, scientific, and technical services	Information	Annual payroll Total (mil dol)	Average per employee dollars
	73	74	75	76	77	78	79	80	81	82	83	84	85
OREGON—Cont'd													
District 3	25 515	381 970	7.6	4.9	5.4	10.4	15.2	5.0	2.2	7.9	2.7	19 343	50 641
District 4	19 344	236 459	12.4	4.8	3.8	15.9	19.0	3.5	1.6	4.0	2.4	9 182	38 832
District 5	21 261	261 782	11.5	6.6	5.3	15.1	16.7	3.5	1.9	4.8	1.4	11 096	42 386
PENNSYLVANIA	299 695	5 306 896	10.4	4.3	4.7	12.5	18.6	5.0	1.2	6.1	2.1	257 627	48 546
District 1	13 961	272 706	5.3	2.9	3.9	10.4	18.7	4.8	2.0	4.8	1.9	12 900	47 302
District 2	14 122	354 970	0.9	1.1	1.1	5.6	25.3	6.9	1.6	10.6	3.3	23 070	64 991
District 3	16 463	267 518	16.3	3.7	3.9	13.1	22.5	3.9	1.0	4.4	1.4	10 332	38 622
District 4	15 810	298 000	13.8	4.6	5.2	13.0	16.3	4.8	1.1	5.6	1.5	13 041	43 760
District 5	15 672	219 805	20.4	3.7	2.6	16.7	17.5	2.5	1.2	3.2	1.5	8 005	36 418
District 6	20 147	363 929	9.0	3.5	6.5	13.7	14.6	8.8	1.1	8.6	2.9	23 031	63 283
District 7	17 900	298 637	8.3	6.1	4.0	10.2	15.7	6.9	1.4	8.7	5.3	18 739	62 748
District 8	21 067	286 996	11.9	6.2	7.5	14.3	16.3	3.4	1.3	6.6	2.0	12 891	44 917
District 9	14 408	212 468	13.9	4.6	3.7	15.8	20.2	2.6	0.7	3.1	1.3	7 622	35 872
District 10	15 876	217 401	16.7	4.6	3.1	16.9	19.6	3.1	1.0	2.8	1.1	7 823	35 985
District 11	14 667	261 381	12.1	3.2	4.4	12.7	18.3	5.3	0.9	4.5	1.8	10 758	41 879
District 12	16 856	247 564	11.6	5.3	3.9	15.0	18.8	3.3	1.1	5.8	1.9	10 758	43 455
District 13	17 742	314 454	6.6	4.4	6.8	16.0	21.4	4.6	1.4	7.1	2.3	17 522	55 721
District 14	19 333	449 041	4.9	3.3	2.9	8.5	19.9	8.6	1.3	8.9	2.4	24 129	53 733
District 15	15 685	304 373	13.4	3.5	6.3	13.1	19.5	3.4	1.0	3.7	1.5	14 872	48 861
District 16	15 612	292 513	16.0	7.7	5.5	12.5	18.0	3.3	1.9	5.0	1.1	12 855	43 948
District 17	14 938	256 892	12.1	2.9	4.4	14.3	20.0	3.7	0.7	2.9	2.2	9 672	37 650
District 18	18 565	319 821	7.8	8.3	5.7	13.2	15.1	3.1	1.2	5.5	1.7	14 954	46 756
RHODE ISLAND	28 387	425 748	9.2	3.9	4.9	11.7	20.4	6.0	1.3	5.4	1.6	19 705	46 283
District 1	13 330	201 213	9.4	4.1	5.1	9.6	19.8	5.6	1.3	5.2	1.3	9 067	45 062
District 2	14 805	219 642	9.2	3.7	4.7	13.9	21.2	6.4	1.3	5.1	1.9	10 376	47 238
SOUTH CAROLINA	103 973	1 662 251	13.5	4.6	4.4	14.3	13.5	4.1	1.5	5.0	2.0	66 120	39 778
District 1	18 510	222 636	4.3	4.8	2.4	18.6	13.3	3.4	2.4	6.1	2.9	8 353	37 519
District 2	13 007	198 015	10.6	5.4	4.3	17.2	13.3	3.2	1.2	4.6	1.6	7 637	38 565
District 3	11 172	172 155	25.9	4.2	3.7	14.4	13.3	2.0	0.8	2.9	0.8	6 239	36 240
District 4	17 766	330 850	15.4	4.2	5.9	12.0	12.2	3.3	1.1	6.0	2.8	14 593	44 108
District 5	11 734	180 774	19.8	4.7	4.9	15.3	11.9	4.3	0.8	4.5	1.7	7 088	39 210
District 6	15 012	280 354	13.2	5.0	5.7	10.2	17.4	7.1	1.6	6.1	2.3	12 428	44 330
District 7	16 227	222 874	11.4	4.4	3.2	18.1	15.5	4.0	2.7	3.2	1.4	7 563	33 934
SOUTH DAKOTA	26 511	353 540	12.8	5.5	5.4	15.1	18.5	7.3	1.1	3.4	1.9	13 813	39 071
At Large	26 511	353 540	12.8	5.5	5.4	15.1	18.5	7.3	1.1	3.4	1.9	13 813	39 071
TENNESSEE	133 344	2 507 205	12.6	4.1	4.6	12.6	16.0	4.7	1.3	4.5	1.9	110 481	44 066
District 1	13 588	234 256	19.3	3.8	2.5	16.2	18.0	3.2	1.4	2.1	1.7	8 626	36 823
District 2	15 667	285 755	8.1	4.0	5.7	14.2	15.9	4.8	1.4	5.1	2.0	11 921	41 717
District 3	14 186	272 440	19.3	4.1	3.0	11.9	14.6	5.3	1.0	6.5	1.4	11 673	42 848
District 4	12 823	230 656	22.4	5.3	5.0	14.4	12.0	4.3	1.0	2.2	1.3	9 079	39 361
District 5	20 430	444 871	5.4	4.1	4.6	9.8	18.8	6.1	1.7	5.9	3.1	23 372	52 536
District 6	13 252	192 795	19.9	4.8	4.0	15.2	15.6	3.3	1.2	3.6	1.3	7 252	37 616
District 7	14 784	223 009	11.2	4.2	2.7	14.6	17.0	6.6	1.2	5.6	2.9	10 537	47 251
District 8	14 754	245 310	13.1	4.1	3.8	13.6	19.6	4.7	1.4	4.0	1.3	10 434	42 534
District 9	13 274	319 883	7.4	3.7	7.9	10.6	14.1	2.8	1.6	3.4	1.6	15 431	48 240
TEXAS	569 091	10 239 710	7.9	6.4	5.1	12.5	14.2	5.0	1.9	6.7	2.3	521 096	50 890
District 1	16 826	262 046	13.4	5.5	3.9	14.2	19.3	4.1	1.5	4.4	1.4	10 400	39 686
District 2	19 705	362 119	11.3	9.2	7.7	11.7	7.5	4.2	1.9	5.8	1.7	20 658	57 048
District 3	20 295	361 991	4.5	3.8	4.7	13.0	12.3	13.2	2.0	9.8	4.8	22 311	61 635
District 4	13 577	195 050	19.2	4.9	3.3	16.2	19.8	3.4	1.0	3.0	1.2	7 118	36 491
District 5	12 462	177 873	12.6	9.5	5.0	17.5	14.9	2.1	1.8	4.1	0.9	6 485	36 456
District 6	13 662	222 756	13.7	5.8	6.5	15.1	13.2	4.4	1.6	3.5	1.4	8 793	39 475
District 7	25 275	464 626	2.6	6.1	4.0	11.1	10.5	6.5	2.9	12.1	2.5	35 234	75 832
District 8	14 292	195 375	9.0	6.7	4.2	15.7	11.6	3.3	1.9	8.0	1.1	11 122	56 925
District 9	12 923	323 758	5.3	4.8	5.0	7.6	32.2	2.2	1.5	8.5	1.3	19 037	58 800
District 10	18 916	284 812	8.3	7.2	5.3	15.4	11.0	4.2	2.0	8.1	3.9	13 826	48 543
District 11	19 189	275 805	6.9	8.3	6.4	13.7	12.5	2.9	2.1	3.8	1.2	13 065	47 372
District 12	17 167	308 480	12.5	5.3	4.0	12.7	14.5	5.9	1.3	5.2	1.6	15 967	51 760
District 13	16 571	223 170	13.5	5.7	5.6	15.2	16.5	4.3	1.4	3.1	1.5	8 883	39 803
District 14	13 595	231 199	13.4	10.6	3.3	14.3	15.6	3.3	2.0	4.9	0.9	11 432	49 445
District 15	12 067	185 065	6.9	3.8	4.6	19.0	24.3	3.4	1.4	3.2	1.6	5 758	31 114
District 16	13 370	217 989	5.7	4.2	4.4	16.9	19.6	2.9	1.8	4.8	4.0	6 966	31 954
District 17	14 352	254 460	11.9	6.8	4.7	13.1	14.4	4.2	1.7	5.0	3.3	10 497	41 254
District 18	16 647	422 211	8.7	5.9	10.8	5.7	7.3	3.9	1.6	9.1	2.4	33 794	80 042
District 19	16 598	238 280	6.4	6.2	5.5	15.4	19.1	4.6	1.5	3.1	2.1	8 785	36 868
District 20	11 255	255 698	3.3	3.1	2.0	14.9	16.5	14.8	1.6	6.9	1.8	10 973	42 914
District 21	26 020	413 255	2.7	6.8	3.3	11.0	15.1	5.1	2.3	10.3	3.9	20 748	50 207
District 22	15 120	199 423	6.9	5.3	3.6	20.6	17.2	2.5	1.5	5.7	1.8	8 581	43 029
District 23	11 134	173 177	5.3	15.2	2.9	17.1	12.4	3.7	1.5	2.5	0.8	6 637	38 326
District 24	27 304	677 799	4.2	5.1	6.5	7.7	6.8	8.6	2.5	10.6	5.2	43 150	63 662
District 25	17 165	212 230	6.7	5.8	5.2	14.4	16.5	4.3	2.2	8.2	2.3	10 614	50 014

1. Specified owner-occupied units; $1,000,000 represents $1,000,000 or more.   2. Specified renter-occupied units.

Table E. Congressional Districts 115th Congress — Land Area and Population Characteristics

					Population and population characteristics, 2015										
					Percent										
					Race alone										
STATE District	Representative, 115th Congress	Land area,[1] 2016 (sq. mi)	Total persons	Per square mile	White	Black	American Indian, Alaska Native	Asian and Pacific Islander	Some other race	Two or more races	Hispanic or Latino[2]	Non-Hispanic White alone	Female	Foreign-born	Born in state of residence
		1	2	3	4	5	6	7	8	9	10	11	12	13	14
TEXAS—Cont'd															
District 26	Michael C. Burgess (R)	907.3	818 125	901.8	78.5	8.2	0.4	6.5	3.3	3.1	17.7	65.3	50.5	12.4	50.5
District 27	Blake Farenthold (R)	9 120.7	734 713	80.6	85.0	5.0	0.5	1.7	5.7	2.2	52.5	40.0	50.8	8.9	75.2
District 28	Henry Cuellar (D)	9 378.9	724 967	77.3	89.2	3.9	0.2	1.1	3.9	1.7	78.2	15.9	51.0	22.2	63.2
District 29	Gene Green (D)	187.1	758 771	4 056.5	77.3	11.0	0.4	1.6	8.2	1.5	77.3	9.6	49.5	33.2	56.8
District 30	Eddie Bernice Johnson (D)	356.3	754 382	2 117.1	48.5	43.6	0.4	1.6	4.1	1.8	39.1	14.9	51.7	18.1	63.4
District 31	John R. Carter (R)	2 154.4	804 974	373.6	76.1	11.4	0.4	5.0	2.7	4.4	24.3	56.7	50.6	10.6	51.0
District 32	Pete Sessions (R)	187.1	748 526	4 001.7	69.1	13.8	0.4	7.8	5.7	3.3	26.0	49.9	50.8	20.7	50.7
District 33	Marc A. Veasey (D)	212.0	740 323	3 492.4	68.0	16.4	0.3	2.0	11.7	1.6	67.0	14.0	49.0	33.5	54.7
District 34	Filemon Vela (D)	8 190.8	730 907	89.2	92.3	1.4	0.3	0.6	4.3	1.0	83.0	14.7	51.1	19.2	71.2
District 35	Lloyd Doggett (D)	593.8	823 909	1 387.5	76.2	8.8	0.7	1.9	10.0	2.4	63.1	25.4	49.3	17.4	63.7
District 36	Brian Babin (R)	7 125.8	731 274	102.6	82.2	9.6	0.5	2.1	3.1	2.5	23.5	62.7	49.6	10.0	68.1
UTAH		82 195.6	2 995 919	36.4	87.2	1.2	1.2	3.1	4.5	2.9	13.7	78.9	49.7	8.2	62.3
District 1	Rob Bishop (R)	19 556.9	740 397	37.9	89.6	1.0	1.1	1.7	3.7	3.0	12.9	81.3	49.8	6.0	64.9
District 2	Chris Stewart (R)	40 015.0	750 207	18.7	83.7	1.2	1.2	4.0	7.0	2.8	15.3	76.7	49.6	9.8	58.1
District 3	Vacant	20 074.0	743 301	37.0	90.5	0.6	1.7	2.7	1.5	3.0	10.2	82.4	49.7	6.7	62.3
District 4	Mia B. Love (R)	2 549.6	762 014	298.9	84.9	1.8	0.8	3.9	5.8	2.8	16.1	75.3	49.8	10.1	63.9
VERMONT		9 217.6	626 042	67.9	94.7	1.3	0.4	1.4	0.3	1.8	1.7	93.4	50.7	4.5	49.9
At Large	Peter Welch (D)	9 217.6	626 042	67.9	94.7	1.3	0.4	1.4	0.3	1.8	1.7	93.4	50.7	4.5	49.9
VIRGINIA		39 481.8	8 382 993	212.3	68.2	19.2	0.3	6.3	2.4	3.5	9.0	62.5	50.8	12.2	49.5
District 1	Robert J. Wittman (R)	4 212.2	771 237	183.1	72.0	17.5	0.3	3.7	2.6	3.9	9.4	66.3	50.8	8.5	46.5
District 2	Scott Taylor (R)	1 103.9	748 489	678.0	66.4	22.0	0.3	5.4	1.5	4.3	8.0	61.3	49.8	7.9	44.0
District 3	Robert C. "Bobby" Scott (D)	625.0	738 228	1 181.2	35.1	57.1	0.7	1.9	1.5	3.7	5.9	31.8	52.0	4.9	61.0
District 4	A. Donald McEachin (D)	3 641.8	753 899	207.0	61.5	31.4	0.3	2.4	1.5	2.9	5.4	58.4	50.5	5.2	65.8
District 5	Thomas A. Garrett, Jr. (R)	10 029.9	736 851	73.5	75.6	19.6	0.1	1.8	0.8	2.0	3.4	73.2	50.8	4.2	65.8
District 6	Bob Goodlatte (R)	5 929.8	745 367	125.7	83.5	10.9	0.2	1.9	0.7	2.7	5.2	79.6	51.1	5.5	63.6
District 7	Dave Brat (R)	3 118.7	778 480	249.6	75.0	15.3	0.3	5.1	1.5	2.9	6.4	70.7	51.6	9.1	55.2
District 8	Donald S. Beyer, Jr. (D)	149.2	808 352	5 416.4	63.5	13.4	0.2	11.9	6.5	4.5	20.0	51.5	50.0	30.2	23.4
District 9	Morgan Griffith (R)	9 113.9	720 447	79.0	90.8	5.6	0.1	1.3	0.7	1.5	2.3	89.2	50.5	2.6	66.3
District 10	Barbara Comstock (R)	1 372.1	807 670	588.6	70.8	6.9	0.3	14.2	2.9	4.9	13.1	61.7	50.5	21.4	36.0
District 11	Gerald E. Connolly (D)	185.2	773 973	4 179.2	56.8	13.5	0.2	18.3	5.8	5.4	18.0	45.9	51.0	31.0	28.4
WASHINGTON		66 453.4	7 170 351	107.9	76.9	3.7	1.3	8.6	4.0	5.5	12.4	69.7	50.0	13.7	47.3
District 1	Suzan K. DelBene (D)	6 185.4	713 051	115.3	79.4	1.2	1.1	10.3	3.6	4.4	9.2	74.7	49.5	16.0	49.1
District 2	Rick Larsen (D)	1 015.4	726 951	715.9	78.3	2.8	1.2	9.2	2.9	5.7	10.5	71.6	50.7	15.0	46.9
District 3	Jaime Herrera Beutler (R)	9 116.1	711 569	78.1	87.0	1.5	0.8	3.6	2.3	4.7	9.4	80.7	50.4	8.1	41.4
District 4	Dan Newsome (R)	19 246.2	709 698	36.9	78.9	0.9	2.3	1.4	12.5	4.0	38.4	54.5	49.5	16.2	56.6
District 5	Cathy McMorris Rodgers (R)	15 473.5	696 426	45.0	88.2	1.5	1.6	2.8	1.6	4.4	6.3	84.0	50.2	5.9	53.2
District 6	Derek Kilmer (D)	6 902.4	680 903	98.6	82.2	3.2	2.1	4.4	1.4	6.6	7.2	77.7	49.7	6.6	48.9
District 7	Pramila Jayapal (D)	144.0	746 317	5 181.4	73.5	4.8	0.7	11.6	2.8	6.5	7.2	70.1	49.6	16.1	39.6
District 8	David G. Reichert (R)	7 359.6	730 327	99.2	77.6	3.0	0.9	9.6	3.3	5.5	11.1	71.2	50.8	13.0	51.8
District 9	Adam Smith (D)	183.6	728 262	3 967.5	52.4	11.0	0.6	23.8	6.0	6.1	12.7	47.2	49.7	28.7	38.7
District 10	Denny Heck (D)	827.3	726 847	878.6	72.7	6.4	1.6	8.1	3.9	7.4	11.8	66.3	49.8	10.1	48.0
WEST VIRGINIA		24 040.9	1 844 128	76.7	93.4	3.9	0.1	0.8	0.2	1.6	1.4	92.3	50.7	1.6	69.7
District 1	David McKinley (R)	6 275.7	614 959	98.0	94.5	2.4	0.1	1.0	0.2	1.8	1.3	93.5	50.4	1.7	68.6
District 2	Alexander X. Mooney (R)	8 019.6	628 879	78.4	91.9	4.9	0.1	0.8	0.3	2.0	2.0	90.4	50.7	2.0	62.4
District 3	Evan H. Jenkins (R)	9 745.6	600 290	61.6	93.9	4.2	0.2	0.5	0.2	1.0	1.0	93.1	51.1	1.1	78.3
WISCONSIN		54 159.9	5 771 337	106.6	86.0	6.3	0.9	2.7	1.8	2.3	6.6	81.8	50.3	4.8	71.4
District 1	Paul Ryan (R)	1 728.1	714 073	413.2	87.5	5.6	0.5	2.3	1.6	2.5	9.8	80.5	50.1	4.7	67.4
District 2	Mark Pocan (D)	4 536.8	750 045	165.3	86.6	4.4	0.4	4.1	1.7	2.9	6.1	82.8	50.5	7.0	64.7
District 3	Ron Kind (D)	11 111.9	719 264	64.7	93.6	1.0	0.6	2.4	0.8	1.6	2.5	92.2	49.8	2.6	71.9
District 4	Gwen Moore (D)	128.5	716 998	5 580.7	52.6	33.4	0.5	3.8	6.0	3.6	16.9	43.1	52.2	9.8	65.6
District 5	F. James Sensenbrenner Jr. (R)	1 890.8	723 853	382.8	91.5	2.4	0.3	2.6	1.0	2.3	5.8	87.4	50.7	4.8	76.5
District 6	Glen Grothman(R)	4 918.7	710 564	144.5	93.2	1.7	0.5	2.6	0.5	1.5	4.5	89.6	49.9	3.6	79.2
District 7	Sean P. Duffy (R)	23 039.1	709 049	30.8	93.5	0.7	1.9	1.7	0.4	1.9	2.2	91.8	49.3	2.3	67.9
District 8	Mike Gallagher (R)	6 806.0	727 491	106.9	89.8	1.3	2.4	2.3	2.2	2.0	5.0	87.2	49.9	3.8	78.4
WYOMING		97 091.2	586 107	6.0	91.5	0.8	2.2	0.9	1.8	2.8	9.9	84.1	49.7	3.8	40.7
At Large	Liz Cheney (R)	97 091.2	586 107	6.0	91.5	0.8	2.2	0.9	1.8	2.8	9.9	84.1	49.7	3.8	40.7

1. Dry land or land partially or temporarily covered by water.   2. May be of any race.

STATE District	Under 5 years	5 to 17 years	18 to 24 years	25 to 34 years	35 to 44 years	45 to 54 years	55 to 64 years	65 to 74 years	75 years and over	Median age	Total Enrollment[1]	High school graduate or more	Bachelor's degree or more
	15	16	17	18	19	20	21	22	23	24	25	26	27
TEXAS—Cont'd													
District 26	6.9	20.5	9.2	14.2	15.7	14.2	10.3	5.9	3.3	34.5	245 524	92.5	41.6
District 27	6.7	18.6	10.2	13.1	12.3	11.8	12.6	8.4	6.3	35.9	183 175	80.9	19.3
District 28	9.1	22.0	10.8	12.2	13.6	11.5	9.5	6.7	4.5	31.9	219 819	70.6	18.4
District 29	8.6	22.9	11.0	15.9	13.3	11.8	9.1	4.9	2.7	29.5	225 844	61.0	9.1
District 30	7.2	20.7	10.0	15.4	13.7	13.0	10.6	5.8	3.6	32.8	205 699	75.6	20.0
District 31	7.3	19.6	9.3	14.9	14.9	12.6	10.2	6.9	4.4	34.2	223 989	92.1	35.2
District 32	7.0	16.9	9.4	16.2	13.5	13.1	11.6	7.7	4.6	35.4	194 899	86.9	43.0
District 33	8.9	22.7	10.5	15.3	13.8	11.8	9.3	4.7	3.2	30.0	214 051	57.6	10.4
District 34	8.4	21.6	10.9	12.5	11.9	11.3	9.8	7.8	5.9	32.2	205 559	66.8	14.6
District 35	7.7	18.1	11.5	18.7	13.6	11.9	9.1	5.7	3.7	31.4	227 749	77.1	18.9
District 36	6.5	18.2	9.8	12.8	12.8	13.3	13.3	8.0	5.4	36.9	182 332	83.9	18.2
UTAH	8.3	22.1	11.4	14.7	13.5	10.3	9.4	6.0	4.2	30.6	954 586	91.5	31.8
District 1	8.4	22.8	11.2	14.5	13.4	10.3	9.6	5.7	4.0	30.3	235 144	92.0	28.7
District 2	7.3	20.5	11.5	15.1	12.9	10.3	10.4	7.7	5.4	32.7	225 967	90.6	31.2
District 3	8.6	22.9	14.8	13.3	12.2	9.9	8.6	5.7	3.8	27.5	265 048	93.4	39.6
District 4	9.1	22.2	9.2	15.8	15.1	10.6	9.2	5.1	3.8	31.2	228 427	90.4	28.6
VERMONT	4.8	14.4	10.7	11.3	11.2	14.5	15.6	10.3	7.2	43.1	150 285	91.7	36.9
At Large	4.8	14.4	10.7	11.3	11.2	14.5	15.6	10.3	7.2	43.1	150 285	91.7	36.9
VIRGINIA	6.1	16.2	9.9	14.0	13.1	13.9	12.6	8.5	5.8	37.8	2 143 693	88.9	37.0
District 1	6.4	18.0	9.0	12.3	13.0	14.6	12.2	8.4	6.0	38.5	205 725	91.0	35.0
District 2	6.5	14.8	11.9	16.6	12.1	12.9	11.8	7.7	5.6	35.1	188 033	91.4	30.9
District 3	6.8	14.9	13.4	17.6	11.1	12.2	12.0	7.0	5.0	33.2	190 162	85.9	24.6
District 4	5.8	17.4	9.0	13.2	12.8	14.6	13.2	8.4	5.6	38.5	196 144	88.8	27.3
District 5	4.8	15.2	9.6	11.8	11.3	13.5	14.8	11.1	7.7	42.6	174 319	85.9	26.5
District 6	5.4	15.0	12.6	11.8	11.3	13.3	13.2	9.9	7.5	39.9	191 871	86.6	26.2
District 7	5.5	17.7	7.9	12.4	13.4	14.7	13.4	9.2	5.9	39.9	196 088	91.4	41.1
District 8	7.3	14.2	7.4	19.8	16.3	13.6	11.0	6.4	4.0	35.5	185 598	90.0	59.6
District 9	5.1	13.8	11.5	11.8	11.5	13.7	14.0	11.0	7.7	42.0	172 222	82.9	20.7
District 10	6.7	20.2	7.5	11.5	15.0	15.9	11.9	7.4	4.1	37.9	229 085	92.3	54.7
District 11	6.6	16.8	9.4	14.8	15.3	14.2	12.0	6.7	4.2	36.4	214 446	91.3	54.7
WASHINGTON	6.2	16.3	9.3	14.7	12.9	13.2	12.9	8.8	5.7	37.5	1 728 161	90.8	34.2
District 1	6.5	16.8	7.2	13.1	14.2	15.1	13.8	8.6	4.6	39.3	172 311	93.7	43.1
District 2	5.7	15.7	10.6	14.8	12.3	12.7	13.1	9.0	6.2	37.4	176 880	92.0	31.0
District 3	6.0	17.9	8.0	12.3	12.7	13.3	13.4	10.2	6.2	39.9	168 928	89.9	24.3
District 4	8.2	21.0	9.3	13.3	12.1	11.7	11.4	7.9	5.2	33.8	190 994	79.1	20.6
District 5	5.8	15.7	11.7	13.8	11.0	12.4	13.5	9.5	6.6	37.6	183 976	92.3	28.2
District 6	5.0	14.2	9.5	12.9	10.9	13.0	15.2	11.8	7.6	42.5	144 338	92.5	28.8
District 7	5.2	10.5	10.5	20.4	15.3	12.8	12.3	7.4	5.7	37.1	159 977	94.8	59.4
District 8	6.2	18.2	8.7	13.2	13.8	14.4	13.0	7.8	4.7	37.4	182 439	90.6	33.3
District 9	6.2	15.8	8.4	17.2	13.9	14.2	11.5	7.3	5.6	36.5	169 163	90.4	41.3
District 10	7.2	17.2	9.6	15.0	12.9	12.7	12.3	7.9	5.4	35.7	179 155	91.3	26.3
WEST VIRGINIA	5.5	15.0	8.9	11.9	12.5	13.4	14.6	10.7	7.5	42.2	399 802	86.0	19.6
District 1	5.0	14.2	10.8	12.3	12.2	13.2	14.1	10.4	7.5	41.4	143 909	88.7	22.5
District 2	5.9	15.8	7.6	12.0	12.6	13.7	14.7	10.6	7.2	42.3	134 833	87.1	21.5
District 3	5.7	15.2	8.3	11.2	12.7	13.2	14.9	11.1	7.8	42.8	121 060	82.2	14.5
WISCONSIN	5.8	16.6	9.7	12.5	12.1	13.9	13.8	8.7	6.8	39.4	1 429 175	91.4	28.4
District 1	5.7	16.9	8.2	11.7	12.1	15.0	14.6	9.0	6.5	41.2	170 814	91.1	26.9
District 2	5.9	15.8	12.3	14.1	12.8	12.8	12.9	7.8	5.7	36.3	201 232	93.5	40.0
District 3	5.5	15.6	13.0	11.8	10.9	12.9	13.5	9.2	7.3	38.5	186 771	92.2	24.5
District 4	7.3	18.1	11.2	16.5	12.6	12.3	11.1	6.2	4.9	32.9	203 856	84.7	27.2
District 5	5.7	16.5	8.5	12.1	12.4	14.6	14.3	8.8	7.3	40.8	178 711	94.1	35.9
District 6	5.2	16.2	9.1	11.6	11.9	14.4	14.4	9.4	7.7	41.8	164 586	91.3	24.6
District 7	5.4	16.3	7.0	10.6	11.5	14.5	15.8	10.8	8.2	44.4	148 987	91.5	22.3
District 8	5.9	17.0	8.3	12.2	12.3	14.3	13.8	9.0	7.0	40.6	174 218	92.5	25.7
WYOMING	6.5	17.3	9.9	14.1	12.3	11.9	13.9	8.4	5.7	36.5	148 772	92.2	26.2
At Large	6.5	17.3	9.9	14.1	12.3	11.9	13.9	8.4	5.7	36.5	148 772	92.2	26.2

1. All persons 3 years old and over enrolled in nursery school through college and graduate or professional school.   2. Persons 25 years old and over.

STATE District	Households, 2015						Group quarters, 2010					
	Number	Average household size	Family households (percent)	Married-couple family (percent)	Female family householder[1]	One person households (percent)	Total in group quarters, 2015	Percent 65 years and over	Persons in correctional institutions	Persons in nursing facilities	Persons in college dormitories	Persons in military quarters
	28	29	30	31	32	33	34	35	36	37	38	39
TEXAS—Cont'd												
District 26	274 216	2.94	75.3	60.7	10.9	18.9	11 905	14.1	1 179	1 636	6 475	0
District 27	263 740	2.73	69.2	49.3	14.0	25.2	14 423	31.7	3 832	4 197	1 365	103
District 28	210 726	3.41	76.9	52.7	18.9	19.5	6 246	32.3	3 252	2 888	740	146
District 29	228 854	3.31	74.2	44.8	20.7	21.6	2 406	36.1	31	1 008	0	0
District 30	259 435	2.84	65.5	37.5	21.2	28.4	18 475	9.2	11 108	2 286	2 507	0
District 31	277 160	2.85	70.7	55.0	11.5	23.6	15 672	16.1	3 442	2 183	2 041	4 084
District 32	282 479	2.63	63.5	48.0	11.0	29.4	5 319	38.4	22	2 226	2 437	0
District 33	219 249	3.35	72.3	43.2	20.3	22.1	6 278	19.3	2 147	1 389	534	0
District 34	212 817	3.34	77.5	53.3	19.1	19.6	19 190	13.7	13 244	2 881	2 180	41
District 35	267 303	3.01	63.9	38.9	17.6	27.0	19 852	9.9	7 971	2 563	5 761	115
District 36	264 815	2.70	69.0	51.7	11.9	26.4	17 360	16.7	12 140	2 926	0	0
UTAH	930 980	3.17	74.5	60.7	9.5	19.8	46 968	10.4	12 666	5 854	15 666	523
District 1	231 359	3.16	76.8	62.7	9.3	18.9	8 688	10.6	1 892	1 190	3 227	488
District 2	251 626	2.93	69.0	55.4	9.5	24.0	12 057	12.1	3 459	1 763	3 443	35
District 3	216 903	3.35	77.7	66.4	8.5	15.9	17 409	7.5	441	1 279	8 960	0
District 4	231 092	3.26	75.0	59.1	10.7	19.7	8 814	12.4	6 874	1 622	36	0
VERMONT	254 865	2.36	59.8	48.5	7.9	30.3	25 439	15.0	1 592	3 588	16 895	5
At Large	254 865	2.36	59.8	48.5	7.9	30.3	25 439	15.0	1 592	3 588	16 895	5
VIRGINIA	3 106 895	2.62	66.1	49.9	11.9	27.1	243 812	12.0	65 240	30 324	84 048	37 568
District 1	271 514	2.77	73.3	58.6	10.4	21.6	19 888	13.8	4 215	2 568	6 380	3 351
District 2	279 059	2.56	65.1	46.7	13.1	27.7	34 193	11.2	1 685	2 534	7 086	7 370
District 3	287 256	2.46	53.8	29.0	19.5	37.0	31 080	5.4	6 045	3 045	11 014	24 287
District 4	270 552	2.68	71.9	51.7	15.5	23.5	27 788	10.2	19 352	2 662	2 942	316
District 5	291 018	2.43	65.4	49.2	12.4	28.1	29 209	13.8	10 972	4 052	12 206	0
District 6	287 061	2.47	63.5	47.3	11.7	29.2	35 522	12.6	4 623	4 349	19 615	1 398
District 7	289 326	2.65	69.9	55.2	10.1	24.7	11 402	19.8	4 500	2 649	3 721	0
District 8	314 949	2.55	56.9	44.2	8.9	33.6	6 743	28.6	944	2 026	1 084	846
District 9	285 298	2.41	64.1	48.6	11.0	30.0	33 527	13.1	10 091	4 288	14 085	0
District 10	264 870	3.02	77.5	65.7	8.0	16.8	6 561	18.7	1 606	907	1 068	0
District 11	265 992	2.88	68.9	54.9	10.2	23.9	7 899	13.6	1 207	1 244	4 847	0
WASHINGTON	2 728 573	2.58	64.5	50.0	10.0	27.0	140 994	18.6	31 960	22 156	35 534	12 385
District 1	266 544	2.64	70.9	59.2	7.5	22.4	8 844	23.7	2 676	1 313	620	0
District 2	278 263	2.57	62.7	47.8	9.8	27.3	12 941	20.5	1 754	2 323	3 862	2 504
District 3	265 756	2.65	67.8	52.2	10.3	25.1	7 277	35.8	1 539	1 617	0	14
District 4	238 724	2.93	73.3	54.1	13.4	20.9	10 560	25.7	4 028	2 246	382	4
District 5	272 518	2.45	63.3	48.3	10.7	30.1	29 544	11.8	5 656	2 927	13 048	513
District 6	270 239	2.46	62.6	48.5	9.6	29.9	17 099	16.0	8 063	3 211	1 022	5 694
District 7	335 747	2.16	48.4	39.1	6.3	36.3	20 990	13.6	1 851	2 700	10 456	362
District 8	258 732	2.80	72.9	58.9	9.8	20.9	6 849	24.8	839	1 305	2 155	0
District 9	274 741	2.60	62.3	46.6	11.0	27.2	12 757	26.9	3 031	2 422	1 348	0
District 10	267 309	2.67	66.6	48.8	13.2	26.4	14 133	17.9	2 523	2 092	2 641	3 294
WEST VIRGINIA	734 536	2.44	64.3	47.8	11.5	30.3	48 188	18.9	16 591	9 748	17 113	79
District 1	243 428	2.44	63.1	47.6	10.9	31.0	21 620	15.8	6 965	3 632	10 300	0
District 2	247 760	2.49	65.9	49.1	11.8	28.6	11 233	23.6	2 583	2 791	3 447	0
District 3	243 348	2.40	63.7	46.8	11.9	31.4	15 335	20.1	7 043	3 325	3 366	79
WISCONSIN	2 319 538	2.42	63.4	49.0	9.8	29.1	148 192	23.1	38 102	33 808	56 773	132
District 1	274 600	2.55	68.6	53.6	10.0	25.3	14 560	21.6	6 723	3 632	2 368	0
District 2	306 443	2.39	59.6	45.8	9.9	29.1	17 970	19.7	2 269	2 791	8 805	0
District 3	282 403	2.44	62.0	50.3	7.3	29.2	31 612	15.5	6 311	3 325	18 297	122
District 4	281 913	2.48	54.1	30.0	18.6	36.5	18 649	17.5	2 539	3 173	9 814	0
District 5	292 232	2.43	65.3	53.4	7.8	28.1	15 165	33.1	1 490	4 832	5 703	0
District 6	290 898	2.36	65.4	53.2	8.4	28.7	23 311	20.2	12 174	5 078	6 097	0
District 7	296 872	2.35	66.0	53.8	7.8	27.7	12 220	42.6	3 541	5 073	1 198	0
District 8	294 177	2.42	65.9	52.0	9.3	27.8	14 705	31.5	3 055	4 742	4 491	10
WYOMING	228 937	2.50	63.5	51.2	7.2	29.9	14 143	18.4	3 576	2 450	4 443	503
At Large	228 937	2.50	63.5	51.2	7.2	29.9	14 143	18.4	3 576	2 450	4 443	503

1. No spouse present.

Table E. Congressional Districts 115th Congress — **Housing and Money Income**

STATE District	Housing units, 2015						Money income, 2015		
			Occupied units				Households		
			Owner-occupied			Renter-occupied			
	Total	Occupied units as a percent of all units	Owner-occupied units as a percent of occupied units	Median value[1] (dollars)	Percent valued at $500,000 or more	Median rent[2]	Per capita income (dollars)	Median income (dollars)	Percent with income of $100,000 or more
	40	41	42	43	44	45	46	47	48
TEXAS—Cont'd									
District 26	287 332	95.4	70.2	216 500	7.2	1 134	35 116	79 738	38.8
District 27	312 509	84.4	61.8	124 500	3.0	877	25 640	50 764	20.8
District 28	239 516	88.0	68.0	110 000	1.7	805	19 474	45 054	17.7
District 29	250 933	91.2	48.5	98 000	1.9	816	16 797	40 871	12.0
District 30	287 232	90.3	50.9	110 700	2.8	913	21 233	42 439	15.2
District 31	302 763	91.5	63.4	200 000	4.6	995	30 093	65 377	28.6
District 32	306 555	92.1	56.6	204 100	17.8	1 084	41 123	66 375	32.2
District 33	241 293	90.9	46.7	87 100	0.6	819	15 701	39 246	9.3
District 34	259 221	82.1	67.2	82 000	1.2	650	16 585	35 642	13.3
District 35	292 148	91.5	47.7	126 800	1.4	952	19 959	43 831	13.9
District 36	302 085	87.7	71.0	124 000	2.1	862	28 219	56 885	25.5
UTAH	1 038 065	89.7	68.9	234 600	8.4	925	25 816	62 912	25.8
District 1	268 208	86.3	71.8	206 600	6.7	832	25 476	63 334	25.0
District 2	288 638	87.2	65.5	216 900	7.9	876	26 024	55 339	21.7
District 3	236 808	91.6	68.8	275 500	13.9	970	26 127	66 007	29.5
District 4	244 411	94.6	69.8	245 700	5.4	1 002	25 638	67 632	27.5
VERMONT	326 874	78.0	70.7	223 700	8.0	923	31 216	56 990	23.0
At Large	326 874	78.0	70.7	223 700	8.0	923	31 216	56 990	23.0
VIRGINIA	3 468 952	89.6	65.0	257 800	18.1	1 144	34 780	66 262	31.8
District 1	307 392	88.3	72.8	305 700	13.7	1 283	34 658	77 593	37.8
District 2	312 967	89.2	60.7	240 700	9.2	1 159	30 688	62 006	24.8
District 3	320 894	89.5	45.5	164 600	3.7	921	23 607	41 152	13.3
District 4	292 721	92.4	69.7	218 400	4.8	1 061	28 529	62 796	26.4
District 5	352 058	82.7	69.5	185 000	10.0	806	28 038	50 612	20.8
District 6	329 045	87.2	65.0	180 300	4.6	805	25 399	49 220	17.0
District 7	311 505	92.9	70.8	264 100	10.5	1 142	37 689	74 889	35.5
District 8	339 999	92.6	50.6	526 300	52.9	1 709	51 753	100 644	50.7
District 9	343 516	83.1	70.9	119 800	2.4	663	23 833	42 174	14.0
District 10	279 775	94.7	78.8	472 000	45.6	1 520	49 662	114 793	57.2
District 11	279 080	95.3	63.7	463 600	43.6	1 752	45 062	105 031	53.4
WASHINGTON	2 991 584	91.2	62.4	284 000	18.8	1 080	33 486	64 129	29.1
District 1	289 273	92.1	72.4	399 100	34.0	1 371	42 527	86 349	42.5
District 2	308 162	90.3	60.2	310 200	14.4	1 132	31 599	65 000	26.9
District 3	292 545	90.8	65.3	237 500	7.5	979	28 710	57 331	24.0
District 4	261 243	91.4	66.2	177 500	3.9	777	23 883	52 351	19.8
District 5	302 936	90.0	61.4	191 400	5.3	769	25 549	47 053	16.8
District 6	319 061	84.7	65.1	253 600	12.3	956	30 645	58 410	22.5
District 7	354 148	94.8	50.4	495 200	49.2	1 338	48 797	80 119	40.6
District 8	286 022	90.5	73.3	321 400	21.3	1 161	35 730	77 320	37.1
District 9	290 404	94.6	55.5	369 700	31.2	1 305	39 045	71 947	35.5
District 10	287 790	92.9	58.6	235 100	6.1	1 055	27 274	56 564	21.8
WEST VIRGINIA	885 539	82.9	72.3	112 100	2.0	675	23 539	42 019	14.3
District 1	289 791	84.0	71.7	112 200	1.9	685	24 740	44 180	15.5
District 2	296 299	83.6	72.3	138 600	3.0	709	25 482	47 045	17.3
District 3	299 449	81.3	73.0	88 700	1.2	616	20 275	35 913	10.0
WISCONSIN	2 656 669	87.3	66.8	168 300	4.1	792	29 563	55 638	21.4
District 1	306 344	89.6	71.1	184 500	3.8	843	30 721	62 206	25.5
District 2	324 773	94.4	61.6	212 100	6.2	905	33 555	61 224	25.6
District 3	322 354	87.6	70.6	148 900	2.7	727	26 694	51 219	17.9
District 4	310 443	90.8	43.9	129 900	3.4	803	23 549	40 748	13.7
District 5	308 561	94.7	68.8	219 800	6.2	894	35 115	66 777	28.8
District 6	322 354	90.2	70.8	155 300	4.4	699	29 993	56 326	20.5
District 7	415 848	71.4	75.5	153 700	3.1	686	28 026	51 863	17.9
District 8	345 992	85.0	71.8	157 100	3.0	716	28 629	56 137	21.1
WYOMING	269 469	85.0	68.0	212 500	6.8	815	31 383	60 214	25.2
At Large	269 469	85.0	68.0	212 500	6.8	815	31 383	60 214	25.2

1. Specified owner-occupied units; $1,000,000 represents $1,000,000 or more.   2. Specified renter-occupied units.

Items 40—48

Table E. Congressional Districts 115th Congress — Poverty, Labor Force, Employment, and Social Security

STATE District	Poverty, 2015 Persons below poverty level (percent)	Families below poverty level (percent)	Percent of households receiving food stamps in past 12 months	Civilian labor force, 2015 Total	Unemployment Total	Rate[1]	Civilian employment,[2] 2015 Total	Percent Management, business, science and arts occupations	Service, sales, and office	Construction and production	Persons under age 65 with no health insurance, 2015 (percent)	Social Security beneficiaries, December 2015 Number	Rate[3]	Supplemental Security Income recipients, December 2015
	49	50	51	52	53	54	55	56	57	58	59	60	61	62
TEXAS—Cont'd														
District 26	7.2	4.8	5.6	448 513	20 252	4.5	428 261	44.7	40.3	15.0	11.8	88 572	108.3	6 410
District 27	17.2	13.8	12.7	351 523	22 692	6.5	328 831	28.7	43.1	28.2	19.5	134 518	183.1	22 132
District 28	25.6	20.9	24.1	314 343	25 968	8.3	288 375	27.4	47.2	25.4	27.1	107 713	148.6	30 965
District 29	25.5	23.7	20.5	352 441	20 927	5.9	331 514	16.1	41.6	42.3	32.2	75 198	99.1	23 064
District 30	24.1	20.1	20.4	359 446	23 052	6.4	336 394	28.7	43.2	28.1	22.8	101 143	134.1	32 984
District 31	10.8	8.0	9.1	396 490	23 395	5.9	373 095	41.5	41.1	17.4	10.5	111 709	138.8	11 521
District 32	12.8	9.8	8.5	413 447	17 288	4.2	396 159	43.5	40.1	16.3	18.1	95 645	127.8	12 182
District 33	24.8	21.8	23.8	345 224	21 411	6.2	323 813	15.8	41.8	42.4	33.6	80 182	108.3	24 411
District 34	29.4	25.9	24.2	285 211	23 656	8.3	261 555	26.2	49.4	24.4	28.3	113 347	155.1	38 270
District 35	20.8	16.6	16.6	416 316	22 674	5.4	393 642	25.7	49.3	25.0	23.0	102 463	124.4	25 123
District 36	13.3	10.0	11.8	344 259	25 735	7.5	318 524	31.0	37.9	31.2	18.0	134 798	184.3	16 567
UTAH	11.3	8.3	7.6	1 472 535	58 198	4.0	1 414 337	36.7	41.5	21.8	11.5	375 685	125.4	31 365
District 1	10.7	8.3	8.3	360 430	16 193	4.5	344 237	35.2	39.3	25.4	9.8	90 768	122.6	7 582
District 2	13.5	9.3	8.5	363 612	14 584	4.0	349 028	35.1	42.5	22.4	14.4	110 352	147.1	9 047
District 3	12.2	9.1	7.0	360 827	13 765	3.8	347 062	41.3	41.3	17.5	10.1	87 858	118.2	6 260
District 4	8.6	6.4	6.4	387 666	13 656	3.5	374 010	35.4	42.7	22.0	11.8	86 707	113.8	8 476
VERMONT	10.2	5.8	11.8	340 689	12 848	3.8	327 841	41.1	38.5	20.5	4.6	142 755	228.0	15 664
At Large	10.2	5.8	11.8	340 689	12 848	3.8	327 841	41.1	38.5	20.5	4.6	142 755	228.0	15 664
VIRGINIA	11.2	7.8	9.2	4 317 898	236 298	5.5	4 081 600	43.0	39.0	18.1	10.5	1 443 127	172.1	156 517
District 1	6.6	4.5	6.8	381 157	18 036	4.7	363 121	43.3	39.3	17.4	8.6	128 498	166.6	8 003
District 2	10.0	7.4	8.1	370 701	21 573	5.8	349 128	38.9	41.9	19.2	11.2	120 501	161.0	11 076
District 3	22.4	17.6	18.5	365 902	33 447	9.1	332 455	31.1	46.9	22.0	13.6	130 228	176.4	31 025
District 4	10.8	8.4	11.1	368 609	22 503	6.1	346 106	36.7	40.9	22.4	8.7	137 554	182.5	15 564
District 5	14.0	9.2	11.1	359 002	19 621	5.5	339 381	36.9	40.2	22.9	11.9	175 977	238.8	18 013
District 6	16.0	10.8	11.1	363 548	19 229	5.3	344 319	33.8	42.0	24.2	12.2	166 202	223.0	16 902
District 7	6.9	4.3	6.1	423 663	21 251	5.0	402 412	44.5	39.5	16.0	9.0	137 887	177.1	8 183
District 8	7.6	5.5	5.4	489 059	22 715	4.6	466 344	56.1	33.0	10.9	10.6	75 444	93.3	7 682
District 9	18.6	13.0	14.7	318 787	20 466	6.4	298 321	33.9	39.2	26.9	11.3	197 816	274.6	25 298
District 10	5.2	3.1	3.3	436 426	15 359	3.5	421 067	53.1	33.7	13.2	8.2	92 981	115.1	5 824
District 11	7.4	4.7	4.5	441 044	22 098	5.0	418 946	53.3	36.1	10.6	10.7	80 039	103.4	8 947
WASHINGTON	12.2	7.9	13.4	3 613 427	215 453	6.0	3 397 974	39.8	38.8	21.4	7.6	1 260 474	175.8	151 062
District 1	7.8	4.6	8.2	373 078	16 055	4.3	357 023	47.4	34.1	18.5	5.7	110 190	154.5	7 774
District 2	11.8	7.9	12.5	372 342	22 195	6.0	350 147	34.3	42.2	23.5	7.9	129 716	178.4	14 228
District 3	12.3	8.0	17.3	334 454	19 665	5.9	314 789	32.4	41.5	26.1	7.5	148 408	208.6	16 440
District 4	17.0	12.7	18.7	326 787	20 642	6.3	306 145	30.0	34.8	35.2	13.5	120 261	169.5	17 143
District 5	16.5	10.6	17.4	321 150	24 116	7.5	297 034	36.6	43.3	20.1	6.4	145 079	208.3	19 169
District 6	11.8	6.8	15.0	308 844	22 462	7.3	286 382	34.7	43.4	22.0	7.9	161 205	236.8	18 579
District 7	10.9	4.8	8.1	459 177	22 159	4.8	437 018	57.8	32.0	10.2	5.4	104 766	140.4	12 850
District 8	8.6	5.4	9.7	376 247	19 445	5.2	356 802	38.8	38.9	22.2	6.2	110 637	151.5	10 658
District 9	11.7	8.2	13.5	398 448	23 155	5.8	375 293	42.8	38.0	19.3	8.2	99 923	137.2	17 660
District 10	14.0	10.0	15.6	342 900	25 555	7.5	317 341	34.9	43.0	22.1	7.6	130 289	179.3	16 561
WEST VIRGINIA	17.9	13.5	16.8	796 708	58 270	7.3	738 438	33.5	43.1	23.4	7.2	468 120	253.8	76 375
District 1	16.9	11.5	14.1	277 637	17 803	6.4	259 834	33.3	43.3	23.3	5.9	147 277	239.5	20 181
District 2	15.1	11.7	15.0	292 527	20 320	6.9	272 207	35.3	41.8	22.9	7.4	152 257	242.1	20 852
District 3	22.1	17.3	21.3	226 544	20 147	8.9	206 397	31.2	44.6	24.2	8.5	168 586	280.8	35 342
WISCONSIN	12.1	7.9	12.2	3 091 421	131 766	4.3	2 959 655	35.2	39.3	25.5	6.6	1 170 705	202.8	118 556
District 1	10.0	7.2	12.1	380 900	18 252	4.8	362 648	34.3	39.6	26.1	6.0	144 144	201.9	13 638
District 2	11.8	6.4	10.6	431 473	18 578	4.3	412 895	44.3	37.8	17.9	5.7	128 078	170.8	11 465
District 3	13.1	7.2	11.0	381 217	14 570	3.8	366 647	32.3	40.0	27.7	7.2	154 410	214.7	12 846
District 4	24.1	20.2	26.3	363 540	27 733	7.6	335 807	34.2	43.8	22.1	10.1	112 836	157.4	39 926
District 5	7.0	4.0	8.0	398 706	11 953	3.0	386 753	40.1	38.7	21.2	4.7	147 286	203.5	7 399
District 6	9.8	6.5	9.9	377 503	14 185	3.8	363 318	31.9	38.4	29.7	4.9	156 240	219.9	9 918
District 7	10.3	6.5	10.9	363 730	12 912	3.5	350 818	31.0	38.2	30.8	7.8	176 727	249.2	11 976
District 8	10.5	7.4	9.3	394 352	13 583	3.4	380 769	32.3	38.3	29.4	6.5	150 984	207.5	11 388
WYOMING	11.1	6.7	4.7	310 369	15 041	4.8	295 328	31.5	39.5	29.0	13.4	103 689	176.9	6 697
At Large	11.1	6.7	4.7	310 369	15 041	4.8	295 328	31.5	39.5	29.0	13.4	103 689	176.9	6 697

1. Percent of civilian labor force.   2. Persons 16 years old and over.   3. Per 1,000 resident population estimated in the 2014 American Community Survey.

Table E. Congressional Districts 115th Congress — **Agriculture**

STATE District	Agriculture, 2012									
	Land in farms				Value of products sold				Government payments	
	Number of farms	Acres	Average size of farm (acres)	Irrigated land (acres)	Total ($1,000)	Average per farm (dollars)	Percent from crops	Percent from livestock and poultry products	Total ($1,000)	Average per farm receiving payments (dollars)
	63	64	65	66	67	68	69	70	71	72
TEXAS—Cont'd										
District 26	3 302	378 816	115	3 483	144 039	43 622	28.8	71.2	1 060	4 400
District 27	12 248	4 802 357	392	136 796	1 227 580	100 227	54.0	46.0	42 540	14 347
District 28	7 794	5 145 001	660	79 700	406 827	52 197	36.3	63.7	11 471	7 439
District 29	100	3 742	37	9	1 099	10 995	81.8	18.3	0	0
District 30	387	38 849	100	1 212	24 876	64 280	95.4	4.6	135	4 657
District 31	4 996	953 480	191	4 435	212 132	42 460	62.2	37.8	5 772	5 305
District 32	220	28 677	130	58	9 079	41 269	40.2	59.8	108	6 012
District 33	107	8 001	75	27	7 499	70 083	96.0	3.9	2	300
District 34	8 326	4 632 760	556	174 856	931 238	111 847	44.1	55.9	17 803	9 825
District 35	1 133	250 124	221	1 547	39 002	34 423	73.0	27.0	873	6 616
District 36	6 888	1 108 089	161	25 421	119 925	17 411	53.7	46.3	5 295	17 534
UTAH	18 027	10 974 396	609	1 104 257	1 816 147	100 746	31.6	68.4	23 898	8 584
District 1	7 334	5 425 669	740	500 075	568 013	77 449	37.1	62.9	12 472	9 805
District 2	4 911	2 536 753	517	404 236	897 850	182 824	24.8	75.2	6 598	7 558
District 3	3 651	2 577 805	706	127 071	205 267	56 222	42.2	57.8	2 877	6 851
District 4	2 131	434 169	204	72 875	145 017	68 051	37.3	62.7	1 950	8 906
VERMONT	7 338	1 251 713	171	3 565	776 105	105 765	22.9	77.1	13 930	8 929
At Large	7 338	1 251 713	171	3 565	776 105	105 765	22.9	77.1	13 930	8 929
VIRGINIA	46 030	8 302 444	180	68 651	3 753 287	81 540	36.2	63.8	82 318	7 719
District 1	2 338	522 532	223	10 540	215 529	92 185	87.3	12.7	8 842	14 495
District 2	567	157 025	277	11 243	280 070	493 951	48.3	51.7	4 246	19 478
District 3	369	104 848	284	3 470	64 905	175 894	81.9	18.1	2 661	19 423
District 4	3 003	766 641	255	7 971	473 780	157 769	61.3	38.7	19 465	14 735
District 5	12 069	2 441 870	202	15 716	613 975	50 872	40.7	59.3	18 392	5 929
District 6	8 195	1 297 577	158	11 153	1 271 186	155 117	9.9	90.1	7 944	6 576
District 7	3 265	523 003	160	4 983	242 528	74 281	68.7	31.3	5 367	10 713
District 8	33	1 227	37	15	1 611	48 818	D	D	D	D
District 9	13 389	2 166 935	162	2 506	487 735	36 428	17.9	82.1	14 226	4 245
District 10	2 775	318 962	115	1 050	100 953	36 379	61.2	38.8	1 150	5 478
District 11	27	1 824	68	4	1 014	37 546	D	D	D	D
WASHINGTON	37 249	14 748 107	396	1 633 571	9 120 749	244 859	71.2	28.8	159 269	22 014
District 1	3 651	215 635	59	44 402	568 090	155 598	45.9	54.1	4 361	10 794
District 2	1 660	124 240	75	19 235	251 457	151 480	61.8	38.2	1 391	10 303
District 3	5 698	888 616	156	53 077	379 033	66 520	44.4	55.6	5 823	11 418
District 4	10 221	7 236 719	708	1 287 721	6 100 198	596 830	73.0	27.0	64 825	25 302
District 5	7 733	5 665 632	733	112 588	1 151 558	148 915	92.9	7.1	79 599	24 364
District 6	2 533	197 926	78	15 406	86 682	34 221	D	D	390	4 432
District 7	196	2 185	11	195	D	D	D	D	38	5 463
District 8	3 967	349 188	88	95 859	413 543	104 246	70.5	29.5	2 648	11 220
District 9	115	1 916	17	282	D	D	D	D	29	4 767
District 10	1 475	66 050	45	4 806	130 983	88 802	43.3	56.7	166	8 316
WEST VIRGINIA	21 489	3 606 674	168	2 064	806 775	37 544	17.2	82.8	7 034	3 203
District 1	8 458	1 305 274	154	D	D	D	D	D	1 923	3 162
District 2	7 563	1 366 085	181	1 238	473 385	62 592	16.2	83.8	3 203	3 632
District 3	5 468	935 315	171	D	D	D	D	D	1 909	2 703
WISCONSIN	69 754	14 568 926	209	421 721	11 744 476	168 370	39.2	60.8	237 304	6 093
District 1	2 667	563 204	211	12 892	485 265	181 952	D	D	D	D
District 2	9 962	2 127 676	214	42 496	1 553 585	155 951	38.1	61.9	44 895	6 876
District 3	19 895	4 295 732	216	218 340	2 936 452	147 597	45.4	54.6	61 572	5 263
District 4	37	455	12	23	4 098	110 746	D	D	D	D
District 5	3 462	635 541	184	11 247	611 624	176 668	43.5	56.5	12 337	6 184
District 6	8 882	1 813 360	204	52 490	1 824 851	205 455	38.0	62.0	34 602	6 824
District 7	16 175	3 418 268	211	70 755	2 438 450	150 754	36.2	63.8	39 552	5 465
District 8	8 674	1 714 690	198	13 478	1 890 152	217 910	28.1	71.9	32 326	6 516
WYOMING	11 736	30 363 641	2 587	1 435 710	1 689 416	143 952	26.0	74.0	28 146	10 027
At Large	11 736	30 363 641	2 587	1 435 710	1 689 416	143 952	26.0	74.0	28 146	10 027

Private nonfarm employment and payroll, 2015

STATE District	Number of establish-ments	Total	Employment — Percent by selected industries									Annual payroll	
			Manufact-uring	Construc-tion	Wholesale trade	Retail trade	Health care and social assistance	Finance and Insurance	Real estate and rental and leasing	Professio-nal, scientific, and technical services	Information	Total (mil dol)	Average per employee dollars
	73	74	75	76	77	78	79	80	81	82	83	84	85
TEXAS—Cont'd													
District 26	14 531	230 020	5.8	5.4	5.2	15.9	11.7	9.0	1.6	4.6	2.0	10 125	44 020
District 27	15 684	248 371	9.3	8.5	4.8	14.9	17.8	2.9	2.3	4.4	1.1	10 606	42 703
District 28	11 122	168 357	2.4	4.5	3.7	18.5	21.9	3.5	1.7	2.4	3.5	5 634	33 462
District 29	10 653	220 469	16.0	12.7	7.7	11.7	5.8	2.3	1.6	4.7	0.7	10 595	48 055
District 30	13 344	324 373	6.7	3.6	4.8	8.8	18.6	6.0	2.7	9.9	3.6	20 976	64 665
District 31	14 671	228 876	6.5	6.3	2.8	16.4	19.9	4.8	1.8	8.3	2.6	10 189	44 518
District 32	21 333	325 576	5.8	3.9	3.5	12.2	16.6	6.7	3.4	10.2	3.5	18 271	56 118
District 33	12 512	270 007	15.7	8.7	11.1	9.8	10.4	1.8	1.8	3.9	1.1	12 307	45 580
District 34	10 620	165 791	4.4	3.2	3.3	17.0	30.4	3.0	1.7	2.9	1.8	4 858	29 303
District 35	15 303	288 619	7.7	7.0	7.5	13.5	12.6	3.1	1.9	5.3	2.7	11 784	40 829
District 36	12 694	246 786	17.4	12.0	3.6	11.7	10.6	1.9	1.4	7.5	0.6	13 413	54 349
UTAH	75 463	1 203 954	9.8	6.1	4.6	12.5	11.1	5.2	1.8	7.8	3.7	51 453	42 737
District 1	17 655	228 627	17.5	6.7	3.4	15.2	12.1	3.7	2.1	6.2	1.4	8 622	37 710
District 2	20 587	359 280	9.9	4.9	5.8	10.9	11.4	6.1	1.4	7.4	3.1	17 040	47 428
District 3	18 513	251 798	5.9	5.7	3.6	13.9	12.3	4.3	2.0	6.8	5.1	10 089	40 069
District 4	18 269	297 665	9.2	8.5	5.5	14.1	11.4	6.1	2.1	9.0	5.6	13 097	44 000
VERMONT	21 121	266 363	11.2	5.2	4.4	15.0	18.1	3.4	1.3	7.1	2.6	10 615	39 852
At Large	21 121	266 363	11.2	5.2	4.4	15.0	18.1	3.4	1.3	7.1	2.6	10 615	39 852
VIRGINIA	197 384	3 198 718	7.4	5.4	3.2	13.3	13.6	4.9	1.7	13.7	3.0	165 789	51 830
District 1	16 805	212 069	5.4	9.9	5.1	17.6	13.1	4.0	1.3	9.5	1.6	8 678	40 921
District 2	16 292	221 726	4.8	5.5	2.5	15.8	12.1	5.7	3.1	10.2	1.8	8 341	37 620
District 3	16 529	335 445	13.9	4.6	3.2	13.4	17.6	3.5	1.6	7.6	2.1	15 156	45 182
District 4	15 513	268 497	8.9	6.7	4.7	11.3	17.1	5.3	1.5	6.3	2.1	12 745	47 469
District 5	16 663	205 526	12.0	6.5	2.8	16.0	18.4	3.6	1.3	5.4	1.8	8 281	40 293
District 6	17 900	303 170	13.7	5.1	3.2	14.3	16.5	4.5	1.4	4.1	1.6	11 568	38 155
District 7	18 776	285 973	3.8	5.4	4.1	15.6	14.0	12.1	1.8	7.9	2.4	13 876	48 523
District 8	20 254	351 230	1.0	4.0	1.5	10.3	9.5	3.2	2.4	24.9	3.2	23 135	65 867
District 9	14 301	211 661	20.1	3.8	4.3	16.6	17.1	2.8	1.0	4.0	1.7	7 791	36 810
District 10	21 771	317 416	5.6	8.0	3.2	12.0	10.2	2.7	1.4	19.6	4.0	18 985	59 811
District 11	21 929	436 487	0.8	2.6	1.6	10.5	10.5	5.8	1.8	31.6	7.0	33 762	77 349
WASHINGTON	182 913	2 602 408	10.1	6.3	5.0	12.7	15.1	3.7	1.8	7.4	4.9	149 259	57 354
District 1	18 891	264 413	10.3	9.1	4.7	9.4	8.7	2.2	1.5	8.6	18.4	21 660	81 918
District 2	19 493	271 300	23.8	7.1	3.3	16.1	13.2	3.8	1.4	4.3	2.0	13 325	49 116
District 3	15 705	186 087	13.1	8.2	4.5	14.6	16.9	3.7	1.7	5.5	2.1	8 565	46 027
District 4	14 005	183 213	12.7	6.1	6.6	16.3	15.3	2.4	1.5	5.7	1.3	7 763	42 374
District 5	16 881	225 334	9.1	5.5	5.4	14.9	20.2	5.3	1.8	4.5	1.9	9 540	42 338
District 6	16 919	190 382	4.9	5.3	2.4	17.2	25.0	3.7	1.9	5.2	1.5	7 891	41 450
District 7	28 394	450 490	3.9	4.2	3.6	9.1	14.7	4.7	2.3	12.8	6.3	33 107	73 492
District 8	15 157	168 279	10.2	9.4	7.9	15.5	12.2	1.8	1.3	3.5	2.1	8 100	48 137
District 9	22 346	430 541	10.3	5.2	6.9	9.2	14.0	3.6	1.9	6.1	5.1	28 264	65 649
District 10	14 549	199 408	7.1	7.4	5.0	16.2	17.0	4.4	2.0	4.4	2.1	8 323	41 737
WEST VIRGINIA	36 993	565 435	8.6	4.3	3.9	15.2	23.1	3.1	1.0	4.7	1.9	22 159	39 189
District 1	13 082	212 349	9.6	4.1	3.0	14.5	23.6	2.6	1.0	4.8	1.6	8 488	39 974
District 2	12 374	185 184	8.8	5.2	5.2	14.9	20.7	4.1	1.2	4.7	2.0	7 378	39 843
District 3	11 242	159 911	7.4	3.5	3.5	17.0	26.4	2.5	0.9	3.3	2.1	5 884	36 797
WISCONSIN	139 500	2 503 532	18.0	4.1	4.7	12.4	15.8	5.5	1.0	4.3	2.3	112 406	44 899
District 1	15 016	243 306	20.5	3.8	5.0	16.1	14.4	2.4	0.9	2.8	1.3	10 149	41 714
District 2	18 901	351 650	11.3	4.5	4.8	12.4	16.1	7.5	1.4	7.1	5.1	17 215	48 956
District 3	16 895	273 183	18.3	3.7	3.9	14.2	16.7	5.0	1.0	3.2	1.9	10 441	38 220
District 4	13 279	322 886	10.2	2.0	4.5	7.3	20.5	9.4	1.2	5.3	2.2	17 288	53 543
District 5	21 113	399 173	17.5	4.5	6.2	12.0	14.9	4.7	1.2	5.0	2.7	19 304	48 359
District 6	16 672	306 734	27.3	4.9	3.4	12.0	13.9	3.7	0.7	3.2	1.0	13 523	44 087
District 7	18 959	248 332	23.2	4.5	4.0	15.9	17.1	4.0	0.7	2.8	1.0	9 433	37 986
District 8	18 182	324 374	20.8	4.6	4.4	12.3	14.0	5.3	0.9	3.4	2.1	13 729	42 326
WYOMING	21 040	219 881	4.5	9.2	3.9	14.7	14.8	3.0	2.2	4.6	1.8	10 094	45 907
At Large	21 040	219 881	4.5	9.2	3.9	14.7	14.8	3.0	2.2	4.6	1.8	10 094	45 907

APPENDIX A
GEOGRAPHIC CONCEPTS AND CODES

GEOGRAPHIC AREAS COVERED

County and City Extra presents data for states (Table A), states and counties (Table B), metropolitan areas (Table C), cities with populations of 25,000 or more in 2010 (Table D), and congressional districts (Table E).

STATES AND COUNTIES

Data are presented for each of the 50 states, the District of Columbia, and the United States as a whole. The states are arranged alphabetically and counties in Table B are arranged alphabetically within each state. Data are presented for 3,142 counties and county equivalents.

County equivalents

In Louisiana, the primary divisions of the state are known as parishes rather than counties. In Alaska, the county equivalents are the organized boroughs, together with the census areas that were developed for general statistical purposes by the state of Alaska and the U.S. Census Bureau. Four states—Maryland, Missouri, Nevada, and Virginia—have one or more incorporated places that are legally independent of any county and thus constitute primary divisions of their states. Within each state, independent cities are listed alphabetically following the list of counties. The District of Columbia is not divided into counties or county equivalents—data for the entire district are presented as a county equivalent. New York City contains five counties: Bronx, Kings, New York, Queens, and Richmond.

County changes since the 2010 census

- The independent city of Bedford, Virginia changed to town status and was added to Bedford County, effective July 1, 2013. In this book, all the data have been updated to reflect this change except the 2012 Census of Governments data in columns 171 through 193, where Bedford county does not include Bedford city.
- Wade Hampton Census Area, AK (02-270) changed its name and FIPS code to Kusilvak Census Area (02-158), effective July 1, 2015.
- Shannon County, SD (46-113) changed its name and FIPS code to Oglala Lakota County (46-102), effective May 1, 2015.
- Petersburg Borough, AK was created from part of Petersburg Census Area and part of Hoonah-Angoon Census Area. Petersburg Borough retains the FIPS code 02-195, formerly used by Petersburg Census Area, effective January 3, 2013.
- Prince of Wales-Hyder Census Area added part of the former Petersburg Census Area, effective January 3, 2013.

County changes since the 2000 census

- Broomfield County, CO, was created from parts of Adams, Boulder, Jefferson, and Weld Counties, effective November 15, 2001. The boundaries of Broomfield County reflect the boundaries of Broomfield city legally in effect on that date.
- Clifton Forge city, VA, formerly an independent city, became a town within Alleghany County, effective July 1, 2001.
- Effective June 20, 2007, the Skagway-Hoonah-Angoon Census Area in Alaska was divided into the Skagway Municipality and the Hoonah-Angoon Census Area.
- In May and June, 2008, the Wrangell-Petersburg and Prince of Wales-Outer Ketchikan Census Areas were dissolved and replaced by Wrangell City and Borough, Petersburg Census Area, and Prince of Wales Census Area. Some territory from the Prince of Wales Outer Ketchikan Census Area became part of the existing Ketchikan Gateway Borough.

METROPOLITAN AREAS

Table C presents data for 382 metropolitan statistical areas and 31 metropolitan divisions, which are located within the 11 largest metropolitan statistical areas. The metropolitan statistical areas are listed alphabetically, and the metropolitan divisions are listed alphabetically under the metropolitan statistical area of which they are components.

The U.S. Office of Management and Budget (OMB) defines metropolitan and micropolitan statistical areas according to published standards. The major purpose of defining these areas is to enable all U.S. government agencies to use the same geographic definitions in tabulating and publishing data. The general concept of a metropolitan or micropolitan statistical area is that of a core area containing a substantial population nucleus, together with adjacent communities that have a high degree of economic and social integration with the core.

New delineations of these Core Based Statistical Areas (CBSAs) based on the 2010 census were released in February 2013 and updated in July 2015. Table C in this book uses these delineations for metropolitan areas and metropolitan divisions. Micropolitan areas are not included in Table C. A few of the data items in Table C were released under the old scheme but have been aggregated from county data to the newly defined metropolitan areas. This results in a higher level of data suppression for those items.

Appendix B lists the metropolitan areas and metropolitan divisions with their component counties and 2010 census populations. Appendix C lists the metropolitan and micropolitan areas, together with their 2010 census populations and their 2016 estimated populations.

Standard definitions of metropolitan areas were first issued in 1949 by the Bureau of the Budget (the predecessor of OMB), under the designation "standard metropolitan area" (SMA). The term was changed to "standard metropolitan statistical area" (SMSA) in 1959, and to "metropolitan statistical area" (MSA) in 1983. The term "metropolitan area" (MA) was adopted in 1990 and referred collectively to metropolitan statistical areas (MSAs), consolidated metropolitan statistical areas (CMSAs), and primary metropolitan statistical areas (PMSAs). The term "core based statistical area" (CBSA) became effective in 2000 and refers collectively to metropolitan and micropolitan statistical areas.

The 2010 standards provide that each CBSA must contain at least one urban area of 10,000 or more population. Each metropolitan statistical area must have at least one urbanized area of 50,000 or more inhabitants. Each micropolitan statistical area must have at least one urban cluster of at least 10,000 but less than 50,000 people.

Under the standards, A metro area contains a core urban area of 50,000 or more population, and a micro area contains an urban core of at least 10,000 (but less than 50,000) population. Each metro or micro area consists of one or more counties and includes the counties containing the core urban area, as well as any adjacent counties that have a high degree of social and economic integration (as measured by commuting to work) with the urban core.

If specified criteria are met, a metropolitan statistical area containing a single core with a population of 2.5 million or more may be subdivided to form smaller groupings of counties referred to as "metropolitan divisions."

As of July 15, 2015, there were 382 metropolitan statistical areas and 556 micropolitan statistical areas in the United States. Table C includes the 382 metropolitan statistical areas and the 31 metropolitan divisions. The metropolitan areas and metropolitan divisions are listed in Appendix B with their 2010 census population counts. The metropolitan areas, metropolitan divisions, and micropolitan areas are listed in Appendix C with their 2010 census populations and their 2016 estimated populations.

The largest city in each metropolitan or micropolitan statistical area is designated a "principal city." Additional cities qualify if specified requirements are met concerning population size and employment. The title of each metropolitan or micropolitan statistical area consists of the names of up to three of its principal cities and the name of each state into which the metropolitan or micropolitan statistical area extends. Titles of metropolitan divisions also typically are based on principal city names, but in certain cases consist of county names. The principal city need not be an incorporated place if it meets the requirements of population size and employment. Usually such a principal city is a census designated place in decennial census data, but it is not included in most other data sources and is not in Table D (Cities) in this volume.

In view of the importance of cities and towns in New England, the 2010 standards also provide for a set of geographic areas that are defined using cities and towns in the six New England states. These New England city and town areas (NECTAs) are not included in this volume.

Appendix B lists the 382 metropolitan statistical areas, together with their component metropolitan divisions, where appropriate, the component counties of each area, and their 2010 census populations Appendix C provides the same information for the 382 metropolitan areas and it also includes the 556 micropolitan statistical areas. Maps showing the metropolitan and micropolitan areas within each state can be found in Appendix D.

CITIES

Table D presents data for 1,437 cities with 2010 census populations of 25,000 or more. Corresponding data for states are also provided. The states are arranged alphabetically and the cities are ordered alphabetically within each state.

As used in this volume, the term *city* refers to places that have been incorporated as cities, boroughs, towns, or villages under the laws of their respective states. Towns in the New England states and New York are treated as minor civil divisions (MCDs) and are not included in the cities database. For Hawaii, data for the census designated places (CDPs) are included in the cities table, since the Census Bureau does not recognize any incorporated places in Hawaii. CDPs are delineated by the Census Bureau, in cooperation with states and localities, as statistical counterparts of incorporated places for purposes of the decennial census. CDPs comprise densely settled concentrations of population that are identifiable by name but are not legally incorporated as places.

Appendix E lists the 1,437 cities followed by the county where each city is located. If a city includes portions of more than one county, the population in each part is specified.

A consolidated city is an incorporated place that has combined its government functions with a county or subcounty entity but contains one or more other semi-independent incorporated places that continue to function as local governments within the consolidated government. Each consolidated city contains a core city, the area of a consolidated city not included in another separately incorporated place. The census geographic term for this core is the "balance" of the consolidated city. Thus the "balance" is essentially the core city of the consolidated government. This volume includes the consolidated city data where possible, but some data sources include numbers only for the "balance" and others do not specify which entity is represented.

Consolidated cities included in this volume are Milford, CT; Athens-Clarke County, GA; Augusta-Richmond County, GA; Indianapolis, IN; Louisville-Jefferson County, KY; Butte-Silver Bow, MT; and Nashville-Davidson, TN.

Appendix E lists these seven consolidated cities, followed by the component places and their 2010 census populations.

On January 1, 2014, Macon, Georgia consolidated with Bibb county. A small portion of Macon that was in Jones county was de-annexed. Data from years prior to 2015 represent the smaller Macon city rather than the consolidated Macon-Bibb County.

CONGRESSIONAL DISTRICTS

The congressional districts shown in this volume are the districts used for the election of the 115th Congress, which convened in January 2017. These are the districts that were established following the 2010 Census and are based on population data from that census. Data are shown for the 435 regular districts plus the District of Columbia, which has a non-voting delegate, but no representative. Corresponding data for each state also are included. States are listed alphabetically and districts numerically within each state. A map showing congressional districts for the 113th Congress is included in Appendix D.

The 115th Congress, which convened in 2017, was the third to reflect the boundaries based on the 2010 census. The Representatives of the 115th Congress are listed. Most of the data in Table E have been collected or updated for the 115th congress, but some sources were collected for the 114th congress or earlier. Boundary changes between the 114th and 115th congresses occurred in Florida, Minnesota, North Carolina, and Virginia.

GEOGRAPHIC CODES

Tables A, B, C, and D provide, in one or more columns at the beginning of the table, a geographic code or codes for each area.

In Table B (States and Counties), a five-digit state and county code is given for each state and county. The first two digits indicate the state; the remaining three represent the county. Within each state, the counties are listed in order, beginning with 001, with even numbers usually omitted. Independent cities follow the counties and begin with the number 510. In the second column of Table B, a five-digit core based statistical area (CBSA) code is given for those counties that are within metropolitan and micro-politan areas. In Table A, a two-digit state code is provided. The state code is a sequential numbering, with some gaps, of the states and the District of Columbia in alphabetical order from Alabama (01) to Wyoming (56).

These codes have been established by the U.S. government as Federal Information Processing Standards and are often referred to as *FIPS codes*. They are used by U.S. government agencies and many other organizations for data presentation. The codes are provided in this volume for use in matching the data given here with other data sources in which counties are identified by FIPS code. The metro area codes will also enable the user to identify the metro area of which a county is a component. Table C (Metropolitan Areas) provides the same metro area codes for each metropolitan area, as well as metropolitan division codes where appropriate.

Table D (Cities) provides, in the first column, a seven-digit state and place code. The first two digits identify the state and are the same as the FIPS codes described above. The remaining five digits are the place FIPS codes established by the U.S. government.

INDEPENDENT CITIES

The following independent cities are not included in any county; their data are presented separately in this volume.

MARYLAND
Baltimore (separate from Baltimore County)

MISSOURI
St. Louis (separate from St. Louis County)

NEVADA
Carson City

VIRGINIA

Alexandria	Manassas
Bristol	Manassas Park
Buena Vista	Martinsville
Charlottesville	Newport News
Chesapeake	Norfolk
Colonial Heights	Norton
Covington	Petersburg
Danville	Poquoson
Emporia	Portsmouth
Fairfax	Radford
Falls Church	Richmond
Franklin	Roanoke
Fredericksburg	Salem
Galax	Staunton
Hampton	Suffolk
Harrisonburg	Virginia Beach
Hopewell	Waynesboro
Lexington	Williamsburg
Lynchburg	Winchester

COUNTY TYPE

Table B (States and Counties) provides, in the third column, a *county type* code that identifies each county by its metropolitan/nonmetropolitan status and its size. These are the "rural-urban continuum codes" developed by the Economic Research Service of the U.S. Department of Agriculture.

The 2013 rural-urban continuum codes form a classification scheme that distinguishes metropolitan counties by size and non-metropolitan counties by degree of urbanization and proximity to metro areas. The standard OMB metro and nonmetro categories have been subdivided into three metro and six nonmetro categories, resulting in a nine-part county codification. This scheme was originally developed in 1974. The codes were updated in 1983, 1993, and 2003 and slightly revised in 1988. The 1988 revision was first published in 1990. This scheme allows researchers to break county data into finer residential groups, beyond metro and nonmetro, particularly for the analysis of trends in nonmetro areas that are related to population density and metro influence. The 2013 and 2003 rural-urban continuum codes are not directly comparable with the codes from previous years because of the new methodology used in developing the 2003 metropolitan areas.

Metropolitan counties
1. Counties in metro areas of 1 million population or more.
2. Counties in metro areas of 250,000 to 1 million population.
3. Counties in metro areas of fewer than 250,000 population.

Nonmetropolitan counties
4. Urban population of 20,000 or more, adjacent to a metro area.
5. Urban population of 20,000 or more, not adjacent to a metro area.

6. Urban population of 2,500 to 19,999, adjacent to a metro area.

7. Urban population of 2,500 to 19,999, not adjacent to a metro area.

8. Completely rural or less than 2,500 urban population, adjacent to a metro area.

9. Completely rural or less than 2,500 urban population, not adjacent to a metro area.

APPENDIX B
METROPOLITAN STATISTICAL AREAS, METROPOLITAN DIVISIONS, AND COMPONENTS
(as defined July 2015)

Core based statistical area	State/ County FIPS code	Title and Geographic Components	2010 Census Population	Core based statistical area	State/ County FIPS code	Title and Geographic Components	2010 Census Population
10180		Abilene, TX...........	165 252	11540		Appleton, WI...........	225 666
	48 059	Callahan County............	13 544		55 015	Calumet County............	48 971
	48 253	Jones County............	20 202		55 087	Outagamie County............	176 695
	48 441	Taylor County............	131 506				
				11700		Asheville, NC...........	424 858
10420		Akron, OH...........	703 200		37 021	Buncombe County............	238 318
	39 133	Portage County............	161 419		37 087	Haywood County............	59 036
	39 153	Summit County............	541 781		37 089	Henderson County............	106 740
					37 115	Madison County............	20 764
10500		Albany, GA...........	157 308				
	13 007	Baker County............	3 451	12020		Athens-Clarke County, GA...........	192 541
	13 095	Dougherty County............	94 565		13 059	Clarke County............	116 714
	13 177	Lee County............	28 298		13 195	Madison County............	28 120
	13 273	Terrell County............	9 315		13 219	Oconee County............	32 808
	13 321	Worth County............	21 679		13 221	Oglethorpe County............	14 899
10540		Albany, OR...........	116 672	12060		Atlanta-Sandy Springs-Roswell, GA	5 286 728
	41 043	Linn County............	116 672		13 013	Barrow County............	69 367
					13 015	Bartow County............	100 157
10580		Albany-Schenectady-Troy, NY	870 716		13 035	Butts County............	23 655
	36 001	Albany County............	304 204		13 045	Carroll County............	110 527
	36 083	Rensselaer County............	159 429		13 057	Cherokee County............	214 346
	36 091	Saratoga County............	219 607		13 063	Clayton County............	259 424
	36 093	Schenectady County............	154 727		13 067	Cobb County............	688 078
	36 095	Schoharie County............	32 749		13 077	Coweta County............	127 317
					13 085	Dawson County............	22 330
10740		Albuquerque, NM	887 077		13 089	DeKalb County............	691 893
	35 001	Bernalillo County............	662 564		13 097	Douglas County............	132 403
	35 043	Sandoval County............	131 561		13 113	Fayette County............	106 567
	35 057	Torrance County............	16 383		13 117	Forsyth County............	175 511
	35 061	Valencia County............	76 569		13 121	Fulton County............	920 581
					13 135	Gwinnett County............	805 321
10780		Alexandria, LA...........	153 922		13 143	Haralson County............	28 780
	22 043	Grant Parish............	22 309		13 149	Heard County............	11 834
	22 079	Rapides Parish............	131 613		13 151	Henry County............	203 922
					13 159	Jasper County............	13 900
10900		Allentown-Bethlehem-Easton, PA-NJ...........	821 173		13 171	Lamar County............	18 317
	34 041	Warren County............	108 692		13 199	Meriwether County............	21 992
	42 025	Carbon County............	65 249		13 211	Morgan County............	17 868
	42 077	Lehigh County............	349 497		13 217	Newton County............	99 958
	42 095	Northampton County............	297 735		13 223	Paulding County............	142 324
					13 227	Pickens County............	29 431
11020		Altoona, PA	127 089		13 231	Pike County............	17 869
	42 013	Blair County............	127 089		13 247	Rockdale County............	85 215
					13 255	Spalding County............	64 073
11100		Amarillo, TX...........	251 933		13 297	Walton County............	83 768
	48 011	Armstrong County............	1 901				
	48 065	Carson County............	6 182	12100		Atlantic City-Hammonton, NJ...........	274 549
	48 359	Oldham County............	2 052		34 001	Atlantic County............	274 549
	48 375	Potter County............	121 073				
	48 381	Randall County............	120 725	12220		Auburn-Opelika, AL...........	140 247
					01 081	Lee County............	140 247
11180		Ames, IA...........	89 542				
	19 169	Story County............	89 542	12260		Augusta-Richmond County, GA-SC...........	564 873
11260		Anchorage, AK...........	380 821		13 033	Burke County............	23 316
	02 020	Anchorage Municipality............	291 826		13 073	Columbia County............	124 053
	02 170	Matanuska-Susitna Borough	88 995		13 181	Lincoln County............	7 996
					13 189	McDuffie County............	21 875
11460		Ann Arbor, MI...........	344 791		13 245	Richmond County............	200 549
	26 161	Washtenaw County............	344 791		45 003	Aiken County............	160 099
					45 037	Edgefield County............	26 985
11500		Anniston-Oxford-Jacksonville, AL	118 572				
	01 015	Calhoun County............	118 572				

Metropolitan Statistical Areas, Metropolitan Divisions, and Components (as defined July 2015)–*Continued*

Core based statistical area	State/ County FIPS code	Title and Geographic Components	2010 Census Population	Core based statistical area	State/ County FIPS code	Title and Geographic Components	2010 Census Population
12420		Austin-Round Rock, TX	1 716 289	13780		Binghamton, NY	251 725
	48 021	Bastrop County	74 171		36 007	Broome County	200 600
	48 055	Caldwell County	38 066		36 107	Tioga County	51 125
	48 209	Hays County	157 107				
	48 453	Travis County	1 024 266	13820		Birmingham-Hoover, AL	1 128 047
	48 491	Williamson County	422 679		01 007	Bibb County	22 915
					01 009	Blount County	57 322
12540		Bakersfield, CA	839 631		01 021	Chilton County	43 643
	06 029	Kern County	839 631		01 073	Jefferson County	658 466
					01 115	St. Clair County	83 593
12580		Baltimore-Columbia-Towson, MD	2 710 489		01 117	Shelby County	195 085
	24 003	Anne Arundel County	537 656		01 127	Walker County	67 023
	24 005	Baltimore County	805 029				
	24 013	Carroll County	167 134	13900		Bismarck, ND	114 778
	24 025	Harford County	244 826		38 015	Burleigh County	81 308
	24 027	Howard County	287 085		38 059	Morton County	27 471
	24 035	Queen Anne's County	47 798		38 065	Oliver County	1 846
	24 510	Baltimore city	620 961		38 085	Sioux County	4 153
12620		Bangor, ME	153 923	13980		Blacksburg-Christiansburg-Radford, VA	178 237
	23 019	Penobscot County	153 923		51 063	Floyd County	15 279
					51 071	Giles County	17 286
12700		Barnstable Town, MA	215 888		51 121	Montgomery County	94 392
	25 001	Barnstable County	215 888		51 155	Pulaski County	34 872
					51 750	Radford city	16 408
12940		Baton Rouge, LA	802 484				
	22 005	Ascension Parish	107 215	14010		Bloomington, IL	186 133
	22 033	East Baton Rouge Parish	440 171		17 039	De Witt County	16 561
	22 037	East Feliciana Parish	20 267		17 113	McLean County	169 572
	22 047	Iberville Parish	33 387				
	22 063	Livingston Parish	128 026	14020		Bloomington, IN	159 549
	22 077	Pointe Coupee Parish	22 802		18 105	Monroe County	137 974
	22 091	St. Helena Parish	11 203		18 119	Owen County	21 575
	22 121	West Baton Rouge Parish	23 788				
	22 125	West Feliciana Parish	15 625	14100		Bloomsburg-Berwick, PA	85 562
					42 037	Columbia County	67 295
12980		Battle Creek, MI	136 146		42 093	Montour County	18 267
	26 025	Calhoun County	136 146				
				14260		Boise City, ID	616 561
13020		Bay City, MI	107 771		16 001	Ada County	392 365
	26 017	Bay County	107 771		16 015	Boise County	7 028
					16 027	Canyon County	188 923
13140		Beaumont-Port Arthur, TX	403 190		16 045	Gem County	16 719
	48 199	Hardin County	54 635		16 073	Owyhee County	11 526
	48 245	Jefferson County	252 273				
	48 351	Newton County	14 445	14460		Boston-Cambridge-Newton, MA-NH	4 552 402
	48 361	Orange County	81 837			Boston, MA Div 14454	1 887 792
					25 021	Norfolk County	670 850
13220		Beckley, WV	124 898		25 023	Plymouth County	494 919
	54 019	Fayette County	46 039		25 025	Suffolk County	722 023
	54 081	Raleigh County	78 859			Cambridge-Newton-Framingham, MA Div 15764	2 246 244
13380		Bellingham, WA	201 140		25 009	Essex County	743 159
	53 073	Whatcom County	201 140		25 017	Middlesex County	1 503 085
						Rockingham County-Strafford County, NH Div 40484	418 366
13460		Bend-Redmond, OR	157 733		33 015	Rockingham County	295 223
	41 017	Deschutes County	157 733		33 017	Strafford County	123 143
13740		Billings, MT	158 934				
	30 009	Carbon County	10 078	14500		Boulder, CO	294 567
	30 037	Golden Valley County	884		08 013	Boulder County	294 567
	30 111	Yellowstone County	147 972				

Core based statistical area	State/ County FIPS code	Title and Geographic Components	2010 Census Population	Core based statistical area	State/ County FIPS code	Title and Geographic Components	2010 Census Population
14540		Bowling Green, KY	158 599	16580		Champaign-Urbana, IL	231 891
	21 003	Allen County	19 956		17 019	Champaign County	201 081
	21 031	Butler County	12 690		17 053	Ford County	14 081
	21 061	Edmonson County	12 161		17 147	Piatt County	16 729
	21 227	Warren County	113 792				
				16620		Charleston, WV	227 078
14740		Bremerton-Silverdale, WA	251 133		54 005	Boone County	24 629
	53 035	Kitsap County	251 133		54 015	Clay County	9 386
					54 039	Kanawha County	193 063
14860		Bridgeport-Stamford-Norwalk, CT	916 829				
	09 001	Fairfield County	916 829	16700		Charleston-North Charleston, SC	664 607
					45 015	Berkeley County	177 843
15180		Brownsville-Harlingen, TX	406 220		45 019	Charleston County	350 209
	48 061	Cameron County	406 220		45 035	Dorchester County	136 555
15260		Brunswick, GA	112 370	16740		Charlotte-Concord-Gastonia, NC-SC	2 217 012
	13 025	Brantley County	18 411		37 025	Cabarrus County	178 011
	13 127	Glynn County	79 626		37 071	Gaston County	206 086
	13 191	McIntosh County	14 333		37 097	Iredell County	159 437
					37 109	Lincoln County	78 265
15380		Buffalo-Cheektowaga-Niagara Falls, NY	1 135 509		37 119	Mecklenburg County	919 628
	36 029	Erie County	919 040		37 159	Rowan County	138 428
	36 063	Niagara County	216 469		37 179	Union County	201 292
					45 023	Chester County	33 140
15500		Burlington, NC	151 131		45 057	Lancaster County	76 652
	37 001	Alamance County	151 131		45 091	York County	226 073
15540		Burlington-South Burlington, VT	211 261	16820		Charlottesville, VA	218 705
	50 007	Chittenden County	156 545		51 003	Albemarle County	98 970
	50 011	Franklin County	47 746		51 029	Buckingham County	17 146
	50 013	Grand Isle County	6 970		51 065	Fluvanna County	25 691
					51 079	Greene County	18 403
15680		California-Lexington Park, MD	105 151		51 125	Nelson County	15 020
	24 037	St. Mary's County	105 151		51 540	Charlottesville city	43 475
15940		Canton-Massillon, OH	404 422	16860		Chattanooga, TN-GA	528 143
	39 019	Carroll County	28 836		13 047	Catoosa County	63 942
	39 151	Stark County	375 586		13 083	Dade County	16 633
					13 295	Walker County	68 756
15980		Cape Coral-Fort Myers, FL	618 754		47 065	Hamilton County	336 463
	12 071	Lee County	618 754		47 115	Marion County	28 237
16020		Cape Girardeau, MO-IL	96 275		47 153	Sequatchie County	14 112
	17 003	Alexander County	8 238	16940		Cheyenne, WY	91 738
	29 017	Bollinger County	12 363		56 021	Laramie County	91 738
	29 031	Cape Girardeau County	75 674				
16060		Carbondale-Marion, IL	126 575				
	17 077	Jackson County	60 218				
	17 199	Williamson County	66 357				
16180		Carson City, NV	55 274				
	32 510	Carson City	55 274				
16220		Casper, WY	75 450				
	56 025	Natrona County	75 450				
16300		Cedar Rapids, IA	257 940				
	19 011	Benton County	26 076				
	19 105	Jones County	20 638				
	19 113	Linn County	211 226				
16540		Chambersburg-Waynesboro, PA	149 618				
	42 055	Franklin County	149 618				

Metropolitan Statistical Areas, Metropolitan Divisions, and Components (as defined July 2015)–*Continued*

Core based statistical area	State/ County FIPS code	Title and Geographic Components	2010 Census Population	Core based statistical area	State/ County FIPS code	Title and Geographic Components	2010 Census Population
16980		Chicago-Naperville-Elgin, IL-IN-WI	9 461 105	17780		College Station-Bryan, TX.............................	228 660
		Chicago-Naperville-Arlington Heights, IL			48 041	Brazos County	194 851
		Div 16974......................................	7 262 718		48 051	Burleson County	17 187
	17 031	Cook County	5 194 675		48 395	Robertson County....................................	16 622
	17 043	DuPage County...................................	916 924				
	17 063	Grundy County	50 063	17820		Colorado Springs, CO................................	645 613
	17 093	Kendall County	114 736		08 041	El Paso County......................................	622 263
	17 111	McHenry County	308 760		08 119	Teller County	23 350
	17 197	Will County	677 560				
		Elgin, IL Div 20994	620 429	17860		Columbia, MO	162 642
	17 037	DeKalb County	105 160		29 019	Boone County	162 642
	17 089	Kane County	515 269				
		Gary, IN Div 23844	708 070	17900		Columbia, SC	767 598
	18 073	Jasper County	33 478		45 017	Calhoun County	15 175
	18 089	Lake County	496 005		45 039	Fairfield County	23 956
	18 111	Newton County..................................	14 244		45 055	Kershaw County	61 697
	18 127	Porter County	164 343		45 063	Lexington County	262 391
		Lake County-Kenosha County, IL-WI Div			45 079	Richland County	384 504
		29404	869 888		45 081	Saluda County	19 875
	17 097	Lake County	703 462				
	55 059	Kenosha County..................................	166 426	17980		Columbus, GA-AL	294 865
					01 113	Russell County	52 947
17020		Chico, CA	220 000		13 053	Chattahoochee County	11 267
	06 007	Butte County	220 000		13 145	Harris County	32 024
17140		Cincinnati, OH-KY-IN	2 114 580		13 197	Marion County	8 742
	18 029	Dearborn County	50 047		13 215	Muscogee County	189 885
	18 115	Ohio County	6 128				
	18 161	Union County	7 516	18020		Columbus, IN..	76 794
	21 015	Boone County	118 811		18 005	Bartholomew County	76 794
	21 023	Bracken County	8 488	18140		Columbus, OH.......................................	1 901 974
	21 037	Campbell County	90 336		39 041	Delaware County	174 214
	21 077	Gallatin County	8 589		39 045	Fairfield County.....................................	146 156
	21 081	Grant County	24 662		39 049	Franklin County	1 163 414
	21 117	Kenton County	159 720		39 073	Hocking County	29 380
	21 191	Pendleton County	14 877		39 089	Licking County	166 492
	39 015	Brown County	44 846		39 097	Madison County	43 435
	39 017	Butler County	368 130		39 117	Morrow County	34 827
	39 025	Clermont County	197 363		39 127	Perry County	36 058
	39 061	Hamilton County	802 374		39 129	Pickaway County	55 698
	39 165	Warren County....................................	212 693		39 159	Union County	52 300
17300		Clarksville, TN-KY	260 625	18580		Corpus Christi, TX...................................	428 185
	21 047	Christian County	73 955		48 007	Aransas County	23 158
	21 221	Trigg County	14 339		48 355	Nueces County	340 223
	47 125	Montgomery County	172 331		48 409	San Patricio County.................................	64 804
17420		Cleveland, TN......................................	115 788	18700		Corvallis, OR	85 579
	47 011	Bradley County	98 963		41 003	Benton County	85 579
	47 139	Polk County	16 825				
				18880		Crestview-Fort Walton Beach-Destin, FL.........	235 865
17460		Cleveland-Elyria, OH...............................	2 077 240		12 091	Okaloosa County	180 822
	39 035	Cuyahoga County..................................	1 280 122		12 131	Walton County	55 043
	39 055	Geauga County....................................	93 389				
	39 085	Lake County	230 041	19060		Cumberland, MD-WV	103 299
	39 093	Lorain County	301 356		24 001	Allegany County.....................................	75 087
	39 103	Medina County....................................	172 332		54 057	Mineral County......................................	28 212
17660		Coeur d'Alene, ID	138 494				
	16 055	Kootenai County	138 494				

Core based statistical area	State/County FIPS code	Title and Geographic Components	2010 Census Population
19100		Dallas-Fort Worth-Arlington, TX	6 426 214
		Dallas-Plano-Irving, TX Div 19124	4 230 520
	48 085	Collin County	782 341
	48 113	Dallas County	2 368 139
	48 121	Denton County	662 614
	48 139	Ellis County	149 610
	48 231	Hunt County	86 129
	48 257	Kaufman County	103 350
	48 397	Rockwall County	78 337
		Fort Worth-Arlington, TX Div 23104	2 195 694
	48 221	Hood County	51 182
	48 251	Johnson County	150 934
	48 367	Parker County	116 927
	48 425	Somervell County	8 490
	48 439	Tarrant County	1 809 034
	48 497	Wise County	59 127
19140		Dalton, GA	142 227
	13 213	Murray County	39 628
	13 313	Whitfield County	102 599
19180		Danville, IL	81 625
	17 183	Vermilion County	81 625
19300		Daphne-Fairhope-Foley, AL	182 265
	01 003	Baldwin County	182 265
19340		Davenport-Moline-Rock Island, IA-IL	379 690
	17 073	Henry County	50 486
	17 131	Mercer County	16 434
	17 161	Rock Island County	147 546
	19 163	Scott County	165 224
19380		Dayton, OH	799 232
	39 057	Greene County	161 573
	39 109	Miami County	102 506
	39 113	Montgomery County	535 153
19460		Decatur, AL	153 829
	01 079	Lawrence County	34 339
	01 103	Morgan County	119 490
19500		Decatur, IL	110 768
	17 115	Macon County	110 768
19660		Deltona-Daytona Beach-Ormond Beach, FL	590 289
	12 035	Flagler County	95 696
	12 127	Volusia County	494 593
19740		Denver-Aurora-Lakewood, CO	2 543 482
	08 001	Adams County	441 603
	08 005	Arapahoe County	572 003
	08 014	Broomfield County	55 889
	08 019	Clear Creek County	9 088
	08 031	Denver County	600 158
	08 035	Douglas County	285 465
	08 039	Elbert County	23 086
	08 047	Gilpin County	5 441
	08 059	Jefferson County	534 543
	08 093	Park County	16 206
19780		Des Moines-West Des Moines, IA	569 633
	19 049	Dallas County	66 135
	19 077	Guthrie County	10 954
	19 121	Madison County	15 679
	19 153	Polk County	430 640
	19 181	Warren County	46 225
19820		Detroit-Warren-Dearborn, MI	4 296 250
		Detroit-Dearborn-Livonia, MI Div 19804	1 820 584
	26 163	Wayne County	1 820 584
		Warren-Troy-Farmington Hills, MI 47664	2 475 666
	26 087	Lapeer County	88 319
	26 093	Livingston County	180 967
	26 099	Macomb County	840 978
	26 125	Oakland County	1 202 362
	26 147	St. Clair County	163 040
20020		Dothan, AL	145 639
	01 061	Geneva County	26 790
	01 067	Henry County	17 302
	01 069	Houston County	101 547
20100		Dover, DE	162 310
	10 001	Kent County	162 310
20220		Dubuque, IA	93 653
	19 061	Dubuque County	93 653
20260		Duluth, MN-WI	279 771
	27 017	Carlton County	35 386
	27 137	St. Louis County	200 226
	55 031	Douglas County	44 159
20500		Durham-Chapel Hill, NC	504 357
	37 037	Chatham County	63 505
	37 063	Durham County	267 587
	37 135	Orange County	133 801
	37 145	Person County	39 464
20700		East Stroudsburg, PA	169 842
	42 089	Monroe County	169 842
20740		Eau Claire, WI	161 151
	55 017	Chippewa County	62 415
	55 035	Eau Claire County	98 736
20940		El Centro, CA	174 528
	06 025	Imperial County	174 528
21060		Elizabethtown-Fort Knox, KY	148 338
	21 093	Hardin County	105 543
	21 123	Larue County	14 193
	21 163	Meade County	28 602
21140		Elkhart-Goshen, IN	197 559
	18 039	Elkhart County	197 559
21300		Elmira, NY	88 830
	36 015	Chemung County	88 830
21340		El Paso, TX	804 123
	48 141	El Paso County	800 647
	48 229	Hudspeth County	3 476

Metropolitan Statistical Areas, Metropolitan Divisions, and Components (as defined July 2015)–*Continued*

Core based statistical area	State/ County FIPS code	Title and Geographic Components	2010 Census Population	Core based statistical area	State/ County FIPS code	Title and Geographic Components	2010 Census Population
21420		Enid, OK...	60 580	23060		Fort Wayne, IN...............................	416 257
	40 047	Garfield County...........................	60 580		18 003	Allen County	355 329
					18 179	Wells County..............................	27 636
21500		Erie, PA..	280 566		18 183	Whitley County..........................	33 292
	42 049	Erie County	280 566				
				23420		Fresno, CA	930 450
21660		Eugene, OR...	351 715		06 019	Fresno County	930 450
	41 039	Lane County	351 715				
				23460		Gadsden, AL	104 430
21780		Evansville, IN-KY...............................	311 552		01 055	Etowah County	104 430
	18 129	Posey County	25 910				
	18 163	Vanderburgh County...................	179 703	23540		Gainesville, FL..............................	264 275
	18 173	Warrick County	59 689		12 001	Alachua County	247 336
	21 101	Henderson County.......................	46 250		12 041	Gilchrist County	16 939
21820		Fairbanks, AK.....................................	97 581	23580		Gainesville, GA.............................	179 684
	02 090	Fairbanks North Star Borough.....	97 581		13 139	Hall County	179 684
22020		Fargo, ND-MN.....................................	208 777	23900		Gettysburg, PA..............................	101 407
	27 027	Clay County	58 999		42 001	Adams County	101 407
	38 017	Cass County	149 778				
				24020		Glens Falls, NY.............................	128 923
22140		Farmington, NM..................................	130 044		36 113	Warren County...........................	65 707
	35 045	San Juan County	130 044		36 115	Washington County	63 216
22180		Fayetteville, NC..................................	366 383	24140		Goldsboro, NC...............................	122 623
	37 051	Cumberland County.....................	319 431		37 191	Wayne County	122 623
	37 093	Hoke County	46 952				
				24220		Grand Forks, ND-MN	98 461
22220		Fayetteville-Springdale-Rogers, AR-MO..........	463 204		27 119	Polk County	31 600
	05 007	Benton County	221 339		38 035	Grand Forks County..................	66 861
	05 087	Madison County...........................	15 717				
	05 143	Washington County	203 065	24260		Grand Island, NE..........................	81 850
	29 119	McDonald County	23 083		31 079	Hall County	58 607
					31 081	Hamilton County	9 124
22380		Flagstaff, AZ.......................................	134 421		31 093	Howard County	6 274
	04 005	Coconino County	134 421		31 121	Merrick County..........................	7 845
22420		Flint, MI...	425 790	24300		Grand Junction, CO	146 723
	26 049	Genesee County	425 790		08 077	Mesa County	146 723
22500		Florence, SC	205 566	24340		Grand Rapids-Wyoming, MI........	988 938
	45 031	Darlington County........................	68 681		26 015	Barry County..............................	59 173
	45 041	Florence County	136 885		26 081	Kent County	602 622
					26 117	Montcalm County.......................	63 342
22520		Florence-Muscle Shoals, AL	147 137		26 139	Ottawa County...........................	263 801
	01 033	Colbert County.............................	54 428				
	01 077	Lauderdale County	92 709	24420		Grants Pass, OR..........................	82 713
					41 033	Josephine County......................	82 713
22540		Fond du Lac, WI.................................	101 633				
	55 039	Fond du Lac County	101 633	24500		Great Falls, MT	81 327
					30 013	Cascade County	81 327
22660		Fort Collins, CO..................................	299 630				
	08 069	Larimer County	299 630	24540		Greeley, CO	252 825
					08 123	Weld County...............................	252 825
22900		Fort Smith, AR-OK	280 467				
	05 033	Crawford County..........................	61 948	24580		Green Bay, WI...............................	306 241
	05 131	Sebastian County	125 744		55 009	Brown County	248 007
	40 079	Le Flore County	50 384		55 061	Kewaunee County......................	20 574
	40 135	Sequoyah County	42 391		55 083	Oconto County...........................	37 660

Core based statistical area	State/ County FIPS code	Title and Geographic Components	2010 Census Population	Core based statistical area	State/ County FIPS code	Title and Geographic Components	2010 Census Population
24660		Greensboro-High Point, NC	723 801	26300		Hot Springs, AR	96 024
	37 081	Guilford County	488 406		05 051	Garland County	96 024
	37 151	Randolph County	141 752				
	37 157	Rockingham County	93 643	26380		Houma-Thibodaux, LA	208 178
24780		Greenville, NC	168 148		22 057	Lafourche Parish	96 318
	37 147	Pitt County	168 148		22 109	Terrebonne Parish	111 860
24860		Greenville-Anderson-Mauldin, SC	824 112	26420		Houston-The Woodlands-Sugar Land, TX	5 920 416
	45 007	Anderson County	187 126		48 015	Austin County	28 417
	45 045	Greenville County	451 225		48 039	Brazoria County	313 166
	45 059	Laurens County	66 537		48 071	Chambers County	35 096
	45 077	Pickens County	119 224		48 157	Fort Bend County	585 375
25060		Gulfport-Biloxi-Pascagoula, MS	370 702		48 167	Galveston County	291 309
	28 045	Hancock County	43 929		48 201	Harris County	4 092 459
	28 047	Harrison County	187 105		48 291	Liberty County	75 643
	28 059	Jackson County	139 668		48 339	Montgomery County	455 746
25180		Hagerstown-Martinsburg, MD-WV	251 599		48 473	Waller County	43 205
	24 043	Washington County	147 430	26580		Huntington-Ashland, WV-KY-OH	364 908
	54 003	Berkeley County	104 169		21 019	Boyd County	49 542
25220		Hammond, LA	121 097		21 089	Greenup County	36 910
	22 105	Tangipahoa Parish	121 097		39 087	Lawrence County	62 450
25260		Hanford-Corcoran, CA	152 982		54 011	Cabell County	96 319
	06 031	Kings County	152 982		54 043	Lincoln County	21 720
25420		Harrisburg-Carlisle, PA	549 475		54 079	Putnam County	55 486
	42 041	Cumberland County	235 406		54 099	Wayne County	42 481
	42 043	Dauphin County	268 100	26620		Huntsville, AL	417 593
	42 099	Perry County	45 969		01 083	Limestone County	82 782
25500		Harrisonburg, VA	125 228		01 089	Madison County	334 811
	51 165	Rockingham County	76 314	26820		Idaho Falls, ID	133 265
	51 660	Harrisonburg city	48 914		16 019	Bonneville County	104 234
25540		Hartford-West Hartford-East Hartford, CT	1 212 381		16 023	Butte County	2 891
	09 003	Hartford County	894 014		16 051	Jefferson County	26 140
	09 007	Middlesex County	165 676	26900		Indianapolis-Carmel-Anderson, IN	1 887 877
	09 013	Tolland County	152 691		18 011	Boone County	56 640
25620		Hattiesburg, MS	142 842		18 013	Brown County	15 242
	28 035	Forrest County	74 934		18 057	Hamilton County	274 569
	28 073	Lamar County	55 658		18 059	Hancock County	70 002
	28 111	Perry County	12 250		18 063	Hendricks County	145 448
					18 081	Johnson County	139 654
25860		Hickory-Lenoir-Morganton, NC	365 497		18 095	Madison County	131 636
	37 003	Alexander County	37 198		18 097	Marion County	903 393
	37 023	Burke County	90 912		18 109	Morgan County	68 894
	37 027	Caldwell County	83 029		18 133	Putnam County	37 963
	37 035	Catawba County	154 358		18 145	Shelby County	44 436
25940		Hilton Head Island-Bluffton-Beaufort, NC	187 010	26980		Iowa City, IA	152 586
	45 013	Beaufort County	162 233		19 103	Johnson County	130 882
	45 053	Jasper County	24 777		19 183	Washington County	21 704
25980		Hinesville, GA	77 917	27060		Ithaca, NY	101 564
	13 179	Liberty County	63 453		36 109	Tompkins County	101 564
	13 183	Long County	14 464	27100		Jackson, MI	160 248
26140		Homosassa Springs, FL	141 236		26 075	Jackson County	160 248
	12 017	Citrus County	141 236				

Core based statistical area	State/County FIPS code	Title and Geographic Components	2010 Census Population	Core based statistical area	State/County FIPS code	Title and Geographic Components	2010 Census Population
27140		Jackson, MS	567 122	28140		Kansas City, MO-KS	2 009 342
	28 029	Copiah County	29 449		20 091	Johnson County	544 179
	28 049	Hinds County	245 285		20 103	Leavenworth County	76 227
	28 089	Madison County	95 203		20 107	Linn County	9 656
	28 121	Rankin County	141 617		20 121	Miami County	32 787
	28 127	Simpson County	27 503		20 209	Wyandotte County	157 505
	28 163	Yazoo County	28 065		29 013	Bates County	17 049
					29 025	Caldwell County	9 424
27180		Jackson, TN	130 011		29 037	Cass County	99 478
	47 023	Chester County	17 131		29 047	Clay County	221 939
	47 033	Crockett County	14 586		29 049	Clinton County	20 743
	47 113	Madison County	98 294		29 095	Jackson County	674 158
					29 107	Lafayette County	33 381
27260		Jacksonville, FL	1 345 596		29 165	Platte County	89 322
	12 003	Baker County	27 115		29 177	Ray County	23 494
	12 019	Clay County	190 865				
	12 031	Duval County	864 263	28420		Kennewick-Richland, WA	253 340
	12 089	Nassau County	73 314		53 005	Benton County	175 177
	12 109	St. Johns County	190 039		53 021	Franklin County	78 163
27340		Jacksonville, NC	177 772	28660		Killeen-Temple, TX	405 300
	37 133	Onslow County	177 772		48 027	Bell County	310 235
					48 099	Coryell County	75 388
27500		Janesville-Beloit, WI	160 331		48 281	Lampasas County	19 677
	55 105	Rock County	160 331				
				28700		Kingsport-Bristol-Bristol, TN-VA	309 544
27620		Jefferson City, MO	149 807		47 073	Hawkins County	56 833
	29 027	Callaway County	44 332		47 163	Sullivan County	156 823
	29 051	Cole County	75 990		51 169	Scott County	23 177
	29 135	Moniteau County	15 607		51 191	Washington County	54 876
	29 151	Osage County	13 878		51 520	Bristol city	17 835
27740		Johnson City, TN	198 716	28740		Kingston, NY	182 493
	47 019	Carter County	57 424		36 111	Ulster County	182 493
	47 171	Unicoi County	18 313				
	47 179	Washington County	122 979	28940		Knoxville, TN	837 571
					47 001	Anderson County	75 129
27780		Johnstown, PA	143 679		47 009	Blount County	123 010
	42 021	Cambria County	143 679		47 013	Campbell County	40 716
					47 057	Grainger County	22 657
27860		Jonesboro, AR	121 026		47 093	Knox County	432 226
	05 031	Craighead County	96 443		47 105	Loudon County	48 556
	05 111	Poinsett County	24 583		47 129	Morgan County	21 987
					47 145	Roane County	54 181
27900		Joplin, MO	175 518		47 173	Union County	19 109
	29 097	Jasper County	117 404				
	29 145	Newton County	58 114	29020		Kokomo, IN	82 752
					18 067	Howard County	82 752
27980		Kahului-Wailuku-Lahaina, HI	154 924				
	15 005	Kalawao County	90	29100		La Crosse-Onalaska, WI-MN	133 665
	15 009	Maui County	154 834		27 055	Houston County	19 027
					55 063	La Crosse County	114 638
28020		Kalamazoo-Portage, MI	326 589				
	26 077	Kalamazoo County	250 331	29180		Lafayette, LA	466 750
	26 159	Van Buren County	76 258		22 001	Acadia Parish	61 773
					22 045	Iberia Parish	73 240
28100		Kankakee, IL	113 449		22 055	Lafayette Parish	221 578
	17 091	Kankakee County	113 449		22 099	St. Martin Parish	52 160
					22 113	Vermilion Parish	57 999
				29200		Lafayette-West Lafayette, IN	201 789
					18 007	Benton County	8 854
					18 015	Carroll County	20 155
					18 157	Tippecanoe County	172 780

Metropolitan Statistical Areas, Metropolitan Divisions, and Components (as defined July 2015)–*Continued*

Core based statistical area	State/County FIPS code	Title and Geographic Components	2010 Census Population	Core based statistical area	State/County FIPS code	Title and Geographic Components	2010 Census Population
29340		Lake Charles, LA	199 607	30780		Little Rock-North Little Rock-Conway, AR	699 757
	22 019	Calcasieu Parish	192 768		05 045	Faulkner County	113 237
	22 023	Cameron Parish	6 839		05 053	Grant County	17 853
					05 085	Lonoke County	68 356
29420		Lake Havasu City-Kingman, AZ	200 186		05 105	Perry County	10 445
	04 015	Mohave County	200 186		05 119	Pulaski County	382 748
					05 125	Saline County	107 118
29460		Lakeland-Winter Haven, FL	602 095				
	12 105	Polk County	602 095	30860		Logan, UT-ID	125 442
					16 041	Franklin County	12 786
29540		Lancaster, PA	519 445		49 005	Cache County	112 656
	42 071	Lancaster County	519 445				
				30980		Longview, TX	214 369
29620		Lansing-East Lansing, MI	464 036		48 183	Gregg County	121 730
	26 037	Clinton County	75 382		48 401	Rusk County	53 330
	26 045	Eaton County	107 759		48 459	Upshur County	39 309
	26 065	Ingham County	280 895				
				31020		Longview, WA	102 410
29700		Laredo, TX	250 304		53 015	Cowlitz County	102 410
	48 479	Webb County	250 304				
				31080		Los Angeles-Long Beach-Anaheim, CA	12 828 837
29740		Las Cruces, NM	209 233			Anaheim-Santa Ana-Irvine, CA Div 11244	3 010 232
	35 013	Dona Ana County	209 233		06 059	Orange County	3 010 232
						Los Angeles-Long Beach-Glendale, CA Div 31084	9 818 605
29820		Las Vegas-Henderson-Paradise, NV	1 951 269				
	32 003	Clark County	1 951 269		06 037	Los Angeles County	9 818 605
29940		Lawrence, KS	110 826	31140		Louisville/Jefferson County, KY-IN	1 235 708
	20 045	Douglas County	110 826		18 019	Clark County	110 232
					18 043	Floyd County	74 578
30020		Lawton, OK	130 291		18 061	Harrison County	39 364
	40 031	Comanche County	124 098		18 143	Scott County	24 181
	40 033	Cotton County	6 193		18 175	Washington County	28 262
					21 029	Bullitt County	74 319
30140		Lebanon, PA	133 568		21 103	Henry County	15 416
	42 075	Lebanon County	133 568		21 111	Jefferson County	741 096
					21 185	Oldham County	60 316
30300		Lewiston, ID-WA	60 888		21 211	Shelby County	42 074
	16 069	Nez Perce County	39 265		21 215	Spencer County	17 061
	53 003	Asotin County	21 623		21 223	Trimble County	8 809
30340		Lewiston-Auburn, ME	107 702	31180		Lubbock, TX	290 805
	23 001	Androscoggin County	107 702		48 107	Crosby County	6 059
					48 303	Lubbock County	278 831
30460		Lexington-Fayette, KY	472 099		48 305	Lynn County	5 915
	21 017	Bourbon County	19 985				
	21 049	Clark County	35 613	31340		Lynchburg, VA	252 634
	21 067	Fayette County	295 803		51 009	Amherst County	32 353
	21 113	Jessamine County	48 586		51 011	Appomattox County	14 973
	21 209	Scott County	47 173		51 019	Bedford County	68 676
	21 239	Woodford County	24 939		51 031	Campbell County	54 842
					51 515	Bedford city	6 222
30620		Lima, OH	106 331		51 680	Lynchburg city	75 568
	39 003	Allen County	106 331				
				31420		Macon, GA	232 293
30700		Lincoln, NE	302 157		13 021	Bibb County	155 547
	31 109	Lancaster County	285 407		13 079	Crawford County	12 630
	31 159	Seward County	16 750		13 169	Jones County	28 669
					13 207	Monroe County	26 424
					13 289	Twiggs County	9 023
				31460		Madera, CA	150 865
					06 039	Madera County	150 865

Metropolitan Statistical Areas, Metropolitan Divisions, and Components (as defined July 2015)–*Continued*

Core based statistical area	State/ County FIPS code	Title and Geographic Components	2010 Census Population	Core based statistical area	State/ County FIPS code	Title and Geographic Components	2010 Census Population
31540		Madison, WI	605 435	33340		Milwaukee-Waukesha-West Allis, WI..............	1 555 908
	55 021	Columbia County	56 833		55 079	Milwaukee County	947 735
	55 025	Dane County.............................	488 073		55 089	Ozaukee County...	86 395
	55 045	Green County	36 842		55 131	Washington County	131 887
	55 049	Iowa County..............................	23 687		55 133	Waukesha County	389 891
31700		Manchester-Nashua, NH...................	400 721	33460		Minneapolis-St. Paul-Bloomington, MN	3 348 859
	33 011	Hillsborough County	400 721		27 003	Anoka County..	330 844
					27 019	Carver County..	91 042
31740		Manhattan, KS............................	92 719		27 025	Chisago County	53 887
	20 149	Pottawatomie County..................	21 604		27 037	Dakota County...	398 552
	20 161	Riley County	71 115		27 053	Hennepin County	1 152 425
					27 059	Isanti County...	37 816
31860		Mankato-North Mankato, MN	96 740		27 079	Le Sueur County..	27 703
	27 013	Blue Earth County	64 013		27 095	Mille Lacs County	26 097
	27 103	Nicollet County...........................	32 727		27 123	Ramsey County..	508 640
					27 139	Scott County..	129 928
31900		Mansfield, OH.............................	124 475		27 141	Sherburne County..	88 499
	39 139	Richland County	124 475		27 143	Sibley County..	15 226
					27 163	Washington County	238 136
32580		McAllen-Edinburg-Mission, TX	774 769		27 171	Wright County	124 700
	48 215	Hidalgo County	774 769		55 093	Pierce County..	41 019
					55 109	St. Croix County	84 345
32780		Medford, OR..............................	203 206				
	41 029	Jackson County	203 206	33540		Missoula, MT...	109 299
					30 063	Missoula County	109 299
32820		Memphis, TN-MS-AR	1 324 829				
	05 035	Crittenden County.......................	50 902	33660		Mobile, AL..	412 992
	28 009	Benton County...........................	8 729		01 097	Mobile County	412 992
	28 033	DeSoto County	161 252				
	28 093	Marshall County	37 144	33700		Modesto, CA...	514 453
	28 137	Tate County	28 886		06 099	Stanislaus County..	514 453
	28 143	Tunica County............................	10 778				
	47 047	Fayette County	38 413	33740		Monroe, LA...	176 441
	47 157	Shelby County............................	927 644		22 073	Ouachita Parish	153 720
	47 167	Tipton County	61 081		22 111	Union Parish	22 721
32900		Merced, CA...............................	255 793	33780		Monroe, MI...	152 021
	06 047	Merced County	255 793		26 115	Monroe County..	152 021
33100		Miami-Fort Lauderdale-West Palm Beach, FL.	5 564 635	33860		Montgomery, AL...	374 536
		Fort Lauderdale-Pompano Beach-Deerfield Beach, FL Div 22744.................................	1 748 066		01 001	Autauga County...	54 571
					01 051	Elmore County...	79 303
	12 011	Broward County	1 748 066		01 085	Lowndes County	11 299
		Miami-Miami Beach-Kendall, FL Div 33124.	2 496 435		01 101	Montgomery County	229 363
	12 086	Miami-Dade County	2 496 435				
		West Palm Beach-Boca Raton-Delray Beach, FL Div 48424..............................	1 320 134	34060		Morgantown, WV..	129 709
					54 061	Monongalia County.......................................	96 189
	12 099	Palm Beach County	1 320 134		54 077	Preston County..	33 520
33140		Michigan City-La Porte, IN	111 467	34100		Morristown, TN..	113 951
	18 091	LaPorte County..........................	111 467		47 063	Hamblen County..	62 544
					47 089	Jefferson County..	51 407
33220		Midland, MI...............................	83 629				
	26 111	Midland County	83 629	34580		Mount Vernon-Anacortes, WA	116 901
					53 057	Skagit County	116 901
33260		Midland, TX...............................	141 671				
	48 317	Martin County	4 799	34620		Muncie, IN..	117 671
	48 329	Midland County..........................	136 872		18 035	Delaware County..	117 671
				34740		Muskegon, MI..	172 188
					26 121	Muskegon County...	172 188

Metropolitan Statistical Areas, Metropolitan Divisions, and Components (as defined July 2015)–*Continued*

Core based statistical area	State/ County FIPS code	Title and Geographic Components	2010 Census Population	Core based statistical area	State/ County FIPS code	Title and Geographic Components	2010 Census Population
34820		Myrtle Beach-Conway-North Myrtle Beach, NC-SC	376 722	35620		New York-Newark-Jersey City, NY-NJ-PA	19 567 410
	37 019	Brunswick County......................................	107 431			Dutchess County-Putnam County, NY Div 20524	397 198
	45 051	Horry County..	269 291		36 027	Dutchess County..................................	297 488
34900		Napa, CA..	136 484		36 079	Putnam County	99 710
	06 055	Napa County..	136 484			Nassau County-Suffolk County, NY Div 35004......	2 832 882
34940		Naples-Immokalee-Marco Island, FL..............	321 520		36 059	Nassau County.....................................	1 339 532
	12 021	Collier County..	321 520		36 103	Suffolk County......................................	1 493 350
34980		Nashville-Davidson—Murfreesboro—Franklin, TN......	1 670 890			Newark, NJ-PA Div 35084........................	2 471 171
	47 015	Cannon County..	13 801		34 013	Essex County..	783 969
	47 021	Cheatham County....................................	39 105		34 019	Hunterdon County.................................	128 349
	47 037	Davidson County	626 681		34 027	Morris County.......................................	492 276
	47 043	Dickson County	49 666		34 035	Somerset County..................................	323 444
	47 081	Hickman County.......................................	24 690		34 037	Sussex County	149 265
	47 111	Macon County...	22 248		34 039	Union County..	536 499
	47 119	Maury County..	80 956		42 103	Pike County..	57 369
	47 147	Robertson County....................................	66 283			New York-Jersey City-White Plains, NY-NJ Div 35614......	13 866 159
	47 149	Rutherford County	262 604		34 003	Bergen County	905 116
	47 159	Smith County	19 166		34 017	Hudson County	634 266
	47 165	Sumner County..	160 645		34 023	Middlesex County..................................	809 858
	47 169	Trousdale County.....................................	7 870		34 025	Monmouth County.................................	630 380
	47 187	Williamson County....................................	183 182		34 029	Ocean County	576 567
	47 189	Wilson County..	113 993		34 031	Passaic County.....................................	501 226
35100		New Bern, NC	126 802		36 005	Bronx County..	1 385 108
	37 049	Craven County...	103 505		36 047	Kings County..	2 504 700
	37 103	Jones County	10 153		36 061	New York County..................................	1 585 873
	37 137	Pamlico County..	13 144		36 071	Orange County.....................................	372 813
35300		New Haven-Milford, CT.............................	862 477		36 081	Queens County.....................................	2 230 722
	09 009	New Haven County...................................	862 477		36 085	Richmond County..................................	468 730
35380		New Orleans-Metairie, LA.........................	1 189 866		36 087	Rockland County...................................	311 687
	22 051	Jefferson Parish......................................	432 552		36 119	Westchester County..............................	949 113
	22 071	Orleans Parish..	343 829	35660		Niles-Benton Harbor, MI...........................	156 813
	22 075	Plaquemines Parish.................................	23 042		26 021	Berrien County......................................	156 813
	22 087	St. Bernard Parish	35 897				
	22 089	St. Charles Parish...................................	52 780	35840		North Port-Sarasota-Bradenton, FL................	702 281
	22 093	St. James Parish	22 102		12 081	Manatee County	322 833
	22 095	St. John the Baptist Parish.......................	45 924		12 115	Sarasota County...................................	379 448
	22 103	St. Tammany Parish.................................	233 740	35980		Norwich-New London, CT...........................	274 055
					09 011	New London County..............................	274 055
				36100		Ocala, FL...	331 298
					12 083	Marion County	331 298
				36140		Ocean City, NJ..	97 265
					34 009	Cape May County..................................	97 265
				36220		Odessa, TX...	137 130
					48 135	Ector County...	137 130
				36260		Ogden-Clearfield, UT	597 159
					49 003	Box Elder County..................................	49 975
					49 011	Davis County..	306 479
					49 029	Morgan County	9 469
					49 057	Weber County.......................................	231 236

Metropolitan Statistical Areas, Metropolitan Divisions, and Components
(as defined July 2015)–*Continued*

Core based statistical area	State/County FIPS code	Title and Geographic Components	2010 Census Population	Core based statistical area	State/County FIPS code	Title and Geographic Components	2010 Census Population
36420		Oklahoma City, OK	1 252 987	37980		Philadelphia-Camden-Wilmington, PA-NJ-DE-MD...............	5 965 343
	40 017	Canadian County...............	115 541			Camden, NJ Div 15804	1 250 679
	40 027	Cleveland County	255 755		34 005	Burlington County...............	448 734
	40 051	Grady County...............	52 431		34 007	Camden County	513 657
	40 081	Lincoln County...............	34 273		34 015	Gloucester County	288 288
	40 083	Logan County...............	41 848			Montgomery County-Bucks County-Chester County, PA Div 33874	1 924 009
	40 087	McClain County...............	34 506		42 017	Bucks County	625 249
	40 109	Oklahoma County...............	718 633		42 029	Chester County	498 886
36500		Olympia-Tumwater, WA	252 264		42 091	Montgomery County...............	799 874
	53 067	Thurston County...............	252 264			Philadelphia, PA Div 37964	2 084 985
36540		Omaha-Council Bluffs, NE-IA...............	865 350		42 045	Delaware County...............	558 979
	19 085	Harrison County...............	14 928		42 101	Philadelphia County...............	1 526 006
	19 129	Mills County...............	15 059			Wilmington, DE-MD-NJ Div 48864	705 670
	19 155	Pottawattamie County...............	93 158		10 003	New Castle County	538 479
	31 025	Cass County	25 241		24 015	Cecil County...............	101 108
	31 055	Douglas County...............	517 110		34 033	Salem County...............	66 083
	31 153	Sarpy County...............	158 840				
	31 155	Saunders County...............	20 780	38060		Phoenix-Mesa-Scottsdale, AZ...............	4 192 887
	31 177	Washington County...............	20 234		04 013	Maricopa County...............	3 817 117
36740		Orlando-Kissimmee-Sanford, FL...............	2 134 411		04 021	Pinal County	375 770
	12 069	Lake County...............	297 052	38220		Pine Bluff, AR...............	100 258
	12 095	Orange County	1 145 956		05 025	Cleveland County	8 689
	12 097	Osceola County...............	268 685		05 069	Jefferson County...............	77 435
	12 117	Seminole County...............	422 718		05 079	Lincoln County...............	14 134
36780		Oshkosh-Neenah, WI...............	166 994	38300		Pittsburgh, PA	2 356 285
	55 139	Winnebago County...............	166 994		42 003	Allegheny County...............	1 223 348
36980		Owensboro, KY...............	114 752		42 005	Armstrong County...............	68 941
	21 059	Daviess County...............	96 656		42 007	Beaver County	170 539
	21 091	Hancock County...............	8 565		42 019	Butler County...............	183 862
	21 149	McLean County...............	9 531		42 051	Fayette County...............	136 606
37100		Oxnard-Thousand Oaks-Ventura, CA...............	823 318		42 125	Washington County...............	207 820
	06 111	Ventura County...............	823 318		42 129	Westmoreland County	365 169
37340		Palm Bay-Melbourne-Titusville, FL	543 376	38340		Pittsfield, MA	131 219
	12 009	Brevard County...............	543 376		25 003	Berkshire County...............	131 219
37460		Panama City, FL...............	184 715	38540		Pocatello, ID...............	82 839
	12 005	Bay County...............	168 852		16 005	Bannock County	82 839
	12 045	Gulf County...............	15 863	38860		Portland-South Portland, ME	514 098
37620		Parkersburg-Vienna, WV...............	92 673		23 005	Cumberland County...............	281 674
	54 105	Wirt County...............	5 717		23 023	Sagadahoc County	35 293
	54 107	Wood County...............	86 956		23 031	York County...............	197 131
37860		Pensacola-Ferry Pass-Brent, FL...............	448 991	38900		Portland-Vancouver-Hillsboro, OR-WA............	2 226 009
	12 033	Escambia County...............	297 619		41 005	Clackamas County...............	375 992
	12 113	Santa Rosa County	151 372		41 009	Columbia County...............	49 351
37900		Peoria, IL...............	379 186		41 051	Multnomah County...............	735 334
	17 123	Marshall County...............	12 640		41 067	Washington County...............	529 710
	17 143	Peoria County...............	186 494		41 071	Yamhill County...............	99 193
	17 175	Stark County...............	5 994		53 011	Clark County...............	425 363
	17 179	Tazewell County...............	135 394		53 059	Skamania County...............	11 066
	17 203	Woodford County...............	38 664	38940		Port St. Lucie, FL...............	424 107
					12 085	Martin County	146 318
					12 111	St. Lucie County...............	277 789
				39140		Prescott, AZ...............	211 033
					04 025	Yavapai County...............	211 033

Core based statistical area	State/ County FIPS code	Title and Geographic Components	2010 Census Population	Core based statistical area	State/ County FIPS code	Title and Geographic Components	2010 Census Population
39300		Providence-Warwick, RI-MA	1 600 852	40220		Roanoke, VA	308 707
	25 005	Bristol County	548 285		51 023	Botetourt County	33 148
	44 001	Bristol County	49 875		51 045	Craig County	5 190
	44 003	Kent County	166 158		51 067	Franklin County	56 159
	44 005	Newport County	82 888		51 161	Roanoke County	92 376
	44 007	Providence County	626 667		51 770	Roanoke city	97 032
	44 009	Washington County	126 979		51 775	Salem city	24 802
39340		Provo-Orem, UT	526 810	40340		Rochester, MN	206 877
	49 023	Juab County	10 246		27 039	Dodge County	20 087
	49 049	Utah County	516 564		27 045	Fillmore County	20 866
					27 109	Olmsted County	144 248
39380		Pueblo, CO	159 063		27 157	Wabasha County	21 676
	08 101	Pueblo County	159 063				
				40380		Rochester, NY	1 079 671
39460		Punta Gorda, FL	159 978		36 051	Livingston County	65 393
	12 015	Charlotte County	159 978		36 055	Monroe County	744 344
					36 069	Ontario County	107 931
39540		Racine, WI	195 408		36 073	Orleans County	42 883
	55 101	Racine County	195 408		36 117	Wayne County	93 772
					36 123	Yates County	25 348
39580		Raleigh, NC	1 130 490				
	37 069	Franklin County	60 619	40420		Rockford, IL	349 431
	37 101	Johnston County	168 878		17 007	Boone County	54 165
	37 183	Wake County	900 993		17 201	Winnebago County	295 266
39660		Rapid City, SD	134 598	40580		Rocky Mount, NC	152 392
	46 033	Custer County	8 216		37 065	Edgecombe County	56 552
	46 093	Meade County	25 434		37 127	Nash County	95 840
	46 103	Pennington County	100 948				
				40660		Rome, GA	96 317
39740		Reading, PA	411 442		13 115	Floyd County	96 317
	42 011	Berks County	411 442				
				40900		Sacramento—Roseville—Arden-Arcade, CA	2 149 127
39820		Redding, CA	177 223		06 017	El Dorado County	181 058
	06 089	Shasta County	177 223		06 061	Placer County	348 432
					06 067	Sacramento County	1 418 788
39900		Reno, NV	425 417		06 113	Yolo County	200 849
	32 029	Storey County	4 010				
	32 031	Washoe County	421 407	40980		Saginaw, MI	200 169
					26 145	Saginaw County	200 169
40060		Richmond, VA	1 208 101				
	51 007	Amelia County	12 690	41060		St. Cloud, MN	189 093
	51 033	Caroline County	28 545		27 009	Benton County	38 451
	51 036	Charles City County	7 256		27 145	Stearns County	150 642
	51 041	Chesterfield County	316 236				
	51 053	Dinwiddie County	28 001	41100		St. George, UT	138 115
	51 075	Goochland County	21 717		49 053	Washington County	138 115
	51 085	Hanover County	99 863				
	51 087	Henrico County	306 935	41140		St. Joseph, MO-KS	127 329
	51 101	King William County	15 935		20 043	Doniphan County	7 945
	51 127	New Kent County	18 429		29 003	Andrew County	17 291
	51 145	Powhatan County	28 046		29 021	Buchanan County	89 201
	51 149	Prince George County	35 725		29 063	DeKalb County	12 892
	51 183	Sussex County	12 087				
	51 570	Colonial Heights city	17 411				
	51 670	Hopewell city	22 591				
	51 730	Petersburg city	32 420				
	51 760	Richmond city	204 214				
40140		Riverside-San Bernardino-Ontario, CA	4 224 851				
	06 065	Riverside County	2 189 641				
	06 071	San Bernardino County	2 035 210				

Metropolitan Statistical Areas, Metropolitan Divisions, and Components (as defined July 2015)–*Continued*

Core based statistical area	State/County FIPS code	Title and Geographic Components	2010 Census Population	Core based statistical area	State/County FIPS code	Title and Geographic Components	2010 Census Population
41180		St. Louis, MO-IL	2 787 701	41940		San Jose-Sunnyvale-Santa Clara, CA	1 836 911
	17 005	Bond County	17 768		06 069	San Benito County	55 269
	17 013	Calhoun County	5 089		06 085	Santa Clara County	1 781 642
	17 027	Clinton County	37 762				
	17 083	Jersey County	22 985	42020		San Luis Obispo-Paso Robles-Arroyo Grande, CA	269 637
	17 117	Macoupin County	47 765		06 079	San Luis Obispo County	269 637
	17 119	Madison County	269 282				
	17 133	Monroe County	32 957	42100		Santa Cruz-Watsonville, CA	262 382
	17 163	St. Clair County	270 056		06 087	Santa Cruz County	262 382
	29 071	Franklin County	101 492				
	29 099	Jefferson County	218 733	42140		Santa Fe, NM	144 170
	29 113	Lincoln County	52 566		35 049	Santa Fe County	144 170
	29 183	St. Charles County	360 485				
	29 189	St. Louis County	998 954	42200		Santa Maria-Santa Barbara, CA	423 895
	29 219	Warren County	32 513		06 083	Santa Barbara County	423 895
	29 510	St. Louis city	319 294				
				42220		Santa Rosa, CA	483 878
41420		Salem, OR	390 738		06 097	Sonoma County	483 878
	41 047	Marion County	315 335				
	41 053	Polk County	75 403	42340		Savannah, GA	347 611
41500		Salinas, CA	415 057		13 029	Bryan County	30 233
	06 053	Monterey County	415 057		13 051	Chatham County	265 128
					13 103	Effingham County	52 250
41540		Salisbury, MD-DE	373 802				
	10 005	Sussex County	197 145	42540		Scranton—Wilkes-Barre—Hazleton, PA	563 631
	24 039	Somerset County	26 470		42 069	Lackawanna County	214 437
	24 045	Wicomico County	98 733		42 079	Luzerne County	320 918
	24 047	Worcester County	51 454		42 131	Wyoming County	28 276
41620		Salt Lake City, UT	1 087 873	42660		Seattle-Tacoma-Bellevue, WA	3 439 809
	49 035	Salt Lake County	1 029 655			Seattle-Bellevue-Everett, WA Div 42644	2 644 584
	49 045	Tooele County	58 218		53 033	King County	1 931 249
					53 061	Snohomish County	713 335
41660		San Angelo, TX	111 823			Tacoma-Lakewood, WA Div 45104	795 225
	48 235	Irion County	1 599		53 053	Pierce County	795 225
	48 451	Tom Green County	110 224				
				42680		Sebastian-Vero Beach, FL	138 028
41700		San Antonio-New Braunfels, TX	2 142 508		12 061	Indian River County	138 028
	48 013	Atascosa County	44 911				
	48 019	Bandera County	20 485	42700		Sebring, FL	98 786
	48 029	Bexar County	1 714 773		12 055	Highlands County	98 786
	48 091	Comal County	108 472				
	48 187	Guadalupe County	131 533	43100		Sheboygan, WI	115 507
	48 259	Kendall County	33 410		55 117	Sheboygan County	115 507
	48 325	Medina County	46 006				
	48 493	Wilson County	42 918	43300		Sherman-Denison, TX	120 877
					48 181	Grayson County	120 877
41740		San Diego-Carlsbad, CA	3 095 313				
	06 073	San Diego County	3 095 313	43340		Shreveport-Bossier City, LA	439 811
					22 015	Bossier Parish	116 979
41860		San Francisco-Oakland-Hayward, CA	4 335 391		22 017	Caddo Parish	254 969
		Oakland-Hayward-Berkeley, CA Div 36084	2 559 296		22 031	De Soto Parish	26 656
	06 001	Alameda County	1 510 271		22 119	Webster Parish	41 207
	06 013	Contra Costa County	1 049 025				
		San Francisco-Redwood City-South San Francisco, CA Div 41884	1 523 686	43420		Sierra Vista-Douglas, AZ	131 346
	06 075	San Francisco County	805 235		04 003	Cochise County	131 346
	06 081	San Mateo County	718 451	43580		Sioux City, IA-NE-SD	168 563
		San Rafael, CA Div 42034	252 409		19 149	Plymouth County	24 986
	06 041	Marin County	252 409		19 193	Woodbury County	102 172
					31 043	Dakota County	21 006
					31 051	Dixon County	6 000
					46 127	Union County	14 399

Core based statistical area	State/County FIPS code	Title and Geographic Components	2010 Census Population	Core based statistical area	State/County FIPS code	Title and Geographic Components	2010 Census Population
43620		Sioux Falls, SD	228 261	45300		Tampa-St. Petersburg-Clearwater, FL	2 783 243
	46 083	Lincoln County	44 828		12 053	Hernando County	172 778
	46 087	McCook County	5 618		12 057	Hillsborough County	1 229 226
	46 099	Minnehaha County	169 468		12 101	Pasco County	464 697
	46 125	Turner County	8 347		12 103	Pinellas County	916 542
43780		South Bend-Mishawaka, IN-MI	319 224	45460		Terre Haute, IN	172 425
	18 141	St. Joseph County	266 931		18 021	Clay County	26 890
	26 027	Cass County	52 293		18 153	Sullivan County	21 475
					18 165	Vermillion County	16 212
43900		Spartanburg, SC	313 268		18 167	Vigo County	107 848
	45 083	Spartanburg County	284 307				
	45 087	Union County	28 961	45500		Texarkana, TX-AR	149 198
					05 081	Little River County	13 171
44060		Spokane-Spokane Valley, WA	527 753		05 091	Miller County	43 462
	53 051	Pend Oreille County	13 001		48 037	Bowie County	92 565
	53 063	Spokane County	471 221	45540		The Villages, FL	93 420
	53 065	Stevens County	43 531		12 119	Sumter County	93 420
44100		Springfield, IL	210 170				
	17 129	Menard County	12 705	45780		Toledo, OH	610 001
	17 167	Sangamon County	197 465		39 051	Fulton County	42 698
					39 095	Lucas County	441 815
44140		Springfield, MA	621 570		39 173	Wood County	125 488
	25 013	Hampden County	463 490				
	25 015	Hampshire County	158 080	45820		Topeka, KS	233 870
					20 085	Jackson County	13 462
44180		Springfield, MO	436 712		20 087	Jefferson County	19 126
	29 043	Christian County	77 422		20 139	Osage County	16 295
	29 059	Dallas County	16 777		20 177	Shawnee County	177 934
	29 077	Greene County	275 174		20 197	Wabaunsee County	7 053
	29 167	Polk County	31 137	45940		Trenton, NJ	366 513
	29 225	Webster County	36 202		34 021	Mercer County	366 513
44220		Springfield, OH	138 333				
	39 023	Clark County	138 333	46060		Tucson, AZ	980 263
					04 019	Pima County	980 263
44300		State College, PA	153 990				
	42 027	Centre County	153 990	46140		Tulsa, OK	937 478
					40 037	Creek County	69 967
44420		Staunton-Waynesboro, VA	118 502		40 111	Okmulgee County	40 069
	51 015	Augusta County	73 750		40 113	Osage County	47 472
	51 790	Staunton city	23 746		40 117	Pawnee County	16 577
	51 820	Waynesboro city	21 006		40 131	Rogers County	86 905
					40 143	Tulsa County	603 403
44700		Stockton-Lodi, CA	685 306		40 145	Wagoner County	73 085
	06 077	San Joaquin County	685 306				
				46220		Tuscaloosa, AL	230 162
44940		Sumter, SC	107 456		01 065	Hale County	15 760
	45 085	Sumter County	107 456		01 107	Pickens County	19 746
					01 125	Tuscaloosa County	194 656
45060		Syracuse, NY	662 577				
	36 053	Madison County	73 442	46340		Tyler, TX	209 714
	36 067	Onondaga County	467 026		48 423	Smith County	209 714
	36 075	Oswego County	122 109				
				46520		Urban Honolulu, HI	953 207
45220		Tallahassee, FL	367 413		15 003	Honolulu County	953 207
	12 039	Gadsden County	46 389				
	12 065	Jefferson County	14 761	46540		Utica-Rome, NY	299 397
	12 073	Leon County	275 487		36 043	Herkimer County	64 519
	12 129	Wakulla County	30 776		36 065	Oneida County	234 878

Metropolitan Statistical Areas,
Metropolitan Divisions,
and Components
(as defined July 2015)–*Continued*

Core based statistical area	State/ County FIPS code	Title and Geographic Components	2010 Census Population	Core based statistical area	State/ County FIPS code	Title and Geographic Components	2010 Census Population
46660		Valdosta, GA	139 588	47900		Washington-Arlington-Alexandria, DC-VA-MD-WV	5 636 232
	13 027	Brooks County	16 243			Silver Spring-Frederick-Rockville, MD Div 43524	1 205 162
	13 101	Echols County..........................	4 034		24 021	Frederick County.....................	233 385
	13 173	Lanier County	10 078		24 031	Montgomery County..................	971 777
	13 185	Lowndes County	109 233			Washington-Arlington-Alexandria, DC-VA-MD-WV Div 47894	4 431 070
46700		Vallejo-Fairfield, CA................	413 344		11 001	District of Columbia.................	601 723
	06 095	Solano County	413 344		24 009	Calvert County	88 737
47020		Victoria, TX............................	94 003		24 017	Charles County	146 551
	48 175	Goliad County	7 210		24 033	Prince George's County...........	863 420
	48 469	Victoria County	86 793		51 013	Arlington County......................	207 627
47220		Vineland-Bridgeton, NJ	156 898		51 043	Clarke County	14 034
	34 011	Cumberland County..................	156 898		51 047	Culpeper County......................	46 689
47260		Virginia Beach-Norfolk-Newport News, VA-NC	1 676 822		51 059	Fairfax County.........................	1 081 726
	37 053	Currituck County	23 547		51 061	Fauquier County......................	65 203
	37 073	Gates County	12 197		51 107	Loudoun County.......................	312 311
	51 073	Gloucester County	36 858		51 153	Prince William County..............	402 002
	51 093	Isle of Wight County	35 270		51 157	Rappahannock County..............	7 373
	51 095	James City County	67 009		51 177	Spotsylvania County................	122 397
	51 115	Mathews County.......................	8 978		51 179	Stafford County	128 961
	51 199	York County	65 464		51 187	Warren County	37 575
	51 550	Chesapeake city......................	222 209		51 510	Alexandria city........................	139 966
	51 650	Hampton city...........................	137 436		51 600	Fairfax city..............................	22 565
	51 700	Newport News city...................	180 719		51 610	Falls Church city	12 332
	51 710	Norfolk city.............................	242 803		51 630	Fredericksburg city..................	24 286
	51 735	Poquoson city..........................	12 150		51 683	Manassas city.........................	37 821
	51 740	Portsmouth city........................	95 535		51 685	Manassas Park city..................	14 273
	51 800	Suffolk city.............................	84 585		54 037	Jefferson County	53 498
	51 810	Virginia Beach city...................	437 994	47940		Waterloo-Cedar Falls, IA..........	167 819
	51 830	Williamsburg city.....................	14 068		19 013	Black Hawk County	131 090
47300		Visalia-Porterville, CA..............	442 179		19 017	Bremer County	24 276
	06 107	Tulare County	442 179		19 075	Grundy County.........................	12 453
47380		Waco, TX...............................	252 772	48060		Watertown-Fort Drum, NY..........	116 229
	48 145	Falls County............................	17 866		36 045	Jefferson County......................	116 229
	48 309	McLennan County	234 906	48140		Wausau, WI.............................	134 063
47460		Walla Walla, WA	62 859		55 073	Marathon County......................	134 063
	53 013	Columbia County	4 078	48260		Weirton-Steubenville, WV-OH.....	124 454
	53 071	Walla Walla County	58 781		39 081	Jefferson County......................	69 709
47580		Warner Robins, GA	179 605		54 009	Brooke County	24 069
	13 153	Houston County.......................	139 900		54 029	Hancock County	30 676
	13 225	Peach County..........................	27 695	48300		Wenatchee, WA.......................	110 884
	13 235	Pulaski County........................	12 010		53 007	Chelan County	72 453
					53 017	Douglas County.......................	38 431
				48540		Wheeling, WV-OH....................	147 950
					39 013	Belmont County	70 400
					54 051	Marshall County.......................	33 107
					54 069	Ohio County............................	44 443
				48620		Wichita, KS.............................	630 919
					20 015	Butler County..........................	65 880
					20 079	Harvey County	34 684
					20 095	Kingman County.......................	7 858
					20 173	Sedgwick County.....................	498 365
					20 191	Sumner County........................	24 132

Metropolitan Statistical Areas, Metropolitan Divisions, and Components (as defined July 2015)–*Continued*

Core based statistical area	State/ County FIPS code	Title and Geographic Components	2010 Census Population	Core based statistical area	State/ County FIPS code	Title and Geographic Components	2010 Census Population
48660		Wichita Falls, TX	151 306	49420		Yakima, WA	243 231
	48 009	Archer County	9 054		53 077	Yakima County	243 231
	48 077	Clay County	10 752				
	48 485	Wichita County	131 500	49620		York-Hanover, PA	434 972
					42 133	York County	434 972
48700		Williamsport, PA	116 111				
	42 081	Lycoming County	116 111	49660		Youngstown-Warren-Boardman, OH-PA	565 773
					39 099	Mahoning County	238 823
48900		Wilmington, NC	254 884		39 155	Trumbull County	210 312
	37 129	New Hanover County	202 667		42 085	Mercer County	116 638
	37 141	Pender County	52 217				
				49700		Yuba City, CA	166 892
49020		Winchester, VA-WV	128 472		06 101	Sutter County	94 737
	51 069	Frederick County	78 305		06 115	Yuba County	72 155
	51 840	Winchester city	26 203				
	54 027	Hampshire County	23 964	49740		Yuma, AZ	195 751
					04 027	Yuma County	195 751
49180		Winston-Salem, NC	640 595				
	37 057	Davidson County	162 878				
	37 059	Davie County	41 240				
	37 067	Forsyth County	350 670				
	37 169	Stokes County	47 401				
	37 197	Yadkin County	38 406				
49340		Worcester, MA-CT	916 980				
	09 015	Windham County	118 428				
	25 027	Worcester County	798 552				

APPENDIX C
CORE BASED STATISTICAL AREAS
(Metropolitan and Micropolitan),
METROPOLITAN DIVISIONS, AND COMPONENTS
(as defined July 2015)

Core Based Statistical Area	State/County FIPS Code	Title and Geographic Components	2010 Census Population	2016 Estimated Population	Core Based Statistical Area	State/County FIPS Code	Title and Geographic Components	2010 Census Population	2016 Estimated Population
10100		Aberdeen, SD Micro area	40 602	43 080	10780		Alexandria, LA Metro area	153 922	154 789
	46013	Brown County, SD	36 531	39 128		22043	Grant Parish, LA	22 309	22 365
	46045	Edmunds County, SD	4 071	3 952		22079	Rapides Parish, LA	131 613	132 424
10140		Aberdeen, WA Micro area	72 797	71 628	10820		Alexandria, MN Micro area	36 009	37 456
	53027	Grays Harbor County, WA	72 797	71 628		27041	Douglas County, MN	36 009	37 456
10180		Abilene, TX Metro area	165 252	170 364	10860		Alice, TX Micro area	40 838	41 149
	48059	Callahan County, TX	13 544	13 820		48249	Jim Wells County, TX	40 838	41 149
	48253	Jones County, TX	20 202	20 009	10900		Allentown-Bethlehem-Easton, PA-NJ Metro area	821 173	835 652
	48441	Taylor County, TX	131 506	136 535		34041	Warren County, NJ	108 692	106 617
10220		Ada, OK Micro area	37 492	38 330		42025	Carbon County, PA	65 249	63 594
	40123	Pontotoc County, OK	37 492	38 330		42077	Lehigh County, PA	349 497	363 147
10300		Adrian, MI Micro area	99 892	98 504		42095	Northampton County, PA	297 735	302 294
	26091	Lenawee County, MI	99 892	98 504	10940		Alma, MI Micro area	42 476	41 202
10420		Akron, OH Metro area	703 200	702 221		26057	Gratiot County, MI	42 476	41 202
	39133	Portage County, OH	161 419	161 921	10980		Alpena, MI Micro area	29 598	28 704
	39153	Summit County, OH	541 781	540 300		26007	Alpena County, MI	29 598	28 704
10460		Alamogordo, NM Micro area	63 797	65 410	11020		Altoona, PA Metro area	127 089	124 650
	35035	Otero County, NM	63 797	65 410		42013	Blair County, PA	127 089	124 650
10500		Albany, GA Metro area	157 308	152 219	11060		Altus, OK Micro area	26 446	25 497
	13007	Baker County, GA	3 451	3 150		40065	Jackson County, OK	26 446	25 497
	13095	Dougherty County, GA	94 565	90 017	11100		Amarillo, TX Metro area	251 933	263 342
	13177	Lee County, GA	28 298	29 337		48011	Armstrong County, TX	1 901	1 876
	13273	Terrell County, GA	9 315	8 967		48065	Carson County, TX	6 182	6 057
	13321	Worth County, GA	21 679	20 748		48359	Oldham County, TX	2 052	2 076
10540		Albany, OR Metro area	116 672	122 849		48375	Potter County, TX	121 073	120 832
	41043	Linn County, OR	116 672	122 849		48381	Randall County, TX	120 725	132 501
10580		Albany-Schenectady-Troy, NY Metro area	870 716	881 839	11140		Americus, GA Micro area	37 829	35 487
	36001	Albany County, NY	304 204	308 846		13249	Schley County, GA	5 010	5 098
	36083	Rensselaer County, NY	159 429	160 070		13261	Sumter County, GA	32 819	30 389
	36091	Saratoga County, NY	219 607	227 053	11180		Ames, IA Metro area	89 542	97 090
	36093	Schenectady County, NY	154 727	154 553		19169	Story County, IA	89 542	97 090
	36095	Schoharie County, NY	32 749	31 317	11220		Amsterdam, NY Micro area	50 219	49 276
10620		Albemarle, NC Micro area	60 585	60 791		36057	Montgomery County, NY	50 219	49 276
	37167	Stanly County, NC	60 585	60 791	11260		Anchorage, AK Metro area	380 821	402 557
10660		Albert Lea, MN Micro area	31 255	30 446		02020	Anchorage Municipality, AK	291 826	298 192
	27047	Freeborn County, MN	31 255	30 446		02170	Matanuska-Susitna Borough, AK	88 995	104 365
10700		Albertville, AL Micro area	93 019	95 157	11380		Andrews, TX Micro area	14 786	17 760
	01095	Marshall County, AL	93 019	95 157		48003	Andrews County, TX	14 786	17 760
10740		Albuquerque, NM Metro area	887 077	909 906	11420		Angola, IN Micro area	34 185	34 116
	35001	Bernalillo County, NM	662 564	676 953		18151	Steuben County, IN	34 185	34 116
	35043	Sandoval County, NM	131 561	142 025	11460		Ann Arbor, MI Metro area	344 791	364 709
	35057	Torrance County, NM	16 383	15 302		26161	Washtenaw County, MI	344 791	364 709
	35061	Valencia County, NM	76 569	75 626	11500		Anniston-Oxford-Jacksonville, AL Metro area	118 572	114 611
10760		Alexander City, AL Micro Area	41 616	40 727		01015	Calhoun County, AL	118 572	114 611
	01123	Tallapoosa County, AL	41 616	40 727					

Core Based Statistical Areas (Metropolitan and Micropolitan), Metropolitan Divisions, and Components (as defined July 2015)–*Continued*

Core Based Statistical Area	State/ County FIPS Code	Title and Geographic Components	2010 Census Population	2016 Estimated Population	Core Based Statistical Area	State/ County FIPS Code	Title and Geographic Components	2010 Census Population	2016 Estimated Population
11540		Appleton, WI Metro area.................	225 666	234 079		13135	Gwinnett County, GA	805 321	907 135
	55015	Calumet County, WI..................	48 971	49 553		13143	Haralson County, GA	28 780	29 042
	55087	Outagamie County, WI................	176 695	184 526		13149	Heard County, GA.......................	11 834	11 487
						13151	Henry County, GA.......................	203 922	221 768
11580		Arcadia, FL Micro area	34 862	35 800		13159	Jasper County, GA.....................	13 900	13 654
	12027	DeSoto County, FL....................	34 862	35 800		13171	Lamar County, GA	18 317	18 469
						13199	Meriwether County, GA	21 992	21 074
11620		Ardmore, OK Micro area.................	47 557	48 556		13211	Morgan County, GA...................	17 868	18 170
	40019	Carter County, OK.......................	47 557	48 556		13217	Newton County, GA	99 958	106 999
						13223	Paulding County, GA.................	142 324	155 825
11660		Arkadelphia, AR Micro area.............	22 995	22 657		13227	Pickens County, GA...................	29 431	30 832
	05019	Clark County, AR	22 995	22 657		13231	Pike County, GA.........................	17 869	17 941
						13247	Rockdale County, GA.................	85 215	89 355
11680		Arkansas City-Winfield, KS Micro area..	36 311	35 753		13255	Spalding County, GA.................	64 073	64 806
	20035	Cowley County, KS	36 311	35 753		13297	Walton County, GA	83 768	90 184
11700		Asheville, NC Metro area.................	424 858	452 319	12100		Atlantic City-Hammonton, NJ Metro area..	274 549	270 991
	37021	Buncombe County, NC	238 318	256 088		34001	Atlantic County, NJ....................	274 549	270 991
	37087	Haywood County, NC..................	59 036	60 682					
	37089	Henderson County, NC................	106 740	114 209	12120		Atmore, AL Micro Area	38 319	37 728
	37115	Madison County, NC...................	20 764	21 340		01053	Escambia County, AL.................	38 319	37 728
11740		Ashland, OH Micro area	53 139	53 652	12140		Auburn, IN Micro area	42 223	42 746
	39005	Ashland County, OH	53 139	53 652		18033	DeKalb County, IN	42 223	42 746
11780		Ashtabula, OH Micro area	101 497	98 231	12180		Auburn, NY Micro area	80 026	77 861
	39007	Ashtabula County, OH	101 497	98 231		36011	Cayuga County, NY	80 026	77 861
11820		Astoria, OR Micro area....................	37 039	38 632	12220		Auburn-Opelika, AL Metro area........	140 247	158 991
	41007	Clatsop County, OR	37 039	38 632		01081	Lee County, AL	140 247	158 991
11860		Atchison, KS Micro area	16 924	16 380	12260		Augusta-Richmond County, GA-SC Metro area...................................	564 873	594 919
	20005	Atchison County, KS	16 924	16 380		13033	Burke County, GA	23 316	22 688
11900		Athens, OH Micro area....................	64 757	66 186		13073	Columbia County, GA	124 053	147 450
	39009	Athens County, OH	64 757	66 186		13181	Lincoln County, GA	7 996	7 828
11940		Athens, TN Micro area....................	52 266	52 850		13189	McDuffie County, GA	21 875	21 490
	47107	McMinn County, TN	52 266	52 850		13245	Richmond County, GA	200 549	201 647
11980		Athens, TX Micro area....................	78 532	79 901		45003	Aiken County, SC......................	160 099	167 458
	48213	Henderson County, TX................	78 532	79 901		45037	Edgefield County, SC.................	26 985	26 358
12020		Athens-Clarke County, GA Metro area..	192 541	205 290	12300		Augusta-Waterville, ME Micro area..	122 151	120 569
	13059	Clarke County, GA	116 714	124 707		23011	Kennebec County, ME	122 151	120 569
	13195	Madison County, GA..................	28 120	28 824	12380		Austin, MN Micro area.....................	39 163	39 163
	13219	Oconee County, GA....................	32 808	36 838		27099	Mower County, MN	39 163	39 163
	13221	Oglethorpe County, GA...............	14 899	14 921	12420		Austin-Round Rock, TX Metro area .	1 716 289	2 056 405
12060		Atlanta-Sandy Springs-Roswell, GA Metro area...................................	5 286 728	5 789 700		48021	Bastrop County, TX....................	74 171	82 733
	13013	Barrow County, GA	69 367	77 126		48055	Caldwell County, TX...................	38 066	41 161
	13015	Bartow County, GA....................	100 157	103 807		48209	Hays County, TX	157 107	204 470
	13035	Butts County, GA	23 655	23 817		48453	Travis County, TX	1 024 266	1 199 323
	13045	Carroll County, GA.....................	110 527	116 261		48491	Williamson County, TX................	422 679	528 718
	13057	Cherokee County, GA................	214 346	241 689	12460		Bainbridge, GA Micro area	27 842	26 822
	13063	Clayton County, GA...................	259 424	279 462		13087	Decatur County, GA...................	27 842	26 822
	13067	Cobb County, GA.......................	688 078	748 150	12540		Bakersfield, CA Metro area	839 631	884 788
	13077	Coweta County, GA	127 317	140 526		06029	Kern County, CA	839 631	884 788
	13085	Dawson County, GA...................	22 330	23 604					
	13089	DeKalb County, GA...................	691 893	740 321					
	13097	Douglas County, GA..................	132 403	142 224					
	13113	Fayette County, GA...................	106 567	111 627					
	13117	Forsyth County, GA...................	175 511	221 009					
	13121	Fulton County, GA.....................	920 581	1 023 336					

Core Based Statistical Area	State/County FIPS Code	Title and Geographic Components	2010 Census Population	2016 Estimated Population
12580		Baltimore-Columbia-Towson, MD Metro area	2 710 489	2 798 886
	24003	Anne Arundel County, MD	537 656	568 346
	24005	Baltimore County, MD	805 029	831 026
	24013	Carroll County, MD	167 134	167 656
	24025	Harford County, MD	244 826	251 032
	24027	Howard County, MD	287 085	317 233
	24035	Queen Anne's County, MD	47 798	48 929
	24510	Baltimore city, MD	620 961	614 664
12620		Bangor, ME Metro area	153 923	151 806
	23019	Penobscot County, ME	153 923	151 806
12660		Baraboo, WI Micro area	61 976	63 949
	55111	Sauk County, WI Micro area	61 976	63 949
12680		Bardstown, KY Micro area	43 437	45 559
	21179	Nelson County, KY	43 437	45 559
12700		Barnstable Town, MA Metro area	215 888	214 276
	25001	Barnstable County, MA	215 888	214 276
12740		Barre, VT Micro area	59 534	58 504
	50023	Washington County, VT	59 534	58 504
12780		Bartlesville, OK Micro area	50 976	52 087
	40147	Washington County, OK	50 976	52 087
12820		Bastrop, LA Micro area	27 979	26 071
	22067	Morehouse Parish, LA	27 979	26 071
12860		Batavia, NY Micro area	60 079	58 482
	36037	Genesee County, NY	60 079	58 482
12900		Batesville, AR Micro area	36 647	37 168
	05063	Independence County, AR	36 647	37 168
12940		Baton Rouge, LA Metro area	802 484	835 175
	22005	Ascension Parish, LA	107 215	121 587
	22033	East Baton Rouge Parish, LA	440 171	447 037
	22037	East Feliciana Parish, LA	20 267	19 683
	22047	Iberville Parish, LA	33 387	32 920
	22063	Livingston Parish, LA	128 026	140 138
	22077	Pointe Coupee Parish, LA	22 802	22 159
	22091	St. Helena Parish, LA	11 203	10 512
	22121	West Baton Rouge Parish, LA	23 788	25 795
	22125	West Feliciana Parish, LA	15 625	15 344
12980		Battle Creek, MI Metro area	136 146	134 386
	26025	Calhoun County, MI	136 146	134 386
13020		Bay City, MI Metro area	107 771	104 747
	26017	Bay County, MI	107 771	104 747
13060		Bay City, TX Micro area	36 702	37 187
	48321	Matagorda County, TX	36 702	37 187
13100		Beatrice, NE Micro area	22 311	21 799
	31067	Gage County, NE Micro area	22 311	21 799
13140		Beaumont-Port Arthur, TX Metro area	403 190	409 968
	48199	Hardin County, TX	54 635	56 322
	48245	Jefferson County, TX	252 273	254 679
	48351	Newton County, TX	14 445	14 003
	48361	Orange County, TX	81 837	84 964
13180		Beaver Dam, WI Micro area	88 759	88 068
	55027	Dodge County, WI	88 759	88 068
13220		Beckley, WV Metro area	124 898	120 924
	54019	Fayette County, WV	46 039	44 323
	54081	Raleigh County, WV	78 859	76 601
13260		Bedford, IN Micro area	46 134	45 518
	18093	Lawrence County, IN	46 134	45 518
13300		Beeville, TX Micro area	31 861	32 750
	48025	Bee County, TX	31 861	32 750
13340		Bellefontaine, OH Micro area	45 858	45 165
	39091	Logan County, OH	45 858	45 165
13380		Bellingham, WA Metro area	201 140	216 800
	53073	Whatcom County, WA	201 140	216 800
13420		Bemidji, MN Micro area	44 442	46 106
	27007	Beltrami County, MN	44 442	46 106
13460		Bend-Redmond, OR Metro area	157 733	181 307
	41017	Deschutes County, OR	157 733	181 307
13500		Bennettsville, SC Micro area	28 933	26 945
	45069	Marlboro County, SC	28 933	26 945
13540		Bennington, VT Micro area	37 125	36 191
	50003	Bennington County, VT	37 125	36 191
13620		Berlin, NH-VT Micro area	39 361	38 215
	33007	Coos County, NH	33 055	32 039
	50009	Essex County, VT	6 306	6 176
13660		Big Rapids, MI Micro area	42 798	43 221
	26107	Mecosta County, MI	42 798	43 221
13700		Big Spring, TX Micro area	36 238	38 022
	48173	Glasscock County, TX	1 226	1 314
	48227	Howard County, TX	35 012	36 708
13720		Big Stone Gap, VA Micro area	61 313	58 060
	51051	Dickenson County, VA	15 903	14 968
	51195	Wise County, VA	41 452	39 228
	51720	Norton city, VA	3 958	3 864
13740		Billings, MT Metro area	158 934	169 728
	30009	Carbon County, MT	10 078	10 460
	30037	Golden Valley County, MT	884	831
	30111	Yellowstone County, MT	147 972	158 437
13780		Binghamton, NY Metro area	251 725	244 094
	36007	Broome County, NY	200 600	195 334
	36107	Tioga County, NY	51 125	48 760
13820		Birmingham-Hoover, AL Metro area	1 128 047	1 147 417
	01007	Bibb County, AL	22 915	22 643
	01009	Blount County, AL	57 322	57 704
	01021	Chilton County, AL	43 643	43 941
	01073	Jefferson County, AL	658 466	659 521
	01115	St. Clair County, AL	83 593	88 019
	01117	Shelby County, AL	195 085	210 622
	01127	Walker County, AL	67 023	64 967
13900		Bismarck, ND Metro area	114 778	131 635
	38015	Burleigh County, ND	81 308	94 487
	38059	Morton County, ND	27 471	30 809
	38065	Oliver County, ND	1 846	1 870
	38085	Sioux County, ND	4 153	4 469

Core Based Statistical Areas (Metropolitan and Micropolitan), Metropolitan Divisions, and Components (as defined July 2015)–*Continued*

Core Based Statistical Area	State/County FIPS Code	Title and Geographic Components	2010 Census Population	2016 Estimated Population	Core Based Statistical Area	State/County FIPS Code	Title and Geographic Components	2010 Census Population	2016 Estimated Population
13940		Blackfoot, ID Micro area	45 607	45 201	14500		Boulder, CO Metro area	294 567	322 226
	16011	Bingham County, ID..........................	45 607	45 201		08013	Boulder County, CO..........................	294 567	322 226
13980		Blacksburg-Christiansburg-Radford, VA Metro area....................................	178 237	182 876	14540		Bowling Green, KY Metro area.........	158 599	171 122
	51063	Floyd County, VA	15 279	15 731		21003	Allen County, KY.............................	19 956	20 631
	51071	Giles County, VA	17 286	16 857		21031	Butler County, KY............................	12 690	12 845
	51121	Montgomery County, VA....................	94 392	98 602		21061	Edmonson County, KY......................	12 161	12 114
	51155	Pulaski County, VA	34 872	34 203		21227	Warren County, KY	113 792	125 532
	51750	Radford city, VA	16 408	17 483	14580		Bozeman, MT Micro area	89 513	104 502
14010		Bloomington, IL Metro area	186 133	188 644		30031	Gallatin County, MT	89 513	104 502
	17039	De Witt County, IL............................	16 561	16 226	14620		Bradford, PA Micro area	43 450	41 883
	17113	McLean County, IL...........................	169 572	172 418		42083	McKean County, PA..........................	43 450	41 883
14020		Bloomington, IN Metro area.............	159 549	166 336	14660		Brainerd, MN Micro area	91 067	92 933
	18105	Monroe County, IN...........................	137 974	145 496		27021	Cass County, MN.............................	28 567	28 993
	18119	Owen County, IN..............................	21 575	20 840		27035	Crow Wing County, MN	62 500	63 940
14100		Bloomsburg-Berwick, PA Metro area..	85 562	84 763	14700		Branson, MO Micro area	83 877	85 782
	42037	Columbia County, PA.......................	67 295	66 420		29209	Stone County, MO Micro area	32 202	31 047
	42093	Montour County, PA.........................	18 267	18 343		29213	Taney County, MO Micro area......	51 675	54 735
14140		Bluefield, WV-VA Micro area...........	107 342	102 618	14720		Breckenridge, CO Micro area..........	27 994	30 374
	51185	Tazewell County, VA........................	45 078	42 150		08117	Summit County, CO..........................	27 994	30 374
	54055	Mercer County, WV..........................	62 264	60 468	14740		Bremerton-Silverdale, WA Metro area..	251 133	264 811
14180		Blytheville, AR Micro area	46 480	42 835		53035	Kitsap County, WA	251 133	264 811
	05093	Mississippi County, AR	46 480	42 835	14780		Brenham, TX Micro area	33 718	35 056
14220		Bogalusa, LA Micro area	47 168	46 310		48477	Washington County, TX....................	33 718	35 056
	22117	Washington Parish, LA.....................	47 168	46 310	14820		Brevard, NC Micro area...................	33 090	33 482
14260		Boise City, ID Metro area	616 561	691 423		37175	Transylvania County, NC	33 090	33 482
	16001	Ada County, ID...............................	392 365	444 028	14860		Bridgeport-Stamford-Norwalk, CT Metro area...................................	916 829	944 177
	16015	Boise County, ID	7 028	7 124		09001	Fairfield County, CT	916 829	944 177
	16027	Canyon County, ID...........................	188 923	211 698	15020		Brookhaven, MS Micro area...........	34 869	34 523
	16045	Gem County, ID...............................	16 719	17 184		28085	Lincoln County, MS.........................	34 869	34 523
	16073	Owyhee County, ID..........................	11 526	11 389	15060		Brookings, OR Micro area	22 364	22 713
14300		Bonham, TX Micro Area	33 915	34 031		41015	Curry County, OR............................	22 364	22 713
	48147	Fannin County, TX............................	33 915	34 031	15100		Brookings, SD Micro area...............	31 965	34 135
14340		Boone, IA Micro area.......................	26 306	26 532		46011	Brookings County, SD....................	31 965	34 135
	19015	Boone County, IA.............................	26 306	26 532	15140		Brownsville, TN Micro Area	18 787	17 853
14380		Boone, NC Micro area	51 079	53 922		47075	Haywood County, TN....................	18 787	17 853
	37189	Watauga County, NC........................	51 079	53 922	15180		Brownsville-Harlingen, TX Metro area..	406 220	422 135
14420		Borger, TX Micro area	22 150	21 511		48061	Cameron County, TX	406 220	422 135
	48233	Hutchinson County, TX.....................	22 150	21 511	15220		Brownwood, TX Micro area	38 106	38 271
14460		Boston-Cambridge Newton, MA-NH Metro area..............................	4 552 402	4 794 447		48049	Brown County, TX...........................	38 106	38 271
		Boston, MA Metro Div 14454........	1 887 792	1 994 976	15260		Brunswick, GA Metro area..............	112 370	116 784
	25021	Norfolk County, MA	670 850	697 181		13025	Brantley County, GA	18 411	18 355
	25023	Plymouth County, MA...............	494 919	513 565		13127	Glynn County, GA	79 626	84 502
	25025	Suffolk County, MA.................	722 023	784 230		13191	McIntosh County, GA.....................	14 333	13 927
14460		Cambridge-Newton-Framingham, MA Metro Div 15764	2 246 244	2 368 792	15340		Bucyrus, OH Micro area.................	43 784	42 083
	25009	Essex County, MA.........................	743 159	779 018		39033	Crawford County, OH......................	43 784	42 083
	25017	Middlesex County, MA..............	1 503 085	1 589 774					
14460		Rockingham County-Strafford County-NH Metro Div 40484........	418 366	430 679					
	33015	Rockingham County, NH...........	295 223	303 251					
	33017	Strafford County, NH..................	123 143	127 428					

Core Based Statistical Areas (Metropolitan and Micropolitan), Metropolitan Divisions, and Components (as defined July 2015)–*Continued*

Core Based Statistical Area	State/County FIPS Code	Title and Geographic Components	2010 Census Population	2016 Estimated Population
15380		Buffalo-Cheektowaga-Niagara Falls, NY Metro area	1 135 509	1 132 804
	36029	Erie County, NY	919 040	921 046
	36063	Niagara County, NY	216 469	211 758
15420		Burley, ID Micro area	43 021	44 120
	16031	Cassia County, ID	22 952	23 504
	16067	Minidoka County, ID	20 069	20 616
15460		Burlington, IA-IL Micro area	47 656	46 608
	17071	Henderson County, IL	7 331	6 869
	19057	Des Moines County, IA	40 325	39 739
15500		Burlington, NC Metro area	151 131	159 688
	37001	Alamance County, NC	151 131	159 688
15540		Burlington-South Burlington, VT Metro area	211 261	217 365
	50007	Chittenden County, VT	156 545	161 531
	50011	Franklin County, VT	47 746	48 915
	50013	Grand Isle County, VT	6 970	6 919
15580		Butte-Silver Bow, MT Micro area	34 200	34 553
	30093	Silver Bow County, MT	34 200	34 553
15620		Cadillac, MI Micro area	47 584	48 265
	26113	Missaukee County, MI	14 849	15 102
	26165	Wexford County, MI	32 735	33 163
15660		Calhoun, GA Micro area	55 186	56 904
	13129	Gordon County, GA	55 186	56 904
15680		California-Lexington Park, MD Metro area	105 151	112 587
	24037	St. Mary's County, MD	105 151	112 587
15700		Cambridge, MD Micro area	32 618	32 258
	24019	Dorchester County, MD	32 618	32 258
15740		Cambridge, OH Micro area	40 087	39 063
	39059	Guernsey County, OH	40 087	39 063
15780		Camden, AR Micro area	31 488	29 242
	05013	Calhoun County, AR	5 368	5 144
	05103	Ouachita County, AR	26 120	24 098
15820		Campbellsville, KY Micro area	24 512	25 397
	21217	Taylor County, KY	24 512	25 397
15860		Cañon City, CO Micro area	46 824	47 446
	08043	Fremont County, CO	46 824	47 446
15900		Canton, IL Micro area	37 069	35 536
	17057	Fulton County, IL	37 069	35 536
15940		Canton-Massillon, OH Metro area	404 422	401 281
	39019	Carroll County, OH	28 836	27 669
	39151	Stark County, OH	375 586	373 612
15980		Cape Coral-Fort Myers, FL Metro area	618 754	722 336
	12071	Lee County, FL	618 754	722 336
16020		Cape Girardeau, MO-IL Metro area	96 275	97 443
	17003	Alexander County, IL	8 238	6 478
	29017	Bollinger County, MO	12 363	12 052
	29031	Cape Girardeau County, MO	75 674	78 913
16060		Carbondale-Marion, IL Metro area	126 575	126 430
	17077	Jackson County, IL	60 218	58 870
	17199	Williamson County, IL	66 357	67 560
16100		Carlsbad-Artesia, NM Micro area	53 829	57 621
	35015	Eddy County, NM	53 829	57 621
16140		Carroll, IA Micro Area	20 816	20 437
	19027	Carroll County, IA	20 816	20 437
16180		Carson City, NV Metro area	55 274	54 742
	32510	Carson City, NV Metro area	55 274	54 742
16220		Casper, WY Metro area	75 450	81 039
	56025	Natrona County, WY	75 450	81 039
16260		Cedar City, UT Micro area	46 163	49 937
	49021	Iron County, UT	46 163	49 937
16300		Cedar Rapids, IA Metro area	257 940	267 799
	19011	Benton County, IA	26 076	25 699
	19105	Jones County, IA	20 638	20 439
	19113	Linn County, IA	211 226	221 661
16340		Cedartown, GA Micro area	41 475	41 776
	13233	Polk County, GA	41 475	41 776
16380		Celina, OH Micro area	40 814	40 909
	39107	Mercer County, OH	40 814	40 909
16420		Central City, KY Micro Area	31 499	31 028
	21177	Muhlenberg County, KY	31 499	31 028
16460		Centralia, IL Micro area	39 437	38 140
	17121	Marion County, IL	39 437	38 140
16500		Centralia, WA Micro area	75 455	77 066
	53041	Lewis County, WA	75 455	77 066
16540		Chambersburg-Waynesboro, PA Metro area	149 618	153 851
	42055	Franklin County, PA	149 618	153 851
16580		Champaign-Urbana, IL Metro area	231 891	238 554
	17019	Champaign County, IL	201 081	208 419
	17053	Ford County, IL	14 081	13 575
	17147	Piatt County, IL	16 729	16 560
16620		Charleston, WV Metro area	227 078	217 916
	54005	Boone County, WV	24 629	22 816
	54015	Clay County, WV	9 386	8 859
	54039	Kanawha County, WV	193 063	186 241
16660		Charleston-Mattoon, IL Micro area	64 921	63 201
	17029	Coles County, IL	53 873	52 343
	17035	Cumberland County, IL	11 048	10 858
16700		Charleston-North Charleston, SC Metro area	664 607	761 155
	45015	Berkeley County, SC	177 843	210 898
	45019	Charleston County, SC	350 209	396 484
	45035	Dorchester County, SC	136 555	153 773

Core Based Statistical Areas (Metropolitan and Micropolitan), Metropolitan Divisions, and Components (as defined July 2015)–*Continued*

Core Based Statistical Area	State/County FIPS Code	Title and Geographic Components	2010 Census Population	2016 Estimated Population	Core Based Statistical Area	State/County FIPS Code	Title and Geographic Components	2010 Census Population	2016 Estimated Population
16740		Charlotte-Concord-Gastonia, NC-SC Metro area..............	2 217 012	2 474 314	17140		Cincinnati, OH-KY-IN Metro area	2 114 580	2 165 139
	37025	Cabarrus County, NC......................	178 011	201 590		18029	Dearborn County, IN	50 047	49 331
	37071	Gaston County, NC.......................	206 086	216 965		18115	Ohio County, IN............................	6 128	5 932
	37097	Iredell County, NC........................	159 437	172 916		18161	Union County, IN..........................	7 516	7 212
	37109	Lincoln County, NC.......................	78 265	81 168		21015	Boone County, KY........................	118 811	128 536
	37119	Mecklenburg County, NC.............	919 628	1 054 835		21023	Bracken County, KY......................	8 488	8 400
	37159	Rowan County, NC.......................	138 428	139 933		21037	Campbell County, KY....................	90 336	92 211
	37179	Union County, NC.........................	201 292	226 606		21077	Gallatin County, KY......................	8 589	8 609
	45023	Chester County, SC......................	33 140	32 181		21081	Grant County, KY.........................	24 662	24 923
	45057	Lancaster County, SC...................	76 652	89 594		21117	Kenton County, KY.......................	159 720	164 945
	45091	York County, SC..........................	226 073	258 526		21191	Pendleton County, KY...................	14 877	14 560
16820		Charlottesville, VA Metro area..........	218 705	231 349		39015	Brown County, OH........................	44 846	43 759
	51003	Albemarle County, VA...................	98 970	106 878		39017	Butler County, OH........................	368 130	377 537
	51029	Buckingham County, VA	17 146	17 048		39025	Clermont County, OH....................	197 363	203 022
	51065	Fluvanna County, VA....................	25 691	26 271		39061	Hamilton County, OH....................	802 374	809 099
	51079	Greene County, VA.......................	18 403	19 371		39165	Warren County, OH......................	212 693	227 063
	51125	Nelson County, VA.......................	15 020	14 869	17200		Claremont-Lebanon, NH-VT Micro area......	218 466	216 307
	51540	Charlottesville city, VA	43 475	46 912		33009	Grafton County, NH......................	89 118	88 888
16860		Chattanooga, TN-GA Metro area	528 143	551 632		33019	Sullivan County, NH.....................	43 742	43 004
	13047	Catoosa County, GA.....................	63 942	66 398		50017	Orange County, VT	28 936	28 919
	13083	Dade County, GA.........................	16 633	16 257		50027	Windsor County, VT	56 670	55 496
	13295	Walker County, GA.......................	68 756	67 896	17220		Clarksburg, WV Micro area	94 196	93 672
	47065	Hamilton County, TN.....................	336 463	357 738		54017	Doddridge County, WV	8 202	8 413
	47115	Marion County, TN........................	28 237	28 446		54033	Harrison County, WV	69 099	68 400
	47153	Sequatchie County, TN.................	14 112	14 897		54091	Taylor County, WV	16 895	16 859
16940		Cheyenne, WY Metro area..............	91 738	98 136	17260		Clarksdale, MS Micro area	26 151	23 809
	56021	Laramie County, WY	91 738	98 136		28027	Coahoma County, MS...................	26 151	23 809
16980		Chicago-Naperville-Elgin, IL-IN-WI Metro area...........................	9 461 105	9 512 999	17300		Clarksville, TN-KY Metro area..........	260 625	282 349
		Chicago-Naperville-Arlington Heights, IL Metro Div 16974	7 262 718	7 304 532		21047	Christian County, KY....................	73 955	72 351
						21221	Trigg County, KY.........................	14 339	14 264
	17031	Cook County, IL...........................	5 194 675	5 203 499		47125	Montgomery County, TN...............	172 331	195 734
	17043	DuPage County, IL	916 924	929 368	17340		Clearlake, CA Micro area	64 665	64 116
	17063	Grundy County, IL........................	50 063	50 437		06033	Lake County, CA..........................	64 665	64 116
	17093	Kendall County, IL........................	114 736	124 695	17380		Cleveland, MS Micro area	34 145	32 737
	17111	McHenry County, IL......................	308 760	307 004		28011	Bolivar County, MS	34 145	32 737
	17197	Will County, IL	677 560	689 529					
16980		Elgin, IL Metro Div 20994	620 429	636 243	17420		Cleveland, TN Metro area	115 788	121 262
	17037	DeKalb County, IL........................	105 160	104 528		47011	Bradley County, TN......................	98 963	104 490
	17089	Kane County, IL...........................	515 269	531 715		47139	Polk County, TN	16 825	16 772
16980		Gary, IN Metro Div 23844	708 070	700 994	17460		Cleveland-Elyria, OH Metro area......	2 077 240	2 055 612
	18073	Jasper County, IN........................	33 478	33 433		39035	Cuyahoga County, OH..................	1 280 122	1 249 352
	18089	Lake County, IN...........................	496 005	485 846		39055	Geauga County, OH.....................	93 389	94 060
	18111	Newton County, IN	14 244	13 924		39085	Lake County, OH.........................	230 041	228 614
	18127	Porter County, IN.........................	164 343	167 791		39093	Lorain County, OH.......................	301 356	306 365
16980		Lake County-Kenosha County, IL-WI Metro Div 29404	869 888	871 230		39103	Medina County, OH......................	172 332	177 221
	17097	Lake County, IL	703 462	703 047	17500		Clewiston, FL Micro area................	39 140	39 290
	55059	Kenosha County, WI.....................	166 426	168 183		12051	Hendry County, FL.......................	39 140	39 290
17020		Chico, CA Metro area	220 000	226 864	17540		Clinton, IA Micro area.....................	49 116	47 309
	06007	Butte County, CA.........................	220 000	226 864		19045	Clinton County, IA	49 116	47 309
17060		Chillicothe, OH Micro area..............	78 064	77 000	17580		Clovis, NM Micro area....................	48 376	50 280
	39141	Ross County, OH	78 064	77 000		35009	Curry County, NM........................	48 376	50 280
					17660		Coeur d'Alene, ID Metro area...........	138 494	154 311
						16055	Kootenai County, ID.....................	138 494	154 311
					17700		Coffeyville, KS Micro area	35 471	32 746
						20125	Montgomery County, KS..............	35 471	32 746

Core Based Statistical Areas (Metropolitan and Micropolitan), Metropolitan Divisions, and Components (as defined July 2015)–*Continued*

Core Based Statistical Area	State/County FIPS Code	Title and Geographic Components	2010 Census Population	2016 Estimated Population
17740		Coldwater, MI Micro area	45 248	43 427
	26023	Branch County, MI	45 248	43 427
17780		College Station-Bryan, TX Metro area	228 660	254 928
	48041	Brazos County, TX	194 851	220 417
	48051	Burleson County, TX	17 187	17 760
	48395	Robertson County, TX	16 622	16 751
17820		Colorado Springs, CO Metro area	645 613	712 327
	08041	El Paso County, CO	622 263	688 284
	08119	Teller County, CO	23 350	24 043
17860		Columbia, MO Metro area	162 642	176 594
	29019	Boone County, MO	162 642	176 594
17900		Columbia, SC Metro area	767 598	817 488
	45017	Calhoun County, SC	15 175	14 796
	45039	Fairfield County, SC	23 956	22 653
	45055	Kershaw County, SC	61 697	64 097
	45063	Lexington County, SC	262 391	286 196
	45079	Richland County, SC	384 504	409 549
	45081	Saluda County, SC	19 875	20 197
17980		Columbus, GA-AL Metro area	294 865	308 755
	01113	Russell County, AL	52 947	58 172
	13053	Chattahoochee County, GA	11 267	10 922
	13145	Harris County, GA	32 024	33 652
	13197	Marion County, GA	8 742	8 524
	13215	Muscogee County, GA	189 885	197 485
18020		Columbus, IN Metro area	76 794	81 402
	18005	Bartholomew County, IN	76 794	81 402
18060		Columbus, MS Micro area	59 779	59 602
	28087	Lowndes County, MS	59 779	59 602
18100		Columbus, NE Micro area	32 237	32 861
	31141	Platte County, NE	32 237	32 861
18140		Columbus, OH Metro area	1 901 974	2 041 520
	39041	Delaware County, OH	174 214	196 463
	39045	Fairfield County, OH	146 156	152 597
	39049	Franklin County, OH	1 163 414	1 264 518
	39073	Hocking County, OH	29 380	28 340
	39089	Licking County, OH	166 492	172 198
	39097	Madison County, OH	43 435	43 419
	39117	Morrow County, OH	34 827	35 036
	39127	Perry County, OH	36 058	35 927
	39129	Pickaway County, OH	55 698	57 565
	39159	Union County, OH	52 300	55 457
18180		Concord, NH Micro area	146 445	148 582
	33013	Merrimack County, NH	146 445	148 582
18220		Connersville, IN Micro area	24 277	23 331
	18041	Fayette County, IN	24 277	23 331
18260		Cookeville, TN Micro area	106 042	109 548
	47087	Jackson County, TN	11 638	11 566
	47133	Overton County, TN	22 083	22 051
	47141	Putnam County, TN	72 321	75 931
18300		Coos Bay, OR Micro area	63 043	63 761
	41011	Coos County, OR	63 043	63 761
18380		Cordele, GA Micro area	23 439	22 721
	13081	Crisp County, GA	23 439	22 721
18420		Corinth, MS Micro area	37 057	37 304
	28003	Alcorn County, MS	37 057	37 304
18460		Cornelia, GA Micro area	43 041	44 246
	13137	Habersham County, GA	43 041	44 246
18500		Corning, NY Micro area	98 990	96 940
	36101	Steuben County, NY	98 990	96 940
18580		Corpus Christi, TX Metro area	428 185	454 726
	48007	Aransas County, TX	23 158	25 721
	48355	Nueces County, TX	340 223	361 350
	48409	San Patricio County, TX	64 804	67 655
18620		Corsicana, TX Micro area	47 735	48 523
	48349	Navarro County, TX	47 735	48 523
18660		Cortland, NY Micro area	49 336	48 070
	36023	Cortland County, NY	49 336	48 070
18700		Corvallis, OR Metro area	85 579	89 385
	41003	Benton County, OR	85 579	89 385
18740		Coshocton, OH Micro area	36 901	36 602
	39031	Coshocton County, OH	36 901	36 602
18780		Craig, CO Micro area	13 795	13 109
	08081	Moffat County, CO	13 795	13 109
18820		Crawfordsville, IN Micro area	38 124	38 074
	18107	Montgomery County, IN	38 124	38 074
18860		Crescent City, CA Micro area	28 610	27 540
	06015	Del Norte County, CA	28 610	27 540
18880		Crestview-Fort Walton Beach-Destin, FL Metro area	235 865	267 059
	12091	Okaloosa County, FL	180 822	201 170
	12131	Walton County, FL	55 043	65 889
18900		Crossville, TN Micro area	56 053	58 655
	47035	Cumberland County, TN	56 053	58 655
18980		Cullman, AL Micro area	80 406	82 471
	01043	Cullman County, AL	80 406	82 471
19000		Cullowhee, NC Micro area	40 271	42 241
	37099	Jackson County, NC	40 271	42 241
19060		Cumberland, MD-WV Metro area	103 299	99 541
	24001	Allegany County, MD	75 087	72 130
	54057	Mineral County, WV	28 212	27 411
19100		Dallas-Fort Worth-Arlington, TX Metro area	6 426 214	7 233 323
		Dallas-Plano-Irving, TX Metro Div 19124	4 230 520	4 793 649
	48085	Collin County, TX	782 341	939 585
	48113	Dallas County, TX	2 368 139	2 574 984
	48121	Denton County, TX	662 614	806 180
	48139	Ellis County, TX	149 610	168 499
	48231	Hunt County, TX	86 129	92 073
	48257	Kaufman County, TX	103 350	118 350
	48397	Rockwall County, TX	78 337	93 978

Core Based Statistical Area	State/ County FIPS Code	Title and Geographic Components	2010 Census Population	2016 Estimated Population	Core Based Statistical Area	State/ County FIPS Code	Title and Geographic Components	2010 Census Population	2016 Estimated Population
19100		Fort Worth-Arlington, TX Metro Div 23104	2 195 694	2 439 674	19740		Denver-Aurora-Lakewood, CO Metro area..........	2 543 482	2 853 077
	48221	Hood County, TX..............	51 182	56 857		08001	Adams County, CO..............	441 603	498 187
	48251	Johnson County, TX..............	150 934	163 274		08005	Arapahoe County, CO..............	572 003	637 068
	48367	Parker County, TX..............	116 927	129 441		08014	Broomfield County, CO..............	55 889	66 529
	48425	Somervell County, TX..............	8 490	8 775		08019	Clear Creek County, CO..............	9 088	9 436
	48439	Tarrant County, TX..............	1 809 034	2 016 872		08031	Denver County, CO..............	600 158	693 060
	48497	Wise County, TX..............	59 127	64 455		08035	Douglas County, CO..............	285 465	328 632
19140		Dalton, GA Metro area..............	142 227	143 904		08039	Elbert County, CO..............	23 086	25 231
	13213	Murray County, GA..............	39 628	39 315		08047	Gilpin County, CO..............	5 441	5 931
	13313	Whitfield County, GA..............	102 599	104 589		08059	Jefferson County, CO..............	534 543	571 837
						08093	Park County, CO..............	16 206	17 166
19180		Danville, IL Metro area..............	81 625	78 111	19760		DeRidder, LA Micro area..............	35 654	36 927
	17183	Vermilion County, IL..............	81 625	78 111		22011	Beauregard Parish, LA..............	35 654	36 927
19220		Danville, KY Micro area..............	53 174	54 390	19780		Des Moines-West Des Moines, IA Metro area..............	569 633	634 725
	21021	Boyle County, KY..............	28 432	30 018		19049	Dallas County, IA..............	66 135	84 516
	21137	Lincoln County, KY..............	24 742	24 372		19077	Guthrie County, IA..............	10 954	10 625
19260		Danville, VA Micro area..............	106 561	103 585		19121	Madison County, IA..............	15 679	15 848
	51143	Pittsylvania County, VA..............	63 506	61 687		19153	Polk County, IA..............	430 640	474 045
	51590	Danville city, VA..............	43 055	41 898		19181	Warren County, IA..............	46 225	49 691
19300		Daphne-Fairhope-Foley, AL Metro area..............	182 265	208 563	19820		Detroit-Warren-Dearborn, MI Metro area..............	4 296 250	4 297 617
	01003	Baldwin County, AL..............	182 265	208 563			Detroit-Dearborn-Livonia, MI Metro Div 19804..............	1 820 584	1 749 366
19340		Davenport-Moline-Rock Island, IA-IL Metro area..............	379 690	382 268		26163	Wayne County, MI..............	1 820 584	1 749 366
	17073	Henry County, IL..............	50 486	49 280	19820		Warren-Troy-Farmington Hills, MI Metro Div 47664..............	2 475 666	2 548 251
	17131	Mercer County, IL..............	16 434	15 730		26087	Lapeer County, MI..............	88 319	88 340
	17161	Rock Island County, IL..............	147 546	144 784		26093	Livingston County, MI..............	180 967	188 624
	19163	Scott County, IA..............	165 224	172 474		26099	Macomb County, MI..............	840 978	867 730
19380		Dayton, OH Metro area..............	799 232	800 683		26125	Oakland County, MI..............	1 202 362	1 243 970
	39057	Greene County, OH..............	161 573	164 765		26147	St. Clair County, MI..............	163 040	159 587
	39109	Miami County, OH..............	102 506	104 679					
	39113	Montgomery County, OH..............	535 153	531 239	19860		Dickinson, ND Micro area..............	24 199	31 199
19420		Dayton, TN Micro area..............	31 809	32 442		38089	Stark County, ND..............	24 199	31 199
	47143	Rhea County, TN..............	31 809	32 442	19940		Dixon, IL Micro area..............	36 031	34 251
19460		Decatur, AL Metro area..............	153 829	152 256		17103	Lee County, IL..............	36 031	34 251
	01079	Lawrence County, AL..............	34 339	33 244	19980		Dodge City, KS Micro area..............	33 848	33 971
	01103	Morgan County, AL..............	119 490	119 012		20057	Ford County, KS..............	33 848	33 971
19500		Decatur, IL Metro area..............	110 768	106 550	20020		Dothan, AL Metro area..............	145 639	147 834
	17115	Macon County, IL..............	110 768	106 550		01061	Geneva County, AL..............	26 790	26 614
19540		Decatur, IN Micro area..............	34 387	35 232		01067	Henry County, AL..............	17 302	17 164
	18001	Adams County, IN..............	34 387	35 232		01069	Houston County, AL..............	101 547	104 056
19580		Defiance, OH Micro area..............	39 037	38 158	20060		Douglas, GA Micro area..............	42 356	43 012
	39039	Defiance County, OH..............	39 037	38 158		13069	Coffee County, GA..............	42 356	43 012
19620		Del Rio, TX Micro area..............	48 879	48 881	20100		Dover, DE Metro area..............	162 310	174 827
	48465	Val Verde County, TX..............	48 879	48 881		10001	Kent County, Delaware..............	162 310	174 827
19660		Deltona-Daytona Beach-Ormond Beach, FL Metro area..............	590 289	637 674	20140		Dublin, GA Micro area..............	58 414	57 021
	12035	Flagler County, FL..............	95 696	108 310		13167	Johnson County, GA..............	9 980	9 505
	12127	Volusia County, FL..............	494 593	529 364		13175	Laurens County, GA..............	48 434	47 516
19700		Deming, NM Micro area..............	25 095	24 450	20180		DuBois, PA Micro area..............	81 642	80 596
	35029	Luna County, NM..............	25 095	24 450		42033	Clearfield County, PA..............	81 642	80 596
					20220		Dubuque, IA Metro area..............	93 653	97 003
						19061	Dubuque County, IA..............	93 653	97 003

Core Based Statistical Areas (Metropolitan and Micropolitan), Metropolitan Divisions, and Components (as defined July 2015)–*Continued*

Core Based Statistical Area	State/ County FIPS Code	Title and Geographic Components	2010 Census Population	2016 Estimated Population	Core Based Statistical Area	State/ County FIPS Code	Title and Geographic Components	2010 Census Population	2016 Estimated Population
20260		Duluth, MN-WI Metro area................	279 771	279 227	21120		Elk City, OK Micro area...................	22 119	22 519
	27017	Carlton County, MN.....................	35 386	35 738		40009	Beckham County, OK....................	22 119	22 519
	27137	St. Louis County, MN....................	200 226	199 980	21140		Elkhart-Goshen, IN Metro area.........	197 559	203 781
	55031	Douglas County, WI	44 159	43 509		18039	Elkhart County, IN.......................	197 559	203 781
20300		Dumas, TX Micro area......................	21 904	22 120	21180		Elkins, WV Micro area...................	29 405	29 006
	48341	Moore County, TX........................	21 904	22 120		54083	Randolph County, WV..................	29 405	29 006
20340		Duncan, OK Micro area...................	45 048	44 090	21220		Elko, NV Micro area......................	50 805	54 085
	40137	Stephens County, OK...................	45 048	44 090		32007	Elko County, NV	48 818	52 168
20380		Dunn, NC Micro area......................	114 678	130 881		32011	Eureka County, NV	1 987	1 917
	37085	Harnett County, NC......................	114 678	130 881	21260		Ellensburg, WA Micro area..............	40 915	44 866
20420		Durango, CO Micro area	51 334	55 623		53037	Kittitas County, WA.....................	40 915	44 866
	08067	La Plata County, CO....................	51 334	55 623	21300		Elmira, NY Metro area....................	88 830	86 322
20460		Durant, OK Micro area....................	42 416	45 573		36015	Chemung County, NY	88 830	86 322
	40013	Bryan County, OK	42 416	45 573	21340		El Paso, TX Metro area..................	804 123	841 971
20500		Durham-Chapel Hill, NC Metro area	504 357	559 535		48141	El Paso County, TX.....................	800 647	837 918
	37037	Chatham County, NC....................	63 505	72 243		48229	Hudspeth County, TX..................	3 476	4 053
	37063	Durham County, NC.....................	267 587	306 212	21380		Emporia, KS Micro area	33 690	33 510
	37135	Orange County, NC.....................	133 801	141 796		20111	Lyon County, KS........................	33 690	33 510
	37145	Person County, NC	39 464	39 284	21420		Enid, OK Metro area.....................	60 580	62 603
20540		Dyersburg, TN Micro area	38 335	37 708		40047	Garfield County, OK....................	60 580	62 603
	47045	Dyer County, TN	38 335	37 708	21460		Enterprise, AL Micro area...............	49 948	51 226
20580		Eagle Pass, TX Micro area..............	54 258	57 685		01031	Coffee County, AL......................	49 948	51 226
	48323	Maverick County, TX....................	54 258	57 685	21500		Erie, PA Metro area......................	280 566	276 207
20660		Easton, MD Micro area...................	37 782	37 278		42049	Erie County, PA.........................	280 566	276 207
	24041	Talbot County, MD	37 782	37 278	21540		Escanaba, MI Micro area................	37 069	36 202
20700		East Stroudsburg, PA Metro area	169 842	166 098		26041	Delta County, MI	37 069	36 202
	42089	Monroe County, PA.....................	169 842	166 098	21580		Española, NM Micro area................	40 246	40 040
20740		Eau Claire, WI Metro area...............	161 151	166 614		35039	Rio Arriba County, NM	40 246	40 040
	55017	Chippewa County, WI	62 415	63 649	21640		Eufaula, AL-GA Micro Area	29 970	28 300
	55035	Eau Claire County, WI	98 736	102 965		01005	Barbour County, AL....................	27 457	25 965
20780		Edwards, CO Micro area	52 197	53 989		13239	Quitman County, GA	2 513	2 335
	08037	Eagle County, CO	52 197	53 989	21660		Eugene, OR Metro area	351 715	369 519
20820		Effingham, IL Micro area.................	34 242	34 386		41039	Lane County, OR	351 715	369 519
	17049	Effingham County, IL....................	34 242	34 386	21700		Eureka-Arcata-Fortuna, CA Micro area	134 623	136 646
20900		El Campo, TX Micro area................	41 280	41 735		06023	Humboldt County, CA	134 623	136 646
	48481	Wharton County, TX	41 280	41 735	21740		Evanston, WY Micro area...............	21 118	20 773
20940		El Centro, CA Metro area...............	174 528	180 883		56041	Uinta County, WY.......................	21 118	20 773
	06025	Imperial County, CA....................	174 528	180 883	21780		Evansville, IN-KY Metro area	311 552	315 948
20980		El Dorado, AR Micro area	41 639	39 887		18129	Posey County, IN	25 910	25 476
	05139	Union County, AR.......................	41 639	39 887		18163	Vanderburgh County, IN	179 703	181 721
21020		Elizabeth City, NC Micro area	64 094	63 617		18173	Warrick County, IN	59 689	62 498
	37029	Camden County, NC....................	9 980	10 418		21101	Henderson County, KY	46 250	46 253
	37139	Pasquotank County, NC...............	40 661	39 864	21820		Fairbanks, AK Metro area...............	97 581	100 605
	37143	Perquimans County, NC	13 453	13 335		02090	Fairbanks North Star Borough, AK................................	97 581	100 605
21060		Elizabethtown-Fort Knox, KY Metro area....................................	148 338	149 538	21840		Fairfield, IA Micro area	16 843	18 090
	21093	Hardin County, KY	105 543	107 316		19101	Jefferson County, IA....................	16 843	18 090
	21123	Larue County, KY.......................	14 193	14 096					
	21163	Meade County, KY	28 602	28 126					

Core Based Statistical Areas (Metropolitan and Micropolitan), Metropolitan Divisions, and Components (as defined July 2015)–*Continued*

Core Based Statistical Area	State/County FIPS Code	Title and Geographic Components	2010 Census Population	2016 Estimated Population	Core Based Statistical Area	State/County FIPS Code	Title and Geographic Components	2010 Census Population	2016 Estimated Population
21860		Fairmont, MN Micro Area	20 840	19 829	22660		Fort Collins, CO Metro area	299 630	339 993
	27091	Martin County, MN	20 840	19 829		08069	Larimer County, CO	299 630	339 993
21900		Fairmont, WV Micro area...............	56 418	56 538	22700		Fort Dodge, IA Micro area...............	38 013	36 769
	54049	Marion County, WV	56 418	56 538		19187	Webster County, IA	38 013	36 769
21980		Fallon, NV Micro area...................	24 877	24 198	22780		Fort Leonard Wood, MO Micro area	52 274	52 654
	32001	Churchill County, NV	24 877	24 198		29169	Pulaski County, MO	52 274	52 654
22020		Fargo, ND-MN Metro area..............	208 777	238 124	22800		Fort Madison-Keokuk, IA-IL-MO Micro area....................................	62 105	59 846
	27027	Clay County, MN	58 999	62 875		17067	Hancock County, IL.......................	19 104	18 508
	38017	Cass County, ND	149 778	175 249		19111	Lee County, IA	35 862	34 615
22060		Faribault-Northfield, MN Micro area .	64 142	65 622		29045	Clark County, MO.........................	7 139	6 723
	27131	Rice County, MN	64 142	65 622	22820		Fort Morgan, CO Micro area	28 159	28 274
22100		Farmington, MO Micro area............	65 359	66 627		08087	Morgan County, CO	28 159	28 274
	29187	St. Francois County, MO..............	65 359	66 627	22840		Fort Payne, AL Micro Area.............	71 109	70 900
22140		Farmington, NM Metro area	130 044	115 079		01049	DeKalb County, AL	71 109	70 900
	35045	San Juan County, NM...................	130 044	115 079	22860		Fort Polk South, LA Micro area........	52 334	50 569
22180		Fayetteville, NC Metro area............	366 383	380 389		22115	Vernon Parish, LA	52 334	50 569
	37051	Cumberland County, NC.............	319 431	327 127	22900		Fort Smith, AR-OK Metro area........	280 467	281 227
	37093	Hoke County, NC	46 952	53 262		05033	Crawford County, AR	61 948	62 267
22220		Fayetteville-Springdale-Rogers, AR-MO Metro area.............................	463 204	525 032		05131	Sebastian County, AR...................	125 744	127 793
	05007	Benton County, AR	221 339	258 291		40079	Le Flore County, OK	50 384	49 873
	05087	Madison County, AR	15 717	16 072		40135	Sequoyah County, OK	42 391	41 294
	05143	Washington County, AR...............	203 065	228 049	23060		Fort Wayne, IN Metro area.............	416 257	431 802
	29119	McDonald County, MO................	23 083	22 620		18003	Allen County, IN	355 329	370 404
22260		Fergus Falls, MN Micro area...........	57 303	58 085		18179	Wells County, IN	27 636	27 949
	27111	Otter Tail County, MN	57 303	58 085		18183	Whitley County, IN	33 292	33 449
22280		Fernley, NV Micro area..................	51 980	53 179	23140		Frankfort, IN Micro area.................	33 224	32 457
	32019	Lyon County, NV	51 980	53 179		18023	Clinton County, IN	33 224	32 457
22300		Findlay, OH Micro area..................	74 782	75 872	23180		Frankfort, KY Micro area	70 706	72 718
	39063	Hancock County, OH	74 782	75 872		21005	Anderson County, KY...................	21 421	22 158
22340		Fitzgerald, GA Micro area...............	17 634	17 243		21073	Franklin County, KY	49 285	50 560
	13017	Ben Hill County, GA	17 634	17 243	23240		Fredericksburg, TX Micro area.........	24 837	26 521
22380		Flagstaff, AZ Metro area................	134 421	140 908		48171	Gillespie County, TX	24 837	26 521
	04005	Coconino County, AZ....................	134 421	140 908	23300		Freeport, IL Micro area..................	47 711	45 624
22420		Flint, MI Metro area	425 790	408 615		17177	Stephenson County, IL..................	47 711	45 624
	26049	Genesee County, MI	425 790	408 615	23340		Fremont, NE Micro area	36 691	36 757
22500		Florence, SC Metro area	205 566	205 976		31053	Dodge County, NE	36 691	36 757
	45031	Darlington County, SC	68 681	67 234	23380		Fremont, OH Micro area.................	60 944	59 330
	45041	Florence County, SC....................	136 885	138 742		39143	Sandusky County, OH...................	60 944	59 330
22520		Florence-Muscle Shoals, AL Metro area......................................	147 137	146 534	23420		Fresno, CA Metro area	930 450	979 915
	01033	Colbert County, AL.......................	54 428	54 216		06019	Fresno County, CA.......................	930 450	979 915
	01077	Lauderdale County, AL	92 709	92 318	23460		Gadsden, AL Metro area	104 430	102 564
22540		Fond du Lac, WI Metro area	101 633	102 144		01055	Etowah County, AL	104 430	102 564
	55039	Fond du Lac County, WI...............	101 633	102 144	23500		Gaffney, SC Micro area..................	55 342	56 646
22580		Forest City, NC Micro area.............	67 810	66 421		45021	Cherokee County, SC	55 342	56 646
	37161	Rutherford County, NC..................	67 810	66 421	23540		Gainesville, FL Metro area	264 275	280 708
22620		Forrest City, AR Micro area.............	28 258	26 196		12001	Alachua County, FL......................	247 336	263 496
	05123	St. Francis County, AR	28 258	26 196		12041	Gilchrist County, FL......................	16 939	17 212
					23580		Gainesville, GA Metro area	179 684	196 637
						13139	Hall County, GA	179 684	196 637

Core Based Statistical Area	State/County FIPS Code	Title and Geographic Components	2010 Census Population	2016 Estimated Population	Core Based Statistical Area	State/County FIPS Code	Title and Geographic Components	2010 Census Population	2016 Estimated Population
23620		Gainesville, TX Micro area	38 437	39 266	24420		Grants Pass, OR Metro area	82 713	85 904
	48097	Cooke County, TX	38 437	39 266		41033	Josephine County, OR	82 713	85 904
23660		Galesburg, IL Micro area	52 919	50 938	24460		Great Bend, KS Micro area	27 674	26 775
	17095	Knox County, IL	52 919	50 938		20009	Barton County, KS	27 674	26 775
23700		Gallup, NM Micro area	71 492	74 923	24500		Great Falls, MT Metro area	81 327	81 755
	35031	McKinley County, NM	71 492	74 923		30013	Cascade County, MT	81 327	81 755
23780		Garden City, KS Micro area	40 753	40 639	24540		Greeley, CO Metro area	252 825	294 932
	20055	Finney County, KS	36 776	36 722		08123	Weld County, CO	252 825	294 932
	20093	Kearny County, KS	3 977	3 917	24580		Green Bay, WI Metro area	306 241	318 236
23820		Gardnerville Ranchos, NV Micro area	46 997	48 020		55009	Brown County, WI	248 007	260 401
	32005	Douglas County, NV	46 997	48 020		55061	Kewaunee County, WI	20 574	20 405
						55083	Oconto County, WI	37 660	37 430
23860		Georgetown, SC Micro area	60 158	61 399	24620		Greeneville, TN Micro area	68 831	68 615
	45043	Georgetown County, SC	60 158	61 399		47059	Greene County, TN	68 831	68 615
23900		Gettysburg, PA Metro area	101 407	102 180	24640		Greenfield Town, MA Micro area	71 372	70 382
	42001	Adams County, PA	101 407	102 180		25011	Franklin County, MA	71 372	70 382
23940		Gillette, WY Micro area	46 133	48 803	24660		Greensboro-High Point, NC Metro area	723 801	756 139
	56005	Campbell County, WY	46 133	48 803		37081	Guilford County, NC	488 406	521 330
23980		Glasgow, KY Micro area	52 272	54 011		37151	Randolph County, NC	141 752	143 416
	21009	Barren County, KY	42 173	43 993		37157	Rockingham County, NC	93 643	91 393
	21169	Metcalfe County, KY	10 099	10 018	24700		Greensburg, IN Micro area	25 740	26 598
24020		Glens Falls, NY Metro area	128 923	126 367		18031	Decatur County, IN	25 740	26 598
	36113	Warren County, NY	65 707	64 567	24740		Greenville, MS Micro area	51 137	47 231
	36115	Washington County, NY	63 216	61 800		28151	Washington County, MS	51 137	47 231
24060		Glenwood Springs, CO Micro area	73 537	76 639	24780		Greenville, NC Metro area	168 148	177 220
	08045	Garfield County, CO	56 389	58 887		37147	Pitt County, NC	168 148	177 220
	08097	Pitkin County, CO	17 148	17 752	24820		Greenville, OH Micro area	52 959	51 778
24100		Gloversville, NY Micro area	55 531	53 828		39037	Darke County, OH	52 959	51 778
	36035	Fulton County, NY	55 531	53 828	24860		Greenville-Anderson-Mauldin, SC Metro area	824 112	884 975
24140		Goldsboro, NC Metro area	122 623	124 150		45007	Anderson County, SC	187 126	196 569
	37191	Wayne County, NC	122 623	124 150		45045	Greenville County, SC	451 225	498 766
24220		Grand Forks, ND-MN Metro area	98 461	102 743		45059	Laurens County, SC	66 537	66 777
	27119	Polk County, MN	31 600	31 660		45077	Pickens County, SC	119 224	122 863
	38035	Grand Forks County, ND	66 861	71 083	24900		Greenwood, MS Micro area	42 914	40 111
24260		Grand Island, NE Metro area	81 850	85 148		28015	Carroll County, MS	10 597	10 255
	31079	Hall County, NE	58 607	61 705		28083	Leflore County, MS	32 317	29 856
	31081	Hamilton County, NE	9 124	9 186	24940		Greenwood, SC Micro area	95 078	95 005
	31093	Howard County, NE	6 274	6 429		45001	Abbeville County, SC	25 417	24 872
	31121	Merrick County, NE	7 845	7 828		45047	Greenwood County, SC	69 661	70 133
24300		Grand Junction, CO Metro area	146 723	150 083	24980		Grenada, MS Micro area	21 906	21 275
	08077	Mesa County, CO	146 723	150 083		28043	Grenada County, MS	21 906	21 275
24330		Grand Rapids, MN Micro Area	45 058	45 242	25060		Gulfport-Biloxi-Pascagoula, MS Metro area	370 702	391 266
	27061	Itasca County, MN	45 058	45 242		28045	Hancock County, MS	43 929	46 791
24340		Grand Rapids-Wyoming, MI Metro area	988 938	1 047 099		28047	Harrison County, MS	187 105	203 234
	26015	Barry County, MI	59 173	59 702		28059	Jackson County, MS	139 668	141 241
	26081	Kent County, MI	602 622	642 173	25100		Guymon, OK Micro area	20 640	21 098
	26117	Montcalm County, MI	63 342	62 974		40139	Texas County, OK	20 640	21 098
	26139	Ottawa County, MI	263 801	282 250					
24380		Grants, NM Micro area	27 213	27 487					
	35006	Cibola County, NM	27 213	27 487					

Core Based Statistical Area	State/County FIPS Code	Title and Geographic Components	2010 Census Population	2016 Estimated Population	Core Based Statistical Area	State/County FIPS Code	Title and Geographic Components	2010 Census Population	2016 Estimated Population
25180		Hagerstown-Martinsburg, MD-WV Metro area............	251 599	263 817		41049	Morrow County, OR	11 173	11 274
	24043	Washington County, MD	147 430	150 292		41059	Umatilla County, OR	75 889	76 456
	54003	Berkeley County, WV..................	104 169	113 525	25860		Hickory-Lenoir-Morganton, NC Metro area...............	365 497	364 187
25200		Hailey, ID Micro area...............	27 701	28 134		37003	Alexander County, NC	37 198	37 428
	16013	Blaine County, ID.......................	21 376	21 791		37023	Burke County, NC	90 912	88 851
	16025	Camas County, ID......................	1 117	1 072		37027	Caldwell County, NC	83 029	81 449
	16063	Lincoln County, ID......................	5 208	5 271		37035	Catawba County, NC	154 358	156 459
25220		Hammond, LA Metro area...............	121 097	130 710	25880		Hillsdale, MI Micro area...............	46 688	45 774
	22105	Tangipahoa Parish, LA................	121 097	130 710		26059	Hillsdale County, MI	46 688	45 774
25260		Hanford-Corcoran, CA Metro area ...	152 982	149 785	25900		Hilo, HI Micro area...............	185 079	198 449
	06031	Kings County, CA.......................	152 982	149 785		15001	Hawaii County, HI	185 079	198 449
25300		Hannibal, MO Micro area...............	38 948	39 118	25940		Hilton Head Island-Bluffton-Beaufort, SC Metro area..................	187 010	211 614
	29127	Marion County, MO.....................	28 781	28 894		45013	Beaufort County, SC	162 233	183 149
	29173	Ralls County, MO........................	10 167	10 224		45053	Jasper County, SC.....................	24 777	28 465
25420		Harrisburg-Carlisle, PA Metro area ..	549 475	568 033	25980		Hinesville, GA Metro area...............	77 917	81 007
	42041	Cumberland County, PA	235 406	248 506		13179	Liberty County, GA....................	63 453	62 570
	42043	Dauphin County, PA....................	268 100	273 707		13183	Long County, GA.......................	14 464	18 437
	42099	Perry County, PA........................	45 969	45 820	26020		Hobbs, NM Micro area.................	64 727	69 749
25460		Harrison, AR Micro area.................	45 233	45 240		35025	Lea County, NM	64 727	69 749
	05009	Boone County, AR	36 903	37 304	26090		Holland, MI Micro area.................	111 408	115 548
	05101	Newton County, AR.....................	8 330	7 936		26005	Allegan County, MI	111 408	115 548
25500		Harrisonburg, VA Metro area...........	125 228	132 822	26140		Homosassa Springs, FL Metro area.	141 236	143 621
	51165	Rockingham County, VA..............	76 314	79 744		12017	Citrus County, FL	141 236	143 621
	51660	Harrisonburg city, VA	48 914	53 078	26220		Hood River, OR Micro area...............	22 346	23 232
25540		Hartford-West Hartford-East Hartford, CT Metro area	1 212 381	1 206 836		41027	Hood River County, OR	22 346	23 232
	09003	Hartford County, CT	894 014	892 389	26260		Hope, AR Micro Area..................	31 606	30 372
	09007	Middlesex County, CT.................	165 676	163 329		05057	Hempstead County, AR	22 609	21 974
	09013	Tolland County, CT.....................	152 691	151 118		05099	Nevada County, AR	8 997	8 398
25580		Hastings, NE Micro area.................	31 364	31 684	26300		Hot Springs, AR Metro area	96 024	97 477
	31001	Adams County, NE.......................	31 364	31 684		05051	Garland County, AR....................	96 024	97 477
25620		Hattiesburg, MS Metro area	142 842	149 138	26340		Houghton, MI Micro area.................	38 784	38 754
	28035	Forrest County, MS	74 934	75 979		26061	Houghton County, MI	36 628	36 555
	28073	Lamar County, MS......................	55 658	60 914		26083	Keweenaw County, MI	2 156	2 199
	28111	Perry County, MS........................	12 250	12 245	26380		Houma-Thibodaux, LA Metro area ...	208 178	211 525
25700		Hays, KS Micro area....................	28 452	28 893		22057	Lafourche Parish, LA...................	96 318	98 305
	20051	Ellis County, KS	28 452	28 893		22109	Terrebonne Parish, LA.................	111 860	113 220
25720		Heber, UT Micro area....................	23 530	30 528	26420		Houston-The Woodlands-Sugar Land, TX Metro area........................	5 920 416	6 772 470
	49051	Wasatch County, UT....................	23 530	30 528		48015	Austin County, TX	28 417	29 758
25740		Helena, MT Micro area...................	74 801	79 135		48039	Brazoria County, TX	313 166	354 195
	30043	Jefferson County, MT...................	11 406	11 853		48071	Chambers County, TX.................	35 096	39 899
	30049	Lewis and Clark County, MT........	63 395	67 282		48157	Fort Bend County, TX	585 375	741 237
25760		Helena-West Helena, AR Micro area..................	21 757	18 975		48167	Galveston County, TX	291 309	329 431
	05107	Phillips County, AR	21 757	18 975		48201	Harris County, TX.......................	4 092 459	4 589 928
25780		Henderson, NC Micro area..............	45 422	44 244		48291	Liberty County, TX	75 643	81 704
	37181	Vance County, NC	45 422	44 244		48339	Montgomery County, TX	455 746	556 203
25820		Hereford, TX Micro area.................	19 372	18 830		48473	Waller County, TX	43 205	50 115
	48117	Deaf Smith County, TX	19 372	18 830	26460		Hudson, NY Micro area..................	63 096	60 989
25840		Hermiston-Pendleton, OR Micro area..................	87 062	87 730		36021	Columbia County, NY..................	63 096	60 989
					26500	42061	Huntingdon, PA Micro area .... Huntingdon County, PA...............	45 913 45 913	45 634 45 634

Core Based Statistical Area	State/County FIPS Code	Title and Geographic Components	2010 Census Population	2016 Estimated Population	Core Based Statistical Area	State/County FIPS Code	Title and Geographic Components	2010 Census Population	2016 Estimated Population
26540		Huntington, IN Micro area................	37 124	36 400	27100		Jackson, MI Metro area..................	160 248	158 460
	18069	Huntington County, IN..................	37 124	36 400		26075	Jackson County, MI......................	160 248	158 460
26580		Huntington-Ashland, WV-KY-OH Metro area................	364 908	359 588	27140		Jackson, MS Metro area................	567 122	579 229
	21019	Boyd County, KY......................	49 542	48 132		28029	Copiah County, MS.....................	29 449	28 482
	21089	Greenup County, KY	36 910	35 893		28049	Hinds County, MS	245 285	241 229
	39087	Lawrence County, OH	62 450	60 872		28089	Madison County, MS	95 203	105 114
	54011	Cabell County, WV	96 319	95 987		28121	Rankin County, MS	141 617	150 228
	54043	Lincoln County, WV	21 720	21 232		28127	Simpson County, MS	27 503	26 912
	54079	Putnam County, WV	55 486	56 941		28163	Yazoo County, MS	28 065	27 264
	54099	Wayne County, WV	42 481	40 531	27160		Jackson, OH Micro area..................	33 225	32 505
26620		Huntsville, AL Metro area	417 593	449 720		39079	Jackson County, OH	33 225	32 505
	01083	Limestone County, AL...................	82 782	92 753	27180		Jackson, TN Metro area................	130 011	129 527
	01089	Madison County, AL...................	334 811	356 967		47023	Chester County, TN	17 131	17 453
26660		Huntsville, TX Micro area	82 446	85 926		47033	Crockett County, TN...................	14 586	14 411
	48455	Trinity County, TX	14 585	14 442		47113	Madison County, TN	98 294	97 663
	48471	Walker County, TX	67 861	71 484	27220		Jackson, WY-ID Micro area.............	31 464	34 151
26700		Huron, SD Micro area....................	17 398	18 101		16081	Teton County, ID	10 170	10 960
	46005	Beadle County, SD......................	17 398	18 101		56039	Teton County, WY	21 294	23 191
26740		Hutchinson, KS Micro area..............	64 511	63 220	27260		Jacksonville, FL Metro area.............	1 345 596	1 478 212
	20155	Reno County, KS	64 511	63 220		12003	Baker County, FL	27 115	27 937
26780		Hutchinson, MN Micro area.............	36 651	35 842		12019	Clay County, FL	190 865	208 311
	27085	McLeod County, MN	36 651	35 842		12031	Duval County, FL	864 263	926 255
26820		Idaho Falls, ID Metro area.............	133 265	142 572		12089	Nassau County, FL	73 314	80 622
	16019	Bonneville County, ID...................	104 234	112 232		12109	St. Johns County, FL	190 039	235 087
	16023	Butte County, ID....................	2 891	2 501	27300		Jacksonville, IL Micro area	40 902	39 330
	16051	Jefferson County, ID	26 140	27 839		17137	Morgan County, IL	35 547	34 277
26860		Indiana, PA Micro area	88 880	86 364		17171	Scott County, IL.......................	5 355	5 053
	42063	Indiana County, PA	88 880	86 364	27340		Jacksonville, NC Metro area............	177 772	187 136
26900		Indianapolis-Carmel-Anderson, IN Metro area..................	1 887 877	2 004 230		37133	Onslow County, NC.....................	177 772	187 136
	18011	Boone County, IN	56 640	64 653	27380		Jacksonville, TX Micro area.............	50 845	51 668
	18013	Brown County, IN	15 242	14 912		48073	Cherokee County, TX..................	50 845	51 668
	18057	Hamilton County, IN	274 569	316 373	27420		Jamestown, ND Micro area	21 100	21 128
	18059	Hancock County, IN	70 002	73 717		38093	Stutsman County, ND	21 100	21 128
	18063	Hendricks County, IN	145 448	160 610	27460		Jamestown-Dunkirk-Fredonia, NY Micro area................................	134 905	129 504
	18081	Johnson County, IN....................	139 654	151 982		36013	Chautauqua County, NY	134 905	129 504
	18095	Madison County, IN....................	131 636	129 296	27500		Janesville-Beloit, WI Metro area.......	160 331	161 620
	18097	Marion County, IN....................	903 393	941 229		55105	Rock County, WI	160 331	161 620
	18109	Morgan County, IN....................	68 894	69 698	27540		Jasper, IN Micro area	54 734	54 983
	18133	Putnam County, IN	37 963	37 436		18037	Dubois County, IN	41 889	42 552
	18145	Shelby County, IN	44 436	44 324		18125	Pike County, IN	12 845	12 431
26940		Indianola, MS Micro area...............	29 450	26 407	27600		Jefferson, GA Micro area................	60 485	64 615
	28133	Sunflower County, MS	29 450	26 407		13157	Jackson County, GA	60 485	64 615
26960		Ionia, MI Micro area...................	63 905	64 232	27620		Jefferson City, MO Metro area	149 807	151 391
	26067	Ionia County, MI.......................	63 905	64 232		29027	Callaway County, MO	44 332	45 078
26980		Iowa City, IA Metro area..................	152 586	168 828		29051	Cole County, MO......................	75 990	76 631
	19103	Johnson County, IA....................	130 882	146 547		29135	Moniteau County, MO	15 607	16 018
	19183	Washington County, IA	21 704	22 281		29151	Osage County, MO	13 878	13 664
27020		Iron Mountain, MI-WI Micro area......	30 591	29 991	27660		Jennings, LA Micro Area	31 594	31 413
	26043	Dickinson County, MI	26 168	25 535		22053	Jefferson Davis Parish, LA............	31 594	31 413
	55037	Florence County, WI	4 423	4 456	27700		Jesup, GA Micro area................	30 099	30 104
27060		Ithaca, NY Metro area	101 564	104 871		13305	Wayne County, GA	30 099	30 104
	36109	Tompkins County, NY	101 564	104 871					

Core Based Statistical Areas (Metropolitan and Micropolitan), Metropolitan Divisions, and Components (as defined July 2015)–*Continued*

Core Based Statistical Area	State/County FIPS Code	Title and Geographic Components	2010 Census Population	2016 Estimated Population
27740		Johnson City, TN Metro area	198 716	201 661
	47019	Carter County, TN........................	57 424	56 502
	47171	Unicoi County, TN........................	18 313	17 719
	47179	Washington County, TN.................	122 979	127 440
27780		Johnstown, PA Metro area	143 679	134 732
	42021	Cambria County, PA	143 679	134 732
27860		Jonesboro, AR Metro area	121 026	129 858
	05031	Craighead County, AR	96 443	105 835
	05111	Poinsett County, AR.....................	24 583	24 023
27900		Joplin, MO Metro area	175 518	177 805
	29097	Jasper County, MO	117 404	119 111
	29145	Newton County, MO.....................	58 114	58 694
27920		Junction City, KS Micro area............	34 362	35 586
	20061	Geary County, KS	34 362	35 586
27940		Juneau, AK Micro area..................	31 275	32 468
	02110	Juneau City and Borough, AK	31 275	32 468
27980		Kahului-Wailuku-Lahaina, HI Metro area..	154 924	165 474
	15005	Kalawao County, HI	90	88
	15009	Maui County, HI	154 834	165 386
28020		Kalamazoo-Portage, MI Metro area .	326 589	336 877
	26077	Kalamazoo County, MI..................	250 331	261 654
	26159	Van Buren County, MI..................	76 258	75 223
28060		Kalispell, MT Micro area.................	90 928	98 082
	30029	Flathead County, MT....................	90 928	98 082
28100		Kankakee, IL Metro area	113 449	110 008
	17091	Kankakee County, IL....................	113 449	110 008
28140		Kansas City, MO-KS Metro area......	2 009 342	2 104 509
	20091	Johnson County, KS	544 179	584 451
	20103	Leavenworth County, KS	76 227	80 204
	20107	Linn County, KS	9 656	9 558
	20121	Miami County, KS	32 787	32 964
	20209	Wyandotte County, KS..................	157 505	163 831
	29013	Bates County, MO.......................	17 049	16 417
	29025	Caldwell County, MO	9 424	9 062
	29037	Cass County, MO........................	99 478	102 845
	29047	Clay County, MO.........................	221 939	239 085
	29049	Clinton County, MO......................	20 743	20 610
	29095	Jackson County, MO.....................	674 158	691 801
	29107	Lafayette County, MO...................	33 381	32 618
	29165	Platte County, MO.......................	89 322	98 309
	29177	Ray County, MO..........................	23 494	22 754
28180		Kapaa, HI Micro area....................	67 091	72 029
	15007	Kauai County, HI.........................	67 091	72 029
28260		Kearney, NE Micro area	52 591	55 935
	31019	Buffalo County, NE......................	46 102	49 383
	31099	Kearney County, NE	6 489	6 552
28300		Keene, NH Micro area	77 117	75 774
	33005	Cheshire County, NH	77 117	75 774
28340		Kendallville, IN Micro area.............	47 536	47 638
	18113	Noble County, IN.........................	47 536	47 638
28380		Kennett, MO Micro area	31 953	30 535
	29069	Dunklin County, MO.....................	31 953	30 535
28420		Kennewick-Richland, WA Metro area...	253 340	283 846
	53005	Benton County, WA......................	175 177	193 686
	53021	Franklin County, WA	78 163	90 160
28500		Kerrville, TX Micro area..................	49 625	51 504
	48265	Kerr County, TX	49 625	51 504
28540		Ketchikan, AK Micro area	13 477	13 746
	02130	Ketchikan Gateway Borough, AK..	13 477	13 746
28580		Key West, FL Micro area.................	73 090	79 077
	12087	Monroe County, FL	73 090	79 077
28620		Kill Devil Hills, NC Micro area	38 327	40 105
	37055	Dare County, NC.........................	33 920	35 964
	37177	Tyrrell County, NC.......................	4 407	4 141
28660		Killeen-Temple, TX Metro area........	405 300	435 857
	48027	Bell County, TX	310 235	340 411
	48099	Coryell County, TX	75 388	74 686
	48281	Lampasas County, TX..................	19 677	20 760
28700		Kingsport-Bristol-Bristol, TN-VA Metro area....................................	309 544	306 334
	47073	Hawkins County, TN	56 833	56 563
	47163	Sullivan County, TN	156 823	156 667
	51169	Scott County, VA.........................	23 177	21 930
	51191	Washington County, VA	54 876	54 214
	51520	Bristol city, VA	17 835	16 960
28740		Kingston, NY Metro area	182 493	179 225
	36111	Ulster County, NY	182 493	179 225
28780		Kingsville, TX Micro area................	32 477	32 094
	48261	Kenedy County, TX......................	416	404
	48273	Kleberg County, TX......................	32 061	31 690
28820		Kinston, NC Micro area	59 495	57 307
	37107	Lenoir County, NC.......................	59 495	57 307
28860		Kirksville, MO Micro area................	30 038	29 753
	29001	Adair County, MO........................	25 607	25 359
	29197	Schuyler County, MO	4 431	4 394
28900		Klamath Falls, OR Micro area	66 380	66 443
	41035	Klamath County, OR	66 380	66 443
28940		Knoxville, TN Metro area.................	837 571	868 546
	47001	Anderson County, TN...................	75 129	75 936
	47009	Blount County, TN.......................	123 010	128 670
	47013	Campbell County, TN...................	40 716	39 714
	47057	Grainger County, TN....................	22 657	23 072
	47093	Knox County, TN.........................	432 226	456 132
	47105	Loudon County, TN......................	48 556	51 454
	47129	Morgan County, TN......................	21 987	21 554
	47145	Roane County, TN	54 181	52 874
	47173	Union County, TN........................	19 109	19 140
29020		Kokomo, IN Metro area	82 752	82 568
	18067	Howard County, IN.......................	82 752	82 568
29060		Laconia, NH Micro area..................	60 088	60 779
	33001	Belknap County, NH.....................	60 088	60 779
29100		La Crosse-Onalaska, WI-MN Metro area...	133 665	136 936
	27055	Houston County, MN....................	19 027	18 814
	55063	La Crosse County, WI..................	114 638	118 122

Core Based Statistical Areas (Metropolitan and Micropolitan), Metropolitan Divisions, and Components (as defined July 2015)–*Continued*

Core Based Statistical Area	State/County FIPS Code	Title and Geographic Components	2010 Census Population	2016 Estimated Population	Core Based Statistical Area	State/County FIPS Code	Title and Geographic Components	2010 Census Population	2016 Estimated Population
29180		Lafayette, LA Metro area..................	466 750	491 528	29940		Lawrence, KS Metro area...............	110 826	119 440
	22001	Acadia Parish, LA........................	61 773	62 645		20045	Douglas County, KS....................	110 826	119 440
	22045	Iberia Parish, LA.........................	73 240	73 273					
	22055	Lafayette Parish, LA....................	221 578	241 398	29980		Lawrenceburg, TN Micro area.........	41 869	43 081
	22099	St. Martin Parish, LA...................	52 160	54 007		47099	Lawrence County, TN	41 869	43 081
	22113	Vermilion Parish, LA....................	57 999	60 205					
					30020		Lawton, OK Metro area	130 291	128 077
29200		Lafayette-West Lafayette, IN Metro				40031	Comanche County, OK................	124 098	122 136
		area..	201 789	216 679		40033	Cotton County, OK......................	6 193	5 941
	18007	Benton County, IN........................	8 854	8 650					
	18015	Carroll County, IN........................	20 155	19 970	30060		Lebanon, MO Micro area................	35 571	35 490
	18157	Tippecanoe County, IN	172 780	188 059		29105	Laclede County, MO	35 571	35 490
29260		La Grande, OR Micro area.............	25 748	26 087	30140		Lebanon, PA Metro area	133 568	138 863
	41061	Union County, OR........................	25 748	26 087		42075	Lebanon County, PA....................	133 568	138 863
29300		LaGrange, GA Micro area	67 044	70 005	30220		Levelland, TX Micro area	22 935	23 275
	13285	Troup County, GA	67 044	70 005		48219	Hockley County, TX	22 935	23 275
29340		Lake Charles, LA Metro area	199 607	207 483	30260		Lewisburg, PA Micro area	44 947	45 565
	22019	Calcasieu Parish, LA....................	192 768	200 601		42119	Union County, PA........................	44 947	45 565
	22023	Cameron Parish, LA....................	6 839	6 882					
					30280		Lewisburg, TN Micro area	30 617	31 915
29380		Lake City, FL Micro area	67 531	69 299		47117	Marshall County, TN	30 617	31 915
	12023	Columbia County, FL	67 531	69 299					
					30300		Lewiston, ID-WA Metro area	60 888	62 675
29420		Lake Havasu City-Kingman, AZ				16069	Nez Perce County, ID	39 265	40 369
		Metro area...................................	200 186	205 249		53003	Asotin County, WA	21 623	22 306
	04015	Mohave County, AZ	200 186	205 249					
					30340		Lewiston-Auburn, ME Metro area.....	107 702	107 319
29460		Lakeland-Winter Haven, FL Metro				23001	Androscoggin County, ME	107 702	107 319
		area..	602 095	666 149					
	12105	Polk County, FL...........................	602 095	666 149	30380		Lewistown, PA Micro area..............	46 682	46 342
						42087	Mifflin County, PA.......................	46 682	46 342
29500		Lamesa, TX Micro area	13 833	13 111					
	48115	Dawson County, TX	13 833	13 111	30420		Lexington, NE Micro area...............	26 370	25 611
						31047	Dawson County, NE	24 326	23 640
29540		Lancaster, PA Metro area...............	519 445	538 500		31073	Gosper County, NE.....................	2 044	1 971
	42071	Lancaster County, PA	519 445	538 500					
					30460		Lexington-Fayette, KY Metro area....	472 099	506 751
29620		Lansing-East Lansing, MI Metro				21017	Bourbon County, KY	19 985	20 030
		area..	464 036	475 099		21049	Clark County, KY........................	35 613	35 819
	26037	Clinton County, MI.......................	75 382	77 888		21067	Fayette County, KY.....................	295 803	318 449
	26045	Eaton County, MI	107 759	109 160		21113	Jessamine County, KY.................	48 586	52 357
	26065	Ingham County, MI.......................	280 895	288 051		21209	Scott County, KY........................	47 173	53 972
						21239	Woodford County, KY	24 939	26 124
29660		Laramie, WY Micro area.................	36 299	38 256					
	56001	Albany County, WY	36 299	38 256	30580		Liberal, KS Micro area..................	22 952	22 709
						20175	Seward County, KS	22 952	22 709
29700		Laredo, TX Metro area	250 304	271 193					
	48479	Webb County, TX.........................	250 304	271 193	30620		Lima, OH Metro area......................	106 331	103 742
						39003	Allen County, OH	106 331	103 742
29740		Las Cruces, NM Metro area	209 233	214 207					
	35013	Doña Ana County, NM..................	209 233	214 207	30660		Lincoln, IL Micro area	30 305	29 527
						17107	Logan County, IL.........................	30 305	29 527
29780		Las Vegas, NM Micro area..............	29 393	27 760					
	35047	San Miguel County, NM...............	29 393	27 760	30700		Lincoln, NE Metro area..................	302 157	326 921
						31109	Lancaster County, NE..................	285 407	309 637
29820		Las Vegas-Henderson-Paradise, NV				31159	Seward County, NE......................	16 750	17 284
		Metro area...................................	1 951 269	2 155 664					
	32003	Clark County, NV	1 951 269	2 155 664	30780		Little Rock-North Little Rock-		
							Conway, AR Metro area	699 757	734 622
29860		Laurel, MS Micro area	84 823	84 531		05045	Faulkner County, AR....................	113 237	122 227
	28061	Jasper County, MS.......................	17 062	16 578		05053	Grant County, AR........................	17 853	18 082
	28067	Jones County, MS........................	67 761	67 953		05085	Lonoke County, AR......................	68 356	72 228
						05105	Perry County, AR	10 445	10 132
29900		Laurinburg, NC Micro area	36 157	35 244		05119	Pulaski County, AR......................	382 748	393 250
	37165	Scotland County, NC....................	36 157	35 244		05125	Saline County, AR.......................	107 118	118 703

Core Based Statistical Area	State/ County FIPS Code	Title and Geographic Components	2010 Census Population	2016 Estimated Population	Core Based Statistical Area	State/ County FIPS Code	Title and Geographic Components	2010 Census Population	2016 Estimated Population
30820		Lock Haven, PA Micro area..............	39 238	39 233	31340		Lynchburg, VA Metro area...............	252 634	260 232
	42035	Clinton County, PA.....................	39 238	39 233		51009	Amherst County, VA....................	32 353	31 633
30860		Logan, UT-ID Metro area...............	125 442	136 159		51011	Appomattox County, VA...............	14 973	15 475
	16041	Franklin County, ID	12 786	13 406		51019	Bedford County, VA....................	68 676	77 960
	49005	Cache County, UT......................	112 656	122 753		51031	Campbell County, VA...................	54 842	54 952
						51680	Lynchburg city, VA	75 568	80 212
30880		Logan, WV Micro area..................	36 743	33 700	31380		Macomb, IL Micro area..................	32 612	30 996
	54045	Logan County, WV	36 743	33 700		17109	McDonough County, IL	32 612	30 996
30900		Logansport, IN Micro area................	38 966	37 946	31420		Macon, GA Metro area..................	232 293	229 182
	18017	Cass County, IN	38 966	37 946		13021	Bibb County, GA	155 547	152 760
30940		London, KY Micro area..................	126 369	128 033		13079	Crawford County, GA....................	12 630	12 322
	21121	Knox County, KY.........................	31 883	31 687		13169	Jones County, GA	28 669	28 623
	21125	Laurel County, KY.......................	58 849	60 250		13207	Monroe County, GA	26 424	27 306
	21235	Whitley County, KY......................	35 637	36 096		13289	Twiggs County, GA	9 023	8 171
30980		Longview, TX Metro area	214 369	217 446	31460		Madera, CA Metro area...................	150 865	154 697
	48183	Gregg County, TX......................	121 730	123 745		06039	Madera County, CA.....................	150 865	154 697
	48401	Rusk County, TX........................	53 330	52 732	31500		Madison, IN Micro area...................	32 428	32 418
	48459	Upshur County, TX......................	39 309	40 969		18077	Jefferson County, IN	32 428	32 418
31020		Longview, WA Metro area	102 410	105 160	31540		Madison, WI Metro area	605 435	648 929
	53015	Cowlitz County, WA......................	102 410	105 160		55021	Columbia County, WI...................	56 833	56 927
31060		Los Alamos, NM Micro area............	17 950	18 147		55025	Dane County, WI.......................	488 073	531 273
	35028	Los Alamos County, NM	17 950	18 147		55045	Green County, WI......................	36 842	37 075
31080		Los Angeles-Long Beach-Anaheim, CA Metro area	12 828 837	13 310 447		55049	Iowa County, WI.......................	23 687	23 654
		Anaheim-Santa Ana-Irvine, CA Metro Div 11244	3 010 232	3 172 532	31580		Madisonville, KY Micro area............	46 920	45 904
	06059	Orange County, CA	3 010 232	3 172 532		21107	Hopkins County, KY....................	46 920	45 904
31080		Los Angeles-Long Beach-Glendale, CA Metro Div 31084	9 818 605	10 137 915	31620		Magnolia, AR Micro area...............	24 552	23 901
	06037	Los Angeles County, CA..............	9 818 605	10 137 915		05027	Columbia County, AR...................	24 552	23 901
31140		Louisville/Jefferson County, KY-IN Metro area.................................	1 235 708	1 283 430	31660		Malone, NY Micro area...................	51 599	50 409
	18019	Clark County, IN..........................	110 232	116 031		36033	Franklin County, NY	51 599	50 409
	18043	Floyd County, IN	74 578	76 990	31680		Malvern, AR Micro area..................	32 923	33 374
	18061	Harrison County, IN.....................	39 364	39 826		05059	Hot Spring County, AR.................	32 923	33 374
	18143	Scott County, IN.........................	24 181	23 730	31700		Manchester-Nashua, NH Metro area	400 721	407 761
	18175	Washington County, IN	28 262	27 670		33011	Hillsborough County, NH..............	400 721	407 761
	21029	Bullitt County, KY........................	74 319	79 151	31740		Manhattan, KS Metro area	92 719	97 004
	21103	Henry County, KY........................	15 416	15 818		20149	Pottawatomie County, KS	21 604	23 661
	21111	Jefferson County, KY	741 096	765 352		20161	Riley County, KS.......................	71 115	73 343
	21185	Oldham County, KY	60 316	65 560	31820		Manitowoc, WI Micro area..............	81 442	79 536
	21211	Shelby County, KY......................	42 074	46 408		55071	Manitowoc County, WI	81 442	79 536
	21215	Spencer County, KY	17 061	18 274	31860		Mankato-North Mankato, MN Metro area	96 740	100 016
	21223	Trimble County, KY......................	8 809	8 620		27013	Blue Earth County, MN	64 013	66 441
31180		Lubbock, TX Metro area..................	290 805	314 840		27103	Nicollet County, MN	32 727	33 575
	48107	Crosby County, TX.......................	6 059	5 992	31900		Mansfield, OH Metro area	124 475	121 107
	48303	Lubbock County, TX.....................	278 831	303 137		39139	Richland County, OH	124 475	121 107
	48305	Lynn County, TX	5 915	5 711	31930		Marietta, OH Micro area	61 778	60 610
31220		Ludington, MI Micro area................	28 705	28 876		39167	Washington County, OH	61 778	60 610
	26105	Mason County, MI.......................	28 705	28 876	31940		Marinette, WI-MI Micro area............	65 778	63 772
31260		Lufkin, TX Micro area	86 771	87 791		26109	Menominee County, MI	24 029	23 281
	48005	Angelina County, TX	86 771	87 791		55075	Marinette County, WI	41 749	40 491
31300		Lumberton, NC Micro area	134 168	133 235	31980		Marion, IN Micro area....................	70 061	66 937
	37155	Robeson County, NC	134 168	133 235		18053	Grant County, IN	70 061	66 937

Core Based Statistical Area	State/County FIPS Code	Title and Geographic Components	2010 Census Population	2016 Estimated Population	Core Based Statistical Area	State/County FIPS Code	Title and Geographic Components	2010 Census Population	2016 Estimated Population
32000		Marion, NC Micro area	44 996	45 075	32820		Memphis, TN-MS-AR Metro area	1 324 829	1 342 842
	37111	McDowell County, NC.................	44 996	45 075		05035	Crittenden County, AR	50 902	49 235
32020		Marion, OH Micro area	66 501	65 096		28009	Benton County, MS	8 729	8 264
	39101	Marion County, OH	66 501	65 096		28033	DeSoto County, MS	161 252	175 611
32100		Marquette, MI Micro area	67 077	66 435		28093	Marshall County, MS	37 144	35 801
	26103	Marquette County, MI..................	67 077	66 435		28137	Tate County, MS	28 886	28 201
32140		Marshall, MN Micro area	25 857	25 699		28143	Tunica County, MS......................	10 778	10 234
	27083	Lyon County, MN	25 857	25 699		47047	Fayette County, TN......................	38 413	39 590
32180		Marshall, MO Micro area	23 370	22 980		47157	Shelby County, TN......................	927 644	934 603
	29195	Saline County, MO	23 370	22 980		47167	Tipton County, TN.......................	61 081	61 303
32220		Marshall, TX Micro area	65 631	66 534	32860		Menomonie, WI Micro area	43 857	44 704
	48203	Harrison County, TX....................	65 631	66 534		55033	Dunn County, WI.........................	43 857	44 704
32260		Marshalltown, IA Micro area............	40 648	40 312	32900		Merced, CA Metro area	255 793	268 672
	19127	Marshall County, IA.....................	40 648	40 312		06047	Merced County, CA......................	255 793	268 672
32280		Martin, TN Micro area......................	35 021	33 507	32940		Meridian, MS Micro area	107 449	103 539
	47183	Weakley County, TN	35 021	33 507		28023	Clarke County, MS.......................	16 732	15 888
32300		Martinsville, VA Micro area.............	67 972	64 890		28069	Kemper County, MS....................	10 456	9 896
	51089	Henry County, VA	54 151	51 445		28075	Lauderdale County, MS	80 261	77 755
	51690	Martinsville city, VA	13 821	13 445	32980		Merrill, WI Micro area	28 743	27 902
32340		Maryville, MO Micro area.................	23 370	22 670		55069	Lincoln County, WI......................	28 743	27 902
	29147	Nodaway County, MO..................	23 370	22 670	33020		Mexico, MO Micro area	25 529	26 021
32380		Mason City, IA Micro area...............	51 749	50 642		29007	Audrain County, MO.....................	25 529	26 021
	19033	Cerro Gordo County, IA	44 151	43 070	33060		Miami, OK Micro area......................	31 848	31 691
	19195	Worth County, IA.........................	7 598	7 572		40115	Ottawa County, OK	31 848	31 691
32460		Mayfield, KY Micro area	37 121	37 182	33100		Miami-Fort Lauderdale-West Palm Beach, FL Metro area...................	5 564 635	6 066 387
	21083	Graves County, KY	37 121	37 182			Fort Lauderdale-Pompano Beach-Deerfield Beach, FL Metro Div 22744...................	1 748 066	1 909 632
32500		Maysville, KY Micro area...............	17 490	17 190		12011	Broward County, FL.................	1 748 066	1 909 632
	21161	Mason County, KY	17 490	17 190	33100		Miami-Miami Beach-Kendall, FL Metro Div 33124	2 496 435	2 712 945
32540		McAlester, OK Micro area...............	45 837	44 173		12086	Miami-Dade County, FL............	2 496 435	2 712 945
	40121	Pittsburg County, OK	45 837	44 173	33100		West Palm Beach-Boca Raton-Delray Beach, FL Metro Div 48424...................	1 320 134	1 443 810
32580		McAllen-Edinburg-Mission, TX Metro area...................	774 769	849 843		12099	Palm Beach County, FL	1 320 134	1 443 810
	48215	Hidalgo County, TX......................	774 769	849 843	33140		Michigan City-La Porte, IN Metro area...................	111 467	110 015
32620		McComb, MS Micro area.................	53 535	52 125		18091	LaPorte County, IN......................	111 467	110 015
	28005	Amite County, MS........................	13 131	12 458	33180		Middlesborough, KY Micro area	28 691	27 117
	28113	Pike County, MS	40 404	39 667		21013	Bell County, KY	28 691	27 117
32660		McMinnville, TN Micro area..............	39 839	40 516	33220		Midland, MI Metro area...................	83 629	83 462
	47177	Warren County, TN	39 839	40 516		26111	Midland County, MI	83 629	83 462
32700		McPherson, KS Micro area..............	29 180	28 804	33260		Midland, TX Metro area...................	141 671	168 288
	20113	McPherson County, KS.................	29 180	28 804		48317	Martin County, TX	4 799	5 723
32740		Meadville, PA Micro area...............	88 765	86 257		48329	Midland County, TX......................	136 872	162 565
	42039	Crawford County, PA	88 765	86 257	33300		Milledgeville, GA Micro area............	55 149	53 784
32780		Medford, OR Metro area.................	203 206	216 527		13009	Baldwin County, GA.....................	45 720	45 144
	41029	Jackson County, OR	203 206	216 527		13141	Hancock County, GA....................	9 429	8 640
					33340		Milwaukee-Waukesha-West Allis, WI Metro area...................	1 555 908	1 572 482

Core Based Statistical Area	State/ County FIPS Code	Title and Geographic Components	2010 Census Population	2016 Estimated Population	Core Based Statistical Area	State/ County FIPS Code	Title and Geographic Components	2010 Census Population	2016 Estimated Population
	55079	Milwaukee County, WI	947 735	951 448	34060		Morgantown, WV Metro area............	129 709	138 380
	55089	Ozaukee County, WI.....................	86 395	88 314		54061	Monongalia County, WV	96 189	104 622
	55131	Washington County, WI	131 887	134 296		54077	Preston County, WV.....................	33 520	33 758
	55133	Waukesha County, WI	389 891	398 424					
33420		Mineral Wells, TX Micro area	28 111	28 053	34100		Morristown, TN Metro area	113 951	117 320
	48363	Palo Pinto County, TX..............	28 111	28 053		47063	Hamblen County, TN....................	62 544	63 785
						47089	Jefferson County, TN	51 407	53 535
33460		Minneapolis-St. Paul-Bloomington, MN Metro area...................	3 348 859	3 551 036	34140		Moscow, ID Micro area....................	37 244	39 196
	27003	Anoka County, MN	330 844	345 957		16057	Latah County, ID	37 244	39 196
	27019	Carver County, MN	91 042	100 262	34180		Moses Lake, WA Micro area	89 120	93 546
	27025	Chisago County, MN.....................	53 887	54 748		53025	Grant County, WA	89 120	93 546
	27037	Dakota County, MN......................	398 552	417 486					
	27053	Hennepin County, MN...................	1 152 425	1 232 483	34220		Moultrie, GA Micro area...................	45 498	45 708
	27059	Isanti County, MN.......................	37 816	39 025		13071	Colquitt County, GA	45 498	45 708
	27079	Le Sueur County, MN	27 703	27 591					
	27095	Mille Lacs County, MN.................	26 097	25 866	34260		Mountain Home, AR Micro area.......	41 513	41 062
	27123	Ramsey County, MN...................	508 640	540 649		05005	Baxter County, AR	41 513	41 062
	27139	Scott County, MN........................	129 928	143 680					
	27141	Sherburne County, MN	88 499	93 528	34300		Mountain Home, ID Micro area	27 038	26 018
	27143	Sibley County, MN.......................	15 226	14 827		16039	Elmore County, ID.......................	27 038	26 018
	27163	Washington County, MN	238 136	253 117					
	27171	Wright County, MN......................	124 700	132 550	34340		Mount Airy, NC Micro area..............	73 673	72 113
	55093	Pierce County, WI	41 019	41 238		37171	Surry County, NC	73 673	72 113
	55109	St. Croix County, WI	84 345	88 029					
					34380		Mount Pleasant, MI Micro area	70 311	71 282
33500		Minot, ND Micro area.....................	69 540	78 723		26073	Isabella County, MI	70 311	71 282
	38049	McHenry County, ND.....................	5 395	5 963					
	38075	Renville County, ND......................	2 470	2 550	34420		Mount Pleasant, TX Micro area.......	32 334	32 592
	38101	Ward County, ND.......................	61 675	70 210		48449	Titus County, TX	32 334	32 592
33540		Missoula, MT Metro area.................	109 299	116 130	34460		Mount Sterling, KY Micro area	44 396	46 506
	30063	Missoula County, MT	109 299	116 130		21011	Bath County, KY.........................	11 591	12 327
						21165	Menifee County, KY	6 306	6 408
33580		Mitchell, SD Micro area	22 835	23 277		21173	Montgomery County, KY	26 499	27 771
	46035	Davison County, SD.....................	19 504	19 903					
	46061	Hanson County, SD	3 331	3 374	34500		Mount Vernon, IL Micro area..........	38 827	38 460
						17081	Jefferson County, IL.....................	38 827	38 460
33620		Moberly, MO Micro area..................	25 414	24 989					
	29175	Randolph County, MO...................	25 414	24 989	34540		Mount Vernon, OH Micro area	60 921	60 814
						39083	Knox County, OH	60 921	60 814
33660		Mobile, AL Metro area....................	412 992	414 836					
	01097	Mobile County, AL.......................	412 992	414 836	34580		Mount Vernon-Anacortes, WA Metro area..	116 901	123 681
33700		Modesto, CA Metro area	514 453	541 560		53057	Skagit County, WA......................	116 901	123 681
	06099	Stanislaus County, CA	514 453	541 560					
					34620		Muncie, IN Metro area.....................	117 671	115 603
33740		Monroe, LA Metro area...................	176 441	179 470		18035	Delaware County, IN....................	117 671	115 603
	22073	Ouachita Parish, LA	153 720	156 983					
	22111	Union Parish, LA	22 721	22 487	34660		Murray, KY Micro area.....................	37 191	38 437
						21035	Calloway County, KY	37 191	38 437
33780		Monroe, MI Metro area....................	152 021	149 208					
	26115	Monroe County, MI......................	152 021	149 208	34700		Muscatine, IA Micro area.................	42 745	42 940
						19139	Muscatine County, IA	42 745	42 940
33860		Montgomery, AL Metro area............	374 536	373 922					
	01001	Autauga County, AL.....................	54 571	55 416	34740		Muskegon, MI Metro area...............	172 188	173 408
	01051	Elmore County, AL......................	79 303	81 799		26121	Muskegon County, MI	172 188	173 408
	01085	Lowndes County, AL....................	11 299	10 358					
	01101	Montgomery County, AL	229 363	226 349	34780		Muskogee, OK Micro area..............	70 990	69 477
						40101	Muskogee County, OK..................	70 990	69 477
33940		Montrose, CO Micro area	41 276	41 471					
	08085	Montrose County, CO	41 276	41 471	34820		Myrtle Beach-Conway-North Myrtle Beach, NC-SC Metro area.............	376 722	449 295
33980		Morehead City, NC Micro area........	66 469	68 890		37019	Brunswick County, NC	107 431	126 953
	37031	Carteret County, NC.....................	66 469	68 890		45051	Horry County, SC	269 291	322 342
34020		Morgan City, LA Micro area............	54 650	52 093	34860		Nacogdoches, TX Micro area..........	64 524	65 806
	22101	St. Mary Parish, LA.....................	54 650	52 093		48347	Nacogdoches County, TX	64 524	65 806

Core Based Statistical Areas (Metropolitan and Micropolitan), Metropolitan Divisions, and Components (as defined July 2015)–*Continued*

Core Based Statistical Area	State/County FIPS Code	Title and Geographic Components	2010 Census Population	2016 Estimated Population	Core Based Statistical Area	State/County FIPS Code	Title and Geographic Components	2010 Census Population	2016 Estimated Population
34900		Napa, CA Metro area	136 484	142 166	35500		Newton, IA Micro area	36 842	36 708
	06055	Napa County, CA	136 484	142 166		19099	Jasper County, IA	36 842	36 708
34940		Naples-Immokalee-Marco Island, FL Metro area	321 520	365 136	35580		New Ulm, MN Micro area	25 893	25 331
	12021	Collier County, FL	321 520	365 136		27015	Brown County, MN	25 893	25 331
34980		Nashville-Davidson—Murfreesboro—Franklin, TN Metro area	1 670 890	1 865 298	35620		New York-Newark-Jersey City, NY-NJ-PA Metro area	19 567 410	20 153 634
	47015	Cannon County, TN	13 801	14 027			Dutchess County-Putnam County, NY Metro Div 20524	397 198	393 373
	47021	Cheatham County, TN	39 105	39 880		36027	Dutchess County, NY	297 488	294 473
	47037	Davidson County, TN	626 681	684 410		36079	Putnam County, NY	99 710	98 900
	47043	Dickson County, TN	49 666	52 170	35620		Nassau County-Suffolk County, NY Metro Div 35004	2 832 882	2 854 083
	47081	Hickman County, TN	24 690	24 295		36059	Nassau County, NY	1 339 532	1 361 500
	47111	Macon County, TN	22 248	23 450		36103	Suffolk County, NY	1 493 350	1 492 583
	47119	Maury County, TN	80 956	89 981	35620		Newark, NJ-PA Metro Div 35084	2 471 171	2 507 478
	47147	Robertson County, TN	66 283	69 165		34013	Essex County, NJ	783 969	796 914
	47149	Rutherford County, TN	262 604	308 251		34019	Hunterdon County, NJ	128 349	124 676
	47159	Smith County, TN	19 166	19 447		34027	Morris County, NJ	492 276	498 423
	47165	Sumner County, TN	160 645	180 063		34035	Somerset County, NJ	323 444	333 751
	47169	Trousdale County, TN	7 870	8 271		34037	Sussex County, NJ	149 265	142 522
	47187	Williamson County, TN	183 182	219 107		34039	Union County, NJ	536 499	555 630
	47189	Wilson County, TN	113 993	132 781		42103	Pike County, PA	57 369	55 562
35020		Natchez, MS-LA Micro area	53 119	51 168	35620		New York-Jersey City-White Plains, NY-NJ Metro Div 35614	13 866 159	14 398 700
	22029	Concordia Parish, LA	20 822	19 920		34003	Bergen County, NJ	905 116	939 151
	28001	Adams County, MS	32 297	31 248		34017	Hudson County, NJ	634 266	677 983
35060		Natchitoches, LA Micro area	39 566	39 162		34023	Middlesex County, NJ	809 858	837 073
	22069	Natchitoches Parish, LA	39 566	39 162		34025	Monmouth County, NJ	630 380	625 846
35100		New Bern, NC Metro area	126 802	126 111		34029	Ocean County, NJ	576 567	592 497
	37049	Craven County, NC	103 505	103 445		34031	Passaic County, NJ	501 226	507 945
	37103	Jones County, NC	10 153	9 845		36005	Bronx County, NY	1 385 108	1 455 720
	37137	Pamlico County, NC	13 144	12 821		36047	Kings County, NY	2 504 700	2 629 150
35140		Newberry, SC Micro area	37 508	38 079		36061	New York County, NY	1 585 873	1 643 734
	45071	Newberry County, SC	37 508	38 079		36071	Orange County, NY	372 813	379 210
35220		New Castle, IN Micro area	49 462	48 521		36081	Queens County, NY	2 230 722	2 333 054
	18065	Henry County, IN	49 462	48 521		36085	Richmond County, NY	468 730	476 015
35260		New Castle, PA Micro area	91 108	87 294		36087	Rockland County, NY	311 687	326 780
	42073	Lawrence County, PA	91 108	87 294		36119	Westchester County, NY	949 113	974 542
35300		New Haven-Milford, CT Metro area	862 477	856 875	35660		Niles-Benton Harbor, MI Metro area	156 813	154 010
	09009	New Haven County, CT	862 477	856 875		26021	Berrien County, MI	156 813	154 010
35380		New Orleans-Metairie, LA Metro area	1 189 866	1 268 883	35700		Nogales, AZ Micro area	47 420	45 985
	22051	Jefferson Parish, LA	432 552	436 523		04023	Santa Cruz County, AZ	47 420	45 985
	22071	Orleans Parish, LA	343 829	391 495	35740		Norfolk, NE Micro area	48 271	48 118
	22075	Plaquemines Parish, LA	23 042	23 464		31119	Madison County, NE	34 876	35 015
	22087	St. Bernard Parish, LA	35 897	45 688		31139	Pierce County, NE	7 266	7 159
	22089	St. Charles Parish, LA	52 780	52 923		31167	Stanton County, NE	6 129	5 944
	22093	St. James Parish, LA	22 102	21 557	35820		North Platte, NE Micro area	37 590	36 815
	22095	St. John the Baptist Parish, LA	45 924	43 631		31111	Lincoln County, NE	36 288	35 550
	22103	St. Tammany Parish, LA	233 740	253 602		31113	Logan County, NE	763	772
35420		New Philadelphia-Dover, OH Micro area	92 582	92 420		31117	McPherson County, NE	539	493
	39157	Tuscarawas County, OH	92 582	92 420	35840		North Port-Sarasota-Bradenton, FL Metro area	702 281	788 457
35440		Newport, OR Micro area	46 034	47 806		12081	Manatee County, FL	322 833	375 888
	41041	Lincoln County, OR	46 034	47 806		12115	Sarasota County, FL	379 448	412 569
35460		Newport, TN Micro area	35 662	35 219	35860		North Vernon, IN Micro area	28 525	27 758
	47029	Cocke County, TN	35 662	35 219		18079	Jennings County, IN	28 525	27 758

Core Based Statistical Area	State/ County FIPS Code	Title and Geographic Components	2010 Census Population	2016 Estimated Population	Core Based Statistical Area	State/ County FIPS Code	Title and Geographic Components	2010 Census Population	2016 Estimated Population
35900		North Wilkesboro, NC Micro area.....	69 340	68 740	36620		Ontario, OR-ID Micro area...............	53 936	53 465
	37193	Wilkes County, NC..............	69 340	68 740		16075	Payette County, ID......................	22 623	23 026
						41045	Malheur County, OR	31 313	30 439
35940		Norwalk, OH Micro area	59 626	58 439					
	39077	Huron County, OH.................	59 626	58 439	36660		Opelousas, LA Micro area..............	83 384	83 883
						22097	St. Landry Parish, LA....................	83 384	83 883
35980		Norwich-New London, CT Metro area............	274 055	269 801	36700		Orangeburg, SC Micro area	92 501	87 903
	09011	New London County, CT..............	274 055	269 801		45075	Orangeburg County, SC..............	92 501	87 903
36020		Oak Harbor, WA Micro area.............	78 506	82 636	36740		Orlando-Kissimmee-Sanford, FL Metro..........	2 134 411	2 441 257
	53029	Island County, WA	78 506	82 636		12069	Lake County, FL..........	297 052	335 396
36100		Ocala, FL Metro area..............	331 298	349 020		12095	Orange County, FL...........	1 145 956	1 314 367
	12083	Marion County, FL..................	331 298	349 020		12097	Osceola County, FL	268 685	336 015
						12117	Seminole County, FL...................	422 718	455 479
36140		Ocean City, NJ Metro area..............	97 265	94 430					
	34009	Cape May County, NJ..................	97 265	94 430	36780		Oshkosh-Neenah, WI Metro area.....	166 994	169 886
						55139	Winnebago County, WI	166 994	169 886
36220		Odessa, TX Metro area	137 130	157 462					
	48135	Ector County, TX..........	137 130	157 462	36820		Oskaloosa, IA Micro area	22 381	22 181
						19123	Mahaska County, IA.....................	22 381	22 181
36260		Ogden-Clearfield, UT Metro area	597 159	654 417					
	49003	Box Elder County, UT	49 975	53 139	36830		Othello, WA Micro area	18 728	19 238
	49011	Davis County, UT.........................	306 479	342 281		53001	Adams County, WA...................	18 728	19 238
	49029	Morgan County, UT......................	9 469	11 437					
	49057	Weber County, UT	231 236	247 560	36840		Ottawa, KS Micro area	25 992	25 560
						20059	Franklin County, KS	25 992	25 560
36300		Ogdensburg-Massena, NY Micro area.............	111 944	110 038	36860		Ottawa-Peru, IL Micro area	154 908	149 612
	36089	St. Lawrence County, NY.............	111 944	110 038		17011	Bureau County, IL......................	34 978	33 359
						17099	LaSalle County, IL.....................	113 924	110 642
36340		Oil City, PA Micro area....................	54 984	52 582		17155	Putnam County, IL	6 006	5 611
	42121	Venango County, PA.................	54 984	52 582					
					36900		Ottumwa, IA Micro area.................	44 378	43 842
36380		Okeechobee, FL Micro area............	39 996	40 314		19051	Davis County, IA	8 753	8 860
	12093	Okeechobee County, FL	39 996	40 314		19179	Wapello County, IA	35 625	34 982
36420		Oklahoma City, OK Metro area	1 252 987	1 373 211	36940		Owatonna, MN Micro area..............	36 576	36 805
	40017	Canadian County, OK..................	115 541	136 532		27147	Steele County, MN.......................	36 576	36 805
	40027	Cleveland County, OK...................	255 755	278 655					
	40051	Grady County, OK.......................	52 431	54 655	36980		Owensboro, KY Metro area..............	114 752	117 959
	40081	Lincoln County, OK.....................	34 273	35 129		21059	Daviess County, KY	96 656	99 674
	40083	Logan County, OK......................	41 848	46 588		21091	Hancock County, KY	8 565	8 810
	40087	McClain County, OK....................	34 506	38 682		21149	McLean County, KY	9 531	9 475
	40109	Oklahoma County, OK	718 633	782 970					
					37020		Owosso, MI Micro area..................	70 648	68 554
36460		Olean, NY Micro area......................	80 317	77 677		26155	Shiawassee County, MI	70 648	68 554
	36009	Cattaraugus County, NY	80 317	77 677					
					37060		Oxford, MS Micro area	47 351	53 796
36500		Olympia-Tumwater, WA Metro area.	252 264	275 222		28071	Lafayette County, MS.................	47 351	53 796
	53067	Thurston County, WA.................	252 264	275 222					
					37080		Oxford, NC Micro area....................	59 916	59 031
36540		Omaha-Council Bluffs, NE-IA Metro area.........	865 350	924 129		37077	Granville County, NC	59 916	59 031
	19085	Harrison County, IA......................	14 928	14 149	37100		Oxnard-Thousand Oaks-Ventura, CA Metro area	823 318	849 738
	19129	Mills County, IA	15 059	14 972					
	19155	Pottawattamie County, IA..............	93 158	93 582		06111	Ventura County, CA	823 318	849 738
	31025	Cass County, NE........................	25 241	25 767					
	31055	Douglas County, NE....................	517 110	554 995	37120		Ozark, AL Micro area....................	50 251	49 226
	31153	Sarpy County, NE	158 840	179 023		01045	Dale County, AL.........................	50 251	49 226
	31155	Saunders County, NE	20 780	21 038					
	31177	Washington County, NE................	20 234	20 603	37140		Paducah, KY-IL Micro area	98 762	97 143
36580		Oneonta, NY Micro area..................	62 259	60 097		17127	Massac County, IL	15 429	14 658
	36077	Otsego County, NY	62 259	60 097		21007	Ballard County, KY......................	8 249	8 054
						21139	Livingston County, KY..................	9 519	9 269
						21145	McCracken County, KY.................	65 565	65 162

Core Based Statistical Areas (Metropolitan and Micropolitan), Metropolitan Divisions, and Components (as defined July 2015)–*Continued*

Core Based Statistical Area	State/County FIPS Code	Title and Geographic Components	2010 Census Population	2016 Estimated Population	Core Based Statistical Area	State/County FIPS Code	Title and Geographic Components	2010 Census Population	2016 Estimated Population
37220		Pahrump, NV Micro area	43 946	43 423	37980		Montgomery County-Bucks County-Chester County, PA Metro Div 33874	1 924 009	1 964 436
	32023	Nye County, NV	43 946	43 423		42017	Bucks County, PA	625 249	626 399
37260		Palatka, FL Micro area	74 364	72 277		42029	Chester County, PA	498 886	516 312
	12107	Putnam County, FL	74 364	72 277		42091	Montgomery County, PA	799 874	821 725
37300		Palestine, TX Micro area	58 458	57 734		53075	Whitman County, WA	44 776	48 851
	48001	Anderson County, TX	58 458	57 734					
37340		Palm Bay-Melbourne-Titusville, FL Metro area	543 376	579 130	39460		Punta Gorda, FL Metro area	159 978	178 465
	12009	Brevard County, FL	543 376	579 130		12015	Charlotte County, FL	159 978	178 465
37420		Pampa, TX Micro area	22 535	22 725	39500		Quincy, IL-MO Micro area	77 314	76 712
	48179	Gray County, TX	22 535	22 725		17001	Adams County, IL	67 103	66 578
37460		Panama City, FL Metro area	184 715	199 964		29111	Lewis County, MO	10 211	10 134
	12005	Bay County, FL	168 852	183 974	39540		Racine, WI Metro area	195 408	195 140
	12045	Gulf County, FL	15 863	15 990		55101	Racine County, WI	195 408	195 140
37500		Paragould, AR Micro area	42 090	44 598	39580		Raleigh, NC Metro area	1 130 490	1 302 946
	05055	Greene County, AR	42 090	44 598		37069	Franklin County, NC	60 619	64 705
37540		Paris, TN Micro area	32 330	32 310		37101	Johnston County, NC	168 878	191 450
	47079	Henry County, TN	32 330	32 310		37183	Wake County, NC	900 993	1 046 791
37580		Paris, TX Micro area	49 793	49 791	39660		Rapid City, SD Metro area	134 598	145 661
	48277	Lamar County, TX	49 793	49 791		46033	Custer County, SD	8 216	8 596
37620		Parkersburg-Vienna, WV Metro area	92 673	91 449		46093	Meade County, SD	25 434	27 693
	54105	Wirt County, WV	5 717	5 806		46103	Pennington County, SD	100 948	109 372
	54107	Wood County, WV	86 956	85 643	39700		Raymondville, TX Micro area	22 134	21 810
37660		Parsons, KS Micro area	21 607	20 444		48489	Willacy County, TX	22 134	21 810
	20099	Labette County, KS	21 607	20 444	39740		Reading, PA Metro area	411 442	414 812
37740		Payson, AZ Micro area	53 597	53 556		42011	Berks County, PA	411 442	414 812
	04007	Gila County, AZ	53 597	53 556	39780		Red Bluff, CA Micro area	63 463	63 276
37780		Pecos, TX Micro area	13 783	14 921		06103	Tehama County, CA	63 463	63 276
	48389	Reeves County, TX	13 783	14 921	39820		Redding, CA Metro area	177 223	179 631
37800		Pella, IA Micro Area	33 309	33 189		06089	Shasta County, CA	177 223	179 631
	19125	Marion County, IA	33 309	33 189	39860		Red Wing, MN Micro area	46 183	46 676
37860		Pensacola-Ferry Pass-Brent, FL Metro area	448 991	485 684		27049	Goodhue County, MN	46 183	46 676
	12033	Escambia County, FL	297 619	315 187	39900		Reno, NV Metro area	425 417	457 667
	12113	Santa Rosa County, FL	151 372	170 497		32029	Storey County, NV	4 010	4 051
37900		Peoria, IL Metro area	379 186	376 246		32031	Washoe County, NV	421 407	453 616
	17123	Marshall County, IL	12 640	11 939	39940		Rexburg, ID Micro area	50 778	51 991
	17143	Peoria County, IL	186 494	185 006		16043	Fremont County, ID	13 242	12 943
	17175	Stark County, IL	5 994	5 776		16065	Madison County, ID	37 536	39 048
	17179	Tazewell County, IL	135 394	134 385	39980		Richmond, IN Micro area	68 917	66 568
	17203	Woodford County, IL	38 664	39 140		18177	Wayne County, IN	68 917	66 568
37940		Peru, IN Micro area	36 903	35 883					
	18103	Miami County, IN	36 903	35 883					
37980		Philadelphia-Camden-Wilmington, PA-NJ-DE-MD Metro area	5 965 343	6 070 500					
		Camden, NJ Metro Div 15804	1 250 679	1 251 764					
	34005	Burlington County, NJ	448 734	449 284					
	34007	Camden County, NJ	513 657	510 150					
	34015	Gloucester County, NJ	288 288	292 330					

Core Based Statistical Areas (Metropolitan and Micropolitan), Metropolitan Divisions, and Components (as defined July 2015)–*Continued*

Core Based Statistical Area	State/County FIPS Code	Title and Geographic Components	2010 Census Population	2016 Estimated Population	Core Based Statistical Area	State/County FIPS Code	Title and Geographic Components	2010 Census Population	2016 Estimated Population
40060		Richmond, VA Metro area	1 208 101	1 281 708	40540		Rock Springs, WY Micro area	43 806	44 165
	51007	Amelia County, VA......................	12 690	12 913		56037	Sweetwater County, WY	43 806	44 165
	51033	Caroline County, VA...................	28 545	30 178					
	51036	Charles City County, VA	7 256	7 071	40580		Rocky Mount, NC Metro area..........	152 392	147 323
	51041	Chesterfield County, VA...............	316 236	339 009		37065	Edgecombe County, NC	56 552	53 318
	51053	Dinwiddie County, VA	28 001	28 144		37127	Nash County, NC	95 840	94 005
	51075	Goochland County, VA.................	21 717	22 668					
	51085	Hanover County, VA	99 863	104 392	40620		Rolla, MO Micro area.....................	45 156	44 608
	51087	Henrico County, VA.....................	306 935	326 501		29161	Phelps County, MO	45 156	44 608
	51101	King William County, VA	15 935	16 334					
	51127	New Kent County, VA	18 429	21 147	40660		Rome, GA Metro area	96 317	96 560
	51145	Powhatan County, VA..................	28 046	28 443		13115	Floyd County, GA.......................	96 317	96 560
	51149	Prince George County, VA...........	35 725	37 845					
	51183	Sussex County, VA	12 087	11 504	40700		Roseburg, OR Micro area...............	107 667	108 457
	51570	Colonial Heights city, VA.............	17 411	17 772		41019	Douglas County, OR	107 667	108 457
	51670	Hopewell city, VA	22 591	22 735					
	51730	Petersburg city, VA	32 420	31 882	40740		Roswell, NM Micro area	65 645	65 282
	51760	Richmond city, VA......................	204 214	223 170		35005	Chaves County, NM....................	65 645	65 282
40080		Richmond-Berea, KY Micro area.....	99 972	106 397	40760		Ruidoso, NM Micro Area	20 497	19 429
	21151	Madison County, KY	82 916	89 547		35027	Lincoln County, NM....................	20 497	19 429
	21203	Rockcastle County, KY	17 056	16 850					
					40780		Russellville, AR Micro area.............	83 939	85 331
40100		Rio Grande City, TX Micro area.......	60 968	64 122		05115	Pope County, AR	61 754	63 779
	48427	Starr County, TX	60 968	64 122		05149	Yell County, AR..........................	22 185	21 552
40140		Riverside-San Bernardino-Ontario, CA	4 224 851	4 527 837	40820		Ruston, LA Micro area.....................	46 735	47 745
						22061	Lincoln Parish, LA	46 735	47 745
	06065	Riverside County, CA...................	2 189 641	2 387 741					
	06071	San Bernardino County, CA..........	2 035 210	2 140 096	40860		Rutland, VT Micro area...................	61 642	59 310
						50021	Rutland County, VT....................	61 642	59 310
40180		Riverton, WY Micro area	40 123	40 242					
	56013	Fremont County, WY....................	40 123	40 242	40900		Sacramento—Roseville—Arden-Arcade, CA Metro area...................	2 149 127	2 296 418
40220		Roanoke, VA Metro area.................	308 707	313 698		06017	El Dorado County, CA.................	181 058	185 625
	51023	Botetourt County, VA	33 148	33 231		06061	Placer County, CA......................	348 432	380 531
	51045	Craig County, VA	5 190	5 158		06067	Sacramento County, CA	1 418 788	1 514 460
	51067	Franklin County, VA	56 159	56 069		06113	Yolo County, CA........................	200 849	215 802
	51161	Roanoke County, VA....................	92 376	94 031					
	51770	Roanoke city, VA........................	97 032	99 660	40940		Safford, AZ Micro area	37 220	37 599
	51775	Salem city, VA	24 802	25 549		04009	Graham County, AZ	37 220	37 599
40260		Roanoke Rapids, NC Micro area......	76 790	71 766	40980		Saginaw, MI Metro area	200 169	192 326
	37083	Halifax County, NC......................	54 691	51 766		26145	Saginaw County, MI....................	200 169	192 326
	37131	Northampton County, NC.............	22 099	20 000					
					41060		St. Cloud, MN Metro area...............	189 093	195 644
40300		Rochelle, IL Micro area..................	53 497	51 273		27009	Benton County, MN....................	38 451	39 992
	17141	Ogle County, IL	53 497	51 273		27145	Stearns County, MN...................	150 642	155 652
40340		Rochester, MN Metro area	206 877	215 884	41100		St. George, UT Metro area..............	138 115	160 245
	27039	Dodge County, MN......................	20 087	20 506		49053	Washington County, UT	138 115	160 245
	27045	Fillmore County, MN....................	20 866	21 003					
	27109	Olmsted County, MN...................	144 248	153 102	41140		St. Joseph, MO-KS Metro area........	127 329	126 565
	27157	Wabasha County, MN..................	21 676	21 273		20043	Doniphan County, KS..................	7 945	7 664
						29003	Andrew County, MO...................	17 291	17 350
40380		Rochester, NY Metro area..............	1 079 671	1 078 879		29021	Buchanan County, MO................	89 201	88 938
	36051	Livingston County, NY.................	65 393	64 257		29063	DeKalb County, MO	12 892	12 613
	36055	Monroe County, NY.....................	744 344	747 727					
	36069	Ontario County, NY.....................	107 931	109 828					
	36073	Orleans County, NY....................	42 883	41 346					
	36117	Wayne County, NY......................	93 772	90 798					
	36123	Yates County, NY........................	25 348	24 923					
40420		Rockford, IL Metro area...................	349 431	339 376					
	17007	Boone County, IL	54 165	53 503					
	17201	Winnebago County, IL..................	295 266	285 873					
40460		Rockingham, NC Micro area	46 639	44 939					
	37153	Richmond County, NC	46 639	44 939					

Core Based Statistical Areas (Metropolitan and Micropolitan), Metropolitan Divisions, and Components (as defined July 2015)–*Continued*

Core Based Statistical Area	State/ County FIPS Code	Title and Geographic Components	2010 Census Population	2016 Estimated Population	Core Based Statistical Area	State/ County FIPS Code	Title and Geographic Components	2010 Census Population	2016 Estimated Population
41180		St. Louis, MO-IL Metro area.............	2 787 701	2 807 002	41780		Sandusky, OH Micro area...............	77 079	75 107
	17005	Bond County, IL........................	17 768	16 824		39043	Erie County, OH.........................	77 079	75 107
	17013	Calhoun County, IL.....................	5 089	4 894					
	17027	Clinton County, IL......................	37 762	37 729	41820		Sanford, NC Micro area..................	57 866	59 616
	17083	Jersey County, IL.......................	22 985	22 025		37105	Lee County, NC...........................	57 866	59 616
	17117	Macoupin County, IL....................	47 765	45 908					
	17119	Madison County, IL.....................	269 282	265 759	41860		San Francisco-Oakland-Hayward, CA Metro area	4 335 391	4 679 166
	17133	Monroe County, IL......................	32 957	34 068			Oakland-Hayward-Berkeley, CA		
	17163	St. Clair County, IL....................	270 056	262 759			Metro Div 36084......................	2 559 296	2 782 831
	29071	Franklin County, MO...................	101 492	102 838		06001	Alameda County, CA.................	1 510 271	1 647 704
	29099	Jefferson County, MO.................	218 733	224 226		06013	Contra Costa County, CA..........	1 049 025	1 135 127
	29113	Lincoln County, MO...................	52 566	55 267	41860		San Francisco-Redwood City-		
	29183	St. Charles County, MO..............	360 485	390 918			South San Francisco, CA Metro		
	29189	St. Louis County, MO.................	998 954	998 581			Div 41884	1 523 686	1 635 684
	29219	Warren County, MO....................	32 513	33 802		06075	San Francisco County, CA........	805 235	870 887
	29510	St. Louis city, MO.....................	319 294	311 404		06081	San Mateo County, CA.............	718 451	764 797
41220		St. Marys, GA Micro area.............	50 513	53 008	41860		San Rafael, CA Metropolitan Div		
	13039	Camden County, GA..................	50 513	53 008			42034....................................	252 409	260 651
41260		St. Marys, PA Micro Area................	31 946	30 480		06041	Marin County, CA	252 409	260 651
	42047	Elk County, PA.........................	31 946	30 480					
41400		Salem, OH Micro area....................	107 841	103 685	41940		San Jose-Sunnyvale-Santa Clara, CA Metro area.........................	1 836 911	1 978 816
	39029	Columbiana County, OH...............	107 841	103 685		06069	San Benito County, CA.................	55 269	59 414
41420		Salem, OR Metro area....................	390 738	418 139		06085	Santa Clara County, CA...............	1 781 642	1 919 402
	41047	Marion County, OR	315 335	336 316	42020		San Luis Obispo-Paso Robles-		
	41053	Polk County, OR	75 403	81 823			Arroyo Grande, CA Metro area	269 637	282 887
41460		Salina, KS Micro area.....................	61 697	61 062		06079	San Luis Obispo County, CA........	269 637	282 887
	20143	Ottawa County, KS......................	6 091	5 920	42100		Santa Cruz-Watsonville, CA Metro		
	20169	Saline County, KS......................	55 606	55 142			area	262 382	274 673
41500		Salinas, CA Metro area	415 057	435 232		06087	Santa Cruz County, CA...............	262 382	274 673
	06053	Monterey County, CA..................	415 057	435 232	42140		Santa Fe, NM Metro area................	144 170	148 651
41540		Salisbury, MD-DE Metro area...........	373 802	400 200		35049	Santa Fe County, NM	144 170	148 651
	10005	Sussex County, DE	197 145	220 251	42200		Santa Maria-Santa Barbara, CA		
	24039	Somerset County, MD.................	26 470	25 928			Metro....................................	423 895	446 170
	24045	Wicomico County, MD.................	98 733	102 577		06083	Santa Barbara County, CA	423 895	446 170
	24047	Worcester County, MD................	51 454	51 444	42220		Santa Rosa, CA Metro area	483 878	503 070
41620		Salt Lake City, UT Metro area...........	1 087 873	1 186 187		06097	Sonoma County, CA	483 878	503 070
	49035	Salt Lake County, UT..................	1 029 655	1 121 354	42300		Sault Ste. Marie, MI Micro area........	38 520	37 724
	49045	Tooele County, UT......................	58 218	64 833		26033	Chippewa County, MI..................	38 520	37 724
41660		San Angelo, TX Metro area..............	111 823	119 943	42340		Savannah, GA Metro area..............	347 611	384 024
	48235	Irion County, TX	1 599	1 557		13029	Bryan County, GA	30 233	36 230
	48451	Tom Green County, TX................	110 224	118 386		13051	Chatham County, GA..................	265 128	289 082
41700		San Antonio-New Braunfels, TX				13103	Effingham County, GA	52 250	58 712
		Metro...................................	2 142 508	2 429 609	42380		Sayre, PA Micro area...................	62 622	60 770
	48013	Atascosa County, TX	44 911	48 797		42015	Bradford County, PA	62 622	60 770
	48019	Bandera County, TX....................	20 485	21 776	42420		Scottsbluff, NE Micro area..............	38 971	38 462
	48029	Bexar County, TX.......................	1 714 773	1 928 680		31007	Banner County, NE.....................	690	798
	48091	Comal County, TX......................	108 472	134 788		31157	Scotts Bluff County, NE	36 970	36 422
	48187	Guadalupe County, TX.................	131 533	155 265		31165	Sioux County, NE.......................	1 311	1 242
	48259	Kendall County, TX.....................	33 410	42 540	42460		Scottsboro, AL Micro area..............	53 227	52 138
	48325	Medina County, TX.....................	46 006	49 283		01071	Jackson County, AL	53 227	52 138
	48493	Wilson County, TX	42 918	48 480	42540		Scranton—Wilkes-Barre—Hazleton,		
41740		San Diego-Carlsbad, CA Metro area	3 095 313	3 317 749			PA Metro area................	563 631	555 225
	06073	San Diego County, CA.................	3 095 313	3 317 749					
41760		Sandpoint, ID Micro area...............	40 877	42 536					
	16017	Bonner County, ID.......................	40 877	42 536					

Core Based Statistical Areas (Metropolitan and Micropolitan), Metropolitan Divisions, and Components (as defined July 2015)–Continued

Core Based Statistical Area	State/County FIPS Code	Title and Geographic Components	2010 Census Population	2016 Estimated Population
	42069	Lackawanna County, PA	214 437	211 321
	42079	Luzerne County, PA	320 918	316 383
	42131	Wyoming County, PA	28 276	27 521
42620		Searcy, AR Micro area	77 076	79 263
	05145	White County, AR	77 076	79 263
42660		Seattle-Tacoma-Bellevue, WA Metro area	3 439 809	3 798 902
		Seattle-Bellevue-Everett, WA Metro Div 42644	2 644 584	2 937 590
	53033	King County, WA	1 931 249	2 149 970
	53061	Snohomish County, WA	713 335	787 620
42660		Tacoma-Lakewood, WA Metro Div 45104	795 225	861 312
	53053	Pierce County, WA	795 225	861 312
42680		Sebastian-Vero Beach, FL Metro area	138 028	151 563
	12061	Indian River County, FL	138 028	151 563
42700		Sebring, FL Metro area	98 786	100 917
	12055	Highlands County, FL	98 786	100 917
42740		Sedalia, MO Micro area	42 201	42 213
	29159	Pettis County, MO	42 201	42 213
42780		Selinsgrove, PA Micro area	39 702	40 468
	42109	Snyder County, PA	39 702	40 468
42820		Selma, AL Micro area	43 820	40 008
	01047	Dallas County, AL	43 820	40 008
42860		Seneca, SC Micro area	74 273	76 355
	45073	Oconee County, SC	74 273	76 355
42900		Seneca Falls, NY Micro area	35 251	34 777
	36099	Seneca County, NY	35 251	34 777
42940		Sevierville, TN Micro area	89 889	96 673
	47155	Sevier County, TN	89 889	96 673
42980		Seymour, IN Micro area	42 376	44 013
	18071	Jackson County, IN	42 376	44 013
43020		Shawano, WI Micro area	46 181	45 595
	55078	Menominee County, WI	4 232	4 533
	55115	Shawano County, WI	41 949	41 062
43060		Shawnee, OK Micro area	69 442	72 290
	40125	Pottawatomie County, OK	69 442	72 290
43100		Sheboygan, WI Metro area	115 507	115 427
	55117	Sheboygan County, WI	115 507	115 427
43140		Shelby, NC Micro area	98 078	97 144
	37045	Cleveland County, NC	98 078	97 144
43180		Shelbyville, TN Micro area	45 058	47 484
	47003	Bedford County, TN	45 058	47 484
43220		Shelton, WA Micro area	60 699	62 198
	53045	Mason County, WA	60 699	62 198
43260		Sheridan, WY Micro area	29 116	30 200
	56033	Sheridan County, WY	29 116	30 200
43300		Sherman-Denison, TX Metro area	120 877	128 235
	48181	Grayson County, TX	120 877	128 235
43320		Show Low, AZ Micro area	107 449	110 026
	04017	Navajo County, AZ	107 449	110 026
43340		Shreveport-Bossier City, LA Metro area	439 811	441 767
	22015	Bossier Parish, LA	116 979	126 057
	22017	Caddo Parish, LA	254 969	248 851
	22031	De Soto Parish, LA	26 656	27 149
	22119	Webster Parish, LA	41 207	39 710
43380		Sidney, OH Micro area	49 423	48 623
	39149	Shelby County, OH	49 423	48 623
43420		Sierra Vista-Douglas, AZ Metro area	131 346	125 770
	04003	Cochise County, AZ	131 346	125 770
43460		Sikeston, MO Micro area	39 191	38 745
	29201	Scott County, MO	39 191	38 745
43500		Silver City, NM Micro area	29 514	28 280
	35017	Grant County, NM	29 514	28 280
43580		Sioux City, IA-NE-SD Metro area	168 563	169 140
	19149	Plymouth County, IA	24 986	25 200
	19193	Woodbury County, IA	102 172	102 779
	31043	Dakota County, NE	21 006	20 465
	31051	Dixon County, NE	6 000	5 762
	46127	Union County, SD	14 399	14 934
43620		Sioux Falls, SD Metro area	228 261	255 729
	46083	Lincoln County, SD	44 828	54 469
	46087	McCook County, SD	5 618	5 625
	46099	Minnehaha County, SD	169 468	187 318
	46125	Turner County, SD	8 347	8 317
43660		Snyder, TX Micro area	16 921	17 333
	48415	Scurry County, TX	16 921	17 333
43700		Somerset, KY Micro area	63 063	63 956
	21199	Pulaski County, KY	63 063	63 956
43740		Somerset, PA Micro area	77 742	75 061
	42111	Somerset County, PA	77 742	75 061
43760		Sonora, CA Micro area	55 365	53 804
	06109	Tuolumne County, CA	55 365	53 804
43780		South Bend-Mishawaka, IN-MI Metro area	319 224	320 740
	18141	St. Joseph County, IN	266 931	269 141
	26027	Cass County, MI	52 293	51 599
43900		Spartanburg, SC Metro area	313 268	329 136
	45083	Spartanburg County, SC	284 307	301 463
	45087	Union County, SC	28 961	27 673
43940		Spearfish, SD Micro area	24 097	25 281
	46081	Lawrence County, SD	24 097	25 281
43980		Spencer, IA Micro area	16 667	16 333
	19041	Clay County, IA	16 667	16 333
44020		Spirit Lake, IA Micro area	16 667	17 243
	19059	Dickinson County, IA	16 667	17 243

Core Based Statistical Areas (Metropolitan and Micropolitan), Metropolitan Divisions, and Components (as defined July 2015)–*Continued*

Core Based Statistical Area	State/County FIPS Code	Title and Geographic Components	2010 Census Population	2016 Estimated Population	Core Based Statistical Area	State/County FIPS Code	Title and Geographic Components	2010 Census Population	2016 Estimated Population
44060		Spokane-Spokane Valley, WA Metro area......	527 753	556 634	44900		Summerville, GA Micro area............	26 015	24 824
	53051	Pend Oreille County, WA...............	13 001	13 123		13055	Chattooga County, GA..................	26 015	24 824
	53063	Spokane County, WA..................	471 221	499 072	44920		Summit Park, UT Micro area...........	36 324	40 307
	53065	Stevens County, WA...................	43 531	44 439		49043	Summit County, UT....................	36 324	40 307
44100		Springfield, IL Metro area	210 170	210 015	44940		Sumter, SC Metro area.................	107 456	107 396
	17129	Menard County, IL.....................	12 705	12 516		45085	Sumter County, SC	107 456	107 396
	17167	Sangamon County, IL	197 465	197 499	44980		Sunbury, PA Micro area	94 528	92 541
44140		Springfield, MA Metro area...............	621 570	630 283		42097	Northumberland County, PA	94 528	92 541
	25013	Hampden County, MA..................	463 490	468 467	45000		Susanville, CA Micro area............	34 895	30 870
	25015	Hampshire County, MA.................	158 080	161 816		06035	Lassen County, CA	34 895	30 870
44180		Springfield, MO Metro area	436 712	458 930	45020		Sweetwater, TX Micro area	15 216	14 993
	29043	Christian County, MO..................	77 422	84 401		48353	Nolan County, TX	15 216	14 993
	29059	Dallas County, MO....................	16 777	16 448	45060		Syracuse, NY Metro area	662 577	656 510
	29077	Greene County, MO...................	275 174	288 690		36053	Madison County, NY	73 442	71 329
	29167	Polk County, MO......................	31 137	31 285		36067	Onondaga County, NY	467 026	466 194
	29225	Webster County, MO...................	36 202	38 106		36075	Oswego County, NY...................	122 109	118 987
44220		Springfield, OH Metro area.............	138 333	134 786	45140		Tahlequah, OK Micro area	46 987	48 700
	39023	Clark County, OH	138 333	134 786		40021	Cherokee County, OK	46 987	48 700
44260		Starkville, MS Micro area................	47 671	49 833	45180		Talladega-Sylacauga, AL Micro area	93 830	90 684
	28105	Oktibbeha County, MS.................	47 671	49 833		01037	Coosa County, AL	11 539	10 581
44300		State College, PA Metro area...........	153 990	161 464		01121	Talladega County, AL..................	82 291	80 103
	42027	Centre County, PA	153 990	161 464	45220		Tallahassee, FL Metro area............	367 413	379 627
44340		Statesboro, GA Micro area..............	70 217	74 722		12039	Gadsden County, FL	46 389	46 006
	13031	Bulloch County, GA....................	70 217	74 722		12065	Jefferson County, FL	14 761	13 906
44420		Staunton-Waynesboro, VA Metro area	118 502	121 247		12073	Leon County, FL.......................	275 487	287 822
	51015	Augusta County, VA...................	73 750	74 997		12129	Wakulla County, FL....................	30 776	31 893
	51790	Staunton city, VA......................	23 746	24 363	45300		Tampa-St. Petersburg-Clearwater, FL Metro area	2 783 243	3 032 171
	51820	Waynesboro city, VA...................	21 006	21 887		12053	Hernando County, FL..................	172 778	182 835
44460		Steamboat Springs, CO Micro area .	23 509	24 648		12057	Hillsborough County, FL...............	1 229 226	1 376 238
	08107	Routt County, CO.....................	23 509	24 648		12101	Pasco County, FL	464 697	512 368
44500		Stephenville, TX Micro area	37 890	41 659		12103	Pinellas County, FL	916 542	960 730
	48143	Erath County, TX......................	37 890	41 659	45340		Taos, NM Micro area...................	32 937	33 065
44540		Sterling, CO Micro area.................	22 709	21 919		35055	Taos County, NM	32 937	33 065
	08075	Logan County, CO	22 709	21 919	45380		Taylorville, IL Micro area	34 800	33 309
44580		Sterling, IL Micro area	58 498	56 536		17021	Christian County, IL....................	34 800	33 309
	17195	Whiteside County, IL...................	58 498	56 536	45460		Terre Haute, IN Metro area	172 425	170 687
44620		Stevens Point, WI Micro area...........	70 019	70 447		18021	Clay County, IN.......................	26 890	26 309
	55097	Portage County, WI....................	70 019	70 447		18153	Sullivan County, IN....................	21 475	20 802
44660		Stillwater, OK Micro area..............	77 350	81 131		18165	Vermillion County, IN	16 212	15 645
	40119	Payne County, OK	77 350	81 131		18167	Vigo County, IN.......................	107 848	107 931
44700		Stockton-Lodi, CA Metro area	685 306	733 709	45500		Texarkana, TX-AR Metro area	149 198	150 098
	06077	San Joaquin County, CA...............	685 306	733 709		05081	Little River County, AR................	13 171	12 451
44740		Storm Lake, IA Micro area..............	20 260	20 332		05091	Miller County, AR	43 462	43 787
	19021	Buena Vista County, IA................	20 260	20 332		48037	Bowie County, TX	92 565	93 860
44780		Sturgis, MI Micro area	61 295	60 853	45520		The Dalles, OR Micro area..............	25 213	26 115
	26149	St. Joseph County, MI.................	61 295	60 853		41065	Wasco County, OR	25 213	26 115
44860		Sulphur Springs, TX Micro area	35 161	36 400	45540		The Villages, FL Metro area............	93 420	123 996
	48223	Hopkins County, TX	35 161	36 400		12119	Sumter County, FL....................	93 420	123 996
					45580		Thomaston, GA Micro area	27 153	26 335
						13293	Upson County, GA....................	27 153	26 335

Core Based Statistical Area	State/County FIPS Code	Title and Geographic Components	2010 Census Population	2016 Estimated Population
45620		Thomasville, GA Micro area	44 720	45 248
	13275	Thomas County, GA	44 720	45 248
45660		Tiffin, OH Micro area	56 745	55 353
	39147	Seneca County, OH	56 745	55 353
45700		Tifton, GA Micro area	40 118	40 828
	13277	Tift County, GA	40 118	40 828
45740		Toccoa, GA Micro area	26 175	25 751
	13257	Stephens County, GA	26 175	25 751
45780		Toledo, OH Metro area	610 001	605 221
	39051	Fulton County, OH	42 698	42 514
	39095	Lucas County, OH	441 815	432 488
	39173	Wood County, OH	125 488	130 219
45820		Topeka, KS Metro area	233 870	233 068
	20085	Jackson County, KS	13 462	13 291
	20087	Jefferson County, KS	19 126	18 897
	20139	Osage County, KS	16 295	15 843
	20177	Shawnee County, KS	177 934	178 146
	20197	Wabaunsee County, KS	7 053	6 891
45860		Torrington, CT Micro area	189 927	182 571
	09005	Litchfield County, CT	189 927	182 571
45900		Traverse City, MI Micro area	143 372	148 684
	26019	Benzie County, MI	17 525	17 572
	26055	Grand Traverse County, MI	86 986	92 084
	26079	Kalkaska County, MI	17 153	17 263
	26089	Leelanau County, MI	21 708	21 765
45940		Trenton, NJ Metro area	366 513	371 023
	34021	Mercer County, NJ	366 513	371 023
45980		Troy, AL Micro area	32 899	33 286
	01109	Pike County, AL	32 899	33 286
46020		Truckee-Grass Valley, CA Micro area	98 764	99 107
	06057	Nevada County, CA	98 764	99 107
46060		Tucson, AZ Metro area	980 263	1 016 206
	04019	Pima County, AZ	980 263	1 016 206
46100		Tullahoma-Manchester, TN Micro area	100 210	102 705
	47031	Coffee County, TN	52 796	54 682
	47051	Franklin County, TN	41 052	41 700
	47127	Moore County, TN	6 362	6 323
46140		Tulsa, OK Metro area	937 478	987 201
	40037	Creek County, OK	69 967	71 312
	40111	Okmulgee County, OK	40 069	39 213
	40113	Osage County, OK	47 472	47 806
	40117	Pawnee County, OK	16 577	16 485
	40131	Rogers County, OK	86 905	91 766
	40143	Tulsa County, OK	603 403	642 940
	40145	Wagoner County, OK	73 085	77 679
46180		Tupelo, MS Micro area	136 268	140 460
	28057	Itawamba County, MS	23 401	23 529
	28081	Lee County, MS	82 910	85 381
	28115	Pontotoc County, MS	29 957	31 550

Core Based Statistical Area	State/County FIPS Code	Title and Geographic Components	2010 Census Population	2016 Estimated Population
46220		Tuscaloosa, AL Metro area	230 162	241 378
	01065	Hale County, AL	15 760	14 952
	01107	Pickens County, AL	19 746	20 324
	01125	Tuscaloosa County, AL	194 656	206 102
46300		Twin Falls, ID Micro area	99 604	106 508
	16053	Jerome County, ID	22 374	22 994
	16083	Twin Falls County, ID	77 230	83 514
46340		Tyler, TX Metro area	209 714	225 290
	48423	Smith County, TX	209 714	225 290
46380		Ukiah, CA Micro area	87 841	87 628
	06045	Mendocino County, CA	87 841	87 628
46460		Union City, TN-KY Micro area	38 620	36 757
	21075	Fulton County, KY	6 813	6 179
	47131	Obion County, TN	31 807	30 578
46500		Urbana, OH Micro area	40 097	38 747
	39021	Champaign County, OH	40 097	38 747
46520		Urban Honolulu, HI Metro area	953 207	992 605
	15003	Honolulu County, HI	953 207	992 605
46540		Utica-Rome, NY Metro area	299 397	293 803
	36043	Herkimer County, NY	64 519	62 613
	36065	Oneida County, NY	234 878	231 190
46620		Uvalde, TX Micro area	26 405	27 285
	48463	Uvalde County, TX	26 405	27 285
46660		Valdosta, GA Metro area	139 588	144 676
	13027	Brooks County, GA	16 243	15 687
	13101	Echols County, GA	4 034	3 962
	13173	Lanier County, GA	10 078	10 399
	13185	Lowndes County, GA	109 233	114 628
46700		Vallejo-Fairfield, CA Metro area	413 344	440 207
	06095	Solano County, CA	413 344	440 207
46740		Valley, AL Micro area	34 215	33 843
	01017	Chambers County, AL	34 215	33 843
46780		Van Wert, OH Micro area	28 744	28 362
	39161	Van Wert County, OH	28 744	28 362
46820		Vermillion, SD Micro area	13 864	14 086
	46027	Clay County, SD	13 864	14 086
46860		Vernal, UT Micro area	32 588	36 373
	49047	Uintah County, UT	32 588	36 373
46900		Vernon, TX Micro area	13 535	12 892
	48487	Wilbarger County, TX	13 535	12 892
46980		Vicksburg, MS Micro area	58 377	56 279
	28021	Claiborne County, MS	9 604	9 139
	28149	Warren County, MS	48 773	47 140
47020		Victoria, TX Metro area	94 003	99 984
	48175	Goliad County, TX	7 210	7 517
	48469	Victoria County, TX	86 793	92 467
47080		Vidalia, GA Micro area	36 346	36 256
	13209	Montgomery County, GA	9 123	9 060
	13279	Toombs County, GA	27 223	27 196

Core Based Statistical Areas (Metropolitan and Micropolitan), Metropolitan Divisions, and Components (as defined July 2015)–*Continued*

Core Based Statistical Area	State/ County FIPS Code	Title and Geographic Components	2010 Census Population	2016 Estimated Population	Core Based Statistical Area	State/ County FIPS Code	Title and Geographic Components	2010 Census Population	2016 Estimated Population
47180		Vincennes, IN Micro area	38 440	37 744	47900		Washington-Arlington-Alexandria, DC-VA-MD-WV Metro area	5 636 232	6 131 977
	18083	Knox County, IN	38 440	37 744			Silver Spring-Frederick-Rockville, MD Metro Div 43524	1 205 162	1 291 454
47220		Vineland-Bridgeton, NJ Metro area	156 898	153 797		24021	Frederick County, MD	233 385	247 591
	34011	Cumberland County, NJ	156 898	153 797		24031	Montgomery County, MD	971 777	1 043 863
47240		Vineyard Haven, MA Micro area	16 535	17 246					
	25007	Dukes County, MA	16 535	17 246	47900		Washington-Arlington-Alexandria, DC-VA-MD-WV Metro Div 47894	4 431 070	4 840 523
47260		Virginia Beach-Norfolk-Newport News, VA-NC Metro area	1 676 822	1 726 907		11001	District of Columbia, DC	601 723	681 170
	37053	Currituck County, NC	23 547	25 809		24009	Calvert County, MD	88 737	91 251
	37073	Gates County, NC	12 197	11 478		24017	Charles County, MD	146 551	157 705
	51073	Gloucester County, VA	36 858	37 214		24033	Prince George's County, MD	863 420	908 049
	51093	Isle of Wight County, VA	35 270	36 596		51013	Arlington County, VA	207 627	230 050
	51095	James City County, VA	67 009	74 404		51043	Clarke County, VA	14 034	14 374
	51115	Mathews County, VA	8 978	8 782		51047	Culpeper County, VA	46 689	50 083
	51199	York County, VA	65 464	67 976		51059	ixFairfax County, VA	1 081 726	1 138 652
	51550	Chesapeake city, VA	222 209	237 940		51061	Fauquier County, VA	65 203	69 069
	51650	Hampton city, VA	137 436	135 410		51107	Loudoun County, VA	312 311	385 945
	51700	Newport News city, VA	180 719	181 825		51153	Prince William County, VA	402 002	455 210
	51710	Norfolk city, VA	242 803	245 115		51157	Rappahannock County, VA	7 373	7 388
	51735	Poquoson city, VA	12 150	12 017		51177	Spotsylvania County, VA	122 397	132 010
	51740	Portsmouth city, VA	95 535	95 252		51179	Stafford County, VA	128 961	144 361
	51800	Suffolk city, VA	84 585	89 273		51187	Warren County, VA	37 575	39 155
	51810	Virginia Beach city, VA	437 994	452 602		51510	Alexandria city, VA	139 966	155 810
	51830	Williamsburg city, VA	14 068	15 214		51600	Fairfax city, VA	22 565	24 164
47300		Visalia-Porterville, CA Metro area	442 179	460 437		51610	Falls Church city, VA	12 332	14 014
	06107	Tulare County, CA	442 179	460 437		51630	Fredericksburg city, VA	24 286	28 297
47340		Wabash, IN Micro area	32 888	31 762		51683	Manassas city, VA	37 821	41 483
	18169	Wabash County, IN	32 888	31 762		51685	Manassas Park city, VA	14 273	15 915
47380		Waco, TX Metro area	252 772	265 207		54037	Jefferson County, WV	53 498	56 368
	48145	Falls County, TX	17 866	17 273	47920		Washington Court House, OH Micro area	29 030	28 676
	48309	McLennan County, TX	234 906	247 934		39047	Fayette County, OH	29 030	28 676
47420		Wahpeton, ND-MN Micro area	22 897	22 711	47940		Waterloo-Cedar Falls, IA Metro area	167 819	170 015
	27167	Wilkin County, MN	6 576	6 358		19013	Black Hawk County, IA	131 090	132 904
	38077	Richland County, ND	16 321	16 353		19017	Bremer County, IA	24 276	24 798
47460		Walla Walla, WA Metro area	62 859	64 278		19075	Grundy County, IA	12 453	12 313
	53013	Columbia County, WA	4 078	3 938	47980		Watertown, SD Micro area	27 227	28 063
	53071	Walla Walla County, WA	58 781	60 340		46029	Codington County, SD	27 227	28 063
47540		Wapakoneta, OH Micro area	45 949	45 894	48020		Watertown-Fort Atkinson, WI Micro area	83 686	84 625
	39011	Auglaize County, OH	45 949	45 894		55055	Jefferson County, WI	83 686	84 625
47580		Warner Robins, GA Metro area	179 605	190 028	48060		Watertown-Fort Drum, NY Metro area	116 229	114 006
	13153	Houston County, GA	139 900	152 122		36045	Jefferson County, NY	116 229	114 006
	13225	Peach County, GA	27 695	26 655					
	13235	Pulaski County, GA	12 010	11 251	48100		Wauchula, FL Micro area	27 731	27 360
47620		Warren, PA Micro area	41 815	40 025		12049	Hardee County, FL	27 731	27 360
	42123	Warren County, PA	41 815	40 025	48140		Wausau, WI Metro area	134 063	135 603
47660		Warrensburg, MO Micro area	52 595	53 942		55073	Marathon County, WI	134 063	135 603
	29101	Johnson County, MO	52 595	53 942	48180		Waycross, GA Micro area	55 070	54 909
47700		Warsaw, IN Micro area	77 358	79 092		13229	Pierce County, GA	18 758	19 171
	18085	Kosciusko County, IN	77 358	79 092		13299	Ware County, GA	36 312	35 738
47780		Washington, IN Micro area	31 648	32 969	48220		Weatherford, OK Micro area	27 469	29 293
	18027	Daviess County, IN	31 648	32 969		40039	Custer County, OK	27 469	29 293
47820		Washington, NC Micro area	47 759	47 526	48260		Weirton-Steubenville, WV-OH Metro area	124 454	119 271
	37013	Beaufort County, NC	47 759	47 526					

Core Based Statistical Areas (Metropolitan and Micropolitan), Metropolitan Divisions, and Components (as defined July 2015)–*Continued*

Core Based Statistical Area	State/ County FIPS Code	Title and Geographic Components	2010 Census Population	2016 Estimated Population	Core Based Statistical Area	State/ County FIPS Code	Title and Geographic Components	2010 Census Population	2016 Estimated Population
	39081	Jefferson County, OH..................	69 709	66 704	49180		Winston-Salem, NC Metro area........	640 595	662 079
	54009	Brooke County, WV.....................	24 069	22 977		37057	Davidson County, NC...................	162 878	164 926
	54029	Hancock County, WV...................	30 676	29 590		37059	Davie County, NC......................	41 240	42 013
48300		Wenatchee, WA Metro area.............	110 884	117 665		37067	Forsyth County, NC....................	350 670	371 511
	53007	Chelan County, WA.....................	72 453	76 338		37169	Stokes County, NC.....................	47 401	46 097
	53017	Douglas County, WA....................	38 431	41 327		37197	Yadkin County, NC....................	38 406	37 532
48460		West Plains, MO Micro area............	40 400	40 210	49220		Wisconsin Rapids-Marshfield, WI Micro area..............................	74 749	73 107
	29091	DHowell County, MO....................	40 400	40 210		55141	Wood County, WI.......................	74 749	73 107
48500		West Point, MS Micro Area.............	20 634	19 850	49260		Woodward, OK Micro area.............	20 081	20 814
	28025	Clay County, MS.......................	20 634	19 850		40153	Woodward County, OK................	20 081	20 814
48540		Wheeling, WV-OH Metro area..........	147 950	142 982	49300		Wooster, OH Micro area................	114 520	116 470
	39013	Belmont County, OH	70 400	68 673		39169	Wayne County, OH	114 520	116 470
	54051	Marshall County, WV...................	33 107	31 793	49340		Worcester, MA-CT Metro area	916 980	935 781
	54069	Ohio County, WV.......................	44 443	42 516		09015	Windham County, CT...................	118 428	116 192
48580		Whitewater-Elkhorn, WI Micro area..	102 228	102 959		25027	Worcester County, MA.................	798 552	819 589
	55127	Walworth County, WI	102 228	102 959	49380		Worthington, MN Micro area...........	21 378	21 848
48620		Wichita, KS Metro area..................	630 919	644 672		27105	Nobles County, MN.....................	21 378	21 848
	20015	Butler County, KS......................	65 880	67 025	49420		Yakima, WA Metro area	243 231	249 636
	20079	Harvey County, KS.....................	34 684	34 913		53077	Yakima County, WA....................	243 231	249 636
	20095	Kingman County, KS....................	7 858	7 467	49460		Yankton, SD Micro area...............	22 438	22 616
	20173	Sedgwick County, KS...................	498 365	511 995		46135	Yankton County, SD....................	22 438	22 616
	20191	Sumner County, KS.....................	24 132	23 272	49620		York-Hanover, PA Metro area	434 972	443 744
48660		Wichita Falls, TX Metro area............	151 306	150 734		42133	York County, PA.......................	434 972	443 744
	48009	Archer County, TX......................	9 054	8 703	49660		Youngstown-Warren-Boardman, OH-PA Metro area..........................	565 773	544 746
	48077	Clay County, TX........................	10 752	10 193		39099	Mahoning County, OH..................	238 823	230 008
	48485	Wichita County, TX	131 500	131 838		39155	Trumbull County, OH	210 312	201 825
48700		Williamsport, PA Metro area............	116 111	115 248		42085	Mercer County, PA.....................	116 638	112 913
	42081	Lycoming County, PA...................	116 111	115 248	49700		Yuba City, CA Metro area	166 892	171 926
48780		Williston, ND Micro area................	22 398	34 337		06101	Sutter County, CA......................	94 737	96 651
	38105	Williams County, ND	22 398	34 337		06115	Yuba County, CA	72 155	75 275
48820		Willmar, MN Micro area.................	42 239	42 495	49740		Yuma, AZ Metro area	195 751	205 631
	27067	Kandiyohi County, MN	42 239	42 495		04027	Yuma County, AZ......................	195 751	205 631
48900		Wilmington, NC Metro area.............	254 884	282 573	49780		Zanesville, OH Micro area..............	86 074	86 068
	37129	New Hanover County, NC.............	202 667	223 483		39119	Muskingum County, OH..............	86 074	86 068
	37141	Pender County, NC....................	52 217	59 090	49820		Zapata, TX Micro area..................	14 018	14 349
48940		Wilmington, OH Micro area.............	42 040	41 902		48505	Zapata County, TX....................	14 018	14 349
	39027	Clinton County, OH....................	42 040	41 902					
48980		Wilson, NC Micro area...................	81 234	81 661					
	37195	Wilson County, NC.....................	81 234	81 661					
49020		Winchester, VA-WV Metro area	128 472	135 238					
	51069	Frederick County, VA...................	78 305	84 421					
	51840	Winchester city, VA....................	26 203	27 516					
	54027	Hampshire County, WV...............	23 964	23 301					
49080		Winnemucca, NV Micro area...........	16 528	16 842					
	32013	Humboldt County, NV	16 528	16 842					
49100		Winona, MN Micro area.................	51 461	50 948					
	27169	Winona County, MN...................	51 461	50 948					

APPENDIX D
MAPS OF CONGRESSIONAL DISTRICTS
AND STATES

Congressional
of

...s of the 113th Congress
...ted States

013 - 2015

4	Congressional District Number
	Congressional District Boundary
	International Boundary
	State Boundary
	County Boundary

An asterisk (*) identifies an incorporated place that is legally independent of any county.

United States™
Census
Bureau

PUERTO RICO and U.S. VIRGIN ISLANDS

ONE RESIDENT COMMISSIONER AT LARGE

ONE DELEGATE AT LARGE

CONGRESSIONAL DISTRICTS OF THE 113TH CONGRESS OF THE UNITED STATES (JANUARY 2013 TO 2015)

ALABAMA - Core Based Statistical Areas (CBSAs) and Counties

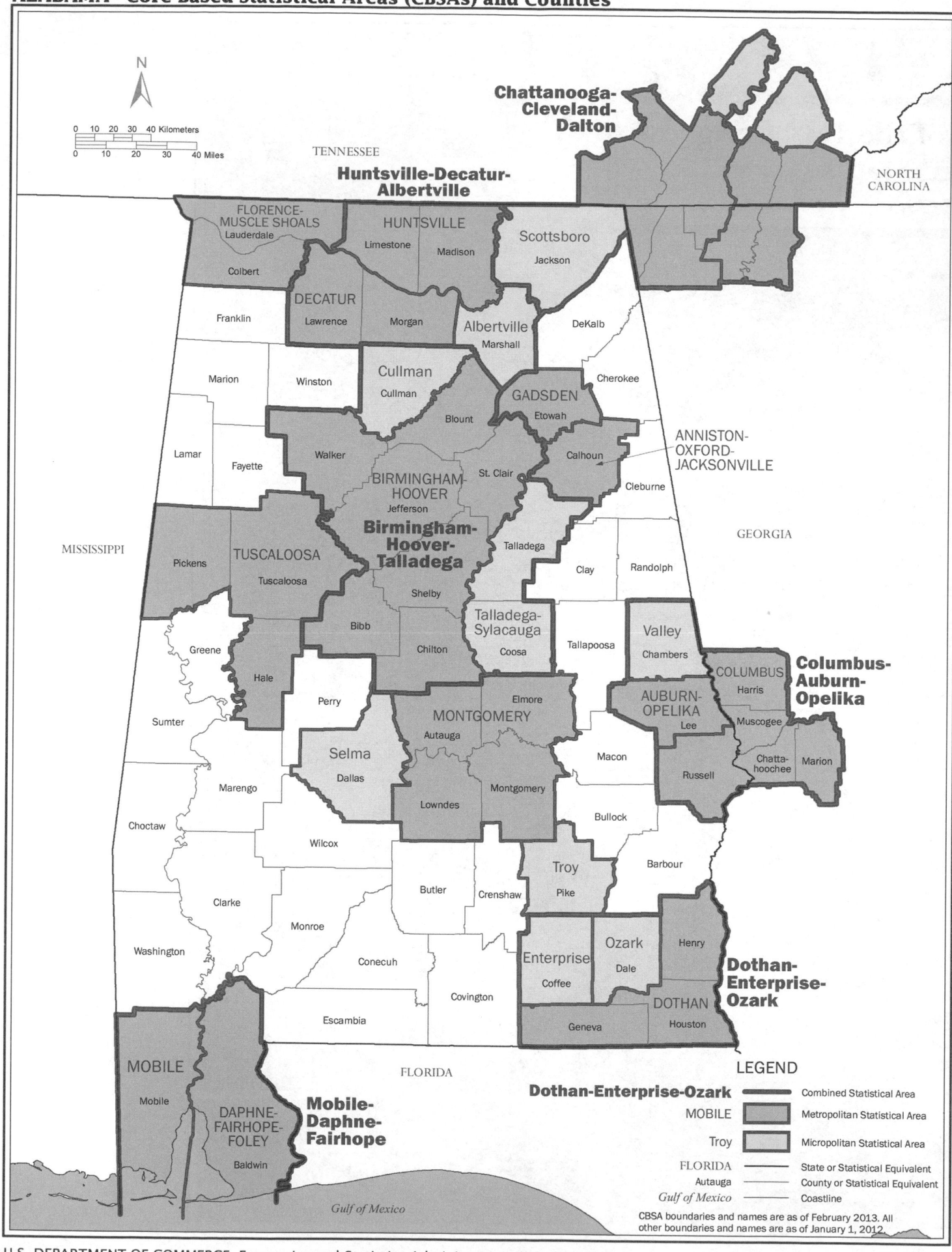

ALASKA - Core Based Statistical Areas (CBSAs) and Counties

CANADA

Prince of Wales-Hyder (pt)

Wrangell

Juneau

Juneau

Skagway

Petersburg

Sitka

Ketchikan Gateway

Prince of Wales-Hyder (pt)

Ketchikan

Haines

Hoonah-Angoon

Yakutat

CANADA

Southeast Fairbanks

Valdez-Cordova

Anchorage

FAIRBANKS

Denali

Yukon-Koyukuk

Fairbanks North Star

ANCHORAGE

Matanuska-Susitna

Kenai Peninsula

North Slope

Northwest Arctic

Arctic Ocean

Nome (pt)

Wade Hampton

Bethel

Dillingham

Bristol Bay

Lake and Peninsula

Kodiak Island

Nome (pt)

RUSSIA

Aleutians East

Pacific Ocean

Aleutians West (pt)

Aleutians West (pt)

LEGEND

FAIRBANKS — Metropolitan Statistical Area

Juneau — Micropolitan Statistical Area

CANADA — International

Bethel — County or Statistical Equivalent

Coastline

Arctic Ocean

CBSA boundaries and names are as of February 2013. All other boundaries and names are as of January 1, 2012.

N

0 75 150 225 300 Kilometers

0 75 150 225 300 Miles

ARIZONA - Core Based Statistical Areas (CBSAs) and Counties

LEGEND

Tucson-Nogales	Combined Statistical Area
YUMA	Metropolitan Statistical Area
Payson	Micropolitan Statistical Area
M E X I C O	International
UTAH	State or Statistical Equivalent
Apache	County or Statistical Equivalent
Pacific Ocean	Coastline

CBSA boundaries and names are as of February 2013. All other boundaries and names are as of January 1, 2012.

COLORADO

NEVADA

UTAH

Las Vegas-Henderson

FLAGSTAFF

Coconino

LAKE HAVASU CITY-KINGMAN

Mohave

Show Low

Navajo

Apache

NEW MEXICO

CALIFORNIA

PRESCOTT

Yavapai

La Paz

Payson

Gila

PHOENIX-MESA-SCOTTSDALE

Maricopa

Pinal

Greenlee

Safford

Graham

YUMA

Yuma

Tucson-Nogales

TUCSON

Pima

SIERRA VISTA-DOUGLAS

Cochise

Pacific Ocean

Nogales

Santa Cruz

M E X I C O

Gulf of California

ARKANSAS - Core Based Statistical Areas (CBSAs) and Counties

KENTUCKY

TENNESSEE

MISSISSIPPI

MISSOURI

OKLAHOMA

LOUISIANA

TEXAS

LEGEND

Combined Statistical Area
Hot Springs-Malvern

Metropolitan Statistical Area
FORT SMITH

Micropolitan Statistical Area
Camden

State or Statistical Equivalent
TEXAS

County or Statistical Equivalent
Arkansas

CBSA boundaries and names are as of February 2013. All other boundaries and names are as of January 1, 2012.

N

40 Miles
40 Kilometers
0 10 20 30 40

Counties and CBSAs (as labeled)

Benton

Fayette

Marshall

Tipton

Memphis-Forrest City

Shelby

MEMPHIS

DeSoto

Tate

Crittenden

Tunica

Blytheville

Mississippi

Clay

Paragould

Greene

Jonesboro-Paragould

Craighead

JONESBORO

Poinsett

Cross

Forrest City

St. Francis

Lee

Helena-West Helena

Phillips

Randolph

Lawrence

Jackson

Woodruff

Monroe

Arkansas

Desha

Chicot

Batesville

Independence

Sharp

Fulton

Izard

Searcy

White

Prairie

Lincoln

Drew

Ashley

Mountain Home

Baxter

Stone

Cleburne

Little Rock-North Little Rock

LITTLE ROCK-NORTH LITTLE ROCK-CONWAY

Lonoke

Jefferson

PINE BLUFF

Marion

Searcy

Van Buren

Faulkner

Pulaski

Cleveland

Bradley

Calhoun

El Dorado

Union

Boone

Harrison

Newton

Pope

Russellville

Conway

Perry

Saline

Grant

Dallas

Camden

Ouachita

Carroll

Madison

Johnson

Yell

HOT SPRINGS

Garland

Hot Springs-Malvern

Malvern

Hot Spring

Arkadelphia

Clark

Nevada

Magnolia

Columbia

McDonald

Benton

FAYETTEVILLE-SPRINGDALE-ROGERS

Washington

Crawford

Franklin

Logan

Montgomery

Pike

Hempstead

Lafayette

Scott

Howard

Miller

Sequoyah

FORT SMITH

Sebastian

Le Flore

Polk

Sevier

Little River

TEXARKANA

Bowie

U.S. DEPARTMENT OF COMMERCE Economics and Statistics Administration U.S. Census Bureau

Appendix D

D-7

CALIFORNIA - Core Based Statistical Areas (CBSAs) and Counties

OREGON

IDAHO

Del Norte
Crescent City
Siskiyou
Modoc

Eureka-Arcata-Fortuna
Humboldt
Trinity

REDDING
Shasta
Redding-Red Bluff

Susanville
Lassen

Red Bluff
Tehama

Plumas

CHICO
Glenn
Butte

Sierra

Ukiah
Mendocino

Clear-lake
Lake
Colusa
Sutter
YUBA CITY
Yuba
Nevada

Truckee-Grass Valley

SANTA ROSA
Sonoma
NAPA
Napa
Yolo
Sacra-mento

Placer

Sacramento-Roseville
SACRAMENTO–ROSEVILLE–ARDEN-ARCADE

El Dorado

San Rafael
SAN FRANCISCO-OAKLAND-HAYWARD
Marin
1
Solano
Contra Costa
2
San Joaquin
STOCKTON-LODI

Calaveras
Amador

Alpine

Sonora
Tuolumne

NEVADA

Mono

San Francisco
San Francisco-Redwood City-South San Francisco
Alameda

San Jose-San Francisco-Oakland
San Mateo
SANTA CRUZ-WATSONVILLE
Santa Clara
3
Santa Cruz

MODESTO
Stanislaus
Merced
Modesto-Merced
MERCED

Mariposa

Madera
MADERA

Fresno-Madera

KEY
1 VALLEJO-FAIRFIELD
2 Oakland-Hayward-Berkeley
3 SAN JOSE-SUNNYVALE-SANTA CLARA

San Benito
SALINAS
Monterey

Fresno
FRESNO

VISALIA-PORTERVILLE
Tulare

Inyo

Visalia-Porterville-Hanford

Kings
HANFORD-CORCORAN

SAN LUIS OBISPO-PASO ROBLES-ARROYO GRANDE

San Luis Obispo

BAKERSFIELD
Kern

Los Angeles-Long Beach

RIVERSIDE-SAN BERNARDINO-ONTARIO
San Bernardino

ARIZONA

Pacific Ocean

Santa Barbara

Ventura

Los Angeles-Long Beach-Glendale

Los Angeles

LOS ANGELES-LONG BEACH-ANAHEIM

SANTA MARIA-SANTA BARBARA

OXNARD-THOUSAND OAKS-VENTURA

Orange

Anaheim-Santa Ana-Irvine
Riverside

SAN DIEGO-CARLSBAD
San Diego

EL CENTRO
Imperial

MEXICO

LEGEND

Fresno-Madera — Combined Statistical Area
NAPA — Metropolitan Statistical Area
Ukiah — Micropolitan Statistical Area
San Rafael ••••• Metropolitan Division
M E X I C O — International
NEVADA — State or Statistical Equivalent
Alameda — County or Statistical Equivalent
Pacific Ocean — Coastline

CBSA boundaries and names are as of February 2013. All other boundaries and names are as of January 1, 2012.

N

0 20 40 60 80 Kilometers
0 20 40 60 80 Miles

COLORADO - Core Based Statistical Areas (CBSAs) and Counties

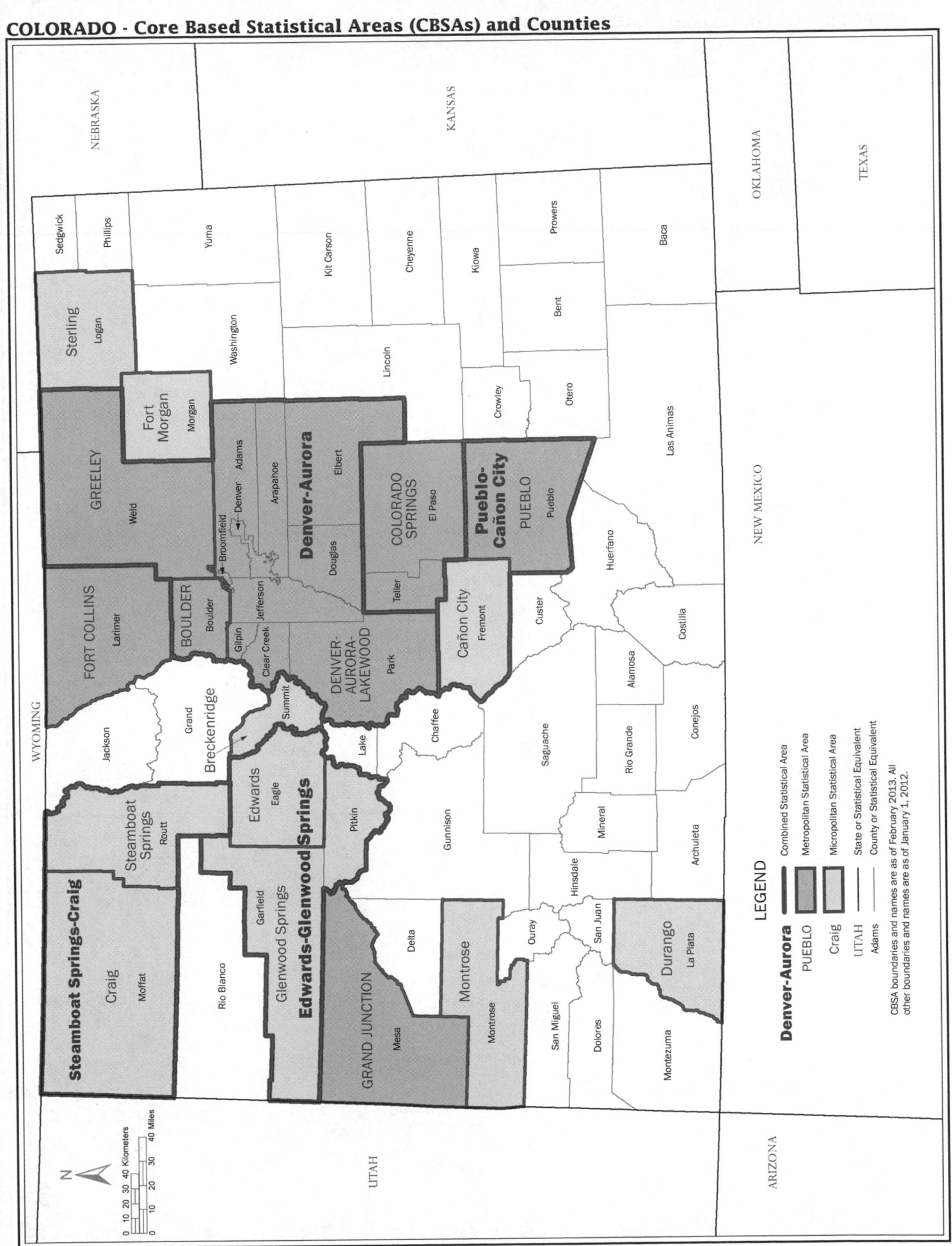

CONNECTICUT - Core Based Statistical Areas (CBSAs) and Counties

RHODE ISLAND

Worcester

Boston-Worcester-Providence (pt)

WORCESTER (pt)

Windham

NORWICH-NEW LONDON

New London

MASSACHUSETTS

Tolland

Hartford-West Hartford

HARTFORD-WEST HARTFORD-EAST HARTFORD

Hartford

Middlesex

NEW HAVEN-MILFORD

New Haven

Long Island Sound

Torrington

Litchfield

New York-Newark (pt)

BRIDGEPORT-STAMFORD-NORWALK

Fairfield

NEW YORK

LEGEND

Combined Statistical Area

Metropolitan Statistical Area

Micropolitan Statistical Area

State or Statistical Equivalent

County or Statistical Equivalent

Coastline

Hartford-West Hartford

NEW HAVEN-MILFORD

Torrington

NEW YORK

Fairfield

Long Island Sound

CBSA boundaries and names are as of February 2013. All other boundaries and names are as of January 1, 2012.

N

0 3 6 9 12 Miles

0 3 6 9 12 Kilometers

Chester

PHILADELPHIA-
CAMDEN-
WILMINGTON
(pt)

Delaware

Burlington

Philadelphia

Camden

PENNSYLVANIA

Wilmington

Gloucester

**Philadelphia-Reading-
Camden (pt)**

Cecil

New
Castle

Salem

NEW JERSEY

DOVER

Kent

Delaware Bay

N

0 3 6 9 12 Kilometers

0 3 6 9 12 Miles

MARYLAND

Atlantic Ocean

Sussex

SALISBURY

Wicomico

Worcester

LEGEND

Philadelphia-Reading-Camden ━━━ Combined Statistical Area

Somerset

DOVER ▭ Metropolitan Statistical Area

Wilmington •••••• Metropolitan Division

MARYLAND ━━━ State or Statistical Equivalent

Kent ─── County or Statistical Equivalent

*Chesapeake
Bay*

Atlantic Ocean ─── Coastline

VIRGINIA

CBSA boundaries and names are as of February 2013. All
other boundaries and names are as of January 1, 2012.

PENNSYLVANIA

WEST VIRGINIA

Frederick

MARYLAND

Jefferson

VIRGINIA

Montgomery

Clarke

Loudoun

Washington-Baltimore-Arlington (pt)

WASHINGTON-ARLINGTON-ALEXANDRIA

Warren

DISTRICT OF COLUMBIA

District of Columbia

Falls Church

Arlington

Washington-Arlington-Alexandria

Fairfax city

Fairfax

Manassas

Alexandria

Fauquier

Manassas Park

Prince George's

Rappahannock

Prince William

Chesapeake Bay

Culpeper

Charles

Calvert

Stafford

N

Fredericksburg

0 4 8 12 16 Kilometers

0 4 8 12 16 Miles

Spotsylvania

LEGEND

Washington-Baltimore-Arlington ——— Combined Statistical Area

WASHINGTON-BALTIMORE-ARLINGTON ▭ Metropolitan Statistical Area

Washington-Arlington-Alexandria ●●●●● Metropolitan Division

VIRGINIA ——— State or Statistical Equivalent

District of Columbia ——— County or Statistical Equivalent

Chesapeake Bay ——— Coastline

CBSA boundaries and names are as of February 2013. All
other boundaries and names are as of January 1, 2012.

FLORIDA - Core Based Statistical Areas (CBSAs) and Counties

LEGEND

Combined Statistical Area
Metropolitan Statistical Area
Micropolitan Statistical Area
Metropolitan Division
State or Statistical Equivalent
County or Statistical Equivalent
Coastline

North Port-Sarasota
OCALA
Arcadia
Miami-Miami Beach-Kendall
GEORGIA
Alachua
Gulf of Mexico

CBSA boundaries and names are as of February 2013. All other boundaries and names are as of January 1, 2012.

GEORGIA - Core Based Statistical Areas (CBSAs) and Counties

TENNESSEE

Chattanooga-Cleveland-Dalton (pt)

NORTH CAROLINA

LEGEND

Rome-Summerville — Combined Statistical Area

ROME — Metropolitan Statistical Area

Jesup — Micropolitan Statistical Area

ALABAMA — State or Statistical Equivalent

Harris — County or Statistical Equivalent

Atlantic Ocean — Coastline

CBSA boundaries and names are as of February 2013. All other boundaries and names are as of January 1, 2012.

Sequatchie

Hamilton

CHATTANOOGA
Marion

Dade

Catoosa

DALTON

Murray

Fannin

Towns

Rabun

Union

Cornelia

Walker

Whitfield

Murray

Gilmer

White

Habersham

Toccoa
Stephens

Summerville

Chattooga

Calhoun
Gordon

Pickens

Lumpkin

Dawson

GAINES-VILLE

Banks

Franklin

Hart

Rome-Summerville

ROME
Floyd

Bartow

Cherokee

Forsyth

Hall

Jefferson
Jackson

Madison

Elbert

SOUTH CAROLINA

Atlanta--Athens-Clarke County--Sandy Springs

Cedartown
Polk

Paulding

Cobb

Gwinnett

Barrow

Clarke

ATHENS-CLARKE COUNTY
Oglethorpe

Wilkes

Lincoln

Edgefield

Aiken

Haralson

Douglas

Fulton

DeKalb

Walton

Oconee

ATLANTA-SANDY SPRINGS-ROSWELL

Carroll

Clayton

Rockdale

Newton

Morgan

Greene

Taliaferro

Warren

McDuffie

Columbia

Richmond

AUGUSTA-RICHMOND COUNTY

ALABAMA

Coweta

Fayette

Henry

Jasper

Putnam

Glascock

Jefferson

Burke

Heard

Spalding

Butts

LaGrange

Meriwether

Pike

Lamar

Monroe

Jones

Baldwin

Milledgeville
Hancock

Washington

Thomaston
Upson

Macon-Warner Robins

MACON
Bibb

Wilkinson

Johnson

Jenkins

Screven

Savannah-Hinesville-Statesboro

Harris

Talbot

Crawford

Twiggs

Dublin

Emanuel

Statesboro
Bulloch

Effingham

Muscogee

Taylor

Peach

WARNER ROBINS
Houston

Bleckley

Laurens

Treutlen

Candler

COLUMBUS
Russell

Chatta-hoochee

Marion

Macon

Schley

Bleckley

Pulaski

Dodge

Wheeler

Montgomery

Vidalia
Toombs

Evans

Tattnall

Bryan

SAVANNAH
Chatham

Columbus-Auburn-Opelika

Stewart

Americus
Sumter

Dooly

Wilcox

Telfair

HINESVILLE

Long

Liberty

Webster

Cordele
Crisp

Ben Hill

Fitzgerald

Jeff Davis

Appling

Jesup
Wayne

McIntosh

Quitman

Randolph

Terrell

Lee

Turner

Irwin

Douglas
Coffee

Bacon

Pierce

BRUNSWICK
Glynn

Clay

Calhoun

Dougherty

Worth

ALBANY

Tifton
Tift

Berrien

Atkinson

Waycross
Ware

Brantley

Atlantic Ocean

Early

Baker

Moultrie
Colquitt

Cook

Lanier

Clinch

St. Marys
Camden

Miller

Mitchell

Seminole

Bainbridge
Decatur

Grady

Thomas-ville
Thomas

Brooks

VALDOSTA

Lowndes

Echols

Charlton

Jacksonville-St. Marys-Palatka (pt)

N

0 10 20 30 40 Kilometers
0 10 20 30 40 Miles

Tallahassee-Bainbridge (pt)

FLORIDA

Hilo
Hawaii

Kalawao
Maui

KAHULUI-
WAILUKU-
LAHAINA

Honolulu
(pt)

URBAN
HONOLULU
(pt)

Kauai

Kapaa

Kapaa

URBAN HONOLULU
(pt)

Honolulu
(pt)

Pacific Ocean

160 Miles

160 Kilometers

120

120

80

80

40

40

0

0

N

LEGEND

URBAN HONOLULU	Metropolitan Statistical Area
Hilo	Micropolitan Statistical Area
Maui	State or Statistical Equivalent
	County or Statistical Equivalent
Pacific Ocean	Coastline

CBSA boundaries and names are as of February 2013. All
other boundaries and names are as of January 1, 2012.

URBAN
HONOLULU
(pt)

Honolulu
(pt)

MIDWAY
ISLANDS
(U.S.
Unincorporated
Territory)

IDAHO - Core Based Statistical Areas (CBSAs) and Counties

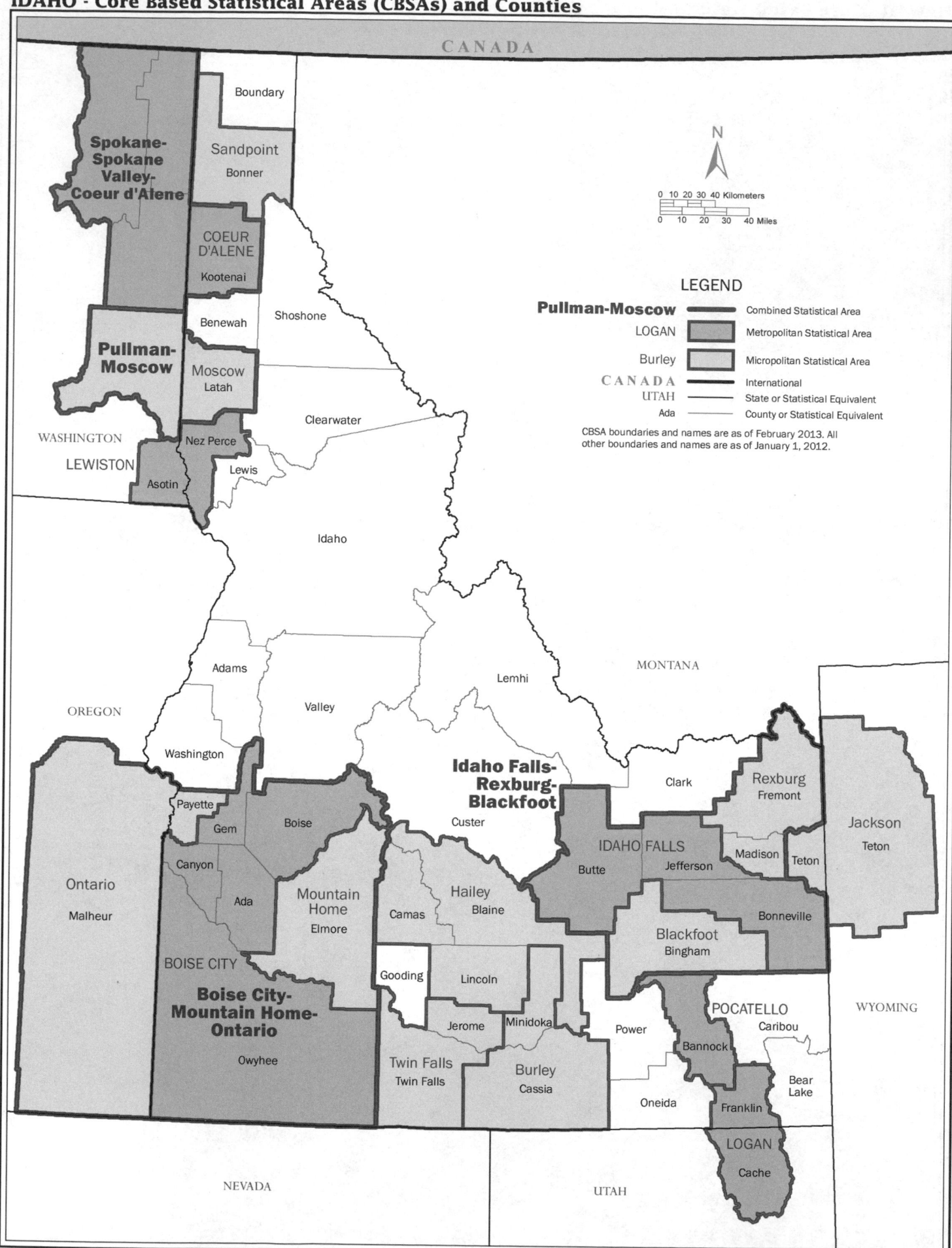

ILLINOIS - Core Based Statistical Areas (CBSAs) and Counties

WISCONSIN

Rockford-Freeport-Rochelle

Freeport
Stephenson

ROCKFORD
Winnebago

Boone

McHenry

Kenosha

Lake County-Kenosha County
Lake

Lake Michigan

Chicago-Naperville

MICHIGAN

Jo Daviess

Carroll

Rochelle
Ogle

Elgin

DeKalb

Kane

CHICAGO-NAPERVILLE-ELGIN

DuPage

Cook

IOWA

Davenport-Moline

Scott

Dixon-Sterling

Sterling
Whiteside

Dixon
Lee

Kendall

Will

Chicago-Naperville-Arlington Heights

Lake

Porter

Rock Island

DAVENPORT-MOLINE-ROCK ISLAND

Henry

Ottawa-Peru
Bureau

LaSalle

Grundy

Newton

Jasper

Mercer

Putnam

KANKAKEE
Kankakee

Burlington
Des Moines

Galesburg
Knox

Stark

Marshall

Pontiac
Livingston

Iroquois

Warren

Henderson

Peoria-Canton

Peoria

Woodford

Lee

Fort Madison-Keokuk

Macomb
McDonough

Canton
Fulton

PEORIA
Tazewell

McLean

Bloomington-Pontiac
BLOOMINGTON

Ford

Clark

Hancock

Mason

Lincoln
Logan

De Witt

CHAMPAIGN-URBANA
Champaign

Piatt

DANVILLE
Vermilion

Lewis

Quincy-Hannibal
Quincy
Adams

Schuyler

Cass

Brown

SPRINGFIELD

Menard

Springfield-Jacksonville-Lincoln

Jacksonville

Sangamon

DECATUR
Macon

Douglas

Charleston-Mattoon
Coles

Edgar

INDIANA

Pike

Scott

Morgan

Taylorville
Christian

Moultrie

Clark

Calhoun

Greene

Macoupin

Montgomery

Shelby

Cumberland

Lincoln

Jersey

ST. LOUIS
Madison

Bond

Fayette

Effingham
Effingham

Jasper

Crawford

MISSOURI

Warren

St. Charles

St. Louis

St. Louis (city)

St. Louis-St. Charles-Farmington

Clinton

Centralia
Marion

Clay

Richland

Lawrence

Wabash

Franklin

St. Clair

Washington

Mount Vernon
Jefferson

Wayne

Edwards

Jefferson

Monroe

Randolph

Perry

Franklin

Hamilton

White

CARBONDALE-MARION
Jackson

Williamson

Saline

Gallatin

CAPE GIRARDEAU
Cape Girardeau

Union

Johnson

Pope

Hardin

Bollinger

Pulaski

Massac

Livingston

KENTUCKY

Paducah
Ballard

McCracken

Cape Girardeau-Sikeston

Paducah-Mayfield

LEGEND

Peoria-Canton ───── Combined Statistical Area

PEORIA ▓▓ Metropolitan Statistical Area

Dixon ☐ Micropolitan Statistical Area

Elgin • • • • Metropolitan Division

IOWA ───── State or Statistical Equivalent

Lee ───── County or Statistical Equivalent

Lake Michigan ───── Coastline

CBSA boundaries and names are as of February 2013. All other boundaries and names are as of January 1, 2012.

TENNESSEE

INDIANA - Core Based Statistical Areas (CBSAs) and Counties

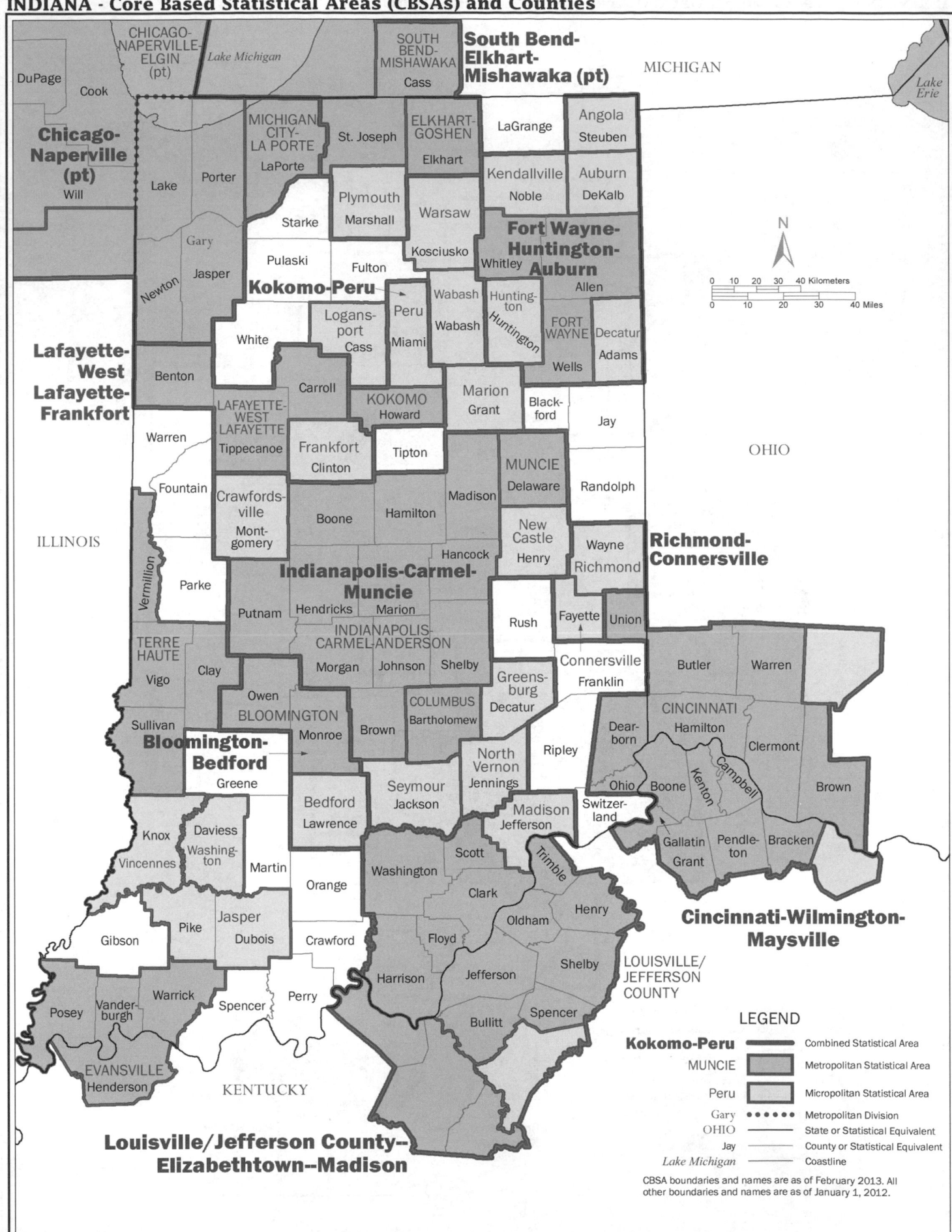

LEGEND

Kokomo-Peru	▬▬▬	Combined Statistical Area
MUNCIE	▨	Metropolitan Statistical Area
Peru	☐	Micropolitan Statistical Area
Gary	••••••	Metropolitan Division
OHIO	▬▬	State or Statistical Equivalent
Jay	▬	County or Statistical Equivalent
Lake Michigan		Coastline

CBSA boundaries and names are as of February 2013. All
other boundaries and names are as of January 1, 2012.

IOWA - Core Based Statistical Areas (CBSAs) and Counties

WISCONSIN

ILLINOIS

MINNESOTA

MISSOURI

KANSAS

NEBRASKA

SOUTH DAKOTA

40 Miles
40 Kilometers
30
20
10
0

N

DAVENPORT-MOLINE-ROCK ISLAND

Jackson

Clinton
Clinton

Scott

Rock Island

Mercer

Henry

DUBUQUE
Dubuque

Cedar Rapids-Iowa City

Allamakee

Clayton

Delaware

Jones

Cedar

Muscatine
Muscatine

Louisa

Henderson

Hancock

Burlington
Des Moines

Fort Madison-Keokuk
Lee

Clark

Winneshiek

Fayette

Buchanan

Linn
CEDAR RAPIDS

Benton

Johnson
IOWA CITY

Washington

Henry

Howard

Chickasaw

Bremer
WATERLOO-CEDAR FALLS
Black Hawk

Iowa

Poweshiek

Keokuk

Fairfield
Jefferson

Van Buren

Mitchell

Floyd

Butler

Grundy

Tama

Oskaloosa
Mahaska

Wapello

Ottumwa
Davis

Worth
Mason City
Cerro Gordo

Franklin

Hardin

Marshall-town
Marshall

Newton
Jasper

Marion

Monroe

Appanoose

Winnebago

Hancock

Wright

Hamilton

AMES
Story

Polk

Warren

Lucas

Wayne

Kossuth

Humboldt

Fort Dodge
Webster

Boone
Boone

DES MOINES-WEST DES MOINES

Madison

Clarke

Decatur

Emmet

Palo Alto

Pocahontas

Calhoun

Greene

Dallas

Guthrie

Adair

Union

Ringgold

Spirit Lake
Dickinson

Spencer
Clay

Storm Lake
Buena Vista

Sac

Carroll

Audubon

Cass

Adams

Taylor

Des Moines-Ames-West Des Moines

Osceola

O'Brien

Cherokee

Ida

Crawford

Shelby

Montgomery

Page

Fremont

Lyon

Sioux

Plymouth

SIOUX CITY
Woodbury

Sioux City-Vermillion

Monona

Harrison

OMAHA-COUNCIL BLUFFS
Pottawattamie

Mills

Union

Dakota

Washington

Douglas

Sarpy

Cass

Dixon

Saunders

Omaha-Council Bluffs-Fremont

LEGEND

Davenport-Moline — Combined Statistical Area

AMES — Metropolitan Statistical Area

Boone — Micropolitan Statistical Area

ILLINOIS — State or Statistical Equivalent

Ida — County or Statistical Equivalent

CBSA boundaries and names are as of February 2013. All other boundaries and names are as of January 1, 2012.

KANSAS - Core Based Statistical Areas (CBSAs) and Counties

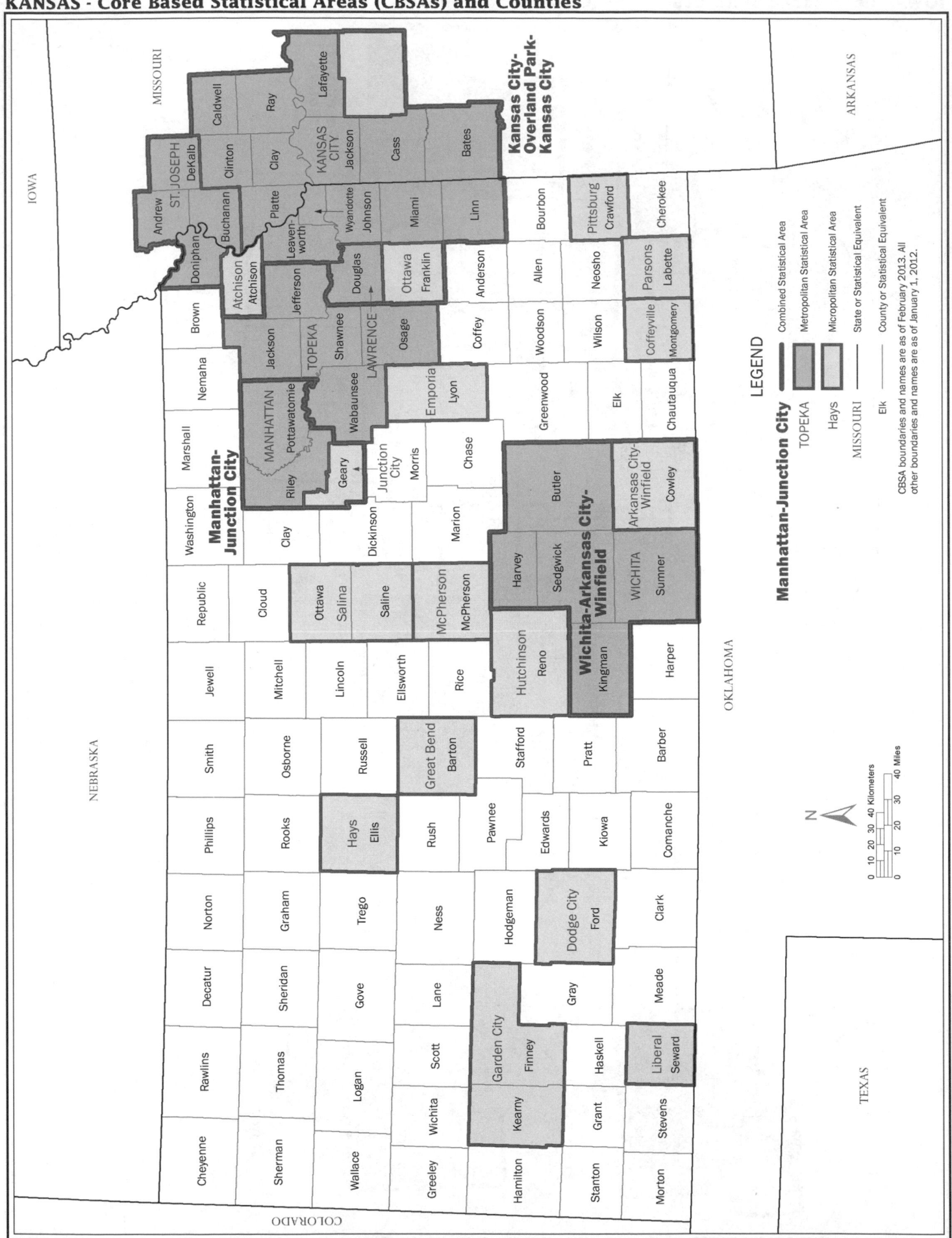

LEGEND

Manhattan-Junction City
TOPEKA
Hays

Combined Statistical Area
Metropolitan Statistical Area
Micropolitan Statistical Area
State or Statistical Equivalent
County or Statistical Equivalent

MISSOURI
Elk

CBSA boundaries and names are as of February 2013. All other boundaries and names are as of January 1, 2012.

KENTUCKY - Core Based Statistical Areas (CBSAs) and Counties

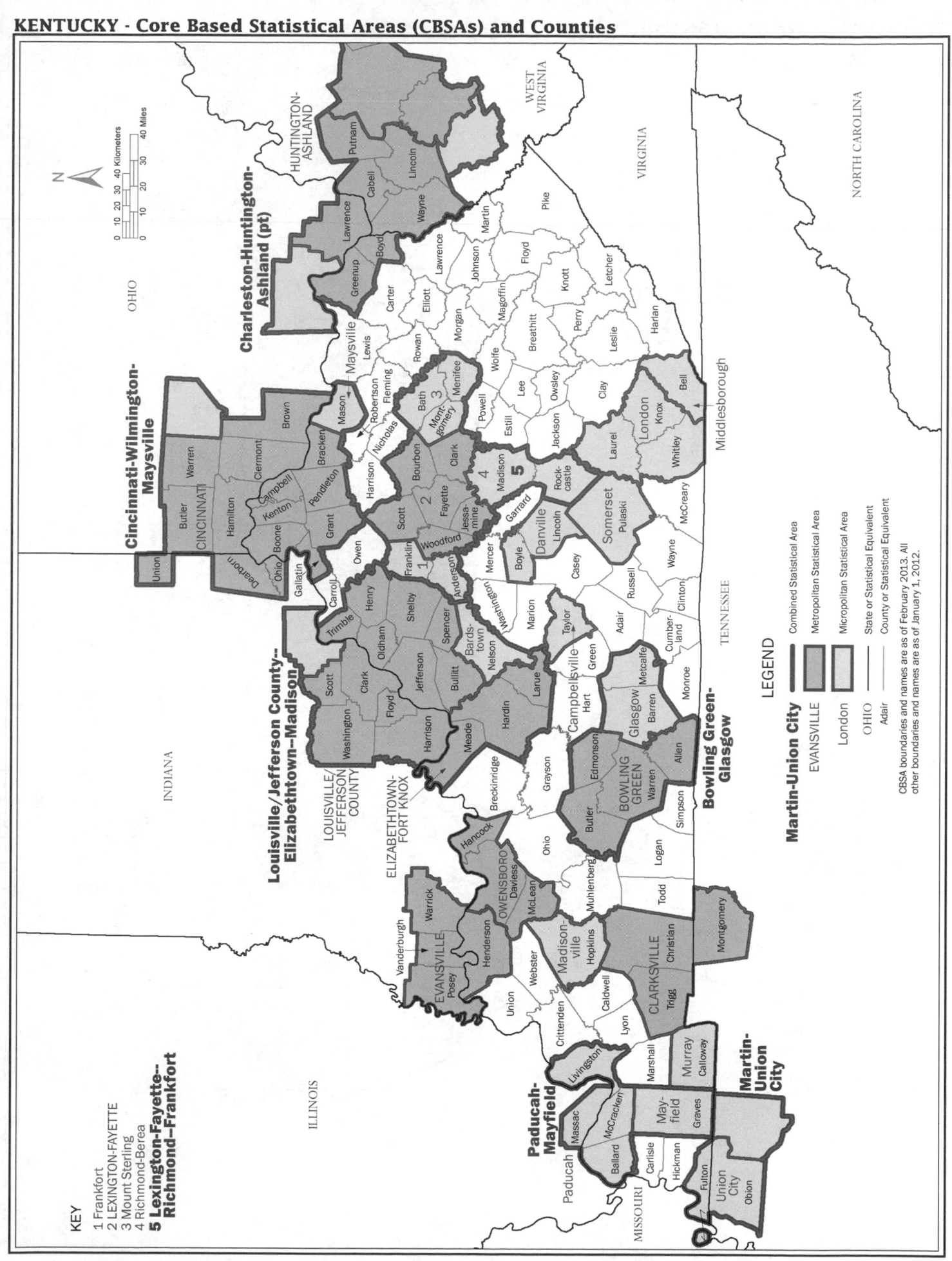

LEGEND

Martin-Union City	Combined Statistical Area
EVANSVILLE	Metropolitan Statistical Area
London	Micropolitan Statistical Area
OHIO	State or Statistical Equivalent
Adair	County or Statistical Equivalent

CBSA boundaries and names are as of February 2013. All other boundaries and names are as of January 1, 2012.

KEY

1 Frankfort
2 LEXINGTON-FAYETTE
3 Mount Sterling
4 Richmond-Berea
5 Lexington-Fayette–Richmond–Frankfort

LOUISIANA - Core Based Statistical Areas (CBSAs) and Counties

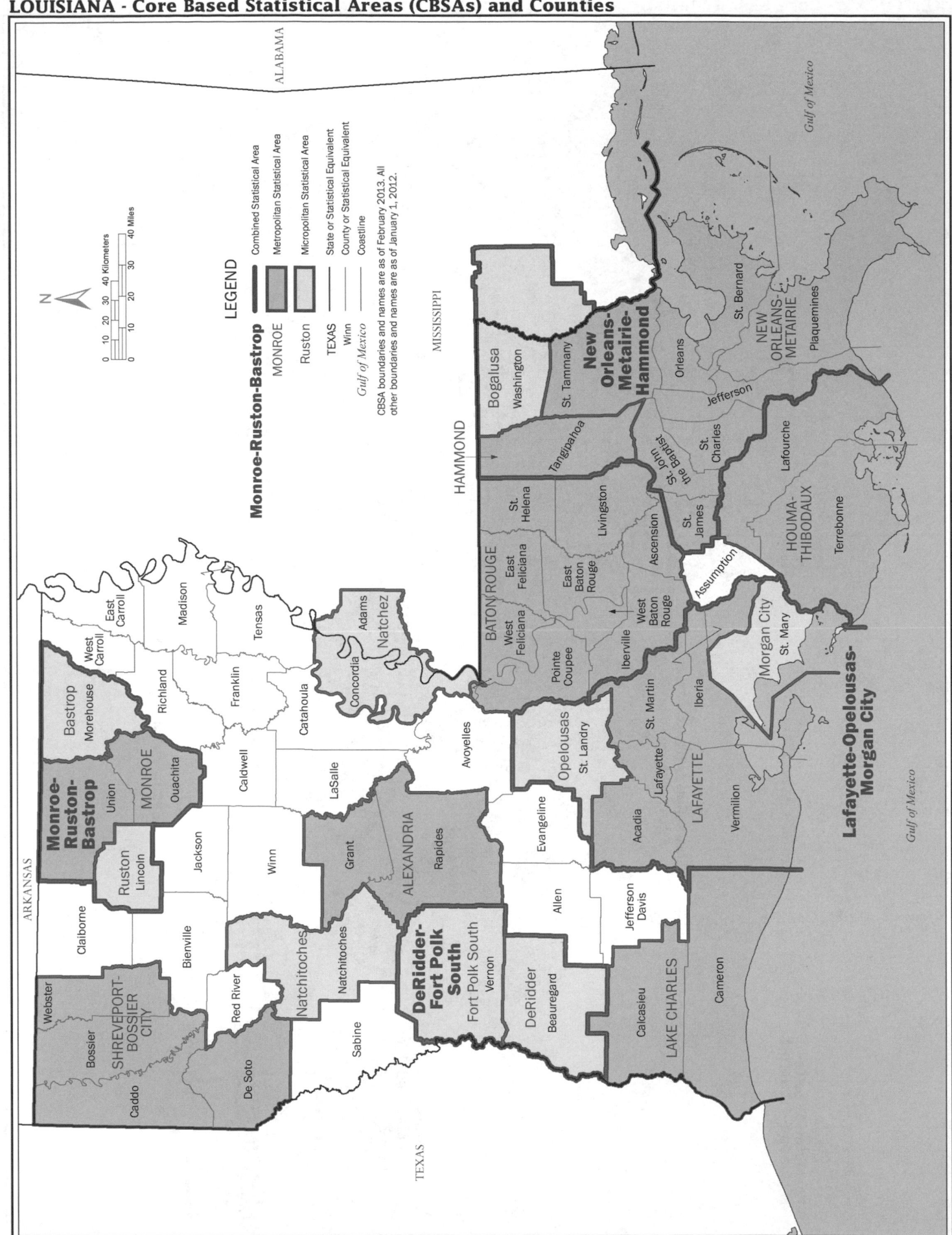

MAINE - Core Based Statistical Areas (CBSAs) and Counties

CANADA

Aroostook

N

0 10 20 30 40 Kilometers
0 10 20 30 40 Miles

Piscataquis

CANADA

Somerset

BANGOR
Penobscot

Franklin

Washington

Oxford

Augusta-
Waterville

Kennebec

Waldo

Hancock

Atlantic Ocean

NEW
HAMPSHIRE

Andro-
scoggin

LEWISTON-
AUBURN

Knox

Lincoln

Sagadahoc

Cumberland

PORTLAND-
SOUTH
PORTLAND

York

Portland-
Lewiston-
South Portland

LEGEND

Portland-Lewiston-South Portland ——— Combined Statistical Area

BANGOR ▭ Metropolitan Statistical Area

Augusta-Waterville ▭ Micropolitan Statistical Area

CANADA ——— International
NEW HAMPSHIRE ——— State or Statistical Equivalent
Knox ——— County or Statistical Equivalent
Atlantic Ocean ——— Coastline

CBSA boundaries and names are as of February 2013. All
other boundaries and names are as of January 1, 2012.

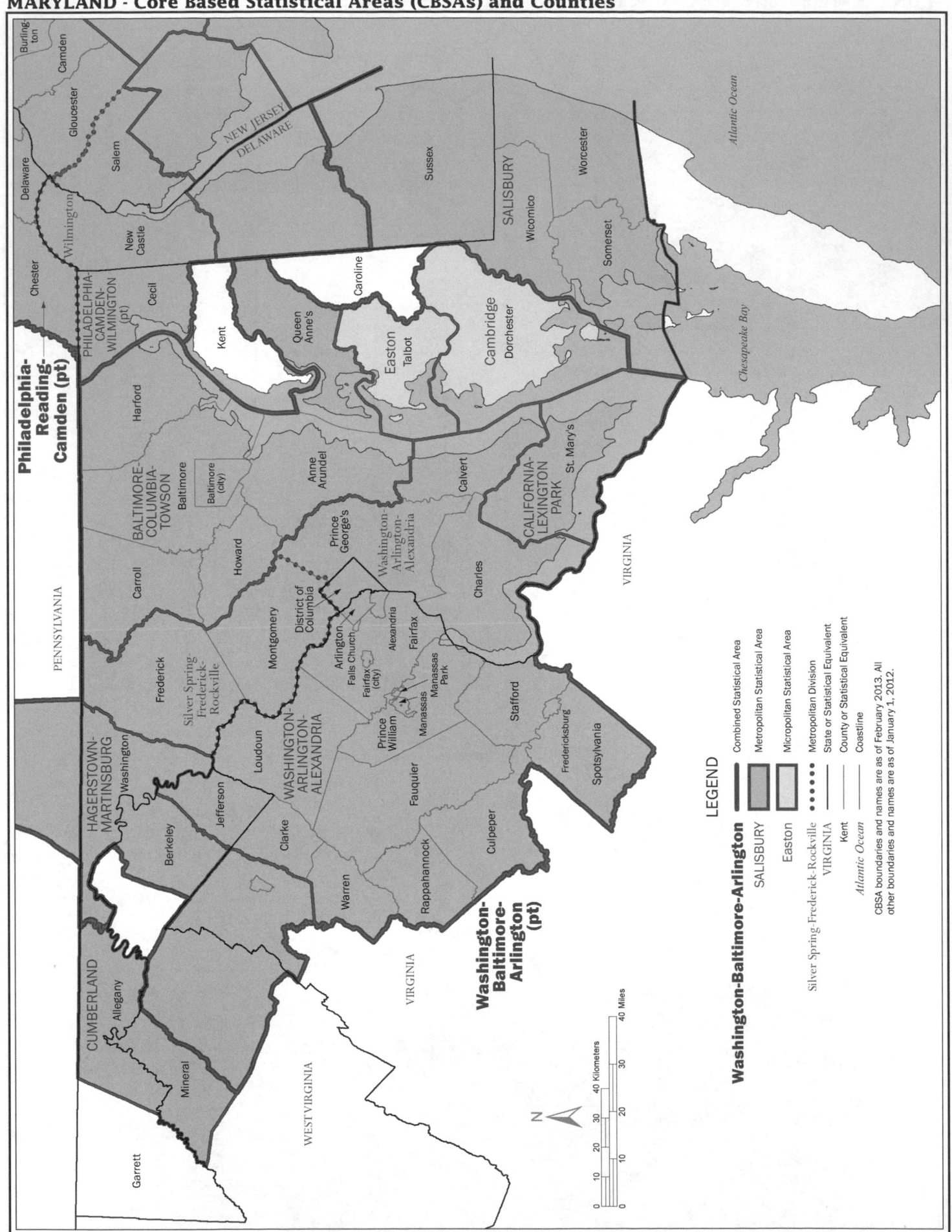

LEGEND

Washington-Baltimore-Arlington

SALISBURY

Easton

Silver Spring-Frederick-Rockville

VIRGINIA

Kent

Atlantic Ocean

Combined Statistical Area

Metropolitan Statistical Area

Micropolitan Statistical Area

Metropolitan Division

State or Statistical Equivalent

County or Statistical Equivalent

Coastline

CBSA boundaries and names are as of February 2013. All other boundaries and names are as of January 1, 2012.

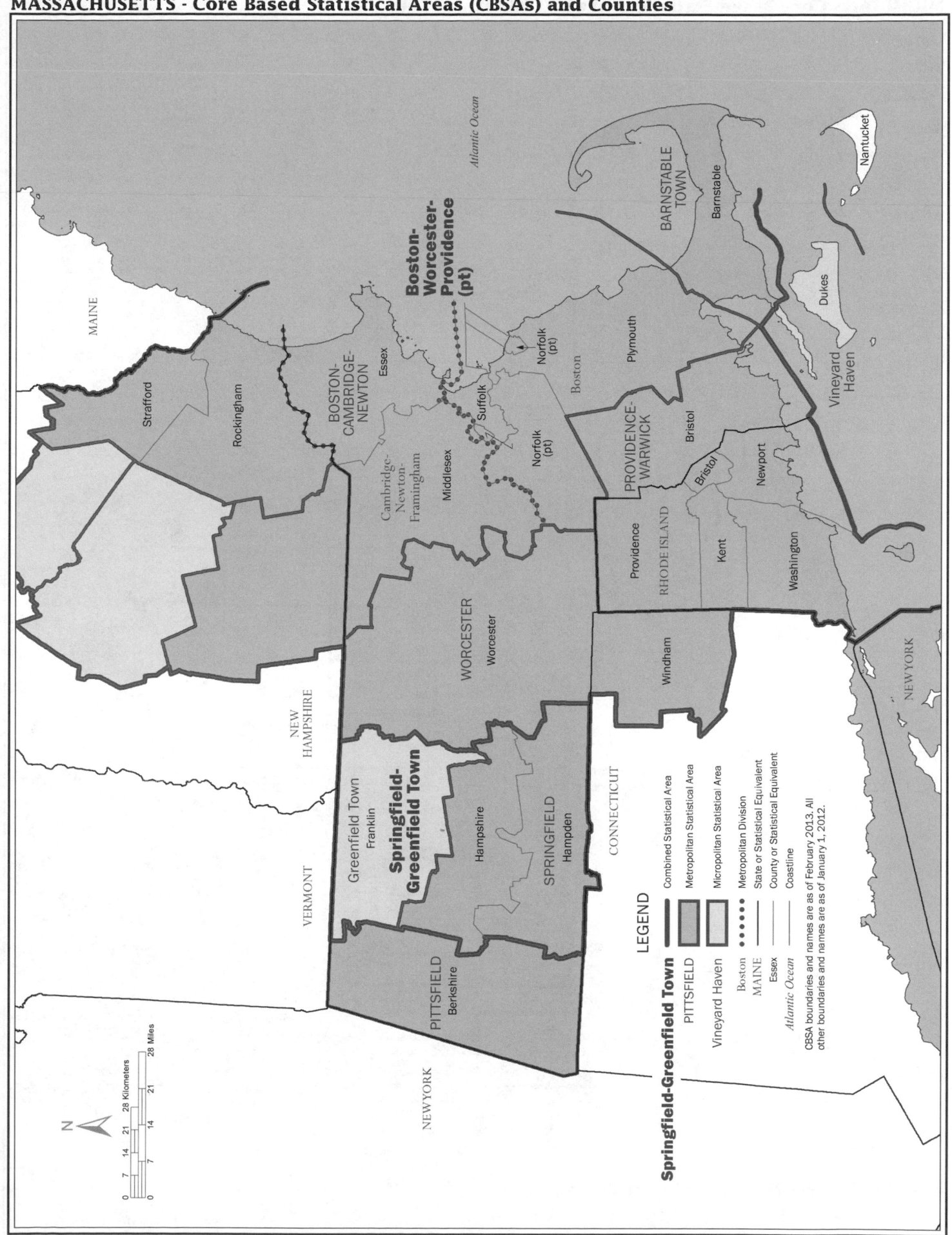

MICHIGAN - Core Based Statistical Areas (CBSAs) and Counties

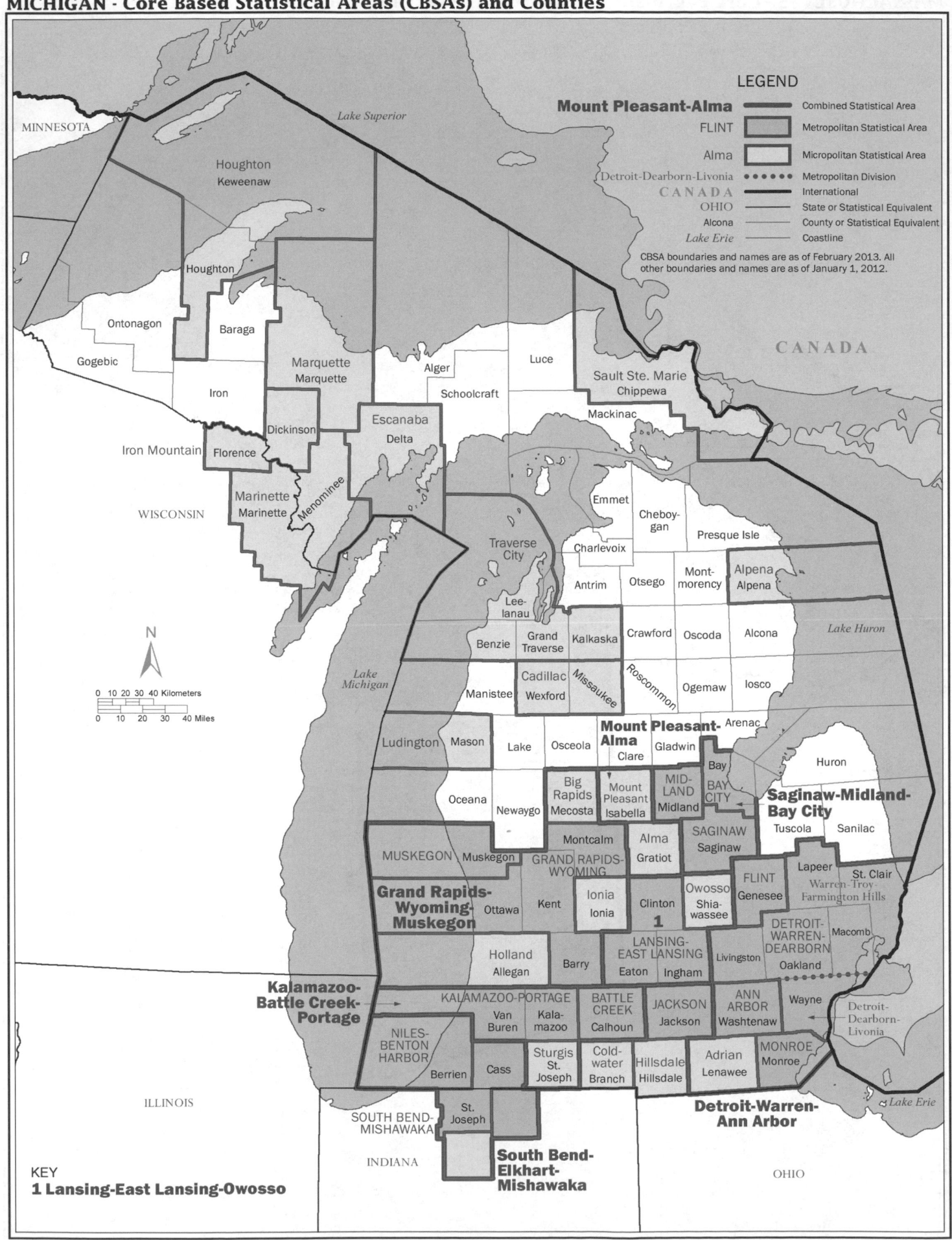

LEGEND

Mount Pleasant-Alma — Combined Statistical Area

FLINT — Metropolitan Statistical Area

Alma — Micropolitan Statistical Area

Detroit-Dearborn-Livonia ••••••• Metropolitan Division

CANADA — International

OHIO —— State or Statistical Equivalent

Alcona —— County or Statistical Equivalent

Lake Erie —— Coastline

CBSA boundaries and names are as of February 2013. All other boundaries and names are as of January 1, 2012.

0 10 20 30 40 Kilometers

0 10 20 30 40 Miles

KEY

1 Lansing-East Lansing-Owosso

MINNESOTA - Core Based Statistical Areas (CBSAs) and Counties

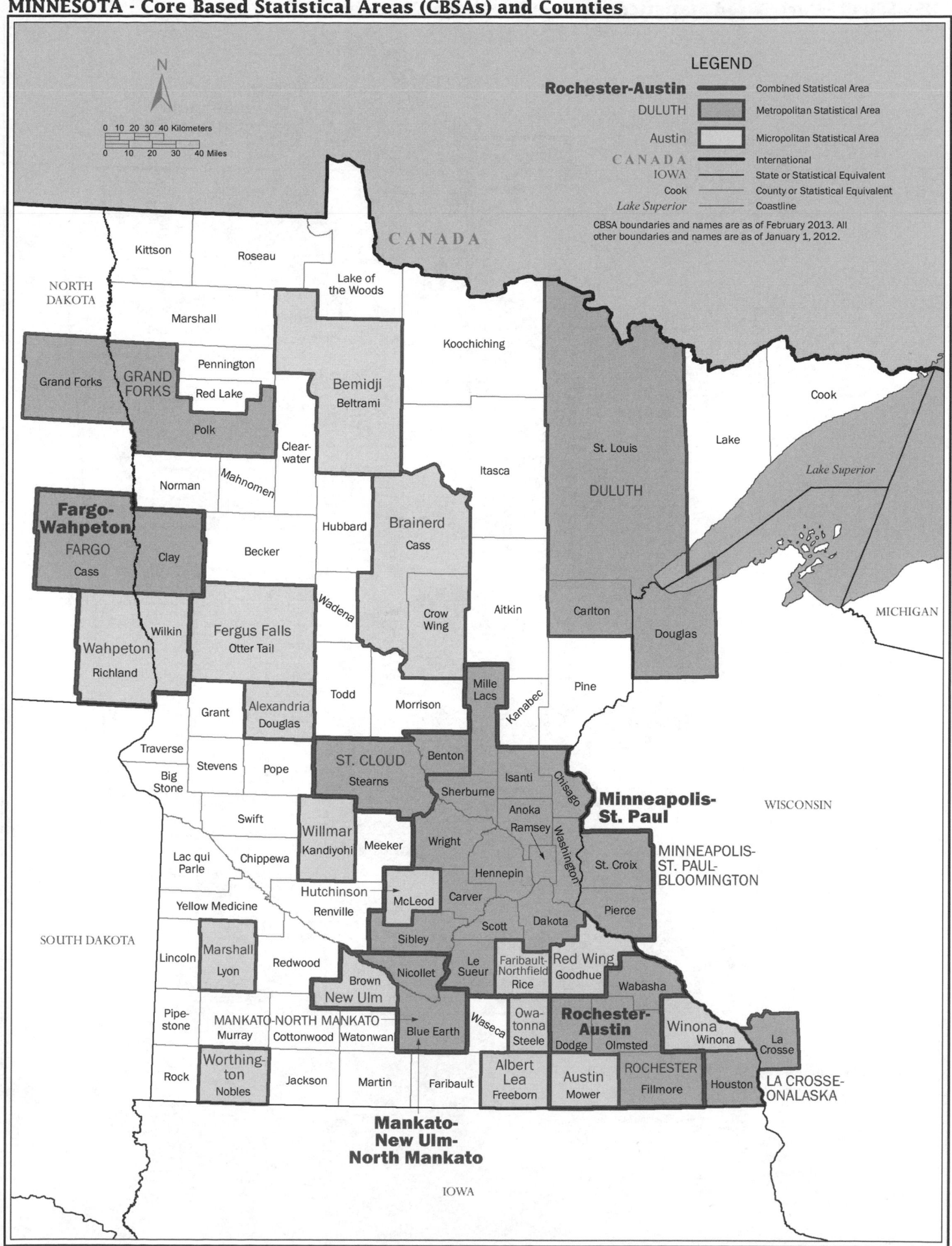

MISSISSIPPI - Core Based Statistical Areas (CBSAs) and Counties

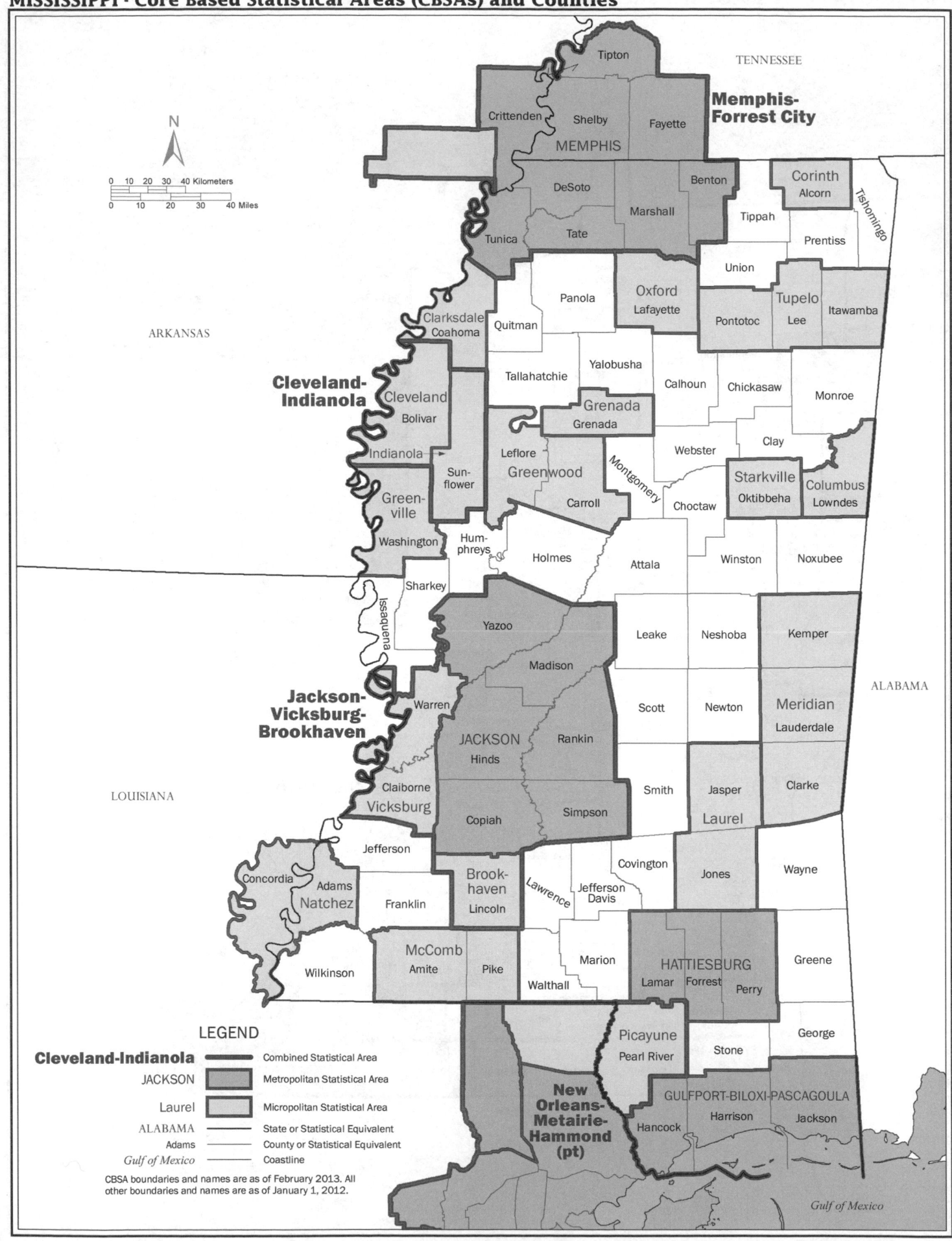

LEGEND

Cleveland-Indianola — Combined Statistical Area

JACKSON — Metropolitan Statistical Area

Laurel — Micropolitan Statistical Area

ALABAMA — State or Statistical Equivalent

Adams — County or Statistical Equivalent

Gulf of Mexico — Coastline

CBSA boundaries and names are as of February 2013. All other boundaries and names are as of January 1, 2012.

MISSOURI - Core Based Statistical Areas (CBSAs) and Counties

U.S. DEPARTMENT OF COMMERCE Economics and Statistics Administration U.S. Census Bureau

Appendix D

MONTANA - Core Based Statistical Areas (CBSAs) and Counties

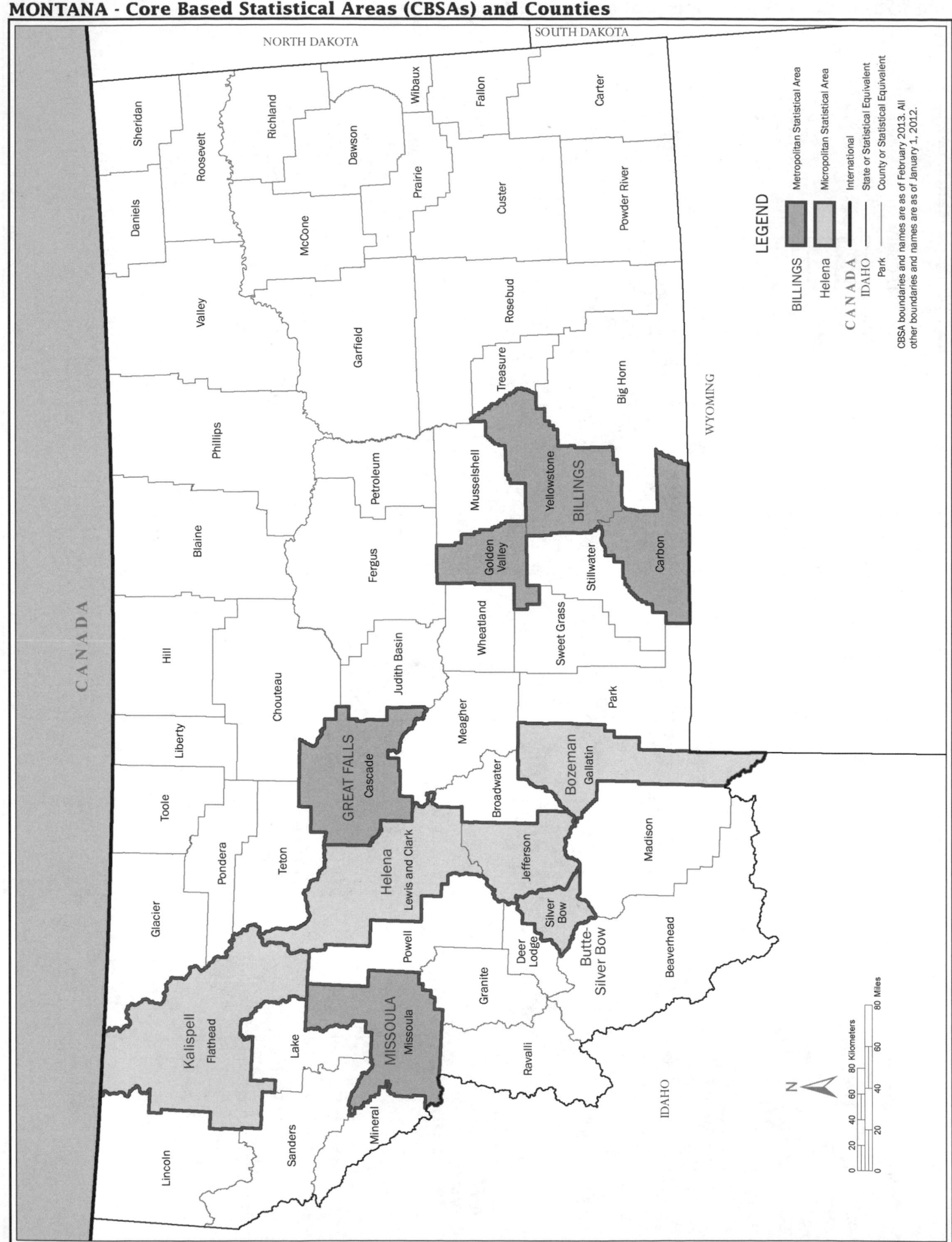

MINNESOTA

IOWA

MISSOURI

Sioux City-Vermillion

Omaha-Council Bluffs-Fremont

Lincoln-Beatrice

SIOUX CITY

Plymouth

Woodbury

Harrison

OMAHA-COUNCIL BLUFFS

Pottawattamie

Mills

Union

Dixon

Dakota

Thurston

Burt

Washington

Douglas

Sarpy

Cass

Otoe

Nemaha

Richardson

Johnson

Pawnee

Cedar

Wayne

Stanton

Colfax

Cuming

Fremont

Dodge

Saunders

LINCOLN

Lancaster

Seward

Beatrice

Gage

Saline

Jefferson

Pierce

Norfolk

Madison

Columbus

Platte

Butler

York

Fillmore

Thayer

Knox

Antelope

Boone

Nance

Polk

Hamilton

Clay

Nuckolls

GRAND ISLAND

Merrick

Wheeler

Greeley

Hall

Hastings

Adams

Webster

KANSAS

Boyd

Holt

Garfield

Valley

Sherman

Howard

Buffalo

Kearney

Kearney

Franklin

Keya Paha

Rock

Loup

Custer

Phelps

Harlan

Brown

Blaine

Dawson

Lexington

Gosper

Furnas

Thomas

Logan

North Platte

Frontier

Red Willow

Cherry

Hooker

McPherson

Lincoln

Hayes

Hitchcock

SOUTH DAKOTA

Grant

Arthur

Keith

Perkins

Chase

Dundy

Sheridan

Garden

Deuel

Dawes

Box Butte

Morrill

Cheyenne

COLORADO

Sioux

Scottsbluff

Scotts Bluff

Banner

Kimball

WYOMING

LEGEND

Lincoln-Beatrice — Combined Statistical Area

LINCOLN — Metropolitan Statistical Area

Norfolk — Micropolitan Statistical Area

IOWA — State or Statistical Equivalent

Adams — County or Statistical Equivalent

CBSA boundaries and names are as of February 2013. All other boundaries and names are as of January 1, 2012.

0 10 20 30 40 Kilometers
0 10 20 30 40 Miles

N

NEVADA - Core Based Statistical Areas (CBSAs) and Counties

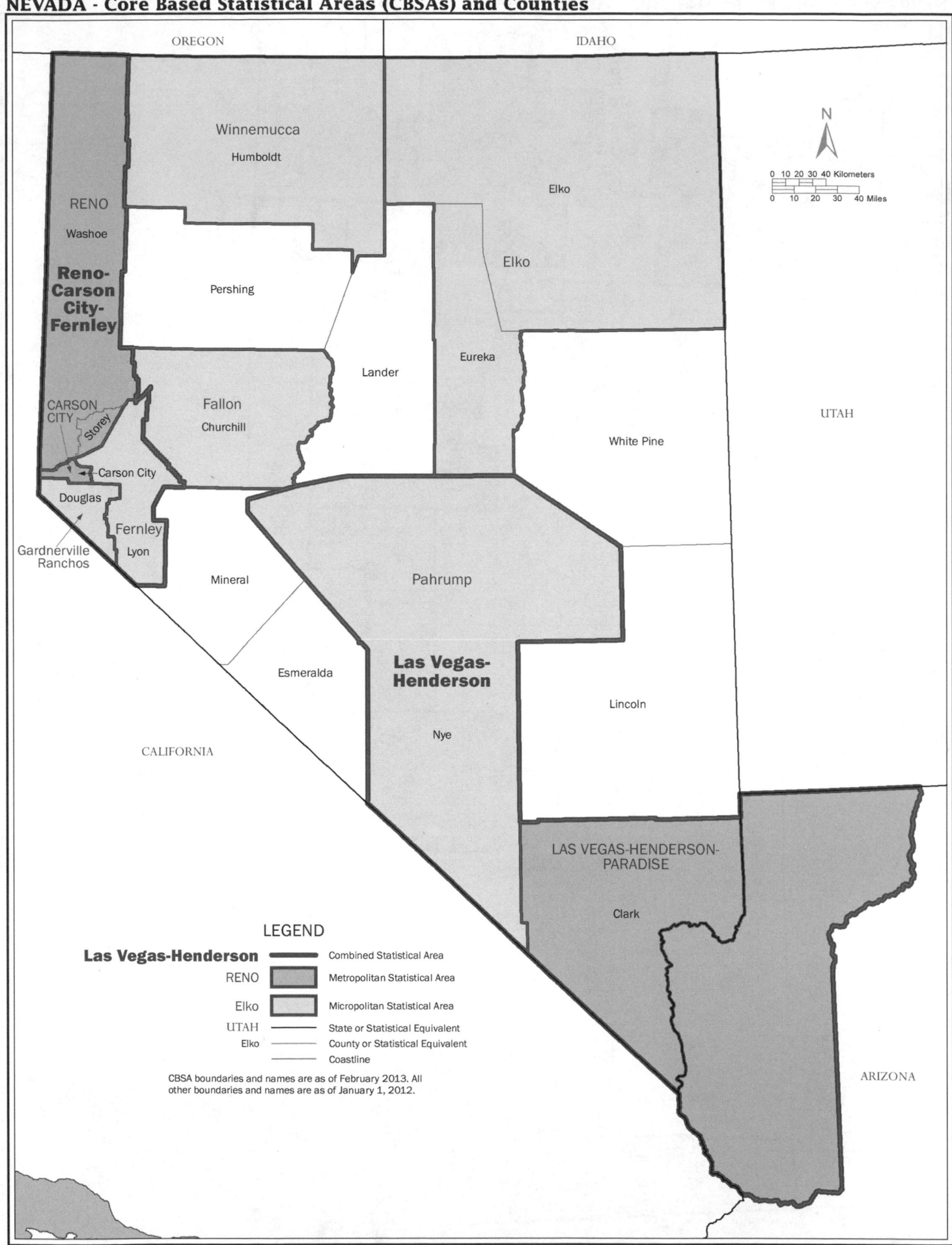

OREGON

IDAHO

Winnemucca

Humboldt

Elko

RENO

Washoe

Elko

Reno-Carson City-Fernley

Pershing

Eureka

UTAH

Lander

CARSON CITY

Storey

Fallon

Churchill

White Pine

Carson City

Douglas

Fernley

Gardnerville Ranchos

Lyon

Mineral

Pahrump

Las Vegas-Henderson

Esmeralda

Lincoln

Nye

CALIFORNIA

LAS VEGAS-HENDERSON-PARADISE

Clark

ARIZONA

N

0 10 20 30 40 Kilometers
0 10 20 30 40 Miles

LEGEND

Las Vegas-Henderson	Combined Statistical Area
RENO	Metropolitan Statistical Area
Elko	Micropolitan Statistical Area
UTAH	State or Statistical Equivalent
Elko	County or Statistical Equivalent
	Coastline

CBSA boundaries and names are as of February 2013. All other boundaries and names are as of January 1, 2012.

NEW HAMPSHIRE - Core Based Statistical Areas (CBSAs) and Counties

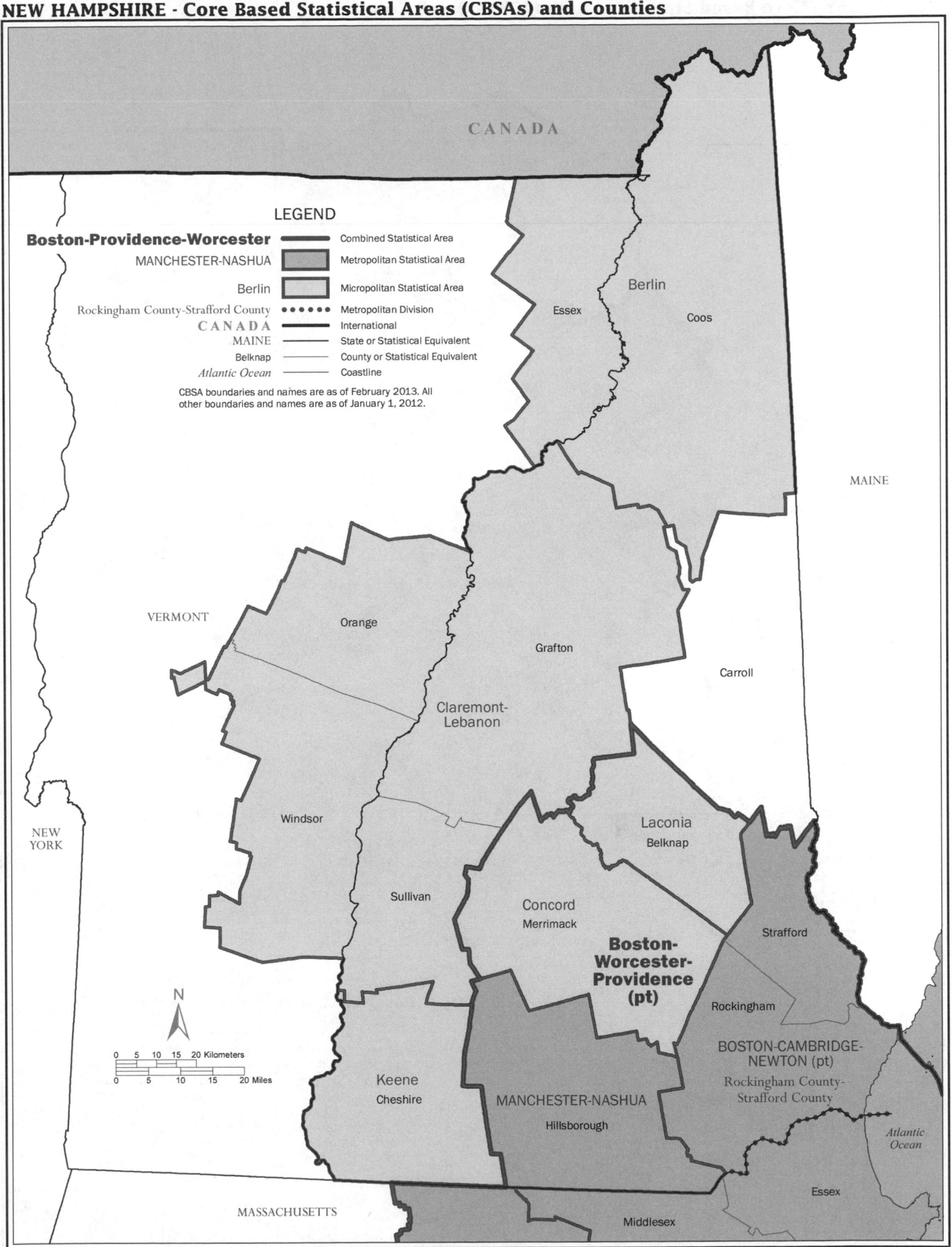

CANADA

LEGEND

Boston-Providence-Worcester ————— Combined Statistical Area

MANCHESTER-NASHUA ▓▓▓ Metropolitan Statistical Area

Berlin ░░░ Micropolitan Statistical Area

Rockingham County-Strafford County •••••• Metropolitan Division

CANADA ————— International

MAINE ——— State or Statistical Equivalent

Belknap ——— County or Statistical Equivalent

Atlantic Ocean ——— Coastline

CBSA boundaries and names are as of February 2013. All
other boundaries and names are as of January 1, 2012.

Essex

Berlin

Coos

MAINE

VERMONT

Orange

Grafton

Carroll

Claremont-
Lebanon

Windsor

Laconia

Belknap

NEW
YORK

Sullivan

Concord

Merrimack

**Boston-
Worcester-
Providence
(pt)**

Strafford

Rockingham

BOSTON-CAMBRIDGE-
NEWTON (pt)

*Rockingham County-
Strafford County*

N

0 5 10 15 20 Kilometers
0 5 10 15 20 Miles

Keene

Cheshire

MANCHESTER-NASHUA

Hillsborough

*Atlantic
Ocean*

MASSACHUSETTS

Middlesex

Essex

NEW JERSEY - Core Based Statistical Areas (CBSAs) and Counties

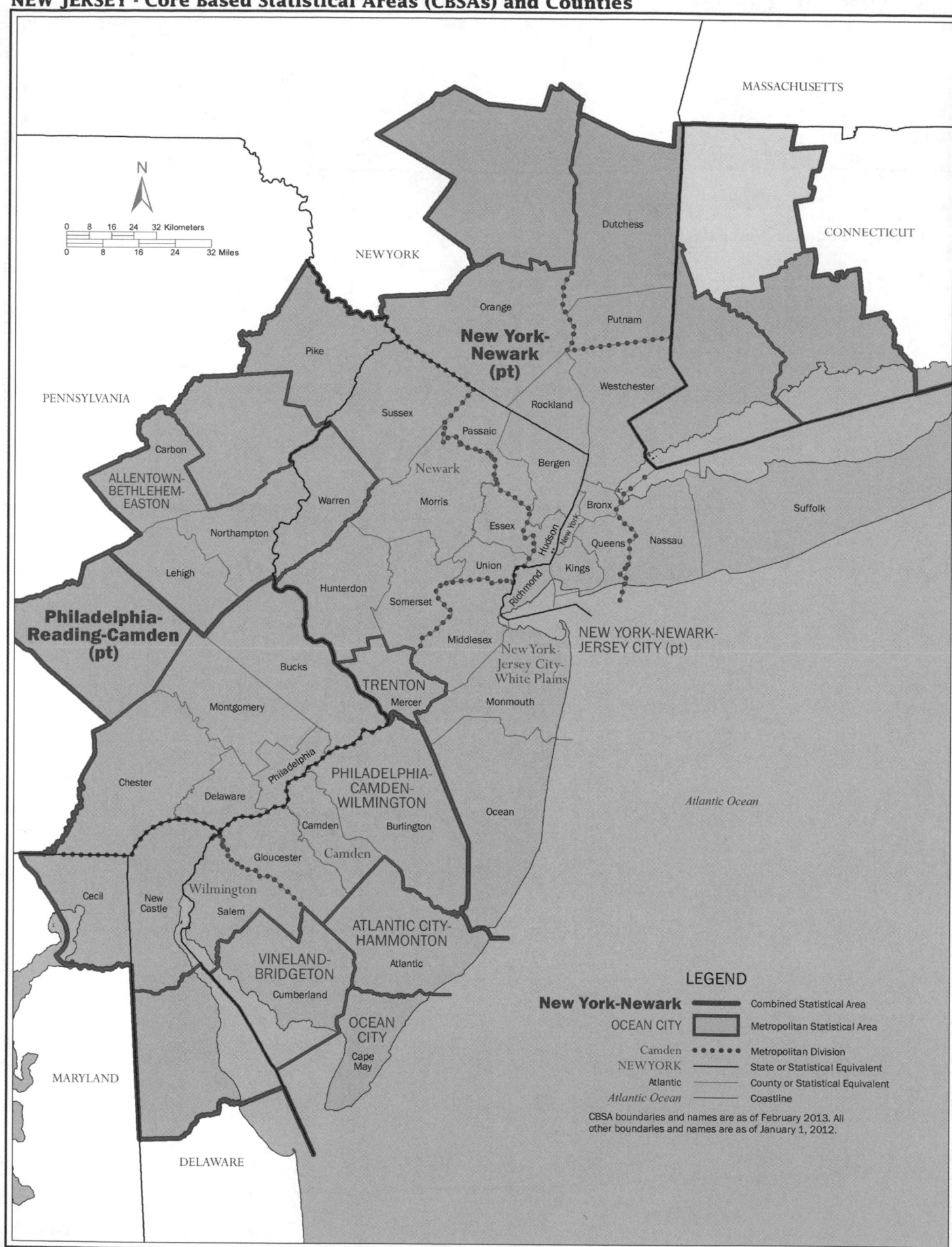

LEGEND

New York-Newark ▬▬▬ Combined Statistical Area

OCEAN CITY ▭ Metropolitan Statistical Area

Camden ●●●●● Metropolitan Division

NEW YORK ▬▬ State or Statistical Equivalent

Atlantic ▬▬ County or Statistical Equivalent

Atlantic Ocean ▬▬ Coastline

CBSA boundaries and names are as of February 2013. All
other boundaries and names are as of January 1, 2012.

NEW MEXICO - Core Based Statistical Areas (CBSAs) and Counties

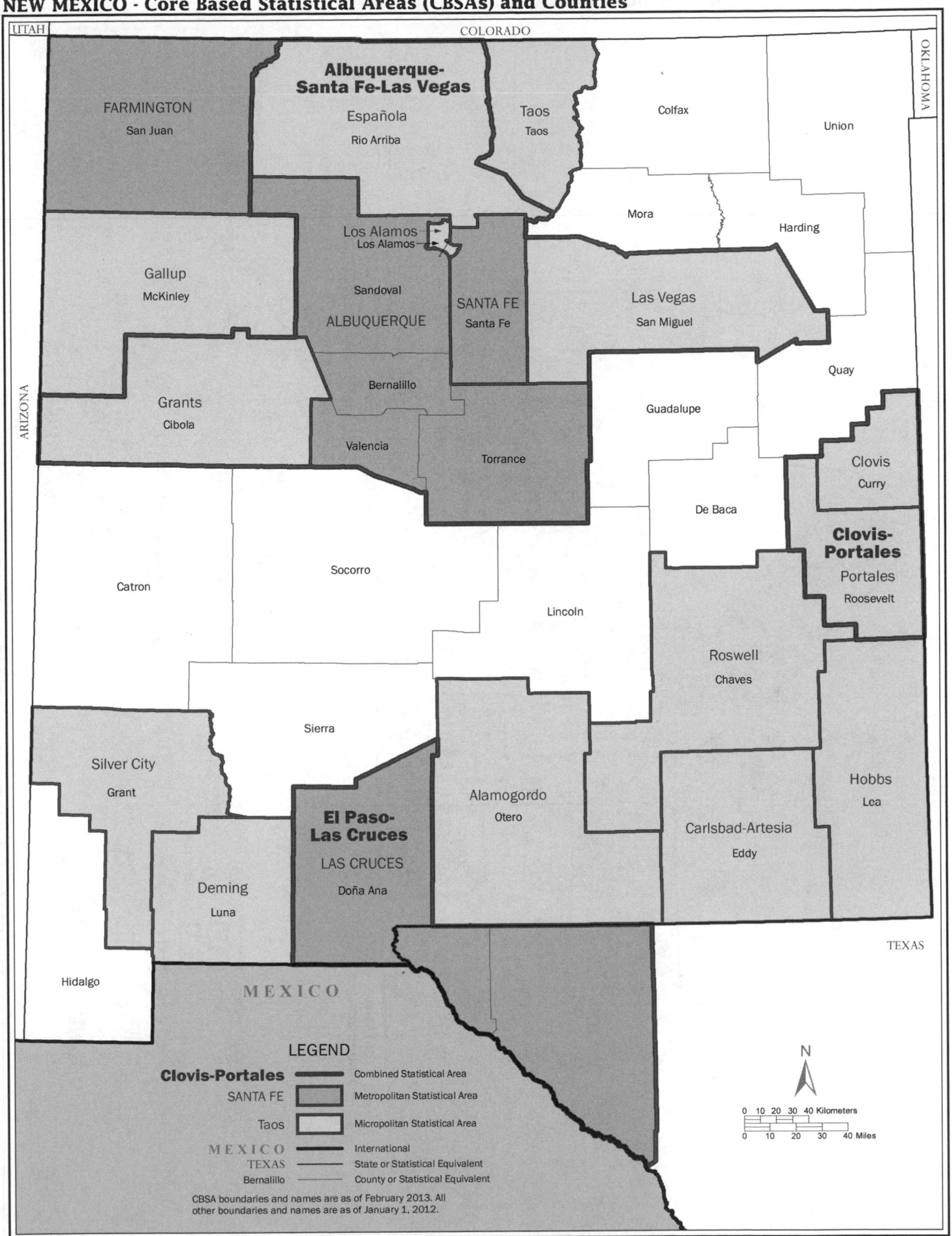

UTAH

COLORADO

OKLAHOMA

ARIZONA

Albuquerque-Santa Fe-Las Vegas

FARMINGTON
San Juan

Española
Rio Arriba

Taos
Taos

Colfax

Union

Los Alamos
Los Alamos

Mora

Harding

Gallup
McKinley

Sandoval

SANTA FE
Santa Fe

Las Vegas
San Miguel

ALBUQUERQUE

Quay

Grants
Cibola

Bernalillo

Guadalupe

Clovis
Curry

Valencia

Torrance

De Baca

Clovis-Portales

Socorro

Lincoln

Portales
Roosevelt

Catron

Roswell
Chaves

Sierra

Silver City
Grant

Alamogordo
Otero

Hobbs
Lea

El Paso-Las Cruces

LAS CRUCES

Carlsbad-Artesia
Eddy

Deming
Luna

Doña Ana

Hidalgo

M E X I C O

TEXAS

LEGEND

Clovis-Portales	Combined Statistical Area
SANTA FE	Metropolitan Statistical Area
Taos	Micropolitan Statistical Area
M E X I C O	International
TEXAS	State or Statistical Equivalent
Bernalillo	County or Statistical Equivalent

CBSA boundaries and names are as of February 2013. All
other boundaries and names are as of January 1, 2012.

N

0 10 20 30 40 Kilometers

0 10 20 30 40 Miles

U.S. DEPARTMENT OF COMMERCE Economics and Statistics Administration U.S. Census Bureau

NEW YORK - Core Based Statistical Areas (CBSAs) and Counties

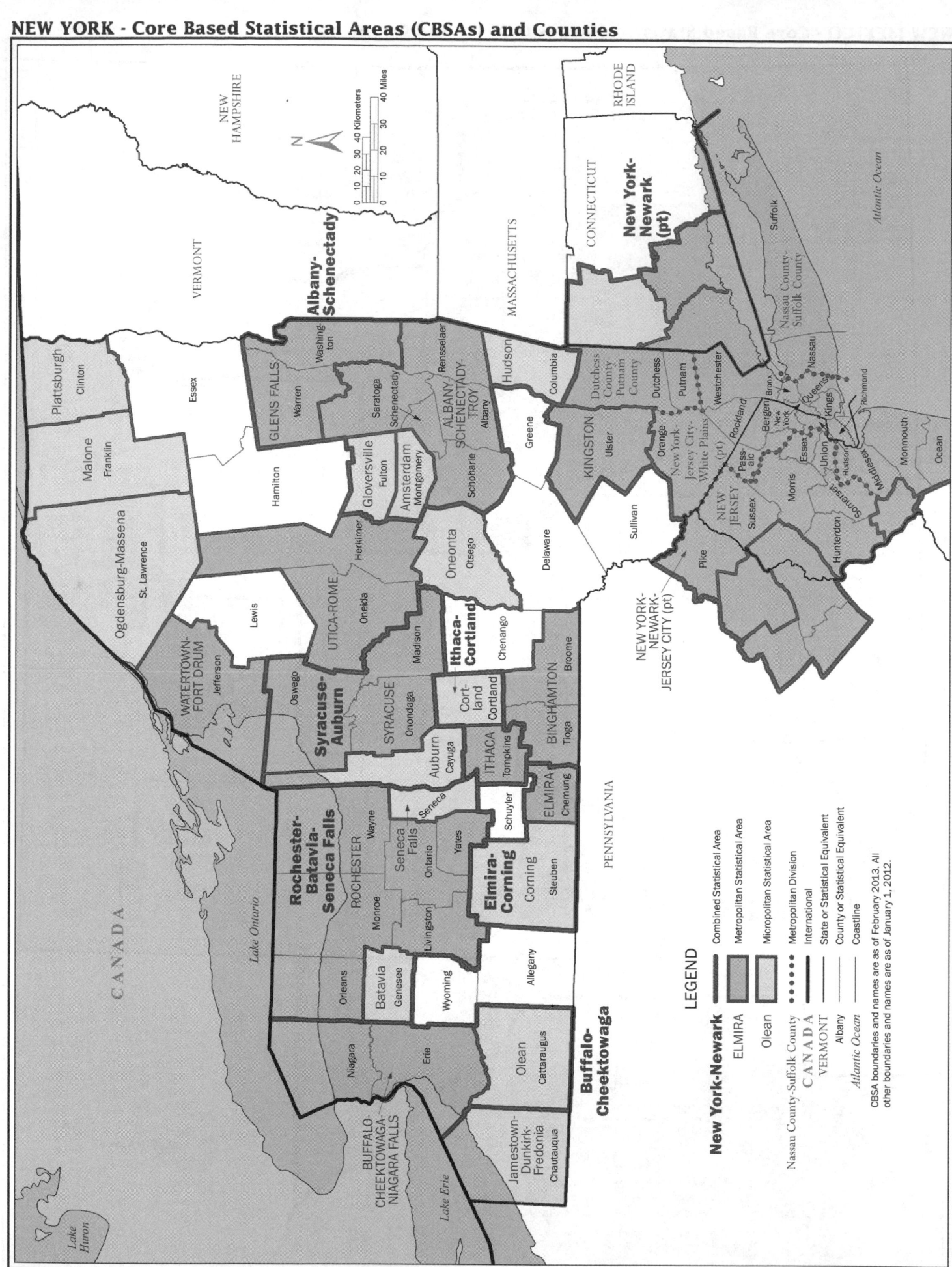

NORTH CAROLINA - Core Based Statistical Areas (CBSAs) and Counties

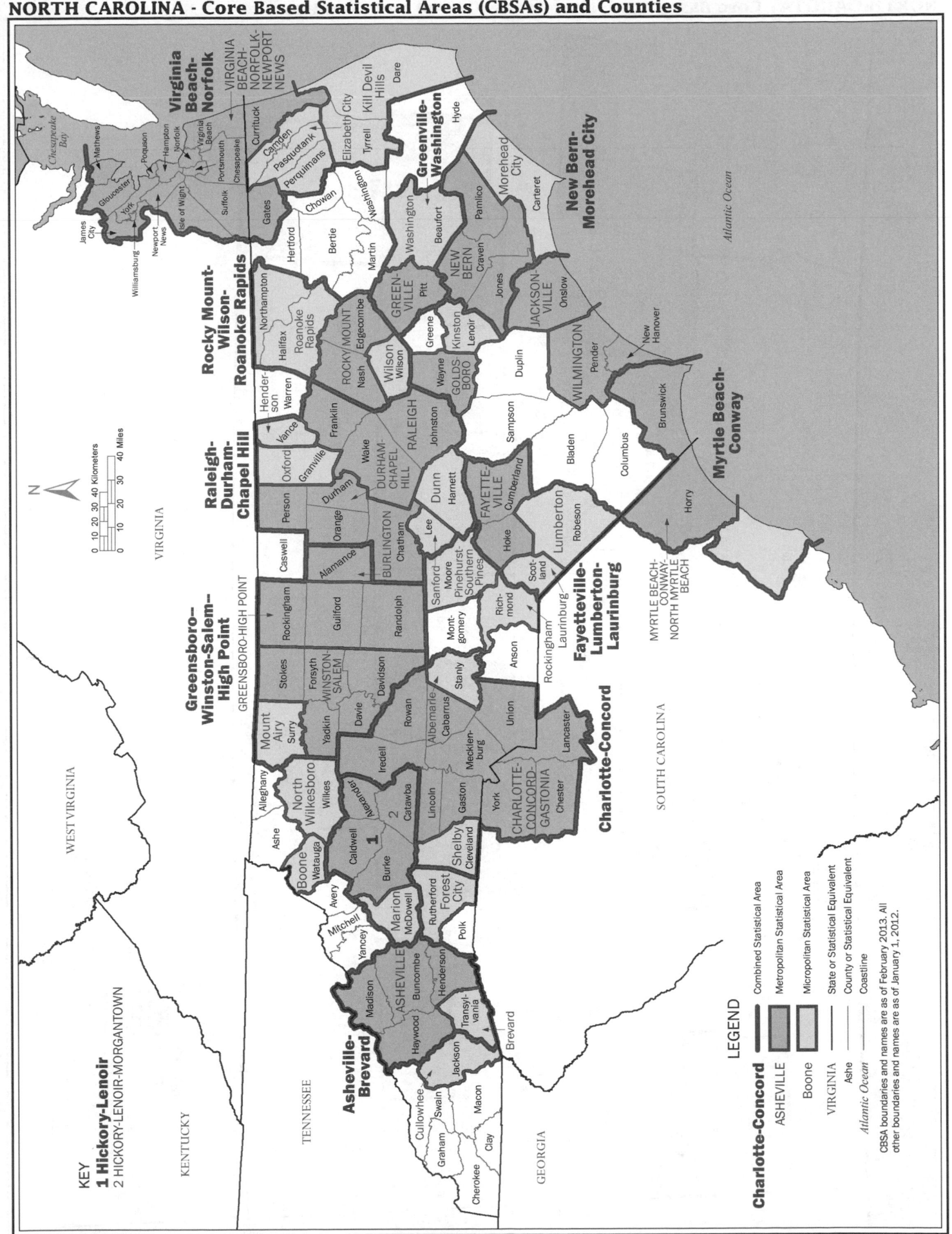

NORTH DAKOTA - Core Based Statistical Areas (CBSAs) and Counties

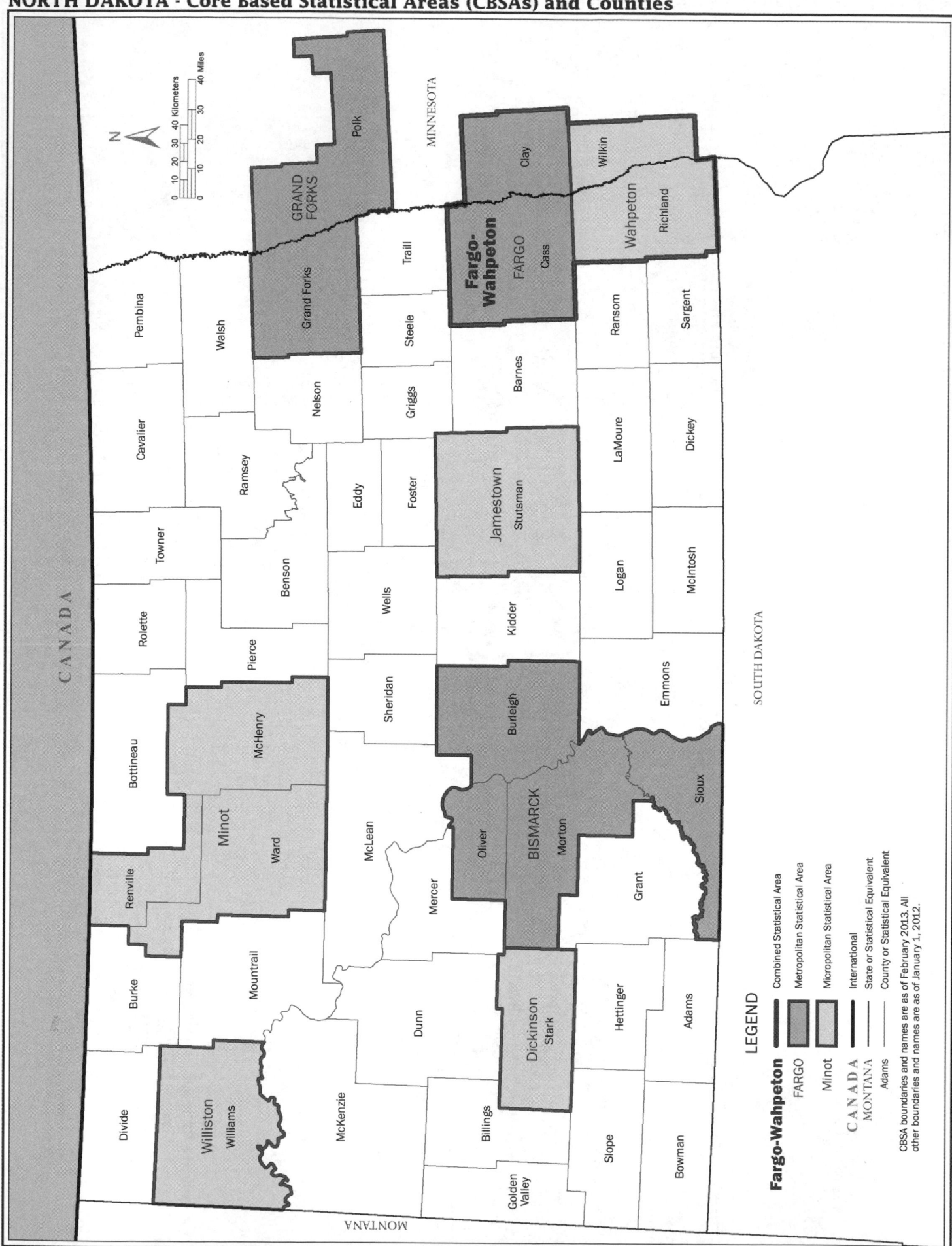

MICHIGAN

CANADA

Lake Erie

PENNSYLVANIA

Cleveland-Akron-Canton

Ashtabula
Ashtabula

Lake

Geauga

CLEVELAND-ELYRIA

Youngstown-Warren

YOUNGSTOWN-WARREN-BOARDMAN

Trumbull

Mercer

Toledo-Port Clinton

Williams

Fulton

Lucas

Ottawa

Port Clinton

Erie

Defiance
Defiance

Henry

TOLEDO
Wood

Fremont
Sandusky

Sandusky

Lorain

Cuyahoga

AKRON
Portage

Summit

Mahoning

Paulding

Putnam

Findlay-Tiffin

Findlay
Hancock

Tiffin
Seneca

Norwalk
Huron

Mansfield-Ashland-Bucyrus

Ash-land
Ashland

Medina

CANTON-MASSILLON

Salem
Columbiana

Pittsburgh-New Castle-Weirton (pt)

Lima-Van Wert-Celina

Van Wert
Van Wert

LIMA
Allen

Wyandot

Bucyrus
Crawford

MANS-FIELD
Richland

Wooster
Wayne

Stark

Carroll

Jefferson

Hancock

Brooke

WEIRTON-STEUBENVILLE

Celina
Mercer

Wapakoneta
Auglaize

Hardin

Marion
Marion

Morrow

Holmes

Tuscarawas
New Philadelphia-Dover

Harrison

Ohio

Sidney
Shelby

Bellefontaine
Logan

Mount Vernon
Knox

Coshocton
Coshocton

WHEELING

Belmont

Greenville
Darke

Urbana
Champaign

Union

Delaware

Columbus-Marion-Zanesville

Licking

Cambridge
Guernsey

Marshall

DAYTON
Miami

SPRINGFIELD
Clark

Madison

COLUMBUS
Franklin

Zanesville
Muskingum

Noble

Monroe

Preble

Dayton-Springfield-Sidney

Greene

Fairfield

Perry

Morgan

Parkersburg-Marietta-Vienna

Union

Montgomery

Washington Court House
Fayette

Pickaway

Marietta
Washington

Cincinnati-Wilmington-Maysville

Wilmington
Clinton

Chillicothe
Ross

Hocking

Butler

Warren

Highland

Vinton

Athens
Athens

Dearborn

CINCINNATI
Hamilton

Clermont

Pike

Jackson
Jackson

Meigs

Ohio

Boone

Kenton

Campbell

Brown

Adams

Portsmouth
Scioto

Point Pleasant

Gallatin

Pendleton

Bracken

Gallia

Mason

WEST VIRGINIA

Grant

INDIANA

Greenup

Lawrence

Putnam

Charleston-Huntington-Ashland

KENTUCKY

Boyd

Cabell

Wayne

Lincoln

HUNTINGTON-ASHLAND

VIRGINIA

N

LEGEND

Findlay-Tiffin	Combined Statistical Area
AKRON	Metropolitan Statistical Area
Athens	Micropolitan Statistical Area
CANADA	International
INDIANA	State or Statistical Equivalent
Adams	County or Statistical Equivalent
Lake Erie	Coastline

CBSA boundaries and names are as of February 2013. All other boundaries and names are as of January 1, 2012.

0 10 20 30 40 Kilometers

0 10 20 30 40 Miles

OKLAHOMA - Core Based Statistical Areas (CBSAs) and Counties

LEGEND

Oklahoma City-Shawnee — Combined Statistical Area
LAWTON — Metropolitan Statistical Area
Bartlesville — Micropolitan Statistical Area
TEXAS — State or Statistical Equivalent
Adair — County or Statistical Equivalent

CBSA boundaries and names are as of February 2013. All other boundaries and names are as of January 1, 2012.

OREGON - Core Based Statistical Areas (CBSAs) and Counties

LEGEND

Medford-Grants Pass Combined Statistical Area
ALBANY Metropolitan Statistical Area
Brookings Micropolitan Statistical Area

NEVADA State or Statistical Equivalent
Baker County or Statistical Equivalent
Pacific Ocean Coastline

CBSA boundaries and names are as of February 2013. All other boundaries and names are as of January 1, 2012.

PENNSYLVANIA - Core Based Statistical Areas (CBSAs) and Counties

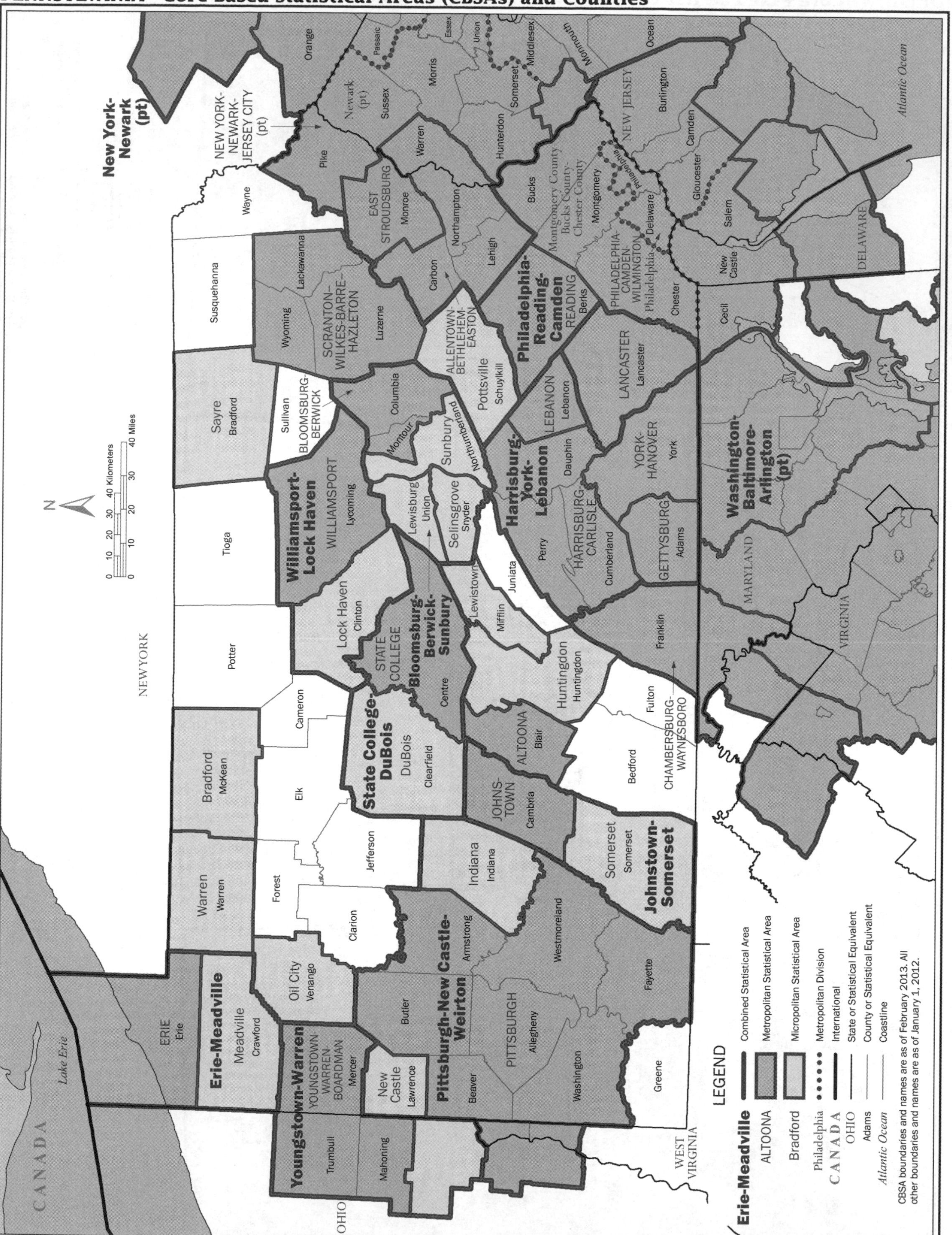

MASSACHUSETTS

Boston-Worcester-Providence (pt)

PROVIDENCE-WARWICK

Providence

Bristol

CONNECTICUT

Kent

Bristol

MASSACHUSETTS

Newport

Washington

N

| 0 | 2 | 4 | 6 | 8 Kilometers |
| 0 | 2 | 4 | 6 | 8 Miles |

LEGEND

Boston-Worcester-Providence ——————— Combined Statistical Area

PROVIDENCE-WARWICK ▭ Metropolitan Statistical Area

MASSACHUSETTS ——————— State or Statistical Equivalent

Bristol ——————— County or Statistical Equivalent

Atlantic Ocean ——————— Coastline

CBSA boundaries and names are as of February 2013. All
other boundaries and names are as of January 1, 2012.

Atlantic Ocean

SOUTH CAROLINA - Core Based Statistical Areas (CBSAs) and Counties

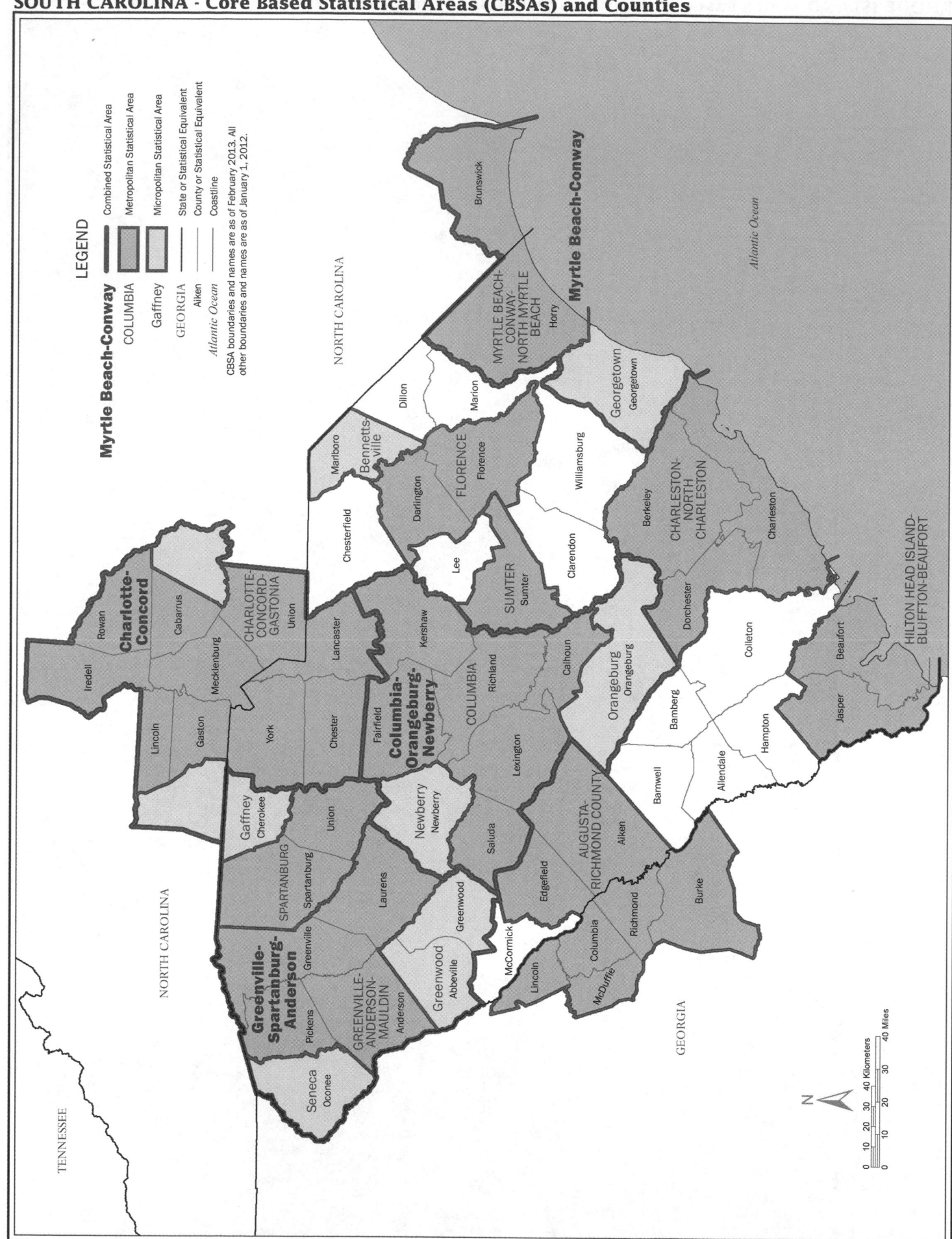

U.S. DEPARTMENT OF COMMERCE Economics and Statistics Administration U.S. Census Bureau

SOUTH DAKOTA - Core Based Statistical Areas (CBSAs) and Counties

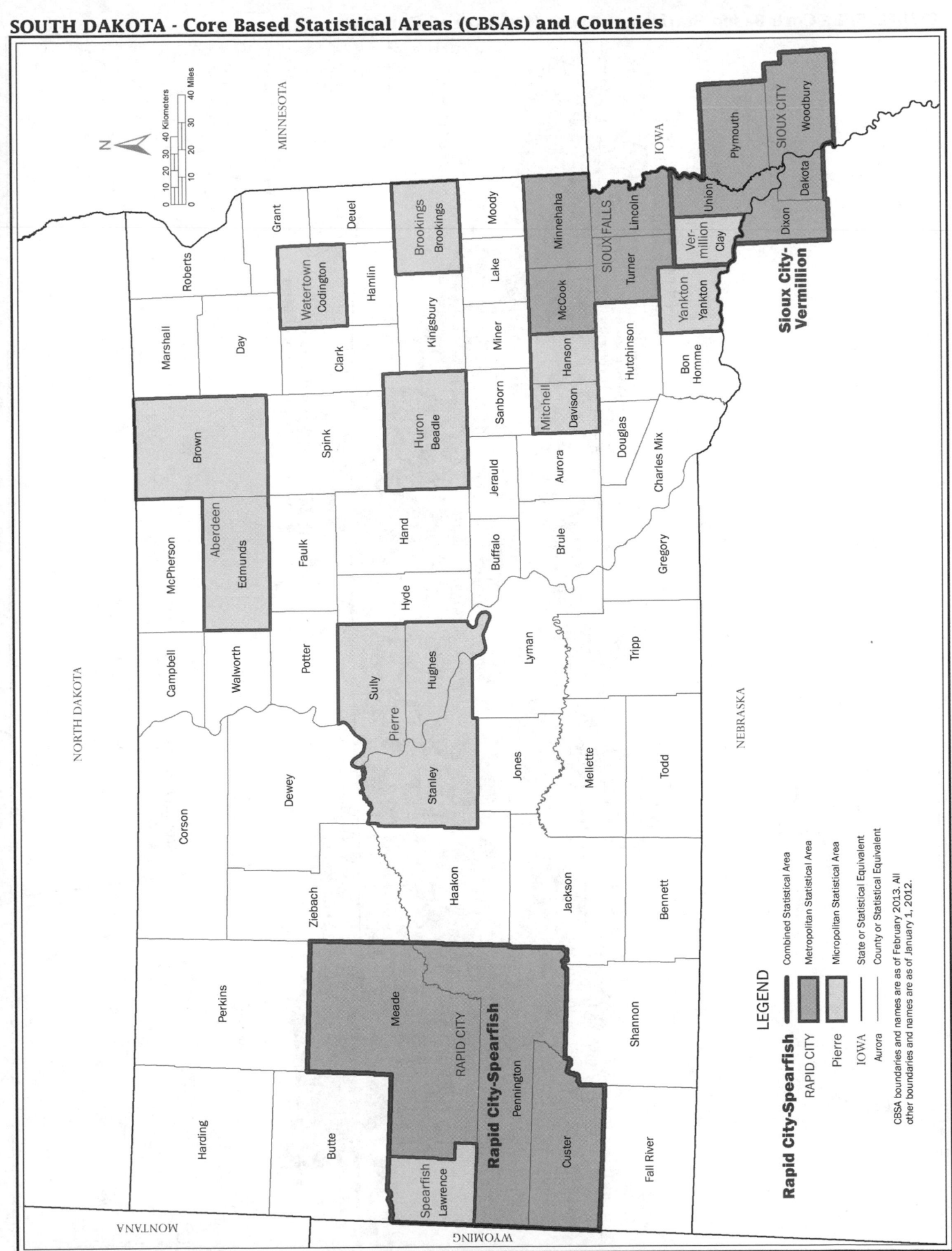

LEGEND

Rapid City-Spearfish — Combined Statistical Area

RAPID CITY — Metropolitan Statistical Area

Pierre — Micropolitan Statistical Area

IOWA — State or Statistical Equivalent

Aurora — County or Statistical Equivalent

CBSA boundaries and names are as of February 2013. All other boundaries and names are as of January 1, 2012.

TENNESSEE - Core Based Statistical Areas (CBSAs) and Counties

OHIO

WEST VIRGINIA

VIRGINIA

KINGSPORT-BRISTOL-BRISTOL

JOHNSON CITY

Johnson City-Kingsport-Bristol

Washington
Bristol
Sullivan
Johnson
Scott
Carter
Unicoi
Hawkins
Greene-ville Greene
Hancock

NORTH CAROLINA

SOUTH CAROLINA

Knoxville-Morristown-Sevierville

Claiborne
Grainger
Hamblen
Jefferson
Cocke
Newport
Sevier-ville Sevier
Union
MORRIS-TOWN
Knox
Blount
KNOXVILLE
Campbell
Anderson
Monroe

KENTUCKY

Scott
Morgan
Roane
Loudon
Meigs

Crossville
Cumberland
Dayton
Rhea
Bledsoe

Athens McMinn
CLEVELAND
Bradley
Polk

Chattanooga-Cleveland-Dalton

Fentress
Overton
Putnam
White
Van Buren
Sequatchie
Marion
Hamilton
CHATTANOOGA
Catoo-sa
Walker
Dade

GEORGIA

Cooke-ville

Pickett
Clay
Jackson
DeKalb
Warren
McMinn-ville
Grundy

Tullahoma-Manchester

Nashville-Davidson—Murfreesboro

NASHVILLE-DAVIDSON—MURFREESBORO—FRANKLIN

Macon
Smith
Cannon
Coffee
Franklin
Moore
Sumner
Trousdale
Wilson
Rutherford
Shelby-ville Bedford
Lewisburg
Lincoln
Robertson
Davidson
Williamson
Maury
Marshall
Cheatham
Giles
Lawrenceburg

Martin-Union City

MEMPHIS

Cookeville

GEORGIA

Bedford

ALABAMA

LEGEND

Combined Statistical Area
Metropolitan Statistical Area
Micropolitan Statistical Area
State or Statistical Equivalent
County or Statistical Equivalent

CBSA boundaries and names are as of February 2013. All other boundaries and names are as of January 1, 2012.

CLARKSVILLE
Christian
Trigg

Montgomery
Dickson
Hickman

Stewart
Houston
Humphreys
Perry
Wayne

Benton
Decatur
Hardin

Lewis
Lawrence

INDIANA

ILLINOIS

MISSOURI

N

0 10 20 30 40 Kilometers
0 10 20 30 40 Miles

Martin-Union City

Paris
Henry
Martin
Weakley
Union City
Obion
Fulton
Lake

Carroll
Gibson
Crockett
Dyersburg
Dyer

Henderson
Chester
JACKSON
Madison
McNairy
Hardeman
Haywood
Lauderdale

ARKANSAS

MEMPHIS
Shelby
Fayette
Tipton
Crittenden

Memphis-Forrest City

Benton
Marshall
DeSoto
Tate
Tunica

MISSISSIPPI

U.S. DEPARTMENT OF COMMERCE Economics and Statistics Administration U.S. Census Bureau

Appendix D

TEXAS - Core Based Statistical Areas (CBSAs) and Counties

Appendix D

KEY
1 DALLAS-FORT WORTH-ARLINGTON
2 Tyler-Jacksonville
3 Jacksonville
4 Nacogdoches

LEGEND

Combined Statistical Area
Metropolitan Statistical Area
Micropolitan Statistical Area
Metropolitan Division
International
State or Statistical Equivalent
County or Statistical Equivalent
Coastline

Dallas-Fort Worth
WACO
Alice

Fort Worth-Arlington
MEXICO
OKLAHOMA
Harris
Gulf of Mexico

CBSA boundaries and names are as of February 2013. All
other boundaries and names are as of January 1, 2012.

N

0 30 60 90 120 Miles
0 30 60 90 120 Kilometers

ARKANSAS
LOUISIANA
OKLAHOMA
NEW MEXICO
MEXICO
Gulf of Mexico

TEXARKANA
Longview-Marshall
Houston-The Woodlands
Victoria-Port Lavaca
Corpus Christi-Kingsville-Alice
Brownsville-Harlingen-Raymondville
McAllen-Edinburg
Dallas-Fort Worth
Sherman-Denison
Wichita Falls
Lubbock-Levelland
Amarillo-Borger
Abilene
San Angelo
Midland-Odessa
El Paso-Las Cruces
Laredo
Del Rio
Killeen-Temple
Austin-Round Rock
San Antonio-New Braunfels
College Station-Bryan
Beaumont-Port Arthur
Houston-The Woodlands-Sugar Land
Corpus Christi
McAllen-Edinburg-Mission
Brownsville-Harlingen
Tyler
Lufkin
Longview
Paris
Waco
Fredericksburg

UTAH - Core Based Statistical Areas (CBSAs) and Counties

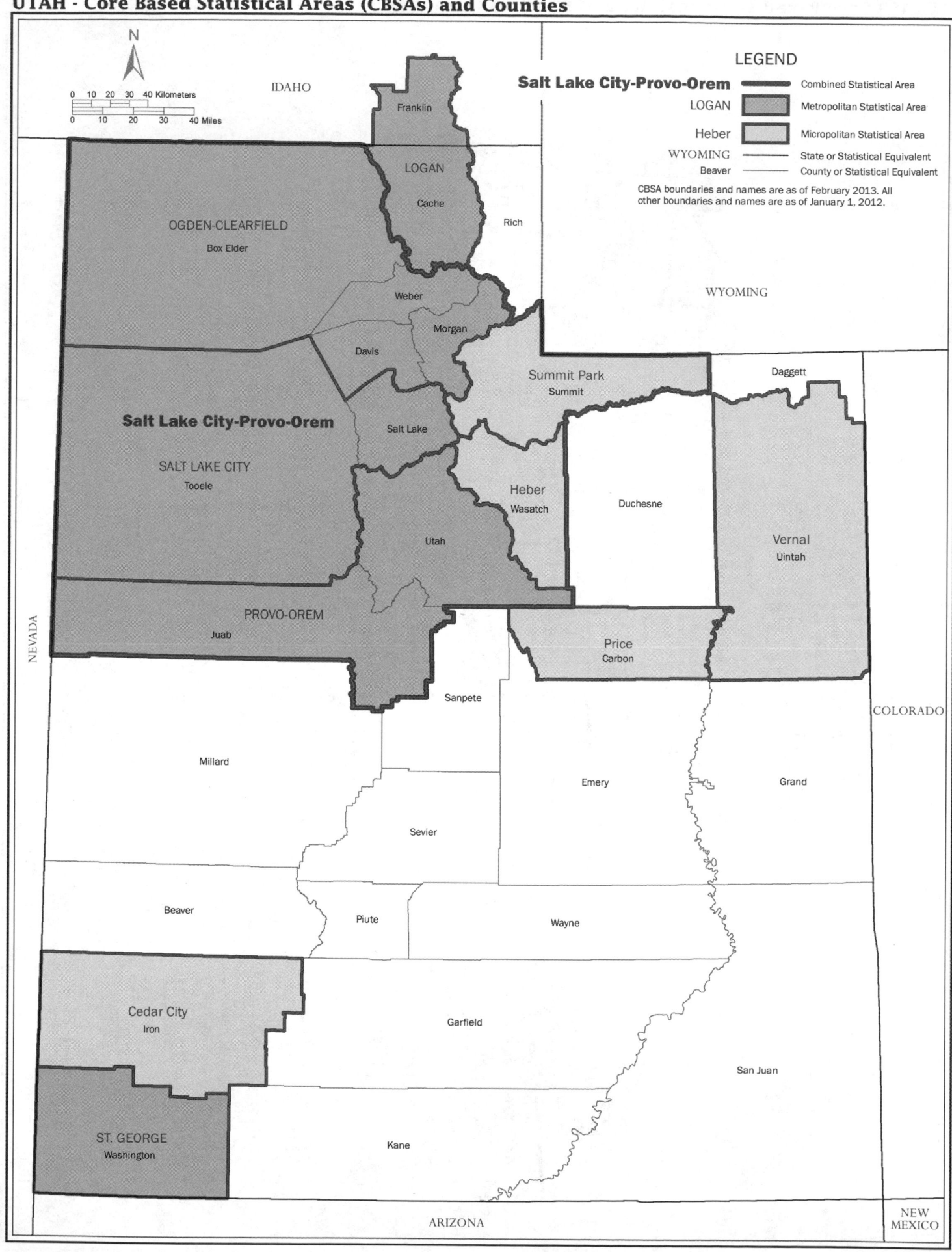

VERMONT - Core Based Statistical Areas (CBSAs) and Counties

N

0 5 10 15 20 Kilometers
0 5 10 15 20 Miles

CANADA

Grand Isle

Franklin

Orleans

BURLINGTON-SOUTH BURLINGTON

Essex

Berlin

Coos

Lamoille

Chittenden

Caledonia

MAINE

Barre
Washington

Addison

Orange

Grafton

NEW YORK

Claremont-Lebanon

Rutland
Rutland

Windsor

NEW HAMPSHIRE

Sullivan

Bennington
Bennington

Windham

LEGEND

BURLINGTON-SOUTH BURLINGTON		Metropolitan Statistical Area
Barre		Micropolitan Statistical Area
CANADA		International
NEW HAMPSHIRE		State or Statistical Equivalent
Addison		County or Statistical Equivalent

CBSA boundaries and names are as of February 2013. All other boundaries and names are as of January 1, 2012.

MASSACHUSETTS

VIRGINIA - Core Based Statistical Areas (CBSAs) and Counties

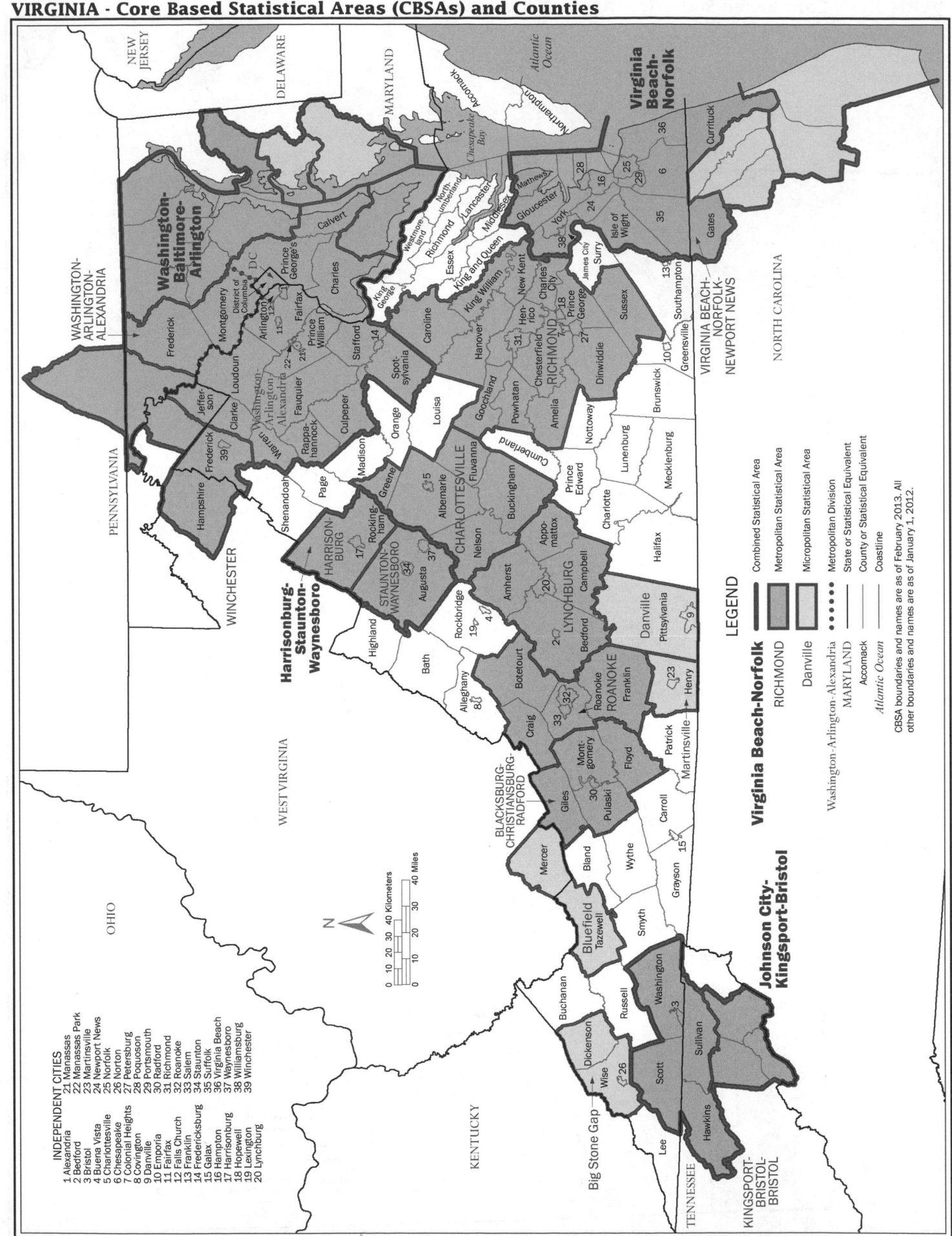

INDEPENDENT CITIES
1 Alexandria
2 Bedford
3 Bristol
4 Buena Vista
5 Charlottesville
6 Chesapeake
7 Colonial Heights
8 Covington
9 Danville
10 Emporia
11 Fairfax
12 Falls Church
13 Franklin
14 Fredericksburg
15 Galax
16 Hampton
17 Harrisonburg
18 Hopewell
19 Lexington
20 Lynchburg
21 Manassas
22 Manassas Park
23 Martinsville
24 Newport News
25 Norfolk
26 Norton
27 Petersburg
28 Poquoson
29 Portsmouth
30 Radford
31 Richmond
32 Roanoke
33 Salem
34 Staunton
35 Suffolk
36 Virginia Beach
37 Waynesboro
38 Williamsburg
39 Winchester

LEGEND

Combined Statistical Area

Metropolitan Statistical Area

Micropolitan Statistical Area

Metropolitan Division

State or Statistical Equivalent

County or Statistical Equivalent

Coastline

Virginia Beach-Norfolk
RICHMOND
Danville
Washington-Arlington-Alexandria
MARYLAND
Accomack
Atlantic Ocean

CBSA boundaries and names are as of February 2013. All
other boundaries and names are as of January 1, 2012.

WASHINGTON - Core Based Statistical Areas (CBSAs) and Counties

CANADA

IDAHO

LEWISTON
Nez Perce

Spokane-
Spokane Valley-
Coeur d'Alene

Pend
Oreille

Spokane

Stevens

SPOKANE-
SPOKANE
VALLEY

Ferry

Lincoln

Pullman-
Moscow

Pullman
Whitman

Aston

Garfield

Columbia

WALLA WALLA

Walla Walla

Moses Lake-
Othello

Othello
Adams

Franklin

Okanogan

Moses Lake
Grant

KENNEWICK-
RICHLAND

Benton

WENATCHEE

Douglas

Chelan

Ellensburg
Kittitas

YAKIMA
Yakima

Klickitat

OREGON

BELLINGHAM
Whatcom

MOUNT VERNON-ANACORTES
Skagit

Oak Harbor
Island

Seattle-Tacoma
SEATTLE-TACOMA-
BELLEVUE
Snohomish

Seattle-Bellevue-Everett
King

Tacoma-Lakewood
Pierce

PORTLAND-
VANCOUVER-
HILLSBORO

Skamania

Portland-
Vancouver-
Salem (pt)

Clackamas

San Juan

Kitsap

Multnomah

Clark

BREMERTON-SILVERDALE
Jefferson

Port Angeles
Clallam

Shelton
Mason

OLYMPIA-
TUMWATER
Thurston

Centralia
Lewis

LONGVIEW
Cowlitz

Washington

Yamhill

Columbia

Aberdeen
Grays Harbor

Pacific

Wahkiakum

Pacific
Ocean

LEGEND

Seattle-Tacoma ▬▬▬ Combined Statistical Area

YAKIMA ▭ Metropolitan Statistical Area

Aberdeen ▭ Micropolitan Statistical Area

Tacoma-Lakewood Metropolitan Division

CANADA •••• International

OREGON State or Statistical Equivalent

Adams County or Statistical Equivalent

Pacific Ocean Coastline

CBSA boundaries and names are as of February 2013. All
other boundaries and names are as of January 1, 2012.

N

0 10 20 30 40 Kilometers
0   10   20   30   40 Miles

WEST VIRGINIA - Core Based Statistical Areas (CBSAs) and Counties

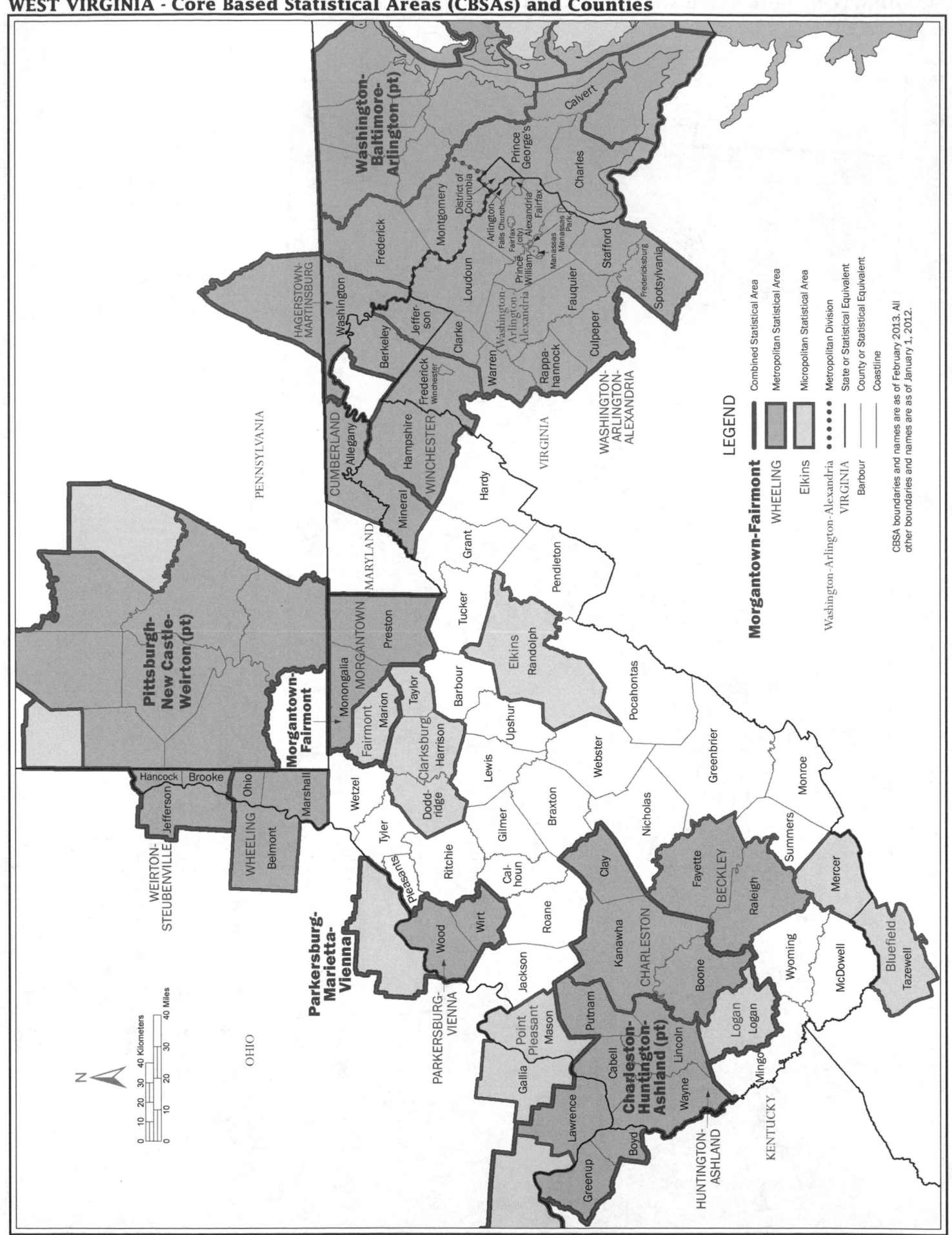

CANADA

Lake Superior

DULUTH
St. Louis

Carlton

Douglas

Bayfield

MICHIGAN

Iron Mountain
Dickinson

MINNESOTA

Mille Lacs

Minneapolis-St. Paul (pt)

Ashland   Iron

Florence

Burnett   Washburn   Sawyer

Vilas

Green Bay-Shawano

Isanti

Sherburne   Chisago

Polk   Barron   Rusk   Price   Oneida   Forest

Marinette
Marinette   Menominee

Wright   Anoka

Merrill
Lincoln

Langlade

Eau Claire-Menomonie

Hennepin   Ramsey

St. Croix

Meno-monie   EAU CLAIRE
Chippewa   Taylor

Wausau-Stevens Point-Wisconsin Rapids
WAUSAU
Marathon

Menominee

Oconto

GREEN BAY

Door

Carver

Dunn

Shawano
Shawano

Scott   Dakota
Pierce   Eau Claire

Clark

Wood   Stevens Point

APPLETON
Outagamie   Brown

Kewaunee

Sibley

Le Sueur

Pepin

Wisconsin Rapids-Marshfield   Portage

Waupaca

Manitowoc

MINNEAPOLIS-ST. PAUL-BLOOMINGTON

Buffalo

Trem-pealeau

Jackson

Appleton-Oshkosh-Neenah

Waushara

OSHKOSH-NEENAH
Winnebago   Calumet

Manitowoc

LA CROSSE-ONALASKA
La Crosse

Monroe

Juneau   Adams   Marquette

Green Lake

FOND DU LAC
Fond du Lac

Sheboygan

SHEBOYGAN

Lake Michigan

Houston

Vernon

Richland

Baraboo
Sauk

Columbia

Beaver Dam
Dodge

Washington   Ozaukee

Milwaukee-Racine-Waukesha

N

IOWA

Crawford

Madison-Janesville-Beloit

MADISON
Iowa   Dane

Watertown-Fort Atkinson   Waukesha

Jefferson

Milwaukee

MILWAUKEE-WAUKESHA-WEST ALLIS

MICHIGAN

0 10 20 30 40 Kilometers
0 10 20 30 40 Miles

Platteville
Grant

Lafayette   Green

JANESVILLE-BELOIT
Rock

Whitewater-Elkhorn
Walworth

RACINE
Racine

Kenosha

Lake County-Kenosha County

ILLINOIS

McHenry   Lake

Chicago-Naperville (pt)

DeKalb   Kane

CHICAGO-NAPERVILLE-ELGIN (pt)
DuPage   Cook

Kendall   Will

INDIANA

Lake   Porter

Grundy

Newton   Jasper

LEGEND

Green Bay-Shawano	Combined Statistical Area
APPLETON	Metropolitan Statistical Area
Baraboo	Micropolitan Statistical Area
Lake County-Kenosha County	•••• Metropolitan Division
CANADA	International
ILLINOIS	State or Statistical Equivalent
Adams	County or Statistical Equivalent
Lake Michigan	Coastline

CBSA boundaries and names are as of February 2013. All other boundaries and names are as of January 1, 2012.

WYOMING - Core Based Statistical Areas (CBSAs) and Counties

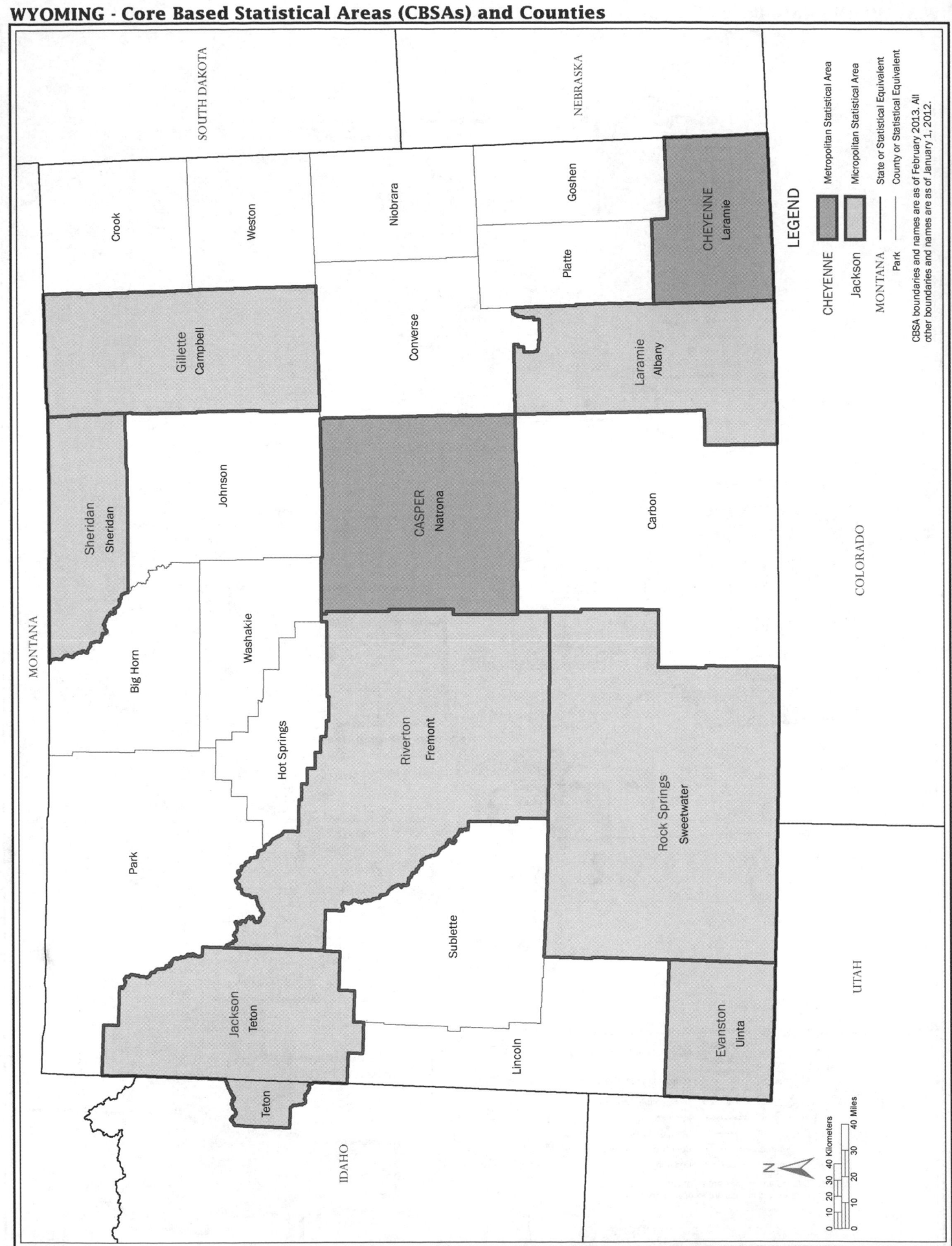

U.S. DEPARTMENT OF COMMERCE Economics and Statistics Administration U.S. Census Bureau

APPENDIX E
CITIES BY COUNTY

The following table is arranged alphabetically by state. Under each state heading are listed all cities with a 2010 census population over 25,000 along with their component counties and the population in each component.

State Code	Place Code	County Code	Geographic Area Name	2010 Census Population	State Code	Place Code	County Code	Geographic Area Name	2010 Census Population
01			**ALABAMA**	4 779 736	01	78552		Vestavia Hills city	34 033
01	00820		Alabaster city	30 352	01	78552	073	Jefferson County	34 019
01	00820	117	Shelby County	30 352	01	78552	117	Shelby County	14
01	03076		Auburn city	53 380	02			**ALASKA**	710 231
01	03076	081	Lee County	53 380	02	03000		Anchorage municipality	291 826
					02	03000	020	Anchorage Municipality	291 826
01	05980		Bessemer city	27 456					
01	05980	073	Jefferson County	27 456	02	24230		Fairbanks city	31 535
					02	24230	090	Fairbanks North Star Borough	31 535
01	07000		Birmingham city	212 237					
01	07000	073	Jefferson County	210 609	02	36400		Juneau city and borough	31 275
01	07000	117	Shelby County	1 628	02	36400	110	Juneau City and Borough	31 275
01	20104		Decatur city	55 683	04			**ARIZONA**	6 392 017
01	20104	083	Limestone County	84	04	02830		Apache Junction city	35 840
01	20104	103	Morgan County	55 599	04	02830	013	Maricopa County	294
					04	02830	021	Pinal County	35 546
01	21184		Dothan city	65 496					
01	21184	045	Dale County	887	04	04720		Avondale city	76 238
01	21184	067	Henry County	5	04	04720	013	Maricopa County	76 238
01	21184	069	Houston County	64 604					
					04	07940		Buckeye town	50 876
01	24184		Enterprise city	26 562	04	07940	013	Maricopa County	50 876
01	24184	031	Coffee County	26 139					
01	24184	045	Dale County	423	04	08220		Bullhead City city	39 540
					04	08220	015	Mohave County	39 540
01	26896		Florence city	39 319					
01	26896	077	Lauderdale County	39 319	04	10530		Casa Grande city	48 571
					04	10530	021	Pinal County	48 571
01	28696		Gadsden city	36 856					
01	28696	055	Etowah County	36 856	04	12000		Chandler city	236 123
					04	12000	013	Maricopa County	236 123
01	35800		Homewood city	25 167					
01	35800	073	Jefferson County	25 167	04	22220		El Mirage city	31 797
					04	22220	013	Maricopa County	31 797
01	35896		Hoover city	81 619					
01	35896	073	Jefferson County	58 582	04	23620		Flagstaff city	65 870
01	35896	117	Shelby County	23 037	04	23620	005	Coconino County	65 870
01	37000		Huntsville city	180 105	04	23760		Florence town	25 536
01	37000	083	Limestone County	1 521	04	23760	021	Pinal County	25 536
01	37000	089	Madison County	178 584					
					04	27400		Gilbert town	208 453
01	45784		Madison city	42 938	04	27400	013	Maricopa County	208 453
01	45784	083	Limestone County	3 453					
01	45784	089	Madison County	39 485	04	27820		Glendale city	226 721
					04	27820	013	Maricopa County	226 721
01	50000		Mobile city	195 111					
01	50000	097	Mobile County	195 111	04	28380		Goodyear city	65 275
					04	28380	013	Maricopa County	65 275
01	51000		Montgomery city	205 764					
01	51000	101	Montgomery County	205 764	04	37620		Kingman city	28 068
					04	37620	015	Mohave County	28 068
01	57048		Opelika city	26 477					
01	57048	081	Lee County	26 477	04	39370		Lake Havasu City city	52 527
					04	39370	015	Mohave County	52 527
01	59472		Phenix City city	32 822					
01	59472	081	Lee County	4 153	04	44270		Marana town	34 961
01	59472	113	Russell County	28 669	04	44270	019	Pima County	34 961
					04	44270	021	Pinal County	0
01	62328		Prattville city	33 960					
01	62328	001	Autauga County	32 168	04	44410		Maricopa city	43 482
01	62328	051	Elmore County	1 792	04	44410	021	Pinal County	43 482
01	77256		Tuscaloosa city	90 468	04	46000		Mesa city	439 041
01	77256	125	Tuscaloosa County	90 468	04	46000	013	Maricopa County	439 041

Cities by County–*Continued*

State Code	Place Code	County Code	Geographic Area Name	2010 Census Population	State Code	Place Code	County Code	Geographic Area Name	2010 Census Population
04	51600		Oro Valley town	41 011	05	41000		Little Rock city	193 524
04	51600	019	Pima County	41 011	05	41000	119	Pulaski County	193 524
04	54050		Peoria city	154 065	05	50450		North Little Rock city	62 304
04	54050	013	Maricopa County	154 058	05	50450	119	Pulaski County	62 304
04	54050	025	Yavapai County	7					
					05	53390		Paragould city	26 113
04	55000		Phoenix city	1 445 632	05	53390	055	Greene County	26 113
04	55000	013	Maricopa County	1 445 632					
					05	55310		Pine Bluff city	49 083
04	57380		Prescott city	39 843	05	55310	069	Jefferson County	49 083
04	57380	025	Yavapai County	39 843					
					05	60410		Rogers city	55 964
04	57450		Prescott Valley town	38 822	05	60410	007	Benton County	55 964
04	57450	025	Yavapai County	38 822					
					05	61670		Russellville city	27 920
04	58150		Queen Creek town	26 361	05	61670	115	Pope County	27 920
04	58150	013	Maricopa County	25 912					
04	58150	021	Pinal County	449	05	63800		Sherwood city	29 523
					05	63800	119	Pulaski County	29 523
04	62140		Sahuarita town	25 259					
04	62140	019	Pima County	25 259	05	66080		Springdale city	69 797
					05	66080	007	Benton County	6 054
04	63470		San Luis city	25 505	05	66080	143	Washington County	63 743
04	63470	027	Yuma County	25 505					
					05	68810		Texarkana city	29 919
04	65000		Scottsdale city	217 385	05	68810	091	Miller County	29 919
04	65000	013	Maricopa County	217 385					
					05	74540		West Memphis city	26 245
04	66820		Sierra Vista city	43 888	05	74540	035	Crittenden County	26 245
04	66820	003	Cochise County	43 888					
					06			**CALIFORNIA**	37 253 956
04	71510		Surprise city	117 517	06	00296		Adelanto city	31 765
04	71510	013	Maricopa County	117 517	06	00296	071	San Bernardino County	31 765
04	73000		Tempe city	161 719	06	00562		Alameda city	73 812
04	73000	013	Maricopa County	161 719	06	00562	001	Alameda County	73 812
04	77000		Tucson city	520 116	06	00884		Alhambra city	83 089
04	77000	019	Pima County	520 116	06	00884	037	Los Angeles County	83 089
04	85540		Yuma city	93 064	06	00947		Aliso Viejo city	47 823
04	85540	027	Yuma County	93 064	06	00947	059	Orange County	47 823
05			**ARKANSAS**	2 915 918	06	02000		Anaheim city	336 265
05	04840		Bella Vista town	26 461	06	02000	059	Orange County	336 265
05	04840	007	Benton County	26 461					
					06	02252		Antioch city	102 372
05	05290		Benton city	30 681	06	02252	013	Contra Costa County	102 372
05	05290	125	Saline County	30 681					
					06	02364		Apple Valley town	69 135
05	05320		Bentonville city	35 301	06	02364	071	San Bernardino County	69 135
05	05320	007	Benton County	35 301					
					06	02462		Arcadia city	56 364
05	15190		Conway city	58 908	06	02462	037	Los Angeles County	56 364
05	15190	045	Faulkner County	58 908					
					06	03064		Atascadero city	28 310
05	23290		Fayetteville city	73 580	06	03064	079	San Luis Obispo County	28 310
05	23290	143	Washington County	73 580					
					06	03162		Atwater city	28 168
05	24550		Fort Smith city	86 209	06	03162	047	Merced County	28 168
05	24550	131	Sebastian County	86 209					
					06	03386		Azusa city	46 361
05	33400		Hot Springs city	35 193	06	03386	037	Los Angeles County	46 361
05	33400	051	Garland County	35 193					
					06	03526		Bakersfield city	347 483
05	34750		Jacksonville city	28 364	06	03526	029	Kern County	347 483
05	34750	119	Pulaski County	28 364					
					06	03666		Baldwin Park city	75 390
05	35710		Jonesboro city	67 263	06	03666	037	Los Angeles County	75 390
05	35710	031	Craighead County	67 263					

Cities by County–*Continued*

State Code	Place Code	County Code	Geographic Area Name	2010 Census Population	State Code	Place Code	County Code	Geographic Area Name	2010 Census Population
06	03820		Banning city	29 603	06	13214		Chino Hills city	74 799
06	03820	065	Riverside County	29 603	06	13214	071	San Bernardino County	74 799
06	04758		Beaumont city	36 877	06	13392		Chula Vista city	243 916
06	04758	065	Riverside County	36 877	06	13392	073	San Diego County	243 916
06	04870		Bell city	35 477	06	13588		Citrus Heights city	83 301
06	04870	037	Los Angeles County	35 477	06	13588	067	Sacramento County	83 301
06	04982		Bellflower city	76 616	06	13756		Claremont city	34 926
06	04982	037	Los Angeles County	76 616	06	13756	037	Los Angeles County	34 926
06	04996		Bell Gardens city	42 072	06	14218		Clovis city	95 631
06	04996	037	Los Angeles County	42 072	06	14218	019	Fresno County	95 631
06	05108		Belmont city	25 835	06	14260		Coachella city	40 704
06	05108	081	San Mateo County	25 835	06	14260	065	Riverside County	40 704
06	05290		Benicia city	26 997	06	14890		Colton city	52 154
06	05290	095	Solano County	26 997	06	14890	071	San Bernardino County	52 154
06	06000		Berkeley city	112 580	06	15044		Compton city	96 455
06	06000	001	Alameda County	112 580	06	15044	037	Los Angeles County	96 455
06	06308		Beverly Hills city	34 109	06	16000		Concord city	122 067
06	06308	037	Los Angeles County	34 109	06	16000	013	Contra Costa County	122 067
06	08100		Brea city	39 282	06	16350		Corona city	152 374
06	08100	059	Orange County	39 282	06	16350	065	Riverside County	152 374
06	08142		Brentwood city	51 481	06	16532		Costa Mesa city	109 960
06	08142	013	Contra Costa County	51 481	06	16532	059	Orange County	109 960
06	08786		Buena Park city	80 530	06	16742		Covina city	47 796
06	08786	059	Orange County	80 530	06	16742	037	Los Angeles County	47 796
06	08954		Burbank city	103 340	06	17568		Culver City city	38 883
06	08954	037	Los Angeles County	103 340	06	17568	037	Los Angeles County	38 883
06	09066		Burlingame city	28 806	06	17610		Cupertino city	58 302
06	09066	081	San Mateo County	28 806	06	17610	085	Santa Clara County	58 302
06	09710		Calexico city	38 572	06	17750		Cypress city	47 802
06	09710	025	Imperial County	38 572	06	17750	059	Orange County	47 802
06	10046		Camarillo city	65 201	06	17918		Daly City city	101 123
06	10046	111	Ventura County	65 201	06	17918	081	San Mateo County	101 123
06	10345		Campbell city	39 349	06	17946		Dana Point city	33 351
06	10345	085	Santa Clara County	39 349	06	17946	059	Orange County	33 351
06	11194		Carlsbad city	105 328	06	17988		Danville town	42 039
06	11194	073	San Diego County	105 328	06	17988	013	Contra Costa County	42 039
06	11530		Carson city	91 714	06	18100		Davis city	65 622
06	11530	037	Los Angeles County	91 714	06	18100	113	Yolo County	65 622
06	12048		Cathedral City city	51 200	06	18394		Delano city	53 041
06	12048	065	Riverside County	51 200	06	18394	029	Kern County	53 041
06	12524		Ceres city	45 417	06	18996		Desert Hot Springs city	25 938
06	12524	099	Stanislaus County	45 417	06	18996	065	Riverside County	25 938
06	12552		Cerritos city	49 041	06	19192		Diamond Bar city	55 544
06	12552	037	Los Angeles County	49 041	06	19192	037	Los Angeles County	55 544
06	13014		Chico city	86 187	06	19766		Downey city	111 772
06	13014	007	Butte County	86 187	06	19766	037	Los Angeles County	111 772
06	13210		Chino city	77 983	06	20018		Dublin city	46 036
06	13210	071	San Bernardino County	77 983	06	20018	001	Alameda County	46 036

Cities by County–*Continued*

State Code	Place Code	County Code	Geographic Area Name	2010 Census Population	State Code	Place Code	County Code	Geographic Area Name	2010 Census Population
06	20956		East Palo Alto city	28 155	06	32548		Hawthorne city	84 293
06	20956	081	San Mateo County	28 155	06	32548	037	Los Angeles County	84 293
06	21712		El Cajon city	99 478	06	33000		Hayward city	144 186
06	21712	073	San Diego County	99 478	06	33000	001	Alameda County	144 186
06	21782		El Centro city	42 598	06	33182		Hemet city	78 657
06	21782	025	Imperial County	42 598	06	33182	065	Riverside County	78 657
06	22020		Elk Grove city	153 015	06	33434		Hesperia city	90 173
06	22020	067	Sacramento County	153 015	06	33434	071	San Bernardino County	90 173
06	22230		El Monte city	113 475	06	33588		Highland city	53 104
06	22230	037	Los Angeles County	113 475	06	33588	071	San Bernardino County	53 104
06	22300		El Paso de Robles (Paso Robles)	29 793	06	34120		Hollister city	34 928
06	22300	079	San Luis Obispo County	29 793	06	34120	069	San Benito County	34 928
06	22678		Encinitas city	59 518	06	36000		Huntington Beach city	189 992
06	22678	073	San Diego County	59 518	06	36000	059	Orange County	189 992
06	22804		Escondido city	143 911	06	36056		Huntington Park city	58 114
06	22804	073	San Diego County	143 911	06	36056	037	Los Angeles County	58 114
06	23042		Eureka city	27 191	06	36294		Imperial Beach city	26 324
06	23042	023	Humboldt County	27 191	06	36294	073	San Diego County	26 324
06	23182		Fairfield city	105 321	06	36448		Indio city	76 036
06	23182	095	Solano County	105 321	06	36448	065	Riverside County	76 036
06	24638		Folsom city	72 203	06	36546		Inglewood city	109 673
06	24638	067	Sacramento County	72 203	06	36546	037	Los Angeles County	109 673
06	24680		Fontana city	196 069	06	36770		Irvine city	212 375
06	24680	071	San Bernardino County	196 069	06	36770	059	Orange County	212 375
06	25338		Foster City city	30 567	06	39220		Laguna Hills city	30 344
06	25338	081	San Mateo County	30 567	06	39220	059	Orange County	30 344
06	25380		Fountain Valley city	55 313	06	39248		Laguna Niguel city	62 979
06	25380	059	Orange County	55 313	06	39248	059	Orange County	62 979
06	26000		Fremont city	214 089	06	39290		La Habra city	60 239
06	26000	001	Alameda County	214 089	06	39290	059	Orange County	60 239
06	27000		Fresno city	494 665	06	39486		Lake Elsinore city	51 821
06	27000	019	Fresno County	494 665	06	39486	065	Riverside County	51 821
06	28000		Fullerton city	135 161	06	39496		Lake Forest city	77 264
06	28000	059	Orange County	135 161	06	39496	059	Orange County	77 264
06	28168		Gardena city	58 829	06	39892		Lakewood city	80 048
06	28168	037	Los Angeles County	58 829	06	39892	037	Los Angeles County	80 048
06	29000		Garden Grove city	170 883	06	40004		La Mesa city	57 065
06	29000	059	Orange County	170 883	06	40004	073	San Diego County	57 065
06	29504		Gilroy city	48 821	06	40032		La Mirada city	48 527
06	29504	085	Santa Clara County	48 821	06	40032	037	Los Angeles County	48 527
06	30000		Glendale city	191 719	06	40130		Lancaster city	156 633
06	30000	037	Los Angeles County	191 719	06	40130	037	Los Angeles County	156 633
06	30014		Glendora city	50 073	06	40340		La Puente city	39 816
06	30014	037	Los Angeles County	50 073	06	40340	037	Los Angeles County	39 816
06	30378		Goleta city	29 888	06	40354		La Quinta city	37 467
06	30378	083	Santa Barbara County	29 888	06	40354	065	Riverside County	37 467
06	31960		Hanford city	53 967	06	40830		La Verne city	31 063
06	31960	031	Kings County	53 967	06	40830	037	Los Angeles County	31 063

Cities by County–*Continued*

State Code	Place Code	County Code	Geographic Area Name	2010 Census Population	State Code	Place Code	County Code	Geographic Area Name	2010 Census Population
06	40886		Lawndale city	32 769	06	48788		Montclair city	36 664
06	40886	037	Los Angeles County	32 769	06	48788	071	San Bernardino County	36 664
06	41124		Lemon Grove city	25 320	06	48816		Montebello city	62 500
06	41124	073	San Diego County	25 320	06	48816	037	Los Angeles County	62 500
06	41474		Lincoln city	42 819	06	48872		Monterey city	27 810
06	41474	061	Placer County	42 819	06	48872	053	Monterey County	27 810
06	41992		Livermore city	80 968	06	48914		Monterey Park city	60 269
06	41992	001	Alameda County	80 968	06	48914	037	Los Angeles County	60 269
06	42202		Lodi city	62 134	06	49138		Moorpark city	34 421
06	42202	077	San Joaquin County	62 134	06	49138	111	Ventura County	34 421
06	42524		Lompoc city	42 434	06	49270		Moreno Valley city	193 365
06	42524	083	Santa Barbara County	42 434	06	49270	065	Riverside County	193 365
06	43000		Long Beach city	462 257	06	49278		Morgan Hill city	37 882
06	43000	037	Los Angeles County	462 257	06	49278	085	Santa Clara County	37 882
06	43280		Los Altos city	28 976	06	49670		Mountain View city	74 066
06	43280	085	Santa Clara County	28 976	06	49670	085	Santa Clara County	74 066
06	44000		Los Angeles city	3 792 621	06	50076		Murrieta city	103 466
06	44000	037	Los Angeles County	3 792 621	06	50076	065	Riverside County	103 466
06	44028		Los Banos city	35 972	06	50258		Napa city	76 915
06	44028	047	Merced County	35 972	06	50258	055	Napa County	76 915
06	44112		Los Gatos town	29 413	06	50398		National City city	58 582
06	44112	085	Santa Clara County	29 413	06	50398	073	San Diego County	58 582
06	44574		Lynwood city	69 772	06	50916		Newark city	42 573
06	44574	037	Los Angeles County	69 772	06	50916	001	Alameda County	42 573
06	45022		Madera city	61 416	06	51182		Newport Beach city	85 186
06	45022	039	Madera County	61 416	06	51182	059	Orange County	85 186
06	45400		Manhattan Beach city	35 135	06	51560		Norco city	27 063
06	45400	037	Los Angeles County	35 135	06	51560	065	Riverside County	27 063
06	45484		Manteca city	67 096	06	52526		Norwalk city	105 549
06	45484	077	San Joaquin County	67 096	06	52526	037	Los Angeles County	105 549
06	46114		Martinez city	35 824	06	52582		Novato city	51 904
06	46114	013	Contra Costa County	35 824	06	52582	041	Marin County	51 904
06	46492		Maywood city	27 395	06	53000		Oakland city	390 724
06	46492	037	Los Angeles County	27 395	06	53000	001	Alameda County	390 724
06	46842		Menifee city	77 519	06	53070		Oakley city	35 432
06	46842	065	Riverside County	77 519	06	53070	013	Contra Costa County	35 432
06	46870		Menlo Park city	32 026	06	53322		Oceanside city	167 086
06	46870	081	San Mateo County	32 026	06	53322	073	San Diego County	167 086
06	46898		Merced city	78 958	06	53896		Ontario city	163 924
06	46898	047	Merced County	78 958	06	53896	071	San Bernardino County	163 924
06	47766		Milpitas city	66 790	06	53980		Orange city	136 416
06	47766	085	Santa Clara County	66 790	06	53980	059	Orange County	136 416
06	48256		Mission Viejo city	93 305	06	54652		Oxnard city	197 899
06	48256	059	Orange County	93 305	06	54652	111	Ventura County	197 899
06	48354		Modesto city	201 165	06	54806		Pacifica city	37 234
06	48354	099	Stanislaus County	201 165	06	54806	081	San Mateo County	37 234
06	48648		Monrovia city	36 590	06	55156		Palmdale city	152 750
06	48648	037	Los Angeles County	36 590	06	55156	037	Los Angeles County	152 750

Cities by County–*Continued*

State Code	Place Code	County Code	Geographic Area Name	2010 Census Population	State Code	Place Code	County Code	Geographic Area Name	2010 Census Population
06	55184		Palm Desert city	48 445	06	60466		Rialto city	99 171
06	55184	065	Riverside County	48 445	06	60466	071	San Bernardino County	99 171
06	55254		Palm Springs city	44 552	06	60620		Richmond city	103 701
06	55254	065	Riverside County	44 552	06	60620	013	Contra Costa County	103 701
06	55282		Palo Alto city	64 403	06	60704		Ridgecrest city	27 616
06	55282	085	Santa Clara County	64 403	06	60704	029	Kern County	27 616
06	55520		Paradise town	26 218	06	62000		Riverside city	303 871
06	55520	007	Butte County	26 218	06	62000	065	Riverside County	303 871
06	55618		Paramount city	54 098	06	62364		Rocklin city	56 974
06	55618	037	Los Angeles County	54 098	06	62364	061	Placer County	56 974
06	56000		Pasadena city	137 122	06	62546		Rohnert Park city	40 971
06	56000	037	Los Angeles County	137 122	06	62546	097	Sonoma County	40 971
06	56700		Perris city	68 386	06	62896		Rosemead city	53 764
06	56700	065	Riverside County	68 386	06	62896	037	Los Angeles County	53 764
06	56784		Petaluma city	57 941	06	62938		Roseville city	118 788
06	56784	097	Sonoma County	57 941	06	62938	061	Placer County	118 788
06	56924		Pico Rivera city	62 942	06	64000		Sacramento city	466 488
06	56924	037	Los Angeles County	62 942	06	64000	067	Sacramento County	466 488
06	57456		Pittsburg city	63 264	06	64224		Salinas city	150 441
06	57456	013	Contra Costa County	63 264	06	64224	053	Monterey County	150 441
06	57526		Placentia city	50 533	06	65000		San Bernardino city	209 924
06	57526	059	Orange County	50 533	06	65000	071	San Bernardino County	209 924
06	57764		Pleasant Hill city	33 152	06	65028		San Bruno city	41 114
06	57764	013	Contra Costa County	33 152	06	65028	081	San Mateo County	41 114
06	57792		Pleasanton city	70 285	06	65042		San Buenaventura (Ventura)	106 433
06	57792	001	Alameda County	70 285	06	65042	111	Ventura County	106 433
06	58072		Pomona city	149 058	06	65070		San Carlos city	28 406
06	58072	037	Los Angeles County	149 058	06	65070	081	San Mateo County	28 406
06	58240		Porterville city	54 165	06	65084		San Clemente city	63 522
06	58240	107	Tulare County	54 165	06	65084	059	Orange County	63 522
06	58520		Poway city	47 811	06	66000		San Diego city	1 307 402
06	58520	073	San Diego County	47 811	06	66000	073	San Diego County	1 307 402
06	59444		Rancho Cordova city	64 776	06	66070		San Dimas city	33 371
06	59444	067	Sacramento County	64 776	06	66070	037	Los Angeles County	33 371
06	59451		Rancho Cucamonga city	165 269	06	67000		San Francisco city	805 235
06	59451	071	San Bernardino County	165 269	06	67000	075	San Francisco County	805 235
06	59514		Rancho Palos Verdes city	41 643	06	67042		San Gabriel city	39 718
06	59514	037	Los Angeles County	41 643	06	67042	037	Los Angeles County	39 718
06	59587		Rancho Santa Margarita city	47 853	06	67112		San Jacinto city	44 199
06	59587	059	Orange County	47 853	06	67112	065	Riverside County	44 199
06	59920		Redding city	89 861	06	68000		San Jose city	945 942
06	59920	089	Shasta County	89 861	06	68000	085	Santa Clara County	945 942
06	59962		Redlands city	68 747	06	68028		San Juan Capistrano city	34 593
06	59962	071	San Bernardino County	68 747	06	68028	059	Orange County	34 593
06	60018		Redondo Beach city	66 748	06	68084		San Leandro city	84 950
06	60018	037	Los Angeles County	66 748	06	68084	001	Alameda County	84 950
06	60102		Redwood City city	76 815	06	68154		San Luis Obispo city	45 119
06	60102	081	San Mateo County	76 815	06	68154	079	San Luis Obispo County	45 119

Cities by County–*Continued*

State Code	Place Code	County Code	Geographic Area Name	2010 Census Population	State Code	Place Code	County Code	Geographic Area Name	2010 Census Population
06	68196		San Marcos city	83 781	06	75630		Suisun City city	28 111
06	68196	073	San Diego County	83 781	06	75630	095	Solano County	28 111
06	68252		San Mateo city	97 207	06	77000		Sunnyvale city	140 081
06	68252	081	San Mateo County	97 207	06	77000	085	Santa Clara County	140 081
06	68294		San Pablo city	29 139	06	78120		Temecula city	100 097
06	68294	013	Contra Costa County	29 139	06	78120	065	Riverside County	100 097
06	68364		San Rafael city	57 713	06	78148		Temple City city	35 558
06	68364	041	Marin County	57 713	06	78148	037	Los Angeles County	35 558
06	68378		San Ramon city	72 148	06	78582		Thousand Oaks city	126 683
06	68378	013	Contra Costa County	72 148	06	78582	111	Ventura County	126 683
06	69000		Santa Ana city	324 528	06	80000		Torrance city	145 438
06	69000	059	Orange County	324 528	06	80000	037	Los Angeles County	145 438
06	69070		Santa Barbara city	88 410	06	80238		Tracy city	82 922
06	69070	083	Santa Barbara County	88 410	06	80238	077	San Joaquin County	82 922
06	69084		Santa Clara city	116 468	06	80644		Tulare city	59 278
06	69084	085	Santa Clara County	116 468	06	80644	107	Tulare County	59 278
06	69088		Santa Clarita city	176 320	06	80812		Turlock city	68 549
06	69088	037	Los Angeles County	176 320	06	80812	099	Stanislaus County	68 549
06	69112		Santa Cruz city	59 946	06	80854		Tustin city	75 540
06	69112	087	Santa Cruz County	59 946	06	80854	059	Orange County	75 540
06	69196		Santa Maria city	99 553	06	80994		Twentynine Palms city	25 048
06	69196	083	Santa Barbara County	99 553	06	80994	071	San Bernardino County	25 048
06	70000		Santa Monica city	89 736	06	81204		Union City city	69 516
06	70000	037	Los Angeles County	89 736	06	81204	001	Alameda County	69 516
06	70042		Santa Paula city	29 321	06	81344		Upland city	73 732
06	70042	111	Ventura County	29 321	06	81344	071	San Bernardino County	73 732
06	70098		Santa Rosa city	167 815	06	81554		Vacaville city	92 428
06	70098	097	Sonoma County	167 815	06	81554	095	Solano County	92 428
06	70224		Santee city	53 413	06	81666		Vallejo city	115 942
06	70224	073	San Diego County	53 413	06	81666	095	Solano County	115 942
06	70280		Saratoga city	29 926	06	82590		Victorville city	115 903
06	70280	085	Santa Clara County	29 926	06	82590	071	San Bernardino County	115 903
06	70742		Seaside city	33 025	06	82954		Visalia city	124 442
06	70742	053	Monterey County	33 025	06	82954	107	Tulare County	124 442
06	72016		Simi Valley city	124 237	06	82996		Vista city	93 834
06	72016	111	Ventura County	124 237	06	82996	073	San Diego County	93 834
06	72520		Soledad city	25 738	06	83332		Walnut city	29 172
06	72520	053	Monterey County	25 738	06	83332	037	Los Angeles County	29 172
06	73080		South Gate city	94 396	06	83346		Walnut Creek city	64 173
06	73080	037	Los Angeles County	94 396	06	83346	013	Contra Costa County	64 173
06	73220		South Pasadena city	25 619	06	83542		Wasco city	25 545
06	73220	037	Los Angeles County	25 619	06	83542	029	Kern County	25 545
06	73262		South San Francisco city	63 632	06	83668		Watsonville city	51 199
06	73262	081	San Mateo County	63 632	06	83668	087	Santa Cruz County	51 199
06	73962		Stanton city	38 186	06	84200		West Covina city	106 098
06	73962	059	Orange County	38 186	06	84200	037	Los Angeles County	106 098
06	75000		Stockton city	291 707	06	84410		West Hollywood city	34 399
06	75000	077	San Joaquin County	291 707	06	84410	037	Los Angeles County	34 399

Cities by County–*Continued*

State Code	Place Code	County Code	Geographic Area Name	2010 Census Population	State Code	Place Code	County Code	Geographic Area Name	2010 Census Population
06	84550		Westminster city	89 701	08	31660		Grand Junction city	58 566
06	84550	059	Orange County	89 701	08	31660	077	Mesa County	58 566
06	84816		West Sacramento city	48 744	08	32155		Greeley city	92 889
06	84816	113	Yolo County	48 744	08	32155	123	Weld County	92 889
06	85292		Whittier city	85 331	08	43000		Lakewood city	142 980
06	85292	037	Los Angeles County	85 331	08	43000	059	Jefferson County	142 980
06	85446		Wildomar city	32 176	08	45255		Littleton city	41 737
06	85446	065	Riverside County	32 176	08	45255	005	Arapahoe County	39 328
					08	45255	035	Douglas County	28
06	85922		Windsor town	26 801	08	45255	059	Jefferson County	2 381
06	85922	097	Sonoma County	26 801	08	45970		Longmont city	86 270
06	86328		Woodland city	55 468	08	45970	013	Boulder County	86 240
06	86328	113	Yolo County	55 468	08	45970	123	Weld County	30
06	86832		Yorba Linda city	64 234	08	46465		Loveland city	66 859
06	86832	059	Orange County	64 234	08	46465	069	Larimer County	66 859
06	86972		Yuba City city	64 925	08	54330		Northglenn city	35 789
06	86972	101	Sutter County	64 925	08	54330	001	Adams County	35 777
					08	54330	123	Weld County	12
06	87042		Yucaipa city	51 367	08	57630		Parker town	45 297
06	87042	071	San Bernardino County	51 367	08	57630	035	Douglas County	45 297
08			**COLORADO**	5 029 196	08	62000		Pueblo city	106 595
08	03455		Arvada city	106 433	08	62000	101	Pueblo County	106 595
08	03455	001	Adams County	2 849	08	77290		Thornton city	118 772
08	03455	059	Jefferson County	103 584	08	77290	001	Adams County	118 772
08	04000		Aurora city	325 078	08	77290	123	Weld County	0
08	04000	001	Adams County	39 871	08	83835		Westminster city	106 114
08	04000	005	Arapahoe County	285 090	08	83835	001	Adams County	63 696
08	04000	035	Douglas County	117	08	83835	059	Jefferson County	42 418
08	07850		Boulder city	97 385	08	84440		Wheat Ridge city	30 166
08	07850	013	Boulder County	97 385	08	84440	059	Jefferson County	30 166
08	08675		Brighton city	33 352	09			**CONNECTICUT**	3 574 097
08	08675	001	Adams County	33 009	09	08000		Bridgeport city	144 229
08	08675	123	Weld County	343	09	08000	001	Fairfield County	144 229
08	09280		Broomfield city	55 889	09	08420		Bristol city	60 477
08	09280	014	Broomfield County	55 889	09	08420	003	Hartford County	60 477
08	12415		Castle Rock town	48 231	09	18430		Danbury city	80 893
08	12415	035	Douglas County	48 231	09	18430	001	Fairfield County	80 893
08	12815		Centennial city	100 377	09	37000		Hartford city	124 775
08	12815	005	Arapahoe County	100 377	09	37000	003	Hartford County	124 775
08	16000		Colorado Springs city	416 427	09	46450		Meriden city	60 868
08	16000	041	El Paso County	416 427	09	46450	009	New Haven County	60 868
08	16495		Commerce City city	45 913	09	47290		Middletown city	47 648
08	16495	001	Adams County	45 913	09	47290	007	Middlesex County	47 648
08	20000		Denver city	600 158	09	49880		Naugatuck borough	31 862
08	20000	031	Denver County	600 158	09	49880	009	New Haven County	31 862
08	24785		Englewood city	30 255	09	50370		New Britain city	73 206
08	24785	005	Arapahoe County	30 255	09	50370	003	Hartford County	73 206
08	27425		Fort Collins city	143 986	09	52000		New Haven city	129 779
08	27425	069	Larimer County	143 986	09	52000	009	New Haven County	129 779
08	27865		Fountain city	25 846	09	52280		New London city	27 620
08	27865	041	El Paso County	25 846	09	52280	011	New London County	27 620

Cities by County–*Continued*

State Code	Place Code	County Code	Geographic Area Name	2010 Census Population	State Code	Place Code	County Code	Geographic Area Name	2010 Census Population
09	55990		Norwalk city	85 603	12	14125		Cooper City city	28 547
09	55990	001	Fairfield County	85 603	12	14125	011	Broward County	28 547
09	56200		Norwich city	40 493	12	14250		Coral Gables city	46 780
09	56200	011	New London County	40 493	12	14250	086	Miami-Dade County	46 780
09	68100		Shelton city	39 559	12	14400		Coral Springs city	121 096
09	68100	001	Fairfield County	39 559	12	14400	011	Broward County	121 096
09	73000		Stamford city	122 643	12	15968		Cutler Bay town	40 286
09	73000	001	Fairfield County	122 643	12	15968	086	Miami-Dade County	40 286
09	76500		Torrington city	36 383	12	16335		Dania Beach city	29 639
09	76500	005	Litchfield County	36 383	12	16335	011	Broward County	29 639
09	80000		Waterbury city	110 366	12	16475		Davie town	91 992
09	80000	009	New Haven County	110 366	12	16475	011	Broward County	91 992
09	82800		West Haven city	55 564	12	16525		Daytona Beach city	61 005
09	82800	009	New Haven County	55 564	12	16525	127	Volusia County	61 005
10			**DELAWARE**	897 934	12	16725		Deerfield Beach city	75 018
10	21200		Dover city	36 047	12	16725	011	Broward County	75 018
10	21200	001	Kent County	36 047					
					12	16875		DeLand city	27 031
10	50670		Newark city	31 454	12	16875	127	Volusia County	27 031
10	50670	003	New Castle County	31 454					
					12	17100		Delray Beach city	60 522
10	77580		Wilmington city	70 851	12	17100	099	Palm Beach County	60 522
10	77580	003	New Castle County	70 851					
					12	17200		Deltona city	85 182
11			**DISTRICT OF COLUMBIA**	601 723	12	17200	127	Volusia County	85 182
11	50000		Washington city	601 723					
11	50000	001	District of Columbia	601 723	12	17935		Doral city	45 704
					12	17935	086	Miami-Dade County	45 704
12			**FLORIDA**	18 801 310					
12	00950		Altamonte Springs city	41 496	12	18575		Dunedin city	35 321
12	00950	117	Seminole County	41 496	12	18575	103	Pinellas County	35 321
12	01700		Apopka city	41 542	12	24000		Fort Lauderdale city	165 521
12	01700	095	Orange County	41 542	12	24000	011	Broward County	165 521
12	02681		Aventura city	35 762	12	24125		Fort Myers city	62 298
12	02681	086	Miami-Dade County	35 762	12	24125	071	Lee County	62 298
12	07300		Boca Raton city	84 392	12	24300		Fort Pierce city	41 590
12	07300	099	Palm Beach County	84 392	12	24300	111	St. Lucie County	41 590
12	07525		Bonita Springs city	43 914	12	25175		Gainesville city	124 354
12	07525	071	Lee County	43 914	12	25175	001	Alachua County	124 354
12	07875		Boynton Beach city	68 217	12	27322		Greenacres city	37 573
12	07875	099	Palm Beach County	68 217	12	27322	099	Palm Beach County	37 573
12	07950		Bradenton city	49 546	12	28452		Hallandale Beach city	37 113
12	07950	081	Manatee County	49 546	12	28452	011	Broward County	37 113
12	10275		Cape Coral city	154 305	12	30000		Hialeah city	224 669
12	10275	071	Lee County	154 305	12	30000	086	Miami-Dade County	224 669
12	11050		Casselberry city	26 241	12	32000		Hollywood city	140 768
12	11050	117	Seminole County	26 241	12	32000	011	Broward County	140 768
12	12875		Clearwater city	107 685	12	32275		Homestead city	60 512
12	12875	103	Pinellas County	107 685	12	32275	086	Miami-Dade County	60 512
12	12925		Clermont city	28 742	12	35000		Jacksonville city	821 784
12	12925	069	Lake County	28 742	12	35000	031	Duval County	821 784
12	13275		Coconut Creek city	52 909	12	35875		Jupiter town	55 156
12	13275	011	Broward County	52 909	12	35875	099	Palm Beach County	55 156

Cities by County–*Continued*

State Code	Place Code	County Code	Geographic Area Name	2010 Census Population	State Code	Place Code	County Code	Geographic Area Name	2010 Census Population
12	36950		Kissimmee city	59 682	12	54075		Palm Beach Gardens city	48 452
12	36950	097	Osceola County	59 682	12	54075	099	Palm Beach County	48 452
12	38250		Lakeland city	97 422	12	54200		Palm Coast city	75 180
12	38250	105	Polk County	97 422	12	54200	035	Flagler County	75 180
12	39075		Lake Worth city	34 910	12	54700		Panama City city	36 484
12	39075	099	Palm Beach County	34 910	12	54700	005	Bay County	36 484
12	39425		Largo city	77 648	12	55775		Pembroke Pines city	154 750
12	39425	103	Pinellas County	77 648	12	55775	011	Broward County	154 750
12	39525		Lauderdale Lakes city	32 593	12	55925		Pensacola city	51 923
12	39525	011	Broward County	32 593	12	55925	033	Escambia County	51 923
12	39550		Lauderhill city	66 887	12	56975		Pinellas Park city	49 079
12	39550	011	Broward County	66 887	12	56975	103	Pinellas County	49 079
12	43125		Margate city	53 284	12	57425		Plantation city	84 955
12	43125	011	Broward County	53 284	12	57425	011	Broward County	84 955
12	43975		Melbourne city	76 068	12	57550		Plant City city	34 721
12	43975	009	Brevard County	76 068	12	57550	057	Hillsborough County	34 721
12	45000		Miami city	399 457	12	58050		Pompano Beach city	99 845
12	45000	086	Miami-Dade County	399 457	12	58050	011	Broward County	99 845
12	45025		Miami Beach city	87 779	12	58575		Port Orange city	56 048
12	45025	086	Miami-Dade County	87 779	12	58575	127	Volusia County	56 048
12	45060		Miami Gardens city	107 167	12	58715		Port St. Lucie city	164 603
12	45060	086	Miami-Dade County	107 167	12	58715	111	St. Lucie County	164 603
12	45100		Miami Lakes town	29 361	12	60975		Riviera Beach city	32 488
12	45100	086	Miami-Dade County	29 361	12	60975	099	Palm Beach County	32 488
12	45975		Miramar city	122 041	12	62100		Royal Palm Beach village	34 140
12	45975	011	Broward County	122 041	12	62100	099	Palm Beach County	34 140
12	49425		North Lauderdale city	41 023	12	62625		St. Cloud city	35 183
12	49425	011	Broward County	41 023	12	62625	097	Osceola County	35 183
12	49450		North Miami city	58 786	12	63000		St. Petersburg city	244 769
12	49450	086	Miami-Dade County	58 786	12	63000	103	Pinellas County	244 769
12	49475		North Miami Beach city	41 523	12	63650		Sanford city	53 570
12	49475	086	Miami-Dade County	41 523	12	63650	117	Seminole County	53 570
12	49675		North Port city	57 357	12	64175		Sarasota city	51 917
12	49675	115	Sarasota County	57 357	12	64175	115	Sarasota County	51 917
12	50575		Oakland Park city	41 363	12	69700		Sunrise city	84 439
12	50575	011	Broward County	41 363	12	69700	011	Broward County	84 439
12	50750		Ocala city	56 315	12	70600		Tallahassee city	181 376
12	50750	083	Marion County	56 315	12	70600	073	Leon County	181 376
12	51075		Ocoee city	35 579	12	70675		Tamarac city	60 427
12	51075	095	Orange County	35 579	12	70675	011	Broward County	60 427
12	53000		Orlando city	238 300	12	71000		Tampa city	335 709
12	53000	095	Orange County	238 300	12	71000	057	Hillsborough County	335 709
12	53150		Ormond Beach city	38 137	12	71900		Titusville city	43 761
12	53150	127	Volusia County	38 137	12	71900	009	Brevard County	43 761
12	53575		Oviedo city	33 342	12	75812		Wellington village	56 508
12	53575	117	Seminole County	33 342	12	75812	099	Palm Beach County	56 508
12	54000		Palm Bay city	103 190	12	76582		Weston city	65 333
12	54000	009	Brevard County	103 190	12	76582	011	Broward County	65 333

Cities by County–*Continued*

State Code	Place Code	County Code	Geographic Area Name	2010 Census Population	State Code	Place Code	County Code	Geographic Area Name	2010 Census Population
12	76600		West Palm Beach city	99 919	13	55020		Newnan city	33 039
12	76600	099	Palm Beach County	99 919	13	55020	077	Coweta County	33 039
12	78250		Winter Garden city	34 568	13	59724		Peachtree City city	34 364
12	78250	095	Orange County	34 568	13	59724	113	Fayette County	34 364
12	78275		Winter Haven city	33 874	13	66668		Rome city	36 303
12	78275	105	Polk County	33 874	13	66668	115	Floyd County	36 303
12	78300		Winter Park city	27 852	13	67284		Roswell city	88 346
12	78300	095	Orange County	27 852	13	67284	121	Fulton County	88 346
12	78325		Winter Springs city	33 282	13	68516		Sandy Springs city	93 853
12	78325	117	Seminole County	33 282	13	68516	121	Fulton County	93 853
13			**GEORGIA**	9 687 653	13	69000		Savannah city	136 286
13	01052		Albany city	77 434	13	69000	051	Chatham County	136 286
13	01052	095	Dougherty County	77 434	13	71492		Smyrna city	51 271
13	01696		Alpharetta city	57 551	13	71492	067	Cobb County	51 271
13	01696	121	Fulton County	57 551					
					13	73256		Statesboro city	28 422
13	04000		Atlanta city	420 003	13	73256	031	Bulloch County	28 422
13	04000	089	DeKalb County	28 292					
13	04000	121	Fulton County	391 711	13	73704		Stockbridge city	25 636
					13	73704	151	Henry County	25 636
13	19000		Columbus city	189 885					
13	19000	215	Muscogee County	189 885	13	78800		Valdosta city	54 518
					13	78800	185	Lowndes County	54 518
13	21380		Dalton city	33 128					
13	21380	313	Whitfield County	33 128	13	80508		Warner Robins city	66 588
					13	80508	153	Houston County	66 224
13	23900		Douglasville city	30 961	13	80508	225	Peach County	364
13	23900	097	Douglas County	30 961					
					15			**HAWAII**	1 360 301
13	24600		Duluth city	26 600	15	06290		East Honolulu CDP	49 914
13	24600	135	Gwinnett County	26 600	15	06290	003	Honolulu County	49 914
13	24768		Dunwoody city	46 267	15	14650		Hilo CDP	43 263
13	24768	089	DeKalb County	46 267	15	14650	001	Hawaii County	43 263
13	25720		East Point city	33 712	15	22700		Kahului CDP	26 337
13	25720	121	Fulton County	33 712	15	22700	009	Maui County	26 337
13	31908		Gainesville city	33 804	15	23150		Kailua CDP	38 635
13	31908	139	Hall County	33 804	15	23150	003	Honolulu County	38 635
13	38964		Hinesville city	33 437	15	28250		Kaneohe CDP	34 597
13	38964	179	Liberty County	33 437	15	28250	003	Honolulu County	34 597
13	42425		Johns Creek city	76 728	15	51050		Mililani Town CDP	27 629
13	42425	121	Fulton County	76 728	15	51050	003	Honolulu County	27 629
13	43192		Kennesaw city	29 783	15	62600		Pearl City CDP	47 698
13	43192	067	Cobb County	29 783	15	62600	003	Honolulu County	47 698
13	44340		LaGrange city	29 588	15	71550		Urban Honolulu CDP	337 256
13	44340	285	Troup County	29 588	15	71550	003	Honolulu County	337 256
13	45488		Lawrenceville city	28 546	15	79700		Waipahu CDP	38 216
13	45488	135	Gwinnett County	28 546	15	79700	003	Honolulu County	38 216
13	49000		Macon city	91 351	16			**IDAHO**	1 567 582
13	49000	021	Bibb County	90 885	16	08830		Boise City city	205 671
13	49000	169	Jones County	466	16	08830	001	Ada County	205 671
13	49756		Marietta city	56 579	16	12250		Caldwell city	46 237
13	49756	067	Cobb County	56 579	16	12250	027	Canyon County	46 237
13	51670		Milton city	32 661	16	16750		Coeur d'Alene city	44 137
13	51670	121	Fulton County	32 661	16	16750	055	Kootenai County	44 137

Cities by County–*Continued*

State Code	Place Code	County Code	Geographic Area Name	2010 Census Population	State Code	Place Code	County Code	Geographic Area Name	2010 Census Population
16	39700		Idaho Falls city	56 813	17	09447		Buffalo Grove village	41 496
16	39700	019	Bonneville County	56 813	17	09447	031	Cook County	13 644
					17	09447	097	Lake County	27 852
16	46540		Lewiston city	31 894					
16	46540	069	Nez Perce County	31 894	17	09642		Burbank city	28 925
					17	09642	031	Cook County	28 925
16	52120		Meridian city	75 092					
16	52120	001	Ada County	75 092	17	10487		Calumet City city	37 042
					17	10487	031	Cook County	37 042
16	56260		Nampa city	81 557					
16	56260	027	Canyon County	81 557	17	11163		Carbondale city	25 902
					17	11163	077	Jackson County	25 902
16	64090		Pocatello city	54 255	17	11163	199	Williamson County	0
16	64090	005	Bannock County	54 239					
16	64090	077	Power County	16	17	11332		Carol Stream village	39 711
					17	11332	043	DuPage County	39 711
16	64810		Post Falls city	27 574					
16	64810	055	Kootenai County	27 574	17	11358		Carpentersville village	37 691
					17	11358	089	Kane County	37 691
16	67420		Rexburg city	25 484					
16	67420	065	Madison County	25 484	17	12385		Champaign city	81 055
					17	12385	019	Champaign County	81 055
16	82810		Twin Falls city	44 125					
16	82810	083	Twin Falls County	44 125	17	14000		Chicago city	2 695 598
					17	14000	031	Cook County	2 695 598
17			**ILLINOIS**	12 830 632	17	14000	043	DuPage County	0
17	00243		Addison village	36 942					
17	00243	043	DuPage County	36 942	17	14026		Chicago Heights city	30 276
					17	14026	031	Cook County	30 276
17	00685		Algonquin village	30 046					
17	00685	089	Kane County	8 433	17	14351		Cicero town	83 891
17	00685	111	McHenry County	21 613	17	14351	031	Cook County	83 891
17	01114		Alton city	27 865	17	15599		Collinsville city	25 579
17	01114	119	Madison County	27 865	17	15599	119	Madison County	22 573
					17	15599	163	St. Clair County	3 006
17	02154		Arlington Heights village	75 101					
17	02154	031	Cook County	75 101	17	17887		Crystal Lake city	40 743
17	02154	097	Lake County	0	17	17887	111	McHenry County	40 743
17	03012		Aurora city	197 899	17	18563		Danville city	33 027
17	03012	043	DuPage County	49 433	17	18563	183	Vermilion County	33 027
17	03012	089	Kane County	130 976					
17	03012	093	Kendall County	6 019	17	18823		Decatur city	76 122
17	03012	197	Will County	11 471	17	18823	115	Macon County	76 122
17	04013		Bartlett village	41 208	17	19161		DeKalb city	43 862
17	04013	031	Cook County	16 797	17	19161	037	DeKalb County	43 862
17	04013	043	DuPage County	24 411					
17	04013	089	Kane County	0	17	19642		Des Plaines city	58 364
					17	19642	031	Cook County	58 364
17	04078		Batavia city	26 045					
17	04078	043	DuPage County	0	17	20591		Downers Grove village	47 833
17	04078	089	Kane County	26 045	17	20591	043	DuPage County	47 833
17	04845		Belleville city	44 478	17	22255		East St. Louis city	27 006
17	04845	163	St. Clair County	44 478	17	22255	163	St. Clair County	27 006
17	05092		Belvidere city	25 585	17	23074		Elgin city	108 188
17	05092	007	Boone County	25 585	17	23074	031	Cook County	24 032
					17	23074	089	Kane County	84 156
17	05573		Berwyn city	56 657					
17	05573	031	Cook County	56 657	17	23256		Elk Grove Village village	33 127
					17	23256	031	Cook County	33 127
17	06613		Bloomington city	76 610	17	23256	043	DuPage County	0
17	06613	113	McLean County	76 610					
					17	23620		Elmhurst city	44 121
17	07133		Bolingbrook village	73 366	17	23620	031	Cook County	0
17	07133	043	DuPage County	1 571	17	23620	043	DuPage County	44 121
17	07133	197	Will County	71 795					
					17	24582		Evanston city	74 486
					17	24582	031	Cook County	74 486

State Code	Place Code	County Code	Geographic Area Name	2010 Census Population
17	27884		Freeport city	25 638
17	27884	177	Stephenson County	25 638
17	28326		Galesburg city	32 195
17	28326	095	Knox County	32 195
17	29730		Glendale Heights village	34 208
17	29730	043	DuPage County	34 208
17	29756		Glen Ellyn village	27 450
17	29756	043	DuPage County	27 450
17	29938		Glenview village	44 692
17	29938	031	Cook County	44 692
17	30926		Granite City city	29 849
17	30926	119	Madison County	29 849
17	32018		Gurnee village	31 295
17	32018	097	Lake County	31 295
17	32746		Hanover Park village	37 973
17	32746	031	Cook County	20 636
17	32746	043	DuPage County	17 337
17	33383		Harvey city	25 282
17	33383	031	Cook County	25 282
17	34722		Highland Park city	29 763
17	34722	097	Lake County	29 763
17	35411		Hoffman Estates village	51 895
17	35411	031	Cook County	51 895
17	35411	089	Kane County	0
17	38570		Joliet city	147 433
17	38570	093	Kendall County	9 749
17	38570	197	Will County	137 684
17	38934		Kankakee city	27 537
17	38934	091	Kankakee County	27 537
17	41183		Lake in the Hills village	28 965
17	41183	111	McHenry County	28 965
17	42028		Lansing village	28 331
17	42028	031	Cook County	28 331
17	44407		Lombard village	43 165
17	44407	043	DuPage County	43 165
17	45694		McHenry city	26 992
17	45694	111	McHenry County	26 992
17	48242		Melrose Park village	25 411
17	48242	031	Cook County	25 411
17	49867		Moline city	43 483
17	49867	161	Rock Island County	43 483
17	51089		Mount Prospect village	54 167
17	51089	031	Cook County	54 167
17	51349		Mundelein village	31 064
17	51349	097	Lake County	31 064
17	51622		Naperville city	141 853
17	51622	043	DuPage County	94 533
17	51622	197	Will County	47 320
17	53000		Niles village	29 803
17	53000	031	Cook County	29 803
17	53234		Normal town	52 497
17	53234	113	McLean County	52 497
17	53481		Northbrook village	33 170
17	53481	031	Cook County	33 170
17	53559		North Chicago city	32 574
17	53559	097	Lake County	32 574
17	54638		Oak Forest city	27 962
17	54638	031	Cook County	27 962
17	54820		Oak Lawn village	56 690
17	54820	031	Cook County	56 690
17	54885		Oak Park village	51 878
17	54885	031	Cook County	51 878
17	55249		O'Fallon city	28 281
17	55249	163	St. Clair County	28 281
17	56640		Orland Park village	56 767
17	56640	031	Cook County	56 583
17	56640	197	Will County	184
17	56887		Oswego village	30 355
17	56887	093	Kendall County	30 355
17	57225		Palatine village	68 557
17	57225	031	Cook County	68 557
17	57225	097	Lake County	0
17	57875		Park Ridge city	37 480
17	57875	031	Cook County	37 480
17	58447		Pekin city	34 094
17	58447	143	Peoria County	0
17	58447	179	Tazewell County	34 094
17	59000		Peoria city	115 007
17	59000	143	Peoria County	115 007
17	60287		Plainfield village	39 581
17	60287	093	Kendall County	2 079
17	60287	197	Will County	37 502
17	62367		Quincy city	40 633
17	62367	001	Adams County	40 633
17	65000		Rockford city	152 871
17	65000	201	Winnebago County	152 871
17	65078		Rock Island city	39 018
17	65078	161	Rock Island County	39 018
17	65442		Romeoville village	39 680
17	65442	197	Will County	39 680
17	66040		Round Lake Beach village	28 175
17	66040	097	Lake County	28 175
17	66703		St. Charles city	32 974
17	66703	043	DuPage County	543
17	66703	089	Kane County	32 431
17	68003		Schaumburg village	74 227
17	68003	031	Cook County	74 227
17	68003	043	DuPage County	0
17	70122		Skokie village	64 784
17	70122	031	Cook County	64 784

State Code	Place Code	County Code	Geographic Area Name	2010 Census Population	State Code	Place Code	County Code	Geographic Area Name	2010 Census Population
17	72000		Springfield city	116 250	18	28386		Goshen city	31 719
17	72000	167	Sangamon County	116 250	18	28386	039	Elkhart County	31 719
17	73157		Streamwood village	39 858	18	29898		Greenwood city	49 791
17	73157	031	Cook County	39 858	18	29898	081	Johnson County	49 791
17	75484		Tinley Park village	56 703	18	31000		Hammond city	80 830
17	75484	031	Cook County	49 236	18	31000	089	Lake County	80 830
17	75484	197	Will County	7 467	18	34114		Hobart city	29 059
17	77005		Urbana city	41 250	18	34114	089	Lake County	29 059
17	77005	019	Champaign County	41 250	18	38358		Jeffersonville city	44 953
17	77694		Vernon Hills village	25 113	18	38358	019	Clark County	44 953
17	77694	097	Lake County	25 113	18	40392		Kokomo city	45 468
17	79293		Waukegan city	89 078	18	40392	067	Howard County	45 468
17	79293	097	Lake County	89 078	18	40788		Lafayette city	67 140
17	80060		West Chicago city	27 086	18	40788	157	Tippecanoe County	67 140
17	80060	043	DuPage County	27 086	18	42426		Lawrence city	46 001
17	81048		Wheaton city	52 894	18	42426	097	Marion County	46 001
17	81048	043	DuPage County	52 894	18	46908		Marion city	29 948
17	81087		Wheeling village	37 648	18	46908	053	Grant County	29 948
17	81087	031	Cook County	37 642	18	48528		Merrillville town	35 246
17	81087	097	Lake County	6	18	48528	089	Lake County	35 246
17	82075		Wilmette village	27 087	18	48798		Michigan City city	31 479
17	82075	031	Cook County	27 087	18	48798	091	LaPorte County	31 479
17	83245		Woodridge village	32 971	18	49932		Mishawaka city	48 252
17	83245	031	Cook County	0	18	49932	141	St. Joseph County	48 252
17	83245	043	DuPage County	32 949	18	51876		Muncie city	70 085
17	83245	197	Will County	22	18	51876	035	Delaware County	70 085
18			**INDIANA**	6 483 802	18	52326		New Albany city	36 372
18	01468		Anderson city	56 129	18	52326	043	Floyd County	36 372
18	01468	095	Madison County	56 129	18	54180		Noblesville city	51 969
18	05860		Bloomington city	80 405	18	54180	057	Hamilton County	51 969
18	05860	105	Monroe County	80 405	18	60246		Plainfield town	27 631
18	10342		Carmel city	79 191	18	60246	063	Hendricks County	27 631
18	10342	057	Hamilton County	79 191	18	61092		Portage city	36 828
18	14734		Columbus city	44 061	18	61092	127	Porter County	36 828
18	14734	005	Bartholomew County	44 061	18	64260		Richmond city	36 812
18	16138		Crown Point city	27 317	18	64260	177	Wayne County	36 812
18	16138	089	Lake County	27 317	18	68220		Schererville town	29 243
18	19486		East Chicago city	29 698	18	68220	089	Lake County	29 243
18	19486	089	Lake County	29 698	18	71000		South Bend city	101 168
18	20728		Elkhart city	50 949	18	71000	141	St. Joseph County	101 168
18	20728	039	Elkhart County	50 949	18	75428		Terre Haute city	60 785
18	22000		Evansville city	117 429	18	75428	167	Vigo County	60 785
18	22000	163	Vanderburgh County	117 429	18	78326		Valparaiso city	31 730
18	23278		Fishers town	76 794	18	78326	127	Porter County	31 730
18	23278	057	Hamilton County	76 794	18	82700		Westfield town	30 068
18	25000		Fort Wayne city	253 691	18	82700	057	Hamilton County	30 068
18	25000	003	Allen County	253 691	18	82862		West Lafayette city	29 596
18	27000		Gary city	80 294	18	82862	157	Tippecanoe County	29 596
18	27000	089	Lake County	80 294					

Cities by County–*Continued*

State Code	Place Code	County Code	Geographic Area Name	2010 Census Population	State Code	Place Code	County Code	Geographic Area Name	2010 Census Population
19			**IOWA**	3 046 355	20	25325		Garden City city	26 658
19	01855		Ames city	58 965	20	25325	055	Finney County	26 658
19	01855	169	Story County	58 965					
					20	33625		Hutchinson city	42 080
19	02305		Ankeny city	45 582	20	33625	155	Reno County	42 080
19	02305	153	Polk County	45 582					
					20	36000		Kansas City city	145 786
19	06355		Bettendorf city	33 217	20	36000	209	Wyandotte County	145 786
19	06355	163	Scott County	33 217					
					20	38900		Lawrence city	87 643
19	09550		Burlington city	25 663	20	38900	045	Douglas County	87 643
19	09550	057	Des Moines County	25 663					
					20	39000		Leavenworth city	35 251
19	11755		Cedar Falls city	39 260	20	39000	103	Leavenworth County	35 251
19	11755	013	Black Hawk County	39 260					
					20	39075		Leawood city	31 867
19	12000		Cedar Rapids city	126 326	20	39075	091	Johnson County	31 867
19	12000	113	Linn County	126 326					
					20	39350		Lenexa city	48 190
19	14430		Clinton city	26 885	20	39350	091	Johnson County	48 190
19	14430	045	Clinton County	26 885					
					20	44250		Manhattan city	52 281
19	16860		Council Bluffs city	62 230	20	44250	149	Pottawatomie County	146
19	16860	155	Pottawattamie County	62 230	20	44250	161	Riley County	52 135
19	19000		Davenport city	99 685	20	52575		Olathe city	125 872
19	19000	163	Scott County	99 685	20	52575	091	Johnson County	125 872
19	21000		Des Moines city	203 433	20	53775		Overland Park city	173 372
19	21000	153	Polk County	203 419	20	53775	091	Johnson County	173 372
19	21000	181	Warren County	14					
					20	62700		Salina city	47 707
19	22395		Dubuque city	57 637	20	62700	169	Saline County	47 707
19	22395	061	Dubuque County	57 637					
					20	64500		Shawnee city	62 209
19	28515		Fort Dodge city	25 206	20	64500	091	Johnson County	62 209
19	28515	187	Webster County	25 206					
					20	71000		Topeka city	127 473
19	38595		Iowa City city	67 862	20	71000	177	Shawnee County	127 473
19	38595	103	Johnson County	67 862					
					20	79000		Wichita city	382 368
19	49485		Marion city	34 768	20	79000	173	Sedgwick County	382 368
19	49485	113	Linn County	34 768					
					21			**KENTUCKY**	4 339 367
19	49755		Marshalltown city	27 552	21	08902		Bowling Green city	58 067
19	49755	127	Marshall County	27 552	21	08902	227	Warren County	58 067
19	50160		Mason City city	28 079	21	17848		Covington city	40 640
19	50160	033	Cerro Gordo County	28 079	21	17848	117	Kenton County	40 640
19	60465		Ottumwa city	25 023	21	24274		Elizabethtown city	28 531
19	60465	179	Wapello County	25 023	21	24274	093	Hardin County	28 531
19	73335		Sioux City city	82 684	21	27982		Florence city	29 951
19	73335	149	Plymouth County	6	21	27982	015	Boone County	29 951
19	73335	193	Woodbury County	82 678					
					21	28900		Frankfort city	25 527
19	79950		Urbandale city	39 463	21	28900	073	Franklin County	25 527
19	79950	049	Dallas County	6 337					
19	79950	153	Polk County	33 126	21	30700		Georgetown city	29 098
					21	30700	209	Scott County	29 098
19	82425		Waterloo city	68 406					
19	82425	013	Black Hawk County	68 406	21	35866		Henderson city	28 757
					21	35866	101	Henderson County	28 757
19	83910		West Des Moines city	56 609					
19	83910	049	Dallas County	11 569	21	37918		Hopkinsville city	31 577
19	83910	153	Polk County	44 999	21	37918	047	Christian County	31 577
19	83910	181	Warren County	41					
					21	40222		Jeffersontown city	26 595
20			**KANSAS**	2 853 118	21	40222	111	Jefferson County	26 595
20	18250		Dodge City city	27 340					
20	18250	057	Ford County	27 340					

Cities by County–*Continued*

State Code	Place Code	County Code	Geographic Area Name	2010 Census Population	State Code	Place Code	County Code	Geographic Area Name	2010 Census Population
21	46027		Lexington-Fayette urban county	295 803	24	04000		Baltimore city	620 961
21	46027	067	Fayette County	295 803	24	04000	510	Baltimore city	620 961
21	56136		Nicholasville city	28 015	24	08775		Bowie city	54 727
21	56136	113	Jessamine County	28 015	24	08775	033	Prince George's County	54 727
21	58620		Owensboro city	57 265	24	18750		College Park city	30 413
21	58620	059	Daviess County	57 265	24	18750	033	Prince George's County	30 413
21	58836		Paducah city	25 024	24	30325		Frederick city	65 239
21	58836	145	McCracken County	25 024	24	30325	021	Frederick County	65 239
21	65226		Richmond city	31 364	24	31175		Gaithersburg city	59 933
21	65226	151	Madison County	31 364	24	31175	031	Montgomery County	59 933
22			**LOUISIANA**	4 533 372	24	36075		Hagerstown city	39 662
22	00975		Alexandria city	47 723	24	36075	043	Washington County	39 662
22	00975	079	Rapides Parish	47 723	24	45900		Laurel city	25 115
22	05000		Baton Rouge city	229 493	24	45900	033	Prince George's County	25 115
22	05000	033	East Baton Rouge Parish	229 493	24	67675		Rockville city	61 209
22	08920		Bossier City city	61 315	24	67675	031	Montgomery County	61 209
22	08920	015	Bossier Parish	61 315	24	69925		Salisbury city	30 343
22	13960		Central city	26 864	24	69925	045	Wicomico County	30 343
22	13960	033	East Baton Rouge Parish	26 864	25			**MASSACHUSETTS**	6 547 629
22	36255		Houma city	33 727	25	00840		Agawam Town city	28 438
22	36255	109	Terrebonne Parish	33 727	25	00840	013	Hampden County	28 438
22	39475		Kenner city	66 702	25	02690		Attleboro city	43 593
22	39475	051	Jefferson Parish	66 702	25	02690	005	Bristol County	43 593
22	40735		Lafayette city	120 623	25	03690		Barnstable Town city	45 193
22	40735	055	Lafayette Parish	120 623	25	03690	001	Barnstable County	45 193
22	41155		Lake Charles city	71 993	25	05595		Beverly city	39 502
22	41155	019	Calcasieu Parish	71 993	25	05595	009	Essex County	39 502
22	51410		Monroe city	48 815	25	07000		Boston city	617 594
22	51410	073	Ouachita Parish	48 815	25	07000	025	Suffolk County	617 594
22	54035		New Iberia city	30 617	25	07740		Braintree Town city	35 744
22	54035	045	Iberia Parish	30 617	25	07740	021	Norfolk County	35 744
22	55000		New Orleans city	343 829	25	09000		Brockton city	93 810
22	55000	071	Orleans Parish	343 829	25	09000	023	Plymouth County	93 810
22	70000		Shreveport city	199 311	25	11000		Cambridge city	105 162
22	70000	015	Bossier Parish	2 702	25	11000	017	Middlesex County	105 162
22	70000	017	Caddo Parish	196 609	25	13205		Chelsea city	35 177
22	70805		Slidell city	27 068	25	13205	025	Suffolk County	35 177
22	70805	103	St. Tammany Parish	27 068	25	13660		Chicopee city	55 298
23			**MAINE**	1 328 361	25	13660	013	Hampden County	55 298
23	02795		Bangor city	33 039	25	21990		Everett city	41 667
23	02795	019	Penobscot County	33 039	25	21990	017	Middlesex County	41 667
23	38740		Lewiston city	36 592	25	23000		Fall River city	88 857
23	38740	001	Androscoggin County	36 592	25	23000	005	Bristol County	88 857
23	60545		Portland city	66 194	25	23875		Fitchburg city	40 318
23	60545	005	Cumberland County	66 194	25	23875	027	Worcester County	40 318
23	71990		South Portland city	25 002	25	25172		Franklin Town city	31 635
23	71990	005	Cumberland County	25 002	25	25172	021	Norfolk County	31 635
24			**MARYLAND**	5 773 552	25	26150		Gloucester city	28 789
24	01600		Annapolis city	38 394	25	26150	009	Essex County	28 789
24	01600	003	Anne Arundel County	38 394					

State Code	Place Code	County Code	Geographic Area Name	2010 Census Population	State Code	Place Code	County Code	Geographic Area Name	2010 Census Population
25	29405		Haverhill city	60 879	25	76030		Westfield city	41 094
25	29405	009	Essex County	60 879	25	76030	013	Hampden County	41 094
25	30840		Holyoke city	39 880	25	77890		West Springfield Town city	28 391
25	30840	013	Hampden County	39 880	25	77890	013	Hampden County	28 391
25	34550		Lawrence city	76 377	25	78972		Weymouth Town city	53 743
25	34550	009	Essex County	76 377	25	78972	021	Norfolk County	53 743
25	35075		Leominster city	40 759	25	81035		Woburn city	38 120
25	35075	027	Worcester County	40 759	25	81035	017	Middlesex County	38 120
25	37000		Lowell city	106 519	25	82000		Worcester city	181 045
25	37000	017	Middlesex County	106 519	25	82000	027	Worcester County	181 045
25	37490		Lynn city	90 329	26			**MICHIGAN**	9 883 640
25	37490	009	Essex County	90 329	26	01380		Allen Park city	28 210
					26	01380	163	Wayne County	28 210
25	37875		Malden city	59 450					
25	37875	017	Middlesex County	59 450	26	03000		Ann Arbor city	113 934
					26	03000	161	Washtenaw County	113 934
25	38715		Marlborough city	38 499					
25	38715	017	Middlesex County	38 499	26	05920		Battle Creek city	52 347
					26	05920	025	Calhoun County	52 347
25	39835		Medford city	56 173					
25	39835	017	Middlesex County	56 173	26	06020		Bay City city	34 932
					26	06020	017	Bay County	34 932
25	40115		Melrose city	26 983					
25	40115	017	Middlesex County	26 983	26	12060		Burton city	29 999
					26	12060	049	Genesee County	29 999
25	40710		Methuen Town city	47 255					
25	40710	009	Essex County	47 255	26	21000		Dearborn city	98 153
					26	21000	163	Wayne County	98 153
25	45000		New Bedford city	95 072					
25	45000	005	Bristol County	95 072	26	21020		Dearborn Heights city	57 774
					26	21020	163	Wayne County	57 774
25	45560		Newton city	85 146					
25	45560	017	Middlesex County	85 146	26	22000		Detroit city	713 777
					26	22000	163	Wayne County	713 777
25	46330		Northampton city	28 549					
25	46330	015	Hampshire County	28 549	26	24120		East Lansing city	48 579
					26	24120	037	Clinton County	1 969
25	52490		Peabody city	51 251	26	24120	065	Ingham County	46 610
25	52490	009	Essex County	51 251					
					26	24290		Eastpointe city	32 442
25	53960		Pittsfield city	44 737	26	24290	099	Macomb County	32 442
25	53960	003	Berkshire County	44 737					
					26	27440		Farmington Hills city	79 740
25	55745		Quincy city	92 271	26	27440	125	Oakland County	79 740
25	55745	021	Norfolk County	92 271					
					26	29000		Flint city	102 434
25	56585		Revere city	51 755	26	29000	049	Genesee County	102 434
25	56585	025	Suffolk County	51 755					
					26	31420		Garden City city	27 692
25	59105		Salem city	41 340	26	31420	163	Wayne County	27 692
25	59105	009	Essex County	41 340					
					26	34000		Grand Rapids city	188 040
25	62535		Somerville city	75 754	26	34000	081	Kent County	188 040
25	62535	017	Middlesex County	75 754					
					26	38640		Holland city	33 051
25	67000		Springfield city	153 060	26	38640	005	Allegan County	7 016
25	67000	013	Hampden County	153 060	26	38640	139	Ottawa County	26 035
25	69170		Taunton city	55 874	26	40680		Inkster city	25 369
25	69170	005	Bristol County	55 874	26	40680	163	Wayne County	25 369
25	72600		Waltham city	60 632	26	41420		Jackson city	33 534
25	72600	017	Middlesex County	60 632	26	41420	075	Jackson County	33 534
25	73440		Watertown Town city	31 915	26	42160		Kalamazoo city	74 262
25	73440	017	Middlesex County	31 915	26	42160	077	Kalamazoo County	74 262

Cities by County–*Continued*

State Code	Place Code	County Code	Geographic Area Name	2010 Census Population	State Code	Place Code	County Code	Geographic Area Name	2010 Census Population
26	42820		Kentwood city	48 707	26	84000		Warren city	134 056
26	42820	081	Kent County	48 707	26	84000	099	Macomb County	134 056
26	46000		Lansing city	114 297	26	86000		Westland city	84 094
26	46000	045	Eaton County	4 734	26	86000	163	Wayne County	84 094
26	46000	065	Ingham County	109 563	26	88900		Wyandotte city	25 883
26	47800		Lincoln Park city	38 144	26	88900	163	Wayne County	25 883
26	47800	163	Wayne County	38 144	26	88940		Wyoming city	72 125
26	49000		Livonia city	96 942	26	88940	081	Kent County	72 125
26	49000	163	Wayne County	96 942	27			**MINNESOTA**	5 303 925
26	50560		Madison Heights city	29 694	27	01486		Andover city	30 598
26	50560	125	Oakland County	29 694	27	01486	003	Anoka County	30 598
26	53780		Midland city	41 863	27	01900		Apple Valley city	49 084
26	53780	017	Bay County	157	27	01900	037	Dakota County	49 084
26	53780	111	Midland County	41 706	27	06382		Blaine city	57 186
26	56020		Mount Pleasant city	26 016	27	06382	003	Anoka County	57 186
26	56020	073	Isabella County	26 016	27	06382	123	Ramsey County	0
26	56320		Muskegon city	38 401	27	06616		Bloomington city	82 893
26	56320	121	Muskegon County	38 401	27	06616	053	Hennepin County	82 893
26	59440		Novi city	55 224	27	07948		Brooklyn Center city	30 104
26	59440	125	Oakland County	55 224	27	07948	053	Hennepin County	30 104
26	59920		Oak Park city	29 319	27	07966		Brooklyn Park city	75 781
26	59920	125	Oakland County	29 319	27	07966	053	Hennepin County	75 781
26	65440		Pontiac city	59 515	27	08794		Burnsville city	60 306
26	65440	125	Oakland County	59 515	27	08794	037	Dakota County	60 306
26	65560		Portage city	46 292	27	13114		Coon Rapids city	61 476
26	65560	077	Kalamazoo County	46 292	27	13114	003	Anoka County	61 476
26	65820		Port Huron city	30 184	27	13456		Cottage Grove city	34 589
26	65820	147	St. Clair County	30 184	27	13456	163	Washington County	34 589
26	69035		Rochester Hills city	70 995	27	17000		Duluth city	86 265
26	69035	125	Oakland County	70 995	27	17000	137	St. Louis County	86 265
26	69800		Roseville city	47 299	27	17288		Eagan city	64 206
26	69800	099	Macomb County	47 299	27	17288	037	Dakota County	64 206
26	70040		Royal Oak city	57 236	27	18116		Eden Prairie city	60 797
26	70040	125	Oakland County	57 236	27	18116	053	Hennepin County	60 797
26	70520		Saginaw city	51 508	27	18188		Edina city	47 941
26	70520	145	Saginaw County	51 508	27	18188	053	Hennepin County	47 941
26	70760		St. Clair Shores city	59 715	27	22814		Fridley city	27 208
26	70760	099	Macomb County	59 715	27	22814	003	Anoka County	27 208
26	74900		Southfield city	71 739	27	31076		Inver Grove Heights city	33 880
26	74900	125	Oakland County	71 739	27	31076	037	Dakota County	33 880
26	74960		Southgate city	30 047	27	35180		Lakeville city	55 954
26	74960	163	Wayne County	30 047	27	35180	037	Dakota County	55 954
26	76460		Sterling Heights city	129 699	27	39878		Mankato city	39 309
26	76460	099	Macomb County	129 699	27	39878	013	Blue Earth County	39 305
26	79000		Taylor city	63 131	27	39878	079	Le Sueur County	4
26	79000	163	Wayne County	63 131	27	39878	103	Nicollet County	0
26	80700		Troy city	80 980	27	40166		Maple Grove city	61 567
26	80700	125	Oakland County	80 980	27	40166	053	Hennepin County	61 567
					27	40382		Maplewood city	38 018
					27	40382	123	Ramsey County	38 018

Cities by County–*Continued*

State Code	Place Code	County Code	Geographic Area Name	2010 Census Population	State Code	Place Code	County Code	Geographic Area Name	2010 Census Population
27	43000		Minneapolis city	382 578	28	36000		Jackson city	173 514
27	43000	053	Hennepin County	382 578	28	36000	049	Hinds County	172 891
					28	36000	089	Madison County	622
27	43252		Minnetonka city	49 734	28	36000	121	Rankin County	1
27	43252	053	Hennepin County	49 734					
					28	46640		Meridian city	41 148
27	43864		Moorhead city	38 065	28	46640	075	Lauderdale County	41 148
27	43864	027	Clay County	38 065					
					28	54040		Olive Branch city	33 484
27	47680		Oakdale city	27 378	28	54040	033	DeSoto County	33 484
27	47680	163	Washington County	27 378					
					28	55760		Pearl city	25 092
27	49300		Owatonna city	25 599	28	55760	121	Rankin County	25 092
27	49300	147	Steele County	25 599					
					28	69280		Southaven city	48 982
27	51730		Plymouth city	70 576	28	69280	033	DeSoto County	48 982
27	51730	053	Hennepin County	70 576					
					28	74840		Tupelo city	34 546
27	54214		Richfield city	35 228	28	74840	081	Lee County	34 546
27	54214	053	Hennepin County	35 228					
					29			**MISSOURI**	5 988 927
27	54880		Rochester city	106 769	29	03160		Ballwin city	30 404
27	54880	109	Olmsted County	106 769	29	03160	189	St. Louis County	30 404
27	55852		Roseville city	33 660	29	06652		Blue Springs city	52 575
27	55852	123	Ramsey County	33 660	29	06652	095	Jackson County	52 575
27	56896		St. Cloud city	65 842	29	11242		Cape Girardeau city	37 941
27	56896	009	Benton County	6 396	29	11242	031	Cape Girardeau County	37 941
27	56896	141	Sherburne County	6 785	29	11242	201	Scott County	0
27	56896	145	Stearns County	52 661					
					29	13600		Chesterfield city	47 484
27	57220		St. Louis Park city	45 250	29	13600	189	St. Louis County	47 484
27	57220	053	Hennepin County	45 250					
					29	15670		Columbia city	108 500
27	58000		St. Paul city	285 068	29	15670	019	Boone County	108 500
27	58000	123	Ramsey County	285 068					
					29	24778		Florissant city	52 158
27	58738		Savage city	26 911	29	24778	189	St. Louis County	52 158
27	58738	139	Scott County	26 911					
					29	27190		Gladstone city	25 410
27	59350		Shakopee city	37 076	29	27190	047	Clay County	25 410
27	59350	139	Scott County	37 076					
					29	31276		Hazelwood city	25 703
27	59998		Shoreview city	25 043	29	31276	189	St. Louis County	25 703
27	59998	123	Ramsey County	25 043					
					29	35000		Independence city	116 830
27	71032		Winona city	27 592	29	35000	047	Clay County	0
27	71032	169	Winona County	27 592	29	35000	095	Jackson County	116 830
27	71428		Woodbury city	61 961	29	37000		Jefferson City city	43 079
27	71428	163	Washington County	61 961	29	37000	027	Callaway County	22
					29	37000	051	Cole County	43 057
28			**MISSISSIPPI**	2 967 297					
28	06220		Biloxi city	44 054	29	37592		Joplin city	50 150
28	06220	047	Harrison County	44 054	29	37592	097	Jasper County	43 955
					29	37592	145	Newton County	6 195
28	14420		Clinton city	25 216					
28	14420	049	Hinds County	25 216	29	38000		Kansas City city	459 787
					29	38000	037	Cass County	197
28	29180		Greenville city	34 400	29	38000	047	Clay County	113 415
28	29180	151	Washington County	34 400	29	38000	095	Jackson County	302 499
					29	38000	165	Platte County	43 676
28	29700		Gulfport city	67 793					
28	29700	047	Harrison County	67 793	29	39044		Kirkwood city	27 540
					29	39044	189	St. Louis County	27 540
28	31020		Hattiesburg city	45 989					
28	31020	035	Forrest County	41 000	29	41348		Lee's Summit city	91 364
28	31020	073	Lamar County	4 989	29	41348	037	Cass County	1 917
					29	41348	095	Jackson County	89 447
28	33700		Horn Lake city	26 066					
28	33700	033	DeSoto County	26 066					

Cities by County–*Continued*

State Code	Place Code	County Code	Geographic Area Name	2010 Census Population	State Code	Place Code	County Code	Geographic Area Name	2010 Census Population
29	42032		Liberty city	29 149	32			**NEVADA**	2 700 551
29	42032	047	Clay County	29 149	32	09700		Carson City	55 274
					32	09700	510	Carson City	55 274
29	46586		Maryland Heights city	27 472					
29	46586	189	St. Louis County	27 472	32	31900		Henderson city	257 729
					32	31900	003	Clark County	257 729
29	54074		O'Fallon city	79 329					
29	54074	183	St. Charles County	79 329	32	40000		Las Vegas city	583 756
					32	40000	003	Clark County	583 756
29	60788		Raytown city	29 526					
29	60788	095	Jackson County	29 526	32	51800		North Las Vegas city	216 961
					32	51800	003	Clark County	216 961
29	64082		St. Charles city	65 794					
29	64082	183	St. Charles County	65 794	32	60600		Reno city	225 221
					32	60600	031	Washoe County	225 221
29	64550		St. Joseph city	76 780					
29	64550	021	Buchanan County	76 780	32	68400		Sparks city	90 264
					32	68400	031	Washoe County	90 264
29	65000		St. Louis city	319 294					
29	65000	510	St. Louis city	319 294	33			**NEW HAMPSHIRE**	1 316 470
					33	14200		Concord city	42 695
29	65126		St. Peters city	52 575	33	14200	013	Merrimack County	42 695
29	65126	183	St. Charles County	52 575					
					33	18820		Dover city	29 987
29	70000		Springfield city	159 498	33	18820	017	Strafford County	29 987
29	70000	043	Christian County	2					
29	70000	077	Greene County	159 496	33	45140		Manchester city	109 565
					33	45140	011	Hillsborough County	109 565
29	75220		University City city	35 371					
29	75220	189	St. Louis County	35 371	33	50260		Nashua city	86 494
					33	50260	011	Hillsborough County	86 494
29	78442		Wentzville city	29 070					
29	78442	183	St. Charles County	29 070	33	65140		Rochester city	29 752
					33	65140	017	Strafford County	29 752
29	79820		Wildwood city	35 517					
29	79820	189	St. Louis County	35 517	34			**NEW JERSEY**	8 791 894
					34	02080		Atlantic City city	39 558
30			**MONTANA**	989 415	34	02080	001	Atlantic County	39 558
30	06550		Billings city	104 170					
30	06550	111	Yellowstone County	104 170	34	03580		Bayonne city	63 024
					34	03580	017	Hudson County	63 024
30	08950		Bozeman city	37 280					
30	08950	031	Gallatin County	37 280	34	05170		Bergenfield borough	26 764
					34	05170	003	Bergen County	26 764
30	32800		Great Falls city	58 505					
30	32800	013	Cascade County	58 505	34	07600		Bridgeton city	25 349
					34	07600	011	Cumberland County	25 349
30	35600		Helena city	28 190					
30	35600	049	Lewis and Clark County	28 190	34	10000		Camden city	77 344
					34	10000	007	Camden County	77 344
30	50200		Missoula city	66 788					
30	50200	063	Missoula County	66 788	34	13690		Clifton city	84 136
					34	13690	031	Passaic County	84 136
31			**NEBRASKA**	1 826 341					
31	03950		Bellevue city	50 137	34	19390		East Orange city	64 270
31	03950	153	Sarpy County	50 137	34	19390	013	Essex County	64 270
31	17670		Fremont city	26 397	34	21000		Elizabeth city	124 969
31	17670	053	Dodge County	26 397	34	21000	039	Union County	124 969
31	19595		Grand Island city	48 520	34	21480		Englewood city	27 147
31	19595	079	Hall County	48 520	34	21480	003	Bergen County	27 147
31	25055		Kearney city	30 787	34	22470		Fair Lawn borough	32 457
31	25055	019	Buffalo County	30 787	34	22470	003	Bergen County	32 457
31	28000		Lincoln city	258 379	34	24420		Fort Lee borough	35 345
31	28000	109	Lancaster County	258 379	34	24420	003	Bergen County	35 345
31	37000		Omaha city	408 958	34	25770		Garfield city	30 487
31	37000	055	Douglas County	408 958	34	25770	003	Bergen County	30 487

State Code	Place Code	County Code	Geographic Area Name	2010 Census Population	State Code	Place Code	County Code	Geographic Area Name	2010 Census Population
34	28680		Hackensack city	43 010	35	16420		Clovis city	37 775
34	28680	003	Bergen County	43 010	35	16420	009	Curry County	37 775
34	32250		Hoboken city	50 005	35	25800		Farmington city	45 877
34	32250	017	Hudson County	50 005	35	25800	045	San Juan County	45 877
34	36000		Jersey City city	247 597	35	32520		Hobbs city	34 122
34	36000	017	Hudson County	247 597	35	32520	025	Lea County	34 122
34	36510		Kearny town	40 684	35	39380		Las Cruces city	97 618
34	36510	017	Hudson County	40 684	35	39380	013	Doña Ana County	97 618
34	40350		Linden city	40 499	35	63460		Rio Rancho city	87 521
34	40350	039	Union County	40 499	35	63460	001	Bernalillo County	130
					35	63460	043	Sandoval County	87 391
34	41310		Long Branch city	30 719					
34	41310	025	Monmouth County	30 719	35	64930		Roswell city	48 366
					35	64930	005	Chaves County	48 366
34	46680		Millville city	28 400					
34	46680	011	Cumberland County	28 400	35	70500		Santa Fe city	67 947
					35	70500	049	Santa Fe County	67 947
34	51000		Newark city	277 140					
34	51000	013	Essex County	277 140	36			**NEW YORK**	19 378 102
					36	01000		Albany city	97 856
34	51210		New Brunswick city	55 181	36	01000	001	Albany County	97 856
34	51210	023	Middlesex County	55 181					
					36	03078		Auburn city	27 687
34	55950		Paramus borough	26 342	36	03078	011	Cayuga County	27 687
34	55950	003	Bergen County	26 342					
					36	06607		Binghamton city	47 376
34	56550		Passaic city	69 781	36	06607	007	Broome County	47 376
34	56550	031	Passaic County	69 781					
					36	11000		Buffalo city	261 310
34	57000		Paterson city	146 199	36	11000	029	Erie County	261 310
34	57000	031	Passaic County	146 199					
					36	24229		Elmira city	29 200
34	58200		Perth Amboy city	50 814	36	24229	015	Chemung County	29 200
34	58200	023	Middlesex County	50 814					
					36	27485		Freeport village	42 860
34	59190		Plainfield city	49 808	36	27485	059	Nassau County	42 860
34	59190	039	Union County	49 808					
					36	29113		Glen Cove city	26 964
34	61530		Rahway city	27 346	36	29113	059	Nassau County	26 964
34	61530	039	Union County	27 346					
					36	32402		Harrison village	27 472
34	65790		Sayreville borough	42 704	36	32402	119	Westchester County	27 472
34	65790	023	Middlesex County	42 704					
					36	33139		Hempstead village	53 891
34	74000		Trenton city	84 913	36	33139	059	Nassau County	53 891
34	74000	021	Mercer County	84 913					
					36	38077		Ithaca city	30 014
34	74630		Union City city	66 455	36	38077	109	Tompkins County	30 014
34	74630	017	Hudson County	66 455					
					36	38264		Jamestown city	31 146
34	76070		Vineland city	60 724	36	38264	013	Chautauqua County	31 146
34	76070	011	Cumberland County	60 724					
					36	42554		Lindenhurst village	27 253
34	79040		Westfield town	30 316	36	42554	103	Suffolk County	27 253
34	79040	039	Union County	30 316					
					36	43335		Long Beach city	33 275
34	79610		West New York town	49 708	36	43335	059	Nassau County	33 275
34	79610	017	Hudson County	49 708					
					36	47042		Middletown city	28 086
35			**NEW MEXICO**	2 059 179	36	47042	071	Orange County	28 086
35	01780		Alamogordo city	30 403					
35	01780	035	Otero County	30 403	36	49121		Mount Vernon city	67 292
					36	49121	119	Westchester County	67 292
35	02000		Albuquerque city	545 852					
35	02000	001	Bernalillo County	545 852	36	50034		Newburgh city	28 866
					36	50034	071	Orange County	28 866
35	12150		Carlsbad city	26 138					
35	12150	015	Eddy County	26 138					

State Code	Place Code	County Code	Geographic Area Name	2010 Census Population	State Code	Place Code	County Code	Geographic Area Name	2010 Census Population
36	50617		New Rochelle city	77 062	37	10740		Cary town	135 234
36	50617	119	Westchester County	77 062	37	10740	037	Chatham County	1 422
					37	10740	183	Wake County	133 812
36	51000		New York city	8 175 133					
36	51000	005	Bronx County	1 385 108	37	11800		Chapel Hill town	57 233
36	51000	047	Kings County	2 504 700	37	11800	063	Durham County	2 836
36	51000	061	New York County	1 585 873	37	11800	135	Orange County	54 397
36	51000	081	Queens County	2 230 722					
36	51000	085	Richmond County	468 730	37	12000		Charlotte city	731 424
					37	12000	119	Mecklenburg County	731 424
36	51055		Niagara Falls city	50 193					
36	51055	063	Niagara County	50 193	37	14100		Concord city	79 066
					37	14100	025	Cabarrus County	79 066
36	53682		North Tonawanda city	31 568					
36	53682	063	Niagara County	31 568	37	19000		Durham city	228 330
					37	19000	063	Durham County	228 300
36	55530		Ossining village	25 060	37	19000	135	Orange County	30
36	55530	119	Westchester County	25 060	37	19000	183	Wake County	0
36	59223		Port Chester village	28 967	37	22920		Fayetteville city	200 564
36	59223	119	Westchester County	28 967	37	22920	051	Cumberland County	200 564
36	59641		Poughkeepsie city	32 736	37	25480		Garner town	25 745
36	59641	027	Dutchess County	32 736	37	25480	183	Wake County	25 745
36	63000		Rochester city	210 565	37	25580		Gastonia city	71 741
36	63000	055	Monroe County	210 565	37	25580	071	Gaston County	71 741
36	63418		Rome city	33 725	37	26880		Goldsboro city	36 437
36	63418	065	Oneida County	33 725	37	26880	191	Wayne County	36 437
36	65255		Saratoga Springs city	26 586	37	28000		Greensboro city	269 666
36	65255	091	Saratoga County	26 586	37	28000	081	Guilford County	269 666
36	65508		Schenectady city	66 135	37	28080		Greenville city	84 554
36	65508	093	Schenectady County	66 135	37	28080	147	Pitt County	84 554
36	70420		Spring Valley village	31 347	37	31060		Hickory city	40 010
36	70420	087	Rockland County	31 347	37	31060	023	Burke County	66
					37	31060	027	Caldwell County	18
36	73000		Syracuse city	145 170	37	31060	035	Catawba County	39 926
36	73000	067	Onondaga County	145 170					
					37	31400		High Point city	104 371
36	75484		Troy city	50 129	37	31400	057	Davidson County	5 310
36	75484	083	Rensselaer County	50 129	37	31400	067	Forsyth County	8
					37	31400	081	Guilford County	99 042
36	76540		Utica city	62 235	37	31400	151	Randolph County	11
36	76540	065	Oneida County	62 235					
					37	33120		Huntersville town	46 773
36	76705		Valley Stream village	37 511	37	33120	119	Mecklenburg County	46 773
36	76705	059	Nassau County	37 511					
					37	33560		Indian Trail town	33 518
36	78608		Watertown city	27 023	37	33560	179	Union County	33 518
36	78608	045	Jefferson County	27 023					
					37	34200		Jacksonville city	70 145
36	81677		White Plains city	56 853	37	34200	133	Onslow County	70 145
36	81677	119	Westchester County	56 853					
					37	35200		Kannapolis city	42 625
37			**NORTH CAROLINA**	9 535 483	37	35200	025	Cabarrus County	33 194
37	01520		Apex town	37 476	37	35200	159	Rowan County	9 431
37	01520	183	Wake County	37 476					
					37	41960		Matthews town	27 198
37	02080		Asheboro city	25 012	37	41960	119	Mecklenburg County	27 198
37	02080	151	Randolph County	25 012					
					37	43920		Monroe city	32 797
37	02140		Asheville city	83 393	37	43920	179	Union County	32 797
37	02140	021	Buncombe County	83 393					
					37	44220		Mooresville town	32 711
37	09060		Burlington city	49 963	37	44220	097	Iredell County	32 711
37	09060	001	Alamance County	49 308					
37	09060	081	Guilford County	655	37	46340		New Bern city	29 524
					37	46340	049	Craven County	29 524

Cities by County—*Continued*

State Code	Place Code	County Code	Geographic Area Name	2010 Census Population	State Code	Place Code	County Code	Geographic Area Name	2010 Census Population
37	55000		Raleigh city	403 892	39	16014		Cleveland Heights city	46 121
37	55000	063	Durham County	1 067	39	16014	035	Cuyahoga County	46 121
37	55000	183	Wake County	402 825					
					39	18000		Columbus city	787 033
37	57500		Rocky Mount city	57 477	39	18000	041	Delaware County	7 245
37	57500	065	Edgecombe County	17 524	39	18000	045	Fairfield County	9 666
37	57500	127	Nash County	39 953	39	18000	049	Franklin County	770 122
37	58860		Salisbury city	33 662	39	19778		Cuyahoga Falls city	49 652
37	58860	159	Rowan County	33 662	39	19778	153	Summit County	49 652
37	59280		Sanford city	28 094	39	21000		Dayton city	141 527
37	59280	105	Lee County	28 094	39	21000	113	Montgomery County	141 527
37	67420		Thomasville city	26 757	39	21434		Delaware city	34 753
37	67420	057	Davidson County	26 493	39	21434	041	Delaware County	34 753
37	67420	151	Randolph County	264					
					39	22694		Dublin city	41 751
37	70540		Wake Forest town	30 117	39	22694	041	Delaware County	4 018
37	70540	069	Franklin County	899	39	22694	049	Franklin County	35 367
37	70540	183	Wake County	29 218	39	22694	159	Union County	2 366
37	74440		Wilmington city	106 476	39	25256		Elyria city	54 533
37	74440	129	New Hanover County	106 476	39	25256	093	Lorain County	54 533
37	74540		Wilson city	49 167	39	25704		Euclid city	48 920
37	74540	195	Wilson County	49 167	39	25704	035	Cuyahoga County	48 920
37	75000		Winston-Salem city	229 617	39	25914		Fairborn city	32 352
37	75000	067	Forsyth County	229 617	39	25914	057	Greene County	32 352
38			**NORTH DAKOTA**	672 591	39	25970		Fairfield city	42 510
38	07200		Bismarck city	61 272	39	25970	017	Butler County	42 510
38	07200	015	Burleigh County	61 272	39	25970	061	Hamilton County	0
38	25700		Fargo city	105 549	39	27048		Findlay city	41 202
38	25700	017	Cass County	105 549	39	27048	063	Hancock County	41 202
38	32060		Grand Forks city	52 838	39	29106		Gahanna city	33 248
38	32060	035	Grand Forks County	52 838	39	29106	049	Franklin County	33 248
38	53380		Minot city	40 888	39	29428		Garfield Heights city	28 849
38	53380	101	Ward County	40 888	39	29428	035	Cuyahoga County	28 849
38	84780		West Fargo city	25 830	39	31860		Green city	25 699
38	84780	017	Cass County	25 830	39	31860	153	Summit County	25 699
39			**OHIO**	11 536 504	39	32592		Grove City city	35 575
39	01000		Akron city	199 110	39	32592	049	Franklin County	35 575
39	01000	153	Summit County	199 110					
					39	33012		Hamilton city	62 477
39	03828		Barberton city	26 550	39	33012	017	Butler County	62 477
39	03828	153	Summit County	26 550					
					39	35476		Hilliard city	28 435
39	04720		Beavercreek city	45 193	39	35476	049	Franklin County	28 435
39	04720	057	Greene County	45 193					
					39	36610		Huber Heights city	38 101
39	07972		Bowling Green city	30 028	39	36610	057	Greene County	0
39	07972	173	Wood County	30 028	39	36610	109	Miami County	959
					39	36610	113	Montgomery County	37 142
39	09680		Brunswick city	34 255					
39	09680	103	Medina County	34 255	39	39872		Kent city	28 904
					39	39872	133	Portage County	28 904
39	12000		Canton city	73 007					
39	12000	151	Stark County	73 007	39	40040		Kettering city	56 163
					39	40040	057	Greene County	467
39	15000		Cincinnati city	296 943	39	40040	113	Montgomery County	55 696
39	15000	061	Hamilton County	296 943					
					39	41664		Lakewood city	52 131
39	16000		Cleveland city	396 815	39	41664	035	Cuyahoga County	52 131
39	16000	035	Cuyahoga County	396 815					

State Code	Place Code	County Code	Geographic Area Name	2010 Census Population	State Code	Place Code	County Code	Geographic Area Name	2010 Census Population
39	41720		Lancaster city	38 780	39	77588		Troy city	25 058
39	41720	045	Fairfield County	38 780	39	77588	109	Miami County	25 058
39	43554		Lima city	38 771	39	79002		Upper Arlington city	33 771
39	43554	003	Allen County	38 771	39	79002	049	Franklin County	33 771
39	44856		Lorain city	64 097	39	80892		Warren city	41 557
39	44856	093	Lorain County	64 097	39	80892	155	Trumbull County	41 557
39	47138		Mansfield city	47 821	39	83342		Westerville city	36 120
39	47138	139	Richland County	47 821	39	83342	041	Delaware County	7 792
					39	83342	049	Franklin County	28 328
39	47754		Marion city	36 837					
39	47754	101	Marion County	36 837	39	83622		Westlake city	32 729
					39	83622	035	Cuyahoga County	32 729
39	48188		Mason city	30 712					
39	48188	165	Warren County	30 712	39	86548		Wooster city	26 119
					39	86548	169	Wayne County	26 119
39	48244		Massillon city	32 149					
39	48244	151	Stark County	32 149	39	86772		Xenia city	25 719
					39	86772	057	Greene County	25 719
39	48790		Medina city	26 678					
39	48790	103	Medina County	26 678	39	88000		Youngstown city	66 982
					39	88000	099	Mahoning County	66 971
39	49056		Mentor city	47 159	39	88000	155	Trumbull County	11
39	49056	085	Lake County	47 159					
					39	88084		Zanesville city	25 487
39	49840		Middletown city	48 694	39	88084	119	Muskingum County	25 487
39	49840	017	Butler County	45 994					
39	49840	165	Warren County	2 700	40			**OKLAHOMA**	3 751 351
					40	04450		Bartlesville city	35 750
39	54040		Newark city	47 573	40	04450	113	Osage County	3
39	54040	089	Licking County	47 573	40	04450	147	Washington County	35 747
39	56882		North Olmsted city	32 718	40	09050		Broken Arrow city	98 850
39	56882	035	Cuyahoga County	32 718	40	09050	143	Tulsa County	80 634
					40	09050	145	Wagoner County	18 216
39	56966		North Ridgeville city	29 465					
39	56966	093	Lorain County	29 465	40	23200		Edmond city	81 405
					40	23200	109	Oklahoma County	81 405
39	57008		North Royalton city	30 444					
39	57008	035	Cuyahoga County	30 444	40	23950		Enid city	49 379
					40	23950	047	Garfield County	49 379
39	61000		Parma city	81 601					
39	61000	035	Cuyahoga County	81 601	40	41850		Lawton city	96 867
					40	41850	031	Comanche County	96 867
39	66390		Reynoldsburg city	35 893					
39	66390	045	Fairfield County	910	40	48350		Midwest City city	54 371
39	66390	049	Franklin County	26 157	40	48350	109	Oklahoma County	54 371
39	66390	089	Licking County	8 826					
					40	49200		Moore city	55 081
39	67468		Riverside city	25 201	40	49200	027	Cleveland County	55 081
39	67468	113	Montgomery County	25 201					
					40	50050		Muskogee city	39 223
39	70380		Sandusky city	25 793	40	50050	101	Muskogee County	39 223
39	70380	043	Erie County	25 793					
					40	52500		Norman city	110 925
39	71682		Shaker Heights city	28 448	40	52500	027	Cleveland County	110 925
39	71682	035	Cuyahoga County	28 448					
					40	55000		Oklahoma City city	579 999
39	74118		Springfield city	60 608	40	55000	017	Canadian County	44 541
39	74118	023	Clark County	60 608	40	55000	027	Cleveland County	63 723
					40	55000	109	Oklahoma County	471 671
39	74944		Stow city	34 837	40	55000	125	Pottawatomie County	64
39	74944	153	Summit County	34 837					
					40	56650		Owasso city	28 915
39	75098		Strongsville city	44 750	40	56650	131	Rogers County	2 614
39	75098	035	Cuyahoga County	44 750	40	56650	143	Tulsa County	26 301
39	77000		Toledo city	287 208	40	59850		Ponca City city	25 387
39	77000	095	Lucas County	287 208	40	59850	071	Kay County	25 387

State Code	Place Code	County Code	Geographic Area Name	2010 Census Population	State Code	Place Code	County Code	Geographic Area Name	2010 Census Population
40	66800		Shawnee city	29 857	41	74950		Tualatin city	26 054
40	66800	125	Pottawatomie County	29 857	41	74950	005	Clackamas County	2 862
					41	74950	067	Washington County	23 192
40	70300		Stillwater city	45 688					
40	70300	119	Payne County	45 688	41	80150		West Linn city	25 109
					41	80150	005	Clackamas County	25 109
40	75000		Tulsa city	391 906					
40	75000	113	Osage County	6 136	42			**PENNSYLVANIA**	12 702 379
40	75000	131	Rogers County	0	42	02000		Allentown city	118 032
40	75000	143	Tulsa County	385 613	42	02000	077	Lehigh County	118 032
40	75000	145	Wagoner County	157					
					42	02184		Altoona city	46 320
41			**OREGON**	3 831 074	42	02184	013	Blair County	46 320
41	01000		Albany city	50 158					
41	01000	003	Benton County	6 463	42	06064		Bethel Park municipality	32 313
41	01000	043	Linn County	43 695	42	06064	003	Allegheny County	32 313
41	05350		Beaverton city	89 803	42	06088		Bethlehem city	74 982
41	05350	067	Washington County	89 803	42	06088	077	Lehigh County	19 343
					42	06088	095	Northampton County	55 639
41	05800		Bend city	76 639					
41	05800	017	Deschutes County	76 639	42	13208		Chester city	33 972
					42	13208	045	Delaware County	33 972
41	15800		Corvallis city	54 462					
41	15800	003	Benton County	54 462	42	21648		Easton city	26 800
					42	21648	095	Northampton County	26 800
41	23850		Eugene city	156 185					
41	23850	039	Lane County	156 185	42	24000		Erie city	101 786
					42	24000	049	Erie County	101 786
41	30550		Grants Pass city	34 533					
41	30550	033	Josephine County	34 533	42	32800		Harrisburg city	49 528
					42	32800	043	Dauphin County	49 528
41	31250		Gresham city	105 594					
41	31250	051	Multnomah County	105 594	42	33408		Hazleton city	25 340
					42	33408	079	Luzerne County	25 340
41	34100		Hillsboro city	91 611					
41	34100	067	Washington County	91 611	42	41216		Lancaster city	59 322
					42	41216	071	Lancaster County	59 322
41	38500		Keizer city	36 478					
41	38500	047	Marion County	36 478	42	42168		Lebanon city	25 477
					42	42168	075	Lebanon County	25 477
41	40550		Lake Oswego city	36 619					
41	40550	005	Clackamas County	34 066	42	50528		Monroeville municipality	28 386
41	40550	051	Multnomah County	2 544	42	50528	003	Allegheny County	28 386
41	40550	067	Washington County	9					
					42	54656		Norristown borough	34 324
41	45000		McMinnville city	32 187	42	54656	091	Montgomery County	34 324
41	45000	071	Yamhill County	32 187					
					42	60000		Philadelphia city	1 526 006
41	47000		Medford city	74 907	42	60000	101	Philadelphia County	1 526 006
41	47000	029	Jackson County	74 907					
					42	61000		Pittsburgh city	305 704
41	55200		Oregon City city	31 859	42	61000	003	Allegheny County	305 704
41	55200	005	Clackamas County	31 859					
					42	61536		Plum borough	27 126
41	59000		Portland city	583 776	42	61536	003	Allegheny County	27 126
41	59000	005	Clackamas County	744					
41	59000	051	Multnomah County	581 485	42	63624		Reading city	88 082
41	59000	067	Washington County	1 547	42	63624	011	Berks County	88 082
41	61200		Redmond city	26 215	42	69000		Scranton city	76 089
41	61200	017	Deschutes County	26 215	42	69000	069	Lackawanna County	76 089
41	64900		Salem city	154 637	42	73808		State College borough	42 034
41	64900	047	Marion County	130 398	42	73808	027	Centre County	42 034
41	64900	053	Polk County	24 239					
					42	85152		Wilkes-Barre city	41 498
41	69600		Springfield city	59 403	42	85152	079	Luzerne County	41 498
41	69600	039	Lane County	59 403					
					42	85312		Williamsport city	29 381
41	73650		Tigard city	48 035	42	85312	081	Lycoming County	29 381
41	73650	067	Washington County	48 035					

Cities by County–*Continued*

State Code	Place Code	County Code	Geographic Area Name	2010 Census Population
42	87048		York city	43 718
42	87048	133	York County	43 718
44			**RHODE ISLAND**	1 052 567
44	19180		Cranston city	80 387
44	19180	007	Providence County	80 387
44	22960		East Providence city	47 037
44	22960	007	Providence County	47 037
44	54640		Pawtucket city	71 148
44	54640	007	Providence County	71 148
44	59000		Providence city	178 042
44	59000	007	Providence County	178 042
44	74300		Warwick city	82 672
44	74300	003	Kent County	82 672
44	80780		Woonsocket city	41 186
44	80780	007	Providence County	41 186
45			**SOUTH CAROLINA**	4 625 364
45	00550		Aiken city	29 524
45	00550	003	Aiken County	29 524
45	01360		Anderson city	26 686
45	01360	007	Anderson County	26 686
45	13330		Charleston city	120 083
45	13330	015	Berkeley County	8 095
45	13330	019	Charleston County	111 988
45	16000		Columbia city	129 272
45	16000	063	Lexington County	559
45	16000	079	Richland County	128 713
45	25810		Florence city	37 056
45	25810	041	Florence County	37 056
45	29815		Goose Creek city	35 938
45	29815	015	Berkeley County	35 933
45	29815	019	Charleston County	5
45	30850		Greenville city	58 409
45	30850	045	Greenville County	58 409
45	30985		Greer city	25 515
45	30985	045	Greenville County	18 635
45	30985	083	Spartanburg County	6 880
45	34045		Hilton Head Island town	37 099
45	34045	013	Beaufort County	37 099
45	48535		Mount Pleasant town	67 843
45	48535	019	Charleston County	67 843
45	49075		Myrtle Beach city	27 109
45	49075	051	Horry County	27 109
45	50875		North Charleston city	97 471
45	50875	015	Berkeley County	0
45	50875	019	Charleston County	78 393
45	50875	035	Dorchester County	19 078
45	61405		Rock Hill city	66 154
45	61405	091	York County	66 154
45	68290		Spartanburg city	37 013
45	68290	083	Spartanburg County	37 013
45	70270		Summerville town	43 392
45	70270	015	Berkeley County	3 643
45	70270	019	Charleston County	1 010
45	70270	035	Dorchester County	38 739
45	70405		Sumter city	40 524
45	70405	085	Sumter County	40 524
46			**SOUTH DAKOTA**	814 180
46	00100		Aberdeen city	26 091
46	00100	013	Brown County	26 091
46	52980		Rapid City city	67 956
46	52980	103	Pennington County	67 956
46	59020		Sioux Falls city	153 888
46	59020	083	Lincoln County	21 095
46	59020	099	Minnehaha County	132 793
47			**TENNESSEE**	6 346 105
47	03440		Bartlett city	54 613
47	03440	157	Shelby County	54 613
47	08280		Brentwood city	37 060
47	08280	187	Williamson County	37 060
47	08540		Bristol city	26 702
47	08540	163	Sullivan County	26 702
47	14000		Chattanooga city	167 674
47	14000	065	Hamilton County	167 674
47	15160		Clarksville city	132 929
47	15160	125	Montgomery County	132 929
47	15400		Cleveland city	41 285
47	15400	011	Bradley County	41 285
47	16420		Collierville town	43 965
47	16420	047	Fayette County	0
47	16420	157	Shelby County	43 965
47	16540		Columbia city	34 681
47	16540	119	Maury County	34 681
47	16920		Cookeville city	30 435
47	16920	141	Putnam County	30 435
47	27740		Franklin city	62 487
47	27740	187	Williamson County	62 487
47	28540		Gallatin city	30 278
47	28540	165	Sumner County	30 278
47	28960		Germantown city	38 844
47	28960	157	Shelby County	38 844
47	33280		Hendersonville city	51 372
47	33280	165	Sumner County	51 372
47	37640		Jackson city	65 211
47	37640	113	Madison County	65 211
47	38320		Johnson City city	63 152
47	38320	019	Carter County	1 252
47	38320	163	Sullivan County	367
47	38320	179	Washington County	61 533
47	39560		Kingsport city	48 205
47	39560	073	Hawkins County	2 854
47	39560	163	Sullivan County	45 351

Cities by County–*Continued*

State Code	Place Code	County Code	Geographic Area Name	2010 Census Population	State Code	Place Code	County Code	Geographic Area Name	2010 Census Population
47	40000		Knoxville city	178 874	48	11428		Burleson city	36 690
47	40000	093	Knox County	178 874	48	11428	251	Johnson County	29 111
					48	11428	439	Tarrant County	7 579
47	41200		La Vergne city	32 588					
47	41200	149	Rutherford County	32 588	48	13024		Carrollton city	119 097
					48	13024	085	Collin County	2
47	41520		Lebanon city	26 190	48	13024	113	Dallas County	49 352
47	41520	189	Wilson County	26 190	48	13024	121	Denton County	69 743
47	46380		Maryville city	27 465	48	13492		Cedar Hill city	45 028
47	46380	009	Blount County	27 465	48	13492	113	Dallas County	44 477
					48	13492	139	Ellis County	551
47	48000		Memphis city	646 889					
47	48000	157	Shelby County	646 889	48	13552		Cedar Park city	48 937
					48	13552	453	Travis County	489
47	50280		Morristown city	29 137	48	13552	491	Williamson County	48 448
47	50280	063	Hamblen County	29 131					
47	50280	089	Jefferson County	6	48	15364		Cleburne city	29 337
					48	15364	251	Johnson County	29 337
47	51560		Murfreesboro city	108 755					
47	51560	149	Rutherford County	108 755	48	15976		College Station city	93 857
					48	15976	041	Brazos County	93 857
47	55120		Oak Ridge city	29 330					
47	55120	001	Anderson County	26 271	48	16432		Conroe city	56 207
47	55120	145	Roane County	3 059	48	16432	339	Montgomery County	56 207
47	69420		Smyrna town	39 974	48	16612		Coppell city	38 659
47	69420	149	Rutherford County	39 974	48	16612	113	Dallas County	37 905
					48	16612	121	Denton County	754
47	70580		Spring Hill city	29 036					
47	70580	119	Maury County	7 023	48	16624		Copperas Cove city	32 032
47	70580	187	Williamson County	22 013	48	16624	027	Bell County	0
					48	16624	099	Coryell County	31 457
48			**TEXAS**	25 145 561	48	16624	281	Lampasas County	575
48	01000		Abilene city	117 063					
48	01000	253	Jones County	5 145	48	17000		Corpus Christi city	305 215
48	01000	441	Taylor County	111 918	48	17000	007	Aransas County	0
					48	17000	273	Kleberg County	0
48	01924		Allen city	84 246	48	17000	355	Nueces County	305 215
48	01924	085	Collin County	84 246	48	17000	409	San Patricio County	0
48	03000		Amarillo city	190 695	48	19000		Dallas city	1 197 816
48	03000	375	Potter County	105 486	48	19000	085	Collin County	46 885
48	03000	381	Randall County	85 209	48	19000	113	Dallas County	1 124 296
					48	19000	121	Denton County	26 579
48	04000		Arlington city	365 438	48	19000	257	Kaufman County	0
48	04000	439	Tarrant County	365 438	48	19000	397	Rockwall County	56
48	05000		Austin city	790 390	48	19624		Deer Park city	32 010
48	05000	209	Hays County	2	48	19624	201	Harris County	32 010
48	05000	453	Travis County	754 691					
48	05000	491	Williamson County	35 697	48	19792		Del Rio city	35 591
					48	19792	465	Val Verde County	35 591
48	06128		Baytown city	71 802					
48	06128	071	Chambers County	4 116	48	19972		Denton city	113 383
48	06128	201	Harris County	67 686	48	19972	121	Denton County	113 383
48	07000		Beaumont city	118 296	48	20092		DeSoto city	49 047
48	07000	245	Jefferson County	118 296	48	20092	113	Dallas County	49 047
48	07132		Bedford city	46 979	48	21628		Duncanville city	38 524
48	07132	439	Tarrant County	46 979	48	21628	113	Dallas County	38 524
48	08236		Big Spring city	27 282	48	21892		Eagle Pass city	26 248
48	08236	227	Howard County	27 282	48	21892	323	Maverick County	26 248
48	10768		Brownsville city	175 023	48	22660		Edinburg city	77 100
48	10768	061	Cameron County	175 023	48	22660	215	Hidalgo County	77 100
48	10912		Bryan city	76 201	48	24000		El Paso city	649 121
48	10912	041	Brazos County	76 201	48	24000	141	El Paso County	649 121

State Code	Place Code	County Code	Geographic Area Name	2010 Census Population	State Code	Place Code	County Code	Geographic Area Name	2010 Census Population
48	24768		Euless city	51 277	48	38632		Keller city	39 627
48	24768	439	Tarrant County	51 277	48	38632	439	Tarrant County	39 627
48	25452		Farmers Branch city	28 616	48	39148		Killeen city	127 921
48	25452	113	Dallas County	28 616	48	39148	027	Bell County	127 921
48	26232		Flower Mound town	64 669	48	39352		Kingsville city	26 213
48	26232	121	Denton County	64 457	48	39352	273	Kleberg County	26 213
48	26232	439	Tarrant County	212					
					48	39952		Kyle city	28 016
48	27000		Fort Worth city	741 206	48	39952	209	Hays County	28 016
48	27000	121	Denton County	7 813					
48	27000	367	Parker County	7	48	40588		Lake Jackson city	26 849
48	27000	439	Tarrant County	733 386	48	40588	039	Brazoria County	26 849
48	27000	497	Wise County	0					
					48	41212		Lancaster city	36 361
48	27648		Friendswood city	35 805	48	41212	113	Dallas County	36 361
48	27648	167	Galveston County	25 510					
48	27648	201	Harris County	10 295	48	41440		La Porte city	33 800
					48	41440	201	Harris County	33 800
48	27684		Frisco city	116 989					
48	27684	085	Collin County	72 489	48	41464		Laredo city	236 091
48	27684	121	Denton County	44 500	48	41464	479	Webb County	236 091
48	28068		Galveston city	47 743	48	41980		League City city	83 560
48	28068	167	Galveston County	47 743	48	41980	167	Galveston County	81 998
					48	41980	201	Harris County	1 562
48	29000		Garland city	226 876					
48	29000	085	Collin County	266	48	42016		Leander city	26 521
48	29000	113	Dallas County	226 608	48	42016	453	Travis County	1 077
48	29000	397	Rockwall County	2	48	42016	491	Williamson County	25 444
48	29336		Georgetown city	47 400	48	42508		Lewisville city	95 290
48	29336	491	Williamson County	47 400	48	42508	113	Dallas County	841
					48	42508	121	Denton County	94 449
48	30464		Grand Prairie city	175 396					
48	30464	113	Dallas County	123 487	48	43012		Little Elm city	25 898
48	30464	139	Ellis County	45	48	43012	121	Denton County	25 898
48	30464	439	Tarrant County	51 864					
					48	43888		Longview city	80 455
48	30644		Grapevine city	46 334	48	43888	183	Gregg County	78 585
48	30644	113	Dallas County	0	48	43888	203	Harrison County	1 870
48	30644	121	Denton County	0					
48	30644	439	Tarrant County	46 334	48	45000		Lubbock city	229 573
					48	45000	303	Lubbock County	229 573
48	30920		Greenville city	25 557					
48	30920	231	Hunt County	25 557	48	45072		Lufkin city	35 067
					48	45072	005	Angelina County	35 067
48	31928		Haltom City city	42 409					
48	31928	439	Tarrant County	42 409	48	45384		McAllen city	129 877
					48	45384	215	Hidalgo County	129 877
48	32312		Harker Heights city	26 700					
48	32312	027	Bell County	26 700	48	45744		McKinney city	131 117
					48	45744	085	Collin County	131 117
48	32372		Harlingen city	64 849					
48	32372	061	Cameron County	64 849	48	46452		Mansfield city	56 368
					48	46452	139	Ellis County	95
48	35000		Houston city	2 099 451	48	46452	251	Johnson County	1 652
48	35000	157	Fort Bend County	38 124	48	46452	439	Tarrant County	54 621
48	35000	201	Harris County	2 057 280					
48	35000	339	Montgomery County	4 047	48	47892		Mesquite city	139 824
					48	47892	113	Dallas County	139 731
48	35528		Huntsville city	38 548	48	47892	257	Kaufman County	93
48	35528	471	Walker County	38 548					
					48	48072		Midland city	111 147
48	35576		Hurst city	37 337	48	48072	317	Martin County	0
48	35576	439	Tarrant County	37 337	48	48072	329	Midland County	111 147
48	37000		Irving city	216 290	48	48768		Mission city	77 058
48	37000	113	Dallas County	216 290	48	48768	215	Hidalgo County	77 058

Cities by County—*Continued*

State Code	Place Code	County Code	Geographic Area Name	2010 Census Population	State Code	Place Code	County Code	Geographic Area Name	2010 Census Population
48	48804		Missouri City city	67 358	48	65600		San Marcos city	44 894
48	48804	157	Fort Bend County	61 755	48	65600	055	Caldwell County	3
48	48804	201	Harris County	5 603	48	65600	187	Guadalupe County	0
					48	65600	209	Hays County	44 891
48	50256		Nacogdoches city	32 996					
48	50256	347	Nacogdoches County	32 996	48	66128		Schertz city	31 465
					48	66128	029	Bexar County	1 157
48	50820		New Braunfels city	57 740	48	66128	091	Comal County	845
48	50820	091	Comal County	47 586	48	66128	187	Guadalupe County	29 463
48	50820	187	Guadalupe County	10 154					
					48	66644		Seguin city	25 175
48	52356		North Richland Hills city	63 343	48	66644	187	Guadalupe County	25 175
48	52356	439	Tarrant County	63 343					
					48	67496		Sherman city	38 521
48	53388		Odessa city	99 940	48	67496	181	Grayson County	38 521
48	53388	135	Ector County	98 270					
48	53388	329	Midland County	1 670	48	68636		Socorro city	32 013
					48	68636	141	El Paso County	32 013
48	55080		Paris city	25 171					
48	55080	277	Lamar County	25 171	48	69032		Southlake city	26 575
					48	69032	121	Denton County	773
48	56000		Pasadena city	149 043	48	69032	439	Tarrant County	25 802
48	56000	201	Harris County	149 043					
					48	70808		Sugar Land city	78 817
48	56348		Pearland city	91 252	48	70808	157	Fort Bend County	78 817
48	56348	039	Brazoria County	86 706					
48	56348	157	Fort Bend County	721	48	72176		Temple city	66 102
48	56348	201	Harris County	3 825	48	72176	027	Bell County	66 102
48	57176		Pflugerville city	46 936	48	72368		Texarkana city	36 411
48	57176	453	Travis County	46 636	48	72368	037	Bowie County	36 411
48	57176	491	Williamson County	300					
					48	72392		Texas City city	45 099
48	57200		Pharr city	70 400	48	72392	071	Chambers County	0
48	57200	215	Hidalgo County	70 400	48	72392	167	Galveston County	45 099
48	58016		Plano city	259 841	48	72530		The Colony city	36 328
48	58016	085	Collin County	254 525	48	72530	121	Denton County	36 328
48	58016	121	Denton County	5 316					
					48	74144		Tyler city	96 900
48	58820		Port Arthur city	53 818	48	74144	423	Smith County	96 900
48	58820	245	Jefferson County	53 814					
48	58820	361	Orange County	4	48	75428		Victoria city	62 592
					48	75428	469	Victoria County	62 592
48	61796		Richardson city	99 223					
48	61796	085	Collin County	28 569	48	76000		Waco city	124 805
48	61796	113	Dallas County	70 654	48	76000	309	McLennan County	124 805
48	62828		Rockwall city	37 490	48	76816		Waxahachie city	29 621
48	62828	397	Rockwall County	37 490	48	76816	139	Ellis County	29 621
48	63284		Rosenberg city	30 618	48	76864		Weatherford city	25 250
48	63284	157	Fort Bend County	30 618	48	76864	367	Parker County	25 250
48	63500		Round Rock city	99 887	48	77272		Weslaco city	35 670
48	63500	453	Travis County	1 362	48	77272	215	Hidalgo County	35 670
48	63500	491	Williamson County	98 525					
					48	79000		Wichita Falls city	104 553
48	63572		Rowlett city	56 199	48	79000	485	Wichita County	104 553
48	63572	113	Dallas County	49 188					
48	63572	397	Rockwall County	7 011	48	80356		Wylie city	41 427
					48	80356	085	Collin County	39 957
48	64472		San Angelo city	93 200	48	80356	113	Dallas County	415
48	64472	451	Tom Green County	93 200	48	80356	397	Rockwall County	1 055
48	65000		San Antonio city	1 327 407	49			**UTAH**	2 763 885
48	65000	029	Bexar County	1 327 381	49	01310		American Fork city	26 263
48	65000	091	Comal County	0	49	01310	049	Utah County	26 263
48	65000	325	Medina County	26					
					49	07690		Bountiful city	42 552
48	65516		San Juan city	33 856	49	07690	011	Davis County	42 552
48	65516	215	Hidalgo County	33 856					

Cities by County–*Continued*

State Code	Place Code	County Code	Geographic Area Name	2010 Census Population	State Code	Place Code	County Code	Geographic Area Name	2010 Census Population
49	11320		Cedar City city	28 857	49	76680		Tooele city	31 605
49	11320	021	Iron County	28 857	49	76680	045	Tooele County	31 605
49	13850		Clearfield city	30 112	49	82950		West Jordan city	103 712
49	13850	011	Davis County	30 112	49	82950	035	Salt Lake County	103 712
49	16270		Cottonwood Heights city	33 433	49	83470		West Valley City city	129 480
49	16270	035	Salt Lake County	33 433	49	83470	035	Salt Lake County	129 480
49	20120		Draper city	42 274	50			**VERMONT**	625 741
49	20120	035	Salt Lake County	40 532	50	10675		Burlington city	42 417
49	20120	049	Utah County	1 742	50	10675	007	Chittenden County	42 417
49	36070		Holladay city	26 472	51			**VIRGINIA**	8 001 024
49	36070	035	Salt Lake County	26 472	51	01000		Alexandria city	139 966
49	40360		Kaysville city	27 300	51	01000	510	Alexandria city	139 966
49	40360	011	Davis County	27 300	51	07784		Blacksburg town	42 620
49	43660		Layton city	67 311	51	07784	121	Montgomery County	42 620
49	43660	011	Davis County	67 311	51	14968		Charlottesville city	43 475
49	44320		Lehi city	47 407	51	14968	540	Charlottesville city	43 475
49	44320	049	Utah County	47 407	51	16000		Chesapeake city	222 209
49	45860		Logan city	48 174	51	16000	550	Chesapeake city	222 209
49	45860	005	Cache County	48 174	51	21344		Danville city	43 055
49	49710		Midvale city	27 964	51	21344	590	Danville city	43 055
49	49710	035	Salt Lake County	27 964	51	35000		Hampton city	137 436
49	53230		Murray city	46 746	51	35000	650	Hampton city	137 436
49	53230	035	Salt Lake County	46 746	51	35624		Harrisonburg city	48 914
49	55980		Ogden city	82 825	51	35624	660	Harrisonburg city	48 914
49	55980	057	Weber County	82 825	51	44984		Leesburg town	42 616
49	57300		Orem city	88 328	51	44984	107	Loudoun County	42 616
49	57300	049	Utah County	88 328	51	47672		Lynchburg city	75 568
49	60930		Pleasant Grove city	33 509	51	47672	680	Lynchburg city	75 568
49	60930	049	Utah County	33 509	51	48952		Manassas city	37 821
49	62470		Provo city	112 488	51	48952	683	Manassas city	37 821
49	62470	049	Utah County	112 488	51	56000		Newport News city	180 719
49	64340		Riverton city	38 753	51	56000	700	Newport News city	180 719
49	64340	035	Salt Lake County	38 753	51	57000		Norfolk city	242 803
49	65110		Roy city	36 884	51	57000	710	Norfolk city	242 803
49	65110	057	Weber County	36 884	51	61832		Petersburg city	32 420
49	65330		St. George city	72 897	51	61832	730	Petersburg city	32 420
49	65330	053	Washington County	72 897	51	64000		Portsmouth city	95 535
49	67000		Salt Lake City city	186 440	51	64000	740	Portsmouth city	95 535
49	67000	035	Salt Lake County	186 440	51	67000		Richmond city	204 214
49	67440		Sandy city	87 461	51	67000	760	Richmond city	204 214
49	67440	035	Salt Lake County	87 461	51	68000		Roanoke city	97 032
49	70850		South Jordan city	50 418	51	68000	770	Roanoke city	97 032
49	70850	035	Salt Lake County	50 418	51	76432		Suffolk city	84 585
49	71290		Spanish Fork city	34 691	51	76432	800	Suffolk city	84 585
49	71290	049	Utah County	34 691	51	82000		Virginia Beach city	437 994
49	72280		Springville city	29 466	51	82000	810	Virginia Beach city	437 994
49	72280	049	Utah County	29 466	51	86720		Winchester city	26 203
49	75360		Taylorsville city	58 652	51	86720	840	Winchester city	26 203
49	75360	035	Salt Lake County	58 652					

Cities by County–*Continued*

State Code	Place Code	County Code	Geographic Area Name	2010 Census Population	State Code	Place Code	County Code	Geographic Area Name	2010 Census Population
53			**WASHINGTON**	6 724 540	53	56625		Pullman city	29 799
53	03180		Auburn city	70 180	53	56625	075	Whitman County	29 799
53	03180	033	King County	62 761					
53	03180	053	Pierce County	7 419	53	56695		Puyallup city	37 022
					53	56695	053	Pierce County	37 022
53	05210		Bellevue city	122 363					
53	05210	033	King County	122 363	53	57535		Redmond city	54 144
					53	57535	033	King County	54 144
53	05280		Bellingham city	80 885					
53	05280	073	Whatcom County	80 885	53	57745		Renton city	90 927
					53	57745	033	King County	90 927
53	07380		Bothell city	33 505					
53	07380	033	King County	17 090	53	58235		Richland city	48 058
53	07380	061	Snohomish County	16 415	53	58235	005	Benton County	48 058
53	07695		Bremerton city	37 729	53	61115		Sammamish city	45 780
53	07695	035	Kitsap County	37 729	53	61115	033	King County	45 780
53	08850		Burien city	33 313	53	62288		SeaTac city	26 909
53	08850	033	King County	33 313	53	62288	033	King County	26 909
53	17635		Des Moines city	29 673	53	63000		Seattle city	608 660
53	17635	033	King County	29 673	53	63000	033	King County	608 660
53	20750		Edmonds city	39 709	53	63960		Shoreline city	53 007
53	20750	061	Snohomish County	39 709	53	63960	033	King County	53 007
53	22640		Everett city	103 019	53	67000		Spokane city	208 916
53	22640	061	Snohomish County	103 019	53	67000	063	Spokane County	208 916
53	23515		Federal Way city	89 306	53	67167		Spokane Valley city	89 755
53	23515	033	King County	89 306	53	67167	063	Spokane County	89 755
53	33805		Issaquah city	30 434	53	70000		Tacoma city	198 397
53	33805	033	King County	30 434	53	70000	053	Pierce County	198 397
53	35275		Kennewick city	73 917	53	73465		University Place city	31 144
53	35275	005	Benton County	73 917	53	73465	053	Pierce County	31 144
53	35415		Kent city	92 411	53	74060		Vancouver city	161 791
53	35415	033	King County	92 411	53	74060	011	Clark County	161 791
53	35940		Kirkland city	48 787	53	75775		Walla Walla city	31 731
53	35940	033	King County	48 787	53	75775	071	Walla Walla County	31 731
53	36745		Lacey city	42 393	53	77105		Wenatchee city	31 925
53	36745	067	Thurston County	42 393	53	77105	007	Chelan County	31 925
53	37900		Lake Stevens city	28 069	53	80010		Yakima city	91 067
53	37900	061	Snohomish County	28 069	53	80010	077	Yakima County	91 067
53	38038		Lakewood city	58 163	54			**WEST VIRGINIA**	1 852 994
53	38038	053	Pierce County	58 163	54	14600		Charleston city	51 400
					54	14600	039	Kanawha County	51 400
53	40245		Longview city	36 648					
53	40245	015	Cowlitz County	36 648	54	39460		Huntington city	49 138
					54	39460	011	Cabell County	45 214
53	40840		Lynnwood city	35 836	54	39460	099	Wayne County	3 924
53	40840	061	Snohomish County	35 836					
					54	55756		Morgantown city	29 660
53	43955		Marysville city	60 020	54	55756	061	Monongalia County	29 660
53	43955	061	Snohomish County	60 020					
					54	62140		Parkersburg city	31 492
53	47560		Mount Vernon city	31 743	54	62140	107	Wood County	31 492
53	47560	057	Skagit County	31 743					
					54	86452		Wheeling city	28 486
53	51300		Olympia city	46 478	54	86452	051	Marshall County	276
53	51300	067	Thurston County	46 478	54	86452	069	Ohio County	28 210
53	53545		Pasco city	59 781					
53	53545	021	Franklin County	59 781					

Cities by County–*Continued*

State Code	Place Code	County Code	Geographic Area Name	2010 Census Population	State Code	Place Code	County Code	Geographic Area Name	2010 Census Population
55			**WISCONSIN**	5 686 986	55	72975		Sheboygan city	49 288
55	02375		Appleton city	72 623	55	72975	117	Sheboygan County	49 288
55	02375	015	Calumet County	11 088					
55	02375	087	Outagamie County	60 045	55	77200		Stevens Point city	26 717
55	02375	139	Winnebago County	1 490	55	77200	097	Portage County	26 717
55	06500		Beloit city	36 966	55	78600		Sun Prairie city	29 364
55	06500	105	Rock County	36 966	55	78600	025	Dane County	29 364
55	10025		Brookfield city	37 920	55	78650		Superior city	27 244
55	10025	133	Waukesha County	37 920	55	78650	031	Douglas County	27 244
55	22300		Eau Claire city	65 883	55	84250		Waukesha city	70 718
55	22300	017	Chippewa County	1 981	55	84250	133	Waukesha County	70 718
55	22300	035	Eau Claire County	63 902	55	84475		Wausau city	39 106
55	25950		Fitchburg city	25 260	55	84475	073	Marathon County	39 106
55	25950	025	Dane County	25 260	55	84675		Wauwatosa city	46 396
55	26275		Fond du Lac city	43 021	55	84675	079	Milwaukee County	46 396
55	26275	039	Fond du Lac County	43 021	55	85300		West Allis city	60 411
55	27300		Franklin city	35 451	55	85300	079	Milwaukee County	60 411
55	27300	079	Milwaukee County	35 451	55	85350		West Bend city	31 078
55	31000		Green Bay city	104 057	55	85350	131	Washington County	31 078
55	31000	009	Brown County	104 057	56			**WYOMING**	563 626
55	31175		Greenfield city	36 720	56	13150		Casper city	55 316
55	31175	079	Milwaukee County	36 720	56	13150	025	Natrona County	55 316
55	37825		Janesville city	63 575	56	13900		Cheyenne city	59 466
55	37825	105	Rock County	63 575	56	13900	021	Laramie County	59 466
55	39225		Kenosha city	99 218	56	31855		Gillette city	29 087
55	39225	059	Kenosha County	99 218	56	31855	005	Campbell County	29 087
55	40775		La Crosse city	51 320	56	45050		Laramie city	30 816
55	40775	063	La Crosse County	51 320	56	45050	001	Albany County	30 816
55	48000		Madison city	233 209					
55	48000	025	Dane County	233 209					
55	48500		Manitowoc city	33 736					
55	48500	071	Manitowoc County	33 736					
55	51000		Menomonee Falls village	35 626					
55	51000	133	Waukesha County	35 626					
55	53000		Milwaukee city	594 833					
55	53000	079	Milwaukee County	594 833					
55	53000	131	Washington County	0					
55	53000	133	Waukesha County	0					
55	54875		Mount Pleasant village	26 197					
55	54875	101	Racine County	26 197					
55	55750		Neenah city	25 501					
55	55750	139	Winnebago County	25 501					
55	56375		New Berlin city	39 584					
55	56375	133	Waukesha County	39 584					
55	58800		Oak Creek city	34 451					
55	58800	079	Milwaukee County	34 451					
55	60500		Oshkosh city	66 083					
55	60500	139	Winnebago County	66 083					
55	66000		Racine city	78 860					
55	66000	101	Racine County	78 860					

Cities by County–*Continued*

The following consolidated cities are included in Table D. They are listed here with their 2010 census populations followed by the separate entities that make up the consolidated city. Data from the American Community Survey include only the "balance," the major city of each consolidated city.

State Code	Place Code	County Code	Geographic Area Name	2010 Census Population	State Code	Place Code	County Code	Geographic Area Name	2010 Census Population
09			**CONNECTICUT**	3 574 097	21	38818		Hurstbourne Acres city	1 811
09	47500		Milford city	52 759	21	39304		Indian Hills city	2 868
			Milford city (balance)	51 271	21	40222		Jeffersontown city	26 595
	88050		Woodmont borough	1 488	21	42598		Kingsley city	381
					21	43900		Langdon Place city	936
13			**GEORGIA**	9 687 653	21	46540		Lincolnshire city	148
13	03436		Athens-Clark county	116 714	21	48006		Louisville/Jefferson County (balance)	597 337
13	03440		Athens-Clark county (balance)	115 452					
13	09068		Bogart town	140	21	48558		Lyndon city	11 002
13	83728		Winterville city	1 122	21	48648		Lynnview city	914
					21	49800		Manor Creek city	140
13	04200		Augusta-Richmond county	200 549	21	50412		Maryhill Estates city	179
13	04204		Augusta-Richmond county (balance)	195 844	21	51193		Meadowbrook Farm city	136
13	09040		Blythe city	694	21	51258		Meadow Vale city	736
13	38040		Hephzibah city	4 011	21	51294		Meadowview Estates city	363
					21	51978		Middletown city	7 218
18			**INDIANA**	6 483 802	21	52842		Mockingbird Valley city	167
18	36000		Indianapolis city	829 718	21	53328		Moorland city	431
18	04204		Beech Grove city	0	21	54660		Murray Hill city	582
18	13492		Clermont town	1 356	21	56550		Norbourne Estates city	441
18	16156		Crows Nest town	73	21	56730		Northfield city	1 020
18	16336		Cumberland town	2 597	21	56928		Norwood city	370
18	34420		Homecroft town	722	21	57658		Old Brownsboro Place city	353
18	36003		Indianapolis city (balance)	820 445	21	59322		Parkway Village city	650
18	42426		Lawrence city	42	21	61554		Plantation city	832
18	48456		Meridian Hills town	1 616	21	62370		Poplar Hills city	362
18	54612		North Crows Nest town	45	21	63264		Prospect city	4 636
18	65556		Rocky Ripple town	606	21	65208		Richlawn city	405
18	72232		Spring Hill town	98	21	65766		Riverwood city	446
18	80234		Warren Park town	1 480	21	66486		Rolling Fields city	646
18	84374		Williams Creek town	407	21	66504		Rolling Hills city	959
18	85742		Wynnedale town	231	21	67944		St. Matthews city	17 472
					21	67998		St. Regis Park city	1 454
21			**KENTUCKY**	4 339 367	21	69384		Seneca Gardens city	696
21	46003		Louisville/Jefferson County	741 096	21	70284		Shively city	15 264
21	01504		Anchorage city	2 348	21	72138		South Park View city	7
21	02656		Audubon Park city	1 473	21	72770		Spring Mill city	287
21	03376		Bancroft city	494	21	72790		Spring Valley city	654
21	03556		Barbourmeade city	1 218	21	74064		Strathmoor Manor city	337
21	05068		Beechwood Village city	1 324	21	74082		Strathmoor Village city	648
21	05392		Bellemeade city	865	21	75190		Sycamore city	160
21	05464		Bellewood city	321	21	75963		Ten Broeck city	103
21	07858		Blue Ridge Manor city	767	21	76380		Thornhill city	178
21	09532		Briarwood city	435	21	80913		Watterson Park city	976
21	09847		Broeck Pointe city	272	21	81372		Wellington city	565
21	10162		Brownsboro Farm city	648	21	81624		West Buechel city	1 230
21	10198		Brownsboro Village city	319	21	82164		Westwood city	634
21	12066		Cambridge city	175	21	83208		Wildwood city	261
21	16395		Coldstream city	1 100	21	83784		Windy Hills city	2 385
21	18270		Creekside city	305	21	84486		Woodland Hills city	696
21	18766		Crossgate city	225	21	84576		Woodlawn Park city	942
21	22204		Douglass Hills city	5 484	21	84891		Worthington Hills city	1 446
21	22474		Druid Hills city	308					
21	27262		Fincastle city	817	30			**MONTANA**	989 415
21	28342		Forest Hills city	444	30	11390		Butte-Silver Bow	34 200
21	31348		Glenview city	531	30	11397		Butte-Silver Bow (balance)	33 525
21	31402		Glenview Hills city	319	30	77650		Walkerville town	675
21	31420		Glenview Manor city	191					
21	31870		Goose Creek city	294	47			**TENNESSEE**	6 346 105
21	32523		Graymoor-Devondale city	2 870	47	52004		Nashville-Davidson	626 681
21	32986		Green Spring city	715	47	04620		Belle Meade city	2 912
21	36102		Heritage Creek city	1 076	47	05140		Berry Hill city	537
21	36374		Hickory Hill city	114	47	27020		Forest Hills city	4 812
21	36865		Hills and Dales city	142	47	29920		Goodlettsville city	10 319
21	37576		Hollow Creek city	783	47	40720		Lakewood city	2 302
21	37630		Hollyvilla city	537	47	52006		Nashville-Davidson (balance)	601 222
21	38170		Houston Acres city	507	47	54780		Oak Hill city	4 529
21	38814		Hurstbourne city	4 216	47	63140		Ridgetop city	48

APPENDIX F
SOURCE NOTES AND EXPLANATIONS

The following documentation is provided in the order in which items appear in the tables. Internet addresses are provided for the sources of the data. Some of the links refer to the specific data tables. Others provide information about the general data source.

TABLE A—STATES

Table A presents 355 items for the United States as a whole, for each individual state, and for the District of Columbia. The states are presented in alphabetical order.

LAND AREA, Items 1 and 4
Source: U.S. Census Bureau—2016 U.S. Gazetteer Files,
http://www.census.gov/geo/maps-data/data/gazetteer2016.html

Land area measurements are shown to the nearest square mile. Land area is an area measurement providing the size, in square miles, of the land portions of each county.

POPULATION AND COMPONENTS OF CHANGE, Items 2–4, 31–41
Source: U.S. Census Bureau—Decennial Censuses and Population Estimates
https://www.census.gov/programs-surveys/popest.html
http://www.census.gov/2010census/data/

The population data for 2016 are Census Bureau estimates of the resident population as of July 1, 2016.

The population data for 1990, 2000, and 2010 are from the decennial censuses and represent the resident population as of April 1 of those years.

The change in population between 2010 and 2016 is made up of (a) natural increase—births minus deaths, and (b) net migration—the difference between the number of persons moving into a particular state and the number of persons moving out of the state. Net migration is composed of internal and international migration.

POPULATION AND POPULATION CHARACTERISTICS, Items 5–23 and 45–63
Source: U.S. Census Bureau—2016 Population Estimates and 2015 American Community Survey
https://www.census.gov/programs-surveys/popest.html
http://www.census.gov/acs/www/

Data on age, sex, race, and Hispanic origin are from the Population Estimates program. Data on place of birth are from the 2015 American Community Survey, a nationwide continuous survey designed to replace the long form questionnaire used in previous censuses.

The concept "race alone or in combination " includes people who reported a single race alone (i.e., Asian) and people who reported that race in combination with one or more of the other major race groups (i.e., White, Black or African American, American Indian and Alaska Native, Native Hawaiian and Other Pacific Islander, and Some Other Race). The "race alone or in combination" concept, therefore, represents the maximum number of people who reported as that race group, either alone, or in combination with another race(s).

The sum of the four individual race alone or in combination categories in this book may add to more than the total population because people who reported more than one race were tallied in each race category. In this book, the Asian group has been combined with the Native Hawaiian and Other Pacific Islander group, causing double-counting of persons who identify with both groups. This is especially pronounced in Hawaii.

Data on race were derived from answers to the question on race that was asked of all persons. The concept of race, as used by the Census Bureau, reflects self-identification by respondents according to the race or races with which they most closely identify. These categories are sociopolitical constructs and should not be interpreted as being scientific or anthropological in nature. Furthermore, the race categories include both racial and national origin groups.

The **White** population is defined as persons who indicated their race as White, as well as persons who did not classify themselves in one of the specific race categories listed on the questionnaire but entered a nationality such as Irish, German, Italian, Lebanese, Near Easterner, Arab, or Polish.

The **Black** population includes persons who indicated their race as "Black, African Am., or Negro," as well as persons who did not classify themselves in one of the specific race categories but reported entries such as African American, Afro American, Kenyan, Nigerian, or Haitian.

The **American Indian or Alaska Native** population includes persons who indicated their race as American Indian or Alaska Native, as well as persons who did not classify themselves in one of the specific race categories but reported entries such as Canadian Indian, French-American Indian, Spanish-American Indian, Eskimo, Aleut, Alaska Indian, or any of the American Indian or Alaska Native tribes.

The **Asian and Pacific Islander** population combines two census groupings: **Asian** and **Native Hawaiian or Other Pacific Islander**. The **Asian** population includes persons who indicated their race as Asian Indian, Chinese, Filipino, Japanese, Korean, Vietnamese, or "Other Asian," as well as persons who provided write-in entries of such groups as Cambodian, Laotian, Hmong, Pakistani, or Taiwanese. The **Native Hawaiian or Other Pacific Islander** population includes persons who indicated their race as "Native Hawaiian," "Guamanian or Chamorro," "Samoan," or "Other Pacific Islander," as well as persons who reported entries such as Part Hawaiian, American Samoan, Fijian, Melanesian, or Tahitian.

The Hispanic population is based on a question that asked respondents "Is this person Spanish/Hispanic/Latino?" Persons marking any one of the four Hispanic categories (i.e., Mexican, Puerto Rican, Cuban, or other Spanish) are collectively referred to as Hispanic.

Age is defined as age at last birthday (number of completed years since birth), as of April 1 of the census year.

The **median age** is the age that divides the population into two equal-size groups. Half of the population is older than the median age and half is younger. Median age is based on a standard distribution of the population by single years of age and is shown to the nearest tenth of a year.

The **female** population is shown as a percentage of total population.

The **foreign-born** population includes all persons who were not U.S. citizens at birth. Foreign-born persons are those who indicated they were either a U.S. citizen by naturalization or were not a citizen of the United States. Neither the census nor the American Community Survey asked about immigration status. The population surveyed included all persons who indicated that the United States was their usual place of residence. The foreign-born population consists of immigrants (legal permanent residents), temporary migrants (students), humanitarian migrants (refugees), and unauthorized migrants (persons illegally residing in the United States).

Percent born in state of residence is shown as a percentage of total population.

IMMIGRANTS, Item 24
Source: Department of Homeland Security, U.S. Citizenship and Immigration Services
http://www.dhs.gov/yearbook-immigration-statistics

The number of immigrants by state of intended residence is summarized from the administrative records of the Citizenship and Immigration Services. This information is compiled from immigrant visas and forms granting legal permanent resident status.

An **immigrant** is an alien admitted to the United States as a lawful permanent resident. Immigrants are those persons lawfully accorded the privilege of residing permanently in the United States. They may be newly arrived individuals who were issued immigrant visas by the Department of State overseas, or they may be U.S. residents who were admitted to permanent resident status in 2015 by the U.S. Citizenship and Immigration Services.

HOUSEHOLDS, Items 25–30 and 64–68
Source: U.S. Census Bureau—2015 American Community Survey
http://www.census.gov/acs/www/

A **household** includes all of the persons who occupy a housing unit. Persons not living in households are classified as living in group quarters. A housing unit is a house, an apartment, a mobile home, a group of rooms, or a single room occupied (or, if vacant, intended for occupancy) as separate living quarters. Separate living quarters are those in which the occupants live separately from

any other persons in the building and have direct access from the outside of the building or through a common hall. The occupants may be a single family, one person living alone, two or more families living together, or any other group of related or unrelated persons who share living quarters. The number of households is the same as the number of year-round occupied housing units.

The measure of **persons per household** is obtained by dividing the number of persons in households by the number of households or householders. One person in each household is designated as the householder. In most cases, this is the person, (or one of the persons) in whose name the house is owned, being bought, or rented. If there is no such person in the household, any adult household member 15 years old and over can be designated as the householder.

A **family** includes a householder and one or more other persons living in the same household who are related to the householder by birth, marriage, or adoption. All persons in a household who are related to the householder are regarded as members of his or her family. A **family household** may contain persons not related to the householder; thus, family households may include more members than families do. A household can contain only one family for the purposes of census tabulations. Not all households contain families, as a household may comprise a group of unrelated persons or one person living alone. Families are classified by type as either a "married couple family" or "other family" according to the presence of a spouse.

The category **female family householder** includes only female-headed family households with no spouse present.

POPULATION PROJECTIONS, Items 42–44
Source: U.S. Census Bureau—Population Projections Branch
www.census.gov/programs-surveys/popproj.html

Projections are estimates of the population for future dates. They illustrate plausible courses of future population change based on assumptions about future births, deaths, international migration, and domestic migration. Projected numbers are based on an estimated population consistent with the most recent decennial census as enumerated. The Census Bureau does not have a current set of state population projections and currently has no plans to produce them. This volume includes projections released in 2005, based on the 2000 census. The Census Bureau notes that these projections should be used with caution because population trends may have changed substantially since their release.

HOUSING, Items 69–92
Source: U.S. Census Bureau—2010 and 2015 American Community Survey
http://www.census.gov/acs/www/

Housing data for 2010 and 2015 are from the American Community Survey, a nationwide continuous survey designed to replace the long form questionnaire used in previous censuses. A sample of households is surveyed to provide estimates.

A **housing unit** is a house, apartment, mobile home or trailer, group of rooms, or single room occupied or, if vacant, intended for occupancy as separate living quarters. Separate living quarters are those in which the occupants do not live and eat with any other person in the structure and which have direct access from the outside of the building or through a common hall. For vacant units, the criteria of separateness and direct access are applied to the intended occupants whenever possible. If that information cannot be obtained, the criteria are applied to the previous occupants.

The occupants of a housing unit may be a single family, one person living alone, two or more families living together, or any other group of related or unrelated persons who share living arrangements. Both occupied and vacant housing units are included in the housing inventory, although recreational vehicles, tents, caves, boats, railroad cars, and the like are included only if they are occupied as a person's usual place of residence.

A housing unit is classified as **occupied** if it is the usual place of residence of the person or group of persons living in it at the time of enumeration, or if the occupants are only temporarily absent (away on vacation). A household consists of all persons who occupy a housing unit as their usual place of residence.

Housing cost, as a percentage of income, is shown separately for owners with mortgages, owners without mortgages, and renters. Also shown is the percentage of mortgaged owners and renters who pay 30 percent or more of household income on selected monthly costs. Rent as a percent of income is a computed ratio of gross rent and monthly household income (total household income divided by 12). Selected owner costs include utilities and fuels, mortgage payments, insurance, taxes, etc. In each case, the ratio of housing cost to income is computed separately for each housing unit. The housing cost ratios for half of all units are above the median shown in this book, and half are below the median. Median monthly housing costs divides the monthly housing costs distribution into two equal parts, one-half of the cases falling below the median monthly housing costs and one-half above the median.

Median value is the dollar amount that divides the distribution of specified owner-occupied housing units into two equal parts, with half of all units below the median value and half above the median value. Value is defined as the respondent's estimate of what the house would sell for if it were for sale. Data are presented for single-family units on fewer than 10 acres of land that have no business or medical office on the property.

Median rent divides the distribution of renter-occupied housing units into two equal parts. The rent concept used in this volume is gross rent, which includes the amount of cash rent a renter pays (contract rent) plus the estimated average cost of utilities and fuels, if these are paid by the renter. The rent is the amount of rent only for living quarters and excludes any business or other space occupied. Single-family houses on lots of 10 or more acres of land are excluded.

Substandard units are occupied units that are overcrowded or lack complete plumbing facilities. For the purposes of this item, "overcrowded" is defined as having 1.01 persons or more per room. Complete plumbing facilities include hot and cold piped water, a flush toilet, and a bathtub or shower. These facilities must be located inside the housing unit, but do not have to be in the same room.

Different house includes all people 1 year old and over who, a year earlier, lived in a different house or apartment from the one they occupied at the time of interview.

BUILDING PERMITS, Items 93–95
Source: U.S. Census Bureau—Building Permits Survey
http://www.census.gov/construction/bps/

These figures represent private residential construction authorized by building permits in approximately 20,000 places in the United States. Valuation represents the expected cost of construction as recorded on the building permit. This figure usually excludes the cost of on-site and off-site development and improvements, as well as the cost of heating, plumbing, electrical, and elevator installations.

National, state, and county totals were obtained by adding the data for permit-issuing places within each jurisdiction. These totals thus are limited to permits issued in the 20,000 place universe covered by the Census Bureau and may not include all permits issued within a state. Current surveys indicate that construction is undertaken for all but a very small percentage of housing units authorized by building permits.

Residential building permits include buildings with any number of housing units. Housing units exclude group quarters (such as dormitories and rooming houses), transient accommodations (such as transient hotels, motels, and tourist courts), "HUD-code" manufactured (mobile) homes, moved or relocated units, and housing units created in an existing residential or nonresidential structure.

MANUFACTURED HOUSING UNITS, Item 96
Source: U.S. Census Bureau—Manufactured Housing Survey
https://www.census.gov/data/tables/2015/econ/mhs/2015-annual-data.html

The Manufactured Housing Survey (MHS) is conducted by the U.S. Census Bureau and sponsored by the Department of Housing and Urban Development (HUD). MHS produces monthly regional estimates of the average sales price of new manufactured homes and more detailed annual estimates including selected characteristics of new manufactured homes. In addition, MHS produces monthly estimates of homes shipped to each state.

A manufactured home is defined as a movable dwelling, 8 feet or more wide and 40 feet or more long, designed to be towed on its own chassis, with transportation gear integral to the unit when it leaves the factory, and without need of a permanent foundation. These manufactured homes include multi-wides and expandable manufactured homes. Excluded are travel trailers, motor homes, and modular housing.

BIRTHS AND DEATHS, Items 97–103
Source: U.S. Centers for Disease Control and Prevention, National Center for Health Statistics
https://www.cdc.gov/nchs/data/nvsr/nvsr66/nvsr66_01.pdf
https://www.cdc.gov/nchs/data/nvsr/nvsr65/nvsr65_04.pdf

The registration of births, deaths, and other vital events in the United States is primarily a state and local function. The civil laws of every state provide for continuous and permanent birth and death registration systems. Through the National Vital Statistics System, the National Center for Health Statistics (NCHS) obtains data on births and deaths from the registration offices of each state, New York City, and the District of Columbia.

Birth and death statistics are limited to events occurring during the year. The data are by place of residence and exclude events for nonresidents of the United States. Births or deaths occurring outside the United States are excluded.

Birth and death rates represent the number of births and deaths per 1,000 resident population enumerated as of April 1 for decennial census years and estimated as of July 1 for other years.

Figures for infant deaths include deaths of children under 1 year of age but exclude fetal deaths. The infant death rate is per 1,000 live births.

The rates of almost all causes of disease, injury, and death vary by age. Age adjustment is a technique for "removing" the effects of age from crude rates, in order to allow meaningful comparisons across populations with different underlying age structures. For example, comparing the crude death rate in Florida to that of California is misleading, since the relatively older population in Florida will lead to a higher crude death rate. For such a comparison, age-adjusted death rates are preferable.

The population estimates were developed by the Census Bureau's Population Division using a traditional cohort component method. Starting with a basic population from the 2000 census, each component of population change—births, deaths, domestic migration, and international migration—is estimated separately for each birth cohort by sex, race, and Hispanic or Latino origin.

Age-adjusted rates are calculated by applying the age-specific rates of various populations to a single standard population. In this volume, the standard population is 2000. Beginning in 2003, The Centers for Disease Control and Prevention switched to the year 2000, after many years of using the year 1940 as the standard population for age-adjusted death rates.

PERSONS LACKING HEALTH INSURANCE, Items 104–105
Source: U.S. Census Bureau—American Community Survey
https://www.census.gov/library/publications/2016/demo/p60–257.html

These estimates are from the American Community Survey, an ongoing nationwide survey that is conducted throughout the year. About 250,000 addresses per month receive the ACS. Respondents are asked whether each household member is currently covered (by specific types of health coverage) at the time of interview. The 2013 estimates were the first to use the ACS. Prior year estimates were based on the Annual Social and Economic Supplement (ASEC) of the Current Population Survey (CPS).

Those lacking coverage are the percentage of the population of each state who were not covered by private health plans purchased directly or provided by an employer, Medicaid, Medicare, or military health care.

MEDICARE BENEFICIARIES, Item 106
Source: U.S. Department of Health and Human Services, Centers for Medicare and Medicaid Services
https://www.cms.gov/Research-Statistics-Data-and-Systems/Statistics-Trends-and-Reports/Medicare-Geographic-Variation/GV_PUF.html

The Centers for Medicare and Medicaid Services (CMS) administers Medicare, which provides health insurance to persons 65 years old and over, persons with permanent kidney failure, and certain persons with disabilities. Medicare has two parts: Hospital Insurance (Part A) and Supplemental Medical Insurance (Part B). The numbers in Table A include persons 65 and older who were enrolled in either or both parts of the program during the year shown.

CRIME, Items 107–110
Source: U.S. Federal Bureau of Investigation—Uniform Crime Reports
https://ucr.fbi.gov/

Crime data are as reported to the Federal Bureau of Investigation (FBI) by law enforcement agencies and have not been adjusted for underreporting. This may affect comparability between geographic areas or over time.

Through the voluntary contribution of crime statistics by law enforcement agencies across the United States, the Uniform Crime Reporting (UCR) Program provides periodic assessments of crime in the nation as measured by offenses that have come to the attention of the law enforcement community. The Committee on Uniform Crime Records of the International Association of Chiefs of Police initiated this voluntary national data-collection effort in 1930. The UCR Program contributors compile and submit their crime data either directly to the FBI or through state-level UCR Programs.

Seven offenses, because of their severity, frequency of occurrence, and likelihood of being reported to police, were initially selected to serve as an index for evaluating fluctuations in the volume of crime. These serious crimes were murder and nonnegligent manslaughter, forcible rape, robbery, aggravated assault, burglary, larceny-theft, and motor vehicle theft. By congressional mandate, arson was added as the eighth index offense in 1979. The totals shown in this volume do not include arson.

In 2004, the FBI discontinued the use of the Crime Index in the UCR Program and its publications, stating that the Crime Index was driven upward by the offense with the highest number of cases (in this case, larceny-theft) creating a bias against jurisdictions with a high number of larceny-thefts but a low number of other serious crimes, such as murder and forcible rape. The FBI is currently publishing a violent crime total and a property crime total until a more viable index is developed.

In 2013, the FBI adopted a new definition of rape. Rape is now defined as, "Penetration, no matter how slight, of the vagina or anus with any body part or object, or oral penetration by a sex organ of another person, without the consent of the victim." The new definition updated the 80-year-old historical definition of rape which was "carnal knowledge of a female forcibly and against her will." Effectively, the revised definition expands rape to include both male and female victims and offenders, and reflects the various forms of sexual penetration understood to be rape, especially non-consenting acts of sodomy, and sexual assaults with objects. **Violent crimes** include four categories of offenses: (1) Murder and non-negligent manslaughter, as defined in the UCR Program, is the willful (non-negligent) killing of one human being by another. This offense excludes deaths caused by negligence, suicide, or accident; justifiable homicides; and attempts to murder or assaults to murder. (2) Rape is the penetration, no matter how slight, of the vagina or anus with any body part or object, or oral penetration by a sex organ of another person, without the consent of the victim. Assaults or attempts to commit rape by force or threat of force are also included; however, statutory rape (without force) and other sex offenses are excluded. (3) Robbery is the taking or attempting to take anything of value from the care, custody, or control of a person or persons by force or threat of force or violence and/or by putting the victim in fear. (4) Aggravated assault is an unlawful attack by one person upon another for the purpose of inflicting severe or aggravated bodily injury. This type of assault is usually accompanied by the use of a weapon or by other means likely to produce death or great bodily harm. Attempts are included, since injury does not necessarily have to result when a gun, knife, or other weapon is used, as these incidents could and probably would result in a serious personal injury if the crime were successfully completed.

Property crimes include three categories: (1) Burglary, or breaking and entering, is the unlawful entry of a structure to commit a felony or theft, even though no force was used to gain entrance. (2) Larceny-theft is the unauthorized taking of the personal property of another, without the use of force. (3) Motor vehicle theft is the unauthorized taking of any motor vehicle.

Rates are based on population estimates provided by the FBI. For some states, reporting is not sufficiently complete to be representative of the state as a whole. The FBI has estimated state totals for those states.

ELEMENTARY AND SECONDARY SCHOOL ENROLLMENT, Items 111 and 112
Source: U.S. Department of Education, National Center for Education Statistics—Common Core of Data
http://nces.ed.gov/ccd/elsi/

Data on public school enrollment is from the Common Core of Data 2014-2015 survey. Public school enrollment includes pre-kindergarten through grade 12 and ungraded students. The student/teacher ratio is calculated by dividing the number of students in all schools by the number of full-time equivalent teachers employed by all schools and agencies.

EDUCATIONAL ATTAINMENT, Items 113–116
Source: U.S. Census Bureau—2010 and 2015 American Community Survey
http://www.census.gov/acs/www/

Data on **educational attainment** are tabulated for the population 25 years old and over. The data were derived from a question that asked respondents for the highest level of school completed or the highest degree received. Persons who had passed a high school equivalency examination were considered high school graduates. Schooling received in foreign schools was to be reported as the equivalent grade or years in the regular American school system. Vocational and technical training, such as barber school training; business, trade, technical, and vocational schools; or other training for a specific trade are specifically excluded.

High school graduate or more. This category includes persons whose highest degree was a high school diploma or its equivalent, and those who reported any level higher than a high school diploma.

Bachelor's degree or more. This category includes persons who have received bachelor's degrees, master's degrees, professional school degrees (such as law school or medical school degrees), and doctoral degrees.

LOCAL GOVERNMENT EDUCATION EXPENDITURES, Items 117 and 118
Source: U.S. Department of Education, National Center for Education Statistics—Common Core of Data
http://nces.ed.gov/ccd/

Total expenditure for education includes provision or support of schools and facilities for elementary and secondary education. It encompasses instructional, support, and auxiliary services (school lunch, student activities, and community service) offered by public school systems. Retirement benefits paid to former education employees and interest payments are not included. Current expenditure includes all components of total expenditure except capital outlay. Expenditure data are obtained by the Census Bureau through its annual survey of government finances and are supplied to the National Center for Education Statistics (NCES). Current expenditure per student is current expenditure divided by the number of students enrolled. The number of students enrolled is based on an annual ''membership'' count of students on or about October 1.

NCES uses the Common Core of Data (CCD) Survey system to acquire and maintain statistical data from each of the 50 states, the District of Columbia, and the outlying areas. State education agencies compile and submit data for approximately 94,000 schools and 17,000 local school districts. Typically, this results in varying interpretation of NCES definitions and different record keeping systems, leading to large amounts of missing data for several states; this absence is reflected in the data in this publication. The numbers in Table A reflect imputations and adjustments as published in *Revenues and Expenditures for Public Elementary and Secondary Education: School Year 2013-2014 (Fiscal Year 2014).*

EXPORTS, Items 119–121
Source: U.S. Department of Commerce, International Trade Administration
http://www.census.gov/foreign-trade/statistics/state/ origin_movement/index.html

The data on exports of goods by state of origin are based on the location of the exporter (the principal party responsible for exportation from the United States). Exporters are often intermediaries, so the data do not necessarily represent the states in which the goods were actually produced. The total includes re-exports of foreign goods.

INCOME AND POVERTY, Items 122–133
Source: U.S. Census Bureau—2015 American Community Survey
http://www.census.gov/acs/www/

The data on income were derived from answers to questions which were asked of the population 15 years old and over. **Total income** is the sum of the amounts reported separately for wage or salary income; net self-employment income; interest, dividends, or net rental or royalty income or income from estates and trusts; Social Security or railroad retirement income; Supplemental Security Income (SSI); public assistance or welfare payments; retirement, survivor, or disability pensions; and all other income. Receipts from the following sources are not included as income: capital gains; money received from the sale of property (unless the recipient was engaged in the business of selling such property); the value of income ''in kind'' from food stamps, public housing subsidies, medical care, employer contributions for individuals, etc.; withdrawal of bank deposits; money borrowed; tax refunds; exchange of money between relatives living in the same household; and gifts and lump-sum inheritances, insurance payments, and other types of lump-sum receipts.

Per capita income is the mean income computed for every man, woman, and child in a particular group. It is derived by dividing the aggregate income of a particular group by the total population in that group. Per capita income is rounded to the nearest whole dollar.

Household income includes the income of the householder and all other individuals 15 years old and over in the household, whether or not they are related to the householder. Since many households consist of only one person, average household income is usually less than average family income. Although the household income statistics cover the past 12 months, the characteristics of individuals and the composition of households refer to the time of enumeration. Thus, the income of the household does not include amounts received by individuals who were members of the household during all or part of the past 12 months if these individuals no longer resided in the household at the time of interview. Similarly, income amounts reported by individuals who did not reside in the household during the past 12 months but who were members of the household at the time of interview are included. However, the composition of most households was the same during the past 12 months as at the time of interview.

Median income divides the income distribution into two equal parts, with half of all cases below the median income level and half of all cases above the median income level. For households and families, the median income is based on the distribution of the total number of households and families, including those with no income. Median income for households is computed on the basis of a standard distribution with a minimum value of less than $2,500 and a maximum value of $200,000 or more and is rounded to the nearest whole dollar.

For **family income**, the incomes of all household members 15 years old and over related to the householder are summed and treated as a single amount. Although the family income statistics cover the past 12 months, the characteristics of individuals and the composition of families refer to the time of interview. Thus, the income of the family does not include amounts received by individuals who were members of the family during all of part of the past 12 months if these individuals no longer resided with the family at the time of interview. Similarly, income amounts reported by individuals who did not reside with the family during the past 12 months but who were members of the family at the time of interview are included. However, the composition of most families was the same during the past 12 months as at the time of interview.

The **poverty status** data were derived from data collected on the number of persons in the household, each person's relationship to the householder, and the income data. The Social Security Administration (SSA) developed the original poverty definition in 1964, which federal interagency committees subsequently revised in 1969 and 1980. The Office of Management and Budget's (OMB) *Directive 14* prescribes the SSA's definition as the official poverty measure for federal agencies to use in their statistical work. Poverty statistics presented in American Community Survey products adhere to the standards defined by OMB in *Directive 14*.

The poverty thresholds vary depending on three criteria: size of family, number of children, and, for one- and two-person families, age of householder. In determining the poverty status of families and unrelated individuals, the Census Bureau uses thresholds (income cutoffs) arranged in a two-dimensional matrix. The matrix consists of family size (from one person to nine or more persons), cross-classified by presence and number of family members under 18 years old (from no children present to eight or more children present). Unrelated individuals and two-person families are further differentiated by age of reference person (under 65 years old and 65 years old and over). To determine a person's poverty status, the person's total family income in the last 12 months is compared to the poverty threshold appropriate for that person's family size and composition. If the total income of that person's family is less than the threshold appropriate for that family, then the person is considered poor or ''below the poverty level,'' together with every member of his or her family. If a person is not living with anyone related by birth, marriage, or adoption, then the person's own income is compared with his or her poverty threshold. The total number of persons below the poverty level is the sum of persons in families and the number of unrelated individuals with incomes below the poverty level in the last 12 months. The average poverty threshold for a four-person family was $24,257 in 2015.

Poverty Thresholds for 2015 by Size of Family and Number of Related Children Under 18 Years

Size of family unit	Weighted average thresholds	Related children under 18 years								
		None	One	Two	Three	Four	Five	Six	Seven	Eight or more
One person (unrelated individual) ...	12,082									
Under 65 years	12,331	12,331								
65 years and over	11,367	11,367								
Two people	15,391									
Householder under 65 years	15,952	15,871	16,337							
Householder 65 years and over...	14,342	14,326	16,275							
Three people.................................	18,871	18,540	19,078	19,096						
Four people..................................	24,257	24,447	24,847	24,036	24,120					
Five people	28,741	29,482	29,911	28,995	28,286	27,853				
Six people	32,542	33,909	34,044	33,342	32,670	31,670	31,078			
Seven people................................	36,998	39,017	39,260	38,421	37,835	36,745	35,473	34,077		
Eight people.................................	41,029	43,637	44,023	43,230	42,536	41,551	40,300	38,999	38,668	
Nine people or more.......................	49,177	52,493	52,747	52,046	51,457	50,490	49,159	47,956	47,658	45,822

Source: U.S. Census Bureau.

The data on **poverty status of households** were derived from answers to the income questions. Since poverty is defined at the family level and not the household level, the poverty status of the household is determined by the poverty status of the householder. Households are classified as poor when the total income of the householder's family in the previous 12 months is below the appropriate poverty threshold. (For nonfamily householders, the person's income is compared with the appropriate threshold.) The income of persons living in the household who are unrelated to the householder is not considered when determining the poverty status of a household, nor does their presence affect the family size in determining the appropriate threshold. The poverty thresholds vary depending upon three criteria: size of family, number of children, and, for one- and two-person families, age of the householder.

Poverty status of children by **family type** is the percentage of children living in that particular type of family that has a family income below the poverty threshold based on family size and composition.

PERSONAL INCOME AND EARNINGS, Items 134–158

Source: U.S. Bureau of Economic Analysis, Regional Economic Accounts
http://www.bea.gov/regional/index.htm#state

Total personal income is the current income received by residents of an area from all sources. It is measured before deductions of income and other personal taxes but after deductions of personal contributions for Social Security, government retirement, and other social insurance programs. It consists of **wage and salary disbursements** (covering all employee earnings, including executive salaries, bonuses, commissions, payments-in-kind, incentive payments, and tips); various types of supplementary earnings, such as employers' contributions to pension funds (termed "other labor income" or "supplements to wages and salaries"); proprietors' income; rental income of persons; dividends; personal interest income; and government and business transfer payments.

Proprietors' income is the monetary income and income-in-kind of proprietorships and partnerships (including the independent professions), and the income of tax-exempt cooperatives. **Dividends** are cash payments by corporations to stockholders who are U.S. residents. **Interest** is the monetary and imputed interest income of persons from all sources. **Rent** is the monetary income of persons from the rental of real property, except the income of persons primarily engaged in the real estate business; the imputed net rental income of owner-occupants of nonfarm dwellings; and the royalties received by persons.

Transfer payments are income for which services are not currently rendered. They consist of both government and business transfer payments. Government transfer payments include payments under the following programs: Federal Old-Age, Survivors, and Disability Insurance ("Social Security"); Medicare and medical vendor payments; unemployment insurance; railroad and government retirement; federal- and state-government-insured workers' compensation; veterans' benefits, including veterans' life insurance; food stamps; black lung payments; Supplemental Security Income; and Temporary Assistance for Needy Families. Government payments to nonprofit institutions, other than for work under research and development contracts, are also included. Business transfer payments consist primarily of liability payments for personal injury and of corporate gifts to nonprofit institutions.

Per capita personal income is based on resident population estimated as of July 1 of the year shown.

Personal tax payments include taxes paid by individuals to federal, state, and local governments. Personal taxes include individual income taxes, estate and gift taxes, motor vehicle license taxes, and personal property taxes. Personal contributions to social insurance ("Social Security taxes") are not included, nor are sales taxes.

Disposable personal income equals personal income less personal tax payments. It is a measure of the income available to persons for spending or saving.

Earnings cover wage and salary disbursements, other labor income, and proprietors' income.

The data for earnings obtained from the Bureau of Economic Analysis (BEA) are based on place of work. In computing personal income, BEA makes an ''adjustment for residence'' to earnings based on commuting patterns; thus, personal income is presented on a place-of-residence basis.

Farm earnings include the income of farm workers (wages and salaries and other labor income) and farm proprietors. Farm proprietors' income includes only the income of sole proprietorships and partnerships.

Farm earnings estimates are benchmarked to data collected in the Census of Agriculture and the revised Department of Agriculture state totals of income and expense items.

Goods-related industries include mining, construction, and manufacturing. **Service-related** and other industries includes private-sector earnings in forestry, related activities, and other; utilities; transportation and warehousing; information; wholesale trade; retail trade; finance and insurance; real estate and rental and leasing; and services, which includes professional, scientific, and technical services; management of companies and enterprises; administrative and waste services; educational services; health care and social assistance; arts, entertainment, and recreation; accommodation and food services; and other services, except public administration. Government earnings include all levels of government. Industries are categorized under the North American Industry Classification System (NAICS), and are not directly comparable to years prior to 2002.

GROSS STATE PRODUCT, Item 159
Source: U.S. Bureau of Economic Analysis, Regional Economic Accounts
http://www.bea.gov/regional/index.htm#state

Gross state product (GSP) for a state is derived as the sum of gross state product originating in all industries in the state. In concept, an industry's GSP, referred to as its ''value added,'' is equivalent to its gross output (sales or receipts and other operating income, commodity taxes, and inventory changes) minus its intermediate inputs (consumption of goods and services purchased from other industries or imported from other countries). As such, it is often referred to as the state counterpart to the nation's gross domestic product (GDP). In practice, GSP estimates are measured as the sum of distributions by industry of the components of gross domestic income—that is, the sum of the costs incurred (such as compensation of employees, net interest, and indirect business taxes) and the profits earned in production.

SOCIAL SECURITY AND SUPPLEMENTAL SECURITY INCOME, Items 160–162
Source: U.S. Social Security Administration
http://www.ssa.gov/policy/docs/statcomps/oasdi_sc/
http://www.ssa.gov/policy/docs/statcomps/ssi_sc/

Social Security beneficiaries are persons receiving benefits under the Old-Age, Survivors, and Disability Insurance Program. These include retired or disabled workers covered by the program,

their spouses and dependent children, and the surviving spouses and dependent children of deceased workers.

Supplemental Security Income (SSI) recipients are persons receiving SSI payments. The SSI program is a cash assistance program that provides monthly benefits to low-income aged, blind, or disabled persons.

Data are as of December of the year shown.

CIVILIAN EMPLOYMENT, Items 163–166
Source: U.S. Census Bureau—2015 American Community Survey
http://www.census.gov/acs/www/
https://www.census.gov/programs-surveys/acs/technical-documentation/code-lists.html

The data on occupation were derived from answers to questions that were asked of all persons 15 years old and over who had worked in the past 5 years. **Occupation** describes the kind of work the person does on the job. For employed persons, the data refer to the person's job during the previous week. For those who worked two or more jobs, the data refer to the job at which the person worked the greatest number of hours. For unemployed persons, the data refer to their last job. The American Community Survey uses the occupational classification system that was developed for the 2000 census and modified in 2002 and again in 2010. This system consists of 539 specific occupational categories for employed persons arranged into 23 major occupational groups. This classification was developed based on the *Standard Occupational Classification (SOC) Manual: 2010*, published by the Executive Office of the President, Office of Management and Budget.

CIVILIAN LABOR FORCE AND UNEMPLOYMENT, Items 167–171
Source: U.S. Bureau of Labor Statistics—Local Area Unemployment Statistics
http://www.bls.gov/lau/#tables

Data for the civilian labor force are the product of a federal-state cooperative program in which state employment security agencies prepare labor force and unemployment estimates under concepts, definitions, and technical procedures established by the Bureau of Labor Statistics (BLS). The **civilian labor force** consists of all civilians 16 years old and over who are either employed or unemployed.

Unemployment includes all persons who did not work during the survey week, made specific efforts to find a job during the prior four weeks, and were available for work during the survey week (except for temporary illness). Persons waiting to be called back to a job from which they had been laid off and those waiting to report to a new job within the next 30 days are included in unemployment figures.

PRIVATE NONFARM EMPLOYMENT AND EARNINGS, Items 172–183

Source: U.S. Bureau of Labor Statistics—Current Employment Survey
http://www.bls.gov/ces/#tables

Data for private nonfarm employment and earnings are compiled from payroll information reported monthly on a voluntary basis to the BLS and its cooperating state agencies. More than 350,000 establishments represent all industries except agriculture.

Employment is the annual average of monthly totals of persons who received pay for any part of the pay period including the 12th day of the month. Included are all full-time and part-time workers in nonfarm establishments. Not covered are government employees, proprietors, the self-employed, unpaid volunteers or family workers, farm workers, and domestic workers in households. The data by industry conform to the definitions established in the North American Industry Classification System (NAICS).

Earnings of **production workers** in **manufacturing** industries are derived from reports of gross payrolls and corresponding paid hours. Payroll is reported before deductions of any kinds. Total hours during the pay period include all hours worked (including overtime hours) and hours paid for holidays, vacations, and sick leave.

AGRICULTURE, ITEMS 184–202

Source: U.S. Department of Agriculture, National Agricultural Statistics Service—2012 Census of Agriculture
https://agcensus.usda.gov/Publications/2012/

The Census Bureau took a census of agriculture every 10 years from 1840 to 1920; since 1925, this census has been taken roughly once every 5 years. The 1997 Census of Agriculture was the first one conducted by the National Agricultural Statistics Service of the U.S. Department of Agriculture. Over time, the definition of a farm has varied. For recent censuses (including the 2012 census), a farm has been defined as any place from which $1,000 or more of agricultural products were produced and sold or normally would have been sold during the census year. Dollar figures are expressed in current dollars and have not been adjusted for inflation or deflation.

The term **operator** refers to a person who operates a farm by either doing the work or making day-to-day decisions about such activities as planting, harvesting, feeding, marketing, etc. The operator may be the owner, a member of the owner's household, a salaried manager, a tenant, a renter, or a sharecropper. If a person rents land to others or has land worked on shares by others, he/she is considered the operator only of the land that is retained for his/her own operation. The census collected information on the total number of operators, the total number of women operators, and demographic information for up to three operators per farm.

Government payments consists of direct payments as defined by the 2002 Farm Bill; payments from Conservation Reserve Program (CRP), Wetlands reserve Program (WRP), Farmable Wetlands Program (FWP), and Conservation Reserve Enhancement Program (CREP); loan deficiency payments; disaster payments; other conservation programs; and all other federal farm programs under which payments were made directly to farm operators. Commodity Credit Corporation (CCC) proceeds, amount from state and local federal crop insurance payments were not included in this category.

The acreage designated as **land in farms** consists primarily of agricultural land used for crops, pasture, or grazing. It also includes woodland and wasteland not actually under cultivation or used for pasture or grazing, provided that this land was part of the farm operator's total operation.

Land in farms is an operating-unit concept and includes all land owned and operated, as well as all land rented from others. Land used rent-free is classified as land rented from others. All land in Indian reservations used for growing crops or grazing livestock is classified as land in farms.

Irrigated land includes all land watered by any artificial or controlled means, such as sprinklers, flooding, furrows or ditches, sub-irrigation, and spreader dikes. Included are supplemental, partial, and preplant irrigation. Each acre was counted only once regardless of the number of times it was irrigated or harvested. Livestock lagoon waste water distributed by sprinkler or flood systems was also included.

Total cropland includes cropland harvested, cropland used only for pasture or grazing, cropland on which all crops failed or were abandoned, cropland in cultivated summer fallow, and cropland idle or used for cover crops or soil improvement but not harvested and not pastured or grazed.

Respondents were asked to report their estimate of the current market **value of land and buildings** owned, rented, or leased from others and rented and leased to others. Market value refers to the respondent's estimate of what the land and buildings would sell for under current market conditions.

The **value of machinery and equipment** was estimated by the respondent as the current market value of all cars, trucks, tractors, combines, balers, irrigation equipment, etc., used on the farm. This value is an estimate of what the machinery and equipment would sell for in its present condition and not the replacement of depreciated value. Share interests are reported at full value at the farm where the equipment and machinery are usually kept. Only equipment that was physically located at the farm on December 31, 2012, is included.

Market **value of agricultural products sold** by farms represents the gross market value before taxes and the production expenses of all agricultural products sold or removed from the place in 2012, regardless of who received the payment. It is equivalent to total sales and it includes sales by the operator as well as the value of any share received by partners, landlords, contractors, and others associated with the operation. It includes value of direct sales and the value of commodities placed in the Commodity Credit Corporation (CCC) loan program. Market value of agricultural products sold does not include payments received for participation in other federal farm programs. Also, it does not include income from farm-related sources such as customwork and other agricultural services, or income from nonfarm sources.

LAND USE, ITEMS 203 to 205

Source: U.S. Department of Agriculture, Natural Resources Conservation Service—2012 National Resources Inventory
http://www.nrcs.usda.gov/technical/NRI/

The National Resources Inventory (NRI) has been conducted every five years since 1982. It provides updated information on the status, condition, and trends of land, soil, water, and related resources on the Nation's non-federal lands. Non-federal lands include privately owned lands, tribal and trust lands, and lands controlled by State and local governments.

The 2012 NRI is based on a sample of about 800,000 locations throughout the United States (excluding Alaska and the District of Columbia). Acreages for federal land and total surface area are established through geospatial processes and administrative records. Total surface area of the contiguous United States is 1,937.7 million acres.

Cropland includes areas used for the production of adapted crops for harvest. Cultivated cropland comprises land in row crops or close-grown crops and also other cultivated cropland, such as hayland or pastureland that is in a rotation with row or close-grown crops. Noncultivated cropland includes permanent hayland and horticultural cropland.

Federally-owned lands include military bases, national forests, wildlife refuges, parks, grassland game preserves, scenic waterways, wilderness areas, monuments, lakeshore, parkways, battlefields, Bureau of Land Management lands, and other federal lands.

Developed land includes any built-up area greater than one fourth of an acre. Built-up areas include residential, industrial, commercial, and institutional land; construction sites; public administrative sites; railroad yards; cemeteries; airports; golf courses; sanitary landfills; sewage treatment plants; water control structures and spillways; other land used for such purpose; small parks (fewer than 10 acres of land) within urban and built-up areas; and highways, railroads, and other transportation facilities that are surrounded by urban areas. Also included are tracts of fewer than 10 acres that do not meet the above definition but are completely surrounded by urban and built-up land, as well as all highways, roads, railroads, and associated rights-of-way outside of urban and built-up areas (including private roads to farmsteads or ranch headquarters, logging roads, and other private roads).

WATER CONSUMPTION, Item 206

Source: U.S. Geological Survey, National Water Use Information Program—2010 Water Use Data
http://water.usgs.gov/watuse/

Every five years, the U.S. Geological Survey compiles national water-use estimates. This volume includes the total fresh and saline water withdrawals expressed as million gallons per day. Estimate of withdrawals of ground and surface water are given for the following categories of use: public water supplies, domestic, commercial, irrigation, livestock, industrial, mining, and thermo-electric power.

MANUFACTURES, Items 207–216

Source: U.S. Census Bureau— 2015 Annual Survey of Manufactures
https://www.census.gov/programs-surveys/asm.html

The Annual Survey of Manufactures (ASM) has been conducted annually every year since 1949, except for years ending in "2" and "7," at which time ASM data are included in the manufacturing sector of the Economic Census. The ASM provides statistics on employment, payroll, worker hours, payroll supplements, cost of materials, value added by manufacturing, capital expenditures, inventories, and energy consumption. It also provides estimates of value of shipments for over 1,400 classes of manufactured products. The Annual Survey of Manufactures includes approximately 50,000 establishments selected from the census universe of 350,000 manufacturing establishments.

The **all employees** number is the average number of production workers for the payroll periods including the 12th of March, May, August, and November plus the number of other employees in mid-March. Included are all persons on paid sick leave, paid holidays, and paid vacations during the pay period. Officers of corporations are included as employees, while proprietors and partners of unincorporated firms are excluded.

Payroll figures include the gross annual earnings of all employees on the payroll of operating manufacturing establishments. The definition, which is the same as the one used for calculating the federal withholding tax, includes all forms of compensation, such as salaries, wages, commissions, dismissal pay, bonuses, vacation and sick leave pay, and compensation-in-kind, prior to such deductions as employees' Social Security contributions, withholding taxes, group insurance, union dues, and savings bonds. The total includes salaries of officers of corporations; it excludes payments to proprietors or partners of unincorporated concerns. Also excluded are payments to members of armed forces and to pensioners carried on the active payrolls of manufacturing establishments.

Production workers include workers (up through the line-supervisor level) engaged in fabricating, processing, assembling, inspecting, receiving, storing, handling, packing, warehousing, shipping (but not delivering), maintenance, repair, janitorial and guard services, product development, auxiliary production for the plant's own use (for example, power plant), record keeping, and other services closely associated with these production operations at the establishment covered by the report. Employees above the working-supervisor level are excluded.

The number of production workers is the average for the payroll periods including the 12th of March, May, August, and November. Not included in this classification are all other employees, defined as non-production employees, including those engaged in factory supervision above the line-supervisor level.

Production worker hours cover hours worked or paid for at the manufacturing plant, including actual overtime hours (not straight-time equivalent hours). The data exclude hours paid for vacations, holidays, or sick leave when the employee is not at the establishment. Production wages represent all compensation paid to production workers.

Value added by manufacture is derived by subtracting the cost of materials, supplies, containers, fuel, purchased electricity, and contract work from the value of shipments (products manufactured plus receipts for services rendered). The result of this calculation is adjusted by the addition of value added by merchandising operations (the difference between the sales value and the cost of merchandise sold without further manufacture, processing, or assembly) plus the net change in finished goods and work-in-process between the beginning- and end-of-year inventories.

Value of shipments covers the received or receivable net selling values; free on board plant (excluding of freight and taxes), of all products shipped, both primary and secondary; and all miscellaneous receipts, such as receipts for contract work performed for others, installation and repair, sales of scrap, and sales of products bought and sold without further processing. Included are all items made by or for the establishments from material owned by it, whether sold, transferred to other plants of the same company, or shipped on consignment. The net selling value of products made in one plant on a contract basis from materials owned by another was reported by the plant providing the materials.

In the case of multi-unit companies, the manufacturer was asked to report the value of products transferred to other establishments of the same company at full economic or commercial value, including both the direct cost of production and a reasonable proportion of ''all other costs'' (including company overhead) and profit (interplant transfers).

The aggregate of the value of shipments figure for industry groups and for all manufacturing industries includes large amounts of duplications, as the products of some industries are used as materials by others. Estimates as to the overall extent of this duplication indicate that the value of manufactured products exclusive of such duplication (the value of finished manufactures) tends to approximate two-thirds of the total value of products reported in the census of manufactures.

Total cost of materials refers to direct charges actually paid or payable for items consumed or put into production during the year, including freight charges and other direct charges incurred by the establishment in acquiring these materials. It includes the cost of materials or fuel consumed, whether purchased by the individual establishment from other companies, transferred to it from other establishments of the same company, or withdrawn from inventory during the year. Included in this item are cost of parts, components, containers, etc.; cost of products bought and sold in the same condition; cost of fuels consumed for heat and power; cost of purchased electricity; and cost of contract work. Aggregate of total cost of materials and total value of shipments includes extensive duplication, since products of some industries are used as materials of others.

2012 ECONOMIC CENSUS: OVERVIEW, Items 217–308

Source: U.S. Census Bureau
https://www.census.gov/programs-surveys/economic-census.html

The Economic Census provides a detailed portrait of the nation's economy, from the national to the local level, once every five years. The 2012 Economic Census covers nearly all of the U.S. economy in its basic collection of establishment statistics. The 1997 Economic Census was the first major data source to use the North American Industry Classification System (NAICS); therefore, data are not comparable to economic data from prior years, which were based on the Standard Industrial Classification (SIC) system.

NAICS, developed in cooperation with Canada and Mexico, classifies North America's economic activities at two-, three-, four-, and five-digit levels of detail; the U.S. version of NAICS further defines industries to a sixth digit. The Economic Census takes advantage of this hierarchy to publish data at these successive levels of detail: sector (two-digit); subsector (three-digit); industry group (four-digit); industry (five-digit); and U.S. industry (six-digit). Information in Table A is at the two-digit level, with a few three- and four-digit items.

Several key statistics are tabulated for all industries included in this volume: number of establishments (or companies); number of employees; payroll; and a measure of output (sales, receipts, revenue, value of shipments, or value of construction work done).

Number of establishments. An establishment is a single physical location at which business is conducted. It is not necessarily identical with a company or enterprise, which may consist of one establishment or more. Economic Census figures represent a summary of reports for individual establishments rather than companies. For cases in which a census report was received, separate information was obtained for each location where business was conducted. When administrative records of other federal agencies were used instead of a census report, no information was available on the number of locations operated. Each Economic Census establishment was tabulated according to the physical location at which the business was conducted. The count of establishments represents those in business at any time during 2012.

When two activities or more were carried on at a single location under a single ownership, all activities were generally grouped together as a single establishment. The entire establishment was classified on the basis of its major activity and all of its data were included in that classification. However, when distinct and separate economic activities (for which different industry classification codes were appropriate) were conducted at a single location under a single ownership, separate establishment reports for each of the different activities were obtained in the census.

Number of employees. Paid employees consist of the full-time and part-time employees, including salaried officers and executives of corporations. Included are employees on paid sick leave, paid holidays, and paid vacations; not included are proprietors and partners of unincorporated businesses. The definition of paid employees is the same as that used by the Internal Revenue Service (IRS) on form 941.

For some industries, the Economic Census gives codes representing the number of employees as a range of numbers (for example, ''100 to 249 employees'' or ''1,000 to 2,499'' employees). In this volume, those codes have been replaced by the standard suppression code ''D.''

Payroll. Payroll includes all forms of compensation, such as salaries, wages, commissions, dismissal pay, bonuses, vacation allowances, sick-leave pay, and employee contributions to qualified pension plans paid during the year to all employees. For corporations, payroll includes amounts paid to officers and executives; for unincorporated businesses, it does not include profit or other compensation of proprietors or partners. Payroll is reported before deductions for Social Security, income tax, insurance, union dues, etc. This definition of payroll is the same as that used on IRS form 941.

Sales, shipments, receipts, revenue, or business done. This measure includes the total sales, shipments, receipts, revenue, or business done by establishments within the scope of the Economic Census. The definition of each of these items is specific to the economic sector measured.

CONSTRUCTION, Items 217–221
Source: U.S. Census Bureau—2012 Economic Census (See Overview of 2012 Economic Census prior to Item 217)

The Construction sector (sector 23) comprises establishments primarily engaged in the construction of buildings and other structures, heavy construction (except buildings), additions, alterations, reconstruction, installation, and maintenance and repairs. Establishments engaged in the demolition or wrecking of buildings and other structures, the clearing of building sites, and the sale of materials from demolished structures are also included. This sector also contains those establishments engaged in blasting, test drilling, landfill, leveling, earthmoving, excavating, land drainage, and other land preparation. The industries within this sector have been defined on the basis of their unique production processes. As with all industries, the production processes are distinguished by their use of specialized human resources and specialized physical capital. Construction activities are generally administered or managed at a relatively fixed place of business, but the actual construction work can be performed at one or more different project sites. This sector is divided into three subsectors of construction activities: (1) building construction and land subdivision and land development; (2) heavy construction (except buildings), such as highways, power plants, and pipelines; and (3) construction activity by special trade contractors.

WHOLESALE TRADE, Items 222–226
Source: U.S. Census Bureau—2012 Economic Census (See Overview of 2012 Economic Census prior to Item 217)

The Wholesale Trade sector (sector 42) comprises establishments engaged in wholesaling merchandise, generally without transformation, and rendering services incidental to the sale of merchandise. The wholesaling process is an intermediate step in the distribution of merchandise. Wholesalers are organized to sell or arrange the purchase or sale of (1) goods for resale (i.e., goods sold to other wholesalers or retailers), (2) capital or durable nonconsumer goods, and (3) raw and intermediate materials and supplies used in production.

Wholesalers sell merchandise to other businesses and normally operate from a warehouse or office. These warehouses and offices are characterized by having little or no display of merchandise. In addition, neither the design nor the location of the premises is intended to solicit walk-in traffic. Wholesalers do not normally use advertising directed to the general public. Customers are generally first reached via telephone, in-person marketing, or by specialized advertising that may include internet and other electronic means. Follow-up orders are either vendor-initiated or

client-initiated, are usually based on previous sales, and typically exhibit strong ties between sellers and buyers. In fact, transactions are often conducted between wholesalers and clients that have long-standing business relationships.

This sector is made up of two main types of wholesalers: those that sell goods on their own account and those that arrange sales and purchases for others for a commission or fee.

(1) Establishments that sell goods on their own account are known as wholesale merchants, distributors, jobbers, drop shippers, import/export merchants, and sales branches. These establishments typically maintain their own warehouse, where they receive and handle goods for their customers. Goods are generally sold without transformation, but may include integral functions, such as sorting, packaging, labeling, and other marketing services.

(2) Establishments arranging for the purchase or sale of goods owned by others or purchasing goods on a commission basis are known as agents and brokers, commission merchants, import/export agents and brokers, auction companies, and manufacturers' representatives. These establishments operate from offices and generally do not own or handle the goods they sell.

Some wholesale establishments may be connected with a single manufacturer and/or promote and sell that particular manufacturer's products to a wide range of other wholesalers or retailers. Other wholesalers may be connected to a retail chain or a limited number of retail chains and only provide a variety of products needed by that particular retail operation(s). These wholesalers may obtain the products from a wide range of manufacturers. Still other wholesalers may not take title to the goods but act as agents and brokers for a commission.

Although, in general, wholesaling normally denotes sales in large volumes, durable nonconsumer goods may be sold in single units. Sales of capital or durable nonconsumer goods used in the production of goods and services, such as farm machinery, medium- and heavy-duty trucks, and industrial machinery, are always included in Wholesale Trade.

RETAIL TRADE, Items 227–235
Source: U.S. Census Bureau—2012 Economic Census (See Overview of 2012 Economic Census prior to Item 217)

The Retail Trade sector (44–45) is made up of establishments engaged in retailing merchandise, generally without transformation, and rendering services incidental to the sale of merchandise.

The retailing process is the final step in the distribution of merchandise; retailers are, therefore, organized to sell merchandise in small quantities to the general public. This sector comprises two main types of retailers: store and nonstore retailers.

Store retailers operate fixed point-of-sale locations, located and designed to attract a high volume of walk-in customers. In general, retail stores have extensive displays of merchandise and use mass-media advertising to attract customers. They typically sell merchandise to the general public for personal or household consumption; some also serve business and institutional clients. These include establishments, such as office supply stores, computer and software stores, building materials dealers, plumbing supply stores, and electrical supply stores. Catalog showrooms, gasoline service stations, automotive dealers, and mobile home dealers are treated as store retailers.

In addition to retailing merchandise, some types of store retailers are also engaged in the provision of after-sales services, such as repair and installation. For example, new automobile dealers, electronic and appliance stores, and musical instrument and supply stores often provide repair services. As a general rule, establishments engaged in retailing merchandise and providing after-sales services are classified in this sector.

Nonstore retailers, like store retailers, are organized to serve the general public, although their retailing methods differ. The establishments of this subsector reach customers and market merchandise with methods, such as the broadcasting of "infomercials," the broadcasting and publishing of direct-response advertising, the publishing of paper and electronic catalogs, door-to-door solicitation, in-home demonstration, selling from portable stalls (street vendors, except food), and distribution through vending machines. Establishments engaged in the direct sale (nonstore) of products, such as home heating oil dealers and home-delivery newspaper routes are included in this sector.

The buying of goods for resale is a characteristic of retail trade establishments that distinguishes them from establishments in the Agriculture, Manufacturing, and Construction sectors. For example, farms that sell their products at or from the point of production are classified in Agriculture instead of in Retail Trade. Similarly, establishments that both manufacture and sell their products to the general public are classified in Manufacturing instead of Retail Trade. However, establishments that engage in processing activities incidental to retailing are classified in retail.

Industries in the **Motor Vehicle and Parts Dealers** subsector (441) retail motor vehicle and parts merchandise from fixed point-of-sale locations. Establishments in this subsector typically operate from a showroom and/or an open lot where the vehicles are on display. The display of vehicles and the related parts require little by way of display equipment. Personnel generally include both sales and sales support staff familiar with the requirements for registering and financing a vehicle as well as a staff of parts experts and mechanics trained to provide vehicle repair and maintenance services. Specific industries have been included in this subsector to identify the type of vehicle being retailed. Sales of capital or durable nonconsumer goods, such as medium and heavy-duty trucks, are always included in the Wholesale Trade sector. These goods are virtually never sold through retail methods.

Industries in the **Food and Beverage Stores** subsector (445) usually retail food and beverage merchandise from fixed point-of-sale locations. Establishments in this subsector have special equipment (e.g., freezers, refrigerated display cases, and refrigerators) for displaying food and beverage goods. They have staff trained in the processing of food products to guarantee the proper storage and sanitary conditions, as mandated by regulatory authority.

Industries in the **Clothing and Clothing Accessories Stores** subsector (448) retail new clothing and clothing accessories merchandise from fixed point-of-sale locations. Establishments in this subsector have similar types of display equipment, as well as employees who are knowledgeable regarding fashion trends and who can match styles, colors, and combinations of clothing and accessories to the characteristics and tastes of the customer.

Industries in the **General Merchandise Stores** subsector (452) retail new general merchandise from fixed point-of-sale locations.

Establishments in this subsector are unique in that they have the equipment and staff capable of retailing a large variety of goods from a single location. This includes a variety of display equipment and staff trained to provide information on many lines of products.

INFORMATION, Items 236–246
Source: U.S. Census Bureau—2012 Economic Census (See Overview of 2012 Economic Census prior to Item 217)

The Information sector (51) comprises establishments engaged in the following processes: (1) producing and distributing information and cultural products, (2) providing the means to transmit or distribute these products as well as data or communications, and (3) processing data.

The main components of this sector are the publishing industries, including software publishing; the motion picture and sound recording industries; the broadcasting and telecommunications industries; and the information services and data processing industries.

For the purpose of NAICS, the transformation of information into a commodity that is produced and distributed by a number of growing industries is at issue. The Information sector groups three types of establishments: (1) those engaged in producing and distributing information and cultural products; (2) those that provide the means to transmit or distribute these products as well as data or communications; and (3) those that process data. Cultural products are those that directly express attitudes, opinions, ideas, values, and artistic creativity; provide entertainment; or offer information and analysis concerning the past and present. Included in this definition are popular, mass-produced products, as well as cultural products that normally have a more limited audience, such as poetry books, literary magazines, or classical records. These activities were formerly classified throughout the existing national classifications. Traditional publishing was in manufacturing; broadcasting in communications; software production in business services; film production in amusement services; and so forth.

Industries in the **Publishing Industries, Except Internet** subsector (511) include establishments engaged in the publishing of newspapers, magazines, other periodicals, and books, as well as database and software publishing. In general, these establishments, which are known as publishers, issue copies of works for which they usually possess copyright. Works may be in one or more formats, including traditional print format, CD-ROM format, or proprietary electronic networks. Publishers may publish works originally created by others for which they have obtained the rights and/or works that they have created in-house. Software publishing is included here because the activity (creation of a copyrighted product and bringing it to market) is equivalent to the creation process for other types of intellectual products.

In NAICS, publishing—the reporting, writing, editing, and other processes that are required to create an edition of a book or a newspaper—is treated as a major economic activity in its own right, rather than as a subsidiary activity to printing, which is a manufacturing activity. Thus, publishing is classified in the Information sector, while printing remains in the NAICS Manufacturing sector. In part, the NAICS classification reflects the fact that publishing increasingly takes place in establishments that are physically separate from the associated printing establishments. More crucially, the NAICS classification of book and newspaper publishing is intended to portray their roles in a modern economy—roles that do not resemble manufacturing activities.

Music publishers are not included in the Publishing Industries subsector, but can be found in the Motion Picture and Sound Recording Industries subsector. Reproduction of prepackaged software is treated in NAICS as a manufacturing activity; online distribution of software products is in the Information sector, and custom design of software to client specifications is included in the Professional, Scientific, and Technical Services sector. These distinctions arise because of the different ways that software is created, reproduced, and distributed.

The Information sector does not include products, such as manifold business forms. Information is not the essential component of these items. Establishments producing these items are included in subsector 323, Printing and Related Support Activities.

Industries in the **Motion Picture and Sound Recording Industries** subsector (512) group establishments involved in the production and distribution of motion pictures and sound recordings. While producers and distributors of motion pictures and sound recordings issue works for sale as traditional publishers do, the processes are different enough to warrant placing the establishments engaged in these activities in separate subsectors. Production is typically a complex process that involves several distinct types of establishments engaged in activities, such as contracting with performers, creating the film or sound content, and providing technical postproduction services. Film distribution is often to exhibitors, such as theaters and broadcasters, rather than to a wholesale or retail distribution chain. When the product is in a mass-produced form, NAICS treats production and distribution as the major economic activity, rather than as a subsidiary activity to the manufacture of such products.

This subsector does not include establishments primarily engaged in the wholesale distribution of video cassettes and sound recordings, such as compact discs and audio tapes; these establishments are included in the Wholesale Trade sector. Reproduction of video cassettes and sound recordings that is carried out separately from establishments engaged in production and distribution is treated in NAICS as a manufacturing activity.

Industries in the **Broadcasting, except Internet** subsector (515) include establishments that create content or acquire the right to distribute and subsequently broadcast content. The industry groups (Radio and Television Broadcasting and Cable and Other Subscription Programming) are based on differences in the methods of communication and the nature of services provided. The Radio and Television Broadcasting industry group includes establishments that operate broadcasting studios and facilities for over-the-air or satellite delivery of radio and television programs, including entertainment, news, and talk programs. These establishments are often engaged in production and purchase of programs and generating revenues from the sale of air time to advertisers, as well as from donations, subsidies, and/or the sale of programs. The Cable and Other Subscription Programming industry group includes establishments that operate studios and facilities for the broadcasting of limited-format programs (such as news, sports, educational, and youth-oriented programs) that are typically narrowly-focused in nature; these programs are usually available on a subscription or fee basis. The distribution of cable and other subscription programming is included in subsector 517, Telecommunications.

Industries in the **Internet Publishing and Broadcasting and Web search portals** subsector (51913) consist of establishments primarily engaged in (1) publishing and/or broadcasting content on the Internet exclusively or (2) operating Web sites that use a search engine to generate and maintain extensive databases of Internet addresses and content in an easily searchable format (and known as Web search portals). The publishing and broadcasting establishments in this industry do not provide traditional (non-Internet) versions of the content that they publish or broadcast. They provide textual, audio, and/or video content of general or specific interest on the Internet exclusively. Establishments known as Web search portals often provide additional Internet services, such as e-mail, connections to other web sites, auctions, news, and other limited content, and serve as a home base for Internet users.

Establishments that are *not* in this group include those primarily engaged in—
- Providing wired broadband Internet access using own operated telecommunications infrastructure—these are classified in Wired Telecommunications Carriers;
- Providing both Internet publishing and other print or electronic (e.g., CD-ROM, diskette) editions in the same establishment or using proprietary networks to distribute content—these are classified in Publishing Industries (except Internet) based on the materials produced;
- Providing Internet access via client-supplied telecommunications connections—these are classified in All Other Telecommunications;
- Providing streaming services on content owned by others—these are classified in Data Processing, Hosting, and Related Services;
- Wholesaling goods on the Internet—these are classified in Wholesale Trade;
- Retailing goods on the Internet—these are classified in Retail Trade;
- Operating stock brokerages, travel reservation systems, purchasing services, and similar activities using the Internet rather than traditional methods—these are classified with the more traditioal establishments providing these services.

Industries in the **Telecommunications** subsector (517) include establishments that provide telecommunications and services related to that activity (e.g., telephony, including Voice over Internet Protocol (VoIP); cable and satellite television distribution services; Internet access; telecommunications reselling services). The Telecommunications subsector is primarily engaged in operating, maintaining, and/or providing access to facilities for the transmission of voice, data, text, sound, and video. A transmission facility may be based on a single technology or a combination of technologies. Establishments primarily engaged as independent contractors in the maintenance and installation of broadcasting and telecommunications systems are classified in sector 23, Construction.

Industries in the **Data processing, hosting, and related services** subsector (518) are establishments primarily engaged in providing infrastructure for hosting or data processing services.

These establishments may provide specialized hosting activities, such as web hosting, streaming services or application hosting; provide application service provisioning; or may provide general time-share mainframe facilities to clients. Data processing establishments provide complete processing and specialized reports from data supplied by clients or provide automated data processing and data entry services.

UTILITIES, Items 247–252

Source: U.S. Census Bureau—2012 Economic Census (See Overview of 2012 Economic Census prior to Item 217)

The Utilities sector (22) comprises establishments engaged in the provision of the following utility services: electric power, natural gas, steam supply, water supply, and sewage removal. Within this sector, the specific activities associated with the utility services provided vary by utility: electric power includes generation, transmission, and distribution; natural gas includes distribution; steam supply includes provision and/or distribution; water supply includes treatment and distribution; and sewage removal includes collection, treatment, and disposal of waste through sewer systems and sewage treatment facilities.

Excluded from this sector are establishments primarily engaged in waste management. These services are classified in subsector 562, Waste Management and Remediation Services, which also collect, treat, and dispose of waste materials; however, establishments in this subsector do not use sewer systems or sewage treatment facilities.

TRANSPORTATION AND WAREHOUSING, Items 252–256

Source: U.S. Census Bureau—2012 Economic Census (See Overview of 2012 Economic Census prior to Item 217)

The Transportation and Warehousing sector (48–49) includes industries that provide transportation of passengers and cargo, warehousing and storage for goods, scenic and sightseeing transportation, and support activities related to modes of transportation. Establishments in these industries use transportation equipment or transportation related facilities as a productive asset. The type of equipment depends on the mode of transportation, which includes air, rail, water, road, and pipeline.

The transportation and warehousing sector distinguishes three basic types of activities: subsectors for each mode of transportation, a subsector for warehousing and storage, and a subsector for establishments providing support activities for transportation. In addition, there are subsectors for establishments that provide passenger transportation for scenic and sightseeing purposes, postal services, and courier services.

FINANCE AND INSURANCE, Items 257–261

Source: U.S. Census Bureau—2012 Economic Census (See Overview of 2012 Economic Census prior to Item 217)

The Finance and Insurance sector (52) comprises establishments primarily engaged in financial transactions (transactions involving the creation, liquidation, or change in ownership of financial assets) and/or in facilitating financial transactions. Three principal types of activities are identified:

(1) Raising funds by taking deposits and/or issuing securities and, in the process, incurring liabilities. Establishments engaged in this activity use raised funds to acquire financial assets by making loans and/or purchasing securities. Putting themselves at risk, they channel funds from lenders to borrowers and transform or repackage the funds with respect to maturity, scale and risk. This activity is known as financial intermediation.

(2) Pooling of risk by underwriting insurance and annuities. Establishments engaged in this activity collect fees, insurance premiums, or annuity considerations; build up reserves; invest those reserves; and make contractual payments. Fees are based on the expected incidence of the insured risk and the expected return on investment.

(3) Providing specialized services facilitating or supporting financial intermediation, insurance, and employee benefit programs.

In addition, monetary authorities charged with monetary control are included in this sector.

REAL ESTATE AND RENTAL AND LEASING, Items 262–266

Source: U.S. Census Bureau—2012 Economic Census (See Overview of 2012 Economic Census prior to Item 217)

The Real Estate and Rental and Leasing sector (53) comprises establishments primarily engaged in renting, leasing, or otherwise allowing the use of tangible or intangible assets, and establishments providing related services. The major portion of this sector comprises establishments that rent, lease, or otherwise allow the use of their own assets by others. The assets may be tangible, such as real estate and equipment, or intangible, such as patents and trademarks.

This sector also includes establishments primarily engaged in managing real estate for others, selling, renting, and/or buying real estate for others, and appraising real estate. These activities are closely related to this sector's main activity. In addition, a substantial proportion of property management is self-performed by lessors.

The main components of this sector are the real estate lessors industries; equipment lessors industries (including motor vehicles, computers, and consumer goods); and lessors of nonfinancial intangible assets (except copyrighted works).

PROFESSIONAL, SCIENTIFIC, AND TECHNICAL SERVICES, Items 267–275

Source: U.S. Census Bureau—2012 Economic Census (See Overview of 2012 Economic Census prior to Item 217)

The Professional, Scientific, and Technical Services sector (54) is made up of establishments that specialize in performing professional, scientific, and technical activities for others. These activities require a high degree of expertise and training. The establishments in this sector specialize according to expertise and provide services to clients in a variety of industries (and, in some cases, to households). Activities performed include legal advice and representation; accounting, bookkeeping, and payroll services; architectural, engineering, and specialized design services; computer services; consulting services; research services; advertising services; photographic services; translation and interpretation services; veterinary services; and other professional, scientific, and technical services.

This sector excludes establishments primarily engaged in providing a range of day-to-day office administrative services, such as financial planning, billing and record keeping, personnel services, and physical distribution and logistics services. These establishments are classified in sector 56, Administrative and Support and Waste Management and Remediation Services.

Legal Services comprises establishments primarily engaged in offering legal services such as offices of lawyers, notaries, title abstract and settlement offices, and all other legal services such as patent agent services, paralegal services, and process serving services.

Accounting, Tax Preparation, Bookkeeping, and Payroll Services comprises establishments primarily engaged in providing services, such as auditing of accounting records, designing accounting systems, preparing financial statements, developing budgets, preparing tax returns, processing payrolls, bookkeeping, and billing.

Architectural, Engineering, and Related Services comprises establishments primarily engaged in offering (1) architectural services for residential, institutional, leisure, commercial, and industrial buildings and structures as well as for landscape purposes; (2) offering engineering services, including drafting services or building inspection services; (3) offering geophysical surveying and mapping services; (4) surveying and mapping services, except geophysical; and (5) offering testing laboratory services except medical and veterinary (the testing can occur in a laboratory or on-site).

Computer Systems Design and Related Services consists of establishments primarily engaged in providing expertise in the field of information technologies through one or more of the following activities: (1) writing, modifying, testing, and supporting software to meet the needs of a particular customer; (2) planning and designing computer systems that integrate computer hardware, software, and communication technologies; (3) on–site management and operation of clients' computer systems and/or data processing facilities; and (4) other professional and technical computer–related advice and services.

HEALTH CARE AND SOCIAL ASSISTANCE, Items 276–289

Source: U.S. Census Bureau—2012 Economic Census (See Overview of 2012 Economic Census prior to Item 217)

The Health Care and Social Assistance sector (62) consists of establishments that provide health care and social assistance services to individuals. The sector includes both health care and social assistance, because it is sometimes difficult to distinguish between the boundaries of these two activities. The industries in this sector are arranged on a continuum starting with those that provide medical care exclusively, continuing with those that provide health care and social assistance, and finishing with those that provide only social assistance. The services provided by establishments in this sector are delivered by trained professionals. All industries in the sector share this commonality of process—namely, labor inputs of health practitioners or social workers with the requisite expertise. Many of the industries in the sector are defined based on the educational degree held by the practitioners included in the industry.

In this volume, taxable and tax-exempt establishments are presented separately.

Excluded from this sector are aerobic classes, which can be found in subsector 713, Amusement, Gambling and Recreation Industries; and nonmedical diet and weight-reducing centers, which can be found in subsector 812, Personal and Laundry Services. Although these can be viewed as health services, they are not typically delivered by health practitioners.

Industries in the **Ambulatory Health Care Services** subsector (621) provide health care services directly or indirectly to ambulatory patients and do not typically provide inpatient services. Health practitioners in this subsector provide outpatient services, and facilities and equipment do not usually play the most significant part in this sector's production process.

Industries in the **Hospitals** subsector (622) provide medical, diagnostic, and treatment services, including physician, nursing, specialized accommodation, and other health services, to inpatients. Hospitals may provide outpatient services as a secondary activity. Many of the services provided by establishments in the Hospitals subsector require the use of specialized facilities and equipment, both of which form a significant and integral part of the production process.

ARTS, ENTERTAINMENT, AND RECREATION, Items 290–294

Source: U.S. Census Bureau—2012 Economic Census (See Overview of 2012 Economic Census prior to Item 217)

The Arts, Entertainment, and Recreation sector (71) includes a wide range of establishments that operate facilities or provide services that meet the diverse cultural, entertainment, and recreational interests of their patrons. This sector is made up of: (1) establishments that are involved in producing, promoting, or participating in live performances, events, or exhibits intended for public viewing; (2) establishments that preserve and exhibit objects and sites of historical, cultural, or educational interest; and (3) establishments that operate facilities or provide services that enable patrons to participate in recreational activities or pursue amusement, hobby, and leisure time interests.

Some establishments that provide cultural, entertainment, or recreational facilities and services are classified in other sectors. Excluded from this sector are: (1) establishments that provide both accommodations and recreational facilities—such as hunting and fishing camps and resort and casino hotels—are classified in subsector 721, Accommodation; (2) restaurants and night clubs that provide live entertainment in addition to the sale of food and beverages are classified in subsector 722, Food Services and Drinking Places; (3) motion picture theaters, libraries and archives, and publishers of newspapers, magazines, books, periodicals, and computer software are classified in sector 51, Information; and (4) establishments that use transportation equipment to provide recreational and entertainment services, such as those operating sightseeing buses, dinner cruises, or helicopter rides, are classified in subsector 487, Scenic and Sightseeing Transportation.

ACCOMMODATION AND FOOD SERVICES, Items 295–300

Source: U.S. Census Bureau—2012 Economic Census (See Overview of 2012 Economic Census prior to Item 217)

The Accommodation and Food Services sector (72) consists of establishments that provide customers with lodging and/or meals, snacks, and beverages for immediate consumption. The sector includes both accommodation and food services establishments because the two activities are often combined at the same establishment. Excluded from this sector are civic and social organizations, amusement and recreation parks, theaters, and other recreation or entertainment facilities providing food and beverage services.

Industries in the **Food Services and Drinking Places** subsector (722) prepare meals, snacks, and beverages to customer order for immediate on-premises and off-premises consumption. There is a wide range of establishments in these industries. Some provide food and drink only; while others provide various combinations of seating space, waiter/waitress services and incidental amenities, such as limited entertainment. The industries in the subsector are grouped based on the type and level of services provided. The industry groups are full-service restaurants; limited-service eating places; special food services, such as food service contractors, caterers, and mobile food services, and drinking places. Food services and drink activities at hotels and motels; amusement parks, theaters, casinos, country clubs, and similar recreational facilities; and civic and social organizations are included in this subsector only if these services are provided by a separate establishment primarily engaged in providing food and beverage services. Excluded from this subsector are establishments operating dinner cruises. These establishments are classified in subsector 487, Scenic and Sightseeing Transportation, because they utilize transportation equipment to provide scenic recreational entertainment.

OTHER SERVICES, EXCEPT PUBLIC ADMINISTRATION Items 301–308

Source: U.S. Census Bureau—2012 Economic Census (See Overview of 2012 Economic Census prior to Item 217)

The Other Services, Except Public Administration sector (81) comprises establishments engaged in providing services not specifically categorized elsewhere in the classification system. Establishments in this sector are primarily engaged in activities such as equipment and machinery repairing, promoting or administering religious activities, grant making, and advocacy; this sector also includes establishments that provide dry-cleaning and laundry services, personal care services, death care services, pet care services, photofinishing services, temporary parking services, and dating services.

Private households that employ workers on or about the premises in activities primarily concerned with the operation of the household are included in this sector.

Excluded from this sector are establishments primarily engaged in retailing new equipment and performing repairs and general maintenance on equipment. These establishments are classified in sector 44–45, Retail Trade.

Industries in the **Repair and Maintenance** subsector (811) restore machinery, equipment, and other products to working order. These establishments also typically provide general or routine maintenance (i.e., servicing) on such products to ensure they work efficiently; this maintenance also helps prevent breakdowns and make certain repairs unnecessary.

The NAICS structure for this subsector brings together most types of repair and maintenance establishments and categorizes them based on production processes (i.e., on the type of repair and maintenance activity performed, and the necessary skills, expertise, and processes required for different repair and maintenance establishments). This NAICS classification does not delineate between repair services provided to businesses versus those provided to households. Although some industries primarily serve either businesses or households, separation by class of customer is limited by the fact that many establishments serve both types. Establishments that repair computers and consumer electronics products are examples of such overlap.

The Repair and Maintenance subsector does not include all establishments engaged in repair and maintenance. For example, a substantial amount of repair is done by establishments that also manufacture machinery, equipment, and other goods. These establishments are included in the Manufacturing sector in NAICS. In addition, the repairing of transportation equipment is often provided by or based at transportation facilities, such as airports and seaports; these activities are included in the Transportation and Warehousing sector.

A particularly unique situation exists with repair of buildings. Plumbing, electrical installation and repair, painting and decorating, and other construction-related establishments are often involved in performing installation or other work on new construction, while also providing repair services on existing structures. Although some establishments do specialize in repair, it is difficult to distinguish between these two types. Thus, all such establishments are included in the Construction sector.

Excluded from this subsector are establishments primarily engaged in rebuilding or remanufacturing machinery and equipment. These are classified in sector 31–33, Manufacturing. Also excluded are retail establishments that provide after-sale services and repair. These are classified in sector 44–45, Retail Trade.

Industries in the **Personal and Laundry Services** subsector (812) include establishments that provide personal and laundry services to individuals, households, and businesses. Services performed include personal care services, death care services, laundry and dry-cleaning services, and a wide range of other personal services, such as pet care (except veterinary) services, photofinishing services, temporary parking services, and dating services.

The Personal and Laundry Services subsector is by no means all-inclusive of the activities that could be termed personal services (i.e., those provided to individuals rather than businesses). There are many other sectors and subsectors that provide services to persons. Establishments providing legal, accounting, tax preparation, architectural, portrait photography, and similar professional services are classified in sector 54, Professional, Scientific, and Technical Services; those providing job placement, travel arrangement, home security, interior and exterior house cleaning, exterminating, lawn and garden care, and similar support services are classified in sector 56, Administrative and Support and Waste Management and Remediation Services; those providing health and social services are classified in sector 62, Health Care and Social Assistance; those providing amusement and recreation services are classified in sector 71, Arts, Entertainment and Recreation; those providing educational instruction are classified in sector 61, Educational Services; those providing repair services are classified in subsector 811, Repair and Maintenance; and those providing spiritual, civic, and advocacy services are classified in subsector 813, Religious, Grantmaking, Civic, Professional, and Similar Organizations.

Industries in the **Religious, Grantmaking, Civic, Professional, and Similar Organizations** subsector (813) include establishments that organize and promote religious activities, support various causes through grant making, advocate various social and political causes, and promote and defend the interests of their members. This category includes only tax-exempt establishments.

The industry groups within the subsector are defined in terms of their activities, separately grouping establishments that provide funding for specific causes or for a variety of charitable causes, establishments that advocate and actively promote causes and beliefs for the public good, and establishments that have an active membership structure to promote causes and represent the interests of their members. Establishments in this subsector may publish newsletters, books, and periodicals for distribution to their membership.

GOVERNMENT EMPLOYMENT, Items 309–311
Source: U.S. Bureau of Economic Analysis—Regional Economic Accounts
http://www.bea.gov/regional/index.htm#state

Employment is measured as the average annual sum of full-time and part-time jobs. The estimates are on a place-of-work basis. Data for federal civilian employment include civilian

employees of the Department of Defense. Military employment includes all persons on active duty status.

STATE GOVERNMENT EMPLOYMENT AND PAYROLL, Items 312–330
Source: U.S. Census Bureau—Annual Survey of Government Employment and Payroll
http://www.census.gov/govs/apes/index.html

The annual Survey of Government Employment and Payroll measures the number of federal, state, and local civilian government employees and their gross monthly payroll for March of the survey year for state and local governments and for the Federal Government.

The survey provides state and local government data on full-time and part-time employment, part-time hours worked, full-time equivalent employment, and payroll statistics by governmental function (i.e., elementary and secondary education, higher education, police protection, fire protection, financial administration, central staff services, judicial and legal, highways, public welfare, solid waste management, sewerage, parks and recreation, health, hospitals, water supply, electric power, gas supply, transit, natural resources, correction, libraries, air transportation, water transport and terminals, other education, state liquor stores, social insurance administration, and housing and community development).

Data have been collected annually since 1957. A census is conducted every five years (years ending in ''2'' and ''7''). A sample of state and local governments is used to collect data in the intervening years. A new sample is selected every five years (years ending in ''4'' and ''9'').

State government employees include all persons paid for personal services performed, including persons paid from federally funded programs, paid elected or appointed officials, persons in a paid leave status, and persons paid on a per meeting, annual, semiannual, or quarterly basis. Unpaid officials, pensioners, persons whose work is performed on a fee basis, and contractors and their employees are excluded from the count of employees. **Full-time employees** are persons employed during the pay period to work the number of hours per week that represents regular full-time employment. Included are full-time temporary or seasonal employees who are working the number of hours that represent full-time employment. **Part-time employees** are persons paid on a part-time basis during the designated pay period. Included are those daily or hourly employees usually engaged for less than the regular full-time workweek, as well as any part-time paid officials. **Full-Time Equivalent employees** is a computed statistic representing the number of full-time employees that could have been employed if the reported number of hours worked by part-time employees had been worked by full-time employees. This statistic is calculated separately for each function of a government by dividing the ''part-time hours paid'' by the standard number of hours for full-time employees in the particular government and then adding the resulting quotient to the number of full-time employees.

Full-time payroll represents gross payroll amounts for the one-month period of March for full-time employees. **Part-time pay** represents gross payroll amounts for the one-month period of March for part-time employees. Gross payroll includes all salaries, wages, fees, commissions, and overtime paid to employees **before** withholdings for taxes, insurance, etc. It also includes incentive payments that are paid at regular pay intervals. It excludes employer share of fringe benefits like retirement, Social Security, health and life insurance, lump sum payments, and so forth.

Administration combines **Financial administration** and **Other government administration**. **Financial administration** includes activities concerned with tax assessment and collection, custody and disbursement of funds, debt management, administration of trust funds, budgeting, and other government-wide financial management activities. This function is not applied to school district or special district governments. **Other government administration** applies to the legislative and government-wide administrative agencies of governments. Included here are overall planning and zoning activities, and central personnel and administrative activities. This function is not applied to school district or special district governments.

Judicial and legal includes all court and court related activities (except probation and parole activities that are included at the "Correction" function), court activities of sheriff's offices, prosecuting attorneys' and public defenders' offices, legal departments, and attorneys providing government-wide legal service.

Police includes all activities concerned, with the enforcement of law and order, including coroner's offices, police training academies, investigation bureaus, and local jails, "lockups," or other detention facilities not intended to serve as correctional facilities.

Corrections includes activities pertaining to the confinement and correction of adults and minors convicted of criminal offenses. Pardon, probation, and parole activities are also included here.

Highways and transportation includes activities associated with the maintenance and operation of streets, roads, sidewalks, bridges, tunnels, toll roads, and ferries. Snow and ice removal, street lighting, and highway and traffic engineering activities are also included here. Also included are the operation, maintenance, and construction of public mass transit systems, including subways, surface rails, and buses, and the provision, construction, operation, maintenance; support of public waterways, harbors, docks, wharves, and related marine terminal facilities; and activities associated with the operation and support of publicly operated airport facilities.

Public welfare includes the administration of various public assistance programs for the needy, veteran services, operation of nursing homes, indigent care institutions, and programs that provide payments for medical care, handicap transportation, and other services for the needy.

Health includes administration of public health programs, community and visiting nurse services, immunization programs, drug abuse rehabilitation programs, health and food inspection activities, operation of outpatient clinics, and environmental pollution control activities.

Hospitals includes only government operated medical care facilities that provide inpatient care. Employees and payrolls of private corporations that lease and operate government-owned hospital facilities are excluded.

Social insurance administration includes the administration of unemployment compensation systems, public employment services, and the Federal Social Security, Medicare, and Railroad Retirement trusts.

Natural resources and Parks includes activities primarily concerned with the conservation and development of natural resources (soil, water, energy, minerals, etc.) and the regulation of industries that develop, utilize, or affect natural resources, as well as the operation and maintenance of parks, playgrounds, swimming pools, public beaches, auditoriums, public golf courses, museums, marinas, botanical gardens, and zoological parks.

Utilities, sewerage, and waste management includes operation, maintenance, and construction of public water supply systems, including production, acquisition, and distribution of water to general public or to other public or private utilities, for residential, commercial, and industrial use; activities associated with the production or acquisition and distribution of electric power; provision, maintenance, and operation of sanitary and storm sewer systems and sewage disposal and treatment facilities; and refuse collection and disposal, operation of sanitary landfills, and street cleaning activities.

Elementary and secondary education and libraries includes activities associated with the operation of public elementary and secondary schools and locally operated vocational-technical schools. Special education programs operated by elementary and secondary school systems are also included as are all ancillary services associated with the operation of schools, such as pupil transportation and food service. Also included are the establishment and provision of libraries for use by the general public and the technical support of privately operated libraries. This category includes classroom teachers, principals, supervisors of instruction, librarians, teacher aides, library aides, and guidance and psychological personnel as well as school superintendents and other administrative personnel, clerical and secretarial staffs, plant operation and maintenance personnel, health and recreation employees, transportation and food service personnel, and any student employees.

Higher education includes state government degree granting institutions that provide academic training above grade 12. This includes persons engaged in teaching and related academic research as well as administrative, clerical, custodial, cafeteria, health personnel, noninstructional employees engaged in organized research, law enforcement personnel, and paid student employees.

STATE GOVERNMENT FINANCES, Items 331–350

Source: U.S. Census Bureau—State Government Finances

http://www.census.gov/govs/state/

Data are from an annual survey conducted by the Census Bureau and pertain to state government fiscal years ending on June 30, except for four states with other ending dates: Alabama and Michigan (September 30), New York (March 31), and Texas (August 31).

The state government finance data presented in this publication may differ from data published by state governments because the

Census Bureau may be using a different definition of which organizations are covered under the term "state government."

For the purpose of Census Bureau statistics, the term "state government" refers not only to the executive, legislative, and judicial branches of a given state, but it also includes agencies, institutions, commissions, and public authorities that operate separately or somewhat autonomously from the central state government but where the state government maintains administrative or fiscal control over their activities as defined by the Census Bureau.

Total **general revenue** includes all revenue except utility, liquor stores, and insurance trust revenue. All tax revenue and intergovernmental revenue, even if designated for employee-retirement or local utility purpose, are classified as general revenue.

Intergovernmental revenue covers amounts received from the federal government as fiscal aid, reimbursements for performance of general government functions and specific services for the paying government, or in lieu of taxes. It excludes any amounts received from other governments from the sale of property, commodities, and utility services.

Taxes consist of compulsory contributions exacted by governments for public purposes. However, this category excludes employer and employee payments for retirement and social insurance purposes, which are classified as insurance trust revenue; it also excludes special assessments, which are classified as non-tax general revenue. Sales and gross receipts taxes do not include dealer discounts, or "commissions" allowed to merchants for collection of taxes from consumers. General sales taxes and selected taxes on sales of motor fuels, tobacco products, and other particular commodities and services are included.

General government expenditure includes capital outlay, a major portion of which is commonly financed by borrowing. Government revenue does not include receipts from borrowing. Among other things, this distorts the relationship between totals of revenue and expenditure figures that are presented and renders it useless as a direct measure of the degree of budgetary "balance" (as that term is generally applied).

Direct general expenditure comprises all expenditures of the state governments, excluding utility, liquor stores, insurance trust expenditures, and any intergovernmental payments.

State government expenditure for **education** is mainly for the provision and general support of schools and other educational facilities and services, including those for educational institutions beyond high school. They cover such related services as student transportation; school lunch and other cafeteria operations; school health, recreation, and library services; and dormitories, dining halls, and bookstores operated by public institutions of higher education.

Health and hospitals expenditure includes health research; clinics; nursing; immunization; other categorical, environmental, and general health services provided by health agencies; establishment and operation of hospital facilities; provision of hospital care; and support of other public and private hospitals.

Highways expenditure is for the provision and maintenance of highway facilities, including toll turnpikes, bridges, tunnels, and ferries, as well as regular roads, highways, and streets. Also included are expenditures for street lighting and for snow and ice removal. Not included are highway policing and traffic control, which are considered part of police protection.

Public safety expenditure includes police and correctional institution expenditures.

Public welfare expenditure covers support of and assistance to needy persons; this aid is contingent upon the person's needs. Included are cash assistance paid directly to needy persons under categorical (Old Age Assistance, Temporary Assistance for Needy Families, Aid to the Blind, and Aid to the Disabled) and other welfare programs; vendor payments made directly to private purveyors for medical care, burials, and other commodities and services provided under welfare programs; welfare institutions; and any intergovernmental or other direct expenditure for welfare purposes. Pensions to former employees and other benefits not contingent on need are excluded.

Natural resources, parks, and recreation includes expenditures for conservation, promotion, and development of natural resources (soil, water, energy, minerals, etc.) and the regulation of industries which develop, utilize, or affect natural resources. It also includes the provision and support of recreational and cultural-scientific facilities, such as golf courses, playgrounds, tennis courts, public beaches, swimming pools, play fields, parks, camping areas, recreational piers and marinas, galleries, museums, zoos, botanical gardens, auditoriums, stadiums, recreational centers, convention centers, exhibition halls, community music, drama, and celebrations.

Debt outstanding includes all long-term debt obligations of the government and its agencies (exclusive of utility debt) and all interest-bearing, short-term (repayable within one year) debt obligations remaining unpaid at the close of the fiscal year. It includes judgments, mortgages, and revenue bonds, as well as general obligation bonds, notes, and interest-bearing warrants. This category consists of non-interest-bearing, short-term obligations; inter-fund obligations; amounts owed in a trust or agency capacity; advances and contingent loans from other governments; and rights of individuals to benefit from government-administered employee-retirement funds.

VOTING AND REGISTRATION, Items 351 and 352
Source: U.S. Census Bureau—Current Population Survey
http://www.census.gov/topics/public-sector/voting.html

These estimates are based on the November 2016 Voting and Registration Supplement to the Current Population Survey (CPS).

Voting rates are calculated using the voting-age population, which includes both citizens and noncitizens. Statistics from surveys are subject to sampling and nonsampling error. The CPS estimate of overall turnout differs from the "official" turnout reported by the Clerk of the House of Representatives.

ELECTION STATISTICS, Items 353–355

Source: U.S. House of Representatives, Statistics of the Presidential and Congressional Election of November 8. 2016
http://history.house.gov/Institution/Election-Statistics/2016election/

Election results show the percentage of the total vote cast for the Democratic and Republican candidates, as well as the combined percentage for all other candidates in the 2016 presidential election. This information was compiled by the Office of the Clerk, U.S. House of Representatives and published on February 22, 2017.

TABLE B—STATES AND COUNTIES

Table B presents 199 items for the United States as a whole, each individual state, and the District of Columbia; and every county, county equivalent, and independent city. The counties are presented in alphabetical order within each state, and the states are also presented in alphabetical order. Independent cities, which are found in Maryland, Missouri, Nevada, and Virginia, are placed in alphabetical order at the end of the list of counties for those states. The District of Columbia is included in Table B as both a county and a state. It is also included as a city in Table D.

LAND AREA, Items 1 and 4

Source: U.S. Census Bureau—2016 U.S. Gazetteer Files,
http://www.census.gov/geo/maps-data/data/gazetteer2016.html

Land area measurements are shown to the nearest square mile. Land area is an area measurement providing the size, in square miles, of the land portions of each county.

POPULATION, Items 2–4

Source: U.S. Census Bureau—Population Estimates
https://www.census.gov/programs-surveys/popest.html

The population data are Census Bureau estimates of the resident population as of July 1 of the year shown. The ranks are shown for counties (including independent cities and the District of Columbia).

POPULATION AND POPULATION CHARACTERISTICS, Items 5–19

Source: U.S. Census Bureau—Population Estimates
https://www.census.gov/programs-surveys/popest.html

The concept of race, as used by the Census Bureau, reflects self-identification by persons according to the race or races with which they most closely identify. These categories are sociopolitical constructs and should not be interpreted as being scientific or anthropological in nature. Furthermore, race categories include both racial and national origin groups.

Beginning with the 2000 census, respondents were offered the option of selecting one or more races. This option was not available in prior censuses; thus, comparisons between censuses should be made with caution. In Table B, Columns 5 through 8 refer to individuals who identified with each racial category, either alone or in combination with other races. The estimates exclude persons of Hispanic or Latino origin from all race groups.

The sum of the four individual race alone or in combination categories in this book will often add to more than the total population because people who reported more than one race were tallied in each race category. In this book, the Asian group has been combined with the Native Hawaiian and Other Pacific Islander group, causing double-counting of persons who identify with both groups. This is especially pronounced in Hawaii.

The **White** population is defined as persons who indicated their race as White, as well as persons who did not classify themselves in one of the specific race categories listed on the questionnaire but entered a nationality such as Irish, German, Italian, Lebanese, Near Easterner, Arab, or Polish.

The **Black** population includes persons who indicated their race as "Black, African Am., or Negro," as well as persons who did not classify themselves in one of the specific race categories but reported entries such as African American, Afro American, Kenyan, Nigerian, or Haitian.

The **American Indian or Alaska Native** population includes persons who indicated their race as American Indian or Alaska Native, as well as persons who did not classify themselves in one of the specific race categories but reported entries such as Canadian Indian, French-American Indian, Spanish-American Indian, Eskimo, Aleut, Alaska Indian, or any of the American Indian or Alaska Native tribes.

The **Asian and Pacific Islander** population combines two census groupings: **Asian** and **Native Hawaiian or Other Pacific Islander**. The **Asian** population includes persons who indicated their race as Asian Indian, Chinese, Filipino, Japanese, Korean, Vietnamese, or "Other Asian," as well as persons who provided write-in entries of such groups as Cambodian, Laotian, Hmong, Pakistani, or Taiwanese. The **Native Hawaiian or Other Pacific Islander** population includes persons who indicated their race as "Native Hawaiian," "Guamanian or Chamorro," "Samoan," or "Other Pacific Islander," as well as persons who reported entries such as Part Hawaiian, American Samoan, Fijian, Melanesian, or Tahitian.

The **Hispanic population** is based on a question that asked respondents "Is this person Spanish/Hispanic/Latino?" Persons marking any one of the four Hispanic categories (i.e., Mexican, Puerto Rican, Cuban, or other Spanish) are collectively referred to as Hispanic.

In the census, the Hispanic origin question was placed before the race question and specific instructions indicated that both questions should be answered. These changes were designed to improve accuracy and may affect comparability with data prior to the 2000 census.

Age is defined as age at last birthday (number of completed years since birth), as of April 1 of the census year. The census also asked for the specific date of birth of the respondent, and census procedures used the birth date for deriving age data. For this reason, it is likely that the data have fewer problems than data from censuses prior to 2000, such as the tendency of respondents to round ages or to report their ages on the date the questionnaire was filled out rather than on April 1.

The **female** population is shown as a percentage of total population.

POPULATION AND COMPONENTS OF CHANGE, Items 20–26
Source: U.S. Census Bureau—Decennial Censuses and Population Estimates
http://www.census.gov/main/www/cen2000.html
https://www.census.gov/programs-surveys/popest.html
http://www.census.gov/2010census/data/

The population data for 2000 and 2010 are from the decennial censuses and represent the resident population as of April 1 of those years. The components of change are based on Census Bureau estimates of the resident population as of July 1, 2016. The change in population between 2010 and 2016 is made up of (a) natural increase—births minus deaths, and (b) net migration—the difference between the number of persons moving into a particular area and the number of persons moving out of the area. Net migration is composed of internal and international migration.

Because the 2016 population estimates are based on a model that begins with a national population estimate, the county components of change do not always exactly add up to the difference between the 2010 census population and the 2016 estimates.

HOUSEHOLDS, Items 27–31
Source: U.S. Census Bureau—American Community Survey, 2015 5-year Estimates
http://www.census.gov/acs/www/

A **household** includes all of the persons who occupy a housing unit. (Persons not living in households are classified as living in group quarters.) A housing unit is a house, an apartment, a mobile home, a group of rooms, or a single room occupied (or, if vacant, intended for occupancy) as separate living quarters. Separate living quarters are those in which the occupants live separately from any other persons in the building and have direct access from the outside of the building or through a common hall. The occupants may be a single family, one person living alone, two or more families living together, or any other group of related or unrelated persons who share living quarters. The number of households is the same as the number of year-round occupied housing units.

A **family** includes a householder and one or more other persons living in the same household who are related to the householder by birth, marriage, or adoption. All persons in a household who are related to the householder are regarded as members of his or her family. A **family household** may contain persons not related to the householder; thus, family households may include more members than families do. A household can contain only one family for the purposes of census tabulations. Not all households contain families, as a household may comprise a group of unrelated persons or of one person living alone. Families are classified by type as either a ''married-couple family'' or ''other family,'' according to the presence or absence of a spouse.

The measure of **persons per household** is obtained by dividing the number of persons in households by the number of households or householders. One person in each household is designated as the householder. In most cases, this is the person (or one of the persons) in whose name the house is owned, being bought, or rented. If there is no such person in the household, any adult household member 15 years old and over can be designated as the householder.

The category **female family householder** includes only female-headed family households with no spouse present.

A nonfamily household consists of a householder living alone or with nonrelatives only. Column 31 shows one-person households as a percentage of all households.

GROUP QUARTERS, Item 32
Source: U.S. Census Bureau—Population Estimates
https://www.census.gov/programs-surveys/popest.html

The Census Bureau classifies all persons not living in households as living in group quarters; this category includes both the institutional and noninstitutional populations. The institutionalized population includes persons under formally authorized, supervised care or custody in institutions, such as correctional institutions, nursing homes, mental (psychiatric) hospitals, and juvenile institutions. The noninstitutionalized population includes persons who live in group quarters other than institutions, such as college dormitories, military quarters, and group homes. This volume includes the total number of persons in group quarters.

DAYTIME POPULATION, Items 33 and 34
Source: U.S. Census Bureau—American Community Survey, 2015 5-year Estimates
http://www.census.gov/acs/www/

Daytime population refers to the number of persons who are present in an area or place during normal business hours, including workers. This can be contrasted with the ''resident'' population, which is present during the evening and nighttime hours. The daytime population estimate is calculated by adding the total resident population and the total workers working in the area/place, and then subtracting the total workers living in the area/place from that result. Information on the expansion or contraction experienced by different communities between their nighttime and daytime populations is important for many planning purposes, especially those concerning transportation, disaster, and relief operations.

The employment/residence ratio is a measure of the total number of workers working in an area or place, relative to the total number of workers living in the area or place. It is often used as a rough indication of the jobs-workers balance in an area/place, although it does not take into account whether the resident workers possess the skills needed for the jobs available in their particular area/place. The employment/residence ratio is calculated by dividing the number of total workers working in an area/place by the number of total workers residing in the area/place.

BIRTHS AND DEATHS, Items 35–38

Source: U.S. Census Bureau—Population Estimates
https://www.census.gov/programs-surveys/popest.html

The numbers of births and deaths are from the Census Bureau's Population Estimates Program. They represent the total number of live births and deaths occurring to residents of an area as estimated using reports from the National Center for Health Statistics (NCHS) and the Federal-State Cooperative for Population Estimates (FSCPE). The rates measure births and deaths during the specified time period as a proportion of an area's population. Rates are expressed per 1,000 population estimated as of July 1. These numbers and rates do not represent the calendar year, but rather the year-long period ending on July 1.

PERSONS UNDER 65 WITH NO HEALTH INSURANCE, Items 39 and 40

Source: U.S. Census Bureau—Small Area Health Insurance Estimates
http://www.census.gov/did/www/sahie/index.html

The Small Area Health Insurance Estimates (SAHIE) program develops model-based estimates of health insurance coverage for counties and states. This developmental program builds on the work of the Small Area Income and Poverty Estimates (SAIPE) program. The SAHIE program models health insurance coverage by combining survey data with population estimates and administrative records. These estimates combine data from administrative records, postcensal population estimates, and the decennial census with direct estimates from the American Community Survey to provide consistent and reliable single-year estimates. These model-based single-year estimates are more reflective of current conditions than multi-year survey estimates.

MEDICARE ENROLLMENT, Items 41–43

Source: U.S. Department of Health and Human Services, Centers for Medicare and Medicaid Services
https://www.cms.gov/Research-Statistics-Data-and-Systems/Statistics-Trends-and-Reports/Medicare-Geographic-Variation/GV_PUF.html

The Centers for Medicare and Medicaid Services (CMS) administers Medicare, which provides health insurance to persons 65 years old and over, persons with permanent kidney failure, and certain persons with disabilities. Original Medicare has two parts: Hospital Insurance and Supplemental Medical Insurance. In recent years, Medicare has been expanded to include two new programs: Medicare Advantage plans and prescription drug coverage. Medicare Advantage Plans are health plan options that are approved by Medicare but run by private companies. Medicare prescription drug plans can be part of Medicare Advantage plans or stand-alone drug plans.

Persons who are eligible for Medicare can enroll in Part A (Hospital Insurance) at no charge, and can choose to pay a monthly premium to enroll in Part B. Most eligible persons are enrolled in Part A, and more than 90 percent of enrollees in Part A are also enrolled in Part B (Supplemental Medical Insurance). This table includes persons who were enrolled in both Part A and Part B during 2014.

Part B beneficiaries can choose to enroll in **Original Medicare**, a fee-for-service plan administered by the Centers for Medicare and Medicaid Services, or in a **Medicare Advantage** plan. Medicare Advantage plans include private fee-for-service plans, preferred provider organizations, health maintenance organizations, medical savings account plans, demonstration plans, and programs for all-inclusive care for the elderly.

CRIME, Items 44–47

Source: U.S. Federal Bureau of Investigation—Uniform Crime Reports
http://www.fbi.gov/ucr/ucr.htm

Crime data are as reported to the Federal Bureau of Investigation (FBI) by law enforcement agencies and have not been adjusted for underreporting. This may affect comparability between geographic areas or over time.

Through the voluntary contribution of crime statistics by law enforcement agencies across the United States, the Uniform Crime Reporting (UCR) Program provides periodic assessments of crime in the nation as measured by offenses that have come to the attention of the law enforcement community. The Committee on Uniform Crime Records of the International Association of Chiefs of Police initiated this voluntary national data collection effort in 1930. The UCR Program contributors compile and submit their crime data either directly to the FBI or through state-level UCR Programs.

Seven offenses, because of their severity, frequency of occurrence, and likelihood of being reported to police, were initially selected to serve as an index for evaluating fluctuations in the volume of crime. These serious crimes were murder and nonnegligent manslaughter, forcible rape, robbery, aggravated assault, burglary, larceny-theft, and motor vehicle theft. By congressional mandate, arson was added as the eighth index offense in 1979. The totals shown in this volume do not include arson.

In 2004, the FBI discontinued the use of the Crime Index in the UCR Program and its publications, stating that the Crime Index was driven upward by the offense with the highest number of cases (in this case, larceny-theft), creating a bias against jurisdictions with a high number of larceny-thefts but a low number of other serious crimes, such as murder and forcible rape. The FBI is currently publishing a violent crime total and property crime total until a more viable index is developed. This book includes the crime total, as well as violent crime and property crime rates.

In 2013, the FBI adopted a new definition of rape. Rape is now defined as, ''Penetration, no matter how slight, of the vagina or anus with any body part or object, or oral penetration by a sex organ of another person, without the consent of the victim.'' The new definition updated the 80-year-old historical definition of rape which was ''carnal knowledge of a female forcibly and against her will.'' Effectively, the revised definition expands rape to include both male and female victims and offenders, and reflects the various forms of sexual penetration understood to be rape, especially nonconsenting acts of sodomy, and sexual assaults with objects.

Violent crimes include four categories of offenses: (1) Murder and nonnegligent manslaughter, as defined in the UCR Program, is the willful (nonnegligent) killing of one human being by another. This offense excludes deaths caused by negligence, suicide, or accident; justifiable homicides; and attempts to murder or assaults to murder. (2) Rape is the penetration, no matter how slight, of the vagina or anus with any body part or object, or oral penetration by a sex organ of another person, without the consent of the victim. Assaults or attempts to commit rape by force or threat of force are also included; however, statutory rape (without force) and other sex offenses are excluded. (3) Robbery is the taking or attempting to take anything of value from the care, custody, or control of a person or persons by force or threat of force or violence and/or by putting the victim in fear. (4) Aggravated assault is an unlawful attack by one person upon another for the purpose of inflicting severe or aggravated bodily injury. This type of assault is usually accompanied by the use of a weapon or by other means likely to produce death or great bodily harm. Attempts are included, since injury does not necessarily have to result when a gun, knife, or other weapon is used, as these incidents could and probably would result in a serious personal injury if the crime were successfully completed.

Property crimes include three categories: (1) Burglary, or breaking and entering, is the unlawful entry of a structure to commit a felony or theft, even though no force was used to gain entrance. (2) Larceny-theft is the unauthorized taking of the personal property of another, without the use of force. (3) Motor vehicle theft is the unauthorized taking of any motor vehicle.

Rates are based on population estimates provided by the FBI. The county totals published in this volume were obtained by aggregating individual reporting units within each county and MSA. If the population total for the units aggregated was less than 75 percent of the county's population (as estimated by the Census Bureau), the total was not considered representative of the county as a whole and was not published. State and U.S. totals include FBI estimates for those areas. State and U.S. totals in this table are the adjusted totals as published in the FBI's *Crime in the United States*.

EDUCATION—SCHOOL ENROLLMENT AND EDUCATIONAL ATTAINMENT, Items 48–51
Source: U.S. Census Bureau—American Community Survey, 2015 5-year Estimates
http://www.census.gov/acs/www/

Data on **school enrollment** are tabulated for the population 3 years old and over. Persons were classified as enrolled in school if they reported attending a "regular" public or private school (or college) during the three months preceding the interview. The instructions were to include only nursery school, kindergarten, elementary school, and schooling which would lead to a high school diploma or a college degree as regular school. The Census Bureau defines a public school as "any school or college controlled and supported by a local, county, state, or federal government." Schools primarily supported and controlled by religious organizations or other private groups are defined as private schools.

Data on **educational attainment** are tabulated for the population 25 years old and over. The data were derived from a question that asked respondents for the highest level of school completed or the highest degree received. Persons who had passed a high school equivalency examination were considered high school graduates. Schooling received in foreign schools was to be reported as the equivalent grade or years in the regular American school system.

Vocational and technical training, such as barber school training; business, trade, technical, and vocational schools; or other training for a specific trade are specifically excluded.

High school graduate or less. This category includes persons whose highest degree was a high school diploma or its equivalent, and those who reported any level lower than a high school diploma.

Bachelor's degree or more. This category includes persons who have received bachelor's degrees, master's degrees, professional school degrees (such as law school or medical school degrees), and doctoral degrees.

LOCAL GOVERNMENT EDUCATION EXPENDITURES, Items 52 and 53
Source: U.S. Department of Education, National Center for Education Statistics, Common Core of Data (CCD), "National Public Education Financial Survey (State Fiscal)," 2013-14 (FY 2014) v.1a; "School District Finance Survey (F-33)," 2013-14 (FY 2014) v.1a

Expenditures are for elementary and secondary Education which includes prekindergarten through twelfth grade regular, special, and vocational education, as well as cocurricular, community service, and adult education programs provided by a public school system. The financial activities of these systems for all instruction, support service, and noninstructional activities are included.

Current spending comprises current operation expenditure, payments made by the state government on behalf of school systems, and transfers made by school systems into their own retirement funds. Current operation expenditures include direct expenditure for salaries, employee benefits, purchased professional and technical services, purchased property and other services, and supplies. It includes gross school system expenditure for instruction, support services, and noninstructional functions. It excludes expenditure for debt service, capital outlay, and reimbursement to other governments (including other school systems).

Current expenditure per student is current expenditure divided by the number of students enrolled. The number of students enrolled is based on an annual "membership" count of students on or about October 1, collected by the National Center for Education Statistics on the Common Core of Data (CCD) agency universe file—"Local Education Agency (School District) Universe Survey."

MONEY INCOME, Items 54–57

Source: U.S. Census Bureau—American Community Survey, 2015 5-year Estimates
http://www.census.gov/acs/www/

Total money income is the sum of the amounts reported separately for wage or salary income; net self-employment income; interest, dividends, or net rental or royalty income or income from estates and trusts; Social Security or railroad retirement income; Supplemental Security Income (SSI); public assistance or welfare payments; retirement, survivor, or disability pensions; and all other income. Receipts from the following sources are not included as income: capital gains; money received from the sale of property (unless the recipient was engaged in the business of selling such property); the value of income "in kind" from food stamps, public housing subsidies, medical care, employer contributions for individuals, etc.; withdrawal of bank deposits; money borrowed; tax refunds; exchange of money between relatives living in the same household; and gifts, lump-sum inheritances, insurance payments, and other types of lump-sum receipts.

Money income differs in definition from personal income (item 62). For example, money income does not include the pension rights, employer provided health insurance, food stamps, or Medicare payments that are included in personal income.

Per capita income is the mean income computed for every man, woman, and child in a particular group. It is derived by dividing the aggregate income of a particular group by the resident population in that group as estimated in the American Community Survey. Per capita income is rounded to the nearest whole dollar.

Household income includes the income of the householder and all other individuals 15 years old and over in the household, whether or not they are related to the householder. Since many households consist of only one person, median household income is usually less than median family income. Although the household income statistics cover the 12 months preceding the interview, the characteristics of individuals and the composition of households refer to the date of interview. Thus, the income of the household does not include amounts received by individuals who were no longer residing in the household at the time of interview. Similarly, income amounts reported by individuals who did not reside in the household during all of the past 12 months but who were members of the household at the time of interview are included. However, the composition of most households was the same during those 12 months as it was at the time of interview.

Median income divides the income distribution into two equal parts, with half of all cases below the median income level and half of all cases above the median income level. For households, the median income is based on the distribution of the total number of households, including those with no income. Median income for households is computed on the basis of a standard distribution with a minimum value of less than $2,500 and a maximum value of $200,000 or more and is rounded to the nearest whole dollar. Median income figures are calculated using linear interpolation if the width of the interval containing the estimate is $2,500 or less. If the width of the interval containing the estimate is greater than $2,500, Pareto interpolation is used.

Income amounts have been adjusted for inflation to represent the final year of multi-year estimates, in this case 2011-2015

estimates. The constant-dollar figures are based on an annual average Consumer Price Index from the Bureau of Labor Statistics. Constant-dollar figures are estimates representing an effort to remove the effects of price changes from statistical series reported in dollar terms. However, the estimates do not reflect the price and cost-of-living differences that may exist between areas.

INCOME AND POVERTY, Items 58–61

Source: U.S. Census Bureau—Small Area Income and Poverty Estimates Program
http://www.census.gov/did/www/saipe/index.html

The annual income and poverty estimates by county are constructed from statistical models that relate income and poverty to indicators based on summary data from federal income tax returns, data about participation in the Food Stamp program, and the previous census. A regression model predicts the number of people in poverty using county-level observations from the current year's American Community Survey (ACS) and administrative records and census data as the predictors. The 2005 estimates were the first to use the ACS. Prior year models were based on the Annual Social and Economic Supplement (ASEC) of the Current Population Survey (CPS). The ACS is a much larger survey than the ASEC, permitting income and poverty estimates based on a single year for many counties, Because of the differences between the two surveys, caution should be used when comparing these estimates with those from earlier years.

The poverty status data were derived from data collected on the number of persons in a household, each person's relationship to the householder, and income data. The Social Security Administration (SSA) developed the original poverty definition in 1964, which federal interagency committees subsequently revised in 1969 and 1980. The Office of Management and Budget's (OMB) Directive 14 prescribes the SSA's definition as the official poverty measure for federal agencies to use in their statistical work. Poverty statistics presented in American Community Survey products adhere to the standards defined by OMB in Directive 14.

Poverty thresholds vary depending on three criteria: size of family, number of children, and, for one- and two-person families, age of householder. In determining the poverty status of families and unrelated individuals, the Census Bureau uses thresholds (income cutoffs) arranged in a two-dimensional matrix. The matrix consists of family size (from one person to nine or more persons), cross-classified by presence and number of family members under 18 years old (from no children present to eight or more children present). Unrelated individuals and two-person families are further differentiated by age of reference person (under 65 years old and 65 years old and over). To determine a person's poverty status, the person's total family income over the previous 12 months is compared with the poverty threshold appropriate for that person's family size and composition. If the total income of that person's family is less than the threshold appropriate for that family, then the person is considered poor or "below the poverty level," together with every member of his or her family. If a person is not living with anyone related by birth, marriage, or adoption, then the person's own income is compared with his or her poverty threshold. The total number of persons below the poverty level is the sum of persons in families

Poverty Thresholds for 2015 by Size of Family and Number of Related Children Under 18 Years

Size of family unit	Weighted average thresholds	Related children under 18 years								
		None	One	Two	Three	Four	Five	Six	Seven	Eight or more
One person (unrelated individual) ...	12,082									
Under 65 years	12,331	12,331								
65 years and over	11,367	11,367								
Two people	15,391									
Householder under 65 years	15,952	15,871	16,337							
Householder 65 years and over...	14,342	14,326	16,275							
Three people....................................	18,871	18,540	19,078	19,096						
Four people.....................................	24,257	24,447	24,847	24,036	24,120					
Five people	28,741	29,482	29,911	28,995	28,286	27,853				
Six people	32,542	33,909	34,044	33,342	32,670	31,670	31,078			
Seven people...................................	36,998	39,017	39,260	38,421	37,835	36,745	35,473	34,077		
Eight people....................................	41,029	43,637	44,023	43,230	42,536	41,551	40,300	38,999	38,668	
Nine people or more........................	49,177	52,493	52,747	52,046	51,457	50,490	49,159	47,956	47,658	45,822

Source: U.S. Census Bureau.

and the number of unrelated individuals with incomes below the poverty level over the previous 12 months.

PERSONAL INCOME AND EARNINGS, Items 62–83

Source: U.S. Bureau of Economic Analysis, Regional Economic Accounts
http://www.bea.gov/regional/index.htm#state

Total personal income is the current income received by residents of an area from all sources. It is measured before deductions of income and other personal taxes, but after deductions of personal contributions for Social Security, government retirement, and other social insurance programs. It consists of **wage and salary disbursements** (covering all employee earnings, including executive salaries, bonuses, commissions, payments-in-kind, incentive payments, and tips); various types of supplementary earnings, such as employers' contributions to pension funds (termed "other labor income" or "supplements to wages and salaries"); proprietors' income; rental income of persons; dividends; personal interest income; and government and business transfer payments.

Per capita personal income is based on the resident population estimated as of July 1 of the year shown.

Proprietors' income is the monetary income and income-in-kind of proprietorships and partnerships (including the independent professions) and the income of tax-exempt cooperatives.

Dividends are cash payments by corporations to stockholders who are U.S. residents. **Interest** is the monetary and imputed interest income of persons from all sources. **Rent** is the monetary income of persons from the rental of real property, except the income of persons primarily engaged in the real estate business; the imputed net rental income of owner-occupants of nonfarm dwellings; and the royalties received by persons.

Transfer payments are income for which services are not currently rendered. They consist of both government and business transfer payments. Government transfer payments include payments under the following programs: Federal Old-Age, Survivors, and Disability Insurance ("Social Security"); Medicare and medical vendor payments; unemployment insurance; railroad and government retirement; federal- and state-government-insured workers' compensation; veterans' benefits, including veterans' life insurance; food stamps; black lung payments; Supplemental Security Income; and Temporary Assistance for Needy Families. Government payments to nonprofit institutions, other than for work under research and development contracts, are also included. Business transfer payments consist primarily of liability payments for personal injury and of corporate gifts to nonprofit institutions.

Personal income differs in definition from money income (items 54–57). For example, personal income includes pension rights, employer-provided health insurance, food stamps, and Medicare. These are not included in the definition of money income.

Earnings cover wage and salary disbursements, other labor income, and proprietors' income.

The data for earnings obtained from the Bureau of Economic Analysis (BEA) are based on place of work. In computing personal income, BEA makes an "adjustment for residence" to earnings, based on commuting patterns; personal income is thus presented on a place-of-residence basis.

Farm earnings include the income of farm workers (wages and salaries and other labor income) and farm proprietors. Farm proprietors' income includes only the income of sole proprietorships and partnerships. Farm earnings estimates are benchmarked to data collected in the Census of Agriculture and the revised Department of Agriculture statistical totals of income and expense items.

Goods-related industries include mining, construction, and manufacturing. **Service-related** and other industries include private-sector earnings in agricultural services, forestry, and fisheries; transportation and public utilities; wholesale trade; retail trade; finance, insurance, and real estate; and services. Government earnings include all levels of government. Industries are categorized under the North American Industry Classification System (NAICS), and are not comparable to years prior to 2002.

SOCIAL SECURITY AND SUPPLEMENTAL SECURITY INCOME, Items 84–86

Source: U.S. Social Security Administration
http://www.ssa.gov/policy/docs/statcomps/oasdi_sc/
http://www.ssa.gov/policy/docs/statcomps/ssi_sc/

Social Security beneficiaries are persons receiving benefits under the Old-Age, Survivors, and Disability Insurance Program. These include retired or disabled workers covered by the program, their spouses and dependent children, and the surviving spouses and dependent children of deceased workers.

Supplemental Security Income (SSI) recipients are persons receiving SSI payments. The SSI program is a cash assistance program that provides monthly benefits to low-income aged, blind, or disabled persons.

Data are as of December of the year shown.

HOUSING, Items 87–96

Source: U.S. Census Bureau—Population Estimates Program
http://www.census.gov/popest/
Source: U.S. Census Bureau—American Community Survey, 2015 5-year Estimates
http://www.census.gov/acs/www/

Housing data for 2016 are from the Population Estimates Program. Housing unit characteristics for 2011-2015 are from the American Community Survey.

A **housing unit** is a house, apartment, mobile home or trailer, group of rooms, or single room occupied or, if vacant, intended for occupancy as separate living quarters. Separate living quarters are those in which the occupants do not live and eat with any other person in the structure and which have direct access from the outside of the building or through a common hall.

The occupants of a housing unit may be a single family, one person living alone, two or more families living together, or any other group of related or unrelated persons who share living quarters. Both occupied and vacant housing units are included in the housing inventory, although recreational vehicles, tents, caves, boats, railroad cars, and the like are included only if they are occupied as a person's usual place of residence.

A housing unit is classified as occupied if it is the usual place of residence of the person or group of persons living in it at the time of enumeration, or if the occupants are only temporarily absent (away on vacation). A household consists of all persons who occupy a housing unit as their usual place of residence. Vacant units for sale or rent include units rented or sold but not occupied and any other units held off the market.

Median value is the dollar amount that divides the distribution of specified owner-occupied housing units into two equal parts, with half of all units below the median value and half of all units above the median value. Value is defined as the respondent's estimate of what the house would sell for if it were for sale. Data are presented for single-family units on fewer than 10 acres of land that have no business or medical offices on the property.

Median rent divides the distribution of renter-occupied housing units into two equal parts. The rent concept used in this volume is gross rent, which includes the amount of cash rent a renter pays (contract rent) plus the estimated average cost of utilities and fuels, if these are paid by the renter. The rent is the amount of rent only for living quarters and excludes amounts paid for any business or other space occupied. Single-family houses on lots of 10 or more acres of land are also excluded.

Housing cost as a percentage of income is shown separately for owners with mortgages, owners without mortgages, and renters. Rent as a percentage of income is a computed ratio of gross rent and monthly household income (total household income divided by 12). Selected owner costs include utilities and fuels, mortgage payments, insurance, taxes, etc. In each case, the ratio of housing cost to income is computed separately for each housing unit. The housing cost ratios for half of all units are above the median shown in this book, and half are below the median shown in the book.

Substandard units are occupied units that are overcrowded or lack complete plumbing facilities. For the purposes of this item, "overcrowded" is defined as having 1.01 persons or more per room. Complete plumbing facilities include hot and cold piped water, a flush toilet, and a bathtub or shower. These facilities must be located inside the housing unit, but do not have to be in the same room.

CIVILIAN LABOR FORCE AND UNEMPLOYMENT, Items 97–100

Source: U.S. Bureau of Labor Statistics—Local Area Unemployment Statistics
http://www.bls.gov/lau/#tables

Data for the civilian labor force are the product of a federal-state cooperative program in which state employment security agencies prepare labor force and unemployment estimates under concepts, definitions, and technical procedures established by the Bureau of Labor Statistics (BLS). The civilian labor force consists of all civilians 16 years old and over who are either employed or unemployed.

Unemployment includes all persons who did not work during the survey week, made specific efforts to find a job during the previous four weeks, and were available for work during the survey week (except for temporary illness). Persons waiting to be called back to a job from which they had been laid off and those waiting to report to a new job within the next 30 days are included in unemployment figures.

Table B includes annual average data for the year shown. The Local Area Unemployment Statistics data are periodically updated to reflect revised inputs, reestimation, and controlling to new statewide totals.

CIVILIAN EMPLOYMENT, Items 101–103

Source: U.S. Census Bureau—American Community Survey, 2015 1-year Estimates
http://www.census.gov/acs/www/

Total employment includes all civilians 16 years old and over who were either (1) "at work"—those who did any work at all during the reference week as paid employees, worked in either their own business or profession, worked on their own farm, or worked 15 hours or more as unpaid workers in a family farm or business; or (2) "with a job, but not at work"—those who had a job but were not at work that week due to illness, weather, industrial dispute, vacation, or other personal reasons.

The **occupational categories** are based on the occupational classification system that was developed for the 2000 census and revised in 2002 and 2010. This system consists of 539 specific occupational categories for employed persons arranged into 23 major occupational groups. This classification was developed based on the *Standard Occupational Classification (SOC) Manual: 2000*, published by the Executive Office of the President, Office of Management and Budget.

Column 102 includes the Management, business, science, and arts occupations category while Column 103 combines the Natural resources, construction, and maintenance occupations and the Production, transportation, and material moving occupations.

PRIVATE NONFARM EMPLOYMENT AND EARNINGS, Items 104–112
Source: U.S. Census Bureau—County Business Patterns
http://www.census.gov/econ/cbp/index.html

Data for private nonfarm employment and earnings are compiled from the payroll information reported monthly in the Census Bureau publication *County Business Patterns*. The estimates are based on surveys conducted by the Census Bureau and administrative records from the Internal Revenue Service (IRS).

The following types of employment are excluded from the tables: government employment, self-employed persons, farm workers, and domestic service workers. Railroad employment jointly covered by Social Security and railroad retirement programs, employment on oceanborne vessels, and employment in foreign countries are also excluded.

Annual payroll is the combined amount of wages paid, tips reported, and other compensation (including salaries, vacation allowances, bonuses, commissions, sick-leave pay, and the value of payments-in-kind such as free meals and lodging) paid to employees before deductions for Social Security, income tax, insurance, union dues, etc. All forms of compensation are included, regardless of whether they are subject to income tax or the Federal Insurance Contributions Act tax, with the exception of annuities, third-party sick pay, and supplemental unemployment compensation benefits (even if income tax was withheld). For corporations, total annual payroll includes compensation paid to officers and executives; for unincorporated businesses, it excludes profit or other compensation of proprietors or partners.

AGRICULTURE, ITEMS 113–132
Source: U.S. Department of Agriculture, National Agricultural Statistics Service—2012 Census of Agriculture
http://agcensus.usda.gov/index.php

Data for the 2012 Census of Agriculture were collected in 2013, but pertain to the year 2012.

The Census Bureau took a census of agriculture every 10 years from 1840 to 1920; since 1925, this census has been taken roughly once every 5 years. The 1997 Census of Agriculture was the first one conducted by the National Agricultural Statistics Service of the U.S. Department of Agriculture. Over time, the definition of a farm has varied. For recent censuses (including the 2012 census), a farm has been defined as any place from which $1,000 or more of agricultural products were produced and sold or normally would have been sold during the census year. Dollar figures are expressed in current dollars and have not been adjusted for inflation or deflation.

The term **operator** refers to a person who operates a farm by either doing the work or making day-to-day decisions about such activities as planting, harvesting, feeding, marketing, etc. The operator may be the owner, a member of the owner's household, a salaried manager, a tenant, a renter, or a sharecropper. If a person rents land to others or has land worked on shares by others, he/she is considered the operator only of the land that is retained for his/her own operation. The census collected information on the total number of operators, the total number of women operators, and demographic information for up to three operators per farm.

The acreage designated as **land in farms** consists primarily of agricultural land used for crops, pasture, or grazing. It also includes woodland and wasteland not actually under cultivation or used for pasture or grazing, provided that this land was part of the farm operator's total operation. Land in farms is an operating-unit concept and includes all land owned and operated, as well as all land rented from others. Land used rent-free is classified as land rented from others. All land in Indian reservations used for growing crops or grazing livestock is classified as land in farms.

Irrigated land includes all land watered by any artificial or controlled means, such as sprinklers, flooding, furrows or ditches, sub-irrigation, and spreader dikes. Included are supplemental, partial, and preplant irrigation. Each acre was counted only once regardless of the number of times it was irrigated or harvested. Livestock lagoon waste water distributed by sprinkler or flood systems was also included.

Total cropland includes cropland harvested, cropland used only for pasture or grazing, cropland on which all crops failed or were abandoned, cropland in cultivated summer fallow, and cropland idle or used for cover crops or soil improvement but not harvested and not pastured or grazed.

Respondents were asked to report their estimate of the current market **value of land and buildings** owned, rented, or leased from others, and rented and leased to others. Market value refers to the respondent's estimate of what the land and buildings would sell for under current market conditions. If the value of land and buildings was not reported, it was estimated during processing by using the average value of land and buildings from similar farms in the same geographic area.

The **value of machinery and equipment** was estimated by the respondent as the current market value of all cars, trucks, tractors, combines, balers, irrigation equipment, etc., used on the farm. This value is an estimate of what the machinery and equipment would sell for in its present condition and not the replacement or depreciated value. Share interests are reported at full value at the farm where the equipment and machinery are usually kept. Only equipment that was physically located at the farm on December 31, 2012, is included.

Market value of agricultural products sold by farms represents the gross market value before taxes and the production expenses of all agricultural products sold or removed from the place in 2012, regardless of who received the payment. It is equivalent to total sales and it includes sales by the operator as well as the value of any share received by partners, landlords, contractors, and others associated with the operation. It includes value of direct sales and the value of commodities placed in the Commodity Credit Corporation (CCC) loan program. Market value of agricultural products sold does not include payments received for participation in other federal farm programs. Also, it does not include income from farm-related sources such as customwork and other agricultural services, or income from non-farm sources.

Government payments consist of direct payments as defined by the 2002 Farm Bill; payments from Conservation Reserve Program (CRP), Wetlands Reserve Program (WRP), Farmable Wetlands Program (FWP), and Conservation Reserve Enhancement Program (CREP); loan deficiency payments; disaster payments; other conservation programs; and all other federal farm programs under which payments were made directly to farm operators. Commodity Credit Corporation (CCC) proceeds, amount from State and local federal crop insurance payments were not included in this category.

WATER CONSUMPTION, Items 133–134
Source: U.S. Geological Survey, National Water-Use Information Program
http://water.usgs.gov/watuse/

Every five years, the U.S. Geological Survey compiles county-level water-use estimates. This volume includes the total fresh and saline withdrawals expressed as million gallons per day. Estimate of withdrawals of ground and surface water are given for the following categories of use: public water supplies, domestic, commercial, irrigation, livestock, industrial, mining, and thermo-electric power. The number of gallons withdrawn per person is based on the county population but the water is not necessarily used locally, providing an indicator of counties that serve as major water sources.

2012 ECONOMIC CENSUS: OVERVIEW, Items 135–166
Source: U.S. Census Bureau
http://www.census.gov/econ/census07/

The Economic Census provides a detailed portrait of the nation's economy, from the national to the local level, once every five years. The 2012 Economic Census covers nearly all of the U.S. economy in its basic collection of establishment statistics. The 1997 Economic Census was the first major data source to use the new North American Industry Classification System (NAICS); therefore, data from this census are not comparable to economic data from prior years, which were based on the Standard Industrial Classification (SIC) system.

NAICS, developed in cooperation with Canada and Mexico, classifies North America's economic activities at two-, three-, four-, and five-digit levels of detail; the U.S. version of NAICS further defines industries to a sixth digit. The Economic Census takes advantage of this hierarchy to publish data at these successive levels of detail: sector (two-digit), subsector (three-digit), industry group (four-digit), industry (five-digit), and U.S. industry (six-digit). Information in Table A is at the two-digit level, with a few three- and four-digit items. The data in Table B are at the two-digit level.

Several key statistics are tabulated for all industries in this volume, including number of establishments (or companies), number of employees, payroll, and certain measures of output (sales, receipts, revenue, value of shipments, or value of construction work done).

Number of establishments. An establishment is a single physical location at which business is conducted. It is not necessarily identical with a company or enterprise, which may consist of one establishment or more. Economic Census figures represent a summary of reports for individual establishments rather than companies. For cases in which a census report was received, separate information was obtained for each location where business was conducted. When administrative records of other federal agencies were used instead of a census report, no information was available on the number of locations operated. Each Economic Census establishment was tabulated according to the physical location at which the business was conducted. The count of establishments represents those in business at any time during 2012.

When two activities or more were carried on at a single location under a single ownership, all activities were generally grouped together as a single establishment. The entire establishment was classified on the basis of its major activity and all of its data were included in that classification. However, when distinct and separate economic activities (for which different industry classification codes were appropriate) were conducted at a single location under a single ownership, separate establishment reports for each of the different activities were obtained in the census.

Number of employees. Paid employees consist of the full-time and part-time employees, including salaried officers and executives of corporations. Included are employees on paid sick leave, paid holidays, and paid vacations; not included are proprietors and partners of unincorporated businesses. The definition of paid employees is the same as that used by the Internal Revenue Service (IRS) on form 941.

For some industries, the Economic Census gives codes representing the number of employees as a range of numbers (for example, ''100 to 249 employees'' or ''1,000 to 2,499'' employees). In this volume, those codes have been replaced by the standard suppression code ''D.''

Payroll. Payroll includes all forms of compensation, such as salaries, wages, commissions, dismissal pay, bonuses, vacation allowances, sick–leave pay, and employee contributions to qualified pension plans paid during the year to all employees. For corporations, payroll includes amounts paid to officers and executives; for unincorporated businesses, it does not include profit or other compensation of proprietors or partners. Payroll is reported before deductions for Social Security, income tax, insurance, union dues, etc. This definition of payroll is the same as that used by on IRS form 941.

Sales, shipments, receipts, revenue, or business done. This measure includes the total sales, shipments, receipts, revenue, or business done by establishments within the scope of the Economic Census. The definition of each of these items is specific to the economic sector measured.

WHOLESALE TRADE, Items 135–138
Source: U.S. Census Bureau—2012 Economic Census (See Overview of 2012 Economic Census prior to Item 135)

The Wholesale Trade sector (sector 42) comprises establishments engaged in wholesaling merchandise, generally without transformation, and rendering services incidental to the sale of merchandise. The wholesaling process is an intermediate step in the distribution of merchandise.

Wholesalers are organized to sell or arrange the purchase or sale of (1) goods for resale (i.e., goods sold to other wholesalers or retailers), (2) capital or durable nonconsumer goods, and (3) raw and intermediate materials and supplies used in production.

Wholesalers sell merchandise to other businesses and normally operate from a warehouse or office. These warehouses and offices are characterized by having little or no display of merchandise. In addition, neither the design nor the location of the premises is intended to solicit walk-in traffic. Wholesalers do not normally use advertising directed to the general public. In general, customers are initially reached via telephone, in-person marketing, or specialized advertising, which may include the internet and other electronic means. Follow-up orders are either vendor-initiated or client-initiated, are usually based on previous sales, and typically exhibit strong ties between sellers and buyers. In fact, transactions are often conducted between wholesalers and clients that have long–standing business relationships.

This sector is made up of two main types of wholesalers: those that sell goods on their own account and those that arrange sales and purchases for others for a commission or fee.

(1) Establishments that sell goods on their own account are known as wholesale merchants, distributors, jobbers, drop shippers, import/export merchants, and sales branches. These establishments typically maintain their own warehouse, where they receive and handle goods for their customers. Goods are generally sold without transformation, but may include integral functions, such as sorting, packaging, labeling, and other marketing services.

(2) Establishments arranging for the purchase or sale of goods owned by others or purchasing goods on a commission basis are known as agents and brokers, commission merchants, import/export agents and brokers, auction companies, and manufacturers' representatives. These establishments operate from offices and generally do not own or handle the goods they sell.

Some wholesale establishments may be connected with a single manufacturer and promote and sell that particular manufacturer's products to a wide range of other wholesalers or retailers. Other wholesalers may be connected to a retail chain or a limited number of retail chains and only provide the products needed by the particular retail operation(s). These wholesalers may obtain the products from a wide range of manufacturers. Still other wholesalers may not take title to the goods, but act instead as agents and brokers for a commission.

Although wholesaling normally denotes sales in large volumes, durable nonconsumer goods may be sold in single units. Sales of capital or durable nonconsumer goods used in the production of goods and services, such as farm machinery, medium- and heavy-duty trucks, and industrial machinery, are always included in Wholesale Trade.

The county table includes only **Merchant wholesalers, except manufacturers' sales branches and offices,** establishments primarily engaged in buying and selling merchandise on their own account. Included here are such types of establishments as wholesale distributors and jobbers, importers, exporters, own-brand importers/marketers, terminal and country grain elevators, and farm products assemblers.

RETAIL TRADE, Items 139–142
Source: U.S. Census Bureau—2012 Economic Census (See Overview of 2012 Economic Census prior to Item 135)

The Retail Trade sector (44–45) is made up of establishments engaged in retailing merchandise, generally without transformation, and rendering services incidental to the sale of merchandise.

The retailing process is the final step in the distribution of merchandise; retailers are therefore organized to sell merchandise in small quantities to the general public. This sector comprises two main types of retailers: store and nonstore retailers.

Store retailers operate fixed point-of-sale locations, located and designed to attract a high volume of walk-in customers. In general, retail stores have extensive displays of merchandise and use mass-media advertising to attract customers. They typically sell merchandise to the general public for personal or household consumption; some also serve business and institutional clients. These include establishments such as office supply stores, computer and software stores, building materials dealers, plumbing supply stores, and electrical supply stores. Catalog showrooms, gasoline service stations, automotive dealers, and mobile home dealers are treated as store retailers.

In addition to retailing merchandise, some types of store retailers are also engaged in the provision of after-sales services, such as repair and installation. For example, new automobile dealers, electronic and appliance stores, and musical instrument and supply stores often provide repair services. As a general rule, establishments engaged in retailing merchandise and providing after-sales services are classified in this sector.

Nonstore retailers, like store retailers, are organized to serve the general public, although their retailing methods differ. The establishments of this subsector reach customers and market merchandise with methods including the broadcasting of "infomercials," the broadcasting and publishing of direct-response advertising, the publishing of paper and electronic catalogs, door-to-door solicitation, in-home demonstration, selling from portable stalls (street vendors, except food), and distribution through vending machines. Establishments engaged in the direct sale (nonstore) of products, such as home heating oil dealers and home-delivery newspaper routes are included in this sector.

The buying of goods for resale is a characteristic of retail trade establishments that distinguishes them from establishments in the Agriculture, Manufacturing, and Construction sectors. For example, farms that sell their products at or from the point of production are classified in Agriculture instead of in Retail Trade. Similarly, establishments that both manufacture and sell their products to the general public are classified in Manufacturing instead of Retail Trade. However, establishments that engage in processing activities incidental to retailing are classified in Retail Trade.

REAL ESTATE AND RENTAL AND LEASING, Items 143–146

Source: U.S. Census Bureau—2012 Economic Census (See Overview of 2012 Economic Census prior to Item 135)

The Real Estate and Rental and Leasing sector (53) comprises establishments primarily engaged in renting, leasing, or otherwise allowing the use of tangible or intangible assets, and establishments providing related services. The major portion of this sector is made up of establishments that rent, lease, or otherwise allow the use of their own assets by others. The assets may be tangible, such as real estate and equipment, or intangible, such as patents and trademarks.

This sector also includes establishments primarily engaged in managing real estate for others, selling, renting, and/or buying real estate for others, and appraising real estate. These activities are closely related to this sector's main activity. In addition, a substantial proportion of property management is self-performed by lessors.

The main components of this sector are the real estate lessors industries; equipment lessors industries (including motor vehicles, computers, and consumer goods); and lessors of nonfinancial intangible assets (except copyrighted works).

PROFESSIONAL, SCIENTIFIC, AND TECHNICAL SERVICES, Items 147–150

Source: U.S. Census Bureau—2012 Economic Census (See Overview of 2012 Economic Census prior to Item 135)

The Professional, Scientific, and Technical Services sector (54) is made up of establishments that specialize in performing professional, scientific, and technical activities for others. These activities require a high degree of expertise and training. The establishments in this sector specialize in one or more areas and provide services to clients in a variety of industries (and, in some cases, to households). Activities performed include legal advice and representation; accounting, bookkeeping, and payroll services; architectural, engineering, and specialized design services; computer services; consulting services; research services; advertising services; photographic services; translation and interpretation services; veterinary services; and other professional, scientific, and technical services.

This sector excludes establishments primarily engaged in providing a range of day-to-day office administrative services, such as financial planning, billing and record keeping, personnel services, and physical distribution and logistics services. These establishments are classified in sector 56, Administrative and Support and Waste Management and Remediation Services.

MANUFACTURING, Items 151–154

Source: U.S. Census Bureau—2012 Economic Census (See Overview of 2012 Economic Census prior to Item 135)

The Manufacturing sector (31–33) is made up of establishments engaged in the mechanical, physical, or chemical transformation of materials, substances, or components into new products. The assembling of component parts of manufactured products is considered manufacturing, except in cases in which the activity is appropriately classified in the Construction sector. Establishments in the Manufacturing sector are often described as plants, factories, or mills, and characteristically use power-driven machines and materials-handling equipment. However, establishments that transform materials or substances into new products by hand or in the worker's home, and establishments engaged in selling to the general public products made on the same premises from which they are sold (such as bakeries, candy stores, and custom tailors) may also be included in this sector. Manufacturing establishments may process materials or contract with other establishments to process their materials for them. Both types of establishments are included in the Manufacturing sector.

The materials, substances, or components transformed by manufacturing establishments are raw materials that are products of agriculture, forestry, fishing, mining, or quarrying, or are products of other manufacturing establishments. The materials used may be purchased directly from producers, obtained through customary trade channels, or secured without recourse to the market by transferring the product from one establishment to another, under the same ownership. The new product of a manufacturing establishment may be finished (in the sense that it is ready for utilization or consumption), or it may be semifinished to become an input for an establishment engaged in further manufacturing. For example, the product of the alumina refinery is the input used in the primary production of aluminum; primary aluminum is the input used in an aluminum wire drawing plant; and aluminum wire is the input used in a fabricated wire product manufacturing establishment.

Data are included for counties with 500 or more employees in the Manufacturing sector.

ACCOMMODATION AND FOOD SERVICES, Items 155–158

Source: U.S. Census Bureau—2012 Economic Census (See Overview of 2012 Economic Census prior to Item 135)

The Accommodation and Food Services sector (72) consists of establishments that provide customers with lodging and/or meals, snacks, and beverages for immediate consumption. This sector includes both accommodation and food services establishments because the two activities are often combined at the same establishment.

Excluded from this sector are civic and social organizations, amusement and recreation parks, theaters, and other recreation or entertainment facilities providing food and beverage services.

HEALTH CARE AND SOCIAL ASSISTANCE, Items 159–162

Source: U.S. Census Bureau—2012 Economic Census (See Overview of 2012 Economic Census prior to Item 135)

The Health Care and Social Assistance sector (62) consists of establishments that provide health care and social assistance services to individuals. The sector includes both health care and social assistance because it is sometimes difficult to distinguish between the boundaries of these two activities. The industries in this sector are arranged on a continuum, starting with establishments that provide medical care exclusively, continuing with those that provide health care and social assistance, and finishing with those that provide only social assistance. The services provided by establishments in this sector are delivered by trained professionals. All industries in the sector share this commonality of process—namely, labor inputs of health practitioners or social workers with the requisite expertise. Many of the industries in the sector are defined based on the educational degree held by the practitioners included in the industry.

Excluded from this sector are aerobic classes, which can be found in subsector 713, Amusement, Gambling, and Recreation Industries; and nonmedical diet and weight-reducing centers, which can be found in subsector 812, Personal and Laundry Services. Although these can be viewed as health services, they are not typically delivered by health practitioners.

OTHER SERVICES, EXCEPT PUBLIC ADMINISTRATION Items 163–166

Source: U.S. Census Bureau—2012 Economic Census (See Overview of 2012 Economic Census prior to Item 135)

The Other Services, Except Public Administration sector (81) comprises establishments engaged in providing services not specifically categorized elsewhere in the classification system. Establishments in this sector are primarily engaged in activities such as equipment and machinery repairing, promoting or administering religious activities, grant making, and advocacy; this sector also includes establishments that provide dry-cleaning and laundry services, personal care services, death care services, pet care services, photofinishing services, temporary parking services, and dating services.

Private households that employ workers on or about the premises in activities primarily concerned with the operation of the household are included in this sector.

Excluded from this sector are establishments primarily engaged in retailing new equipment and performing repairs and general maintenance on equipment. These establishments are classified in sector 44–45, Retail Trade.

NONEMPLOYER BUSINESSES, Items 167 and 168

Source: U.S. Census Bureau—Nonemployer Statistics http://www.census.gov/econ/nonemployer/

Nonemployer Statistics is an annual series that provides subnational economic data for businesses that have no paid employees and are subject to federal income tax. The data consist of the number of businesses and total receipts by industry. Most nonemployers are self-employed individuals operating unincorporated businesses (known as sole proprietorships), which may or may not be the owner's principal source of income.

The majority of all business establishments in the United States are nonemployers, yet these firms average less than 4 percent of all sales and receipts nationally. Due to their small economic impact, these firms are excluded from most other Census Bureau business statistics (the primary exception being the Survey of Business Owners). The Nonemployers Statistics series is the primary resource available to study the scope and activities of nonemployers at a detailed geographic level.

BUILDING PERMITS, Items 169 and 170

Source: U.S. Census Bureau—Building Permits Survey http://www.census.gov/construction/bps/

These figures represent private residential construction authorized by building permits in approximately 20,000 places in the United States. Valuation represents the expected cost of construction as recorded on the building permit. This figure usually excludes the cost of on-site and off-site development and improvements, as well as the cost of heating, plumbing, electrical, and elevator installations.

National, state, and county totals were obtained by adding the data for permit-issuing places within each jurisdiction. Not all areas of the country require a building or zoning permit. The statistics only represent those areas that do require a permit. These totals thus are limited to permits issued in the 20,000 place universe covered by the Census Bureau and may not include all permits issued within a state. Current surveys indicate that construction is undertaken for all but a very small percentage of housing units authorized by building permits.

Residential building permits include buildings with any number of housing units. Housing units exclude group quarters (such as dormitories and rooming houses), transient accommodations (such as transient hotels, motels, and tourist courts), ''HUD-code'' manufactured (mobile) homes, moved or relocated units, and housing units created in an existing residential or nonresidential structure.

COUNTY AREA LOCAL GOVERNMENT EMPLOYMENT AND PAYROLL, Items 171-179

Source: U.S. Census Bureau—2012 Census of Governments
http://www.census.gov/govs/cog2012/

These items include data for all local governments (i.e., counties, municipalities, townships, special districts, and school districts) located within the county. The Census of Governments identifies the scope and nature of the nation's state and local government sector; provides authoritative benchmark figures of public finance and public employment; classifies local government organizations, powers, and activities; and measures federal, state, and local fiscal relationships. The Employment component was mailed March 2012 to collect information on the number of state and local government civilian employees and their payrolls.

Government employees include all persons paid for personal services performed, including persons paid from federally funded programs, paid elected or appointed officials, persons in a paid leave status, and persons paid on a per meeting, annual, semiannual, or quarterly basis. Unpaid officials, pensioners, persons whose work is performed on a fee basis, and contractors and their employees are excluded from the count of employees. **Full-Time Equivalent employees** is a computed statistic representing the number of full-time employees that could have been employed if the reported number of hours worked by part-time employees had been worked by full-time employees. This statistic is calculated separately for each function of a government by dividing the ''part-time hours paid'' by the standard number of hours for full-time employees in the particular government and then adding the resulting quotient to the number of full-time employees.

March payroll represents gross payroll amounts for the one-month period of March for full-time and part-time employees. Gross payroll includes all salaries, wages, fees, commissions, and overtime paid to employees **before** withholdings for taxes, insurance, etc. It also includes incentive payments that are paid at regular pay intervals. It excludes employer share of fringe benefits like retirement, Social Security, health and life insurance, lump sum payments, and so forth.

Administration and Judicial and Legal combines **Financial administration**, **Other government administration, and Judicial and Legal** activities. **Financial administration** includes activities concerned with tax assessment and collection, custody and disbursement of funds, debt management, administration of trust funds, budgeting, and other government-wide financial management activities. This function is not applied to school district or special district governments. **Other government administration** applies to the legislative and government-wide administrative agencies of governments. Included here are overall planning and zoning activities, and central personnel and administrative activities. This function is not applied to school district or special district governments. **Judicial and legal** includes all court and court related activities (except probation and parole activities that are included at the ''Correction'' function), court activities of sheriff's offices, prosecuting attorneys' and public defenders' offices, legal departments, and attorneys providing government-wide legal service.

Police and Corrections includes all activities concerned, with the enforcement of law and order, including coroner's offices, police training academies, investigation bureaus, and local jails, ''lockups,'' or other detention facilities not intended to serve as correctional facilities. **Corrections** includes activities pertaining to the confinement and correction of adults and minors convicted of criminal offenses. Pardon, probation, and parole activities are also included here.

Fire protection includes local government fire protection and prevention activities plus any ambulance, rescue, or other auxiliary services provided by a fire protection agency. Volunteer firefighters, if remunerated for their services on a ''per fire'' or some other basis, are included as part-time employees.

Highways and transportation includes activities associated with the maintenance and operation of streets, roads, sidewalks, bridges, tunnels, toll roads, and ferries. Snow and ice removal, street lighting, and highway and traffic engineering activities are also included here. Also included are the operation, maintenance, and construction of public mass transit systems, including subways, surface rails, and buses, and the provision, construction, operation, maintenance; support of public waterways, harbors, docks, wharves, and related marine terminal facilities; and activities associated with the operation and support of publicly operated airport facilities.

Health and Welfare includes **Health, Hospitals, and Public welfare.** **Health** includes administration of public health programs, community and visiting nurse services, immunization programs, drug abuse rehabilitation programs, health and food inspection activities, operation of outpatient clinics, and environmental pollution control activities. **Hospitals** includes only government operated medical care facilities that provide inpatient care. Employees and payrolls of private corporations that lease and operate government-owned hospital facilities are excluded.

Public Welfare includes the administration of various public assistance programs for the needy, veteran services, operation of nursing homes, indigent care institutions, and programs that provide payments for medical care, handicap transportation, and other services for the needy.

Natural resources and Utilities includes activities primarily concerned with the conservation and development of natural resources (soil, water, energy, minerals, etc.) and the regulation of industries that develop, utilize, or affect natural resources, as well as the operation and maintenance of **parks**, playgrounds, swimming pools, public beaches, auditoriums, public golf courses, museums, marinas, botanical gardens, and zoological parks. **Utilities, sewerage, and waste management** includes operation, maintenance, and construction of public water supply systems, including production, acquisition, and distribution of water to general public or to other public or private utilities, for residential, commercial, and industrial use; activities associated with the production or acquisition and distribution of electric power; provision, maintenance, and operation of sanitary and storm sewer systems and sewage disposal and treatment facilities; and refuse collection and disposal, operation of sanitary landfills, and street cleaning activities.

Education and libraries includes activities associated with the operation of public elementary and secondary schools and locally operated vocational-technical schools. Special education programs operated by elementary and secondary school systems are also included as are all ancillary services associated with the operation of schools, such as pupil transportation and food service. Also included are the establishment and provision of libraries for use by the general public and the technical support of privately operated libraries. This category includes classroom teachers, principals, supervisors of instruction, librarians, teacher aides, library aides, and guidance and psychological personnel as well as school superintendents and other administrative personnel, clerical and secretarial staffs, plant operation and maintenance personnel, health and recreation employees, transportation and food service personnel, and any student employees. Also included are any degree granting institutions that provide academic training above grade 12.

LOCAL GOVERNMENT FINANCES, Items 180–193

Source: U.S. Census Bureau—2012 Census of Governments
http://www.census.gov/govs/cog/

Data on local government finances are based on result of the 2012 Census of Governments. For each county area, the financial data comprise amounts for all local governments—not only the county government, but also any municipalities, townships, school districts, and special districts within the county. Statistics from governmental units located in two or more county areas are assigned to the county area containing the administrative office.

Revenue and expenditure items include all amounts of money received and paid out, respectively, by a government and its agencies (net of correcting transactions such as recoveries of refunds), with the exception of amounts for debt issuance and retirement and for loan and investment, agency, and private transactions.

Payments among the various funds and agencies of a particular government are excluded from revenue and expenditure items as representing internal transfers. Therefore, a government's contribution to a retirement fund that it administers is not counted as expenditure, nor is the receipt of this contribution by the retirement fund counted as revenue.

Total **general revenue** includes all revenue except utility, liquor stores, and insurance trust revenue. All tax revenue and intergovernmental revenue, even if designated for employee-retirement or local utility purpose, are classified as general revenue.

Intergovernmental revenue covers amounts received from the federal government as fiscal aid, reimbursements for performance of general government functions and specific services for the paying government, or in lieu of taxes. It excludes any amounts received from other governments from the sale of property, commodities, and utility services.

Taxes consist of compulsory contributions exacted by governments for public purposes. However, this category excludes employer and employee payments for retirement and social insurance purposes, which are classified as insurance trust revenue; it also excludes special assessments, which are classified as non-tax general revenue. Property taxes are taxes conditioned on ownership of property and assessed by its value. Sales and gross receipts taxes do not include dealer discounts, or "commissions" allowed to merchants for collection of taxes from consumers.

General sales taxes and selected taxes on sales of motor fuels, tobacco products, and other particular commodities and services are included.

General government expenditure includes capital outlay, a major portion of which is commonly financed by borrowing. Government revenue does not include receipts from borrowing. Among other things, this distorts the relationship between totals of revenue and expenditure figures that are presented and renders it useless as a direct measure of the degree of budgetary "balance" (as that term is generally applied).

Direct general expenditure comprises all expenditures of the local governments, excluding utility, liquor stores, insurance trust expenditures, and any intergovernmental payments.

Local government expenditure for **education** is mainly for the provision and general support of schools and other educational facilities and services, including those for educational institutions beyond high school. They cover such related services as student transportation; school lunch and other cafeteria operations; school health, recreation, and library services; and dormitories, dining halls, and bookstores operated by public institutions of higher education.

Health and hospital expenditure includes health research; clinics; nursing; immunization; other categorical, environmental, and general health services provided by health agencies; establishment and operation of hospital facilities; provision of hospital care; and support of other public and private hospitals.

Police protection expenditure includes police activities such as patrols, communications, custody of persons awaiting trial, and vehicular inspection.

Public welfare expenditure covers support of and assistance to needy persons; this aid is contingent upon the person's needs. Included are cash assistance paid directly to needy persons under categorical (Old Age Assistance, Temporary Assistance for Needy Families, Aid to the Blind, and Aid to the Disabled) and other welfare programs; vendor payments made directly to private purveyors for medical care, burials, and other commodities and services provided under welfare programs; welfare institutions; and any intergovernmental or other direct expenditure for welfare purposes. Pensions to former employees and other benefits not contingent on need are excluded.

Highway expenditure is for the provision and maintenance of highway facilities, including toll turnpikes, bridges, tunnels, and ferries, as well as regular roads, highways, and streets. Also included are expenditures for street lighting and for snow and ice removal. Not included are highway policing and traffic control, which are considered part of police protection.

Debt outstanding includes all long-term debt obligations of the government and its agencies (exclusive of utility debt) and all interest-bearing, short-term (repayable within one year) debt obligations remaining unpaid at the close of the fiscal year. It includes judgments, mortgages, and revenue bonds, as well as general obligation bonds, notes, and interest-bearing warrants. This category consists of non-interest-bearing, short-term obligations; inter-fund obligations; amounts owed in a trust or agency capacity; advances and contingent loans from other governments; and rights of individuals to benefit from government-administered employee-retirement funds.

GOVERNMENT EMPLOYMENT, Items 194–196

Source: U.S. Bureau of Economic Analysis—Regional Economic Accounts
http://www.bea.gov/regional/index.htm#state

Employment is measured as the average annual sum of full-time and part-time jobs. The estimates are on a place-of-work basis. State and local government employment includes person employed in all state and local government agencies and enterprises. Data for federal civilian employment include civilian employees of the federal government, including civilian employees of the Department of Defense. Military employment includes all persons on active duty status.

INDIVIDUAL INCOME TAX RETURNS, Items 197–199

Source: U.S. Internal Revenue Servicw, Statistics of Income Program
https://www.irs.gov/uac/soi-tax-stats-county-data-2014

The Revenue Act of 1916 mandated the annual publication of statistics related to ''the operations of the internal revenue laws'' as they affect individuals, all forms of businesses, estates. nonprofit organizations, trusts, and investments abroad and foreign investments in the United States. The Statistics of Income (SOI) division fulfills this function by collecting and processing data so that they become informative and by sharing information about how the tax system works with other government agencies and the general public. Publication types include traditional print sources, Internet files, CD-ROMs, and files sent via e-mail. SOI has an information office, Statistical Information Services, to facilitate the dissemination of SOI data.

SOI bases its county data on administrative records of individual income tax returns (Forms 1040) from the Internal Revenue Service (IRS) Individual Master File (IMF) system. Included in these data are returns filed during the 12-month period, January 1, 2015 to December 31, 2015. While the bulk of returns filed during the 12-month period are primarily for Tax Year 2014, the IRS received a limited number of returns for tax years before 2014 and these have been included within the county data.

Data do not represent the full U.S. population because many individuals are not required to file an individual income tax return. The address shown on the tax return may differ from the taxpayer's actual residence. State and county codes were based on the ZIP code shown on the return. Excluded were tax returns filed without a ZIP code and returns filed with a ZIP code that did not match the State code shown on the return.

SOI did not attempt to correct any ZIP codes on the returns; however, it did take the following precautions to avoid disclosing information about specific taxpayers: Excluded from the data are items with less than 20 returns within a county. Also excluded are tax returns representing a specified percentage of the total of any particular cell. For example, if one return represented 75 percent of the value of a given cell, the return was suppressed from the county detail. The actual threshold percentage used cannot be released.

Column 197 show the number of returns. Column 198 shows the mean Adjusted Gross Income for the county and column 199 shows the mean income tax (line 56 on Form 1040). for the county.

TABLE C—METROPOLITAN AREAS

Table C presents 199 items for the 382 metropolitan statistical areas (MSAs) and 31 metropolitan divisions in the United States. The metropolitan areas are presented in alphabetical order, and the metropolitan divisions are presented in alphabetical order within the appropriate metropolitan area. For some data items, the metropolitan area data have been aggregated from county data sources.

LAND AREA, Items 1 and 4

Source: U.S. Census Bureau—2016 U.S. Gazetteer Files,
http://www.census.gov/geo/maps-data/data/gazetteer2016.html

Land area measurements are shown to the nearest square mile. Land area is an area measurement providing the size, in square miles, of the land portions of each county.

POPULATION, Items 2–4

Source: U.S. Census Bureau—Population Estimates
https://www.census.gov/programs-surveys/popest.html

The population data are Census Bureau estimates of the resident population as of July 1 of the year shown. The ranks are shown for metropolitan statistical areas, but exclude metropolitan divisions.

POPULATION AND POPULATION CHARACTERISTICS, Items 5–19

Source: U.S. Census Bureau—Population Estimates
http://www.census.gov/popest/estimates.html

The concept of race, as used by the Census Bureau, reflects self-identification by persons according to the race or races with which they most closely identify. These categories are sociopolitical constructs and should not be interpreted as being scientific or anthropological in nature. Furthermore, race categories include both racial and national origin groups.

Beginning with the 2000 census, respondents were offered the option of selecting one or more races. This option was not available in prior censuses; thus, comparisons between censuses should be made with caution. In Table C, Columns 5 through 8 refer to individuals who identified with each racial category, either alone or in combination with other races. The estimates exclude persons of Hispanic or Latino origin from all race groups. Because respondents could include as many categories as they wished, and because the columns refer to the percentage of the population, the total will often exceed 100 percent.

The **White** population is defined as persons who indicated their race as White, as well as persons who did not classify themselves in one of the specific race categories listed on the questionnaire but entered a nationality such as Irish, German, Italian, Lebanese, Near Easterner, Arab, or Polish.

The **Black** population includes persons who indicated their race as "Black, African Am., or Negro," as well as persons who did not classify themselves in one of the specific race categories but reported entries such as African American, Afro American, Kenyan, Nigerian, or Haitian.

The **American Indian or Alaska Native** population includes persons who indicated their race as American Indian or Alaska Native, as well as persons who did not classify themselves in one of the specific race categories but reported entries such as Canadian Indian, French-American Indian, Spanish-American Indian, Eskimo, Aleut, Alaska Indian, or any of the American Indian or Alaska Native tribes.

The **Asian and Pacific Islander** population combines two census groupings: **Asian** and **Native Hawaiian or Other Pacific Islander**. The **Asian** population includes persons who indicated their race as Asian Indian, Chinese, Filipino, Japanese, Korean, Vietnamese, or "Other Asian," as well as persons who provided write-in entries of such groups as Cambodian, Laotian, Hmong, Pakistani, or Taiwanese. The **Native Hawaiian or Other Pacific Islander** population includes persons who indicated their race as "Native Hawaiian," "Guamanian or Chamorro," "Samoan," or "Other Pacific Islander," as well as persons who reported entries such as Part Hawaiian, American Samoan, Fijian, Melanesian, or Tahitian.

The sum of the four individual race alone or in combination categories in this book will often add to more than the total population because people who reported more than one race were tallied in each race category. In this book, the Asian group has been combined with the Native Hawaiian and Other Pacific Islander group, causing double-counting of persons who identify with both groups. This is especially pronounced in Hawaii.

The **Hispanic population** is based on a complete-count question that asked respondents "Is this person Spanish/Hispanic/Latino?" Persons marking any one of the four Hispanic categories (i.e., Mexican, Puerto Rican, Cuban, or other Spanish) are collectively referred to as Hispanic.

In the 2000 census, the Hispanic origin question was placed before the race question and specific instructions indicated that both questions should be answered. These changes were designed to improve accuracy and may affect comparability with 1990 data.

Age is defined as age at last birthday (number of completed years since birth), as of April 1 of the census year. The 2000 census also asked for the specific date of birth of the respondent, and 2000 census procedures used the birth date for deriving age data. For this reason, it is likely that the 2000 data have fewer problems than data from prior censuses, such as the tendency of respondents to round ages or to report their ages on the date the questionnaire was filled out rather than on April 1.

The **female** population is shown as a percentage of total population.

POPULATION AND COMPONENTS OF CHANGE, Items 20–26
Source: U.S. Census Bureau—Decennial Censuses and Population Estimates
http://www.census.gov/main/www/cen2000.html
https://www.census.gov/programs-surveys/popest.html
http://www.census.gov/2010census/data/

The population data for 2000 and 2010 are from the decennial censuses and represent the resident population as of April 1 of those years. The components of change are based on Census Bureau estimates of the resident population as of July 1 of 2016. The change in population between 2010 and 2016 is made up of (a) natural increase—births minus deaths, and (b) net migration—the difference between the number of persons moving into a particular area and the number of persons moving out of the area. Net migration is composed of internal and international migration.

Because the 2016 population estimates are based on a model that begins with a national population estimate, the county and msa components of change do not always exactly add up to the difference between the 2010 census population and the 2016 estimates.

HOUSEHOLDS, Items 27–31
Source: U.S. Census Bureau—American Community Survey, 2015 1-year Estimates
http://www.census.gov/acs/www/

A **household** includes all of the persons who occupy a housing unit. (Persons not living in households are classified as living in group quarters.) A housing unit is a house, an apartment, a mobile home, a group of rooms, or a single room occupied (or, if vacant, intended for occupancy) as separate living quarters. Separate living quarters are those in which the occupants live separately from any other persons in the building and have direct access from the outside of the building or through a common hall. The occupants may be a single family, one person living alone, two or more families living together, or any other group of related or unrelated persons who share living quarters. The number of households is the same as the number of year-round occupied housing units.

A **family** includes a householder and one or more other persons living in the same household who are related to the householder by birth, marriage, or adoption. All persons in a household who are related to the householder are regarded as members of his or her family. A **family household** may contain persons not related to the householder; thus, family households may include more members than families do. A household can contain only one family for the purposes of census tabulations. Not all households contain families, as a household may comprise a group of unrelated persons or of one person living alone. Families are classified by type as either a "husband-wife family" or "other family," according to the presence or absence of a spouse.

The measure of **persons per household** is obtained by dividing the number of persons in households by the number of households or householders. One person in each household is designated as the householder. In most cases, this is the person (or one of the persons) in whose name the house is owned, being bought, or rented. If there is no such person in the household, any adult household member 15 years old and over can be designated as the householder.

The category **female family householder** includes only female-headed family households with no spouse present.

GROUP QUARTERS, Item 32
Source: U.S. Census Bureau—Population Estimates
https://www.census.gov/programs-surveys/popest.html

The Census Bureau classifies all persons not living in households as living in group quarters; this category includes both the institutional and noninstitutional populations. The institutionalized population includes persons under formally authorized, supervised care or custody in institutions, such as correctional institutions, nursing homes, mental (psychiatric) hospitals, and juvenile institutions. The noninstitutionalized population includes persons who live in group quarters other than institutions, such as college dormitories, military quarters, and group homes. This volume includes the total number of persons in group quarters.

DAYTIME POPULATION, Items 33 and 34
Source: U.S. Census Bureau—American Community Survey, 2015 1-year Estimates
http://www.census.gov/acs/www/

Daytime population refers to the number of persons who are present in an area or place during normal business hours, including workers. This can be contrasted with the "resident" population, which is present during the evening and nighttime hours. The daytime population estimate is calculated by adding the total resident population and the total workers working in the area/place, and then subtracting the total workers living in the area/place from that result. Information on the expansion or contraction experienced by different communities between their nighttime and daytime populations is important for many planning purposes, especially those concerning transportation, disaster, and relief operations.

The employment/residence ratio is a measure of the total number of workers working in an area or place, relative to the total number of workers living in the area or place. It is often used as a rough indication of the jobs-workers balance in an area/place, although it does not take into account whether the resident workers possess the skills needed for the jobs available in their particular area/place. The employment/residence ratio is calculated by dividing the number of total workers working in an area/place by the number of total workers residing in the area/place.

BIRTHS AND DEATHS, Items 35–38
Source: U.S. Census Bureau—Population Estimates
https://www.census.gov/programs-surveys/popest.html

The numbers of births and deaths are from the Census Bureau's Population Estimates Program. They represent the total number of live births and deaths occurring to residents of an area as estimated using reports from the National Center for Health Statistics (NCHS) and the Federal-State Cooperative for Population Estimates (FSCPE). The rates measure births and deaths during the specified time period as a proportion of an area's population. Rates are expressed per 1,000 population estimated as of July 1. These numbers and rates do not represent the calendar year, but rather the year-long period ending on July 1.

PERSONS UNDER 65 WITH NO HEALTH INSURANCE, Items 39 and 40
Source: U.S. Census Bureau—Small Area Health Insurance Estimates
http://www.census.gov/did/www/sahie/index.html

The Small Area Health Insurance Estimates (SAHIE) program develops model-based estimates of health insurance coverage for counties and states. This developmental program builds on the work of the Small Area Income and Poverty Estimates (SAIPE) program. The SAHIE program models health insurance coverage by combining survey data with population estimates and administrative records. These estimates combine data from administrative records, postcensal population estimates, and the decennial census with direct estimates from the American Community Survey to provide consistent and reliable single-year estimates. These model-based single-year estimates are more reflective of current conditions than multi-year survey estimates. The metropolitan area estimates have been aggregated from the county estimates.

MEDICARE ENROLLMENT, Items 41–43
Source: U.S. Department of Health and Human Services, Centers for Medicare and Medicaid Services
https://www.cms.gov/Research-Statistics-Data-and-Systems/Statistics-Trends-and-Reports/Medicare-Geographic-Variation/GV_PUF.html

The Centers for Medicare and Medicaid Services (CMS) administers Medicare, which provides health insurance to persons 65 years old and over, persons with permanent kidney failure, and certain persons with disabilities. Original Medicare has two parts: Hospital Insurance and Supplemental Medical Insurance. In recent years, Medicare has been expanded to include two new programs: Medicare Advantage plans and prescription drug coverage. Medicare Advantage Plans are health plan options that are approved by Medicare but run by private companies. Medicare prescription drug plans can be part of Medicare Advantage plans or stand-alone drug plans.

Persons who are eligible for Medicare can enroll in Part A (Hospital Insurance) at no charge, and can choose to pay a monthly premium to enroll in Part B. Most eligible persons are enrolled in Part A, and more than 90 percent of enrollees in Part A are also enrolled in Part B (Supplemental Medical Insurance). This table includes persons who were enrolled in both Part A and Part B during 2014.

Part B beneficiaries can choose to enroll in **Original Medicare**, a fee-for-service plan administered by the Centers for Medicare and Medicaid Services, or in a **Medicare Advantage** plan.

Medicare Advantage plans include private fee-for-service plans, preferred provider organizations, health maintenance organizations, medical savings account plans, demonstration plans, and programs for all-inclusive care for the elderly.

CRIME, Items 44–47

Source: U.S. Federal Bureau of Investigation—
Uniform Crime Reports
http://www.fbi.gov/ucr/ucr.htm

Crime data are as reported to the Federal Bureau of Investigation (FBI) by law enforcement agencies and have not been adjusted for underreporting. This may affect comparability between geographic areas or over time.

Through the voluntary contribution of crime statistics by law enforcement agencies across the United States, the Uniform Crime Reporting (UCR) Program provides periodic assessments of crime in the nation as measured by offenses that have come to the attention of the law enforcement community. The Committee on Uniform Crime Records of the International Association of Chiefs of Police initiated this voluntary national data collection effort in 1930. The UCR Program contributors compile and submit their crime data either directly to the FBI or through state-level UCR Programs.

Seven offenses, because of their severity, frequency of occurrence, and likelihood of being reported to police, were initially selected to serve as an index for evaluating fluctuations in the volume of crime. These serious crimes were murder and nonnegligent manslaughter, forcible rape, robbery, aggravated assault, burglary, larceny-theft, and motor vehicle theft. By congressional mandate, arson was added as the eighth index offense in 1979. The totals shown in this volume do not include arson.

In 2004, the FBI discontinued the use of the Crime Index in the UCR Program and its publications, stating that the Crime Index was driven upward by the offense with the highest number of cases (in this case, larceny-theft), creating a bias against jurisdictions with a high number of larceny-thefts but a low number of other serious crimes, such as murder and forcible rape. The FBI is currently publishing a violent crime total and property crime total until a more viable index is developed. This book includes the crime total, as well as violent crime and property crime rates.

In 2013, the FBI adopted a new definition of rape. Rape is now defined as, "Penetration, no matter how slight, of the vagina or anus with any body part or object, or oral penetration by a sex organ of another person, without the consent of the victim." The new definition updated the 80-year-old historical definition of rape which was "carnal knowledge of a female forcibly and against her will." Effectively, the revised definition expands rape to include both male and female victims and offenders, and reflects the various forms of sexual penetration understood to be rape, especially nonconsenting acts of sodomy, and sexual assaults with objects.

Violent crimes include four categories of offenses: (1) Murder and nonnegligent manslaughter, as defined in the UCR Program, is the willful (nonnegligent) killing of one human being by another. This offense excludes deaths caused by negligence, suicide, or accident; justifiable homicides; and attempts to murder or assaults to murder. (2) Rape is the penetration, no matter how slight, of the vagina or anus with any body part or object, or oral penetration by a sex organ of another person, without the consent of the victim. Assaults or attempts to commit rape by force or threat of force are also included; however, statutory rape (without force) and other sex offenses are excluded. (3) Robbery is the

taking or attempting to take anything of value from the care, custody, or control of a person or persons by force or threat of force or violence and/or by putting the victim in fear. (4) Aggravated assault is an unlawful attack by one person upon another for the purpose of inflicting severe or aggravated bodily injury. This type of assault is usually accompanied by the use of a weapon or by other means likely to produce death or great bodily harm. Attempts are included, since injury does not necessarily have to result when a gun, knife, or other weapon is used, as these incidents could and probably would result in a serious personal injury if the crime were successfully completed.

Property crimes include three categories: (1) Burglary, or breaking and entering, is the unlawful entry of a structure to commit a felony or theft, even though no force was used to gain entrance. (2) Larceny-theft is the unauthorized taking of the personal property of another, without the use of force. (3) Motor vehicle theft is the unauthorized taking of any motor vehicle.

Rates are based on population estimates provided by the FBI. The county totals published in this volume were obtained by aggregating individual reporting units within each county and MSA. If the population total for the units aggregated was less than 75 percent of the county's population (as estimated by the Census Bureau), the total was not considered representative of the county as a whole and was not published. State and U.S. totals include FBI estimates for those areas. State and U.S. totals in this table are the adjusted totals as published in the FBI's *Crime in the United States*.

EDUCATION—SCHOOL ENROLLMENT AND EDUCATIONAL ATTAINMENT, Items 48–51

Source: U.S. Census Bureau—American Community
Survey, 2015 1-year Estimates
http://www.census.gov/acs/www/

Data on **school enrollment** and educational attainment were derived from a sample of the population. Persons were classified as enrolled in school if they reported attending a "regular" public or private school (or college) during the three months prior to the survey. The instructions were to "include only nursery school, kindergarten, elementary school, and schooling which would lead to a high school diploma or a college degree" as regular school. The Census Bureau defines a public school as "any school or college controlled and supported by a local, county, state, or federal government." Schools primarily supported and controlled by religious organizations or other private groups are defined as private schools.

Data on **educational attainment** are tabulated for the population 25 years old and over. The data were derived from a question that asked respondents for the highest level of school completed or the highest degree received. Persons who had passed a high school equivalency examination were considered high school graduates. Schooling received in foreign schools was to be reported as the equivalent grade or years in the regular American school system.

Vocational and technical training, such as barber school training; business, trade, technical, and vocational schools; or other training for a specific trade are specifically excluded.

High school graduate or less. This category includes persons whose highest degree was a high school diploma or its equivalent,

F-38   Table C—Metropolitan Areas

Appendix F

and those who reported any level lower than a high school diploma.

Bachelor's degree or more. This category includes persons who have received bachelor's degrees, master's degrees, professional school degrees (such as law school or medical school degrees), and doctoral degrees.

LOCAL GOVERNMENT EDUCATION EXPENDITURES, Items 52 and 53

U.S. Department of Education, National Center for Education Statistics, Common Core of Data (CCD), "National Public Education Financial Survey (State Fiscal)," 2013-14 (FY 2014) v.1a; "School District Finance Survey (F-33)," 2013-14 (FY 2014) v.1a

Expenditures are for elementary and secondary Education which includes prekindergarten through twelfth grade regular, special, and vocational education, as well as cocurricular, community service, and adult education programs provided by a public school system. The financial activities of these systems for all instruction, support service, and noninstructional activities are included.

Current Spending comprises current operation expenditure, payments made by the state government on behalf of school systems, and transfers made by school systems into their own retirement funds. Current operation expenditures include direct expenditure for salaries, employee benefits, purchased professional and technical services, purchased property and other services, and supplies. It includes gross school system expenditure for instruction, support services, and noninstructional functions. It excludes expenditure for debt service, capital outlay, and reimbursement to other governments (including other school systems).

Current expenditure per student is current expenditure divided by the number of students enrolled. The number of students enrolled is based on an annual "membership" count of students on or about October 1.

INCOME AND POVERTY Items 54–61

Source: U.S. Census Bureau—American Community Survey, 2015 1-year Estimates
http://www.census.gov/acs/www/

The data on income were derived from responses of a sample of persons 15 years old and over. **Total money income** is the sum of the amounts reported separately for wage or salary income; net self-employment income; interest, dividends, or net rental or royalty income or income from estates and trusts; Social Security or railroad retirement income; Supplemental Security Income (SSI); public assistance or welfare payments; retirement, survivor, or disability pensions; and all other income. Receipts from the following sources are not included as income: capital gains; money received from the sale of property (unless the recipient was engaged in the business of selling such property); the value of income "in kind" from food stamps, public housing subsidies, medical care, employer contributions for individuals, etc.; withdrawal of bank deposits; money borrowed; tax refunds; exchange of money between relatives living in the same household; and gifts, lump-sum inheritances, insurance payments, and other types of lump-sum receipts.

Money income differs in definition from personal income (item 62). For example, money income does not include the pension rights, employer provided health insurance, food stamps, or Medicare payments that are included in personal income.

Per capita income is the mean income computed for every man, woman, and child in a particular group. It is derived by dividing the aggregate income of a particular group by the resident population in that group in the survey year. Per capita income is rounded to the nearest whole dollar.

Household income includes the income of the householder and all other individuals 15 years old and over in the household, whether or not they are related to the householder. Since many households consist of only one person, median household income is usually less than median family income. Although the household income statistics cover the year preceding the survey, the characteristics of individuals and the composition of households refer to the date of the survey. Thus, the income of the household does not include amounts received by individuals who were members of the household during the year if these individuals were no longer residing in the household at the time of the survey. Similarly, income amounts reported by individuals who did not reside in the household during the year but who were members of the household at the time of the survey are included. However, the composition of most households was the same during the year as it was at the time of the survey.

Mean household income is the amount obtained by dividing the aggregate income of all households by the total number of households. The mean is based on the distribution of the total number of households including those with no income. Mean income is rounded to the nearest whole dollar. Care should be exercised in using and interpreting mean income values for small subgroups of the population. Because the mean is influenced strongly by extreme values in the distribution, it is especially susceptible to the effects of sampling variability, misreporting, and processing errors. The median, which is not affected by extreme values, is, therefore, a better measure than the mean when the population base is small.

Median income divides the income distribution into two equal parts, with half of all cases below the median income level and half of all cases above the median income level. For households, the median income is based on the distribution of the total number of households, including those with no income. Median income for households is computed on the basis of a standard distribution with a minimum value of less than $2,500 and a maximum value of $200,000 or more and is rounded to the nearest whole dollar. Median income figures are calculated using linear interpolation if the width of the interval containing the estimate is $2,500 or less. If the width of the interval containing the estimate is greater than $2,500, Pareto interpolation is used.

Income components were reported for the 12 months preceding the interview month. Monthly Consumer Price Indices (CPI) factors were used to inflation-adjust these components to a reference calendar year (January through December). For example, a household interviewed in March 2012 reports their income for March 2011 through February 2012. Their income is adjusted to the 2012 reference calendar year by multiplying their reported income by 2012 average annual CPI (January-December 2008) and then

Poverty Thresholds for 2015 by Size of Family and Number of Related Children Under 18 Years

Size of family unit	Weighted average thresholds	Related children under 18 years								
		None	One	Two	Three	Four	Five	Six	Seven	Eight or more
One person (unrelated individual) ...	12,082									
Under 65 years	12,331	12,331								
65 years and over	11,367	11,367								
Two people	15,391									
Householder under 65 years	15,952	15,871	16,337							
Householder 65 years and over...	14,342	14,326	16,275							
Three people................................	18,871	18,540	19,078	19,096						
Four people..................................	24,257	24,447	24,847	24,036	24,120					
Five people	28,741	29,482	29,911	28,995	28,286	27,853				
Six people	32,542	33,909	34,044	33,342	32,670	31,670	31,078			
Seven people................................	36,998	39,017	39,260	38,421	37,835	36,745	35,473	34,077		
Eight people.................................	41,029	43,637	44,023	43,230	42,536	41,551	40,300	38,999	38,668	
Nine people or more.......................	49,177	52,493	52,747	52,046	51,457	50,490	49,159	47,956	47,658	45,822

Source: U.S. Census Bureau.

dividing by the average CPI for March 2011–February 2012. However, the estimates do not reflect the price and cost-of-living differences that may exist between areas.

The **poverty status** data were derived from data collected on the number of persons in a household, each person's relationship to the householder, and income data. The Social Security Administration (SSA) developed the original poverty definition in 1964, which federal interagency committees subsequently revised in 1969 and 1980. The Office of Management and Budget's (OMB) *Directive 14* prescribes the SSA's definition as the official poverty measure for federal agencies to use in their statistical work. Poverty statistics presented in American Community Survey products adhere to the standards defined by OMB in *Directive 14*.

Poverty thresholds vary depending on three criteria: size of family, number of children, and, for one- and two-person families, age of householder. In determining the poverty status of families and unrelated individuals, the Census Bureau uses thresholds (income cutoffs) arranged in a two-dimensional matrix. The matrix consists of family size (from one person to nine or more persons), cross-classified by presence and number of family members under 18 years old (from no children present to eight or more children present). Unrelated individuals and two-person families are further differentiated by age of reference person (under 65 years old and 65 years old and over). To determine a person's poverty status, the person's total family income over the previous 12 months is compared with the poverty threshold appropriate for that person's family size and composition. If the total income of that person's family is less than the threshold appropriate for that family, then the person is considered poor or "below the poverty level," together with every member of his or her family. If a person is not living with anyone related by birth, marriage, or adoption, then the person's own income is compared with his or her poverty threshold. The total number of persons below the poverty level is the sum of persons in families and the number of unrelated individuals with incomes below the poverty level over the previous 12 months.

PERSONAL INCOME AND EARNINGS, Items 62–83

Source: U.S. Bureau of Economic Analysis, Regional Economic Accounts
http://www.bea.gov/regional/index.htm#state

Total personal income is the current income received by residents of an area from all sources. It is measured before deductions of income and other personal taxes, but after deductions of personal contributions for Social Security, government retirement, and other social insurance programs. It consists of **wage and salary disbursements** (covering all employee earnings, including executive salaries, bonuses, commissions, payments-in-kind, incentive payments, and tips); various types of supplementary earnings, such as employers' contributions to pension funds (termed "other labor income" or "supplements to wages and salaries"); proprietors' income; rental income of persons; dividends; personal interest income; and government and business transfer payments.

Per capita personal income is based on the resident population estimated as of July 1 of the year shown.

Proprietors' income is the monetary income and income-in-kind of proprietorships and partnerships (including the independent professions) and the income of tax-exempt cooperatives. **Dividends** are cash payments by corporations to stockholders who are U.S. residents. **Interest** is the monetary and imputed interest income of persons from all sources. **Rent** is the monetary income of persons from the rental of real property, except the income of persons primarily engaged in the real estate business; the imputed net rental income of owner-occupants of nonfarm dwellings; and the royalties received by persons.

Transfer payments are income for which services are not currently rendered. They consist of both government and business transfer payments. Government transfer payments include payments under the following programs: Federal Old-Age, Survivors, and Disability Insurance ("Social Security"); Medicare and medical vendor payments; unemployment insurance; railroad and government retirement; federal- and state-government-insured workers' compensation; veterans' benefits, including veterans' life insurance; food stamps; black lung payments; Supplemental Security Income; and Temporary Assistance for Needy Families. Government payments to nonprofit institutions, other than for work under research and development contracts, are also included. Business transfer payments consist primarily of liability payments for personal injury and of corporate gifts to nonprofit institutions.

Personal income differs in definition from money income (items 54–57). For example, personal income includes pension rights, employer-provided health insurance, food stamps, and Medicare. These are not included in the definition of money income.

Earnings cover wage and salary disbursements, other labor income, and proprietors' income.

The data for earnings obtained from the Bureau of Economic Analysis (BEA) are based on place of work. In computing personal income, BEA makes an "adjustment for residence" to earnings, based on commuting patterns; personal income is thus presented on a place-of-residence basis.

Farm earnings include the income of farm workers (wages and salaries and other labor income) and farm proprietors. Farm proprietors' income includes only the income of sole proprietorships and partnerships. Farm earnings estimates are benchmarked to data collected in the Census of Agriculture and the revised Department of Agriculture statistical totals of income and expense items.

Goods-related industries include mining, construction, and manufacturing. **Service-related** and other industries include private-sector earnings in agricultural services, forestry, and fisheries; transportation and public utilities; wholesale trade; retail trade; finance, insurance, and real estate; and services. Government earnings include all levels of government. Industries are categorized under the North American Industry Classification System (NAICS), and are not comparable to years prior to 2002.

SOCIAL SECURITY AND SUPPLEMENTAL SECURITY INCOME, Items 84–86
Source: U.S. Social Security Administration
http://www.ssa.gov/policy/docs/statcomps/oasdi_sc/
http://www.ssa.gov/policy/docs/statcomps/ssi_sc/

Social Security beneficiaries are persons receiving benefits under the Old-Age, Survivors, and Disability Insurance Program. These include retired or disabled workers covered by the program, their spouses and dependent children, and the surviving spouses and dependent children of deceased workers.

Supplemental Security Income (SSI) recipients are persons receiving SSI payments. The SSI program is a cash assistance program that provides monthly benefits to low-income aged, blind, or disabled persons.

Data are as of December of the year shown.

HOUSING, Items 87–96
Source: U.S. Census Bureau—Population Estimates Program
https://www.census.gov/programs-surveys/popest.html
Source: U.S. Census Bureau—American Community Survey. 2015 1-year Estimates
http://www.census.gov/acs/www/

Housing data for 2016 are from the Population Estimates Program. Housing unit characteristics for 2015 are from the American Community Survey.

A **housing unit** is a house, apartment, mobile home or trailer, group of rooms, or single room occupied or, if vacant, intended for occupancy as separate living quarters. Separate living quarters are those in which the occupants do not live and eat with any other person in the structure and which have direct access from the outside of the building through a common hall.

The occupants of a housing unit may be a single family, one person living alone, two or more families living together, or any other group of related or unrelated persons who share living quarters. Both occupied and vacant housing units are included in the housing inventory, although recreational vehicles, tents, caves, boats, railroad cars, and the like are included only if they are occupied as a person's usual place of residence.

A housing unit is classified as occupied if it is the usual place of residence of the person or group of persons living in it at the time of enumeration, or if the occupants are only temporarily absent (away on vacation). A household consists of all persons who occupy a housing unit as their usual place of residence. Vacant units for sale or rent include units rented or sold but not occupied and any other units held off the market.

Median value is the dollar amount that divides the distribution of specified owner-occupied housing units into two equal parts, with half of all units below the median value and half of all units above the median value. Value is defined as the respondent's estimate of what the house would sell for if it were for sale. Data are presented for single-family units on fewer than 10 acres of land that have no business or medical offices on the property.

Median rent divides the distribution of renter-occupied housing units into two equal parts. The rent concept used in this volume is gross rent, which includes the amount of cash rent a renter pays (contract rent) plus the estimated average cost of utilities and fuels, if these are paid by the renter. The rent is the amount of rent only for living quarters and excludes amounts paid for any business or other space occupied. Single-family houses on lots of 10 or more acres of land are also excluded.

Housing cost as a percentage of income is shown separately for owners with mortgages, owners without mortgages, and renters. Rent as a percentage of income is a computed ratio of gross rent and monthly household income (total household income in the past 12 months divided by 12). Selected owner costs include utilities and fuels, mortgage payments, insurance, taxes, etc. In each case, the ratio of housing cost to income is computed separately for each housing unit. The housing cost ratios for half of all units are above the median shown in this book, and half are below the median shown in the book.

The proportion of **Households that have a computer** includes households with desktop or laptop computers, handheld computers, or some other type of computer.

CIVILIAN LABOR FORCE AND UNEMPLOYMENT, Items 97–100
Source: U.S. Bureau of Labor Statistics—Local Area Unemployment Statistics
http://www.bls.gov/lau/#tables

Data for the civilian labor force are the product of a federal-state cooperative program in which state employment security agencies prepare labor force and unemployment estimates under concepts, definitions, and technical procedures established by the Bureau of Labor Statistics (BLS). The civilian labor force consists of all civilians 16 years old and over who are either employed or unemployed.

Unemployment includes all persons who did not work during the survey week, made specific efforts to find a job during the previous four weeks, and were available for work during the survey week (except for temporary illness). Persons waiting to be called back to a job from which they had been laid off and those waiting to report to a new job within the next 30 days are included in unemployment figures.

Table C includes annual average data for the year shown. The Local Area Unemployment Statistics data are periodically updated to reflect revised inputs, reestimation, and controlling to new statewide totals.

CIVILIAN EMPLOYMENT, Items 101–103
Source: U.S. Census Bureau—American Community Survey. 2015 1-year Estimates
http://www.census.gov/acs/www/

Total employment includes all civilians 16 years old and over who were either (1) "at work"—those who did any work at all during the reference week as paid employees, worked in either their own business or profession, worked on their own farm, or worked 15 hours or more as unpaid workers in a family farm or business; or (2) "with a job, but not at work"—those who had a job but were not at work that week due to illness, weather, industrial dispute, vacation, or other personal reasons.

The **occupational categories** are based on the occupational classification system that was developed for the 2000 census. This system consists of 509 specific occupational categories for employed persons arranged into 23 major occupational groups. This classification was developed based on the *Standard Occupational Classification (SOC) Manual: 2000*, published by the Executive Office of the President, Office of Management and Budget.

Column 102 includes the Management, business, science, and arts occupations category while Column 103 combines the Natural resources, construction, and maintenance occupations and the Production, transportation, and material moving occupations.

PRIVATE NONFARM EMPLOYMENT AND EARNINGS, Items 104–112
Source: U.S. Census Bureau—County Business Patterns
http://www.census.gov/econ/cbp/index.html

Data for private nonfarm employment and earnings are compiled from the payroll information reported monthly in the Census Bureau publication *County Business Patterns*. The estimates are based on surveys conducted by the Census Bureau and administrative records from the Internal Revenue Service (IRS).

The following types of employment are excluded from the tables: government employment, self-employed persons, farm workers, and domestic service workers. Railroad employment jointly covered by Social Security and railroad retirement programs, employment on oceanborne vessels, and employment in foreign countries are also excluded.

Annual payroll is the combined amount of wages paid, tips reported, and other compensation (including salaries, vacation allowances, bonuses, commissions, sick-leave pay, and the value of payments-in-kind such as free meals and lodging) paid to employees before deductions for Social Security, income tax, insurance, union dues, etc. All forms of compensation are included, regardless of whether they are subject to income tax or the Federal Insurance Contributions Act tax, with the exception of annuities, third-party sick pay, and supplemental unemployment compensation benefits (even if income tax was withheld). For corporations, total annual payroll includes compensation paid to officers and executives; for unincorporated businesses, it excludes profit or other compensation of proprietors or partners.

AGRICULTURE, ITEMS 113–132
Source: U.S. Department of Agriculture, National Agricultural Statistics Service—2012 Census of Agriculture
http://agcensus.usda.gov/index.php

Data for the 2012 Census of Agriculture were collected in 2013, but pertain to the year 2012.

The Census Bureau took a census of agriculture every 10 years from 1840 to 1920; since 1925, this census has been taken roughly once every 5 years. The 1997 Census of Agriculture was the first one conducted by the National Agricultural Statistics Service of the U.S. Department of Agriculture. Over time, the definition of a farm has varied. For recent censuses (including the 2012 census), a farm has been defined as any place from which $1,000 or more of agricultural products were produced and sold or normally would have been sold during the census year. Dollar figures are expressed in current dollars and have not been adjusted for inflation or deflation.

The term **operator** refers to a person who operates a farm by either doing the work or making day-to-day decisions about such activities as planting, harvesting, feeding, marketing, etc. The operator may be the owner, a member of the owner's household, a salaried manager, a tenant, a renter, or a sharecropper. If a person rents land to others or has land worked on shares by others, he/she is considered the operator only of the land that is retained for his/her own operation. The census collected information on the total number of operators, the total number of women operators, and demographic information for up to three operators per farm.

The acreage designated as **land in farms** consists primarily of agricultural land used for crops, pasture, or grazing. It also includes woodland and wasteland not actually under cultivation or used for pasture or grazing, provided that this land was part of the farm operator's total operation. Land in farms is an operating-unit concept and includes all land owned and operated, as well as all land rented from others. Land used rent-free is classified as land rented from others. All land in Indian reservations used for growing crops or grazing livestock is classified as land in farms.

Irrigated land includes all land watered by any artificial or controlled means, such as sprinklers, flooding, furrows or ditches, sub-irrigation, and spreader dikes. Included are supplemental, partial, and preplant irrigation. Each acre was counted only once regardless of the number of times it was irrigated or harvested. Livestock lagoon waste water distributed by sprinkler or flood systems was also included.

Total cropland includes cropland harvested, cropland used only for pasture or grazing, cropland on which all crops failed or were abandoned, cropland in cultivated summer fallow, and cropland idle or used for cover crops or soil improvement but not harvested and not pastured or grazed.

Respondents were asked to report their estimate of the current market **value of land and buildings** owned, rented, or leased from others, and rented and leased to others. Market value refers to the respondent's estimate of what the land and buildings would sell for under current market conditions. If the value of land and buildings was not reported, it was estimated during processing by using the average value of land and buildings from similar farms in the same geographic area.

The **value of machinery and equipment** was estimated by the respondent as the current market value of all cars, trucks, tractors, combines, balers, irrigation equipment, etc., used on the farm. This value is an estimate of what the machinery and equipment would sell for in its present condition and not the replacement or depreciated value. Share interests are reported at full value at the farm where the equipment and machinery are usually kept. Only equipment that was physically located at the farm on December 31, 2012, is included.

Market value of agricultural products sold by farms represents the gross market value before taxes and the production expenses of all agricultural products sold or removed from the place in 2012, regardless of who received the payment. It is equivalent to total sales and it includes sales by the operator as well as the value of any share received by partners, landlords, contractors, and others associated with the operation. It includes value of direct sales and the value of commodities placed in the Commodity Credit Corporation (CCC) loan program. Market value of agricultural products sold does not include payments received for participation in other federal farm programs. Also, it does not include income from farm-related sources such as custom work and other agricultural services, or income from nonfarm sources.

Government payments consists of direct payments as defined by the 2002 Farm Bill; payments from Conservation Reserve Program (CRP), Wetlands Reserve Program (WRP), Farmable

Wetlands Program (FWP), and Conservation Reserve Enhancement Program (CREP); loan deficiency payments; disaster payments; other conservation programs; and all other federal farm programs under which payments were made directly to farm operators. Commodity Credit Corporation (CCC) proceeds, amount from State and local federal crop insurance payments were not included in this category.

WATER CONSUMPTION, Items 133–134
Source: U.S. Geological Survey, National Water-Use Information Program
http://water.usgs.gov/watuse/

Every five years, the U.S. Geological Survey compiles county-level water-use estimates. This volume includes the total fresh and saline withdrawals expressed as million gallons per day. Estimate of withdrawals of ground and surface water are given for the following categories of use: public water supplies, domestic, commercial, irrigation, livestock, industrial, mining, and thermo-electric power. The number of gallons withdrawn per person is based on the metropolitan area population but the water is not necessarily used locally, providing an indicator of metropolitan areas that serve as major water sources.

2012 Economic CENSUS: OVERVIEW, Items 135–166
Source: U.S. Census Bureau
http://www.census.gov/econ/census07/

The Economic Census provides a detailed portrait of the nation's economy, from the national to the local level, once every five years. The 2012 Economic Census covers nearly all of the U.S. economy in its basic collection of establishment statistics. The 1997 Economic Census was the first major data source to use the new North American Industry Classification System (NAICS); therefore, data from this census are not comparable to economic data from prior years, which were based on the Standard Industrial Classification (SIC) system.

NAICS, developed in cooperation with Canada and Mexico, classifies North America's economic activities at two-, three-, four-, and five-digit levels of detail; the U.S. version of NAICS further defines industries to a sixth digit. The Economic Census takes advantage of this hierarchy to publish data at these successive levels of detail: sector (two-digit), subsector (three-digit), industry group (four-digit), industry (five-digit), and U.S. industry (six-digit). Information in Table A is at the two-digit level, with a few three- and four-digit items. The data in Tables B and C are at the two-digit level.

Several key statistics are tabulated for all industries in this volume, including number of establishments (or companies), number of employees, payroll, and certain measures of output (sales, receipts, revenue, value of shipments, or value of construction work done).

Number of establishments. An establishment is a single physical location at which business is conducted. It is not necessarily identical with a company or enterprise, which may consist of one establishment or more. Economic Census figures represent a summary of reports for individual establishments rather than companies. For cases in which a census report was received, separate information was obtained for each location where business was conducted. When administrative records of other federal agencies were used instead of a census report, no information was available on the number of locations operated. Each Economic Census establishment was tabulated according to the physical location at which the business was conducted. The count of establishments represents those in business at any time during 2002.

When two activities or more were carried on at a single location under a single ownership, all activities were generally grouped together as a single establishment. The entire establishment was classified on the basis of its major activity and all of its data were included in that classification. However, when distinct and separate economic activities (for which different industry classification codes were appropriate) were conducted at a single location under a single ownership, separate establishment reports for each of the different activities were obtained in the census.

Number of employees. Paid employees consist of the full-time and part-time employees, including salaried officers and executives of corporations. Included are employees on paid sick leave, paid holidays, and paid vacations; not included are proprietors and partners of unincorporated businesses. The definition of paid employees is the same as that used by the Internal Revenue Service (IRS) on form 941.

For some industries, the Economic Census gives codes representing the number of employees as a range of numbers (for example, ''100 to 249 employees'' or ''1,000 to 2,499'' employees). In this volume, those codes have been replaced by the standard suppression code ''D.''

Payroll. Payroll includes all forms of compensation, such as salaries, wages, commissions, dismissal pay, bonuses, vacation allowances, sick-leave pay, and employee contributions to qualified pension plans paid during the year to all employees. For corporations, payroll includes amounts paid to officers and executives; for unincorporated businesses, it does not include profit or other compensation of proprietors or partners. Payroll is reported before deductions for Social Security, income tax, insurance, union dues, etc. This definition of payroll is the same as that used by on IRS form 941.

Sales, shipments, receipts, revenue, or business done. This measure includes the total sales, shipments, receipts, revenue, or business done by establishments within the scope of the Economic Census. The definition of each of these items is specific to the economic sector measured.

WHOLESALE TRADE, Items 135–138
Source: U.S. Census Bureau—2012 Economic Census (See Overview of 2012 Economic Census prior to Item 135)

The Wholesale Trade sector (sector 42) comprises establishments engaged in wholesaling merchandise, generally without transformation, and rendering services incidental to the sale of merchandise. The wholesaling process is an intermediate step in the distribution of merchandise.

Wholesalers are organized to sell or arrange the purchase or sale of (1) goods for resale (i.e., goods sold to other wholesalers or retailers), (2) capital or durable nonconsumer goods, and (3) raw and intermediate materials and supplies used in production.

Wholesalers sell merchandise to other businesses and normally operate from a warehouse or office. These warehouses and offices are characterized by having little or no display of merchandise. In addition, neither the design nor the location of the premises is intended to solicit walk-in traffic. Wholesalers do not normally use advertising directed to the general public. In general, customers are initially reached via telephone, in-person marketing, or specialized advertising, which may include the internet and other electronic means. Follow-up orders are either vendor-initiated or client-initiated, are usually based on previous sales, and typically exhibit strong ties between sellers and buyers. In fact, transactions are often conducted between wholesalers and clients that have long-standing business relationships.

This sector is made up of two main types of wholesalers: those that sell goods on their own account and those that arrange sales and purchases for others for a commission or fee.

(1) Establishments that sell goods on their own account are known as wholesale merchants, distributors, jobbers, drop shippers, import/export merchants, and sales branches. These establishments typically maintain their own warehouse, where they receive and handle goods for their customers. Goods are generally sold without transformation, but may include integral functions, such as sorting, packaging, labeling, and other marketing services.

(2) Establishments arranging for the purchase or sale of goods owned by others or purchasing goods on a commission basis are known as agents and brokers, commission merchants, import/export agents and brokers, auction companies, and manufacturers' representatives. These establishments operate from offices and generally do not own or handle the goods they sell.

Some wholesale establishments may be connected with a single manufacturer and promote and sell that particular manufacturer's products to a wide range of other wholesalers or retailers. Other wholesalers may be connected to a retail chain or a limited number of retail chains and only provide the products needed by the particular retail operation(s). These wholesalers may obtain the products from a wide range of manufacturers. Still other wholesalers may not take title to the goods, but act instead as agents and brokers for a commission.

Although wholesaling normally denotes sales in large volumes, durable nonconsumer goods may be sold in single units. Sales of capital or durable nonconsumer goods used in the production of goods and services, such as farm machinery, medium- and heavy-duty trucks, and industrial machinery, are always included in Wholesale Trade.

The metropolitan area table includes only **Merchant wholesalers, except manufacturers' sales branches and offices,** establishments primarily engaged in buying and selling merchandise on their own account. Included here are such types of establishments as wholesale distributors and jobbers, importers, exporters, own-brand importers/marketers, terminal and country grain elevators, and farm products assemblers.

RETAIL TRADE, Items 139–142

Source: U.S. Census Bureau—2012 Economic Census (See Overview of 2012 Economic Census prior to Item 135)

The Retail Trade sector (44–45) is made up of establishments engaged in retailing merchandise, generally without transformation, and rendering services incidental to the sale of merchandise.

The retailing process is the final step in the distribution of merchandise; retailers are therefore organized to sell merchandise in small quantities to the general public. This sector comprises two main types of retailers: store and nonstore retailers.

Store retailers operate fixed point-of-sale locations, located and designed to attract a high volume of walk-in customers. In general, retail stores have extensive displays of merchandise and use mass-media advertising to attract customers. They typically sell merchandise to the general public for personal or household consumption; some also serve business and institutional clients. These include establishments such as office supply stores, computer and software stores, building materials dealers, plumbing supply stores, and electrical supply stores. Catalog showrooms, gasoline service stations, automotive dealers, and mobile home dealers are treated as store retailers.

In addition to retailing merchandise, some types of store retailers are also engaged in the provision of after-sales services, such as repair and installation. For example, new automobile dealers, electronic and appliance stores, and musical instrument and supply stores often provide repair services. As a general rule, establishments engaged in retailing merchandise and providing after-sales services are classified in this sector.

Nonstore retailers, like store retailers, are organized to serve the general public, although their retailing methods differ. The establishments of this subsector reach customers and market merchandise with methods including the broadcasting of ''infomercials,'' the broadcasting and publishing of direct-response advertising, the publishing of paper and electronic catalogs, door-to-door solicitation, in-home demonstration, selling from portable stalls (street vendors, except food), and distribution through vending machines. Establishments engaged in the direct sale (nonstore) of products, such as home heating oil dealers and home-delivery newspaper routes are included in this sector.

The buying of goods for resale is a characteristic of retail trade establishments that distinguishes them from establishments in the Agriculture, Manufacturing, and Construction sectors. For example, farms that sell their products at or from the point of production are classified in Agriculture instead of in Retail Trade. Similarly, establishments that both manufacture and sell their products to the general public are classified in Manufacturing instead of Retail Trade. However, establishments that engage in processing activities incidental to retailing are classified in Retail Trade.

REAL ESTATE AND RENTAL AND LEASING, Items 143–146

Source: U.S. Census Bureau—2012 Economic Census (See Overview of 2012 Economic Census prior to Item 135)

The Real Estate and Rental and Leasing sector (53) comprises establishments primarily engaged in renting, leasing, or otherwise allowing the use of tangible or intangible assets, and establishments providing related services. The major portion of this sector is made up of establishments that rent, lease, or otherwise allow the use of their own assets by others. The assets may be tangible, such as real estate and equipment, or intangible, such as patents and trademarks.

This sector also includes establishments primarily engaged in managing real estate for others, selling, renting, and/or buying real estate for others, and appraising real estate. These activities are closely related to this sector's main activity. In addition, a substantial proportion of property management is self-performed by lessors.

The main components of this sector are the real estate lessors industries; equipment lessors industries (including motor vehicles, computers, and consumer goods); and lessors of nonfinancial intangible assets (except copyrighted works).

PROFESSIONAL, SCIENTIFIC, AND TECHNICAL SERVICES, Items 147–150

Source: U.S. Census Bureau—2012 Economic Census (See Overview of 2012 Economic Census prior to Item 135)

The Professional, Scientific, and Technical Services sector (54) is made up of establishments that specialize in performing professional, scientific, and technical activities for others. These activities require a high degree of expertise and training. The establishments in this sector specialize in one or more areas and provide services to clients in a variety of industries (and, in some cases, to households). Activities performed include legal advice and representation; accounting, bookkeeping, and payroll services; architectural, engineering, and specialized design services; computer services; consulting services; research services; advertising services; photographic services; translation and interpretation services; veterinary services; and other professional, scientific, and technical services.

This sector excludes establishments primarily engaged in providing a range of day-to-day office administrative services, such as financial planning, billing and record keeping, personnel services, and physical distribution and logistics services. These establishments are classified in sector 56, Administrative and Support and Waste Management and Remediation Services.

MANUFACTURING, Items 151–154

Source: U.S. Census Bureau—2012 Economic Census (See Overview of 2012 Economic Census prior to Item 135)

The Manufacturing sector (31–33) is made up of establishments engaged in the mechanical, physical, or chemical transformation of materials, substances, or components into new products. The assembling of component parts of manufactured products is considered manufacturing, except in cases in which the activity is appropriately classified in the Construction sector. Establishments in the Manufacturing sector are often described as plants, factories, or mills, and characteristically use power-driven machines and materials-handling equipment. However, establishments that transform materials or substances into new products by hand or in the worker's home, and establishments engaged in selling to the general public products made on the same premises from which they are sold (such as bakeries, candy stores, and custom tailors) may also be included in this sector. Manufacturing establishments may process materials or contract with other establishments to process their materials for them. Both types of establishments are included in the Manufacturing sector.

The materials, substances, or components transformed by manufacturing establishments are raw materials that are products of agriculture, forestry, fishing, mining, or quarrying, or are products of other manufacturing establishments. The materials used may be purchased directly from producers, obtained through customary trade channels, or secured without recourse to the market by transferring the product from one establishment to another, under the same ownership. The new product of a manufacturing establishment may be finished (in the sense that it is ready for utilization or consumption), or it may be semifinished to become an input for an establishment engaged in further manufacturing. For example, the product of the alumina refinery is the input used in the primary production of aluminum; primary aluminum is the input used in an aluminum wire drawing plant; and aluminum wire is the input used in a fabricated wire product manufacturing establishment.

Data are included for counties with 500 or more employees in the Manufacturing sector.

ACCOMMODATION AND FOOD SERVICES, Items 155–158

Source: U.S. Census Bureau—2012 Economic Census (See Overview of 2012 Economic Census prior to Item 135)

The Accommodation and Food Services sector (72) consists of establishments that provide customers with lodging and/or meals, snacks, and beverages for immediate consumption. This sector includes both accommodation and food services establishments because the two activities are often combined at the same establishment.

Excluded from this sector are civic and social organizations, amusement and recreation parks, theaters, and other recreation or entertainment facilities providing food and beverage services.

HEALTH CARE AND SOCIAL ASSISTANCE, Items 159–162

Source: U.S. Census Bureau—2012 Economic Census (See Overview of 2012 Economic Census prior to Item 135)

The Health Care and Social Assistance sector (62) consists of establishments that provide health care and social assistance services to individuals. The sector includes both health care and social assistance because it is sometimes difficult to distinguish between the boundaries of these two activities. The industries in this sector are arranged on a continuum, starting with establishments that provide medical care exclusively, continuing with those that provide health care and social assistance, and finishing with those that provide only social assistance. The services provided by establishments in this sector are delivered by trained professionals. All industries in the sector share this commonality of process—namely, labor inputs of health practitioners or social workers with the requisite expertise. Many of the industries in the sector are defined based on the educational degree held by the practitioners included in the industry.

Excluded from this sector are aerobic classes, which can be found in subsector 713, Amusement, Gambling, and Recreation Industries; and nonmedical diet and weight-reducing centers, which can be found in subsector 812, Personal and Laundry Services. Although these can be viewed as health services, they are not typically delivered by health practitioners.

OTHER SERVICES, EXCEPT PUBLIC ADMINISTRATION Items 163–166

Source: U.S. Census Bureau—2012 Economic Census (See Overview of 2012 Economic Census prior to Item 135)

The Other Services, Except Public Administration sector (81) comprises establishments engaged in providing services not specifically categorized elsewhere in the classification system. Establishments in this sector are primarily engaged in activities such as equipment and machinery repairing, promoting or administering religious activities, grant making, and advocacy; this sector also includes establishments that provide dry-cleaning and laundry services, personal care services, death care services, pet care services, photofinishing services, temporary parking services, and dating services.

Private households that employ workers on or about the premises in activities primarily concerned with the operation of the household are included in this sector.

Excluded from this sector are establishments primarily engaged in retailing new equipment and performing repairs and general maintenance on equipment. These establishments are classified in sector 44–45, Retail Trade.

NONEMPLOYER BUSINESSES, Items 167 and 168

Source: U.S. Census Bureau—Nonemployer Statistics
http://www.census.gov/econ/nonemployer/

Nonemployer Statistics is an annual series that provides subnational economic data for businesses that have no paid employees and are subject to federal income tax. The data consist of the number of businesses and total receipts by industry. Most nonemployers are self-employed individuals operating unincorporated businesses (known as sole proprietorships), which may or may not be the owner's principal source of income.

The majority of all business establishments in the United States are nonemployers, yet these firms average less than 4 percent of all sales and receipts nationally. Due to their small economic impact, these firms are excluded from most other Census Bureau business statistics (the primary exception being the Survey of Business Owners). The Nonemployers Statistics series is the primary resource available to study the scope and activities of nonemployers at a detailed geographic level.

BUILDING PERMITS, Items 169 and 170

Source: U.S. Census Bureau—Building Permits Survey
http://www.census.gov/construction/bps/

These figures represent private residential construction authorized by building permits in approximately 20,000 places in the United States. Valuation represents the expected cost of construction as recorded on the building permit. This figure usually excludes the cost of on-site and off-site development and improvements, as well as the cost of heating, plumbing, electrical, and elevator installations.

National, state, and county totals were obtained by adding the data for permit-issuing places within each jurisdiction. Not all areas of the country require a building or zoning permit. The statistics only represent those areas that do require a permit. These totals thus are limited to permits issued in the 20,000 place universe covered by the Census Bureau and may not include all permits issued within a state. Current surveys indicate that construction is undertaken for all but a very small percentage of housing units authorized by building permits.

Residential building permits include buildings with any number of housing units. Housing units exclude group quarters (such as dormitories and rooming houses), transient accommodations (such as transient hotels, motels, and tourist courts), "HUD-code" manufactured (mobile) homes, moved or relocated units, and housing units created in an existing residential or nonresidential structure.

METROPOLITAN AREA LOCAL GOVERNMENT EMPLOYMENT AND PAYROLL, Items 171-179

Source: U.S. Census Bureau—2012 Census of Governments
http://www.census.gov/govs/cog2012/

These items include data for all local governments (i.e., counties, municipalities, townships, special districts, and school districts) located within the metropolitan area. The Census of Governments identifies the scope and nature of the nation's state and local government sector; provides authoritative benchmark figures of public finance and public employment; classifies local government organizations, powers, and activities; and measures federal, state, and local fiscal relationships. The Employment component was mailed March 2012 to collect information on the number of state and local government civilian employees and their payrolls.

Government employees include all persons paid for personal services performed, including persons paid from federally funded programs, paid elected or appointed officials, persons in a paid leave status, and persons paid on a per meeting, annual, semiannual, or quarterly basis. Unpaid officials, pensioners, persons whose work is performed on a fee basis, and contractors and their employees are excluded from the count of employees. **Full-Time Equivalent employees** is a computed statistic representing the number of full-time employees that could have been employed if the reported number of hours worked by part-time employees had been worked by full-time employees. This statistic is calculated separately for each function of a government by dividing the "part-time hours paid" by the standard number of hours for full-time employees in the particular government and then adding the resulting quotient to the number of full-time employees.

March payroll represents gross payroll amounts for the one-month period of March for full-time and part-time employees. Gross payroll includes all salaries, wages, fees, commissions, and overtime paid to employees **before** withholdings for taxes, insurance, etc. It also includes incentive payments that are paid at regular pay intervals. It excludes employer share of fringe benefits like retirement, Social Security, health and life insurance, lump sum payments, and so forth.

Administration and Judicial and Legal combines **Financial administration, Other government administration, and Judicial and Legal** activities. **Financial administration** includes activities concerned with tax assessment and collection, custody and disbursement of funds, debt management, administration of trust funds, budgeting, and other government-wide financial management activities. This function is not applied to school district or special district governments. **Other government administration** applies to the legislative and government-wide administrative agencies of governments. Included here are overall planning and zoning activities, and central personnel and administrative activities. This function is not applied to school district or special district governments. **Judicial and legal** includes all court and court related activities (except probation and parole activities that are included at the "Correction" function), court activities of sheriff's offices, prosecuting attorneys' and public defenders' offices, legal departments, and attorneys providing government-wide legal service.

Police and Corrections includes all activities concerned, with the enforcement of law and order, including coroner's offices, police training academies, investigation bureaus, and local jails, "lockups," or other detention facilities not intended to serve as correctional facilities. **Corrections** includes activities pertaining to the confinement and correction of adults and minors convicted of criminal offenses. Pardon, probation, and parole activities are also included here.

Fire protection includes local government fire protection and prevention activities plus any ambulance, rescue, or other auxiliary services provided by a fire protection agency. Volunteer firefighters, if remunerated for their services on a "per fire" or some other basis, are included as part-time employees.

Highways and transportation includes activities associated with the maintenance and operation of streets, roads, sidewalks, bridges, tunnels, toll roads, and ferries. Snow and ice removal, street lighting, and highway and traffic engineering activities are also included here. Also included are the operation, maintenance, and construction of public mass transit systems, including subways, surface rails, and buses, and the provision, construction, operation, maintenance; support of public waterways, harbors, docks, wharves, and related marine terminal facilities; and activities associated with the operation and support of publicly operated airport facilities.

Health and Welfare includes **Health, Hospitals, and Public welfare. Health** includes administration of public health programs, community and visiting nurse services, immunization programs, drug abuse rehabilitation programs, health and food inspection activities, operation of outpatient clinics, and environmental pollution control activities. **Hospitals** includes only government operated medical care facilities that provide inpatient care. Employees and payrolls of private corporations that lease and operate government-owned hospital facilities are excluded.

Public Welfare includes the administration of various public assistance programs for the needy, veteran services, operation of nursing homes, indigent care institutions, and programs that provide payments for medical care, handicap transportation, and other services for the needy.

Natural resources and Utilities includes activities primarily concerned with the conservation and development of natural resources (soil, water, energy, minerals, etc.) and the regulation of industries that develop, utilize, or affect natural resources, as well as the operation and maintenance of **parks**, playgrounds, swimming pools, public beaches, auditoriums, public golf courses, museums, marinas, botanical gardens, and zoological parks. **Utilities, sewerage, and waste management** includes operation, maintenance, and construction of public water supply systems, including production, acquisition, and distribution of water to general public or to other public or private utilities, for residential, commercial, and industrial use; activities associated with the production or acquisition and distribution of electric power; provision, maintenance, and operation of sanitary and storm sewer systems and sewage disposal and treatment facilities; and refuse collection and disposal, operation of sanitary landfills, and street cleaning activities.

Education and libraries includes activities associated with the operation of public elementary and secondary schools and locally operated vocational-technical schools. Special education programs operated by elementary and secondary school systems are also included as are all ancillary services associated with the operation of schools, such as pupil transportation and food service. Also included are the establishment and provision of libraries for use by the general public and the technical support of privately operated libraries. This category includes classroom teachers, principals, supervisors of instruction, librarians, teacher aides, library aides, and guidance and psychological personnel as well as school superintendents and other administrative personnel, clerical and secretarial staffs, plant operation and maintenance personnel, health and recreation employees, transportation and food service personnel, and any student employees. Also included are any degree granting institutions that provide academic training above grade 12.

LOCAL GOVERNMENT FINANCES, Items 180–193
Source: U.S. Census Bureau—2012 Census of Governments
http://www.census.gov/govs/cog/

Data on local government finances are based on result of the 2012 Census of Governments. For each metropolitan area, the data are aggregated from its component counties, and the financial data comprise amounts for all local governments—not only the county governments, but also any municipalities, townships, school districts, and special districts within the county. Statistics from governmental units located in two or more county areas are assigned to the county area containing the administrative office.

Revenue and expenditure items include all amounts of money received and paid out, respectively, by a government and its agencies (net of correcting transactions such as recoveries of refunds), with the exception of amounts for debt issuance and retirement and for loan and investment, agency, and private transactions.

Payments among the various funds and agencies of a particular government are excluded from revenue and expenditure items as representing internal transfers. Therefore, a government's contribution to a retirement fund that it administers is not counted as expenditure, nor is the receipt of this contribution by the retirement fund counted as revenue.

Total **general revenue** includes all revenue except utility, liquor stores, and insurance trust revenue. All tax revenue and intergovernmental revenue, even if designated for employee-retirement or local utility purpose, are classified as general revenue.

Intergovernmental revenue covers amounts received from the federal government as fiscal aid, reimbursements for performance of general government functions and specific services for the paying government, or in lieu of taxes. It excludes any amounts received from other governments from the sale of property, commodities, and utility services.

Taxes consist of compulsory contributions exacted by governments for public purposes. However, this category excludes employer and employee payments for retirement and social insurance purposes, which are classified as insurance trust revenue; it also excludes special assessments, which are classified as non-tax general revenue. Property taxes are taxes conditioned on ownership of property and assessed by its value. Sales and gross receipts taxes do not include dealer discounts, or "commissions" allowed to merchants for collection of taxes from consumers. General sales taxes and selected taxes on sales of motor fuels, tobacco products, and other particular commodities and services are included.

General government expenditure includes capital outlay, a major portion of which is commonly financed by borrowing. Government revenue does not include receipts from borrowing. Among other things, this distorts the relationship between totals of revenue and expenditure figures that are presented and renders it useless as a direct measure of the degree of budgetary "balance" (as that term is generally applied).

Direct general expenditure comprises all expenditures of the local governments, excluding utility, liquor stores, insurance trust expenditures, and any intergovernmental payments.

Local government expenditure for **education** is mainly for the provision and general support of schools and other educational facilities and services, including those for educational institutions beyond high school. They cover such related services as student transportation; school lunch and other cafeteria operations; school health, recreation, and library services; and dormitories, dining halls, and bookstores operated by public institutions of higher education.

Health and hospital expenditure includes health research; clinics; nursing; immunization; other categorical, environmental, and general health services provided by health agencies; establishment and operation of hospital facilities; provision of hospital care; and support of other public and private hospitals.

Police protection expenditure includes police activities such as patrols, communications, custody of persons awaiting trial, and vehicular inspection.

Public welfare expenditure covers support of and assistance to needy persons; this aid is contingent upon the person's needs. Included are cash assistance paid directly to needy persons under categorical (Old Age Assistance, Temporary Assistance for Needy Families, Aid to the Blind, and Aid to the Disabled) and other welfare programs; vendor payments made directly to private purveyors for medical care, burials, and other commodities and services provided under welfare programs; welfare institutions; and any intergovernmental or other direct expenditure for welfare purposes. Pensions to former employees and other benefits not contingent on need are excluded.

Highway expenditure is for the provision and maintenance of highway facilities, including toll turnpikes, bridges, tunnels, and ferries, as well as regular roads, highways, and streets. Also included are expenditures for street lighting and for snow and ice removal. Not included are highway policing and traffic control, which are considered part of police protection.

Debt outstanding includes all long-term debt obligations of the government and its agencies (exclusive of utility debt) and all interest-bearing, short-term (repayable within one year) debt obligations remaining unpaid at the close of the fiscal year. It includes judgments, mortgages, and revenue bonds, as well as general obligation bonds, notes, and interest-bearing warrants. This category consists of non-interest-bearing, short-term obligations; inter-fund obligations; amounts owed in a trust or agency capacity; advances and contingent loans from other governments; and rights of individuals to benefit from government-administered employee-retirement funds.

GOVERNMENT EMPLOYMENT, Items 194–196

Source: U.S. Bureau of Economic Analysis—Regional Economic Accounts
http://www.bea.gov/regional/index.htm#state

Employment is measured as the average annual sum of full-time and part-time jobs. The estimates are on a place-of-work basis. The estimates are on a place-of-work basis. State and local government employment includes person employed in all state and local government agencies and enterprises. Data for federal civilian employment include civilian employees of the federal government, including civilian employees of the Department of Defense. Military employment includes all persons on active duty status.

INDIVIDUAL INCOME TAX RETURNS, Items 197–199

Source: U.S. Internal Revenue Servicw, Statistics of Income Program
https://www.irs.gov/uac/soi-tax-stats-county-data-2014

The Revenue Act of 1916 mandated the annual publication of statistics related to "the operations of the internal revenue laws" as they affect individuals, all forms of businesses, estates. nonprofit organizations, trusts, and investments abroad and foreign investments in the United States. The Statistics of Income (SOI) division fulfills this function by collecting and processing data so that they become informative and by sharing information about how the tax system works with other government agencies and the general public. Publication types include traditional print sources, Internet files, CD-ROMs, and files sent via e-mail. SOI has an information office, Statistical Information Services, to facilitate the dissemination of SOI data.

SOI bases its county data on administrative records of individual income tax returns (Forms 1040) from the Internal Revenue Service (IRS) Individual Master File (IMF) system. Included in these data are returns filed during the 12-month period, January 1, 2015 to December 31, 2015. While the bulk of returns filed during the 12-month period are primarily for Tax Year 2014, the IRS received a limited number of returns for tax years before 2014 and these have been included within the county data.

Data do not represent the full U.S. population because many individuals are not required to file an individual income tax return. The address shown on the tax return may differ from the taxpayer's actual residence. State and county codes were based on the ZIP code shown on the return. Excluded were tax returns filed without a ZIP code and returns filed with a ZIP code that did not match the State code shown on the return.

SOI did not attempt to correct any ZIP codes on the returns; however, it did take the following precautions to avoid disclosing information about specific taxpayers: Excluded from the data are items with less than 20 returns within a county. Also excluded are tax returns representing a specified percentage of the total of any particular cell. For example, if one return represented 75 percent of the value of a given cell, the return was suppressed from the county detail. The actual threshold percentage used cannot be released.

Column 197 show the number of returns. Column 198 shows the mean Adjusted Gross Income for the county and column 199 shows the mean income tax (line 56 on Form 1040). for the county.

TABLE D—CITIES

Table D present 146 items of data for cities with populations of 25,000 or more at the time of the 2010 census.

LAND AREA, Items 1 and 4
Source: U.S. Census Bureau—2016 U.S. Gazetteer Files,
http://www.census.gov/geo/maps-data/data/gazetteer2016.html

Land area measurements are shown to the nearest square mile. Land area is an area measurement providing the size, in square miles, of the land portions of each county.

POPULATION, Items 2–4
Source: U.S. Census Bureau—Population Estimates
https://www.census.gov/programs-surveys/popest.html

The population data are Census Bureau estimates of the resident population as of July 1 of the year shown.

POPULATION CHARACTERISTICS, Items 5–22
Source: U.S. Census Bureau—American Community Survey 2015 1-year Supplemental Estimates
http://www.census.gov/acs/www/

Data on age, sex, race, Hispanic origin, and place of birth are from the 2015 American Community Survey, a nationwide continuous survey designed to replace the long form questionnaire used in previous censuses.

Data on race were derived from answers to the question on race that was asked of all persons. The concept of race, as used by the Census Bureau, reflects self-identification by respondents according to the race or races with which they most closely identify. These categories are sociopolitical constructs and should not be interpreted as being scientific or anthropological in nature. Furthermore, the race categories include both racial and national origin groups.

On the American Community Survey, respondents were offered the option of selecting one or more races. This option was not available prior to the 2000 census; thus, comparisons between censuses should be made with caution. In this table, Columns 5 through 10 refer to individuals who identified with one specific racial category, while Column 11 includes those who selected more than one race.

The **White** population is defined as persons who indicated their race as White, as well as persons who did not classify themselves in one of the specific race categories listed on the questionnaire but entered a nationality such as Irish, German, Italian, Lebanese, Near Easterner, Arab, or Polish.

The **Black** population includes persons who indicated their race as ''Black, African Am., or Negro,'' as well as persons who did not classify themselves in one of the specific race categories but reported entries such as African American, Afro American, Kenyan, Nigerian, or Haitian.

The **American Indian or Alaska Native** population includes persons who indicated their race as American Indian or Alaska Native, as well as persons who did not classify themselves in one of the specific race categories but reported entries such as Canadian Indian, French-American Indian, Spanish-American Indian, Eskimo, Aleut, Alaska Indian, or any of the American Indian or Alaska Native tribes.

The **Asian** population includes persons who indicated their race as Asian Indian, Chinese, Filipino, Japanese, Korean, Vietnamese, or ''Other Asian,'' as well as persons who provided write-in entries of such groups as Cambodian, Laotian, Hmong, Pakistani, or Taiwanese.

The **Native Hawaiian or Other Pacific Islander** population includes persons who indicated their race as ''Native Hawaiian,'' ''Guamanian or Chamorro,'' ''Samoan,'' or ''Other Pacific Islander,'' as well as persons who reported entries such as Part Hawaiian, American Samoan, Fijian, Melanesian, or Tahitian.

Some Other Race includes all other responses not included in the ''White,'' ''Black or African American,'' ''American Indian or Alaska Native,'' ''Asian,'' and ''Native Hawaiian or Other Pacific Islander'' race categories described above. Respondents reporting entries such as multiracial, mixed, interracial, or a Hispanic, Latino, or Spanish group (for example, Mexican, Puerto Rican, Cuban, or Spanish) in response to the race question are included in this category.

Two or More Races. People may choose to provide two or more races either by checking two or more race response check boxes, by providing multiple responses, or by some combination of check boxes and other responses. The race response categories shown on the questionnaire are collapsed into the five minimum race groups identified by OMB, and the Census Bureau's ''Some Other Race'' category.

The **Hispanic population** is based on a separate question that asked respondents ''Is this person Spanish/Hispanic/Latino?'' Persons marking any one of the four Hispanic categories (i.e., Mexican, Puerto Rican, Cuban, or other Spanish) are collectively referred to as Hispanic.

The Hispanic origin question was placed before the race question and specific instructions indicated that both questions should be answered.

The **foreign-born** population includes all persons who were not U.S. citizens at birth. Foreign-born persons are those who indicated they were either a U.S. citizen by naturalization or were not a citizen of the United States. The foreign-born population consists of immigrants (legal permanent residents), temporary migrants (students), humanitarian migrants (refugees), and unauthorized migrants (persons illegally residing in the United States).

Age is defined as age at last birthday (number of completed years since birth), at the time of the interview. The American Community Survey also asked for the specific date of birth of the respondent. Both age and date of birth are used in combination to calculate the most accurate age at the time of the interview.

The **female** population is shown as a percentage of total population.

POPULATION CHANGE, Items 23–26

Source: U.S. Census Bureau—Decennial Censuses
U.S. Census Bureau—Population Estimates
http://www.census.gov/main/www/cen2000.html
http://www.census.gov/2010census/data/
https://www.census.gov/programs-surveys/
popest.html

The population data for 2000 and 2010 are from the decennial censuses and represent the resident population as of April 1 of those years. The data for 2016 are from the Census Bureau's Population Estimates Program and represent the estimated resident population as of July 1.

The change in population from 2010 to 2016 is calculated from census data based on city boundaries as they existed in 2000 and 2010, respectively. No attempt was made to adjust the data to reflect boundary changes.

HOUSEHOLDS, Items 27–30

Source: U.S. Census Bureau—American Community
Survey, 2015 1-year Supplemental Estimates
http://www.census.gov/acs/www/

A **household** includes all of the persons who occupy a housing unit. (Persons not living in households are classified as living in group quarters.) A housing unit is a house, an apartment, a mobile home, a group of rooms, or a single room occupied (or, if vacant, intended for occupancy) as separate living quarters. Separate living quarters are those in which the occupants live separately from any other persons in the building and have direct access from the outside of the building or through a common hall. The occupants may be a single family, one person living alone, two or more families living together, or any other group of related or unrelated persons who share living quarters. The number of households is the same as the number of year-round occupied housing units.

A **family** includes a householder and one or more other persons living in the same household who are related to the householder by birth, marriage, or adoption. All persons in a household who are related to the householder are regarded as members of his or her family. A **family household** may contain persons not related to the householder; thus, family households may include more members than families do. A household can contain only one family for the purposes of census tabulations. Not all households contain families, as a household may comprise a group of unrelated persons or of one person living alone. Families are classified by type as either a "husband-wife family" or "other family," according to the presence or absence of a spouse.

The measure of **persons per household** is obtained by dividing the number of persons in households by the number of households or householders. One person in each household is designated as the householder. In most cases, this is the person (or one of the persons) in whose name the house is owned, being bought, or rented. If there is no such person in the household, any adult household member 15 years old and over can be designated as the householder.

The category **female family householder** includes only female-headed family households with no spouse present.

GROUP QUARTERS, Item 31–34

Source: U.S. Census Bureau—2010 Census of
Population and Housing
http://www.census.gov/2010census/data/

The Census Bureau classifies all persons not living in households as living in group quarters; this category includes both the institutional and noninstitutional populations. This volume includes the total number of persons in group quarters and in selected types of group quarters.

The **institutionalized population** includes persons who are primarily ineligible, unable, or unlikely to participate in the labor force while residents, including those in correctional institutions, skilled-nursing facilities, mental (psychiatric) hospitals, and juvenile institutions.

Nursing facilities include facilities licensed to provide medical care with 7-day, 24-hour coverage for people requiring long-term non-acute care. People in these facilities require nursing care, regardless of age. Included in this category are skilled-nursing facilities, intermediate-care facilities, long-term care rooms in wards or buildings on the grounds of hospitals, or long-term care rooms/nursing wings in congregate housing facilities. Also included are nursing, convalescent, and rest homes, such as soldiers', veterans', and fraternal or religious homes for the aged, with or without nursing care.

The **noninstitutionalized population** includes persons who live in group quarters other than institutions, such as college dormitories, military quarters, and group homes.

CRIME, Items 35–38

Source: U.S. Federal Bureau of Investigation—
Uniform Crime Reports
http://www.fbi.gov/ucr/ucr.htm

Crime data are as reported to the Federal Bureau of Investigation (FBI) by law enforcement agencies and have not been adjusted for underreporting. This may affect comparability between geographic areas or over time.

Through the voluntary contribution of crime statistics by law enforcement agencies across the United States, the Uniform Crime Reporting (UCR) Program provides periodic assessments of crime in the nation as measured by offenses that have come to the attention of the law enforcement community. The Committee on Uniform Crime Records of the International Association of Chiefs of Police initiated this voluntary national data collection effort in 1930. The UCR Program contributors compile and submit their crime data either directly to the FBI or through state-level UCR Programs.

Seven offenses, because of their severity, frequency of occurrence, and likelihood of being reported to police, were initially selected to serve as an index for evaluating fluctuations in the volume of crime. These serious crimes were murder and nonnegligent manslaughter, forcible rape, robbery, aggravated assault, burglary, larceny-theft, and motor vehicle theft. By congressional mandate, arson was added as the eighth index offense in 1979. The totals shown in this volume do not include arson.

In 2004, the FBI discontinued the use of the Crime Index in the UCR Program and its publications, stating that the Crime Index was driven upward by the offense with the highest number of cases (in this case, larceny-theft), creating a bias against jurisdictions with a high number of larceny-thefts but a low number of other serious crimes, such as murder and forcible rape. The FBI is currently publishing a violent crime total and property crime total until a more viable index is developed. This book includes the total Crime Index, as well as violent crime and property crime rates.

In 2013, the FBI adopted a new definition of rape. Rape is now defined as, "Penetration, no matter how slight, of the vagina or anus with any body part or object, or oral penetration by a sex organ of another person, without the consent of the victim." The new definition updated the 80-year-old historical definition of rape which was "carnal knowledge of a female forcibly and against her will." Effectively, the revised definition expands rape to include both male and female victims and offenders, and reflects the various forms of sexual penetration understood to be rape, especially nonconsenting acts of sodomy, and sexual assaults with objects.

Violent crimes include four categories of offenses: (1) Murder and nonnegligent manslaughter, as defined in the UCR Program, is the willful (nonnegligent) killing of one human being by another. This offense excludes deaths caused by negligence, suicide, or accident; justifiable homicides; and attempts to murder or assaults to murder. (2) Rape is the penetration, no matter how slight, of the vagina or anus with any body part or object, or oral penetration by a sex organ of another person, without the consent of the victim Assaults or attempts to commit rape by force or threat of force are also included; however, statutory rape (without force) and other sex offenses are excluded. (3) Robbery is the taking or attempting to take anything of value from the care, custody, or control of a person or persons by force or threat of force or violence and/or by putting the victim in fear. (4) Aggravated assault is an unlawful attack by one person upon another for the purpose of inflicting severe or aggravated bodily injury. This type of assault is usually accompanied by the use of a weapon or by other means likely to produce death or great bodily harm. Attempts are included, since injury does not necessarily have to result when a gun, knife, or other weapon is used, as these incidents could and probably would result in a serious personal injury if the crime were successfully completed.

Property crimes include three categories: (1) Burglary, or breaking and entering, is the unlawful entry of a structure to commit a felony or theft, even though no force was used to gain entrance. (2) Larceny-theft is the unauthorized taking of the personal property of another, without the use of force. (3) Motor vehicle theft is the unauthorized taking of any motor vehicle.

Rates are based on population estimates provided by the FBI. If a city is not in the UCR database, or if the population total for the units aggregated was less than 75 percent of the city's population (as estimated by the Census Bureau), the total was not considered representative of the city as a whole and was not published. State and U.S. totals include FBI estimates for those areas.

EDUCATIONAL ATTAINMENT, Items 39–41
Source: U.S. Census Bureau—American Community Survey, 2015 1-year Supplemental Estimates
http://www.census.gov/acs/www/

Data on **educational attainment** are tabulated for the population 25 years old and over. The data were derived from a question that asked respondents for the highest level of school completed or the highest degree received. Persons who had passed a high school equivalency examination were considered high school graduates. Schooling received in foreign schools was to be reported as the equivalent grade or years in the regular American school system.

Vocational and technical training, such as barber school training; business, trade, technical, and vocational schools; or other training for a specific trade are specifically excluded.

High school graduate or less. This category includes persons whose highest degree was a high school diploma or its equivalent, and those who reported any level lower than a high school diploma.

Bachelor's degree or more. This category includes persons who have received bachelor's degrees, master's degrees, professional school degrees (such as law school or medical school degrees), and doctoral degrees.

INCOME AND POVERTY, Items 42–46
Source: U.S. Census Bureau—American Community Survey, 2015 1-year Supplemental Estimates
http://www.census.gov/acs/www/

Total money income is the sum of the amounts reported separately for wage or salary income; net self-employment income; interest, dividends, or net rental or royalty income or income from estates and trusts; Social Security or railroad retirement income; Supplemental Security Income (SSI); public assistance or welfare payments; retirement, survivor, or disability pensions; and all other income. Receipts from the following sources are not included as income: capital gains; money received from the sale of property (unless the recipient was engaged in the business of selling such property); the value of income "in kind" from food stamps, public housing subsidies, medical care, employer contributions for individuals, etc.; withdrawal of bank deposits; money borrowed; tax refunds; exchange of money between relatives living in the same household; and gifts, lump-sum inheritances, insurance payments, and other types of lump-sum receipts.

Household income includes the income of the householder and all other individuals 15 years old and over in the household, whether or not they are related to the householder. Since many households consist of only one person, median household income is usually less than median family income. Although the household income statistics cover the twelve months prior to the survey, the characteristics of individuals and the composition of households refer to the date of the interview. Thus, the income of the household does not include amounts received by individuals who were members of the household during all or part of the year if these individuals were no longer residing in the household at the time of the interview. Similarly, income amounts reported by individuals who did not reside in the household during full year but who were members of the household at the time of the interview are included. However, the composition of most households was the same during the year as it was at the time of the interview.

Median income divides the income distribution into two equal parts, with half of all cases below the median income level and half of all cases above the median income level. For households, the median income is based on the distribution of the total number of households, including those with no income. Median income for households is computed on the basis of a standard distribution with a minimum value of less than $2,500 and a maximum value of $200,000 or more and is rounded to the nearest whole dollar. Median income figures are calculated using linear interpolation if the width of the interval containing the estimate is $2,500 or less. If the width of the interval containing the estimate is greater than $2,500, Pareto interpolation is used.

Income components were reported for the 12 months preceding the interview month. Monthly Consumer Price Index (CPI) factors were used to inflation-adjust these components to a reference calendar year (January through December). For example, a household interviewed in March 2012 reports their income for March 2011 through February 2012. Their income is adjusted to the 2012 reference calendar year by multiplying their reported income by 2012 average annual CPI (January-December 2012) and then dividing by the average CPI for March 2006-February 2012. In addition, the 3-year estimates are inflation-adjusted to the final year. However, the estimates do not reflect the price and cost-of-living differences that may exist between areas.

The **poverty status** data were derived from data collected on the number of persons in a household, each person's relationship to the householder, and each person's income during the past twelve months. The Social Security Administration (SSA) developed the original poverty definition in 1964, which federal interagency committees subsequently revised in 1969 and 1980. The Office of Management and Budget's (OMB) *Directive 14* prescribes the SSA's definition as the official poverty measure for federal agencies to use in their statistical work.

Poverty thresholds vary depending on three criteria: size of family, number of children, and, for one- and two-person families, age of householder. In determining the poverty status of families and unrelated individuals, the Census Bureau uses thresholds (income cutoffs) arranged in a two-dimensional matrix. The matrix consists of family size (from one person to nine or more persons), cross-classified by presence and number of family members under 18 years old (from no children present to eight or more children present). Unrelated individuals and two-person families are further differentiated by age of reference person (under 65 years old and 65 years old and over). To determine a person's poverty status, the person's total family income over the previous 12 months is compared with the poverty threshold appropriate for that person's family size and composition. If the total income of that person's family is less than the threshold appropriate for that family, then the person is considered poor or "below the poverty level," together with every member of his or her family. If a person is not living with anyone related by birth, marriage, or adoption, then the person's own income is compared with his or her poverty threshold. The total number of persons below the poverty level is the sum of persons in families and the number of unrelated individuals with incomes below the poverty level.

HOUSING, Items 47–54
Source: U.S. Census Bureau—2010 Census of Population and Housing
http://www.census.gov/2010census/data/
Source: U.S. Census Bureau—American Community Survey, 2015 1-year Supplemental Estimates
http://www.census.gov/acs/www/

The housing unit counts in columns 47 through 49 are from the 2010 census. The characteristics of occupied housing units are from the 2010-2014 American Community Survey.

A **housing unit** is a house, apartment, mobile home or trailer, group of rooms, or single room occupied or, if vacant, intended for occupancy as separate living quarters. Separate living quarters are those in which the occupants do not live and eat with any other person in the structure and which have direct access from the outside of the building through a common hall. For vacant units, the criteria of separateness and direct access are applied to the intended occupants whenever possible. If that information cannot be obtained, the criteria are applied to the previous occupants.

The occupants of a housing unit may be a single family, one person living alone, two or more families living together, or any other group of related or unrelated persons who share living quarters. Both occupied and vacant housing units are included in the housing inventory, although recreational vehicles, tents, caves, boats, railroad cars, and the like are included only if they are occupied as a person's usual place of residence.

A housing unit is classified as occupied if it is the usual place of residence of the person or group of persons living in it at the time of enumeration, or if the occupants are only temporarily absent (away on vacation). A household consists of all persons who occupy a housing unit as their usual place of residence. Vacant units for sale or rent include units rented or sold but not occupied and any other units held off the market.

The percent change represents the difference in the number of total housing units in a specified area from 2000 to 2010.

A housing unit is **owner occupied** if the owner or co-owner lives in the unit, even if it is mortgaged or not fully paid for. The owner or co-owner must live in the unit and is usually the first person listed on the census or ACS questionnaire.

All occupied housing units that are not owner occupied, whether they are rented for cash rent or occupied without payment of cash rent, are classified as **renter occupied**.

Median value is the dollar amount that divides the distribution of specified owner-occupied housing units into two equal parts, with half of all units below the median value and half of all units above the median value. Value is defined as the respondent's estimate of what the house would sell for if it were for sale. Data are presented for single-family units on fewer than 10 acres of land that have no business or medical offices on the property.

Median rent divides the distribution of renter-occupied housing units into two equal parts. The rent concept used in this volume is gross rent, which includes the amount of cash rent a renter pays (contract rent) plus the estimated average cost of utilities and fuels, if these are paid by the renter. The rent is the amount of rent only for living quarters and excludes amounts paid for any business or other space occupied. Single-family houses on lots of 10 or more acres of land are also excluded.

COMMUTING, Items 55 and 56

Source: U.S. Census Bureau—American Community Survey, 2015 1-year Supplemental Estimates
http://www.census.gov/acs/www/

Means of transportation to work refers to the principal mode of travel or type of conveyance that a worker usually used to get from home to work during the reference week. This question was asked of people who indicated that they worked at some time during the reference week. People who used different means of transportation on different days of the week were asked to specify the one they used most often, that is, the greatest number of days. People who used more than one means of transportation to get to work each day were asked to report the one used for the longest distance during the work trip. The category, ''Car, truck, or van,'' includes workers using a car (including company cars but excluding taxicabs), a truck of one-ton capacity or less, or a van. The category, ''**Drove alone**,'' includes people who usually drove alone to work as well as people who were driven to work by someone who then drove back home or to a non-work destination.

The question on **travel time to work** was asked of people who indicated that they worked at some time during the reference week, and who reported that they worked outside their home. Travel time to work refers to the total number of minutes that it usually took the worker to get from home to work during the reference week. The elapsed time includes time spent waiting for public transportation, picking up passengers in carpools, and time spent in other activities related to getting to work.

COMPUTER AND INTERNET USE, Items 57 and 58

Source: U.S. Census Bureau—American Community Survey, 2015 1-year Supplemental Estimates
http://www.census.gov/acs/www/

The **computer use** question asked if anyone in the household owned or used a computer and included three response categories for a desktop/laptop, a handheld computer, or some other type of computer. Respondents could select all categories that applied.

Another question asked if any member of the household accesses the **internet**. ''Access'' refers to whether or not someone in the household uses or connects to the Internet, regardless of whether or not they pay for the service. Respondents were to select only ONE of the following choices:

• Yes, with a subscription to an Internet service—This category includes housing units where someone pays to access the Internet through a service such as a data plan for a mobile phone, a cable modem, DSL or other type of service. This will normally refer to a service that someone is billed for directly for Internet alone or sometimes as part of a bundle.

• Yes, without a subscription to an Internet service—Some respondents may live in a city or town that provides free Internet services for their residents. In addition, some colleges or universities provide Internet services. These are examples of cases where respondents may be able to access the Internet without a subscription.

• No Internet access at this house, apartment, or mobile home—This category includes housing units where no one connects to or uses the Internet using a paid service or any free services.

MIGRATION, Items 59 and 60

Source: U.S. Census Bureau—American Community Survey, 2015 1-year Supplemental Estimates
http://www.census.gov/acs/www/

Residence one year ago is used in conjunction with location of current residence to determine the extent of residential mobility of the population and the resulting redistribution of the population across the various states, metropolitan areas, and regions of the country. **Same house** includes all people 1 year old and over who, a year before the survey date, lived in the same house or apartment that they occupied at the time of interview.

The **percent who lived outside** current **county** includes all persons who did not live in their current county 1 year before the interview. However, they may have lived outside their current city but still in the same county.

CIVILIAN LABOR FORCE AND UNEMPLOYMENT, Items 61–64

Source: U.S. Bureau of Labor Statistics—Local Areas Unemployment Statistics
http://www.bls.gov/lau/#tables

Data for the civilian labor force are the product of a federal-state cooperative program in which state employment security agencies prepare labor force and unemployment estimates under concepts, definitions, and technical procedures established by the Bureau of Labor Statistics (BLS). The civilian labor force consists of all civilians 16 years old and over who are either employed or unemployed.

Unemployment includes all persons who did not work during the survey week, made specific efforts to find a job during the previous four weeks, and were available for work during the survey week (except for temporary illness). Persons waiting to be called back to a job from which they had been laid off and those waiting to report to a new job within the next 30 days are included in unemployment figures.

Table D includes annual average data for the year shown. The Local Area Unemployment Statistics data are periodically updated to reflect revised inputs, reestimation, and controlling to new statewide totals.

EMPLOYMENT, Items 65–68

Source: U.S. Census Bureau—American Community Survey, 2015 1-year Supplemental Estimates
http://www.census.gov/acs/www/

The **labor force** includes all persons 16 years old and over who were either (1) ''at work''—those who did any work at all during the reference week as paid employees, worked in either their own business or profession, worked on their own farm, or worked 15 hours or more as unpaid workers in a family farm or business; or (2) ''with a job, but not at work''—those who had a job but were not at work that week due to illness, weather, industrial dispute, vacation, or other personal reasons.

Full-year, Full-Time Workers includes people 16 to 64 years old who usually worked 35 hours or more per week for 50 to 52 weeks in the past 12 months.

BUILDING PERMITS, Items 69–71

Source: U.S. Census Bureau—Building Permits Survey
http://www.census.gov/const/www/permitsindex.html

These figures represent private residential construction authorized by building permits in approximately 20,000 places in the United States. Valuation represents the expected cost of construction as recorded on the building permit. This figure usually excludes the cost of on-site and off-site development and improvements, as well as the cost of heating, plumbing, electrical, and elevator installations.

National, state, and county totals were obtained by adding the data for permit-issuing places within each jurisdiction. These totals thus are limited to permits issued in the 20,000 place universe covered by the Census Bureau and may not include all permits issued within a state. Current surveys indicate that construction is undertaken for all but a very small percentage of housing units authorized by building permits.

Residential building permits include buildings with any number of housing units. Housing units exclude group quarters (such as dormitories and rooming houses), transient accommodations (such as transient hotels, motels, and tourist courts), ''HUD-code'' manufactured (mobile) homes, moved or relocated units, and housing units created in an existing residential or nonresidential structure.

2012 Economic CENSUS: OVERVIEW, Items 72–107

Source: U.S. Census Bureau
http://www.census.gov/econ/census07/

The Economic Census provides a detailed portrait of the nation's economy, from the national to the local level, once every five years. The 2012 Economic Census covers nearly all of the U.S. economy in its basic collection of establishment statistics. The 1997 Economic Census was the first major data source to use the new North American Industry Classification System (NAICS); therefore, data from this census are not comparable to economic data from prior years, which were based on the Standard Industrial Classification (SIC) system.

NAICS, developed in cooperation with Canada and Mexico, classifies North America's economic activities at two-, three-, four-, and five-digit levels of detail; the U.S. version of NAICS further defines industries to a sixth digit. The Economic Census takes advantage of this hierarchy to publish data at these successive levels of detail: sector (two-digit), subsector (three-digit), industry group (four-digit), industry (five-digit), and U.S. industry (six-digit). Information in Table A is at the two-digit level, with a few three- and four-digit items. The data in Table D are at the two-digit level.

Several key statistics are tabulated for all industries in this volume, including number of establishments (or companies), number of employees, payroll, and certain measures of output (sales, receipts, revenue, value of shipments, or value of construction work done).

Number of establishments. An establishment is a single physical location at which business is conducted. It is not necessarily identical with a company or enterprise, which may consist of one establishment or more. Economic Census figures represent a summary of reports for individual establishments rather than companies. For cases in which a census report was received, separate information was obtained for each location where business was conducted. When administrative records of other federal agencies were used instead of a census report, no information was available on the number of locations operated. Each Economic Census establishment was tabulated according to the physical location at which the business was conducted. The count of establishments represents those in business at any time during 2002.

When two activities or more were carried on at a single location under a single ownership, all activities were generally grouped together as a single establishment. The entire establishment was classified on the basis of its major activity and all of its data were included in that classification. However, when distinct and separate economic activities (for which different industry classification codes were appropriate) were conducted at a single location under a single ownership, separate establishment reports for each of the different activities were obtained in the census.

Number of employees. Paid employees consist of the full-time and part-time employees, including salaried officers and executives of corporations. Included are employees on paid sick leave, paid holidays, and paid vacations; not included are proprietors and partners of unincorporated businesses. The definition of paid employees is the same as that used by the Internal Revenue Service (IRS) on form 941. For some industries, the Economic Census gives codes representing the number of employees as a range of numbers (for example, ''100 to 249 employees'' or ''1,000 to 2,499'' employees). In this volume, those codes have been replaced by the standard suppression code ''D.''

Payroll. Payroll includes all forms of compensation, such as salaries, wages, commissions, dismissal pay, bonuses, vacation allowances, sick-leave pay, and employee contributions to qualified pension plans paid during the year to all employees. For corporations, payroll includes amounts paid to officers and executives; for unincorporated businesses, it does not include profit or other compensation of proprietors or partners. Payroll is reported before deductions for Social Security, income tax, insurance, union dues, etc. This definition of payroll is the same as that used by on IRS form 941.

Sales, shipments, receipts, revenue, or business done. This measure includes the total sales, shipments, receipts, revenue, or business done by establishments within the scope of the Economic Census. The definition of each of these items is specific to the economic sector measured.

WHOLESALE TRADE, Items 72–75

Source: U.S. Census Bureau—2012 Economic Census (See Overview of 2012 Economic Census prior to Item 72)

The Wholesale Trade sector (sector 42) comprises establishments engaged in wholesaling merchandise, generally without transformation, and rendering services incidental to the sale of merchandise. The wholesaling process is an intermediate step in the distribution of merchandise.

Wholesalers are organized to sell or arrange the purchase or sale of (1) goods for resale (i.e., goods sold to other wholesalers or retailers), (2) capital or durable nonconsumer goods, and (3) raw and intermediate materials and supplies used in production.

Wholesalers sell merchandise to other businesses and normally operate from a warehouse or office. These warehouses and offices are characterized by having little or no display of merchandise. In addition, neither the design nor the location of the premises is intended to solicit walk-in traffic. Wholesalers do not normally use advertising directed to the general public. In general, customers are initially reached via telephone, in-person marketing, or specialized advertising, which may include the internet and other electronic means. Follow-up orders are either vendor-initiated or client-initiated, are usually based on previous sales, and typically exhibit strong ties between sellers and buyers. In fact, transactions are often conducted between wholesalers and clients that have long-standing business relationships.

This sector is made up of two main types of wholesalers: those that sell goods on their own account and those that arrange sales and purchases for others for a commission or fee.

(1) Establishments that sell goods on their own account are known as wholesale merchants, distributors, jobbers, drop shippers, import/export merchants, and sales branches. These establishments typically maintain their own warehouse, where they receive and handle goods for their customers. Goods are generally sold without transformation, but may include integral functions, such as sorting, packaging, labeling, and other marketing services.

(2) Establishments arranging for the purchase or sale of goods owned by others or purchasing goods on a commission basis are known as agents and brokers, commission merchants, import/export agents and brokers, auction companies, and manufacturers' representatives. These establishments operate from offices and generally do not own or handle the goods they sell.

Some wholesale establishments may be connected with a single manufacturer and promote and sell that particular manufacturer's products to a wide range of other wholesalers or retailers. Other wholesalers may be connected to a retail chain or a limited number of retail chains and only provide the products needed by the particular retail operation(s). These wholesalers may obtain the products from a wide range of manufacturers. Still other wholesalers may not take title to the goods, but act instead as agents and brokers for a commission.

Although wholesaling normally denotes sales in large volumes, durable nonconsumer goods may be sold in single units. Sales of capital or durable nonconsumer goods used in the production of goods and services, such as farm machinery, medium- and heavy-duty trucks, and industrial machinery, are always included in Wholesale Trade.

The city table includes only **Merchant wholesalers, except manufacturers' sales branches and offices,** establishments primarily engaged in buying and selling merchandise on their own account. Included here are such types of establishments as wholesale distributors and jobbers, importers, exporters, own-brand importers/marketers, terminal and country grain elevators, and farm products assemblers.

RETAIL TRADE, Items 76–79
Source: U.S. Census Bureau—2012 Economic Census (See Overview of 2012 Economic Census prior to Item 72)

The Retail Trade sector (44–45) is made up of establishments engaged in retailing merchandise, generally without transformation, and rendering services incidental to the sale of merchandise.

The retailing process is the final step in the distribution of merchandise; retailers are therefore organized to sell merchandise in small quantities to the general public. This sector comprises two main types of retailers: store and nonstore retailers.

Store retailers operate fixed point-of-sale locations, located and designed to attract a high volume of walk-in customers. In general, retail stores have extensive displays of merchandise and use mass-media advertising to attract customers. They typically sell merchandise to the general public for personal or household consumption; some also serve business and institutional clients. These include establishments such as office supply stores, computer and software stores, building materials dealers, plumbing supply stores, and electrical supply stores. Catalog showrooms, gasoline service stations, automotive dealers, and mobile home dealers are treated as store retailers.

In addition to retailing merchandise, some types of store retailers are also engaged in the provision of after-sales services, such as repair and installation. For example, new automobile dealers, electronic and appliance stores, and musical instrument and supply stores often provide repair services. As a general rule, establishments engaged in retailing merchandise and providing after-sales services are classified in this sector.

Nonstore retailers, like store retailers, are organized to serve the general public, although their retailing methods differ. The establishments of this subsector reach customers and market merchandise with methods including the broadcasting of "infomercials," the broadcasting and publishing of direct-response advertising, the publishing of paper and electronic catalogs, door-to-door solicitation, in-home demonstration, selling from portable stalls (street vendors, except food), and distribution through vending machines. Establishments engaged in the direct sale (nonstore) of products, such as home heating oil dealers and home-delivery newspaper routes are included in this sector.

The buying of goods for resale is a characteristic of retail trade establishments that distinguishes them from establishments in the Agriculture, Manufacturing, and Construction sectors. For example, farms that sell their products at or from the point of production are classified in Agriculture instead of in Retail Trade. Similarly, establishments that both manufacture and sell their products to the general public are classified in Manufacturing instead of Retail Trade. However, establishments that engage in processing activities incidental to retailing are classified in Retail Trade.

REAL ESTATE AND RENTAL AND LEASING, Items 80–83

Source: U.S. Census Bureau—2012 Economic Census (See Overview of 2012 Economic Census prior to Item 72)

The Real Estate and Rental and Leasing sector (53) comprises establishments primarily engaged in renting, leasing, or otherwise allowing the use of tangible or intangible assets, and establishments providing related services. The major portion of this sector is made up of establishments that rent, lease, or otherwise allow the use of their own assets by others. The assets may be tangible, such as real estate and equipment, or intangible, such as patents and trademarks.

This sector also includes establishments primarily engaged in managing real estate for others, selling, renting, and/or buying real estate for others, and appraising real estate. These activities are closely related to this sector's main activity. In addition, a substantial proportion of property management is self-performed by lessors.

The main components of this sector are the real estate lessors industries; equipment lessors industries (including motor vehicles, computers, and consumer goods); and lessors of nonfinancial intangible assets (except copyrighted works).

PROFESSIONAL, SCIENTIFIC, AND TECHNICAL SERVICES, Items 84–87

Source: U.S. Census Bureau—2012 Economic Census (See Overview of 2012 Economic Census prior to Item 72)

The Professional, Scientific, and Technical Services sector (54) is made up of establishments that specialize in performing professional, scientific, and technical activities for others. These activities require a high degree of expertise and training. The establishments in this sector specialize in one or more areas and provide services to clients in a variety of industries (and, in some cases, to households). Activities performed include legal advice and representation; accounting, bookkeeping, and payroll services; architectural, engineering, and specialized design services; computer services; consulting services; research services; advertising services; photographic services; translation and interpretation services; veterinary services; and other professional, scientific, and technical services.

Table D includes only those establishments subject to federal income tax.

This sector excludes establishments primarily engaged in providing a range of day-to-day office administrative services, such as financial planning, billing and record keeping, personnel services, and physical distribution and logistics services. These establishments are classified in sector 56, Administrative and Support and Waste Management and Remediation Services.

MANUFACTURING, Items 88–91

Source: U.S. Census Bureau—2012 Economic Census (See Overview of 2012 Economic Census prior to Item 72)

The Manufacturing sector (31–33) is made up of establishments engaged in the mechanical, physical, or chemical transformation of materials, substances, or components into new products. The assembling of component parts of manufactured products is considered manufacturing, except in cases in which the activity is appropriately classified in the Construction sector. Establishments in the Manufacturing sector are often described as plants, factories, or mills, and characteristically use power-driven machines and materials-handling equipment. However, establishments that transform materials or substances into new products by hand or in the worker's home, and establishments engaged in selling to the general public products made on the same premises from which they are sold (such as bakeries, candy stores, and custom tailors) may also be included in this sector. Manufacturing establishments may process materials or contract with other establishments to process their materials for them. Both types of establishments are included in the Manufacturing sector.

The materials, substances, or components transformed by manufacturing establishments are raw materials that are products of agriculture, forestry, fishing, mining, or quarrying, or are products of other manufacturing establishments. The materials used may be purchased directly from producers, obtained through customary trade channels, or secured without recourse to the market by transferring the product from one establishment to another, under the same ownership. The new product of a manufacturing establishment may be finished (in the sense that it is ready for utilization or consumption), or it may be semifinished to become an input for an establishment engaged in further manufacturing. For example, the product of the alumina refinery is the input used in the primary production of aluminum; primary aluminum is the input used in an aluminum wire drawing plant; and aluminum wire is the input used in a fabricated wire product manufacturing establishment.

Data are included for cities with 500 or more employees in the Manufacturing sector.

ACCOMMODATION AND FOOD SERVICES, Items 92–95

Source: U.S. Census Bureau—2012 Economic Census (See Overview of 2012 Economic Census prior to Item 72)

The Accommodation and Food Services sector (72) consists of establishments that provide customers with lodging and/or meals, snacks, and beverages for immediate consumption. This sector includes both accommodation and food services establishments because the two activities are often combined at the same establishment.

Excluded from this sector are civic and social organizations, amusement and recreation parks, theaters, and other recreation or entertainment facilities providing food and beverage services.

ARTS, ENTERTAINMENT, AND RECREATION, Items 96–99

Source: U.S. Census Bureau—2012 Economic Census (See Overview of 2012 Economic Census prior to Item 72)

The Arts, Entertainment, and Recreation sector (71) includes a wide range of establishments that operate facilities or provide services that meet the diverse cultural, entertainment, and recreational interests of their patrons. This sector is made up of: (1) establishments that are involved in producing, promoting, or participating in live performances, events, or exhibits intended for public viewing; (2) establishments that preserve and exhibit objects and sites of historical, cultural, or educational interest; and (3) establishments that operate facilities or provide services that enable patrons to participate in recreational activities or pursue amusement, hobby, and leisure time interests.

Some establishments that provide cultural, entertainment, or recreational facilities and services are classified in other sectors. Excluded from this sector are: (1) establishments that provide both accommodations and recreational facilities—such as hunting and fishing camps and resort and casino hotels—are classified in subsector 721, Accommodation; (2) restaurants and night clubs that provide live entertainment in addition to the sale of food and beverages are classified in subsector 722, Food Services and Drinking Places; (3) motion picture theaters, libraries and archives, and publishers of newspapers, magazines, books, periodicals, and computer software are classified in sector 51, Information; and (4) establishments that use transportation equipment to provide recreational and entertainment services, such as those operating sightseeing buses, dinner cruises, or helicopter rides, are classified in subsector 487, Scenic and Sightseeing Transportation.

Table D includes only those establishments subject to federal tax.

HEALTH CARE AND SOCIAL ASSISTANCE, Items 100–103

Source: U.S. Census Bureau—2012 Economic Census (See Overview of 2012 Economic Census prior to Item 72)

The Health Care and Social Assistance sector (62) consists of establishments that provide health care and social assistance services to individuals. The sector includes both health care and social assistance because it is sometimes difficult to distinguish between the boundaries of these two activities. The industries in this sector are arranged on a continuum, starting with establishments that provide medical care exclusively, continuing with those that provide health care and social assistance, and finishing with those that provide only social assistance. The services provided by establishments in this sector are delivered by trained professionals. All industries in the sector share this commonality of process—namely, labor inputs of health practitioners or social workers with the requisite expertise. Many of the industries in the sector are defined based on the educational degree held by the practitioners included in the industry.

Excluded from this sector are aerobic classes, which can be found in subsector 713, Amusement, Gambling, and Recreation

Industries; and nonmedical diet and weight-reducing centers, which can be found in subsector 812, Personal and Laundry Services. Although these can be viewed as health services, they are not typically delivered by health practitioners.

Table D includes only those establishments subject to federal tax.

OTHER SERVICES, EXCEPT PUBLIC ADMINISTRATION Items 104–107

Source: U.S. Census Bureau—2012 Economic Census (See Overview of 2012 Economic Census prior to Item 72)

The Other Services, Except Public Administration sector (81) comprises establishments engaged in providing services not specifically categorized elsewhere in the classification system. Establishments in this sector are primarily engaged in activities such as equipment and machinery repairing, promoting or administering religious activities, grant making, and advocacy; this sector also includes establishments that provide dry-cleaning and laundry services, personal care services, death care services, pet care services, photofinishing services, temporary parking services, and dating services.

Private households that employ workers on or about the premises in activities primarily concerned with the operation of the household are included in this sector.

In Table D, only firms subject to federal tax are included.

Excluded from this sector are establishments primarily engaged in retailing new equipment and performing repairs and general maintenance on equipment. These establishments are classified in sector 44–45, Retail Trade.

CITY GOVERNMENT EMPLOYMENT AND PAYROLL, Items 171-179

Source: U.S. Census Bureau—2012 Census of Governments
http://www.census.gov/govs/cog2012/

These items include data for municipal governments only. They do not include any special district government entities within the city. The Census of Governments identifies the scope and nature of the nation's state and local government sector; provides authoritative benchmark figures of public finance and public employment; classifies local government organizations, powers, and activities; and measures federal, state, and local fiscal relationships. The Employment component was mailed March 2012 to collect information on the number of state and local government civilian employees and their payrolls.

Government employees include all persons paid for personal services performed, including persons paid from federally funded programs, paid elected or appointed officials, persons in a paid leave status, and persons paid on a per meeting, annual, semiannual, or quarterly basis. Unpaid officials, pensioners, persons whose work is performed on a fee basis, and contractors and their employees are excluded from the count of employees. **Full-Time Equivalent employees** is a computed statistic representing the number of full-time employees that could have been employed if the reported number of hours worked by part-time employees had been worked by full-time employees. This statistic is calculated separately for each function of a government by dividing the "part-time hours paid" by the standard number of hours for full-time employees in the particular government and then adding the resulting quotient to the number of full-time employees.

March payroll represents gross payroll amounts for the one-month period of March for full-time and part-time employees. Gross payroll includes all salaries, wages, fees, commissions, and overtime paid to employees **before** withholdings for taxes, insurance, etc. It also includes incentive payments that are paid at regular pay intervals. It excludes employer share of fringe benefits like retirement, Social Security, health and life insurance, lump sum payments, and so forth.

Administration and Judicial and Legal combines **Financial administration, Other government administration, and Judicial and Legal** activities. **Financial administration** includes activities concerned with tax assessment and collection, custody and disbursement of funds, debt management, administration of trust funds, budgeting, and other government-wide financial management activities. This function is not applied to school district or special district governments. **Other government administration** applies to the legislative and government-wide administrative agencies of governments. Included here are overall planning and zoning activities, and central personnel and administrative activities. This function is not applied to school district or special district governments. **Judicial and legal** includes all court and court related activities (except probation and parole activities that are included at the "Correction" function), court activities of sheriff's offices, prosecuting attorneys' and public defenders' offices, legal departments, and attorneys providing government-wide legal service.

Police and Corrections includes all activities concerned, with the enforcement of law and order, including coroner's offices, police training academies, investigation bureaus, and local jails, "lockups," or other detention facilities not intended to serve as correctional facilities. **Corrections** includes activities pertaining to the confinement and correction of adults and minors convicted of criminal offenses. Pardon, probation, and parole activities are also included here.

Fire protection includes local government fire protection and prevention activities plus any ambulance, rescue, or other auxiliary services provided by a fire protection agency. Volunteer firefighters, if remunerated for their services on a "per fire" or some other basis, are included as part-time employees.

Highways and transportation includes activities associated with the maintenance and operation of streets, roads, sidewalks, bridges, tunnels, toll roads, and ferries. Snow and ice removal, street lighting, and highway and traffic engineering activities are also included here. Also included are the operation, maintenance, and construction of public mass transit systems, including subways, surface rails, and buses, and the provision, construction, operation, maintenance; support of public waterways, harbors, docks, wharves, and related marine terminal facilities; and activities associated with the operation and support of publicly operated airport facilities.

Health and Welfare includes **Health, Hospitals, and Public welfare. Health** includes administration of public health programs, community and visiting nurse services, immunization programs, drug abuse rehabilitation programs, health and food

inspection activities, operation of outpatient clinics, and environmental pollution control activities. **Hospitals** includes only government operated medical care facilities that provide inpatient care. Employees and payrolls of private corporations that lease and operate government-owned hospital facilities are excluded.

Public Welfare includes the administration of various public assistance programs for the needy, veteran services, operation of nursing homes, indigent care institutions, and programs that provide payments for medical care, handicap transportation, and other services for the needy.

Natural resources and Utilities includes activities primarily concerned with the conservation and development of natural resources (soil, water, energy, minerals, etc.) and the regulation of industries that develop, utilize, or affect natural resources, as well as the operation and maintenance of **parks**, playgrounds, swimming pools, public beaches, auditoriums, public golf courses, museums, marinas, botanical gardens, and zoological parks. **Utilities, sewerage, and waste management** includes operation, maintenance, and construction of public water supply systems, including production, acquisition, and distribution of water to general public or to other public or private utilities, for residential, commercial, and industrial use; activities associated with the production or acquisition and distribution of electric power; provision, maintenance, and operation of sanitary and storm sewer systems and sewage disposal and treatment facilities; and refuse collection and disposal, operation of sanitary landfills, and street cleaning activities.

Education and libraries includes activities associated with the operation of public elementary and secondary schools and locally operated vocational-technical schools. Special education programs operated by elementary and secondary school systems are also included as are all ancillary services associated with the operation of schools, such as pupil transportation and food service. Also included are the establishment and provision of libraries for use by the general public and the technical support of privately operated libraries. This category includes classroom teachers, principals, supervisors of instruction, librarians, teacher aides, library aides, and guidance and psychological personnel as well as school superintendents and other administrative personnel, clerical and secretarial staffs, plant operation and maintenance personnel, health and recreation employees, transportation and food service personnel, and any student employees. Also included are any degree granting institutions that provide academic training above grade 12.

CITY GOVERNMENT FINANCES, Items 117–139
Source: U.S. Census Bureau—2012 Census of Governments
http://www.census.gov/govs/cog

Revenue and expenditure data are included in Table D for municipal governments only. The data do not include funds of any special district governments located in the city. For example, if a city's school district is a separate governmental unit, it is not included.

Total **general revenue** includes all revenue except utility, liquor stores, and insurance trust revenue. All tax revenue and intergovernmental revenue, even if designated for employee-retirement or local utility purpose, are classified as general revenue.

Intergovernmental revenue covers amounts received from other governments as fiscal aid in the form of shared revenues and grants-in-aid, as reimbursements for the performance of general government functions and specific services for the paying government (for example, care of prisoners or contractual research), or in lieu of taxes. It excludes any amounts received from other governments from the sale of property, commodities, and utility services. All intergovernmental revenue is classified as general revenue. Intergovernmental revenue from the state governments includes amounts originally from the federal government but channeled through the state.

Taxes consist of compulsory contributions exacted by governments for public purposes. However, this category excludes employer and employee payments for retirement and social insurance purposes, which are classified as insurance trust revenue. All tax revenue is classified as general revenue and comprises amounts received (including interest and penalties, but excluding protested amounts and refunds) from all taxes imposed by a government. Note that local government tax revenue excludes any amounts from shares of state-imposed and collected taxes, which are classified as intergovernmental revenue.

Property taxes are based on ownership of property and measured by its value. They include general property taxes related to property as a whole—real and personal, tangible or intangible—whether taxed at a single rate or at classified rates. Also included are taxes on selected types of property, such as motor vehicles or certain or all intangibles.

Sales and gross receipts taxes include "licenses" at more than nominal rates, based on volume or value of transfers of goods or services; taxes upon gross receipts or upon gross income; and related taxes based upon the use, storage, production (other than the severance of natural resources), importation, or consumption of goods. Dealer discounts "commissions," which are allowed to merchants for the collection of taxes from consumers, are excluded.

Total **general expenditure** includes all city expenditure other than specifically enumerated kinds of expenditure, including utility, liquor store, and employee-retirement and other insurance trust expenditures.

Capital outlays are direct expenditures for contract of force account construction or buildings, roads, and other improvements, and for purchases of equipment, land, and existing structures. They include amounts for additions, replacements, and major alterations to fixed work and structures. Expenditures for repair to such works and structures, however, is classified as current operation expenditure.

A major portion of capital outlay is commonly financed by borrowing, while governmental revenue does not include receipts from borrowing. Among other things, this distorts the relationship between the totals presented for revenue and expenditure and renders this relationship useless as a direct measure of the degree of budgetary "balance" (as that term is generally applied).

Public welfare expenditure covers support of and assistance to needy persons; this aid is contingent upon the person's needs. Included are cash assistance paid directly to needy persons; vendor payments made directly to private purveyors for medical care, burials, and other commodities and services provided under welfare programs; welfare institutions; and any intergovernmental or other direct expenditure for welfare purposes. Pensions to former employees and other benefits not contingent on need are excluded.

Highway expenditure is for the provision and maintenance of highway facilities, including toll turnpikes, bridges, tunnels, and ferries, as well as regular roads, highways, and streets. Also included are expenditures for street lighting and for snow and ice removal. Not included are highway policing and traffic control, which are considered part of police protection.

Parking facilities include the construction, purchase, maintenance, and operation of public-use parking lots, garages, parking meters, and other distinctive parking facilities on a commercial basis.

Education is mainly for the provision and general support of schools and other educational facilities and services, including those for educational institutions beyond high school. Elementary and secondary education includes the provision of public kindergarten through high school education by local governments. It encompasses instructional, support, and auxiliary services (school lunch, student activities, and community services) offered by public school systems. Higher education consists of all local institutions of higher education.

Health expenditures include outpatient health services other than hospital care, such as public health administration; research and education; categorical health programs; treatment and immunization clinics; nursing; environmental health activities, such as air and water pollution control; ambulance service if provided separately from fire protection services; and other general public health activities, such as mosquito abatement. School health services provided by health agencies (rather than school agencies) are included here. Not included are sewage treatment operations, which are classified as part of sewerage and sanitation. **Hospital expenditures** include financing, construction, acquisition, maintenance and operation of hospital facilities, provision of hospital care, and support of public or private hospitals.

Police protection encompasses expenditures for the preservation of law and order, as well as for traffic safety. It includes police patrols and communications, crime prevention activities, detention and custody of persons awaiting trial, traffic safety, and vehicular inspection.

Sewerage and recreation include sanitary and storm sewers, sewage disposal facilities and services, and other government activities for such purposes. Street cleaning and the collection and disposal of garbage and other waste are also included.

Parks and recreation includes cultural and scientific activities, such as museums and art galleries; organized recreation, including playgrounds and playing fields, swimming pools, and bathing beaches; and municipal parks and special recreation facilities, such as auditoriums, stadiums, auto camps, recreation piers, and boat harbors.

Housing and community development includes city housing and redevelopment projects and the regulation, promotion, and support of private housing and redevelopment activities. Data from Arizona, Kentucky, Michigan, New Mexico, New York, and Virginia generally include municipal housing authorities. Housing authorities for other cities are usually classified as independent governments, and data from them are not included.

Interest on debt is the amount paid for the use of borrowed money.

Total **debt outstanding** is the total of debt obligations remaining unpaid on the date specified. **Debt issued during the year** is the amount of the outstanding debt that was recently borrowed.

CLIMATE, Items 140–146

Source: National Oceanic and Atmospheric Administration
https://www.ncdc.noaa.gov/data-access/land-based-station-data/land-based-datasets/climate-normals

All climate data are average values for the 30-year period from 1971 to 2000.

Mean temperatures for January and July were determined by adding the average daily maximum temperatures and the average daily minimum temperatures and dividing by two.

Temperature limits represent average daily minimum for January and average daily maximum for July.

Annual precipitation values are the average annual water equivalent of all precipitation for the 30-year period.

Heating and cooling degree days are used as relative measures of the energy required for heating and cooling buildings. One heating degree day is accumulated for each whole degree that the mean daily temperature is below 65 degrees Fahrenheit (a mean daily temperature of 62 degrees Fahrenheit will produce three heating degree days). Cooling degree days are accumulated in similar fashion for deviations of the mean daily temperature above 65 degrees Fahrenheit.

TABLE E—CONGRESSIONAL DISTRICTS OF THE 115TH CONGRESS

Members of the House of Representatives are for the 115th Congress.

LAND AREA, Items 1–3

Source: U.S. Census Bureau—2016 U.S. Gazetteer Files,
http://www.census.gov/geo/maps-data/data/gazetteer2016.html

Land area measurements are shown to the nearest square mile. Land area is an area measurement providing the size, in square miles, of the land portions of each county.

POPULATION, Items 2–3

Source: U.S. Census Bureau—American Community Survey
http://www.census.gov/acs/www/

The population data are estimates from the American Community Survey.

POPULATION AND POPULATION CHARACTERISTICS, Items 4–24

Source: U.S. Census Bureau—American Community Survey
http://www.census.gov/acs/www/

Data on age, sex, race, Hispanic origin foreign-born residents, and percent born in state of residence are from the 2015 American Community Survey.

Data on race were derived from answers to the question on race that was asked of all respondents. The concept of race, as used by the Census Bureau, reflects self-identification by people according to the race or races with which they most closely identify. These categories are sociopolitical constructs and should not be interpreted as being scientific or anthropological in nature. Furthermore, the race categories include both racial and national origin groups.

In Table E, Columns 4 through 8 refer to individuals who identified with each racial category alone, while column 9 includes persons who identified with two or more races.

The **White** population is defined as persons who indicated their race as White, as well as persons who did not classify themselves in one of the specific race categories listed on the questionnaire but entered a nationality such as Irish, German, Italian, Lebanese, Near Easterner, Arab, or Polish.

The **Black** population includes persons who indicated their race as "Black, African Am., or Negro," as well as persons who did not classify themselves in one of the specific race categories but reported entries such as African American, Afro American, Kenyan, Nigerian, or Haitian.

The **American Indian or Alaska Native** population includes persons who indicated their race as American Indian or Alaska Native, as well as persons who did not classify themselves in one of the specific race categories but reported entries such as Canadian Indian, French-American Indian, Spanish-American Indian, Eskimo, Aleut, Alaska Indian, or any of the American Indian or Alaska Native tribes.

The **Asian and Pacific Islander** population combines two census groupings: **Asian** and **Native Hawaiian or Other Pacific Islander**. The **Asian** population includes persons who indicated their race as Asian Indian, Chinese, Filipino, Japanese, Korean, Vietnamese, or "Other Asian," as well as persons who provided write-in entries of such groups as Cambodian, Laotian, Hmong, Pakistani, or Taiwanese. The **Native Hawaiian or Other Pacific Islander** population includes persons who indicated their race as "Native Hawaiian," "Guamanian or Chamorro," "Samoan," or "Other Pacific Islander," as well as persons who reported entries such as Part Hawaiian, American Samoan, Fijian, Melanesian, or Tahitian.

The **Hispanic population** is based on a question that asked respondents "Is this person Spanish/Hispanic/Latino?" Persons marking any one of the four Hispanic categories (i.e., Mexican, Puerto Rican, Cuban, or other Spanish) are collectively referred to as Hispanic.

The **Non-Hispanic White alone** number in Column 11 includes only those persons who were not Hispanic and whose race was "White only."

The **female** population is shown as a percentage of total population.

The **foreign-born** population includes all persons who were not U.S. citizens at birth. Foreign-born persons are those who indicated they were either a U.S. citizen by naturalization or were not a citizen of the United States. The foreign-born population consists of immigrants (legal permanent residents), temporary migrants (students), humanitarian migrants (refugees), and unauthorized migrants (persons illegally residing in the United States).

Percent born in state of residence is shown as a percentage of total population.

Age is defined as age at last birthday (number of completed years since birth).

EDUCATION—SCHOOL ENROLLMENT AND EDUCATIONAL ATTAINMENT, Items 25–27
Source: U.S. Census Bureau—American Community Survey
http://www.census.gov/acs/www/

Data on school enrollment and educational attainment were derived from a sample of the population. Persons were classified as enrolled in school if they reported attending a ''regular'' public or private school (or college) during the year. The instructions were to ''include only nursery school, kindergarten, elementary school, and schooling which would lead to a high school diploma or a college degree'' as regular school. The Census Bureau defines a public school as ''any school or college controlled and supported by a local, county, state, or federal government.'' Schools primarily supported and controlled by religious organizations or other private groups are defined as private schools.

Data on **educational attainment** are tabulated for the population 25 years old and over. The data were derived from a question that asked respondents for the highest level of school completed or the highest degree received. Persons who had passed a high school equivalency examination were considered high school graduates. Schooling received in foreign schools was to be reported as the equivalent grade or years in the regular American school system.

Vocational and technical training, such as barber school training; business, trade, technical, and vocational schools; or other training for a specific trade are specifically excluded.

High school graduate or more. This category includes persons who have received a high school diploma or its equivalent, and those who reported any level higher than a high school diploma.

Bachelor's degree or more. This category includes persons who have received bachelor's degrees, master's degrees, professional school degrees (such as law school or medical school degrees), and doctoral degrees.

HOUSEHOLDS, Items 28–33
Source: U.S. Census Bureau—American Community Survey
http://www.census.gov/acs/www/

A **household** includes all persons who occupy a housing unit. (Persons not living in households are classified as living in group quarters.) A housing unit is a house, an apartment, a mobile home, a group of rooms, or a single room occupied (or, if vacant, intended for occupancy) as separate living quarters. Separate living quarters are those in which the occupants live separately from any other persons in the building and have direct access from the outside of the building or through a common hall. The occupants may be a single family, one person living alone, two or more families living together, or any other group of related or unrelated persons who share living quarters. The number of households is the same as the number of year-round occupied housing units.

A **family** includes a householder and one or more other persons living in the same household who are related to the householder by birth, marriage, or adoption. All persons in a household who are related to the householder are regarded as members of his or her family. A **family household** may contain persons not related to the householder; thus, family households may include more members than families do. A household can contain only one family for the purposes of census tabulations. Not all households contain families, as a household may comprise a group of unrelated persons or of one person living alone. Families are classified by type as either a ''husband-wife family'' or ''other family,'' according to the presence or absence of a spouse.

The measure of **persons per household** is obtained by dividing the number of persons in households by the number of households or householders. One person in each household is designated as the householder. In most cases, this is the person (or one of the persons) in whose name the house is owned, being bought, or rented. If there is no such person in the household, any adult household member 15 years old and over can be designated as the householder.

The category **female family householder** includes only female-headed family households with no spouse present.

GROUP QUARTERS, Items 34–39
Source: U.S. Census Bureau—American Community Survey
http://www.census.gov/acs/www/

The Census Bureau classifies all people not living in households as living in **group quarters**. There are two types of group quarters: institutional, including **correctional facilities**, **nursing homes**, and mental hospitals; and non-institutional, including **college dormitories**, **military quarters**, group homes, missions, and shelters.

HOUSING, Items 40—45
Source: U.S. Census Bureau—American Community Survey
http://www.census.gov/acs/www/

A **housing unit** is a house, apartment, mobile home or trailer, group of rooms, or single room occupied or, if vacant, intended for occupancy as separate living quarters. Separate living quarters are those in which the occupants do not live and eat with any other person in the structure and which have direct access from the outside of the building or through a common hall. For vacant units, the criteria of separateness and direct access are applied to the intended occupants whenever possible. If that information cannot be obtained, the criteria are applied to the previous occupants.

The occupants of a housing unit may be a single family, one person living alone, two or more families living together, or any other group of related or unrelated persons who share living quarters. Both occupied and vacant housing units are included in the housing inventory, although recreational vehicles, tents, caves, boats, railroad cars, and the like are included only if they are occupied as a person's usual place of residence.

A housing unit is classified as **occupied** if it is the usual place of residence of the person or group of persons living in it at the time of interview, or if the occupants are only temporarily absent (away on vacation). A household consists of all persons who occupy a housing unit as their usual place of residence. Vacant units for sale or rent include units rented or sold but not occupied and any other units held off the market.

A housing unit is **owner occupied** if the owner or co-owner lives in the unit, even if it is mortgaged or not fully paid for. The owner or co-owner must live in the unit and is usually the first person listed on the census questionnaire.

All occupied housing units that are not owner occupied, whether they are rented for cash rent or occupied without payment of cash rent, are classified as **renter occupied**.

Median value is the dollar amount that divides the distribution of specified owner-occupied housing units into two equal parts, with half of all units below the median value and half of all units above the median value. Value is defined as the respondent's estimate of what the house would sell for if it was for sale. Data are presented for single-family units on fewer than 10 acres of land that have no business or medical offices on the property.

Median rent divides the distribution of renter-occupied housing units into two equal parts. The rent concept used in this volume is gross rent, which includes the amount of cash rent a renter pays (contract rent) plus the estimated average cost of utilities and fuels, if these are paid by the renter. The rent is the amount of rent only for living quarters and excludes amounts paid for any business or other space occupied. Single-family houses on lots of 10 or more acres of land are also excluded.

Housing cost as a percentage of income is shown separately for owners with mortgages, owners without mortgages, and renters. Rent as a percentage of income is a computed ratio of gross rent and monthly household income (total household income the past 12 months divided by 12). Selected owner costs include utilities and fuels, mortgage payments, insurance, taxes, etc. In each case, the ratio of housing cost to income is computed separately for each housing unit. The housing cost ratios for half of all units are above the median shown in this book, and half are below the median shown in the book.

Substandard units are occupied units that are overcrowded or lack complete plumbing facilities. For the purposes of this item, "overcrowded" is defined as having 1.01 persons or more per room. Complete plumbing facilities include hot and cold piped water, a flush toilet, and a bathtub or shower. These facilities must be located inside the housing unit, but do not have to be in the same room.

INCOME AND POVERTY, Items 46–51
Source: U.S. Census Bureau—American Community Survey
http://www.census.gov/acs/www/

The data on income were derived from responses of a sample of persons 15 years old and over. **Total money income** is the sum of the amounts reported separately for wage or salary income; net self-employment income; interest, dividends, or net rental or royalty income or income from estates and trusts; Social Security or railroad retirement income; Supplemental Security Income (SSI); public assistance or welfare payments; retirement, survivor, or disability pensions; and all other income. Receipts from the following sources are not included as income: capital gains; money received from the sale of property (unless the recipient was engaged in the business of selling such property); the value of income "in kind" from food stamps, public housing subsidies, medical care, employer contributions for individuals, etc.; withdrawal of bank deposits; money borrowed; tax refunds; exchange of money between relatives living in the same household; and gifts, lump-sum inheritances, insurance payments, and other types of lump-sum receipts.

Per capita income is the mean income computed for every man, woman, and child in a particular group. It is derived by dividing the aggregate income of a particular group by the resident population in that group. Per capita income is rounded to the nearest whole dollar.

Household income includes the income of the householder and all other individuals 15 years old and over in the household, whether or not they are related to the householder. Since many households consist of only one person, median household income is usually less than median family income.

The **poverty status** data were derived from data collected on the number of persons in a household, from questionnaire item 3, which provided data on each person's relationship to the householder, and questionnaire items 41 and 42, which were also used to derive the income data. The Social Security Administration (SSA) developed the original poverty definition in 1964, which federal interagency committees subsequently revised in 1969 and 1980. The Office of Management and Budget's (OMB) *Directive 14* prescribes the SSA's definition as the official poverty measure for federal agencies to use in their statistical work. Poverty statistics presented in American Community Survey products adhere to the standards defined by OMB in *Directive 14*.

Poverty thresholds vary depending on three criteria: size of family, number of children, and, for one- and two-person families, age of householder. In determining the poverty status of families and unrelated individuals, the Census Bureau uses thresholds (income cutoffs) arranged in a two-dimensional matrix. The matrix consists of family size (from one person to nine or more persons), cross-classified by presence and number of family members under 18 years old (from no children present to eight or more children present). Unrelated individuals and two-person families are further differentiated by age of reference person (under 65 years old and 65 years old and over). To determine a person's poverty status, the person's total family income over the previous 12 months is compared with the poverty threshold appropriate for that person's family size and composition. If the total income of that person's family is less than the threshold

Poverty Thresholds for 2015 by Size of Family and Number of Related Children Under 18 Years

Size of family unit	Weighted average thresholds	Related children under 18 years								
		None	One	Two	Three	Four	Five	Six	Seven	Eight or more
One person (unrelated individual) ...	12,082									
Under 65 years	12,331	12,331								
65 years and over	11,367	11,367								
Two people	15,391									
Householder under 65 years	15,952	15,871	16,337							
Householder 65 years and over...	14,342	14,326	16,275							
Three people................................	18,871	18,540	19,078	19,096						
Four people..................................	24,257	24,447	24,847	24,036	24,120					
Five people	28,741	29,482	29,911	28,995	28,286	27,853				
Six people	32,542	33,909	34,044	33,342	32,670	31,670	31,078			
Seven people...............................	36,998	39,017	39,260	38,421	37,835	36,745	35,473	34,077		
Eight people.................................	41,029	43,637	44,023	43,230	42,536	41,551	40,300	38,999	38,668	
Nine people or more.....................	49,177	52,493	52,747	52,046	51,457	50,490	49,159	47,956	47,658	45,822

Source: U.S. Census Bureau.

appropriate for that family, then the person is considered poor or "below the poverty level," together with every member of his or her family. If a person is not living with anyone related by birth, marriage, or adoption, then the person's own income is compared with his or her poverty threshold. The total number of persons below the poverty level is the sum of persons in families and the number of unrelated individuals with incomes below the poverty level over the previous 12 months. The average poverty threshold for a four-person family was $24,257 in 2015.

The data on participation in the Food Stamp Program are designed to identify households in which one or more of the current members received food stamps during the past 12 months. Once a food stamp household was identified, a question was asked about the total value of all food stamps received by the household during that 12-month period. The Food Stamp Act of 1977 defines this federally funded program as one intended to "permit low-income households to obtain a more nutritious diet" (from title XIII of P.L. 95-113, The Food Stamp Act of 1977, declaration of policy). Providing eligible households with coupons that can be used to purchase food increases food purchasing power. The Food and Nutrition Service (FNS) of the U.S. Department of Agriculture (USDA) administers the Food Stamp program through state and local welfare offices. The Food Stamp program is the major national income support program to which all low-income and low-resource households, regardless of household characteristics, are eligible.

CIVILIAN LABOR FORCE, UNEMPLOYMENT, AND EMPLOYMENT, Items 52–58
Source: U.S. Census Bureau—American Community Survey
http://www.census.gov/acs/www/

The **civilian labor force** consists of all civilians 16 years old and over who are either employed or unemployed.

Unemployment includes all persons who did not work during the survey week, made specific efforts to find a job during the previous four weeks, and were available for work during the survey week (except for temporary illness). Persons waiting to

be called back to a job from which they had been laid off and those waiting to report to a new job within the next 30 days are included in unemployment figures.

Total employment includes all civilians 16 years old and over who were either (1) "at work"—those who did any work at all during the reference week as paid employees, worked in either their own business or profession, worked on their own farm, or worked 15 hours or more as unpaid workers in a family farm or business; or (2) "with a job, but not at work"—those who had a job but were not at work that week due to illness, weather, industrial dispute, vacation, or other personal reasons.

The **occupational categories** are based on the occupational classification system that was developed for the 2000 census. This system consists of 539 specific occupational categories for employed persons arranged into 23 major occupational groups. This classification was developed based on the *Standard Occupational Classification (SOC) Manual: 2010*, published by the Executive Office of the President, Office of Management and Budget.

PERSONS WITH NO HEALTH INSURANCE, Item 59
Source: U.S. Census Bureau—American Community Survey
http://www.census.gov/acs/www/

The percentage of persons under age 65 with no **health insurance** shows the percentage of the population of each congressional district who were not covered by private health plans purchased directly or provided by an employer, Medicaid, Medicare, or military health care.

SOCIAL SECURITY AND SUPPLEMENTAL SECURITY INCOME, Items 60–62
Source: U.S. Social Security Administration
http://www.ssa.gov/policy/docs/factsheets/cong_stats/

Social Security beneficiaries are persons receiving benefits under the Old-Age, Survivors, and Disability Insurance Program.

These include retired or disabled workers covered by the program, their spouses and dependent children, and the surviving spouses and dependent children of deceased workers.

Supplemental Security Income (SSI) recipients are persons receiving SSI payments. The SSI program is a cash assistance program that provides monthly benefits to low-income aged, blind, or disabled persons.

Data are as of December of the year shown.

AGRICULTURE, ITEMS 63–72
Source: U.S. Department of Agriculture, National Agricultural Statistics Service—2012 Census of Agriculture
http://agcensus.usda.gov/index.php

The Census Bureau took a census of agriculture every 10 years from 1840 to 1920; since 1925, this census has been taken roughly once every 5 years. The 1997 Census of Agriculture was the first one conducted by the National Agricultural Statistics Service of the U.S. Department of Agriculture. Over time, the definition of a farm has varied. For recent censuses (including the 2012 census), a farm has been defined as any place from which $1,000 or more of agricultural products were produced and sold or normally would have been sold during the census year. Dollar figures are expressed in current dollars and have not been adjusted for inflation or deflation.

The acreage designated as **land in farms** consists primarily of agricultural land used for crops, pasture, or grazing. It also includes woodland and wasteland not actually under cultivation or used for pasture or grazing, provided that this land was part of the farm operator's total operation.

Land in farms is an operating-unit concept and includes all land owned and operated, as well as all land rented from others. Land used rent-free is classified as land rented from others. All land in Indian reservations used for growing crops or grazing livestock is classified as land in farms.

The **value of farm products sold** by farms represents the gross market value before taxes and the production expenses of all agricultural products sold or removed from the place in 2012, regardless of who received the payment. It includes sales by the operator as well as the value of any share received by partners, landlords, contractors, and others associated with the operation. It represents the sum of all crops, including nursery products sold and livestock and poultry and their products sold.

The value of crops sold in 2012 does not necessarily represent the sales from crops harvested that year. The data include sales from crops produced in earlier years and exclude some crops that were produced in 2012 but held in storage and not sold during the census year. For crops sold through a co-op that made payments in several installments, only the total value received in the census year was reported.

Government payments consists of government payments received from the Conservation Reserve Program (CRP) and Wetlands Reserve Program (WRP), plus government payments received from federal programs other than the CRP, WRP, and Commodity Credit Corporation (CCC).

PRIVATE NONFARM EMPLOYMENT AND EARNINGS, Items 73-85
Source: U.S. Census Bureau—County Business Patterns
https://www.census.gov/programs-surveys/cbp.html

Data for private nonfarm employment and earnings are compiled from the payroll information reported monthly in the Census Bureau publication *County Business Patterns*. The estimates are based on surveys conducted by the Census Bureau and administrative records from the Internal Revenue Service (IRS).

The following types of employment are excluded from the tables: government employment, self-employed persons, farm workers, and domestic service workers. Railroad employment jointly covered by Social Security and railroad retirement programs, employment on oceanborne vessels, and employment in foreign countries are also excluded.

Annual payroll is the combined amount of wages paid, tips reported, and other compensation (including salaries, vacation allowances, bonuses, commissions, sick-leave pay, and the value of payments-in-kind such as free meals and lodging) paid to employees before deductions for Social Security, income tax, insurance, union dues, etc. All forms of compensation are included, regardless of whether they are subject to income tax or the Federal Insurance Contributions Act tax, with the exception of annuities, third-party sick pay, and supplemental unemployment compensation benefits (even if income tax was withheld). For corporations, total annual payroll includes compensation paid to officers and executives; for unincorporated businesses, it excludes profit or other compensation of proprietors or partners.